# This certifies that

AND

WERE UNITED IN

# HOLY MATRIMONY

ON THE DAY OF

IN THE YEAR OF OUR LORD NINETEEN HUNDRED AND

AT

BY

WITNESS

WITNESS

# HUSBAND'S FAMILY TREE

NAME

DATE BORN

PLACE

BROTHERS, SISTERS

FATHER

DATE BORN

PLACE

BROTHERS, SISTERS

MOTHER

DATE BORN

PLACE

BROTHERS, SISTERS

FATHER

DATE BORN

PLACE

BROTHERS, SISTERS

MOTHER

DATE BORN

PLACE

BROTHERS, SISTERS

FATHER

DATE BORN

PLACE

BROTHERS, SISTERS

MOTHER

DATE BORN

PLACE

BROTHERS, SISTERS

FATHER

FATHER

FATHER

MOTHER

MOTHER

FATHER

MOTHER

FATHER

FATHER

MOTHER

MOTHER

FATHER

MOTHER

FATHER

FATHER

FATHER

MOTHER

MOTHER

FATHER

MOTHER

MOTHER

FATHER

FATHER

MOTHER

MOTHER

FATHER

MOTHER

FATHER

FATHER

FATHER

MOTHER

MOTHER

FATHER

MOTHER

MOTHER

FATHER

FATHER

MOTHER

MOTHER

FATHER

MOTHER

FATHER

FATHER

FATHER

MOTHER

MOTHER

FATHER

MOTHER

MOTHER

FATHER

FATHER

MOTHER

MOTHER

FATHER

MOTHER

# WIFE'S FAMILY TREE

NAME

DATE BORN

PLACE

BROTHERS, SISTERS

FATHER

DATE BORN

PLACE

BROTHERS, SISTERS

MOTHER

DATE BORN

PLACE

BROTHERS, SISTERS

FATHER

DATE BORN

PLACE

BROTHERS, SISTERS

MOTHER

DATE BORN

PLACE

BROTHERS, SISTERS

FATHER

DATE BORN

PLACE

BROTHERS, SISTERS

MOTHER

DATE BORN

PLACE

BROTHERS, SISTERS

FATHER

FATHER

MOTHER

FATHER

MOTHER

FATHER

MOTHER

MOTHER

FATHER

MOTHER

FATHER

MOTHER

FATHER

MOTHER

FATHER

FATHER

MOTHER

FATHER

MOTHER

FATHER

MOTHER

MOTHER

FATHER

MOTHER

FATHER

MOTHER

FATHER

MOTHER

FATHER

FATHER

MOTHER

FATHER

MOTHER

FATHER

MOTHER

MOTHER

FATHER

MOTHER

FATHER

MOTHER

FATHER

MOTHER

FATHER

FATHER

MOTHER

FATHER

MOTHER

FATHER

MOTHER

MOTHER

FATHER

MOTHER

FATHER

MOTHER

FATHER

MOTHER

# OUR CHILDREN AND

NAME
BORN PLACE
NAME
BORN PLACE
NAME
BORN PLACE
NAME
BORN PLACE
NAME
BORN PLACE

NAME
BORN PLACE
MARRIED TO

NAME
BORN PLACE
NAME
BORN PLACE
NAME
BORN PLACE
NAME
BORN PLACE
NAME
BORN PLACE

NAME
BORN PLACE
MARRIED TO

NAME
BORN PLACE
NAME
BORN PLACE
NAME
BORN PLACE
NAME
BORN PLACE

NAME
BORN PLACE
MARRIED TO

# GRANDCHILDREN

NAME
BORN PLACE
MARRIED TO

NAME
BORN PLACE
NAME
BORN PLACE
NAME
BORN PLACE
NAME
BORN PLACE
NAME
BORN PLACE

NAME
BORN PLACE
MARRIED TO

NAME
BORN PLACE
NAME
BORN PLACE
NAME
BORN PLACE
NAME
BORN PLACE
NAME
BORN PLACE

NAME
BORN PLACE
MARRIED TO

NAME
BORN PLACE
NAME
BORN PLACE
NAME
BORN PLACE
NAME
BORN PLACE

# EVENTS TO REMEMBER

## in the life of our family

# SPECIAL PICTURE MEMORIES

# SPECIAL PICTURE MEMORIES

# CHURCH RECORD

FATHER'S PARENTS

FIRST GENERATION: FATHER AND MOTHER

OUR CHILDREN

OUR GRANDCHILDREN

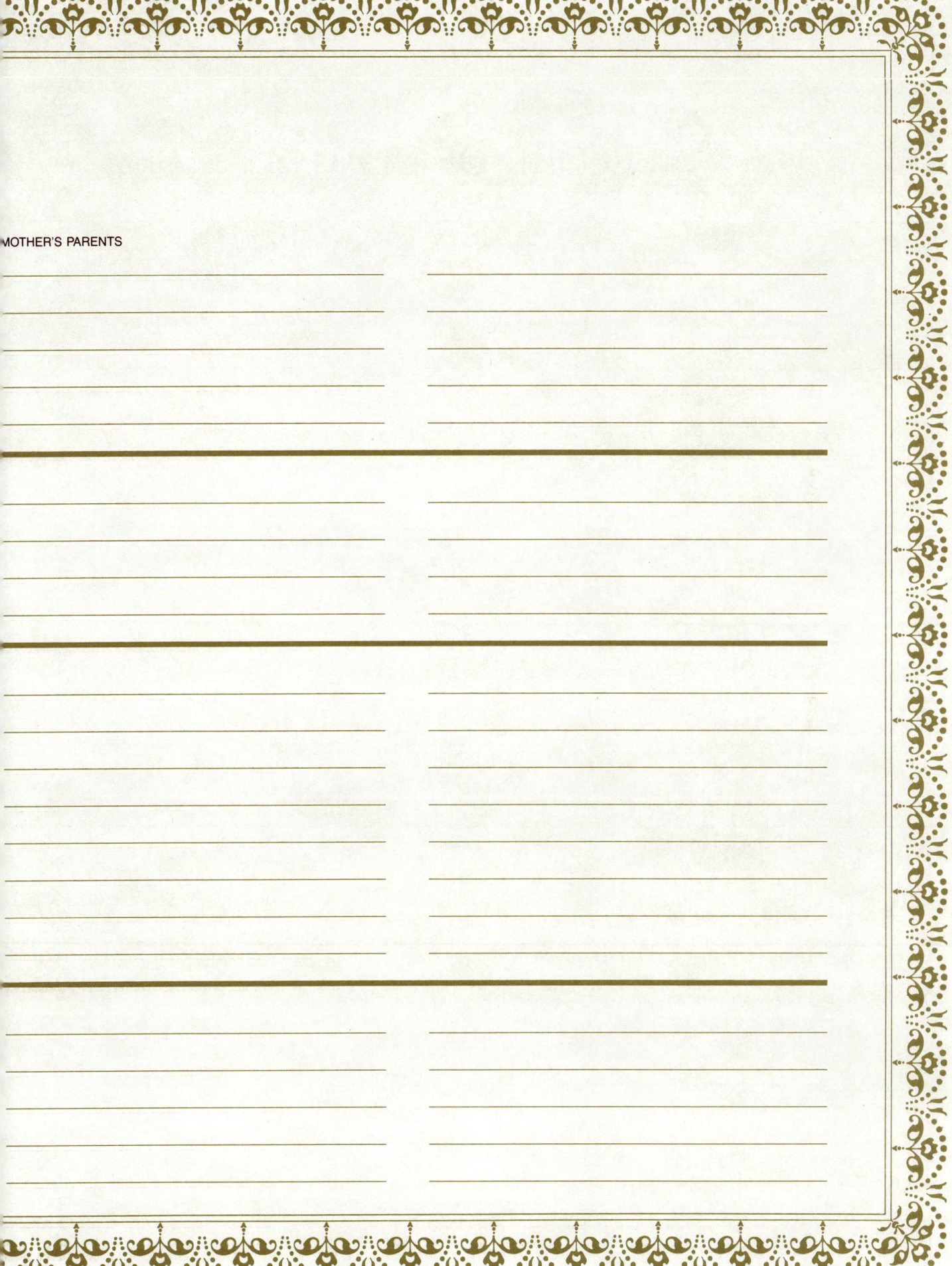

MOTHER'S PARENTS

# RECORD OF DEATHS

NAME

DATE PLACE

NAME

DATE PLACE

NAME

DATE PLACE

NAME

DATE PLACE

NAME

DATE PLACE

NAME

DATE PLACE

NAME

DATE PLACE

NAME

DATE PLACE

NAME

DATE PLACE

NAME

DATE PLACE

NAME

DATE PLACE

NAME

DATE PLACE

NAME

DATE PLACE

NAME

DATE PLACE

NAME

DATE PLACE

NAME

DATE PLACE

NAME

DATE PLACE

NAME

DATE PLACE

NAME

DATE PLACE

NAME

DATE PLACE

NAME

DATE PLACE

NAME

DATE PLACE

# HOLY BIBLE

Containing the Old and New Testaments

New King James Version
Red Letter Edition

FAMILY REFERENCE EDITION

THOMAS NELSON PUBLISHERS
Nashville • Camden • New York

Title page logo: The triquetra (from a Latin word meaning "three-cornered") is an ancient symbol for the Trinity. It comprises three interwoven arcs, distinct yet equal and inseparable, symbolizing that the Father, Son, and Holy Spirit are three distinct yet equal Persons and indivisibly One God.

***Printed in the United States of America***

1 2 3 4 5 6 7 8 9 10 11 12 13 14 15 16 17 18 19 20 — 89 88 87 86 85

# PREFACE

## Purpose

In the preface to the 1611 edition, the translators of the Authorized Version, known popularly as the King James Bible, state that it was not their purpose "to make a new translation . . . but to make a good one better." Indebted to the earlier work of William Tyndale and others, they saw their best contribution to consist in revising and enhancing the excellence of the English versions which had sprung from the Reformation of the sixteenth century. In harmony with the purpose of the King James scholars, the translators and editors of the present work have not pursued a goal of innovation. They have perceived the Holy Bible, New King James Version, as a continuation of the labors of the earlier translators, thus unlocking for today's readers the spiritual treasures found especially in the Authorized Version of the Holy Scriptures.

## A Living Legacy

For nearly four hundred years, and throughout several revisions of its English form, the King James Bible has been deeply revered among the English-speaking peoples of the world. The precision of translation for which it is historically renowned, and its majesty of style, have enabled that monumental version of the Word of God to become the mainspring of the religion, language, and legal foundations of our civilization.

Although the Elizabethan period and our own era share in zeal for technical advance, the former period was more aggressively devoted to classical learning. Along with this awakened concern for the classics came a flourishing companion interest in the Scriptures, an interest that was enlivened by the conviction that the manuscripts were providentially handed down and were a trustworthy record of the inspired Word of God. The King James translators were committed to producing an English Bible that would be a precise translation, and by no means a paraphrase or a broadly approximate rendering. On the one hand, the scholars were almost as familiar with the original languages of the Bible as with their native English. On the other hand, their reverence for the divine Author and His Word assured a translation of the Scriptures in which only a principle of utmost accuracy could be accepted.

In 1786 Catholic scholar Alexander Geddes said of the King James Bible, "If accuracy and strictest attention to the letter of the text be supposed to constitute an excellent version, this is of all versions the most excellent." George Bernard Shaw became a literary legend in our century because of his severe and often humorous criticisms of our most cherished values. Surprisingly, however, Shaw pays the following tribute to the scholars commissioned by King James: "The translation was extraordinarily well done because to the translators what they were translating was not merely a curious collection of ancient books written by different authors in different stages of culture, but the Word of God divinely revealed through His chosen and expressly inspired scribes. In this conviction they carried out their work with boundless reverence and care and achieved a beautifully artistic result." History agrees with these estimates. Therefore, while seeking to unveil the excellent *form* of the traditional English Bible, special care has also been taken in the present edition to preserve the work of *precision* which is the legacy of the 1611 translators.

## Complete Equivalence in Translation

Where new translation has been necessary in the New King James Version, the most complete representation of the original has been rendered by considering the history of usage and etymology of words in their contexts. This principle of complete equivalence seeks to preserve *all* of the information in the text, while presenting it in good literary form. Dynamic equivalence, a recent procedure in Bible translation, commonly results in paraphrasing where a more literal rendering is needed to reflect a specific and vital sense. For example, a completely equivalent rendering of 1 Samuel 15:33 would read, "and Samuel hacked [or hewed] Agag in pieces. . . ." However, one contemporary translation needlessly softens the statement: "and Samuel put Agag to death. . . ." The latter rendering does not accurately translate the language of the text, following the principle of dynamic equivalence, the procedure rather widely followed throughout that version.

In keeping with the principle of complete equivalence, it is the policy to translate interjections which are commonly omitted in modern language renderings of the Bible. As an example, the interjection *behold,* in the older King James editions, continues to have a place in English usage, especially in dramatically calling attention to a spectacular scene, or an event of profound importance such as the Immanuel prophecy of Isaiah 7:14. Consequently, *behold* is retained for these occasions in the present edition. However, the Hebrew and Greek originals for this word can be translated variously, depending on the circumstances in the passage. Therefore, in addition to *behold,* words such as *indeed, look, see,* and *surely* are also rendered to convey the appropriate sense suggested by the context in each case.

In faithfulness to God and to our readers, it was deemed appropriate that all participating scholars sign a statement affirming their belief in the verbal and plenary inspiration of Scripture, and in the inerrancy of the original autographs.

## Devotional Quality

The King James scholars readily appreciated the intrinsic beauty of divine revelation. They accordingly disciplined their talents to render well-chosen English words of their time, as well as a graceful, often musical arrangement of language, which has stirred the hearts of Bible readers through the years. The translators, the committees, and the editors of the present edition, while sensitive to the late-twentieth-century English idiom, and while adhering faithfully to the Hebrew, Aramaic, and Greek texts, have sought to maintain those lyrical and devotional qualities that are so highly regarded in the Authorized Version. This devotional quality is especially apparent in the poetic and prophetic books, although even the relatively plain style of the Gospels and Epistles cannot strictly be likened, as sometimes suggested, to modern newspaper style. The Koine Greek of the New Testament is influenced by the Hebrew background of the writers, for whom even the Gospel narratives were not merely flat utterance, but often song in various degrees of rhythm.

### The Style

Students of the Bible applaud the timeless devotional character of our historic Bible. Yet it is also universally understood that our language, like all living languages, has undergone profound change since 1611. Subsequent revisions of the King James Bible have sought to keep abreast of changes in English speech. The present work is a further step toward this objective. Where obsolescence and other reading difficulties exist, present-day vocabulary, punctuation, and grammar have been carefully integrated. Words representing ancient objects, such as *chariot* and *phylactery,* have no modern substitutes and are therefore retained.

A special feature of the New King James Version is its conformity to the thought flow of the 1611 Bible. The reader discovers that the sequence and selection of words, phrases, and clauses of the new edition, while much clearer, are so close to the traditional that there is remarkable ease in listening to the reading of either edition while following with the other.

In the discipline of translating biblical and other ancient languages, a standard method of transliteration, that is, the English spelling of untranslated words, such as names of persons and places, has never been commonly adopted. In keeping with the design of the present work, the King James spelling of untranslated words is retained, although made uniform throughout. For example, instead of the spellings *Isaiah* and *Elijah* in the Old Testament, and *Esaias* and *Elias* in the New Testament, *Isaiah* and *Elijah* now appear in both Testaments.

King James doctrinal and theological terms, for example, *propitiation, justification,* and *sanctification,* are generally familiar to English-speaking peoples. Such terms have been retained except where the original language indicates need for a more precise translation.

Readers of the Authorized Version will immediately be struck by the absence of several pronouns: *thee, thou,* and *ye* are replaced by the simple *you,* while *your* and *yours* are substituted for *thy* and *thine* as applicable. *Thee, thou, thy,* and *thine* were once forms of address to express a special relationship to human as well as divine persons. These pronouns are no longer part of our language. However, reverence for God in the present work is preserved by capitalizing pronouns, including *You, Your,* and *Yours,* which refer to Him. Additionally, capitalization of these pronouns benefits the reader by clearly distinguishing divine and human persons referred to in a passage. Without such capitalization the distinction is often obscure, because the antecedent of a pronoun is not always clear in the English translation.

In addition to the pronoun usages of the seventeenth century, the *-eth* and *-est* verb endings, so familiar in the earlier King James editions, are now obsolete. Unless a speaker is schooled in these verb endings, there is common difficulty in selecting the correct form to be used with a given subject of the verb in vocal prayer. That is, should we use *love, loveth,* or *lovest? do, doeth, doest,* or *dost? have, hath,* or *hast?* Because these forms are obsolete, contemporary English usage has been substituted for the previous verb endings.

In older editions of the King James Version, the frequency of the connective *and* far exceeded the limits of present English usage. Also, biblical linguists agree that the Hebrew and Greek original words for this conjunction may commonly be translated otherwise, depending on the immediate context. Therefore, instead of *and,* alternatives such as *also, but, however, now, so, then,* and *thus* are accordingly rendered in the present edition, when the original language permits.

The real character of the Authorized Version does not reside in its archaic pronouns or verbs or other grammatical forms of the seventeenth century, but rather in the care taken by its scholars to impart the letter and spirit of the original text in a majestic and reverent style.

### The Format

The format of the New King James Version is designed to enhance the vividness and devotional quality of the Holy Scriptures:

— Subject headings assist the reader to identify topics and transitions in the biblical content.
— Words or phrases in *italics* indicate expressions in the original language which require clarification by additional English words, as also done throughout the history of the King James Bible.
— Verse numbers in bold type indicate the beginning of a paragraph.
— *Oblique type* in the New Testament indicates a quotation from the Old Testament.
— Poetry is structured as contemporary verse to reflect the poetic form and beauty of the passage in the original language.
— The covenant name of God was usually translated from the Hebrew as "LORD" or "GOD" (using capital letters as shown) in the King James Old Testament. This tradition is maintained. In the present edition the name is so capitalized whenever the covenant name is quoted in the New Testament from a passage in the Old Testament.

### The Old Testament Text

The Hebrew Bible has come down to us through the scrupulous care of ancient scribes who copied the original text in successive generations. By the sixth century A.D. the scribes were succeeded by a group known as the Masoretes, who continued to preserve the sacred Scriptures for another five hundred years in a form known as the Masoretic Text. Babylonia, Palestine, and Tiberias were the main centers of Masoretic activity; but by the tenth century A.D. the Masoretes of Tiberias, led by the family of ben Asher, gained the ascendancy. Through subsequent editions, the ben Asher text became in the twelfth century the only recognized form of the Hebrew Scriptures.

Daniel Bomberg printed the first Rabbinic Bible in 1516–17; that work was followed in 1524–25 by a second edition prepared by Jacob ben Chayyim and also published by Bomberg. The text of ben Chayyim was adopted in most subsequent Hebrew Bibles, including those used by the King James translators. The ben Chayyim text was also used for the first two editions of Rudolph Kittel's *Biblia Hebraica* of 1906 and 1912. In 1937 Paul Kahle published a third edition of *Biblia Hebraica*. This edition was based on the oldest dated manuscript of the ben Asher text, the Leningrad Manuscript B19a (A.D. 1008), which Kahle regarded as superior to that used by ben Chayyim.

For the New King James Version the text used was the 1967/1977 Stuttgart edition of the *Biblia Hebraica*, with frequent comparisons being made with the Bomberg edition of 1524–25. The Septuagint (Greek) Version of the Old Testament and the Latin Vulgate also were consulted. In addition to referring to a variety of ancient versions of the Hebrew Scriptures, the New King James Version draws on the resources of relevant manuscripts from the Dead Sea caves. In the few places where the Hebrew was so obscure that the 1611 King James was compelled to follow one of the versions, but where information is now available to resolve the problems, the New King James Version follows the Hebrew text. Significant variations are recorded in the center reference column.

**The New Testament Text**

There is more manuscript support for the New Testament than for any other body of ancient literature. Over five thousand Greek, eight thousand Latin, and many more manuscripts in other languages attest the integrity of the New Testament. There is only one basic New Testament used by Protestants, Roman Catholics, and Orthodox, by conservatives and liberals. Minor variations in hand copying have appeared through the centuries, before mechanical printing began about A.D. 1450.

Some variations exist in the spelling of Greek words, in word order, and in similar details. These ordinarily do not show up in translation and do not affect the sense of the text in any way.

Other manuscript differences such as omission or inclusion of a word or a clause, and two paragraphs in the Gospels, should not overshadow the overwhelming degree of *agreement* which exists among the ancient records. Bible readers may be assured that the most important differences in English New Testaments of today are due, not to manuscript divergence, but to the way in which translators view the task of translation: How literally should the text be rendered? How does the translator view the matter of biblical inspiration? Does the translator adopt a paraphrase when a literal rendering would be quite clear and more to the point? The New King James Version follows the historic precedent of the Authorized Version in maintaining a literal approach to translation, except where the idiom of the original language cannot be translated directly into our tongue.

The King James New Testament was based on the traditional text of the Greek-speaking churches, first published in 1516, and later called the Textus Receptus or Received Text. Although based on the relatively few available manuscripts, these were representative of many more which existed at the time but only became known later. In the late nineteenth century, B. Westcott and F. Hort taught that this text had been officially edited by the fourth-century church, but a total lack of historical evidence for this event has forced a revision of the theory. It is now widely held that the Byzantine Text that largely supports the Textus Receptus has as much right as the Alexandrian or any other tradition to be weighed in determining the text of the New Testament. Those readings in the Textus Receptus which have weak support are indicated in the center reference column as being opposed by both Critical and Majority Texts (see "Center-Column Notes," below).

Since the 1880s most contemporary translations of the New Testament have relied upon a relatively few manuscripts discovered chiefly in the late nineteenth and early twentieth centuries. Such translations depend primarily on two manuscripts, Codex Vaticanus and Codex Sinaiticus, because of their greater age. The Greek text obtained by using these sources and the related papyri (our most ancient manuscripts) is known as the Alexandrian Text. However, some scholars have grounds for doubting the faithfulness of Vaticanus and Sinaiticus, since they often disagree with one another, and Sinaiticus exhibits excessive omission.

A third viewpoint of New Testament scholarship holds that the best text is based on the consensus of the majority of existing Greek manuscripts. This text is called the Majority Text. Most of these manuscripts are in substantial agreement. Even though many are late, and none is earlier than the fifth century, usually their readings are verified by papyri, ancient versions, quotations from the early church fathers, or a combination of these. The Majority Text is similar to the Textus Receptus, but it corrects those readings which have little or no support in the Greek manuscript tradition.

Today, scholars agree that the science of New Testament textual criticism is in a state of flux. Very few scholars still favor the Textus Receptus as such, and then often for its historical prestige as the text of Luther, Calvin, Tyndale, and the King James Version. For about a century most have followed a Critical Text—so called because it is edited according to specific principles of textual criticism—which depends heavily upon the Alexandrian type of text. More recently many have abandoned this Critical Text (which is quite similar to the one edited by Westcott and Hort) for one that is more eclectic. Finally, a small but growing number of scholars prefer the Majority Text, which is close to the traditional text except in the Revelation.

In light of these facts, and also because the New King James Version is the fifth revision of a historic document translated from specific Greek texts, the editors decided to retain the traditional text in the body of the New Testament and to indicate major Critical and Majority Text variant readings in the center reference column. Although these variations are duly indicated in the center-column notes of the present edition, it is most important to emphasize that fully eighty-five percent of the New Testament text is the same in the Textus Receptus, the Alexandrian Text, and the Majority Text.

**Center-Column Notes**

Significant explanatory notes, alternate translations, and cross-references, as well as New Testament citations of Old Testament passages, are supplied in the center reference column.

Important textual variants in the Old Testament are identified in a standard form.

The textual notes in the present edition of the New Testament make no evaluation of readings, but do clearly indicate the manuscript sources of readings. They objectively present the facts without such tendentious remarks as "the best manuscripts omit" or "the most reliable manuscripts read." Such notes are value judgments that differ according to varying viewpoints on the text. By giving a clearly defined set of variants the New King James Version benefits readers of all textual persuasions.

Where significant variations occur in the New Testament Greek manuscripts, textual notes are classified as follows:

1. NU-Text
   These variations from the traditional text generally represent the Alexandrian or Egyptian type of text described previously in "The New Testament Text." They are found in the Critical Text published in the twenty-sixth edition of the Nestle-Aland Greek New Testament (N) and in the United Bible Societies' third edition (U), hence the acronym, "NU-Text."
2. M-Text
   This symbol indicates points of variation in the Majority Text from the traditional text, as also previously discussed in "The New Testament Text." It should be noted that M stands for whatever reading is printed in the published *Greek New Testament According to the Majority Text,* whether supported by overwhelming, strong, or only a divided majority textual tradition.

The textual notes reflect the scholarship of the past 150 years and will assist the reader to observe the variations between the different manuscript traditions of the New Testament. Such information is generally not available in English translations of the New Testament.

# GETTING THE MOST FROM YOUR CENTER-COLUMN REFERENCE BIBLE

The center column of your family Bible contains a wealth of information—over 60,000 references, including 10,000 translation notes, to enhance your study of God's Word. Take a few minutes to learn how to interpret the various types of notes you will find there.

**THE RAISED a's, b's, AND c's** in the text key you to cross-references in the center column.

**WHEN YOU SEE A RAISED 1, 2, OR 3** in the text you know to expect a note or translation in the center column.

**LITERAL TRANSLATIONS:** exact translations; reproduced word for word

**CROSS-REFERENCES** point out verses that will explain the referenced word or phrase in the text.

**EXPLANATORY NOTES** shed light on words or phrases in the text, not translated from the original languages.

**TEXTUAL NOTES** point out significant textual variants in both the Old and New Testaments (see page x for abbreviations and for definitions of the various texts).

**ALTERNATE TRANSLATIONS:** different from those in the text but justified by the original languages

**EQUIVALENT TRANSLATIONS:** roughly similar in meaning to the translations in the text and helpful in clarifying them

**REFERENCES ENCLOSED IN SQUARE BRACKETS:** passages similar in theme to the referenced passage in the text

*The Birth of Jesus Christ*

THE book of the [a]genealogy[1] of Jesus Christ,
[b]the Son of David, [c]the Son of Abraham:
2 [a]Abraham begot Isaac, [b]Isaac begot Jacob,
and Jacob begot [c]Judah and his brothers.
3 [a]Judah begot Perez and Zerah by Tamar,
[b]Perez begot Hezron, and Hezron begot Ram.
4 Ram begot Amminadab, Amminadab begot
Nahshon, and Nahshon begot Salmon.
5 Salmon begot [a]Boaz by Rahab, Boaz begot
Obed by Ruth, Obed begot Jesse,
6 and [a]Jesse begot David the king.
[b]David the king begot Solomon by her [1]*who
had been the wife* of Uriah.
7 [a]Solomon begot Rehoboam, Rehoboam begot
[b]Abijah, and Abijah begot [1]Asa.
8 Asa begot [a]Jehoshaphat, Jehoshaphat begot
Joram, and Joram begot [b]Uzziah.
9 Uzziah begot Jotham, Jotham begot [a]Ahaz,
and Ahaz begot Hezekiah.
10 [a]Hezekiah begot Manasseh, Manasseh begot
[1]Amon, and Amon begot [b]Josiah.
11 [a]Josiah begot [1]Jeconiah and his brothers about
the time they were [b]carried away to Babylon.
12 And after they were brought to Babylon,
[a]Jeconiah begot Shealtiel, and Shealtiel begot
[b]Zerubbabel.
13 Zerubbabel begot Abiud, Abiud begot Eliakim,
and Eliakim begot Azor.
14 Azor begot Zadok, Zadok begot Achim, and
Achim begot Eliud.
15 Eliud begot Eleazar, Eleazar begot Matthan,
and Matthan begot Jacob.
16 And Jacob begot Joseph the husband of
[a]Mary, of whom was born Jesus who is called
Christ.
17 So all the generations from Abraham to David
*are* fourteen generations, from David until the
captivity in Babylon *are* fourteen generations, and
from the captivity in Babylon until the Christ *are*
fourteen generations.
18 Now the [a]birth of Jesus Christ was as follows:
After His mother Mary was betrothed to Joseph,
before they came together, she was found with
child [b]of the Holy Spirit.
19 Then Joseph her husband, being [1]a just *man*,
and not wanting [a]to make her a public example,
was minded to put her away secretly.
20 But while he thought about these things,
behold, an angel of the Lord appeared to him in a
dream, saying, "Joseph, son of David, do not be
afraid to take to you Mary your wife, [a]for that
which is [1]conceived in her is of the Holy Spirit.
21 [a]"And she will bring forth a Son, and you shall
call His name [1]JESUS, [b]for He will save His people
from their sins."
22 So all this was done that it might be fulfilled
which was spoken by the Lord through the
prophet, saying:

CHAPTER 1
1 [a]Luke 3:23 [b]John 7:42 [c]Gen. 12:3; 22:18 [1]Lit. *generation*
2 [a]Gen. 21:2, 12 [b]Gen. 25:26; 28:14 [c]Gen. 29:35
3 [a]Gen. 38:27; 49:10 [b]Ruth 4:18–22
5 [a]Ruth 2:1; 4:1–13
6 [a]1 Sam. 16:1 [b]2 Sam. 7:12; 12:24 [1]Words in italic type have been added for clarity. They are not found in the original Greek.
7 [a]1 Chr. 3:10 [b]2 Chr. 11:20 [1]NU *Asaph*
8 [a]1 Chr. 3:10 [b]2 Kin. 15:13
9 [a]2 Kin. 15:38
10 [a]2 Kin. 20:21 [b]1 Kin. 13:2 [1]NU *Amos*
11 [a]1 Chr. 3:15, 16 [b]2 Kin. 24:14–16 [1]Or *Coniah* or *Jehoiachin*
12 [a]1 Chr. 3:17 [b]Ezra 3:2
16 [a]Matt. 13:55
18 [a]Luke 1:27 [b]Luke 1:35
19 [a]Deut. 24:1 [1]*an upright*
20 [a]Luke 1:35 [1]Lit. *begotten*
21 [a]Luke 1:31; 2:21 [b]John 1:29 [1]Lit. *Savior*
23 [a]Is. 7:14 [1]Words in oblique type in the New Testament are quoted from the Old Testament.
25 [a]Luke 2:7, 21 [1]Kept her a virgin [2]NU *a Son*

CHAPTER 2
1 [a]Luke 2:4–7 [b]Gen. 25:6 [1]Gr. *magoi*
2 [a]Luke 2:11 [b][Num. 24:17]
4 [a]2 Chr. 36:14 [b]2 Chr. 34:13 [c]Mal. 2:7
6 [a]Mic. 5:2

30 "For in the resurrection they neither marry
nor are given in marriage, but [a]are like angels [1]of
God in heaven.
31 "But concerning the resurrection of the dead,
have you not read what was spoken to you by
God, saying,
32 [a]*'I am the God of Abraham, the God of Isaac,*
*and the God of Jacob'*? God is not the God of the
dead, but of the living."
33 And when the multitudes heard *this,* [a]they
were astonished at His teaching.
**34** [a]But when the Pharisees heard that He had
silenced the Sadducees, they gathered together.
35 Then one of them, [a]a lawyer, asked *Him* a
*question,* testing Him, and saying,
36 "Teacher, which *is* the great commandment in
the law?"
37 Jesus said to him, [a]" *'You shall love the* LORD
*your God with all your heart, with all your soul,*
*and with all your mind.'*
38 "This is *the* first and great commandment.
39 "And *the* second *is* like it: [a]*'You shall love*
*your neighbor as yourself.'*
40 [a]"On these two commandments hang all the
Law and the Prophets."
**41** [a]While the Pharisees were gathered together,
Jesus asked them,
42 saying, "What do you think about the Christ?
Whose Son is He?" They said to Him, "*The* [a]Son of
David."
43 He said to them, "How then does David in the
Spirit call Him *'Lord,'* saying:

44 *'The[a]* LORD *said to my Lord,*
*"Sit at My right hand,*
*Till I make Your enemies Your footstool" '*?

45 "If David then calls Him *'Lord,'* how is He his
Son?"
46 [a]And no one was able to answer Him a word,
[b]nor from that day on did anyone dare question
Him anymore.

## *Jesus Rebukes the Scribes and Pharisees*

**23** Then Jesus spoke to the multitudes and to
His disciples,
2 saying: [a]"The scribes and the Pharisees sit in
Moses' seat.
3 "Therefore whatever they tell you [1]to observe,
*that* observe and do, but do not do according to
their works; for [a]they say, and do not do.
4 [a]"For they bind heavy burdens, hard to bear,
and lay *them* on men's shoulders; but they *them-*
*selves* will not move them with one of their
fingers.
5 "But all their works they do to [a]be seen by
men. They make their phylacteries broad and
enlarge the borders of their garments.
6 [a]"They love the [1]best places at feasts, the best
seats in the synagogues,
7 "greetings in the marketplaces, and to be
called by men, 'Rabbi, Rabbi.'
8 [a]"But you, do not be called 'Rabbi'; for One is
your [1]Teacher, [2]the Christ, and you are all brethren.
9 "Do not call anyone on earth your father; [a]for
One is your Father, He who is in heaven.

**4** [a]Prov. 9:2
**6** [1]*insolently*
**7** [a][Dan. 9:26]
**8** [a]Matt. 10:11
**10** [a]Matt. 13:38, 47, 48
**11** [a][Col. 3:10, 12]
**12** [a][Rom. 3:19]
**13** [a]Matt. 8:12; 25:30 [1]NU omits *take him away and*
**14** [a]Matt. 20:16
**15** [a]Mark 12:13–17
**16** [a]Mark 3:6; 8:15; 12:13 [1]Lit. *look at the face of*
**18** [1]*knew*
**21** [a]Matt. 17:25 [b][Rom. 13:1–7] [c][1 Cor. 3:23; 6:19, 20; 12:27] [1]*Pay*
**23** [a]Luke 20:27–40 [b]Acts 23:8
**24** [a]Deut. 25:5
**29** [a]John 20:9 [1]*deceived*
**30** [a][1 John 3:2] [1]NU omits *of God*
**32** [a]Ex. 3:6, 15
**33** [a]Matt. 7:28
**34** [a]Mark 12:28–31
**35** [a]Luke 7:30; 10:25; 11:45, 46, 52; 14:3
**37** [a]Deut. 6:5; 10:12; 30:6
**39** [a]Lev. 19:18
**40** [a][Matt. 7:12]
**41** [a]Luke 20:41–44
**42** [a]Matt. 1:1; 21:9
**44** [a]Ps. 110:1
**46** [a]Luke 14:6 [b]Mark 12:34

CHAPTER 23
**2** [a]Neh. 8:4, 8
**3** [a][Rom. 2:19] [1]NU omits *to observe*
**4** [a]Luke 11:46
**5** [a][Matt. 6:1–6, 16–18]
**6** [a]Luke 11:43; 20:46 [1]Or *place of honor*
**8** [a][James 3:1] [1]*Leader* [2]NU

QUOTATION MARKS in the text follow modern English usage. For easier reading, only the marks denoting the most recently opened quotation are repeated in a new paragraph.

OBLIQUE TYPE in the New Testament indicates a quotation from the Old Testament. The sources of the quotations are found in cross-references.

PERSONAL PRONOUNS and certain nouns are capitalized when they refer to Deity.

THE COVENANT NAME OF GOD in the Old Testament, represented by the Hebrew consonants YHWH, is translated "LORD" or "GOD" (using capital letters as shown), as it has been throughout the history of the King James Bible. In this edition the capitalized form is also used whenever the covenant name is quoted in the New Testament from a passage in the Old Testament.

A BOLD-FACE VERSE NUMERAL in the text indicates a paragraph break. When a new paragraph begins within a verse, the new paragraph is indented (see, for example, Nehemiah 13:22).

POETRY is structured as contemporary verse to reflect the poetic form and beauty of the original language.

SUBJECT HEADINGS have been added to help you follow the flow of thought in the biblical material.

ITALIC TYPE in the text indicates words that the original texts do not contain but which English requires for clarity.

# TABLE OF CONTENTS


Preface . . . iii
Getting the Most from Your Center-Column Reference Bible . . . vii
List of Abbreviations . . . x

## Old Testament

Genesis . . . 1
Exodus . . . 36
Leviticus . . . 66
Numbers . . . 87
Deuteronomy . . . 118
Joshua . . . 144
Judges . . . 161
Ruth . . . 179
1 Samuel . . . 181
2 Samuel . . . 203
1 Kings . . . 223
2 Kings . . . 245
1 Chronicles . . . 266
2 Chronicles . . . 286
Ezra . . . 310
Nehemiah . . . 317
Esther . . . 328
Job . . . 333
Psalms . . . 355
Proverbs . . . 411
Ecclesiastes . . . 431
Song of Solomon . . . 437
Isaiah . . . 441
Jeremiah . . . 486
Lamentations . . . 531
Ezekiel . . . 535
Daniel . . . 572
Hosea . . . 584
Joel . . . 590
Amos . . . 593
Obadiah . . . 598
Jonah . . . 599
Micah . . . 601
Nahum . . . 605
Habakkuk . . . 607
Zephaniah . . . 609
Haggai . . . 611
Zechariah . . . 612
Malachi . . . 619

How to Establish Your Family Devotional Time . . . 623
Read Your Bible Through in a Year . . . 631

## New Testament

Matthew . . . 635
Mark . . . 658
Luke . . . 672
John . . . 697
Acts . . . 715
Romans . . . 739
1 Corinthians . . . 748
2 Corinthians . . . 758
Galatians . . . 764
Ephesians . . . 767
Philippians . . . 770
Colossians . . . 773
1 Thessalonians . . . 775
2 Thessalonians . . . 777
1 Timothy . . . 778
2 Timothy . . . 781
Titus . . . 783
Philemon . . . 784
Hebrews . . . 784
James . . . 792
1 Peter . . . 794
2 Peter . . . 797
1 John . . . 798
2 John . . . 801
3 John . . . 802
Jude . . . 802
Revelation . . . 803

Harmony of the Gospels . . . 815
The Jewish Calendar . . . 820

# ABBREVIATIONS OF BIBLE BOOKS

|  |  |
|---|---|
| Acts | Acts |
| Amos | Amos |
| 1 Chronicles | 1 Chr. |
| 2 Chronicles | 2 Chr. |
| Colossians | Col. |
| 1 Corinthians | 1 Cor. |
| 2 Corinthians | 2 Cor. |
| Daniel | Dan. |
| Deuteronomy | Deut. |
| Ecclesiastes | Eccl. |
| Ephesians | Eph. |
| Esther | Esth. |
| Exodus | Ex. |
| Ezekiel | Ezek. |
| Ezra | Ezra |
| Galatians | Gal. |
| Genesis | Gen. |
| Habakkuk | Hab. |
| Haggai | Hag. |
| Hebrews | Heb. |
| Hosea | Hos. |
| Isaiah | Is. |
| James | James |
| Jeremiah | Jer. |
| Job | Job |
| Joel | Joel |
| John | John |
| 1 John | 1 John |
| 2 John | 2 John |
| 3 John | 3 John |
| Jonah | Jon. |
| Joshua | Josh. |
| Jude | Jude |
| Judges | Judg. |
| 1 Kings | 1 Kin. |
| 2 Kings | 2 Kin. |
| Lamentations | Lam. |
| Leviticus | Lev. |
| Luke | Luke |
| Malachi | Mal. |
| Mark | Mark |
| Matthew | Matt. |
| Micah | Mic. |
| Nahum | Nah. |
| Nehemiah | Neh. |
| Numbers | Num. |
| Obadiah | Obad. |
| 1 Peter | 1 Pet. |
| 2 Peter | 2 Pet. |
| Philemon | Philem. |
| Philippians | Phil. |
| Proverbs | Prov. |
| Psalms | Ps. |
| Revelation | Rev. |
| Romans | Rom. |
| Ruth | Ruth |
| 1 Samuel | 1 Sam. |
| 2 Samuel | 2 Sam. |
| Song of Solomon | Song |
| 1 Thessalonians | 1 Thess. |
| 2 Thessalonians | 2 Thess. |
| 1 Timothy | 1 Tim. |
| 2 Timothy | 2 Tim. |
| Titus | Titus |
| Zechariah | Zech. |
| Zephaniah | Zeph. |

# SPECIAL ABBREVIATIONS

|  |  |
|---|---|
| Arab. | Arabic |
| Aram. | Aramaic |
| Bg. | the 1524–25 edition of the Hebrew Old Testament published by Daniel Bomberg (see Preface, "The Old Testament Text") |
| cf. | compare |
| ch., chs. | chapter, chapters |
| DSS | Dead Sea Scrolls |
| fem. | feminine |
| f., ff. | following verse, following verses |
| Gr. | Greek |
| Heb. | Hebrew |
| i.e. | that is |
| Kt. | Kethib (literally, in Aramaic, "written")—the written words of the Hebrew Old Testament preserved by the Masoretes (see "Qr." below) |
| Lat. | Latin |
| Lit. | Literally |
| LXX | Septuagint—an ancient translation of the Old Testament into Greek |
| M | Majority Text (see Preface, "The New Testament Text") |
| ms., mss. | manuscript, manuscripts |
| masc. | masculine |
| MT | Masoretic Text—the traditional Hebrew Old Testament (see Preface, "The Old Testament Text") |
| NU | the most prominent modern Critical Text of the Greek New Testament, published in the twenty-sixth edition of the Nestle-Aland (N) Greek New Testament and in the third edition of the United Bible Societies' (U) Greek New Testament (see Preface, "The New Testament Text") |
| pl. | plural |
| Qr. | Qere (literally, in Aramaic, "read")—certain words read aloud, differing from the written words, in the Masoretic tradition of the Hebrew Old Testament (see "Kt." above) |
| Sam. | Samaritan Pentateuch—a variant Hebrew edition of the books of Moses, used by the Samaritan community |
| sing. | singular |
| Syr. | Syriac |
| Tg. | Targum—an Aramaic paraphrase of the Old Testament |
| TR | Textus Receptus or Received Text (see Preface, "The New Testament Text") |
| v., vv. | verse, verses |
| vss. | versions—ancient translations of the Bible |
| Vg. | Vulgate—an ancient translation of the Bible into Latin, translated and edited by Jerome |

# THE OLD TESTAMENT

*The First Book of Moses Called*

# GENESIS

## *The Creation*

IN the [a]beginning [b]God created the heavens and
the earth.
2 The earth was [a]without form, and void; and
darkness [1]*was* on the face of the deep. [b]And the
Spirit of God was hovering over the face of the
waters.
3 [a]Then God said, [b]"Let there be [c]light"; and
there was light.
4 And God saw the light, that *it was* good; and
God divided the light from the darkness.
5 God called the light Day, and the [a]darkness He
called Night. [1]So the evening and the morning
were the first day.
**6** Then God said, [a]"Let there be a [1]firmament in
the midst of the waters, and let it divide the
waters from the waters."
7 Thus God made the firmament, [a]and divided
the waters which *were* under the firmament from
the waters which *were* [b]above the firmament; and
it was so.
8 And God called the firmament Heaven. So the
evening and the morning were the second day.
**9** Then God said, [a]"Let the waters under the
heavens be gathered together into one place, and
[b]let the dry *land* appear"; and it was so.
10 And God called the dry *land* Earth, and the
gathering together of the waters He called Seas.
And God saw that *it was* good.
11 Then God said, "Let the earth [a]bring forth
grass, the herb *that* yields seed, *and* the [b]fruit tree
*that* yields fruit according to its kind, whose seed
*is* in itself, on the earth"; and it was so.
12 And the earth brought forth grass, the herb
*that* yields seed according to its kind, and the tree
*that* yields fruit, whose seed *is* in itself according
to its kind. And God saw that *it was* good.
13 So the evening and the morning were the
third day.
**14** Then God said, "Let there be [a]lights in the
firmament of the heavens to divide the day from
the night; and let them be for signs and [b]seasons,
and for days and years;
15 "and let them be for lights in the firmament of
the heavens to give light on the earth"; and it was
so.
16 Then God made two great [1]lights: the [a]greater
light to rule the day, and the [b]lesser light to rule
the night. *He made* [c]the stars also.
17 God set them in the firmament of the [a]heavens
to give light on the earth,
18 and to [a]rule over the day and over the night,
and to divide the light from the darkness. And
God saw that *it was* good.
19 So the evening and the morning were the
fourth day.
**20** Then God said, "Let the waters abound with
an abundance of living [1]creatures, and let birds fly
above the earth across the face of the [2]firmament
of the heavens."
21 So [a]God created great sea creatures and every
living thing that moves, with which the waters
abounded, according to their kind, and every
winged bird according to its kind. And God saw
that *it was* good.
22 And God blessed them, saying, [a]"Be fruitful
and multiply, and fill the waters in the seas, and
let birds multiply on the earth."
23 So the evening and the morning were the fifth
day.
**24** Then God said, "Let the earth bring forth the
living creature according to its kind: cattle and
creeping thing and beast of the earth, *each* according to its kind"; and it was so.
25 And God made the beast of the earth according to its kind, cattle according to its kind, and
everything that creeps on the earth according to
its kind. And God saw that *it was* good.
**26** Then God said, [a]"Let Us make man in Our
image, according to Our likeness; [b]let them have
dominion over the fish of the sea, over the birds of
the air, and over the cattle, over [1]all the earth and
over every creeping thing that creeps on the
earth."
27 So God created man [a]in His *own* image; in the
image of God He created him; [b]male and female
He created them.
28 Then God blessed them, and God said to them,
[a]"Be fruitful and multiply; fill the earth and [b]sub-
due it; have dominion over the fish of the sea, over
the birds of the air, and over every living thing
that [1]moves on the earth."
**29** And God said, "See, I have given you every
herb *that* yields seed which *is* on the face of all the
earth, and every tree whose fruit yields seed; [a]to
you it shall be for food.
30 "Also, to [a]every beast of the earth, to every
[b]bird of the air, and to everything that creeps on
the earth, in which *there is* [1]life, *I have given*
every green herb for food"; and it was so.
31 Then [a]God saw everything that He had made,
and indeed *it was* very good. So the evening and
the morning were the sixth day.

## *The Garden of Eden*

**2** Thus the heavens and the earth, and [a]all the
host of them, were finished.
2 [a]And on the seventh day God ended His work
which He had done, and He rested on the seventh
day from all His work which He had done.
3 Then God [a]blessed the seventh day and sanctified it, because in it He rested from all His work
which God had created and made.
**4** [a]This *is* the [1]history of the heavens and the
earth when they were created, in the day that the
LORD God made the earth and the heavens,
5 before any [a]plant of the field was in the earth
and before any herb of the field had grown. For
the LORD God had not [b]caused it to rain on the
earth, and *there was* no man [c]to till the ground;
6 but a mist went up from the earth and watered
the whole face of the ground.
7 And the LORD God formed man *of* the [a]dust of
the ground, and [b]breathed into his [c]nostrils the
breath of life; and [d]man became a living being.
**8** The LORD God planted [a]a garden [b]eastward in
[c]Eden, and there He put the man whom He had
formed.
9 And out of the ground the LORD God made
[a]every tree grow that is pleasant to the sight and
good for food. [b]The tree of life *was* also in the
midst of the garden, and the tree of the knowledge
of good and [c]evil.

CHAPTER 1

**1** [a][John 1:1–3] [b]Acts 17:24
**2** [a]Jer. 4:23 [b]Is. 40:13, 14 [1]Words in italic type have been added for clarity. They are not found in the original Hebrew or Aramaic.
**3** [a]Ps. 33:6, 9 [b]2 Cor. 4:6 [c][Heb. 11:3]
**5** [a]Ps. 19:2; 33:6; 74:16; 104:20; 136:5 [1]Lit. *And evening was, and morning was, a day, one.*
**6** [a]Jer. 10:12 [1]*expanse*
**7** [a]Prov. 8:27–29 [b]Ps. 148:4
**9** [a]Job 26:10 [b]Ps. 24:1, 2; 33:7; 95:5
**11** [a]Heb. 6:7 [b]2 Sam. 16:1
**14** [a]Ps. 74:16; 136:5–9 [b]Ps. 104:19
**16** [a]Ps. 136:8 [b]Ps. 8:3 [c]Job 38:7 [1]*luminaries*
**17** [a]Gen. 15:5
**18** [a]Jer. 31:35
**20** [1]*souls* [2]*expanse*
**21** [a]Ps. 104:25–28
**22** [a]Gen. 8:17
**26** [a][Eph. 4:24] [b]Gen. 9:2 [1]Syr. *all the wild animals of*
**27** [a]Gen. 5:2 [b]Matt. 19:4
**28** [a]Gen. 9:1, 7 [b]1 Cor. 9:27 [1]*moves about on*
**29** [a]Gen. 9:3
**30** [a]Ps. 145:15 [b]Job 38:41 [1]*a living soul*
**31** [a][Ps. 104:24]

CHAPTER 2

**1** [a]Ps. 33:6
**2** [a]Ex. 20:9–11; 31:17
**3** [a][Is. 58:13]
**4** [a]Gen. 1:1 [1]Heb. *toledoth,* lit. *generations*
**5** [a]Gen. 1:11, 12 [b]Gen. 7:4 [c]Gen. 3:23
**7** [a]Gen. 3:19, 23 [b]Job 33:4 [c]Gen. 7:22 [d]1 Cor. 15:45
**8** [a]Is. 51:3 [b]Gen. 3:23, 24 [c]Gen. 4:16
**9** [a]Ezek. 31:8 [b][Gen. 3:22] [c][Deut. 1:39]

**10** Now a river went out of Eden to water the
garden, and from there it parted and became four
riverheads.
11 The name of the first *is* Pishon; it *is* the one
which skirts [a]the whole land of Havilah, where
*there is* gold.
12 And the gold of that land *is* good. [a]Bdellium
and the onyx stone *are* there.
13 The name of the second river *is* Gihon; it *is* the
one which goes around the whole land of Cush.
14 The name of the third river *is* [a]Hiddekel;[1] it *is*
the one which goes toward the east of [2]Assyria.
The fourth river *is* the Euphrates.
**15** Then the LORD God took [1]the man and put
him in the garden of Eden to [2]tend and keep it.
16 And the LORD God commanded the man, saying, "Of every tree of the garden you may freely
eat;
17 "but of the tree of the knowledge of good and
evil [a]you shall not eat, for in the day that you eat
of it [b]you[1] shall surely [c]die."
**18** And the LORD God said, "*It is* not good that
man should be alone; [a]I will make him a helper
comparable to him."
19 [a]Out of the ground the LORD God formed
every beast of the field and every bird of the air,
and [b]brought *them* to [1]Adam to see what he would
call them. And whatever Adam called each living
creature, that *was* its name.
20 So Adam gave names to all cattle, to the birds
of the air, and to every beast of the field. But for
Adam there was not found a helper comparable to
him.
21 And the LORD God caused a [a]deep sleep to fall
on Adam, and he slept; and He took one of his
ribs, and closed up the flesh in its place.
22 Then the rib which the LORD God had taken
from man He [1]made into a woman, [a]and He
[b]brought her to the man.
23 And Adam said:

"This *is* now [a]bone of my bones
And flesh of my flesh;
She shall be called [1]Woman,
Because she was [b]taken out of [2]Man."

24 [a]Therefore a man shall leave his father and
mother and [b]be[1] joined to his wife, and they shall
become one flesh.
25 [a]And they were both naked, the man and his
wife, and were not [b]ashamed.

## *The Fall of Man*

**3** Now [a]the serpent was [b]more cunning than any
beast of the field which the LORD God had
made. And he said to the woman, "Has God
indeed said, 'You shall not eat of every tree of the
garden'?"
2 And the woman said to the serpent, "We may
eat the [a]fruit of the trees of the garden;
3 "but of the fruit of the tree which *is* in the
midst of the garden, God has said, 'You shall not
eat it, nor shall you [a]touch it, lest you die.' "
4 [a]Then the serpent said to the woman, "You
will not surely die.
5 "For God knows that in the day you eat of it
your eyes will be opened, and you will be like God,
knowing good and evil."
6 So when the woman [a]saw that the tree *was*
good for food, that it *was* [1]pleasant to the eyes,
and a tree desirable to make *one* wise, she took of
its fruit [b]and ate. She also gave to her husband
with her, and he ate.
7 Then the eyes of both of them were opened,
[a]and they knew that they *were* naked; and they
sewed fig leaves together and made themselves
[1]coverings.
8 And they heard [a]the [1]sound of the LORD God
walking in the garden in the [2]cool of the day, and
Adam and his wife [b]hid themselves from the
presence of the LORD God among the trees of the
garden.
**9** Then the LORD God called to Adam and said to
him, "Where *are* you?"
10 So he said, "I heard Your voice in the garden,
[a]and I was afraid because I was naked; and I hid
myself."
11 And He said, "Who told you that you *were*
naked? Have you eaten from the tree of which I
commanded you that you should not eat?"
12 Then the man said, [a]"The woman whom You
gave *to be* with me, she gave me of the tree, and I
ate."
13 And the LORD God said to the woman, "What
*is* this you have done?" The woman said, [a]"The
serpent deceived me, and I ate."
14 So the LORD God said to the serpent:

"Because you have done this,
You *are* cursed more than all cattle,
And more than every beast of the field;
On your belly you shall go,
And [a]you shall eat dust
All the days of your life.
15 And I will put enmity
Between you and the woman,
And between [a]your seed and [b]her Seed;
[c]He shall bruise your head,
And you shall bruise His heel."

16 To the woman He said:

"I will greatly multiply
your sorrow and your conception;
[a]In pain you shall bring forth children;
[b]Your desire *shall be* [1]for your husband,
And he shall [c]rule over you."

17 Then to Adam He said, [a]"Because you have
heeded the voice of your wife, and have eaten
from the tree [b]of which I commanded you, saying,
'You shall not eat of it':

[c]"Cursed *is* the ground for your sake;
[d]In toil you shall eat *of* it
All the days of your life.
18 Both thorns and thistles
it shall [1]bring forth for you,
And [a]you shall eat the herb of the field.
19 [a]In the sweat of your face you shall eat bread
Till you return to the ground,
For out of it you were taken;
[b]For dust you *are,*
And [c]to dust you shall return."

**20** And Adam called his wife's name [a]Eve,[1] because she was the mother of all living.
21 Also for Adam and his wife the LORD God
made tunics of skin, and clothed them.
**22** Then the LORD God said, "Behold, the man has
become like one of Us, to know good and evil.
And now, lest he put out his hand and take also of
the tree of life, and eat, and live forever"—
23 therefore the LORD God sent him out of the

**11** [a]Gen. 25:18
**12** [a]Num. 11:7
**14** [a]Dan. 10:4 [1]Or *Tigris* [2]Heb. *Ashshur*
**15** [1]Or *Adam* [2]*cultivate*
**17** [a]Gen. 3:1, 3, 11, 17 [b]Gen. 3:3, 19 [c]Rom. 5:12 [1]Lit. *dying you shall die*
**18** [a]1 Cor. 11:8, 9
**19** [a]Gen. 1:20, 24 [b]Ps. 8:6 [1]Or *the man*
**21** [a]1 Sam. 26:12
**22** [a]1 Tim. 2:13 [b]Heb. 13:4 [1]Lit. *built*
**23** [a]Gen. 29:14 [b]1 Cor. 11:8, 9 [1]Heb. *Ishshah* [2]Heb. *Ish*
**24** [a]Matt. 19:5 [b]Mark 10:6–8 [1]Lit. *cling*
**25** [a]Gen. 3:7, 10 [b]Is. 47:3

CHAPTER 3
**1** [a]1 Chr. 21:1 [b]2 Cor. 11:3
**2** [a]Gen. 2:16, 17
**3** [a]Ex. 19:12, 13
**4** [a][2 Cor. 11:3]
**6** [a]1 John 2:16 [b]1 Tim. 2:14 [1]Lit. *a desirable thing*
**7** [a]Gen. 2:25 [1]*girding coverings*
**8** [a]Job 38:1 [b]Job 31:33 [1]Or *voice* [2]Or *wind, breeze*
**10** [a]Gen. 2:25
**12** [a][Prov. 28:13]
**13** [a]2 Cor. 11:3
**14** [a]Deut. 28:15–20
**15** [a]John 8:44 [b]Is. 7:14 [c]Rom. 16:20
**16** [a]John 16:21 [b]Gen. 4:7 [c]1 Cor. 11:3 [1]Lit. *toward*
**17** [a]1 Sam. 15:23 [b]Gen. 2:17 [c]Rom. 8:20–22 [d]Eccl. 2:23
**18** [a]Ps. 104:14 [1]*cause to grow*
**19** [a]2 Thess. 3:10 [b]Gen. 2:7; 5:5 [c]Job 21:26
**20** [a]2 Cor. 11:3 [1]Lit. *Life* or *Living*

garden of Eden [a]to till the ground from which he
was taken.
24 So [a]He drove out the man; and He placed
[b]cherubim [c]at the east of the garden of Eden, and
a flaming sword which turned every way, to guard
the way to the tree of [d]life.

### *Cain and Abel*

**4** Now Adam knew Eve his wife, and she conceived and bore [1]Cain, and said, "I have acquired a man from the LORD."
2 Then she bore again, this time his brother
[1]Abel. Now [a]Abel was a keeper of sheep, but Cain
was a tiller of the ground.
3 And [1]in the process of time it came to pass
that Cain brought an offering of the fruit [a]of the
ground to the LORD.
4 Abel also brought of [a]the firstborn of his flock
and of [b]their fat. And the LORD [c]respected Abel
and his offering,
5 but He did not respect Cain and his offering.
And Cain was very angry, and his countenance
fell.
6 So the LORD said to Cain, "Why are you
angry? And why has your countenance fallen?
7 "If you do well, will you not be accepted? And
if you do not do well, sin lies at the door. And its
desire *is* [1]for you, but you should rule over it."
8 Now Cain [1]talked with Abel his [2]brother; and
it came to pass, when they were in the field, that
Cain rose up against Abel his brother and [a]killed
him.
**9** Then the LORD said to Cain, "Where *is* Abel
your brother?" He said, [a]"I do not know. *Am* I [b]my
brother's keeper?"
10 And He said, "What have you done? The voice
of your brother's blood [a]cries out to Me from the
ground.
11 "So now [a]you *are* cursed from the earth,
which has opened its mouth to receive your
brother's blood from your hand.
12 "When you till the ground, it shall no longer
yield its strength to you. A fugitive and a vagabond you shall be on the earth."
13 And Cain said to the LORD, "My [1]punishment
*is* greater than I can bear!
14 "Surely You have driven me out this day from
the face of the ground; [a]I shall be [b]hidden from
Your face; I shall be a fugitive and a vagabond on
the earth, and it will happen *that* [c]anyone who
finds me will kill me."
15 And the LORD said to him, [1]"Therefore, whoever kills Cain, vengeance shall be taken on him
[a]sevenfold." And the LORD set a [b]mark on Cain,
lest anyone finding him should kill him.
**16** Then Cain [a]went out from the [b]presence of the
LORD and dwelt in the land of [1]Nod on the east of
Eden.
17 And Cain knew his wife, and she conceived
and bore Enoch. And he built a city, [a]and called
the name of the city after the name of his son—
Enoch.
18 To Enoch was born Irad; and Irad begot Mehujael, and Mehujael begot Methushael, and Methushael begot Lamech.
**19** Then Lamech took for himself [a]two wives: the
name of one *was* Adah, and the name of the
second *was* Zillah.
20 And Adah bore Jabal. He was the father of
those who dwell in tents and have livestock.
21 His brother's name *was* Jubal. He was the
father of all those who play the harp and [1]flute.
22 And as for Zillah, she also bore Tubal-Cain, an
instructor of every craftsman in bronze and iron.
And the sister of Tubal-Cain *was* Naamah.
23 Then Lamech said to his wives:

"Adah and Zillah, hear my voice;
Wives of Lamech, listen to my speech!
For I have [1]killed a man for wounding me,
Even a young man [2]for hurting me.
24 [a]If Cain shall be avenged sevenfold,
Then Lamech seventy-sevenfold."

**25** And Adam knew his wife again, and she bore a
son and [a]named him [1]Seth, "For God has appointed another seed for me instead of Abel,
whom Cain killed."
26 And as for Seth, [a]to him also a son was born;
and he named him [1]Enosh. Then *men* began [b]to
call on the name of the LORD.

### *The Family of Adam*

**5** This is the book of the [a]genealogy of Adam. In
the day that God created man, He made him in
[b]the likeness of God.
2 He created them [a]male and female, and
[b]blessed them and called them Mankind in the day
they were created.
3 And Adam lived one hundred and thirty years,
and begot *a son* [a]in his own likeness, after his
image, and [b]named him Seth.
4 After he begot Seth, [a]the days of Adam were
eight hundred years; [b]and he had sons and daughters.
5 So all the days that Adam lived were nine
hundred and thirty years; [a]and he died.
**6** Seth lived one hundred and five years, and
begot [a]Enosh.
7 After he begot Enosh, Seth lived eight hundred and seven years, and had sons and daughters.
8 So all the days of Seth were nine hundred and
twelve years; and he died.
**9** Enosh lived ninety years, and begot [1]Cainan.
10 After he begot Cainan, Enosh lived eight
hundred and fifteen years, and had sons and
daughters.
11 So all the days of Enosh were nine hundred
and five years; and he died.
**12** Cainan lived seventy years, and begot Mahalalel.
13 After he begot Mahalalel, Cainan lived eight
hundred and forty years, and had sons and daughters.
14 So all the days of Cainan were nine hundred
and ten years; and he died.
**15** Mahalalel lived sixty-five years, and begot
Jared.
16 After he begot Jared, Mahalalel lived eight
hundred and thirty years, and had sons and
daughters.
17 So all the days of Mahalalel were eight hundred and ninety-five years; and he died.
**18** Jared lived one hundred and sixty-two years,
and begot [a]Enoch.
19 After he begot Enoch, Jared lived eight hundred years, and had sons and daughters.
20 So all the days of Jared were nine hundred and
sixty-two years; and he died.
**21** Enoch lived sixty-five years, and begot Methuselah.
22 After he begot Methuselah, Enoch [a]walked
with God three hundred years, and had sons and
daughters.

---

**23** [a]Gen. 4:2; 9:20
**24** [a]Ezek. 31:3, 11 [b]Ps. 104:4 [c]Gen. 2:8 [d]Gen. 2:9

CHAPTER 4

**1** [1]Lit. *Acquire*
**2** [a]Luke 11:50, 51 [1]Lit. *Breath* or *Nothing*
**3** [a]Num. 18:12 [1]Lit. *at the end of days*
**4** [a]Num. 18:17 [b]Lev. 3:16 [c]Heb. 11:4
**7** [1]Lit. *toward*
**8** [a][1 John 3:12–15] [1]Lit. *said to* [2]Sam., LXX, Syr., Vg. add *"Let us go out to the field."*
**9** [a]John 8:44 [b]1 Cor. 8:11–13
**10** [a]Heb. 12:24
**11** [a]Gen. 3:14
**13** [1]*iniquity*
**14** [a]Ps. 51:11 [b]Is. 1:15 [c]Num. 35:19, 21, 27
**15** [a]Gen. 4:24 [b]Ezek. 9:4, 6 [1]So with MT, Tg.; LXX, Syr., Vg. *Not so;*
**16** [a]2 Kin. 13:23; 24:20 [b]Jon. 1:3 [1]Lit. *Wandering*
**17** [a]Ps. 49:11
**19** [a]Gen. 2:24; 16:3
**21** [1]*pipe*
**23** [1]*slain a man for my wound* [2]*for my hurt*
**24** [a]Gen. 4:15
**25** [a]Gen. 5:3 [1]Lit. *Appointed*
**26** [a]Gen. 5:6 [b]Zeph. 3:9 [1]Gr. *Enos,* Luke 3:38

CHAPTER 5

**1** [a]Gen. 2:4; 6:9 [b]Gen. 1:26; 9:6
**2** [a]Mark 10:6 [b]Gen. 1:28; 9:1
**3** [a]1 Cor. 15:48, 49 [b]Gen. 4:25
**4** [a]Luke 3:36–38 [b]Gen. 1:28; 4:25
**5** [a][Heb. 9:27]
**6** [a]Gen. 4:26
**9** [1]Heb. *Qenan*
**18** [a]Jude 14, 15
**22** [a]Gen. 6:9; 17:1; 24:40; 48:15

23 So all the days of Enoch were three hundred and sixty-five years.
24 And [a]Enoch walked with God; and he *was* not, for God [b]took him.
**25** Methuselah lived one hundred and eighty-seven years, and begot Lamech.
26 After he begot Lamech, Methuselah lived seven hundred and eighty-two years, and had sons and daughters.
27 So all the days of Methuselah were nine hundred and sixty-nine years; and he died.
**28** Lamech lived one hundred and eighty-two years, and had a son.
29 And he called his name [a]Noah,[1] saying, "This *one* will comfort us concerning our work and the toil of our hands, because of the ground [b]which the LORD has cursed."
30 After he begot Noah, Lamech lived five hundred and ninety-five years, and had sons and daughters.
31 So all the days of Lamech were seven hundred and seventy-seven years; and he died.
**32** And Noah was five hundred years old, and Noah begot [a]Shem, Ham, [b]and Japheth.

## *Noah Makes the Ark*

**6** Now it came to pass, [a]when men began to multiply on the face of the earth, and daughters were born to them,
2 that the sons of God saw the daughters of men, that they *were* beautiful; and they [a]took wives for themselves of all whom they chose.
3 And the LORD said, [a]"My Spirit shall not [b]strive[1] with man forever, [c]for he *is* indeed flesh; yet his days shall be one hundred and twenty years."
4 There were [1]giants on the earth in those [a]days, and also afterward, when the sons of God came in to the daughters of men and they bore *children* to them. Those *were* the mighty men who *were* of old, men of renown.
**5** Then [1]the LORD saw that the wickedness of man *was* great in the earth, and *that* every [a]intent[2] of the thoughts of his heart *was* only evil [3]continually.
6 And [a]the LORD was sorry that He had made man on the earth, and [b]He was grieved in His [c]heart.
7 So the LORD said, "I will [a]destroy man whom I have created from the face of the earth, both man and beast, creeping thing and birds of the air, for I am sorry that I have made them."
8 But Noah [a]found grace in the eyes of the LORD.
**9** This is the genealogy of Noah. [a]Noah was a just man, [1]perfect in his generations. Noah [b]walked with God.
10 And Noah begot three sons: [a]Shem, Ham, and Japheth.
**11** The earth also was corrupt [a]before God, and the earth was [b]filled with violence.
12 So God [a]looked upon the earth, and indeed it was corrupt; for [b]all flesh had corrupted their way on the earth.
13 And God said to Noah, [a]"The end of all flesh has come before Me, for the earth is filled with violence through them; [b]and behold, [c]I will destroy them with the earth.
**14** "Make yourself an ark of gopherwood; make [1]rooms in the ark, and cover it inside and outside with pitch.
15 "And this is how you shall make it: The length of the ark *shall be* three hundred [1]cubits, its width fifty cubits, and its height thirty cubits.
16 "You shall make a window for the ark, and you shall finish it to a cubit from above; and set the door of the ark in its side. You shall make it *with* lower, second, and third *decks*.
17 [a]"And behold, I Myself am bringing [b]floodwaters on the earth, to destroy from under heaven all flesh in which *is* the breath of life; everything that *is* on the earth shall [c]die.
18 "But I will establish My [a]covenant with you; and [b]you shall go into the ark—you, your sons, your wife, and your sons' wives with you.
19 "And of every living thing of all flesh you shall bring [a]two of every *sort* into the ark, to keep *them* alive with you; they shall be male and female.
20 "Of the birds after their kind, of animals after their kind, and of every creeping thing of the earth after its kind, two of every *kind* [a]will come to you to keep *them* alive.
21 "And you shall take for yourself of all food that is eaten, and you shall gather *it* to yourself; and it shall be food for you and for them."
**22** [a]Thus Noah did; [b]according to all that [c]God commanded him, so he did.

## *The Flood*

**7** Then the [a]LORD said to Noah, [b]"Come into the ark, you and all your household, because I have seen *that* [c]you *are* righteous before Me in this generation.
2 "You shall take with you seven each of every [a]clean animal, a male and his female; [b]two each of animals that *are* unclean, a male and his female;
3 "also seven each of birds of the air, male and female, to keep [1]the species alive on the face of all the earth.
4 "For after [a]seven more days I will cause it to rain on the earth [b]forty days and forty nights, and I will [1]destroy from the face of the earth all living things that I have made."
5 [a]And Noah did according to all that the LORD commanded him.
6 Noah *was* [a]six hundred years old when the floodwaters were on the earth.
**7** [a]So Noah, with his sons, his wife, and his sons' wives, went into the ark because of the waters of the flood.
8 Of clean animals, of animals that *are* unclean, of birds, and of everything that creeps on the earth,
9 two by two they went into the ark to Noah, male and female, as God had commanded Noah.
10 And it came to pass after seven days that the waters of the flood were on the earth.
11 In the six hundredth year of Noah's life, in the second month, the seventeenth day of the month, on [a]that day all [b]the fountains of the great deep were broken up, and the [c]windows of heaven were opened.
12 [a]And the rain was on the earth forty days and forty nights.
**13** On the very same day Noah and Noah's sons, Shem, Ham, and Japheth, and Noah's wife and the three wives of his sons with them, entered the ark—
14 [a]they and every beast after its kind, all cattle after their kind, every creeping thing that creeps on the earth after its kind, and every bird after its kind, every bird of every [b]sort.

**24** [a]2 Kin. 2:11 [b]Heb. 11:5
**29** [a]Luke 3:36 [b]Gen. 3:17–19; 4:11 [1]Lit. *Rest*
**32** [a]Gen. 6:10; 7:13 [b]Gen. 10:21

CHAPTER 6
**1** [a]Gen. 1:28
**2** [a]Deut. 7:3, 4
**3** [a][Gal. 5:16, 17] [b]2 Thess. 2:7 [c]Ps. 78:39 [1]LXX, Syr., Tg., Vg. *abide*
**4** [a]Num. 13:32, 33 [1]Heb. *nephilim, fallen* or *mighty ones*
**5** [a]Gen. 8:21 [1]So with MT, Tg.; Vg. *God;* LXX *LORD God* [2]*thought* [3]*all the day*
**6** [a]1 Sam. 15:11, 29 [b]Is. 63:10 [c]Mark 3:5
**7** [a]Gen. 7:4, 23
**8** [a]Gen. 19:19
**9** [a]2 Pet. 2:5 [b]Gen. 5:22, 24 [1]*blameless* or *having integrity*
**10** [a]Gen. 5:32; 7:13
**11** [a]Rom. 2:13 [b]Ezek. 8:17
**12** [a]Ps. 14:2; 53:2, 3 [b]Ps. 14:1–3
**13** [a]1 Pet. 4:7 [b]Gen. 6:17 [c]2 Pet. 2:4–10
**14** [1]Lit. *compartments* or *nests*
**15** [1]A cubit is about 18 inches.
**17** [a]2 Pet. 2:5 [b]2 Pet. 3:6 [c]Luke 16:22
**18** [a]Gen. 8:20—9:17; 17:7 [b]Gen. 7:1, 7, 13
**19** [a]Gen. 7:2, 8, 9, 14–16
**20** [a]Gen. 7:9, 15
**22** [a]Gen. 7:5; 12:4, 5 [b]Gen. 7:5, 9, 16 [c][1 John 5:3]

CHAPTER 7
**1** [a]Matt. 11:28 [b]Matt. 24:38 [c]Gen. 6:9
**2** [a]Lev. 11 [b]Lev. 10:10
**3** [1]Lit. *seed*
**4** [a]Gen. 7:10 [b]Gen. 7:12, 17 [1]Lit. *blot out*
**5** [a]Gen. 6:22
**6** [a]Gen. 5:4, 32
**7** [a]Matt. 24:38
**11** [a]Matt. 24:39 [b]Gen. 8:2 [c]Ps. 78:23
**12** [a]Gen. 7:4, 17
**14** [a]Gen. 6:19 [b]Gen. 1:21

15 And they [a]went into the ark to Noah, two by two, of all flesh in which *is* the breath of life.
16 So those that entered, male and female of all flesh, went in [a]as God had commanded him; and the LORD shut him in.
**17** [a]Now the flood was on the earth forty days. The waters increased and lifted up the ark, and it rose high above the earth.
18 The waters prevailed and greatly increased on the earth, [a]and the ark moved about on the surface of the waters.
19 And the waters prevailed exceedingly on the earth, and all the high hills under the whole heaven were covered.
20 The waters prevailed fifteen cubits upward, and the mountains were covered.
21 [a]And all flesh died that moved on [1]the earth: birds and cattle and beasts and every creeping thing that creeps on the earth, and every man.
22 All in [a]whose nostrils *was* the breath [1]of the spirit of life, all that *was* on the dry *land,* died.
23 So He destroyed all living things which were on the face of the ground: both man and cattle, creeping thing and bird of the air. They were destroyed from the earth. Only [a]Noah and those who *were* with him in the ark remained *alive.*
24 [a]And the waters prevailed on the earth one hundred and fifty days.

### *The Flood Waters Recede*

**8** Then God [a]remembered Noah, and every living thing, and all the animals that *were* with him in the ark. [b]And God made a wind to pass over the earth, and the waters subsided.
2 [a]The fountains of the deep and the windows of heaven were also [b]stopped, and [c]the rain from heaven was restrained.
3 And the waters receded continually from the earth. At the end [a]of the hundred and fifty days the waters decreased.
4 Then the ark rested in the seventh month, the seventeenth day of the month, on the mountains of Ararat.
5 And the waters decreased continually until the tenth month. In the tenth *month,* on the first *day* of the month, the tops of the mountains were seen.
**6** So it came to pass, at the end of forty days, that Noah opened [a]the window of the ark which he had made.
7 Then he sent out a raven, which kept going to and fro until the waters had dried up from the earth.
8 He also sent out from himself a dove, to see if the waters had receded from the face of the ground.
9 But the dove found no resting place for the sole of her foot, and she returned into the ark to him, for the waters *were* on the face of the whole earth. So he put out his hand and took her, and drew her into the ark to himself.
10 And he waited yet another seven days, and again he sent the dove out from the ark.
11 Then the dove came to him in the evening, and behold, a freshly plucked olive leaf *was* in her mouth; and Noah knew that the waters had receded from the earth.
12 So he waited yet another seven days and sent out the dove, which did not return again to him anymore.
**13** And it came to pass in the six hundred and first year, in the first *month,* the first *day* of the month, that the waters were dried up from the earth; and Noah removed the covering of the ark and looked, and indeed the surface of the ground was dry.
14 And in the second month, on the twenty-seventh day of the month, the earth was dried.
**15** Then God spoke to Noah, saying,
16 "Go out of the ark, [a]you and your wife, and your sons and your sons' wives with you.
17 "Bring out with you every living thing of all flesh that *is* with you: birds and cattle and every creeping thing that creeps on the earth, so that they may abound on the earth, and [a]be fruitful and multiply on the earth."
18 So Noah went out, and his sons and his wife and his sons' wives with him.
19 Every animal, every creeping thing, every bird, *and* whatever creeps on the earth, according to their families, went out of the ark.
**20** Then Noah built an [a]altar to the LORD, and took of [b]every clean animal and of every clean bird, and offered [c]burnt offerings on the altar.
21 And the LORD smelled [a]a soothing aroma. Then the LORD said in His heart, "I will never again [b]curse the ground for man's sake, although the [c]imagination[1] of man's heart *is* evil from his youth; [d]nor will I again destroy every living thing as I have done.

22 "While the earth [a]remains,
Seedtime and harvest,
Cold and heat,
Winter and summer,
And [b]day and night
Shall not cease."

### *God's Promise to Noah*

**9** So God blessed Noah and his sons, and said to them: [a]"Be fruitful and multiply, and fill the earth.
2 [a]"And the fear of you and the dread of you shall be on every beast of the earth, on every bird of the air, on all that move *on* the earth, and on all the fish of the sea. They are given into your hand.
3 [a]"Every moving thing that lives shall be food for you. I have given you [b]all things, even as the [c]green herbs.
4 [a]"But you shall not eat flesh with its life, *that is,* its blood.
5 "Surely for your lifeblood I will demand *a reckoning;* [a]from the hand of every beast I will require it, and [b]from the hand of man. From the hand of every [c]man's brother I will require the life of man.

6 "Whoever [a]sheds man's blood,
By man his blood shall be shed;
[b]For in the image of God
He made man.
7 And as for you, [a]be fruitful and multiply;
Bring forth abundantly in the earth
And multiply in it."

**8** Then God spoke to Noah and to his sons with him, saying:
9 "And as for Me, [a]behold, I establish [b]My covenant with you and with your [1]descendants after you,
10 [a]"and with every living creature that *is* with you: the birds, the cattle, and every beast of the

**15** [a]Gen. 6:19, 20; 7:9 **16** [a]Gen. 7:2, 3 **17** [a]Gen. 7:4, 12; 8:6 **18** [a]Ps. 104:26 **21** [a]Gen. 6:7, 13, 17; 7:4 [1]*the land* **22** [a]Gen. 2:7 [1]LXX, Vg. omit *of the spirit* **23** [a]Matt. 24:38, 39; Luke 17:26, 27; Heb. 11:7; 1 Pet. 3:20; 2 Pet. 2:5 **24** [a]Gen. 8:3, 4

CHAPTER 8
**1** [a]Gen. 19:29; Ex. 2:24; 1 Sam. 1:19; Ps. 105:42; 106:4 [b]Ex. 14:21; 15:10; Job 12:15; Ps. 29:10; Is. 44:27; Nah. 1:4 **2** [a]Gen. 7:11 [b]Deut. 11:17 [c]Gen. 7:4, 12; Job 38:37 **3** [a]Gen. 7:24 **6** [a]Gen. 6:16 **16** [a]Gen. 7:13 **17** [a]Gen. 1:22, 28; 9:1, 7 **20** [a]Gen. 12:7; Ex. 29:18, 25 [b]Gen. 7:2; Lev. 11 [c]Gen. 22:2; Ex. 10:25 **21** [a]Ex. 29:18, 25; Lev. 1:9; Ezek. 20:41; 2 Cor. 2:15; Eph. 5:2 [b]Gen. 3:17; 6:7, 13, 17; Is. 54:9 [c]Gen. 6:5; 11:6; Job 14:4; Ps. 51:5; Jer. 17:9; Rom. 1:21; 3:23; Eph. 2:1–3 [d]Gen. 9:11, 15 [1]*intent* or *thought* **22** [a]Is. 54:9 [b]Ps. 74:16; Jer. 33:20, 25

CHAPTER 9
**1** [a]Gen. 1:28, 29; 8:17; 9:7, 19; 10:32 **2** [a]Gen. 1:26, 28; Ps. 8:6 **3** [a]Deut. 12:15; 14:3, 9, 11; Acts 10:12, 13 [b]Rom. 14:14, 20; 1 Cor. 10:23, 26; Col. 2:16; [1 Tim. 4:3, 4] [c]Gen. 1:29 **4** [a]Lev. 7:26; 17:10–16; 19:26; Deut. 12:16, 23; 15:23; 1 Sam. 14:33, 34; Acts 15:20, 29 **5** [a]Ex. 21:28 [b]Gen. 4:9, 10; Ps. 9:12 [c]Acts 17:26 **6** [a]Ex. 21:12–14; Lev. 24:17; Num. 35:33; Matt. 26:52 [b]Gen. 1:26, 27 **7** [a]Gen. 9:1, 19 **9** [a]Gen. 6:18 [b]Is. 54:9 [1]Lit. *seed* **10** [a]Ps. 145:9

earth with you, of all that go out of the ark, every
beast of the earth.
11 "Thus [a]I establish My covenant with you:
Never again shall all flesh be cut off by the waters
of the flood; never again shall there be a flood to
destroy the earth."
12 And God said: [a]"This *is* the sign of the covenant which I make between Me and you, and
every living creature that *is* with you, for perpetual generations:
13 "I set [a]My rainbow in the cloud, and it shall be
for the sign of the covenant between Me and the
earth.
14 "It shall be, when I bring a cloud over the
earth, that the rainbow shall be seen in the cloud;
15 "and [a]I will remember My covenant which *is*
between Me and you and every living creature of
all flesh; the waters shall never again become a
flood to destroy all flesh.
16 "The rainbow shall be in the cloud, and I will
look on it to remember [a]the everlasting covenant
between God and every living creature of all flesh
that *is* on the earth."
17 And God said to Noah, "This *is* the sign of the
covenant which I have established between Me
and all flesh that *is* on the earth."
**18** Now the sons of Noah who went out of the
ark were Shem, Ham, and Japheth. [a]And Ham *was*
the father of Canaan.
19 [a]These three *were* the sons of Noah, [b]and from
these the whole earth was populated.
**20** And Noah began *to be* [a]a farmer, and he
planted a vineyard.
21 Then he drank of the wine [a]and was drunk,
and became uncovered in his tent.
22 And Ham, the father of Canaan, saw the
nakedness of his father, and told his two brothers
outside.
23 [a]But Shem and Japheth took a garment, laid *it*
on both their shoulders, and went backward and
covered the nakedness of their father. Their faces
*were* [1]turned away, and they did not see their
father's nakedness.
**24** So Noah awoke from his wine, and knew what
his younger son had done to him.
25 Then he said:

[a]"Cursed *be* Canaan;
A [b]servant of servants
He shall be to his brethren."

26 And he said:

[a]"Blessed *be* the LORD,
The God of Shem,
And may Canaan be his servant.
27 May God [a]enlarge Japheth,
[b]And may he dwell in the tents of Shem;
And may Canaan be his servant."

**28** And Noah lived after the flood three hundred
and fifty years.
29 So all the days of Noah were nine hundred and
fifty years; and he died.

### *Nations That Descended from Noah*

**10** Now this *is* the genealogy of the sons of
Noah: Shem, Ham, and Japheth. [a]And sons
were born to them after the flood.
**2** [a]The sons of Japheth *were* Gomer, Magog,
Madai, Javan, Tubal, Meshech, and Tiras.
3 The sons of Gomer *were* Ashkenaz, [1]Riphath,
and Togarmah.
4 The sons of Javan *were* Elishah, Tarshish,
Kittim, and [1]Dodanim.
5 From these [a]the coastland *peoples* of the
Gentiles were separated into their lands, everyone
according to his language, according to their
families, into their nations.
**6** [a]The sons of Ham *were* Cush, Mizraim, [1]Put,
and Canaan.
7 The sons of Cush *were* Seba, Havilah, Sabtah,
Raamah, and Sabtechah; and the sons of Raamah
*were* Sheba and Dedan.
8 Cush begot [a]Nimrod; he began to be a mighty
one on the earth.
9 He was a mighty [a]hunter [b]before the LORD;
therefore it is said, "Like Nimrod the mighty
hunter before the LORD."
10 [a]And the beginning of his kingdom was [b]Babel,
Erech, Accad, and Calneh, in the land of Shinar.
11 From that land he went [a]to Assyria and built
Nineveh, Rehoboth Ir, Calah,
12 and Resen between Nineveh and Calah (that
*is* the principal city).
13 Mizraim begot Ludim, Anamim, Lehabim,
Naphtuhim,
14 Pathrusim, and Casluhim [a](from whom came
the Philistines and Caphtorim).
**15** Canaan begot Sidon his firstborn, and [a]Heth;
16 [a]the Jebusite, the Amorite, and the Girgashite;
17 the Hivite, the Arkite, and the Sinite;
18 the Arvadite, the Zemarite, and the Hamathite. Afterward the families of the Canaanites were
dispersed.
19 [a]And the border of the Canaanites was from
Sidon as you go toward Gerar, as far as Gaza;
then as you go toward Sodom, Gomorrah, Admah,
and Zeboiim, as far as Lasha.
20 These *were* the sons of Ham, according to
their families, according to their languages, in
their lands *and* in their nations.
**21** And *children* were born also to Shem, the
father of all the children of Eber, [1]the brother of
Japheth the elder.
22 The [a]sons of Shem *were* Elam, Asshur, [b]Ar-
phaxad, Lud, and Aram.
23 The sons of Aram *were* Uz, Hul, Gether, and
[1]Mash.
24 [1]Arphaxad begot [a]Salah, and Salah begot Eber.
25 [a]To Eber were born two sons: the name of one
*was* [1]Peleg, for in his days the earth was divided;
and his brother's name *was* Joktan.
26 Joktan begot Almodad, Sheleph, Hazarmaveth, Jerah,
27 Hadoram, Uzal, Diklah,
28 [1]Obal, Abimael, Sheba,
29 Ophir, Havilah, and Jobab. All these *were* the
sons of Joktan.
30 And their dwelling place was from Mesha as
you go toward Sephar, the mountain of the east.
31 These *were* the sons of Shem, according to
their families, according to their languages, in
their lands, according to their nations.
**32** [a]These *were* the families of the sons of Noah,
according to their generations, in their nations;
[b]and from these the nations were divided on the
earth after the flood.

### *The Tower of Babel*

**11** Now the whole earth had one language and
one [1]speech.
2 And it came to pass, as they journeyed from

11 [a]Is. 54:9
12 [a]Gen. 9:13, 17; 17:11
13 [a]Ezek. 1:28
15 [a]Lev. 26:42, 45
16 [a]Gen. 17:13, 19
18 [a]Gen. 9:25–27; 10:6
19 [a]Gen. 5:32 [b]1 Chr. 1:4
20 [a]Gen. 3:19, 23; 4:2
21 [a]Prov. 20:1
23 [a]Ex. 20:12 [1]Lit. *backwards*
25 [a]Deut. 27:16 [b]Josh. 9:23
26 [a]Gen. 14:20; 24:27
27 [a]Gen. 10:2–5; 39:3 [b]Eph. 2:13, 14; 3:6

CHAPTER 10
1 [a]Gen. 9:1, 7, 19
2 [a]1 Chr. 1:5–7
3 [1]*Diphath,* 1 Chr. 1:6
4 [1]Sam. *Rodanim* and 1 Chr. 1:7
5 [a]Ps. 72:10
6 [a]1 Chr. 1:8–16 [1]Or *Phut*
8 [a]Mic. 5:6
9 [a]Jer. 16:16 [b]Gen. 21:20
10 [a]Mic. 5:6 [b]Gen. 11:9
11 [a]Mic. 5:6
14 [a]1 Chr. 1:12
15 [a]Gen. 23:3
16 [a]Gen. 14:7; 15:19–21
19 [a]Num. 34:2–12
21 [1]Or *the older brother of Japheth*
22 [a]1 Chr. 1:17–28 [b]Luke 3:36
23 [1]LXX *Meshech* and 1 Chr. 1:17
24 [a]Gen. 11:12 [1]So with MT, Vg., Tg.; LXX *Arphaxad begot Cainan, and Cainan begot Salah* (cf. Luke 3:35, 36)
25 [a]1 Chr. 1:19 [1]Lit. *Division*
28 [1]*Ebal,* 1 Chr. 1:22
32 [a]Gen. 10:1 [b]Gen. 9:19; 11:8

CHAPTER 11
1 [1]Lit. *lip*

the east, that they found a plain in the land [a]of
Shinar, and they dwelt there.
3 Then they said to one another, "Come, let us
make bricks and [1]bake *them* thoroughly." They
had brick for stone, and they had asphalt for
mortar.
4 And they said, "Come, let us build ourselves a
city, and a tower [a]whose top *is* in the heavens; let
us make a [b]name for ourselves, lest we [c]be scattered abroad over the face of the whole earth."
5 [a]But the LORD came down to see the city and
the tower which the sons of men had built.
6 And the LORD said, "Indeed [a]the people *are*
one and they all have [b]one language, and this is
what they begin to do; now nothing that they
[c]propose to do will be withheld from them.
7 "Come, [a]let Us go down and there [b]confuse
their language, that they may not understand one
another's speech."
8 So [a]the LORD scattered them abroad from
there [b]over the face of all the earth, and they
ceased building the city.
9 Therefore its name is called [1]Babel, [a]because
there the LORD confused the language of all the
earth; and from there the LORD scattered them
abroad over the face of all the earth.
**10** [a]This *is* the genealogy of Shem: Shem *was* one
hundred years old, and begot Arphaxad two years
after the flood.
11 After he begot Arphaxad, Shem lived five
hundred years, and begot sons and daughters.
**12** Arphaxad lived thirty-five years, [a]and begot
Salah.
13 After he begot Salah, Arphaxad lived four
hundred and three years, and begot sons and
daughters.
**14** Salah lived thirty years, and begot Eber.
15 After he begot Eber, Salah lived four hundred
and three years, and begot sons and daughters.
**16** [a]Eber lived thirty-four years, and begot [b]Peleg.
17 After he begot Peleg, Eber lived four hundred
and thirty years, and begot sons and daughters.
**18** Peleg lived thirty years, and begot Reu.
19 After he begot Reu, Peleg lived two hundred
and nine years, and begot sons and daughters.
**20** Reu lived thirty-two years, and begot [a]Serug.
21 After he begot Serug, Reu lived two hundred
and seven years, and begot sons and daughters.
**22** Serug lived thirty years, and begot Nahor.
23 After he begot Nahor, Serug lived two hundred years, and begot sons and daughters.
**24** Nahor lived twenty-nine years, and begot
[a]Terah.
25 After he begot Terah, Nahor lived one hundred and nineteen years, and begot sons and
daughters.
**26** Now Terah lived seventy years, and [a]begot
[1]Abram, Nahor, and Haran.
**27** This *is* the genealogy of Terah: Terah begot
[a]Abram, Nahor, and Haran. Haran begot Lot.
28 And Haran died before his father Terah in his
native land, in Ur of the Chaldeans.
29 Then Abram and Nahor took wives: the name
of Abram's wife *was* [a]Sarai,[1] and the name of
Nahor's wife, [b]Milcah, the daughter of Haran the
father of Milcah and the father of Iscah.
30 But [a]Sarai was barren; she had no child.
**31** And Terah [a]took his son Abram and his grandson Lot, the son of Haran, and his daughter-in-law
Sarai, his son Abram's wife, and they went out
with them from [b]Ur of the Chaldeans to go to [c]the
land of Canaan; and they came to Haran and
dwelt there.
32 So the days of Terah were two hundred and
five years, and Terah died in Haran.

### *God Speaks to Abram*

# 12

Now the [a]LORD had said to Abram:

"Get [b]out of your country,
From your family
And from your father's house,
To a land that I will show you.
2 [a]I will make you a great nation;
[b]I will bless you
And make your name great;
[c]And you shall be a blessing.
3 [a]I will bless those who bless you,
And I will curse him who curses you;
And in [b]you all the families
of the earth shall be [c]blessed."

**4** So Abram departed as the LORD had spoken to
him, and Lot went with him. And Abram *was*
seventy-five years old when he departed from
Haran.
5 Then Abram took Sarai his wife and Lot his
brother's son, and all their possessions that they
had gathered, and [a]the [1]people whom they had
acquired [b]in Haran, and they [c]departed to go to
the land of Canaan. So they came to the land of
Canaan.
6 Abram [a]passed through the land to the place
of Shechem, [b]as far as [1]the terebinth tree of
Moreh. [c]And the Canaanites *were* then in the
land.
7 [a]Then the LORD appeared to Abram and said,
[b]"To your [1]descendants I will give this land." And
there he built an [c]altar to the LORD, who had
appeared to him.
8 And he moved from there to the mountain
east of Bethel, and he pitched his tent *with* Bethel
on the west and Ai on the east; there he built an
altar to the LORD and [a]called on the name of the
LORD.
9 So Abram journeyed, [a]going on still toward
the [1]South.
**10** Now there was [a]a famine in the land, and
Abram [b]went down to Egypt to dwell there, for
the famine *was* [c]severe in the land.
11 And it came to pass, when he was close to
entering Egypt, that he said to Sarai his wife,
"Indeed I know that you *are* [a]a woman of beautiful countenance.
12 "Therefore it will happen, when the Egyptians
see you, that they will say, 'This *is* his wife'; and
they [a]will kill me, but they will let you live.
13 [a]"Please say you *are* my [b]sister, that it may be
well with me for your sake, and that [1]I may live
because of you."
**14** So it was, when Abram came into Egypt, that
the Egyptians saw the woman, that she *was* very
beautiful.
15 The princes of Pharaoh also saw her and
commended her to Pharaoh. And the woman was
taken to Pharaoh's house.
16 He [a]treated Abram well for her sake. He [b]had
sheep, oxen, male donkeys, male and female
servants, female donkeys, and camels.
17 But the LORD [a]plagued Pharaoh and his house
with great plagues because of Sarai, Abram's wife.
18 And Pharaoh called Abram and said, [a]"What *is*

**2** [a]Gen. 10:10; 14:1
**3** [1]Lit. *burn*
**4** [a]Deut. 1:28; 9:1 [b]Gen. 6:4 [c]Deut. 4:27
**5** [a]Gen. 18:21
**6** [a]Gen. 9:19 [b]Gen. 11:1 [c]Ps. 2:1
**7** [a]Gen. 1:26 [b]Ex. 4:11
**8** [a][Luke 1:51] [b]Gen. 10:25, 32
**9** [a]1 Cor. 14:23 [1]Lit. *Confusion,* Babylon
**10** [a]Gen. 10:22–25
**12** [a]Luke 3:35
**16** [a]1 Chr. 1:19 [b]Luke 3:35
**20** [a]Luke 3:35
**24** [a]Josh. 24:2
**26** [a]1 Chr. 1:26 [1]*Abraham,* Gen. 17:5
**27** [a]Gen. 11:31; 17:5
**29** [a]Gen. 17:15; 20:12 [b]Gen. 22:20, 23; 24:15 [1]*Sarah,* Gen. 17:15
**30** [a]Gen. 16:1, 2
**31** [a]Gen. 12:1 [b]Acts 7:4 [c]Gen. 10:19

CHAPTER 12

**1** [a]Acts 7:2, 3 [b]Gen. 13:9
**2** [a]Deut. 26:5 [b]Gen. 22:17; 24:35 [c]Gen. 28:4
**3** [a]Num. 24:9 [b]Acts 3:25 [c]Is. 41:27
**5** [a]Gen. 14:14 [b]Gen. 11:31 [c]Gen. 13:18 [1]Lit. *souls*
**6** [a]Heb. 11:9 [b]Deut. 11:30 [c]Gen. 10:18, 19 [1]Or *Alon Moreh*
**7** [a]Gen. 17:1; 18:1 [b]Gen. 13:15; 15:18; 17:8 [c]Gen. 13:4, 18; 22:9 [1]Lit. *seed*
**8** [a]Gen. 4:26; 13:4; 21:33
**9** [a]Gen. 13:1, 3; 20:1; 24:62 [1]Heb. *Negev*
**10** [a]Gen. 26:1 [b]Ps. 105:13 [c]Gen. 43:1
**11** [a]Gen. 12:14; 26:7; 29:17
**12** [a]Gen. 20:11; 26:7
**13** [a]Gen. 20:1–18; 26:6–11 [b]Gen. 20:12 [1]Lit. *my soul*
**16** [a]Gen. 20:14 [b]Gen. 13:2
**17** [a]1 Chr. 16:21
**18** [a]Gen. 20:9, 10; 26:10

this you have done to me? Why did you not tell
me that she *was* your wife?
19 "Why did you say, 'She *is* my sister'? I might
have taken her as my wife. Now therefore, here is
your wife; take *her* and go your way."
20 [a]So Pharaoh commanded *his* men concerning
him; and they sent him away, with his wife and all
that he had.

### *Abram Inherits Canaan*

**13** Then Abram went up from Egypt, he and
his wife and all that he had, and [a]Lot with
him, [b]to the [1]South.
2 [a]Abram *was* very rich in livestock, in silver,
and in gold.
3 And he went on his journey [a]from the South
as far as Bethel, to the place where his tent had
been at the beginning, between Bethel and Ai,
4 to the [a]place of the altar which he had made
there at first. And there Abram [b]called on the
name of the LORD.
**5** Lot also, who went with Abram, had flocks
and herds and tents.
6 Now [a]the land was not able to [1]support them,
that they might dwell together, for their possessions were so great that they could not dwell
together.
7 And there was [a]strife between the herdsmen
of Abram's livestock and the herdsmen of Lot's
livestock. [b]The Canaanites and the Perizzites then
dwelt in the land.
8 So Abram said to Lot, [a]"Please let there be no
strife between you and me, and between my
herdsmen and your herdsmen; for we *are* brethren.
9 [a]"*Is* not the whole land before you? Please
[b]separate from me. [c]If *you take* the left, then I will
go to the right; or, if *you go* to the right, then I
will go to the left."
10 And Lot lifted his eyes and saw all [a]the plain of
Jordan, that it *was* well watered everywhere
(before the LORD [b]destroyed Sodom and Gomorrah) [c]like the garden of the LORD, like the land of
Egypt as you go toward [d]Zoar.
11 Then Lot chose for himself all the plain of
Jordan, and Lot journeyed east. And they separated from each other.
12 Abram dwelt in the land of Canaan, and Lot
[a]dwelt in the cities of the plain and [b]pitched *his*
tent even as far as Sodom.
13 But the men of Sodom [a]*were* exceedingly
wicked and [b]sinful against the LORD.
**14** And the LORD said to Abram, after Lot [a]had
separated from him: "Lift your eyes now and look
from the place where you are—[b]northward, southward, eastward, and westward;
15 "for all the land which you see [a]I give to you
and [b]your [1]descendants forever.
16 "And [a]I will make your descendants as the
dust of the earth; so that if a man could number
the dust of the earth, *then* your descendants also
could be numbered.
17 "Arise, walk in the land through its length and
its width, for I give it to you."
18 [a]Then Abram moved *his* tent, and went and
[b]dwelt by [1]the terebinth trees of Mamre, [c]which
*are* in Hebron, and built an [d]altar there to the
LORD.

### *Lot's Capture and Rescue*

**14** And it came to pass in the days of Amraphel
king [a]of Shinar, Arioch king of Ellasar,
Chedorlaomer king of [b]Elam, and Tidal king of
[1]nations,
2 *that* they made war with Bera king of Sodom,
Birsha king of Gomorrah, Shinab king of [a]Admah,
Shemeber king of Zeboiim, and the king of Bela
(that is, [b]Zoar).
3 All these joined together in the Valley of
Siddim [a](that is, the Salt Sea).
4 Twelve years [a]they served Chedorlaomer, and
in the thirteenth year they rebelled.
**5** In the fourteenth year Chedorlaomer and the
kings that *were* with him came and attacked [a]the
Rephaim in Ashteroth Karnaim, [b]the Zuzim in
Ham, [c]the Emim in Shaveh Kiriathaim,
6 [a]and the Horites in their mountain of Seir, as
far as El Paran, which *is* by the wilderness.
7 Then they turned back and came to En Mishpat (that *is,* Kadesh), and attacked all the country
of the Amalekites, and also the Amorites who
dwelt [a]in Hazezon Tamar.
8 And the king of Sodom, the king of Gomorrah,
the king of Admah, the king of Zeboiim, and the
king of Bela (that *is,* Zoar) went out and joined
together in battle in the Valley of Siddim
9 against Chedorlaomer king of Elam, Tidal king
of [1]nations, Amraphel king of Shinar, and Arioch
king of Ellasar—four kings against five.
10 Now the Valley of Siddim *was full of* [a]asphalt
pits; and the kings of Sodom and Gomorrah fled;
*some* fell there, and the remainder fled [b]to the
mountains.
11 Then they took [a]all the goods of Sodom and
Gomorrah, and all their provisions, and went their
way.
12 They also took Lot, Abram's [a]brother's son
[b]who dwelt in Sodom, and his goods, and departed.
**13** Then one who had escaped came and told
Abram the [a]Hebrew, for [b]he dwelt by [1]the terebinth trees of Mamre the Amorite, brother of
Eshcol and brother of Aner; [c]and they *were* allies
with Abram.
14 Now [a]when Abram heard that [b]his brother was
taken captive, he armed his three hundred and
eighteen trained *servants* who were [c]born in his
own house, and went in pursuit [d]as far as Dan.
15 He divided his forces against them by night,
and he and his servants [a]attacked them and
pursued them as far as Hobah, which *is* [1]north of
Damascus.
16 So he [a]brought back all the goods, and also
brought back his brother Lot and his goods, as
well as the women and the people.
**17** And the king of Sodom [a]went out to meet him
at the Valley of Shaveh (that *is,* the [b]King's
Valley), [c]after his return from [1]the defeat of
Chedorlaomer and the kings who *were* with him.
**18** Then [a]Melchizedek king of Salem brought out
[b]bread and wine; he *was* [c]the priest of [d]God Most
High.
19 And he blessed him and said:

[a]"Blessed be Abram of God Most High,
[b]Possessor of heaven and earth;
20 And [a]blessed be God Most High,
Who has delivered your enemies
into your hand."

And he [b]gave him [1]a tithe of all.

---

**12:20** [a][Prov. 21:1]

CHAPTER 13
**1** [a]Gen. 12:4; 14:12, 16 [b]Gen. 12:9 [1]Heb. *Negev*
**2** [a]Gen. 24:35; 26:14
**3** [a]Gen. 12:8, 9
**4** [a]Gen. 12:7, 8; 21:33 [b]Ps. 116:17
**6** [a]Gen. 36:7 [1]Lit. *bear*
**7** [a]Gen. 26:20 [b]Gen. 12:6; 15:20, 21
**8** [a]1 Cor. 6:7
**9** [a]Gen. 20:15; 34:10 [b]Gen. 13:11, 14 [c][Rom. 12:18]
**10** [a]Gen. 19:17–29 [b]Gen. 19:24 [c]Gen. 2:8, 10 [d]Deut. 34:3
**12** [a]Gen. 19:24, 25, 29 [b]Gen. 14:12, 19
**13** [a]Gen. 18:20, 21 [b]Gen. 6:11; 39:9
**14** [a]Gen. 13:11 [b]Gen. 28:14
**15** [a]Acts 7:5 [b]2 Chr. 20:7 [1]Lit. *seed*
**16** [a]Gen. 22:17
**18** [a]Gen. 26:17 [b]Gen. 14:13 [c]Gen. 23:2; 35:27 [d]Gen. 8:20; 22:8, 9 [1]Or *Alon Mamre*

CHAPTER 14
**1** [a]Gen. 10:10; 11:2 [b]Is. 11:11; 21:2 [1]Heb. *goyim*
**2** [a]Deut. 29:23 [b]Gen. 13:10; 19:22
**3** [a]Num. 34:12
**4** [a]Gen. 9:26
**5** [a]Gen. 15:20 [b]Deut. 2:20 [c]Deut. 2:10
**6** [a]Deut. 2:12, 22
**7** [a]2 Chr. 20:2
**9** [1]Heb. *goyim*
**10** [a]Gen. 11:3 [b]Gen. 19:17, 30
**11** [a]Gen. 14:16, 21
**12** [a]Gen. 11:27; 12:5 [b]Gen. 13:12
**13** [a]Gen. 39:14; 40:15 [b]Gen. 13:18 [c]Gen. 14:24; 21:27, 32 [1]Or *Alon Mamre*
**14** [a]Gen. 19:29 [b]Gen. 13:8; 14:12 [c]Gen. 12:5; 15:3; 17:27 [d]Deut. 34:1
**15** [a]Is. 41:2, 3 [1]Lit. *on the left hand of*
**16** [a]Gen. 31:18
**17** [a]1 Sam. 18:6 [b]2 Sam. 18:18 [c]Heb. 7:1 [1]Lit. *striking*
**18** [a]Heb. 7:1–10 [b]Gen. 18:5 [c]Ps. 110:4 [d]Acts 16:17
**19** [a]Ruth 3:10 [b]Gen. 14:22
**20** [a]Gen. 24:27 [b]Heb. 7:4 [1]*one-tenth*

**21** Now the king of Sodom said to Abram, "Give me the [1]persons, and take the goods for yourself."

22 But Abram [a]said to the king of Sodom, "I [b]have raised my hand to the LORD, God Most High, [c]the Possessor of heaven and earth,

23 "that [a]I *will take* nothing, from a thread to a sandal strap, and that I will not take anything that *is* yours, lest you should say, 'I have made Abram rich'—

24 "except only what the young men have eaten, and the portion of the men who went with me: Aner, Eshcol, and Mamre; let them take their portion."

### *God's Promise to Abram*

**15** After these things the word of the LORD came to Abram [a]in a vision, saying, [b]"Do not be afraid, Abram. I *am* your [c]shield, [1]your exceedingly [d]great reward."

2 [a]But Abram said, "Lord GOD, what will You give me, [b]seeing I [1]go childless, and the heir of my house *is* Eliezer of Damascus?"

3 Then Abram said, "Look, You have given me no offspring; indeed [a]one[1] born in my house is my heir!"

4 And behold, the word of the LORD *came* to him, saying, "This one shall not be your heir, but one who [a]will come from your own body shall be your heir."

5 Then He brought him outside and said, "Look now toward heaven, and [a]count the [b]stars if you are able to number them." And He said to him, [c]"So shall your [d]descendants be."

6 And he [a]believed in the LORD, and He [b]accounted it to him for righteousness.

**7** Then He said to him, "I *am* the LORD, who [a]brought you out of [b]Ur of the Chaldeans, [c]to give you this land to inherit it."

8 And he said, "Lord GOD, [a]how shall I know that I will inherit it?"

9 So He said to him, "Bring Me a three-year-old heifer, a three-year-old female goat, a three-year-old ram, a turtledove, and a young pigeon."

10 Then he brought all these to Him and [a]cut them in two, down the middle, and placed each piece opposite the other; but he did not cut [b]the birds in two.

11 And when the vultures came down on the carcasses, Abram drove them away.

**12** Now when the sun was going down, [a]a deep sleep fell upon Abram; and behold, horror *and* great darkness fell upon him.

13 Then He said to Abram: "Know certainly [a]that your descendants will be strangers in a land *that is* not theirs, and will serve them, and [b]they will afflict them four hundred years.

14 "And also the nation whom they serve [a]I will judge; afterward [b]they shall come out with great possessions.

15 "Now as for you, [a]you shall [1]go [b]to your fathers in peace; [c]you shall be buried at a good old age.

16 "But [a]in the fourth generation they shall return here, for the iniquity [b]of the Amorites [c]*is* not yet complete."

**17** And it came to pass, when the sun went down and it was dark, that behold, there appeared a smoking oven and a burning torch that [a]passed between those pieces.

18 On the same day the LORD [a]made a covenant with Abram, saying:

[b]"To your descendants I have given this land, from the river of Egypt to the great river, the River Euphrates—

19 "the Kenites, the Kenezzites, the Kadmonites,

20 "the Hittites, the Perizzites, the Rephaim,

21 "the Amorites, the Canaanites, the Girgashites, and the Jebusites."

### *Hagar and Ishmael*

**16** Now Sarai, Abram's wife, [a]had borne him no *children.* And she had [b]an Egyptian maidservant whose name was [c]Hagar.

2 [a]So Sarai said to Abram, "See now, the LORD [b]has restrained me from bearing *children.* Please, [c]go in to my maid; perhaps I shall [1]obtain children by her." And Abram [d]heeded the voice of Sarai.

3 Then Sarai, Abram's wife, took Hagar her maid, the Egyptian, and gave her to her husband Abram to be his wife, after Abram [a]had dwelt ten years in the land of Canaan.

4 So he went in to Hagar, and she conceived. And when she saw that she had conceived, her mistress became [a]despised in her [1]eyes.

5 Then Sarai said to Abram, [1]"My wrong *be* upon you! I gave my maid into your embrace; and when she saw that she had conceived, I became despised in her eyes. [a]The LORD judge between you and me."

6 [a]So Abram said to Sarai, "Indeed your maid *is* in your hand; do to her as you please." And when Sarai dealt harshly with her, [b]she fled from her presence.

**7** Now the [a]Angel of the LORD found her by a spring of water in the wilderness, [b]by the spring on the way to [c]Shur.

8 And He said, "Hagar, Sarai's maid, where have you come from, and where are you going?" She said, "I am fleeing from the presence of my mistress Sarai."

9 The Angel of the LORD said to her, "Return to your mistress, and [a]submit yourself under her hand."

10 Then the Angel of the LORD said to her, [a]"I will multiply your descendants exceedingly, so that they shall not be counted for multitude."

11 And the Angel of the LORD said to her:

"Behold, you *are* with child,
[a]And you shall bear a son.
You shall call his name [1]Ishmael,
Because the LORD has heard your affliction.

12 [a]He shall be a wild man;
His hand *shall be* against every man,
And every man's hand against him.
[b]And he shall dwell in the presence
of all his brethren."

13 Then she called the name of the LORD who spoke to her, You-Are-[1]the-God-Who-Sees; for she said, "Have I also here [2]seen Him [a]who sees me?"

14 Therefore the well was called [a]Beer Lahai Roi;[1] observe, *it is* [b]between Kadesh and Bered.

**15** So [a]Hagar bore Abram a son; and Abram named his son, whom Hagar bore, Ishmael.

16 Abram *was* eighty-six years old when Hagar bore Ishmael to Abram.

### *The Sign of God's Promise to Abraham*

**17** When Abram was ninety-nine years old, the LORD [a]appeared to Abram and said to him, [b]"I *am* [1]Almighty God; [c]walk before Me and be [d]blameless.

---

**21** [1]Lit. *souls* **22** [a]Gen. 14:2, 8, 10 [b]Dan. 12:7 [c]Gen. 14:19 **23** [a]2 Kin. 5:16

CHAPTER 15

**1** [a]Dan. 10:1 [b]Gen. 21:17; 26:24 [c]Deut. 33:29 [d]Prov. 11:18 [1]Or *your reward shall be very great* **2** [a]Gen. 17:18 [b]Acts 7:5 [1]*am childless* **3** [a]Gen. 14:14 [1]*a servant* **4** [a]2 Sam. 7:12 **5** [a]Ps. 147:4 [b]Jer. 33:22 [c]Ex. 32:13 [d]Gen. 17:19 **6** [a]Rom. 4:3, 9, 22 [b]Ps. 32:2; 106:31 **7** [a]Gen. 12:1 [b]Gen. 11:28, 31 [c]Ps. 105:42, 44 **8** [a]Luke 1:18 **10** [a]Jer. 34:18 [b]Lev. 1:17 **12** [a]Gen. 2:21; 28:11 **13** [a]Ex. 1:11 [b]Ex. 12:40 **14** [a]Ex. 6:6 [b]Ex. 12:36 **15** [a]Job 5:26 [b]Gen. 25:8; 47:30 [c]Gen. 25:8 [1]Die and join your ancestors **16** [a]Ex. 12:41 [b]1 Kin. 21:26 [c]Matt. 23:32 **17** [a]Jer. 34:18, 19 **18** [a]Gen. 24:7 [b]Gen. 12:7; 17:8

CHAPTER 16

**1** [a]Gen. 11:30; 15:2, 3 [b]Gen. 12:16; 21:9 [c]Gal. 4:24 **2** [a]Gen. 30:3 [b]Gen. 20:18 [c]Gen. 30:3, 9 [d]Gen. 3:17 [1]Lit. *be built up from* **3** [a]Gen. 12:4, 5 **4** [a][Prov. 30:21, 23] [1]*sight* **5** [a]Gen. 31:53 [1]*The wrong done to me be* **6** [a]1 Pet. 3:7 [b]Ex. 2:15 **7** [a]Gen. 21:17, 18; 22:11, 15; 31:11 [b]Gen. 20:1; 25:18 [c]Ex. 15:22 **9** [a][Titus 2:9] **10** [a]Gen. 17:20 **11** [a]Luke 1:13, 31 [1]Lit. *God Hears* **12** [a]Gen. 21:20 [b]Gen. 25:18 **13** [a]Gen. 31:42 [1]Heb. *El Roi* [2]Seen the back of **14** [a]Gen. 24:62 [b]Num. 13:26 [1]Lit. *Well of the One Who Lives and Sees Me* **15** [a]Gal. 4:22

CHAPTER 17

**1** [a]Gen. 12:7; 18:1 [b]Gen. 28:3; 35:11 [c]2 Kin. 20:3 [d]Deut. 18:13 [1]Heb. *El Shaddai*

2 “And I will make My [a]covenant between Me
and you, and [b]will multiply you exceedingly.”
3 Then Abram fell on his face, and God talked
with him, saying:
4 “As for Me, behold, My covenant is with you,
and you shall be [a]a father of [1]many nations.
5 “No longer shall [a]your name be called [1]Abram,
but your name shall be [2]Abraham; [b]for I have
made you a father of [3]many nations.
6 “I will make you exceedingly fruitful; and I
will make [a]nations of you, and [b]kings shall come
from you.
7 “And I will [a]establish My covenant between
Me and you and your descendants after you in
their generations, for an everlasting covenant, [b]to
be God to you and [c]your descendants after you.
8 “Also [a]I give to you and your descendants
after you the land [b]in[1] which you are a stranger,
all the land of Canaan, as an everlasting possession; and [c]I will be their God.”
**9** And God said to Abraham: “As for you, [a]you
shall keep My covenant, you and your descendants after you throughout their generations.
10 “This *is* My covenant which you shall keep,
between Me and you and your descendants after
you: [a]Every male child among you shall be circumcised;
11 “and you shall be circumcised in the flesh of
your foreskins, and it shall be [a]a sign of the
covenant between Me and you.
12 “He who is eight days old among you [a]shall be
circumcised, every male child in your generations,
he who is born in your house or bought with
money from any foreigner who is not your descendant.
13 “He who is born in your house and he who is
bought with your money must be circumcised,
and My covenant shall be in your flesh for an
everlasting covenant.
14 “And the uncircumcised male child, who is not
circumcised in the flesh of his foreskin, that
person [a]shall be cut off from his people; he has
broken My covenant.”
**15** Then God said to Abraham, “As for Sarai your
wife, you shall not call her name Sarai, but [1]Sarah
*shall be* her name.
16 “And I will bless her [a]and also give you a son
by her; then I will bless her, and she shall be *a
mother* [b]*of* nations; [c]kings of peoples shall be from
her.”
17 Then Abraham fell on his face [a]and laughed,
and said in his heart, “Shall *a child* be born to a
man who is one hundred years old? And shall
Sarah, who is ninety years old, bear *a child?*”
18 And Abraham [a]said to God, “Oh, that Ishmael
might live before You!”
19 Then God said: “No, [a]Sarah your wife shall
bear you a son, and you shall call his name Isaac;
I will establish My [b]covenant with him for an
everlasting covenant, *and* with his descendants
after him.
20 “And as for Ishmael, I have heard you. Behold,
I have blessed him, and will make him fruitful,
and [a]will multiply him exceedingly. He shall beget
[b]twelve princes, [c]and I will make him a great
nation.
21 “But My [a]covenant I will establish with Isaac,
[b]whom Sarah shall bear to you at this [c]set time
next year.”
22 Then He finished talking with him, and God
went up from Abraham.
**23** So Abraham took Ishmael his son, all who
were born in his house and all who were bought
with his money, every male among the men of
Abraham’s house, and circumcised the flesh of
their foreskins that very same day, as God had
said to him.
24 Abraham *was* ninety-nine years old when he
was circumcised in the flesh of his foreskin.
25 And Ishmael his son *was* thirteen years old
when he was circumcised in the flesh of his
foreskin.
26 That very same day Abraham was circumcised, and his son Ishmael;
27 and [a]all the men of his house, born in the
house or bought with money from a foreigner,
were circumcised with him.

### *A Son Is Promised*

**18** Then the LORD appeared to him by [1]the
[a]terebinth trees of Mamre, as he was sitting
in the tent door in the heat of the day.
2 [a]So he lifted his eyes and looked, and behold,
three men were standing by him; [b]and when he
saw *them,* he ran from the tent door to meet
them, and bowed himself to the ground,
3 and said, “My Lord, if I have now found favor
in Your sight, do not pass on by Your servant.
4 “Please let [a]a little water be brought, and wash
your feet, and rest yourselves under the tree.
5 “And [a]I will bring a morsel of bread, that [b]you
may refresh your hearts. After that you may pass
by, [c]inasmuch as you have come to your servant.”
They said, “Do as you have said.”
6 So Abraham hurried into the tent to Sarah
and said, “Quickly, make ready three measures of
fine meal; knead *it* and make cakes.”
7 And Abraham ran to the herd, took a tender
and good calf, gave *it* to a young man, and he
hastened to prepare it.
8 So [a]he took butter and milk and the calf which
he had prepared, and set *it* before them; and he
stood by them under the tree as they ate.
**9** Then they said to him, “Where *is* Sarah your
wife?” So he said, “Here, [a]in the tent.”
10 And He said, “I will certainly return to you
[a]according to the time of life, and behold, [b]Sarah
your wife shall have a son.” (Sarah was listening
in the tent door which *was* behind him.)
11 Now [a]Abraham and Sarah were old, well advanced in age; *and* [1]Sarah [b]had passed the age of
childbearing.
12 Therefore Sarah [a]laughed within herself, saying, [b]“After I have grown old, shall I have pleasure, my [c]lord being old also?”
13 And the LORD said to Abraham, “Why did
Sarah laugh, saying, ‘Shall I surely bear *a child,*
since I am old?’
14 [a]“Is anything too hard for the LORD? [b]At the
appointed time I will return to you, according to
the time of life, and Sarah shall have a son.”
15 But Sarah denied *it,* saying, “I did not laugh,”
for she was afraid. And He said, “No, but you did
laugh!”
**16** Then the men rose from there and looked
toward Sodom, and Abraham went with them [a]to
send them on the way.
17 And the LORD said, [a]“Shall I hide from Abraham what I am doing,
18 “since Abraham shall surely become a great
and mighty nation, and all the nations of the earth
shall be [a]blessed in him?
19 “For I have known him, in order [a]that he may

**2** [a]Gen. 15:18 [b]Gen. 12:2; 13:16; 15:5; 18:18
**4** [a][Rom. 4:11, 12, 16] [1]Lit. *multitude of nations*
**5** [a]Neh. 9:7 [b]Rom. 4:17 [1]Lit. *Exalted Father* [2]Lit. *Father of a Multitude* [3]*multitude of*
**6** [a]Gen. 17:16; 35:11 [b]Matt. 1:6
**7** [a][Gal. 3:17] [b]Gen. 26:24; 28:13 [c]Rom. 9:8
**8** [a]Acts 7:5 [b]Gen. 23:4; 28:4 [c]Lev. 26:12 [1]Lit. *of your sojournings*
**9** [a]Ex. 19:5
**10** [a]Acts 7:8
**11** [a]Ex. 12:13, 48
**12** [a]Lev. 12:3
**14** [a]Ex. 4:24–26
**15** [1]Lit. *Princess*
**16** [a]Gen. 18:10 [b]Gen. 35:11 [c]Gen. 17:6; 36:31
**17** [a]Gen. 17:3; 18:12; 21:6
**18** [a]Gen. 18:23
**19** [a]Gen. 18:10; 21:2 [b]Gen. 22:16
**20** [a]Gen. 16:10 [b]Gen. 25:12–16 [c]Gen. 21:13, 18
**21** [a]Gen. 26:2–5 [b]Gen. 21:2 [c]Gen. 18:14
**27** [a]Gen. 18:19

CHAPTER 18
**1** [a]Gen. 13:18; 14:13 [1]Or *Alon Mamre*
**2** [a]Heb. 13:2 [b]Gen. 19:1
**4** [a]Gen. 19:2; 24:32; 43:24
**5** [a]Judg. 6:18, 19; 13:15, 16 [b]Judg. 19:5 [c]Gen. 19:8; 33:10
**8** [a]Gen. 19:3
**9** [a]Gen. 24:67
**10** [a]2 Kin. 4:16 [b]Rom. 9:9
**11** [a]Gen. 17:17 [b]Gen. 31:35 [1]Lit. *the manner of women had ceased to be with Sarah*
**12** [a]Gen. 17:17 [b]Luke 1:18 [c]1 Pet. 3:6
**14** [a]Jer. 32:17 [b]Gen. 17:21; 18:10
**16** [a]Rom. 15:24
**17** [a]Ps. 25:14
**18** [a][Acts 3:25, 26]
**19** [a][Deut. 4:9, 10; 6:6, 7]

command his children and his household after
him, that they keep the way of the LORD, to do
righteousness and justice, that the LORD may
bring to Abraham what He has spoken to him."
20 And the LORD said, "Because [a]the outcry
against Sodom and Gomorrah is great, and because their [b]sin is very grave,
21 [a]"I will go down now and see whether they
have done altogether according to the outcry
against it that has come to Me; and if not, [b]I will
know."
**22** Then the men turned away from there [a]and
went toward Sodom, but Abraham still stood
before the LORD.
23 And Abraham [a]came near and said, [b]"Would
You also [c]destroy the [d]righteous with the wicked?
24 "Suppose there were fifty righteous within the
city; would You also destroy the place and not
spare *it* for the fifty righteous that were in it?
25 "Far be it from You to do such a thing as this,
to slay the righteous with the wicked, so [a]that the
righteous should be as the wicked; far be it from
You! [b]Shall not the Judge of all the earth do
right?"
26 So the LORD said, [a]"If I find in Sodom fifty
righteous within the city, then I will spare all the
place for their sakes."
27 Then Abraham answered and said, "Indeed
now, I who *am* [a]*but* dust and ashes have taken it
upon myself to speak to the Lord:
28 "Suppose there were five less than the fifty
righteous; would You destroy all of the city for
*lack of* five?" So He said, "If I find there forty-five,
I will not destroy *it*."
29 And he spoke to Him yet again and said,
"Suppose there should be forty found there?" So
He said, "I will not do *it* for the sake of forty."
30 Then he said, "Let not the Lord be angry, and
I will speak: Suppose thirty should be found
there?" So He said, "I will not do *it* if I find thirty
there."
31 And he said, "Indeed now, I have taken it
upon myself to speak to the Lord: Suppose twenty
should be found there?" So He said, "I will not
destroy *it* for the sake of twenty."
32 Then he said, [a]"Let not the Lord be angry, and
I will speak but once more: Suppose ten should be
found there?" [b]And He said, "I will not destroy *it*
for the sake of ten."
33 So the LORD went His way as soon as He had
finished speaking with Abraham; and Abraham
returned to his place.

## *Two Evil Cities Destroyed*

**19** Now [a]the two angels came to Sodom in the
evening, and [b]Lot was sitting in the gate of
Sodom. When Lot saw *them,* he rose to meet
them, and he bowed himself with his face toward
the ground.
2 And he said, "Here now, my lords, please [a]turn
in to your servant's house and spend the night,
and [b]wash your feet; then you may rise early and
go on your way." And they said, [c]"No, but we will
spend the night in the open square."
3 But he insisted strongly; so they turned in to
him and entered his house. [a]Then he made them a
feast, and baked [b]unleavened bread, and they ate.
**4** Now before they lay down, the men of the
city, the men of Sodom, both old and young, all
the people from every quarter, surrounded the
house.
5 [a]And they called to Lot and said to him,
"Where are the men who came to you tonight?
[b]Bring them out to us that we [c]may know them
*carnally.*"
6 So [a]Lot went out to them through the doorway, shut the door behind him,
7 and said, "Please, my brethren, do not do so
wickedly!
8 [a]"See now, I have two daughters who have
not known a man; please, let me bring them out to
you, and you may do to them as you wish; only do
nothing to these men, [b]since this is the reason
they have come under the shadow of my roof."
9 And they said, "Stand back!" Then they said,
"This one [a]came in to [1]stay *here,* [b]and he keeps
acting as a judge; now we will deal worse with
you than with them." So they pressed hard
against the man Lot, and came near to break
down the door.
10 But the men reached out their hands and
pulled Lot into the house with them, and shut the
door.
11 And they [a]struck the men who *were* at the
doorway of the house with blindness, both small
and great, so that they became weary *trying* to
find the door.
**12** Then the men said to Lot, "Have you anyone
else here? Son-in-law, your sons, your daughters,
and whomever you have in the city—[a]take *them*
out of this place!
13 "For we will destroy this place, because the
[a]outcry against them has grown great before the
face of the LORD, and [b]the LORD has sent us to
destroy it."
14 So Lot went out and spoke to his sons-in-law,
[a]who had married his daughters, and said, [b]"Get
up, get out of this place; for the LORD will destroy
this city!" [c]But to his sons-in-law he seemed to be
joking.
**15** When the morning dawned, the angels urged
Lot to hurry, saying, [a]"Arise, take your wife and
your two daughters who are here, lest you be
consumed in the punishment of the city."
16 And while he lingered, the men [a]took hold of
his hand, his wife's hand, and the hands of his two
daughters, the [b]LORD being merciful to him, [c]and
they brought him out and set him outside the city.
17 So it came to pass, when they had brought
them outside, that [1]he said, [a]"Escape for your life!
[b]Do not look behind you nor stay anywhere in the
plain. Escape [c]to the mountains, lest you be [2]de-
stroyed."
18 Then Lot said to them, "Please, [a]no, my lords!
19 "Indeed now, your servant has found favor in
your sight, and you have increased your mercy
which you have shown me by saving my life; but I
cannot escape to the mountains, lest some evil
overtake me and I die.
20 "See now, this city *is* near *enough* to flee to,
and it *is* a little one; please let me escape there (*is*
it not a little one?) and my soul shall live."
21 And he said to him, "See, [a]I have favored you
concerning this thing also, in that I will not
overthrow this city for which you have spoken.
22 "Hurry, escape there. For [a]I cannot do anything until you arrive there." Therefore [b]the name
of the city was called [1]Zoar.
**23** The sun had risen upon the earth when Lot
entered Zoar.
24 Then the LORD rained [a]brimstone and [b]fire on
Sodom and Gomorrah, from the LORD out of the
heavens.

**20** [a]Gen. 4:10; 19:13 [b]Gen. 13:13
**21** [a]Gen. 11:5 [b]Deut. 8:2; 13:3
**22** [a]Gen. 18:16; 19:1
**23** [a][Heb. 10:22] [b]Num. 16:22 [c]Job 9:22 [d]Gen. 20:4
**25** [a]Is. 3:10, 11 [b]Deut. 1:16, 17; 32:4
**26** [a]Jer. 5:1
**27** [a][Gen. 3:19]
**32** [a]Judg. 6:39 [b]James 5:16

CHAPTER 19

**1** [a]Gen. 18:2, 16, 22 [b]Gen. 18:1–5
**2** [a][Heb. 13:2] [b]Gen. 18:4; 24:32 [c]Luke 24:28
**3** [a]Gen. 18:6–8 [b]Ex. 12:8
**5** [a]Is. 3:9 [b]Judg. 19:22 [c]Gen. 4:1
**6** [a]Judg. 19:23
**8** [a]Judg. 19:24 [b]Gen. 18:5
**9** [a]2 Pet. 2:7, 8 [b]Ex. 2:14 [1]As a resident alien
**11** [a]Gen. 20:17
**12** [a]2 Pet. 2:7, 9
**13** [a]Gen. 18:20 [b]1 Chr. 21:15
**14** [a]Matt. 1:18 [b]Num. 16:21, 24, 26, 45 [c]Ex. 9:21
**15** [a]Rev. 18:4
**16** [a]2 Pet. 2:7 [b]Luke 18:13 [c]Ps. 34:22
**17** [a]Jer. 48:6 [b]Matt. 24:16–18 [c]Gen. 14:10 [1]LXX, Syr., Vg. *they* [2]Lit. *swept away*
**18** [a]Acts 10:14
**21** [a]Job 42:8, 9
**22** [a]Ex. 32:10 [b]Gen. 13:10; 14:2 [1]Lit. *Little* or *Insignificant*
**24** [a]Deut. 29:23 [b]Lev. 10:2

25 So He [1]overthrew those cities, all the plain, all the inhabitants of the cities, and [a]what grew on the ground.

26 But his wife looked back behind him, and she became [a]a pillar of salt.

**27** And Abraham went early in the morning to the place where [a]he had stood before the LORD.

28 Then he looked toward Sodom and Gomorrah, and toward all the land of the plain; and he saw, and behold, [a]the smoke of the land which went up like the smoke of a furnace.

**29** And it came to pass, when God destroyed the cities of the plain, that God [a]remembered Abraham, and sent Lot out of the midst of the overthrow, when He overthrew the cities in which Lot had dwelt.

**30** Then Lot went up out of Zoar and [a]dwelt in the mountains, and his two daughters were with him; for he was afraid to dwell in Zoar. And he and his two daughters dwelt in a cave.

31 Now the firstborn said to the younger, "Our father *is* old, and *there is* no man on the earth [a]to come in to us as is the custom of all the earth.

32 "Come, let us make our father drink wine, and we will lie with him, that we [a]may preserve the [1]lineage of our father."

33 So they made their father drink wine that night. And the firstborn went in and lay with her father, and he did not know when she lay down or when she arose.

34 It happened on the next day that the firstborn said to the younger, "Indeed I lay with my father last night; let us make him drink wine tonight also, and you go in *and* lie with him, that we may preserve the [1]lineage of our father."

35 Then they made their father drink wine that night also. And the younger arose and lay with him, and he did not know when she lay down or when she arose.

**36** Thus both the daughters of Lot were with child by their father.

37 The firstborn bore a son and called his name Moab; [a]he *is* the father of the Moabites to this day.

38 And the younger, she also bore a son and called his name Ben-Ammi; [a]he *is* the father of the people of Ammon to this day.

### *Abraham and Abimelech*

**20** And Abraham journeyed from [a]there to the South, and dwelt between [b]Kadesh and Shur, and [c]stayed in Gerar.

2 Now Abraham said of Sarah his wife, [a]"She *is* my sister." And Abimelech king of Gerar sent and [b]took Sarah.

3 But [a]God came to Abimelech [b]in a dream by night, and said to him, [c]"Indeed you *are* a dead man because of the woman whom you have taken, for she *is* [1]a man's wife."

4 But Abimelech had not come near her; and he said, "Lord, [a]will You slay a righteous nation also?

5 "Did he not say to me, 'She *is* my sister'? And she, even she herself said, 'He *is* my brother.' [a]In the [1]integrity of my heart and innocence of my hands I have done this."

6 And God said to him in a dream, "Yes, I know that you did this in the integrity of your heart. For [a]I also withheld you from sinning [b]against Me; therefore I did not let you touch her.

7 "Now therefore, restore the man's wife; [a]for he *is* a prophet, and he will pray for you and you shall live. But if you do not restore *her*, [b]know that you shall surely die, you [c]and all who *are* yours."

8 So Abimelech rose early in the morning, called all his servants, and told all these things in their hearing; and the men were very much afraid.

9 And Abimelech called Abraham and said to him, "What have you done to us? How have I [1]offended you, [a]that you have brought on me and on my kingdom a great sin? You have done deeds to me [b]that ought not to be done."

10 Then Abimelech said to Abraham, "What did you have in view, that you have done this thing?"

11 And Abraham said, "Because I thought, surely [a]the fear of God *is* not in this place; and [b]they will kill me on account of my wife.

12 "But indeed [a]*she is* truly my sister. She *is* the daughter of my father, but not the daughter of my mother; and she became my wife.

13 "And it came to pass, when [a]God caused me to wander from my father's house, that I said to her, 'This *is* your kindness that you should do for me: in every place, wherever we go, [b]say of me, "He *is* my brother." ' "

**14** Then Abimelech [a]took sheep, oxen, and male and female servants, and gave *them* to Abraham; and he restored Sarah his wife to him.

15 And Abimelech said, "See, [a]my land *is* before you; dwell where it pleases you."

16 Then to Sarah he said, "Behold, I have given your brother a thousand *pieces* of silver; [a]indeed this [1]vindicates you [b]before all who *are* with you and before everybody." Thus she was [2]rebuked.

**17** So Abraham [a]prayed to God; and God [b]healed Abimelech, his wife, and his female servants. Then they bore *children;*

18 for the LORD [a]had closed up all the wombs of the house of Abimelech because of Sarah, Abraham's wife.

### *Isaac Is Born*

**21** And the LORD [a]visited Sarah as He had said, and the LORD did for Sarah [b]as He had spoken.

2 For Sarah [a]conceived and bore Abraham a son in his old age, [b]at the set time of which God had spoken to him.

3 And Abraham called the name of his son who was born to him—whom Sarah bore to him—[a]Isaac.[1]

4 Then Abraham [a]circumcised his son Isaac when he was eight days old, [b]as God had commanded him.

5 Now [a]Abraham was one hundred years old when his son Isaac was born to him.

6 And Sarah said, [a]"God has [1]made me laugh, *and* all who hear [b]will laugh with me."

7 She also said, "Who would have said to Abraham that Sarah would nurse children? [a]For I have borne *him* a son in his old age."

**8** So the child grew and was weaned. And Abraham made a great feast on the same day that Isaac was weaned.

9 And Sarah saw the son of Hagar [a]the Egyptian, whom she had borne to Abraham, [b]scoffing.[1]

10 Therefore she said to Abraham, [a]"Cast out this bondwoman and her son; for the son of this bondwoman shall not be heir with my son, *namely* with Isaac."

11 And the matter was very [1]displeasing in Abraham's sight [a]because of his son.

12 But God said to Abraham, "Do not let it be

---

**25** [a]Ps. 107:34 [1]*devastated* **26** [a]Luke 17:32 **27** [a]Gen. 18:22 **28** [a]Rev. 9:2; 18:9 **29** [a]Gen. 8:1; 18:23 **30** [a]Gen. 19:17, 19 **31** [a]Gen. 16:2, 4; 38:8, 9 **32** [a][Mark 12:19] [1]Lit. *seed* **34** [1]Lit. *seed* **37** [a]Deut. 2:9 **38** [a]Deut. 2:19

CHAPTER 20

**1** [a]Gen. 18:1 [b]Gen. 12:9; 16:7, 14 [c]Gen. 26:1, 6 **2** [a]Gen. 12:11–13; 26:7 [b]Gen. 12:15 **3** [a]Ps. 105:14 [b]Job 33:15 [c]Gen. 20:7 [1]Lit. *married to a husband* **4** [a]Gen. 18:23–25 **5** [a]2 Kin. 20:3 [1]*innocence* **6** [a]1 Sam. 25:26, 34 [b]Gen. 39:9 **7** [a]1 Sam. 7:5 [b]Gen. 2:17 [c]Num. 16:32, 33 **9** [a]Gen. 26:10; 39:9 [b]Gen. 34:7 [1]*sinned against* **11** [a]Prov. 16:6 [b]Gen. 12:12; 26:7 **12** [a]Gen. 11:29 **13** [a]Gen. 12:1–9, 11 [b]Gen. 12:13; 20:5 **14** [a]Gen. 12:16 **15** [a]Gen. 13:9; 34:10; 47:6 **16** [a]Gen. 26:11 [b]Gen. 24:65 [1]Lit. *is a covering of the eyes for you to all* [2]Or *justified* **17** [a]Job 42:9 [b]Gen. 21:2 **18** [a]Gen. 12:17

CHAPTER 21

**1** [a]1 Sam. 2:21 [b][Gal. 4:23, 28] **2** [a]Heb. 11:11, 12 [b]Gen. 17:21; 18:10, 14 **3** [a]Gen. 17:19, 21 [1]Lit. *Laughter* **4** [a]Acts 7:8 [b]Gen. 17:10, 12 **5** [a]Gen. 17:1, 17 **6** [a]Is. 54:1 [b]Luke 1:58 [1]Lit. *made laughter for me* **7** [a]Gen. 18:11, 12 **9** [a]Gen. 16:1, 4, 15 [b][Gal. 4:29] [1]Lit. *laughing* **10** [a]Gal. 3:18; 4:30 **11** [a]Gen. 17:18 [1]*distressing*

displeasing in your sight because of the lad or
because of your bondwoman. Whatever Sarah has
said to you, listen to her voice; for [a]in Isaac your
seed shall be called.
13 "Yet I will also make [a]a nation of the son of
the bondwoman, because he *is* your [1]seed."
14 So Abraham rose early in the morning, and
took bread and [1]a skin of water; and putting *it* on
her shoulder, he gave *it* and the boy to Hagar, and
[a]sent her away. Then she departed and wandered
in the Wilderness of Beersheba.
**15** And the water in the skin was used up, and
she placed the boy under one of the shrubs.
16 Then she went and sat down across from *him*
at a distance of about a bowshot; for she said to
herself, "Let me not see the death of the boy." So
she sat opposite *him,* and lifted her voice and
wept.
17 And [a]God heard the voice of the lad. Then the
[b]angel of God called to Hagar out of heaven, and
said to her, "What ails you, Hagar? Fear not, for
God has heard the voice of the lad where he *is.*
18 "Arise, lift up the lad and hold him with your
hand, for [a]I will make him a great nation."
19 Then [a]God opened her eyes, and she saw a
well of water. And she went and filled the skin
with water, and gave the lad a drink.
20 So God [a]was with the lad; and he grew and
dwelt in the wilderness, [b]and became an archer.
21 He dwelt in the Wilderness of Paran; and his
mother [a]took a wife for him from the land of
Egypt.
**22** And it came to pass at that time that [a]Abim-
elech and Phichol, the commander of his army,
spoke to Abraham, saying, [b]"God *is* with you in all
that you do.
23 "Now therefore, [a]swear[1] to me by God that
you will not deal falsely with me, with my offspring, or with my posterity; but that according to
the kindness that I have done to you, you will do
to me and to the land in which you have dwelt."
24 And Abraham said, "I will swear."
**25** Then Abraham rebuked Abimelech because of
a well of water which Abimelech's servants [a]had
seized.
26 And Abimelech said, "I do not know who has
done this thing; you did not tell me, nor had I
heard *of it* until today."
27 So Abraham took sheep and oxen and gave
them to Abimelech, and the two of them [a]made a
[1]covenant.
28 And Abraham set seven ewe lambs of the
flock by themselves.
29 Then Abimelech asked Abraham, [a]"What *is
the meaning of* these seven ewe lambs which you
have set by themselves?"
30 And he said, "You will take *these* seven ewe
lambs from my hand, that [a]they may be my
witness that I have dug this well."
31 Therefore he [a]called that place [1]Beersheba,
because the two of them swore an oath there.
32 Thus they made a covenant at Beersheba. So
Abimelech rose with Phichol, the commander of
his army, and they returned to the land of the
Philistines.
33 Then *Abraham* planted a tamarisk tree in
Beersheba, and [a]there called on the name of the
LORD, [b]the Everlasting God.
34 And Abraham stayed in the land of the Philistines many days.

12 [a][Rom. 9:7, 8]
13 [a]Gen. 16:10; 17:20; 21:18; 25:12–18 [1]*descendant*
14 [a]John 8:35 [1]A water bottle made of skins
17 [a]Ex. 3:7 [b]Gen. 22:11
18 [a]Gen. 16:10; 21:13; 25:12–16
19 [a]Num. 22:31
20 [a]Gen. 28:15; 39:2, 3, 21 [b]Gen. 16:12
21 [a]Gen. 24:4
22 [a]Gen. 20:2, 14; 26:26 [b]Gen. 26:28
23 [a]Josh. 2:12 [1]*take an oath*
25 [a]Gen. 26:15, 18, 20–22
27 [a]Gen. 26:31; 31:44 [1]*treaty*
29 [a]Gen. 33:8
30 [a]Gen. 31:48, 52
31 [a]Gen. 21:14; 26:33 [1]Lit. *Well of the Oath* or *Well of the Seven*
33 [a]Gen. 4:26; 12:8; 13:4; 26:25 [b]Deut. 32:40; 33:27

CHAPTER 22
1 [a]Heb. 11:17
2 [a]Gen. 22:12, 16 [b]John 5:20 [c]2 Chr. 3:1 [d]Gen. 8:20; 31:54
5 [a][Heb. 11:19] [1]Or *young man*
6 [a]John 19:17
7 [1]Or *goat*
8 [a]John 1:29, 36 [b]Ex. 12:3–6
9 [a][Heb. 11:17–19]
11 [a]Gen. 16:7–11; 21:17, 18; 31:11
12 [a]1 Sam. 15:22 [b]James 2:21, 22 [c]Gen. 22:2, 16
14 [1]Heb. *YHWH Yireh*
16 [a]Ps. 105:9
17 [a]Gen. 17:16; 26:3, 24 [b]Gen. 15:5; 26:4 [c]Gen. 13:16; 32:12 [d]Gen. 24:60
18 [a]Gen. 12:3; 18:18; 26:4 [b]Gen. 18:19; 22:3, 10; 26:5
19 [a]Gen. 21:31
20 [a]Gen. 11:29; 24:15
21 [a]Job 1:1 [b]Job 32:2

## *Abraham Commanded to Offer Isaac*

**22** Now it came to pass after these things that
[a]God tested Abraham, and said to him,
"Abraham!" And he said, "Here I am."
2 Then He said, "Take now your son, [a]your only
*son* Isaac, whom you [b]love, and go [c]to the land of
Moriah, and offer him there as a [d]burnt offering on
one of the mountains of which I shall tell you."
**3** So Abraham rose early in the morning and
saddled his donkey, and took two of his young
men with him, and Isaac his son; and he split the
wood for the burnt offering, and arose and went
to the place of which God had told him.
4 Then on the third day Abraham lifted his eyes
and saw the place afar off.
5 And Abraham said to his young men, "Stay
here with the donkey; the [1]lad and I will go
yonder and worship, and we will [a]come back to
you."
6 So Abraham took the wood of the burnt offering and [a]laid *it* on Isaac his son; and he took the
fire in his hand, and a knife, and the two of them
went together.
7 But Isaac spoke to Abraham his father and
said, "My father!" And he said, "Here I am, my
son." Then he said, "Look, the fire and the wood,
but where *is* the [1]lamb for a burnt offering?"
8 And Abraham said, "My son, God will provide
for Himself the [a]lamb for a [b]burnt offering." So the
two of them went together.
**9** Then they came to the place of which God had
told him. And Abraham built an altar there and
placed the wood in order; and he bound Isaac his
son and [a]laid him on the altar, upon the wood.
10 And Abraham stretched out his hand and took
the knife to slay his son.
11 But the [a]Angel of the LORD called to him from
heaven and said, "Abraham, Abraham!" So he
said, "Here I am."
12 And He said, [a]"Do not lay your hand on the
lad, or do anything to him; for [b]now I know that
you fear God, since you have not [c]withheld your
son, your only *son,* from Me."
13 Then Abraham lifted his eyes and looked, and
there behind *him was* a ram caught in a thicket by
its horns. So Abraham went and took the ram,
and offered it up for a burnt offering instead of his
son.
14 And Abraham called the name of the place,
[1]The-LORD-Will-Provide; as it is said *to* this day,
"In the Mount of the LORD it shall be provided."
**15** Then the Angel of the LORD called to Abraham
a second time out of heaven,
16 and said: [a]"By Myself I have sworn, says the
LORD, because you have done this thing, and have
not withheld your son, your only *son*—
17 "blessing I will [a]bless you, and multiplying I
will multiply your descendants [b]as the stars of the
heaven [c]and as the sand which *is* on the seashore;
and [d]your descendants shall possess the gate of
their enemies.
18 [a]"In your seed all the nations of the earth shall
be blessed, [b]because you have obeyed My voice."
19 So Abraham returned to his young men, and
they rose and went together to [a]Beersheba; and
Abraham dwelt at Beersheba.
**20** Now it came to pass after these things that it
was told Abraham, saying, "Indeed [a]Milcah also
has borne children to your brother Nahor:
21 [a]"Huz his firstborn, Buz his brother, Kemuel
the father [b]of Aram,

22 "Chesed, Hazo, Pildash, Jidlaph, and Bethuel."
23 And [a]Bethuel begot [1]Rebekah. These eight
Milcah bore to Nahor, Abraham's brother.
24 His concubine, whose name was Reumah, also
bore Tebah, Gaham, Thahash, and Maachah.

### *Death and Burial of Sarah*

**23** Sarah lived one hundred and twenty-seven
years; *these were* the years of the life of
Sarah.
2 So Sarah died in [a]Kirjath Arba (that *is,* [b]He-
bron) in the land of Canaan, and Abraham came
to mourn for Sarah and to weep for her.
3 Then Abraham stood up from before his dead,
and spoke to the sons of [a]Heth, saying,
4 [a]"I *am* a foreigner and a visitor among you.
[b]Give me property for a burial place among you,
that I may bury my dead out of my sight."
5 And the sons of Heth answered Abraham,
saying to him,
6 "Hear us, my lord: You *are* [a]a [1]mighty prince
among us; bury your dead in the choicest of our
burial places. None of us will withhold from you
his burial place, that you may bury your dead."
7 Then Abraham stood up and bowed himself to
the people of the land, the sons of Heth.
8 And he spoke with them, saying, "If it is your
wish that I bury my dead out of my sight, hear
me, and [1]meet with Ephron the son of Zohar for
me,
9 "that he may give me the cave of [a]Machpelah
which he has, which *is* at the end of his field. Let
him give it to me at the full price, as property for a
burial place among you."
10 Now Ephron dwelt among the sons of Heth;
and Ephron the Hittite answered Abraham in the
presence of the sons of Heth, all who [a]entered at
the gate of his city, saying,
11 [a]"No, my lord, hear me: I give you the field
and the cave that *is* in it; I give it to you in the
presence of the sons of my people. I give it to you.
Bury your dead!"
12 Then Abraham bowed himself down before
the people of the land;
13 and he spoke to Ephron in the hearing of the
people of the land, saying, "If you *will give it,*
please hear me. I will give you money for the field;
take *it* from me and I will bury my dead there."
14 And Ephron answered Abraham, saying to
him,
15 "My lord, listen to me; the land *is worth* four
hundred [a]shekels of silver. What *is* that between
you and me? So bury your dead."
16 And Abraham listened to Ephron; and Abraham [a]weighed out the silver for Ephron which he
had named in the hearing of the sons of Heth, four
hundred shekels of silver, currency of the merchants.
**17** So [a]the field of Ephron which *was* in Machpelah, which *was* before Mamre, the field and the
cave which *was* in it, and all the trees that *were* in
the field, which *were* within all the surrounding
borders, were deeded
18 to Abraham as a possession in the presence of
the sons of Heth, before all who went in at the
gate of his city.
19 And after this, Abraham buried Sarah his wife
in the cave of the field of Machpelah, before
Mamre (that *is,* Hebron) in the land of Canaan.
20 So the field and the cave that *is* in it [a]were
deeded to Abraham by the sons of Heth as property for a burial place.

### *Rebekah Chosen as a Wife for Isaac*

**24** Now Abraham [a]was old, well advanced in
age; and the LORD [b]had blessed Abraham in
all things.
2 So Abraham said [a]to the oldest servant of his
house, who [b]ruled over all that he had, "Please,
[c]put your hand under my thigh,
3 "and I will make you [a]swear[1] by the LORD, the
God of heaven and the God of the earth, that [b]you
will not take a wife for my son from the daughters
of the Canaanites, among whom I dwell;
4 [a]"but you shall go [b]to my country and to my
family, and take a wife for my son Isaac."
5 And the servant said to him, "Perhaps the
woman will not be willing to follow me to this
land. Must I take your son back to the land from
which you came?"
6 But Abraham said to him, "Beware that you
do not take my son back there.
7 "The LORD God of heaven, who [a]took me from
my father's house and from the land of my family,
and who spoke to me and swore to me, saying,
[b]'To your [1]descendants I give this land,' [c]He will
send His angel before you, and you shall take a
wife for my son from there.
8 "And if the woman is not willing to follow
you, then [a]you will be released from this oath;
only do not take my son back there."
9 So the servant put his hand under the thigh of
Abraham his master, and swore to him concerning
this matter.
**10** Then the servant took ten of his master's
camels and departed, [a]for all his master's goods
*were in* his hand. And he arose and went to
Mesopotamia, to [b]the city of Nahor.
11 And he made his camels kneel down outside
the city by a well of water at evening time, the
time [a]when women go out to draw *water.*
12 Then he [a]said, "O LORD God of my master
Abraham, please [b]give me success this day, and
show kindness to my master Abraham.
13 "Behold, here [a]I stand by the well of water,
and [b]the daughters of the men of the city are
coming out to draw water.
14 "Now let it be that the young woman to whom
I say, 'Please let down your pitcher that I may
drink,' and she says, 'Drink, and I will also give
your camels a drink'—*let* her *be the one* You have
appointed for Your servant Isaac. And [a]by this I
will know that You have shown kindness to my
master."
**15** And it happened, [a]before he had finished
speaking, that behold, [b]Rebekah,[1] who was born
to Bethuel, son of [c]Milcah, the wife of Nahor,
Abraham's brother, came out with her pitcher on
her shoulder.
16 Now the young woman [a]*was* very beautiful to
behold, a virgin; no man had known her. And she
went down to the well, filled her pitcher, and
came up.
17 And the servant ran to meet her and said,
"Please let me drink a little water from your
pitcher."
18 [a]So she said, "Drink, my lord." Then she
quickly let her pitcher down to her hand, and gave
him a drink.
19 And when she had finished giving him a drink,

---

**23** [a]Gen. 24:15 [1]*Rebecca,* Rom. 9:10

CHAPTER 23

**2** [a]Josh. 14:15; 15:13; 21:11 [b]Gen. 13:18; 23:19
**3** [a]Gen. 10:15; 15:20
**4** [a][Gen. 17:8] [b]Acts 7:5, 16
**6** [a]Gen. 13:2; 14:14; 24:35 [1]Lit. *prince of God*
**8** [1]*approach*
**9** [a]Gen. 25:9
**10** [a]Gen. 23:18; 34:20, 24
**11** [a]2 Sam. 24:21–24
**15** [a]Ex. 30:13
**16** [a]Jer. 32:9, 10
**17** [a]Gen. 25:9; 49:29–32; 50:13
**20** [a]Jer. 32:10, 11

CHAPTER 24

**1** [a]Gen. 18:11; 21:5 [b]Gen. 12:2; 13:2; 24:35
**2** [a]Gen. 15:2 [b]Gen. 24:10; 39:4–6 [c]Gen. 47:29
**3** [a]Gen. 14:19, 22 [b]Deut. 7:3 [1]*take an oath*
**4** [a]Gen. 28:2 [b]Gen. 12:1
**7** [a]Gen. 12:1; 24:3 [b]Gen. 12:7; 13:15; 15:18; 17:8 [c]Ex. 23:20, 23; 33:2 [1]Lit. *seed*
**8** [a]Josh. 2:17–20
**10** [a]Gen. 24:2, 22 [b]Gen. 11:31, 32; 22:20; 27:43; 29:5
**11** [a]Ex. 2:16
**12** [a]Ex. 3:6, 15 [b]Neh. 1:11
**13** [a]Gen. 24:43 [b]Ex. 2:16
**14** [a]Judg. 6:17, 37
**15** [a]Is. 65:24 [b]Gen. 24:45; 25:20 [c]Gen. 22:20, 23 [1]*Rebecca,* Rom. 9:10
**16** [a]Gen. 12:11; 26:7; 29:17
**18** [a][1 Pet. 3:8, 9]

she said, "I will draw *water* for your camels also,
until they have finished drinking."
20 Then she quickly emptied her pitcher into the
trough, ran back to the well to draw *water,* and
drew for all his camels.
21 And the man, wondering at her, remained
silent so as to know whether [a]the LORD had made
his journey prosperous or not.
**22** So it was, when the camels had finished drinking, that the man took a golden [a]nose ring weighing half a shekel, and two bracelets for her wrists
weighing ten *shekels* of gold,
23 and said, "Whose daughter *are* you? Tell me,
please, is there room *in* your father's house for us
[1]to lodge?"
24 So she said to him, [a]"I *am* the daughter of
Bethuel, Milcah's son, whom she bore to Nahor."
25 Moreover she said to him, "We have both
straw and feed enough, and room to lodge."
26 Then the man [a]bowed down his head and
worshiped the LORD.
27 And he said, [a]"Blessed *be* the LORD God of my
master Abraham, who has not forsaken [b]His
mercy and His truth toward my master. As for me,
being on the way, the LORD [c]led me to the house
of my master's brethren."
28 So the young woman ran and told her mother's household these things.
**29** Now Rebekah had a brother whose name *was*
[a]Laban, and Laban ran out to the man by the well.
30 So it came to pass, when he saw the nose ring,
and the bracelets on his sister's wrists, and when
he heard the words of his sister Rebekah, saying,
"Thus the man spoke to me," that he went to the
man. And there he stood by the camels at the well.
31 And he said, "Come in, [a]O blessed of the LORD!
Why do you stand outside? For I have prepared
the house, and a place for the camels."
**32** Then the man came to the house. And he
unloaded the camels, and [a]provided straw and
feed for the camels, and water to [b]wash his feet
and the feet of the men who *were* with him.
33 *Food* was set before him to eat, but he said, [a]"I
will not eat until I have told about my errand."
And he said, "Speak on."
34 So he said, "I *am* Abraham's servant.
35 "The LORD [a]has blessed my master greatly,
and he has become great; and He has given him
flocks and herds, silver and gold, male and female
servants, and camels and donkeys.
36 "And Sarah my master's wife [a]bore a son to
my master when she was old; and [b]to him he has
given all that he has.
37 "Now my master [a]made me swear, saying,
'You shall not take a wife for my son from the
daughters of the Canaanites, in whose land I
dwell;
38 [a]'but you shall go to my father's house and to
my family, and take a wife for my son.'
39 [a]"And I said to my master, 'Perhaps the
woman will not follow me.'
40 [a]"But he said to me, 'The LORD, [b]before whom
I walk, will send His angel with you and [1]prosper
your way; and you shall take a wife for my son
from my family and from my father's house.
41 [a]'You will be clear from this oath when you
arrive among my family; for if they will not give
*her* to you, then you will be released from my
oath.'
**42** "And this day I came to the well and said, [a]'O
LORD God of my master Abraham, if You will now
prosper the way in which I go,

43 [a]'behold, I stand by the well of water; and it
shall come to pass that when the virgin comes out
to draw *water,* and I say to her, "Please give me a
little water from your pitcher to drink,"
44 'and she says to me, "Drink, and I will draw
for your camels also,"—*let* her *be* the woman
whom the LORD has appointed for my master's
son.'
**45** [a]"But before I had finished [b]speaking in my
heart, there was Rebekah, coming out with her
pitcher on her shoulder; and she went down to the
well and drew *water.* And I said to her, 'Please let
me drink.'
46 "And she made haste and let her pitcher down
from her *shoulder,* and said, 'Drink, and I will give
your camels a drink also.' So I drank, and she
gave the camels a drink also.
47 "Then I asked her, and said, 'Whose daughter
*are* you?' And she said, 'The daughter of Bethuel,
Nahor's son, whom Milcah bore to him.' So I put
the nose ring on her nose and the bracelets on her
wrists.
48 [a]"And I bowed my head and worshiped the
LORD, and blessed the LORD God of my master
Abraham, who had led me in the way of truth to
[b]take the daughter of my master's brother for his
son.
49 "Now if you will [a]deal kindly and truly with
my master, tell me. And if not, tell me, that I may
turn to the right hand or to the left."
**50** Then Laban and Bethuel answered and said,
[a]"The thing comes from the LORD; we cannot
[b]speak to you either bad or good.
51 [a]"Here *is* Rebekah before you; take *her* and
go, and let her be your master's son's wife, as the
LORD has spoken."
**52** And it came to pass, when Abraham's servant
heard their words, that [a]he worshiped the LORD,
*bowing himself* to the earth.
53 Then the servant brought out [a]jewelry of
silver, jewelry of gold, and clothing, and gave
*them* to Rebekah. He also gave [b]precious things to
her brother and to her mother.
54 And he and the men who *were* with him ate
and drank and stayed all night. Then they arose in
the morning, and he said, [a]"Send me away to my
master."
55 But her brother and her mother said, "Let the
young woman stay with us *a few* days, at least
ten; after that she may go."
56 And he said to them, "Do not [1]hinder me, since
the LORD has prospered my way; send me away so
that I may go to my master."
57 So they said, "We will call the young woman
and ask her personally."
58 Then they called Rebekah and said to her,
"Will you go with this man?" And she said, "I will
go."
59 So they sent away Rebekah their sister [a]and
her nurse, and Abraham's servant and his men.
60 And they blessed Rebekah and said to her:

"Our sister, *may* you *become*
[a]*The mother of* thousands of ten thousands;
[b]And may your descendants possess
The gates of those who hate them."

**61** Then Rebekah and her maids arose, and they
rode on the camels and followed the man. So the
servant took Rebekah and departed.
62 Now Isaac came from the way of [a]Beer Lahai
Roi, for he dwelt in the South.

**21** [a]Gen. 24:12–14, 27, 52
**22** [a]Gen. 24:47; Ex. 32:2, 3; Is. 3:19–21
**23** [1]*to spend the night*
**24** [a]Gen. 22:23; 24:15
**26** [a]Gen. 24:48, 52; Ex. 4:31
**27** [a]Gen. 24:12, 42, 48; Ex. 18:10; Ruth 4:14; 1 Sam. 25:32, 39; 2 Sam. 18:28; Luke 1:68 [b]Gen. 32:10; Ps. 98:3 [c]Gen. 24:21, 48
**29** [a]Gen. 29:5, 13
**31** [a]Gen. 26:29; Judg. 17:2; Ruth 3:10; Ps. 115:15
**32** [a]Gen. 43:24; Judg. 19:21 [b]Gen. 19:2; John 13:5, 13–15
**33** [a]Job 23:12; John 4:34; Eph. 6:5–7
**35** [a]Gen. 13:2; 24:1
**36** [a]Gen. 21:1–7 [b]Gen. 21:10; 25:5
**37** [a]Gen. 24:2–4
**38** [a]Gen. 24:4
**39** [a]Gen. 24:5
**40** [a]Gen. 24:7 [b]Gen. 5:22, 24; 17:1; 1 Kin. 8:23 [1]*make your way successful*
**41** [a]Gen. 24:8
**42** [a]Gen. 24:12
**43** [a]Gen. 24:13
**45** [a]Gen. 24:15 [b]1 Sam. 1:13
**48** [a]Gen. 24:26, 52 [b]Gen. 22:23; 24:27; Ps. 32:8; 48:14; Is. 48:17
**49** [a]Gen. 47:29; Josh. 2:14
**50** [a]Ps. 118:23; Matt. 21:42; Mark 12:11 [b]Gen. 31:24, 29
**51** [a]Gen. 20:15
**52** [a]Gen. 24:26, 48
**53** [a]Gen. 24:10, 22; Ex. 3:22; 11:2; 12:35 [b]2 Chr. 21:3; Ezra 1:6
**54** [a]Gen. 24:56, 59; 30:25
**56** [1]*delay*
**59** [a]Gen. 35:8
**60** [a]Gen. 17:16 [b]Gen. 22:17; 28:14
**62** [a]Gen. 16:14; 25:11

63 And Isaac went out [a]to meditate in the field in
the evening; and he lifted his eyes and looked, and
there, the camels *were* coming.
64 Then Rebekah lifted her eyes, and when she
saw Isaac [a]she dismounted from her camel;
65 for she had said to the servant, "Who *is* this
man walking in the field to meet us?" The servant
said, "It *is* my master." So she took a veil and
covered herself.
66 And the servant told Isaac all the things that
he had done.
67 Then Isaac brought her into his mother Sarah's tent; and he [a]took Rebekah and she became
his wife, and he loved her. So Isaac [b]was comforted after his mother's *death*.

### *Birth of Esau and Jacob*

**25** Abraham again took a wife, and her name
*was* [a]Keturah.
2 And [a]she bore him Zimran, Jokshan, Medan,
Midian, Ishbak, and Shuah.
3 Jokshan begot Sheba and Dedan. And the
sons of Dedan were Asshurim, Letushim, and
Leummim.
4 And the sons of Midian *were* Ephah, Epher,
Hanoch, Abidah, and Eldaah. All these *were* the
children of Keturah.
5 And [a]Abraham gave all that he had to Isaac.
6 But Abraham gave gifts to the sons of the
concubines which Abraham had; and while he
was still living he [a]sent them eastward, away from
Isaac his son, to [b]the country of the east.
**7** This *is* the sum of the years of Abraham's life
which he lived: one hundred and seventy-five
years.
8 Then Abraham breathed his last and [a]died in a
good old age, an old man and full *of years*, and
[b]was gathered to his people.
9 And [a]his sons Isaac and Ishmael buried him in
the cave of [b]Machpelah, which *is* before Mamre, in
the field of Ephron the son of Zohar the Hittite,
10 [a]the field which Abraham purchased from the
sons of Heth. [b]There Abraham was buried, and
Sarah his wife.
11 And it came to pass, after the death of Abraham, that God blessed his son Isaac. And Isaac
dwelt at [a]Beer Lahai Roi.
**12** Now this *is* the [a]genealogy of Ishmael, Abraham's son, whom Hagar the Egyptian, Sarah's
maidservant, bore to Abraham.
13 And [a]these *were* the names of the sons of
Ishmael, by their names, according to their generations: The firstborn of Ishmael, Nebajoth; then
Kedar, Adbeel, Mibsam,
14 Mishma, Dumah, Massa,
15 [1]Hadar, Tema, Jetur, Naphish, and Kedemah.
16 These *were* the sons of Ishmael and these
*were* their names, by their towns and their [1]settle-
ments, [a]twelve princes according to their nations.
17 These *were* the years of the life of Ishmael:
one hundred and thirty-seven years; and [a]he
breathed his last and died, and was gathered to his
people.
18 [a](They dwelt from Havilah as far as Shur,
which *is* east of Egypt as you go toward Assyria.)
He [1]died [b]in the presence of all his brethren.
**19** This *is* the [a]genealogy of Isaac, Abraham's
son. [b]Abraham begot Isaac.
20 Isaac was forty years old when he took Rebekah as wife, [a]the daughter of Bethuel the Syrian
of Padan Aram, [b]the sister of Laban the Syrian.
21 Now Isaac pleaded with the LORD for his wife,
because she *was* barren; [a]and the LORD granted
his plea, [b]and Rebekah his wife conceived.
22 But the children struggled together within
her; and she said, "If *all is* well, why *am I like*
this?" [a]So she went to inquire of the LORD.
23 And the LORD said to her:

[a]"Two nations *are* in your womb,
Two peoples shall be separated
from your body;
*One* people shall be stronger than [b]the other,
[c]And the older shall serve the younger."

24 So when her days were fulfilled *for her* to give
birth, indeed *there were* twins in her womb.
25 And the first came out red. *He was* [a]like a
hairy garment all over; so they called his name
[1]Esau.
26 Afterward his brother came out, and [a]his hand
took hold of Esau's heel; so [b]his name was called
[1]Jacob. Isaac *was* sixty years old when she bore
them.
**27** So the boys grew. And Esau was [a]a skillful
hunter, a man of the field; but Jacob was [b]a [1]mild
man, [c]dwelling in tents.
28 And Isaac loved Esau because he [a]ate *of his*
game, [b]but Rebekah loved Jacob.
**29** Now Jacob cooked a stew; and Esau came in
from the field, and he *was* weary.
30 And Esau said to Jacob, "Please feed me with
that same red *stew*, for I *am* weary." Therefore his
name was called [1]Edom.
31 But Jacob said, "Sell me your birthright as of
this day."
32 And Esau said, "Look, I *am* about to die; so
[a]what *is* this birthright to me?"
33 Then Jacob said, [1]"Swear to me as of this
day." So he swore to him, and [a]sold his birthright
to Jacob.
34 And Jacob gave Esau bread and stew of lentils; then [a]he ate and drank, arose, and went his
way. Thus Esau [b]despised *his* birthright.

### *Isaac and Abimelech*

**26** There was a famine in the land, besides [a]the
first famine that was in the days of Abraham. And Isaac went to [b]Abimelech king of the
Philistines, in Gerar.
2 Then the LORD appeared to him and said: [a]"Do
not go down to Egypt; live in [b]the land of which I
shall tell you.
3 [a]"Dwell in this land, and [b]I will be with you
and [c]bless you; for to you and your descendants [d]I
give all these lands, and I will perform [e]the oath
which I swore to Abraham your father.
4 "And [a]I will make your descendants multiply
as the stars of heaven; I will give to your descendants all these lands; [b]and in your seed all the
nations of the earth shall be blessed;
5 [a]"because Abraham obeyed My voice and kept
My charge, My commandments, My statutes, and
My laws."
**6** So Isaac dwelt in Gerar.
7 And the men of the place asked about his wife.
And [a]he said, "She *is* my sister"; for [b]he was afraid
to say, "*She is* my wife," *because he thought*, "lest
the men of the place kill me for Rebekah, because
she *is* [c]beautiful to behold."
8 Now it came to pass, when he had been there
a long time, that Abimelech king of the Philistines

**63** [a]Josh. 1:8
**64** [a]Josh. 15:18
**67** [a]Gen. 25:20; 29:20 [b]Gen. 23:1, 2; 38:12

CHAPTER 25
**1** [a]1 Chr. 1:32, 33
**2** [a]1 Chr. 1:32, 33
**5** [a]Gen. 24:35, 36
**6** [a]Gen. 21:14 [b]Judg. 6:3
**8** [a]Gen. 15:15; 47:8, 9 [b]Gen. 25:17; 35:29; 49:29, 33
**9** [a]Gen. 35:29; 50:13 [b]Gen. 23:9, 17; 49:30
**10** [a]Gen. 23:3–16 [b]Gen. 49:31
**11** [a]Gen. 16:14
**12** [a]Gen. 11:10, 27; 16:15
**13** [a]1 Chr. 1:29–31
**15** [1]MT *Hadad*
**16** [a]Gen. 17:20 [1]*camps*
**17** [a]Gen. 25:8; 49:33
**18** [a]1 Sam. 15:7 [b]Gen. 16:12 [1]*fell*
**19** [a]Gen. 36:1, 9 [b]Matt. 1:2
**20** [a]Gen. 22:23; 24:15, 29, 67 [b]Gen. 24:29
**21** [a]1 Chr. 5:20 [b]Rom. 9:10–13
**22** [a]1 Sam. 1:15; 9:9; 10:22
**23** [a]Gen. 17:4–6, 16; 24:60 [b]2 Sam. 8:14 [c]Rom. 9:12
**25** [a]Gen. 27:11, 16, 23 [1]Lit. *Hairy*
**26** [a]Hos. 12:3 [b]Gen. 27:36 [1]*Supplanter* or *Deceitful*, lit. *One Who Takes the Heel*
**27** [a]Gen. 27:3, 5 [b]Job 1:1, 8 [c]Heb. 11:9 [1]Lit. *complete*
**28** [a]Gen. 27:4, 19, 25, 31 [b]Gen. 27:6–10
**30** [1]Lit. *Red*
**32** [a]Mark 8:36, 37
**33** [a]Heb. 12:16 [1]*Take an oath*
**34** [a]Eccl. 8:15 [b]Heb. 12:16, 17

CHAPTER 26
**1** [a]Gen. 12:10 [b]Gen. 20:1, 2
**2** [a]Gen. 12:7; 17:1; 18:1; 35:9 [b]Gen. 12:1
**3** [a]Heb. 11:9 [b]Gen. 28:13, 15 [c]Gen. 12:2 [d]Gen. 12:7; 13:15; 15:18 [e]Gen. 22:16
**4** [a]Gen. 15:5; 22:17 [b]Gen. 12:3; 22:18
**5** [a]Gen. 22:16, 18
**7** [a]Gen. 12:13; 20:2, 12, 13 [b]Prov. 29:25 [c]Gen. 12:11; 24:16; 29:17

looked through a window, and saw, and there was
Isaac, [1]showing endearment to Rebekah his wife.
9 Then Abimelech called Isaac and said, "Quite
obviously she *is* your wife; so how could you say,
'She *is* my sister'?" Isaac said to him, "Because I
said, 'Lest I die on account of her.' "
10 And Abimelech said, "What *is* this you have
done to us? One of the people might soon have
lain with your wife, and [a]you would have brought
guilt on us."
11 So Abimelech charged all *his* people, saying,
"He who [a]touches this man or his wife shall surely
be put to death."
**12** Then Isaac sowed in that land, and reaped in
the same year [a]a hundredfold; and the LORD
[b]blessed him.
13 The man [a]began to prosper, and continued
prospering until he became very prosperous;
14 for he had possessions of flocks and possessions of herds and a great number of servants. So
the Philistines [a]envied him.
15 Now the Philistines had stopped up all the
wells [a]which his father's servants had dug in the
days of Abraham his father, and they had filled
them with earth.
16 And Abimelech said to Isaac, "Go away from
us, for [a]you are much mightier than we."
**17** Then Isaac departed from there and [1]pitched
his tent in the Valley of Gerar, and dwelt there.
18 And Isaac dug again the wells of water which
they had dug in the days of Abraham his father,
for the Philistines had stopped them up after the
death of Abraham. [a]He called them by the names
which his father had called them.
19 Also Isaac's servants dug in the valley, and
found a well of running water there.
20 But the herdsmen of Gerar [a]quarreled with
Isaac's herdsmen, saying, "The water *is* ours." So
he called the name of the well [1]Esek, because they
quarreled with him.
21 Then they dug another well, and they quarreled over that *one* also. So he called its name
[1]Sitnah.
22 And he moved from there and dug another
well, and they did not quarrel over it. So he called
its name [1]Rehoboth, because he said, "For now
the LORD has made room for us, and we shall [a]be
fruitful in the land."
**23** Then he went up from there to Beersheba.
24 And the LORD [a]appeared to him the same night
and said, [b]"I *am* the God of your father Abraham;
[c]do not fear, for [d]I *am* with you. I will bless you
and multiply your descendants for My servant
Abraham's sake."
25 So he [a]built an altar there and [b]called on the
name of the LORD, and he pitched his tent there;
and there Isaac's servants dug a well.
**26** Then Abimelech came to him from Gerar with
Ahuzzath, one of his friends, [a]and Phichol the
commander of his army.
27 And Isaac said to them, "Why have you come
to me, [a]since you hate me and have [b]sent me away
from you?"
28 But they said, "We have certainly seen that
the LORD [a]is with you. So we said, 'Let there now
be an oath between us, between you and us; and
let us make a [1]covenant with you,
29 'that you will do us no harm, since we have
not touched you, and since we have done nothing
to you but good and have sent you away in peace.
[a]You *are* now the blessed of the LORD.' "
30 [a]So he made them a feast, and they ate and
drank.
31 Then they arose early in the morning and
[a]swore an oath with one another; and Isaac sent
them away, and they departed from him in peace.
32 It came to pass the same day that Isaac's
servants came and told him about the well which
they had dug, and said to him, "We have found
water."
33 So he called it [1]Shebah. [a]Therefore the name
of the city *is* [2]Beersheba to this day.
**34** [a]When Esau was forty years old, he took as
wives Judith the daughter of Beeri the Hittite, and
Basemath the daughter of Elon the Hittite.
35 And [a]they were a grief of mind to Isaac and
Rebekah.

## *Jacob Receives Isaac's Blessing*

**27** Now it came to pass, when Isaac was [a]old
and [b]his eyes were so dim that he could not
see, that he called Esau his older son and said to
him, "My son." And he answered him, "Here I
am."
2 Then he said, "Behold now, I am old. I [a]do not
know the day of my death.
3 [a]"Now therefore, please take your weapons,
your quiver and your bow, and go out to the field
and hunt game for me.
4 "And make me [1]savory food, such as I love,
and bring *it* to me that I may eat, that my soul
[a]may bless you before I die."
**5** Now Rebekah was listening when Isaac spoke
to Esau his son. And Esau went to the field to
hunt game and to bring *it*.
6 So Rebekah spoke to Jacob her son, saying,
"Indeed I heard your father speak to Esau your
brother, saying,
7 'Bring me game and make [1]savory food for me,
that I may eat it and bless you in the presence of
the LORD before my death.'
8 "Now therefore, my son, [a]obey my voice according to what I command you.
9 "Go now to the flock and bring me from there
two choice kids of the goats, and I will make
[a]savory food from them for your father, such as he
loves.
10 "Then you shall take *it* to your father, that he
may eat *it*, and that he [a]may bless you before his
death."
11 And Jacob said to Rebekah his mother, "Look,
[a]Esau my brother *is* a hairy man, and I *am* a
smooth-*skinned* man.
12 "Perhaps my father will [a]feel me, and I shall
seem to be a deceiver to him; and I shall bring [b]a
curse on myself and not a blessing."
13 But his mother said to him, [a]"*Let* your curse
*be* on me, my son; only obey my voice, and go, get
*them* for me."
14 And he went and got *them* and brought *them*
to his mother, and his mother [a]made [1]savory food,
such as his father loved.
15 Then Rebekah took [a]the choice clothes of her
elder son Esau, which *were* with her in the house,
and put them on Jacob her younger son.
16 And she put the skins of the kids of the goats
on his hands and on the smooth part of his neck.
17 Then she gave the savory food and the bread,
which she had prepared, into the hand of her son
Jacob.
**18** So he went to his father and said, "My father."
And he said, "Here I am. Who *are* you, my son?"
19 Jacob said to his father, "I *am* Esau your

8 [1]*caressing*
10 [a]Gen. 20:9
11 [a]Ps. 105:15
12 [a]Matt. 13:8, 23; Mark 4:8 [b]Gen. 24:1; 25:3, 11; 26:3; Job 42:12; Prov. 10:22
13 [a]Gen. 24:35; [Prov. 10:22]
14 [a]Gen. 37:11; Eccl. 4:4
15 [a]Gen. 21:25, 30
16 [a]Ex. 1:9
17 [1]*camped*
18 [a]Gen. 21:31
20 [a]Gen. 21:25 [1]Lit. *Quarrel*
21 [1]Lit. *Enmity*
22 [a]Gen. 17:6; 28:3; 41:52; Ex. 1:7 [1]Lit. *Spaciousness*
24 [a]Gen. 26:2 [b]Gen. 17:7, 8; 24:12; Ex. 3:6; Acts 7:32 [c]Gen. 15:1 [d]Gen. 26:3, 4
25 [a]Gen. 12:7, 8; 13:4, 18; 22:9; 33:20 [b]Gen. 21:33; Ps. 116:17
26 [a]Gen. 21:22
27 [a]Judg. 11:7 [b]Gen. 26:16
28 [a]Gen. 21:22, 23 [1]*treaty*
29 [a]Gen. 24:31; Ps. 115:15
30 [a]Gen. 19:3
31 [a]Gen. 21:31
33 [a]Gen. 21:31; 28:10 [1]Lit. *Oath* or *Seven* [2]Lit. *Well of the Oath* or *Well of the Seven*
34 [a]Gen. 28:8; 36:2
35 [a]Gen. 27:46; 28:1, 8

CHAPTER 27

1 [a]Gen. 35:28 [b]Gen. 48:10; 1 Sam. 3:2
2 [a][Prov. 27:1; James 4:14]
3 [a]Gen. 25:27, 28
4 [a]Gen. 27:19, 25, 27, 31; 48:9, 15, 16; 49:28; Deut. 33:1; Heb. 11:20 [1]*tasty*
7 [1]*tasty*
8 [a]Gen. 27:13, 43
9 [a]Gen. 27:4
10 [a]Gen. 27:4; 48:16
11 [a]Gen. 25:25
12 [a]Gen. 27:21, 22 [b]Gen. 9:25; Deut. 27:18
13 [a]Gen. 43:9; 1 Sam. 25:24; 2 Sam. 14:9; Matt. 27:25
14 [a]Prov. 23:3; Luke 21:34 [1]*tasty*
15 [a]Gen. 27:27

firstborn; I have done just as you told me; please
arise, sit and eat of my game, [a]that your soul may
bless me."
20 But Isaac said to his son, "How *is it* that you
have found *it* so quickly, my son?" And he said,
"Because the LORD your God brought *it* to me."
21 Then Isaac said to Jacob, "Please come near,
that I [a]may feel you, my son, whether you *are*
really my son Esau or not."
22 So Jacob went near to Isaac his father, and he
felt him and said, "The voice *is* Jacob's voice, but
the hands *are* the hands of Esau."
23 And he did not recognize him, because [a]his
hands were hairy like his brother Esau's hands; so
he blessed him.
24 Then he said, "*Are* you really my son Esau?"
He said, "I *am.*"
25 He said, "Bring *it* near to me, and I will eat of
my son's game, so [a]that my soul may bless you."
So he brought *it* near to him, and he ate; and he
brought him wine, and he drank.
26 Then his father Isaac said to him, "Come near
now and kiss me, my son."
27 And he came near and [a]kissed him; and he
smelled the smell of his clothing, and blessed him
and said:

"Surely, [b]the smell of my son
*Is* like the smell of a field
Which the LORD has blessed.
28 Therefore may [a]God give you
Of [b]the dew of heaven,
Of [c]the fatness of the earth,
And [d]plenty of grain and wine.
29 [a]Let peoples serve you,
And nations bow down to you.
Be master over your brethren,
And [b]let your mother's sons
bow down to you.
[c]Cursed *be* everyone who curses you,
And blessed *be* those who bless you!"

**30** Now it happened, as soon as Isaac had finished blessing Jacob, and Jacob had scarcely gone
out from the presence of Isaac his father, that
Esau his brother came in from his hunting.
31 He also had made [1]savory food, and brought it
to his father, and said to his father, "Let my father
arise and [a]eat of his son's game, that your soul
may bless me."
32 And his father Isaac said to him, "Who *are*
you?" So he said, "I *am* your son, your firstborn,
Esau."
33 Then Isaac trembled exceedingly, and said,
"Who? Where *is* the one who hunted game and
brought *it* to me? I ate all *of it* before you came,
and I have blessed him—[a]*and* indeed he shall be
blessed."
34 When Esau heard the words of his father, [a]he
cried with an exceedingly great and bitter cry, and
said to his father, "Bless me—me also, O my
father!"
35 But he said, "Your brother came with deceit
and has taken away your blessing."
36 And *Esau* said, [a]"Is he not rightly named
[1]Jacob? For he has supplanted me these two times.
He took away my birthright, and now look, he has
taken away my blessing!" And he said, "Have you
not reserved a blessing for me?"
37 Then Isaac answered and said to Esau, [a]"Indeed I have made him your master, and all his
brethren I have given to him as servants; with
[b]grain and wine I have [1]sustained him. What shall
I do now for you, my son?"
38 And Esau said to his father, "Have you only
one blessing, my father? Bless me—me also, O my
father!" And Esau lifted up his voice [a]and wept.
**39** Then Isaac his father answered and said to
him:

"Behold, [a]your dwelling shall be
of the [1]fatness of the earth,
And of the dew of heaven from above.
40 By your sword you shall live,
And [a]you shall serve your brother;
And [b]it shall come to pass,
when you become restless,
That you shall break his yoke
from your neck."

**41** So Esau [a]hated Jacob because of the blessing
with which his father blessed him, and Esau said
in his heart, [b]"The days of mourning for my father
[1]are at hand; [c]then I will kill my brother Jacob."
42 And the words of Esau her older son were told
to Rebekah. So she sent and called Jacob her
younger son, and said to him, "Surely your
brother Esau [a]comforts himself concerning you *by
intending* to kill you.
43 "Now therefore, my son, obey my voice: arise,
flee to my brother Laban [a]in Haran.
44 "And stay with him a [a]few days, until your
brother's fury turns away,
45 "until your brother's anger turns away from
you, and he forgets what you have done to him;
then I will send and bring you from there. Why
should I be bereaved also of you both in one day?"
46 And Rebekah said to Isaac, [a]"I am weary of
my life because of the daughters of Heth; [b]if Jacob
takes a wife of the daughters of Heth, like these
*who are* the daughters of the land, what good will
my life be to me?"

### *Jacob Sent to His Uncle Laban*

**28** Then Isaac called Jacob and [a]blessed him,
and [1]charged him, and said to him: [b]"You
shall not take a wife from the daughters of Canaan.
2 [a]"Arise, go to [b]Padan Aram, to the house of
[c]Bethuel your mother's father; and take yourself a
wife from there of the daughters of [d]Laban your
mother's brother.

3 "May [a]God Almighty bless you,
And make you [b]fruitful and multiply you,
That you may be an assembly of peoples;
4 And give you [a]the blessing of Abraham,
To you and your descendants with you,
That you may inherit the land
[b]In[1] which you are a stranger,
Which God gave to Abraham."

5 So Isaac sent Jacob away, and he went to
Padan Aram, to Laban the son of Bethuel the
Syrian, the brother of Rebekah, the mother of
Jacob and Esau.
**6** Esau saw that Isaac had blessed Jacob and
sent him away to Padan Aram to take himself a
wife from there, *and that* as he blessed him he
gave him a charge, saying, "You shall not take a
wife from the daughters of Canaan,"
7 and that Jacob had obeyed his father and his
mother and had gone to Padan Aram.
8 Also Esau saw [a]that the daughters of Canaan
did not please his father Isaac.

**19** [a]Gen. 27:4
**21** [a]Gen. 27:12
**23** [a]Gen. 27:16
**25** [a]Gen. 27:4, 10, 19, 31
**27** [a]Gen. 29:13 [b]Song 4:11; Hos. 14:6
**28** [a]Heb. 11:20 [b]Gen. 27:39; Deut. 33:13, 28; 2 Sam. 1:21; Ps. 133:3; Prov. 3:20; Mic. 5:7; Zech. 8:12 [c]Gen. 45:18; Num. 18:12 [d]Deut. 7:13; 33:28
**29** [a]Gen. 9:25; 25:23; Is. 45:14; 49:7; 60:12, 14 [b]Gen. 37:7, 10; 49:8 [c]Gen. 12:2, 3; Zeph. 2:8, 9
**31** [a]Gen. 27:4 [1]*tasty*
**33** [a]Gen. 25:23; 28:3, 4; Num. 23:20; Rom. 11:29
**34** [a][Heb. 12:17]
**36** [a]Gen. 25:26, 32–34 [1]*Supplanter* or *Deceitful,* lit. *One Who Takes the Heel*
**37** [a]2 Sam. 8:14 [b]Gen. 27:28, 29 [1]*provided support for*
**38** [a]Heb. 12:17
**39** [a]Gen. 27:28; Heb. 11:20 [1]*fertility*
**40** [a]Gen. 25:23; 27:29; 2 Sam. 8:14; [Obad. 18–20] [b]2 Kin. 8:20–22
**41** [a]Gen. 26:27; 32:3–11; 37:4, 5, 8 [b]Gen. 50:2–4, 10 [c]Obad. 10 [1]*are soon here*
**42** [a]Ps. 64:5
**43** [a]Gen. 11:31; 25:20; 28:2, 5
**44** [a]Gen. 31:41
**46** [a]Gen. 26:34, 35; 28:8 [b]Gen. 24:3

CHAPTER 28
**1** [a]Gen. 27:33 [b]Gen. 24:3 [1]*commanded*
**2** [a]Hos. 12:12 [b]Gen. 25:20 [c]Gen. 22:23 [d]Gen. 24:29; 27:43; 29:5
**3** [a]Gen. 17:16; 35:11; 48:3 [b]Gen. 26:4, 24
**4** [a]Gen. 12:2, 3; 22:17; Gal. 3:8 [b]Gen. 17:8; 23:4; 36:7; 1 Chr. 29:15; Ps. 39:12 [1]Lit. *Of your sojournings*
**8** [a]Gen. 24:3; 26:34, 35; 27:46

9 So Esau went to Ishmael and [a]took [b]Mahalath
the daughter of Ishmael, Abraham's son, [c]the
sister of Nebajoth, to be his wife in addition to the
wives he had.
**10** Now Jacob [a]went out from Beersheba and
went toward [b]Haran.
11 So he came to a certain place and stayed there
all night, because the sun had set. And he took
one of the stones of that place and put it at his
head, and he lay down in that place to sleep.
12 Then he [a]dreamed, and behold, a ladder *was*
set up on the earth, and its top reached to heaven;
and there [b]the angels of God were ascending and
descending on it.
13 [a]And behold, the LORD stood above it and said:
[b]"I *am* the LORD God of Abraham your father and
the God of Isaac; [c]the land on which you lie I will
give to you and your descendants.
14 "Also your [a]descendants shall be as the dust of
the earth; you shall spread abroad [b]to the west
and the east, to the north and the south; and in
you and [c]in your seed all the families of the earth
shall be blessed.
15 "Behold, [a]I *am* with you and will [b]keep[1] you
wherever you go, and will [c]bring you back to this
land; for [d]I will not leave you [e]until I have done
what I have spoken to you."
16 Then Jacob awoke from his sleep and said,
"Surely the LORD is in [a]this place, and I did not
know *it.*"
17 And he was afraid and said, "How awesome *is*
this place! This *is* none other than the house of
God, and this *is* the gate of heaven!"
**18** Then Jacob rose early in the morning, and
took the stone that he had put at his head, [a]set it
up as a pillar, [b]and poured oil on top of it.
19 And he called the name of [a]that place [1]Bethel;
but the name of that city had been Luz previously.
20 [a]Then Jacob made a vow, saying, "If [b]God will
be with me, and keep me in this way that I am
going, and give me [c]bread to eat and clothing to
put on,
21 "so that [a]I come back to my father's house in
peace, [b]then the LORD shall be my God.
22 "And this stone which I have set as a pillar
[a]shall be God's house, [b]and of all that You give me
I will surely give a [1]tenth to You."

### *Jacob Marries Leah and Rachel*

**29** So Jacob went on his journey [a]and came to
the land of the people of the East.
2 And he looked, and saw a [a]well in the field;
and behold, there *were* three flocks of sheep lying
by it; for out of that well they watered the flocks.
A large stone *was* on the well's mouth.
3 Now all the flocks would be gathered there;
and they would roll the stone from the well's
mouth, water the sheep, and put the stone back in
its place on the well's mouth.
**4** And Jacob said to them, "My brethren, where
*are* you from?" And they said, "We *are* from
[a]Haran."
5 Then he said to them, "Do you know [a]Laban
the son of Nahor?" And they said, "We know
him."
6 So he said to them, [a]"Is he well?" And they
said, "*He is* well. And look, his daughter Rachel [b]is
coming with the sheep."
7 Then he said, "Look, *it is* still [1]high day; *it is*
not time for the cattle to be gathered together.
Water the sheep, and go and feed *them.*"
8 But they said, "We cannot until all the flocks
are gathered together, and they have rolled the
stone from the well's mouth; then we water the
sheep."
**9** Now while he was still speaking with them,
[a]Rachel came with her father's sheep, for she was
a shepherdess.
10 And it came to pass, when Jacob saw Rachel
the daughter of Laban his mother's brother, and
the sheep of Laban his mother's brother, that
Jacob went near and [a]rolled the stone from the
well's mouth, and watered the flock of Laban his
mother's brother.
11 Then Jacob [a]kissed Rachel, and lifted up his
voice and wept.
12 And Jacob told Rachel that he *was* [a]her father's relative and that he *was* Rebekah's son. [b]So
she ran and told her father.
**13** Then it came to pass, when Laban heard the
report about Jacob his sister's son, that [a]he ran to
meet him, and embraced him and kissed him, and
brought him to his house. So he told Laban all
these things.
14 And Laban said to him, [a]"Surely you *are* my
bone and my flesh." And he stayed with him for a
month.
**15** Then Laban said to Jacob, "Because you *are*
my relative, should you therefore serve me for
nothing? Tell me, [a]what *should* your wages *be?*"
16 Now Laban had two daughters: the name of
the elder *was* Leah, and the name of the younger
*was* Rachel.
17 Leah's eyes *were* [1]delicate, but Rachel was
[a]beautiful of form and appearance.
18 Now Jacob loved Rachel; so he said, [a]"I will
serve you seven years for Rachel your younger
daughter."
19 And Laban said, "*It is* better that I give her to
you than that I should give her to another man.
Stay with me."
20 So Jacob [a]served seven years for Rachel, and
they seemed *only* a few days to him because of the
love he had for her.
**21** Then Jacob said to Laban, "Give *me* my wife,
for my days are fulfilled, that I may [a]go in to her."
22 And Laban gathered together all the men of
the place and [a]made a feast.
23 Now it came to pass in the evening, that he
took Leah his daughter and brought her to Jacob;
and he went in to her.
24 And Laban gave his maid [a]Zilpah to his daughter Leah *as* a maid.
25 So it came to pass in the morning, that behold,
it *was* Leah. And he said to Laban, "What is this
you have done to me? Was it not for Rachel that I
served you? Why then have you [a]deceived me?"
26 And Laban said, "It must not be done so in our
[1]country, to give the younger before the firstborn.
27 [a]"Fulfill her week, and we will give you this
one also for the service which you will serve with
me still another seven years."
28 Then Jacob did so and fulfilled her week. So he
gave him his daughter Rachel as wife also.
29 And Laban gave his maid [a]Bilhah to his daughter Rachel as a maid.
30 Then *Jacob* also went in to Rachel, and he also
[a]loved Rachel more than Leah. And he served
with Laban [b]still another seven years.
**31** When the LORD [a]saw that Leah *was* [1]unloved,
He [b]opened her womb; but Rachel *was* barren.
32 So Leah conceived and bore a son, and she

**9** [a]Gen. 26:34, 35 [b]Gen. 36:2, 3 [c]Gen. 25:13
**10** [a]Hos. 12:12 [b]Gen. 12:4, 5; 27:43; 29:4
**12** [a]Gen. 31:10; 41:1 [b]John 1:51
**13** [a]Gen. 35:1; 48:3 [b]Gen. 26:24 [c]Gen. 13:15, 17; 26:3; 35:12
**14** [a]Gen. 13:16; 22:17 [b]Gen. 13:14, 15 [c]Gen. 12:3; 18:18; 22:18; 26:4
**15** [a]Gen. 26:3, 24; 31:3 [b]Gen. 48:16 [c]Gen. 35:6; 48:21 [d]Deut. 7:9; 31:6, 8 [e]Num. 23:19 [1]*protect*
**16** [a]Ex. 3:5
**18** [a]Gen. 31:13, 45 [b]Lev. 8:10–12
**19** [a]Judg. 1:23, 26 [1]Lit. *House of God*
**20** [a]Judg. 11:30 [b]Gen. 28:15 [c]1 Tim. 6:8
**21** [a]Judg. 11:31 [b]Deut. 26:17
**22** [a]Gen. 35:7, 14 [b]Gen. 14:20 [1]*tithe*

CHAPTER 29

**1** [a]Num. 23:7
**2** [a]Gen. 24:10, 11
**4** [a]Gen. 11:31; 28:10
**5** [a]Gen. 24:24, 29; 28:2
**6** [a]Gen. 43:27 [b]Ex. 2:16, 17
**7** [1]*early in the day*
**9** [a]Ex. 2:16
**10** [a]Ex. 2:17
**11** [a]Gen. 33:4; 45:14, 15
**12** [a]Gen. 13:8; 14:14, 16; 28:5 [b]Gen. 24:28
**13** [a]Gen. 24:29–31
**14** [a]Gen. 2:23; 37:27
**15** [a]Gen. 30:28; 31:41
**17** [a]Gen. 12:11, 14; 26:7 [1]Or *weak*
**18** [a]Gen. 31:41
**20** [a]Gen. 30:26
**21** [a]Judg. 15:1
**22** [a]John 2:1, 2
**24** [a]Gen. 30:9, 10
**25** [a]1 Sam. 28:12
**26** [1]Lit. *place*
**27** [a]Judg. 14:2
**29** [a]Gen. 30:3–5
**30** [a]Deut. 21:15–17 [b]Gen. 30:26; 31:41
**31** [a]Ps. 127:3 [b]Gen. 30:1 [1]Lit. *hated*

called his name [1]Reuben; for she said, "The LORD
has surely [a]looked on my affliction. Now therefore, my husband will love me."
33 Then she conceived again and bore a son, and
said, "Because the LORD has heard that I *am*
[1]unloved, He has therefore given me this *son*
also." And she called his name [2]Simeon.
34 She conceived again and bore a son, and said,
"Now this time my husband will become attached
to me, because I have borne him three sons."
Therefore his name was called [1]Levi.
35 And she conceived again and bore a son, and
said, "Now I will praise the LORD." Therefore she
called his name [a]Judah.[1] Then she stopped bearing.

### *Jacob's Children*

**30** Now when Rachel saw that [a]she bore Jacob
no children, Rachel [b]envied her sister, and
said to Jacob, "Give me children, [c]or else I die!"
2 And Jacob's anger was aroused against Rachel, and he said, [a]"*Am* I in the place of God, who
has withheld from you the fruit of the womb?"
3 So she said, "Here is [a]my maid Bilhah; go in to
her, [b]and she will bear *a child* on my knees, [c]that I
also may [1]have children by her."
4 Then she gave him Bilhah her maid [a]as wife,
and Jacob went in to her.
5 And Bilhah conceived and bore Jacob a son.
6 Then Rachel said, "God has [a]judged my case;
and He has also heard my voice and given me a
son." Therefore she called his name [1]Dan.
7 And Rachel's maid Bilhah conceived again and
bore Jacob a second son.
8 Then Rachel said, "With [1]great wrestlings I
have wrestled with my sister, *and* indeed I have
prevailed." So she called his name [2]Naphtali.
9 When Leah saw that she had stopped bearing,
she took Zilpah her maid and [a]gave her to Jacob
as wife.
10 And Leah's maid Zilpah bore Jacob a son.
11 Then Leah said, [1]"A troop comes!" So she
called his name [2]Gad.
12 And Leah's maid Zilpah bore Jacob a second
son.
13 Then Leah said, "I am happy, for the daughters [a]will call me blessed." So she called his name
[1]Asher.
14 Now Reuben went in the days of wheat harvest and found mandrakes in the field, and
brought them to his mother Leah. Then Rachel
said to Leah, [a]"Please give me *some* of your son's
mandrakes."
15 But she said to her, [a]"*Is it* a small matter that
you have taken away my husband? Would you
take away my son's mandrakes also?" And Rachel
said, "Therefore he will lie with you tonight for
your son's mandrakes."
16 When Jacob came out of the field in the
evening, Leah went out to meet him and said,
"You must come in to me, for I have surely hired
you with my son's mandrakes." And he lay with
her that night.
17 And God listened to Leah, and she conceived
and bore Jacob a fifth son.
18 Leah said, "God has given me my wages,
because I have given my maid to my husband." So
she called his name [1]Issachar.
19 Then Leah conceived again and bore Jacob a
sixth son.
20 And Leah said, "God has endowed me *with* a
good endowment; now my husband will dwell
with me, because I have borne him six sons." So
she called his name [1]Zebulun.
21 Afterward she bore a [a]daughter, and called her
name [1]Dinah.
22 Then God [a]remembered Rachel, and God listened to her and [b]opened her womb.
23 And she conceived and bore a son, and said,
"God has taken away [a]my reproach."
24 So she called his name [1]Joseph, and said, [a]"The
LORD shall add to me another son."
25 And it came to pass, when Rachel had borne
Joseph, that Jacob said to Laban, [a]"Send me away,
that I may go to [b]my own place and to my country.
26 "Give *me* my wives and my children [a]for
whom I have served you, and let me go; for you
know my service which I have done for you."
27 And Laban said to him, "Please *stay,* if I have
found favor in your eyes, *for* [a]I have learned by
experience that the LORD has blessed me for your
sake."
28 Then he said, [a]"Name me your wages, and I
will give *it.*"
29 So *Jacob* said to him, [a]"You know how I have
served you and how your livestock has been with
me.
30 "For what you had before I *came was* little,
and it has increased to a great amount; the LORD
has blessed you [1]since my coming. And now, when
shall I also [a]provide for my own house?"
31 So he said, "What shall I give you?" And
Jacob said, "You shall not give me anything. If
you will do this thing for me, I will again feed and
keep your flocks:
32 "Let me pass through all your flock today,
removing from there all the speckled and spotted
sheep, and all the brown ones among the lambs,
and the spotted and speckled among the goats;
and [a]*these* shall be my wages.
33 "So my [a]righteousness will answer for me in
time to come, when the subject of my wages
comes before you: every one that *is* not speckled
and spotted among the goats, and brown among
the lambs, will be considered stolen, if *it is* with
me."
34 And Laban said, "Oh, that it were according to
your word!"
35 So he removed that day the male goats that
were [a]speckled and spotted, all the female goats
that were speckled and spotted, every one that
had *some* white in it, and all the brown ones
among the lambs, and gave *them* into the hand of
his sons.
36 Then he put three days' journey between
himself and Jacob, and Jacob fed the rest of
Laban's flocks.
37 Now [a]Jacob took for himself rods of green
poplar and of the almond and chestnut trees,
peeled white strips in them, and exposed the white
which *was* in the rods.
38 And the rods which he had peeled, he set
before the flocks in the gutters, in the watering
troughs where the flocks came to drink, so that
they should conceive when they came to drink.
39 So the flocks conceived before the rods, and
the flocks brought forth streaked, speckled, and
spotted.
40 Then Jacob separated the lambs, and made the
flocks face toward the streaked and all the brown
in the flock of Laban; but he put his own flocks by
themselves and did not put them with Laban's
flock.

32 [a]Gen. 16:11; 31:42; Ex. 3:7; 4:31; Deut. 26:7; Ps. 25:18 [1]Lit. *See, a Son*
33 [1]Lit. *hated* [2]Lit. *Heard*
34 [1]Lit. *Attached*
35 [a]Gen. 49:8; Matt. 1:2 [1]Lit. *Praise*

CHAPTER 30
1 [a]Gen. 16:1, 2; 29:31 [b]Gen. 37:11 [c]1 Sam. 1:5, 6; [Job 5:2]
2 [a]Gen. 16:2; 1 Sam. 1:5
3 [a]Gen. 16:2 [b]Gen. 50:23; Job 3:12 [c]Gen. 16:2, 3 [1]Lit. *be built up by her*
4 [a]Gen. 16:3, 4
6 [a]Gen. 18:25; Ps. 35:24; 43:1; Lam. 3:59 [1]Lit. *Judge*
8 [1]Lit. *wrestlings of God* [2]Lit. *My Wrestling*
9 [a]Gen. 30:4
11 [1]So with Qr., Syr., Tg.; Kt.; LXX, Vg. *in fortune* [2]Lit. *Troop* or *Fortune*
13 [a]Prov. 31:28; Luke 1:48 [1]Lit. *Happy*
14 [a]Gen. 25:30
15 [a][Num. 16:9, 13]
18 [1]Lit. *Hire*
20 [1]Lit. *Dwelling*
21 [a]Gen. 34:1 [1]Lit. *Judgment*
22 [a]Gen. 19:29; 1 Sam. 1:19, 20 [b]Gen. 29:31
23 [a]1 Sam. 1:6; Is. 4:1; Luke 1:25
24 [a]Gen. 35:16–18 [1]Lit. *He Will Add*
25 [a]Gen. 24:54, 56 [b]Gen. 18:33
26 [a]Gen. 29:18–20, 27, 30; Hos. 12:12
27 [a]Gen. 26:24; 39:3; Is. 61:9
28 [a]Gen. 29:15; 31:7, 41
29 [a]Gen. 31:6, 38–40; Matt. 24:45; Titus 2:10
30 [a][1 Tim. 5:8] [1]Lit. *at my foot*
32 [a]Gen. 31:8
33 [a]Ps. 37:6
35 [a]Gen. 31:9–12
37 [a]Gen. 31:9–12

41 And it came to pass, whenever the stronger
livestock conceived, that Jacob placed the rods
before the eyes of the livestock in the gutters, that
they might conceive among the rods.
42 But when the flocks were feeble, he did not
put *them* in; so the feebler were Laban's and the
stronger Jacob's.
43 Thus the man [a]became exceedingly prosperous, and [b]had large flocks, female and male servants, and camels and donkeys.

### *Jacob Leaves Laban*

**31** Now *Jacob* heard the words of Laban's
sons, saying, "Jacob has taken away all that
was our father's, and from what was our father's
he has acquired all this [a]wealth."
2 And Jacob saw the [a]countenance of Laban,
and indeed it *was* not [b]*favorable* toward him as
before.
3 Then the LORD said to Jacob, [a]"Return to the
land of your fathers and to your family, and I will
[b]be with you."
4 So Jacob sent and called Rachel and Leah to
the field, to his flock,
5 and said to them, [a]"I see your father's [1]counte-
nance, that it *is* not *favorable* toward me as
before; but the God of my father [b]has been with
me.
6 "And [a]you know that with all my might I have
served your father.
7 "Yet your father has deceived me and
[a]changed my wages [b]ten times, but God [c]did not
allow him to hurt me.
8 "If he said thus: [a]'The speckled shall be your
wages,' then all the flocks bore speckled. And if he
said thus: 'The streaked shall be your wages,' then
all the flocks bore streaked.
9 "So God has [a]taken away the livestock of your
father and given *them* to me.
10 "And it happened, at the time when the flocks
conceived, that I lifted my eyes and saw in a
dream, and behold, the rams which leaped upon
the flocks *were* streaked, speckled, and gray-
spotted.
11 "Then [a]the Angel of God spoke to me in a
dream, saying, 'Jacob.' And I said, 'Here I am.'
12 "And He said, 'Lift your eyes now and see, all
the rams which leap on the flocks *are* streaked,
speckled, and gray-spotted; for [a]I have seen all
that Laban is doing to you.
13 'I *am* the God of Bethel, [a]where you anointed
the pillar *and* where you made a vow to Me. Now
[b]arise, get out of this land, and return to the land
of your family.' "
14 Then Rachel and Leah answered and said to
him, [a]"Is there still any portion or inheritance for
us in our father's house?
15 "Are we not considered strangers by him? For
[a]he has sold us, and also completely consumed our
money.
16 "For all these riches which God has taken
from our father are *really* ours and our children's;
now then, whatever God has said to you, do it."
**17** Then Jacob rose and set his sons and his wives
on camels.
18 And he carried away all his livestock and all
his possessions which he had gained, his acquired
livestock which he had gained in Padan Aram, to
go to his father Isaac in the land of [a]Canaan.
19 Now Laban had gone to shear his sheep, and
Rachel had stolen the [a]household[1] idols that were
her father's.
20 And Jacob stole away, unknown to Laban the
Syrian, in that he did not tell him that he intended
to flee.
21 So he fled with all that he had. He arose and
crossed the river, and [a]headed[1] toward the mountains of Gilead.
**22** And Laban was told on the third day that
Jacob had fled.
23 Then he took [a]his brethren with him and
pursued him for seven days' journey, and he
overtook him in the mountains of Gilead.
24 But God [a]had come to Laban the Syrian in a
dream by night, and said to him, "Be careful that
you [b]speak to Jacob neither good nor bad."
**25** So Laban overtook Jacob. Now Jacob had
pitched his tent in the mountains, and Laban with
his brethren pitched in the mountains of Gilead.
26 And Laban said to Jacob: "What have you
done, that you have stolen away unknown to me,
and [a]carried away my daughters like captives
*taken* with the sword?
27 "Why did you flee away secretly, and steal
away from me, and not tell me; for I might have
sent you away with joy and songs, with timbrel
and harp?
28 "And you did not allow me [a]to kiss my sons
and my daughters. Now [b]you have done foolishly
in *so* doing.
29 "It is in my power to do you harm, but the
[a]God of your father spoke to me [b]last night,
saying, 'Be careful that you speak to Jacob neither
good nor bad.'
30 "And now you have surely gone because you
greatly long for your father's house, *but* why did
you [a]steal my gods?"
31 Then Jacob answered and said to Laban, "Because I was [a]afraid, for I said, 'Perhaps you would
take your daughters from me by force.'
32 "With whomever you find your gods, [a]do not
let him live. In the presence of our brethren,
identify what I have of yours and take *it* with
you." For Jacob did not know that Rachel had
stolen them.
**33** And Laban went into Jacob's tent, into Leah's
tent, and into the two maids' tents, but he did not
find *them*. Then he went out of Leah's tent and
entered Rachel's tent.
34 Now Rachel had taken the [1]household idols,
put them in the camel's saddle, and sat on them.
And Laban [2]searched all about the tent but did not
find *them*.
35 And she said to her father, "Let it not displease my lord that I cannot [a]rise before you, for
the manner of women *is* with me." And he
searched but did not find the [1]household idols.
**36** Then Jacob was angry and rebuked Laban,
and Jacob answered and said to Laban: "What *is*
my [1]trespass? What *is* my sin, that you have so
hotly pursued me?
37 "Although you have searched all my things,
what part of your household things have you
found? Set *it* here before my brethren and your
brethren, that they may judge between us both!
38 "These twenty years I *have been* with you;
your ewes and your female goats have not miscar-
ried their young, and I have not eaten the rams of
your flock.
39 [a]"That which was torn *by beasts* I did not
bring to you; I bore the loss of it. [b]You required it

**43** [a]Gen. 12:16; 30:30 [b]Gen. 13:2; 24:35; 26:13, 14

CHAPTER 31

**1** [a]Ps. 49:16
**2** [a]Gen. 4:5 [b]Deut. 28:54
**3** [a]Gen. 28:15, 20, 21; 32:9 [b]Gen. 46:4
**5** [a]Gen. 31:2, 3 [b]Gen. 21:22; 28:13, 15; 31:29, 42, 53; Is. 41:10; Heb. 13:5 [1]Lit. *face*
**6** [a]Gen. 30:29; 31:38–41
**7** [a]Gen. 29:25; 31:41 [b]Num. 14:22; Neh. 4:12; Job 19:3; Zech. 8:23 [c]Gen. 15:1; 20:6; 31:29; Job 1:10; Ps. 37:28; 105:14
**8** [a]Gen. 30:32
**9** [a]Gen. 31:1, 16
**11** [a]Gen. 16:7–11; 22:11, 15; 31:13; 48:16
**12** [a]Gen. 31:42; Ex. 3:7; Ps. 139:3; Eccl. 5:8
**13** [a]Gen. 28:16–22; 35:1, 6, 15 [b]Gen. 31:3; 32:9
**14** [a]Gen. 2:24
**15** [a]Gen. 29:15, 20, 23, 27; Neh. 5:8
**18** [a]Gen. 17:8; 33:18; 35:27
**19** [a]Gen. 31:30, 34; 35:2; Judg. 17:5; 1 Sam. 19:13; Hos. 3:4 [1]Heb. *teraphim*
**21** [a]Gen. 46:28; 2 Kin. 12:17; Luke 9:51, 53 [1]Lit. *set his face toward*
**23** [a]Gen. 13:8
**24** [a]Gen. 20:3; 31:29; 46:2–4; Job 33:15; Matt. 1:20 [b]Gen. 24:50; 31:7, 29
**26** [a]1 Sam. 30:2
**28** [a]Gen. 31:55; Ruth 1:9, 14; 1 Kin. 19:20; Acts 20:37 [b]1 Sam. 13:13
**29** [a]Gen. 28:13; 31:5, 24, 42, 53 [b]Gen. 31:24
**30** [a]Gen. 31:19; Josh. 24:2; Judg. 17:5; 18:24
**31** [a]Gen. 26:7; 32:7, 11
**32** [a]Gen. 44:9
**34** [1]Heb. *teraphim* [2]Lit. *felt*
**35** [a]Ex. 20:12; Lev. 19:32 [1]Heb. *teraphim*
**36** [1]*transgression*
**39** [a]Ex. 22:10 [b]Ex. 22:10–13

from my hand, *whether* stolen by day or stolen by
night.
40 "*There* I was! In the day the drought consumed me, and the frost by night, and my sleep
departed from my eyes.
41 "Thus I have been in your house twenty years;
I [a]served you fourteen years for your two daughters, and six years for your flock, and [b]you have
changed my wages ten times.
42 [a]"Unless the God of my father, the God of
Abraham and [b]the Fear of Isaac, had been with
me, surely now you would have sent me away
empty-handed. [c]God has seen my affliction and
the labor of my hands, and [d]rebuked *you* last
night."
**43** And Laban answered and said to Jacob,
"*These* daughters *are* my daughters, and *these*
children *are* my children, and *this* flock *is* my
flock; all that you see *is* mine. But what can I do
this day to these my daughters or to their children
whom they have borne?
44 "Now therefore, come, [a]let us make a [1]cov-
enant, [b]you and I, and let it be a witness between
you and me."
45 So Jacob [a]took a stone and set it up *as* a pillar.
46 Then Jacob said to his brethren, "Gather
stones." And they took stones and made a heap,
and they ate there on the heap.
47 Laban called it [1]Jegar Sahadutha, but Jacob
called it [2]Galeed.
48 And Laban said, [a]"This heap *is* a witness
between you and me this day." Therefore its name
was called Galeed,
49 also [a]Mizpah,[1] because he said, "May the LORD
watch between you and me when we are absent
one from another.
50 "If you afflict my daughters, or if you take
*other* wives besides my daughters, *although* no
man *is* with us—see, God *is* witness between you
and me!"
**51** Then Laban said to Jacob, "Here is this heap
and here is *this* pillar, which I have placed between you and me.
52 "This heap *is* a witness, and *this* pillar *is* a
witness, that I will not pass beyond this heap to
you, and you will not pass beyond this heap and
this pillar to me, for harm.
53 "The God of Abraham, the God of Nahor, and
the God of their father [a]judge between us." And
Jacob [b]swore by [c]the [1]Fear of his father Isaac.
54 Then Jacob offered a sacrifice on the mountain, and called his brethren to eat bread. And
they ate bread and stayed all night on the mountain.
55 And early in the morning Laban arose, and
[a]kissed his sons and daughters and [b]blessed them.
Then Laban departed and [c]returned to his place.

### *Jacob Prepares to Meet Esau*

**32** So Jacob went on his way, and [a]the angels
of God met him.
2 When Jacob saw them, he said, "This *is* God's
[a]camp." And he called the name of that place
[1]Mahanaim.
**3** Then Jacob sent messengers before him to
Esau his brother [a]in the land of Seir, [b]the [1]country
of Edom.
4 And he commanded them, saying, [a]"Speak
thus to my lord Esau, 'Thus your servant Jacob
says: "I have dwelt with Laban and stayed there
until now.
5 [a]"I have oxen, donkeys, flocks, and male and
female servants; and I have sent to tell my lord,
that [b]I may find favor in your sight." ' "
**6** Then the messengers returned to Jacob, saying, "We came to your brother Esau, and [a]he also
is coming to meet you, and four hundred men *are*
with him."
7 So Jacob was greatly afraid and [a]distressed;
and he divided the people that *were* with him, and
the flocks and herds and camels, into two companies.
8 And he said, "If Esau comes to the one company and [1]attacks it, then the other company
which is left will escape."
**9** [a]Then Jacob said, [b]"O God of my father Abraham and God of my father Isaac, the LORD [c]who
said to me, 'Return to your country and to your
family, and I will deal well with you':
10 "I am not worthy of the least of all the [a]mer-
cies and of all the truth which You have shown
Your servant; for I crossed over this Jordan with
[b]my staff, and now I have become two companies.
11 [a]"Deliver me, I pray, from the hand of my
brother, from the hand of Esau; for I fear him, lest
he come and [1]attack me *and* [b]the mother with the
children.
12 "For [a]You said, 'I will surely treat you well,
and make your descendants as the [b]sand of the
sea, which cannot be numbered for multitude.' "
**13** So he lodged there that same night, and took
what [1]came to his hand as [a]a present for Esau his
brother:
14 two hundred female goats and twenty male
goats, two hundred ewes and twenty rams,
15 thirty milk camels with their colts, forty cows
and ten bulls, twenty female donkeys and ten
foals.
16 Then he delivered *them* to the hand of his
servants, every drove by itself, and said to his
servants, "Pass over before me, and put some
distance between successive droves."
17 And he commanded the first one, saying,
"When Esau my brother meets you and asks you,
saying, 'To whom do you belong, and where are
you going? Whose *are* these in front of you?'
18 "then you shall say, 'They *are* your servant
Jacob's. It *is* a present sent to my lord Esau; and
behold, he also *is* behind us.' "
19 So he commanded the second, the third, and
all who followed the droves, saying, "In this
manner you shall speak to Esau when you find
him;
20 "and also say, 'Behold, your servant Jacob *is*
behind us.' " For he said, "I will [a]appease him with
the present that goes before me, and afterward I
will see his face; perhaps he will accept me."
21 So the present went on over before him, but
he himself lodged that night in the camp.
**22** And he arose that night and took his two
wives, his two female servants, and his eleven
sons, [a]and crossed over the ford of Jabbok.
23 He took them, sent them [1]over the brook, and
sent over what he had.
24 Then Jacob was left alone; and [a]a Man wrestled with him until the [1]breaking of day.
25 Now when He saw that He did not prevail
against him, He [1]touched the socket of his hip;
and [a]the socket of Jacob's hip was out of joint as
He wrestled with him.
26 And [a]He said, "Let Me go, for the day breaks."
But he said, [b]"I will not let You go unless You
bless me!"

**41** [a]Gen. 29:20, 27–30 [b]Gen. 31:7
**42** [a]Gen. 31:5, 29, 53; Ps. 124:1, 2 [b]Gen. 31:53; Is. 8:13 [c]Gen. 29:32; Ex. 3:7 [d]Gen. 31:24, 29; 1 Chr. 12:17
**44** [a]Gen. 21:27, 32; 26:28 [b]Josh. 24:27 [1]*treaty*
**45** [a]Gen. 28:18; 35:14; Josh. 24:26, 27
**47** [1]Lit., in Aram., *Heap of Witness* [2]Lit., in Heb., *Heap of Witness*
**48** [a]Josh. 24:27
**49** [a]Judg. 10:17; 11:29; 1 Sam. 7:5, 6 [1]Lit. *Watch*
**53** [a]Gen. 16:5 [b]Gen. 21:23 [c]Gen. 31:42 [1]A reference to God
**55** [a]Gen. 29:11, 13; 31:28, 43 [b]Gen. 28:1 [c]Gen. 18:33; 30:25; Num. 24:25

CHAPTER 32

**1** [a]Num. 22:31; 2 Kin. 6:16, 17; [Ps. 34:7; 91:1; Heb. 1:14]
**2** [a]Josh. 5:14; Ps. 103:21; 148:2; Luke 2:13 [1]Lit. *Double Camp*
**3** [a]Gen. 14:6; 33:14, 16 [b]Gen. 25:30; 36:6–9; Deut. 2:5; Josh. 24:4 [1]Lit. *field*
**4** [a]Prov. 15:1
**5** [a]Gen. 30:43 [b]Gen. 33:8, 15
**6** [a]Gen. 33:1
**7** [a]Gen. 32:11; 35:3
**8** [1]Lit. *strikes*
**9** [a][Ps. 50:15] [b]Gen. 28:13; 31:42 [c]Gen. 31:3, 13
**10** [a]Gen. 24:27 [b]Job 8:7
**11** [a]Ps. 59:1, 2 [b]Hos. 10:14 [1]Lit. *strike*
**12** [a]Gen. 28:13–15 [b]Gen. 22:17
**13** [a]Gen. 43:11 [1]*he had received*
**20** [a][Prov. 21:14]
**22** [a]Num. 21:24; Deut. 3:16; Josh. 12:2
**23** [1]*across*
**24** [a]Josh. 5:13–15; Hos. 12:2–4 [1]*dawn*
**25** [a]Matt. 26:41; 2 Cor. 12:7 [1]*struck*
**26** [a]Luke 24:28 [b]Hos. 12:4

27 So He said to him, "What *is* your name?" He
said, "Jacob."
28 And He said, [a]"Your name shall no longer be
called Jacob, but [1]Israel; for you have [b]struggled
with God and [c]with men, and have prevailed."
29 Then Jacob asked, saying, "Tell *me* Your
name, I pray." And He said, [a]"Why *is* it *that* you
ask about My name?" And He [b]blessed him there.
30 So Jacob called the name of the place [1]Peniel:
"For [a]I have seen God face to face, and my life is
preserved."
31 Just as he crossed over [1]Penuel the sun rose
on him, and he limped on his hip.
32 Therefore to this day the children of Israel do
not eat the muscle that shrank, which *is* on the
hip socket, because He [1]touched the socket of
Jacob's hip in the muscle that shrank.

### *Jacob and Esau Make Peace*

**33** Now Jacob lifted his eyes and looked, and
there, [a]Esau was coming, and with him were
four hundred men. So he divided the children
among Leah, Rachel, and the two maidservants.
2 And he put the maidservants and their children in front, Leah and her children behind, and
Rachel and Joseph last.
3 Then he crossed over before them and [a]bowed
himself to the ground seven times, until he came
near to his brother.
4 [a]But Esau ran to meet him, and embraced him,
[b]and fell on his neck and kissed him, and they
wept.
5 And he lifted his eyes and saw the women and
children, and said, "Who *are* these with you?" So
he said, "The children [a]whom God has graciously
given your servant."
6 Then the maidservants came near, they and
their children, and bowed down.
7 And Leah also came near with her children,
and they bowed down. Afterward Joseph and
Rachel came near, and they bowed down.
8 Then Esau said, "What *do* you *mean by* [a]all
this company which I met?" And he said, "*These
are* [b]to find favor in the sight of my lord."
9 But Esau said, "I have enough, my brother;
keep what you have for yourself."
10 And Jacob said, "No, please, if I have now
found favor in your sight, then receive my present
from my hand, inasmuch as I [a]have seen your face
as though I had seen the face of God, and you
were pleased with me.
11 "Please, take [a]my blessing that is brought to
you, because God has dealt [b]graciously with me,
and because I have [1]enough." [c]So he urged him,
and he took *it*.
12 Then Esau said, "Let us take our journey; let
us go, and I will go before you."
13 But Jacob said to him, "My lord knows that
the children *are* weak, and the flocks and herds
which are nursing *are* with me. And if the men
should drive them hard one day, all the flock will
die.
14 "Please let my lord go on ahead before his
servant. I will lead on slowly at a pace which the
livestock that go before me, and the children, [1]are
able to endure, until I come to my lord [a]in Seir."
15 And Esau said, "Now let me leave with you
*some* of the people who *are* with me." But he said,
"What need is there? [a]Let me find favor in the
sight of my lord."
16 So Esau returned that day on his way to Seir.
17 And Jacob journeyed to [a]Succoth, built himself a house, and made [1]booths for his livestock.
Therefore the name of the place is called [2]Succoth.
18 Then Jacob came [1]safely to [a]the city of [b]She-
chem, which *is* in the land of Canaan, when he
came from Padan Aram; and he pitched his tent
before the city.
19 And [a]he bought the parcel of [1]land, where he
had pitched his tent, from the children of Hamor,
Shechem's father, for one hundred pieces of
money.
20 Then he erected an altar there and called it
[a]El[1] Elohe Israel.

### *What Dinah's Brothers Did*

**34** Now [a]Dinah the daughter of Leah, whom
she had borne to Jacob, went out to see the
daughters of the land.
2 And when Shechem the son of Hamor the
Hivite, prince of the country, saw her, he [a]took
her and lay with her, and violated her.
3 His soul [1]was strongly attracted to Dinah the
daughter of Jacob, and he loved the young woman
and spoke [2]kindly to the young woman.
4 So Shechem [a]spoke to his father Hamor, saying, "Get me this young woman as a wife."
5 And Jacob heard that he had defiled Dinah his
daughter. Now his sons were with his livestock in
the field; so Jacob [a]held[1] his peace until they came.
6 Then Hamor the father of Shechem went out
to Jacob to speak with him.
7 And the sons of Jacob came in from the field
when they heard *it;* and the men were grieved and
very angry, because he [a]had done a disgraceful
thing in Israel by lying with Jacob's daughter, [b]a
thing which ought not to be done.
8 But Hamor spoke with them, saying, "The
soul of my son Shechem longs for your daughter.
Please give her to him as a wife.
9 "And make marriages with us; give your
daughters to us, and take our daughters to yourselves.
10 "So you shall dwell with us, and the land shall
be before you. Dwell and trade in it, and acquire
possessions for yourselves in it."
11 Then Shechem said to her father and her
brothers, "Let me find favor in your eyes, and
whatever you say to me I will give.
12 "Ask me ever so much [a]dowry[1] and gift, and I
will give according to what you say to me; but
give me the young woman as a wife."
13 But the sons of Jacob answered Shechem and
Hamor his father, and spoke [a]deceitfully, because
he had defiled Dinah their sister.
14 And they said to them, "We cannot do this
thing, to give our sister to one who is [a]uncircum-
cised, for [b]that *would be* a reproach to us.
15 "But on this *condition* we will consent to you:
If you will become as we *are*, if every male of you
is circumcised,
16 "then we will give our daughters to you, and
we will take your daughters to us; and we will
dwell with you, and we will become one people.
17 "But if you will not heed us and be circumcised, then we will take our daughter and be
gone."
18 And their words pleased Hamor and Shechem,
Hamor's son.
19 So the young man did not delay to do the
thing, because he delighted in Jacob's daughter.

**28** [a]Gen. 35:10; 1 Kin. 18:31; 2 Kin. 17:34 [b]Hos. 12:3, 4 [c]Gen. 25:31; 27:33 [1]Lit. *Prince with God*
**29** [a]Judg. 13:17, 18 [b]Gen. 35:9
**30** [a]Gen. 16:13; Ex. 24:10, 11; 33:20; Num. 12:8; Deut. 5:24; Judg. 6:22; Is. 6:5; [Matt. 5:8; 1 Cor. 13:12] [1]Lit. *Face of God*
**31** [1]Lit. *Face of God;* same as *Peniel*, v. 30
**32** [1]*struck*

CHAPTER 33
**1** [a]Gen. 32:6
**3** [a]Gen. 18:2; 42:6
**4** [a]Gen. 32:28 [b]Gen. 45:14, 15
**5** [a]Gen. 48:9; [Ps. 127:3]; Is. 8:18
**8** [a]Gen. 32:13–16 [b]Gen. 32:5
**10** [a]Gen. 43:3; 2 Sam. 3:13; 14:24, 28, 32
**11** [a]Judg. 1:15; 1 Sam. 25:27; 30:26 [b]Gen. 30:43; Ex. 33:19 [c]2 Kin. 5:23 [1]Lit. *all*
**14** [a]Gen. 32:3; 36:8 [1]*can stand it*
**15** [a]Gen. 34:11; 47:25; Ruth 2:13
**17** [a]Josh. 13:27; Judg. 8:5; Ps. 60:6 [1]*shelters* [2]Lit. *Booths*
**18** [a]John 3:23 [b]Gen. 12:6; 35:4; Josh. 24:1; Judg. 9:1; Ps. 60:6 [1]Or *to Shalem, a city of*
**19** [a]Josh. 24:32; John 4:5 [1]Lit. *the field*
**20** [a]Gen. 35:7 [1]Lit. *God, the God of Israel*

CHAPTER 34
**1** [a]Gen. 30:21
**2** [a]Gen. 20:2
**3** [1]Lit. *clung to* [2]*tenderly*
**4** [a]Judg. 14:2
**5** [a]2 Sam. 13:22 [1]*kept silent*
**7** [a]Deut. 22:20–30; Josh. 7:15; Judg. 20:6 [b]Deut. 23:17; 2 Sam. 13:12
**12** [a]Ex. 22:16, 17; Deut. 22:29 [1]*bride-price*
**13** [a]Gen. 31:7; Ex. 8:29
**14** [a]Ex. 12:48 [b]Josh. 5:2–9

He *was* [a]more honorable than all the household of
his father.
20 And Hamor and Shechem his son came to the
[a]gate of their city, and spoke with the men of their
city, saying:
21 "These men *are* at peace with us. Therefore let
them dwell in the land and trade in it. For indeed
the land *is* large enough for them. Let us take
their daughters to us as wives, and let us give
them our daughters.
22 "Only on this *condition* will the men consent
to dwell with us, to be one people: if every male
among us is circumcised as they *are* circumcised.
23 "*Will* not their livestock, their property, and
every animal of theirs *be* ours? Only let us consent
to them, and they will dwell with us."
24 And all who went out of the gate of his city
heeded Hamor and Shechem his son; every male
was circumcised, all who [a]went out of the gate of
his city.
**25** Now it came to pass on the third day, when
they were in pain, that two of the sons of Jacob,
[a]Simeon and Levi, Dinah's brothers, each took his
sword and came boldly upon the city and killed all
the males.
26 And they [a]killed Hamor and Shechem his son
with the edge of the sword, and took Dinah from
Shechem's house, and went out.
27 The sons of Jacob came upon the slain, and
plundered the city, because their sister had been
defiled.
28 They took their sheep, their oxen, and their
donkeys, what *was* in the city and what *was* in
the field,
29 and all their wealth. All their little ones and
their wives they took captive; and they plundered
even all that *was* in the houses.
30 Then Jacob said to Simeon and Levi, [a]"You
have [b]troubled me [c]by making me obnoxious
among the inhabitants of the land, among the
Canaanites and the Perizzites; [d]and since I *am* few
in number, they will gather themselves together
against me and kill me. I shall be destroyed, my
household and I."
31 But they said, "Should he treat our sister like a
harlot?"

## *God Blesses Jacob at Bethel*

**35** Then God said to Jacob, "Arise, go up to
[a]Bethel and dwell there; and make an altar
there to God, [b]who appeared to you [c]when you
fled from the face of Esau your brother."
2 And Jacob said to his [a]household and to all
who *were* with him, "Put away [b]the foreign gods
that *are* among you, [c]purify yourselves, and
change your garments.
3 "Then let us arise and go up to Bethel; and I
will make an altar there to God, [a]who answered
me in the day of my distress [b]and has been with
me in the way which I have gone."
4 So they gave Jacob all the foreign [1]gods which
*were* in their hands, and *all* the [a]earrings which
*were* in their ears; and Jacob hid them under [b]the
terebinth tree which *was* by Shechem.
**5** And they journeyed, and [a]the terror of God
was upon the cities that *were* all around them,
and they did not pursue the sons of Jacob.
6 So Jacob came to [a]Luz (that *is,* Bethel), which
*is* in the land of Canaan, he and all the people who
*were* with him.
7 And he [a]built an altar there and called the
place [1]El Bethel, because [b]there God appeared to
him when he fled from the face of his brother.
8 Now [a]Deborah, Rebekah's nurse, died, and she
was buried below Bethel under the terebinth tree.
So the name of it was called [1]Allon Bachuth.
9 Then [a]God appeared to Jacob again, when he
came from Padan Aram, and [b]blessed him.
10 And God said to him, "Your name *is* Jacob;
[a]your name shall not be called Jacob anymore,
[b]but Israel shall be your name." So He called his
name Israel.
11 Also God said to him: [a]"I *am* God Almighty.
[b]Be fruitful and multiply; [c]a nation and a company
of nations shall proceed from you, and kings shall
come from your body.
12 "The [a]land which I gave Abraham and Isaac I
give to you; and to your descendants after you I
give this land."
13 Then God [a]went[1] up from him in the place
where He talked with him.
14 So Jacob [a]set up a pillar in the place where He
talked with him, a pillar of stone; and he poured a
drink offering on it, and he poured oil on it.
15 And Jacob called the name of the place where
God spoke with him, [a]Bethel.
**16** Then they journeyed from Bethel. And when
there was but a little distance to go to Ephrath,
Rachel labored *in childbirth,* and she had hard
labor.
17 Now it came to pass, when she was in hard
labor, that the midwife said to her, "Do not fear;
[a]you will have this son also."
18 And so it was, as her soul was departing (for
she died), that she called his name [1]Ben-Oni; but
his father called him [2]Benjamin.
19 So [a]Rachel died and was buried on the way to
[b]Ephrath (that *is,* Bethlehem).
20 And Jacob set a pillar on her grave, which *is*
the pillar of Rachel's grave [a]to this day.
**21** Then Israel journeyed and pitched his tent
beyond [a]the tower of Eder.
22 And it happened, when Israel dwelt in that
land, that Reuben went and [a]lay with Bilhah his
father's concubine; and Israel heard *about it.*
Now the sons of Jacob were twelve:
23 the sons of Leah *were* [a]Reuben, Jacob's firstborn, and Simeon, Levi, Judah, Issachar, and
Zebulun;
24 the sons of Rachel *were* Joseph and Benjamin;
25 the sons of Bilhah, Rachel's maidservant, *were*
Dan and Naphtali;
26 and the sons of Zilpah, Leah's maidservant,
*were* Gad and Asher. These *were* the sons of
Jacob who were born to him in Padan Aram.
**27** Then Jacob came to his father Isaac at
[a]Mamre, or [b]Kirjath Arba[1] (that *is,* Hebron), where
Abraham and Isaac had dwelt.
28 Now the days of Isaac were one hundred and
eighty years.
29 So Isaac breathed his last and died, and [a]was
[1]gathered to his people, *being* old and full of days.
And [b]his sons Esau and Jacob buried him.

## *The Family of Esau*

**36** Now this *is* the genealogy of Esau, [a]who is
Edom.
2 [a]Esau took his wives from the daughters of
Canaan: Adah the daughter of Elon the [b]Hittite;
[c]Aholibamah[1] the daughter of Anah, the daughter
of Zibeon the Hivite;
3 and [a]Basemath, Ishmael's daughter, sister of
Nebajoth.

**19** [a]1 Chr. 4:9
**20** [a]Ruth 4:1, 11
**24** [a]Gen. 23:10, 18
**25** [a]Gen. 29:33, 34; 42:24; 49:5–7
**26** [a]Gen. 49:5, 6
**30** [a]Gen. 49:6 [b]Josh. 7:25 [c]Ex. 5:21 [d]Deut. 4:27

CHAPTER 35

**1** [a]Gen. 28:19; 31:13 [b]Gen. 28:13 [c]Gen. 27:43
**2** [a]Josh. 24:15 [b]Josh. 24:2, 14, 23 [c]Ex. 19:10, 14
**3** [a]Gen. 32:7, 24 [b]Gen. 28:15, 20; 31:3, 42
**4** [a]Hos. 2:13 [b]Josh. 24:26 [1]*idols*
**5** [a]Ex. 15:16; 23:27
**6** [a]Gen. 28:19, 22; 48:3
**7** [a]Eccl. 5:4 [b]Gen. 28:13 [1]Lit. *God of the House of God*
**8** [a]Gen. 24:59 [1]Lit. *Terebinth of Weeping*
**9** [a]Josh. 5:13 [b]Gen. 32:29
**10** [a]Gen. 17:5 [b]Gen. 32:28
**11** [a]Ex. 6:3 [b]Gen. 9:1, 7 [c]Gen. 17:5, 6, 16; 28:3; 48:4
**12** [a]Gen. 12:7; 13:15; 26:3, 4; 28:13; 48:4
**13** [a]Gen. 17:22; 18:33 [1]*departed*
**14** [a]Gen. 28:18, 19; 31:45
**15** [a]Gen. 28:19
**17** [a]Gen. 30:24
**18** [1]Lit. *Son of My Sorrow* [2]Lit. *Son of the Right Hand*
**19** [a]Gen. 48:7 [b]Mic. 5:2
**20** [a]1 Sam. 10:2
**21** [a]Mic. 4:8
**22** [a]Gen. 49:4
**23** [a]Ex. 1:1–4
**27** [a]Gen. 13:18; 18:1; 23:19 [b]Josh. 14:15 [1]Lit. *Town* or *City of Arba*
**29** [a]Gen. 15:15; 25:8; 49:33 [b]Gen. 25:9; 49:31 [1]Joined his ancestors

CHAPTER 36

**1** [a]Gen. 25:30
**2** [a]Gen. 26:34; 28:9 [b]2 Kin. 7:6 [c]Gen. 36:25 [1]Or *Oholibamah*
**3** [a]Gen. 28:9

4 Now [a]Adah bore Eliphaz to Esau, and Basemath bore Reuel.
5 And [1]Aholibamah bore Jeush, Jaalam, and
Korah. These *were* the sons of Esau who were
born to him in the land of Canaan.
6 Then Esau took his wives, his sons, his daughters, and all the persons of his household, his
cattle and all his animals, and all his goods which
he had gained in the land of Canaan, and went to
a country away from the presence of his brother
Jacob.
7 [a]For their possessions were too great for them
to dwell together, and [b]the land where they were
strangers could not support them because of their
livestock.
8 So Esau dwelt in [a]Mount Seir. [b]Esau *is* Edom.
**9** And this *is* the genealogy of Esau the father of
the Edomites in Mount Seir.
10 These *were* the names of Esau's sons: [a]Eliphaz
the son of Adah the wife of Esau, and Reuel the
son of Basemath the wife of Esau.
11 And the sons of Eliphaz were Teman, Omar,
[1]Zepho, Gatam, and Kenaz.
12 Now Timna was the concubine of Eliphaz,
Esau's son, and she bore [a]Amalek to Eliphaz.
These *were* the sons of Adah, Esau's wife.
13 These *were* the sons of Reuel: Nahath, Zerah,
Shammah, and Mizzah. These were the sons of
Basemath, Esau's wife.
14 These were the sons of [1]Aholibamah, Esau's
wife, the daughter of Anah, the daughter of
Zibeon. And she bore to Esau: Jeush, Jaalam, and
Korah.
**15** These *were* the chiefs of the sons of Esau. The
sons of Eliphaz, the firstborn *son* of Esau, were
Chief Teman, Chief Omar, Chief Zepho, Chief
Kenaz,
16 [1]Chief Korah, Chief Gatam, *and* Chief Amalek.
These *were* the chiefs of Eliphaz in the land of
Edom. They *were* the sons of Adah.
**17** These *were* the sons of Reuel, Esau's son:
Chief Nahath, Chief Zerah, Chief Shammah, and
Chief Mizzah. These *were* the chiefs of Reuel in
the land of Edom. These *were* the sons of Basemath, Esau's wife.
**18** And these *were* the sons of [1]Aholibamah,
Esau's wife: Chief Jeush, Chief Jaalam, and Chief
Korah. These *were* the chiefs *who descended* from
Aholibamah, Esau's wife, the daughter of Anah.
19 These *were* the sons of Esau, who is Edom,
and these *were* their chiefs.
**20** [a]These *were* the sons of Seir [b]the Horite who
inhabited the land: Lotan, Shobal, Zibeon, Anah,
21 Dishon, Ezer, and Dishan. These *were* the
chiefs of the Horites, the sons of Seir, in the land
of Edom.
22 And the sons of Lotan were Hori and [1]Hemam.
Lotan's sister *was* Timna.
23 These *were* the sons of Shobal: [1]Alvan, Manahath, Ebal, [2]Shepho, and Onam.
24 These *were* the sons of Zibeon: both Ajah and
Anah. This *was the* Anah who found the [1]water in
the wilderness as he pastured [a]the donkeys of his
father Zibeon.
25 These *were* the children of Anah: Dishon and
[1]Aholibamah the daughter of Anah.
26 These *were* the sons of [1]Dishon: [2]Hemdan,
Eshban, Ithran, and Cheran.
27 These *were* the sons of Ezer: Bilhan, Zaavan,
and [1]Akan.
28 These *were* the sons of Dishan: [a]Uz and Aran.
**29** These *were* the chiefs of the Horites: Chief
Lotan, Chief Shobal, Chief Zibeon, Chief Anah,
30 Chief Dishon, Chief Ezer, and Chief Dishan.
These *were* the chiefs of the Horites, according to
their chiefs in the land of Seir.
**31** [a]Now these *were* the kings who reigned in the
land of Edom before any king reigned over the
children of Israel:
32 Bela the son of Beor reigned in Edom, and the
name of his city *was* Dinhabah.
33 And when Bela died, Jobab the son of Zerah of
Bozrah reigned in his place.
34 When Jobab died, Husham of the land of the
Temanites reigned in his place.
35 And when Husham died, Hadad the son of
Bedad, who attacked Midian in the field of Moab,
reigned in his place. And the name of his city *was*
Avith.
36 When Hadad died, Samlah of Masrekah
reigned in his place.
37 And when Samlah died, Saul of [a]Rehoboth-*by*-
the-River reigned in his place.
38 When Saul died, Baal-Hanan the son of Achbor reigned in his place.
39 And when Baal-Hanan the son of Achbor died,
[1]Hadar reigned in his place; and the name of his
city *was* [2]Pau. His wife's name *was* Mehetabel, the
daughter of Matred, the daughter of Mezahab.
**40** And these *were* the names of the chiefs of
Esau, according to their families and their places,
by their names: Chief Timnah, Chief [1]Alvah, Chief
Jetheth,
41 Chief [1]Aholibamah, Chief Elah, Chief Pinon,
42 Chief Kenaz, Chief Teman, Chief Mibzar,
43 Chief Magdiel, and Chief Iram. These *were* the
chiefs of Edom, according to their dwelling places
in the land of their possession. Esau *was* the
father of [1]the Edomites.

### *Joseph's Dreams*

**37** Now Jacob dwelt in the land [a]where his
father was a [1]stranger, in the land of Canaan.
2 This *is* the history of Jacob. Joseph, *being*
seventeen years old, was feeding the flock with his
brothers. And the lad *was* with the sons of Bilhah
and the sons of Zilpah, his father's wives; and
Joseph brought [a]a bad report of them to his father.
3 Now Israel loved Joseph more than all his
children, because he *was* [a]the son of his old age.
Also he [b]made him a tunic of *many* colors.
4 But when his brothers saw that their father
loved him more than all his brothers, they [a]hated
him and could not speak peaceably to him.
**5** Now Joseph had a dream, and he told *it* to his
brothers; and they hated him even more.
6 So he said to them, "Please hear this dream
which I have dreamed:
7 [a]"There we were, binding sheaves in the field.
Then behold, my sheaf arose and also stood upright; and indeed your sheaves stood all around
and bowed down to my sheaf."
8 And his brothers said to him, "Shall you
indeed reign over us? Or shall you indeed have
dominion over us?" So they hated him even more
for his dreams and for his words.
**9** Then he dreamed still another dream and told
it to his brothers, and said, "Look, I have dreamed
another dream. And this time, [a]the sun, the moon,
and the eleven stars bowed down to me."
10 So he told *it* to his father and his brothers; and

4 [a]1 Chr. 1:35
5 [1]Or *Oholibamah*
7 [a]Gen. 13:6, 11 [b]Gen. 17:8; 28:4; Heb. 11:9
8 [a]Gen. 32:3; Deut. 2:5; Josh. 24:4 [b]Gen. 36:1, 19
10 [a]1 Chr. 1:35
11 [1]*Zephi,* 1 Chr. 1:36
12 [a]Ex. 17:8–16; Num. 24:20; Deut. 25:17–19; 1 Sam. 15:2, 3
14 [1]Or *Oholibamah*
16 [1]Sam. omits *Chief Korah*
18 [1]Or *Oholibamah*
20 [a]1 Chr. 1:38–42 [b]Gen. 14:6; Deut. 2:12, 22
22 [1]*Homam,* 1 Chr. 1:39
23 [1]*Alian,* 1 Chr. 1:40 [2]*Shephi,* 1 Chr. 1:40
24 [a]Lev. 19:19 [1]So with MT, Vg. (*hot springs*); LXX *Jamin;* Tg. *mighty men;* Talmud *mules*
25 [1]Or *Oholibamah*
26 [1]Heb. *Dishan* [2]*Hamran,* 1 Chr. 1:41
27 [1]*Jaakan,* 1 Chr. 1:42
28 [a]Job 1:1
31 [a]Gen. 17:6, 16; 35:11; 1 Chr. 1:43
37 [a]Gen. 10:11
39 [1]Sam., Syr. *Hadad* and 1 Chr. 1:50 [2]*Pai,* 1 Chr. 1:50
40 [1]*Aliah,* 1 Chr. 1:51
41 [1]Or *Oholibamah*
43 [1]Heb. *Edom*

CHAPTER 37
1 [a]Gen. 17:8; 23:4; 28:4; 36:7; Heb. 11:9 [1]*sojourner,* temporary resident
2 [a]Gen. 35:25, 26; 1 Sam. 2:22–24
3 [a]Gen. 44:20 [b]Gen. 37:23, 32; Judg. 5:30; 1 Sam. 2:19
4 [a]Gen. 27:41; 49:23; 1 Sam. 17:28; John 15:18–20
7 [a]Gen. 42:6, 9; 43:26; 44:14
9 [a]Gen. 46:29; 47:25

his father rebuked him and said to him, "What *is*
this dream that you have dreamed? Shall your
mother and I and [a]your brothers indeed come to
bow down to the earth before you?"
11 And [a]his brothers envied him, but his father
[b]kept the matter *in mind.*
**12** Then his brothers went to feed their father's
flock in [a]Shechem.
13 And Israel said to Joseph, "Are not your
brothers feeding *the flock* in Shechem? Come, I
will send you to them." So he said to him, "Here I
am."
14 Then he said to him, "Please go and see if it is
well with your brothers and well with the flocks,
and bring back word to me." So he sent him out of
the Valley of [a]Hebron, and he went to Shechem.
15 Now a certain man found him, and there he
was, wandering in the field. And the man asked
him, saying, "What are you seeking?"
16 So he said, "I am seeking my brothers. [a]Please
tell me where they are feeding *their flocks.*"
17 And the man said, "They have departed from
here, for I heard them say, 'Let us go to Dothan.' "
So Joseph went after his brothers and found them
in [a]Dothan.
**18** Now when they saw him afar off, even before
he came near them, [a]they conspired against him
to kill him.
19 Then they said to one another, "Look, this
[1]dreamer is coming!
20 [a]"Come therefore, let us now kill him and cast
him into some pit; and we shall say, 'Some wild
beast has devoured him.' We shall see what will
become of his dreams!"
21 But [a]Reuben heard *it,* and he delivered him out
of their hands, and said, "Let us not kill him."
22 And Reuben said to them, "Shed no blood, *but*
cast him into this pit which *is* in the wilderness,
and do not lay a hand on him"—that he might
deliver him out of their hands, and bring him back
to his father.
**23** So it came to pass, when Joseph had come to
his brothers, that they [a]stripped Joseph *of* his
tunic, the tunic of *many* colors that *was* on him.
24 Then they took him and cast him into a pit.
And the pit *was* empty; *there was* no water in it.
25 [a]And they sat down to eat a meal. Then they
lifted their eyes and looked, and there was a
company of [b]Ishmaelites, coming from Gilead
with their camels, bearing spices, [c]balm, and
myrrh, on their way to carry *them* down to Egypt.
26 So Judah said to his brothers, "What profit *is*
*there* if we kill our brother and [a]conceal his blood?
27 "Come and let us sell him to the Ishmaelites,
and [a]let not our hand be upon him, for he *is* [b]our
brother *and* [c]our flesh." And his brothers listened.
28 Then [a]Midianite traders passed by; so *the*
*brothers* pulled Joseph up and lifted him out of the
pit, [b]and sold him to the Ishmaelites for [c]twenty
*shekels* of silver. And they took Joseph to Egypt.
**29** Then Reuben returned to the pit, and indeed
Joseph *was* not in the pit; and he [a]tore his clothes.
30 And he returned to his brothers and said, "The
lad [a]*is* no *more;* and I, where shall I go?"
31 So they took [a]Joseph's tunic, killed a kid of the
goats, and dipped the tunic in the blood.
32 Then they sent the tunic of *many* colors, and
they brought *it* to their father and said, "We have
found this. Do you know whether it *is* your son's
tunic or not?"
33 And he recognized it and said, "*It is* my son's
tunic. A [a]wild beast has devoured him. Without
doubt Joseph is torn to pieces."
34 Then Jacob [a]tore his clothes, put sackcloth on
his waist, and [b]mourned for his son many days.
35 And all his sons and all his daughters [a]arose to
comfort him; but he refused to be comforted, and
he said, "For [b]I shall go down into the grave to my
son in mourning." Thus his father wept for him.
36 Now [a]the [1]Midianites had sold him in Egypt to
Potiphar, an officer of Pharaoh *and* captain of the
guard.

### *Sons of Judah*

**38** It came to pass at that time that Judah
departed from his brothers, and [a]visited a
certain Adullamite whose name *was* Hirah.
2 And Judah [a]saw there a daughter of a certain
Canaanite whose name *was* [b]Shua, and he married her and went in to her.
3 So she conceived and bore a son, and he called
his name [a]Er.
4 She conceived again and bore a son, and she
called his name [a]Onan.
5 And she conceived yet again and bore a son,
and called his name [a]Shelah. He was at Chezib
when she bore him.
6 Then Judah [a]took a wife for Er his firstborn,
and her name *was* [b]Tamar.
7 But [a]Er, Judah's firstborn, was wicked in the
sight of the LORD, [b]and the LORD killed him.
8 And Judah said to Onan, "Go in to [a]your
brother's wife and marry her, and raise up an heir
to your brother."
9 But Onan knew that the heir would not be
[a]his; and it came to pass, when he went in to his
brother's wife, that he emitted on the ground, lest
he should give an heir to his brother.
10 And the thing which he did [1]displeased the
LORD; therefore He killed [a]him also.
11 Then Judah said to Tamar his daughter-in-
law, [a]"Remain a widow in your father's house till
my son Shelah is grown." For he said, "Lest he
also die like his brothers." And Tamar went and
dwelt [b]in her father's house.
**12** Now in the process of time the daughter of
Shua, Judah's wife, died; and Judah [a]was comforted, and went up to his sheepshearers at Timnah, he and his friend Hirah the Adullamite.
13 And it was told Tamar, saying, "Look, your
father-in-law is going up [a]to Timnah to shear his
sheep."
14 So she took off her widow's garments, covered
*herself* with a veil and wrapped herself, and [a]sat in
an open place which *was* on the way to Timnah;
for she saw [b]that Shelah was grown, and she was
not given to him as a wife.
15 When Judah saw her, he thought she *was* a
harlot, because she had covered her face.
16 Then he turned to her by the way, and said,
"Please let me come in to you"; for he did not
know that she *was* his daughter-in-law. So she
said, "What will you give me, that you may come
in to me?"
17 And he said, [a]"I will send a young goat from
the flock." So she said, [b]"Will you give *me* a
pledge till you send *it?* "
18 Then he said, "What pledge shall I give you?"
So she said, [a]"Your signet and cord, and your staff
that *is* in your hand." Then he gave *them* to her,
and went in to her, and she conceived by him.
19 So she arose and went away, and [a]laid aside

**10** [a]Gen. 27:29
**11** [a]Matt. 27:17, 18; Acts 7:9 [b]Dan. 7:28; Luke 2:19, 51
**12** [a]Gen. 33:18–20
**14** [a]Gen. 13:18; 23:2, 19; 35:27; Josh. 14:14, 15; Judg. 1:10
**16** [a]Song 1:7
**17** [a]2 Kin. 6:13
**18** [a]1 Sam. 19:1; Ps. 31:13; 37:12, 32; Matt. 21:38; 26:3, 4; 27:1; Mark 14:1; John 11:53; Acts 23:12
**19** [1]Lit. *master of dreams*
**20** [a]Gen. 37:22; Prov. 1:11
**21** [a]Gen. 42:22
**23** [a]Matt. 27:28
**25** [a]Prov. 30:20 [b]Gen. 16:11, 12; 37:28, 36; 39:1 [c]Jer. 8:22
**26** [a]Gen. 37:20
**27** [a]1 Sam. 18:17 [b]Gen. 42:21 [c]Gen. 29:14
**28** [a]Gen. 37:25; Judg. 6:1–3; 8:22, 24 [b]Gen. 45:4, 5; Ps. 105:17; Acts 7:9 [c]Matt. 27:9
**29** [a]Gen. 37:34; 44:13; Job 1:20
**30** [a]Gen. 42:13, 36
**31** [a]Gen. 37:3, 23
**33** [a]Gen. 37:20
**34** [a]Gen. 37:29; 2 Sam. 3:31 [b]Gen. 50:10
**35** [a]2 Sam. 12:17 [b]Gen. 25:8; 35:29; 42:38; 44:29, 31
**36** [a]Gen. 39:1 [1]MT *Medanites*

CHAPTER 38
**1** [a]2 Kin. 4:8
**2** [a]Gen. 34:2 [b]1 Chr. 2:3
**3** [a]Gen. 46:12; Num. 26:19
**4** [a]Gen. 46:12; Num. 26:19
**5** [a]Num. 26:20
**6** [a]Gen. 21:21 [b]Ruth 4:12
**7** [a]Gen. 46:12; Num. 26:19 [b]1 Chr. 2:3
**8** [a]Deut. 25:5, 6; Matt. 22:24
**9** [a]Deut. 25:6
**10** [a]Gen. 46:12; Num. 26:19 [1]Lit. *was evil in the eyes of*
**11** [a]Ruth 1:12, 13 [b]Lev. 22:13
**12** [a]2 Sam. 13:39
**13** [a]Josh. 15:10, 57; Judg. 14:1
**14** [a]Prov. 7:12 [b]Gen. 38:11, 26
**17** [a]Judg. 15:1; Ezek. 16:33 [b]Gen. 38:20
**18** [a]Gen. 38:25; 41:42
**19** [a]Gen. 38:14

her veil and put on the garments of her widowhood.
20 And Judah sent the young goat by the hand of
his friend the Adullamite, to receive *his* pledge
from the woman's hand, but he did not find her.
21 Then he asked the men of that place, saying,
"Where is the harlot who *was* [1]openly by the
roadside?" And they said, "There was no harlot in
this *place.*"
22 So he returned to Judah and said, "I cannot
find her. Also, the men of the place said there was
no harlot in this *place.*"
23 Then Judah said, "Let her take *them* for
herself, lest we be shamed; for I sent this young
goat and you have not found her."
**24** And it came to pass, about three months after,
that Judah was told, saying, "Tamar your daughter-in-law has [a]played the harlot; furthermore she
*is* [1]with child by harlotry." So Judah said, "Bring
her out [b]and let her be burned!"
25 When she *was* brought out, she sent to her
father-in-law, saying, "By the man to whom these
belong, I *am* with child." And she said, [a]"Please
determine whose these *are*—the signet and cord,
and staff."
26 So Judah [a]acknowledged *them* and said, [b]"She
has been more righteous than I, because [c]I did not
give her to Shelah my son." And he [d]never knew
her again.
**27** Now it came to pass, at the time for giving
birth, that behold, twins *were* in her womb.
28 And so it was, when she was giving birth, that
*the one* put out *his* hand; and the midwife took a
scarlet *thread* and bound it on his hand, saying,
"This one came out first."
29 Then it happened, as he drew back his hand,
that his brother came out unexpectedly; and she
said, "How did you break through? *This* breach *be*
upon you!" Therefore his name was called [a]Perez.[1]
30 Afterward his brother came out who had the
scarlet *thread* on his hand. And his name was
called [a]Zerah.

### *Joseph's Advancement*

**39** Now Joseph had been taken [a]down to
Egypt. And [b]Potiphar, an officer of Pharaoh,
captain of the guard, an Egyptian, [c]bought him
from the Ishmaelites who had taken him down
there.
2 [a]The LORD was with Joseph, and he was a
successful man; and he was in the house of his
master the Egyptian.
3 And his master saw that the LORD *was* with
him and that the LORD [a]made all he did [1]to prosper
in his hand.
4 So Joseph [a]found favor in his sight, and served
him. Then he made him [b]overseer of his house,
and all *that* he had he put [1]under his authority.
5 So it was, from the time *that* he had made him
overseer of his house and all that he had, that [a]the
LORD blessed the Egyptian's house for Joseph's
sake; and the blessing of the LORD was on all that
he had in the house and in the field.
6 Thus he left all that he had in Joseph's [1]hand,
and he did not know what he had except for the
[2]bread which he ate. Now Joseph [a]was handsome
in form and appearance.
**7** And it came to pass after these things that his
master's wife [1]cast longing eyes on Joseph, and
she said, [a]"Lie with me."
8 But he refused and said to his master's wife,
"Look, my master does not know what *is* with me
in the house, and he has committed all that he has
to my hand.
9 "*There is* no one greater in this house than I,
nor has he kept back anything from me but you,
because you *are* his wife. [a]How then can I do this
great wickedness, and [b]sin against God?"
10 So it was, as she spoke to Joseph day by day,
that he [a]did not heed her, to lie with her *or* to be
with her.
11 But it happened about this time, when Joseph
went into the house to do his work, and none of
the men of the house *was* inside,
12 that she [a]caught him by his garment, saying,
"Lie with me." But he left his garment in her
hand, and fled and ran outside.
13 And so it was, when she saw that he had left
his garment in her hand and fled outside,
14 that she called to the men of her house and
spoke to them, saying, "See, he has brought in to
us a [a]Hebrew to [1]mock us. He came in to me to lie
with me, and I cried out with a loud voice.
15 "And it happened, when he heard that I lifted
my voice and cried out, that he left his garment
with me, and fled and went outside."
16 So she kept his garment with her until his
master came home.
17 Then she [a]spoke to him with words like these,
saying, "The Hebrew servant whom you brought
to us came in to me to mock me;
18 "so it happened, as I lifted my voice and cried
out, that he left his garment with me and fled
outside."
**19** So it was, when his master heard the words
which his wife spoke to him, saying, "Your servant did to me after this manner," that his [a]anger
was aroused.
20 Then Joseph's master took him and [a]put him
into the [b]prison, a place where the king's prisoners
*were* confined. And he was there in the prison.
**21** But the LORD was with Joseph and showed
him mercy, and He [a]gave[1] him favor in the sight of
the keeper of the prison.
22 And the keeper of the prison [a]committed to
Joseph's hand all the prisoners who *were* in the
prison; whatever they did there, it was his doing.
23 The keeper of the prison did not look into
anything *that was* under [1]*Joseph's* authority,
because [a]the LORD was with him; and whatever he
did, the LORD made *it* prosper.

### *Joseph Interprets Dreams*

**40** It came to pass after these things *that* the
[a]butler and the baker of the king of Egypt
offended their lord, the king of Egypt.
2 And Pharaoh was [a]angry with his two officers,
the chief butler and the chief baker.
3 [a]So he put them in custody in the house of the
captain of the guard, in the prison, the place
where Joseph *was* confined.
4 And the captain of the guard charged Joseph
with them, and he served them; so they were in
custody for a while.
**5** Then the butler and the baker of the king of
Egypt, who *were* confined in the prison, [a]had a
dream, both of them, each man's dream in one
night *and* each man's dream with its *own* interpretation.
6 And Joseph came in to them in the morning
and looked at them, and saw that they *were* [1]sad.
7 So he asked Pharaoh's officers who *were* with

**21** [1]*in full view*
**24** [a]Judg. 19:2 [b]Lev. 20:14; 21:9; Deut. 22:21 [1]*pregnant*
**25** [a]Gen. 37:32; 38:18
**26** [a]Gen. 37:33 [b]1 Sam. 24:17 [c]Gen. 38:14 [d]Job 34:31, 32
**29** [a]Gen. 46:12; Num. 26:20; Ruth 4:12; 1 Chr. 2:4; Matt. 1:3 [1]Lit. *Breach* or *Breakthrough*
**30** [a]Gen. 46:12; 1 Chr. 2:4; Matt. 1:3

CHAPTER 39

**1** [a]Gen. 12:10; 43:15 [b]Gen. 37:36; Ps. 105:17 [c]Gen. 37:28; 45:4
**2** [a]Gen. 26:24, 28; 28:15; 35:3; 39:3, 21, 23; 1 Sam. 16:18; 18:14, 28; Acts 7:9
**3** [a]Ps. 1:3 [1]*to be a success*
**4** [a]Gen. 18:3; 19:19; 39:21 [b]Gen. 24:2, 10; 39:8, 22; 41:40 [1]Lit. *in his hand*
**5** [a]Gen. 18:26; 30:27; 2 Sam. 6:11
**6** [a]Gen. 29:17; 1 Sam. 16:12 [1]Care [2]Food
**7** [a]2 Sam. 13:11 [1]Lit. *lifted up her eyes toward*
**9** [a]Lev. 20:10; Prov. 6:29, 32 [b]Gen. 20:6; 42:18; 2 Sam. 12:13; Ps. 51:4
**10** [a]Prov. 1:10
**12** [a]Prov. 7:13
**14** [a]Gen. 14:13; 41:12 [1]*laugh at*
**17** [a]Ex. 23:1; Ps. 120:3; Prov. 26:28
**19** [a]Prov. 6:34, 35
**20** [a]Ps. 105:18; [1 Pet. 2:19] [b]Gen. 40:3, 15; 41:14
**21** [a]Gen. 39:2; Ex. 3:21; Ps. 105:19; [Prov. 16:7]; Dan. 1:9; Acts 7:9, 10 [1]Caused him to be viewed with favor by
**22** [a]Gen. 39:4; 40:3, 4
**23** [a]Gen. 39:2, 3 [1]Lit. *his hand*

CHAPTER 40

**1** [a]Gen. 40:11, 13; Neh. 1:11
**2** [a]Prov. 16:14
**3** [a]Gen. 39:1, 20, 23; 41:10
**5** [a]Gen. 37:5; 41:1
**6** [1]*dejected*

him in the custody of his lord's house, saying,
[a]"Why do you look *so* sad today?"
8 And they said to him, [a]"We each have had a
dream, and *there is* no interpreter of it." So Joseph
said to them, [b]"Do not interpretations belong to
God? Tell *them* to me, please."
**9** Then the chief butler told his dream to Joseph,
and said to him, "Behold, in my dream a vine *was*
before me,
10 "and in the vine *were* three branches; it *was*
as though it budded, its blossoms shot forth, and
its clusters brought forth ripe grapes.
11 "Then Pharaoh's cup *was* in my hand; and I
took the grapes and pressed them into Pharaoh's
cup, and placed the cup in Pharaoh's hand."
12 And Joseph said to him, [a]"This *is* the interpretation of it: The three branches [b]*are* three days.
13 "Now within three days Pharaoh will [a]lift up
your head and restore you to your [1]place, and you
will put Pharaoh's cup in his hand according to
the former manner, when you were his butler.
14 "But [a]remember me when it is well with you,
and [b]please show kindness to me; make mention
of me to Pharaoh, and get me out of this house.
15 "For indeed I was [a]stolen away from the land
of the Hebrews; [b]and also I have done nothing
here that they should put me into the dungeon."
**16** When the chief baker saw that the interpretation was good, he said to Joseph, "I also *was* in
my dream, and there were three [1]white baskets on
my head.
17 "In the uppermost basket *were* all kinds of
baked goods for Pharaoh, and the birds ate them
out of the basket on my head."
18 So Joseph answered and said, [a]"This *is* the
interpretation of it: The three baskets *are* three
days.
19 [a]"Within three days Pharaoh will lift [1]off your
head from you and [b]hang you on a tree; and the
birds will eat your flesh from you."
**20** Now it came to pass on the third day, *which*
*was* Pharaoh's [a]birthday, that he [b]made a feast for
all his servants; and he [c]lifted up the head of the
chief butler and of the chief baker among his
servants.
21 Then he [a]restored the chief butler to his but-
lership again, and [b]he placed the cup in Pharaoh's
hand.
22 But he [a]hanged the chief baker, as Joseph had
interpreted to them.
23 Yet the chief butler did not remember Joseph,
but [a]forgot him.

### *Pharaoh's Dreams*

**41** Then it came to pass, at the end of two full
years, that [a]Pharaoh had a dream; and behold, he stood by the river.
2 Suddenly there came up out of the river seven
cows, fine looking and fat; and they fed in the
meadow.
3 Then behold, seven other cows came up after
them out of the river, ugly and gaunt, and stood
by the *other* cows on the bank of the river.
4 And the ugly and gaunt cows ate up the seven
fine looking and fat cows. So Pharaoh awoke.
5 He slept and dreamed a second time; and
suddenly seven heads of grain came up on one
stalk, plump and good.
6 Then behold, seven thin heads, blighted by the
[a]east wind, sprang up after them.
7 And the seven thin heads devoured the seven
plump and full heads. So Pharaoh awoke, and
indeed, *it was* a dream.
8 Now it came to pass in the morning [a]that his
spirit was troubled, and he sent and called for all
[b]the magicians of Egypt and all its [c]wise men. And
Pharaoh told them his dreams, but *there was* no
one who could interpret them for Pharaoh.
**9** Then the [a]chief butler spoke to Pharaoh, saying: "I remember my faults this day.
10 "When Pharaoh was [a]angry with his servants,
[b]and put me in custody in the house of the captain
of the guard, *both* me and the chief baker,
11 [a]"we each had a dream in one night, he and I.
Each of us dreamed according to the interpretation of his *own* dream.
12 "Now there *was* a young [a]Hebrew man with
us there, a [b]servant of the captain of the guard.
And we told him, and he [c]interpreted our dreams
for us; to each man he interpreted according to his
*own* dream.
13 "And it came to pass, just [a]as he interpreted
for us, so it happened. He restored me to my office,
and he hanged him."
**14** [a]Then Pharaoh sent and called Joseph, and
they [b]brought him quickly [c]out of the dungeon;
and he shaved, [d]changed his clothing, and came to
Pharaoh.
15 And Pharaoh said to Joseph, "I have had a
dream, and *there is* no one who can interpret it.
[a]But I have heard it said of you *that* you can
understand a dream, to interpret it."
16 So Joseph answered Pharaoh, saying, [a]"*It is*
not in me; [b]God will give Pharaoh an answer of
peace."
17 Then Pharaoh said to Joseph: "Behold, [a]in my
dream I stood on the bank of the river.
18 "Suddenly seven cows came up out of the
river, fine looking and fat; and they fed in the
meadow.
19 "Then behold, seven other cows came up after
them, poor and very ugly and gaunt, such ugliness
as I have never seen in all the land of Egypt.
20 "And the gaunt and ugly cows ate up the first
seven, the fat cows.
21 "When they had eaten them up, no one would
have known that they had eaten them, for they
*were* just as ugly as at the beginning. So I awoke.
22 "Also I saw in my dream, and suddenly seven
[1]heads came up on one stalk, full and good.
23 "Then behold, seven heads, withered, thin,
*and* blighted by the east wind, sprang up after
them.
24 "And the thin heads devoured the seven good
heads. So [a]I told *this* to the magicians, but *there*
*was* no one who could explain *it* to me."
**25** Then Joseph said to Pharaoh, "The dreams of
Pharaoh *are* one; [a]God has shown Pharaoh what
He *is* about to do:
26 "The seven good cows *are* seven years, and
the seven good [1]heads *are* seven years; the dreams
*are* one.
27 "And the seven thin and ugly cows which
came up after them *are* seven years, and the seven
empty heads blighted by the east wind are [a]seven
years of famine.
28 [a]"This *is* the thing which I have spoken to
Pharaoh. God has shown Pharaoh what He *is*
about to do.
29 "Indeed [a]seven years of great plenty will come
throughout all the land of Egypt;
30 "but after them seven years of famine will
[a]arise, and all the plenty will be forgotten in the

**7** [a]Neh. 2:2
**8** [a]Gen. 41:15 [b][Dan. 2:11, 20–22, 27, 28, 47]
**12** [a]Dan. 2:36; 4:18, 19 [b]Gen. 40:18; 42:17
**13** [a]2 Kin. 25:27 [1]*position*
**14** [a]Luke 23:42 [b]Josh. 2:12
**15** [a]Gen. 37:26–28 [b]Gen. 39:20
**16** [1]Or *baskets of white bread*
**18** [a]Gen. 40:12
**19** [a]Gen. 40:13 [b]Deut. 21:22 [1]Lit. *up*
**20** [a]Matt. 14:6–10 [b]Mark 6:21 [c]Gen. 40:13, 19
**21** [a]Gen. 40:13 [b]Neh. 2:1
**22** [a]Gen. 40:19
**23** [a]Eccl. 9:15, 16

CHAPTER 41

**1** [a]Gen. 40:5
**6** [a]Ex. 10:13
**8** [a]Dan. 2:1, 3; 4:5, 19 [b]Ex. 7:11, 22 [c]Matt. 2:1
**9** [a]Gen. 40:1, 14, 23
**10** [a]Gen. 40:2, 3 [b]Gen. 39:20
**11** [a]Gen. 40:5
**12** [a]Gen. 39:14; 43:32 [b]Gen. 37:36 [c]Gen. 40:12
**13** [a]Gen. 40:21, 22
**14** [a]Ps. 105:20 [b]Dan. 2:25 [c][1 Sam. 2:8] [d]2 Kin. 25:27–29
**15** [a]Dan. 5:16
**16** [a]Dan. 2:30 [b]Dan. 2:22, 28, 47
**17** [a]Gen. 41:1
**22** [1]Heads of grain
**24** [a]Is. 8:19
**25** [a]Dan. 2:28, 29, 45
**26** [1]Heads of grain
**27** [a]2 Kin. 8:1
**28** [a][Gen. 41:25, 32]
**29** [a]Gen. 41:47
**30** [a]Gen. 41:54, 56

land of Egypt; and the famine [b]will deplete the land.
31 "So the plenty will not be known in the land because of the famine following, for it *will be* very severe.
32 "And the dream was repeated to Pharaoh twice because the [a]thing *is* established by God, and God will shortly bring it to pass.
33 "Now therefore, let Pharaoh select a discerning and wise man, and set him over the land of Egypt.
34 "Let Pharaoh do *this,* and let him appoint [1]officers over the land, [a]to collect one-fifth *of the produce* of the land of Egypt in the seven plentiful years.
35 "And [a]let them gather all the food of those good years that are coming, and store up grain under the [1]authority of Pharaoh, and let them keep food in the cities.
36 "Then that food shall be as a [1]reserve for the land for the seven years of famine which shall be in the land of Egypt, that the land [a]may not [2]perish during the famine."
**37** So [a]the advice was good in the eyes of Pharaoh and in the eyes of all his servants.
38 And Pharaoh said to his servants, "Can we find *such a one* as this, a man [a]in whom *is* the Spirit of God?"
39 Then Pharaoh said to Joseph, "Inasmuch as God has shown you all this, *there is* no one as discerning and wise as you.
40 [a]"You shall be [1]over my house, and all my people shall be ruled according to your word; only in regard to the throne will I be greater than you."
41 And Pharaoh said to Joseph, "See, I have [a]set you over all the land of Egypt."
42 Then Pharaoh [a]took his signet ring off his hand and put it on Joseph's hand; and he [b]clothed him in garments of fine linen [c]and put a gold chain around his neck.
43 And he had him ride in the second [a]chariot which he had; [b]and they cried out before him, "Bow the knee!" So he set him [c]over all the land of Egypt.
44 Pharaoh also said to Joseph, "I *am* Pharaoh, and without your consent no man may lift his hand or foot in all the land of Egypt."
45 And Pharaoh called Joseph's name [1]Zaphnath-Paaneah. And he gave him as a wife [a]Asenath, the daughter of Poti-Pherah priest of On. So Joseph went out over *all* the land of Egypt.
**46** Joseph was thirty years old when he [a]stood before Pharaoh king of Egypt. And Joseph went out from the presence of Pharaoh, and went throughout all the land of Egypt.
47 Now in the seven plentiful years the ground brought forth [1]abundantly.
48 So he gathered up all the food of the seven years which were in the land of Egypt, and laid up the food in the cities; he laid up in every city the food of the fields which surrounded them.
49 Joseph gathered very much grain, [a]as the sand of the sea, until he stopped counting, for *it was* immeasurable.
**50** [a]And to Joseph were born two sons before the years of famine came, whom Asenath, the daughter of Poti-Pherah priest of On, bore to him.
51 Joseph called the name of the firstborn [1]Manasseh: "For God has made me forget all my toil and all my [a]father's house."
52 And the name of the second he called [1]Ephraim: "For God has caused me to be [a]fruitful in the land of my affliction."
**53** Then the seven years of plenty which were in the land of Egypt ended,
54 [a]and the seven years of famine began to come, [b]as Joseph had said. The famine was in all lands, but in all the land of Egypt there was bread.
55 So when all the land of Egypt was famished, the people cried to Pharaoh for bread. Then Pharaoh said to all the Egyptians, "Go to Joseph; [a]whatever he says to you, do."
56 The famine was over all the face of the earth, and Joseph opened [1]all the storehouses and [a]sold to the Egyptians. And the famine became severe in the land of Egypt.
57 [a]So all countries came to Joseph in Egypt to [b]buy *grain,* because the famine was severe in all lands.

### *Joseph's Brothers Go to Egypt*

**42** When [a]Jacob saw that there was grain in Egypt, Jacob said to his sons, "Why do you look at one another?"
2 And he said, "Indeed I have heard that there is grain in Egypt; go down to that place and buy for us there, that we may [a]live and not die."
3 So Joseph's ten brothers went down to buy grain in Egypt.
4 But Jacob did not send Joseph's brother Benjamin with his brothers, for he said, [a]"Lest some calamity befall him."
5 And the sons of Israel went to buy *grain* among those who journeyed, for the famine was [a]in the land of Canaan.
**6** Now Joseph *was* governor [a]over the land; and it was he who sold to all the people of the land. And Joseph's brothers came and [b]bowed down before him with *their* faces to the earth.
7 Joseph saw his brothers and recognized them, but he acted as [a]a stranger to them and spoke [1]roughly to them. Then he said to them, "Where do you come from?" And they said, "From the land of Canaan to buy food."
8 So Joseph recognized his brothers, but they did not recognize him.
9 Then Joseph [a]remembered the dreams which he had dreamed about them, and said to them, "You *are* spies! You have come to see the [1]nakedness of the land!"
10 And they said to him, "No, my lord, but your servants have come to buy food.
11 "We *are* all one man's sons; we *are* honest *men;* your servants are not spies."
12 But he said to them, "No, but you have come to see the nakedness of the land."
13 And they said, "Your servants *are* twelve brothers, the sons of one man in the land of Canaan; and in fact, the youngest *is* with our father today, and one [a]*is* no more."
14 But Joseph said to them, "It *is* as I spoke to you, saying, 'You *are* spies!'
15 "In this *manner* you shall be tested: [a]By the life of Pharaoh, you shall not leave this place unless your youngest brother comes here.
16 "Send one of you, and let him bring your brother; and you shall be [1]kept in prison, that your words may be tested to see whether *there is* any truth in you; or else, by the life of Pharaoh, surely you *are* spies!"
17 So he [1]put them all together in prison [a]three days.

30 [b]Gen. 47:13; Ps. 105:16
32 [a]Gen. 41:25, 28; Num. 23:19; Is. 46:10, 11
34 [a][Prov. 6:6–8] [1]*overseers*
35 [a]Gen. 41:48 [1]Lit. *hand*
36 [a]Gen. 47:15, 19 [1]Lit. *supply* [2]*be cut off*
37 [a]Ps. 105:19; Acts 7:10
38 [a]Num. 27:18; [Job 32:8; Prov. 2:6]; Dan. 4:8, 9, 18; 5:11, 14; 6:3
40 [a]Ps. 105:21; Acts 7:10 [1]In charge of
41 [a]Gen. 42:6; Ps. 105:21; Dan. 6:3; Acts 7:10
42 [a]Esth. 3:10 [b]Esth. 8:2, 15 [c]Dan. 5:7, 16, 29
43 [a]Gen. 46:29 [b]Esth. 6:9 [c]Gen. 42:6
45 [a]Gen. 46:20 [1]Probably Egyptian for *God Speaks and He Lives*
46 [a]1 Sam. 16:21; 1 Kin. 12:6, 8; Dan. 1:19
47 [1]Lit. *by handfuls*
49 [a]Gen. 22:17; Judg. 7:12; 1 Sam. 13:5
50 [a]Gen. 46:20; 48:5
51 [a]Ps. 45:10 [1]Lit. *Making Forgetful*
52 [a]Gen. 17:6; 28:3; 49:22 [1]Lit. *Fruitfulness*
54 [a]Ps. 105:16; Acts 7:11 [b]Gen. 41:30
55 [a]John 2:5
56 [a]Gen. 42:6 [1]Lit. *all that was in them*
57 [a]Ezek. 29:12 [b]Gen. 27:28, 37; 42:3

CHAPTER 42
1 [a]Acts 7:12
2 [a]Gen. 43:8; Ps. 33:18, 19; Is. 38:1
4 [a]Gen. 42:38
5 [a]Gen. 12:10; 26:1; 41:57; Acts 7:11
6 [a]Gen. 41:41, 55 [b]Gen. 37:7–10; 41:43; Is. 60:14
7 [a]Gen. 45:1, 2 [1]*harshly*
9 [a]Gen. 37:5–9 [1]Exposed parts
13 [a]Gen. 37:30; 42:32; 44:20; Lam. 5:7
15 [a]1 Sam. 1:26; 17:55
16 [1]Lit. *bound*
17 [a]Gen. 40:4, 7, 12 [1]Lit. *gathered*

18 Then Joseph said to them the third day, "Do
this and live, [a]*for* I fear God:
19 "If you *are* honest *men,* let one of your brothers be confined to your prison house; but you, go
and carry grain for the famine of your houses.
20 "And [a]bring your youngest brother to me; so
your words will be verified, and you shall not die."
And they did so.
21 Then they said to one another, [a]"We *are* truly
guilty concerning our brother, for we saw the
anguish of his soul when he pleaded with us, and
we would not hear; [b]therefore this distress has
come upon us."
22 And Reuben answered them, saying, [a]"Did I
not speak to you, saying, 'Do not sin against the
boy'; and you would not listen? Therefore behold,
his blood is now [b]required of us."
23 But they did not know that Joseph understood
*them,* for he spoke to them through an interpreter.
24 And he turned himself away from them and
[a]wept. Then he returned to them again, and talked
with them. And he took [b]Simeon from them and
bound him before their eyes.
**25** Then Joseph [a]gave a command to fill their
sacks with grain, to [b]restore every man's money to
his sack, and to give them provisions for the
journey. [c]Thus he did for them.
26 So they loaded their donkeys with the grain
and departed from there.
27 But as [a]one *of them* opened his sack to give his
donkey feed at the encampment, he saw his
money; and there it was, in the mouth of his sack.
28 So he said to his brothers, "My money has
been restored, and there it is, in my sack!" Then
their hearts [1]failed *them* and they were afraid,
saying to one another, "What *is* this *that* God has
done to us?"
**29** Then they went to Jacob their father in the
land of Canaan and told him all that had happened to them, saying:
30 "The man *who is* lord of the land [a]spoke
[1]roughly to us, and took us for spies of the country.
31 "But we said to him, 'We *are* honest *men;* we
are not spies.
32 'We *are* twelve brothers, sons of our father;
one *is* no *more,* and the youngest *is* with our
father this day in the land of Canaan.'
33 "Then the man, the lord of the country, said to
us, [a]'By this I will know that you *are* honest *men:*
Leave one of your brothers *here* with me, take
*food for* the famine of your households, and be
gone.
34 'And bring your [a]youngest brother to me; so I
shall know that you *are* not spies, but *that* you *are*
honest *men.* I will grant your brother to you, and
you may [b]trade in the land.' "
**35** Then it happened as they emptied their sacks,
that surprisingly [a]each man's bundle of money
*was* in his sack; and when they and their father
saw the bundles of money, they were afraid.
36 And Jacob their father said to them, "You
have [a]bereaved me: Joseph is no *more,* Simeon is
no *more,* and you want to take [b]Benjamin. All
these things are against me."
37 Then Reuben spoke to his father, saying, "Kill
my two sons if I do not bring him *back* to you; put
him in my hands, and I will bring him back to
you."
38 But he said, "My son shall not go down with
you, for [a]his brother is dead, and he is left alone.
[b]If any calamity should befall him along the way
in which you go, then you would [c]bring down my
gray hair with sorrow to the grave."

### *Joseph's Brothers Return with Benjamin*

**43** Now the famine *was* [a]severe in the land.
2 And it came to pass, when they had eaten
up the grain which they had brought from Egypt,
that their father said to them, "Go [a]back, buy us a
little food."
3 But Judah spoke to him, saying, "The man
solemnly warned us, saying, 'You shall not see my
face unless your [a]brother *is* with you.' "
4 "If you send our brother with us, we will go
down and buy you food.
5 "But if you will not send *him,* we will not go
down; for the man said to us, 'You shall not see
my face unless your brother *is* with you.' "
6 And Israel said, "Why did you deal *so* [1]wrong-
fully with me *as* to tell the man whether you had
still *another* brother?"
7 But they said, "The man asked us pointedly
about ourselves and our family, saying, '*Is* your
father still alive? Have you *another* brother?' And
we told him according to these words. Could we
possibly have known that he would say, 'Bring
your brother down'?"
**8** Then Judah said to Israel his father, "Send the
lad with me, and we will arise and go, that we may
[a]live and not die, both we and you *and* also our
little ones.
9 "I myself will be surety for him; from my hand
you shall require him. [a]If I do not bring him *back*
to you and set him before you, then let me bear
the blame forever.
10 "For if we had not lingered, surely by now we
would have returned this second time."
11 And their father Israel said to them, "If *it
must be* so, then do this: Take some of the best
fruits of the land in your vessels and [a]carry down
a present for the man—a little [b]balm and a little
honey, spices and myrrh, pistachio nuts and almonds.
12 "Take double money in your hand, and take
back in your hand the money [a]that was returned
in the mouth of your sacks; perhaps it was an
oversight.
13 "Take your brother also, and arise, go back to
the man.
14 "And may God [a]Almighty [b]give you mercy
before the man, that he may release your other
brother and Benjamin. [c]If I am bereaved, I am
bereaved!"
**15** So the men took that present and Benjamin,
and they took double money in their hand, and
arose and went [a]down to Egypt; and they stood
before Joseph.
16 When Joseph saw Benjamin with them, he
said to the [a]steward of his house, "Take *these* men
to my home, and slaughter [1]an animal and make
ready; for *these* men will dine with me at noon."
17 Then the man did as Joseph ordered, and the
man brought the men into Joseph's house.
18 Now the men were [a]afraid because they were
brought into Joseph's house; and they said, "*It is*
because of the money, which was returned in our
sacks the first time, that we are brought in, so that
he may [1]make a case against us and seize us, to
take us as slaves with our donkeys."
19 When they drew near to the steward of

**18** [a]Gen. 22:12; 39:9; Ex. 1:17; Lev. 25:43; Neh. 5:15; Prov. 1:7; 9:10
**20** [a]Gen. 42:34; 43:5; 44:23
**21** [a]Gen. 37:26–28; 44:16; 45:3; Job 36:8, 9; Hos. 5:15 [b]Prov. 21:13; Matt. 7:2
**22** [a]Gen. 37:21, 22, 29 [b]Gen. 9:5, 6; 1 Kin. 2:32; 2 Chr. 24:22; Ps. 9:12; Luke 11:50, 51
**24** [a]Gen. 43:30; 45:14, 15 [b]Gen. 34:25, 30; 43:14, 23
**25** [a]Gen. 44:1 [b]Gen. 43:12 [c][Matt. 5:44; Rom. 12:17, 20, 21; 1 Pet. 3:9]
**27** [a]Gen. 43:21, 22
**28** [1]*sank*
**30** [a]Gen. 42:7 [1]*harshly*
**33** [a]Gen. 42:15, 19, 20
**34** [a]Gen. 42:20; 43:3, 5 [b]Gen. 34:10
**35** [a]Gen. 43:12, 15, 21
**36** [a]Gen. 43:14 [b]Gen. 35:18; [Rom. 8:28, 31]
**38** [a]Gen. 37:22; 42:13; 44:20, 28 [b]Gen. 42:4; 44:29 [c]Gen. 37:35; 44:31

CHAPTER 43

**1** [a]Gen. 41:54, 57; 42:5; 45:6, 11
**2** [a]Gen. 42:2; 44:25
**3** [a]Gen. 42:20; 43:5; 44:23
**6** [1]Lit. *wickedly*
**8** [a]Gen. 42:2; 47:19
**9** [a]Gen. 42:37; 44:32; Philem. 18, 19
**11** [a]Gen. 32:20; 33:10; 43:25, 26; [Prov. 18:16] [b]Gen. 37:25; Jer. 8:22; Ezek. 27:17
**12** [a]Gen. 42:25, 35; 43:21, 22
**14** [a]Gen. 17:1; 28:3; 35:11; 48:3 [b]Gen. 39:21; Ps. 106:46 [c]Gen. 42:36; Esth. 4:16
**15** [a]Gen. 39:1; 46:3, 6
**16** [a]Gen. 24:2; 39:4; 44:1 [1]Lit. *a slaughter*
**18** [a]Gen. 42:28 [1]Lit. *roll himself upon us*

Joseph's house, they talked with him at the door
of the house,
20 and said, "O sir, [a]we indeed came down the
first time to buy food;
21 "but [a]it happened, when we came to the encampment, that we opened our sacks, and there,
*each* man's money *was* in the mouth of his sack,
our money in full weight; so we have brought it
back in our hand.
22 "And we have brought down other money in
our hands to buy food. We do not know who put
our money in our sacks."
23 But he said, "Peace *be* with you, do not be
afraid. Your God and the God of your father has
given you treasure in your sacks; I had your
money." Then he brought [a]Simeon out to them.
24 So the man brought the men into Joseph's
house and [a]gave *them* water, and they washed
their feet; and he gave their donkeys feed.
25 Then they made the present ready for Joseph's
coming at noon, for they heard that they would
eat bread there.
**26** And when Joseph came home, they brought
him the present which *was* in their hand into the
house, and [a]bowed down before him to the earth.
27 Then he asked them about *their* well-being,
and said, "*Is* your father well, the old man [a]of
whom you spoke? *Is* he still alive?"
28 And they answered, "Your servant our father
*is* in good health; he *is* still alive." [a]And they
bowed their heads down and prostrated themselves.
29 Then he lifted his eyes and saw his brother
Benjamin, [a]his mother's son, and said, "*Is* this
your younger brother [b]of whom you spoke to
me?" And he said, "God be gracious to you, my
son."
30 Now [a]his heart yearned for his brother; so
Joseph made haste and sought *somewhere* to
weep. And he went into *his* chamber and [b]wept
there.
31 Then he washed his face and came out; and he
restrained himself, and said, "Serve the [a]bread."
32 So they set him a place by himself, and them
by themselves, and the Egyptians who ate with
him by themselves; because the Egyptians could
not eat food with the [a]Hebrews, for that *is* [b]an
abomination to the Egyptians.
33 And they sat before him, the firstborn according to his [a]birthright and the youngest according
to his youth; and the men looked in astonishment
at one another.
34 Then he took servings to them from before
him, but Benjamin's serving was [a]five times as
much as any of theirs. So they drank and were
merry with him.

### *Joseph's Final Test of His Brothers*

**44** And he commanded [1]the [a]steward of his
house, saying, [b]"Fill the men's sacks with
food, as much as they can carry, and put each
man's money in the mouth of his sack.
2 "Also put my cup, the silver cup, in the mouth
of the sack of the youngest, and his grain money."
So he did according to the word that Joseph had
spoken.
3 As soon as the morning dawned, the men were
sent away, they and their donkeys.
4 When they had gone out of the city, *and* were
not *yet* far off, Joseph said to his steward, "Get up,
follow the men; and when you overtake them, say
to them, 'Why have you [a]repaid evil for good?
5 '*Is* not this *the one* from which my lord drinks,
and with which he indeed practices divination?
You have done evil in so doing.'"
**6** So he overtook them, and he spoke to them
these same words.
7 And they said to him, "Why does my lord say
these words? Far be it from us that your servants
should do such a thing.
8 "Look, we brought back to you from the land
of Canaan [a]the money which we found in the
mouth of our sacks. How then could we steal
silver or gold from your lord's house?
9 "With whomever of your servants it is found,
[a]let him die, and we also will be my lord's slaves."
10 And he said, "Now also *let* it *be* according to
your words; he with whom it is found shall be my
slave, and you shall be blameless."
11 Then each man speedily let down his sack to
the ground, and each opened his sack.
12 So he searched. He began with the oldest and
[1]left off with the youngest; and the cup was found
in Benjamin's sack.
13 Then they [a]tore their clothes, and each man
loaded his donkey and returned to the city.
**14** So Judah and his brothers came to Joseph's
house, and he *was* still there; and they [a]fell before
him on the ground.
15 And Joseph said to them, "What deed *is* this
you have done? Did you not know that such a
man as I can certainly practice divination?"
16 Then Judah said, "What shall we say to my
lord? What shall we speak? Or how shall we clear
ourselves? God has [a]found out the iniquity of your
servants; here [b]we are, my lord's slaves, both we
and *he* also with whom the cup was found."
17 But he said, [a]"Far be it from me that I should
do so; the man in whose hand the cup was found,
he shall be my slave. And as for you, go up in
peace to your father."
**18** Then Judah came near to him and said: "O my
lord, please let your servant speak a word in my
lord's hearing, and [a]do not let your anger burn
against your servant; for you *are* even like Pharaoh.
19 "My lord asked his servants, saying, 'Have you
a father or a brother?'
20 "And we said to my lord, 'We have a father, an
old man, and [a]a child of *his* old age, *who is* young;
his brother is [b]dead, and he [c]alone is left of his
mother's children, and his [d]father loves him.'
21 "Then you said to your servants, [a]'Bring him
down to me, that I may set my eyes on him.'
22 "And we said to my lord, 'The lad cannot leave
his father, for *if* he should leave his father, *his
father* would die.'
23 "But you said to your servants, [a]'Unless your
youngest brother comes down with you, you shall
see my face no more.'
24 "So it was, when we went up to your servant
my father, that we told him the words of my lord.
25 "And [a]our father said, 'Go back *and* buy us a
little food.'
26 "But we said, 'We cannot go down; if our
youngest brother is with us, then we will go down;
for we may not see the man's face unless our
youngest brother *is* with us.'
27 "Then your servant my father said to us, 'You
know that [a]my wife bore me two sons;
28 'and the one went out from me, and I said,

20 [a]Gen. 42:3, 10
21 [a]Gen. 42:27, 35
23 [a]Gen. 42:24
24 [a]Gen. 18:4; 19:2; 24:32
26 [a]Gen. 37:7, 10; 42:6; 44:14
27 [a]Gen. 29:6; 42:11, 13; 43:7; 45:3; 2 Kin. 4:26
28 [a]Gen. 37:7, 10
29 [a]Gen. 35:17, 18 [b]Gen. 42:13
30 [a]1 Kin. 3:26 [b]Gen. 42:24; 45:2, 14, 15; 46:29
31 [a]Gen. 43:25
32 [a]Gen. 41:12; Ex. 1:15 [b]Gen. 46:34; Ex. 8:26
33 [a]Gen. 27:36; 42:7; Deut. 21:16, 17
34 [a]Gen. 35:24; 45:22

CHAPTER 44

1 [a]Gen. 43:16 [b]Gen. 42:25 [1]Lit. *the one over*
4 [a]1 Sam. 25:21
8 [a]Gen. 43:21
9 [a]Gen. 31:32
12 [1]*finished with*
13 [a]Gen. 37:29, 34; Num. 14:6; 2 Sam. 1:11
14 [a]Gen. 37:7, 10
16 [a][Num. 32:23] [b]Gen. 44:9
17 [a]Prov. 17:15
18 [a]Gen. 18:30, 32; Ex. 32:22
20 [a]Gen. 37:3; 43:8; 44:30 [b]Gen. 42:38 [c]Gen. 46:19 [d]Gen. 42:4
21 [a]Gen. 42:15, 20
23 [a]Gen. 43:3, 5
25 [a]Gen. 43:2
27 [a]Gen. 30:22-24; 35:16-18; 46:19

[a]"Surely he is torn to pieces"; and I have not seen
him since.
29 'But if you [a]take this one also from me, and
calamity befalls him, you shall bring down my
gray hair with sorrow to the grave.'
30 "Now therefore, when I come to your servant
my father, and the lad *is* not with us, since [a]his life
is bound up in the lad's life,
31 "it will happen, when he sees that the lad *is*
not *with us,* that he will die. So your servants will
bring down the gray hair of your servant our
father with sorrow to the grave.
32 "For your servant became surety for the lad to
my father, saying, [a]'If I do not bring him *back* to
you, then I shall bear the blame before my father
forever.'
33 "Now therefore, please [a]let your servant remain instead of the lad as a slave to my lord, and
let the lad go up with his brothers.
34 "For how shall I go up to my father if the lad
*is* not with me, lest perhaps I see the evil that
would [1]come upon my father?"

### *Joseph Sends for Jacob*

**45** Then Joseph could not restrain himself
before all those who stood by him, and he
cried out, "Make everyone go out from me!" So no
one stood with him [a]while Joseph made himself
known to his brothers.
2 And he [a]wept aloud, and the Egyptians and
the house of Pharaoh heard *it.*
3 Then Joseph said to his brothers, [a]"I *am*
Joseph; does my father still live?" But his brothers
could not answer him, for they were dismayed in
his presence.
4 And Joseph said to his brothers, "Please come
near to me." So they came near. Then he said: "I
*am* Joseph your brother, [a]whom you sold into
Egypt.
5 "But now, do not therefore be grieved or
angry with yourselves because you sold me here;
[a]for God sent me before you to preserve life.
6 "For these two years the [a]famine *has been* in
the land, and *there are* still five years in which
*there will be* neither plowing nor harvesting.
7 "And God [a]sent me before you to preserve a
[1]posterity for you in the earth, and to save your
lives by a great deliverance.
8 "So now *it was* not you *who* sent me here, but
[a]God; and He has made me [b]a father to Pharaoh,
and lord of all his house, and a [c]ruler throughout
all the land of Egypt.
9 "Hurry and go up to my father, and say to
him, 'Thus says your son Joseph: "God has made
me lord of all Egypt; come down to me, do not
[1]tarry.
10 [a]"You shall dwell in the land of Goshen, and
you shall be near to me, you and your children,
your children's children, your flocks and your
herds, and all that you have.
11 "There I will [a]provide for you, lest you and
your household, and all that you have, come to
poverty; for *there are* still five years of famine." '
12 "And behold, your eyes and the eyes of my
brother Benjamin see that *it is* [a]my mouth that
speaks to you.
13 "So you shall tell my father of all my glory in
Egypt, and of all that you have seen; and you shall
hurry and [a]bring my father down here."
14 Then he fell on his brother Benjamin's neck
and wept, and Benjamin wept on his neck.
15 Moreover he [a]kissed all his brothers and wept
over them, and after that his brothers talked with
him.
**16** Now the report of it was heard in Pharaoh's
house, saying, "Joseph's brothers have come." So
it pleased Pharaoh and his servants well.
17 And Pharaoh said to Joseph, "Say to your
brothers, 'Do this: Load your animals and depart;
go to the land of Canaan.
18 'Bring your father and your households and
come to me; I will give you the best of the land of
Egypt, and you will eat [a]the [1]fat of the land.
19 'Now you are commanded—do this: Take
carts out of the land of Egypt for your little ones
and your wives; bring your father and come.
20 'Also do not be concerned about your goods,
for the best of all the land of Egypt *is* yours.' "
**21** Then the sons of Israel did so; and Joseph
gave them [a]carts,[1] according to the command of
Pharaoh, and he gave them provisions for the
journey.
22 He gave to all of them, to each man, [a]changes
of garments; but to Benjamin he gave three
hundred *pieces* of silver and [b]five changes of
garments.
23 And he sent to his father these *things:* ten
donkeys loaded with the good things of Egypt,
and ten female donkeys loaded with grain, bread,
and food for his father for the journey.
24 So he sent his brothers away, and they departed; and he said to them, "See that you do not
become troubled along the way."
**25** Then they went up out of Egypt, and came to
the land of Canaan to Jacob their father.
26 And they told him, saying, "Joseph *is* still
alive, and he *is* governor over all the land of
Egypt." [a]And Jacob's heart stood still, because he
did not believe them.
27 But when they told him all the words which
Joseph had said to them, and when he saw the
carts which Joseph had sent to carry him, the
spirit [a]of Jacob their father revived.
28 Then Israel said, "*It is* enough. Joseph my son
*is* still alive. I will go and see him before I die."

### *Jacob Goes to Egypt*

**46** So Israel took his journey with all that he
had, and came to [a]Beersheba, and offered
sacrifices [b]to the God of his father Isaac.
2 Then God spoke to Israel [a]in the visions of the
night, and said, "Jacob, Jacob!" And he said,
"Here I am."
3 So He said, "I *am* God, [a]the God of your
father; do not fear to go down to Egypt, for I will
[b]make of you a great nation there.
4 [a]"I will go down with you to Egypt, and I will
also surely [b]bring you up *again;* and [c]Joseph [1]will
put his hand on your eyes."
5 Then [a]Jacob arose from Beersheba; and the
sons of Israel carried their father Jacob, their little
ones, and their wives, in the [1]carts [b]which Pharaoh had sent to carry him.
6 So they took their livestock and their goods,
which they had acquired in the land of Canaan,
and went to Egypt, [a]Jacob and all his descendants
with him.
7 His sons and his sons' sons, his daughters and
his sons' daughters, and all his descendants he
brought with him to Egypt.
8 Now [a]these *were* the names of the children of

**28** [a]Gen. 37:31–35
**29** [a]Gen. 42:36, 38; 44:31
**30** [a][1 Sam. 18:1; 25:29]
**32** [a]Gen. 43:9
**33** [a]Ex. 32:32
**34** [1]Lit. *find*

CHAPTER 45
**1** [a]Acts 7:13
**2** [a]Gen. 43:30; 46:29
**3** [a]Gen. 43:27; Acts 7:13
**4** [a]Gen. 37:28; 39:1; Ps. 105:17
**5** [a]Gen. 45:7, 8; 50:20; Ps. 105:16, 17
**6** [a]Gen. 43:1; 47:4, 13
**7** [a]Gen. 45:5; 50:20 [1]*remnant*
**8** [a][Rom. 8:28] [b]Judg. 17:10; Is. 22:21 [c]Gen. 41:43; 42:6
**9** [1]*delay*
**10** [a]Gen. 46:28, 34; 47:1, 6; Ex. 9:26
**11** [a]Gen. 47:12
**12** [a]Gen. 42:23
**13** [a]Gen. 46:6–28; Acts 7:14
**15** [a]Gen. 48:10
**18** [a]Gen. 27:28; 47:6; Deut. 32:9–14 [1]The choicest produce
**21** [a]Gen. 45:19; 46:5 [1]*wagons*
**22** [a]2 Kin. 5:5 [b]Gen. 43:34
**26** [a]Job 29:24; Ps. 126:1; Luke 24:11, 41
**27** [a]Judg. 15:19; Is. 40:29

CHAPTER 46
**1** [a]Gen. 21:31, 33; 26:32, 33; 28:10 [b]Gen. 26:24, 25; 28:13; 31:42; 32:9
**2** [a]Gen. 15:1; 22:11; 31:11; Num. 12:6; Job 33:14, 15
**3** [a]Gen. 17:1; 28:13 [b]Gen. 12:2; Ex. 1:9; 12:37; Deut. 26:5
**4** [a]Gen. 28:15; 31:3; 48:21; Ex. 3:12 [b]Gen. 15:16; 50:12, 24, 25; Ex. 3:8 [c]Gen. 50:1 [1]Will close your eyes when you die
**5** [a]Gen. 47:9; Acts 7:15 [b]Gen. 45:19–21 [1]*wagons*
**6** [a]Deut. 26:5; Josh. 24:4; Ps. 105:23; Is. 52:4; Acts 7:15
**8** [a]Ex. 1:1–4

Israel, Jacob and his sons, who went to Egypt:
[b]Reuben *was* Jacob's firstborn.
9 The [a]sons of Reuben *were* Hanoch, Pallu,
Hezron, and Carmi.
10 [a]The sons of Simeon *were* [1]Jemuel, Jamin,
Ohad, [2]Jachin, [3]Zohar, and Shaul, the son of a
Canaanite woman.
11 The sons of [a]Levi *were* Gershon, Kohath, and
Merari.
12 The sons of [a]Judah *were* [b]Er, Onan, Shelah,
Perez, and Zerah (but Er and Onan died in the
land of Canaan). [c]The sons of Perez were Hezron
and Hamul.
13 The sons of Issachar *were* Tola, [1]Puvah, [2]Job,
and Shimron.
14 The [a]sons of Zebulun *were* Sered, Elon, and
Jahleel.
15 These *were* the [a]sons of Leah, whom she bore
to Jacob in Padan Aram, with his daughter Dinah.
All the persons, his sons and his daughters, *were*
thirty-three.
**16** The sons of Gad *were* [1]Ziphion, Haggi, Shuni,
[2]Ezbon, Eri, [3]Arodi, and Areli.
17 [a]The sons of Asher *were* Jimnah, Ishuah, Isui,
Beriah, and Serah, their sister. And the sons of
Beriah *were* Heber and Malchiel.
18 [a]These *were* the sons of Zilpah, [b]whom Laban
gave to Leah his daughter; and these she bore to
Jacob: sixteen persons.
**19** The [a]sons of Rachel, [b]Jacob's wife, *were*
Joseph and Benjamin.
20 [a]And to Joseph in the land of Egypt were born
Manasseh and Ephraim, whom Asenath, the
daughter of Poti-Pherah priest of On, bore to him.
21 [a]The sons of Benjamin *were* Belah, Becher,
Ashbel, Gera, Naaman, [b]Ehi, Rosh, [c]Muppim,
[1]Huppim, and Ard.
22 These *were* the sons of Rachel, who were born
to Jacob: fourteen persons in all.
**23** The son of Dan *was* [1]Hushim.
24 [a]The sons of Naphtali *were* [1]Jahzeel, Guni,
Jezer, and [2]Shillem.
25 [a]These *were* the sons of Bilhah, [b]whom Laban
gave to Rachel his daughter, and she bore these to
Jacob: seven persons in all.
**26** [a]All the persons who went with Jacob to
Egypt, who came from his body, [b]besides Jacob's
sons' wives, *were* sixty-six persons in all.
27 And the sons of Joseph who were born to him
in Egypt *were* two persons. [a]All the persons of the
house of Jacob who went to Egypt were seventy.
**28** Then he sent Judah before him to Joseph, [a]to
point out before him *the way* to Goshen. And they
came [b]to the land of Goshen.
29 So Joseph made ready his [a]chariot and went
up to Goshen to meet his father Israel; and he
presented himself to him, and [b]fell on his neck and
wept on his neck a good while.
30 And Israel said to Joseph, [a]"Now let me die,
since I have seen your face, because you *are* still
alive."
31 Then Joseph said to his brothers and to his
father's household, [a]"I will go up and tell Pharaoh,
and say to him, 'My brothers and those of my
father's house, who *were* in the land of Canaan,
have come to me.
32 'And the men *are* [a]shepherds, for their occupation has been to feed livestock; and they have
brought their flocks, their herds, and all that they
have.'
33 "So it shall be, when Pharaoh calls you and
says, [a]'What is your occupation?'

8 [b]Num. 26:4, 5
9 [a]Ex. 6:14
10 [a]Ex. 6:15 [1]*Nemuel,* 1 Chr. 4:24 [2]*Jarib,* 1 Chr. 4:24 [3]*Zerah,* 1 Chr. 4:24
11 [a]1 Chr. 6:1, 16
12 [a]1 Chr. 2:3; 4:21 [b]Gen. 38:3, 7, 10 [c]Gen. 38:29
13 [1]*Puah,* Num. 26:23; 1 Chr. 7:1 [2]*Jashub,* Num. 26:24; 1 Chr. 7:1
14 [a]Num. 26:26
15 [a]Gen. 35:23; 49:31
16 [1]Sam., LXX *Zephon* and Num. 26:15 [2]*Ozni,* Num. 26:16 [3]*Arod,* Num. 26:17
17 [a]1 Chr. 7:30
18 [a]Gen. 30:10; 37:2 [b]Gen. 29:24
19 [a]Gen. 35:24 [b]Gen. 44:27
20 [a]Gen. 41:45, 50–52; 48:1
21 [a]1 Chr. 7:6; 8:1 [b]Num. 26:38 [c]Num. 26:39 [1]*Hupham,* Num. 26:39
23 [1]*Shuham,* Num. 26:42
24 [a]Num. 26:48 [1]*Jahziel,* 1 Chr. 7:13 [2]*Shallum,* 1 Chr. 7:13
25 [a]Gen. 30:5, 7 [b]Gen. 29:29
26 [a]Ex. 1:5 [b]Gen. 35:11
27 [a]Deut. 10:22
28 [a]Gen. 31:21 [b]Gen. 47:1
29 [a]Gen. 41:43 [b]Gen. 45:14, 15
30 [a]Luke 2:29, 30
31 [a]Gen. 47:1
32 [a]Gen. 47:3
33 [a]Gen. 47:2, 3
34 [a]Gen. 47:3 [b]Gen. 30:35; 34:5; 37:17 [c]Gen. 43:32 [1]*loathsome*

CHAPTER 47
1 [a]Gen. 46:31 [b]Gen. 45:10; 46:28; 50:8
2 [a]Acts 7:13
3 [a]Gen. 46:33 [b]Gen. 46:32, 34
4 [a]Deut. 26:5 [b]Gen. 43:1 [c]Gen. 46:34
6 [a]Gen. 20:15; 45:10, 18; 47:11 [b]Gen. 47:4
7 [a]Gen. 47:10; 48:15, 20
9 [a][Heb. 11:9, 13] [b]Gen. 47:28 [c][Job 14:1] [d]Gen. 5:5; 11:10, 11; 25:7, 8; 35:28 [1]Lit. *sojourning*
10 [a]Gen. 47:7
11 [a]Ex. 1:11; 12:37 [b]Gen. 47:6, 27
12 [a]Gen. 45:11; 50:21

34 "that you shall say, 'Your servants' [a]occupa-
tion has been with livestock [b]from our youth even
till now, both we *and* also our fathers,' that you
may dwell in the land of Goshen; for every shepherd *is* [c]an[1] abomination to the Egyptians."

### *Joseph Is Governor of Egypt*

**47** Then Joseph [a]went and told Pharaoh, and
said, "My father and my brothers, their
flocks and their herds and all that they possess,
have come from the land of Canaan; and indeed
they *are* in [b]the land of Goshen."
2 And he took five men from among his brothers and [a]presented them to Pharaoh.
3 Then Pharaoh said to his brothers, [a]"What *is*
your occupation?" And they said to Pharaoh,
[b]"Your servants *are* shepherds, both we *and* also
our fathers."
4 And they said to Pharaoh, [a]"We have come to
dwell in the land, because your servants have no
pasture for their flocks, [b]for the famine *is* severe in
the land of Canaan. Now therefore, please let your
servants [c]dwell in the land of Goshen."
5 Then Pharaoh spoke to Joseph, saying, "Your
father and your brothers have come to you.
6 [a]"The land of Egypt *is* before you. Have your
father and brothers dwell in the best of the land;
let them dwell [b]in the land of Goshen. And if you
know *any* competent men among them, then
make them chief herdsmen over my livestock."
**7** Then Joseph brought in his father Jacob and
set him before Pharaoh; and Jacob [a]blessed Pharaoh.
8 Pharaoh said to Jacob, "How old *are* you?"
9 And Jacob said to Pharaoh, [a]"The days of the
years of my [1]pilgrimage *are* [b]one hundred and
thirty years; [c]few and evil have been the days of
the years of my life, and [d]they have not attained
to the days of the years of the life of my fathers in
the days of their pilgrimage."
10 So Jacob [a]blessed Pharaoh, and went out from
before Pharaoh.
**11** And Joseph situated his father and his brothers, and gave them a possession in the land of
Egypt, in the best of the land, in the land of
[a]Rameses, [b]as Pharaoh had commanded.
12 Then Joseph provided [a]his father, his brothers,
and all his father's household with bread, according to the number in *their* families.
**13** Now *there was* no bread in all the land; for the
famine *was* very severe, [a]so that the land of Egypt
and the land of Canaan languished because of the
famine.
14 [a]And Joseph gathered up all the money that
was found in the land of Egypt and in the land of
Canaan, for the grain which they bought; and
Joseph brought the money into Pharaoh's house.
15 So when the money failed in the land of Egypt
and in the land of Canaan, all the Egyptians came
to Joseph and said, "Give us bread, for [a]why
should we die in your presence? For the money
has failed."
16 Then Joseph said, "Give your livestock, and I
will give you *bread* for your livestock, if the
money is gone."
17 So they brought their livestock to Joseph, and
Joseph gave them bread *in exchange* for the
horses, the flocks, the cattle of the herds, and for

13 [a]Gen. 41:30; Acts 7:11
14 [a]Gen. 41:56; 42:6
15 [a]Gen. 47:19

the donkeys. Thus he [1]fed them with bread *in
exchange* for all their livestock that year.
18 When that year had ended, they came to him
the next year and said to him, "We will not hide
from my lord that our money is gone; my lord also
has our herds of livestock. There is nothing left in
the sight of my lord but our bodies and our lands.
19 "Why should we die before your eyes, both we
and our land? Buy us and our land for bread, and
we and our land will be servants of Pharaoh; give
*us* seed, that we may [a]live and not die, that the
land may not be desolate."
**20** Then Joseph [a]bought all the land of Egypt for
Pharaoh; for every man of the Egyptians sold his
field, because the famine was severe upon them.
So the land became Pharaoh's.
21 And as for the people, he [1]moved them into
the cities, from *one* end of the borders of Egypt to
the *other* end.
22 [a]Only the land of the [b]priests he did not buy;
for the priests had rations *allotted to them* by
Pharaoh, and they ate their rations which Pharaoh gave them; therefore they did not sell their
lands.
23 Then Joseph said to the people, "Indeed I have
bought you and your land this day for Pharaoh.
Look, *here is* seed for you, and you shall sow the
land.
24 "And it shall come to pass in the harvest that
you shall give one-fifth to Pharaoh. Four-fifths
shall be your own, as seed for the field and for
your food, for those of your households and as
food for your little ones."
25 So they said, "You have saved [a]our lives; let us
find favor in the sight of my lord, and we will be
Pharaoh's servants."
26 And Joseph made it a law over the land of
Egypt to this day, *that* Pharaoh should have one-
fifth, [a]except for the land of the priests only,
*which* did not become Pharaoh's.
**27** So Israel [a]dwelt in the land of Egypt, in the
country of Goshen; and they had possessions
there and [b]grew and multiplied exceedingly.
28 And Jacob lived in the land of Egypt seventeen years. So the length of Jacob's life was one
hundred and forty-seven years.
29 When the time [a]drew near that Israel must
die, he called his son Joseph and said to him,
"Now if I have found favor in your sight, please
[b]put your hand under my thigh, and [c]deal kindly
and truly with me. [d]Please do not bury me in
Egypt,
30 "but [a]let me lie with my fathers; you shall
carry me out of Egypt and [b]bury me in their burial
place." And he said, "I will do as you have said."
31 Then he said, "Swear to me." And he swore to
him. So [a]Israel bowed himself on the head of the
bed.

### *Jacob Blesses Joseph's Sons*

**48** Now it came to pass after these things that
Joseph was told, "Indeed your father *is*
sick"; and he took with him his two sons, [a]Manas-
seh and Ephraim.
2 And Jacob was told, "Look, your son Joseph is
coming to you"; and Israel [1]strengthened himself
and sat up on the bed.
3 Then Jacob said to Joseph: "God [a]Almighty
appeared to me at [b]Luz in the land of Canaan and
blessed me,
4 "and said to me, 'Behold, I will [a]make you
fruitful and multiply you, and I will make of you a
multitude of people, and [b]give this land to your
descendants after you [c]*as* an everlasting possession.'
5 "And now your [a]two sons, Ephraim and Manasseh, who were born to you in the land of Egypt
before I came to you in Egypt, *are* mine; as
Reuben and Simeon, they shall be mine.
6 "Your [1]offspring [2]whom you beget after them
shall be yours; they will be called by the name of
their brothers in their inheritance.
7 "But as for me, when I came from Padan,
[a]Rachel died beside me in the land of Canaan on
the way, when *there was* but a little distance to go
to Ephrath; and I buried her there on the way to
Ephrath (that is, Bethlehem)."
**8** Then Israel saw Joseph's sons, and said, "Who
*are* these?"
9 And Joseph said to his father, "They *are* my
sons, whom God has given me in this *place*." And
he said, "Please bring them to me, and [a]I will bless
them."
10 Now [a]the eyes of Israel were dim with age, *so
that* he could not see. Then Joseph brought them
near him, and he [b]kissed them and embraced
them.
11 And Israel said to Joseph, [a]"I had not thought
to see your face; but in fact, God has also shown
me your offspring!"
12 So Joseph brought them from beside his
knees, and he bowed down with his face to the
earth.
13 And Joseph took them both, Ephraim with his
right hand toward Israel's left hand, and Manasseh with his left hand toward Israel's right hand,
and brought *them* near him.
14 Then Israel stretched out his right hand and
[a]laid *it* on Ephraim's head, who *was* the younger,
and his left hand on Manasseh's head, [b]guiding his
hands knowingly, for Manasseh *was* the [c]first-
born.
15 And [a]he blessed Joseph, and said:

"God, [b]before whom my fathers
  Abraham and Isaac walked,
The God who has fed me
  all my life long to this day,
16 The Angel [a]who has redeemed me
  from all evil,
Bless the lads;
Let [b]my name be named upon them,
And the name of my fathers
  Abraham and Isaac;
And let them [c]grow into a multitude
  in the midst of the earth."

**17** Now when Joseph saw that his father [a]laid his
right hand on the head of Ephraim, it displeased
him; so he took hold of his father's hand to
remove it from Ephraim's head to Manasseh's
head.
18 And Joseph said to his father, "Not so, my
father, for this *one is* the firstborn; put your right
hand on his head."
19 But his father refused and said, [a]"I know, my
son, I know. He also shall become a people, and he
also shall be great; but truly [b]his younger brother
shall be greater than he, and his descendants shall
become a multitude of nations."
20 So he blessed them that day, saying, [a]"By you
Israel will bless, saying, 'May God make you as
Ephraim and as Manasseh!' " And thus he set
Ephraim before Manasseh.

**17** [1]*supplied*
**19** [a]Gen. 43:8
**20** [a]Jer. 32:43
**21** [1]So with MT, Tg.; Sam., LXX *made the people virtual slaves* (cf. Vg.)
**22** [a]Lev. 25:34; Ezra 7:24 [b]Gen. 41:45
**25** [a]Gen. 33:15
**26** [a]Gen. 47:22
**27** [a]Gen. 47:11 [b]Gen. 17:6; 26:4; 35:11; 46:3; Ex. 1:7; Deut. 26:5; Acts 7:17
**29** [a]Deut. 31:14; 1 Kin. 2:1 [b]Gen. 24:2–4 [c]Gen. 24:49; Josh. 2:14 [d]Gen. 50:25
**30** [a]2 Sam. 19:37 [b]Gen. 49:29; 50:5–13; Heb. 11:21
**31** [a]Gen. 48:2; 1 Kin. 1:47; Heb. 11:21

CHAPTER 48
**1** [a]Gen. 41:51, 56; 46:20; 50:23; Josh. 14:4
**2** [1]Collected his strength
**3** [a]Gen. 43:14; 49:25 [b]Gen. 28:13, 19; 35:6, 9
**4** [a]Gen. 46:3 [b]Gen. 35:12; Ex. 6:8 [c]Gen. 17:8
**5** [a]Gen. 41:50; 46:20; 48:8; Josh. 13:7; 14:4
**6** [1]*children* [2]Who are born to you
**7** [a]Gen. 35:9, 16, 19, 20
**9** [a]Gen. 27:4; 47:15
**10** [a]Gen. 27:1; 1 Sam. 3:2 [b]Gen. 27:27; 45:15; 50:1
**11** [a]Gen. 45:26
**14** [a]Matt. 19:15; Mark 10:16 [b]Gen. 48:19 [c]Gen. 41:51, 52; Josh. 17:1
**15** [a]Gen. 47:7, 10; 49:24; [Heb. 11:21] [b]Gen. 17:1; 24:40; 2 Kin. 20:3
**16** [a]Gen. 22:11, 15–18; 28:13–15; 31:11; [Ps. 34:22; 121:7] [b]Amos 9:12; Acts 15:17 [c]Num. 26:34, 37
**17** [a]Gen. 48:14
**19** [a]Gen. 48:14 [b]Num. 1:33, 35; Deut. 33:17
**20** [a]Ruth 4:11, 12

21 Then Israel said to Joseph, "Behold, I am
dying, but [a]God will be with you and bring you
back to the land of your fathers.
22 "Moreover [a]I have given to you one [1]portion
above your brothers, which I took from the hand
[b]of the Amorite with my sword and my bow."

### *Jacob's Prophecy Concerning His Sons*

**49** And Jacob called his sons and said, "Gather
together, that I may [a]tell you what shall
befall you [b]in the last days:

2 "Gather together and hear, you sons of Jacob,
And listen to Israel your father.

3 "Reuben, you are [a]my firstborn,
My might and the beginning of my strength,
The excellency of dignity
and the excellency of power.
4 Unstable as water, you shall not excel,
Because you [a]went up to your father's bed;
Then you defiled *it*—
He went up to my couch.

5 "Simeon and Levi *are* brothers;
Instruments of [1]cruelty
*are in* their dwelling place.
6 [a]Let not my soul enter their council;
Let not my honor be united
[b]to their assembly;
[c]For in their anger they slew a man,
And in their self-will they [1]hamstrung an ox.
7 Cursed *be* their anger, for *it is* fierce;
And their wrath, for it is cruel!
[a]I will divide them in Jacob
And scatter them in Israel.

8 "Judah,[a] you *are he* whom
your brothers shall praise;
[b]Your hand *shall be* on the neck
of your enemies;
[c]Your father's children
shall bow down before you.
9 Judah *is* [a]a lion's whelp;
From the prey, my son, you have gone up.
[b]He [1]bows down, he lies down as a lion;
And as a lion, who shall rouse him?
10 [a]The [1]scepter shall not depart from Judah,
Nor [b]a lawgiver from between his feet,
[c]Until Shiloh comes;
[d]And to Him *shall be*
the obedience of the people.
11 Binding his donkey to the vine,
And his donkey's colt to the choice vine,
He washed his garments in wine,
And his clothes in the blood of grapes.
12 His eyes *are* darker than wine,
And his teeth whiter than milk.

13 "Zebulun[a] shall dwell by the haven of the sea;
He *shall become* a haven for ships,
And his border shall [b]adjoin Sidon.

14 "Issachar[a] is a strong donkey,
Lying down between two burdens;
15 He saw that rest *was* good,
And that the land *was* pleasant;
He bowed [a]his shoulder to bear *a burden*,
And became a band of slaves.

16 "Dan[a] shall judge his people
As one of the tribes of Israel.
17 [a]Dan shall be a serpent by the way,
A viper by the path,
That bites the horse's heels
So that its rider shall fall backward.

18 [a]I have waited for your salvation, O LORD!

19 "Gad,[a1] a troop shall [2]tramp upon him,
But he shall [2]triumph at last.

20 "Bread from [a]Asher *shall be* rich,
And he shall yield royal dainties.

21 "Naphtali[a] *is* a deer let loose;
He uses [1]beautiful words.

22 "Joseph *is* a fruitful bough,
A fruitful bough by a well;
His branches run over the wall.
23 The archers have [a]bitterly grieved him,
Shot *at him* and hated him.
24 But his [a]bow remained in strength,
And the arms of his hands were [1]made strong
By the hands of [b]the Mighty *God* of Jacob
[c](From there [d]*is* the Shepherd,
[e]the Stone of Israel),
25 [a]By the God of your father who will help you,
[b]And by the Almighty [c]who will bless you
*With* blessings of heaven above,
Blessings of the deep that lies beneath,
Blessings of the breasts and of the womb.
26 The blessings of your father
Have excelled the blessings of my ancestors,
[a]Up to the utmost bound of the everlasting
hills.
[b]They shall be on the head of Joseph,
And on the crown of the head of him who
was separate from his brothers.

27 "Benjamin is a [a]ravenous wolf;
In the morning he shall devour the prey,
[b]And at night he shall divide the spoil."

**28** All these *are* the twelve tribes of Israel, and
this *is* what their father spoke to them. And he
blessed them; he blessed each one according to his
own blessing.
**29** Then he charged them and said to them: "I
[a]am to be gathered to my people; [b]bury me with
my fathers [c]in the cave that *is* in the field of
Ephron the Hittite,
30 "in the cave that *is* in the field of Machpelah,
which *is* before Mamre in the land of Canaan,
[a]which Abraham bought with the field of Ephron
the Hittite as a possession for a burial place.
31 [a]"There they buried Abraham and Sarah his
wife, [b]there they buried Isaac and Rebekah his
wife, and there I buried Leah.
32 "The field and the cave that *is* there *were*
purchased from the sons of Heth."
33 And when Jacob had finished commanding his
sons, he drew his feet up into the bed and
breathed his last, and was gathered to his people.

### *Burial of Jacob*

**50** Then Joseph [a]fell on his father's face, and
[b]wept over him, and kissed him.
2 And Joseph commanded his servants the physicians to [a]embalm his father. So the physicians
embalmed Israel.
3 Forty days were required for him, for such are
the days required for those who are embalmed;
and the Egyptians [a]mourned[1] for him seventy
days.
4 Now when the days of his mourning were
past, Joseph spoke to [a]the household of Pharaoh,
saying, "If now I have found favor in your eyes,
please speak in the hearing of Pharaoh, saying,
5 [a]'My father made me swear, saying, "Behold, I

**21** [a]Gen. 28:15; 46:4; 50:24
**22** [a]Josh. 24:32 [b]Gen. 34:28 [1]Lit. *shoulder*

CHAPTER 49
**1** [a]Deut. 33:1, 6–25 [b]Is. 2:2; 39:6
**3** [a]Gen. 29:32
**4** [a]Gen. 35:22
**5** [1]*violence*
**6** [a]Prov. 1:15, 16 [b]Ps. 26:9 [c]Gen. 34:26 [1]*lamed*
**7** [a]Josh. 19:1, 9; 21:1–42
**8** [a]Deut. 33:7 [b]Ps. 18:40 [c]1 Chr. 5:2
**9** [a][Rev. 5:5] [b]Num. 23:24; 24:9 [1]*couches*
**10** [a]Num. 24:17 [b]Ps. 60:7 [c]Is. 11:1 [d]Ps. 2:6–9; 72:8–11 [1]A symbol of kingship
**13** [a]Deut. 33:18, 19 [b]Gen. 10:19
**14** [a]1 Chr. 12:32
**15** [a]1 Sam. 10:9
**16** [a]Deut. 33:22
**17** [a]Judg. 18:27
**18** [a]Is. 25:9
**19** [a]Deut. 33:20 [1]Lit. *Troop* [2]Lit. *raid*
**20** [a]Deut. 33:24
**21** [a]Deut. 33:23
**23** [a]Gen. 37:4, 24
**24** [a]Job 29:20 [b]Ps. 132:2, 5 [c]Gen. 45:11; 47:12 [d][Ps. 23:1; 80:1] [e]Is. 28:16 [1]Or *supple*
**25** [a]Gen. 28:13; 32:9; 35:3; 43:23; 50:17 [b]Gen. 17:1; 35:11 [c]Deut. 33:13
**26** [a]Deut. 33:15 [b]Deut. 33:16
**27** [a]Judg. 20:21, 25 [b]Zech. 14:1
**29** [a]Gen. 15:15; 25:8; 35:29 [b]Gen. 47:30 [c]Gen. 23:16–20; 50:13
**30** [a]Gen. 23:3–20
**31** [a]Gen. 23:19, 20; 25:9 [b]Gen. 35:29; 50:13

CHAPTER 50
**1** [a]Gen. 46:4, 29 [b]2 Kin. 13:14
**2** [a]Gen. 50:26
**3** [a]Deut. 34:8 [1]Lit. *wept*
**4** [a]Esth. 4:2
**5** [a]Gen. 47:29–31

am dying; in my grave [b]which I dug for myself in
the land of Canaan, there you shall bury me."
Now therefore, please let me go up and bury my
father, and I will come back.' "
6 And Pharaoh said, "Go up and bury your
father, as he made you swear."
**7** So Joseph went up to bury his father; and with
him went up all the servants of Pharaoh, the
elders of his house, and all the elders of the land of
Egypt,
8 as well as all the house of Joseph, his brothers,
and his father's house. Only their little ones, their
flocks, and their herds they left in the land of
Goshen.
9 And there went up with him both chariots and
horsemen, and it was a very great gathering.
10 Then they came to the threshing floor of Atad,
which *is* beyond the Jordan, and they [a]mourned
there with a great and very solemn lamentation.
[b]He observed seven days of mourning for his
father.
11 And when the inhabitants of the land, the
Canaanites, saw the mourning at the threshing
floor of Atad, they said, "This *is* a deep mourning
of the Egyptians." Therefore its name was called
[1]Abel Mizraim, which *is* beyond the Jordan.
**12** So his sons did for him just as he had commanded them.
13 For [a]his sons carried him to the land of Canaan, and buried him in the cave of the field of
Machpelah, before Mamre, which Abraham
[b]bought with the field from Ephron the Hittite as
property for a burial place.
14 And after he had buried his father, Joseph
returned to Egypt, he and his brothers and all who
went up with him to bury his father.
**15** When Joseph's brothers saw that their father
was dead, [a]they said, "Perhaps Joseph will hate us,
and may [1]actually repay us for all the evil which
we did to him."
16 So they sent *messengers* to Joseph, saying,
"Before your father died he commanded, saying,
17 'Thus you shall say to Joseph: "I beg you,
please forgive the trespass of your brothers and
their sin; [a]for they did evil to you." ' Now, please,
forgive the trespass of the servants of [b]the God of
your father." And Joseph wept when they spoke
to him.
18 Then his brothers also went and [a]fell down
before his face, and they said, "Behold, we *are*
your servants."
19 Joseph said to them, [a]"Do not be afraid, [b]for
*am* I in the place of God?
20 [a]"But as for you, you meant evil against me;
*but* [b]God meant it for good, in order to bring it
about as *it is* this day, to save many people alive.
21 "Now therefore, do not be afraid; [a]I will provide for you and your little ones." And he comforted them and spoke [1]kindly to them.
**22** So Joseph dwelt in Egypt, he and his father's
household. And Joseph lived one hundred and ten
years.
23 Joseph saw Ephraim's children [a]to the third
*generation.* [b]The children of Machir, the son of
Manasseh, [c]were also brought up on Joseph's
knees.
24 And Joseph said to his brethren, "I am dying;
but [a]God will surely visit you, and bring you out of
this land to the land [b]of which He swore to
Abraham, to Isaac, and to Jacob."
25 Then [a]Joseph took an oath from the children
of Israel, saying, "God will surely [1]visit you, and
[b]you shall carry up my [c]bones from here."
26 So Joseph died, *being* one hundred and ten
years old; and they embalmed him, and he was put
in a coffin in Egypt.

5 [b]Is. 22:16
10 [a]Acts 8:2 [b]1 Sam. 31:13
11 [1]Lit. *Mourning of Egypt*
13 [a]Acts 7:16 [b]Gen. 23:16–20
15 [a][Job 15:21] [1]*fully*
17 [a][Prov. 28:13] [b]Gen. 49:25
18 [a]Gen. 37:7–10; 41:43; 44:14
19 [a]Gen. 45:5 [b]2 Kin. 5:7
20 [a]Ps. 56:5 [b][Acts 3:13–15]
21 [a][Matt. 5:44] [1]Lit. *to their hearts*
23 [a]Job 42:16 [b]Num. 26:29; 32:39 [c]Gen. 30:3
24 [a]Ex. 3:16, 17 [b]Gen. 26:3; 35:12; 46:4
25 [a]Ex. 13:19 [b]Deut. 1:8; 30:1–8 [c]Ex. 13:19 [1]*give attention to*

*The Second Book of Moses Called*

# EXODUS

## *Israel's Suffering in Egypt*

NOW [a]these *are* the names of the children of
Israel who came to Egypt; each man and
his household came with Jacob:
2 Reuben, Simeon, Levi, and Judah;
3 Issachar, Zebulun, and Benjamin;
4 Dan, Naphtali, Gad, and Asher.
5 All those [1]who were descendants of Jacob
were [a]seventy[2] persons (for Joseph was in Egypt
*already*).
6 And [a]Joseph died, all his brothers, and all that
generation.
7 [a]But the children of Israel were fruitful and
increased abundantly, multiplied and [1]grew exceedingly mighty; and the land was filled with
them.
**8** Now there arose a new king over Egypt, [a]who
did not know Joseph.
9 And he said to his people, "Look, the people of
the children of Israel *are* more and [a]mightier than
we;
10 [a]"come, let us [b]deal shrewdly with them, lest
they multiply, and it happen, in the event of war,
that they also join our enemies and fight against
us, and *so* go up out of the land."
11 Therefore they set taskmasters over them [a]to
afflict them with their [b]burdens. And they built for
Pharaoh [c]supply cities, Pithom [d]and Raamses.
12 But the more they afflicted them, the more
they multiplied and grew. And they were in dread
of the children of Israel.
13 So the Egyptians made the children of Israel
[a]serve with [1]rigor.
14 And they [a]made their lives bitter with hard
bondage—[b]in mortar, in brick, and in all manner
of service in the field. All their service in which
they made them serve *was* with rigor.
**15** Then the king of Egypt spoke to the [a]Hebrew
midwives, of whom the name of one *was* Shiphrah
and the name of the other Puah;
16 and he said, "When you do the duties of a
midwife for the Hebrew women, and see *them* on
the birthstools, if it *is* a [a]son, then you shall kill
him; but if it *is* a daughter, then she shall live."
17 But the midwives [a]feared God, and did not do

CHAPTER 1
1 [a]Gen. 46:8–27
5 [a]Gen. 46:26, 27 [1]Lit. *who came from the loins of* [2]DSS, LXX *seventy-five;* cf. Acts 7:14
6 [a]Gen. 50:26
7 [a]Acts 7:17 [1]*became very numerous*
8 [a]Acts 7:18, 19
9 [a]Gen. 26:16
10 [a]Ps. 83:3, 4 [b]Acts 7:19
11 [a]Ex. 3:7; 5:6 [b]Ex. 1:14; 2:11; 5:4–9; 6:6 [c]1 Kin. 9:19 [d]Gen. 47:11
13 [a]Gen. 15:13 [1]*harshness*
14 [a]Num. 20:15 [b]Ps. 81:6
15 [a]Ex. 2:6
16 [a]Acts 7:19
17 [a]Prov. 16:6

[b]as the king of Egypt commanded them, but saved
the male children alive.
18 So the king of Egypt called for the midwives
and said to them, "Why have you done this thing,
and saved the male children alive?"
19 And [a]the midwives said to Pharaoh, "Because
the Hebrew women *are* not like the Egyptian
women; for they [1]*are* lively and give birth before
the midwives come to them."
20 [a]Therefore God dealt well with the midwives,
and the people multiplied and [1]grew very mighty.
21 And so it was, because the midwives feared
God, [a]that He [1]provided households for them.
22 So Pharaoh commanded all his people, saying,
[a]"Every son who is [1]born you shall cast into the
river, and every daughter you shall save alive."

### *Birth of Moses*

**2** And [a]a man of the house of Levi went and
took *as wife* a daughter of Levi.
2 So the woman conceived and bore a son. And
[a]when she saw that he *was* a beautiful *child,* she
hid him three months.
3 But when she could no longer hide him, she
took an ark of [a]bulrushes for him, daubed it with
[b]asphalt and [c]pitch, put the child in it, and laid *it* in
the reeds [d]by the river's bank.
4 [a]And his sister stood afar off, to know what
would be done to him.
5 Then the [a]daughter of Pharaoh came down to
bathe at the river. And her maidens walked along
the riverside; and when she saw the ark among
the reeds, she sent her maid to get it.
6 And when she opened *it,* she saw the child,
and behold, the baby wept. So she had compassion
on him, and said, "This is one of the Hebrews'
children."
7 Then his sister said to Pharaoh's daughter,
"Shall I go and call a nurse for you from the
Hebrew women, that she may nurse the child for
you?"
8 And Pharaoh's daughter said to her, "Go." So
the maiden went and called the child's mother.
9 Then Pharaoh's daughter said to her, "Take
this child away and nurse him for me, and I will
give *you* your wages." So the woman took the
child and nursed him.
10 And the child grew, and she brought him to
Pharaoh's daughter, and he became [a]her son. So
she called his name [1]Moses, saying, "Because I
drew him out of the water."
11 Now it came to pass in those days, [a]when
Moses was grown, that he went out to his brethren and looked at their burdens. And he saw an
Egyptian beating a Hebrew, one of his brethren.
12 So he looked this way and that way, and when
he saw no one, he [a]killed the Egyptian and hid him
in the sand.
13 And [a]when he went out the second day, behold, two Hebrew men [b]were fighting, and he said
to the one who did the wrong, "Why are you
striking your companion?"
14 Then he said, [a]"Who made you a prince and a
judge over us? Do you intend to kill me as you
killed the Egyptian?" So Moses [b]feared and said,
"Surely this thing is known!"
15 When Pharaoh heard of this matter, he sought
to kill Moses. But [a]Moses fled from [1]the face of
Pharaoh and dwelt in the land of [b]Midian; and he
sat down by [c]a well.
16 [a]Now the priest of Midian had seven daughters. [b]And they came and drew water, and they
filled the [c]troughs to water their father's flock.
17 Then the [a]shepherds came and [b]drove them
away; but Moses stood up and helped them, and
[c]watered their flock.
18 When they came to [a]Reuel[1] their father, [b]he
said, "How *is it that* you have come so soon
today?"
19 And they said, "An Egyptian delivered us from
the hand of the shepherds, and he also drew
enough water for us and watered the flock."
20 So he said to his daughters, "And where *is* he?
Why *is* it *that* you have left the man? Call him,
that he may [a]eat bread."
21 Then Moses was content to live with the man,
and he gave [a]Zipporah his daughter to Moses.
22 And she bore *him* a son. He called his name
[a]Gershom,[1] for he said, "I have been [b]a [2]stranger
in a foreign land."
23 Now it happened [a]in the process of time that
the king of Egypt died. Then the children of Israel
[b]groaned because of the bondage, and they cried
out; and [c]their cry came up to God because of the
bondage.
24 So God [a]heard their groaning, and God [b]re-
membered His [c]covenant with Abraham, with
Isaac, and with Jacob.
25 And God [a]looked upon the children of Israel,
and God [b]acknowledged *them.*

### *Moses at the Burning Bush*

**3** Now Moses was tending the flock of [a]Jethro
his father-in-law, [b]the priest of Midian. And he
led the flock to the back of the desert, and came to
[c]Horeb, [d]the mountain of God.
2 And [a]the Angel of the LORD appeared to him in
a flame of fire from the midst of a bush. So he
looked, and behold, the bush was burning with
fire, but the bush *was* not consumed.
3 Then Moses said, "I will now turn aside and
see this [a]great sight, why the bush does not burn."
4 So when the LORD saw that he turned aside to
look, God called [a]to him from the midst of the
bush and said, "Moses, Moses!" And he said,
"Here I am."
5 Then He said, "Do not draw near this place.
[a]Take your sandals off your feet, for the place
where you stand *is* holy ground."
6 Moreover He said, [a]"I *am* the God of your
father—the God of Abraham, the God of Isaac,
and the God of Jacob." And Moses hid his face, for
[b]he was afraid to look upon God.
7 And the LORD said: [a]"I have surely seen the
oppression of My people who *are* in Egypt, and
have heard their cry [b]because of their taskmasters, [c]for I know their [1]sorrows.
8 "So [a]I have come down to [b]deliver them out of
the hand of the Egyptians, and to bring them up
from that land [c]to a good and large land, to a land
[d]flowing with milk and honey, to the place of [e]the
Canaanites and the Hittites and the Amorites and
the Perizzites and the Hivites and the Jebusites.
9 "Now therefore, behold, [a]the cry of the children of Israel has come to Me, and I have also
seen the [b]oppression with which the Egyptians
oppress them.
10 [a]"Come now, therefore, and I will send you to

**17** [b]Dan. 3:16, 18
**19** [a]Josh. 2:4 [1]*have vigor of life,* bear quickly, easily
**20** [a][Prov. 11:18] [1]*became very numerous*
**21** [a]1 Sam. 2:35 [1]*gave them families*
**22** [a]Acts 7:19 [1]Sam., LXX, Tg. add *to the Hebrews*

CHAPTER 2
**1** [a]Ex. 6:16–20
**2** [a]Acts 7:20
**3** [a]Is. 18:2 [b]Gen. 14:10 [c]Gen. 6:14 [d]Is. 19:6
**4** [a]Num. 26:59
**5** [a]Acts 7:21
**10** [a]Acts 7:21 [1]Heb. *Mosheh,* lit. *Drawn Out*
**11** [a]Heb. 11:24–26
**12** [a]Acts 7:24, 25
**13** [a]Acts 7:26–28 [b]Prov. 25:8
**14** [a]Acts 7:27, 28 [b]Judg. 6:27
**15** [a]Acts 7:29 [b]Ex. 3:1 [c]Gen. 24:11; 29:2 [1]*the presence of Pharaoh*
**16** [a]Ex. 3:1; 4:18; 18:12 [b]Gen. 24:11, 13, 19; 29:6–10 [c]Gen. 30:38
**17** [a]Gen. 47:3 [b]Gen. 26:19–21 [c]Gen. 29:3, 10
**18** [a]Num. 10:29 [b]Ex. 3:1; 4:18 [1]*Jethro,* Ex. 3:1
**20** [a]Gen. 31:54; 43:25
**21** [a]Ex. 4:25; 18:2
**22** [a]Ex. 4:20; 18:3, 4 [b]Acts 7:29 [1]Lit. *Stranger There* [2]*sojourner,* temporary resident
**23** [a]Acts 7:34 [b]Deut. 26:7 [c]James 5:4
**24** [a]Ex. 6:5 [b]Gen. 15:13; 22:16–18; 26:2–5; 28:13–15 [c]Gen. 12:1–3; 15:14; 17:1–14
**25** [a]Ex. 4:31 [b]Ex. 3:7

CHAPTER 3
**1** [a]Ex. 4:18 [b]Ex. 2:16 [c]Ex. 18:5 [d]Ex. 17:6
**2** [a]Deut. 33:16
**3** [a]Acts 7:31
**4** [a]Deut. 33:16
**5** [a]Josh. 5:15
**6** [a][Matt. 22:32] [b]1 Kin. 19:13
**7** [a]Ex. 2:23–25 [b]Ex. 1:11 [c]Ex. 2:25 [1]*pain*

**8** [a]Gen. 15:13–16; 46:4; 50:24, 25 [b]Ex. 6:6–8; 12:51 [c]Num. 13:27; Deut. 1:25; 8:7–9; Josh. 3:17 [d]Ex. 3:17; 13:5; Jer. 11:5; Ezek. 20:6 [e]Gen. 15:19–21; Josh. 24:11
**9** [a]Ex. 2:23 [b]Ex. 1:11, 13, 14
**10** [a]Gen. 15:13, 14; Ex. 12:40, 41; [Mic. 6:4]; Acts 7:6, 7

Pharaoh that you may bring My people, the
children of Israel, out of Egypt."
11 But Moses said to God, [a]"Who *am* I that I
should go to Pharaoh, and that I should bring the
children of Israel out of Egypt?"
12 So He said, [a]"I will certainly be with you. And
this *shall be* a [b]sign to you that I have sent you:
When you have brought the people out of Egypt,
you shall serve God on this mountain."
**13** Then Moses said to God, "Indeed, *when* I
come to the children of Israel and say to them,
'The God of your fathers has sent me to you,' and
they say to me, 'What *is* His name?' what shall I
say to them?"
14 And God said to Moses, "I AM WHO I AM."
And He said, "Thus you shall say to the children
of Israel, [a]'I AM has sent me to you.' "
15 Moreover God said to Moses, "Thus you shall
say to the children of Israel: 'The LORD God of
your fathers, the God of Abraham, the God of
Isaac, and the God of Jacob, has sent me to you.
This *is* [a]My name forever, and this *is* My memorial
to all generations.'
16 "Go and [a]gather the elders of Israel together,
and say to them, 'The LORD God of your fathers,
the God of Abraham, of Isaac, and of Jacob,
appeared to me, saying, [b]"I have surely visited you
and *seen* what is done to you in Egypt;
17 "and I have said [a]I will bring you up out of the
affliction of Egypt to the land of the Canaanites
and the Hittites and the Amorites and the Perizzites and the Hivites and the Jebusites, to a land
flowing with milk and honey." '
18 "Then [a]they will heed your voice; and [b]you
shall come, you and the elders of Israel, to the
king of Egypt; and you shall say to him, 'The LORD
God of the Hebrews has [c]met with us; and now,
please, let us go three days' journey into the
wilderness, that we may sacrifice to the LORD our
God.'
19 "But I am sure that the king of Egypt [a]will not
let you go, no, not even by a mighty hand.
20 "So I will [a]stretch out My hand and strike
Egypt with [b]all My wonders which I will do in its
midst; and [c]after that he will let you go.
21 "And [a]I will give this people favor in the sight
of the Egyptians; and it shall be, when you go,
that you shall not go empty-handed.
22 [a]"But every woman shall ask of her neighbor,
namely, of her who dwells near her house, [b]arti-
cles of silver, articles of gold, and clothing; and
you shall put *them* on your sons and on your
daughters. So [c]you shall plunder the Egyptians."

### *Moses Returns to Egypt*

**4** Then Moses answered and said, "But suppose
they will not believe me or listen to my voice;
suppose they say, 'The LORD has not appeared to
you.' "
2 So the LORD said to him, "What *is* that in your
hand?" He said, "A rod."
3 And He said, "Cast it on the ground." So he
cast it on the ground, and it became a serpent; and
Moses fled from it.
4 Then the LORD said to Moses, "Reach out your
hand and take *it* by the tail" (and he reached out
his hand and caught it, and it became a rod in his
hand),
5 "that they may [a]believe that the [b]LORD God of
their fathers, the God of Abraham, the God of
Isaac, and the God of Jacob, has appeared to you."
6 Furthermore the LORD said to him, "Now put
your hand in your bosom." And he put his hand in
his bosom, and when he took it out, behold, his
hand *was* leprous, [a]like snow.
7 And He said, "Put your hand in your bosom
again." So he put his hand in his bosom again, and
drew it out of his bosom, and behold, [a]it was
restored like his *other* flesh.
8 "Then it will be, if they do not believe you, nor
heed the message of the [a]first sign, that they may
believe the message of the latter sign.
9 "And it shall be, if they do not believe even
these two signs, or listen to your voice, that you
shall take water from [1]the river and pour *it* on the
dry *land*. [a]The water which you take from the
river will become blood on the dry *land*."
**10** Then Moses said to the LORD, "O my Lord, I
*am* not eloquent, neither before nor since You
have spoken to Your servant; but [a]I *am* slow of
speech and [1]slow of tongue."
11 So the LORD said to him, [a]"Who has made
man's mouth? Or who makes the mute, the deaf,
the seeing, or the blind? *Have* not I, the LORD?
12 "Now therefore, go, and I will be [a]with your
mouth and teach you what you shall say."
13 But he said, "O my Lord, [a]please send by the
hand of whomever *else* You may send."
14 So [a]the anger of the LORD was kindled against
Moses, and He said: "Is not Aaron the Levite your
[b]brother? I know that he can speak well. And
look, [c]he is also coming out to meet you. When he
sees you, he will be glad in his heart.
15 "Now [a]you shall speak to him and [b]put the
words in his mouth. And I will be with your
mouth and with his mouth, and [c]I will teach you
what you shall do.
16 "So he shall be your spokesman to the people.
And he himself shall be as a mouth for you, and
[a]you shall be to him as God.
17 "And you shall take this rod in your hand,
with which you shall do the signs."
**18** So Moses went and returned to [a]Jethro his
father-in-law, and said to him, "Please let me go
and return to my brethren who *are* in Egypt, and
see whether they are still alive." And Jethro said
to Moses, [b]"Go in peace."
19 Now the LORD said to Moses in [a]Midian, "Go,
return to [b]Egypt; for [c]all the men who sought your
life are dead."
20 Then Moses [a]took his wife and his sons and set
them on a donkey, and he returned to the land of
Egypt. And Moses took [b]the rod of God in his
hand.
21 And the LORD said to Moses, "When you go
back to Egypt, see that you do all those [a]wonders
before Pharaoh which I have put in your hand.
But [b]I will harden his heart, so that he will not let
the people go.
22 "Then you shall [a]say to Pharaoh, 'Thus says
the LORD: [b]"Israel *is* My son, [c]My firstborn.
23 "So I say to you, let My son go that he may
serve Me. But if you refuse to let him go, indeed [a]I
will kill your son, your firstborn." ' "
**24** And it came to pass on the way, at the [a]en-
campment, that the LORD [b]met him and sought to
[c]kill him.
25 Then [a]Zipporah took [b]a sharp stone and cut
off the foreskin of her son and [1]cast *it* at [2]*Moses'*
feet, and said, "Surely you *are* a husband of blood
to me!"
26 So He let him go. Then she said, "*You are* a
[1]husband of blood!"—because of the circumcision.
**27** And the LORD said to Aaron, "Go into the

11 [a]Ex. 4:10; 6:12
12 [a]Gen. 31:3 [b]Ex. 4:8; 19:3
14 [a][John 8:24, 28, 58]
15 [a]Ps. 30:4; 97:12; 102:12; 135:13
16 [a]Ex. 4:29 [b]Ex. 2:25; 4:31
17 [a]Gen. 15:13–21; 46:4; 50:24, 25
18 [a]Ex. 4:31 [b]Ex. 5:1, 3 [c]Num. 23:3, 4, 15, 16
19 [a]Ex. 5:2
20 [a]Ex. 6:6; 9:15 [b]Deut. 6:22 [c]Ex. 11:1; 12:31–37
21 [a]Ex. 11:3; 12:36
22 [a]Ex. 11:2 [b]Ex. 33:6 [c]Job 27:17

CHAPTER 4

5 [a]Ex. 4:31; 19:9 [b]Ex. 3:6, 15
6 [a]Num. 12:10
7 [a]Deut. 32:39
8 [a]Ex. 7:6–13
9 [a]Ex. 7:19, 20 [1]The Nile
10 [a]Ex. 3:11; 4:1; 6:12 [1]*heavy* or *dull of tongue;* cannot talk very well
11 [a]Ps. 94:9; 146:8
12 [a]Is. 50:4
13 [a]Jon. 1:3
14 [a]Num. 11:1, 33 [b]Num. 26:59 [c]Ex. 4:27
15 [a]Ex. 4:12, 30; 7:1, 2 [b]Num. 23:5, 12 [c]Deut. 5:31
16 [a]Ex. 7:1, 2
18 [a]Ex. 2:21; 3:1; 4:18 [b]Judg. 18:6
19 [a]Ex. 3:1; 18:1 [b]Gen. 46:3, 6 [c]Ex. 2:15, 23
20 [a]Ex. 18:2–5 [b]Num. 20:8, 9, 11
21 [a]Ex. 3:20; 11:9, 10 [b]John 12:40
22 [a]Ex. 5:1 [b]Hos. 11:1 [c]Jer. 31:9
23 [a]Ex. 11:5; 12:29
24 [a]Gen. 42:27 [b]Num. 22:22 [c]Gen. 17:14
25 [a]Ex. 2:21; 18:2 [b]Josh. 5:2, 3 [1]Lit. *made it touch* [2]Lit. *his*
26 [1]*bridegroom*

wilderness [a]to meet Moses." So he went and met
him on [b]the mountain of God, and kissed him.
28 So Moses [a]told Aaron all the words of the
LORD who had sent him, and all the [b]signs which
He had commanded him.
29 Then Moses and Aaron [a]went and gathered
together all the elders of the children of Israel.
30 [a]And Aaron spoke all the words which the
LORD had spoken to Moses. Then he did the signs
in the sight of the people.
31 So the people [a]believed; and when they heard
that the LORD had [b]visited the children of Israel
and that He [c]had looked on their affliction, then
[d]they bowed their heads and worshiped.

## *Let My People Go*

**5** Afterward Moses and Aaron went in and told
Pharaoh, "Thus says the LORD God of Israel:
'Let My people go, that they may [1]hold [a]a feast to
Me in the wilderness.' "
2 And Pharaoh said, [a]"Who *is* the LORD, that I
should obey His voice to let Israel go? I do not
know the LORD, [b]nor will I let Israel go."
3 So they said, [a]"The God of the Hebrews has
[b]met with us. Please, let us go three days' journey
into the desert and sacrifice to the LORD our God,
lest He fall upon us with [c]pestilence or with the
sword."
4 Then the king of Egypt said to them, "Moses
and Aaron, why do you take the people from their
work? Get *back* to your [a]labor."
5 And Pharaoh said, "Look, the people of the
land *are* [a]many now, and you make them rest
from their labor!"
6 So the same day Pharaoh commanded the
[a]taskmasters of the people and their officers,
saying,
7 "You shall no longer give the people straw to
make [a]brick as before. Let them go and gather
straw for themselves.
8 "And you shall lay on them the quota of bricks
which they made before. You shall not reduce it.
For they are idle; therefore they cry out, saying,
'Let us go *and* sacrifice to our God.'
9 "Let more work be laid on the men, that they
may labor in it, and let them not regard false
words."
**10** And the taskmasters of the people and their
officers went out and spoke to the people, saying,
"Thus says Pharaoh: 'I will not give you straw.
11 'Go, get yourselves straw where you can find
it; yet none of your work will be reduced.' "
12 So the people were scattered abroad throughout all the land of Egypt to gather stubble instead
of straw.
13 And the taskmasters forced *them* to hurry,
saying, "Fulfill your work, *your* daily quota, as
when there was straw."
14 Also the [a]officers of the children of Israel,
whom Pharaoh's taskmasters had set over them,
were [b]beaten *and* were asked, "Why have you not
fulfilled your task in making brick both yesterday
and today, as before?"
**15** Then the officers of the children of Israel came
and cried out to Pharaoh, saying, "Why are you
dealing thus with your servants?
16 "There is no straw given to your servants, and
they say to us, 'Make brick!' And indeed your
servants *are* beaten, but the fault *is* in your *own*
people."

**27** [a]Ex. 4:14 [b]Ex. 3:1; 18:5; 24:13
**28** [a]Ex. 4:15, 16 [b]Ex. 4:8, 9
**29** [a]Ex. 3:16; 12:21
**30** [a]Ex. 4:15, 16
**31** [a]Ex. 3:18; 4:8, 9; 19:9 [b]Gen. 50:24 [c]Ex. 2:25; 3:7 [d]Gen. 24:26

CHAPTER 5

**1** [a]Ex. 3:18; 7:16; 10:9 [1]*keep a pilgrim-feast*
**2** [a]2 Kin. 18:35 [b]Ex. 3:19; 7:14
**3** [a]Ex. 3:18; 7:16 [b]Num. 23:3 [c]Ex. 9:15
**4** [a]Ex. 1:11; 2:11; 6:6
**5** [a]Ex. 1:7, 9
**6** [a]Ex. 1:11; 3:7; 5:10, 13, 14
**7** [a]Ex. 1:14
**14** [a]Ex. 5:6 [b]Is. 10:24
**21** [a]Ex. 6:9; 14:11; 15:24; 16:2 [1]Lit. *our scent to stink before*

CHAPTER 6

**1** [a]Ex. 3:19 [b]Ex. 12:31, 33, 39
**2** [1]Heb. *YHWH*
**3** [a]Gen. 17:1; 35:9; 48:3 [b]Gen. 28:3; 35:11 [c]Ps. 68:4; 83:18 [1]Heb. *YHWH,* traditionally *Jehovah*
**4** [a]Gen. 12:7; 15:18; 17:4, 7, 8; 26:3; 28:4, 13 [b]Lev. 25:23 [c]Gen. 28:4 [1]*made* or *ratified* [2]*sojournings* [3]*sojourners,* temporary residents
**5** [a]Ex. 2:24
**6** [a]Deut. 6:12 [b]Deut. 26:8 [c]Deut. 7:8 [1]Mighty power
**7** [a]2 Sam. 7:24 [b]Ex. 29:45, 46 [c]Ex. 5:4, 5
**8** [a]Gen. 15:18; 26:3 [1]*promised,* lit. *lifted up my hand*
**9** [a]Ex. 5:21 [b]Ex. 2:23 [1]Lit. *shortness*
**12** [a]Jer. 1:6 [1]One who does not speak well
**13** [a]Deut. 31:14 [1]*charge*
**14** [a]Gen. 46:9
**15** [a]Gen. 46:10 [1]*Nemuel,* Num. 26:12

17 But he said, "You *are* idle! Idle! Therefore you
say, 'Let us go *and* sacrifice to the LORD.'
18 "Therefore go now *and* work; for no straw
shall be given you, yet you shall deliver the quota
of bricks."
19 And the officers of the children of Israel saw
*that* they *were* in trouble after it was said, "You
shall not reduce *any* bricks from your daily
quota."
**20** Then, as they came out from Pharaoh, they
met Moses and Aaron who stood there to meet
them.
21 [a]And they said to them, "Let the LORD look on
you and judge, because you have made [1]us abhor-
rent in the sight of Pharaoh and in the sight of his
servants, to put a sword in their hand to kill us."
**22** So Moses returned to the LORD and said,
"Lord, why have You brought trouble on this
people? Why *is* it You have sent me?
23 "For since I came to Pharaoh to speak in Your
name, he has done evil to this people; neither have
You delivered Your people at all."

## *God Renews His Promise to Israel*

**6** Then the LORD said to Moses, "Now you shall
see what I will do to Pharaoh. For [a]with a
strong hand he will let them go, and with a strong
hand [b]he will drive them out of his land."
**2** And God spoke to Moses and said to him: "I
*am* [1]the LORD.
3 [a]"I appeared to Abraham, to Isaac, and to
Jacob, as [b]God Almighty, but *by* My name [c]LORD[1]
I was not known to them.
4 [a]"I have also [1]established My covenant with
them, [b]to give them the land of Canaan, the land
of their [2]pilgrimage, [c]in which they were [3]strang-
ers.
5 "And [a]I have also heard the groaning of the
children of Israel whom the Egyptians keep in
bondage, and I have remembered My covenant.
6 "Therefore say to the children of Israel: [a]'I *am*
the LORD; [b]I will bring you out from under the
burdens of the Egyptians, I will [c]rescue you from
their bondage, and I will redeem you with [1]an
outstretched arm and with great judgments.
7 'I will [a]take you as My people, and [b]I will be
your God. Then you shall know that I *am* the
LORD your God who brings you out [c]from under
the burdens of the Egyptians.
8 'And I will bring you into the land which I
[a]swore[1] to give to Abraham, Isaac, and Jacob; and
I will give it to you *as* a heritage: I *am* the LORD.' "
9 So Moses spoke thus to the children of Israel;
[a]but they did not heed Moses, because of [b]anguish[1]
of spirit and cruel bondage.
**10** And the LORD spoke to Moses, saying,
11 "Go in, tell Pharaoh king of Egypt to let the
children of Israel go out of his land."
12 And Moses spoke before the LORD, saying,
"The children of Israel have not heeded me. How
then shall Pharaoh heed me, for [a]I *am* [1]of uncircumcised lips?"
13 Then the LORD spoke to Moses and Aaron, and
gave them a [a]command[1] for the children of Israel
and for Pharaoh king of Egypt, to bring the
children of Israel out of the land of Egypt.
**14** These *are* the heads of their fathers' houses:
[a]The sons of Reuben, the firstborn of Israel, *were*
Hanoch, Pallu, Hezron, and Carmi. These are the
families of Reuben.
15 [a]And the sons of Simeon *were* [1]Jemuel, Jamin,

Ohad, Jachin, Zohar, and Shaul the son of a Canaanite woman. These *are* the families of Simeon.

16 These *are* the names of [a]the sons of Levi according to their generations: Gershon, Kohath, and Merari. And the years of the life of Levi *were* one hundred and thirty-seven.

17 [a]The sons of Gershon *were* Libni and Shimi according to their families.

18 And [a]the sons of Kohath *were* Amram, Izhar, Hebron, and Uzziel. And the years of the life of Kohath *were* one hundred and thirty-three.

19 [a]The sons of Merari *were* Mahli and Mushi. These *are* the families of Levi according to their generations.

**20** Now [a]Amram took for himself [b]Jochebed, his father's sister, as wife; and she bore him [c]Aaron and Moses. And the years of the life of Amram *were* one hundred and thirty-seven.

21 [a]The sons of Izhar *were* Korah, Nepheg, and Zichri.

22 And [a]the sons of Uzziel *were* Mishael, Elzaphan, and Zithri.

23 Aaron took to himself Elisheba, daughter of [a]Amminadab, sister of Nahshon, as wife; and she bore him [b]Nadab, Abihu, [c]Eleazar, and Ithamar.

24 And [a]the sons of Korah *were* Assir, Elkanah, and Abiasaph. These are the families of the Korahites.

25 Eleazar, Aaron's son, took for himself one of the daughters of Putiel as wife; and [a]she bore him Phinehas. These *are* the heads of the fathers' houses of the Levites according to their families.

**26** These *are the same* Aaron and Moses to whom the LORD said, "Bring out the children of Israel from the land of Egypt according to their [a]armies."[1]

27 These *are* the ones who spoke to Pharaoh king of Egypt, [a]to bring out the children of Israel from Egypt. These *are the same* Moses and Aaron.

**28** And it came to pass, on the day the LORD spoke to Moses in the land of Egypt,

29 that the LORD spoke to Moses, saying, "I *am* the LORD. [a]Speak to Pharaoh king of Egypt all that I say to you."

30 But Moses said before the LORD, "Behold, [a]I *am* [1]of uncircumcised lips, and how shall Pharaoh heed me?"

### *Moses Before Pharaoh*

**7** So the LORD said to Moses: "See, I have made you [a]*as* God to Pharaoh, and Aaron your brother shall be [b]your prophet.

2 "You [a]shall speak all that I command you. And Aaron your brother shall tell Pharaoh to send the children of Israel out of his land.

3 "And [a]I will harden Pharaoh's heart, and [b]multiply My [c]signs and My wonders in the land of Egypt.

4 "But [a]Pharaoh will not heed you, so [b]that I may lay My hand on Egypt and bring My [1]armies *and* My people, the children of Israel, out of the land of Egypt [c]by great judgments.

5 "And the Egyptians [a]shall know that I *am* the LORD, when I [b]stretch out My hand on Egypt and [c]bring out the children of Israel from among them."

6 Then Moses and Aaron [a]did *so;* just as the LORD commanded them, so they did.

7 And Moses *was* [a]eighty years old and [b]Aaron eighty-three years old when they spoke to Pharaoh.

**8** Then the LORD spoke to Moses and Aaron, saying,

9 "When Pharaoh speaks to you, saying, [a]'Show a miracle for yourselves,' then you shall say to Aaron, [b]'Take your rod and cast *it* before Pharaoh, *and* let it become a serpent.' "

10 So Moses and Aaron went in to Pharaoh, and they did so, just [a]as the LORD commanded. And Aaron cast down his rod before Pharaoh and before his servants, and it [b]became a serpent.

11 But Pharaoh also [a]called the wise men and [b]the [1]sorcerers; so the magicians of Egypt, they also [c]did in like manner with their [2]enchantments.

12 For every man threw down his rod, and they became serpents. But Aaron's rod swallowed up their rods.

13 And Pharaoh's heart grew hard, and he did not heed them, as the LORD had said.

**14** So the LORD said to Moses: [a]"Pharaoh's heart *is* hard; he refuses to let the people go.

15 "Go to Pharaoh in the morning, when he goes out to the [a]water, and you shall stand by the river's bank to meet him; and [b]the rod which was turned to a serpent you shall take in your hand.

16 "And you shall say to him, [a]'The LORD God of the Hebrews has sent me to you, saying, "Let My people go, [b]that they may [1]serve Me in the wilderness"; but indeed, until now you would not hear!

17 'Thus says the LORD: "By this [a]you shall know that I *am* the LORD. Behold, I will strike the waters which *are* in the river with the rod that *is* in my hand, and [b]they shall be turned [c]to blood.

18 "And the fish that *are* in the river shall die, the river shall stink, and the Egyptians will [a]loathe[1] to drink the water of the river." ' "

**19** Then the LORD spoke to Moses, "Say to Aaron, 'Take your rod and [a]stretch out your hand over the waters of Egypt, over their streams, over their rivers, over their ponds, and over all their pools of water, that they may become blood. And there shall be blood throughout all the land of Egypt, both in *buckets of* wood and *pitchers of* stone.' "

20 And Moses and Aaron did so, just as the LORD commanded. So he [a]lifted up the rod and struck the waters that *were* in the river, in the sight of Pharaoh and in the sight of his servants. And all the [b]waters that *were* in the river were turned to blood.

21 The fish that *were* in the river died, the river stank, and the Egyptians [a]could not drink the water of the river. So there was blood throughout all the land of Egypt.

22 [a]Then the magicians of Egypt did [b]so with their [1]enchantments; and Pharaoh's heart grew hard, and he did not heed them, [c]as the LORD had said.

23 And Pharaoh turned and went into his house. Neither was his heart moved by this.

24 So all the Egyptians dug all around the river for water to drink, because they could not drink the water of the river.

25 And seven days passed after the LORD had struck the river.

### *The Plagues of Frogs, Lice, and Flies*

**8** And the LORD spoke to Moses, "Go to Pharaoh and say to him, 'Thus says the LORD: "Let My people go, [a]that they may serve Me.

2 "But if you [a]refuse to let *them* go, behold, I will smite all your territory with [b]frogs.

**16** [a]Gen. 46:11
**17** [a]1 Chr. 6:17
**18** [a]1 Chr. 6:2, 18
**19** [a]1 Chr. 6:19; 23:21
**20** [a]Ex. 2:1, 2 [b]Num. 26:59 [c]Num. 26:59
**21** [a]1 Chr. 6:37, 38
**22** [a]Lev. 10:4
**23** [a]Ruth 4:19, 20 [b]Lev. 10:1 [c]Ex. 28:1
**24** [a]Num. 26:11
**25** [a]Num. 25:7, 11
**26** [a]Ex. 7:4; 12:17, 51 [1]*hosts*
**27** [a]Ps. 77:20
**29** [a]Ex. 6:11; 7:2
**30** [a]Ex. 4:10; 6:12 [1]One who does not speak well

CHAPTER 7
**1** [a]Ex. 4:16 [b]Ex. 4:15, 16
**2** [a]Ex. 4:15
**3** [a]Ex. 4:21; 9:12 [b]Ex. 11:9 [c]Deut. 4:34
**4** [a]Ex. 3:19, 20; 10:1; 11:9 [b]Ex. 9:14 [c]Ex. 6:6; 12:12 [1]*hosts*
**5** [a]Ps. 9:16 [b]Ex. 9:15 [c]Ex. 3:20; 6:6; 12:51
**6** [a]Ex. 7:2
**7** [a]Deut. 29:5; 31:2; 34:7 [b]Num. 33:39
**9** [a]Is. 7:11 [b]Ex. 4:2, 3, 17
**10** [a]Ex. 7:9 [b]Ex. 4:3
**11** [a]Gen. 41:8 [b]2 Tim. 3:8 [c]Ex. 7:22; 8:7, 18 [1]*soothsayers* [2]*secret arts*
**14** [a]Ex. 8:15; 10:1, 20, 27
**15** [a]Ex. 2:5; 8:20 [b]Ex. 4:2, 3; 7:10
**16** [a]Ex. 3:13, 18; 4:22 [b]Ex. 3:12, 18; 4:23; 5:1, 3; 8:1 [1]*worship*
**17** [a]Ex. 5:2; 7:5; 10:2 [b]Ex. 4:9; 7:20 [c]Rev. 11:6; 16:4, 6
**18** [a]Ex. 7:24 [1]*be weary of drinking*
**19** [a]Ex. 8:5, 6, 16; 9:22; 10:12, 21; 14:21, 26
**20** [a]Ex. 17:5 [b]Ps. 78:44; 105:29, 30
**21** [a]Ex. 7:18
**22** [a]Ex. 7:11 [b]Ex. 8:7 [c]Ex. 3:19; 7:3 [1]*secret arts*

CHAPTER 8
**1** [a]Ex. 3:12, 18; 4:23; 5:1, 3
**2** [a]Ex. 7:14; 9:2 [b]Rev. 16:13

3 "So the river shall bring forth frogs abundantly, which shall go up and come into your
house, into your [a]bedroom, on your bed, into the
houses of your servants, on your people, into your
ovens, and into your kneading bowls.
4 "And the frogs shall come up on you, on your
people, and on all your servants." ' "
**5** Then the LORD spoke to Moses, "Say to Aaron,
[a]'Stretch out your hand with your rod over the
streams, over the rivers, and over the ponds, and
cause frogs to come up on the land of Egypt.' "
6 So Aaron stretched out his hand over the
waters of Egypt, and [a]the frogs came up and
covered the land of Egypt.
7 [a]And the magicians did so with their [1]enchant-
ments, and brought up frogs on the land of Egypt.
**8** Then Pharaoh called for Moses and Aaron,
and said, [a]"Entreat[1] the LORD that He may take
away the frogs from me and from my people; and
I will let the people [b]go, that they may sacrifice to
the LORD."
9 And Moses said to Pharaoh, "Accept the
honor of saying when I shall intercede for you, for
your servants, and for your people, to destroy the
frogs from you and your houses, *that* they may
remain in the river only."
10 So he said, "Tomorrow." And he said, "*Let it
be* according to your word, that you may know
that [a]*there is* no one like the LORD our God.
11 "And the frogs shall depart from you, from
your houses, from your servants, and from your
people. They shall remain in the river only."
12 Then Moses and Aaron went out from Pharaoh. And Moses [a]cried out to the LORD concerning the frogs which He had brought against Pharaoh.
13 So the LORD did according to the word of
Moses. And the frogs died out of the houses, out
of the courtyards, and out of the fields.
14 They gathered them together in heaps, and
the land stank.
15 But when Pharaoh saw that there was [a]relief,
[b]he hardened his heart and did not heed them, as
the LORD had said.
**16** So the LORD said to Moses, "Say to Aaron,
'Stretch out your rod, and strike the dust of the
land, so that it may become [1]lice throughout all
the land of Egypt.' "
17 And they did so. For Aaron stretched out his
hand with his rod and struck the dust of the earth,
and [a]it became lice on man and beast. All the dust
of the land became lice throughout all the land of
Egypt.
18 Now [a]the magicians so worked with their
[1]enchantments to bring forth lice, but they [b]could
not. So there were lice on man and beast.
19 Then the magicians said to Pharaoh, "This *is*
[a]the[1] finger of God." But Pharaoh's [b]heart grew
hard, and he did not heed them, just as the LORD
had said.
**20** And the LORD said to Moses, [a]"Rise early in
the morning and stand before Pharaoh as he
comes out to the water. Then say to him, 'Thus
says the LORD: [b]"Let My people go, that they may
serve Me.
21 "Or else, if you will not let My people go,
behold, I will send swarms *of flies* on you and your
servants, on your people and into your houses.
The houses of the Egyptians shall be full of
swarms *of flies,* and also the ground on which
they *stand.*

3 [a]Ps. 105:30
5 [a]Ex. 7:19
6 [a]Ps. 78:45; 105:30
7 [a]Ex. 7:11, 22 [1]*secret arts*
8 [a]Ex. 8:28; 9:28; 10:17; Num. 21:7; 1 Kin. 13:6 [b]Ex. 10:8, 24 [1]*Pray to, Make supplication to*
10 [a]Ex. 9:14; 15:11; Deut. 4:35, 39; 33:26; 2 Sam. 7:22; 1 Chr. 17:20; Ps. 86:8; Is. 46:9; [Jer. 10:6, 7]
12 [a]Ex. 8:30; 9:33; 10:18; 32:11; [James 5:16–18]
15 [a]Eccl. 8:11 [b]Ex. 7:14, 22; 9:34; 1 Sam. 6:6
16 [1]*gnats*
17 [a]Ps. 105:31
18 [a]Ex. 7:11, 12; 8:7 [b]Dan. 5:8; 2 Tim. 3:8, 9 [1]*secret arts*
19 [a]Ex. 7:5; 10:7; 1 Sam. 6:3, 9; Ps. 8:3; Luke 11:20 [b]Ex. 8:15 [1]An act of God
20 [a]Ex. 7:15; 9:13 [b]Ex. 3:18; 4:23; 5:1, 3; 8:1
22 [a]Ex. 9:4, 6, 26; 10:23; 11:6, 7; 12:13 [b]Gen. 50:8 [c]Ex. 7:5, 17; 10:2; 14:4 [d]Ex. 9:29
23 [a]Ex. 4:8 [1]Lit. *set a ransom,* Ex. 9:4; 11:7
24 [a]Ps. 78:45; 105:31
26 [a]Gen. 43:32; 46:34; [Deut. 7:25, 26; 12:31] [1]Put us to death by stoning
27 [a]Ex. 3:18; 5:3 [b]Ex. 3:12
28 [a]Ex. 8:8, 15, 29, 32; 9:28; 1 Kin. 13:6
29 [a]Ex. 8:8, 15
30 [a]Ex. 8:12
32 [a]Ex. 4:21; 8:8, 15; Ps. 52:2

CHAPTER 9

1 [a]Ex. 4:23; 8:1 [b]Ex. 7:16
2 [a]Ex. 8:2
3 [a]Ex. 7:4; 1 Sam. 5:6; Ps. 39:10; Acts 13:11
4 [a]Ex. 8:22
6 [a]Ex. 9:19, 20, 25; Ps. 78:48, 50
7 [a]Ex. 7:14; 8:32

22 "And in that day [a]I will set apart the land of
[b]Goshen, in which My people dwell, that no
swarms *of flies* shall be there, in order that you
may [c]know that I *am* the LORD in the midst of the
[d]land.
23 "I will [1]make a difference between My people
and your people. Tomorrow this [a]sign shall be." ' "
24 And the LORD did so. [a]Thick swarms *of flies*
came into the house of Pharaoh, *into* his servants'
houses, and into all the land of Egypt. The land
was corrupted because of the swarms *of flies.*
**25** Then Pharaoh called for Moses and Aaron,
and said, "Go, sacrifice to your God in the land."
26 And Moses said, "It is not right to do so, for
we would be sacrificing [a]the abomination of the
Egyptians to the LORD our God. If we sacrifice the
abomination of the Egyptians before their eyes,
then will they not [1]stone us?
27 "We will go [a]three days' journey into the
wilderness and sacrifice to the LORD our God as
[b]He will command us."
28 So Pharaoh said, "I will let you go, that you
may sacrifice to the LORD your God in the wilderness; only you shall not go very far away. [a]Inter-
cede for me."
29 Then Moses said, "Indeed I am going out from
you, and I will entreat the LORD, that the swarms
*of flies* may depart tomorrow from Pharaoh, from
his servants, and from his people. But let Pharaoh
not [a]deal deceitfully anymore in not letting the
people go to sacrifice to the LORD."
30 So Moses went out from Pharaoh and [a]en-
treated the LORD.
31 And the LORD did according to the word of
Moses; He removed the swarms *of flies* from
Pharaoh, from his servants, and from his people.
Not one remained.
32 But Pharaoh [a]hardened his heart at this time
also; neither would he let the people go.

### *The Plague on the Cattle; the Plagues of Boils and Hail*

**9** Then the LORD said to Moses, [a]"Go in to
Pharaoh and tell him, 'Thus says the LORD
God of the Hebrews: "Let My people go, that they
may [b]serve Me.
2 "For if you [a]refuse to let *them* go, and still
hold them,
3 "behold, the [a]hand of the LORD will be on your
cattle in the field, on the horses, on the donkeys,
on the camels, on the oxen, and on the sheep—a
very severe pestilence.
4 "And [a]the LORD will make a difference between the livestock of Israel and the livestock of
Egypt. So nothing shall die of all *that* belongs to
the children of Israel." ' "
5 Then the LORD appointed a set time, saying,
"Tomorrow the LORD will do this thing in the
land."
6 So the LORD did this thing on the next day,
and [a]all the livestock of Egypt died; but of the
livestock of the children of Israel, not one died.
7 Then Pharaoh sent, and indeed, not even one
of the livestock of the Israelites was dead. But the
[a]heart of Pharaoh became hard, and he did not let
the people go.
**8** So the LORD said to Moses and Aaron, "Take
for yourselves handfuls of ashes from a furnace,
and let Moses scatter it toward the heavens in the
sight of Pharaoh.
9 "And it will become fine dust in all the land of

Egypt, and it will cause [a]boils that break out in
sores on man and beast throughout all the land of
Egypt."
10 Then they took ashes from the furnace and
stood before Pharaoh, and Moses scattered *them*
toward heaven. And *they* caused [a]boils that break
out in sores on man and beast.
11 And the [a]magicians could not stand before
Moses because of the [b]boils, for the boils were on
the magicians and on all the Egyptians.
12 But the LORD hardened the heart of Pharaoh;
and he [a]did not heed them, just [b]as the LORD had
spoken to Moses.
**13** Then the LORD said to Moses, [a]"Rise early in
the morning and stand before Pharaoh, and say to
him, 'Thus says the LORD God of the Hebrews:
"Let My people go, that they may [b]serve Me,
14 "for at this time I will send all My plagues to
your very heart, and on your servants and on your
people, [a]that you may know that *there is* none like
Me in all the earth.
15 "Now if I had [a]stretched out My hand and
struck you and your people with [b]pestilence, then
you would have been cut off from the earth.
16 "But indeed for [a]this *purpose* I have raised you
up, that I may [b]show My power *in* you, and that
My [c]name may be declared in all the earth.
17 "As yet you exalt yourself against My people
in that you will not let them go.
18 "Behold, tomorrow about this time I will cause
very heavy hail to rain down, such as has not been
in Egypt since its founding until now.
19 "Therefore send now *and* gather your livestock and all that you have in the field, for the hail
shall come down on every man and every animal
which is found in the field and is not brought
home; and they shall die." ' "
20 He who [a]feared the word of the LORD among
the [b]servants of Pharaoh made his servants and
his livestock flee to the houses.
21 But he who did not regard the word of the
LORD left his servants and his livestock in the
field.
**22** Then the LORD said to Moses, "Stretch out
your hand toward heaven, that there may be [a]hail
in all the land of Egypt—on man, on beast, and on
every herb of the field, throughout the land of
Egypt."
23 And Moses stretched out his rod toward
heaven; and [a]the LORD sent thunder and hail, and
fire darted to the ground. And the LORD rained
hail on the land of Egypt.
24 So there was hail, and fire mingled with the
hail, so very heavy that there was none like it in
all the land of Egypt since it became a nation.
25 And the [a]hail struck throughout the whole
land of Egypt, all that *was* in the field, both man
and beast; and the hail struck every herb of the
field and broke every tree of the field.
26 [a]Only in the land of Goshen, where the children of Israel *were*, there was no hail.
**27** And Pharaoh sent and [a]called for Moses and
Aaron, and said to them, [b]"I have sinned this time.
[c]The LORD *is* righteous, and my people and I *are*
wicked.
28 [a]"Entreat[1] the LORD, that there may be no
*more* [2]mighty thundering and hail, for *it is*
enough. I will let you [b]go, and you shall stay no
longer."
29 So Moses said to him, "As soon as I have gone
out of the city, I will [a]spread out my hands to the
LORD; the thunder will cease, and there will be no
more hail, that you may know that the [b]earth *is*
the LORD's.
30 "But as for you and your servants, [a]I know
that you will not yet fear the LORD God."
31 Now the flax and the barley were struck, [a]for
the barley *was* in the head and the flax *was* in
bud.
32 But the wheat and the spelt were not struck,
for they *are* [1]late crops.
33 So Moses went out of the city from Pharaoh
and [a]spread out his hands to the LORD; then the
thunder and the hail ceased, and the rain was not
poured on the earth.
34 And when Pharaoh saw that the rain, the hail,
and the thunder had ceased, he sinned yet more;
and he hardened his heart, he and his servants.
35 So [a]the heart of Pharaoh was hard; neither
would he let the children of Israel go, as the LORD
had spoken by Moses.

### *The Plagues of Locusts and Darkness*

**10** Now the LORD said to Moses, "Go in to
Pharaoh; [a]for I have hardened his heart and
the hearts of his servants, [b]that I may show these
signs of Mine before him,
2 "and that [a]you may tell in the hearing of your
son and your son's son the mighty things I have
done in Egypt, and My signs which I have done
among them, that you may [b]know that I *am* the
LORD."
**3** So Moses and Aaron came in to Pharaoh and
said to him, "Thus says the LORD God of the
Hebrews: 'How long will you refuse to [a]humble
yourself before Me? Let My people go, that they
may [b]serve Me.
4 'Or else, if you refuse to let My people go,
behold, tomorrow I will bring [a]locusts into your
territory.
5 'And they shall cover the face of the earth, so
that no one will be able to see the earth; and [a]they
shall eat the residue of what is left, which remains
to you from the hail, and they shall eat every tree
which grows up for you out of the field.
6 'They shall [a]fill your houses, the houses of all
your servants, and the houses of all the Egyptians—which neither your fathers nor your fathers' fathers have seen, since the day that they
were on the earth to this day.' " And he turned
and went out from Pharaoh.
7 Then Pharaoh's [a]servants said to him, "How
long shall this man be [b]a snare to us? Let the men
go, that they may serve the LORD their God. Do
you not yet know that Egypt is destroyed?"
8 So Moses and Aaron were brought again to
Pharaoh, and he said to them, "Go, serve the LORD
your God. Who *are* the ones that are going?"
9 And Moses said, "We will go with our young
and our old; with our sons and our daughters,
with our flocks and our herds we will go, for [a]we
must hold a feast to the LORD."
10 Then he said to them, "The LORD had better be
with you when I let you and your little ones go!
Beware, for evil is ahead of you.
11 "Not so! Go now, you *who are* men, and serve
the LORD, for that is what you desired." And they
were driven [a]out from Pharaoh's presence.
**12** Then the LORD said to Moses, [a]"Stretch out
your hand over the land of Egypt for the locusts,
that they may come upon the land of Egypt, and

9 [a]Rev. 16:2
10 [a]Deut. 28:27
11 [a][Ex. 8:18, 19] [b]Job 2:7
12 [a]Ex. 7:13 [b]Ex. 4:21
13 [a]Ex. 8:20 [b]Ex. 9:1
14 [a]Ex. 8:10
15 [a]Ex. 3:20; 7:5 [b]Ex. 5:3
16 [a][Rom. 9:17, 18 [b]Ex. 7:4, 5; 10:1; 11:9; 14:17 [c]1 Kin. 8:43
20 [a][Prov. 13:13] [b]Ex. 8:19; 10:7
22 [a]Rev. 16:21
23 [a]Josh. 10:11
25 [a]Ps. 78:47, 48; 105:32, 33
26 [a]Ex. 8:22, 23; 9:4, 6; 10:23; 11:7; 12:13
27 [a]Ex. 8:8 [b]Ex. 9:34; 10:16, 17 [c]2 Chr. 12:6
28 [a]Ex. 8:8, 28; 10:17 [b]Ex. 8:25; 10:8, 24 [1]*Pray to, Make supplication to* [2]Lit. *voices of God* or *sounds of God*
29 [a]Is. 1:15 [b]Ps. 24:1
30 [a][Is. 26:10]
31 [a]Ruth 1:22; 2:23
32 [1]Lit. *darkened*
33 [a]Ex. 8:12; 9:29
35 [a]Ex. 4:21

CHAPTER 10
1 [a]John 12:40 [b]Ex. 7:4; 9:16
2 [a]Joel 1:3 [b]Ex. 7:5, 17; 8:22
3 [a][1 Kin. 21:29] [b]Ex. 4:23; 8:1; 9:1
4 [a]Rev. 9:3
5 [a]Ex. 9:32
6 [a]Ex. 8:3, 21
7 [a]Ex. 7:5; 8:19; 9:20; 12:33 [b]Ex. 23:33
9 [a]Ex. 5:1; 7:16
11 [a]Ex. 10:28
12 [a]Ex. 7:19

[b]eat every herb of the land—all that the hail has left."

13 So Moses stretched out his rod over the land of Egypt, and the LORD brought an east wind on the land all that day and all *that* night. When it was morning, the east wind brought the locusts.

14 And [a]the locusts went up over all the land of Egypt and rested on all the territory of Egypt. *They were* very severe; [b]previously there had been no such locusts as they, nor shall there be such after them.

15 For they [a]covered the face of the whole earth, so that the land was darkened; and they [b]ate every herb of the land and all the fruit of the trees which the hail had left. So there remained nothing green on the trees or on the plants of the field throughout all the land of Egypt.

**16** Then Pharaoh called [a]for Moses and Aaron in haste, and said, [b]"I have sinned against the LORD your God and against you.

17 "Now therefore, please forgive my sin only this once, and [a]entreat[1] the LORD your God, that He may take away from me this death only."

18 So he [a]went out from Pharaoh and entreated the LORD.

19 And the LORD turned a very strong west wind, which took the locusts away and blew them [a]into the Red Sea. There remained not one locust in all the territory of Egypt.

20 But the LORD [a]hardened Pharaoh's heart, and he did not let the children of Israel go.

**21** Then the LORD said to Moses, [a]"Stretch out your hand toward heaven, that there may be darkness over the land of Egypt, [1]darkness *which* may even be felt."

22 So Moses stretched out his hand toward heaven, and there was [a]thick darkness in all the land of Egypt [b]three days.

23 They did not see one another; nor did anyone rise from his place for three days. [a]But all the children of Israel had light in their dwellings.

**24** Then Pharaoh called to Moses and [a]said, "Go, serve the LORD; only let your flocks and your herds be kept back. Let your [b]little ones also go with you."

25 But Moses said, "You must also give [1]us sacrifices and burnt offerings, that we may sacrifice to the LORD our God.

26 "Our [a]livestock also shall go with us; not a hoof shall be left behind. For we must take some of them to serve the LORD our God, and even we do not know with what we must serve the LORD until we arrive there."

**27** But the LORD [a]hardened Pharaoh's heart, and he would not let them go.

28 Then Pharaoh said to him, [a]"Get away from me! Take heed to yourself and see my face no more! For in the day you see my face you shall die!"

29 So Moses said, "You have spoken well. [a]I will never see your face again."

### *God's Warning About Egypt's Firstborn*

**11** And the LORD said to Moses, "I will bring one more plague on Pharaoh and on Egypt. [a]Afterward he will let you go from here. [b]When he lets *you* go, he will surely drive you out of here altogether.

2 "Speak now in the hearing of the people, and let every man ask from his neighbor and every woman from her neighbor, [a]articles of silver and articles of gold."

3 [a]And the LORD gave the people favor in the sight of the Egyptians. Moreover the man [b]Moses *was* very great in the land of Egypt, in the sight of Pharaoh's servants and in the sight of the people.

**4** Then Moses said, "Thus says the LORD: [a]'About midnight I will go out into the midst of Egypt;

5 'and [a]all the firstborn in the land of Egypt shall die, from the firstborn of Pharaoh who sits on his throne, even to the firstborn of the female servant who *is* behind the handmill, and all the firstborn of the animals.

6 [a]'Then there shall be a great cry throughout all the land of Egypt, [b]such as was not like it *before,* nor shall be like it again.

7 [a]'But against none of the children of Israel [b]shall a dog [1]move its tongue, against man or beast, that you may know that the LORD does make a difference between the Egyptians and Israel.'

8 "And [a]all these your servants shall come down to me and bow down to me, saying, 'Get out, and all the people who follow you!' After that I will go out." [b]Then he went out from Pharaoh in great anger.

**9** But the LORD said to Moses, [a]"Pharaoh will not heed you, so that [b]My wonders may be multiplied in the land of Egypt."

10 So Moses and Aaron did all these wonders before Pharaoh; [a]and the LORD hardened Pharaoh's heart, and he did not let the children of Israel go out of his land.

### *God Establishes the Passover*

**12** Now the LORD spoke to Moses and Aaron in the land of Egypt, saying,

2 [a]"This month *shall be* your beginning of months; it *shall be* the first month of the year to you.

3 "Speak to all the congregation of Israel, saying: 'On the [a]tenth of this month every man shall take for himself a lamb, according to the house of *his* father, a lamb for a household.

4 'And if the household is too small for the lamb, let him and his neighbor next to his house take *it* according to the number of the persons; according to each man's need you shall make your count for the lamb.

5 'Your lamb shall be [a]without[1] blemish, a male [2]of the first year. You may take *it* from the sheep or from the goats.

6 'Now you shall keep it until the [a]fourteenth day of the same month. Then the whole assembly of the congregation of Israel shall kill it at twilight.

7 'And they shall take *some* of the blood and put *it* on the two doorposts and on the lintel of the houses where they eat it.

8 'Then they shall eat the flesh on that [a]night; [b]roasted in fire, with [c]unleavened bread *and* with bitter *herbs* they shall eat it.

9 'Do not eat it raw, nor boiled at all with water, but [a]roasted in fire—its head with its legs and its entrails.

10 [a]'You shall let none of it remain until morning, and what remains of it until morning you shall burn with fire.

11 'And thus you shall eat it: [1]*with* a belt on your waist, your sandals on your feet, and your staff in

---

12 [b]Ex. 10:5, 15
14 [a]Ps. 78:46; 105:34 [b]Joel 1:4, 7; 2:1–11
15 [a]Ex. 10:5 [b]Ps. 105:35
16 [a]Ex. 8:8 [b]Ex. 9:27
17 [a]1 Kin. 13:6 [1]*make supplication to*
18 [a]Ex. 8:30
19 [a]Joel 2:20
20 [a]Ex. 4:21; 10:1; 11:10
21 [a]Ex. 9:22 [1]Lit. *that one may feel the darkness*
22 [a]Ps. 105:28 [b]Ex. 3:18
23 [a]Ex. 8:22, 23
24 [a]Ex. 8:8, 25; 10:8 [b]Ex. 10:10
25 [1]Lit. *into our hands*
26 [a]Ex. 10:9
27 [a]Ex. 4:21; 10:1, 20; 14:4, 8
28 [a]Ex. 10:11
29 [a]Heb. 11:27

CHAPTER 11
1 [a]Ex. 12:31, 33, 39 [b]Ex. 6:1; 12:39
2 [a]Ex. 3:22; 12:35, 36
3 [a]Ex. 3:21; 12:36 [b]Deut. 34:10–12
4 [a]Ex. 12:12, 23, 29
5 [a]Ex. 4:23; 12:12, 29
6 [a]Ex. 12:30 [b]Ex. 10:14
7 [a]Ex. 8:22 [b]Josh. 10:21 [1]*sharpen*
8 [a]Ex. 12:31–33 [b]Heb. 11:27
9 [a]Ex. 3:19; 7:4; 10:1 [b]Ex. 7:3; 9:16
10 [a]Rom. 2:5

CHAPTER 12
2 [a]Deut. 16:1
3 [a]Josh. 4:19
5 [a][1 Pet. 1:19] [1]*perfect* or *sound* [2]*a year old*
6 [a]Lev. 23:5
8 [a]Num. 9:12 [b]Deut. 16:7 [c]1 Cor. 5:8
9 [a]Deut. 16:7
10 [a]Ex. 16:19; 23:18; 34:25
11 [1]Made ready to travel

your hand. So you shall eat it in haste. [a]It *is* the
LORD's Passover.
12 'For I [a]will pass through the land of Egypt on
that night, and will strike all the firstborn in the
land of Egypt, both man and beast; and [b]against
all the gods of Egypt I will execute judgment: [c]I
*am* the LORD.
13 'Now the blood shall be a sign for you on the
houses where you *are.* And when I see the blood,
I will pass over you; and the plague shall not be on
you to destroy *you* when I strike the land of
Egypt.
14 'So this day shall be to you [a]a memorial; and
you shall keep it as a [b]feast to the LORD throughout your generations. You shall keep it as a feast
[c]by an everlasting ordinance.
15 [a]'Seven days you shall eat unleavened bread.
On the first day you shall remove leaven from
your houses. For whoever eats leavened bread
from the first day until the seventh day, [b]that
[1]person shall be [2]cut off from Israel.
16 'On the first day *there shall be* [a]a holy convocation, and on the seventh day there shall be a
holy convocation for you. No manner of work
shall be done on them; but *that* which everyone
must eat—that only may be prepared by you.
17 'So you shall observe *the Feast of* Unleavened
Bread, for [a]on this same day I will have brought
your [1]armies [b]out of the land of Egypt. Therefore
you shall observe this day throughout your generations as an everlasting ordinance.
18 [a]'In the first *month,* on the fourteenth day of
the month at evening, you shall eat unleavened
bread, until the twenty-first day of the month at
evening.
19 'For [a]seven days no leaven shall be found in
your houses, since whoever eats what is leavened,
that same person shall be cut off from the congregation of Israel, whether *he is* a stranger or a
native of the land.
20 'You shall eat nothing leavened; in all your
dwellings you shall eat unleavened bread.' "
**21** Then [a]Moses called for all the [b]elders of Israel
and said to them, [c]"Pick out and take lambs for
yourselves according to your families, and kill the
Passover *lamb.*
22 [a]"And you shall take a bunch of hyssop, dip *it*
in the blood that *is* in the basin, and [b]strike the
lintel and the two doorposts with the blood that *is*
in the basin. And none of you shall go out of the
door of his house until morning.
23 [a]"For the LORD will pass through to strike the
Egyptians; and when He sees the [b]blood on the
[1]lintel and on the two doorposts, the LORD will
pass over the door and [c]not allow [d]the destroyer to
come into your houses to strike *you.*
24 "And you shall [a]observe this thing as an
ordinance for you and your sons forever.
25 "It will come to pass when you come to the
land which the LORD will give you, [a]just as He
promised, that you shall keep this service.
26 [a]"And it shall be, when your children say to
you, 'What do you mean by this service?'
27 "that you shall say, [a]'It *is* the Passover sacrifice of the LORD, who passed over the houses of
the children of Israel in Egypt when He struck the
Egyptians and delivered our households.' " So the
people [b]bowed their heads and worshiped.
28 Then the children of Israel went away and [a]did
*so;* just as the LORD had commanded Moses and
Aaron, so they did.
**29** [a]And it came to pass at midnight that [b]the
LORD struck all the firstborn in the land of Egypt,
from the firstborn of Pharaoh who sat on his
throne to the firstborn of the captive who *was* [1]in
the dungeon, and all the firstborn of [c]livestock.
30 So Pharaoh rose in the night, he, all his servants, and all the Egyptians; and there was a great
cry in Egypt, for *there was* not a house where
*there was* not one dead.
**31** Then he [a]called for Moses and Aaron by night,
and said, "Rise, go out from among my people,
[b]both you and the children of Israel. And go, serve
the LORD as you have [c]said.
32 [a]"Also take your flocks and your herds, as you
have said, and be gone; and bless me also."
33 [a]And the Egyptians [b]urged the people, that
they might send them out of the land in haste. For
they said, "We *shall* all *be* dead."
34 So the people took their dough before it was
leavened, having their kneading bowls bound up
in their clothes on their shoulders.
35 Now the children of Israel had done according
to the word of Moses, and they had asked from
the Egyptians [a]articles of silver, articles of gold,
and clothing.
36 [a]And the LORD had given the people favor in
the sight of the Egyptians, so that they granted
them *what they requested.* Thus [b]they plundered
the Egyptians.
**37** Then [a]the children of Israel journeyed from
[b]Rameses to Succoth, about [c]six hundred thousand men on foot, besides children.
38 A [a]mixed multitude went up with them also,
and flocks and herds—a great deal of [b]livestock.
39 And they baked unleavened cakes of the
dough which they had brought out of Egypt; for it
was not leavened, because [a]they were driven out
of Egypt and could not wait, nor had they prepared provisions for themselves.
**40** Now the [1]sojourn of the children of Israel who
lived in [2]Egypt *was* [a]four hundred and thirty
years.
41 And it came to pass at the end of the four
hundred and thirty years—on that very same
day—it came to pass that [a]all the armies of the
LORD went out from the land of Egypt.
42 It *is* [a]a [1]night of solemn observance to the
LORD for bringing them out of the land of Egypt.
This *is* that night of the LORD, a solemn observance for all the children of Israel throughout
their generations.
**43** And the LORD said to Moses and Aaron, "This
*is* [a]the ordinance of the Passover: No foreigner
shall eat it.
44 "But every man's servant who is bought for
money, when you have [a]circumcised him, then he
may eat it.
45 [a]"A sojourner and a hired servant shall not eat
it.
46 "In one house it shall be eaten; you shall not
carry any of the flesh outside the house, [a]nor shall
you break one of its bones.
47 [a]"All the congregation of Israel shall keep it.
48 "And [a]when a stranger [1]dwells with you *and*
*wants* to keep the Passover to the LORD, let all his
males be circumcised, and then let him come near
and keep it; and he shall be as a native of the land.
For no uncircumcised person shall eat it.
49 [a]"One law shall be for the native-born and for
the stranger who dwells among you."

11 [a]Ex. 12:13, 21, 27, 43
12 [a]Ex. 11:4, 5 [b]Num. 33:4 [c]Ex. 6:2
14 [a]Ex. 13:9 [b]Lev. 23:4, 5 [c]Ex. 12:17, 24; 13:10
15 [a]Lev. 23:6 [b]Gen. 17:14 [1]*soul* [2]Put to death
16 [a]Lev. 23:2, 7, 8
17 [a]Ex. 12:14; 13:3, 10 [b]Num. 33:1 [1]*hosts*
18 [a]Lev. 23:5–8
19 [a]Ex. 12:15; 23:15; 34:18
21 [a][Heb. 11:28] [b]Ex. 3:16 [c]Num. 9:4
22 [a]Heb. 11:28 [b]Ex. 12:7
23 [a]Ex. 11:4; 12:12, 13 [b]Ex. 24:8 [c]Rev. 7:3; 9:4 [d]Heb. 11:28 [1]Cross-piece at top of door
24 [a]Ex. 12:14, 17; 13:5, 10
25 [a]Ex. 3:8, 17
26 [a]Ex. 10:2; 13:8, 14, 15
27 [a]Ex. 12:11 [b]Ex. 4:31
28 [a][Heb. 11:28]
29 [a]Ex. 11:4, 5 [b]Num. 8:17; 33:4 [c]Ex. 9:6 [1]*in prison*
31 [a]Ex. 10:28, 29 [b]Ex. 8:25; 11:1 [c]Ex. 10:9
32 [a]Ex. 10:9, 26
33 [a]Ex. 10:7 [b]Ps. 105:38
35 [a]Ex. 3:21, 22; 11:2, 3
36 [a]Ex. 3:21 [b]Gen. 15:14
37 [a]Num. 33:3, 5 [b]Gen. 47:11 [c]Ex. 38:26
38 [a]Num. 11:4 [b]Deut. 3:19
39 [a]Ex. 6:1; 11:1; 12:31–33
40 [a]Acts 7:6 [1]Length of the stay [2]Sam., LXX *Egypt and Canaan*
41 [a]Ex. 3:8, 10; 6:6; 7:4
42 [a]Deut. 16:1, 6 [1]*night of vigil*
43 [a]Num. 9:14
44 [a]Gen. 17:12, 13
45 [a]Lev. 22:10
46 [a][John 19:33, 36]
47 [a]Ex. 12:6
48 [a]Num. 9:14 [1]As a resident alien
49 [a]Num. 15:15, 16

**50** Thus all the children of Israel did; as the LORD commanded Moses and Aaron, so they did.
51 [a]And it came to pass, on that very same day, that the LORD brought the children of Israel out of the land of Egypt [b]according to their armies.

### *How Israel Remembered the Exodus*

**13** Then the LORD spoke to Moses, saying,
2 [a]"Consecrate[1] to Me all the firstborn, whatever opens the womb among the children of Israel, *both* of man and beast; it is Mine."
**3** And Moses said to the people: [a]"Remember this day in which you went out of Egypt, out of the house of [1]bondage; for [b]by strength of hand the LORD brought you out of this *place.* [c]No leavened bread shall be eaten.
4 [a]"On this day you are going out, in the month Abib.
5 "And it shall be, when the LORD [a]brings you into the [b]land of the Canaanites and the Hittites and the Amorites and the Hivites and the Jebusites, which He [c]swore to your fathers to give you, a land flowing with milk and honey, [d]that you shall keep this service in this month.
6 [a]"Seven days you shall eat unleavened bread, and on the seventh day *there shall be* a feast to the LORD.
7 "Unleavened bread shall be eaten seven days. And [a]no leavened bread shall be seen among you, nor shall leaven be seen among you in all your quarters.
8 "And you shall [a]tell your son in that day, saying, '*This is done* because of what the LORD did for me when I came up from Egypt.'
9 "It shall be as [a]a sign to you on your hand and as a memorial between your eyes, that the LORD's law may be in your mouth; for with a strong hand the LORD has brought you out of Egypt.
10 [a]"You shall therefore keep this [1]ordinance in its season from year to year.
**11** "And it shall be, when the LORD [a]brings you into the land of the [b]Canaanites, as He swore to you and your fathers, and gives it to you,
12 [a]"that you shall [1]set apart to the LORD all that open the womb, that is, every firstborn that comes from an animal which you have; the males *shall be* the LORD's.
13 "But [a]every firstborn of a donkey you shall redeem with a lamb; and if you will not redeem *it,* then you shall break its neck. And all the firstborn of man among your sons [b]you shall redeem.
14 [a]"So it shall be, when your son asks you in time to come, saying, 'What *is* this?' that you shall say to him, [b]'By strength of hand the LORD brought us out of Egypt, out of the house of bondage.
15 'And it came to pass, when Pharaoh was stubborn about letting us go, that [a]the LORD killed all the firstborn in the land of Egypt, both the firstborn of man and the firstborn of beast. Therefore I sacrifice to the LORD all males that open the womb, but all the firstborn of my sons I redeem.'
16 "It shall be as [a]a sign on your hand and as frontlets between your eyes, for by strength of hand the LORD brought us out of Egypt."
**17** Then it came to pass, when Pharaoh had let the people go, that God did not lead them *by* way of the land of the Philistines, although that *was* near; for God said, "Lest perhaps the people [a]change their minds when they see war, and [b]return to Egypt."

**51** [a]Ex. 12:41; 20:2 [b]Ex. 6:26

CHAPTER 13

**2** [a]Luke 2:23 [1]*Set apart*
**3** [a]Deut. 16:3 [b]Ex. 3:20; 6:1 [c]Ex. 12:8, 19 [1]Lit. *slaves*
**4** [a]Ex. 12:2; 23:15; 34:18
**5** [a]Ex. 3:8, 17 [b]Gen. 17:8 [c]Ex. 6:8 [d]Ex. 12:25, 26
**6** [a]Ex. 12:15–20
**7** [a]Ex. 12:19
**8** [a]Ex. 10:2; 12:26; 13:14
**9** [a]Deut. 6:8; 11:18
**10** [a]Ex. 12:14, 24 [1]*regulation*
**11** [a]Ex. 13:5 [b]Num. 21:3
**12** [a]Lev. 27:26 [1]Lit. *cause to pass over*
**13** [a]Ex. 34:20 [b]Num. 3:46, 47; 18:15, 16
**14** [a]Deut. 6:20 [b]Ex. 13:3, 9
**15** [a]Ex. 12:29
**16** [a]Ex. 13:9
**17** [a]Ex. 14:11 [b]Deut. 17:16
**18** [a]Num. 33:6
**19** [a]Gen. 50:24, 25 [b]Ex. 1:6; Deut. 33:13–17 [c]Ex. 4:31 [1]*give attention to*
**20** [a]Num. 33:6–8 [b]Ex. 12:37
**21** [a]Deut. 1:33

CHAPTER 14

**2** [a]Ex. 13:18 [b]Num. 33:7 [c]Jer. 44:1
**3** [a]Ps. 71:11
**4** [a]Ex. 4:21; 7:3; 14:17 [b]Ex. 9:16; 14:17, 18, 23 [c]Ex. 7:5; 14:25
**5** [a]Ps. 105:25
**6** [1]*harnessed*
**7** [a]Ex. 15:4
**8** [a]Ex. 14:4 [b]Num. 33:3
**9** [a]Josh. 24:6
**10** [a]Neh. 9:9
**11** [a]Ps. 106:7, 8
**12** [a]Ex. 5:21; 6:9
**13** [a]2 Chr. 20:15, 17 [b]Ps. 46:10, 11 [c]Ex. 14:30; 15:2 [d]Deut. 28:68 [1]*deliverance*
**14** [a]Deut. 1:30; 3:22 [b][Is. 30:15] [1]Lit. *be quiet*

18 So God [a]led the people around *by* way of the wilderness of the Red Sea. And the children of Israel went up in orderly ranks out of the land of Egypt.
19 And Moses took the [a]bones of [b]Joseph with him, for he had placed the children of Israel under solemn oath, saying, [c]"God will surely [1]visit you, and you shall carry up my bones from here with you."
20 So [a]they took their journey from [b]Succoth and camped in Etham at the edge of the wilderness.
21 And [a]the LORD went before them by day in a pillar of cloud to lead the way, and by night in a pillar of fire to give them light, so as to go by day and night.
22 He did not take away the pillar of cloud by day or the pillar of fire by night *from* before the people.

### *Crossing the Red Sea*

**14** Now the LORD spoke to Moses, saying:
2 "Speak to the children of Israel, [a]that they turn and camp before [b]Pi Hahiroth, between [c]Migdol and the sea, opposite Baal Zephon; you shall camp before it by the sea.
3 "For Pharaoh will say of the children of Israel, [a]'They *are* bewildered by the land; the wilderness has closed them in.'
4 "Then [a]I will harden Pharaoh's heart, so that he will pursue them; and I [b]will gain honor over Pharaoh and over all his army, [c]that the Egyptians may know that I *am* the LORD." And they did so.
**5** Now it was told the king of Egypt that the people had fled, and [a]the heart of Pharaoh and his servants was turned against the people; and they said, "Why have we done this, that we have let Israel go from serving us?"
6 So he [1]made ready his chariot and took his people with him.
7 Also, he took [a]six hundred choice chariots, and all the chariots of Egypt with captains over every one of them.
8 And the LORD [a]hardened the heart of Pharaoh king of Egypt, and he pursued the children of Israel; and [b]the children of Israel went out with boldness.
9 So the [a]Egyptians pursued them, all the horses *and* chariots of Pharaoh, his horsemen and his army, and overtook them camping by the sea beside Pi Hahiroth, before Baal Zephon.
**10** And when Pharaoh drew near, the children of Israel lifted their eyes, and behold, the Egyptians marched after them. So they were very afraid, and the children of Israel [a]cried out to the LORD.
11 [a]Then they said to Moses, "Because *there were* no graves in Egypt, have you taken us away to die in the wilderness? Why have you so dealt with us, to bring us up out of Egypt?
12 [a]"*Is* this not the word that we told you in Egypt, saying, 'Let us alone that we may serve the Egyptians?' For *it would have been* better for us to serve the Egyptians than that we should die in the wilderness."
13 And Moses said to the people, [a]"Do not be afraid. [b]Stand still, and see the [c]salvation[1] of the LORD, which He will accomplish for you today. For the Egyptians whom you see today, you shall [d]see again no more forever.
14 [a]"The LORD will fight for you, and you shall [b]hold[1] your peace."

**15** And the LORD said to Moses, "Why do you cry
to Me? Tell the children of Israel to go forward.
16 "But [a]lift up your rod, and stretch out your
hand over the sea and divide it. And the children
of Israel shall go on dry *ground* through the midst
of the sea.
17 "And I indeed will [a]harden the hearts of the
Egyptians, and they shall follow them. So I will
[b]gain honor over Pharaoh and over all his army,
his chariots, and his horsemen.
18 "Then the Egyptians shall know that I *am* the
LORD, when I have gained honor for Myself over
Pharaoh, his chariots, and his horsemen."
**19** And the Angel of God, [a]who went before the
camp of Israel, moved and went behind them; and
the pillar of cloud went from before them and
stood behind them.
20 So it came between the camp of the Egyptians
and the camp of Israel. Thus it was a cloud and
darkness *to the one,* and it gave light by night *to*
*the other,* so that the one did not come near the
other all that night.
**21** Then Moses stretched out his hand over the
sea; and the LORD caused the sea to go *back* by a
strong east wind all that night, and [a]made the sea
into dry *land,* and the waters were [b]divided.
22 So [a]the children of Israel went into the midst
of the sea on the dry *ground,* and the waters *were*
[b]a wall to them on their right hand and on their
left.
23 And the Egyptians pursued and went after
them into the midst of the sea, all Pharaoh's
horses, his chariots, and his horsemen.
24 Now it came to pass, in the morning [a]watch,
that [b]the LORD looked down upon the army of the
Egyptians through the pillar of fire and cloud, and
He [1]troubled the army of the Egyptians.
25 And He [1]took off their chariot wheels, so that
they drove them with difficulty; and the Egyptians
said, "Let us flee from the face of Israel, for the
LORD [a]fights for them against the Egyptians."
**26** Then the LORD said to Moses, "Stretch out
your hand over the sea, that the waters may come
back upon the Egyptians, on their chariots, and on
their horsemen."
27 And Moses stretched out his hand over the
sea; and when the morning appeared, the sea
[a]returned to its full depth, while the Egyptians
were fleeing into it. So the LORD [b]overthrew[1] the
Egyptians in the midst of the sea.
28 Then [a]the waters returned and covered the
chariots, the horsemen, *and* all the army of Pharaoh that came into the sea after them. Not so
much as one of them remained.
29 But [a]the children of Israel had walked on dry
*land* in the midst of the sea, and the waters *were* a
wall to them on their right hand and on their left.
**30** So the LORD [a]saved[1] Israel that day out of the
hand of the Egyptians, and Israel [b]saw the Egyptians dead on the seashore.
31 Thus Israel saw the great [1]work which the
LORD had done in Egypt; so the people feared the
LORD, and [a]believed the LORD and His servant
Moses.

## *The Song of Moses*

**15** Then [a]Moses and the children of Israel sang
this song to the LORD, and spoke, saying:

"I will [b]sing to the LORD,
For He has triumphed gloriously!
The horse and its rider
He has thrown into the sea!
2 The LORD *is* my strength and [a]song,
And He has become my salvation;
He *is* my God, and [b]I will praise Him;
My [c]father's God, and I [d]will exalt Him.
3 The LORD *is* a man of [a]war;
The LORD *is* His [b]name.
4 [a]Pharaoh's chariots and his army
He has cast into the sea;
[b]His chosen captains also
are drowned in the Red Sea.
5 The depths have covered them;
[a]They sank to the bottom like a stone.

6 "Your [a]right hand, O LORD,
has become glorious in power;
Your right hand, O LORD,
has dashed the enemy in pieces.
7 And in the greatness of Your [a]excellence
You have overthrown those
who rose against You;
You sent forth [b]Your wrath;
It [c]consumed them [d]like stubble.
8 And [a]with the blast of Your nostrils
The waters were gathered together;
[b]The floods stood upright like a heap;
The depths [1]congealed
in the heart of the sea.
9 [a]The enemy said, 'I will pursue,
I will overtake,
I will [b]divide the spoil;
My desire shall be satisfied on them.
I will draw my sword,
My hand shall destroy them.'
10 You blew with Your wind,
The sea covered them;
They sank like lead in the mighty waters.

11 "Who[a] *is* like You, O LORD, among the [1]gods?
Who *is* like You, [b]glorious in holiness,
Fearful in [c]praises, [d]doing wonders?
12 You stretched out Your right hand;
The earth swallowed them.
13 You in Your mercy have [a]led forth
The people whom You have redeemed;
You have guided *them* in Your strength
To [b]Your holy habitation.

14 "The [a]people will hear *and* be afraid;
[b]Sorrow[1] will take hold of the inhabitants of
[2]Philistia.
15 [a]Then [b]the chiefs of Edom will be dismayed;
[c]The mighty men of Moab,
Trembling will take hold of them;
[d]All the inhabitants of Canaan
will [e]melt away.
16 [a]Fear and dread will fall on them;
By the greatness of Your arm
They will be [b]*as* still as a stone,
Till Your people pass over, O LORD,
Till the people pass over
[c]Whom You have purchased.
17 You will bring them in and [a]plant them
In the [b]mountain of Your inheritance,
*In* the place, O LORD, *which* You have made
For Your own dwelling,
The [c]sanctuary, O LORD,
*which* Your hands have established.

18 "The[a] LORD shall reign forever and ever."

19 For the [a]horses of Pharaoh went with his
chariots and his horsemen into the sea, and [b]the

**16** [a]Num. 20:8, 9, 11
**17** [a]Ex. 14:8 [b]Ex. 14:4
**19** [a][Is. 63:9]
**21** [a]Ps. 66:6; 106:9; 136:13, 14 [b]Is. 63:12, 13
**22** [a]Ex. 15:19 [b]Ex. 14:29; 15:8
**24** [a]Judg. 7:19 [b]Ex. 13:21 [1]*confused*
**25** [a]Ex. 7:5; 14:4, 14, 18 [1]Sam., LXX, Syr. *bound*
**27** [a]Josh. 4:18 [b]Ex. 15:1, 7 [1]Lit. *shook off*
**28** [a]Ps. 78:53; 106:11
**29** [a]Ps. 66:6; 78:52, 53
**30** [a]Ps. 106:8, 10 [b]Ps. 58:10; 59:10 [1]*delivered*
**31** [a]John 2:11; 11:45 [1]Lit. *hand with which the LORD worked*

CHAPTER 15

**1** [a]Ps. 106:12 [b]Is. 12:1–6
**2** [a]Is. 12:2 [b]Gen. 28:21, 22 [c]Ex. 3:6, 15, 16 [d]Is. 25:1
**3** [a]Rev. 19:11 [b]Ps. 24:8; 83:18
**4** [a]Ex. 14:28 [b]Ex. 14:7
**5** [a]Neh. 9:11
**6** [a]Ps. 17:7; 118:15
**7** [a]Deut. 33:26 [b]Ps. 78:49, 50 [c]Ps. 59:13 [d]Is. 5:24
**8** [a]Ex. 14:21, 22, 29 [b]Ps. 78:13 [1]*became firm*
**9** [a]Judg. 5:30 [b]Is. 53:12
**11** [a]1 Kin. 8:23 [b]Is. 6:3 [c]1 Chr. 16:25 [d]Ps. 77:11, 14 [1]*mighty ones*
**13** [a][Ps. 77:20] [b]Ps. 78:54
**14** [a]Josh. 2:9 [b]Ps. 48:6 [1]*anguish* [2]*Philistia*
**15** [a]Gen. 36:15, 40 [b]Deut. 2:4 [c]Num. 22:3, 4 [d]Josh. 5:1 [e]Josh. 2:9–11, 24
**16** [a]Josh. 2:9 [b]1 Sam. 25:37 [c]Jer. 31:11
**17** [a]Ps. 44:2; 80:8, 15 [b]Ps. 2:6; 78:54, 68 [c]Ps. 68:16; 76:2; 132:13, 14
**18** [a]Is. 57:15
**19** [a]Ex. 14:23 [b]Ex. 14:28

LORD brought back the waters of the sea upon
them. But the children of Israel went on dry *land*
in the midst of the sea.
**20** Then Miriam [a]the prophetess, [b]the sister of
Aaron, [c]took the timbrel in her hand; and all the
women went out after her [d]with timbrels and with
dances.
21 And Miriam [a]answered them:

[b]"Sing to the LORD,
For He has triumphed gloriously!
The horse and its rider
He has thrown into the sea!"

**22** So Moses brought Israel from the Red Sea;
then they went out into the Wilderness of [a]Shur.
And they went three days in the wilderness and
found no [b]water.
23 Now when they came to [a]Marah, they could
not drink the waters of Marah, for they *were*
bitter. Therefore the name of it was called [1]Marah.
24 And the people [a]complained against Moses,
saying, "What shall we drink?"
25 So he cried out to the LORD, and the LORD
showed him a tree. [a]When he cast *it* into the
waters, the waters were made sweet. There He
[b]made a statute and an [1]ordinance for them, and
there [c]He tested them,
26 and said, [a]"If you diligently heed the voice of
the LORD your God and do what is right in His
sight, give ear to His commandments and keep all
His statutes, I will put none of the [b]diseases on
you which I have brought on the Egyptians. For I
*am* the LORD [c]who heals you."
**27** [a]Then they came to Elim, where there *were*
twelve wells of water and seventy palm trees; so
they camped there by the waters.

### *God Sends Quails and Manna*

**16** And they [a]journeyed from Elim, and all the
congregation of the children of Israel came
to the Wilderness of Sin, which is between Elim
and [b]Sinai, on the fifteenth day of the second
month after they departed from the land of Egypt.
2 Then the whole congregation of the children
of Israel [a]complained against Moses and Aaron in
the wilderness.
3 And the children of Israel said to them, [a]"Oh,
that we had died by the hand of the LORD in the
land of Egypt, [b]when we sat by the pots of meat
*and* when we ate bread to the full! For you have
brought us out into this wilderness to kill this
whole assembly with hunger."
**4** Then the LORD said to Moses, "Behold, I will
rain [a]bread from heaven for you. And the people
shall go out and gather [1]a certain quota every day,
that I may [b]test them, whether they will [c]walk in
My law or not.
5 "And it shall be on the sixth day that they
shall prepare what they bring in, and [a]it shall be
twice as much as they gather daily."
6 Then Moses and Aaron said to all the children
of Israel, [a]"At evening you shall know that the
LORD has brought you out of the land of Egypt.
7 "And in the morning you shall see [a]the glory
of the LORD; for He [b]hears your complaints against
the LORD. But [c]what *are* we, that you complain
against us?"
8 Also Moses said, "*This shall be seen* when the
LORD gives you meat to eat in the evening, and in
the morning bread to the full; for the LORD hears
your complaints which you make against Him.
And what *are* we? Your complaints *are* not
against us but [a]against the LORD."
**9** Then Moses spoke to Aaron, "Say to all the
congregation of the children of Israel, [a]'Come near
before the LORD, for He has heard your complaints.' "
10 Now it came to pass, as Aaron spoke to the
whole congregation of the children of Israel, that
they looked toward the wilderness, and behold,
the glory of the LORD [a]appeared in the cloud.
11 And the LORD spoke to Moses, saying,
12 [a]"I have heard the complaints of the children
of Israel. Speak to them, saying, [b]'At twilight you
shall eat meat, and [c]in the morning you shall be
filled with bread. And you shall know that I *am*
the LORD your God.' "
**13** So it was that [a]quails came up at evening and
covered the camp, and in the morning [b]the dew
lay all around the camp.
14 And when the layer of dew lifted, there, on the
surface of the wilderness, was [a]a small round
[b]substance, *as* fine as frost on the ground.
15 So when the children of Israel saw *it,* they said
to one another, "What is it?" For they did not
know what it *was.* And Moses said to them, [a]"This
*is* the bread which the LORD has given you to eat.
16 "This is the thing which the LORD has commanded: 'Let every man gather it [a]according to
each one's need, one [b]omer for each person,
*according to the* number of persons; let every man
take for *those* who *are* in his tent.' "
17 Then the children of Israel did so and gathered, some more, some less.
18 So when they measured *it* by omers, [a]he who
gathered much had nothing left over, and he who
gathered little had no lack. Every man had gathered according to each one's need.
19 And Moses said, "Let no one [a]leave any of it
till morning."
20 Notwithstanding they did not [1]heed Moses.
But some of them left part of it until morning, and
it bred worms and stank. And Moses was angry
with them.
21 So they gathered it every morning, every man
according to his need. And when the sun became
hot, it melted.
**22** And so it was, on the sixth day, *that* they
gathered twice as much bread, two omers for each
one. And all the rulers of the congregation came
and told Moses.
23 Then he said to them, "This *is what* the LORD
has said: 'Tomorrow *is* [a]a Sabbath rest, a holy
Sabbath to the LORD. Bake what you will bake
*today,* and boil what you will boil; and lay up for
yourselves all that remains, to be kept until morning.' "
24 So they laid it up till morning, as Moses
commanded; and it did not [a]stink, nor were there
any worms in it.
25 Then Moses said, "Eat that today, for today *is*
a Sabbath to the LORD; today you will not find it in
the field.
26 [a]"Six days you shall gather it, but on the
seventh day, the Sabbath, there will be none."
27 Now it happened *that some* of the people went
out on the seventh day to gather, but they found
none.
28 And the LORD said to Moses, "How long [a]do
you refuse to keep My commandments and My
laws?
29 "See! For the LORD has given you the Sabbath;

**20** [a]Judg. 4:4 [b]Num. 26:59 [c]1 Sam. 18:6 [d]Judg. 11:34; 21:21
**21** [a]1 Sam. 18:7 [b]Ex. 15:1
**22** [a]Gen. 16:7; 20:1; 25:18 [b]Num. 20:2
**23** [a]Num. 33:8 [1]Lit. *Bitter*
**24** [a]Ex. 14:11; 16:2
**25** [a]2 Kin. 2:21 [b]Josh. 24:25 [c]Deut. 8:2, 16 [1]*regulation*
**26** [a]Deut. 7:12, 15 [b]Deut. 28:27, 58, 60 [c]Ex. 23:25
**27** [a]Num. 33:9

CHAPTER 16
**1** [a]Num. 33:10, 11 [b]Ex. 12:6, 51; 19:1
**2** [a]1 Cor. 10:10
**3** [a]Lam. 4:9 [b]Num. 11:4, 5
**4** [a][John 6:31–35] [b]Deut. 8:2, 16 [c]Judg. 2:22 [1]Lit. *the portion of a day in its day*
**5** [a]Lev. 25:21
**6** [a]Ex. 6:7
**7** [a]John 11:4, 40 [b]Num. 14:27; 17:5 [c]Num. 16:11
**8** [a]1 Sam. 8:7
**9** [a]Num. 16:16
**10** [a]Num. 16:19
**12** [a]Ex. 16:8 [b]Ex. 16:6 [c]Ex. 16:7
**13** [a]Num. 11:31 [b]Num. 11:9
**14** [a]Num. 11:7, 8 [b]Ps. 147:16
**15** [a]1 Cor. 10:3
**16** [a]Ex. 12:4 [b]Ex. 16:32, 36
**18** [a]2 Cor. 8:15
**19** [a]Ex. 12:10; 16:23; 23:18
**20** [1]*listen to*
**23** [a]Gen. 2:3
**24** [a]Ex. 16:20
**26** [a]Ex. 20:9, 10
**28** [a]2 Kin. 17:14

therefore He gives you on the sixth day bread for
two days. Let every man remain in his place; let
no man go out of his place on the seventh day."
30 So the people rested on the seventh day.
31 And the house of Israel called its name
[1]Manna. And [a]it *was* like white coriander seed,
and the taste of it *was* like wafers *made* with
honey.
**32** Then Moses said, "This *is* the thing which the
LORD has commanded: 'Fill an omer with it, to be
kept for your generations, that they may see the
bread with which I fed you in the wilderness,
when I brought you out of the land of Egypt.' "
33 And Moses said to Aaron, [a]"Take a pot and
put an omer of manna in it, and lay it up before
the LORD, to be kept for your generations."
34 As the LORD commanded Moses, so Aaron laid
it up [a]before the Testimony, to be kept.
35 And the children of Israel [a]ate manna [b]forty
years, [c]until they came to an inhabited land; they
ate manna until they came to the border of the
land of Canaan.
36 Now an omer *is* one-tenth of an ephah.

### *God Gives the People Water*

**17** Then [a]all the congregation of the children of
Israel set out on their journey from the
Wilderness of [b]Sin, according to the commandment of the LORD, and camped in Rephidim; but
*there was* no water for the people to [c]drink.
2 [a]Therefore the people contended with Moses,
and said, "Give us water, that we may drink." So
Moses said to them, "Why do you contend with
me? Why do you [b]tempt the LORD?"
3 And the people thirsted there for water, and
the people [a]complained against Moses, and said,
"Why *is* it you have brought us up out of Egypt,
to kill us and our children and our [b]livestock with
thirst?"
4 So Moses [a]cried out to the LORD, saying,
"What shall I do with this people? They are
almost ready to [b]stone[1] me!"
5 And the LORD said to Moses, [a]"Go on before
the people, and take with you some of the elders
of Israel. Also take in your hand your rod with
which [b]you struck the river, and go.
6 [a]"Behold, I will stand before you there on the
rock in Horeb; and you shall strike the rock, and
water will come out of it, that the people may
drink." And Moses did so in the sight of the elders
of Israel.
7 So he called the name of the place [a]Massah[1]
and [2]Meribah, because of the contention of the
children of Israel, and because they [3]tempted the
LORD, saying, "Is the LORD among us or not?"
**8** [a]Now Amalek came and fought with Israel in
Rephidim.
9 And Moses said to Joshua, "Choose us some
men and go out, fight with Amalek. Tomorrow I
will stand on the top of the hill with [a]the rod of
God in my hand."
10 So Joshua did as Moses said to him, and
fought with Amalek. And Moses, Aaron, and Hur
went up to the top of the hill.
11 And so it was, when Moses [a]held up his hand,
that Israel prevailed; and when he let down his
hand, Amalek prevailed.
12 But Moses' hands *became* [1]heavy; so they took
a stone and put *it* under him, and he sat on it. And
Aaron and Hur supported his hands, one on one
side, and the other on the other side; and his
hands were steady until the going down of the
sun.
13 So Joshua defeated Amalek and his people
with the edge of the sword.
**14** Then the LORD said to Moses, [a]"Write this *for*
a memorial in the book and recount *it* in the
hearing of Joshua, that [b]I will utterly blot out the
remembrance of Amalek from under heaven."
15 And Moses built an altar and called its name,
[1]The-LORD-Is-My-Banner;
16 for he said, "Because [1]the LORD has [a]sworn:
the LORD *will have* war with Amalek from generation to generation."

### *The Appointment of Judges*

**18** And [a]Jethro, the priest of Midian, Moses'
father-in-law, heard of all that [b]God had
done for Moses and for Israel His people—that the
LORD had brought Israel out of Egypt.
2 Then Jethro, Moses' father-in-law, took [a]Zip-
porah, Moses' wife, after he had sent her back,
3 with her [a]two sons, of whom the [b]name of one
*was* [1]Gershom (for he said, "I have been a [2]stran-
ger in a foreign land")
4 and the name of the other *was* [1]Eliezer (for *he
said,* "The God of my father *was* my [a]help, and
delivered me from the sword of Pharaoh");
5 and Jethro, Moses' father-in-law, came with
his sons and his wife to Moses in the wilderness,
where he was encamped at [a]the mountain of God.
6 Now he had said to Moses, "I, your father-in-
law Jethro, am coming to you with your wife and
her two sons with her."
**7** So Moses [a]went out to meet his father-in-law,
bowed down, and [b]kissed him. And they asked
each other about *their* well-being, and they went
into the tent.
8 And Moses told his father-in-law all that the
LORD had done to Pharaoh and to the Egyptians
for Israel's sake, all the hardship that had come
upon them on the way, and *how* the LORD had
[a]delivered them.
9 Then Jethro rejoiced for all the [a]good which
the LORD had done for Israel, whom He had
delivered out of the hand of the Egyptians.
10 And Jethro said, [a]"Blessed *be* the LORD, who
has delivered you out of the hand of the Egyptians
and out of the hand of Pharaoh, *and* who has
delivered the people from under the hand of the
Egyptians.
11 "Now I know that the LORD *is* [a]greater than all
the gods; [b]for in the very thing in which they
[1]behaved [c]proudly, *He was* above them."
12 Then Jethro, Moses' father-in-law, [1]took a
burnt [a]offering and *other* sacrifices *to offer* to God.
And Aaron came with all the elders of Israel [b]to
eat bread with Moses' father-in-law before God.
**13** And so it was, on the next day, that Moses [a]sat
to judge the people; and the people stood before
Moses from morning until evening.
14 So when Moses' father-in-law saw all that he
did for the people, he said, "What *is* this thing that
you are doing for the people? Why do you alone
[1]sit, and all the people stand before you from
morning until evening?"
15 And Moses said to his father-in-law, "Because
[a]the people come to me to inquire of God.
16 "When they have [a]a [1]difficulty, they come to
me, and I judge between one and another; and I
make known the statutes of God and His laws."

**31** [a]Num. 11:7–9 [1]Lit. *What,* Ex. 16:15
**33** [a]Heb. 9:4
**34** [a]Num. 17:10
**35** [a]Deut. 8:3, 16 [b]Num. 33:38 [c]Josh. 5:12

CHAPTER 17
**1** [a]Ex. 16:1 [b]Num. 33:11–15 [c]Ex. 15:22
**2** [a]Num. 20:2, 3, 13 [b][Deut. 6:16]
**3** [a]Ex. 16:2, 3 [b]Ex. 12:38
**4** [a]Ex. 14:15 [b]John 8:59; 10:31 [1]Put me to death by stoning
**5** [a]Ezek. 2:6 [b]Num. 20:8
**6** [a]Num. 20:10, 11
**7** [a]Num. 20:13, 24; 27:14 [1]Lit. *Tempted* [2]Lit. *Contention* [3]*tested*
**8** [a]Gen. 36:12
**9** [a]Ex. 4:20
**11** [a][James 5:16]
**12** [1]Weary of being held up
**14** [a]Ex. 24:4; 34:27 [b]1 Sam. 15:3
**15** [1]Heb. *YHWH Nissi*
**16** [a]Gen. 22:14–16 [1]Lit. *a hand is upon the throne of the LORD*

CHAPTER 18
**1** [a]Ex. 2:16, 18; 3:1 [b][Ps. 106:2, 8]
**2** [a]Ex. 2:21; 4:20–26
**3** [a]Acts 7:29 [b]Ex. 2:22 [1]Lit. *Stranger There* [2]*sojourner,* temporary resident
**4** [a]Gen. 49:25 [1]Lit. *My God Is Help*
**5** [a]Ex. 3:1, 12; 4:27; 24:13
**7** [a]Gen. 18:2 [b]Ex. 4:27
**8** [a]Ex. 15:6, 16
**9** [a][Is. 63:7–14]
**10** [a]Gen. 14:20
**11** [a]2 Chr. 2:5 [b]Ex. 1:10, 16, 22; 5:2, 7 [c]Luke 1:51 [1]*acted presumptuously*
**12** [a]Ex. 24:5 [b]Deut. 12:7 [1]So with MT, LXX; Syr., Tg., Vg. *offered*
**13** [a]Matt. 23:2
**14** [1]Sit as judge
**15** [a]Lev. 24:12
**16** [a]Ex. 24:14 [1]*dispute*

17 So Moses' father-in-law said to him, "The
thing that you do *is* not good.
18 "Both you and these people who *are* with you
will surely wear yourselves out. For this thing *is*
too much for you; [a]you are not able to perform it
by yourself.
19 "Listen now to my voice; I will give you
[1]counsel, and God will be with you: Stand [a]before
God for the people, so that you may [b]bring the
difficulties to God.
20 "And you shall [a]teach them the statutes and
the laws, and show them the way in which they
must walk and [b]the work they must do.
21 "Moreover you shall select from all the people
[a]able men, such as [b]fear God, [c]men of truth,
[d]hating covetousness; and place *such* over them *to
be* rulers of thousands, rulers of hundreds, rulers
of fifties, and rulers of tens.
22 "And let them judge the people at all times.
[a]Then it will be *that* every great matter they shall
bring to you, but every small matter they themselves shall judge. So it will be easier for you, for
[b]they will bear *the burden* with you.
23 "If you do this thing, and God so commands
you, then you will be able to endure, and all this
people will also go to their [a]place in peace."
**24** So Moses heeded the voice of his father-in-law
and did all that he had said.
25 And [a]Moses chose able men out of all Israel,
and made them heads over the people: rulers of
thousands, rulers of hundreds, rulers of fifties, and
rulers of tens.
26 So they judged the people at all times; the
[a]hard[1] cases they brought to Moses, but they
judged every small case themselves.
27 Then Moses let his father-in-law depart, and
[a]he went his way to his own land.

### *Israel at Mount Sinai*

**19** In the third month after the children of
Israel had gone out of the land of Egypt, on
the same day, [a]they came *to* the Wilderness of
Sinai.
2 For they had departed from [a]Rephidim, had
come *to* the Wilderness of Sinai, and camped in
the wilderness. So Israel camped there before [b]the
mountain.
3 And [a]Moses went up to God, and the LORD
[b]called to him from the mountain, saying, "Thus
you shall say to the house of Jacob, and tell the
children of Israel:
4 [a]'You have seen what I did to the Egyptians,
and *how* [b]I [1]bore you on eagles' wings and
brought you to Myself.
5 'Now [a]therefore, if you will indeed obey My
voice and [b]keep My covenant, then [c]you shall be a
special treasure to Me above all people; for all the
earth *is* [d]Mine.
6 'And you shall be to Me a [a]kingdom of priests
and a [b]holy nation.' These *are* the words which
you shall speak to the children of Israel."
**7** So Moses came and called for the [a]elders of
the people, and [1]laid before them all these words
which the LORD commanded him.
8 Then [a]all the people answered together and
said, "All that the LORD has spoken we will do."
So Moses brought back the words of the people to
the LORD.
9 And the LORD said to Moses, "Behold, I come
to you [a]in the thick cloud, [b]that the people may
hear when I speak with you, and believe you
forever." So Moses told the words of the people to
the LORD.
**10** Then the LORD said to Moses, "Go to the
people and [a]consecrate them today and tomorrow,
and let them wash their clothes.
11 "And let them be ready for the third day. For
on the third day the LORD will come down upon
Mount Sinai in the sight of all the people.
12 "You shall set bounds for the people all
around, saying, 'Take heed to yourselves *that* you
do *not* go up to the mountain or touch its base.
[a]Whoever touches the mountain shall surely be
put to death.
13 'Not a hand shall touch him, but he shall
surely be stoned or shot *with an arrow;* whether
man or beast, he shall not live.' When the trumpet
sounds long, they shall come near the mountain."
**14** So Moses went down from the mountain to
the people and sanctified the people, and they
washed their clothes.
15 And he said to the people, "Be ready for the
third day; [a]do not come near *your* wives."
**16** Then it came to pass on the third day, in the
morning, that there were [a]thunderings and lightnings, and a thick cloud on the mountain; and the
sound of the trumpet was very loud, so that all the
people who *were* in the camp [b]trembled.
17 And [a]Moses brought the people out of the
camp to meet with God, and they stood at the foot
of the mountain.
18 Now [a]Mount Sinai *was* completely in smoke,
because the LORD descended upon [b]it in fire. [c]Its
smoke ascended like the smoke of a furnace, and
[1]the [d]whole mountain quaked greatly.
19 And when the blast of the trumpet sounded
long and became louder and louder, [a]Moses spoke,
and [b]God answered him by voice.
20 Then the LORD came down upon Mount Sinai,
on the top of the mountain. And the LORD called
Moses to the top of the mountain, and Moses
went up.
21 And the LORD said to Moses, "Go down and
warn the people, lest they break through [a]to gaze
at the LORD, and many of them perish.
22 "Also let the [a]priests who come near the LORD
[b]consecrate themselves, lest the LORD [c]break out
against them."
23 But Moses said to the LORD, "The people
cannot come up to Mount Sinai; for You warned
us, saying, [a]'Set bounds around the mountain and
consecrate it.'"
24 Then the LORD said to him, "Away! Get down
and then come up, you and Aaron with you. But
do not let the priests and the people break
through to come up to the LORD, lest He break out
against them."
25 So Moses went down to the people and spoke
to them.

### *The Ten Commandments*

**20** And God spoke [a]all these words, saying:
2 [a]"I *am* the LORD your God, who brought
you out of the land of Egypt, [b]out of the
house of [1]bondage.
**3** [a]"You shall have no other gods before Me.
**4** [a]"You shall not make for yourself a carved
image—any likeness *of anything* that *is* in
heaven above, or that *is* in the earth beneath, or that *is* in the water under the
earth;

**18** [a]Num. 11:14, 17
**19** [a]Ex. 4:16; 20:19 [b]Num. 9:8; 27:5 [1]*advice*
**20** [a]Deut. 5:1 [b]Deut. 1:18
**21** [a]Acts 6:3 [b]2 Sam. 23:3 [c]Ezek. 18:8 [d]Deut. 16:19
**22** [a]Deut. 1:17 [b]Num. 11:17
**23** [a]Ex. 16:29
**25** [a]Deut. 1:15
**26** [a]Job 29:16 [1]*difficult matters*
**27** [a]Num. 10:29, 30

CHAPTER 19

**1** [a]Num. 33:15
**2** [a]Ex. 17:1 [b]Ex. 3:1, 12; 18:5
**3** [a]Acts 7:38 [b]Ex. 3:4
**4** [a]Deut. 29:2 [b]Is. 63:9 [1]*sustained*
**5** [a]Ex. 15:26; 23:22 [b]Deut. 5:2 [c]Ps. 135:4 [d]Ex. 9:29
**6** [a][1 Pet. 2:5, 9] [b]Deut. 7:6; 14:21; 26:19
**7** [a]Ex. 4:29, 30 [1]*set*
**8** [a]Deut. 5:27; 26:17
**9** [a]Ex. 19:16; 20:21; 24:15 [b]Deut. 4:12, 36
**10** [a]Lev. 11:44, 45
**12** [a]Heb. 12:20
**15** [a][1 Cor. 7:5]
**16** [a]Heb. 12:18, 19 [b]Heb. 12:21
**17** [a]Deut. 4:10
**18** [a]Deut. 4:11 [b]Ex. 3:2; 24:17 [c]Gen. 15:17; 19:28 [d]Ps. 68:8 [1]LXX *all the people*
**19** [a]Heb. 12:21 [b]Ps. 81:7
**21** [a]1 Sam. 6:19
**22** [a]Ex. 19:24; 24:5 [b]Lev. 10:3; 21:6–8 [c]2 Sam. 6:7, 8
**23** [a]Ex. 19:12

CHAPTER 20

**1** [a]Deut. 5:22
**2** [a]Hos. 13:4 [b]Ex. 13:3 [1]*slaves*
**3** [a]Jer. 25:6; 35:15
**4** [a]Deut. 4:15–19; 27:15

5 [a]you shall not bow down to them nor
[1]serve them. [b]For I, the LORD your God,
*am* a jealous God, [c]visiting[2] the iniquity of
the fathers upon the children to the third
and fourth *generations* of those who hate
Me,
6 but [a]showing mercy to thousands, to those
who love Me and keep My commandments.
7 [a]"You shall not take the name of the LORD
your God in vain, for the LORD [b]will not
hold *him* guiltless who takes His name in
vain.
8 [a]"Remember the Sabbath day, to keep it holy.
9 [a]Six days you shall labor and do all your
work,
10 but the [a]seventh day *is* the Sabbath of the
LORD your God. *In it* you shall do no work:
you, nor your son, nor your daughter, nor
your male servant, nor your female servant, nor your cattle, [b]nor your stranger
who *is* within your gates.
11 For [a]*in* six days the LORD made the heavens and the earth, the sea, and all that *is* in
them, and rested the seventh day. Therefore the LORD blessed the Sabbath day and
hallowed it.
12 [a]"Honor your father and your mother, that
your days may be [b]long upon the land
which the LORD your God is giving you.
13 [a]"You shall not murder.
14 [a]"You shall not commit [b]adultery.
15 [a]"You shall not steal.
16 [a]"You shall not bear false witness against your
neighbor.
17 [a]"You shall not covet your neighbor's house;
[b]you shall not covet your neighbor's wife,
nor his male servant, nor his female servant, nor his ox, nor his donkey, nor anything that *is* your neighbor's."
18 Now [a]all the people [b]witnessed the thunderings, the lightning flashes, the sound of the trumpet, and the mountain [c]smoking; and when the
people saw *it*, they trembled and stood afar off.
19 Then they said to Moses, [a]"You speak with us,
and we will hear; but [b]let not God speak with us,
lest we die."
20 And Moses said to the people, [a]"Do not fear;
[b]for God has come to test you, and [c]that His fear
may be before you, so that you may not sin."
21 So the people stood afar off, but Moses drew
near [a]the thick darkness where God *was*.
22 Then the LORD said to Moses, "Thus you shall
say to the children of Israel: 'You have seen that I
have talked with you [a]from heaven.
23 'You shall not make *anything to be* [a]with
Me—gods of silver or gods of gold you shall not
make for yourselves.
24 'An altar of [a]earth you shall make for Me, and
you shall sacrifice on it your burnt offerings and
your peace offerings, [b]your sheep and your oxen.
In every [c]place where I [1]record My name I will
come to you, and I will [d]bless you.
25 'And [a]if you make Me an altar of stone, you
shall not build it of hewn stone; for if you [b]use
your tool on it, you have profaned it.
26 'Nor shall you go up by steps to My altar, that
your [a]nakedness may not be exposed on it.'

## *The Treatment of Servants*

**21** "Now these *are* the [1]judgments which you
shall [a]set before them:
2 [a]"If you buy a Hebrew servant, he shall serve
six years; and in the seventh he shall go out free
and pay nothing.
3 "If he comes in by himself, he shall go out by
himself; if he *comes in* married, then his wife shall
go out with him.
4 "If his master has given him a wife, and she
has borne him sons or daughters, the wife and her
children shall be her master's, and he shall go out
by himself.
5 [a]"But if the servant plainly says, 'I love my
master, my wife, and my children; I will not go out
free,'
6 "then his master shall bring him to the
[a]judges. He shall also bring him to the door, or to
the doorpost, and his master shall pierce his ear
with an awl; and he shall serve him forever.
7 "And if a man [a]sells his daughter to be a
female servant, she shall not go out as the male
servants do.
8 "If she [1]does not please her master, who has
betrothed her to himself, then he shall let her be
redeemed. He shall have no right to sell her to a
foreign people, since he has dealt deceitfully with
her.
9 "And if he has betrothed her to his son, he
shall deal with her according to the custom of
daughters.
10 "If he takes another *wife*, he shall not diminish her food, her clothing, [a]and her marriage
rights.
11 "And if he does not do these three for her,
then she shall go out free, without *paying* money.
12 [a]"He who strikes a man so that he dies shall
surely be put to death.
13 "However, [a]if he did not lie in wait, but God
[b]delivered *him* into his hand, then [c]I will appoint
for you a place where he may flee.
14 "But if a man acts with [a]premeditation against
his neighbor, to kill him by treachery, [b]you shall
take him from My altar, that he may die.
15 "And he who strikes his father or his mother
shall surely be put to death.
16 [a]"He who kidnaps a man and [b]sells him, or if
he is [c]found in his hand, shall surely be put to
death.
17 "And [a]he who curses his father or his mother
shall surely be put to death.
18 "If men contend with each other, and one
strikes the other with a stone or with *his* fist, and
he does not die but is confined to *his* bed,
19 "if he rises again and walks about outside
[a]with his staff, then he who struck *him* shall be
[1]acquitted. He shall only pay *for* the loss of his
time, and shall provide *for him* to be thoroughly
healed.
20 "And if a man beats his male or female servant
with a rod, so that he dies under his hand, he shall
surely be punished.
21 "Notwithstanding, if he remains alive a day or
two, he shall not be punished; for he *is* his [a]prop-
erty.
22 "If men [1]fight, and hurt a woman with child,
so that [2]she gives birth prematurely, yet no harm
follows, he shall surely be punished accordingly as

**5** [a]Is. 44:15, 19 [b]Deut. 4:24 [c]Num. 14:18, 33 [1]*worship* [2]*punishing*
**6** [a]Deut. 7:9
**7** [a]Lev. 19:12 [b]Mic. 6:11
**8** [a]Lev. 26:2
**9** [a]Luke 13:14
**10** [a]Gen. 2:2, 3 [b]Neh. 13:16–19
**11** [a]Ex. 31:17
**12** [a]Lev. 19:3 [b]Deut. 5:16, 33; 6:2; 11:8, 9
**13** [a]Rom. 13:9
**14** [a]Matt. 5:27 [b]Deut. 5:18
**15** [a]Lev. 19:11, 13
**16** [a]Deut. 5:20
**17** [a][Eph. 5:3, 5] [b][Matt. 5:28]
**18** [a]Heb. 12:18, 19 [b]Rev. 1:10, 12 [c]Ex. 19:16, 18
**19** [a]Heb. 12:19 [b]Deut. 5:5, 23–27
**20** [a][Is. 41:10, 13] [b][Deut. 13:3] [c]Is. 8:13
**21** [a]Ex. 19:16
**22** [a]Deut. 4:36; 5:24, 26
**23** [a]Ex. 32:1, 2, 4
**24** [a]Ex. 20:25; 27:1–8 [b]Ex. 24:5 [c]2 Chr. 6:6 [d]Gen. 12:2 [1]*cause my name to be remembered*
**25** [a]Deut. 27:5 [b]Josh. 8:30, 31
**26** [a]Ex. 28:42, 43

CHAPTER 21

**1** [a]Deut. 4:14; 6:1 [1]*ordinances*
**2** [a]Jer. 34:14
**5** [a]Deut. 15:16, 17
**6** [a]Ex. 12:12; 22:8, 9
**7** [a]Neh. 5:5
**8** [1]Lit. *is evil in the eyes of*
**10** [a][1 Cor. 7:3, 5]
**12** [a][Matt. 26:52]
**13** [a]Deut. 19:4, 5 [b]1 Sam. 24:4, 10, 18 [c]Num. 35:11
**14** [a]Deut. 19:11, 12 [b]1 Kin. 2:28–34
**16** [a]Deut. 24:7 [b]Gen. 37:28 [c]Ex. 22:4
**17** [a]Mark 7:10
**19** [a]2 Sam. 3:29 [1]*exempt from punishment*
**21** [a]Lev. 25:44–46
**22** [1]*struggle* [2]Lit. *her children come out*

the woman's husband imposes on him; and he shall [a]pay as the judges *determine*.
23 "But if *any* harm follows, then you shall give life for life,
24 [a]"eye for eye, tooth for tooth, hand for hand, foot for foot,
25 "burn for burn, wound for wound, stripe for stripe.
**26** "If a man strikes the eye of his male or female servant, and destroys it, he shall let him go free for the sake of his eye.
27 "And if he knocks out the tooth of his male or female servant, he shall let him go free for the sake of his tooth.
**28** "If an ox gores a man or a woman to death, then [a]the ox shall surely be stoned, and its flesh shall not be eaten; but the owner of the ox *shall be* [1]acquitted.
29 "But if the ox [1]tended to thrust with its horn in times past, and it has been made known to his owner, and he has not kept it confined, so that it has killed a man or a woman, the ox shall be stoned and its owner also shall be put to death.
30 "If there is imposed on him a sum of money, then he shall pay [a]to redeem his life, whatever is imposed on him.
31 "Whether it has gored a son or gored a daughter, according to this judgment it shall be done to him.
32 "If the ox gores a male or female servant, he shall give to their master [a]thirty shekels of silver, and the [b]ox shall be stoned.
**33** "And if a man opens a pit, or if a man digs a pit and does not cover it, and an ox or a donkey falls in it,
34 "the owner of the pit shall make *it* good; he shall give money to their owner, but the dead *animal* shall be his.
**35** "If one man's ox hurts another's, so that it dies, then they shall sell the live ox and divide the money from it; and the dead *ox* they shall also divide.
36 "Or if it was known that the ox tended to thrust in time past, and its owner has not kept it confined, he shall surely pay ox for ox, and the dead animal shall be his own.

### *Responsibility for Property*

**22** "If a man steals an ox or a sheep, and slaughters it or sells it, he shall [a]restore five oxen for an ox and four sheep for a sheep.
2 "If the thief is found [a]breaking in, and he is struck so that he dies, *there shall be* [b]no guilt for his bloodshed.
3 "If the sun has risen on him, *there shall be* guilt for his bloodshed. He should make full restitution; if he has nothing, then he shall be [a]sold[1] for his theft.
4 "If the theft is certainly [a]found alive in his hand, whether it is an ox or donkey or sheep, he shall [b]restore double.
**5** "If a man causes a field or vineyard to be grazed, and lets loose his animal, and it feeds in another man's field, he shall make restitution from the best of his own field and the best of his own vineyard.
**6** "If fire breaks out and catches in thorns, so that stacked grain, standing grain, or the field is consumed, he who kindled the fire shall surely make restitution.
7 "If a man [a]delivers to his neighbor money or articles to keep, and it is stolen out of the man's house, [b]if the thief is found, he shall pay double.
8 "If the thief is not found, then the master of the house shall be brought to the [a]judges *to see* whether he has put his hand into his neighbor's goods.
**9** "For any kind of trespass, *whether it concerns* an ox, a donkey, a sheep, or clothing, *or* for any kind of lost thing which *another* claims to be his, the [a]cause of both parties shall come before the judges; *and* whomever the judges condemn shall pay double to his neighbor.
**10** "If a man delivers to his neighbor a donkey, an ox, a sheep, or any animal to keep, and it dies, is hurt, or driven away, no one seeing *it*,
11 "*then* an [a]oath of the LORD shall be between them both, that he has not put his hand into his neighbor's goods; and the owner of it shall accept *that*, and he shall not make *it* good.
12 "But [a]if, in fact, it is stolen from him, he shall make restitution to the owner of it.
13 "If it is [a]torn to pieces *by a beast, then* he shall bring it as evidence, *and* he shall not make good what was torn.
**14** "And if a man borrows *anything* from his neighbor, and it becomes injured or dies, the owner of it not *being* with it, he shall surely make *it* good.
15 "If its owner *was* with it, he shall not make *it* good; if it *was* hired, it came for its hire.
**16** "[a]If a man entices a virgin who is not betrothed, and lies with her, he shall surely pay the bride-price for her *to be* his wife.
17 "If her father utterly refuses to give her to him, he shall pay money according to the [a]bride-price of virgins.
**18** [a]"You shall not permit a sorceress to live.
**19** [a]"Whoever lies with an animal shall surely be put to death.
**20** [a]"He who sacrifices to *any* god, except to the LORD only, he shall be utterly destroyed.
**21** [a]"You shall neither mistreat a [1]stranger nor oppress him, for you were strangers in the land of Egypt.
**22** [a]"You shall not afflict any widow or fatherless child.
23 "If you afflict them in any way, *and* they [a]cry at all to Me, I will surely [b]hear their cry;
24 "and My [a]wrath will become hot, and I will kill you with the sword; [b]your wives shall be widows, and your children fatherless.
**25** [a]"If you lend money to *any of* My people *who are* poor among you, you shall not be like a moneylender to him; you shall not charge him [b]interest.
26 [a]"If you ever take your neighbor's garment as a pledge, you shall return it to him before the sun goes down.
27 "For that *is* his only covering, it *is* his garment for his skin. What will he sleep in? And it will be that when he cries to Me, I will hear, for I *am* [a]gracious.
**28** [a]"You shall not revile God, nor curse a [b]ruler of your people.
**29** "You shall not delay *to offer* [a]the first of your ripe produce and your juices. [b]The firstborn of your sons you shall give to Me.
30 [a]"Likewise you shall do with your oxen *and* your sheep. It shall be with its mother [b]seven days; on the eighth day you shall give it to Me.
**31** "And you shall be [a]holy men to Me: [b]you shall

**22** [a]Ex. 18:21, 22; 21:30
**24** [a]Lev. 24:20
**28** [a]Gen. 9:5 [1]*exempt from punishment*
**29** [1]*was inclined*
**30** [a]Num. 35:31
**32** [a]Zech. 11:12, 13 [b]Ex. 21:28

CHAPTER 22
**1** [a]2 Sam. 12:6
**2** [a]Matt. 6:19; 24:43 [b]Num. 35:27
**3** [a]Ex. 21:2 [1]Sold as a slave
**4** [a]Ex. 21:16 [b]Prov. 6:31
**7** [a]Lev. 6:1–7 [b]Ex. 22:4
**8** [a]Ex. 21:6, 22; 22:28
**9** [a]Deut. 25:1
**11** [a]Heb. 6:16
**12** [a]Gen. 31:39
**13** [a]Gen. 31:39
**16** [a]Deut. 22:28, 29
**17** [a]Gen. 34:12
**18** [a]1 Sam. 28:3–10
**19** [a]Lev. 18:23; 20:15, 16
**20** [a]Ex. 32:8; 34:15
**21** [a]Deut. 10:19 [1]*sojourner*
**22** [a][James 1:27]
**23** [a][Luke 18:7] [b]Ps. 18:6
**24** [a]Ps. 69:24 [b]Ps. 109:9
**25** [a]Lev. 25:35–37 [b]Ps. 15:5
**26** [a]Deut. 24:6, 10–13
**27** [a]Ex. 34:6, 7
**28** [a]Eccl. 10:20 [b]Acts 23:5
**29** [a]Ex. 23:16, 19 [b]Ex. 13:2, 12, 15
**30** [a]Deut. 15:19 [b]Lev. 22:27
**31** [a]Lev. 11:44; 19:2 [b]Ezek. 4:14

not eat meat torn *by beasts* in the field; you shall
throw it to the dogs.

### *The LORD's Angel Sent to Lead Israel*

**23** "You [a]shall not circulate a false report. Do
not put your hand with the wicked to be an
[b]unrighteous witness.
2 [a]"You shall not follow a crowd to do evil; [b]nor
shall you testify in a dispute so as to turn aside
after many to pervert *justice.*
3 "You shall not show partiality to a [a]poor man
in his dispute.
**4** [a]"If you meet your enemy's ox or his donkey
going astray, you shall surely bring it back to him
again.
5 [a]"If you see the donkey of one who hates you
lying under its burden, and you would refrain
from helping it, you shall surely help him with it.
**6** [a]"You shall not pervert the judgment of your
poor in his dispute.
7 [a]"Keep yourself far from a false matter; [b]do
not kill the innocent and righteous. For [c]I will not
justify the wicked.
8 "And [a]you shall take no bribe, for a bribe
blinds the discerning and perverts the words of
the righteous.
9 "Also [a]you shall not oppress a [1]stranger, for
you know the heart of a stranger, because you
were strangers in the land of Egypt.
**10** [a]"Six years you shall sow your land and gather
in its produce,
11 "but the seventh *year* you shall let it rest and
lie fallow, that the poor of your people may eat;
and what they leave, the beasts of the field may
eat. In like manner you shall do with your vineyard *and* your [1]olive grove.
12 [a]"Six days you shall do your work, and on the
seventh day you shall rest, that your ox and your
donkey may rest, and the son of your female
servant and the stranger may be refreshed.
13 "And in all that I have said to you, [a]be circum-
spect and [b]make no mention of the name of other
gods, nor let it be heard from your mouth.
**14** [a]"Three times you shall keep a feast to Me in
the year:
15 [a]"You shall keep the Feast of Unleavened
Bread (you shall eat unleavened bread seven days,
as I commanded you, at the time appointed in the
month of Abib, for in it you came out of Egypt;
[b]none shall appear before Me empty);
16 [a]"and the Feast of Harvest, the firstfruits of
your labors which you have sown in the field; and
[b]the Feast of Ingathering at the end of the year,
when you have gathered in *the fruit of* your labors
from the field.
17 [a]"Three times in the year all your males shall
appear before the Lord [1]GOD.
18 [a]"You shall not offer the blood of My sacrifice
with leavened [b]bread; nor shall the fat of My
[1]sacrifice remain until morning.
19 [a]"The first of the firstfruits of your land you
shall bring into the house of the LORD your God.
[b]You shall not boil a young goat in its mother's
milk.
**20** [a]"Behold, I send an Angel before you to keep
you in the way and to bring you into the place
which I have prepared.
21 "Beware of Him and obey His voice; [a]do not
provoke Him, for He will [b]not pardon your transgressions; for [c]My name *is* in Him.
22 "But if you indeed obey His voice and do all
that I speak, then [a]I will be an enemy to your
enemies and an adversary to your adversaries.
23 [a]"For My Angel will go before you and [b]bring
you in to the Amorites and the Hittites and the
Perizzites and the Canaanites and the Hivites and
the Jebusites; and I will [1]cut them off.
24 "You shall not [a]bow down to their gods, nor
serve them, [b]nor do according to their works; [c]but
you shall utterly overthrow them and completely
break down their *sacred* pillars.
25 "So you shall [a]serve the LORD your God, and
[b]He will bless your bread and your water. And [c]I
will take sickness away from the midst of you.
26 [a]"No one shall suffer miscarriage or be barren
in your land; I will [b]fulfill the number of your
days.
**27** "I will send [a]My fear before you, I will [b]cause
confusion among all the people to whom you
come, and will make all your enemies turn *their*
backs to you.
28 "And [a]I will send hornets before you, which
shall drive out the Hivite, the Canaanite, and the
Hittite from before you.
29 [a]"I will not drive them out from before you in
one year, lest the land become desolate and the
beasts of the field become too numerous for you.
30 "Little by little I will drive them out from
before you, until you have increased, and you
inherit the land.
31 "And [a]I will set your [1]bounds from the Red
Sea to the sea, Philistia, and from the desert to the
[2]River. For I will [b]deliver the inhabitants of the
land into your hand, and you shall drive them out
before you.
32 [a]"You shall make no [1]covenant with them, nor
with their gods.
33 "They shall not dwell in your land, lest they
make you sin against Me. For *if* you serve their
gods, [a]it will surely be a snare to you."

### *Moses and the Elders on Mount Sinai*

**24** Now He said to Moses, "Come up to the
LORD, you and Aaron, [a]Nadab and Abihu,
[b]and seventy of the elders of Israel, and worship
from afar.
2 "And Moses alone shall come near the LORD,
but they shall not come near; nor shall the people
go up with him."
**3** So Moses came and told the people all the
words of the LORD and all the [1]judgments. And all
the people answered with one voice and said, [a]"All
the words which the LORD has said we will do."
4 And Moses [a]wrote all the words of the LORD.
And he rose early in the morning, and built an
altar at the foot of the mountain, and twelve
[b]pillars according to the twelve tribes of Israel.
5 Then he sent young men of the children of
Israel, who offered [a]burnt offerings and sacrificed
peace offerings of oxen to the LORD.
6 And Moses [a]took half the blood and put *it* in
basins, and half the blood he sprinkled on the
altar.
7 Then he [a]took the Book of the Covenant and
read in the hearing of the people. And they said,
"All that the LORD has said we will do, and be
obedient."
8 And Moses took the blood, sprinkled *it* on the
people, and said, "This is [a]the blood of the covenant which the LORD has made with you according to all these words."

CHAPTER 23
1 [a]Ps. 101:5 [b]Deut. 19:16–21
2 [a]Gen. 7:1 [b]Lev. 19:5
3 [a]Deut. 1:17; 16:19
4 [a][Rom. 12:20]
5 [a]Deut. 22:4
6 [a]Eccl. 5:8
7 [a]Eph. 4:25 [b]Matt. 27:4 [c]Rom. 1:18
8 [a]Prov. 15:27; 17:8, 23
9 [a]Ex. 22:21 [1]*sojourner*
10 [a]Lev. 25:1–7
11 [1]*olive yards*
12 [a]Luke 13:14
13 [a]1 Tim. 4:16 [b]Josh. 23:7
14 [a]Ex. 23:17; 34:22–24
15 [a]Ex. 12:14–20 [b]Ex. 22:29; 34:20
16 [a]Ex. 34:22 [b]Deut. 16:13
17 [a]Deut. 16:16 [1]Heb. *YHWH,* usually translated *LORD*
18 [a]Ex. 34:25 [b]Deut. 16:4 [1]*feast*
19 [a]Deut. 26:2, 10 [b]Deut. 14:21
20 [a]Ex. 3:2; 13:15; 14:19
21 [a]Ps. 78:40, 56 [b]Deut. 18:19 [c]Is. 9:6
22 [a]Deut. 30:7
23 [a]Ex. 23:20 [b]Josh. 24:8, 11 [1]*annihilate them*
24 [a]Ex. 20:5; 23:13, 33 [b]Deut. 12:30, 31 [c]Num. 33:52
25 [a]Deut. 6:13 [b]Deut. 28:5 [c]Ex. 15:26
26 [a]Deut. 7:14; 28:4 [b]1 Chr. 23:1
27 [a]Ex. 15:16 [b]Deut. 7:23
28 [a]Josh. 24:12
29 [a]Deut. 7:22
31 [a]Gen. 15:18 [b]Josh. 21:44 [1]*boundaries* [2]Heb. *Nahar,* the Euphrates
32 [a]Ex. 34:12, 15 [1]*treaty*
33 [a]Ps. 106:36

CHAPTER 24
1 [a]Lev. 10:1, 2 [b]Num. 11:16
3 [a]Ex. 19:8; 24:7 [1]*ordinances*
4 [a]Deut. 31:9 [b]Gen. 28:18
5 [a]Ex. 18:12; 20:24
6 [a]Heb. 9:18
7 [a]Heb. 9:19
8 [a][Luke 22:20]

9 Then Moses went up, also Aaron, Nadab, and
Abihu, and seventy of the elders of Israel,
10 and they [a]saw the God of Israel. And *there*
*was* under His feet as it were a paved work of
[b]sapphire stone, and it was like the [c]very[1] heavens
in *its* clarity.
11 But on the nobles of the children of Israel He
[a]did not [1]lay His hand. So [b]they saw God, and they
[c]ate and drank.
**12** Then the LORD said to Moses, [a]"Come up to
Me on the mountain and be there; and I will give
you [b]tablets of stone, and the law and commandments which I have written, that you may teach
them."
13 So Moses arose with [a]his assistant Joshua, and
Moses went up to the mountain of God.
14 And he said to the elders, "Wait here for us
until we come back to you. Indeed, Aaron and
[a]Hur *are* with you. If any man has a difficulty, let
him go to them."
15 Then Moses went up into the mountain, and [a]a
cloud covered the mountain.
16 Now [a]the glory of the LORD rested on Mount
Sinai, and the cloud covered it six days. And on
the seventh day He called to Moses out of the
midst of the cloud.
17 The sight of the glory of the LORD *was* like [a]a
consuming fire on the top of the mountain in the
eyes of the children of Israel.
18 So Moses went into the midst of the cloud and
went up into the mountain. And [a]Moses was on
the mountain forty days and forty nights.

### *The Ark of the Testimony*

**25** Then the LORD spoke to Moses, saying:
2 "Speak to the children of Israel, that they
bring Me an [1]offering. [a]From everyone who gives
it willingly with his heart you shall take My
offering.
3 "And this *is* the offering which you shall take
from them: gold, silver, and bronze;
4 "blue, purple, and scarlet *thread,* fine linen,
and goats' *hair;*
5 "ram skins dyed red, [1]badger skins, and acacia
wood;
6 [a]"oil for the light, and [b]spices for the anointing
oil and for the sweet incense;
7 "onyx stones, and stones to be set in the
[a]ephod and in the breastplate.
8 "And let them make Me a [a]sanctuary,[1] that [b]I
may dwell among them.
9 "According to all that I show you, *that is,* the
pattern of the tabernacle and the pattern of all its
furnishings, just so you shall make *it.*
**10** [a]"And they shall make an ark of acacia wood;
two and a half cubits *shall be* its length, a cubit
and a half its width, and a cubit and a half its
height.
11 "And you shall overlay it with pure gold,
inside and out you shall overlay it, and shall make
on it a molding of [a]gold all around.
12 "You shall cast four rings of gold for it, and
put *them* in its four corners; two rings *shall be* on
one side, and two rings on the other side.
13 "And you shall make poles *of* acacia wood,
and overlay them with gold.
14 "You shall put the poles into the rings on the
sides of the ark, that the ark may be carried by
them.
15 [a]"The poles shall be in the rings of the ark;
they shall not be taken from it.
16 "And you shall put into the ark [a]the Testimony which I will give you.
17 [a]"You shall make a mercy seat of pure gold;
two and a half cubits *shall be* its length and a
cubit and a half its width.
18 "And you shall make two cherubim of gold; of
hammered work you shall make them at the two
ends of the mercy seat.
19 "Make one cherub at one end, and the other
cherub at the other end; you shall make the
cherubim at the two ends of it *of one piece* with
the mercy seat.
20 "And [a]the cherubim shall stretch out *their*
wings above, covering the mercy seat with their
wings, and they shall face one another; the faces
of the cherubim *shall be* toward the mercy seat.
21 [a]"You shall put the mercy seat on top of the
ark, and [b]in the ark you shall put the Testimony
that I will give you.
22 "And [a]there I will meet with you, and I will
speak with you from above the mercy seat, from
[b]between the two cherubim which *are* on the ark
of the Testimony, about everything which I will
give you in commandment to the children of
Israel.
**23** [a]"You shall also make a table of acacia wood;
two cubits *shall be* its length, a cubit its width,
and a cubit and a half its height.
24 "And you shall overlay it with pure gold, and
make a molding of gold all around.
25 "You shall make for it a frame of a handbreadth all around, and you shall make a gold
molding for the frame all around.
26 "And you shall make for it four rings of gold,
and put the rings on the four corners that *are* at
its four legs.
27 "The rings shall be close to the frame, as
holders for the poles to bear the table.
28 "And you shall make the poles of acacia wood,
and overlay them with gold, that the table may be
carried with them.
29 "You shall make [a]its dishes, its pans, its pitchers, and its bowls for pouring. You shall make
them of pure gold.
30 "And you shall set the [a]showbread on the
table before Me always.
**31** [a]"You shall also make a lampstand of pure
gold; the lampstand shall be of hammered work.
Its shaft, its branches, its bowls, its *ornamental*
knobs, and flowers shall be *of one piece.*
32 "And six branches shall come out of its sides:
three branches of the lampstand out of one side,
and three branches of the lampstand out of the
other side.
33 [a]"Three bowls *shall be* made like almond
*blossoms* on one branch, *with* an *ornamental*
knob and a flower, and three bowls made like
almond *blossoms* on the other branch, *with* an
*ornamental* knob and a flower—and so for the six
branches that come out of the lampstand.
34 [a]"On the lampstand itself four bowls *shall be*
made like almond *blossoms, each with* its *orna-*
*mental* knob and flower.
35 "And *there shall be* a knob under the *first* two
branches of the same, a knob under the *second*
two branches of the same, and a knob under the
*third* two branches of the same, according to the
six branches that extend from the lampstand.
36 "Their knobs and their branches *shall be of*
*one piece;* all of it *shall be* one hammered piece of
pure gold.

**10** [a][John 1:18; 6:46] [b]Ezek. 1:26 [c]Matt. 17:2 [1]Lit. *substance of heaven*
**11** [a]Ex. 19:21 [b]Gen. 32:30 [c]1 Cor. 10:18 [1]*stretch out His*
**12** [a]Ex. 24:2, 15 [b]Ex. 31:18; 32:15
**13** [a]Ex. 32:17
**14** [a]Ex. 17:10, 12
**15** [a]Ex. 19:9
**16** [a]Ex. 16:10; 33:18
**17** [a]Deut. 4:26, 36; 9:3
**18** [a]Ex. 34:28

CHAPTER 25

**2** [a]Ex. 35:4–9, 21 [1]*heave offering*
**5** [1]Or *dolphin*
**6** [a]Ex. 27:20 [b]Ex. 30:23
**7** [a]Ex. 28:4, 6–14
**8** [a]Heb. 9:1, 2 [b][2 Cor. 6:16] [1]*sacred place*
**10** [a]Ex. 37:1–9
**11** [a]Ex. 37:2
**15** [a]1 Kin. 8:8
**16** [a]Heb. 9:4
**17** [a]Ex. 37:6
**20** [a]1 Kin. 8:7
**21** [a]Ex. 26:34; 40:20 [b]Ex. 25:16
**22** [a]Ex. 29:42, 43; 30:6, 36 [b]Num. 7:89
**23** [a]Ex. 37:10–16
**29** [a]Ex. 37:16
**30** [a]Lev. 24:5–9
**31** [a]Zech. 4:2
**33** [a]Ex. 37:19
**34** [a]Ex. 37:20–22

37 "You shall make seven lamps for it, and [a]they
shall arrange its lamps so that they [b]give light in
front of it.
38 "And its wick-trimmers and their trays *shall
be* of pure gold.
39 "It shall be made of a talent of pure gold, with
all these utensils.
40 "And [a]see to it that you make *them* according
to the pattern which was shown you on the
mountain.

### *The Tabernacle*

**26** "Moreover [a]you shall make the tabernacle
*with* ten curtains *of* fine woven linen and
blue, purple, and scarlet *thread;* with artistic
designs of cherubim you shall weave them.
2 "The length of each curtain *shall be* twenty-
eight cubits, and the width of each curtain four
cubits. And every one of the curtains shall have
[1]the same measurements.
3 "Five curtains shall be coupled to one another,
and *the other* five curtains *shall be* coupled to one
another.
4 "And you shall make loops of blue *yarn* on the
edge of the curtain on the selvedge of *one* set, and
likewise you shall do on the outer edge of *the
other* curtain of the second set.
5 "Fifty loops you shall make in the one curtain,
and fifty loops you shall make on the edge of the
curtain that *is* on the end of the second set, that
the loops may be clasped to one another.
6 "And you shall make fifty clasps of gold, and
couple the curtains together with the clasps, so
that it may be one tabernacle.
7 [a]"You shall also make curtains of goats' *hair,*
to be a tent over the tabernacle. You shall make
eleven curtains.
8 "The length of each curtain *shall be* thirty
cubits, and the width of each curtain four cubits;
and the eleven curtains shall all have the same
measurements.
9 "And you shall couple five curtains by themselves and six curtains by themselves, and you
shall double over the sixth curtain at the forefront
of the tent.
10 "You shall make fifty loops on the edge of the
curtain that is outermost in *one* set, and fifty loops
on the edge of the curtain of the second set.
11 "And you shall make fifty bronze clasps, put
the clasps into the loops, and couple the tent
together, that it may be one.
12 "The remnant that remains of the curtains of
the tent, the half curtain that remains, shall hang
over the back of the tabernacle.
13 "And a cubit on one side and a cubit on the
other side, of what remains of the length of the
curtains of the tent, shall hang over the sides of
the tabernacle, on this side and on that side, to
cover it.
14 [a]"You shall also make a covering of ram skins
dyed red for the tent, and a covering of badger
skins above that.
**15** "And for the tabernacle you shall [a]make the
boards of acacia wood, standing upright.
16 "Ten cubits *shall be* the length of a board, and
a cubit and a half *shall be* the width of each board.
17 "Two [1]tenons *shall be* in each board for binding one to another. Thus you shall make for all the
boards of the tabernacle.
18 "And you shall make the boards for the tabernacle, twenty boards for the south side.

**37** [a]Ex. 27:21; 30:8; Lev. 24:3, 4; 2 Chr. 13:11 [b]Num. 8:2
**40** [a]Ex. 25:9; 26:30; Num. 8:4; 1 Chr. 28:11, 19; Acts 7:44; [Heb. 8:5]

CHAPTER 26
**1** [a]Ex. 36:8–19
**2** [1]Lit. *one measure*
**7** [a]Ex. 36:14
**14** [a]Ex. 35:7, 23; 36:19
**15** [a]Ex. 36:20–34
**17** [1]Projections for joining, lit. *hands*
**24** [1]Lit. *doubled*
**28** [a]Ex. 36:33
**30** [a]Ex. 25:9, 40; 27:8; 39:32; Num. 8:4; Acts 7:44; [Heb. 8:2, 5]
**31** [a]Ex. 27:21; 36:35–38; Lev. 16:2; 2 Chr. 3:14; Matt. 27:51; Heb. 9:3; 10:20
**33** [a]Ex. 25:10–16; 40:21 [b]Lev. 16:2; Heb. 9:2, 3
**34** [a]Ex. 25:17–22; 40:20; Heb. 9:5
**35** [a]Ex. 40:22; Heb. 9:2 [b]Ex. 40:24
**36** [a]Ex. 36:37
**37** [a]Ex. 36:38

CHAPTER 27
**1** [a]Ex. 38:1; Ezek. 43:13

19 "You shall make forty sockets of silver under
the twenty boards: two sockets under each of the
boards for its two tenons.
20 "And for the second side of the tabernacle, the
north side, *there shall be* twenty boards
21 "and their forty sockets of silver: two sockets
under each of the boards.
22 "For the far side of the tabernacle, westward,
you shall make six boards.
23 "And you shall also make two boards for the
two back corners of the tabernacle.
24 "They shall be [1]coupled together at the bottom
and they shall be coupled together at the top by
one ring. Thus it shall be for both of them. They
shall be for the two corners.
25 "So there shall be eight boards with their
sockets of silver—sixteen sockets—two sockets
under each of the boards.
**26** "And you shall make bars of acacia wood: five
for the boards on one side of the tabernacle,
27 "five bars for the boards on the other side of
the tabernacle, and five bars for the boards of the
side of the tabernacle, for the far side westward.
28 "The [a]middle bar shall pass through the midst
of the boards from end to end.
29 "You shall overlay the boards with gold, make
their rings of gold *as* holders for the bars, and
overlay the bars with gold.
30 "And you shall raise up the tabernacle [a]ac-
cording to its pattern which you were shown on
the mountain.
**31** [a]"You shall make a veil woven of blue, purple,
and scarlet *thread,* and fine woven linen. It shall
be woven with an artistic design of cherubim.
32 "You shall hang it upon the four pillars of
acacia *wood* overlaid with gold. Their hooks *shall
be* gold, upon four sockets of silver.
33 "And you shall hang the veil from the clasps.
Then you shall bring [a]the ark of the Testimony in
there, behind the veil. The veil shall be a divider
for you between [b]the holy *place* and the Most
Holy.
34 [a]"You shall put the mercy seat upon the ark of
the Testimony in the Most Holy.
35 [a]"You shall set the table outside the veil, and
[b]the lampstand across from the table on the side
of the tabernacle toward the south; and you shall
put the table on the north side.
**36** [a]"You shall make a screen for the door of the
tabernacle, *woven of* blue, purple, and scarlet
*thread,* and fine woven linen, made by a weaver.
37 "And you shall make for the screen [a]five
pillars of acacia *wood,* and overlay them with
gold; their hooks *shall be* gold, and you shall cast
five sockets of bronze for them.

### *The Altar of the Burnt Offering*

**27** "You shall make [a]an altar of acacia wood,
five cubits long and five cubits wide—the
altar shall be square—and its height *shall be* three
cubits.
2 "You shall make its horns on its four corners;
its horns shall be of one piece with it. And you
shall overlay it with bronze.
3 "Also you shall make its pans to receive its
ashes, and its shovels and its basins and its forks
and its firepans; you shall make all its utensils of
bronze.
4 "You shall make a grate for it, a network of
bronze; and on the network you shall make four
bronze rings at its four corners.

5 "You shall put it under the rim of the altar beneath, that the network may be midway up the altar.

6 "And you shall make poles for the altar, poles of acacia wood, and overlay them with bronze.

7 "The poles shall be put in the rings, and the poles shall be on the two sides of the altar to bear it.

8 "You shall make it hollow with boards; [a]as it was shown you on the mountain, so shall they make *it*.

**9** [a]"You shall also make the court of the tabernacle. For the south side *there shall be* hangings for the court *made of* fine woven linen, one hundred cubits long for one side.

10 "And its twenty pillars and their twenty sockets *shall be* bronze. The hooks of the pillars and their bands *shall be* silver.

11 "Likewise along the length of the north side *there shall be* hangings one hundred *cubits* long, with its twenty pillars and their twenty sockets of bronze, and the hooks of the pillars and their bands of silver.

**12** "And along the width of the court on the west side *shall be* hangings of fifty cubits, with their ten pillars and their ten sockets.

13 "The width of the court on the east side *shall be* fifty cubits.

14 "The hangings on *one* side *of the gate shall be* fifteen cubits, *with* their three pillars and their three sockets.

15 "And on the other side *shall be* hangings of fifteen *cubits, with* their three pillars and their three sockets.

**16** "For the gate of the court *there shall be* a screen twenty cubits long, *woven of* blue, purple, and scarlet *thread,* and fine woven linen, made by a weaver. It *shall have* four pillars and four sockets.

17 "All the pillars around the court shall have bands of silver; their [a]hooks *shall be* of silver and their sockets of bronze.

18 "The length of the court *shall be* one hundred cubits, the width fifty throughout, and the height five cubits, *woven of* fine linen thread, and its sockets of bronze.

19 "All the utensils of the tabernacle for all its service, all its pegs, and all the pegs of the court, *shall be* of bronze.

**20** "And [a]you shall command the children of Israel that they bring you pure oil of pressed olives for the light, to cause the lamp to [1]burn continually.

21 "In the tabernacle of meeting, [a]outside the veil which *is* before the Testimony, [b]Aaron and his sons shall tend it from evening until morning before the LORD. [c]*It shall be* a statute forever to their generations on behalf of the children of Israel.

### *How the Priests Were Dressed*

**28** "Now take [a]Aaron your brother, and his sons with him, from among the children of Israel, that he may minister to Me as [b]priest, Aaron *and* Aaron's sons: [c]Nadab, Abihu, [d]Eleazar, and Ithamar.

2 "And [a]you shall make [1]holy garments for Aaron your brother, for glory and for beauty.

3 "So [a]you shall speak to all *who are* gifted artisans, [b]whom I have filled with the spirit of wisdom, that they may make Aaron's garments, to consecrate him, that he may minister to Me as priest.

4 "And these *are* the garments which they shall make: [a]a breastplate, [b]an [1]ephod, [c]a robe, [d]a skillfully woven tunic, a turban, and [e]a sash. So they shall make holy garments for Aaron your brother and his sons, that he may minister to Me as priest.

**5** "They shall take the gold, blue, purple, and scarlet *thread,* and the fine linen,

6 [a]"and they shall make the ephod of gold, blue, purple, *and* scarlet *thread,* and fine woven linen, artistically worked.

7 "It shall have two shoulder straps joined at its two edges, and *so* it shall be joined together.

8 "And the [1]intricately woven band of the ephod, which *is* on it, shall be of the same workmanship, *made of* gold, blue, purple, and scarlet *thread,* and fine woven linen.

9 "Then you shall take two onyx [a]stones and engrave on them the names of the sons of Israel:

10 "six of their names on one stone and six names on the other stone, in order of their [a]birth.

11 "With the work of an [a]engraver in stone, *like* the engravings of a signet, you shall engrave the two stones with the names of the sons of Israel. You shall set them in settings of gold.

12 "And you shall put the two stones on the shoulders of the ephod *as* memorial stones for the sons of Israel. So [a]Aaron shall bear their names before the LORD on his two shoulders [b]as a memorial.

13 "You shall also make settings of gold,

14 "and you shall make two chains of pure gold like braided cords, and fasten the braided chains to the settings.

**15** [a]"You shall make the breastplate of judgment. Artistically woven according to the workmanship of the ephod you shall make it: of gold, blue, purple, and scarlet *thread,* and fine woven linen, you shall make it.

16 "It shall be doubled into a square: a span *shall be* its length, and a span *shall be* its width.

17 [a]"And you shall put settings of stones in it, four rows of stones: *The first* row *shall be* a [1]sardius, a topaz, and an emerald; *this shall be* the first row;

18 "the second row *shall be* a turquoise, a sapphire, and a diamond;

19 "the third row, a [1]jacinth, an agate, and an amethyst;

20 "and the fourth row, a [1]beryl, an [2]onyx, and a jasper. They shall be set in gold settings.

21 "And the stones shall have the names of the sons of Israel, twelve according to their names, *like* the engravings of a signet, each one with its own name; they shall be according to the twelve tribes.

**22** "You shall make chains for the breastplate at the end, like braided cords of pure gold.

23 "And you shall make two rings of gold for the breastplate, and put the two rings on the two ends of the breastplate.

24 "Then you shall put the two braided *chains* of gold in the two rings which are on the ends of the breastplate;

25 "and the *other* two ends of the two braided *chains* you shall fasten to the two settings, and put them on the shoulder straps of the ephod in the front.

**26** "You shall make two rings of gold, and put

---

**8** [a]Ex. 25:40; 26:30; Acts 7:44; [Heb. 8:5]
**9** [a]Ex. 38:9–20
**17** [a]Ex. 38:19
**20** [a]Ex. 35:8, 28; Lev. 24:1–4 [1]Lit. *ascend*
**21** [a]Ex. 26:31, 33 [b]Ex. 30:8; 1 Sam. 3:3; 2 Chr. 13:11 [c]Ex. 28:43; 29:9; Lev. 3:17; 16:34; Num. 18:23; 19:21; 1 Sam. 30:25

CHAPTER 28

**1** [a]Num. 3:10; 18:7 [b]Ps. 99:6; Heb. 5:4 [c]Ex. 24:1, 9; Lev. 10:1 [d]Ex. 6:23; Lev. 10:6, 16
**2** [a]Ex. 29:5, 29; 31:10; 39:1–31; Lev. 8:7–9, 30 [1]*sacred*
**3** [a]Ex. 31:6; 36:1 [b]Ex. 31:3; 35:30, 31; Is. 11:2; Eph. 1:17
**4** [a]Ex. 28:15 [b]Ex. 28:6 [c]Ex. 28:31 [d]Ex. 28:39 [e]Lev. 8:7 [1]Ornamented vest
**6** [a]Ex. 39:2–7; Lev. 8:7
**8** [1]*ingenious work of*
**9** [a]Ex. 35:27
**10** [a]Gen. 29:31—30:24; 35:16–18
**11** [a]Ex. 35:35
**12** [a]Ex. 28:29, 30; 39:6, 7 [b]Lev. 24:7; Num. 31:54; Josh. 4:7; Zech. 6:14; 1 Cor. 11:24
**15** [a]Ex. 39:8–21
**17** [a]Ex. 39:10 [1]Or *ruby*
**19** [1]Or *amber*
**20** [1]Or *yellow jasper* [2]Or *carnelian*

them on the two ends of the breastplate, on the edge of it, which is on the inner side of the ephod.
27 "And two *other* rings of gold you shall make, and put them on the two shoulder straps, underneath the ephod toward its front, right at the seam above the [1]intricately woven band of the ephod.
28 "They shall bind the breastplate by means of its rings to the rings of the ephod, using a blue cord, so that it is above the intricately woven band of the ephod, and so that the breastplate does not come loose from the ephod.
29 "So Aaron shall [a]bear the names of the sons of Israel on the breastplate of judgment over his heart, when he goes into the holy *place,* as a memorial before the LORD continually.
30 "And [a]you shall put in the breastplate of judgment the [1]Urim and the Thummim, and they shall be over Aaron's heart when he goes in before the LORD. So Aaron shall bear the judgment of the children of Israel over his heart before the LORD continually.
**31** [a]"You shall make the robe of the ephod all of blue.
32 "There shall be an opening for his head in the middle of it; it shall have a woven binding all around its opening, like the opening in a coat of mail, so that it does not tear.
**33** "And upon its hem you shall make pomegranates of blue, purple, and scarlet, all around its hem, and bells of gold between them all around:
34 "a golden bell and a pomegranate, a golden bell and a pomegranate, upon the hem of the robe all around.
35 "And it shall be upon Aaron when he ministers, and its sound will be heard when he goes into the holy *place* before the LORD and when he comes out, that he may not die.
**36** [a]"You shall also make a plate of pure gold and engrave on it, *like* the engraving of a signet:

HOLINESS TO THE LORD.

37 "And you shall put it on a blue cord, that it may be on the turban; it shall be on the front of the turban.
38 "So it shall be on Aaron's forehead, that Aaron may [a]bear the iniquity of the holy things which the children of Israel hallow in all their [1]holy gifts; and it shall always be on his forehead, that they may be [b]accepted before the LORD.
**39** "You shall [a]skillfully weave the tunic of fine linen *thread,* you shall make the turban of fine linen, and you shall make the sash of woven work.
**40** [a]"For Aaron's sons you shall make tunics, and you shall make sashes for them. And you shall make [1]hats for them, for glory and [b]beauty.
41 "So you shall put them on Aaron your brother and on his sons with him. You shall [a]anoint them, [b]consecrate them, and [1]sanctify them, that they may minister to Me as priests.
42 "And you shall make [a]for them linen trousers to cover their [1]nakedness; they shall [2]reach from the waist to the thighs.
43 "They shall be on Aaron and on his sons when they come into the tabernacle of meeting, or when they come near [a]the altar to minister in the holy *place,* that they [b]do not incur [1]iniquity and die. [c]*It shall be* a statute forever to him and his descendants after him.

*How the Sacrifices Were Made*

**29** "And this is what you shall do to them to hallow them for ministering to Me as priests: [a]Take one young bull and two rams without blemish,
2 "and [a]unleavened bread, unleavened cakes mixed with oil, and unleavened wafers anointed with oil (you shall make them of wheat flour).
3 "You shall put them in one basket and bring them in the basket, with the bull and the two rams.
4 "And Aaron and his sons you shall bring to the door of the tabernacle of meeting, [a]and you shall wash them with water.
5 [a]"Then you shall take the garments, put the tunic on Aaron, and the robe of the ephod, the ephod, and the breastplate, and gird him with [b]the intricately woven band of the ephod.
6 [a]"You shall put the turban on his head, and put the holy crown on the turban.
7 "And you shall take the anointing [a]oil, pour *it* on his head, and anoint him.
8 "Then [a]you shall bring his sons and put tunics on them.
9 "And you shall gird them with sashes, Aaron and his sons, and put the hats on them. [a]The priesthood shall be theirs for a perpetual statute. So you shall [b]consecrate Aaron and his sons.
**10** "You shall also have the bull brought before the tabernacle of meeting, and [a]Aaron and his sons shall put their hands on the head of the bull.
11 "Then you shall kill the bull before the LORD, *by* the door of the tabernacle of meeting.
12 "You shall take *some* of the blood of the bull and put *it* on [a]the horns of the altar with your finger, and [b]pour all the blood beside the base of the altar.
13 "And [a]you shall take all the fat that covers the entrails, the fatty lobe *attached* to the liver, and the two kidneys and the fat that *is* on them, and burn *them* on the altar.
14 "But [a]the flesh of the bull, with its skin and its offal, you shall burn with fire outside the camp. It *is* a sin offering.
**15** [a]"You shall also take one ram, and Aaron and his sons shall [b]put their hands on the head of the ram;
16 "and you shall kill the ram, and you shall take its blood and [a]sprinkle *it* all around on the altar.
17 "Then you shall cut the ram in pieces, wash its entrails and its legs, and put *them* with its pieces and with its head.
18 "And you shall burn the whole ram on the altar. It *is* a [a]burnt offering to the LORD; it *is* a sweet aroma, an offering made by fire to the LORD.
**19** [a]"You shall also take the other ram, and Aaron and his sons shall put their hands on the head of the ram.
20 "Then you shall kill the ram, and take some of its blood and put *it* on the tip of the right ear of Aaron and on the tip of the right ear of his sons, on the thumb of their right hand and on the big toe of their right foot, and sprinkle the blood all around on the altar.
21 "And you shall take some of the blood that is on the altar, and some of [a]the anointing oil, and sprinkle *it* on Aaron and on his garments, on his sons and on the garments of his sons with him;

**27** [1]*ingenious work of* **29** [a]Ex. 28:12 **30** [a]Lev. 8:8; Num. 27:21; Deut. 33:8; 1 Sam. 28:6; Ezra 2:63; Neh. 7:65 [1]Lit. *Lights and the Perfections* **31** [a]Ex. 39:22–26 **36** [a]Ex. 39:30, 31; Lev. 8:9; Zech. 14:20 **38** [a]Ex. 28:43; Lev. 10:17; 22:9, 16; Num. 18:1; [Is. 53:11]; Ezek. 4:4–6; [John 1:29; Heb. 9:28; 1 Pet. 2:24] [b]Lev. 1:4; 22:27; 23:11; Is. 56:7 [1]*sacred* **39** [a]Ex. 35:35; 39:27–29 **40** [a]Ex. 28:4; 39:27–29, 41; Ezek. 44:17, 18 [b]Ex. 28:2 [1]*headgear* or *turbans* **41** [a]Ex. 29:7–9; 30:30; 40:15; Lev. 10:7 [b]Ex. 29:9; Lev. 8; Heb. 7:28 [1]*set them apart* **42** [a]Ex. 39:28; Lev. 6:10; 16:4; Ezek. 44:18 [1]*bare flesh* [2]Lit. *be* **43** [a]Ex. 20:26 [b]Lev. 5:1, 17; 20:19, 20; 22:9; Num. 9:13; 18:22 [c]Ex. 27:21; Lev. 17:7 [1]*guilt*

CHAPTER 29

**1** [a]Lev. 8; [Heb. 7:26–28] **2** [a]Lev. 2:4; 6:19–23 **4** [a]Ex. 40:12; Lev. 8:6; [Heb. 10:22] **5** [a]Ex. 28:2; Lev. 8:7 [b]Ex. 28:8 **6** [a]Ex. 28:36, 37; Lev. 8:9 **7** [a]Ex. 25:6; 30:25–31; Lev. 8:12; 10:7; 21:10; Num. 35:25; Ps. 133:2 **8** [a]Ex. 28:39, 40; Lev. 8:13 **9** [a]Ex. 40:15; Num. 3:10; 18:7; 25:13; Deut. 18:5 [b]Ex. 28:41; Lev. 8 **10** [a]Lev. 1:4; 8:14 **12** [a]Lev. 8:15 [b]Ex. 27:2; 30:2; Lev. 4:7 **13** [a]Lev. 1:8; 3:3, 4 **14** [a]Lev. 4:11, 12, 21; Heb. 13:11 **15** [a]Lev. 8:18 [b]Lev. 1:4–9 **16** [a]Ex. 24:6; Lev. 1:5, 11 **18** [a]Ex. 20:24 **19** [a]Lev. 8:22 **21** [a]Ex. 30:25, 31

and [b]he and his garments shall be hallowed, and his sons and his sons' garments with him.
22 "Also you shall take the fat of the ram, the fat tail, the fat that covers the entrails, the fatty lobe *attached to* the liver, the two kidneys and the fat on them, the right thigh (for it *is* a ram of consecration),
23 [a]"one loaf of bread, one cake *made with* oil, and one wafer from the basket of the unleavened bread that *is* before the LORD;
24 "and you shall put all these in the hands of Aaron and in the hands of his sons, and you shall [a]wave them *as* a wave offering before the LORD.
25 [a]"You shall receive them back from their hands and burn *them* on the altar as a burnt offering, as a sweet aroma before the LORD. It *is* an offering made by fire to the LORD.
26 "Then you shall take [a]the breast of the ram of Aaron's consecration and wave it *as* a wave offering before the LORD; and it shall be your portion.
27 "And from the ram of the consecration you shall consecrate [a]the breast of the wave offering which is waved, and the thigh of the heave offering which is raised, of *that* which *is* for Aaron and of *that* which is for his sons.
28 "It shall be from the children of Israel *for* Aaron and his sons [a]by a statute forever. For it is a heave offering; [b]it shall be a heave offering from the children of Israel from the sacrifices of their peace offerings, *that is,* their heave offering to the LORD.
**29** "And the [a]holy garments of Aaron [b]shall be his sons' after him, [c]to be anointed in them and to be consecrated in them.
30 [a]"That son who becomes priest in his place shall put them on for [b]seven days, when he enters the tabernacle of meeting to minister in the [1]holy *place.*
**31** "And you shall take the ram of the consecration and [a]boil its flesh in the holy place.
32 "Then Aaron and his sons shall eat the flesh of the ram, and the [a]bread that *is* in the basket, *by* the door of the tabernacle of meeting.
33 [a]"They shall eat those things with which the atonement was made, to consecrate *and* to sanctify them; [b]but an outsider shall not eat *them,* because they *are* holy.
34 "And if any of the flesh of the consecration offerings, or of the bread, remains until the morning, then [a]you shall burn the remainder with fire. It shall not be eaten, because it *is* holy.
**35** "Thus you shall do to Aaron and his sons, according to all that I have commanded you. [a]Seven days you shall consecrate them.
36 "And you [a]shall offer a bull every day *as* a sin offering for atonement. [b]You shall cleanse the altar when you make atonement for it, and you shall anoint it to sanctify it.
37 "Seven days you shall make atonement for the altar and sanctify it. And the altar shall be most holy. [a]Whatever touches the altar must be holy.
**38** "Now this *is* what you shall offer on the altar: [a]two lambs of the first year, [b]day by day continually.
39 "One lamb you shall offer [a]in the morning, and the other lamb you shall offer [1]at twilight.
40 "With the one lamb shall be one-tenth *of an ephah* of flour mixed with one-fourth of a hin of pressed oil, and one-fourth of a hin of wine *as* a drink offering.
41 "And the other lamb you shall [a]offer [1]at twilight; and you shall offer with it the grain offering and the drink offering, as in the morning, for a sweet aroma, an offering made by fire to the LORD.
42 "*This shall be* [a]a continual burnt offering throughout your generations *at* the door of the tabernacle of meeting before the LORD, [b]where I will meet you to speak with you.
43 "And there I will meet with the children of Israel, and *the tabernacle* [a]shall be sanctified by My glory.
44 "So I will consecrate the tabernacle of meeting and the altar. I will also [a]consecrate both Aaron and his sons to minister to Me as priests.
45 [a]"I will dwell among the children of Israel and will [b]be their God.
46 "And they shall know that [a]I *am* the LORD their God, who [b]brought them up out of the land of Egypt, that I may dwell among them. I *am* the LORD their God.

### *The Altar of Incense*

**30** "You shall make [a]an altar to burn incense on; you shall make it of acacia wood.
2 "A cubit *shall be* its length and a cubit its width—it shall be square—and two cubits *shall be* its height. Its horns *shall be* of one piece with it.
3 "And you shall overlay its top, its sides all around, and its horns with pure gold; and you shall make for it a [1]molding of gold all around.
4 "Two gold rings you shall make for it, under the molding on both its sides. You shall place *them* on its two sides, and they will be holders for the poles with which to bear it.
5 "You shall make the poles of acacia wood, and overlay them with gold.
6 "And you shall put it before the [a]veil that *is* before the ark of the Testimony, before the [b]mercy seat that *is* over the Testimony, where I will meet with you.
7 "Aaron shall burn on it [a]sweet incense every morning; when [b]he tends the lamps, he shall burn incense on it.
8 "And when Aaron lights the lamps [1]at twilight, he shall burn incense on it, a perpetual incense before the LORD throughout your generations.
9 "You shall not offer [a]strange incense on it, or a burnt offering, or a grain offering; nor shall you pour a drink offering on it.
10 "And [a]Aaron shall make atonement upon its horns once a year with the blood of the sin offering of atonement; once a year he shall make atonement upon it throughout your generations. It *is* most holy to the LORD."
**11** Then the LORD spoke to Moses, saying:
12 [a]"When you take the census of the children of Israel for their number, then every man shall give [b]a[1] ransom for himself to the LORD, when you number them, that there may be no [c]plague among them when *you* number them.
13 [a]"This is what everyone among those who are numbered shall give: half a shekel according to the shekel of the sanctuary [b](a shekel *is* twenty gerahs). [c]The half-shekel *shall be* an offering to the LORD.
14 "Everyone included among those who are numbered, from twenty years old and above, shall give an [1]offering to the LORD.
15 "The [a]rich shall not give more and the poor shall not give less than half a shekel, when *you*

21 [b][Heb. 9:22]
23 [a]Lev. 8:26
24 [a]Lev. 7:30; 10:14
25 [a]Lev. 8:28
26 [a]Lev. 7:31, 34; 8:29
27 [a]Num. 18:11, 18
28 [a]Lev. 10:15 [b]Lev. 3:1; 7:34
29 [a]Ex. 28:2 [b]Num. 20:26, 28 [c]Num. 18:8
30 [a]Num. 20:28 [b]Lev. 8:35 [1]*sanctuary*
31 [a]Lev. 8:31
32 [a]Matt. 12:4
33 [a]Lev. 10:14, 15, 17 [b]Lev. 22:10
34 [a]Lev. 7:18; 8:32
35 [a]Lev. 8:33–35
36 [a]Heb. 10:11 [b]Ex. 30:26–29; 40:10, 11
37 [a]Num. 4:15; Hag. 2:11–13; Matt. 23:19
38 [a]Num. 28:3–31; 29:6–38 [b]Dan. 12:11
39 [a]Ezek. 46:13–15 [1]Lit. *between the two evenings*
41 [a]2 Kin. 16:15 [1]Lit. *between the two evenings*
42 [a]Ex. 30:8 [b]Ex. 25:22; 33:7, 9
43 [a]1 Kin. 8:11
44 [a]Lev. 21:15
45 [a][Rev. 21:3] [b]Gen. 17:8
46 [a]Ex. 16:12; 20:2 [b]Lev. 11:45

CHAPTER 30
1 [a]Ex. 37:25–29
3 [1]*border*
6 [a]Ex. 26:31–35 [b]Ex. 25:21, 22
7 [a]1 Sam. 2:28 [b]Ex. 27:20, 21
8 [1]Lit. *between the two evenings*
9 [a]Lev. 10:1
10 [a]Lev. 16:3–34
12 [a]Num. 1:2; 26:2 [b][1 Pet. 1:18, 19] [c]2 Sam. 24:15 [1]*the price of a life*
13 [a]Matt. 17:24 [b]Num. 3:47 [c]Ex. 38:26
14 [1]*contribution*
15 [a][Eph. 6:9]

give an offering to the LORD, to make atonement
for yourselves.
16 "And you shall take the atonement money of
the children of Israel, and [a]shall [1]appoint it for the
service of the tabernacle of meeting, that it may
be [b]a memorial for the children of Israel before the
LORD, to make atonement for yourselves."
17 Then the LORD spoke to Moses, saying:
18 [a]"You shall also make a [1]laver of bronze, with
its base also of bronze, for washing. You shall [b]put
it between the tabernacle of meeting and the
altar. And you shall put water in it,
19 "for Aaron and his sons [a]shall wash their
hands and their feet in water from it.
20 "When they go into the tabernacle of meeting,
or when they come near the altar to minister, to
burn an offering made by fire to the LORD, they
shall wash with water, lest they die.
21 "So they shall wash their hands and their feet,
lest they die. And [a]it shall be a [1]statute forever to
them—to him and his descendants throughout
their generations."
22 Moreover the LORD spoke to Moses, saying:
23 "Also take for yourself [a]quality spices—five
hundred *shekels* of liquid [b]myrrh, half as much
sweet-smelling cinnamon (two hundred and fifty
*shekels*), two hundred and fifty *shekels* of sweet-
smelling [c]cane,
24 "five hundred *shekels* of [a]cassia, according to
the shekel of the sanctuary, and a [b]hin of olive oil.
25 "And you shall make from these a holy anointing oil, an ointment compounded according to the
art of the perfumer. It shall be [a]a holy anointing
oil.
26 [a]"With it you shall anoint the tabernacle of
meeting and the ark of the Testimony;
27 "the table and all its utensils, the lampstand
and its utensils, and the altar of incense;
28 "the altar of burnt offering with all its utensils,
and the laver and its base.
29 "You shall consecrate them, that they may be
most holy; [a]whatever touches them must be holy.
30 [a]"And you shall anoint Aaron and his sons,
and consecrate them, that *they* may minister to
Me as priests.
31 "And you shall speak to the children of Israel,
saying: 'This shall be a holy anointing oil to Me
throughout your generations.
32 'It shall not be poured on man's flesh; nor shall
you make *any other* like it, according to its
composition. [a]It *is* holy, *and* it shall be holy to you.
33 [a]'Whoever [1]compounds *any* like it, or whoever
puts *any* of it on an outsider, [b]shall be [2]cut off
from his people.' "
34 And the LORD said to Moses: [a]"Take sweet
spices, stacte and onycha and galbanum, and pure
frankincense with *these* sweet spices; there shall
be equal amounts of each.
35 "You shall make of these an incense, a com-
pound [a]according to the art of the perfumer,
salted, pure, *and* holy.
36 "And you shall beat *some* of it very fine, and
put some of it before the Testimony in the tabernacle of meeting [a]where I will meet with you. [b]It
shall be most holy to you.
37 "But *as for* the incense which you shall make,
[a]you shall not make any for yourselves, according
to its [1]composition. It shall be to you holy for the
LORD.
38 [a]"Whoever makes *any* like it, to smell it, he
shall be cut off from his people."

### *The Sabbath as a Sign*

31 Then the LORD spoke to Moses, saying:
2 [a]"See, I have called by name Bezalel the
[b]son of Uri, the son of Hur, of the tribe of Judah.
3 "And I have [a]filled him with the Spirit of God,
in wisdom, in understanding, in knowledge, and in
all *kinds of* workmanship,
4 "to design artistic works, to work in gold, in
silver, in bronze,
5 "in cutting jewels for setting, in carving wood,
and to work in all *kinds of* workmanship.
6 "And I, indeed I, have appointed with him
[a]Aholiab the son of Ahisamach, of the tribe of
Dan; and I have put wisdom in the hearts of all
the [b]gifted artisans, that they may make all that I
have commanded you:
7 [a]"the tabernacle of meeting, [b]the ark of the
Testimony and [c]the mercy seat that *is* on it, and
all the furniture of the tabernacle—
8 [a]"the table and its utensils, [b]the pure *gold*
lampstand with all its utensils, the altar of incense,
9 [a]"the altar of burnt offering with all its utensils, and [b]the laver and its base—
10 [a]"the [1]garments of ministry, the holy garments
for Aaron the priest and the garments of his sons,
to minister as priests,
11 [a]"and the anointing oil and [b]sweet incense for
the holy *place*. According to all that I have commanded you they shall do."
12 And the LORD spoke to Moses, saying,
13 "Speak also to the children of Israel, saying:
[a]'Surely My Sabbaths you shall keep, for it *is* a
sign between Me and you throughout your generations, that *you* may know that I *am* the LORD
who [b]sanctifies[1] you.
14 [a]'You shall keep the Sabbath, therefore, for *it*
*is* holy to you. Everyone who [1]profanes it shall
surely be put to death; for [b]whoever does *any*
work on it, that person shall be cut off from
among his people.
15 'Work shall be done for [a]six days, but the
[b]seventh *is* the Sabbath of rest, holy to the LORD.
Whoever does *any* work on the Sabbath day, he
shall surely be put to death.
16 'Therefore the children of Israel shall keep the
Sabbath, to observe the Sabbath throughout their
generations *as* a perpetual covenant.
17 'It *is* [a]a sign between Me and the children of
Israel forever; for [b]*in* six days the LORD made the
heavens and the earth, and on the seventh day He
rested and was refreshed.' "
18 And when He had made an end of speaking
with him on Mount Sinai, He gave Moses [a]two
tablets of the Testimony, tablets of stone, written
with the finger of God.

### *The Golden Calf*

32 Now when the people saw that Moses [a]de-
layed coming down from the mountain, the
people [b]gathered together to Aaron, and said to
him, [c]"Come, make us [1]gods that shall [d]go before
us; for *as for* this Moses, the man who [e]brought us
up out of the land of Egypt, we do not know what
has become of him."
2 And Aaron said to them, "Break off the
[a]golden earrings which *are* in the ears of your

16 [a]Ex. 38:25–31 [b]Num. 16:40 [1]*give*
18 [a]Ex. 38:8 [b]Ex. 40:30 [1]*basin*
19 [a]Ex. 40:31, 32
21 [a]Ex. 28:43 [1]*requirement*
23 [a]Ezek. 27:22 [b]Prov. 7:17 [c]Song 4:14
24 [a]Ps. 45:8 [b]Ex. 29:40
25 [a]Ex. 37:29; 40:9
26 [a]Lev. 8:10
29 [a]Ex. 29:37; Num. 4:15; Hag. 2:11–13
30 [a]Lev. 8:12
32 [a]Ex. 30:25, 37
33 [a]Ex. 30:38 [b]Gen. 17:14 [1]*mixes* [2]Put to death
34 [a]Ex. 25:6; 37:29
35 [a]Ex. 30:25
36 [a]Ex. 29:42 [b]Lev. 2:3
37 [a]Ex. 30:32 [1]Lit. *proportion*
38 [a]Ex. 30:33

CHAPTER 31
2 [a]Ex. 35:30—36:1 [b]1 Chr. 2:20
3 [a]1 Kin. 7:14
6 [a]Ex. 35:34 [b]Ex. 28:3; 35:10, 35; 36:1
7 [a]Ex. 36:8 [b]Ex. 37:1–5 [c]Ex. 37:6–9
8 [a]Ex. 37:10–16 [b]Ex. 37:17–24
9 [a]Ex. 38:1–7 [b]Ex. 38:8
10 [a]Ex. 39:1, 41 [1]Or *woven garments*
11 [a]Ex. 30:23–33 [b]Ex. 30:34–38
13 [a]Ezek. 20:12, 20 [b]Lev. 20:8 [1]*consecrates*
14 [a]Ex. 20:8 [b]Num. 15:32–36 [1]*defiles*
15 [a]Ex. 20:9–11 [b]Gen. 2:2
17 [a]Ex. 31:13 [b]Gen. 1:31; 2:2, 3
18 [a][Ex. 24:12; 32:15, 16]

CHAPTER 32
1 [a]Ex. 24:18; Deut. 9:9–12 [b]Ex. 17:1–3 [c]Acts 7:40 [d]Ex. 13:21 [e]Ex. 32:8 [1]Or *a god*
2 [a]Ex. 11:2; 35:22

wives, your sons, and your daughters, and bring
*them* to me."
3 So all the people broke off the golden earrings
which *were* in their ears, and brought *them* to
Aaron.
4 [a]And he received *the gold* from their hand, and
he fashioned it with an engraving tool, and made
a molded calf. Then they said, "This *is* your god, O
Israel, that [b]brought you out of the land of
Egypt!"
5 So when Aaron saw *it,* he built an altar before
it. And Aaron made a [a]proclamation and said,
"Tomorrow *is* a feast to the LORD."
6 Then they rose early on the next day, offered
burnt offerings, and brought peace offerings; and
the people [a]sat down to eat and drink, and rose up
to play.
**7** And the LORD said to Moses, [a]"Go, get down!
For your people whom you brought out of the
land of Egypt [b]have corrupted *themselves.*
8 "They have turned aside quickly out of the
way which [a]I commanded them. They have made
themselves a molded calf, and worshiped it and
sacrificed to it, and said, [b]'This *is* your god, O
Israel, that brought you out of the land of
Egypt!' "
9 And the LORD said to Moses, [a]"I have seen this
people, and indeed it *is* a [1]stiff-necked people!
10 "Now therefore, [a]let Me alone, that [b]My wrath
may burn hot against them and I may [1]consume
them. And [c]I will make of you a great nation."
**11** [a]Then Moses pleaded with [1]the LORD his God,
and said: "LORD, why does Your wrath burn hot
against Your people whom You have brought out
of the land of Egypt with great power and with a
mighty hand?
12 [a]"Why should the Egyptians speak, and say,
'He brought them out to harm them, to kill them
in the mountains, and to consume them from the
face of the earth'? Turn from Your fierce wrath,
and [b]relent from this harm to Your people.
13 "Remember Abraham, Isaac, and Israel, Your
servants, to whom You [a]swore by Your own self,
and said to them, [b]'I will multiply your descendants as the stars of heaven; and all this land that
I have spoken of I give to your descendants, and
they shall inherit *it* forever.' "
14 So the LORD [a]relented from the harm which
He said He would do to His people.
**15** And [a]Moses turned and went down from the
mountain, and the two tablets of the Testimony
*were* in his hand. The tablets *were* written on both
sides; on the one *side* and on the other they were
written.
16 Now the [a]tablets *were* the work of God, and
the writing *was* the writing of God engraved on
the tablets.
17 And when Joshua heard the noise of the
people as they shouted, he said to Moses, "*There
is* a noise of war in the camp."
18 But he said:

"*It is* not the noise of the shout of victory,
Nor the noise of the cry of defeat,
*But* the sound of singing I hear."

**19** So it was, as soon as he came near the camp,
that [a]he saw the calf *and* the dancing. So Moses'
anger became hot, and he cast the tablets out of
his hands and broke them at the foot of the
mountain.
20 [a]Then he took the calf which they had made,
burned *it* in the fire, and ground *it* to powder; and
he scattered *it* on the water and made the children
of Israel drink *it.*
21 And Moses said to Aaron, [a]"What did this
people do to you that you have brought *so* great a
sin upon them?"
22 So Aaron said, "Do not let the anger of my
lord become hot. [a]You know the people, that they
*are set* on evil.
23 "For they said to me, 'Make us gods that shall
go before us; *as for* this Moses, the man who
brought us out of the land of Egypt, we do not
know what has become of him.'
24 "And I said to them, 'Whoever has any gold,
let them break *it* off.' So they gave *it* to me, and I
cast it into the fire, and this calf came out."
**25** Now when Moses saw that the people *were*
[a]unrestrained (for Aaron [b]had not restrained
them, to *their* shame among their enemies),
26 then Moses stood in the entrance of the camp,
and said, "Whoever *is* on the LORD's side—*come*
to me!" And all the sons of Levi gathered themselves together to him.
27 And he said to them, "Thus says the LORD God
of Israel: 'Let every man put his sword on his side,
and go in and out from entrance to entrance
throughout the camp, and [a]let every man kill his
brother, every man his companion, and every man
his neighbor.' "
28 So the sons of Levi did according to the word
of Moses. And about three thousand men of the
people fell that day.
29 [a]Then Moses said, [1]"Consecrate yourselves
today to the LORD, that He may bestow on you a
blessing this day, for every man has opposed his
son and his brother."
**30** Now it came to pass on the next day that
Moses said to the people, [a]"You have committed a
great sin. So now I will go up to the LORD;
[b]perhaps I can [c]make atonement for your sin."
31 Then Moses [a]returned to the LORD and said,
"Oh, these people have committed a great sin, and
have [b]made for themselves a god of gold!
32 "Yet now, if You will forgive their sin—but if
not, I pray, [a]blot me [b]out of Your book which You
have written."
33 And the LORD said to Moses, [a]"Whoever has
sinned against Me, I will [b]blot him out of My book.
34 "Now therefore, go, lead the people to *the
place* of which I have [a]spoken to you. [b]Behold, My
Angel shall go before you. Nevertheless, [c]in the
day when I [d]visit for punishment, I will visit
punishment upon them for their sin."
**35** So the LORD plagued the people because of
[a]what they did with the calf which Aaron made.

### *Moses Prays for God's Presence*

**33** Then the LORD said to Moses, "Depart *and*
go up from here, you [a]and the people whom
you have brought out of the land of Egypt, to the
land of which I swore to Abraham, Isaac, and
Jacob, saying, [b]'To your descendants I will give it.'
2 [a]"And I will send *My* Angel before you, [b]and I
will drive out the Canaanite and the Amorite and
the Hittite and the Perizzite and the Hivite and
the Jebusite.
3 "*Go up* [a]to a land flowing with milk and
honey; for I will not go up in your midst, lest [b]I
[1]consume you on the way, for you *are* a [c]stiff-
necked[2] people."

---

4 [a]Ex. 20:3, 4, 23 [b]Ex. 29:45, 46
5 [a]2 Kin. 10:20
6 [a]Num. 25:2
7 [a]Deut. 9:8–21 [b]Gen. 6:11, 12
8 [a]Ex. 20:3, 4, 23 [b]1 Kin. 12:28
9 [a][Acts 7:51] [1]*stubborn*
10 [a]Deut. 9:14, 19 [b]Ex. 22:24 [c]Num. 14:12 [1]*destroy*
11 [a]Deut. 9:18, 26–29 [1]Lit. *the face of the LORD*
12 [a]Num. 14:13–19 [b]Ex. 32:14
13 [a][Heb. 6:13] [b]Gen. 12:7; 13:15; 15:7, 18; 22:17; 26:4; 35:11, 12
14 [a]2 Sam. 24:16
15 [a]Deut. 9:15
16 [a]Ex. 31:18
19 [a]Deut. 9:16, 17
20 [a]Deut. 9:21
21 [a]Gen. 26:10
22 [a]Deut. 9:24
25 [a]Ex. 33:4, 5 [b]2 Chr. 28:19
27 [a]Num. 25:5–13
29 [a]Ex. 28:41 [1]Lit. *Fill your hand*
30 [a]1 Sam. 12:20, 23 [b]2 Sam. 16:12 [c]Num. 25:13
31 [a]Deut. 9:18 [b]Ex. 20:23
32 [a]Ps. 69:28 [b]Dan. 12:1
33 [a][Ezek. 18:4; 33:2, 14, 15] [b]Ex. 17:14
34 [a]Ex. 3:17 [b]Ex. 23:20 [c]Deut. 32:35 [d]Ps. 89:32
35 [a]Neh. 9:18

CHAPTER 33
1 [a]Ex. 32:1, 7, 13 [b]Gen. 12:7
2 [a]Ex. 32:34 [b]Josh. 24:11
3 [a]Ex. 3:8 [b]Num. 16:21, 45 [c]Ex. 32:9; 33:5 [1]*destroy* [2]*stubborn*

4 And when the people heard this bad news,
[a]they mourned, [b]and no one put on his ornaments.
5 For the LORD had said to Moses, "Say to the
children of Israel, 'You *are* a stiff-necked people. I
could come up into your midst in one moment and
consume you. Now therefore, take off your [1]orna-
ments, that I may [a]know what to do to you.' "
6 So the children of Israel stripped themselves
of their ornaments by Mount Horeb.
7 Moses took his tent and pitched it outside the
camp, far from the camp, and [a]called it the tabernacle of meeting. And it came to pass *that* everyone who [b]sought the LORD went out to the tabernacle of meeting which *was* outside the camp.
8 So it was, whenever Moses went out to the
tabernacle, *that* all the people rose, and each man
stood [a]*at* his tent door and watched Moses until
he had gone into the tabernacle.
9 And it came to pass, when Moses entered the
tabernacle, that the pillar of cloud descended and
stood *at* the door of the tabernacle, and [1]*the LORD*
[a]talked with Moses.
10 All the people saw the pillar of cloud standing
*at* the tabernacle door, and all the people rose and
[a]worshiped, each man *in* his tent door.
11 So [a]the LORD spoke to Moses face to face, as a
man speaks to his friend. And he would return to
the camp, but [b]his servant Joshua the son of Nun,
a young man, did not depart from the tabernacle.
12 Then Moses said to the LORD, "See, [a]You say
to me, 'Bring up this people.' But You have not let
me know whom You will send with me. Yet You
have said, [b]'I know you by name, and you have
also found grace in My sight.'
13 "Now therefore, I pray, [a]if I have found grace
in Your sight, [b]show me now Your way, that I
may know You and that I may find grace in Your
sight. And consider that this nation *is* [c]Your
people."
14 And He said, [a]"My Presence will go *with you*,
and I will give you [b]rest."
15 Then he said to Him, [a]"If Your Presence does
not go *with us*, do not bring us up from here.
16 "For how then will it be known that Your
people and I have found grace in Your sight,
[a]except You go with us? So we [b]shall be separate,
Your people and I, from all the people who *are*
upon the face of the earth."
17 So the LORD said to Moses, [a]"I will also do this
thing that you have spoken; for you have found
grace in My sight, and I know you by name."
18 And he said, "Please, show me [a]Your glory."
19 Then He said, "I will make all My [a]goodness
pass before you, and I will proclaim the name of
the LORD before you. [b]I will be gracious to whom I
will be [c]gracious, and I will have compassion on
whom I will have compassion."
20 But He said, "You cannot see My face; for [a]no
man shall see Me, and live."
21 And the LORD said, "Here is a place by Me, and
you shall stand on the rock.
22 "So it shall be, while My glory passes by, that
I will put you [a]in the cleft of the rock, and will
[b]cover you with My hand while I pass by.
23 "Then I will take away My hand, and you shall
see My back; but My face shall [a]not be seen."

### *How the Law Was Recorded*

**34** And the LORD said to Moses, [a]"Cut two
tablets of stone like the first *ones*, and [b]I will
write on *these* tablets the words that were on the
first tablets which you broke.
2 "So be ready in the morning, and come up in
the morning to Mount Sinai, and present yourself
to Me there [a]on the top of the mountain.
3 "And no man shall [a]come up with you, and let
no man be seen throughout all the mountain; let
neither flocks nor herds feed before that mountain."
4 So he cut two tablets of stone like the first
*ones*. Then Moses rose early in the morning and
went up Mount Sinai, as the LORD had commanded him; and he took in his hand the two
tablets of stone.
5 Now the LORD descended in the [a]cloud and
stood with him there, and [b]proclaimed the name
of the LORD.
6 And the LORD passed before him and proclaimed, "The LORD, the LORD [a]God, merciful and
gracious, longsuffering, and abounding in [b]good-
ness and [c]truth,
7 [a]"keeping mercy for thousands, [b]forgiving
iniquity and transgression and sin, [c]by no means
clearing *the guilty*, visiting the iniquity of the
fathers upon the children and the children's children to the third and the fourth generation."
8 So Moses made haste and [a]bowed his head
toward the earth, and worshiped.
9 Then he said, "If now I have found grace in
Your sight, O Lord, [a]let my Lord, I pray, go among
us, even though we *are* a [b]stiff-necked[1] people;
and pardon our iniquity and our sin, and take us
as [c]Your inheritance."
10 And He said: "Behold, [a]I make a covenant.
Before all your people I will [b]do [1]marvels such as
have not been done in all the earth, nor in any
nation; and all the people among whom you *are*
shall see the work of the LORD. For it *is* [c]an
awesome thing that I will do with you.
11 [a]"Observe what I command you this day.
Behold, [b]I am driving out from before you the
Amorite and the Canaanite and the Hittite and
the Perizzite and the Hivite and the Jebusite.
12 [a]"Take heed to yourself, lest you make a
covenant with the inhabitants of the land where
you are going, lest it be a snare in your midst.
13 "But you shall [a]destroy their altars, break their
*sacred* pillars, and [b]cut down their wooden images
14 "(for you shall worship [a]no other god, for the
LORD, whose [b]name *is* Jealous, *is* a [c]jealous God),
15 "lest you make a covenant with the inhabitants of the land, and they [a]play the harlot with
their gods and make sacrifice to their gods, and
*one of them* [b]invites you and you [c]eat of his
sacrifice,
16 "and you take of [a]his daughters for your sons,
and his daughters [b]play the harlot with their gods
and make your sons play the harlot with their
gods.
17 [a]"You shall make no molded gods for yourselves.
18 "The Feast of [a]Unleavened Bread you shall
keep. Seven days you shall eat unleavened bread,
as I commanded you, in the appointed time of the

4 [a]Num. 14:1, 39 [b]Ezra 9:3
5 [a][Ps. 139:23] [1]*jewelry*
7 [a]Ex. 29:42, 43 [b]Deut. 4:29
8 [a]Num. 16:27
9 [a]Ps. 99:7 [1]Lit. *He*
10 [a]Ex. 4:31
11 [a]Num. 12:8 [b]Ex. 24:13
12 [a]Ex. 3:10; 32:34 [b]Ex. 33:17
13 [a]Ex. 34:9 [b]Ps. 25:4; 27:11; 86:11; 119:33 [c]Deut. 9:26, 29
14 [a]Is. 63:9 [b]Josh. 21:44; 22:4
15 [a]Ex. 33:3
16 [a]Num. 14:14 [b]Ex. 34:10
17 [a][James 5:16]
18 [a][1 Tim. 6:16]
19 [a]Ex. 34:6, 7 [b][Rom. 9:15, 16, 18] [c][Rom. 4:4, 16]
20 [a][Gen. 32:30]
22 [a]Is. 2:21 [b]Ps. 91:1, 4
23 [a][John 1:18]

CHAPTER 34

1 [a][Ex. 24:12; 31:18; 32:15, 16, 19] [b]Deut. 10:2, 4
2 [a]Ex. 19:11, 18, 20
3 [a]Ex. 19:12, 13; 24:9–11
5 [a]Ex. 19:9 [b]Ex. 33:19
6 [a]Neh. 9:17 [b]Rom. 2:4 [c]Ps. 108:4
7 [a]Ex. 20:6 [b]Ps. 103:3, 4 [c]Job 10:14
8 [a]Ex. 4:31
9 [a]Ex. 33:12–16 [b]Ex. 33:3 [c]Ps. 33:12; 94:14 [1]*stubborn*
10 [a]Deut. 5:2 [b]Ps. 77:14 [c]Ps. 145:6 [1]*wonderful acts*
11 [a]Deut. 6:25 [b]Ex. 23:20–33; 33:2
12 [a]Ex. 23:32, 33
13 [a]Deut. 12:3 [b]2 Kin. 18:4
14 [a][Ex. 20:3–5] [b][Is. 9:6; 57:15] [c][Deut. 4:24]
15 [a]Judg. 2:17 [b]Num. 25:1, 2 [c]1 Cor. 8:4, 7, 10
16 [a]Gen. 28:1 [b]Num. 25:1, 2
17 [a]Ex. 20:4, 23; 32:8
18 [a]Ex. 12:15, 16

month of Abib; for in the [b]month of Abib you
came out from Egypt.
19 [a]"All [1]that open the womb *are* Mine, and every
male firstborn among your livestock, *whether* ox
or sheep.
20 "But [a]the firstborn of a donkey you shall
redeem with a lamb. And if you will not redeem
*him,* then you shall break his neck. All the firstborn of your sons you shall redeem. And none
shall appear before Me [b]empty-handed.
**21** [a]"Six days you shall work, but on the seventh
day you shall rest; in plowing time and in harvest
you shall rest.
22 "And you shall observe the Feast of Weeks, of
the firstfruits of wheat harvest, and the Feast of
Ingathering at the year's end.
23 [a]"Three times in the year all your men shall
appear before the Lord, the LORD God of Israel.
24 "For I will [a]cast out the nations before you
and enlarge your borders; neither will any man
covet your land when you go up to appear before
the LORD your God three times in the year.
**25** "You shall not offer the blood of My sacrifice
with leaven, [a]nor shall the sacrifice of the Feast of
the Passover be left until morning.
26 [a]"The first of the firstfruits of your land you
shall bring to the house of the LORD your God.
You shall not boil a young goat in its mother's
milk."
**27** Then the LORD said to Moses, "Write [a]these
words, for according to the tenor of these words I
have made a covenant with you and with Israel."
28 [a]So he was there with the LORD forty days and
forty nights; he neither ate bread nor drank water.
And [b]He wrote on the tablets the words of the
covenant, the [1]Ten Commandments.
**29** Now it was so, when Moses came down from
Mount Sinai (and the [a]two tablets of the Testimony *were* in Moses' hand when he came down
from the mountain), that Moses did not know that
[b]the skin of his face shone while he talked with
Him.
30 So when Aaron and all the children of Israel
saw Moses, behold, the skin of his face shone, and
they were afraid to come near him.
31 Then Moses called to them, and Aaron and all
the rulers of the congregation returned to him;
and Moses talked with them.
32 Afterward all the children of Israel came near,
[a]and he gave them as commandments all that the
LORD had spoken with him on Mount Sinai.
33 And when Moses had finished speaking with
them, he put [a]a veil on his face.
34 But [a]whenever Moses went in before the LORD
to speak with Him, he would take the veil off until
he came out; and he would come out and speak to
the children of Israel whatever he had been commanded.
35 And whenever the children of Israel saw the
face of Moses, that the skin of Moses' face shone,
then Moses would put the veil on his face again,
until he went in to speak with Him.

### *Sabbath Regulations*

**35** Then Moses gathered all the congregation
of the children of Israel together, and said
to them, [a]"These *are* the words which the LORD
has commanded *you* to do:
2 "Work shall be done for [a]six days, but the
seventh day shall be a holy day for you, a Sabbath
of rest to the LORD. Whoever does any work on it
shall be put to [b]death.
3 [a]"You shall kindle no fire throughout your
dwellings on the Sabbath day."
**4** And Moses spoke to all the congregation of
the children of Israel, saying, [a]"This *is* the thing
which the LORD commanded, saying:
5 'Take from among you an offering to the
LORD. [a]Whoever *is* of a willing heart, let him bring
it as an offering to the LORD: [b]gold, silver, and
bronze;
6 [a]'blue, purple, and scarlet *thread,* fine linen,
and [b]goats' *hair;*
7 'ram skins dyed red, badger skins, and acacia
wood;
8 'oil for the light, [a]and spices for the anointing
oil and for the sweet incense;
9 'onyx stones, and stones to be set in the ephod
and in the breastplate.
**10** [a]'All *who are* gifted artisans among you shall
come and make all that the LORD has commanded:
11 [a]'the tabernacle, its tent, its covering, its
clasps, its boards, its bars, its pillars, and its
sockets;
12 [a]'the ark and its poles, *with* the mercy seat,
and the veil of the covering;
13 'the [a]table and its poles, all its utensils, [b]and
the showbread;
14 'also [a]the lampstand for the light, its utensils,
its lamps, and the oil for the light;
15 [a]'the incense altar, its poles, [b]the anointing oil,
[c]the sweet incense, and the screen for the door at
the entrance of the tabernacle;
16 [a]'the altar of burnt offering with its bronze
grating, its poles, all its utensils, *and* the laver and
its base;
17 [a]'the hangings of the court, its pillars, their
sockets, and the screen for the gate of the court;
18 'the pegs of the tabernacle, the pegs of the
court, and their cords;
19 [a]'the [1]garments of ministry, for ministering in
the holy *place*—the holy garments for Aaron the
priest and the garments of his sons, to minister as
priests.' "
**20** And all the congregation of the children of
Israel departed from the presence of Moses.
21 Then everyone came [a]whose heart [1]was
stirred, and everyone whose spirit was willing, *and*
they [b]brought the LORD's offering for the work of
the tabernacle of meeting, for all its service, and
for the holy garments.
22 They came, both men and women, as many as
had a willing heart, *and* brought [a]earrings and
nose rings, rings and necklaces, all [b]jewelry of
gold, that is, every man who *made* an offering of
gold to the LORD.
23 And [a]every man, with whom was found blue,
purple, and scarlet *thread,* fine linen, and goats'
*hair,* red skins of rams, and [1]badger skins, brought
*them.*
24 Everyone who offered an offering of silver or
bronze brought the LORD's offering. And everyone
with whom was found acacia wood for any work
of the service, brought *it.*
25 All the women *who were* [a]gifted artisans spun
yarn with their hands, and brought what they had
spun, of blue, purple, *and* scarlet, and fine linen.
26 And all the women whose hearts [1]stirred with
wisdom spun yarn of goats' *hair.*
27 [a]The rulers brought onyx stones, and the

**18** [b]Ex. 12:2; 13:4
**19** [a]Ex. 13:2; 22:29 [1]*the firstborn*
**20** [a]Ex. 13:13 [b]Ex. 22:29; 23:15; Deut. 16:16
**21** [a]Ex. 20:9; 23:12; 31:15; 35:2; Lev. 23:3; Deut. 5:13
**23** [a]Ex. 23:14–17
**24** [a][Ex. 33:2]; Josh. 11:23; 1 Kin. 4:21; 2 Chr. 36:14–16; Ps. 78:55
**25** [a]Ex. 12:10
**26** [a]Ex. 23:19; Deut. 26:2
**27** [a]Ex. 17:14; 24:4; Deut. 31:9
**28** [a]Ex. 24:18 [b]Ex. 34:1, 4; Deut. 4:31; 10:2, 4 [1]Lit. *Ten Words*
**29** [a]Ex. 32:15 [b]Matt. 17:2; 2 Cor. 3:7
**32** [a]Ex. 24:3
**33** [a][2 Cor. 3:13, 14]
**34** [a][2 Cor. 3:13–16]

CHAPTER 35
**1** [a]Ex. 34:32
**2** [a]Ex. 20:9, 10; Lev. 23:3; Deut. 5:13 [b]Num. 15:32–36
**3** [a]Ex. 12:16; 16:23
**4** [a]Ex. 25:1, 2
**5** [a]Ex. 25:2; 1 Chr. 29:14; Mark 12:41–44; 2 Cor. 8:10–12; 9:7 [b]Ex. 38:24
**6** [a]Ex. 36:8 [b]Ex. 36:14
**8** [a]Ex. 25:6; 30:23–25
**10** [a]Ex. 31:2–6; 36:1, 2
**11** [a]Ex. 26:1, 2; 36:14
**12** [a]Ex. 25:10–22
**13** [a]Ex. 25:23 [b]Ex. 25:30; Lev. 24:5, 6
**14** [a]Ex. 25:31
**15** [a]Ex. 30:1 [b]Ex. 30:25 [c]Ex. 30:34–38
**16** [a]Ex. 27:1–8
**17** [a]Ex. 27:9–18
**19** [a]Ex. 31:10; 39:1, 41 [1]Or *woven garments*
**21** [a]Ex. 25:2; 35:5, 22, 26, 29; 36:2 [b]Ex. 35:24 [1]Lit. *lifted him up*
**22** [a]Ex. 32:2, 3 [b]Ex. 11:2
**23** [a]1 Chr. 29:8 [1]Or *dolphin*
**25** [a]Ex. 28:3; 31:6; 36:1
**26** [1]Lit. *lifted them up*
**27** [a]1 Chr. 29:6; Ezra 2:68

stones to be set in the ephod and in the breastplate,

28 and [a]spices and oil for the light, for the anointing oil, and for the sweet incense.

29 The children of Israel brought a [a]freewill offering to the LORD, all the men and women whose hearts were willing to bring *material* for all kinds of work which the LORD, by the hand of Moses, had commanded to be done.

**30** And Moses said to the children of Israel, "See, [a]the LORD has called by name Bezalel the son of Uri, the son of Hur, of the tribe of Judah;

31 "and He has filled him with the Spirit of God, in wisdom and understanding, in knowledge and all manner of workmanship,

32 "to design artistic works, to work in gold and silver and bronze,

33 "in cutting jewels for setting, in carving wood, and to work in all manner of artistic workmanship.

34 "And He has put in his heart the ability to teach, *in* him and [a]Aholiab the son of Ahisamach, of the tribe of Dan.

35 "He has [a]filled them with skill to do all manner of work of the engraver and the designer and the tapestry maker, in blue, purple, and scarlet *thread,* and fine linen, and of the weaver—those who do every work and those who design artistic works.

### *Building the Tabernacle*

**36** "And Bezalel and Aholiab, and every [a]gifted artisan in whom the LORD has put wisdom and understanding, to know how to do all manner of work for the service of the [b]sanctuary,[1] shall do according to all that the LORD has commanded."

**2** Then Moses called Bezalel and Aholiab, and every gifted artisan in whose heart the LORD had put wisdom, everyone [a]whose heart [1]was stirred, to come and do the work.

3 And they received from Moses all the [a]offering which the children of Israel [b]had brought for the work of the service of making the sanctuary. So they continued bringing to him freewill offerings every morning.

4 Then all the craftsmen who were doing all the work of the sanctuary came, each from the work he was doing,

5 and they spoke to Moses, saying, [a]"The people bring much more than enough for the service of the work which the LORD commanded *us* to do."

6 So Moses gave a commandment, and they caused it to be proclaimed throughout the camp, saying, "Let neither man nor woman do any more work for the offering of the sanctuary." And the people were restrained from bringing,

7 for the material they had was sufficient for all the work to be done—indeed too [a]much.

**8** [a]Then all the gifted artisans among them who worked on the tabernacle made ten curtains woven of fine linen, and of blue, purple, and scarlet *thread; with* artistic designs of cherubim they made them.

9 The length of each curtain *was* twenty-eight cubits, and the width of each curtain four cubits; the curtains *were* all the same size.

10 And he coupled five curtains to one another, and *the other* five curtains he coupled to one another.

11 He made loops of blue *yarn* on the edge of the curtain on the selvedge of one set; likewise he did on the outer edge of *the other* curtain of the second set.

12 [a]Fifty loops he made on one curtain, and fifty loops he made on the edge of the curtain on the end of the second set; the loops held one *curtain* to another.

13 And he made fifty clasps of gold, and coupled the curtains to one another with the clasps, that it might be one tabernacle.

**14** [a]He made curtains of goats' *hair* for the tent over the tabernacle; he made eleven curtains.

15 The length of each curtain *was* thirty cubits, and the width of each curtain four cubits; the eleven curtains *were* the same size.

16 He coupled five curtains by themselves and six curtains by themselves.

17 And he made fifty loops on the edge of the curtain that is outermost in one set, and fifty loops he made on the edge of the curtain of the second set.

18 He also made fifty bronze clasps to couple the tent together, that it might be one.

19 [a]Then he made a covering for the tent of ram skins dyed red, and a covering of [1]badger skins above *that.*

**20** For the tabernacle [a]he made boards of acacia wood, standing upright.

21 The length of each board *was* ten cubits, and the width of each board a cubit and a half.

22 Each board had two [1]tenons [a]for binding one to another. Thus he made for all the boards of the tabernacle.

23 And he made boards for the tabernacle, twenty boards for the south side.

24 Forty sockets of silver he made to go under the twenty boards: two sockets under each of the boards for its two tenons.

25 And for the other side of the tabernacle, the north side, he made twenty boards

26 and their forty sockets of silver: two sockets under each of the boards.

27 For the west side of the tabernacle he made six boards.

28 He also made two boards for the two back corners of the tabernacle.

29 And they were coupled at the bottom and [1]coupled together at the top by one ring. Thus he made both of them for the two corners.

30 So there were eight boards and their sockets—sixteen sockets of silver—two sockets under each of the boards.

**31** And he made [a]bars of acacia wood: five for the boards on one side of the tabernacle,

32 five bars for the boards on the other side of the tabernacle, and five bars for the boards of the tabernacle on the far side westward.

33 And he made the middle bar to pass through the boards from one end to the other.

34 He overlaid the boards with gold, made their rings of gold *to be* holders for the bars, and overlaid the bars with gold.

**35** And he made [a]a veil of blue, purple, and scarlet *thread,* and fine woven linen; it was worked *with* an artistic design of cherubim.

36 He made for it four pillars of acacia *wood,* and overlaid them with gold, with their hooks of gold; and he cast four sockets of silver for them.

**37** He also made a [a]screen for the tabernacle door, of blue, purple, and scarlet *thread,* and fine woven linen, made by a [1]weaver,

38 and its five pillars with their hooks. And he

**28** [a]Ex. 30:23
**29** [a]Ex. 35:5, 21; 36:3; 1 Chr. 29:9
**30** [a]Ex. 31:1–6
**34** [a]Ex. 31:6
**35** [a]Ex. 31:3, 6; 35:31; 1 Kin. 7:14; 2 Chr. 2:14; Is. 28:26

CHAPTER 36
**1** [a]Ex. 28:3; 31:6; 35:10, 35 [b]Ex. 25:8 [1]*holy place*
**2** [a]Ex. 35:21, 26; 1 Chr. 29:5, 9, 17 [1]*lifted him up*
**3** [a]Ex. 35:5 [b]Ex. 35:27
**5** [a]2 Chr. 24:14; 31:6–10; [2 Cor. 8:2, 3]
**7** [a]1 Kin. 8:64
**8** [a]Ex. 26:1–14
**12** [a]Ex. 26:5
**14** [a]Ex. 26:7
**19** [a]Ex. 26:14 [1]Or *dolphin*
**20** [a]Ex. 26:15–29
**22** [a]Ex. 26:17 [1]Projections for joining, lit. *hands*
**29** [1]Lit. *doubled*
**31** [a]Ex. 26:26–29
**35** [a]Ex. 26:31–37
**37** [a]Ex. 26:36 [1]Lit. *variegator,* a weaver in colors

overlaid their capitals and their rings with gold, but their five sockets *were* bronze.

### *The Furniture of the Tabernacle*

**37** Then [a]Bezalel made [b]the ark of acacia wood; two and a half cubits *was* its length, a cubit and a half its width, and a cubit and a half its height.

2 He overlaid it with pure gold inside and outside, and made a molding of gold all around it.

3 And he cast for it four rings of gold *to be set* in its four corners: two rings on one side, and two rings on the other side of it.

4 He made poles of acacia wood, and overlaid them with gold.

5 And he put the poles into the rings at the sides of the ark, to bear the ark.

6 He also made the [a]mercy seat of pure gold; two and a half cubits *was* its length and a cubit and a half its width.

7 He made two cherubim of beaten gold; he made them of one piece at the two ends of the mercy seat:

8 one cherub at one end on this side, and the other cherub at the *other* end on that side. He made the cherubim at the two ends *of one piece* with the mercy seat.

9 The cherubim spread out *their* wings above, *and* covered the [a]mercy seat with their wings. They faced one another; the faces of the cherubim were toward the mercy seat.

**10** He made [a]the table of acacia wood; two cubits *was* its length, a cubit its width, and a cubit and a half its height.

11 And he overlaid it with pure gold, and made a molding of gold all around it.

12 Also he made a frame of a handbreadth all around it, and made a molding of gold for the frame all around it.

13 And he cast for it four rings of gold, and put the rings on the four corners that *were* at its four legs.

14 The rings were close to the frame, as holders for the poles to bear the table.

15 And he made the poles of acacia wood to bear the table, and overlaid them with gold.

16 He made of pure gold the utensils which were on the table: its [a]dishes, its cups, its bowls, and its pitchers for pouring.

17 He also made the [a]lampstand of pure gold; of hammered work he made the lampstand. Its shaft, its branches, its bowls, its *ornamental* knobs, and its flowers were of the same piece.

18 And six branches came out of its sides: three branches of the lampstand out of one side, and three branches of the lampstand out of the other side.

19 There were three bowls made like almond *blossoms* on one branch, with an *ornamental* knob and a flower, and three bowls made like almond *blossoms* on the other branch, with an *ornamental* knob and a flower—and so for the six branches coming out of the lampstand.

20 And on the lampstand itself *were* four bowls made like almond *blossoms, each with* its *ornamental* knob and flower.

21 *There was* a knob under the *first* two branches of the same, a knob under the *second* two branches of the same, and a knob under the *third* two branches of the same, according to the six branches extending from it.

22 Their knobs and their branches were of one piece; all of it *was* one hammered piece of pure gold.

23 And he made its seven lamps, its [a]wick-trimmers, and its trays of pure gold.

24 Of a talent of pure gold he made it, with all its utensils.

**25** [a]He made the incense altar of acacia wood. Its length *was* a cubit and its width a cubit—*it was* square—and two cubits *was* its height. Its horns were *of one piece* with it.

26 And he overlaid it with pure gold: its top, its sides all around, and its horns. He also made for it a molding of gold all around it.

27 He made two rings of gold for it under its molding, by its two corners on both sides, as holders for the poles with which to bear it.

28 And he [a]made the poles of acacia wood, and overlaid them with gold.

**29** He also made [a]the holy anointing oil and the pure incense of sweet spices, according to the work of the perfumer.

### *The Court of the Tabernacle*

**38** He made [a]the altar of burnt offering of acacia wood; five cubits *was* its length and five cubits its width—*it was* square—and its height *was* three cubits.

2 He made its horns on its four corners; the horns were *of one piece* with it. And he overlaid it with bronze.

3 He made all the utensils for the altar: the pans, the shovels, the basins, the forks, and the firepans; all its utensils he made of bronze.

4 And he made a grate of bronze network for the altar, under its rim, midway from the bottom.

5 He cast four rings for the four corners of the bronze grating, *as* holders for the poles.

6 And he made the poles of acacia wood, and overlaid them with bronze.

7 Then he put the poles into the rings on the sides of the altar, with which to bear it. He made the altar hollow with boards.

**8** He made [a]the laver of bronze and its base of bronze, from the bronze mirrors of the serving women who assembled at the door of the tabernacle of meeting.

**9** Then he made [a]the court on the south side; the hangings of the court *were of* fine woven linen, one hundred cubits long.

10 There *were* twenty pillars for them, with twenty bronze sockets. The hooks of the pillars and their bands *were* silver.

11 On the north side *the hangings were* one hundred cubits *long,* with twenty pillars and their twenty bronze sockets. The hooks of the pillars and their bands *were* silver.

12 And on the west side *there were* hangings of fifty cubits, with ten pillars and their ten sockets. The hooks of the pillars and their bands *were* silver.

13 For the east side *the hangings were* fifty cubits.

14 The hangings of one side *of the gate were* fifteen cubits *long, with* their three pillars and their three sockets,

15 and the same for the other side of the court gate; on this side and that *were* hangings of fifteen cubits, *with* their three pillars and their three sockets.

CHAPTER 37
1 [a]Ex. 35:30; 36:1 [b]Ex. 25:10–20
6 [a]Ex. 25:17
9 [a]Ex. 25:20
10 [a]Ex. 25:23–29
16 [a]Ex. 25:29
17 [a]Ex. 25:31–39
23 [a]Num. 4:9
25 [a]Ex. 30:1–5
28 [a]Ex. 30:5
29 [a]Ex. 30:23–25

CHAPTER 38
1 [a]Ex. 27:1–8
8 [a]Ex. 30:18
9 [a]Ex. 27:9–19

16 All the hangings of the court all around *were*
*of* fine woven linen.
17 The sockets for the pillars *were* bronze, the
hooks of the pillars and their bands *were* silver,
and the overlay of their capitals *was* silver; and all
the pillars of the court had bands of silver.
18 The screen for the gate of the court *was*
woven of blue, purple, and scarlet *thread,* and of
fine woven linen. The length *was* twenty cubits,
and the height along its width *was* five cubits,
corresponding to the hangings of the court.
19 And *there were* four pillars *with* their four
sockets of bronze; their hooks *were* silver, and the
overlay of their capitals and their bands *was*
silver.
20 All the [a]pegs of the tabernacle, and of the
court all around, *were* bronze.
**21** [1]This is the inventory of the tabernacle, [a]the
tabernacle of the Testimony, which was counted
according to the commandment of Moses, for the
service of the Levites, [b]by the hand of [c]Ithamar,
son of Aaron the priest.
22 [a]Bezalel the son of Uri, the son of Hur, of the
tribe of Judah, made all that the LORD had commanded Moses.
23 And with him *was* [a]Aholiab the son of Ahisamach, of the tribe of Dan, an engraver and [1]de-
signer, a weaver of blue, purple, and scarlet
*thread,* and of fine linen.
**24** All the gold that was used in all the work of
the holy *place,* that is, the gold of the [a]offering,
was twenty-nine talents and seven hundred and
thirty shekels, according to [b]the shekel of the
sanctuary.
25 And the silver from those who were [a]num-
bered of the congregation *was* one hundred
talents and one thousand seven hundred and
seventy-five shekels, according to the shekel of
the sanctuary:
26 [a]a bekah for [1]each man (*that is,* half a shekel,
according to the shekel of the sanctuary), for
everyone included in the numbering from twenty
years old and above, for [b]six hundred and three
thousand, five hundred and fifty *men.*
27 And from the hundred talents of silver were
cast [a]the sockets of the sanctuary and the bases of
the veil: one hundred sockets from the hundred
talents, one talent for each socket.
28 Then from the one thousand seven hundred
and seventy-five *shekels* he made hooks for the
pillars, overlaid their capitals, and [a]made bands for
them.
**29** The offering of bronze *was* seventy talents
and two thousand four hundred shekels.
30 And with it he made the sockets for the door
of the tabernacle of meeting, the bronze altar, the
bronze grating for it, and all the utensils for the
altar,
31 the sockets for the court all around, the bases
for the court gate, all the pegs for the tabernacle,
and all the pegs for the court all around.

### *How the Priests Were Dressed*

**39** Of the [a]blue, purple, and scarlet *thread* they
made [b]garments[1] of ministry, for ministering in the [2]holy *place,* and made the holy garments for Aaron, [c]as the LORD had commanded
Moses.
**2** [a]He made the [b]ephod of gold, blue, purple, and
scarlet *thread,* and of fine woven linen.
3 And they beat the gold into thin sheets and
cut *it into* threads, to work *it* in *with* the blue,
purple, and scarlet *thread,* and the fine linen, *into*
artistic designs.
4 They made shoulder straps for it to couple *it*
together; it was coupled together at its two edges.
5 And the intricately woven band of his ephod
that *was* on it *was* of the same workmanship,
*woven of* gold, blue, purple, and scarlet *thread,*
and *of* fine woven linen, as the LORD had commanded Moses.
**6** [a]And they set onyx stones, enclosed in [1]set-
tings of gold; they were engraved, as signets are
engraved, with the names of the sons of Israel.
7 He put them on the shoulders of the ephod *as*
[a]memorial stones for the sons of Israel, as the
LORD had commanded Moses.
**8** [a]And he made the breastplate, artistically
woven like the workmanship of the ephod, of
gold, blue, purple, and scarlet *thread,* and of fine
woven linen.
9 They made the breastplate square by doubling
it; a span *was* its length and a span its width when
doubled.
10 [a]And they set in it four rows of stones: a row
with a sardius, a topaz, and an emerald was the
first row;
11 the second row, a turquoise, a sapphire, and a
diamond;
12 the third row, a jacinth, an agate, and an
amethyst;
13 the fourth row, a beryl, an onyx, and a jasper.
*They were* enclosed in settings of gold in their
mountings.
14 *There were* [a]twelve stones according to the
names of the sons of Israel: according to their
names, *engraved like* a signet, each one with its
own name according to the twelve tribes.
15 And they made chains for the breastplate at
the ends, like braided cords of pure gold.
16 They also made two settings of gold and two
gold rings, and put the two rings on the two ends
of the breastplate.
17 And they put the two braided *chains* of gold in
the two rings on the ends of the breastplate.
18 The two ends of the two braided *chains* they
fastened in the two settings, and put them on the
shoulder straps of the ephod in the front.
19 And they made two rings of gold and put *them*
on the two ends of the breastplate, on the edge of
it, which *was* on the inward side of the ephod.
20 They made two *other* gold rings and put them
on the two shoulder straps, underneath the ephod
toward its front, right at the seam above the
intricately woven band of the ephod.
21 And they bound the breastplate by means of
its rings to the rings of the ephod with a blue cord,
so that it would be above the intricately woven
band of the ephod, and that the breastplate would
not come loose from the ephod, as the LORD had
commanded Moses.
**22** [a]He made the [b]robe of the ephod of woven
work, all of blue.
23 And *there was* an opening in the middle of the
robe, like the opening in a coat of mail, *with* a
woven binding all around the opening, so that it
would not tear.
24 They made on the hem of the robe pomegranates of blue, purple, and scarlet, and of fine woven
*linen.*
25 And they made [a]bells of pure gold, and put the

**20** [a]Ex. 27:19
**21** [a]Num. 1:50, 53; 9:15; 10:11; 17:7, 8; 2 Chr. 24:6; Acts 7:44 [b]Num. 4:28, 33 [c]Ex. 28:1; Lev. 10:6, 16 [1]Lit. *These are the things appointed for*
**22** [a]Ex. 31:2, 6; 1 Chr. 2:18–20
**23** [a]Ex. 31:6; 36:1 [1]*skillful workman*
**24** [a]Ex. 35:5, 22 [b]Ex. 30:13, 24; Lev. 5:15; 27:3, 25; Num. 3:47; 18:16
**25** [a]Ex. 30:11–16; Num. 1:2
**26** [a]Ex. 30:13, 15 [b]Ex. 12:37; Num. 1:46; 26:51 [1]Lit. *a head*
**27** [a]Ex. 26:19, 21, 25, 32
**28** [a]Ex. 27:17
CHAPTER 39
**1** [a]Ex. 25:4; 35:23 [b]Ex. 31:10; 35:19 [c]Ex. 28:4 [1]Or *woven garments* [2]*sanctuary*
**2** [a]Ex. 28:6–14 [b]Lev. 8:7
**6** [a]Ex. 28:9–11 [1]*plaited work*
**7** [a]Ex. 28:12, 29; Josh. 4:7
**8** [a]Ex. 28:15–30
**10** [a]Ex. 28:17
**14** [a]Rev. 21:12
**22** [a]Ex. 28:31–35 [b]Ex. 29:5; Lev. 8:7
**25** [a]Ex. 28:33

bells between the pomegranates on the hem of the
robe all around between the pomegranates:
26 a bell and a pomegranate, a bell and a pomegranate, all around the hem of the robe to [1]minis-
ter in, as the LORD had commanded Moses.
**27** [a]They made tunics, artistically woven of fine
linen, for Aaron and his sons,
28 [a]a turban of fine linen, exquisite hats of fine
linen, [b]short trousers of fine woven linen,
29 [a]and a sash of fine woven linen with blue,
purple, and scarlet *thread,* made by a weaver, as
the LORD had commanded Moses.
**30** [a]Then they made the plate of the holy crown
of pure gold, and wrote on it an inscription *like*
the engraving of a signet:

[b]HOLINESS TO THE LORD.

31 And they tied to it a blue cord, to fasten *it*
above on the turban, as the LORD had commanded
Moses.
**32** Thus all the work of the tabernacle of the tent
of meeting was [a]finished. And the children of
Israel did [b]according to all that the LORD had
commanded Moses; so they did.
33 And they brought the tabernacle to Moses, the
tent and all its furnishings: its clasps, its boards,
its bars, its pillars, and its sockets;
34 the covering of ram skins dyed red, the covering of badger skins, and the veil of the covering;
35 the ark of the Testimony with its poles, and
the mercy seat;
36 the table, all its utensils, and the [a]showbread;
37 the pure *gold* lampstand with its lamps (the
lamps set in order), all its utensils, and the oil for
light;
38 the gold altar, the anointing oil, and the sweet
incense; the screen for the tabernacle door;
39 the bronze altar, its grate of bronze, its poles,
and all its utensils; the laver with its base;
40 the hangings of the court, its pillars and its
sockets, the screen for the court gate, its cords,
and its pegs; all the utensils for the service of the
tabernacle, for the tent of meeting;
41 and the [1]garments of ministry, to [2]minister in
the holy *place:* the holy garments for Aaron the
priest, and his sons' garments, to minister as
priests.
**42** According to all that the LORD had commanded Moses, so the children of Israel [a]did all
the work.
43 Then Moses looked over all the work, and
indeed they had done it; as the LORD had commanded, just so they had done it. And Moses
[a]blessed them.

## *The Tabernacle Finished*

**40** Then the LORD [a]spoke to Moses, saying:
2 "On the first day of the [a]first month you
shall set up [b]the tabernacle of the tent of meeting.
3 [a]"You shall put in it the ark of the Testimony,
and [1]partition off the ark with the veil.
4 [a]"You shall bring in the table and [b]arrange the
things that are to be set in order on it; [c]and you
shall bring in the lampstand and [1]light its lamps.
5 [a]"You shall also set the altar of gold for the
incense before the ark of the Testimony, and put
up the screen for the door of the tabernacle.
6 "Then you shall set the [a]altar of the burnt
offering before the door of the tabernacle of the
tent of meeting.
7 "And [a]you shall set the laver between the
tabernacle of meeting and the altar, and put water
in it.
8 "You shall set up the court all around, and
hang up the screen at the court gate.
9 "And you shall take the anointing oil, and
[a]anoint the tabernacle and all that *is* in it; and you
shall hallow it and all its utensils, and it shall be
holy.
10 "You shall [a]anoint the altar of the burnt
offering and all its utensils, and consecrate the
altar. [b]The altar shall be most holy.
11 "And you shall anoint the laver and its base,
and consecrate it.
12 [a]"Then you shall bring Aaron and his sons to
the door of the tabernacle of meeting and wash
them with water.
13 "You shall put the holy [a]garments on Aaron,
[b]and anoint him and consecrate him, that he may
minister to Me as priest.
14 "And you shall bring his sons and clothe them
with tunics.
15 "You shall anoint them, as you anointed their
father, that they may minister to Me as priests; for
their anointing shall surely be [a]an everlasting
priesthood throughout their generations."
16 Thus Moses did; according to all that the LORD
had commanded him, so he did.
**17** And it came to pass in the first month of the
second year, on the first *day* of the month, *that*
the [a]tabernacle was [1]raised up.
18 So Moses raised up the tabernacle, fastened its
sockets, set up its boards, put in its bars, and
raised up its pillars.
19 And he spread out the tent over the tabernacle
and put the covering of the tent on top of it, as the
LORD had commanded Moses.
20 He took [a]the Testimony and put *it* into the
ark, inserted the poles through the rings of the
ark, and put the mercy seat on top of the ark.
21 And he brought the ark into the tabernacle,
[a]hung up the veil of the covering, and partitioned
off the ark of the Testimony, as the LORD had
commanded Moses.
22 [a]He put the table in the tabernacle of meeting,
on the north side of the tabernacle, outside the
veil;
23 [a]and he set the bread in order upon it before
the LORD, as the LORD had commanded Moses.
24 [a]He put the lampstand in the tabernacle of
meeting, across from the table, on the south side
of the tabernacle;
25 and [a]he lit the lamps before the LORD, as the
LORD had commanded Moses.
26 [a]He put the gold altar in the tabernacle of
meeting in front of the veil;
27 [a]and he burned sweet incense on it, as the
LORD had commanded Moses.
28 [a]He hung up the screen *at* the door of the
tabernacle.
29 [a]And he put the altar of burnt offering *before*
the door of the tabernacle of the tent of meeting,
and [b]offered upon it the burnt offering and the
grain offering, as the LORD had commanded Moses.
30 [a]He set the laver between the tabernacle of
meeting and the altar, and put water there for
washing;
31 and Moses, Aaron, and his sons would [a]wash
their hands and their feet *with water* from it.
32 Whenever they went into the tabernacle of

**26** [1]*serve*
**27** [a]Ex. 28:39, 40
**28** [a]Ex. 28:4, 39; Lev. 8:9; Ezek. 44:18 [b]Ex. 28:42; Lev. 6:10
**29** [a]Ex. 28:39
**30** [a]Ex. 28:36, 37 [b]Zech. 14:20
**32** [a]Ex. 40:17 [b]Ex. 25:40; 39:42, 43
**36** [a]Ex. 25:23–30
**41** [1]Or *woven garments* [2]*serve*
**42** [a]Ex. 35:10
**43** [a]Lev. 9:22, 23; Num. 6:23–26; Josh. 22:6; 2 Sam. 6:18; 1 Kin. 8:14; 2 Chr. 30:27

CHAPTER 40
**1** [a]Ex. 25:1—31:18
**2** [a]Ex. 12:2; 13:4 [b]Ex. 26:1, 30; 40:17
**3** [a]Ex. 26:33; 40:21; Lev. 16:2; Num. 4:5 [1]*screen*
**4** [a]Ex. 26:35; 40:22 [b]Ex. 25:30; 40:23 [c]Ex. 40:24, 25 [1]*set up*
**5** [a]Ex. 40:26
**6** [a]Ex. 39:39
**7** [a]Ex. 30:18; 40:30
**9** [a]Ex. 30:26; Lev. 8:10
**10** [a]Ex. 30:26–30 [b]Ex. 29:36, 37
**12** [a]Ex. 29:4–9; Lev. 8:1–13
**13** [a]Ex. 29:5; 39:1, 41 [b][Ex. 28:41]; Lev. 8:12
**15** [a]Ex. 29:9; Num. 25:13
**17** [a]Ex. 40:2; Num. 7:1 [1]*erected*
**20** [a]Ex. 25:16; Deut. 10:5; 1 Kin. 8:9; 2 Chr. 5:10; Heb. 9:4
**21** [a]Ex. 26:33
**22** [a]Ex. 26:35
**23** [a]Ex. 40:4; Lev. 24:5, 6
**24** [a]Ex. 26:35
**25** [a]Ex. 25:37; 30:7, 8; 40:4; Lev. 24:3, 4
**26** [a]Ex. 30:1, 6; 40:5
**27** [a]Ex. 30:7
**28** [a]Ex. 26:36; 40:5
**29** [a]Ex. 40:6 [b]Ex. 29:38–42
**30** [a]Ex. 30:18; 40:7
**31** [a]Ex. 30:19, 20; John 13:8

meeting, and when they came near the altar, they
washed, [a]as the LORD had commanded Moses.
33 [a]And he raised up the court all around the
tabernacle and the altar, and hung up the screen
of the court gate. So Moses [b]finished the work.
34 [a]Then the [b]cloud covered the tabernacle of
meeting, and the [c]glory of the LORD filled the
tabernacle.
35 And Moses [a]was not able to enter the tabernacle of meeting, because the cloud rested above it,
and the glory of the LORD filled the tabernacle.
36 [a]Whenever the cloud was taken up from
above the tabernacle, the children of Israel would
[1]go onward in all their journeys.
37 But [a]if the cloud was not taken up, then they
did not journey till the day that it was taken up.
38 For [a]the cloud of the LORD *was* above the
tabernacle by day, and fire was over it by night, in
the sight of all the house of Israel, throughout all
their journeys.

32 [a]Ex. 30:19
33 [a]Ex. 27:9–18; 40:8 [b][Heb. 3:2–5]
34 [a]Num. 9:15 [b]1 Kin. 8:10, 11 [c]Lev. 9:6, 23
35 [a]1 Kin. 8:11
36 [a]Num. 9:17 [1]*journey*
37 [a]Num. 9:19–22
38 [a]Ex. 13:21

*The Third Book of Moses Called*

# LEVITICUS

### *The Burnt Offering*

NOW the LORD [a]called to Moses, and spoke to
him [b]from the tabernacle of meeting, saying,
2 "Speak to the children of Israel, and say to
them: [a]'When any one of you brings an offering to
the LORD, you shall bring your offering of the
livestock—of the herd and of the flock.
3 'If his offering *is* a burnt sacrifice of the herd,
let him offer a male [a]without blemish; he shall
offer it of his own free will at the door of the
tabernacle of meeting before the LORD.
4 [a]'Then he shall put his hand on the head of the
burnt offering, and it will be [b]accepted on his
behalf [c]to make atonement for him.
5 'He shall kill the [a]bull before the LORD; [b]and
the priests, Aaron's sons, shall bring the blood
[c]and sprinkle the blood all around on the altar that
*is* by the door of the tabernacle of meeting.
6 'And he shall [a]skin the burnt offering and cut
it into its pieces.
7 'The sons of Aaron the priest shall put [a]fire on
the altar, and [b]lay the wood in order on the fire.
8 'Then the priests, Aaron's sons, shall lay the
parts, the head, and the fat in order on the wood
that *is* on the fire upon the altar;
9 'but he shall wash its entrails and its legs with
water. And the priest shall burn all on the altar as
a burnt sacrifice, an offering made by fire, a
[a]sweet[1] aroma to the LORD.
10 'If his offering *is* of the flocks—of the sheep or
of the goats—as a burnt sacrifice, he shall bring a
male [a]without blemish.
11 [a]'He shall kill it on the north side of the altar
before the LORD; and the priests, Aaron's sons,
shall sprinkle its blood all around on the altar.
12 'And he shall cut it into its pieces, with its
head and its fat; and the priest shall lay them in
order on the wood that *is* on the fire upon the
altar;
13 'but he shall wash the entrails and the legs
with water. Then the priest shall bring *it* all and
burn *it* on the altar; it *is* a burnt sacrifice, an
[a]offering made by fire, a sweet aroma to the LORD.
14 'And if the burnt sacrifice of his offering to the
LORD *is* of birds, then he shall bring his offering of
[a]turtledoves or young pigeons.
15 'The priest shall bring it to the altar, [1]wring off
its head, and burn *it* on the altar; its blood shall be
drained out at the side of the altar.
16 'And he shall remove its crop with its feathers
and cast it [a]beside the altar on the east side, into
the place for ashes.
17 'Then he shall split it at its wings, *but* [a]shall
not divide *it* completely; and the priest shall burn
it on the altar, on the wood that *is* on the fire. [b]It
*is* a burnt sacrifice, an offering made by fire, a
[1]sweet aroma to the LORD.

### *The Grain Offering*

2 'When anyone offers [a]a grain offering to the
LORD, his offering shall be *of* fine flour. And he
shall pour oil on it, and put [b]frankincense on it.
2 'He shall bring it to Aaron's sons, the priests,
one of whom shall take from it his handful of fine
flour and oil with all the frankincense. And the
priest shall burn [a]*it as* a memorial on the altar, an
offering made by fire, a sweet aroma to the LORD.
3 [a]'The rest of the grain offering *shall be* Aaron's
and his [b]sons'. [c]*It is* most holy of the offerings to
the LORD made by fire.
4 'And if you bring as an offering a grain offering baked in the oven, *it shall be* unleavened
cakes of fine flour mixed with oil, or unleavened
wafers [a]anointed[1] with oil.
5 'But if your offering *is* a grain offering *baked*
in a [1]pan, *it shall be of* fine flour, unleavened,
mixed with oil.
6 'You shall break it in pieces and pour oil on it;
it *is* a grain offering.
7 'If your offering *is* a grain offering *baked* in a
[a]covered pan, it shall be made *of* fine flour with oil.
8 'You shall bring the grain offering that is made
of these things to the LORD. And when it is
presented to the priest, he shall bring it to the
altar.
9 'Then the priest shall take from the grain
offering [a]a memorial portion, and burn *it* on the
altar. *It is* an [b]offering made by fire, a sweet aroma
to the LORD.
10 'And [a]what is left of the grain offering *shall be*
Aaron's and his sons'. *It is* most holy of the
offerings to the LORD made by fire.
11 'No grain offering which you bring to the
LORD shall be made with [a]leaven, for you shall
burn no leaven nor any honey in any offering to
the LORD made by fire.
12 [a]'As for the offering of the firstfruits, you shall
offer them to the LORD, but they shall not be
burned on the altar for a sweet aroma.
13 'And every offering of your grain offering [a]you
shall season with salt; you shall not allow [b]the salt

CHAPTER 1
1 [a]Ex. 19:3; 25:22 [b]Ex. 40:34
2 [a]Lev. 22:18, 19
3 [a]Eph. 5:27
4 [a]Lev. 3:2, 8, 13; 4:15 [b][Rom. 12:1] [c]2 Chr. 29:23, 24
5 [a]Mic. 6:6 [b]2 Chr. 35:11 [c][Heb. 12:24]
6 [a]Lev. 7:8
7 [a]Mal. 1:10 [b]Gen. 22:9
9 [a]Gen. 8:21 [1]*soothing* or *pleasing aroma*
10 [a]Lev. 1:3
11 [a]Lev. 1:5
13 [a]Num. 15:4–7; 28:12–14
14 [a]Lev. 5:7, 11; 12:8
15 [1]Lit. *nip* or *chop off*
16 [a]Lev. 6:10
17 [a]Gen. 15:10 [b]Lev. 1:9, 13 [1]*soothing* or *pleasing aroma*

CHAPTER 2
1 [a]Num. 15:4 [b]Lev. 5:11
2 [a]Lev. 2:9; 5:12; 6:15; 24:7
3 [a]Lev. 7:9 [b]Lev. 6:6; 10:12, 13 [c]Num. 18:9
4 [a]Ex. 29:2 [1]*spread*
5 [1]*flat plate* or *griddle*
7 [a]Lev. 7:9
9 [a]Lev. 2:2, 16; 5:12; 6:15 [b]Ex. 29:18
10 [a]Lev. 2:3; 6:16
11 [a]Lev. 6:16, 17
12 [a]Lev. 23:10, 11, 17, 18
13 [a][Col. 4:6] [b]Num. 18:19

of the covenant of your God to be lacking from your grain offering. [c]With all your offerings you shall offer salt.

14 'If you offer a grain offering of your firstfruits to the LORD, [a]you shall offer for the grain offering of your firstfruits green heads of grain roasted on the fire, grain beaten from [b]full heads.

15 'And [a]you shall put oil on it, and lay frankincense on it. It *is* a grain offering.

16 'Then the priest shall burn [a]the memorial portion: *part* of its beaten grain and *part* of its oil, with all the frankincense, as an offering made by fire to the LORD.

## *The Peace Offering*

**3** 'When his offering *is* a [a]sacrifice of a peace offering, if he offers *it* of the herd, whether male or female, he shall offer it [b]without [1]blemish before the LORD.

2 'And [a]he shall lay his hand on the head of his offering, and kill it *at* the door of the tabernacle of meeting; and Aaron's sons, the priests, shall [b]sprinkle the blood all around on the altar.

3 'Then he shall offer from the sacrifice of the peace offering an offering made by fire to the LORD. [a]The fat that covers the entrails and all the fat that *is* on the entrails,

4 'the two kidneys and the fat that *is* on them by the flanks, and the fatty lobe *attached* to the liver above the kidneys, he shall remove;

5 'and Aaron's sons [a]shall burn it on the altar upon the [b]burnt sacrifice, which *is* on the wood that *is* on the fire, *as* an [c]offering made by fire, a [d]sweet aroma to the LORD.

6 'If his offering as a sacrifice of a peace offering to the LORD *is* of the flock, *whether* male or female, [a]he shall offer it without blemish.

7 'If he offers a [a]lamb as his offering, then he shall [b]offer it [c]before the LORD.

8 'And he shall lay his hand on the head of his offering, and kill it before the tabernacle of meeting; and Aaron's sons shall sprinkle its blood all around on the altar.

9 'Then he shall offer from the sacrifice of the peace offering, as an offering made by fire to the LORD, its fat *and* the whole fat tail which he shall remove close to the backbone. And the fat that covers the entrails and all the fat that *is* on the entrails,

10 'the two kidneys and the fat that *is* on them by the flanks, and the fatty lobe *attached* to the liver above the kidneys, he shall remove;

11 'and the priest shall burn *them* on the altar *as* [a]food, an offering made by fire to the LORD.

12 'And if his [a]offering *is* a goat, then [b]he shall offer it before the LORD.

13 'He shall lay his hand on its head and kill it before the tabernacle of meeting; and the sons of Aaron shall sprinkle its blood all around on the altar.

14 'Then he shall offer from it his offering, as an offering made by fire to the LORD. The fat that covers the entrails and all the fat that *is* on the entrails,

15 'the two kidneys and the fat that *is* on them by the flanks, and the fatty lobe *attached* to the liver above the kidneys, he shall remove;

16 'and the priest shall burn them on the altar *as* food, an offering made by fire for a sweet aroma; [a]all the fat *is* the LORD's.

17 '*This shall be* a [a]perpetual[1] statute throughout your generations in all your dwellings: you shall eat neither fat nor [b]blood.' "

## *The Sin Offering*

**4** Now the LORD spoke to Moses, saying,

2 "Speak to the children of Israel, saying: [a]'If a person sins [1]unintentionally against any of the commandments of the LORD *in anything* which ought not to be done, and does any of them,

3 [a]'if the anointed priest sins, bringing guilt on the people, then let him offer to the LORD for his sin which he has sinned [b]a young bull without blemish as a [c]sin offering.

4 'He shall bring the bull [a]to the door of the tabernacle of meeting before the LORD, lay his hand on the bull's head, and kill the bull before the LORD.

5 'Then the anointed priest [a]shall take some of the bull's blood and bring it to the tabernacle of meeting.

6 'The priest shall dip his finger in the blood and sprinkle some of the blood seven times before the LORD, in front of the [a]veil of the sanctuary.

7 'And the priest shall [a]put some of the blood on the horns of the altar of sweet incense before the LORD, which is in the tabernacle of meeting; and he shall pour [b]the remaining blood of the bull at the base of the altar of the burnt offering, which is at the door of the tabernacle of meeting.

8 'He shall take from it all the fat of the bull as the sin offering. The fat that covers the entrails and all the fat which *is* on the entrails,

9 'the two kidneys and the fat that *is* on them by the flanks, and the fatty lobe *attached* to the liver above the kidneys, he shall remove,

10 [a]'as it was taken from the bull of the sacrifice of the peace offering; and the priest shall burn them on the altar of the burnt offering.

11 [a]'But the bull's hide and all its flesh, with its head and legs, its entrails and offal—

12 'the whole bull he shall carry outside the camp to a clean place, [a]where the ashes are poured out, and [b]burn it on wood with fire; where the ashes are poured out it shall be burned.

13 'Now [a]if the whole congregation of Israel sins unintentionally, [b]and the thing is hidden from the eyes of the assembly, and they have done *something against* any of the commandments of the LORD *in anything* which should not be done, and are guilty;

14 'when the sin which they have committed becomes known, then the assembly shall offer a young bull for the sin, and bring it before the tabernacle of meeting.

15 'And the elders of the congregation [a]shall lay their hands on the head of the bull before the LORD. Then the bull shall be killed before the LORD.

16 [a]'The anointed priest shall bring some of the bull's blood to the tabernacle of meeting.

17 'Then the priest shall dip his finger in the blood and sprinkle *it* seven times before the LORD, in front of the veil.

18 'And he shall put *some* of the blood on the horns of the altar which *is* before the LORD, which *is* in the tabernacle of meeting; and he shall pour the remaining blood at the base of the altar of burnt offering, which is at the door of the tabernacle of meeting.

19 'He shall take all the fat from it and burn *it* on the altar.

13 [c]Ezek. 43:24
14 [a]Lev. 23:10, 14 [b]2 Kin. 4:42
15 [a]Lev. 2:1
16 [a]Lev. 2:2

CHAPTER 3
1 [a]Lev. 7:11, 29 [b]Lev. 1:3; 22:20–24 [1]*imperfection* or *defect*
2 [a]Ex. 29:10, 11, 16, 20; Lev. 1:4, 5; 16:21 [b]Lev. 1:5
3 [a]Ex. 29:13, 22; Lev. 1:8; 3:16; 4:8, 9
5 [a]Ex. 29:13; Lev. 6:12; 7:28–34 [b]2 Chr. 35:14 [c]Num. 28:3–10 [d]Num. 15:8–10
6 [a]Lev. 3:1; 22:20–24
7 [a]Num. 15:4, 5 [b]1 Kin. 8:62 [c]Lev. 17:8, 9
11 [a]Lev. 21:6, 8, 17, 21, 22; 22:25; Num. 28:2; [Ezek. 44:7; Mal. 1:7, 12]
12 [a]Num. 15:6–11 [b]Lev. 3:1, 7
16 [a]Lev. 7:23–25; 1 Sam. 2:15; 2 Chr. 7:7
17 [a]Lev. 6:18; 7:36; 17:7; 23:14 [b]Gen. 9:4; Lev. 7:23, 26; 17:10, 14; 1 Sam. 14:33 [1]*everlasting* or *never-ending*

CHAPTER 4
2 [a]Lev. 5:15–18; Num. 15:22–30; 1 Sam. 14:27; Acts 3:17 [1]*through error*
3 [a]Ex. 40:15; Lev. 8:12 [b]Lev. 3:1; 9:2 [c]Lev. 9:7
4 [a]Lev. 1:3, 4; 4:15; Num. 8:12
5 [a]Lev. 16:14; Num. 19:4
6 [a]Ex. 40:21, 26
7 [a]Lev. 4:18, 25, 30, 34; 8:15; 9:9; 16:18 [b]Lev. 5:9; Ex. 40:5, 6
10 [a]Lev. 3:3–5
11 [a]Ex. 29:14; Lev. 9:11; Num. 19:5
12 [a]Lev. 4:21; 6:10, 11; 16:27 [b][Heb. 13:11, 12]
13 [a]Num. 15:24–26; Josh. 7:11 [b]Lev. 5:2–4, 17
15 [a]Lev. 1:3, 4
16 [a]Lev. 4:5; [Heb. 9:12–14]

20 'And he shall do [a]with the bull as he did [b]with the bull as a sin offering; thus he shall do with it. So the priest shall make [1]atonement for them, and it shall be forgiven them.

21 'Then he shall carry the bull outside the camp, and burn it as he burned the first bull. It *is* a sin offering for the assembly.

**22** 'When a [1]ruler has sinned, and [a]done *something* unintentionally *against* any of the commandments of the LORD his God *in anything* which should not be done, and is guilty,

23 'or [a]if his sin which he has committed [1]comes to his knowledge, he shall bring as his offering a kid of the goats, a male without blemish.

24 'And [a]he shall lay his hand on the head of the goat, and kill it at the place where they kill the burnt offering before the LORD. It *is* a sin offering.

25 [a]'The priest shall take some of the blood of the sin offering with his finger, put *it* on the horns of the altar of burnt offering, and pour its blood at the base of the altar of burnt offering.

26 'And he shall burn all its fat on the altar, like [a]the fat of the sacrifice of the peace offering. [b]So the priest shall make [1]atonement for him concerning his sin, and it shall be forgiven him.

**27** [a]'If [1]anyone of the [2]common people sins unintentionally by doing *something against* any of the commandments of the LORD *in anything* which ought not to be done, and is guilty,

28 'or [a]if his sin which he has committed comes to his knowledge, then he shall bring as his offering a kid of the goats, a female without blemish, for his sin which he has committed.

29 [a]'And he shall lay his hand on the head of the sin offering, and kill the sin offering at the place of the burnt offering.

30 'Then the priest shall take *some* of its blood with his finger, put *it* on the horns of the altar of burnt offering, and pour all *the remaining* blood at the base of the altar.

31 [a]'He shall remove all its fat, [b]as fat is removed from the sacrifice of the peace offering; and the priest shall burn it on the altar for a [c]sweet aroma to the LORD. [d]So the priest shall make atonement for him, and it shall be forgiven him.

**32** 'If he brings a lamb as his sin offering, [a]he shall bring a female without blemish.

33 'Then he shall [a]lay his hand on the head of the sin offering, and kill it as a sin offering at the place where they kill the burnt offering.

34 'The priest shall take *some* of the blood of the sin offering with his finger, put *it* on the horns of the altar of burnt offering, and pour all *the remaining* blood at the base of the altar.

35 'He shall remove all its fat, as the fat of the lamb is removed from the sacrifice of the peace offering. Then the priest shall burn it on the altar, [a]according to the offerings made by fire to the LORD. [b]So the priest shall make atonement for his sin that he has committed, and it shall be forgiven him.

## *The Trespass Offering*

**5** 'If a person sins in [a]hearing the utterance of an oath, and *is* a witness, whether he has seen or known *of the matter*—if he does not tell *it*, he [b]bears [1]guilt.

2 'Or [a]if a person touches any unclean thing, whether *it is* the carcass of an unclean beast, or the carcass of unclean livestock, or the carcass of unclean creeping things, and he is unaware of it, he also shall be unclean and [b]guilty.

3 'Or if he touches [a]human uncleanness—whatever uncleanness with which a man may be defiled, and he is unaware of it—when he realizes *it*, then he shall be guilty.

4 'Or if a person [1]swears, speaking thoughtlessly with *his* lips [a]to do evil or [b]to do good, whatever *it is* that a man may pronounce by an oath, and he is unaware of it—when he realizes *it*, then he shall be guilty in any of these *matters*.

5 'And it shall be, when he is guilty in any of these *matters*, that he shall [a]confess that he has sinned in that *thing;*

6 'and he shall bring his trespass offering to the LORD for his sin which he has committed, a female from the flock, a lamb or a kid of the goats as a sin offering. So the priest shall make atonement for him concerning his sin.

**7** [a]'If he is not able to bring a lamb, then he shall bring to the LORD, for his trespass which he has committed, two [b]turtledoves or two young pigeons: one as a sin offering and the other as a burnt offering.

8 'And he shall bring them to the priest, who shall offer *that* which *is* for the sin offering first, and [a]wring off its head from its neck, but shall not divide *it* [1]completely.

9 'Then he shall sprinkle *some* of the blood of the sin offering on the side of the altar, and the [a]rest of the blood shall be drained out at the base of the altar. It *is* a sin offering.

10 'And he shall offer the second *as* a burnt offering according to the [a]prescribed manner. So [b]the priest shall make atonement on his behalf for his sin which he has committed, and it shall be forgiven him.

**11** 'But if he is [a]not able to bring two turtledoves or two young pigeons, then he who sinned shall bring for his offering one-tenth of an ephah of fine flour as a sin offering. [b]He shall put no oil on it, nor shall he put frankincense on it, for it *is* a sin offering.

12 'Then he shall bring it to the priest, and the priest shall take his handful of it [a]as a memorial portion, and burn *it* on the altar [b]according to the offerings made by fire to the LORD. It *is* a sin offering.

13 [a]'The priest shall make atonement for him, [1]for his sin that he has committed in any of these matters; and it shall be forgiven him. [b]*The rest* shall be the priest's as a grain offering.' "

**14** Then the LORD spoke to Moses, saying:

15 [a]"If a person commits a trespass, and sins unintentionally in regard to the holy things of the LORD, then [b]he shall bring to the LORD as his trespass offering a ram without blemish from the flocks, with your valuation in shekels of silver according to [c]the shekel of the sanctuary, as a trespass offering.

16 "And he shall make restitution for the harm that he has done in regard to the holy thing, [a]and shall add one-fifth to it and give it to the priest. [b]So the priest shall make atonement for him with the ram of the trespass offering, and it shall be forgiven him.

**17** "If a person sins, and commits any of these things which are forbidden to be done by the commandments of the LORD, [a]though he does not know *it*, yet he is [b]guilty and shall bear his [1]iniquity.

**20** [a]Lev. 4:3 [b]Lev. 1:4; Num. 19:5 [1]Lit. *covering*
**22** [a]Lev. 4:2, 13, 27 [1]*leader*
**23** [a]Lev. 4:14; 5:4 [1]*is made known to him*
**24** [a]Lev. 4:4; [Is. 53:6]
**25** [a]Lev. 4:7, 18, 30, 34
**26** [a]Lev. 3:3–5 [b]Lev. 4:20; Num. 15:28 [1]Lit. *covering*
**27** [a]Lev. 4:2; Num. 15:27 [1]Lit. *any soul* [2]Lit. *people of the land*
**28** [a]Lev. 4:23
**29** [a]Lev. 1:4; 4:4, 24
**31** [a]Lev. 3:14 [b]Lev. 3:3, 4 [c]Gen. 8:21; Ex. 29:18; Lev. 1:9, 13; 2:2, 9, 12 [d]Lev. 4:26
**32** [a]Lev. 4:28
**33** [a]Lev. 1:4; Num. 8:12
**35** [a]Lev. 3:5 [b]Lev. 4:26, 31

CHAPTER 5
**1** [a]Prov. 29:24; [Jer. 23:10] [b]Lev. 5:17; 7:18; 17:16; 19:8; 20:17; Num. 9:13 [1]*his iniquity*
**2** [a]Lev. 11:24, 28, 31, 39; Num. 19:11–16; Deut. 14:8 [b]Lev. 5:17
**3** [a]Lev. 5:12, 13, 15
**4** [a]1 Sam. 25:22; Acts 23:12 [b][Matt. 5:33–37]; Mark 6:23; [James 5:12] [1]*vows*
**5** [a]Lev. 16:21; 26:40; Num. 5:7; Ezra 10:11, 12; Ps. 32:5; Prov. 28:13
**7** [a]Lev. 12:6, 8; 14:21 [b]Lev. 1:14
**8** [a]Lev. 1:15–17 [1]Lit. *apart*
**9** [a]Lev. 4:7, 18, 30, 34
**10** [a]Lev. 1:14–17 [b]Lev. 4:20, 26; 5:13, 16
**11** [a]Lev. 14:21–32 [b]Lev. 2:1, 2; 6:15; Num. 5:15
**12** [a]Lev. 2:2 [b]Lev. 4:35
**13** [a]Lev. 4:26 [b]Lev. 2:3; 6:17, 26 [1]*concerning his sin*
**15** [a]Lev. 4:2; 22:14; Num. 5:5–8 [b]Ezra 10:19 [c]Ex. 30:13; Lev. 27:25
**16** [a]Lev. 6:5; 22:14; 27:13, 15, 27, 31; Num. 5:7 [b]Lev. 4:26
**17** [a]Lev. 4:2, 13, 22, 27 [b]Lev. 5:1, 2 [1]*punishment*

18 [a]"And he shall bring to the priest a ram without blemish from the flock, with your valuation,
as a trespass offering. So the priest shall make
atonement for him regarding his ignorance in
which he erred and did not know *it*, and it shall be
forgiven him.
19 "It is a trespass offering; [a]he has certainly
trespassed against the LORD."

## *Laws About the Burnt Offering, the Grain Offering, and the Sin Offering*

**6** And the LORD spoke to Moses, saying:
2 "If a person sins and [a]commits a trespass
against the LORD by [b]lying[1] to his neighbor about
[c]what was delivered to him for safekeeping, or
about [2]a pledge, or about a robbery, or if he has
[d]extorted from his neighbor,
3 "or if he [a]has found what was lost and lies
concerning it, and [b]swears falsely—in any one of
these things that a man may do in which he sins:
4 "then it shall be, because he has sinned and is
guilty, that he shall [1]restore [a]what he has stolen,
or the thing which he has extorted, or what was
delivered to him for safekeeping, or the lost thing
which he found,
5 "or all that about which he has sworn falsely.
He shall [a]restore its full value, add one-fifth more
to it, *and* give it to whomever it belongs, on the
day of his trespass offering.
6 "And he shall bring his trespass offering to the
LORD, [a]a ram without blemish from the flock, with
your [1]valuation, as a trespass offering, to the
priest.
7 [a]"So the priest shall make atonement for him
before the LORD, and he shall be forgiven for any
one of these things that he may have done in
which he trespasses."
**8** Then the LORD spoke to Moses, saying,
9 "Command Aaron and his sons, saying, 'This
*is* the [a]law of the burnt offering: The burnt offering *shall be* on the hearth upon the altar all night
until morning, and the fire of the altar shall be
kept burning on it.
10 [a]'And the priest shall put on his linen garment,
and his linen trousers he shall put on his body, and
take up the ashes of the burnt offering which the
fire has consumed on the altar, and he shall put
them [b]beside the altar.
11 'Then [a]he shall take off his garments, put on
other garments, and carry the ashes outside the
camp [b]to a clean place.
12 'And the fire on the altar shall be kept burning
on it; it shall not be put out. And the priest shall
burn wood on it every morning, and lay the burnt
offering in order on it; and he shall burn on it [a]the
fat of the peace offerings.
13 'A fire shall always be burning on the [a]altar; it
shall never go out.
**14** 'This *is* the law of the grain offering: The sons
of Aaron shall offer it on the altar before the
LORD.
15 'He shall take from it his handful of the fine
flour of the grain offering, with its oil, and all the
frankincense which *is* on the grain offering, and
shall burn *it* on the altar *for* a sweet aroma, as a
memorial to the LORD.
16 'And the remainder of it Aaron and his sons
shall eat; with unleavened bread it shall be eaten
in a holy place; in the court of the tabernacle of
meeting they shall eat it.
17 'It shall not be baked with leaven. I have given
it *as* their [1]portion of My offerings made by fire; it
*is* most holy, like the sin offering and the [a]trespass
offering.
18 [a]'All the males among the children of Aaron
may eat it. [b]*It shall be* a statute forever in your
generations concerning the offerings made by fire
to the LORD. [c]Everyone who touches them must
be holy.' "
**19** And the LORD spoke to Moses, saying,
20 [a]"This *is* the offering of Aaron and his sons,
which they shall offer to the LORD, *beginning* on
the day when he is anointed: one-tenth of an
[b]ephah of fine flour as a daily grain offering, half
of it in the morning and half of it at night.
21 "It shall be made in a [a]pan with oil. *When it is*
mixed, you shall bring it in. The baked pieces of
the grain offering you shall offer *for* a [1]sweet
aroma to the LORD.
22 "The priest from among his sons, [a]who is
anointed in his place, shall offer it. *It is* a statute
forever to the LORD. [b]It shall be [1]wholly burned.
23 "For every grain offering for the priest shall be
wholly burned. It shall not be eaten."
**24** Also the LORD spoke to Moses, saying,
25 "Speak to Aaron and to his sons, saying, 'This
*is* the law of the sin offering: [a]In the place where
the burnt offering is killed, the sin offering shall be
killed before the LORD. It *is* most holy.
26 [a]'The priest who offers it for sin shall eat it. In
a holy place it shall be eaten, in the court of the
tabernacle of meeting.
27 [a]'Everyone who touches its flesh [1]must be
holy. And when its blood is sprinkled on any
garment, you shall wash that on which it was
sprinkled, in a holy place.
28 'But the earthen vessel in which it is boiled
[a]shall be broken. And if it is boiled in a bronze pot,
it shall be both scoured and rinsed in water.
29 'All the males among the priests may eat it. It
*is* most holy.
30 [a]'But no sin offering from which *any* of the
blood is brought into the tabernacle of meeting, to
make atonement in [1]the holy [b]*place,* shall be
[c]eaten. It shall be [d]burned in the fire.

## *Laws About the Trespass Offering and the Peace Offerings*

**7** 'Likewise [a]this *is* the law of the trespass offering (it *is* most holy):
2 'In the place where they kill the burnt offering
they shall kill the trespass offering. And its blood
he shall sprinkle all around on the altar.
3 'And he shall offer from it all its fat. The fat
tail and the fat that covers the entrails,
4 'the two kidneys and the fat that *is* on them by
the flanks, and the fatty lobe *attached* to the liver
above the kidneys, he shall remove;
5 'and the priest shall burn them on the altar *as*
an offering made by fire to the LORD. It *is* a
trespass offering.
6 [a]'Every male among the priests may eat it. It
shall be eaten in a holy place. [b]It *is* most holy.
7 [a]'The trespass offering *is* like the sin offering;
*there is* one law for them both: the priest who
makes atonement with it shall have *it*.
8 'And the priest who offers anyone's burnt
offering, that priest shall have for himself the skin
of the burnt offering which he has offered.
9 'Also [a]every grain offering that is baked in the
oven and all that is prepared in the covered pan,
or [1]in a pan, shall be the priest's who offers it.

---

**18** [a]Lev. 5:15
**19** [a]Ezra 10:2

CHAPTER 6
**2** [a]Num. 5:6 [b]Lev. 19:11; Acts 5:4; Col. 3:9 [c]Ex. 22:7, 10 [d]Prov. 24:28 [1]*deceiving his associate* [2]*an entrusted security*
**3** [a]Ex. 23:4; Deut. 22:1–4 [b]Ex. 22:11; Lev. 19:12; Jer. 7:9; Zech. 5:4
**4** [a]Lev. 24:18, 21 [1]*return*
**5** [a]Lev. 5:16; Num. 5:7, 8; 2 Sam. 12:6
**6** [a]Lev. 1:3; 5:15 [1]*appraisal*
**7** [a]Lev. 4:26
**9** [a]Ex. 29:38–42; Num. 28:3–10
**10** [a]Ex. 28:39–43; Lev. 16:4; Ezek. 44:7, 18 [b]Lev. 1:16
**11** [a]Ezek. 44:19 [b]Lev. 4:12
**12** [a]Lev. 3:3, 5, 9, 14
**13** [a]Lev. 1:7
**17** [a]Lev. 7:7 [1]*share*
**18** [a]Lev. 6:29; 7:6; Num. 18:10; 1 Cor. 9:13 [b]Lev. 3:17 [c]Ex. 29:37; Lev. 22:3–7; Num. 4:15; Hag. 2:11–13
**20** [a]Ex. 29:2 [b]Ex. 16:36
**21** [a]Lev. 2:5; 7:9 [1]*pleasing*
**22** [a]Lev. 4:3 [b]Ex. 29:25 [1]*completely*
**25** [a]Lev. 1:1, 3, 5, 11
**26** [a][Lev. 10:17, 18]; Num. 18:9, 10; [Ezek. 44:28, 29]
**27** [a]Ex. 29:37; Num. 4:15; Hag. 2:11–13 [1]Lit. *shall*
**28** [a]Lev. 11:33; 15:12
**30** [a]Lev. 4:7, 11, 12, 18, 21; 10:18; 16:27; [Heb. 13:11, 12] [b]Ex. 26:33 [c]Lev. 6:16, 23, 26 [d]Lev. 16:27 [1]*The Most Holy Place* when capitalized

CHAPTER 7
**1** [a]Lev. 5:14—6:7
**6** [a]Lev. 6:16–18, 29; Num. 18:9 [b]Lev. 2:3
**7** [a]Lev. 6:24–30; 14:13
**9** [a]Lev. 2:3, 10; Num. 18:9; Ezek. 44:29 [1]*on a griddle*

10 ‘Every grain offering, *whether* mixed with oil,
or dry, shall belong to all the sons of Aaron, to one
*as much* as the other.
**11** [a]‘This *is* the law of the sacrifice of peace
offerings which he shall offer to the LORD:
12 ‘If he offers it for a thanksgiving, then he shall
offer, with the sacrifice of thanksgiving, unleavened cakes mixed with oil, unleavened wafers
[a]anointed with oil, or cakes of blended flour mixed
with oil.
13 ‘Besides the cakes, *as* his offering he shall offer
[a]leavened bread with the sacrifice of thanksgiving
of his peace offering.
14 ‘And from it he shall offer one cake from each
offering *as* a heave offering to the LORD. [a]It shall
belong to the priest who sprinkles the blood of the
peace offering.
**15** [a]‘The flesh of the sacrifice of his peace offering
for thanksgiving shall be eaten the same day it is
offered. He shall not leave any of it until morning.
16 ‘But [a]if the sacrifice of his offering *is* a vow or
a voluntary offering, it shall be eaten the same day
that he offers his sacrifice; but on the next day the
remainder of it also may be eaten;
17 ‘the remainder of the flesh of the sacrifice on
the third day must be burned with fire.
18 ‘And if *any* of the flesh of the sacrifice of his
peace offering is eaten at all on the third day, it
shall not be accepted, nor shall it be [a]imputed to
him; it shall be an [b]abomination *to* him who offers
it, and the person who eats of it shall bear [1]guilt.
**19** ‘The flesh that touches any unclean thing shall
not be eaten. It shall be burned with fire. And as
for the *clean* flesh, all who are [1]clean may eat of it.
20 ‘But the person who eats the flesh of the
sacrifice of the peace offering that *belongs* to the
[a]LORD, [b]while he is unclean, that person [c]shall be
cut off from his people.
21 ‘Moreover the person who touches any unclean thing, *such as* [a]human uncleanness, *an*
[b]unclean animal, or any [c]abominable[1] unclean
thing, and who eats the flesh of the sacrifice of the
peace offering that *belongs* to the LORD, that
person [d]shall be cut off from his people.’ ”
**22** And the LORD spoke to Moses, saying,
23 “Speak to the children of Israel, saying: [a]‘You
shall not eat any fat, of ox or sheep or goat.
24 ‘And the fat of an animal that dies *naturally*,
and the fat of what is torn by wild beasts, may be
used in any other way; but you shall by no means
eat it.
25 ‘For whoever eats the fat of the animal of
which men offer an offering made by fire to the
LORD, the person who eats *it* shall be cut off from
his people.
26 [a]‘Moreover you shall not eat any blood in any
of your dwellings, *whether* of bird or beast.
27 ‘Whoever eats any blood, that person shall be
cut off from his people.’ ”
**28** Then the LORD spoke to Moses, saying,
29 “Speak to the children of Israel, saying: [a]‘He
who offers the sacrifice of his peace offering to the
LORD shall bring his offering to the LORD from the
sacrifice of his peace offering.
30 [a]‘His own hands shall bring the offerings made
by fire to the LORD. The fat with the breast he
shall bring, that the [b]breast may be waved *as* a
wave offering before the LORD.
31 [a]‘And the priest shall burn the fat on the altar,
but the [b]breast shall be Aaron’s and his sons’.
32 [a]‘Also the right thigh you shall give to the
priest *as* a heave offering from the sacrifices of
your peace offerings.
33 ‘He among the sons of Aaron, who offers the
blood of the peace offering and the fat, shall have
the right thigh for *his* part.
34 ‘For [a]the breast of the wave offering and the
thigh of the heave offering I have taken from the
children of Israel, from the sacrifices of their
peace offerings, and I have given them to Aaron
the priest and to his sons from the children of
Israel by a statute forever.’ ”
**35** This *is* the consecrated portion for Aaron and
his sons, from the offerings made by fire to the
LORD, on the day when *Moses* presented them to
[1]minister to the LORD as priests.
36 The LORD commanded this to be given to them
by the children of Israel, [a]on the day that He
anointed them, *by* a statute forever throughout
their generations.
**37** This *is* the law [a]of the burnt offering, [b]the
grain offering, [c]the sin offering, [d]the trespass
offering, [e]the consecrations, and [f]the sacrifice of
the peace offering,
38 which the LORD commanded Moses on Mount
Sinai, on the day when He commanded the children of Israel [a]to offer their offerings to the LORD
in the Wilderness of Sinai.

### *The Priests’ Offerings*

**8** And the LORD spoke to Moses, saying:
2 [a]“Take Aaron and his sons with him, and
[b]the garments, [c]the anointing oil, a [d]bull as the sin
offering, two [e]rams, and a basket of unleavened
bread;
3 “and gather all the congregation together at
the door of the tabernacle of meeting.”
4 So Moses did as the LORD commanded him.
And the congregation was gathered together at
the door of the tabernacle of meeting.
5 And Moses said to the congregation, “This *is*
what the LORD commanded to be done.”
**6** Then Moses brought Aaron and his sons and
[a]washed them with water.
7 And he [a]put the tunic on him, girded him with
the sash, clothed him with the robe, and put the
ephod on him; and he girded him with the intricately woven band of the ephod, and with it tied
*the ephod* on him.
8 Then he put the breastplate on him, and he
[a]put the [1]Urim and the Thummim in the breastplate.
9 [a]And he put the turban on his head. Also on
the turban, on its front, he put the golden plate,
the holy crown, as the LORD had commanded
Moses.
**10** [a]Also Moses took the anointing oil, and
anointed the tabernacle and all that *was* in it, and
consecrated them.
11 He sprinkled some of it on the altar seven
times, anointed the altar and all its utensils, and
the laver and its base, to [1]consecrate them.
12 And he [a]poured some of the anointing oil on
Aaron’s head and anointed him, to consecrate
him.
13 [a]Then Moses brought Aaron’s sons and put
tunics on them, girded them with sashes, and put
[1]hats on them, as the LORD had commanded
Moses.
**14** [a]And he brought the bull for the sin offering.
Then Aaron and his sons [b]laid their hands on the
head of the bull for the sin offering,

**11** [a]Lev. 3:1; 22:18, 21
**12** [a]Num. 6:15
**13** [a]Amos 4:5
**14** [a]Num. 18:8, 11, 19
**15** [a]Lev. 22:29, 30
**16** [a]Lev. 19:5–8
**18** [a]Num. 18:27 [b]Lev. 11:10, 11, 41; 19:7 [1]*his iniquity*
**19** [1]*pure*
**20** [a][Heb. 2:17] [b]Num. 19:13 [c]Gen. 17:14
**21** [a]Lev. 5:2, 3, 5 [b]Lev. 11:24, 28 [c]Ezek. 4:14 [d]Lev. 7:20 [1]So with MT, LXX, Vg.; Sam., Syr., Tg. *swarming thing* (cf. 5:2)
**23** [a]Lev. 3:17; 17:10–15
**26** [a]Acts 15:20, 29
**29** [a]Lev. 3:1; 22:21
**30** [a]Lev. 3:3, 4, 9, 14 [b]Ex. 29:24, 27
**31** [a]Lev. 3:5, 11, 16 [b]Deut. 18:3
**32** [a]Num. 6:20
**34** [a]Lev. 10:14, 15
**35** [1]*serve*
**36** [a]Lev. 8:12, 30
**37** [a]Lev. 6:9 [b]Lev. 6:14 [c]Lev. 6:25 [d]Lev. 7:1 [e]Ex. 29:1 [f]Lev. 7:11
**38** [a]Lev. 1:1, 2

CHAPTER 8
**2** [a]Ex. 29:1–3 [b]Ex. 28:2, 4 [c]Ex. 30:24, 25 [d]Ex. 29:10 [e]Ex. 29:15, 19
**6** [a]Heb. 10:22
**7** [a]Ex. 39:1–31
**8** [a]Ex. 28:30 [1]Lit. *Lights and the Perfections,* Ex. 28:30
**9** [a]Ex. 28:36, 37; 29:6
**10** [a]Ex. 30:26–29; 40:10, 11
**11** [1]*set them apart* for the LORD
**12** [a]Ps. 133:2
**13** [a]Ex. 29:8, 9 [1]*head pieces*
**14** [a]Ezek. 43:19 [b]Lev. 4:4

15 and Moses killed *it*. [a]Then he took the blood, and put *some* on the horns of the altar all around with his finger, and purified the altar. And he poured the blood at the base of the altar, and consecrated it, to make [1]atonement for it.

16 [a]Then he took all the fat that *was* on the entrails, the fatty lobe *attached to* the liver, and the two kidneys with their fat, and Moses burned *them* on the altar.

17 But the bull, its hide, its flesh, and its offal, he burned with fire outside the camp, as the LORD [a]had commanded Moses.

**18** [a]Then he brought the ram as the burnt offering. And Aaron and his sons laid their hands on the head of the ram,

19 and Moses killed *it*. Then he sprinkled the blood all around on the altar.

20 And he cut the ram into pieces; and Moses [a]burned the head, the pieces, and the fat.

21 Then he washed the entrails and the legs in water. And Moses burned the whole ram on the altar. It *was* a burnt sacrifice for a [1]sweet aroma, an offering made by fire to the LORD, [a]as the LORD had commanded Moses.

**22** And [a]he brought the second ram, the ram of consecration. Then Aaron and his sons laid their hands on the head of the ram,

23 and Moses killed *it*. Also he took *some* of [a]its blood and put it on the tip of Aaron's right ear, on the thumb of his right hand, and on the big toe of his right foot.

24 Then he brought Aaron's sons. And Moses put *some* of the [a]blood on the tips of their right ears, on the thumbs of their right hands, and on the big toes of their right feet. And Moses sprinkled the blood all around on the altar.

25 [a]Then he took the fat and the fat tail, all the fat that *was* on the entrails, the fatty lobe *attached to* the liver, the two kidneys and their fat, and the right thigh;

26 [a]and from the basket of unleavened bread that was before the LORD he took one unleavened cake, a cake of bread *anointed with* oil, and one wafer, and put *them* on the fat and on the right thigh;

27 and he put all *these* [a]in Aaron's hands and in his sons' hands, and waved them *as* a wave offering before the LORD.

28 [a]Then Moses took them from their hands and burned *them* on the altar, on the burnt offering. They *were* consecration offerings for a sweet aroma. That *was* an offering made by fire to the LORD.

29 And [a]Moses took the [b]breast and waved it *as* a wave offering before the LORD. It was Moses' [c]part of the ram of consecration, as the LORD had commanded Moses.

**30** Then [a]Moses took some of the anointing oil and some of the blood which *was* on the altar, and sprinkled *it* on Aaron, on his garments, on his sons, and on the garments of his sons with him; and he consecrated Aaron, his garments, his sons, and the garments of his sons with him.

31 And Moses said to Aaron and his sons, [a]"Boil the flesh *at* the door of the tabernacle of meeting, and eat it there with the bread that *is* in the basket of consecration offerings, as I commanded, saying, 'Aaron and his sons shall eat it.'

32 [a]"What remains of the flesh and of the bread you shall burn with fire.

33 "And you shall not go outside the door of the tabernacle of meeting *for* seven days, until the days of your consecration are ended. For [a]seven days he shall consecrate you.

34 [a]"As he has done this day, *so* the LORD has commanded to do, to make atonement for you.

35 "Therefore you shall stay *at* the door of the tabernacle of meeting day and night for seven days, and [a]keep the [1]charge of the LORD, so that you may not die; for so I have been commanded."

36 So Aaron and his sons did all the things that the LORD had commanded by the hand of Moses.

### *The First Offerings of Aaron*

**9** It came to pass on the [a]eighth day that Moses called Aaron and his sons and the elders of Israel.

2 And he said to Aaron, "Take for yourself a young [a]bull as a sin offering and a ram as a burnt offering, without blemish, and offer *them* before the LORD.

3 "And to the children of Israel you shall speak, saying, [a]'Take a kid of the goats as a sin offering, and a calf and a lamb, *both* of the first year, without blemish, as a burnt offering,

4 'also a bull and a ram as peace offerings, to sacrifice before the LORD, and [a]a grain offering mixed with oil; for [b]today the LORD will appear to you.' "

**5** So they brought what Moses commanded before the tabernacle of meeting. And all the congregation drew near and stood [1]before the LORD.

6 Then Moses said, "This *is* the thing which the LORD commanded you to do, and the glory of the LORD will appear to you."

7 And Moses said to Aaron, "Go to the altar, [a]offer your sin offering and your burnt offering, and make atonement for yourself and for the people. [b]Offer the offering of the people, and make atonement for them, as the LORD commanded."

**8** Aaron therefore went to the altar and killed the calf of the sin offering, which *was* for himself.

9 Then the sons of Aaron brought the blood to him. And he dipped his finger in the blood, put *it* on the horns of the altar, and poured the blood at the base of the altar.

10 [a]But the fat, the kidneys, and the fatty lobe from the liver of the sin offering he burned on the altar, as the LORD had commanded Moses.

11 [a]The flesh and the hide he burned with fire outside the camp.

**12** And he killed the burnt offering; and Aaron's sons presented to him the blood, [a]which he sprinkled all around on the altar.

13 [a]Then they presented the burnt offering to him, with its pieces and head, and he burned *them* on the altar.

14 [a]And he washed the entrails and the legs, and burned *them* with the burnt offering on the altar.

**15** [a]Then he brought the people's offering, and took the goat, which *was* the sin offering for the people, and killed it and offered it for sin, like the first one.

16 And he brought the burnt offering and offered it [a]according to the [1]prescribed manner.

17 Then he brought the grain offering, took a handful of it, and burned *it* on the altar, [a]besides the burnt sacrifice of the morning.

**18** He also killed the bull and the ram *as* [a]sacrifices of peace offerings, which *were* for the people.

**15** [a]Ex. 29:12, 36; Lev. 4:7; Ezek. 43:20, 26; [Heb. 9:22] [1]Lit. *covering*
**16** [a]Ex. 29:13; Lev. 4:8
**17** [a]Ex. 29:14; Lev. 4:11, 12
**18** [a]Ex. 29:15
**20** [a]Lev. 1:8
**21** [a]Ex. 29:18 [1]*pleasing*
**22** [a]Ex. 29:19, 31; Lev. 8:2
**23** [a]Ex. 29:20, 21; Lev. 14:14
**24** [a][Heb. 9:13, 14, 18–23]
**25** [a]Ex. 29:22
**26** [a]Ex. 29:23
**27** [a]Ex. 29:24; Lev. 7:30, 34
**28** [a]Ex. 29:25
**29** [a]Ps. 99:6 [b]Ex. 29:27 [c]Ex. 29:26
**30** [a]Ex. 29:21; 30:30; Num. 3:3
**31** [a]Ex. 29:31, 32
**32** [a]Ex. 29:34
**33** [a]Ex. 29:30, 35; Lev. 10:7; Ezek. 43:25, 26
**34** [a][Heb. 7:16]
**35** [a]Num. 1:53; 3:7; 9:19; Deut. 11:1; 1 Kin. 2:3; Ezek. 48:11 [1]*office*

CHAPTER 9

**1** [a]Ezek. 43:27
**2** [a]Ex. 29:21; Lev. 4:1–12
**3** [a]Lev. 4:23, 28; Ezra 6:17; 10:19
**4** [a]Lev. 2:4 [b]Ex. 29:43; Lev. 9:6, 23
**5** [1]*in the presence of*
**7** [a]Lev. 4:3; 1 Sam. 3:14; [Heb. 5:3–5; 7:27] [b]Lev. 4:16, 20; Heb. 5:1
**10** [a]Ex. 23:18; Lev. 8:16
**11** [a]Lev. 4:11, 12; 8:17
**12** [a]Lev. 1:5; 8:19
**13** [a]Lev. 8:20
**14** [a]Lev. 8:21
**15** [a][Is. 53:10; Heb. 2:17; 5:3]
**16** [a]Lev. 1:1–13 [1]*ordinance*
**17** [a]Ex. 29:38, 39
**18** [a]Lev. 3:1–11

And Aaron's sons presented to him the blood, which he sprinkled all around on the altar,
19 and the fat from the bull and the ram—the fatty tail, what covers *the entrails* and the kidneys, and the fatty lobe *attached to* the liver;
20 and they put the fat on the breasts. [a]Then he burned the fat on the altar;
21 but the breasts and the right thigh Aaron waved [a]*as* a wave offering before the LORD, as Moses had commanded.
**22** Then Aaron lifted his hand toward the people, [a]blessed them, and came down from offering the sin offering, the burnt offering, and peace offerings.
23 And Moses and Aaron went into the tabernacle of meeting, and came out and blessed the people. Then the glory of the LORD appeared to all the people,
24 and [a]fire came out from before the LORD and consumed the burnt offering and the fat on the altar. When all the people saw *it,* they [b]shouted and fell on their [c]faces.

### *The Conduct of the Priests*

**10** [a]Nadab and Abihu, the sons of Aaron, [b]each took his censer and put fire in it, put incense on it, and offered [c]profane fire before the LORD, which He had not commanded them.
2 So [a]fire went out from the LORD and devoured them, and they died before the LORD.
3 And Moses said to Aaron, "This is what the LORD spoke, saying:

'By those [a]who come near Me
I must be regarded as holy;
And before all the people
I must be glorified.' "

So Aaron held his peace.
4 Then Moses called Mishael and Elzaphan, the sons of Uzziel the uncle of Aaron, and said to them, "Come near, [a]carry your brethren from [1]before the sanctuary out of the camp."
5 So they went near and carried them by their tunics out of the camp, as Moses had said.
6 And Moses said to Aaron, and to Eleazar and Ithamar, his sons, "Do not [1]uncover your heads nor tear your clothes, lest you die, and [a]wrath come upon all the people. But let your brethren, the whole house of Israel, [2]bewail the burning which the LORD has kindled.
7 [a]"You shall not go out from the door of the tabernacle of meeting, lest you die, [b]for the anointing oil of the LORD *is* upon you." And they did according to the word of Moses.
8 Then the LORD spoke to Aaron, saying:
9 [a]"Do not drink wine or intoxicating drink, you, nor your sons with you, when you go into the tabernacle of meeting, lest you die. *It shall be* a statute forever throughout your generations,
10 "that you may [a]distinguish between holy and unholy, and between unclean and clean,
11 [a]"and that you may teach the children of Israel all the statutes which the LORD has spoken to them by the hand of Moses."
**12** And Moses spoke to Aaron, and to Eleazar and Ithamar, his sons who were left: [a]"Take the grain offering that remains of the offerings made by fire to the LORD, and eat it without leaven beside the altar; [b]for it *is* most holy.
13 "You shall eat it in a [a]holy place, because it *is* your [1]due and your sons' due, of the sacrifices made by fire to the LORD; for [b]so I have been commanded.
14 [a]"The breast of the wave offering and the thigh of the heave offering you shall eat in a clean place, you, your sons, and your [b]daughters with you; for *they are* your due and your sons' [c]due, *which* are given from the sacrifices of peace offerings of the children of Israel.
15 [a]"The thigh of the heave offering and the breast of the wave offering they shall bring with the offerings of fat made by fire, to offer *as* a wave offering before the LORD. And it shall be yours and your sons' with you, by a statute forever, as the LORD has commanded."
**16** Then Moses made careful inquiry about [a]the goat of the sin offering, and there it was—burned up. And he was angry with Eleazar and Ithamar, the sons of Aaron *who were* left, saying,
17 [a]"Why have you not eaten the sin offering in a holy place, since it *is* most holy, and [1]*God* has given it to you to bear [b]the guilt of the congregation, to make atonement for them before the LORD?
18 "See! [a]Its blood was not brought inside [1]the holy *place;* indeed you should have eaten it in a holy *place,* [b]as I commanded."
19 And Aaron said to Moses, "Look, [a]this day they have offered their sin offering and their burnt offering before the LORD, and such things have befallen me! *If* I had eaten the sin offering today, [b]would it have been accepted in the sight of the LORD?"
20 So when Moses heard *that,* he was content.

### *Clean and Unclean Animals*

**11** Now the LORD spoke to Moses and Aaron, saying to them,
2 "Speak to the children of Israel, saying, [a]'These *are* the animals which you may eat among all the animals that *are* on the earth:
3 'Among the animals, whatever divides the hoof, having cloven hooves *and* chewing the cud—that you may eat.
4 'Nevertheless these you shall [a]not eat among those that chew the cud or those that have cloven hooves: the camel, because it chews the cud but does not have cloven hooves, is [1]unclean to you;
5 'the [1]rock hyrax, because it chews the cud but does not have cloven hooves, *is* [2]unclean to you;
6 'the hare, because it chews the cud but does not have cloven hooves, *is* unclean to you;
7 'and the swine, though it divides the hoof, having cloven hooves, yet does not chew the cud, [a]*is* unclean to you.
8 'Their flesh you shall not eat, and their carcasses you shall not touch. [a]They *are* unclean to you.
9 [a]'These you may eat of all that *are* in the water: whatever in the water has fins and scales, whether in the seas or in the rivers—that you may eat.
10 'But all in the seas or in the rivers that do not have fins and scales, all that move in the water or any living thing which *is* in the water, they *are* [1]an [a]abomination to you.
11 'They shall be an abomination to you; you shall not eat their flesh, but you shall regard their carcasses as an abomination.
12 'Whatever in the water does not have fins or scales—that *shall be* an abomination to you.

**20** [a]Lev. 3:5, 16
**21** [a]Lev. 7:30–34
**22** [a]Luke 24:50
**24** [a]Judg. 6:21 [b]Ezra 3:11 [c]1 Kin. 18:38, 39

CHAPTER 10
**1** [a]Num. 3:2–4 [b]Lev. 16:12 [c]Ex. 30:9
**2** [a]Num. 11:1; 16:35
**3** [a]Ex. 19:22
**4** [a]Acts 5:6, 10 [1]*in front of*
**6** [a]2 Sam. 24:1 [1]An act of mourning [2]*weep bitterly*
**7** [a]Lev. 8:33; 21:12 [b]Lev. 8:30
**9** [a]Ezek. 44:21
**10** [a]Ezek. 22:26; 44:23
**11** [a]Deut. 24:8
**12** [a]Num. 18:9 [b]Lev. 21:22
**13** [a]Num. 18:10 [b]Lev. 2:3; 6:16 [1]*portion*
**14** [a]Num. 18:11 [b]Lev. 22:13 [c]Num. 18:10
**15** [a]Lev. 7:29, 30, 34
**16** [a]Lev. 9:3, 15
**17** [a]Lev. 6:24–30 [b]Ex. 28:38
**18** [a]Lev. 6:30 [b]Lev. 6:26, 30 [1]*The Most Holy Place* when capitalized
**19** [a]Lev. 9:8, 12 [b][Is. 1:11–15]

CHAPTER 11
**2** [a]Deut. 14:4
**4** [a]Acts 10:14 [1]*impure*
**5** [1]*rock badger* [2]*impure*
**7** [a]Is. 65:4; 66:3, 17
**8** [a]Is. 52:11
**9** [a]Deut. 14:9
**10** [a]Lev. 7:18, 21 [1]*detestable*

**13** [a]'And these you shall regard as an abomination among the birds; they shall not be eaten, they
*are* an abomination: the eagle, the vulture, the
buzzard,
14 'the kite, and the falcon after its kind;
15 'every raven after its kind,
16 'the ostrich, the short-eared owl, the seagull,
and the hawk after its kind;
17 'the little owl, the fisher owl, and the screech
owl;
18 'the white owl, the jackdaw, and the carrion
vulture;
19 'the stork, the heron after its kind, the hoopoe,
and the bat.
**20** 'All flying insects that creep on *all* fours *shall
be* an abomination to you.
21 'Yet these you may eat of every flying insect
that creeps on *all* fours: those which have jointed
legs above their feet with which to leap on the
earth.
22 'These you may eat: [a]the locust after its kind,
the destroying locust after its kind, the cricket
after its kind, and the grasshopper after its kind.
23 'But all *other* flying insects which have four
feet *shall be* an abomination to you.
**24** 'By these you shall become [1]unclean; whoever
touches the carcass of any of them shall be
unclean until evening;
25 'whoever carries part of the carcass of any of
them [a]shall wash his clothes and be unclean until
evening:
26 '*The carcass* of any animal which divides the
foot, but is not cloven-hoofed or does not chew
the cud, *is* unclean to you. Everyone who touches
it shall be unclean.
27 'And whatever goes on its paws, among all
kinds of animals that go on *all* fours, those *are*
unclean to you. Whoever touches any such carcass shall be unclean until evening.
28 'Whoever carries *any such* carcass shall wash
his clothes and be unclean until evening. It *is*
unclean to you.
**29** 'These also *shall be* unclean to you among the
creeping things that creep on the earth: the mole,
[a]the mouse, and the large lizard after its kind;
30 'the gecko, the monitor lizard, the sand reptile,
the sand lizard, and the chameleon.
31 'These *are* unclean to you among all that
creep. Whoever [a]touches them when they are
dead shall be unclean until evening.
32 'Anything on which *any* of them falls, when
they are dead shall be [1]unclean, whether *it is* any
item of wood or clothing or skin or sack, whatever
item *it is*, in which *any* work is done, [a]it must be
put in water. And it shall be unclean until evening; then it shall be clean.
33 'Any [a]earthen vessel into which *any* of them
falls [b]you shall break; and whatever *is* in it shall be
unclean:
34 'in such a vessel, any edible food upon which
water falls becomes unclean, and any drink that
may be drunk from it becomes unclean.
35 'And everything on which *a part* of *any such*
carcass falls shall be unclean; *whether it is* an
oven or cooking stove, it shall be broken down;
*for* they *are* unclean, and shall be unclean to you.
36 'Nevertheless a spring or a cistern, *in which
there is* plenty of water, shall be clean, but whatever touches any such carcass becomes unclean.
37 'And if a part of *any such* carcass falls on any
planting seed which is to be sown, it *remains*
clean.
38 'But if water is put on the seed, and if *a part* of
*any such* carcass falls on it, it *becomes* [1]unclean to
you.
**39** 'And if any animal which you may eat dies, he
who touches its carcass shall be [a]unclean until
evening.
40 [a]'He who eats of its carcass shall wash his
clothes and be unclean until evening. He also who
carries its carcass shall wash his clothes and be
unclean until evening.
**41** 'And every creeping thing that creeps on the
earth *shall be* [1]an abomination. It shall not be
eaten.
42 'Whatever crawls on its belly, whatever goes
on *all* fours, or whatever has many feet among all
creeping things that creep on the earth—these
you shall not eat, for they *are* an abomination.
43 [a]'You shall not make [1]yourselves [2]abominable
with any creeping thing that creeps; nor shall you
make yourselves unclean with them, lest you be
defiled by them.
44 'For I *am* the LORD your [a]God. You shall
therefore consecrate yourselves, and [b]you shall be
holy; for I *am* holy. Neither shall you defile
yourselves with any creeping thing that creeps on
the earth.
45 [a]'For I *am* the LORD who brings you up out of
the land of Egypt, to be your God. [b]You shall
therefore be holy, for I *am* holy.
**46** 'This *is* the law [1]of the animals and the birds
and every living creature that moves in the waters, and of every creature that creeps on the
earth,
47 [a]'to distinguish between the unclean and the
clean, and between the animal that may be eaten
and the animal that may not be eaten.' "

### *The Purification of Women*

**12** Then the LORD spoke to Moses, saying,
2 "Speak to the children of Israel, saying:
'If a [a]woman has conceived, and borne a male
child, then [b]she shall be [1]unclean seven days; [c]as in
the days of her customary impurity she shall be
unclean.
3 'And on the [a]eighth day the flesh of his foreskin shall be circumcised.
4 'She shall then continue in the blood of *her*
purification thirty-three days. She shall not touch
any [1]hallowed thing, nor come into the sanctuary
until the days of her purification are fulfilled.
5 'But if she bears a female child, then she shall
be unclean two weeks, as in her customary impurity, and she shall continue in the blood of *her*
purification sixty-six days.
**6** [a]'When the days of her purification are fulfilled, whether for a son or a daughter, she shall
bring to the priest a [b]lamb [1]of the first year as a
burnt offering, and a young pigeon or a turtledove
as a [c]sin offering, to the door of the tabernacle of
meeting.
7 'Then he shall offer it before the LORD, and
make [1]atonement for her. And she shall be clean
from the flow of her blood. This *is* the law for her
who has borne a male or a female.
8 [a]'And if she is not able to bring a lamb, then
she may bring two turtledoves or two young
pigeons—one as a burnt offering and the other as

**13** [a]Deut. 14:12–19; Is. 66:17
**22** [a]Matt. 3:4; Mark 1:6
**24** [1]*impure*
**25** [a]Lev. 14:8; 15:5; Num. 19:10, 21, 22; 31:24; Zech. 13:1; [Heb. 9:10; 10:22; Rev. 7:14]
**29** [a]Is. 66:17
**31** [a]Hag. 2:13
**32** [a]Lev. 15:12 [1]*impure*
**33** [a]Lev. 6:28 [b]Lev. 15:12; Ps. 2:9; Jer. 48:38; [2 Tim. 2:21]; Rev. 2:27
**38** [1]*impure*
**39** [a]Hag. 2:11–13
**40** [a]Ex. 22:31; Lev. 17:15; 22:8; Deut. 14:21; Ezek. 4:14; 44:31
**41** [1]*detestable*
**43** [a]Lev. 20:25 [1]Lit. *your souls* [2]*impure*
**44** [a]Ex. 6:7; Lev. 22:33; 25:38; 26:45 [b]Ex. 19:6; Lev. 19:2; 20:7, 26; [Amos 3:3]; Matt. 5:48; 1 Thess. 4:7; 1 Pet. 1:15, 16; [Rev. 22:11, 14]
**45** [a]Ex. 6:7; 20:2; Lev. 22:33; 25:38; 26:45; Ps. 105:43–45; Hos. 11:1 [b]Lev. 11:44
**46** [1]*concerning*
**47** [a]Lev. 10:10; Ezek. 44:23; Mal. 3:18

CHAPTER 12

**2** [a]Lev. 15:19; [Job 14:4; Ps. 51:5] [b]Ex. 22:30; Lev. 8:33; 13:4; Luke 2:22 [c]Lev. 18:19 [1]*impure*
**3** [a]Gen. 17:12; Luke 1:59; 2:21; John 7:22, 23; Gal. 5:3
**4** [1]*consecrated*
**6** [a]Luke 2:22 [b][John 1:29; 1 Pet. 1:18, 19] [c]Lev. 5:7 [1]Lit. *a son of his year*
**7** [1]Lit. *covering*
**8** [a]Lev. 5:7; Luke 2:22–24

a sin offering. [b]So the priest shall make atonement for her, and she will be [1]clean.' "

## *Signs and Treatment of Leprosy*

**13** And the LORD spoke to Moses and Aaron, saying:

2 "When a man has on the skin of his body a swelling, [a]a scab, or a bright spot, and it becomes on the skin of his body *like* a [1]leprous sore, [b]then he shall be brought to Aaron the priest or to one of his sons the priests.

3 "The priest shall examine the sore on the skin of the body; and if the hair on the sore has turned white, and the sore appears *to be* deeper than the skin of his body, it *is* a leprous sore. Then the priest shall examine him, and pronounce him [1]unclean.

4 "But if the bright spot *is* white on the skin of his body, and does not appear *to be* deeper than the skin, and its hair has not turned white, then the priest shall isolate *the one who has* the sore [a]seven days.

5 "And the priest shall examine him on the seventh day; and indeed *if* the sore appears to be as it was, *and* the sore has not spread on the skin, then the priest shall isolate him another seven days.

6 "Then the priest shall examine him again on the seventh day; and indeed *if* the sore has faded, *and* the sore has not spread on the skin, then the priest shall pronounce him clean; it *is only* a scab, and he [a]shall wash his clothes and be clean.

7 "But if the scab should at all spread over the skin, after he has been seen by the priest for his cleansing, he shall be seen by the priest again.

8 "And *if* the priest sees that the scab has indeed spread on the skin, then the priest shall pronounce him [1]unclean. It *is* leprosy.

**9** "When the leprous sore is on a person, then he shall be brought to the priest.

10 [a]"And the priest shall examine *him;* and indeed *if* the swelling on the skin *is* white, and it has turned the hair white, and *there is* a spot of raw flesh in the swelling,

11 "it *is* an old leprosy on the skin of his body. The priest shall pronounce him [1]unclean, and shall not isolate him, for he *is* unclean.

**12** "And if leprosy breaks out all over the skin, and the leprosy covers all the skin of *the one who has* the sore, from his head to his foot, wherever the priest looks,

13 "then the priest shall consider; and indeed *if* the leprosy has covered all his body, he shall pronounce *him* clean *who has* the sore. It has all turned [a]white. He *is* clean.

14 "But when raw flesh appears on him, he shall be unclean.

15 "And the priest shall examine the raw flesh and pronounce him to be unclean; *for* the raw flesh *is* unclean. It *is* leprosy.

16 "Or if the raw flesh changes and turns white again, he shall come to the priest.

17 "And the priest shall examine him; and indeed *if* the sore has turned white, then the priest shall pronounce *him* clean *who has* the sore. He *is* clean.

**18** "If the body develops a [a]boil in the skin, and it is healed,

19 "and in the place of the boil there comes a white swelling or a bright spot, reddish-white, then it shall be shown to the priest;

20 "and *if,* when the priest sees it, it indeed *appears* deeper than the skin, and its hair has turned white, the priest shall pronounce him unclean. It *is* a leprous sore which has broken out of the boil.

21 "But if the priest examines it, and indeed *there are* no white hairs in it, and it *is* not deeper than the skin, but has faded, then the priest shall isolate him seven days;

22 "and if it should at all spread over the skin, then the priest shall pronounce him unclean. It *is* a [1]leprous sore.

23 "But if the bright spot stays in one place, *and* has not spread, it *is* the scar of the boil; and the priest shall pronounce him clean.

**24** "Or if the body receives a [a]burn on its skin by fire, and the raw *flesh* of the burn becomes a bright spot, reddish-white or white,

25 "then the priest shall examine it; and indeed *if* the hair of the bright spot has turned white, and it appears deeper than the skin, it *is* leprosy broken out in the burn. Therefore the priest shall pronounce him unclean. It *is* a leprous sore.

26 "But if the priest examines it, and indeed *there are* no white hairs in the bright spot, and it *is* not deeper than the skin, but has faded, then the priest shall isolate him seven days.

27 "And the priest shall examine him on the seventh day. If it has at all spread over the skin, then the priest shall pronounce him unclean. It *is* a leprous sore.

28 "But if the bright spot stays in one place, *and* has not spread on the skin, but has faded, it *is* a swelling from the burn. The priest shall pronounce him clean, for it *is* the scar from the burn.

**29** "If a man or woman has a sore on the head or the beard,

30 "then the priest shall examine the sore; and indeed if it appears deeper than the skin, *and there is* in it thin yellow hair, then the priest shall pronounce him unclean. It *is* a scaly leprosy of the head or beard.

31 "But if the priest examines the scaly sore, and indeed it does not appear deeper than the skin, and *there is* no black hair in it, then the priest shall isolate *the one who has* the scale seven days.

32 "And on the seventh day the priest shall examine the sore; and indeed *if* the scale has not spread, and there is no yellow hair in it, and the scale does not appear deeper than the skin,

33 "he shall shave himself, but the scale he shall not shave. And the priest shall isolate *the one who has* the scale another seven days.

34 "On the seventh day the priest shall examine the scale; and indeed *if* the scale has not spread over the skin, and does not appear deeper than the skin, then the priest shall pronounce him clean. He shall wash his clothes and be clean.

35 "But if the scale should at all spread over the skin after his cleansing,

36 "then the priest shall examine him; and indeed *if* the scale has spread over the skin, the priest need not seek for yellow hair. He *is* unclean.

37 "But if the scale appears to be at a standstill, and there is black hair grown up in it, the scale has healed. He *is* clean, and the priest shall pronounce him clean.

**38** "If a man or a woman has bright spots on the skin of the body, *specifically* white bright spots,

39 "then the priest shall look; and indeed *if* the bright spots on the skin of the body *are* dull white,

**8** [b]Lev. 4:26 [1]*pure*

CHAPTER 13

**2** [a]Deut. 28:27; Is. 3:17 [b]Deut. 17:8, 9; 24:8; Mal. 2:7; Luke 17:14 [1]Heb. *saraath,* disfiguring skin diseases, including leprosy, and so in vv. 2–46 and 14:1–32

**3** [1]*defiled*

**4** [a]Lev. 14:8

**6** [a]Lev. 11:25; 14:8; [John 13:8, 10]

**8** [1]*defiled*

**10** [a]Num. 12:10, 12; 2 Kin. 5:27; 2 Chr. 26:19, 20

**11** [1]*defiled*

**13** [a]Ex. 4:6

**18** [a]Ex. 9:9; 15:26

**22** [1]*infection*

**24** [a]Is. 3:24

it *is* a white spot *that* grows on the skin. He *is*
clean.
40 "As for the man whose hair has fallen from his
head, he *is* bald, *but* he *is* clean.
41 "He whose hair has fallen from his forehead,
he *is* bald on the forehead, *but* he *is* clean.
42 "And if there is on the bald head or bald
[a]forehead a reddish-white sore, it *is* leprosy breaking out on his bald head or his bald forehead.
43 "Then the priest shall examine it; and indeed *if*
the swelling of the sore *is* reddish-white on his
bald head or on his bald forehead, as the appearance of leprosy on the skin of the body,
44 "he is a leprous man. He *is* unclean. The priest
shall surely pronounce him [1]unclean; his sore *is* on
his [a]head.
45 "Now the leper on whom the sore *is*, his
clothes shall be torn and his head [a]bare; and he
shall [b]cover his mustache, and cry, [c]'Unclean!
Unclean!'
46 "He shall be unclean. All the days he has the
sore he shall be unclean. He *is* unclean, and he
shall [1]dwell alone; his dwelling *shall be* [a]outside
the camp.
**47** "Also, if a garment has a [1]leprous plague in it,
*whether it is* a woolen garment or a linen garment,
48 "whether *it is* in the warp or woof of linen or
wool, whether in leather or in anything made of
leather,
49 "and if the plague is greenish or reddish in the
garment or in the leather, whether in the warp or
in the woof, or in anything made of leather, it *is* a
leprous [1]plague and shall be shown to the priest.
50 "The priest shall examine the plague and
isolate *that which has* the plague seven days.
51 "And he shall examine the plague on the
seventh day. If the plague has spread in the
garment, either in the warp or in the woof, in
the leather *or* in anything made of leather, the
plague *is* [a]an active leprosy. It *is* unclean.
52 "He shall therefore burn that garment in
which is the plague, whether warp or woof, in
wool or in linen, or anything of leather, for it *is* an
active leprosy; *the garment* shall be burned in the
fire.
**53** "But if the priest examines *it*, and indeed the
plague has not spread in the garment, either in the
warp or in the woof, or in anything made of
leather,
54 "then the priest shall command that they
wash *the thing* in which *is* the plague; and he shall
isolate it another seven days.
55 "Then the priest shall examine the plague
after it has been washed; and indeed *if* the plague
has not changed its color, though the plague has
not spread, it *is* unclean, and you shall burn it in
the fire; it continues eating away, *whether* the
damage *is* outside or inside.
56 "If the priest examines *it*, and indeed the
plague has faded after washing it, then he shall
tear it out of the garment, whether out of the
warp or out of the woof, or out of the leather.
57 "But if it appears again in the garment, either
in the warp or in the woof, or in anything made of
leather, it *is* a spreading *plague*; you shall burn
with fire that in which is the plague.
58 "And if you wash the garment, either warp or
woof, or whatever is made of leather, if the plague
has disappeared from it, then it shall be washed a
second time, and shall be clean.

**42** [a]2 Chr. 26:19
**44** [a]Is. 1:5 [1]*altogether defiled*
**45** [a]Lev. 10:6; 21:10 [b]Ezek. 24:17, 22; Mic. 3:7 [c]Is. 6:5; 64:6; Lam. 4:15; Luke 5:8
**46** [a]Num. 5:1–4; 12:14; 2 Kin. 7:3; 15:5; 2 Chr. 26:21; Ps. 38:11; Luke 17:12 [1]*live alone*
**47** [1]A mold, fungus, or similar infestation, and so in vv. 47–59
**49** [1]*mark*
**51** [a]Lev. 14:44
CHAPTER 14
**2** [a]Matt. 8:2, 4; Mark 1:40, 44; Luke 5:12, 14; 17:14 [1]See note at 13:2
**3** [1]Heb. *saraath*, disfiguring skin diseases, including leprosy, and so in vv. 1–32
**4** [a]Lev. 14:6, 49, 51, 52; Num. 19:6; Heb. 9:19 [b]Ex. 25:4 [c]Ex. 12:22; Ps. 51:7
**7** [a]Num. 19:18, 19; [Heb. 9:13, 21; 12:24] [b]2 Kin. 5:10, 14; Ps. 51:2
**8** [a]Lev. 11:25; 13:6; Num. 8:7 [b]Lev. 11:25; [Eph. 5:26; Heb. 10:22; Rev. 1:5, 6] [c]Lev. 13:5; Num. 5:2, 3; 12:14, 15; 2 Chr. 26:21
**9** [a]Num. 19:19
**10** [a]Matt. 8:4; Mark 1:44; Luke 5:14 [b]Lev. 2:1; Num. 15:4
**12** [a]Lev. 5:6, 18; 6:6; 14:19 [b]Ex. 29:22–24, 26
**13** [a]Ex. 29:11; Lev. 1:5, 11; 4:4, 24 [b]Lev. 6:24–30; 7:7 [c]Lev. 2:3; 7:6; 21:22
**14** [a]Ex. 29:20; Lev. 8:23, 24
**16** [a]Lev. 4:6

**59** "This *is* the law of the leprous plague in a
garment of wool or linen, either in the warp or
woof, or in anything made of leather, to pronounce it clean or to pronounce it unclean."

## *The Cleansing of Lepers*

**14** Then the LORD spoke to Moses, saying,
2 "This shall be the law of the [1]leper for the
day of his cleansing: He [a]shall be brought to the
priest.
3 "And the priest shall go out of the camp, and
the priest shall examine *him;* and indeed, *if* the
[1]leprosy is healed in the leper,
4 "then the priest shall command to take for
him who is to be cleansed two living *and* clean
birds, [a]cedar wood, [b]scarlet, and [c]hyssop.
5 "And the priest shall command that one of the
birds be killed in an earthen vessel over running
water.
6 "As for the living bird, he shall take it, the
cedar wood and the scarlet and the hyssop, and
dip them and the living bird in the blood of the
bird *that was* killed over the running water.
7 "And he shall [a]sprinkle it [b]seven times on him
who is to be cleansed from the leprosy, and shall
pronounce him clean, and shall let the living bird
loose in the open field.
8 "He who is to be cleansed [a]shall wash his
clothes, shave off all his hair, and [b]wash himself in
water, that he may be clean. After that he shall
come into the camp, and [c]shall stay outside his
tent seven days.
9 "But on the [a]seventh day he shall shave all the
hair off his head and his beard and his eyebrows—
all his hair he shall shave off. He shall wash his
clothes and wash his body in water, and he shall
be clean.
**10** "And on the eighth day [a]he shall take two
male lambs without blemish, one ewe lamb of the
first year without blemish, three-tenths *of an*
*ephah* of fine flour mixed with oil as [b]a grain
offering, and one log of oil.
11 "Then the priest who makes *him* clean shall
present the man who is to be made clean, and
those things, before the LORD, *at* the door of the
tabernacle of meeting.
12 "And the priest shall take one male lamb and
[a]offer it as a trespass offering, and the log of oil,
and [b]wave them *as* a wave offering before the
LORD.
13 "Then he shall kill the lamb [a]in the place
where he kills the sin offering and the burnt
offering, in a holy place; for [b]as the sin offering *is*
the priest's, so *is* the trespass offering. [c]It *is* most
holy.
14 "The priest shall take *some* of the blood of the
trespass offering, and the priest shall put *it* [a]on the
tip of the right ear of him who is to be cleansed,
on the thumb of his right hand, and on the big toe
of his right foot.
15 "And the priest shall take *some* of the log of
oil, and pour *it* into the palm of his own left hand.
16 "Then the priest shall dip his right finger in
the oil that *is* in his left hand, and shall [a]sprinkle
some of the oil with his finger seven times before
the LORD.
17 "And of the rest of the oil in his hand, the
priest shall put *some* on the tip of the right ear of
him who is to be cleansed, on the thumb of his
right hand, and on the big toe of his right foot, on
the blood of the trespass offering.

18 "The rest of the oil that *is* in the priest's hand he shall put on the head of him who is to be cleansed. [a]So the priest shall make [1]atonement for him before the LORD.
19 "Then the priest shall offer [a]the sin offering, and make atonement for him who is to be cleansed from his uncleanness. Afterward he shall kill the burnt offering.
20 "And the priest shall offer the burnt offering and the grain offering on the altar. So the priest shall make atonement for him, and he shall be [a]clean.
**21** "But [a]if he *is* poor and cannot afford it, then he shall take one male lamb *as* a trespass offering to be waved, to make atonement for him, [1]one-tenth *of an ephah* of fine flour mixed with oil as a grain offering, a log of oil,
22 [a]"and two turtledoves or two young pigeons, such as he is able to afford: one shall be a sin offering and the other a burnt offering.
23 [a]"He shall bring them to the priest on the eighth day for his cleansing, to the door of the tabernacle of meeting, before the LORD.
24 [a]"And the priest shall take the lamb of the trespass offering and the log of oil, and the priest shall wave them *as* a wave offering before the LORD.
25 "Then he shall kill the lamb of the trespass offering, [a]and the priest shall take *some* of the blood of the trespass offering and put *it* on the tip of the right ear of him who is to be cleansed, on the thumb of his right hand, and on the big toe of his right foot.
26 "And the priest shall pour some of the oil into the palm of his own left hand.
27 "Then the priest shall sprinkle with his right finger *some* of the oil that *is* in his left hand seven times before the LORD.
28 "And the priest shall put *some* of the oil that *is* in his hand on the tip of the right ear of him who is to be cleansed, on the thumb of the right hand, and on the big toe of his right foot, on the place of the blood of the trespass offering.
29 "The rest of the oil that *is* in the priest's hand he shall put on the head of him who is to be cleansed, to make atonement for him before the LORD.
30 "And he shall offer one of [a]the turtledoves or young pigeons, such as he can afford—
31 "such as he is able to afford, the one *as* a sin offering and the other *as* a burnt offering, with the grain offering. So the priest shall make atonement for him who is to be cleansed before the LORD.
32 "This *is* the law *for one* who had a leprous sore, who cannot afford [a]the usual cleansing."
**33** And the LORD spoke to Moses and Aaron, saying:
34 [a]"When you have come into the land of Canaan, which I give you as a possession, and [b]I put the [1]leprous plague in a house in the land of your possession,
35 "and he who owns the house comes and tells the priest, saying, 'It seems to me that *there is* [a]some plague in the house,'
36 "then the priest shall command that they empty the house, before the priest goes *into it* to examine the plague, that all that *is* in the house may not be made unclean; and afterward the priest shall go in to examine the house.
37 "And he shall examine the plague; and indeed *if* the plague *is* on the walls of the house with ingrained streaks, greenish or reddish, which appear to be [1]deep in the wall,
38 "then the priest shall go out of the house, to the door of the house, and [1]shut up the house seven days.
39 "And the priest shall come again on the seventh day and look; and indeed *if* the plague has spread on the walls of the house,
40 "then the priest shall command that they take away the stones in which *is* the plague, and they shall cast them into an unclean place outside the city.
41 "And he shall cause the house to be scraped inside, all around, and the dust that they scrape off they shall pour out in an unclean place outside the city.
42 "Then they shall take other stones and put *them* in the place of *those* stones, and he shall take other mortar and plaster the house.
**43** "Now if the plague comes back and breaks out in the house, after he has taken away the stones, after he has scraped the house, and after it is plastered,
44 "then the priest shall come and look; and indeed *if* the plague has spread in the house, it *is* [a]an active leprosy in the house. It *is* unclean.
45 "And he shall break down the house, its stones, its timber, and all the plaster of the house, and he shall carry *them* outside the city to an unclean place.
46 "Moreover he who goes into the house at all while it is shut up shall be [1]unclean [a]until evening.
47 "And he who lies down in the house shall [a]wash his clothes, and he who eats in the house shall wash his clothes.
**48** "But if the priest comes in and examines *it*, and indeed the plague has not spread in the house after the house was plastered, then the priest shall pronounce the house clean, because the plague is healed.
49 "And [a]he shall take, to cleanse the house, two birds, cedar wood, scarlet, and hyssop.
50 "Then he shall kill one of the birds in an earthen vessel over running water;
51 "and he shall take the cedar wood, the hyssop, the scarlet, and the living bird, and dip them in the blood of the slain bird and in the running water, and sprinkle the house seven times.
52 "And he shall [1]cleanse the house with the blood of the bird and the running water and the living bird, with the cedar wood, the hyssop, and the scarlet.
53 "Then he shall let the living bird loose outside the city in the open field, and [a]make atonement for the house, and it shall be clean.
**54** "This *is* the law for any [a]leprous sore and scale,
55 "for the [a]leprosy of a garment [b]and of a house,
56 [a]"for a swelling and a scab and a bright spot,
57 "to [a]teach when *it is* unclean and when *it is* clean. This *is* the law of leprosy."

### *Unclean Discharges from the Body*

**15** And the LORD spoke to Moses and Aaron, saying,
2 "Speak to the children of Israel, and say to them: [a]'When any man has a discharge from his body, his discharge *is* unclean.
3 'And this shall be his uncleanness in regard to his discharge—whether his body runs with his

**18** [a]Lev. 4:26; 5:6; Num. 15:28; [Heb. 2:17] [1]Lit. *covering*
**19** [a]Lev. 5:1, 6; 12:7; [2 Cor. 5:21]
**20** [a]Lev. 14:8, 9
**21** [a]Lev. 5:7, 11; 12:8; 27:8 [1]Approximately two dry quarts
**22** [a]Lev. 12:8; 15:14, 15
**23** [a]Lev. 14:10, 11
**24** [a]Lev. 14:12
**25** [a]Lev. 14:14, 17
**30** [a]Lev. 14:22; 15:14, 15
**32** [a]Lev. 14:10
**34** [a]Gen. 12:7; 13:17; 17:8; Num. 32:22; Deut. 7:1; 32:49 [b][Prov. 3:33] [1]Decomposition by mildew, mold, dry rot, etc., and so in vv. 34–53
**35** [a][Ps. 91:9, 10; Prov. 3:33; Zech. 5:4]
**37** [1]Lit. *lower than the wall*
**38** [1]*quarantine*
**44** [a]Lev. 13:51; [Zech. 5:4]
**46** [a]Lev. 11:24; 15:5 [1]*defiled*
**47** [a]Lev. 14:8
**49** [a]Lev. 14:4
**52** [1]*ceremonially cleanse*
**53** [a]Lev. 14:20
**54** [a]Lev. 13:30; 26:21
**55** [a]Lev. 13:47–52 [b]Lev. 14:34
**56** [a]Lev. 13:2
**57** [a]Lev. 11:47; 20:25; Deut. 24:8; Ezek. 44:23

CHAPTER 15
**2** [a]Lev. 22:4; Num. 5:2; 2 Sam. 3:29

discharge, or his body is stopped up by his discharge, it *is* his uncleanness.
4 ‘Every bed is [1]unclean on which he who has the discharge lies, and everything on which he sits shall be unclean.
5 ‘And whoever [a]touches his bed shall [b]wash his clothes and [c]bathe in water, and be unclean until evening.
6 ‘He who sits on anything on which he who has the [a]discharge sat shall wash his clothes and bathe in water, and be unclean until evening.
7 ‘And he who touches the body of him who has the discharge shall wash his clothes and bathe in water, and be unclean until evening.
8 ‘If he who has the discharge [a]spits on him who is clean, then he shall wash his clothes and bathe in water, and be unclean until evening.
9 ‘Any saddle on which he who has the discharge rides shall be unclean.
10 ‘Whoever touches anything that was under him shall be unclean until evening. He who carries *any of* those things shall wash his clothes and bathe in water, and be unclean until evening.
11 ‘And whomever the one who has the discharge touches, and has not rinsed his hands in water, he shall wash his clothes and bathe in water, and be unclean until evening.
12 ‘The [a]vessel of earth that he who has the discharge touches shall be broken, and every vessel of wood shall be rinsed in water.
**13** ‘And when he who has a discharge is cleansed of his discharge, then [a]he shall count for himself seven days for his cleansing, wash his clothes, and bathe his body in running water; then he shall be clean.
14 ‘On the eighth day he shall take for himself [a]two turtledoves or two young pigeons, and come before the LORD, to the door of the tabernacle of meeting, and give them to the priest.
15 ‘Then the priest shall offer them, [a]the one *as* a sin offering and the other *as* a burnt offering. [b]So the priest shall make [1]atonement for him before the LORD because of his discharge.
**16** [a]‘If any man has an emission of semen, then he shall wash all his body in water, and be unclean until evening.
17 ‘And any garment and any leather on which there is semen, it shall be washed with water, and be unclean until evening.
18 ‘Also, when a woman lies with a man, and *there is* an emission of semen, they shall bathe in water, and [a]be unclean until evening.
**19** [a]‘If a woman has a discharge, *and* the discharge from her body is blood, she shall be [1]set apart seven days; and whoever touches her shall be unclean until evening.
20 ‘Everything that she lies on during her impurity shall be unclean; also everything that she sits on shall be unclean.
21 ‘Whoever touches her bed shall wash his clothes and bathe in water, and be unclean until evening.
22 ‘And whoever touches anything that she sat on shall wash his clothes and bathe in water, and be unclean until evening.
23 ‘If *anything* is on *her* bed or on anything on which she sits, when he touches it, he shall be unclean until evening.
24 ‘And [a]if any man lies with her at all, so that her impurity is on him, he shall be [1]unclean seven days; and every bed on which he lies shall be unclean.
**25** ‘If [a]a woman has a discharge of blood for many days, other than at the time of her *customary* impurity, or if it runs beyond her *usual time of* impurity, all the days of her unclean discharge shall be as the days of her *customary* impurity. She *shall be* unclean.
26 ‘Every bed on which she lies all the days of her discharge shall be to her as the bed of her impurity; and whatever she sits on shall be unclean, as the uncleanness of her impurity.
27 ‘Whoever touches those things shall be unclean; he shall wash his clothes and bathe in water, and be unclean until evening.
**28** ‘But [a]if she is cleansed of her discharge, then she shall count for herself seven days, and after that she shall be clean.
29 ‘And on the eighth day she shall take for herself two turtledoves or two young pigeons, and bring them to the priest, to the door of the tabernacle of meeting.
30 ‘Then the priest shall offer the one *as* a sin offering and the other *as* a [a]burnt offering, and the priest shall make atonement for her before the LORD for the discharge of her uncleanness.
**31** ‘Thus you shall [a]separate the children of Israel from their uncleanness, lest they die in their uncleanness when they [b]defile My tabernacle that *is* among them.
32 [a]‘This *is* the law for one who has a discharge, [b]and *for him* who emits semen and is unclean thereby,
33 [a]‘and for her who is indisposed because of her *customary* impurity, and for one who has a discharge, either man [b]or woman, [c]and for him who lies with her who is unclean.’ ”

### *The Day of Atonement*

**16** Now the LORD spoke to Moses after [a]the death of the two sons of Aaron, when they offered *profane fire* before the LORD, and died;
2 and the LORD said to Moses: “Tell Aaron your brother [a]not to come at *just* any time into the Holy *Place* inside the veil, before the mercy seat which *is* on the ark, lest he die; for [b]I will appear in the cloud above the mercy seat.
3 [1]“Thus Aaron shall [a]come into the Holy *Place:* [b]with *the blood of* a young bull as a sin offering, and *of* a ram as a burnt offering.
4 “He shall put the [a]holy linen tunic and the linen trousers on his body; he shall be girded with a linen sash, and with the linen turban he shall be attired. These *are* holy garments. Therefore [b]he shall wash his body in water, and put them on.
5 “And he shall take from [a]the congregation of the children of Israel two kids of the goats as a sin offering, and one ram as a burnt offering.
**6** “Aaron shall offer the bull as a sin offering, which *is* for himself, and [a]make atonement for himself and for his house.
7 “He shall take the two goats and present them before the LORD *at* the door of the tabernacle of meeting.
8 “Then Aaron shall cast lots for the two goats: one lot for the LORD and the other lot for the scapegoat.
9 “And Aaron shall bring the goat on which the LORD’s lot fell, and offer it *as* a sin offering.
10 “But the goat on which the lot fell to be the scapegoat shall be presented alive before the

**4** [1]*defiled*
**5** [a]Lev. 5:2; 14:46 [b]Lev. 14:8, 47 [c]Lev. 11:25; 17:15
**6** [a]Lev. 15:10; Deut. 23:10
**8** [a]Num. 12:14
**12** [a]Lev. 6:28; 11:32, 33
**13** [a]Lev. 14:8; 15:28; Num. 19:11, 12
**14** [a]Lev. 14:22, 23, 30, 31
**15** [a]Lev. 14:30, 31 [b]Lev. 14:19, 31 [1]Lit. *covering*
**16** [a]Lev. 22:4; Deut. 23:10, 11
**18** [a][Ex. 19:15; 1 Sam. 21:4; 1 Cor. 6:18]
**19** [a]Lev. 12:2 [1]Lit. *in her impurity*
**24** [a]Lev. 18:19; 20:18 [1]*defiled*
**25** [a]Matt. 9:20; Mark 5:25; Luke 8:43
**28** [a]Lev. 15:13–15
**30** [a]Lev. 5:7
**31** [a]Lev. 11:47; 14:57; 22:2; Deut. 24:8; Ezek. 44:23; [Heb. 12:15] [b]Lev. 20:3; Num. 5:3; 19:13, 20; Ezek. 5:11; 23:38; 36:17
**32** [a]Lev. 15:2 [b]Lev. 15:16
**33** [a]Lev. 15:19 [b]Lev. 15:25 [c]Lev. 15:24

CHAPTER 16

**1** [a]Lev. 10:1, 2; 2 Sam. 6:6–8
**2** [a]Ex. 30:10; Lev. 16:34; 23:27; [Heb. 6:19; 9:7, 8, 12; 10:19] [b]Ex. 25:21, 22; 40:34; 1 Kin. 8:10–12
**3** [a]Lev. 4:1–12; 16:6; [Heb. 9:7, 12, 24, 25] [b]Lev. 4:3 [1]Lit. *With this*
**4** [a]Ex. 28:39, 42, 43; Lev. 6:10; Ezek. 44:17, 18 [b]Ex. 30:20; Lev. 8:6, 7
**5** [a]Lev. 4:14; Num. 29:11; 2 Chr. 29:21; Ezra 6:17; Ezek. 45:22, 23
**6** [a]Lev. 9:7; [Heb. 5:3; 7:27, 28; 9:7]

LORD, to make [a]atonement upon it, *and* to let it go
as the scapegoat into the wilderness.
**11** "And Aaron shall bring the bull of the sin
offering, which is for [a]himself, and make atonement for himself and for his house, and shall kill
the bull as the sin offering which *is* for himself.
12 "Then he shall take [a]a censer full of burning
coals of fire from the altar before the LORD, with
his hands full of [b]sweet incense beaten fine, and
bring *it* inside the veil.
13 [a]"And he shall put the incense on the fire
before the LORD, that the cloud of incense may
cover the [b]mercy seat that *is* on the Testimony,
lest he [c]die.
14 [a]"He shall take some of the blood of the bull
and [b]sprinkle *it* with his finger on the mercy seat
on the east *side;* and before the mercy seat he
shall sprinkle some of the blood with his finger
seven times.
**15** [a]"Then he shall kill the goat of the sin offering,
which *is* for the people, bring its blood [b]inside the
veil, do with that blood as he did with the blood of
the bull, and sprinkle it on the mercy seat and
before the mercy seat.
16 "So he shall [a]make atonement for the Holy
*Place,* because of the uncleanness of the children
of Israel, and because of their transgressions, for
all their sins; and so he shall do for the tabernacle
of meeting which remains among them in the
midst of their uncleanness.
17 "There shall be [a]no man in the tabernacle of
meeting when he goes in to make atonement in
the Holy *Place,* until he comes out, that he may
make atonement for himself, for his household,
and for all the assembly of Israel.
18 "And he shall go out to the altar that *is* before
the LORD, and make atonement for [a]it, and shall
take some of the blood of the bull and some of the
blood of the goat, and put it on the horns of the
altar all around.
19 "Then he shall sprinkle some of the blood on it
with his finger seven times, cleanse it, and [a]conse-
crate[1] it from the [2]uncleanness of the children of
Israel.
**20** "And when he has made an end of atoning for
the Holy *Place,* the tabernacle of meeting, and the
altar, he shall bring the live goat.
21 "Aaron shall lay both his hands on the head of
the live goat, [a]confess over it all the iniquities of
the children of Israel, and all their transgressions,
concerning all their sins, [b]putting them on the
head of the goat, and shall send *it* away into the
wilderness by the hand of a suitable man.
22 "The goat [1]shall [a]bear on itself all their iniquities to an [2]uninhabited land; and he shall [b]release
the goat in the wilderness.
**23** "Then Aaron shall come into the tabernacle of
meeting, [a]shall take off the linen garments which
he put on when he went into the Holy *Place,* and
shall leave them there.
24 "And he shall wash his body with water in a
holy place, put on his garments, come out and
offer his burnt offering and the burnt offering of
the people, and make [1]atonement for himself and
for the people.
25 [a]"The fat of the sin offering he shall burn on
the altar.
26 "And he who released the goat as the scapegoat shall wash his clothes [a]and bathe his body in
water, and afterward he may come into the camp.
27 [a]"The bull *for* the sin offering and the goat *for*
the sin offering, whose blood was brought in to
make atonement in the Holy *Place,* shall be carried outside the camp. And they shall burn in the
fire their skins, their flesh, and their offal.
28 "Then he who burns them shall wash his
clothes and bathe his body in water, and afterward he may come into the camp.
**29** "*This* shall be a statute forever for you: [a]In the
seventh month, on the tenth *day* of the month,
you shall [1]afflict your souls, and do no work at all,
*whether* a native of your own country or a stranger who [2]dwells among you.
30 "For on that day *the priest* shall make [1]atone-
ment for you, to [a]cleanse you, *that* you may be
clean from all your sins before the LORD.
31 [a]"It *is* a sabbath of solemn rest for you, and
you shall afflict your souls. *It is* a statute forever.
32 [a]"And the priest, who is anointed and [b]conse-
crated to minister as priest in his father's place,
shall make atonement, and put on the linen
clothes, the holy garments;
33 "then he shall make [1]atonement for [2]the Holy
Sanctuary, and he shall make atonement for the
tabernacle of meeting and for the altar, and he
shall make atonement for the priests and for all
the people of the assembly.
34 [a]"This shall be an everlasting statute for you,
to make atonement for the children of Israel, for
all their sins, [b]once a year." And he did as the
LORD commanded Moses.

## *One Place of Sacrifice*

**17** And the LORD spoke to Moses, saying,
2 "Speak to Aaron, to his sons, and to all
the children of Israel, and say to them, 'This *is* the
thing which the LORD has commanded, saying:
3 "Whatever man of the house of Israel, [a]kills an
ox or lamb or goat in the camp, or who kills *it*
outside the camp,
4 "and does not bring it to the door of the
tabernacle of meeting, to offer an offering to the
LORD before the tabernacle of the LORD, the guilt
of bloodshed shall be [a]imputed to that man. He
has shed blood; and that man shall be [1]cut off
from among his people,
5 "to the end that the children of Israel may
bring their sacrifices [a]which they offer in the open
field, that they may bring them to the LORD at the
door of the tabernacle of meeting, to the priest,
and offer them *as* peace offerings to the LORD.
6 "And the priest [a]shall sprinkle the blood on the
altar of the LORD *at* the door of the tabernacle of
meeting, and [b]burn the fat for a sweet aroma to
the LORD.
7 "They shall no more offer their sacrifices [a]to
[1]demons, after whom they [b]have played the harlot.
This shall be a statute forever for them throughout their generations." '
8 "Also you shall say to them: 'Whatever man of
the house of Israel, or of the strangers who dwell
among you, [a]who offers a burnt offering or sacrifice,
9 'and does not [a]bring it to the door of the
tabernacle of meeting, to offer it to the LORD, that
man shall be [1]cut off from among his people.
**10** [a]'And whatever man of the house of Israel, or
of the strangers who dwell among you, who eats
any blood, [b]I will set My face against that person
who eats blood, and will cut him off from among
his people.
11 'For the [a]life of the flesh *is* in the blood, and I

**10** [a][1 John 2:2]
**11** [a][Heb. 7:27; 9:7]
**12** [a]Lev. 10:1 [b]Ex. 30:34–38
**13** [a]Ex. 30:7, 8 [b]Ex. 25:21 [c]Ex. 28:43
**14** [a][Heb. 9:25; 10:4] [b]Lev. 4:6, 17
**15** [a][Heb. 2:17] [b][Heb. 6:19; 7:27; 9:3, 7, 12]
**16** [a]Ex. 29:36; 30:10
**17** [a]Luke 1:10
**18** [a]Ex. 29:36
**19** [a]Ezek. 43:20 [1]*set it apart* [2]*impurity*
**21** [a]Lev. 5:5; 26:40 [b][Is. 53:6]
**22** [a][Is. 53:6, 11, 12] [b]Lev. 14:7 [1]*shall carry* [2]*solitary land*
**23** [a]Ezek. 42:14; 44:19
**24** [1]Lit. *covering*
**25** [a]Lev. 1:8; 4:10
**26** [a]Lev. 15:5
**27** [a]Heb. 13:11
**29** [a]Lev. 23:27–32 [1]*humble yourselves* [2]As a resident alien
**30** [a]Jer. 33:8 [1]Lit. *covering*
**31** [a]Lev. 23:27, 32
**32** [a]Lev. 4:3, 5, 16; 21:10 [b]Ex. 29:29, 30
**33** [1]Lit. *covering* [2]The Most Holy Place
**34** [a]Lev. 23:31 [b][Heb. 9:7, 25, 28]

CHAPTER 17
**3** [a]Deut. 12:5, 15, 21
**4** [a]Rom. 5:13 [1]Put to death
**5** [a]Deut. 12:1–27
**6** [a]Lev. 3:2 [b]Num. 18:17
**7** [a]Deut. 32:17 [b]Ezek. 23:8 [1]Having the form of a goat or satyr
**8** [a]Lev. 1:2, 3; 18:26
**9** [a]Lev. 14:23 [1]Put to death
**10** [a]Gen. 9:4 [b]Lev. 20:3, 5, 6
**11** [a]Gen. 9:4

have given it to you upon the altar [b]to make
atonement for your souls; for [c]it *is* the blood *that*
makes atonement for the soul.'
12 "Therefore I said to the children of Israel, 'No
one among you shall eat blood, nor shall any
stranger who dwells among you eat blood.'
13 "Whatever man of the children of Israel, or of
the strangers who dwell among you, who [a]hunts
and catches any animal or bird that may be eaten,
he shall [b]pour out its blood and [c]cover it with dust;
14 [a]"for *it is* the life of all flesh. Its blood sustains
its life. Therefore I said to the children of Israel,
'You shall not eat the blood of any flesh, for the
life of all flesh is its blood. Whoever eats it shall be
cut off.'
15 [a]"And every person who eats what died *natu-*
*rally* or what was torn *by beasts, whether he is* a
native of your own country or a stranger, [b]he shall
both wash his clothes and [c]bathe in water, and be
unclean until evening. Then he shall be clean.
16 "But if he does not wash *them* or bathe his
body, then [a]he shall bear his [1]guilt."

## *Immorality Is Forbidden*

18 Then the LORD spoke to Moses, saying,
2 "Speak to the children of Israel, and say
to them: [a]'I am the LORD your God.
3 [a]'According to [1]the doings of the land of
Egypt, where you dwelt, you shall not do; and
[b]according to the doings of the land of Canaan,
where I am bringing you, you shall not do; nor
shall you walk in their [2]ordinances.
4 [a]'You shall observe My judgments and keep
My ordinances, to walk in them: I *am* the LORD
your God.
5 'You shall therefore keep My statutes and My
judgments, which if a man does, he shall live by
them: I *am* the LORD.
6 'None of you shall approach anyone who is
near of kin to him, to uncover his nakedness: I *am*
the LORD.
7 'The nakedness of your father or the nakedness of your mother you shall not uncover. She *is*
your mother; you shall not uncover her nakedness.
8 'The nakedness of your [a]father's wife you shall
not uncover; it *is* your father's nakedness.
9 [a]'The nakedness of your sister, the daughter of
your father, or the daughter of your mother,
*whether* born at home or elsewhere, their nakedness you shall not uncover.
10 'The nakedness of your son's daughter or your
daughter's daughter, their nakedness you shall
not uncover; for theirs *is* your own nakedness.
11 'The nakedness of your father's wife's daughter, begotten by your father—she *is* your sister—
you shall not uncover her nakedness.
12 [a]'You shall not uncover the nakedness of your
father's sister; she *is* near of kin to your father.
13 'You shall not uncover the nakedness of your
mother's sister, for she *is* near of kin to your
mother.
14 [a]'You shall not uncover the nakedness of your
father's brother. You shall not approach his wife;
she *is* your aunt.
15 'You shall not uncover the nakedness of your
daughter-in-law—she *is* your son's wife—you
shall not uncover her nakedness.
16 'You shall not uncover the nakedness of your
brother's wife; it *is* your brother's nakedness.
17 'You shall not uncover the nakedness of a
woman and her [a]daughter, nor shall you take her
son's daughter or her daughter's daughter, to
uncover her nakedness. They *are* near of kin to
her. It *is* wickedness.
18 'Nor shall you take a woman [a]as a rival to her
sister, to uncover her nakedness while the other is
alive.
19 'Also you shall not approach a woman to
uncover her nakedness as [a]long as she is in her
[b]*customary* impurity.
20 [a]'Moreover you shall not lie carnally with your
[b]neighbor's wife, to defile yourself with her.
21 'And you shall not let any of your descendants
[a]pass through [b]*the fire* to [c]Molech, nor shall you
profane the name of your God: I *am* the LORD.
22 'You shall not lie with [a]a male as with a
woman. It *is* an abomination.
23 'Nor shall you mate with any [a]animal, to defile
yourself with it. Nor shall any woman stand
before an animal to mate with it. It *is* perversion.
24 [a]'Do not defile yourselves with any of these
things; [b]for by all these the nations are defiled,
which I am casting out before you.
25 'For [a]the land is defiled; therefore I [b]visit[1] the
punishment of its iniquity upon it, and the land
[c]vomits out its inhabitants.
26 [a]'You shall therefore [1]keep My statutes and
My judgments, and shall not commit *any* of these
abominations, *either* any of your own nation or
any stranger who dwells among you
27 '(for all these abominations the men of the
land have done, who *were* before you, and thus
the land is defiled),
28 'lest [a]the land vomit you out also when you
defile it, as it vomited out the nations that *were*
before you.
29 'For whoever commits any of these abominations, the persons who commit *them* shall be [1]cut
off from among their people.
30 'Therefore you shall keep My [1]ordinance, so
[a]that *you* do not commit *any* of these abominable
customs which were committed before you, and
that you do not defile yourselves by them: [b]I *am*
the LORD your God.' "

## *Moral and Ceremonial Laws*

19 And the LORD spoke to Moses, saying,
2 "Speak to all the congregation of the
children of Israel, and say to them: [a]'You shall be
holy, for I the LORD your God *am* holy.
3 [a]'Every one of you shall revere his mother and
his father, and [b]keep My Sabbaths: I *am* the LORD
your God.
4 [a]'Do not turn to idols, [b]nor make for yourselves [1]molded gods: I *am* the LORD your God.
5 'And [a]if you offer a sacrifice of a peace offering
to the LORD, you shall offer it of your own free
will.
6 'It shall be eaten the same day you offer *it,* and
on the next day. And if any remains until the third
day, it shall be burned in the fire.
7 'And if it is eaten at all on the third day, it *is* an
abomination. It shall not be accepted.
8 'Therefore *everyone* who eats it shall bear his
iniquity, because he has profaned the hallowed
*offering* of the LORD; and that person shall be cut
off from his people.
9 [a]'When you reap the harvest of your land, you
shall not wholly reap the corners of your field, nor
shall you gather the gleanings of your harvest.
10 'And you shall not glean your vineyard, nor

11 [b][Matt. 26:28] [c][Heb. 9:22]
13 [a]Lev. 7:26 [b]Deut. 12:16, 24 [c]Ezek. 24:7
14 [a]Gen. 9:4
15 [a]Ex. 22:31 [b]Lev. 11:25 [c]Lev. 15:5
16 [a]Lev. 5:1 [1]*iniquity*

CHAPTER 18
2 [a]Ex. 6:7
3 [a]Ezek. 20:7, 8 [b]Lev. 18:24–30; 20:23 [1]*what is done in* [2]*statutes*
4 [a]Ezek. 20:19
8 [a]Gen. 35:22
9 [a]Deut. 27:22
12 [a]Lev. 20:19
14 [a]Lev. 20:20
17 [a]Lev. 20:14
18 [a]1 Sam. 1:6, 8
19 [a]Ezek. 18:6 [b]Lev. 15:24; 20:18
20 [a][Prov. 6:25–33] [b]Lev. 20:10
21 [a]Lev. 20:2–5 [b]2 Kin. 16:3 [c]1 Kin. 11:7, 33
22 [a]Lev. 20:13
23 [a]Ex. 22:19
24 [a]Matt. 15:18–20 [b]Deut. 18:12
25 [a]Num. 35:33, 34 [b]Jer. 5:9 [c]Lev. 18:28; 20:22 [1]*bring judgment for*
26 [a]Lev. 18:5, 30 [1]*obey*
28 [a]Jer. 9:19
29 [1]Put to death
30 [a]Lev. 18:3; 22:9 [b]Lev. 18:2 [1]*charge*

CHAPTER 19
2 [a]Lev. 11:44; 20:7, 26
3 [a]Ex. 20:12 [b]Ex. 16:23; 20:8; 31:13
4 [a]Ex. 20:4 [b]Ex. 34:17 [1]*molten*
5 [a]Lev. 7:16
9 [a]Deut. 24:19–22

shall you gather *every* grape of your vineyard;
you shall leave them for the poor and the stranger: I *am* the LORD your God.
11 [a]'You shall not steal, nor deal falsely, [b]nor lie
to one another.
12 'And you shall not [a]swear by My name falsely,
[b]nor shall you profane the name of your God: I *am*
the LORD.
**13** [a]'You shall not cheat your neighbor, nor rob
*him.* [b]The wages of him who is hired shall not
remain with you all night until morning.
14 'You shall not curse the deaf, [a]nor put a
stumblingblock before the blind, but shall fear
your God: I *am* the LORD.
**15** 'You shall do no injustice in [a]judgment. You
shall not [b]be partial to the poor, nor honor the
person of the mighty. In righteousness you shall
judge your neighbor.
16 'You shall not go about *as* a [a]talebearer among
your people; nor shall you [b]take a stand against
the life of your neighbor: I *am* the LORD.
**17** [a]'You shall not hate your brother in your
heart. [b]You shall surely [1]rebuke your neighbor,
and not bear sin because of him.
18 [a]'You shall not take vengeance, nor bear any
grudge against the children of your people, [b]but
you shall love your neighbor as yourself: I *am* the
LORD.
**19** 'You shall keep My statutes. You shall not let
your livestock breed with another kind. You shall
not sow your field with mixed seed. Nor shall a
garment of mixed linen and wool come upon you.
20 'Whoever lies carnally with a woman who *is*
[a]betrothed to a man as a concubine, and who has
not at all been redeemed nor given her freedom,
for this there shall be [1]scourging; *but* they shall
not be put to death, because she was not free.
21 'And he shall bring his trespass offering to the
LORD, to the door of the tabernacle of meeting, a
ram as a trespass offering.
22 'The priest shall make [1]atonement for him
with the ram of the trespass offering before the
LORD for his sin which he has committed. And the
sin which he has committed shall be forgiven him.
**23** 'When you come into the land, and have
planted all kinds of trees for food, then you shall
count their fruit as [1]uncircumcised. Three years it
shall be as uncircumcised to you. *It* shall not be
eaten.
24 'But in the fourth year all its fruit shall be
holy, a praise to the LORD.
25 'And in the fifth year you may eat its fruit,
that it may yield to you its increase: I *am* the
LORD your God.
**26** 'You shall not eat *anything* with the blood,
nor shall you practice divination or soothsaying.
27 'You shall not shave around the sides of your
head, nor shall you disfigure the edges of your
beard.
28 'You shall not [a]make any cuttings in your
flesh for the dead, nor tattoo any marks on you: I
*am* the LORD.
**29** [a]'Do not prostitute your daughter, to cause her
to be a harlot, lest the land fall into harlotry, and
the land become full of wickedness.
**30** 'You shall [1]keep My Sabbaths and [a]reverence
My sanctuary: I *am* the LORD.
**31** 'Give no regard to mediums and familiar spirits; do not seek after [a]them, to be defiled by them:
I *am* the LORD your God.
**32** [a]'You shall [1]rise before the gray headed and
honor the presence of an old man, and [b]fear your
God: I *am* the LORD.
**33** 'And [a]if a stranger dwells with you in your
land, you shall not mistreat him.
34 [a]'The stranger who dwells among you shall be
to you as [1]one born among you, and [b]you shall
love him as yourself; for you were strangers in the
land of Egypt: I *am* the LORD your God.
**35** 'You shall do no injustice in judgment, in
measurement of length, weight, or volume.
36 'You shall have [a]honest scales, honest weights,
an honest ephah, and an honest hin: I *am* the
LORD your God, who brought you out of the land
of Egypt.
**37** [a]'Therefore you shall observe all My statutes
and all My judgments, and perform them: I *am*
the LORD.' "

### *Penalties for Breaking the Law*

**20** Then the LORD spoke to Moses, saying,
2 [a]"Again, you shall say to the children of
Israel: [b]'Whoever of the children of Israel, or of
the strangers who [1]dwell in Israel, who gives *any*
of his descendants to Molech, he shall surely be
put to death. The people of the land shall [c]stone
him with stones.
3 [a]'I will set My face against that man, and will
[1]cut him off from his people, because he has given
*some* of his descendants to Molech, to defile My
sanctuary and profane My holy name.
4 'And if the people of the land should in any
way [1]hide their eyes from the man, when he gives
*some* of his descendants to Molech, and they do
not kill him,
5 'then I will set My face against that man and
against his family; and I will cut him off from his
people, and all who prostitute themselves with
him to commit harlotry with Molech.
**6** 'And [a]the person who turns to mediums and
familiar spirits, to prostitute himself with them, I
will set My face against that person and cut him
off from his people.
7 [a]'Consecrate[1] yourselves therefore, and be
holy, for I *am* the LORD your God.
**8** 'And you shall keep [a]My statutes, and perform
them: [b]I *am* the LORD who [1]sanctifies you.
9 'For [a]everyone who curses his father or his
mother shall surely be put to death. He has cursed
his father or his mother. [b]His blood *shall be* upon
him.
10 [a]'The man who commits adultery with *another*
man's wife, *he* who commits adultery with his
neighbor's wife, the adulterer and the adulteress,
shall surely be put to death.
11 'The man who lies with his [a]father's wife has
uncovered his father's nakedness; both of them
shall surely be put to death. Their blood *shall be*
upon them.
12 'If a man lies with his [a]daughter-in-law, both
of them shall surely be put to death. They have
committed perversion. Their blood *shall be* upon
them.
13 [a]'If a man lies with a male as he lies with a
woman, both of them have committed an abomination. They shall surely be put to death. Their
blood *shall be* upon them.
14 'If a man marries a woman and her [a]mother, it
*is* wickedness. They shall be burned with fire, both
he and they, that there may be no wickedness
among you.
15 'If a man mates with an [a]animal, he shall

11 [a]Ex. 20:15, 16 [b]Eph. 4:25
12 [a]Deut. 5:11 [b]Lev. 18:21
13 [a]Ex. 22:7–15, 21–27 [b]Deut. 24:15
14 [a]Deut. 27:18
15 [a]Deut. 16:19 [b]Ex. 23:3, 6
16 [a]Prov. 11:13; 18:8; 20:19 [b]1 Kin. 21:7–19
17 [a][1 John 2:9, 11; 3:15] [b]Matt. 18:15 [1]*reprove*
18 [a][Deut. 32:35] [b]Mark 12:31
20 [a]Deut. 22:23–27 [1]*punishment*
22 [1]Lit. *covering*
23 [1]*unclean*
28 [a]Jer. 16:6
29 [a]Deut. 22:21; 23:17, 18
30 [a]Lev. 26:2 [1]*observe*
31 [a]Lev. 20:6, 27
32 [a]1 Tim. 5:1 [b]Lev. 19:14 [1]*rise to give honor*
33 [a]Ex. 22:21
34 [a]Ex. 12:48 [b]Deut. 10:19 [1]*native among you*
36 [a]Deut. 25:13–15
37 [a]Lev. 18:4, 5

CHAPTER 20
2 [a]Lev. 18:2 [b]Lev. 18:21 [c]Deut. 17:2–5 [1]*As resident aliens*
3 [a]Lev. 17:10 [1]Put him to death
4 [1]*disregard*
6 [a]Lev. 19:31
7 [a]Lev. 19:2 [1]*Set yourselves apart* for the LORD
8 [a]Lev. 19:19, 37 [b]Ex. 31:13 [1]*sets you apart*
9 [a]Ex. 21:17 [b]2 Sam. 1:16
10 [a]Ex. 20:14
11 [a]Lev. 18:7, 8
12 [a]Lev. 18:15
13 [a]Lev. 18:22
14 [a]Lev. 18:17
15 [a]Lev. 18:23

surely be put to death, and you shall kill the animal.

16 'If a woman approaches any animal and mates with it, you shall kill the woman and the animal. They shall surely be put to death. Their blood *is* upon them.

17 'If a man takes his [a]sister, his father's daughter or his mother's daughter, and sees her nakedness and she sees his nakedness, it *is* a wicked thing. And they shall be [1]cut off in the sight of their people. He has uncovered his sister's nakedness. He shall bear his [2]guilt.

18 [a]'If a man lies with a woman during her [1]sickness and uncovers her nakedness, he has [2]exposed her flow, and she has uncovered the flow of her blood. Both of them shall be [3]cut off from their people.

19 'You shall not uncover the nakedness of your [a]mother's sister nor of your [b]father's sister, for that would uncover his near of kin. They shall bear their guilt.

20 'If a man lies with his [a]uncle's wife, he has uncovered his uncle's nakedness. They shall bear their sin; they shall die childless.

21 'If a man takes his [a]brother's wife, it *is* an [1]unclean thing. He has uncovered his brother's nakedness. They shall be childless.

**22** 'You shall therefore keep all My [a]statutes and all My judgments, and perform them, that the land where I am bringing you to dwell [b]may not vomit you out.

23 [a]'And you shall not walk in the statutes of the nation which I am casting out before you; for they commit all these things, and [b]therefore I abhor them.

24 'But [a]I have said to you, "You shall inherit their land, and I will give it to you to possess, a land flowing with milk and honey." I *am* the LORD your God, [b]who has separated you from the peoples.

25 [a]'You shall therefore distinguish between clean animals and unclean, between unclean birds and clean, [b]and you shall not make yourselves [1]abominable by beast or by bird, or by any kind of living thing that creeps on the ground, which I have separated from you as [2]unclean.

26 'And you shall be holy to Me, [a]for I the LORD *am* holy, and have separated you from the peoples, that you should be Mine.

**27** [a]'A man or a woman who is a medium, or who has familiar spirits, shall surely be put to death; they shall stone them with stones. Their blood *shall be* upon them.' "

### *The Holiness of the Priests*

**21** And the LORD said to Moses, "Speak to the priests, the sons of Aaron, and say to them: [a]'None shall defile himself for the dead among his people,

2 'except for his relatives who are nearest to him: his mother, his father, his son, his daughter, and his brother;

3 'also his virgin sister who is near to him, who has had no husband, for her he may defile himself.

4 '*Otherwise* he shall not defile himself, *being* a [1]chief man among his people, to profane himself.

**5** [a]'They shall not make any bald *place* on their heads, nor shall they shave the edges of their beards nor make any cuttings in their flesh.

6 'They shall be [a]holy to their God and not profane the name of their God, for they offer the offerings of the LORD made by fire, *and* the [b]bread of their God; [c]therefore they shall be holy.

7 [a]'They shall not take a wife *who is* a harlot or a defiled woman, nor shall they take a woman [b]divorced from her husband; for [1]*the priest* is holy to his God.

8 'Therefore you shall [1]consecrate him, for he offers the bread of your God. He shall be holy to you, for [a]I the LORD, who [b]sanctify you, *am* holy.

9 'The daughter of any priest, if she profanes herself by playing the harlot, she profanes her father. She shall be [a]burned with fire.

**10** '*He who is* the high priest among his brethren, on whose head the anointing oil was [a]poured and who is consecrated to wear the garments, shall not [b]uncover[1] his head nor tear his clothes;

11 'nor shall he go [a]near any dead body, nor defile himself for his father or his mother;

12 [a]'nor shall he go out of the sanctuary, nor profane the sanctuary of his God; for the [b]consecration of the anointing oil of his God *is* upon him: I *am* the LORD.

13 'And he shall take a wife in her virginity.

14 'A widow or a divorced woman or a defiled woman *or* a harlot—these he shall not marry; but he shall take a virgin of his own people as wife.

15 'Nor shall he profane his posterity among his people, for I the LORD sanctify him.' "

**16** And the LORD spoke to Moses, saying,

17 "Speak to Aaron, saying: 'No man of your descendants in *succeeding* generations, who has *any* defect, may approach to offer the bread of his God.

18 'For any man who has a [a]defect shall not approach: a man blind or lame, who has a marred *face* or any *limb* [b]too long,

19 'a man who has a broken foot or broken hand,

20 'or is a hunchback or a dwarf, or *a man* who has a defect in his eye, or eczema or scab, or is a eunuch.

21 'No man of the descendants of Aaron the priest, who has a defect, shall come near to offer the offerings made by fire to the LORD. He has a defect; he shall not come near to offer the bread of his God.

22 'He may eat the bread of his God, *both* the most holy and the holy;

23 'only he shall not go near the [a]veil or approach the altar, because he has a defect, lest [b]he profane My sanctuaries; for I the LORD sanctify them.' "

24 And Moses told *it* to Aaron and his sons, and to all the children of Israel.

### *The Holiness of the Offerings*

**22** Then the LORD spoke to Moses, saying,

2 "Speak to Aaron and his sons, that they [a]separate[1] themselves from the holy things of the children of Israel, and that they [b]do not profane My holy name *by* what they [c]dedicate to Me: I *am* the LORD.

3 "Say to them: 'Whoever of all your descendants throughout your generations, who goes near the holy things which the children of Israel dedicate to the LORD, [a]while he has [1]uncleanness upon him, that person shall be cut off from My presence: I *am* the LORD.

4 'Whatever man of the descendants of Aaron, who *is* a [a]leper or has [b]a discharge, shall not eat the holy offerings [c]until he is clean. And [d]whoever touches anything made unclean *by* a corpse, or [e]a man who has had an emission of semen,

---

17 [a]Lev. 18:9; Deut. 27:22 [1]Put to death [2]*iniquity*
18 [a]Lev. 15:24; 18:19 [1]Or *customary impurity* [2]Lit. *made bare* [3]Put to death
19 [a]Lev. 18:13 [b]Lev. 18:12
20 [a]Lev. 18:14
21 [a]Lev. 18:16; Matt. 14:3, 4 [1]*indecent, impure*
22 [a]Lev. 18:26; 19:37 [b]Lev. 18:25, 28; 2 Chr. 36:14–16
23 [a]Lev. 18:3, 24 [b]Deut. 9:5
24 [a]Ex. 3:17; 6:8; 13:5; 33:1–3 [b]Ex. 19:5; 33:16; Lev. 20:26; Deut. 7:6; 14:2; 1 Kin. 8:53
25 [a]Lev. 10:10; 11:1–47; Deut. 14:3–21 [b]Lev. 11:43 [1]*detestable* or *loathsome* [2]*defiled*
26 [a]Lev. 19:2; 1 Pet. 1:16
27 [a]Lev. 19:31; 1 Sam. 28:9

CHAPTER 21
1 [a]Lev. 19:28; Ezek. 44:25
4 [1]Lit. *master* or *husband*
5 [a]Lev. 19:27; Deut. 14:1; Ezek. 44:20
6 [a]Ex. 22:31 [b]Lev. 3:11 [c]Is. 52:11
7 [a]Ezek. 44:22 [b]Deut. 24:1, 2 [1]Lit. *he*
8 [a]Lev. 11:44, 45 [b]Lev. 8:12, 30 [1]*set him apart*
9 [a]Deut. 22:21
10 [a]Lev. 8:12 [b]Lev. 10:6, 7 [1]In mourning
11 [a]Num. 19:14
12 [a]Lev. 10:7 [b]Ex. 29:6, 7
18 [a]Lev. 22:19–25 [b]Lev. 22:23
23 [a]Lev. 16:2 [b]Lev. 21:12

CHAPTER 22
2 [a]Num. 6:3 [b]Lev. 18:21 [c]Ex. 28:38; Lev. 16:19; 25:10; Num. 18:32; Deut. 15:19 [1]*keep themselves apart from*
3 [a]Lev. 7:20, 21; Num. 19:13 [1]*defilement*
4 [a]Num. 5:2 [b]Lev. 15:2 [c]Lev. 14:2; 15:13 [d]Lev. 11:24–28, 39, 40; Num. 19:11 [e]Lev. 15:16, 17

5 ‘or [a]whoever touches any creeping thing by
which he would be made unclean, or [b]any person
by whom he would become unclean, whatever his
uncleanness may be—
6 ‘the person who has touched any such thing
shall be unclean until evening, and shall not eat
the holy *offerings* unless he [a]washes his body with
water.
7 ‘And when the sun goes down he shall be
clean; and afterward he may eat the holy *offer-*
*ings,* because [a]it *is* his food.
8 [a]‘Whatever dies *naturally* or is torn *by beasts*
he shall not eat, to defile himself with it: I *am* the
LORD.
9 ‘They shall therefore keep [a]My [1]ordinance,
[b]lest they bear sin for it and die thereby, if they
profane it: I the LORD sanctify them.
**10** [a]‘No outsider shall eat the holy *offering;* one
who [1]dwells with the priest, or a hired servant,
shall not eat the holy thing.
11 ‘But if the priest [a]buys a person with his
money, he may eat it; and one who is born in his
house may eat his food.
12 ‘If the priest’s daughter is married to an outsider, she may not eat of the holy offerings.
13 ‘But if the priest’s daughter is a widow or
divorced, and has no child, and has returned to
her father’s house as in her youth, she may eat her
father’s food; but no outsider shall eat it.
**14** ‘And if a man eats the holy *offering* unintentionally, then he shall restore a holy *offering* to
the priest, and add one-fifth to it.
15 ‘They shall not profane the [a]holy *offerings* of
the children of Israel, which they offer to the
LORD,
16 ‘or allow them to bear the guilt of trespass
when they eat their holy *offerings;* for I the LORD
sanctify them.’ ”
**17** And the LORD spoke to Moses, saying,
18 “Speak to Aaron and his sons, and to all the
children of Israel, and say to them: [a]‘Whatever
man of the house of Israel, or of the strangers in
Israel, who [1]offers his sacrifice for any of his vows
or for any of his freewill offerings, which they
offer to the LORD as a burnt offering—
19 [a]‘*you shall offer* of your own free will a male
without blemish from the cattle, from the sheep,
or from the goats.
20 [a]‘Whatever has a defect, you shall not offer,
for it shall not be acceptable on your behalf.
21 ‘And [a]whoever offers a sacrifice of a peace
offering to the LORD, [b]to fulfill *his* vow, or a
freewill offering from the cattle or the sheep, it
must be perfect to be accepted; there shall be no
defect in it.
22 [a]‘Those *that are* blind or broken or maimed, or
have an [1]ulcer or eczema or scabs, you shall not
offer to the LORD, nor make [b]an offering by fire of
them on the altar to the LORD.
23 ‘Either a bull or a lamb that has any limb [a]too
long or too short you may offer *as* a freewill
offering, but for a vow it shall not be accepted.
24 ‘You shall not offer to the LORD what is
bruised or crushed, or torn or cut; nor shall you
make *any offering of them* in your land.
25 ‘Nor [a]from a foreigner’s hand shall you offer
any of these as [b]the bread of your God, because
their [c]corruption *is* in them, *and* defects *are* in
them. They shall not be accepted on your behalf.’ ”
**26** And the LORD spoke to Moses, saying:

27 [a]“When a bull or a sheep or a goat is born, it
shall be seven days with its mother; and from the
eighth day and thereafter it shall be accepted as
an offering made by fire to the LORD.
28 “*Whether it is* a cow or ewe, do not kill both
her [a]and her young on the same day.
29 “And when you [a]offer a sacrifice of thanksgiving to the LORD, offer *it* of your own free will.
30 “On the same day it shall be eaten; you shall
leave [a]none of it until morning: I *am* the LORD.
**31** [a]“Therefore you shall keep My commandments, and perform them: I *am* the LORD.
32 [a]“You shall not profane My holy name, but [b]I
will be [1]hallowed among the children of Israel. I
*am* the LORD who [c]sanctifies you,
33 [a]“who brought you out of the land of Egypt, to
be your God: I *am* the LORD.”

### *The Regular Feasts*

**23** And the LORD spoke to Moses, saying,
2 “Speak to the children of Israel, and say
to them: ‘The feasts of the LORD, which you shall
proclaim *to be* [a]holy convocations, these *are* My
feasts.
**3** [a]‘Six days shall work be done, but the seventh
day *is* a Sabbath of solemn rest, a holy convocation. You shall do no work *on it;* it *is* the Sabbath
of the LORD in all your dwellings.
**4** [a]‘These *are* the feasts of the LORD, holy convocations which you shall proclaim at their appointed times.
5 [a]‘On the fourteenth *day* of the first month at
twilight *is* the LORD’s Passover.
6 ‘And on the fifteenth day of the same month *is*
the Feast of Unleavened Bread to the LORD; seven
days you must eat unleavened bread.
7 [a]‘On the first day you shall have a holy convocation; you shall do no [1]customary work on it.
8 ‘But you shall offer an offering made by fire to
the LORD for seven days. The seventh day *shall be*
a holy convocation; you shall do no customary
work *on it.*’ ”
**9** And the LORD spoke to Moses, saying,
10 “Speak to the children of Israel, and say to
them: [a]‘When you come into the land which I give
to you, and reap its harvest, then you shall bring a
sheaf of [b]the firstfruits of your harvest to the
priest.
11 ‘He shall [a]wave the sheaf before the LORD, to
be accepted on your behalf; on the day after the
Sabbath the priest shall wave it.
12 ‘And you shall offer on that day, when you
wave the sheaf, a male lamb of the first year,
without blemish, as a burnt offering to the LORD.
13 ‘Its grain offering *shall be* two-tenths *of an*
*ephah* of fine flour mixed with oil, an offering
made by fire to the LORD, for a [1]sweet aroma; and
its drink offering *shall be* of wine, one-fourth of a
hin.
14 ‘You shall eat neither bread nor parched grain
nor fresh grain until the same day that you have
brought an offering to your God; *it shall be* a
statute forever throughout your generations in all
your dwellings.
**15** ‘And you shall count for yourselves from the
day after the Sabbath, from the day that you
brought the sheaf of the wave offering: seven
Sabbaths shall be completed.
16 ‘Count [a]fifty days to the day after the seventh
Sabbath; then you shall offer [b]a new grain offering
to the LORD.

**5** [a]Lev. 11:23–28 [b]Lev. 15:7, 19
**6** [a]Lev. 15:5
**7** [a]Lev. 21:22; Num. 18:11, 13
**8** [a]Ex. 22:31; Lev. 7:24; 11:39, 40; 17:15; Ezek. 44:31
**9** [a]Lev. 18:30 [b]Ex. 28:43; Lev. 22:16; Num. 18:22 [1]*charge*
**10** [a]Ex. 29:33; Lev. 22:13; Num. 3:10 [1]As a visitor
**11** [a]Ex. 12:44
**15** [a]Num. 18:32
**18** [a]Lev. 1:2, 3, 10 [1]*brings his offering*
**19** [a]Lev. 1:3; Deut. 15:21
**20** [a]Deut. 15:21; 17:1; Mal. 1:8, 14; [Eph. 5:27; Heb. 9:14; 1 Pet. 1:19]
**21** [a]Lev. 3:1, 6 [b]Num. 15:3, 8; Ps. 61:8; 65:1; Eccl. 5:4, 5
**22** [a]Lev. 22:20; Mal. 1:8 [b]Lev. 1:9, 13; 3:3, 5 [1]*running sore*
**23** [a]Lev. 21:18
**25** [a]Num. 15:15, 16 [b]Lev. 21:6, 17 [c]Mal. 1:14
**27** [a]Ex. 22:30
**28** [a]Deut. 22:6, 7
**29** [a]Lev. 7:12; Ps. 107:22; 116:17; Amos 4:5
**30** [a]Lev. 7:15
**31** [a]Lev. 19:37; Num. 15:40; Deut. 4:40
**32** [a]Lev. 18:21 [b]Lev. 10:3; Matt. 6:9; Luke 11:2 [c]Lev. 20:8 [1]*treated as holy*
**33** [a]Lev. 19:36, 37; Num. 15:40; Deut. 4:40

CHAPTER 23
**2** [a]Ex. 12:16
**3** [a]Ex. 20:9; 23:12; 31:15; Lev. 19:3; Deut. 5:13, 14; Luke 13:14
**4** [a]Ex. 23:14–16; Lev. 23:2, 37
**5** [a]Ex. 12:1–28; Num. 9:1–5; 28:16–25; Deut. 16:1–8; Josh. 5:10
**7** [a]Ex. 12:16; Num. 28:18, 25 [1]*occupational*
**10** [a]Ex. 23:19; 34:26 [b][Rom. 11:16]; James 1:18; Rev. 14:4
**11** [a]Ex. 29:24
**13** [1]*pleasing*
**16** [a]Acts 2:1 [b]Num. 28:26

17 'You shall bring from your dwellings two wave *loaves* of two-tenths *of an ephah*. They shall be of fine flour; they shall be baked with leaven. *They are* [a]the firstfruits to the LORD.

18 'And you shall offer with the bread seven lambs of the first year, without blemish, one young bull, and two rams. They shall be *as* a burnt offering to the LORD, with their grain offering and their drink offerings, an offering made by fire for a sweet aroma to the LORD.

19 'Then you shall sacrifice [a]one kid of the goats as a sin offering, and two male lambs of the first year as a sacrifice of a [b]peace offering.

20 'The priest shall wave them with the bread of the firstfruits *as* a wave offering before the LORD, with the two lambs. [a]They shall be holy to the LORD for the priest.

21 'And you shall proclaim on the same day *that* it is a holy convocation to you. You shall do no customary work *on it. It shall be* a statute forever in all your dwellings throughout your generations.

**22** [a]'When you reap the harvest of your land, you shall not wholly reap the corners of your field when you reap, nor shall you gather any gleaning from your harvest. You shall leave them for the poor and for the stranger: I *am* the LORD your God.' "

**23** Then the LORD spoke to Moses, saying,

24 "Speak to the children of Israel, saying: 'In the [a]seventh month, on the first *day* of the month, you shall have a sabbath-*rest*, [b]a memorial of blowing of trumpets, a holy convocation.

25 'You shall do no customary work *on it;* and you shall offer an offering made by fire to the LORD.' "

**26** And the LORD spoke to Moses, saying:

27 [a]"Also the tenth *day* of this seventh month *shall be* the Day of Atonement. It shall be a holy convocation for you; you shall afflict your souls, and offer an offering made by fire to the LORD.

28 "And you shall do no work on that same day, for it *is* the Day of Atonement, [a]to make atonement for you before the LORD your God.

29 "For any person who is not [a]afflicted *in soul* on that same day [b]shall be cut off from his people.

30 "And any person who does any work on that same day, [a]that person I will destroy from among his people.

31 "You shall do no manner of work; *it shall be* a statute forever throughout your generations in all your dwellings.

32 "It *shall be* to you a sabbath of *solemn* rest, and you shall [1]afflict your souls; on the ninth *day* of the month at evening, from evening to evening, you shall [2]celebrate your sabbath."

**33** Then the LORD spoke to Moses, saying,

34 "Speak to the children of Israel, saying: [a]'The fifteenth day of this seventh month *shall be* the Feast of Tabernacles *for* seven days to the LORD.

35 'On the first day *there shall be* a holy convocation. You shall do no customary work *on it.*

36 '*For* seven days you shall offer an [a]offering made by fire to the LORD. [b]On the eighth day you shall have a holy convocation, and you shall offer an offering made by fire to the LORD. It *is* a [c]sacred[1] assembly, *and* you shall do no customary work *on it.*

37 [a]'These *are* the feasts of the LORD which you shall proclaim *to be* holy convocations, to offer an offering made by fire to the LORD, a burnt offering and a grain offering, a sacrifice and drink offerings, everything on its day—

38 [a]'besides the Sabbaths of the LORD, besides your gifts, besides all your vows, and besides all your freewill offerings which you give to the LORD.

**39** 'Also on the fifteenth day of the seventh month, when you have [a]gathered in the fruit of the land, you shall keep the feast of the LORD *for* seven days; on the first day *there shall be* a sabbath-*rest,* and on the eighth day a sabbath-*rest.*

40 'And [a]you shall take for yourselves on the first day the [1]fruit of beautiful trees, branches of palm trees, the boughs of leafy trees, and willows of the brook; [b]and you shall rejoice before the LORD your God for seven days.

41 [a]'You shall keep it as a feast to the LORD for seven days in the year. *It shall be* a statute forever in your generations. You shall celebrate it in the seventh month.

42 [a]'You shall dwell in [1]booths for seven days. [b]All who are native Israelites shall dwell in booths,

43 [a]'that your generations may [b]know that I made the children of Israel dwell in booths when [c]I brought them out of the land of Egypt: I *am* the LORD your God.' "

**44** So Moses [a]declared to the children of Israel the feasts of the LORD.

### *The Punishment for Blasphemy*

**24** Then the LORD spoke to Moses, saying:
2 [a]"Command the children of Israel that they bring to you pure oil of pressed olives for the light, to make the lamps burn continually.

3 "Outside the veil of the Testimony, in the tabernacle of meeting, Aaron shall be in charge of it from evening until morning before the LORD continually; *it shall be* a statute forever in your generations.

4 "He shall [1]be in charge of the lamps on [a]the pure *gold* lampstand before the LORD continually.

**5** "And you shall take fine flour and bake twelve [a]cakes with it. Two-tenths *of an ephah* shall be in each cake.

6 "You shall set them in two rows, six in a row, [a]on the pure *gold* table before the LORD.

7 "And you shall put pure frankincense on *each* row, that it may be on the bread for a [a]memorial, an offering made by fire to the LORD.

8 [a]"Every Sabbath he shall set it in order before the LORD continually, *being taken* from the children of Israel by an everlasting covenant.

9 "And [a]it shall be for Aaron and his sons, [b]and they shall eat it in a holy place; for it *is* most holy to him from the offerings of the LORD made by fire, by a perpetual statute."

**10** Now the son of an Israelite woman, whose father *was* an Egyptian, went out among the children of Israel; and this Israelite *woman's* son and a man of Israel fought each other in the camp.

11 And the Israelite woman's son [a]blasphemed the name *of the LORD* and [b]cursed; and so they [c]brought him to Moses. (His mother's name *was* Shelomith the daughter of Dibri, of the tribe of Dan.)

12 Then they [a]put him [1]in custody, [b]that [2]the mind of the LORD might be shown to them.

**13** And the LORD spoke to Moses, saying,

14 "Take outside the camp him who has cursed;

---

17 [a]Num. 15:17–21
19 [a]Num. 28:30 [b]Lev. 3:1
20 [a]Deut. 18:4
22 [a]Lev. 19:9, 10
24 [a]Num. 29:1 [b]Lev. 25:9
27 [a]Num. 29:7
28 [a]Lev. 16:34
29 [a]Jer. 31:9 [b]Num. 5:2
30 [a]Lev. 20:3–6
32 [1]*humble yourselves* [2]*observe your sabbath*
34 [a]Num. 29:12
36 [a]Num. 29:12–34 [b]Num. 29:35–38 [c]Deut. 16:8 [1]*solemn*
37 [a]Lev. 23:2, 4
38 [a]Num. 29:39
39 [a]Ex. 23:16
40 [a]Neh. 8:15 [b]Deut. 12:7; 16:14, 15 [1]*foliage*
41 [a]Num. 29:12
42 [a][Is. 4:6] [b]Neh. 8:14–16 [1]*tabernacles;* shelters made of boughs
43 [a]Deut. 31:13 [b]Ex. 10:2 [c]Lev. 22:33
44 [a]Lev. 23:2

CHAPTER 24
2 [a]Ex. 27:20, 21
4 [a]Ex. 25:31; 31:8; 37:17 [1]*arrange* or *set in order*
5 [a]Ex. 25:30; 39:36; 40:23
6 [a]1 Kin. 7:48
7 [a]Lev. 2:2, 9, 16
8 [a]1 Chr. 9:32
9 [a]Matt. 12:4 [b]Ex. 29:33
11 [a]Ex. 22:28 [b]Is. 8:21 [c]Ex. 18:22, 26
12 [a]Num. 15:34 [b]Num. 27:5 [1]*under guard* [2]Lit. *it might be declared to them from the mouth of the LORD*

then let all who heard *him* [a]lay their hands on his
head, and let all the congregation stone him.
15 "Then you shall speak to the children of Israel,
saying: 'Whoever curses his God [a]shall [1]bear his
sin.
16 'And whoever [a]blasphemes the name of the
LORD shall surely be put to death. All the congregation shall certainly stone him, the stranger as
well as him who is born in the land. When he
blasphemes the name *of the LORD,* he shall be put
to death.
**17** [a]'Whoever kills any man shall surely be put to
death.
18 [a]'Whoever kills an animal shall make it good,
animal for animal.
19 'If a man causes disfigurement of his neighbor,
as [a]he has done, so shall it be done to him—
20 'fracture for [a]fracture, [b]eye for eye, tooth for
tooth; as he has caused disfigurement of a man, so
shall it be done to him.
21 'And whoever kills an animal shall restore it;
but whoever kills a man shall be put to death.
22 'You shall have [a]the[1] same law for the stranger
and for one from your own country; for I *am* the
LORD your God.' "
**23** Then Moses spoke to the children of Israel;
and they took outside the camp him who had
cursed, and stoned him with stones. So the children of Israel did as the LORD commanded Moses.

## *The Seventh Year and the Jubilee Year*

**25** And the LORD spoke to Moses on Mount
[a]Sinai, saying,
2 "Speak to the children of Israel, and say to
them: 'When you come into the land which I give
you, then the land shall [a]keep a sabbath to the
LORD.
3 'Six years you shall sow your field, and six
years you shall prune your vineyard, and gather
its fruit;
4 'but in the [a]seventh year there shall be a
sabbath of solemn [b]rest for the land, a sabbath to
the LORD. You shall neither sow your field nor
prune your vineyard.
5 [a]'What grows of its own accord of your harvest you shall not reap, nor gather the grapes of
your untended vine, *for* it is a year of rest for the
land.
6 'And the sabbath *produce* of the land shall be
food for you: for you, your male and female
servants, your hired man, and the stranger who
dwells with you,
7 'for your livestock and the beasts that *are* in
your land—all its produce shall be for food.
**8** 'And you shall count seven sabbaths of years
for yourself, seven times seven years; and the time
of the seven sabbaths of years shall be to you
forty-nine years.
9 'Then you shall cause the trumpet of the
Jubilee to sound on the tenth *day* of the seventh
month; [a]on the Day of Atonement you shall make
the trumpet to sound throughout all your land.
10 'And you shall consecrate the fiftieth year, and
[a]proclaim liberty throughout *all* the land to all its
inhabitants. It shall be a Jubilee for you; [b]and each
of you shall return to his possession, and each of
you shall return to his family.
11 'That fiftieth year shall be a Jubilee to you; in
it [a]you shall neither sow nor reap what grows of
its own accord, nor gather *the grapes* of your
untended vine.
12 'For it *is* the Jubilee; it shall be holy to you;
[a]you shall eat its produce from the field.
**13** [a]'In this Year of Jubilee, each of you shall
return to his possession.
14 'And if you sell anything to your neighbor or
buy from your neighbor's hand, you shall not
[a]oppress one another.
15 [a]'According to the number of years after the
Jubilee you shall buy from your neighbor, and
according to the number of years of crops he shall
sell to you.
16 'According to the multitude of years you shall
increase its price, and according to the fewer
number of years you shall diminish its price; for
he sells to you *according* to the number *of the
years* of the crops.
17 'Therefore [a]you shall not [1]oppress one another,
[b]but you shall fear your God; for I *am* the LORD
your God.
**18** [a]'So you shall observe My statutes and keep
My judgments, and perform them; [b]and you will
dwell in the land in safety.
19 'Then the land will yield its fruit, and [a]you will
eat your fill, and dwell there in safety.
20 'And if you say, [a]"What shall we eat in the
seventh year, since [b]we shall not sow nor gather
in our produce?"
21 'Then I will [a]command My blessing on you in
the [b]sixth year, and it will bring forth produce
enough for three years.
22 [a]'And you shall sow in the eighth year, and eat
[b]old produce until the ninth year; until its produce
comes in, you shall eat *of* the old *harvest.*
**23** 'The land shall not be sold permanently, for
[a]the land *is* Mine; for you *are* [b]strangers and
sojourners with Me.
24 'And in all the land of your possession you
shall grant redemption of the land.
**25** [a]'If one of your brethren becomes poor, and
has sold *some* of his possession, and if [b]his redeeming relative comes to redeem it, then he may
redeem what his brother sold.
26 'Or if the man has no one to redeem it, but he
himself becomes able to redeem it,
27 'then [a]let him count the years since its sale,
and restore the remainder to the man to whom he
sold it, that he may return to his possession.
28 'But if he is not able to have *it* restored to
himself, then what was sold shall remain in the
hand of him who bought it until the Year of
Jubilee; [a]and in the Jubilee it shall be released, and
he shall return to his possession.
29 'If a man sells a house in a walled city, then he
may redeem it within a whole year after it is sold;
*within* a full year he may redeem it.
30 'But if it is not redeemed within the space of a
full year, then the house in the walled city shall
belong permanently to him who bought it,
throughout his generations. It shall not be released in the Jubilee.
31 'However the houses of villages which have no
wall around them shall be counted as the fields of
the country. They may be redeemed, and they
shall be released in the Jubilee.
32 'Nevertheless [a]the cities of the Levites, *and* the
houses in the cities of their possession, the Levites
may redeem at any time.
33 'And if a man purchases a house from the
Levites, then the house that was sold in the city of
his possession shall be released in the Jubilee; for

**14** [a]Deut. 13:9; 17:7
**15** [a]Lev. 20:17; Num. 9:13 [1]*be responsible for*
**16** [a]Ex. 20:7; 1 Kin. 21:10, 13; [Matt. 12:31; Mark 3:28, 29]
**17** [a]Gen. 9:6; Ex. 21:12; Num. 35:30, 31; Deut. 19:11, 12; 27:24
**18** [a]Lev. 24:21
**19** [a]Ex. 21:24
**20** [a]Ex. 21:23; Deut. 19:21 [b][Matt. 5:38, 39]
**22** [a]Ex. 12:49; Lev. 19:33–37; Num. 9:14; 15:15, 16, 29 [1]*one standard of judgment*

CHAPTER 25
**1** [a]Lev. 26:46
**2** [a]Lev. 26:34, 35
**4** [a]Deut. 15:1; Neh. 10:31 [b][Heb. 4:9]
**5** [a]2 Kin. 19:29
**9** [a]Lev. 23:24, 27
**10** [a]Is. 61:2; 63:4; Jer. 34:8, 15, 17; [Luke 4:19] [b]Lev. 25:13, 28, 54; Num. 36:4
**11** [a]Lev. 25:5
**12** [a]Lev. 25:6, 7
**13** [a]Lev. 25:10; 27:24; Num. 36:4
**14** [a]Lev. 19:13
**15** [a]Lev. 27:18, 23
**17** [a]Lev. 25:14; Prov. 14:31; 22:22; Jer. 7:5, 6; 1 Thess. 4:6 [b]Lev. 19:14, 32; 25:43 [1]*mistreat*
**18** [a]Lev. 19:37 [b]Lev. 26:5; Deut. 12:10; Ps. 4:8; Jer. 23:6
**19** [a]Lev. 26:5; Ezek. 34:25
**20** [a]Matt. 6:25, 31 [b]Lev. 25:4, 5
**21** [a]Deut. 28:8 [b]Ex. 16:29
**22** [a]2 Kin. 19:29 [b]Lev. 26:10; Josh. 5:11
**23** [a]Ex. 19:5; 2 Chr. 7:20 [b]Gen. 23:4; Ex. 6:4; 1 Chr. 29:15; Ps. 39:12; Heb. 11:13; 1 Pet. 2:11
**25** [a]Ruth 2:20; 4:4, 6 [b]Num. 5:8; Ruth 3:2, 9, 12; [Job 19:25]; Jer. 32:7, 8
**27** [a]Lev. 25:50–52
**28** [a]Lev. 25:10, 13
**32** [a]Num. 35:1–8; Josh. 21:2

the houses in the cities of the Levites *are* their
possession among the children of Israel.
34 'But [a]the field of the common-land of their
cities may not be [b]sold, for it *is* their perpetual
possession.
**35** 'If one of your brethren becomes poor, and
[1]falls into poverty among you, then you shall [a]help
him, like a stranger or a sojourner, that he may
live with you.
36 [a]'Take no usury or interest from him; but [b]fear
your God, that your brother may live with you.
37 'You shall not lend him your money for usury,
nor lend him your food at a profit.
38 [a]'I *am* the LORD your God, who brought you
out of the land of Egypt, to give you the land of
Canaan *and* to be your God.
**39** 'And if *one of* your brethren *who dwells* by
you becomes poor, and sells himself to you, you
shall not compel him to serve as a slave.
40 'As a hired servant *and* a sojourner he shall be
with you, *and* shall serve you until the Year of
Jubilee.
41 'And *then* he shall depart from you—he and
his children [a]with him—and shall return to his
own family. He shall return to the possession of
his fathers.
42 'For they *are* [a]My servants, whom I brought
out of the land of Egypt; they shall not be sold as
slaves.
43 [a]'You shall not rule over him [b]with [1]rigor, but
you [c]shall fear your God.
44 'And as for your male and female slaves whom
you may have—from the nations that are around
you, from them you may buy male and female
slaves.
45 'Moreover you may buy [a]the children of the
strangers who dwell among you, and their families
who are with you, which they beget in your land;
and they shall become your property.
46 'And [a]you may take them as an inheritance for
your children after you, to inherit *them as* a
possession; they shall be your permanent slaves.
But regarding your brethren, the children of
Israel, you shall not rule over one another with
rigor.
**47** 'Now if a sojourner or stranger close to you
becomes rich, and *one of* your brethren *who
dwells* by him becomes poor, and sells himself to
the stranger *or* sojourner close to you, or to a
member of the stranger's family,
48 'after he is sold he may be redeemed again.
One of his brothers may redeem him;
49 'or his uncle or his uncle's son may redeem
him; or *anyone* who is near of kin to him in his
family may redeem him; or if he is able he may
redeem himself.
50 'Thus he shall reckon with him who bought
him: The price of his release shall be according to
the number of years, from the year that he was
sold to him until the Year of Jubilee; *it shall be*
[a]according to the time of a hired servant for him.
51 'If *there are* still many years *remaining,* according to them he shall repay the price of his
redemption from the money with which he was
bought.
52 'And if there remain but a few years until the
Year of Jubilee, then he shall reckon with him,
*and* according to his years he shall repay him the
price of his redemption.
53 'He shall be with him as a yearly hired servant,
and he shall not rule with rigor over him in your
sight.
54 'And if he is not redeemed in these *years,* then
he shall be released in the Year of Jubilee—he and
his children with him.
55 'For the children of Israel *are* servants to Me;
they *are* My servants whom I brought out of the
land of Egypt: I *am* the LORD your God.

### *Promise of Blessing and Judgment*

**26** 'You shall [a]not make idols for yourselves;
Neither a carved image nor a *sacred* pillar
shall you rear up for yourselves;
nor shall you set up an engraved stone in
your land, to bow down to it;
for I *am* the LORD your God.
2 [a]You shall [1]keep My Sabbaths and reverence
My sanctuary:
I *am* the LORD.

**3** [a]'If you walk in My statutes and keep My
commandments, and perform them,
4 [a]then I will give you rain in its season, [b]the
land shall yield its produce, and the trees
of the field shall yield their fruit.
5 [a]Your threshing shall last till the time of
vintage, and the vintage shall last till the
time of sowing;
you shall eat your bread to the full, and
[b]dwell in your land safely.
6 [a]I will give peace in the land, and [b]you shall
lie down, and none will make *you* afraid;
I will rid the land of [c]evil[1] beasts,
and [d]the sword will not go through your
land.
7 You will chase your enemies, and they shall
fall by the sword before you.
8 [a]Five of you shall chase a hundred, and a
hundred of you shall put ten thousand to
flight;
your enemies shall fall by the sword before
you.

**9** 'For I will [a]look on you favorably and [b]make
you fruitful, multiply you and confirm My
[c]covenant with you.
10 You shall eat the [a]old harvest, and clear out
the old because of the new.
11 [a]I will set My [1]tabernacle among you, and
My soul shall not abhor you.
12 [a]I will walk among you and be your God, and
you shall be My people.
13 I *am* the LORD your God, who brought you
out of the land of Egypt, that *you* should
not be their slaves;
I have broken the bands of your [a]yoke and
made you walk [1]upright.

**14** 'But if you do not obey Me, and do not
observe all these commandments,
15 and if you despise My statutes, or if your
soul abhors My judgments, so that you do
not perform all My commandments, *but*
break My covenant,
16 I also will do this to you:
I will even appoint terror over you, [a]wasting
disease and fever which shall [b]consume
the eyes and [c]cause sorrow of heart.
And [d]you shall sow your seed [1]in vain, for
your enemies shall eat it.

**34** [a]Num. 35:2–5 [b]Acts 4:36, 37
**35** [a]Deut. 15:7–11; 24:14, 15; Luke 6:35; 1 John 3:17 [1]Lit. *his hand fails*
**36** [a]Ex. 22:25; Deut. 23:19, 20 [b]Neh. 5:9
**38** [a]Lev. 11:45; 22:32, 33
**41** [a]Ex. 21:3
**42** [a]Lev. 25:55; [Rom. 6:22; 1 Cor. 7:22, 23]
**43** [a]Eph. 6:9; Col. 4:1 [b]Ex. 1:13, 14; Lev. 25:46, 53; Ezek. 34:4 [c]Ex. 1:17; Deut. 25:18; Mal. 3:5 [1]*severity*
**45** [a][Is. 56:3, 6, 7]
**46** [a]Is. 14:2
**50** [a]Job 7:1; Is. 16:14

CHAPTER 26

**1** [a]Ex. 20:4, 5; Deut. 4:15–18; 5:8
**2** [a]Lev. 19:30 [1]*observe*
**3** [a]Deut. 28:1–14
**4** [a]Is. 30:23 [b]Ps. 67:6
**5** [a]Deut. 11:15; Joel 2:19, 26; Amos 9:13 [b]Lev. 25:18, 19; Ezek. 34:25
**6** [a]Is. 45:7 [b]Job 11:19; Ps. 4:8; Zeph. 3:13 [c]2 Kin. 17:25; Hos. 2:18 [d]Ezek. 14:17 [1]*wild beasts*
**8** [a]Deut. 32:30; Judg. 7:7–12
**9** [a]Ex. 2:25; 2 Kin. 13:23 [b]Gen. 17:6, 7; Ps. 107:38 [c]Gen. 17:1–7
**10** [a]Lev. 25:22
**11** [a]Ex. 25:8; 29:45, 46; Josh. 22:19; Ps. 76:2; Ezek. 37:26; Rev. 21:3 [1]*dwelling place*
**12** [a]Deut. 23:14; [2 Cor. 6:16]
**13** [a]Gen. 27:40 [1]*erect*
**16** [a]Deut. 28:22 [b]1 Sam. 2:33 [c]Ezek. 24:23; 33:10 [d]Judg. 6:3–6; Job 31:8; Mic. 6:15 [1]*without profit*

17 I will [1]set [a]My face against you, and [b]you
shall be defeated by your enemies.
[c]Those who hate you shall reign over you, and
you shall [d]flee when no one pursues you.

18 'And after all this, if you do not obey Me,
then I will punish you [a]seven times more
for your sins.
19 I will [a]break the pride of your power;
I [b]will make your heavens like iron and your
earth like bronze.
20 And your [a]strength shall be spent in vain;
for your [b]land shall not yield its produce, nor
shall the trees of the land yield their fruit.

21 'Then, if you walk contrary to Me, and are
not willing to obey Me, I will bring on you
seven times more plagues, according to
your sins.
22 [a]I will also send wild beasts among you,
which shall rob you of your children,
destroy your livestock, and make you few
in number;
and [b]your highways shall be desolate.

23 'And if [a]by these things you are not reformed
by Me, but walk contrary to Me,
24 [a]then I also will walk contrary to you, and I
will punish you yet seven times for your
sins.
25 And [a]I will bring a sword against you that
will execute the vengeance of the covenant;
when you are gathered together within your
cities [b]I will send pestilence among you;
and you shall be delivered into the hand of
the enemy.
26 [a]When I have cut off your supply of bread,
ten women shall bake your bread in one
oven, and they shall bring back your
bread by weight, [b]and you shall eat and
not be satisfied.

27 'And after all this, if you do not obey Me, but
walk contrary to Me,
28 then I also will walk contrary to you in fury;
and I, even I, will chastise you seven times
for your sins.
29 [a]You[1] shall eat the flesh of your sons, and
you shall eat the flesh of your daughters.
30 [a]I will destroy your high places, cut down
your incense altars, and cast your carcasses on the lifeless forms of your idols;
and My soul shall abhor you.
31 I will lay your [a]cities waste and [b]bring your
sanctuaries to desolation, and I will not
[c]smell the fragrance of your [1]sweet aro-
mas.
32 [a]I will bring the land to desolation, and your
enemies who dwell in it shall be astonished at it.
33 [a]I will scatter you among the nations and
draw out a sword after you;
your land shall be desolate and your cities
waste.
34 [a]Then the land shall enjoy its sabbaths as
long as it lies desolate and you *are* in your
enemies' land;
then the land shall rest and enjoy its sabbaths.
35 As long as *it* lies desolate it shall rest—
for the time it did not rest on your [a]sabbaths
when you dwelt in it.

36 'And as for those of you who are left, I will
send [a]faintness[1] into their hearts in the
lands of their enemies;
the sound of a shaken leaf shall cause them
to flee;
they shall flee as though fleeing from a
sword, and they shall fall when no one
pursues.
37 [a]They shall stumble over one another, as it
were before a sword, when no one pursues;
and [b]you shall have no *power* to stand
before your enemies.
38 You shall [a]perish among the nations, and
the land of your enemies shall eat you up.
39 And those of you who are left [a]shall [1]waste
away in their iniquity in your enemies'
lands;
also in their [b]fathers' iniquities, which are
with them, they shall waste away.

40 '*But* [a]if they confess their iniquity and the
iniquity of their fathers, with their unfaithfulness in which they were unfaithful
to Me, and that they also have walked
contrary to Me,
41 and *that* I also have walked contrary to
them and have brought them into the
land of their enemies;
if their [a]uncircumcised hearts are [b]humbled,
and they [c]accept their guilt—
42 then I will [a]remember My covenant with
Jacob, and My covenant with Isaac and
My covenant with Abraham I will remember;
I will [b]remember the land.
43 [a]The land also shall be left empty by them,
and will enjoy its sabbaths while it lies
desolate without them;
they will accept their guilt, because they
[b]despised My judgments and because
their soul abhorred My statutes.
44 Yet for all that, when they are in the land of
their enemies, [a]I will not cast them away,
nor shall I abhor them, to utterly destroy
them and break My covenant with them;
for I *am* the LORD their God.
45 But [a]for their sake I will remember the
covenant of their ancestors, [b]whom I
brought out of the land of Egypt [c]in the
sight of the nations, that I might be their
God:
I *am* the LORD.' "

46 [a]These *are* the statutes and judgments and
laws which the LORD made between Himself and
the children of Israel [b]on Mount Sinai by the hand
of Moses.

## *Persons and Property Dedicated to God*

**27** Now the LORD spoke to Moses, saying,
2 "Speak to the children of Israel, and say
to them: [a]'When a man [1]consecrates by a vow
certain persons to the LORD, according to your
[2]valuation,
3 'if your valuation is of a male from twenty
years old up to sixty years old, then your valuation shall be fifty shekels of silver, [a]according to
the shekel of the sanctuary.
4 'If it *is* a female, then your valuation shall be
thirty shekels;
5 'and if from five years old up to twenty years

17 [a]Ps. 34:16 [b]Deut. 28:25 [c]Ps. 106:41 [d]Prov. 28:1 [1]*oppose you*
18 [a]1 Sam. 2:5
19 [a]Is. 25:11 [b]Deut. 28:23
20 [a]Ps. 127:1 [b]Gen. 4:12
22 [a]Deut. 32:24 [b]Judg. 5:6
23 [a]Amos 4:6–12
24 [a]Lev. 26:28, 41
25 [a]Ezek. 5:17 [b]Deut. 28:21
26 [a]Ps. 105:16 [b]Mic. 6:14
29 [a]2 Kin. 6:28, 29 [1]In time of famine
30 [a]2 Chr. 34:3
31 [a]2 Kin. 25:4, 10 [b]Ps. 74:7 [c]Is. 1:11–15 [1]*pleasing*
32 [a]Jer. 9:11; 18:16
33 [a]Deut. 4:27
34 [a]2 Chr. 36:21
35 [a]Lev. 25:2
36 [a]Ezek. 21:7, 12, 15 [1]*fear*
37 [a]1 Sam. 14:15, 16 [b]Josh. 7:12, 13
38 [a]Deut. 4:26
39 [a]Ezek. 4:17; 33:10 [b]Ex. 34:7 [1]*rot away*
40 [a]Neh. 9:2
41 [a]Acts 7:51 [b]2 Chr. 12:6, 7, 12 [c]Dan. 9:7
42 [a]Ex. 2:24; 6:5 [b]Ps. 136:23
43 [a]Lev. 26:34, 35 [b]Lev. 26:15
44 [a]Deut. 4:31
45 [a][Rom. 11:28] [b]Lev. 22:33; 25:38 [c]Ps. 98:2
46 [a][John 1:17] [b]Lev. 25:1

CHAPTER 27

2 [a]Num. 6:2 [1]Or *makes a difficult* or *extraordinary vow* [2]*appraisal*
3 [a]Ex. 30:13

old, then your valuation for a male shall be twenty
shekels, and for a female ten shekels;
6 ‘and if from a month old up to five years old,
then your valuation for a male shall be five shekels of silver, and for a female your valuation shall
be three shekels of silver;
7 ‘and if from sixty years old and above, if *it is* a
male, then your valuation shall be fifteen shekels,
and for a female ten shekels.
8 ‘But if he is too poor to pay your valuation,
then he shall present himself before the priest, and
the priest shall set a value for [a]him; according to
the ability of him who vowed, the priest shall
value him.
**9** ‘If *it is* an animal that men may bring as an
offering to the LORD, all that *anyone* gives to the
LORD shall be holy.
10 ‘He shall not substitute it or exchange it, good
for bad or bad for good; and if he at all exchanges
animal for animal, then both it and the one exchanged for it shall be [a]holy.
11 ‘If *it is* an unclean animal which they do not
offer as a sacrifice to the LORD, then he shall
present the animal before the priest;
12 ‘and the priest shall set a value for it, whether
it is good or bad; as you, the priest, value it, so it
shall be.
13 [a]‘But if he *wants* at all *to* redeem it, then he
must add one-fifth to your valuation.
**14** ‘And when a man [1]dedicates his house *to be*
holy to the LORD, then the priest shall set a value
for it, whether it is good or bad; as the priest
values it, so it shall stand.
15 ‘If he who dedicated it *wants to* [1]redeem his
house, then he must add one-fifth of the money of
your valuation to it, and it shall be his.
**16** ‘If a man [1]dedicates to the LORD *part* of a field
of his possession, then your valuation shall be
according to the seed for it. A homer of barley
seed *shall be valued* at fifty shekels of silver.
17 ‘If he dedicates his field from the Year of
Jubilee, according to your valuation it shall stand.
18 ‘But if he dedicates his field after the Jubilee,
then the priest shall [a]reckon to him the money
due according to the years that remain till the
Year of Jubilee, and it shall be deducted from your
valuation.
19 ‘And if he who dedicates the field ever wishes
to redeem it, then he must add one-fifth of the
money of your valuation to it, and it shall belong
to him.
20 ‘But if he does not want to redeem the field, or
if he has sold the field to another man, it shall not
be redeemed anymore;
21 ‘but the field, [a]when it is released in the Jubilee, shall be holy to the LORD, as a [b]devoted field; it
shall be [c]the possession of the priest.
22 ‘And if a man dedicates to the LORD a field
which he has bought, which is not the field of [a]his
possession,
23 ‘then the priest shall reckon to him the worth
of your valuation, up to the Year of Jubilee, and
he shall give your valuation on that day *as* a holy
*offering* to the LORD.
24 [a]‘In the Year of Jubilee the field shall return to
him from whom it was bought, to the one who
*owned* the land as a possession.
25 ‘And all your valuations shall be according to
the shekel of the sanctuary: [a]twenty gerahs to the
shekel.
**26** ‘But the [a]firstborn of the animals, which
should be the LORD’s firstborn, no man shall
dedicate; whether *it is* an ox or sheep, it *is* the
LORD’s.
27 ‘And if *it is* an unclean animal, then he shall
redeem *it* according to your valuation, and [a]shall
add one-fifth to it; or if it is not redeemed, then it
shall be sold according to your valuation.
**28** [a]‘Nevertheless no [1]devoted *offering* that a man
may devote to the LORD of all that he has, *both*
man and beast, or the field of his possession, shall
be sold or redeemed; every devoted *offering is*
most holy to the LORD.
29 [a]‘No person under the ban, who may become
doomed to destruction among men, shall be redeemed, *but* shall surely be put to death.
30 ‘And [a]all the tithe of the land, *whether* of the
seed of the land *or* of the fruit of the tree, *is* the
LORD’s. It *is* holy to the LORD.
31 [a]‘If a man wants at all to redeem *any* of his
tithes, he shall add one-fifth to it.
32 ‘And concerning the tithe of the herd or the
flock, of whatever [a]passes under the rod, the tenth
one shall be holy to the LORD.
33 ‘He shall not inquire whether it is good or bad,
[a]nor shall he exchange it; and if he exchanges it at
all, then both it and the one exchanged for it shall
be holy; it shall not be redeemed.’ ”
**34** [a]These *are* the commandments which the
LORD commanded Moses for the children of Israel
on Mount [b]Sinai.

**8** [a]Lev. 5:11; 14:21–24
**10** [a]Lev. 27:33
**13** [a]Lev. 6:5; 22:14; 27:15, 19
**14** [1]*sets apart*
**15** [1]*buy back*
**16** [1]*sets apart*
**18** [a]Lev. 25:15, 16, 28
**21** [a]Lev. 25:10, 28, 31 [b]Lev. 27:28 [c]Num. 18:14; Ezek. 44:29
**22** [a]Lev. 25:10, 25
**24** [a]Lev. 25:10–13, 28
**25** [a]Ex. 30:13; Lev. 27:3; Num. 3:47; 18:16; Ezek. 45:12
**26** [a]Ex. 13:2, 12; 22:30
**27** [a]Lev. 27:11, 12
**28** [a]Lev. 27:21; Num. 18:14; Josh. 6:17–19 [1]*Given exclusively and irrevocably*
**29** [a]Num. 21:2
**30** [a]Gen. 28:22; Num. 18:21, 24; 2 Chr. 31:5, 6, 12; Neh. 13:12; Mal. 3:8
**31** [a]Lev. 27:13
**32** [a]Jer. 33:13; Ezek. 20:37; Mic. 7:14
**33** [a]Lev. 27:10
**34** [a]Lev. 26:46; Deut. 4:5; Mal. 4:4 [b]Ex. 19:1–6, 25; [Heb. 12:18–29]

*The Fourth Book of Moses Called*

# NUMBERS

### *The First Census of Israel*

NOW the LORD spoke to Moses [a]in the Wilderness of Sinai, [b]in the tabernacle of
meeting, on the [c]first *day* of the second
month, in the second year after they had come out
of the land of Egypt, saying:
2 [a]“Take a census of all the congregation of the
children of Israel, by their families, by their
fathers’ houses, according to the number of
names, every male [b]individually,
3 “from [a]twenty years old and above—all who
*are able to* go to war in Israel. You and Aaron
shall number them by their armies.
4 “And with you there shall be a man from
every tribe, each one the head of his father’s
house.
**5** “These are the names of the men who shall
stand with you: from Reuben, Elizur the son of
Shedeur;
6 “from Simeon, Shelumiel the son of Zurishaddai;

CHAPTER 1
**1** [a]Ex. 19:1; Num. 10:11, 12 [b]Ex. 25:22 [c]Ex. 40:2, 17; Num. 9:1; 10:11
**2** [a]Ex. 30:12; Num. 26:2, 63, 64; 2 Sam. 24:2; 1 Chr. 21:2 [b]Ex. 30:12, 13; 38:26
**3** [a]Ex. 30:14; 38:26

7 "from Judah, Nahshon the son of Amminadab;
8 "from Issachar, Nethanel the son of Zuar;
9 "from Zebulun, Eliab the son of Helon;
10 "from the sons of Joseph: from Ephraim, Elishama the son of Ammihud; from Manasseh, Gamaliel the son of Pedahzur;
11 "from Benjamin, Abidan the son of Gideoni;
12 "from Dan, Ahiezer the son of Ammishaddai;
13 "from Asher, Pagiel the son of Ocran;
14 "from Gad, Eliasaph the son of [a]Deuel;[1]
15 "from Naphtali, Ahira the son of Enan."
16 [a]These *were* [b]chosen[1] from the congregation, leaders of their fathers' tribes, [c]heads of the divisions in Israel.
**17** Then Moses and Aaron took these men who had been [1]mentioned [a]by name,
18 and they assembled all the congregation together on the first *day* of the second month; and they recited their [a]ancestry by families, by their fathers' houses, according to the number of names, from twenty years old and above, each one individually.
19 As the LORD commanded Moses, so he numbered them in the Wilderness of Sinai.
20 Now the [a]children of Reuben, Israel's oldest son, their genealogies by their families, by their fathers' house, according to the number of names, every male individually, from twenty years old and above, all who *were able to* go to war:
21 those who were numbered of the tribe of Reuben *were* forty-six thousand five hundred.
**22** From the [a]children of Simeon, their genealogies by their families, by their fathers' house, of those who were numbered, according to the number of names, every male individually, from twenty years old and above, all who *were able to* go to war:
23 those who were numbered of the tribe of Simeon *were* fifty-nine thousand three hundred.
**24** From the [a]children of Gad, their genealogies by their families, by their fathers' house, according to the number of names, from twenty years old and above, all who *were able to* go to war:
25 those who were numbered of the tribe of Gad *were* forty-five thousand six hundred and fifty.
**26** From the [a]children of Judah, their genealogies by their families, by their fathers' house, according to the number of names, from twenty years old and above, all who *were able to* go to war:
27 those who were numbered of the tribe of Judah *were* [a]seventy-four thousand six hundred.
**28** From the [a]children of Issachar, their genealogies by their families, by their fathers' house, according to the number of names, from twenty years old and above, all who *were able to* go to war:
29 those who were numbered of the tribe of Issachar *were* fifty-four thousand four hundred.
**30** From the [a]children of Zebulun, their genealogies by their families, by their fathers' house, according to the number of names, from twenty years old and above, all who *were able to* go to war:
31 those who were numbered of the tribe of Zebulun *were* fifty-seven thousand four hundred.
**32** From the sons of Joseph, the [a]children of Ephraim, their genealogies by their families, by their fathers' house, according to the number of names, from twenty years old and above, all who *were able to* go to war:
33 those who were numbered of the tribe of Ephraim *were* forty thousand five hundred.
**34** From the [a]children of Manasseh, their genealogies by their families, by their fathers' house, according to the number of names, from twenty years old and above, all who *were able to* go to war:
35 those who were numbered of the tribe of Manasseh *were* thirty-two thousand two hundred.
**36** From the [a]children of Benjamin, their genealogies by their families, by their fathers' house, according to the number of names, from twenty years old and above, all who *were able to* go to war:
37 those who were numbered of the tribe of Benjamin *were* thirty-five thousand four hundred.
**38** From the [a]children of Dan, their genealogies by their families, by their fathers' house, according to the number of names, from twenty years old and above, all who *were able to* go to war:
39 those who were numbered of the tribe of Dan *were* sixty-two thousand seven hundred.
**40** From the [a]children of Asher, their genealogies by their families, by their fathers' house, according to the number of names, from twenty years old and above, all who *were able to* go to war:
41 those who were numbered of the tribe of Asher *were* forty-one thousand five hundred.
**42** From the children of Naphtali, their genealogies by their families, by their fathers' house, according to the number of names, from twenty years old and above, all who *were able to* go to war:
43 those who were numbered of the tribe of Naphtali *were* fifty-three thousand four hundred.
**44** [a]These are the ones who were numbered, whom Moses and Aaron numbered, with the leaders of Israel, twelve men, each one representing his father's house.
45 So all who were numbered of the children of Israel, by their fathers' houses, from twenty years old and above, all who *were able to* go to war in Israel—
46 all who were numbered were [a]six hundred and three thousand five hundred and fifty.
**47** But [a]the Levites were not numbered among them by their fathers' tribe;
48 for the LORD had spoken to Moses, saying:
49 [a]"Only the tribe of Levi you shall not number, nor take a census of them among the children of Israel;
50 [a]"but you shall appoint the Levites over the tabernacle of the Testimony, over all its furnishings, and over all things that belong to it; they shall carry the tabernacle and all its furnishings; they shall attend to it [b]and camp around the tabernacle.
51 [a]"And when the tabernacle is to go forward, the Levites shall take it down; and when the tabernacle is to be set up, the Levites shall set it [b]up. [c]The outsider who comes near shall be put to death.
52 "The children of Israel shall pitch their tents, [a]everyone by his own camp, everyone by his own standard, according to their armies;
53 [a]"but the Levites shall camp around the tabernacle of the Testimony, that there may be no [b]wrath on the congregation of the children of Israel; and the Levites shall [c]keep[1] charge of the tabernacle of the Testimony."

**14** [a]Num. 7:42 [1]*Reuel,* Num. 2:14
**16** [a]Ex. 18:21; Num. 7:2; 1 Chr. 27:16–22 [b]Num. 16:2 [c]Ex. 18:21, 25; Jer. 5:5; Mic. 3:1, 9; 5:2 [1]*called*
**17** [a]Is. 43:1 [1]*designated*
**18** [a]Ezra 2:59; Heb. 7:3
**20** [a]Num. 2:10, 11; 26:5–11; 32:6, 15, 21, 29
**22** [a]Num. 2:12, 13; 26:12–14
**24** [a]Gen. 30:11; Num. 26:15–18; Josh. 4:12; Jer. 49:1
**26** [a]Gen. 29:35; Num. 26:19–22; 2 Sam. 24:9; Ps. 78:68; Matt. 1:2
**27** [a]2 Chr. 17:14
**28** [a]Num. 2:5, 6
**30** [a]Num. 2:7, 8; 26:26, 27
**32** [a]Gen. 48:1–22; Num. 26:28–37; Deut. 33:13–17; Jer. 7:15; Obad. 19
**34** [a]Num. 2:20, 21; 26:28–34
**36** [a]Gen. 49:27; Num. 26:38–41; 2 Chr. 17:17; Rev. 7:8
**38** [a]Gen. 30:6; 46:23; Num. 2:25, 26; 26:42, 43
**40** [a]Num. 2:27, 28; 26:44–47
**44** [a]Num. 26:64
**46** [a]Ex. 12:37; 38:26; Num. 2:32; 26:51, 63; Heb. 11:12; Rev. 7:4–8
**47** [a]Num. 2:33; 3:14–22; 26:57–62; 1 Chr. 6:1–47; 21:6
**49** [a]Num. 2:33; 26:62
**50** [a]Ex. 38:21; Num. 3:7, 8; 4:15, 25–27, 33 [b]Num. 3:23, 29, 35, 38
**51** [a]Num. 4:5–15; 10:17, 21 [b]Num. 10:21 [c]Num. 3:10, 38; 4:15, 19, 20; 18:22
**52** [a]Num. 2:2, 34; 24:2
**53** [a]Num. 1:50 [b]Lev. 10:6; Num. 8:19; 16:46; 18:5; 1 Sam. 6:19 [c]Num. 8:24; 18:2–4; 1 Chr. 23:32 [1]*have in their care*

54 Thus the children of Israel did; according to all
that the LORD commanded Moses, so they did.

### *The Camps and Leaders of the Tribes*

2 And the LORD spoke to Moses and Aaron,
saying:
2 [a]"Everyone of the children of Israel shall camp
by his own [1]standard, beside the emblems of his
father's house; they shall camp [b]some distance
from the tabernacle of meeting.
3 "On the [a]east side, toward the rising of the
sun, those of the standard of the forces with
Judah shall camp according to their armies; and
[b]Nahshon the son of Amminadab *shall be* the
leader of the children of Judah."
4 And his army was numbered at seventy-four
thousand six hundred.
5 "Those who camp next to him *shall be* the
tribe of Issachar, and Nethanel the son of Zuar
*shall be* the leader of the children of Issachar."
6 And his army was numbered at fifty-four
thousand four hundred.
7 "Then *comes* the tribe of Zebulun, and Eliab
the son of Helon *shall be* the leader of the children
of Zebulun."
8 And his army was numbered at fifty-seven
thousand four hundred.
9 "All who were numbered according to their
armies of the forces with Judah, one hundred and
eighty-six thousand four hundred—[a]these shall
[1]break camp first.
**10** "On the [a]south side *shall be* the standard of
the forces with Reuben according to their armies,
and the leader of the children of Reuben *shall be*
Elizur the son of Shedeur."
11 And his army was numbered at forty-six thousand five hundred.
12 "Those who camp next to him *shall be* the
tribe of Simeon, and the leader of the children of
Simeon *shall be* Shelumiel the son of Zurishaddai."
13 And his army was numbered at fifty-nine
thousand three hundred.
14 "Then *comes* the tribe of Gad, and the leader
of the children of Gad *shall be* Eliasaph the son of
[1]Reuel."
15 And his army was numbered at forty-five
thousand six hundred and fifty.
16 "All who were numbered according to their
armies of the forces with Reuben, one hundred
and fifty-one thousand four hundred and fifty—
[a]they shall [1]be the second to break camp.
17 [a]"And the tabernacle of meeting shall move
out with the [1]camp of the Levites [b]in the middle of
the [2]camps; as they camp, so they shall move out,
everyone in his place, by their [3]standards.
**18** "On the west side *shall be* the standard of the
forces with Ephraim according to their armies,
and the leader of the children of Ephraim *shall be*
Elishama the son of Ammihud."
19 And his army was numbered at forty thousand
five hundred.
20 "Next to him *comes* the tribe of Manasseh,
and the leader of the children of Manasseh *shall*
*be* Gamaliel the son of Pedahzur."
21 And his army was numbered at thirty-two
thousand two hundred.
22 "Then *comes* the tribe of Benjamin, and the
leader of the children of Benjamin *shall be* Abidan
the son of Gideoni."

CHAPTER 2
**2** [a]Num. 1:52; 24:2 [b]Josh. 3:4 [1]*banner*
**3** [a]Num. 10:5 [b]Num. 1:7; 7:12; 10:14; Ruth 4:20; 1 Chr. 2:10; Matt. 1:4; Luke 3:32, 33
**9** [a]Num. 10:14 [1]Lit. *set forth*
**10** [a]Num. 10:6
**14** [1]*Deuel,* Num. 1:14; 7:42
**16** [a]Num. 10:18 [1]Lit. *set forth second*
**17** [a]Num. 10:17, 21 [b]Num. 1:53 [1]*company* [2]*whole company* [3]*banners*
**24** [a]Num. 10:22 [1]Lit. *set forth third*
**25** [1]*banner*
**31** [a]Num. 10:25 [1]Lit. *set forth last* [2]*banners*
**32** [a]Ex. 38:26; Num. 1:46; 11:21
**33** [a]Num. 1:47; 26:57–62
**34** [a]Num. 1:54 [b]Num. 24:2, 5, 6 [1]*banners*

CHAPTER 3
**1** [a]Ex. 6:16–27 [1]Lit. *generations*
**2** [a]Ex. 6:23 [b]Lev. 10:1, 2; Num. 26:60, 61; 1 Chr. 24:2
**3** [a]Ex. 28:41; Lev. 8 [1]Lit. *whose hands he filled*
**4** [a]Lev. 10:1, 2; Num. 26:61; 1 Chr. 24:2
**6** [a]Num. 8:6–22; 18:1–7; Deut. 10:8; 33:8–11
**7** [a]Num. 1:50; 8:11, 15, 24, 26
**9** [a]Num. 8:19; 18:6, 7 [1]Sam., LXX *Me*

23 And his army was numbered at thirty-five
thousand four hundred.
24 "All who were numbered according to their
armies of the forces with Ephraim, one hundred
and eight thousand one hundred—[a]they shall [1]be
the third to break camp.
**25** "The [1]standard of the forces with Dan *shall be*
on the north side according to their armies, and
the leader of the children of Dan *shall be* Ahiezer
the son of Ammishaddai."
26 And his army was numbered at sixty-two
thousand seven hundred.
27 "Those who camp next to him *shall be* the
tribe of Asher, and the leader of the children of
Asher *shall be* Pagiel the son of Ocran."
28 And his army was numbered at forty-one
thousand five hundred.
29 "Then *comes* the tribe of Naphtali, and the
leader of the children of Naphtali *shall be* Ahira
the son of Enan."
30 And his army was numbered at fifty-three
thousand four hundred.
31 "All who were numbered of the forces with
Dan, one hundred and fifty-seven thousand six
hundred—[a]they shall [1]break camp last, with their
[2]standards."
**32** These *are* the ones who were numbered of the
children of Israel by their fathers' houses. [a]All
who were numbered according to their armies of
the forces *were* six hundred and three thousand
five hundred and fifty.
33 But [a]the Levites were not numbered among
the children of Israel, just as the LORD commanded Moses.
34 Thus the children of Israel [a]did according to
all that the LORD commanded Moses; [b]so they
camped by their [1]standards and so they broke
camp, each one by his family, according to their
fathers' houses.

### *The Number and Duties of the Levites*

3 Now these *are* the [a]records[1] of Aaron and
Moses when the LORD spoke with Moses on
Mount Sinai.
2 And these *are* the names of the sons of Aaron:
Nadab, the [a]firstborn, and [b]Abihu, Eleazar, and
Ithamar.
3 These *are* the names of the sons of Aaron, [a]the
anointed priests, [1]whom he consecrated to minister as priests.
4 [a]Nadab and Abihu had died before the LORD
when they offered profane fire before the LORD in
the Wilderness of Sinai; and they had no children.
So Eleazar and Ithamar ministered as priests in
the presence of Aaron their father.
**5** And the LORD spoke to Moses, saying:
6 [a]"Bring the tribe of Levi near, and present
them before Aaron the priest, that they may serve
him.
7 "And they shall attend to his needs and the
needs of the whole congregation before the tabernacle of meeting, to do [a]the work of the tabernacle.
8 "Also they shall attend to all the furnishings of
the tabernacle of meeting, and to the needs of the
children of Israel, to do the work of the tabernacle.
9 "And [a]you shall give the Levites to Aaron and
his sons; they *are* given entirely to [1]him from
among the children of Israel.

10 "So you shall appoint Aaron and his sons, [a]and they shall attend to their priesthood; [b]but the outsider who comes near shall be put to death."
11 Then the LORD spoke to Moses, saying:
12 "Now behold, [a]I Myself have taken the Levites from among the children of Israel instead of every firstborn who opens the womb among the children of Israel. Therefore the Levites shall be [b]Mine,
13 "because [a]all the firstborn *are* Mine. [b]On the day that I struck all the firstborn in the land of Egypt, I sanctified to Myself all the firstborn in Israel, both man and beast. They shall be Mine: I *am* the LORD."
**14** Then the LORD spoke to Moses in the Wilderness of Sinai, saying:
15 "Number the children of Levi by their fathers' houses, by their families; you shall number [a]every male from a month old and above."
16 So Moses numbered them according to the [1]word of the LORD, as he was commanded.
17 [a]These were the sons of Levi by their names: Gershon, Kohath, and Merari.
18 And these *are* the names of the sons of [a]Gershon by their families: [b]Libni and Shimei.
19 And the sons of [a]Kohath by their families: [b]Amram, Izehar, Hebron, and Uzziel.
20 [a]And the sons of Merari by their families: Mahli and Mushi. These *are* the families of the Levites by their fathers' houses.
21 From Gershon *came* the family of the Libnites and the family of the Shimites; these *were* the families of the Gershonites.
22 Those who were numbered, according to the number of all the males from a month old and above—of those who were numbered *there were* seven thousand five hundred.
23 [a]The families of the Gershonites were to camp behind the tabernacle westward.
24 And the leader of the father's house of the Gershonites *was* Eliasaph the son of Lael.
25 [a]The duties of the children of Gershon in the tabernacle of meeting *included* [b]the tabernacle, [c]the tent with [d]its covering, [e]the screen for the door of the tabernacle of meeting,
26 [a]the screen for the door of the court, [b]the hangings of the court which *are* around the tabernacle and the altar, and [c]their cords, according to all the work relating to them.
**27** [a]From Kohath *came* the family of the Amramites, the family of the Izharites, the family of the Hebronites, and the family of the Uzzielites; these *were* the families of the Kohathites.
28 According to the number of all the males, from a month old and above, *there were* eight thousand [1]six hundred [2]keeping charge of the sanctuary.
29 [a]The families of the children of Kohath were to camp on the south side of the tabernacle.
30 And the leader of the fathers' house of the families of the Kohathites *was* Elizaphan the son of [a]Uzziel.
31 [a]Their duty *included* [b]the ark, [c]the table, [d]the lampstand, [e]the altars, the utensils of the sanctuary with which they ministered, [f]the screen, and all the work relating to them.
32 And Eleazar the son of Aaron the priest *was to be* chief over the leaders of the Levites, *with* oversight of those who kept charge of the sanctuary.

10 [a]Ex. 29:9; Num. 18:7 [b]Num. 1:51; 3:38; 16:40
12 [a]Num. 3:41; 8:16; 18:6 [b]Ex. 13:2; Num. 3:45; 8:14
13 [a]Ex. 13:2; Lev. 27:26; Num. 8:16, 17; Neh. 10:36; Luke 2:23 [b]Ex. 13:12, 15; Num. 8:17
15 [a]Num. 3:39; 26:62
16 [1]Lit. *mouth*
17 [a]Gen. 46:11; Ex. 6:16–22; Num. 26:57; 1 Chr. 6:1, 16; 23:6
18 [a]Num. 4:38–41 [b]Ex. 6:17
19 [a]Num. 4:34–37 [b]Ex. 6:18
20 [a]Ex. 6:19; Num. 4:42–45
23 [a]Num. 1:53
25 [a]Num. 4:24–26 [b]Ex. 25:9 [c]Ex. 26:1 [d]Ex. 26:7, 14 [e]Ex. 26:36
26 [a]Ex. 27:9, 12, 14, 15 [b]Ex. 27:16 [c]Ex. 35:18
27 [a]1 Chr. 26:23
28 [1]Some LXX mss. *three* [2]*taking care of*
29 [a]Ex. 6:18; Num. 1:53
30 [a]Lev. 10:4
31 [a]Num. 4:15 [b]Ex. 25:10 [c]Ex. 25:23 [d]Ex. 25:31 [e]Ex. 27:1; 30:1 [f]Ex. 26:31–33
35 [a]Num. 1:53; 2:25
36 [a]Num. 4:31, 32
38 [a]Num. 1:53 [b]Num. 18:5 [c]Num. 3:7, 8 [d]Num. 3:10
39 [a]Num. 3:43; 4:48; 26:62
40 [a]Num. 3:15 [1]*Take a census of*
41 [a]Num. 3:12, 45
45 [a]Num. 3:12, 41
46 [a]Ex. 13:13, 15; Num. 18:15, 16 [b]Num. 3:39, 43
47 [a]Lev. 27:6; Num. 18:16 [b]Num. 1:2, 18, 20 [c]Ex. 30:13
50 [a]Num. 3:46, 47
51 [a]Num. 3:48

**33** From Merari *came* the family of the Mahlites and the family of the Mushites; these *were* the families of Merari.
34 And those who were numbered, according to the number of all the males from a month old and above, *were* six thousand two hundred.
35 The leader of the fathers' house of the families of Merari *was* Zuriel the son of Abihail. [a]These *were* to camp on the north side of the tabernacle.
36 And [a]the appointed duty of the children of Merari *included* the boards of the tabernacle, its bars, its pillars, its sockets, its utensils, all the work relating to them,
37 and the pillars of the court all around, with their sockets, their pegs, and their cords.
**38** [a]Moreover those who were to camp before the tabernacle on the east, before the tabernacle of meeting, *were* Moses, Aaron, and his sons, [b]keeping charge of the sanctuary, [c]to meet the needs of the children of Israel; but [d]the outsider who came near was to be put to death.
39 [a]All who were numbered of the Levites, whom Moses and Aaron numbered at the commandment of the LORD, by their families, all the males from a month old and above, *were* twenty-two thousand.
**40** Then the LORD said to Moses: [a]"Number[1] all the firstborn males of the children of Israel from a month old and above, and take the number of their names.
41 [a]"And you shall take the Levites for Me—I *am* the LORD—instead of all the firstborn among the children of Israel, and the livestock of the Levites instead of all the firstborn among the livestock of the children of Israel."
42 So Moses numbered all the firstborn among the children of Israel, as the LORD commanded him.
43 And all the firstborn males, according to the number of names from a month old and above, of those who were numbered of them, were twenty-two thousand two hundred and seventy-three.
**44** Then the LORD spoke to Moses, saying:
45 [a]"Take the Levites instead of all the firstborn among the children of Israel, and the livestock of the Levites instead of their livestock. The Levites shall be Mine: I *am* the LORD.
46 "And for [a]the redemption of the two hundred and seventy-three of the firstborn of the children of Israel, [b]who are more than the number of the Levites,
47 "you shall take [a]five shekels for each one [b]individually; you shall take *them* in the currency of the shekel of the sanctuary, [c]the shekel of twenty gerahs.
48 "And you shall give the money, with which the excess number of them is redeemed, to Aaron and his sons."
49 So Moses took the redemption money from those who were over and above those who were redeemed by the Levites.
50 From the firstborn of the children of Israel he took the money, [a]one thousand three hundred and sixty-five *shekels,* according to the shekel of the sanctuary.
51 And Moses [a]gave their redemption money to Aaron and his sons, according to the word of the LORD, as the LORD commanded Moses.

### *The Tasks Assigned to the Levites*

4 Then the LORD spoke to Moses and Aaron,
saying:
2 "Take a census of the sons of [a]Kohath from
among the children of Levi, by their families, by
their fathers' house,
3 [a]"from thirty years old and above, even to fifty
years old, all who enter the service to do the work
in the tabernacle of meeting.
4 [a]"This *is* the service of the sons of Kohath in
the tabernacle of meeting, *relating to* [b]the most
holy things:
5 "When the camp prepares to journey, Aaron
and his sons shall come, and they shall take down
[a]the covering veil and cover the [b]ark of the Testimony with it.
6 "Then they shall put on it a covering of badger
skins, and spread over *that* a cloth entirely of
[a]blue; and they shall insert [b]its poles.
7 "On the [a]table of showbread they shall spread
a blue cloth, and put on it the dishes, the pans, the
bowls, and the [1]pitchers for pouring; and the
[b]showbread[2] shall be on it.
8 "They shall spread over them a scarlet cloth,
and cover the same with a covering of badger
skins; and they shall insert its poles.
9 "And they shall take a blue cloth and cover
the [a]lampstand of the light, [b]with its lamps, its
wick-trimmers, its trays, and all its oil vessels,
with which they service it.
10 "Then they shall put it with all its utensils in a
covering of badger skins, and put *it* on a carrying
beam.
11 "Over [a]the golden altar they shall spread a
blue cloth, and cover it with a covering of badger
skins; and they shall insert its poles.
12 "Then they shall take all the [a]utensils of
service with which they minister in the sanctuary,
put *them* in a blue cloth, cover them with a
covering of badger skins, and put *them* on a
carrying beam.
13 "Also they shall take away the ashes from the
altar, and spread a purple cloth over it.
14 "They shall put on it all its implements with
which they minister there—the firepans, the
forks, the shovels, the [1]basins, and all the utensils
of the altar—and they shall spread on it a covering of badger skins, and insert its poles.
15 "And when Aaron and his sons have finished
covering the sanctuary and all the furnishings of
the sanctuary, when the camp is set to go, then
[a]the sons of Kohath shall come to carry *them;* [b]but
they shall not touch any holy thing, lest they die.
[c]These *are* the things in the tabernacle of meeting
which the sons of Kohath are to carry.
16 "The appointed duty of Eleazar the son of
Aaron the priest *is* [a]the oil for the light, the [b]sweet
incense, [c]the daily grain offering, the [d]anointing
oil, the oversight of all the tabernacle, of all that *is*
in it, with the sanctuary and its furnishings."
17 Then the LORD spoke to Moses and Aaron,
saying:
18 "Do not cut off the tribe of the families of the
Kohathites from among the Levites;
19 "but do this in regard to them, that they may
live and not die when they approach [a]the most
holy things: Aaron and his sons shall go in and
[1]appoint each of them to his service and his task.
20 [a]"But they shall not go in to watch while the
holy things are being covered, lest they die."
21 Then the LORD spoke to Moses, saying:
22 "Also take a census of the sons of [a]Gershon,
by their fathers' house, by their families.
23 [a]"From thirty years old and above, even to
fifty years old, you shall number them, all who
enter to perform the service, to do the work in the
tabernacle of meeting.
24 "This *is* the [a]service of the families of the
Gershonites, in serving and carrying:
25 [a]"They shall carry the [b]curtains of the tabernacle and the tabernacle of meeting *with* its
covering, the covering of [c]badger skins that *is* on
it, the screen for the door of the tabernacle of
meeting,
26 "the screen for the door of the gate of the
court, the hangings of the court which *are* around
the tabernacle and altar, and their cords, all the
furnishings for their service and all that is made
for these things: so shall they serve.
27 "Aaron and his sons shall [1]assign all the service of the sons of the Gershonites, all their tasks
and all their service. And you shall [2]appoint to
them all their tasks as their duty.
28 "This *is* the service of the families of the sons
of Gershon in the tabernacle of meeting. And their
duties *shall be* [a]under the [1]authority of Ithamar
the son of Aaron the priest.
29 "*As for* the sons of [a]Merari, you shall number
them by their families and by their fathers' house.
30 [a]"From thirty years old and above, even to
fifty years old, you shall number them, everyone
who enters the service to do the work of the
tabernacle of meeting.
31 "And [a]this *is* [b]what they must carry as all their
service for the tabernacle of meeting: [c]the boards
of the tabernacle, its bars, its pillars, its sockets,
32 "and the pillars around the court with their
sockets, pegs, and cords, with all their furnishings
and all their service; and you shall [a]assign *to each*
*man* by name the items he must carry.
33 "This *is* the service of the families of the sons
of Merari, as all their service for the tabernacle of
meeting, under the [1]authority of Ithamar the son
of Aaron the priest."
34 [a]And Moses, Aaron, and the leaders of the
congregation numbered the sons of the Kohathites by their families and by their fathers' house,
35 from thirty [a]years old and above, even to fifty
years old, everyone who entered the service for
work in the tabernacle of meeting;
36 and those who were numbered by their families were two thousand seven hundred and fifty.
37 These *were* the ones who were numbered of
the families of the Kohathites, all who might serve
in the tabernacle of meeting, whom Moses and
Aaron numbered according to the commandment
of the LORD by the hand of Moses.
38 And those who were numbered of the sons of
Gershon, by their families and by their fathers'
house,
39 from thirty years old and above, even to fifty
years old, everyone who entered the service for
work in the tabernacle of meeting—
40 those who were numbered by their families, by
their fathers' house, were two thousand six hundred and thirty.
41 [a]These *are* the ones who were numbered of
the families of the sons of Gershon, of all who
might serve in the tabernacle of meeting, whom

CHAPTER 4
2 [a]Num. 3:27–32
3 [a]Num. 4:23, 30, 35; 8:24; 1 Chr. 23:3, 24, 27; Ezra 3:8
4 [a]Num. 4:15 [b]Num. 4:19
5 [a]Ex. 26:31; Heb. 9:3 [b]Ex. 25:10, 16
6 [a]Ex. 39:1 [b]Ex. 25:13; 1 Kin. 8:7, 8
7 [a]Ex. 25:23, 29, 30 [b]Lev. 24:5–9 [1]*jars for the drink offering* [2]Lit. *continual bread*
9 [a]Ex. 25:31 [b]Ex. 25:37, 38
11 [a]Ex. 30:1–5
12 [a]Ex. 25:9; 1 Chr. 9:29
14 [1]*bowls*
15 [a]Num. 7:9; 10:21; Deut. 31:9; Josh. 4:10; 2 Sam. 6:13; 1 Chr. 15:2, 15 [b]2 Sam. 6:6, 7; 1 Chr. 13:9, 10 [c]Num. 3:31
16 [a]Ex. 25:6; Lev. 24:2 [b]Ex. 30:34 [c]Ex. 29:38 [d]Ex. 30:23–25
19 [a]Num. 4:4 [1]*assign*
20 [a]Ex. 19:21; 1 Sam. 6:19
22 [a]Num. 3:22
23 [a]Num. 4:3; 1 Chr. 23:3, 24, 27
24 [a]Num. 7:7
25 [a]Num. 3:25, 26 [b]Ex. 36:8 [c]Ex. 26:14
27 [1]*command* [2]*assign*
28 [a]Num. 4:33 [1]Lit. *hand*
29 [a]Num. 3:33–37
30 [a]Num. 4:3; 8:24–26
31 [a]Num. 3:36, 37 [b]Num. 7:8 [c]Ex. 26:15
32 [a]Ex. 25:9; 38:21
33 [1]Lit. *hand*
34 [a]Num. 4:2
35 [a]Num. 4:47
41 [a]Num. 4:22

Moses and Aaron numbered according to the
commandment of the LORD.
**42** Those of the families of the sons of Merari
who were numbered, by their families, by their
fathers' [1]house,
43 from thirty years old and above, even to fifty
years old, everyone who entered the service for
work in the tabernacle of meeting—
44 those who were numbered by their families
were three thousand two hundred.
45 These *are* the ones who were numbered of the
families of the sons of Merari, whom Moses and
Aaron numbered [a]according to the word of the
LORD by the hand of Moses.
**46** All who were [a]numbered of the Levites, whom
Moses, Aaron, and the leaders of Israel numbered,
by their families and by their fathers' houses,
47 [a]from thirty years old and above, even to fifty
years old, everyone who came to do the work of
service and the work of bearing burdens in the
tabernacle of meeting—
48 those who were numbered were eight thousand five hundred and eighty.
49 According to the commandment of the LORD
they were numbered by the hand of Moses, [a]each
according to his service and according to his task;
thus were they numbered by him, [b]as the LORD
commanded Moses.

### *The Law Concerning Jealousy*

**5** And the LORD spoke to Moses, saying:
2 "Command the children of Israel that they
put out of the camp every [a]leper, everyone who
has a [b]discharge, and whoever becomes [c]defiled
[1]by a corpse.
3 "You shall put out both male and female; you
shall put them outside the camp, that they may
not defile their camps [a]in the midst of which I
dwell."
4 And the children of Israel did so, and put them
outside the camp; as the LORD spoke to Moses, so
the children of Israel did.
**5** Then the LORD spoke to Moses, saying,
6 "Speak to the children of Israel: [a]'When a man
or woman commits any sin that men commit in
unfaithfulness against the LORD, and that person
is guilty,
7 [a]'then he shall confess the sin which he has
committed. He shall make restitution for his
trespass [b]in full, plus one-fifth of it, and give *it* to
the one he has wronged.
8 'But if the man has no [1]relative to whom
restitution may be made for the wrong, the restitution for the wrong *must go* to the LORD for the
priest, in addition to [a]the ram of the atonement
with which atonement is made for him.
9 'Every [a]offering[1] of all the holy things of the
children of Israel, which they bring to the priest,
shall be [b]his.
10 'And every man's [1]holy things shall be his;
whatever any man gives the priest shall be [a]his.' "
**11** And the LORD spoke to Moses, saying,
12 "Speak to the children of Israel, and say to
them: 'If any man's wife goes astray and behaves
unfaithfully toward him,
13 'and a man [a]lies with her carnally, and it is
hidden from the eyes of her husband, and it is
concealed that she has defiled herself, and *there
was* no witness against her, nor was she [b]caught—
14 'if the spirit of jealousy comes upon him and
he becomes [a]jealous of his wife, who has defiled
herself; or if the spirit of jealousy comes upon him
and he becomes jealous of his wife, although she
has not defiled herself—
15 'then the man shall bring his wife to the priest.
He shall [a]bring the offering required for her, one-
tenth of an ephah of barley meal; he shall pour no
oil on it and put no frankincense on it, because it
*is* a grain offering of jealousy, an offering for
remembering, for [b]bringing iniquity to remembrance.
**16** 'And the priest shall bring her near, and set
her before the LORD.
17 'The priest shall take holy water in an earthen
vessel, and take some of the dust that is on the
floor of the tabernacle and put *it* into the water.
18 'Then the priest shall stand the woman before
the [a]LORD, uncover the woman's head, and put the
offering for remembering in her hands, which *is*
the grain offering of jealousy. And the priest shall
have in his hand the bitter water that brings a
curse.
19 'And the priest shall put her under oath, and
say to the woman, "If no man has lain with you,
and if you have not gone astray to uncleanness
*while* under your husband's *authority*, be free
from this bitter water that brings a curse.
20 "But if you have gone astray *while* under your
husband's *authority*, and if you have defiled yourself and some man other than your husband has
lain with you"—
21 'then the priest shall [a]put the woman under
the oath of the curse, and he shall say to the
woman—[b]"the LORD make you a curse and an
oath among your people, when the LORD makes
your thigh [1]rot and your belly swell;
22 "and may this water that causes the curse [a]go
into your stomach, and make *your* belly swell and
*your* thigh rot." [b]Then the woman shall say,
"Amen, so be it."
**23** 'Then the priest shall write these curses in a
book, and he shall scrape *them* off into the bitter
water.
24 'And he shall make the woman drink the bitter
water that brings a curse, and the water that
brings the curse shall enter her *to become* bitter.
25 [a]'Then the priest shall take the grain offering
of jealousy from the woman's hand, shall [b]wave
the offering before the LORD, and bring it to the
altar;
26 'and the priest shall take a handful of the
offering, [a]as its memorial portion, burn *it* on
the altar, and afterward make the woman drink
the water.
27 'When he has made her drink the water, then
it shall be, if she has defiled herself and behaved
unfaithfully toward her husband, that the water
that brings a [a]curse will enter her *and become*
bitter, and her belly will swell, her thigh will rot,
and the woman [b]will become a curse among her
people.
28 'But if the woman has not defiled herself, and
is clean, then she shall be free and may conceive
children.
**29** 'This *is* the law of jealousy, when a wife, *while*
under her husband's *authority*, [a]goes astray and
defiles herself,
30 'or when the spirit of jealousy comes upon a
man, and he becomes jealous of his wife; then he
shall stand the woman before the LORD, and the
priest shall execute all this law upon her.

**42** [1]*household*
**45** [a]Num. 4:29
**46** [a]Num. 3:39; 26:57–62; 1 Chr. 23:3–23
**47** [a]Num. 4:3, 23, 30
**49** [a]Num. 4:15, 24, 31 [b]Num. 4:1, 21

CHAPTER 5

**2** [a]Lev. 13:3, 8, 46; Num. 12:10, 14, 15 [b]Lev. 15:2 [c]Lev. 21:1; Num. 9:6, 10; 19:11, 13; 31:19 [1]*by contact with*
**3** [a]Lev. 26:11, 12; Num. 35:34; [2 Cor. 6:16]
**6** [a]Lev. 5:14—6:7
**7** [a]Lev. 5:5; 26:40, 41; Josh. 7:19; Ps. 32:5; 1 John 1:9 [b]Lev. 6:4, 5
**8** [a]Lev. 5:15; 6:6, 7; 7:7 [1]*redeemer,* Heb. *goel*
**9** [a]Ex. 29:28; Lev. 6:17, 18, 26; 7:6–14 [b]Lev. 7:32–34; 10:14, 15 [1]*heave offering*
**10** [a]Lev. 10:13 [1]*consecrated*
**13** [a]Lev. 18:20; 20:10 [b]John 8:4
**14** [a]Prov. 6:34; Song 8:6
**15** [a]Lev. 5:11 [b]1 Kin. 17:18; Ezek. 29:16; Heb. 10:3
**18** [a]Heb. 13:4
**21** [a]Josh. 6:26; 1 Sam. 14:24; Neh. 10:29 [b]Jer. 29:22 [1]Lit. *fall away*
**22** [a]Ps. 109:18 [b]Deut. 27:15–26
**25** [a]Lev. 8:27 [b]Lev. 2:2, 9
**26** [a]Lev. 2:2, 9
**27** [a]Deut. 28:37; Is. 65:15; Jer. 24:9; 29:18, 22; 42:18 [b]Num. 5:21
**29** [a]Num. 5:19

31 ‘Then the man shall be free from [1]iniquity, but that woman [a]shall bear her [2]guilt.’ ”

### *The Law for the Nazirite*

**6** Then the LORD spoke to Moses, saying,
2 “Speak to the children of Israel, and say to them: ‘When either a man or woman [1]consecrates an offering to take the vow of a Nazirite, [a]to separate himself to the LORD,
3 [a]‘he shall separate himself from wine and *similar* drink; he shall drink neither vinegar made from wine nor vinegar made from *similar* drink; neither shall he drink any grape juice, nor eat fresh grapes or raisins.
4 ‘All the days of his [1]separation he shall eat nothing that is produced by the grapevine, from seed to skin.
5 ‘All the days of the vow of his separation no [a]razor shall come upon his head; until the days are fulfilled for which he separated himself to the LORD, he shall be holy. *Then* he shall let the locks of the hair of his head grow.
6 ‘All the days that he separates himself to the LORD [a]he shall not go near a dead body.
7 [a]‘He shall not [1]make himself unclean even for his father or his mother, for his brother or his sister, when they die, because his separation to God *is* on his head.
8 [a]‘All the days of his separation he shall be holy to the LORD.
**9** ‘And if anyone dies very suddenly beside him, and he defiles his consecrated head, then he shall [a]shave his head on the day of his cleansing; on the seventh day he shall shave it.
10 ‘Then [a]on the eighth day he shall bring two turtledoves or two young pigeons to the priest, to the door of the tabernacle of meeting;
11 ‘and the priest shall offer one as a sin offering and *the* other as a burnt offering, and make atonement for him, because he sinned in regard to the corpse; and he shall sanctify his head that same day.
12 ‘He shall consecrate to the LORD the days of his separation, and bring a male lamb in its first year [a]as a trespass offering; but the former days shall be [1]lost, because his separation was defiled.
**13** ‘Now this *is* the law of the Nazirite: [a]When the days of his separation are fulfilled, he shall be brought to the door of the tabernacle of meeting.
14 ‘And he shall present his offering to the LORD: one male lamb in its first year without blemish as a burnt offering, one ewe lamb in its first year without blemish [a]as a sin offering, one ram without blemish [b]as a peace offering,
15 ‘a basket of unleavened bread, [a]cakes of fine flour mixed with oil, unleavened wafers [b]anointed with oil, and their grain offering with their [c]drink offerings.
16 ‘Then the priest shall bring *them* before the LORD and offer his sin offering and his burnt offering;
17 ‘and he shall offer the ram as a sacrifice of a peace offering to the LORD, with the basket of unleavened bread; the priest shall also offer its grain offering and its drink offering.
18 [a]‘Then the Nazirite shall shave his consecrated head *at* the door of the tabernacle of meeting, and shall take the hair from his consecrated head and put *it* on the fire which is under the sacrifice of the peace offering.
19 ‘And the priest shall take the [a]boiled shoulder of the ram, one [b]unleavened cake from the basket, and one unleavened wafer, and [c]put *them* upon the hands of the Nazirite after he has shaved his consecrated *hair,*
20 ‘and the priest shall wave them as a wave offering before the LORD; [a]they *are* holy for the priest, together with the breast of the wave offering and the thigh of the heave offering. After that the Nazirite may drink wine.’
**21** “This is the law of the Nazirite who vows to the LORD the offering for his separation, and besides that, whatever else his hand is able to provide; according to the vow which he takes, so he must do according to the law of his separation.”
**22** And the LORD spoke to Moses, saying:
23 “Speak to Aaron and his sons, saying, ‘This is the way you shall bless the children of Israel. Say to them:

24 “The LORD [a]bless you and [b]keep you;
25 The LORD [a]make His face shine upon you,
And [b]be gracious to you;
26 [a]The LORD [1]lift up His countenance upon you,
And [b]give you peace.” ’

27 [a]“So they shall [1]put My name on the children of Israel, and [b]I will bless them.”

### *Offerings for the Dedication of the Altar*

**7** Now it came to pass, when Moses had finished [a]setting up the tabernacle, that he [b]anointed it and consecrated it and all its furnishings, and the altar and all its utensils; so he anointed them and consecrated them.
2 Then [a]the leaders of Israel, the heads of their fathers’ houses, who *were* the leaders of the tribes [1]and over those who were numbered, made an offering.
3 And they brought their offering before the LORD, six covered carts and twelve oxen, a cart for *every* two of the leaders, and for each one an ox; and they presented them before the tabernacle.
4 Then the LORD spoke to Moses, saying,
5 “Accept *these* from them, that they may be used in doing the work of the tabernacle of meeting; and you shall give them to the Levites, *to* every man according to his service.”
6 So Moses took the carts and the oxen, and gave them to the Levites.
7 Two carts and four oxen [a]he gave to the sons of Gershon, according to their service;
8 [a]and four carts and eight oxen he gave to the sons of Merari, according to their service, under the [1]authority of Ithamar the son of Aaron the priest.
9 But to the sons of Kohath he gave none, because theirs *was* [a]the service of the holy things, [b]*which* they carried on their shoulders.
**10** Now the leaders offered [a]the dedication *offering* for the altar when it was anointed; so the leaders offered their offering before the altar.
11 For the LORD said to Moses, “They shall offer their offering, one leader each day, for the dedication of the altar.”
**12** And the one who offered his offering on the first day *was* [a]Nahshon the son of Amminadab, from the tribe of Judah.
13 His offering *was* one silver platter, the weight of which *was* one hundred and thirty *shekels,* and one silver bowl of seventy shekels, according to

---

**31** [a]Lev. 20:17, 19, 20 [1]*guilt* [2]*iniquity*

CHAPTER 6

**2** [a]Lev. 27:2; Judg. 13:5; [Lam. 4:7; Amos 2:11, 12]; Acts 21:23; Rom. 1:1 [1]Or *makes a difficult vow*
**3** [a]Lev. 10:9; Amos 2:12; Luke 1:15
**4** [1]Separation as a Nazirite
**5** [a]Judg. 13:5; 16:17; 1 Sam. 1:11
**6** [a]Lev. 21:1–3, 11; Num. 19:11–22
**7** [a]Lev. 21:1, 2, 11; Num. 9:6 [1]By touching a dead body
**8** [a][2 Cor. 6:17, 18]
**9** [a]Lev. 14:8, 9; Acts 18:18; 21:24
**10** [a]Lev. 5:7; 14:22; 15:14, 29
**12** [a]Lev. 5:6 [1]*void*
**13** [a]Acts 21:26
**14** [a]Lev. 4:2, 27, 32 [b]Lev. 3:6
**15** [a]Lev. 2:4 [b]Ex. 29:2 [c]Num. 15:5, 7, 10
**18** [a]Num. 6:9; Acts 21:23, 24
**19** [a]1 Sam. 2:15 [b]Ex. 29:23, 24 [c]Lev. 7:30
**20** [a]Ex. 29:27, 28
**24** [a]Deut. 28:3–6 [b]Ps. 121:7; John 7:11
**25** [a]Ps. 31:16; 67:1; 80:3, 7, 19; 119:135; Dan. 9:17 [b]Gen. 43:29; Ex. 33:19; Mal. 1:9
**26** [a]Ps. 4:6; 89:15 [b]Lev. 26:6; Is. 26:3, 12; John 14:27; Phil. 4:7 [1]Look upon you with favor
**27** [a]Deut. 28:10; 2 Sam. 7:23; 2 Chr. 7:14; Is. 43:7; Dan. 9:18, 19 [b]Ex. 20:24; Num. 23:20; Ps. 5:12; 67:7; 115:12, 13; Eph. 1:3 [1]*invoke*

CHAPTER 7

**1** [a]Ex. 40:17–33 [b]Lev. 8:10, 11
**2** [a]Num. 1:4 [1]Lit. *who stood over*
**7** [a]Num. 4:24–28
**8** [a]Num. 4:29–33 [1]Lit. *hand*
**9** [a]Num. 4:15 [b]Num. 4:6–14
**10** [a]Num. 7:1; Deut. 20:5; 1 Kin. 8:63; 2 Chr. 7:5, 9; Ezra 6:16; Neh. 12:27
**12** [a]Num. 2:3

[a]the shekel of the sanctuary, both of them full of fine flour mixed with oil as a [b]grain offering;

14 one gold pan of ten *shekels,* full of [a]incense;

15 [a]one young bull, one ram, and one male lamb [b]in its first year, as a burnt offering;

16 one kid of the goats as a [a]sin offering;

17 and for [a]the sacrifice of peace offerings: two oxen, five rams, five male goats, and five male lambs in their first year. This *was* the offering of Nahshon the son of Amminadab.

**18** On the second day Nethanel the son of Zuar, leader of Issachar, presented *an offering.*

19 *For* his offering he offered one silver platter, the weight of which *was* one hundred and thirty *shekels,* and one silver bowl of seventy shekels, according to the shekel of the sanctuary, both of them full of fine flour mixed with oil as a grain offering;

20 one gold pan of ten *shekels,* full of incense;

21 one young bull, one ram, and one male lamb in its first year, as a burnt offering;

22 one kid of the goats as a sin offering;

23 and as the sacrifice of peace offerings: two oxen, five rams, five male goats, and five male lambs in their first year. This *was* the offering of Nethanel the son of Zuar.

**24** On the third day Eliab the son of Helon, leader of the children of Zebulun, *presented an offering.*

25 His offering *was* one silver platter, the weight of which *was* one hundred and thirty *shekels,* and one silver bowl of seventy shekels, according to the shekel of the sanctuary, both of them full of fine flour mixed with oil as a grain offering;

26 one gold pan of ten *shekels,* full of incense;

27 one young bull, one ram, and one male lamb in its first year, as a burnt offering;

28 one kid of the goats as a sin offering;

29 and for the sacrifice of peace offerings: two oxen, five rams, five male goats, and five male lambs in their first year. This *was* the offering of Eliab the son of Helon.

**30** On the fourth day [a]Elizur the son of Shedeur, leader of the children of Reuben, *presented an offering.*

31 His offering *was* one silver platter, the weight of which *was* one hundred and thirty *shekels,* and one silver bowl of seventy shekels, according to the shekel of the sanctuary, both of them full of fine flour mixed with oil as a grain offering;

32 one gold pan of ten *shekels,* full of incense;

33 one young bull, one ram, and one male lamb in its first year, as a burnt offering;

34 one kid of the goats as a sin offering;

35 and as the sacrifice of peace offerings: two oxen, five rams, five male goats, and five male lambs in their first year. This *was* the offering of Elizur the son of Shedeur.

**36** On the fifth day [a]Shelumiel the son of Zurishaddai, leader of the children of Simeon, *presented an offering.*

37 His offering *was* one silver platter, the weight of which *was* one hundred and thirty *shekels,* and one silver bowl of seventy shekels, according to the shekel of the sanctuary, both of them full of fine flour mixed with oil as a grain offering;

38 one gold pan of ten *shekels,* full of incense;

39 one young bull, one ram, and one male lamb in its first year, as a burnt offering;

40 one kid of the goats as a sin offering;

41 and as the sacrifice of peace offerings: two oxen, five rams, five male goats, and five male lambs in their first year. This *was* the offering of Shelumiel the son of Zurishaddai.

**42** On the sixth day [a]Eliasaph the son of [1]Deuel, leader of the children of Gad, *presented an offering.*

43 His offering *was* one silver platter, the weight of which *was* one hundred and thirty *shekels,* and one silver bowl of seventy shekels, according to the shekel of the sanctuary, both of them full of fine flour mixed with oil as a grain offering;

44 one gold pan of ten *shekels,* full of incense;

45 one young bull, one ram, and one male lamb in its first year, as [a]a burnt offering;

46 one kid of the goats as a sin offering;

47 and as the sacrifice of peace offerings: two oxen, five rams, five male goats, and five male lambs in their first year. This *was* the offering of Eliasaph the son of Deuel.

**48** On the seventh day [a]Elishama the son of Ammihud, leader of the children of Ephraim, *presented an offering.*

49 His offering *was* one silver platter, the weight of which *was* one hundred and thirty *shekels,* and one silver bowl of seventy shekels, according to the shekel of the sanctuary, both of them full of fine flour mixed with oil as a grain offering;

50 one gold pan of ten *shekels,* full of incense;

51 one young bull, one ram, and one male lamb in its first year, as a burnt offering;

52 one kid of the goats as a sin offering;

53 and as the sacrifice of peace offerings: two oxen, five rams, five male goats, and five male lambs in their first year. This *was* the offering of Elishama the son of Ammihud.

**54** On the eighth day [a]Gamaliel the son of Pedahzur, leader of the children of Manasseh, *presented an offering.*

55 His offering *was* one silver platter, the weight of which *was* one hundred and thirty *shekels,* and one silver bowl of seventy shekels, according to the shekel of the sanctuary, both of them full of fine flour mixed with oil as a grain offering;

56 one gold pan of ten *shekels,* full of incense;

57 one young bull, one ram, and one male lamb in its first year, as a burnt offering;

58 one kid of the goats as a sin offering;

59 and as the sacrifice of peace offerings: two oxen, five rams, five male goats, and five male lambs in their first year. This *was* the offering of Gamaliel the son of Pedahzur.

**60** On the ninth day [a]Abidan the son of Gideoni, leader of the children of Benjamin, *presented an offering.*

61 His offering *was* one silver platter, the weight of which *was* one hundred and thirty *shekels,* and one silver bowl of seventy shekels, according to the shekel of the sanctuary, both of them full of fine flour mixed with oil as a grain offering;

62 one gold pan of ten *shekels,* full of incense;

63 one young bull, one ram, and one male lamb in its first year, as a burnt offering;

64 one kid of the goats as a sin offering;

65 and as the sacrifice of peace offerings: two oxen, five rams, five male goats, and five male lambs in their first year. This *was* the offering of Abidan the son of Gideoni.

**66** On the tenth day [a]Ahiezer the son of Ammishaddai, leader of the children of Dan, *presented an offering.*

**13** [a]Ex. 30:13 [b]Lev. 2:1
**14** [a]Ex. 30:34
**15** [a]Lev. 1:2 [b]Ex. 12:5
**16** [a]Lev. 4:23
**17** [a]Lev. 3:1
**30** [a]Num. 1:5; 2:10
**36** [a]Num. 1:6; 2:12; 7:41
**42** [a]Num. 1:14; 2:14; 10:20 [1]*Reuel,* Num. 2:14
**45** [a]Ps. 40:6
**48** [a]Num. 1:10; 2:18; 1 Chr. 7:26
**54** [a]Num. 1:10; 2:20
**60** [a]Num. 1:11; 2:22
**66** [a]Num. 1:12; 2:25

67 His offering *was* one silver platter, the weight
of which *was* one hundred and thirty *shekels,* and
one silver bowl of seventy shekels, according to
the shekel of the sanctuary, both of them full of
fine flour mixed with oil as a grain offering;
68 one gold pan of ten *shekels,* full of incense;
69 one young bull, one ram, and one male lamb in
its first year, as a burnt offering;
70 one kid of the goats as a sin offering;
71 and as the sacrifice of peace offerings: two
oxen, five rams, five male goats, and five male
lambs in their first year. This *was* the offering of
Ahiezer the son of Ammishaddai.
**72** On the eleventh day [a]Pagiel the son of Ocran,
leader of the children of Asher, *presented an
offering.*
73 His offering *was* one silver platter, the weight
of which *was* one hundred and thirty *shekels,* and
one silver bowl of seventy shekels, according to
the shekel of the sanctuary, both of them full of
fine flour mixed with oil as a grain offering;
74 one gold pan of ten *shekels,* full of incense;
75 one young bull, one ram, and one male lamb in
its first year, as a burnt offering;
76 one kid of the goats as a sin offering;
77 and as the sacrifice of peace offerings: two
oxen, five rams, five male goats, and five male
lambs in their first year. This *was* the offering of
Pagiel the son of Ocran.
**78** On the twelfth day [a]Ahira the son of Enan,
leader of the children of Naphtali, *presented an
offering.*
79 His offering *was* one silver platter, the weight
of which *was* one hundred and thirty *shekels,* and
one silver bowl of seventy shekels, according to
the shekel of the sanctuary, both of them full of
fine flour mixed with oil as a grain offering;
80 one gold pan of ten *shekels,* full of incense;
81 one young bull, one ram, and one male lamb in
its first year, as a burnt offering;
82 one kid of the goats as a sin offering;
83 and as the sacrifice of peace offerings: two
oxen, five rams, five male goats, and five male
lambs in their first year. This *was* the offering of
Ahira the son of Enan.
**84** This *was* [a]the dedication *offering* for the altar
from the leaders of Israel, when it was anointed:
twelve silver platters, twelve silver bowls, and
twelve gold pans.
85 Each silver platter *weighed* one hundred and
thirty *shekels* and each bowl seventy *shekels.* All
the silver of the vessels *weighed* two thousand
four hundred *shekels,* according to the shekel of
the sanctuary.
86 The twelve gold pans full of incense *weighed*
ten *shekels* apiece, according to the shekel of the
sanctuary; all the gold of the pans *weighed* one
hundred and twenty *shekels.*
87 All the oxen for the burnt offering *were* twelve
young bulls, the rams twelve, the male lambs in
their first year twelve, with their grain offering,
and the kids of the goats as a sin offering twelve.
88 And all the oxen for the sacrifice of peace
offerings were twenty-four bulls, the rams sixty,
the male goats sixty, and the lambs in their first
year sixty. This *was* the dedication *offering* for the
altar after it was [a]anointed.
**89** Now when Moses went into the tabernacle of
meeting [a]to speak with Him, he heard [b]the voice
of One speaking to him from above the mercy seat
that *was* on the ark of the Testimony, from
[c]between the two cherubim; thus He spoke to him.

*The Cleansing of the Levites*

**8** And the LORD spoke to Moses, saying:
2 "Speak to Aaron, and say to him, 'When you
[a]arrange the lamps, the seven [b]lamps shall give
light in front of the lampstand.' "
3 And Aaron did so; he arranged the lamps to
face toward the front of the lampstand, as the
LORD commanded Moses.
4 [a]Now this workmanship of the lampstand *was*
hammered gold; from its shaft to its flowers it *was*
[b]hammered work. [c]According to the pattern
which the LORD had shown Moses, so he made the
lampstand.
**5** Then the LORD spoke to Moses, saying:
6 "Take the Levites from among the children of
Israel and cleanse them *ceremonially.*
7 "Thus you shall do to them to cleanse them:
Sprinkle [a]water of purification on them, and [b]let[1]
them shave all their body, and let them wash their
clothes, and *so* make themselves clean.
8 "Then let them take a young bull with [a]its
grain offering of fine flour mixed with oil, and you
shall take another young bull as a sin offering.
9 [a]"And you shall bring the Levites before the
tabernacle of meeting, [b]and you shall gather
together the whole congregation of the children
of Israel.
10 "So you shall bring the Levites before the
LORD, and the children of Israel [a]shall lay their
hands on the Levites;
11 "and Aaron shall [1]offer the Levites before the
LORD *like* a [a]wave offering from the children of
Israel, that they may perform the work of the
LORD.
12 [a]"Then the Levites shall lay their hands on the
heads of the young bulls, and you shall offer one
as a sin offering and the other as a burnt offering
to the LORD, to make atonement for the Levites.
13 "And you shall stand the Levites before Aaron
and his sons, and then offer them *like* a wave
offering to the LORD.
14 "Thus you shall [a]separate the Levites from
among the children of Israel, and the Levites shall
be [b]Mine.
15 "After that the Levites shall go in to service
the tabernacle of meeting. So you shall cleanse
them and [a]offer them *like* a wave offering.
16 "For they *are* [a]wholly given to Me from
among the children of Israel; I have taken them
for Myself [b]instead of all who open the womb, the
firstborn of all the children of Israel.
17 [a]"For all the firstborn among the children of
Israel *are* Mine, *both* man and beast; on the day
that I struck all the firstborn in the land of Egypt
I [1]sanctified them to Myself.
18 "I have taken the Levites instead of all the
firstborn of the children of Israel.
19 "And [a]I have given the Levites as a gift to
Aaron and his sons from among the children of
Israel, to do the work for the children of Israel in
the tabernacle of meeting, and to make atonement for the children of Israel, [b]that there be no
plague among the children of Israel when the
children of Israel come near the sanctuary."
**20** Thus Moses and Aaron and all the congregation of the children of Israel did to the Levites;
according to all that the LORD commanded Moses

**72** [a]Num. 1:13; 2:27
**78** [a]Num. 1:15; 2:29
**84** [a]Num. 7:10
**88** [a]Num. 7:1, 10
**89** [a][Ex. 33:9, 11]; Num. 12:8 [b]Ex. 25:21, 22 [c]Ps. 80:1; 99:1

CHAPTER 8

**2** [a]Lev. 24:2–4 [b]Ex. 25:37; 40:25
**4** [a]Ex. 25:31 [b]Ex. 25:18 [c]Ex. 25:40; Acts 7:44
**7** [a]Num. 19:9, 13, 17, 20; Ps. 51:2, 7; [Heb. 9:13, 14] [b]Lev. 14:8, 9 [1]Heb. *let them cause a razor to pass over*
**8** [a]Lev. 2:1; Num. 15:8–10
**9** [a]Ex. 29:4; 40:12 [b]Lev. 8:3
**10** [a]Lev. 1:4
**11** [a]Num. 18:6 [1]*present*
**12** [a]Ex. 29:10
**14** [a]Num. 16:9 [b]Num. 3:12, 45; 16:9
**15** [a]Num. 8:11, 13
**16** [a]Num. 3:9 [b]Ex. 13:2; Num. 3:12, 45
**17** [a]Ex. 12:2, 12, 13, 15; Num. 3:13; Luke 2:23 [1]*set them apart*
**19** [a]Num. 3:9 [b]Num. 1:53; 16:46; 18:5; 2 Chr. 26:16

concerning the Levites, so the children of Israel
did to them.
21 [a]And the Levites purified themselves and
washed their clothes; then Aaron presented them
*like* a wave offering before the LORD, and Aaron
made atonement for them to cleanse them.
22 [a]After that the Levites went in to do their
work in the tabernacle of meeting before Aaron
and his sons; [b]as the LORD commanded Moses
concerning the Levites, so they did to them.
**23** Then the LORD spoke to Moses, saying,
24 "This *is* what *pertains* to the Levites: [a]From
twenty-five years old and above one may enter to
perform service in the work of the tabernacle of
meeting;
25 "and at the age of fifty years they must cease
performing this work, and shall work no more.
26 "They may minister with their brethren in the
tabernacle of meeting, [a]to attend to needs, but
they *themselves* shall do no work. Thus you shall
do to the Levites regarding their duties."

## *How the Passover Was Kept*

**9** Now the LORD spoke to Moses in the Wilderness of Sinai, in the first month of the second
year after they had come out of the land of Egypt,
saying:
2 "Let the children of Israel keep [a]the Passover
at its appointed [b]time.
3 "On the fourteenth day of this month, [1]at
twilight, you shall [2]keep it at its appointed time.
According to all its [3]rites and ceremonies you shall
keep it."
4 So Moses told the children of Israel that they
should keep the Passover.
5 And [a]they kept the Passover on the fourteenth
day of the first month, at twilight, in the Wilderness of Sinai; according to all that the LORD
commanded Moses, so the children of Israel did.
**6** Now there were *certain* men who were [a]de-
filed by a human corpse, so that they could not
keep the Passover on that day; [b]and they came
before Moses and Aaron that day.
7 And those men said to him, "We *became*
defiled by a human corpse. Why are we kept from
presenting the offering of the LORD at its appointed time among the children of Israel?"
8 And Moses said to them, "Stand still, that [a]I
may hear what the LORD will command concerning you."
**9** Then the LORD spoke to Moses, saying,
10 "Speak to the children of Israel, saying: 'If
anyone of you or your [1]posterity is unclean because of a corpse, or *is* far away on a journey, he
may still keep the LORD's Passover.
11 'On [a]the fourteenth day of the second month,
at twilight, they may keep it. They shall [b]eat it
with unleavened bread and bitter herbs.
12 [a]'They shall leave none of it until morning,
[b]nor break one of its bones. [c]According to all the
[1]ordinances of the Passover they shall keep it.
13 'But the man who *is* clean and is not on a
journey, and ceases to keep the Passover, that
same person [a]shall be cut off from among his
people, because he [b]did not bring the offering of
the LORD at its appointed time; that man shall
[c]bear his sin.
14 'And if a stranger [1]dwells among you, and
would keep the LORD's Passover, he must do so
according to the rite of the Passover and according to its ceremony; [a]you shall have one [2]ordi-
nance, both for the stranger and the native of the
land.' "
**15** Now [a]on the day that the tabernacle was
raised up, the cloud [b]covered the tabernacle, the
tent of the Testimony; [c]from evening until morning it was above the tabernacle like the appearance of fire.
16 So it was always: the cloud covered it *by day*,
and the appearance of fire by night.
17 Whenever the cloud [a]was [1]taken up from
above the tabernacle, after that the children of
Israel would journey; and in the place where the
cloud settled, there the children of Israel would
pitch their tents.
18 At the [1]command of the LORD the children of
Israel would journey, and at the command of the
LORD they would camp; [a]as long as the cloud
stayed above the tabernacle they remained encamped.
19 Even when the cloud continued long, many
days above the tabernacle, the children of Israel
[a]kept the charge of the LORD and did not journey.
20 So it was, when the cloud was above the
tabernacle a few days: according to the command
of the LORD they would remain encamped, and
according to the command of the LORD they
would journey.
21 So it was, when the cloud remained only from
evening until morning: when the cloud was taken
up in the morning, then they would journey;
whether by day or by night, whenever the cloud
was taken up, they would journey.
22 *Whether it was* two days, a month, or a year
that the cloud remained above the tabernacle, the
children of Israel [a]would remain encamped and
not journey; but when it was taken up, they
would journey.
23 At the command of the LORD they remained
encamped, and at the command of the LORD they
journeyed; they [a]kept the charge of the LORD, at
the command of the LORD by the hand of Moses.

## *The Israelites Leave Mount Sinai*

**10** And the LORD spoke to Moses, saying:
2 "Make two silver trumpets for yourself;
you shall make them of hammered work; you
shall use them for [a]calling the congregation and
for directing the movement of the camps.
3 "When [a]they blow both of them, all the congregation shall gather before you at the door of
the tabernacle of meeting.
4 "But if they blow *only* one, then the leaders,
the [a]heads of the divisions of Israel, shall gather to
you.
5 "When you sound the [a]advance, [b]the camps
that lie on the east side shall then begin their
journey.
6 "When you sound the advance the second
time, then the camps that lie [a]on the south side
shall begin their journey; they shall sound the call
for them to begin their journeys.
7 "And when the assembly is to be gathered
together, [a]you shall blow, but not [b]sound the
advance.
8 [a]"The sons of Aaron, the priests, shall blow the
trumpets; and these shall be to you as an [1]ordi-
nance forever throughout your generations.
9 [a]"When you go to war in your land against the
enemy who [b]oppresses you, then you shall sound
an alarm with the trumpets, and you will be

---

**21** [a]Num. 8:7
**22** [a]Num. 8:15 [b]Num. 8:5
**24** [a]Num. 4:3; 1 Chr. 23:3, 24, 27
**26** [a]Num. 1:53

CHAPTER 9

**2** [a]Ex. 12:1–16; Lev. 23:5; Num. 28:16; Deut. 16:1, 2 [b]2 Chr. 30:1–15; Luke 22:7; [1 Cor. 5:7, 8]
**3** [1]Lit. *between the evenings* [2]*observe* [3]*statutes*
**5** [a]Josh. 5:10
**6** [a]Num. 5:2; 19:11–22; John 18:28 [b]Ex. 18:15, 19, 26; Num. 27:2
**8** [a]Ex. 18:22; Num. 27:5
**10** [1]*descendants*
**11** [a]2 Chr. 30:2, 15 [b]Ex. 12:8
**12** [a]Ex. 12:10 [b]Ex. 12:46; [John 19:36] [c]Ex. 12:43 [1]*statutes*
**13** [a]Gen. 17:14; Ex. 12:15, 47 [b]Num. 9:7 [c]Num. 5:31
**14** [a]Ex. 12:49; Lev. 24:22; Num. 15:15, 16, 29 [1]As a resident alien [2]*statute*
**15** [a]Ex. 40:33, 34; Neh. 9:12, 19; Ps. 78:14 [b]Is. 4:5 [c]Ex. 13:21, 22; 40:38
**17** [a]Ex. 40:36–38; Num. 10:11, 12, 33, 34; Ps. 80:1 [1]*lifted up*
**18** [a]1 Cor. 10:1 [1]Lit. *mouth*
**19** [a]Num. 1:53; 3:8
**22** [a]Ex. 40:36, 37
**23** [a]Num. 9:19

CHAPTER 10

**2** [a]Is. 1:13
**3** [a]Jer. 4:5; Joel 2:15
**4** [a]Ex. 18:21; Num. 1:16; 7:2
**5** [a]Joel 2:1 [b]Num. 2:3
**6** [a]Num. 2:10
**7** [a]Num. 10:3 [b]Joel 2:1
**8** [a]Num. 31:6; Josh. 6:4; 1 Chr. 15:24; 2 Chr. 13:12 [1]*statute*
**9** [a]Num. 31:6; Josh. 6:5; 2 Chr. 13:14 [b]Judg. 2:18; 4:3; 6:9; 10:8, 12

[c]remembered before the LORD your God, and you
will be saved from your enemies.
10 "Also [a]in the day of your gladness, in your
appointed feasts, and at the beginning of your
months, you shall blow the trumpets over
your burnt offerings and over the sacrifices of
your peace offerings; and they shall be [b]a memorial for you before your God: I *am* the LORD your
God."
11 Now it came to pass on the twentieth *day* of
the second month, in the second year, that the
cloud [a]was taken up from above the tabernacle of
the Testimony.
12 And the children of Israel set out from the
[a]Wilderness of Sinai on [b]their journeys; then the
cloud settled down in the [c]Wilderness of Paran.
13 So they started out for the first time [a]accord-
ing to the command of the LORD by the hand of
Moses.
**14** The [1]standard of the camp of the children of
Judah [a]set out first according to their armies; over
their army was [b]Nahshon the son of Amminadab.
15 Over the army of the tribe of the children of
Issachar *was* Nethanel the son of Zuar.
16 And over the army of the tribe of the children
of Zebulun *was* Eliab the son of Helon.
17 Then [a]the tabernacle was taken down; and the
sons of Gershon and the sons of Merari set out,
[b]carrying the tabernacle.
**18** And [a]the standard of the camp of Reuben set
out according to their armies; over their army *was*
Elizur the son of Shedeur.
19 Over the army of the tribe of the children of
Simeon *was* Shelumiel the son of Zurishaddai.
20 And over the army of the tribe of the children
of Gad *was* Eliasaph the son of Deuel.
21 Then the Kohathites set out, carrying the
[a]holy things. (The tabernacle would be [1]prepared
for their arrival.)
**22** And [a]the standard of the camp of the children
of Ephraim set out according to their armies; over
their army *was* Elishama the son of Ammihud.
23 Over the army of the tribe of the children of
Manasseh *was* Gamaliel the son of Pedahzur.
24 And over the army of the tribe of the children
of Benjamin *was* Abidan the son of Gideoni.
**25** Then [a]the standard of the camp of the children
of Dan (the rear guard of all the camps), set out
according to their armies; over their army *was*
Ahiezer the son of Ammishaddai.
26 Over the army of the tribe of the children of
Asher *was* Pagiel the son of Ocran.
27 And over the army of the tribe of the children
of Naphtali *was* Ahira the son of Enan.
28 [a]Thus *was* the order of march of the children
of Israel, according to their armies, when they
began their journey.
**29** Now Moses said to [a]Hobab the son of [b]Reuel[1]
the Midianite, Moses' father-in-law, "We are
setting out for the place of which the LORD said,
[c]'I will give it to you.' Come with us, and [d]we will
treat you well; for [e]the LORD has promised good
things to Israel."
30 And he said to him, "I will not go, but I will
depart to my *own* land and to my relatives."
31 So [1]*Moses* said, "Please do not leave, inasmuch
as you know how we are to camp in the wilderness, and you can [2]be our [a]eyes.
32 "And it shall be, if you go with us—indeed it
shall be—that [a]whatever good the LORD will do to
us, the same we will do to you."

**33** So they departed from [a]the mountain of the
LORD on a journey of three days; and the ark of
the covenant of the LORD [b]went before them for
the three days' journey, to search out a resting
place for them.
34 And [a]the cloud of the LORD *was* above them
by day when they went out from the camp.
35 So it was, whenever the ark set out, that
Moses said:

[a]"Rise up, O LORD!
Let Your enemies be scattered,
And let those who hate You
flee before You."

36 And when it rested, he said:

"Return, O LORD,
*To* the many thousands of Israel."

## *The Seventy Elders*

**11** Now [a]*when* the people complained, it displeased the LORD; [b]for the LORD heard *it,*
and His anger was aroused. So the [c]fire of the
LORD burned among them, and consumed *some* in
the outskirts of the camp.
2 Then the people [a]cried out to Moses, and when
Moses [b]prayed to the LORD, the fire was
[1]quenched.
3 So he called the name of the place [1]Taberah,
because the fire of the LORD had burned among
them.
**4** Now the [a]mixed multitude who were among
them [1]yielded to [b]intense craving; so the children
of Israel also wept again and said: [c]"Who will give
us meat to eat?
5 [a]"We remember the fish which we ate freely in
Egypt, the cucumbers, the melons, the leeks, the
onions, and the garlic;
6 "but now [a]our whole being *is* dried up; *there is*
nothing at all except this manna *before* our eyes!"
7 Now [a]the manna *was* like coriander seed, and
its color like the color of bdellium.
8 The people went about and gathered *it,*
ground *it* on millstones or beat *it* in the mortar,
cooked *it* in pans, and made cakes of it; and [a]its
taste was like the taste of pastry prepared with oil.
9 And [a]when the dew fell on the camp in the
night, the manna fell on it.
**10** Then Moses heard the people weeping
throughout their families, everyone at the door of
his tent; and [a]the anger of the LORD was greatly
aroused; Moses also was displeased.
11 [a]So Moses said to the LORD, "Why have You
afflicted Your servant? And why have I not found
favor in Your sight, that You have laid the [1]bur-
den of all these people on me?
12 "Did I conceive all these people? Did I beget
them, that You should say to me, [a]'Carry them in
your bosom, as a [b]guardian carries a nursing
child,' to the land which You [c]swore[1] to their
fathers?
13 [a]"Where am I to get meat to give to all these
people? For they weep all over me, saying, 'Give
us meat, that we may eat.'
14 [a]"I am not able to bear all these people alone,
because the burden *is* too heavy for me.
15 "If You treat me like this, please kill me here
and now—if I have found favor in Your sight—
and [a]do not let me see my wretchedness!"
**16** So the LORD said to Moses: "Gather to Me
[a]seventy men of the elders of Israel, whom you

**9** [c]Gen. 8:1; Ps. 106:4
**10** [a]Lev. 23:24; Num. 29:1; 1 Chr. 15:24; 2 Chr. 5:12; Ps. 81:3 [b]Lev. 23:24; Num. 10:9
**11** [a]Num. 9:17
**12** [a]Ex. 19:1; Num. 1:1; 9:5 [b]Ex. 40:36 [c]Gen. 21:21; Num. 12:16; Deut. 1:1
**13** [a]Num. 10:5, 6
**14** [a]Num. 2:3–9 [b]Num. 1:7 [1]*banner*
**17** [a]Num. 1:51 [b]Num. 4:21–32; 7:7–9
**18** [a]Num. 2:10–16
**21** [a]Num. 4:4–20; 7:9 [1]Prepared by the Gershonites and the Merarites
**22** [a]Num. 2:18–24
**25** [a]Num. 2:25–31; Josh. 6:9
**28** [a]Num. 2:34
**29** [a]Judg. 4:11 [b]Ex. 2:18; 3:1; 18:12 [c]Gen. 12:7; Ex. 6:4–8 [d]Judg. 1:16 [e]Gen. 32:12; Ex. 3:8 [1]*Jethro,* Ex. 3:1; LXX *Raguel*
**31** [a]Job 29:15 [1]Lit. *he* [2]Act as our guide
**32** [a]Ex. 18:9; Lev. 19:34; Judg. 1:16
**33** [a]Ex. 3:1; Deut. 1:6 [b]Deut. 1:33; Josh. 3:3–6; Ezek. 20:6
**34** [a]Ex. 13:21; Neh. 9:12, 19
**35** [a]Ps. 68:1, 2; 132:8; Is. 17:12–14

CHAPTER 11

**1** [a]Num. 14:2; 16:11; 17:5; Deut. 9:22 [b]Ps. 78:21 [c]Lev. 10:2; 2 Kin. 1:12
**2** [a]Num. 12:11, 13; 21:7 [b][James 5:16] [1]*extinguished*
**3** [1]Lit. *Burning*
**4** [a]Ex. 12:38 [b]1 Cor. 10:6 [c][Ps. 78:18] [1]Lit. *lusted intensely*
**5** [a]Ex. 16:3
**6** [a]Num. 21:5
**7** [a]Ex. 16:14, 31
**8** [a]Ex. 16:31
**9** [a]Ex. 16:13, 14
**10** [a]Ps. 78:21
**11** [a]Ex. 5:22; Deut. 1:12 [1]*responsibility*
**12** [a]Is. 40:11 [b]Is. 49:23; 1 Thess. 2:7 [c]Gen. 26:3 [1]*solemnly promised*
**13** [a]Matt. 15:33; Mark 8:4
**14** [a]Ex. 18:18; Deut. 1:12
**15** [a]Rev. 3:17
**16** [a]Ex. 18:25; 24:1, 9

know to be the elders of the people and [b]officers
over them; bring them to the tabernacle of meeting, that they may stand there with you.
17 "Then I will come down and talk with you
there. [a]I will take of the Spirit that *is* upon you
and will put *the same* upon them; and they shall
bear the burden of the people with you, that you
may not bear *it* yourself alone.
18 "Then you shall say to the people, [1]'Consecrate yourselves for tomorrow, and you shall eat
meat; for you have wept [a]in the hearing of the
LORD, saying, "Who will give us meat to eat? For
*it was* well with us in Egypt." Therefore the LORD
will give you meat, and you shall eat.
19 'You shall eat, not one day, nor two days, nor
five days, nor ten days, nor twenty days,
20 [a]'but *for* a whole month, until it comes out of
your nostrils and becomes loathsome to you,
because you have [b]despised the LORD who is
among you, and have wept before Him, saying,
[c]"Why did we ever come up out of Egypt?" ' "
21 And Moses said, [a]"The people whom I *am*
among *are* six hundred thousand men on foot; yet
You have said, 'I will give them meat, that they
may eat *for* a whole month.'
22 [a]"Shall flocks and herds be slaughtered for
them, to provide enough for them? Or shall all the
fish of the sea be gathered together for them, to
provide enough for them?"
23 And the LORD said to Moses, [a]"Has[1] the LORD's
arm been shortened? Now you shall see whether
[b]what I say will happen to you or not."
**24** So Moses went out and told the people the
words of the LORD, and he [a]gathered the seventy
men of the elders of the people and placed them
around the tabernacle.
25 Then the LORD came down in the cloud, and
spoke to him, and took of the Spirit that *was* upon
him, and placed *the same* upon the seventy elders;
and it happened, [a]when the Spirit rested upon
them, that [b]they prophesied, [1]although they never
did *so* again.
**26** But two men had remained in the camp: the
name of one *was* Eldad, and the name of the other
Medad. And the Spirit rested upon them. Now
they *were* among those listed, but who [a]had not
gone out to the tabernacle; yet they prophesied in
the camp.
27 And a young man ran and told Moses, and
said, "Eldad and Medad are prophesying in the
camp."
28 So Joshua the son of Nun, Moses' assistant,
*one* of his choice men, answered and said, "Moses
my lord, [a]forbid them!"
29 Then Moses said to him, "Are you [1]zealous for
my sake? [a]Oh, that all the LORD's people were
prophets *and* that the LORD would put His Spirit
upon them!"
30 And Moses returned to the camp, he and the
elders of Israel.
**31** Now a [a]wind went out from the LORD, and it
brought quail from the sea and left *them* fluttering
near the camp, about a day's journey on this side
and about a day's journey on the other side, all
around the camp, and about two cubits above the
surface of the ground.
32 And the people stayed up all that day, all
night, and all the next day, and gathered the quail
(he who gathered least gathered ten [a]homers);
and they spread *them* out for themselves all
around the camp.
33 But while the [a]meat *was* still between their
teeth, before it was chewed, the wrath of the LORD
was aroused against the people, and the LORD
struck the people with a very great plague.
34 So he called the name of that place [1]Kibroth
Hattaavah, because there they buried the people
who had yielded to craving.
35 [a]From Kibroth Hattaavah the people moved to
Hazeroth, and camped at Hazeroth.

### *Miriam and Aaron Speak Against Moses*

**12** Then [a]Miriam and Aaron [1]spoke [b]against
Moses because of the [2]Ethiopian woman
whom he had married; for [c]he had married an
Ethiopian woman.
2 So they said, "Has the LORD indeed spoken
only through [a]Moses? [b]Has He not spoken
through us also?" And the LORD [c]heard *it.*
3 (Now the man Moses *was* very humble, more
than all men who *were* on the face of the earth.)
4 [a]Suddenly the LORD said to Moses, Aaron, and
Miriam, "Come out, you three, to the tabernacle
of meeting!" So the three came out.
5 [a]Then the LORD came down in the pillar of
cloud and stood *in* the door of the tabernacle, and
called Aaron and Miriam. And they both went
forward.
6 Then He said, "Hear now My words:

If there is a prophet among you,
*I*, the LORD, make Myself known
  to him [a]in a vision;
I speak to him [b]in a dream.
7 Not so with [a]My servant Moses;
[b]He *is* faithful in all [c]My house.
8 I speak with him [a]face to face,
Even [b]plainly,[1] and not in [2]dark sayings;
And he sees [c]the form of the LORD.
Why then [d]were you not afraid
To speak against My servant Moses?"

**9** So the anger of the LORD was aroused against
them, and He departed.
10 And when the cloud departed from above the
tabernacle, [a]suddenly Miriam *became* [b]leprous, as
*white as* snow. Then Aaron turned toward Miriam, and there she was, a leper.
11 So Aaron said to Moses, "Oh, my lord! Please
[a]do not lay [1]*this* sin on us, in which we have done
foolishly and in which we have sinned.
12 "Please [a]do not let her be as one dead, whose
flesh is half consumed when he comes out of his
mother's womb!"
13 So Moses cried out to the LORD, saying,
"Please [a]heal her, O God, I pray!"
**14** Then the LORD said to Moses, "If her father
had but [a]spit in her face, would she not be shamed
seven days? Let her be [b]shut[1] out of the camp
seven days, and afterward she may be received
*again.*"
15 [a]So Miriam was shut out of the camp seven
days, and the people did not journey till Miriam
was brought in *again.*
16 And afterward the people moved from [a]Haze-
roth and camped in the Wilderness of Paran.

### *The Twelve Spies Sent to Canaan*

**13** And the LORD spoke to Moses, saying,
2 [a]"Send men to spy out the land of Canaan, which I am giving to the children of Israel;
from each tribe of their fathers you shall send a
man, every one a leader among them."

**16** [b]Deut. 16:18
**17** [a]1 Sam. 10:6
**18** [a]Ex. 16:7 [1]*Set yourselves apart*
**20** [a]Ps. 78:29; 106:15 [b]1 Sam. 10:19 [c]Num. 21:5
**21** [a]Gen. 12:2
**22** [a]2 Kin. 7:2
**23** [a]Is. 50:2; 59:1 [b]Num. 23:19 [1]*Is the* LORD*'s power limited?*
**24** [a]Num. 11:16
**25** [a]2 Kin. 2:15 [b]Joel 2:28 [1]Tg., Vg. *and they did not cease*
**26** [a]Jer. 36:5
**28** [a][Mark 9:38–40]
**29** [a]1 Cor. 14:5 [1]*jealous*
**31** [a]Ex. 16:13
**32** [a]Ezek. 45:11
**33** [a]Ps. 78:29–31; 106:15
**34** [1]Lit. *Graves of Craving*
**35** [a]Num. 33:17

CHAPTER 12

**1** [a]Num. 20:1 [b]Num. 11:1 [c]Ex. 2:21 [1]*criticized* [2]*Cushite*
**2** [a]Num. 16:3 [b]Mic. 6:4 [c]Ezek. 35:12, 13
**4** [a][Ps. 76:9]
**5** [a]Ex. 19:9; 34:5
**6** [a]Gen. 46:2 [b]Gen. 31:10
**7** [a]Josh. 1:1 [b]Heb. 3:2, 5 [c]1 Tim. 1:12
**8** [a]Deut. 34:10 [b][1 Cor. 13:12] [c]Ex. 33:19–23 [d]2 Pet. 2:10 [1]*appearing* [2]*riddles*
**10** [a]Deut. 24:9 [b]2 Kin. 5:27; 15:5
**11** [a]2 Sam. 19:19; 24:10 [1]*the penalty for this*
**12** [a]Ps. 88:4
**13** [a]Ps. 103:3
**14** [a]Deut. 25:9 [b]Lev. 13:46 [1]*exiled*
**15** [a]Deut. 24:9
**16** [a]Num. 11:35; 33:17, 18

CHAPTER 13

**2** [a]Deut. 1:22; 9:23

3 So Moses sent them [a]from the Wilderness of
Paran according to the command of the LORD, all
of them men who *were* heads of the children of
Israel.
4 Now these *were* their names: from the tribe
of Reuben, Shammua the son of Zaccur;
5 from the tribe of Simeon, Shaphat the son
of Hori;
6 [a]from the tribe of Judah, [b]Caleb the son of
Jephunneh;
7 from the tribe of Issachar, Igal the son of
Joseph;
8 from the tribe of Ephraim, [1]Hoshea the son
of Nun;
9 from the tribe of Benjamin, Palti the son of
Raphu;
10 from the tribe of Zebulun, Gaddiel the son
of Sodi;
11 from the tribe of Joseph, *that is,* from the tribe
of Manasseh, Gaddi the son of Susi;
12 from the tribe of Dan, Ammiel the son of
Gemalli;
13 from the tribe of Asher, Sethur the son
of Michael;
14 from the tribe of Naphtali, Nahbi the son of
Vophsi;
15 from the tribe of Gad, Geuel the son of Machi.
16 These *are* the names of the men whom Moses
sent to [1]spy out the land. And Moses called [a]Ho-
shea[2] the son of Nun, Joshua.
**17** Then Moses sent them to spy out the land of
Canaan, and said to them, "Go up this *way* into
the South, and go up to [a]the mountains,
18 "and see what the land is like: whether the
people who dwell in it *are* strong or weak, few or
many;
19 "whether the land they dwell in *is* good or bad;
whether the cities they inhabit *are* like camps or
strongholds;
20 "whether the land *is* [1]rich or poor; and
whether there are forests there or not. [a]Be of good
courage. And bring some of the fruit of the land."
Now the time *was* the season of the first ripe
grapes.
**21** So they went up and spied out the land [a]from
the Wilderness of Zin as far as [b]Rehob, near the
entrance of [c]Hamath.
22 And they went up through the South and
came to [a]Hebron; Ahiman, Sheshai, and Talmai,
the descendants of [b]Anak, *were* there. (Now Hebron was built seven years before Zoan in Egypt.)
23 [a]Then they came to the [1]Valley of Eshcol, and
there cut down a branch with one cluster of
grapes; they carried it between two of them on a
pole. *They* also *brought* some of the pomegranates
and figs.
24 The place was called the Valley of [1]Eshcol,
because of the cluster which the men of Israel cut
down there.
25 And they returned from spying out the land
after forty days.
**26** Now they departed and came back to Moses
and Aaron and all the congregation of the children of Israel in the Wilderness of Paran, at
[a]Kadesh; they brought back word to them and to
all the congregation, and showed them the fruit of
the land.
27 Then they told him, and said: "We went to the
land where you sent us. It truly [1]flows with [a]milk
and honey, [b]and this *is* its fruit.
28 "Nevertheless the [a]people who dwell in the
land *are* strong; the cities *are* fortified *and* very
large; moreover we saw the descendants of [b]Anak
there.
29 [a]"The Amalekites dwell in the land of the
South; the Hittites, the Jebusites, and the Amorites dwell in the mountains; and the Canaanites
dwell by the sea and along the banks of the
Jordan."
**30** Then [a]Caleb quieted the people before Moses,
and said, "Let us go up at once and take possession, for we are well able to overcome it."
31 [a]But the men who had gone up with him said,
"We are not able to go up against the people, for
they *are* stronger than we."
32 And they [a]gave the children of Israel a bad
report of the land which they had spied out,
saying, "The land through which we have gone as
spies *is* a land that devours its inhabitants, and [b]all
the people whom we saw in it *are* men of *great*
stature.
33 "There we saw the [1]giants ([a]the descendants
of Anak came from the giants); and we were [b]like[2]
grasshoppers in our own sight, and so we were [c]in
their sight."

## *God Punishes Israel*

**14** So all the congregation lifted up their voices
and cried, and the people [a]wept that night.
2 [a]And all the children of Israel complained
against Moses and Aaron, and the whole congregation said to them, "If only we had died in the
land of Egypt! Or if only we had died in this
wilderness!
3 "Why has the LORD brought us to this land to
[1]fall by the sword, that our wives and [a]children
should become victims? Would it not be better for
us to return to Egypt?"
4 So they said to one another, [a]"Let us select a
leader and [b]return to Egypt."
5 Then Moses and Aaron [1]fell on their faces
before all the assembly of the congregation of the
children of Israel.
**6** But Joshua the son of Nun and Caleb the son
of Jephunneh, *who were* among those who had
spied out the land, tore their clothes;
7 and they spoke to all the congregation of the
children of Israel, saying: [a]"The land we passed
through to spy out *is* an exceedingly good land.
8 "If the LORD [a]delights in us, then He will bring
us into this land and give it to us, [b]'a land which
flows with milk and honey.'
9 "Only [a]do not rebel against the LORD, [b]nor fear
the people of the land, for [c]they[1] *are* our bread;
their protection has departed from them, [d]and the
LORD *is* with us. Do not fear them."
10 [a]And all the congregation said to stone them
with stones. Now [b]the glory of the LORD appeared
in the tabernacle of meeting before all the children of Israel.
**11** Then the LORD said to Moses: "How long will
these people [a]reject[1] Me? And how long will they
not [b]believe Me, with all the [2]signs which I have
performed among them?
12 "I will strike them with the pestilence and
disinherit them, and I will [a]make of you a nation
greater and mightier than they."
**13** And [a]Moses said to the LORD: [b]"Then the
Egyptians will hear *it,* for by Your might You
brought these people up from among them,
14 "and they will tell *it* to the inhabitants of this
land. They have [a]heard that You, LORD, *are*

3 [a]Num. 12:16; 32:8
6 [a]Num. 34:19 [b]Josh. 14:6, 7
8 [1]LXX, Vg. *Oshea*
16 [a]Ex. 17:9 [1]*secretly search* [2]LXX, Vg. *Oshea*
17 [a]Judg. 1:9
20 [a]Deut. 31:6, 7, 23 [1]*fertile or barren*
21 [a]Num. 20:1; 27:14; 33:36 [b]Josh. 19:28 [c]Josh. 13:5
22 [a]Josh. 15:13, 14 [b]Josh. 11:21, 22
23 [a]Deut. 1:24, 25 [1]*Wadi*
24 [1]Lit. *Cluster*
26 [a]Deut. 1:19
27 [a]Ex. 3:8, 17; 13:5; 33:3 [b]Deut. 1:25 [1]Has an abundance of food
28 [a]Deut. 1:28; 9:1, 2 [b]Josh. 11:21, 22
29 [a]Judg. 6:3
30 [a]Num. 14:6, 24
31 [a]Deut. 1:28; 9:1–3
32 [a]Num. 14:36, 37 [b]Amos 2:9
33 [a]Deut. 1:28; 9:2 [b]Is. 40:22 [c]1 Sam. 17:42 [1]Heb. *nephilim* [2]As mere insects

CHAPTER 14
1 [a]Deut. 1:45
2 [a]Ex. 16:2; 17:3
3 [a]Deut. 1:39 [1]*be killed in battle*
4 [a]Neh. 9:17 [b]Acts 7:39
5 [1]*prostrated themselves*
7 [a]Num. 13:27
8 [a]Deut. 10:15 [b]Num. 13:27
9 [a]Deut. 1:26; 9:7, 23, 24 [b]Deut. 7:18 [c]Num. 24:8 [d]Deut. 20:1, 3, 4; 31:6–8 [1]They shall be as food for our consumption.
10 [a]Ex. 17:4 [b]Ex. 16:10
11 [a]Heb. 3:8 [b]Deut. 9:23 [1]*despise* [2]*miraculous signs*
12 [a]Ex. 32:10
13 [a]Ps. 106:23 [b]Ex. 32:12
14 [a]Deut. 2:25

among these people; that You, LORD, are seen face
to face and Your cloud stands above them, and
You go before them in a pillar of cloud by day and
in a pillar of fire by night.
15 "Now *if* You kill these people as one man,
then the nations which have heard of Your fame
will speak, saying,
16 'Because the LORD was not [a]able to bring this
people to the land which He swore to give them,
therefore He killed them in the wilderness.'
17 "And now, I pray, let the power of my Lord be
great, just as You have spoken, saying,
18 [a]'The LORD is longsuffering and abundant in
mercy, forgiving iniquity and transgression; but
He by no means clears *the guilty,* [b]visiting the
iniquity of the fathers on the children to the third
and fourth *generation.*'
19 [a]"Pardon the iniquity of this people, I pray,
[b]according to the greatness of Your mercy, just
[c]as You have forgiven this people, from Egypt
even until now."
**20** Then the LORD said: "I have pardoned, [a]ac-
cording to your word;
21 "but truly, as I live, [a]all the earth shall be filled
with the glory of the LORD—
22 [a]"because all these men who have seen My
glory and the signs which I did in Egypt and in the
wilderness, and have put Me to the test now
[b]these ten times, and have not heeded My voice,
23 "they certainly shall not [a]see the land of which
I [1]swore to their fathers, nor shall any of those
who rejected Me see it.
24 "But My servant [a]Caleb, because he has a
different spirit in him and [b]has followed Me fully, I
will bring into the land where he went, and his
descendants shall inherit it.
25 "Now the Amalekites and the Canaanites
dwell in the valley; tomorrow turn and [a]move out
into the wilderness by the Way of the Red Sea."
**26** And the LORD spoke to Moses and Aaron,
saying,
27 [a]"How long *shall I bear with* this evil congregation who complain against Me? [b]I have heard
the complaints which the children of Israel make
against Me.
28 "Say to them, [a]'As I live,' says the LORD, 'just
as you have spoken in My hearing, so I will do to
you:
29 'The carcasses of you who have complained
against Me shall fall in this wilderness, [a]all of you
who were numbered, according to your entire
number, from twenty years old and above.
30 [a]'Except for Caleb the son of Jephunneh and
Joshua the son of Nun, you shall by no means
enter the land which I [1]swore I would make you
dwell in.
31 [a]'But your little ones, whom you said would be
victims, I will bring in, and they shall [1]know the
land which [b]you have despised.
32 'But *as for* you, [a]your[1] carcasses shall fall in
this wilderness.
33 'And your sons shall [a]be [1]shepherds in the
wilderness [b]forty years, and [c]bear the brunt of
your infidelity, until your carcasses are consumed
in the wilderness.
34 [a]'According to the number of the days in
which you spied out the land, [b]forty days, for each
day you shall bear your [1]guilt one year, *namely*
forty years, [c]and you shall know My [2]rejection.
35 [a]'I the LORD have spoken this. I will surely do
so to all [b]this evil congregation who are gathered
together against Me. In this wilderness they shall
be consumed, and there they shall die.'"
36 Now the men whom Moses sent to spy out the
land, who returned and made all the congregation
complain against him by bringing a bad report of
the land,
37 those very men who brought the evil report
about the land, [a]died by the plague before the
LORD.
38 [a]But Joshua the son of Nun and Caleb the son
of Jephunneh remained alive, of the men who
went to spy out the land.
**39** Then Moses told these words to all the children of Israel, [a]and the people mourned greatly.
40 And they rose early in the morning and went
up to the top of the mountain, saying, [a]"Here we
are, and we will go up to the place which the LORD
has promised, for we have sinned!"
41 And Moses said, "Now why do you [1]transgress
the command of the LORD? For this will not
succeed.
42 [a]"Do not go up, lest you be defeated by your
enemies, for the LORD *is* not among you.
43 "For the Amalekites and the Canaanites *are*
there before you, and you shall fall by the sword;
[a]because you have turned away from the LORD,
the LORD will not be with you."
44 [a]But they presumed to go up to the mountaintop. Nevertheless, neither the ark of the covenant
of the LORD nor Moses departed from the camp.
45 Then the Amalekites and the Canaanites who
dwelt in that mountain came down and attacked
them, and drove them back as far as [a]Hormah.

### *Laws Concerning Offerings*

**15** And the LORD spoke to Moses, saying,
2 [a]"Speak to the children of Israel, and say
to them: 'When you have come into the land you
are to inhabit, which I am giving to you,
3 'and you [a]make an offering by fire to the LORD,
a burnt offering or a sacrifice, [b]to fulfill a vow or
as a freewill offering or [c]in your appointed feasts,
to make a [d]sweet[1] aroma to the LORD, from the
herd or the flock,
4 'then [a]he who presents his offering to the
LORD shall bring [b]a grain offering of one-tenth *of
an ephah* of fine flour mixed [c]with one-fourth of a
hin of oil;
5 [a]'and one-fourth of a hin of wine as a drink
offering you shall prepare with the burnt offering
or the sacrifice, for each [b]lamb.
6 [a]'Or for a ram you shall prepare as a grain
offering two-tenths *of an ephah* of fine flour
mixed with one-third of a hin of oil;
7 'and as a drink offering you shall offer one-
third of a hin of wine as a sweet aroma to the
LORD.
8 'And when you prepare a young bull as a
burnt offering, or as a sacrifice to fulfill a vow, or
as a [a]peace offering to the LORD,
9 'then shall be offered [a]with the young bull a
grain offering of three-tenths *of an ephah* of fine
flour mixed with half a hin of oil;
10 'and you shall bring as the drink offering half a
hin of wine as an offering made by fire, a sweet
aroma to the LORD.
11 [a]'Thus it shall be done for each young bull, for
each ram, or for each lamb or young goat.
12 'According to the number that you prepare, so
you shall do with everyone according to their
number.

**16** [a]Deut. 9:28
**18** [a]Ex. 34:6, 7 [b]Ex. 20:5
**19** [a]Ex. 32:32; 34:9 [b]Ps. 51:1; 106:45 [c]Ps. 78:38
**20** [a]Mic. 7:18–20
**21** [a]Ps. 72:19
**22** [a]Deut. 1:35 [b]Gen. 31:7
**23** [a]Num. 26:65; 32:11 [1]*solemnly promised*
**24** [a]Josh. 14:6, 8, 9 [b]Num. 32:12
**25** [a]Deut. 1:40
**27** [a]Ex. 16:28 [b]Ex. 16:12
**28** [a]Heb. 3:16–19
**29** [a]Num. 1:45, 46; 26:64
**30** [a]Deut. 1:36–38 [1]*solemnly promised*
**31** [a]Deut. 1:39 [b]Ps. 106:24 [1]*be acquainted with*
**32** [a]Num. 26:64, 65; 32:13 [1]You shall die
**33** [a]Ps. 107:40 [b]Deut. 2:14 [c]Ezek. 23:35 [1]Vg. *wanderers*
**34** [a]Num. 13:25 [b]Ezek. 4:6 [c][Heb. 4:1] [1]*iniquity* [2]*opposition*
**35** [a]Num. 23:19 [b]1 Cor. 10:5
**37** [a][1 Cor. 10:10]
**38** [a]Josh. 14:6, 10
**39** [a]Ex. 33:4
**40** [a]Deut. 1:41–44
**41** [1]*overstep*
**42** [a]Deut. 1:42; 31:17
**43** [a]2 Chr. 15:2
**44** [a]Deut. 1:43
**45** [a]Num. 21:3

CHAPTER 15
**2** [a]Lev. 23:10
**3** [a]Lev. 1:2, 3 [b]Lev. 7:16; 22:18, 21 [c]Lev. 23:2, 8, 12, 38 [d]Ex. 29:18 [1]*pleasing aroma*
**4** [a]Lev. 2:1; 6:14 [b]Ex. 29:40 [c]Num. 28:5
**5** [a]Num. 28:7, 14 [b]Lev. 1:10; 3:6
**6** [a]Num. 28:12, 14
**8** [a]Lev. 7:11
**9** [a]Num. 28:12, 14
**11** [a]Num. 28

13 'All who are native-born shall do these things in this manner, in presenting an offering made by fire, a sweet aroma to the LORD.

14 'And if a stranger [1]dwells with you, or whoever *is* among you throughout your generations, and would present an offering made by fire, a sweet aroma to the LORD, just as you do, so shall he do.

15 [a]'One [1]ordinance *shall be* for you of the assembly and for the stranger who dwells *with you,* an ordinance forever throughout your generations; as you are, so shall the stranger be before the LORD.

16 'One law and one custom shall be for you and for the stranger who dwells with you.' "

**17** Again the LORD spoke to Moses, saying,

18 [a]"Speak to the children of Israel, and say to them: 'When you come into the land to which I bring you,

19 'then it will be, when you eat of [a]the bread of the land, that you shall offer up a heave offering to the LORD.

20 [a]'You shall offer up a cake of the first of your ground meal *as* a heave offering; as [b]a heave offering of the threshing floor, so shall you offer it up.

21 'Of the first of your ground meal you shall give to the LORD a heave offering throughout your generations.

**22** [a]'If you sin unintentionally, and do not observe all these commandments which the LORD has spoken to Moses—

23 'all that the LORD has commanded you by the hand of Moses, from the day the LORD gave commandment and onward throughout your generations—

24 'then it will be, [a]if it is unintentionally committed, [1]without the knowledge of the congregation, that the whole congregation shall offer one young bull as a burnt offering, as a sweet aroma to the LORD, [b]with its grain offering and its drink offering, according to the ordinance, and [c]one kid of the goats as a sin offering.

25 [a]'So the priest shall make atonement for the whole congregation of the children of Israel, and it shall be forgiven them, for it was unintentional; they shall bring their offering, an offering made by fire to the LORD, and their sin offering before the LORD, for their unintended sin.

26 'It shall be forgiven the whole congregation of the children of Israel and the stranger who dwells among them, because all the people *did it* unintentionally.

**27** 'And [a]if a person sins unintentionally, then he shall bring a female goat in its first year as a sin offering.

28 [a]'So the priest shall make atonement for the person who sins unintentionally, when he sins unintentionally before the LORD, to make atonement for him; and it shall be forgiven him.

29 [a]'You shall have one law for him who sins unintentionally, *for* him who is native-born among the children of Israel and for the stranger who dwells among them.

**30** [a]'But the person who does *anything* [1]presumptuously, *whether he is* native-born or a stranger, that one [2]brings reproach on the LORD, and he shall be [3]cut off from among his people.

31 'Because he has [a]despised the word of the LORD, and has broken His commandment, that person shall be completely cut off; his [1]guilt *shall be* upon him.' "

**32** Now while the children of Israel were in the wilderness, [a]they found a man gathering sticks on the Sabbath day.

33 And those who found him gathering sticks brought him to Moses and Aaron, and to all the congregation.

34 They put him [a]under guard, because it had not been explained what should be done to him.

35 Then the LORD said to Moses, [a]"The man must surely be put to death; all the congregation shall [b]stone him with stones outside the camp."

36 So, as the LORD commanded Moses, all the congregation brought him outside the camp and stoned him with stones, and he died.

**37** Again the LORD spoke to Moses, saying,

38 "Speak to the children of Israel: Tell [a]them to make tassels on the corners of their garments throughout their generations, and to put a blue thread in the tassels of the corners.

39 "And you shall have the tassel, that you may look upon it and [a]remember all the commandments of the LORD and do them, and that you [b]*may* not [c]follow the harlotry to which your own heart and your own eyes are inclined,

40 "and that you may remember and do all My commandments, and be [a]holy for your God.

41 "I *am* the LORD your God, who brought you out of the land of Egypt, to be your God: I *am* the LORD your God."

### *Korah's Rebellion*

**16** Now [a]Korah the son of Izhar, the son of Kohath, the son of Levi, with [b]Dathan and Abiram the sons of Eliab, and On the son of Peleth, sons of Reuben, took *men;*

2 and they rose up before Moses with some of the children of Israel, two hundred and fifty leaders of the congregation, [a]representatives of the congregation, men of renown.

3 [a]They gathered together against Moses and Aaron, and said to them, "*You* [1]*take* too much upon yourselves, for [b]all the congregation *is* holy, every one of them, [c]and the LORD *is* among them. Why then do you exalt yourselves above the assembly of the LORD?"

4 So when Moses heard *it,* he [a]fell on his face;

5 and he spoke to Korah and all his company, saying, "Tomorrow morning the LORD will show who *is* [a]His and *who is* [b]holy,[1] and will cause *him* to come near to Him. That one whom He chooses He will cause to [c]come near to Him.

6 "Do this: Take censers, Korah and all your company;

7 "put fire in them and put incense in them before the LORD tomorrow, and it shall be *that* the man whom the LORD chooses *is* the holy one. *You take* too much upon yourselves, you sons of Levi!"

8 Then Moses said to Korah, "Hear now, you sons of Levi:

9 "*Is it* [a]a small thing to you that the God of Israel has [b]separated you from the congregation of Israel, to bring you near to Himself, to do the work of the tabernacle of the LORD, and to stand before the congregation to serve them;

10 "and that He has brought you near *to Himself,* you and all your brethren, the sons of Levi, with you? And are you seeking the priesthood also?

11 "Therefore you and all your company *are*

**14** [1]As a resident alien
**15** [a]Ex. 12:49; Num. 9:14; 15:29 [1]*statute*
**18** [a]Num. 15:2; Deut. 26:1
**19** [a]Josh. 5:11, 12
**20** [a]Ex. 34:26; Lev. 23:10, 14, 17; Deut. 26:2, 10; Prov. 3:9, 10 [b]Lev. 2:14; 23:10, 16
**22** [a]Lev. 4:2
**24** [a]Lev. 4:13 [b]Num. 15:8–10 [c]Lev. 4:23 [1]Lit. *away from the eyes*
**25** [a]Lev. 4:20; [Heb. 2:17]
**27** [a]Lev. 4:27–31
**28** [a]Lev. 4:35
**29** [a]Num. 15:15
**30** [a]Num. 14:40–44; Deut. 1:43; 17:12; Ps. 19:13; Heb. 10:26 [1]*defiantly,* lit. *with a high hand* [2]*blasphemes* [3]Put to death
**31** [a]2 Sam. 12:9; Prov. 13:13 [1]*iniquity*
**32** [a]Ex. 31:14, 15; 35:2, 3
**34** [a]Lev. 24:12
**35** [a]Ex. 31:14, 15 [b]Lev. 24:14; Deut. 21:21; 1 Kin. 21:13; Acts 7:58
**38** [a]Deut. 22:12; Matt. 23:5
**39** [a]Ps. 103:18 [b]Deut. 29:19 [c]Ps. 73:27; 106:39; James 4:4
**40** [a][Lev. 11:44, 45; Rom. 12:1; Col. 1:22; 1 Pet. 1:15, 16]

CHAPTER 16

**1** [a]Ex. 6:21 [b]Num. 26:9; Deut. 11:6
**2** [a]Num. 1:16; 26:9
**3** [a]Num. 12:2; 14:2; Ps. 106:16 [b]Ex. 19:6 [c]Ex. 29:45 [1]*assume too much for*
**4** [a]Num. 14:5; 20:6
**5** [a][2 Tim. 2:19] [b]Lev. 21:6–8, 12 [c]Ezek. 40:46; 44:15, 16 [1]*set aside* for His use only
**9** [a]1 Sam. 18:23; Is. 7:13 [b]Num. 3:41, 45; 8:13–16; Deut. 10:8

gathered together against the LORD. [a]And what *is*
Aaron that you complain against him?"
**12** And Moses sent to call Dathan and Abiram
the sons of Eliab, but they said, "We will not come
up!
13 "*Is it* a small thing that you have brought us
up out of [a]a land flowing with milk and honey, to
kill us in the wilderness, that you should [b]keep
acting like a prince over us?
14 "Moreover [a]you have not brought us into [b]a
land flowing with milk and honey, nor given us
inheritance of fields and vineyards. Will you put
out the eyes of these men? We will not come up!"
**15** Then Moses was very angry, and said to the
LORD, [a]"Do not [1]respect their offering. [b]I have not
taken one donkey from them, nor have I hurt one
of them."
16 And Moses said to Korah, "Tomorrow, you
and all your company be present [a]before the
LORD—you and they, as well as Aaron.
17 "Let each take his censer and put incense in it,
and each of you bring his censer before the LORD,
two hundred and fifty censers; both you and
Aaron, each *with* his censer."
18 So every man took his censer, put fire in it,
laid incense on it, and stood at the door of the
tabernacle of meeting with Moses and Aaron.
19 And Korah gathered all the congregation
against them at the door of the tabernacle of
meeting. Then [a]the glory of the LORD appeared to
all the congregation.
**20** And the LORD spoke to Moses and Aaron,
saying,
21 [a]"Separate yourselves from among this congregation, that I may [b]consume them in a moment."
22 Then they [a]fell[1] on their faces, and said, "O
God, [b]the God of the spirits of all flesh, shall one
man sin, and You be angry with all the [c]congrega-
tion?"
23 So the LORD spoke to Moses, saying,
24 "Speak to the congregation, saying, 'Get away
from the tents of Korah, Dathan, and Abiram.' "
25 Then Moses rose and went to Dathan and
Abiram, and the elders of Israel followed him.
26 And he spoke to the congregation, saying,
[a]"Depart now from the tents of these wicked men!
Touch nothing of theirs, lest you be consumed in
all their sins."
27 So they got away from around the tents of
Korah, Dathan, and Abiram; and Dathan and
Abiram came out and stood at the door of their
tents, with their wives, their sons, and their little
[a]children.
28 And Moses said: [a]"By this you shall know that
the LORD has sent me to do all these works, for *I
have* not *done them* [b]of my own will.
29 "If these men die naturally like all men, or if
they are [a]visited by the common fate of all men,
*then* the LORD has not sent me.
30 "But if the LORD creates [a]a new thing, and the
earth opens its mouth and swallows them up with
all that belongs to them, and they [b]go down alive
into the pit, then you will understand that these
men have rejected the LORD."
**31** [a]Now it came to pass, as he finished speaking
all these words, that the ground split apart under
them,
32 and the earth opened its mouth and swallowed
them up, with their households and [a]all the men
with Korah, with all *their* goods.

11 [a]Ex. 16:7, 8
13 [a]Ex. 16:3; Num. 11:4–6 [b]Ex. 2:14; Acts 7:27, 35
14 [a]Num. 14:1–4 [b]Ex. 3:8; Lev. 20:24
15 [a]Gen. 4:4, 5 [b]1 Sam. 12:3; Acts 20:33 [1]*graciously regard*
16 [a]1 Sam. 12:3, 7
19 [a]Ex. 16:7, 10; Lev. 9:6, 23; Num. 14:10
21 [a]Gen. 19:17; Jer. 51:6 [b]Ex. 32:10; 33:5
22 [a]Num. 14:5 [b]Num. 27:16; Job 12:10; Eccl. 12:7; Heb. 12:9 [c]Gen. 18:23–32; 20:4 [1]*prostrated themselves*
26 [a]Gen. 19:12, 14, 15, 17
27 [a]Ex. 20:5; Num. 26:11
28 [a]Ex. 3:12; John 5:36 [b]Num. 24:13; John 5:30
29 [a]Ex. 20:5; Job 35:15; Is. 10:3
30 [a]Job 31:3; Is. 28:21 [b][Ps. 55:15]
31 [a]Num. 26:10; Ps. 106:17
32 [a]Num. 26:11; 1 Chr. 6:22, 37
35 [a]Lev. 10:2; Num. 11:1–3; 26:10; Ps. 106:18
37 [a]Lev. 27:28
38 [a]Prov. 20:2; Hab. 2:10 [b]Num. 17:10; Ezek. 14:8 [1]Or *at the cost of their own lives*
40 [a]Num. 3:10; 2 Chr. 26:18 [1]*reminder*
41 [a]Num. 14:2; Ps. 106:25
42 [a]Ex. 40:34
46 [a]Lev. 10:6; Num. 18:5 [1]Lit. *covering*
48 [a]Num. 25:8; Ps. 106:30

33 So they and all those with them went down
alive into the pit; the earth closed over them, and
they perished from among the assembly.
34 Then all Israel who *were* around them fled at
their cry, for they said, "Lest the earth swallow us
up *also!*"
35 And [a]a fire came out from the LORD and
consumed the two hundred and fifty men who
were offering incense.
**36** Then the LORD spoke to Moses, saying:
37 "Tell Eleazar, the son of Aaron the priest, to
pick up the censers out of the blaze, for [a]they are
holy, and scatter the fire some distance away.
38 "The censers of [a]these men who sinned
[1]against their own souls, let them be made into
hammered plates as a covering for the altar.
Because they presented them before the LORD,
therefore they are holy; [b]and they shall be a sign
to the children of Israel."
39 So Eleazar the priest took the bronze censers,
which those who were burned up had presented,
and they were hammered out as a covering on the
altar,
40 *to be* a [1]memorial to the children of Israel
[a]that no outsider, who *is* not a descendant of
Aaron, should come near to offer incense before
the LORD, that he might not become like Korah
and his companions, just as the LORD had said to
him through Moses.
**41** On the next day [a]all the congregation of the
children of Israel complained against Moses and
Aaron, saying, "You have killed the people of the
LORD."
42 Now it happened, when the congregation had
gathered against Moses and Aaron, that they
turned toward the tabernacle of meeting; and
suddenly [a]the cloud covered it, and the glory of
the LORD appeared.
43 Then Moses and Aaron came before the tabernacle of meeting.
44 And the LORD spoke to Moses, saying,
45 "Get away from among this congregation,
that I may consume them in a moment." And they
fell on their faces.
**46** So Moses said to Aaron, "Take a censer and
put fire in it from the altar, put incense *on it,* and
take it quickly to the congregation and make
[1]atonement for them; [a]for wrath has gone out
from the LORD. The plague has begun."
47 Then Aaron took *it* as Moses commanded, and
ran into the midst of the assembly; and already
the plague had begun among the people. So he put
in the incense and made atonement for the people.
48 And he stood between the dead and the living;
so [a]the plague was stopped.
49 Now those who died in the plague were fourteen thousand seven hundred, besides those who
died in the Korah incident.
50 So Aaron returned to Moses at the door of the
tabernacle of meeting, for the plague had stopped.

### *Aaron's Rod*

**17** And the LORD spoke to Moses, saying:
2 "Speak to the children of Israel, and get
from them a rod from each father's house, all their
leaders according to their fathers' houses—twelve
rods. Write each man's name on his rod.
3 "And you shall write Aaron's name on the rod
of Levi. For there shall be one rod for the head of
*each* father's house.
4 "Then you shall place them in the tabernacle

of meeting before [a]the Testimony, [b]where I meet
with you.
5 "And it shall be *that* the rod of the man
[a]whom I choose will blossom; thus I will rid
Myself of the complaints of the children of Israel,
[b]which they make against you."
**6** So Moses spoke to the children of Israel, and
each of their leaders gave him a rod apiece, for
each leader according to their fathers' houses,
twelve rods; and the rod of Aaron *was* among
their rods.
7 And Moses placed the rods before the LORD in
[a]the tabernacle of witness.
**8** Now it came to pass on the next day that
Moses went into the tabernacle of witness, and
behold, the [a]rod of Aaron, of the house of Levi,
had sprouted and put forth buds, had produced
blossoms and yielded ripe almonds.
9 Then Moses brought out all the rods from
before the LORD to all the children of Israel; and
they looked, and each man took his rod.
**10** And the LORD said to Moses, "Bring [a]Aaron's
rod back before the Testimony, to be kept [b]as a
sign against the rebels, [c]that you may put their
complaints away from Me, lest they die."
11 Thus did Moses; just as the LORD had commanded him, so he did.
**12** So the children of Israel spoke to Moses,
saying, "Surely we die, we perish, we all perish!
13 [a]"Whoever even comes near the tabernacle of
the LORD must die. Shall we all utterly die?"

### *Duties of Priests and Levites; How They Were Supported*

**18** Then the LORD said to Aaron: [a]"You and
your sons and your father's house with you
shall [b]bear the [1]iniquity *related to* the sanctuary,
and you and your sons with you shall bear the
iniquity *associated with* your priesthood.
2 "Also bring with you your brethren of the
[a]tribe of Levi, the tribe of your father, that they
may be [b]joined with you and serve you while you
and your sons *are* with you before the tabernacle
of [1]witness.
3 "They shall attend to your [1]needs and [a]all the
needs of the tabernacle; [b]but they shall not come
near the articles of the sanctuary and the altar,
[c]lest they die—they and you also.
4 "They shall be joined with you and attend to
the needs of the tabernacle of meeting, for all the
work of the tabernacle; [a]but an outsider shall not
come near you.
5 "And you shall attend to [a]the duties of the
sanctuary and the duties of the altar, [b]that there
*may* be no more wrath on the children of Israel.
6 "Behold, I Myself have [a]taken your brethren
the Levites from among the children of Israel;
[b]*they are* a gift to you, given by the LORD, to do
the work of the tabernacle of meeting.
7 "Therefore [a]you and your sons with you shall
attend to your priesthood for everything at the
altar and [b]behind the veil; and you shall serve. I
give your priesthood *to you* as a [c]gift for service,
but the outsider who comes near shall be put to
death."
**8** And the LORD spoke to Aaron: "Here, [a]I Myself have also given you [1]charge of My heave
offerings, all the holy gifts of the children of
Israel; I have given them [b]as a portion to you and
your sons, as an ordinance forever.
9 "This shall be yours of the most holy things
*reserved* from the fire: every offering of theirs,
every [a]grain offering and every [b]sin offering and
every [c]trespass offering which they render to Me,
*shall be* most holy for you and your sons.
10 [a]"In a most holy *place* you shall eat it; every
male shall eat it. It shall be holy to you.
11 "This also *is* yours: [a]the heave offering of their
gift, with all the wave offerings of the children of
Israel; I have given them to you, and your sons
and daughters with you, as an ordinance forever.
[b]Everyone who is [1]clean in your house may eat it.
12 [a]"All the [1]best of the oil, all the best of the new
wine and the grain, [b]their firstfruits which they
offer to the LORD, I have given them to you.
13 "Whatever first ripe fruit is in their land,
[a]which they bring to the LORD, shall be yours.
Everyone who is clean in your house may eat it.
14 [a]"Every [1]devoted thing in Israel shall be yours.
15 "Everything that first opens [a]the womb of all
flesh, which they bring to the LORD, whether man
or beast, shall be yours; nevertheless [b]the firstborn
of man you shall surely redeem, and the firstborn
of unclean animals you shall redeem.
16 "And those redeemed of the devoted things
you shall redeem when one month old, [a]according
to your valuation, for five shekels of silver, according to the shekel of the sanctuary, which *is*
[b]twenty gerahs.
17 [a]"But the firstborn of a cow, the firstborn of a
sheep, or the firstborn of a goat you shall not
redeem; they *are* holy. [b]You shall sprinkle their
blood on the altar, and burn their fat *as* an
offering made by fire for a sweet aroma to the
LORD.
18 "And their flesh shall be yours, just as the
[a]wave[1] breast and the right thigh are yours.
19 "All the heave offerings of the holy things,
which the children of Israel offer to the LORD, I
have given to you and your sons and daughters
with you as an ordinance forever; [a]it *is* a covenant
of salt forever before the LORD with you and your
descendants with you."
20 Then the LORD said to Aaron: "You shall have
[a]no inheritance in their land, nor shall you have
any portion among them; [b]I *am* your portion and
your inheritance among the children of Israel.
**21** "Behold, [a]I have given the children of Levi all
the tithes in Israel as [1]an inheritance in return for
the work which they perform, [b]the work of the
tabernacle of meeting.
22 [a]"Hereafter the children of Israel shall not
come near the tabernacle of meeting, [b]lest they
bear sin and die.
23 "But the Levites shall perform the work of the
tabernacle of meeting, and they shall bear their
iniquity; *it shall be* a statute forever, throughout
your generations, that among the children of
Israel they shall have no inheritance.
24 "For the tithes of the children of Israel, which
they offer up *as* a heave offering to the LORD, I
have given to the Levites [1]as an inheritance;
therefore I have said to them, 'Among the children of Israel they shall have no inheritance.'"
**25** Then the LORD spoke to Moses, saying,
26 "Speak thus to the Levites, and say to them:
'When you take from the children of Israel the
tithes which I have given you from them as your
inheritance, then you shall offer up a heave offering of it to the LORD, [a]a tenth of the tithe.
27 'And your heave offering shall be reckoned to

CHAPTER 17
**4** [a]Ex. 25:16 [b]Ex. 25:22; 29:42, 43; 30:36
**5** [a]Num. 16:5 [b]Num. 16:11
**7** [a]Ex. 38:21
**8** [a][Ezek. 17:24]
**10** [a]Heb. 9:4 [b]Deut. 9:7, 24 [c]Num. 17:5
**13** [a]Num. 1:51, 53; 18:4, 7

CHAPTER 18
**1** [a]Num. 17:13 [b]Ex. 28:38 [1]*guilt*
**2** [a]Num. 1:47 [b]Num. 3:5–10 [1]*testimony*
**3** [a]Num. 3:25, 31, 36 [b]Num. 16:40 [c]Num. 4:15 [1]*service*
**4** [a]Num. 3:10
**5** [a]Lev. 24:3 [b]Num. 8:19; 16:46
**6** [a]Num. 3:12, 45 [b]Num. 3:9
**7** [a]Num. 3:10; 18:5 [b]Heb. 9:3, 6 [c]1 Pet. 5:2, 3
**8** [a]Lev. 6:16, 18; 7:28–34 [b]Ex. 29:29; 40:13, 15 [1]*custody*
**9** [a]Lev. 2:2, 3; 10:12, 13 [b]Lev. 6:25, 26 [c]Lev. 7:7
**10** [a]Lev. 6:16, 26
**11** [a]Deut. 18:3–5 [b]Lev. 22:1–16 [1]*purified*
**12** [a]Ex. 23:19 [b]Ex. 22:29 [1]Lit. *fat*
**13** [a]Ex. 22:29; 23:19; 34:26
**14** [a]Lev. 27:1–33 [1]*consecrated*
**15** [a]Ex. 13:2 [b]Ex. 13:12–15
**16** [a]Lev. 27:6 [b]Ex. 30:13
**17** [a]Deut. 15:19 [b]Lev. 3:2, 5
**18** [a]Ex. 29:26–28 [1]*breast of the wave offering*
**19** [a]2 Chr. 13:5
**20** [a]Josh. 13:14, 33 [b]Ezek. 44:28
**21** [a]Lev. 27:30–33 [b]Num. 3:7, 8 [1]*a possession*
**22** [a]Num. 1:51 [b]Lev. 22:9
**24** [1]*for a possession*
**26** [a]Neh. 10:38

you as though *it were* the grain of the [a]threshing
floor and as the fullness of the winepress.
28 'Thus you shall also offer a heave offering to
the LORD from all your tithes which you receive
from the children of Israel, and you shall give the
LORD's heave offering from it to Aaron the priest.
29 'Of all your gifts you shall offer up every heave
offering due to the LORD, from all the [1]best of
them, the consecrated part of them.'
30 "Therefore you shall say to them: 'When you
have lifted up the best of it, then *the rest* shall be
accounted to the Levites as the produce of the
threshing floor and as the produce of the winepress.
31 'You may eat it in any place, you and your
households, for it *is* [a]your [1]reward for your work
in the tabernacle of meeting.
32 'And you shall [a]bear no sin because of it, when
you have lifted up the best of it. But you shall not
[b]profane the holy gifts of the children of Israel,
lest you die.' "

## *The Purification of the Unclean*

**19** Now the LORD spoke to Moses and Aaron,
saying,
2 "This *is* the [1]ordinance of the law which the
LORD has commanded, saying: 'Speak to the children of Israel, that they bring you a red heifer
without [2]blemish, in which there *is* no [a]defect [b]*and*
on which a yoke has never come.
3 'You shall give it to Eleazar the priest, that he
may take it [a]outside the camp, and it shall be
slaughtered before him;
4 'and Eleazar the priest shall take some of its
blood with his finger, and [a]sprinkle some of its
blood seven times directly in front of the tabernacle of meeting.
5 'Then the heifer shall be burned in his sight:
[a]its hide, its flesh, its blood, and its offal shall be
burned.
6 'And the priest shall take [a]cedar wood and
[b]hyssop and scarlet, and cast *them* into the midst
of the fire burning the heifer.
7 [a]'Then the priest shall wash his clothes, he
shall bathe in water, and afterward he shall come
into the camp; the priest shall be unclean until
evening.
8 'And the one who burns it shall wash his
clothes in water, bathe in water, and shall be
unclean until evening.
9 'Then a man *who is* clean shall gather up [a]the
ashes of the heifer, and store *them* outside the
camp in a clean place; and they shall be kept for
the congregation of the children of Israel [b]for the
water of [1]purification; it *is* for purifying from sin.
10 'And the one who gathers the ashes of the
heifer shall wash his clothes, and be unclean until
evening. It shall be a statute forever to the children of Israel and to the stranger who dwells
among them.
11 [a]'He who touches the dead [1]body of anyone
shall be unclean seven days.
12 [a]'He shall purify himself with the water on the
third day and on the seventh day; *then* he will be
clean. But if he does not purify himself on the
third day and on the seventh day, he will not be
clean.
13 'Whoever touches the body of anyone who
has died, and [a]does not purify himself, [b]defiles the
tabernacle of the LORD. That person shall be cut
off from Israel. He shall be unclean, because [c]the
water of purification was not sprinkled on him;
[d]his uncleanness *is* still on him.
14 'This *is* the law when a man dies in a tent: All
who come into the tent and all who *are* in the tent
shall be unclean seven days;
15 'and every [a]open vessel, which has no cover
fastened on it, *is* unclean.
16 [a]'Whoever in the open field touches one who is
slain by a sword or who has died, or a bone of a
man, or a grave, shall be unclean seven days.
17 'And for an unclean *person* they shall take
some of the [a]ashes of the heifer burnt for purification from sin, and [1]running water shall be put on
them in a vessel.
18 'A clean person shall take [a]hyssop and dip *it* in
the water, sprinkle *it* on the tent, on all the
vessels, on the persons who were there, or on the
one who touched a bone, the slain, the dead, or a
grave.
19 'The clean *person* shall sprinkle the unclean
on the third day and on the seventh day; [a]and on
the seventh day he shall purify himself, wash his
clothes, and bathe in water; and at evening he
shall be clean.
20 'But the man who is unclean and does not
purify himself, that person shall be cut off from
among the assembly, because he has [a]defiled the
sanctuary of the LORD. The water of purification
has not been sprinkled on him; he *is* unclean.
21 'It shall be a perpetual statute for them. He
who sprinkles the water of purification shall wash
his clothes; and he who touches the water of
purification shall be unclean until evening.
22 [a]'Whatever the unclean *person* touches shall
be unclean; and [b]the person who touches *it* shall
be unclean until evening.' "

## *Edom Refuses Passage to Israel*

**20** Then[a] the children of Israel, the whole
congregation, came into the Wilderness of
Zin in the first month, and the people stayed in
[b]Kadesh; and [c]Miriam died there and was buried
there.
2 [a]Now there was no water for the congregation; [b]so they gathered together against Moses
and Aaron.
3 And the people [a]contended with Moses and
spoke, saying: "If only we had died [b]when our
brethren died before the LORD!
4 [a]"Why have you brought up the assembly of
the LORD into this wilderness, that we and our
animals should die here?
5 "And why have you made us come up out of
Egypt, to bring us to this evil place? It *is* not a
place of grain or figs or vines or pomegranates;
nor *is* there any water to drink."
6 So Moses and Aaron went from the presence
of the assembly to the door of the tabernacle of
meeting, and [a]they [1]fell on their faces. And [b]the
glory of the LORD appeared to them.
7 Then the LORD spoke to Moses, saying,
8 [a]"Take the rod; you and your brother Aaron
gather the congregation together. Speak to the
rock before their eyes, and it will yield its water;
thus [b]you shall bring water for them out of the
rock, and give drink to the congregation and their
animals."

**27** [a]Num. 15:20; [2 Cor. 8:12]
**29** [1]Lit. *fat*
**31** [a][Matt. 10:10; Luke 10:7]; 1 Cor. 9:13; [1 Tim. 5:18] [1]*wages*
**32** [a]Lev. 19:8; 22:16; Ezek. 22:26 [b]Lev. 22:2, 15

CHAPTER 19
**2** [a]Lev. 22:20–25 [b]Deut. 21:3; 1 Sam. 6:7 [1]*statute* [2]*defect*
**3** [a]Lev. 4:12, 21; Num. 19:9; Heb. 13:11
**4** [a]Lev. 4:6; Heb. 9:13
**5** [a]Ex. 29:14; Lev. 4:11, 12; 9:11
**6** [a]Lev. 14:4, 6, 49 [b]Ex. 12:22; 1 Kin. 4:33
**7** [a]Lev. 11:25; 15:5; 16:26, 28
**9** [a][Heb. 9:13, 14] [b]Num. 19:13, 20, 21 [1]Lit. *impurity*
**11** [a]Lev. 21:1, 11; Num. 5:2; 6:6; 9:6, 10; 31:19; Lam. 4:14; Hag. 2:13 [1]Lit. *soul of man*
**12** [a]Num. 19:19; 31:19
**13** [a]Lev. 22:3–7 [b]Lev. 15:31 [c]Num. 8:7; 19:9 [d]Lev. 7:20; 22:3
**15** [a]Lev. 11:32; Num. 31:20
**16** [a]Num. 19:11; 31:19
**17** [a]Num. 19:9 [1]Lit. *living*
**18** [a]Ps. 51:7
**19** [a]Lev. 14:9
**20** [a]Num. 19:13
**22** [a]Hag. 2:11–13 [b]Lev. 15:5

CHAPTER 20
**1** [a]Num. 13:21; 33:36 [b]Num. 13:26 [c]Ex. 15:20; Num. 26:59
**2** [a]Ex. 17:1 [b]Num. 16:19, 42
**3** [a]Ex. 17:2; Num. 14:2 [b]Num. 11:1, 33; 14:37; 16:31–35, 49
**4** [a]Ex. 17:3
**6** [a]Num. 14:5; 16:4, 22, 45 [b]Num. 14:10 [1]*prostrated themselves*
**8** [a]Ex. 4:17, 20; 17:5, 6 [b]Neh. 9:15; Ps. 78:15, 16; 105:41; Is. 43:20; 48:21; [1 Cor. 10:4]

9 So Moses took the rod [a]from before the LORD as He commanded him.

10 And Moses and Aaron gathered the assembly together before the rock; and he said to them, [a]"Hear now, you rebels! Must we bring water for you out of this rock?"

11 Then Moses lifted his hand and struck the rock twice with his rod; [a]and water came out abundantly, and the congregation and their animals drank.

**12** Then the LORD spoke to Moses and Aaron, "Because [a]you did not believe Me, to [b]hallow Me in the eyes of the children of Israel, therefore you shall not bring this assembly into the land which I have given them."

13 [a]This *was* the water of [1]Meribah, because the children of Israel contended with the LORD, and He was hallowed among them.

**14** [a]Now Moses sent messengers from Kadesh to the king of [b]Edom. [c]"Thus says your brother Israel: 'You know all the hardship that has befallen us,

15 [a]'how our fathers went down to Egypt, [b]and we dwelt in Egypt a long time, [c]and the Egyptians [1]afflicted us and our fathers.

16 [a]'When we cried out to the LORD, He heard our voice and [b]sent the Angel and brought us up out of Egypt; now here we are in Kadesh, a city on the edge of your border.

17 'Please [a]let us pass through your country. We will not pass through fields or vineyards, nor will we drink water from wells; we will go along the King's Highway; we will not turn aside to the right hand or to the left until we have passed through your territory.' "

18 Then [a]Edom said to him, "You shall not pass through my *land,* lest I come out against you with the sword."

19 So the children of Israel said to him, "We will go by the Highway, and if I or my livestock drink any of your water, [a]then I will pay for it; let me only pass through on foot, nothing *more.*"

20 Then he said, [a]"You shall not pass through." So Edom came out against them with many men and with a strong hand.

21 Thus Edom [a]refused to give Israel passage through his territory; so Israel [b]turned away from him.

**22** Now the children of Israel, the whole congregation, journeyed from [a]Kadesh [b]and came to Mount Hor.

23 And the LORD spoke to Moses and Aaron in Mount Hor by the border of the land of Edom, saying:

24 "Aaron shall [1]be [a]gathered to his people, for he shall not enter the land which I have given to the children of Israel, because you rebelled against My word at the water of Meribah.

25 [a]"Take Aaron and Eleazar his son, and bring them up to Mount Hor;

26 "and strip Aaron of his garments and put them on Eleazar his son; for Aaron shall be gathered *to his people* and die there."

27 So Moses did just as the LORD commanded, and they went up to Mount Hor in the sight of all the congregation.

28 [a]Moses stripped Aaron of his garments and put them on Eleazar his son; and [b]Aaron died there on the top of the mountain. Then Moses and Eleazar came down from the mountain.

29 Now when all the congregation saw that Aaron was dead, all the house of Israel mourned for Aaron [a]thirty days.

### *The Fiery Serpents*

**21** The [a]king of Arad, the Canaanite, who dwelt in the South, heard that Israel was coming on the road to Atharim. Then he fought against Israel and took *some* of them prisoners.

2 [a]So Israel made a vow to the LORD, and said, "If You will indeed deliver this people into my hand, then [b]I will utterly destroy their cities."

3 And the LORD listened to the voice of Israel and delivered up the Canaanites, and they utterly destroyed them and their cities. So the name of that place was called [1]Hormah.

**4** Then they journeyed from Mount Hor by the Way of the Red Sea, to [a]go around the land of Edom; and the soul of the people became very [1]discouraged on the way.

5 And the people [a]spoke against God and against Moses: "Why have you brought us up out of Egypt to die in the wilderness? For *there is* no food and no water, and our soul [1]loathes this worthless bread."

6 So [a]the LORD sent [b]fiery serpents among the people, and they bit the people; and many of the people of Israel died.

**7** [a]Therefore the people came to Moses, and said, "We have [b]sinned, for we have spoken against the LORD and against you; [c]pray to the LORD that He take away the serpents from us." So Moses prayed for the people.

8 Then the LORD said to Moses, [a]"Make a [b]fiery *serpent,* and set it on a pole; and it shall be that everyone who is bitten, when he looks at it, shall live."

9 So [a]Moses made a bronze serpent, and put it on a pole; and so it was, if a serpent had bitten anyone, when he looked at the bronze serpent, he lived.

**10** Now the children of Israel moved on and [a]camped in Oboth.

11 And they journeyed from Oboth and camped at [1]Ije Abarim, in the wilderness which *is* east of Moab, toward the sunrise.

12 [a]From there they moved and camped in the Valley of Zered.

13 From there they moved and camped on the other side of the Arnon, which *is* in the wilderness that extends from the border of the Amorites; for [a]the Arnon *is* the border of Moab, between Moab and the Amorites.

14 Therefore it is said in the Book of the Wars of the LORD:

[1]"Waheb in Suphah,
The brooks of the Arnon,
15 And the slope of the brooks
That reaches to the dwelling of [a]Ar,
And lies on the border of Moab."

**16** From there *they went* [a]to Beer, which *is* the well where the LORD said to Moses, "Gather the people together, and I will give them water."

17 [a]Then Israel sang this song:

"Spring up, O well!
All of you sing to it—
18 The well the leaders sank,
Dug by the nation's nobles,
By the [a]lawgiver, with their staves."

And from the wilderness *they went* to Mattanah,

9 [a]Num. 17:10
10 [a]Ps. 106:33
11 [a][1 Cor. 10:4]
12 [a]Deut. 1:37; 3:26, 27; 34:5 [b]Lev. 10:3
13 [a]Deut. 33:8 [1]Lit. *Contention*
14 [a]Judg. 11:16, 17 [b]Gen. 36:31–39 [c]Deut. 2:4
15 [a]Gen. 46:6 [b]Ex. 12:40 [c]Deut. 26:6 [1]*did evil to*
16 [a]Ex. 2:23; 3:7 [b]Ex. 3:2; 14:19
17 [a]Num. 21:22
18 [a]Num. 24:18
19 [a]Deut. 2:6, 28
20 [a]Judg. 11:17
21 [a]Deut. 2:27, 30 [b]Judg. 11:18
22 [a]Num. 33:37 [b]Num. 21:4
24 [a]Gen. 25:8 [1]Die and join his ancestors
25 [a]Num. 33:38
28 [a]Ex. 29:29, 30 [b]Num. 33:38
29 [a]Deut. 34:8

CHAPTER 21
1 [a]Judg. 1:16
2 [a]Gen. 28:20 [b]Deut. 2:34
3 [1]Lit. *Utter Destruction*
4 [a]Judg. 11:18 [1]*impatient*
5 [a]Num. 20:4, 5 [1]*detests*
6 [a]1 Cor. 10:9 [b]Deut. 8:15
7 [a]Num. 11:2 [b]Lev. 26:40 [c]Ex. 8:8
8 [a][John 3:14, 15] [b]Is. 14:29; 30:6
9 [a]John 3:14, 15
10 [a]Num. 33:43, 44
11 [1]Lit. *The Heaps of Abarim*
12 [a]Deut. 2:13
13 [a]Num. 22:36
14 [1]Ancient unknown places; Vg. *What He did in the Red Sea*
15 [a]Deut. 2:9, 18, 29
16 [a]Judg. 9:21
17 [a]Ex. 15:1
18 [a]Is. 33:22

19 from Mattanah to Nahaliel, from Nahaliel to
Bamoth,
20 and from Bamoth, *in* the valley that *is* in the
[1]country of Moab, to the top of Pisgah which
looks [a]down on the [2]wasteland.
21 Then [a]Israel sent messengers to Sihon king of
the Amorites, saying,
22 [a]"Let me pass through your land. We will not
turn aside into fields or vineyards; we will not
drink water from wells. We will go by the King's
Highway until we have passed through your
territory."
23 [a]But Sihon would not allow Israel to pass
through his territory. So Sihon gathered all his
people together and [1]went out against Israel in the
wilderness, [b]and he came to Jahaz and fought
against Israel.
24 Then [a]Israel defeated him with the edge of the
sword, and took possession of his land from the
Arnon to the Jabbok, as far as the people of
Ammon; for the border of the people of Ammon
*was* fortified.
25 So Israel took all these cities, and Israel [a]dwelt
in all the cities of the Amorites, in Heshbon and in
all its villages.
26 For Heshbon *was* the city of Sihon king of the
Amorites, who had fought against the former king
of Moab, and had taken all his land from his hand
as far as the Arnon.
27 Therefore those who speak in [1]proverbs say:

"Come to Heshbon, let it be built;
Let the city of Sihon be repaired.

28 "For [a]fire went out from Heshbon,
A flame from the city of Sihon;
It consumed [b]Ar of Moab,
The lords of the [c]heights of the Arnon.
29 Woe to you, [a]Moab!
You have perished, O people of [b]Chemosh!
He has given his [c]sons as fugitives,
And his [d]daughters into captivity,
To Sihon king of the Amorites.

30 "But we have shot at them;
Heshbon has perished [a]as far as Dibon.
Then we laid waste as far as Nophah,
Which *reaches* to [b]Medeba."

31 Thus Israel dwelt in the land of the Amorites.
32 Then Moses sent to [1]spy out [a]Jazer; and they
took its villages and drove out the Amorites who
*were* there.
33 [a]And they turned and went up by the way to
[b]Bashan. So Og king of Bashan went out against
them, he and all his people, to battle [c]at Edrei.
34 Then the LORD said to Moses, [a]"Do not fear
him, for I have [1]delivered him into your hand,
with all his people and his land; and [b]you shall do
to him as you did to Sihon king of the Amorites,
who dwelt at Heshbon."
35 [a]So they defeated him, his sons, and all his
people, until there was no survivor left him; and
they took possession of his land.

### *Balak Sends for Balaam*

22 Then [a]the children of Israel moved, and
camped in the plains of Moab on the side of
the Jordan *across from* Jericho.
2 Now [a]Balak the son of Zippor saw all that
Israel had done to the Amorites.
3 And [a]Moab was exceedingly afraid of the
people because they *were* many, and Moab was
sick with dread because of the children of Israel.
4 So Moab said to [a]the elders of Midian, "Now
this company will [1]lick up everything around us,
as an ox licks up the grass of the field." And Balak
the son of Zippor *was* king of the Moabites at that
time.
5 Then [a]he sent messengers to Balaam the son
of Beor at [b]Pethor, which *is* near [1]the River in the
land of [2]the sons of his people, to call him, saying:
"Look, a people has come from Egypt. See, they
cover the face of the earth, and are settling next
to me!
6 [a]"Therefore please come at once, [b]curse this
people for me, for they *are* too mighty for me.
Perhaps I shall be able to defeat them and drive
them out of the land, for I know that he whom
you bless *is* blessed, and he whom you curse is
cursed."
7 So the elders of Moab and the elders of Midian
departed with [a]the diviner's fee in their hand, and
they came to Balaam and spoke to him the words
of Balak.
8 And he said to them, [a]"Lodge here tonight,
and I will bring back word to you, as the LORD
speaks to me." So the princes of Moab stayed with
Balaam.
9 [a]Then God came to Balaam and said, "Who
*are* these men with you?"
10 So Balaam said to God, "Balak the son of
Zippor, king of Moab, has sent to me, *saying,*
11 'Look, a people has come out of Egypt, and
they cover the face of the earth. Come now, curse
them for me; perhaps I shall be able to overpower
them and drive them out.' "
12 And God said to Balaam, "You shall not go
with them; you shall not curse the people, for
[a]they *are* blessed."
13 So Balaam rose in the morning and said to the
princes of Balak, "Go back to your land, for the
LORD has refused to give me permission to go with
you."
14 And the princes of Moab rose and went to
Balak, and said, "Balaam refuses to come with
us."
15 Then Balak again sent princes, more numerous and more [1]honorable than they.
16 And they came to Balaam and said to him,
"Thus says Balak the son of Zippor: 'Please let
nothing hinder you from coming to me;
17 'for I will certainly [a]honor you greatly, and I
will do whatever you say to me. [b]Therefore please
come, curse this people for me.' "
18 Then Balaam answered and said to the servants of Balak, [a]"Though Balak were to give me
his house full of silver and gold, [b]I could not go
beyond the word of the LORD my God, to do less
or more.
19 "Now therefore, please, you also [a]stay here
tonight, that I may know what more the LORD will
say to me."
20 [a]And God came to Balaam at night and said to
him, "If the men come to call you, rise *and* go
with them; but [b]only the word which I speak to
you—that you shall do."
21 So Balaam rose in the morning, saddled his
donkey, and went with the princes of Moab.
22 Then God's anger was aroused because he
went, [a]and the Angel of the LORD took His stand
in the way as an adversary against him. And he

20 [a]Num. 23:28 [1]Lit. *field* [2]Or *Jeshimon*
21 [a]Num. 32:33; Deut. 2:26–37; Judg. 11:19
22 [a]Num. 20:16, 17
23 [a]Deut. 29:7 [b]Deut. 2:32; Judg. 11:20 [1]*attacked*
24 [a]Deut. 2:33; Josh. 12:1; Neh. 9:22; Ps. 135:10; 136:19; Amos 2:9
25 [a]Amos 2:10
27 [1]*parables*
28 [a]Jer. 48:45, 46 [b]Deut. 2:9, 18; Is. 15:1 [c]Num. 22:41; 33:52
29 [a]Jer. 48:46 [b]Judg. 11:24; 1 Kin. 11:33; 2 Kin. 23:13 [c]Is. 15:2, 5 [d]Is. 16:2
30 [a]Num. 32:3, 34; Jer. 48:18, 22 [b]Is. 15:2
32 [a]Num. 32:1, 3, 35; Jer. 48:32 [1]*secretly search*
33 [a]Deut. 29:7 [b]Deut. 3:1 [c]Josh. 13:12
34 [a]Deut. 3:2 [b]Num. 21:24; Ps. 135:10; 136:20 [1]*given you victory over him*
35 [a]Deut. 3:3, 4; 29:7; Josh. 13:12

CHAPTER 22
1 [a]Num. 33:48, 49
2 [a]Josh. 24:9; Judg. 11:25; Mic. 6:5; Rev. 2:14
3 [a]Ex. 15:15
4 [a]Num. 25:15–18; 31:1–3; Josh. 13:21 [1]*consume*
5 [a]Num. 31:8, 16; Deut. 23:4; Josh. 13:22; 24:9; Neh. 13:1, 2; Mic. 6:5; 2 Pet. 2:15; Jude 11; Rev. 2:14 [b]Deut. 23:4 [1]The Euphrates [2]Or *the people of Amau*
6 [a]Num. 22:17; 23:7, 8 [b]Num. 22:12; 24:9
7 [a]1 Sam. 9:7, 8
8 [a]Num. 22:19
9 [a]Gen. 20:3
12 [a]Num. 23:20; [Rom. 11:28]
15 [1]*distinguished*
17 [a]Num. 24:11 [b]Num. 22:6
18 [a]Num. 22:38; 24:13 [b]1 Kin. 22:14; 2 Chr. 18:13
19 [a]Num. 22:8
20 [a]Num. 22:9 [b]Num. 22:35; 23:5, 12, 16, 26; 24:13
22 [a]Ex. 4:24

was riding on his donkey, and his two servants
*were* with him.
23 Now [a]the donkey saw the Angel of the LORD
standing in the way with His drawn sword in His
hand, and the donkey turned aside out of the way
and went into the field. So Balaam struck the
donkey to turn her back onto the road.
24 Then the Angel of the LORD stood in a narrow
path between the vineyards, *with* a wall on this
side and a wall on that side.
25 And when the donkey saw the Angel of the
LORD, she pushed herself against the wall and
crushed Balaam's foot against the wall; so he
struck her again.
26 Then the Angel of the LORD went further, and
stood in a narrow place where there *was* no way
to turn either to the right hand or to the left.
27 And when the donkey saw the Angel of the
LORD, she lay down under Balaam; so Balaam's
anger was aroused, and he struck the donkey with
his staff.
28 Then the LORD [a]opened the mouth of the
donkey, and she said to Balaam, "What have I
done to you, that you have struck me these three
times?"
29 And Balaam said to the donkey, "Because you
have [1]abused me. I wish there were a sword in my
hand, [a]for now I would kill you!"
30 [a]So the donkey said to Balaam, "*Am* I not
your donkey on which you have ridden, ever since
*I became* yours, to this day? Was I ever [1]disposed
to do this to you?" And he said, "No."
**31** Then the LORD [a]opened Balaam's eyes, and he
saw the Angel of the LORD standing in the way
with His drawn sword in His hand; and he bowed
his head and fell flat on his face.
32 And the Angel of the LORD said to him, "Why
have you struck your donkey these three times?
Behold, I have come out [1]to stand against you,
because *your* way is [a]perverse[2] before Me.
33 "The donkey saw Me and turned aside from
Me these three times. If she had not turned aside
from Me, surely I would also have killed you by
now, and let her live."
34 And Balaam said to the Angel of the LORD, [a]"I
have sinned, for I did not know You stood in the
way against me. Now therefore, if it [1]displeases
You, I will turn back."
35 Then the Angel of the LORD said to Balaam,
"Go with the men, [a]but only the word that I speak
to you, that you shall speak." So Balaam went
with the princes of Balak.
**36** Now when Balak heard that Balaam was coming, [a]he went out to meet him at the city of Moab,
[b]which *is* on the border at the Arnon, the boundary of the territory.
37 Then Balak said to Balaam, "Did I not earnestly send to you, calling for you? Why did you
not come to me? Am I not able [a]to honor you?"
38 And Balaam said to Balak, "Look, I have come
to you! Now, have I any power at all to say
anything? [a]The word that God puts in my mouth,
that I must speak."
39 So Balaam went with Balak, and they came to
Kirjath Huzoth.
40 Then Balak offered oxen and sheep, and he
sent *some* to Balaam and to the princes who *were*
with him.
**41** So it was, the next day, that Balak took
Balaam and brought him up to the [a]high places of
Baal, that from there he might observe [1]the extent
of the people.

### *The Prophecies of Balaam*

**23** Then Balaam said to Balak, [a]"Build seven
altars for me here, and prepare for me here
seven bulls and seven rams."
2 And Balak did just as Balaam had spoken, and
Balak and Balaam [a]offered a bull and a ram on
*each* altar.
3 Then Balaam said to Balak, [a]"Stand by your
burnt offering, and I will go; perhaps the LORD will
come [b]to meet me, and whatever He shows me I
will tell you." So he went to a desolate height.
4 [a]And God met Balaam, and he said to Him, "I
have prepared the seven altars, and I have offered
on *each* altar a bull and a ram."
5 Then the LORD [a]put a word in Balaam's mouth,
and said, "Return to Balak, and thus you shall
speak."
6 So he returned to him, and there he was,
standing by his burnt offering, he and all the
princes of Moab.
7 And he [a]took up his [1]oracle and said:

"Balak the king of Moab
has brought me from Aram,
From the mountains of the east.
[b]'Come, curse Jacob for me,
And come, [c]denounce Israel!'

8 "How[a] shall I curse
whom God has not cursed?
And how shall I denounce
*whom* the LORD has not denounced?
9 For from the top of the rocks I see him,
And from the hills I behold him;
There! [a]A people dwelling alone,
[b]Not reckoning itself among the nations.

10 "Who[a] can count the [1]dust of Jacob,
Or number one-fourth of Israel?
Let me die [b]the death of the righteous,
And let my end be like his!"

**11** Then Balak said to Balaam, "What have you
done to me? [a]I took you to curse my enemies, and
look, you have blessed *them* bountifully!"
12 So he answered and said, [a]"Must I not take
heed to speak what the LORD has put in my
mouth?"
**13** Then Balak said to him, "Please come with me
to another place from which you may see them;
you shall see only the outer part of them, and shall
not see them all; curse them for me from there."
14 So he brought him to the field of Zophim, to
the top of Pisgah, [a]and built seven altars, and
offered a bull and a ram on *each* altar.
15 And he said to Balak, "Stand here by your
burnt offering while I [1]meet *the LORD* over there."
16 Then the LORD met Balaam, and [a]put a word in
his mouth, and said, "Go back to Balak, and thus
you shall speak."
17 So he came to him, and there he was, standing
by his burnt offering, and the princes of Moab
were with him. And Balak said to him, "What has
the LORD spoken?"
18 Then he took up his oracle and said:

[a]"Rise up, Balak, and hear!
Listen to me, son of Zippor!

19 "God[a] *is* not a man, that He should lie,
Nor a son of man, that He should repent.
Has He [b]said, and will He not do?

**23** [a]Josh. 5:13; 2 Kin. 6:17; Dan. 10:7; Acts 22:9
**28** [a]2 Pet. 2:16
**29** [a][Prov. 12:10; Matt. 15:19] [1]*mocked*
**30** [a]2 Pet. 2:16 [1]*accustomed*
**31** [a]Gen. 21:19; 2 Kin. 6:17; Luke 24:16, 31
**32** [a][2 Pet. 2:14, 15] [1]*as an adversary* [2]*contrary*
**34** [a]1 Sam. 15:24, 30; 26:21; 2 Sam. 12:13 [1]Lit. *is evil in your eyes*
**35** [a]Num. 22:20
**36** [a]Gen. 14:17 [b]Num. 21:13
**37** [a]Num. 22:17; 24:11
**38** [a]Num. 23:26; 24:13; 1 Kin. 22:14; 2 Chr. 18:13
**41** [a]Num. 21:28; Deut. 12:2 [1]*the farthest extent*

CHAPTER 23
**1** [a]Num. 23:29
**2** [a]Num. 23:14, 30
**3** [a]Num. 23:15 [b]Num. 23:4, 16
**4** [a]Num. 23:16
**5** [a]Num. 22:20, 35, 38; 23:16; Deut. 18:18; Jer. 1:9
**7** [a]Deut. 23:4; Job 27:1; 29:1; Ps. 78:2 [b]Num. 22:6, 11, 17 [c]1 Sam. 17:10 [1]*prophetic discourse*
**8** [a]Num. 22:12
**9** [a]Deut. 32:8; 33:28; Josh. 11:23 [b]Ex. 33:16; Ezra 9:2; [Eph. 2:14]
**10** [a]Gen. 13:16; 22:17; 28:14; 2 Chr. 1:9 [b]Ps. 116:15 [1]Or *dust cloud*
**11** [a]Num. 22:11
**12** [a]Num. 22:38
**14** [a]Num. 23:1, 2
**15** [1]So with MT, Tg., Vg.; Syr. *call;* LXX *go and ask God*
**16** [a]Num. 22:35; 23:5
**18** [a]Judg. 3:20
**19** [a]1 Sam. 15:29; Mal. 3:6; James 1:17 [b]Num. 11:23; 1 Kin. 8:56

Or has He spoken,
and will He not make it good?
20 Behold, I have received *a command* to bless;
[a]He has blessed, and I cannot reverse it.

21 "He[a] has not observed iniquity in Jacob,
Nor has He seen [1]wickedness in Israel.
The LORD his God *is* with him,
[b]And the shout of a King *is* among them.
22 [a]God brings them out of Egypt;
He has [b]strength like a wild ox.

23 "For *there is* no [1]sorcery against Jacob,
Nor any [2]divination against Israel.
It now must be said of Jacob
And of Israel, 'Oh, [a]what God has done!'
24 Look, a people rises [a]like a lioness,
And lifts itself up like a lion;
[b]It shall not lie down
until it devours the prey,
And drinks the blood of the slain."

**25** Then Balak said to Balaam, "Neither curse
them at all, nor bless them at all!"
26 So Balaam answered and said to Balak, "Did I
not tell you, saying, [a]'All that the LORD speaks,
that I must do'?"
**27** Then Balak said to Balaam, "Please come, I
will take you to another place; perhaps it will
please God that you may curse them for me from
there."
28 So Balak took Balaam to the top of Peor, that
[a]overlooks [1]the wasteland.
29 Then Balaam said to Balak, "Build for me here
seven altars, and prepare for me here seven bulls
and seven rams."
30 And Balak did as Balaam had said, and offered
a bull and a ram on *every* altar.

### *Balaam Foretells the Happiness of Israel*

**24** Now when Balaam saw that it pleased the
LORD to bless Israel, he did not go as at
[a]other times, to seek to use [1]sorcery, but he set his
face toward the wilderness.
2 And Balaam raised his eyes, and saw Israel
[a]encamped according to their tribes; and [b]the
Spirit of God came upon him.
3 [a]Then he took up his oracle and said:

"The utterance of Balaam the son of Beor,
The utterance of the man
whose eyes are opened,
4 The utterance of him
who hears the words of God,
Who sees the vision of the Almighty,
Who [a]falls down, with eyes wide open:

5 "How lovely are your tents, O Jacob!
Your dwellings, O Israel!
6 Like valleys that stretch out,
Like gardens by the riverside,
[a]Like aloes [b]planted by the LORD,
Like cedars beside the waters.
7 He shall pour water from his buckets,
And his seed *shall be* [a]in many waters.

"His king shall be higher than [b]Agag,
And his [c]kingdom shall be exalted.

8 "God[a] brings him out of Egypt;
He has strength like a wild ox;
He shall [b]consume the nations, his enemies;
He shall [c]break their bones
And [d]pierce *them* with his arrows.

**20** [a]Gen. 12:2; 22:17; Num. 22:12
**21** [a]Ps. 32:2; [Rom. 4:7, 8] [b]Ps. 89:15–18 [1]*trouble*
**22** [a]Num. 24:8 [b]Deut. 33:17; Job 39:10
**23** [a]Ps. 31:19; 44:1 [1]*enchantment* [2]*fortune-telling*
**24** [a]Gen. 49:9 [b]Gen. 49:27; Josh. 11:23
**26** [a]Num. 22:38
**28** [a]Num. 21:20 [1]Or *Jeshimon*

CHAPTER 24

**1** [a]Num. 23:3, 15 [1]*enchantments*
**2** [a]Num. 2:2, 34 [b]Num. 11:25; 1 Sam. 10:10; 19:20, 23; 2 Chr. 15:1
**3** [a]Num. 23:7, 18
**4** [a]Ezek. 1:28
**6** [a]Ps. 1:3; Jer. 17:8 [b]Ps. 104:16
**7** [a]Jer. 51:13; Rev. 17:1, 15 [b]1 Sam. 15:8, 9 [c]2 Sam. 5:12; 1 Chr. 14:2
**8** [a]Num. 23:22 [b]Num. 14:9; 23:24 [c]Ps. 2:9; Jer. 50:17 [d]Ps. 45:5
**9** [a]Gen. 49:9; Num. 23:24 [b]Gen. 12:3; 27:29
**10** [a]Ezek. 21:14, 17 [b]Num. 23:11; Neh. 13:2
**11** [a]Num. 22:17, 37
**14** [a][Mic. 6:5] [b]Gen. 49:1; Deut. 4:30; Dan. 2:28
**17** [a]Rev. 1:7; Matt. 1:2; Luke 3:34 [b]Matt. 2:2 [c]Gen. 49:10 [1]*shatter the forehead* [2]Or *Sheth,* Jer. 48:45
**18** [a]2 Sam. 8:14 [1]*mightily*
**19** [a]Gen. 49:10; Amos 9:11, 12 [1]*shall rule*
**24** [a]Gen. 10:4; Ezek. 27:6; Dan. 11:30 [b]Gen. 10:21, 25 [1]Heb. *Kittim* [2]Lit. *he* or *that one*
**25** [a]Num. 21:34; 31:8

CHAPTER 25

**1** [a]Num. 33:49; Josh. 2:1 [b]Rev. 2:14 [1]Heb. *Shittim*

9 'He[a] bows down, he lies down as a lion;
And as a lion, who will rouse him?'

[b]"Blessed *is* he who blesses you,
And cursed *is* he who curses you."

**10** Then Balak's anger was aroused against Balaam, and he [a]struck his hands together; and
Balak said to Balaam, [b]"I called you to curse my
enemies, and look, you have bountifully blessed
*them* these three times!
11 "Now therefore, flee to your place. [a]I said I
would greatly honor you, but in fact, the LORD has
kept you back from honor."
12 So Balaam said to Balak, "Did I not also speak
to your messengers whom you sent to me, saying,
13 'If Balak were to give me his house full of
silver and gold, I could not go beyond the word of
the LORD, to do good or bad of my own will. What
the LORD says, that I must speak'?
14 "And now, indeed, I am going to my people.
Come, [a]I will advise you what this people will do
to your people in the [b]latter days."
**15** So he took up his oracle and said:

"The utterance of Balaam the son of Beor,
And the utterance of the man
whose eyes are opened;
16 The utterance of him
who hears the words of God,
And has the knowledge of the Most High,
*Who* sees the vision of the Almighty,
*Who* falls down, with eyes wide open:

17 "I[a] see Him, but not now;
I behold Him, but not near;
[b]A Star shall come out of Jacob;
[c]A Scepter shall rise out of Israel,
And [1]batter the brow of Moab,
And destroy all the sons of [2]tumult.

18 "And [a]Edom shall be a possession;
Seir also, his enemies, shall be a possession,
While Israel does [1]valiantly.
19 [a]Out of Jacob One [1]shall have dominion,
And destroy the remains of the city."

**20** Then he looked on Amalek, and he took up his
oracle and said:

"Amalek *was* first among the nations,
But *shall be* last until he perishes."

**21** Then he looked on the Kenites, and he took up
his oracle and said:

"Firm is your dwelling place,
And your nest is set in the rock;
22 Nevertheless Kain shall be burned.
How long until Asshur
carries you away captive?"

**23** Then he took up his oracle and said:

"Alas! Who shall live when God does this?
24 But ships *shall come*
from the coasts of [a]Cyprus,[1]
And they shall afflict Asshur and afflict [b]Eber,
And so shall [2]*Amalek,* until he perishes."

25 So Balaam rose and departed and [a]returned to
his place; Balak also went his way.

### *The Zeal of Phinehas*

**25** Now Israel remained in [a]Acacia Grove,[1] and
the [b]people began to commit harlotry with
the women of Moab.

2 [a]They invited the people to [b]the sacrifices of
their gods, and the people ate and [c]bowed down to
their gods.
3 So Israel was joined to Baal of Peor, and [a]the
anger of the LORD was aroused against Israel.
4 Then the LORD said to Moses, [a]"Take all the
leaders of the people and hang the offenders
before the LORD, out in the sun, [b]that the fierce
anger of the LORD may turn away from Israel."
5 So Moses said to [a]the judges of Israel, [b]"Every
one of you kill his men who were joined to Baal of
Peor."
**6** And indeed, one of the children of Israel came
and presented to his brethren a Midianite woman
in the sight of Moses and in the sight of all the
congregation of the children of Israel, [a]who *were*
weeping at the door of the tabernacle of meeting.
7 Now [a]when Phinehas [b]the son of Eleazar, the
son of Aaron the priest, saw *it*, he rose from
among the congregation and took a javelin in his
hand;
8 and he went after the man of Israel into the
tent and thrust both of them through, the man of
Israel, and the woman through her body. So [a]the
plague was [b]stopped among the children of Israel.
9 And [a]those who died in the plague were
twenty-four thousand.
**10** Then the LORD spoke to Moses, saying:
11 [a]"Phinehas the son of Eleazar, the son of
Aaron the priest, has turned back My wrath from
the children of Israel, because he was zealous
with My zeal among them, so that I did not
consume the children of Israel in [b]My zeal.
12 "Therefore say, [a]'Behold, I give to him My
[b]covenant of peace;
13 'and it shall be to him and [a]his descendants
after him a covenant of [b]an everlasting priesthood, because he was [c]zealous for his God, and
[d]made [1]atonement for the children of Israel.' "
**14** Now the name of the Israelite who was killed,
who was killed with the Midianite woman, *was*
Zimri the son of Salu, a leader of a father's house
among the Simeonites.
15 And the name of the Midianite woman who
was killed *was* Cozbi the daughter of [a]Zur; he *was*
head of the people of a father's house in Midian.
**16** Then the LORD spoke to Moses, saying:
17 [a]"Harass the Midianites, and [1]attack them;
18 "for they harassed you with their [a]schemes[1] by
which they seduced you in the matter of Peor and
in the matter of Cozbi, the daughter of a leader of
Midian, their sister, who was killed in the day of
the plague because of Peor."

### *The Second Census of Israel*

**26** And it came to pass, after the [a]plague, that
the LORD spoke to Moses and Eleazar the
son of Aaron the priest, saying:
2 [a]"Take a census of all the congregation of the
children of Israel [b]from twenty years old and
above, by their fathers' houses, all who are able to
go to war in Israel."
3 So Moses and Eleazar the priest spoke with
them [a]in the plains of Moab by the Jordan, *across*
*from* Jericho, saying:
4 "*Take a census of the people* from twenty
years old and above, just as the LORD [a]com-
manded Moses and the children of Israel who
came out of the land of Egypt."
**5** [a]Reuben *was* the firstborn of Israel. The children of Reuben *were: of* Hanoch, the family of the
Hanochites; *of* Pallu, the family of the Palluites;
6 *of* Hezron, the family of the Hezronites; *of*
Carmi, the family of the Carmites.
7 These *are* the families of the Reubenites: those
who were numbered of them were forty-three
thousand seven hundred and thirty.
8 And the son of Pallu *was* Eliab.
9 The sons of Eliab *were* Nemuel, Dathan, and
Abiram. These *are* the Dathan and Abiram, [a]repre-
sentatives of the congregation, who contended
against Moses and Aaron in the company of
Korah, when they contended against the LORD;
10 [a]and the earth opened its mouth and swallowed them up together with Korah when that
company died, when the fire devoured two hundred and fifty men; [b]and they became a sign.
11 Nevertheless [a]the children of Korah did not
die.
**12** The sons of Simeon according to their families
*were: of* Nemuel, the family of the Nemuelites; *of*
[1]Jamin, the family of the Jaminites; *of* [2]Jachin, the
family of the Jachinites;
13 *of* [1]Zerah, the family of the Zarhites; *of* Shaul,
the family of the Shaulites.
14 These *are* the families of the Simeonites:
twenty-two thousand two hundred.
**15** The sons of Gad according to their families
*were: of* [1]Zephon, the family of the Zephonites; *of*
Haggi, the family of the Haggites; *of* Shuni, the
family of the Shunites;
16 *of* [1]Ozni, the family of the Oznites; *of* Eri, the
family of the Erites;
17 *of* [1]Arod, the family of the Arodites; *of* Areli,
the family of the Arelites.
18 These *are* the families of the sons of Gad
according to those who were numbered of them:
forty thousand five hundred.
**19** [a]The sons of Judah *were* Er and Onan; and Er
and Onan died in the land of Canaan.
20 And [a]the sons of Judah according to their
families were: *of* Shelah, the family of the Shelan-
ites; *of* Perez, the family of the Parzites; *of* Zerah,
the family of the Zarhites.
21 And the sons of Perez were: *of* Hezron, the
family of the Hezronites; *of* Hamul, the family of
the Hamulites.
22 These *are* the families of Judah according to
those who were numbered of them: seventy-six
thousand five hundred.
**23** The sons of Issachar according to their families *were: of* Tola, the family of the Tolaites; of
[1]Puah, the family of the [2]Punites;
24 of [1]Jashub, the family of the Jashubites; of
Shimron, the family of the Shimronites.
25 These *are* the families of Issachar according to
those who were numbered of them: sixty-four
thousand three hundred.
**26** [a]The sons of Zebulun according to their families *were:* of Sered, the family of the Sardites; of
Elon, the family of the Elonites; of Jahleel, the
family of the Jahleelites.
27 These *are* the families of the Zebulunites
according to those who were numbered of them:
sixty thousand five hundred.
**28** [a]The sons of Joseph according to their families, by Manasseh and Ephraim, *were:*
29 The sons of [a]Manasseh: of [b]Machir, the family
of the Machirites; and Machir begot Gilead; of
Gilead, the family of the Gileadites.
30 These *are* the sons of Gilead: *of* [1]Jeezer, the

**2** [a]Hos. 9:10 [b]Ex. 34:15 [c]Ex. 20:5
**3** [a]Ps. 106:28, 29
**4** [a]Deut. 4:3 [b]Num. 25:11
**5** [a]Ex. 18:21 [b]Deut. 13:6, 9
**6** [a]Joel 2:17
**7** [a]Ps. 106:30 [b]Ex. 6:25
**8** [a]Ps. 106:30 [b]Num. 16:46–48
**9** [a]Deut. 4:3
**11** [a]Ps. 106:30 [b][Ex. 20:5]
**12** [a][Mal. 2:4, 5; 3:1] [b]Is. 54:10
**13** [a]1 Chr. 6:4 [b]Ex. 40:15 [c]Acts 22:3 [d][Heb. 2:17] [1]Lit. *covering*
**15** [a]Num. 31:8
**17** [a]Num. 31:1–3 [1]*be hostile toward*
**18** [a]Rev. 2:14 [1]*tricks*

CHAPTER 26
**1** [a]Num. 25:9
**2** [a]Num. 1:2; 14:29 [b]Num. 1:3
**3** [a]Num. 22:1; 31:12; 33:48; 35:1
**4** [a]Num. 1:1
**5** [a]Ex. 6:14
**9** [a]Num. 1:16; 16:1, 2
**10** [a]Num. 16:32–35 [b]Num. 16:38–40
**11** [a]Ex. 6:24
**12** [1]*Jemuel,* Gen. 46:10; Ex. 6:15 [2]*Jarib,* 1 Chr. 4:24
**13** [1]*Zohar,* Gen. 46:10
**15** [1]*Ziphion,* Gen. 46:16
**16** [1]*Ezbon,* Gen. 46:16
**17** [1]Sam., Syr. *Arodi* and Gen. 46:16
**19** [a]Gen. 38:2; 46:12
**20** [a]1 Chr. 2:3
**23** [1]So with Sam., LXX, Syr., Vg.; Heb. *Puvah,* Gen. 46:13; 1 Chr. 7:1 [2]Sam., LXX, Syr., Vg. *Puaites*
**24** [1]*Job,* Gen. 46:13
**26** [a]Gen. 46:14
**28** [a]Gen. 46:20
**29** [a]Josh. 17:1 [b]1 Chr. 7:14, 15
**30** [1]*Abiezer,* Josh. 17:2

family of the Jeezerites; of Helek, the family of the
Helekites;
31 *of* Asriel, the family of the Asrielites; *of* Shechem, the family of the Shechemites;
32 *of* Shemida, the family of the Shemidaites; *of*
Hepher, the family of the Hepherites.
33 Now [a]Zelophehad the son of Hepher had no
sons, but daughters; and the names of the daughters of Zelophehad *were* Mahlah, Noah, Hoglah,
Milcah, and Tirzah.
34 These *are* the families of Manasseh; and those
who were numbered of them *were* fifty-two thousand seven hundred.
**35** These *are* the sons of Ephraim according to
their families: of Shuthelah, the family of the
Shuthalhites; of [1]Becher, the family of the Bach-
rites; of Tahan, the family of the Tahanites.
36 And these *are* the sons of Shuthelah: of Eran,
the family of the Eranites.
37 These *are* the families of the sons of Ephraim
according to those who were numbered of them:
thirty-two thousand five hundred. These *are* the
sons of Joseph according to their families.
**38** [a]The sons of Benjamin according to their
families were: of Bela, the family of the Belaites; of
Ashbel, the family of the Ashbelites; of [b]Ahiram,
the family of the Ahiramites;
39 of [a]Shupham,[1] the family of the Shuphamites;
of [2]Hupham, the family of the Huphamites.
40 And the sons of Bela were [1]Ard and Naaman:
[a]*of Ard,* the family of the Ardites; of Naaman, the
family of the Naamites.
41 These *are* the sons of Benjamin according to
their families; and those who were numbered of
them *were* forty-five thousand six hundred.
**42** These *are* the sons of Dan according to their
families: of [1]Shuham, the family of the Shuhamites. These *are* the families of Dan according to
their families.
43 All the families of the Shuhamites, according
to those who were numbered of them, *were* sixty-
four thousand four hundred.
**44** [a]The sons of Asher according to their families
*were:* of Jimna, the family of the Jimnites; of
Jesui, the family of the Jesuites; of Beriah, the
family of the Beriites.
45 Of the sons of Beriah: of Heber, the family of
the Heberites; of Malchiel, the family of the
Malchielites.
46 And the name of the daughter of Asher *was*
Serah.
47 These *are* the families of the sons of Asher
according to those who were numbered of them:
fifty-three thousand four hundred.
**48** [a]The sons of Naphtali according to their families *were:* of [1]Jahzeel, the family of the Jahzeel-
ites; of Guni, the family of the Gunites;
49 of Jezer, the family of the Jezerites; of [a]Shil-
lem, the family of the Shillemites.
50 These *are* the families of Naphtali according to
their families; and those who were numbered of
them *were* forty-five thousand four hundred.
**51** [a]These *are* those who were numbered of the
children of Israel: six hundred and one thousand
seven hundred and thirty.
**52** Then the LORD spoke to Moses, saying:
53 [a]"To these the land shall be [b]divided as an
inheritance, according to the number of names.
54 [a]"To a large *tribe* you shall give a larger
inheritance, and to a small *tribe* you shall give a
smaller inheritance. Each shall be given its inheritance according to those who were numbered of
them.
55 "But the land shall be [a]divided by lot; they
shall inherit according to the names of the tribes
of their fathers.
56 "According to the lot their inheritance shall be
divided between the larger and the smaller."
**57** [a]And these *are* those who were numbered of
the Levites according to their families: of Gershon, the family of the Gershonites; of Kohath,
the family of the Kohathites; of Merari, the family
of the Merarites.
58 These *are* the families of the Levites: the
family of the Libnites, the family of the Hebronites, the family of the Mahlites, the family of the
Mushites, and the family of the Korathites. And
Kohath begot Amram.
59 The name of Amram's wife *was* [a]Jochebed the
daughter of Levi, who was born to Levi in Egypt;
and to Amram she bore Aaron and Moses and
their sister Miriam.
60 [a]To Aaron were born Nadab and Abihu, Eleazar and Ithamar.
61 And [a]Nadab and Abihu died when they offered
profane fire before the LORD.
62 [a]Now those who were numbered of them were
twenty-three thousand, every male from a month
old and above; [b]for they were not numbered
among the other children of Israel, because there
was [c]no inheritance given to them among the
children of Israel.
**63** These *are* those who were numbered by Moses
and Eleazar the priest, who numbered the children of Israel [a]in the plains of Moab by the Jordan,
*across from* Jericho.
64 [a]But among these there was not a man of
those who were numbered by Moses and Aaron
the priest when they numbered the children of
Israel in the [b]Wilderness of Sinai.
65 For the LORD had said of them, "They [a]shall
surely die in the wilderness." So there was not left
a man of them, [b]except Caleb the son of Jephunneh and Joshua the son of Nun.

### *The Law of Inheritance*

**27** Then came the daughters of [a]Zelophehad
the son of Hepher, the son of Gilead, the son
of Machir, the son of Manasseh, from the families
of Manasseh the son of Joseph; and these *were*
the names of his daughters: Mahlah, Noah, Hoglah, Milcah, and Tirzah.
2 And they stood before Moses, before Eleazar
the priest, and before the leaders and all the
congregation, *by* the doorway of the tabernacle of
meeting, saying:
3 "Our father [a]died in the wilderness; but he was
not in the company of those who gathered together against the LORD, [b]in company with Korah,
but he died in his own sin; and he had no sons.
4 "Why should the name of our father be [a]re-
moved[1] from among his family because he had no
son? [b]Give us a [2]possession among our father's
brothers."
5 So Moses [a]brought their case before the LORD.
**6** And the LORD spoke to Moses, saying:
7 "The daughters of Zelophehad speak *what is*
right; [a]you shall surely give them a possession of
inheritance among their father's brothers, and
cause the inheritance of their father to pass to
them.
8 "And you shall speak to the children of Israel,

**33** [a]Num. 27:1; 36:11
**35** [1]*Bered,* 1 Chr. 7:20
**38** [a]Gen. 46:21; 1 Chr. 7:6 [b]Gen. 46:21; 1 Chr. 8:1, 2
**39** [a]1 Chr. 7:12 [1]MT *Shephupham; Shephuphan,* 1 Chr. 8:5 [2]*Huppim,* Gen. 46:21
**40** [a]1 Chr. 8:3 [1]*Addar,* 1 Chr. 8:3
**42** [1]*Hushim,* Gen. 46:23
**44** [a]Gen. 46:17; 1 Chr. 7:30
**48** [a]Gen. 46:24; 1 Chr. 7:13 [1]*Jahziel,* 1 Chr. 7:13
**49** [a]1 Chr. 7:13
**51** [a]Ex. 12:37; 38:26; Num. 1:46; 11:21
**53** [a]Josh. 11:23; 14:1 [b]Num. 33:54
**54** [a]Num. 33:54
**55** [a]Num. 33:54; 54:13; Josh. 11:23; 14:2
**57** [a]Gen. 46:11; Ex. 6:16–19; Num. 3:15; 1 Chr. 6:1, 16
**59** [a]Ex. 2:1, 2; 6:20
**60** [a]Num. 3:2
**61** [a]Lev. 10:1, 2; Num. 3:3, 4; 1 Chr. 24:2
**62** [a]Num. 3:39 [b]Num. 1:49 [c]Num. 18:20, 23, 24
**63** [a]Num. 26:3
**64** [a]Num. 14:29–35; Deut. 2:14–16; Heb. 3:17 [b]Num. 1:1–46
**65** [a]Num. 14:26–35; [1 Cor. 10:5, 6] [b]Num. 14:30

CHAPTER 27
**1** [a]Num. 26:33; 36:1, 11; Josh. 17:3
**3** [a]Num. 14:35; 26:64, 65 [b]Num. 16:1, 2
**4** [a]Deut. 25:6 [b]Josh. 17:4 [1]*withdrawn* [2]*inheritance*
**5** [a]Ex. 18:13–26
**7** [a]Num. 36:2; Josh. 17:4

saying: 'If a man dies and has no son, then you
shall cause his inheritance to pass to his daughter.
9 'If he has no daughter, then you shall give his
inheritance to his brothers.
10 'If he has no brothers, then you shall give his
inheritance to his father's brothers.
11 'And if his father has no brothers, then you
shall give his inheritance to the relative closest to
him in his family, and he shall possess it.' " And it
shall be to the children of Israel [a]a statute of
judgment, just as the LORD commanded Moses.
**12** Now the LORD said to Moses: [a]"Go up into this
Mount Abarim, and see the land which I have
given to the children of Israel.
13 "And when you have seen it, you also [a]shall
[1]be gathered to your people, as Aaron your
brother was gathered.
14 "For in the Wilderness of Zin, during the strife
of the congregation, you [a]rebelled against My
command to hallow Me at the waters before their
eyes." (These *are* the [b]waters of Meribah, at
Kadesh in the Wilderness of Zin.)
**15** Then Moses spoke to the LORD, saying:
16 "Let the LORD, [a]the God of the spirits of all
flesh, set a man over the congregation,
17 [a]"who may go out before them and go in
before them, who may lead them out and bring
them in, that the congregation of the LORD may
not be [b]like sheep which have no shepherd."
**18** And the LORD said to Moses: "Take Joshua the
son of Nun with you, a man [a]in whom *is* the Spirit,
and [b]lay your hand on him;
19 "set him before Eleazar the priest and before
all the congregation, and [a]inaugurate[1] him in their
sight.
20 "And [a]you shall give *some* of your authority to
him, that all the congregation of the children of
Israel [b]may be obedient.
21 [a]"He shall stand before Eleazar the priest, who
shall inquire before the LORD for him [b]by the
judgment of the Urim; [c]at his word they shall go
out, and at his word they shall come in, *both* he
and all the children of Israel with him, all the
congregation."
22 So Moses did as the LORD commanded him. He
took Joshua and set him before Eleazar the priest
and before all the congregation.
23 And he laid his hands on him [a]and [1]inaugu-
rated him, just as the LORD commanded by the
hand of Moses.

### *The Daily, Sabbath, and Monthly Offerings*

**28** Now the LORD spoke to Moses, saying,
2 "Command the children of Israel, and say
to them, 'My offering, [a]My food for My offerings
made by fire as a sweet aroma to Me, you shall be
careful to offer to Me at their appointed time.'
3 "And you shall say to them, [a]'This *is* the
offering made by fire which you shall offer to the
LORD: two male lambs in their first year without
blemish, day by day, as a regular burnt offering.
4 'The one lamb you shall offer in the morning,
the other lamb you shall offer in the evening,
5 'and [a]one-tenth of an ephah of fine flour as a
[b]grain offering mixed with one-fourth of a hin of
pressed oil.
6 '*It is* [a]a regular burnt offering which was
ordained at Mount Sinai for a sweet aroma, an
offering made by fire to the LORD.
7 'And its drink offering *shall be* one-fourth of a
hin for each lamb; [a]in a holy *place* you shall pour
out the drink to the LORD as an offering.
8 'The other lamb you shall offer in the evening;
as the morning grain offering and its drink offering, you shall offer *it* as an offering made by fire, a
[1]sweet aroma to the LORD.
**9** 'And on the Sabbath day two lambs in their
first year, without blemish, and two-tenths *of an
ephah* of fine flour as a grain offering, mixed with
oil, with its drink offering—
10 '*this is* [a]the burnt offering for every Sabbath,
besides the regular burnt offering with its drink
offering.
**11** [a]'At the beginnings of your months you shall
present a burnt offering to the LORD: two young
bulls, one ram, and seven lambs in their first year,
without blemish;
12 [a]'three-tenths *of an ephah* of fine flour as a
grain offering, mixed with oil, for each bull; two-
tenths *of an ephah* of fine flour as a grain offering,
mixed with oil, for the one ram;
13 'and one-tenth *of an ephah* of fine flour, mixed
with oil, as a grain offering for each lamb, as a
burnt offering of sweet aroma, an offering made
by fire to the LORD.
14 'Their drink offering shall be half a hin of wine
for a bull, one-third of a hin for a ram, and one-
fourth of a hin for a lamb; this *is* the burnt
offering for each month throughout the months of
the year.
15 'Also [a]one kid of the goats as a sin offering to
the LORD shall be offered, besides the regular
burnt offering and its drink offering.
**16** [a]'On the fourteenth day of the first month *is*
the Passover of the LORD.
17 [a]'And on the fifteenth day of this month *is* the
feast; unleavened bread shall be eaten for seven
days.
18 'On the [a]first day *you shall have* a holy [1]convo-
cation. You shall do no [2]customary work.
19 'And you shall present an offering made by fire
as a burnt offering to the LORD: two young bulls,
one ram, and seven lambs in their first year. [a]Be
sure they are without blemish.
20 'Their grain offering shall be of fine flour
mixed with oil: three-tenths *of an ephah* you shall
offer for a bull, and two-tenths for a ram;
21 'you shall offer one-tenth *of an ephah* for each
of the seven lambs;
22 'also [a]one goat *as* a sin offering, to make
[1]atonement for you.
23 'You shall offer these besides the burnt offering of the morning, which *is* for a regular burnt
offering.
24 'In this manner you shall offer the food of the
offering made by fire daily for seven days, as a
sweet aroma to the LORD; it shall be offered
besides the regular burnt offering and its drink
offering.
25 'And [a]on the seventh day you shall have a holy
convocation. You shall do no customary work.
**26** 'Also [a]on the day of the firstfruits, when you
bring a new grain offering to the LORD at your
*Feast of* Weeks, you shall have a holy convocation. You shall do no customary work.
27 'You shall present a burnt offering as a sweet
aroma to the LORD: [a]two young bulls, one ram,
and seven lambs in their first year,
28 'with their grain offering of fine flour mixed
with oil: three-tenths *of an ephah* for each bull,
two-tenths for the one ram,

11 [a]Num. 35:29
12 [a]Num. 33:47
13 [a]Deut. 10:6; 34:5, 6 [1]Die and join your ancestors
14 [a]Ps. 106:32, 33 [b]Ex. 17:7
16 [a]Num. 16:22
17 [a]Deut. 31:2 [b]Zech. 10:2
18 [a]Gen. 41:38 [b]Deut. 34:9
19 [a]Deut. 3:28; 31:3, 7, 8, 23 [1]*commission*
20 [a]Num. 11:17 [b]Josh. 1:16–18
21 [a]1 Sam. 23:9; 30:7 [b]Ex. 28:30 [c]1 Sam. 22:10
23 [a]Deut. 3:28; 31:7, 8 [1]*commissioned*

CHAPTER 28
2 [a]Lev. 3:11; 21:6, 8
3 [a]Ex. 29:38–42
5 [a]Ex. 16:36 [b]Lev. 2:1
6 [a]Ex. 29:42
7 [a]Ex. 29:42
8 [1]*pleasing*
10 [a]Ezek. 46:4
11 [a]Num. 10:10
12 [a]Num. 15:4–12
15 [a]Num. 15:24; 28:3, 22
16 [a]Lev. 23:5–8
17 [a]Lev. 23:6
18 [a]Lev. 23:7 [1]*assembly* or *gathering* [2]*occupational*
19 [a]Deut. 15:21
22 [a]Num. 28:15 [1]Lit. *covering*
25 [a]Lev. 23:8
26 [a]Deut. 16:9–12
27 [a]Lev. 23:18, 19

29 'and one-tenth for each of the seven lambs;
30 '*also* one kid of the goats, to make [1]atonement
for you.
31 [a]'Be sure they are without [1]blemish. You shall
present *them* with their drink offerings, besides
the regular burnt offering with its grain offering.

### *Offerings at the Regular Feasts*

**29** 'And in the seventh month, on the first *day*
of the month, you shall have a holy convocation. You shall do no customary work. For you
[a]it is a day of blowing the trumpets.
2 'You shall offer a burnt offering as a sweet
aroma to the LORD: one young bull, one ram, *and*
seven lambs in their first year, without blemish.
3 'Their grain offering *shall be* fine flour mixed
with oil: three-tenths *of an ephah* for the bull,
two-tenths for the ram,
4 'and one-tenth for each of the seven lambs;
5 'also one kid of the goats *as* a sin offering, to
make atonement for you;
6 'besides [a]the burnt offering with its grain
offering for the New Moon, [b]the regular burnt
offering with its grain offering, and their drink
offerings, [c]according to their ordinance, as a sweet
aroma, an offering made by fire to the LORD.
**7** [a]'On the tenth *day* of this seventh month you
shall have a holy convocation. You shall [b]afflict
your souls; you shall not do any work.
8 'You shall present a burnt offering to the LORD
*as* a sweet aroma: one young bull, one ram, *and*
seven lambs in their first year. [a]Be sure they are
without blemish.
9 'Their grain offering *shall be of* fine flour
mixed with oil: three-tenths *of an ephah* for the
bull, two-tenths for the one ram,
10 'and one-tenth for each of the seven lambs;
11 'also one kid of the goats *as* a sin offering,
besides [a]the sin offering for atonement, the regular burnt offering with its grain offering, and their
drink offerings.
**12** [a]'On the fifteenth day of the seventh month
you shall have a holy convocation. You shall do
no customary work, and you shall keep a feast to
the LORD seven days.
13 [a]'You shall present a burnt offering, an offering made by fire as a sweet aroma to the LORD:
thirteen young bulls, two rams, *and* fourteen
lambs in their first year. They shall be without
blemish.
14 'Their grain offering *shall be of* fine flour
mixed with oil: three-tenths *of an ephah* for each
of the thirteen bulls, two-tenths for each of the
two rams,
15 'and one-tenth for each of the fourteen lambs;
16 'also one kid of the goats *as* a sin offering,
besides the regular burnt offering, its grain offering, and its drink offering.
**17** 'On the [a]second day *present* twelve young
bulls, two rams, fourteen lambs in their first year
without blemish,
18 'and their grain offering and their drink offerings for the bulls, for the rams, and for the lambs,
by their number, [a]according to the ordinance;
19 'also one kid of the goats *as* a sin offering,
besides the regular burnt offering with its grain
offering, and their drink offerings.
**20** 'On the third day *present* eleven bulls, two
rams, fourteen lambs in their first year without
blemish,
21 'and their grain offering and their drink offerings for the bulls, for the rams, and for the lambs,
by their number, [a]according to the ordinance;
22 'also one goat *as* a sin offering, besides the
regular burnt offering, its grain offering, and its
drink offering.
**23** 'On the fourth day *present* ten bulls, two rams,
*and* fourteen lambs in their first year, without
blemish,
24 'and their grain offering and their drink offerings for the bulls, for the rams, and for the lambs,
by their number, according to the ordinance;
25 'also one kid of the goats *as* a sin offering,
besides the regular burnt offering, its grain offering, and its drink offering.
**26** 'On the fifth day *present* nine bulls, two rams,
*and* fourteen lambs in their first year without
blemish,
27 'and their grain offering and their drink offerings for the bulls, for the rams, and for the lambs,
by their number, according to the ordinance;
28 'also one goat *as* a sin offering, besides the
regular burnt offering, its grain offering, and its
drink offering.
**29** 'On the sixth day *present* eight bulls, two
rams, *and* fourteen lambs in their first year without blemish,
30 'and their grain offering and their drink offerings for the bulls, for the rams, and for the lambs,
by their number, according to the ordinance;
31 'also one goat *as* a sin offering, besides the
regular burnt offering, its grain offering, and its
drink offering.
**32** 'On the seventh day *present* seven bulls, two
rams, *and* fourteen lambs in their first year without blemish,
33 'and their grain offering and their drink offerings for the bulls, for the rams, and for the lambs,
by their number, according to the ordinance;
34 'also one goat *as* a sin offering, besides the
regular burnt offering, its grain offering, and its
drink offering.
**35** 'On the eighth day you shall have a [a]sacred[1]
assembly. You shall do no customary work.
36 'You shall present a burnt offering, an offering
made by fire as a sweet aroma to the LORD: one
bull, one ram, seven lambs in their first year
without blemish,
37 'and their grain offering and their drink offerings for the bull, for the ram, and for the lambs, by
their number, according to the ordinance;
38 'also one goat *as* a sin offering, besides the
regular burnt offering, its grain offering, and its
drink offering.
**39** 'These you shall present to the LORD at your
[a]appointed feasts (besides your [b]vowed offerings
and your freewill offerings) as your burnt offerings and your grain offerings, as your drink offerings and your peace offerings.' "
**40** So Moses told the children of Israel everything, just as the LORD commanded Moses.

### *The Law Concerning Vows*

**30** Then Moses spoke to [a]the heads of the
tribes concerning the children of Israel,
saying, "This *is* the thing which the LORD has
commanded:
2 [a]"If a man makes a vow to the LORD, or
[b]swears an oath to bind himself by some agreement, he shall not break his word; he shall [c]do
according to all that proceeds out of his mouth.
**3** "Or if a woman makes a vow to the LORD, and

**30** [1]Lit. *covering*
**31** [a]Num. 28:3, 19 [1]*defect*

CHAPTER 29

**1** [a]Ex. 23:16; 34:22; Lev. 23:23–25
**6** [a]Num. 28:11–15 [b]Num. 28:3 [c]Num. 15:11, 12
**7** [a]Lev. 16:29–34; 23:26–32 [b]Ps. 35:13; Is. 58:5
**8** [a]Num. 28:19
**11** [a]Lev. 16:3, 5
**12** [a]Lev. 23:33–35; Deut. 16:13–15; Ezek. 45:25
**13** [a]Ezra 3:4
**17** [a]Lev. 23:36
**18** [a]Num. 15:12; 28:7, 14; 29:3, 4, 9, 10
**21** [a]Num. 29:18
**35** [a]Lev. 23:36 [1]*solemn*
**39** [a]Lev. 23:1–44; 1 Chr. 23:31; 2 Chr. 31:3; Ezra 3:5; Neh. 10:33; Is. 1:14 [b]Lev. 7:16; 22:18, 21, 23; 23:38

CHAPTER 30

**1** [a]Num. 1:4, 16; 7:2
**2** [a]Lev. 27:2; Deut. 23:21–23; Judg. 11:30, 31, 35; Eccl. 5:4 [b]Lev. 5:4; Matt. 14:9; Acts 23:14 [c]Job 22:27; Ps. 22:25; 50:14; 66:13, 14; Nah. 1:15

binds *herself* by some agreement while in her father's house in her youth,

4 "and her father hears her vow and the agreement by which she has bound herself, and her father [1]holds his peace, then all her vows shall stand, and every agreement with which she has bound herself shall stand.

5 "But if her father overrules her on the day that he hears, then none of her vows nor her agreements by which she has bound herself shall stand; and the LORD will release her, because her father overruled her.

**6** "If indeed she takes a husband, while bound by her vows or by a rash utterance from her lips by which she bound herself,

7 "and her husband hears *it*, and makes no response to her on the day that he hears, then her vows shall stand, and her agreements by which she bound herself shall stand.

8 "But if her husband [a]overrules her on the day that he hears *it*, he shall make void her vow which she took and what she uttered with her lips, by which she bound herself, and the LORD will release her.

**9** "Also any vow of a widow or a divorced woman, by which she has bound herself, shall stand against her.

**10** "If she vowed in her husband's house, or bound herself by an agreement with an oath,

11 "and her husband heard *it*, and made no response to her *and* did not overrule her, then all her vows shall stand, and every agreement by which she bound herself shall stand.

12 "But if her husband truly made them void on the day he heard *them*, then whatever proceeded from her lips concerning her vows or concerning the agreement binding her, it shall not stand; her husband has made them [1]void, and the LORD will release her.

13 "Every vow and every binding oath to afflict her soul, her husband may confirm it, or her husband may make it void.

14 "Now if her husband makes no response whatever to her from day to day, then he confirms all her vows or all the agreements that bind her; he confirms them, because he made no response to her on the day that he heard *them*.

15 "But if he does make them void after he has heard *them*, then he shall bear her guilt."

**16** These *are* the statutes which the LORD commanded Moses, between a man and his wife, and between a father and his daughter in her youth in her father's house.

### *The Midianites Conquered*

**31** And the LORD spoke to Moses, saying:

2 [a]"Take vengeance on the Midianites for the children of Israel. Afterward you shall [b]be gathered to your people."

3 So Moses spoke to the people, saying, "Arm some of yourselves for war, and let them go against the Midianites to take vengeance for the LORD on [a]Midian.

4 "A thousand from each tribe of all the tribes of Israel you shall send to the war."

5 So there were recruited from the divisions of Israel one thousand from *each* tribe, twelve thousand armed for war.

6 Then Moses sent them to the war, one thousand from *each* tribe; he sent them to the war with Phinehas the son of Eleazar the priest, with the holy articles and [a]the signal trumpets in his hand.

7 And they warred against the Midianites, just as the LORD commanded Moses, and [a]they killed all the [b]males.

8 They killed the kings of Midian with *the rest of* those who were killed—[a]Evi, Rekem, [b]Zur, Hur, and Reba, the five kings of Midian. [c]Balaam the son of Beor they also killed with the sword.

9 And the children of Israel took the women of Midian captive, with their little ones, and took as spoil all their cattle, all their flocks, and all their goods.

10 They also burned with fire all the cities where they dwelt, and all their forts.

11 And [a]they took all the spoil and all the booty—of man and beast.

**12** Then they brought the captives, the booty, and the spoil to Moses, to Eleazar the priest, and to the congregation of the children of Israel, to the camp in the plains of Moab by the Jordan, *across from* Jericho.

13 And Moses, Eleazar the priest, and all the leaders of the congregation, went to meet them outside the camp.

14 But Moses was angry with the officers of the army, *with* the captains over thousands and captains over hundreds, who had come from the battle.

15 And Moses said to them: "Have you kept [a]all the women alive?

16 "Look, [a]these *women* caused the children of Israel, through the [b]counsel of Balaam, to trespass against the LORD in the incident of Peor, and [c]there was a plague among the congregation of the LORD.

17 "Now therefore, [a]kill every male among the little ones, and kill every woman who has known a man intimately.

18 "But keep alive [a]for yourselves all the young girls who have not known a man intimately.

19 "And as for you, [a]remain outside the camp seven days; whoever has killed any person, and [b]whoever has touched any slain, purify yourselves and your captives on the third day and on the seventh day.

20 "Purify every garment, everything made of leather, everything woven of goats' *hair*, and everything made of wood."

**21** Then Eleazar the priest said to the men of war who had gone to the battle, "This *is* the [1]ordinance of the law which the LORD commanded Moses:

22 "Only the gold, the silver, the bronze, the iron, the tin, and the lead,

23 "everything that can endure fire, you shall put through the fire, and it shall be clean; and it shall be purified [a]with the water of purification. But all that cannot endure fire you shall put through water.

24 [a]"And you shall wash your clothes on the seventh day and be clean, and afterward you may come into the camp."

**25** Now the LORD spoke to Moses, saying:

26 "Count up the plunder that was [1]taken—of man and beast—you and Eleazar the priest and the chief fathers of the congregation;

27 "and [a]divide the plunder into two parts, between those who took part in the war, who went out to battle, and all the congregation.

28 "And levy a [1]tribute for the LORD on the men

**4** [1]*says nothing* to interfere
**8** [a][Gen. 3:16]
**12** [1]*annulled* or *invalidated*

CHAPTER 31
**2** [a]Num. 25:17 [b]Num. 25:12, 13
**3** [a]Josh. 13:21
**6** [a]Num. 10:9
**7** [a]Deut. 20:13; Judg. 21:11; 1 Sam. 27:9; 1 Kin. 11:15, 16 [b]Gen. 34:25
**8** [a]Josh. 13:21 [b]Num. 25:15 [c]Num. 31:16; Josh. 13:22
**11** [a]Deut. 20:14
**15** [a]Deut. 20:14
**16** [a]Num. 25:2 [b]Num. 24:14; 2 Pet. 2:15; Rev. 2:14 [c]Num. 25:9
**17** [a]Deut. 7:2; 20:16–18; Judg. 21:11
**18** [a]Deut. 21:10–14
**19** [a]Num. 5:2 [b]Num. 19:11–22
**21** [1]*statute*
**23** [a]Num. 19:9, 17
**24** [a]Lev. 11:25
**26** [1]*captured*
**27** [a]Josh. 22:8; 1 Sam. 30:24
**28** [1]*tax*

of war who went out to battle: [a]one of every five
hundred of the persons, the cattle, the donkeys,
and the sheep;
29 "take *it* from their half, and [a]give *it* to Eleazar
the priest as a heave offering to the LORD.
30 "And from the children of Israel's half you
shall take [a]one of every fifty, drawn from the
persons, the cattle, the donkeys, and the sheep,
from all the livestock, and give them to the
Levites [b]who [1]keep charge of the tabernacle of the
LORD."
31 So Moses and Eleazar the priest did as the
LORD commanded Moses.
**32** The booty remaining from the plunder, which
the men of war had taken, was six hundred and
seventy-five thousand sheep,
33 seventy-two thousand cattle,
34 sixty-one thousand donkeys,
35 and thirty-two thousand persons in all, of
women who had not known a man intimately.
36 And the half, the portion for those who had
gone out to war, was in number three hundred
and thirty-seven thousand five hundred sheep;
37 and the LORD's [1]tribute of the sheep was six
hundred and seventy-five.
38 The cattle *were* thirty-six thousand, of which
the LORD's tribute *was* seventy-two.
39 The donkeys *were* thirty thousand five hundred, of which the LORD's tribute *was* sixty-one.
40 The persons *were* sixteen thousand, of which
the LORD's tribute *was* thirty-two persons.
41 So Moses gave the tribute *which was* the
LORD's heave offering to Eleazar the priest, [a]as the
LORD commanded Moses.
**42** And from the children of Israel's half, which
Moses separated from the men who fought—
43 now the half belonging to the congregation
was three hundred and thirty-seven thousand five
hundred sheep,
44 thirty-six thousand cattle,
45 thirty thousand five hundred donkeys,
46 and sixteen thousand persons—
47 and [a]from the children of Israel's half Moses
took one of every fifty, drawn from man and
beast, and gave them to the Levites, who kept
charge of the tabernacle of the LORD, as the LORD
commanded Moses.
**48** Then the officers who *were* over thousands of
the army, the captains of thousands and captains
of hundreds, came near to Moses;
49 and they said to Moses, "Your servants have
taken a count of the men of war who *are* under
our command, and not a man of us is missing.
50 "Therefore we have brought an offering for
the LORD, what every man found of ornaments of
gold: armlets and bracelets and signet rings and
earrings and necklaces, [a]to make [1]atonement for
ourselves before the LORD."
51 So Moses and Eleazar the priest received the
gold from them, all the fashioned ornaments.
52 And all the gold of the offering that they
offered to the LORD, from the captains of thousands and captains of hundreds, was sixteen
thousand seven hundred and fifty shekels.
53 [a](The men of war had taken spoil, every man
for himself.)
54 And Moses and Eleazar the priest received the
gold from the captains of thousands and of hundreds, and brought it into the tabernacle of meeting [a]as a memorial for the children of Israel before
the LORD.

### *Reuben and Gad Inherit East of Jordan*

**32** Now the children of Reuben and the children of Gad had a very great multitude of
livestock; and when they saw the land of [a]Jazer
and the land of [b]Gilead, that indeed the region
*was* a place for livestock,
2 the children of Gad and the children of Reuben came and spoke to Moses, to Eleazar the
priest, and to the leaders of the congregation,
saying,
3 "Ataroth, Dibon, Jazer, [a]Nimrah, [b]Heshbon,
Elealeh, [c]Shebam, Nebo, and [d]Beon,
4 "the country [a]which the LORD defeated before
the congregation of Israel, *is* a land for livestock,
and your servants have livestock."
5 Therefore they said, "If we have found favor
in your sight, let this land be given to your
servants as a possession. Do not take us over the
Jordan."
**6** And Moses said to the children of Gad and to
the children of Reuben: "Shall your brethren go to
war while you sit here?
7 "Now why will you [a]discourage the heart of
the children of Israel from going over into the
land which the LORD has given them?
8 "Thus your fathers did [a]when I sent them
away from Kadesh Barnea [b]to see the land.
9 "For [a]when they went up to the Valley of
Eshcol and saw the land, they discouraged the
heart of the children of Israel, so that they did not
go into the land which the LORD had given them.
10 [a]"So the LORD's anger was aroused on that
day, and He swore an oath, saying,
11 'Surely none of the men who came up from
Egypt, [a]from twenty years old and above, shall see
the land of which I swore to Abraham, Isaac, and
Jacob, because [b]they have not wholly followed
Me,
12 'except Caleb the son of Jephunneh, the Kenizzite, and Joshua the son of Nun, [a]for they have
wholly followed the LORD.'
13 "So the LORD's anger was aroused against
Israel, and He made them [a]wander in the wilderness forty years, until [b]all the generation that had
done evil in the sight of the LORD was gone.
14 "And look! You have risen in your fathers'
place, a brood of sinful men, to increase still more
the [a]fierce anger of the LORD against Israel.
15 "For if you [a]turn away from following Him, He
will once again leave them in the wilderness, and
you will destroy all these people."
**16** Then they came near to him and said: "We
will build sheepfolds here for our livestock, and
cities for our little ones,
17 "but [a]we ourselves will be armed, ready *to go*
before the children of Israel until we have brought
them to their place; and our little ones will dwell
in the fortified cities because of the inhabitants of
the land.
18 [a]"We will not return to our homes until every
one of the children of Israel has [1]received his
inheritance.
19 "For we will not inherit with them on the
other side of the Jordan and beyond, [a]because our
inheritance has fallen to us on this eastern side of
the Jordan."
**20** Then [a]Moses said to them: "If you do this

---

**28** [a]Num. 31:30, 47
**29** [a]Deut. 18:1–5
**30** [a]Num. 31:42–47 [b]Num. 3:7, 8, 25, 31, 36; 18:3, 4 [1]*perform the service*
**37** [1]*tax*
**41** [a]Num. 5:9, 10; 18:8, 19
**47** [a]Num. 31:30
**50** [a]Ex. 30:12–16 [1]Lit. *covering*
**53** [a]Num. 31:32; Deut. 20:14
**54** [a]Ex. 30:16

CHAPTER 32

**1** [a]Num. 21:32; Josh. 13:25; 2 Sam. 24:5 [b]Deut. 3:13
**3** [a]Num. 32:36 [b]Josh. 13:17, 26 [c]Num. 32:38 [d]Num. 32:38
**4** [a]Num. 21:24, 34, 35
**7** [a]Num. 13:27—14:4
**8** [a]Num. 13:3, 26 [b]Deut. 1:19–25
**9** [a]Num. 13:24, 31; Deut. 1:24, 28
**10** [a]Num. 14:11; Deut. 1:34–36
**11** [a]Num. 14:28, 29; 26:63–65; Deut. 1:35 [b]Num. 14:24, 30
**12** [a]Num. 14:6–9, 24, 30; Deut. 1:36; Josh. 14:8, 9
**13** [a]Num. 14:33–35 [b]Num. 26:64, 65
**14** [a]Num. 11:1; Deut. 1:34
**15** [a]Deut. 30:17, 18; Josh. 22:16–18; 2 Chr. 7:19; 15:2
**17** [a]Josh. 4:12, 13
**18** [a]Josh. 22:1–4 [1]*possessed*
**19** [a]Josh. 12:1; 13:8
**20** [a]Deut. 3:18; Josh. 1:14

thing, if you arm yourselves before the LORD for
the war,
21 "and all your armed men cross over the Jordan before the LORD until He has driven out His
enemies from before Him,
22 "and [a]the land is subdued before the LORD,
then afterward [b]you may return and be blameless
before the LORD and before Israel; and [c]this land
shall be your possession before the LORD.
23 "But if you do not do so, then take note, you
have sinned against the LORD; and be sure [a]your
sin will find you out.
24 [a]"Build cities for your little ones and folds for
your sheep, and do [1]what has proceeded out of
your mouth."
25 And the children of Gad and the children of
Reuben spoke to Moses, saying: "Your servants
will do as my lord commands.
26 [a]"Our little ones, our wives, our flocks, and all
our livestock will be there in the cities of Gilead;
27 [a]"but your servants will cross over, every man
armed for war, before the LORD to battle, just as
my lord says."
**28** So Moses gave command [a]concerning them to
Eleazar the priest, to Joshua the son of Nun, and
to the chief fathers of the tribes of the children of
Israel.
29 And Moses said to them: "If the children of
Gad and the children of Reuben cross over the
Jordan with you, every man armed for battle
before the LORD, and the land is subdued before
you, then you shall give them the land of Gilead as
a possession.
30 "But if they do not cross over armed with you,
they shall have possessions among you in the land
of Canaan."
31 Then the children of Gad and the children of
Reuben answered, saying: "As the LORD has said
to your servants, so we will do.
32 "We will cross over armed before the LORD
into the land of Canaan, but the possession of our
inheritance *shall remain* with us on this side of
the Jordan."
**33** So [a]Moses gave to the children of Gad, to the
children of Reuben, and to half the tribe of Manasseh the son of Joseph, [b]the kingdom of Sihon king
of the Amorites and the kingdom of Og king of
Bashan, the land with its cities within the borders,
the cities of the surrounding country.
34 And the children of Gad built [a]Dibon and
Ataroth and [b]Aroer,
35 Atroth and Shophan and [a]Jazer and Jogbehah,
36 [a]Beth Nimrah and Beth Haran, [b]fortified cities,
and folds for sheep.
37 And the children of Reuben built [a]Heshbon
and Elealeh and Kirjathaim,
38 [a]Nebo and [b]Baal Meon [c](*their* names being
changed) and Shibmah; and they gave *other*
names to the cities which they built.
39 And the children of [a]Machir the son of Manasseh went to Gilead and took it, and [1]dispossessed
the Amorites who *were* in it.
40 So Moses [a]gave Gilead to Machir the son of
Manasseh, and he dwelt in it.
41 Also [a]Jair the son of Manasseh went and took
its small towns, and called them [b]Havoth Jair.[1]
42 Then Nobah went and took Kenath and its
villages, and he called it Nobah, after his own
name.

*The Wilderness Journeys*

**33** These *are* the journeys of the children of
Israel, who went out of the land of Egypt by
their armies under the [a]hand of Moses and Aaron.
2 Now Moses wrote down the starting points of
their journeys at the command of the LORD. And
these *are* their journeys according to their starting points:
3 They [a]departed from Rameses in [b]the first
month, on the fifteenth day of the first month; on
the day after the Passover the children of Israel
went out [c]with boldness in the sight of all the
Egyptians.
4 For the Egyptians were burying all *their* firstborn, [a]whom the LORD had killed among them.
Also [b]on their gods the LORD had executed judgments.
**5** [a]Then the children of Israel moved from Rameses and camped at Succoth.
6 They departed from [a]Succoth and camped at
Etham, which *is* on the edge of the wilderness.
7 [a]They moved from Etham and turned back to
Pi Hahiroth, which *is* east of Baal Zephon; and
they camped near Migdol.
8 They departed [1]from before Hahiroth and
[a]passed through the midst of the sea into the
wilderness, went three days' journey in the Wilderness of Etham, and camped at Marah.
9 They moved from Marah and [a]came to Elim.
At Elim *were* twelve springs of water and seventy
palm trees; so they camped there.
10 They moved from Elim and camped by the
Red Sea.
11 They moved from the Red Sea and camped in
the [a]Wilderness of Sin.
12 They journeyed from the Wilderness of Sin
and camped at Dophkah.
13 They departed from Dophkah and camped at
Alush.
14 They moved from Alush and camped at
[a]Rephidim, where there was no water for the
people to drink.
15 They departed from Rephidim and camped in
the [a]Wilderness of Sinai.
16 They moved from the Wilderness of Sinai and
camped [a]at [1]Kibroth Hattaavah.
17 They departed from Kibroth Hattaavah and
[a]camped at Hazeroth.
18 They departed from Hazeroth and camped at
[a]Rithmah.
19 They departed from Rithmah and camped at
Rimmon Perez.
20 They departed from Rimmon Perez and
camped at Libnah.
21 They moved from Libnah and camped at Rissah.
22 They journeyed from Rissah and camped at
Kehelathah.
23 They went from Kehelathah and camped at
Mount Shepher.
24 They moved from Mount Shepher and camped
at Haradah.
25 They moved from Haradah and camped at
Makheloth.
26 They moved from Makheloth and camped
at Tahath.
27 They departed from Tahath and camped at
Terah.

**22** [a]Deut. 3:20; Josh. 11:23 [b]Josh. 22:4 [c]Deut. 3:12, 15, 16, 18; Josh. 1:15; 13:8, 32; 22:4, 9
**23** [a]Gen. 4:7; 44:16; Josh. 7:1–26; Is. 59:12; [Gal. 6:7]
**24** [a]Num. 32:16 [1]*what you said you would do*
**26** [a]Josh. 1:14
**27** [a]Josh. 4:12
**28** [a]Josh. 1:13
**33** [a]Deut. 3:8–17; 29:8; Josh. 12:1–6; 13:8–31; 22:4 [b]Num. 21:24, 33, 35
**34** [a]Num. 33:45, 46 [b]Deut. 2:36
**35** [a]Num. 32:1, 3
**36** [a]Num. 32:3 [b]Num. 32:24
**37** [a]Num. 21:27
**38** [a]Is. 46:1 [b]Ezek. 25:9 [c]Ex. 23:13; Josh. 23:7
**39** [a]Gen. 50:23; Num. 27:1; 36:1 [1]*drove out*
**40** [a]Deut. 3:12, 13, 15; Josh. 13:31
**41** [a]Deut. 3:14; Josh. 13:30 [b]Judg. 10:4; 1 Kin. 4:13 [1]Lit. *Towns of Jair*

CHAPTER 33

**1** [a]Ps. 77:20
**3** [a]Ex. 12:37 [b]Ex. 12:2; 13:4 [c]Ex. 14:8
**4** [a]Ex. 12:29 [b][Ex. 12:12; 18:11]; Is. 19:1
**5** [a]Ex. 12:37
**6** [a]Ex. 13:20
**7** [a]Ex. 14:1, 2, 9
**8** [a]Ex. 14:22; 15:22, 23 [1]Heb. mss., Sam., Syr., Tg., Vg. *from Pi Hahiroth*; cf. Num. 33:7
**9** [a]Ex. 15:27
**11** [a]Ex. 16:1
**14** [a]Ex. 17:1; 19:2
**15** [a]Ex. 16:1; 19:1, 2
**16** [a]Num. 11:34 [1]Lit. *Graves of Craving*
**17** [a]Num. 11:35
**18** [a]Num. 12:16

28 They moved from Terah and camped at Mithkah.
29 They went from Mithkah and camped at
Hashmonah.
30 They departed from Hashmonah and [a]camped
at Moseroth.
31 They departed from Moseroth and camped at
Bene Jaakan.
32 They moved from [a]Bene Jaakan and [b]camped
at Hor Hagidgad.
33 They went from Hor Hagidgad and camped
at Jotbathah.
34 They moved from Jotbathah and camped at
Abronah.
35 They departed from Abronah [a]and camped at
Ezion Geber.
36 They moved from Ezion Geber and camped in
the [a]Wilderness of Zin, which *is* Kadesh.
37 They moved from [a]Kadesh and camped at
Mount Hor, on the boundary of the land of Edom.
**38** Then [a]Aaron the priest went up to Mount Hor
at the command of the LORD, and died there in the
fortieth year after the children of Israel had come
out of the land of Egypt, on the first *day* of the
fifth month.
39 Aaron *was* one hundred and twenty-three
years old when he died on Mount Hor.
**40** Now [a]the king of Arad, the Canaanite, who
dwelt in the South in the land of Canaan, heard of
the coming of the children of Israel.
**41** So they departed from Mount Hor and camped
at Zalmonah.
42 They departed from Zalmonah and camped at
Punon.
43 They departed from Punon and [a]camped at
Oboth.
44 [a]They departed from Oboth and camped at Ije
Abarim, at the border of Moab.
45 They departed from [1]Ijim and camped [a]at
Dibon Gad.
46 They moved from Dibon Gad and camped at
[a]Almon Diblathaim.
47 They moved from Almon Diblathaim [a]and
camped in the mountains of Abarim, before Nebo.
48 They departed from the mountains of Abarim
and [a]camped in the plains of Moab by the Jordan,
*across from* Jericho.
49 They camped by the Jordan, from Beth Jesi-
moth as far as the [a]Abel Acacia Grove[1] in the
plains of Moab.
**50** Now the LORD spoke to Moses in the plains of
Moab by the Jordan, *across from* Jericho, saying,
51 "Speak to the children of Israel, and say to
them: [a]'When you have crossed the Jordan into
the land of Canaan,
52 [a]'then you shall drive out all the inhabitants of
the land from before you, destroy all their engraved stones, destroy all their molded images,
and demolish all their [1]high places;
53 'you shall dispossess *the inhabitants of* the
land and dwell in it, for I have given you the land
to [a]possess.
54 'And [a]you shall divide the land by lot as an
inheritance among your families; to the larger you
shall give a larger inheritance, and to the smaller
you shall give a smaller inheritance; there everyone's *inheritance* shall be whatever falls to him by
lot. You shall inherit according to the tribes of
your fathers.
55 'But if you do not drive out the inhabitants of
the land from before you, then it shall be that
those whom you let remain *shall be* [a]irritants in
your eyes and thorns in your sides, and they shall
harass you in the land where you dwell.
56 'Moreover it shall be *that* I will do to you as I
thought to do to them.' "

## *The Borders of Canaan*

**34** Then the LORD spoke to Moses, saying,
2 "Command the children of Israel, and say
to them: 'When you come into [a]the land of Canaan, this *is* the land that shall fall to you as an
inheritance—the land of Canaan to its boundaries.
3 [a]'Your southern border shall be from the Wilderness of Zin along the border of Edom; then
your southern border shall extend eastward to the
end of [b]the Salt Sea;
4 'your border shall turn from the southern side
of [a]the Ascent of Akrabbim, continue to Zin, and
be on the south of [b]Kadesh Barnea; then it shall go
on to [c]Hazar Addar, and continue to Azmon;
5 'the border shall turn from Azmon [a]to the
Brook of Egypt, and it shall end at the Sea.
**6** 'As for the [a]western border, you shall have the
Great Sea for a border; this shall be your western
border.
**7** 'And this shall be your northern border: From
the Great Sea you shall mark out your *border* line
to [a]Mount Hor;
8 'from Mount Hor you shall mark out *your
border* [a]to the entrance of Hamath; then the
direction of the border shall be toward [b]Zedad;
9 'the border shall proceed to Ziphron, and it
shall end at [a]Hazar Enan. This shall be your
northern border.
**10** 'You shall mark out your eastern border from
Hazar Enan to Shepham;
11 'the border shall go down from Shepham [a]to
Riblah on the east side of Ain; the border shall go
down and reach to the eastern [1]side of the Sea [b]of
Chinnereth;
12 'the border shall go down along the Jordan,
and it shall end at [a]the Salt Sea. This shall be your
land with its surrounding boundaries.' "
**13** Then Moses commanded the children of Israel, saying: [a]"This *is* the land which you shall
inherit by lot, which the LORD has commanded to
give to the nine tribes and to the half-tribe.
14 [a]"For the tribe of the children of Reuben
according to the house of their fathers, and the
tribe of the children of Gad according to the house
of their fathers, have received *their inheritance;*
and the half-tribe of Manasseh has received its
inheritance.
15 "The two tribes and the half-tribe have received their inheritance on this side of the Jordan,
*across from* Jericho eastward, toward the sunrise."
**16** And the LORD spoke to Moses, saying,
17 "These *are* the names of the men who shall
divide the land among you as an inheritance:
[a]Eleazar the priest and Joshua the son of Nun.
18 "And you shall take one [a]leader of every tribe
to divide the land for the inheritance.
19 "These *are* the names of the men: from the
tribe of Judah, Caleb the son of Jephunneh;
20 "from the tribe of the children of Simeon,
Shemuel the son of Ammihud;
21 "from the tribe of Benjamin, Elidad the son of
Chislon;

**30** [a]Deut. 10:6
**32** [a]Deut. 10:6 [b]Deut. 10:7
**35** [a]Deut. 2:8; 1 Kin. 9:26; 22:48
**36** [a]Num. 20:1; 27:14
**37** [a]Num. 20:22, 23; 21:4
**38** [a]Num. 20:25, 28; Deut. 10:6; 32:50
**40** [a]Num. 21:1
**43** [a]Num. 21:10
**44** [a]Num. 21:11
**45** [a]Num. 32:34 [1]Same as *Ije Abarim,* v. 44
**46** [a]Jer. 48:22; Ezek. 6:14
**47** [a]Num. 21:20; Deut. 32:49
**48** [a]Num. 22:1; 31:12; 35:1
**49** [a]Num. 25:1; Josh. 2:1 [1]Heb. *Abel Shittim*
**51** [a]Deut. 7:1, 2; 9:1; Josh. 3:17
**52** [a]Ex. 23:24, 33; 34:13; Deut. 7:2, 5; 12:3; Judg. 2:2; Ps. 106:34–36 [1]Places for pagan worship
**53** [a]Deut. 11:31; Josh. 21:43
**54** [a]Num. 26:53–56
**55** [a]Josh. 23:13; Judg. 2:3

CHAPTER 34
**2** [a]Gen. 17:8; Deut. 1:7, 8; Ps. 78:54, 55; 105:11
**3** [a]Josh. 15:1–3; Ezek. 47:13, 19 [b]Gen. 14:3; Josh. 15:2
**4** [a]Josh. 15:3 [b]Num. 13:26; 32:8 [c]Josh. 15:3, 4
**5** [a]Gen. 15:18; Josh. 15:4, 47; 1 Kin. 8:65; Is. 27:12
**6** [a]Ex. 23:31; Josh. 15:12; Ezek. 47:20
**7** [a]Num. 33:37
**8** [a]Num. 13:21; Josh. 13:5; 2 Kin. 14:25 [b]Ezek. 47:15
**9** [a]Ezek. 47:17
**11** [a]2 Kin. 23:33; Jer. 39:5, 6 [b]Deut. 3:17; Josh. 11:2; 12:3; 13:27; 19:35; Matt. 14:34; Luke 5:1 [1]Lit. *shoulder*
**12** [a]Num. 34:3
**13** [a]Gen. 15:18; Num. 26:52–56; Deut. 11:24; Josh. 14:1–5
**14** [a]Num. 32:33
**17** [a]Josh. 14:1, 2; 19:51
**18** [a]Num. 1:4, 16

22 "a leader from the tribe of the children of Dan,
Bukki the son of Jogli;
23 "from the sons of Joseph: a leader from the
tribe of the children of Manasseh, Hanniel the son
of Ephod,
24 "and a leader from the tribe of the children
of Ephraim, Kemuel the son of Shiphtan;
25 "a leader from the tribe of the children of
Zebulun, Elizaphan the son of Parnach;
26 "a leader from the tribe of the children
of Issachar, Paltiel the son of Azzan;
27 "a leader from the tribe of the children of
Asher, Ahihud the son of Shelomi;
28 "and a leader from the tribe of the children
of Naphtali, Pedahel the son of Ammihud."
29 These *are* the ones the LORD commanded to
[1]divide the inheritance among the children of
Israel in the land of Canaan.

### *The Laws Concerning Murder and Bloodshed*

**35** And the LORD spoke to Moses in [a]the plains
of Moab by the Jordan *across from* Jericho,
saying:
2 [a]"Command the children of Israel that they
give the Levites cities to dwell in from the inheritance of their possession, and you shall *also* give
the Levites [b]common-land around the cities.
3 "They shall have the cities to dwell in; and
their common-land shall be for their cattle, for
their herds, and for all their animals.
4 "The common-land of the cities which you
will give the Levites *shall extend* from the wall of
the city outward a thousand cubits all around.
5 "And you shall measure outside the city on
the east side two thousand cubits, on the south
side two thousand cubits, on the west side two
thousand cubits, and on the north side two thousand cubits. The city *shall be* in the middle. This
shall belong to them as common-land for the
cities.
6 "Now among the cities which you will give to
the Levites *you shall appoint* [a]six cities of refuge,
to which a manslayer may flee. And to these you
shall add forty-two cities.
7 "So all the cities you will give to the Levites
*shall be* [a]forty-eight; these *you shall give* with
their common-land.
8 "And the cities which you will give *shall be*
[a]from the possession of the children of Israel;
[b]from the larger *tribe* you shall give many, from
the smaller you shall give few. Each shall give
some of its cities to the Levites, in proportion to
the inheritance that each receives."
**9** Then the LORD spoke to Moses, saying,
10 "Speak to the children of Israel, and say to
them: [a]'When you cross the Jordan into the land
of Canaan,
11 'then [a]you shall appoint cities to be cities of
refuge for you, that the manslayer who kills any
person accidentally may flee there.
12 [a]'They shall be cities of refuge for you from
the avenger, that the manslayer may not die until
he stands before the congregation in judgment.
13 'And of the cities which you give, you shall
have [a]six cities of refuge.
14 [a]'You shall appoint three cities on this side of
the Jordan, and three cities you shall appoint in
the land of Canaan, *which* will be cities of refuge.
15 'These six cities shall be for refuge for the
children of Israel, [a]for the stranger, and for the
sojourner among them, that anyone who kills a
person accidentally may flee there.
**16** [a]'But if he strikes him with an iron implement,
so that he dies, he *is* a murderer; the murderer
shall surely be put to death.
17 'And if he strikes him with a stone in the hand,
by which one could die, and he does die, he *is* a
murderer; the murderer shall surely be put to
death.
18 'Or *if* he strikes him with a wooden hand
weapon, by which one could die, and he does die,
he *is* a murderer; the murderer shall surely be put
to death.
19 [a]'The[1] avenger of blood himself shall put the
murderer to death; when he meets him, he shall
put him to death.
20 [a]'If he pushes him out of hatred or, [b]while
lying in wait, hurls something at him so that he
dies,
21 'or in enmity he strikes him with his hand so
that he dies, the one who struck *him* shall surely
be put to death; he *is* a murderer. The avenger of
blood shall put the murderer to death when he
meets him.
**22** 'However, if he pushes him suddenly [a]without
enmity, or throws anything at him without lying
in wait,
23 'or uses a stone, by which a man could die,
throwing *it* at him without seeing *him*, so that he
dies, while he was not his enemy or seeking his
harm,
24 'then [a]the congregation shall judge between
the manslayer and the avenger of blood according
to these judgments.
25 'So the congregation shall deliver the manslayer from the hand of the avenger of blood, and
the congregation shall return him to the city of
refuge where he had fled, and [a]he shall remain
there until the death of the high priest [b]who was
anointed with the holy oil.
26 'But if the manslayer at any time goes outside
the limits of the city of refuge where he fled,
27 'and the avenger of blood finds him outside
the limits of his city of refuge, and the avenger of
blood kills the manslayer, he shall not be guilty of
[1]blood,
28 'because he should have remained in his city
of refuge until the death of the high priest. But
after the death of the high priest the manslayer
may return to the land of his possession.
**29** 'And these *things* shall be [a]a statute of judgment to you throughout your generations in all
your dwellings.
30 'Whoever kills a person, the murderer shall be
put to death on the [a]testimony of witnesses; but
one witness is not *sufficient* testimony against a
person for the death *penalty*.
31 'Moreover you shall take no ransom for the
life of a murderer who *is* guilty of death, but he
shall surely be put to death.
32 'And you shall take no ransom for him who
has fled to his city of refuge, that he may return to
dwell in the land before the death of the priest.
33 'So you shall not pollute the land where you
*are*; for blood [a]defiles the land, and no [1]atone-
ment can be made for the land, for the blood
that is shed on it, except [b]by the blood of him who
shed it.

**29** [1]*apportion*

CHAPTER 35
**1** [a]Num. 33:50
**2** [a]Josh. 14:3, 4; 21:2, 3; Ezek. 45:1; 48:10–20 [b]Lev. 25:22–34
**6** [a]Deut. 4:41; Josh. 20:2, 7, 8; 21:3, 13
**7** [a]Josh. 21:41
**8** [a]Josh. 21:3 [b]Num. 26:54; 33:54
**10** [a]Deut. 19:2; Josh. 20:1–9
**11** [a]Ex. 21:13; Num. 35:22–25; Deut. 19:1–13
**12** [a]Deut. 19:6; Josh. 20:3, 5, 6
**13** [a]Num. 35:6
**14** [a]Deut. 4:41; Josh. 20:8
**15** [a]Num. 15:16
**16** [a]Ex. 21:12, 14; Lev. 24:17; Deut. 19:11, 12
**19** [a]Num. 35:21, 24, 27; Deut. 19:6, 12 [1]A family member who is to avenge the victim
**20** [a]Gen. 4:8; 2 Sam. 3:27; 20:10; 1 Kin. 2:31, 32 [b]Ex. 21:14; Deut. 19:11, 12
**22** [a]Ex. 21:13
**24** [a]Num. 35:12; Josh. 20:6
**25** [a]Josh. 20:6 [b]Ex. 29:7; Lev. 4:3; 21:10
**27** [1]Murder
**29** [a]Num. 27:11
**30** [a]Deut. 17:6; 19:15; Matt. 18:16; John 7:51; 8:17, 18; 2 Cor. 13:1; Heb. 10:28
**33** [a]Deut. 21:7, 8; Ps. 106:38 [b]Gen. 9:6 [1]Lit. *covering*

34 'Therefore [a]do not defile the land which you
inhabit, in the midst of which I dwell; for [b]I the
LORD dwell among the children of Israel.' "

### *Marriage Within the Tribe*

**36** Now the chief fathers of the families of the
[a]children of Gilead the son of Machir, the
son of Manasseh, of the families of the sons of
Joseph, came near and [b]spoke before Moses and
before the leaders, the chief fathers of the children
of Israel.
2 And they said: [a]"The LORD commanded my
lord *Moses* to give the land as an inheritance by
lot to the children of Israel, and [b]my lord was
commanded by the LORD to give the inheritance
of our brother Zelophehad to his daughters.
3 "Now if they are married to any of the sons of
the *other* tribes of the children of Israel, then their
inheritance will be [a]taken from the inheritance of
our fathers, and it will be added to the inheritance
of the tribe into which they marry; so it will be
taken from the lot of our inheritance.
4 "And when [a]the Jubilee of the children of
Israel comes, then their inheritance will be added
to the inheritance of the tribe into which they
marry; so their inheritance will be taken away
from the inheritance of the tribe of our fathers."
**5** Then Moses commanded the children of Israel
according to the word of the LORD, saying: [a]"What
the tribe of the sons of Joseph speaks is right.
6 "This *is* what the LORD commands concerning
the daughters of Zelophehad, saying, 'Let them
[1]marry whom they think best, [a]but they may
marry only within the family of their father's
tribe.'
7 "So the inheritance of the children of Israel
shall not change hands from tribe to tribe, for
every one of the children of Israel shall [a]keep the
inheritance of the tribe of his fathers.
8 "And [a]every daughter who possesses an inheritance in any tribe of the children of Israel shall be
the wife of one of the family of her father's tribe,
so that the children of Israel each may possess the
inheritance of his fathers.
9 "Thus no inheritance shall change hands from
*one* tribe to another, but every tribe of the children of Israel shall keep its own inheritance."
**10** Just as the LORD commanded Moses, so did
the daughters of Zelophehad;
**11** [a]for Mahlah, Tirzah, Hoglah, Milcah, and
Noah, the daughters of Zelophehad, were married
to the sons of their father's brothers.
**12** They were married into the families of the
children of Manasseh the son of Joseph, and their
inheritance remained in the tribe of their father's
family.
**13** These *are* the commandments and the judgments which the LORD commanded the children of
Israel by the hand of Moses [a]in the plains of Moab
by the Jordan, *across from* Jericho.

**34** [a]Lev. 18:24, 25; Deut. 21:23 [b]Ex. 29:45, 46

CHAPTER 36

**1** [a]Num. 26:29 [b]Num. 27:1–11
**2** [a]Num. 26:55; 33:54; Josh. 17:4 [b]Num. 27:1, 5–7
**3** [a]Num. 27:4
**4** [a]Lev. 25:10
**5** [a]Num. 27:7
**6** [a]Num. 36:11, 12 [1]Lit. *be wives to*
**7** [a]1 Kin. 21:3
**8** [a]1 Chr. 23:22
**11** [a]Num. 26:33; 27:1
**13** [a]Num. 26:3; 33:50

*The Fifth Book of Moses Called*

# DEUTERONOMY

### *Moses Reviews Israel's Disobedience*

THESE *are* the words which Moses spoke to
all Israel [a]on this side of the Jordan in the
wilderness, in the [1]plain opposite [2]Suph,
between Paran, Tophel, Laban, Hazeroth, and
Dizahab.
2 *It is* eleven days' *journey* from Horeb by way
of Mount Seir [a]to Kadesh Barnea.
3 Now it came to pass [a]in the fortieth year, in
the eleventh month, on the first *day* of the month,
*that* Moses spoke to the children of Israel according to all that the LORD had given him as commandments to them,
4 [a]after he had killed Sihon king of the Amorites, who dwelt in Heshbon, and Og king of
Bashan, who dwelt at Ashtaroth [b]in[1] Edrei.
5 On this side of the Jordan in the land of Moab,
Moses began to explain this law, saying,
6 "The LORD our God spoke to us [a]in Horeb,
saying: 'You have dwelt long [b]enough at this
mountain.
7 'Turn and take your journey, and go to the
mountains of the Amorites, to all the neighboring
*places* in the [1]plain, in the mountains and in the
lowland, in the South and on the seacoast, to the
land of the Canaanites and to Lebanon, as far as
the great river, the River Euphrates.
8 'See, I have set the land before you; go in and
possess the land which the LORD [1]swore to your
fathers—to [a]Abraham, Isaac, and Jacob—to give
to them and their descendants after them.'
**9** "And [a]I spoke to you at that time, saying: 'I
[1]alone am not able to bear you.
10 'The LORD your God has multiplied you, [a]and
here you *are* today, as the stars of heaven in
multitude.
11 [a]'May the LORD God of your fathers make you
a thousand times more numerous than you are,
and bless you [b]as He has promised you!
12 [a]'How can I alone bear your problems and
your burdens and your complaints?
13 'Choose wise, understanding, and knowledgeable men from among your tribes, and I will make
them [1]heads over you.'
14 "And you answered me and said, 'The thing
which you have told *us* to do *is* good.'
15 "So I took [a]the heads of your tribes, wise and
knowledgeable men, and [1]made them heads over
you, leaders of thousands, leaders of hundreds,
leaders of fifties, leaders of tens, and officers for
your tribes.
16 "Then I commanded your judges at that time,
saying, 'Hear *the cases* between your brethren,
and [a]judge righteously between a man and his
[b]brother or the stranger who is with him.
17 [a]'You shall not show partiality in judgment;
you shall hear the small as well as the great; you
shall not be afraid in any man's presence, for [b]the
judgment *is* God's. The case that is too hard for
you, [c]bring to me, and I will hear it.'
18 "And I commanded you at that time all the
things which you should do.

CHAPTER 1

**1** [a]Deut. 4:44–46 [1]Heb. *arabah* [2]LXX ms., Tg., Vg. *Red Sea*
**2** [a]Num. 13:26; 32:8
**3** [a]Num. 33:38
**4** [a]Num. 21:23, 24, 33–35 [b]Josh. 13:12 [1]LXX, Syr., Vg. *and;* cf. Josh. 12:4
**6** [a]Ex. 3:1, 12 [b]Ex. 19:1, 2
**7** [1]Heb. *arabah*
**8** [a]Gen. 12:7; 15:5; 22:17; 26:3; 28:13 [1]*promised*
**9** [a]Ex. 18:18, 24 [1]*am not able to bear you by myself*
**10** [a]Gen. 15:5; 22:17
**11** [a]2 Sam. 24:3 [b]Gen. 15:5
**12** [a]1 Kin. 3:8, 9
**13** [1]*rulers*
**15** [a]Ex. 18:25 [1]*appointed*
**16** [a]Deut. 16:18 [b]Lev. 24:22
**17** [a]Prov. 24:23–26 [b]2 Chr. 19:6 [c]Ex. 18:22, 26

**19** "So we departed from Horeb, [a]and went through all that great and terrible wilderness which you saw on the way to the mountains of the Amorites, as the LORD our God had commanded us. Then [b]we came to Kadesh Barnea.
20 "And I said to you, 'You have come to the mountains of the Amorites, which the LORD our God is giving us.
21 'Look, the LORD your God has set the land before you; go up *and* possess *it*, as the LORD God of your fathers has spoken to you; [a]do not fear or be discouraged.'
22 "And every one of you came near to me and said, 'Let us send men before us, and let them search out the land for us, and bring back word to us of the way by which we should go up, and of the cities into which we shall come.'
23 "The plan pleased me well; so [a]I took twelve of your men, one man from *each* tribe.
24 [a]"And they departed and went up into the mountains, and came to the Valley of Eshcol, and spied it out.
25 "They also took *some* of the fruit of the land in their hands and brought *it* down to us; and they brought back word to us, saying, '*It is* a [a]good land which the LORD our God is giving us.'
**26** [a]"Nevertheless you would not go up, but rebelled against the command of the LORD your God;
27 "and you [a]complained in your tents, and said, 'Because the LORD [b]hates us, He has brought us out of the land of Egypt to deliver us into the hand of the Amorites, to destroy us.
28 'Where can we go up? Our brethren have [1]discouraged our hearts, saying, [a]"The people *are* greater and taller than we; the cities *are* great and fortified up to heaven; moreover we have seen the sons of the [b]Anakim there." '
29 "Then I said to you, 'Do not be terrified, [a]or afraid of them.
30 [a]'The LORD your God, who goes before you, He will fight for you, according to all He did for you in Egypt before your eyes,
31 'and in the wilderness where you saw how the LORD your God carried you, as a [a]man carries his son, in all the way that you went until you came to this place.'
32 "Yet, for all that, [a]you did not believe the LORD your God,
33 [a]"who went in the way before you [b]to search out a place for you to pitch your tents, to show you the way you should go, in the fire by night and in the cloud by day.
**34** "And the LORD heard the sound of your words, and was angry, [a]and took an oath, saying,
35 [a]'Surely not one of these men of this evil generation shall see that good land of which I [1]swore to give to your fathers,
36 [a]'except Caleb the son of Jephunneh; he shall see it, and to him and his children I am giving the land on which he walked, because [b]he [1]wholly followed the LORD.'
37 [a]"The LORD was also angry with me for your sakes, saying, 'Even you shall not go in there.
38 [a]'Joshua the son of Nun, [b]who stands before you, he shall go in there. [c]Encourage him, for he shall cause Israel to inherit it.
39 [a]'Moreover your little ones and your children, who [b]you say will be victims, who today [c]have no knowledge of good and evil, they shall go in there; to them I will give it, and they shall possess it.

**19** [a]Deut. 2:7; 8:15; 32:10 [b]Num. 13:26
**21** [a]Josh. 1:6, 9
**23** [a]Num. 13:2, 3
**24** [a]Num. 13:21–25
**25** [a]Num. 13:27
**26** [a]Num. 14:1–4
**27** [a]Ps. 106:25 [b]Deut. 9:28
**28** [a]Deut. 9:1, 2 [b]Num. 13:28 [1]Lit. *melted*
**29** [a]Num. 14:9
**30** [a]Ex. 14:14
**31** [a]Is. 46:3, 4; 63:9
**32** [a]Jude 5
**33** [a]Ex. 13:21 [b]Num. 10:33
**34** [a]Deut. 2:14, 15
**35** [a]Num. 14:22, 23 [1]*promised*
**36** [a][Josh. 14:9] [b]Num. 32:11, 12 [1]*fully*
**37** [a]Deut. 3:26; 4:21; 34:4
**38** [a]Num. 14:30 [b]1 Sam. 16:22 [c]Deut. 31:7, 23
**39** [a]Num. 14:31 [b]Num. 14:3 [c]Is. 7:15, 16
**40** [a]Num. 14:25
**41** [a]Num. 14:40
**42** [a]Num. 14:41–43
**43** [a]Num. 14:44 [b]Deut. 17:12, 13 [1]*willfully*
**44** [a]Ps. 118:12
**46** [a]Deut. 2:7, 14

CHAPTER 2
**1** [a]Deut. 1:40 [b]Num. 14:25 [1]*circled around*
**3** [a]Deut. 2:7, 14
**4** [a]Num. 20:14–21 [b]Deut. 23:7
**5** [a]Gen. 36:8
**7** [a]Deut. 8:2–4 [1]Lit. *goings*
**8** [a]Judg. 11:18 [b]Num. 21:4
**9** [a]Deut. 2:18, 29 [b]Gen. 19:36–38
**10** [a]Gen. 14:5 [b]Deut. 9:2
**11** [1]Heb. *rephaim*
**12** [a]Deut. 2:22 [1]*stead*
**13** [a]Num. 21:12 [1]*Wadi* or *Brook*

40 [a]'But *as for* you, turn and take your journey into the wilderness by the Way of the Red Sea.'
**41** "Then you answered and said to me, [a]'We have sinned against the LORD; we will go up and fight, just as the LORD our God commanded us.' And when everyone of you had girded on his weapons of war, you were ready to go up into the mountain.
42 "And the LORD said to me, 'Tell them, [a]"Do not go up nor fight, for I *am* not among you; lest you be defeated before your enemies." '
43 "So I spoke to you; yet you would not listen, but [a]rebelled against the command of the LORD, and [b]presumptuously[1] went up into the mountain.
44 "And the Amorites who dwelt in that mountain came out against you and chased you [a]as bees do, and drove you back from Seir to Hormah.
45 "Then you returned and wept before the LORD, but the LORD would not listen to your voice nor give ear to you.
46 [a]"So you remained in Kadesh many days, according to the days that you spent *there*.

### *The Desert Years*

**2** "Then we turned and [a]journeyed into the wilderness of the Way of the Red Sea, [b]as the LORD spoke to me, and we [1]skirted Mount Seir for many days.
2 "And the LORD spoke to me, saying:
3 'You have skirted this mountain [a]long enough; turn northward.
4 'And command the people, saying, [a]"You *are about to* pass through the territory of [b]your brethren, the descendants of Esau, who live in Seir; and they will be afraid of you. Therefore watch yourselves carefully.
5 "Do not meddle with them, for I will not give you *any* of their land, no, not so much as one footstep, [a]because I have given Mount Seir to Esau *as* a possession.
6 "You shall buy food from them with money, that you may eat; and you shall also buy water from them with money, that you may drink.
7 "For the LORD your God has blessed you in all the work of your hand. He knows your [1]trudging through this great wilderness. [a]These forty years the LORD your God *has been* with you; you have lacked nothing." '
**8** "And when we passed beyond our brethren, the descendants of Esau who dwell in Seir, away from the road of the plain, away from [a]Elath and Ezion Geber, we [b]turned and passed by way of the Wilderness of Moab.
9 "Then the LORD said to me, 'Do not harass Moab, nor contend with them in battle, for I will not give you *any* of their land *as* a possession, because I have given [a]Ar to [b]the descendants of Lot *as* a possession.' "
10 [a](The Emim had dwelt there in times past, a people as great and numerous and tall as [b]the Anakim.
11 They were also regarded as [1]giants, like the Anakim, but the Moabites call them Emim.
12 [a]The Horites formerly dwelt in Seir, but the descendants of Esau dispossessed them and destroyed them from before them, and dwelt in their [1]place, just as Israel did to the land of their possession which the LORD gave them.)
13 " 'Now rise and cross over [a]the [1]Valley of the Zered.' So we crossed over the Valley of the Zered.

14 "And the time we took to come [a]from Kadesh
Barnea until we crossed over the Valley of the
Zered *was* thirty-eight years, [b]until all the generation of the men of war [1]was consumed from the
midst of the camp, [c]just as the LORD had sworn to
them.
15 "For indeed the hand of the LORD was against
them, to destroy them from the midst of the camp
until they [1]were consumed.
**16** "So it was, when all the men of war had finally
perished from among the people,
17 "that the LORD spoke to me, saying:
18 'This day you are to cross over at Ar, the
boundary of Moab.
19 'And *when* you come near the people of Ammon, do not harass them or meddle with them, for
I will not give you *any* of the land of the people of
Ammon *as* a possession, because I have given it to
[a]the descendants of Lot *as* a possession.' "
20 (That was also regarded as a land of [1]giants;
giants formerly dwelt there. But the Ammonites
call them [a]Zamzummim,
21 [a]a people as great and numerous and tall as
the Anakim. But the LORD destroyed them before
them, and they dispossessed them and dwelt in
their place,
22 just as He had done for the descendants of
Esau, [a]who dwelt in Seir, when He destroyed [b]the
Horites from before them. They dispossessed them
and dwelt in their place, even to this day.
23 And [a]the Avim, who dwelt in villages as far as
Gaza—[b]the Caphtorim, who came from Caphtor,
destroyed them and dwelt in their place.)
**24** " 'Rise, take your journey, and [a]cross over the
River Arnon. Look, I have given into your hand
[b]Sihon the Amorite, king of Heshbon, and his
land. Begin [1]to possess *it,* and engage him in
battle.
25 [a]'This day I will begin to put the dread and
fear of you upon the nations [1]under the whole
heaven, who shall hear the report of you, and shall
[b]tremble and be in anguish because of you.'
**26** "And I [a]sent messengers from the Wilderness
of Kedemoth to Sihon king of Heshbon, [b]with
words of peace, saying,
27 [a]'Let me pass through your land; I will keep
strictly to the road, and I will turn neither to the
right nor to the left.
28 'You shall sell me food for money, that I may
eat, and give me water for money, that I may
drink; [a]only let me pass through on foot,
29 [a]'just as the descendants of Esau who dwell in
Seir and the Moabites who dwell in Ar did for me,
until I cross the Jordan to the land which the
LORD our God is giving us.'
30 [a]"But Sihon king of Heshbon would not let us
pass through, for [b]the LORD your God [c]hardened
his spirit and made his heart obstinate, that He
might deliver him into your hand, as *it is* this day.
31 "And the LORD said to me, 'See, I have begun
to [a]give Sihon and his land over to you. Begin to
possess *it,* that you may inherit his land.'
32 [a]"Then Sihon and all his people came out
against us to fight at Jahaz.
33 "And [a]the LORD our God delivered him [1]over
to us; so [b]we defeated him, his sons, and all his
people.
34 "We took all his cities at that time, and we
[a]utterly destroyed the men, women, and little ones
of every city; we left none remaining.
35 "We took only the livestock as plunder for
ourselves, with the spoil of the cities which we
took.
36 [a]"From Aroer, which *is* on the bank of the
River Arnon, and *from* [b]the city that *is* in the
ravine, as far as Gilead, there was not one city
too strong for us; [c]the LORD our God delivered all
to us.
37 "Only you did not go near the land of the
people of Ammon—anywhere along the River
[a]Jabbok, or to the cities of the mountains, or
[b]wherever the LORD our God had forbidden us.

### *Israel Conquers Og of Bashan*

**3** "Then we turned and went up the road to
Bashan; and [a]Og king of Bashan came out
against us, he and all his people, to battle [b]at
Edrei.
2 "And the LORD said to me, 'Do not fear him,
for I have delivered him and all his people and his
land into your hand; you shall do to him as you
did to [a]Sihon king of the Amorites, who dwelt at
Heshbon.'
3 "So the LORD our God also delivered into our
hands Og king of Bashan, with all his people, and
we [1]attacked him until he had no survivors remaining.
4 "And we took all his cities at that time; there
was not a city which we did not take from them:
sixty cities, [a]all the region of Argob, the kingdom
of Og in Bashan.
5 "All these cities *were* fortified with high walls,
gates, and bars, besides a great many rural towns.
6 "And we utterly destroyed them, as we did to
Sihon king [a]of Heshbon, utterly destroying the
men, women, and children of every city.
7 "But all the livestock and the spoil of the cities
we took as booty for ourselves.
8 "And at that time we took the [a]land from the
hand of the two kings of the Amorites who *were*
on this side of the Jordan, from the River Arnon to
Mount [b]Hermon
9 "(the Sidonians call [a]Hermon Sirion, and the
Amorites call it Senir),
10 [a]"all the cities of the plain, all Gilead, and [b]all
Bashan, as far as Salcah and Edrei, cities of the
kingdom of Og in Bashan.
11 [a]"For only Og king of Bashan remained of the
remnant of [b]the [1]giants. Indeed his bedstead *was*
an iron bedstead. (*Is* it not in [c]Rabbah of the
people of Ammon?) Nine cubits *is* its length and
four cubits its width, according to the standard
cubit.
**12** "And this [a]land, *which* we possessed at that
time, [b]from Aroer, which *is* by the River Arnon,
and half the mountains of Gilead and [c]its cities, I
gave to the Reubenites and the Gadites.
13 [a]"The rest of Gilead, and all Bashan, the
kingdom of Og, I gave to half the tribe of Manasseh. (All the region of Argob, with all Bashan, was
called the land of the [1]giants.
14 [a]"Jair the son of Manasseh took all the region
of Argob, [b]as far as the border of the Geshurites
and the Maachathites, and [c]called Bashan after his
own name, [1]Havoth Jair, to this day.)
15 "Also I gave [a]Gilead to Machir.
16 "And to the Reubenites [a]and the Gadites I
gave from Gilead as far as the River Arnon, the
middle of the river as *the* border, as far as the
River Jabbok, [b]the border of the people of Ammon;
17 "the plain also, with the Jordan as *the* border,

**14** [a]Num. 13:26 [b]Deut. 1:34, 35 [c]Num. 14:35 [1]*perished*
**15** [1]*perished*
**19** [a]Gen. 19:38
**20** [a]Gen. 14:5 [1]Heb. *rephaim*
**21** [a]Deut. 2:10
**22** [a]Gen. 36:8 [b]Gen. 14:6; 36:20–30
**23** [a]Josh. 13:3 [b]Gen. 10:14
**24** [a]Judg. 11:18 [b]Deut. 1:4 [1]*to take possession*
**25** [a]Ex. 23:27 [b]Ex. 15:14–16 [1]*everywhere under the heavens*
**26** [a]Num. 21:21–32 [b]Deut. 20:10
**27** [a]Judg. 11:19
**28** [a]Num. 20:19
**29** [a]Deut. 23:3, 4
**30** [a]Num. 21:23 [b]Josh. 11:20 [c]Ex. 4:21
**31** [a]Deut. 1:3, 8
**32** [a]Num. 21:23
**33** [a]Deut. 7:2 [b]Num. 21:24 [1]Lit. *before us*
**34** [a]Lev. 27:28
**36** [a]Deut. 3:12; 4:48 [b]Josh. 13:9, 16 [c]Ps. 44:3
**37** [a]Gen. 32:22 [b]Deut. 2:5, 9, 19

CHAPTER 3
**1** [a]Num. 21:33–35 [b]Deut. 1:4
**2** [a]Num. 21:34
**3** [1]*struck*
**4** [a]Deut. 3:13, 14
**6** [a]Deut. 2:24, 34, 35
**8** [a]Josh. 12:6; 13:8–12 [b]Deut. 4:48
**9** [a]1 Chr. 5:23
**10** [a]Deut. 4:49 [b]Josh. 12:5; 13:11
**11** [a]Amos 2:9 [b]Deut. 2:11, 20 [c]Jer. 49:2 [1]Heb. *rephaim*
**12** [a]Num. 32:33 [b]Deut. 2:36 [c]Num. 34:14
**13** [a]Josh. 13:29–31; 17:1 [1]Heb. *rephaim*
**14** [a]1 Chr. 2:22 [b]Josh. 13:13 [c]Num. 32:41 [1]Lit. *Towns of Jair*
**15** [a]Num. 32:39, 40
**16** [a]2 Sam. 24:5 [b]Num. 21:24

from Chinnereth [a]as far as the east side of the Sea
of the Arabah [b](the Salt Sea), below the slopes of
Pisgah.
**18** "Then I commanded you at that time, saying:
'The LORD your God has given you this land to
possess. [a]All you men of valor shall cross over
armed before your brethren, the children of Israel.
19 'But your wives, your little ones, and your
livestock (I know that you have much livestock)
shall stay in your cities which I have given you,
20 'until the LORD has given [a]rest to your brethren as to you, and they also possess the land
which the LORD your God is giving them beyond
the Jordan. Then each of you may [b]return to his
possession which I have given you.'
21 "And [a]I commanded Joshua at that time,
saying, 'Your eyes have seen all that the LORD
your God has done to these two kings; so will the
LORD do to all the kingdoms through which you
pass.
22 'You must not fear them, for [a]the LORD your
God Himself fights for you.'
**23** "Then [a]I pleaded with the LORD at that time,
saying:
24 'O Lord GOD, You have begun to show Your
servant [a]Your greatness and Your [1]mighty hand,
for [b]what god *is there* in heaven or on earth who
can do *anything* like Your works and Your
mighty *deeds?*
25 'I pray, let me cross over and see [a]the good
land beyond the Jordan, those pleasant mountains, and Lebanon.'
26 "But the LORD [a]was angry with me on your
account, and would not listen to me. So the LORD
said to me: 'Enough of that! Speak no more to Me
of this matter.
27 [a]'Go up to the top of Pisgah, and lift your eyes
toward the west, the north, the south, and the
east; behold *it* with your eyes, for you shall not
cross over this Jordan.
28 'But [a]command[1] Joshua, and encourage him
and strengthen him; for he shall go over before
this people, and he shall cause them to inherit the
land which you will see.'
29 "So we stayed in [a]the valley opposite Beth
Peor.

### *Warning Against Idolatry*

**4** "Now, O Israel, listen to [a]the statutes and the
judgments which I teach you to observe, that
you may live, and go in and [1]possess the land
which the LORD God of your fathers is giving you.
2 [a]"You shall not add to the word which I
command you, nor take from it, that you may
keep the commandments of the LORD your God
which I command you.
3 "Your eyes have seen what the LORD did at
[a]Baal Peor; for the LORD your God has destroyed
from among you all the men who followed Baal of
Peor.
4 "But you who held fast to the LORD your God
*are* alive today, every one of you.
5 "Surely I have taught you statutes and judgments, just as the LORD my God commanded me,
that you should act according *to them* in the land
which you go to possess.
6 "Therefore be careful to observe *them;* for this
*is* [a]your wisdom and your understanding in the
sight of the peoples who will hear all these statutes, and say, 'Surely this great nation *is* a wise
and understanding people.'
7 "For [a]what great nation *is there* that has [b]God[1]
*so* near to it, as the LORD our God *is* to us, for
whatever *reason* we may call upon Him?
8 "And what great nation *is there* that has *such*
statutes and righteous judgments as are in all this
law which I set before you this day?
**9** "Only take heed to yourself, and diligently
[a]keep yourself, lest you [b]forget the things your
eyes have seen, and lest they depart from your
heart all the days of your life. And [c]teach them to
your children and your grandchildren,
10 "*especially concerning* [a]the day you stood
before the LORD your God in Horeb, when the
LORD said to me, 'Gather the people to Me, and I
will let them hear My words, that they may learn
to fear Me all the days they live on the earth, and
*that* they may teach their children.'
11 "Then you came near and stood at the foot of
the mountain, and the mountain burned with fire
to the midst of heaven, with darkness, cloud, and
thick darkness.
12 [a]"And the LORD spoke to you out of the midst
of the fire. You heard the sound of the words, but
saw no [1]form; [b]*you* only *heard* a voice.
13 [a]"So He declared to you His covenant which
He commanded you to perform, [b]the Ten Commandments; and [c]He wrote them on two tablets of
stone.
14 "And [a]the LORD commanded me at that time
to teach you statutes and judgments, that you
might [1]observe them in the land which you cross
over to possess.
**15** [a]"Take careful heed to yourselves, for you saw
no [b]form when the LORD spoke to you at Horeb
out of the midst of the fire,
16 "lest you [a]act corruptly and [b]make for yourselves a carved image in the [1]form of any figure:
[c]the likeness of male or female,
17 "the likeness of any animal that *is* on the
earth or the likeness of any winged bird that flies
in the air,
18 "the likeness of anything that creeps on the
ground or the likeness of any fish that *is* in the
water beneath the earth.
19 "And *take heed,* lest you [a]lift your eyes to
heaven, and *when* you see the sun, the moon, and
the stars, [b]all the host of heaven, you feel driven
to [c]worship them and serve them, which the LORD
your God has [1]given to all the peoples under the
whole heaven as a heritage.
20 "But the LORD has taken you and [a]brought
you out of the iron furnace, out of Egypt, to be
[b]His people, an inheritance, as you are this day.
21 "Furthermore [a]the LORD was angry with me
for your sakes, and swore that [b]I would not cross
over the Jordan, and that I would not enter the
good land which the LORD your God is giving you
as an inheritance.
22 "But [a]I must die in this land, [b]I must not cross
over the Jordan; but you shall cross over and
[1]possess [c]that good land.
23 "Take heed to yourselves, lest you forget the
covenant of the LORD your God which He made
with you, [a]and make for yourselves a carved
image in the form of anything which the LORD
your God has forbidden you.
24 "For [a]the LORD your God *is* a consuming fire,
[b]a jealous God.
**25** "When you beget children and grandchildren
and have grown old in the land, and act corruptly
and make a carved image in the form of anything,

**17** [a]Num. 34:11, 12 [b]Gen. 14:3
**18** [a]Num. 32:20
**20** [a]Deut. 12:9, 10 [b]Josh. 22:4
**21** [a][Num. 27:22, 23]
**22** [a]Ex. 14:14
**23** [a][2 Cor. 12:8, 9]
**24** [a]Deut. 5:24; 11:2 [b]2 Sam. 7:22 [1]*strong*
**25** [a]Deut. 4:22
**26** [a]Num. 20:12; 27:14
**27** [a]Num. 23:14; 27:12
**28** [a]Num. 27:18, 23 [1]*charge*
**29** [a]Deut. 4:46; 34:6

CHAPTER 4

**1** [a][Rom. 10:5] [1]*take possession of*
**2** [a]Prov. 30:6
**3** [a]Num. 25:1–9
**6** [a][2 Tim. 3:15]
**7** [a][2 Sam. 7:23] [b][Is. 55:6] [1]Or *a god*
**9** [a]Prov. 4:23 [b]Deut. 29:2–8 [c]Gen. 18:19
**10** [a]Ex. 19:9, 16, 17
**12** [a]Deut. 5:4, 22 [b]1 Kin. 19:11–18 [1]*similitude*
**13** [a]Deut. 9:9, 11 [b]Ex. 34:28 [c]Ex. 24:12
**14** [a]Ex. 21:1 [1]*do* or *perform*
**15** [a]Josh. 23:11 [b]Is. 40:18
**16** [a]Deut. 9:12; 31:29 [b]Ex. 20:4, 5 [c]Rom. 1:23 [1]*similitude*
**19** [a]Deut. 17:3 [b]2 Kin. 21:3 [c][Rom. 1:25] [1]*divided*
**20** [a]Jer. 11:4 [b]Deut. 7:6; 27:9
**21** [a]Num. 20:12 [b]Num. 27:13, 14
**22** [a]2 Pet. 1:13–15 [b]Deut. 3:27 [c]Deut. 3:25 [1]*take possession of*
**23** [a]Deut. 4:16
**24** [a]Deut. 9:3 [b]Ex. 20:5; 34:14

and [a]do evil in the sight of the LORD your God to
provoke Him to anger,
26 [a]"I call heaven and earth to witness against
you this day, that you will soon utterly perish
from the land which you cross over the Jordan to
possess; you will not [1]prolong *your* days in it, but
will be utterly destroyed.
27 "And the LORD [a]will scatter you among the
peoples, and you will be left few in number among
the nations where the LORD will drive you.
28 "And [a]there you will serve gods, the work of
men's hands, wood and stone, [b]which neither see
nor hear nor eat nor smell.
29 [a]"But from there you will seek the LORD your
God, and you will find *Him* if you seek Him with
all your heart and with all your soul.
30 "When you are in [1]distress, and all these
things come upon you in the [a]latter days, when
you [b]turn to the LORD your God and obey His
voice
31 "(for the LORD your God *is* a merciful God), He
will not forsake you nor [a]destroy you, nor forget
the covenant of your fathers which He swore to
them.
**32** "For [a]ask now concerning the days that are
past, which were before you, since the day that
God created man on the earth, and *ask* [b]from one
end of heaven to the other, whether *any* great
*thing* like this has happened, or *anything* like it
has been heard.
33 [a]"Did *any* people *ever* hear the voice of God
speaking out of the midst of the fire, as you have
heard, and live?
34 "Or did God *ever* try to go *and* take for
Himself a nation from the midst of *another* nation,
[a]by trials, [b]by signs, by wonders, by war, [c]by a
mighty hand and [d]an outstretched arm, [e]and by
great [1]terrors, according to all that the LORD your
God did for you in Egypt before your eyes?
35 "To you it was shown, that you might know
that the LORD Himself *is* God; [a]*there is* none other
besides Him.
36 [a]"Out of heaven He let you hear His voice,
that He might instruct you; on earth He showed
you His great fire, and you heard His words out of
the midst of the fire.
37 "And because [a]He loved your fathers, therefore He chose their [1]descendants after them; and
[b]He brought you out of Egypt with His Presence,
with His mighty power,
38 [a]"driving out from before you nations greater
and mightier than you, to bring you in, to give you
their land *as* an inheritance, as *it is* this day.
39 "Therefore know this day, and consider *it* in
your heart, that [a]the LORD Himself *is* God in
heaven above and on the earth beneath; *there is*
no other.
40 [a]"You shall therefore keep His statutes and
His commandments which I command you today,
that [1]it may go well with you and with your
children after you, and that you may [2]prolong
*your* days in the land which the LORD your God is
giving you for all time."
**41** Then Moses [a]set apart three cities on this side
of the Jordan, toward the rising of the sun,
42 [a]that the manslayer might flee there, who kills
his neighbor unintentionally, without having
hated him in time past, and that by fleeing to one
of these cities he might live:
43 [a]Bezer in the wilderness on the plateau for the

25 [a]2 Kin. 17:17
26 [a]Deut. 30:18, 19 [1]*live long on it*
27 [a]Deut. 28:62
28 [a]Jer. 16:13 [b]Ps. 115:4–7; 135:15–17
29 [a][2 Chr. 15:4]
30 [a]Hos. 3:5 [b]Joel 2:12 [1]*tribulation*
31 [a]Jer. 30:11
32 [a]Job 8:8 [b]Matt. 24:31
33 [a]Deut. 5:24–26
34 [a]Deut. 7:19 [b]Ex. 7:3 [c]Ex. 13:3 [d]Ex. 6:6 [e]Deut. 26:8 [1]*calamities*
35 [a]Mark 12:32
36 [a]Heb. 12:19, 25
37 [a]Deut. 7:7, 8; 10:15; 33:3 [b]Ex. 13:3, 9, 14 [1]Lit. *seed*
38 [a]Deut. 7:1
39 [a]Josh. 2:11
40 [a]Lev. 22:31 [1]*you may prosper* [2]*live long*
41 [a]Num. 35:6
42 [a]Deut. 19:4
43 [a]Josh. 20:8
46 [a]Deut. 3:29 [b]Num. 21:24 [1]*struck*
47 [a]Num. 21:33–35 [1]*east*
48 [a]Deut. 2:36; 3:12 [b]Deut. 3:9 [1]Syr. *Sirion*
49 [a]Deut. 3:17

CHAPTER 5

2 [a]Ex. 19:5
3 [a]Heb. 8:9
4 [a]Ex. 19:9
5 [a]Gal. 3:19 [b]Ex. 19:16
6 [a]Ex. 20:2–17 [1]*slavery*
7 [a]Hos. 13:4 [1]*besides*
8 [a]Ex. 20:4
9 [a]Ex. 34:7, 14–16 [1]*worship them* [2]*punishing*
10 [a]Dan. 9:4 [1]*observe*
11 [a]Ex. 20:7 [1]*innocent*
12 [a]Ex. 20:8 [1]*sanctify it*
13 [a]Ex. 23:12; 35:2
14 [a][Heb. 4:4]

Reubenites, Ramoth in Gilead for the Gadites, and
Golan in Bashan for the Manassites.
**44** Now this *is* the law which Moses set before
the children of Israel.
45 These *are* the testimonies, the statutes, and
the judgments which Moses spoke to the children
of Israel after they came out of Egypt,
46 on this side of the Jordan, [a]in the valley
opposite Beth Peor, in the land of Sihon king of
the Amorites, who dwelt at Heshbon, whom Moses and the children of Israel [b]defeated[1] after they
came out of Egypt.
47 And they took possession of his land and the
land [a]of Og king of Bashan, two kings of the
Amorites, who *were* on this side of the Jordan,
toward the [1]rising of the sun,
48 [a]from Aroer, which *is* on the bank of the River
Arnon, even to Mount [1]Sion (that is, [b]Hermon),
49 and all the plain on the east side of the Jordan
as far as the Sea of the Arabah, below the [a]slopes
of Pisgah.

## *The Ten Commandments*

**5** And Moses called all Israel, and said to them:
"Hear, O Israel, the statutes and judgments
which I speak in your hearing today, that you
may learn them and be careful to observe them.
2 [a]"The LORD our God made a covenant with us
in Horeb.
3 "The LORD [a]did not make this covenant with
our fathers, but with us, those who *are* here today,
all of us who *are* alive.
4 [a]"The LORD talked with you face to face on
the mountain from the midst of the fire.
5 [a]"I stood between the LORD and you at that
time, to declare to you the word of the LORD; for
[b]you were afraid because of the fire, and you did
not go up the mountain. *He* said:
**6** [a]'I *am* the LORD your God who brought you
out of the land of Egypt, out of the house
of [1]bondage.
**7** [a]'You shall have no other gods [1]before Me.
**8** [a]'You shall not make for yourself a carved
image—any likeness *of anything* that *is* in
heaven above, or that *is* in the earth beneath, or that *is* in the water under the
earth;
9 you shall not [a]bow[1] down to them nor
serve them. For I, the LORD your God, *am*
a jealous God, [2]visiting the iniquity of the
fathers upon the children to the third and
fourth *generations* of those who hate Me,
10 [a]but showing mercy to thousands, to those
who love Me and [1]keep My commandments.
**11** [a]'You shall not take the name of the LORD
your God in vain, for the LORD will not
hold *him* [1]guiltless who takes His name in
vain.
**12** [a]'Observe the Sabbath day, to [1]keep it holy, as
the LORD your God commanded you.
13 [a]Six days you shall labor and do all your
work,
14 but the seventh day *is* the [a]Sabbath of the
LORD your God. *In it* you shall do no work:
you, nor your son, nor your daughter, nor
your male servant, nor your female servant, nor your ox, nor your donkey, nor
any of your cattle, nor your stranger who
*is* within your gates, that your male ser-

vant and your female servant may rest as
well as you.
15 [a]And remember that you were a slave in
the land of Egypt, and the LORD your God
brought you out from there [b]by a mighty
hand and by an outstretched arm; therefore the LORD your God commanded you
to keep the Sabbath day.
16 [a]'Honor your father and your mother, as the
LORD your God has commanded you, [b]that
your days may be long, and that it may be
well with [c]you in the land which the LORD
your God is giving you.
17 [a]'You shall not murder.
18 [a]'You shall not commit adultery.
19 [a]'You shall not steal.
20 [a]'You shall not bear false witness against your
neighbor.
21 [a]'You shall not covet your neighbor's wife; and
you shall not desire your neighbor's house,
his field, his male servant, his female servant, his ox, his donkey, or anything that
*is* your neighbor's.'
22 "These words the LORD spoke to all your
assembly, in the mountain from the midst of the
fire, the cloud, and the thick darkness, with a loud
voice; and He added no more. And [a]He wrote them
on two tablets of stone and gave them to me.
23 [a]"So it was, when you heard the voice from
the midst of the darkness, while the mountain was
burning with fire, that you came near to me, all
the heads of your tribes and your elders.
24 "And you said: 'Surely the LORD our God has
shown us His glory and His greatness, and [a]we
have heard His voice from the midst of the fire.
We have seen this day that God speaks with man;
yet he [b]*still* lives.
25 'Now therefore, why should we die? For this
great fire will consume us; [a]if we hear the voice of
the LORD our God anymore, then we shall die.
26 [a]'For who *is there* of all flesh who has heard
the voice of the living God speaking from the
midst of the fire, as we *have,* and lived?
27 'You go near and hear all that the LORD our
God may say, and [a]tell us all that the LORD our
God says to you, and we will hear and do *it.*'
28 "Then the LORD heard the voice of your words
when you spoke to me, and the LORD said to me: 'I
have heard the voice of the words of this people
which they have spoken to you. [a]They are right *in*
all that they have spoken.
29 [a]'Oh, that they had such a heart in them that
they would fear Me and [b]always keep all My
commandments, [c]that it might be well with them
and with their children forever!
30 'Go and say to them, "Return to your tents."
31 'But as for you, stand here by Me, [a]and I will
speak to you all the commandments, the statutes,
and the judgments which you shall teach them,
that they may observe *them* in the land which I
am giving them to possess.'
32 "Therefore you shall [1]be careful to do as the
LORD your God has commanded you; [a]you shall
not turn aside to the right hand or to the left.
33 "You shall walk in [a]all the ways which the
LORD your God has commanded you, that you
may live [b]and *that it may be* well with you, and
*that* you may prolong *your* days in the land which
you shall possess.

### *The Great Commandment*

6 "Now this *is* [a]the commandment, *and these*
*are* the statutes and judgments which the
LORD your God has commanded to teach you, that
you may observe *them* in the land which you are
crossing over to possess,
2 [a]"that you may fear the LORD your God, to
keep all His statutes and His commandments
which I command you, you and your son and your
grandson, all the days of your life, [b]and that your
days may be prolonged.
3 "Therefore hear, O Israel, and [1]be careful to
observe *it,* that it may be well with you, and that
you may [a]multiply greatly [b]as the LORD God of
your fathers has promised you—[c]'a land flowing
with milk and honey.'
4 [a]"Hear, O Israel: [1]The LORD our God, the LORD
*is* one!
5 [a]"You shall love the LORD your God with all
your heart, [b]with all your soul, and with all your
strength.
6 "And [a]these words which I command you
today shall be in your heart.
7 [a]"You shall teach them diligently to your
children, and shall talk of them when you sit in
your house, when you walk by the way, when you
lie down, and when you rise up.
8 [a]"You shall bind them as a sign on your hand,
and they shall be as frontlets between your eyes.
9 [a]"You shall write them on the doorposts of
your house and on your gates.
10 "So it shall be, when the LORD your God
brings you into the land of which He [1]swore to
your fathers, to Abraham, Isaac, and Jacob, to
give you large and beautiful cities [a]which you did
not build,
11 "houses full of all good things, which you did
not fill, hewn-out wells which you did not dig,
vineyards and olive trees which you did not
plant—[a]when you have eaten and are full—
12 "*then* beware, lest you forget the [a]LORD who
brought you out of the land of Egypt, from the
house of bondage.
13 "You shall [a]fear the LORD your God and serve
Him, and [b]shall take oaths in His name.
14 "You shall not go after other gods, [a]the gods
of the peoples who *are* all around you
15 "(for [a]the LORD your God *is* a jealous God
[b]among you), lest the anger of the LORD your God
be aroused against you and destroy you from the
face of the earth.
16 [a]"You shall not [1]tempt the LORD your God [b]as
you [2]tempted *Him* in Massah.
17 "You shall [a]diligently keep the commandments of the LORD your God, His testimonies, and
His statutes which He has commanded you.
18 "And you [a]shall do *what is* right and good in
the sight of the LORD, that it may be well with
you, and that you may go in and possess the good
land of which the LORD swore to your fathers,
19 [a]"to cast out all your enemies from before you,
as the LORD has spoken.
20 [a]"When your son asks you in time to come,
saying, 'What *is the meaning of* the testimonies,
the statutes, and the judgments which the LORD
our God has commanded you?'
21 "then you shall say to your son: 'We were

15 [a]Deut. 15:15 [b]Deut. 4:34, 37
16 [a]Lev. 19:3 [b]Deut. 6:2 [c]Deut. 4:40
17 [a]Matt. 5:21
18 [a]Ex. 20:14
19 [a][Rom. 13:9]
20 [a]Ex. 20:16; 23:1
21 [a]Ex. 20:17
22 [a]Deut. 4:13
23 [a]Ex. 20:18, 19
24 [a]Ex. 19:19 [b]Deut. 4:33
25 [a]Deut. 18:16
26 [a]Deut. 4:33
27 [a]Ex. 20:19
28 [a]Deut. 18:17
29 [a]Ps. 81:13 [b]Deut. 11:1 [c]Deut. 4:40
31 [a][Gal. 3:19]
32 [a]Deut. 17:20; 28:14 [1]*observe*
33 [a]Deut. 10:12 [b]Deut. 4:40

CHAPTER 6

1 [a]Deut. 12:1
2 [a][Eccl. 12:13] [b]Deut. 4:40
3 [a]Deut. 7:13 [b]Gen. 22:17 [c]Ex. 3:8, 17 [1]Lit. *observe to do*
4 [a][1 Cor. 8:4, 6] [1]Or *The LORD is our God, the LORD alone,* i.e., the only one
5 [a]Matt. 22:37 [b]2 Kin. 23:25
6 [a]Deut. 11:18–20
7 [a]Deut. 4:9; 11:19
8 [a]Prov. 3:3; 6:21; 7:3
9 [a]Deut. 11:20
10 [a]Josh. 24:13 [1]*promised*
11 [a]Deut. 8:10; 11:15; 14:29
12 [a]Deut. 8:11–18
13 [a]Matt. 4:10 [b]Deut. 5:11
14 [a]Deut. 13:7
15 [a]Ex. 20:5 [b]Ex. 33:3
16 [a]Luke 4:12 [b][1 Cor. 10:9] [1]*test* [2]*tested*
17 [a]Deut. 11:22
18 [a]Ex. 15:26
19 [a]Num. 33:52, 53
20 [a]Ex. 13:8, 14

slaves of Pharaoh in Egypt, and the LORD brought
us out of Egypt [a]with a mighty hand;
22 'and the LORD showed signs and wonders
before our eyes, great and severe, against Egypt,
Pharaoh, and all his household.
23 'Then He brought us out from there, that He
might bring us in, to give us the land of which He
[1]swore to our fathers.
24 'And the LORD commanded us to [1]observe all
these [2]statutes, [a]to fear the LORD our God, [b]for our
good always, that [c]He might preserve us alive, as
*it is* [3]this day.
25 'Then [a]it will be righteousness for us, if we are
careful to observe all these commandments before
the LORD our God, as He has commanded us.'

### *The Blessings of Obedience*

7 "When the LORD your God brings you into the
land which you go to [a]possess, and has cast
out many [b]nations before you, [c]the Hittites and
the Girgashites and the Amorites and the Canaanites and the Perizzites and the Hivites and the
Jebusites, seven nations greater and mightier than
you,
2 "and when the LORD your God delivers [a]them
over to you, you shall conquer them *and* utterly
destroy them. [b]You shall make no covenant with
them nor show mercy to them.
3 [a]"Nor shall you make marriages with them.
You shall not give your daughter to their son, nor
take their daughter for your son.
4 "For they will turn your sons away from
following Me, to serve other gods; [a]so the anger of
the LORD will be aroused against you and destroy
you suddenly.
5 "But thus you shall deal with them: you shall
[a]destroy their altars, and break down their *sacred*
pillars, and cut down their [1]wooden images, and
burn their carved images with fire.
6 "For you *are* a [1]holy people to the LORD your
God; [a]the LORD your God has chosen you to be a
people for Himself, a special treasure above all the
peoples on the face of the earth.
7 "The LORD did not set His [a]love on you nor
choose you because you were more in number
than any other people, for you were [b]the least of
all peoples;
8 "but [a]because the LORD loves you, and because He would keep [b]the oath which He swore to
your fathers, [c]the LORD has brought you out with
a mighty hand, and redeemed you from the house
of [1]bondage, from the hand of Pharaoh king of
Egypt.
9 "Therefore know that the LORD your God, He
*is* God, [a]the faithful God [b]who keeps covenant and
mercy for a thousand generations with those who
love Him and keep His commandments;
10 "and He repays those who hate Him to their
face, to destroy them. He will not [1]be [a]slack with
him who hates Him; He will repay him to his face.
11 "Therefore you shall keep the commandment,
the statutes, and the judgments which I command
you today, to observe them.
12 "Then it shall come to pass, because you listen
to these judgments, and keep and do them, that
the LORD your God will keep with you the covenant and the mercy which He swore to your
fathers.
13 "And He will [a]love you and bless you and
[1]multiply you; [b]He will also bless the fruit of your
womb and the fruit of your land, your grain and

21 [a]Ex. 13:3
23 [1]*promised*
24 [a]Deut. 6:2 [b]Jer. 32:39 [c]Deut. 4:1 [1]*do* [2]*ordinances* [3]*today*
25 [a][Rom. 10:3, 5]

CHAPTER 7
1 [a]Deut. 6:10 [b]Gen. 15:19–21 [c]Ex. 33:2
2 [a]Num. 31:17 [b]Josh. 2:14
3 [a]1 Kin. 11:2
4 [a]Deut. 6:15
5 [a]Ex. 23:24; 34:13 [1]Or *Asherim,* Canaanite deities
6 [a]Ex. 19:5, 6 [1]*set-apart*
7 [a]Deut. 4:37 [b]Deut. 10:22
8 [a]Deut. 10:15 [b]Luke 1:55, 72, 73 [c]Ex. 13:3, 14 [1]*slavery*
9 [a]1 Cor. 1:9 [b]Neh. 1:5
10 [a][2 Pet. 3:10] [1]*delay*
13 [a]John 14:21 [b]Deut. 28:4 [1]*cause you to increase* [2]*promised*
14 [a]Ex. 23:26
15 [a]Ex. 9:14; 15:26
16 [a]Judg. 8:27 [1]*consume*
18 [a]Ps. 105:5
19 [a]Deut. 4:34; 29:3
20 [a]Josh. 24:12
22 [a]Ex. 23:29, 30 [1]*consume*
24 [a]Josh. 10:24, 42; 12:1–24 [b]Josh. 23:9 [1]*before*
25 [a]Prov. 23:6 [1]*desire*
26 [a]Deut. 13:17 [1]*devoted* or *banned*

CHAPTER 8
1 [a]Deut. 4:1; 6:24 [b]Deut. 30:16 [1]*observe to do* [2]*increase in number* [3]*promised*
2 [a]Amos 2:10 [b]Ex. 16:4 [c][John 2:25]
3 [a]Ex. 16:2, 3 [b]Ex. 16:12, 14, 35 [c]Matt. 4:4
4 [a]Neh. 9:21
5 [a]2 Sam. 7:14 [1]*consider*

your new wine and your oil, the increase of your
cattle and the offspring of your flock, in the land
of which He [2]swore to your fathers to give you.
14 "You shall be blessed above all peoples; there
shall not be a male or female [a]barren among you
or among your livestock.
15 "And the LORD will take away from you all
sickness, and will afflict you with none of the
[a]terrible diseases of Egypt which you have known,
but will lay *them* on all those who hate you.
16 "Also you shall [1]destroy all the peoples whom
the LORD your God delivers over to you; your eye
shall have no pity on them; nor shall you serve
their gods, for that *will* [a]*be* a snare to you.
17 "If you should say in your heart, 'These nations are greater than I; how can I dispossess
them?'—
18 "you shall not be afraid of them, *but* you shall
[a]remember well what the LORD your God did to
Pharaoh and to all Egypt:
19 [a]"the great trials which your eyes saw, the
signs and the wonders, the mighty hand and the
outstretched arm, by which the LORD your God
brought you out. So shall the LORD your God do to
all the peoples of whom you are afraid.
20 [a]"Moreover the LORD your God will send the
hornet among them until those who are left, who
hide themselves from you, are destroyed.
21 "You shall not be terrified of them; for the
LORD your God, the great and awesome God, *is*
among you.
22 "And the LORD your God will drive out those
nations before you [a]little by little; you will be
unable to [1]destroy them at once, lest the beasts of
the field become *too* numerous for you.
23 "But the LORD your God will deliver them over
to you, and will inflict defeat upon them until they
are destroyed.
24 "And [a]He will deliver their kings into your
hand, and you will destroy their name from under
heaven; [b]no one shall be able to stand [1]against you
until you have destroyed them.
25 "You shall burn the carved images of their
gods with fire; you shall not [a]covet[1] the silver or
gold *that is* on them, nor take *it* for yourselves,
lest you be snared by it; for it *is* an abomination to
the LORD your God.
26 "Nor shall you bring an abomination into your
house, lest you be doomed to destruction like it.
You shall utterly detest it and utterly abhor it, [a]for
it *is* an [1]accursed thing.

### *Warnings Against Forgetting the LORD*

8 "Every commandment which I command you
today [a]you must [1]be careful to observe, that
you may live and [b]multiply,[2] and go in and possess
the land of which the LORD [3]swore to your fathers.
2 "And you shall remember that the LORD your
God [a]led you all the way these forty years in the
wilderness, to humble you *and* [b]test you, [c]to know
what *was* in your heart, whether you would keep
His commandments or not.
3 "So He humbled you, [a]allowed you to hunger,
and [b]fed you with manna which you did not know
nor did your fathers know, that He might make
you know that man shall [c]not live by bread alone;
but man lives by every *word* that proceeds from
the mouth of the LORD.
4 [a]"Your garments did not wear out on you, nor
did your foot swell these forty years.
5 [a]"You should [1]know in your heart that as a

man chastens his son, *so* the LORD your God
chastens you.
6 "Therefore you shall keep the commandments
of the LORD your God, [a]to walk in His ways and to
fear Him.
7 "For the LORD your God is bringing you into a
good land, [a]a land of brooks of water, of fountains
and springs, that flow out of valleys and hills;
8 "a land of wheat and barley, of vines and fig
trees and pomegranates, a land of olive oil and
honey;
9 "a land in which you will eat bread without
scarcity, in which you will lack nothing; a land
whose stones *are* iron and out of whose hills you
can dig copper.
10 [a]"When you have eaten and are full, then you
shall bless the LORD your God for the good land
which He has given you.
**11** "Beware that you do not forget the LORD your
God by not keeping His commandments, His
judgments, and His statutes which I command
you today,
12 [a]"lest—*when* you have eaten and are [1]full, and
have built beautiful houses and dwell *in them;*
13 "and *when* your herds and your flocks multiply, and your silver and your gold are [1]multiplied,
and all that you have is multiplied;
14 [a]"when your heart [1]is lifted up, and you [b]forget
the LORD your God who brought you out of the
land of Egypt, from the house of bondage;
15 "who [a]led you through that great and terrible
wilderness, [b]*in which were* fiery serpents and
scorpions and thirsty land where there was no
water; [c]who brought water for you out of the
flinty rock;
16 "who fed you in the wilderness with [a]manna,
which your fathers did not know, that He might
humble you and that He might test you, [b]to do
you good in the end—
17 "then you say in your heart, 'My power and
the might of my hand have gained me this
wealth.'
18 "And you shall remember the LORD your God,
[a]for *it is* He who gives you power to get wealth,
[b]that He may [1]establish His covenant which He
swore to your fathers, as *it is* this day.
19 "Then it shall be, if you by any means forget
the LORD your God, and follow other gods, and
serve them and worship them, [a]I testify against
you this day that you shall surely perish.
20 "As the nations which the LORD destroys
before you, [a]so you shall perish, because you
would not be obedient to the voice of the LORD
your God.

### *Israel's Rebellion at Horeb*

**9** "Hear, O Israel: You *are* to cross over the
Jordan today, and go in to dispossess nations
greater and mightier than yourself, cities great
and fortified up to heaven,
2 "a people great and tall, the [a]descendants of
the Anakim, whom you know, and *of whom* you
heard *it said,* 'Who can stand before the descendants of Anak?'
3 "Therefore understand today that the LORD
your God *is* He who [a]goes over before you *as* a
[b]consuming fire. [c]He will destroy them and bring
them down before you; [d]so you shall drive them
out and destroy them quickly, as the LORD has
said to you.
4 [a]"Do not think in your heart, after the LORD
your God has cast them out before you, saying,
'Because of my righteousness the LORD has
brought me in to possess this land'; but *it is*
[b]because of the wickedness of these nations *that*
the LORD is driving them out from before you.
5 [a]"*It is* not because of your righteousness or
the uprightness of your heart *that* you go in to
possess their land, but because of the wickedness
of these nations *that* the LORD your God drives
them out from before you, and that He may [1]fulfill
the [b]word which the LORD swore to your fathers,
to Abraham, Isaac, and Jacob.
6 "Therefore understand that the LORD your
God is not giving you this good land to possess
because of your righteousness, for you *are* a [a]stiff-
necked[1] people.
7 "Remember! Do not forget how you [a]provoked
the LORD your God to wrath in the wilderness.
[b]From the day that you departed from the land of
Egypt until you came to this place, you have been
rebellious against the LORD.
8 "Also [a]in Horeb you provoked the LORD to
wrath, so that the LORD was angry *enough* with
you to have destroyed you.
9 [a]"When I went up into the mountain to receive the tablets of stone, the tablets of the
covenant which the LORD made with you, then I
stayed on the mountain forty days and [b]forty
nights. I neither ate bread nor drank water.
10 [a]"Then the LORD delivered to me two tablets
of stone written with the finger of God, and on
them *were* all the words which the LORD had
spoken to you on the mountain from the midst of
the fire [b]in[1] the day of the assembly.
11 "And it came to pass, at the end of forty days
and forty nights, *that* the LORD gave me the two
tablets of stone, the tablets of the covenant.
12 "Then the LORD said to me, [a]'Arise, go down
quickly from here, for your people whom you
brought out of Egypt have acted corruptly; they
have [b]quickly turned aside from the way which I
commanded them; they have made themselves a
molded image.'
**13** "Furthermore [a]the LORD spoke to me, saying,
'I have seen this people, and indeed [b]they are a
[1]stiff-necked people.
14 [a]'Let Me alone, that I may destroy them and
[b]blot out their name from under heaven; [c]and I
will make of you a nation mightier and greater
than they.'
15 [a]"So I turned and came down from the mountain, and [b]the mountain burned with fire; and the
two tablets of the covenant *were* in my two
hands.
16 "And [a]I looked, and behold, you had sinned
against the LORD your God—had made for yourselves a molded calf! You had turned aside quickly
from the way which the LORD had commanded
you.
17 "Then I took the two tablets and threw them
out of my two hands and [a]broke them before your
eyes.
18 "And I [a]fell[1] down before the LORD, as at the
first, forty days and forty nights; I neither ate
bread nor drank water, because of all your sin
which you committed in doing wickedly in the
sight of the LORD, to provoke Him to anger.
19 [a]"For I was afraid of the anger and hot displeasure with which the LORD was angry with
you, to destroy you. [b]But the LORD listened to me
at that time also.

**6** [a][Deut. 5:33]
**7** [a]Deut. 11:9–12; Jer. 2:7
**10** [a]Deut. 6:11, 12
**12** [a]Deut. 28:47; Prov. 30:9; Hos. 13:6 [1]*satisfied*
**13** [1]*increased*
**14** [a]1 Cor. 4:7 [b]Deut. 8:11; Ps. 106:21 [1]*becomes proud*
**15** [a]Is. 63:12–14 [b]Num. 21:6 [c]Ex. 17:6; Num. 20:11
**16** [a]Ex. 16:15 [b]Jer. 24:5, 6; [Heb. 12:11]
**18** [a]Prov. 10:22; Hos. 2:8 [b]Deut. 7:8, 12 [1]*confirm*
**19** [a]Deut. 4:26; 30:18
**20** [a][Dan. 9:11, 12]

CHAPTER 9
**2** [a]Num. 13:22, 28, 33; Josh. 11:21, 22
**3** [a]Deut. 1:33; 31:3; Josh. 3:11; 5:14; John 10:4 [b]Deut. 4:24; Heb. 12:29 [c]Deut. 7:24 [d]Ex. 23:31
**4** [a]Deut. 8:17; [Rom. 11:6, 20; 1 Cor. 4:4, 7] [b]Gen. 15:16; Lev. 18:3, 24–30; Deut. 12:31; 18:9–14
**5** [a][Titus 3:5] [b]Gen. 50:24 [1]*perform*
**6** [a]Ex. 34:9; Deut. 31:27 [1]*stubborn* or *rebellious*
**7** [a]Num. 14:22 [b]Ex. 14:11
**8** [a]Ex. 32:1–8; Ps. 106:19
**9** [a]Ex. 24:12, 15; Deut. 5:2–22 [b]Ex. 24:18
**10** [a]Ex. 31:18; Deut. 4:13 [b]Ex. 19:17 [1]*when you were all gathered together*
**12** [a]Ex. 32:7, 8 [b]Deut. 31:29
**13** [a]Ex. 32:9 [b]Deut. 9:6 [1]*stubborn* or *rebellious*
**14** [a]Ex. 32:10 [b]Deut. 29:20 [c]Num. 14:12
**15** [a]Ex. 32:15–19 [b]Ex. 19:18
**16** [a]Ex. 32:19
**17** [a]Ex. 32:19
**18** [a]Ex. 34:28; Ps. 106:23 [1]*prostrated myself*
**19** [a]Ex. 32:10, 11; Heb. 12:21 [b]Ex. 32:14

20 "And the LORD was very angry with Aaron
*and* would have destroyed him; so I prayed for
Aaron also at the same time.
21 "Then I took your sin, the calf which you had
made, and burned it with fire and crushed it *and*
ground *it* very small, until it was as fine as dust;
and I [a]threw its dust into the brook that descended from the mountain.
**22** "Also at [a]Taberah and [b]Massah and [c]Kibroth
Hattaavah you [1]provoked the LORD to wrath.
23 "Likewise, [a]when the LORD sent you from
Kadesh Barnea, saying, 'Go up and possess the
land which I have given you,' then you rebelled
against the commandment of the LORD your God,
and [b]you did not believe Him nor obey His voice.
24 [a]"You have been rebellious against the LORD
from the day that I knew you.
**25** [a]"Thus I [1]prostrated myself before the LORD;
forty days and forty nights I kept prostrating
myself, because the LORD had said He would
destroy you.
26 "Therefore I prayed to the LORD, and said: 'O
Lord GOD, do not destroy Your people and [a]Your
inheritance whom You have redeemed through
Your greatness, whom You have brought out of
Egypt with a mighty hand.
27 'Remember Your servants, Abraham, Isaac,
and Jacob; do not look on the stubbornness of this
people, or on their wickedness or their sin,
28 'lest the land from which You brought us
should say, "Because the LORD was not able to
bring them to the land which He promised them,
and because He hated them, He has brought them
out to kill them in the wilderness."
29 'Yet they *are* Your people and Your inheritance, whom You brought out by Your mighty
power and by Your outstretched arm.'

### *The Second Pair of Stone Tablets*

**10** "At that time the LORD said to me, [1]'Hew for
yourself two tablets of stone like the first,
and come up to Me on the mountain and make
yourself an [a]ark of wood.
2 'And I will write on the tablets the words that
were on the first tablets, which you broke; and
[a]you shall put them in the ark.'
3 "So I made an ark of acacia wood, hewed two
tablets of stone like the first, and went up the
mountain, having the two tablets in my hand.
4 "And He wrote on the tablets according to the
first writing, the Ten [1]Commandments, [a]which the
LORD had spoken to you in the mountain from
the midst of the fire in the day of the assembly;
and the LORD gave them to me.
5 "Then I turned and [a]came down from the
mountain, and [b]put the tablets in the ark which I
had made; [c]and there they are, just as the LORD
commanded me."
**6** (Now the children of Israel journeyed from
the wells of Bene Jaakan to Moserah, where
Aaron [a]died, and where he was buried; and Eleazar his son ministered as priest in his [1]stead.
7 [a]From there they journeyed to Gudgodah, and
from Gudgodah to Jotbathah, a land of [1]rivers of
water.
8 At that time [a]the LORD [1]separated the tribe of
Levi [b]to bear the ark of the covenant of the LORD,
[c]to stand before the LORD to minister to Him and
[d]to bless in His name, to this day.
9 [a]Therefore Levi has no portion nor inheritance
with his brethren; the LORD *is* his inheritance, just
as the LORD your God promised him.)
10 "As at the first time, [a]I stayed in the mountain
forty days and forty nights; [b]the LORD also heard
me at that time, *and* the LORD chose not to
destroy you.
11 [a]"Then the LORD said to me, 'Arise, begin *your*
journey before the people, that they may go in
and possess the land which I swore to their
fathers to give them.'
**12** "And now, Israel, [a]what does the LORD your
God require of you, but to fear the LORD your
God, to walk in all His ways and to [b]love Him, to
serve the LORD your God with all your heart and
with all your soul,
13 "*and* to keep the commandments of the LORD
and His statutes which I command you today [a]for
your [1]good?
14 "Indeed heaven and the highest heavens belong to the [a]LORD your God, *also* the earth with all
that *is* in it.
15 "The LORD delighted only in your fathers, to
love them; and He chose their [1]descendants after
them, you above all peoples, as *it is* this day.
16 "Therefore circumcise the foreskin of your
[a]heart, and be [b]stiff-necked[1] no longer.
17 "For the LORD your God *is* [a]God of gods and
[b]Lord of lords, the great God, [c]mighty and awesome, who [d]shows no partiality nor takes a bribe.
18 [a]"He administers justice for the fatherless and
the widow, and loves the stranger, giving him
food and clothing.
19 "Therefore love the stranger, for you were
strangers in the land of Egypt.
20 [a]"You shall fear the LORD your God; you shall
serve Him, and to Him you shall hold fast, and
take oaths in His name.
21 "He *is* your praise, and He *is* your God, who
has done for you these great and awesome things
which your eyes have seen.
22 "Your fathers went down to Egypt with seventy persons, and now the LORD your God has
made you as the stars of heaven in multitude.

### *The Blessings of the Promised Land*

**11** "Therefore you shall love the LORD your
God, and keep His charge, His statutes, His
judgments, and His commandments always.
2 "Know today that *I do* not *speak* with your
children, who have not known and who have not
seen the [1]chastening of the LORD your God, His
greatness and His mighty hand and His outstretched arm—
3 "His signs and His acts which He did in the
midst of Egypt, to Pharaoh king of Egypt, and to
all his land;
4 "what He did to the army of Egypt, to their
horses and their chariots: [a]how He made the
waters of the Red Sea overflow them as they
pursued you, and *how* the LORD has destroyed
them to this day;
5 "what He did for you in the wilderness until
you came to this place;
6 "and [a]what He did to Dathan and Abiram the
sons of Eliab, the son of Reuben: how the earth
opened its mouth and swallowed them up, their
households, their tents, and all the substance that
*was* [1]in their possession, in the midst of all Israel—
7 "but your eyes have [a]seen every great [1]act of
the LORD which He did.

---

**21** [a]Ex. 32:20
**22** [a]Num. 11:1, 3 [b]Ex. 17:7 [c]Num. 11:4, 34 [1]*caused the LORD to be angry*
**23** [a]Num. 13:3 [b]Ps. 106:24, 25
**24** [a]Deut. 9:7; 31:27
**25** [a]Deut. 9:18 [1]*fell down*
**26** [a]Deut. 32:9

CHAPTER 10

**1** [a]Ex. 25:10 [1]*Cut out*
**2** [a]Ex. 25:16, 21
**4** [a]Ex. 20:1; 34:28 [1]Lit. *Words*
**5** [a]Ex. 34:29 [b]Ex. 40:20 [c]1 Kin. 8:9
**6** [a]Num. 20:25–28; 33:38 [1]*place*
**7** [a]Num. 33:32–34 [1]*brooks*
**8** [a]Num. 3:6 [b]Num. 4:5, 15; 10:21 [c]Deut. 18:5 [d]Num. 6:23 [1]*set apart*
**9** [a]Num. 18:20, 24; Deut. 18:1, 2; Ezek. 44:28
**10** [a]Ex. 34:28; Deut. 9:18 [b]Ex. 32:14
**11** [a]Ex. 33:1
**12** [a]Mic. 6:8 [b]Deut. 6:5; Matt. 22:37; 1 Tim. 1:5
**13** [a]Deut. 6:24 [1]*benefit* or *welfare*
**14** [a][Neh. 9:6; Ps. 68:33; 115:16]
**15** [1]Lit. *seed*
**16** [a]Lev. 26:41; Deut. 30:6; Jer. 4:4; Rom. 2:28, 29 [b]Deut. 9:6, 13 [1]*rebellious*
**17** [a]Deut. 4:35, 39; Is. 44:8; 46:9; Dan. 2:47; 1 Cor. 8:5, 6 [b]Rev. 19:16 [c]Deut. 7:21 [d]Acts 10:34
**18** [a]Ex. 22:22–24; Ps. 68:5; 146:9
**20** [a]Matt. 4:10

CHAPTER 11

**2** [1]*discipline*
**4** [a]Ex. 14:28; Ps. 106:11
**6** [a]Num. 16:1–35; Ps. 106:16–18 [1]*at their feet*
**7** [a]Deut. 10:21; 29:2 [1]*work*

8 "Therefore you shall keep every commandment which I command you today, that you may [a]be strong, and go in and possess the land which you cross over to possess,

9 "and [a]that you may prolong *your* days in the land [b]which the LORD [1]swore to give your fathers, to them and their descendants, [c]'a land flowing with milk and honey.'

10 "For the land which you go to possess *is* not like the land of Egypt from which you have come, where you sowed your seed and watered *it* by foot, as a vegetable garden;

11 [a]"but the land which you cross over to possess *is* a land of hills and valleys, which drinks water from the rain of heaven,

12 "a land for which the LORD your God cares; [a]the eyes of the LORD your God *are* always on it, from the beginning of the year to the very end of the year.

**13** 'And it shall be that if you earnestly [1]obey My commandments which I command you today, to love the LORD your God and serve Him with all your heart and with all your soul,

14 'then [a]I[1] will give *you* the rain for your land in its season, [b]the early rain and the latter rain, that you may gather in your grain, your new wine, and your oil.

15 [a]'And I will send grass in your fields for your livestock, that you may [b]eat and be [1]filled.'

16 "Take heed to yourselves, [a]lest your heart be deceived, and you turn aside and [b]serve other gods and worship them,

17 "lest [a]the LORD's anger be aroused against you, and He [b]shut up the heavens so that there be no rain, and the land yield no produce, and [c]you perish quickly from the good land which the LORD is giving you.

**18** "Therefore [a]you shall [1]lay up these words of mine in your heart and in your [b]soul, and [c]bind them as a sign on your hand, and they shall be as frontlets between your eyes.

19 [a]"You shall teach them to your children, speaking of them when you sit in your house, when you walk by the way, when you lie down, and when you rise up.

20 [a]"And you shall write them on the doorposts of your house and on your gates,

21 "that [a]your days and the days of your children may be multiplied in the land of which the LORD swore to your fathers to give them, like [b]the days of the heavens above the earth.

**22** "For if [a]you carefully keep all these commandments which I command you to do—to love the LORD your God, to walk in all His ways, and [b]to hold fast to Him—

23 "then the LORD will [a]drive out all these nations from before you, and you will [b]dispossess greater and mightier nations than yourselves.

24 [a]"Every place on which the sole of your foot treads shall be yours: [b]from the wilderness and Lebanon, from the river, the River Euphrates, even to the [1]Western Sea, shall be your territory.

25 "No man shall be able to [a]stand [1]against you; the LORD your God will put the [b]dread of you and the fear of you upon all the land where you tread, just as He has said to you.

**26** [a]"Behold, I set before you today a blessing and a curse:

27 [a]"the blessing, if you obey the commandments of the LORD your God which I command you today;

28 "and the [a]curse, if you do not obey the commandments of the LORD your God, but turn aside from the way which I command you today, to go after other gods which you have not known.

29 "Now it shall be, when the LORD your God has brought you into the land which you go to possess, that you shall put the [a]blessing on Mount Gerizim and the [b]curse on Mount Ebal.

30 "*Are* they not on the other side of the Jordan, toward the setting sun, in the land of the Canaanites who dwell in the plain opposite Gilgal, [a]beside the terebinth trees of Moreh?

31 "For you will cross over the Jordan and go in to possess the land which the LORD your God is giving you, and you will possess it and dwell in it.

32 "And you shall be careful to observe all the statutes and judgments which I set before you today.

### *Only One Place of Worship*

**12** "These [a]*are* the statutes and judgments which you shall be careful to observe in the land which the LORD God of your fathers is giving you to possess, [b]all[1] the days that you live on the earth.

2 [a]"You shall utterly destroy all the places where the nations which you shall dispossess served their gods, [b]on the high mountains and on the hills and under every green tree.

3 "And [a]you shall destroy their altars, break their *sacred* pillars, and burn their [1]wooden images with fire; you shall cut down the carved images of their gods and destroy their names from that place.

4 "You shall not [a]worship the LORD your God *with* such *things.*

5 "But you shall seek the [a]place where the LORD your God chooses, out of all your tribes, to put His name for His [b]dwelling[1] place; and there you shall go.

6 [a]"There you shall take your burnt offerings, your sacrifices, your tithes, the heave offerings of your hand, your vowed offerings, your freewill offerings, and the [b]firstborn of your herds and flocks.

7 "And [a]there you shall eat before the LORD your God, and [b]you shall rejoice in [1]all to which you have put your hand, you and your households, in which the LORD your God has blessed you.

8 "You shall not at all do as we are doing here today—[a]every man doing whatever *is* right in his own eyes—

9 "for as yet you have not come to the [a]rest[1] and the inheritance which the LORD your God is giving you.

10 "But *when* you cross over the Jordan and dwell in the land which the LORD your God is giving you to inherit, and He gives you [a]rest from all your enemies round about, so that you dwell in safety,

11 "then there will be the place where the LORD your God chooses to make His name abide. There you shall bring all that I command you: your burnt offerings, your sacrifices, your tithes, the heave offerings of your hand, and all your choice offerings which you vow to the LORD.

12 "And [a]you shall rejoice before the LORD your God, you and your sons and your daughters, your male and female servants, and the [b]Levite who *is*

---

8 [a]Josh. 1:6, 7
9 [a]Deut. 4:40; 5:16, 33; 6:2 [b]Deut. 9:5 [c]Ex. 3:8 [1]*promised*
11 [a]Deut. 8:7
12 [a]1 Kin. 9:3
13 [1]Lit. *listen to*
14 [a]Deut. 28:12 [b]Joel 2:23 [1]So with MT, Tg.; Sam., LXX, Vg. *He*
15 [a]Ps. 104:14 [b]Deut. 6:11 [1]*satisfied*
16 [a]Job 31:27 [b]Deut. 8:19
17 [a]Deut. 6:15; 9:19 [b]2 Chr. 6:26; 7:13 [c]Deut. 4:26
18 [a]Deut. 6:6–9 [b]Ps. 119:2, 34 [c]Deut. 6:8 [1]Lit. *put*
19 [a]Deut. 4:9, 10; 6:7
20 [a]Deut. 6:9
21 [a]Deut. 4:40 [b]Ps. 72:5; 89:29
22 [a]Deut. 11:1 [b]Deut. 10:20
23 [a]Deut. 4:38 [b]Deut. 9:1
24 [a]Josh. 1:3; 14:9 [b]Gen. 15:18 [1]Mediterranean
25 [a]Deut. 7:24 [b]Deut. 2:25 [1]*before*
26 [a]Deut. 30:1, 15, 19
27 [a]Deut. 28:1–14
28 [a]Deut. 28:15–68
29 [a]Josh. 8:33 [b]Deut. 27:13–26
30 [a]Gen. 12:6

CHAPTER 12
1 [a]Deut. 6:1 [b]Deut. 4:9, 10 [1]As long as
2 [a]Ex. 34:13 [b]2 Kin. 16:4; 17:10, 11
3 [a]Num. 33:52 [1]Or *Asherim*
4 [a]Deut. 12:31
5 [a]Ex. 20:24 [b]Ex. 15:13 [1]*home*
6 [a]Lev. 17:3, 4 [b]Deut. 14:23
7 [a]Deut. 14:26 [b]Deut. 12:12, 18 [1]*all that you undertake*
8 [a]Judg. 17:6; 21:25
9 [a]Deut. 3:20; 25:19 [1]Or *place of rest*
10 [a]Josh. 11:23
12 [a]Deut. 12:18; 26:11 [b]Deut. 10:9; 14:29

within your gates, since he has no portion nor
inheritance with you.
13 "Take heed to yourself that you do not offer
your burnt offerings in every place that you see;
14 "but in the place which the LORD chooses, in
one of your tribes, there you shall offer your burnt
offerings, and there you shall do all that I command you.
**15** "However, [a]you may slaughter and eat meat
within all your gates, whatever your heart desires,
according to the blessing of the LORD your God
which He has given you; [b]the unclean and the
clean may eat of it, [c]of the gazelle and the deer
alike.
16 [a]"Only you shall not eat the blood; you shall
pour it on the earth like water.
17 "You may not eat within your gates the tithe
of your grain or your new wine or your oil, of the
firstborn of your herd or your flock, of any of your
offerings which you vow, of your freewill offerings, or of the [1]heave offering of your hand.
18 "But you must eat them before the LORD your
God in the place which the LORD your God
chooses, you and your son and your daughter,
your male servant and your female servant, and
the Levite who *is* within your gates; and you shall
rejoice before the LORD your God in [1]all to which
you put your hands.
19 [1]"Take heed to yourself that you do not forsake the Levite as long as you live in your land.
**20** "When the LORD your God [a]enlarges your
border as He has promised you, and you say, 'Let
me eat meat,' because you long to eat meat, you
may eat as much meat as your heart desires.
21 "If the place where the LORD your God
chooses to put His name is too far from [a]you, then
you may slaughter from your herd and from your
flock which the LORD has given you, just as I have
commanded you, and you may eat within your
gates as much as your heart desires.
22 "Just as the gazelle and the deer are eaten, so
you may eat them; the unclean and the clean alike
may eat them.
23 "Only be sure that you do not eat the blood,
[a]for the blood *is* the life; you may not eat the life
with the meat.
24 "You shall not eat it; you shall pour it on the
earth like water.
25 "You shall not eat it, [a]that it may go well with
you and your children after you, [b]when you do
*what is* right in the sight of the LORD.
26 "Only the [a]holy things which you have, and
your vowed offerings, you shall take and go to the
place which the LORD chooses.
27 "And [a]you shall offer your burnt offerings, the
meat and the blood, on the altar of the LORD your
God; and the blood of your sacrifices shall be
poured out on the altar of the LORD your God, and
you shall eat the meat.
28 "Observe and obey all these words which I
command you, [a]that it may go well with you and
your children after you forever, when you do
*what is* good and right in the sight of the LORD
your God.
**29** "When [a]the LORD your God cuts off from
before you the nations which you go to dispossess,
and you displace them and dwell in their land,
30 "take heed to yourself that you are not ensnared to follow them, after they are destroyed
from before you, and that you do not inquire after
their gods, saying, 'How did these nations serve
their gods? I also will do likewise.'
31 [a]"You shall not worship the LORD your God in
that way; for every [1]abomination to the LORD
which He hates they have done to their gods; for
[b]they burn even their sons and daughters in the
fire to their gods.
32 "Whatever I command you, be careful to
observe it; [a]you shall not add to it nor take away
from it.

## *Idol-Worshipers Will Be Punished*

**13** "If there arises among you a prophet or a
[a]dreamer of dreams, [b]and he gives you
a sign or a wonder,
2 "and [a]the sign or the wonder comes to pass, of
which he spoke to you, saying, 'Let us go after
other gods'—which you have not known—'and let
us serve them,'
3 "you shall not listen to the words of that
prophet or that dreamer of dreams, for the LORD
your God [a]is testing you to know whether you
love the LORD your God with all your heart and
with all your soul.
4 "You shall [a]walk[1] after the LORD your God and
fear Him, and keep His commandments and obey
His voice; you shall serve Him and [b]hold fast to
Him.
5 "But [a]that prophet or that dreamer of dreams
shall be put to death, because he has spoken in
order to turn *you* away from the LORD your God,
who brought you out of the land of Egypt and
redeemed you from the house of bondage, to
entice you from the way in which the LORD your
God commanded you to walk. [b]So you shall [1]put
away the evil from your midst.
**6** [a]"If your brother, the son of your mother, your
son or your daughter, [b]the wife [1]of your bosom, or
your friend [c]who is as your own soul, secretly
entices you, saying, 'Let us go and serve other
gods,' which you have not known, neither you nor
your fathers,
7 "of the gods of the people which *are* all around
you, near to you or far off from you, from *one* end
of the earth to the *other* end of the earth,
8 "you shall [a]not [1]consent to him or listen to
him, nor shall your eye pity him, nor shall you
spare him or conceal him;
9 "but you shall surely kill him; your hand shall
be first against him to put him to [a]death, and
afterward the hand of all the people.
10 "And you shall stone him with stones until he
dies, because he sought to entice you away from
the LORD your God, who brought you out of the
land of Egypt, from the house of bondage.
11 "So all Israel shall hear and [a]fear, and not
again do such wickedness as this among you.
**12** [a]"If you hear someone in one of your cities,
which the LORD your God gives you to dwell in,
saying,
13 [1]'Corrupt men have gone out from among you
and enticed the inhabitants of their city, saying,
"Let us go and serve other gods" '—which you
have not known—
14 "then you shall inquire, search out, and ask
diligently. And *if it is* indeed true *and* certain *that*
such an [1]abomination was committed among you,
15 "you shall surely strike the inhabitants of that
city with the edge of the sword, utterly destroying
it, all that is in it and its livestock—with the edge
of the sword.

**15** [a]Deut. 12:21 [b]Deut. 12:22 [c]Deut. 14:5
**16** [a]Gen. 9:4; Lev. 7:26; 17:10–12; 1 Sam. 14:33; Acts 15:20, 29
**17** [1]*contribution*
**18** [1]*all your undertakings*
**19** [1]*Be careful*
**20** [a]Gen. 15:18; Ex. 34:24; Deut. 11:24; 19:8
**21** [a]Deut. 14:24
**23** [a]Gen. 9:4; Lev. 17:10–14; Deut. 12:16
**25** [a]Deut. 4:40; 6:18; Is. 3:10 [b]Ex. 15:26; 1 Kin. 11:38
**26** [a]Num. 5:9, 10; 18:19
**27** [a]Lev. 1:5, 9, 13, 17
**28** [a]Deut. 12:25
**29** [a]Ex. 23:23; Deut. 19:1; Josh. 23:4
**31** [a]Lev. 18:3, 26, 30; 20:1, 2 [b]Deut. 18:10; Ps. 106:37; Jer. 32:35 [1]*detestable action*
**32** [a]Deut. 4:2; 13:18; Josh. 1:7; Prov. 30:6; Rev. 22:18, 19

CHAPTER 13
**1** [a]Num. 12:6; Jer. 23:28; Zech. 10:2 [b]Matt. 24:24; Mark 13:22; 2 Thess. 2:9
**2** [a]Deut. 18:22
**3** [a]Ex. 20:20; Deut. 8:2, 16
**4** [a]Deut. 10:12, 20; 2 Kin. 23:3 [b]Deut. 30:20 [1]*follow the LORD*
**5** [a]Deut. 18:20; Jer. 14:15 [b]Deut. 17:5, 7; 1 Cor. 5:13 [1]*exterminate*
**6** [a]Deut. 17:2 [b]Gen. 16:5 [c]1 Sam. 18:1, 3 [1]Whom you cherish
**8** [a]Deut. 7:16; Prov. 1:10 [1]*yield*
**9** [a]Lev. 24:14; Deut. 17:7
**11** [a]Deut. 17:13
**12** [a]Judg. 20:1–48
**13** [1]Lit. *Sons of Belial*
**14** [1]*detestable action*

16 "And you shall gather all its plunder into the
middle of the street, and [1]completely [a]burn with
fire the city and all its plunder, for the LORD your
God. It shall be [b]a [2]heap forever; it shall not be
built again.
17 [a]"So none of the accursed things shall remain
in your hand, that the LORD may [b]turn from the
fierceness of His anger and show you mercy, have
compassion on you and [1]multiply you, just as He
swore to your fathers,
18 "because you have listened to the voice of the
LORD your God, [a]to keep all His commandments
which I command you today, to do *what is* right
in the eyes of the LORD your God.

### *Clean and Unclean Food*

**14** "You *are* [a]the children of the LORD your
God; [b]you shall not cut yourselves nor
[1]shave the front of your head for the dead.
2 [a]"For you *are* a holy people to the LORD your
God, and the LORD has chosen you to be a people
for Himself, a special treasure above all the peoples who *are* on the face of the earth.
**3** [a]"You shall not eat any [1]detestable thing.
4 [a]"These *are* the animals which you may eat:
the ox, the sheep, the goat,
5 "the deer, the gazelle, the roe deer, the wild
goat, the [1]mountain goat, the antelope, and the
mountain sheep.
6 "And you may eat every animal with cloven
hooves, having the hoof split into two parts, *and
that* chews the cud, among the animals.
7 "Nevertheless, of those that chew the cud or
have cloven hooves, you shall not eat, *such as*
these: the camel, the hare, and the rock hyrax; for
they chew the cud but do not have cloven hooves;
they *are* unclean for you.
8 "Also the swine is unclean for you, because it
has cloven hooves, yet *does* not *chew* the cud; you
shall not eat their flesh [a]or touch their dead
carcasses.
**9** [a]"These you may eat of all that *are* in the
waters: you may eat all that have fins and scales.
10 "And whatever does not have fins and scales
you shall not eat; it *is* unclean for you.
**11** "All clean birds you may eat.
12 [a]"But these you shall not eat: the eagle, the
vulture, the buzzard,
13 "the red kite, the falcon, and the kite after
their kinds;
14 "every raven after its kind;
15 "the ostrich, the short-eared owl, the seagull,
and the hawk after their kinds;
16 "the little owl, the screech owl, the white owl,
17 "the jackdaw, the carrion vulture, the fisher
owl,
18 "the stork, the heron after its kind, and the
hoopoe and the bat.
19 "Also [a]every [1]creeping thing that flies is unclean for you; [b]they shall not be eaten.
20 "You may eat all clean birds.
**21** [a]"You shall not eat anything that dies *of itself;*
you may give it to the alien who *is* within your
gates, that he may eat it, or you may sell it to a
foreigner; [b]for you *are* a holy people to the LORD
your God. [c]You shall not boil a young goat in its
mother's milk.
**22** [a]"You shall truly tithe all the increase of your
grain that the field produces year by year.
23 [a]"And you shall eat before the LORD your God,
in the place where He chooses to make His name
abide, the tithe of your grain and your new wine
and your oil, of [b]the firstborn of your herds and
your flocks, that you may learn to fear the LORD
your God always.
24 "But if the journey is too long for you, so that
you are not able to carry *the tithe, or* [a]if the place
where the LORD your God chooses to put His
name is too far from you, when the LORD your
God has blessed you,
25 "then you shall exchange *it* for money, take
the money in your hand, and go to the place
which the LORD your God chooses.
26 "And you shall spend that money for whatever your heart desires: for oxen or sheep, for
wine or similar drink, for whatever your heart
desires; you shall eat there before the LORD your
God, and you shall [a]rejoice, you and your household.
27 "You shall not [1]forsake the [a]Levite who *is*
within your gates, for he has no part nor inheritance with you.
**28** [a]"At the end of *every* third year you shall
bring out the [b]tithe of your produce of that year
and store *it* up within your gates.
29 "And the Levite, because he has no portion
nor inheritance with you, and the stranger and
the fatherless and the widow who *are* within your
gates, may come and eat and be satisfied, that the
LORD your God may bless you in all the work of
your hand which you do.

### *The Year of Release*

**15** "At the end of [a]*every* seven years you shall
grant a [1]release *of debts.*
2 "And this *is* the form of the release: Every
creditor who has lent *anything* to his neighbor
shall [1]release *it;* he shall not [2]require *it* of his
neighbor or his brother, because it is called the
LORD's release.
3 "Of a foreigner you may require *it;* but you
shall give up your claim to what is owed by your
brother,
4 "except when there may be no poor among
you; for the LORD will greatly [a]bless you in the
land which the LORD your God is giving you to
possess *as* an inheritance—
5 "only if you carefully obey the voice of the
LORD your God, to observe with care all these
commandments which I command you today.
6 "For the LORD your God will bless you just as
He promised you; [a]you shall lend to many nations,
but you shall not borrow; you shall reign over
many nations, but they shall not reign over you.
**7** "If there is among you a poor man of your
brethren, within any of the [1]gates in your land
which the LORD your God is giving you, [a]you shall
not harden your heart nor shut your hand from
your poor brother,
8 "but [a]you shall [1]open your hand wide to him
and willingly lend him sufficient for his need,
whatever he needs.
9 "Beware lest there be a wicked thought in
your heart, saying, 'The seventh year, the year of
release, is at hand,' and your [a]eye be evil against
your poor brother and you give him nothing, and
[b]he cry out to the LORD against you, and [c]it
become sin among you.
10 "You shall surely give to him, and [a]your heart
should not be grieved when you give to him,
because [b]for this thing the LORD your God will

**16** [a]Josh. 6:24 [b]Josh. 8:28; Is. 17:1; 25:2; Jer. 49:2 [1]Or *as a whole-offering* [2]Lit. *mound* or *ruin*
**17** [a]Josh. 6:18 [b]Josh. 7:26 [1]*increase*
**18** [a]Deut. 12:25, 28, 32

CHAPTER 14

**1** [a][Rom. 8:16; Gal. 3:26] [b]Lev. 19:28; 21:1–5 [1]*make any baldness between your eyes*
**2** [a]Lev. 20:26; Deut. 7:6; [Rom. 12:1]
**3** [a]Ezek. 4:14 [1]*abominable*
**4** [a]Lev. 11:2–45
**5** [1]Or *addax*
**8** [a]Lev. 11:26, 27
**9** [a]Lev. 11:9
**12** [a]Lev. 11:13
**19** [a]Lev. 11:20 [b]Lev. 11:23 [1]*swarming*
**21** [a]Lev. 17:15; 22:8; Ezek. 4:14; 44:31 [b]Deut. 14:2 [c]Ex. 23:19; 34:26
**22** [a]Lev. 27:30; Deut. 12:6, 17; Neh. 10:37
**23** [a]Deut. 12:5–7 [b]Deut. 15:19, 20
**24** [a]Deut. 12:5, 21
**26** [a]Deut. 12:7
**27** [a]Deut. 12:12 [1]*neglect*
**28** [a]Deut. 26:12; Amos 4:4 [b]Num. 18:21–24

CHAPTER 15

**1** [a]Ex. 21:2; 23:10, 11; Lev. 25:4; Jer. 34:14 [1]*remission*
**2** [1]*cancel the debt* [2]*exact it*
**4** [a]Deut. 7:13
**6** [a]Deut. 28:12, 44
**7** [a]Ex. 23:6; Lev. 25:35–37; Deut. 24:12–14; [1 John 3:17] [1]*towns*
**8** [a]Matt. 5:42; Gal. 2:10 [1]*freely open*
**9** [a]Deut. 28:54, 56 [b]Ex. 22:23; Deut. 24:15; Job 34:28; Ps. 12:5; James 5:4 [c][Matt. 25:41, 42]
**10** [a]2 Cor. 9:5, 7 [b]Deut. 14:29; Ps. 41:1; Prov. 22:9

bless you in all your works and in all to which you
put your hand.
11 “For [a]the poor will never cease from the land;
therefore I command you, saying, ‘You shall [1]open
your hand wide to your brother, to your poor and
your needy, in your land.’
**12** [a]“If your brother, a Hebrew man, or a Hebrew
woman, is [b]sold to you and serves you six years,
then in the seventh year you shall let him go free
from you.
13 “And when you [1]send him away free from you,
you shall not let him go away empty-handed;
14 “you shall supply him liberally from your
flock, from your threshing floor, and from your
winepress. *From what* the LORD has [a]blessed you
with, you shall give to him.
15 [a]“You shall remember that you were a slave in
the land of Egypt, and the LORD your God redeemed you; therefore I command you this thing
today.
16 “And [a]if it happens that he says to you, ‘I will
not go away from you,’ because he loves you and
your house, since he prospers with you,
17 “then you shall take an awl and thrust *it*
through his ear to the door, and he shall be your
servant forever. Also to your female servant you
shall do likewise.
18 “It shall not seem hard to you when you send
him away free from you; for he has been worth [a]a
double hired servant in serving you six years.
Then the LORD your God will bless you in all that
you do.
**19** [a]“All the firstborn males that come from your
herd and your flock you shall [1]sanctify to the
LORD your God; you shall do no work with the
firstborn of your herd, nor shear the firstborn of
your flock.
20 [a]“You and your household shall eat *it* before
the LORD your God year by year in the place
which the LORD chooses.
21 [a]“But if there is a defect in it, *if it is* lame or
blind *or has* any serious defect, you shall not
sacrifice it to the LORD your God.
22 “You may eat it within your gates; [a]the unclean and the clean *person* alike *may eat it,* as *if it*
*were* a gazelle or a deer.
23 “Only you shall not eat its blood; you shall
pour it on the ground like water.

## *The Three Appointed Feasts*

**16** “Observe the [a]month of Abib, and keep the
Passover to the LORD your God, for [b]in the
month of Abib the LORD your God brought you
out of Egypt by night.
2 “Therefore you shall sacrifice the Passover to
the LORD your God, from the flock and [a]the herd,
in the [b]place where the LORD chooses to put His
name.
3 “You shall eat no leavened bread with it;
[a]seven days you shall eat unleavened bread with
it, *that is,* the bread of affliction (for you came out
of the land of Egypt in haste), that you may
[b]remember the day in which you came out of the
land of Egypt all the days of your life.
4 [a]“And no leaven shall be seen among you in all
your territory for seven days, nor shall *any* of the
meat which you sacrifice the first day at twilight
remain overnight until [b]morning.
5 “You may not sacrifice the Passover within
any of your gates which the LORD your God gives
you;
6 “but at the place where the LORD your God
chooses to make His name abide, there you shall
sacrifice the Passover [a]at twilight, at the going
down of the sun, at the time you came out of
Egypt.
7 “And you shall roast and eat *it* [a]in the place
which the LORD your God chooses, and in the
morning you shall turn and go to your tents.
8 “Six days you shall eat unleavened bread, and
[a]on the seventh day there *shall be* a [1]sacred
assembly to the LORD your God. You shall do no
work *on it.*
**9** “You shall count seven weeks for yourself;
begin to count the seven weeks from *the time* you
begin *to put* the sickle to the grain.
10 “Then you shall keep the [a]Feast of Weeks to
the LORD your God with the tribute of a freewill
offering from your hand, which you shall give [b]as
the LORD your God blesses you.
11 [a]“You shall rejoice before the LORD your God,
you and your son and your daughter, your male
servant and your female servant, the Levite who
*is* within your gates, the stranger and the fatherless and the widow who *are* among you, at the
place where the LORD your God chooses to make
His name abide.
12 [a]“And you shall remember that you were a
slave in Egypt, and you shall be careful to observe
these statutes.
**13** [a]“You shall observe the Feast of Tabernacles
seven days, when you have gathered from your
threshing floor and from your winepress.
14 “And [a]you shall rejoice in your feast, you and
your son and your daughter, your male servant
and your female servant and the Levite, the
stranger and the fatherless and the widow, who
*are* within your [1]gates.
15 [a]“Seven days you shall keep a sacred feast to
the LORD your God in the place which the LORD
chooses, because the LORD your God will bless
you in all your produce and in all the work of your
hands, so that you surely rejoice.
16 [a]“Three times a year all your males shall
appear before the LORD your God in the place
which He chooses: at the Feast of Unleavened
Bread, at the Feast of Weeks, and at the Feast of
Tabernacles; and [b]they shall not appear before the
LORD empty-handed.
17 “Every man *shall give* as he is able, [a]according
to the blessing of the LORD your God which He
has given you.
**18** “You shall appoint [a]judges and officers in all
your [1]gates, which the LORD your God gives you,
according to your tribes, and they shall judge the
people with just judgment.
19 [a]“You shall not pervert justice; [b]you shall not
[1]show partiality, [c]nor take a bribe, for a bribe
blinds the eyes of the wise and [2]twists the words
of the righteous.
20 “You shall follow what is altogether just, that
you may [a]live and inherit the land which the LORD
your God is giving you.
**21** [a]“You shall not plant for yourself any tree, as
a [1]wooden image, near the altar which you build
for yourself to the LORD your God.
22 [a]“You shall not set up a sacred pillar, which
the LORD your God hates.

## *Various Instructions*

**17** “You [a]shall not sacrifice to the LORD your
God a bull or sheep which has any [1]blemish

---

**11** [a]Matt. 26:11; Mark 14:7; John 12:8 [1]*freely open*
**12** [a]Ex. 21:2–6; Jer. 34:14 [b]Lev. 25:39–46
**13** [1]*set him free*
**14** [a]Prov. 10:22
**15** [a]Deut. 5:15
**16** [a]Ex. 21:5, 6
**18** [a]Is. 16:14
**19** [a]Ex. 13:2, 12 [1]*set apart* or *consecrate*
**20** [a]Lev. 7:15–18; Deut. 12:5; 14:23
**21** [a]Lev. 22:19–25; Deut. 17:1
**22** [a]Deut. 12:15, 16, 22

CHAPTER 16

**1** [a]Ex. 12:2 [b]Ex. 13:4
**2** [a]Num. 28:19 [b]Deut. 12:5, 26; 15:20
**3** [a]Num. 29:12 [b]Ex. 13:3; Deut. 4:9
**4** [a]Ex. 13:7 [b]Num. 9:12
**6** [a]Ex. 12:7–10
**7** [a]2 Kin. 23:23
**8** [a]Ex. 12:16; 13:6; Lev. 23:8, 36 [1]Lit. *restraint*
**10** [a]Ex. 34:22; Lev. 23:15, 16; Num. 28:26 [b]1 Cor. 16:2
**11** [a]Deut. 16:14
**12** [a]Deut. 15:15
**13** [a]Ex. 23:16
**14** [a]Neh. 8:9 [1]*towns*
**15** [a]Lev. 23:39–41
**16** [a]Ex. 23:14–17; 34:22–24 [b]Ex. 23:15
**17** [a]Lev. 14:30, 31; Deut. 16:10
**18** [a]Ex. 23:1–8; Deut. 1:16, 17; John 7:24 [1]*towns*
**19** [a]Ex. 23:2, 6 [b]Deut. 1:17 [c]Ex. 23:8 [1]Lit. *regard faces* [2]*perverts*
**20** [a]Ezek. 18:5–9
**21** [a]Ex. 34:13 [1]Or *Asherah*
**22** [a]Lev. 26:1

CHAPTER 17

**1** [a]Deut. 15:21; Mal. 1:8, 13 [1]Lit. *evil thing*

*or* defect, for that *is* an [2]abomination to the LORD
your God.
**2** [a]"If there is found among you, within any of
your [1]gates which the LORD your God gives you, a
man or a woman who has been wicked in the
sight of the LORD your God, [b]in transgressing His
covenant,
3 "who has gone and served other gods and
worshiped them, either [a]the sun or moon or any of
the host of heaven, [b]which I have not commanded,
4 [a]"and it is told you, and you hear *of it,* then
you shall inquire diligently. And if *it is* indeed true
*and* certain that such an [1]abomination has been
committed in Israel,
5 "then you shall bring out to your gates that
man or woman who has committed that wicked
thing, and [a]shall stone [b]to death that man or
woman with stones.
6 "Whoever is deserving of death shall be put to
death on the testimony of two or three [a]witnesses;
he shall not be put to death on the testimony of
one witness.
7 "The hands of the witnesses shall be the first
against him to put him to death, and afterward
the hands of all the people. So you shall put away
the evil from among [a]you.
**8** [a]"If a matter arises which is too hard for you
to judge, between degrees of guilt for bloodshed,
between one judgment or another, or between
one punishment or another, matters of controversy within your gates, then you shall arise and
go up to the [b]place which the LORD your God
chooses.
9 "And [a]you shall come to the priests, the Levites, and [b]to the judge *there* in those days, and
inquire *of them;* [c]they shall pronounce upon you
the sentence of judgment.
10 "You shall do according to the sentence which
they pronounce upon you in that place which the
LORD chooses. And you shall be careful to do
according to all that they order you.
11 "According to the sentence of the law in
which they instruct you, according to the judgment which they tell you, you shall do; you shall
not turn aside *to* the right hand or *to* the left from
the sentence which they pronounce upon you.
12 "Now [a]the man who acts presumptuously and
will not heed the priest who stands to minister
there before the LORD your God, or the judge, that
man shall die. So you shall put away the evil from
Israel.
13 [a]"And all the people shall hear and fear, and
no longer act presumptuously.
**14** "When you come to the land which the LORD
your God is giving you, and possess it and dwell in
it, and say, [a]'I will set a king over me like all the
nations that *are* around me,'
15 "you shall surely set a king over you [a]whom
the LORD your God chooses; *one* [b]from among
your brethren you shall set as king over you; you
may not set a foreigner over you, who *is* not your
brother.
16 "But he shall not multiply [a]horses for himself,
nor cause the people [b]to return to Egypt to multiply horses, for [c]the LORD has said to you, [d]'You
shall not return that way again.'
17 "Neither shall he multiply wives for himself,
lest his heart turn away; nor shall he greatly
multiply silver and [a]gold for himself.
**18** "Also it shall be, when he sits on the throne of
his kingdom, that he shall write for himself a copy
of this law in a book, from *the one* [a]before the
priests, the Levites.
19 "And [a]it shall be with him, and he shall read it
all the days of his life, that he may learn to fear
the LORD his God and be careful to observe all the
words of this law and these statutes,
20 "that his heart may not [1]be lifted above his
brethren, that he [a]may not turn aside from the
commandment *to* the right hand or *to* the left, and
that he may [2]prolong *his* days in his kingdom, he
and his children in the midst of Israel.

### *The Levites' Share; a New Prophet Is Coming*

**18** "The priests, the Levites—all the tribe of
Levi—shall have [1]no part nor [a]inheritance
with Israel; they shall eat the offerings of the
LORD made by fire, and His portion.
2 "Therefore they shall have no inheritance
among their brethren; the LORD is their inheritance, as He said to them.
**3** "And this shall be the priest's [a]due[1] from the
people, from those who offer a sacrifice, whether
*it is* bull or sheep: they shall give to the priest the
shoulder, the cheeks, and the stomach.
4 [a]"The firstfruits of your grain and your new
wine and your oil, and the first of the fleece of
your sheep, you shall give him.
5 "For [a]the LORD your God has chosen him out
of all your tribes [b]to stand to minister in the name
of the LORD, him and his sons forever.
**6** "So if a Levite comes from any of your [1]gates,
from where he [a]dwells among all Israel, and comes
with all the desire of his mind [b]to the place which
the LORD chooses,
7 "then he may serve in the name of the LORD
his God [a]as all his brethren the Levites *do,* who
stand there before the LORD.
8 "They shall have equal [a]portions to eat, besides what comes from the sale of his inheritance.
**9** "When you come into the land which the
LORD your God is giving you, [a]you shall not learn
to follow the [1]abominations of those nations.
10 "There shall not be found among you *anyone*
who makes his son or his daughter [a]pass[1] through
the fire, [b]*or one* who practices witchcraft, *or* a
soothsayer, or one who interprets omens, or a
sorcerer,
11 [a]"or one who conjures spells, or a medium, or
a spiritist, or [b]one who calls up the dead.
12 "For all who do these things *are* [1]an abomination to the LORD, and [a]because of these abominations the LORD your God drives them out from
before you.
13 "You shall be [1]blameless before the LORD your
God.
14 "For these nations which you will dispossess
listened to soothsayers and diviners; but as for
you, the LORD your God has not [1]appointed such
for you.
**15** [a]"The LORD your God will raise up for you a
Prophet like me from your midst, from your
brethren. Him you shall hear,
16 "according to all you desired of the LORD your
God in Horeb [a]in the day of the assembly, saying,
[b]'Let me not hear again the voice of the LORD my
God, nor let me see this great fire anymore, lest I
die.'
17 "And the LORD said to me: [a]'What they have
spoken is good.

**1** [2]*detestable thing*
**2** [a]Deut. 13:6 [b]Josh. 7:11 [1]*towns*
**3** [a]Deut. 4:19 [b]Jer. 7:22
**4** [a]Deut. 13:12, 14 [1]*detestable thing*
**5** [a]Lev. 24:14–16 [b]Deut. 13:6–18
**6** [a]Num. 35:30
**7** [a]Deut. 13:5; 19:19
**8** [a]Deut. 1:17 [b]Deut. 12:5; 16:2
**9** [a]Jer. 18:18 [b]Deut. 19:17–19 [c]Ezek. 44:24
**12** [a]Num. 15:30
**13** [a]Deut. 13:11
**14** [a]1 Sam. 8:5, 19, 20; 10:19
**15** [a]1 Sam. 9:15, 16; 10:24; 16:12, 13 [b]Jer. 30:21
**16** [a]1 Kin. 4:26; 10:26–29 [b]Ezek. 17:15 [c]Ex. 13:17, 18 [d]Deut. 28:68
**17** [a]1 Kin. 10:14
**18** [a]Deut. 31:24–26
**19** [a]Ps. 119:97, 98
**20** [a]Deut. 5:32 [1]*become proud* [2]*continue long in his kingdom*

CHAPTER 18
**1** [a]Deut. 10:9 [1]*no portion*
**3** [a]Lev. 7:32–34; 1 Sam. 2:13–16, 29 [1]*right*
**4** [a]Ex. 22:29
**5** [a]Ex. 28:1 [b]Deut. 10:8
**6** [a]Num. 35:2 [b]Deut. 12:5; 14:23 [1]*towns*
**7** [a]2 Chr. 31:2
**8** [a]2 Chr. 31:4
**9** [a]Deut. 12:29, 30; 20:16–18 [1]*detestable acts*
**10** [a]Deut. 12:31 [b]Is. 8:19 [1]Be burned as an offering to an idol
**11** [a]Lev. 20:27 [b]1 Sam. 28:7
**12** [a]Lev. 18:24 [1]*detestable*
**13** [1]Lit. *perfect*
**14** [1]*allowed you to do so*
**15** [a]Acts 3:22
**16** [a]Deut. 5:23–27 [b]Ex. 20:18, 19
**17** [a]Deut. 5:28

18 [a]'I will raise up for them a Prophet like you
from among their brethren, and [b]will put My
words in His mouth, [c]and He shall speak to them
all that I command Him.
19 [a]'And it shall be *that* whoever will not hear My
words, which He speaks in My name, I will require
*it* of him.
20 'But [a]the prophet who presumes to speak a
word in My name, which I have not commanded
him to speak, or [b]who speaks in the name of other
gods, that prophet shall die.'
21 "And if you say in your heart, 'How shall we
know the word which the LORD has not spoken?'—
22 [a]"when a prophet speaks in the name of the
LORD, [b]if the thing does not happen or come to
pass, that *is* the thing which the LORD has not
spoken; the prophet has spoken it [c]presumptu-
ously; you shall not be afraid of him.

## *Cities of Safety*

**19** "When the LORD your God [a]has cut off the
nations whose land the LORD your God is
giving you, and you dispossess them and dwell in
their cities and in their houses,
2 [a]"you shall separate three cities for yourself in
the midst of your land which the LORD your God is
giving you to possess.
3 "You shall prepare roads for yourself, and
divide into three parts the territory of your land
which the LORD your God is giving you to inherit,
that any manslayer may flee there.
4 "And [a]this *is* the case of the manslayer who
flees there, that he may live: Whoever kills his
neighbor [1]unintentionally, not having hated him
in time past—
5 "as when *a man* goes to the woods with his
neighbor to cut timber, and his hand swings a
stroke with the ax to cut down the tree, and the
head slips from the handle and strikes his neighbor so that he dies—he shall flee to one of these
cities and live;
6 [a]"lest the avenger of blood, while his anger is
hot, pursue the manslayer and overtake him,
because the way is long, and kill him, though he
*was* not deserving of death, since he had not
hated the victim in time past.
7 "Therefore I command you, saying, 'You shall
separate three cities for yourself.'
8 "Now if the LORD your God [a]enlarges your
territory, as He swore to [b]your fathers, and gives
you the land which He promised to give to your
fathers,
9 "and if you keep all these commandments and
do them, which I command you today, to love the
LORD your God and to walk always in His ways,
[a]then you shall add three more cities for yourself
besides these three,
10 [a]"lest innocent blood be shed in the midst of
your land which the LORD your God is giving you
*as* an inheritance, and *thus* guilt of bloodshed be
upon you.
**11** "But [a]if anyone hates his neighbor, lies in wait
for him, rises against him and strikes him mortally, so that he dies, and he flees to one of these
cities,
12 "then the elders of his city shall send and
bring him from there, and deliver him over to the
hand of the avenger of blood, that he may die.
13 [a]"Your eye shall not pity him, [b]but you shall
[1]put away *the guilt of* innocent blood from Israel,
that it may go well with you.
**14** [a]"You shall not remove your neighbor's landmark, which the men of old have set, in your
inheritance which you will inherit in the land that
the LORD your God is giving you to possess.
**15** [a]"One witness shall not rise against a man
concerning any iniquity or any sin that he commits; by the mouth of two or three witnesses the
matter shall be established.
16 "If a false witness [a]rises against any man to
testify against him of wrongdoing,
17 "then both men in the controversy shall stand
before the LORD, [a]before the priests and the judges
who serve in those days.
18 "And the judges shall make careful inquiry,
and indeed, *if* the witness *is* a false witness, who
has testified falsely against his brother,
19 [a]"then you shall do to him as he thought to
have done to his brother; so [b]you shall put away
the evil from among you.
20 [a]"And those who remain shall hear and fear,
and hereafter they shall not again commit such
evil among you.
21 [a]"Your eye shall not pity: [b]life *shall be* for life,
eye for eye, tooth for tooth, hand for hand, foot
for foot.

## *Laws Concerning War*

**20** "When you go out to battle against your
enemies, and see [a]horses and chariots *and*
people more numerous than you, do not be [b]afraid
of them; for the LORD your God *is* [c]with you, who
brought you up from the land of Egypt.
2 "So it shall be, when you are on the verge of
battle, that the priest shall approach and speak to
the people.
3 "And he shall say to them, 'Hear, O Israel:
Today you are on the verge of battle with your
enemies. Do not let your heart faint, do not be
afraid, and do not tremble or be terrified because
of them;
4 'for the LORD your God *is* He who goes with
you, [a]to fight for you against your enemies, to
save you.'
5 "Then the officers shall speak to the people,
saying: 'What man *is there* who has built a new
house and has not [a]dedicated it? Let him go and
return to his house, lest he die in the battle and
another man dedicate it.
6 'Also what man *is there* who has planted a
vineyard and has not eaten of it? Let him go and
return to his house, lest he die in the battle and
another man eat of it.
7 [a]'And what man *is there* who is betrothed to a
woman and has not married her? Let him go and
return to his house, lest he die in the battle and
another man marry her.'
8 "The officers shall speak further to the people,
and say, [a]'What man *is there who is* fearful and
fainthearted? Let him go and return to his house,
[1]lest the heart of his brethren faint like his heart.'
9 "And so it shall be, when the officers have
finished speaking to the people, that they shall
make captains of the armies to lead the people.
**10** "When you go near a city to fight against it,
[a]then proclaim an offer of peace to it.
11 "And it shall be that if they accept your offer
of peace, and open to you, then all the people *who
are* found in it shall be placed under tribute to
you, and serve you.

**18** [a]Deut. 34:10; John 1:45; Acts 3:22 [b]Num. 23:5; Is. 49:2; 51:16; John 17:8 [c][John 4:25; 8:28]
**19** [a]Acts 3:23; [Heb. 12:25]
**20** [a]Deut. 13:5; Jer. 14:14, 15; Zech. 13:2–5 [b]Deut. 13:1–3; Jer. 2:8
**22** [a]Jer. 28:9 [b]Deut. 13:2 [c]Deut. 18:20

CHAPTER 19
**1** [a]Deut. 12:29
**2** [a]Ex. 21:13; Num. 35:10–15; Deut. 4:41; Josh. 20:2
**4** [a]Num. 35:9–34; Deut. 4:42 [1]*ignorantly,* lit. *without knowledge*
**6** [a]Num. 35:12
**8** [a]Deut. 12:20 [b]Gen. 15:18–21
**9** [a]Josh. 20:7–9
**10** [a]Num. 35:33; Deut. 21:1–9
**11** [a]Num. 35:16, 24; Deut. 27:24; [1 John 3:15]
**13** [a]Deut. 13:8 [b]Num. 35:33, 34; 1 Kin. 2:31 [1]*purge the blood of the innocent*
**14** [a]Deut. 27:17; Job 24:2; Prov. 22:28; Hos. 5:10
**15** [a]Num. 35:30; Deut. 17:6; Matt. 18:16; John 8:17; 2 Cor. 13:1; 1 Tim. 5:19; Heb. 10:28
**16** [a]Ex. 23:1; Ps. 27:12; 35:11
**17** [a]Deut. 17:8–11; 21:5
**19** [a]Prov. 19:5; Dan. 6:24 [b]Deut. 13:5; 17:7; 21:21; 22:21
**20** [a]Deut. 17:13; 21:21
**21** [a]Deut. 19:13 [b]Ex. 21:23, 24; Lev. 24:20; Matt. 5:38, 39

CHAPTER 20
**1** [a]Ps. 20:7; Is. 31:1 [b]Deut. 7:18 [c]Num. 23:21; Deut. 5:6; 31:6, 8; 2 Chr. 13:12; 32:7, 8; Ps. 23:4; Is. 41:10
**4** [a]Deut. 1:30; 3:22; Josh. 23:10
**5** [a]Neh. 12:27
**7** [a]Deut. 24:5
**8** [a]Judg. 7:3 [1]So with MT, Tg.; Sam., LXX, Syr., Vg. *lest he make his brother's heart faint*
**10** [a]2 Sam. 10:19

12 "Now if the city will not make peace with you, but makes war against you, then you shall besiege it.

13 "And when the LORD your God delivers it into your hands, [a]you shall strike every male in it with the edge of the sword.

14 "But the women, the little ones, [a]the livestock, and all that is in the city, all its spoil, you shall plunder for yourself; and [b]you shall eat the enemies' plunder which the LORD your God gives you.

15 "Thus you shall do to all the cities *which are* very far from you, which *are* not of the cities of these nations.

16 "But [a]of the cities of these peoples which the LORD your God gives you *as* an inheritance, you shall let nothing that breathes remain alive,

17 "but you shall utterly destroy them: the Hittite and the Amorite and the Canaanite and the Perizzite and the Hivite and the Jebusite, just as the LORD your God has commanded you,

18 "lest [a]they teach you to do according to all their [1]abominations which they have done for their gods, and you [b]sin against the LORD your God.

**19** "When you besiege a city for a long time, while making war against it to take it, you shall not destroy its trees by wielding an ax against them; if you can eat of them, do not cut them down to use in the siege, for the tree of the field *is* man's *food.*

20 "Only the trees which you know *are* not trees for food you may destroy and cut down, to build siegeworks against the city that makes war with you, until it is subdued.

## *Unsolved Murder and Other Regulations*

**21** "If *anyone* is found slain, lying in the field in the land which the LORD your God is giving you to possess, *and* it is not known who killed him,

2 "then your elders and your judges shall go out and measure *the distance* from the slain man to the surrounding cities.

3 "And it shall be *that* the elders of the city nearest to the slain man will take a heifer which has not been worked *and* which has not pulled with a [a]yoke.

4 "The elders of that city shall bring the heifer down to a valley with flowing water, which is neither plowed nor sown, and they shall break the heifer's neck there in the valley.

5 "Then the priests, the sons of Levi, shall come near, for [a]the LORD your God has chosen them to minister to Him and to bless in the name of the LORD; [b]by their word every controversy and every [1]assault shall be *settled.*

6 "And all the elders of that city nearest to the slain *man* [a]shall wash their hands over the heifer whose neck was broken in the valley.

7 "Then they shall answer and say, 'Our hands have not shed this blood, nor have our eyes seen *it.*

8 'Provide atonement, O LORD, for Your people Israel, whom You have redeemed, [a]and do not lay innocent blood to the charge of Your people Israel.' And atonement shall be provided on their behalf for the blood.

9 "So [a]you shall put away the *guilt of* innocent blood from among you when you do *what is* right in the sight of the LORD.

**10** "When you go out to war against your enemies, and the LORD your God delivers them into your hand, and you take them captive,

11 "and you see among the captives a beautiful woman, and desire her and would take her for your [a]wife,

12 "then you shall bring her home to your house, and she shall [a]shave her head and trim her nails.

13 "She shall put off the clothes of her captivity, remain in your house, and [a]mourn her father and her mother a full month; after that you may go in to her and be her husband, and she shall be your wife.

14 "And it shall be, if you have no delight in her, then you shall set her free, but you certainly shall not sell her for money; you shall not treat her brutally, because you have [a]humbled her.

**15** "If a man has two wives, one loved [a]and the other unloved, and they have borne him children, *both* the loved and the unloved, and *if* the firstborn son is of her who is unloved,

16 "then it shall be, [a]on the day he bequeaths his possessions to his sons, *that* he must not bestow firstborn status on the son of the loved wife in preference to the son of the unloved, the *true* firstborn.

17 "But he shall acknowledge the son of the unloved wife *as* the firstborn [a]by giving him a double portion of all that he has, for he [b]*is* the beginning of his strength; [c]the right of the firstborn *is* his.

**18** "If a man has a stubborn and rebellious son who will not obey the voice of his father or the voice of his mother, and *who,* when they have chastened him, will not heed them,

19 "then his father and his mother shall take hold of him and bring him out to the elders of his city, to the gate of his city.

20 "And they shall say to the elders of his city, 'This son of ours is stubborn and rebellious; he will not obey our voice; he is a glutton and a drunkard.'

21 "Then all the men of his city shall stone him to death with stones; [a]so you shall put away the evil from among you, [b]and all Israel shall hear and fear.

**22** "If a man has committed a sin [a]deserving of death, and he is put to death, and you hang him on a tree,

23 [a]"his body shall not remain overnight on the tree, but you shall surely bury him that day, so that [b]you do not defile the land which the LORD your God is giving you *as* an inheritance; for [c]he who is hanged *is* accursed of God.

## *Various Laws of Morality*

**22** "You [a]shall not see your brother's ox or his sheep going astray, and [1]hide yourself from them; you shall certainly bring them back to your brother.

2 "And if your brother *is* not near you, or if you do not know him, then you shall bring it to your own house, and it shall remain with you until your brother seeks it; then you shall restore it to him.

3 "You shall do the same with his donkey, and so shall you do with his garment; with any lost thing of your brother's, which he has lost and you have found, you shall do likewise; you [1]must not hide yourself.

4 [a]"You shall not see your brother's donkey or his ox fall down along the road, and hide yourself

---

13 [a]Num. 31:7
14 [a]Josh. 8:2 [b]1 Sam. 14:30
16 [a]Ex. 23:31–33; Num. 21:2, 3; Deut. 7:1–5; Josh. 11:14
18 [a]Ex. 34:12–16; Deut. 7:4; 12:30; 18:9 [b]Ex. 23:33; 2 Kin. 21:3–15; Ps. 106:34–41 [1]*detestable things*

CHAPTER 21
3 [a]Num. 19:2
5 [a]Deut. 10:8; 1 Chr. 23:13 [b]Deut. 17:8, 9 [1]Lit. *stroke*
6 [a]Ps. 19:12; 26:6; Matt. 27:24
8 [a]Deut. 19:10, 13; Jon. 1:14
9 [a]Deut. 19:13
11 [a]Num. 31:18
12 [a]Lev. 14:8, 9; Num. 6:9
13 [a]Ps. 45:10
14 [a]Gen. 34:2; Deut. 22:29; Judg. 19:24
15 [a]Gen. 29:33
16 [a]1 Chr. 5:2; 26:10
17 [a]2 Kin. 2:9 [b]Gen. 49:3 [c]Gen. 25:31, 33
21 [a]Deut. 13:5; 19:19, 20; 22:21, 24 [b]Deut. 13:11
22 [a]Deut. 22:26; Matt. 26:66; Mark 14:64; Acts 23:29
23 [a]Josh. 8:29; 10:26, 27; John 19:31 [b]Lev. 18:25; Num. 35:34 [c]Gal. 3:13

CHAPTER 22
1 [a]Ex. 23:4 [1]*ignore them*
3 [1]*may not avoid responsibility*
4 [a]Ex. 23:5

from them; you shall surely help him lift *them* up
again.
5 "A woman shall not wear anything that pertains to a man, nor shall a man put on a woman's
garment, for all who do so *are* [1]an abomination to
the LORD your God.
6 "If a bird's nest happens to be before you
along the way, in any tree or on the ground, with
young ones or eggs, with the mother sitting on the
young or on the eggs, [a]you shall not take the
mother with the young;
7 "you shall surely let the mother go, and take
the young for yourself, [a]that it may be well with
you and *that* you may prolong *your* days.
8 "When you build a new house, then you shall
make a parapet for your roof, that you may not
bring guilt of bloodshed on your household if
anyone falls from it.
9 [a]"You shall not sow your vineyard with different kinds of seed, lest the yield of the seed which
you have sown and the fruit of your vineyard be
defiled.
10 [a]"You shall not plow with an ox and a donkey
together.
11 [a]"You shall not wear a garment of different
sorts, *such as* wool and linen mixed together.
12 "You shall make [a]tassels on the four corners
of the clothing with which you cover *yourself*.
13 "If any man takes a wife, and goes in to her,
and [a]detests her,
14 "and charges her with shameful conduct, and
brings a bad name on her, and says, 'I took this
woman, and when I came to her I found she *was*
not a virgin,'
15 "then the father and mother of the young
woman shall take and bring out *the evidence of*
the young woman's virginity to the elders of the
city at the gate.
16 "And the young woman's father shall say to
the elders, 'I gave my daughter to this man as
wife, and he detests her.
17 'Now he has charged her with shameful conduct, saying, "I found your daughter *was* not a
virgin," and yet these *are the evidences of* my
daughter's virginity.' And they shall spread the
cloth before the elders of the city.
18 "Then the elders of that city shall take that
man and punish him;
19 "and they shall fine him one hundred *shekels*
of silver and give *them* to the father of the young
woman, because he has brought a bad name on a
virgin of Israel. And she shall be his wife; he
cannot divorce her all his days.
20 "But if the thing is true, *and evidences of*
virginity are not found for the young woman,
21 "then they shall bring out the young woman
to the door of her father's house, and the men of
her city shall stone her to death with [a]stones,
because she has [b]done a disgraceful thing in
Israel, to play the harlot in her father's house. [c]So
you shall [1]put away the evil from among you.
22 [a]"If a man is found lying with a woman married to a husband, then both of them shall die—
the man that lay with the woman, and the
woman; so you shall put away the evil from Israel.
23 "If a young woman *who is* a virgin is [a]be-
trothed to a husband, and a man finds her in the
city and lies with her,
24 "then you shall bring them both out to the
gate of that city, and you shall stone them to
death with stones, the young woman because she
did not cry out in the city, and the man because
he [a]humbled his neighbor's wife; [b]so you shall put
away the evil from among you.
25 "But if a man finds a betrothed young woman
in the countryside, and the man forces her and lies
with her, then only the man who lay with her
shall die.
26 "But you shall do nothing to the young
woman; *there is* in the young woman no sin
*deserving* of death, for just as when a man rises
against his neighbor and kills him, even so *is* this
matter.
27 "For he found her in the countryside, *and* the
betrothed young woman cried out, but *there was*
no one to save her.
28 [a]"If a man finds a young woman *who is* a
virgin, who is not betrothed, and he seizes her and
lies with her, and they are found out,
29 "then the man who lay with her shall give to
the young woman's father [a]fifty *shekels* of silver,
and she shall be his wife [b]because he has humbled
her; he shall not be permitted to divorce her all his
days.
30 [a]"A man shall not take his father's wife, nor
[b]uncover his father's bed.

### *Those Excluded from the Congregation*

23 "He who is emasculated by crushing or
mutilation shall [a]not enter the assembly of
the LORD.
2 "One of illegitimate birth shall not enter the
assembly of the LORD; even to the tenth generation none of his *descendants* shall enter the
assembly of the LORD.
3 [a]"An Ammonite or Moabite shall not enter the
assembly of the LORD; even to the tenth generation none of his *descendants* shall enter the
assembly of the LORD forever,
4 [a]"because they did not meet you with bread
and water on the road when you came out of
Egypt, and [b]because they hired against you Balaam the son of Beor from Pethor of [1]Mesopota-
mia, to curse you.
5 "Nevertheless the LORD your God would not
listen to Balaam, but the LORD your God turned
the curse into a blessing for you, because the
LORD your God [a]loves you.
6 [a]"You shall not seek their peace nor their
prosperity all your days forever.
7 "You shall not abhor an Edomite, [a]for he *is*
your brother. You shall not abhor an Egyptian,
because [b]you were an alien in his land.
8 "The children of the third generation born to
them may enter the assembly of the LORD.
9 "When the army goes out against your enemies, then keep yourself from every wicked
thing.
10 [a]"If there is any man among you who becomes
unclean by some occurrence in the night, then he
shall go outside the camp; he shall not come inside
the camp.
11 "But it shall be, when evening comes, that [a]he
shall wash with water; and when the sun sets, he
may come into the camp.
12 "Also you shall have a place outside the camp,
where you may go out;
13 "and you shall have an implement among
your equipment, and when you sit down outside,
you shall dig with it and turn and cover your
refuse.
14 "For the LORD your God [a]walks in the midst of

5 [1]*detestable*
6 [a]Lev. 22:28
7 [a]Deut. 4:40
9 [a]Lev. 19:19
10 [a][2 Cor. 6:14–16]
11 [a]Lev. 19:19
12 [a]Num. 15:37–41; Matt. 23:5
13 [a]Deut. 21:15; 24:3
21 [a]Deut. 21:21 [b]Gen. 34:7; Judg. 20:5–10; 2 Sam. 13:12, 13 [c]Deut. 13:5 [1]*purge the evil person*
22 [a]Lev. 20:10; Num. 5:22–27; Ezek. 16:38; [Matt. 5:27, 28]; John 8:5; [1 Cor. 6:9; Heb. 13:4]
23 [a]Lev. 19:20–22; Matt. 1:18, 19
24 [a]Deut. 21:14 [b]Deut. 22:21, 22; 1 Cor. 5:2, 13
28 [a]Ex. 22:16, 17
29 [a]Ex. 22:16, 17 [b]Deut. 22:24
30 [a]Lev. 18:8; 20:11; Deut. 27:20; 1 Cor. 5:1 [b]Ruth 3:9; Ezek. 16:8

CHAPTER 23
1 [a]Lev. 21:20; 22:24
3 [a]Neh. 13:1, 2
4 [a]Deut. 2:27–30 [b]Num. 22:5, 6; 23:7; Josh. 24:9; 2 Pet. 2:15; Jude 11 [1]Heb. *Aram Naharaim*
5 [a]Deut. 4:37
6 [a]Ezra 9:12
7 [a]Gen. 25:24–26; Deut. 2:4, 8; Amos 1:11; Obad. 10, 12 [b]Ex. 22:21; 23:9; Lev. 19:34; Deut. 10:19
10 [a]Lev. 15:16
11 [a]Lev. 15:5
14 [a]Lev. 26:12; Deut. 7:21

your camp, to deliver you and give your enemies
over to you; therefore your camp shall be holy,
that He may see no unclean thing among you, and
turn away from you.
15 [a]"You shall not give back to his master the
slave who has escaped from his master to you.
16 "He may dwell with you in your midst, in the
place which he chooses within one of your gates,
where it [1]seems best to him; [a]you shall not oppress
him.
17 "There shall be no *ritual* [1]harlot [a]of the daughters of Israel, or a [b]perverted[2] one of the sons of
Israel.
18 "You shall not bring the wages of a harlot or
the price of a dog to the house of the LORD your
God for any vowed offering, for both of these *are*
[1]an abomination to the LORD your God.
19 [a]"You shall not charge interest to your
brother—interest on money *or* food *or* anything
that is lent out at interest.
20 [a]"To a foreigner you may charge interest, but
to your brother you shall not charge interest, [b]that
the LORD your God may bless you in all to which
you set your hand in the land which you are
entering to possess.
21 [a]"When you make a vow to the LORD your
God, you shall not delay to pay it; for the LORD
your God will surely require it of you, and it would
be sin to you.
22 "But if you abstain from vowing, it shall not
be sin to you.
23 [a]"That which has gone from your lips you
shall keep and perform, for you voluntarily vowed
to the LORD your God what you have promised
with your mouth.
24 "When you come into your neighbor's vineyard, you may eat your fill of grapes at your
pleasure, but you shall not put *any* in your container.
25 "When you come into your neighbor's standing grain, [a]you may pluck the heads with your
hand, but you shall not use a sickle on your
neighbor's standing grain.

## *Laws Concerning the Family*

24 "When a [a]man takes a wife and marries her,
and it happens that she finds no favor in his
eyes because he has found some [1]uncleanness in
her, and he writes her a [b]certificate of divorce,
puts *it* in her hand, and sends her out of his house,
2 "when she has departed from his house, and
goes and becomes another man's *wife,*
3 "*if* the latter husband detests her and writes
her a certificate of divorce, puts *it* in her hand, and
sends her out of his house, or if the latter husband
dies who took her as his wife,
4 [a]"*then* her former husband who divorced her
must not take her back to be his wife after she has
been defiled; for that *is* [1]an abomination before
the LORD, and you shall not bring sin on the land
which the LORD your God is giving you *as* an
inheritance.
5 [a]"When a man has taken a new wife, he shall
not go out to war or be charged with any business; he shall be free at home one year, and [b]bring
happiness to his wife whom he has taken.
6 "No man shall take the lower or the upper
millstone in pledge, for he takes [1]*one's* living in
pledge.
7 "If a man is [a]found [1]kidnapping any of his
brethren of the children of Israel, and mistreats
him or sells him, then that kidnapper shall die;
[b]and you shall put away the evil from among you.
8 "Take heed in [a]an outbreak of leprosy, that
you carefully observe and do according to all that
the priests, the Levites, shall teach you; just as I
commanded them, *so* you shall be careful to do.
9 [a]"Remember what the LORD your God did [b]to
Miriam on the way when you came out of Egypt.
10 "When you [a]lend your brother anything, you
shall not go into his house to get his pledge.
11 "You shall stand outside, and the man to
whom you lend shall bring the pledge out to you.
12 "And if the man *is* poor, you shall not [1]keep
his pledge overnight.
13 [a]"You shall in any case return the pledge to
him again when the sun goes down, that he may
sleep in his own garment and [b]bless you; and [c]it
shall be righteousness to you before the LORD
your God.
14 "You shall not [a]oppress a hired servant *who is*
poor and needy, *whether* one of your brethren or
one of the aliens who *is* in your land within your
gates.
15 "Each day [a]you shall give *him* his wages, and
not let the sun go down on it, for he *is* poor and
has set his heart on it; [b]lest he cry out against you
to the LORD, and it be sin to you.
16 [a]"Fathers shall not be put to death for *their*
children, nor shall children be put to death for
*their* fathers; a person shall be put to death for his
own sin.
17 [a]"You shall not pervert justice due the stranger or the fatherless, [b]nor take a widow's garment
as a pledge.
18 "But [a]you shall remember that you were a
slave in Egypt, and the LORD your God redeemed
you from there; therefore I command you to do
this thing.
19 [a]"When you reap your harvest in your field,
and forget a sheaf in the field, you shall not go
back to get it; it shall be for the stranger, the
fatherless, and the widow, that the LORD your God
may [b]bless you in all the work of your hands.
20 "When you beat your olive trees, you shall not
go over the boughs again; it shall be for the
stranger, the fatherless, and the widow.
21 "When you gather the grapes of your vineyard, you shall not glean *it* afterward; it shall be
for the stranger, the fatherless, and the widow.
22 "And you shall remember that you were a
slave in the land of Egypt; therefore I command
you to do this thing.

## *Laws of Social Responsibility*

25 "If there is a [a]dispute between men, and
they come to [1]court, that *the judges* may
judge them, and they [b]justify the righteous and
condemn the wicked,
2 "then it shall be, if the wicked man [a]deserves
to be beaten, that the judge will cause him to lie
down [b]and be beaten in his presence, according to
his guilt, with a certain number of blows.
3 [a]"Forty blows he may give him *and* no more,
lest he should exceed this and beat him with many
blows above these, and your brother [b]be humiliated in your sight.
4 [a]"You shall not muzzle an ox while it [1]treads
out *the grain.*
5 [a]"If brothers dwell together, and one of them
dies and has no son, the widow of the dead man
shall not be *married* to a stranger outside *the*

15 [a]1 Sam. 30:15
16 [a]Ex. 22:21 [1]*pleases him best*
17 [a]Lev. 19:29 [b]2 Kin. 23:7 [1]Heb. *qedeshah,* fem. of *qedesh* (note 2) [2]Heb. *qedesh,* one practicing sodomy and prostitution in religious rituals
18 [1]*detestable*
19 [a]Ex. 22:25
20 [a]Deut. 15:3 [b]Deut. 15:10
21 [a]Eccl. 5:4, 5
23 [a]Ps. 66:13, 14
25 [a]Luke 6:1

CHAPTER 24

1 [a][Matt. 5:31; 19:7] [b][Jer. 3:8] [1]*indecency,* lit. *nakedness of a thing*
4 [a][Jer. 3:1] [1]*a detestable thing*
5 [a]Deut. 20:7 [b]Prov. 5:18
6 [1]*life*
7 [a]Ex. 21:16 [b]Deut. 19:19 [1]Lit. *stealing*
8 [a]Lev. 13:2; 14:2
9 [a][1 Cor. 10:6] [b]Num. 12:10
10 [a]Matt. 5:42
12 [1]Lit. *sleep with his pledge*
13 [a]Ex. 22:26 [b]2 Tim. 1:18 [c]Deut. 6:25
14 [a][Mal. 3:5]
15 [a]Lev. 19:13 [b]James 5:4
16 [a]Ezek. 18:20
17 [a]Ex. 23:6 [b]Ex. 22:26
18 [a]Deut. 24:22
19 [a]Lev. 19:9, 10 [b]Ps. 41:1

CHAPTER 25

1 [a]Deut. 17:8–13; 19:17 [b]Prov. 17:15 [1]Lit. *the judgment*
2 [a]Prov. 19:29 [b]Matt. 10:17
3 [a]2 Cor. 11:24 [b]Job 18:3
4 [a][Prov. 12:10] [1]*threshes*
5 [a]Matt. 22:24

*family;* her husband's brother shall go in to her,
take her as his wife, and perform the duty of a
husband's brother to her.
6 "And it shall be *that* the firstborn son which
she bears [a]will succeed to the name of his dead
brother, that [b]his name may not be blotted out of
Israel.
7 "But if the man does not want to take his
brother's wife, then let his brother's wife go up to
the [a]gate to the elders, and say, 'My husband's
brother refuses to raise up a name to his brother
in Israel; he will not perform the duty of my
husband's brother.'
8 "Then the elders of his city shall call him and
speak to him. But *if* he stands firm and says, [a]'I do
not want to take her,'
9 "then his brother's wife shall come to him in
the presence of the elders, [a]remove his sandal
from his foot, spit in his face, and answer and say,
'So shall it be done to the man who will not [b]build
up his brother's house.'
10 "And his name shall be called in Israel, 'The
house of him who had his sandal removed.'
**11** "If *two* men fight together, and the wife of one
draws near to rescue her husband from the hand
of the one attacking him, and puts out her hand
and seizes him by the genitals,
12 "then you shall cut off her hand; [a]your eye
shall not pity *her.*
**13** [a]"You shall not have in your bag differing
weights, a heavy and a light.
14 "You shall not have in your house differing
measures, a large and a small.
15 "You shall have a perfect and just weight, a
perfect and just measure, [a]that your days may be
lengthened in the land which the LORD your God
is giving you.
16 "For [a]all who do such things, all who behave
unrighteously, *are* [1]an abomination to the LORD
your God.
**17** [a]"Remember what Amalek did to you on the
way as you were coming out of Egypt,
18 "how he met you on the way and attacked
your rear ranks, all the stragglers at your rear,
when you *were* tired and weary; and he [a]did not
fear God.
19 "Therefore it shall be, [a]when the LORD your
God has given you rest from your enemies all
around, in the land which the LORD your God is
giving you to possess *as* an inheritance, *that* you
will [b]blot out the remembrance of Amalek from
under heaven. You shall not forget.

### *The Offerings of Firstfruits and Tithes*

**26** "And it shall be, when you come into the
land which the LORD your God is giving
you *as* an inheritance, and you possess it and
dwell in it,
2 [a]"that you shall take some of the first of all the
produce of the ground, which you shall bring from
your land that the LORD your God is giving you,
and put *it* in a basket and [b]go to the place where
the LORD your God chooses to make His name
abide.
3 "And you shall go to the one who is priest in
those days, and say to him, 'I declare today to the
LORD [1]your God that I have come to the country
which the LORD swore to our fathers to give us.'
4 "Then the priest shall take the basket out of
your hand and set it down before the altar of the
LORD your God.
5 "And you shall answer and say before the
LORD your God: 'My father *was* [a]a [1]Syrian, [b]about
to perish, and [c]he went down to Egypt and [2]dwelt
there, [d]few in number; and there he became a
nation, [e]great, mighty, and populous.
6 'But the [a]Egyptians mistreated us, afflicted us,
and laid hard bondage on us.
7 [a]'Then we cried out to the LORD God of our
fathers, and the LORD heard our voice and looked
on our affliction and our labor and our oppression.
8 'So [a]the LORD brought us out of Egypt with a
mighty hand and with an outstretched arm, [b]with
great terror and with signs and wonders.
9 'He has brought us to this place and has given
us this land, [a]"a land flowing with milk and
honey";
10 'and now, behold, I have brought the firstfruits of the land which you, O LORD, have given
me.' Then you shall set it before the LORD your
God, and worship before the LORD your God.
11 "So [a]you shall rejoice in every good *thing*
which the LORD your God has given to you and
your house, you and the Levite and the stranger
who *is* among you.
**12** "When you have finished laying aside all the
[a]tithe of your increase in the third year—[b]the year
of tithing—and have given *it* to the Levite, the
stranger, the fatherless, and the widow, so that
they may eat within your gates and be filled,
13 "then you shall say before the LORD your God:
'I have removed the [1]holy *tithe* from *my* house,
and also have given them to the Levite, the
stranger, the fatherless, and the widow, according
to all Your commandments which You have commanded me; I have not transgressed Your commandments, [a]nor have I forgotten *them.*
14 [a]'I have not eaten any of it [1]when in mourning,
nor have I removed *any* of it [2]for an unclean *use,*
nor given *any* of it for the dead. I have obeyed the
voice of the LORD my God, and have done according to all that You have commanded me.
15 [a]'Look down from Your holy [1]habitation, from
heaven, and bless Your people Israel and the land
which You have given us, just as You swore to
our fathers, [b]"a land flowing with milk and
honey." '
**16** "This day the LORD your God commands you
to observe these statutes and judgments; therefore you shall be careful to observe them with all
your heart and with all your soul.
17 "Today you have [a]proclaimed the LORD to be
your God, and that you will walk in His ways and
keep His statutes, His commandments, and His
judgments, and that you will [b]obey His voice.
18 "Also today [a]the LORD has proclaimed you to
be His special people, just as He promised you,
that *you* should keep all His commandments,
19 "and that He will set you [a]high above all
nations which He has made, in praise, in name,
and in honor, and that you may be [b]a [1]holy people
to the LORD your God, just as He has spoken."

### *The Curses at Mount Ebal*

**27** Now Moses, with the elders of Israel, commanded the people, saying: "Keep all the
commandments which I command you today.
2 "And it shall be, on the day [a]when you cross
over the Jordan to the land which the LORD your
God is giving you, that [b]you shall set up for
yourselves large stones, and whitewash them with
lime.

**6** [a]Gen. 38:9 [b]Ruth 4:5, 10
**7** [a]Ruth 4:1, 2
**8** [a]Ruth 4:6
**9** [a]Ruth 4:7, 8 [b]Ruth 4:11
**12** [a]Deut. 7:2; 19:13
**13** [a]Lev. 19:35–37; Prov. 11:1; 20:23; Ezek. 45:10; Mic. 6:11
**15** [a]Ex. 20:12
**16** [a]Prov. 11:1; [1 Thess. 4:6] [1]*detestable*
**17** [a]Ex. 17:8–16; 1 Sam. 15:1–3
**18** [a][Ps. 36:1]; Rom. 3:18
**19** [a]1 Sam. 15:3 [b]Ex. 17:14

CHAPTER 26
**2** [a]Ex. 22:29; 23:16, 19; Num. 18:13; Deut. 16:10; Prov. 3:9 [b]Deut. 12:5
**3** [1]LXX *my*
**5** [a]Gen. 25:20; Hos. 12:12 [b]Gen. 43:1, 2; 45:7, 11 [c]Gen. 46:1, 6; Acts 7:15 [d]Gen. 46:27; Deut. 10:22 [e]Deut. 1:10 [1]Or *Aramean* [2]As a resident alien
**6** [a]Ex. 1:8–11, 14
**7** [a]Ex. 2:23–25; 3:9; 4:31
**8** [a]Ex. 12:37, 51; 13:3, 14, 16; Deut. 5:15 [b]Deut. 4:34; 34:11, 12
**9** [a]Ex. 3:8, 17
**11** [a]Deut. 12:7; 16:11; Eccl. 3:12, 13; 5:18–20
**12** [a]Lev. 27:30; Num. 18:24 [b]Deut. 14:28, 29
**13** [a]Ps. 119:141, 153, 176 [1]*hallowed things*
**14** [a]Lev. 7:20; Jer. 16:7; Hos. 9:4 [1]Lit. *in my mourning* [2]Or *while I was unclean*
**15** [a]Ps. 80:14; Is. 63:15; Zech. 2:13 [b]Ex. 3:8 [1]*home*
**17** [a]Ex. 20:19 [b]Deut. 15:5
**18** [a]Ex. 6:7; 19:5; Deut. 7:6; 14:2; 28:9; [Titus 2:14; 1 Pet. 2:9]
**19** [a]Deut. 4:7, 8; 28:1 [b]Ex. 19:6; Deut. 7:6; 28:9; Is. 62:12; [1 Pet. 2:9] [1]*consecrated*

CHAPTER 27
**2** [a]Josh. 4:1 [b]Josh. 8:32

3 "You shall write on them all the words of this
law, when you have crossed over, that you may
enter the land which the LORD your God is giving
you, [a]'a land flowing with milk and honey,' just as
the LORD God of your fathers promised you.
4 "Therefore it shall be, when you have crossed
over the Jordan, *that* [a]on Mount Ebal you shall set
up these stones, which I command you today, and
you shall whitewash them with lime.
5 "And there you shall build an altar to the
LORD your God, an altar of stones; [a]you shall not
use an iron *tool* on them.
6 "You shall build with [1]whole stones the altar
of the LORD your God, and offer burnt offerings on
it to the LORD your God.
7 "You shall offer peace offerings, and shall eat
there, and [a]rejoice before the LORD your God.
8 "And you shall [a]write very plainly on the
stones all the words of this law."
**9** Then Moses and the priests, the Levites, spoke
to all Israel, saying, "Take heed and listen, O
Israel: [a]This day you have become the people of
the LORD your God.
10 "Therefore you shall obey the voice of the
LORD your God, and observe His commandments
and His statutes which I command you today."
**11** And Moses commanded the people on the
same day, saying,
12 "These shall stand [a]on Mount Gerizim to bless
the people, when you have crossed over the
Jordan: Simeon, Levi, Judah, Issachar, Joseph,
and Benjamin;
13 "and [a]these shall stand on Mount Ebal to
curse: Reuben, Gad, Asher, Zebulun, Dan, and
Naphtali.
**14** "And [a]the Levites shall speak with a loud
voice and say to all the men of Israel:
15 [a]'Cursed *is* the one who makes a carved or
molded image, [1]an abomination to the LORD, the
work of the hands of the craftsman, and sets *it* up
in secret.'
[b]And all the people shall answer and say,
'Amen!'
16 [a]'Cursed *is* the one who treats his father or his
mother with contempt.'
And all the people shall say, 'Amen!'
17 [a]'Cursed *is* the one who moves his neighbor's
landmark.'
And all the people shall say, 'Amen!'
18 [a]'Cursed *is* the one who makes the blind to
wander off the road.'
And all the people shall say, 'Amen!'
19 [a]'Cursed *is* the one who perverts the justice
due the stranger, the fatherless, and widow.'
And all the people shall say, 'Amen!'
20 [a]'Cursed *is* the one who lies with his father's
wife, because he has uncovered his father's bed.'
And all the people shall say, 'Amen!'
21 [a]'Cursed *is* the one who lies with any kind of
animal.'
And all the people shall say, 'Amen!'
22 [a]'Cursed *is* the one who lies with his sister, the
daughter of his father or the daughter of his
mother.'
And all the people shall say, 'Amen!'
23 [a]'Cursed *is* the one who lies with his mother-
in-law.'
And all the people shall say, 'Amen!'
24 [a]'Cursed *is* the one who attacks his neighbor
secretly.'
And all the people shall say, 'Amen!'
25 [a]'Cursed *is* the one who takes a bribe to slay
an innocent person.'
And all the people shall say, 'Amen!'
26 [a]'Cursed *is* the one who does not confirm *all*
the words of this law.'
And all the people shall say, 'Amen!'

### *The Consequences of Disobedience*

**28** "Now it shall come to pass, [a]if you diligently
obey the voice of the LORD your God, to
observe carefully all His commandments which I
command you today, that the LORD your God [b]will
set you high above all nations of the earth.
2 "And all these blessings shall come upon you
and [a]overtake you, because you obey the voice of
the LORD your God:
3 [a]"Blessed *shall* you *be* in the city, and blessed
*shall* you *be* [b]in the country.
4 "Blessed *shall be* [a]the [1]fruit of your body, the
produce of your ground and the increase of your
herds, the increase of your cattle and the offspring
of your flocks.
5 "Blessed *shall be* your basket and your kneading bowl.
6 [a]"Blessed *shall* you *be* when you come in, and
blessed *shall* you *be* when you go out.
**7** "The LORD [a]will cause your enemies who rise
against you to be defeated before your face; they
shall come out against you one way and flee
before you seven ways.
8 "The LORD will [a]command the blessing on you
in your storehouses and in all to which you [b]set
your hand, and He will bless you in the land which
the LORD your God is giving you.
9 [a]"The LORD will establish you as a holy people
to Himself, just as He has sworn to you, if you
keep the commandments of the LORD your God
and walk in His ways.
10 "Then all peoples of the earth shall see that
you are [a]called by the name of the LORD, and they
shall be [b]afraid of you.
11 "And [a]the LORD will grant you plenty of goods,
in the fruit of your body, in the increase of your
livestock, and in the produce of your ground, in
the land of which the LORD [1]swore to your fathers
to give you.
12 "The LORD will open to you His good [1]trea-
sure, the heavens, [a]to give the rain to your land in
its season, and [b]to bless all the work of your hand.
[c]You shall lend to many nations, but you shall not
borrow.
13 "And the LORD will make [a]you the head and
not the tail; you shall be above only, and not be
beneath, if you [1]heed the commandments of the
LORD your God, which I command you today, and
are careful to observe *them*.
14 [a]"So you shall not turn aside from any of the
words which I command you this day, *to* the right
or the left, to go after other gods to serve them.
**15** "But it shall come to pass, [a]if you do not obey
the voice of the LORD your God, to observe carefully all His commandments and His statutes
which I command you today, that all these curses
will come upon you and overtake you:
16 "Cursed *shall* you *be* in the city, and cursed
*shall* you *be* in the country.
17 "Cursed *shall be* your basket and your kneading bowl.
18 "Cursed *shall be* the [1]fruit of your body and
the produce of your land, the increase of your
cattle and the offspring of your flocks.

**3** [a]Ex. 3:8
**4** [a]Deut. 11:29; Josh. 8:30, 31
**5** [a]Ex. 20:25; Josh. 8:31
**6** [1]*uncut*
**7** [a]Deut. 26:11
**8** [a]Josh. 8:32
**9** [a]Deut. 26:18
**12** [a]Deut. 11:29; Josh. 8:33; Judg. 9:7
**13** [a]Deut. 11:29; Josh. 8:33
**14** [a]Deut. 33:10; Josh. 8:33; Dan. 9:11
**15** [a]Ex. 20:4, 23; 34:17; Lev. 19:4; 26:1; Deut. 4:16, 23; Is. 44:9; Hos. 13:2 [b]Num. 5:22; Jer. 11:5; 1 Cor. 14:16 [1]*a detestable thing*
**16** [a]Ex. 20:12; Lev. 19:3; 20:9; Deut. 5:16; 21:18–21; Ezek. 22:7
**17** [a]Deut. 19:14; Prov. 22:28
**18** [a]Lev. 19:14
**19** [a]Ex. 22:21, 22; 23:9; Lev. 19:33; Deut. 10:18; 24:17
**20** [a]Lev. 18:8; 20:11; Deut. 22:30; 1 Cor. 5:1
**21** [a]Ex. 22:19; Lev. 18:23; 20:15, 16
**22** [a]Lev. 18:9
**23** [a]Lev. 18:17; 20:14
**24** [a]Ex. 20:13; 21:12; Lev. 24:17; Num. 35:30, 31
**25** [a]Ex. 23:7; Ps. 15:5; Ezek. 22:12
**26** [a]Ps. 119:21; Jer. 11:3; Gal. 3:10

CHAPTER 28
**1** [a]Ex. 15:26; Lev. 26:3–13; Deut. 7:12–26; 11:13 [b]Deut. 26:19; 1 Chr. 14:2
**2** [a]Deut. 28:15
**3** [a]Ps. 128:1, 4 [b]Gen. 39:5
**4** [a]Gen. 22:17 [1]*offspring*
**6** [a]Ps. 121:8
**7** [a]Lev. 26:7, 8
**8** [a]Lev. 25:21 [b]Deut. 15:10
**9** [a]Ex. 19:5, 6
**10** [a]Num. 6:27; 2 Chr. 7:14; Is. 63:19; Dan. 9:18, 19 [b]Deut. 11:25
**11** [a]Deut. 30:9 [1]*promised*
**12** [a]Lev. 26:4; Deut. 11:14 [b]Deut. 14:29 [c]Deut. 15:6 [1]*storehouse*
**13** [a][Is. 9:14, 15] [1]*listen to*
**14** [a]Deut. 5:32; Josh. 1:7
**15** [a]Lev. 26:14–39; Josh. 23:15; Dan. 9:10–14; Mal. 2:2
**18** [1]*offspring*

19 "Cursed *shall* you *be* when you come in, and cursed *shall* you *be* when you go out.

**20** "The LORD will send on you [a]cursing, [b]confusion, and [c]rebuke in all that you set your hand to do, until you are destroyed and until you perish quickly, because of the wickedness of your doings in which you have forsaken Me.

21 "The LORD will make the [1]plague cling to you until He has consumed you from the land which you are going to possess.

22 [a]"The LORD will strike you with consumption, with fever, with inflammation, with severe burning fever, with the sword, with [b]scorching,[1] and with mildew; they shall pursue you until you perish.

23 "And [a]your heavens which *are* over your head shall be bronze, and the earth which is under you *shall be* iron.

24 "The LORD will change the rain of your land to powder and dust; from the heaven it shall come down on you until you are destroyed.

25 [a]"The LORD will cause you to be defeated before your enemies; you shall go out one way against them and flee seven ways before them; and you shall become [1]troublesome to all the kingdoms of the earth.

26 [a]"Your carcasses shall be food for all the birds of the air and the beasts of the earth, and no one shall frighten *them* away.

27 "The LORD will strike you with [a]the boils of Egypt, with [b]tumors, with the scab, and with the itch, from which you cannot be healed.

28 "The LORD will strike you with madness and blindness and [a]confusion of heart.

29 "And you shall [a]grope at noonday, as a blind man gropes in darkness; you shall not prosper in your ways; you shall be only oppressed and plundered continually, and no one shall save *you.*

30 [a]"You shall betroth a wife, but another man shall lie with her; [b]you shall build a house, but you shall not dwell in it; [c]you shall plant a vineyard, but shall not gather its grapes.

31 "Your ox *shall be* slaughtered before your eyes, but you shall not eat of it; your donkey *shall be* violently taken away from before you, and shall not be restored to you; your sheep *shall be* given to your enemies, and you shall have no one to rescue *them.*

32 "Your sons and your daughters *shall be* given to [a]another people, and your eyes shall look and [b]fail *with longing* for them all day long; and *there shall be* [1]no strength in your [c]hand.

33 "A nation whom you have not known shall eat [a]the fruit of your land and the produce of your labor, and you shall be only oppressed and crushed continually.

34 "So you shall be driven mad because of the sight which your eyes see.

35 "The LORD will strike you in the knees and on the legs with severe boils which cannot be healed, and from the sole of your foot to the top of your head.

36 "The LORD will [a]bring you and the king whom you set over you to a nation which neither you nor your fathers have known, and [b]there you shall serve other gods—wood and stone.

37 "And you shall become [a]an[1] astonishment, a proverb, [b]and a byword among all nations where the LORD will drive you.

38 [a]"You shall carry much seed out to the field but gather little in, for [b]the locust shall [1]consume it.

39 "You shall plant vineyards and tend *them,* but you shall neither drink *of* the [a]wine nor gather the *grapes;* for the worms shall eat them.

40 "You shall have olive trees throughout all your territory, but you shall not anoint *yourself* with the oil; for your olives shall drop off.

41 "You shall beget sons and daughters, but they shall not be yours; for [a]they shall go into captivity.

42 "Locusts shall [1]consume all your trees and the produce of your land.

43 "The alien who *is* among you shall rise higher and higher above you, and you shall come down lower and lower.

44 "He shall lend to you, but you shall not lend to him; he shall be the head, and you shall be the tail.

45 "Moreover all these curses shall come upon you and pursue and overtake you, until you are destroyed, because you [1]did not obey the voice of the LORD your God, to keep His commandments and His statutes which He commanded you.

46 "And they shall be upon [a]you for a sign and a wonder, and on your descendants forever.

**47** [a]"Because you did not serve the LORD your God with joy and gladness of heart, [b]for the abundance of everything,

48 "therefore you shall serve your enemies, whom the LORD will send against you, in [a]hunger, in thirst, in nakedness, and in need of everything; and He [b]will put a yoke of iron on your neck until He has destroyed you.

49 [a]"The LORD will bring a nation against you from afar, from the end of the earth, [b]*as swift* as the eagle flies, a nation whose language you will not understand,

50 "a nation of fierce countenance, [a]which does not respect the elderly nor show favor to the young.

51 "And they shall eat the increase of your livestock and the produce of your land, until you are destroyed; they shall not leave you grain or new wine or oil, *or* the increase of your cattle or the offspring of your flocks, until they have destroyed you.

52 "They shall [a]besiege you at all your gates until your high and fortified walls, in which you trust, come down throughout all your land; and they shall besiege you at all your gates throughout all your land which the LORD your God has given you.

53 [a]"You shall eat the [1]fruit of your own body, the flesh of your sons and your daughters whom the LORD your God has given you, in the siege and desperate straits in which your enemy shall distress you.

54 "The [1]sensitive and very refined man among you [a]will[2] be hostile toward his brother, toward [b]the wife of his bosom, and toward the rest of his children whom he leaves behind,

55 "so that he will not give any of them the flesh of his children whom he will eat, because he has nothing left in the siege and desperate straits in which your enemy shall distress you at all your gates.

56 "The [1]tender and [2]delicate woman among you, who would not venture to set the sole of her foot on the ground because of her delicateness and sensitivity, [3]will refuse to the husband of her bosom, and to her son and her daughter,

57 "her [1]placenta which comes out [a]from be-

**20** [a]Mal. 2:2 [b]Is. 65:14 [c]Ps. 80:16; Is. 30:17
**21** [1]*pestilence*
**22** [a]Lev. 26:16 [b]Amos 4:9 [1]*blight*
**23** [a]Lev. 26:19
**25** [a]Deut. 32:30 [1]*a terror*
**26** [a]1 Sam. 17:44; Ps. 79:2
**27** [a]Ex. 15:26 [b]1 Sam. 5:6
**28** [a]Jer. 4:9
**29** [a]Job 5:14
**30** [a]2 Sam. 12:11; Job 31:10; Jer. 8:10 [b]Amos 5:11; Zeph. 1:13 [c]Deut. 20:6; Job 31:8; Jer. 12:13; Mic. 6:15
**32** [a]2 Chr. 29:9 [b]Ps. 119:82 [c]Neh. 5:5 [1]*nothing you can do*
**33** [a]Lev. 26:16; Jer. 5:15, 17
**36** [a]2 Kin. 17:4, 6; 24:12, 14; 25:7, 11; 2 Chr. 36:1–21; Jer. 39:1–9 [b]Deut. 4:28; Jer. 16:13
**37** [a]1 Kin. 9:7, 8; Jer. 24:9; 25:9 [b]Ps. 44:14 [1]*a thing of horror*
**38** [a]Mic. 6:15; Hag. 1:6 [b]Ex. 10:4; Joel 1:4 [1]*devour*
**39** [a]Zeph. 1:13
**41** [a]Lam. 1:5
**42** [1]*possess*
**45** [1]*did not listen to*
**46** [a]Num. 26:10; Is. 8:18; Ezek. 14:8
**47** [a]Deut. 12:7; Neh. 9:35–37 [b]Deut. 32:15
**48** [a]Lam. 4:4–6 [b]Jer. 28:13, 14
**49** [a]Is. 5:26–30; 7:18–20; Jer. 5:15 [b]Jer. 48:40; 49:22; Lam. 4:19; Hos. 8:1
**50** [a]2 Chr. 36:17
**52** [a]2 Kin. 25:1, 2, 4
**53** [a]Lev. 26:29; 2 Kin. 6:28, 29; Jer. 19:9; Lam. 2:20; 4:10 [1]*offspring*
**54** [a]Deut. 15:9 [b]Deut. 13:6 [1]Lit. *tender* [2]Lit. *his eye shall be evil toward*
**56** [1]*sensitive* [2]*refined* [3]Lit. *her eye shall be evil toward*
**57** [a]Gen. 49:10 [1]*afterbirth*

tween her feet and her children whom she bears;
for she will eat them secretly for lack of everything in the siege and desperate straits in which
your enemy shall distress you at all your gates.
**58** "If you do not carefully observe all the words
of this law that are written in this book, that you
may fear [a]this glorious and awesome name, THE
LORD YOUR GOD,
59 "then the LORD will bring upon you and your
descendants [a]extraordinary plagues—great and
prolonged plagues—and serious and prolonged
sicknesses.
60 "Moreover He will bring back on you all [a]the
diseases of Egypt, of which you were afraid, and
they shall cling to you.
61 "Also every sickness and every plague, which
*is* not written in this Book of the Law, will the
LORD bring upon you until you are destroyed.
62 "You [a]shall be left few in number, whereas
you were [b]as the stars of heaven in multitude,
because you would not obey the voice of the LORD
your God.
63 "And it shall be, *that* just as the LORD [a]re-
joiced over you to do you good and multiply you,
so the LORD [b]will rejoice over you to destroy you
and bring you to nothing; and you shall be
[c]plucked[1] from off the land which you go to
possess.
**64** "Then the LORD [a]will scatter you among all
peoples, from one end of the earth to the other,
and [b]there you shall serve other gods, which
neither you nor your fathers have known—wood
and stone.
65 "And [a]among those nations you shall find no
rest, nor shall the sole of your foot have a resting
place; [b]but there the LORD will give you a [1]trem-
bling heart, failing eyes, and [c]anguish of soul.
66 "Your life shall hang in doubt before you; you
shall fear day and night, and have no assurance of
life.
67 [a]"In the morning you shall say, 'Oh, that it
were evening!' And at evening you shall say, 'Oh,
that it were morning!' because of the fear which
terrifies your heart, and [b]because of the sight
which your eyes see.
68 "And the LORD [a]will take you back to Egypt in
ships, by the way of which I said to you, [b]'You
shall never see it again.' And there you shall be
offered for sale to your enemies as male and
female slaves, but no one will buy *you*."

### *God Renews His Promise to Israel*

**29** These *are* the words of the covenant which
the LORD commanded Moses to make with
the children of Israel in the land of Moab, besides
the [a]covenant which He made with them in
Horeb.
**2** Now Moses called all Israel and said to them:
[a]"You have seen all that the LORD did before your
eyes in the land of Egypt, to Pharaoh and to all his
servants and to all his land—
3 [a]"the great trials which your eyes have seen,
the signs, and those great wonders.
4 "Yet [a]the LORD has not given you a heart to
[1]perceive and eyes to see and ears to hear, to this
*very* day.
5 [a]"And I have led you forty years in the wilderness. [b]Your clothes have not worn out on you, and
your sandals have not worn out on your feet.
6 [a]"You have not eaten bread, nor have you
drunk wine or *similar* drink, that you may know
that I *am* the LORD your God.
7 "And when you came to this place, [a]Sihon
king of Heshbon and Og king of Bashan came out
against us to battle, and we conquered them.
8 "We took their land and [a]gave it as an inheritance to the Reubenites, to the Gadites, and to
half the tribe of Manasseh.
9 "Therefore [a]keep the words of this covenant,
and do them, that you may [b]prosper in all that you
do.
**10** "All of you stand today before the LORD your
God: your leaders and your tribes and your elders
and your officers, all the men of Israel,
11 "your little ones and your wives—also the
stranger who *is* in your camp, from [a]the one who
cuts your wood to the one who draws your water—
12 "that you may enter into covenant with the
LORD your God, and [a]into His oath, which the
LORD your God makes with you today,
13 "that He may [a]establish you today as a people
for Himself, and *that* He may be God to you, [b]just
as He has spoken to you, and [c]just as He has
sworn to your fathers, to Abraham, Isaac, and
Jacob.
**14** "I make this covenant and this oath, [a]not with
you alone,
15 "but with *him* who stands here with us today
before the LORD our God, [a]as well as with *him* who
*is* not here with us today
16 (for you know that we dwelt in the land of
Egypt and that we came through the nations
which you passed by,
17 and you saw their [1]abominations and their
idols which *were* among them—wood and stone
and silver and gold);
18 "so that there may not be among you man or
woman or family or tribe, [a]whose heart turns
away today from the LORD our God, to go *and*
serve the gods of these nations, [b]and that there
may not be among you a root bearing [c]bitterness
or wormwood;
19 "and so it may not happen, when he hears the
words of this curse, that he blesses himself in his
heart, saying, 'I shall have peace, even though I
[1]follow the [a]dictates of my heart'—[b]as though the
drunkard could be included with the sober.
20 [a]"The LORD would not spare him; for then [b]the
anger of the LORD and [c]His jealousy would burn
against that man, and every curse that is written
in this book would settle on him, and the LORD
[d]would blot out his name from under heaven.
21 "And the LORD [a]would separate him from all
the tribes of Israel for adversity, according to all
the curses of the covenant that are written in this
Book of the [b]Law,
22 "so that the coming generation of your children who rise up after you, and the foreigner who
comes from a far land, would say, when they [a]see
the plagues of that land and the sicknesses which
the LORD has laid on it:
23 'The whole land *is* brimstone, [a]salt, and burning; it is not sown, nor does it bear, nor does any
grass grow there, [b]like the overthrow of Sodom
and Gomorrah, Admah, and Zeboiim, which the
LORD overthrew in His anger and His wrath.'
24 "All nations would say, [a]'Why has the LORD
done so to this land? What does the heat of this
great anger mean?'
25 "Then *people* would say: 'Because they have

**58** [a]Ex. 6:3
**59** [a]Dan. 9:12
**60** [a]Deut. 7:15
**62** [a]Deut. 4:27 [b]Deut. 10:22; Neh. 9:23
**63** [a]Deut. 30:9; Jer. 32:41 [b]Prov. 1:26; [Is. 1:24] [c]Jer. 12:14; 45:4 [1]*torn*
**64** [a]Lev. 26:33; Deut. 4:27, 28; Neh. 1:8; Jer. 16:13; Amos 9:9 [b]Deut. 28:36
**65** [a]Lam. 1:3; Amos 9:4 [b]Lev. 26:36 [c]Lev. 26:16 [1]*anxious*
**67** [a]Job 7:4 [b]Deut. 28:34
**68** [a]Jer. 43:7; Hos. 8:13 [b]Deut. 17:16

CHAPTER 29

**1** [a]Lev. 26:46; Deut. 5:2, 3
**2** [a]Ex. 19:4; Deut. 11:7
**3** [a]Deut. 4:34; 7:19
**4** [a][Is. 6:9, 10; Ezek. 12:2]; Matt. 13:14; [Acts 28:26, 27]; Rom. 11:8; [Eph. 4:18] [1]*understand* or *know*
**5** [a]Deut. 1:3; 8:2 [b]Deut. 8:4
**6** [a]Ex. 16:12; Deut. 8:3
**7** [a]Num. 21:23, 24; Deut. 2:26—3:3
**8** [a]Num. 32:33; Deut. 3:12, 13
**9** [a]Deut. 4:6; 1 Kin. 2:3 [b]Josh. 1:7
**11** [a]Josh. 9:21, 23, 27
**12** [a]Neh. 10:29
**13** [a]Deut. 28:9 [b]Ex. 6:7 [c]Gen. 17:7, 8
**14** [a][Jer. 31:31; Heb. 8:7, 8]
**15** [a]Acts 2:39
**17** [1]*detestable things*
**18** [a]Deut. 11:16 [b]Heb. 12:15 [c]Deut. 32:32; Acts 8:23
**19** [a]Jer. 3:17; 7:24 [b]Is. 30:1 [1]*walk in the stubbornness* or *imagination*
**20** [a]Ezek. 14:7 [b]Ps. 74:1 [c]Ps. 79:5; Ezek. 23:25 [d]Ex. 32:33; Deut. 9:14; 2 Kin. 14:27
**21** [a][Matt. 24:51] [b]Deut. 30:10
**22** [a]Jer. 19:8; 49:17; 50:13
**23** [a]Jer. 17:6; Zeph. 2:9 [b]Gen. 19:24, 25; Is. 1:9; Jer. 20:16; Hos. 11:8
**24** [a]1 Kin. 9:8; Jer. 22:8

forsaken the covenant of the LORD God of their fathers, which He made with them when He brought them out of the land of Egypt;
26 'for they went and served other gods and worshiped them, gods that they did not know and that He had not given to them.
27 'Then the anger of the LORD was aroused against this land, [a]to bring on it every curse that is written in this book.
28 'And the LORD [a]uprooted them from their land in anger, in wrath, and in great indignation, and cast them into another land, as *it is* this day.'
29 "The secret *things belong* to the LORD our God, but those *things which are* revealed *belong* to us and to our children forever, that *we* may do all the words of this law.

### *The Blessing of Returning to God*

**30** "Now [a]it shall come to pass, when [b]all these things come upon you, the blessing and the [c]curse which I have set before you, and [d]you [1]call *them* to mind among all the nations where the LORD your God drives you,
2 "and you [a]return to the LORD your God and obey His voice, according to all that I command you today, you and your children, with all your heart and with all your soul,
3 [a]"that the LORD your God will bring you back from captivity, and have compassion on you, and [b]gather you again from all the nations where the LORD your God has scattered you.
4 [a]"If *any* of you are driven out to the farthest *parts* under heaven, from there the LORD your God will gather you, and from there He will bring you.
5 "Then the LORD your God will bring you to the land which your fathers possessed, and you shall possess it. He will prosper you and multiply you more than your fathers.
6 "And [a]the LORD your God will circumcise your heart and the heart of your descendants, to love the LORD your God with all your heart and with all your soul, that you may live.
7 "Also the LORD your God will put all these [a]curses on your enemies and on those who hate you, who persecuted you.
8 "And you will [a]again obey the voice of the LORD and do all His commandments which I command you today.
9 [a]"The LORD your God will make you abound in all the work of your hand, in the [1]fruit of your body, in the increase of your livestock, and in the produce of your land for good. For the LORD will again [b]rejoice over you for good as He rejoiced over your fathers,
10 "if you obey the voice of the LORD your God, to keep His commandments and His statutes which are written in this Book of the Law, *and* if you turn to the LORD your God with all your heart and with all your soul.
**11** "For this commandment which I command you today [a]*is* [1]not *too* mysterious for you, nor *is* it far off.
12 [a]"It *is* not in heaven, that you should say, 'Who will ascend into heaven for us and bring it to us, that we may hear it and do it?'
13 "Nor *is* it beyond the sea, that you should say, 'Who will go over the sea for us and bring it to us, that we may hear it and do it?'
14 "But the word *is* very near you, [a]in your mouth and in your heart, that you may do it.
**15** "See, [a]I have set before you today life and good, death and evil,
16 "in that I command you today to love the LORD your God, to walk in His ways, and to keep His commandments, His statutes, and His judgments, that you may live and multiply; and the LORD your God will bless you in the land which you go to possess.
17 "But if your heart turns away so that you do not hear, and are drawn away, and worship other gods and serve them,
18 [a]"I announce to you today that you shall surely perish; you shall not prolong *your* days in the land which you cross over the Jordan to go in and possess.
19 [a]"I call heaven and earth as witnesses today against you, *that* [b]I have set before you life and death, blessing and cursing; therefore choose life, that both you and your descendants may live;
20 "that you may love the LORD your God, that you may obey His voice, and that you may cling to Him, for He *is* your [a]life and the length of your days; and that you may dwell in the land which the LORD swore to your fathers, to Abraham, Isaac, and Jacob, to give them."

### *Joshua the New Leader of Israel*

**31** Then Moses went and spoke these words to all Israel.
2 And he said to them: "I [a]*am* one hundred and twenty years old today. I can no longer [b]go out and come in. Also the LORD has said to me, [c]'You shall not cross over this Jordan.'
3 "The LORD your God [a]Himself crosses over before you; He will destroy these nations from before you, and you shall dispossess them. [b]Joshua himself crosses over before you, just [c]as the LORD has said.
4 [a]"And the LORD will do to them [b]as He did to Sihon and Og, the kings of the Amorites and their land, when He destroyed them.
5 [a]"The LORD will give them over to you, that you may do to them according to every commandment which I have commanded you.
6 [a]"Be strong and of good courage, [b]do not fear nor be afraid of them; for the LORD your God, [c]He *is* the One who goes with you. [d]He will not leave you nor forsake you."
**7** Then Moses called Joshua and said to him in the sight of all Israel, [a]"Be strong and of good courage, for you must go with this people to the land which the LORD has sworn to their fathers to give them, and you shall cause them to inherit it.
8 "And the LORD, [a]He *is* the One who goes before you. [b]He will be with you, He will not leave you nor forsake you; do not fear nor be dismayed."
**9** So Moses wrote this law [a]and delivered it to the priests, the sons of Levi, [b]who bore the ark of the covenant of the LORD, and to all the elders of Israel.
10 And Moses commanded them, saying: "At the end of *every* seven years, at the appointed time in the [a]year of release, [b]at the Feast of Tabernacles,
11 "when all Israel comes to [a]appear before the LORD your God in the [b]place which He chooses, [c]you shall read this law before all Israel in their hearing.
12 [a]"Gather the people together, men and women and little ones, and the stranger who *is* within your gates, that they may hear and that they may

---

**27** [a]Dan. 9:11
**28** [a]1 Kin. 14:15; 2 Chr. 7:20; Ps. 52:5; Prov. 2:22

CHAPTER 30
**1** [a]Lev. 26:40 [b]Deut. 28:2 [c]Deut. 28:15–45 [d]Deut. 4:29, 30 [1]Lit. *cause them to return to your heart*
**2** [a]Deut. 4:29, 30; Neh. 1:9; Is. 55:7; Lam. 3:40; Joel 2:12
**3** [a]Ps. 106:45; Jer. 29:14; Lam. 3:22, 32 [b]Ps. 147:2; Jer. 32:37; Ezek. 34:13
**4** [a]Deut. 28:64; Neh. 1:9; Is. 62:11
**6** [a]Deut. 10:16; Jer. 32:39; Ezek. 11:19
**7** [a]Is. 54:15–17; Jer. 30:16, 20
**8** [a]Zeph. 3:20
**9** [a]Deut. 28:11 [b]Deut. 28:63; Jer. 32:41 [1]*offspring*
**11** [a]Is. 45:19 [1]*not hidden from*
**12** [a]Prov. 30:4; Rom. 10:6–8
**14** [a]Rom. 10:8
**15** [a]Deut. 30:1, 19
**18** [a]Deut. 4:26; 8:19
**19** [a]Deut. 4:26 [b]Deut. 30:15
**20** [a]Ps. 27:1; [John 11:25; 14:6; Col. 3:4]

CHAPTER 31
**2** [a]Ex. 7:7; Deut. 34:7 [b]Num. 27:17; 1 Kin. 3:7 [c]Num. 20:12
**3** [a]Deut. 9:3; Josh. 11:23 [b]Num. 27:18 [c]Num. 27:21
**4** [a]Deut. 3:21 [b]Num. 21:24, 33
**5** [a]Deut. 7:2; 20:10–20
**6** [a]Josh. 10:25; 1 Chr. 22:13 [b]Deut. 1:29 [c]Deut. 20:4 [d]Josh. 1:5; Heb. 13:5
**7** [a]Num. 27:19; Deut. 31:23; Josh. 1:6
**8** [a]Ex. 13:21 [b]Deut. 31:6; Josh. 1:5; 1 Chr. 28:20; Heb. 13:5
**9** [a]Deut. 17:18; 31:25, 26 [b]Num. 4:5, 6, 15; Deut. 10:8; 31:25, 26; Josh. 3:3
**10** [a]Deut. 15:1, 2 [b]Lev. 23:34; Deut. 16:13
**11** [a]Deut. 16:16 [b]Deut. 12:5 [c]Josh. 8:34; 2 Kin. 23:2
**12** [a]Deut. 4:10

learn to fear the LORD your God and carefully
observe all the words of this law,
13 "and *that* their children, [a]who have not known
it, [b]may hear and learn to fear the LORD your God
as long as you live in the land which you cross the
Jordan to possess."
**14** Then the LORD said to Moses, [a]"Behold, the
days approach when you must die; call Joshua,
and present yourselves in the tabernacle of meeting, that [b]I may [1]inaugurate him." So Moses and
Joshua went and presented themselves in the
tabernacle of meeting.
15 Now [a]the LORD appeared at the tabernacle in a
pillar of cloud, and the pillar of cloud stood above
the door of the tabernacle.
**16** And the LORD said to Moses: "Behold, you will
[1]rest with your fathers; and this people will [a]rise
and [b]play the harlot with the gods of the foreigners of the land, where they go *to be* among them,
and they will [c]forsake Me and [d]break My covenant
which I have made with them.
17 "Then My anger shall be [a]aroused against
them in that day, and [b]I will forsake them, and I
will [c]hide My face from them, and they shall be
[1]devoured. And many evils and troubles shall
befall them, so that they will say in that day,
[d]'Have not these evils come upon us because our
God *is* [e]not among us?'
18 "And [a]I will surely hide My face in that day
because of all the evil which they have done, in
that they have turned to other gods.
19 "Now therefore, write down this song for
yourselves, and teach it to the children of Israel;
put it in their mouths, that this song may be [a]a
witness for Me against the children of Israel.
20 "When I have brought them to the land flowing with milk and honey, of which I swore to their
fathers, and they have eaten and filled themselves
[a]and grown fat, [b]then they will turn to other gods
and serve them; and they will provoke Me and
break My covenant.
21 "Then it shall be, [a]when many evils and troubles have come upon them, that this song will
testify against them as a witness; for it will not be
forgotten in the mouths of their descendants, for
[b]I know the inclination [c]of their behavior today,
even before I have brought them to the land of
which I swore *to give them.*"
**22** Therefore Moses wrote this song the same
day, and taught it to the children of Israel.
23 [a]Then He inaugurated Joshua the son of Nun,
and said, [b]"Be strong and of good courage; for you
shall bring the children of Israel into the land of
which I swore to them, and I will be with you."
**24** So it was, when Moses had completed writing
the words of this law in a book, when they were
finished,
25 that Moses commanded the Levites, who bore
the ark of the covenant of the LORD, saying:
26 "Take this Book of the Law, [a]and put it beside
the ark of the covenant of the LORD your God,
that it may be there [b]as a witness against you;
27 [a]"for I know your rebellion and your [b]stiff
neck. *If* today, while I am yet alive with you, you
have been rebellious against the LORD, then how
much more after my death?
28 "Gather to me all the elders of your tribes, and
your officers, that I may speak these words in
their hearing [a]and call heaven and earth to witness against them.
29 "For I know that after my death you will

**13** [a]Deut. 11:2 [b]Ps. 78:6, 7
**14** [a]Num. 27:13 [b]Num. 27:19; Deut. 3:28 [1]*commission*
**15** [a]Ex. 33:9
**16** [a]Deut. 29:22 [b]Ex. 34:15; Deut. 4:25–28; Judg. 2:11, 12, 17 [c]Deut. 32:15 [d]Judg. 2:20 [1]Die and join your ancestors
**17** [a]Judg. 2:14; 6:13 [b]2 Chr. 15:2 [c]Deut. 32:20 [d]Judg. 6:13 [e]Num. 14:42 [1]*consumed*
**18** [a]Deut. 31:17; [Is. 1:15, 16]
**19** [a]Deut. 31:22, 26
**20** [a]Deut. 32:15–17 [b]Deut. 31:16
**21** [a]Deut. 31:17 [b]Hos. 5:3 [c]Amos 5:25, 26
**23** [a]Num. 27:23; Deut. 31:14 [b]Deut. 31:7
**26** [a]2 Kin. 22:8 [b]Deut. 31:19
**27** [a]Deut. 9:7, 24 [b]Ex. 32:9; Deut. 9:6, 13
**28** [a]Deut. 30:19
**29** [a]Deut. 32:5; Judg. 2:19; [Acts 20:29, 30] [b]Deut. 28:15 [c]Gen. 49:1; Deut. 4:30

CHAPTER 32
**1** [a]Deut. 4:26; Ps. 50:4; Is. 1:2 [b]Jer. 6:19
**2** [a]Is. 55:10, 11 [b]Ps. 72:6 [1]*doctrine*
**3** [a]Deut. 28:58 [b]1 Chr. 29:11
**4** [a]Deut. 32:15, 18, 30; Ps. 18:2 [b]2 Sam. 22:31 [c]Deut. 7:9; Is. 65:16; Jer. 10:10 [d]Job 34:10
**5** [a]Deut. 4:25; 31:29 [b]Phil. 2:15
**6** [a]Ps. 116:12 [b]Ex. 4:22; Deut. 1:31; Is. 63:16 [c]Ps. 74:2 [d]Deut. 32:15 [1]*repay the*
**7** [a]Ps. 44:1 [b]Ex. 12:26; 13:14; Ps. 78:5–8
**8** [a]Acts 17:26 [b]Gen. 11:8 [1]LXX, DSS *angels of God;* Symmachus, Lat. *sons of God*
**9** [a]Ex. 19:5
**10** [a]Jer. 2:6; Hos. 13:5 [b]Ps. 17:8; Prov. 7:2; Zech. 2:8 [1]*pupil*
**11** [a]Is. 31:5
**13** [a]Is. 58:14
**14** [a]Ps. 81:16 [b]Gen. 49:11
**15** [a]Deut. 31:20 [b]Is. 1:4 [c]Is. 51:13

[a]become utterly corrupt, and turn aside from the
way which I have commanded you. And [b]evil will
befall you [c]in the latter days, because you will do
evil in the sight of the LORD, to provoke Him to
anger through the work of your hands."
**30** Then Moses spoke in the hearing of all the
assembly of Israel the words of this song until
they were ended:

### *The Song of Moses*

**32** "Give [a]ear, O heavens, and I will speak;
And hear, O [b]earth,
the words of my mouth.
2 Let [a]my [1]teaching drop as the rain,
My speech distill as the dew,
[b]As raindrops on the tender herb,
And as showers on the grass.
3 For I proclaim the [a]name of the LORD:
[b]Ascribe greatness to our God.
4 *He is* [a]the Rock, [b]His work *is* perfect;
For all His ways *are* justice,
[c]A God of truth and [d]without injustice;
Righteous and upright *is* He.

5 "They[a] have corrupted themselves;
*They are* not His children,
Because of their blemish:
A [b]perverse and crooked generation.
6 Do you thus [a]deal[1] with the LORD,
O foolish and unwise people?
*Is* He not [b]your Father, *who* [c]bought you?
Has He not [d]made you and established you?

7 "Remember[a] the days of old,
Consider the years of many generations.
[b]Ask your father, and he will show you;
Your elders, and they will tell you:
8 When the Most High [a]divided their
inheritance to the nations,
When He [b]separated the sons of Adam,
He set the boundaries of the peoples
According to the number of the [1]children of
Israel.
9 For [a]the LORD's portion *is* His people;
Jacob *is* the place of His inheritance.

10 "He found him [a]in a desert land
And in the wasteland, a howling wilderness;
He encircled him, He instructed him,
He [b]kept him as the [1]apple of His eye.
11 [a]As an eagle stirs up its nest,
Hovers over its young,
Spreading out its wings, taking them up,
Carrying them on its wings,
12 *So* the LORD alone led him,
And *there was* no foreign god with him.

13 "He[a] made him ride in the heights
of the earth,
That he might eat the produce of the fields;
He made him draw honey from the rock,
And oil from the flinty rock;
14 Curds from the cattle, and milk of the flock,
[a]With fat of lambs;
And rams of the breed of Bashan, and goats,
With the choicest wheat;
And you drank wine,
the [b]blood of the grapes.

**15** "But Jeshurun grew fat and kicked;
[a]You grew fat, you grew thick,
You are obese!
Then he [b]forsook God *who* [c]made him,

And scornfully esteemed
the [d]Rock of his salvation.
16 [a]They provoked Him to jealousy
with foreign *gods;*
With [1]abominations they provoked Him to
anger.
17 [a]They sacrificed to demons, not to God,
*To gods* they did not know,
To new *gods,* new arrivals
That your fathers did not fear.
18 [a]Of the Rock *who* begot you,
you are unmindful,
And have [b]forgotten the God
who fathered you.

**19** "And[a] when the LORD saw *it,*
He spurned *them,*
Because of the provocation of His sons and
His daughters.
20 And He said: 'I will hide My face from them,
I will see what their end *will be,*
For they *are* a perverse generation,
[a]Children in whom *is* no faith.
21 [a]They have provoked Me to jealousy
by *what* is not God;
They have moved Me to anger
[b]by their [1]foolish idols.
But [c]I will provoke them to jealousy
by *those who are* not a nation;
I will move them to anger
by a foolish nation.
22 For [a]a fire is kindled in My anger,
And shall burn to the [1]lowest [2]hell;
It shall consume the earth with her increase,
And set on fire
the foundations of the mountains.

**23** 'I will [a]heap disasters on them;
[b]I will spend My arrows on them.
24 *They shall be* wasted with hunger,
Devoured by pestilence and bitter
destruction;
I will also send against them
the [a]teeth of beasts,
With the poison of serpents of the dust.
25 The sword shall destroy outside;
*There shall be* terror within
For the young man and virgin,
The nursing child with the man of gray hairs.
26 [a]I would have said,
"I will dash them in pieces,
I will make the memory of them
to cease from among men,"
27 Had I not feared the wrath of the enemy,
Lest their adversaries should misunderstand,
Lest they should say, [a]"Our hand *is* high;
And it is not the LORD
who has done all this." '

**28** "For they *are* a nation void of counsel,
Nor *is there any* understanding in them.
29 [a]Oh, that they were wise,
*that* they understood this,
*That* they would consider their [b]latter end!
30 How could one chase a thousand,
And two put ten thousand to flight,
Unless their Rock [a]had sold them,
And the LORD had surrendered them?
31 For their rock *is* not like our Rock,
[a]Even our enemies themselves *being* judges.
32 For [a]their vine *is* of the vine of Sodom
And of the fields of Gomorrah;
Their grapes *are* grapes of gall,
Their clusters *are* bitter.
33 Their wine *is* [a]the poison of serpents,
And the cruel [b]venom of cobras.

**34** '*Is* this not [a]laid up in store with Me,
Sealed up among My treasures?
35 [a]Vengeance is Mine, and recompense;
Their foot shall slip in *due* time;
[b]For the day of their calamity *is* at hand,
And the things to come hasten upon them.'

36 "For[a] the LORD will judge His people
[b]And have compassion on His servants,
When He sees that *their* power is gone,
And [c]*there is* no one *remaining,* bond or free.
37 He will say: [a]'Where *are* their gods,
The rock in which they sought refuge?
38 Who ate the fat of their sacrifices,
*And* drank the wine of their drink offering?
Let them rise and help you,
*And* be your refuge.

39 'Now see that [a]I, *even* I, *am* He,
And [b]*there is* no God besides Me;
[c]I kill and I make alive;
I wound and I heal;
Nor *is there any*
who can deliver from My hand.
40 For I raise My hand to heaven,
And say, "*As* I live forever,
41 [a]If I [1]whet My glittering sword,
And My hand takes hold on judgment,
I will render vengeance to My enemies,
And repay those who hate Me.
42 I will make My arrows drunk with blood,
And My sword shall devour flesh,
With the blood of the slain and the captives,
From the heads
of the leaders of the enemy." '

43 "Rejoice,[a] O Gentiles, *with* His [1]people;
For He will [b]avenge
the blood of His servants,
And render vengeance to His adversaries;
He [c]will provide atonement for His land *and*
His people."

**44** So Moses came with [1]Joshua the son of Nun
and spoke all the words of this song in the hearing
of the people.
45 Moses finished speaking all these words to all
Israel,
46 and he said to them: [a]"Set your hearts on all
the words which I testify among you today, which
you shall command your [b]children to be careful to
observe—all the words of this law.
47 "For it *is* not a [1]futile thing for you, because it
*is* your [a]life, and by this word you shall prolong
*your* days in the land which you cross over the
Jordan to possess."
**48** Then the LORD spoke to Moses that very same
day, saying:
49 [a]"Go up this mountain of the Abarim, Mount
Nebo, which *is* in the land of Moab, across from
Jericho; view the land of Canaan, which I give to
the children of Israel as a possession;
50 "and die on the mountain which you ascend,
and be [1]gathered to your people, just as [a]Aaron
your brother died on Mount Hor and was gathered
to his people;
51 "because [a]you trespassed against Me among
the children of Israel at the waters of [1]Meribah
Kadesh, in the Wilderness of Zin, because you [b]did

**15** [d]Ps. 95:1
**16** [a]Ps. 78:58; 1 Cor. 10:22 [1]*detestable acts*
**17** [a]Rev. 9:20
**18** [a]Is. 17:10 [b]Jer. 2:32
**19** [a]Judg. 2:14
**20** [a]Matt. 17:17
**21** [a]Ps. 78:58 [b]Ps. 31:6 [c]Rom. 10:19 [1]*foolishness,* lit. *vanities*
**22** [a]Num. 16:33–35; Ps. 18:7, 8; Lam. 4:11 [1]*lowest part of* [2]Or *Sheol*
**23** [a]Ex. 32:12; Deut. 29:21, 24 [b]Ps. 7:12, 13
**24** [a]Lev. 26:22
**26** [a]Ezek. 20:23
**27** [a]Is. 10:12–15
**29** [a]Ps. 81:13; [Luke 19:42] [b]Deut. 31:29
**30** [a]Judg. 2:14; Ps. 44:12
**31** [a][1 Sam 4:7, 8; Jer. 40:2, 3]
**32** [a]Is. 1:8–10
**33** [a]Ps. 58:4 [b]Rom. 3:13
**34** [a][Jer. 2:22]
**35** [a]Ps. 94:1; Rom. 12:19; Heb. 10:30 [b]2 Pet. 2:3
**36** [a]Ps. 135:14; Heb. 10:30 [b]Ps. 106:45; Jer. 31:20 [c]2 Kin. 14:26
**37** [a]Judg. 10:14; Jer. 2:28
**39** [a]Is. 41:4; 43:10 [b]Deut. 32:12; Is. 45:5 [c]1 Sam. 2:6; Ps. 68:20
**41** [a]Is. 1:24; 66:16; Jer. 50:28–32 [1]*sharpen*
**43** [a]Rom. 15:10 [b]2 Kin. 9:7; Rev. 6:10; 19:2 [c]Ps. 65:3; 79:9; 85:1 [1]DSS add *And let all the gods (angels) worship Him;* cf. LXX and Heb. 1:6
**44** [1]Heb. *Hoshea,* Num. 13:8, 16
**46** [a]Ezek. 40:4; 44:5 [b]Deut. 11:19
**47** [a]Deut. 8:3; 30:15–20 [1]*vain*
**49** [a]Num. 27:12–14; Deut. 3:27
**50** [a]Num. 20:25, 28; 33:38 [1]Join your ancestors
**51** [a]Num. 20:11–13 [b]Lev. 10:3 [1]Lit. *Contention at Kadesh*

not hallow Me in the midst of the children of Israel.
52 [a]"Yet you shall see the land before *you*,
though you shall not go there, into the land which
I am giving to the children of Israel."

## *Moses' Final Blessing on Israel*

**33** Now this *is* [a]the blessing with which Moses [b]the man of God blessed the children of Israel before his death.
2 And he said:

[a]"The LORD came from Sinai,
And dawned on them from [b]Seir;
He shone forth from [c]Mount Paran,
And He came with [d]ten thousands of saints;
From His right hand
*Came* a fiery law for them.
3 Yes, [a]He loves the people;
[b]All His saints *are* in Your hand;
They [c]sit down at Your feet;
*Everyone* [d]receives Your words.
4 [a]Moses [1]commanded a law for us,
[b]A heritage of the congregation of Jacob.
5 And He was [a]King in [b]Jeshurun,
When the leaders of the people
were gathered,
All the tribes of Israel together.

**6** "Let [a]Reuben live, and not die,
*Nor* let his men be few."

**7** And this he said of [a]Judah:

"Hear, LORD, the voice of Judah,
And bring him to his people;
[b]Let his hands be sufficient for him,
And may You be [c]a help
against his enemies."

**8** And of [a]Levi he said:

[b]"*Let* Your [1]Thummim and Your Urim
*be* with Your holy one,
[c]Whom You tested at Massah,
And with whom You contended
at the waters of Meribah,
9 [a]Who says of his father and mother,
'I have not [b]seen them';
[c]Nor did he acknowledge his brothers,
Or know his own children;
For [d]they have observed Your word
And kept Your covenant.
10 [a]They shall teach Jacob Your judgments,
And Israel Your law.
They shall put incense before You,
[b]And a whole burnt sacrifice on Your altar.
11 Bless his substance, LORD,
And [a]accept the work of his hands;
Strike the loins of those
who rise against him,
And of those who hate him,
that they rise not again."

**12** Of Benjamin he said:

"The beloved of the LORD
shall dwell in safety by Him,
*Who* shelters him all the day long;
And he shall dwell between His shoulders."

**13** And of Joseph he said:

[a]"Blessed of the LORD *is* his land,
With the precious things of heaven, with the
[b]dew,
And the deep lying beneath,
14 With the precious fruits of the sun,
With the precious produce of the months,
15 With the best things
of [a]the ancient mountains,
With the precious things
[b]of the everlasting hills,
16 With the precious things
of the earth and its fullness,
And the favor of [a]Him
who dwelt in the bush.
Let *the blessing* come
[b]'on the head of Joseph,
And on the crown of the head of him *who*
*was* separate from his brothers.'
17 His glory *is like* a [a]firstborn bull,
And his horns *like* the [b]horns of the wild ox;
Together with them
[c]He shall push the peoples
To the ends of the earth;
[d]They *are* the ten thousands of Ephraim,
And they *are* the thousands of Manasseh."

**18** And of Zebulun he said:

[a]"Rejoice, Zebulun, in your going out,
And Issachar in your tents!
19 They shall [a]call the peoples *to* the mountain;
There [b]they shall offer sacrifices
of righteousness;
For they shall partake
*of* the abundance of the seas
And *of* treasures hidden in the sand."

**20** And of Gad he said:

"Blessed *is* he who [a]enlarges Gad;
He dwells as a lion,
And tears the arm and the crown of his head.
21 [a]He provided the first *part* for himself,
Because a lawgiver's portion
was reserved there.
[b]He came *with* the heads of the people;
He administered the justice of the LORD,
And His judgments with Israel."

**22** And of Dan he said:

"Dan *is* a lion's whelp;
[a]He shall leap from Bashan."

**23** And of Naphtali he said:

"O Naphtali, [a]satisfied with favor,
And full of the blessing of the LORD,
[b]Possess the west and the south."

**24** And of Asher he said:

[a]"Asher *is* most blessed of sons;
Let him be favored by his brothers,
And let him [b]dip his foot in oil.
25 Your sandals *shall be* [a]iron and bronze;
As your days, *so shall* your strength *be*.

26 "*There is* [a]no one like the God of [b]Jeshurun,
[c]*Who* rides the heavens to help you,
And in His excellency on the clouds.
27 The eternal God *is your* [a]refuge,
And underneath *are* the everlasting arms;
[b]He will thrust out the enemy
from before you,
And will say, 'Destroy!'
28 Then [a]Israel shall dwell in safety,
[b]The fountain of Jacob [c]alone,
In a land of grain and new wine;
His [d]heavens shall also drop dew.

**32:52** [a]Num. 27:12; Deut. 34:1–5

CHAPTER 33
**1** [a]Gen. 49:28 [b]Ps. 90
**2** [a]Ex. 19:18, 20; Ps. 68:8, 17; Hab. 3:3 [b]Deut. 2:1, 4 [c]Num. 10:12 [d]Dan. 7:10; Acts 7:53; Rev. 5:11
**3** [a]Ps. 47:4; Hos. 11:1 [b]1 Sam. 2:9 [c][Luke 10:39] [d]Prov. 2:1
**4** [a]Deut. 4:2; John 1:17; 7:19 [b]Ps. 119:111 [1]*charged us with*
**5** [a]Ex. 15:18 [b]Deut. 32:15
**6** [a]Gen. 49:3, 4
**7** [a]Gen. 49:8–12 [b]Gen. 49:8 [c]Ps. 146:5
**8** [a]Gen. 49:5 [b]Ex. 28:30; Lev. 8:8 [c]Num. 20:2–13; Deut. 6:2, 3, 16; Ps. 81:7 [1]Lit. *Perfections and Your Lights*
**9** [a][Num. 25:5–8; Matt. 10:37; 19:29] [b][Gen. 29:32] [c]Ex. 32:26–28 [d]Mal. 2:5, 6
**10** [a]Lev. 10:11; Deut. 31:9–13; Mal. 2:7 [b]Lev. 1:9; Ps. 51:19
**11** [a]2 Sam. 24:23; Ezek. 20:40
**13** [a]Gen. 49:22–26 [b]Gen. 27:28
**15** [a]Gen. 49:26 [b]Hab. 3:6
**16** [a]Ex. 3:2–4; Acts 7:30–35 [b]Gen. 49:26
**17** [a]1 Chr. 5:1 [b]Num. 23:22 [c]1 Kin. 22:11; Ps. 44:5 [d]Gen. 48:19
**18** [a]Gen. 49:13–15
**19** [a]Ex. 15:17; Ps. 2:6; Is. 2:3 [b]Ps. 4:5; 51:19
**20** [a]1 Chr. 12:8
**21** [a]Num. 32:16, 17 [b]Josh. 4:12
**22** [a]Gen. 49:16, 17; Josh. 19:47
**23** [a]Gen. 49:21 [b]Josh. 19:32
**24** [a]Gen. 49:20 [b]Job 29:6
**25** [a]Deut. 8:9
**26** [a]Ex. 15:11; Deut. 4:35; Ps. 86:8; Jer. 10:6 [b]Deut. 32:15 [c]Deut. 10:14; Ps. 68:3, 33, 34; 104:3
**27** [a][Ps. 90:1; 91:2, 9] [b]Deut. 9:3–5
**28** [a]Deut. 33:12; Jer. 23:6; 33:16 [b]Deut. 8:7, 8 [c]Num. 23:9 [d]Gen. 27:28

29 [a]Happy *are* you, O Israel!
[b]Who *is* like you, a people saved by the LORD,
[c]The shield of your help
And the sword of your majesty!
Your enemies [d]shall submit to you,
And [e]you shall tread down
their [1]high places."

### *Moses Dies on Mount Nebo*

34 Then Moses went up from the plains of
Moab [a]to Mount Nebo, to the top of Pisgah,
which is across from Jericho. And the LORD
showed him all the land of Gilead as far as Dan,
2 all Naphtali and the land of Ephraim and
Manasseh, all the land of Judah as far as the
[1]Western Sea,
3 the South, and the plain of the Valley of
Jericho, [a]the city of palm trees, as far as Zoar.
4 Then the LORD said to him, [a]"This *is* the land
of which I swore to give Abraham, Isaac, and
Jacob, saying, 'I will give it to your descendants.'
[b]I have caused you to see *it* with your eyes, but
you shall not cross over there."
5 [a]So Moses the servant of the LORD died there
in the land of Moab, according to the word of the
LORD.
6 And He buried him in a valley in the land of
Moab, opposite Beth Peor; but [a]no one knows his
grave to this day.
7 [a]Moses *was* one hundred and twenty years old
when he died. [b]His [1]eyes were not dim nor his
natural vigor [2]diminished.
8 And the children of Israel wept for Moses in
the plains of Moab [a]thirty days. So the days of
weeping *and* mourning for Moses ended.
9 Now Joshua the son of Nun was full of the
[a]spirit of wisdom, for [b]Moses had laid his hands on
him; so the children of Israel heeded him, and did
as the LORD had commanded Moses.
10 But since then there [a]has not arisen in Israel a
prophet like Moses, [b]whom the LORD knew face to
face,
11 in all [a]the signs and wonders which the LORD
sent him to do in the land of Egypt, before Pharaoh, before all his servants, and in all his land,
12 and by all that mighty power and all the great
terror which Moses performed in the sight of all
Israel.

29 [a]Ps. 144:15 [b]2 Sam. 7:23 [c]Ps. 115:9 [d]Ps. 18:44; 66:3 [e]Num. 33:52 [1]Places for pagan worship

CHAPTER 34
1 [a]Deut. 32:49
2 [1]Mediterranean
3 [a]2 Chr. 28:15
4 [a]Gen. 12:7 [b]Deut. 3:27
5 [a]Deut. 32:50; Josh. 1:1, 2
6 [a]Jude 9
7 [a]Deut. 31:2 [b]Gen. 27:1; 48:10 [1]*eyesight was not weakened* [2]*reduced*
8 [a]Gen. 50:3, 10
9 [a]Is. 11:2 [b]Num. 27:18, 23
10 [a]Deut. 18:15, 18 [b]Ex. 33:11
11 [a]Deut. 7:19

*The Book of*

# JOSHUA

### *Joshua Commanded to Cross the Jordan*

AFTER the death of Moses the servant of the
LORD, it came to pass that the LORD spoke
to Joshua the son of Nun, Moses' [a]assis-
tant, saying:
2 [a]"Moses My servant is dead. Now therefore,
arise, go over this Jordan, you and all this people,
to the land which I am giving to them—the
children of Israel.
3 [a]"Every place that the sole of your foot will
tread upon I have given you, as I said to Moses.
4 [a]"From the wilderness and this Lebanon as far
as the great river, the River Euphrates, all the land
of the Hittites, and to the Great Sea toward the
going down of the sun, shall be your territory.
5 [a]"No man shall *be able to* stand before you all
the days of your life; [b]as I was with Moses, *so* [c]I
will be with you. [d]I will not leave you nor forsake
you.
6 [a]"Be strong and of good courage, for to this
people you shall [1]divide as an inheritance the land
which I swore to their fathers to give them.
7 "Only be strong and very courageous, that
you may observe to do according to all the law
[a]which Moses My servant commanded you; [b]do
not turn from it to the right hand or to the left,
that you may [1]prosper wherever you go.
8 [a]"This Book of the Law shall not depart from
your mouth, but [b]you[1] shall meditate in it day and
night, that you may observe to do according to all
that is written in it. For then you will make your
way prosperous, and then you will have good
success.
9 [a]"Have I not commanded you? Be strong and
of good courage; [b]do not be afraid, nor be dismayed, for the LORD your God *is* with you wherever you go."
10 Then Joshua commanded the officers of the
people, saying,
11 "Pass through the camp and command the
people, saying, 'Prepare provisions for yourselves,
for [a]within three days you will cross over this
Jordan, to go in to possess the land which the
LORD your God is giving you to possess.' "
12 And to the Reubenites, the Gadites, and half
the tribe of Manasseh Joshua spoke, saying,
13 "Remember [a]the word which Moses the servant of the LORD commanded you, saying, 'The
LORD your God is giving you rest and is giving you
this land.'
14 "Your wives, your little ones, and your livestock shall remain in the land which Moses gave
you on this side of the Jordan. But you shall [1]pass
before your brethren armed, all your mighty men
of valor, and help them,
15 "until the LORD has given your brethren rest,
as He *gave* you, and they also have taken possession of the land which the LORD your God is
giving them. [a]Then you shall return to the land of
your possession and enjoy it, which Moses the
LORD's servant gave you on this side of the Jordan
toward the sunrise."
16 So they answered Joshua, saying, "All that
you command us we will do, and wherever you
send us we will go.
17 "Just as we heeded Moses in all things, so we
will heed you. Only the LORD your God [a]be with
you, as He was with Moses.
18 "Whoever rebels against your command and
does not heed your words, in all that you command him, shall be put to death. Only be strong
and of good courage."

CHAPTER 1
1 [a]Ex. 24:13; Num. 13:16; 14:6, 29, 30, 37, 38; Deut. 1:38; Acts 7:45
2 [a]Num. 12:7; Deut. 34:5
3 [a]Deut. 11:24; Josh. 11:23
4 [a]Gen. 15:18; Ex. 23:31; Num. 34:3–12
5 [a]Deut. 7:24 [b]Ex. 3:12 [c]Deut. 31:8, 23 [d]Deut. 31:6, 7; Heb. 13:5
6 [a]Deut. 31:7, 23 [1]*give as a possession*
7 [a]Num. 27:23; Deut. 31:7; Josh. 11:15 [b]Deut. 5:32 [1]*have success* or *act wisely*
8 [a]Deut. 17:18, 19; 31:24, 26; Josh. 8:34 [b]Deut. 29:9; Ps. 1:1–3 [1]*you shall be constantly in*
9 [a]Deut. 31:7 [b]Ps. 27:1
11 [a]Deut. 9:1; Josh. 3:17
13 [a]Num. 32:20–28
14 [1]*cross over ahead of*
15 [a]Josh. 22:1–4
17 [a]1 Sam. 20:13; 1 Kin. 1:37

## *Rahab Hides the Spies*

2 Now Joshua the son of Nun sent out two men
[a]from [1]Acacia Grove to spy secretly, saying,
"Go, view the land, especially Jericho." So they
went, and [b]came to the house of a harlot named
[c]Rahab, and [2]lodged there.
2 And [a]it was told the king of Jericho, saying,
"Behold, men have come here tonight from the
children of Israel to search out the country."
3 So the king of Jericho sent to Rahab, saying,
"Bring out the men who have come to you, who
have entered your house, for they have come to
search out all the country."
4 [a]Then the woman took the two men and hid
them. So she said, "Yes, the men came to me, but
I did not know where they *were* from.
5 "And it happened as the gate was being shut,
when it was dark, that the men went out. Where
the men went I do not know; pursue them
quickly, for you may overtake them."
6 (But [a]she had brought them up to the roof and
hidden them with the stalks of flax, which she had
laid in order on the roof.)
7 Then the men pursued them by the road to the
Jordan, to the fords. And as soon as those who
pursued them had gone out, they shut the gate.
**8** Now before they lay down, she came up to
them on the roof,
9 and said to the men: [a]"I know that the LORD
has given you the land, that [b]the terror of you has
fallen on us, and that all the inhabitants of the
land [c]are fainthearted because of you.
10 "For we have heard how the LORD [a]dried up
the water of the Red Sea for you when you came
out of Egypt, and [b]what you did to the two kings
of the Amorites who *were* on the other side of the
Jordan, Sihon and Og, whom you [c]utterly destroyed.
11 "And as soon as we [a]heard *these things*, [b]our
hearts melted; neither did there remain any more
courage in anyone because of you, for [c]the LORD
your God, He *is* God in heaven above and on earth
beneath.
12 "Now therefore, I beg you, [a]swear to me by
the LORD, since I have shown you kindness, that
you also will show kindness to [b]my father's house,
and [c]give me [1]a true token,
13 "and [a]spare my father, my mother, my brothers, my sisters, and all that they have, and deliver
our lives from death."
14 So the men answered her, "Our lives for yours,
if none of you tell this business of ours. And it
shall be, when the LORD has given us the land,
that [a]we will deal kindly and truly with you."
**15** Then she [a]let them down by a rope through
the window, for her house *was* on the city wall;
she dwelt on the wall.
16 And she said to them, "Get to the mountain,
lest the pursuers meet you. Hide there three days,
until the pursuers have returned. Afterward you
may go your way."
17 So the men said to her: "We *will be* [a]blame-
less[1] of this oath of yours which you have made us
swear,
18 [a]"unless, *when* we come into the land, you
bind this line of scarlet cord in the window
through which you let us down, [b]and unless you
[1]bring your father, your mother, your brothers,
and all your father's household to your own home.
19 "So it shall be *that* whoever goes outside the
doors of your house into the street, his blood *shall*
*be* on his own head, and we *will be* [1]guiltless. And
whoever is with you in the house, [a]his [2]blood *shall*
*be* on our head if a hand is laid on him.
20 "And if you tell this business of ours, then we
will be [1]free from your oath which you made us
swear."
21 Then she said, "According to your words, so
*be* it." And she sent them away, and they departed. And she bound the scarlet cord in the
window.
**22** They departed and went to the mountain, and
stayed there three days until the pursuers returned. The pursuers sought *them* all along the
way, but did not find *them*.
23 So the two men returned, descended from the
mountain, and crossed over; and they came to
Joshua the son of Nun, and told him all that had
befallen them.
24 And they said to Joshua, "Truly [a]the LORD has
delivered all the land into our hands, for indeed all
the inhabitants of the country are fainthearted
because of us."

## *Israel Crosses the Jordan*

3 Then Joshua rose early in the morning; and
they set out [a]from [1]Acacia Grove and came to
the Jordan, he and all the children of Israel, and
lodged there before they crossed over.
2 So it was, [a]after three days, that the officers
went through the camp;
3 and they commanded the people, saying,
[a]"When you see the ark of the covenant of the
LORD your God, [b]and the priests, the Levites,
[1]bearing it, then you shall set out from your place
and go after it.
4 [a]"Yet there shall be a space between you and
it, about two thousand cubits by measure. Do not
come near it, that you may know the way by
which you must go, for you have not passed *this*
way before."
5 And Joshua said to the people, [a]"Sanctify[1]
yourselves, for tomorrow the LORD will do wonders among you."
6 Then Joshua spoke to the priests, saying,
[a]"Take up the ark of the covenant and cross over
before the people." So they took up the ark of the
covenant and went before the people.
**7** And the LORD said to Joshua, "This day I will
begin to [a]exalt[1] you in the sight of all Israel, that
they may know that, [b]as I was with Moses, *so* I
will be with you.
8 "You shall command [a]the priests who bear the
ark of the covenant, saying, 'When you have
come to the edge of the water of the Jordan, [b]you
shall stand in the Jordan.' "
**9** So Joshua said to the children of Israel, "Come
here, and hear the words of the LORD your God."
10 And Joshua said, "By this you shall know that
[a]the living God *is* among you, and *that* He will
without fail [b]drive out from before you the [c]Ca-
naanites and the Hittites and the Hivites and the
Perizzites and the Girgashites and the Amorites
and the Jebusites:
11 "Behold, the ark of the covenant of [a]the Lord
of all the earth is crossing over before you into the
Jordan.
12 "Now therefore, [a]take for yourselves twelve
men from the tribes of Israel, one man from every
tribe.
13 "And it shall come to pass, [a]as soon as the
soles of the feet of the priests who bear the ark of

CHAPTER 2
1 [a]Num. 25:1 [b]James 2:25 [c]Matt. 1:5 [1]Heb. *Shittim* [2]Lit. *lay down*
2 [a]Josh. 2:22
4 [a]2 Sam. 17:19, 20
6 [a]Ex. 1:17
9 [a]Deut. 1:8 [b]Deut. 2:25; 11:25 [c]Josh. 5:1
10 [a]Ex. 14:21 [b]Num. 21:21–35 [c]Josh. 6:21
11 [a]Ex. 15:14, 15 [b]Josh. 5:1; 7:5 [c]Deut. 4:39
12 [a]1 Sam. 20:14, 15, 17 [b]1 Tim. 5:8 [c]Josh. 2:18 [1]*a pledge of truth*
13 [a]Josh. 6:23–25
14 [a]Judg. 1:24
15 [a]Acts 9:25
17 [a]Ex. 20:7 [1]*free from obligation to this oath*
18 [a]Josh. 2:12 [b]Josh. 6:23 [1]Lit. *gather*
19 [a]1 Kin. 2:32 [1]*free from obligation* [2]*guilt of bloodshed*
20 [1]*free from obligation to*
24 [a]Ex. 23:31

CHAPTER 3
1 [a]Josh. 2:1 [1]Heb. *Shittim*
2 [a]Josh. 1:10, 11
3 [a]Num. 10:33 [b]Deut. 31:9, 25 [1]*carrying*
4 [a]Ex. 19:12
5 [a]Josh. 7:13 [1]*Consecrate*
6 [a]Num. 4:15
7 [a]Josh. 4:14 [b]Josh. 1:5, 9 [1]*make you great*
8 [a]Josh. 3:3 [b]Josh. 3:17
10 [a]1 Thess. 1:9 [b]Ex. 33:2 [c]Acts 13:19
11 [a]Zech. 4:14; 6:5
12 [a]Josh. 4:2, 4
13 [a]Josh. 3:15, 16

the LORD, [b]the Lord of all the earth, shall rest in
the waters of the Jordan, *that* the waters of the
Jordan shall be cut off, the waters that come down
from upstream, and they [c]shall stand as a heap."
**14** So it was, when the people set out from their
camp to cross over the Jordan, with the priests
bearing the [a]ark of the covenant before the people,
15 and as those who bore the ark came to the
Jordan, and [a]the feet of the priests who bore
the ark dipped in the edge of the water (for the
[b]Jordan overflows all its banks [c]during the whole
time of harvest),
16 that the waters which came down from upstream stood *still, and* rose in a heap very far
away [1]at Adam, the city that *is* beside [a]Zaretan. So
the waters that went down [b]into the Sea of the
Arabah, [c]the Salt Sea, failed, *and* were cut off; and
the people crossed over opposite Jericho.
17 Then the priests who bore the ark of the
covenant of the LORD stood firm on dry ground in
the midst of the Jordan; [a]and all Israel crossed
over on dry ground, until all the people had
crossed completely over the Jordan.

## *The Twelve Stones Taken from the Jordan*

**4** And it came to pass, when all the people had
completely crossed [a]over the Jordan, that the
LORD spoke to Joshua, saying:
2 [a]"Take for yourselves twelve men from the
people, one man from every tribe,
3 "and command them, saying, 'Take for yourselves twelve stones from here, out of the midst of
the Jordan, from the place where [a]the priests' feet
stood firm. You shall carry them over with you
and leave them in [b]the lodging place where you
lodge tonight.' "
4 Then Joshua called the twelve men whom he
had appointed from the children of Israel, one
man from every tribe;
5 and Joshua said to them: "Cross over before
the ark of the LORD your God into the midst of the
Jordan, and each one of you take up a stone on his
shoulder, according to the number of the tribes of
the children of Israel,
6 "that this may be [a]a sign among you [b]when
your children ask in time to come, saying, 'What
do these stones *mean* to you?'
7 "Then you shall answer them that [a]the waters
of the Jordan were cut off before the ark of the
covenant of the LORD; when it crossed over the
Jordan, the waters of the Jordan were cut off. And
these stones shall be for [b]a memorial to the
children of Israel forever."
**8** And the children of Israel did so, just as
Joshua commanded, and took up twelve stones
from the midst of the Jordan, as the LORD had
spoken to Joshua, according to the number of the
tribes of the children of Israel, and carried them
over with them to the place where they lodged,
and laid them down there.
9 Then Joshua set up twelve stones in the midst
of the Jordan, in the place where the feet of the
priests who bore the ark of the covenant stood;
and they are there to this day.
**10** So the priests who bore the ark stood in the
midst of the Jordan until everything was finished
that the LORD had commanded Joshua to speak to
the people, according to all that Moses had commanded Joshua; and the people hurried and
crossed over.
11 Then it came to pass, when all the people had
completely crossed over, that the [a]ark of the LORD
and the priests crossed over in the presence of the
people.
12 And [a]the men of Reuben, the men of Gad, and
half the tribe of Manasseh crossed over armed
before the children of Israel, as Moses had spoken
to them.
13 About forty thousand [1]prepared for war
crossed over before the LORD for battle, to the
plains of Jericho.
14 On that day the LORD [a]exalted[1] Joshua in the
sight of all Israel; and they feared him, as they had
feared Moses, all the days of his life.
**15** Then the LORD spoke to Joshua, saying,
16 "Command the priests who bear [a]the ark of
the Testimony to come up from the Jordan."
17 Joshua therefore commanded the priests, saying, "Come up from the Jordan."
18 And it came to pass, when the priests who
bore the ark of the covenant of the LORD had
come from the midst of the Jordan, *and* the soles
of the priests' feet touched the dry land, that the
waters of the Jordan returned to their place [a]and
overflowed all its banks as before.
**19** Now the people came up from the Jordan on
the tenth *day* of the first month, and they camped
[a]in Gilgal on the east border of Jericho.
20 And [a]those twelve stones which they took out
of the Jordan, Joshua set up in Gilgal.
21 Then he spoke to the children of Israel, saying: [a]"When your children ask their fathers in
time to come, saying, 'What *are* these stones?'
22 "then you shall let your children know, saying, [a]'Israel crossed over this Jordan on [b]dry land';
23 "for the LORD your God dried up the waters of
the Jordan before you until you had crossed over,
as the LORD your God did to the Red Sea, [a]which
He dried up before us until we had crossed over,
24 [a]"that all the peoples of the earth may know
the hand of the LORD, that it *is* [b]mighty, that you
may [c]fear the LORD your God [1]forever."

## *The Circumcision and Passover at Gilgal*

**5** So it was, when all the kings of the Amorites
who *were* on the west side of the Jordan, and
all the kings of the Canaanites [a]who *were* by the
sea, [b]heard that the LORD had dried up the waters
of the Jordan from before the children of Israel
until [1]we had crossed over, that [2]their heart
melted; [c]and there was no spirit in them any
longer because of the children of Israel.
**2** At that time the LORD said to Joshua, "Make
[a]flint knives for yourself, and circumcise the sons
of Israel again the second time."
3 So Joshua made flint knives for himself, and
circumcised the sons of Israel at [1]the hill of the
foreskins.
4 And this *is* the reason why Joshua circumcised
them: [a]All the people who came out of Egypt *who*
*were* males, all the men of war, had died in the
wilderness on the way, after they had come out of
Egypt.
5 For all the people who came out had been
circumcised, but all the people born in the wilderness, on the way as they came out of Egypt, had
not been circumcised.
6 For the children of Israel walked [a]forty years
in the wilderness, till all the people *who were* men
of war, who came out of Egypt, were [1]consumed,
because they did not obey the voice of the LORD—

**13** [b]Josh. 3:11 [c]Ps. 78:13; 114:3
**14** [a]Ps. 132:8; Acts 7:44, 45
**15** [a]Josh. 3:13 [b]1 Chr. 12:15; Jer. 12:5; 49:19 [c]Josh. 4:18; 5:10, 12
**16** [a]1 Kin. 4:12; 7:46 [b]Deut. 3:17 [c]Gen. 14:3; Num. 34:3 [1]Many mss., vss., and Qr. *from Adam*
**17** [a]Gen. 50:24; Ex. 3:8; 6:1–8; 14:21, 22, 29; 33:1; Deut. 6:10; Heb. 11:29

CHAPTER 4
**1** [a]Deut. 27:2; Josh. 3:17
**2** [a]Josh. 3:12
**3** [a]Josh. 3:13 [b]Josh. 4:19, 20
**6** [a]Deut. 27:2; Ps. 103:2 [b]Ex. 12:26; 13:14; Deut. 6:20
**7** [a]Josh. 3:13, 16 [b]Ex. 12:14; Num. 16:40
**11** [a]Josh. 3:11; 6:11
**12** [a]Num. 32:17, 20, 27, 28; Josh. 1:14
**13** [1]*equipped*
**14** [a]Josh. 3:7; 1 Chr. 29:25 [1]*made Joshua great*
**16** [a]Ex. 25:16, 22
**18** [a]Josh. 3:15; 1 Chr. 12:15
**19** [a]Josh. 5:9
**20** [a]Deut. 11:30; Josh. 4:3; 5:9, 10
**21** [a]Josh. 4:6
**22** [a]Ex. 12:26, 27; 13:8–14; Deut. 26:5–9 [b]Josh. 3:17
**23** [a]Ex. 14:21
**24** [a]1 Kin. 8:42; 2 Kin. 19:19; Ps. 106:8 [b]Ex. 15:16; 1 Chr. 29:12; Ps. 89:13 [c]Ex. 14:31; Deut. 6:2; Ps. 76:7; Jer. 10:7 [1]Lit. *all days*

CHAPTER 5
**1** [a]Num. 13:29 [b]Ex. 15:14, 15 [c]Josh. 2:10, 11; 9:9; 1 Kin. 10:5 [1]Qr., some Heb. mss. and editions, LXX, Syr., Tg., Vg. *they* [2]*their courage failed*
**2** [a]Ex. 4:25
**3** [1]Or *Gibeath Haaraloth*
**4** [a]Num. 14:29; 26:64, 65; Deut. 2:14–16
**6** [a]Num. 14:33; Deut. 1:3; 29:5 [1]*destroyed*

to whom the LORD swore that [b]He would not show
them the land which the LORD had sworn to their
fathers that He would give us, [c]"a land flowing
with milk and honey."
7 Then Joshua circumcised [a]their sons *whom* He
raised up in their place; for they were uncircumcised, because they had not been circumcised on
the way.
8 So it was, when they had finished circumcis-
ing all the people, that they stayed in their places
in the camp [a]till they were healed.
9 Then the LORD said to Joshua, "This day I
have rolled away [a]the reproach of Egypt from
you." Therefore the name of the place is called
[b]Gilgal[1] to this day.
**10** Now the children of Israel camped in Gilgal,
and kept the Passover [a]on the fourteenth day of
the month at twilight on the plains of Jericho.
11 And they ate of the produce of the land on the
day after the Passover, unleavened bread and
[1]parched grain, on the very same day.
12 Then [a]the manna ceased on the day after they
had eaten the produce of the land; and the children of Israel no longer had manna, but they ate
the food of the land of Canaan that year.
**13** And it came to pass, when Joshua was by
Jericho, that he lifted his eyes and looked, and
behold, [a]a Man stood opposite him [b]with His
sword drawn in His hand. And Joshua went to
Him and said to Him, "*Are* You for us or for our
adversaries?"
14 So He said, "No, but *as* Commander of the
army of the LORD I have now come." And Joshua
[a]fell on his face to the earth and [b]worshiped, and
said to Him, "What does my Lord say to His
servant?"
15 Then the Commander of the LORD's army said
to Joshua, [a]"Take your sandal off your foot, for
the place where you stand *is* holy." And Joshua
did so.

## *The Fall of Jericho*

**6** Now [a]Jericho was securely shut up because of
the children of Israel; none went out, and
none came in.
2 And the LORD said to Joshua: "See! [a]I have
given Jericho into your hand, its [b]king, *and* the
mighty men of valor.
3 "You shall march around the city, all *you* men
of war; you shall go all around the city once. This
you shall do six days.
4 "And seven priests shall bear seven [a]trumpets
of rams' horns before the ark. But the seventh day
you shall march around the city [b]seven times, and
[c]the priests shall blow the trumpets.
5 "It shall come to pass, when they make a long
*blast* with the ram's horn, *and* when you hear the
sound of the trumpet, that all the people shall
shout with a great shout; then the wall of the city
will fall down flat. And the people shall go up
every man straight before him."
**6** Then Joshua the son of Nun called the priests
and said to them, "Take up the ark of the covenant, and let seven priests bear seven trumpets
of rams' horns before the ark of the LORD."
7 And he said to the people, "Proceed, and
march around the city, and let him who is armed
advance before the ark of the LORD."
**8** So it was, when Joshua had spoken to the
people, that the seven priests bearing the seven
trumpets of rams' horns before the LORD advanced and blew the trumpets, and the ark of the
covenant of the LORD followed them.
9 The armed men went before the priests who
blew the trumpets, [a]and the rear guard came after
the ark, while *the priests* continued blowing the
trumpets.
10 Now Joshua had commanded the people, saying, "You shall not shout or make any noise with
your voice, nor shall a word proceed out of your
mouth, until the day I say to you, 'Shout!' Then
you shall shout."
11 So he had [a]the ark of the LORD circle the city,
going around *it* once. Then they came into the
camp and [1]lodged in the camp.
**12** And Joshua rose early in the morning, [a]and
the priests took up the ark of the LORD.
13 Then seven priests bearing seven trumpets of
rams' horns before the ark of the LORD went on
continually and blew with the trumpets. And the
armed men went before them. But the rear guard
came after the ark of the LORD, while *the priests*
continued blowing the trumpets.
14 And the second day they marched around the
city once and returned to the camp. So they did
six days.
**15** But it came to pass on the seventh day that
they rose early, about the dawning of the day, and
marched around the city seven times in the same
manner. On that day only they marched around
the city seven times.
16 And the seventh time it happened, when the
priests blew the trumpets, that Joshua said to
the people: "Shout, for the LORD has given you the
city!
17 "Now the city shall be [a]doomed by the LORD to
destruction, it and all who *are* in it. Only [b]Rahab
the harlot shall live, she and all who *are* with her
in the house, because [c]she hid the messengers that
we sent.
18 "And you, [a]by all means abstain from the
accursed things, lest you become accursed when
you take of the accursed things, and make the
camp of Israel a curse, [b]and trouble it.
19 "But all the silver and gold, and vessels of
bronze and iron, *are* [1]consecrated to the LORD;
they [2]shall come into the treasury of the LORD."
20 So the people shouted when *the priests* blew
the trumpets. And it happened when the people
heard the sound of the trumpet, and the people
shouted with a great shout, that [a]the wall fell
down flat. Then the people went up into the city,
every man straight before him, and they took the
city.
21 And they [a]utterly destroyed all that *was* in the
city, both man and woman, young and old, ox and
sheep and donkey, with the edge of the sword.
**22** But Joshua had said to the two men who had
spied out the country, "Go into the harlot's house,
and from there bring out the woman and all that
she has, [a]as you swore to her."
23 And the young men who had been spies went
in and brought out Rahab, [a]her father, her mother,
her brothers, and all that she had. So they brought
out all her relatives and left them outside the
camp of Israel.
24 But they burned the city and all that *was* in it
with fire. Only the silver and gold, and the vessels
of bronze and iron, they put into the treasury of
the house of the LORD.
25 And Joshua spared Rahab the harlot, her
father's household, and all that she had. So [a]she

**6** [b]Num. 14:23, 29–35; 26:23–65; Heb. 3:11 [c]Ex. 3:8
**7** [a]Num. 14:31; Deut. 1:39
**8** [a]Gen. 34:25
**9** [a]Gen. 34:14 [b]Josh. 4:19 [1]Lit. *Rolling*
**10** [a]Ex. 12:6; Num. 9:5
**11** [1]*roasted*
**12** [a]Ex. 16:35
**13** [a]Gen. 18:1, 2; 32:24, 30; Ex. 23:23; Num. 22:31; Zech. 1:8; Acts 1:10 [b]Num. 22:23; 1 Chr. 21:16
**14** [a]Gen. 17:3; Num. 20:6 [b]Ex. 34:8
**15** [a]Ex. 3:5; Acts 7:33

CHAPTER 6
**1** [a]Josh. 2:1
**2** [a]Josh. 2:9, 24; 8:1 [b]Deut. 7:24
**4** [a]Lev. 25:9; Judg. 7:16, 22 [b]1 Kin. 18:43; 2 Kin. 4:35; 5:10 [c]Num. 10:8
**9** [a]Num. 10:25
**11** [a]Josh. 4:11 [1]*spent the night*
**12** [a]Deut. 31:25
**17** [a]Deut. 13:17; Josh. 7:1 [b]Josh. 2:1; Matt. 1:5 [c]Josh. 2:4, 6
**18** [a]Deut. 7:26 [b]Josh. 7:1, 12, 25; 1 Kin. 18:17, 18; [Jon. 1:12]
**19** [1]*set apart* [2]*shall go*
**20** [a]Heb. 11:30
**21** [a]Deut. 7:2; 20:16, 17
**22** [a]Josh. 2:12–19; Heb. 11:31
**23** [a]Josh. 2:13
**25** [a][Matt. 1:5]

dwells in Israel to this day, because she hid the
messengers whom Joshua sent to spy out Jericho.
**26** Then Joshua [1]charged *them* at that time,
saying, [a]"Cursed *be* the man before the LORD who
rises up and builds this city Jericho; he shall lay its
foundation with his firstborn, and with his youngest he shall set up its gates."
27 So the LORD was with Joshua, and his fame
spread throughout all the country.

## *The Sin of Achan*

**7** But the children of Israel [1]committed a [a]tres-
pass regarding the [b]accursed[2] things, for
[c]Achan the son of Carmi, the son of [3]Zabdi, the
son of Zerah, of the tribe of Judah, took of the
accursed things; so the anger of the LORD burned
against the children of Israel.
2 Now Joshua sent men from Jericho to Ai,
which *is* beside Beth Aven, on the east side of
Bethel, and spoke to them, saying, "Go up and spy
out the country." So the men went up and spied
out Ai.
3 And they returned to Joshua and said to him,
"Do not let all the people go up, but let about two
or three thousand men go up and attack Ai. Do
not weary all the people there, for *the people of Ai
are* few."
4 So about three thousand men went up there
from the people, [a]but they fled before the men of
Ai.
5 And the men of Ai struck down about thirty-
six men, for they chased them *from* before the
gate as far as Shebarim, and struck them down on
the descent; therefore [a]the[1] hearts of the people
melted and became like water.
**6** Then Joshua [a]tore his clothes, and fell to the
earth on his face before the ark of the LORD until
evening, he and the elders of Israel; and they [b]put
dust on their heads.
7 And Joshua said, "Alas, Lord [1]GOD, [a]why have
You brought this people over the Jordan at all—to
deliver us into the hand of the Amorites, to
destroy us? Oh, that we had been content, and
dwelt on the other side of the Jordan!
8 "O Lord, what shall I say when Israel turns its
[1]back before its enemies?
9 "For the Canaanites and all the inhabitants of
the land will hear *it,* and surround us, and [a]cut off
our name from the earth. Then [b]what will You do
for Your great name?"
**10** So the LORD said to Joshua: "Get up! Why do
you lie thus on your face?
11 "Israel has sinned, and they have also transgressed My covenant which I commanded them.
[a]For they have even taken some of the [1]accursed
things, and have both stolen and [b]deceived; and
they have also put *it* among their own stuff.
12 [a]"Therefore the children of Israel could not
stand before their enemies, *but* turned *their* backs
before their enemies, because [b]they have become
doomed to destruction. Neither will I be with you
anymore, unless you destroy the accursed from
among you.
13 "Get up, [a]sanctify[1] the people, and say, [b]'Sanctify yourselves for tomorrow, because thus says
the LORD God of Israel: *"There is* an accursed
thing in your midst, O Israel; you cannot stand
before your enemies until you take away the
accursed thing from among you."
14 'In the morning therefore you shall be brought
according to your tribes. And it shall be *that* the
tribe which [a]the LORD takes shall come according
to families; and the family which the LORD takes
shall come by households; and the household
which the LORD takes shall come man by man.
15 [a]'Then it shall be *that* he who is taken with the
accursed thing shall be burned with fire, he and all
that he has, because he has [b]transgressed[1] the
covenant of the LORD, and because he [c]has done a
disgraceful thing in Israel.' "
**16** So Joshua rose early in the morning and
brought Israel by their tribes, and the tribe of
Judah was taken.
17 He brought the clan of Judah, and he took the
family of the Zarhites; and he brought the family
of the Zarhites man by man, and Zabdi was taken.
18 Then he brought his household man by man,
and Achan the son of Carmi, the son of Zabdi, the
son of Zerah, of the tribe of Judah, [a]was taken.
19 Now Joshua said to Achan, "My son, I beg
you, [a]give glory to the LORD God of Israel, [b]and
make confession to Him, and [c]tell me now what
you have done; do not hide *it* from me."
20 And Achan answered Joshua and said, "Indeed [a]I have sinned against the LORD God of
Israel, and this is what I have done:
21 "When I saw among the spoils a beautiful
Babylonian garment, two hundred shekels of
silver, and a wedge of gold weighing fifty shekels,
I [1]coveted them and took them. And there they
are, hidden in the earth in the midst of my tent,
with the silver under it."
**22** So Joshua sent messengers, and they ran to
the tent; and there it was, hidden in his tent, with
the silver under it.
23 And they took them from the midst of the
tent, brought them to Joshua and to all the
children of Israel, and laid them out before
the LORD.
24 Then Joshua, and all Israel with him, took
Achan the son of Zerah, the silver, the garment,
the wedge of gold, his sons, his daughters, his
oxen, his donkeys, his sheep, his tent, and [a]all that
he had, and they brought them to [b]the Valley of
Achor.
25 And Joshua said, [a]"Why have you troubled us?
The LORD will trouble you this day." [b]So all Israel
stoned him with stones; and they burned them
with fire after they had stoned them with stones.
26 Then they [a]raised over him a great heap of
stones, still there to this day. So [b]the LORD turned
from the fierceness of His anger. Therefore the
name of that place has been called [c]the Valley of
[1]Achor to this day.

## *The Capture and Destruction of Ai*

**8** Now the LORD said to Joshua: [a]"Do not be
afraid, nor be dismayed; take all the people of
war with you, and arise, go up to Ai. See, [b]I have
given into your hand the king of Ai, his people, his
city, and his land.
2 "And you shall do to Ai and its king as you did
to [a]Jericho and its king. Only [b]its spoil and its
cattle you shall take as booty for yourselves. Lay
an ambush for the city behind it."
**3** So Joshua arose, and all the people of war, to
go up against Ai; and Joshua chose thirty thousand mighty men of valor and sent them away by
night.
4 And he commanded them, saying: "Behold,
[a]you shall lie in ambush against the city, behind

**26** [a]1 Kin. 16:34 [1]*warned*

CHAPTER 7

**1** [a]Josh. 7:20, 21 [b]Josh. 6:17–19 [c]Josh. 22:20 [1]*acted unfaithfully* [2]*devoted* [3]*Zimri,* 1 Chr. 2:6
**4** [a]Lev. 26:17; Deut. 28:25
**5** [a]Lev. 26:36; Josh. 2:9, 11 [1]*the people's courage failed*
**6** [a]Gen. 37:29, 34 [b]1 Sam. 4:12
**7** [a]Ex. 17:3; Num. 21:5 [1]Heb. *YHWH,* LORD
**8** [1]Lit. *neck*
**9** [a]Deut. 32:26 [b]Ex. 32:12; Num. 14:13
**11** [a]Josh. 6:17–19 [b]Acts 5:1, 2 [1]*devoted*
**12** [a]Judg. 2:14 [b]Deut. 7:26; [Hag. 2:13, 14]
**13** [a]Ex. 19:10 [b]Josh. 3:5 [1]*set apart*
**14** [a][Prov. 16:33]
**15** [a]1 Sam. 14:38, 39 [b]Josh. 7:11 [c]Gen. 34:7; Judg. 20:6 [1]*overstepped*
**18** [a]1 Sam. 14:42
**19** [a]1 Sam. 6:5; Jer. 13:16; John 9:24 [b]Num. 5:6, 7; 2 Chr. 30:22; Ezra 10:10, 11; Ps. 32:5; Prov. 28:13; Jer. 3:12, 13; Dan. 9:4 [c]1 Sam. 14:43
**20** [a]Num. 22:34; 1 Sam. 15:24
**21** [1]*desired*
**24** [a]Num. 16:32, 33; Dan. 6:24 [b]Josh. 7:26; 15:7
**25** [a]Josh. 6:18; 1 Chr. 2:7; [Gal. 5:12] [b]Deut. 17:5
**26** [a]Josh. 8:29; 2 Sam. 18:17; Lam. 3:53 [b]Deut. 13:17 [c]Josh. 7:24; Is. 65:10; Hos. 2:15 [1]Lit. *Trouble*

CHAPTER 8

**1** [a]Deut. 1:21; 7:18; 31:8; Josh. 1:9; 10:8 [b]Josh. 6:2
**2** [a]Josh. 6:21 [b]Deut. 20:14; Josh. 8:27
**4** [a]Judg. 20:29

# THE OLD TESTAMENT ILLUSTRATED

Out of God's measureless love flows a plan to bring sinful man to forgiving fellowship with Himself. This design of God was born of infinite concern, and nourished in providential care.

Our first parents, Adam and Eve, decided, as we do, to live their lives away from the will of God. Tempted by Satan, they yielded to sin and lost their eternal birthright.

When sin invaded the human race God's plan to redeem man was set in motion. The Old Testament shows varied examples of God, in His holiness, seeking sinful man.

God first acted through Abraham's seed. Israel is His chosen people. They were the custodians of His Word and redemption. From this people the Messiah was born.

The Old Testament is not always an encouraging story. It tells of the rebellion of God's people. It shows open, willful sin in the face of a long-suffering God. But the Old Testament is salvation in process.

God worked through Israel's deceit and idolatry. He guided. He chastised. He forgave. In God's patience we see the hope of a fallen world.

Abraham, Isaac, Jacob, Moses, Joseph—all stand as reeds in the wind of temptation. Empowered by God's truth, they gradually moved God's nation and purpose forward.

The Old Testament is as human as sin, and as divine as unconditioned love. The thread which runs through Genesis to Malachi is clearly seen by the believing eye: it is Christ, the Messiah.

It was a weary road from Eden to Bethlehem. Nevertheless, in traveling this road, salvation in process became salvation realized.

To make the Old Testament live for the reader, the publishers have spared neither time nor effort to reproduce these matchless paintings by great artists. To view all of the original paintings would require a small fortune and a trip around the world. In the next few pages the reader can actually live the events of the Old Testament.

*THE GARDEN OF EDEN. Field. Genesis 2:8*

*NOAH BUILDING THE ARK, Bianchini*

*THE TOWER OF BABEL. Valkenborgh. Genesis 11:4* ➧

# ABRAHAM OFFERS ISAAC AS A SACRIFICE

Abraham and Sarah had only one son. His name was Isaac. He was their pride and joy because he was the son of the promise. God was going to make him a great nation. Abraham also had another son by his maid, Hagar; and Sarah was jealous of Hagar's son. So Abraham asked Hagar and Ishmael to leave his household. Then Isaac was the only son who remained with Abraham.

Soon thereafter God appeared to Abraham to test him. He told Abraham to take his only son, Isaac, whom he loved, to the top of the mountain and offer him there as a sacrifice. Upon hearing these words, Abraham's heart was saddened. He obeyed God, however. Early in the morning, he took his son and his servants and traveled toward the mountain. Before they came to the mountain, Abraham told his servants to wait while he and his son went to worship God on the mountain. He said that when they were through, they would come back.

Abraham carried the fire and his son carried the wood, and they started toward the mountain. Isaac looked at his father and said, "Father, we have the fire and we have the wood. Where is the lamb for a burnt offering?" Abraham answered and said, "God will provide Himself a lamb for a burnt offering."

When they got to the top, Abraham took his son, tied him with a rope and put him on top of the wood. He drew his knife to kill his son as God had commanded him. As Abraham lifted the knife, he heard the voice of God saying, "Abraham, do your son no harm for now I know that you believe in God." Abraham turned, looked, and saw a ram caught in the bush. He took his son from the altar and made an offering of the ram instead. This was a great moment of testing for Abraham, but he obeyed God. God was pleased with Abraham because he believed.

*THE SACRIFICE OF ISAAC. Rembrandt. Genesis 22:10-13* ➤

◀ *JACOB'S DREAM. Feti. Genesis 28:10-12*

*JACOB WRESTLES WITH THE ANGEL, Francken*

*JACOB'S DESPAIR. Ribera. Genesis 31:2-12*

*JOSEPH SOLD BY HIS BROTHERS. Castillo. Genesis 37:28*

*JACOB AND JOSEPH MEET. Moeyaert. Genesis 46:29*

*MOSES SAVED FROM THE RIVER. Largillierre. Exodus 2:5-10*

*MOSES BEFORE THE BURNING BUSH. Feti. Exodus 3:2-5*

*THE EGYPTIANS STRICKEN BY THE PLAGUE. Poussin. Exodus 12:21-32*

*MOSES DIVIDING THE RED SEA. Eckersberg. Exodus 14:21*

*SAMSON IN THE TREADMILL. Bloch. Judges 16:21*

*DAVID WITH THE HEAD OF GOLIATH. Gentileschi. 1 Samuel 17:51*

*ABIGAIL MEETS DAVID WITH PRESENTS. Rubens. I Samuel 25:18-35*

*KING SOLOMON'S JUDGMENT. Rubens. 1 Kings 3:16-28*

*THE VISION OF EZEKIEL, THE RESURRECTION OF THE FLESH. Callantes. Ezekiel 37:1-14*

*DANIEL'S ANSWER TO THE KING.*
*Rivere. Daniel 6:21, 22*

the city. Do not go very far from the city, but all
of you be ready.
5 "Then I and all the people who *are* with me
will approach the city; and it will come about,
when they come out against us as at the first, that
[a]we shall flee before them.
6 "For they will come out after us till we have
drawn them from the city, for they will say, '*They
are* fleeing before us as at the first.' Therefore we
will flee before them.
7 "Then you shall rise from the ambush and
seize the city, for the LORD your God will deliver it
into your hand.
8 "And it will be, when you have taken the city,
*that* you shall set the city on fire. According to the
commandment of the LORD you shall do. [a]See, I
have commanded you."
**9** Joshua therefore sent them out; and they
went to lie in ambush, and stayed between Bethel
and Ai, on the west side of Ai; but Joshua lodged
that night among the people.
10 Then Joshua rose up early in the morning and
mustered the people, and went up, he and the
elders of Israel, before the people to Ai.
11 [a]And all the people of war who *were* with him
went up and drew near; and they came before the
city and camped on the north side of Ai. Now a
valley *lay* between them and Ai.
12 So he took about five thousand men and set
them in ambush between Bethel and Ai, on the
west side of [1]the city.
13 And when they had set the people, all the
army that *was* on the north of the city, and its
rear guard on the west of the city, Joshua went
that night into the midst of the valley.
**14** Now it happened, when the king of Ai saw *it*,
that the men of the city hurried and rose early and
went out against Israel to battle, he and all his
people, at an appointed place before the plain. But
he [a]did not know that *there was* an ambush
against him behind the city.
15 And Joshua and all Israel [a]made as if they
were beaten before them, and fled by the way of
the wilderness.
16 So all the people who *were* in Ai were called
together to pursue them. And they pursued
Joshua and were drawn away from the city.
17 There was not a man left in Ai or Bethel who
did not go out after Israel. So they left the city
open and pursued Israel.
**18** Then the LORD said to Joshua, "Stretch out
the spear that *is* in your hand toward Ai, for I will
give it into your hand." And Joshua stretched out
the spear that *was* in his hand toward the city.
19 So *those in* ambush arose quickly out of their
place; they ran as soon as he had stretched out his
hand, and they entered the city and took it, and
hurried to set the city on fire.
20 And when the men of Ai looked behind them,
they saw, and behold, the smoke of the city
ascended to heaven. So they had no power to flee
this way or that way, and the people who had fled
to the wilderness turned back on the pursuers.
21 Now when Joshua and all Israel saw that the
ambush had taken the city and that the smoke of
the city ascended, they turned back and struck
down the men of Ai.
22 Then the others came out of the city against
them; so they were *caught* in the midst of Israel,
some on this side and some on that side. And they

5 [a]Josh. 7:5; Judg. 20:32
8 [a]2 Sam. 13:28
11 [a]Josh. 8:5
12 [1]Ai
14 [a]Judg. 20:34; Eccl. 9:12
15 [a]Judg. 20:36
22 [a]Deut. 7:2
26 [a]Josh. 6:21
27 [a]Num. 31:22, 26 [b]Josh. 8:2
28 [a]Deut. 13:16
29 [a]Josh. 10:26 [b]Deut. 21:22, 23; Josh. 10:27 [c]Josh. 7:26; 10:27
30 [a]Deut. 27:4–8
31 [a]Ex. 20:25; Deut. 27:5, 6 [b]Ex. 20:24
32 [a]Deut. 27:2, 3, 8
33 [a]Deut. 31:9, 25 [b]Deut. 31:12 [c]Deut. 11:29; 27:12
34 [a]Deut. 31:11; Neh. 8:3 [b]Deut. 28:2, 15, 45; 29:20, 21; 30:19 [c]Josh. 1:8
35 [a]Ex. 12:38; Deut. 31:12 [b]Josh. 8:33

CHAPTER 9
1 [a]Num. 13:29; Josh. 3:10 [b]Num. 34:6 [c]Ex. 3:17; 23:23
2 [a]Josh. 10:5; Ps. 83:3, 5 [1]Lit. *mouth*
3 [a]Josh. 9:17, 22; 10:2; 21:17; 2 Sam. 21:1, 2 [b]Josh. 6:27
4 [1]*acted as envoys*

struck them down, so that they [a]let none of them
remain or escape.
23 But the king of Ai they took alive, and
brought him to Joshua.
**24** And it came to pass when Israel had made an
end of slaying all the inhabitants of Ai in the field,
in the wilderness where they pursued them, and
when they all had fallen by the edge of the sword
until they were consumed, that all the Israelites
returned to Ai and struck it with the edge of the
sword.
25 So it was *that* all who fell that day, both men
and women, *were* twelve thousand—all the people
of Ai.
26 For Joshua did not draw back his hand, with
which he stretched out the spear, until he had
[a]utterly destroyed all the inhabitants of Ai.
27 [a]Only the livestock and the spoil of that city
Israel took as booty for themselves, according to
the word of the LORD which He had [b]commanded
Joshua.
28 So Joshua burned Ai and made it [a]a heap
forever, a desolation to this day.
29 [a]And the king of Ai he hanged on a tree until
evening. [b]And as soon as the sun was down,
Joshua commanded that they should take his
corpse down from the tree, cast it at the entrance
of the gate of the city, and [c]raise over it a great
heap of stones *that remains* to this day.
**30** Now Joshua built an altar to the LORD God of
Israel [a]in Mount Ebal,
31 as Moses the servant of the LORD had commanded the children of Israel, as it is written in
the Book of the Law of Moses: [a]"an altar of whole
stones over which no man has wielded an iron
*tool.*" And [b]they offered on it burnt offerings to
the LORD, and sacrificed peace offerings.
32 And there, in the presence of the children of
Israel, [a]he wrote on the stones a copy of the law of
Moses, which he had written.
33 Then all Israel, with their elders and officers
and judges, stood on either side of the ark before
the priests, the Levites, [a]who bore the ark of the
covenant of the LORD, [b]the stranger as well as he
who was born among them. Half of them *were* in
front of Mount Gerizim and half of them in front
of Mount Ebal, [c]as Moses the servant of the LORD
had commanded before, that they should bless the
people of Israel.
34 And afterward [a]he read all the words of the
law, [b]the blessings and the cursings, according to
all that is written in the [c]Book of the Law.
35 There was not a word of all that Moses had
commanded which Joshua did not read before all
the assembly of Israel, [a]with the women, the little
ones, [b]and the strangers who were living among
them.

### *The Deceit of the Gibeonites*

**9** And it came to pass when [a]all the kings who
*were* on this side of the Jordan, in the hills and
in the lowland and in all the coasts of [b]the Great
Sea toward Lebanon—[c]the Hittite, the Amorite,
the Canaanite, the Perizzite, the Hivite, and the
Jebusite—heard *about it*,
2 that they [a]gathered together to fight with
Joshua and Israel with one [1]accord.
3 But when the inhabitants of [a]Gibeon [b]heard
what Joshua had done to Jericho and Ai,
4 they worked craftily, and went and [1]pretended

to be ambassadors. And they took old sacks on
their donkeys, old wineskins torn and [2]mended,
5 old and patched sandals on their feet, and old
garments on themselves; and all the bread of their
provision was dry *and* moldy.
6 And they went to Joshua, [a]to the camp at
Gilgal, and said to him and to the men of Israel,
"We have come from a far country; now therefore, make a [1]covenant with us."
7 Then the men of Israel said to the [a]Hivites,
"Perhaps you dwell among us; so [b]how can we
make a covenant with you?"
8 But they said to Joshua, [a]"We *are* your servants." And Joshua said to them, "Who *are* you,
and where do you come from?"
9 So they said to him: [a]"From a very far country
your servants have come, because of the name of
the LORD your God; for we have [b]heard of His
fame, and all that He did in Egypt,
10 "and [a]all that He did to the two kings of the
Amorites who *were* beyond the Jordan—to Sihon
king of Heshbon, and Og king of Bashan, who was
at Ashtaroth.
11 "Therefore our elders and all the inhabitants
of our country spoke to us, saying, 'Take provisions with you for the journey, and go to meet
them, and say to them, "We *are* your servants;
now therefore, make a covenant with us." '
12 "This bread of ours we took hot *for* our provision from our houses on the day we departed to
come to you. But now look, it is dry and moldy.
13 "And these wineskins which we filled *were*
new, and see, they are torn; and these our garments and our sandals have become old because
of the very long journey."
14 Then the men of Israel took some of their
provisions; [a]but they [1]did not ask counsel of the
LORD.
15 So Joshua [a]made peace with them, and made a
covenant with them to let them live; and the
rulers of the congregation swore to them.
**16** And it happened at the end of three days, after
they had made a covenant with them, that they
heard that they *were* their neighbors who dwelt
near them.
17 Then the children of Israel journeyed and
came to their cities on the third day. Now their
cities *were* [a]Gibeon, Chephirah, Beeroth, and
Kirjath Jearim.
18 But the children of Israel did not [1]attack them,
[a]because the rulers of the congregation had sworn
to them by the LORD God of Israel. And all the
congregation complained against the rulers.
19 Then all the rulers said to all the congregation,
"We have sworn to them by the LORD God of
Israel; now therefore, we may not touch them.
20 "This we will do to them: We will let them live,
lest [a]wrath be upon us because of the oath which
we swore to them."
21 And the rulers said to them, "Let them live,
but let them be [a]woodcutters and water carriers
for all the congregation, as the rulers had [b]prom-
ised them."
**22** Then Joshua called for them, and he spoke to
them, saying, "Why have you deceived us, saying,
[a]'We *are* very far from you,' when [b]you dwell near
us?
23 "Now therefore, you *are* [a]cursed, and none of
you shall be freed from being slaves—woodcutters
and water carriers for the house of my God."
24 So they answered Joshua and said, "Because
your servants were clearly told that the LORD your
God [a]commanded His servant Moses to give you
all the land, and to destroy all the inhabitants of
the land from before you; therefore [b]we were very
much afraid for our lives because of you, and have
done this thing.
25 "And now, here we are, [a]in your hands; do
with us as it seems good and right to do to us."
26 So he did to them, and delivered them out of
the hand of the children of Israel, so that they did
not kill them.
27 And that day Joshua made them [a]woodcutters
and water carriers for the congregation and for
the altar of the LORD, [b]in the place which He
would choose, even to this day.

### *The Sun Stands Still*

**10** Now it came to pass when Adoni-Zedek
king of Jerusalem [a]heard how Joshua had
taken [b]Ai and had utterly destroyed it—[c]as he had
done to Jericho and its king, so he had done to [d]Ai
and its king—and [e]how the inhabitants of Gibeon
had made peace with Israel and were among
them,
2 that they [a]feared greatly, because Gibeon *was*
a great city, like one of the royal cities, and
because it *was* greater than Ai, and all its men
*were* mighty.
3 Therefore Adoni-Zedek king of Jerusalem sent
to Hoham king of Hebron, Piram king of Jarmuth,
Japhia king of Lachish, and Debir king of Eglon,
saying,
4 "Come up to me and help me, that we may
attack Gibeon, for [a]it has made peace with Joshua
and with the children of Israel."
5 Therefore the five kings of the [a]Amorites, the
king of Jerusalem, the king of Hebron, the king of
Jarmuth, the king of Lachish, *and* the king of
Eglon, [b]gathered together and went up, they and
all their armies, and camped before Gibeon and
made war against it.
**6** And the men of Gibeon sent to Joshua at the
camp [a]at Gilgal, saying, "Do not forsake your
servants; come up to us quickly, save us and help
us, for all the kings of the Amorites who dwell in
the mountains have gathered together against
us."
7 So Joshua ascended from Gilgal, he and [a]all
the people of war with him, and all the mighty
men of valor.
8 And the LORD said to Joshua, [a]"Do not fear
them, for I have delivered them into your hand;
[b]not a man of them shall [c]stand before you."
9 Joshua therefore came upon them suddenly,
having marched all night from Gilgal.
10 So the LORD [a]routed them before Israel, killed
them with a great slaughter at Gibeon, chased
them along the road that goes [b]to Beth Horon, and
struck them down as far as [c]Azekah and Makkedah.
11 And it happened, as they fled before Israel *and*
were on the descent of Beth Horon, [a]that the LORD
cast down large hailstones from heaven on them
as far as Azekah, and they died. *There were* more
who died from the hailstones than the children of
Israel killed with the sword.
**12** Then Joshua spoke to the LORD in the day
when the LORD delivered up the Amorites before
the children of Israel, and he said in the sight of
Israel:

**4** [2]Lit. *tied up*
**6** [a]Josh. 5:10 [1]*treaty*
**7** [a]Josh. 9:1; 11:19 [b]Ex. 23:32; Deut. 7:2
**8** [a]Deut. 20:11; 2 Kin. 10:5
**9** [a]Deut. 20:15 [b]Ex. 15:14; Josh. 2:9, 10; 5:1
**10** [a]Num. 21:24, 33
**14** [a]Num. 27:21; Is. 30:1 [1]Lit. *did not inquire at the mouth of*
**15** [a]2 Sam. 21:2
**17** [a]Josh. 18:25
**18** [a]Ps. 15:4 [1]*strike*
**20** [a]2 Sam. 21:1, 2, 6; Ezek. 17:13, 15
**21** [a]Deut. 29:11 [b]Josh. 9:15
**22** [a]Josh. 9:6, 9 [b]Josh. 9:16
**23** [a]Gen. 9:25
**24** [a]Ex. 23:31–33; Deut. 7:1, 2 [b]Ex. 15:14
**25** [a]Gen. 16:6
**27** [a]Josh. 9:21, 23 [b]Deut. 12:5

CHAPTER 10

**1** [a]Josh. 9:1 [b]Josh. 8:1 [c]Josh. 6:21 [d]Josh. 8:22, 26, 28 [e]Josh. 9:15
**2** [a]Ex. 15:14–16; Deut. 11:25; 1 Chr. 14:17
**4** [a]Josh. 9:15; 10:1
**5** [a]Num. 13:29 [b]Josh. 9:2
**6** [a]Josh. 5:10; 9:6
**7** [a]Josh. 8:1
**8** [a]Josh. 11:6; Judg. 4:14 [b]Josh. 1:5, 9 [c]Josh. 21:44
**10** [a]Judg. 4:15; 1 Sam. 7:10, 12; Is. 28:21 [b]Josh. 16:3, 5 [c]Josh. 15:35
**11** [a]Is. 30:30; Rev. 16:21

[a]"Sun, stand still over Gibeon;
And Moon, in the Valley of [b]Aijalon."
13 So the sun stood still,
And the moon stopped,
Till the people had revenge
Upon their enemies.
[a]*Is* this not written in the Book of Jasher? So the
sun stood still in the midst of heaven, and did not
hasten to go *down* for about a whole day.
14 And there has been [a]no day like that, before it
or after it, that the LORD heeded the voice of a
man; for [b]the LORD fought for Israel.
15 [a]Then Joshua returned, and all Israel with
him, to the camp at Gilgal.
**16** But these five kings had fled and hidden themselves in a cave at Makkedah.
17 And it was told Joshua, saying, "The five kings
have been found hidden in the cave at Makkedah."
18 So Joshua said, "Roll large stones against the
mouth of the cave, and set men by it to guard
them.
19 "And do not stay *there* yourselves, *but* pursue
your enemies, and attack their rear guard. Do not
allow them to enter their cities, for the LORD your
God has delivered them into your hand."
20 Then it happened, while Joshua and the children of Israel made an end of slaying them with a
very great slaughter, till they had finished, that
those who escaped entered fortified cities.
21 And all the people returned to the camp, to
Joshua at Makkedah, in peace. [a]No one [1]moved
his tongue against any of the children of Israel.
**22** Then Joshua said, "Open the mouth of the
cave, and bring out those five kings to me from
the cave."
23 And they did so, and brought out those five
kings to him from the cave: the king of Jerusalem,
the king of Hebron, the king of Jarmuth, the king
of Lachish, *and* the king of Eglon.
24 So it was, when they brought out those kings
to Joshua, that Joshua called for all the men of
Israel, and said to the captains of the men of war
who went with him, "Come near, put your feet on
the necks of these kings." And they drew near and
[a]put their feet on their necks.
25 Then Joshua said to [1]them, [a]"Do not be afraid,
nor be dismayed; be strong and of good courage,
for [b]thus the LORD will do to all your enemies
against whom you fight."
26 And afterward Joshua struck [1]them and killed
them, and hanged them on five trees; and they
[a]were hanging on the trees until evening.
27 So it was at the time of the going down of the
sun *that* Joshua commanded, and they [a]took them
down from the trees, cast them into the cave
where they had been hidden, and laid large stones
against the cave's mouth, *which remain* until this
very day.
**28** On that day Joshua took Makkedah, and
struck it and its king with the edge of the sword.
He utterly [a]destroyed [1]them—all the people who
*were* in it. He let none remain. He also did to the
king of Makkedah [b]as he had done to the king of
Jericho.
**29** Then Joshua passed from Makkedah, and all
Israel with him, to [a]Libnah; and they fought
against Libnah.
30 And the LORD also delivered it and its king
into the hand of Israel; he struck it and all the
people who *were* in it with the edge of the sword.
He let none remain in it, but did to its king as he
had done to the king of Jericho.
**31** Then Joshua passed from Libnah, and all
Israel with him, to Lachish; and they encamped
against it and fought against it.
32 And the LORD delivered Lachish into the hand
of Israel, who took it on the second day, and
struck it and all the people who *were* in it with the
edge of the sword, according to all that he had
done to Libnah.
33 Then Horam king of Gezer came up to help
Lachish; and Joshua struck him and his people,
until he left him none remaining.
**34** From Lachish Joshua passed to Eglon, and all
Israel with him; and they encamped against it and
fought against it.
35 They took it on that day and struck it with the
edge of the sword; all the people who *were* in it he
utterly destroyed that day, according to all that he
had done to Lachish.
**36** So Joshua went up from Eglon, and all Israel
with him, to [a]Hebron; and they fought against it.
37 And they took it and struck it with the edge of
the sword—its king, all its cities, and all the people
who *were* in it; he left none remaining, according
to all that he had done to Eglon, but utterly
destroyed it and all the people who *were* in it.
**38** Then Joshua returned, and all Israel with him,
to [a]Debir; and they fought against it.
39 And he took it and its king and all its cities;
they struck them with the edge of the sword and
utterly destroyed all the people who *were* in it. He
left none remaining; as he had done to Hebron, so
he did to Debir and its king, as he had done also to
Libnah and its king.
**40** So Joshua conquered all the land: the [a]moun-
tain country and the [1]South and the lowland and
the wilderness slopes, and [b]all their kings; he left
none remaining, but [c]utterly destroyed all that
breathed, as the LORD God of Israel had commanded.
41 And Joshua conquered them from [a]Kadesh
Barnea as far as [b]Gaza, [c]and all the country of
Goshen, even as far as Gibeon.
42 All these kings and their land Joshua took at
one time, [a]because the LORD God of Israel fought
for Israel.
43 Then Joshua returned, and all Israel with him,
to the camp at Gilgal.

### *Joshua Conquers the Entire Land*

**11** And it came to pass, when Jabin king of
Hazor heard *these things,* that he [a]sent to
Jobab king of Madon, to the king [b]of Shimron, to
the king of Achshaph,
2 and to the kings who *were* from the north, in
the mountains, in the plain south of [a]Chinneroth,
in the lowland, and in the heights [b]of Dor on the
west,
3 to the Canaanites in the east and in the west,
the [a]Amorite, the Hittite, the Perizzite, the Jebusite in the mountains, [b]and the Hivite below
[c]Hermon [d]in the land of Mizpah.
4 So they went out, they and all their armies
with them, *as* many people [a]*as* the sand that *is* on
the seashore in multitude, with very many horses
and chariots.
5 And when all these kings had [1]met together,
they came and camped together at the waters of
Merom to fight against Israel.
**6** But the LORD said to Joshua, [a]"Do not be

**12** [a]Is. 28:21; Hab. 3:11 [b]Judg. 12:12
**13** [a]2 Sam. 1:18
**14** [a]Is. 38:7, 8 [b]Ex. 14:14; Deut. 1:30; 20:4; Josh. 10:42; 23:3
**15** [a]Josh. 10:43
**21** [a]Ex. 11:7 [1]*criticized,* lit. *sharpened his tongue*
**24** [a]Ps. 107:40; Is. 26:5, 6; Mal. 4:3
**25** [a]Deut. 31:6–8; Josh. 1:9 [b]Deut. 3:21; 7:19 [1]The captains
**26** [a]Josh. 8:29; 2 Sam. 21:9 [1]The kings
**27** [a]Deut. 21:22, 23; Josh. 8:29
**28** [a]Deut. 7:2, 16 [b]Josh. 6:21 [1]So with MT and most authorities; many Heb. mss., some mss. of LXX, and some mss. of Tg. *it*
**29** [a]Josh. 15:42; 21:13; 2 Kin. 8:22; 19:8
**36** [a]Num. 13:22; Josh. 14:13–15; 15:13; Judg. 1:10, 20; 2 Sam. 5:1, 3, 5, 13; 2 Chr. 11:10
**38** [a]Josh. 15:15; Judg. 1:11; 1 Chr. 6:58
**40** [a]Deut. 1:7 [b]Deut. 7:24 [c]Deut. 20:16, 17 [1]Heb. *Negev,* and so throughout the book
**41** [a]Num. 13:26; Deut. 9:23 [b]Gen. 10:19; Josh. 11:22 [c]Josh. 11:16; 15:51
**42** [a]Josh. 10:14

CHAPTER 11

**1** [a]Josh. 10:3 [b]Josh. 19:15
**2** [a]Num. 34:11 [b]Josh. 17:11; Judg. 1:27; 1 Kin. 4:11
**3** [a]Josh. 9:1 [b]Deut. 7:1; Judg. 3:3, 5; 1 Kin. 9:20 [c]Josh. 11:17; 13:5, 11 [d]Gen. 31:49
**4** [a]Gen. 22:17; 32:12; Judg. 7:12; 1 Sam. 13:5
**5** [1]Lit. *assembled by appointment*
**6** [a]Josh. 10:8

afraid because of them, for tomorrow about this
time I will deliver all of them slain before Israel.
You shall [b]hamstring their horses and burn their
chariots with fire."
7 So Joshua and all the people of war with him
came against them suddenly by the waters of
Merom, and they attacked them.
8 And the LORD delivered them into the hand of
Israel, who defeated them and chased them to
[1]Greater [a]Sidon, to the [2]Brook [b]Misrephoth, and to
the Valley of Mizpah eastward; they attacked
them until they left none of them remaining.
9 So Joshua did to them as the LORD had told
him: he hamstrung their horses and burned their
chariots with fire.
**10** Joshua turned back at that time and took
Hazor, and struck its king with the sword; for
Hazor was formerly the head of all those kingdoms.
11 And they struck all the people who *were* in it
with the edge of the sword, [a]utterly destroying
*them.* There was none left [b]breathing. Then he
burned Hazor with fire.
12 So all the cities of those kings, and all their
kings, Joshua took and struck with the edge of
the sword. He utterly destroyed them, [a]as Moses
the servant of the LORD had commanded.
13 But *as for* the cities that stood on their
[1]mounds, Israel burned none of them, except
Hazor only, *which* Joshua burned.
14 And all the [a]spoil of these cities and the
livestock, the children of Israel took as booty for
themselves; but they struck every man with the
edge of the sword until they had destroyed them,
and they left none breathing.
15 [a]As the LORD had commanded Moses his servant, so [b]Moses commanded Joshua, and [c]so
Joshua did. [1]He left nothing undone of all that the
LORD had commanded Moses.
**16** Thus Joshua took all this land: [a]the mountain
country, all the South, [b]all the land of Goshen, the
lowland, and the Jordan [1]plain—the mountains of
Israel and its lowlands,
17 [a]from [1]Mount Halak and the ascent to Seir,
even as far as Baal Gad in the Valley of Lebanon
below Mount Hermon. He captured [b]all their
kings, and struck them down and killed them.
18 Joshua made war a long time with all those
kings.
19 There was not a city that made peace with the
children of Israel, except [a]the Hivites, the inhabitants of Gibeon. All *the others* they took in battle.
20 For [a]it was of the LORD [1]to harden their hearts,
that they should come against Israel in battle,
that He might utterly destroy them, *and* that they
might receive no mercy, but that He might destroy them, [b]as the LORD had commanded Moses.
**21** And at that time Joshua came and cut off [a]the
Anakim from the mountains: from Hebron, from
Debir, from Anab, from all the mountains of
Judah, and from all the mountains of Israel;
Joshua utterly destroyed them with their cities.
22 None of the Anakim were left in the land of
the children of Israel; they remained only [a]in
Gaza, in Gath, [b]and in Ashdod.
23 So Joshua took the whole land, [a]according to
all that the LORD had said to Moses; and Joshua
gave it as an inheritance to Israel [b]according to
their divisions by their tribes. Then the land
[c]rested from war.

### *The Kings Defeated by Joshua*

**12** These *are* the kings of the land whom the
children of Israel defeated, and whose land
they possessed on the other side of the Jordan
toward the rising of the sun, [a]from the River
Arnon [b]to Mount Hermon, and all the eastern
Jordan plain:
2 *One king was* [a]Sihon king of the Amorites,
who dwelt in Heshbon *and* ruled half of Gilead,
from Aroer, which is on the bank of the River
Arnon, from the middle of that river, even as far
as the River Jabbok, *which is* the border of the
Ammonites,
3 and [a]the eastern Jordan plain from the [1]Sea of
Chinneroth as far as the [2]Sea of the Arabah (the
Salt Sea), [b]the road to Beth Jeshimoth, and [3]south-
ward below [c]the[4] slopes of Pisgah.
4 *The other king was* [a]Og king of Bashan and his
territory, *who was* of [b]the remnant of the giants,
[c]who dwelt at Ashtaroth and at Edrei,
5 and reigned over [a]Mount Hermon, [b]over Salcah, over all Bashan, [c]as far as the border of the
Geshurites and the Maachathites, and over half of
Gilead *to* the border of Sihon king of Heshbon.
6 [a]These Moses the servant of the LORD and the
children of Israel had conquered; and [b]Moses the
servant of the LORD had given it *as* a possession to
the Reubenites, the Gadites, and half the tribe of
Manasseh.
**7** And these *are* the kings of the country [a]which
Joshua and the children of Israel conquered on
this side of the Jordan, on the west, from Baal Gad
in the Valley of Lebanon as far as [1]Mount Halak
and the ascent to [b]Seir, which Joshua [c]gave to the
tribes of Israel *as* a possession according to their
divisions,
8 [a]in the mountain country, in the lowlands, in
the *Jordan* plain, in the slopes, in the wilderness,
and in the South—[b]the Hittites, the Amorites, the
Canaanites, the Perizzites, the Hivites, and the
Jebusites:
9 [a]the king of Jericho, one; [b]the king of Ai,
which *is* beside Bethel, one;
10 [a]the king of Jerusalem, one; the king of Hebron, one;
11 the king of Jarmuth, one; the king of Lachish,
one;
12 the king of Eglon, one; [a]the king of Gezer, one;
13 [a]the king of Debir, one; the king of Geder, one;
14 the king of Hormah, one; the king of Arad,
one;
15 [a]the king of Libnah, one; the king of Adullam,
one;
16 [a]the king of Makkedah, one; [b]the king of
Bethel, one;
17 the king of Tappuah, one; [a]the king of Hepher,
one;
18 the king of Aphek, one; the king of [1]Lasharon,
one;
19 the king of Madon, one; [a]the king of Hazor,
one;
20 the king of [a]Shimron Meron, one; the king of
Achshaph, one;
21 the king of Taanach, one; the king of Megiddo,
one;
22 [a]the king of Kedesh, one; the king of Jokneam
in Carmel, one;

**6** [b]2 Sam. 8:4
**8** [a]Gen. 49:13 [b]Josh. 13:6 [1]Heb. *Sidon Rabbah* [2]Heb. *Misrephoth Maim,* lit. *Burnings of Water*
**11** [a]Deut. 20:16 [b]Josh. 10:40
**12** [a]Num. 33:50–56
**13** [1]Heb. *tel,* a heap of successive city ruins
**14** [a]Deut. 20:14–18
**15** [a]Ex. 34:10–17 [b]Deut. 31:7, 8 [c]Josh. 1:7 [1]Lit. *He turned aside from nothing*
**16** [a]Josh. 12:8 [b]Josh. 10:40, 41 [1]Heb. *arabah*
**17** [a]Josh. 12:7 [b]Deut. 7:24 [1]Lit. *The Smooth* or *Bald Mountain*
**19** [a]Josh. 9:3–7
**20** [a]Deut. 2:30 [b]Deut. 20:16, 17 [1]Lit. *to make strong*
**21** [a]Num. 13:22, 33
**22** [a]1 Sam. 17:4 [b]Josh. 15:46
**23** [a]Num. 34:2–15 [b]Num. 26:53 [c]Deut. 12:9, 10; 25:19

CHAPTER 12
**1** [a]Num. 21:24 [b]Deut. 3:8
**2** [a]Deut. 2:24–27
**3** [a]Deut. 3:17 [b]Josh. 13:20 [c]Deut. 3:17; 4:49 [1]Sea of Galilee [2]Lit. *Sea of the Plain,* The Dead Sea [3]Or *Teman* [4]Or *Ashdoth Pisgah*
**4** [a]Num. 21:33 [b]Deut. 3:11 [c]Deut. 1:4
**5** [a]Deut. 3:8 [b]Deut. 3:10 [c]Deut. 3:14
**6** [a]Num. 21:24, 35 [b]Num. 32:29–33
**7** [a]Josh. 11:17 [b]Gen. 14:6; 32:3 [c]Josh. 11:23 [1]Lit. *The Bald Mountain*
**8** [a]Josh. 10:40; 11:16 [b]Ex. 3:8; 23:23
**9** [a]Josh. 6:2 [b]Josh. 8:29
**10** [a]Josh. 10:23
**12** [a]Josh. 10:33
**13** [a]Josh. 10:38, 39
**15** [a]Josh. 10:29, 30
**16** [a]Josh. 10:28 [b]Judg. 1:22
**17** [a]1 Kin. 4:10
**18** [1]Or *Sharon*
**19** [a]Josh. 11:10
**20** [a]Josh. 11:1; 19:15
**22** [a]Josh. 19:37; 20:7; 21:32

23 the king of Dor in the [a]heights of Dor, one; the
king of [b]the people of Gilgal, one;
24 the king of Tirzah, one—[a]all the kings, thirty-
one.

### *The Land East of the Jordan*

**13** Now Joshua [a]was old, advanced in years.
And the LORD said to him: "You are old,
advanced in years, and there remains very much
land yet to be possessed.
2 [a]"This is the land that yet remains: [b]all the
territory of the Philistines and all [c]*that of* the
Geshurites,
3 [a]"from Sihor, which *is* east of Egypt, as far as
the border of Ekron northward (*which* is counted
as Canaanite); the [b]five lords of the Philistines—
the Gazites, the Ashdodites, the Ashkelonites, the
Gittites, and the Ekronites; also [c]the Avites;
4 "from the south, all the land of the Canaanites, and Mearah that belongs to the Sidonians [a]as
far as Aphek, to the border of [b]the Amorites;
5 "the land of [a]the [1]Gebalites, and all Lebanon,
toward the sunrise, [b]from Baal Gad below Mount
Hermon as far as the entrance to Hamath;
6 "all the inhabitants of the mountains from
Lebanon as far as [a]the [1]Brook Misrephoth, *and* all
the Sidonians—them [b]I will drive out from before
the children of Israel; only [c]divide[2] it by lot to
Israel as an inheritance, as I have commanded
you.
7 "Now therefore, divide this land as an inheritance to the nine tribes and half the tribe of
Manasseh."
**8** With the other half tribe the Reubenites and
the Gadites received their inheritance, [a]which
Moses had given them, [b]beyond the Jordan eastward, as Moses the servant of the LORD had given
them:
9 from Aroer which *is* on the bank of the River
Arnon, and the town that *is* in the midst of the
ravine, [a]and all the plain of Medeba as far as
Dibon;
10 [a]all the cities of Sihon king of the Amorites,
who reigned in Heshbon, as far as the border of
the children of Ammon;
11 [a]Gilead, and the border of the Geshurites and
Maachathites, all Mount Hermon, and all Bashan
as far as Salcah;
12 all the kingdom of Og in Bashan, who reigned
in Ashtaroth and Edrei, who remained of [a]the
remnant of the giants; [b]for Moses had [1]defeated
and [2]cast out these.
13 Nevertheless the children of Israel [a]did not
drive out the Geshurites or the Maachathites, but
the Geshurites and the Maachathites dwell among
the Israelites until this day.
14 [a]Only to the tribe of Levi he had given [1]no
inheritance; the sacrifices of the LORD God of
Israel made by fire *are* their inheritance, [b]as He
said to them.
**15** [a]And Moses had given to the tribe of the
children of Reuben *an inheritance* according to
their families.
16 Their territory was [a]from Aroer, which *is* on
the bank of the River Arnon, [b]and the city that *is*
in the midst of the ravine, [c]and all the plain by
Medeba;
17 [a]Heshbon and all its cities that *are* in the plain:
Dibon, Bamoth Baal, Beth Baal Meon,
18 [a]Jahaza, Kedemoth, Mephaath,
19 [a]Kirjathaim, [b]Sibmah, Zereth Shahar on the
mountain of the valley,
20 Beth Peor, [a]the slopes of Pisgah, and Beth
Jeshimoth—
21 [a]all the cities of the plain and all the kingdom
of Sihon king of the Amorites, who reigned in
Heshbon, [b]whom Moses had struck [c]with the
princes of Midian: Evi, Rekem, Zur, Hur, and
Reba, who *were* princes of Sihon dwelling in the
country.
22 The children of Israel also killed with the
sword [a]Balaam the son of Beor, the [1]soothsayer,
among those who were killed by them.
23 And the border of the children of Reuben was
the bank of the Jordan. This *was* the inheritance
of the children of Reuben according to their
families, the cities and their villages.
**24** [a]Moses also had given *an inheritance* to the
tribe of Gad, to the children of Gad according to
their families.
25 [a]Their territory was Jazer, and all the cities of
Gilead, [b]and half the land of the Ammonites as far
as Aroer, which *is* before [c]Rabbah,
26 and from Heshbon to Ramath Mizpah and
Betonim, and from Mahanaim to the border of
Debir,
27 and in the valley [a]Beth Haram, Beth Nimrah,
[b]Succoth, and Zaphon, the rest of the kingdom of
Sihon king of Heshbon, with the Jordan as *its*
border, as far as the edge [c]of the [1]Sea of Chinnereth, on the other side of the Jordan eastward.
28 This *is* the inheritance of the children of Gad
according to their families, the cities and their
villages.
**29** [a]Moses also had given *an inheritance* to half
the tribe of Manasseh; it was for half the tribe of
the children of Manasseh according to their families:
30 Their territory was from Mahanaim, all Bashan, all the kingdom of Og king of Bashan, and
[a]all the towns of Jair which are in Bashan, sixty
cities;
31 half of Gilead, and [a]Ashtaroth and Edrei, cities
of the kingdom of Og in Bashan, *were* for the
[b]children of Machir the son of Manasseh, for half
of the children of Machir according to their families.
32 These *are the areas* which Moses had [1]distrib-
uted as an inheritance in the plains of Moab on
the other side of the Jordan, by Jericho eastward.
33 [a]But to the tribe of Levi Moses had given no
inheritance; the LORD God of Israel *was* their
inheritance, [b]as He had said to them.

### *The Land West of the Jordan; Hebron Given to Caleb*

**14** These *are the areas* which the children of
Israel inherited in the land of Canaan,
[a]which Eleazar the priest, Joshua the son of Nun,
and the heads of the fathers of the tribes of the
children of Israel distributed as an inheritance to
them.
2 Their inheritance *was* [a]by lot, as the LORD had
commanded by the hand of Moses, for the nine
tribes and the half-tribe.
3 [a]For Moses had given the inheritance of the
two tribes and the half-tribe on the other side of
the Jordan; but to the Levites he had given no
inheritance among them.
4 For [a]the children of Joseph were two tribes:
Manasseh and Ephraim. And they gave no part to

**23** [a]Josh. 11:2 [b]Is. 9:1
**24** [a]Deut. 7:24

CHAPTER 13
**1** [a]Josh. 14:10; 23:1, 2
**2** [a]Judg. 3:1–3 [b]Joel 3:4 [c]2 Sam. 3:3
**3** [a]Jer. 2:18 [b]Judg. 3:3 [c]Deut. 2:23
**4** [a]Josh. 12:18; 19:30 [b]Judg. 1:34
**5** [a]1 Kin. 5:18; Ezek. 27:9 [b]Josh. 12:7 [1]Or *Giblites*
**6** [a]Josh. 11:8 [b]Josh. 23:13 [c]Josh. 14:1, 2 [1]Heb. *Misrephoth Maim* [2]*apportion*
**8** [a]Num. 32:33 [b]Josh. 12:1–6
**9** [a]Num. 21:30
**10** [a]Num. 21:24, 25
**11** [a]Josh. 12:5
**12** [a]Deut. 3:11 [b]Num. 21:24, 34, 35 [1]Lit. *struck* [2]*dispossessed*
**13** [a]Josh. 13:11
**14** [a]Josh. 14:3, 4 [b]Josh. 13:33 [1]*no land as a possession*
**15** [a]Num. 34:14
**16** [a]Josh. 12:2 [b]Num. 21:28 [c]Num. 21:30
**17** [a]Num. 21:28, 30
**18** [a]Num. 21:23
**19** [a]Num. 32:37 [b]Num. 32:38
**20** [a]Deut. 3:17
**21** [a]Deut. 3:10 [b]Num. 21:24 [c]Num. 31:8
**22** [a]Num. 22:5; 31:8 [1]*diviner*
**24** [a]Num. 34:14
**25** [a]Num. 32:1, 35 [b]Judg. 11:13, 15 [c]Deut. 3:11
**27** [a]Num. 32:36 [b]Gen. 33:17 [c]Num. 34:11 [1]Sea of Galilee
**29** [a]Num. 34:14
**30** [a]Num. 32:41
**31** [a]Josh. 9:10; 12:4; 13:12 [b]Num. 32:39, 40
**32** [1]*apportioned*
**33** [a]Josh. 13:14; 18:7 [b]Num. 18:20

CHAPTER 14
**1** [a]Num. 34:16–29
**2** [a]Num. 26:55; 33:54; 34:13
**3** [a]Josh. 13:8, 32, 33
**4** [a]2 Chr. 30:1

the Levites in the land, except [b]cities to dwell *in,* with their common-lands for their livestock and their property.

5 [a]As the LORD had commanded Moses, so the children of Israel did; and they divided the land.

**6** Then the children of Judah came to Joshua in Gilgal. And Caleb the son of Jephunneh the [a]Kenizzite said to him: "You know [b]the word which the LORD said to Moses the man of God concerning [c]you and me in Kadesh Barnea.

7 "I *was* forty years old when Moses the servant of the LORD [a]sent me from Kadesh Barnea to spy out the land, and I brought back word to him as *it was* in my heart.

8 "Nevertheless [a]my brethren who went up with me made the [1]heart of the people melt, but I wholly [b]followed the LORD my God.

9 "So Moses swore on that day, saying, [a]'Surely the land [b]where your foot has trodden shall be your inheritance and your children's forever, because you have wholly followed the LORD my God.'

10 "And now, behold, the LORD has kept me [a]alive, [b]as He said, these forty-five years, ever since the LORD spoke this word to Moses while Israel [1]wandered in the wilderness; and now, here I am this day, eighty-five years old.

11 [a]"As yet I *am as* strong this day as on the day that Moses sent me; just as my strength *was* then, so now *is* my strength for war, both [b]for going out and for coming in.

12 "Now therefore, give me this mountain of which the LORD spoke in that day; for you heard in that day how [a]the Anakim *were* there, and *that* the cities *were* great *and* fortified. [b]It may be that the LORD *will be* with me, and [c]I shall be able to drive them out as the LORD said."

**13** And Joshua [a]blessed him, [b]and gave Hebron to Caleb the son of Jephunneh as an inheritance.

14 [a]Hebron therefore became the inheritance of Caleb the son of Jephunneh the Kenizzite to this day, because he [b]wholly followed the LORD God of Israel.

15 And [a]the name of Hebron formerly was Kirjath Arba (*Arba was* the greatest man among the Anakim). [b]Then the land had rest from war.

### *The Cities of Judah*

**15** So *this* was the [1]lot of the tribe of the children of Judah according to their families: [a]The border of Edom at the [b]Wilderness of Zin southward *was* the extreme southern boundary.

2 And their [a]southern border began at the shore of the Salt Sea, from the bay that faces southward.

3 Then it went out to the southern side of [a]the Ascent of Akrabbim, passed along to Zin, ascended on the south side of Kadesh Barnea, passed along to Hezron, went up to Adar, and went around to Karkaa.

4 *From there* it passed [a]toward Azmon and went out to the Brook of Egypt; and the border ended at the sea. This shall be your southern border.

5 The east border *was* the Salt Sea as far as the mouth of the Jordan. And the [a]border on the northern quarter *began* at the bay of the sea at the mouth of the Jordan.

6 The border went up to [a]Beth Hoglah and passed north of Beth Arabah; and the border went up [b]to the stone of Bohan the son of Reuben.

7 Then the border went up toward [a]Debir from [b]the Valley of Achor, and it turned northward toward Gilgal, which *is* before the Ascent of Adummim, which *is* on the south side of the valley. The border continued toward the waters of En Shemesh and ended at [c]En Rogel.

8 And the border went up [a]by the Valley of the Son of Hinnom to the southern slope of the [b]Jebusite *city* (which *is* Jerusalem). The border went up to the top of the mountain that *lies* before the Valley of Hinnom westward, which *is* at the end of the Valley [c]of [1]Rephaim northward.

9 Then the border went around from the top of the hill to [a]the fountain of the water of Nephtoah, and extended to the cities of Mount Ephron. And the border went around [b]to Baalah (which *is* [c]Kirjath Jearim).

10 Then the border [1]turned westward from Baalah to Mount Seir, passed along to the side of Mount Jearim on the north (which *is* Chesalon), went down to Beth Shemesh, and passed on to [a]Timnah.

11 And the border went out to the side of [a]Ekron northward. Then the border went around to Shicron, passed along to Mount Baalah, and extended to Jabneel; and the border ended at the sea.

12 The west border *was* [a]the coastline of the Great Sea. This *is* the boundary of the children of Judah all around according to their families.

**13** [a]Now to Caleb the son of Jephunneh he gave a share among the children of [b]Judah, according to the commandment of the LORD to Joshua, *namely,* [c]Kirjath Arba, which *is* Hebron (*Arba was* the father of Anak).

14 Caleb drove out [a]the three sons of Anak from there: [b]Sheshai, Ahiman, and Talmai, the children of Anak.

15 Then [a]he went up from there to the inhabitants of Debir (formerly the name of Debir *was* Kirjath Sepher).

**16** [a]And Caleb said, "He who [1]attacks Kirjath Sepher and takes it, to him I will give Achsah my daughter as wife."

17 So [a]Othniel the [b]son of Kenaz, the brother of Caleb, took it; and he gave him [c]Achsah his daughter as wife.

18 [a]Now it was so, when she came *to him,* that she persuaded him to ask her father for a field. So [b]she dismounted from *her* donkey, and Caleb said to her, "What do you wish?"

19 She answered, "Give me a [a]blessing; since you have given me land in the South, give me also springs of water." So he gave her the upper springs and the lower springs.

**20** This *was* the inheritance of the tribe of the children of Judah according to their families:

21 The cities at the limits of the tribe of the children of Judah, toward the border of Edom in the South, were Kabzeel, [a]Eder, Jagur,

22 Kinah, Dimonah, Adadah,

23 Kedesh, Hazor, Ithnan,

24 [a]Ziph, Telem, Bealoth,

25 Hazor, Hadattah, Kerioth, Hezron (which *is* Hazor),

26 Amam, Shema, Moladah,

27 Hazar Gaddah, Heshmon, Beth Pelet,

28 Hazar Shual, [a]Beersheba, Bizjothjah,

29 Baalah, Ijim, Ezem,

30 Eltolad, Chesil, [a]Hormah,

31 [a]Ziklag, Madmannah, Sansannah,

32 Lebaoth, Shilhim, Ain, and [a]Rimmon: all the cities *are* twenty-nine, with their villages.

---

**4** [b]Num. 35:2–8
**5** [a]Josh. 21:2
**6** [a]Num. 32:11, 12 [b]Num. 14:24, 30 [c]Num. 13:26
**7** [a]Num. 13:6, 17; 14:6
**8** [a]Num. 13:31, 32 [b]Num. 14:24 [1]*courage of the people fail*
**9** [a]Num. 14:23, 24 [b]Deut. 1:36
**10** [a]Num. 14:24, 30, 38 [b]Josh. 5:6 [1]Lit. *walked*
**11** [a]Deut. 34:7 [b]Deut. 31:2
**12** [a]Num. 13:28, 33 [b]Rom. 8:31 [c]Josh. 15:14
**13** [a]Josh. 22:6 [b]Josh. 10:37; 15:13
**14** [a]Josh. 21:12 [b]Josh. 14:8, 9
**15** [a]Gen. 23:2 [b]Josh. 11:23

CHAPTER 15

**1** [a]Num. 34:3 [b]Num. 33:36 [1]*allotment*
**2** [a]Num. 34:3, 4
**3** [a]Num. 34:4
**4** [a]Num. 34:5
**5** [a]Josh. 18:15–19
**6** [a]Josh. 18:19, 21 [b]Josh. 18:17
**7** [a]Josh. 13:26 [b]Josh. 7:26 [c]2 Sam. 17:17
**8** [a]Josh. 18:16 [b]Judg. 1:21; 19:10 [c]Josh. 18:16 [1]Lit. *Giants*
**9** [a]Josh. 18:15 [b]1 Chr. 13:6 [c]Judg. 18:12
**10** [a]Gen. 38:13 [1]*turned around*
**11** [a]Josh. 19:43
**12** [a]Num. 34:6, 7
**13** [a]Josh. 14:13 [b]Num. 13:6 [c]Josh. 14:15
**14** [a]Judg. 1:10, 20 [b]Num. 13:22
**15** [a]Judg. 1:11
**16** [a]Judg. 1:12 [1]Lit. *strikes*
**17** [a]Judg. 1:13; 3:9 [b]Num. 32:12 [c]Judg. 1:12
**18** [a]Judg. 1:14 [b]Gen. 24:64
**19** [a]Gen. 33:11
**21** [a]Gen. 35:21
**24** [a]1 Sam. 23:14
**28** [a]Gen. 21:31
**30** [a]Josh. 19:4
**31** [a]1 Sam. 27:6; 30:1
**32** [a]Judg. 20:45, 47

**33** In the lowland: [a]Eshtaol, Zorah, Ashnah,
34 Zanoah, En Gannim, Tappuah, Enam,
35 Jarmuth, [a]Adullam, Socoh, Azekah,
36 Sharaim, Adithaim, Gederah, and Gedero-
thaim: fourteen cities with their villages;
37 Zenan, Hadashah, Migdal Gad,
38 Dilean, Mizpah, [a]Joktheel,
39 [a]Lachish, Bozkath, [b]Eglon,
40 Cabbon, [1]Lahmas, Kithlish,
41 Gederoth, Beth Dagon, Naamah, and Makkedah: sixteen cities with their villages;
42 [a]Libnah, Ether, Ashan,
43 Jiphtah, Ashnah, Nezib,
44 Keilah, Achzib, and Mareshah: nine cities with
their villages;
45 Ekron, with its towns and villages;
46 from Ekron to the sea, all that *lay* near [a]Ash-
dod, with their villages;
47 Ashdod with its towns and villages, Gaza with
its towns and villages—as far as [a]the Brook of
Egypt and [b]the Great Sea with *its* coastline.
**48** And in the mountain country: Shamir, Jattir,
Sochoh,
49 Dannah, Kirjath Sannah (which *is* Debir),
50 Anab, Eshtemoh, Anim,
51 [a]Goshen, Holon, and Giloh: eleven cities with
their villages;
52 Arab, Dumah, Eshean,
53 Janum, Beth Tappuah, Aphekah,
54 Humtah, [a]Kirjath Arba (which *is* Hebron), and
Zior: nine cities with their villages;
55 [a]Maon, Carmel, Ziph, Juttah,
56 Jezreel, Jokdeam, Zanoah,
57 Kain, Gibeah, and Timnah: ten cities with
their villages;
58 Halhul, Beth Zur, Gedor,
59 Maarath, Beth Anoth, and Eltekon: six cities
with their villages;
60 [a]Kirjath Baal (which *is* Kirjath Jearim) and
Rabbah: two cities with their villages.
**61** In the wilderness: Beth Arabah, Middin, Seca-
cah,
62 Nibshan, the City of Salt, and [a]En Gedi: six
cities with their villages.
63 As for the Jebusites, the inhabitants of Jerusalem, [a]the children of Judah could not drive them
out; [b]but the Jebusites dwell with the children of
Judah at Jerusalem to this day.

### *The Borders of Ephraim*

**16** The lot [1]fell to the children of Joseph from
the Jordan, by Jericho, to the waters of
Jericho on the east, to the [a]wilderness that goes
up from Jericho through the mountains to [2]Bethel,
2 then went out [1]from [a]Bethel to Luz, passed
along to the border of the Archites at Ataroth,
3 and went down westward to the boundary of
the Japhletites, [a]as far as the boundary of Lower
Beth Horon to [b]Gezer; and [1]it ended at the sea.
4 [a]So the children of Joseph, Manasseh and
Ephraim, took their [1]inheritance.
**5** [a]The border of the children of Ephraim, according to their families, was *thus:* The border of
their inheritance on the east side was [b]Ataroth
Addar [c]as far as Upper Beth Horon.
6 And the border went out toward the sea on
the north side of [a]Michmethath; then the border
went around eastward to Taanath Shiloh, and
passed by it on the east of Janohah.
7 Then it went down from Janohah to Ataroth

**33** [a]Judg. 13:25; 16:31
**35** [a]1 Sam. 22:1
**38** [a]2 Kin. 14:7
**39** [a]2 Kin. 14:19 [b]Josh. 10:3
**40** [1]Or *Lahmam*
**42** [a]Josh. 21:13
**46** [a]Josh. 11:22
**47** [a]Josh. 15:4 [b]Num. 34:6
**51** [a]Josh. 10:41; 11:16
**54** [a]Josh. 14:15
**55** [a]1 Sam. 23:24, 25
**60** [a]Josh. 18:14; 1 Sam. 7:1, 2
**62** [a]1 Sam. 23:29; Ezek. 47:10
**63** [a]Judg. 1:8, 21; 2 Sam. 5:6; 1 Chr. 11:4 [b]Judg. 1:21

CHAPTER 16
**1** [a]Josh. 8:15; 18:12 [1]Lit. *went out* [2]LXX *Bethel Luz*
**2** [a]Josh. 18:13; Judg. 1:26 [1]LXX *to Bethel,*
**3** [a]Josh. 18:13; 1 Kin. 9:17; 2 Chr. 8:5 [b]Josh. 21:21; 1 Kin. 9:15; 1 Chr. 7:28 [1]Lit. *the goings out of it were at the sea*
**4** [a]Josh. 17:14 [1]*possession*
**5** [a]Judg. 1:29; 1 Chr. 7:28, 29 [b]Josh. 18:13 [c]2 Chr. 8:5
**6** [a]Josh. 17:7
**7** [1]*Naaran,* 1 Chr. 7:28
**8** [a]Josh. 17:8 [b]Josh. 17:9 [1]Lit. *the goings out of it were at the sea*
**9** [a]Josh. 17:9
**10** [a]Josh. 15:63; 17:12, 13; Judg. 1:29; 1 Kin. 9:16

CHAPTER 17
**1** [a]Gen. 41:51; 46:20; 48:18 [b]Gen. 50:23; Judg. 5:14 [c]Deut. 3:15
**2** [a]Num. 26:29–33 [b]1 Chr. 7:18 [c]Num. 26:31 [d]Num. 26:32 [1]*Jeezer,* Num. 26:30
**3** [a]Num. 26:33; 27:1; 36:2
**4** [a]Josh. 14:1 [b]Num. 27:2–11 [1]*possession*
**5** [a]Josh. 22:7
**7** [a]Josh. 16:6
**8** [a]Josh. 16:8
**9** [a]Josh. 16:9 [1]*boundary* [2]*Wadi*
**11** [a]1 Chr. 7:29 [b]Judg. 1:27; 1 Sam. 31:10; 1 Kin. 4:12
**12** [a]Judg. 1:19, 27, 28

and [1]Naarah, reached to Jericho, and came out at
the Jordan.
8 The border went out from [a]Tappuah westward
to the [b]Brook Kanah, and [1]it ended at the sea. This
*was* the inheritance of the tribe of the children of
Ephraim according to their families.
9 [a]The separate cities for the children of
Ephraim *were* among the inheritance of the children of Manasseh, all the cities with their villages.
10 [a]And they did not drive out the Canaanites
who dwelt in Gezer; but the Canaanites dwell
among the Ephraimites to this day and have
become forced laborers.

### *The Territory of Manasseh*

**17** There was also a lot for the tribe of Manasseh, for he *was* the [a]firstborn of Joseph:
*namely* for [b]Machir the firstborn of Manasseh, the
father of Gilead, because he was a man of war;
therefore he was given [c]Gilead and Bashan.
2 And there was *a lot* for [a]the rest of the children of Manasseh according to their families: [b]for
the children of [1]Abiezer, the children of Helek,
[c]the children of Asriel, the children of Shechem,
[d]the children of Hepher, and the children of Shemida; these *were* the male children of Manasseh
the son of Joseph according to their families.
**3** But [a]Zelophehad the son of Hepher, the son of
Gilead, the son of Machir, the son of Manasseh,
had no sons, but only daughters. And these *are*
the names of his daughters: Mahlah, Noah, Hoglah, Milcah, and Tirzah.
4 And they came near before [a]Eleazar the priest,
before Joshua the son of Nun, and before the
rulers, saying, [b]"The LORD commanded Moses to
give us an [1]inheritance among our brothers."
Therefore, according to the commandment of the
LORD, he gave them an inheritance among their
father's brothers.
5 Ten shares fell to [a]Manasseh, besides the land
of Gilead and Bashan, which *were* on the other
side of the Jordan,
6 because the daughters of Manasseh received
an inheritance among his sons; and the rest of
Manasseh's sons had the land of Gilead.
**7** And the territory of Manasseh was from Asher
to [a]Michmethath, that *lies* east of Shechem; and
the border went along south to the inhabitants of
En Tappuah.
8 Manasseh had the land of Tappuah, but [a]Tap-
puah on the border of Manasseh *belonged* to the
children of Ephraim.
9 And the [1]border descended to the [2]Brook
Kanah, southward to the brook. [a]These cities of
Ephraim *are* among the cities of Manasseh. The
border of Manasseh *was* on the north side of the
brook; and it ended at the sea.
10 Southward *it was* Ephraim's, northward *it was*
Manasseh's, and the sea was its border. Manasseh's territory was adjoining Asher on the north
and Issachar on the east.
11 And in Issachar and in Asher, [a]Manasseh had
[b]Beth Shean and its towns, Ibleam and its towns,
the inhabitants of Dor and its towns, the inhabitants of En Dor and its towns, the inhabitants of
Taanach and its towns, and the inhabitants of
Megiddo and its towns—three hilly regions.
12 Yet [a]the children of Manasseh could not drive
out *the inhabitants of* those cities, but the Canaanites were determined to dwell in that land.
13 And it happened, when the children of Israel

grew strong, that they put the Canaanites to
[a]forced labor, but did not utterly drive them out.
14 [a]Then the children of Joseph spoke to Joshua,
saying, "Why have you given us *only* [b]one [1]lot and
one share to inherit, since we *are* [c]a great people,
inasmuch as the LORD has blessed us until now?"
15 So Joshua answered them, "If you *are* a great
people, *then* go up to the forest *country* and clear
a place for yourself there in the land of the
Perizzites and the giants, since the mountains of
Ephraim are too confined for you."
16 But the children of Joseph said, "The mountain country is not enough for us; and all the
Canaanites who dwell in the land of the valley
have [a]chariots of iron, *both those* who *are* of Beth
Shean and its towns and *those* who *are* [b]of the
Valley of Jezreel."
17 And Joshua spoke to the house of Joseph—to
Ephraim and Manasseh—saying, "You *are* a great
people and have great power; you shall not have
*only* one [1]lot,
18 "but the mountain country shall be yours.
Although it *is* wooded, you shall cut it down, and
its [1]farthest extent shall be yours; for you shall
drive out the Canaanites, [a]though they have iron
chariots *and* are strong."

### *The Land Described and Divided*

**18** Now the whole congregation of the children
of Israel assembled together [a]at Shiloh, and
[b]set up the tabernacle of meeting there. And the
land was subdued before them.
2 But there remained among the children of
Israel seven tribes which had not yet received
their inheritance.
3 Then Joshua said to the children of Israel:
[a]"How long will you neglect to go and possess the
land which the LORD God of your fathers has
given you?
4 "Pick out from among you three men for *each*
tribe, and I will send them; they shall rise and go
through the land, survey it according to their
inheritance, and come *back* to me.
5 "And they shall divide it into seven parts.
[a]Judah shall remain in their territory on the south,
and the [b]house of Joseph shall remain in their
territory on the north.
6 "You shall therefore [1]survey the land in seven
parts and bring *the survey* here to me, [a]that I may
cast lots for you here before the LORD our God.
7 [a]"But the Levites have no part among you, for
the priesthood of the LORD *is* their inheritance.
[b]And Gad, Reuben, and half the tribe of Manasseh
have received their inheritance beyond the Jordan
on the east, which Moses the servant of the LORD
gave them."
8 Then the men arose to go away; and Joshua
charged those who went to [1]survey the land,
saying, "Go, walk [a]through the land, survey it, and
come back to me, that I may cast lots for you here
before the LORD in Shiloh."
9 So the men went, passed through the land,
and [1]wrote the survey in a book in seven parts by
cities; and they came to Joshua at the camp in
Shiloh.
10 Then Joshua cast [a]lots for them in Shiloh
before the LORD, and there [b]Joshua divided the
land to the children of Israel according to their
[1]divisions.
11 [a]Now the lot of the tribe of the children of
Benjamin came up according to their families, and
the territory of their lot came out between the
children of Judah and the children of Joseph.
12 [a]Their border on the north side began at the
Jordan, and the border went up to the side of
Jericho on the north, and went up through the
mountains westward; it ended at the Wilderness
of Beth Aven.
13 The border went over from there toward Luz,
to the side of Luz [a](which *is* Bethel) southward;
and the border descended to Ataroth Addar, near
the hill that *lies* on the south side [b]of Lower Beth
Horon.
14 Then the border extended around the west
side to the south, from the hill that *lies* before
Beth Horon southward; and [1]it ended at [a]Kirjath
Baal (which *is* Kirjath Jearim), a city of the
children of Judah. This *was* the west side.
15 The south side *began* at the end of Kirjath
Jearim, and the border extended on the west and
went out to [a]the spring of the waters of Nephtoah.
16 Then the border came down to the end of the
mountain that *lies* before [a]the Valley of the Son of
Hinnom, which *is* in the Valley of the [1]Rephaim
on the north, descended to the Valley of Hinnom,
to the side of the Jebusite *city* on the south, and
descended to [b]En Rogel.
17 And it went around from the north, went out
to En Shemesh, and extended toward Geliloth,
which is before the Ascent of Adummim, and
descended to [a]the stone of Bohan the son of
Reuben.
18 Then it passed along toward the north side of
[1]Arabah, and went down to Arabah.
19 And the border passed along to the north side
of Beth Hoglah; then [1]the border ended at the
north bay at the [a]Salt Sea, at the south end of the
Jordan. This *was* the southern boundary.
20 The Jordan was its border on the east side.
This *was* the inheritance of the children of Benjamin, according to its boundaries all around, according to their families.
21 Now the cities of the tribe of the children of
Benjamin, according to their families, were Jericho, Beth Hoglah, Emek Keziz,
22 Beth Arabah, Zemaraim, Bethel,
23 Avim, Parah, Ophrah,
24 Chephar Haammoni, Ophni, and Gaba: twelve
cities with their villages;
25 [a]Gibeon, [b]Ramah, Beeroth,
26 Mizpah, Chephirah, Mozah,
27 Rekem, Irpeel, Taralah,
28 Zelah, Eleph, [a]Jebus (which *is* Jerusalem),
Gibeath, *and* Kirjath: fourteen cities with their
villages. This was the inheritance of the children
of Benjamin according to their families.

### *The Remainder of the Land Divided*

**19** The [a]second lot came out for Simeon, for
the tribe of the children of Simeon according to their families. [b]And their inheritance was
within the inheritance of the children of Judah.
2 [a]They had in their inheritance Beersheba
(Sheba), Moladah,
3 Hazar Shual, Balah, Ezem,
4 Eltolad, Bethul, Hormah,
5 Ziklag, Beth Marcaboth, Hazar Susah,
6 Beth Lebaoth, and Sharuhen: thirteen cities
and their villages;
7 Ain, Rimmon, Ether, and Ashan: four cities
and their villages;
8 and all the villages that *were* all around these

13 [a]Josh. 16:10
14 [a]Josh. 16:4 [b]Gen. 48:22 [c]Gen. 48:19; Num. 26:34, 37 [1]*allotment*
16 [a]Josh. 17:18; Judg. 1:19; 4:3 [b]Josh. 19:18; 1 Kin. 4:12
17 [1]*allotment*
18 [a]Deut. 20:1 [1]Lit. *goings out*

CHAPTER 18

1 [a]Josh. 19:51; 21:2; 22:9; Jer. 7:12 [b]Judg. 18:31; 1 Sam. 1:3, 24; 4:3, 4
3 [a]Judg. 18:9
5 [a]Josh. 15:1 [b]Josh. 16:1—17:18
6 [a]Josh. 14:2; 18:10 [1]*describe in writing*
7 [a]Num. 18:7, 20; Josh. 13:33 [b]Josh. 13:8
8 [a]Gen. 13:17 [1]*describe in writing*
9 [1]*described it in writing*
10 [a]Acts 13:19 [b]Num. 34:16–29; Josh. 19:51 [1]*portions*
11 [a]Judg. 1:21
12 [a]Josh. 16:1
13 [a]Gen. 28:19; Josh. 16:2; Judg. 1:23 [b]Josh. 16:3
14 [a]Josh. 15:9 [1]Lit. *its goings out were*
15 [a]Josh. 15:9
16 [a]Josh. 15:8 [b]Josh. 15:7 [1]Lit. *Giants*
17 [a]Josh. 15:6
18 [1]*Beth Arabah,* Josh. 15:6; 18:22
19 [a]Josh. 15:2, 5 [1]Lit. *the goings out of the border were*
25 [a]Josh. 11:19; 21:17; 1 Kin. 3:4, 5 [b]Jer. 31:15
28 [a]Josh. 15:8, 63

CHAPTER 19

1 [a]Judg. 1:3 [b]Josh. 19:9
2 [a]1 Chr. 4:28

cities as far as Baalath Beer, [a]Ramah of the South.
This *was* the inheritance of the tribe of the children of Simeon according to their families.
9 The inheritance of the children of Simeon *was*
*included* in the share of the children of Judah, for
the share of the children of Judah was [1]too much
for them. [a]Therefore the children of Simeon had
*their* inheritance within the inheritance of [2]that
people.
**10** The third lot came out for the children of
Zebulun according to their families, and the border of their inheritance was as far as Sarid.
11 [a]Their border went toward the west and to
Maralah, went to Dabbasheth, and extended along
the brook that is [b]east of Jokneam.
12 Then from Sarid it went eastward toward the
sunrise along the border of Chisloth Tabor, and
went out toward [a]Daberath, bypassing Japhia.
13 And from there it passed along on the east of
[a]Gath Hepher, toward Eth Kazin, and extended to
Rimmon, which borders on Neah.
14 Then the border went around it on the north
side of Hannathon, and [1]it ended in the Valley of
Jiphthah El.
15 Included were Kattath, Nahallal, Shimron,
Idalah, and Bethlehem: twelve cities with their
villages.
16 This *was* the inheritance of the children of
Zebulun according to their families, these cities
with their villages.
**17** The fourth lot came out to Issachar, for the
children of Issachar according to their families.
18 And their territory went to Jezreel, and *in-*
*cluded* Chesulloth, Shunem,
19 Haphraim, Shion, Anaharath,
20 Rabbith, Kishion, Abez,
21 Remeth, En Gannim, En Haddah, and Beth
Pazzez.
22 And the border reached to Tabor, Shahazi-
mah, and [a]Beth Shemesh; their border ended at
the Jordan: sixteen cities with their villages.
23 This *was* the inheritance of the tribe of the
children of Issachar according to their families,
the cities and their villages.
**24** [a]The fifth lot came out for the tribe of the
children of Asher according to their families.
25 And their territory included Helkath, Hali,
Beten, Achshaph,
26 Alammelech, Amad, and Mishal; it reached to
[a]Mount Carmel westward, along *the Brook* Shihor
Libnath.
27 It turned toward the sunrise to Beth Dagon;
and it reached to Zebulun and to the Valley of
Jiphthah El, then northward beyond Beth Emek
and Neiel, bypassing [a]Cabul *which was* on the left,
28 including [1]Ebron, Rehob, Hammon, and
Kanah, [a]as far as Greater Sidon.
29 And the border turned to Ramah and to the
fortified city of Tyre; then the border turned to
Hosah, and ended at the sea by the region of
[a]Achzib.
30 Also Ummah, Aphek, and Rehob *were in-*
*cluded:* twenty-two cities with their villages.
31 This *was* the inheritance of the tribe of the
children of Asher according to their families, these
cities with their villages.
**32** [a]The sixth lot came out to the children of
Naphtali, for the children of Naphtali according to
their families.
33 And their border began at Heleph, enclosing
the territory from the terebinth tree in Zaanan-
nim, Adami Nekeb, and Jabneel, as far as Lak-
kum; [1]it ended at the Jordan.
34 [a]From Heleph the border extended westward
to Aznoth Tabor, and went out from there toward
Hukkok; it adjoined Zebulun on the south side
and Asher on the west side, and ended at Judah by
the Jordan toward the sunrise.
35 And the fortified cities *are* Ziddim, Zer, Hammath, Rakkath, Chinnereth,
36 Adamah, Ramah, Hazor,
37 [a]Kedesh, Edrei, En Hazor,
38 Iron, Migdal El, Horem, Beth Anath, and Beth
Shemesh: nineteen cities with their villages.
39 This *was* the inheritance of the tribe of the
children of Naphtali according to their families,
the cities and their villages.
**40** [a]The seventh lot came out for the tribe of the
children of Dan according to their families.
41 And the territory of their inheritance was
Zorah, [a]Eshtaol, Ir Shemesh,
42 [a]Shaalabbin, [b]Aijalon, Jethlah,
43 Elon, Timnah, [a]Ekron,
44 Eltekeh, Gibbethon, Baalath,
45 Jehud, Bene Berak, Gath Rimmon,
46 Me Jarkon, and Rakkon, with the region [1]near
[2]Joppa.
47 And the [a]border of the children of Dan went
beyond these, because the children of Dan went
up to fight against Leshem and took it; and they
struck it with the edge of the sword, took possession of it, and dwelt in it. They called Leshem,
[b]Dan, after the name of Dan their father.
48 This *is* the inheritance of the tribe of the
children of Dan according to their families, these
cities with their villages.
**49** When they had [1]made an end of dividing the
land as an inheritance according to their borders,
the children of Israel gave an inheritance among
them to Joshua the son of Nun.
50 According to the word of the LORD they gave
him the city which he asked for, [a]Timnath [b]Serah
in the mountains of Ephraim; and he built the city
and dwelt in it.
51 [a]These *were* the inheritances which Eleazar
the priest, Joshua the son of Nun, and the heads of
the fathers of the tribes of the children of Israel
divided as an inheritance by lot [b]in Shiloh before
the LORD, at the door of the tabernacle of meeting.
So they made an end of dividing the country.

## *Six Cities of Safety*

**20** The LORD also spoke to Joshua, saying,
2 "Speak to the children of Israel, saying:
[a]'Appoint[1] for yourselves cities of refuge, of which
I spoke to you through Moses,
3 'that the slayer who kills a person accidentally
*or* unintentionally may flee there; and they shall
be your refuge from the avenger of blood.
4 'And when he flees to one of those cities, and
stands at the entrance of the gate of the city, and
[1]declares his case in the hearing of the elders of
that city, they shall take him into the city as one
of them, and give him a place, that he may dwell
among them.
5 [a]'Then if the avenger of blood pursues him,
they shall not deliver the slayer into his hand,
because he struck his neighbor unintentionally,
but did not hate him beforehand.
6 'And he shall dwell in that city [a]until he stands
before the congregation for judgment, *and* until
the death of the one who is high priest in those

8 [a]1 Sam. 30:27
9 [a]Josh. 19:1 [1]*too large* [2]Lit. *them*
11 [a]Gen. 49:13 [b]Josh. 12:22
12 [a]1 Chr. 6:72
13 [a]2 Kin. 14:25
14 [1]Lit. *the goings out of it were*
22 [a]Josh. 15:10; Judg. 1:33
24 [a]Judg. 1:31, 32
26 [a]1 Sam. 15:12; 1 Kin. 18:20; Is. 33:9; 35:2; Jer. 46:18
27 [a]1 Kin. 9:13
28 [a]Gen. 10:19; Josh. 11:8; Judg. 1:31; Acts 27:3 [1]So with MT, Tg., Vg.; a few Heb. mss. *Abdon* (cf. 21:30 and 1 Chr. 6:74)
29 [a]Judg. 1:31
32 [a]Josh. 19:32–39; Judg. 1:33
33 [1]Lit. *its goings out were*
34 [a]Deut. 33:23
37 [a]Josh. 20:7
40 [a]Josh. 19:40–48; Judg. 1:34–36
41 [a]Josh. 15:33
42 [a]Judg. 1:35; 1 Kin. 4:9 [b]Josh. 10:12; 21:24
43 [a]Josh. 15:11; Judg. 1:18
46 [1]*over against* [2]Heb. *Japho*
47 [a]Judg. 18 [b]Judg. 18:29
49 [1]*finished*
50 [a]Josh. 24:30 [b]1 Chr. 7:24
51 [a]Num. 34:17; Josh. 14:1 [b]Josh. 18:1, 10

CHAPTER 20
2 [a]Ex. 21:13; Num. 35:6–34; Deut. 19:2, 9 [1]*Designate*
4 [1]*states*
5 [a]Num. 35:12
6 [a]Num. 35:12, 24, 25

days. Then the slayer may return and come to his
own city and his own house, to the city from
which he fled.' "
7 So they appointed [a]Kedesh in Galilee, in the
mountains of Naphtali, [b]Shechem in the mountains of Ephraim, and [c]Kirjath Arba (which *is*
Hebron) in [d]the mountains of Judah.
8 And on the other side of the Jordan, by Jericho eastward, they assigned [a]Bezer in the wilderness on the plain, from the tribe of Reuben,
[b]Ramoth in Gilead, from the tribe of Gad, and
[c]Golan in Bashan, from the tribe of Manasseh.
9 [a]These were the cities appointed for all the
children of Israel and for the stranger who [1]dwelt
among them, that whoever killed a person accidentally might flee there, and not die by the hand
of the avenger of blood [b]until he stood before the
congregation.

### *The Cities of the Levites*

**21** Then the heads of the fathers' *houses* of the
[a]Levites came near to [b]Eleazar the priest, to
Joshua the son of Nun, and to the heads of the
fathers' *houses* of the tribes of the children of
Israel.
2 And they spoke to them at [a]Shiloh in the land
of Canaan, saying, [b]"The LORD commanded
through Moses to give us cities to dwell in, with
their common-lands for our livestock."
3 So the children of Israel gave to the Levites
from their inheritance, at the commandment of
the LORD, these cities and their common-lands:
4 Now the lot came out for the families of the
Kohathites. And [a]the children of Aaron the priest,
*who were* of the Levites, [b]had thirteen cities by lot
from the tribe of Judah, from the tribe of Simeon,
and from the tribe of Benjamin.
5 [a]The rest of the children of Kohath had ten
cities by lot from the families of the tribe of
Ephraim, from the tribe of Dan, and from the half-
tribe of Manasseh.
6 And [a]the children of Gershon had thirteen
cities by lot from the families of the tribe of
Issachar, from the tribe of Asher, from the tribe of
Naphtali, and from the half-tribe of Manasseh in
Bashan.
7 [a]The children of Merari according to their
families had twelve cities from the tribe of Reuben, from the tribe of Gad, and from the tribe of
Zebulun.
8 [a]And the children of Israel gave these cities
with their common-lands by lot to the Levites, [b]as
the LORD had commanded by the hand of Moses.
**9** So they gave from the tribe of the children of
Judah and from the tribe of the children of Simeon these cities which are [1]designated by name,
10 which were for the children of Aaron, one of
the families of the Kohathites, *who were* of the
children of Levi; for the lot was theirs first.
11 [a]And they gave them [1]Kirjath Arba (*Arba was*
the father of [b]Anak), [c]which *is* Hebron, in the
mountains of Judah, with the common-land surrounding it.
12 But [a]the fields of the city and its villages they
gave to Caleb the son of Jephunneh as his possession.
**13** Thus [a]to the children of Aaron the priest they
gave [b]Hebron with its common-land (a city of
refuge for the slayer), [c]Libnah with its common-
land,
14 [a]Jattir with its common-land, [b]Eshtemoa with
its common-land,
15 [a]Holon with its common-land, [b]Debir with its
common-land,
16 [a]Ain with its common-land, [b]Juttah with its
common-land, and [c]Beth Shemesh with its
common-land: nine cities from those two tribes;
17 and from the tribe of Benjamin, [a]Gibeon with
its common-land, [b]Geba with its common-land,
18 Anathoth with its common-land, and [a]Almon
with its common-land: four cities.
19 All the cities of the children of Aaron, the
priests, *were* thirteen cities with their common-
lands.
**20** [a]And the families of the children of Kohath,
the Levites, the rest of the children of Kohath,
even they had the cities of their [1]lot from the tribe
of Ephraim.
21 For they gave them [a]Shechem with its
common-land in the mountains of Ephraim (a city
of refuge for the slayer), [b]Gezer with its common-
land,
22 Kibzaim with its common-land, and Beth Horon with its common-land: four cities;
23 and from the tribe of Dan, Eltekeh with its
common-land, Gibbethon with its common-land,
24 [a]Aijalon with its common-land, *and* Gath
Rimmon with its common-land: four cities;
25 and from the half-tribe of Manasseh, Tanach
with its common-land and Gath Rimmon with its
common-land: two cities.
26 All the ten cities with their common-lands
were for the rest of the families of the children of
Kohath.
**27** [a]Also to the children of Gershon, of the families of the Levites, from the *other* half-tribe of
Manasseh, *they gave* [b]Golan in Bashan with its
common-land (a city of refuge for the slayer), and
Be Eshterah with its common-land: two cities;
28 and from the tribe of Issachar, Kishion with its
common-land, Daberath with its common-land,
29 Jarmuth with its common-land, *and* En Gannim with its common-land: four cities;
30 and from the tribe of Asher, Mishal with its
common-land, Abdon with its common-land,
31 Helkath with its common-land, and Rehob
with its common-land: four cities;
32 and from the tribe of Naphtali, [a]Kedesh in
Galilee with its common-land (a city of refuge for
the slayer), Hammoth Dor with its common-land,
and Kartan with its common-land: three cities.
33 All the cities of the Gershonites according to
their families *were* thirteen cities with their
common-lands.
**34** [a]And to the families of the children of Merari,
the rest of the Levites, from the tribe of Zebulun,
Jokneam with its common-land, Kartah with its
common-land,
35 Dimnah with its common-land, *and* Nahalal
with its common-land: four cities;
36 [1]and from the tribe of Reuben, [a]Bezer with its
common-land, Jahaz with its common-land,
37 Kedemoth with its common-land, and Mephaath with its common-land: four cities;
38 and from the tribe of Gad, [a]Ramoth in Gilead
with its common-land (a city of refuge for the
slayer), Mahanaim with its common-land,
39 Heshbon with its common-land, *and* Jazer
with its common-land: four cities in all.
40 So all the cities for the children of Merari

**7** [a]Josh. 21:32; 1 Chr. 6:76 [b]Josh. 21:21; 2 Chr. 10:1 [c]Josh. 14:15; 21:11, 13 [d]Luke 1:39
**8** [a]Deut. 4:43; Josh. 21:36; 1 Chr. 6:78 [b]Josh. 21:38; 1 Kin. 22:3 [c]Josh. 21:27
**9** [a]Num. 35:15 [b]Josh. 20:6 [1]As a resident alien

CHAPTER 21

**1** [a]Num. 35:1–8 [b]Num. 34:16–29; Josh. 14:1; 17:4
**2** [a]Josh. 18:1 [b]Num. 35:2
**4** [a]Josh. 21:8, 19 [b]Josh. 19:51
**5** [a]Josh. 21:20
**6** [a]Josh. 21:27
**7** [a]Josh. 21:34
**8** [a]Josh. 21:3 [b]Num. 35:2
**9** [1]Lit. *called*
**11** [a]Josh. 20:7; 1 Chr. 6:55 [b]Josh. 14:15; 15:13, 14 [c]Josh. 20:7; Luke 1:39 [1]Lit. *City of Arba*
**12** [a]Josh. 14:14; 1 Chr. 6:56
**13** [a]1 Chr. 6:57 [b]Josh. 15:54; 20:2, 7 [c]Josh. 15:42; 2 Kin. 8:22
**14** [a]Josh. 15:48 [b]Josh. 15:50
**15** [a]1 Chr. 6:58 [b]Josh. 15:49
**16** [a]1 Chr. 6:59 [b]Josh. 15:55 [c]Josh. 15:10
**17** [a]Josh. 18:25 [b]Josh. 18:24
**18** [a]1 Chr. 6:60
**20** [a]1 Chr. 6:66 [1]*allotment*
**21** [a]Josh. 20:7 [b]Judg. 1:29
**24** [a]Josh. 10:12
**27** [a]Josh. 21:6; 1 Chr. 6:71 [b]Josh. 20:8
**32** [a]Josh. 20:7
**34** [a]Josh. 21:7; 1 Chr. 6:77–81
**36** [a]Deut. 4:43; Josh. 20:8 [1]So with LXX, Vg. (cf. 1 Chr. 6:78, 79); MT, Bg., Tg. omit vv. 36, 37
**38** [a]Josh. 20:8

according to their families, the rest of the families of the Levites, were *by* their lot twelve cities.
41 [a]All the cities of the Levites within the possession of the children of Israel *were* forty-eight cities with their common-lands.
42 Every one of these cities had its common-land surrounding it; thus *were* all these cities.
**43** So the LORD gave to Israel [a]all the land of which He had sworn to give to their fathers, and they [b]took possession of it and dwelt in it.
44 [a]The LORD gave them [b]rest all around, according to all that He had sworn to their fathers. And [c]not a man of all their enemies stood against them; the LORD delivered all their enemies into their hand.
45 [a]Not a word failed of any good thing which the LORD had spoken to the house of Israel. All came to pass.

### *An Altar by the Jordan*

**22** Then Joshua called the Reubenites, the Gadites, and half the tribe of Manasseh,
2 and said to them: "You have kept [a]all that Moses the servant of the LORD commanded you, [b]and have obeyed my voice in all that I commanded you.
3 "You have not [1]left your brethren these many days, up to this day, but have kept the charge of the commandment of the LORD your God.
4 "And now the LORD your God has given [a]rest to your brethren, as He promised them; now therefore, return and go to your tents *and* to the land of your possession, [b]which Moses the servant of the LORD gave you on the other side of the Jordan.
5 "But [a]take[1] careful heed to do the commandment and the law which Moses the servant of the LORD commanded you, [b]to love the LORD your God, to walk in all His ways, to keep His commandments, to hold fast to Him, and to serve Him with all your heart and with all your soul."
6 So Joshua [a]blessed them and sent them away, and they went to their tents.
**7** Now to half the tribe of Manasseh Moses had given a possession in Bashan, [a]but to the *other* half of it Joshua gave *a possession* among their brethren on this side of the Jordan, westward. And indeed, when Joshua sent them away to their tents, he blessed them,
8 and spoke to them, saying, "Return with much riches to your tents, with very much livestock, with silver, with gold, with bronze, with iron, and with very much clothing. [a]Divide the [1]spoil of your enemies with your brethren."
9 So the children of Reuben, the children of Gad, and half the tribe of Manasseh returned, and departed from the children of Israel at Shiloh, which *is* in the land of Canaan, to go to [a]the country of Gilead, to the land of their possession, which they had obtained according to the word of the LORD by the hand of Moses.
**10** And when they came to the region of the Jordan which *is* in the land of Canaan, the children of Reuben, the children of Gad, and half the tribe of Manasseh built an altar there by the Jordan—a great, impressive altar.
11 Now the children of Israel [a]heard *someone* say, "Behold, the children of Reuben, the children of Gad, and half the tribe of Manasseh have built an altar on the [1]frontier of the land of Canaan, in the region of the Jordan—on the children of Israel's side."
12 And when the children of Israel heard *of it,* [a]the whole congregation of the children of Israel gathered together at Shiloh to go to war against them.
**13** Then the children of Israel [a]sent [b]Phinehas the son of Eleazar the priest to the children of Reuben, to the children of Gad, and to half the tribe of Manasseh, into the land of Gilead,
14 and with him ten rulers, one ruler each from the chief house of every tribe of Israel; and [a]each one *was* the head of the house of his father among the [1]divisions of Israel.
15 Then they came to the children of Reuben, to the children of Gad, and to half the tribe of Manasseh, to the land of Gilead, and they spoke with them, saying,
16 "Thus says the whole congregation of the LORD: 'What [a]treachery[1] *is* this that you have committed against the God of Israel, to turn away this day from following the LORD, in that you have built for yourselves an altar, [b]that you might rebel this day against the LORD?
17 '*Is* the iniquity [a]of Peor not enough for us, from which we are not cleansed till this day, although there was a plague in the congregation of the LORD,
18 'but that you must turn away this day from following the LORD? And it shall be, if you rebel today against the LORD, that tomorrow [a]He will be angry with the whole congregation of Israel.
19 [1]'Nevertheless, if the land of your possession *is* unclean, *then* cross over to the land of the possession of the LORD, [a]where the LORD's tabernacle stands, and take possession among us; but do not rebel against the LORD, nor rebel against us, by building yourselves an altar besides the altar of the LORD our God.
20 [a]'Did not Achan the son of Zerah [1]commit a trespass in the [2]accursed thing, and wrath fell on all the congregation of Israel? And that man did not perish alone in his iniquity.' "
21 Then the children of Reuben, the children of Gad, and half the tribe of Manasseh answered and said to the heads of the [1]divisions of Israel:
22 "The LORD [a]God of gods, the LORD God of gods, He [b]knows, and let Israel itself know—if *it is* in rebellion, or if in treachery against the LORD, do not save us this day.
23 "If we have built ourselves an altar to turn from following the LORD, or if to offer on it burnt offerings or grain offerings, or if to offer peace offerings on it, let the LORD Himself [a]require *an account.*
24 "But in fact we have done it [1]for fear, for a reason, saying, 'In time to come your descendants may speak to our descendants, saying, "What have you to do with the LORD God of Israel?
25 "For the LORD has made the Jordan a border between you and us, *you* children of Reuben and children of Gad. You have no part in the LORD." So your descendants would make our descendants cease fearing the LORD.'
26 "Therefore we said, 'Let us now prepare to build ourselves an altar, not for burnt offering nor for sacrifice,
27 'but *that* it *may be* [a]a [1]witness between you and us and our generations after us, that we may [b]perform the service of the LORD before Him with our burnt offerings, with our sacrifices, and with

**41** [a]Num. 35:7
**43** [a]Gen. 12:7; 26:3, 4; 28:4, 13, 14 [b]Num. 33:53; Josh. 1:11
**44** [a]Deut. 7:23, 24; Josh. 11:23; 22:4 [b]Josh. 1:13, 15; 11:23 [c]Deut. 7:24
**45** [a][Num. 23:19]; Josh. 23:14; 1 Kin. 8:56

CHAPTER 22
**2** [a]Num. 32:20–22; Deut. 3:18 [b]Josh. 1:12–18
**3** [1]*forsaken*
**4** [a]Josh. 21:44 [b]Num. 32:33
**5** [a]Deut. 6:6, 17; 11:22; Jer. 12:16 [b]Deut. 10:12; 11:13, 22 [1]*be very careful to do*
**6** [a]Gen. 47:7; Ex. 39:43; Josh. 14:13; 2 Sam. 6:18; Luke 24:50
**7** [a]Josh. 17:1–13
**8** [a]Num. 31:27; 1 Sam. 30:24 [1]*plunder*
**9** [a]Num. 32:1, 26, 29
**11** [a]Deut. 13:12–18; Judg. 20:12, 13 [1]Lit. *front*
**12** [a]Josh. 18:1; Judg. 20:1
**13** [a]Deut. 13:14; Judg. 20:12 [b]Ex. 6:25; Num. 25:7, 11–13
**14** [a]Num. 1:4 [1]Lit. *thousands*
**16** [a]Deut. 12:5–14 [b]Lev. 17:8, 9 [1]*unfaithful act*
**17** [a]Num. 25:1–9; Deut. 4:3
**18** [a]Num. 16:22
**19** [a]Josh. 18:1 [1]*However*
**20** [a]Josh. 7:1–26 [1]*act unfaithfully* [2]*devoted thing*
**21** [1]Lit. *thousands*
**22** [a]Deut. 4:35; 10:17; Is. 44:8; 45:5; 46:9; [1 Cor. 8:5, 6] [b][Job 10:7; 23:10; Jer. 12:3; 2 Cor. 11:11, 31]
**23** [a]Deut. 18:19; 1 Sam. 20:16
**24** [1]Lit. *from fear*
**27** [a]Gen. 31:48; Josh. 22:34; 24:27 [b]Deut. 12:5, 14 [1]*testimony*

our peace offerings; that your descendants may not say to our descendants in time to come, "You have no part in the LORD." '

28 "Therefore we said that it will be, when they say *this* to us or to our generations in time to come, that we may say, 'Here is the replica of the altar of the LORD which our fathers made, though not for burnt offerings nor for sacrifices; but it *is* a witness between you and us.'

29 "Far be it from us that we should rebel against the LORD, and turn from following the LORD this day, [a]to build an altar for burnt offerings, for grain offerings, or for sacrifices, besides the altar of the LORD our God which *is* before His tabernacle."

**30** Now when Phinehas the priest and the rulers of the congregation, the heads of the [1]divisions of Israel who *were* with him, heard the words that the children of Reuben, the children of Gad, and the children of Manasseh spoke, it pleased them.

31 Then Phinehas the son of Eleazar the priest said to the children of Reuben, the children of Gad, and the children of Manasseh, "This day we perceive that the LORD *is* [a]among us, because you have not committed this treachery against the LORD. Now you have delivered the children of Israel out of the hand of the LORD."

**32** And Phinehas the son of Eleazar the priest, and the rulers, returned from the children of Reuben and the children of Gad, from the land of Gilead to the land of Canaan, to the children of Israel, and brought back word to them.

33 So the thing pleased the children of Israel, and the children of Israel [a]blessed God; they spoke no more of going against them in battle, to destroy the land where the children of Reuben and Gad dwelt.

34 The children of Reuben and the children of [1]Gad called the altar, *Witness,* "For *it is* a witness between us that the LORD *is* God."

## *Joshua's Farewell Address*

**23** Now it came to pass, a long time after the LORD [a]had given rest to Israel from all their enemies round about, that Joshua [b]was old, advanced in age.

2 And Joshua [a]called for all Israel, for their elders, for their heads, for their judges, and for their officers, and said to them: "I am old, advanced in age.

3 "You have seen all that the [a]LORD your God has done to all these nations because of you, for the [b]LORD your God *is* He who has fought for you.

4 "See, [a]I have divided to you by lot these nations that remain, to be an inheritance for your tribes, from the Jordan, with all the nations that I have cut off, as far as the Great Sea westward.

5 "And the LORD your God [a]will expel them from before you and drive them out of your sight. So you shall possess their land, [b]as the LORD your God promised you.

6 [a]"Therefore be very courageous to keep and to do all that is written in the Book of the Law of Moses, [b]lest you turn aside from it to the right hand or to the left,

7 "*and* lest you [a]go[1] among these nations, these who remain among you. You shall not [b]make mention of the name of their gods, nor cause *anyone* to [c]swear *by them;* you shall not [d]serve them nor bow down to them,

8 "but you shall [a]hold fast to the LORD your God, as you have done to this day.

9 [a]"For the LORD has [1]driven out from before you great and strong nations; but *as for* you, no one has been able to stand against you to this day.

10 [a]"One man of you shall chase a thousand, for the LORD your God *is* He who fights for you, [b]as He promised you.

11 [a]"Therefore take careful heed to yourselves, that you love the LORD your God.

12 "Or else, if indeed you do [a]go back, and cling to the remnant of these nations—these that remain among you—and [b]make marriages with them, and go in to them and they to you,

13 "know for certain that [a]the LORD your God will no longer drive out these nations from before you. [b]But they shall be snares and traps to you, and scourges on your sides and thorns in your eyes, until you perish from this good land which the LORD your God has given you.

**14** "Behold, this day [a]I[1] *am* going the way of all the earth. And you know in all your hearts and in all your souls that [b]not one thing has failed of all the good things which the LORD your God spoke concerning you. All have come to pass for you; not one word of them has failed.

15 [a]"Therefore it shall come to pass, that as all the good things have come upon you which the LORD your God promised you, so the LORD will bring upon you [b]all harmful things, until He has destroyed you from this good land which the LORD your God has given you.

16 [1]"When you have transgressed the covenant of the LORD your God, which He commanded you, and have gone and served other gods, and bowed down to them, then the [a]anger of the LORD will burn against you, and you shall perish quickly from the good land which He has given you."

## *The Covenant at Shechem*

**24** Then Joshua gathered all the tribes of Israel to [a]Shechem and [b]called for the elders of Israel, for their heads, for their judges, and for their officers; and they [c]presented themselves before God.

2 And Joshua said to all the people, "Thus says the LORD God of Israel: [a]'Your fathers, *including* Terah, the father of Abraham and the father of Nahor, dwelt on the other side of [1]the River in old times; and [b]they served other gods.

3 [a]'Then I took your father Abraham from the other side of [1]the River, led him throughout all the land of Canaan, and multiplied his [2]descendants and [b]gave him Isaac.

4 'To Isaac I gave [a]Jacob and Esau. To [b]Esau I gave the mountains of Seir to possess, [c]but Jacob and his children went down to Egypt.

5 [a]'Also I sent Moses and Aaron, and [b]I plagued Egypt, according to what I did among them. Afterward I brought you out.

6 'Then I [a]brought your fathers out of Egypt, and you came to the sea; and the Egyptians pursued your fathers with chariots and horsemen to the Red Sea.

7 'So they cried out to the LORD; and He put [a]darkness between you and the Egyptians, brought the sea upon them, and covered them. And [b]your eyes saw what I did in Egypt. Then you dwelt in the wilderness [c]a long time.

8 'And I brought you into the land of the Amorites, who dwelt on the other side of the Jordan, [a]and they fought with you. But I gave them into

29 [a]Deut. 12:13, 14
30 [1]Lit. *thousands*
31 [a]Lev. 26:11, 12
33 [a]1 Chr. 29:20
34 [1]LXX adds *and half the tribe of Manasseh*

CHAPTER 23

1 [a]Josh. 21:44; 22:4 [b]Josh. 13:1; 24:29
2 [a]Deut. 31:28
3 [a]Ps. 44:3 [b]Deut. 1:30
4 [a]Josh. 13:2, 6; 18:10
5 [a]Ex. 23:30; 33:2 [b]Num. 33:53
6 [a]Josh. 1:7 [b]Deut. 5:32
7 [a]Deut. 7:2, 3 [b]Ex. 23:13 [c]Deut. 6:13; 10:20 [d]Ex. 20:5 [1]*associate with*
8 [a]Deut. 10:20
9 [a]Deut. 7:24; 11:23 [1]*dispossessed*
10 [a]Lev. 26:8 [b]Ex. 14:14
11 [a]Josh. 22:5
12 [a][2 Pet. 2:20, 21] [b]Deut. 7:3, 4
13 [a]Judg. 2:3 [b]Ex. 23:33; 34:12
14 [a]1 Kin. 2:2 [b]Josh. 21:45 [1]I am going to die.
15 [a]Deut. 28:63 [b]Deut. 28:15–68
16 [a]Deut. 4:24–28 [1]Or *If ever*

CHAPTER 24

1 [a]Gen. 35:4 [b]Josh. 23:2 [c]1 Sam. 10:19
2 [a]Gen. 11:7–32 [b]Josh. 24:14 [1]The Euphrates
3 [a]Gen. 12:1Acts 7:2, 3 [b][Ps. 127:3] [1]The Euphrates [2]Lit. *seed*
4 [a]Gen. 25:24–26 [b]Deut. 2:5 [c]Gen. 46:1, 3, 6
5 [a]Ex. 3:10 [b]Ex. 7—10
6 [a]Ex. 12:37, 51; 14:2–31
7 [a]Ex. 14:20 [b]Deut. 4:34 [c]Josh. 5:6
8 [a]Num. 21:21–35

your hand, that you might possess their land, and
I destroyed them from before you.
9 'Then [a]Balak the son of Zippor, king of Moab,
arose to make war against Israel, and [b]sent and
called Balaam the son of Beor to curse you.
10 [a]'But I would not listen to Balaam; [b]therefore
he continued to bless you. So I delivered you out
of his hand.
11 'Then [a]you went over the Jordan and came to
Jericho. And [b]the men of Jericho fought against
you—*also* the Amorites, the Perizzites, the Canaanites, the Hittites, the Girgashites, the Hivites,
and the Jebusites. But I delivered them into your
hand.
12 [a]'I sent the hornet before you which drove
them out from before you, *also* the two kings of
the Amorites, *but* [b]not with your sword or with
your bow.
13 'I have given you a land for which you did not
labor, and [a]cities which you did not build, and you
dwell in them; you eat of the vineyards and olive
groves which you did not plant.'
**14** [a]"Now therefore, fear the LORD, serve Him in
[b]sincerity and in truth, and [c]put away the gods
which your fathers served on the other side of [1]the
River and [d]in Egypt. Serve the LORD!
15 "And if it seems evil to you to serve the LORD,
[a]choose for yourselves this day whom you will
serve, whether [b]the gods which your fathers
served that *were* on the other side of [1]the River, or
[c]the gods of the Amorites, in whose land you
dwell. [d]But as for me and my house, we will serve
the LORD."
16 So the people answered and said: "Far be it
from us that we should forsake the LORD to serve
other gods;
17 "for the LORD our God *is* He who brought us
and our fathers up out of the land of Egypt, from
the house of bondage, who did those great signs in
our sight, and preserved us in all the way that we
went and among all the people through whom we
passed.
18 "And the LORD drove out from before us all
the people, including the Amorites who dwelt in
the land. [a]We also will serve the LORD, for He *is*
our God."
19 But Joshua said to the people, [a]"You cannot
serve the LORD, for He *is* a [b]holy God. He *is* [c]a
jealous God; [d]He will not forgive your transgressions nor your sins.
20 [a]"If you forsake the LORD and serve foreign
gods, [b]then He will turn and do you harm and
consume you, after He has done you good."
21 And the people said to Joshua, "No, but we
will serve the LORD!"
22 So Joshua said to the people, "You *are* witnesses against yourselves that [a]you have chosen
the LORD for yourselves, to serve Him." And they
said, "*We are* witnesses!"
23 "Now therefore," *he said,* [a]"put away the
foreign gods which *are* among you, and [b]incline
your heart to the LORD God of Israel."
24 And the people [a]said to Joshua, "The LORD our
God we will serve, and His voice we will obey!"
25 So Joshua [a]made[1] a covenant with the people
that day, and made for them a statute and an
ordinance [b]in Shechem.
**26** Then Joshua [a]wrote these words in the Book
of the Law of God. And he took [b]a large stone, and
[c]set it up there [d]under the oak that *was* by the
sanctuary of the LORD.
27 And Joshua said to all the people, "Behold,
this stone shall be [a]a witness to us, for [b]it has
heard all the words of the LORD which He spoke to
us. It shall therefore be a witness to you, lest you
deny your God."
28 So [a]Joshua let the people depart, each to his
own inheritance.
**29** [a]Now it came to pass after these things that
Joshua the son of Nun, the servant of the LORD,
died, *being* one hundred and ten years old.
30 And they buried him within the border of his
inheritance at [a]Timnath Serah, which *is* in the
mountains of Ephraim, on the north side of Mount
Gaash.
31 [a]Israel served the LORD all the days of Joshua,
and all the days of the elders who outlived Joshua,
who had [b]known all the works of the LORD which
He had done for Israel.
**32** [a]The bones of Joseph, which the children of
Israel had brought up out of Egypt, they buried at
Shechem, in the plot of ground [b]which Jacob had
bought from the sons of Hamor the father of
Shechem for one hundred [1]pieces of silver, and
which had become an inheritance of the children
of Joseph.
33 And [a]Eleazar the son of Aaron died. They
buried him in a hill *belonging to* [b]Phinehas his son,
which was given to him in the mountains of
Ephraim.

**9** [a]Judg. 11:25 [b]Num. 22:2–14
**10** [a]Deut. 23:5 [b]Num. 23:11, 20; 24:10
**11** [a]Josh. 3:14, 17 [b]Josh. 6:1; 10:1
**12** [a]Ex. 23:28 [b]Ps. 44:3
**13** [a]Deut. 6:10, 11
**14** [a]1 Sam. 12:24 [b]2 Cor. 1:12 [c]Ezek. 20:18 [d]Ezek. 20:7, 8 [1]The Euphrates
**15** [a]1 Kin. 18:21 [b]Josh. 24:2 [c]Ex. 23:24, 32 [d]Gen. 18:19 [1]The Euphrates
**18** [a]Ps. 116:16
**19** [a]Matt. 6:24 [b]1 Sam. 6:20 [c]Ex. 20:5 [d]Ex. 23:21
**20** [a]Ezra 8:22 [b]Deut. 4:24–26
**22** [a]Ps. 119:173
**23** [a]Gen. 35:2 [b]1 Kin. 8:57, 58
**24** [a]Deut. 5:24–27
**25** [a]Ex. 15:25 [b]Josh. 24:1 [1]Lit. *cut a covenant*
**26** [a]Deut. 31:24 [b]Judg. 9:6 [c]Gen. 28:18 [d]Gen. 35:4
**27** [a]Gen. 31:48 [b]Deut. 32:1
**28** [a]Judg. 2:6, 7
**29** [a]Judg. 2:8
**30** [a]Josh. 19:50
**31** [a]Judg. 2:7 [b]Deut. 11:2
**32** [a]Gen. 50:25 [b]Gen. 33:19 [1]Heb. *qesitah,* an unknown ancient measure of weight
**33** [a]Ex. 28:1 [b]Ex. 6:25

# *The Book of* JUDGES

### *The Continuing Conquest of Canaan*

CHAPTER 1

NOW after the [a]death of Joshua it came to
pass that the children of Israel [b]asked the
LORD, saying, "Who shall be first to go up
for us against the [c]Canaanites to fight against
them?"
2 And the LORD said, [a]"Judah shall go up. Indeed I have delivered the land into his hand."
3 So Judah said to [a]Simeon his brother, "Come
up with me to my allotted territory, that we may
fight against the Canaanites; and [b]I will likewise
go with you to your allotted territory." And
Simeon went with him.
4 Then Judah went up, and the LORD delivered
the Canaanites and the Perizzites into their hand;
and they killed ten thousand men at [a]Bezek.
5 And they found Adoni-Bezek in Bezek, and
fought against him; and they defeated the Canaanites and the Perizzites.
6 Then Adoni-Bezek fled, and they pursued him
and caught him and cut off his thumbs and big
toes.

**1** [a]Josh. 24:29 [b]Num. 27:21 [c]Josh. 17:12, 13
**2** [a]Gen. 49:8, 9
**3** [a]Josh. 19:1 [b]Judg. 1:17
**4** [a]1 Sam. 11:8

7 And Adoni-Bezek said, "Seventy kings with
their thumbs and big toes cut off used to gather
*scraps* under my table; [a]as I have done, so God has
repaid me." Then they brought him to Jerusalem,
and there he died.
**8** Now [a]the children of Judah fought against
Jerusalem and took it; they struck it with the edge
of the sword and set the city on fire.
9 [a]And afterward the children of Judah went
down to fight against the Canaanites who dwelt in
the mountains, in the [1]South, and in the lowland.
10 Then Judah [1]went against the Canaanites who
dwelt in [a]Hebron. (Now the name of Hebron *was*
formerly [b]Kirjath Arba.) And they killed Sheshai,
Ahiman, and Talmai.
11 [a]From there they went against the inhabitants
of Debir. (The name of Debir *was* formerly Kirjath
Sepher.)
12 [a]Then Caleb said, "Whoever attacks Kirjath
Sepher and takes it, to him I will give my daughter Achsah as wife."
13 And Othniel the son of Kenaz, [a]Caleb's younger brother, took it; so he gave him his daughter
Achsah as wife.
14 [a]Now it happened, when she came *to him,* that
[1]she urged him to ask her father for a field. And
she dismounted from *her* donkey, and Caleb said
to her, "What do you wish?"
15 So she said to him, [a]"Give me a blessing; since
you have given me land in the South, give me also
springs of water." And Caleb gave her the upper
springs and the lower springs.
**16** [a]Now the children of the Kenite, Moses' father-in-law, went up [b]from the City of Palms with
the children of Judah into the Wilderness of
Judah, which *lies* in the South *near* [c]Arad; [d]and
they went and dwelt among the people.
17 [a]And Judah went with his brother Simeon, and
they attacked the Canaanites who inhabited Ze-
phath, and utterly destroyed it. So the name of the
city was called [b]Hormah.
18 Also Judah took [a]Gaza with its territory,
Ashkelon with its territory, and Ekron with its
territory.
19 So the LORD was with Judah. And they drove
out the mountaineers, but they could not drive
out the inhabitants of the lowland, because they
had [a]chariots of iron.
20 [a]And they gave Hebron to Caleb, as Moses had
said. Then he [1]expelled from there the [b]three sons
of Anak.
21 [a]But the children of Benjamin did not drive
out the Jebusites who inhabited Jerusalem; so the
Jebusites dwell with the children of Benjamin in
Jerusalem to this day.
**22** And the [1]house of Joseph also went up against
Bethel, [a]and the LORD *was* with them.
23 So the [1]house of Joseph [a]sent men to spy out
Bethel. (The name of the city *was* formerly [b]Luz.)
24 And when the spies saw a man coming out of
the city, they said to him, "Please show us the
entrance to the city, and [a]we will show you
mercy."
25 So he showed them the entrance to the city,
and they struck the city with the edge of the
sword; but they let the man and all his family go.
26 And the man went to the land of the Hittites,
built a city, and called its name Luz, which *is* its
name to this day.
**27** [a]However, Manasseh did not drive out *the
inhabitants of* Beth Shean and its villages, or
[b]Taanach and its villages, or the inhabitants of
[c]Dor and its villages, or the inhabitants of Ibleam
and its villages, or the inhabitants of Megiddo and
its villages; for the Canaanites were determined to
dwell in that land.
28 And it came to pass, when Israel was strong,
that they put the Canaanites [1]under tribute, but
did not completely drive them out.
**29** [a]Nor did Ephraim drive out the Canaanites
who dwelt in Gezer; so the Canaanites dwelt in
Gezer among them.
**30** Nor did [a]Zebulun drive out the inhabitants of
Kitron or the inhabitants of Nahalol; so the Canaanites dwelt among them, and [1]were put under
tribute.
**31** [a]Nor did Asher drive out the inhabitants of
Acco or the inhabitants of Sidon, or of Ahlab,
Achzib, Helbah, Aphik, or Rehob.
32 So the Asherites [a]dwelt among the Canaanites, the inhabitants of the land; for they did not
drive them out.
**33** [a]Nor did Naphtali drive out the inhabitants of
Beth Shemesh or the inhabitants of Beth Anath;
but they dwelt among the Canaanites, the inhabitants of the land. Nevertheless the inhabitants of
Beth Shemesh and Beth Anath were put under
tribute to them.
**34** And the Amorites forced the children of Dan
into the mountains, for they would not allow
them to come down to the valley;
35 and the Amorites were determined to dwell in
Mount Heres, [a]in Aijalon, and in [1]Shaalbim; yet
when the strength of the house of Joseph became
greater, they [2]were put under tribute.
36 Now the boundary of the Amorites *was* [a]from
the Ascent of Akrabbim, from Sela, and upward.

### *Israel's Unfaithfulness*

**2** Then the Angel of the LORD came up from
Gilgal to Bochim, and said: [a]"I led you up from
Egypt and [b]brought you to the land of which I
swore to your fathers; and [c]I said, 'I will never
break My covenant with you.
2 'And [a]you shall make no [1]covenant with the
inhabitants of this land; [b]you shall tear down their
altars.' [c]But you have not obeyed My voice. Why
have you done this?
3 "Therefore I also said, 'I will not drive them
out before you; but they shall be [a]*thorns*[1] in your
side, and [b]their gods shall [2]be a [c]snare to you.' "
4 So it was, when the Angel of the LORD spoke
these words to all the children of Israel, that the
people lifted up their voices and wept.
5 Then they called the name of that place [1]Bo-
chim; and they sacrificed there to the LORD.
6 And when [a]Joshua had dismissed the people,
the children of Israel went each to his own inheritance to possess the land.
**7** [a]So the people served the LORD all the days of
Joshua, and all the days of the elders who outlived
Joshua, who had seen all the great works of the
LORD which He had done for Israel.
8 Now [a]Joshua the son of Nun, the servant of
the LORD, died *when he was* one hundred and ten
years old.
9 [a]And they buried him within the border of his
inheritance at [b]Timnath Heres, in the mountains
of Ephraim, on the north side of Mount Gaash.
10 When all that generation had [1]been gathered
to their fathers, another generation arose after
them who [a]did not know the LORD nor the work
which He had done for Israel.

**7** [a]Lev. 24:19
**8** [a]Josh. 15:63
**9** [a]Josh. 10:36; 11:21; 15:13 [1]Heb. *Negev,* and so throughout the book
**10** [a]Josh. 15:13–19 [b]Josh. 14:15 [1]*attacked*
**11** [a]Josh. 15:15
**12** [a]Josh. 15:16, 17
**13** [a]Judg. 3:9
**14** [a]Josh. 15:18, 19 [1]LXX, Vg. *he urged her*
**15** [a]Gen. 33:11
**16** [a]Num. 10:29–32 [b]Deut. 34:3 [c]Josh. 12:14 [d]1 Sam. 15:6
**17** [a]Judg. 1:3 [b]Num. 21:3
**18** [a]Josh. 11:22
**19** [a]Josh. 17:16, 18
**20** [a]Josh. 14:9, 14 [b]Josh. 15:14 [1]*drove out from there*
**21** [a]Josh. 15:63
**22** [a]Judg. 1:19 [1]*family*
**23** [a]Josh. 2:1; 7:2 [b]Gen. 28:19 [1]*family*
**24** [a]Josh. 2:12, 14
**27** [a]Josh. 17:11–13 [b]Josh. 21:25 [c]Josh. 17:11
**28** [1]*to forced labor*
**29** [a]Josh. 16:10
**30** [a]Josh. 19:10–16 [1]*became forced laborers*
**31** [a]Josh. 19:24–31
**32** [a]Ps. 106:34, 35
**33** [a]Josh. 19:32–39
**35** [a]Josh. 19:42 [1]*Shaalabbin,* Josh. 19:42 [2]*became forced laborers*
**36** [a]Josh. 15:3

CHAPTER 2
**1** [a]Ex. 20:2 [b]Deut. 1:8 [c]Gen. 17:7, 8
**2** [a]Deut. 7:2 [b]Deut. 12:3 [c]Ps. 106:34 [1]*treaty*
**3** [a]Josh. 23:13 [b]Judg. 3:6 [c]Ps. 106:36 [1]LXX, Tg., Vg. *enemies to you* [2]*entrap you*
**5** [1]Lit. *Weeping*
**6** [a]Josh. 22:6; 24:28–31
**7** [a]Josh. 24:31
**8** [a]Josh. 24:29
**9** [a]Josh. 24:30 [b]Josh. 19:49, 50
**10** [a]1 Sam. 2:12 [1]Died and joined their ancestors

11 Then the children of Israel did [a]evil in the
sight of the LORD, and served the Baals;
12 and they [a]forsook the LORD God of their fathers, who had brought them out of the land of
Egypt; and they followed [b]other gods from *among*
the gods of the people who *were* all around them,
and they [c]bowed down to them; and they provoked the LORD to anger.
13 They forsook the LORD [a]and served [1]Baal and
the [2]Ashtoreths.
14 [a]And the anger of the LORD was hot against
Israel. So He [b]delivered them into the hands of
plunderers who despoiled them; and [c]He sold them
into the hands of their enemies all around, so that
they [d]could no longer stand before their enemies.
15 Wherever they went out, the hand of the LORD
was against them for calamity, as the LORD had
said, and as the LORD had [a]sworn to them. And
they were greatly distressed.
16 Nevertheless, [a]the LORD raised up judges who
delivered them out of the hand of those who
plundered them.
17 Yet they would not listen to their judges, but
they [a]played the harlot with other gods, and
bowed down to them. They turned quickly from
the way in which their fathers walked, in obeying
the commandments of the LORD; they did not do
so.
18 And when the LORD raised up judges for them,
[a]the LORD was with the judge and delivered them
out of the hand of their enemies all the days of the
judge; [b]for the LORD was moved to pity by their
groaning because of those who oppressed them
and harassed them.
19 And it came to pass, [a]when the judge was
dead, that they reverted and behaved more corruptly than their fathers, by following other gods,
to serve them and bow down to them. They did
not cease from their own doings nor from their
stubborn way.
20 Then the anger of the LORD was hot against
Israel; and He said, "Because this nation has
[a]transgressed My covenant which I commanded
their fathers, and has not heeded My voice,
21 "I also will no longer drive out before them
any of the nations which Joshua [a]left when he
died,
22 "so [a]that through them I may [b]test Israel,
whether they will keep the ways of the LORD, to
walk in them as their fathers kept *them*, or not."
23 Therefore the LORD left those nations, without
driving them out immediately; nor did He deliver
them into the hand of Joshua.

## *Ehud Saves Israel from Moab*

**3** Now these *are* [a]the nations which the LORD
left, that He might test Israel by them, *that is*,
all who had not [1]known any of the wars in Canaan
2 (*this was* only so that the generations of the
children of Israel might be taught to know war, at
least those who had not formerly known it),
3 *namely*, [a]five lords of the Philistines, all the
Canaanites, the Sidonians, and the Hivites who
dwelt in Mount Lebanon, from Mount Baal Hermon to the entrance of Hamath.
4 And they were *left, that He might* test Israel
by them, to [1]know whether they would obey the
commandments of the LORD, which He had commanded their fathers by the hand of Moses.
5 [a]Thus the children of Israel dwelt among the
Canaanites, the Hittites, the Amorites, the Perizzites, the Hivites, and the Jebusites.
6 And [a]they took their daughters to be their
wives, and gave their daughters to their sons; and
they served their gods.
7 So the children of Israel did [a]evil in the sight
of the LORD. They [b]forgot the LORD their God, and
served the Baals and [1]Asherahs.
8 Therefore the anger of the LORD was hot
against Israel, and He [a]sold them into the hand of
[b]Cushan-Rishathaim king of Mesopotamia; and
the children of Israel served Cushan-Rishathaim
eight years.
9 When the children of Israel [a]cried out to the
LORD, the LORD [b]raised up a deliverer for the
children of Israel, who delivered them: [c]Othniel
the son of Kenaz, Caleb's younger brother.
10 [a]The Spirit of the LORD came upon him, and he
judged Israel. He went out to war, and the LORD
delivered Cushan-Rishathaim king of Mesopotamia into his hand; and his hand prevailed over
Cushan-Rishathaim.
11 So the land had rest for forty years. Then
Othniel the son of Kenaz died.
12 [a]And the children of Israel again did evil in the
sight of the LORD. So the LORD strengthened
[b]Eglon king of Moab against Israel, because they
had done evil in the sight of the LORD.
13 Then he gathered to himself the people of
Ammon and [a]Amalek, went and [1]defeated Israel,
and took possession of [b]the City of Palms.
14 So the children of Israel [a]served Eglon king of
Moab eighteen years.
15 But when the children of Israel [a]cried out to
the LORD, the LORD raised up a deliverer for them:
Ehud the son of Gera, the Benjamite, a [b]left-
handed man. By him the children of Israel sent
tribute to Eglon king of Moab.
16 Now Ehud made himself a dagger (it was
double-edged and a cubit in length) and fastened
it under his clothes on his right thigh.
17 So he brought the tribute to Eglon king of
Moab. (Now Eglon *was* a very fat man.)
18 And when he had finished presenting the
tribute, he sent away the people who had carried
the tribute.
19 But he himself turned back [a]from the [1]stone
images that *were* at Gilgal, and said, "I have a
secret message for you, O king." He said, "Keep
silence!" And all who attended him went out from
him.
20 So Ehud came to him (now he was sitting
upstairs in his cool private chamber). Then Ehud
said, "I have a message from God for you." So he
arose from *his* seat.
21 Then Ehud reached with his left hand, took
the dagger from his right thigh, and thrust it into
his belly.
22 Even the [1]hilt went in after the blade, and the
fat closed over the blade, for he did not draw the
dagger out of his belly; and his entrails came out.
23 Then Ehud went out through the porch and
shut the doors of the upper room behind him and
locked them.
24 When he had gone out, [1]*Eglon's* servants came
to look, and *to their* surprise, the doors of the
upper room were locked. So they said, "He is
probably [a]attending[2] to his needs in the cool
chamber."
25 So they waited till they were [a]embarrassed,
and still he had not opened the doors of the upper

11 [a]Judg. 3:7, 12; 4:1; 6:1
12 [a]Deut. 31:16; Judg. 8:33; 10:6 [b]Deut. 6:14 [c]Ex. 20:5
13 [a]Judg. 10:6; Ps. 106:36 [1]A Canaanite god [2]Canaanite goddesses
14 [a]Deut. 31:17; Judg. 3:8; Ps. 106:40–42 [b]2 Kin. 17:20 [c]Is. 50:1 [d]Lev. 26:37; Josh. 7:12, 13
15 [a]Lev. 26:14–26; Deut. 28:15–68
16 [a]Judg. 3:9, 10, 15; Ps. 106:43–45
17 [a]Ex. 34:15
18 [a]Josh. 1:5 [b]Gen. 6:6
19 [a]Judg. 3:12
20 [a][Josh. 23:16]
21 [a]Josh. 23:4, 5, 13
22 [a]Judg. 3:1, 4 [b]Deut. 8:2, 16; 13:3

CHAPTER 3

1 [a]Judg. 1:1; 2:21, 22 [1]*experienced*
3 [a]Josh. 13:3
4 [1]*find out*
5 [a]Ps. 106:35
6 [a]Ex. 34:15, 16; Deut. 7:3, 4; Josh. 23:12
7 [a]Judg. 2:11 [b]Deut. 32:18 [1]Name or symbol for Canaanite goddesses
8 [a]Deut. 32:30; Judg. 2:14 [b]Hab. 3:7
9 [a]Judg. 3:15 [b]Judg. 2:16 [c]Judg. 1:13
10 [a]Num. 27:18; 1 Sam. 11:6; 2 Chr. 15:1
12 [a]Judg. 2:19 [b]1 Sam. 12:9
13 [a]Judg. 5:14 [b]Deut. 34:3; Judg. 1:16; 2 Chr. 28:15 [1]*struck*
14 [a]Deut. 28:48
15 [a]Ps. 78:34 [b]Judg. 20:16
19 [a]Josh. 4:20 [1]Tg. *quarries*
22 [1]*handle*
24 [a]1 Sam. 24:3 [1]Lit. *his* [2]Lit. *covering his feet*
25 [a]2 Kin. 2:17; 8:11

room. Therefore they took the key and opened
*them.* And there was their master, fallen dead on
the floor.
**26** But Ehud had escaped while they delayed, and
passed beyond the [1]stone images and escaped to
Seirah.
27 And it happened, when he arrived, that [a]he
blew the trumpet in the [b]mountains of Ephraim,
and the children of Israel went down with him
from the mountains; and [1]he led them.
28 Then he said to them, "Follow *me,* for [a]the
LORD has delivered your enemies the Moabites
into your hand." So they went down after him,
seized the [b]fords of the Jordan leading to Moab,
and did not allow anyone to cross over.
29 And at that time they killed about ten thousand men of Moab, all stout men of valor; not a
man escaped.
30 So Moab was subdued that day under the
hand of Israel. And [a]the land had rest for eighty
years.
**31** After him was [a]Shamgar the son of Anath,
who killed six hundred men of the Philistines
[b]with an ox goad; [c]and he also delivered [d]Israel.

### *Deborah and Barak Defend Israel*

**4** When Ehud was dead, [a]the children of Israel
again did [b]evil in the sight of the LORD.
2 So the LORD [a]sold them into the hand of Jabin
king of Canaan, who reigned in [b]Hazor. The
commander of his army *was* [c]Sisera, who dwelt in
[d]Harosheth Hagoyim.
3 And the children of Israel cried out to the
LORD; for Jabin had nine hundred [a]chariots of
iron, and for twenty years [b]he had harshly oppressed the children of Israel.
4 Now Deborah, a prophetess, the wife of Lapi-
doth, was judging Israel at that time.
5 [a]And she would sit under the palm tree of
Deborah between Ramah and Bethel in the mountains of Ephraim. And the children of Israel came
up to her for judgment.
6 Then she sent and called for [a]Barak the son of
Abinoam from [b]Kedesh in Naphtali, and said to
him, "Has not the LORD God of Israel commanded,
'Go and [1]deploy *troops* at Mount [c]Tabor; take with
you ten thousand men of the sons of Naphtali and
of the sons of Zebulun;
7 'and against you [a]I will deploy Sisera, the
commander of Jabin's army, with his chariots and
his multitude at the [b]River Kishon; and I will
[1]deliver him into your hand'?"
8 And Barak said to her, "If you will go with me,
then I will go; but if you will not go with me, I will
not go!"
9 So she said, "I will surely go with you; nevertheless there will be no glory for you in the
journey you are taking, for the LORD will [a]sell
Sisera into the hand of a woman." Then Deborah
arose and went with Barak to Kedesh.
10 And Barak called [a]Zebulun and Naphtali to
Kedesh; he went up with ten thousand men [b]un-
der[1] his command, and Deborah went up with
him.
**11** Now Heber [a]the Kenite, of the children of
[b]Hobab the father-in-law of Moses, had separated
himself from the Kenites and pitched his tent near
the terebinth tree at Zaanaim, [c]which *is* beside
Kedesh.
12 And they reported to Sisera that Barak the son
of Abinoam had gone up to Mount Tabor.
13 So Sisera gathered together all his chariots,
nine hundred chariots of iron, and all the people
who *were* with him, from Harosheth Hagoyim to
the River Kishon.
14 Then Deborah said to Barak, [1]"Up! For this *is*
the day in which the LORD has delivered Sisera
into your hand. [a]Has not the LORD gone out before
you?" So Barak went down from Mount Tabor
with ten thousand men following him.
15 And the LORD routed Sisera and all *his* chariots and all *his* army with the edge of the sword
before Barak; and Sisera alighted from *his* chariot
and fled away on foot.
16 But Barak pursued the chariots and the army
as far as Harosheth Hagoyim, and all the army of
Sisera fell by the edge of the sword; not a man
was [a]left.
**17** However, Sisera had fled away on foot to the
tent of [a]Jael, the wife of Heber the Kenite; for
*there was* peace between Jabin king of Hazor and
the house of Heber the Kenite.
18 And Jael went out to meet Sisera, and said to
him, "Turn aside, my lord, turn aside to me; do not
fear." And when he had turned aside with her into
the tent, she covered him with a [1]blanket.
19 Then he said to her, "Please give me a little
water to drink, for I am thirsty." So she opened [a]a
jug of milk, gave him a drink, and covered him.
20 And he said to her, "Stand at the door of the
tent, and if any man comes and inquires of you,
and says, 'Is there any man here?' you shall say,
'No.' "
21 Then Jael, Heber's wife, [a]took a tent peg and
took a hammer in her hand, and went softly to
him and drove the peg into his temple, and it went
down into the ground; for he was fast asleep and
weary. So he died.
22 And then, as Barak pursued Sisera, Jael came
out to meet him, and said to him, "Come, I will
show you the man whom you seek." And when he
went into her *tent,* there lay Sisera, dead with the
peg in his temple.
**23** So on that day God subdued Jabin king of
Canaan in the presence of the children of Israel.
24 And the hand of the children of Israel grew
stronger and stronger against Jabin king of Canaan, until they had destroyed Jabin king of
Canaan.

### *The Song of Deborah and Barak*

**5** Then Deborah and Barak the son of Abinoam
[a]sang on that day, saying:

2 "When[1] leaders [a]lead in Israel,
[b]When the people [2]willingly offer themselves,
Bless the LORD!

3 "Hear,[a] O kings! Give ear, O princes!
I, *even* [b]I, will sing to the LORD;
I will sing praise to the LORD God of Israel.

4 "LORD, [a]when You went out from Seir,
When You marched from [b]the field of Edom,
The earth trembled and the heavens poured,
The clouds also poured water;
5 [a]The mountains [1]gushed before the LORD,
[b]This Sinai, before the LORD God of Israel.

6 "In the days of [a]Shamgar, son of Anath,
In the days of [b]Jael,
[c]The highways were deserted,
And the travelers walked along the byways.

**26** [1]Tg. *quarries*
**27** [a]Judg. 6:34; 1 Sam. 13:3 [b]Josh. 17:15 [1]Lit. *he went before them*
**28** [a]Judg. 7:9, 15; 1 Sam. 17:47 [b]Josh. 2:7; Judg. 12:5
**30** [a]Judg. 3:11
**31** [a]Judg. 5:6 [b]1 Sam. 17:47 [c]Judg. 2:16 [d]1 Sam. 4:1

CHAPTER 4

**1** [a]Judg. 2:19 [b]Judg. 2:11
**2** [a]Judg. 2:14 [b]Josh. 11:1, 10 [c]1 Sam. 12:9; Ps. 83:9 [d]Judg. 4:13, 16
**3** [a]Deut. 20:1; Judg. 1:19 [b]Ps. 106:42
**5** [a]Gen. 35:8
**6** [a]Heb. 11:32 [b]Josh. 19:37; 21:32 [c]Judg. 8:18 [1]*march*
**7** [a]Ex. 14:4 [b]Judg. 5:21; 1 Kin. 18:40; Ps. 83:9, 10 [1]Lit. *draw*
**9** [a]Judg. 2:14
**10** [a]Judg. 5:18 [b]Ex. 11:8; 1 Kin. 20:10 [1]Lit. *at his feet*
**11** [a]Judg. 1:16 [b]Num. 10:29 [c]Judg. 4:6
**14** [a]Deut. 9:3; 31:3; 2 Sam. 5:24; Ps. 68:7; Is. 52:12 [1]*Arise!*
**16** [a]Ex. 14:28; Ps. 83:9
**17** [a]Judg. 5:6
**18** [1]*rug*
**19** [a]Judg. 5:24–27
**21** [a]Judg. 5:24–27

CHAPTER 5

**1** [a]Ex. 15:1; Judg. 4:4
**2** [a]Ps. 18:47 [b]2 Chr. 17:16 [1]Or *When locks are loosed* [2]*volunteer*
**3** [a]Deut. 32:1, 3 [b]Ps. 27:6
**4** [a]Deut. 33:2; Ps. 68:7 [b]Ps. 68:8
**5** [a]Ps. 97:5 [b]Ex. 19:18 [1]*flowed*
**6** [a]Judg. 3:31 [b]Judg. 4:17 [c]Is. 33:8

7 Village life ceased, it ceased in Israel,
Until I, Deborah, arose,
Arose a mother in Israel.
8 They chose [a]new gods;
Then *there was* war in the gates;
Not a shield or spear was seen among forty
thousand in Israel.
9 My heart *is* with the rulers of Israel
Who offered themselves willingly
with the people.
Bless the LORD!

10 "Speak, you who ride on white [a]donkeys,
Who sit in judges' attire,
And who walk along the road.
11 Far from the noise of the archers, among the
watering places,
There they shall recount
the righteous acts of the LORD,
The righteous acts *for* His villagers in Israel;
Then the people of the LORD
shall go down to the gates.

12 "Awake,[a] awake, Deborah!
Awake, awake, sing a song!
Arise, Barak, and lead your captives away,
O son of Abinoam!

13 "Then the survivors came down,
the people against the nobles;
The LORD came down for me
against the mighty.
14 From Ephraim *were* those
whose roots were in [a]Amalek.
After you, Benjamin, with your peoples,
From Machir rulers came down,
And from Zebulun
those who bear the recruiter's staff.
15 And [1]the princes of Issachar
*were* with Deborah;
As Issachar, so *was* Barak
Sent into the valley [2]under his command;
Among the divisions of Reuben
*There were* great resolves of heart.
16 Why did you sit among the sheepfolds,
To hear the pipings for the flocks?
The divisions of Reuben
have great searchings of heart.
17 [a]Gilead stayed beyond the Jordan,
And why did Dan remain [1]on ships?
[b]Asher continued at the seashore,
And stayed by his inlets.
18 [a]Zebulun *is* a people *who* jeopardized their
lives to the point of death,
Naphtali also, on the heights
of the battlefield.

19 "The kings came *and* fought,
Then the kings of Canaan fought
In [a]Taanach, by the waters of Megiddo;
They took no spoils of silver.
20 They fought from the heavens;
The stars from their courses fought against
Sisera.
21 [a]The torrent of Kishon swept them away,
That ancient torrent, the torrent of Kishon.
O my soul, march on in strength!
22 Then the horses' hooves pounded,
The galloping, galloping of his steeds.
23 'Curse Meroz,' said the [1]angel of the LORD,
'Curse its inhabitants bitterly,
Because they did not come
to the help of the LORD,
To the help of the LORD against the mighty.'

**8** [a]Deut. 32:17
**10** [a]Judg. 10:4; 12:14
**12** [a]Ps. 57:8
**14** [a]Judg. 3:13
**15** [1]So with LXX, Syr., Tg., Vg.; MT *And my princes in Issachar* [2]Lit. *at his feet*
**17** [a]Josh. 22:9 [b]Josh. 19:29, 31 [1]Or *at ease*
**18** [a]Judg. 4:6, 10
**19** [a]Judg. 1:27
**21** [a]Judg. 4:7
**23** [1]Or *Angel*
**24** [a][Luke 1:28]
**27** [a]Judg. 4:18–21
**29** [1]*princesses* [2]Lit. *repeats her words to herself*
**31** [a]Ps. 92:9 [b]2 Sam. 23:4 [c]Ps. 37:6; 89:36, 37 [d]Ps. 19:5
CHAPTER 6
**1** [a]Judg. 2:11 [b]Num. 22:4; 31:1–3
**2** [a]1 Sam. 13:6; Heb. 11:38
**3** [a]Judg. 7:12
**4** [a]Lev. 26:16 [b]Deut. 28:31
**5** [1]*innumerable*
**6** [a]Ps. 50:15; Hos. 5:15
**8** [a]Josh. 24:17 [1]*slavery*
**9** [a]Ps. 44:2, 3
**10** [a]2 Kin. 17:35, 37, 38; Jer. 10:2 [b]Judg. 2:1, 2
**11** [a]Josh. 17:2; Judg. 6:15

24 "Most blessed among women is Jael,
The wife of Heber the Kenite;
[a]Blessed is she among women in tents.
25 He asked for water, she gave milk;
She brought out cream in a lordly bowl.
26 She stretched her hand to the tent peg,
Her right hand to the workmen's hammer;
She pounded Sisera, she pierced his head,
She split and struck through his temple.
27 At her feet he sank, he fell, he lay still;
At her feet he sank, he fell;
Where he sank, there he fell [a]dead.

28 "The mother of Sisera looked
through the window,
And cried out through the lattice,
'Why is his chariot *so* long in coming?
Why tarries the clatter of his chariots?'
29 Her wisest [1]ladies answered her,
Yes, she [2]answered herself,
30 'Are they not finding and dividing the spoil:
To every man a girl *or* two;
For Sisera, plunder of dyed garments,
Plunder of garments embroidered and dyed,
Two pieces of dyed embroidery
for the neck of the looter?'

31 "Thus let all Your enemies [a]perish, O LORD!
But *let* those who love Him *be* [b]like the [c]sun
When it comes out in full [d]strength."

So the land had rest for forty years.

### *Gideon Called to Service*

**6** Then the children of Israel did [a]evil in the
sight of the LORD. So the LORD delivered them
into the hand of [b]Midian for seven years,
2 and the hand of Midian prevailed against
Israel. Because of the Midianites, the children of
Israel made for themselves the dens, [a]the caves,
and the strongholds which *are* in the mountains.
3 So it was, whenever Israel had sown, Midianites would come up; also Amalekites and the
[a]people of the East would come up against them.
4 Then they would encamp against them and
[a]destroy the produce of the earth as far as Gaza,
and leave no sustenance for Israel, neither sheep
nor ox nor [b]donkey.
5 For they would come up with their livestock
and their tents, coming in as numerous as locusts;
both they and their camels were [1]without number;
and they would enter the land to destroy it.
6 So Israel was greatly impoverished because of
the Midianites, and the children of Israel [a]cried
out to the LORD.
**7** And it came to pass, when the children of
Israel cried out to the LORD because of the Midianites,
8 that the LORD sent a prophet to the children of
Israel, who said to them, "Thus says the LORD God
of Israel: 'I brought you up from Egypt and
brought you out of the [a]house of [1]bondage;
9 'and I delivered you out of the hand of the
Egyptians and out of the hand of all who oppressed you, and [a]drove them out before you and
gave you their land.
10 'Also I said to you, "I *am* the LORD your God;
[a]do not fear the gods of the Amorites, in whose
land you dwell. But you have not obeyed My
[b]voice." ' "
**11** Now the Angel of the LORD came and sat
under the terebinth tree which *was* in Ophrah,
which *belonged* to Joash [a]the Abiezrite, while his

son [b]Gideon threshed wheat in the winepress, in
order to hide *it* from the Midianites.
12 And the [a]Angel of the LORD appeared to him,
and said to him, "The LORD *is* [b]with you, you
mighty man of valor!"
13 Gideon said to Him, "O [1]my lord, if the LORD is
with us, why then has all this happened to us?
And [a]where *are* all His miracles [b]which our fathers
told us about, saying, 'Did not the LORD bring us
up from Egypt?' But now the LORD has [c]forsaken
us and delivered us into the hands of the Midianites."
14 Then the LORD turned to him and said, [a]"Go in
this might of yours, and you shall save Israel from
the hand of the Midianites. [b]Have I not sent you?"
15 So he said to Him, "O [1]my Lord, how can I
save Israel? Indeed [a]my clan *is* the weakest in
Manasseh, and I *am* the least in my father's
house."
16 And the LORD said to him, [a]"Surely I will be
with you, and you shall [1]defeat the Midianites as
one man."
17 Then he said to Him, "If now I have found
favor in Your sight, then [a]show me a sign that it is
You who talk with me.
18 [a]"Do not depart from here, I pray, until I come
to You and bring out my offering and set *it* before
You." And He said, "I will wait until you come
back."
**19** [a]So Gideon went in and prepared a young
goat, and unleavened bread from an ephah of
flour. The meat he put in a basket, and he put the
broth in a pot; and he brought *them* out to Him
under the terebinth tree and presented *them.*
20 The Angel of God said to him, "Take the meat
and the unleavened bread and [a]lay *them* on this
rock, and [b]pour out the broth." And he did so.
**21** Then the Angel of the LORD put out the end of
the staff that *was* in His hand, and touched the
meat and the unleavened bread; and [a]fire rose out
of the rock and consumed the meat and the
unleavened bread. And the Angel of the LORD
departed out of his sight.
22 Now Gideon [a]perceived that He *was* the Angel
of the LORD. So Gideon said, "Alas, O Lord GOD!
[b]For I have seen the Angel of the LORD face to
face."
23 Then the LORD said to him, [a]"Peace *be* with
you; do not fear, you shall not die."
24 So Gideon built an altar there to the LORD, and
called it [1]The-LORD-*Is*-Peace. To this day it *is* still
[a]in Ophrah of the Abiezrites.
**25** Now it came to pass the same night that the
LORD said to him, "Take your father's young bull,
the second bull of seven years old, and [a]tear down
the altar of [b]Baal that your father has, and [c]cut
down the [1]wooden image that *is* beside it;
26 "and build an altar to the LORD your God on
top of this [1]rock in the proper arrangement, and
take the second bull and offer a burnt sacrifice
with the wood of the image which you shall cut
down."
27 So Gideon took ten men from among his
servants and did as the LORD had said to him. But
because he feared his father's household and the
men of the city too much to do *it* by day, he did *it*
by night.
**28** And when the men of the city arose early in
the morning, there was the altar of Baal, torn
down; and the wooden image that *was* beside it
was cut down, and the second bull was being
offered on the altar *which had been* built.
29 So they said to one another, "Who has done
this thing?" And when they had inquired and
asked, they said, "Gideon the son of Joash has
done this thing."
30 Then the men of the city said to Joash, "Bring
out your son, that he may die, because he has torn
down the altar of Baal, and because he has cut
down the wooden image that *was* beside it."
31 But Joash said to all who stood against him,
"Would you [1]plead for Baal? Would you save him?
Let the one who would plead for him be put to
death by morning! If he *is* a god, let him plead for
himself, because his altar has been torn down!"
32 Therefore on that day he called him [a]Jerub-
baal,[1] saying, "Let Baal plead against him, because
he has torn down his altar."
**33** Then all [a]the Midianites and Amalekites, the
people of the East, gathered together; and they
crossed over and encamped in [b]the Valley of
Jezreel.
34 But [a]the Spirit of the LORD came upon Gideon;
then he [b]blew the trumpet, and the Abiezrites
gathered behind him.
35 And he sent messengers throughout all Manasseh, who also gathered behind him. He also
sent messengers to [a]Asher, [b]Zebulun, and Naphtali; and they came up to meet them.
**36** So Gideon said to God, "If You will save Israel
by my hand as You have said—
37 [a]"look, I shall put a fleece of wool on the
threshing floor; if there is dew on the fleece only,
and *it is* dry on all the ground, then I shall know
that You will save Israel by my hand, as You have
said."
38 And it was so. When he rose early the next
morning and squeezed the fleece together, he
wrung the dew out of the fleece, a bowlful of
water.
39 Then Gideon said to God, [a]"Do not be angry
with me, but let me speak just once more: Let me
test, I pray, just once more with the fleece; let it
now be dry only on the fleece, but on all the
ground let there be dew."
40 And God did so that night. It was dry on the
fleece only, but there was dew on all the ground.

## *Gideon's Three Hundred Men*

**7** Then [a]Jerubbaal (that *is,* Gideon) and all the
people who *were* with him rose early and
encamped beside the well of Harod, so that the
camp of the Midianites was on the north side of
them by the hill of Moreh in the valley.
**2** And the LORD said to Gideon, "The people
who *are* with you *are* too many for Me to give the
Midianites into their hands, lest Israel [a]claim glory
for itself against Me, saying, 'My own hand has
saved me.'
3 "Now therefore, proclaim in the hearing of the
people, saying, [a]'Whoever *is* fearful and afraid, let
him turn and depart at once from Mount Gilead.' "
And twenty-two thousand of the people returned,
and ten thousand remained.
**4** But the LORD said to Gideon, "The people *are*
still *too* many; bring them down to the water, and
I will test them for you there. Then it will be, *that*
of whom I say to you, 'This one shall go with you,'
the same shall go with you; and of whomever I
say to you, 'This one shall not go with you,' the
same shall not go."
5 So he brought the people down to the water.
And the LORD said to Gideon, "Everyone who laps

11 [b]Judg. 7:1; Heb. 11:32
12 [a]Judg. 13:3; Luke 1:11, 28 [b]Josh. 1:5
13 [a][Is. 59:1] [b]Josh. 4:6, 21; Ps. 44:1 [c]Deut. 31:17; 2 Chr. 15:2; Ps. 44:9–16 [1]Heb. *adoni,* used of man
14 [a]1 Sam. 12:11 [b]Josh. 1:9
15 [a]1 Sam. 9:21 [1]Heb. *Adonai,* used of God
16 [a]Ex. 3:12; Josh. 1:5 [1]Lit. *strike*
17 [a]Judg. 6:36, 37; 2 Kin. 20:8; Ps. 86:17; Is. 7:11; 38:7, 8
18 [a]Gen. 18:3, 5
19 [a]Gen. 18:6–8
20 [a]Judg. 13:19 [b]1 Kin. 18:33, 34
21 [a]Lev. 9:24
22 [a]Gen. 32:30; Ex. 33:20; Judg. 13:21, 22 [b]Gen. 16:13
23 [a]Dan. 10:19
24 [a]Judg. 8:32 [1]Heb. *YHWH Shalom*
25 [a]Judg. 2:2 [b]Judg. 3:7 [c]Ex. 34:13; Deut. 7:5 [1]Or *Asherah,* a Canaanite goddess
26 [1]*stronghold*
31 [1]*contend*
32 [a]Judg. 7:1; 1 Sam. 12:11; 2 Sam. 11:21 [1]Lit. *Let Baal Plead*
33 [a]Judg. 6:3 [b]Josh. 17:16; Hos. 1:5
34 [a]Judg. 3:10; 1 Chr. 12:18; 2 Chr. 24:20 [b]Num. 10:3; Judg. 3:27
35 [a]Judg. 5:17; 7:23 [b]Judg. 4:6, 10; 5:18
37 [a][Ex. 4:3–7]
39 [a]Gen. 18:32

CHAPTER 7

1 [a]Judg. 6:32
2 [a]Deut. 8:17; Is. 10:13
3 [a]Deut. 20:8

from the water with his tongue, as a dog laps, you
shall set apart by himself; likewise everyone who
gets down on his knees to drink."
6 And the number of those who lapped, *putting*
their hand to their mouth, was three hundred
men; but all the rest of the people got down on
their knees to drink water.
7 Then the LORD said to Gideon, [a]"By the three
hundred men who lapped I will save you, and
deliver the Midianites into your hand. Let all the
*other* people go, every man to his [1]place."
8 So the people took provisions and their trumpets in their hands. And he sent away all *the rest
of* Israel, every man to his tent, and retained those
three hundred men. Now the camp of Midian was
below him in the valley.
**9** It happened on the same [a]night that the LORD
said to him, "Arise, go down against the camp, for
I have delivered it into your hand.
10 "But if you are afraid to go down, go down to
the camp with Purah your servant,
11 "and you shall [a]hear what they say; and afterward [1]your hands shall be strengthened to go
down against the camp." Then he went down with
Purah his servant to the outpost of the armed men
who *were* in the camp.
12 Now the Midianites and Amalekites, [a]all the
people of the East, were lying in the valley [b]as
numerous as locusts; and their camels *were* [1]with-
out number, as the sand by the seashore in multitude.
13 And when Gideon had come, there was a man
telling a dream to his companion. He said, "I have
had a dream: *To my* surprise, a loaf of barley bread
tumbled into the camp of Midian; it came to a tent
and struck it so that it fell and overturned, and the
tent collapsed."
14 Then his companion answered and said, "This
*is* nothing else but the sword of Gideon the son of
Joash, a man of Israel! Into his hand [a]God has
delivered Midian and the whole camp."
**15** And so it was, when Gideon heard the telling
of the dream and its interpretation, that he worshiped. He returned to the camp of Israel, and
said, "Arise, for the LORD has delivered the camp
of Midian into your hand."
16 Then he divided the three hundred men *into*
three companies, and he put a trumpet into every
man's hand, with empty pitchers, and torches
inside the pitchers.
17 And he said to them, "Look at me and do
likewise; watch, and when I come to the edge of
the camp you shall do as I do:
18 "When I blow the trumpet, I and all who *are*
with me, then you also blow the trumpets on
every side of the whole camp, and say, '*The sword
of* the LORD and of Gideon!' "
**19** So Gideon and the hundred men who *were*
with him came to the outpost of the camp at the
beginning of the middle watch, just as they had
posted the watch; and they blew the trumpets and
broke the pitchers that *were* in their hands.
20 Then the three companies blew the trumpets
and broke the pitchers—they held the torches in
their left hands and the trumpets in their right
hands for blowing—and they cried, "The sword of
the LORD and of Gideon!"
21 And [a]every man stood in his place all around
the camp; [b]and the whole army ran and cried out
and fled.
22 When the three hundred [a]blew the trumpets,
[b]the LORD set [c]every man's sword against his
companion throughout the whole camp; and the
army fled to [1]Beth Acacia, toward Zererah, as far
as the border of [d]Abel Meholah, by Tabbath.
23 And the men of Israel gathered together from
[a]Naphtali, Asher, and all Manasseh, and pursued
the Midianites.
**24** Then Gideon sent messengers throughout
all the [a]mountains of Ephraim, saying, "Come
down against the Midianites, and seize from them
the watering places as far as Beth Barah and the
Jordan." Then all the men of Ephraim gathered
together and [b]seized the watering places as far as
[c]Beth Barah and the Jordan.
25 And they captured [a]two princes of the Midianites, [b]Oreb and Zeeb. They killed Oreb at the rock
of Oreb, and Zeeb they killed at the winepress of
Zeeb. They pursued Midian and brought the heads
of Oreb and Zeeb to Gideon on the [c]other side of
the Jordan.

### *Gideon Conquers Midian's Kings*

**8** Now [a]the men of Ephraim said to him, "Why
have you done this to us by not calling us
when you went to fight with the Midianites?" And
they reprimanded him sharply.
2 So he said to them, "What have I done now in
comparison with you? *Is* not the [1]gleaning *of the
grapes* of Ephraim better than [2]the vintage of
[a]Abiezer?
3 [a]"God has delivered into your hands the
princes of Midian, Oreb and Zeeb. And what was I
able to do in comparison with you?" Then their
[b]anger toward him subsided when he said that.
**4** When Gideon came [a]to the Jordan, he and [b]the
three hundred men who *were* with him crossed
over, exhausted but still in pursuit.
5 Then he said to the men of [a]Succoth, "Please
give loaves of bread to the people who follow me,
for they are exhausted, and I am pursuing Zebah
and Zalmunna, kings of Midian."
6 And the leaders of Succoth said, [a]"*Are*[1] the
hands of Zebah and Zalmunna now in your hand,
that [b]we should give bread to your army?"
7 So Gideon said, "For this cause, when the
LORD has delivered Zebah and Zalmunna into my
hand, [a]then I will tear your flesh with the thorns
of the wilderness and with briers!"
8 Then he went up from there [a]to Penuel and
spoke to them in the same way. And the men of
Penuel answered him as the men of Succoth had
answered.
9 So he also spoke to the men of Penuel, saying,
"When I [a]come back in peace, [b]I will tear down
this tower!"
**10** Now Zebah and Zalmunna *were* at Karkor,
and their armies with them, about fifteen thousand, all who were left of [a]all the army of the
people of the East; for [b]one hundred and twenty
thousand men who drew the sword had fallen.
11 Then Gideon went up by the road of those
who dwell in tents on the east of [a]Nobah and
Jogbehah; and he [1]attacked the army while the
camp felt [b]secure.
12 When Zebah and Zalmunna fled, he pursued
them; and he [a]took the two kings of Midian,
Zebah and Zalmunna, and routed the whole army.
**13** Then Gideon the son of Joash returned from
battle, from the Ascent of Heres.
14 And he caught a young man of the men of
Succoth and interrogated him; and he wrote down
for him the leaders of Succoth and its elders,
seventy-seven men.

**7** [a]1 Sam. 14:6 [1]*home*
**9** [a]Gen. 46:2, 3; Judg. 6:25
**11** [a]Gen. 24:14; 1 Sam. 14:9, 10 [1]*you shall be encouraged*
**12** [a]Judg. 6:3, 33; 8:10 [b]Judg. 6:5 [1]*innumerable*
**14** [a]Judg. 6:14, 16
**21** [a]Ex. 14:13, 14; 2 Chr. 20:17 [b]2 Kin. 7:7
**22** [a]Josh. 6:4, 16, 20 [b]Ps. 83:9; Is. 9:4 [c]1 Sam. 14:20; 2 Chr. 20:23 [d]1 Kin. 4:12 [1]Heb. *Beth Shittah*
**23** [a]Judg. 6:35
**24** [a]Judg. 3:27 [b]Judg. 3:28 [c]John 1:28
**25** [a]Judg. 8:3 [b]Ps. 83:11; Is. 10:26 [c]Judg. 8:4

CHAPTER 8
**1** [a]Judg. 12:1; 2 Sam. 19:41
**2** [a]Judg. 6:11 [1]Few grapes left after the harvest [2]The whole harvest
**3** [a]Judg. 7:24, 25 [b]Prov. 15:1
**4** [a]Judg. 7:25 [b]Judg. 7:6
**5** [a]Gen. 33:17; Ps. 60:6
**6** [a]1 Kin. 20:11; Judg. 8:15 [b]1 Sam. 25:11 [1]Lit. *Is the palm*
**7** [a]Judg. 8:16
**8** [a]Gen. 32:30, 31; 1 Kin. 12:25
**9** [a]1 Kin. 22:27 [b]Judg. 8:17
**10** [a]Judg. 7:12 [b]Judg. 6:5
**11** [a]Num. 32:35, 42 [b]Judg. 18:27; [1 Thess. 5:3] [1]Lit. *struck*
**12** [a]Ps. 83:11

15 Then he came to the men of Succoth and said,
"Here are Zebah and Zalmunna, about whom you
[a]ridiculed me, saying, '*Are* the hands of Zebah and
Zalmunna now in your hand, that we should give
bread to your weary men?' "
16 [a]And he took the elders of the city, and thorns
of the wilderness and briers, and with them he
[1]taught the men of Succoth.
17 [a]Then he tore down the tower of [b]Penuel and
killed the men of the city.
**18** And he said to Zebah and Zalmunna, "What
kind of men *were they* whom you killed at [a]Ta-
bor?" So they answered, "As you *are,* so *were*
they; each one resembled the son of a king."
19 Then he said, "They *were* my brothers, the
sons of my mother. *As* the LORD lives, if you had
let them live, I would not kill you."
20 And he said to Jether his firstborn, "Rise, kill
them!" But the youth would not draw his sword;
for he was afraid, because he *was* still a youth.
21 So Zebah and Zalmunna said, "Rise yourself,
and kill us; for as a man *is, so is* his strength." So
Gideon arose and [a]killed Zebah and Zalmunna,
and took the crescent ornaments that *were* on
their camels' necks.
**22** Then the men of Israel said to Gideon, [a]"Rule
over us, both you and your son, and your grandson also; for you have [b]delivered us from the hand
of Midian."
23 But Gideon said to them, "I will not rule over
you, nor shall my son rule over you; [a]the LORD
shall rule over you."
24 Then Gideon said to them, "I would like to
[1]make a request of you, that each of you would
give me the earrings from his plunder." For they
had golden earrings, [a]because they *were* Ishmaelites.
25 So they answered, "We will gladly give *them.*"
And they spread out a garment, and each man
threw into it the earrings from his plunder.
26 Now the weight of the gold earrings that he
requested was one thousand seven hundred *shekels* of gold, besides the crescent ornaments, pendants, and purple robes which *were* on the kings
of Midian, and besides the chains that *were*
around their camels' necks.
27 Then Gideon [a]made it into an ephod and set it
up in his city, [b]Ophrah. And all Israel [c]played the
harlot with it there. It became [d]a snare to Gideon
and to his house.
28 Thus Midian was subdued before the children
of Israel, so that they lifted their heads no more.
[a]And the country was quiet for forty years in the
days of Gideon.
**29** Then [a]Jerubbaal the son of Joash went and
dwelt in his own house.
30 Gideon had [a]seventy sons who were his own
offspring, for he had many wives.
31 [a]And his concubine who *was* in Shechem also
bore him a son, whose name he called Abimelech.
32 Now Gideon the son of Joash died [a]at a good
old age, and was buried in the tomb of Joash his
father, [b]in Ophrah of the Abiezrites.
**33** So it was, [a]as soon as Gideon was dead, that
the children of Israel again [b]played the harlot with
the Baals, [c]and made Baal-Berith their god.
34 Thus the children of Israel [a]did not remember
the LORD their God, who had delivered them from
the hands of all their enemies on every side;
35 [a]nor did they show kindness to the house of
Jerubbaal (Gideon) in accordance with the good
he had done for Israel.

### *Abimelech's Wickedness and Downfall*

**9** Then Abimelech the son of Jerubbaal went to
Shechem, to [a]his mother's brothers, and spoke
with them and with all the family of the house of
his mother's father, saying,
2 "Please speak in the hearing of all the men of
Shechem: 'Which is better for you, that all [a]sev-
enty of the sons of Jerubbaal reign over you, or
that one reign over you?' Remember that I *am*
your own flesh and [b]bone."
3 And his mother's brothers spoke all these
words concerning him in the hearing of all the
men of Shechem; and their heart was inclined to
follow Abimelech, for they said, "He is our
[a]brother."
4 So they gave him seventy *shekels* of silver
from the temple of [a]Baal-Berith, with which Abimelech hired [b]worthless and reckless men; and they
followed him.
5 Then he went to his father's house [a]at Ophrah
and [b]killed his brothers, the seventy sons of
Jerubbaal, on one stone. But Jotham the youngest
son of Jerubbaal was left, because he hid himself.
6 And all the men of Shechem gathered together, all of Beth Millo, and they went and made
Abimelech king beside the terebinth tree at the
pillar that *was* in Shechem.
**7** Now when they told Jotham, he went and
stood on top of [a]Mount Gerizim, and lifted his
voice and cried out. And he said to them:

"Listen to me, you men of Shechem,
That God may listen to you!

8 "The[a] trees once went forth
to anoint a king over them.
And they said to the olive tree,
[b]'Reign over us!'
9 But the olive tree said to them,
'Should I cease giving my oil,
[a]With which they honor God and men,
And go to sway over trees?'

10 "Then the trees said to the fig tree,
'You come *and* reign over us!'
11 But the fig tree said to them,
'Should I cease my sweetness
and my good fruit,
And go to sway over trees?'

12 "Then the trees said to the vine,
'You come *and* reign over us!'
13 But the vine said to them,
'Should I cease my new wine,
[a]Which cheers *both* God and men,
And go to sway over trees?'

14 "Then all the trees said to the bramble,
'You come *and* reign over us!'
15 And the bramble said to the trees,
'If in truth you anoint me as king over you,
*Then* come *and* take shelter in my [a]shade;
But if not, [b]let fire come out of the bramble
And devour the [c]cedars of Lebanon!'

**16** "Now therefore, if you have acted in truth and
sincerity in making Abimelech king, and if you
have dealt well with Jerubbaal and his house, and
have done to him [a]as[1] he deserves—
17 "for my [a]father fought for you, risked his life,
and [b]delivered you out of the hand of Midian;
18 [a]"but you have risen up against my father's
house this day, and killed his seventy sons on one
stone, and made Abimelech, the son of his [b]female

---

**15** [a]Judg. 8:6
**16** [a]Judg. 8:7 [1]*disciplined*
**17** [a]Judg. 8:9 [b]1 Kin. 12:25
**18** [a]Judg. 4:6; Ps. 89:12
**21** [a]Ps. 83:11
**22** [a][Judg. 9:8] [b]Judg. 3:9; 9:17
**23** [a]1 Sam. 8:7; 10:19; 12:12; Ps. 10:16
**24** [a]Gen. 37:25, 28 [1]Lit. *request a request*
**27** [a]Judg. 17:5 [b]Judg. 6:11, 24 [c][Ps. 106:39] [d]Deut. 7:16
**28** [a]Judg. 5:31
**29** [a]Judg. 6:32; 7:1
**30** [a]Judg. 9:2, 5
**31** [a]Judg. 9:1
**32** [a]Gen. 25:8; Job 5:26 [b]Judg. 6:24; 8:27
**33** [a]Judg. 2:19 [b]Judg. 2:17 [c]Judg. 9:4, 46
**34** [a]Deut. 4:9; Judg. 3:7; Ps. 78:11, 42; 106:13, 21
**35** [a]Judg. 9:16–18

CHAPTER 9

**1** [a]Judg. 8:31, 35
**2** [a]Judg. 8:30; 9:5, 18 [b]Gen. 29:14
**3** [a]Gen. 29:15
**4** [a]Judg. 8:33 [b]Judg. 11:3; 2 Chr. 13:7; Acts 17:5
**5** [a]Judg. 6:24 [b]Judg. 8:30; 9:2, 18; 2 Kin. 11:1, 2
**7** [a]Deut. 11:29; 27:12; Josh. 8:33; John 4:20
**8** [a]2 Kin. 14:9 [b]Judg. 8:22, 23
**9** [a][John 5:23]
**13** [a]Ps. 104:15
**15** [a]Is. 30:2; Dan. 4:12; Hos. 14:7 [b]Num. 21:28; Judg. 9:20; Ezek. 19:14 [c]2 Kin. 14:9; Is. 2:13; Ezek. 31:3
**16** [a]Judg. 8:35 [1]Lit. *according to the doing of his hands*
**17** [a]Judg. 7 [b]Judg. 8:22
**18** [a]Judg. 8:30, 35; 9:2, 5, 6 [b]Judg. 8:31

servant, king over the men of Shechem, because
he is your brother—
19 "if then you have acted in truth and sincerity
with Jerubbaal and with his house this day, *then*
[a]rejoice in Abimelech, and let him also rejoice in
you.
20 "But if not, [a]let fire come from Abimelech and
devour the men of Shechem and Beth Millo; and
let fire come from the men of Shechem and from
Beth Millo and devour Abimelech!"
21 And Jotham ran away and fled; and he went to
[a]Beer and dwelt there, for fear of Abimelech his
brother.
**22** After Abimelech had reigned over Israel three
years,
23 [a]God sent a [b]spirit of ill will between Abimelech and the men of Shechem; and the men of
Shechem [c]dealt treacherously with Abimelech,
24 [a]that the crime *done* to the seventy sons of
Jerubbaal might be settled and their [b]blood be laid
on Abimelech their brother, who killed them, and
on the men of Shechem, who aided him in the
killing of his brothers.
25 And the men of Shechem set [1]men in ambush
against him on the tops of the mountains, and
they robbed all who passed by them along that
way; and it was told Abimelech.
**26** Now Gaal the son of Ebed came with his
brothers and went over to Shechem; and the men
of Shechem put their confidence in him.
27 So they went out into the fields, and gathered
*grapes* from their vineyards and trod *them*, and
[1]made merry. And they went into [a]the house of
their god, and ate and drank, and cursed Abimelech.
28 Then Gaal the son of Ebed said, [a]"Who *is*
Abimelech, and who *is* Shechem, that we should
serve him? *Is he* not the son of Jerubbaal, and *is*
*not* Zebul his officer? Serve the men of [b]Hamor the
father of Shechem; but why should we serve him?
29 [a]"If only this people were under my [1]authority!
Then I would remove Abimelech." So [2]he said to
Abimelech, "Increase your army and come out!"
**30** When Zebul, the ruler of the city, heard the
words of Gaal the son of Ebed, his anger was
aroused.
31 And he sent messengers to Abimelech secretly, saying, "Take note! Gaal the son of Ebed
and his brothers have come to Shechem; and here
they are, fortifying the city against you.
32 "Now therefore, get up by night, you and the
people who *are* with you, and [1]lie in wait in the
field.
33 "And it shall be, as soon as the sun is up in the
morning, *that* you shall rise early and rush upon
the city; and *when* he and the people who are with
him come out against you, you may then do to
them [1]as you find opportunity."
**34** So Abimelech and all the people who *were*
with him rose by night, and [1]lay in wait against
Shechem in four companies.
35 When Gaal the son of Ebed went out and
stood in the entrance to the city gate, Abimelech
and the people who *were* with him rose from lying
in wait.
36 And when Gaal saw the people, he said to
Zebul, "Look, people are coming down from the
tops of the mountains!" But Zebul said to him,
"You see the shadows of the mountains as *if they*
*were* men."
37 So Gaal spoke again and said, "See, people are
coming down from the center of the land, and

**19** [a]Is. 8:6; [Phil. 3:3]
**20** [a]Judg. 9:15, 45, 56, 57
**21** [a]Num. 21:16
**23** [a]1 Kin. 12:15; Is. 19:14 [b]1 Sam. 16:14; 18:9, 10; 1 Kin. 22:22; 2 Chr. 18:22 [c]Is. 33:1
**24** [a]1 Kin. 2:32; Esth. 9:25; Matt. 23:35, 36 [b]Num. 35:33
**25** [1]Lit. *liers-in-wait for*
**27** [a]Judg. 9:4 [1]*rejoiced*
**28** [a]1 Sam. 25:10; 1 Kin. 12:16 [b]Gen. 34:2, 6; Josh. 24:32
**29** [a]2 Sam. 15:4 [1]Lit. *hand* [2]So with MT, Tg., [Vg.]; DSS *they;* LXX *I*
**32** [1]Set up an ambush
**33** [1]Lit. *as your hand can find*
**34** [1]Set up an ambush
**37** [1]Heb. *Meonenim*
**38** [a]Judg. 9:28, 29
**41** [1]*exiled*
**43** [1]Lit. *struck*
**45** [a]Judg. 9:20 [b]Deut. 29:23; 2 Kin. 3:25
**46** [a]Judg. 8:33 [1]*fortified room*
**48** [a]Ps. 68:14
**49** [1]*fortified room*
**50** [1]*besieged*
**53** [a]2 Sam. 11:21
**54** [a]1 Sam. 31:4
**55** [1]*home*
**56** [a]Judg. 9:24; Job 31:3; Prov. 5:22

another company is coming from the [1]Diviners'
Terebinth Tree."
38 Then Zebul said to him, "Where indeed *is* your
mouth now, with which you [a]said, 'Who is Abimelech, that we should serve him?' *Are* not these
the people whom you despised? Go out, if you will,
and fight with them now."
39 So Gaal went out, leading the men of Shechem, and fought with Abimelech.
40 And Abimelech chased him, and he fled from
him; and many fell wounded, to the *very* entrance
of the gate.
41 Then Abimelech dwelt at Arumah, and Zebul
[1]drove out Gaal and his brothers, so that they
would not dwell in Shechem.
**42** And it came about on the next day that the
people went out into the field, and they told
Abimelech.
43 So he took his people, divided them into three
companies, and lay in wait in the field. And he
looked, and there were the people, coming out of
the city; and he rose against them and [1]attacked
them.
44 Then Abimelech and the company that *was*
with him rushed forward and stood at the entrance of the gate of the city; and the *other* two
companies rushed upon all who *were* in the fields
and killed them.
45 So Abimelech fought against the city all that
day; [a]he took the city and killed the people who
*were* in it; and he [b]demolished the city and sowed
it with salt.
**46** Now when all the men of the tower of Shechem had heard *that,* they entered the [1]stronghold
of the temple [a]of the god Berith.
47 And it was told Abimelech that all the men of
the tower of Shechem were gathered together.
48 Then Abimelech went up to Mount [a]Zalmon,
he and all the people who *were* with him. And
Abimelech took an ax in his hand and cut down a
bough from the trees, and took it and laid *it* on his
shoulder; then he said to the people who were
with him, "What you have seen me do, make
haste *and* do as I *have done.*"
49 So each of the people likewise cut down his
own bough and followed Abimelech, put *them*
against the [1]stronghold, and set the stronghold on
fire above them, so that all the people of the tower
of Shechem died, about a thousand men and
women.
**50** Then Abimelech went to Thebez, and he [1]en-
camped against Thebez and took it.
51 But there was a strong tower in the city, and
all the men and women—all the people of the
city—fled there and shut themselves in; then they
went up to the top of the tower.
52 So Abimelech came as far as the tower and
fought against it; and he drew near the door of the
tower to burn it with fire.
53 But a certain woman [a]dropped an upper millstone on Abimelech's head and crushed his skull.
54 Then [a]he called quickly to the young man, his
armorbearer, and said to him, "Draw your sword
and kill me, lest men say of me, 'A woman killed
him.'" So his young man thrust him through, and
he died.
55 And when the men of Israel saw that Abimelech was dead, they departed, every man to his
[1]place.
**56** [a]Thus God repaid the wickedness of Abimelech, which he had done to his father by killing
his seventy brothers.

57 And all the evil of the men of Shechem God returned on their own heads, and on them came [a]the curse of Jotham the son of Jerubbaal.

### *Israel Humiliated*

**10** After Abimelech there [a]arose to save Israel Tola the son of Puah, the son of Dodo, a man of Issachar; and he dwelt in Shamir in the mountains of Ephraim.
2 He judged Israel twenty-three years; and he died and was buried in Shamir.
**3** After him arose Jair, a Gileadite; and he judged Israel twenty-two years.
4 Now he had thirty sons who [a]rode on thirty donkeys; they also had thirty towns, [b]which are called [1]"Havoth Jair" to this day, which *are* in the land of Gilead.
5 And Jair died and was buried in Camon.
**6** Then [a]the children of Israel again did evil in the sight of the LORD, and [b]served the Baals and the Ashtoreths, [c]the gods of Syria, the gods of [d]Sidon, the gods of Moab, the gods of the people of Ammon, and the gods of the Philistines; and they forsook the LORD and did not serve Him.
7 So the anger of the LORD was hot against Israel; and He [a]sold them into the hands of the [b]Philistines and into the hands of the people of [c]Ammon.
8 From that year they [1]harassed and oppressed the children of Israel for eighteen years—all the children of Israel who *were* on the other side of the Jordan in the [a]land of the Amorites, in Gilead.
9 Moreover the people of Ammon crossed over the Jordan to fight against Judah also, against Benjamin, and against the house of Ephraim, so that Israel was severely distressed.
**10** [a]And the children of Israel cried out to the LORD, saying, "We have [b]sinned against You, because we have both forsaken our God and served the Baals!"
11 So the LORD said to the children of Israel, "*Did I* not *deliver you* [a]from the Egyptians and [b]from the Amorites and [c]from the people of Ammon and [d]from the Philistines?
12 "Also [a]the Sidonians [b]and Amalekites and [1]Maonites [c]oppressed you; and you cried out to Me, and I delivered you from their hand.
13 [a]"Yet you have forsaken Me and served other gods. Therefore I will deliver you no more.
14 "Go and [a]cry out to the gods which you have chosen; let them deliver you in your time of distress."
**15** And the children of Israel said to the LORD, "We have sinned! [a]Do to us whatever seems best to You; only deliver us this day, we pray."
16 [a]So they put away the foreign gods from among them and served the LORD. And [b]His soul could no longer endure the misery of Israel.
**17** Then the people of Ammon gathered together and encamped in Gilead. And the children of Israel assembled together and encamped in [a]Mizpah.
18 And the people, the leaders of Gilead, said to one another, "Who *is* the man who will begin the fight against the people of Ammon? He shall [a]be head over all the inhabitants of Gilead."

### *Jephthah Defends Israel*

**11** Now [a]Jephthah the Gileadite was [b]a mighty man of valor, but he *was* the son of a harlot; and Gilead begot Jephthah.
2 Gilead's wife bore sons; and when his wife's sons grew up, they drove Jephthah out, and said to him, "You shall have [a]no inheritance in our father's house, for you *are* the son of another woman."
3 Then Jephthah fled from his brothers and dwelt in the land of [a]Tob; and [b]worthless men banded together with Jephthah and went out *raiding* with him.
**4** It came to pass after a time that the [a]people of Ammon made war against Israel.
5 And so it was, when the people of Ammon made war against Israel, that the elders of Gilead went to get Jephthah from the land of Tob.
6 Then they said to Jephthah, "Come and be our commander, that we may fight against the people of Ammon."
7 So Jephthah said to the elders of Gilead, [a]"Did you not hate me, and expel me from my father's house? Why have you come to me now when you are in [1]distress?"
8 [a]And the elders of Gilead said to Jephthah, "That is why we have [b]turned[1] again to you now, that you may go with us and fight against the people of Ammon, and be [c]our head over all the inhabitants of Gilead."
9 So Jephthah said to the elders of Gilead, "If you take me back home to fight against the people of Ammon, and the LORD delivers them to me, shall I be your head?"
10 And the elders of Gilead said to Jephthah, [a]"The LORD will be a witness between us, if we do not do according to your words."
11 Then Jephthah went with the elders of Gilead, and the people made him [a]head and commander over them; and Jephthah spoke all his words [b]before the LORD in Mizpah.
**12** Now Jephthah sent messengers to the king of the people of Ammon, saying, [a]"What do you have against me, that you have come to fight against me in my land?"
13 And the king of the people of Ammon answered the messengers of Jephthah, [a]"Because Israel took away my land when they came up out of Egypt, from [b]the Arnon as far as [c]the Jabbok, and to the Jordan. Now therefore, restore those *lands* peaceably."
14 So Jephthah again sent messengers to the king of the people of Ammon,
15 and said to him, "Thus says Jephthah: [a]'Israel did not take away the land of Moab, nor the land of the people of Ammon;
16 'for when Israel came up from Egypt, they walked through the wilderness as far as the Red Sea and [a]came to Kadesh.
17 'Then [a]Israel sent messengers to the king of Edom, saying, "Please let me pass through your land." [b]But the king of Edom would not heed. And in like manner they sent to the [c]king of Moab, but he would not *consent.* So Israel [d]remained in Kadesh.
18 'And they [a]went along through the wilderness and [b]bypassed the land of Edom and the land of Moab, came to the east side of the land of Moab, and encamped on the other side of the Arnon. But they did not enter the border of Moab, for the Arnon *was* the border of Moab.
19 'Then [a]Israel sent messengers to Sihon king of the Amorites, king of Heshbon; and Israel said to him, "Please [b]let us pass through your land into our place."

**57** [a]Judg. 9:20

CHAPTER 10
**1** [a]Judg. 2:16
**4** [a]Judg. 5:10; 12:14 [b]Deut. 3:14 [1]Lit. *Towns of Jair,* Num. 32:41; Deut. 3:14
**6** [a]Judg. 2:11; 3:7; 6:1; 13:1 [b]Judg. 2:13 [c]Judg. 2:12 [d]1 Kin. 11:33; Ps. 106:36
**7** [a]Judg. 2:14; 4:2; 1 Sam. 12:9 [b]Judg. 13:1 [c]Judg. 3:13
**8** [a]Num. 32:33 [1]Lit. *shattered*
**10** [a]Judg. 6:6; 1 Sam. 12:10 [b]Deut. 1:41
**11** [a]Ex. 14:30 [b]Num. 21:21, 24, 25 [c]Judg. 3:12, 13 [d]Judg. 3:31
**12** [a]Judg. 1:31; 5:19 [b]Judg. 6:3; 7:12 [c]Ps. 106:42, 43 [1]LXX mss. *Midianites*
**13** [a][Deut. 32:15; Judg. 2:12; Jer. 2:13]
**14** [a]Deut. 32:37, 38
**15** [a]1 Sam. 3:18; 2 Sam. 15:26
**16** [a]2 Chr. 7:14; Jer. 18:7, 8 [b]Ps. 106:44, 45; Is. 63:9
**17** [a]Gen. 31:49; Judg. 11:11, 29
**18** [a]Judg. 11:8, 11

CHAPTER 11
**1** [a]Heb. 11:32 [b]Judg. 6:12; 2 Kin. 5:1
**2** [a]Gen. 21:10; Deut. 23:2
**3** [a]2 Sam. 10:6, 8 [b]1 Sam. 22:2
**4** [a]Judg. 10:9, 17
**7** [a]Gen. 26:27 [1]*trouble*
**8** [a]Judg. 10:18 [b][Luke 17:4] [c]Judg. 10:18 [1]*returned*
**10** [a]Gen. 31:49, 50; Jer. 29:23; 42:5
**11** [a]Judg. 11:8 [b]Judg. 10:17; 20:1; 1 Sam. 10:17
**12** [a]2 Sam. 16:10
**13** [a]Num. 21:24–26 [b]Josh. 13:9 [c]Gen. 32:22
**15** [a]Deut. 2:9, 19
**16** [a]Num. 13:26; 20:1
**17** [a]Num. 20:14 [b]Num. 20:14–21 [c]Josh. 24:9 [d]Num. 20:1
**18** [a]Deut. 2:9, 18, 19 [b]Num. 21:4
**19** [a]Num. 21:21; Deut. 2:26–36 [b]Num. 21:22; Deut. 2:27

20 [a]'But Sihon did not trust Israel to pass through his territory. So Sihon gathered all his people together, encamped in Jahaz, and fought against Israel.

21 'And the LORD God of Israel [a]delivered Sihon and all his people into the hand of Israel, and they [b]defeated[1] them. Thus Israel gained possession of all the land of the Amorites, who inhabited that country.

22 'They took possession of [a]all the territory of the Amorites, from the Arnon to the Jabbok and from the wilderness to the Jordan.

23 'And now the LORD God of Israel has [1]dispossessed the Amorites from before His people Israel; should you then possess it?

24 'Will you not possess whatever [a]Chemosh your god gives you to possess? So whatever [b]the LORD our God takes possession of before us, we will possess.

25 'And now, *are* you any better than [a]Balak the son of Zippor, king of Moab? Did he ever strive against Israel? Did he ever fight against them?

26 'While Israel dwelt in [a]Heshbon and its villages, in [b]Aroer and its villages, and in all the cities along the banks of the Arnon, for three hundred years, why did you not recover *them* within that time?

27 'Therefore I have not sinned against you, but you wronged me by fighting against me. May the LORD, [a]the Judge, [b]render judgment this day between the children of Israel and the people of Ammon.' "

28 However, the king of the people of Ammon did not heed the words which Jephthah sent him.

**29** Then [a]the Spirit of the LORD came upon Jephthah, and he passed through Gilead and Manasseh, and passed through Mizpah of Gilead; and from Mizpah of Gilead he advanced *toward* the people of Ammon.

30 And Jephthah [a]made a vow to the LORD, and said, "If You will indeed deliver the people of Ammon into my hands,

31 "then it will be that whatever comes out of the doors of my house to meet me, when I return in peace from the people of Ammon, [a]shall surely be the LORD's, [b]and I will offer it up as a burnt offering."

**32** So Jephthah advanced toward the people of Ammon to fight against them, and the LORD delivered them into his hands.

33 And he [1]defeated them from Aroer as far as [a]Minnith—twenty cities—and to [2]Abel Keramim, with a very great slaughter. Thus the people of Ammon were subdued before the children of Israel.

**34** When Jephthah came to his house at [a]Mizpah, there was [b]his daughter, coming out to meet him with timbrels and dancing; and she *was his* only child. Besides her he had neither son nor daughter.

35 And it came to pass, when he saw her, that he [a]tore his clothes, and said, "Alas, my daughter! You have brought me very low! You are among those who trouble me! For I [b]have [1]given my word to the LORD, and [c]I cannot [2]go back on it."

36 So she said to him, "My father, *if* you have given your word to the LORD, [a]do to me according to what has gone out of your mouth, because [b]the LORD has avenged you of your enemies, the people of Ammon."

37 Then she said to her father, "Let this thing be done for me: let me alone for two months, that I may go and wander on the mountains and [1]bewail my virginity, my [2]friends and I."

38 So he said, "Go." And he sent her away *for* two months; and she went with her friends, and bewailed her virginity on the mountains.

39 And it was so at the end of two months that she returned to her father, and he [a]carried out his vow with her which he had vowed. She [1]knew no man. And it became a custom in Israel

40 *that* the daughters of Israel went four days each year to [1]lament the daughter of Jephthah the Gileadite.

## *Ephraimites Slain by Jephthah*

**12** Then [a]the men of Ephraim [1]gathered together, crossed over toward Zaphon, and said to Jephthah, "Why did you cross over to fight against the people of Ammon, and did not call us to go with you? We will burn your house down on you with fire!"

2 And Jephthah said to them, "My people and I were in a great struggle with the people of Ammon; and when I called you, you did not deliver me out of their hands.

3 "So when I saw that you would not deliver *me*, I [a]took my life in my hands and crossed over against the people of Ammon; and the LORD delivered them into my hand. Why then have you come up to me this day to fight against me?"

4 Now Jephthah gathered together all the men of Gilead and fought against Ephraim. And the men of Gilead defeated Ephraim, because they said, "You Gileadites [a]*are* fugitives of Ephraim among the Ephraimites *and* among the Manassites."

5 The Gileadites seized the [a]fords of the Jordan before the Ephraimites *arrived*. And when *any* Ephraimite who escaped said, "Let me cross over," the men of Gilead would say to him, "*Are* you an Ephraimite?" If he said, "No,"

6 then they would say to him, "Then say, [a]'Shibboleth'!"[1] And he would say, "Sibboleth," for he could not [2]pronounce *it* right. Then they would take him and kill him at the fords of the Jordan. There fell at that time forty-two thousand Ephraimites.

7 And Jephthah judged Israel six years. Then Jephthah the Gileadite died and was buried in among the cities of Gilead.

**8** After him, Ibzan of Bethlehem judged Israel.

9 He had thirty sons. And he gave away thirty daughters in marriage, and brought in thirty daughters from elsewhere for his sons. He judged Israel seven years.

10 Then Ibzan died and was buried at Bethlehem.

**11** After him, Elon the Zebulunite judged Israel. He judged Israel ten years.

12 And Elon the Zebulunite died and was buried at Aijalon in the country of Zebulun.

**13** After him, Abdon the son of Hillel the Pirathonite judged Israel.

14 He had forty sons and thirty grandsons, who [a]rode on seventy young donkeys. He judged Israel eight years.

15 Then Abdon the son of Hillel the Pirathonite died and was buried in Pirathon in the land of Ephraim, [a]in the mountains of the Amalekites.

**20** [a]Num. 21:23; Deut. 2:27
**21** [a]Josh. 24:8 [b]Num. 21:24, 25 [1]Lit. *struck*
**22** [a]Deut. 2:36, 37
**23** [1]*driven out*
**24** [a]Num. 21:29; 1 Kin. 11:7; Jer. 48:7 [b][Deut. 9:4, 5; Josh. 3:10]
**25** [a]Num. 22:2; Josh. 24:9; Mic. 6:5
**26** [a]Num. 21:25, 26 [b]Deut. 2:36
**27** [a]Gen. 18:25 [b]Gen. 16:5; 31:53; [1 Sam. 24:12, 15]
**29** [a]Judg. 3:10
**30** [a]Gen. 28:20; Num. 30:2; 1 Sam. 1:11
**31** [a]Lev. 27:2, 3, 28; 1 Sam. 1:11 [b]Ps. 66:13
**33** [a]Ezek. 27:17 [1]Lit. *struck* [2]Lit. *Plain of Vineyards*
**34** [a]Judg. 10:17; 11:11 [b]Ex. 15:20; 1 Sam. 18:6; Ps. 68:25; Jer. 31:4
**35** [a]Gen. 37:29, 34 [b]Eccl. 5:2, 4, 5 [c]Num. 30:2 [1]Lit. *opened my mouth* [2]Lit. *take it back*
**36** [a]Num. 30:2 [b]2 Sam. 18:19, 31
**37** [1]*lament* [2]*companions*
**39** [a]Judg. 11:31 [1]Remained a virgin
**40** [1]*commemorate*

CHAPTER 12

**1** [a]Judg. 8:1 [1]*were summoned*
**3** [a]1 Sam. 19:5; 28:21; Job 13:14
**4** [a]1 Sam. 25:10
**5** [a]Josh. 22:11
**6** [a]Ps. 69:2, 15 [1]Lit. *a flowing stream;* used as a test of dialect [2]Lit. *speak so*
**14** [a]Judg. 5:10; 10:4
**15** [a]Judg. 3:13, 27; 5:14

## *The Birth of Samson*

**13** Again the children of Israel [a]did evil in the sight of the LORD, and the LORD delivered them [b]into the hand of the Philistines for forty years.

**2** Now there was a certain man from [a]Zorah, of the family of the Danites, whose name *was* Manoah; and his wife *was* barren and had no children.

3 And the [a]Angel of the LORD appeared to the woman and said to her, "Indeed now, you are barren and have borne no children, but you shall conceive and bear a son.

4 "Now therefore, please be careful [a]not to drink wine or *similar* drink, and not to eat anything unclean.

5 "For behold, you shall conceive and bear a son. And no [a]razor shall come upon his head, for the child shall be [b]a Nazirite to God from the womb; and he shall [c]begin to deliver Israel out of the hand of the Philistines."

**6** So the woman came and told her husband, saying, [a]"A Man of God came to me, and His [b]countenance[1] *was* like the countenance of the Angel of God, very awesome; but I [c]did not ask Him where He *was* from, and He did not tell me His name.

7 "And He said to me, 'Behold, you shall conceive and bear a son. Now drink no wine or *similar* drink, nor eat anything unclean, for the child shall be a Nazirite to God from the womb to the day of his death.' "

**8** Then Manoah prayed to the LORD, and said, "O my Lord, please let the Man of God whom You sent come to us again and teach us what we shall do for the child who will be born."

9 And God listened to the voice of Manoah, and the Angel of God came to the woman again as she was sitting in the field; but Manoah her husband *was* not with her.

10 Then the woman ran in haste and told her husband, and said to him, "Look, the Man who came to me the *other* day has just now appeared to me!"

11 So Manoah arose and followed his wife. When he came to the Man, he said to Him, "Are You the Man who spoke to this woman?" And He said, "I *am.*"

12 Manoah said, "Now let Your words come *to pass!* What will be the boy's rule of life, and his work?"

13 So the Angel of the LORD said to Manoah, "Of all that I said to the woman let her be careful.

14 "She may not eat anything that comes from the vine, [a]nor may she drink wine or *similar* drink, nor eat anything unclean. All that I commanded her let her observe."

**15** Then Manoah said to the Angel of the LORD, "Please [a]let us detain You, and we will prepare a young goat for You."

16 And the Angel of the LORD said to Manoah, "Though you detain Me, I will not eat your food. But if you offer a burnt offering, you must offer it to the LORD." (For Manoah did not know He *was* the Angel of the LORD.)

17 Then Manoah said to the Angel of the LORD, "What *is* Your name, that when Your words come *to pass* we may honor You?"

18 And the Angel of the LORD said to him, [a]"Why do you ask My name, seeing it *is* wonderful?"

19 So Manoah took the young goat with the grain offering, [a]and offered it upon the rock to the LORD. And He did a wondrous thing while Manoah and his wife looked on—

20 it happened as the flame went up toward heaven from the altar—the Angel of the LORD ascended in the flame of the altar! When Manoah and his wife saw *this,* they [a]fell on their faces to the ground.

21 When the Angel of the LORD appeared no more to Manoah and his wife, [a]then Manoah knew that He *was* the Angel of the LORD.

22 And Manoah said to his wife, [a]"We shall surely die, because we have seen God!"

23 But his wife said to him, "If the LORD had desired to kill us, He would not have accepted a burnt offering and a grain offering from our hands, nor would He have shown us all these *things,* nor would He have told us *such things* as these at this time."

**24** So the woman bore a son and called his name [a]Samson; and [b]the child grew, and the LORD blessed him.

25 [a]And the Spirit of the LORD began to move upon him at [1]Mahaneh Dan [b]between Zorah and [c]Eshtaol.

## *Samson's Feast and Riddle*

**14** Now Samson went down [a]to Timnah, and [b]saw a woman in Timnah of the daughters of the Philistines.

2 So he went up and told his father and mother, saying, "I have seen a woman in Timnah of the daughters of the Philistines; now therefore, [a]get her for me as a wife."

3 Then his father and mother said to him, "*Is there* no woman among the daughters of [a]your brethren, or among all my people, that you must go and get a wife from the [b]uncircumcised Philistines?" And Samson said to his father, "Get her for me, for [1]she pleases me well."

4 But his father and mother did not know that it was [a]of the LORD—that He was seeking an occasion to move against the Philistines. For at that time [b]the Philistines had dominion over Israel.

5 So Samson went down to Timnah with his father and mother, and came to the vineyards of Timnah.

Now *to his* surprise, a young lion *came* roaring against him.

6 And [a]the Spirit of the LORD came mightily upon him, and he tore the lion apart as one would have torn apart a young goat, though *he had* nothing in his hand. But he did not tell his father or his mother what he had done.

7 Then he went down and talked with the woman; and she pleased Samson well.

8 After some time, when he returned to get her, he turned aside to see the carcass of the lion. And behold, a swarm of bees and honey *were* in the carcass of the lion.

9 He took some of it in his hands and went along, eating. When he came to his father and mother, he gave *some* to them, and they also ate. But he did not tell them that he had taken the honey out of the [a]carcass of the lion.

**10** So his father went down to the woman. And Samson gave a feast there, for young men used to do so.

11 And it happened, when they saw him, that they brought thirty companions to be with him.

CHAPTER 13

**1** [a]Judg. 2:11 [b]Judg. 10:7; 1 Sam. 12:9
**2** [a]Josh. 19:41; Judg. 16:31
**3** [a]Judg. 6:12
**4** [a]Num. 6:2, 3, 20; Judg. 13:4; Luke 1:15
**5** [a]Num. 6:5; 1 Sam. 1:11 [b]Num. 6:2 [c]1 Sam. 7:13; 2 Sam. 8:1; 1 Chr. 18:1
**6** [a]Gen. 32:24–30 [b]Matt. 28:3; Luke 9:29; Acts 6:15 [c]Judg. 13:17, 18 [1]*appearance*
**14** [a]Num. 6:3, 4; Judg. 13:4
**15** [a]Gen. 18:5; Judg. 6:18
**18** [a]Gen. 32:29
**19** [a]Judg. 6:19–21
**20** [a]Lev. 9:24; 1 Chr. 21:16; Ezek. 1:28; Matt. 17:6
**21** [a]Judg. 6:22
**22** [a]Gen. 32:30; Ex. 33:20; Deut. 5:26; Judg. 6:22, 23
**24** [a]Heb. 11:32 [b]1 Sam. 3:19; Luke 1:80
**25** [a]Judg. 3:10; 1 Sam. 11:6; Matt. 4:1 [b]Josh. 15:33; Judg. 18:11 [c]Judg. 16:31 [1]Lit. *Camp of Dan,* Judg. 18:12

CHAPTER 14

**1** [a]Gen. 38:13; Josh. 15:10, 57 [b]Gen. 34:2
**2** [a]Gen. 21:21
**3** [a]Gen. 24:3, 4 [b]Gen. 34:14; Ex. 34:16; Deut. 7:3 [1]Lit. *she is right in my eyes*
**4** [a]Josh. 11:20; 1 Kin. 12:15; 2 Kin. 6:33; 2 Chr. 10:15 [b]Deut. 28:48; Judg. 13:1
**6** [a]Judg. 3:10
**9** [a]Lev. 11:27

12 Then Samson said to them, "Let me [a]pose a riddle to you. If you can correctly solve and explain it to me [b]within the seven days of the feast, then I will give you thirty linen garments and thirty [c]changes of clothing.
13 "But if you cannot explain *it* to me, then you shall give me thirty linen garments and thirty changes of clothing." And they said to him, [a]"Pose your riddle, that we may hear it."
14 So he said to them:

"Out of the eater came something to eat,
And out of the strong
came something sweet."

Now for three days they could not explain the riddle.
**15** But it came to pass on the [1]seventh day that they said to Samson's wife, [a]"Entice your husband, that he may explain the riddle to us, [b]or else we will burn you and your father's house with fire. Have you invited us in order to take what is ours? *Is that* not *so?*"
16 Then Samson's wife wept on him, and said, [a]"You only hate me! You do not love me! You have posed a riddle to the sons of my people, but you have not explained *it* to me." And he said to her, "Look, I have not explained *it* to my father or my mother; so should I explain *it* to you?"
17 Now she had wept on him the seven days while their feast lasted. And it happened on the seventh day that he told her, because she pressed him so much. Then she explained the riddle to the sons of her people.
18 So the men of the city said to him on the seventh day before the sun went down:

"What *is* sweeter than honey?
And what *is* stronger than a lion?"

And he said to them:

"If you had not plowed with my heifer,
You would not have solved my riddle!"

**19** Then [a]the Spirit of the LORD came upon him mightily, and he went down to Ashkelon and killed thirty of their men, took their apparel, and gave the changes *of clothing* to those who had explained the riddle. So his anger was aroused, and he went back up to his father's house.
20 And Samson's wife [a]was *given* to his companion, who had been [b]his best man.

### *Samson Burns the Philistines' Corn*

**15** After a while, in the time of wheat harvest, it happened that Samson visited his wife with a [a]young goat. And he said, "Let me go in to my wife, into *her* room." But her father would not permit him to go in.
2 Her father said, "I really thought that you thoroughly [a]hated her; therefore I gave her to your companion. *Is* not her younger sister better than she? Please, take her instead."
3 And Samson said to them, "This time I shall be blameless regarding the Philistines if I harm them!"
4 Then Samson went and caught three hundred foxes; and he took torches, turned *the foxes* tail to tail, and put a torch between each pair of tails.
5 When he had set the torches on fire, he let *the foxes* go into the standing grain of the Philistines, and burned up both the shocks and the standing grain, as well as the vineyards *and* olive groves.
6 Then the Philistines said, "Who has done this?" And they answered, "Samson, the son-in-law of the Timnite, because he has taken his wife and given her to his companion." [a]So the Philistines came up and burned her and her father with fire.
7 Samson said to them, "Since you would do a thing like this, I will surely take revenge on you, and after that I will cease."
8 So he attacked them hip and thigh with a great slaughter; then he went down and dwelt in the cleft of the rock of [a]Etam.
**9** Now the Philistines went up, encamped in Judah, and deployed themselves [a]against Lehi.
10 And the men of Judah said, "Why have you come up against us?" So they answered, "We have come up to [1]arrest Samson, to do to him as he has done to us."
11 Then three thousand men of Judah went down to the cleft of the rock of Etam, and said to Samson, "Do you not know that the Philistines [a]rule over us? What *is* this you have done to us?" And he said to them, "As they did to me, so I have done to them."
12 But they said to him, "We have come down to arrest you, that we may deliver you into the hand of the Philistines." Then Samson said to them, "Swear to me that you will not kill me yourselves."
13 So they spoke to him, saying, "No, but we will tie you securely and deliver you into their hand; but we will surely not kill you." And they bound him with two [a]new ropes and brought him up from the rock.
**14** When he came to Lehi, the Philistines came shouting against him. Then [a]the Spirit of the LORD came mightily upon him; and the ropes that *were* on his arms became like flax that is burned with fire, and his bonds [1]broke loose from his hands.
15 He found a fresh jawbone of a donkey, reached out his hand and took it, and [a]killed a thousand men with it.
16 Then Samson said:

"With the jawbone of a donkey,
Heaps upon heaps,
With the jawbone of a donkey
I have slain a thousand men!"

17 And so it was, when he had finished speaking, that he threw the jawbone from his hand, and called that place [1]Ramath Lehi.
**18** Then he became very thirsty; so he cried out to the LORD and said, [a]"You have given this great deliverance by the hand of Your servant; and now shall I die of thirst and fall into the hand of the uncircumcised?"
19 So God split the hollow place that *is* in [1]Lehi, and water came out, and he drank; and [a]his spirit returned, and he revived. Therefore he called its name [2]En Hakkore, which is in Lehi to this day.
20 And [a]he judged Israel [b]twenty years [c]in the days of the Philistines.

### *Samson and Delilah*

**16** Now Samson went to [a]Gaza and saw a harlot there, and went in to her.
2 *When* the Gazites *were told,* "Samson has come here!" they [a]surrounded *the place* and lay in wait for him all night at the gate of the city. They were quiet all night, saying, "In the morning, when it is daylight, we will kill him."

---

12 [a]1 Kin. 10:1; Ezek. 17:2 [b]Gen. 29:27 [c]Gen. 45:22; 2 Kin. 5:22
13 [a]Ezek. 17:2
15 [a]Judg. 16:5 [b]Judg. 15:6 [1]So with MT, Tg., Vg.; LXX, [Syr.] *fourth*
16 [a]Judg. 16:15
19 [a]Judg. 3:10; 13:25
20 [a]Judg. 15:2 [b]John 3:29

CHAPTER 15
1 [a]Gen. 38:17
2 [a]Judg. 14:20
6 [a]Judg. 14:15
8 [a]2 Chr. 11:6
9 [a]Judg. 15:19
10 [1]Lit. *bind*
11 [a]Lev. 26:25; Deut. 28:43; Judg. 13:1; 14:4; Ps. 106:40–42
13 [a]Judg. 16:11, 12
14 [a]Judg. 3:10; 14:6 [1]Lit. *were melted*
15 [a]Lev. 26:8; Josh. 23:10; Judg. 3:31
17 [1]Lit. *Jawbone Height*
18 [a]Ps. 3:7
19 [a]Gen. 45:27; Is. 40:29 [1]Lit. *Jawbone,* Judg. 15:14 [2]Lit. *Spring of the Caller*
20 [a]Judg. 10:2; 12:7–14 [b]Judg. 16:31 [c]Judg. 13:1

CHAPTER 16
1 [a]Josh. 15:47
2 [a]1 Sam. 23:26; Ps. 118:10–12

3 And Samson lay *low* till midnight; then he arose at midnight, took hold of the doors of the gate of the city and the two gateposts, pulled them up, bar and all, put *them* on his shoulders, and carried them to the top of the hill that faces Hebron.

**4** Afterward it happened that he loved a woman in the Valley of Sorek, whose name *was* Delilah.

5 And the [a]lords of the Philistines came up to her and said to her, [b]"Entice him, and find out where his great strength *lies,* and by what *means* we may overpower him, that we may bind him to afflict him; and every one of us will give you eleven hundred *pieces* of silver."

**6** So Delilah said to Samson, "Please tell me where your great strength *lies,* and with what you may be bound to afflict you."

7 And Samson said to her, "If they bind me with seven fresh bowstrings, not yet dried, then I shall become weak, and be like any *other* man."

8 So the lords of the Philistines brought up to her seven fresh bowstrings, not yet dried, and she bound him with them.

9 Now *men were* lying in wait, staying with her in the room. And she said to him, "The Philistines *are* upon you, Samson!" But he broke the bowstrings as a strand of yarn breaks when it touches fire. So the secret of his strength was not known.

**10** Then Delilah said to Samson, "Look, you have mocked me and told me lies. Now, please tell me what you may be bound with."

11 So he said to her, "If they bind me securely with [a]new ropes [1]that have never been used, then I shall become weak, and be like any *other* man."

12 Therefore Delilah took new ropes and bound him with them, and said to him, "The Philistines *are* upon you, Samson!" And *men were* lying in wait, staying in the room. But he broke them off his arms like a thread.

**13** Delilah said to Samson, "Until now you have mocked me and told me lies. Tell me what you may be bound with." And he said to her, "If you weave the seven locks of my head into the web of the loom"—

14 So she wove *it* tightly with the batten of the loom, and said to him, "The Philistines *are* upon you, Samson!" But he awoke from his sleep, and pulled out the batten and the web from the loom.

**15** Then she said to him, [a]"How can you say, 'I love you,' when your heart *is* not with me? You have mocked me these three times, and have not told me where your great strength *lies.*"

16 And it came to pass, when she pestered him daily with her words and pressed him, *so* that his soul was [1]vexed to death,

17 that he [a]told her all his heart, and said to her, [b]"No razor has ever come upon my head, for I *have been* a Nazirite to God from my mother's womb. If I am shaven, then my strength will leave me, and I shall become weak, and be like any *other* man."

**18** When Delilah saw that he had told her all his heart, she sent and called for the lords of the Philistines, saying, "Come up once more, for he has told me all his heart." So the lords of the Philistines came up to her and brought the money in their hand.

19 [a]Then she lulled him to sleep on her knees, and called for a man and had him shave off the seven locks of his head. Then [1]she began to torment him, and his strength left him.

20 And she said, "The Philistines *are* upon you, Samson!" So he awoke from his sleep, and said, "I will go out as before, at other times, and shake myself free!" But he did not know that the LORD [a]had departed from him.

**21** Then the Philistines took him and [1]put out his [a]eyes, and brought him down to Gaza. They bound him with bronze fetters, and he became a grinder in the prison.

22 However, the hair of his head began to grow again after it had been shaven.

**23** Now the lords of the Philistines gathered together to offer a great sacrifice to [a]Dagon their god, and to rejoice. And they said:

"Our god has delivered into our hands
Samson our enemy!"

24 When the people saw him, they [a]praised their god; for they said:

"Our god has delivered into our hands our enemy,
The destroyer of our land,
And the one who multiplied our dead."

25 So it happened, when their hearts were [a]merry, that they said, "Call for Samson, that he may perform for us." So they called for Samson from the prison, and he performed for them. And they stationed him between the pillars.

26 Then Samson said to the lad who held him by the hand, "Let me feel the pillars which support the temple, so that I can lean on them."

27 Now the temple was full of men and women. All the lords of the Philistines *were* there—about three thousand men and women on the [a]roof watching while Samson performed.

**28** Then Samson called to the LORD, saying, "O Lord GOD, [a]remember me, I pray! Strengthen me, I pray, just this once, O God, that I may with one *blow* take vengeance on the Philistines for my two eyes!"

29 And Samson took hold of the two middle pillars which supported the temple, and he braced himself against them, one on his right and the other on his left.

30 Then Samson said, "Let me die with the Philistines!" And he pushed with *all his* might, and the temple fell on the lords and all the people who *were* in it. So the dead that he killed at his death were more than he had killed in his life.

31 And his brothers and all his father's household came down and took him, and brought *him* up and [a]buried him between Zorah and Eshtaol in the tomb of his father Manoah. He had judged Israel [b]twenty years.

### *Micah's Idols*

**17** Now there was a man from the mountains of Ephraim, whose name *was* [a]Micah.

2 And he said to his mother, "The eleven hundred *shekels* of silver that were taken from you, and on which you [a]put a curse, even saying it in my ears—here *is* the silver with me; I took it." And his mother said, [b]"*May you be* blessed by the LORD, my son!"

3 So when he had returned the eleven hundred *shekels* of silver to his mother, his mother said, "I had wholly dedicated the silver from my hand to the LORD for my son, to [a]make a carved image and a molded image; now therefore, I will return it to you."

**5** [a]Josh. 13:3 [b]Judg. 14:15
**11** [a]Judg. 15:13 [1]Lit. *with which work has never been done*
**15** [a]Judg. 14:16
**16** [1]Lit. *impatient to the point of*
**17** [a][Mic. 7:5] [b]Num. 6:5; Judg. 13:5
**19** [a]Prov. 7:26, 27 [1]So with MT, Tg., Vg.; LXX *he began to be weak,*
**20** [a]Num. 14:9, 42, 43; [Josh. 7:12]; 1 Sam. 16:14; 18:12; 28:15, 16; 2 Chr. 15:2
**21** [a]2 Kin. 25:7 [1]Lit. *bored out*
**23** [a]1 Sam. 5:2
**24** [a]Dan. 5:4
**25** [a]Judg. 9:27
**27** [a]Deut. 22:8
**28** [a]Jer. 15:15
**31** [a]Judg. 13:25 [b]Judg. 15:20

CHAPTER 17
**1** [a]Judg. 18:2
**2** [a]Lev. 5:1 [b]Gen. 14:19
**3** [a]Ex. 20:4, 23; 34:17; Lev. 19:4

4 Thus he returned the silver to his mother. Then his mother [a]took two hundred *shekels* of silver and gave them to the silversmith, and he made it into a carved image and a molded image; and they were in the house of Micah.
5 The man Micah had a [a]shrine, and made an [b]ephod and [c]household[1] idols; and he consecrated one of his sons, who became his priest.
6 [a]In those days *there was* no king in Israel; [b]everyone did *what was* right in his own eyes.
**7** Now there was a young man from [a]Bethlehem in Judah, of the family of Judah; he *was* a Levite, and [b]was staying there.
8 The man departed from the city of Bethlehem in Judah to stay wherever he could find *a place*. Then he came to the mountains of Ephraim, to the house of Micah, as he journeyed.
9 And Micah said to him, "Where do you come from?" So he said to him, "I *am* a Levite from Bethlehem in Judah, and I am on my way to find *a place* to stay."
10 Micah said to him, "Dwell with me, [a]and be a [b]father and a priest to me, and I will give you ten *shekels* of silver per year, a suit of clothes, and your sustenance." So the Levite went in.
11 Then the Levite was content to dwell with the man; and the young man became like one of his sons to him.
12 So Micah [a]consecrated[1] the Levite, and the young man [b]became his priest, and lived in the house of Micah.
13 Then Micah said, "Now I know that the LORD will be good to me, since I have a Levite as [a]priest!"

### *Micah and the Danites*

**18** In [a]those days *there was* no king in Israel. And in those days [b]the tribe of the Danites was seeking an inheritance for itself to dwell in; for until that day *their* inheritance among the tribes of Israel had not fallen to them.
2 So the children of Dan sent five men of their family from their territory, men of valor from [a]Zorah and Eshtaol, [b]to spy out the land and search it. They said to them, "Go, search the land." So they went to the mountains of Ephraim, to the [c]house of Micah, and lodged there.
3 While they *were* at the house of Micah, they recognized the voice of the young Levite. They turned aside and said to him, "Who brought you here? What are you doing in this *place?* What do you have here?"
4 He said to them, "Thus and so Micah did for me. He has [a]hired me, and I have become his priest."
5 So they said to him, "Please [a]inquire [b]of God, that we may know whether the journey on which we go will be prosperous."
6 And the priest said to them, [a]"Go in peace. [1]The presence of the LORD *be* with you on your way."
**7** So the five men departed and went to [a]Laish. They saw the people who *were* there, [b]how they dwelt safely, in the manner of the Sidonians, quiet and secure. *There were* no rulers in the land who might put *them* to shame for anything. They *were* far from the [c]Sidonians, and they had no ties [1]with anyone.
8 Then [1]*the spies* came back to their brethren at [a]Zorah and Eshtaol, and their brethren said to them, "What *is* your *report?"*
9 So they said, [a]"Arise, let us go up against them. For we have seen the land, and indeed it *is* very good. *Would* you [b]*do* nothing? Do not hesitate to go, *and* enter to possess the land.
10 "When you go, you will come to a [a]secure people and a large land. For God has given it into your hands, [b]a place where *there is* no lack of anything that *is* on the earth."
**11** And six hundred men of the family of the Danites went from there, from Zorah and Eshtaol, armed with weapons of war.
12 Then they went up and encamped in [a]Kirjath Jearim in Judah. (Therefore they call that place [b]Mahaneh Dan[1] to this day. There *it is,* west of Kirjath Jearim.)
13 And they passed from there to the mountains of Ephraim, and came to [a]the house of Micah.
**14** [a]Then the five men who had gone to spy out the country of Laish answered and said to their brethren, "Do you know that [b]there are in these houses an ephod, household idols, a carved image, and a molded image? Now therefore, consider what you should do."
15 So they turned aside there, and came to the house of the young Levite man—to the house of Micah—and greeted him.
16 The [a]six hundred men armed with their weapons of war, who *were* of the children of Dan, stood by the entrance of the gate.
17 Then [a]the five men who had gone to spy out the land went up. Entering there, they took [b]the carved image, the ephod, the household idols, and the molded image. The priest stood at the entrance of the gate with the six hundred men *who were* armed with weapons of war.
18 When these went into Micah's house and took the carved image, the ephod, the household idols, and the molded image, the priest said to them, "What are you doing?"
19 And they said to him, "Be quiet, [a]put your hand over your mouth, and come with us; [b]be a father and a priest to us. *Is it* better for you to be a priest to the household of one man, or that you be a priest to a tribe and a family in Israel?"
20 So the priest's heart was glad; and he took the ephod, the household idols, and the carved image, and took his place among the people.
21 Then they turned and departed, and put the little ones, the livestock, and the goods in front of them.
**22** When they were a good way from the house of Micah, the men who *were* in the houses near Micah's house gathered together and overtook the children of Dan.
23 And they called out to the children of Dan. So they turned around and said to Micah, [a]"What ails you, that you have gathered such a company?"
24 So he said, "You have [a]taken away my [1]gods which I made, and the priest, and you have gone away. Now what more do I have? How can you say to me, 'What ails you?' "
25 And the children of Dan said to him, "Do not let your voice be heard among us, lest [1]angry men fall upon you, and you lose your life, with the lives of your household!"
26 Then the children of Dan went their way. And when Micah saw that they *were* too strong for him, he turned and went back to his house.
**27** So they took *the things* Micah had made, and the priest who had belonged to him, and went to Laish, to a people quiet and secure; [a]and they

**4** [a]Is. 46:6
**5** [a]Judg. 18:24 [b]Judg. 8:27; 18:14 [c]Gen. 31:19, 30; Hos. 3:4 [1]Heb. *teraphim*
**6** [a]Judg. 18:1; 19:1 [b]Deut. 12:8; Judg. 21:25
**7** [a]Josh. 19:15; Judg. 19:1; Ruth 1:1, 2; Mic. 5:2; Matt. 2:1, 5, 6 [b]Deut. 18:6
**10** [a]Judg. 18:19 [b]Gen. 45:8; Job 29:16
**12** [a]Judg. 17:5 [b]Judg. 18:30 [1]Lit. *filled the hand of*
**13** [a]Judg. 18:4

CHAPTER 18
**1** [a]Judg. 17:6; 19:1; 21:25 [b]Josh. 19:40–48
**2** [a]Judg. 13:25 [b]Num. 13:17; Josh. 2:1 [c]Judg. 17:1
**4** [a]Judg. 17:10, 12
**5** [a]1 Kin. 22:5; [Is. 30:1]; Hos. 4:12 [b]Judg. 1:1; 17:5; 18:14
**6** [a]1 Kin. 22:6 [1]Lit. *The* LORD *is before the way in which you go*
**7** [a]Josh. 19:47 [b]Judg. 18:27–29 [c]Judg. 10:12 [1]So with MT, Tg., Vg.; LXX *with Syria*
**8** [a]Judg. 18:2 [1]Lit. *they*
**9** [a]Num. 13:30; Josh. 2:23, 24 [b]1 Kin. 22:3
**10** [a]Judg. 18:7, 27 [b]Deut. 8:9
**12** [a]Josh. 15:60 [b]Judg. 13:25 [1]Lit. *Camp of Dan*
**13** [a]Judg. 18:2
**14** [a]1 Sam. 14:28 [b]Judg. 17:5
**16** [a]Judg. 18:11
**17** [a]Judg. 18:2, 14 [b]Judg. 17:4, 5
**19** [a]Job 21:5; 29:9; 40:4; Mic. 7:16 [b]Judg. 17:10
**23** [a]2 Kin. 6:28
**24** [a]Gen. 31:30; Judg. 17:5 [1]*idols*
**25** [1]Lit. *bitter of soul*
**27** [a]Josh. 19:47

struck them with the edge of the sword and
burned the city with fire.
28 *There was* no deliverer, because it *was* [a]far
from Sidon, and they had no ties with anyone. It
was in the valley that belongs [b]to Beth Rehob. So
they rebuilt the city and dwelt there.
29 And [a]they called the name of the city [b]Dan,
after the name of Dan their father, who was born
to Israel. However, the name of the city formerly
*was* Laish.
**30** Then the children of Dan set up for themselves the carved image; and Jonathan the son of
Gershom, the son of [1]Manasseh, and his sons were
priests to the tribe of Dan [a]until the day of the
captivity of the land.
31 So they set up for themselves Micah's carved
image which he made, [a]all the time that the house
of God was in Shiloh.

### *The Levite and His Concubine*

**19** And it came to pass in those days, [a]when
*there was* no king in Israel, that there was a
certain Levite staying in the remote mountains of
Ephraim. He took for himself a concubine from
[b]Bethlehem in Judah.
2 But his concubine played the harlot against
him, and went away from him to her father's
house at Bethlehem in Judah, and was there four
whole months.
3 Then her husband arose and went after her, to
[a]speak [1]kindly to her *and* bring her back, having
his servant and a couple of donkeys with him. So
she brought him into her father's house; and when
the father of the young woman saw him, he was
glad to meet him.
4 Now his father-in-law, the young woman's
father, detained him; and he stayed with him
three days. So they ate and drank and lodged
there.
**5** Then it came to pass on the fourth day that
they arose early in the morning, and he stood to
depart; but the young woman's father said to his
son-in-law, [a]"Refresh your heart with a morsel of
bread, and afterward go your way."
6 So they sat down, and the two of them ate and
drank together. Then the young woman's father
said to the man, "Please be content to stay all
night, and let your heart be merry."
7 And when the man stood to depart, his father-
in-law urged him; so he lodged there again.
8 Then he arose early in the morning on the
fifth day to depart, but the young woman's father
said, "Please refresh your heart." So they delayed
until afternoon; and both of them ate.
9 And when the man stood to depart—he and
his concubine and his servant—his father-in-law,
the young woman's father, said to him, "Look, the
day is now drawing toward evening; please spend
the night. See, the day is coming to an end; lodge
here, that your heart may be merry. Tomorrow go
your way early, so that you may get [1]home."
**10** However, the man was not willing to spend
that night; so he rose and departed, and came to
opposite [a]Jebus (that *is*, Jerusalem). With him
were the two saddled donkeys; his concubine *was*
also with him.
11 They *were* near Jebus, and the day was far
spent; and the servant said to his master, "Come,
please, and let us turn aside into this city [a]of the
Jebusites and lodge in it."
12 But his master said to him, "We will not turn
aside here into a city of foreigners, who *are* not of
the children of Israel; we will go on [a]to Gibeah."
13 So he said to his servant, "Come, let us draw
near to one of these places, and spend the night in
Gibeah or in [a]Ramah."
14 And they passed by and went their way; and
the sun went down on them near Gibeah, which
belongs to Benjamin.
15 They turned aside there to go in to lodge in
Gibeah. And when he went in, he sat down in the
open square of the city, for no one would [a]take
them into *his* house to spend the night.
**16** Just then an old man came in from [a]his work
in the field at evening, who also *was* from the
mountains of Ephraim; he was staying in Gibeah,
whereas the men of the place *were* Benjamites.
17 And when he raised his eyes, he saw the
traveler in the open square of the city; and the old
man said, "Where are you going, and where do
you come from?"
18 So he said to him, "We *are* passing from
Bethlehem in Judah toward the remote mountains
of Ephraim; I *am* from there. I went to Bethlehem
in Judah; *now* I am going to [a]the house of the
LORD. But there *is* no one who will take me into
his house,
19 "although we have both straw and fodder for
our donkeys, and bread and wine for myself, for
your female servant, and for the young man *who
is* with your servant; *there is* no lack of anything."
20 And the old man said, [a]"Peace *be* with you!
However, *let* all your needs *be* my responsibility;
[b]only do not spend the night in the open square."
21 [a]So he brought him into his house, and gave
fodder to the donkeys. [b]And they washed their
feet, and ate and drank.
**22** As they were [a]enjoying themselves, suddenly
[b]certain men of the city, [c]perverted[1] men, surrounded the house *and* beat on the door. They
spoke to the master of the house, the old man,
saying, [d]"Bring out the man who came to your
house, that we may know him *carnally!*"
23 But [a]the man, the master of the house, went
out to them and said to them, "No, my brethren! I
beg you, do not act *so* wickedly! Seeing this man
has come into my house, [b]do not commit this
outrage.
24 [a]"Look, *here is* my virgin daughter and [1]*the
man's* concubine; let me bring them out now.
[b]Humble them, and do with them as you please;
but to this man do not do such a vile thing!"
25 But the men would not heed him. So the man
took his concubine and brought *her* out to them.
And they [a]knew her and abused her all night until
morning; and when the day began to break, they
let her go.
26 Then the woman came as the day was dawning, and fell down at the door of the man's house
where her master *was,* till it was light.
**27** When her master arose in the morning, and
opened the doors of the house and went out to go
his way, there was his concubine, fallen *at* the
door of the house with her hands on the threshold.
28 And he said to her, "Get up and let us be
going." But [a]there was no answer. So the man
lifted her onto the donkey; and the man got up
and went to his place.
**29** When he entered his house he took a knife,
laid hold of his concubine, and [a]divided her into
twelve pieces, [1]limb by limb, and sent her throughout all the territory of Israel.

**28** [a]Judg. 18:7 [b]Num. 13:21; 2 Sam. 10:6
**29** [a]Josh. 19:47 [b]Judg. 20:1; 1 Kin. 12:29, 30; 15:20
**30** [a]2 Kin. 15:29 [1]LXX, Vg. *Moses*
**31** [a]Deut. 12:1–32; Josh. 18:1, 8; Judg. 19:18; 21:12

CHAPTER 19

**1** [a]Judg. 17:6; 18:1; 21:25 [b]Judg. 17:7; Ruth 1:1
**3** [a]Gen. 34:3; 50:21 [1]Lit. *to her heart*
**5** [a]Gen. 18:5; Judg. 19:8; Ps. 104:15
**9** [1]Lit. *to your tent*
**10** [a]Josh. 18:28; 1 Chr. 11:4, 5
**11** [a]Josh. 15:8, 63; Judg. 1:21; 2 Sam. 5:6
**12** [a]Josh. 18:28
**13** [a]Josh. 18:25
**15** [a]Matt. 25:43
**16** [a]Ps. 104:23
**18** [a]Josh. 18:1; Judg. 18:31; 20:18; 1 Sam. 1:3, 7
**20** [a]Gen. 43:23; Judg. 6:23; 1 Sam. 25:6 [b]Gen. 19:2
**21** [a]Gen. 24:32; 43:24 [b]Gen. 18:4; John 13:5
**22** [a]Judg. 16:25; 19:6, 9 [b]Gen. 19:4, 5; Judg. 20:5; Hos. 9:9; 10:9 [c]Deut. 13:13; 1 Sam. 2:12; 1 Kin. 21:10; [2 Cor. 6:15] [d]Gen. 19:5; [Rom. 1:26, 27] [1]Lit. *sons of Belial*
**23** [a]Gen. 19:6, 7 [b]Gen. 34:7; Deut. 22:21; Judg. 20:6, 10; 2 Sam. 13:12
**24** [a]Gen. 19:8 [b]Gen. 34:2; Deut. 21:14 [1]Lit. *his*
**25** [a]Gen. 4:1
**28** [a]Judg. 20:5
**29** [a]Judg. 20:6; 1 Sam. 11:7 [1]Lit. *with her bones*

30 And so it was that all who saw it said, "No
such deed has been done or seen from the day
that the children of Israel came up from the land
of Egypt until this day. Consider it, [a]confer, and
speak up!"

### *The War Against the Benjamites*

**20** So [a]all the children of Israel came out, from
[b]Dan to [c]Beersheba, as well as from the land
of Gilead, and the congregation gathered together
as one man before the LORD [d]at Mizpah.
2 And the leaders of all the people, all the tribes
of Israel, presented themselves in the assembly of
the people of God, four hundred thousand foot
soldiers [a]who drew the sword.
3 (Now the children of Benjamin heard that the
children of Israel had gone up to Mizpah.) Then
the children of Israel said, "Tell *us,* how did this
wicked deed happen?"
4 So the Levite, the husband of the woman who
was murdered, answered and said, "My concubine
and [a]I went into Gibeah, which belongs to Benjamin, to spend the night.
5 [a]"And the men of Gibeah rose against me, and
surrounded the house at night because of me.
They intended to kill me, [b]but instead they ravished my concubine so that she died.
6 "So [a]I took hold of my concubine, cut her in
pieces, and sent her throughout all the territory of
the inheritance of Israel, because they [b]committed
lewdness and outrage in Israel.
7 "Look! All of you *are* children of Israel; [a]give
your advice and counsel here and now!"
**8** So all the people arose as one man, saying,
"None *of us* will go to his tent, nor will any turn
back to his house;
9 "but now this *is* the thing which we will do to
Gibeah: *We will go up* [a]against it by lot.
10 "We will take ten men out of *every* hundred
throughout all the tribes of Israel, a hundred out
of *every* thousand, and a thousand out of *every*
ten thousand, to make provisions for the people,
that when they come to Gibeah in Benjamin, they
may repay all the vileness that they have done in
Israel."
11 So all the men of Israel were gathered against
the city, united together as one man.
**12** [a]Then the tribes of Israel sent men through all
the tribe of Benjamin, saying, "What *is* this wickedness that has occurred among you?
13 "Now therefore, deliver up the men, [a]the
[1]perverted men who *are* in Gibeah, that we may
put them to death and [b]remove the evil from
Israel!" But the children of Benjamin would not
listen to the voice of their brethren, the children
of Israel.
14 Instead, the children of Benjamin gathered
together from their cities to Gibeah, to go to
battle against the children of Israel.
15 And from their cities at that time [a]the children
of Benjamin numbered twenty-six thousand men
who drew the sword, besides the inhabitants of
Gibeah, who numbered seven hundred select men.
16 Among all this people *were* seven hundred
select men *who were* [a]left-handed; every one
could sling a stone at a hair's *breadth* and not
miss.
17 Now besides Benjamin, the men of Israel
numbered four hundred thousand men who drew
the sword; all of these *were* men of war.
**18** Then the children of Israel arose and [a]went up
to [1]the house of God to [b]inquire of God. They said,
"Which of us shall go up first to battle against the
children of Benjamin?" The LORD said, [c]"Judah
first!"
19 So the children of Israel rose in the morning
and encamped against Gibeah.
20 And the men of Israel went out to battle
against Benjamin, and the men of Israel put
themselves in battle array to fight against them at
Gibeah.
21 Then [a]the children of Benjamin came out of
Gibeah, and on that day cut down to the ground
twenty-two thousand men of the Israelites.
22 And the people, that is, the men of Israel,
encouraged themselves and again formed the
battle line at the place where they had put themselves in array on the first day.
23 [a]Then the children of Israel went up and wept
before the LORD until evening, and asked counsel
of the LORD, saying, "Shall I again draw near for
battle against the children of my brother Benjamin?" And the LORD said, "Go up against him."
**24** So the children of Israel approached the children of Benjamin on the second day.
25 And [a]Benjamin went out against them from
Gibeah on the second day, and cut down to the
ground eighteen thousand more of the children of
Israel; all these drew the sword.
**26** Then all the children of Israel, that is, all the
people, [a]went up and came to [1]the house of God
and wept. They sat there before the LORD and
fasted that day until evening; and they offered
burnt offerings and peace offerings before the
LORD.
27 So the children of Israel inquired of the LORD
([a]the ark of the covenant of God *was* there in
those days,
28 [a]and Phinehas the son of Eleazar, the son of
Aaron, [b]stood before it in those days), saying,
"Shall I yet again go out to battle against the
children of my brother Benjamin, or shall I
cease?" And the LORD said, "Go up, for tomorrow
I will deliver them into your hand."
**29** Then Israel [a]set men in ambush all around
Gibeah.
30 And the children of Israel went up against the
children of Benjamin on the third day, and put
themselves in battle array against Gibeah as at
the other times.
31 So the children of Benjamin went out against
the people, *and* were drawn away from the city.
They began to strike down *and* kill some of the
people, as at the other times, in the highways
[a](one of which goes up to Bethel and the other to
Gibeah) and in the field, about thirty men of
Israel.
32 And the children of Benjamin said, "They *are*
defeated before us, as at first." But the children of
Israel said, "Let us flee and draw them away from
the city to the highways."
33 So all the men of Israel rose from their place
and put themselves in battle array at Baal Tamar.
Then Israel's men in ambush burst forth from
their position in the plain of Geba.
34 And ten thousand select men from all Israel
came against Gibeah, and the battle was fierce.
[a]But [1]*the Benjamites* did not know that disaster
*was* upon them.
35 The LORD [1]defeated Benjamin before Israel.
And the children of Israel destroyed that day
twenty-five thousand one hundred Benjamites; all
these drew the sword.

**30** [a]Judg. 20:7; Prov. 13:10

CHAPTER 20

**1** [a]Josh. 22:12; Judg. 20:11; 21:5 [b]Judg. 18:29; 1 Sam. 3:20; 2 Sam. 3:10; 24:2 [c]Josh. 19:2 [d]Judg. 10:17; 1 Sam. 7:5
**2** [a]Judg. 8:10
**4** [a]Judg. 19:15
**5** [a]Judg. 19:22 [b]Judg. 19:25, 26
**6** [a]Judg. 19:29 [b]Josh. 7:15
**7** [a]Judg. 19:30
**9** [a]Judg. 1:3
**12** [a]Deut. 13:14; Josh. 22:13, 16
**13** [a]Deut. 13:13; Judg. 19:22 [b]Deut. 17:12; 1 Cor. 5:13 [1]Lit. *sons of Belial*
**15** [a]Num. 1:36, 37; 2:23; 26:41
**16** [a]Judg. 3:15; 1 Chr. 12:2
**18** [a]Judg. 20:23, 26 [b]Num. 27:21 [c]Judg. 1:1, 2 [1]Or *Bethel*
**21** [a][Gen. 49:27]
**23** [a]Judg. 20:26, 27
**25** [a]Judg. 20:21
**26** [a]Judg. 20:18, 23; 21:2 [1]Or *Bethel*
**27** [a]Josh. 18:1; 1 Sam. 1:3; 3:3; 4:3, 4
**28** [a]Num. 25:7, 13; Josh. 24:33 [b]Deut. 10:8; 18:5
**29** [a]Josh. 8:4
**31** [a]Judg. 21:19
**34** [a]Josh. 8:14; Job 21:13; Is. 47:11 [1]Lit. *they*
**35** [1]Lit. *struck*

**36** So the children of Benjamin saw that they
were defeated. [a]The men of Israel had given
ground to the Benjamites, because they relied on
the men in ambush whom they had set against
Gibeah.
37 [a]And the men in ambush quickly rushed upon
Gibeah; the men in ambush spread out and struck
the whole city with the edge of the sword.
38 Now the appointed signal between the men of
Israel and the men in ambush was that they
would make a great cloud of [a]smoke rise up from
the city,
39 whereupon the men of Israel would turn in
battle. Now Benjamin had begun [1]to strike *and*
kill about thirty of the men of Israel. For they
said, "Surely they are defeated before us, as *in* the
first battle."
40 But when the cloud began to rise from the city
in a column of smoke, the Benjamites [a]looked
behind them, and there was the whole city going
up *in smoke* to heaven.
41 And when the men of Israel turned back, the
men of Benjamin panicked, for they saw that
disaster had come upon them.
42 Therefore they [1]turned *their backs* before the
men of Israel in the direction of the wilderness;
but the battle overtook them, and whoever *came*
out of the cities they destroyed in their midst.
43 They surrounded the Benjamites, chased
them, *and* easily trampled them down as far as the
front of Gibeah toward the east.
44 And eighteen thousand men of Benjamin fell;
all these *were* men of valor.
45 Then [1]they turned and fled toward the wilderness to the rock of [a]Rimmon; and they cut down
five thousand of them on the highways. Then they
pursued them relentlessly up to Gidom, and killed
two thousand of them.
46 So all who fell of Benjamin that day were
twenty-five thousand men who drew the sword;
all these *were* [1]men of valor.
47 [a]But six hundred men turned and fled toward
the wilderness to the rock of Rimmon, and they
stayed at the rock of Rimmon for four months.
48 And the men of Israel turned back against the
children of Benjamin, and struck them down with
the edge of the sword—from *every* city, men and
beasts, all who were found. They also set fire to all
the cities they came to.

### *Wives for the Benjamites*

**21** Now [a]the men of Israel had sworn an oath
at Mizpah, saying, "None of us shall give his
daughter to Benjamin as a wife."
2 Then the people came [a]to [1]the house of God,
and remained there before God till evening. They
lifted up their voices and wept bitterly,
3 and said, "O LORD God of Israel, why has this
come to pass in Israel, that today there should be
one tribe *missing* in Israel?"
4 So it was, on the next morning, that the
people rose early and [a]built an altar there, and
offered burnt offerings and peace offerings.
5 The children of Israel said, "Who *is there*
among all the tribes of Israel who did not come up
with the assembly to the LORD?" [a]For they had
made a great oath concerning anyone who had
not come up to the LORD at Mizpah, saying, "He
shall surely be put to death."
6 And the children of Israel grieved for Benjamin their brother, and said, "One tribe is cut off
from Israel today.
7 "What shall we do for wives for those who
remain, seeing we have sworn by the LORD that
we will not give them our daughters as wives?"
8 And they said, "What one *is there* from the
tribes of Israel who did not come up to Mizpah to
the LORD?" And, in fact, no one had come to the
camp from [a]Jabesh Gilead to the assembly.
9 For when the people were counted, indeed,
not one of the inhabitants of Jabesh Gilead *was*
there.
10 So the congregation sent out there twelve
thousand of their most valiant men, and commanded them, saying, [a]"Go and strike the inhabitants of Jabesh Gilead with the edge of the sword,
including the women and children.
11 "And this *is* the thing that you shall do: [a]You
shall utterly destroy every male, and every
woman who has known a man intimately."
12 So they found among the inhabitants of Jabesh Gilead four hundred young virgins who had
not known a man intimately; and they brought
them to the camp at [a]Shiloh, which is in the land
of Canaan.
**13** Then the whole congregation sent *word* to the
children of Benjamin [a]who *were* at the rock of
Rimmon, and announced peace to them.
14 So Benjamin came back at that time, and they
gave them the women whom they had saved alive
of the women of Jabesh Gilead; and yet they had
not found enough for them.
15 And the people [a]grieved for Benjamin, because
the LORD had made a void in the tribes of Israel.
**16** Then the elders of the congregation said,
"What shall we do for wives for those who remain, since the women of Benjamin have been
destroyed?"
17 And they said, "*There must be* an inheritance
for the survivors of Benjamin, that a tribe may not
be destroyed from Israel.
18 "However, we cannot give them wives from
our daughters, [a]for the children of Israel have
sworn an oath, saying, 'Cursed *be* the one who
gives a wife to Benjamin.' "
19 Then they said, "In fact, *there is* a yearly
[a]feast of the LORD in [b]Shiloh, which *is* north of
Bethel, on the east side of the [c]highway that goes
up from Bethel to Shechem, and south of Lebo-
nah."
20 Therefore they instructed the children of Benjamin, saying, "Go, lie in wait in the vineyards,
21 "and watch; and just when the daughters of
Shiloh come out [a]to perform their dances, then
come out from the vineyards, and every man
catch a wife for himself from the daughters of
Shiloh; then go to the land of Benjamin.
22 "Then it shall be, when their fathers or their
brothers come to us to complain, that we will say
to them, 'Be kind to them for our sakes, because
we did not take a wife for any of them in the war;
for *it is* not *as though* you have given the *women*
to them at this time, making yourselves guilty of
your oath.' "
**23** And the children of Benjamin did so; they
took enough wives for their number from those
who danced, whom they caught. Then they went
and returned to their inheritance, and they [a]re-
built the cities and dwelt in them.
24 So the children of Israel departed from there
at that time, every man to his tribe and family;
they went out from there, every man to his
inheritance.
**25** [a]In those days *there was* no king in Israel;
[b]everyone did *what was* right in his own eyes.

**36** [a]Josh. 8:15
**37** [a]Josh. 8:19
**38** [a]Josh. 8:20
**39** [1]Lit. *to strike the slain ones*
**40** [a]Josh. 8:20
**42** [1]*fled*
**45** [a]Josh. 15:32; 1 Chr. 6:77; Zech. 14:10 [1]LXX *the rest*
**46** [1]*valiant warriors*
**47** [a]Judg. 21:13

CHAPTER 21
**1** [a]Judg. 20:1
**2** [a]Judg. 20:18, 26 [1]Or *Bethel*
**4** [a]Deut. 12:5; 2 Sam. 24:25
**5** [a]Judg. 20:1–3
**8** [a]1 Sam. 11:1; 31:11
**10** [a]Num. 31:17; Judg. 5:23; 1 Sam. 11:7
**11** [a]Num. 31:17; Deut. 20:13, 14
**12** [a]Josh. 18:1; Judg. 18:31
**13** [a]Judg. 20:47
**15** [a]Judg. 21:6
**18** [a]Judg. 11:35; 21:1
**19** [a]Lev. 23:2 [b]Deut. 12:5; Josh. 18:1; Judg. 18:31; 1 Sam. 1:3 [c]Judg. 20:31
**21** [a]Ex. 15:20; Judg. 11:34; 1 Sam. 18:6
**23** [a]Judg. 20:48
**25** [a]Judg. 17:6; 18:1; 19:1 [b]Deut. 12:8; Judg. 17:6

*The Book of*

# RUTH

### *Naomi and Ruth Return from Moab*

NOW it came to pass, in the days when [a]the
judges [1]ruled, that there was [b]a famine in
the land. And a certain man of [c]Bethlehem,
Judah, went to [2]dwell in the country of [d]Moab, he
and his wife and his two sons.
2 The name of the man *was* Elimelech, the
name of his wife *was* Naomi, and the names of his
two sons *were* Mahlon and Chilion—[a]Ephrathites
of Bethlehem, Judah. And they went [b]to the
country of Moab and remained there.
3 Then Elimelech, Naomi's husband, died; and
she was left, and her two sons.
4 Now they took wives of the women of Moab:
the name of the one *was* Orpah, and the name of
the other Ruth. And they [1]dwelt there about ten
years.
5 Then both Mahlon and Chilion also died; so
the woman survived her two sons and her husband.
**6** Then she arose with her daughters-in-law that
she might return from the country of Moab, for
she had heard in the country of Moab that the
LORD had [a]visited[1] His people by [b]giving them
bread.
7 Therefore she went out from the place where
she was, and her two daughters-in-law with her;
and they went on the way to return to the land of
Judah.
8 And Naomi said to her two daughters-in-law,
[a]"Go, return each to her mother's house. [b]The
LORD deal kindly with you, as you have dealt
[c]with the dead and with me.
9 "The LORD grant that you may find [a]rest, each
in the house of her husband." So she kissed them,
and they lifted up their voices and wept.
10 And they said to her, "Surely we will return
with you to your people."
11 But Naomi said, "Turn back, my daughters;
why will you go with me? *Are* there still sons in
my womb, [a]that they may be your husbands?
12 "Turn back, my daughters, go—for I am too
old to have a husband. If I should say I have hope,
*if* I should have a husband tonight and should also
bear sons,
13 "would you wait for them till they were
grown? Would you restrain yourselves from having husbands? No, my daughters; for it grieves me
very much for your sakes that [a]the hand of the
LORD has gone out against me!"
14 Then they lifted up their voices and wept
again; and Orpah kissed her mother-in-law, but
Ruth [a]clung to her.
**15** And she said, "Look, your sister-in-law has
gone back to [a]her people and to her gods; [b]return
after your sister-in-law."
16 But Ruth said:

[a]"Entreat[1] me not to leave you,
*Or to* turn back from following after you;
For wherever you go, I will go;
And wherever you lodge, I will lodge;
[b]Your people *shall be* my people,
And your God, my God.
17 Where you die, I will die,
And there will I be buried.
[a]The LORD do so to me, and more also,
If *anything but* death parts you and me."

18 [a]When she saw that she [1]was determined to go
with her, she stopped speaking to her.
**19** Now the two of them went until they came to
Bethlehem. And it happened, when they had come
to Bethlehem, that [a]all the city was excited because of them; and the women said, [b]"*Is* this
Naomi?"
20 But she said to them, "Do not call me [1]Naomi;
call me [2]Mara, for the Almighty has dealt very
bitterly with me.
21 "I went out full, [a]and the LORD has brought
me home again empty. Why do you call me Naomi, since the LORD has testified against me, and
[1]the Almighty has afflicted me?"
**22** So Naomi returned, and Ruth the Moabitess
her daughter-in-law with her, who returned from
the country of Moab. Now they came to Bethlehem [a]at the beginning of barley harvest.

### *Ruth Meets Boaz*

**2** There was a [a]relative of Naomi's husband, a
man of great wealth, of the family of [b]Elim-
elech. His name *was* [c]Boaz.
2 So Ruth the Moabitess said to Naomi, "Please
let me go to the [a]field, and glean heads of grain
after *him* in whose sight I may find favor." And
she said to her, "Go, my daughter."
3 Then she left, and went and gleaned in the
field after the reapers. And she happened to come
to the part of the field *belonging* to Boaz, who *was*
of the family of Elimelech.
**4** Now behold, Boaz came from [a]Bethlehem, and
said to the reapers, [b]"The LORD *be* with you!" And
they answered him, "The LORD bless you!"
5 Then Boaz said to his servant who was in
charge of the reapers, "Whose young woman *is*
this?"
6 So the servant who was in charge of the
reapers answered and said, "It *is* the young Moabite woman [a]who came back with Naomi from the
country of Moab.
7 "And she said, 'Please let me glean and gather
after the reapers among the sheaves.' So she came
and has continued from morning until now,
though she rested a little in the house."
**8** Then Boaz said to Ruth, "You will listen, my
daughter, will you not? Do not go to glean in
another field, nor go from here, but stay close by
my young women.
9 "*Let* your eyes *be* on the field which they reap,
and go after them. Have I not commanded the
young men not to touch you? And when you are
thirsty, go to the vessels and drink from what the
young men have drawn."
10 So she [a]fell on her face, bowed down to the
ground, and said to him, "Why have I found
[b]favor in your eyes, that you should take notice of
me, since I *am* a foreigner?"
11 And Boaz answered and said to her, "It has
been fully reported to me, [a]all that you have done
for your mother-in-law since the death of your
husband, and *how* you have left your father and
your mother and the land of your birth, and have
come to a people whom you did not know before.

CHAPTER 1

**1** [a]Judg. 2:16–18 [b]Gen. 12:10; 26:1; 2 Kin. 8:1 [c]Judg. 17:8; Mic. 5:2 [d]Gen. 19:37 [1]Lit. *judged* [2]As a resident alien
**2** [a]Gen. 35:19; 1 Sam. 1:1; 1 Kin. 11:26 [b]Judg. 3:30
**4** [1]*lived*
**6** [a]Ex. 3:16; 4:31; Jer. 29:10; Zeph. 2:7; Luke 1:68 [b]Ps. 132:15; Matt. 6:11 [1]*attended to*
**8** [a]Josh. 24:15 [b]2 Tim. 1:16–18 [c]Ruth 2:20
**9** [a]Ruth 3:1
**11** [a]Gen. 38:11; Deut. 25:5
**13** [a]Judg. 2:15; Job 19:21; Ps. 32:4; 38:2
**14** [a][Prov. 17:17]
**15** [a]Judg. 11:24 [b]Josh. 1:15
**16** [a]2 Kin. 2:2, 4, 6 [b]Ruth 2:11, 12 [1]*Urge me not*
**17** [a]1 Sam. 3:17; 2 Sam. 19:13; 2 Kin. 6:31
**18** [a]Acts 21:14 [1]Lit. *made herself strong to go*
**19** [a]Matt. 21:10 [b]Is. 23:7; Lam. 2:15
**20** [1]Lit. *Pleasant* [2]Lit. *Bitter*
**21** [a]Job 1:21 [1]Heb. *Shaddai*
**22** [a]Ruth 2:23; 2 Sam. 21:9

CHAPTER 2

**1** [a]Ruth 3:2, 12 [b]Ruth 1:2 [c]Ruth 4:21
**2** [a]Lev. 19:9, 10; 23:22; Deut. 24:19
**4** [a]Ruth 1:1 [b]Ps. 129:7, 8; Luke 1:28; 2 Thess. 3:16
**6** [a]Ruth 1:22
**10** [a]1 Sam. 25:23 [b]1 Sam. 1:18
**11** [a]Ruth 1:14–18

12 [a]"The LORD repay your work, and a full reward be given you by the LORD God of Israel, [b]under whose wings you have come for refuge."

13 Then she said, [a]"Let me find favor in your sight, my lord; for you have comforted me, and have spoken [1]kindly to your maidservant, [b]though I am not like one of your maidservants."

**14** Now Boaz said to her at mealtime, "Come here, and eat of the bread, and dip your piece of bread in the vinegar." So she sat beside the reapers, and he passed parched *grain* to her; and she ate and [a]was satisfied, and kept some back.

15 And when she rose up to [1]glean, Boaz commanded his young men, saying, "Let her glean even among the sheaves, and do not [2]reproach her.

16 "Also let *grain* from the bundles fall purposely for her; leave *it* that she may glean, and do not rebuke her."

**17** So she gleaned in the field until evening, and beat out what she had gleaned, and it was about an ephah of [a]barley.

18 Then she took *it* up and went into the city, and her mother-in-law saw what she had gleaned. So she brought out and gave to her [a]what she had kept back after she had been satisfied.

19 And her mother-in-law said to her, "Where have you gleaned today? And where did you work? Blessed be the one who [a]took notice of you." So she told her mother-in-law with whom she had worked, and said, "The man's name with whom I worked today *is* Boaz."

20 Then Naomi said to her daughter-in-law, [a]"Blessed *be* he of the LORD, who [b]has not forsaken His kindness to the living and the dead!" And Naomi said to her, "This man *is* a relation of ours, [c]one of [1]our close relatives."

21 Ruth the Moabitess said, "He also said to me, 'You shall stay close by my young men until they have finished all my harvest.' "

22 And Naomi said to Ruth her daughter-in-law, "*It is* good, my daughter, that you go out with his young women, and that people do not [1]meet you in any other field."

23 So she stayed close by the young women of Boaz, to glean until the end of barley harvest and wheat harvest; and she dwelt with her mother-in-law.

## *Boaz Is Ruth's Relative*

**3** Then Naomi her mother-in-law said to her, "My daughter, [a]shall I not seek [b]security[1] for you, that it may be well with you?

2 "Now Boaz, [a]whose young women you were with, *is he* not our relative? In fact, he is winnowing barley tonight at the threshing floor.

3 "Therefore wash yourself and [a]anoint yourself, put on your *best* garment and go down to the threshing floor; *but* do not make yourself known to the man until he has finished eating and drinking.

4 "Then it shall be, when he lies down, that you shall notice the place where he lies; and you shall go in, uncover his feet, and lie down; and he will tell you what you should do."

5 And she said to her, "All that you say to me I will do."

**6** So she went down to the threshing floor and did according to all that her mother-in-law instructed her.

7 And after Boaz had eaten and drunk, and [a]his heart was cheerful, he went to lie down at the end of the heap of grain; and she came softly, uncovered his feet, and lay down.

**8** Now it happened at midnight that the man was startled, and turned himself; and there, a woman was lying at his feet.

9 And he said, "Who *are* you?" So she answered, "I *am* Ruth, your maidservant. [a]Take[1] your maidservant under your wing, for you are [b]a [2]close relative."

10 Then he said, [a]"Blessed *are* you of the LORD, my daughter! For you have shown more kindness at the end than [b]at the beginning, in that you did not go after young men, whether poor or rich.

11 "And now, my daughter, do not fear. I will do for you all that you request, for all the people of my town know that you *are* [a]a virtuous woman.

12 "Now it is true that I *am* a [a]close relative; however, [b]there is a relative closer than I.

13 "Stay this night, and in the morning it shall be *that* if he will [a]perform the duty of a close relative for you—good; let him do it. But if he does not want to perform the duty for you, then I will perform the duty for you, [b]*as* the LORD lives! Lie down until morning."

**14** So she lay at his feet until morning, and she arose before one could recognize another. Then he said, [a]"Do not let it be known that the woman came to the threshing floor."

15 Also he said, "Bring the [1]shawl that *is* on you and hold it." And when she held it, he measured six *ephahs* of barley, and laid *it* on her. Then [2]she went into the city.

16 When she came to her mother-in-law, she said, [1]"*Is* that you, my daughter?" Then she told her all that the man had done for her.

17 And she said, "These six *ephahs* of barley he gave me; for he said to me, 'Do not go empty-handed to your mother-in-law.' "

18 Then she said, [a]"Sit still, my daughter, until you know how the matter will turn out; for the man will not rest until he has concluded the matter this day."

## *Boaz Marries Ruth*

**4** Now Boaz went up to the gate and sat down there; and behold, [a]the close relative of whom Boaz had spoken came by. So Boaz said, "Come aside, [1]friend, sit down here." So he came aside and sat down.

2 And he took ten men of [a]the elders of the city, and said, "Sit down here." So they sat down.

3 Then he said to the close relative, "Naomi, who has come back from the country of Moab, sold the piece of land [a]which *belonged* to our brother Elimelech.

4 "And I thought to [1]inform you, saying, [a]'Buy *it* back [b]in the presence of the inhabitants and the elders of my people. If you will redeem *it*, redeem *it*; but if [2]you will not redeem *it*, *then* tell me, that I may know; [c]for *there is* no one but you to redeem *it*, and I *am* next after you.' " And he said, "I will redeem *it*."

5 Then Boaz said, "On the day you buy the field from the hand of Naomi, you must also buy *it* from Ruth the Moabitess, the wife of the dead, [a]to [1]perpetuate the name of the dead through his inheritance."

6 [a]And the close relative said, "I cannot redeem *it* for myself, lest I ruin my own inheritance. You

---

**12** [a]1 Sam. 24:19; Ps. 58:11 [b]Ruth 1:16; Ps. 17:8; 36:7; 57:1; 61:4; 63:7; 91:4
**13** [a]Gen. 33:15; 1 Sam. 1:18 [b]1 Sam. 25:41 [1]Lit. *to the heart of*
**14** [a]Ruth 2:18
**15** [1]Gather after the reapers [2]*rebuke*
**17** [a]Ruth 1:22
**18** [a]Ruth 2:14
**19** [a]Ruth 2:10; [Ps. 41:1]
**20** [a]Ruth 3:10; 2 Sam. 2:5 [b]Prov. 17:17 [c]Ruth 3:9; 4:4, 6 [1]*our redeemers*, Heb. *goalenu*
**22** [1]*encounter*

CHAPTER 3

**1** [a]1 Cor. 7:36; 1 Tim. 5:8 [b]Ruth 1:9 [1]Lit. *rest*
**2** [a]Ruth 2:3, 8
**3** [a]2 Sam. 14:2
**7** [a]Judg. 19:6, 9, 22; 2 Sam. 13:28; Esth. 1:10
**9** [a]Ezek. 16:8 [b]Ruth 2:20; 3:12 [1]Or *Spread the corner of your garment over your maidservant* [2]*redeemer*, Heb. *goel*
**10** [a]Ruth 2:20 [b]Ruth 1:8
**11** [a]Prov. 12:4; 31:10–31
**12** [a]Ruth 3:9 [b]Ruth 4:1
**13** [a]Deut. 25:5–10; Ruth 4:5, 10; Matt. 22:24 [b]Judg. 8:19; Jer. 4:2; 12:16
**14** [a][Rom. 12:17; 14:16; 1 Cor. 10:32; 2 Cor. 8:21; 1 Thess. 5:22]
**15** [1]*cloak* [2]Many Heb. mss., Syr., Vg. *she;* MT, LXX, Tg. *he*
**16** [1]Or *How are you,*
**18** [a][Ps. 37:3, 5]

CHAPTER 4

**1** [a]Ruth 3:12 [1]Lit. *so and so*, Heb. *peloni almoni*
**2** [a]1 Kin. 21:8; Prov. 31:23
**3** [a]Lev. 25:25
**4** [a]Jer. 32:7, 8 [b]Gen. 23:18 [c]Lev. 25:25 [1]Lit. *uncover your ear* [2]So with many Heb. mss., LXX, Syr., Tg., Vg.; MT *he*
**5** [a]Gen. 38:8; Deut. 25:5, 6; Ruth 3:13; Matt. 22:24 [1]Lit. *raise up*
**6** [a]Ruth 3:12, 13; Job 19:14

redeem my right of redemption for yourself, for I
cannot redeem *it*."
7 [a]Now this *was the custom* in former times in
Israel concerning redeeming and exchanging, to
confirm anything: one man took off his sandal and
gave *it* to the other, and this *was* a confirmation
in Israel.
8 Therefore the close relative said to Boaz,
"Buy *it* for yourself." So he took off his sandal.
9 And Boaz said to the elders and all the people,
"You *are* witnesses this day that I have bought all
that was Elimelech's, and all that *was* Chilion's
and Mahlon's, from the hand of Naomi.
10 "Moreover, Ruth the Moabitess, the widow of
Mahlon, I have acquired as my wife, to perpetuate
the name of the dead through his inheritance,
[a]that the name of the dead may not be cut off
from among his brethren and from [1]his position at
the gate. You *are* witnesses this day."
11 And all the people who *were* at the gate, and
the elders, said, "*We are* witnesses. [a]The LORD
make the woman who is coming to your house
like Rachel and Leah, the two who [b]built the
house of Israel; and may you prosper in [c]Ephra-
thah and be famous in [d]Bethlehem.
12 "May your house be like the house of [a]Perez,
[b]whom Tamar bore to Judah, because of [c]the
offspring which the LORD will give you from this
young woman."
13 So Boaz [a]took Ruth and she became his wife;
and when he went in to her, [b]the LORD gave her
conception, and she bore a son.
14 Then [a]the women said to Naomi, "Blessed *be*
the LORD, who has not left you this day without a
[1]close relative; and may his name be famous in
Israel!
15 "And may he be to you a restorer of life and a
[1]nourisher of your old age; for your daughter-in-
law, who loves you, who is [a]better to you than
seven sons, has borne him."
16 Then Naomi took the child and laid him on her
bosom, and became a nurse to him.
17 [a]Also the neighbor women gave him a name,
saying, "There is a son born to Naomi." And they
called his name Obed. He *is* the father of Jesse, the
father of David.
18 [a]Now this *is* the genealogy of Perez: [b]Perez
begot Hezron;
19 Hezron begot Ram, and Ram begot Amminadab;
20 Amminadab begot [a]Nahshon, and Nahshon
begot [b]Salmon;[1]
21 Salmon begot Boaz, and Boaz begot Obed;
22 Obed begot Jesse, and Jesse begot [a]David.

7 [a]Deut. 25:7–10
10 [a]Deut. 25:6 [1]Probably his civic office
11 [a]Ps. 127:3; 128:3 [b]Gen. 29:25–30 [c]Gen. 35:16–18 [d]Mic. 5:2
12 [a]Matt. 1:3 [b]Gen. 38:6–29 [c]1 Sam. 2:20
13 [a]Ruth 3:11 [b]Gen. 29:31; 33:5
14 [a]Luke 1:58 [1]*redeemer,* Heb. *goel*
15 [a]1 Sam. 1:8 [1]*sustainer*
17 [a]Luke 1:58
18 [a]1 Chr. 2:4, 5 [b]Num. 26:20, 21
20 [a]Num. 1:7 [b]Matt. 1:4 [1]Heb. *Salmah*
22 [a]Matt. 1:6

*The First Book of*

# SAMUEL

## *The Birth of Samuel*

NOW there was a certain man of Ramathaim
Zophim, of the [a]mountains of Ephraim,
and his name *was* [b]Elkanah the son of
Jeroham, the son of [1]Elihu, the son of [2]Tohu, the
son of Zuph, [c]an Ephraimite.
2 And he had [a]two wives: the name of one *was*
Hannah, and the name of the other Peninnah.
Peninnah had children, but Hannah had no children.
3 This man went up from his city [a]yearly [b]to
worship and sacrifice to the LORD of hosts in
[c]Shiloh. Also the two sons of Eli, Hophni and
Phinehas, the priests of the LORD, *were* there.
4 And whenever the time came for Elkanah to
make an [a]offering, he would give portions to
Peninnah his wife and to all her sons and daughters.
5 But to Hannah he would give a double portion,
for he loved Hannah, [a]although the LORD had
closed her womb.
6 And her rival also [a]provoked her severely, to
make her miserable, because the LORD had closed
her womb.
7 So it was, year by year, when she went up to
the house of the LORD, that she provoked her;
therefore she wept and did not eat.
8 Then Elkanah her husband said to her, "Hannah, why do you weep? Why do you not eat? And
why is your heart grieved? *Am* I not [a]better to you
than ten sons?"
9 So Hannah arose after they had finished eating and drinking in Shiloh. Now Eli the priest was
sitting on the seat by the doorpost of [a]the [1]taber-
nacle of the LORD.
10 [a]And she *was* in bitterness of soul, and prayed
to the LORD and [1]wept in anguish.
11 Then she [a]made a vow and said, "O LORD of
hosts, if You will indeed [b]look on the affliction of
Your maidservant and [c]remember me, and not
forget Your maidservant, but will give Your maidservant a male child, then I will give him to the
LORD all the days of his life, and [d]no razor shall
come upon his head."
12 And it happened, as she continued praying
before the LORD, that Eli watched her mouth.
13 Now Hannah spoke in her heart; only her lips
moved, but her voice was not heard. Therefore Eli
thought she was drunk.
14 So Eli said to her, "How long will you be
drunk? Put your wine away from you!"
15 But Hannah answered and said, "No, my lord,
I *am* a woman of sorrowful spirit. I have drunk
neither wine nor intoxicating drink, but have
[a]poured out my soul before the LORD.
16 "Do not consider your maidservant a [a]wicked[1]
woman, for out of the abundance of my complaint
and grief I have spoken until now."
17 Then Eli answered and said, [a]"Go in peace,
and [b]the God of Israel grant your petition which
you have asked of Him."
18 And she said, [a]"Let your maidservant find
favor in your sight." So the woman [b]went her way
and ate, and her face was no longer *sad*.
19 Then they rose early in the morning and
worshiped before the LORD, and returned and
came to their house at Ramah. And Elkanah

CHAPTER 1
1 [a]Josh. 17:17, 18; 24:33 [b]1 Chr. 6:27, 33–38 [c]Ruth 1:2 [1]*Eliel,* 1 Chr. 6:34 [2]*Toah,* 1 Chr. 6:34
2 [a]Deut. 21:15–17
3 [a]Luke 2:41 [b]Deut. 12:5–7; 16:16 [c]Josh. 18:1
4 [a]Deut. 12:17, 18
5 [a]Gen. 16:1; 30:1, 2
6 [a]Job 24:21
8 [a]Ruth 4:15
9 [a]1 Sam. 3:3 [1]*palace* or *temple,* Heb. *heykal*
10 [a]Job 7:11 [1]Lit. *wept greatly*
11 [a]Num. 30:6–11 [b]Ps. 25:18 [c]Gen. 8:1 [d]Num. 6:5
15 [a]Ps. 42:4; 62:8
16 [a]Deut. 13:13 [1]Lit. *daughter of Belial*
17 [a]Mark 5:34 [b]Ps. 20:3–5
18 [a]Ruth 2:13 [b]Rom. 15:13

[a]knew Hannah his wife, and the LORD [b]remem-
bered her.
20 So it came to pass in the process of time that
Hannah conceived and bore a son, and called his
name [1]Samuel, *saying,* "Because I have asked for
him from the LORD."
21 Now the man Elkanah and all his house [a]went
up to offer to the LORD the yearly sacrifice and his
vow.
22 But Hannah did not go up, for she said to her
husband, "*Not* until the child is weaned; then I
will [a]take him, that he may appear before the
LORD and [b]remain there [c]forever."
23 So [a]Elkanah her husband said to her, "Do
what seems best to you; wait until you have
weaned him. Only let the LORD [1]establish [2]His
word." Then the woman stayed and nursed her
son until she had weaned him.
**24** Now when she had weaned him, she [a]took him
up with her, with [1]three bulls, one ephah of flour,
and a skin of wine, and brought him to [b]the house
of the LORD in Shiloh. And the child *was* young.
25 Then they slaughtered a bull, and [a]brought the
child to Eli.
26 And she said, "O my lord! [a]As your soul lives,
my lord, I *am* the woman who stood by you here,
praying to the LORD.
27 [a]"For this child I prayed, and the LORD has
granted me my petition which I asked of Him.
28 "Therefore I also have lent him to the LORD;
as long as he lives he shall be [1]lent to the LORD."
So they [a]worshiped the LORD there.

### *The Sins of Eli's Sons*

**2** And Hannah [a]prayed and said:

[b]"My heart rejoices in the LORD;
[c]My [1]horn is exalted in the LORD.
[2]I smile at my enemies,
Because I [d]rejoice in Your salvation.

2 "No[a] one is holy like the LORD,
For *there is* [b]none besides You,
Nor *is there* any [c]rock like our God.

3 "Talk no more so very proudly;
[a]Let no arrogance come from your mouth,
For the LORD *is* the God of [b]knowledge;
And by Him actions are weighed.

4 "The[a] bows of the mighty men *are* broken,
And those who stumbled
are girded with strength.
5 *Those who were* full
have hired themselves out for bread,
And the hungry have ceased *to hunger.*
Even [a]the barren has borne seven,
And [b]she who has many children has become
feeble.

6 "The[a] LORD kills and makes alive;
He brings down to the grave and brings up.
7 The LORD [a]makes poor and makes rich;
[b]He brings low and lifts up.
8 [a]He raises the poor from the dust
*And* lifts the beggar from the ash heap,
[b]To set *them* among princes
And make them inherit the throne of glory.

[c]"For the pillars of the earth *are* the LORD's,
And He has set the world upon them.
9 [a]He will guard the feet of His saints,
But the [b]wicked shall be silent in darkness.

"For by strength no man shall prevail.

10 The adversaries of the LORD
shall be [a]broken in pieces;
[b]From heaven He will thunder against them.
[c]The LORD will judge the ends of the earth.

[d]"He will give [e]strength to His king,
And [f]exalt the [1]horn of His anointed."

11 Then Elkanah went to his house at Ramah.
But the child [1]ministered to the LORD before Eli
the priest.
**12** Now the sons of Eli *were* [a]corrupt;[1] [b]they did
not know the LORD.
13 And the priests' custom with the people *was
that* when any man offered a sacrifice, the priest's
servant would come with a three-pronged fleshhook in his hand while the meat was boiling.
14 Then he would thrust *it* into the pan, or kettle,
or caldron, or pot; and the priest would take for
himself all that the fleshhook brought up. So they
did in [a]Shiloh to all the Israelites who came there.
15 Also, before they [a]burned the fat, the priest's
servant would come and say to the man who
sacrificed, "Give meat for roasting to the priest,
for he will not take boiled meat from you, but
raw."
16 And *if* the man said to him, "They should
really burn the fat first; *then* you may take *as
much* as your heart desires," he would then
answer him, "*No,* but you must give *it* now; and if
not, I will take *it* by force."
17 Therefore the sin of the young men was very
great [a]before the LORD, for men [b]abhorred[1] the
offering of the LORD.
**18** [a]But Samuel ministered before the LORD, *even
as* a child, [b]wearing a linen ephod.
19 Moreover his mother used to make him a little
robe, and bring *it* to him year by year when she
[a]came up with her husband to offer the yearly
sacrifice.
20 And Eli [a]would bless Elkanah and his wife, and
say, "The LORD give you descendants from this
woman for the [1]loan that was [b]given to the LORD."
Then they would go to their own home.
21 And the LORD [a]visited[1] Hannah, so that she
conceived and bore three sons and two daughters.
Meanwhile the child Samuel [b]grew before the
LORD.
**22** Now Eli was very old; and he heard everything
his sons did to all Israel, [1]and how they lay with
[a]the women who assembled at the door of the
tabernacle of meeting.
23 So he said to them, "Why do you do such
things? For I hear of your evil dealings from all
the people.
24 "No, my sons! For *it is* not a good report that I
hear. You make the LORD's people transgress.
25 "If one man sins against another, [a]God[1] will
judge him. But if a man [b]sins against the LORD,
who will intercede for him?" Nevertheless they
did not heed the voice of their father, [c]because the
LORD desired to kill them.
26 And the child Samuel [a]grew in stature, and [b]in
favor both with the LORD and men.
**27** Then a [a]man of God came to Eli and said to
him, "Thus says the LORD: [b]'Did I not clearly
reveal Myself to the house of your father when
they were in Egypt in Pharaoh's house?
28 'Did I not [a]choose him out of all the tribes of
Israel *to be* My priest, to offer upon My altar, to
burn incense, and to wear an ephod before Me?

**19** [a]Gen. 4:1 [b]Gen. 21:1; 30:22
**20** [1]Lit. *Heard by God*
**21** [a]1 Sam. 1:3
**22** [a]Luke 2:22 [b]1 Sam. 1:11, 28 [c]Ex. 21:6
**23** [a]Num. 30:7, 10, 11 [1]*confirm* [2]So with MT, Tg., Vg.; DSS, LXX, Syr. *your*
**24** [a]Num. 15:9, 10 [b]Josh. 18:1 [1]DSS, LXX, Syr. *a three-year-old bull*
**25** [a]Luke 2:22
**26** [a]2 Kin. 2:2, 4, 6; 4:30
**27** [a][Matt. 7:7]
**28** [a]Gen. 24:26, 52 [1]*granted*

CHAPTER 2
**1** [a]Phil. 4:6 [b]Luke 1:46–55 [c]Ps. 75:10; 89:17, 24; 92:10; 112:9 [d]Ps. 9:14; 13:5; 35:9 [1]Strength [2]Lit. *My mouth is enlarged*
**2** [a]Ex. 15:11 [b]Deut. 4:35 [c]Deut. 32:4, 30, 31
**3** [a]Ps. 94:4 [b]1 Sam. 16:7
**4** [a]Ps. 37:15; 46:9
**5** [a]Ps. 113:9 [b]Is. 54:1
**6** [a]Deut. 32:39
**7** [a]Deut. 8:17, 18 [b]Ps. 75:7
**8** [a]Luke 1:52 [b]Job 36:7 [c]Job 38:4–6
**9** [a][1 Pet. 1:5] [b][Rom. 3:19]
**10** [a]Ps. 2:9 [b]Ps. 18:13, 14 [c]Ps. 96:13; 98:9 [d][Matt. 28:18] [e]Ps. 21:1, 7 [f]Ps. 89:24 [1]Strength
**11** [1]*served*
**12** [a]Deut. 13:13 [b]Judg. 2:10 [1]Lit. *sons of Belial*
**14** [a]1 Sam. 1:3
**15** [a]Lev. 3:3–5, 16
**17** [a]Gen. 6:11 [b][Mal. 2:7–9] [1]*despised*
**18** [a]1 Sam. 2:11; 3:1 [b]Ex. 28:4
**19** [a]1 Sam. 1:3, 21
**20** [a]Gen. 14:19 [b]1 Sam. 1:11, 27, 28 [1]*gift*
**21** [a]Gen. 21:1 [b]1 Sam. 2:26; 3:19–21 [1]*attended to*
**22** [a]Ex. 38:8 [1]So with MT, Tg., Vg.; DSS, LXX omit rest of verse
**25** [a]Deut. 1:17; 25:1, 2 [b]Num. 15:30 [c]Josh. 11:20 [1]Tg. *the Judge*
**26** [a]1 Sam. 2:21 [b]Prov. 3:4
**27** [a]Deut. 33:1; Judg. 13:6; 1 Sam. 9:6; 1 Kin. 13:1 [b]Ex. 4:14–16; 12:1
**28** [a]Ex. 28:1, 4; Num. 16:5

And [b]did I not give to the house of your father all
the offerings of the children of Israel made by fire?
29 'Why do you [a]kick at My sacrifice and My
offering which I have commanded *in My* [b]dwelling
place, and honor your sons more than [c]Me, to
make yourselves fat with the best of all the
offerings of Israel My people?'
30 "Therefore the LORD God of Israel says: [a]'I
said indeed *that* your house and the house of your
father would walk before Me forever.' But now
the LORD says: [b]'Far be it from Me; for those who
honor Me I will honor, and [c]those who despise Me
shall be lightly esteemed.
31 'Behold, [a]the days are coming that I will cut
off your [1]arm and the arm of your father's house,
so that there will not be an old man in your house.
32 'And you will see an enemy *in My* dwelling
place, *despite* all the good which God does for
Israel. And there shall not be [a]an old man in your
house forever.
33 'But any of your men *whom* I do not cut off
from My altar shall consume your eyes and grieve
your heart. And all the descendants of your house
shall die in the flower of their age.
34 'Now this *shall be* [a]a sign to you that will come
upon your two sons, on Hophni and Phinehas: [b]in
one day they shall die, both of them.
35 'Then [a]I will raise up for Myself a faithful
priest *who* shall do according to what *is* in My
heart and in My mind. [b]I will build him a sure
house, and he shall walk before [c]My anointed
forever.
36 [a]'And it shall come to pass that everyone who
is left in your house will come *and* bow down to
him for a piece of silver and a morsel of bread, and
say, "Please, [1]put me in one of the priestly positions, that I may eat a piece of bread." ' "

## *Samuel Warns Eli*

**3** Now [a]the boy Samuel ministered to the LORD
before Eli. And [b]the word of the LORD was rare
in those days; *there was* no widespread revelation.
2 And it came to pass at that time, while Eli *was*
lying down in his place, and when his eyes had
begun to grow [a]so dim that he could not see,
3 and before [a]the lamp of God went out in the
[1]tabernacle of the LORD where the ark of God *was*,
and while Samuel was lying down,
4 that the LORD called Samuel. And he answered, "Here I am!"
5 So he ran to Eli and said, "Here I am, for you
called me." And he said, "I did not call; lie down
again." And he went and lay down.
6 Then the LORD called yet again, "Samuel!" So
Samuel arose and went to Eli, and said, "Here I
am, for you called me." He answered, "I did not
call, my son; lie down again."
7 (Now Samuel [a]did not yet know the LORD, nor
was the word of the LORD yet revealed to him.)
8 And the LORD called Samuel again the third
time. So he arose and went to Eli, and said, "Here
I am, for you did call me." Then Eli perceived that
the LORD had called the boy.
9 Therefore Eli said to Samuel, "Go, lie down;
and it shall be, if He calls you, that you must say,
[a]'Speak, LORD, for Your servant hears.' " So Samuel went and lay down in his place.
**10** Now the LORD came and stood and called as at
other times, "Samuel! Samuel!" And Samuel answered, "Speak, for Your servant hears."
11 Then the LORD said to Samuel: "Behold, I will
do something in Israel [a]at which both ears of
everyone who hears it will tingle.
12 "In that day I will perform against Eli [a]all that
I have spoken concerning his house, from beginning to end.
13 [a]"For I have told him that I will [b]judge his
house forever for the iniquity which he knows,
because [c]his sons made themselves vile, and he
[d]did not [1]restrain them.
14 "And therefore I have sworn to the house of
Eli that the iniquity of Eli's house [a]shall not be
atoned for by sacrifice or offering forever."
**15** So Samuel lay down until [1]morning, and
opened the doors of the house of the LORD. And
Samuel was afraid to tell Eli the vision.
16 Then Eli called Samuel and said, "Samuel, my
son!" He answered, "Here I am."
17 And he said, "What *is* the word that *the* LORD
spoke to you? Please do not hide *it* from me. [a]God
do so to you, and more also, if you hide anything
from me of all the things that He said to you."
18 Then Samuel told him everything, and hid
nothing from him. And he said, [a]"It *is* the LORD.
Let Him do what seems good to Him."
**19** So Samuel [a]grew, and [b]the LORD was with him
[c]and let none of his words [1]fall to the ground.
20 And all Israel [a]from Dan to Beersheba knew
that Samuel *had been* [1]established as a prophet of
the LORD.
21 Then the LORD appeared again in Shiloh. For
the LORD revealed Himself to Samuel in Shiloh by
[a]the word of the LORD.

## *The Death of Eli*

**4** And the word of Samuel came to all [1]Israel.
Now Israel went out to battle against the
Philistines, and encamped beside [a]Ebenezer; and
the Philistines encamped in Aphek.
2 Then the [a]Philistines put themselves in battle
array against Israel. And when they joined battle,
Israel was [1]defeated by the Philistines, who killed
about four thousand men of the army in the field.
3 And when the people had come into the camp,
the elders of Israel said, "Why has the LORD
defeated us today before the Philistines? [a]Let us
bring the ark of the covenant of the LORD from
Shiloh to us, that when it comes among us it may
save us from the hand of our enemies."
4 So the people sent to Shiloh, that they might
bring from there the ark of the covenant of the
LORD of hosts, [a]who dwells *between* [b]the cherubim. And the [c]two sons of Eli, Hophni and Phinehas, *were* there with the ark of the covenant of
God.
**5** And when the ark of the covenant of the LORD
came into the camp, all Israel shouted so loudly
that the earth shook.
6 Now when the Philistines heard the noise of
the shout, they said, "What *does* the sound of this
great shout in the camp of the Hebrews *mean?*"
Then they understood that the ark of the LORD
had come into the camp.
7 So the Philistines were afraid, for they said,
"God has come into the camp!" And they said,
[a]"Woe to us! For such a thing has never happened
before.
8 "Woe to us! Who will deliver us from the hand
of these mighty gods? These *are* the gods who
struck the Egyptians with all the plagues in the
wilderness.
9 [a]"Be strong and conduct yourselves like men,

**28** [b]Num. 5:9
**29** [a]Deut. 32:15 [b]Deut. 12:5 [c]Matt. 10:37
**30** [a]Ex. 29:9 [b]Jer. 18:9, 10 [c]Mal. 2:9–12
**31** [a]1 Kin. 2:27, 35 [1]*strength*
**32** [a]Zech. 8:4
**34** [a]1 Kin. 13:3 [b]1 Sam. 4:11, 17
**35** [a]1 Kin. 2:35 [b]1 Kin. 11:38 [c]Ps. 18:50
**36** [a]1 Kin. 2:27 [1]*assign*

CHAPTER 3

**1** [a]1 Sam. 2:11, 18 [b]Ps. 74:9
**2** [a]1 Sam. 4:15
**3** [a]Ex. 27:20, 21 [1]*palace* or *temple*
**7** [a]1 Sam. 2:12
**9** [a]1 Kin. 2:17
**11** [a]2 Kin. 21:12
**12** [a]1 Sam. 2:27–36
**13** [a]1 Sam. 2:29–31 [b]1 Sam. 2:22 [c]1 Sam. 2:12, 17, 22 [d]1 Sam. 2:23, 25 [1]Lit. *rebuke*
**14** [a]Num. 15:30, 31
**15** [1]So with MT, Tg., Vg.; LXX adds *and he arose in the morning*
**17** [a]Ruth 1:17
**18** [a]Is. 39:8
**19** [a]1 Sam. 2:21 [b]Gen. 21:22; 28:15; 39:2, 21, 23 [c]1 Sam. 9:6 [1]*fail*
**20** [a]Judg. 20:1 [1]*confirmed*
**21** [a]1 Sam. 3:1, 4

CHAPTER 4

**1** [a]1 Sam. 7:12 [1]So with MT, Tg.; LXX, Vg. add *And it came to pass in those days that the Philistines gathered themselves together to fight;* LXX adds further *against Israel*
**2** [a]1 Sam. 12:9 [1]Lit. *struck*
**3** [a]Josh. 6:6–21
**4** [a]1 Sam. 6:2 [b]Num. 7:89 [c]1 Sam. 2:12
**7** [a]Ex. 15:14
**9** [a]1 Cor. 16:13

you Philistines, that you do not become servants of the Hebrews, [b]as they have been to you. [1]Conduct yourselves like men, and fight!"
10 So the Philistines fought, and [a]Israel was [1]defeated, and every man fled to his tent. There was a very great slaughter, and there fell of Israel thirty thousand foot soldiers.
11 Also [a]the ark of God was captured; and [b]the two sons of Eli, Hophni and Phinehas, died.
**12** Then a man of Benjamin ran from the battle line the same day, and [a]came to Shiloh with his clothes torn and [b]dirt on his head.
13 Now when he came, there was Eli, sitting on [a]a seat [1]by the wayside watching, for his heart [2]trembled for the ark of God. And when the man came into the city and told *it,* all the city cried out.
14 When Eli heard the noise of the outcry, he said, "What *does* the sound of this tumult *mean?*" And the man came quickly and told Eli.
15 Eli was ninety-eight years old, and [a]his eyes were so [1]dim that he could not see.
16 Then the man said to Eli, "I *am* he who came from the battle. And I fled today from the battle line." And he said, [a]"What happened, my son?"
17 So the messenger answered and said, "Israel has fled before the Philistines, and there has been a great slaughter among the people. Also your two sons, Hophni and Phinehas, are dead; and the ark of God has been captured."
18 Then it happened, when he made mention of the ark of God, that Eli fell off the seat backward by the side of the gate; and his neck was broken and he died, for the man was old and heavy. And he had judged Israel forty years.
**19** Now his daughter-in-law, Phinehas' wife, was with child, *due* to be delivered; and when she heard the news that the ark of God was captured, and that her father-in-law and her husband were dead, she bowed herself and gave birth, for her labor pains came upon her.
20 And about the time of her death [a]the women who stood by her said to her, "Do not fear, for you have borne a son." But she did not answer, nor did she [1]regard *it.*
21 Then she named the child [a]Ichabod,[1] saying, [b]"The glory has departed from Israel!" because the ark of God had been captured and because of her father-in-law and her husband.
22 And she said, "The glory has departed from Israel, for the ark of God has been captured."

### *The Philistines and the Ark of God*

**5** Then the Philistines took the ark of God and brought it [a]from Ebenezer to Ashdod.
2 When the Philistines took the ark of God, they brought it into the house of [a]Dagon[1] and set it by Dagon.
3 And when the people of Ashdod arose early in the morning, there was Dagon, [a]fallen on its face to the earth before the ark of the LORD. So they took Dagon and [b]set it in its place again.
4 And when they arose early the next morning, there was Dagon, fallen on its face to the ground before the ark of the LORD. [a]The head of Dagon and both the palms of its hands *were* broken off on the threshold; only [1]Dagon's torso was left of it.
5 Therefore neither the priests of Dagon nor any who come into Dagon's house [a]tread on the threshold of Dagon in Ashdod to this day.
**6** But the [a]hand of the LORD was heavy on the people of Ashdod, and He [b]ravaged them and struck them with [c]tumors,[1] *both* Ashdod and its [d]territory.
7 And when the men of Ashdod saw how *it was,* they said, "The ark of the [a]God of Israel must not remain with us, for His hand is harsh toward us and Dagon our god."
8 Therefore they sent and gathered to themselves all the [a]lords of the Philistines, and said, "What shall we do with the ark of the God of Israel?" And they answered, "Let the ark of the God of Israel be carried away to [b]Gath." So they carried the ark of the God of Israel away.
9 So it was, after they had carried it away, that [a]the hand of the LORD was against the city with a very great destruction; and He struck the men of the city, both small and great, [1]and tumors broke out on them.
**10** Therefore they sent the ark of God to Ekron. So it was, as the ark of God came to Ekron, that the Ekronites cried out, saying, "They have brought the ark of the God of Israel to us, to kill us and our people!"
11 So they sent and gathered together all the lords of the Philistines, and said, "Send away the ark of the God of Israel, and let it go back to its own place, so that it does not kill us and our people." For there was a deadly destruction throughout all the city; the hand of God was very heavy there.
12 And the men who did not die were stricken with the tumors, and the [a]cry of the city went up to heaven.

### *The Philistines Return the Ark*

**6** Now the ark of the LORD was in the country of the Philistines seven months.
2 And the Philistines [a]called for the priests and the diviners, saying, "What shall we do with the ark of the LORD? Tell us how we should send it to its place."
3 So they said, "If you send away the ark of the God of Israel, do not send it [a]empty; but by all means return *it* to Him *with* [b]a trespass offering. Then you will be healed, and it will be known to you why His hand is not removed from you."
4 Then they said, "What *is* the trespass offering which we shall return to Him?" They answered, [a]"Five golden tumors and five golden rats, *according to* the number of the lords of the Philistines. For the same plague *was* on all of [1]you and on your lords.
5 "Therefore you shall make images of your tumors and images of your rats that [a]ravage the land, and you shall [b]give glory to the God of Israel; perhaps He will [c]lighten[1] His hand from you, from [d]your gods, and from your land.
6 "Why then do you harden your hearts [a]as the Egyptians and Pharaoh hardened their hearts? When He did mighty things among them, [b]did they not let the people go, that they might depart?
7 "Now therefore, make [a]a new cart, take two milk cows [b]which have never been yoked, and hitch the cows to the cart; and take their calves home, away from them.
8 "Then take the ark of the LORD and set it on the cart; and put [a]the articles of gold which you are returning to Him *as* a trespass offering in a chest by its side. Then send it away, and let it go.
9 "And watch: if it goes up the road to its own territory, to [a]Beth Shemesh, *then* He has done [1]us

**9** [b]Judg. 13:1 [1]Lit. *Be men*
**10** [a]Deut. 28:15, 25 [1]Lit. *struck down*
**11** [a]Ps. 78:60, 61 [b]1 Sam. 2:34
**12** [a]2 Sam. 1:2 [b]Josh. 7:6
**13** [a]1 Sam. 1:9; 4:18 [1]So with MT, Vg.; LXX *beside the gate watching the road* (cf. Tg.) [2]*trembled with anxiety*
**15** [a]1 Sam. 3:2 [1]*fixed*
**16** [a]2 Sam. 1:4
**20** [a]Gen. 35:16–19 [1]*pay any attention to*
**21** [a]1 Sam. 14:3 [b]Ps. 26:8; 78:61 [1]Lit. *Inglorious*

CHAPTER 5
**1** [a]1 Sam. 4:1; 7:12
**2** [a]1 Chr. 10:8–10 [1]A Philistine idol
**3** [a]Is. 19:1; 46:1, 2 [b]Is. 46:7
**4** [a]Mic. 1:7 [1]So with LXX, Syr., Tg., Vg.; MT *Dagon*
**5** [a]Zeph. 1:9
**6** [a]Ex. 9:3; [b]1 Sam. 6:5 [c]Deut. 28:27; Ps. 78:66 [d]Josh. 15:46, 47 [1]Probably bubonic plague. LXX, Vg. add *And in the midst of their land rats sprang up, and there was a great death panic in the city*
**7** [a]1 Sam. 6:5
**8** [a]1 Sam. 6:4 [b]Josh. 11:22
**9** [a]Deut. 2:15 [1]Vg. *and they had tumors in their secret parts*
**12** [a]Jer. 14:2

CHAPTER 6
**2** [a]Gen. 41:8
**3** [a]Deut. 16:16 [b]Lev. 5:15, 16
**4** [a]1 Sam. 5:6, 9, 12; 6:17 [1]Lit. *them*
**5** [a]1 Sam. 5:6 [b]Josh. 7:19 [c]1 Sam. 5:6, 11 [d]1 Sam. 5:3, 4, 7 [1]*ease*
**6** [a]Ex. 7:13; 8:15; 9:34; 14:17 [b]Ex. 12:31
**7** [a]2 Sam. 6:3 [b]Num. 19:2
**8** [a]1 Sam. 6:4, 5
**9** [a]Josh. 15:10; 21:16 [1]*this calamity to us*

this great evil. But if not, then [b]we shall know that
*it is* not His hand *that* struck us—it happened to
us by chance."
**10** Then the men did so; they took two milk cows
and hitched them to the cart, and shut up their
calves at home.
11 And they set the ark of the LORD on the cart,
and the chest with the gold rats and the images of
their tumors.
12 Then the cows headed straight for the road to
Beth Shemesh, *and* went along the [a]highway,
lowing as they went, and did not turn aside to the
right hand or the left. And the lords of the Philistines went after them to the border of Beth
Shemesh.
13 Now *the people of* Beth Shemesh *were* reaping
their [a]wheat harvest in the valley; and they lifted
their eyes and saw the ark, and rejoiced to see *it.*
14 Then the cart came into the field of Joshua of
Beth Shemesh, and stood there; a large stone *was*
there. So they split the wood of the cart and
offered the cows as a burnt offering to the LORD.
15 The Levites took down the ark of the LORD
and the chest that *was* with it, in which *were* the
articles of gold, and put *them* on the large stone.
Then the men of Beth Shemesh offered burnt
offerings and made sacrifices the same day to the
LORD.
16 So when [a]the five lords of the Philistines had
seen *it,* they returned to Ekron the same day.
**17** [a]These *are* the golden tumors which the Philistines returned *as* a trespass offering to the LORD:
one for Ashdod, one for Gaza, one for Ashkelon,
one for [b]Gath, one for Ekron;
18 and the golden rats, *according to* the number
of all the cities of the Philistines *belonging* to the
five lords, *both* fortified cities and country villages, even as far as the large *stone of* Abel on
which they set the ark of the LORD, *which stone
remains* to this day in the field of Joshua of Beth
Shemesh.
19 Then [a]He struck the men of Beth Shemesh,
because they had looked into the ark of the LORD.
[1]He [b]struck fifty thousand and seventy men of the
people, and the people lamented because the LORD
had struck the people with a great slaughter.
**20** And the men of Beth Shemesh said, [a]"Who is
able to stand before this holy LORD God? And to
whom shall it go up from us?"
21 So they sent messengers to the inhabitants of
[a]Kirjath Jearim, saying, "The Philistines have
brought back the ark of the LORD; come down *and*
take it up with you."

## *Israel Defeats the Philistines*

**7** Then the men of [a]Kirjath Jearim came and
took the ark of the LORD, and brought it into
the house of [b]Abinadab on the hill, and [c]conse-
crated Eleazar his son to keep the ark of the LORD.
**2** So it was that the ark remained in Kirjath
Jearim a long time; it was there twenty years. And
all the house of Israel lamented after the LORD.
3 Then Samuel spoke to all the house of Israel,
saying, "If you [a]return to the LORD with all your
hearts, *then* [b]put away the foreign gods and the
[c]Ashtoreths[1] from among you, and [d]prepare your
hearts for the LORD, and [e]serve Him only; and He
will deliver you from the hand of the Philistines."
4 So the children of Israel put away the [a]Baals
and the [1]Ashtoreths, and served the LORD only.
5 And Samuel said, [a]"Gather all Israel to Mizpah, and [b]I will pray to the LORD for you."
6 So they gathered together at Mizpah, [a]drew
water, and poured *it* out before the LORD. And
they [b]fasted that day, and said there, [c]"We have
sinned against the LORD." And Samuel judged the
children of Israel at Mizpah.
7 Now when the Philistines heard that the children of Israel had gathered together at Mizpah,
the lords of the Philistines went up against Israel.
And when the children of Israel heard *of it,* they
were afraid of the Philistines.
8 So the children of Israel said to Samuel, [a]"Do
not cease to cry out to the LORD our God for us,
that He may save us from the hand of the Philistines."
**9** And Samuel took a [a]suckling lamb and offered
*it as* a whole burnt offering to the LORD. Then
[b]Samuel cried out to the LORD for Israel, and the
LORD answered him.
10 Now as Samuel was offering up the burnt
offering, the Philistines drew near to battle
against Israel. [a]But the LORD thundered with a
loud thunder upon the Philistines that day, and so
confused them that they were overcome before
Israel.
11 And the men of Israel went out of Mizpah and
pursued the Philistines, and [1]drove them back as
far as below Beth Car.
12 Then Samuel [a]took a stone and set *it* up
between Mizpah and Shen, and called its name
[1]Ebenezer, saying, "Thus far the LORD has helped
us."
**13** [a]So the Philistines were subdued, and they [b]did
not come anymore into the territory of Israel. And
the hand of the LORD was against the Philistines
all the days of Samuel.
14 Then the cities which the Philistines had
taken from Israel were restored to Israel, from
Ekron to Gath; and Israel recovered its territory
from the hands of the Philistines. Also there was
peace between Israel and the Amorites.
**15** And Samuel [a]judged Israel all the days of his
life.
16 He went from year to year on a circuit to
Bethel, Gilgal, and Mizpah, and judged Israel in all
those places.
17 But [a]he always returned to Ramah, for his
home *was* there. There he judged Israel, and there
he [b]built an altar to the LORD.

## *Israel Asks for a King*

**8** Now it came to pass when Samuel was [a]old
that he [b]made his [c]sons judges over Israel.
2 The name of his firstborn was Joel, and the
name of his second, Abijah; *they were* judges in
Beersheba.
3 But his sons [a]did not walk in his ways; they
turned aside [b]after dishonest gain, [c]took bribes,
and perverted justice.
4 Then all the elders of Israel gathered together
and came to Samuel at Ramah,
5 and said to him, "Look, you are old, and your
sons do not walk in your ways. Now [a]make us a
king to judge us like all the nations."
**6** But the thing [a]displeased Samuel when they
said, "Give us a king to judge us." So Samuel
[b]prayed to the LORD.
7 And the LORD said to Samuel, "Heed the voice
of the people in all that they say to you; for [a]they

**9** [b]1 Sam. 6:3
**12** [a]Num. 20:19
**13** [a]1 Sam. 12:17
**16** [a]Josh. 13:3
**17** [a]1 Sam. 6:4 [b]1 Sam. 5:8
**19** [a]Ex. 19:21 [b]2 Sam. 6:7 [1]Or *He struck seventy men of the people and fifty oxen of a man*
**20** [a]Mal. 3:2
**21** [a]1 Chr. 13:5, 6

CHAPTER 7
**1** [a]1 Sam. 6:21 [b]2 Sam. 6:3, 4 [c]Lev. 21:8
**3** [a]Deut. 30:2–10 [b]Gen. 35:2 [c]Judg. 2:13 [d]Job 11:13 [e]Luke 4:8 [1]Images of Canaanite goddesses
**4** [a]Judg. 2:11; 10:16 [1]Images of Canaanite goddesses
**5** [a]Judg. 10:17; 20:1 [b]1 Sam. 12:17–19
**6** [a]2 Sam. 14:14 [b]Neh. 9:1, 2 [c]1 Sam. 12:10
**8** [a]Is. 37:4
**9** [a]Lev. 22:27 [b]1 Sam. 12:18
**10** [a]2 Sam. 22:14, 15
**11** [1]*struck them down*
**12** [a]Josh. 4:9; 24:26 [1]Lit. *Stone of Help*
**13** [a]Judg. 13:1 [b]1 Sam. 13:5
**15** [a]1 Sam. 12:11
**17** [a]1 Sam. 8:4 [b]Judg. 21:4

CHAPTER 8
**1** [a]1 Sam. 12:2 [b]Deut. 16:18, 19 [c]Judg. 10:4
**3** [a]Jer. 22:15–17 [b]Ex. 18:21 [c]Ex. 23:6–8
**5** [a]Deut. 17:14, 15
**6** [a]1 Sam. 12:17 [b]1 Sam. 7:9
**7** [a]Ex. 16:8

have not rejected you, but [b]they have rejected Me,
that I should not reign over them.
8 "According to all the works which they have
done since the day that I brought them up out of
Egypt, even to this day—with which they have
forsaken Me and served other gods—so they are
doing to you also.
9 "Now therefore, heed their voice. However,
you shall solemnly forewarn them, and [a]show
them the behavior of the king who will reign over
them."
**10** So Samuel told all the words of the LORD to
the people who asked him for a king.
11 And he said, [a]"This will be the behavior of the
king who will reign over you: He will take your
[b]sons and appoint *them* for his own [c]chariots and
*to be* his horsemen, and *some* will run before his
chariots.
12 "He will [a]appoint captains over his thousands
and captains over his fifties, *will set some* to plow
his ground and reap his harvest, and *some* to
make his weapons of war and equipment for his
chariots.
13 "He will take your daughters *to be* perfumers,
cooks, and bakers.
14 "And [a]he will take the best of your fields, your
vineyards, and your olive groves, and give *them* to
his servants.
15 "He will take a tenth of your grain and your
vintage, and give it to his officers and servants.
16 "And he will take your male servants, your
female servants, your finest [1]young men, and your
donkeys, and put *them* to his work.
17 "He will take a tenth of your sheep. And you
will be his servants.
18 "And you will cry out in that day because of
your king whom you have chosen for yourselves,
and the LORD [a]will not hear you in that day."
**19** Nevertheless the people [a]refused to obey the
voice of Samuel; and they said, "No, but we will
have a king over us,
20 that we also may be [a]like all the nations, and
that our king may judge us and go out before us
and fight our battles."
21 And Samuel heard all the words of the people,
and he repeated them in the hearing of the LORD.
22 So the LORD said to Samuel, [a]"Heed their
voice, and make them a king." And Samuel said to
the men of Israel, "Every man go to his city."

### *Saul Chosen King*

**9** There was a man of Benjamin whose name
*was* [a]Kish the son of Abiel, the son of Zeror,
the son of Bechorath, the son of Aphiah, a Benjamite, a mighty man of [1]power.
2 And he had a choice and handsome son whose
name *was* Saul. *There was* not a more handsome
person than he among the children of Israel.
[a]From his shoulders upward *he was* taller than
any of the people.
3 Now the donkeys of Kish, Saul's father, were
lost. And Kish said to his son Saul, "Please take
one of the servants with you, and arise, go and
look for the donkeys."
4 So he passed through the mountains of
Ephraim and through the land of [a]Shalisha, but
they did not find *them*. Then they passed through
the land of Shaalim, and *they were* not *there*.
Then he passed through the land of the Benjamites, but they did not find *them*.
**5** When they had come to the land of [a]Zuph,
Saul said to his servant who *was* with him,
"Come, let [b]us return, lest my father cease *caring*
about the donkeys and become worried about us."
6 And he said to him, "Look now, *there is* in this
city [a]a man of God, and *he is* an honorable man;
[b]all that he says surely comes to pass. So let us go
there; perhaps he can show us the way that we
should go."
7 Then Saul said to his servant, "But look, *if* we
go, [a]what shall we bring the man? For the bread in
our vessels is all gone, and *there is* no present to
bring to the man of God. What do we have?"
8 And the servant answered Saul again and said,
"Look, I have here at hand one fourth of a shekel
of silver. I will give *that* to the man of God, to tell
us our way."
9 (Formerly in Israel, when a man [a]went [1]to
inquire of God, he spoke thus: "Come, let us go to
the seer"; for *he who is* now *called* a prophet was
formerly called [b]a seer.)
10 Then Saul said to his servant, [1]"Well said;
come, let us go." So they went to the city where
the man of God *was*.
**11** As they went up the hill to the city, [a]they met
some young women going out to draw water, and
said to them, "Is the seer here?"
12 And they answered them and said, "Yes, there
he is, just ahead of you. Hurry now; for today he
came to this city, because [a]there is a sacrifice of
the people today [b]on the high place.
13 "As soon as you come into the city, you will
surely find him before he goes up to the high place
to eat. For the people will not eat until he comes,
because he must bless the sacrifice; afterward
those who are invited will eat. Now therefore, go
up, for about this time you will find him."
14 So they went up to the city. As they were
coming into the city, there was Samuel, coming
out toward them on his way up to the high place.
**15** [a]Now the LORD had told Samuel in his ear the
day before Saul came, saying,
16 "Tomorrow about this time [a]I will send you a
man from the land of Benjamin, [b]and you shall
anoint him [1]commander over My people Israel,
that he may save My people from the hand of the
Philistines; for I have [c]looked upon My people,
because their cry has come to Me."
17 So when Samuel saw Saul, the LORD said to
him, [a]"There he is, the man of whom I spoke to
you. This one shall reign over My people."
18 Then Saul drew near to Samuel in the gate,
and said, "Please tell me, where *is* the seer's
house?"
19 Samuel answered Saul and said, "I *am* the
seer. Go up before me to the high place, for you
shall eat with me today; and tomorrow I will let
you go and will tell you all that *is* in your heart.
20 "But as for [a]your donkeys that were lost three
days ago, do not be anxious about them, for they
have been found. And [1]on whom [b]*is* all the desire
of Israel? *Is it* not on you and on all your father's
house?"
21 And Saul answered and said, [a]"*Am* I not a
Benjamite, of the [b]smallest of the tribes of Israel,
and [c]my family the least of all the families of the
[1]tribe of Benjamin? Why then do you speak like
this to me?"
22 Now Samuel took Saul and his servant and
brought them into the hall, and had them sit in
the place of honor among those who were invited;
there *were* about thirty persons.

**7** [b]1 Sam. 10:19
**9** [a]1 Sam. 8:11–18
**11** [a]Deut. 17:14–20 [b]1 Sam. 14:52 [c]2 Sam. 15:1
**12** [a]1 Sam. 22:7
**14** [a]1 Kin. 21:7; [Ezek. 46:18]
**16** [1]LXX *cattle*
**18** [a]Prov. 1:25–28; Is. 1:15; Mic. 3:4
**19** [a]Is. 66:4; Jer. 44:16
**20** [a]1 Sam. 8:5
**22** [a]1 Sam. 8:7; Hos. 13:11

CHAPTER 9

**1** [a]1 Sam. 14:51; 1 Chr. 8:33; 9:36–39 [1]*wealth*
**2** [a]1 Sam. 10:23
**4** [a]2 Kin. 4:42
**5** [a]1 Sam. 1:1 [b]1 Sam. 10:2
**6** [a]Deut. 33:1; 1 Kin. 13:1; 2 Kin. 5:8 [b]1 Sam. 3:19
**7** [a]Judg. 6:18; 13:17; 1 Kin. 14:3; 2 Kin. 4:42; 8:8
**9** [a]Gen. 25:22 [b]2 Sam. 24:11; 2 Kin. 17:13; 1 Chr. 26:28; 29:29; 2 Chr. 16:7, 10; Is. 30:10; Amos 7:12 [1]Lit. *to seek God*
**10** [1]Lit. *Your word is good*
**11** [a]Gen. 24:11, 15; 29:8, 9; Ex. 2:16
**12** [a]Gen. 31:54; 1 Sam. 16:2 [b]1 Sam. 7:17; 10:5; 1 Kin. 3:2
**15** [a]1 Sam. 15:1
**16** [a]Deut. 17:15 [b]1 Sam. 10:1 [c]Ex. 2:23–25; 3:7, 9 [1]*prince* or *ruler*
**17** [a]1 Sam. 16:12; Hos. 13:11
**20** [a]1 Sam. 9:3 [b]1 Sam. 8:5, 19; 12:13 [1]*for whom*
**21** [a]1 Sam. 15:17 [b]Judg. 20:46–48; Ps. 68:27 [c]Judg. 6:15 [1]Lit. *tribes*

23 And Samuel said to the cook, "Bring the portion which I gave you, of which I said to you, 'Set it apart.' "

24 So the cook took up [a]the thigh with its upper part and set *it* before Saul. And *Samuel* said, "Here it is, what was kept back. *It* was set apart for you. Eat; for until this time it has been kept for you, since I said I invited the people." So Saul ate with Samuel that day.

**25** When they had come down from the high place into the city, [1]*Samuel* spoke with Saul on [a]the top of the house.

26 They arose early; and it was about the dawning of the day that Samuel called to Saul on the top of the house, saying, "Get up, that I may send you on your way." And Saul arose, and both of them went outside, he and Samuel.

**27** As they were going down to the outskirts of the city, Samuel said to Saul, "Tell the servant to go on ahead of us." And he went on. "But you stand here [1]awhile, that I may announce to you the word of God."

### *Samuel Anoints Saul*

**10** Then [a]Samuel took a flask of oil and poured *it* on his head, [b]and kissed him and said: "*Is it* not because [c]the LORD has anointed you commander over [d]His [1]inheritance?

2 "When you have departed from me today, you will find two men by [a]Rachel's tomb in the territory of Benjamin [b]at Zelzah; and they will say to you, 'The donkeys which you went to look for have been found. And now your father has ceased caring about the donkeys and is worrying about [c]you, saying, "What shall I do about my son?" '

3 "Then you shall go on forward from there and come to the terebinth tree of Tabor. There three men going up [a]to God at Bethel will meet you, one carrying three young goats, another carrying three loaves of bread, and another carrying a skin of wine.

4 "And they will [1]greet you and give you two *loaves* of bread, which you shall receive from their hands.

5 "After that you shall come to the hill of God [a]where the Philistine garrison *is*. And it will happen, when you have come there to the city, that you will meet a group of prophets coming down [b]from the high place with a stringed instrument, a tambourine, a flute, and a harp before them; [c]and they will be prophesying.

6 "Then [a]the Spirit of the LORD will come upon you, and [b]you will prophesy with them and be turned into another man.

7 "And let it be, when these [a]signs come to you, *that* you do as the occasion demands; for [b]God *is* with you.

8 "You shall go down before me [a]to Gilgal; and surely I will come down to you to offer burnt offerings *and* make sacrifices of peace offerings. [b]Seven days you shall wait, till I come to you and show you what you should do."

**9** So it was, when he had turned his back to go from Samuel, that God [1]gave him another heart; and all those signs came to pass that day.

10 [a]When they came there to the hill, there was [b]a group of prophets to meet him; then the Spirit of God came upon him, and he prophesied among them.

11 And it happened, when all who knew him formerly saw that he indeed prophesied among the prophets, that the people said to one another, "What *is* this *that* has come upon the son of Kish? [a]*Is* Saul also among the prophets?"

12 Then a man from there answered and said, "But [a]who *is* their father?" Therefore it became a proverb: "*Is* Saul also among the prophets?"

13 And when he had finished prophesying, he went to the high place.

**14** Then Saul's [a]uncle said to him and his servant, "Where did you go?" So he said, "To look for the donkeys. When we saw that *they were* nowhere *to be found*, we went to Samuel."

15 And Saul's uncle said, "Tell me, please, what Samuel said to you."

16 So Saul said to his uncle, "He told us plainly that the donkeys had been [a]found." But about the matter of the kingdom, he did not tell him what Samuel had said.

**17** Then Samuel called the people together [a]to the LORD [b]at Mizpah,

18 and said to the children of Israel, [a]"Thus says the LORD God of Israel: 'I brought up Israel out of Egypt, and delivered you from the hand of the Egyptians *and* from the hand of all kingdoms and from those who oppressed you.'

19 [a]"But you have today rejected your God, who Himself saved you from all your adversities and your tribulations; and you have said to Him, 'No, set a king over us!' Now therefore, present yourselves before the LORD by your tribes and by your [1]clans."

20 And when Samuel had [a]caused all the tribes of Israel to come near, the tribe of Benjamin was chosen.

21 When he had caused the tribe of Benjamin to come near by their families, the family of Matri was chosen. And Saul the son of Kish was chosen. But when they sought him, he could not be found.

22 Therefore they [a]inquired of the LORD further, "Has the man come here yet?" And the LORD answered, "There he is, hidden among the equipment."

23 So they ran and brought him from there; and when he stood among the people, [a]he was taller than any of the people from his shoulders upward.

24 And Samuel said to all the people, "Do you see him [a]whom the LORD has chosen, that *there is* no one like him among all the people?" So all the people shouted and said, [b]"Long[1] live the king!"

**25** Then Samuel explained to the people [a]the behavior of royalty, and wrote *it* in a book and laid *it* up before the LORD. And Samuel sent all the people away, every man to his house.

26 And Saul also went home [a]to Gibeah; and valiant *men* went with him, whose hearts God had touched.

27 [a]But some [b]rebels said, "How can this man save us?" So they despised him, [c]and brought him no presents. But he [1]held his peace.

### *Saul Defeats the Ammonites*

**11** Then [a]Nahash the Ammonite came up and [1]encamped against [b]Jabesh Gilead; and all the men of Jabesh said to Nahash, [c]"Make a covenant with us, and we will serve you."

2 And Nahash the Ammonite answered them, "On this *condition* I will make *a covenant* with

**24** [a]Lev. 7:32, 33
**25** [a]Deut. 22:8 [1]So with MT, Tg.; LXX omits *He spoke with Saul on top of the house;* LXX, Vg. afterward add *And he prepared a bed for Saul on top of the house, and he slept*
**27** [1]*now*

CHAPTER 10

**1** [a]2 Kin. 9:3, 6 [b]Ps. 2:12 [c]Acts 13:21 [d]Deut. 32:9 [1]So with MT, Tg., Vg.; LXX *people Israel; and you shall rule the people of the Lord;* LXX, Vg. add *And you shall deliver His people from the hands of their enemies all around them. And this shall be a sign to you, that God has anointed you to be a prince*
**2** [a]Gen. 35:16–20; 48:7 [b]Josh. 18:28 [c]1 Sam. 9:3–5
**3** [a]Gen. 28:22; 35:1, 3, 7
**4** [1]*ask you about your welfare*
**5** [a]1 Sam. 13:2, 3 [b]1 Sam. 19:12, 20 [c]2 Kin. 3:15
**6** [a]Num. 11:25, 29 [b]1 Sam. 10:10; 19:23, 24
**7** [a]Ex. 4:8 [b]Judg. 6:12
**8** [a]1 Sam. 11:14, 15; 13:8 [b]1 Sam. 13:8–10
**9** [1]*changed his heart*
**10** [a]1 Sam. 10:5 [b]1 Sam. 19:20
**11** [a]Matt. 13:54–57
**12** [a]John 5:30, 36
**14** [a]1 Sam. 14:50
**16** [a]1 Sam. 9:20
**17** [a]Judg. 20:1 [b]1 Sam. 7:5, 6
**18** [a]Judg. 6:8, 9
**19** [a]1 Sam. 8:7, 19; 12:12 [1]*thousands*
**20** [a]Acts 1:24, 26
**22** [a]1 Sam. 23:2, 4, 10, 11
**23** [a]1 Sam. 9:2
**24** [a]2 Sam. 21:6 [b]1 Kin. 1:25, 39 [1]Lit. *May the king live*
**25** [a]1 Sam. 8:11–18
**26** [a]Judg. 20:14
**27** [a]1 Sam. 11:12 [b]Deut. 13:13; 1 Sam. 25:17 [c]2 Sam. 8:2; 1 Kin. 4:21; 10:25; 2 Chr. 17:5; Matt. 2:11 [1]*kept silent*

CHAPTER 11

**1** [a]1 Sam. 12:12 [b]Judg. 21:8; 1 Sam. 31:11 [c]Gen. 26:28; 1 Kin. 20:34; Job 41:4; Ezek. 17:13 [1]*besieged*

you, that I may put out all your right eyes, and
bring [a]reproach on all Israel."
3 Then the elders of Jabesh said to him, "Hold
off for seven days, that we may send messengers
to all the territory of Israel. And then, if *there is*
no one to [1]save us, we will come out to you."
**4** So the messengers came [a]to Gibeah of Saul
and told the news in the hearing of the people.
And [b]all the people lifted up their voices and wept.
5 Now there was Saul, coming behind the herd
from the field; and Saul said, "What *troubles* the
people, that they weep?" And they told him the
words of the men of Jabesh.
6 [a]Then the Spirit of God came upon Saul when
he heard this news, and his anger was greatly
aroused.
7 So he took a yoke of oxen and [a]cut them in
pieces, and sent *them* throughout all the territory
of Israel by the hands of messengers, saying,
[b]"Whoever does not go out with Saul and Samuel
to battle, so it shall be done to his oxen." And the
fear of the LORD fell on the people, and they came
out [1]with one consent.
8 When he numbered them in [a]Bezek, the children [b]of Israel were three hundred thousand, and
the men of Judah thirty thousand.
9 And they said to the messengers who came,
"Thus you shall say to the men of Jabesh Gilead:
'Tomorrow, by *the time* the sun is hot, you shall
have help.' " Then the messengers came and
reported *it* to the men of Jabesh, and they were
glad.
10 Therefore the men of Jabesh said, "Tomorrow
we will come out to you, and you may do with us
whatever seems good to you."
11 So it was, on the next day, that [a]Saul put the
people [b]in three companies; and they came into
the midst of the camp in the morning watch, and
killed Ammonites until the heat of the day. And it
happened that those who survived were scattered,
so that no two of them were left together.
**12** Then the people said to Samuel, [a]"Who *is* he
who said, 'Shall Saul reign over us?' [b]Bring the
men, that we may put them to death."
13 But Saul said, [a]"Not a man shall be put to
death this day, for today [b]the LORD has accomplished salvation in Israel."
14 Then Samuel said to the people, "Come, let us
go [a]to Gilgal and renew the kingdom there."
15 So all the people went to Gilgal, and there
they made Saul king [a]before the LORD in Gilgal.
[b]There they made sacrifices of peace offerings
before the LORD, and there Saul and all the men of
Israel rejoiced greatly.

### *Samuel's Address to the People*

**12** Now Samuel said to all Israel: "Indeed I
have [1]heeded [a]your voice in all that you said
to me, and [b]have made a king over you.
2 "And now here is the king, [a]walking before
you; [b]and I am old and grayheaded, and look, my
sons *are* with you. I have walked before you from
my childhood to this day.
3 "Here I am. Witness against me before the
LORD and before [a]His anointed: [b]Whose ox have I
taken, or whose donkey have I taken, or whom
have I cheated? Whom have I oppressed, or from
whose hand have I received *any* [c]bribe with which
to [d]blind my eyes? I will restore *it* to you."
4 And they said, [a]"You have not cheated us or
oppressed us, nor have you taken anything from
any man's hand."
5 Then he said to them, "The LORD *is* witness
against you, and His anointed *is* witness this day,
[a]that you have not found anything [b]in my hand."
And they answered, "*He is* witness."
**6** Then Samuel said to the people, [a]"*It is* the
LORD who raised up Moses and Aaron, and who
brought your fathers up from the land of Egypt.
7 "Now therefore, stand still, that I may [a]reason
with you before the LORD concerning all the
[b]righteous acts of the LORD which He did to you
and your fathers:
8 [a]"When Jacob had gone into [1]Egypt, and your
fathers [b]cried out to the LORD, then the LORD [c]sent
Moses and Aaron, who brought your fathers out
of Egypt and made them dwell in this place.
9 "And when they [a]forgot the LORD their God,
He sold them into the hand of [b]Sisera, commander
of the army of Hazor, into the hand of the [c]Philis-
tines, and into the hand of the king of [d]Moab; and
they fought against them.
10 "Then they cried out to the LORD, and said,
[a]'We have sinned, because we have forsaken the
LORD [b]and served the Baals and [1]Ashtoreths; but
now deliver us from the hand of our enemies, and
we will serve You.'
11 "And the LORD sent [1]Jerubbaal, [2]Bedan, [a]Jeph-
thah, and [b]Samuel, and delivered you out of the
hand of your enemies on every side; and you
dwelt in safety.
12 "And when you saw that [a]Nahash king of the
Ammonites came against you, [b]you said to me,
'No, but a king shall reign over us,' when [c]the
LORD your God *was* your king.
13 "Now therefore, [a]here is the king [b]whom you
have chosen *and* whom you have desired. And
take note, [c]the LORD has set a king over you.
14 "If you [a]fear the LORD and serve Him and obey
His voice, and do not rebel against the commandment of the LORD, then both you and the king
who reigns over you will continue following the
LORD your God.
15 "However, if you do [a]not obey the voice of the
LORD, but [b]rebel against the commandment of the
LORD, then the hand of the LORD will be against
you, as *it was* against your fathers.
**16** "Now therefore, [a]stand and see this great
thing which the LORD will do before your eyes:
17 "*Is* today not the [a]wheat harvest? [b]I will call to
the LORD, and He will send thunder and [c]rain, that
you may perceive and see that [d]your wickedness
*is* great, which you have done in the sight of the
LORD, in asking a king for yourselves."
18 So Samuel called to the LORD, and the LORD
sent thunder and rain that day; and [a]all the people
greatly feared the LORD and Samuel.
**19** And all the people said to Samuel, [a]"Pray for
your servants to the LORD your God, that we may
not die; for we have added to all our sins the evil
of asking a king for ourselves."
20 Then Samuel said to the people, "Do not fear.
You have done all this wickedness; [a]yet do not
turn aside from following the LORD, but serve the
LORD with all your heart.
21 "And [a]do not turn aside; [b]for *then you would*
go after empty things which cannot profit or
deliver, for they *are* nothing.
22 "For [a]the LORD will not forsake [b]His people,
[c]for His great name's sake, because [d]it has pleased
the LORD to make you His people.

**2** [a]Gen. 34:14
**3** [1]*deliver*
**4** [a]1 Sam. 10:26; 15:34 [b]Judg. 2:4; 20:23, 26; 21:2
**6** [a]Judg. 3:10; 6:34; 11:29; 13:25; 14:6
**7** [a]Judg. 19:29 [b]Judg. 21:5, 8, 10 [1]Lit. *as one man*
**8** [a]Judg. 1:5 [b]2 Sam. 24:9
**11** [a]1 Sam. 31:11 [b]Judg. 7:16, 20
**12** [a]1 Sam. 10:27 [b]Luke 19:27
**13** [a]2 Sam. 19:22 [b]Ex. 14:13, 30
**14** [a]1 Sam. 7:16; 10:8
**15** [a]1 Sam. 10:17 [b]1 Sam. 10:8

CHAPTER 12
**1** [a]1 Sam. 8:5, 7, 9, 20, 22 [b]1 Sam. 10:24; 11:14, 15 [1]*listened to*
**2** [a]Num. 27:17 [b]1 Sam. 8:1, 5
**3** [a]1 Sam. 10:1; 24:6 [b]Num. 16:15 [c]Ex. 23:8 [d]Deut. 16:19
**4** [a]Lev. 19:13
**5** [a]Acts 23:9; 24:20 [b]Ex. 22:4
**6** [a]Mic. 6:4
**7** [a]Is. 1:18 [b]Judg. 5:11
**8** [a]Gen. 46:5, 6 [b]Ex. 2:23–25 [c]Ex. 3:10; 4:14–16 [1]So with MT, Tg., Vg.; LXX adds *and the Egyptians afflicted them*
**9** [a]Judg. 3:7 [b]Judg. 4:2 [c]Judg. 3:31; 10:7; 13:1 [d]Judg. 3:12–30
**10** [a]Judg. 10:10 [b]Judg. 2:13; 3:7 [1]Images of Canaanite goddesses
**11** [a]Judg. 11:1 [b]1 Sam. 7:13 [1]Syr. *Deborah; Tg. Gideon* [2]LXX, Syr. *Barak;* Tg. *Simson* [3]Syr. *Simson*
**12** [a]1 Sam. 11:1, 2 [b]1 Sam. 8:5, 19, 20 [c]Judg. 8:23
**13** [a]1 Sam. 10:24 [b]1 Sam. 8:5; 12:17, 19 [c]Hos. 13:11
**14** [a]Josh. 24:14
**15** [a]Deut. 28:15 [b]Is. 1:20
**16** [a]Ex. 14:13, 31
**17** [a]Gen. 30:14 [b][James 5:16–18] [c]Ezra 10:9 [d]1 Sam. 8:7
**18** [a]Ex. 14:31
**19** [a]Ex. 9:28
**20** [a]Deut. 11:16
**21** [a]2 Chr. 25:15 [b]Is. 41:29; Jer. 16:19; Hab. 2:18; 1 Cor. 8:4
**22** [a]Deut. 31:6; 1 Kin. 6:13 [b]Is. 43:21 [c]Ex. 32:12; Num. 14:13; Josh. 7:9; Ps. 106:8; Jer. 14:21 [d]Deut. 7:6–11; 1 Pet. 2:9

23 "Moreover, as for me, far be it from me that I
should sin against the LORD [a]in ceasing to pray for
you; but [b]I will teach you the [c]good and the right
way.
24 [a]"Only fear the LORD, and serve Him in truth
with all your heart; for [b]consider what [c]great
things He has done for you.
25 "But if you still do wickedly, [a]you shall be
swept away, [b]both you and your king."

## *Israel in Distress*

**13** Saul [1]reigned one year; and when he had
reigned two years over Israel,
2 Saul chose for himself three thousand *men* of
Israel. Two thousand were with Saul in [a]Mich-
mash and in the mountains of Bethel, and a
thousand were with [b]Jonathan in [c]Gibeah of
Benjamin. The rest of the people he sent away,
every man to his tent.
3 And Jonathan attacked [a]the garrison of the
Philistines that *was* in [b]Geba, and the Philistines
heard *of it.* Then Saul blew the trumpet throughout all the land, saying, "Let the Hebrews hear!"
4 Now all Israel heard it said *that* Saul had
attacked a garrison of the Philistines, and *that*
Israel had also become [1]an abomination to the
Philistines. And the people were called together to
Saul at Gilgal.
**5** Then the Philistines gathered together to fight
with Israel, [1]thirty thousand chariots and six
thousand horsemen, and people [a]as the sand
which *is* on the seashore in multitude. And they
came up and encamped in Michmash, to the east
of [b]Beth Aven.
6 When the men of Israel saw that they were in
danger (for the people were distressed), then the
people [a]hid in caves, in thickets, in rocks, in holes,
and in pits.
7 And *some of* the Hebrews crossed over the
Jordan to the [a]land of Gad and Gilead. As for Saul,
he *was* still in Gilgal, and all the people followed
him trembling.
**8** [a]Then he waited seven days, according to the
time set by Samuel. But Samuel did not come to
Gilgal; and the people were scattered from him.
9 So Saul said, "Bring a burnt offering and peace
offerings here to me." And he offered the burnt
offering.
10 Now it happened, as soon as he had finished
presenting the burnt offering, that Samuel came;
and Saul went out to meet him, that he might
[1]greet him.
**11** And Samuel said, "What have you done?"
Saul said, "When I saw that the people were
scattered from me, and *that* you did not come
within the days appointed, and *that* the Philistines
gathered together at Michmash,
12 "then I said, 'The Philistines will now come
down on me at Gilgal, and I have not made
supplication to the LORD.' Therefore I felt compelled, and offered a burnt offering."
13 And Samuel said to Saul, [a]"You have done
foolishly. [b]You have not kept the commandment
of the LORD your God, which He commanded you.
For now the LORD would have established your
kingdom over Israel forever.
14 [a]"But now your kingdom shall not continue.
[b]The LORD has sought for Himself a man [c]after His
own heart, and the LORD has commanded him *to
be* commander over His people, because you have
[d]not kept what the LORD commanded you."
15 Then Samuel arose and went up from Gilgal to
Gibeah of [1]Benjamin. And Saul numbered the
people present with him, [a]about six hundred men.
**16** Saul, Jonathan his son, and the people present
with them remained in [1]Gibeah of Benjamin. But
the Philistines encamped in Michmash.
17 Then raiders came out of the camp of the
Philistines in three companies. One company
turned onto the road to [a]Ophrah, to the land of
Shual,
18 another company turned to the road *to* [a]Beth
Horon, and another company turned *to* the road
of the border that overlooks the Valley of [b]Zeboim
toward the wilderness.
**19** Now [a]there was no blacksmith to be found
throughout all the land of Israel, for the Philistines said, "Lest the Hebrews make swords or
spears."
20 But all the Israelites would go down to the
Philistines to sharpen each man's plowshare, his
mattock, his ax, and his sickle;
21 and the charge for a sharpening was a [1]pim for
the plowshares, the mattocks, the forks, and the
axes, and to set the points of the goads.
22 So it came about, on the day of battle, that
[a]there was neither sword nor spear found in the
hand of any of the people who *were* with Saul and
Jonathan. But they were found with Saul and
Jonathan his son.
23 [a]And the garrison of the Philistines went out
to the pass of Michmash.

## *Saul's Curse*

**14** Now it happened one day that Jonathan the
son of Saul said to the young man who
[1]bore his armor, "Come, let us go over to the
Philistines' garrison that *is* on the other side." But
he did not tell his father.
2 And Saul was sitting in the outskirts of [a]Gib-
eah under a pomegranate tree which *is* in Migron.
The people who *were* with him *were* about six
hundred men.
3 [a]Ahijah the son of Ahitub, [b]Ichabod's brother,
the son of Phinehas, the son of Eli, the LORD's
priest in Shiloh, was [c]wearing an ephod. But the
people did not know that Jonathan had gone.
**4** Between the passes, by which Jonathan
sought to go over [a]to the Philistines' garrison,
*there was* a sharp rock on one side and a sharp
rock on the other side. And the name of one *was*
Bozez, and the name of the other Seneh.
5 The front of one faced northward opposite
Michmash, and the other southward opposite
Gibeah.
**6** Then Jonathan said to the young man who
bore his armor, "Come, let us go over to the
garrison of these [a]uncircumcised; it may be that
the LORD will work for us. For nothing restrains
the LORD [b]from saving by many or by few."
7 So his armorbearer said to him, "Do all that is
in your heart. Go then; here I am with you,
according to your heart."
8 Then Jonathan said, "Very well, let us cross
over to *these* men, and we will show ourselves to
them.
9 "If they say thus to us, 'Wait until we come to
you,' then we will stand still in our place and not
go up to them.
10 "But if they say thus, 'Come up to us,' then we
will go up. For the LORD has delivered them into
our hand, and [a]this *will be* a sign to us."
11 So both of them showed themselves to the
garrison of the Philistines. And the Philistines

**23** [a]Rom. 1:9 [b]Ps. 34:11 [c]1 Kin. 8:36
**24** [a]Eccl. 12:13 [b]Is. 5:12 [c]Deut. 10:21
**25** [a]Josh. 24:20 [b]Deut. 28:36

CHAPTER 13
**1** [1]Heb. is difficult; cf. 2 Sam. 5:4; 1 Kin. 14:2; see also 2 Sam. 2:10, Acts 13:21
**2** [a]1 Sam. 14:5, 31 [b]1 Sam. 14:1 [c]1 Sam. 10:26
**3** [a]1 Sam. 10:5 [b]2 Sam. 5:25
**4** [1]*odious*
**5** [a]Judg. 7:12 [b]Josh. 7:2 [1]So with MT, LXX, Tg., Vg.; Syr. and some mss. of LXX *three thousand*
**6** [a]Judg. 6:2
**7** [a]Num. 32:1–42
**8** [a]1 Sam. 10:8
**10** [1]Lit. *bless him*
**13** [a]2 Chr. 16:9 [b]1 Sam. 5:11, 22, 28
**14** [a]1 Sam. 15:28; 31:6 [b]1 Sam. 16:1 [c]Acts 7:46; 13:22 [d]1 Sam. 15:11, 19
**15** [a]1 Sam. 13:2, 6, 7; 14:2 [1]So with MT, Tg.; [LXX], Vg. add *And the rest of the people went up after Saul to meet the people who fought against them, going from Gilgal to Gibeah in the hill of Benjamin.*
**16** [1]Heb. *Geba*
**17** [a]Josh. 18:23
**18** [a]Josh. 16:3; 18:13, 14 [b]Neh. 11:34
**19** [a]Judg. 5:8
**21** [1]About two-thirds shekel weight
**22** [a]Judg. 5:8
**23** [a]1 Sam. 14:1, 4

CHAPTER 14
**1** [1]*carried*
**2** [a]1 Sam. 13:15, 16
**3** [a]1 Sam. 22:9, 11, 20 [b]1 Sam. 4:21 [c]1 Sam. 2:28
**4** [a]1 Sam. 13:23
**6** [a]1 Sam. 17:26, 36 [b]Judg. 7:4, 7
**10** [a]Gen. 24:14

said, "Look, the Hebrews are coming out of the holes where they have [a]hidden."

12 Then the men of the garrison called to Jonathan and his armorbearer, and said, "Come up to us, and we will [1]show you something." Jonathan said to his armorbearer, "Come up after me, for the LORD has delivered them into the hand of Israel."

13 And Jonathan climbed up on his hands and knees with his armorbearer after him; and they [a]fell before Jonathan. And as he came after him, his armorbearer killed them.

14 That first slaughter which Jonathan and his armorbearer made was about twenty men within about [1]half an acre of land.

**15** And [a]there was [1]trembling in the camp, in the field, and among all the people. The garrison and [b]the raiders also trembled; and the earth quaked, so that it was [c]a very great trembling.

16 Now the watchmen of Saul in Gibeah of Benjamin looked, and *there* was the multitude, melting away; and they [a]went here and there.

17 Then Saul said to the people who *were* with him, "Now call the roll and see who has gone from us." And when they had called the roll, surprisingly, Jonathan and his armorbearer *were* not *there.*

18 And Saul said to Ahijah, "Bring the [1]ark of God here" (for at that time the [2]ark of God was with the children of Israel).

19 Now it happened, while Saul [a]talked to the priest, that the noise which *was* in the camp of the Philistines continued to increase; so Saul said to the priest, "Withdraw your hand."

20 Then Saul and all the people who *were* with him assembled, and they went to the battle; and indeed [a]every man's sword was against his neighbor, *and there was* very great confusion.

21 Moreover the Hebrews *who* were with the Philistines before that time, who went up with them into the camp *from the* surrounding *country,* they also joined the Israelites who *were* with Saul and Jonathan.

22 Likewise all the men of Israel who [a]had hidden in the mountains of Ephraim, *when* they heard that the Philistines fled, they also followed hard after them in the battle.

23 [a]So the LORD saved Israel that day, and the battle shifted [b]to Beth Aven.

**24** And the men of Israel were distressed that day, for Saul had [a]placed the people under oath, saying, "Cursed *is* the man who eats *any* food until evening, before I have taken vengeance on my enemies." So none of the people tasted food.

25 [a]Now all *the people* of the land came to a forest; and there was [b]honey on the ground.

26 And when the people had come into the woods, there was the honey, dripping; but no one put his hand to his mouth, for the people feared the oath.

27 But Jonathan had not heard his father charge the people with the oath; therefore he stretched out the end of the rod that *was* in his hand and dipped it in a honeycomb, and put his hand to his mouth; and his [1]countenance brightened.

28 Then one of the people said, "Your father strictly charged the people with an oath, saying, 'Cursed *is* the man who eats food this day.'" And the people were faint.

29 But Jonathan said, "My father has troubled the land. Look now, how my countenance has brightened because I tasted a little of this honey.

30 "How much better if the people had eaten freely today of the spoil of their enemies which they found! For now would there not have been a much greater slaughter among the Philistines?"

**31** Now they had [1]driven back the Philistines that day from Michmash to Aijalon. So the people were very faint.

32 And the people rushed on the [1]spoil, and took sheep, oxen, and calves, and slaughtered *them* on the ground; and the people ate *them* [a]with the blood.

33 Then they told Saul, saying, "Look, the people are sinning against the LORD by eating with the blood!" So he said, "You have dealt treacherously; roll a large stone to me this day."

34 Then Saul said, "Disperse yourselves among the people, and say to them, 'Bring me here every man's ox and every man's sheep, slaughter *them* here, and eat; and do not sin against the LORD by eating with the blood.'" So every one of the people brought his ox with him that night, and slaughtered *it* there.

35 Then Saul [a]built an altar to the LORD. This was the first altar that he built to the LORD.

**36** Now Saul said, "Let us go down after the Philistines by night, and plunder them until the morning light; and let us not leave a man of them." And they said, "Do whatever seems good to you." Then the priest said, "Let us draw near to God here."

37 So Saul [a]asked counsel of God, "Shall I go down after the Philistines? Will You deliver them into the hand of Israel?" But [b]He did not answer him that day.

38 And Saul said, [a]"Come over here, all you chiefs of the people, and know and see what this sin was today.

39 "For [a]*as* the LORD lives, who saves Israel, though it be in Jonathan my son, he shall surely die." But not a man among all the people answered him.

40 Then he said to all Israel, "You be on one side, and my son Jonathan and I will be on the other side." And the people said to Saul, "Do what seems good to you."

41 Therefore Saul said to the LORD God of Israel, [a]"Give[1] a perfect *lot.*" [b]So Saul and Jonathan were taken, but the people escaped.

42 And Saul said, "Cast *lots* between my son Jonathan and me." So Jonathan was taken.

43 Then Saul said to Jonathan, [a]"Tell me what you have done." And Jonathan told him, and said, [b]"I only tasted a little honey with the end of the rod that *was* in my hand. So now I must die!"

44 Saul answered, [a]"God do so and more also; [b]for you shall surely die, Jonathan."

45 But the people said to Saul, "Shall Jonathan die, who has accomplished this great deliverance in Israel? Certainly not! [a]*As* the LORD lives, not one hair of his head shall fall to the ground, for he has worked [b]with God this day." So the people rescued Jonathan, and he did not die.

46 Then Saul returned from pursuing the Philistines, and the Philistines went to their own place.

**47** So Saul established his sovereignty over Israel, and fought against all his enemies on every side, against Moab, against the people of [a]Ammon, against Edom, against the kings of [b]Zobah, and against the Philistines. Wherever he turned, he [1]harassed *them.*

48 And he gathered an army and [a]attacked[1] the

**11** [a]1 Sam. 13:6; 14:22
**12** [1]*teach*
**13** [a]Lev. 26:8; Josh. 23:10
**14** [1]Lit. *half the area plowed by a yoke* of oxen in a day
**15** [a]Deut. 28:7; 2 Kin. 7:6, 7; Job 18:11 [b]1 Sam. 13:17 [c]Gen. 35:5 [1]*terror*
**16** [a]1 Sam. 14:20
**18** [1]So with MT, Tg., Vg.; LXX *ephod* [2]See preceding note
**19** [a]Num. 27:21
**20** [a]Judg. 7:22; 2 Chr. 20:23
**22** [a]1 Sam. 13:6
**23** [a]Ex. 14:30; 2 Chr. 32:22; Hos. 1:7 [b]1 Sam. 13:5
**24** [a]Josh. 6:26
**25** [a]Deut. 9:28; Matt. 3:5 [b]Ex. 3:8; Num. 13:27; Matt. 3:4
**27** [1]Lit. *eyes*
**31** [1]Lit. *struck*
**32** [a]Gen. 9:4; Lev. 3:17; 17:10–14; 19:26; Deut. 12:16, 23, 24; Acts 15:20 [1]*plunder*
**35** [a]1 Sam. 7:12, 17; 2 Sam. 24:25
**37** [a]Judg. 20:18 [b]1 Sam. 28:6
**38** [a]Josh. 7:14; 1 Sam. 10:19
**39** [a]1 Sam. 14:24, 44; 2 Sam. 12:5
**41** [a]Prov. 16:33; Acts 1:24–26 [b]Josh. 7:16; 1 Sam. 10:20, 21 [1]So with MT, Tg.; LXX, [Vg.] *Why do you not answer Your servant today? If the injustice is with me or Jonathan my son, O LORD God of Israel, give proof; and if You say it is with Your people Israel, give holiness.*
**43** [a]Josh. 7:19 [b]1 Sam. 14:27
**44** [a]Ruth 1:17; 1 Sam. 25:22 [b]1 Sam. 14:39
**45** [a]2 Sam. 14:11; 1 Kin. 1:52; Luke 21:18; Acts 27:34 [b][2 Cor. 6:1; Phil. 2:12, 13]
**47** [a]1 Sam. 11:1–13 [b]2 Sam. 10:6 [1]LXX, [Tg.], Vg. *prospered.*
**48** [a]Ex. 17:16; 1 Sam. 15:3–7 [1]Lit. *struck*

Amalekites, and delivered Israel from the hands of
those who plundered them.
49 [a]The sons of Saul were Jonathan, [1]Jishui, and
Malchishua. And the names of his two daughters
*were these:* the name of the firstborn Merab, and
the name of the younger [b]Michal.
50 The name of Saul's wife *was* Ahinoam the
daughter of Ahimaaz. And the name of the commander of his army *was* Abner the son of Ner,
Saul's [a]uncle.
51 [a]Kish *was* the father of Saul, and Ner the
father of Abner *was* the son of Abiel.
**52** Now there was fierce war with the Philistines
all the days of Saul. And when Saul saw any
strong man or any valiant man, [a]he took him for
himself.

## *God Rejects Saul*

**15** Samuel also said to Saul, [a]"The LORD sent
me to anoint you king over His people, over
Israel. Now therefore, heed the voice of the words
of the LORD.
2 "Thus says the LORD of hosts: 'I will punish
what Amalek did to Israel, [a]how he ambushed him
on the way when he came up from Egypt.
3 'Now go and [a]attack[1] Amalek, and [b]utterly
destroy all that they have, and do not spare them.
But kill both man and woman, infant and nursing
child, ox and sheep, camel and donkey.' "
4 So Saul gathered the people together and
numbered them in Telaim, two hundred thousand
foot soldiers and ten thousand men of Judah.
5 And Saul came to a city of Amalek, and lay in
wait in the valley.
**6** Then Saul said to [a]the Kenites, [b]"Go, depart,
get down from among the Amalekites, lest I
destroy you with them. For [c]you showed kindness
to all the children of Israel when they came up out
of Egypt." So the Kenites departed from among
the Amalekites.
7 [a]And Saul attacked the Amalekites, from
[b]Havilah all the way to [c]Shur, which is east of
Egypt.
8 [a]He also took Agag king of the Amalekites
alive, and [b]utterly destroyed all the people with
the edge of the sword.
9 But Saul and the people [a]spared Agag and the
best of the sheep, the oxen, the fatlings, the lambs,
and all *that was* good, and were unwilling to
utterly destroy them. But everything despised and
worthless, that they utterly destroyed.
**10** Now the word of the LORD came to Samuel,
saying,
11 [a]"I greatly regret that I have set up Saul *as*
king, for he has [b]turned back from following Me,
[c]and has not performed My commandments." And
it [d]grieved Samuel, and he cried out to the LORD
all night.
12 So when Samuel rose early in the morning to
meet Saul, it was told Samuel, saying, "Saul went
to [a]Carmel, and indeed, he set up a monument for
himself; and he has gone on around, passed by,
and gone down to Gilgal."
13 Then Samuel went to Saul, and Saul said to
him, [a]"Blessed *are* you of the LORD! I have performed the commandment of the LORD."
14 But Samuel said, "What then *is* this bleating
of the sheep in my ears, and the lowing of the
oxen which I hear?"
15 And Saul said, "They have brought them from
the Amalekites; [a]for the people spared the best of
the sheep and the oxen, to sacrifice to the LORD
your God; and the rest we have utterly destroyed."
16 Then Samuel said to Saul, "Be quiet! And I
will tell you what the LORD said to me last night."
And he said to him, "Speak on."
**17** So Samuel said, [a]"When you *were* little in
your own eyes, *were* you not head of the tribes of
Israel? And did not the LORD anoint you king over
Israel?
18 "Now the LORD sent you on a mission, and
said, 'Go, and utterly destroy the sinners, the
Amalekites, and fight against them until they are
[1]consumed.'
19 "Why then did you not obey the voice of the
LORD? Why did you swoop down on the [1]spoil, and
do evil in the sight of the LORD?"
20 And Saul said to Samuel, [a]"But I have obeyed
the voice of the LORD, and gone on the mission on
which the LORD sent me, and brought back Agag
king of Amalek; I have utterly destroyed the
Amalekites.
21 [a]"But the people took of the plunder, sheep
and oxen, the best of the things which should
have been utterly destroyed, to sacrifice to the
LORD your God in Gilgal."
22 So Samuel said:

[a]"Has the LORD *as great* delight
 in burnt offerings and sacrifices,
As in obeying the voice of the LORD?
Behold, [b]to obey is better than sacrifice,
*And* to heed than the fat of rams.
23 For rebellion *is as* the sin of [1]witchcraft,
And stubbornness *is as* iniquity and idolatry.
Because you have rejected
 the word of the LORD,
[a]He also has rejected you from *being* king."

**24** [a]Then Saul said to Samuel, "I have sinned, for
I have transgressed the commandment of the
LORD and your words, because I [b]feared the people
and obeyed their voice.
25 "Now therefore, please pardon my sin, and
return with me, that I may worship the LORD."
26 But Samuel said to Saul, "I will not return
with you, [a]for you have rejected the word of the
LORD, and the LORD has rejected you from being
king over Israel."
27 And as Samuel turned around to go away,
[a]*Saul* seized the edge of his robe, and it tore.
28 So Samuel said to him, [a]"The LORD has torn
the kingdom of Israel from you today, and has
given it to a neighbor of yours, *who is* better than
you.
29 "And also the Strength of Israel [a]will not lie
nor relent. For He *is* not a man, that He should
relent."
30 Then he said, "I have sinned; *yet* [a]honor me
now, please, before the elders of my people and
before Israel, and return with me, that I may
worship the LORD your God."
31 So Samuel turned back after Saul, and Saul
worshiped the LORD.
**32** Then Samuel said, "Bring Agag king of the
Amalekites here to me." So Agag came to him
cautiously. And Agag said, "Surely the bitterness
of death is past."
33 But Samuel said, [a]"As your sword has made
women childless, so shall your mother be childless
among women." And Samuel hacked Agag in
pieces before the LORD in Gilgal.

**49** [a]1 Sam. 31:2 [b]1 Sam. 18:17–20, 27; 19:12 [1]*Abinadab,* 1 Chr. 8:33; 9:39
**50** [a]1 Sam. 10:14
**51** [a]1 Sam. 9:1, 21
**52** [a]1 Sam. 8:11

CHAPTER 15

**1** [a]1 Sam. 9:16; 10:1
**2** [a]Deut. 25:17–19
**3** [a]Deut. 25:19 [b]Num. 24:20 [1]Lit. *strike*
**6** [a]Num. 24:21 [b]Gen. 18:25; 19:12, 14 [c]Ex. 18:10, 19
**7** [a]1 Sam. 14:48 [b]Gen. 2:11; 25:17, 18 [c]Gen. 16:7
**8** [a]1 Sam. 15:32, 33 [b]1 Sam. 27:8, 9
**9** [a]1 Sam. 15:3, 15, 19
**11** [a]Gen. 6:6, 7 [b]1 Kin. 9:6 [c]1 Sam. 13:13; 15:3, 9 [d]1 Sam. 15:35; 16:1
**12** [a]Josh. 15:55
**13** [a]Judg. 17:2
**15** [a]Gen. 3:12, 131 Sam. 15:9, 21
**17** [a]1 Sam. 9:21; 10:22
**18** [1]*exterminated*
**19** [1]*plunder*
**20** [a]1 Sam. 15:13
**21** [a]1 Sam. 15:15
**22** [a][Is. 1:11–17] [b][Hos. 6:6]
**23** [a]1 Sam. 13:14; 16:1 [1]*divination*
**24** [a]Josh. 7:20 [b][Is. 51:12, 13]
**26** [a]1 Sam. 2:30
**27** [a]1 Kin. 11:30, 31
**28** [a]1 Kin. 11:31
**29** [a]Num. 23:19
**30** [a][John 5:44; 12:43]
**33** [a][Gen. 9:6]

**34** Then Samuel went to [a]Ramah, and Saul went
up to his house at [b]Gibeah of Saul.
35 And [a]Samuel went no more to see Saul until
the day of his death. Nevertheless Samuel
mourned for Saul, and the LORD regretted that He
had made Saul king over Israel.

## *David Anointed King*

**16** Now the LORD said to Samuel, [a]"How long
will you mourn for Saul, seeing I have
rejected him from reigning over Israel? [b]Fill your
horn with oil, and go; I am sending you to [c]Jesse
the Bethlehemite. For [d]I have [1]provided Myself a
king among his sons."
2 And Samuel said, "How can I go? If Saul hears
*it,* he will kill me." But the LORD said, "Take a
heifer with you, and say, [a]'I have come to sacrifice
to the LORD.'
3 "Then invite Jesse to the sacrifice, and I will
show you what you shall do; you shall anoint for
Me the one I name to you."
4 So Samuel did what the LORD said, and went
to Bethlehem. And the elders of the town [a]trem-
bled at his coming, and said, [b]"Do you come
peaceably?"
5 And he said, "Peaceably; I have come to
sacrifice to the LORD. [a]Sanctify[1] yourselves, and
come with me to the sacrifice." Then he consecrated Jesse and his sons, and invited them to the
sacrifice.
**6** So it was, when they came, that he looked at
[a]Eliab and [b]said, "Surely the LORD's anointed *is*
before Him!"
7 But the LORD said to Samuel, [a]"Do not look at
his appearance or at his physical stature, because
I have [1]refused him. [b]For[2] *the LORD does* not *see*
as man sees; for man [c]looks at the outward appearance, but the LORD looks at the [d]heart."
8 So Jesse called Abinadab, and made him pass
before Samuel. And he said, "Neither has the
LORD chosen this one."
9 Then Jesse made Shammah pass by. And he
said, "Neither has the LORD chosen this one."
10 Thus Jesse made seven of his sons pass before
Samuel. And Samuel said to Jesse, "The LORD has
not chosen these."
11 And Samuel said to Jesse, "Are all the young
men here?" Then he said, "There remains yet the
youngest, and there he is, keeping the [a]sheep."
And Samuel said to Jesse, "Send and bring him.
For we will not [1]sit down till he comes here."
12 So he sent and brought him in. Now he *was*
[a]ruddy, [b]with [1]bright eyes, and good-looking. [c]And
the LORD said, "Arise, anoint him; for this *is* the
one!"
13 Then Samuel took the horn of oil and
anointed him in the midst of his brothers; and [a]the
Spirit of the LORD came upon David from that day
forward. So Samuel arose and went to Ramah.
**14** [a]But the Spirit of the LORD departed from Saul,
and [b]a distressing spirit from the LORD troubled
him.
15 And Saul's servants said to him, "Surely, a
distressing spirit from God is troubling you.
16 "Let our master now command your servants,
*who are* before you, to seek out a man *who is* a
skillful player on the harp. And it shall be that he
will [a]play it with his hand when the [1]distressing
spirit from God is upon you, and you shall be
well."

**34** [a]1 Sam. 7:17 [b]1 Sam. 11:4
**35** [a]1 Sam. 19:24

CHAPTER 16

**1** [a]1 Sam. 15:23, 35 [b]1 Sam. 9:16; 10:1 [c]Ruth 4:18–22 [d]Acts 13:22 [1]Lit. *seen*
**2** [a]1 Sam. 9:12
**4** [a]1 Sam. 21:1 [b]1 Kin. 2:13
**5** [a]Ex. 19:10 [1]*Consecrate*
**6** [a]1 Sam. 17:13, 28 [b]1 Kin. 12:26
**7** [a]Ps. 147:10 [b]Is. 55:8, 9 [c]2 Cor. 10:7 [d]1 Kin. 8:39 [1]*rejected* [2]LXX *For God does not see as man sees;* Tg. *It is not by the appearance of a man;* Vg. *Nor do I judge according to the looks of a man*
**11** [a]2 Sam. 7:8 [1]So with LXX, Vg.; MT *turn around;* Tg., Syr. *turn away*
**12** [a]1 Sam. 17:42 [b]Gen. 39:6 [c]1 Sam. 9:17 [1]Lit. *beautiful*
**13** [a]Num. 27:18
**14** [a]Judg. 16:20 [b]Judg. 9:23
**16** [a]1 Sam. 18:10; 19:9 [1]Lit. *evil*
**17** [1]Lit. *Look now for a man for me*
**18** [a]1 Sam. 3:19; 18:12, 14
**20** [a]1 Sam. 10:4, 27
**21** [a]Gen. 41:46

CHAPTER 17

**1** [a]Josh. 15:35
**4** [a]2 Sam. 21:19 [b]Josh. 11:21, 22
**5** [1]*clothed with scaled body armor*
**8** [a]1 Sam. 8:17
**9** [a]1 Sam. 11:1
**10** [a]1 Sam. 17:26, 36, 45
**12** [a]Ruth 4:22 [b]Gen. 35:19 [c]1 Sam. 16:10, 11
**13** [a]1 Sam. 16:6, 8, 9

17 So Saul said to his servants, [1]"Provide me now
a man who can play well, and bring *him* to me."
18 Then one of the servants answered and said,
"Look, I have seen a son of Jesse the Bethlehemite, *who is* skillful in playing, a mighty man of
valor, a man of war, prudent in speech, and a
handsome person; and [a]the LORD *is* with him."
**19** Therefore Saul sent messengers to Jesse, and
said, "Send me your son David, who *is* with the
sheep."
20 And Jesse [a]took a donkey *loaded with* bread, a
skin of wine, and a young goat, and sent *them* by
his son David to Saul.
21 So David came to Saul and [a]stood before him.
And he loved him greatly, and he became his
armorbearer.
22 Then Saul sent to Jesse, saying, "Please let
David stand before me, for he has found favor in
my sight."
23 And so it was, whenever the spirit from God
was upon Saul, that David would take a harp and
play *it* with his hand. Then Saul would become
refreshed and well, and the distressing spirit
would depart from him.

## *David Kills Goliath*

**17** Now the Philistines gathered their armies
together to battle, and were gathered at
[a]Sochoh, which *belongs* to Judah; they encamped
between Sochoh and Azekah, in Ephes Dammim.
2 And Saul and the men of Israel were gathered
together, and they encamped in the Valley of
Elah, and drew up in battle array against the
Philistines.
3 The Philistines stood on a mountain on one
side, and Israel stood on a mountain on the other
side, with a valley between them.
4 And a champion went out from the camp of
the Philistines, named [a]Goliath, from [b]Gath,
whose height *was* six cubits and a span.
5 *He had* a bronze helmet on his head, and he
*was* [1]armed with a coat of mail, and the weight of
the coat *was* five thousand shekels of bronze.
6 And *he had* bronze armor on his legs and a
bronze javelin between his shoulders.
7 Now the staff of his spear *was* like a weaver's
beam, and his iron spearhead *weighed* six hundred
shekels; and a shield-bearer went before him.
8 Then he stood and cried out to the armies of
Israel, and said to them, "Why have you come out
to line up for battle? *Am* I not a Philistine, and
you the [a]servants of Saul? Choose a man for
yourselves, and let him come down to me.
9 "If he is able to fight with me and kill him, then
we will be your servants. But if I prevail against
him and kill him, then you shall be our servants
and [a]serve us."
10 And the Philistine said, "I [a]defy the armies of
Israel this day; give me a man, that we may fight
together."
11 When Saul and all Israel heard these words of
the Philistine, they were dismayed and greatly
afraid.
**12** Now David *was* [a]the son of that [b]Ephrathite of
Bethlehem Judah, whose name *was* Jesse, and
who had [c]eight sons. And the man was old, advanced *in years,* in the days of Saul.
13 The three oldest sons of Jesse had gone to
follow Saul to the battle. The [a]names of his three
sons who went to the battle *were* Eliab the first-

born, next to him Abinadab, and the third Shammah.

14 David *was* the youngest. And the three oldest followed Saul.

15 But David occasionally went and returned from Saul [a]to feed his father's sheep at Bethlehem.

16 And the Philistine drew near and presented himself forty days, morning and evening.

17 Then Jesse said to his son David, "Take now for your brothers an ephah of this dried *grain* and these ten loaves, and run to your brothers at the camp.

18 "And carry these ten cheeses to the captain of *their* thousand, and [a]see how your brothers fare, and bring back news of them."

19 Now Saul and they and all the men of Israel *were* in the Valley of Elah, fighting with the Philistines.

**20** So David rose early in the morning, left the sheep with a keeper, and took *the things* and went as Jesse had commanded him. And he came to the camp as the army was going out to the fight and shouting for the battle.

21 For Israel and the Philistines had drawn up in battle array, army against army.

22 And David left his supplies in the hand of the supply keeper, ran to the army, and came and greeted his brothers.

23 Then as he talked with them, there was the champion, the Philistine of Gath, Goliath by name, coming up from the armies of the Philistines; and he spoke [a]according to the same words. So David heard *them*.

24 And all the men of Israel, when they saw the man, fled from him and were dreadfully afraid.

25 So the men of Israel said, "Have you seen this man who has come up? Surely he has come up to defy Israel; and it shall be *that* the man who kills him the king will enrich with great riches, [a]will give him his daughter, and give his father's house exemption *from taxes* in Israel."

26 Then David spoke to the men who stood by him, saying, "What shall be done for the man who kills this Philistine and takes away [a]the reproach from Israel? For who *is* this [b]uncircumcised Philistine, that he should [c]defy the armies of [d]the living God?"

27 And the people answered him in this manner, saying, [a]"So shall it be done for the man who kills him."

**28** Now Eliab his oldest brother heard when he spoke to the men; and Eliab's [a]anger was aroused against David, and he said, "Why did you come down here? And with whom have you left those few sheep in the wilderness? I know your pride and the insolence of your heart, for you have come down to see the battle."

29 And David said, "What have I done now? [a]*Is*[1] *there* not a cause?"

30 Then he turned from him toward another and [a]said the same thing; and these people answered him as the first ones *did*.

**31** Now when the words which David spoke were heard, they reported *them* to Saul; and he sent for him.

32 Then David said to Saul, [a]"Let no man's heart fail because of him; [b]your servant will go and fight with this Philistine."

33 And Saul said to David, [a]"You are not able to go against this Philistine to fight with him; for you *are* a youth, and he a man of war from his youth."

34 But David said to Saul, "Your servant used to keep his father's sheep, and when a [a]lion or a bear came and took a lamb out of the flock,

35 I went out after it and struck it, and delivered *the lamb* from its mouth; and when it arose against me, I caught *it* by its beard, and struck and killed it.

36 "Your servant has killed both lion and bear; and this uncircumcised Philistine will be like one of them, seeing he has defied the armies of the living God."

37 Moreover David said, [a]"The LORD, who delivered me from the paw of the lion and from the paw of the bear, He will deliver me from the hand of this Philistine." And Saul said to David, [b]"Go, and the LORD be with you!"

**38** So Saul clothed David with his [1]armor, and he put a bronze helmet on his head; he also clothed him with a coat of mail.

39 David fastened his sword to his armor and tried to walk, for he had not tested *them*. And David said to Saul, "I cannot walk with these, for I have not tested *them*." So David took them off.

**40** Then he took his staff in his hand; and he chose for himself five smooth stones from the brook, and put them in a shepherd's bag, in a pouch which he had, and his sling was in his hand. And he drew near to the Philistine.

41 So the Philistine came, and began drawing near to David, and the man who bore the shield *went* before him.

42 And when the Philistine looked about and saw David, he [a]disdained[1] him; for he was *only* a youth, [b]ruddy and good-looking.

43 So the Philistine [a]said to David, "*Am* I a dog, that you come to me with sticks?" And the Philistine cursed David by his gods.

44 And the Philistine [a]said to David, "Come to me, and I will give your flesh to the birds of the air and the beasts of the field!"

45 Then David said to the Philistine, "You come to me with a sword, with a spear, and with a javelin. [a]But I come to you in the name of the LORD of hosts, the God of the armies of Israel, whom you have [b]defied.

46 "This day the LORD will deliver you into my hand, and I will strike you and take your head from you. And this day I will give [a]the carcasses of the camp of the Philistines to the birds of the air and the wild beasts of the earth, [b]that all the earth may know that there is a God in Israel.

47 "Then all this assembly shall know that the LORD [a]does not save with sword and spear; for [b]the battle *is* the LORD's, and He will give you into our hands."

**48** So it was, when the Philistine arose and came and drew near to meet David, that David hurried and [a]ran toward the army to meet the Philistine.

49 Then David put his hand in his bag and took out a stone; and he slung *it* and struck the Philistine in his forehead, so that the stone sank into his forehead, and he fell on his face to the earth.

50 So David prevailed over the Philistine with a [a]sling and a stone, and struck the Philistine and killed him. But *there was* no sword in the hand of David.

51 Therefore David ran and stood over the Philistine, took his [a]sword and drew it out of its sheath and killed him, and cut off his head with it. And when the Philistines saw that their champion was dead, [b]they fled.

**15** [a]1 Sam. 16:11, 19; 2 Sam. 7:8

**18** [a]Gen. 37:13, 14

**23** [a]1 Sam. 17:8–10

**25** [a]Josh. 15:16

**26** [a]1 Sam. 11:2 [b]1 Sam. 14:6; 17:36; Jer. 9:25, 26 [c]1 Sam. 17:10 [d]Deut. 5:26; 2 Kin. 19:4; Jer. 10:10

**27** [a]1 Sam. 17:25

**28** [a]Gen. 37:4, 8–36; [Prov. 18:19; Matt. 10:36]

**29** [a]1 Sam. 17:17 [1]Lit. *Is it not a word* or *matter*

**30** [a]1 Sam. 17:26, 27

**32** [a]Deut. 20:1–4 [b]1 Sam. 16:18

**33** [a]Num. 13:31; Deut. 9:2

**34** [a]Judg. 14:5

**37** [a][2 Cor. 1:10; 2 Tim. 4:17, 18] [b]1 Sam. 20:13; 1 Chr. 22:11, 16

**38** [1]Lit. *clothes*

**42** [a][Ps. 123:4; Prov. 16:18; 1 Cor. 1:27, 28] [b]1 Sam. 16:12 [1]*belittled*

**43** [a]1 Sam. 24:14; 2 Sam. 3:8; 9:8; 16:9; 2 Kin. 8:13

**44** [a]1 Sam. 17:46; 1 Kin. 20:10, 11

**45** [a]2 Sam. 22:33, 35; 2 Chr. 32:8; Ps. 124:8; [2 Cor. 10:4]; Heb. 11:33, 34 [b]1 Sam. 17:10

**46** [a]Deut. 28:26 [b]Josh. 4:24; 1 Kin. 8:43; 18:36; 2 Kin. 19:19; Is. 52:10

**47** [a]1 Sam. 14:6; 2 Chr. 14:11; 20:15; Ps. 44:6; Hos. 1:7; Zech. 4:6 [b]2 Chr. 20:15

**48** [a]Ps. 27:3

**50** [a]Judg. 3:31; 15:15; 20:16

**51** [a]1 Sam. 21:9; 2 Sam. 23:21 [b]Heb. 11:34

52 Now the men of Israel and Judah arose and shouted, and pursued the Philistines as far as the entrance of [1]the valley and to the gates of Ekron. And the wounded of the Philistines fell along the road to [a]Shaaraim, even as far as Gath and Ekron.

53 Then the children of Israel returned from chasing the Philistines, and they plundered their tents.

54 And David took the head of the Philistine and brought it to Jerusalem, but he put his armor in his tent.

**55** When Saul saw David going out against the Philistine, he said to [a]Abner, the commander of the army, "Abner, [b]whose son *is* this youth?" And Abner said, "As your soul lives, O king, I do not know."

56 So the king said, "Inquire whose son this young man *is*."

57 Then, as David returned from the slaughter of the Philistine, Abner took him and brought him before Saul [a]with the head of the Philistine in his hand.

58 And Saul said to him, "Whose son *are* you, young man?" So David answered, [a]"*I am* the son of your servant Jesse the Bethlehemite."

## *Saul Becomes Jealous of David*

**18** Now when he had finished speaking to Saul, [a]the [1]soul of Jonathan was knit to the soul of David, [b]and Jonathan loved him as his own soul.

2 Saul took him that day, [a]and would not let him go home to his father's house anymore.

3 Then Jonathan and David made a [a]covenant, because he loved him as his own soul.

4 And Jonathan took off the robe that *was* on him and gave it to David, with his armor, even to his sword and his bow and his belt.

**5** So David went out wherever Saul sent him, *and* [1]behaved wisely. And Saul set him over the men of war, and he was accepted in the sight of all the people and also in the sight of Saul's servants.

6 Now it had happened as they were coming *home,* when David was returning from the slaughter of the [1]Philistine, that [a]the women had come out of all the cities of Israel, singing and dancing, to meet King Saul, with tambourines, with joy, and with musical instruments.

7 So the women [a]sang as they danced, and said:

> [b]"Saul has slain his thousands,
> And David his ten thousands."

8 Then Saul was very angry, and the saying [a]displeased him; and he said, "They have ascribed to David ten thousands, and to me they have ascribed *only* thousands. Now *what* more can he have but [b]the kingdom?"

9 So Saul [1]eyed David from that day forward.

**10** And it happened on the next day that [a]the distressing spirit from God came upon Saul, [b]and he prophesied inside the house. So David [c]played *music* with his hand, as at other times; [d]but *there was* a spear in Saul's hand.

11 And Saul [a]cast the spear, for he said, "I will pin David to the wall!" But David escaped his presence twice.

**12** Now Saul was [a]afraid of David, because [b]the LORD was with him, but had [c]departed from Saul.

13 Therefore Saul removed him from [1]his presence, and made him his captain over a thousand; and [a]he went out and came in before the people.

14 And David behaved wisely in all his ways, and [a]the LORD *was* with him.

15 Therefore, when Saul saw that he behaved very wisely, he was afraid of him.

16 But [a]all Israel and Judah loved David, because he went out and came in before them.

**17** Then Saul said to David, "Here is my older daughter Merab; [a]I will give her to you as a wife. Only be valiant for me, and fight [b]the LORD's battles." For Saul thought, [c]"Let my hand not be against him, but let the hand of the Philistines be against him."

18 So David said to Saul, [a]"Who *am* I, and what *is* my life *or* my father's family in Israel, that I should be son-in-law to the king?"

19 But it happened at the time when Merab, Saul's daughter, should have been given to David, that she was given to [a]Adriel the [b]Meholathite as a wife.

20 [a]Now Michal, Saul's daughter, loved David. And they told Saul, and the thing pleased him.

21 So Saul said, "I will give her to him, that she may [1]be a snare to him, and that [a]the hand of the Philistines may be against him." Therefore Saul said to David a second time, [b]"You shall be my son-in-law today."

**22** And Saul commanded his servants, "Communicate with David secretly, and say, 'Look, the king has delight in you, and all his servants love you. Now therefore, become the king's son-in-law.' "

23 So Saul's servants spoke those words in the hearing of David. And David said, "Does it seem to you *a* light *thing* to be a king's son-in-law, seeing I *am* a poor and lightly esteemed man?"

24 And the servants of Saul told him, saying, [1]"In this manner David spoke."

25 Then Saul said, "Thus you shall say to David: 'The king does not desire any [a]dowry but one hundred foreskins of the Philistines, to take [b]vengeance on the king's enemies.' " But Saul [c]thought to make David fall by the hand of the Philistines.

26 So when his servants told David these words, it pleased David well to become the king's son-in-law. Now [a]the days had not expired;

27 therefore David arose and went, he and [a]his men, and killed two hundred men of the Philistines. And [b]David brought their foreskins, and they gave them in full count to the king, that he might become the king's son-in-law. Then Saul gave him Michal his daughter as a wife.

**28** Thus Saul saw and knew that the LORD *was* with David, and *that* Michal, Saul's daughter, loved him;

29 and Saul was still more afraid of David. So Saul became David's enemy [1]continually.

30 Then the princes of the Philistines [a]went out *to war.* And so it was, whenever they went out, *that* David [b]behaved more wisely than all the servants of Saul, so that his name became highly esteemed.

## *Saul Seeks to Kill David*

**19** Now Saul spoke to Jonathan his son and to all his servants, that they should kill [a]David; but Jonathan, Saul's son, [b]delighted greatly in David.

2 So Jonathan told David, saying, "My father Saul seeks to kill you. Therefore please be on your guard until morning, and stay in a secret *place* and hide.

---

**52** [a]Josh. 15:36 [1]So with MT, Syr., Tg., Vg.; LXX *Gath*
**55** [a]1 Sam. 14:50 [b]1 Sam. 16:21, 22
**57** [a]1 Sam. 17:54
**58** [a]1 Sam. 17:12

CHAPTER 18

**1** [a]Gen. 44:30 [b]1 Sam. 20:17 [1]*life of Jonathan was bound up with the life of*
**2** [a]1 Sam. 17:15
**3** [a]1 Sam. 20:8–17
**5** [1]Or *prospered*
**6** [a]Ex. 15:20, 21 [1]*Philistines*
**7** [a]Ex. 15:21 [b]1 Sam. 21:11; 29:5
**8** [a]Eccl. 4:4 [b]1 Sam. 15:28
**9** [1]Viewed with suspicion
**10** [a]1 Sam. 16:14 [b]1 Sam. 19:24 [c]1 Sam. 16:23 [d]1 Sam. 19:9, 10
**11** [a]1 Sam. 19:10; 20:33
**12** [a]1 Sam. 18:15, 29 [b]1 Sam. 16:13, 18 [c]1 Sam. 16:14; 28:15
**13** [a]Num. 27:17 [1]Lit. *himself*
**14** [a]Josh. 6:27
**16** [a]1 Sam. 18:5
**17** [a]1 Sam. 14:49; 17:25 [b]Num. 32:20, 27, 29 [c]1 Sam. 18:21, 25
**18** [a]2 Sam. 7:18
**19** [a]2 Sam. 21:8 [b]Judg. 7:22
**20** [a]1 Sam. 18:28
**21** [a]1 Sam. 18:17 [b]1 Sam. 18:26 [1]*be bait for*
**24** [1]Lit. *According to these words*
**25** [a]Ex. 22:17 [b]1 Sam. 14:24 [c]1 Sam. 18:17
**26** [a]1 Sam. 18:21
**27** [a]1 Sam. 18:13 [b]2 Sam. 3:14
**29** [1]*all the days*
**30** [a]2 Sam. 11:1 [b]1 Sam. 18:5

CHAPTER 19

**1** [a]1 Sam. 8:8, 9 [b]1 Sam. 18:1

3 "And I will go out and stand beside my father
in the field where you *are,* and I will speak with
my father about you. Then what I observe, I will
tell [a]you."
4 Thus Jonathan [a]spoke well of David to Saul
his father, and said to him, "Let not the king [b]sin
against his servant, against David, because he has
not sinned against you, and because his works
*have been* very good toward you.
5 "For he took his [a]life in his hands and [b]killed
the Philistine, and [c]the LORD brought about a
great deliverance for all Israel. You saw *it* and
rejoiced. [d]Why then will you [e]sin against innocent
blood, to kill David without a cause?"
6 So Saul heeded the voice of Jonathan, and
Saul swore, "*As* the LORD lives, he shall not be
killed."
7 Then Jonathan called David, and Jonathan
told him all these things. So Jonathan brought
David to Saul, and he was in his presence [a]as in
times past.
8 And there was war again; and David went out
and fought with the Philistines, [a]and struck them
with a mighty blow, and they fled from him.
9 Now [a]the distressing spirit from the LORD
came upon Saul as he sat in his house with his
spear in his hand. And David was playing *music*
with *his* hand.
10 Then Saul sought to pin David to the wall
with the spear, but he slipped away from Saul's
presence; and he drove the spear into the wall. So
David fled and escaped that night.
11 [a]Saul also sent messengers to David's house to
watch him and to kill him in the morning. And
Michal, David's wife, told him, saying, "If you do
not save your life tonight, tomorrow you will be
killed."
12 So Michal [a]let David down through a window.
And he went and fled and escaped.
13 And Michal took [1]an image and laid *it* in the
bed, put a cover of goats' *hair* for his head, and
covered *it* with clothes.
14 So when Saul sent messengers to take David,
she said, "He *is* sick."
15 Then Saul sent the messengers *back* to see
David, saying, "Bring him up to me in the bed,
that I may kill him."
16 And when the messengers had come in, there
was the image in the bed, with a cover of goats'
*hair* for his head.
17 Then Saul said to Michal, "Why have you
deceived me like this, and sent my enemy away,
so that he has escaped?" And Michal answered
Saul, "He said to me, 'Let me go! [a]Why should I
kill you?' "
18 So David fled and escaped, and went to [a]Sam-
uel at [b]Ramah, and told him all that Saul had done
to him. And he and Samuel went and stayed in
Naioth.
19 Now it was told Saul, saying, "Take note,
David *is* at Naioth in Ramah!"
20 Then [a]Saul sent messengers to take David.
[b]And when they saw the group of prophets prophesying, and Samuel standing *as* leader over them,
the Spirit of God came upon the messengers of
Saul, and they also [c]prophesied.
21 And when Saul was told, he sent other messengers, and they prophesied likewise. Then Saul
sent messengers again the third time, and they
prophesied also.
22 Then he also went to Ramah, and came to the
great well that *is* at Sechu. So he asked, and said,
"Where *are* Samuel and David?" And *someone*
said, "Indeed *they are* at Naioth in Ramah."
23 So he went there to Naioth in Ramah. Then
[a]the Spirit of God was upon him also, and he went
on and prophesied until he came to Naioth in
Ramah.
24 [a]And he also stripped off his clothes and
prophesied before Samuel in like manner, and lay
down [b]naked all that day and all that night.
Therefore they say, [c]"*Is* Saul also among the
prophets?"

### *Jonathan's Covenant with David*

**20** Then David fled from Naioth in Ramah, and
went and said to Jonathan, "What have I
done? What *is* my iniquity, and what *is* my sin
before your father, that he seeks my life?"
2 So Jonathan said to him, "By no means! You
shall not die! Indeed, my father will do nothing
either great or small without first telling me. And
why should my father hide this thing from me? It
*is* not *so!*"
3 Then David took an oath again, and said,
"Your father certainly knows that I have found
favor in your eyes, and he has said, 'Do not let
Jonathan know this, lest he be grieved.' But [a]truly,
*as* the LORD lives and *as* your soul lives, *there is*
but a step between me and death."
4 So Jonathan said to David, "Whatever you
yourself desire, I will do *it* for you."
5 And David said to Jonathan, "Indeed tomorrow *is* the [a]New Moon, and I should not fail to sit
with the king to eat. But let me go, that I may
[b]hide in the field until the third *day* at evening.
6 "If your father misses me at all, then say,
'David earnestly asked *permission* of me that he
might run over [a]to Bethlehem, his city, for *there is*
a yearly sacrifice there for all the family.'
7 [a]"If he says thus: '*It is* well,' your servant will
be safe. But if he is very angry, be sure that [b]evil is
determined by him.
8 "Therefore you shall [a]deal kindly with your
servant, for [b]you have brought your servant into a
covenant of the LORD with you. Nevertheless, [c]if
there is iniquity in me, kill me yourself, for why
should you bring me to your father?"
9 But Jonathan said, "Far be it from you! For if I
knew certainly that evil was determined by my
father to come upon you, then would I not tell
you?"
10 Then David said to Jonathan, "Who will tell
me, or what *if* your father answers you roughly?"
11 And Jonathan said to David, "Come, let us go
out into the field." So both of them went out into
the field.
12 Then Jonathan said to David: "The LORD God
of Israel *is witness!* When I have [1]sounded out my
father sometime tomorrow, *or* the third *day,* and
indeed *there is* good toward David, and I do not
send to you and tell you,
13 "may [a]the LORD do so and much more to
Jonathan. But if it pleases my father *to do* you
evil, then I will report it to you and send you
away, that you may go in safety. And [b]the LORD
be with you as He has [c]been with my father.
14 "And you shall not only show me the kindness
of the LORD while I still live, that I may not die;
15 "but [a]you shall not [1]cut off your kindness from
my [2]house forever, no, not when the LORD has cut

3 [a]1 Sam. 20:8–13
4 [a]1 Sam. 20:32; [Prov. 31:8, 9] [b]Gen. 42:22; [Prov. 17:13]; Jer. 18:20
5 [a]Judg. 9:17; 12:3 [b]1 Sam. 17:49, 50 [c]1 Sam. 11:13; 1 Chr. 11:14 [d]1 Sam. 20:32 [e][Deut. 19:10–13]
7 [a]1 Sam. 16:21; 18:2, 10, 13
8 [a]1 Sam. 18:27; 23:5
9 [a]1 Sam. 16:14; 18:10, 11
11 [a]Judg. 16:2; Ps. 59:title
12 [a]Josh. 2:15; Acts 9:25; 2 Cor. 11:33
13 [1]*household idols,* Heb. *teraphim*
17 [a]2 Sam. 2:22
18 [a]1 Sam. 16:13 [b]1 Sam. 7:17
20 [a]1 Sam. 19:11, 14; John 7:32 [b]1 Sam. 10:5, 6, 10; [1 Cor. 14:3, 24, 25] [c]Num. 11:25; Joel 2:28
23 [a]1 Sam. 10:10
24 [a]Is. 20:2 [b]Mic. 1:8 [c]1 Sam. 10:10–12

CHAPTER 20
3 [a]1 Sam. 27:1; 2 Kin. 2:6
5 [a]Num. 10:10; 28:11–15 [b]1 Sam. 19:2, 3
6 [a]1 Sam. 16:4; 17:12; John 7:42
7 [a]Deut. 1:23; 2 Sam. 17:4 [b]1 Sam. 25:17; Esth. 7:7
8 [a]Josh. 2:14 [b]1 Sam. 18:3; 20:16; 23:18 [c]2 Sam. 14:32
12 [1]*searched out*
13 [a]Ruth 1:17; 1 Sam. 3:17 [b]Josh. 1:5; 1 Sam. 17:37; 18:12; 1 Chr. 22:11, 16 [c]1 Sam. 10:7
15 [a]1 Sam. 24:21; 2 Sam. 9:1, 3, 7; 21:7 [1]*stop being kind* [2]*family*

off every one of the enemies of David from the
face of the earth."
16 So Jonathan made *a covenant* with the [1]house
of David, *saying,* [a]"Let the LORD require *it* at the
hand of David's enemies."
17 Now Jonathan again caused David to vow,
because he loved him; [a]for he loved him as he
loved his own soul.
18 Then Jonathan said to David, [a]"Tomorrow *is*
the New Moon; and you will be missed, because
your seat will be empty.
19 "And *when* you have stayed three days, go
down quickly and come to [a]the place where you
hid on the day of the deed; and remain by the
stone Ezel.
20 "Then I will shoot three arrows to the side, as
though I shot at a target;
21 "and there I will send a lad, *saying,* 'Go, find
the arrows.' If I expressly say to the lad, 'Look,
the arrows *are* on this side of you; get them and
come'—then, [a]as the LORD lives, *there is* safety for
you and no harm.
22 "But if I say thus to the young man, 'Look, the
arrows *are* beyond you'—go your way, for the
LORD has sent you away.
23 "And as for [a]the matter which you and I have
spoken of, indeed the LORD *be* between you and
me forever."
24 Then David hid in the field. And when the
New Moon had come, the king sat down to eat the
feast.
25 Now the king sat on his seat, as at other times,
on a seat by the wall. And [1]Jonathan arose, and
Abner sat by Saul's side, but David's place was
empty.
26 Nevertheless Saul did not say anything that
day, for he thought, "Something has happened to
him; he *is* unclean, surely he *is* [a]unclean."
27 And it happened the next day, the second *day*
of the month, that David's place was empty. And
Saul said to Jonathan his son, "Why has the son
of Jesse not come to eat, either yesterday or
today?"
28 So Jonathan [a]answered Saul, "David earnestly
asked *permission* of me *to* go to Bethlehem.
29 "And he said, 'Please let me go, for our family
has a sacrifice in the city, and my brother has
commanded me *to be there.* And now, if I have
found favor in your eyes, please let me get away
and see my brothers.' Therefore he has not come
to the king's table."
30 Then Saul's anger was aroused against Jonathan, and he said to him, "You son of a perverse,
rebellious *woman!* Do I not know that you have
chosen the son of Jesse to your own shame and to
the shame of your mother's nakedness?
31 "For as long as the son of Jesse lives on the
earth, you shall not be established, nor your
kingdom. Now therefore, send and bring him to
me, for he [1]shall surely die."
32 And Jonathan answered Saul his father, and
said to him, [a]"Why should he be killed? What has
he done?"
33 Then Saul [a]cast a spear at him to [1]kill him, [b]by
which Jonathan knew that it was determined by
his father to kill David.
34 So Jonathan arose from the table in fierce
anger, and ate no food the second day of the
month, for he was grieved for David, because his
father had treated him shamefully.
35 And so it was, in the morning, that Jonathan
went out into the field at the time appointed with
David, and a little lad *was* with him.
36 Then he said to his lad, "Now run, find the
arrows which I shoot." As the lad ran, he shot an
arrow beyond him.
37 When the lad had come to the place where the
arrow was which Jonathan had shot, Jonathan
cried out after the lad and said, "*Is* not the arrow
beyond you?"
38 And Jonathan cried out after the lad, "Make
haste, hurry, do not delay!" So Jonathan's lad
gathered up the arrows and came back to his
master.
39 But the lad did not know anything. Only
Jonathan and David knew of the matter.
40 Then Jonathan gave his [1]weapons to his lad,
and said to him, "Go, carry *them* to the city."
41 As soon as the lad had gone, David arose from
*a place* toward the south, fell on his face to the
ground, and bowed down three times. And they
kissed one another; and they wept together, but
David more so.
42 Then Jonathan said to David, [a]"Go in peace,
since we have both sworn in the name of the
LORD, saying, 'May the LORD be between you and
me, and between your descendants, and my descendants, forever.' " So he arose and departed,
and Jonathan went into the city.

### *David Flees to Nob and Then to Gath*

21 Now David came to Nob, to Ahimelech the
priest. And [a]Ahimelech was [b]afraid when he
met David, and said to him, "Why *are* you alone,
and no one is with you?"
2 So David said to Ahimelech the priest, "The
king has ordered me on some business, and said to
me, 'Do not let anyone know anything about the
business on which I send you, or what I have
commanded you.' And I have directed *my* young
men to such and such a place.
3 "Now therefore, what have you on hand? Give
*me* five *loaves of* bread in my hand, or whatever
can be found."
4 And the priest answered David and said,
"*There is* no [1]common bread on hand; but there is
[a]holy[2] bread, [b]if the young men have at least kept
themselves from women."
5 Then David answered the priest, and said to
him, "Truly, women *have been* kept from us about
three days since I came out. And [1]the [a]vessels of
the young men are holy, and *the bread is* in effect
common, even though it was consecrated [b]in the
vessel this day."
6 So the priest [a]gave him holy *bread;* for there
was no bread there but the showbread [b]which had
been taken from before the LORD, in order to put
hot bread *in its place* on the day when it was
taken away.
7 Now a certain man of the servants of Saul *was*
there that day, detained before the LORD. And his
name *was* [a]Doeg, an Edomite, the chief of the
herdsmen who *belonged* to Saul.
8 And David said to Ahimelech, "Is there not
here on hand a spear or a sword? For I have
brought neither my sword nor my weapons with
me, because the king's business required haste."
9 So the priest said, "The sword of Goliath the
Philistine, whom you killed in [a]the Valley of Elah,
[b]there it is, wrapped in a cloth behind the ephod. If
you will take that, take *it.* For *there is* no other

16 [a]Deut. 23:21; 1 Sam. 25:22; 31:2; 2 Sam. 4:7; 21:8 [1]*family*
17 [a]1 Sam. 18:1
18 [a]1 Sam. 20:5, 24
19 [a]1 Sam. 19:2
21 [a]Jer. 4:2
23 [a]1 Sam. 20:14, 15
25 [1]So with MT, Syr., Tg., Vg.; LXX *he sat across from Jonathan*
26 [a]Lev. 7:20, 21; 15:5
28 [a]1 Sam. 20:6
31 [1]Lit. *is a son of death*
32 [a]Gen. 31:36; 1 Sam. 19:5; [Prov. 31:9]; Matt. 27:23; Luke 23:22
33 [a]1 Sam. 18:11; 19:10 [b]1 Sam. 20:7 [1]*strike him down*
40 [1]*equipment*
42 [a]1 Sam. 1:17

CHAPTER 21

1 [a]1 Sam. 14:3; Mark 2:26 [b]1 Sam. 16:4
4 [a]Ex. 25:30; Lev. 24:5–9; Matt. 12:4 [b]Ex. 19:15 [1]*ordinary* [2]*consecrated*
5 [a]Ex. 19:14, 15; 1 Thess. 4:4 [b]Lev. 8:26 [1]The young men are ceremonially undefiled
6 [a]Matt. 12:3, 4; Mark 2:25, 26; Luke 6:3, 4 [b]Lev. 24:8, 9
7 [a]1 Sam. 14:47; 22:9; Ps. 52:title
9 [a]1 Sam. 17:2, 50 [b]1 Sam. 31:10

except that one here." And David said, "*There is* none like it; give it to me."

**10** Then David arose and fled that day from before Saul, and went to Achish the king of Gath.

11 And [a]the servants of Achish said to him, [b]"*Is* this not David the king of the land? Did they not sing of him to one another in dances, saying:

[c]'Saul has slain his thousands,
And David his ten thousands'?"

12 Now David [a]took these words [1]to heart, and was very much afraid of Achish the king of Gath.

13 So [a]he changed his behavior before them, pretended [1]madness in their hands, [2]scratched on the doors of the gate, and let his saliva fall down on his beard.

14 Then Achish said to his servants, "Look, you see the man is insane. Why have you brought him to me?

15 "Have I need of madmen, that you have brought this *fellow* to play the madman in my presence? Shall this *fellow* come into my house?"

## *Saul Kills the Priests of Nob*

**22** David therefore departed from there and [a]escaped [b]to the cave of Adullam. So when his brothers and all his father's house heard *it*, they went down there to him.

2 [a]And everyone *who was* in distress, everyone who *was* in debt, and everyone *who was* [1]discontented gathered to him. So he became captain over them. And there were about [b]four hundred men with him.

**3** Then David went from there to Mizpah of [a]Moab; and he said to the king of Moab, "Please let my father and mother come here with you, till I know what God will do for me."

4 So he brought them before the king of Moab, and they dwelt with him all the time that David was in the stronghold.

5 Now the prophet [a]Gad said to David, "Do not stay in the stronghold; depart, and go to the land of Judah." So David departed and went into the forest of Hereth.

**6** When Saul heard that David and the men who *were* with him had been discovered—now Saul was staying in [a]Gibeah under a tamarisk tree in Ramah, with his spear in his hand, and all his servants standing about him—

7 then Saul said to his servants who stood about him, "Hear now, you Benjamites! Will the son of Jesse [a]give every one of you fields and vineyards, *and* make you all captains of thousands and captains of hundreds?

8 "All of you have conspired against me, and *there is* no one who reveals to me that [a]my son has made a covenant with the son of Jesse; and *there is* not one of you who is sorry for me or reveals to me that my son has stirred up my servant against me, to lie in wait, as *it is* this day."

**9** Then answered [a]Doeg the Edomite, who was set over the servants of Saul, and said, "I saw the son of Jesse going to Nob, to [b]Ahimelech the son of [c]Ahitub.

10 [a]"And he inquired of the LORD for him, [b]gave him provisions, and gave him the sword of Goliath the Philistine."

**11** So the king sent to call Ahimelech the priest, the son of Ahitub, and all his father's house, the priests who *were* in Nob. And they all came to the king.

12 And Saul said, "Hear now, son of Ahitub!" He answered, "Here I am, my lord."

13 Then Saul said to him, "Why have you conspired against me, you and the son of Jesse, in that you have given him bread and a sword, and have inquired of God for him, that he should rise against me, to lie in wait, as it is this day?"

14 So Ahimelech answered the king and said, "And who among all your servants *is as* [a]faithful as David, who is the king's son-in-law, who goes at your bidding, and is honorable in your house?

15 "Did I then begin to inquire of God for him? Far be it from me! Let not the king impute anything to his servant, *or* to any in the house of my father. For your servant knew nothing of all this, little or much."

16 And the king said, "You shall surely die, Ahimelech, you and all [a]your father's house!"

17 Then the king said to the guards who stood about him, "Turn and kill the priests of the LORD, because their hand also *is* with David, and because they knew when he fled and did not tell it to me." But the servants of the king [a]would not lift their hands to strike the priests of the LORD.

18 And the king said to Doeg, "You turn and kill the priests!" So Doeg the Edomite turned and [1]struck the priests, and [a]killed on that day eighty-five men who wore a linen ephod.

19 [a]Also Nob, the city of the priests, he struck with the edge of the sword, both men and women, children and nursing infants, oxen and donkeys and sheep—with the edge of the sword.

**20** [a]Now one of the sons of Ahimelech the son of Ahitub, named Abiathar, [b]escaped and fled after David.

21 And Abiathar told David that Saul had killed the LORD's priests.

22 So David said to Abiathar, "I knew that day, when Doeg the Edomite *was* there, that he would surely tell Saul. I have caused *the death* of all the persons of your father's [1]house.

23 "Stay with me; do not fear. [a]For he who seeks my life seeks your life, but with me you *shall be* safe."

## *David Escapes to the Wilderness*

**23** Then they told David, saying, "Look, the Philistines are fighting against [a]Keilah, and they are robbing the threshing floors."

2 Therefore David [a]inquired of the LORD, saying, "Shall I go and [1]attack these Philistines?" And the LORD said to David, "Go and attack the Philistines, and save Keilah."

3 But David's men said to him, "Look, we are afraid here in Judah. How much more then if we go to Keilah against the armies of the Philistines?"

4 Then David inquired of the LORD once again. And the LORD answered him and said, "Arise, go down to Keilah. For I will deliver the Philistines into your hand."

5 And David and his men went to Keilah and [a]fought with the Philistines, struck them with a mighty blow, and took away their livestock. So David saved the inhabitants of Keilah.

**6** Now it happened, when Abiathar the son of Ahimelech [a]fled to David at Keilah, *that* he went down *with* an ephod in his hand.

7 And Saul was told that David had gone to Keilah. So Saul said, "God has delivered him into my hand, for he has shut himself in by entering a town that has gates and bars."

**11** [a]Ps. 56:title [b]1 Sam. 18:6–8; 29:5
**12** [a]Luke 2:19 [1]Lit. *in his heart*
**13** [a]Ps. 34:title [1]*insanity* [2]*scribbled*

CHAPTER 22

**1** [a]Ps. 57:title; 142:title [b]Josh. 12:15; 15:35; 2 Sam. 23:13
**2** [a]Judg. 11:3 [b]1 Sam. 25:13 [1]Lit. *bitter of soul*
**3** [a]2 Sam. 8:2
**5** [a]2 Sam. 24:11; 1 Chr. 21:9; 29:29; 2 Chr. 29:25
**6** [a]1 Sam. 15:34
**7** [a]1 Sam. 8:14
**8** [a]1 Sam. 18:3; 20:16, 30
**9** [a]1 Sam. 21:7; 22:22; Ps. 52:title [b]1 Sam. 21:1 [c]1 Sam. 14:3
**10** [a]Num. 27:21; 1 Sam. 10:22 [b]1 Sam. 21:6, 9
**14** [a]1 Sam. 19:4, 5; 20:32; 24:11
**16** [a]Deut. 24:16
**17** [a]Ex. 1:17
**18** [a]1 Sam. 2:31 [1]*attacked*
**19** [a]Josh. 21:1–45; 1 Sam. 22:9, 11
**20** [a]1 Sam. 23:6, 9; 30:7; 1 Kin. 2:26, 27 [b]1 Sam. 2:33
**22** [1]*family*
**23** [a]1 Kin. 2:26

CHAPTER 23

**1** [a]Josh. 15:44; Neh. 3:17, 18
**2** [a]1 Sam. 22:10; 23:4, 6, 9; 28:6; 30:8; 2 Sam. 5:19, 23 [1]Lit. *strike*
**5** [a]1 Sam. 19:8; 2 Sam. 5:20
**6** [a]1 Sam. 22:20

8 Then Saul called all the people together for
war, to go down to Keilah to besiege David and
his men.
**9** When David knew that Saul plotted evil
against him, [a]he said to Abiathar the priest, "Bring
the ephod here."
10 Then David said, "O LORD God of Israel, Your
servant has certainly heard that Saul seeks to
come to Keilah [a]to destroy the city for my sake.
11 "Will the men of Keilah deliver me into his
hand? Will Saul come down, as Your servant has
heard? O LORD God of Israel, I pray, tell Your
servant." And the LORD said, "He will come
down."
12 Then David said, "Will the men of Keilah
[1]deliver me and my men into the hand of Saul?"
And the LORD said, "They will deliver *you.*"
13 So David and his men, [a]about six hundred,
arose and departed from Keilah and went wherever they could go. Then it was told Saul that
David had escaped from Keilah; so he halted the
expedition.
**14** And David stayed in strongholds in the wilderness, and remained in [a]the mountains in the
Wilderness of [b]Ziph. Saul [c]sought him every day,
but God did not deliver him into his hand.
15 So David saw that Saul had come out to seek
his life. And David *was* in the Wilderness of Ziph
[1]in a forest.
16 Then Jonathan, Saul's son, arose and went to
David in the woods and [1]strengthened his hand in
God.
17 And he said to him, [a]"Do not fear, for the hand
of Saul my father shall not find you. You shall be
king over Israel, and I shall be next to you. [b]Even
my father Saul knows that."
18 So the two of them [a]made a covenant before
the LORD. And David stayed in the woods, and
Jonathan went to his own house.
**19** Then the Ziphites [a]came up to Saul at Gibeah,
saying, "Is David not hiding with us in strongholds in the woods, in the hill of Hachilah, which
*is* on the south of Jeshimon?
20 "Now therefore, O king, come down according
to all the desire of your soul to come down; and
[a]our part *shall be* to deliver him into the king's
hand."
21 And Saul said, "Blessed *are* you of the LORD,
for you have compassion on me.
22 "Please go and find out for sure, and see the
place where his hideout is, *and* who has seen him
there. For I am told he is very crafty.
23 "See therefore, and take knowledge of all the
lurking places where he hides; and come back to
me with certainty, and I will go with you. And it
shall be, if he is in the land, that I will search for
him throughout all the [1]clans of Judah."
**24** So they arose and went to Ziph before Saul.
But David and his men *were* in the Wilderness [a]of
Maon, in the plain on the south of Jeshimon.
25 When Saul and his men went to seek *him,*
they told David. Therefore he went down [1]to the
rock, and stayed in the Wilderness of Maon. And
when Saul heard *that,* he pursued David in the
Wilderness of Maon.
26 Then Saul went on one side of the mountain,
and David and his men on the other side of the
mountain. [a]So David made haste to get away from
Saul, for Saul and his men [b]were encircling David
and his men to take them.
**27** [a]But a messenger came to Saul, saying, "Hurry
and come, for the Philistines have invaded the
land!"
28 Therefore Saul returned from pursuing David,
and went against the Philistines; so they called
that place [1]the Rock of Escape.
29 Then David went up from there and dwelt in
strongholds at [a]En Gedi.

### *David Spares Saul's Life*

**24** Now it happened, [a]when Saul had returned
from following the Philistines, that it was
told him, saying, "Take note! David *is* in the
Wilderness of En Gedi."
2 Then Saul took three thousand chosen men
from all Israel, and [a]went to seek David and his
men on the Rocks of the Wild Goats.
3 So he came to the sheepfolds by the road,
where there *was* a cave; and [a]Saul went in to
[b]attend to his needs. ([c]David and his men were
staying in the recesses of the cave.)
4 [a]Then the men of David said to him, "This is
the day of which the LORD said to you, 'Behold, I
will deliver your enemy into your hand, that you
may do to him as it seems good to you.' " And
David arose and secretly cut off a corner of Saul's
robe.
5 Now it happened afterward that [a]David's
heart troubled him because he had cut Saul's *robe.*
6 And he said to his men, [a]"The LORD forbid that
I should do this thing to my master, the LORD's
anointed, to stretch out my hand against him,
seeing he *is* the anointed of the LORD."
7 So David [a]restrained his servants with *these*
words, and did not allow them to rise against Saul.
And Saul got up from the cave and went on *his*
way.
**8** David also arose afterward, went out of the
cave, and called out to Saul, saying, "My lord the
king!" And when Saul looked behind him, David
stooped with his face to the earth, and bowed
down.
9 And David said to Saul: [a]"Why do you listen to
the words of men who say, 'Indeed David seeks
your harm'?
10 "Look, this day your eyes have seen that the
LORD delivered you today into my hand in the
cave, and *someone* urged *me* to kill you. But *my*
*eye* spared you, and I said, 'I will not stretch out
my hand against my lord, for he *is* the LORD's
anointed.'
11 "Moreover, my father, see! Yes, see the corner
of your robe in my hand! For in that I cut off the
corner of your robe, and did not kill you, know
and see that *there is* [a]neither evil nor rebellion in
my hand, and I have not sinned against you. Yet
you [b]hunt my life to take it.
12 [a]"Let the LORD judge between you and me,
and let the LORD avenge me on you. But my hand
shall not be against you.
13 "As the proverb of the ancients says, [a]'Wickedness proceeds from the wicked.' But my hand
shall not be against you.
14 "After whom has the king of Israel come out?
Whom do you pursue? [a]A dead dog? [b]A flea?
15 [a]"Therefore let the LORD be judge, and judge
between you and me, and [b]see and [c]plead my case,
and deliver me out of your hand."
**16** So it was, when David had finished speaking
these words to Saul, that Saul said, [a]"*Is* this your
voice, my son David?" And Saul lifted up his voice
and wept.

9 [a]Num. 27:21; 1 Sam. 23:6; 30:7
10 [a]1 Sam. 22:19
12 [1]Lit. *shut up*
13 [a]1 Sam. 22:2; 25:13
14 [a]Ps. 11:1 [b]Josh. 15:55; 2 Chr. 11:8 [c]Ps. 32:7; 54:3, 4
15 [1]Or *in Horesh*
16 [1]*encouraged him*
17 [a][Ps. 27:1–3; Heb. 13:6] [b]1 Sam. 20:31; 24:20
18 [a]1 Sam. 18:3; 20:12–17, 42; 2 Sam. 9:1; 21:7
19 [a]1 Sam. 26:1; Ps. 54:title
20 [a]Ps. 54:3
23 [1]*thousands*
24 [a]Josh. 15:55; 1 Sam. 25:2
25 [1]Or *from the rock*
26 [a]Ps. 31:22 [b]Ps. 17:9
27 [a]2 Kin. 19:9
28 [1]Heb. *Sela Hammahlekoth*
29 [a]Josh. 15:62; 2 Chr. 20:2

CHAPTER 24

1 [a]1 Sam. 23:19, 28, 29
2 [a]1 Sam. 26:2; Ps. 38:12
3 [a]1 Sam. 24:10 [b]Judg. 3:24 [c]Ps. 57:title; 142:title
4 [a]1 Sam. 26:8–11
5 [a]2 Sam. 24:10
6 [a]1 Sam. 26:11
7 [a]Ps. 7:4; [Matt. 5:44; Rom. 12:17, 19]
9 [a]Ps. 141:6; [Prov. 16:28; 17:9]
11 [a]Judg. 11:27; Ps. 7:3; 35:7 [b]1 Sam. 26:20
12 [a]Gen. 16:5; Judg. 11:27; 1 Sam. 26:10–23; Job 5:8
13 [a][Matt. 7:16–20]
14 [a]1 Sam. 17:43; 2 Sam. 9:8 [b]1 Sam. 26:20
15 [a]1 Sam. 24:12 [b]2 Chr. 24:22 [c]Ps. 35:1; 43:1; 119:154; Mic. 7:9
16 [a]1 Sam. 26:17

17 [a]Then he said to David: "You *are* [b]more righteous than I; for [c]you have rewarded me with
good, whereas I have rewarded you with evil.
18 "And you have shown this day how you have
dealt well with me; for when [a]the LORD delivered
me into your hand, you did not kill me.
19 "For if a man finds his enemy, will he let him
get away safely? Therefore may the LORD reward
you with good for what you have done to me this
day.
20 "And now [a]I know indeed that you shall
surely be king, and that the kingdom of Israel
shall be established in your hand.
21 [a]"Therefore swear now to me by the LORD
[b]that you will not cut off my descendants after me,
and that you will not destroy my name from my
father's house."
22 So David swore to Saul. And Saul went home,
but David and his men went up to [a]the stronghold.

### *David Befriends Abigail*

**25** Then [a]Samuel died; and the Israelites gathered together and [b]lamented for him, and
buried him at his home in Ramah. And David
arose and went down [c]to the Wilderness of [1]Paran.
2 Now *there was* a man [a]in Maon whose business *was* in [b]Carmel, and the man *was* very rich.
He had three thousand sheep and a thousand
goats. And he was shearing his sheep in Carmel.
3 The name of the man *was* Nabal, and the
name of his wife Abigail. And *she was* a woman of
good understanding and beautiful appearance; but
the man *was* harsh and evil in *his* doings. He *was*
*of the house of* [a]Caleb.
4 When David heard in the wilderness that
Nabal was [a]shearing his sheep,
5 David sent ten young men; and David said to
the young men, "Go up to Carmel, go to Nabal,
and greet him in my name.
6 "And thus you shall say to him who lives *in*
*prosperity:* [a]'Peace *be* to you, peace to your house,
and peace to all that you have!
7 'Now I have heard that you have shearers.
Your shepherds were with us, and we did not hurt
them, [a]nor was there anything missing from them
all the while they were in Carmel.
8 'Ask your young men, and they will tell you.
Therefore [1]let *my* young men find favor in your
eyes, for we come on [a]a feast day. Please give
whatever comes to your hand to your servants
and to your son David.' "
9 So when David's young men came, they spoke
to Nabal according to all these words in the name
of David, and waited.
**10** Then Nabal answered David's servants, and
said, [a]"Who *is* David, and who *is* the son of Jesse?
There are many servants nowadays who break
away each one from his master.
11 [a]"Shall I then take my bread and my water
and my [1]meat that I have killed for my shearers,
and give *it* to men when I do not know where
they *are* from?"
12 So David's young men turned on their heels
and went back; and they came and told him all
these words.
13 Then David said to his men, "Every man gird
on his sword." So every man girded on his sword,
and David also girded on his sword. And about
four hundred men went with David, and two
hundred [a]stayed with the supplies.
**14** Now one of the young men told Abigail, Nabal's wife, saying, "Look, David sent messengers
from the wilderness to greet our master; and he
[1]reviled them.
15 "But the men *were* very good to us, and [a]we
were not hurt, nor did we miss anything as long as
we accompanied them, when we were in the
fields.
16 "They were [a]a wall to us both by night and
day, all the time we were with them keeping the
sheep.
17 "Now therefore, know and consider what you
will do, for [a]harm is determined against our master and against all his household. For he *is such* a
[b]scoundrel[1] that *one* cannot speak to him."
**18** Then Abigail made haste and [a]took two hundred *loaves* of bread, two skins of wine, five sheep
already dressed, five seahs of roasted *grain*, one
hundred clusters of raisins, and two hundred
cakes of figs, and loaded *them* on donkeys.
19 And she said to her servants, [a]"Go on before
me; see, I am coming after you." But she did not
tell her husband Nabal.
20 So it was, *as* she rode on the donkey, that she
went down under cover of the hill; and there were
David and his men, coming down toward her, and
she met them.
21 Now David had said, "Surely in vain I have
protected all that this *fellow* has in the wilderness,
so that nothing was missed of all that *belongs* to
him. And he has [a]repaid me evil for good.
22 [a]"May God do so, and more also, to the enemies of David, if I [b]leave [c]one male of all who
*belong* to him by morning light."
**23** Now when Abigail saw David, she [a]dis-
mounted quickly from the donkey, fell on her face
before David, and bowed down to the ground.
24 So she fell at his feet and said: "On me, my
lord, *on me let* this iniquity *be!* And please let your
maidservant [1]speak in your ears, and hear the
words of your maidservant.
25 "Please, let not my lord [1]regard this scoundrel
Nabal. For as his name *is*, so *is* he: [2]Nabal *is* his
name, and folly *is* with him! But I, your maidservant, did not see the young men of my lord whom
you sent.
26 "Now therefore, my lord, [a]*as* the LORD lives
and *as* your soul lives, since the LORD has [b]held
you back from coming to bloodshed and from
[c]avenging[1] yourself with your own hand, now
then, [d]let your enemies and those who seek harm
for my lord be as Nabal.
27 "And now [a]this present which your maidservant has brought to my lord, let it be given to the
young men who follow my lord.
28 "Please forgive the trespass of your maidservant. For [a]the LORD will certainly make for my
lord an enduring house, because my lord [b]fights
the battles of the LORD, [c]and evil is not found in
you throughout your days.
29 "Yet a man has risen to pursue you and seek
your life, but the life of my lord shall be [a]bound in
the bundle of the living with the LORD your God;
and the lives of your enemies He shall [b]sling out,
*as from* the pocket of a sling.
30 "And it shall come to pass, when the LORD has
done for my lord according to all the good that He
has spoken concerning you, and has appointed
you [a]ruler over Israel,
31 "that this will be no grief to you, nor offense of
heart to my lord, either that you have shed blood
without cause, or that my lord has avenged

**17** [a]1 Sam. 26:21 [b]Gen. 38:26 [c][Matt. 5:44]
**18** [a]1 Sam. 26:23
**20** [a]1 Sam. 23:17
**21** [a]Gen. 21:23 [b]2 Sam. 21:6–8
**22** [a]1 Sam. 23:29

CHAPTER 25

**1** [a]1 Sam. 28:3 [b]Deut. 34:8 [c]Gen. 21:21 [1]So with MT, Syr., Tg., Vg.; LXX *Maon*
**2** [a]1 Sam. 23:24 [b]Josh. 15:55
**3** [a]Josh. 15:13
**4** [a]Gen. 38:13
**6** [a]1 Chr. 12:18
**7** [a]1 Sam. 25:15, 21
**8** [a]Esth. 8:17; 9:19, 22 [1]*be gracious to the young men*
**10** [a]Judg. 9:28
**11** [a]Judg. 8:6, 15 [1]Lit. *slaughter*
**13** [a]1 Sam. 30:24
**14** [1]*scolded* or *scorned at*
**15** [a]1 Sam. 25:7, 21
**16** [a]Ex. 14:22
**17** [a]1 Sam. 20:7 [b]Deut. 13:13 [1]Lit. *son of Belial*
**18** [a]Gen. 32:13
**19** [a]Gen. 32:16, 20
**21** [a]Ps. 109:5
**22** [a]1 Sam. 3:17; 20:13, 16 [b]1 Sam. 25:34 [c]1 Kin. 14:10; 21:21
**23** [a]Judg. 1:14
**24** [1]*speak to you*
**25** [1]*pay attention to* [2]Lit. *Fool*
**26** [a]2 Kin. 2:2 [b]Gen. 20:6 [c][Rom. 12:19] [d]2 Sam. 18:32 [1]Lit. *saving yourself*
**27** [a]Gen. 33:11
**28** [a]2 Sam. 7:11–16, 27 [b]1 Sam. 18:17 [c]1 Sam. 24:11
**29** [a][Col. 3:3] [b]Jer. 10:18
**30** [a]1 Sam. 13:14; 15:28

himself. But when the LORD has dealt well with
my lord, then remember your maidservant."
**32** Then David said to Abigail: [a]"Blessed *is* the
LORD God of Israel, who sent you this day to meet
me!
33 "And blessed *is* your advice and blessed *are*
you, because you have [a]kept me this day from
coming to bloodshed and from avenging myself
with my own hand.
34 "For indeed, *as* the LORD God of Israel lives,
who has [a]kept me back from hurting you, unless
you had hurried and come to meet me, surely [b]by
morning light no males would have been left to
Nabal!"
35 So David received from her hand what she
had brought him, and said to her, [a]"Go up in peace
to your house. See, I have heeded your voice and
[b]respected your person."
**36** Now Abigail went to Nabal, and there he was,
[a]holding a feast in his house, like the feast of a
king. And Nabal's heart *was* merry within him, for
he *was* very drunk; therefore she told him nothing, little or much, until morning light.
37 So it was, in the morning, when the wine had
gone from Nabal, and his wife had told him these
things, that his heart died within him, and he
became *like* a stone.
38 Then it happened, *after* about ten days, that
the LORD [a]struck Nabal, and he died.
**39** So when David heard that Nabal was dead, he
said, [a]"Blessed *be* the LORD, who has [b]pleaded the
cause of my reproach from the hand of Nabal, and
has [c]kept His servant from evil! For the LORD has
[d]returned the wickedness of Nabal on his own
head." And David sent and proposed to Abigail, to
take her as his wife.
40 When the servants of David had come to
Abigail at Carmel, they spoke to her saying,
"David sent us to you, to ask you to become his
wife."
41 Then she arose, bowed her face to the earth,
and said, "Here is your maidservant, a servant to
[a]wash the feet of the servants of my lord."
42 So Abigail rose in haste and rode on a donkey,
[1]attended by five of her maidens; and she followed
the messengers of David, and became his wife.
43 David also took Ahinoam [a]of Jezreel, [b]and so
both of them were his wives.
**44** But Saul had given [a]Michal his daughter,
David's wife, to [1]Palti the son of Laish, who *was*
from [b]Gallim.

### *David Spares Saul's Life Again*

**26** Now the Ziphites came to Saul at Gibeah,
saying, [a]"Is David not hiding in the hill of
Hachilah, opposite Jeshimon?"
2 Then Saul arose and went down to the Wilderness of Ziph, having [a]three thousand chosen men
of Israel with him, to seek David in the Wilderness
of Ziph.
3 And Saul encamped in the hill of Hachilah,
which *is* opposite Jeshimon, by the road. But
David stayed in the wilderness, and he saw that
Saul came after him into the wilderness.
4 David therefore sent out spies, and understood
that Saul had indeed come.
**5** So David arose and came to the place where
Saul had encamped. And David saw the place
where Saul lay, and [a]Abner the son of Ner, the
commander of his army. Now Saul lay within the
camp, with the people encamped all around him.
6 Then David answered, and said to Ahimelech
the Hittite and to Abishai [a]the son of Zeruiah,
brother of [b]Joab, saying, "Who will [c]go down with
me to Saul in the camp?" And [d]Abishai said, "I will
go down with you."
7 So David and Abishai came to the people by
night; and there Saul lay sleeping within the
camp, with his spear stuck in the ground by his
head. And Abner and the people lay all around
him.
8 Then Abishai said to David, [a]"God has delivered your enemy into your hand this day. Now
therefore, please, let me strike him [1]at once with
the spear, right to the earth; and I will not *have to*
*strike* him a second time!"
9 But David said to Abishai, "Do not destroy
him; [a]for who can stretch out his hand against the
LORD's anointed, and be guiltless?"
10 David said furthermore, "*As* the LORD lives,
[a]the LORD shall strike him, or [b]his day shall come
to die, or he shall [c]go out to battle and perish.
11 [a]"The LORD forbid that I should stretch out my
hand against the LORD's anointed. But please, take
now the spear and the jug of water that *are* by his
head, and let us go."
12 So David took the spear and the jug of water
*by* Saul's head, and they got away; and no man
saw or knew *it* or awoke. For they *were* all asleep,
because [a]a deep sleep from the LORD had fallen on
them.
**13** Now David went over to the other side, and
stood on the top of a hill afar off, a great distance
*being* between them.
14 And David called out to the people and to
Abner the son of Ner, saying, "Do you not answer,
Abner?" Then Abner answered and said, "Who
*are* you, calling out to the king?"
15 So David said to Abner, "*Are* you not a man?
And who *is* like you in Israel? Why then have you
not guarded your lord the king? For one of the
people came in to destroy your lord the king.
16 "This thing that you have done *is* not good. *As*
the LORD lives, you deserve to die, because you
have not guarded your master, the LORD's
anointed. And now see where the king's spear *is*,
and the jug of water that *was* by his head."
**17** Then Saul knew David's voice, and said, [a]"*Is*
that your voice, my son David?" David said, "*It is*
my voice, my lord, O king."
18 And he said, [a]"Why does my lord thus pursue
his servant? For what have I done, or what evil *is*
in my hand?
19 "Now therefore, please, let my lord the king
hear the words of his servant: If the LORD has
[a]stirred you up against me, let Him accept an
offering. But if *it is* the children of men, *may* they
*be* cursed before the LORD, [b]for they have driven
me out this day from sharing in the [c]inheritance of
the LORD, saying, 'Go, serve other gods.'
20 "So now, do not let my blood fall to the earth
before the face of the LORD. For the king of Israel
has come out to seek [a]a flea, as when one hunts a
partridge in the mountains."
**21** Then Saul said, [a]"I have sinned. Return, my
son David. For I will harm you no more, because
my life was precious in your eyes this day. Indeed
I have played the fool and erred exceedingly."
22 And David answered and said, "Here is the
king's spear. Let one of the young men come over
and get it.
23 [a]"May the LORD [b]repay every man *for* his

**32** [a]Gen. 24:27; Ex. 18:10; 1 Kin. 1:48; Ps. 41:13; 72:18; 106:48; Luke 1:68
**33** [a]1 Sam. 25:26
**34** [a]1 Sam. 25:26 [b]1 Sam. 25:22
**35** [a]1 Sam. 20:42; 2 Sam. 15:9; 2 Kin. 5:19; Luke 7:50; 8:48 [b]Gen. 19:21
**36** [a]2 Sam. 13:28; Prov. 20:1; Is. 5:11; Dan. 5:1; [Hos. 4:11]
**38** [a]1 Sam. 26:10; 2 Sam. 6:7; Ps. 104:29
**39** [a]1 Sam. 25:32 [b]1 Sam. 24:15; Prov. 22:23 [c]1 Sam. 25:26, 34 [d]1 Kin. 2:44
**41** [a][Prov. 15:33]; Luke 7:38, 44
**42** [1]Lit. *with five of her maidens at her feet*
**43** [a]Josh. 15:56 [b]1 Sam. 27:3; 30:5
**44** [a]1 Sam. 18:20; 2 Sam. 3:14 [b]Is. 10:30 [1]*Paltiel,* 2 Sam. 3:15

CHAPTER 26
**1** [a]1 Sam. 23:19; Ps. 54:title
**2** [a]1 Sam. 13:2; 24:2
**5** [a]1 Sam. 14:50, 51; 17:55
**6** [a]1 Chr. 2:16 [b]2 Sam. 2:13 [c]Judg. 7:10, 11 [d]2 Sam. 2:18, 24
**8** [a]1 Sam. 24:4 [1]Or *one time*
**9** [a]1 Sam. 24:6, 7; 2 Sam. 1:14, 16
**10** [a][Deut. 32:35]; 1 Sam. 25:26, 38; [Luke 18:7; Rom. 12:19; Heb. 10:30] [b]Gen. 47:29; Deut. 31:14; [Job 7:1; 14:5]; Ps. 37:13 [c]1 Sam. 31:6
**11** [a]1 Sam. 24:6–12; [Rom. 12:17, 19]
**12** [a]Gen. 2:21; 15:12; Is. 29:10
**17** [a]1 Sam. 24:16
**18** [a]1 Sam. 24:9, 11–14
**19** [a]2 Sam. 16:11; 24:1 [b]Deut. 4:27, 28 [c]2 Sam. 14:16; 20:19
**20** [a]1 Sam. 24:14
**21** [a]Ex. 9:27; 1 Sam. 15:24, 30; 24:17; 2 Sam. 12:13
**23** [a]1 Sam. 24:19; Ps. 7:8; 18:20; 62:12 [b]2 Sam. 22:21

righteousness and his faithfulness; for the LORD
delivered you into *my* hand today, but I would not
stretch out my hand against the LORD's anointed.
24 "And indeed, as your life was valued much
this day in my eyes, so let my life be valued much
in the eyes of the LORD, and let Him deliver me
out of all tribulation."
25 Then Saul said to David, "*May* you *be* blessed,
my son David! You shall both do great things and
also still [a]prevail." So David went on his way, and
Saul returned to his place.

### *David and Achish*

**27** And David said in his heart, "Now I shall
perish someday by the hand of Saul. *There*
*is* nothing better for me than that I should speedily escape to the land of the Philistines; and Saul
will [1]despair of me, to seek me anymore in any
part of Israel. So I shall escape out of his hand."
2 Then David arose [a]and went over with the six
hundred men who *were* with him [b]to Achish the
son of Maoch, king of Gath.
3 So David dwelt with Achish at Gath, he and
his men, each man with his household, *and* David
[a]with his two wives, Ahinoam the Jezreelitess, and
Abigail the Carmelitess, Nabal's widow.
4 And it was told Saul that David had fled to
Gath; so he sought him no more.
5 Then David said to Achish, "If I have now
found favor in your eyes, let them give me a place
in some town in the country, that I may dwell
there. For why should your servant dwell in the
royal city with you?"
6 So Achish gave him Ziklag that day. Therefore
[a]Ziklag has belonged to the kings of Judah to this
day.
7 Now [1]the time that David [a]dwelt in the country of the Philistines was one full year and four
months.
8 And David and his men went up and raided
[a]the Geshurites, [b]the [1]Girzites, and the [c]Amalek-
ites. For those nations were the inhabitants of the
land from [2]of old, [d]as you go to Shur, even as far
as the land of Egypt.
9 Whenever David [1]attacked the land, he left
neither man nor woman alive, but took away the
sheep, the oxen, the donkeys, the camels, and the
apparel, and returned and came to Achish.
10 Then Achish would say, "Where have you
made a raid today?" And David would say,
"Against the southern *area* of Judah, or against
the southern *area* of [a]the Jerahmeelites, or against
the southern *area* of [b]the Kenites."
11 David would save neither man nor woman
alive, to bring *news* to Gath, saying, "Lest they
should inform on us, saying, 'Thus David did.' "
And thus *was* his behavior all the time he dwelt in
the country of the Philistines.
12 So Achish believed David, saying, "He has
made his people Israel utterly abhor him; therefore he will be my servant forever."

### *Saul Consults a Medium*

**28** Now [a]it happened in those days that the
Philistines gathered their armies together
for war, to fight with Israel. And Achish said to
David, "You assuredly know that you will go out
with me to battle, you and your men."
2 So David said to Achish, "Surely you know
what your servant can do." And Achish said to
David, "Therefore I will make you one of my chief
guardians forever."
3 Now [a]Samuel had died, and all Israel had
lamented for him and buried him in [b]Ramah, in his
own city. And Saul had put [c]the mediums and the
spiritists out of the land.
4 Then the Philistines gathered together, and
came and encamped at [a]Shunem. So Saul gathered all Israel together, and they encamped at
[b]Gilboa.
5 When Saul saw the army of the Philistines, he
was [a]afraid, and his heart trembled greatly.
6 And when Saul inquired of the LORD, [a]the
LORD did not answer him, either by [b]dreams or [c]by
Urim or by the prophets.
7 Then Saul said to his servants, "Find me a
woman who is a medium, [a]that I may go to her
and inquire of her." And his servants said to him,
"In fact, *there is* a woman who is a medium at En
Dor."
8 So Saul disguised himself and put on other
clothes, and he went, and two men with him; and
they came to the woman by night. And [a]he said,
"Please conduct a séance for me, and bring up for
me the one I shall name to you."
9 Then the woman said to him, "Look, you
know what Saul has done, how he has [a]cut off the
mediums and the spiritists from the land. Why
then do you lay a snare for my life, to cause me to
die?"
10 And Saul swore to her by the LORD, saying,
"*As* the LORD lives, no punishment shall come
upon you for this thing."
11 Then the woman said, "Whom shall I bring up
for you?" And he said, "Bring up Samuel for me."
12 When the woman saw Samuel, she cried out
with a loud voice. And the woman spoke to Saul,
saying, "Why have you deceived me? For you *are*
Saul!"
13 And the king said to her, "Do not be afraid.
What did you see?" And the woman said to Saul,
"I saw [a][1] spirit ascending out of the earth."
14 So he said to her, "What *is* his form?" And she
said, "An old man is coming up, and he *is* covered
with [a]a mantle." And Saul perceived that it *was*
Samuel, and he stooped with *his* face to the
ground and bowed down.
15 Now Samuel said to Saul, "Why have you
[a]disturbed me by bringing me up?" And Saul
answered, "I am deeply distressed; for the Philistines make war against me, and [b]God has departed
from me and [c]does not answer me anymore,
neither by prophets nor by dreams. Therefore I
have called you, that you may reveal to me what I
should do."
16 Then Samuel said: "So why do you ask me,
seeing the LORD has departed from you and has
become your enemy?
17 "And the LORD has done for [1]Himself [a]as He
spoke by me. For the LORD has torn the kingdom
out of your hand and given it to your neighbor,
David.
18 [a]"Because you did not obey the voice of the
LORD nor execute His fierce wrath upon [b]Amalek,
therefore the LORD has done this thing to you this
day.
19 "Moreover the LORD will also deliver Israel
with you into the hand of the Philistines. And
tomorrow you and your sons *will be* with [a]me. The
LORD will also deliver the army of Israel into the
hand of the Philistines."

25 [a]Gen. 32:28; 1 Sam. 24:20

CHAPTER 27

1 [1]*despair of searching for*
2 [a]1 Sam. 25:13 [b]1 Sam. 21:10; 1 Kin. 2:39
3 [a]1 Sam. 25:42, 43
6 [a]Josh. 15:31; 19:5; 1 Chr. 12:1; Neh. 11:28
7 [a]1 Sam. 29:3 [1]Lit. *the number of days*
8 [a]Josh. 13:2, 13 [b]Josh. 16:10; Judg. 1:29 [c]Ex. 17:8, 16; 1 Sam. 15:7, 8 [d]Gen. 25:18; Ex. 15:22 [1]Or *Gezrites* [2]*ancient times*
9 [1]Lit. *struck*
10 [a]1 Chr. 2:9, 25 [b]Judg. 1:16

CHAPTER 28

1 [a]1 Sam. 29:1, 2
3 [a]1 Sam. 25:1 [b]1 Sam. 1:19 [c]Ex. 22:18; Lev. 19:31; 20:27; Deut. 18:10, 11; 1 Sam. 15:23; 28:9
4 [a]Josh. 19:18; 1 Sam. 28:4; 1 Kin. 1:3; 2 Kin. 4:8 [b]1 Sam. 31:1
5 [a]Job 18:11; [Is. 57:20]
6 [a]1 Sam. 14:37; Prov. 1:28; Lam. 2:9 [b]Num. 12:6; Joel 2:28 [c]Ex. 28:30; Num. 27:21; Deut. 33:8
7 [a]1 Chr. 10:13
8 [a]Deut. 18:10, 11; 1 Chr. 10:13; Is. 8:19
9 [a]1 Sam. 28:3
13 [a]Ex. 22:28; Ps. 138:1 [1]Heb. *elohim*
14 [a]1 Sam. 15:27; 2 Kin. 2:8, 13
15 [a]Is. 14:9 [b]1 Sam. 16:14; 18:12 [c]1 Sam. 28:6
17 [a]1 Sam. 15:28 [1]Or *him*, David
18 [a]1 Sam. 13:9–13; 15:1–26; 1 Kin. 20:42; 1 Chr. 10:13; Jer. 48:10 [b]1 Sam. 15:3–9
19 [a]1 Sam. 31:1–6; Job 3:17–19

**20** Immediately Saul fell full length on the ground, and was dreadfully afraid because of the words of Samuel. And there was no strength in him, for he had eaten no food all day or all night.
21 And the woman came to Saul and saw that he was severely troubled, and said to him, "Look, your maidservant has obeyed your voice, and I have [a]put my life in my hands and heeded the words which you spoke to me.
22 "Now therefore, please, heed also the voice of your maidservant, and let me set a piece of bread before you; and eat, that you may have strength when you go on *your* way."
23 But he refused and said, "I will not eat." So his servants, together with the woman, urged him; and he heeded their voice. Then he arose from the ground and sat on the bed.
24 Now the woman had a fatted calf in the house, and she hastened to kill it. And she took flour and kneaded *it*, and baked unleavened bread from it.
25 So she brought *it* before Saul and his servants, and they ate. Then they rose and went away that night.

### *The Philistines Distrust David*

**29** Then [a]the Philistines gathered together all their armies [b]at Aphek, and the Israelites encamped by a fountain which *is* in Jezreel.
2 And the [a]lords of the Philistines [1]passed in review by hundreds and by thousands, but [b]David and his men passed in review at the rear with Achish.
3 Then the princes of the Philistines said, "What *are* these Hebrews *doing here?*" And Achish said to the princes of the Philistines, "*Is* this not David, the servant of Saul king of Israel, who has been with me [a]these days, or these years? And to this day I have [b]found no fault in him since he defected *to me.*"
4 But the princes of the Philistines were angry with him; so the princes of the Philistines said to him, [a]"Make this fellow return, that he may go back to the place which you have appointed for him, and do not let him go down with us to [b]battle, lest [c]in the battle he become our adversary. For with what could he reconcile himself to his master, if not with the heads of these [d]men?
5 "*Is* this not David, [a]of whom they sang to one another in dances, saying:

[b]'Saul has slain his thousands,
And David his ten thousands'?"

**6** Then Achish called David and said to him, "Surely, *as* the LORD lives, you have been upright, and [a]your going out and your coming in with me in the army *is* good in my sight. For to this day [b]I have not found evil in you since the day of your coming to me. Nevertheless the lords do not favor you.
7 "Therefore return now, and go in peace, that you may not displease the lords of the Philistines."
**8** So David said to Achish, "But what have I done? And to this day what have you found in your servant as long as I have been with you, that I may not go and fight against the enemies of my lord the king?"
9 Then Achish answered and said to David, "I know that you *are* as good in my sight [a]as an angel of God; nevertheless [b]the princes of the Philistines have said, 'He shall not go up with us to the battle.'
10 "Now therefore, rise early in the morning with your master's servants [a]who have come with [1]you. And as soon as you are up early in the morning and have light, depart."
11 So David and his men rose early to depart in the morning, to return to the land of the Philistines. [a]And the Philistines went up to Jezreel.

### *David Defeats the Amalekites*

**30** Now it happened, when David and his men came to [a]Ziklag, on the third day, that the [b]Amalekites had invaded the South and Ziklag, attacked Ziklag and burned it with fire,
2 and had taken captive the [a]women and those who *were* there, from small to great; they did not kill anyone, but carried *them* away and went their way.
3 So David and his men came to the city, and there it was, burned with fire; and their wives, their sons, and their daughters had been taken captive.
4 Then David and the people who *were* with him lifted up their voices and wept, until they had no more power to weep.
5 And David's two [a]wives, Ahinoam the Jezreelitess, and Abigail the widow of Nabal the Carmelite, had been taken captive.
6 Now David was greatly distressed, for [a]the people spoke of stoning him, because the soul of all the people was [1]grieved, every man for his sons and his daughters. [b]But David strengthened himself in the LORD his God.
**7** [a]Then David said to Abiathar the priest, Ahimelech's son, "Please bring the ephod here to me." And [b]Abiathar brought the ephod to David.
8 [a]So David inquired of the LORD, saying, "Shall I pursue this troop? Shall I overtake them?" And He answered him, "Pursue, for you shall surely overtake *them* and without fail recover *all.*"
9 So David went, he and the six hundred men who *were* with him, and came to the Brook Besor, where those stayed who were left behind.
10 But David pursued, he and four hundred men; [a]for two hundred stayed *behind,* who were so weary that they could not cross the Brook Besor.
**11** Then they found an Egyptian in the field, and brought him to David; and they gave him bread and he ate, and they let him drink water.
12 And they gave him a piece of [a]a cake of figs and two clusters of raisins. So [b]when he had eaten, his strength came back to him; for he had eaten no bread nor drunk water for three days and three nights.
13 Then David said to him, "To whom do you *belong,* and where *are* you from?" And he said, "I *am* a young man from Egypt, servant of an Amalekite; and my master left me behind, because three days ago I fell sick.
14 "We made an invasion of the southern *area* of [a]the Cherethites, in the *territory* which *belongs* to Judah, and of the southern *area* [b]of Caleb; and we burned Ziklag with fire."
15 And David said to him, "Can you take me down to this troop?" So he said, "Swear to me by God that you will neither kill me nor deliver me into the hands of my [a]master, and I will take you down to this troop."
**16** And when he had brought him down, there they were, spread out over all the land, [a]eating and drinking and dancing, because of all the great

**21** [a]Judg. 12:3; 1 Sam. 19:5; Job 13:14

CHAPTER 29

**1** [a]1 Sam. 28:1 [b]Josh. 12:18; 19:30; 1 Sam. 4:1; 1 Kin. 20:30
**2** [a]1 Sam. 6:4; 7:7 [b]1 Sam. 28:1, 2 [1]*passed on in the rear*
**3** [a]1 Sam. 27:7 [b]1 Sam. 27:1–6; 1 Chr. 12:19, 20; Dan. 6:5
**4** [a]1 Sam. 27:6 [b]1 Sam. 14:21 [c]1 Sam. 29:9 [d]1 Chr. 12:19, 20
**5** [a]1 Sam. 21:11 [b]1 Sam. 18:7
**6** [a]2 Sam. 3:25; 2 Kin. 19:27 [b]1 Sam. 29:3
**9** [a]2 Sam. 14:17, 20; 19:27 [b]1 Sam. 29:4
**10** [a]1 Chr. 12:19, 22 [1]So with MT, Tg., Vg.; LXX adds *and go to the place which I have selected for you there; and set no bothersome word in your heart, for you are good before me. And rise on your way*
**11** [a]2 Sam. 4:4

CHAPTER 30

**1** [a]1 Sam. 27:6 [b]1 Sam. 15:7; 27:8
**2** [a]1 Sam. 27:2, 3
**5** [a]1 Sam. 25:42, 43
**6** [a]Ex. 17:4; John 8:59 [b]1 Sam. 23:16; Is. 25:4; Hab. 3:17–19 [1]Lit. *bitter*
**7** [a]1 Sam. 23:2–9 [b]1 Sam. 23:6
**8** [a]1 Sam. 23:2, 4; Ps. 50:15; 91:15
**10** [a]1 Sam. 30:9, 21
**12** [a]1 Sam. 25:18; 1 Kin. 20:7 [b]Judg. 15:19; 1 Sam. 14:27
**14** [a]2 Sam. 8:18; 1 Kin. 1:38, 44; Ezek. 25:16; Zeph. 2:5 [b]Josh. 14:13; 15:13
**15** [a]Deut. 23:15
**16** [a]1 Thess. 5:3

spoil which they had taken from the land of the Philistines and from the land of Judah.
17 Then David attacked them from twilight until the evening of the next day. Not a man of them escaped, except four hundred young men who rode on camels and fled.
18 So David recovered all that the Amalekites had carried away, and David rescued his two wives.
19 And nothing of theirs was lacking, either small or great, sons or daughters, spoil or anything which they had taken from them; [a]David recovered all.
20 Then David took all the flocks and herds they had driven before those *other* livestock, and said, "This *is* David's spoil."
**21** Now David came to the [a]two hundred men who had been so weary that they could not follow David, whom they also had made to stay at the Brook Besor. So they went out to meet David and to meet the people who *were* with him. And when David came near the people, he [1]greeted them.
22 Then all the wicked and [a]worthless[1] men of those who went with David answered and said, "Because they did not go with us, we will not give them *any* of the spoil that we have recovered, except for every man's wife and children, that they may lead *them* away and depart."
23 But David said, "My brethren, you shall not do so with what the LORD has given us, who has preserved us and delivered into our hand the troop that came against us.
24 "For who will heed you in this matter? But [a]as his part *is* who goes down to the battle, so *shall* his part *be* who stays by the supplies; they shall share alike."
25 So it was, from that day forward; he made it a statute and an ordinance for Israel to this day.
**26** Now when David came to Ziklag, he sent *some* of the [1]spoil to the elders of Judah, to his friends, saying, "Here is a present for you from the spoil of the enemies of the LORD"—
27 to *those* who *were* in Bethel, *those* who *were* in [a]Ramoth of the South, *those* who *were* in [b]Jattir,
28 *those* who *were* in [a]Aroer, *those* who *were* in [b]Siphmoth, *those* who *were* in [c]Eshtemoa,
29 *those* who *were* in Rachal, *those* who *were* in the cities of [a]the Jerahmeelites, *those* who *were* in the cities of the [b]Kenites,
30 *those* who *were* in [a]Hormah, *those* who *were* in [1]Chorashan, *those* who *were* in Athach,
31 *those* who *were* in [a]Hebron, and to all the places where David himself and his men were accustomed to [b]rove.

### *The Death of Saul and His Sons*

**31** Now [a]the Philistines fought against Israel; and the men of Israel fled from before the Philistines, and fell slain on Mount [b]Gilboa.
2 Then the Philistines followed hard after Saul and his sons. And the Philistines killed [a]Jonathan, Abinadab, and Malchishua, Saul's sons.
3 [a]The battle became fierce against Saul. The archers [1]hit him, and he was severely wounded by the archers.
4 [a]Then Saul said to his armorbearer, "Draw your sword, and thrust me through with it, lest [b]these uncircumcised men come and thrust me through and [1]abuse me." But his armorbearer would not, [c]for he was greatly afraid. Therefore Saul took a sword and [d]fell on it.
5 And when his armorbearer saw that Saul was dead, he also fell on his sword, and died with him.
6 So Saul, his three sons, his armorbearer, and all his men died together that same day.
7 And when the men of Israel who *were* on the other side of the valley, and *those* who *were* on the other side of the Jordan, saw that the men of Israel had fled and that Saul and his sons were dead, they forsook the cities and fled; and the Philistines came and dwelt in them.
8 So it happened the next day, when the Philistines came to strip the slain, that they found Saul and his three sons fallen on Mount Gilboa.
9 And they cut off his head and stripped off his armor, and sent *word* throughout the land of the Philistines, to [a]proclaim *it in* the temple of their idols and among the people.
10 [a]Then they put his armor in the temple of the [b]Ashtoreths, and [c]they fastened his body to the wall of [d]Beth[1] Shan.
**11** [a]Now when the inhabitants of Jabesh Gilead heard what the Philistines had done to Saul,
12 [a]all the valiant men arose and traveled all night, and took the body of Saul and the bodies of his sons from the wall of Beth Shan; and they came to Jabesh and [b]burned them there.
13 Then they took their bones and [a]buried *them* under the tamarisk tree at Jabesh, [b]and fasted seven days.

**19** [a]1 Sam. 30:8
**21** [a]1 Sam. 30:10 [1]*asked them concerning their welfare*
**22** [a]Deut. 13:13 [1]Lit. *men of Belial*
**24** [a]Josh. 22:8
**26** [1]*booty*
**27** [a]Josh. 19:8 [b]Josh. 15:48; 21:14
**28** [a]Josh. 13:16 [b]1 Chr. 27:27 [c]Josh. 15:50
**29** [a]1 Sam. 27:10 [b]Judg. 1:16
**30** [a]Judg. 1:17 [1]Or *Borashan*
**31** [a]2 Sam. 2:1 [b]1 Sam. 23:22

CHAPTER 31

**1** [a]1 Chr. 10:1–12 [b]1 Sam. 28:4
**2** [a]1 Sam. 14:49
**3** [a]2 Sam. 1:6 [1]Lit. *found him*
**4** [a]Judg. 9:54 [b]1 Sam. 14:6; 17:26, 36 [c]2 Sam. 1:14 [d]2 Sam. 1:6, 10 [1]*torture*
**9** [a]2 Sam. 1:20
**10** [a]1 Sam. 21:9 [b]Judg. 2:13 [c]2 Sam. 21:12 [d]Judg. 1:27 [1]*Beth Shean*, Josh. 17:11
**11** [a]1 Sam. 11:1–13
**12** [a]2 Sam. 2:4–7 [b]2 Chr. 16:14
**13** [a]2 Sam. 2:4, 5; 21:12–14 [b]Gen. 50:10

# *The Second Book of*
# SAMUEL

### *David Learns of Saul's Death*

NOW it came to pass after the [a]death of Saul, when David had returned from [b]the slaughter of the Amalekites, and David had stayed two days in Ziklag,
2 on the third day, behold, it happened that [a]a man came from Saul's camp [b]with his clothes [1]torn and dust on his head. So it was, when he came to David, that he [c]fell to the ground and prostrated himself.
3 And David said to him, "Where have you come from?" So he said to him, "I have escaped from the camp of Israel."
4 Then David said to him, [a]"How did the matter go? Please tell me." And he answered, "The people have fled from the battle, many of the people are fallen and dead, and Saul and [b]Jonathan his son are dead also."
5 So David said to the young man who told him, "How do you know that Saul and Jonathan his son are dead?"

CHAPTER 1

**1** [a]1 Sam. 31:6 [b]1 Sam. 30:1, 17, 26
**2** [a]2 Sam. 4:10 [b]1 Sam. 4:12 [c]1 Sam. 25:23 [1]To show grief
**4** [a]1 Sam. 4:16; 31:3 [b]1 Sam. 31:2

6 Then the young man who told him said, "As I
happened by chance *to be* on [a]Mount Gilboa,
there was [b]Saul, leaning on his spear; and indeed
the chariots and horsemen followed hard after
him.
7 "Now when he looked behind him, he saw me
and called to me. And I answered, 'Here I am.'
8 "And he said to me, 'Who *are* you?' So I
answered him, 'I *am* an Amalekite.'
9 "He said to me again, 'Please stand over me
and kill me, for [1]anguish has come upon me, but
my life still *remains* in me.'
10 "So I stood over him and [a]killed him, because I
was sure that he could not live after he had fallen.
And I took the crown that *was* on his head and
the bracelet that *was* on his arm, and have
brought them here to my lord."
**11** Therefore David took hold of his own clothes
and [a]tore them, and *so did* all the men who *were*
with him.
12 And they [a]mourned and wept and [b]fasted until
evening for Saul and for Jonathan his son, for the
[c]people of the LORD and for the house of Israel,
because they had fallen by the sword.
13 Then David said to the young man who told
him, "Where *are* you from?" And he answered, "I
*am* the son of an alien, an Amalekite."
14 So David said to him, "How [a]was it you were
not [b]afraid to [c]put forth your hand to destroy the
LORD's anointed?"
15 Then [a]David called one of the young men and
said, "Go near, *and* execute him!" And he struck
him so that he died.
16 So David said to him, [a]"Your blood *is* on your
own head, for [b]your own mouth has testified
against you, saying, 'I have killed the LORD's
anointed.'"
**17** Then David lamented with this lamentation
over Saul and over Jonathan his son,
18 [a]and he told *them* to teach the children of
Judah *the Song of* the Bow; indeed *it is* written [b]in
the Book [1]of Jasher:

19 "The beauty of Israel is slain
on your high places!
[a]How the mighty have fallen!
20 [a]Tell *it* not in Gath,
Proclaim *it* not in the streets of [b]Ashkelon—
Lest [c]the daughters of the Philistines rejoice,
Lest the daughters of [d]the uncircumcised
triumph.

21 "O [a]mountains of Gilboa,
[b]*Let there be* no dew nor rain upon you,
Nor fields of offerings.
For the shield of the mighty
is [1]cast away there!
The shield of Saul, not [c]anointed with oil.
22 From the blood of the slain,
From the fat of the mighty,
[a]The bow of Jonathan did not turn back,
And the sword of Saul did not return empty.

23 "Saul and Jonathan *were* beloved
and pleasant in their lives,
And in their [a]death they were not divided;
They were swifter than eagles,
They were [b]stronger than lions.

24 "O daughters of Israel, weep over Saul,
Who clothed you in scarlet, with luxury;
Who put ornaments of gold on your apparel.

25 "How the mighty have fallen
in the midst of the battle!
Jonathan *was* slain in your high places.
26 I am distressed for you,
my brother Jonathan;
You have been very pleasant to me;
[a]Your love to me was wonderful,
Surpassing the love of women.

27 "How[a] the mighty have fallen,
And the weapons of war perished!"

### *Israel and Judah at War*

**2** It happened after this that David [a]inquired of
the LORD, saying, "Shall I go up to any of the
cities of Judah?" And the LORD said to him, "Go
up." David said, "Where shall I go up?" And He
said, "To [b]Hebron."
2 So David went up there, and his [a]two wives
also, Ahinoam the Jezreelitess, and Abigail the
widow of Nabal the Carmelite.
3 And David brought up [a]the men who *were*
with him, every man with his household. So they
dwelt in the cities of Hebron.
**4** [a]Then the men of Judah came, and there they
[b]anointed David king over the house of Judah.
And they told David, saying, [c]"The men of Jabesh
Gilead *were the ones* who buried Saul."
5 So David sent messengers to the men of Jabesh Gilead, and said to them, [a]"You *are* blessed
of the LORD, for you have shown this kindness to
your lord, to Saul, and have buried him.
6 "And now may [a]the LORD show kindness and
truth to you. I also will repay you this kindness,
because you have done this thing.
7 "Now therefore, let your hands be
strengthened, and be valiant; for your master Saul
is dead, and also the house of Judah has anointed
me king over them."
**8** But [a]Abner the son of Ner, commander of
Saul's army, took [1]Ishbosheth the son of Saul and
brought him over to [b]Mahanaim;
9 and he made him king over [a]Gilead, over the
[b]Ashurites, over [c]Jezreel, over Ephraim, over
Benjamin, and over all Israel.
10 Ishbosheth, Saul's son, *was* forty years old
when he began to reign over Israel, and he
reigned two years. Only the house of Judah followed David.
11 And [a]the [1]time that David was king in Hebron
over the house of Judah was seven years and six
months.
**12** Now Abner the son of Ner, and the servants of
Ishbosheth the son of Saul, went out from Mahanaim to [a]Gibeon.
13 And [a]Joab the son of Zeruiah, and the servants of David, went out and met them by [b]the
pool of Gibeon. So they sat down, one on one side
of the pool and the other on the other side of the
pool.
14 Then Abner said to Joab, "Let the young men
now arise and compete before us." And Joab said,
"Let them arise."
15 So they arose and went over by number,
twelve from Benjamin, *followers* of Ishbosheth
the son of Saul, and twelve from the servants of
David.
16 And each one grasped his opponent by the
head and *thrust* his sword in his opponent's side;
so they fell down together. Therefore that place

**6** [a]1 Sam. 31:1 [b]1 Sam. 31:2–4
**9** [1]*agony*
**10** [a]Judg. 9:54
**11** [a]2 Sam. 3:31; 13:31
**12** [a]2 Sam. 3:31 [b]1 Sam. 31:13 [c]2 Sam. 6:21
**14** [a]Num. 12:8 [b]1 Sam. 31:4 [c]1 Sam. 24:6; 26:9
**15** [a]2 Sam. 4:10, 12
**16** [a]1 Kin. 2:32–37 [b]Luke 19:22
**18** [a]1 Sam. 31:3 [b]Josh. 10:13 [1]Lit. *of the Upright*
**19** [a]2 Sam. 1:27
**20** [a]Mic. 1:10 [b]Jer. 25:20 [c]Ex. 15:20 [d]1 Sam. 31:4
**21** [a]1 Sam. 31:1 [b]Ezek. 31:15 [c]1 Sam. 10:1 [1]Lit. *defiled*
**22** [a]1 Sam. 18:4
**23** [a]1 Sam. 31:2–4 [b]Judg. 14:18
**26** [a]1 Sam. 18:1–4; 19:2; 20:17
**27** [a]2 Sam. 1:19, 25

CHAPTER 2

**1** [a]Judg. 1:1 [b]1 Sam. 30:31
**2** [a]1 Sam. 25:42, 43; 30:5
**3** [a]1 Chr. 12:1
**4** [a]1 Sam. 30:26 [b]1 Sam. 16:13 [c]1 Sam. 31:11–13
**5** [a]Ruth 2:20; 3:10
**6** [a]2 Tim. 1:16, 18
**8** [a]1 Sam. 14:50 [b]2 Sam. 17:24 [1]*Esh-Baal*, 1 Chr. 8:33; 9:39
**9** [a]Josh. 22:9 [b]Judg. 1:32 [c]1 Sam. 29:1
**11** [a]2 Sam. 5:5 [1]Lit. *number of days*
**12** [a]Josh. 10:2–12; 18:25
**13** [a]1 Chr. 2:16; 11:6 [b]Jer. 41:12

was called [1]the Field of Sharp Swords, which *is* in Gibeon.
17 So there was a very fierce battle that day, and Abner and the men of Israel were beaten before the servants of David.
**18** Now the [a]three sons of Zeruiah were there: Joab and Abishai and Asahel. And Asahel *was* [b]*as* fleet of foot [c]as a wild gazelle.
19 So Asahel pursued Abner, and in going he did not turn to the right hand or to the left from following Abner.
20 Then Abner looked behind him and said, "*Are* you Asahel?" He answered, "I *am*."
21 And Abner said to him, "Turn aside to your right hand or to your left, and lay hold on one of the young men and take his armor for yourself." But Asahel would not turn aside from following him.
22 So Abner said again to Asahel, "Turn aside from following me. Why should I strike you to the ground? How then could I face your brother Joab?"
23 However, he refused to turn aside. Therefore Abner struck him [a]in the stomach with the blunt end of the spear, so that the spear came out of his back; and he fell down there and died on the spot. So it was *that* as many as came to the place where Asahel fell down and died, stood [b]still.
**24** Joab and Abishai also pursued Abner. And the sun was going down when they came to the hill of Ammah, which *is* before Giah by the road to the Wilderness of Gibeon.
25 Now the children of Benjamin gathered together behind Abner and became [1]a unit, and took their stand on top of a hill.
26 Then Abner called to Joab and said, "Shall the sword devour forever? Do you not know that it will be bitter in the latter end? How long will it be then until you tell the people to return from pursuing their brethren?"
27 And Joab said, "*As* God lives, [1]unless [a]you had spoken, surely then by morning all the people would have given up pursuing their brethren."
28 So Joab blew a trumpet; and all the people stood still and did not pursue Israel anymore, nor did they fight anymore.
29 Then Abner and his men went on all that night through the plain, crossed over the Jordan, and went through all Bithron; and they came to Mahanaim.
**30** So Joab returned from pursuing Abner. And when he had gathered all the people together, there were missing of David's servants nineteen men and Asahel.
31 But the servants of David had struck down, of Benjamin and Abner's men, three hundred and sixty men who died.
32 Then they took up Asahel and buried him in his father's tomb, which *was in* [a]Bethlehem. And Joab and his men went all night, and they came to Hebron at daybreak.

### *Joab Kills Abner*

**3** Now there was a long [a]war between the house of Saul and the house of David. But David grew stronger and stronger, and the house of Saul grew weaker and weaker.
**2** Sons were born [a]to David in Hebron: His firstborn was Amnon [b]by Ahinoam the Jezreelitess;
3 his second, [1]Chileab, by Abigail the widow of Nabal the Carmelite; the third, [a]Absalom the son of Maacah, the daughter of Talmai, king [b]of Geshur;
4 the fourth, [a]Adonijah the son of Haggith; the fifth, Shephatiah the son of Abital;
5 and the sixth, Ithream, by David's wife Eglah. These were born to David in Hebron.
**6** Now it was so, while there was war between the house of Saul and the house of David, that Abner was strengthening *his hold* on the house of Saul.
7 And Saul had a concubine, whose name *was* [a]Rizpah, the daughter of Aiah. So *Ishbosheth* said to Abner, "Why have you [b]gone in to my father's concubine?"
8 Then Abner became very angry at the words of Ishbosheth, and said, "*Am* I [a]a dog's head that belongs to Judah? Today I show loyalty to the house of Saul your father, to his brothers, and to his friends, and have not delivered you into the hand of David; and you charge me today with a fault concerning this woman?
9 [a]"May God do so to Abner, and more also, if I do not do for David [b]as the LORD has sworn to him—
10 "to transfer the kingdom from the [1]house of Saul, and set up the throne of David over Israel and over Judah, [a]from Dan to Beersheba."
11 And he could not answer Abner another word, because he feared him.
**12** Then Abner sent messengers on his behalf to David, saying, "Whose *is* the land?" saying *also,* "Make your covenant with me, and indeed my hand *shall be* with you to bring all Israel to you."
13 And *David* said, "Good, I will make a covenant with you. But one thing I require of you: [a]you shall not see my face unless you first bring [b]Michal, Saul's daughter, when you come to see my face."
14 So David sent messengers to [a]Ishbosheth, Saul's son, saying, "Give *me* my wife Michal, whom I betrothed to myself [b]for a hundred foreskins of the Philistines."
15 And Ishbosheth sent and took her from *her* husband, from [1]Paltiel the son of Laish.
16 Then her husband went along with her to [a]Bahurim, [1]weeping behind her. So Abner said to him, "Go, return!" And he returned.
**17** Now Abner had communicated with the elders of Israel, saying, "In time past you were seeking for David *to be* king over you.
18 "Now then, do *it!* [a]For the LORD has spoken of David, saying, 'By the hand of My servant David, [1]I will save My people Israel from the hand of the Philistines and the hand of all their enemies.' "
19 And Abner also spoke in the hearing of [a]Benjamin. Then Abner also went to speak in the hearing of David in Hebron all that seemed good to Israel and the whole house of Benjamin.
20 So Abner and twenty men with him came to David at Hebron. And David made a feast for Abner and the men who *were* with him.
21 Then Abner said to David, "I will arise and go, and [a]gather all Israel to my lord the king, that they may make a covenant with you, and that you may [b]reign over all that your heart desires." So David sent Abner away, and he went in peace.
**22** At that moment the servants of David and Joab came from a raid and brought much [1]spoil with them. But Abner *was* not with David in

---

**16** [1]Heb. *Helkath Hazzurim*
**18** [a]1 Chr. 2:16 [b]1 Chr. 12:8; Hab. 3:19 [c]Ps. 18:33
**23** [a]2 Sam. 3:27; 4:6; 20:10 [b]2 Sam. 20:12
**25** [1]*one band*
**27** [a]2 Sam. 2:14 [1]*if you had not spoken*
**32** [a]1 Sam. 20:6

CHAPTER 3

**1** [a]1 Kin. 14:30; [Ps. 46:9]
**2** [a]1 Chr. 3:1–4 [b]1 Sam. 25:42, 43
**3** [a]2 Sam. 15:1–10 [b]Josh. 13:13; 1 Sam. 27:8; 2 Sam. 13:37; 14:32; 15:8 [1]*Daniel,* 1 Chr. 3:1
**4** [a]1 Kin. 1:5
**7** [a]2 Sam. 21:8–11 [b]2 Sam. 16:21
**8** [a]Deut. 23:18; 1 Sam. 24:14; 2 Sam. 9:8; 16:9
**9** [a]Ruth 1:17; 1 Kin. 19:2 [b]1 Sam. 15:28; 16:1, 12; 28:17; 1 Chr. 12:23
**10** [a]Judg. 20:1; 1 Sam. 3:20; 2 Sam. 17:11; 1 Kin. 4:25 [1]*family*
**13** [a]Gen. 43:3 [b]1 Sam. 18:20; 19:11; 25:44; 2 Sam. 6:16
**14** [a]2 Sam. 2:10 [b]1 Sam. 18:25–27
**15** [1]*Palti,* 1 Sam. 25:44
**16** [a]2 Sam. 16:5; 19:16 [1]Lit. *going and weeping*
**18** [a]2 Sam. 3:9 [1]So with many Heb. mss., LXX, Syr., Tg.; MT *he*
**19** [a]1 Sam. 10:20, 21; 1 Chr. 12:29
**21** [a]2 Sam. 3:10, 12 [b]1 Kin. 11:37
**22** [1]*booty*

Hebron, for he had sent him away, and he had gone in peace.

23 When Joab and all the troops that *were* with him had come, they told Joab, saying, "Abner the son of Ner came to the king, and he sent him away, and he has gone in peace."

24 Then Joab came to the king and said, "What have you done? Look, Abner came to you; why *is* it *that* you sent him away, and he has already gone?

25 "Surely you realize that Abner the son of Ner came to deceive you, to know [a]your going out and your coming in, and to know all that you are doing."

26 And when Joab had gone from David's presence, he sent messengers after Abner, who brought him back from the well of Sirah. But David did not know *it.*

27 Now when Abner had returned to Hebron, Joab [a]took him aside in the gate to speak with him privately, and there [1]stabbed him [b]in the stomach, so that he died for the blood of [c]Asahel his brother.

**28** Afterward, when David heard *it,* he said, "My kingdom and I *are* [1]guiltless before the LORD forever of the blood of Abner the son of Ner.

29 [a]"Let it rest on the head of Joab and on all his father's house; and let there never fail to be in the [1]house of Joab one [b]who has a discharge or is a leper, who leans on a staff or falls by the sword, or who lacks bread."

30 So Joab and Abishai his brother killed Abner, because he had killed their brother [a]Asahel at Gibeon in the battle.

**31** Then David said to Joab and to all the people who were with him, [a]"Tear your clothes, [b]gird yourselves with sackcloth, and mourn for Abner." And King David followed the coffin.

32 So they buried Abner in Hebron; and the king lifted up his voice and wept at the grave of Abner, and all the people wept.

33 And the king sang *a lament* over Abner and said:

"Should Abner die as a [a]fool dies?
34 Your hands were not bound
Nor your feet put into fetters;
As a man falls before wicked men,
*so* you fell."

Then all the people wept over him again.

35 And when all the people came [a]to persuade David to eat food while it was still day, David took an oath, saying, [b]"God do so to me, and more also, if I taste bread or anything else [c]till the sun goes down!"

36 Now all the people took note *of it,* and it pleased them, since whatever the king did pleased all the people.

37 For all the people and all Israel understood that day that it had not been the king's *intent* to kill Abner the son of Ner.

38 Then the king said to his servants, "Do you not know that a prince and a great man has fallen this day in Israel?

39 "And I *am* weak today, though anointed king; and these men, the sons of Zeruiah, [a]*are* too harsh for me. [b]The LORD shall repay the evildoer according to his wickedness."

### *Ishbosheth Is Murdered*

**4** When Saul's [1]son heard that Abner had died in Hebron, [a]he[2] lost heart, and all Israel was [b]troubled.

2 Now Saul's son *had* two men *who were* captains of troops. The name of one *was* Baanah and the name of the other Rechab, the sons of Rimmon the Beerothite, of the children of Benjamin. (For [a]Beeroth also was [1]*part* of Benjamin,

3 because the Beerothites fled to [a]Gittaim and have been sojourners there until this day.)

4 [a]Jonathan, Saul's son, had a son *who was* lame in *his* feet. He was five years old when the news about Saul and Jonathan came [b]from Jezreel; and his nurse took him up and fled. And it happened, as she made haste to flee, that he fell and became lame. His name *was* [c]Mephibosheth.[1]

5 Then the sons of Rimmon the Beerothite, Rechab and Baanah, set out and came at about the heat of the day to the [a]house of Ishbosheth, who was lying on his bed at noon.

6 And they came there, all the way into the house, *as though* to get wheat, and they [1]stabbed him [a]in the stomach. Then Rechab and Baanah his brother escaped.

7 For when they came into the house, he was lying on his bed in his bedroom; then they struck him and killed him, beheaded him and took his head, and were all night escaping through the plain.

8 And they brought the head of Ishbosheth to David at Hebron, and said to the king, "Here is the head of Ishbosheth, the son of Saul your enemy, [a]who sought your life; and the LORD has avenged my lord the king this day of Saul and his descendants."

**9** But David answered Rechab and Baanah his brother, the sons of Rimmon the Beerothite, and said to them, "*As* the LORD lives, [a]who has redeemed my life from all adversity,

10 "when [a]someone told me, saying, 'Look, Saul is dead,' thinking to have brought good news, I arrested him and had him executed in Ziklag—the one who *thought* I would give him a reward for *his* news.

11 "How much more, when wicked men have killed a righteous person in his own house on his bed? Therefore, shall I not now [a]require his [1]blood at your hand and [2]remove you from the earth?"

12 So David [a]commanded his young men, and they executed them, cut off their hands and feet, and hanged *them* by the pool in Hebron. But they took the head of Ishbosheth and buried *it* in the [b]tomb of Abner in Hebron.

### *David Reigns over All Israel*

**5** Then all the tribes of Israel [a]came to David at Hebron and spoke, saying, "Indeed [b]we *are* your bone and your flesh.

2 "Also, in time past, when Saul was king over us, [a]you were the one who led Israel out and brought them in; and the LORD said to you, [b]'You shall shepherd My people Israel, and be ruler over Israel.' "

3 [a]Therefore all the elders of Israel came to the king at Hebron, [b]and King David made a covenant with them at Hebron [c]before the LORD. And they anointed David king over Israel.

---

25 [a]Deut. 28:6; 1 Sam. 29:6; Is. 37:28
27 [a]2 Sam. 20:9, 10; 1 Kin. 2:5 [b]2 Sam. 4:6 [c]2 Sam. 2:23 [1]Lit. *struck*
28 [1]*innocent*
29 [a]Deut. 21:6–9; 1 Kin. 2:32, 33 [b]Lev. 15:2 [1]*family*
30 [a]2 Sam. 2:23
31 [a]Josh. 7:6; 2 Sam. 1:2, 11 [b]Gen. 37:34
33 [a]2 Sam. 13:12, 13
35 [a]2 Sam. 12:17; Jer. 16:7, 8 [b]Ruth 1:17 [c]Judg. 20:26; 2 Sam. 1:12
39 [a]2 Sam. 19:5–7 [b]1 Kin. 2:5, 6, 32–34; 2 Tim. 4:14

CHAPTER 4

1 [a]Ezra 4:4; Is. 13:7 [b]Matt. 2:3 [1]Ishbosheth [2]Lit. *his hands dropped*
2 [a]Josh. 18:25 [1]*considered part of*
3 [a]Neh. 11:33
4 [a]2 Sam. 9:3 [b]1 Sam. 29:1, 11 [c]2 Sam. 9:6 [1]*Merib-Baal,* 1 Chr. 8:34; 9:40
5 [a]2 Sam. 2:8, 9
6 [a]2 Sam. 2:23; 20:10 [1]Lit. *struck*
8 [a]1 Sam. 19:2, 10, 11; 23:15; 25:29
9 [a]Gen. 48:16; 1 Kin. 1:29; Ps. 31:7
10 [a]2 Sam. 1:2–16
11 [a][Gen. 9:5, 6; Ps. 9:12] [1]Or *bloodshed* [2]Lit. *consume you*
12 [a]2 Sam. 1:15 [b]2 Sam. 3:32

CHAPTER 5

1 [a]1 Chr. 11:1–3 [b]Gen. 29:14; Judg. 9:2; 2 Sam. 19:12, 13
2 [a]1 Sam. 18:5, 13, 16 [b]1 Sam. 16:1
3 [a]2 Sam. 3:17; 1 Chr. 11:3 [b]2 Sam. 2:4; 3:21; 2 Kin. 11:17 [c]Judg. 11:11; 1 Sam. 23:18

4 David *was* [a]thirty years old when he began to reign, *and* [b]he reigned forty years.

5 In Hebron he reigned over Judah [a]seven years and six months, and in Jerusalem he reigned thirty-three years over all Israel and Judah.

**6** [a]And the king and his men went to Jerusalem against [b]the Jebusites, the inhabitants of the land, who spoke to David, saying, "You shall not come in here; but the blind and the lame will repel you," thinking, "David cannot come in here."

7 Nevertheless David took the stronghold of Zion [a](that *is*, the City of David).

8 Now David said on that day, "Whoever climbs up by way of the water shaft and defeats the Jebusites (the lame and the blind, *who are* hated by David's soul), [a]*he shall be chief and captain.*" Therefore they say, "The blind and the lame shall not come into the house."

9 Then David dwelt in the stronghold, and called it [a]the City of David. And David built all around from [1]the Millo and inward.

10 So David went on and became great, and [a]the LORD God of hosts *was* with [b]him.

**11** Then [a]Hiram [b]king of Tyre sent messengers to David, and cedar trees, and carpenters and masons. And they built David a house.

12 So David knew that the LORD had established him as king over Israel, and that He had [a]exalted His kingdom [b]for the sake of His people Israel.

13 And [a]David took more concubines and wives from Jerusalem, after he had come from Hebron. Also more sons and daughters were born to David.

14 Now [a]these *are* the names of those who were born to him in Jerusalem: [1]Shammua, Shobab, Nathan, [b]Solomon,

15 Ibhar, [1]Elishua, Nepheg, Japhia,

16 Elishama, Eliada, and Eliphelet.

**17** [a]Now when the Philistines heard that they had anointed David king over Israel, all the Philistines went up to search for David. And David heard *of it* [b]and went down to the stronghold.

18 The Philistines also went and deployed themselves in [a]the Valley of Rephaim.

19 So David [a]inquired of the LORD, saying, "Shall I go up against the Philistines? Will You deliver them into my hand?" And the LORD said to David, "Go up, for I will doubtless deliver the Philistines into your hand."

20 So David went to [a]Baal Perazim, and David defeated them there; and he said, "The LORD has broken through my enemies before me, like a breakthrough of water." Therefore he called the name of that place [1]Baal Perazim.

21 And they left their [1]images there, and David and his men [a]carried them away.

**22** [a]Then the Philistines went up once again and deployed themselves in the Valley of Rephaim.

23 Therefore [a]David inquired of the LORD, and He said, "You shall not go up; circle around behind them, and come upon them in front of the mulberry trees.

24 "And it shall be, when you [a]hear the sound of marching in the tops of the mulberry trees, then you shall advance quickly. For then [b]the LORD will go out before you to strike the camp of the Philistines."

25 And David did so, as the LORD commanded him; and he drove back the Philistines from [a]Geba[1] as far as [b]Gezer.

### *David Brings Back the Ark*

**6** Again David gathered all *the* choice *men* of Israel, thirty thousand.

2 And [a]David arose and went with all the people who *were* with him from [1]Baale Judah to bring up from there the ark of God, whose name is called [2]by the Name, the LORD of Hosts, [b]who dwells *between* the cherubim.

3 So they set the ark of God on a new cart, and brought it out of the house of Abinadab, which *was* on [a]the hill; and Uzzah and Ahio, the sons of Abinadab, drove the new [1]cart.

4 And they brought it out of [a]the house of Abinadab, which *was* on the hill, accompanying the ark of God; and Ahio went before the ark.

5 Then David and all the house of Israel [a]played *music* before the LORD on all kinds of *instruments of* fir wood, on harps, on stringed instruments, on tambourines, on sistrums, and on cymbals.

**6** And when they came to [a]Nachon's threshing floor, Uzzah put out *his* [b]*hand* to the ark of God and [1]took hold of it, for the oxen stumbled.

7 Then the anger of the LORD was aroused against Uzzah, and God struck him there for *his* [1]error; and he died there by the ark of God.

8 And David became angry because of the LORD's outbreak against Uzzah; and he called the name of the place [1]Perez Uzzah to this day.

9 [a]David was afraid of the LORD that day; and he said, "How can the ark of the LORD come to me?"

10 So David would not move the ark of the LORD with him into the [a]City of David; but David took it aside into the house of Obed-Edom the [b]Gittite.

11 [a]The ark of the LORD remained in the house of Obed-Edom the Gittite three months. And the LORD [b]blessed Obed-Edom and all his household.

**12** Now it was told King David, saying, "The LORD has blessed the house of Obed-Edom and all that *belongs* to him, because of the ark of God." [a]So David went and brought up the ark of God from the house of Obed-Edom to the City of David with gladness.

13 And so it was, when [a]those bearing the ark of the LORD had gone six paces, that he sacrificed [b]oxen and fatted sheep.

14 Then David [a]danced[1] before the LORD with all *his* might; and David *was* wearing [b]a linen ephod.

15 [a]So David and all the house of Israel brought up the ark of the LORD with shouting and with the sound of the trumpet.

**16** Now as the ark of the LORD came into the City of David, [a]Michal, Saul's daughter, looked through a window and saw King David leaping and whirling before the LORD; and she despised him in her heart.

17 So [a]they brought the ark of the LORD, and set it in [b]its place in the midst of the tabernacle that David had erected for it. Then David [c]offered burnt offerings and peace offerings before the LORD.

18 And when David had finished offering burnt offerings and peace offerings, [a]he blessed the people in the name of the LORD of hosts.

19 [a]Then he distributed among all the people, among the whole multitude of Israel, both the

---

4 [a]Gen. 41:46 [b]1 Chr. 26:31; 29:27
5 [a]2 Sam. 2:11
6 [a]Judg. 1:21 [b]Josh. 15:63
7 [a]1 Kin. 2:10; 8:1; 9:24
8 [a]1 Chr. 11:6–9
9 [a]2 Sam. 5:7 [1]Lit. *The Landfill*
10 [a]1 Sam. 17:45 [b]1 Sam. 18:12, 28
11 [a]1 Kin. 5:1–18 [b]1 Chr. 14:1
12 [a]Num. 24:7 [b]Is. 45:4
13 [a][Deut. 17:17]
14 [a]1 Chr. 3:5–8 [b]2 Sam. 12:24 [1]*Shimea,* 1 Chr. 3:5
15 [1]*Elishama,* 1 Chr. 3:6
17 [a]1 Chr. 11:16 [b]2 Sam. 23:14
18 [a]1 Chr. 11:15
19 [a]1 Sam. 23:2
20 [a]Is. 28:21 [1]Lit. *Master of Breakthroughs*
21 [a]Deut. 7:5, 25 [1]*idols*
22 [a]1 Chr. 14:13
23 [a]2 Sam. 5:19
24 [a]1 Chr. 14:15 [b]Judg. 4:14
25 [a]1 Chr. 14:16 [b]Josh. 16:10 [1]So with MT, Tg., Vg.; LXX *Gibeon*

CHAPTER 6
2 [a]1 Chr. 13:5, 6 [b]Ps. 80:1 [1]*Baalah, Kirjath Jearim,* Josh. 15:9; 1 Chr. 13:6 [2]LXX, Tg., Vg. omit *by the Name;* many Heb. mss., [Syr.] *there*
3 [a]1 Sam. 26:1 [1]LXX adds *with the ark*
4 [a]1 Sam. 7:1
5 [a]1 Sam. 18:6, 7
6 [a]1 Chr. 13:9 [b]Num. 4:15, 19, 20 [1]*held it*
7 [1]Or *irreverence*
8 [1]Lit. *Outburst Against Uzzah*
9 [a]Ps. 119:120
10 [a]2 Sam. 5:7 [b]1 Chr. 13:13; 26:4–8
11 [a]1 Chr. 13:14 [b]Gen. 30:27; 39:5
12 [a]1 Chr. 15:25—16:3
13 [a]Josh. 3:3 [b]1 Kin. 8:5
14 [a]Ps. 30:11; 149:3 [b]1 Sam. 2:18, 28 [1]*whirled about*
15 [a]1 Chr. 15:28
16 [a]2 Sam. 3:14
17 [a]1 Chr. 16:1 [b]1 Chr. 15:1; 2 Chr. 1:4 [c]1 Kin. 8:5, 62, 63
18 [a]1 Kin. 8:14, 15, 55
19 [a]1 Chr. 16:3

women and the men, to everyone a loaf of bread, a
piece *of meat,* and a cake of raisins. So all the
people departed, everyone to his house.
**20** [a]Then David returned to bless his household.
And Michal the daughter of Saul came out to
meet David, and said, "How glorious was the king
of Israel today, [b]uncovering himself today in the
eyes of the maids of his servants, as one of the
[c]base fellows [1]shamelessly uncovers himself!"
21 So David said to Michal, "*It was* before the
LORD, [a]who chose me instead of your father and
all his house, to appoint me ruler over the [b]people
of the LORD, over Israel. Therefore I will play
*music* before the LORD.
22 "And I will be even more undignified than
this, and will be humble in my own sight. But as
for the maidservants of whom you have spoken,
by them I will be held in honor."
23 Therefore Michal the daughter of Saul had no
children [a]to the day of her death.

## *God's Promise to David*

**7** Now it came to pass [a]when the king was
dwelling in his house, and the LORD had given
him rest from all his enemies all around,
2 that the king said to Nathan the prophet, "See
now, I dwell in [a]a house of cedar, [b]but the ark of
God dwells inside tent [c]curtains."
3 Then Nathan said to the king, "Go, do all that
*is* in your [a]heart, for the LORD *is* with you."
**4** But it happened that night that the word of
the LORD came to Nathan, saying,
5 "Go and tell My servant David, 'Thus says the
LORD: [a]"Would you build a house for Me to dwell
in?
6 "For I have not dwelt in a house [a]since the
time that I brought the children of Israel up from
Egypt, even to this day, but have moved about in
[b]a tent and in a tabernacle.
7 "Wherever I have [a]moved about with all the
children of Israel, have I ever spoken a word to
anyone from the tribes of Israel, whom I commanded [b]to shepherd My people Israel, saying,
'Why have you not built Me a house of cedar?' " '
8 "Now therefore, thus shall you say to My
servant David, 'Thus says the LORD of hosts: [a]"I
took you from the sheepfold, from following the
sheep, to be ruler over My people, over Israel.
9 "And [a]I have been with you wherever you
have gone, [b]and have [1]cut off all your enemies
from before you, and have made you a great
name, like the name of the great men who *are* on
the earth.
10 "Moreover I will appoint a place for My people
Israel, and will [a]plant them, that they may dwell in
a place of their own and move no more; [b]nor shall
the sons of wickedness oppress them anymore, as
previously,
11 [a]"since the time that I commanded judges *to
be* over My people Israel, and have caused you to
rest from all your enemies. Also the LORD [1]tells
you [b]that He will make you a [2]house.
**12** [a]"When your days are fulfilled and you [b]rest
with your fathers, [c]I will set up your seed after
you, who will come from your body, and I will
establish his kingdom.
13 [a]"He shall build a house for My name, and I
will [b]establish the throne of his kingdom forever.
14 [a]"I will be his Father, and he shall be [b]My son.
If he commits iniquity, I will chasten him with the
rod of men and with the [1]blows of the sons of men.
15 "But My mercy shall not depart from him, [a]as
I took *it* from Saul, whom I removed from before
you.
16 "And [a]your house and your kingdom shall be
established forever before [1]you. Your throne shall
be established forever." ' "
17 According to all these words and according to
all this vision, so Nathan spoke to David.
**18** Then King David went in and sat before the
LORD; and he said: [a]"Who *am* I, O Lord GOD? And
what is my house, that You have brought me this
far?
19 "And yet this was a small thing in Your sight,
O Lord GOD; and You have also spoken of Your
servant's house for a great while to come. [a]*Is* this
the manner of man, O Lord GOD?
20 "Now what more can David say to You? For
You, Lord GOD, [a]know Your servant.
21 "For Your word's sake, and according to Your
own heart, You have done all these great things,
to make Your servant know *them.*
22 "Therefore [a]You are great, [1]O Lord GOD. For
[b]*there is* none like You, nor *is there any* God
besides You, according to all that we have heard
with our [c]ears.
23 "And who *is* like Your people, like Israel, [a]the
one nation on the earth whom God went to
redeem for Himself as a people, to make for
Himself a name—and to do for Yourself great and
awesome deeds for Your land—before [b]Your people whom You redeemed for Yourself from Egypt,
the nations, and their gods?
24 "For [a]You have made Your people Israel Your
very own people forever; [b]and You, LORD, have
become their God.
25 "Now, O LORD God, the word which You have
spoken concerning Your servant and concerning
his house, establish *it* forever and do as You have
said.
26 "So let Your name be magnified forever, saying, 'The LORD of hosts *is* the God over Israel.'
And let the house of Your servant David be
established before You.
27 "For You, O LORD of hosts, God of Israel, have
revealed *this* to Your servant, saying, 'I will build
you a house.' Therefore Your servant has found it
in his heart to pray this prayer to You.
28 "And now, O Lord GOD, You are God, and
[a]Your words are true, and You have promised this
goodness to Your servant.
29 "Now therefore, let it please You to bless the
house of Your servant, that it may continue
before You forever; for You, O Lord GOD, have
spoken *it,* and with Your blessing let the house of
Your servant be blessed [a]forever."

## *David Extends His Kingdom*

**8** After this it came to pass that David [1]attacked
the Philistines and subdued them. And David
took [2]Metheg Ammah from the hand of the Philistines.
2 Then [a]he defeated Moab. Forcing them down
to the ground, he measured them off with a line.
With two lines he measured off those to be put to
death, and with one full line those to be kept alive.
So the Moabites became David's [b]servants, *and*
[c]brought tribute.
**3** David also defeated Hadadezer the son of
Rehob, king of [a]Zobah, as he went to recover [b]his
territory at the River Euphrates.
4 David took from him one thousand *chariots,*
[1]seven hundred horsemen, and twenty thousand
foot soldiers. Also David [a]hamstrung all the

**20** [a]Ps. 30:title [b]2 Sam. 6:14, 16 [c]Judg. 9:4 [1]*openly*
**21** [a]1 Sam. 13:14; 15:28 [b]2 Kin. 11:17
**23** [a]Is. 22:14

CHAPTER 7

**1** [a]1 Chr. 17:1–27
**2** [a]2 Sam. 5:11 [b]Acts 7:46 [c]Ex. 26:1
**3** [a]1 Kin. 8:17, 18
**5** [a]1 Kin. 5:3, 4; 8:19
**6** [a]1 Kin. 8:16 [b]Ex. 40:18, 34
**7** [a]Lev. 26:11, 12 [b]2 Sam. 5:2
**8** [a]1 Sam. 16:11, 12
**9** [a]2 Sam. 5:10 [b]1 Sam. 31:6 [1]*destroyed*
**10** [a]Ps. 44:2; 80:8 [b]Ps. 89:22, 23
**11** [a]Judg. 2:14–16 [b]2 Sam. 7:27 [1]*declares to you* [2]Royal dynasty
**12** [a]1 Kin. 2:1 [b]Deut. 31:16 [c]Ps. 132:11
**13** [a]1 Kin. 5:5; 8:19 [b][Is. 9:7; 49:8]
**14** [a][Heb. 1:5] [b][Ps. 2:7; 89:26, 27, 30] [1]*strokes*
**15** [a]1 Sam. 15:23, 28; 16:14
**16** [a]2 Sam. 7:13 [1]LXX *Me*
**18** [a]Ex. 3:11
**19** [a][Is. 55:8, 9]
**20** [a]John 21:17
**22** [a]Deut. 10:17 [b]Ex. 15:11 [c]Ex. 10:2 [1]Tg., Syr. *O LORD God*
**23** [a]Ps. 147:20 [b]Deut. 9:26; 33:29
**24** [a][Deut. 26:18] [b]Ps. 48:14
**28** [a]John 17:17
**29** [a]2 Sam. 22:51

CHAPTER 8

**1** [1]Lit. *struck* [2]Lit. *The Bridle of the Mother City*
**2** [a]Num. 24:17 [b]2 Sam. 12:31 [c]1 Kin. 4:21
**3** [a]1 Sam. 14:47 [b]2 Sam. 10:15–19
**4** [a]Josh. 11:6, 9 [1]*seven thousand,* 1 Chr. 18:4

chariot horses, except that he spared *enough* of
them for one hundred chariots.
5 [a]When the Syrians of Damascus came to help
Hadadezer king of Zobah, David killed twenty-
two thousand of the Syrians.
6 Then David put garrisons in Syria of Damascus; and the Syrians became David's servants, *and*
brought tribute. So [a]the LORD preserved David
wherever he went.
7 And David took [a]the shields of gold that had
belonged to the servants of Hadadezer, and
brought them to Jerusalem.
8 Also from [1]Betah and from [a]Berothai,[2] cities of
Hadadezer, King David took a large amount of
bronze.
**9** When [1]Toi king of [a]Hamath heard that David
had defeated all the army of Hadadezer,
10 then Toi sent [1]Joram his son to King David, to
[2]greet him and bless him, because he had fought
against Hadadezer and defeated him (for Hadadezer had been at war with Toi); and *Joram* brought
with him articles of silver, articles of gold, and
articles of bronze.
11 King David also [a]dedicated these to the LORD,
along with the silver and gold that he had dedicated from all the nations which he had subdued—
12 from [1]Syria, from Moab, from the people of
Ammon, from the [a]Philistines, from Amalek, and
from the spoil of Hadadezer the son of Rehob,
king of Zobah.
13 And David made *himself* a [a]name when he
returned from killing [b]eighteen thousand [1]Syrians
in [c]the Valley of Salt.
14 He also put garrisons in Edom; throughout all
Edom he put garrisons, and [a]all the Edomites
became David's servants. And the LORD preserved
David wherever he went.
**15** So David reigned over all Israel; and David
administered judgment and justice to all his
people.
16 [a]Joab the son of Zeruiah *was* over the army;
[b]Jehoshaphat the son of Ahilud *was* recorder;
17 [a]Zadok the son of Ahitub and Ahimelech the
son of Abiathar *were* the priests; [1]Seraiah *was* the
[2]scribe;
18 [a]Benaiah the son of Jehoiada *was over* both
the [b]Cherethites and the Pelethites; and David's
sons were [1]chief ministers.

### *David's Kindness to Mephibosheth*

**9** Now David said, "Is there still anyone who is
left of the house of Saul, that I may [a]show him
[1]kindness for Jonathan's sake?"
2 And *there was* a servant of the house of Saul
whose name *was* [a]Ziba. So when they had called
him to David, the king said to him, "*Are* you
Ziba?" He said, "At your service!"
3 Then the king said, "*Is* there not still someone
of the house of Saul, to whom I may show [a]the
kindness of God?" And Ziba said to the king,
"There is still a son of Jonathan *who is* [b]lame in
*his* feet."
4 So the king said to him, "Where *is* he?" And
Ziba said to the king, "Indeed he *is* in the house of
[a]Machir the son of Ammiel, in Lo Debar."
**5** Then King David sent and brought him out of
the house of Machir the son of Ammiel, from Lo
Debar.
6 Now when [a]Mephibosheth[1] the son of Jonathan, the son of Saul, had come to David, he fell
on his face and prostrated himself. Then David
said, "Mephibosheth?" And he answered, "Here is
your servant!"
7 So David said to him, "Do not fear, for I will
surely show you kindness for Jonathan your
father's sake, and will restore to you all the land of
Saul your grandfather; and you shall eat bread at
my table continually."
8 Then he bowed himself, and said, "What *is*
your servant, that you should look upon such [a]a
dead dog as I?"
**9** And the king called to Ziba, Saul's servant,
and said to him, [a]"I have given to your master's
son all that belonged to Saul and to all his house.
10 "You therefore, and your sons and your servants, shall work the land for him, and you shall
bring in *the harvest*, that your master's son may
have food to eat. But Mephibosheth your master's
son [a]shall eat bread at my table always." Now
Ziba had [b]fifteen sons and twenty servants.
11 Then Ziba said to the king, "According to all
that my lord the king has commanded his servant,
so will your servant do." "As for Mephibosheth,"
*said the king*, "he shall eat at [1]my table like one of
the king's sons."
12 Mephibosheth had a young son [a]whose name
*was* Micha. And all who dwelt in the house of
Ziba *were* servants of Mephibosheth.
13 So Mephibosheth dwelt in Jerusalem, [a]for he
ate continually at the king's table. And he [b]was
lame in both his feet.

### *The Defeat of the Ammonites and Syrians*

**10** It happened after this that the [a]king of the
people of Ammon died, and Hanun his son
reigned in his place.
2 Then David said, "I will show [a]kindness to
Hanun the son of [b]Nahash, as his father showed
kindness to me." So David sent by the hand of his
servants to comfort him concerning his father.
And David's servants came into the land of the
people of Ammon.
3 And the princes of the people of Ammon said
to Hanun their lord, "Do you think that David
really honors your father because he has sent
comforters to you? Has David not *rather* sent his
servants to you to search the city, to spy it out,
and to overthrow it?"
4 Therefore Hanun took David's servants,
shaved off half of their beards, cut off their garments in the middle, [a]at their buttocks, and sent
them away.
5 When they told David, he sent to meet them,
because the men were greatly [1]ashamed. And the
king said, "Wait at Jericho until your beards have
grown, and *then* return."
**6** When the people of Ammon saw that they
[a]had made themselves repulsive to David, the
people of Ammon sent and hired [b]the Syrians of
[c]Beth Rehob and the Syrians of Zoba, twenty
thousand foot soldiers; and from the king of
[d]Maacah one thousand men, and from [e]Ish-Tob
twelve thousand men.
7 Now when David heard *of it*, he sent Joab and
all the army of [a]the mighty men.
8 Then the people of Ammon came out and put
themselves in battle array at the entrance of the
gate. And [a]the Syrians of Zoba, Beth Rehob, Ish-
Tob, and Maacah *were* by themselves in the field.
**9** When Joab saw that the battle line was
against him before and behind, he chose some of
Israel's best and put *them* in battle array against
the Syrians.

**5** [a]1 Kin. 11:23–25
**6** [a]2 Sam. 7:9; 8:14
**7** [a]1 Kin. 10:16
**8** [a]Ezek. 47:16 [1]*Tibhath,* 1 Chr. 18:8 [2]*Chun,* 1 Chr. 18:8
**9** [a]1 Kin. 8:65 [1]*Tou,* 1 Chr. 18:9
**10** [1]*Hadoram,* 1 Chr. 18:10 [2]Lit. *ask him of his welfare*
**11** [a]1 Kin. 7:51
**12** [a]2 Sam. 5:17–25 [1]LXX, Syr., Heb. mss. *Edom*
**13** [a]2 Sam. 7:9 [b]2 Kin. 14:7 [c]1 Chr. 18:12 [1]LXX, Syr., Heb. mss. *Edomites* and 1 Chr. 18:12
**14** [a]Gen. 27:29, 37–40
**16** [a]2 Sam. 19:13; 20:23 [b]1 Kin. 4:3
**17** [a]1 Chr. 6:4–8; 24:3 [1]*Shavsha,* 1 Chr. 18:16 [2]*secretary*
**18** [a]1 Chr. 18:17 [b]1 Sam. 30:14 [1]Lit. *priests*

CHAPTER 9

**1** [a]1 Sam. 18:3; 20:14–16 [1]*covenant faithfulness*
**2** [a]2 Sam. 16:1–4; 19:17, 29
**3** [a]1 Sam. 20:14 [b]2 Sam. 4:4
**4** [a]2 Sam. 17:27–29
**6** [a]2 Sam. 16:4; 19:24–30 [1]Or *Merib-Baal*
**8** [a]2 Sam. 16:9
**9** [a]2 Sam. 16:4; 19:29
**10** [a]2 Sam. 9:7, 11, 13; 19:28 [b]2 Sam. 19:17
**11** [1]LXX *David's table*
**12** [a]1 Chr. 8:34
**13** [a]2 Sam. 9:7, 10, 11 [b]2 Sam. 9:3

CHAPTER 10

**1** [a]1 Chr. 19:1
**2** [a]2 Sam. 9:1 [b]1 Sam. 11:1
**4** [a]Is. 20:4; 47:2
**5** [1]*humiliated*
**6** [a]Gen. 34:30 [b]2 Sam. 8:3, 5 [c]Judg. 18:28 [d]Deut. 3:14 [e]Judg. 11:3, 5
**7** [a]2 Sam. 23:8
**8** [a]2 Sam. 10:6

10 And the rest of the people he put under the command of [a]Abishai his brother, that he might set *them* in battle array against the people of Ammon.
11 Then he said, "If the Syrians are too strong for me, then you shall help me; but if the people of Ammon are too strong for you, then I will come and help you.
12 [a]"Be of good courage, and let us [b]be strong for our people and for the cities of our God. And may [c]the LORD do *what is* good in His sight."
13 So Joab and the people who *were* with him drew near for the battle against the Syrians, and they fled before him.
14 When the people of Ammon saw that the Syrians were fleeing, they also fled before Abishai, and entered the city. So Joab returned from the people of Ammon and went to [a]Jerusalem.
**15** When the Syrians saw that they had been defeated by Israel, they gathered together.
16 Then [1]Hadadezer sent and brought out the Syrians who *were* beyond [2]the River, and they came to Helam. And [3]Shobach the commander of Hadadezer's army *went* before them.
17 When it was told David, he gathered all Israel, crossed over the Jordan, and came to Helam. And the Syrians set themselves in battle array against David and fought with him.
18 Then the Syrians fled before Israel; and David killed seven hundred charioteers and forty thousand [a]horsemen of the Syrians, and struck Shobach the commander of their army, who died there.
19 And when all the kings *who were* servants to [1]Hadadezer saw that they were defeated by Israel, they made peace with Israel and [a]served them. So the Syrians were afraid to help the people of Ammon anymore.

## *David and Bathsheba*

**11** It happened in the spring of the year, at the [a]time when kings go out *to battle,* that [b]David sent Joab and his servants with him, and all Israel; and they destroyed the people of Ammon and besieged [c]Rabbah. But David remained at Jerusalem.
2 Then it happened one evening that David arose from his bed [a]and walked on the roof of the king's house. And from the roof he [b]saw a woman bathing, and the woman *was* very beautiful to behold.
3 So David sent and inquired about the woman. And *someone* said, "*Is* this not [1]Bathsheba, the daughter of [2]Eliam, the wife [a]of Uriah the [b]Hittite?"
4 Then David sent messengers, and took her; and she came to him, and [a]he lay with her, for she was [b]cleansed from her impurity; and she returned to her house.
5 And the woman conceived; so she sent and told David, and said, "I *am* with child."
**6** Then David sent to Joab, *saying,* "Send me Uriah the Hittite." And Joab sent Uriah to David.
7 When Uriah had come to him, David asked how Joab was doing, and how the people were doing, and how the war prospered.
8 And David said to Uriah, "Go down to your house and [a]wash your feet." So Uriah departed from the king's house, and a gift *of food* from the king followed him.
9 But Uriah slept at the [a]door of the king's house with all the servants of his lord, and did not go down to his house.
10 So when they told David, saying, "Uriah did not go down to his house," David said to Uriah, "Did you not come from a journey? Why did you not go down to your house?"
11 And Uriah said to David, [a]"The ark and Israel and Judah are dwelling in tents, and [b]my lord Joab and the servants of my lord are encamped in the open fields. Shall I then go to my house to eat and drink, and to lie with my wife? *As* you live, and *as* your soul lives, I will not do this thing."
12 Then David said to Uriah, "Wait here today also, and tomorrow I will let you depart." So Uriah remained in Jerusalem that day and the next.
13 Now when David called him, he ate and drank before him; and he made him [a]drunk. And at evening he went out to lie on his bed [b]with the servants of his lord, but he did not go down to his house.
**14** In the morning it happened that David [a]wrote a letter to Joab and sent *it* by the hand of Uriah.
15 And he wrote in the letter, saying, "Set Uriah in the forefront of the [1]hottest battle, and retreat from him, that he may [a]be struck down and die."
16 So it was, while Joab besieged the city, that he assigned Uriah to a place where he knew there *were* valiant men.
17 Then the men of the city came out and fought with Joab. And *some* of the people of the servants of David fell; and Uriah the Hittite died also.
**18** Then Joab sent and told David all the things concerning the war,
19 and charged the messenger, saying, "When you have finished telling the matters of the war to the king,
20 if it happens that the king's wrath rises, and he says to you: 'Why did you approach so near to the city when you fought? Did you not know that they would shoot from the wall?
21 'Who struck [a]Abimelech the son of [1]Jerubbesheth? Was it not a woman who cast a piece of a millstone on him from the wall, so that he died in Thebez? Why did you go near the wall?'—then you shall say, 'Your servant Uriah the Hittite is dead also.' "
**22** So the messenger went, and came and told David all that Joab had sent by him.
23 And the messenger said to David, "Surely the men prevailed against us and came out to us in the field; then we drove them back as far as the entrance of the gate.
24 "The archers shot from the wall at your servants; and *some* of the king's servants are dead, and your servant Uriah the Hittite is dead also."
25 Then David said to the messenger, "Thus you shall say to Joab: 'Do not let this thing [1]displease you, for the sword devours one as well as another. Strengthen your attack against the city, and overthrow it.' So encourage him."
**26** When the wife of Uriah heard that Uriah her husband was dead, she mourned for her husband.
27 And when her mourning was over, David sent and brought her to his house, and she [a]became his wife and bore him a son. But the thing that David had done [b]displeased[1] the LORD.

## *Nathan Rebukes David*

**12** Then the LORD sent Nathan to David. And [a]he came to him, and [b]said to him: "There were two men in one city, one rich and the other poor.

---

10 [a]1 Sam. 26:6; 2 Sam. 3:30
12 [a]Deut. 31:6; Josh. 1:6, 7, 9; Neh. 4:14 [b]1 Sam. 4:9; 1 Cor. 16:13 [c]1 Sam. 3:18
14 [a]2 Sam. 11:1
16 [1]Heb. *Hadarezer* [2]The Euphrates [3]*Shophach,* 1 Chr. 19:16
18 [a]1 Chr. 19:18
19 [a]2 Sam. 8:6 [1]Heb. *Hadarezer*

CHAPTER 11

1 [a]1 Kin. 20:22–26 [b]1 Chr. 20:1 [c]2 Sam. 12:26; Jer. 49:2, 3; Amos 1:14
2 [a]Deut. 22:8; 1 Sam. 9:25; Matt. 24:17; Acts 10:9 [b]Gen. 34:2; [Ex. 20:17]; Job 31:1; [Matt. 5:28]
3 [a]2 Sam. 23:39 [b]1 Sam. 26:6 [1]*Bathshua,* 1 Chr. 3:5 [2]*Ammiel,* 1 Chr. 3:5
4 [a][Lev. 20:10; Deut. 22:22]; Ps. 51:title; [James 1:14, 15] [b]Lev. 15:19, 28
8 [a]Gen. 18:4; 19:2
9 [a]1 Kin. 14:27, 28
11 [a]2 Sam. 7:2, 6 [b]2 Sam. 20:6–22
13 [a]Gen. 19:33, 35 [b]2 Sam. 11:9
14 [a]1 Kin. 21:8, 9
15 [a]2 Sam. 12:9 [1]*fiercest*
21 [a]Judg. 9:50–54 [1]*Jerubbaal,* Gideon, Judg. 6:32
25 [1]Lit. *be evil in your sight*
27 [a]2 Sam. 12:9 [b]1 Chr. 21:7; [Heb. 13:4] [1]Lit. *was evil in the eyes of*

CHAPTER 12

1 [a]Ps. 51:title [b]1 Kin. 20:35–41

2 "The rich *man* had exceedingly many flocks
and herds.
3 "But the poor *man* had nothing, except one
little ewe lamb which he had bought and nourished; and it grew up together with him and with
his children. It ate of his own food and drank from
his own cup and lay in his bosom; and it was like
a daughter to him.
4 "And a traveler came to the rich man, who
refused to take from his own flock and from his
own herd to prepare one for the wayfaring man
who had come to him; but he took the poor man's
lamb and prepared it for the man who had come
to him."
5 So David's anger was greatly aroused against
the man, and he said to Nathan, "*As* the LORD
lives, the man who has done this [1]shall surely die!
6 "And he shall restore [a]fourfold for the lamb,
because he did this thing and because he had no
pity."
7 Then Nathan said to David, "You *are* the man!
Thus says the LORD God of Israel: 'I [a]anointed you
king over Israel, and I delivered you from the
hand of Saul.
8 'I gave you your master's house and your
master's wives into your keeping, and gave you
the house of Israel and Judah. And if *that had
been* too little, I also would have given you much
more!
9 [a]'Why have you [b]despised the commandment
of the LORD, to do evil in His sight? [c]You have
killed Uriah the Hittite with the sword; you have
taken his wife *to be* your wife, and have killed him
with the sword of the people of Ammon.
10 'Now therefore, [a]the sword shall never depart
from your house, because you have despised Me,
and have taken the wife of Uriah the Hittite to be
your wife.'
11 "Thus says the LORD: 'Behold, I will raise up
adversity against you from your own house; and I
will [a]take your wives before your eyes and give
*them* to your neighbor, and he shall lie with your
wives in the sight of this sun.
12 'For you did *it* secretly, [a]but I will do this thing
before all Israel, before the sun.' "
13 [a]So David said to Nathan, [b]"I have sinned
against the LORD." And Nathan said to David,
"The LORD also has [c]put away your sin; you shall
not die.
14 "However, because by this deed you have
given great occasion to the enemies of the LORD
[a]to blaspheme, the child also *who is* born to you
shall surely die."
15 Then Nathan departed to his house.
And the [a]LORD struck the child that Uriah's
wife bore to David, and it became ill.
16 David therefore pleaded with God for the
child, and David fasted and went in and [a]lay all
night on the ground.
17 So the elders of his house arose *and went* to
him, to raise him up from the ground. But he
would not, nor did he eat food with them.
18 Then on the seventh day it came to pass that
the child died. And the servants of David were
afraid to tell him that the child was dead. For they
said, "Indeed, while the child was alive, we spoke
to him, and he would not heed our voice. How can
we tell him that the child is dead? He may do some
harm!"
19 When David saw that his servants were whispering, David perceived that the child was dead.
Therefore David said to his servants, "Is the child
dead?" And they said, "He is dead."
20 So David arose from the ground, washed and
[a]anointed himself, and changed his clothes; and he
went into the house of the LORD and [b]worshiped.
Then he went to his own house; and when he
requested, they set food before him, and he ate.
21 Then his servants said to him, "What *is* this
that you have done? You fasted and wept for the
child *while he was* alive, but when the child died,
you arose and ate food."
22 And he said, "While the child was alive, I
fasted and wept; [a]for I said, 'Who can tell *whether*
[1]the LORD will be gracious to me, that the child
may live?'
23 "But now he is dead; why should I fast? Can I
bring him back again? I shall go [a]to him, but [b]he
shall not return to me."
**24** Then David comforted Bathsheba his wife,
and went in to her and lay with her. So [a]she bore a
son, and [b]he[1] called his name Solomon. Now the
LORD loved him,
25 and He sent *word* by the hand of Nathan the
prophet: So [1]he called his name [2]Jedidiah, because
of the LORD.
**26** Now [a]Joab fought against [b]Rabbah of the
people of Ammon, and took the royal city.
27 And Joab sent messengers to David, and said,
"I have fought against Rabbah, and I have taken
the city's water *supply*.
28 "Now therefore, gather the rest of the people
together and encamp against the city and take it,
lest I take the city and it be called after my name."
29 So David gathered all the people together and
went to Rabbah, fought against it, and took it.
30 [a]Then he took their king's crown from his
head. Its weight *was* a talent of gold, with precious stones. And it was *set* on David's head. Also
he brought out the [1]spoil of the city in great
abundance.
31 And he brought out the people who *were* in it,
and put *them to work* with saws and iron picks
and iron axes, and made them cross over to the
brick works. So he did to all the cities of the
people of Ammon. Then David and all the people
returned to Jerusalem.

### *Amnon's Sin Against Tamar*

**13** After this [a]Absalom the son of David had a
lovely sister, whose name *was* [b]Tamar; and
[c]Amnon the son of David loved her.
2 Amnon was so distressed over his sister Tamar
that he became sick; for she *was* a virgin. And it
was improper for Amnon to do anything to her.
3 But Amnon had a friend whose name *was*
Jonadab [a]the son of Shimeah, David's brother.
Now Jonadab *was* a very crafty man.
4 And he said to him, "Why *are* you, the king's
son, becoming thinner day after day? Will you not
tell me?" Amnon said to him, "I love Tamar, my
brother Absalom's sister."
5 So Jonadab said to him, "Lie down on your
bed and pretend to be ill. And when your father
comes to see you, say to him, 'Please let my sister
Tamar come and give me food, and prepare the
food in my sight, that I may see *it* and eat it from
her hand.' "
6 Then Amnon lay down and pretended to be ill;
and when the king came to see him, Amnon said
to the king, "Please let Tamar my sister come and

**5** [1]*deserves to die,* lit. *is a son of death*
**6** [a][Ex. 22:1]; Luke 19:8
**7** [a]1 Sam. 16:13; 2 Sam. 5:3
**9** [a]1 Sam. 15:19 [b]Num. 15:31 [c]2 Sam. 11:14–17, 27
**10** [a]2 Sam. 13:28; 18:14; 1 Kin. 2:25; [Amos 7:9]
**11** [a]Deut. 28:30; 2 Sam. 16:21, 22
**12** [a]2 Sam. 16:22
**13** [a]1 Sam. 15:24 [b]2 Sam. 24:10; Job 7:20; Ps. 51; Luke 18:13 [c]2 Sam. 24:10; Job 7:21; [Ps. 32:1–5; Prov. 28:13; Mic. 7:18]; Zech. 3:4
**14** [a]Is. 52:5; [Ezek. 36:20, 23]; Rom. 2:24
**15** [a]1 Sam. 25:38
**16** [a]2 Sam. 13:31
**20** [a]Ruth 3:3; Matt. 6:17 [b]Job 1:20
**22** [a]Is. 38:1–5; Joel 2:14; Jon. 3:9 [1]Heb. mss., Syr. *God*
**23** [a]Gen. 37:35 [b]Job 7:8–10
**24** [a]Matt. 1:6 [b]1 Chr. 22:9 [1]So with Kt., LXX, Vg.; Qr., a few Heb. mss., Syr., Tg. *she*
**25** [1]Qr., some Heb. mss., Syr., Tg. *she* [2]Lit. *Beloved of the LORD*
**26** [a]1 Chr. 20:1 [b]Deut. 3:11; 2 Sam. 11:1
**30** [a]1 Chr. 20:2 [1]*plunder*

CHAPTER 13
**1** [a]2 Sam. 3:2, 3; 1 Chr. 3:2 [b]1 Chr. 3:9 [c]2 Sam. 3:2
**3** [a]1 Sam. 16:9

[a]make a couple of cakes for me in my sight, that I
may eat from her hand."
7 And David sent home to Tamar, saying, "Now
go to your brother Amnon's house, and prepare
food for him."
8 So Tamar went to her brother Amnon's house;
and he was lying down. Then she took flour and
kneaded *it*, made cakes in his sight, and baked the
cakes.
9 And she took the pan and placed *them* out
before him, but he refused to eat. Then Amnon
said, [a]"Have everyone go out from me." And they
all went out from him.
10 Then Amnon said to Tamar, "Bring the food
into the bedroom, that I may eat from your hand."
And Tamar took the cakes which she had made,
and brought *them* to Amnon her brother in the
bedroom.
11 Now when she had brought *them* to him to
eat, [a]he took hold of her and said to her, "Come,
lie with me, my sister."
12 But she answered him, "No, my brother, do
not [1]force me, for [a]no such thing should be done in
Israel. Do not do this [b]disgraceful thing!
13 "And I, where could I take my shame? And as
for you, you would be like one of the fools in
Israel. Now therefore, please speak to the king;
[a]for he will not withhold me from you."
14 However, he would not heed her voice; and
being stronger than she, he [a]forced her and lay
with her.
**15** Then Amnon hated her [1]exceedingly, so that
the hatred with which he hated her *was* greater
than the love with which he had loved her. And
Amnon said to her, "Arise, be gone!"
16 So she said to him, "No, indeed! This evil of
sending me away *is* worse than the other that you
did to me." But he would not listen to her.
17 Then he called his servant who attended him,
and said, "Here! Put this *woman* out, away from
me, and bolt the door behind her."
18 Now she had on [a]a robe of many colors, for the
king's virgin daughters wore such apparel. And
his servant put her out and bolted the door behind
her.
**19** Then Tamar put [a]ashes on her head, and tore
her robe of many colors that *was* on her, and [b]laid
her hand on her head and went away crying
bitterly.
20 And Absalom her brother said to her, "Has
Amnon your brother been with you? But now hold
your peace, my sister. He *is* your brother; do not
take this thing to heart." So Tamar remained
desolate in her brother Absalom's house.
**21** But when King David heard of all these things,
he was very angry.
22 And Absalom spoke to his brother Amnon
[a]neither good nor bad. For Absalom [b]hated Amnon, because he had forced his sister Tamar.
**23** And it came to pass, after two full years, that
Absalom [a]had sheepshearers in Baal Hazor, which
*is* near Ephraim; so Absalom invited all the king's
sons.
24 Then Absalom came to the king and said,
"Kindly note, your servant has sheepshearers;
please, let the king and his servants go with your
servant."
25 But the king said to Absalom, "No, my son, let
us not all go now, lest we be a burden to you."
Then he urged him, but he would not go; and he
blessed him.
26 Then Absalom said, "If not, please let my
brother Amnon go with us." And the king said to
him, "Why should he go with you?"
27 But Absalom urged him; so he let Amnon and
all the king's sons go with him.
**28** Now Absalom had commanded his servants,
saying, "Watch now, when Amnon's [a]heart is
merry with wine, and when I say to you, 'Strike
Amnon!' then kill him. Do not be afraid. Have I
not commanded you? Be courageous and [1]val-
iant."
29 So the servants of Absalom [a]did to Amnon as
Absalom had commanded. Then all the king's
sons arose, and each one got on [b]his mule and fled.
**30** And it came to pass, while they were on the
way, that news came to David, saying, "Absalom
has killed all the king's sons, and not one of them
is left!"
31 So the king arose and [a]tore his garments and
[b]lay on the ground, and all his servants stood by
with their clothes torn.
32 Then [a]Jonadab the son of Shimeah, David's
brother, answered and said, "Let not my lord
suppose they have killed all the young men, the
king's sons, for only Amnon is dead. For by the
command of Absalom this has been determined
from the day that he forced his sister Tamar.
33 "Now therefore, [a]let not my lord the king take
the thing to his heart, to think that all the king's
sons are dead. For only Amnon is dead."
**34** [a]Then Absalom fled. And the young man who
was keeping watch lifted his eyes and looked, and
there, many people were coming from the road on
the hillside behind [1]him.
35 And Jonadab said to the king, "Look, the
king's sons are coming; as your servant said, so it
is."
36 So it was, as soon as he had finished speaking,
that the king's sons indeed came, and they lifted
up their voice and wept. Also the king and all his
servants wept very bitterly.
37 But Absalom fled and went to [a]Talmai the son
of Ammihud, king of Geshur. And *David* mourned
for his son every day.
38 So Absalom fled and went to [a]Geshur, and was
there three years.
39 And [1]King David [2]longed to go to Absalom.
For he had been [a]comforted concerning Amnon,
because he was dead.

### *Joab's Scheme for Absalom's Return*

**14** So Joab the son of Zeruiah perceived that
the king's heart *was* concerned [a]about Absalom.
2 And Joab sent to [a]Tekoa and brought from
there a wise woman, and said to her, "Please
pretend to be a mourner, [b]and put on mourning
apparel; do not anoint yourself with oil, but act
like a woman who has been mourning a long time
for the dead.
3 "Go to the king and speak to him in this
manner." So Joab [a]put the words in her mouth.
**4** And when the woman of Tekoa [1]spoke to the
king, she [a]fell on her face to the ground and
prostrated herself, and said, [b]"Help, O king!"
5 Then the king said to her, "What troubles
you?" And she answered, [a]"Indeed I *am* a widow,
my husband is dead.
6 "Now your maidservant had two sons; and the
two fought with each other in the field, and *there*

**6** [a]Gen. 18:6
**9** [a]Gen. 45:1
**11** [a]Gen. 39:12; [Deut. 27:22]; Ezek. 22:11
**12** [a][Lev. 18:9–11; 20:17] [b]Gen. 34:7; Judg. 19:23; 20:6 [1]Lit. *humble me*
**13** [a]Gen. 20:12
**14** [a]Lev. 18:9; [Deut. 22:25; 27:22]; 2 Sam. 12:11
**15** [1]*with a very great hatred*
**18** [a]Gen. 37:3; Judg. 5:30; Ps. 45:13–14
**19** [a]Josh. 7:6; 2 Sam. 1:2; Job 2:12; 42:6 [b]Jer. 2:37
**22** [a]Gen. 24:50; 31:24 [b][Lev. 19:17, 18; 1 John 2:9, 11; 3:10, 12, 15]
**23** [a]Gen. 38:12, 13; 1 Sam. 25:4
**28** [a]Judg. 19:6, 9, 22; Ruth 3:7; 1 Sam. 25:36; Esth. 1:10 [1]Lit. *sons of valor*
**29** [a]2 Sam. 12:10 [b]2 Sam. 18:9; 1 Kin. 1:33, 38
**31** [a]2 Sam. 1:11 [b]2 Sam. 12:16
**32** [a]2 Sam. 13:3–5
**33** [a]2 Sam. 19:19
**34** [a]2 Sam. 13:37, 38 [1]LXX adds *And the watchman went and told the king, and said, "I see men from the way of Horonaim, from the regions of the mountains."*
**37** [a]2 Sam. 3:3; 1 Chr. 3:2
**38** [a]2 Sam. 14:23, 32; 15:8
**39** [a]Gen. 38:12; 2 Sam. 12:19, 23 [1]So with MT, Syr., Vg.; LXX *the spirit of the king;* Tg. *the soul of King David* [2]So with MT, Tg.; LXX, Vg. *ceased to pursue after*

CHAPTER 14
**1** [a]2 Sam. 13:39
**2** [a]2 Sam. 23:26; 2 Chr. 11:6; Amos 1:1 [b]Ruth 3:3
**3** [a]Ex. 4:15; 2 Sam. 14:19
**4** [a]1 Sam. 20:41; 25:23; 2 Sam. 1:2 [b]2 Kin. 6:26, 28 [1]Many Heb. mss., LXX, Syr., Vg. *came*
**5** [a][Zech. 7:10]

*was* no one to part them, but the one struck the
other and killed him.
7 “And now the whole family has risen up
against your maidservant, and they said, ‘Deliver
him who struck his brother, that we may execute
him [a]for the life of his brother whom he killed; and
we will destroy the heir also.’ So they would
extinguish my ember that is left, and leave to my
husband *neither* name nor remnant on the earth.”
**8** Then the king said to the woman, “Go to your
house, and I will give orders concerning you.”
9 And the woman of Tekoa said to the king,
“My lord, O king, *let* [a]the [1]iniquity *be* on me and
on my father’s house, [b]and the king and his throne
*be* guiltless.”
10 So the king said, “Whoever says *anything* to
you, bring him to me, and he shall not touch you
anymore.”
11 Then she said, “Please let the king remember
the LORD your God, and do not permit [a]the
avenger of blood to destroy anymore, lest they
destroy my son.” And he said, [b]“As the LORD lives,
not one hair of your son shall fall to the ground.”
**12** Therefore the woman said, “Please, let your
maidservant speak *another* word to my lord the
king.” And he said, “Say on.”
13 So the woman said: “Why then have you
schemed such a thing against [a]the people of God?
For the king speaks this thing as one who is
guilty, *in that* the king does not bring [b]his banished one home again.
14 “For we [a]will surely die and *become* like water
spilled on the ground, which cannot be gathered
up again. Yet God does not [b]take away a life; but
He [c]devises means, so that His banished ones are
not [1]expelled from Him.
15 “Now therefore, I have come to speak of this
thing to my lord the king because the people have
made me afraid. And your maidservant said, ‘I will
now speak to the king; it may be that the king will
perform the request of his maidservant.
16 ‘For the king will hear and deliver his maidservant from the hand of the man *who would* destroy
me and my son together from the [a]inheritance of
God.’
17 “Your maidservant said, ‘The word of my lord
the king will now be comforting; for [a]as the angel
of God, so *is* my lord the king in [b]discerning good
and evil. And may the LORD your God be with
you.’ ”
**18** Then the king answered and said to the
woman, “Please do not hide from me anything
that I ask you.” And the woman said, “Please, let
my lord the king speak.”
19 So the king said, “*Is* the hand of Joab with you
in all this?” And the woman answered and said,
“*As* you live, my lord the king, no one can turn to
the right hand or to the left from anything that
my lord the king has spoken. For your servant
Joab commanded me, and [a]he put all these words
in the mouth of your maidservant.
20 “To bring about this change of affairs your
servant Joab has done this thing; but my lord *is*
wise, [a]according to the wisdom of the angel of
God, to know everything that *is* in the earth.”
21 And the king said to Joab, “All right, I have
granted this thing. Go therefore, bring back the
young man Absalom.”
22 Then Joab fell to the ground on his face and
bowed himself, and [1]thanked the king. And Joab
said, “Today your servant knows that I have
found favor in your sight, my lord, O king, in that
the king has fulfilled the request of his servant.”
23 So Joab arose [a]and went to Geshur, and
brought Absalom to Jerusalem.
24 And the king said, “Let him return to his own
house, but [a]do not let him see my face.” So
Absalom returned to his own house, but did not
see the king’s face.
**25** Now in all Israel there was no one who was
praised as much as Absalom for his good looks.
[a]From the sole of his foot to the crown of his head
there was no blemish in him.
26 And when he cut the hair of his head—at the
end of every year he cut *it* because it was heavy
on him—when he cut it, he weighed the hair of his
head at two hundred shekels according to the
king’s standard.
27 [a]To Absalom were born three sons, and one
daughter whose name *was* Tamar. She was a
woman of beautiful appearance.
**28** And Absalom dwelt two full years in Jerusalem, [a]but did not see the king’s face.
29 Therefore Absalom sent for Joab, to send him
to the king, but he would not come to him. And
when he sent again the second time, he would not
come.
30 So he said to his servants, “See, Joab’s field is
near mine, and he has barley there; go and set it
on fire.” And Absalom’s servants set the field on
fire.
31 Then Joab arose and came to Absalom’s
house, and said to him, “Why have your servants
set my field on fire?”
32 And Absalom answered Joab, “Look, I sent to
you, saying, ‘Come here, so that I may send you to
the king, to say, “Why have I come from Geshur?
*It would be* better for me *to be* there still.” ’ Now
therefore, let me see the king’s face; but [a]if there is
iniquity in me, let him execute me.”
33 So Joab went to the king and told him. And
when he had called for Absalom, he came to the
king and bowed himself on his face to the ground
before the king. Then the king [a]kissed Absalom.

### *David Flees from Jerusalem*

**15** After this [a]it happened that Absalom [b]pro-
vided himself with chariots and horses, and
fifty men to run before him.
2 Now Absalom would rise early and stand
beside the way to the gate. *So* it was, whenever
anyone who had a [a]lawsuit[1] came to the king for a
decision, that Absalom would call to him and say,
“What city *are* you from?” And he would say,
“Your servant *is* from such and such a tribe of
Israel.”
3 Then Absalom would say to him, “Look, your
[1]case *is* good and right; but *there is* no [2]deputy of
the king to hear you.”
4 Moreover Absalom would say, [a]“Oh, that I
were made judge in the land, and everyone who
has any suit or cause would come to me; then I
would give him justice.”
5 And *so* it was, whenever anyone came near to
bow down to him, that he would put out his hand
and take him and [a]kiss him.
6 In this manner Absalom acted toward all
Israel who came to the king for judgment. [a]So
Absalom stole the hearts of the men of Israel.
**7** Now it came to pass [a]after [1]forty years that
Absalom said to the king, “Please, let me go to

**7** [a]Num. 35:19; Deut. 19:12, 13
**9** [a]Gen. 27:13; 43:9; 1 Sam. 25:24; Matt. 27:25 [b]2 Sam. 3:28, 29; 1 Kin. 2:33 [1]*guilt*
**11** [a]Num. 35:19, 21; [Deut. 19:4–10] [b]1 Sam. 14:45; 1 Kin. 1:52; Matt. 10:30; Acts 27:34
**13** [a]Judg. 20:2 [b]2 Sam. 13:37, 38
**14** [a]Job 30:23; 34:15; [Heb. 9:27] [b]Job 34:19; Matt. 22:16; Acts 10:34; Rom. 2:11 [c]Num. 35:15 [1]*cast out*
**16** [a]Deut. 32:9; 1 Sam. 26:19; 2 Sam. 20:19
**17** [a]1 Sam. 29:9; 2 Sam. 19:27 [b]1 Kin. 3:9
**19** [a]2 Sam. 14:3
**20** [a]2 Sam. 14:17; 19:27
**22** [1]Lit. *blessed*
**23** [a]2 Sam. 13:37, 38
**24** [a]Gen. 43:3; 2 Sam. 3:13
**25** [a]Deut. 28:35; Job 2:7; Is. 1:6
**27** [a]2 Sam. 13:1; 18:18
**28** [a]2 Sam. 14:24
**32** [a]1 Sam. 20:8; [Prov. 28:13]
**33** [a]Gen. 33:4; 45:15; Luke 15:20

CHAPTER 15

**1** [a]2 Sam. 12:11 [b]1 Kin. 1:5
**2** [a]Deut. 19:17 [1]Lit. *controversy*
**3** [1]Lit. *words* [2]Lit. *listener*
**4** [a]Judg. 9:29
**5** [a]2 Sam. 14:33; 20:9
**6** [a][Rom. 16:18]
**7** [a][Deut. 23:21] [1]LXX mss., Syr., Josephus *four*

[b]Hebron and pay the vow which I made to the
LORD.
8 [a]"For your servant [b]took a vow [c]while I dwelt
at Geshur in Syria, saying, 'If the LORD indeed
brings me back to Jerusalem, then I will serve the
LORD.' "
9 And the king said to him, "Go in peace." So he
arose and went to Hebron.
**10** Then Absalom sent spies throughout all the
tribes of Israel, saying, "As soon as you hear the
sound of the trumpet, then you shall say, 'Absalom [a]reigns in Hebron!' "
11 And with Absalom went two hundred men
[a]invited from Jerusalem, and they [b]went along
innocently and did not know anything.
12 Then Absalom sent for Ahithophel the Gilonite, [a]David's counselor, from his city—from [b]Gi-
loh—while he offered sacrifices. And the conspiracy grew strong, for the people with Absalom
[c]continually increased in number.
**13** Now a messenger came to David, saying,
[a]"The hearts of the men of Israel are [1]with Absalom."
14 So David said to all his servants who *were*
with him at Jerusalem, "Arise, and let us [a]flee, or
we shall not escape from Absalom. Make haste to
depart, lest he overtake us suddenly and bring
disaster upon us, and strike the city with the edge
of the sword."
15 And the king's servants said to the king, "We
*are* your servants, *ready to do* whatever my lord
the king commands."
16 Then [a]the king went out with all his household
after him. But the king left [b]ten women, concubines, to keep the house.
17 And the king went out with all the people
after him, and stopped at the outskirts.
18 Then all his servants passed [1]before him; [a]and
all the Cherethites, all the Pelethites, and all the
Gittites, [b]six hundred men who had followed him
from Gath, passed before the king.
**19** Then the king said to [a]Ittai the Gittite, "Why
are you also going with us? Return and remain
with the king. For you *are* a foreigner and also an
exile from your own place.
20 "In fact, you came *only* yesterday. Should I
make you wander up and down with us today,
since I go [a]I know not where? Return, and take
your brethren back. Mercy and truth *be* with
you."
21 But Ittai answered the king and said, [a]"*As* the
LORD lives, and *as* my lord the king lives, surely in
whatever place my lord the king shall be, whether
in death or life, even there also your servant will
be."
22 So David said to Ittai, "Go, and cross over."
Then Ittai the Gittite and all his men and all the
little ones who *were* with him crossed over.
23 And all the country wept with a loud voice,
and all the people crossed over. The king himself
also crossed over the Brook Kidron, and all the
people crossed over toward the way of the [a]wilder-
ness.
**24** There was [a]Zadok also, and all the Levites
with him, bearing the [b]ark of the covenant of God.
And they set down the ark of God, and [c]Abiathar
went up until all the people had finished crossing
over from the city.
25 Then the king said to Zadok, "Carry the ark of
God back into the city. If I find favor in the eyes
of the LORD, He [a]will bring me back and show me
*both* it and [b]His dwelling place.
26 "But if He says thus: 'I have no [a]delight in
you,' here I am, [b]let Him do to me as seems good
to Him."
27 The king also said to Zadok the priest, "*Are*
you *not* a [a]seer?[1] Return to the city in peace, and
[b]your two sons with you, Ahimaaz your son, and
Jonathan the son of Abiathar.
28 "See, [a]I will wait in the plains of the wilderness until word comes from you to inform me."
29 Therefore Zadok and Abiathar carried the ark
of God back to Jerusalem. And they remained
there.
**30** So David went up by the Ascent of the *Mount*
*of* Olives, and wept as he went up; and he [a]had his
head covered and went [b]barefoot. And all the
people who *were* with him [c]covered their heads
and went up, [d]weeping as they went up.
31 Then *someone* told David, saying, [a]"Ahithophel *is* among the conspirators with Absalom."
And David said, "O LORD, I pray, [b]turn the counsel
of Ahithophel into foolishness!"
**32** Now it happened when David had come to the
top *of the mountain*, where he worshiped God—
there was Hushai the [a]Archite coming to meet
him [b]with his robe torn and dust on his head.
33 David said to him, "If you go on with me, then
you will become [a]a burden to me.
34 "But if you return to the city, and say to
Absalom, [a]'I will be your servant, O king; *as* I *was*
your father's servant previously, so I *will* now also
*be* your servant,' then you may defeat the counsel
of Ahithophel for me.
35 "And *do* you not *have* Zadok and Abiathar the
priests with you there? Therefore it will be *that*
whatever you hear from the king's house, you
shall tell to [a]Zadok and Abiathar the priests.
36 "Indeed *they have* there [a]with them their two
sons, Ahimaaz, Zadok's *son*, and Jonathan, Abiathar's *son*; and by them you shall send me
everything you hear."
37 So Hushai, [a]David's friend, went into the city.
[b]And Absalom came into Jerusalem.

### *Absalom Enters Jerusalem*

**16** When[a] David was a little past the top *of the*
*mountain*, there was [b]Ziba the servant of
Mephibosheth, who met him with a couple of
saddled donkeys, and on them two hundred *loaves*
of bread, one hundred clusters of raisins, one
hundred summer fruits, and a skin of wine.
2 And the king said to Ziba, "What do you mean
to do with these?" So Ziba said, "The donkeys *are*
for the king's household to ride on, the bread and
summer fruit for the young men to eat, and the
wine for [a]those who are faint in the wilderness to
drink."
3 Then the king said, "And where *is* your [a]mas-
ter's son?" [b]And Ziba said to the king, "Indeed he
is staying in Jerusalem, for he said, 'Today the
house of Israel will restore the kingdom of my
father to me.' "
4 So the king said to Ziba, "Here, all that *be-*
*longs* to Mephibosheth *is* yours." And Ziba said, "I
humbly bow before you, *that* I may find favor in
your sight, my lord, O king!"
**5** Now when King David came to [a]Bahurim,
there was a man from the family of the house of
Saul, whose name *was* [b]Shimei the son of Gera,

**7** [b]2 Sam. 3:2, 3
**8** [a]1 Sam. 16:2 [b]Gen. 28:20, 21 [c]2 Sam. 13:38
**10** [a]1 Kin. 1:34; 2 Kin. 9:13
**11** [a]1 Sam. 16:3, 5 [b]Gen. 20:5
**12** [a]2 Sam. 16:15; 1 Chr. 27:33; Ps. 41:9; 55:12–14 [b]Josh. 15:51 [c]Ps. 3:1
**13** [a]Judg. 9:3; 2 Sam. 15:6 [1]Lit. *after*
**14** [a]2 Sam. 12:11; Ps. 3:title
**16** [a]Ps. 3:title [b]2 Sam. 12:11; 16:21, 22
**18** [a]2 Sam. 8:18 [b]1 Sam. 23:13; 25:13; 30:1, 9 [1]Lit. *by his hand*
**19** [a]2 Sam. 18:2
**20** [a]1 Sam. 23:13
**21** [a]Ruth 1:16, 17; [Prov. 17:17]
**23** [a]2 Sam. 15:28; 16:2
**24** [a]2 Sam. 8:17 [b]Num. 4:15; 1 Sam. 4:4 [c]1 Sam. 22:20
**25** [a][Ps. 43:3] [b]Ex. 15:13; Jer. 25:30
**26** [a]Num. 14:8; 2 Sam. 22:20; 1 Kin. 10:9; 2 Chr. 9:8; Is. 62:4 [b]1 Sam. 3:18
**27** [a]1 Sam. 9:6–9 [b]2 Sam. 17:17–20 [1]*prophet*
**28** [a]Josh. 5:10; 2 Sam. 17:16
**30** [a]2 Sam. 19:4; Esth. 6:12; Ezek. 24:17, 23 [b]Is. 20:2–4 [c]Jer. 14:3, 4 [d][Ps. 126:6]
**31** [a]Ps. 3:1, 2; 55:12 [b]2 Sam. 16:23; 17:14, 23
**32** [a]Josh. 16:2 [b]2 Sam. 1:2
**33** [a]2 Sam. 19:35
**34** [a]2 Sam. 16:19
**35** [a]2 Sam. 17:15, 16
**36** [a]2 Sam. 15:27
**37** [a]2 Sam. 16:16; 1 Chr. 27:33 [b]2 Sam. 16:15

CHAPTER 16
**1** [a]2 Sam. 15:30, 32 [b]2 Sam. 9:2; 19:17, 29
**2** [a]2 Sam. 15:23; 17:29
**3** [a]2 Sam. 9:9, 10 [b]2 Sam. 19:27
**5** [a]2 Sam. 3:16 [b]2 Sam. 19:21; 1 Kin. 2:8, 9, 44–46

coming from there. He came out, cursing continuously as he came.
6 And he threw stones at David and at all the servants of King David. And all the people and all the mighty men *were* on his right hand and on his left.
7 Also Shimei said thus when he cursed: "Come out! Come out! You [1]bloodthirsty man, [a]you [2]rogue!
8 "The LORD has [a]brought upon you all [b]the blood of the house of Saul, in whose place you have reigned; and the LORD has delivered the kingdom into the hand of Absalom your son. So now you *are caught* in your own evil, because you are a [1]bloodthirsty man!"
**9** Then Abishai the son of Zeruiah said to the king, "Why should this [a]dead dog [b]curse my lord the king? Please, let me go over and take off his head!"
10 But the king said, [a]"What have I to do with you, you sons of Zeruiah? So let him curse, because [b]the LORD has said to him, 'Curse David.' [c]Who then shall say, 'Why have you done so?' "
11 And David said to Abishai and all his servants, "See how [a]my son who [b]came from my own body seeks my life. How much more now *may this* Benjamite? Let him alone, and let him curse; for so the LORD has ordered him.
12 "It may be that the LORD will look on [1]my affliction, and that the LORD will [a]repay me with [b]good for his cursing this day."
13 And as David and his men went along the road, Shimei went along the hillside opposite him and cursed as he went, threw stones at him and [1]kicked up dust.
14 Now the king and all the people who *were* with him became weary; so they refreshed themselves there.
**15** Meanwhile [a]Absalom and all the people, the men of Israel, came to Jerusalem; and Ahithophel *was* with him.
16 And so it was, when Hushai the Archite, [a]David's friend, came to Absalom, that [b]Hushai said to Absalom, "*Long* live the king! *Long* live the king!"
17 So Absalom said to Hushai, "*Is* this your loyalty to your friend? [a]Why did you not go with your friend?"
18 And Hushai said to Absalom, "No, but whom the LORD and this people and all the men of Israel choose, his I will be, and with him I will remain.
19 "Furthermore, [a]whom should I serve? *Should I* not *serve* in the presence of his son? As I have served in your father's presence, so will I be in your presence."
**20** Then Absalom said to [a]Ahithophel, "Give advice as to what we should do."
21 And Ahithophel said to Absalom, "Go in to your father's [a]concubines, whom he has left to keep the house; and all Israel will hear that you [b]are abhorred by your father. Then [c]the hands of all who are with you will be strong."
22 So they pitched a tent for Absalom on the top of the house, and Absalom went in to his father's concubines [a]in the sight of all Israel.
23 Now the advice of Ahithophel, which he gave in those days, *was* as if one had inquired at the oracle of God. So *was* all the advice of Ahithophel [a]both with David and with Absalom.

**7** [a]Deut. 13:13 [1]Lit. *man of bloodshed* [2]*worthless man*
**8** [a]Judg. 9:24, 56, 57; 1 Kin. 2:32, 33 [b]2 Sam. 1:16; 3:28, 29; 4:11, 12 [1]Lit. *man of bloodshed*
**9** [a]1 Sam. 24:14; 2 Sam. 9:8 [b]Ex. 22:28
**10** [a]2 Sam. 3:39; 19:22; [1 Pet. 2:23] [b]2 Kin. 18:25; [Lam. 3:38] [c][Rom. 9:20]
**11** [a]2 Sam. 12:11 [b]Gen. 15:4
**12** [a]Deut. 23:5; Neh. 13:2; Prov. 20:22 [b]Deut. 23:5; [Rom. 8:28; Heb. 12:10, 11] [1]So with Kt., LXX, Syr., Vg.; Qr. *my eyes;* Tg. *tears of my eyes*
**13** [1]Lit. *dusted him with dust*
**15** [a]2 Sam. 15:12, 37
**16** [a]2 Sam. 15:37 [b]2 Sam. 15:34
**17** [a]2 Sam. 19:25; [Prov. 17:17]
**19** [a]2 Sam. 15:34
**20** [a]2 Sam. 15:12
**21** [a]2 Sam. 15:16; 20:3 [b]Gen. 34:30; 1 Sam. 13:4 [c]2 Sam. 2:7; Zech. 8:13
**22** [a]2 Sam. 12:11, 12
**23** [a]2 Sam. 15:12

CHAPTER 17
**2** [a]Deut. 25:18; 2 Sam. 16:14 [b]Zech. 13:7 [1]*tremble with fear*
**4** [a]2 Sam. 5:3; 19:11
**5** [a]2 Sam. 15:32–34
**8** [a]Hos. 13:8
**10** [a]Josh. 2:11
**11** [a]Judg. 20:1; 2 Sam. 3:10 [b]Gen. 22:17; Josh. 11:4; 1 Kin. 20:10
**13** [a]Mic. 1:6
**14** [a]2 Sam. 15:31, 34
**15** [a]2 Sam. 15:35, 36
**16** [a]2 Sam. 15:28
**17** [a]2 Sam. 15:27, 36; 1 Kin. 1:42, 43 [b]Josh. 2:4–6 [c]Josh. 15:7; 18:16
**18** [a]2 Sam. 3:16; 16:5
**19** [a]Josh. 2:4–6

### *The Advice of Ahithophel and Hushai*

**17** Moreover Ahithophel said to Absalom, "Now let me choose twelve thousand men, and I will arise and pursue David tonight.
2 "I will come upon him while he *is* [a]weary and weak, and make him [1]afraid. And all the people who *are* with him will flee, and I will [b]strike only the king.
3 "Then I will bring back all the people to you. When all return except the man whom you seek, all the people will be at peace."
4 And the saying pleased Absalom and all the [a]elders of Israel.
**5** Then Absalom said, "Now call Hushai the Archite also, and let us hear what he [a]says too."
6 And when Hushai came to Absalom, Absalom spoke to him, saying, "Ahithophel has spoken in this manner. Shall we do as he says? If not, speak up."
7 So Hushai said to Absalom: "The advice that Ahithophel has given *is* not good at this time.
8 "For," said Hushai, "you know your father and his men, that they *are* mighty men, and they *are* enraged in their minds, like [a]a bear robbed of her cubs in the field; and your father *is* a man of war, and will not camp with the people.
9 "Surely by now he is hidden in some pit, or in some *other* place. And it will be, when some of them are overthrown at the first, that whoever hears *it* will say, 'There is a slaughter among the people who follow Absalom.'
10 "And even he *who is* valiant, whose heart *is* like the heart of a lion, will [a]melt completely. For all Israel knows that your father *is* a mighty man, and *those* who *are* with him *are* valiant men.
11 "Therefore I advise that all Israel be fully gathered to you, [a]from Dan to Beersheba, [b]like the sand that *is* by the sea for multitude, and that you go to battle in person.
12 "So we will come upon him in some place where he may be found, and we will fall on him as the dew falls on the ground. And of him and all the men who *are* with him there shall not be left so much as one.
13 "Moreover, if he has withdrawn into a city, then all Israel shall bring ropes to that city; and we will [a]pull it into the river, until there is not one small stone found there."
14 So Absalom and all the men of Israel said, "The advice of Hushai the Archite *is* better than the advice of Ahithophel." For [a]the LORD had purposed to defeat the good advice of Ahithophel, to the intent that the LORD might bring disaster on Absalom.
**15** [a]Then Hushai said to Zadok and Abiathar the priests, "Thus and so Ahithophel advised Absalom and the elders of Israel, and thus and so I have advised.
16 "Now therefore, send quickly and tell David, saying, 'Do not spend this night [a]in the plains of the wilderness, but speedily cross over, lest the king and all the people who *are* with him be swallowed up.' "
17 [a]Now Jonathan and Ahimaaz [b]stayed at [c]En Rogel, for they dared not be seen coming into the city; so a female servant would come and tell them, and they would go and tell King David.
18 Nevertheless a lad saw them, and told Absalom. But both of them went away quickly and came to a man's house [a]in Bahurim, who had a well in his court; and they went down into it.
19 [a]Then the woman took and spread a covering

over the well's mouth, and spread ground grain on
it; and the thing was not known.
20 And when Absalom's servants came to the
woman at the house, they said, "Where *are* Ahimaaz and Jonathan?" So [a]the woman said to them,
"They have gone over the water brook." And
when they had searched and could not find *them,*
they returned to Jerusalem.
21 Now it came to pass, after they had departed,
that they came up out of the well and went and
told King David, and said to David, [a]"Arise and
cross over the water quickly. For thus has Ahithophel advised against you."
22 So David and all the people who *were* with
him arose and crossed over the Jordan. By morning light not one of them was left who had not
gone over the Jordan.
**23** Now when Ahithophel saw that his advice was
not followed, he saddled a donkey, and arose and
went home to [a]his house, to his city. Then he [1]put
his [b]household in order, and [c]hanged himself, and
died; and he was buried in his father's tomb.
**24** Then David went to [a]Mahanaim. And Absalom
crossed over the Jordan, he and all the men of
Israel with him.
25 And Absalom made [a]Amasa captain of the
army instead of Joab. This Amasa *was* the son of a
man whose name *was* [1]Jithra, an [2]Israelite, who
had gone in to [b]Abigail the daughter of Nahash,
sister of Zeruiah, Joab's mother.
26 So Israel and Absalom encamped in the land
of Gilead.
**27** Now it happened, when David had come to
Mahanaim, that [a]Shobi the son of Nahash from
Rabbah of the people of Ammon, [b]Machir the son
of Ammiel from Lo Debar, and [c]Barzillai the
Gileadite from Rogelim,
28 brought beds and basins, earthen vessels and
wheat, barley and flour, parched *grain* and beans,
lentils and parched *seeds,*
29 honey and curds, sheep and cheese of the
herd, for David and the people who *were* with him
to eat. For they said, "The people are hungry and
weary and thirsty [a]in the wilderness."

### *Absalom Murdered by Joab*

**18** And David [1]numbered the people who *were*
with him, and [a]set captains of thousands
and captains of hundreds over them.
2 Then David sent out one third of the people
under the hand of Joab, [a]one third under the hand
of Abishai the son of Zeruiah, Joab's brother, and
one third under the hand of [b]Ittai the Gittite. And
the king said to the people, "I also will surely go
out with you myself."
3 [a]But the people answered, "You shall not go
out! For if we flee away, they will not care about
us; nor if half of us die, will they care about us.
But *you are* worth ten thousand of us now. For
you are now more help to us in the city."
4 Then the king said to them, "Whatever seems
best to you I will do." So the king stood beside the
gate, and all the people went out by hundreds and
by thousands.
5 Now the king had commanded Joab, Abishai,
and Ittai, saying, "*Deal* gently for my sake with
the young man Absalom." [a]And all the people
heard when the king gave all the captains orders
concerning Absalom.
**6** So the people went out into the field of battle
against Israel. And the battle was in the [a]woods of
Ephraim.
7 The people of Israel were overthrown there
before the servants of David, and a great slaughter of twenty thousand took place there that day.
8 For the battle there was scattered over the
face of the whole countryside, and the woods
devoured more people that day than the sword
devoured.
**9** Then Absalom met the servants of David.
Absalom rode on a mule. The mule went under
the thick boughs of a great terebinth tree, and [a]his
head caught in the terebinth; so he was left
hanging between heaven and earth. And the mule
which *was* under him went on.
10 Now a certain man saw *it* and told Joab, and
said, "I just saw Absalom hanging in a terebinth
tree!"
11 So Joab said to the man who told him, "You
just saw *him!* And why did you not strike him
there to the ground? I would have given you ten
*shekels* of silver and a belt."
12 But the man said to Joab, "Though I were to
receive a thousand *shekels* of silver in my hand, I
would not raise my hand against the king's son.
[a]For in our hearing the king commanded you and
Abishai and Ittai, saying, [1]'Beware lest anyone
*touch* the young man Absalom!'
13 "Otherwise I would have dealt falsely against
my own life. For there is nothing hidden from the
king, and you yourself would have set yourself
against *me.*"
14 Then Joab said, "I cannot linger with you."
And he took three spears in his hand and thrust
them through Absalom's heart, while he was *still*
alive in the midst of the terebinth tree.
15 And ten young men who bore Joab's armor
surrounded Absalom, and struck and killed him.
**16** So Joab blew the trumpet, and the people
returned from pursuing Israel. For Joab held back
the people.
17 And they took Absalom and cast him into a
large pit in the woods, and [a]laid a very large heap
of stones over him. Then all Israel [b]fled, everyone
to his tent.
18 Now Absalom in his lifetime had taken and set
up a [1]pillar for himself, which *is* in [a]the King's
Valley. For he said, [b]"I have no son to keep my
name in remembrance." He called the pillar after
his own name. And to this day it is called Absalom's Monument.
**19** Then [a]Ahimaaz the son of Zadok said, "Let me
run now and take the news to the king, how the
LORD has [1]avenged him of his enemies."
20 And Joab said to him, "You shall not take the
news this day, for you shall take the news another
day. But today you shall take no news, because
the king's son is dead."
21 Then Joab said to the Cushite, "Go, tell the
king what you have seen." So the Cushite bowed
himself to Joab and ran.
22 And Ahimaaz the son of Zadok said again to
Joab, "But [1]whatever happens, please let me also
run after the Cushite." So Joab said, "Why will
you run, my son, since you have no news ready?"
23 "But whatever happens," *he said,* "let me
run." So he said to him, "Run." Then Ahimaaz ran
by way of the plain, and outran the Cushite.
**24** Now David was sitting between the [a]two
gates. And the watchman went up to the roof over

**20** [a]Ex. 1:19; [Lev. 19:11]; Josh. 2:3–5
**21** [a]2 Sam. 17:15, 16
**23** [a]2 Sam. 15:12 [b]2 Kin. 20:1 [c]Matt. 27:5 [1]Lit. *gave charge concerning his house*
**24** [a]Gen. 32:2; Josh. 13:26; 2 Sam. 2:8; 19:32
**25** [a]2 Sam. 19:13; 20:9–12; 1 Kin. 2:5, 32 [b]1 Chr. 2:16 [1]*Jether,* 1 Chr. 2:17 [2]So with MT, some mss. of LXX, Tg.; some mss. of LXX *Ishmaelite* (cf. 1 Chr. 2:17); Vg. *of Jezrael*
**27** [a]1 Sam. 11:1; 2 Sam. 10:1; 12:29 [b]2 Sam. 9:4 [c]2 Sam. 19:31, 32; 1 Kin. 2:7
**29** [a]2 Sam. 16:2, 14

CHAPTER 18

**1** [a]Ex. 18:25; Num. 31:14; 1 Sam. 22:7 [1]Lit. *attended to*
**2** [a]Judg. 7:16; 1 Sam. 11:11 [b]2 Sam. 15:19–22
**3** [a]2 Sam. 21:17
**5** [a]2 Sam. 18:12
**6** [a]Josh. 17:15, 18; 2 Sam. 17:26
**9** [a]2 Sam. 14:26
**12** [a]2 Sam. 18:5 [1]Vss. *'Protect the young man Absalom for me!'*
**17** [a]Deut. 21:20, 21; Josh. 7:26; 8:29 [b]2 Sam. 19:8; 20:1, 22
**18** [a]Gen. 14:17 [b]2 Sam. 14:27 [1]*monument*
**19** [a]2 Sam. 15:36; 17:17 [1]*vindicated*
**22** [1]Lit. *be what may*
**24** [a]Judg. 5:11; 2 Sam. 13:34; 2 Kin. 9:17

the gate, to the wall, lifted his eyes and looked,
and there was a man, running alone.
25 Then the watchman cried out and told the
king. And the king said, "If he *is* alone, *there is*
news in his mouth." And he came rapidly and
drew near.
26 Then the watchman saw *another* man running, and the watchman called to the gatekeeper
and said, "There is *another* man, running alone!"
And the king said, "He also brings news."
27 So the watchman said, [1]"I think the running
of the first is like the running of Ahimaaz the son
of Zadok." And the king said, "He *is* a good man,
and comes with [a]good news."
28 So Ahimaaz called out and said to the king,
[1]"All is well!" Then he bowed down with his face
to the earth before the king, and said, [a]"Blessed *be*
the LORD your God, who has delivered up the men
who raised their hand against my lord the king!"
29 The king said, "Is the young man Absalom
safe?" Ahimaaz answered, "When Joab sent the
king's servant and *me* your servant, I saw a great
tumult, but I did not know what *it was about.*"
30 And the king said, "Turn aside *and* stand
here." So he turned aside and stood still.
31 Just then the Cushite came, and the Cushite
said, "There is good news, my lord the king! For
the LORD has avenged you this day of all those
who rose against you."
32 And the king said to the Cushite, "Is the
young man Absalom safe?" So the Cushite answered, "May the enemies of my lord the king,
and all who rise against you to do harm, be like
*that* young man!"
**33** Then the king was deeply moved, and went up
to the chamber over the gate, and wept. And as he
went, he said thus: [a]"O my son Absalom—my son,
my son Absalom—if only I had died in your place!
O Absalom my son, [b]my son!"

### *David Returns to Jerusalem*

**19** And Joab was told, "Behold, the king is
weeping and [a]mourning for Absalom."
2 So the victory that day was *turned* into
[a]mourning for all the people. For the people heard
it said that day, "The king is grieved for his son."
3 And the people [1]stole back [a]into the city that
day, as people who are ashamed steal away when
they flee in battle.
4 But the king [a]covered his face, and the king
cried out with a loud voice, [b]"O my son Absalom!
O Absalom, my son, my son!"
5 Then [a]Joab came into the house to the king,
and said, "Today you have disgraced all your
servants who today have saved your life, the lives
of your sons and daughters, the lives of your
wives and the lives of your concubines,
6 "in that you love your enemies and hate your
friends. For you have declared today that you
[1]regard neither princes nor servants; for today I
perceive that if Absalom had lived and all of us
had died today, then it would have pleased you
well.
7 "Now therefore, arise, go out and speak [1]com-
fort to your servants. For I swear by the LORD, if
you do not go out, not one will stay with you this
night. And that will be worse for you than all the
evil that has befallen you from your youth until
now."
8 Then the king arose and sat in the [a]gate. And
they told all the people, saying, "There is the king,
sitting in the gate." So all the people came before
the king. For everyone of Israel had [b]fled to his
tent.
**9** Now all the people were in a dispute throughout all the tribes of Israel, saying, "The king saved
us from the hand of our [a]enemies, he delivered us
from the hand of the [b]Philistines, and now he has
[c]fled from the land because of Absalom.
10 "But Absalom, whom we anointed over us, has
died in battle. Now therefore, why do you say
nothing about bringing back the king?"
**11** So King David sent to [a]Zadok and Abiathar
the priests, saying, "Speak to the elders of Judah,
saying, 'Why are you the last to bring the king
back to his house, since the words of all Israel
have come to the king, to his *very* house?
12 'You *are* my brethren, you *are* [a]my bone and
my flesh. Why then are you the last to bring back
the king?'
13 [a]"And say to Amasa, '*Are* you not my bone
and my flesh? [b]God do so to me, and more also, if
you are not commander of the army before me
[1]continually in place of Joab.' "
14 So he swayed the hearts of all the men of
Judah, [a]just as *the heart of* one man, so that they
sent *this word* to the king: "Return, you and all
your servants!"
15 Then the king returned and came to the Jordan. And Judah came to [a]Gilgal, to go to meet the
king, to escort the king [b]across the Jordan.
16 And [a]Shimei the son of Gera, a Benjamite,
who *was* from Bahurim, hurried and came down
with the men of Judah to meet King David.
17 *There were* a thousand men of [a]Benjamin with
him, and [b]Ziba the servant of the house of Saul,
and his fifteen sons and his twenty servants with
him; and they went over the Jordan before the
king.
18 Then a ferryboat went across to carry over the
king's household, and to do what he thought
good.
Now Shimei the son of Gera fell down before
the king when he had crossed the Jordan.
19 Then he said to the king, [a]"Do not let my lord
[1]impute iniquity to me, or remember what [b]wrong
your servant did on the day that my lord the king
left Jerusalem, that the king should [c]take *it* to
heart.
20 "For I, your servant, know that I have sinned.
Therefore here I am, the first to come today of all
[a]the house of Joseph to go down to meet my lord
the king."
21 But Abishai the son of Zeruiah answered and
said, "Shall not Shimei be put to death for this,
[a]because he [b]cursed the LORD's anointed?"
22 And David said, [a]"What have I to do with you,
you sons of Zeruiah, that you should be adversaries to me today? [b]Shall any man be put to death
today in Israel? For do I not know that today I *am*
king over Israel?"
23 Therefore [a]the king said to Shimei, "You shall
not die." And the king swore to him.
**24** Now [a]Mephibosheth the son of Saul came
down to meet the king. And he had not cared for
his feet, nor trimmed his mustache, nor washed
his clothes, from the day the king departed until
the day he returned in peace.
25 So it was, when he had come to Jerusalem to
meet the king, that the king said to him, [a]"Why
did you not go with me, Mephibosheth?"
26 And he answered, "My lord, O king, my ser-

**27** [a]1 Kin. 1:42 [1]Lit. *I see the running*
**28** [a]2 Sam. 16:12 [1]*Peace be to you*
**33** [a]2 Sam. 12:10 [b]2 Sam. 19:4

CHAPTER 19

**1** [a]Jer. 14:2
**2** [a]Esth. 4:3
**3** [a]2 Sam. 17:24, 27; 19:32 [1]*went by stealth*
**4** [a]2 Sam. 15:30 [b]2 Sam. 18:33
**5** [a]2 Sam. 18:14
**6** [1]*have no respect for*
**7** [1]Lit. *to the heart of*
**8** [a]2 Sam. 15:2; 18:24 [b]2 Sam. 18:17
**9** [a]2 Sam. 8:1–14 [b]2 Sam. 3:18 [c]2 Sam. 15:14
**11** [a]2 Sam. 15:24
**12** [a]2 Sam. 5:1; 1 Chr. 11:1
**13** [a]2 Sam. 17:25; 1 Chr. 2:17 [b]Ruth 1:17 [1]*permanently*
**14** [a]Judg. 20:1
**15** [a]Josh. 5:9; 1 Sam. 11:14, 15 [b]2 Sam. 17:22
**16** [a]2 Sam. 16:5; 1 Kin. 2:8
**17** [a]2 Sam. 3:19; 1 Kin. 12:21 [b]2 Sam. 9:2, 10; 16:1, 2
**19** [a]1 Sam. 22:15 [b]2 Sam. 16:5, 6 [c]2 Sam. 13:33 [1]*charge me with iniquity*
**20** [a]Judg. 1:22; 1 Kin. 11:28
**21** [a][Ex. 22:28] [b][1 Sam. 26:9]
**22** [a]2 Sam. 3:39; 16:10 [b]1 Sam. 11:13
**23** [a]1 Kin. 2:8, 9, 37, 46
**24** [a]2 Sam. 9:6; 21:7
**25** [a]2 Sam. 16:7

vant deceived me. For your servant said, 'I will
saddle a donkey for myself, that I may ride on it
and go to the king,' because your servant *is* lame.
27 "And [a]he has slandered your servant to my
lord the king, [b]but my lord the king *is* like the
angel of God. Therefore do *what is* good in your
eyes.
28 "For all my father's house were but dead men
before my lord the king. [a]Yet you set your servant
among those who eat at your own table. Therefore what right have I still to [1]cry out anymore to
the king?"
29 So the king said to him, "Why do you speak
anymore of your matters? I have said, 'You and
Ziba divide the land.'"
30 Then Mephibosheth said to the king, "Rather,
let him take it all, inasmuch as my lord the king
has come back in peace to his own house."
**31** And [a]Barzillai the Gileadite came down from
Rogelim and went across the Jordan with the
king, to escort him across the Jordan.
32 Now Barzillai was a very aged man, eighty
years old. And [a]he had provided the king with
supplies while he stayed at Mahanaim, for he *was*
a very rich man.
33 And the king said to Barzillai, "Come across
with me, and I will provide for you while you are
with me in Jerusalem."
34 But Barzillai said to the king, "How long have
I to live, that I should go up with the king to
Jerusalem?
35 "I *am* today [a]eighty years old. Can I discern
between the good and bad? Can your servant
taste what I eat or what I drink? Can I hear any
longer the voice of singing men and singing
women? Why then should your servant be a
further burden to my lord the king?
36 "Your servant will go a little way across the
Jordan with the king. And why should the king
repay me *with* such a reward?
37 "Please let your servant turn back again, that
I may die in my own city, near the grave of my
father and mother. But here is your servant
[a]Chimham; let him cross over with my lord the
king, and do for him what seems good to you."
38 And the king answered, "Chimham shall cross
over with me, and I will do for him what seems
good to you. Now whatever you request of me, I
will do for you."
39 Then all the people went over the Jordan. And
when the king had crossed over, the king [a]kissed
Barzillai and blessed him, and he returned to his
own place.
**40** Now the king went on to Gilgal, and [1]Chim-
ham went on with him. And all the people of
Judah escorted the king, and also half the people
of Israel.
41 Just then all the men of Israel came to the
king, and said to the king, "Why have our brethren, the men of Judah, stolen you away and
[a]brought the king, his household, and all David's
men with him across the Jordan?"
42 So all the men of Judah answered the men of
Israel, "Because the king *is* [a]a close relative of
ours. Why then are you angry over this matter?
Have we ever eaten at the king's *expense?* Or has
he given us any gift?"
43 And the men of Israel answered the men of
Judah, and said, "We have [a]ten shares in the king;
therefore we also have more *right* to David than
you. Why then do you despise us—were we not
the first to advise bringing back our king?" Yet
[b]the words of the men of Judah were [1]fiercer than
the words of the men of Israel.

### *Sheba Revolts Against David*

**20** And there happened to be there a [1]rebel,
whose name *was* Sheba the son of Bichri, a
Benjamite. And he blew a trumpet, and said:

[a]"We have no share in David,
Nor do we have inheritance
in the son of Jesse;
[b]Every man to his tents, O Israel!"

2 So every man of Israel deserted David, *and*
followed Sheba the son of Bichri. But the [a]men of
Judah, from the Jordan as far as Jerusalem, remained loyal to their king.
**3** Now David came to his house at Jerusalem.
And the king took the ten women, [a]his concubines
whom he had left to keep the house, and put them
in seclusion and supported them, but did not go in
to them. So they were shut up to the day of their
death, living in widowhood.
**4** And the king said to Amasa, [a]"Assemble the
men of Judah for me within three days, and be
present here yourself."
5 So Amasa went to assemble *the men of* Judah.
But he delayed longer than the set time which
David had appointed him.
6 And David said to [a]Abishai, "Now Sheba the
son of Bichri will do us more harm than Absalom.
Take [b]your lord's servants and pursue him, lest he
find for himself fortified cities, and escape us."
7 So Joab's men, with the [a]Cherethites, the
Pelethites, and [b]all the mighty men, went out after
him. And they went out of Jerusalem to pursue
Sheba the son of Bichri.
8 When they *were* at the large stone which *is* in
Gibeon, Amasa came before them. Now Joab was
dressed in battle armor; on it was a belt *with* a
sword fastened in its sheath at his hips; and as he
was going forward, it fell out.
9 Then Joab said to Amasa, "*Are* you in health,
my brother?" [a]And Joab took Amasa by the beard
with his right hand to kiss him.
10 But Amasa did not notice the sword that *was*
in Joab's hand. And [a]he struck him with it [b]in the
stomach, and his entrails poured out on the
ground; and he did not *strike* him again. Thus he
died. Then Joab and Abishai his brother pursued
Sheba the son of Bichri.
11 Meanwhile one of Joab's men stood near
Amasa, and said, "Whoever favors Joab and whoever *is* for David—follow Joab!"
12 But Amasa wallowed in *his* blood in the middle of the highway. And when the man saw that
all the people stood still, he moved Amasa from
the highway to the field and threw a garment over
him, when he saw that everyone who came upon
him halted.
13 When he was removed from the highway, all
the people went on after Joab to pursue Sheba the
son of Bichri.
**14** And he went through all the tribes of Israel to
[a]Abel and Beth Maachah and all the Berites. So
they were gathered together and also went after
[1]*Sheba.*
15 Then they came and besieged him in Abel of
Beth Maachah; and they [a]cast up a siege mound
against the city, and it stood by the rampart. And

**27** [a]2 Sam. 16:3, 4 [b]2 Sam. 14:17, 20
**28** [a]2 Sam. 9:7–13 [1]*complain*
**31** [a]2 Sam. 17:27–29; 1 Kin. 2:7
**32** [a]2 Sam. 17:27–29
**35** [a]Ps. 90:10
**37** [a]2 Sam. 19:40; Jer. 41:17
**39** [a]Gen. 31:55; Ruth 1:14; 2 Sam. 14:33
**40** [1]MT *Chimhan*
**41** [a]2 Sam. 19:15
**42** [a]2 Sam. 19:12
**43** [a]1 Kin. 11:30, 31 [b]Judg. 8:1; 12:1 [1]*harsher*

CHAPTER 20
**1** [a]2 Sam. 19:43; 1 Kin. 12:16 [b]1 Sam. 13:2; 2 Sam. 18:17; 2 Chr. 10:16 [1]Lit. *man of Belial*
**2** [a]2 Sam. 19:14
**3** [a]2 Sam. 15:16; 16:21, 22
**4** [a]2 Sam. 17:25; 19:13
**6** [a]2 Sam. 21:17 [b]2 Sam. 11:11; 1 Kin. 1:33
**7** [a]2 Sam. 8:18; 1 Kin. 1:38, 44 [b]2 Sam. 15:18
**9** [a]Matt. 26:49; Luke 22:47
**10** [a]2 Sam. 3:27; 1 Kin. 2:5 [b]2 Sam. 2:23
**14** [a]1 Kin. 15:20; 2 Kin. 15:29; 2 Chr. 16:4 [1]Lit. *him*
**15** [a]2 Kin. 19:32; Ezek. 4:2

all the people who *were* with Joab battered the
wall to throw it down.
**16** Then a wise woman cried out from the city,
"Hear, hear! Please say to Joab, 'Come nearby,
that I may speak with you.' "
17 When he had come near to her, the woman
said, "*Are* you Joab?" He answered, "I *am.*" Then
she said to him, "Hear the words of your maidservant." And he answered, "I am listening."
18 So she spoke, saying, "They used to talk in
former times, saying, 'They shall surely seek
*guidance* at Abel,' and so they would end *disputes.*
19 "I *am among the* peaceable *and* faithful in
Israel. You seek to destroy a city and a mother in
Israel. Why would you swallow up [a]the inheritance of the LORD?"
20 And Joab answered and said, "Far be it, far be
it from me, that I should swallow up or destroy!
21 "That *is* not so. But a man from the mountains
of Ephraim, Sheba the son of Bichri by name, has
raised his hand against the king, against David.
Deliver him only, and I will depart from the city."
So the woman said to Joab, "Watch, his head will
be thrown to you over the wall."
22 Then the woman [a]in her wisdom went to all
the people. And they cut off the head of Sheba the
son of Bichri, and threw *it* out to Joab. Then he
blew a trumpet, and they withdrew from the city,
every man to his tent. So Joab returned to the
king at Jerusalem.
**23** And [a]Joab *was* over all the army of Israel;
Benaiah the son of Jehoiada *was* over the Cherethites and the Pelethites;
24 Adoram *was* [a]in charge of revenue; [b]Jehosha-
phat the son of Ahilud *was* recorder;
25 Sheva *was* scribe; [a]Zadok and Abiathar *were*
the priests;
26 [a]and Ira the Jairite was [1]a chief minister under
David.

## *Seven Sons of Saul Hanged*

**21** Now there was a famine in the days of
David for three years, year after year; and
David [a]inquired of the LORD. And the LORD answered, "*It is* because of Saul and *his* [1]bloodthirsty
house, because he killed the Gibeonites."
2 So the king called the Gibeonites and spoke to
them. Now the Gibeonites *were* not of the children of Israel, but [a]of the remnant of the Amorites; the children of Israel had sworn protection
to them, but Saul had sought to kill them [b]in his
zeal for the children of Israel and Judah.
3 Therefore David said to the Gibeonites, "What
shall I do for you? And with what shall I make
atonement, that you may bless [a]the inheritance of
the LORD?"
4 And the Gibeonites said to him, "We will have
no silver or gold from Saul or from his house, nor
shall you kill any man in Israel for us." So he said,
"Whatever you say, I will do for you."
5 Then they answered the king, "As for the man
who consumed us and plotted against us, *that* we
should be destroyed from remaining in any of the
territories of Israel,
6 "let seven men of his descendants be delivered
[a]to us, and we will hang them before the LORD [b]in
Gibeah of Saul, [c]*whom* the LORD chose." And the
king said, "I will give *them.*"
7 But the king spared [a]Mephibosheth the son of
Jonathan, the son of Saul, because of [b]the LORD's
oath that *was* between them, between David and
Jonathan the son of Saul.
8 So the king took Armoni and Mephibosheth,
the two sons of [a]Rizpah the daughter of Aiah,
whom she bore to Saul, and the five sons of
[1]Michal the daughter of Saul, whom she [2]brought
up for Adriel the son of Barzillai the Meholathite;
9 and he delivered them into the hands of the
Gibeonites, and they hanged them on the hill
[a]before the LORD. So they fell, *all* seven together,
and were put to death in the days of harvest, in
the first *days,* in the beginning of barley harvest.
**10** Now [a]Rizpah the daughter of Aiah took sackcloth and spread it for herself on the rock, [b]from
the beginning of harvest until the late rains
poured on them from heaven. And she did not
allow the birds of the air to rest on them by day
nor the beasts of the field by night.
11 And David was told what Rizpah the daughter
of Aiah, the concubine of Saul, had done.
12 Then David went and took the bones of Saul,
and the bones of Jonathan his son, from the men
of [a]Jabesh Gilead who had stolen them from the
street of [1]Beth Shan, where the [b]Philistines had
hung them up, after the Philistines had struck
down Saul in Gilboa.
13 So he brought up the bones of Saul and the
bones of Jonathan his son from there; and they
gathered the bones of those who had been
hanged.
14 They buried the bones of Saul and Jonathan
his son in the country of Benjamin in [a]Zelah, in
the tomb of Kish his father. So they performed all
that the king commanded. And after that [b]God
heeded the prayer for the land.
**15** When the Philistines were at war again with
Israel, David and his servants with him went
down and fought against the Philistines; and
David grew faint.
16 Then Ishbi-Benob, who *was* one of the sons of
[1]the [a]giant, the weight of whose bronze spear *was*
three hundred *shekels,* who was bearing a new
*sword,* thought he could kill David.
17 But [a]Abishai the son of Zeruiah came to his
aid, and struck the Philistine and killed him. Then
the men of David swore to him, saying, [b]"You
shall go out no more with us to battle, lest you
quench the [c]lamp of Israel."
**18** [a]Now it happened afterward that there was
again a battle with the Philistines at Gob. Then
[b]Sibbechai the Hushathite killed [1]Saph, who *was*
one of the sons of [2]the giant.
19 Again there was war at Gob with the Philistines, where [a]Elhanan the son of [1]Jaare-Oregim
the Bethlehemite killed [b]*the brother of* Goliath the
Gittite, the shaft of whose spear *was* like a weaver's beam.
20 Yet again [a]there was war at Gath, where there
was a man of *great* stature, who had six fingers on
each hand and six toes on each foot, twenty-four
in number; and he also was born to [1]the giant.
21 So when he [a]defied Israel, Jonathan the son of
[1]Shimea, David's brother, killed him.
22 [a]These four were born to [1]the giant in Gath,
and fell by the hand of David and by the hand of
his servants.

## *David's Song of Deliverance*

**22** Then David [a]spoke to the LORD the words of
this song, on the day when the LORD had
[b]delivered him from the hand of all his enemies,
and from the hand of Saul.

**19** [a]1 Sam. 26:19; 2 Sam. 14:16; 21:3
**22** [a]2 Sam. 20:16; [Eccl. 9:13–16]
**23** [a]2 Sam. 8:16–18; 1 Kin. 4:3–6
**24** [a]1 Kin. 4:6 [b]2 Sam. 8:16; 1 Kin. 4:3
**25** [a]2 Sam. 8:17; 1 Kin. 4:4
**26** [a]2 Sam. 8:18 [1]Or *David's priest*

CHAPTER 21
**1** [a]Num. 27:21; 2 Sam. 5:19 [1]Lit. *house of bloodshed*
**2** [a]Josh. 9 [b][Ex. 34:11–16]
**3** [a]1 Sam. 26:19; 2 Sam. 20:19
**6** [a]Num. 25:4 [b]1 Sam. 10:26 [c]1 Sam. 10:24; [Hos. 13:11]
**7** [a]2 Sam. 4:4; 9:10 [b]1 Sam. 18:3; 20:12–17; 23:18; 2 Sam. 9:1–7
**8** [a]2 Sam. 3:7 [1]*Merab,* 1 Sam. 18:19; 25:44; 2 Sam. 3:14; 6:23 [2]Lit. *bore to Adriel*
**9** [a]2 Sam. 6:17
**10** [a]2 Sam. 3:7; 21:8 [b]Deut. 21:23
**12** [a]1 Sam. 31:11–13 [b]1 Sam. 31:8 [1]*Beth Shean,* Josh. 17:11
**14** [a]Josh. 18:28 [b]Josh. 7:26; 2 Sam. 24:25
**16** [a]Num. 13:22, 28; Josh. 15:14; 2 Sam. 21:18–22 [1]Or *Rapha*
**17** [a]2 Sam. 20:6–10 [b]2 Sam. 18:3 [c]2 Sam. 22:29; 1 Kin. 11:36
**18** [a]1 Chr. 20:4–8 [b]1 Chr. 11:29; 27:11 [1]*Sippai,* 1 Chr. 20:4 [2]Or *Rapha*
**19** [a]2 Sam. 23:24 [b]1 Sam. 17:4; 1 Chr. 20:5 [1]*Jair,* 1 Chr. 20:5
**20** [a]1 Chr. 20:6 [1]Or *Rapha*
**21** [a]1 Sam. 17:10 [1]*Shammah,* 1 Sam. 16:9 and elsewhere
**22** [a]1 Chr. 20:8 [1]Or *Rapha*

CHAPTER 22
**1** [a]Ex. 15:1; Deut. 31:30; Judg. 5:1 [b]Ps. 18:title; 34:19

2 And he [a]said:

[b]"The LORD *is* my rock and
my [c]fortress and my deliverer;
3 The God of my strength,
[a]in whom I will trust;
My [b]shield and the [c]horn[1] of my salvation,
My [d]stronghold and my [e]refuge;
My Savior, You save me from violence.
4 I will call upon the LORD,
*who is worthy* to be praised;
So shall I be saved from my enemies.

5 "When the waves of death surrounded me,
The floods of ungodliness [1]made me afraid.
6 The [a]sorrows of Sheol surrounded me;
The snares of death confronted me.
7 In my distress [a]I called upon the LORD,
And cried out to my God;
He [b]heard my voice from His temple,
And my cry *entered* His ears.

8 "Then [a]the earth shook and trembled;
[b]The foundations of [1]heaven
quaked and were shaken,
Because He was angry.
9 Smoke went up from His nostrils,
And devouring [a]fire from His mouth;
Coals were kindled by it.
10 He [a]bowed the heavens also, and came down
With [b]darkness under His feet.
11 He rode upon a cherub, and flew;
And He [1]was seen [a]upon the wings
of the wind.
12 He made [a]darkness canopies around Him,
Dark waters *and* thick clouds of the skies.
13 From the brightness before Him
Coals of fire were kindled.

14 "The LORD [a]thundered from heaven,
And the Most High uttered His voice.
15 He sent out [a]arrows and scattered them;
Lightning bolts, and He vanquished them.
16 Then the channels of the sea
[a]were seen,
The foundations of the world
were uncovered,
At the [b]rebuke of the LORD,
At the blast of the breath of His nostrils.

17 "He[a] sent from above, He took me,
He drew me out of many waters.
18 He delivered me from my strong enemy,
From those who hated me;
For they were too strong for me.
19 They confronted me in the day
of my calamity,
But the LORD was my [a]support.
20 [a]He also brought me out into a broad place;
He delivered me because He [b]delighted in me.

21 "The[a] LORD rewarded me
according to my righteousness;
According to the [b]cleanness of my hands
He has recompensed me.
22 For I have [a]kept the ways of the LORD,
And have not wickedly departed
from my God.
23 For all His [a]judgments *were* before me;
And *as for* His statutes,
I did not depart from them.
24 I was also [a]blameless before Him,
And I kept myself from my iniquity.

2 [a]Ps. 18 [b]Deut. 32:4 [c]Ps. 91:2
3 [a]Heb. 2:13 [b]Gen. 15:1 [c]Luke 1:69 [d]Prov. 18:10 [e]Ps. 9:9; 46:1, 7, 11 [1]Strength
5 [1]Or *overwhelmed*
6 [a]Ps. 116:3
7 [a]Ps. 116:4; 120:1 [b]Ex. 3:7
8 [a]Judg. 5:4 [b]Job 26:11 [1]So with MT, LXX, Tg.; Syr., Vg. *hills* (cf. Ps. 18:7)
9 [a]Heb. 12:29
10 [a]Is. 64:1 [b]Ex. 20:21
11 [a]Ps. 104:3 [1]So with MT, LXX; many Heb. mss., Syr., Vg. *flew* (cf. Ps. 18:10); Tg. *spoke with power*
12 [a]Job 36:29
14 [a]Job 37:2–5
15 [a]Deut. 32:23
16 [a]Nah. 1:4 [b]Ex. 15:8
17 [a]Ps. 144:7
19 [a]Is. 10:20
20 [a]Ps. 31:8; 118:5 [b]2 Sam. 15:26
21 [a]1 Sam. 26:23 [b]Ps. 24:4
22 [a]Ps. 119:3
23 [a][Deut. 6:6–9; 7:12]
24 [a][Eph. 1:4]
25 [a]2 Sam. 22:21 [1]*rewarded* [2]LXX, Syr., Vg. *the cleanness of my hands in His sight* (cf. Ps. 22:24); Tg. *my cleanness before His word*
26 [a][Matt. 5:7]
27 [a][Lev. 26:23, 24]
28 [a]Ps. 72:12 [b]Job 40:11 [1]*afflicted*
29 [a]Ps. 119:105; 132:17
30 [a]2 Sam. 5:6–8
31 [a][Matt. 5:48] [b]Ps. 12:6
32 [a]Is. 45:5, 6
33 [a]Ps. 27:1 [b][Heb. 13:21] [c]Ps. 101:2, 6 [1]DSS, LXX, Syr., Vg. *It is God who arms me with strength* (cf. Ps. 22:24); Tg. *It is God who sustains me with strength* [2]So with Qr., LXX, Syr., Tg., Vg. (cf. Ps. 18:32); Kt. *His*
34 [a]2 Sam. 2:18 [b]Is. 33:16 [1]So with Qr., LXX, Syr., Tg., Vg. (cf. Ps. 18:33); Kt. *His*
35 [1]Lit. *for the war*
37 [a]Prov. 4:12
39 [a]Mal. 4:3

25 Therefore [a]the LORD has [1]recompensed me
according to my righteousness,
According to [2]my cleanness in His eyes.

26 "With [a]the merciful
You will show Yourself merciful;
With a blameless man
You will show Yourself blameless;
27 With the pure You will show Yourself pure;
And [a]with the devious
You will show Yourself shrewd.
28 You will save the [a]humble[1] people;
But Your eyes *are* on [b]the haughty,
*that* You may bring *them* down.

29 "For You *are* my [a]lamp, O LORD;
The LORD shall enlighten my darkness.
30 For by You I can run against a troop;
By my God I can leap over a [a]wall.
31 *As for* God, [a]His way *is* perfect;
[b]The word of the LORD *is* proven;
He *is* a shield to all who trust in Him.

32 "For [a]who *is* God, except the LORD?
And who *is* a rock, except our God?
33 [1]God *is* my [a]strength *and* power,
And He [b]makes [2]my way [c]perfect.
34 He makes [1]my feet [a]like the *feet* of deer,
And [b]sets me on my high places.
35 He teaches my hands [1]to make war,
So that my arms can bend a bow of bronze.

36 "You have also given me
the shield of Your salvation;
Your gentleness has made me great.
37 You [a]enlarged my path under me;
So my feet did not slip.

38 "I have pursued my enemies
and destroyed them;
Neither did I turn back again
till they were destroyed.
39 And I have destroyed them
and wounded them,
So that they could not rise;
They have fallen [a]under my feet.
40 For You have [a]armed me with strength for
the battle;
You have [1]subdued under me [b]those
who rose against me.
41 You have also [1]given me
the [a]necks of my enemies,
So that I destroyed those who hated me.
42 They looked, but *there was* none to save;
*Even* [a]to the LORD,
but He did not answer them.
43 Then I beat them as fine [a]as the dust of the
earth;
I trod them [b]like dirt in the streets,
*And* I [1]spread them out.

44 "You[a] have also delivered me
from the [1]strivings of my people;
You have kept me
as the [b]head of the nations.
[c]A people I have not known shall serve me.
45 The foreigners submit to me;
As soon as they hear, they obey me.
46 The foreigners fade away,
And [1]come frightened [a]from their hideouts.

40 [a][Ps. 18:32] [b][Ps. 44:5] [1]Lit. *caused to bow down*
41 [a]Gen. 49:8; Josh. 10:24 [1]*given me victory over*
42 [a]1 Sam. 28:6; Prov. 1:28; Is. 1:15
43 [a]2 Kin. 13:7; Ps. 18:42 [b]Is. 10:6 [1]*scattered*
44 [a]2 Sam. 3:1 [b]Deut. 28:13 [c][Is. 55:5] [1]*contentions*
46 [a]1 Sam. 14:11; [Mic. 7:17] [1]So with LXX, Tg., Vg. (cf. Ps. 18:45); MT *gird themselves*

47 "The LORD lives!
Blessed *be* my Rock!
Let God be exalted,
The [a]Rock of my salvation!
48 *It is* God who avenges me,
And [a]subdues the peoples under me;
49 He delivers me from my enemies.
You also lift me up
above those who rise against me;
You have delivered me
from the [a]violent man.
50 Therefore I will give thanks to You,
O LORD, among [a]the Gentiles,
And sing praises to Your [b]name.

51 [a]*He is* the tower of salvation to His king,
And shows mercy to His [b]anointed,
To David and [c]his descendants forevermore."

## *David's Mighty Men*

**23** Now these *are* the last words of David.

*Thus* says David the son of Jesse;
*Thus* says [a]the man raised up on high,
[b]The anointed of the God of Jacob,
And the sweet psalmist of Israel:

2 "The[a] Spirit of the LORD spoke by me,
And His word *was* on my tongue.
3 The God of Israel said,
[a]The Rock of Israel spoke to me:
'He who rules over men *must be* just,
Ruling [b]in the fear of God.
4 And [a]*he shall be* like the light
of the morning *when* the sun rises,
A morning without clouds,
*Like* the tender grass
*springing* out of the earth,
By clear shining after rain.'

5 "Although my house *is* not so with God,
[a]Yet He has made with me
an everlasting covenant,
Ordered in all *things* and secure.
For *this is* all my salvation and all *my* desire;
Will He not make *it* increase?
6 But *the sons* of rebellion *shall* all *be*
as thorns thrust away,
Because they cannot be taken with hands.
7 But the man *who* touches them
Must be [1]armed with iron
and the shaft of a spear,
And they shall be utterly burned
with fire in *their* place."

8 These *are* the names of the mighty men whom David had: [1]Josheb-Basshebeth the Tachmonite, chief among [2]the captains. He was called Adino the Eznite, because he had killed eight hundred men at one time.
9 And after him *was* [a]Eleazar the son of [1]Dodo, the Ahohite, *one* of the three mighty men with David when they defied the Philistines *who* were gathered there for battle, and the men of Israel had retreated.
10 He arose and attacked the Philistines until his hand was [a]weary, and his hand stuck to the sword. The LORD brought about a great victory that day; and the people returned after him only to [b]plunder.
11 And after him *was* [a]Shammah the son of Agee the Hararite. [b]The Philistines had gathered together into a troop where there was a piece of ground full of lentils. So the people fled from the Philistines.
12 But he stationed himself in the middle of the field, defended it, and killed the Philistines. So the LORD brought about a great victory.
**13** Then [a]three of the thirty chief men went down at harvest time and came to David at [b]the cave of Adullam. And the troop of Philistines encamped in [c]the Valley of Rephaim.
14 David *was* then in [a]the stronghold, and the garrison of the Philistines *was* then *in* Bethlehem.
15 And David said with longing, "Oh, that someone would give me a drink of the water from the well of Bethlehem, which *is* by the gate!"
16 So the three mighty men broke through the camp of the Philistines, drew water from the well of Bethlehem that *was* by the gate, and took it and brought *it* to David. Nevertheless he would not drink it, but poured it out to the LORD.
17 And he said, "Far be it from me, O LORD, that I should do this! Is *this not* [a]the blood of the men who went in *jeopardy of* their lives?" Therefore he would not drink it. These things were done by the three mighty men.
**18** Now [a]Abishai the brother of Joab, the son of Zeruiah, was chief of [1]*another* three. He lifted his spear against three hundred *men*, killed *them*, and won a name among *these* three.
19 Was he not the most honored of three? Therefore he became their captain. However, he did not attain to the *first* three.
**20** Benaiah *was* the son of Jehoiada, the son of a valiant man from [a]Kabzeel, [1]who had done many deeds. [b]He had killed two lion-like heroes of Moab. He also had gone down and killed a lion in the midst of a pit on a snowy day.
21 And he killed an Egyptian, [1]a spectacular man. The Egyptian *had* a spear in his hand; so he went down to him with a staff, wrested the spear out of the Egyptian's hand, and killed him with his own spear.
22 These *things* Benaiah the son of Jehoiada did, and won a name among three mighty men.
23 He was more honored than the thirty, but he did not attain to the *first* three. And David appointed him [a]over his guard.
**24** [a]Asahel the brother of Joab *was* one of the thirty; Elhanan the son of Dodo of Bethlehem,
25 [a]Shammah the Harodite, Elika the Harodite,
26 Helez the Paltite, Ira the son of Ikkesh the Tekoite,
27 Abiezer the Anathothite, Mebunnai the Hushathite,
28 Zalmon the Ahohite, Maharai the Netophathite,
29 Heleb the son of Baanah (the Netophathite), Ittai the son of Ribai from Gibeah of the children of Benjamin,
30 Benaiah a Pirathonite, Hiddai from the brooks of [a]Gaash,
31 Abi-Albon the Arbathite, Azmaveth the Barhumite,
32 Eliahba the Shaalbonite (of the sons of Jashen), Jonathan,
33 [a]Shammah the [1]Hararite, Ahiam the son of Sharar the Hararite,
34 Eliphelet the son of Ahasbai, the son of the Maachathite, Eliam the son of [a]Ahithophel the Gilonite,
35 [1]Hezrai the Carmelite, Paarai the Arbite,
36 Igal the son of Nathan of [a]Zobah, Bani the Gadite,

**47** [a][2 Sam. 22:3]; Ps. 89:26
**48** [a]1 Sam. 24:12; Ps. 144:2
**49** [a]Ps. 140:1, 4, 11
**50** [a]2 Sam. 8:1–14 [b]Ps. 57:7; Rom. 15:9
**51** [a]Ps. 144:10 [b]Ps. 89:20 [c]2 Sam. 7:12–16; Ps. 89:29

CHAPTER 23
**1** [a]2 Sam. 7:8, 9; Ps. 78:70, 71 [b]1 Sam. 16:12, 13; Ps. 89:20
**2** [a]Matt. 22:43; [2 Pet. 1:21]
**3** [a][Deut. 32:4] [b]Ex. 18:21; [Is. 11:1–5]
**4** [a]Ps. 89:36; Is. 60:1
**5** [a]2 Sam. 7:12; Ps. 89:29; Is. 55:3
**7** [1]Lit. *filled*
**8** [1]Lit. *One Who Sits in the Seat* (1 Chr. 11:11) [2]So with MT, Tg.; LXX, Vg. *the three*
**9** [a]1 Chr. 11:12; 27:4 [1]*Dodai,* 1 Chr. 27:4
**10** [a]Judg. 8:4 [b]1 Sam. 30:24, 25
**11** [a]1 Chr. 11:27 [b]1 Chr. 11:13, 14
**13** [a]1 Chr. 11:15 [b]1 Sam. 22:1 [c]2 Sam. 5:18
**14** [a]1 Sam. 22:4, 5
**17** [a][Lev. 17:10]
**18** [a]2 Sam. 21:17; 1 Chr. 11:20 [1]So with MT, LXX, Vg.; some Heb. mss., Syr. *thirty;* Tg. *the mighty men*
**20** [a]Josh. 15:21 [b]Ex. 15:15 [1]Lit. *great of acts*
**21** [1]Lit. *a man of appearance*
**23** [a]2 Sam. 8:18; 20:23
**24** [a]2 Sam. 2:18; 1 Chr. 27:7
**25** [a]1 Chr. 11:27
**30** [a]Judg. 2:9
**33** [a]2 Sam. 23:11 [1]Or *Ararite*
**34** [a]2 Sam. 15:12
**35** [1]*Hezro,* 1 Chr. 11:37
**36** [a]2 Sam. 8:3

37 Zelek the Ammonite, Naharai the Beerothite
(armorbearer of Joab the son of Zeruiah),
38 [a]Ira the Ithrite, Gareb the Ithrite,
39 *and* [a]Uriah the Hittite: thirty-seven in all.

### *God Punishes David*

**24** Again [a]the anger of the LORD was aroused
against Israel, and He moved David against
them to say, [b]"Go, [1]number Israel and Judah."
2 So the king said to Joab the commander of the
army who *was* with him, "Now go throughout all
the tribes of Israel, [a]from Dan to Beersheba, and
count the people, that [b]I may know the number of
the people."
3 And Joab said to the king, "Now may the
LORD your God [a]add to the people a hundred times
more than there are, and may the eyes of my lord
the king see *it.* But why does my lord the king
desire this thing?"
4 Nevertheless the king's word [1]prevailed
against Joab and against the captains of the army.
Therefore Joab and the captains of the army went
out from the presence of the king to count the
people of Israel.
5 And they crossed over the Jordan and camped
in [a]Aroer, on the right side of the town which *is* in
the midst of the ravine of Gad, and toward [b]Jazer.
6 Then they came to Gilead and to the land of
Tahtim Hodshi; they came to [a]Dan Jaan and
around to [b]Sidon;
7 and they came to the stronghold of [a]Tyre and
to all the cities of the [b]Hivites and the Canaanites.
Then they went out to South Judah *as far as*
Beersheba.
8 So when they had gone through all the land,
they came to Jerusalem at the end of nine months
and twenty days.
9 Then Joab gave the sum of the number of the
people to the king. [a]And there were in Israel eight
hundred thousand valiant men who drew the
sword, and the men of Judah were five hundred
thousand men.
10 And [a]David's heart condemned him after he
had numbered the people. So [b]David said to the
LORD, [c]"I have sinned greatly in what I have done;
but now, I pray, O LORD, take away the iniquity of
Your servant, for I have [d]done very foolishly."
11 Now when David arose in the morning, the
word of the LORD came to the prophet [a]Gad,
David's [b]seer, saying,
12 "Go and tell David, 'Thus says the LORD: "I
offer you three *things;* choose one of them for
yourself, that I may do *it* to you." ' "
13 So Gad came to David and told him; and he
said to him, "Shall [a]seven[1] years of famine come to
you in your land? Or shall you flee three months
before your enemies, while they pursue you? Or
shall there be three days' plague in your land?
Now consider and see what answer I should take
back to Him who sent me."
14 And David said to Gad, "I am in great distress.
Please let us fall into the hand of the LORD, [a]for
His mercies *are* great; but [b]do not let me fall into
the hand of man."
15 So [a]the LORD sent a plague upon Israel from
the morning till the appointed time. From Dan to
Beersheba seventy thousand men of the people
died.
16 [a]And when the [1]angel stretched out his hand
over Jerusalem to destroy it, [b]the LORD relented
from the destruction, and said to the [1]angel who
was destroying the people, "It is enough; now
restrain your hand." And the [1]angel of the LORD
was by the threshing floor of [2]Araunah the Jebusite.
17 Then David spoke to the LORD when he saw
the angel who was striking the people, and said,
"Surely [a]I have sinned, and I have done wickedly;
but these sheep, what have they done? Let Your
hand, I pray, be against me and against my father's house."
18 And Gad came that day to David and said to
him, [a]"Go up, erect an altar to the LORD on the
threshing floor of Araunah the Jebusite."
19 So David, according to the word of Gad, went
up as the LORD commanded.
20 Now Araunah looked, and saw the king and
his servants coming toward him. So Araunah
went out and bowed before the king with his face
to the ground.
21 Then Araunah said, "Why has my lord the
king come to his servant?" [a]And David said, "To
buy the threshing floor from you, to build an altar
to the LORD, that [b]the plague may be withdrawn
from the people."
22 Now Araunah said to David, "Let my lord the
king take and offer up whatever *seems* good to
him. [a]Look, *here are* oxen for burnt sacrifice, and
threshing implements and the yokes of the oxen
for wood.
23 "All these, O king, Araunah has given to the
king." And Araunah said to the king, "May the
LORD your God [a]accept you."
24 Then the king said to Araunah, "No, but I will
surely buy *it* from you for a price; nor will I offer
burnt offerings to the LORD my God with that
which costs me nothing." So [a]David bought the
threshing floor and the oxen for fifty shekels of
silver.
25 And David built there an altar to the LORD,
and offered burnt offerings and peace offerings.
[a]So the LORD heeded the prayers for the land, and
[b]the plague was withdrawn from Israel.

**38** [a]1 Cor. 11:28
**39** [a]2 Sam. 11:3, 6

CHAPTER 24

**1** [a]2 Sam. 21:1, 2 [b]Num. 26:2; 1 Chr. 27:23, 24 [1]*take a census of*
**2** [a]Judg. 20:1; 2 Sam. 3:10 [b][Jer. 17:5]
**3** [a]Deut. 1:11
**4** [1]*overruled*
**5** [a]Deut. 2:36; Josh. 13:9, 16 [b]Num. 32:1, 3
**6** [a]Josh. 19:47; Judg. 18:29 [b]Josh. 19:28; Judg. 18:28
**7** [a]Josh. 19:29 [b]Josh. 11:3; Judg. 3:3
**9** [a]1 Chr. 21:5
**10** [a]1 Sam. 24:5 [b]2 Sam. 23:1 [c]2 Sam. 12:13 [d]1 Sam. 13:13; [2 Chr. 16:9]
**11** [a]1 Sam. 22:5 [b]1 Sam. 9:9; 1 Chr. 29:29
**13** [a]Ezek. 14:21 [1]So with MT, Syr., Tg., Vg.; LXX *three* (1 Chr. 21:12)
**14** [a][Ps. 51:1; 103:8, 13, 14; 119:156; 130:4, 7] [b][Is. 47:6; Zech. 1:15]
**15** [a]1 Chr. 21:14
**16** [a]Ex. 12:23; 2 Kin. 19:35; Acts 12:23 [b]Gen. 6:6; 1 Sam. 15:11 [1]Or *Angel* [2]*Ornan,* 1 Chr. 21:15
**17** [a]2 Sam. 7:8; 1 Chr. 21:17; Ps. 74:1
**18** [a]1 Chr. 21:18
**21** [a]Gen. 23:8–16 [b]Num. 16:48, 50
**22** [a]1 Sam. 6:14; 1 Kin. 19:21
**23** [a][Ezek. 20:40, 41]
**24** [a]1 Chr. 21:24, 25
**25** [a]2 Sam. 21:14 [b]2 Sam. 24:21

*The First Book of the*

# KINGS

CHAPTER 1

### *Solomon Made King*

NOW King David was [a]old, [1]advanced in
years; and they put covers on him, but he
could not get warm.
2 Therefore his servants said to him, "Let a
young woman, a virgin, be sought for our lord the
king, and let her [1]stand before the king, and let
her care for him; and let her lie in your bosom,
that our lord the king may be warm."
3 So they sought for a lovely young woman
throughout all the territory of Israel, and found
[a]Abishag the [b]Shunammite, and brought her to
the king.
4 The young woman *was* very lovely; and she
cared for the king, and served him; but the king
did not know her.
**5** Then [a]Adonijah the [1]son of Haggith exalted
himself, saying, "I will [2]be king"; and [b]he prepared
for himself chariots and horsemen, and fifty men
to run before him.
6 (And his father had not [1]rebuked him at any
time by saying, "Why have you done so?" He *was*
also very good-looking. [a]*His mother* had borne
him after Absalom.)
7 Then he conferred with [a]Joab the son of
Zeruiah and with [b]Abiathar the priest, and [c]they
followed and helped Adonijah.
8 But [a]Zadok the priest, [b]Benaiah the son of
Jehoiada, [c]Nathan the prophet, [d]Shimei, Rei, and
[e]the mighty men who *belonged* to David were not
with Adonijah.
9 And Adonijah sacrificed sheep and oxen and
fattened cattle by the stone of [1]Zoheleth, which *is*
by [a]En Rogel;[2] he also invited all his brothers, the
king's sons, and all the men of Judah, the king's
servants.
10 But he did not invite Nathan the prophet,
Benaiah, the mighty men, or [a]Solomon his
brother.
**11** So Nathan spoke to Bathsheba the mother of
Solomon, saying, "Have you not heard that Adonijah the son of [a]Haggith has become king, and
David our lord does not know *it?*
12 "Come, please, let me now give you advice,
that you may save your own life and the life of
your son Solomon.
13 "Go immediately to King David and say to
him, 'Did you not, my lord, O king, swear to your
maidservant, saying, [a]"Assuredly your son Solomon shall reign after me, and he shall sit on my
throne"? Why then has Adonijah become king?'
14 "Then, while you are still talking there with
the king, I also will come in after you and confirm
your words."
**15** So Bathsheba went into the chamber to the
king. (Now the king was very old, and Abishag
the Shunammite was serving the king.)
16 And Bathsheba bowed and did homage to the
king. Then the king said, "What is your wish?"
17 Then she said to him, "My lord, [a]you swore by
the LORD your God to your maidservant, *saying,*
'Assuredly Solomon your son shall reign after me,
and he shall sit on my throne.'
18 "So now, look! Adonijah has become king;
and now, my lord the king, you do not know
about *it.*
19 [a]"He has sacrificed oxen and fattened cattle
and sheep in abundance, and has invited all the
sons of the king, Abiathar the priest, and Joab the
commander of the army; but Solomon your servant he has not invited.
20 "And as for you, my lord, O king, the eyes of
all Israel *are* on you, that you should tell them
who will sit on the throne of my lord the king
after him.
21 "Otherwise it will happen, when my lord the
king [a]rests with his fathers, that I and my son
Solomon will be counted as offenders."
**22** And just then, while she was still talking with
the king, Nathan the prophet also came in.
23 So they told the king, saying, "Here is Nathan
the prophet." And when he came in before the
king, he bowed down before the king with his face
to the ground.
24 And Nathan said, "My lord, O king, have you
said, 'Adonijah shall reign after me, and he shall
sit on my throne'?
25 [a]"For he has gone down today, and has sacrificed oxen and fattened cattle and sheep in abundance, and has invited all the king's sons, and the
commanders of the army, and Abiathar the priest;
and look! They are eating and drinking before
him; and they say, [b]'*Long*[1] live King Adonijah!'
26 "But he has not invited me—me your servant—nor Zadok the priest, nor Benaiah the son
of Jehoiada, nor your servant Solomon.
27 "Has this thing been done by my lord the king,
and you have not told your servant who should sit
on the throne of my lord the king after him?"
**28** Then King David answered and said, "Call
Bathsheba to me." So she came into the king's
presence and stood before the king.
29 And the king took an oath and said, [a]"*As* the
LORD lives, who has redeemed my life from every
distress,
30 [a]"just as I swore to you by the LORD God of
Israel, saying, 'Assuredly Solomon your son shall
be king after me, and he shall sit on my throne in
my place,' so I certainly will do this day."
31 Then Bathsheba bowed with *her* face to the
earth, and paid homage to the king, and said,
[a]"Let my lord King David live forever!"
**32** And King David said, "Call to me Zadok the
priest, Nathan the prophet, and Benaiah the son of
Jehoiada." So they came before the king.
33 The king also said to them, [a]"Take with you
the servants of your lord, and have Solomon my
son ride on my own [b]mule, and take him down to
[c]Gihon.[1]
34 "There let Zadok the priest and Nathan the
prophet [a]anoint him king over Israel; and [b]blow
the horn, and say, [1]'*Long* live King Solomon!'
35 "Then you shall come up after him, and he
shall come and sit on my throne, and he shall be
king in my place. For I have appointed him to be
ruler over Israel and Judah."
36 Benaiah the son of Jehoiada answered the
king and said, [a]"Amen! May the LORD God of my
lord the king say so *too.*
37 [a]"As the LORD has been with my lord the king,
even so may He be with Solomon, and [b]make his
throne greater than the throne of my lord King
David."

**1** [a]1 Chr. 23:1 [1]70 years
**2** [1]Or *serve*
**3** [a]1 Kin. 2:17 [b]Josh. 19:18; 1 Sam. 28:4
**5** [a]2 Sam. 3:4 [b]2 Sam. 15:1 [1]The fourth son [2]Lit. *reign*
**6** [a]2 Sam. 3:3, 4; 1 Chr. 3:2 [1]Lit. *pained*
**7** [a]1 Chr. 11:6 [b]2 Sam. 20:25 [c]1 Kin. 2:22, 28
**8** [a]1 Kin. 2:35 [b]1 Kin. 2:25; 2 Sam. 8:18 [c]2 Sam. 12:1 [d]1 Kin. 4:18 [e]2 Sam. 23:8
**9** [a]Josh. 15:7; 18:16; 2 Sam. 17:17 [1]Lit. *Serpent* [2]A spring south of Jerusalem in the Kidron Valley
**10** [a]2 Sam. 12:24
**11** [a]2 Sam. 3:4
**13** [a]1 Kin. 1:30; 1 Chr. 22:9–13
**17** [a]1 Kin. 1:13, 30
**19** [a]1 Kin. 1:7–9, 25
**21** [a]Deut. 31:16; 2 Sam. 7:12; 1 Kin. 2:10
**25** [a]1 Kin. 1:9, 19 [b]1 Sam. 10:24 [1]Lit. *Let King Adonijah live*
**29** [a]2 Sam. 4:9; 12:5
**30** [a]1 Kin. 1:13, 17
**31** [a]Neh. 2:3; Dan. 2:4; 3:9
**33** [a]2 Sam. 20:6 [b]Esth. 6:8 [c]2 Chr. 32:30; 33:14 [1]A spring east of Jerusalem in the Kidron Valley
**34** [a]1 Sam. 10:1; 16:3, 12; 2 Sam. 2:4; 5:3; 1 Kin. 19:16; 2 Kin. 9:3; 11:12; 1 Chr. 29:22 [b]2 Sam. 15:10; 2 Kin. 9:13; 11:14 [1]Lit. *Let King Solomon live*
**36** [a]Jer. 28:6
**37** [a]Josh. 1:5, 17; 1 Sam. 20:13 [b]1 Kin. 1:47

**38** So Zadok the priest, Nathan the prophet,
[a]Benaiah the son of Jehoiada, the [b]Cherethites,
and the Pelethites went down and had Solomon
ride on King David's mule, and took him to Gihon.
39 Then Zadok the priest took a horn of [a]oil from
the tabernacle and [b]anointed Solomon. And they
blew the horn, [c]and all the people said, [1]"Long live
King Solomon!"
40 And all the people went up after him; and the
people played the flutes and rejoiced with great
joy, so that the earth *seemed to* split with their
sound.
**41** Now Adonijah and all the guests who *were*
with him heard *it* as they finished eating. And
when Joab heard the sound of the horn, he said,
"Why *is* the city in such a noisy uproar?"
42 While he was still speaking, there came [a]Jonathan,
the son of Abiathar the priest. And Adonijah
said to him, "Come in, for [b]you *are* a prominent
man, and bring good news."
43 Then Jonathan answered and said to Adonijah,
"No! Our lord King David has made Solomon
king.
44 "The king has sent with him Zadok the priest,
Nathan the prophet, Benaiah the son of Jehoiada,
the Cherethites, and the Pelethites; and they have
made him ride on the king's mule.
45 "So Zadok the priest and Nathan the prophet
have anointed him king at Gihon; and they have
gone up from there rejoicing, so that the city is in
an uproar. This *is* the noise that you have heard.
46 "Also Solomon [a]sits on the throne of the
kingdom.
47 "And moreover the king's servants have gone
to bless our lord King David, saying, [a]'May God
make the name of Solomon better than your
name, and may He make his throne greater than
your throne.' [b]Then the king bowed himself on the
bed.
48 "Also the king said thus, 'Blessed *be* the LORD
God of Israel, who has [a]given *one* to sit on my
throne this day, while my eyes see [b]*it!*' "
49 So all the guests who were with Adonijah
were afraid, and arose, and each one went his
way.
**50** Now Adonijah was afraid of Solomon; so he
arose, and went and [a]took hold of the horns of the
altar.
51 And it was told Solomon, saying, "Indeed
Adonijah is afraid of King Solomon; for look, he
has taken hold of the horns of the altar, saying,
'Let King Solomon swear to me today that he will
not put his servant to death with the sword.' "
52 Then Solomon said, "If he proves himself a
worthy man, [a]not one hair of him shall fall to the
earth; but if wickedness is found in him, he shall
die."
53 So King Solomon sent them to bring him
down from the altar. And he came and fell down
before King Solomon; and Solomon said to him,
"Go to your house."

### *David's Instructions to Solomon*

**2** Now [a]the days of David drew near that he
should die, and he [1]charged Solomon his son,
saying:
2 [a]"I go the way of all the earth; [b]be strong,
therefore, and prove yourself a man.
3 "And keep the charge of the LORD your God:
to walk in His ways, to keep His statutes, His
commandments, His judgments, and His testimonies,
as it is written in the Law of Moses, that you
may [a]prosper in all that you do and wherever you
turn;
4 "that the LORD may [a]fulfill His word which He
spoke concerning me, saying, [b]'If your sons take
heed to their way, to [c]walk before Me in truth
with all their heart and with all their soul,' He
said, [d]'you shall not lack a man on the throne of
Israel.'
5 "Moreover you know also what Joab the son
of Zeruiah [a]did to me, *and* what he did to the two
commanders of the armies of Israel, to [b]Abner the
son of Ner and [c]Amasa the son of Jether, whom he
killed. And he shed the blood of war in peacetime,
and put the blood of war on his belt that *was*
around his waist, and on his sandals that *were* on
his feet.
6 "Therefore do [a]according to your wisdom, and
do not let his gray hair go down to the grave in
peace.
7 "But show kindness to the sons of [a]Barzillai
the Gileadite, and let them be among those who
[b]eat at your table, for so [c]they came to me when I
fled from Absalom your brother.
8 "And see, *you have* with you [a]Shimei the son
of Gera, a Benjamite from Bahurim, who cursed
me with a malicious curse in the day when I went
to Mahanaim. But [b]he came down to meet me at
the Jordan, and [c]I swore to him by the LORD,
saying, 'I will not put you to death with the
sword.'
9 "Now therefore, [a]do not hold him guiltless, for
you *are* a wise man and know what you ought to
do to him; but [b]bring his gray hair down to the
grave with blood."
**10** So [a]David [1]rested with his fathers, and was
buried in [b]the City of David.
11 The period that David [a]reigned over Israel *was*
forty years; seven years he reigned in Hebron, and
in Jerusalem he reigned thirty-three years.
12 [a]Then Solomon sat on the throne of his father
David; and his kingdom was [b]firmly established.
**13** Now Adonijah the son of Haggith came to
Bathsheba the mother of Solomon. So she said,
[a]"Do you come peaceably?" And he said, "Peaceably."
14 Moreover he said, "I have something *to say* to
you." And she said, "Say it."
15 Then he said, "You know that the kingdom
was [a]mine, and all Israel had set their expectations
on me, that I should reign. However, the kingdom
has been turned over, and has become my brother's;
for [b]it was his from the LORD.
16 "Now I ask one petition of you; do not [1]deny
me." And she said to him, "Say it."
17 Then he said, "Please speak to King Solomon,
for he will not refuse you, that he may give me
[a]Abishag the Shunammite as wife."
18 So Bathsheba said, "Very well, I will speak for
you to the king."
**19** Bathsheba therefore went to King Solomon, to
speak to him for Adonijah. And the king rose up
to meet her and [a]bowed down to her, and sat
down on his throne and had a throne set for the
king's mother; [b]so she sat at his right hand.
20 Then she said, "I desire one small petition of
you; do not [1]refuse me." And the king said to her,
"Ask it, my mother, for I will not refuse you."
21 So she said, "Let Abishag the Shunammite be
given to Adonijah your brother as wife."
22 And King Solomon answered and said to his

---

**38** [a]2 Sam. 8:18; 23:20–23 [b]2 Sam. 20:7; 1 Chr. 18:17
**39** [a]Ex. 30:23, 25, 32; Ps. 89:20 [b]1 Chr. 29:22 [c]1 Sam. 10:24 [1]Lit. *Let King Solomon live*
**42** [a]2 Sam. 17:17, 20 [b]2 Sam. 18:27
**46** [a]1 Kin. 2:12; 1 Chr. 29:23
**47** [a]1 Kin. 1:37 [b]Gen. 47:31
**48** [a]1 Kin. 3:6; [Ps. 132:11, 12] [b]2 Sam. 7:12
**50** [a]Ex. 27:2; 30:10; 1 Kin. 2:28
**52** [a]1 Sam. 14:45; 2 Sam. 14:11; Acts 27:34

CHAPTER 2

**1** [a]Gen. 47:29; Deut. 31:14 [1]*commanded*
**2** [a]Josh. 23:14 [b]Deut. 31:7, 23; 1 Chr. 22:13
**3** [a][Deut. 29:9; Josh. 1:7]; 1 Chr. 22:12, 13
**4** [a]2 Sam. 7:25 [b][Ps. 132:12] [c]2 Kin. 20:3 [d]2 Sam. 7:12, 13; 1 Kin. 8:25
**5** [a]2 Sam. 3:39; 18:5, 12, 14 [b]2 Sam. 3:27; 1 Kin. 2:32 [c]2 Sam. 20:10
**6** [a]1 Kin. 2:9; Prov. 20:26
**7** [a]2 Sam. 19:31–39 [b]2 Sam. 9:7, 10; 19:28 [c]2 Sam. 17:17–29
**8** [a]2 Sam. 16:5–13 [b]2 Sam. 19:18 [c]2 Sam. 19:23
**9** [a]Ex. 20:7; Job 9:28 [b]Gen. 42:38; 44:31
**10** [a]1 Kin. 1:21; Acts 2:29; 13:36 [b]2 Sam. 5:7; 1 Kin. 3:1 [1]Died and joined his ancestors
**11** [a]2 Sam. 5:4, 5; 1 Chr. 3:4; 29:26, 27
**12** [a]1 Kin. 1:46; 1 Chr. 29:23 [b]1 Kin. 2:46; 2 Chr. 1:1
**13** [a]1 Sam. 16:4, 5
**15** [a]1 Kin. 1:11, 18 [b]1 Chr. 22:9, 10; 28:5–7; [Dan. 2:21]
**16** [1]Lit. *turn away the face*
**17** [a]1 Kin. 1:3, 4
**19** [a][Ex. 20:12] [b]Ps. 45:9
**20** [1]Lit. *turn away the face*

mother, "Now why do you ask Abishag the Shunammite for Adonijah? Ask for him the kingdom also—for he *is* my [a]older brother—for him, and for [b]Abiathar the priest, and for Joab the son of Zeruiah."

23 Then King Solomon swore by the LORD, saying, [a]"May God do so to me, and more also, if Adonijah has not spoken this word against his own life!

24 "Now therefore, *as* the LORD lives, who has confirmed me and set me on the throne of David my father, and who has established a [1]house for me, as He [a]promised, Adonijah shall be put to death today!"

25 So King Solomon sent by the hand of [a]Benaiah the son of Jehoiada; and he struck him down, and he died.

**26** And to Abiathar the priest the king said, "Go to [a]Anathoth, to your own fields, for [1]you *are* deserving of death; but I will not put you to death at this time, [b]because you carried the ark of the Lord GOD before my father David, and because you were afflicted every time my father was afflicted."

27 So Solomon removed Abiathar from being priest to the LORD, that he might [a]fulfill the word of the LORD which He spoke concerning the house of Eli at Shiloh.

**28** Then news came to Joab, for Joab [a]had defected to Adonijah, though he had not defected to Absalom. So Joab fled to the tabernacle of the LORD, and [b]took hold of the horns of the altar.

29 And King Solomon was told, "Joab has fled to the tabernacle of the LORD; there *he is,* by the altar." Then Solomon sent Benaiah the son of Jehoiada, saying, "Go, [a]strike him down."

30 So Benaiah went to the tabernacle of the LORD, and said to him, "Thus says the king, [a]'Come out!'" And he said, "No, but I will die here." And Benaiah brought back word to the king, saying, "Thus said Joab, and thus he answered me."

31 Then the king said to him, [a]"Do as he has said, and strike him down and bury him, [b]that you may take away from me and from the house of my father the innocent blood which Joab shed.

32 "So the LORD [a]will return his [1]blood on his head, because he struck down two men more righteous [b]and better than he, and killed them with the sword—[c]Abner the son of Ner, the commander of the army of Israel, and [d]Amasa the son of Jether, the commander of the army of Judah—though my father David did not know *it.*

33 "Their blood shall therefore return upon the head of Joab and [a]upon the head of his descendants forever. [b]But upon David and his descendants, upon his house and his throne, there shall be peace forever from the LORD."

34 So Benaiah the son of Jehoiada went up and struck and killed him; and he was buried in his own house in the wilderness.

35 The king put Benaiah the son of Jehoiada in his place over the army, and the king put [a]Zadok the priest in the place of [b]Abiathar.

**36** Then the king sent and called for [a]Shimei, and said to him, "Build yourself a house in Jerusalem and dwell there, and do not go out from there anywhere.

37 "For it shall be, on the day you go out and cross [a]the Brook Kidron, know for certain you shall surely die; [b]your [1]blood shall be on your own head."

38 And Shimei said to the king, "The saying *is* good. As my lord the king has said, so your servant will do." So Shimei dwelt in Jerusalem many days.

**39** Now it happened at the end of three years, that two slaves of Shimei ran away to [a]Achish the son of Maachah, king of Gath. And they told Shimei, saying, "Look, your slaves *are* in Gath!"

40 So Shimei arose, saddled his donkey, and went to Achish at Gath to seek his slaves. And Shimei went and brought his slaves from Gath.

41 And Solomon was told that Shimei had gone from Jerusalem to Gath and had come back.

42 Then the king sent and called for Shimei, and said to him, "Did I not make you swear by the LORD, and warn you, saying, 'Know for certain that on the day you go out and travel anywhere, you shall surely die'? And you said to me, 'The word I have heard *is* good.'

43 "Why then have you not kept the oath of the LORD and the commandment that I gave you?"

44 The king said moreover to Shimei, "You know, as your heart acknowledges, [a]all the wickedness that you did to my father David; therefore the LORD will [b]return your wickedness on your own head.

45 "But King Solomon *shall be* blessed, and [a]the throne of David shall be established before the LORD forever."

46 So the king commanded Benaiah the son of Jehoiada; and he went out and struck him down, and he died. Thus the [a]kingdom was established in the hand of Solomon.

## *Solomon Prays for Wisdom*

**3** Now [a]Solomon made [1]a treaty with Pharaoh king of Egypt, and married Pharaoh's daughter; then he brought her [b]to the City of David until he had finished building his [c]own house, and [d]the house of the LORD, and [e]the wall all around Jerusalem.

2 [a]Meanwhile the people sacrificed at the high places, because there was no house built for the name of the LORD until those days.

3 And Solomon [a]loved the LORD, [b]walking in the statutes of his father David, except that he sacrificed and burned incense at the high places.

**4** Now [a]the king went to Gibeon to sacrifice there, [b]for that *was* the great high place: Solomon offered a thousand burnt offerings on that altar.

5 [a]At Gibeon the LORD appeared to Solomon [b]in a dream by night; and God said, "Ask! What shall I give you?"

6 [a]And Solomon said: "You have shown great mercy to Your servant David my father, because he [b]walked before You in truth, in righteousness, and in uprightness of heart with You; You have continued this great kindness for him, and You [c]have given him a son to sit on his throne, as *it is* this day.

7 "Now, O LORD my God, You have made Your servant king instead of my father David, but I *am* a [a]little child; I do not know *how* [b]to go out or come in.

8 "And Your servant *is* in the midst of Your people whom You [a]have chosen, a great people, [b]too numerous to be numbered or counted.

9 [a]"Therefore give to Your servant an [1]understanding heart [b]to judge Your people, that I may

**22** [a]1 Chr. 3:2, 5 [b]1 Kin. 1:7
**23** [a]Ruth 1:17
**24** [a]2 Sam. 7:11, 13 [1]Royal dynasty
**25** [a]2 Sam. 8:18
**26** [a]Josh. 21:18 [b]2 Sam. 15:14, 29 [1]Lit. *you are a man of death*
**27** [a]1 Sam. 2:31–35
**28** [a]1 Kin. 1:7 [b]1 Kin. 1:50
**29** [a]1 Kin. 2:5, 6
**30** [a][Ex. 21:14]
**31** [a][Ex. 21:14] [b][Num. 35:33]
**32** [a]Judg. 9:24, 57 [b]2 Chr. 21:13, 14 [c]2 Sam. 3:27 [d]2 Sam. 20:9, 10 [1]Or *bloodshed*
**33** [a]2 Sam. 3:29 [b][Prov. 25:5]
**35** [a]1 Sam. 2:35 [b]1 Kin. 2:27
**36** [a]1 Kin. 2:8
**37** [a]2 Sam. 15:23 [b]Josh. 2:19 [1]Or *bloodshed*
**39** [a]1 Sam. 27:2
**44** [a]2 Sam. 16:5–13 [b]1 Sam. 25:39
**45** [a][Prov. 25:5]
**46** [a]2 Chr. 1:1

CHAPTER 3

**1** [a]1 Kin. 7:8; 9:24 [b]2 Sam. 5:7 [c]1 Kin. 7:1 [d]1 Kin. 6 [e]1 Kin. 9:15, 19 [1]*an alliance*
**2** [a][Deut. 12:2–5, 13, 14]
**3** [a][Rom. 8:28] [b][1 Kin. 3:6, 14]
**4** [a]2 Chr. 1:3 [b]1 Chr. 16:39; 21:29
**5** [a]1 Kin. 9:2; 11:9 [b]Num. 12:6
**6** [a]2 Chr. 1:8 [b]1 Kin. 2:4; 9:4 [c]1 Kin. 1:48
**7** [a]Jer. 1:6, 7 [b]Num. 27:17
**8** [a][Deut. 7:6] [b]Gen. 13:6; 15:5; 22:17
**9** [a]2 Chr. 1:10 [b]Ps. 72:1, 2 [1]Lit. *hearing*

[c]discern between good and evil. For who is able to judge this great people of Yours?"

**10** The speech pleased the LORD, that Solomon had asked this thing.

11 Then God said to him: "Because you have asked this thing, and have [a]not asked long life for yourself, nor have asked riches for yourself, nor have asked the life of your enemies, but have asked for yourself understanding to discern justice,

12 [a]"behold, I have done according to your words; [b]see, I have given you a wise and understanding heart, so that there has not been anyone like you before you, nor shall any like you arise after you.

13 "And I have also [a]given you what you have not asked: both [b]riches and honor, so that there shall not be anyone like you among the kings all your days.

14 "So [a]if you walk in My ways, to keep My statutes and My commandments, [b]as your father David walked, then I will [c]lengthen[1] your days."

15 Then Solomon [a]awoke; and indeed it had been a dream. And he came to Jerusalem and stood before the ark of the covenant of the LORD, offered up burnt offerings, offered peace offerings, and [b]made a feast for all his servants.

**16** Now two women *who were* harlots came to the king, and [a]stood before him.

17 And one woman said, "O my lord, this woman and I dwell in the same house; and I gave birth while she *was* in the house.

18 "Then it happened, the third day after I had given birth, that this woman also gave birth. And we *were* together; [1]no one *was* with us in the house, except the two of us in the house.

19 "And this woman's son died in the night, because she lay on him.

20 "So she arose in the middle of the night and took my son from my side, while your maidservant slept, and laid him in her bosom, and laid her dead child in my bosom.

21 "And when I rose in the morning to nurse my son, there he was, dead. But when I had examined him in the morning, indeed, he was not my son whom I had borne."

22 Then the other woman said, "No! But the living one *is* my son, and the dead one *is* your son." And the first woman said, "No! But the dead one *is* your son, and the living one *is* my son." Thus they spoke before the king.

**23** And the king said, "The one says, 'This *is* my son, who lives, and your son *is* the dead one'; and the other says, 'No! But your son *is* the dead one, and my son *is* the living one.' "

24 Then the king said, "Bring me a sword." So they brought a sword before the king.

25 And the king said, "Divide the living child in two, and give half to one, and half to the other."

26 Then the woman whose son *was* living spoke to the king, for [a]she yearned with compassion for her son; and she said, "O my lord, give her the living child, and by no means kill him!" But the other said, "Let him be neither mine nor yours, *but* divide *him*."

27 So the king answered and said, "Give the first woman the living child, and by no means kill him; she *is* his mother."

28 And all Israel heard of the judgment which the king had rendered; and they feared the king, for they saw that the [a]wisdom of God *was* in him to administer justice.

## *Solomon's Princes and Officers*

**4** So King Solomon was king over all Israel.

2 And these *were* his officials: Azariah the son of Zadok, the priest;

3 Elihoreph and Ahijah, the sons of Shisha, [1]scribes; [a]Jehoshaphat the son of Ahilud, the recorder;

4 [a]Benaiah the son of Jehoiada, over the army; Zadok and [b]Abiathar, the priests;

5 Azariah the son of Nathan, over [a]the officers; Zabud the son of Nathan, [b]a priest *and* [c]the king's friend;

6 Ahishar, over the household; and [a]Adoniram the son of Abda, over the labor force.

7 And Solomon had twelve governors over all Israel, who provided food for the king and his household; each one made provision for one month of the year.

8 These *are* their names: [1]Ben-Hur, in the mountains of Ephraim;

9 [1]Ben-Deker, in Makaz, Shaalbim, Beth Shemesh, and Elon Beth Hanan;

10 [1]Ben-Hesed, in Arubboth; to him *belonged* Sochoh and all the land of Hepher;

11 [1]Ben-Abinadab, *in* all the regions of Dor; he had Taphath the daughter of Solomon as wife;

12 Baana the son of Ahilud, *in* Taanach, Megiddo, and all Beth Shean, which *is* beside Zaretan below Jezreel, from Beth Shean to Abel Meholah, as far as the other side of Jokneam;

13 [1]Ben-Geber, in Ramoth Gilead; to him *belonged* [a]the towns of Jair the son of Manasseh, in Gilead; to him *also belonged* [b]the region of Argob in Bashan—sixty large cities with walls and bronze gate-bars;

14 Ahinadab the son of Iddo, *in* Mahanaim;

15 [a]Ahimaaz, in Naphtali; he also took Basemath the daughter of Solomon as wife;

16 Baanah the son of [a]Hushai, in Asher and Aloth;

17 Jehoshaphat the son of Paruah, in Issachar;

18 [a]Shimei the son of Elah, in Benjamin;

19 Geber the son of Uri, in the land of Gilead, *in* [a]the country of Sihon king of the Amorites, and of Og king of Bashan. *He was* the only governor who *was* in the land.

**20** Judah and Israel *were* as numerous [a]as the sand by the sea in multitude, [b]eating and drinking and rejoicing.

21 So [a]Solomon reigned over all kingdoms from [b]the[1] River *to* the land of the Philistines, as far as the border of Egypt. [c]*They* brought tribute and served Solomon all the days of his life.

**22** [a]Now Solomon's [1]provision for one day was thirty [2]kors of fine flour, sixty kors of meal,

23 ten fatted oxen, twenty oxen from the pastures, and one hundred sheep, besides deer, gazelles, roebucks, and fatted fowl.

24 For he had dominion over all *the region* on this side of [1]the River from Tiphsah even to Gaza, namely over [a]all the kings on this side of the River; and [b]he had peace on every side all around him.

25 And Judah and Israel [a]dwelt[1] safely, [b]each man under his vine and his fig tree, [c]from Dan as far as Beersheba, all the days of Solomon.

**26** [a]Solomon had [1]forty thousand stalls of [b]horses for his chariots, and twelve thousand horsemen.

---

**9** [c][Heb. 5:14]
**11** [a][James 4:3]
**12** [a][1 John 5:14, 15] [b]Eccl. 1:16
**13** [a][Matt. 6:33] [b]1 Kin. 4:21, 24; 10:23
**14** [a][1 Kin. 6:12] [b]1 Kin. 15:5 [c]Ps. 91:16 [1]*prolong*
**15** [a]Gen. 41:7 [b]1 Kin. 8:65
**16** [a]Num. 27:2
**18** [1]Lit. *no stranger*
**26** [a]Jer. 31:20
**28** [a]1 Kin. 3:9, 11, 12

CHAPTER 4

**3** [a]2 Sam. 8:16; 20:24 [1]*secretaries*
**4** [a]1 Kin. 2:35 [b]1 Kin. 2:27
**5** [a]1 Kin. 4:7 [b]2 Sam. 8:18; 20:26 [c]2 Sam. 15:37; 16:16
**6** [a]1 Kin. 5:14
**8** [1]Lit. *Son of Hur*
**9** [1]Lit. *Son of Deker*
**10** [1]Lit. *Son of Hesed*
**11** [1]Lit. *Son of Abinadab*
**13** [a]Num. 32:41 [b]Deut. 3:4 [1]Lit. *Son of Geber*
**15** [a]2 Sam. 15:27
**16** [a]1 Chr. 27:33
**18** [a]1 Kin. 1:8
**19** [a]Deut. 3:8–10
**20** [a]Gen. 22:17; 32:12 [b]Mic. 4:4
**21** [a]Ps. 72:8 [b]Gen. 15:18 [c]Ps. 68:29 [1]The Euphrates
**22** [a]Neh. 5:18 [1]Lit. *bread* [2]Each about 5 bushels
**24** [a]Ps. 72:11 [b]1 Chr. 22:9 [1]The Euphrates
**25** [a][Jer. 23:6] [b][Mic. 4:4] [c]Judg. 20:1 [1]*lived in safety*
**26** [a]1 Kin. 10:26 [b][Deut. 17:16] [1]So with MT, most other authorities; some LXX mss. *four thousand* (cf. 2 Chr. 9:25)

27 And [a]these governors, each man in his month,
provided food for King Solomon and for all who
came to King Solomon's table. There was no lack
in their supply.
28 They also brought barley and straw to the
proper place, for the horses and steeds, each man
according to his charge.
**29** And [a]God gave Solomon wisdom and exceedingly great understanding, and largeness of heart
like the sand on the seashore.
30 Thus Solomon's wisdom excelled the wisdom
of all the men [a]of the East and all [b]the wisdom of
Egypt.
31 For he was [a]wiser than all men—[b]than Ethan
the Ezrahite, [c]and Heman, Chalcol, and Darda, the
sons of Mahol; and his fame was in all the surrounding nations.
32 [a]He spoke three thousand proverbs, and his
[b]songs were one thousand and five.
33 Also he spoke of trees, from the cedar tree of
Lebanon even to the hyssop that springs out
of the wall; he spoke also of animals, of birds, of
creeping things, and of fish.
34 And men of all nations, from all the kings of
the earth who had heard of his wisdom, [a]came to
hear the wisdom of Solomon.

### *Solomon's Agreement with King Hiram*

**5** Now [a]Hiram king of Tyre sent his servants to
Solomon, because he heard that they had
anointed him king in place of his father, [b]for
Hiram had always loved David.
2 Then [a]Solomon sent to Hiram, saying:

3 [a]You know how my father David could not
build a house for the name of the LORD his
God [b]because of the wars which were fought
against him on every side, until the LORD put
[1]*his foes* under the soles of his feet.
4 But now the LORD my God has given me
[a]rest[1] on every side; *there is* neither
adversary nor [2]evil occurrence.
5 [a]And behold, [1]I propose to build a house for
the name of the LORD my God, [b]as the LORD
spoke to my father David, saying, "Your son,
whom I will set on your throne in your place,
he shall build the house for My name."
6 Now therefore, command that they cut down
[a]cedars for me from Lebanon; and my
servants will be with your servants, and I
will pay you wages for your servants
according to whatever you say. For you
know *there is* none among us who has skill
to cut timber like the Sidonians.

7 So it was, when Hiram heard the words of
Solomon, that he rejoiced greatly and said,

Blessed *be* the LORD this day, for He has
given David a wise son over this great
people!

8 Then Hiram sent to Solomon, saying:

I have considered *the message* which you
sent me, *and* I will do all you desire
concerning the cedar and cypress logs.
9 My servants shall bring *them* down [a]from
Lebanon to the sea; I will float them in rafts
by sea to the place you indicate to me, and
will have them broken apart there; then you
can take *them* away. And you shall fulfill my
desire [b]by giving food for my household.

10 Then Hiram gave Solomon cedar and cypress
logs *according to* all his desire.
11 [a]And Solomon gave Hiram twenty thousand
[1]kors of wheat *as* food for his household, and
[2]twenty kors of pressed oil. Thus Solomon gave to
Hiram year by year.
12 So the LORD gave Solomon wisdom, [a]as He
had promised him; and there was peace between
Hiram and Solomon, and the two of them made a
treaty together.
**13** Then King Solomon raised up a labor force out
of all Israel; and the labor force was thirty thousand men.
14 And he sent them to Lebanon, ten thousand a
month in shifts: they were one month in Lebanon
*and* two months at home; [a]Adoniram *was* in
charge of the labor force.
15 [a]Solomon had seventy thousand who carried
burdens, and eighty thousand who quarried *stone*
in the mountains,
16 besides three thousand [1]three hundred from
the [a]chiefs of Solomon's deputies, who supervised
the people who labored in the work.
17 And the king commanded them to quarry
large stones, costly stones, *and* [a]hewn stones, to
lay the foundation of the [1]temple.
18 So Solomon's builders, Hiram's builders, and
the Gebalites quarried *them;* and they prepared
timber and stones to build the [1]temple.

### *Solomon Builds the Temple*

**6** And [a]it came to pass in the four hundred and
[1]eightieth year after the children of Israel had
come out of the land of Egypt, in the fourth year
of Solomon's reign over Israel, in the month of
[2]Ziv, which *is* the second month, [b]that he began to
build the house of the LORD.
2 Now [a]the house which King Solomon built for
the LORD, its length *was* sixty cubits, its width
twenty, and its height thirty cubits.
3 The vestibule in front of the [1]sanctuary of the
house *was* [2]twenty cubits long across the width of
the house, *and* the width of [3]*the vestibule extended* [4]ten cubits from the front of the house.
4 And he made for the house [a]windows with
beveled frames.
**5** Against the wall of the [1]temple he built [a]cham-
bers all around, *against* the walls of the temple, all
around the sanctuary [b]and the [2]inner sanctuary.
Thus he made side chambers all around it.
6 The lowest chamber *was* five cubits wide, the
middle *was* six cubits wide, and the third *was*
seven cubits wide; for he made narrow ledges
around the outside of the temple, so that *the
support beams* would not be fastened into the
walls of the [1]temple.
7 And [a]the temple, when it was being built, was
built with stone finished at the quarry, so that no
hammer or chisel *or* any iron tool was heard in the
temple while it was being built.
8 The doorway for the [1]middle story *was* on the
right side of the temple. They went up by stairs to
the middle *story,* and from the middle to the third.
9 [a]So he built the [1]temple and finished it, and he
paneled the temple with beams and boards of
cedar.
10 And he built side chambers against the entire
temple, each five cubits high; they were attached
to the temple with cedar beams.
**11** Then the word of the LORD came to Solomon,
saying:

---

**27** [a]1 Kin. 4:7
**29** [a]1 Kin. 3:12
**30** [a]Gen. 25:6 [b]Is. 19:11, 12
**31** [a]1 Kin. 3:12 [b]1 Chr. 15:19 [c]1 Chr. 2:6
**32** [a]Eccl. 12:9 [b]Song 1:1
**34** [a]1 Kin. 10:1

CHAPTER 5
**1** [a]2 Chr. 2:3 [b]2 Sam. 5:11
**2** [a]2 Chr. 2:3
**3** [a]1 Chr. 28:2, 3 [b]1 Chr. 22:8; 28:3 [1]Lit. *them*
**4** [a]1 Kin. 4:24 [1]*peace* [2]*misfortune*
**5** [a]2 Chr. 2:4 [b]2 Sam. 7:12, 13 [1]Lit. *I am saying*
**6** [a]2 Chr. 2:8, 10
**9** [a]Ezra 3:7 [b]Ezek. 27:17
**11** [a]2 Chr. 2:10 [1]Each about 5 bushels [2]So with MT, Tg., Vg.; LXX, [Syr.] *twenty thousand kors*
**12** [a]1 Kin. 3:12
**14** [a]1 Kin. 12:18
**15** [a]2 Chr. 2:17, 18
**16** [a]1 Kin. 9:23 [1]So with MT, Tg., Vg.; LXX *six hundred*
**17** [a]1 Kin. 6:7 [1]Lit. *house*
**18** [1]Lit. *house*

CHAPTER 6
**1** [a]2 Chr. 3:1, 2 [b]Acts 7:47 [1]So with MT, Tg., Vg.; LXX *fortieth* [2]Or *Ayyar,* April or May
**2** [a]Ezek. 41:1
**3** [1]Heb. *heykal;* here the main room of the temple; elsewhere called *the Holy Place,* Ex. 26:33; Ezek. 41:1 [2]About 30 feet [3]Lit. *it* [4]About 15 feet
**4** [a]Ezek. 40:16; 41:16
**5** [a]Ezek. 41:6 [b]1 Kin. 6:16, 19–21, 31 [1]Lit. *house* [2]Heb. *debir;* here the inner room of the temple; elsewhere called *the Most Holy Place,* v. 16
**6** [1]Lit. *house*
**7** [a]Deut. 27:5, 6
**8** [1]So with MT, Vg.; LXX *upper story;* Tg. *ground story*
**9** [a]1 Kin. 6:14, 38 [1]Lit. *house*

12 "*Concerning* this [1]temple which you are building, [a]if you walk in My statutes, execute My
judgments, keep all My commandments, and walk
in them, then I will perform My [2]word with you,
[b]which I spoke to your father David.
13 "And [a]I will dwell among the children of
Israel, and will not [b]forsake My people Israel."
**14** So Solomon built the temple and finished it.
15 And he built the inside walls of the temple
with cedar boards; from the floor of the temple to
the ceiling he paneled the inside with wood; and
he covered the floor of the temple with planks of
cypress.
16 Then he built the twenty-cubit room at the
rear of the temple, from floor to ceiling, with cedar
boards; he built *it* inside as the inner sanctuary, as
the [a]Most Holy *Place.*
17 And in front of it the temple sanctuary was
forty cubits *long.*
18 The inside of the temple was cedar, carved
with ornamental buds and open flowers. All *was*
cedar; there was no stone *to be* seen.
19 And he prepared the [1]inner sanctuary inside
the temple, to set the ark of the covenant of the
LORD there.
20 The inner sanctuary *was* twenty cubits long,
twenty cubits wide, and twenty cubits high. He
overlaid it with pure gold, and overlaid the altar of
cedar.
21 So Solomon overlaid the inside of the temple
with pure gold. He stretched gold chains across
the front of the inner sanctuary, and overlaid it
with gold.
22 The whole temple he overlaid with gold, until
he had finished all the temple; also he overlaid
with gold [a]the entire altar that *was* by the inner
sanctuary.
**23** Inside the inner sanctuary [a]he made two
cherubim *of* olive wood, *each* ten cubits high.
24 One wing of the cherub *was* five cubits, and
the other wing of the cherub five cubits: ten cubits
from the tip of one wing to the tip of the other.
25 And the other cherub *was* ten cubits; both
cherubim *were* of the same size and shape.
26 The height of one cherub *was* ten cubits, and
so *was* the other cherub.
27 Then he set the cherubim inside the inner
[1]room; and [a]they stretched out the wings of the
cherubim so that the wing of the one touched *one*
wall, and the wing of the other cherub touched
the other wall. And their wings touched each
other in the middle of the room.
28 Also he overlaid the cherubim with gold.
**29** Then he carved all the walls of the temple all
around, both the inner and outer *sanctuaries,*
with carved [a]figures of cherubim, palm trees, and
open flowers.
30 And the floor of the temple he overlaid with
gold, both the inner and outer *sanctuaries.*
**31** For the entrance of the inner sanctuary he
made doors *of* olive wood; the lintel *and* doorposts
*were* [1]one-fifth *of the wall.*
32 The two doors *were of* olive wood; and he
carved on them figures of cherubim, palm trees,
and open flowers, and overlaid *them* with gold;
and he spread gold on the cherubim and on the
palm trees.
33 So for the door of the [1]sanctuary he also made
doorposts *of* olive wood, [2]one-fourth *of the wall.*
34 And the two doors *were of* cypress wood; [a]two
panels *comprised* one folding door, and two panels
*comprised* the other folding door.
35 Then he carved cherubim, palm trees, and
open flowers *on them,* and overlaid *them* with
gold applied evenly on the carved work.
**36** And he built the [a]inner court with three rows
of hewn stone and a row of cedar beams.
**37** [a]In the fourth year the foundation of the
house of the LORD was laid, in the month of [1]Ziv.
38 And in the eleventh year, in the month of [1]Bul,
which is the eighth month, the house was finished
in all its details and according to all its plans. So
he was [a]seven years in building it.

### *The Construction and Furniture of the Temple*

**7** But Solomon took [a]thirteen years to build his
own house; so he finished all his house.
**2** He also built the [a]House of the Forest of
Lebanon; its length *was* [1]one hundred cubits, its
width [2]fifty cubits, and its height thirty cubits,
with four rows of cedar pillars, and cedar beams
on the pillars.
3 And *it was* paneled with cedar above the
beams that *were* on forty-five pillars, fifteen *to* a
row.
4 *There were* windows *with beveled frames in*
three rows, and window *was* opposite window *in*
three tiers.
5 And all the doorways and doorposts *had* rec-
tangular frames; and window *was* opposite window *in* three tiers.
**6** He also made the Hall of Pillars: its length *was*
fifty cubits, and its width thirty cubits; and in
front of them *was* a portico with pillars, and a
canopy *was* in front of them.
7 Then he made a hall for the throne, the Hall of
Judgment, where he might judge; and *it was*
paneled with cedar from floor to [1]ceiling.
8 And the house where he dwelt *had* another
court inside the hall, of like workmanship. Solomon also made a house like this hall for Pharaoh's
daughter, [a]whom he had taken *as wife.*
**9** All these *were of* costly stones cut to size,
trimmed with saws, inside and out, from the
foundation to the eaves, and also on the outside to
the great court.
10 The foundation *was of* costly stones, large
stones, some ten cubits and some eight cubits.
11 And above *were* costly stones, hewn to size,
and cedar wood.
12 The great court *was* enclosed with three rows
of hewn stones and a row of cedar beams. So were
the [a]inner court of the house of the LORD [b]and the
vestibule of the temple.
**13** Now King Solomon sent and brought [1]Huram
from Tyre.
14 [a]He *was* the son of a widow from the tribe of
Naphtali, and [b]his father *was* a man of Tyre, a
bronze worker; [c]he was filled with wisdom and
understanding and skill in working with all kinds
of bronze work. So he came to King Solomon and
did all his work.
**15** And he [1]cast [a]two pillars of bronze, each one
eighteen cubits high, and a line of twelve cubits
measured the circumference of each.
16 Then he made two capitals *of* cast bronze, to
set on the tops of the pillars. The height of one
capital *was* five cubits, and the height of the other
capital *was* five cubits.
17 *He made* a lattice network, with wreaths of

**12** [a]1 Kin. 2:4; 9:4 [b][2 Sam. 7:13; 1 Chr. 22:10] [1]Lit. *house* [2]*promise*
**13** [a]Ex. 25:8; Lev. 26:11; [2 Cor. 6:16; Rev. 21:3] [b][Deut. 31:6]
**16** [a]Ex. 26:33; Lev. 16:2; 1 Kin. 8:6; 2 Chr. 3:8; Ezek. 45:3; Heb. 9:3
**19** [1]The Most Holy Place
**22** [a]Ex. 30:1, 3, 6
**23** [a]Ex. 37:7–9; 2 Chr. 3:10–12
**27** [a]Ex. 25:20; 37:9; 1 Kin. 8:7; 2 Chr. 5:8 [1]Lit. *house*
**29** [a]Ex. 36:8, 35
**31** [1]Or *five-sided*
**33** [1]*temple* [2]Or *four-sided*
**34** [a]Ezek. 41:23–25
**36** [a]1 Kin. 7:12; Jer. 36:10
**37** [a]1 Kin. 6:1 [1]Or *Ayyar,* April or May
**38** [a]2 Sam. 7:13; 1 Kin. 5:5; 6:1; 8:19 [1]Or *Heshvan,* October or November

CHAPTER 7

**1** [a]1 Kin. 3:1; 9:10; 2 Chr. 8:1
**2** [a]1 Kin. 10:17, 21; 2 Chr. 9:16 [1]About 150 feet [2]About 75 feet
**7** [1]Lit. *floor* of the upper level
**8** [a]1 Kin. 3:1; 9:24; 11:1; 2 Chr. 8:11
**12** [a]1 Kin. 6:36 [b]John 10:23; Acts 3:11
**13** [1]*Hiram,* 2 Chr. 2:13, 14
**14** [a]2 Chr. 2:14 [b]2 Chr. 4:16 [c]Ex. 31:3; 36:1
**15** [a]2 Kin. 25:17; 2 Chr. 3:15; 4:12; Jer. 52:21 [1]*fashioned*

chainwork, for the capitals which *were* on top of
the pillars: seven chains for one capital and seven
for the other capital.
18 So he made the pillars, and two rows of pomegranates above the network all around to cover
the capitals that *were* on top; and thus he did for
the other capital.
19 The capitals which *were* on top of the pillars
in the hall *were* in the shape of lilies, four cubits.
20 The capitals on the two pillars also *had pomegranates* above, by the convex surface which *was*
next to the network; and there *were* [a]two hundred
such pomegranates in rows on each of the capitals
all around.
21 [a]Then he set up the pillars by the vestibule of
the temple; he set up the pillar on the right and
called its name [1]Jachin, and he set up the pillar on
the left and called its name [2]Boaz.
22 The tops of the pillars were in the shape of
lilies. So the work of the pillars was finished.
**23** And he made [a]the Sea of cast bronze, ten
cubits from one brim to the other; *it was* completely round. Its height *was* five cubits, and a line
of thirty cubits measured its circumference.
24 Below its brim *were* ornamental buds encircling it all around, ten to a cubit, [a]all the way
around the Sea. The ornamental buds *were* cast in
two rows when it was cast.
25 It stood on [a]twelve oxen: three looking toward
the north, three looking toward the west, three
looking toward the south, and three looking
toward the east; the Sea *was set* upon them, and
all their back parts *pointed* inward.
26 It *was* a handbreadth thick; and its brim was
shaped like the brim of a cup, *like* a lily blossom. It
contained [1]two thousand baths.
**27** He also made ten [1]carts of bronze; four cubits
*was* the length of each cart, four cubits its width,
and three cubits its height.
28 And this *was* the design of the carts: They had
panels, and the panels *were* between frames;
29 on the panels that *were* between the frames
*were* lions, oxen, and cherubim. And on the
frames *was* a pedestal on top. Below the lions and
oxen *were* wreaths of plaited work.
30 Every cart had four bronze wheels and axles
of bronze, and its four feet had supports. Under
the laver *were* supports of cast *bronze* beside each
wreath.
31 Its opening inside the crown at the top *was*
one cubit in diameter; and the opening *was* round,
shaped *like* a pedestal, one and a half cubits in
outside diameter; and also on the opening *were*
engravings, but the panels were square, not
round.
32 Under the panels *were* the four wheels, and
the axles of the wheels *were joined* to the cart.
The height of a wheel *was* one and a half cubits.
33 The workmanship of the wheels *was* like the
workmanship of a chariot wheel; their axle pins,
their rims, their spokes, and their hubs *were* all of
cast *bronze*.
34 And *there were* four supports at the four
corners of each cart; its supports *were* part of the
cart itself.
35 On the top of the cart, at the height of half a
cubit, *it was* perfectly round. And on the top of
the cart, its flanges and its panels *were* of the
same casting.
36 On the plates of its flanges and on its panels he
engraved cherubim, lions, and palm trees, wherever there was a clear space on each, with
wreaths all around.
37 Thus he made the ten carts. All of them were
of [1]the same mold, one measure, *and* one shape.
**38** Then [a]he made ten lavers of bronze; each laver
contained [1]forty baths, *and* each laver *was* four
cubits. On each of the ten carts *was* a laver.
39 And he put five carts on the right side of the
house, and five on the left side of the house. He set
the Sea on the right side of the house, toward the
southeast.
**40** [a]Huram[1] made the lavers and the shovels and
the bowls. So Huram finished doing all the work
that he was to do for King Solomon *for* the house
of the LORD:
41 the two pillars, the *two* bowl-shaped capitals
that *were* on top of the two pillars; the two
[a]networks covering the two bowl-shaped capitals
which *were* on top of the pillars;
42 [a]four hundred pomegranates for the two networks (two rows of pomegranates for each network, to cover the two bowl-shaped capitals that
*were* on top of the pillars);
43 the ten carts, and ten lavers on the carts;
44 one Sea, and twelve oxen under the Sea;
45 [a]the pots, the shovels, and the bowls. All these
articles which [1]Huram made for King Solomon *for*
the house of the LORD *were of* burnished bronze.
46 [a]In the plain of Jordan the king had them cast
in clay molds, between [b]Succoth and [c]Zaretan.
47 And Solomon did not weigh all the articles,
because *there were* so many; the weight of the
bronze was not [a]determined.
48 Thus Solomon had all the furnishings made
for the house of the LORD: [a]the altar of gold, and
[b]the table of gold on which *was* [c]the showbread;
49 the lampstands of pure gold, five on the right
*side* and five on the left in front of the inner
sanctuary, with the flowers and the lamps and the
wick-trimmers of gold;
50 the basins, the trimmers, the bowls, the ladles,
and the [1]censers of pure gold; and the hinges of
gold, *both* for the doors of the inner room (the
Most Holy *Place*) *and* for the doors of the main
hall of the temple.
51 So all the work that King Solomon had done
for the house of the LORD was finished; and
Solomon brought in the things [a]which his father
David had dedicated: the silver and the gold and
the furnishings. He put them in the treasuries of
the house of the LORD.

## *The Ark Brought into the Temple*

**8** Now [a]Solomon assembled the elders of Israel
and all the heads of the tribes, the chief
fathers of the children of Israel, to King Solomon
in Jerusalem, [b]that they might bring [c]up the ark of
the covenant of the LORD from the City of David,
which *is* Zion.
2 Therefore all the men of Israel assembled with
King Solomon at the [a]feast in the month of [1]Etha-
nim, which *is* the seventh month.
3 So all the elders of Israel came, [a]and the
priests took up the ark.
4 Then they brought up the ark of the LORD,
[a]the [1]tabernacle of meeting, and all the holy
furnishings that *were* in the tabernacle. The
priests and the Levites brought them up.
5 Also King Solomon, and all the congregation
of Israel who were assembled with him, *were* with
him before the ark, [a]sacrificing sheep and oxen

**20** [a]2 Chr. 3:16; 4:13; Jer. 52:23
**21** [a]2 Chr. 3:17 [1]Lit. *He Shall Establish* [2]Lit. *In It Is Strength*
**23** [a]2 Kin. 25:13; 2 Chr. 4:2; Jer. 52:17
**24** [a]2 Chr. 4:3
**25** [a]2 Chr. 4:4, 5; Jer. 52:20
**26** [1]About 12,000 gallons; *three thousand,* 2 Chr. 4:5
**27** [1]Or *stands*
**37** [1]*one*
**38** [a]Ex. 30:18; 2 Chr. 4:6 [1]About 240 gallons
**40** [a]2 Chr. 4:11—5:1 [1]Heb. *Hiram;* cf. 2 Chr. 2:13, 14
**41** [a]1 Kin. 7:17, 18
**42** [a]1 Kin. 7:20
**45** [a]Ex. 27:3; 2 Chr. 4:16 [1]Heb. *Hiram;* cf. 2 Chr. 2:13, 14
**46** [a]2 Chr. 4:17 [b]Gen. 33:17; Josh. 13:27 [c]Josh. 3:16
**47** [a]1 Chr. 22:3, 14
**48** [a]Ex. 37:25, 26; 2 Chr. 4:8 [b]Ex. 37:10, 11 [c]Lev. 24:5–8
**50** [1]*fire pans*
**51** [a]2 Sam. 8:11; 1 Chr. 18:11; 2 Chr. 5:1

CHAPTER 8

**1** [a]Num. 1:4; 7:2; 2 Chr. 5:2–14 [b]2 Sam. 6:12–17; 1 Chr. 15:25–29 [c]2 Sam. 5:7; 6:12, 16
**2** [a]Lev. 23:34; 1 Kin. 8:65; 2 Chr. 7:8–10 [1]Or *Tishri,* September or October
**3** [a]Num. 4:15; 7:9; Deut. 31:9; Josh. 3:3, 6
**4** [a]1 Kin. 3:4; 2 Chr. 1:3 [1]*tent*
**5** [a]2 Sam. 6:13; 2 Chr. 1:6

that could not be counted or numbered for multitude.
6 Then the priests [a]brought in the ark of the
covenant of the LORD to [b]its place, into the inner
sanctuary of the temple, to the Most Holy *Place,*
[c]under the wings of the cherubim.
7 For the cherubim spread *their* two wings over
the place of the ark, and the cherubim overshadowed the ark and its poles.
8 The poles [a]extended so that the [1]ends of the
poles could be seen from the holy *place,* in front of
the inner sanctuary; but they could not be seen
from outside. And they are there to this day.
9 [a]Nothing *was* in the ark [b]except the two
tablets of stone which Moses [c]put there at Horeb,
[d]when the LORD made *a covenant* with the children of Israel, when they came out of the land of
Egypt.
10 And it came to pass, when the priests came
out of the holy *place,* that the cloud [a]filled the
house of the LORD,
11 so that the priests could not continue ministering because of the cloud; for the [a]glory of the
LORD filled the house of the LORD.
**12** [a]Then Solomon spoke:

"The LORD said He would dwell [b]in the dark
cloud.
13 [a]I have surely built You an exalted house,
[b]And a place for You to dwell in forever."

**14** Then the king turned around and [a]blessed the
whole assembly of Israel, while all the assembly of
Israel was standing.
15 And he said: [a]"Blessed *be* the LORD God of
Israel, who [b]spoke with His mouth to my father
David, and with His hand has fulfilled *it,* saying,
16 'Since the day that I brought My people Israel
out of Egypt, I have chosen no city from any tribe
of Israel *in which* to build a house, that [a]My name
might be there; but I chose [b]David to be over My
people Israel.'
17 "Now [a]it was in the heart of my father David
to build a [1]temple for the name of the LORD God of
Israel.
18 [a]"But the LORD said to my father David,
'Whereas it was in your heart to build a temple for
My name, you did well that it was in your heart.
19 'Nevertheless [a]you shall not build the temple,
but your son who will come from your body, he
shall build the temple for My name.'
20 "So the LORD has fulfilled His word which He
spoke; and I have [1]filled the position of my father
David, and sit on the throne of Israel, [a]as the LORD
promised; and I have built a temple for the name
of the LORD God of Israel.
21 "And there I have made a place for the ark, in
which *is* [a]the covenant of the LORD which He
made with our fathers, when He brought them out
of the land of Egypt."
**22** Then Solomon stood before [a]the altar of the
LORD in the presence of all the assembly of Israel,
and [b]spread out his hands toward heaven;
23 and he said: "LORD God of Israel, [a]*there is* no
God in heaven above or on earth below like You,
[b]who keep *Your* covenant and mercy with Your
servants who [c]walk before You with all their
hearts.
24 "You have kept what You promised Your
servant David my father; You have both spoken
with Your mouth and fulfilled *it* with Your hand,
as *it is* this day.

25 "Therefore, LORD God of Israel, now keep
what You promised Your servant David my father, saying, [a]'You shall not fail to have a man sit
before Me on the throne of Israel, only if your
sons take heed to their way, that they walk before
Me as you have walked before Me.'
26 [a]"And now I pray, O God of Israel, let Your
word come true, which You have spoken to Your
servant David my father.
27 "But [a]will God indeed dwell on the earth?
Behold, heaven and the [b]heaven of heavens cannot contain You. How much less this temple
which I have built!
28 "Yet regard the prayer of Your servant and his
supplication, O LORD my God, and listen to the cry
and the prayer which Your servant is praying
before You today:
29 "that Your eyes may be open toward this
[1]temple night and day, toward the place of which
You said, [a]'My name shall be [b]there,' that You
may hear the prayer which Your servant makes
[c]toward this place.
30 [a]"And may You hear the supplication of Your
servant and of Your people Israel, when they pray
toward this place. Hear in heaven Your dwelling
place; and when You hear, forgive.
**31** "When anyone sins against his neighbor, and
is forced to take [a]an oath, and comes *and* takes an
oath before Your altar in this temple,
32 "then hear in heaven, and act, and judge Your
servants, [a]condemning the wicked, bringing his
way on his head, and justifying the righteous by
giving him according to his righteousness.
**33** [a]"When Your people Israel are defeated before
an enemy because they have sinned against You,
and [b]when they turn back to You and confess
Your name, and pray and make supplication to
You in this temple,
34 "then hear in heaven, and forgive the sin of
Your people Israel, and bring them back to the
land which You gave to their [a]fathers.
**35** [a]"When the heavens are shut up and there is
no rain because they have sinned against You,
when they pray toward this place and confess
Your name, and turn from their sin because You
afflict them,
36 "then hear in heaven, and forgive the sin of
Your servants, Your people Israel, that You may
[a]teach them [b]the good way in which they should
walk; and send rain on Your land which You have
given to Your people as an inheritance.
**37** [a]"When there is famine in the land, pestilence
*or* blight *or* mildew, locusts *or* grasshoppers; when
their enemy besieges them in the land of their
[1]cities; whatever plague or whatever sickness
*there is;*
38 "whatever prayer, whatever supplication is
made by anyone, *or* by all Your people Israel,
when each one knows the plague of his own
heart, and spreads out his hands toward this
temple:
39 "then hear in heaven Your dwelling place, and
forgive, and act, and give to everyone according
to all his ways, whose heart You know (for You
alone [a]know the hearts of all the sons of men),
40 [a]"that they may fear You all the days that
they live in the land which You gave to our
fathers.
**41** "Moreover, concerning a foreigner, who *is* not
of Your people Israel, but has come from a far
country for Your name's sake

**6** [a]2 Sam. 6:17 [b]1 Kin. 6:19 [c]1 Kin. 6:27
**8** [a]Ex. 25:13–15; 37:4, 5 [1]*heads*
**9** [a]Ex. 25:21 [b]Deut. 10:5 [c]Ex. 24:7, 8; 40:20 [d]Ex. 34:27, 28
**10** [a]Ex. 40:34, 35
**11** [a]2 Chr. 7:1, 2
**12** [a]2 Chr. 6:1 [b]Ps. 18:11; 97:2
**13** [a]2 Sam. 7:13 [b]Ps. 132:14
**14** [a]2 Sam. 6:18
**15** [a]Luke 1:68 [b]2 Sam. 7:2, 12, 13, 25
**16** [a]1 Kin. 8:29 [b]2 Sam. 7:8
**17** [a]2 Sam. 7:2, 3 [1]Lit. *house,* and so in vv. 18–20
**18** [a]2 Chr. 6:8, 9
**19** [a]2 Sam. 7:5, 12, 13
**20** [a]1 Chr. 28:5, 6 [1]*risen in the place of*
**21** [a]Deut. 31:26
**22** [a]2 Chr. 6:12 [b]Ezra 9:5
**23** [a]Ex. 15:11 [b][Neh. 1:5] [c][Gen. 17:1]
**25** [a]1 Kin. 2:4; 9:5
**26** [a]2 Sam. 7:25
**27** [a][Acts 7:49; 17:24] [b]2 Cor. 12:2
**29** [a]Deut. 12:11 [b]1 Kin. 9:3 [c]Dan. 6:10 [1]Lit. *house*
**30** [a]Neh. 1:6
**31** [a]Ex. 22:8–11
**32** [a]Deut. 25:1
**33** [a]Deut. 28:25 [b]Lev. 26:39, 40
**34** [a][Lev. 26:40–42]
**35** [a]Deut. 28:23
**36** [a]Ps. 25:4; 27:11; 94:12 [b]1 Sam. 12:23
**37** [a]Lev. 26:16, 25, 26 [1]Lit. *gates*
**39** [a][1 Sam. 16:7]
**40** [a][Ps. 130:4]

42 "(for they will hear of Your great name and
Your [a]strong hand and Your outstretched arm),
when he comes and prays toward this temple,
43 "hear in heaven Your dwelling place, and do
according to all for which the foreigner calls to
You, [a]that all peoples of the earth may know Your
name and [b]fear You, as *do* Your people Israel, and
that they may know that this temple which I have
built is called by Your name.
**44** "When Your people go out to battle against
their enemy, wherever You send them, and when
they pray to the LORD toward the city which You
have chosen and the temple which I have built for
Your name,
45 "then hear in heaven their prayer and their
supplication, and maintain their [1]cause.
**46** "When they sin against You [a](for *there is* no
one who does not sin), and You become angry
with them and deliver them to the enemy, and
they take them captive [b]to the land of the enemy,
far or near;
47 [a]"*yet* when they [1]come to themselves in the
land where they were carried captive, and repent,
and make supplication to You in the land of those
who took them captive, [b]saying, 'We have sinned
and done wrong, we have committed wickedness';
48 "and *when* they [a]return to You with all their
heart and with all their soul in the land of their
enemies who led them away captive, and [b]pray to
You toward their land which You gave to their
fathers, the city which You have chosen and the
temple which I have built for Your name:
49 "then hear in heaven Your dwelling place
their prayer and their supplication, and maintain
their [1]cause,
50 "and forgive Your people who have sinned
against You, and all their transgressions which
they have transgressed against You; and [a]grant
them compassion before those who took them
captive, that they may have compassion on them
51 "(for [a]they *are* Your people and Your inheritance, whom You brought out of Egypt, [b]out of
the iron furnace),
52 [a]"that Your eyes may be open to the supplication of Your servant and the supplication of Your
people Israel, to listen to them whenever they call
to You.
53 "For You separated them from among all the
peoples of the earth *to be* Your inheritance, [a]as
You spoke by Your servant Moses, when You
brought our fathers out of Egypt, O Lord GOD."
**54** [a]And so it was, when Solomon had finished
praying all this prayer and supplication to the
LORD, that he arose from before the altar of the
LORD, from kneeling on his knees with his hands
spread up to heaven.
55 Then he stood [a]and blessed all the assembly of
Israel with a loud voice, saying:
56 "Blessed *be* the LORD, who has given [a]rest[1] to
His people Israel, according to all that He promised. [b]There has not failed one word of all His good
promise, which He promised through His servant
Moses.
57 "May the LORD our God be with us, as He was
with our fathers. [a]May He not leave us nor forsake
us,
58 "that He may [a]incline our hearts to Himself, to
walk in all His ways, and to keep His commandments and His statutes and His judgments, which
He commanded our fathers.
59 "And may these words of mine, with which I
have made supplication before the LORD, be near
the LORD our God day and night, that He may
maintain the cause of His servant and the cause of
His people Israel, as each day may require,
60 [a]"that all the peoples of the earth may know
that [b]the LORD *is* God; *there is* no other.
61 "Let your [a]heart therefore be [1]loyal to the
LORD our God, to walk in His statutes and keep
His commandments, as at this day."
**62** Then [a]the king and all Israel with him offered
sacrifices before the LORD.
63 And Solomon offered a sacrifice of peace
offerings, which he offered to the LORD, twenty-
two thousand bulls and one hundred and twenty
thousand sheep. So the king and all the children
of Israel dedicated the house of the LORD.
64 On [a]the same day the king consecrated the
middle of the court that *was* in front of the house
of the LORD; for there he offered burnt offerings,
grain offerings, and the fat of the peace offerings,
because the [b]bronze altar that *was* before the
LORD *was* too small to receive the burnt offerings,
the grain offerings, and the fat of the peace
offerings.
65 At that time Solomon held [a]a feast, and all
Israel with him, a great assembly from [b]the entrance of Hamath to [c]the Brook of Egypt, before
the LORD our God, [d]seven days and seven *more*
days—fourteen days.
66 [a]On the eighth day he sent the people away;
and they [1]blessed the king, and went to their tents
joyful and glad of heart for all the good that the
LORD had done for His servant David, and for
Israel His people.

## *God's Promise to Solomon*

**9** And [a]it came to pass, when Solomon had
finished building the house of the LORD [b]and
the king's house, and [c]all Solomon's desire which
he wanted to do,
2 that the LORD appeared to Solomon the second time, [a]as He had appeared to him at Gibeon.
3 And the LORD said to him: [a]"I have heard your
prayer and your supplication that you have made
before Me; I have consecrated this house which
you have built [b]to put My name there forever,
[c]and My eyes and My heart will be there perpetually.
4 "Now if you [a]walk before Me [b]as your father
David walked, in integrity of heart and in uprightness, to do according to all that I have commanded you, *and* if you [c]keep My statutes and My
judgments,
5 "then I will establish the throne of your kingdom over Israel forever, [a]as I promised David your
father, saying, 'You shall not fail to have a man on
the throne of Israel.'
6 [a]"But if you or your sons at all [1]turn from
following Me, and do not keep My commandments *and* My statutes which I have set before
you, but go and serve other gods and worship
them,
7 [a]"then I will [1]cut off Israel from the land
which I have given them; and this house which I
have consecrated [b]for My name I will cast out of
My sight. [c]Israel will be a proverb and a byword
among all peoples.
8 "And *as for* [a]this house, *which* is exalted,
everyone who passes by it will be astonished and
will hiss, and say, [b]'Why has the LORD done thus
to this land and to this house?'

**42** [a]Deut. 3:24
**43** [a][1 Sam. 17:46] [b]Ps. 102:15
**45** [1]*justice*
**46** [a]Ps. 130:3 [b]Lev. 26:34, 44
**47** [a][Lev. 26:40–42] [b]Dan. 9:5 [1]Lit. *bring back to their heart*
**48** [a]Jer. 29:12–14 [b]Dan. 6:10
**49** [1]*justice*
**50** [a]Ps. 106:46
**51** [a]Deut. 9:26–29 [b]Jer. 11:4
**52** [a]1 Kin. 8:29
**53** [a]Ex. 19:5, 6
**54** [a]2 Chr. 7:1
**55** [a]2 Sam. 6:18
**56** [a]1 Chr. 22:18 [b]Deut. 12:10 [1]*peace*
**57** [a]Deut. 31:6
**58** [a]Ps. 119:36
**60** [a]1 Sam. 17:46 [b]Deut. 4:35, 39
**61** [a]Deut. 18:13 [1]Lit. *at peace with*
**62** [a]2 Chr. 7:4–10
**64** [a]2 Chr. 7:7 [b]2 Chr. 4:1
**65** [a]Lev. 23:34 [b]Num. 34:8 [c]Gen. 15:18 [d]2 Chr. 7:8
**66** [a]2 Chr. 7:9 [1]*thanked*

CHAPTER 9

**1** [a]2 Chr. 7:11 [b]1 Kin. 7:1 [c]2 Chr. 8:6
**2** [a]1 Kin. 3:5; 11:9
**3** [a]Ps. 10:17 [b]1 Kin. 8:29 [c]Deut. 11:12
**4** [a]Gen. 17:1 [b]1 Kin. 11:4, 6; 15:5 [c]1 Kin. 8:61
**5** [a]2 Sam. 7:12, 16
**6** [a]2 Sam. 7:14–16 [1]*turn back*
**7** [a][Lev. 18:24–29] [b][Jer. 7:4–14] [c]Ps. 44:14 [1]*destroy*
**8** [a]2 Chr. 7:21 [b][Deut. 29:24–26]

9 "Then they will answer, 'Because they forsook
the LORD their God, who brought their fathers out
of the land of Egypt, and have embraced other
gods, and worshiped them and served them; therefore the LORD has brought all this [a]calamity on
them.' "
**10** Now [a]it happened at the end of twenty years,
when Solomon had built the two houses, the
house of the LORD and the king's house
11 [a](Hiram the king of Tyre had supplied Solomon with cedar and cypress and gold, as much as
he desired), *that* King Solomon then gave Hiram
twenty cities in the land of Galilee.
12 Then Hiram went from Tyre to see the cities
which Solomon had given him, but they did not
please him.
13 So he said, "What *kind of* cities *are* these
which you have given me, my brother?" [a]And he
called them the land of [1]Cabul, as they are to this
day.
14 Then Hiram sent the king one hundred and
twenty talents of gold.
**15** And this *is* the reason for [a]the labor force
which King Solomon raised: to build the house of
the LORD, his own house, [1]the [b]Millo, the wall of
Jerusalem, [c]Hazor, [d]Megiddo, and [e]Gezer.
16 (Pharaoh king of Egypt had gone up and
taken Gezer and burned it with fire, [a]had killed
the Canaanites who dwelt in the city, and had
given it *as* a dowry to his daughter, Solomon's
wife.)
17 And Solomon built Gezer, Lower [a]Beth Horon,
18 [a]Baalath, and Tadmor in the wilderness, in the
land *of Judah,*
19 all the storage cities that Solomon had, cities
for [a]his chariots and cities for his [b]cavalry, and
whatever Solomon [c]desired to build in Jerusalem,
in Lebanon, and in all the land of his dominion.
**20** [a]All the people *who were* left of the Amorites,
Hittites, Perizzites, Hivites, and Jebusites, who
*were* not of the children of Israel—
21 that is, their descendants [a]who were left in the
land after them, [b]whom the children of Israel had
not been able to destroy completely—[c]from these
Solomon raised [d]forced labor, as it is to this day.
22 But of the children of Israel Solomon [a]made
no forced laborers, because they *were* men of war
and his servants: his officers, his captains, commanders of his chariots, and his cavalry.
**23** Others *were* chiefs of the officials who *were*
over Solomon's work: [a]five hundred and fifty, who
ruled over the people who did the work.
**24** But [a]Pharaoh's daughter came up from the
City of David to [b]her house which [1]*Solomon* had
built for her. [c]Then he built the Millo.
**25** [a]Now three times a year Solomon offered
burnt offerings and peace offerings on the altar
which he had built for the LORD, and he burned
incense with them *on the altar* that *was* before
the LORD. So he finished the temple.
**26** [a]King Solomon also built a fleet of ships at
[b]Ezion Geber, which *is* near [1]Elath on the shore of
the Red Sea, in the land of Edom.
27 [a]Then Hiram sent his servants with the fleet,
seamen who knew the sea, to work with the
servants of Solomon.
28 And they went to [a]Ophir, and acquired four
hundred and twenty talents of gold from there,
and brought *it* to King Solomon.

### *Solomon's Wealth and Fame*

**10** Now when the [a]queen of Sheba heard of the
fame of Solomon concerning the name of
the LORD, she came [b]to test him with hard questions.
2 She came to Jerusalem with a very great
[1]retinue, with camels that bore spices, very much
gold, and precious stones; and when she came to
Solomon, she spoke with him about all that was in
her heart.
3 So Solomon answered all her questions; there
was nothing [1]so difficult for the king that he could
not explain *it* to her.
4 And when the queen of Sheba had seen all the
wisdom of Solomon, the house that he had built,
5 the food on his table, the seating of his servants, the service of his waiters and their apparel,
his cupbearers, [a]and his entryway by which he
went up to the house of the LORD, there was no
more spirit in her.
6 Then she said to the king: "It was a true
report which I heard in my own land about your
words and your wisdom.
7 "However I did not believe the words until I
came and saw with my own eyes; and indeed the
half was not told me. Your wisdom and prosperity
exceed the fame of which I heard.
8 [a]"Happy *are* your men and happy *are* these
your servants, who stand continually before you
*and* hear your wisdom!
9 [a]"Blessed be the LORD your God, who [b]de-
lighted in you, setting you on the throne of Israel!
Because the LORD has loved Israel forever, therefore He made you king, [c]to do justice and righteousness."
10 Then she [a]gave the king one hundred and
twenty talents of gold, spices in great quantity,
and precious stones. There never again came such
abundance of spices as the queen of Sheba gave to
King Solomon.
**11** [a]Also, the ships of Hiram, which brought gold
from Ophir, brought great *quantities* of [1]almug
wood and precious stones from Ophir.
12 [a]And the king made [1]steps of the almug wood
for the house of the LORD and for the king's
house, also harps and stringed instruments for
singers. There never again came such [b]almug
wood, nor has the like been seen to this day.
13 Now King Solomon gave the queen of Sheba
all she desired, whatever she asked, besides what
Solomon had given her according to the royal
generosity. So she turned and went to her own
country, she and her servants.
**14** The weight of gold that came to Solomon
yearly was six hundred and sixty-six talents of
gold,
15 besides *that* from the [a]traveling merchants,
from the income of traders, [b]from all the kings of
Arabia, and from the governors of the country.
**16** And King Solomon made two hundred large
shields *of* hammered gold; six hundred *shekels* of
gold went into each shield.
17 He also *made* [a]three hundred shields *of* hammered gold; three minas of gold went into each
shield. The king put them in the [b]House of the
Forest of Lebanon.
**18** [a]Moreover the king made a great throne of
ivory, and overlaid it with pure gold.

**9** [a][Deut. 29:25–28]
**10** [a]1 Kin. 6:37, 38; 7:1; 2 Chr. 8:1
**11** [a]1 Kin. 5:1
**13** [a]Josh. 19:27 [1]Lit. *Good for Nothing*
**15** [a]1 Kin. 5:13 [b]2 Sam. 5:9; 1 Kin. 9:24 [c]Josh. 11:1; 19:36 [d]Josh. 17:11 [e]Josh. 16:10 [1]Lit. *The Landfill*
**16** [a]Josh. 16:10; Judg. 1:29
**17** [a]Josh. 10:10; 16:3; 21:22; 2 Chr. 8:5
**18** [a]Josh. 19:44; 2 Chr. 8:4
**19** [a]1 Kin. 10:26; 2 Chr. 1:14 [b]1 Kin. 4:26 [c]1 Kin. 9:1
**20** [a]2 Chr. 8:7
**21** [a]Judg. 1:21–36; 3:1 [b]Josh. 15:63; 17:12, 13 [c]Judg. 1:28, 35 [d]Ezra 2:55, 58; Neh. 7:57
**22** [a][Lev. 25:39]
**23** [a]2 Chr. 8:10
**24** [a]1 Kin. 3:1 [b]1 Kin. 7:8 [c]2 Sam. 5:9; 1 Kin. 11:27; 2 Chr. 32:5 [1]Lit. *he;* cf. 2 Chr. 8:11
**25** [a]Ex. 23:14–17; Deut. 16:16; 2 Chr. 8:12, 13
**26** [a]2 Chr. 8:17, 18 [b]Num. 33:35; Deut. 2:8; 1 Kin. 22:48 [1]Heb. *Eloth*
**27** [a]1 Kin. 5:6, 9; 10:11
**28** [a]Job 22:24

CHAPTER 10
**1** [a]2 Chr. 9:1; Matt. 12:42; Luke 11:31 [b]Judg. 14:12; Ps. 49:4; Prov. 1:6
**2** [1]*company*
**3** [1]*too*
**5** [a]1 Chr. 26:16; 2 Chr. 9:4
**8** [a]Prov. 8:34
**9** [a]1 Kin. 5:7 [b]2 Sam. 22:20 [c]2 Sam. 8:15; Ps. 72:2; [Prov. 8:15]
**10** [a]Ps. 72:10, 15
**11** [a]1 Kin. 9:27, 28; Job 22:24 [1]*algum,* 2 Chr. 9:10–11
**12** [a]2 Chr. 9:11 [b]2 Chr. 9:10 [1]Or *supports*
**15** [a]2 Chr. 1:16 [b]2 Chr. 9:24; Ps. 72:10
**17** [a]1 Kin. 14:26 [b]1 Kin. 7:2
**18** [a]1 Kin. 10:22; 2 Chr. 9:17; Ps. 45:8

19 The throne had six steps, and the top of the
throne *was* round at the back; *there were* armrests on either side of the place of the seat, and
two lions stood beside the armrests.
20 Twelve lions stood there, one on each side of
the six steps; nothing like *this* had been made for
any *other* kingdom.
**21** [a]All King Solomon's drinking vessels *were*
gold, and all the vessels of the House of the Forest
of Lebanon *were* pure gold. Not *one was* silver, for
this was accounted as nothing in the days of
Solomon.
22 For the king had [a]merchant[1] ships at sea with
the fleet of Hiram. Once every three years the
merchant [b]ships came bringing gold, silver, ivory,
apes, and [2]monkeys.
23 So [a]King Solomon surpassed all the kings of
the earth in riches and wisdom.
**24** Now all the earth sought the presence of
Solomon to hear his wisdom, which God had put
in his heart.
25 Each man brought his present: articles of
silver and gold, garments, armor, spices, horses,
and mules, at a set rate year by year.
**26** [a]And Solomon [b]gathered chariots and horsemen; he had one thousand four hundred chariots
and twelve thousand horsemen, whom he [1]sta-
tioned in the chariot cities and with the king at
Jerusalem.
27 [a]The king made silver *as common* in Jerusalem as stones, and he made cedar trees as abundant as the sycamores which *are* in the lowland.
**28** [a]Also Solomon had horses imported from
Egypt and Keveh; the king's merchants bought
them in Keveh at the *current* price.
29 Now a chariot that was imported from Egypt
cost six hundred *shekels* of silver, and a horse one
hundred and fifty; [a]and [1]thus, through their
agents, they exported *them* to all the kings of the
Hittites and the kings of Syria.

## *Solomon Turns Away from the LORD*

**11** But [a]King Solomon loved [b]many foreign
women, as well as the daughter of Pharaoh:
women of the Moabites, Ammonites, Edomites,
Sidonians, *and* Hittites—
2 from the nations of whom the LORD had said
to the children of Israel, [a]"You shall not inter-
marry with them, nor they with you. Surely they
will turn away your hearts after their gods."
Solomon clung to these in love.
3 And he had seven hundred wives, princesses,
and three hundred concubines; and his wives
turned away his heart.
4 For it was so, when Solomon was old, [a]that his
wives turned his heart after other gods; and his
[b]heart was not [1]loyal to the LORD his God, [c]as *was*
the heart of his father David.
5 For Solomon went after [a]Ashtoreth the goddess of the Sidonians, and after [b]Milcom[1] the
abomination of the [c]Ammonites.
6 Solomon did evil in the sight of the LORD, and
did not fully follow the LORD, as *did* his father
David.
7 [a]Then Solomon built a [1]high place for [b]Che-
mosh the abomination of Moab, on [c]the hill that *is*
east of Jerusalem, and for Molech the abomination of the people of Ammon.
8 And he did likewise for all his foreign wives,
who burned incense and sacrificed to their gods.
**9** So the LORD became angry with Solomon,
because his heart had turned from the LORD God
of Israel, [a]who had appeared to him twice,
10 and [a]had commanded him concerning this
thing, that he should not go after other gods; but
he did not keep what the LORD had commanded.
11 Therefore the LORD said to Solomon, "Because
you have done this, and have not kept My covenant and My statutes, which I have commanded
you, [a]I will surely tear the kingdom away from
you and give it to your [b]servant.
12 "Nevertheless I will not do it in your days, for
the sake of your father David; I will tear it out of
the hand of your son.
13 [a]"However I will not tear away the whole
kingdom; I will give [b]one tribe to your son [c]for the
sake of my servant David, and for the sake of
Jerusalem [d]which I have chosen."
**14** Now the LORD [a]raised up an adversary against
Solomon, Hadad the Edomite; he *was* a descendant of the king in Edom.
15 [a]For it happened, when David was in Edom,
and Joab the commander of the army had gone up
to bury the slain, [b]after he had killed every male in
Edom
16 (because for six months Joab remained there
with all Israel, until he had cut down every male
in Edom),
17 that Hadad fled to go to Egypt, he and certain
Edomites of his father's servants with him. Hadad
*was* still a little child.
18 Then they arose from Midian and came to
Paran; and they took men with them from Paran
and came to Egypt, to Pharaoh king of Egypt,
who gave him a house, apportioned food for him,
and gave him land.
19 And Hadad found great favor in the sight of
Pharaoh, so that he gave him as wife the sister of
his own wife, that is, the sister of Queen Tahpenes.
20 Then the sister of Tahpenes bore him Genubath his son, whom Tahpenes weaned in Pharaoh's house. And Genubath was in Pharaoh's
household among the sons of Pharaoh.
21 [a]So when Hadad heard in Egypt that David
[1]rested with his fathers, and that Joab the commander of the army was dead, Hadad said to
Pharaoh, [2]"Let me depart, that I may go to my
own country."
22 Then Pharaoh said to him, "But what have
you lacked with me, that suddenly you seek to go
to your own country?" So he answered, "Nothing,
but do let me go anyway."
**23** And God raised up *another* adversary against
him, Rezon the son of Eliadah, who had fled from
his lord, [a]Hadadezer king of Zobah.
24 So he gathered men to him and became captain over a band *of raiders*, [a]when David killed
those *of Zobah*. And they went to Damascus and
dwelt there, and reigned in Damascus.
25 He was an adversary of Israel all the days of
Solomon (besides the trouble that Hadad *caused*);
and he abhorred Israel, and reigned over Syria.
**26** Then Solomon's servant, [a]Jeroboam the son of
Nebat, an Ephraimite from Zereda, whose mother's name *was* Zeruah, a widow, [b]also [c]rebelled
against the king.
27 And this *is* what caused him to rebel against
the king: [a]Solomon had built the Millo *and* [1]re-
paired the damages to the City of David his father.
28 The man Jeroboam *was* a mighty man of
valor; and Solomon, seeing that the young man

**21** [a]2 Chr. 9:20
**22** [a]Gen. 10:4; 2 Chr. 20:36 [b]1 Kin. 9:26–28; 22:48; Ps. 72:10 [1]Lit. *ships of Tarshish,* deep-sea vessels [2]Or *peacocks*
**23** [a]1 Kin. 3:12, 13; 4:30; 2 Chr. 1:12
**26** [a]1 Kin. 4:26; 2 Chr. 1:14; 9:25 [b][Deut. 17:16]; 1 Kin. 9:19 [1]So with LXX, Syr., Tg., Vg. (cf. 2 Chr. 9:25); MT *led*
**27** [a][Deut. 17:17]; 2 Chr. 1:15–17
**28** [a][Deut. 17:16]; 2 Chr. 1:16; 9:28
**29** [a]Josh. 1:4; 2 Kin. 7:6, 7 [1]Lit. *by their hands*

CHAPTER 11
**1** [a][Neh. 13:26] [b][Deut. 17:17]; 1 Kin. 3:1
**2** [a]Ex. 34:16; [Deut. 7:3, 4]
**4** [a][Deut. 17:17; Neh. 13:26] [b]1 Kin. 8:61 [c]1 Kin. 9:4 [1]Lit. *at peace with*
**5** [a]Judg. 2:13; 1 Kin. 11:33 [b][Lev. 20:2–5] [c]2 Kin. 23:13 [1]Or *Molech*
**7** [a]Num. 33:52 [b]Num. 21:29; Judg. 11:24 [c]2 Kin. 23:13 [1]A place for pagan worship
**9** [a]1 Kin. 3:5; 9:2
**10** [a]1 Kin. 6:12; 9:6, 7
**11** [a]1 Kin. 11:31; 12:15, 16 [b]1 Kin. 11:31, 37
**13** [a]2 Sam. 7:15; 1 Chr. 17:13; Ps. 89:33 [b]1 Kin. 12:20 [c]2 Sam. 7:15, 16 [d]Deut. 12:11; 1 Kin. 9:3; 14:21
**14** [a]1 Chr. 5:26
**15** [a]2 Sam. 8:14; 1 Chr. 18:12, 13 [b]Num. 24:18, 19; [Deut. 20:13]
**21** [a]1 Kin. 2:10, 34 [1]Died and joined his ancestors [2]Lit. *Send me away*
**23** [a]2 Sam. 8:3; 10:16
**24** [a]2 Sam. 8:3; 10:8, 18
**26** [a]1 Kin. 12:2 [b]1 Kin. 11:11; 2 Chr. 13:6 [c]2 Sam. 20:21
**27** [a]1 Kin. 9:15, 24 [1]Lit. *closed up the breaches*

was [a]industrious, made him the officer over all the
labor force of the house of Joseph.
29 Now it happened at that time, when Jeroboam
went out of Jerusalem, that the prophet [a]Ahijah
the Shilonite met him on the way; and he had
clothed himself with a new garment, and the two
*were* alone in the field.
30 Then Ahijah took hold of the new garment
that *was* on him, and [a]tore it *into* twelve pieces.
31 And he said to Jeroboam, "Take for yourself
ten pieces, for [a]thus says the LORD, the God of
Israel: 'Behold, I will tear the kingdom out of the
hand of Solomon and will give ten tribes to you
32 '(but he shall have one tribe for the sake of My
servant David, and for the sake of Jerusalem, the
city which I have chosen out of all the tribes of
Israel),
33 [a]'because [1]they have forsaken Me, and worshiped Ashtoreth the goddess of the Sidonians,
Chemosh the god of the Moabites, and Milcom the
god of the people of Ammon, and have not walked
in My ways to do *what is* right in My eyes and
*keep* My statutes and My judgments, as *did* his
father David.
34 'However I will not take the whole kingdom
out of his hand, because I have made him ruler all
the days of his life for the sake of My servant
David, whom I chose because he kept My commandments and My statutes.
35 'But [a]I will take the kingdom out of his son's
hand and give it to you—ten tribes.
36 'And to his son I will give one tribe, that [a]My
servant David may always have a lamp before Me
in Jerusalem, the city which I have chosen for
Myself, to put My name there.
37 'So I will take you, and you shall reign over all
your heart desires, and you shall be king over
Israel.
38 'Then it shall be, if you heed all that I command you, walk in My ways, and do *what is* right
in My sight, to keep My statutes and My commandments, as My servant David did, then [a]I will
be with you and [b]build for you an enduring house,
as I built for David, and will give Israel to you.
39 'And I will afflict the descendants of David
because of this, but not forever.' "
40 Solomon therefore sought to kill Jeroboam.
But Jeroboam arose and fled to Egypt, to [a]Shishak
king of Egypt, and was in Egypt until the death of
Solomon.
**41** Now [a]the rest of the acts of Solomon, all that
he did, and his wisdom, *are* they not written in the
book of the acts of Solomon?
42 [a]And the period that Solomon reigned in Jerusalem over all Israel *was* forty years.
43 [a]Then Solomon [1]rested with his fathers, and
was buried in the City of David his father. And
Rehoboam his son reigned in his [b]place.

### *Rehoboam Made King*

**12** And [a]Rehoboam went to [b]Shechem, for all
Israel had gone to Shechem to make him
king.
2 So it happened, when [a]Jeroboam the son of
Nebat heard *it* (he was still in [b]Egypt, for he had
fled from the presence of King Solomon and had
been dwelling in Egypt),
3 that they sent and called him. Then Jeroboam
and the whole assembly of Israel came and spoke
to Rehoboam, saying,
4 "Your father made our [a]yoke [1]heavy; now
therefore, lighten the burdensome service of your
father, and his heavy yoke which he put on us,
and we will serve you."
5 So he said to them, "Depart *for* three days,
then come back to me." And the people departed.
**6** Then King Rehoboam consulted the elders
who stood before his father Solomon while he still
lived, and he said, "How do you advise *me* to
answer these people?"
7 And they spoke to him, saying, [a]"If you will be
a servant to these people today, and serve them,
and answer them, and speak good words to them,
then they will be your servants forever."
8 But he rejected the advice which the elders
had given him, and consulted the young men who
had grown up with him, who stood before him.
9 And he said to them, "What advice do you
give? How should we answer this people who
have spoken to me, saying, 'Lighten the yoke
which your father put on us'?"
10 Then the young men who had grown up with
him spoke to him, saying, "Thus you should speak
to this people who have spoken to you, saying,
'Your father made our yoke heavy, but you make
*it* lighter on us'—thus you shall say to them: 'My
little *finger* shall be thicker than my father's waist!
11 'And now, whereas my father put a heavy
yoke on you, I will add to your yoke; my father
chastised you with whips, but I will chastise you
with [1]scourges!' "
**12** So Jeroboam and all the people came to Rehoboam the third day, as the king had directed,
saying, "Come back to me the third day."
13 Then the king answered the people [1]roughly,
and rejected the [2]advice which the elders had
given him;
14 and he spoke to them according to the advice
of the young men, saying, "My father made your
yoke heavy, but I will add to your yoke; my father
chastised you with whips, but I will chastise you
with [1]scourges!"
15 So the king did not listen to the people; for
[a]the turn *of events* was from the LORD, that He
might fulfill His word, which the LORD had [b]spo-
ken by Ahijah the Shilonite to Jeroboam the son
of Nebat.
**16** Now when all Israel saw that the king did not
listen to them, the people answered the king,
saying:

> [a]"What share have we in David?
> *We have* no inheritance in the son of Jesse.
> To your tents, O Israel!
> Now see to your own house, O David!"

So Israel departed to their tents.
17 But Rehoboam reigned over [a]the children of
Israel who dwelt in the cities of Judah.
18 Then King Rehoboam [a]sent Adoram, who *was*
in charge of the revenue; but all Israel stoned him
with stones, and he died. Therefore King Rehoboam mounted his chariot in haste to flee to
Jerusalem.
19 So [a]Israel has been in rebellion against the
house of David to this day.
20 Now it came to pass when all Israel heard that
Jeroboam had come back, they sent for him and
called him to the congregation, and made him
king over all [a]Israel. There was none who followed
the house of David, but the tribe of Judah [b]only.
**21** And when [a]Rehoboam came to Jerusalem, he
assembled all the house of Judah with the tribe of

**28** [a][Prov. 22:29]
**29** [a]1 Kin. 12:15; 14:2; 2 Chr. 9:29
**30** [a]1 Sam. 15:27, 28; 24:5
**31** [a]1 Kin. 11:11, 13
**33** [a]1 Sam. 7:3; 1 Kin. 11:5–8 [1]So with MT, Tg.; LXX, Syr., Vg. *he has*
**35** [a]1 Kin. 12:16, 17
**36** [a][1 Kin. 15:4; 2 Kin. 8:19]
**38** [a]Deut. 31:8; Josh. 1:5 [b]2 Sam. 7:11, 27
**40** [a]1 Kin. 11:17; 14:25; 2 Chr. 12:2–9
**41** [a]2 Chr. 9:29
**42** [a]2 Chr. 9:30
**43** [a]1 Kin. 2:10; 2 Chr. 9:31 [b]1 Kin. 14:21; 2 Chr. 10:1 [1]Died and joined his ancestors

CHAPTER 12

**1** [a]2 Chr. 10:1 [b]Judg. 9:6
**2** [a]1 Kin. 11:26 [b]1 Kin. 11:40
**4** [a]1 Sam. 8:11–18; 1 Kin. 4:7; 5:13–15 [1]*hard*
**7** [a]2 Chr. 10:7; [Prov. 15:1]
**11** [1]Scourges with points or barbs, lit. *scorpions*
**13** [1]*harshly* [2]*advice*
**14** [1]Lit. *scorpions*
**15** [a]Deut. 2:30; Judg. 14:4; 1 Kin. 12:24; 2 Chr. 10:15 [b]1 Kin. 11:11, 29, 31
**16** [a]2 Sam. 20:1
**17** [a]1 Kin. 11:13, 36; 2 Chr. 11:14–17
**18** [a]1 Kin. 4:6; 5:14
**19** [a]2 Kin. 17:21
**20** [a]2 Kin. 17:21 [b]1 Kin. 11:13, 32, 36
**21** [a]2 Chr. 11:1–4

[b]Benjamin, one hundred and eighty thousand
chosen *men* who were warriors, to fight against
the house of Israel, that he might restore the
kingdom to Rehoboam the son of Solomon.
22 But [a]the word of God came to Shemaiah the
man of God, saying,
23 "Speak to Rehoboam the son of Solomon, king
of Judah, to all the house of Judah and Benjamin,
and to the rest of the people, saying,
24 'Thus says the LORD: "You shall not go up nor
fight against your brethren the children of Israel.
Let every man return to his house, [a]for this thing
is from Me."'" Therefore they obeyed the word of
the LORD, and turned back, according to the word
of the LORD.
**25** Then Jeroboam [a]built[1] Shechem in the mountains of Ephraim, and dwelt there. Also he went
out from there and built [b]Penuel.
26 And Jeroboam said in his heart, "Now the
kingdom may return to the house of David:
27 "If these people [a]go up to offer sacrifices in the
house of the LORD at Jerusalem, then the heart of
this people will turn back to their lord, Rehoboam
king of Judah, and they will kill me and go back to
Rehoboam king of Judah."
28 Therefore the king asked advice, [a]made two
calves of gold, and said to the people, "It is too
much for you to go up to Jerusalem. [b]Here are
your gods, O Israel, which brought you up from
the land of Egypt!"
29 And he set up one in [a]Bethel, and the other he
put in [b]Dan.
30 Now this thing became [a]a sin, for the people
went *to worship* before the one as far as Dan.
31 He made [1]shrines on the high places, [a]and
made priests from every class of people, who were
not of the sons of Levi.
32 Jeroboam [1]ordained a feast on the fifteenth
day of the eighth month, like [a]the feast that *was*
in Judah, and offered sacrifices on the altar. So he
did at Bethel, sacrificing to the calves that he had
made. [b]And at Bethel he installed the priests of the
high places which he had made.
33 So he made offerings on the altar which he
had made at Bethel on the fifteenth day of the
eighth month, in the month which he had [a]devised
in his own heart. And he [1]ordained a feast for the
children of Israel, and offered sacrifices on the
altar and [b]burned incense.

## *A Prophet of Judah Warns Jeroboam*

**13** And behold, [a]a man of God went from Judah to Bethel [1]by the word of the LORD,
[b]and Jeroboam stood by the altar to burn incense.
2 Then he cried out against the altar [1]by the
word of the LORD, and said, "O altar, altar! Thus
says the LORD: 'Behold, a child, [a]Josiah by name,
shall be born to the house of David; and on you he
shall sacrifice the priests of the high places who
burn incense on you, and men's bones shall be
[b]burned on you.'"
3 And he gave [a]a sign the same day, saying,
"This *is* the sign which the LORD has spoken:
Surely the altar shall split apart, and the ashes on
it shall be poured out."
4 So it came to pass when King Jeroboam heard
the saying of the man of God, who cried out
against the altar in Bethel, that he stretched out
his hand from the altar, saying, "Arrest him!"
Then his hand, which he stretched out toward
him, withered, so that he could not pull it back to
himself.
5 The altar also was split apart, and the ashes
poured out from the altar, according to the sign
which the man of God had given by the word of
the LORD.
6 Then the king answered and said to the man
of God, "Please [a]entreat the favor of the LORD
your God, and pray for me, that my hand may be
restored to me." So the man of God entreated the
LORD, and the king's hand was restored to him,
and became as before.
7 Then the king said to the man of God, "Come
home with me and refresh yourself, and [a]I will
give you a reward."
8 But the man of God said to the king, [a]"If you
were to give me half your house, I would not go in
with you; nor would I eat bread nor drink water in
this place.
9 "For so it was commanded me by the word of
the LORD, saying, [a]'You shall not eat bread, nor
drink water, nor return by the same way you
came.'"
10 So he went another way and did not return by
the way he came to Bethel.
**11** Now an [a]old prophet dwelt in Bethel, and his
[1]sons came and told him all the works that the
man of God had done that day in Bethel; they also
told their father the words which he had spoken
to the king.
12 And their father said to them, "Which way did
he go?" For his sons [1]had seen which way the man
of God went who came from Judah.
13 Then he said to his sons, "Saddle the donkey
for me." So they saddled the donkey for him; and
he rode on it,
14 and went after the man of God, and found him
sitting under an oak. Then he said to him, "*Are*
you the man of God who came from Judah?" And
he said, "I *am.*"
15 Then he said to him, "Come home with me
and eat bread."
16 And he said, [a]"I cannot return with you nor go
in with you; neither can I eat bread nor drink
water with you in this place.
17 "For [1]I have been told [a]by the word of the
LORD, 'You shall not eat bread nor drink water
there, nor return by going the way you came.'"
18 He said to him, "I too *am* a prophet as you *are,*
and an angel spoke to me by the word of the
LORD, saying, 'Bring him back with you to your
house, that he may eat bread and drink water.'"
(He was lying to him.)
19 So he went back with him, and ate bread in his
house, and drank water.
**20** Now it happened, as they sat at the table, that
the word of the LORD came to the prophet who
had brought him back;
21 and he cried out to the man of God who came
from Judah, saying, "Thus says the LORD: 'Because you have disobeyed the word of the LORD,
and have not kept the commandment which the
LORD your God commanded you,
22 'but you came back, ate bread, and drank
water in the [a]place of which *the LORD* said to you,
"Eat no bread and drink no water," your corpse
shall not come to the tomb of your fathers.'"
**23** So it was, after he had eaten bread and after
he had drunk, that he saddled the donkey for him,
the prophet whom he had brought back.
24 When he was gone, [a]a lion met him on the

**21** [b]2 Sam. 19:17
**22** [a]2 Chr. 11:2; 12:5–7
**24** [a]1 Kin. 12:15
**25** [a]Gen. 12:6; Judg. 9:45–49; 1 Kin. 12:1 [b]Gen. 32:30, 31; Judg. 8:8, 17 [1]*fortified*
**27** [a][Deut. 12:5–7, 14]
**28** [a]2 Kin. 10:29; 17:16; [Hos. 8:4–7] [b]Ex. 32:4, 8
**29** [a]Gen. 28:19 [b]Judg. 18:26–31
**30** [a]1 Kin. 13:34; 2 Kin. 17:21
**31** [a][Num. 3:10; 17:1–11]; Judg. 17:5; 1 Kin. 13:33; 2 Kin. 17:32; 2 Chr. 11:14, 15 [1]Lit. *house,* cf. 1 Kin. 13:32 lit. *houses*
**32** [a]Lev. 23:33, 34; Num. 29:12; 1 Kin. 8:2, 5 [b]Amos 7:10–13 [1]*instituted*
**33** [a]Num. 15:39 [b]1 Kin. 13:1 [1]*instituted*

CHAPTER 13
**1** [a]2 Kin. 23:17 [b]1 Kin. 12:32, 33 [1]*at the LORD's command*
**2** [a]2 Kin. 23:15, 16 [b][Lev. 26:30] [1]*at the LORD's command*
**3** [a]Ex. 4:1–5; Judg. 6:17; Is. 7:14; 38:7; John 2:18; 1 Cor. 1:22
**6** [a]Ex. 8:8; 9:28; 10:17; Num. 21:7; Jer. 37:3; Acts 8:24; [James 5:16]
**7** [a]1 Sam. 9:7; 2 Kin. 5:15
**8** [a]Num. 22:18; 24:13; 1 Kin. 13:16, 17
**9** [a][1 Cor. 5:11]
**11** [a]1 Kin. 13:25 [1]Lit. *son*
**12** [1]LXX, Syr., Tg., Vg. *showed him*
**16** [a]1 Kin. 13:8, 9
**17** [a]1 Kin. 20:35; 1 Thess. 4:15 [1]Lit. *a command came to me by*
**22** [a]1 Kin. 13:9
**24** [a]1 Kin. 20:36

road and killed him. And his corpse was thrown on the road, and the donkey stood by it. The lion also stood by the corpse.
25 And there, men passed by and saw the corpse thrown on the road, and the lion standing by the corpse. Then they went and told *it* in the city where the old prophet dwelt.
26 Now when the prophet who had brought him back from the way heard *it,* he said, "It *is* the man of God who was disobedient to the word of the LORD. Therefore the LORD has delivered him to the lion, which has torn him and killed him, according to the word of the LORD which He spoke to him."
27 And he spoke to his sons, saying, "Saddle the donkey for me." So they saddled *it.*
28 Then he went and found his corpse thrown on the road, and the donkey and the lion standing by the corpse. The lion had not eaten the corpse nor torn the donkey.
29 And the prophet took up the corpse of the man of God, laid it on the donkey, and brought it back. So the old prophet came to the city to mourn, and to bury him.
30 Then he laid the corpse in his own tomb; and they mourned over him, *saying,* [a]"Alas, my brother!"
31 So it was, after he had buried him, that he spoke to his sons, saying, "When I am dead, then bury me in the tomb where the man of God *is* buried; [a]lay my bones beside his bones.
32 [a]"For the [1]saying which he cried out by the word of the LORD against the altar in Bethel, and against all the [2]shrines on the high places which *are* in the cities of [b]Samaria, will surely come to pass."
**33** [a]After this event Jeroboam did not turn from his evil way, but again he made priests from every class of people for the high places; whoever wished, he consecrated him, and he became *one* of the priests of the high places.
34 [a]And this thing was the sin of the house of Jeroboam, so as [b]to exterminate and destroy *it* from the face of the earth.

### *Ahijah's Prophecy Against Jeroboam*

**14** At that time Abijah the son of Jeroboam became sick.
2 And Jeroboam said to his wife, "Please arise, and disguise yourself, that they may not recognize you as the wife of Jeroboam, and go to Shiloh. Indeed, Ahijah the prophet *is* there, who told me that [a]*I would be* king over this people.
3 [a]"Also take [1]with you ten loaves, *some* cakes, and a jar of honey, and go to him; he will tell you what will become of the child."
4 And Jeroboam's wife did so; she arose [a]and went to Shiloh, and came to the house of Ahijah. But Ahijah could not see, for his eyes were [1]glazed by reason of his age.
**5** Now the LORD had said to Ahijah, "Here is the wife of Jeroboam, coming to ask you something about her son, for he *is* sick. Thus and thus you shall say to her; for it will be, when she comes in, that she will pretend *to be* another *woman.*"
6 And so it was, when Ahijah heard the sound of her footsteps as she came through the door, he said, "Come in, wife of Jeroboam. Why do you pretend *to be* another *person?* For I *have been* sent to you *with* bad *news.*
7 "Go, tell Jeroboam, 'Thus says the LORD God of Israel: [a]"Because I exalted you from among the people, and made you ruler over My people Israel,
8 "and [a]tore the kingdom away from the house of David, and gave it to you; and *yet* you have not been as My servant David, [b]who kept My commandments and who followed Me with all his heart, to do only *what was* right in My eyes;
9 "but you have done more evil than all who were before you, [a]for you have gone and made for yourself other gods and molded images to provoke Me to anger, and [b]have cast Me behind your back—
10 "therefore behold! [a]I will bring disaster on the house of Jeroboam, and [b]will cut off from Jeroboam every male in Israel, [c]bond and free; I will take away the remnant of the house of Jeroboam, as one takes away refuse until it is all gone.
11 "The dogs shall eat [a]whoever belongs to Jeroboam and dies in the city, and the birds of the air shall eat whoever dies in the field; for the LORD has spoken!" '
12 "Arise therefore, go to your own house. [a]When your feet enter the city, the child shall die.
13 "And all Israel shall mourn for him and bury him, for he is the only one of Jeroboam who shall [1]come to the grave, because in him [a]there is found something good toward the LORD God of Israel in the house of Jeroboam.
14 [a]"Moreover the LORD will raise up for Himself a king over Israel who shall cut off the house of Jeroboam; [1]this is the day. What? Even now!
15 "For the LORD will strike Israel, as a reed is shaken in the water. He will [a]uproot Israel from this [b]good land which He gave to their fathers, and will scatter them [c]beyond [1]the River, [d]because they have made their [2]wooden images, provoking the LORD to anger.
16 "And He will give Israel up because of the sins of Jeroboam, [a]who sinned and who made Israel sin."
**17** Then Jeroboam's wife arose and departed, and came to [a]Tirzah. [b]When she came to the threshold of the house, the child died.
18 And they buried him; and all Israel mourned for him, [a]according to the word of the LORD which He spoke through His servant Ahijah the prophet.
**19** Now the rest of the acts of Jeroboam, how he [a]made war and how he reigned, indeed they *are* written in the book of the chronicles of the kings of Israel.
20 The period that Jeroboam reigned *was* twenty-two years. So he rested with his fathers. Then [a]Nadab his son reigned in his place.
**21** And Rehoboam the son of Solomon reigned in Judah. [a]Rehoboam *was* forty-one years old when he became king. He reigned seventeen years in Jerusalem, the city [b]which the LORD had chosen out of all the tribes of Israel, to put His name there. [c]His mother's name *was* Naamah, an Ammonitess.
22 [a]Now Judah did evil in the sight of the LORD, and they [b]provoked Him to jealousy with their sins which they committed, more than all that their fathers had done.
23 For they also built for themselves [a]high[1] places, [b]*sacred* pillars, and [c]wooden images on every high hill and [d]under every green tree.
24 [a]And there were also [1]perverted persons in the land. They did according to all the [b]abominations of the nations which the LORD had cast out before the children of [c]Israel.

**30** [a]Jer. 22:18
**31** [a]2 Kin. 23:17, 18
**32** [a]2 Kin. 23:16, 19 [b]1 Kin. 16:24 [1]Lit. *word* [2]Lit. *houses*
**33** [a]1 Kin. 12:31, 32
**34** [a]1 Kin. 12:30 [b][1 Kin. 14:10; 15:29, 30]

CHAPTER 14

**2** [a]1 Kin. 11:29–31
**3** [a]1 Sam. 9:7, 8 [1]Lit. *in your hand*
**4** [a]1 Kin. 11:29 [1]Lit. *set*
**7** [a]1 Kin. 16:2
**8** [a]1 Kin. 11:31 [b]1 Kin. 11:33, 38; 15:5
**9** [a]1 Kin. 12:28 [b]Ps. 50:17
**10** [a]1 Kin. 15:29 [b]1 Kin. 21:21 [c]Deut. 32:36
**11** [a]1 Kin. 16:4; 21:24
**12** [a]1 Kin. 14:17
**13** [a]2 Chr. 12:12; 19:3 [1]Be buried
**14** [a]1 Kin. 15:27–29 [1]Or *this day and from now on*
**15** [a]2 Kin. 17:6 [b][Josh. 23:15, 16] [c]2 Kin. 15:29 [d][Ex. 34:13, 14] [1]The Euphrates [2]Or *Asherim,* Canaanite deities
**16** [a]1 Kin. 12:30; 13:34; 15:30, 34; 16:2
**17** [a]Song 6:4 [b]1 Kin. 14:12
**18** [a]1 Kin. 14:13
**19** [a]2 Chr. 13:2–20
**20** [a]1 Kin. 15:25
**21** [a]2 Chr. 12:13 [b]1 Kin. 11:32, 36 [c]1 Kin. 14:31
**22** [a]2 Chr. 12:1, 14 [b]Deut. 32:21
**23** [a]Deut. 12:2 [b][Deut. 16:22] [c][2 Kin. 17:9, 10] [d]Is. 57:5 [1]Places for pagan worship
**24** [a]Deut. 23:17 [b]Deut. 20:18 [c][Deut. 9:4, 5] [1]Heb. *qedeshim,* those practicing sodomy and prostitution in religious rituals

**25** [a]It happened in the fifth year of King Rehoboam *that* Shishak king of Egypt came up against
Jerusalem.
26 [a]And he took away the treasures of the house
of the LORD and the treasures of the king's house;
he took away everything. He also took away all
the gold shields [b]which Solomon had made.
27 Then King Rehoboam made bronze shields in
their place, and [1]committed *them* to the hands of
the captains of the [2]guard, who guarded the
doorway of the king's house.
28 And whenever the king entered the house of
the LORD, the guards carried them, then brought
them back into the guardroom.
**29** [a]Now the rest of the acts of Rehoboam, and all
that he did, *are* they not written in the book of the
chronicles of the kings of Judah?
30 And there was [a]war between Rehoboam and
Jeroboam all *their* days.
31 [a]So Rehoboam [1]rested with his fathers, and
was buried with his fathers in the City of David.
[b]His mother's name *was* Naamah, an Ammonitess.
Then [c]Abijam[2] his son reigned in his place.

## *The Reigns of Abijam, Asa, Nadab, and Baasha*

**15** [a]In the eighteenth year of King Jeroboam
the son of Nebat, Abijam became king over
Judah.
2 He reigned three years in Jerusalem. [a]His
mother's name *was* [b]Maachah the granddaughter
of [c]Abishalom.
3 And he walked in all the sins of his father,
which he had done before him; [a]his heart was not
[1]loyal to the LORD his God, as was the heart of his
father David.
4 Nevertheless [a]for David's sake the LORD his
God gave him a lamp in Jerusalem, by setting up
his son after him and by establishing Jerusalem;
5 because David [a]did *what was* right in the eyes
of the LORD, and had not turned aside from
anything that He commanded him all the days of
his life, [b]except in the matter of Uriah the Hittite.
6 [a]And there was war between [1]Rehoboam and
Jeroboam all the days of his life.
7 [a]Now the rest of the acts of Abijam, and all
that he did, *are* they not written in the book of the
chronicles of the kings of Judah? And there was
war between Abijam and Jeroboam.
8 [a]So Abijam [1]rested with his fathers, and they
buried him in the City of David. Then Asa his son
reigned in his place.
**9** In the twentieth year of Jeroboam king of
Israel, Asa became king over Judah.
10 And he reigned forty-one years in Jerusalem.
His grandmother's name *was* Maachah the granddaughter of Abishalom.
11 [a]Asa did *what was* right in the eyes of the
LORD, as *did* his father David.
12 [a]And he banished the [1]perverted persons from
the land, and removed all the idols that his fathers
had made.
13 Also he removed [a]Maachah his grandmother
from *being* queen mother, because she had made
an obscene image of [1]Asherah. And Asa cut down
her obscene image and [b]burned *it* by the Brook
Kidron.
14 [a]But the [1]high places were not removed. Nevertheless Asa's [b]heart was loyal to the LORD all his
days.
15 He also brought into the house of the LORD
the things which his father [a]had dedicated, and
the things which he himself had dedicated: silver
and gold and utensils.
**16** Now there was war between Asa and Baasha
king of Israel all their days.
17 And [a]Baasha king of Israel came up against
Judah, and built [b]Ramah, [c]that he might let none
go out or come in to Asa king of Judah.
18 Then Asa took all the silver and gold *that was*
left in the treasuries of the house of the LORD and
the treasuries of the king's house, and delivered
them into the hand of his servants. And King Asa
sent them to [a]Ben-Hadad the son of Tabrimmon,
the son of Hezion, king of Syria, who dwelt in
[b]Damascus, saying,
19 "*Let there be* a treaty between you and me, as
there was between my father and your father. See,
I have sent you a present of silver and gold. Come
and break your treaty with Baasha king of Israel,
so that he will withdraw from me."
20 So Ben-Hadad heeded King Asa, and [a]sent the
captains of his armies against the cities of Israel.
He attacked [b]Ijon, [c]Dan, [d]Abel Beth Maachah, and
all Chinneroth, with all the land of Naphtali.
21 Now it happened, when Baasha heard *it*, that
he stopped building Ramah, and remained in
[a]Tirzah.
22 [a]Then King Asa made a proclamation
throughout all Judah; none *was* exempted. And
they took away the stones and timber of Ramah,
which Baasha had used for building; and with
them King Asa built [b]Geba of Benjamin, and
[c]Mizpah.
**23** The rest of all the acts of Asa, all his might, all
that he did, and the cities which he built, *are* they
not written in the book of the chronicles of the
kings of Judah? But [a]in the time of his old age he
was diseased in his feet.
24 So Asa [1]rested with his fathers, and was buried
with his fathers in the City of David his father.
[a]Then [b]Jehoshaphat his son reigned in his place.
**25** Now [a]Nadab the son of Jeroboam became king
over Israel in the second year of Asa king of
Judah, and he reigned over Israel two years.
26 And he did evil in the sight of the LORD, and
walked in the way of his father, and in [a]his sin by
which he had made Israel sin.
27 [a]Then Baasha the son of Ahijah, of the house
of Issachar, conspired against him. And Baasha
killed him at [b]Gibbethon, which *belonged* to the
Philistines, while Nadab and all Israel laid siege to
Gibbethon.
28 Baasha killed him in the third year of Asa king
of Judah, and reigned in his place.
29 And it was so, when he became king, *that* he
killed all the house of Jeroboam. He did not leave
to Jeroboam anyone that breathed, until he had
destroyed him, according to [a]the word of the LORD
which He had spoken by His servant Ahijah the
Shilonite,
30 [a]because of the sins of Jeroboam, which he
had sinned and by which he had made Israel sin,
because of his provocation with which he had
provoked the LORD God of Israel to anger.
**31** Now the rest of the acts of Nadab, and all that
he did, *are* they not written in the book of the
chronicles of the kings of Israel?
32 [a]And there was war between Asa and Baasha
king of Israel all their days.
**33** In the third year of Asa king of Judah, Baasha

**25** [a]1 Kin. 11:40
**26** [a]2 Chr. 12:9–11 [b]1 Kin. 10:17
**27** [1]*entrusted* [2]Lit. *runners*
**29** [a]2 Chr. 12:15, 16
**30** [a]1 Kin. 12:21–24; 15:6
**31** [a]2 Chr. 12:16 [b]1 Kin. 14:21 [c]2 Chr. 12:16 [1]Died and joined his ancestors [2]*Abijah,* 2 Chr. 12:16

CHAPTER 15
**1** [a]2 Chr. 13:1
**2** [a]2 Chr. 11:20–22 [b]2 Chr. 13:2 [c]2 Chr. 11:21
**3** [a]Ps. 119:80 [1]Lit. *at peace with*
**4** [a]2 Sam. 21:17
**5** [a]1 Kin. 9:4; 14:8 [b]2 Sam. 11:3, 15–17; 12:9, 10
**6** [a]1 Kin. 14:30 [1]So with MT, LXX, Tg., Vg.; some Heb. mss., Syr. *Abijam*
**7** [a]2 Chr. 13:2–22
**8** [a]2 Chr. 14:1 [1]Died and joined his ancestors
**11** [a]2 Chr. 14:2
**12** [a]1 Kin. 14:24; 22:46 [1]Heb. *qedeshim,* those practicing sodomy and prostitution in religious rituals
**13** [a]2 Chr. 15:16–18 [b]Ex. 32:20 [1]A Canaanite goddess
**14** [a]1 Kin. 3:2; 22:43 [b]1 Kin. 8:61; 15:3 [1]Places for pagan worship
**15** [a]1 Kin. 7:51
**17** [a]2 Chr. 16:1–6 [b]Josh. 18:25 [c]1 Kin. 12:26–29
**18** [a]2 Chr. 16:2 [b]1 Kin. 11:23, 24
**20** [a]1 Kin. 20:1 [b]2 Kin. 15:29 [c]Judg. 18:29 [d]2 Sam. 20:14, 15
**21** [a]1 Kin. 14:17; 16:15–18
**22** [a]2 Chr. 16:6 [b]Josh. 21:17 [c]Josh. 18:26
**23** [a]2 Chr. 16:11–14
**24** [a]2 Chr. 17:1 [b]Matt. 1:8 [1]Died and joined his ancestors
**25** [a]1 Kin. 14:20
**26** [a]1 Kin. 12:28–33; 14:16
**27** [a]1 Kin. 14:14 [b]Josh. 19:44; 21:23
**29** [a]1 Kin. 14:10–14
**30** [a]1 Kin. 14:9, 16
**32** [a]1 Kin. 15:16

the son of Ahijah became king over all Israel in
Tirzah, and *reigned* twenty-four years.
34 He did evil in the sight of the LORD, and
walked in [a]the way of Jeroboam, and in his sin by
which he had made Israel sin.

### *The Reigns of Elah, Zimri, Omri, and Ahab*

**16** Then the word of the LORD came to [a]Jehu
the son of [b]Hanani, against [c]Baasha, saying:
2 [a]"Inasmuch as I lifted you out of the dust and
made you ruler over My people Israel, and [b]you
have walked in the way of Jeroboam, and have
made My people Israel sin, to provoke Me to
anger with their sins,
3 "surely I will [a]take[1] away the posterity of
Baasha and the posterity of his house, and I will
make your house like [b]the house of Jeroboam the
son of Nebat.
4 "The dogs shall eat [a]whoever belongs to Baasha and dies in the city, and the birds of the air
shall eat whoever dies in the fields."
**5** Now the rest of the acts of Baasha, what he
did, and his might, [a]*are* they not written in the
book of the chronicles of the kings of Israel?
6 So Baasha [1]rested with his fathers and was
buried in [a]Tirzah. Then Elah his son reigned in his
place.
7 And also the word of the LORD came by the
prophet [a]Jehu the son of Hanani against Baasha
and his house, because of all the evil that he did in
the sight of the LORD in provoking Him to anger
with the work of his hands, in being like the house
of Jeroboam, and because [b]he killed them.
**8** In the twenty-sixth year of Asa king of Judah,
Elah the son of Baasha became king over Israel,
*and reigned* two years in Tirzah.
9 [a]Now his servant Zimri, commander of half *his*
chariots, conspired against him as he was in
Tirzah drinking himself drunk in the house of
Arza, [b]steward[1] of *his* house in Tirzah.
10 And Zimri went in and struck him and killed
him in the twenty-seventh year of Asa king of
Judah, and reigned in his place.
11 Then it came to pass, when he began to reign,
as soon as he was seated on his throne, *that* he
killed all the household of Baasha; he [a]did not
leave him one male, neither of his relatives nor of
his friends.
12 Thus Zimri destroyed all the household of
Baasha, [a]according to the word of the LORD,
which He spoke against Baasha by Jehu the
prophet,
13 for all the sins of Baasha and the sins of Elah
his son, by which they had sinned and by which
they had made Israel sin, in provoking the LORD
God of Israel to anger [a]with their [1]idols.
**14** Now the rest of the acts of Elah, and all that
he did, *are* they not written in the book of the
chronicles of the kings of Israel?
**15** In the twenty-seventh year of Asa king of
Judah, Zimri had reigned in Tirzah seven days.
And the people *were* encamped [a]against Gibbethon, which *belonged* to the Philistines.
16 Now the people *who were* encamped heard it
said, "Zimri has conspired and also has killed the
king." So all Israel made Omri, the commander of
the army, king over Israel that day in the camp.
17 Then Omri and all Israel with him went up
from Gibbethon, and they besieged Tirzah.
18 And it happened, when Zimri saw that the city
was [1]taken, that he went into the citadel of the
king's house and burned the king's house [2]down
upon himself with fire, and died,
19 because of the sins which he had committed in
doing evil in the sight of the LORD, [a]in walking in
the [b]way of Jeroboam, and in his sin which he had
committed to make Israel sin.
**20** Now the rest of the acts of Zimri, and the
treason he committed, *are* they not written in the
book of the chronicles of the kings of Israel?
**21** Then the people of Israel were divided into
two parts: half of the people followed Tibni the
son of Ginath, to make him king, and half followed Omri.
22 But the people who followed Omri prevailed
over the people who followed Tibni the son of
Ginath. So Tibni died and Omri reigned.
23 In the thirty-first year of Asa king of Judah,
Omri became king over Israel, *and reigned* twelve
years. Six years he reigned in [a]Tirzah.
24 And he bought the hill of Samaria from Shemer for two talents of silver; then he built on the
hill, and called the name of the city which he built,
[a]Samaria,[1] after the name of Shemer, owner of the
hill.
25 [a]Omri did evil in the eyes of the LORD, and did
worse than all who *were* before him.
26 For he [a]walked in all the ways of Jeroboam the
son of Nebat, and in his sin by which he had made
Israel sin, provoking the LORD God of Israel to
anger with their [b]idols.[1]
**27** Now the rest of the acts of Omri which he did,
and the might that he showed, *are* they not
written in the book of the chronicles of the kings
of Israel?
28 So Omri rested with his fathers and was buried
in Samaria. Then Ahab his son reigned in his
place.
**29** In the thirty-eighth year of Asa king of Judah,
Ahab the son of Omri became king over Israel;
and Ahab the son of Omri reigned over Israel in
Samaria twenty-two years.
30 Now Ahab the son of Omri did evil in the sight
of the LORD, more than all who *were* before him.
31 And it came to pass, as though it had been a
trivial thing for him to walk in the sins of Jeroboam the son of Nebat, [a]that he took as wife
Jezebel the daughter of Ethbaal, king of the
[b]Sidonians; [c]and he went and served Baal and
worshiped him.
32 Then he set up an altar for Baal in [a]the temple
of Baal, which he had built in Samaria.
33 [a]And Ahab made a [1]wooden image. Ahab [b]did
more to provoke the LORD God of Israel to anger
than all the kings of Israel who were before him.
34 In his days Hiel of Bethel built Jericho. He laid
its foundation [1]with Abiram his firstborn, and with
his youngest *son* Segub he set up its gates, [a]ac-
cording to the word of the LORD, which He had
spoken through Joshua the son of Nun.

### *Elijah Raises the Widow's Son*

**17** And Elijah the Tishbite, of the [a]inhabitants
of Gilead, said to Ahab, [b]"*As* the LORD God
of Israel lives, [c]before whom I stand, [d]there shall
not be dew nor rain [e]these years, except at my
word."
2 Then the word of the LORD came to him,
saying,
3 "Get away from here and turn eastward, and
hide by the Brook Cherith, which flows into the
Jordan.

**34** [a]1 Kin. 13:33; 14:16

CHAPTER 16

**1** [a]1 Kin. 16:7; 2 Chr. 19:2; 20:34 [b]2 Chr. 16:7–10 [c]1 Kin. 15:27
**2** [a]1 Sam. 2:8; 1 Kin. 14:7 [b]1 Kin. 12:25–33; 15:34
**3** [a]1 Kin. 16:11; 21:21 [b]1 Kin. 14:10; 15:29 [1]*consume*
**4** [a]1 Kin. 14:11; 21:24
**5** [a]2 Chr. 16:11
**6** [a]1 Kin. 14:17; 15:21 [1]Died and joined his ancestors
**7** [a]1 Kin. 16:1 [b]1 Kin. 15:27, 29
**9** [a]2 Kin. 9:30–33 [b]Gen. 24:2; 39:4; 1 Kin. 18:3 [1]Lit. *who was over the house*
**11** [a]1 Sam. 25:22
**12** [a]1 Kin. 16:3
**13** [a]Deut. 32:21; 1 Sam. 12:21; [Is. 41:29; Jon. 2:8; 1 Cor. 8:4; 10:19] [1]Lit. *vanities*
**15** [a]1 Kin. 15:27
**18** [1]*captured* [2]Lit. *over him*
**19** [a]1 Kin. 15:26, 34 [b]1 Kin. 12:25–33
**23** [a]1 Kin. 15:21; 2 Kin. 15:14
**24** [a]1 Kin. 13:32; 2 Kin. 17:24; John 4:4 [1]Heb. *Shomeron*
**25** [a]Mic. 6:16
**26** [a]1 Kin. 16:19 [b]1 Kin. 16:13 [1]Lit. *vanities*
**31** [a]Deut. 7:3 [b]Judg. 18:7; 1 Kin. 11:1–5 [c]1 Kin. 21:25, 26; 2 Kin. 10:18; 17:16
**32** [a]2 Kin. 10:21, 26, 27
**33** [a]2 Kin. 13:6 [b]1 Kin. 14:9; 16:29, 30; 21:25 [1]Or *Asherah,* a Canaanite goddess
**34** [a]Josh. 6:26 [1]At the cost of the life of

CHAPTER 17

**1** [a]Judg. 12:4 [b]1 Kin. 18:10; 22:14; 2 Kin. 3:14; 5:20 [c]Deut. 10:8 [d]1 Kin. 18:1; James 5:17 [e]Luke 4:25

4 "And it will be *that* you shall drink from the
brook, and I have commanded the [a]ravens to feed
you there."
5 So he went and did according to the word of
the LORD, for he went and stayed by the Brook
Cherith, which flows into the Jordan.
6 The ravens brought him bread and meat in the
morning, and bread and meat in the evening; and
he drank from the brook.
7 And it happened after a while that the brook
dried up, because there had been no rain in the
land.
**8** Then the word of the LORD came to him,
saying,
9 "Arise, go to [a]Zarephath, which *belongs* to
[b]Sidon, and dwell there. See, I have commanded a
widow there to provide for you."
10 So he arose and went to Zarephath. And when
he came to the gate of the city, indeed a widow
*was* there gathering sticks. And he called to her
and said, "Please bring me a little water in a cup,
that I may drink."
11 And as she was going to get *it,* he called to her
and said, "Please bring me a morsel of bread in
your hand."
12 So she said, "As the LORD your God lives, I do
not have bread, only a handful of flour in a bin,
and a little oil in a [1]jar; and see, I *am* gathering a
couple of sticks that I may go in and prepare it for
myself and my son, that we may eat it, and [a]die."
13 And Elijah said to her, "Do not fear; go *and* do
as you have said, but make me a small cake from
it first, and bring *it* to me; and afterward make
*some* for yourself and your son.
14 "For thus says the LORD God of Israel: 'The
bin of flour shall not be used up, nor shall the jar
of oil run dry, until the day the LORD sends rain on
the earth.' "
15 So she went away and did according to the
word of Elijah; and she and he and her household
ate for *many* days.
16 The bin of flour was not used up, nor did the
jar of oil run dry, according to the word of the
LORD which He spoke by Elijah.
**17** Now it happened after these things *that* the
son of the woman who owned the house became
sick. And his sickness was so [1]serious that [2]there
was no breath left in him.
18 So she said to Elijah, [a]"What have I to do with
you, O man of God? Have you come to me to
bring my sin to remembrance, and to kill my son?"
19 And he said to her, "Give me your son." So he
took him out of her arms and carried him to the
upper room where he was staying, and laid him on
his own bed.
20 Then he cried out to the LORD and said, "O
LORD my God, have You also brought tragedy on
the widow with whom I lodge, by killing her son?"
21 [a]And he stretched himself out on the child
three times, and cried out to the LORD and said, "O
LORD my God, I pray, let this child's soul come
back to him."
22 Then the LORD heard the voice of Elijah; and
the soul of the child came back to him, and he
[a]revived.
23 And Elijah took the child and brought him
down from the upper room into the house, and
gave him to his mother. And Elijah said, "See,
your son lives!"
24 Then the woman said to Elijah, "Now by this
[a]I know that you *are* a man of God, *and* that the
word of the LORD in your mouth *is* the truth."

## *The Contest on Mount Carmel*

**18** And it came to pass *after* [a]many days that
the word of the LORD came to Elijah, in the
third year, saying, "Go, present yourself to Ahab,
and [b]I will send rain on the earth."
2 So Elijah went to present himself to Ahab; and
*there was* a severe famine in Samaria.
3 And Ahab had called Obadiah, who *was* [1]in
charge of *his* house. (Now Obadiah feared the
LORD greatly.
4 For so it was, while Jezebel [1]massacred the
prophets of the LORD, that Obadiah had taken one
hundred prophets and hidden them, fifty to a
cave, and had fed them with bread and water.)
5 And Ahab had said to Obadiah, "Go into the
land to all the springs of water and to all
the brooks; perhaps we may find grass to keep the
horses and mules alive, so that we will not have to
kill any livestock."
6 So they divided the land between them to
explore it; Ahab went one way by himself, and
Obadiah went another way by himself.
**7** Now as Obadiah was on his way, suddenly
Elijah met him; and he [a]recognized him, and fell
on his face, and said, "*Is* that you, my lord Elijah?"
8 And he answered him, "*It is* I. Go, tell your
master, 'Elijah *is here.*' "
9 So he said, "How have I sinned, that you are
delivering your servant into the hand of Ahab, to
kill me?
10 "*As* the LORD your God lives, there is no
nation or kingdom where my master has not sent
someone to hunt for you; and when they said, '*He
is* not *here,*' he took an oath from the kingdom or
nation that they could not find you.
11 "And now you say, 'Go, tell your master,
"Elijah *is here*" '!
12 "And it shall come to pass, *as soon as* I am
gone from you, that [a]the Spirit of the LORD will
carry you to a place I do not know; so when I go
and tell Ahab, and he cannot find you, he will kill
me. But I your servant have feared the LORD from
my youth.
13 "Was it not reported to my lord what I did
when Jezebel killed the prophets of the LORD, how
I hid one hundred men of the LORD's prophets,
fifty to a cave, and fed them with bread and
water?
14 "And now you say, 'Go, tell your master,
"Elijah *is here.*" ' He will kill me!"
15 Then Elijah said, "*As* the LORD of hosts lives,
before whom I stand, I will surely present myself
to him today."
16 So Obadiah went to meet Ahab, and told him;
and Ahab went to meet Elijah.
**17** Then it happened, when Ahab saw Elijah, that
Ahab said to him, [a]"*Is that* you, O [b]troubler of
Israel?"
18 And he answered, "I have not troubled Israel,
but you and your father's house *have,* [a]in that you
have forsaken the commandments of the LORD
and have followed the Baals.
19 "Now therefore, send *and* gather all Israel to
me on Mount [a]Carmel, the four hundred and fifty
prophets of Baal, [b]and the four hundred prophets
of [1]Asherah, who [2]eat at Jezebel's table."
**20** So Ahab sent for all the children of Israel, and

**4** [a]Job 38:41
**9** [a]Obad. 20; Luke 4:25, 26 [b]2 Sam. 24:6
**12** [a]Deut. 28:23, 24 [1]Lit. *pitcher* or *water jar*
**17** [1]*severe* [2]He died.
**18** [a]Luke 5:8
**21** [a]2 Kin. 4:34, 35; Acts 20:10
**22** [a]Luke 7:14, 15; Heb. 11:35
**24** [a]John 2:11; 3:2; 16:30

CHAPTER 18

**1** [a]1 Kin. 17:1; Luke 4:25; James 5:17 [b]Deut. 28:12
**3** [1]Lit. *over the house*
**4** [1]Lit. *cut off*
**7** [a]2 Kin. 1:6–8
**12** [a]2 Kin. 2:16; Ezek. 3:12, 14; Matt. 4:1; Acts 8:39
**17** [a]1 Kin. 21:20 [b]Josh. 7:25; Acts 16:20
**18** [a]1 Kin. 16:30–33; [2 Chr. 15:2]
**19** [a]Josh. 19:26; 2 Kin. 2:25 [b]1 Kin. 16:33 [1]A Canaanite goddess [2]Are provided for by Jezebel

[a]gathered the prophets together on Mount Carmel.
21 And Elijah came to all the people, and said,
[a]"How long will you falter between two opinions?
If the LORD *is* God, follow Him; but if Baal, [b]follow
him." But the people answered him not a word.
22 Then Elijah said to the people, [a]"I alone am
left a prophet of the LORD; [b]but Baal's prophets
*are* four hundred and fifty men.
23 "Therefore let them give us two bulls; and let
them choose one bull for themselves, cut it in
pieces, and lay *it* on the wood, but put no fire
*under it;* and I will prepare the other bull, and lay
*it* on the wood, but put no fire *under it.*
24 "Then you call on the name of your gods, and
I will call on the name of the LORD; and the God
who [a]answers by fire, He is God." So all the people
answered and said, [1]"It is well spoken."
**25** Now Elijah said to the prophets of Baal,
"Choose one bull for yourselves and prepare *it*
first, for you *are* many; and call on the name of
your god, but put no fire *under it.*"
26 So they took the bull which was given them,
and they prepared *it,* and called on the name of
Baal from morning even till noon, saying, "O Baal,
[1]hear us!" But *there was* [a]no voice; no one answered. Then they [2]leaped about the altar which
they had made.
27 And so it was, at noon, that Elijah mocked
them and said, "Cry [1]aloud, for he *is* a god; either
he is meditating, or he is busy, or he is on a
journey, *or* perhaps he is sleeping and must be
awakened."
28 So they cried aloud, and [a]cut themselves, as
was their custom, with [1]knives and lances, until
the blood gushed out on them.
29 And when midday was past, [a]they prophesied
until the *time* of the offering of the *evening*
sacrifice. But *there was* [b]no voice; no one answered, no one paid attention.
**30** Then Elijah said to all the people, "Come near
to me." So all the people came near to him. [a]And
he repaired the altar of the LORD *that was* broken
down.
31 And Elijah took twelve stones, according to
the number of the tribes of the sons of Jacob, to
whom the word of the LORD had come, saying,
[a]"Israel shall be your name."
32 Then with the stones he built an altar [a]in the
name of the LORD; and he made a trench around
the altar large enough to hold two seahs of seed.
33 And he [a]put the wood in order, cut the bull in
pieces, and laid *it* on the wood, and said, "Fill four
waterpots with water, and [b]pour *it* on the burnt
sacrifice and on the wood."
34 Then he said, "Do *it* a second time," and they
did *it* a second time; and he said, "Do *it* a third
time," and they did *it* a third time.
35 So the water ran all around the altar; and he
also filled [a]the trench with water.
36 And it came to pass, at *the time of* the offering
of the *evening* sacrifice, that Elijah the prophet
came near and said, "LORD [a]God of Abraham,
Isaac, and Israel, [b]let it be known this day that
You *are* God in Israel and I *am* Your servant, and
*that* [c]I have done all these things at Your word.
37 "Hear me, O LORD, hear me, that this people
may know that You *are* the LORD God, and *that*
You have turned their hearts back *to You* again."
38 Then [a]the fire of the LORD fell and consumed
the burnt sacrifice, and the wood and the stones
and the dust, and it licked up the water that *was*
in the trench.
39 Now when all the people saw *it,* they fell on
their faces; and they said, [a]"The LORD, He *is* God!
The LORD, He *is* God!"
40 And Elijah said to them, [a]"Seize the prophets
of Baal! Do not let one of them escape!" So they
seized them; and Elijah brought them down to the
Brook [b]Kishon and [c]executed them there.
**41** Then Elijah said to Ahab, "Go up, eat and
drink; for *there is* the sound of abundance of
rain."
42 So Ahab went up to eat and drink. And Elijah
went up to the top of Carmel; [a]then he bowed
down on the ground, and put his face between his
knees,
43 and said to his servant, "Go up now, look
toward the sea." So he went up and looked, and
said, "*There is* nothing." And seven times he said,
"Go again."
44 Then it came to pass the seventh *time,* that he
said, "There is a cloud, as small as a man's hand,
rising out of the sea!" So he said, "Go up, say to
Ahab, [1]'Prepare *your chariot,* and go down before
the rain stops you.' "
45 Now it happened in the meantime that the sky
became black with clouds and wind, and there
was a heavy rain. So Ahab rode away and went to
Jezreel.
46 Then the [a]hand of the LORD came upon Elijah;
and he [b]girded[1] up his loins and ran ahead of Ahab
to the entrance of Jezreel.

### *Elijah Flees to Horeb*

**19** And Ahab told Jezebel all that Elijah had
done, also how he had [a]executed all the
prophets with the sword.
2 Then Jezebel sent a messenger to Elijah, saying, [a]"So let the gods do *to me,* and more also, if I
do not make your life as the life of one of them by
tomorrow about this time."
3 And when he saw *that,* he arose and ran for
his life, and went to Beersheba, which *belongs* to
Judah, and left his servant there.
4 But he himself went a day's journey into the
wilderness, and came and sat down under a
[1]broom tree. And he [a]prayed that he might die,
and said, "It is enough! Now, LORD, take my life,
for I *am* no better than my fathers!"
5 Then as he lay and slept under a broom tree,
suddenly an angel touched him, and said to him,
"Arise *and* eat."
6 Then he looked, and there by his head *was* a
cake baked on [1]coals, and a jar of water. So he ate
and drank, and lay down again.
7 And the angel of the LORD came back the
second time, and touched him, and said, "Arise
*and* eat, because the journey *is* too great for you."
8 So he arose, and ate and drank; and he went in
the strength of that food forty days and [a]forty
nights as far as [b]Horeb, the mountain of God.
**9** And there he went into a cave, and spent the
night in that place; and behold, the word of the
LORD *came* to him, and He said to him, "What are
you doing here, Elijah?"
10 So he said, [a]"I have been very [b]zealous for the
LORD God of hosts; for the children of Israel have
forsaken Your covenant, torn down Your altars,
and [c]killed Your prophets with the sword. [d]I alone
am left; and they seek to take my life."
**11** Then He said, "Go out, and stand [a]on the

**20** [a]1 Kin. 22:6
**21** [a]2 Kin. 17:41; [Matt. 6:24] [b]Josh. 24:15
**22** [a]1 Kin. 19:10, 14 [b]1 Kin. 18:19
**24** [a]1 Kin. 18:38; 1 Chr. 21:26 [1]Lit. *The word is good*
**26** [a]Ps. 115:5; Jer. 10:5; [1 Cor. 8:4] [1]*answer* [2]Lit. *limped about, leaped in dancing around*
**27** [1]*with a loud voice*
**28** [a][Lev. 19:28; Deut. 14:1] [1]*swords*
**29** [a]Ex. 29:39, 41 [b]1 Kin. 18:26
**30** [a]1 Kin. 19:10, 14; 2 Chr. 33:16
**31** [a]Gen. 32:28; 35:10; 2 Kin. 17:34
**32** [a][Ex. 20:25; Col. 3:17]
**33** [a]Gen. 22:9; Lev. 1:6–8 [b]Judg. 6:20
**35** [a]1 Kin. 18:32, 38
**36** [a]Gen. 28:13; Ex. 3:6; 4:5; [Matt. 22:32] [b]1 Kin. 8:43; 2 Kin. 19:19 [c]Num. 16:28
**38** [a]Gen. 15:17; Lev. 9:24; 10:1, 2; Judg. 6:21; 2 Kin. 1:12; 1 Chr. 21:26; 2 Chr. 7:1; Job 1:16
**39** [a]1 Kin. 18:21, 24
**40** [a]2 Kin. 10:25 [b]Judg. 4:7; 5:21 [c][Deut. 13:5; 18:20]
**42** [a]James 5:17, 18
**44** [1]Lit. *Bind* or *Harness*
**46** [a]2 Kin. 3:15; Is. 8:11; Ezek. 3:14 [b]2 Kin. 4:29; 9:1; Jer. 1:17; 1 Pet. 1:13 [1]Tucked the skirts of his robe in his belt in preparation for quick travel

CHAPTER 19
**1** [a]1 Kin. 18:40
**2** [a]Ruth 1:17; 1 Kin. 20:10; 2 Kin. 6:31
**4** [a]Num. 11:15; Jer. 20:14–18; Jon. 4:3, 8 [1]*juniper*
**6** [1]*hot stones*
**8** [a]Ex. 24:18; 34:28; Deut. 9:9–11, 18; Matt. 4:2 [b]Ex. 3:1; 4:27
**10** [a]Rom. 11:3 [b]Num. 25:11, 13; Ps. 69:9 [c]1 Kin. 18:4 [d]1 Kin. 18:22; Rom. 11:3
**11** [a]Ex. 19:20; 24:12, 18

mountain before the LORD.” And behold, the LORD
[b]passed by, and [c]a great and strong wind tore into
the mountains and broke the rocks in pieces
before the LORD, *but* the LORD *was* not in the
wind; and after the wind an earthquake, *but* the
LORD *was* not in the earthquake;
12 and after the earthquake a fire, *but* the LORD
*was* not in the fire; and after the fire [1]a still small
voice.
13 So it was, when Elijah heard *it,* that [a]he
wrapped his face in his mantle and went out and
stood in the entrance of the cave. [b]Suddenly a
voice *came* to him, and said, “What are you doing
here, Elijah?”
14 [a]And he said, “I have been very zealous for the
LORD God of hosts; because the children of Israel
have forsaken Your covenant, torn down Your
altars, and killed Your prophets with the sword. I
alone am left; and they seek to take my life.”
15 Then the LORD said to him: “Go, return on
your way to the Wilderness of Damascus; [a]and
when you arrive, anoint Hazael *as* king over
Syria.
16 “Also you shall anoint [a]Jehu the son of Nimshi
*as* king over Israel. And [b]Elisha the son of Shaphat of Abel Meholah you shall anoint *as* prophet
in your place.
17 [a]“It shall be *that* whoever escapes the sword
of Hazael, Jehu will [b]kill; and whoever escapes the
sword of Jehu, [c]Elisha will kill.
18 [a]“Yet I have reserved seven thousand in Israel, all whose knees have not bowed to Baal, [b]and
every mouth that has not kissed him.”
**19** So he departed from there, and found Elisha
the son of Shaphat, who *was* plowing *with* twelve
yoke *of oxen* before him, and he was with the
twelfth. Then Elijah passed by him and threw his
[a]mantle on him.
20 And he left the oxen and ran after Elijah, and
said, [a]“Please let me kiss my father and my
mother, and *then* I will follow you.” And he said
to him, “Go back again, for what have I done to
you?”
21 So *Elisha* turned back from him, and took a
yoke of oxen and slaughtered them and [a]boiled
their flesh, using the oxen’s equipment, and gave
it to the people, and they ate. Then he arose and
followed Elijah, and became his servant.

### *Ahab Defeats the Syrians*

**20** Now [a]Ben-Hadad the king of Syria gathered
all his forces together; thirty-two kings
*were* with him, with horses and chariots. And he
went up and besieged [b]Samaria, and made war
against it.
2 Then he sent messengers into the city to Ahab
king of Israel, and said to him, “Thus says Ben-
Hadad:
3 ‘Your silver and your gold *are* mine; your
loveliest wives and children are mine.’ ”
4 And the king of Israel answered and said, “My
lord, O king, just as you say, I and all that I have
*are* yours.”
5 Then the messengers came back and said,
“Thus speaks Ben-Hadad, saying, ‘Indeed I have
sent to you, saying, “You shall deliver to me your
silver and your gold, your wives and your children”;
6 ‘but I will send my servants to you tomorrow
about this time, and they shall search your house
and the houses of your servants. And it shall be,
*that* whatever is [1]pleasant in your eyes, they will
put *it* in their hands and take *it.*’ ”
**7** So the king of Israel called all the elders of the
land, and said, “Notice, please, and see how this
*man* seeks trouble, for he sent to me for my wives,
my children, my silver, and my gold; and I did not
deny him.”
8 And all the elders and all the people said to
him, “Do not listen or consent.”
9 Therefore he said to the messengers of Ben-
Hadad, “Tell my lord the king, ‘All that you sent
for to your servant the first time I will do, but this
thing I cannot do.’ ” And the messengers departed
and brought back word to him.
10 Then Ben-Hadad sent to him and said, [a]“The
gods do so to me, and more also, if enough dust is
left of Samaria for a handful for each of the people
[1]who follow me.”
11 So the king of Israel answered and said, “Tell
*him,* ‘Let not the one who puts on *his armor*
[a]boast like the one who takes *it off.*’ ”
12 And it happened when *Ben-Hadad* heard this
message, as he and the kings *were* [a]drinking at the
[1]command post, that he said to his servants, “Get
ready.” And they got ready to attack the city.
**13** Suddenly a prophet approached Ahab king of
Israel, saying, “Thus says the LORD: ‘Have you
seen all this great multitude? Behold, [a]I will
deliver it into your hand today, and you shall
know that I *am* the LORD.’ ”
14 So Ahab said, “By whom?” And he said, “Thus
says the LORD: ‘By the young leaders of the
provinces.’ ” Then he said, “Who will set the
battle in order?” And he answered, “You.”
15 Then he mustered the young leaders of the
provinces, and there were two hundred and thirty-
two; and after them he mustered all the people, all
the children of Israel—seven thousand.
16 So they went out at noon. Meanwhile Ben-
Hadad and the thirty-two kings helping him were
[a]getting drunk at the command post.
17 The young leaders of the provinces went out
first. And Ben-Hadad sent out *a patrol,* and they
told him, saying, “Men are coming out of Samaria!”
18 So he said, “If they have come out for peace,
take them alive; and if they have come out for
war, take them alive.”
19 Then these young leaders of the provinces
went out of the city with the army which followed
them.
20 And each one killed his man; so the Syrians
fled, and Israel pursued them; and Ben-Hadad the
king of Syria escaped on a horse with the cavalry.
21 Then the king of Israel went out and attacked
the horses and chariots, and killed the Syrians
with a great slaughter.
22 And the prophet came to the king of Israel
and said to him, “Go, strengthen yourself; take
note, and see what you should do, [a]for [1]in the
spring of the year the king of Syria will come up
against you.”
**23** Then the servants of the king of Syria said to
him, “Their gods *are* gods of the hills. Therefore
they were stronger than we; but if we fight
against them in the plain, surely we will be stronger than they.
24 “So do this thing: Dismiss the kings, each
from his position, and put captains in their [1]places;
25 “and you shall muster an army like the army
[1]that you have lost, horse for horse and chariot for

11 [b]Ex. 33:21, 22 [c]Ezek. 1:4; 37:7
12 [1]*a delicate whispering voice*
13 [a]Ex. 3:6; Is. 6:2 [b]1 Kin. 19:9
14 [a]1 Kin. 19:10
15 [a]2 Kin. 8:8–15
16 [a]2 Kin. 9:1–10 [b]1 Kin. 19:19–21; 2 Kin. 2:9–15
17 [a]2 Kin. 8:12; 13:3, 22 [b]2 Kin. 9:14—10:28 [c][Hos. 6:5]
18 [a]Rom. 11:4 [b]Hos. 13:2
19 [a]1 Sam. 28:14; 2 Kin. 2:8, 13, 14
20 [a][Matt. 8:21, 22; Luke 9:61, 62]; Acts 20:37
21 [a]2 Sam. 24:22 [1]Lit. *he*

CHAPTER 20

1 [a]1 Kin. 15:18, 20; 2 Kin. 6:24 [b]1 Kin. 16:24; 2 Kin. 6:24
6 [1]*pleasing*
10 [a]1 Kin. 19:2; 2 Kin. 6:31 [1]Lit. *at my feet*
11 [a]Prov. 27:1; [Eccl. 7:8]
12 [a]1 Kin. 20:16 [1]Lit. *booths* or *shelters*
13 [a]1 Kin. 20:28
16 [a]1 Kin. 16:9; 20:12; [Prov. 20:1]
22 [a]2 Sam. 11:1; 1 Kin. 20:26 [1]Lit. *at the return*
24 [1]*positions*
25 [1]Lit. *that fell from you*

chariot. Then we will fight against them in the plain; surely we will be stronger than they." And he listened to their voice and did so.

26 So it was, in the spring of the year, that Ben-Hadad mustered the Syrians and went up to [a]Aphek to fight against Israel.

27 And the children of Israel were mustered and given provisions, and they went against them. Now the children of Israel encamped before them like two little flocks of goats, while the Syrians filled the [a]countryside.

**28** Then a [a]man of God came and spoke to the king of Israel, and said, "Thus says the LORD: 'Because the Syrians have said, "The LORD *is* God of the hills, but He *is* not God of the valleys," therefore [b]I will deliver all this great multitude into your hand, and you shall know that I *am* the LORD.' "

29 And they encamped opposite each other for seven days. So it was that on the seventh day the battle was joined; and the children of Israel killed one hundred thousand foot soldiers *of* the Syrians in one day.

30 But the rest fled to Aphek, into the city; then a wall fell on twenty-seven thousand of the men *who were* left. And Ben-Hadad fled and went into the city, into an inner chamber.

**31** Then his servants said to him, "Look now, we have heard that the kings of the house of Israel *are* merciful kings. Please, let us [a]put sackcloth around our waists and ropes around our heads, and go out to the king of Israel; perhaps he will spare your life."

32 So they wore sackcloth around their waists and *put* ropes around their heads, and came to the king of Israel and said, "Your servant Ben-Hadad says, 'Please let me live.' " And he said, "*Is* he still alive? He *is* my brother."

33 Now the men were watching closely to see whether *any sign of mercy would come* from him; and they quickly grasped *at this word* and said, "Your brother Ben-Hadad." So he said, "Go, bring him." Then Ben-Hadad came out to him; and he had him come up into the chariot.

34 So *Ben-Hadad* said to him, [a]"The cities which my father took from your father I will restore; and you may set up marketplaces for yourself in Damascus, as my father did in Samaria." Then *Ahab said,* "I will send you away with this treaty." So he made a treaty with him and sent him away.

**35** Now a certain man of [a]the sons of the prophets said to his neighbor [b]by the word of the LORD, "Strike me, please." And the man refused to strike him.

36 Then he said to him, "Because you have not obeyed the voice of the LORD, surely, as soon as you depart from me, a lion shall kill you." And as soon as he left him, [a]a lion found him and killed him.

37 And he found another man, and said, "Strike me, please." So the man struck him, inflicting a wound.

38 Then the prophet departed and waited for the king by the road, and disguised himself with a bandage over his eyes.

39 Now [a]as the king passed by, he cried out to the king and said, "Your servant went out into the midst of the battle; and there, a man came over and brought a man to me, and said, 'Guard this man; if by any means he is missing, [b]your life shall be for his life, or else you shall [1]pay a talent of silver.'

40 "While your servant was busy here and there, he was gone." Then the king of Israel said to him, "So *shall* your judgment *be;* you yourself have decided *it.*"

41 And he hastened to take the bandage away from his eyes; and the king of Israel recognized him as one of the prophets.

42 Then he said to him, "Thus says the LORD: [a]'Because you have let slip out of *your* hand a man whom I appointed to utter destruction, therefore your life shall go for his life, and your people for his people.' "

43 So the king of Israel [a]went to his house sullen and displeased, and came to Samaria.

### *Elijah Pronounces Ahab's Doom*

**21** And it came to pass after these things *that* Naboth the Jezreelite had a vineyard which *was* in [a]Jezreel, next to the palace of Ahab king of Samaria.

2 So Ahab spoke to Naboth, saying, "Give me your [a]vineyard, that I may have it for a vegetable garden, because it *is* near, next to my house; and for it I will give you a vineyard better than it. *Or,* if it seems good to you, I will give you its worth in money."

3 But Naboth said to Ahab, "The LORD forbid [a]that I should give the inheritance of my fathers to you!"

4 So Ahab went into his house sullen and displeased because of the word which Naboth the Jezreelite had spoken to him; for he had said, "I will not give you the inheritance of my fathers." And he lay down on his bed, and turned away his face, and would eat no food.

**5** But [a]Jezebel his wife came to him, and said to him, "Why is your spirit so sullen that you eat no food?"

6 He said to her, "Because I spoke to Naboth the Jezreelite, and said to him, 'Give me your vineyard for money; or else, if it pleases you, I will give you *another* vineyard for it.' And he answered, 'I will not give you my vineyard.' "

7 Then Jezebel his wife said to him, "You now exercise authority over Israel! Arise, eat food, and let your heart be cheerful; I will give you the vineyard of Naboth the Jezreelite."

8 And she wrote letters in Ahab's name, sealed *them* with his seal, and sent the letters to the elders and the nobles who *were* dwelling in the city with Naboth.

9 She wrote in the letters, saying, "Proclaim a fast, and seat Naboth [1]with high honor among the people;

10 "and seat two men, scoundrels, before him to bear witness against him, saying, 'You have [a]blasphemed God and the king.' *Then* take him out, and [b]stone him, that he may die."

**11** So the men of his city, the elders and nobles who were inhabitants of his city, did as Jezebel had sent to them, as it *was* written in the letters which she had sent to them.

12 [a]They proclaimed a fast, and seated Naboth with high honor among the people.

13 And two men, scoundrels, came in and sat before him; and the scoundrels [a]witnessed against him, against Naboth, in the presence of the people, saying, "Naboth has blasphemed God and the

26 [a]Josh. 13:4; 2 Kin. 13:17
27 [a]Judg. 6:3–5; 1 Sam. 13:5–8
28 [a]1 Kin. 17:18 [b]1 Kin. 20:13
31 [a]Gen. 37:34; 2 Sam. 3:31
34 [a]1 Kin. 15:20
35 [a]2 Kin. 2:3, 5, 7, 15 [b]1 Kin. 13:17, 18
36 [a]1 Kin. 13:24
39 [a]2 Sam. 12:1 [b]2 Kin. 10:24 [1]Lit. *weigh*
42 [a]1 Kin. 22:31–37
43 [a]1 Kin. 21:4

CHAPTER 21

1 [a]Judg. 6:33; 1 Kin. 18:45, 46
2 [a]1 Sam. 8:14
3 [a][Lev. 25:23; Num. 36:7; Ezek. 46:18]
5 [a]1 Kin. 19:1, 2
9 [1]Lit. *at the head*
10 [a][Ex. 22:28; Lev. 24:15, 16]; Acts 6:11 [b][Lev. 24:14]
12 [a]Is. 58:4
13 [a][Ex. 20:16; 23:1, 7]

king!" [b]Then they took him outside the city and
stoned him with stones, so that he died.
14 Then they sent to Jezebel, saying, "Naboth
has been stoned and is dead."
**15** And it came to pass, when Jezebel heard that
Naboth had been stoned and was dead, that
Jezebel said to Ahab, "Arise, take possession of
the vineyard of Naboth the Jezreelite, which he
refused to give you for money; for Naboth is not
alive, but dead."
16 So it was, when Ahab heard that Naboth was
dead, that Ahab got up and went down to take
possession of the vineyard of Naboth the Jezreelite.
**17** [a]Then the word of the LORD came to [b]Elijah
the Tishbite, saying,
18 "Arise, go down to meet Ahab king of Israel,
[a]who *lives* in Samaria. There *he is,* in the vineyard
of Naboth, where he has gone down to take
possession of it.
19 "You shall speak to him, saying, 'Thus says
the LORD: "Have you murdered and also taken
possession?" ' And you shall speak to him, saying,
'Thus says the LORD: [a]"In the place where dogs
licked the blood of Naboth, dogs shall lick your
blood, even yours." ' "
20 So Ahab said to Elijah, [a]"Have you found me,
O my enemy?" And he answered, "I have found
*you,* because [b]you have sold yourself to do evil in
the sight of the LORD:
21 'Behold, [a]I will bring calamity on you. I will
take away your [b]posterity, and will cut off from
Ahab [c]every male in Israel, both [d]bond and free.
22 'I will make your house like the house of
[a]Jeroboam the son of Nebat, and like the house of
[b]Baasha the son of Ahijah, because of the provocation with which you have provoked *Me* to
anger, and made Israel sin.'
23 "And [a]concerning Jezebel the LORD also
spoke, saying, 'The dogs shall eat Jezebel by the
[1]wall of Jezreel.'
24 "The dogs shall eat [a]whoever belongs to Ahab
and dies in the city, and the birds of the air shall
eat whoever dies in the field."
**25** But [a]there was no one like Ahab who sold
himself to do wickedness in the sight of the LORD,
[b]because Jezebel his wife [1]stirred him up.
26 And he behaved very abominably in following
idols, according to all [a]*that* the Amorites had
done, whom the LORD had cast out before the
children of Israel.
**27** So it was, when Ahab heard those words, that
he tore his clothes and [a]put sackcloth on his body,
and fasted and lay in sackcloth, and went about
mourning.
28 And the word of the LORD came to Elijah the
Tishbite, saying,
29 "See how Ahab has humbled himself before
Me? Because he [a]has humbled himself before Me, I
will not bring the calamity in his days. [b]In the
days of his son I will bring the calamity on his
house."

## *Micaiah's True Prophecy*

**22** Now three years passed without war between Syria and Israel.
2 Then it came to pass, in the third year, that
[a]Jehoshaphat the king of Judah went down to
*visit* the king of Israel.
3 And the king of Israel said to his servants, "Do
you know that [a]Ramoth in Gilead *is* ours, but we

**13** [b]2 Chr. 24:21; Acts 7:58, 59; Heb. 11:37
**17** [a][Ps. 9:12] [b]1 Kin. 19:1
**18** [a]1 Kin. 13:32; 2 Chr. 22:9
**19** [a]1 Kin. 22:38; 2 Kin. 9:26
**20** [a]1 Kin. 18:17 [b]1 Kin. 21:25; 2 Kin. 17:17; [Rom. 7:14]
**21** [a]1 Kin. 14:10; 2 Kin. 9:8 [b]2 Kin. 10:10 [c]1 Sam. 25:22 [d]1 Kin. 14:10
**22** [a]1 Kin. 15:29 [b]1 Kin. 16:3, 11
**23** [a]2 Kin. 9:10, 30–37 [1]So with MT, LXX; some Heb. mss., Syr., Tg., Vg. *plot of ground* instead of *wall* (cf. 2 Kin. 9:36)
**24** [a]1 Kin. 14:11; 16:4
**25** [a]1 Kin. 16:30–33; 21:20 [b]1 Kin. 16:31 [1]*incited him*
**26** [a]Gen. 15:16; [Lev. 18:25–30]; 2 Kin. 21:11
**27** [a]Gen. 37:34; 2 Sam. 3:31; 2 Kin. 6:30
**29** [a][2 Kin. 22:19] [b]2 Kin. 9:25; 10:11, 17

CHAPTER 22
**2** [a]1 Kin. 15:24; 2 Chr. 18:2
**3** [a]Deut. 4:43; Josh. 21:38; 1 Kin. 4:13
**4** [a]2 Kin. 3:7
**5** [a]2 Kin. 3:11
**6** [a]1 Kin. 18:19 [1]The false prophets
**7** [a]2 Kin. 3:11 [1]Or *him*
**11** [a]Zech. 1:18–21 [b]Deut. 33:17
**14** [a]Num. 22:38; 24:13
**17** [a]Num. 27:17; 1 Kin. 22:34–36; 2 Chr. 18:16; Matt. 9:36; Mark 6:34
**19** [a]Is. 6:1; Ezek. 1:26–28; Dan. 7:9 [b]Job 1:6; 2:1; Ps. 103:20; Dan. 7:10; Zech. 1:10; [Matt. 18:10; Heb. 1:7, 14]

hesitate to take it out of the hand of the king of
Syria?"
4 So he said to Jehoshaphat, "Will you go with
me to fight at Ramoth Gilead?" Jehoshaphat said
to the king of Israel, [a]"I *am* as you *are,* my people
as your people, my horses as your horses."
**5** Also Jehoshaphat said to the king of Israel,
[a]"Please inquire for the word of the LORD today."
6 Then the king of Israel [a]gathered [1]the prophets together, about four hundred men, and said to
them, "Shall I go against Ramoth Gilead to fight,
or shall I refrain?" So they said, "Go up, for the
Lord will deliver *it* into the hand of the king."
7 And [a]Jehoshaphat said, "*Is there* not still a
prophet of the LORD here, that we may inquire of
[1]Him?"
8 So the king of Israel said to Jehoshaphat,
"*There is* still one man, Micaiah the son of Imlah,
by whom we may inquire of the LORD; but I hate
him, because he does not prophesy good concerning me, but evil." And Jehoshaphat said, "Let not
the king say such things!"
9 Then the king of Israel called an officer and
said, "Bring Micaiah the son of Imlah quickly!"
10 The king of Israel and Jehoshaphat the king of
Judah, having put on *their* robes, sat each on his
throne, at a threshing floor at the entrance of the
gate of Samaria; and all the prophets prophesied
before them.
11 Now Zedekiah the son of Chenaanah had
made [a]horns of iron for himself; and he said,
"Thus says the LORD: 'With these you shall [b]gore
the Syrians until they are destroyed.' "
12 And all the prophets prophesied so, saying,
"Go up to Ramoth Gilead and prosper, for the
LORD will deliver *it* into the king's hand."
**13** Then the messenger who had gone to call
Micaiah spoke to him, saying, "Now listen, the
words of the prophets with one accord encourage
the king. Please, let your word be like the word of
one of them, and speak encouragement."
14 And Micaiah said, "*As* the LORD lives, [a]what-
ever the LORD says to me, that I will speak."
15 Then he came to the king; and the king said to
him, "Micaiah, shall we go to war against Ramoth
Gilead, or shall we refrain?" And he answered
him, "Go and prosper, for the LORD will deliver *it*
into the hand of the king!"
16 So the king said to him, "How many times
shall I make you swear that you tell me nothing
but the truth in the name of the LORD?"
**17** Then he said, "I saw all Israel [a]scattered on
the mountains, as sheep that have no shepherd.
And the LORD said, 'These have no master. Let
each return to his house in peace.' "
18 And the king of Israel said to Jehoshaphat,
"Did I not tell you he would not prophesy good
concerning me, but evil?"
19 Then *Micaiah* said, "Therefore hear the word
of the LORD: [a]I saw the LORD sitting on His throne,
[b]and all the host of heaven standing by, on His
right hand and on His left.
20 "And the LORD said, 'Who will persuade Ahab
to go up, that he may fall at Ramoth Gilead?' So
one spoke in this manner, and another spoke in
that manner.
21 "Then a spirit came forward and stood before
the LORD, and said, 'I will persuade him.'
22 "The LORD said to him, 'In what way?' So he
said, 'I will go out and be a lying spirit in the
mouth of all his prophets.' And the LORD said,

[a]'You shall persuade *him,* and also prevail. Go out
and do so.'
23 [a]"Therefore look! The LORD has put a lying
spirit in the mouth of all these prophets of yours,
and the LORD has declared disaster against you."
**24** Now Zedekiah the son of Chenaanah went
near and [a]struck Micaiah on the cheek, and said,
[b]"Which way did the spirit from the LORD go from
me to speak to you?"
25 And Micaiah said, "Indeed, you shall see on
that day when you go into an [a]inner chamber to
hide!"
26 So the king of Israel said, "Take Micaiah, and
return him to Amon the governor of the city and
to Joash the king's son;
27 "and say, 'Thus says the king: "Put this *fellow*
in [a]prison, and feed him with bread of affliction
and water of affliction, until I come in peace." ' "
28 But Micaiah said, "If you ever return in peace,
[a]the LORD has not spoken by me." And he said,
"Take heed, all you people!"
**29** So the king of Israel and Jehoshaphat the king
of Judah went up to Ramoth Gilead.
30 And the king of Israel said to Jehoshaphat, "I
will disguise myself and go into battle; but you put
on your robes." So the king of Israel [a]disguised
himself and went into battle.
31 Now the [a]king of Syria had commanded the
thirty-two [b]captains of his chariots, saying, "Fight
with no one small or great, but only with the king
of Israel."
32 So it was, when the captains of the chariots
saw Jehoshaphat, that they said, "Surely it *is* the
king of Israel!" Therefore they turned aside to
fight against him, and Jehoshaphat [a]cried out.
33 And it happened, when the captains of the
chariots saw that it *was* not the king of Israel,
that they turned back from pursuing him.
34 Now a *certain* man drew a bow at random,
and struck the king of Israel between the joints of
his armor. So he said to the driver of his chariot,
"Turn around and take me out of the battle, for I
am wounded."
35 The battle increased that day; and the king
was propped up in his chariot, facing the Syrians,
and died at evening. The blood ran out from the
wound onto the floor of the chariot.
36 Then, as the sun was going down, a shout
went throughout the army, saying, "Every man to
his city, and every man to his own country!"
**37** So the king died, and was brought to Samaria.
And they buried the king in Samaria.
38 Then *someone* washed the chariot at a pool in
Samaria, and the dogs licked up his blood while
[1]the harlots bathed, according [a]to the word of the
LORD which He had spoken.
39 Now the rest of the acts of Ahab, and all that
he did, [a]the ivory house which he built and all the
cities that he built, *are* they not written in the
book of the chronicles of the kings of Israel?
40 So Ahab [1]rested with his fathers. Then [a]Aha-
ziah his son reigned in his place.
**41** [a]Jehoshaphat the son of Asa had become king
over Judah in the fourth year of Ahab king of
Israel.
42 Jehoshaphat *was* thirty-five years old when he
became king, and he reigned twenty-five years in
Jerusalem. His mother's name *was* Azubah the
daughter of Shilhi.
43 And [a]he walked in all the ways of his father
Asa. He did not turn aside from them, doing *what*
*was* right in the eyes of the LORD. Nevertheless
[b]the high places were not taken away, *for* the
people offered sacrifices and burned incense on
the high places.
44 Also [a]Jehoshaphat made [b]peace with the king
of Israel.
**45** Now the rest of the acts of Jehoshaphat, the
might that he showed, and how he made war, *are*
they not written [a]in the book of the chronicles of
the kings of Judah?
46 [a]And the rest of the [1]perverted persons, who
remained in the days of his father Asa, he banished from the land.
47 [a]*There was* then no king in Edom, only a
deputy of the king.
48 [a]Jehoshaphat [b]made [1]merchant ships to go to
[c]Ophir for gold; [d]but they never sailed, for the
ships were wrecked at [e]Ezion Geber.
49 Then Ahaziah the son of Ahab said to Jehoshaphat, "Let my servants go with your servants in the ships." But Jehoshaphat would not.
50 And [a]Jehoshaphat [1]rested with his fathers, and
was buried with his fathers in the City of David
his father. Then Jehoram his son reigned in his
place.
**51** [a]Ahaziah the son of Ahab became king over
Israel in Samaria in the seventeenth year of
Jehoshaphat king of Judah, and reigned two years
over Israel.
52 He did evil in the sight of the LORD, and
[a]walked in the way of his father and in the way of
his mother and in the way of Jeroboam the son of
Nebat, who had made Israel sin;
53 for [a]he served Baal and worshiped him, and
provoked the LORD God of Israel to anger, [b]ac-
cording[1] to all that his father had done.

**22** [a]Judg. 9:23; 1 Sam. 16:14; 18:10; 19:9; Job 12:16; [Ezek. 14:9; 2 Thess. 2:11]
**23** [a][Ezek. 14:9]
**24** [a]Jer. 20:2 [b]2 Chr. 18:23
**25** [a]1 Kin. 20:30
**27** [a]2 Chr. 16:10; 18:25–27
**28** [a]Num. 16:29; Deut. 18:20–22
**30** [a]2 Chr. 35:22
**31** [a]1 Kin. 20:1 [b]1 Kin. 20:24; 2 Chr. 18:30
**32** [a]2 Chr. 18:31
**38** [a]1 Kin. 21:19 [1]Tg., Syr. *they washed his armor*
**39** [a]Ps. 45:8; Amos 3:15
**40** [a]2 Kin. 1:2, 18 [1]Died and joined his ancestors
**41** [a]2 Chr. 20:31
**43** [a]2 Chr. 17:3; 20:32, 33 [b]1 Kin. 14:23; 15:14; 2 Kin. 12:3
**44** [a]2 Chr. 19:2 [b]2 Chr. 18:1
**45** [a]2 Chr. 20:34
**46** [a]Gen. 19:5; Deut. 23:17; 1 Kin. 14:24; 15:12; 2 Kin. 23:7; Jude 7 [1]Heb. *qadesh,* those practicing sodomy and prostitution in religious rituals
**47** [a]2 Sam. 8:14; 2 Kin. 3:9; 8:20
**48** [a]2 Chr. 20:35–37 [b]1 Kin. 10:22 [c]1 Kin. 9:28 [d]2 Chr. 20:37 [e]1 Kin. 9:26 [1]Or *ships of Tarshish*
**50** [a]2 Chr. 21:1 [1]Died and joined his ancestors
**51** [a]1 Kin. 22:40
**52** [a]1 Kin. 15:26; 21:25
**53** [a]Judg. 2:11 [b]1 Kin. 16:30–32 [1]In the same way that

## *The Second Book of the*

# KINGS

### *The Death of Ahaziah*

MOAB [a]rebelled against Israel [b]after the
death of Ahab.
2 Now [a]Ahaziah fell through the lattice
of his upper room in Samaria, and was injured; so
he sent messengers and said to them, "Go, inquire
of [b]Baal-Zebub,[1] the god of [c]Ekron, whether I shall
recover from this injury."
3 But the [1]angel of the LORD said to Elijah the
Tishbite, "Arise, go up to meet the messengers of
the king of Samaria, and say to them, *'Is it*
because *there is* no God in Israel *that* you are
going to inquire of Baal-Zebub, the god of Ekron?'
4 "Now therefore, thus says the LORD: 'You
shall not come down from the bed to which you
have gone up, but you shall surely die.' " So Elijah
departed.
**5** And when the messengers returned to [1]him,
he said to them, "Why have you come back?"
6 So they said to him, "A man came up to meet
us, and said to us, 'Go, return to the king who sent
you, and say to him, "Thus says the LORD: *'Is it*
because *there is* no God in Israel *that* you are
sending to inquire of Baal-Zebub, the god of
Ekron? Therefore you shall not come down from
the bed to which you have gone up, but you shall
surely die.' " ' "
7 Then he said to them, "What kind of man *was*
*it* who came up to meet you and told you these
words?"
8 So they answered him, "[a]A hairy man wearing
a leather belt around his waist." And he said, [b]"It
*is* Elijah the Tishbite."
**9** Then the king sent to him a captain of fifty
with his fifty men. So he went up to him; and
there he was, sitting on the top of a hill. And he
spoke to him: "Man of God, the king has said,
'Come down!' "
10 So Elijah answered and said to the captain of
fifty, "If I *am* a man of God, then [a]let fire come
down from heaven and consume you and your
fifty men." And fire came down from heaven and
consumed him and his fifty.
11 Then he sent to him another captain of fifty
with his fifty men. And he answered and said to
him: "Man of God, thus has the king said, 'Come
down quickly!' "
12 So Elijah answered and said to them, "If I *am*
a man of God, let fire come down from heaven
and consume you and your fifty men." And the
fire of God came down from heaven and consumed him and his fifty.
**13** Again, he sent a third captain of fifty with his
fifty men. And the third captain of fifty went up,
and came and [1]fell on his knees before Elijah, and
pleaded with him, and said to him: "Man of God,
please let my life and the life of these fifty servants of yours [a]be precious in your sight.
14 "Look, fire has come down from heaven and
burned up the first two captains of fifties with
their fifties. But let my life now be precious in
your sight."
15 And the [1]angel of the LORD said to Elijah, "Go
down with him; do not be afraid of him." So he
arose and went down with him to the king.
16 Then he said to him, "Thus says the LORD:
'Because you have sent messengers to inquire of
Baal-Zebub, the god of Ekron, *is it* because *there*
*is* no God in Israel to inquire of His word? Therefore you shall not come down from the bed to
which you have gone up, but you shall surely
die.' "
**17** So *Ahaziah* died according to the word of the
LORD which Elijah had spoken. Because he had no
son, [a]Jehoram[1] became king in his place, in the
second year of Jehoram the son of Jehoshaphat,
king of Judah.
18 Now the rest of the acts of Ahaziah which he
did, *are* they not written in the book of the
chronicles of the kings of Israel?

### *Elijah Divides the Jordan*

**2** And it came to pass, when the LORD was about
to [a]take up Elijah into heaven by a whirlwind,
that Elijah went with [b]Elisha from Gilgal.
2 Then Elijah said to Elisha, [a]"Stay here, please,
for the LORD has sent me on to Bethel." But Elisha
said, "*As* the LORD lives, and [b]*as* your soul lives, I
will not leave you!" So they went down to Bethel.
3 Now [a]the sons of the prophets who *were* at
Bethel came out to Elisha, and said to him, "Do
you know that the LORD will take away your
master [1]from over you today?" And he said, "Yes,
I know; keep silent!"
**4** Then Elijah said to him, "Elisha, stay here,
please, for the LORD has sent me on to Jericho."
But he said, "*As* the LORD lives, and *as* your soul
lives, I will not leave you!" So they came to
Jericho.
5 Now the sons of the prophets who *were* at
Jericho came to Elisha and said to him, "Do you
know that the LORD will take away your master
from over you today?" So he answered, "Yes, I
know; keep silent!"
6 Then Elijah said to him, "Stay here, please, for
the LORD has sent me on to the Jordan." But he
said, "*As* the LORD lives, and *as* your soul lives, I
will not leave you!" So the two of them went on.
7 And fifty men of the sons of the prophets went
and stood facing *them* at a distance, while the two
of them stood by the Jordan.
8 Now Elijah took his mantle, rolled *it* up, and
struck the water; and [a]it was divided this way and
that, so that the two of them crossed over on dry
[b]ground.
**9** And so it was, when they had crossed over,
that Elijah said to Elisha, "Ask! What may I do for
you, before I am taken away from you?" Elisha
said, "Please let a double portion of your spirit be
upon me."
10 So he said, "You have asked a hard thing.
*Nevertheless,* if you see me *when I am* taken from
you, it shall be so for you; but if not, it shall not be
so."
11 Then it happened, as they continued on and
talked, that suddenly [a]a chariot of fire *appeared*
with horses of fire, and separated the two of them;
and Elijah [b]went up by a whirlwind into heaven.
**12** And Elisha saw *it,* and he cried out, [a]"My
father, my father, the chariot of Israel and its
horsemen!" So he saw him no more. And he took
hold of his own clothes and tore them into two
pieces.

CHAPTER 1
1 [a]2 Sam. 8:2 [b]2 Kin. 3:5
2 [a]1 Kin. 22:40 [b]2 Kin. 1:3, 6, 16; Matt. 10:25; Mark 3:22 [c]1 Sam. 5:10 [1]Lit. *Lord of Flies*
3 [1]Or *Angel*
5 [1]Ahaziah
8 [a]Zech. 13:4; Matt. 3:4; Mark 1:6 [b]1 Kin. 18:7
10 [a]1 Kin. 18:36–38; Luke 9:54
13 [a]1 Sam. 26:21; Ps. 72:14 [1]Lit. *bowed down*
15 [1]Or *Angel*
17 [a]1 Kin. 22:50; 2 Kin. 8:16; Matt. 1:8 [1]The son of Ahab king of Israel, 2 Kin. 3:1

CHAPTER 2
1 [a]Gen. 5:24; [Heb. 11:5] [b]1 Kin. 19:16–21
2 [a]Ruth 1:15, 16 [b]1 Sam. 1:26; 2 Kin. 2:4, 6; 4:30
3 [a]1 Kin. 20:35; 2 Kin. 2:5, 7, 15; 4:1, 38; 9:1 [1]Lit. *from your head*
8 [a]Ex. 14:21, 22; Josh. 3:16; 2 Kin. 2:14 [b]Josh. 3:17
11 [a]2 Kin. 6:17; Ps. 104:4 [b]Gen. 5:24; Heb. 11:5
12 [a]2 Kin. 13:14

13 He also took up the mantle of Elijah that had
fallen from him, and went back and stood by the
bank of the Jordan.
14 Then he took the mantle of Elijah that had
fallen from him, and struck the water, and said,
"Where *is* the LORD God of Elijah?" And when he
also had struck the water, [a]it was divided this way
and that; and Elisha crossed over.
15 Now when the sons of the prophets who *were*
[a]from[1] Jericho saw him, they said, "The spirit of
Elijah rests on Elisha." And they came to meet
him, and bowed to the ground before him.
16 Then they said to him, "Look now, there are
fifty strong men with your servants. Please let
them go and search for your master, [a]lest perhaps
the Spirit of the LORD has taken him up and cast
him upon some mountain or into some valley."
And he said, "You shall not send anyone."
17 But when they urged him till he was
[a]ashamed, he said, "Send *them!*" Therefore they
sent fifty men, and they searched for three days
but did not find him.
18 And when they came back to him, for he had
stayed in Jericho, he said to them, "Did I not say
to you, 'Do not go'?"
**19** Then the men of the city said to Elisha,
"Please notice, the situation of this city *is* pleasant, as my lord sees; but the water *is* bad, and the
ground barren."
20 And he said, "Bring me a new bowl, and put
salt in it." So they brought *it* to him.
21 Then he went out to the source of the water,
and [a]cast in the salt there, and said, "Thus says
the LORD: 'I have [1]healed this water; from it there
shall be no more death or barrenness.' "
22 So the water remains [a]healed to this day,
according to the word of Elisha which he spoke.
**23** Then he went up from there to Bethel; and as
he was going up the road, some youths came from
the city and mocked him, and said to him, "Go up,
you baldhead! Go up, you baldhead!"
24 So he turned around and looked at them, and
[a]pronounced a curse on them in the name of the
LORD. And two female bears came out of the
woods and mauled forty-two of the youths.
25 Then he went from there to [a]Mount Carmel,
and from there he returned to Samaria.

### *Elisha Predicts Victory over Moab*

**3** Now [a]Jehoram the son of Ahab became king
over Israel at Samaria in the eighteenth year
of Jehoshaphat king of Judah, and reigned twelve
years.
2 And he did evil in the sight of the LORD, but
not like his father and mother; for he put away
the *sacred* pillar of Baal [a]that his father had made.
3 Nevertheless he persisted in [a]the sins of Jeroboam the son of Nebat, who had made Israel sin;
he did not depart from them.
**4** Now Mesha king of Moab was a sheepbreeder,
and he [a]regularly paid the king of Israel one
hundred thousand [b]lambs and the wool of one
hundred thousand rams.
5 But it happened, when [a]Ahab died, that the
king of Moab rebelled against the king of Israel.
**6** So King Jehoram went out of Samaria at that
time and mustered all Israel.
7 Then he went and sent to Jehoshaphat king of
Judah, saying, "The king of Moab has rebelled
against me. Will you go with me to fight against
Moab?" And he said, "I will go up; [a]I *am* as you
*are,* my people as your people, my horses as your
horses."
8 Then he said, "Which way shall we go up?"
And he answered, "By way of the Wilderness of
Edom."
9 So the king of Israel went with the king of
Judah and the king of Edom, and they marched on
that roundabout route seven days; and there was
no water for the army, nor for the animals that
followed them.
10 And the king of Israel said, "Alas! For the
LORD has called these three kings together to
deliver them into the hand of Moab."
11 But [a]Jehoshaphat said, "*Is there* no prophet of
the LORD here, that we may inquire of the LORD
by him?" So one of the servants of the king of
Israel answered and said, "Elisha the son of
Shaphat *is* here, who [b]poured[1] water on the hands
of Elijah."
12 And Jehoshaphat said, "The word of the LORD
is with him." So the king of Israel and Jehoshaphat and the king of Edom [a]went down to him.
**13** Then Elisha said to the king of Israel, [a]"What
have I to do with you? [b]Go to [c]the prophets of
your father and the [d]prophets of your mother."
But the king of Israel said to him, "No, for the
LORD has called these three kings *together* to
deliver them into the hand of Moab."
14 And Elisha said, [a]"*As* the LORD of hosts lives,
before whom I stand, surely were it not that I
regard the presence of Jehoshaphat king of Judah,
I would not look at you, nor see you.
15 "But now bring me [a]a musician." Then it
happened, when the musician [b]played, that [c]the
hand of the LORD came upon him.
16 And he said, "Thus says the LORD: [a]'Make this
valley full of [1]ditches.'
17 "For thus says the LORD: 'You shall not see
wind, nor shall you see rain; yet that valley shall
be filled with water, so that you, your cattle, and
your animals may drink.'
18 "And this is a simple matter in the sight of the
LORD; He will also deliver the Moabites into your
hand.
19 "Also you shall attack every fortified city and
every choice city, and shall cut down every good
tree, and stop up every spring of water, and ruin
every good piece of land with stones."
**20** Now it happened in the morning, when [a]the
grain offering was offered, that suddenly water
came by way of Edom, and the land was filled
with water.
21 And when all the Moabites heard that the
kings had come up to fight against them, all who
were able to bear arms and older were [1]gathered;
and they stood at the border.
22 Then they rose up early in the morning, and
the sun was shining on the water; and the Moabites saw the water on the other side *as* red as
blood.
23 And they said, "This is blood; the kings have
surely struck swords and have killed one another;
now therefore, Moab, to the spoil!"
24 So when they came to the camp of Israel,
Israel rose up and attacked the Moabites, so that
they fled before them; and they entered *their* land,
killing the Moabites.
25 Then they destroyed the cities, and each man
threw a stone on every good piece of land and
filled it; and they stopped up all the springs of
water and cut down all the good trees. But they

**14** [a]2 Kin. 2:8
**15** [a]2 Kin. 2:7 [1]Or *at Jericho opposite him saw*
**16** [a]1 Kin. 18:12; Ezek. 8:3; Acts 8:39
**17** [a]2 Kin. 8:11
**21** [a]Ex. 15:25, 26; 2 Kin. 4:41; 6:6; John 9:6 [1]*purified*
**22** [a]Ezek. 47:8, 9
**24** [a]Deut. 27:13–26
**25** [a]1 Kin. 18:19, 20; 2 Kin. 4:25

CHAPTER 3
**1** [a]2 Kin. 1:17
**2** [a]1 Kin. 16:31, 32
**3** [a]1 Kin. 12:28–32
**4** [a]2 Sam. 8:2 [b]Is. 16:1, 2
**5** [a]2 Kin. 1:1
**7** [a]1 Kin. 22:4
**11** [a]1 Kin. 22:7 [b]1 Kin. 19:21; [John 13:4, 5, 13, 14] [1]Was the personal servant of
**12** [a]2 Kin. 2:25
**13** [a][Ezek. 14:3] [b]Judg. 10:14; Ruth 1:15 [c]1 Kin. 22:6–11 [d]1 Kin. 18:19
**14** [a]1 Kin. 17:1; 2 Kin. 5:16
**15** [a]1 Sam. 10:5 [b]1 Sam. 16:16, 23; 1 Chr. 25:1 [c]Ezek. 1:3; 3:14, 22; 8:1
**16** [a]Jer. 14:3 [1]*water canals*
**20** [a]Ex. 29:39, 40
**21** [1]*summoned*

left the stones of [a]Kir Haraseth *intact.* However
the slingers surrounded and attacked it.
**26** And when the king of Moab saw that the
battle was too fierce for him, he took with him
seven hundred men who drew swords, to break
through to the king of Edom, but they could not.
27 Then [a]he took his eldest son who would have
reigned in his place, and offered him *as* a burnt
offering upon the wall; and there was great [1]indig-
nation against Israel. [b]So they departed from him
and returned to *their own* land.

### *Elisha and the Shunammite Woman*

**4** A certain woman of the wives of [a]the sons of
the prophets cried out to Elisha, saying, "Your
servant my husband is dead, and you know that
your servant feared the LORD. And the creditor is
coming [b]to take my two sons to be his slaves."
2 So Elisha said to her, "What shall I do for you?
Tell me, what do you have in the house?" And she
said, "Your maidservant has nothing in the house
but a jar of oil."
3 Then he said, "Go, borrow vessels from everywhere, from all your neighbors—empty vessels;
[a]do not gather just a few.
4 "And when you have come in, you shall shut
the door behind you and your sons; then pour it
into all those vessels, and set aside the full ones."
5 So she went from him and shut the door
behind her and her sons, who brought *the vessels*
to her; and she poured *it* out.
6 Now it came to pass, when the vessels were
full, that she said to her son, "Bring me another
vessel." And he said to her, "*There is* not another
vessel." So the oil ceased.
7 Then she came and told the man of God. And
he said, "Go, sell the oil and pay your debt; and
you *and* your sons live on the rest."
**8** Now it happened one day that Elisha went to
[a]Shunem, where there *was* a [1]notable woman, and
she [2]persuaded him to eat some food. So it was, as
often as he passed by, he would turn in there to
eat some food.
9 And she said to her husband, "Look now, I
know that this *is* a holy man of God, who passes
by us regularly.
10 "Please, let us make [1]a small upper room on
the wall; and let us put a bed for him there, and a
table and a chair and a lampstand; so it will be,
whenever he comes to us, he can turn in there."
11 And it happened one day that he came there,
and he turned in to the upper room and lay down
there.
12 Then he said to [a]Gehazi his servant, "Call this
Shunammite woman." When he had called her,
she stood before him.
13 And he said to him, "Say now to her, 'Look,
you have been concerned for us with all this care.
What *can I* do for you? Do you want me to speak
on your behalf to the king or to the commander of
the army?'" She answered, "I dwell among my
own people."
14 So he said, "What then *is* to be done for her?"
And Gehazi answered, "Actually, she has no son,
and her husband is old."
15 So he said, "Call her." When he had called her,
she stood in the doorway.
16 Then he said, [1]"About this time next year you
shall embrace a son." And she said, "No, my lord.
Man of God, [a]do not lie to your maidservant!"
17 But the woman conceived, and bore a son
when the appointed time had come, of which
Elisha had told her.
**18** And the child grew. Now it happened one day
that he went out to his father, to the reapers.
19 And he said to his father, "My head, my head!"
So he said to a servant, "Carry him to his mother."
20 When he had taken him and brought him to
his mother, he sat on her knees till noon, and *then*
died.
21 And she went up and laid him on the bed of
the man of God, shut *the door* upon him, and went
out.
22 Then she called to her husband, and said,
"Please send me one of the young men and one of
the donkeys, that I may run to the man of God
and come back."
23 So he said, "Why are you going to him today?
*It is* neither the [a]New Moon nor the Sabbath."
And she said, [1]"*It is* well."
24 Then she saddled a donkey, and said to her
servant, "Drive, and go forward; do not slacken
the pace for me unless I tell you."
25 And so she departed, and went to the man of
God [a]at Mount Carmel.
So it was, when the man of God saw her afar
off, that he said to his servant Gehazi, "Look, the
Shunammite woman!
26 "Please run now to meet her, and say to her,
'*Is it* well with you? *Is it* well with your husband?
*Is it* well with the child?'" And she answered, "*It
is* well."
27 Now when she came to the man of God at the
hill, she caught him by the feet, but Gehazi came
near to push her away. But the man of God said,
"Let her alone; for her soul *is* in deep distress, and
the LORD has hidden *it* from me, and has not told
me."
28 So she said, "Did I ask a son of my lord? [a]Did I
not say, 'Do not deceive me'?"
29 Then he said to Gehazi, [a]"Get[1] yourself ready,
and take my staff in your hand, and be on your
way. If you meet anyone, [b]do not greet him; and if
anyone greets you, do not answer him; but [c]lay
my staff on the face of the child."
30 And the mother of the child said, [a]"*As* the
LORD lives, and *as* your soul lives, I will not [b]leave
you." So he arose and followed her.
31 Now Gehazi went on ahead of them, and laid
the staff on the face of the child; but *there was*
neither voice nor hearing. Therefore he went back
to meet him, and told him, saying, "The child has
[a]not awakened."
**32** When Elisha came into the house, there was
the child, lying dead on his bed.
33 He [a]went in therefore, shut the door behind
the two of them, [b]and prayed to the LORD.
34 And he went up and lay on the child, and put
his mouth on his mouth, his eyes on his eyes, and
his hands on his hands; and [a]he stretched himself
out on the child, and the flesh of the child became
warm.
35 He returned and walked back and forth in the
house, and again went up [a]and stretched himself
out on him; then [b]the child sneezed seven times,
and the child opened his eyes.
36 And he called Gehazi and said, "Call this
Shunammite woman." So he called her. And when
she came in to him, he said, "Pick up your son."
37 So she went in, fell at his feet, and bowed to
the ground; then she [a]picked up her son and went
out.

**25** [a]Is. 16:7, 11; Jer. 48:31, 36
**27** [a][Deut. 18:10; Amos 2:1; Mic. 6:7] [b]2 Kin. 8:20 [1]*wrath*

CHAPTER 4

**1** [a]1 Kin. 20:35; 2 Kin. 2:3 [b][Lev. 25:39–41, 48]; 1 Sam. 22:2; Neh. 5:2–5; Matt. 18:25
**3** [a]2 Kin. 3:16
**8** [a]Josh. 19:18 [1]Lit. *great* [2]Lit. *laid hold on him*
**10** [1]Or *a small walled upper chamber*
**12** [a]2 Kin. 4:29–31; 5:20–27; 8:4, 5
**16** [a]2 Kin. 4:28 [1]Lit. *About this season, as the time of life*
**23** [a]Num. 10:10; 28:11; 1 Chr. 23:31 [1]Or *It will be well*
**25** [a]2 Kin. 2:25
**28** [a]2 Kin. 4:16
**29** [a]1 Kin. 18:46; 2 Kin. 9:1 [b]Luke 10:4 [c]Ex. 7:19; 14:16; 2 Kin. 2:8, 14; Acts 19:12 [1]Lit. *Gird up your loins.* The skirt of the robe was wrapped around the legs and tucked in the belt to gain freedom of movement.
**30** [a]2 Kin. 2:2 [b]2 Kin. 2:4
**31** [a]John 11:11
**33** [a]2 Kin. 4:4; [Matt. 6:6]; Luke 8:51 [b]1 Kin. 17:20
**34** [a]1 Kin. 17:21–23; Acts 20:10
**35** [a]1 Kin. 17:21 [b]2 Kin. 8:1, 5
**37** [a]1 Kin. 17:23; [Heb. 11:35]

38 And Elisha returned to [a]Gilgal, and *there was*
a [b]famine in the land. Now the sons of the prophets *were* [c]sitting before him; and he said to his
servant, "Put on the large pot, and boil stew for
the sons of the prophets."
39 So one went out into the field to gather herbs,
and found a wild vine, and gathered from it a
lapful of wild gourds, and came and sliced *them*
into the pot of stew, though they did not know
*what they were.*
40 Then they served it to the men to eat. Now it
happened, as they were eating the stew, that they
cried out and said, "Man of God, *there is* [a]death in
the pot!" And they could not eat *it.*
41 So he said, "Then bring some flour." And [a]he
put *it* into the pot, and said, "Serve *it* to the
people, that they may eat." And there was nothing harmful in the pot.
42 Then a man came from [a]Baal Shalisha, [b]and
brought the man of God bread of the firstfruits,
twenty loaves of barley bread, and newly ripened
grain in his knapsack. And he said, "Give *it* to the
people, that they may eat."
43 But his servant said, [a]"What? Shall I set this
before one hundred men?" He said again, "Give it
to the people, that they may eat; for thus says the
LORD: [b]'They shall eat and have *some* left over.' "
44 So he set *it* before them; and they ate [a]and had
*some* left over, according to the word of the LORD.

## *The Cure of Naaman's Leprosy*

5 Now [a]Naaman, commander of the army of the
king of Syria, was [b]a great and honorable man
in the eyes of his master, because by him the LORD
had given victory to Syria. He was also a mighty
man of valor, *but* a leper.
2 And the Syrians had gone out [a]on[1] raids, and
had brought back captive a young girl from the
land of Israel. She [2]waited on Naaman's wife.
3 Then she said to her mistress, "If only my
master *were* with the prophet who *is* in Samaria!
For he would heal him of his leprosy."
4 And *Naaman* went in and told his master,
saying, "Thus and thus said the girl who *is* from
the land of Israel."
5 Then the king of Syria said, "Go now, and I
will send a letter to the king of Israel." So he
departed and [a]took with him ten talents of silver,
six thousand *shekels* of gold, and ten changes of
clothing.
6 Then he brought the letter to the king of
Israel, which said,

> Now be advised, when this letter comes to
> you, that I have sent Naaman my servant to
> you, that you may heal him of his leprosy.

7 And it happened, when the king of Israel read
the letter, that he tore his clothes and said, "*Am* I
[a]God, to kill and make alive, that this man sends a
man to me to heal him of his leprosy? Therefore
please consider, and see how he seeks a quarrel
with me."
8 So it was, when Elisha the man of God heard
that the king of Israel had torn his clothes, that he
sent to the king, saying, "Why have you torn your
clothes? Please let him come to me, and he shall
know that there is a prophet in Israel."
9 Then Naaman went with his horses and
chariot, and he stood at the door of Elisha's house.
10 And Elisha sent a messenger to him, saying,
"Go and [a]wash in the Jordan seven times, and
your flesh shall be restored to you, and *you shall*
be clean."
11 But Naaman became furious, and went away
and said, "Indeed, I said to myself, 'He will surely
come out *to me,* and stand and call on the name of
the LORD his God, and wave his hand over the
place, and heal the leprosy.'
12 "*Are* not the [1]Abanah and the Pharpar, the
rivers of Damascus, better than all the waters of
Israel? Could I not wash in them and be clean?"
So he turned and went away in a rage.
13 And his [a]servants came near and spoke to him,
and said, "My father, *if* the prophet had told you
*to do* something great, would you not have done
*it?* How much more then, when he says to you,
'Wash, and be clean'?"
14 So he went down and dipped seven times in
the Jordan, according to the saying of the man of
God; and his [a]flesh was restored like the flesh of a
little child, and [b]he was clean.
15 And he returned to the man of God, he and all
his aides, and came and stood before him; and he
said, "Indeed, now I know that *there is* [a]no God in
all the earth, except in Israel; now therefore,
please take [b]a gift from your servant."
16 But he said, [a]"*As* the LORD lives, before whom
I stand, [b]I will receive nothing." And he urged him
to take *it,* but he refused.
17 So Naaman said, "Then, if not, please let your
servant be given two mule-loads of earth; for your
servant will no longer offer either burnt offering
or sacrifice to other gods, but to the LORD.
18 "Yet in this thing may the LORD pardon your
servant: when my master goes into the temple of
Rimmon to worship there, and [a]he leans on my
hand, and I bow down in the temple of Rimmon—
when I bow down in the temple of Rimmon, may
the LORD please pardon your servant in this
thing."
19 Then he said to him, "Go in peace." So he
departed from him a short distance.
20 But [a]Gehazi, the servant of Elisha the man of
God, said, "Look, my master has spared Naaman
this Syrian, while not receiving from his hands
what he brought; but *as* the LORD lives, I will run
after him and take something from him."
21 So Gehazi pursued Naaman. When Naaman
saw *him* running after him, he got down from the
chariot to meet him, and said, "*Is* all well?"
22 And he said, "All *is* [a]well. My master has sent
me, saying, 'Indeed, just now two young men of
the sons of the prophets have come to me from
the mountains of Ephraim. Please give them a
talent of silver and two changes of garments.' "
23 So Naaman said, "Please, take two talents."
And he urged him, and bound two talents of silver
in two bags, with two changes of garments, and
handed *them* to two of his servants; and they
carried *them* on ahead of him.
24 When he came to [1]the citadel, he took *them*
from their hand, and stored *them* away in the
house; then he let the men go, and they departed.
25 Now he went in and stood before his master.
Elisha said to him, "Where *did you go,* Gehazi?"
And he said, "Your servant did not go anywhere."
26 Then he said to him, "Did not my heart go
*with you* when the man turned back from his
chariot to meet you? *Is it* [a]time to receive money
and to receive clothing, olive groves and vineyards, sheep and oxen, male and female servants?
27 "Therefore the leprosy of Naaman [a]shall cling

38 [a]2 Kin. 2:1 [b]2 Kin. 8:1 [c]Luke 10:39; Acts 22:3
40 [a]Ex. 10:17
41 [a]Ex. 15:25; 2 Kin. 2:21
42 [a]1 Sam. 9:4 [b]1 Sam. 9:7; [1 Cor. 9:11; Gal. 6:6]
43 [a]Luke 9:13; John 6:9 [b]Luke 9:17; John 6:11
44 [a]Matt. 14:20; 15:37; John 6:13

CHAPTER 5

1 [a]Luke 4:27 [b]Ex. 11:3
2 [a]2 Kin. 6:23; 13:20 [1]Or *in bands* [2]Served, lit. *was before*
5 [a]1 Sam. 9:8; 2 Kin. 8:8, 9
7 [a][Gen. 30:2; Deut. 32:39; 1 Sam. 2:6]
10 [a]2 Kin. 4:41; John 9:7
12 [1]So with Kt., LXX, Vg.; Qr., Syr., Tg. *Amanah*
13 [a]1 Sam. 28:23
14 [a]2 Kin. 5:10; Job 33:25 [b]Luke 4:27; 5:13
15 [a]Dan. 2:47; 3:29; 6:26, 27 [b]Gen. 33:11
16 [a]2 Kin. 3:14 [b]Gen. 14:22, 23; 2 Kin. 5:20, 26; [Matt. 10:8]; Acts 8:18, 20
18 [a]2 Kin. 7:2, 17
20 [a]2 Kin. 4:12; 8:4, 5
22 [a]2 Kin. 4:26
24 [1]Lit. *the hill*
26 [a][Eccl. 3:1, 6]
27 [a][1 Tim. 6:10]

to you and your descendants forever." And he
went out from his presence [b]leprous, *as white* as
snow.

### *Elisha and the Syrians*

**6** And [a]the sons of the prophets said to Elisha,
"See now, the place where we dwell with you
is too small for us.
2 "Please, let us go to the Jordan, and let every
man take a beam from there, and let us make
there a place where we may dwell." So he answered, "Go."
3 Then one said, [a]"Please consent to go with
your servants." And he answered, "I will go."
4 So he went with them. And when they came
to the Jordan, they cut down trees.
5 But as one was cutting down a tree, the iron
*ax head* fell into the water; and he cried out and
said, "Alas, master! For it was [a]borrowed."
6 So the man of God said, "Where did it fall?"
And he showed him the place. So [a]he cut off a
stick, and threw *it* in there; and he made the iron
float.
7 Therefore he said, "Pick *it* up for yourself." So
he reached out his hand and took it.
**8** Now the [a]king of Syria was making war
against Israel; and he consulted with his servants,
saying, "My camp *will be* in such and such a
place."
9 And the man of God sent to the king of Israel,
saying, "Beware that you do not pass this place,
for the Syrians are coming down there."
10 Then the king of Israel sent *someone* to the
place of which the man of God had told him. Thus
he warned him, and he was watchful there, not
just once or twice.
11 Therefore the heart of the king of Syria was
greatly troubled by this thing; and he called his
servants and said to them, "Will you not show me
which of us *is* for the king of Israel?"
12 And one of his servants said, "None, my lord,
O king; but Elisha, the prophet who *is* in Israel,
tells the king of Israel the words that you speak in
your bedroom."
**13** So he said, "Go and see where he *is*, that I
may send and get him." And it was told him,
saying, "Surely *he is* in [a]Dothan."
14 Therefore he sent horses and chariots and a
great army there, and they came by night and
surrounded the city.
15 And when the servant of the man of God arose
early and went out, there was an army, surrounding the city with horses and chariots. And his
servant said to him, "Alas, my master! What shall
we do?"
16 So he answered, [a]"Do not fear, for [b]those who
*are* with us *are* more than those who *are* with
them."
17 And Elisha prayed, and said, "LORD, I pray,
open his eyes that he may see." Then the LORD
[a]opened the eyes of the young man, and he saw.
And behold, the mountain *was* full of [b]horses and
chariots of fire all around Elisha.
18 So when *the Syrians* came down to him,
Elisha prayed to the LORD, and said, "Strike this
people, I pray, with blindness." And [a]He struck
them with blindness according to the word of
Elisha.
**19** Now Elisha said to them, "This *is* not the way,
nor *is* this the city. Follow me, and I will bring you
to the man whom you seek." But he led them to
Samaria.
20 So it was, when they had come to Samaria,
that Elisha said, "LORD, open the eyes of these
*men*, that they may see." And the LORD opened
their eyes, and they saw; and there *they were*,
inside Samaria!
21 Now when the king of Israel saw them, he said
to Elisha, "My [a]father, shall I kill *them?* Shall I kill
*them?*"
22 But he answered, "You shall not kill *them*.
Would you kill those whom you have taken captive with your sword and your bow? [a]Set food and
water before them, that they may eat and drink
and go to their master."
23 Then he prepared a great feast for them; and
after they ate and drank, he sent them away and
they went to their master. So [a]the bands of Syrian
*raiders* came no more into the land of Israel.
**24** And it happened after this that [a]Ben-Hadad
king of Syria gathered all his army, and went up
and besieged Samaria.
25 And there was a great [a]famine in Samaria; and
indeed they besieged it until a donkey's head was
*sold* for eighty *shekels* of silver, and one-fourth of
a [1]kab of dove droppings for five *shekels* of silver.
26 Then, as the king of Israel was passing by on
the wall, a woman cried out to him, saying, "Help,
my lord, O king!"
27 And he said, "If the LORD does not help you,
where can I find help for you? From the threshing
floor or from the winepress?"
28 Then the king said to her, "What is troubling
you?" And she answered, "This woman said to
me, 'Give your son, that we may eat him today,
and we will eat my son tomorrow.'
29 "So [a]we boiled my son, and ate him. And I said
to her on the next day, 'Give your son, that we
may eat him'; but she has hidden her son."
**30** Now it happened, when the king heard the
words of the woman, that he [a]tore his clothes; and
as he passed by on the wall, the people looked,
and there underneath *he had* sackcloth on his
body.
31 Then he said, [a]"God do so to me and more
also, if the head of Elisha the son of Shaphat
remains on him today!"
32 But Elisha was sitting in his house, and [a]the
elders were sitting with him. And *the king* sent a
man ahead of him, but before the messenger came
to him, he said to the elders, [b]"Do you see how
this son of [c]a murderer has sent someone to take
away my head? Look, when the messenger comes,
shut the door, and hold him fast at the door. *Is* not
the sound of his master's feet behind him?"
33 And while he was still talking with them, there
was the messenger, coming down to him; and
then *the king* said, "Surely this calamity *is* from
the LORD; [a]why should I wait for the LORD any
longer?"

### *The Syrians Flee*

**7** Then Elisha said, "Hear the word of the LORD.
Thus says the LORD: [a]'Tomorrow about this
time a [1]seah of fine flour *shall be sold* for a shekel,
and two seahs of barley for a shekel, at the gate of
Samaria.' "
2 [a]So an officer on whose hand the king leaned
answered the man of God and said, "Look, [b]*if* the
LORD would make windows in heaven, could this

---

**27** [b]Ex. 4:6; Num. 12:10; 2 Kin. 15:5

CHAPTER 6

**1** [a]2 Kin. 4:38
**3** [a]2 Kin. 5:23
**5** [a][Ex. 22:14]
**6** [a]Ex. 15:25; 2 Kin. 2:21; 4:41
**8** [a]2 Kin. 8:28, 29
**13** [a]Gen. 37:17
**16** [a]Ex. 14:13; 1 Kin. 17:13 [b]2 Chr. 32:7; Ps. 55:18; [Rom. 8:31]
**17** [a]Num. 22:31; Luke 24:31 [b]2 Kin. 2:11; Ps. 34:7; 68:17; Zech. 1:8; 6:1–7
**18** [a]Gen. 19:11; Acts 13:11
**21** [a]2 Kin. 2:12; 5:13; 8:9
**22** [a][Rom. 12:20]
**23** [a]2 Kin. 5:2; 6:8, 9
**24** [a]1 Kin. 20:1
**25** [a]2 Kin. 4:38; 8:1 [1]Approximately 1 pint
**29** [a]Lev. 26:27–29; Deut. 28:52–57; Lam. 4:10
**30** [a]1 Kin. 21:27
**31** [a]Ruth 1:17; 1 Kin. 19:2
**32** [a]Ezek. 8:1; 14:1; 20:1 [b]Luke 13:32 [c]1 Kin. 18:4, 13, 14; 21:10, 13
**33** [a]Job 2:9

CHAPTER 7

**1** [a]2 Kin. 7:18, 19 [1]A third of an ephah, or about 8 gallons
**2** [a]2 Kin. 5:18; 7:17, 19, 20 [b]Gen. 7:11; Mal. 3:10

thing be?" And he said, "In fact, you shall see *it* with your eyes, but you shall not eat of it."

**3** Now there were four leprous men [a]at the entrance of the gate; and they said to one another, "Why are we sitting here until we die?

4 "If we say, 'We will enter the city,' the famine *is* in the city, and we shall die there. And if we sit here, we die also. Now therefore, come, let us surrender to the [a]army of the Syrians. If they keep us alive, we shall live; and if they kill us, we shall only die."

5 And they rose at twilight to go to the camp of the Syrians; and when they had come to the outskirts of the Syrian camp, to their surprise no one *was* there.

6 For the LORD had caused the army of the Syrians [a]to hear the noise of chariots and the noise of horses—the noise of a great army; so they said to one another, "Look, the king of Israel has hired against us [b]the kings of the Hittites and the kings of the Egyptians to attack us!"

7 Therefore they [a]arose and fled at twilight, and left the camp intact—their tents, their horses, and their donkeys—and they fled for their lives.

8 And when these lepers came to the outskirts of the camp, they went into one tent and ate and drank, and carried from it silver and gold and clothing, and went and hid *them;* then they came back and entered another tent, and carried *some* from there *also,* and went and hid *it.*

**9** Then they said to one another, "We are not doing right. This day *is* a day of good news, and we remain silent. If we wait until morning light, some [1]punishment will come upon us. Now therefore, come, let us go and tell the king's household."

10 So they went and called to the gatekeepers of the city, and told them, saying, "We went to the Syrian camp, and surprisingly no one *was* there, not a human sound—only horses and donkeys tied, and the tents intact."

11 And the gatekeepers called out, and they told *it* to the king's household inside.

**12** So the king arose in the night and said to his servants, "Let me now tell you what the Syrians have done to us. They know that we *are* [a]hungry; therefore they have gone out of the camp to [1]hide themselves in the field, saying, 'When they come out of the city, we shall catch them alive, and get into the city.' "

13 And one of his servants answered and said, "Please, let several *men* take five of the remaining horses which are left in the city. Look, they *may either become* like all the multitude of Israel that are left in it; or indeed, *I say,* they *may become* like all the multitude of Israel left from those who are consumed; so let us send them and see."

14 Therefore they took two chariots with horses; and the king sent them in the direction of the Syrian army, saying, "Go and see."

15 And they went after them to the Jordan; and indeed all the road *was* full of garments and weapons which the Syrians had thrown away in their haste. So the messengers returned and told the king.

16 Then the people went out and plundered the tents of the Syrians. So a seah of fine flour was *sold* for a shekel, and two seahs of barley for a shekel, [a]according to the word of the LORD.

**17** Now the king had appointed the officer on whose hand he leaned to have charge of the gate. But the people trampled him in the gate, and he died, just [a]as the man of God had said, who spoke when the king came down to him.

18 So it happened just as the man of God had spoken to the king, saying, [a]"Two seahs of barley for a shekel, and a seah of fine flour for a shekel, shall be *sold* tomorrow about this time in the gate of Samaria."

19 Then that officer had answered the man of God, and said, "Now look, *if* the LORD would make windows in heaven, could such a thing be?" And he had said, "In fact, you shall see *it* with your eyes, but you shall not eat of it."

20 And so it happened to him, for the people trampled him in the gate, and he died.

### *The King Restores the Shunammite's Land*

**8** Then Elisha spoke to the woman [a]whose son he had restored to life, saying, "Arise and go, you and your household, and stay wherever you can; for the LORD [b]has called for a [c]famine, and furthermore, it will come upon the land for seven years."

2 So the woman arose and did according to the saying of the man of God, and she went with her household and dwelt in the land of the Philistines seven years.

3 It came to pass, at the end of seven years, that the woman returned from the land of the Philistines; and she went to make an appeal to the king for her house and for her land.

4 Then the king talked with [a]Gehazi, the servant of the man of God, saying, "Tell me, please, all the great things Elisha has done."

5 Now it happened, as he was telling the king how he had restored the dead to life, that there was the woman whose son he had [a]restored to life, appealing to the king for her house and for her land. And Gehazi said, "My lord, O king, this *is* the woman, and this *is* her son whom Elisha restored to life."

6 And when the king asked the woman, she told him. So the king appointed a certain officer for her, saying, "Restore all that *was* hers, and all the proceeds of the field from the day that she left the land until now."

**7** Then Elisha went to Damascus, and [a]Ben-Hadad king of Syria was sick; and it was told him, saying, "The man of God has come here."

8 And the king said to [a]Hazael, [b]"Take a present in your hand, and go to meet the man of God, and [c]inquire of the LORD by him, saying, 'Shall I recover from this disease?' "

9 So [a]Hazael went to meet him and took a present with him, of every good thing of Damascus, forty camel-loads; and he came and stood before him, and said, "Your son Ben-Hadad king of Syria has sent me to you, saying, 'Shall I recover from this disease?' "

10 And Elisha said to him, "Go, say to him, 'You shall certainly recover.' However the LORD has shown me that [a]he will really die."

11 Then he [1]set his countenance in a stare until he was ashamed; and the man of God [a]wept.

12 And Hazael said, "Why is my lord weeping?" He answered, "Because I know [a]the evil that you will do to the children of Israel: Their strongholds you will set on fire, and their young men you will kill with the sword; and you [b]will dash their children, and rip open their women with child."

13 So Hazael said, "But what [a]*is* your servant—a

---

**3** [a][Lev. 13:45, 46; Num. 5:2–4; 12:10–14]
**4** [a]2 Kin. 6:24
**6** [a]2 Sam. 5:24; 2 Kin. 19:7; Job 15:21 [b]1 Kin. 10:29
**7** [a]Ps. 48:4–6; [Prov. 28:1]
**9** [1]Calamity
**12** [a]2 Kin. 6:24–29 [1]Hide themselves in ambush
**16** [a]2 Kin. 7:1
**17** [a]2 Kin. 6:32; 7:2
**18** [a]2 Kin. 7:1

CHAPTER 8

**1** [a]2 Kin. 4:18, 31–35 [b]Ps. 105:16; Hag. 1:11 [c]2 Sam. 21:1; 1 Kin. 18:2; 2 Kin. 4:38; 6:25
**4** [a]2 Kin. 4:12; 5:20–27
**5** [a]2 Kin. 4:35
**7** [a]2 Kin. 6:24
**8** [a]1 Kin. 19:15 [b]1 Sam. 9:7; 1 Kin. 14:3; 2 Kin. 5:5 [c]2 Kin. 1:2
**9** [a]1 Kin. 19:15
**10** [a]2 Kin. 8:15
**11** [a]Luke 19:41 [1]*fixed his gaze*
**12** [a]2 Kin. 10:32; 12:17; 13:3, 7; Amos 1:3, 4 [b]2 Kin. 15:16; Hos. 13:16; Amos 1:13; Nah. 3:10
**13** [a]1 Sam. 17:43; 2 Sam. 9:8

dog, that he should do this gross thing?" And
Elisha answered, [b]"The LORD has shown me that
you *will become* king over Syria."
14 Then he departed from Elisha, and came to his
master, who said to him, "What did Elisha say to
you?" And he answered, "He told me you would
surely recover."
15 But it happened on the next day that he took a
thick cloth and dipped *it* in water, and spread *it*
over his face so that he died; and Hazael reigned
in his place.
**16** Now [a]in the fifth year of Joram the son of
Ahab, king of Israel, Jehoshaphat *having been*
king of Judah, [b]Jehoram the son of Jehoshaphat
began to reign as [1]king of Judah.
17 He was [a]thirty-two years old when he became
king, and he reigned eight years in Jerusalem.
18 And he walked in the way of the kings of
Israel, just as the house of Ahab had done, for [a]the
daughter of Ahab was his wife; and he did evil in
the sight of the LORD.
19 Yet the LORD would not destroy Judah, for the
sake of his servant David, [a]as He promised him to
give a lamp to him *and* his sons forever.
20 In his days [a]Edom revolted against Judah's
authority, [b]and made a king over themselves.
21 So [1]Joram went to Zair, and all his chariots
with him. Then he rose by night and attacked the
Edomites who had surrounded him and the captains of the chariots; and the troops fled to their
tents.
22 Thus Edom has been in revolt against Judah's
authority to this day. [a]And Libnah revolted at that
time.
**23** Now the rest of the acts of [1]Joram, and all that
he did, *are* they not written in the book of the
chronicles of the kings of Judah?
24 So Joram [1]rested with his fathers, and was
buried with his fathers in the City of David. Then
[a]Ahaziah[2] his son reigned in his place.
**25** In the twelfth year of Joram the son of Ahab,
king of Israel, Ahaziah the son of Jehoram, king
of Judah, began to reign.
26 Ahaziah *was* [a]twenty-two years old when he
became king, and he reigned one year in Jerusalem. His mother's name *was* Athaliah the granddaughter of Omri, king of Israel.
27 [a]And he walked in the way of the house of
Ahab, and did evil in the sight of the LORD, like
the house of Ahab, for he *was* the son-in-law of
the house of Ahab.
**28** Now he went [a]with Joram the son of Ahab to
war against Hazael king of Syria at [b]Ramoth
Gilead; and the Syrians wounded Joram.
29 Then [a]King Joram went back to Jezreel to
recover from the wounds which the Syrians had
inflicted on him at [1]Ramah, when he fought
against Hazael king of Syria. [b]And Ahaziah the
son of Jehoram, king of Judah, went down to see
Joram the son of Ahab in Jezreel, because he was
sick.

## *The Violent Deaths of Joram, Ahaziah, and Jezebel*

**9** And Elisha the prophet called one of [a]the sons
of the prophets, and said to him, [b]"Get[1] yourself ready, take this flask of oil in your hand, [c]and
go to Ramoth Gilead.
2 "Now when you arrive at that place, look
there for Jehu the son of Jehoshaphat, the son of
Nimshi, and go in and make him rise up from

13 [b]1 Kin. 19:15
16 [a]2 Kin. 1:17; 3:1 [b]2 Chr. 21:3 [1]Co-regent with his father
17 [a]2 Chr. 21:5–10
18 [a]2 Kin. 8:26, 27
19 [a]2 Sam. 7:13; 1 Kin. 11:36; 15:4; 2 Chr. 21:7
20 [a]Gen. 27:40; 2 Chr. 21:8–10 [b]1 Kin. 22:47
21 [1]*Jehoram,* v. 16
22 [a]Josh. 21:13; 2 Kin. 19:8; 2 Chr. 21:10
23 [1]*Jehoram,* v. 16
24 [a]2 Chr. 22:1, 7 [1]Died and joined his ancestors [2]Or *Azariah* or *Jehoahaz*
26 [a]2 Chr. 22:2
27 [a]2 Chr. 22:3, 4
28 [a]2 Chr. 22:5 [b]1 Kin. 22:3, 29
29 [a]2 Kin. 9:15 [b]2 Kin. 9:16; 2 Chr. 22:6, 7 [1]*Ramoth,* v. 28

CHAPTER 9
1 [a]1 Kin. 20:35 [b]2 Kin. 4:29; Jer. 1:17 [c]2 Kin. 8:28, 29 [1]Lit. *Gird up your loins*
2 [a]2 Kin. 9:5, 11
3 [a]1 Kin. 19:16
6 [a]1 Sam. 2:7, 8; 1 Kin. 19:16; 2 Kin. 9:3; 2 Chr. 22:7
7 [a][Deut. 32:35, 41] [b]1 Kin. 18:4; 21:15
8 [a]1 Kin. 14:10; 21:21; 2 Kin. 10:17 [b]1 Sam. 25:22 [c]Deut. 32:36; 2 Kin. 14:26
9 [a]1 Kin. 14:10; 15:29; 21:22 [b]1 Kin. 16:3, 11
10 [a]1 Kin. 21:23; 2 Kin. 9:35, 36
11 [a]Jer. 29:26; Hos. 9:7; Mark 3:21; John 10:20; Acts 26:24; [1 Cor. 4:10]
13 [a]Matt. 21:7, 8; Mark 11:7, 8 [1]Lit. *under his feet*
14 [a]2 Kin. 8:28
15 [a]2 Kin. 8:29 [1]*Jehoram,* v. 24
16 [a]2 Kin. 8:29
17 [1]Are you peaceful?
18 [1]Lit. *Turn behind me*

among [a]his associates, and take him to an inner
room.
3 "Then [a]take the flask of oil, and pour *it* on his
head, and say, 'Thus says the LORD: "I have
anointed you king over Israel." ' Then open the
door and flee, and do not delay."
4 So the young man, the servant of the prophet,
went to Ramoth Gilead.
5 And when he arrived, there *were* the captains
of the army sitting; and he said, "I have a message
for you, commander." Jehu said, "For which *one*
of us?" And he said, "For you, commander."
6 Then he arose and went into the house. And
he poured the oil on his head, and said to him,
[a]"Thus says the LORD God of Israel: 'I have
anointed you king over the people of the LORD,
over Israel.
7 'You shall strike down the house of Ahab your
master, that I may [a]avenge the blood of My
servants the prophets, and the blood of all the
servants of the LORD, [b]at the hand of Jezebel.
8 'For the whole house of Ahab shall perish; and
[a]I will cut off from Ahab all [b]the males in Israel,
both [c]bond and free.
9 'So I will make the house of Ahab like the
house of [a]Jeroboam the son of Nebat, and like the
house of [b]Baasha the son of Ahijah.
10 [a]'The dogs shall eat Jezebel on the plot *of
ground* at Jezreel, and *there shall be* none to bury
*her.*' " And he opened the door and fled.
**11** Then Jehu came out to the servants of his
master, and *one* said to him, "*Is* all well? Why did
[a]this madman come to you?" And he said to them,
"You know the man and his babble."
12 And they said, "A lie! Tell us now." So he said,
"Thus and thus he spoke to me, saying, 'Thus says
the LORD: "I have anointed you king over Israel." ' "
13 Then each man hastened [a]to take his garment
and put *it* [1]under him on the top of the steps; and
they blew trumpets, saying, "Jehu is king!"
**14** So Jehu the son of Jehoshaphat, the son of
Nimshi, conspired against [a]Joram. (Now Joram
had been defending Ramoth Gilead, he and all
Israel, against Hazael king of Syria.
15 But [a]King [1]Joram had returned to Jezreel to
recover from the wounds which the Syrians had
inflicted on him when he fought with Hazael king
of Syria.) And Jehu said, "If you are so minded, let
no one leave *or* escape from the city to go and tell
*it* in Jezreel."
16 So Jehu rode in a chariot and went to Jezreel,
for Joram was laid up there; [a]and Ahaziah king of
Judah had come down to see Joram.
**17** Now a watchman stood on the tower in Jezreel, and he saw the company of Jehu as he came,
and said, "I see a company of men." And Joram
said, "Get a horseman and send him to meet them,
and let him say, [1]'*Is it* peace?' "
18 So the horseman went to meet him, and said,
"Thus says the king: '*Is it* peace?' " And Jehu said,
"What have you to do with peace? [1]Turn around
and follow me." So the watchman reported, saying, "The messenger went to them, but is not
coming back."
19 Then he sent out a second horseman who
came to them, and said, "Thus says the king: '*Is it*
peace?' " And Jehu answered, "What have you to
do with peace? Turn around and follow me."
20 So the watchman reported, saying, "He went
up to them and is not coming back; and the

driving *is* like the driving of Jehu the son of
Nimshi, for he drives furiously!"
21 Then Joram said, [1]"Make ready." And his
chariot was made ready. Then [a]Joram king of
Israel and Ahaziah king of Judah went out, each
in his chariot; and they went out to meet Jehu,
and [2]met him [b]on the property of Naboth the
Jezreelite.
22 Now it happened, when Joram saw Jehu, that
he said, "*Is it* peace, Jehu?" So he answered,
"What peace, as long as the harlotries of your
mother Jezebel and her witchcraft *are* so many?"
23 Then Joram turned around and fled, and said
to Ahaziah, "Treachery, Ahaziah!"
24 Now Jehu [1]drew his bow with full strength
and shot Jehoram between his arms; and the
arrow came out at his heart, and he sank down in
his chariot.
25 Then *Jehu* said to Bidkar his captain, "Pick
*him* up, *and* throw him into the tract of the field of
Naboth the Jezreelite; for remember, when you
and I were riding together behind Ahab his father,
that [a]the LORD laid this [b]burden upon him:
26 'Surely I saw yesterday the blood of Naboth
and the blood of his sons,' says the LORD, [a]'and I
will repay you [1]in this plot,' says the LORD. Now
therefore, take *and* throw him on the plot *of
ground,* according to the word of the LORD."
27 But when Ahaziah king of Judah saw *this,* he
fled by the road to [1]Beth Haggan. So Jehu pursued
him, and said, [2]"Shoot him also in the chariot."
*And they shot him* at the Ascent of Gur, which is
by Ibleam. Then he fled to [a]Megiddo, and died
there.
28 And his servants carried him in the chariot to
Jerusalem, and buried him in his tomb with his
fathers in the City of David.
29 In the eleventh year of Joram the son of Ahab,
Ahaziah had become king over Judah.
30 Now when Jehu had come to Jezreel, Jezebel
heard *of it;* [a]and she put paint on her eyes and
adorned her head, and looked through a window.
31 Then, as Jehu entered at the gate, she said,
[a]"*Is it* peace, Zimri, murderer of your master?"
32 And he looked up at the window, and said,
"Who *is* on my side? Who?" So two *or* three
eunuchs looked out at him.
33 Then he said, "Throw her down." So they
threw her down, and *some* of her blood spattered
on the wall and on the horses; and he trampled
her underfoot.
34 And when he had gone in, he ate and drank.
Then he said, "Go now, see to this accursed
*woman,* and bury her, for [a]she was a king's daughter."
35 So they went to bury her, but they found no
more of her than the skull and the feet and the
palms of *her* hands.
36 Therefore they came back and told him. And
he said, "This *is* the word of the LORD, which He
spoke by His servant Elijah the Tishbite, saying,
[a]'On the plot *of ground* at Jezreel dogs shall eat
the flesh of Jezebel;
37 'and the corpse of Jezebel shall be [a]as refuse
on the surface of the field, in the plot at Jezreel, so
that they shall not say, "Here *lies* Jezebel." ' "

**21** [a]1 Kin. 19:17; 2 Chr. 22:7 [b]1 Kin. 21:1–14 [1]*Harness up* [2]Lit. *found*
**24** [1]Lit. *filled his hand*
**25** [a]1 Kin. 21:19, 24–29 [b]Is. 13:1
**26** [a]1 Kin. 21:13, 19 [1]*on this property*
**27** [a]2 Chr. 22:7, 9 [1]Lit. *The Garden House* [2]Lit. *Strike*
**30** [a][Jer. 4:30]; Ezek. 23:40
**31** [a]1 Kin. 16:9–20; 2 Kin. 9:18–22
**34** [a][Ex. 22:28]; 1 Kin. 16:31
**36** [a]1 Kin. 21:23
**37** [a]Ps. 83:10

CHAPTER 10

**1** [1]So with MT, Syr., Tg.; LXX *Samaria;* Vg. *city* [2]*the guardians of*
**3** [1]*most upright*
**4** [a]2 Kin. 9:24, 27 [1]Lit. *stand before*
**7** [a]Judg. 9:5; 1 Kin. 21:21; 2 Kin. 11:1
**9** [a]2 Kin. 9:14–24
**10** [a]1 Sam. 3:19; 1 Kin. 8:56; Jer. 44:28 [b]1 Kin. 21:17–24, 29
**12** [1]Lit. *The Shearing House*
**13** [a]2 Chr. 22:8
**14** [a]2 Chr. 22:8 [1]Lit. *The Shearing House*
**15** [a]Jer. 35:6 [b]1 Chr. 2:55 [c]Ezra 10:19; Ezek. 17:18 [1]Lit. *found*

## *Ahab's Seventy Sons Killed*

10 Now Ahab had seventy sons in Samaria.
And Jehu wrote and sent letters to Samaria,
to the rulers of [1]Jezreel, to the elders, and to
[2]those who reared Ahab's *sons,* saying:

2 Now as soon as this letter comes to you,
since your master's sons *are* with you, and
you have chariots and horses, a fortified city
also, and weapons,
3 choose the [1]best qualified of your master's
sons, set *him* on his father's throne, and fight
for your master's house.

4 But they were exceedingly afraid, and said,
"Look, [a]two kings could not [1]stand up to him; how
then can we stand?"
5 And he who *was* in charge of the house, and
he who *was* in charge of the city, the elders also,
and those who reared *the sons,* sent to Jehu,
saying, "We *are* your servants, we will do all you
tell us; but we will not make anyone king. Do
*what is* good in your sight."
6 Then he wrote a second letter to them, saying:

If you *are* for me and will obey my voice,
take the heads of the men, your master's
sons, and come to me at Jezreel by this time
tomorrow.

Now the king's sons, seventy persons, *were* with
the great men of the city, *who* were rearing them.
7 So it was, when the letter came to them, that
they took the king's sons and [a]slaughtered seventy persons, put their heads in baskets and sent
*them* to him at Jezreel.
8 Then a messenger came and told him, saying,
"They have brought the heads of the king's sons."
And he said, "Lay them in two heaps at the
entrance of the gate until morning."
9 So it was, in the morning, that he went out
and stood, and said to all the people, "You *are*
righteous. Indeed [a]I conspired against my master
and killed him; but who killed all these?
10 "Know now that nothing shall [a]fall to the
earth of the word of the LORD which the LORD
spoke concerning the house of Ahab; for the LORD
has done what He spoke [b]by His servant Elijah."
11 So Jehu killed all who remained of the house
of Ahab in Jezreel, and all his great men and his
close acquaintances and his priests, until he left
him none remaining.
12 And he arose and departed and went to Samaria. On the way, at [1]Beth Eked of the Shepherds,
13 [a]Jehu met with the brothers of Ahaziah king
of Judah, and said, "Who *are* you?" So they
answered, "We *are* the brothers of Ahaziah; we
have come down to greet the sons of the king and
the sons of the queen mother."
14 And he said, "Take them alive!" So they took
them alive, and [a]killed them at the well of [1]Beth
Eked, forty-two men; and he left none of them.
15 Now when he departed from there, he [1]met
[a]Jehonadab the son of [b]Rechab, *coming* to meet
him; and he greeted him and said to him, "Is your
heart right, as my heart *is* toward your heart?"
And Jehonadab answered, "It is." *Jehu said,* "If it
is, [c]give *me* your hand." So he gave *him* his hand,
and he took him up to him into the chariot.

16 Then he said, "Come with me, and see my [a]zeal for the LORD." So they had him ride in his chariot.
17 And when he came to Samaria, [a]he killed all who remained to Ahab in Samaria, till he had destroyed them, according to the word of the LORD [b]which He spoke to Elijah.
**18** Then Jehu gathered all the people together, and said to them, [a]"Ahab served Baal a little, Jehu will serve him much.
19 "Now therefore, call to me all the [a]prophets of Baal, all his servants, and all his priests. Let no one be missing, for I have a great sacrifice for Baal. Whoever is missing shall not live." But Jehu acted deceptively, with the intent of destroying the worshipers of Baal.
20 And Jehu said, [1]"Proclaim a solemn assembly for Baal." So they proclaimed *it.*
21 Then Jehu sent throughout all Israel; and all the worshipers of Baal came, so that there was not a man left who did not come. So they came into the [1]temple of Baal, and the [a]temple of Baal was full from one end to the other.
22 And he said to the one in charge of the wardrobe, "Bring out vestments for all the worshipers of Baal." So he brought out vestments for them.
23 Then Jehu and Jehonadab the son of Rechab went into the temple of Baal, and said to the worshipers of Baal, "Search and see that no servants of the LORD are here with you, but only the worshipers of Baal."
24 So they went in to offer sacrifices and burnt offerings. Now Jehu had appointed for himself eighty men on the outside, and had said, "*If* any of the men whom I have brought into your hands escapes, *whoever lets him escape, it shall be* [a]his life for the life of the other."
25 Now it happened, as soon as he had made an end of offering the burnt offering, that Jehu said to the guard and to the captains, "Go in *and* kill them; let no one come out!" And they killed them with the edge of the sword; then the guards and the officers threw *them* out, and went into the [1]inner room of the temple of Baal.
26 And they brought the [a]*sacred* pillars out of the temple of Baal and burned them.
27 Then they broke down the *sacred* pillar of Baal, and tore down the [1]temple of Baal and [a]made it a refuse dump to this day.
28 Thus Jehu destroyed Baal from Israel.
**29** However Jehu did not turn away from the sins of Jeroboam the son of Nebat, who had made Israel sin, *that is,* from [a]the golden calves that *were* at Bethel and Dan.
30 And the LORD [a]said to Jehu, "Because you have done well in doing *what is* right in My sight, *and* have done to the house of Ahab all that *was* in My heart, [b]your sons shall sit on the throne of Israel to the fourth *generation.*"
31 But Jehu [1]took no heed to walk in the law of the LORD God of Israel with all his heart; for he did not depart from [a]the sins of Jeroboam, who had made Israel sin.
**32** In those days the LORD began to cut off *parts* of Israel; and [a]Hazael conquered them in all the territory of Israel.
33 from the Jordan eastward: all the land of Gilead—Gad, Reuben, and Manasseh—from [a]Aroer, which *is* by the River Arnon, including [b]Gilead and Bashan.
**34** Now the rest of the acts of Jehu, all that he

**16** [a]1 Kin. 19:10
**17** [a]2 Kin. 9:8; 2 Chr. 22:8 [b]1 Kin. 21:21, 29
**18** [a]1 Kin. 16:31, 32
**19** [a]1 Kin. 18:19; 22:6
**20** [1]*Consecrate*
**21** [a]1 Kin. 16:32; 2 Kin. 11:18 [1]Lit. *house*
**24** [a]1 Kin. 20:39
**25** [1]Lit. *city*
**26** [a][Deut. 7:5, 25]; 1 Kin. 14:23; 2 Kin. 3:2
**27** [a]Ezra 6:11; Dan. 2:5; 3:29 [1]Lit. *house*
**29** [a]1 Kin. 12:28–30; 13:33, 34
**30** [a]2 Kin. 9:6, 7 [b]2 Kin. 13:1, 10; 14:23; 15:8, 12
**31** [a]1 Kin. 14:16 [1]*was not careful*
**32** [a]1 Kin. 19:17; 2 Kin. 8:12; 13:22
**33** [a]Deut. 2:36 [b]Amos 1:3–5
**35** [a]2 Kin. 13:1 [1]Died and joined his ancestors

CHAPTER 11

**1** [a]2 Chr. 22:10 [b]2 Kin. 8:26 [c]2 Kin. 9:27
**2** [a]2 Kin. 8:25 [1]*Jehoshabeath,* 2 Chr. 22:11 [2]Or *Jehoash*
**4** [a]2 Kin. 12:2; 2 Chr. 23:1 [1]*guards*
**5** [a]1 Chr. 9:25 [1]Lit. *enter in*
**7** [1]*companies*
**9** [a]2 Chr. 23:8
**10** [a]2 Sam. 8:7; 1 Chr. 18:7
**11** [1]Lit. *shoulder*
**12** [a]Ex. 25:16; 31:18 [b]1 Sam. 10:24 [1]Law, Ex. 25:16, 21; Deut. 31:9
**13** [a]2 Kin. 8:26; 2 Chr. 23:12
**14** [a]2 Kin. 23:3; 2 Chr. 34:31

did, and all his might, *are* they not written in the book of the chronicles of the kings of Israel?
35 So Jehu [1]rested with his fathers, and they buried him in Samaria. Then [a]Jehoahaz his son reigned in his place.
36 And the period that Jehu reigned over Israel in Samaria *was* twenty-eight years.

### *Joash Crowned King of Judah*

**11** When [a]Athaliah [b]the mother of Ahaziah saw that her son was [c]dead, she arose and destroyed all the royal heirs.
2 But [1]Jehosheba, the daughter of King Joram, sister of [a]Ahaziah, took [2]Joash the son of Ahaziah, and stole him away from among the king's sons *who were* being murdered; and they hid him and his nurse in the bedroom, from Athaliah, so that he was not killed.
3 So he was hidden with her in the house of the LORD for six years, while Athaliah reigned over the land.
**4** In [a]the seventh year Jehoiada sent and brought the captains of hundreds—of the bodyguards and the [1]escorts—and brought them into the house of the LORD to him. And he made a covenant with them and took an oath from them in the house of the LORD, and showed them the king's son.
5 Then he commanded them, saying, "This *is* what you shall do: One-third of you who [1]come on duty [a]on the Sabbath shall be keeping watch over the king's house,
6 "one-third *shall be* at the gate of Sur, and one-third at the gate behind the escorts. You shall keep the watch of the house, lest it be broken down.
7 "The two [1]contingents of you who go off duty on the Sabbath shall keep the watch of the house of the LORD for the king.
8 "But you shall surround the king on all sides, every man with his weapons in his hand; and whoever comes within range, let him be put to death. You are to be with the king as he goes out and as he comes in."
**9** [a]So the captains of the hundreds did according to all that Jehoiada the priest commanded. Each of them took his men who were to be on duty on the Sabbath, with those who were going off duty on the Sabbath, and came to Jehoiada the priest.
10 And the priest gave the captains of hundreds the spears and shields which *had belonged* to King David, [a]that were in the temple of the LORD.
11 Then the escorts stood, every man with his weapons in his hand, all around the king, from the right [1]side of the temple to the left side of the temple, by the altar and the house.
12 And he brought out the king's son, put the crown on him, and *gave him* the [a]Testimony;[1] they made him king and anointed him, and they clapped their hands and said, [b]"Long live the king!"
**13** [a]Now when Athaliah heard the noise of the escorts *and* the people, she came to the people *in* the temple of the LORD.
14 When she looked, there was the king standing by [a]a pillar according to custom; and the leaders and the trumpeters were by the king. All the people of the land were rejoicing and blowing trumpets. So Athaliah tore her clothes and cried out, "Treason! Treason!"
15 And Jehoiada the priest commanded the

captains of the hundreds, the officers of the army,
and said to them, "Take her outside [1]under guard,
and slay with the sword whoever follows her." For
the priest had said, "Do not let her be killed in the
house of the LORD."
16 So they seized her; and she went by way of the
horses' entrance *into* the king's house, and there
she was killed.
**17** [a]Then Jehoiada [b]made a covenant between the
LORD, the king, and the people, that they should
be the LORD's people, and *also* [c]between the king
and the people.
18 And all the people of the land went to the
[a]temple of Baal, and tore it down. They thoroughly [b]broke in pieces its altars and [1]images, and
[c]killed Mattan the priest of Baal before the altars.
And [d]the priest appointed [2]officers over the house
of the LORD.
19 Then he took the captains of hundreds, the
bodyguards, the escorts, and all the people of
the land; and they brought the king down from
the house of the LORD, and went by way of the
gate of the escorts to the king's house. Then he
sat on the throne of the kings.
20 So all the people of the land rejoiced; and the
city was quiet, for they had slain Athaliah with
the sword *in* the king's house.
21 Jehoash *was* [a]seven years old when he became
king.

### *Jehoash Reigns over Judah*

**12** In the seventh year of Jehu, [a]Jehoash[1] became king, and he reigned forty years in
Jerusalem. His mother's name *was* Zibiah of
Beersheba.
2 Jehoash did *what was* right in the sight of the
LORD all the days in which [a]Jehoiada the priest
instructed him.
3 But [a]the [1]high places were not taken away; the
people still sacrificed and burned incense on the
high places.
4 And Jehoash said to the priests, [a]"All the
money of the dedicated gifts that are brought into
the house of the LORD—each man's [b]census[1]
money, each man's [c]assessment money—*and* all
the money that [2]a man purposes in his heart to
bring into the house of the LORD,
5 "let the priests take *it* themselves, each from
his constituency; and let them repair the [1]damages
of the temple, wherever any dilapidation is
found."
6 Now it was so, by the twenty-third year of
King Jehoash, [a]*that* the priests had not repaired
the damages of the temple.
7 [a]So King Jehoash called Jehoiada the priest
and the *other* priests, and said to them, "Why
have you not repaired the damages of the temple?
Now therefore, do not take *more* money from
your constituency, but deliver it for repairing the
damages of the temple."
8 And the priests agreed that they would neither
receive *more* money from the people, nor repair
the damages of the temple.
**9** Then Jehoiada the priest took [a]a chest, bored a
hole in its lid, and set it beside the altar, on the
right side as one comes into the house of the
LORD; and the priests who [1]kept the door put
[b]there all the money brought into the house of the
LORD.
10 So it was, whenever they saw that *there was*
much money in the chest, that the king's [a]scribe[1]
and the high priest came up and [2]put it in bags,
and counted the money that was found in the
house of the LORD.
11 Then they gave the money, which had been
apportioned, into the hands of those who did the
work, who had the oversight of the house of the
LORD; and they [1]paid it out to the carpenters and
builders who worked on the house of the LORD,
12 and to masons and stonecutters, and for buy-
ing timber and hewn stone, to [a]repair the damage
of the house of the LORD, and for all that was paid
out to repair the temple.
13 However [a]there were not made for the house
of the LORD basins of silver, trimmers, sprinkling-
bowls, trumpets, any articles of gold or articles of
silver, from the money brought into the house of
the LORD.
14 But they gave that to the workmen, and they
repaired the house of the LORD with it.
15 Moreover [a]they did not require an account
from the men into whose hand they delivered the
money to be paid to workmen, for they dealt
faithfully.
16 [a]The money from the trespass offerings and
the money from the sin offerings was not brought
into the house of the LORD. [b]It belonged to the
priests.
**17** [a]Hazael king of Syria went up and fought
against Gath, and took it; then [b]Hazael set his face
to [1]go up to Jerusalem.
18 And Jehoash king of Judah [a]took all the sacred things that his fathers, Jehoshaphat and
Jehoram and Ahaziah, kings of Judah, had dedicated, and his own sacred things, and all the gold
found in the treasuries of the house of the LORD
and in the king's house, and sent *them* to Hazael
king of Syria. Then he went away from Jerusalem.
**19** Now the rest of the acts of [1]Joash, and all that
he did, *are* they not written in the book of the
chronicles of the kings of Judah?
20 And [a]his servants arose and formed a conspiracy, and killed Joash in the house of [1]the Millo,
which goes down to Silla.
21 For [1]Jozachar the son of Shimeath and Jehozabad the son of [2]Shomer, his servants, struck
him. So he died, and they buried him with his
fathers in the City of David. Then [a]Amaziah his
son reigned in his place.

### *Elisha's Final Prophecy and Death*

**13** In the twenty-third year of [a]Joash[1] the son
of Ahaziah, king of Judah, [b]Jehoahaz the
son of Jehu became king over Israel in Samaria,
*and reigned* seventeen years.
2 And he did evil in the sight of the LORD, and
followed the [a]sins of Jeroboam the son of Nebat,
who had made Israel sin. He did not [1]depart from
them.
**3** Then [a]the anger of the LORD was aroused
against Israel, and He delivered them into the
hand of [b]Hazael king of Syria, and into the hand
of [c]Ben-Hadad the son of Hazael, all *their* days.
4 So Jehoahaz [a]pleaded with the LORD, and the
LORD listened to him; for [b]He saw the oppression
of Israel, because the king of Syria oppressed
them.
5 [a]Then the LORD gave Israel a deliverer, so that
they escaped from under the hand of the Syrians;
and the children of Israel dwelt in their tents as
before.
6 Nevertheless they did not depart from the sins

**15** [1]Lit. *between ranks*
**17** [a]2 Chr. 23:16 [b]Josh. 24:24, 25 [c]2 Sam. 5:3
**18** [a]2 Kin. 10:26, 27 [b][Deut. 12:3] [c]1 Kin. 18:40 [d]2 Chr. 23:18 [1]Idols [2]Lit. *offices*
**21** [a]2 Chr. 24:1–14

CHAPTER 12
**1** [a]2 Chr. 24:1 [1]*Joash,* 2 Kin. 11:2ff.
**2** [a]2 Kin. 11:4
**3** [a]2 Kin. 14:4; 15:35 [1]Places for pagan worship
**4** [a]2 Kin. 22:4 [b]Ex. 30:13–16; Lev. 27:2–28 [c]Ex. 35:5 [1]Lit. *the money coming over* [2]*any man's heart prompts him to bring*
**5** [1]Lit. *breaches*
**6** [a]2 Chr. 24:5
**7** [a]2 Chr. 24:6
**9** [a]2 Chr. 23:1; 24:8 [b]Mark 12:41 [1]*guarded at the door*
**10** [a]2 Sam. 8:17 [1]*secretary* [2]*tied it up*
**11** [1]Lit. *weighed*
**12** [a]2 Kin. 22:5, 6
**13** [a]2 Chr. 24:14
**15** [a]2 Kin. 22:7
**16** [a][Lev. 5:15, 18] [b][Num. 18:9]
**17** [a]2 Kin. 8:12 [b]2 Chr. 24:23 [1]Advance upon
**18** [a]1 Kin. 15:18
**19** [1]*Jehoash,* vv. 1–18
**20** [a]2 Kin. 14:5 [1]Lit. *The Landfill*
**21** [a]2 Chr. 24:27 [1]*Zabad,* 2 Chr. 24:26 [2]*Shimrith,* 2 Chr. 24:26

CHAPTER 13
**1** [a]2 Kin. 12:1 [b]2 Kin. 10:35 [1]*Jehoash,* 2 Kin. 12:1–18
**2** [a]1 Kin. 12:26–33 [1]Lit. *turn*
**3** [a]Judg. 2:14 [b]2 Kin. 8:12 [c]Amos 1:4
**4** [a][Ps. 78:34] [b][Ex. 3:7, 9]
**5** [a]2 Kin. 13:25; 14:25, 27

of the house of Jeroboam, who had made Israel
sin, *but* walked in them; [a]and the [1]wooden image
also remained in Samaria.
7 For He left of the army of Jehoahaz only fifty
horsemen, ten chariots, and ten thousand foot
soldiers; for the king of Syria had destroyed them
[a]and made them [b]like the dust at threshing.
**8** Now the rest of the acts of Jehoahaz, all that
he did, and his might, *are* they not written in the
book of the chronicles of the kings of Israel?
9 So Jehoahaz [1]rested with his fathers, and they
buried him in Samaria. Then [2]Joash his son
reigned in his place.
**10** In the thirty-seventh year of Joash king of
Judah, [1]Jehoash the son of Jehoahaz became king
over Israel in Samaria, *and reigned* sixteen years.
11 And he did evil in the sight of the LORD. He did
not depart from all the sins of Jeroboam the son of
Nebat, who made Israel sin, *but* walked in them.
**12** [a]Now the rest of the acts of Joash, [b]all that he
did, and [c]his might with which he fought against
Amaziah king of Judah, *are* they not written in
the book of the chronicles of the kings of Israel?
13 So Joash [a]rested[1] with his fathers. Then Jeroboam sat on his throne. And Joash was buried in
Samaria with the kings of Israel.
**14** Elisha had become sick with the illness of
which he would die. Then Joash the king of Israel
came down to him, and wept over his face, and
said, "O my father, my father, [a]the chariots of
Israel and their horsemen!"
15 And Elisha said to him, "Take a bow and some
arrows." So he took himself a bow and some
arrows.
16 Then he said to the king of Israel, "Put your
hand on the bow." So he put his hand *on it,* and
Elisha put his hands on the king's hands.
17 And he said, "Open the east window"; and he
opened *it.* Then Elisha said, "Shoot"; and he shot.
And he said, "The arrow of the LORD's deliverance
and the arrow of deliverance from Syria; for you
must strike the Syrians at [a]Aphek till you have
destroyed *them.*"
18 Then he said, "Take the arrows"; so he took
*them.* And he said to the king of Israel, "Strike the
ground"; so he struck three times, and stopped.
19 And the man of God was angry with him, and
said, "You should have struck five or six times;
then you would have struck Syria till you had
destroyed *it!* [a]But now you will strike Syria *only*
three times."
**20** Then Elisha [1]died, and they buried him. And
the [a]*raiding* bands from Moab invaded the land in
the spring of the year.
21 So it was, as they were burying a man, that
suddenly they spied a band *of raiders;* and they
put the man in the tomb of Elisha; and when the
man was let down and touched the bones of
Elisha, he revived and stood on his feet.
**22** And [a]Hazael king of Syria oppressed Israel all
the days of Jehoahaz.
23 But the LORD was [a]gracious to them, had
compassion on them, and [b]regarded them, [c]be-
cause of His covenant with Abraham, Isaac, and
Jacob, and would not yet destroy them or cast
them from His presence.
**24** Now Hazael king of Syria died. Then Ben-
Hadad his son reigned in his place.
25 And [1]Jehoash the son of Jehoahaz recaptured
from the hand of Ben-Hadad, the son of Hazael,
the cities which he had taken out of the hand of
Jehoahaz his father by war. [a]Three times Joash
defeated him and recaptured the cities of Israel.

### *Amaziah Reigns over Judah*

**14** In [a]the second year of Joash the son of
Jehoahaz, king of Israel, [b]Amaziah the son
of Joash, king of Judah, became king.
2 He was twenty-five years old when he became
king, and he reigned twenty-nine years in Jerusalem. His mother's name was Jehoaddan of Jerusalem.
3 And he did *what was* right in the sight of the
LORD, yet not like his father David; he did everything [a]as his father Joash had done.
4 [a]However the [1]high places were not taken
away, and the people still sacrificed and burned
incense on the high places.
**5** Now it happened, as soon as the kingdom was
established in his hand, that he executed his
servants [a]who had murdered his father the king.
6 But the children of the murderers he did not
execute, according to what is written in the Book
of the Law of Moses, in which the LORD commanded, saying, [a]"Fathers shall not be put to
death for their children, nor shall children be put
to death for their fathers; but a person shall be put
to death for his own sin."
7 [a]He killed ten thousand Edomites in [b]the Valley of Salt, and took [1]Sela by war, [c]and called its
name Joktheel to this day.
**8** [a]Then Amaziah sent messengers to [1]Jehoash
the son of Jehoahaz, the son of Jehu, king of
Israel, saying, "Come, let us face one another *in
battle.*"
9 And Jehoash king of Israel sent to Amaziah
king of Judah, saying, [a]"The thistle that *was* in
Lebanon sent to the [b]cedar that *was* in Lebanon,
saying, 'Give your daughter to my son as wife';
and a wild beast that *was* in Lebanon passed by
and trampled the thistle.
10 "You have indeed defeated Edom, and [a]your
heart has [1]lifted you up. Glory *in that,* and stay at
home; for why should you meddle with trouble so
that you fall—you and Judah with you?"
11 But Amaziah would not heed. Therefore Jehoash king of Israel went out; so he and Amaziah
king of Judah faced one another at [a]Beth Shemesh, which *belongs* to Judah.
12 And Judah was defeated by Israel, and every
man fled to his tent.
13 Then Jehoash king of Israel captured Amaziah
king of Judah, the son of Jehoash, the son of
Ahaziah, at Beth Shemesh; and he went to Jerusalem, and broke down the wall of Jerusalem from
[a]the Gate of Ephraim to [b]the Corner Gate—[1]four
hundred cubits.
14 And he took all [a]the gold and silver, all the
articles that were found in the house of the LORD
and in the treasuries of the king's house, and
hostages, and returned to Samaria.
**15** [a]Now the rest of the acts of Jehoash which he
did—his might, and how he fought with Amaziah
king of Judah—*are* they not written in the book of
the chronicles of the kings of Israel?
16 So Jehoash [1]rested with his fathers, and was
buried in Samaria with the kings of Israel. Then
Jeroboam his son reigned in his place.
**17** [a]Amaziah the son of Joash, king of Judah,
lived fifteen years after the death of Jehoash the
son of Jehoahaz, king of Israel.
18 Now the rest of the acts of Amaziah, *are* they

**6** [a]1 Kin. 16:33 [1]Or *Asherah,* a Canaanite goddess
**7** [a]2 Kin. 10:32 [b][Amos 1:3]
**9** [1]Died and joined his ancestors [2]Or *Jehoash*
**10** [1]*Joash,* v. 9
**12** [a]2 Kin. 14:8–15 [b]2 Kin. 13:14–19, 25 [c]2 Kin. 14:9; 2 Chr. 25:17–25
**13** [a]2 Kin. 14:16 [1]Died and joined his ancestors
**14** [a]2 Kin. 2:12
**17** [a]1 Kin. 20:26
**19** [a]2 Kin. 13:25
**20** [a]2 Kin. 3:5; 24:2 [1]Having prophesied at least 55 years
**22** [a]2 Kin. 8:12, 13
**23** [a]2 Kin. 14:27 [b][Ex. 2:24, 25] [c]Gen. 13:16, 17; 17:2–7; Ex. 32:13
**25** [a]2 Kin. 13:18, 19 [1]*Joash,* vv. 12–14, 25

CHAPTER 14
**1** [a]2 Kin. 13:10 [b]2 Chr. 25:1, 2
**3** [a]2 Kin. 12:2
**4** [a]2 Kin. 12:3 [1]Places for pagan worship
**5** [a]2 Kin. 12:20
**6** [a]Deut. 24:16; [Jer. 31:30; Ezek. 18:4, 20]
**7** [a]2 Chr. 25:5–16 [b]2 Sam. 8:13; 1 Chr. 18:12; Ps. 60:title [c]Josh. 15:38 [1]Lit. *The Rock;* the city of Petra
**8** [a]2 Chr. 25:17, 18 [1]*Joash,* 2 Kin. 13:9, 12–14, 25; 2 Chr. 25:17ff.
**9** [a]Judg. 9:8–15 [b]1 Kin. 4:33
**10** [a]Deut. 8:14; 2 Chr. 32:25; [Ezek. 28:2, 5, 17; Hab. 2:4] [1]Made you proud
**11** [a]Josh. 19:38; 21:16
**13** [a]Neh. 8:16; 12:39 [b]Jer. 31:38; Zech. 14:10 [1]About 600 feet
**14** [a]1 Kin. 7:51; 2 Kin. 12:18; 16:8
**15** [a]2 Kin. 13:12, 13
**16** [1]Died and joined his ancestors
**17** [a]2 Chr. 25:25–28

not written in the book of the chronicles of the
kings of Judah?
19 And [a]they formed a conspiracy against him in
Jerusalem, and he fled to [b]Lachish; but they sent
after him to Lachish and killed him there.
20 Then they brought him on horses, and he was
buried at Jerusalem with his fathers in the City of
David.
**21** And all the people of Judah took [a]Azariah,[1]
who *was* sixteen years old, and made him king
instead of his father Amaziah.
22 He built [a]Elath[1] and restored it to Judah, after
[2]the king rested with his fathers.
**23** In the fifteenth year of Amaziah the son of
Joash, king of Judah, Jeroboam the son of Joash,
king of Israel, became king in Samaria, *and
reigned* forty-one years.
24 And he did evil in the sight of the LORD; he did
not depart from all the [a]sins of Jeroboam the son
of Nebat, who had made Israel sin.
25 He [a]restored the [1]territory of Israel [b]from the
entrance of Hamath to [c]the[2] Sea of the Arabah,
according to the word of the LORD God of Israel,
which He had spoken through His servant [d]Jonah
the son of Amittai, the prophet who *was* from
[e]Gath Hepher.
26 For the LORD [a]saw *that* the affliction of Israel
*was* very bitter; and whether bond or free, [b]there
was no helper for Israel.
27 [a]And the LORD did not say that He would blot
out the name of Israel from under heaven; but He
saved them by the hand of Jeroboam the son of
Joash.
**28** Now the rest of the acts of Jeroboam, and all
that he did—his might, how he made war, and
how he recaptured for Israel, from [a]Damascus and
Hamath, [b]*what had belonged* to Judah—*are* they
not written in the book of the chronicles of the
kings of Israel?
29 So Jeroboam [1]rested with his fathers, the
kings of Israel. Then [a]Zechariah his son reigned in
his place.

## *The Kings Who Ruled over Israel and Judah*

**15** In the twenty-seventh year of Jeroboam
king of Israel, [a]Azariah the son of Amaziah,
king of Judah, [b]became king.
2 He was sixteen years old when he became
king, and he reigned fifty-two years in Jerusalem.
His mother's name *was* Jecholiah of Jerusalem.
3 And he did *what was* right in the sight of the
LORD, according to all that his father Amaziah had
done,
4 [a]except that the [1]high places were not removed; the people still sacrificed and burned
incense on the high places.
5 Then the LORD [a]struck the king, so that he
was a leper until the day of his [b]death; so he
[c]dwelt in an isolated house. And Jotham the king's
son *was* over the *royal* house, judging the people
of the land.
**6** Now the rest of the acts of Azariah, and all
that he did, *are* they not written in the book of the
chronicles of the kings of Judah?
7 So Azariah [1]rested with his fathers, and [a]they
buried him with his fathers in the City of David.
Then Jotham his son reigned in his place.
**8** In the thirty-eighth year of Azariah king of
Judah, [a]Zechariah the son of Jeroboam reigned
over Israel in Samaria six months.
9 And he did evil in the sight of the LORD, [a]as his
fathers had done; he did not depart from the sins
of Jeroboam the son of Nebat, who had made
Israel sin.
10 Then Shallum the son of Jabesh conspired
against him, and [a]struck and killed him in front of
the people; and he reigned in his place.
**11** Now the rest of the acts of Zechariah, indeed
they *are* written in the book of the chronicles of
the kings of Israel.
12 This *was* the word of the LORD which He
spoke to Jehu, saying, [a]"Your sons shall sit on the
throne of Israel to the fourth *generation.*" And so
it was.
**13** Shallum the son of Jabesh became king in the
thirty-ninth year of [1]Uzziah king of Judah; and he
reigned a full month in Samaria.
14 For Menahem the son of Gadi went up from
[a]Tirzah, came to Samaria, and struck Shallum the
son of Jabesh in Samaria and killed him; and he
reigned in his place.
**15** Now the rest of the acts of Shallum, and the
conspiracy which he [1]led, indeed they *are* written
in the book of the chronicles of the kings of Israel.
16 Then from Tirzah, Menahem attacked [a]Tiph-
sah, all who *were* there, and its territory. Because
they did not surrender, therefore he attacked *it.*
All [b]the women there who were with child he
ripped open.
**17** In the thirty-ninth year of Azariah king of
Judah, Menahem the son of Gadi became king
over Israel, *and reigned* ten years in Samaria.
18 And he did evil in the sight of the LORD; he did
not depart all his days from the sins of Jeroboam
the son of Nebat, who had made Israel sin.
19 [a]Pul[1] king of Assyria came against the land;
and Menahem gave Pul a thousand talents of
silver, that his [2]hand might be with him to
[b]strengthen the kingdom under his control.
20 And Menahem [a]exacted[1] the money from Israel, from all the very wealthy, from each man
fifty shekels of silver, to give to the king of
Assyria. So the king of Assyria turned back, and
did not stay there in the land.
**21** Now the rest of the acts of Menahem, and all
that he did, *are* they not written in the book of the
chronicles of the kings of Israel?
22 So Menahem [1]rested with his fathers. Then
Pekahiah his son reigned in his place.
**23** In the fiftieth year of Azariah king of Judah,
Pekahiah the son of Menahem became king over
Israel in Samaria, *and reigned* two years.
24 And he did evil in the sight of the LORD; he did
not depart from the sins of Jeroboam the son of
Nebat, who had made Israel sin.
25 Then Pekah the son of Remaliah, an officer of
his, conspired against him and [1]killed him in
Samaria, in the [a]citadel of the king's house, along
with Argob and Arieh; and with him were fifty
men of Gilead. He killed him and reigned in his
place.
**26** Now the rest of the acts of Pekahiah, and all
that he did, indeed they *are* written in the book of
the chronicles of the kings of Israel.
**27** In the fifty-second year of Azariah king of
Judah, [a]Pekah the son of Remaliah became king
over Israel in Samaria, *and reigned* twenty years.
28 And he did evil in the sight of the LORD; he did
not depart from the sins of Jeroboam the son of
Nebat, who had made Israel sin.
29 In the days of Pekah king of Israel, [1]Tiglath-
Pileser king of Assyria [a]came and took [b]Ijon, Abel

**19** [a]2 Chr. 25:27 [b]Josh. 10:31
**21** [a]2 Kin. 15:13; 2 Chr. 26:1 [1]*Uzziah,* 2 Chr. 26:1ff.; Is. 6:1; etc.
**22** [a]1 Kin. 9:26; 2 Kin. 16:6; 2 Chr. 8:17 [1]Heb. *Eloth* [2]Amaziah died and joined his ancestors.
**24** [a]1 Kin. 12:26–33
**25** [a]2 Kin. 10:32; 13:5, 25 [b]Num. 13:21; 34:8; 1 Kin. 8:65 [c]Deut. 3:17 [d]Jon. 1:1; Matt. 12:39, 40 [e]Josh. 19:13 [1]*border* [2]The Dead Sea
**26** [a]Ex. 3:7; 2 Kin. 13:4; Ps. 106:44 [b]Deut. 32:36
**27** [a][2 Kin. 13:5, 23]
**28** [a]1 Kin. 11:24 [b]2 Sam. 8:6; 1 Kin. 11:24; 2 Chr. 8:3
**29** [a]2 Kin. 15:8 [1]Died and joined his ancestors

CHAPTER 15
**1** [a]2 Kin. 15:13, 30 [b]2 Kin. 14:21; 2 Chr. 26:1, 3, 4
**4** [a]2 Kin. 12:3; 14:4; 15:35 [1]Places for pagan worship
**5** [a]2 Chr. 26:19–23; Ps. 78:31 [b]Is. 6:1 [c][Lev. 13:46]; Num. 12:14
**7** [a]2 Chr. 26:23 [1]Died and joined his ancestors
**8** [a]2 Kin. 14:29
**9** [a]2 Kin. 14:24
**10** [a]Amos 7:9
**12** [a]2 Kin. 10:30
**13** [1]*Azariah,* 2 Kin. 14:21ff.; 15:1ff.
**14** [a]1 Kin. 14:17; Song 6:4
**15** [1]Lit. *conspired*
**16** [a]1 Kin. 4:24 [b]2 Kin. 8:12; Hos. 13:16
**19** [a]1 Chr. 5:26; 66:19; Hos. 8:9 [b]2 Kin. 14:5 [1]Tiglath-Pileser III, v. 29 [2]Support
**20** [a]2 Kin. 23:35 [1]*took*
**22** [1]Died and joined his ancestors
**25** [a]1 Kin. 16:18 [1]Lit. *struck*
**27** [a]2 Chr. 28:6; Is. 7:1
**29** [a]2 Kin. 16:7, 10; 1 Chr. 5:26 [b]1 Kin. 15:20 [1]A later name of *Pul,* v. 19

Beth Maachah, Janoah, Kedesh, Hazor, Gilead,
and Galilee, all the land of Naphtali; and he
[c]carried them captive to Assyria.
30 Then Hoshea the son of Elah led a conspiracy
against Pekah the son of Remaliah, and struck
and killed him; so he [a]reigned in his place in the
twentieth year of Jotham the son of Uzziah.
**31** Now the rest of the acts of Pekah, and all that
he did, indeed they *are* written in the book of the
chronicles of the kings of Israel.
**32** In the second year of Pekah the son of Remaliah, king of Israel, [a]Jotham the son of Uzziah,
king of Judah, began to reign.
33 He was twenty-five years old when he became
king, and he reigned sixteen years in Jerusalem.
His mother's name *was* [1]Jerusha the daughter of
Zadok.
34 And he did *what was* right in the sight of the
LORD; he did [a]according to all that his father
Uzziah had done.
35 [a]However the [1]high places were not removed;
the people still sacrificed and burned incense on
the high places. [b]He built the Upper Gate of the
house of the LORD.
**36** Now the rest of the acts of Jotham, and all
that he did, *are* they not written in the book of the
chronicles of the kings of Judah?
37 In those days the LORD began to send [a]Rezin
king of Syria and [b]Pekah the son of Remaliah
against Judah.
38 So Jotham [1]rested with his fathers, and was
buried with his fathers in the City of David his
father. Then Ahaz his son reigned in his place.

### *Ahaz and Hezekiah Reign over Judah*

**16** In the seventeenth year of Pekah the son of
Remaliah, Ahaz the son of Jotham, king of
Judah, began to reign.
2 Ahaz *was* twenty years old when he became
king, and he reigned sixteen years in Jerusalem;
and he did not do *what was* right in the sight of
the LORD his God, as his father David *had done.*
3 But he walked in the way of the kings of
Israel; indeed [a]he made his son pass through the
fire, according to the [b]abominations of the nations
whom the LORD had cast out from before the
children of Israel.
4 And he sacrificed and burned incense on the
[a]high places, [b]on the hills, and under every green
tree.
**5** [a]Then Rezin king of Syria and Pekah the son
of Remaliah, king of Israel, came up to Jerusalem
to *make* war; and they besieged Ahaz but could
not overcome *him.*
6 At that time Rezin king of Syria [a]captured
[1]Elath for Syria, and drove the men of Judah from
Elath. Then the [2]Edomites went to Elath, and
dwell there to this day.
**7** So Ahaz sent messengers to [a]Tiglath-Pileser[1]
king of Assyria, saying, "I *am* your servant and
your son. Come up and save me from the hand of
the king of Syria and from the hand of the king of
Israel, who rise up against me."
8 And Ahaz [a]took the silver and gold that was
found in the house of the LORD, and in the treasuries of the king's house, and sent *it as* a present to
the king of Assyria.
9 So the king of Assyria heeded him; for the
king of Assyria went up against [a]Damascus and
[b]took it, carried *its people* captive to [c]Kir, and
killed Rezin.
**10** Now King Ahaz went to Damascus to meet
Tiglath-Pileser king of Assyria, and saw an altar
that *was* at Damascus; and King Ahaz sent to
Urijah the priest the design of the altar and its
pattern, according to all its workmanship.
11 Then [a]Urijah the priest built an altar according to all that King Ahaz had sent from Damascus. So Urijah the priest made *it* before King Ahaz
came back from Damascus.
12 And when the king came back from Damascus, the king saw the altar; and [a]the king approached the altar and made offerings on it.
13 So he burned his burnt offering and his grain
offering; and he poured his drink offering and
sprinkled the blood of his peace offerings on the
altar.
14 He also brought [a]the bronze altar which *was*
before the LORD, from the front of the [1]temple—
from between the *new* altar and the house of the
LORD—and put it on the north side of the *new*
altar.
15 Then King Ahaz commanded Urijah the
priest, saying, "On the great *new* altar burn [a]the
morning burnt offering, the evening grain offering, the king's burnt sacrifice, and his grain offering, with the burnt offering of all the people of the
land, their grain offering, and their drink offerings;
and sprinkle on it all the blood of the burnt
offering and all the blood of the sacrifice. And the
bronze altar shall be for me to inquire *by.*"
16 Thus did Urijah the priest, according to all
that King Ahaz commanded.
**17** [a]And King Ahaz cut off [b]the panels of the
carts, and removed the lavers from them; and he
took down [c]the Sea from the bronze oxen that
*were* under it, and put it on a pavement of stones.
18 Also he removed the Sabbath pavilion which
they had built in the temple, and he removed the
king's outer entrance from the house of the LORD,
on account of the king of Assyria.
**19** Now the rest of the acts of Ahaz which he did,
*are* they not written in the book of the chronicles
of the kings of Judah?
20 So Ahaz rested with his fathers, and [a]was
buried with his fathers in the City of David. Then
Hezekiah his son reigned in his place.

### *Assyria Conquers Israel*

**17** In the twelfth year of Ahaz king of Judah,
[a]Hoshea the son of Elah became king of
Israel in Samaria, *and he reigned* nine years.
2 And he did evil in the sight of the LORD, but
not as the kings of Israel who were before him.
3 [a]Shalmaneser king of Assyria came up against
him; and Hoshea [b]became his vassal, and paid him
tribute money.
4 And the king of Assyria uncovered a conspiracy by Hoshea; for he had sent messengers to So,
king of Egypt, and brought no tribute to the king
of Assyria, as *he had done* year by year. Therefore
the king of Assyria shut him up, and bound him in
prison.
**5** Now [a]the king of Assyria went throughout all
the land, and went up to Samaria and besieged it
for three years.
6 [a]In the ninth year of Hoshea, the king of
Assyria took Samaria and [b]carried Israel away to
Assyria, [c]and placed them in Halah and by the
Habor, the River of Gozan, and in the cities of the
Medes.
**7** For [a]so it was that the children of Israel had

**29** [c]2 Kin. 17:6
**30** [a]2 Kin. 17:1; [Hos. 10:3, 7, 15]
**32** [a]2 Chr. 27:1
**33** [1]*Jerushah,* 2 Chr. 27:1
**34** [a]2 Kin. 15:3, 4; 2 Chr. 26:4, 5
**35** [a]2 Kin. 15:4 [b]2 Chr. 23:20; 27:3 [1]Places for pagan worship
**37** [a]2 Kin. 16:5–9; Is. 7:1–17 [b]2 Kin. 15:26, 27
**38** [1]Died and joined his ancestors

CHAPTER 16
**3** [a][Lev. 18:21]; 2 Kin. 17:17; 2 Chr. 28:3; Ps. 106:37, 38; Is. 1:1 [b][Deut. 12:31]; 2 Kin. 21:2, 11
**4** [a]2 Kin. 15:34, 35 [b][Deut. 12:2]; 1 Kin. 14:23
**5** [a]2 Kin. 15:37; Is. 7:1, 4
**6** [a]2 Kin. 14:22; 2 Chr. 26:2 [1]Lit. *Large Tree;* sing. of *Eloth* [2]A few ancient mss. *Syrians*
**7** [a]2 Kin. 15:29; 1 Chr. 5:26; 2 Chr. 28:20 [1]A later name of *Pul,* 2 Kin. 15:19
**8** [a]2 Kin. 12:17, 18; 2 Chr. 28:21
**9** [a]2 Kin. 14:28 [b]Amos 1:5 [c]Is. 22:6; Amos 9:7
**11** [a]Is. 8:2
**12** [a]2 Chr. 26:16, 19
**14** [a]Ex. 27:1, 2; 40:6, 29; 2 Chr. 4:1 [1]Lit. *house*
**15** [a]Ex. 29:39–41
**17** [a]2 Chr. 28:24 [b]1 Kin. 7:27–29 [c]1 Kin. 7:23–25
**20** [a]2 Chr. 28:27

CHAPTER 17
**1** [a]2 Kin. 15:30
**3** [a]2 Kin. 18:9–12 [b]2 Kin. 24:1
**5** [a]2 Kin. 18:9; Hos. 13:16
**6** [a]2 Kin. 18:10, 11; Is. 7:7–9; Hos. 1:4; 13:16; Amos 4:2 [b]Lev. 26:32, 33; [Deut. 28:36, 64; 29:27, 28] [c]1 Chr. 5:26
**7** [a][Josh. 23:16]

sinned against the LORD their God, who had
brought them up out of the land of Egypt, from
under the hand of Pharaoh king of Egypt; and
they had [b]feared other gods,
8 and [a]had walked in the statutes of the nations
whom the LORD had cast out from before the
children of Israel, and of the kings of Israel, which
they had made.
9 Also the children of Israel secretly did against
the LORD their God things that *were* not right, and
they built for themselves [1]high places in all their
cities, [a]from watchtower to fortified city.
10 [a]They set up for themselves *sacred* pillars and
[b]wooden images[1] [c]on every high hill and under
every green tree.
11 There they burned incense on all the high
places, like the nations whom the LORD had
carried away before them; and they did wicked
things to provoke the LORD to anger,
12 for they served idols, [a]of which the LORD had
said to them, [b]"You shall not do this thing."
13 Yet the LORD testified against Israel and
against Judah, by all of His [a]prophets, [b]every seer,
saying, [c]"Turn from your evil ways, and keep My
commandments *and* My statutes, according to all
the law which I commanded your fathers, and
which I sent to you by My servants the prophets."
14 Nevertheless they would not hear, but [a]stif-
fened their necks, like the necks of their fathers,
who [b]did not believe in the LORD their God.
15 And they [a]rejected His statutes [b]and His covenant that He had made with their fathers, and
His testimonies which He had testified against
them; they followed [c]idols, [d]became idolaters, and
*went* after the nations who *were* all around them,
*concerning* whom the LORD had charged them
that they should [e]not do like them.
16 So they left all the commandments of the
LORD their God, [a]made for themselves a molded
image *and* two calves, [b]made a wooden image and
worshiped all the [c]host of heaven, [d]and served
Baal.
17 [a]And they caused their sons and daughters to
pass through the fire, [b]practiced witchcraft and
soothsaying, and [c]sold themselves to do evil in the
sight of the LORD, to provoke Him to anger.
18 Therefore the LORD was very angry with Israel, and removed them from His sight; there was
none left [a]but the tribe of Judah alone.
**19** Also [a]Judah did not keep the commandments
of the LORD their God, but walked in the statutes
of Israel which they made.
20 And the LORD rejected all the descendants of
Israel, afflicted them, and [a]delivered them into the
hand of plunderers, until He had cast them from
His [b]sight.
21 For [a]He tore Israel from the house of David,
and [b]they made Jeroboam the son of Nebat king.
Then Jeroboam drove Israel from following the
LORD, and made them commit a great sin.
22 For the children of Israel walked in all the sins
of Jeroboam which he did; they did not depart
from them,
23 until the LORD removed Israel out of His sight,
[a]as He had said by all His servants the prophets.
[b]So Israel was carried away from their own land
to Assyria, *as it is* to this day.
**24** [a]Then the king of Assyria brought *people* from
Babylon, Cuthah, [b]Ava, Hamath, and from Sepharvaim, and placed *them* in the cities of Samaria
instead of the children of Israel; and they took
possession of Samaria and dwelt in its cities.
25 And it was so, at the beginning of their dwelling there, *that* they did not fear the LORD; therefore the LORD sent lions among them, which killed
*some* of them.
26 So they spoke to the king of Assyria, saying,
"The nations whom you have removed and placed
in the cities of Samaria do not know the rituals of
the God of the land; therefore He has sent lions
among them, and indeed, they are killing them
because they do not know the rituals of the God
of the land."
27 Then the king of Assyria commanded, saying,
"Send there one of the priests whom you brought
from there; let him go and dwell there, and let him
teach them the rituals of the God of the land."
28 Then one of the priests whom they had carried
away from Samaria came and dwelt in Bethel, and
taught them how they should fear the LORD.
**29** However every nation continued to make
gods of its own, and put *them* [a]in the shrines on
the high places which the Samaritans had made,
*every* nation in the cities where they dwelt.
30 The men of [a]Babylon made Succoth Benoth,
the men of Cuth made Nergal, the men of Hamath
made Ashima,
31 [a]and the Avites made Nibhaz and Tartak; and
the Sepharvites [b]burned their children in fire to
Adrammelech and Anammelech, the gods of
Sepharvaim.
32 So they feared the LORD, [a]and from every class
they appointed for themselves priests of the [1]high
places, who sacrificed for them in the shrines of
the high places.
33 [a]They feared the LORD, yet served their own
gods—according to the rituals of the nations from
among whom they were carried away.
34 To this day they continue practicing the former rituals; they do not fear the LORD, nor do they
follow their statutes or their ordinances, or the
law and commandment which the LORD had commanded the children of Jacob, [a]whom He named
Israel,
35 with whom the LORD had made a covenant
and charged them, saying: [a]"You shall not fear
other gods, nor [b]bow down to them nor serve
them nor sacrifice to them;
36 "but the LORD, who [a]brought you up from the
land of Egypt with great power and [b]an outstretched arm, [c]Him you shall fear, Him you shall
worship, and to Him you shall offer sacrifice.
37 "And the statutes, the ordinances, the law,
and the commandment which He wrote for you,
[a]you shall be careful to observe forever; you shall
not fear other gods.
38 "And the covenant that I have made with you,
[a]you shall not forget, nor shall you fear other
gods.
39 "But the LORD your God you shall fear; and He
will deliver you from the hand of all your enemies."
40 However they did not obey, but they followed
their former rituals.
41 [a]So these nations feared the LORD, yet served
their carved images; also their children and their

**7** [b]Judg. 6:10 **8** [a][Lev. 18:3; Deut. 18:9]; 2 Kin. 16:3 **9** [a]2 Kin. 18:8 [1]Places for pagan worship **10** [a]1 Kin. 14:23; Is. 57:5 [b][Ex. 34:12–14; Deut. 16:21]; Mic. 5:14 [c][Deut. 12:2]; 2 Kin. 16:4 [1]Or *Asherim,* Canaanite deities **12** [a][Ex. 20:3–5; Lev. 26:1; Deut. 5:7, 8] [b][Deut. 4:19] **13** [a]Neh. 9:29, 30 [b]1 Sam. 9:9 [c][Jer. 18:11; 25:5; 35:15; Ezek. 18:31] **14** [a]Ex. 32:9; 33:3; Deut. 31:27; [Prov. 29:1; Acts 7:51] [b]Deut. 9:23; Ps. 78:22 **15** [a]Jer. 44:3 [b]Ex. 24:6–8; Deut. 29:25 [c]Deut. 32:21; 1 Kin. 16:31; [1 Cor. 8:4] [d]2 Chr. 13:7; Jer. 2:5; [Rom. 1:21–23] [e][Deut. 12:30, 31] **16** [a]Ex. 32:8; 1 Kin. 12:28 [b][1 Kin. 14:15] [c][Deut. 4:19] [d]1 Kin. 16:31; 22:53 **17** [a][Lev. 18:21]; 2 Kin. 16:3; Ezek. 23:37 [b][Lev. 19:26; Deut. 18:10–12] [c]1 Kin. 21:20 **18** [a]1 Kin. 11:13, 32 **19** [a]Jer. 3:8 **20** [a]Judg. 2:14; 2 Kin. 13:3; 15:29 [b]2 Kin. 24:20 **21** [a]1 Kin. 11:11, 31 [b]1 Kin. 12:20, 28 **23** [a]1 Kin. 14:16; Is. 8:4 [b]2 Kin. 17:6 **24** [a]Ezra 4:2, 10 [b]2 Kin. 18:34 **29** [a]1 Kin. 12:31; 13:32 **30** [a]2 Kin. 17:24 **31** [a]Ezra 4:9 [b][Lev. 18:21; Deut. 12:31] **32** [a]1 Kin. 12:31; 13:33 [1]Places for pagan worship **33** [a]Zeph. 1:5 **34** [a]Gen. 32:28; 35:10 **35** [a]Judg. 6:10 [b][Ex. 20:5] **36** [a]Ex. 14:15–30 [b]Ex. 6:6; 9:15 [c][Deut. 10:20] **37** [a]Deut. 5:32 **38** [a]Deut. 4:23; 6:12 **41** [a]2 Kin. 17:32, 33

children's children have continued doing as their
fathers did, even to this day.

### *Sennacherib Invades Judah*

**18** Now it came to pass in the third year of
[a]Hoshea the son of Elah, king of Israel, *that*
[b]Hezekiah the son of Ahaz, king of Judah, began
to reign.
2 He was twenty-five years old when he became
king, and he reigned twenty-nine years in Jerusalem. His mother's name *was* [a]Abi[1] the daughter of
Zechariah.
3 And he did *what was* right in the sight of the
LORD, according to all that his father David had
done.
**4** [a]He removed the [1]high places and broke the
*sacred* pillars, cut down the [2]wooden image and
broke in pieces the [b]bronze serpent that Moses
had made; for until those days the children of
Israel burned incense to it, and called it [3]Nehush-
tan.
5 He [a]trusted in the LORD God of Israel, [b]so that
after him was none like him among all the kings
of Judah, nor who were before him.
6 For he [a]held fast to the LORD; he did not
depart from following Him, but kept His commandments, which the LORD had commanded
Moses.
7 The LORD [a]was with him; he [b]prospered wherever he went. And he [c]rebelled against the king of
Assyria and did not serve him.
8 [a]He [1]subdued the Philistines, as far as Gaza
and its territory, [b]from watchtower to fortified
city.
**9** Now [a]it came to pass in the fourth year of
King Hezekiah, which *was* the seventh year of
Hoshea the son of Elah, king of Israel, *that* Shalmaneser king of Assyria came up against Samaria
and besieged it.
10 And at the end of three years they took it. In
the sixth year of Hezekiah, that *is,* [a]the ninth year
of Hoshea king of Israel, Samaria was taken.
11 [a]Then the king of Assyria carried Israel away
captive to Assyria, and put them [b]in Halah and by
the Habor, the River of Gozan, and in the cities of
the Medes,
12 because they [a]did not obey the voice of the
LORD their God, but transgressed His covenant
*and* all that Moses the servant of the LORD had
commanded; and they would neither hear nor do
*them.*
**13** And [a]in the fourteenth year of King Hezekiah,
Sennacherib king of Assyria came up against all
the fortified cities of Judah and took them.
14 Then Hezekiah king of Judah sent to the king
of Assyria at Lachish, saying, "I have done wrong;
turn away from me; whatever you impose on me I
will pay." And the king of Assyria assessed Hezekiah king of Judah three hundred talents of silver
and thirty talents of gold.
15 So Hezekiah [a]gave *him* all the silver that was
found in the house of the LORD and in the treasuries of the king's house.
16 At that time Hezekiah stripped *the gold from*
the doors of the temple of the LORD, and *from* the
pillars which Hezekiah king of Judah had overlaid, and gave [1]it to the king of Assyria.
**17** Then the king of Assyria sent *the* [1]Tartan, *the*
[2]Rabsaris, *and the* [3]Rabshakeh from Lachish, with
a great army against Jerusalem, to King Hezekiah.
And they went up and came to Jerusalem. When
they had come up, they went and stood by the
[a]aqueduct from the upper pool, [b]which *was* on the
highway to the Fuller's Field.
18 And when they had called to the king, [a]Elia-
kim the son of Hilkiah, who *was* over the household, Shebna the [1]scribe, and Joah the son of
Asaph, the recorder, came out to them.
19 Then *the* Rabshakeh said to them, "Say now
to Hezekiah, 'Thus says the great king, the king of
Assyria: [a]"What confidence *is* this in which you
trust?
20 "You speak of *having* plans and power for
war; but *they are* [1]mere words. And in whom do
you trust, that you rebel against me?
21 [a]"Now look! You are trusting in the staff of
this broken reed, Egypt, on which if a man leans,
it will go into his hand and pierce it. So *is* Pharaoh
king of Egypt to all who trust in him.
22 "But if you say to me, 'We trust in the LORD
our God,' *is* it not He [a]whose [1]high places and
whose altars Hezekiah has taken away, and said
to Judah and Jerusalem, 'You shall worship before
this altar in Jerusalem'?" '
23 "Now therefore, I urge you, give a pledge to
my master the king of Assyria, and I will give you
two thousand horses—if you are able on your part
to put riders on them!
24 "How then will you repel one captain of the
least of my master's servants, and put your trust
in Egypt for chariots and horsemen?
25 "Have I now come up without the LORD
against this place to destroy it? The LORD said to
me, 'Go up against this land, and destroy it.' "
**26** [a]Then Eliakim the son of Hilkiah, Shebna, and
Joah said to *the* Rabshakeh, "Please speak to your
servants in [b]Aramaic, for we understand *it;* and do
not speak to us in [1]Hebrew in the hearing of the
people who *are* on the wall."
27 But *the* Rabshakeh said to them, "Has my
master sent me to your master and to you to
speak these words, and not to the men who sit on
the wall, who will eat and drink their own waste
with you?"
28 Then *the* Rabshakeh stood and called out with
a loud voice in [1]Hebrew, and spoke, saying, "Hear
the word of the great king, the king of Assyria!
29 "Thus says the king: [a]'Do not let Hezekiah
deceive you, for he shall not be able to deliver you
from his hand;
30 'nor let Hezekiah make you trust in the LORD,
saying, "The LORD will surely deliver us; this city
shall not be given into the hand of the king of
Assyria." '
31 "Do not listen to Hezekiah; for thus says the
king of Assyria: 'Make *peace* with me [1]by a
present and come out to me; and every one of you
eat from his own [a]vine and every one from his
own fig tree, and every one of you drink the
waters of his own cistern;
32 'until I come and take you away to a land like
your own land, [a]a land of grain and new wine, a
land of bread and vineyards, a land of olive groves
and honey, that you may live and not die. But do
not listen to Hezekiah, lest he persuade you,
saying, "The LORD will deliver us."
33 [a]'Has any of the gods of the nations at all
delivered its land from the hand of the king of
Assyria?
34 'Where *are* the gods of [a]Hamath and Arpad?
Where *are* the gods of Sepharvaim and Hena and

CHAPTER 18
**1** [a]2 Kin. 17:1 [b]2 Chr. 28:27; 29:1
**2** [a]Is. 38:5 [1]*Abijah,* 2 Chr. 29:1ff.
**4** [a]2 Chr. 31:1 [b]Num. 21:5–9 [1]Places for pagan worship [2]Or *Asherah,* a Canaanite goddess [3]Lit. *Bronze Thing,* also similar to Heb. *nahash, serpent*
**5** [a]2 Kin. 19:10; [Job 13:15; Ps. 13:5] [b]2 Kin. 23:25
**6** [a]Deut. 10:20; Josh. 23:8
**7** [a][2 Chr. 15:2] [b]Gen. 39:2, 3; 1 Sam. 18:5, 14; Ps. 60:12 [c]2 Kin. 16:7
**8** [a]1 Chr. 4:41; 2 Chr. 28:18; Is. 14:29 [b]2 Kin. 17:9 [1]Lit. *struck*
**9** [a]2 Kin. 17:3
**10** [a]2 Kin. 17:6
**11** [a]2 Kin. 17:6; Hos. 1:4; Amos 4:2 [b]1 Chr. 5:26
**12** [a]2 Kin. 17:7–18
**13** [a]2 Chr. 32:1; Is. 36:1—39:8
**15** [a]1 Kin. 15:18, 19; 2 Kin. 12:18; 16:8
**16** [1]Lit. *them*
**17** [a]2 Kin. 20:20 [b]Is. 7:3 [1]A title, probably *Commander in Chief* [2]A title, probably *Chief Officer* [3]A title, probably *Chief of Staff* or *Governor*
**18** [a]2 Kin. 19:2; Is. 22:20 [1]*secretary*
**19** [a]2 Chr. 32:10; [Ps. 118:8, 9]
**20** [1]Lit. *a word of the lips*
**21** [a]Is. 30:2–7; Ezek. 29:6, 7
**22** [a]2 Kin. 18:4; 2 Chr. 31:1; 32:12 [1]Places for pagan worship
**26** [a]Is. 36:11—39:8 [b]Ezra 4:7; Dan. 2:4 [1]Lit. *Judean*
**28** [1]Lit. *Judean*
**29** [a]2 Chr. 32:15
**31** [a]1 Kin. 4:20, 25 [1]By paying tribute
**32** [a]Deut. 8:7–9; 11:12
**33** [a]2 Kin. 19:12; Is. 10:10, 11
**34** [a]2 Kin. 19:13

[b]Ivah? Indeed, have they delivered Samaria from
my hand?
35 'Who among all the gods of the lands have
delivered their countries from my hand, [a]that the
LORD should deliver Jerusalem from my hand?' "
**36** But the people held their peace and answered
him not a word; for the king's commandment was,
"Do not answer him."
37 Then Eliakim the son of Hilkiah, who *was*
over the household, Shebna the scribe, and Joah
the son of Asaph, the recorder, came to Hezekiah
[a]with *their* clothes torn, and told him the words of
*the* Rabshakeh.

### *Isaiah's Prophecy and Judah's Deliverance*

**19** And [a]so it was, when King Hezekiah heard
*it*, that he tore his clothes, covered himself
with [b]sackcloth, and went into the house of the
LORD.
2 Then he sent Eliakim, who *was* over the
household, Shebna the scribe, and the elders of
the priests, covered with sackcloth, to Isaiah the
prophet, the son of Amoz.
3 And they said to him, "Thus says Hezekiah:
'This day *is* a day of trouble, and rebuke, and
blasphemy; for the children have come to birth,
but *there is* no strength to [1]bring them forth.
4 [a]'It may be that the LORD your God will hear
all the words of *the* Rabshakeh, whom his master
the king of Assyria has sent to [b]reproach the
living God, and will [c]rebuke the words which the
LORD your God has heard. Therefore lift up *your*
prayer for the remnant that is left.' "
**5** So the servants of King Hezekiah came to
Isaiah.
6 [a]And Isaiah said to them, "Thus you shall say
to your master, 'Thus says the LORD: "Do not be
[b]afraid of the words which you have heard, with
which the [c]servants of the king of Assyria have
blasphemed Me.
7 "Surely I will send [a]a spirit upon him, and he
shall hear a rumor and return to his own land; and
I will cause him to fall by the sword in his own
land." ' "
**8** Then *the* Rabshakeh returned and found the
king of Assyria warring against Libnah, for he
heard that he had departed [a]from Lachish.
9 And [a]the king heard concerning Tirhakah
king of Ethiopia, "Look, he has come out to make
war with you." So he again sent messengers to
Hezekiah, saying,
10 "Thus you shall speak to Hezekiah king of
Judah, saying: 'Do not let your God [a]in whom you
trust deceive you, saying, "Jerusalem shall not be
given into the hand of the king of Assyria."
11 'Look! You have heard what the kings of
Assyria have done to all lands by utterly destroying them; and shall you be delivered?
12 [a]'Have the gods of the nations delivered those
whom my fathers have destroyed, Gozan and
Haran and Rezeph, and the people of [b]Eden who
*were* in Telassar?
13 [a]'Where *is* the king of Hamath, the king of
Arpad, and the king of the city of Sepharvaim,
Hena, and Ivah?' "
**14** [a]And Hezekiah received the letter from the
hand of the messengers, and read it; and Hezekiah
went up to the house of the LORD, and spread it
before the LORD.
15 Then Hezekiah prayed before the LORD, and
said: "O LORD God of Israel, *the One* [a]who dwells
*between* the cherubim, [b]You are God, You alone,
of all the kingdoms of the earth. You have made
heaven and earth.
16 [a]"Incline Your ear, O LORD, and hear; [b]open
Your eyes, O LORD, and see; and hear the words of
Sennacherib, [c]which he has sent to reproach the
living God.
17 "Truly, LORD, the kings of Assyria have laid
waste the nations and their lands,
18 "and have cast their gods into the fire; for they
*were* [a]not gods, but [b]the work of men's hands—
wood and stone. Therefore they destroyed them.
19 "Now therefore, O LORD our God, I pray, save
us from his hand, [a]that all the kingdoms of the
earth may [b]know that You *are* the LORD God, You
alone."
**20** Then Isaiah the son of Amoz sent to Hezekiah, saying, "Thus says the LORD God of Israel:
[a]'Because you have prayed to Me against Sennacherib king of Assyria, [b]I have heard.'
21 "This *is* the word which the LORD has spoken
concerning him:

'The virgin, [a]the daughter of Zion,
Has despised you, laughed you to scorn;
The daughter of Jerusalem
[b]Has shaken *her* head behind your back!

**22** 'Whom have you reproached
and blasphemed?
Against whom have you raised *your* voice,
And lifted up your eyes on high?
Against [a]the Holy *One* of Israel.
23 [a]By your messengers you have reproached the
Lord,
And said: [b]"By the multitude of my chariots
I have come up
to the height of the mountains,
To the limits of Lebanon;
I will cut down its tall cedars
*And* its choice cypress trees;
I will enter the extremity of its borders,
*To* its fruitful forest.
24 I have dug and drunk strange water,
And with the soles of my feet
I have [a]dried up
All the brooks of defense."

**25** 'Did you not hear long ago
*How* [a]I made it,
From ancient times that I formed it?
Now I have brought it to pass,
That [b]you should be
For crushing fortified cities
*into* heaps of ruins.
26 Therefore their inhabitants had little power;
They were dismayed and confounded;
They were *as* the grass of the field
And the green herb,
*As* [a]the grass on the housetops
And *grain* blighted before it is grown.

**27** 'But [a]I know your dwelling place,
Your going out and your coming in,
And your rage against Me.
28 Because your rage against Me
and your tumult
Have come up to My ears,
Therefore [a]I will put My hook in your nose
And My bridle in your lips,
And I will turn you back
[b]By the way which you came.

**34** [b]2 Kin. 17:24
**35** [a]Dan. 3:15
**37** [a]Is. 33:7

CHAPTER 19

**1** [a]2 Kin. 18:13; 2 Chr. 32:20–22; Is. 37:1 [b]Ps. 69:11
**3** [1]*give birth*
**4** [a]2 Sam. 16:12 [b]2 Kin. 18:35 [c]Ps. 50:21
**6** [a]Is. 37:6 [b][Ps. 112:7] [c]2 Kin. 18:17
**7** [a]2 Kin. 19:35–37; Jer. 51:1
**8** [a]2 Kin. 18:14, 17
**9** [a]1 Sam. 23:27; Is. 37:9
**10** [a]2 Kin. 18:5
**12** [a]2 Kin. 18:33, 34 [b]Ezek. 27:23
**13** [a]2 Kin. 18:34
**14** [a]Is. 37:14
**15** [a]Ex. 25:22; Ps. 80:1; Is. 37:16 [b][Is. 44:6]
**16** [a]Ps. 31:2; Is. 37:17 [b]1 Kin. 8:29; 2 Chr. 6:40 [c]2 Kin. 19:4
**18** [a][Is. 44:9–20; Jer. 10:3–5] [b]Ps. 115:4; Jer. 10:3; [Acts 17:29]
**19** [a]Ps. 83:18 [b]1 Kin. 8:42, 43
**20** [a]Is. 37:21 [b]2 Kin. 20:5; Ps. 65:2
**21** [a]Jer. 14:17; Lam. 2:13 [b]Ps. 22:7, 8
**22** [a]Jer. 51:5
**23** [a]2 Kin. 18:17 [b]Ps. 20:7
**24** [a]Is. 19:6
**25** [a][Is. 45:7] [b]Is. 10:5, 6
**26** [a]Ps. 129:6
**27** [a]Ps. 139:1–3; Is. 37:28
**28** [a]Job 41:2; Ezek. 29:4; 38:4; Amos 4:2 [b]2 Kin. 19:33, 36

29 'This *shall be* a [a]sign to you:

You shall eat this year
such as grows [1]of itself,
And in the second year
what springs from the same;
Also in the third year sow and reap,
Plant vineyards and eat the fruit of them.
30 [a]And the remnant who have escaped
of the house of Judah
Shall again take root downward,
And bear fruit upward.
31 For out of Jerusalem shall go a remnant,
And those who escape from Mount Zion.
[a]The zeal of the LORD [1]of hosts will do this.'

32 "Therefore thus says the LORD concerning the
king of Assyria:

'He shall [a]not come into this city,
Nor shoot an arrow there,
Nor come before it with shield,
Nor build a siege mound against it.
33 By the way that he came,
By the same shall he return;
And he shall not come into this city,'
Says the LORD.
34 'For [a]I will [b]defend this city, to save it
For My own sake
and [c]for My servant David's sake.' "

35 And [a]it came to pass on a certain night that
the [1]angel of the LORD went out, and killed in the
camp of the Assyrians one hundred and eighty-
five thousand; and when *people* arose early in the
morning, there were the corpses—all dead.
36 So Sennacherib king of Assyria departed and
went away, returned *home*, and remained at
[a]Nineveh.
37 Now it came to pass, as he was worshiping in
the temple of Nisroch his god, that his sons
[a]Adrammelech and Sharezer [b]struck him down
with the sword; and they escaped into the land of
Ararat. Then [c]Esarhaddon his son reigned in his
place.

### *Hezekiah's Sickness and Recovery*

**20** In [a]those days Hezekiah was sick and near
death. And Isaiah the prophet, the son of
Amoz, went to him and said to him, "Thus says
the LORD: 'Set your house in order, for you shall
die, and not live.' "
2 Then he turned his face toward the wall, and
prayed to the LORD, saying,
3 [a]"Remember now, O LORD, I pray, how I have
walked before You in truth and with a loyal heart,
and have done *what was* good in Your sight." And
Hezekiah wept bitterly.
4 And it happened, before Isaiah had gone out
into the middle court, that the word of the LORD
came to him, saying,
5 "Return and tell Hezekiah [a]the leader of My
people, 'Thus says the LORD, the God of David
your father: [b]"I have heard your prayer, I have
seen [c]your tears; surely I will heal you. On the
third day you shall go up to the house of the LORD.
6 "And I will add to your days fifteen years. I
will deliver you and this city from the hand of the
king of Assyria; and [a]I will defend this city for My
own sake, and for the sake of My servant David." ' "
7 Then [a]Isaiah said, "Take a lump of figs." So
they took and laid *it* on the boil, and he recovered.
8 And Hezekiah said to Isaiah, [a]"What *is* the
sign that the LORD will heal me, and that I shall go
up to the house of the LORD the third day?"
9 Then Isaiah said, [a]"This is the sign to you from
the LORD, that the LORD will do the thing which
He has spoken: *shall* the shadow go forward ten
degrees or go backward ten degrees?"
10 And Hezekiah answered, "It is an easy thing
for the shadow to go down ten [1]degrees; no, but
let the shadow go backward ten degrees."
11 So Isaiah the prophet cried out to the LORD,
and [a]He brought the shadow ten [1]degrees backward, by which it had gone down on the sundial of
Ahaz.
12 [a]At that time [1]Berodach-Baladan the son of
Baladan, king of Babylon, sent letters and a present to Hezekiah, for he heard that Hezekiah had
been sick.
13 And [a]Hezekiah was attentive to them, and
showed them all the house of his treasures—the
silver and gold, the spices and precious ointment,
and [1]all [2]his armory—all that was found among
his treasures. There was nothing in his house or in
all his dominion that Hezekiah did not show them.
14 Then Isaiah the prophet went to King Hezekiah, and said to him, "What did these men say,
and from where did they come to you?" So Hezekiah said, "They came from a far country, from
Babylon."
15 And he said, "What have they seen in your
house?" So Hezekiah answered, [a]"They have seen
all that *is* in my house; there is nothing among my
treasures that I have not shown them."
16 Then Isaiah said to Hezekiah, "Hear the word
of the LORD:
17 'Behold, the days are coming when all that *is*
in your house, and what your fathers have accu-
mulated until this day, [a]shall be carried to Babylon; nothing shall be left,' says the LORD.
18 'And [a]they shall take away some of your sons
who will [1]descend from you, whom you will beget;
[b]and they shall be [c]eunuchs in the palace of the
king of Babylon.' "
19 So Hezekiah said to Isaiah, [a]"The word of the
LORD which you have spoken *is* good!" For he
said, "Will there not be peace and truth at least in
my days?"
20 [a]Now the rest of the acts of Hezekiah—all his
might, and how he [b]made a [c]pool and a [1]tunnel
and [d]brought water into the city—*are* they not
written in the book of the chronicles of the kings
of Judah?
21 So [a]Hezekiah [1]rested with his fathers. Then
Manasseh his son reigned in his place.

### *Manasseh and Amon Reign over Judah*

**21** Manasseh [a]*was* twelve years old when he
became king, and he reigned fifty-five years
in Jerusalem. His mother's name *was* Hephzibah.
2 And he did evil in the sight of the LORD,
[a]according to the abominations of the nations
whom the LORD had cast out before the children
of Israel.
3 For he rebuilt the [1]high places [a]which Hezekiah his father had destroyed; he raised up altars
for Baal, and made a [2]wooden image, [b]as Ahab
king of Israel had done; and he [c]worshiped all [3]the
host of heaven and served them.
4 [a]He also built altars in the house of the LORD,
of which the LORD had said, [b]"In Jerusalem I will
put My name."

**29** [a]2 Kin. 20:8, 9 [1]Without cultivation
**30** [a]2 Chr. 32:22, 23
**31** [a]Is. 9:7 [1]So with many Heb. mss. and ancient vss. (cf. Is. 37:32); MT omits *of hosts*
**32** [a]Is. 8:7–10
**34** [a]2 Kin. 20:6 [b]Is. 31:5 [c]1 Kin. 11:12, 13
**35** [a]Is. 10:12–19; 37:36 [1]Or *Angel*
**36** [a]Gen. 10:11
**37** [a]2 Kin. 17:31 [b]2 Kin. 19:7 [c]Ezra 4:2

CHAPTER 20
**1** [a]Is. 38:1–22
**3** [a]Neh. 13:22
**5** [a]1 Sam. 9:16; 10:1 [b]Ps. 65:2 [c]Ps. 39:12; 56:8
**6** [a]2 Kin. 19:34
**7** [a]Is. 38:21
**8** [a]Judg. 6:17, 37, 39
**9** [a]Is. 38:7, 8
**10** [1]Lit. *steps*
**11** [a]Is. 38:8 [1]Lit. *steps*
**12** [a]Is. 39:1–8 [1]*Merodach-Baladan,* Is. 39:1
**13** [a]2 Chr. 32:27, 31 [1]So with many Heb. mss., Syr., Tg.; MT omits *all* [2]Lit. *the house of his armor*
**15** [a]2 Kin. 20:13
**17** [a]Jer. 27:21, 22; 52:17
**18** [a]2 Kin. 24:12 [b]Dan. 1:3–7 [c]Dan. 1:11, 18 [1]*be born from*
**19** [a]1 Sam. 3:18
**20** [a]2 Chr. 32:32 [b]Neh. 3:16 [c]Is. 7:3 [d]2 Chr. 32:3, 30 [1]*aqueduct*
**21** [a]2 Chr. 32:33 [1]Died and joined his ancestors

CHAPTER 21
**1** [a]2 Chr. 33:1–9
**2** [a]2 Kin. 16:3
**3** [a]2 Kin. 18:4, 22 [b]1 Kin. 16:31–33 [c][Deut. 4:19; 17:2–5] [1]Places for pagan worship [2]Or *Asherah,* a Canaanite goddess [3]The gods of the Assyrians
**4** [a]Jer. 7:30; 32:34 [b]1 Kin. 11:13

5 And he built altars for all the host of heaven in
the [a]two courts of the house of the LORD.
6 [a]Also he made his son pass through the fire,
practiced [b]soothsaying, used witchcraft, and consulted spiritists and mediums. He did much evil in
the sight of the LORD, to provoke *Him* to anger.
7 He even set a carved image of [1]Asherah that
he had made, in the [2]house of which the LORD had
said to David and to Solomon his son, [a]"In this
house and in Jerusalem, which I have chosen out
of all the tribes of Israel, I will put My name
forever;
8 [a]"and I will not make the feet of Israel wander
anymore from the land which I gave their fathers—only if they are careful to do according to
all that I have commanded them, and according to
all the law that My servant Moses commanded
them."
9 But they paid no attention, and Manasseh
[a]seduced them to do more evil than the nations
whom the LORD had destroyed before the children
of Israel.
**10** And the LORD spoke [a]by His servants the
prophets, saying,
11 [a]"Because Manasseh king of Judah has done
these abominations ([b]he has acted more wickedly
than all the [c]Amorites who *were* before him, and
[d]has also made Judah sin with his idols),
12 "therefore thus says the LORD God of Israel:
'Behold, *I* am bringing *such* calamity upon Jerusalem and Judah, that whoever hears of it, both [a]his
ears will tingle.
13 'And I will stretch over Jerusalem [a]the measuring line of Samaria and the plummet of the
house of Ahab; [b]I will wipe Jerusalem as *one*
wipes a dish, wiping *it* and turning *it* upside down.
14 'So I will forsake the [a]remnant of My inheritance and deliver them into the hand of their
enemies; and they shall become victims of plunder
to all their enemies,
15 'because they have done evil in My sight, and
have provoked Me to anger since the day their
fathers came out of Egypt, even to this day.' "
16 [a]Moreover Manasseh shed very much innocent blood, till he had filled Jerusalem from one
end to another, besides his sin by which he made
Judah sin, in doing evil in the sight of the LORD.
**17** Now [a]the rest of the acts of [b]Manasseh—all
that he did, and the sin that he committed—*are*
they not written in the book of the chronicles of
the kings of Judah?
18 So [a]Manasseh [1]rested with his fathers, and was
buried in the garden of his own house, in the
garden of Uzza. Then his son Amon reigned in his
place.
**19** [a]Amon *was* twenty-two years old when he
became king, and he reigned two years in Jerusalem. His mother's name *was* Meshullemeth the
daughter of Haruz of Jotbah.
20 And he did evil in the sight of the LORD, [a]as his
father Manasseh had done.
21 So he walked in all the ways that his father
had walked; and he served the idols that his father
had served, and worshiped them.
22 He [a]forsook the LORD God of his fathers, and
did not walk in the way of the LORD.
**23** [a]Then the servants of Amon [b]conspired
against him, and killed the king in his own house.
24 But the people of the land [a]executed all those
who had conspired against King Amon. Then the
people of the land made his son Josiah king in his
place.
**25** Now the rest of the acts of Amon which he
did, *are* they not written in the book of the
chronicles of the kings of Judah?
26 And he was buried in his tomb in the garden of
Uzza. Then Josiah his son reigned in his place.

### *Hilkiah Finds the Book of the Law*

**22** Josiah [a]*was* eight years old when he became
king, and he reigned thirty-one years in
Jerusalem. His mother's name *was* Jedidah the
daughter of Adaiah of [b]Bozkath.
2 And he did *what was* right in the sight of the
LORD, and walked in all the ways of his father
David; he [a]did not turn aside to the right hand or
to the left.
**3** [a]Now it came to pass, in the eighteenth year of
King Josiah, *that* the king sent Shaphan the
scribe, the son of Azaliah, the son of Meshullam,
to the house of the LORD, saying:
4 "Go up to Hilkiah the high priest, that he may
count the money which has been [a]brought into
the house of the LORD, which [b]the doorkeepers
have gathered from the people.
5 "And let them [a]deliver it into the hand of
those doing the work, who are the overseers in
the house of the LORD; let them give it to those
who *are* in the house of the LORD doing the work,
to repair the damages of the house—
6 "to carpenters and builders and masons—and
to buy timber and hewn stone to repair the house.
7 "However [a]there need be no accounting made
with them of the money delivered into their hand,
because they deal faithfully."
**8** Then Hilkiah the high priest said to Shaphan
the scribe, [a]"I have found the Book of the Law in
the house of the LORD." And Hilkiah gave the
book to Shaphan, and he read it.
9 So Shaphan the scribe went to the king, bringing the king word, saying, "Your servants have
[1]gathered the money that was found in the house,
and have delivered it into the hand of those who
do the work, who oversee the house of the LORD."
10 Then Shaphan the scribe showed the king,
saying, "Hilkiah the priest has given me a book."
And Shaphan read it before the king.
**11** Now it happened, when the king heard the
words of the Book of the Law, that he tore his
clothes.
12 Then the king commanded Hilkiah the priest,
[a]Ahikam the son of Shaphan, [1]Achbor the son of
Michaiah, Shaphan the scribe, and Asaiah a servant of the king, saying,
13 "Go, inquire of the LORD for me, for the people
and for all Judah, concerning the words of this
book that has been found; for great *is* [a]the wrath
of the LORD that is aroused against us, because
our fathers have not obeyed the words of this
book, to do according to all that is written concerning us."
**14** So Hilkiah the priest, Ahikam, Achbor, Shaphan, and Asaiah went to Huldah the prophetess,
the wife of Shallum the son of [a]Tikvah, the son of
Harhas, keeper of the wardrobe. (She dwelt in
Jerusalem in the Second Quarter.) And they spoke
with her.
15 Then she said to them, "Thus says the LORD
God of Israel, 'Tell the man who sent you to Me,
16 "Thus says the LORD: 'Behold, [a]I will bring
calamity on this place and on its inhabitants—all

**5** [a]1 Kin. 6:36; 7:12; 2 Kin. 23:12
**6** [a][Lev. 18:21; 20:2]; 2 Kin. 16:3; 17:17 [b]Lev. 19:26, 31; [Deut. 18:10–14]; 2 Kin. 17:17
**7** [a]2 Sam. 7:13; 1 Kin. 8:29; 9:3; 2 Kin. 23:27; 2 Chr. 7:12, 16; Jer. 32:34 [1]A Canaanite goddess [2]Temple
**8** [a]2 Sam. 7:10; [2 Kin. 18:11, 12]
**9** [a][Prov. 29:12]
**10** [a]2 Kin. 17:13
**11** [a]2 Kin. 23:26, 27; 24:3, 4 [b]1 Kin. 21:26 [c]Gen. 15:16 [d]2 Kin. 21:9
**12** [a]1 Sam. 3:11; Jer. 19:3
**13** [a]Lam. 2:8; Amos 7:7, 8 [b]2 Kin. 22:16–19; 25:4–11
**14** [a]Jer. 6:9
**16** [a]2 Kin. 24:4
**17** [a]2 Chr. 33:11–19 [b]2 Kin. 20:21
**18** [a]2 Chr. 33:20 [1]Died and joined his ancestors
**19** [a]2 Chr. 33:21–23
**20** [a]2 Kin. 21:2–6, 11, 16
**22** [a]Judg. 2:12, 13; 1 Kin. 11:33; 1 Chr. 28:9
**23** [a]1 Chr. 3:14; 2 Chr. 33:24, 25; Matt. 1:10 [b]2 Kin. 12:20; 14:19
**24** [a]2 Kin. 14:5

CHAPTER 22

**1** [a]1 Kin. 13:2; 2 Chr. 34:1 [b]Josh. 15:39
**2** [a]Deut. 5:32; Josh. 1:7
**3** [a]2 Chr. 34:8
**4** [a]2 Kin. 12:4 [b]2 Kin. 12:9, 10
**5** [a]2 Kin. 12:11–14
**7** [a]2 Kin. 12:15; [1 Cor. 4:2]
**8** [a]Deut. 31:24–26; 2 Chr. 34:14
**9** [1]Lit. *poured out*
**12** [a]2 Kin. 25:22; Jer. 26:24 [1]*Abdon the son of Micah,* 2 Chr. 34:20
**13** [a][Deut. 29:23–28; 31:17, 18]
**14** [a]2 Chr. 34:22
**16** [a]Deut. 29:27; [Dan. 9:11–14]

the words of the book which the king of Judah
has read—
17 [a]'because they have forsaken Me and burned
incense to other gods, that they might provoke
Me to anger with all the works of their hands.
Therefore My wrath shall be aroused against this
place and shall not be quenched.' " '
18 "But as for [a]the king of Judah, who sent you
to inquire of the LORD, in this manner you shall
speak to him, 'Thus says the LORD God of Israel:
"*Concerning* the words which you have heard—
19 "because your [a]heart was tender, and you
[b]humbled yourself before the LORD when you
heard what I spoke against this place and against
its inhabitants, that they would become [c]a desolation and [d]a curse, and you tore your clothes and
wept before Me, I also have heard *you*," says the
LORD.
20 "Surely, therefore, I will [1]gather you to your
fathers, and you [a]shall [2]be gathered to your grave
in peace; and your eyes shall not see all the
calamity which I will bring on this place." ' " So
they brought back word to the king.

### *Josiah Restores True Worship*

**23** Now [a]the king sent them to gather all the
elders of Judah and Jerusalem to him.
2 The king went up to the house of the LORD
with all the men of Judah, and with him all the
inhabitants of Jerusalem—the priests and the
prophets and all the people, both small and great.
And he [a]read in their hearing all the words of the
Book of the Covenant [b]which had been found in
the house of the LORD.
**3** Then the king [a]stood by a pillar and made a
[b]covenant before the LORD, to follow the LORD and
to keep His commandments and His testimonies
and His statutes, with all *his* heart and all *his* soul,
to perform the words of this covenant that were
written in this book. And all the people took a
stand for the covenant.
4 And the king commanded Hilkiah the high
priest, the [a]priests of the second order, and the
doorkeepers, to bring [b]out of the temple of the
LORD all the articles that were made for Baal, for
[1]Asherah, and for all [2]the host of heaven; and he
burned them outside Jerusalem in the fields of
Kidron, and carried their ashes to Bethel.
5 Then he removed the idolatrous priests whom
the kings of Judah had ordained to burn incense
on the high places in the cities of Judah and in the
places all around Jerusalem, and those who
burned incense to Baal, to the sun, to the moon, to
the [1]constellations, and to [a]all the host of heaven.
6 And he brought out the [a]wooden[1] image from
the house of the LORD, to the Brook Kidron
outside Jerusalem, burned it at the Brook Kidron
and ground *it* to [b]ashes, and threw its ashes on
[c]the graves of the common people.
7 Then he tore down the *ritual* [1]booths [a]of the
[2]perverted persons that *were* in the house of
the LORD, [b]where the [c]women wove hangings for
the wooden image.
8 And he brought all the priests from the cities
of Judah, and defiled the high places where the
priests had burned incense, from [a]Geba to Beersheba; also he broke down the high places at the
gates which *were* at the entrance of the Gate of
Joshua the governor of the city, which *were* to the
left of the city gate.
9 [a]Nevertheless the priests of the high places did
not come up to the altar of the LORD in Jerusalem,
[b]but they ate unleavened bread among their
brethren.
10 And he defiled [a]Topheth, which *is* in [b]the
Valley of the [1]Son of Hinnom, [c]that no man might
make his son or his daughter [d]pass through the
fire to Molech.
11 Then he removed the horses that the kings of
Judah had [1]dedicated to the sun, at the entrance
to the house of the LORD, by the chamber of
Nathan-Melech, the officer who *was* in the court;
and he burned the chariots of the sun with fire.
12 The altars that *were* [a]on the roof, the upper
chamber of Ahaz, which the kings of Judah had
made, and the altars which [b]Manasseh had made
in the two courts of the house of the LORD, the
king broke down and pulverized there, and threw
their dust into the Brook Kidron.
13 Then the king defiled the [1]high places that
*were* east of Jerusalem, which *were* on the [2]south
of [3]the Mount of Corruption, which [a]Solomon
king of Israel had built for Ashtoreth the abomination of the Sidonians, for Chemosh the abomination of the Moabites, and for Milcom the
abomination of the people of Ammon.
14 And he [a]broke in pieces the *sacred* pillars and
cut down the wooden images, and filled their
places with the bones of men.
**15** Moreover the altar that *was* at Bethel, *and* the
[1]high place [a]which Jeroboam the son of Nebat,
who made Israel sin, had made, both that altar
and the high place he broke down; and he burned
the high place *and* crushed *it* to powder, and
burned the wooden image.
16 As Josiah turned, he saw the tombs that *were*
there on the mountain. And he sent and took the
bones out of the tombs and burned *them* on
the altar, and defiled it according to the [a]word of
the LORD which the man of God proclaimed, who
proclaimed these words.
17 Then he said, "What gravestone *is* this that I
see?" So the men of the city told him, "*It is* [a]the
tomb of the man of God who came from Judah
and proclaimed these things which you have done
against the altar of Bethel."
18 And he said, "Let him alone; let no one move
his bones." So they let his bones alone, with the
bones of [a]the prophet who came from Samaria.
19 Now Josiah also took away all the [1]shrines of
the [2]high places that *were* [a]in the cities of Samaria, which the kings of Israel had made to
provoke [3]the LORD to anger; and he did to them
according to all the deeds he had done in Bethel.
20 [a]He [b]executed all the priests of the [1]high places
who *were* there, on the altars, and [c]burned men's
bones on them; and he returned to Jerusalem.
**21** Then the king commanded all the people,
saying, [a]"Keep the Passover to the LORD your
God, [b]as *it is* written in this Book of the Covenant."
22 [a]Such a Passover surely had never been held
since the days of the judges who judged Israel,
nor in all the days of the kings of Israel and the
kings of Judah.
23 But in the eighteenth year of King Josiah this
Passover was held before the LORD in Jerusalem.
24 Moreover Josiah put away those who consulted mediums and spiritists, the household gods
and idols, all the abominations that were seen in
the land of Judah and in Jerusalem, that he might
perform the words of [a]the law which were written

**17** [a]Deut. 29:25–27
**18** [a]2 Chr. 34:26
**19** [a][Ps. 51:17] [b]1 Kin. 21:29 [c]Lev. 26:31, 32 [d]Jer. 26:6; 44:22
**20** [a][Is. 57:1, 2] [1]Cause you to join your ancestors in death [2]Die a natural death

CHAPTER 23
**1** [a]2 Chr. 34:29, 30
**2** [a]Deut. 31:10–13 [b]2 Kin. 22:8
**3** [a]2 Kin. 11:14 [b]2 Kin. 11:17
**4** [a]2 Kin. 25:18 [b]2 Kin. 21:3–7 [1]A Canaanite goddess [2]The gods of the Assyrians
**5** [a]2 Kin. 21:3 [1]Of the Zodiac
**6** [a]2 Kin. 21:7 [b]Ex. 32:20 [c]2 Chr. 34:4 [1]Or *Asherah,* a Canaanite goddess
**7** [a]1 Kin. 14:24; 15:12 [b]Ezek. 16:16 [c]Ex. 38:8 [1]Lit. *houses* [2]Heb. *qedeshim,* those practicing sodomy and prostitution in religious rituals
**8** [a]Josh. 21:17
**9** [a][Ezek. 44:10–14] [b]1 Sam. 2:36
**10** [a]Is. 30:33 [b]Josh. 15:8 [c][Lev. 18:21] [d]2 Kin. 21:6 [1]Kt. *Sons*
**11** [1]*given*
**12** [a]Jer. 19:13 [b]2 Kin. 21:5
**13** [a]1 Kin. 11:5–7 [1]Places for pagan worship [2]Lit. *right of* [3]The Mount of Olives
**14** [a][Ex. 23:24]
**15** [a]1 Kin. 12:28–33 [1]A place for pagan worship
**16** [a]1 Kin. 13:2
**17** [a]1 Kin. 13:1, 30, 31
**18** [a]1 Kin. 13:11, 31
**19** [a]2 Chr. 34:6, 7 [1]Lit. *houses* [2]Places for pagan worship [3]So with LXX, Syr., Vg.; MT, Tg. omit *the* LORD
**20** [a]1 Kin. 13:2 [b]2 Kin. 10:25; 11:18 [c]2 Chr. 34:5 [1]Places for pagan worship
**21** [a]2 Chr. 35:1 [b]Deut. 16:2–8
**22** [a]2 Chr. 35:18, 19
**24** [a][Lev. 19:31; 20:27]

in the book [b]that Hilkiah the priest found in the
house of the LORD.
25 [a]Now before him there was no king like him,
who turned to the LORD with all his heart, with all
his soul, and with all his might, according to all
the Law of Moses; nor after him did *any* arise like
him.
**26** Nevertheless the LORD did not turn from the
fierceness of His great wrath, with which His
anger was aroused against Judah, [a]because of all
the provocations with which Manasseh had provoked Him.
27 And the LORD said, "I will also remove Judah
from My sight, as [a]I have removed Israel, and will
cast off this city Jerusalem which I have chosen,
and the house of which I said, [b]'My name shall be
there.' "
**28** Now the rest of the acts of Josiah, and all that
he did, *are* they not written in the book of the
chronicles of the kings of Judah?
29 [a]In his days Pharaoh Necho king of Egypt
went [1]to the aid of the king of Assyria, to the
River Euphrates; and King Josiah went against
him. And *Pharaoh Necho* killed him at [b]Megiddo
when he [c]confronted him.
30 [a]Then his servants moved his body in a chariot
from Megiddo, brought him to Jerusalem, and
buried him in his own tomb. And [b]the people of
the land took Jehoahaz the son of Josiah,
anointed him, and made him king in his father's
place.
**31** [a]Jehoahaz *was* twenty-three years old when
he became king, and he reigned three months in
Jerusalem. His mother's name *was* [b]Hamutal the
daughter of Jeremiah of Libnah.
32 And he did evil in the sight of the LORD,
according to all that his fathers had done.
33 Now Pharaoh Necho put him in prison [a]at
Riblah in the land of Hamath, that he might not
reign in Jerusalem; and he imposed on the land a
tribute of one hundred talents of silver and a
talent of gold.
34 Then [a]Pharaoh Necho made Eliakim the son of
Josiah king in place of his father Josiah, and
[b]changed his name to [c]Jehoiakim. And *Pharaoh*
took Jehoahaz [d]and went to Egypt, and [1]he died
there.
**35** So Jehoiakim gave [a]the silver and gold to
Pharaoh; but he taxed the land to give money
according to the command of Pharaoh; he exacted
the silver and gold from the people of the land,
from every one according to his assessment, to
give *it* to Pharaoh Necho.
36 [a]Jehoiakim *was* twenty-five years old when he
became king, and he reigned eleven years in
Jerusalem. His mother's name *was* Zebudah the
daughter of Pedaiah of Rumah.
37 And he did evil in the sight of the LORD,
according to all that his fathers had done.

### *Jehoiachin Taken Captive to Babylon*

**24** In [a]his days Nebuchadnezzar king of [b]Baby-
lon came up, and Jehoiakim became his
vassal *for* three years. Then he turned and rebelled against him.
2 [a]And the LORD sent against him *raiding* [1]bands
of Chaldeans, bands of Syrians, bands of Moabites, and bands of the people of Ammon; He sent
them against Judah to destroy it, [b]according to
the word of the LORD which He had spoken by His
servants the prophets.
3 Surely at the commandment of the LORD *this*
came upon Judah, to remove *them* from His sight
[a]because of the sins of Manasseh, according to all
that he had done,
4 [a]and also because of the innocent blood that
he had shed; for he had filled Jerusalem with
innocent blood, which the LORD would not pardon.
**5** Now the rest of the acts of Jehoiakim, and all
that he did, *are* they not written in the book of the
chronicles of the kings of Judah?
6 [a]So Jehoiakim rested with his fathers. Then
Jehoiachin his son reigned in his place.
7 And [a]the king of Egypt did not come out of his
land anymore, for [b]the king of Babylon had taken
all that belonged to the king of Egypt from the
Brook of Egypt to the River Euphrates.
**8** [a]Jehoiachin[1] *was* eighteen years old when he
became king, and he reigned in Jerusalem three
months. His mother's name *was* Nehushta the
daughter of Elnathan of Jerusalem.
9 And he did evil in the sight of the LORD,
according to all that his father had done.
**10** [a]At that time the servants of Nebuchadnezzar
king of Babylon came up against Jerusalem, and
the city [1]was besieged.
11 And Nebuchadnezzar king of Babylon came
against the city, as his servants were besieging it.
12 [a]Then Jehoiachin king of Judah, his mother,
his servants, his princes, and his officers went out
to the king of Babylon; and the king of Babylon,
[b]in the eighth year of his reign, took him prisoner.
**13** [a]And he carried out from there all the treasures of the house of the LORD and the treasures
of the king's house, and he [b]cut in pieces all the
articles of gold which Solomon king of Israel had
made in the temple of the LORD, [c]as the LORD had
said.
14 Also [a]he carried into captivity all Jerusalem:
all the captains and all the mighty men of valor,
[b]ten thousand captives, and [c]all the craftsmen and
smiths. None remained except [d]the poorest people
of the land.
15 And [a]he carried Jehoiachin captive to Babylon.
The king's mother, the king's wives, his officers,
and the mighty of the land he carried into captivity from Jerusalem to Babylon.
16 [a]All the valiant men, seven thousand, and
craftsmen and smiths, one thousand, all *who were*
strong *and* fit for war, these the king of Babylon
brought captive to Babylon.
17 Then [a]the king of Babylon made Mattaniah,
[b]*Jehoiachin's*[1] uncle, king in his place, and
[c]changed his name to Zedekiah.
**18** [a]Zedekiah *was* twenty-one years old when he
became king, and he reigned eleven years in
Jerusalem. His mother's name *was* [b]Hamutal the
daughter of Jeremiah of Libnah.
19 [a]He also did evil in the sight of the LORD,
according to all that Jehoiakim had done.
20 For because of the anger of the LORD *this*
happened in Jerusalem and Judah, that He finally
cast them out from His presence. [a]Then Zedekiah
rebelled against the king of Babylon.

### *The Captivity of Judah*

**25** Now it came to pass [a]in the ninth year of his
reign, in the tenth month, on the tenth *day*
of the month, *that* Nebuchadnezzar king of Babylon and all his army came against Jerusalem and

**24** [b]2 Kin. 22:8
**25** [a]2 Kin. 18:5
**26** [a]Jer. 15:4
**27** [a]2 Kin. 17:18, 20; 18:11; 21:13 [b]1 Kin. 8:29; 9:3
**29** [a]Jer. 2:16; 46:2 [b]Zech. 12:11 [c]2 Kin. 14:8 [1]Or *to attack*, Heb. *al* can mean *together with* or *against*
**30** [a]2 Chr. 35:24 [b]2 Chr. 36:1–4
**31** [a]Jer. 22:11 [b]2 Kin. 24:18
**33** [a]2 Kin. 25:6
**34** [a]2 Chr. 36:4 [b]Dan. 1:7 [c]Matt. 1:11 [d]Ezek. 19:3, 4 [1]Jehoahaz
**35** [a]2 Kin. 23:33
**36** [a]2 Chr. 36:5

CHAPTER 24

**1** [a]Dan. 1:1 [b]2 Kin. 20:14
**2** [a]Jer. 25:9; 32:28; 35:11 [b]2 Kin. 20:17; 21:12–14; 23:27 [1]*troops*
**3** [a]2 Kin. 21:2, 11; 23:26
**4** [a]2 Kin. 21:16
**6** [a]Jer. 22:18, 19
**7** [a]Jer. 37:57 [b]Jer. 46:2
**8** [a]2 Chr. 36:9 [1]*Jeconiah*, 1 Chr. 3:16; Jer. 24:1; or *Coniah*, Jer. 22:24, 28
**10** [a]Dan. 1:1 [1]Lit. *came into siege*
**12** [a]Jer. 22:24–30; 24:1; 29:1, 2 [b]2 Chr. 36:10
**13** [a]Is. 39:6 [b]Dan. 5:2, 3 [c]Jer. 20:5
**14** [a]Jer. 24:1 [b]2 Kin. 24:16 [c]1 Sam. 13:19 [d]2 Kin. 25:12
**15** [a]Jer. 22:24–28
**16** [a]Jer. 52:28
**17** [a]Jer. 37:1 [b]2 Chr. 36:10 [c]2 Chr. 36:4 [1]Lit. *his*
**18** [a]Jer. 52:1 [b]2 Kin. 23:31
**19** [a]2 Chr. 36:12
**20** [a]Ezek. 17:15

CHAPTER 25

**1** [a]Jer. 6:6; 34:2

encamped against it; and they built a siege wall
against it all around.
2 So the city was besieged until the eleventh
year of King Zedekiah.
3 By the ninth *day* of the [a]*fourth* month the
famine had become so severe in the city that there
was no food for the people of the land.
**4** Then [a]the city wall was broken through, and
all the men of war *fled* at night by way of the gate
between two walls, which was by the king's
garden, even though the Chaldeans *were* still
encamped all around against the city. And [b]*the
king*[1] went by way of the [2]plain.
5 But the army of the Chaldeans pursued the
king, and they overtook him in the plains of
Jericho. All his army was scattered from him.
6 So they took the king and brought him up to
the king of Babylon [a]at Riblah, and they pronounced judgment on him.
7 Then they killed the sons of Zedekiah before
his eyes, [a]put[1] out the eyes of Zedekiah, bound
him with bronze fetters, and took him to Babylon.
**8** And in the fifth month, [a]on the seventh *day* of
the month (which *was* [b]the nineteenth year of
King Nebuchadnezzar king of Babylon), [c]Nebu-
zaradan the captain of the guard, a servant of the
king of Babylon, came to Jerusalem.
9 [a]He burned the house of the LORD [b]and the
king's house; all the houses of Jerusalem, that is,
all the houses of the great, [c]he burned with fire.
10 And all the army of the Chaldeans who *were
with* the captain of the guard [a]broke down the
walls of Jerusalem all around.
**11** Then Nebuzaradan the captain of the guard
carried away captive [a]the rest of the people *who*
remained in the city and the defectors who had
deserted to the king of Babylon, with the rest of
the multitude.
12 But the captain of the guard [a]left *some* of the
poor of the land as vinedressers and farmers.
13 [a]The bronze [b]pillars that *were* in the house of
the LORD, and [c]the carts and [d]the bronze Sea that
*were* in the house of the LORD, the Chaldeans
broke in pieces, and [e]carried their bronze to
Babylon.
14 They also took away [a]the pots, the shovels,
the trimmers, the spoons, and all the bronze
utensils with which the priests ministered.
15 The firepans and the basins, the things of solid
gold and solid silver, the captain of the guard took
away.
16 The two pillars, one Sea, and the carts, which
Solomon had made for the house of the LORD, [a]the
bronze of all these articles was beyond measure.
17 [a]The height of one pillar *was* [1]eighteen cubits,
and the capital on it *was* of bronze. The height of
the capital was three cubits, and the network and
pomegranates all around the capital were all of
bronze. The second pillar was the same, with a
network.
**18** [a]And the captain of the guard took [b]Seraiah
the chief priest, [c]Zephaniah the second priest, and
the three doorkeepers.
19 He also took out of the city an officer who had
charge of the men of war, [a]five men of [1]the king's
close associates who were found in the city, the
chief recruiting officer of the army, who mustered
the people of the land, and sixty men of the people
of the land *who were* found in the city.
20 So Nebuzaradan, captain of the guard, took
these and brought them to the king of Babylon at
Riblah.
21 Then the king of Babylon struck them and put
them to death at Riblah in the land of Hamath.
[a]Thus Judah was carried away captive from its
own land.
**22** Then he made Gedaliah the son of [a]Ahikam,
the son of Shaphan, governor over [b]the people
who remained in the land of Judah, whom Nebuchadnezzar king of Babylon had left.
23 Now when all the [a]captains of the armies, they
and *their* men, heard that the king of Babylon had
made Gedaliah governor, they came to Gedaliah
at Mizpah—Ishmael the son of Nethaniah, Johanan the son of Careah, Seraiah the son of Tanhumeth the Netophathite, and [1]Jaazaniah the son
of a Maachathite, they and their men.
24 And Gedaliah took an oath before them and
their men, and said to them, "Do not be afraid of
the servants of the Chaldeans. Dwell in the land
and serve the king of Babylon, and it shall be well
with you."
**25** But [a]it happened in the seventh month that
Ishmael the son of Nethaniah, the son of Elishama, of the royal family, came with ten men and
struck and killed Gedaliah, the Jews, as well as the
Chaldeans who were with him at Mizpah.
26 And all the people, small and great, and the
captains of the armies, arose [a]and went to Egypt;
for they were afraid of the Chaldeans.
**27** [a]Now it came to pass in the thirty-seventh
year of the captivity of Jehoiachin king of Judah,
in the twelfth month, on the twenty-seventh *day*
of the month, *that* [1]Evil-Merodach king of Babylon, in the year that he began to reign, [b]released
Jehoiachin king of Judah from prison.
28 He spoke kindly to him, and gave him a more
prominent seat than those of the kings who *were*
with him in Babylon.
29 So Jehoiachin changed from his prison garments, and he [a]ate [1]bread regularly before the
king all the days of his life.
30 And as for his [1]provisions, *there was* a [2]regular
ration given him by the king, a portion for each
day, all the days of his life.

**3** [a]2 Kin. 6:24, 25; Is. 3:1; Jer. 39:2; Lam. 4:9, 10
**4** [a]Jer. 39:2 [b]Jer. 39:4–7; Ezek. 12:12 [1]Lit. *he* [2]Or *Arabah,* The Jordan Valley
**6** [a]2 Kin. 23:33; Jer. 52:9
**7** [a]Jer. 39:7; Ezek. 17:16 [1]*blinded*
**8** [a]Jer. 52:12 [b]2 Kin. 24:12 [c]Jer. 39:9
**9** [a]2 Kin. 25:13; 2 Chr. 36:19; Ps. 79:1; Jer. 7:14 [b]Jer. 39:8 [c]Jer. 17:27
**10** [a]2 Kin. 14:13; Neh. 1:3
**11** [a]Is. 1:9; Jer. 5:19; 39:9
**12** [a]2 Kin. 24:14; Jer. 39:10; 40:7; 52:16
**13** [a]Jer. 52:17 [b]1 Kin. 7:15 [c]1 Kin. 7:27 [d]1 Kin. 7:23 [e]2 Kin. 20:17; Jer. 27:19–22
**14** [a]Ex. 27:3; 1 Kin. 7:45
**16** [a]1 Kin. 7:47
**17** [a]1 Kin. 7:15–22; Jer. 52:21 [1]About 27 feet
**18** [a]Jer. 39:9–13; 52:12–16, 24 [b]1 Chr. 6:14; Ezra 7:1 [c]Jer. 21:1; 29:25, 29
**19** [a]Esth. 1:14; Jer. 52:25 [1]Lit. *those seeing the king's face*
**21** [a]Lev. 26:33; Deut. 28:36, 64; 2 Kin. 23:27
**22** [a]2 Kin. 22:12 [b]Is. 1:9; Jer. 40:5
**23** [a]Jer. 40:7–9 [1]*Jezaniah,* Jer. 40:8
**25** [a]Jer. 41:1–3
**26** [a]2 Kin. 19:31; Jer. 43:4–7
**27** [a]2 Kin. 24:12, 15; Jer. 52:31–34 [b]Gen. 40:13, 20 [1]Lit. *The Man of Marduk*
**29** [a]2 Sam. 9:7 [1]Food
**30** [1]Lit. *allowance* [2]Lit. *allowance*

*The First Book of the*

# CHRONICLES

## *The Family of Adam—from Seth to Esau*

ADAM,[a] [b]Seth, Enosh,
2 Cainan, Mahalalel, Jared,
3 Enoch, Methuselah, Lamech,
4 [a]Noah,[1] Shem, Ham, and Japheth.
**5** [a]The sons of Japheth *were* Gomer, Magog, Madai, Javan, Tubal, Meshech, and Tiras.
6 The sons of Gomer *were* Ashkenaz, [1]Diphath, and Togarmah.
7 The sons of Javan *were* Elishah, [1]Tarshishah, Kittim, and [2]Rodanim.
**8** [a]The sons of Ham *were* Cush, Mizraim, Put, and Canaan.
9 The sons of Cush *were* Seba, Havilah, [1]Sabta, [2]Raama, and Sabtecha. The sons of Raama *were* Sheba and Dedan.
10 Cush [a]begot Nimrod; he began to be a mighty one on the earth.
11 Mizraim begot Ludim, Anamim, Lehabim, Naphtuhim,
12 Pathrusim, Casluhim (from whom came the Philistines and the [a]Caphtorim).
13 [a]Canaan begot Sidon, his firstborn, and Heth;
14 the Jebusite, the Amorite, and the Girgashite;
15 the Hivite, the Arkite, and the Sinite;
16 the Arvadite, the Zemarite, and the Hamathite.
**17** The sons of [a]Shem *were* Elam, Asshur, [b]Arphaxad, Lud, Aram, Uz, Hul, Gether, and [1]Meshech.
18 Arphaxad begot Shelah, and Shelah begot Eber.
19 To Eber were born two sons: the name of one *was* [1]Peleg, for in his days the [2]earth was divided; and his brother's name *was* Joktan.
20 [a]Joktan begot Almodad, Sheleph, Hazarmaveth, Jerah,
21 Hadoram, Uzal, Diklah,
22 [1]Ebal, Abimael, Sheba,
23 Ophir, Havilah, and Jobab. All these *were* the sons of Joktan.
**24** [a]Shem, Arphaxad, Shelah,
25 [a]Eber, Peleg, Reu,
26 Serug, Nahor, Terah,
27 and [a]Abram, who *is* Abraham.
28 [a]The sons of Abraham *were* [b]Isaac and [c]Ishmael.
**29** These *are* their genealogies: The [a]firstborn of Ishmael *was* Nebajoth; then Kedar, Adbeel, Mibsam,
30 Mishma, Dumah, Massa, [1]Hadad, Tema,
31 Jetur, Naphish, and Kedemah. These *were* the sons of Ishmael.
**32** Now [a]the sons born to Keturah, Abraham's concubine, *were* Zimran, Jokshan, Medan, Midian, Ishbak, and Shuah. The sons of Jokshan *were* Sheba and Dedan.
33 The sons of Midian *were* Ephah, Epher, Hanoch, Abida, and Eldaah. All these were the children of Keturah.
**34** And [a]Abraham begot Isaac. [b]The sons of Isaac *were* Esau and Israel.
35 The sons of [a]Esau *were* Eliphaz, Reuel, Jeush, Jaalam, and Korah.
36 And the sons of Eliphaz *were* Teman, Omar, [1]Zephi, Gatam, *and* Kenaz; and *by* [a]Timna, Amalek.
37 The sons of Reuel *were* Nahath, Zerah, Shammah, and Mizzah.
**38** [a]The sons of Seir *were* Lotan, Shobal, Zibeon, Anah, Dishon, Ezer, and Dishan.
39 And the sons of Lotan *were* Hori and [1]Homam; Lotan's sister *was* Timna.
40 The sons of Shobal *were* [1]Alian, Manahath, Ebal, [2]Shephi, and Onam. The sons of Zibeon *were* Ajah and Anah.
41 The son of Anah *was* [a]Dishon. The sons of Dishon *were* [1]Hamran, Eshban, Ithran, and Cheran.
42 The sons of Ezer *were* Bilhan, Zaavan, *and* [1]Jaakan. The sons of Dishan *were* Uz and Aran.
**43** Now these *were* the [a]kings who reigned in the land of Edom before a king reigned over the children of Israel: Bela the son of Beor, and the name of his city was Dinhabah.
44 And when Bela died, Jobab the son of Zerah of Bozrah reigned in his place.
45 When Jobab died, Husham of the land of the Temanites reigned in his place.
46 And when Husham died, Hadad the son of Bedad, who [1]attacked Midian in the field of Moab, reigned in his place. The name of his city *was* Avith.
47 When Hadad died, Samlah of Masrekah reigned in his place.
48 [a]And when Samlah died, Saul of Rehoboth-by-the-River reigned in his place.
49 When Saul died, Baal-Hanan the son of Achbor reigned in his place.
50 And when Baal-Hanan died, [1]Hadad reigned in his place; and the name of his city was [2]Pai. His wife's name was Mehetabel the daughter of Matred, the daughter of Mezahab.
51 Hadad died also. And the chiefs of Edom were Chief Timnah, Chief [1]Aliah, Chief Jetheth,
52 Chief Aholibamah, Chief Elah, Chief Pinon,
53 Chief Kenaz, Chief Teman, Chief Mibzar,
54 Chief Magdiel, and Chief Iram. These *were* the chiefs of Edom.

## *The Family of Israel*

**2** These *were* the [a]sons of [1]Israel: [b]Reuben, Simeon, Levi, Judah, Issachar, Zebulun,
2 Dan, Joseph, Benjamin, Naphtali, Gad, and Asher.
**3** The sons of [a]Judah *were* Er, Onan, and Shelah. *These* three were born to him by the daughter of [b]Shua, the Canaanitess. [c]Er, the firstborn of Judah, was wicked in the sight of the LORD; so He killed him.
4 And [a]Tamar, his daughter-in-law, [b]bore him Perez and Zerah. All the sons of Judah *were* five.
5 The sons of [a]Perez *were* Hezron and Hamul.
6 The sons of Zerah *were* [1]Zimri, [a]Ethan, Heman, Calcol, and [2]Dara—five of them in all.
7 The son of [a]Carmi *was* [1]Achar, the troubler of Israel, who transgressed in the [b]accursed[2] thing.
8 The son of Ethan *was* Azariah.
**9** Also the sons of Hezron who were born to him *were* Jerahmeel, [1]Ram, and [2]Chelubai.

CHAPTER 1
**1** [a]Gen. 1:27; 2:7; 5:1, 2, 5 [b]Gen. 4:25, 26; 5:3–9
**4** [a]Gen. 5:28—10:1 [1]So with MT, Vg.; LXX adds *the sons of Noah*
**5** [a]Gen. 10:2–4
**6** [1]*Riphath,* Gen. 10:3
**7** [1]*Dodanim,* Gen. 10:4 [2]*Tarshish,* Gen. 10:4
**8** [a]Gen. 10:6
**9** [1]*Sabtah,* Gen. 10:7 [2]*Raamah,* Gen. 10:7
**10** [a]Gen. 10:8–10, 13
**12** [a]Deut. 2:23
**13** [a]Gen. 9:18, 25–27; 10:15
**17** [a]Gen. 10:22–29; 11:10 [b]Luke 3:36 [1]*Mash,* Gen. 10:23
**19** [1]Lit. *Division,* Gen. 10:25 [2]Or *land*
**20** [a]Gen. 10:26
**22** [1]*Obal,* Gen. 10:28
**24** [a]Luke 3:34–36
**25** [a]Gen. 11:15
**27** [a]Gen. 17:5
**28** [a]Gen. 21:2, 3 [b]Gen. 21:2 [c]Gen. 16:11, 15
**29** [a]Gen. 25:13–16
**30** [1]*Hadar,* Gen. 25:15
**32** [a]Gen. 25:1–4
**34** [a]Gen. 21:2 [b]Gen. 25:9, 25, 26, 29; 32:28
**35** [a]Gen. 36:10–19
**36** [a]Gen. 36:12 [1]*Zepho,* Gen. 36:11
**38** [a]Gen. 36:20–28
**39** [1]*Hemam* or *Heman,* Gen. 36:22
**40** [1]*Alvan,* Gen. 36:23 [2]*Shepho,* Gen. 36:23
**41** [a]Gen. 36:25 [1]*Hemdan,* Gen. 36:26
**42** [1]*Akan,* Gen. 36:27
**43** [a]Gen. 36:31–43
**46** [1]Lit. *struck*
**48** [a]Gen. 36:37
**50** [1]*Hadar,* Gen. 36:39 [2]*Pau,* Gen. 36:39
**51** [1]*Alvah,* Gen. 36:40

CHAPTER 2
**1** [a]Gen. 29:32–35; 35:23, 26; 46:8–27 [b]Gen. 29:32; 35:22 [1]*Jacob,* Gen. 32:28
**3** [a]Num. 26:19 [b]Gen. 38:2 [c]Gen. 38:7
**4** [a]Gen. 38:6 [b]Matt. 1:3
**5** [a]Ruth 4:18
**6** [a]1 Kin. 4:31 [1]*Zabdi,* Josh. 7:1 [2]*Darda,* 1 Kin. 4:31
**7** [a]1 Chr. 4:1 [b]Josh. 6:18 [1]*Achan,* Josh. 7:1 [2]*banned* or *devoted*
**9** [1]*Aram,* Matt. 1:3, 4 [2]*Caleb,* vv. 18, 42

10 Ram [a]begot Amminadab, and Amminadab
begot Nahshon, [b]leader of the children of Judah;
11 Nahshon begot [1]Salma, and Salma begot Boaz;
12 Boaz begot Obed, and Obed begot Jesse;
13 [a]Jesse begot Eliab his firstborn, Abinadab the
second, [1]Shimea the third,
14 Nethanel the fourth, Raddai the fifth,
15 Ozem the sixth, *and* David the [a]seventh.
16 Now their sisters *were* Zeruiah and Abigail.
[a]And the sons of Zeruiah *were* Abishai, Joab, and
Asahel—three.
17 Abigail bore Amasa; and the father of Amasa
*was* [1]Jether the Ishmaelite.
**18** Caleb the son of Hezron had children by
Azubah, *his* wife, and by Jerioth. Now these were
her sons: Jesher, Shobab, and Ardon.
19 When Azubah died, Caleb [1]took [a]Ephrath[2] as
his wife, who bore him Hur.
20 And Hur begot Uri, and Uri begot [a]Bezalel.
**21** Now afterward Hezron went in to the daughter of [a]Machir the father of Gilead, whom he
married when he *was* sixty years old; and she bore
him Segub.
22 Segub begot [a]Jair,[1] who had twenty-three
cities in the land of Gilead.
23 [a](Geshur and Syria took from them the towns
of Jair, with Kenath and its towns—sixty towns.)
All these *belonged to* the sons of Machir the father
of Gilead.
24 After Hezron died in Caleb Ephrathah, Hezron's wife Abijah bore him [a]Ashhur the father of
Tekoa.
**25** The sons of Jerahmeel, the firstborn of Hezron, *were* Ram, the firstborn, and Bunah, Oren,
Ozem, *and* Ahijah.
26 Jerahmeel had another wife, whose name was
Atarah; she was the mother of Onam.
27 The sons of Ram, the firstborn of Jerahmeel,
were Maaz, Jamin, and Eker.
28 The sons of Onam were Shammai and Jada.
The sons of Shammai *were* Nadab and Abishur.
29 And the name of the wife of Abishur *was*
Abihail, and she bore him Ahban and Molid.
30 The sons of Nadab *were* Seled and Appaim;
Seled died without children.
31 The son of Appaim *was* Ishi, the son of Ishi
*was* Sheshan, and [a]Sheshan's son *was* Ahlai.
32 The sons of Jada, the brother of Shammai,
*were* Jether and Jonathan; Jether died without
children.
33 The sons of Jonathan *were* Peleth and Zaza.
These were the sons of Jerahmeel.
**34** Now Sheshan had no sons, only daughters.
And Sheshan had an Egyptian servant whose
name *was* Jarha.
35 Sheshan gave his daughter to Jarha his servant as wife, and she bore him Attai.
36 Attai begot Nathan, and Nathan begot [a]Zabad;
37 Zabad begot Ephlal, and Ephlal begot [a]Obed;
38 Obed begot Jehu, and Jehu begot Azariah;
39 Azariah begot Helez, and Helez begot Eleasah;
40 Eleasah begot Sismai, and Sismai begot Shallum;
41 Shallum begot Jekamiah, and Jekamiah begot
Elishama.
**42** The descendants of Caleb the brother of Jerahmeel *were* Mesha, his firstborn, who was the
father of Ziph, and the sons of Mareshah the
father of Hebron.
43 The sons of Hebron *were* Korah, Tappuah,
Rekem, and Shema.
44 Shema begot Raham the father of Jorkoam,
and Rekem begot Shammai.
45 And the son of Shammai *was* Maon, and
Maon *was* the father of Beth Zur.
46 Ephah, Caleb's concubine, bore Haran, Moza,
and Gazez; and Haran begot Gazez.
47 And the sons of Jahdai *were* Regem, Jotham,
Geshan, Pelet, Ephah, and Shaaph.
48 Maachah, Caleb's concubine, bore Sheber and
Tirhanah.
49 She also bore Shaaph the father of Madmannah, Sheva the father of Machbenah and the
father of Gibea. And the daughter of Caleb *was*
[a]Achsah.[1]
**50** These were the descendants of Caleb: The
sons of [a]Hur, the firstborn of [1]Ephrathah, *were*
Shobal the father of [b]Kirjath Jearim,
51 Salma the father of Bethlehem, *and* Hareph
the father of Beth Gader.
52 And Shobal the father of Kirjath Jearim had
descendants: [1]Haroeh, *and* half of the [2]families of
Manuhoth.
53 The families of Kirjath Jearim *were* the Ith-
rites, the Puthites, the Shumathites, and the
Mishraites. From these came the Zorathites and
the Eshtaolites.
54 The sons of Salma *were* Bethlehem, the Netophathites, [1]Atroth Beth Joab, half of the Manahethites, and the Zorites.
55 And the families of the scribes who dwelt at
Jabez *were* the Tirathites, the Shimeathites, *and*
the Suchathites. These *were* the [a]Kenites who
came from Hammath, the father of the house of
[b]Rechab.

### *The Family of David*

**3** Now these were the sons of David who were
born to him in Hebron: The firstborn *was*
[a]Amnon, by [b]Ahinoam the [c]Jezreelitess; the second, [1]Daniel, by [d]Abigail the Carmelitess;
2 the third, [a]Absalom the son of Maacah, the
daughter of Talmai, king of Geshur; the fourth,
[b]Adonijah the son of Haggith;
3 the fifth, Shephatiah, by Abital; the sixth,
Ithream, by his wife [a]Eglah.
4 *These* six were born to him in Hebron. [a]There
he reigned seven years and six months, and [b]in
Jerusalem he reigned thirty-three years.
5 [a]And these were born to him in Jerusalem:
[1]Shimea, Shobab, Nathan, and [b]Solomon—four by
[2]Bathshua the daughter of [3]Ammiel.
6 Also *there* were Ibhar, [1]Elishama, [2]Eliphelet,
7 Nogah, Nepheg, Japhia,
8 Elishama, [1]Eliada, and Eliphelet—[a]nine *in all.*
9 *These were* all the sons of David, besides the
sons of the concubines, and [a]Tamar their sister.
**10** Solomon's son *was* [a]Rehoboam; [1]Abijah *was*
his son, Asa his son, Jehoshaphat his son,
11 [1]Joram his son, [2]Ahaziah his son, [3]Joash his
son,
12 Amaziah his son, [1]Azariah his son, Jotham his
son,
13 Ahaz his son, Hezekiah his son, Manasseh his
son,
14 Amon his son, *and* Josiah his son.
15 The sons of Josiah *were* Johanan the firstborn,
the second [1]Jehoiakim, the third Zedekiah, and
the fourth [2]Shallum.

**10** [a]Matt. 1:4 [b]Num. 1:7; 2:3
**11** [1]*Salmon,* Ruth 4:21; Luke 3:32
**13** [a]1 Sam. 16:6 [1]*Shammah,* 1 Sam. 16:9
**15** [a]1 Sam. 16:10, 11; 17:12
**16** [a]2 Sam. 2:18
**17** [1]*Jithra the Israelite,* 2 Sam. 17:25
**19** [a]1 Chr. 2:50 [1]Lit. *took to himself* [2]Or *Ephrathah*
**20** [a]Ex. 31:2; 38:22
**21** [a]Num. 27:1
**22** [a]Judg. 10:3 [1]Reckoned to Manasseh through the daughter of Machir, Num. 32:41; Deut. 3:14; 25:5, 6; 1 Kin. 4:13; 1 Chr. 7:14
**23** [a]Deut. 3:14
**24** [a]1 Chr. 4:5
**31** [a]1 Chr. 2:34, 35
**36** [a]1 Chr. 11:41
**37** [a]2 Chr. 23:1
**49** [a]Josh. 15:17 [1]Or *Achsa*
**50** [a]1 Chr. 4:4 [b]Josh. 9:17; 18:14 [1]*Ephrath,* v. 19
**52** [1]*Reaiah,* 1 Chr. 4:2 [2]Or *Manuhothites,* same as *Manahethites,* v. 54
**54** [1]Or *Ataroth of the house of Joab*
**55** [a]Judg. 1:16 [b]Jer. 35:2

CHAPTER 3

**1** [a]2 Sam. 3:2–5 [b]1 Sam. 25:43 [c]Josh. 15:56 [d]1 Sam. 25:39–42 [1]*Chileab,* 2 Sam. 3:3
**2** [a]2 Sam. 13:37; 15:1 [b]1 Kin. 1:5
**3** [a]2 Sam. 3:5
**4** [a]2 Sam. 2:11 [b]2 Sam. 5:5
**5** [a]1 Chr. 14:4–7 [b]2 Sam. 12:24, 25 [1]*Shammua,* 1 Chr. 14:4; 2 Sam. 5:14 [2]*Bathsheba,* 2 Sam. 11:3 [3]*Eliam,* 2 Sam. 11:3
**6** [1]*Elishua,* 1 Chr. 14:5; 2 Sam. 5:15 [2]*Elpelet,* 1 Chr. 14:5
**8** [a]2 Sam. 5:14–16 [1]*Beeliada,* 1 Chr. 14:5
**9** [a]2 Sam. 13:1
**10** [a]1 Kin. 11:43 [1]*Abijam,* 1 Kin. 15:1

**11** [1]*Jehoram,* 2 Kin. 1:17; 8:16 [2]Or *Azariah* or *Jehoahaz* [3]*Jehoash,* 2 Kin. 12:1
**12** [1]*Uzziah,* Is. 6:1
**15** [1]*Eliakim,* 2 Kin. 23:34 [2]*Jehoahaz,* 2 Kin. 23:31

16 The sons of [a]Jehoiakim *were* [1]Jeconiah his son
*and* [2]Zedekiah his son.
**17** And the sons of [1]Jeconiah [2]*were* Assir, Shealtiel [a]his son,
18 *and* Malchiram, Pedaiah, Shenazzar, Jeca-
miah, Hoshama, and Nedabiah.
19 The sons of Pedaiah *were* Zerubbabel and
Shimei. The sons of Zerubbabel *were* Meshullam,
Hananiah, Shelomith their sister,
20 and Hashubah, Ohel, Berechiah, Hasadiah,
and Jushab-Hesed—five *in all.*
21 The sons of Hananiah *were* Pelatiah and Jeshaiah, the sons of Rephaiah, the sons of Arnan,
the sons of Obadiah, and the sons of Shechaniah.
22 The son of Shechaniah was Shemaiah. The
sons of Shemaiah *were* [a]Hattush, Igal, Bariah,
Neariah, and Shaphat—six *in all.*
23 The sons of Neariah *were* Elioenai, Hezekiah,
and Azrikam—three *in all.*
24 The sons of Elioenai *were* Hodaviah, Eliashib,
Pelaiah, Akkub, Johanan, Delaiah, and Anani—
seven *in all.*

### *The Family of Judah*

**4** The sons of Judah *were* [a]Perez, Hezron,
[1]Carmi, Hur, and Shobal.
2 And [1]Reaiah the son of Shobal begot Jahath,
and Jahath begot Ahumai and Lahad. These *were*
the families of the Zorathites.
3 These *were* the sons *of the father* of Etam:
Jezreel, Ishma, and Idbash; and the name of their
sister *was* Hazelelponi;
4 and Penuel *was* the father of Gedor, and Ezer
*was the* father of Hushah. These *were* the sons of
[a]Hur, the firstborn of Ephrathah the father of
Bethlehem.
5 And [a]Ashhur the father of Tekoa had two
wives, Helah and Naarah.
6 Naarah bore him Ahuzzam, Hepher, Temeni,
and Haahashtari. These *were* the sons of Naarah.
7 The sons of Helah *were* Zereth, Zohar, and
Ethnan;
8 and Koz begot Anub, Zobebah, and the families of Aharhel the son of Harum.
**9** Now Jabez was [a]more honorable than his
brothers, and his mother called his name [1]Jabez,
saying, "Because I bore *him* in pain."
10 And Jabez called on the God of Israel saying,
"Oh, that You would bless me indeed, and enlarge
my [1]territory, that Your hand would be with me,
and that You would keep *me* from evil, that I may
not cause pain!" So God granted him what he
requested.
**11** Chelub the brother of [a]Shuhah begot Mehir,
who *was* the father of Eshton.
12 And Eshton begot Beth-Rapha, Paseah, and
Tehinnah the father of [1]Ir-Nahash. These *were* the
men of Rechah.
**13** The sons of Kenaz *were* [a]Othniel and Seraiah.
The sons of Othniel *were* [1]Hathath,
14 and Meonothai *who* begot Ophrah. Seraiah
begot Joab the father of [a]Ge Harashim,[1] for they
were craftsmen.
15 The sons of [a]Caleb the son of Jephunneh *were*
Iru, Elah, and Naam. The son of Elah *was* [1]Kenaz.
16 The sons of Jehallelel *were* Ziph, Ziphah, Tiria,
and Asarel.
17 The sons of Ezrah *were* Jether, Mered, Epher,
and Jalon. And [1]*Mered's wife bore* Miriam, Shammai, and Ishbah the father of Eshtemoa.
18 ([1]His wife Jehudijah bore Jered the father of
Gedor, Heber the father of Sochoh, and Jekuthiel
the father of Zanoah.) And these were the sons of
Bithiah the daughter of Pharaoh, whom Mered
took.
19 The sons of Hodiah's wife, the sister of Na-
ham, *were* the fathers of Keilah the Garmite and
of Eshtemoa the [a]Maachathite.
20 And the sons of Shimon *were* Amnon, Rinnah,
Ben-Hanan, and Tilon. And the sons of Ishi *were*
Zoheth and Ben-Zoheth.
21 The sons of [a]Shelah [b]the son of Judah *were* Er
the father of Lecah, Laadah the father of Mareshah, and the families of the house of the linen
workers of the house of Ashbea;
22 also Jokim, the men of Chozeba, and Joash;
Saraph, who ruled in Moab, and Jashubi-Lehem.
Now the [1]records are ancient.
23 These *were* the potters and those who dwell at
[1]Netaim and [2]Gederah; there they dwelt with the
king for his work.
**24** The [a]sons of Simeon *were* [1]Nemuel, Jamin,
[2]Jarib, [3]Zerah, *and* Shaul,
25 Shallum his son, Mibsam his son, and Mishma
his son.
26 And the sons of Mishma *were* Hamuel his son,
Zacchur his son, and Shimei his son.
27 Shimei had sixteen sons and six daughters; but
his brothers did not have many children, [a]nor did
any of their families multiply as much as the
children of Judah.
**28** They dwelt at Beersheba, Moladah, Hazar
Shual,
29 [1]Bilhah, Ezem, [2]Tolad,
30 Bethuel, Hormah, Ziklag,
31 Beth Marcaboth, [1]Hazar Susim, Beth Biri, and
at Shaaraim. These *were* their cities until the
reign of David.
32 And their villages *were* [1]Etam, Ain, Rimmon,
Tochen, and Ashan—five cities—
33 and all the villages that *were* around these
cities as far as [1]Baal. These *were* their dwelling
places, and they maintained their genealogy:
34 Meshobab, Jamlech, and Joshah the son of
Amaziah;
35 Joel, and Jehu the son of Joshibiah, the son of
Seraiah, the son of Asiel;
36 Elioenai, Jaakobah, Jeshohaiah, Asaiah, Adiel,
Jesimiel, and Benaiah;
37 Ziza the son of Shiphi, the son of Allon, the
son of Jedaiah, the son of Shimri, the son of
Shemaiah—
38 these mentioned by name *were* leaders in their
families, and their father's house increased
greatly.
**39** So they went to the entrance of Gedor, as far
as the east side of the valley, to seek pasture for
their flocks.
40 And they found rich, good pasture, and the
land *was* broad, quiet, and peaceful; for some
Hamites formerly lived there.
41 These recorded by name came in the days of
Hezekiah king of Judah; and they [a]attacked[1] their
tents and the Meunites who were found there, and
[b]utterly destroyed them, as it is to this day. So
they dwelt in their place, because *there was*
pasture for their flocks there.
42 Now *some* of them, five hundred men of the
sons of Simeon, went to Mount Seir, having as
their captains Pelatiah, Neariah, Rephaiah, and
Uzziel, the sons of Ishi.
43 And they [1]defeated [a]the rest of the Amalekites
who had escaped. They have dwelt there to this
day.

**16** [a]Matt. 1:11 [1]*Jehoiachin,* 2 Kin. 24:8, or *Coniah,* Jer. 22:24 [2]*Mattaniah,* 2 Kin. 24:17
**17** [a]Matt. 1:12 [1]*Jehoiachin,* 2 Kin. 24:8, or *Coniah,* Jer. 22:24 [2]Or *the captive were*
**22** [a]Ezra 8:2

CHAPTER 4

**1** [a]Gen. 38:29; 46:12 [1]*Chelubai,* 1 Chr. 2:9 or *Caleb,* 1 Chr. 2:18
**2** [1]*Haroeh,* 1 Chr. 2:52
**4** [a]Ex. 31:2; 1 Chr. 2:50
**5** [a]1 Chr. 2:24
**9** [a]Gen. 34:19 [1]Lit. *He Will Cause Pain*
**10** [1]*border*
**11** [a]Gen. 38:1–5
**12** [1]Lit. *City of Nahash*
**13** [a]Josh. 15:17; Judg. 3:9, 11 [1]LXX, Vg. add *and Meonothai*
**14** [a]Neh. 11:35 [1]Lit. *Valley of Craftsmen*
**15** [a]Josh. 14:6, 14; 15:13, 17; 1 Chr. 6:56 [1]Or *Uknaz*
**17** [1]Lit. *she*
**18** [1]Or *His Judean wife*
**19** [a]2 Kin. 25:23
**21** [a]Gen. 38:11, 14 [b]Gen. 38:1–5; 46:12
**22** [1]Lit. *words*
**23** [1]Lit. *Plants* [2]Lit. *Hedges*
**24** [a]Num. 26:12–14 [1]*Jemuel,* Gen. 46:10; Ex. 6:15; Num. 26:12 [2]*Jachin,* Gen. 46:10; Num. 26:12 [3]*Zohar,* Gen. 46:10; Ex. 6:15
**27** [a]Num. 2:9
**29** [1]*Balah,* Josh. 19:3 [2]*Eltolad,* Josh. 19:4
**31** [1]*Hazar Susah,* Josh. 19:5
**32** [1]*Ether,* Josh. 19:7
**33** [1]*Baalath Beer,* Josh. 19:8
**41** [a]2 Kin. 18:8 [b]2 Kin. 19:11 [1]Lit. *struck*
**43** [a]Ex. 17:14; 1 Sam. 15:8; 30:17 [1]Lit. *struck*

### *The Families of Reuben, Gad, and Manasseh (East)*

**5** Now the sons of Reuben the firstborn of Israel—[a]he *was* indeed the firstborn, but because he [b]defiled his father's bed, [c]his birthright
was given to the sons of Joseph, the son of Israel,
so that the genealogy is not listed according to the
birthright;
2 yet [a]Judah prevailed over his brothers, and
from him *came* a [b]ruler, although [1]the birthright
was Joseph's—
3 the sons of [a]Reuben the firstborn of Israel
were Hanoch, Pallu, Hezron, and Carmi.
4 The sons of Joel *were* Shemaiah his son, Gog
his son, Shimei his son,
5 Micah his son, Reaiah his son, Baal his son,
6 and Beerah his son, whom [1]Tiglath-Pileser
king of Assyria [a]carried into captivity. He *was*
leader of the Reubenites.
7 And his brethren by their families, [a]when the
genealogy of their generations was registered: the
chief, Jeiel, and Zechariah,
8 and Bela the son of Azaz, the son of Shema,
the son of Joel, who dwelt in [a]Aroer, as far as
Nebo and Baal Meon.
9 Eastward they settled as far as the [1]entrance
of the wilderness this side of the River Euphrates,
because their cattle had [2]multiplied [a]in the land of
Gilead.
10 Now in the days of Saul they made war [a]with
the Hagrites, who fell by their hand; and they
dwelt in their tents throughout the entire *area*
east of Gilead.
11 And the [a]children of Gad dwelt next to them
in the land of [b]Bashan as far as [c]Salcah:
12 Joel *was* the chief, Shapham the next, then
Jaanai and Shaphat in Bashan,
13 and their brethren of their father's house:
Michael, Meshullam, Sheba, Jorai, Jachan, Zia,
and Heber—seven *in all.*
14 These *were* the children of Abihail the son of
Huri, the son of Jaroah, the son of Gilead, the son
of Michael, the son of Jeshishai, the son of Jahdo,
the son of Buz;
15 Ahi the son of Abdiel, the son of Guni, *was*
chief of their father's house.
16 And *the Gadites* dwelt in Gilead, in Bashan
and in its villages, and in all the [1]common-lands of
[a]Sharon within their borders.
17 All these were registered by genealogies in the
days of [a]Jotham king of Judah, and in the days of
[b]Jeroboam king of Israel.
18 The sons of Reuben, the Gadites, and half the
tribe of Manasseh *had* forty-four thousand seven
hundred and sixty valiant men, men able to bear
shield and sword, to shoot with the bow, and
skillful in war, who went to war.
19 They made war with the Hagrites, [a]Jetur,
Naphish, and Nodab.
20 And [a]they were helped against them, and the
Hagrites were delivered into their hand, and all
who *were* with them, for they [b]cried out to God in
the battle. He [1]heeded their prayer, because they
[c]put their trust in Him.
21 Then they took away their livestock—fifty
thousand of their camels, two hundred and fifty
thousand of their sheep, and two thousand of
their donkeys—also one hundred thousand of
their men;
22 for many fell dead, because the war [a]*was*
God's. And they dwelt in their place until [b]the
captivity.

CHAPTER 5
1 [a]Gen. 29:32; 49:3 [b]Gen. 35:22; 49:4 [c]Gen. 48:15, 22
2 [a]Gen. 49:8, 10 [b]Mic. 5:2 [1]*the right of the firstborn*
3 [a]Ex. 6:14
6 [a]2 Kin. 18:11 [1]Heb. *Tilgath Pilneser*
7 [a]1 Chr. 5:17
8 [a]Josh. 12:2; 13:15, 16
9 [a]Josh. 22:8, 9 [1]*beginning* [2]*increased*
10 [a]Gen. 25:12
11 [a]Num. 26:15–18 [b]Josh. 13:11, 24–28 [c]Deut. 3:10
16 [a]1 Chr. 27:29 [1]*open lands*
17 [a]2 Kin. 15:5, 32 [b]2 Kin. 14:16, 28
19 [a]Gen. 25:15
20 [a][1 Chr. 5:22] [b]2 Chr. 14:11–13 [c]Ps. 9:10; 20:7, 8; 22:4, 5 [1]Lit. *was entreated for them*
22 [a][Josh. 23:10] [b]2 Kin. 15:29; 17:6
23 [a]Deut. 3:9
25 [a]2 Kin. 17:7
26 [a]2 Kin. 15:19 [b]2 Kin. 15:29 [c]2 Kin. 17:6; 18:11 [1]Heb. *Tilgath Pilneser*

CHAPTER 6
1 [a]Ex. 6:16 [1]Or *Gershom,* v. 16
2 [a]1 Chr. 6:18, 22
3 [a]Lev. 10:1, 2
8 [a]2 Sam. 8:17 [b]2 Sam. 15:27
10 [a]2 Chr. 26:17, 18 [b]1 Kin. 6:1 [1]Lit. *house*
11 [a]Ezra 7:3 [b]2 Chr. 19:11
12 [1]*Meshullam,* 1 Chr. 9:11
14 [a]Neh. 11:11
15 [a]2 Kin. 25:21
16 [a]Ex. 6:16 [1]Heb. *Gershom,* an alternate spelling for *Gershon,* vv. 17, 20, 43, 62, 71
20 [a]1 Chr. 6:42
21 [1]*Ethan,* v. 42 [2]*Adaiah,* v. 41 [3]*Ethni,* v. 41
22 [a]Num. 16:1 [1]*Izhar,* vv. 2, 18

23 So the children of the half-tribe of Manasseh
dwelt in the land. Their *numbers* increased from
Bashan to Baal Hermon, that is, to [a]Senir, or
Mount Hermon.
24 These *were* the heads of their fathers' houses:
Epher, Ishi, Eliel, Azriel, Jeremiah, Hodaviah, and
Jahdiel. They were mighty men of valor, famous
men, *and* heads of their fathers' houses.
25 And they were unfaithful to the God of their
fathers, and [a]played the harlot after the gods of
the peoples of the land, whom God had destroyed
before them.
26 So the God of Israel stirred up the spirit of [a]Pul
king of Assyria, that is, [b]Tiglath-Pileser[1] king of
Assyria. He carried the Reubenites, the Gadites,
and the half-tribe of Manasseh into captivity. He
took them to [c]Halah, Habor, Hara, and the river of
Gozan to this day.

### *The Family of Levi*

**6** The sons of Levi *were* [a]Gershon,[1] Kohath, and
Merari.
2 The sons of Kohath *were* Amram, [a]Izhar,
Hebron, and Uzziel.
3 The children of Amram *were* Aaron, Moses,
and Miriam. And the sons of Aaron *were* [a]Nadab,
Abihu, Eleazar, and Ithamar.
4 Eleazar begot Phinehas, *and* Phinehas begot
Abishua;
5 Abishua begot Bukki, and Bukki begot Uzzi;
6 Uzzi begot Zerahiah, and Zerahiah begot
Meraioth;
7 Meraioth begot Amariah, and Amariah begot
Ahitub;
8 [a]Ahitub begot [b]Zadok, and Zadok begot Ahimaaz;
9 Ahimaaz begot Azariah, and Azariah begot
Johanan;
10 Johanan begot Azariah (it was he [a]who ministered as priest in the [b]temple[1] that Solomon built
in Jerusalem);
11 [a]Azariah begot [b]Amariah, and Amariah begot
Ahitub;
12 Ahitub begot Zadok, and Zadok begot [1]Shal-
lum;
13 Shallum begot Hilkiah, and Hilkiah begot
Azariah;
14 Azariah begot [a]Seraiah, and Seraiah begot
Jehozadak.
15 Jehozadak went *into captivity* [a]when the
LORD carried Judah and Jerusalem into captivity
by the hand of Nebuchadnezzar.
16 The sons of Levi *were* [a]Gershon,[1] Kohath, and
Merari.
17 These are the names of the sons of Gershon:
Libni and Shimei.
18 The sons of Kohath *were* Amram, Izhar, Hebron, and Uzziel.
19 The sons of Merari *were* Mahli and Mushi.
Now these *are* the families of the Levites according to their fathers:
20 Of Gershon *were* Libni his son, Jahath his son,
[a]Zimmah his son,
21 [1]Joah his son, [2]Iddo his son, Zerah his son, *and*
[3]Jeatherai his son.
22 The sons of Kohath *were* [1]Amminadab his son,
[a]Korah his son, Assir his son,
23 Elkanah his son, Ebiasaph his son, Assir his
son,
24 Tahath his son, Uriel his son, Uzziah his son,
and Shaul his son.

25 The sons of Elkanah *were* [a]Amasai and Ahimoth.
26 *As for* Elkanah, the sons of Elkanah *were* [1]Zophai his son, [2]Nahath his son,
27 [1]Eliab his son, Jeroham his son, *and* Elkanah his son.
28 The sons of Samuel *were* [1]*Joel* the firstborn, and Abijah [2]the second.
29 The sons of Merari *were* Mahli, Libni his son, Shimei his son, Uzzah his son,
30 Shimea his son, Haggiah his son, *and* Asaiah his son.
**31** Now these are [a]the men whom David appointed over the service of song in the house of the LORD, after the [b]ark came to rest.
32 They were ministering with music before the dwelling place of the tabernacle of meeting, until Solomon had built the house of the LORD in Jerusalem, and they served in their office according to their order.
**33** And these *are* the ones who [1]ministered with their sons: Of the sons of the [a]Kohathites *were* Heman the singer, the son of Joel, the son of Samuel,
34 the son of Elkanah, the son of Jeroham, the son of [1]Eliel, the son of [2]Toah,
35 the son of Zuph, the son of Elkanah, the son of Mahath, the son of Amasai,
36 the son of Elkanah, the son of Joel, the son of Azariah, the son of Zephaniah,
37 the son of Tahath, the son of Assir, the son of [a]Ebiasaph, the son of Korah,
38 the son of Izhar, the son of Kohath, the son of Levi, the son of Israel.
39 And his brother [a]Asaph, who stood at his right hand, *was* Asaph the son of Berachiah, the son of Shimea,
40 the son of Michael, the son of Baaseiah, the son of Malchijah,
41 the son of [a]Ethni, the son of Zerah, the son of Adaiah,
42 the son of Ethan, the son of Zimmah, the son of Shimei,
43 the son of Jahath, the son of Gershon, the son of Levi.
**44** Their brethren, the sons of Merari, on the left hand, *were* [1]Ethan the son of [2]Kishi, the son of Abdi, the son of Malluch,
45 the son of Hashabiah, the son of Amaziah, the son of Hilkiah,
46 the son of Amzi, the son of Bani, the son of Shamer,
47 the son of Mahli, the son of Mushi, the son of Merari, the son of Levi.
48 And their brethren, the Levites, *were* appointed to every [a]kind of service of the tabernacle of the house of God.
**49** [a]But Aaron and his sons offered sacrifices [b]on the altar of burnt offering and [c]on the altar of incense, for all the work of the Most Holy *Place*, and to make atonement for Israel, according to all that Moses the servant of God had commanded.
50 Now these *are* the [a]sons of Aaron: Eleazar his son, Phinehas his son, Abishua his son,
51 Bukki his son, Uzzi his son, Zerahiah his son,
52 Meraioth his son, Amariah his son, Ahitub his son,
53 Zadok his son, *and* Ahimaaz his son.
**54** [a]Now these *are* their dwelling places throughout their settlements in their territory, for they were *given* by lot to the sons of Aaron, of the family of the Kohathites:

55 [a]They gave them Hebron in the land of Judah, with its surrounding [1]common-lands.
56 [a]But the fields of the city and its villages they gave to Caleb the son of Jephunneh.
57 And [a]to the sons of Aaron they gave *one of* the cities of refuge, Hebron; also Libnah with its common-lands, Jattir, Eshtemoa with its common-lands,
58 [1]Hilen with its common-lands, Debir with its common-lands,
59 [1]Ashan with its common-lands, and Beth Shemesh with its common-lands.
60 And from the tribe of Benjamin: Geba with its common-lands, [1]Alemeth with its common-lands, and Anathoth with its common-lands. All their cities among their families *were* thirteen.
**61** [a]To the rest of the family of the tribe of the Kohathites *they gave* [b]by lot ten cities from half the tribe of Manasseh.
62 And to the sons of Gershon, throughout their families, *they gave* thirteen cities from the tribe of Issachar, from the tribe of Asher, from the tribe of Naphtali, and from the tribe of Manasseh in Bashan.
63 To the sons of Merari, throughout their families, *they gave* [a]twelve cities from the tribe of Reuben, from the tribe of Gad, and from the tribe of Zebulun.
64 So the children of Israel gave *these* cities with their [1]common-lands to the Levites.
65 And they gave by lot from the tribe of the children of Judah, from the tribe of the children of Simeon, and from the tribe of the children of Benjamin these cities which are called by *their* names.
**66** Now [a]some of the families of the sons of Kohath *were given* cities as their territory from the tribe of Ephraim.
67 [a]And they gave them *one of* the cities of refuge, Shechem with its common-lands, in the mountains of Ephraim, also Gezer with its common-lands,
68 [a]Jokmeam with its common-lands, Beth Horon with its common-lands,
69 Aijalon with its common-lands, and Gath Rimmon with its common-lands.
70 And from the half-tribe of Manasseh: Aner with its common-lands and Bileam with its common-lands, for the rest of the family of the sons of Kohath.
**71** From the family of the half-tribe of Manasseh the sons of Gershon *were given* Golan in Bashan with its common-lands and [1]Ashtaroth with its common-lands.
72 And from the tribe of Issachar: [1]Kedesh with its common-lands, Daberath with its common-lands,
73 Ramoth with its common-lands, and Anem with its common-lands.
74 And from the tribe of Asher: Mashal with its common-lands, Abdon with its common-lands,
75 Hukok with its common-lands, and Rehob with its common-lands.
76 And from the tribe of Naphtali: Kedesh in Galilee with its common-lands, Hammon with its common-lands, and Kirjathaim with its common-lands.
**77** From the tribe of Zebulun the rest of the children of Merari *were given* [1]Rimmon with its common-lands and Tabor with its common-lands.
78 And on the other side of the Jordan, across from Jericho, on the east side of the Jordan, *they*

**25** [a]1 Chr. 6:35, 36
**26** [1]*Zuph,* v. 35; 1 Sam. 1:1 [2]*Toah,* v. 34
**27** [1]*Eliel,* v. 34
**28** [1]So with LXX, Syr., Arab.; cf. v. 33 and 1 Sam. 8:2 [2]Heb. *Vashni*
**31** [a]1 Chr. 15:16–22, 27; 16:4–6 [b]2 Sam. 6:17; 1 Kin. 8:4; 1 Chr. 15:25—16:1
**33** [a]Num. 26:57 [1]Lit. *stood with*
**34** [1]*Elihu,* 1 Sam. 1:1 [2]*Tohu,* 1 Sam. 1:1
**37** [a]Ex. 6:24
**39** [a]2 Chr. 5:12
**41** [a]1 Chr. 6:21
**44** [1]*Jeduthun,* 1 Chr. 9:16; 25:1, 3, 6; 2 Chr. 35:15; Ps. 62:title [2]Or *Kushaiah*
**48** [a]1 Chr. 9:14–34
**49** [a]Ex. 28:1; [Num. 18:1–8] [b]Lev. 1:8, 9 [c]Ex. 30:7
**50** [a]1 Chr. 6:4–8; Ezra 7:5
**54** [a]Josh. 21
**55** [a]Josh. 14:13; 21:11, 12 [1]*open lands*
**56** [a]Josh. 14:13; 15:13
**57** [a]Josh. 21:13, 19
**58** [1]*Holon,* Josh. 21:15
**59** [1]*Ain,* Josh. 21:16
**60** [1]*Almon,* Josh. 21:18
**61** [a]1 Chr. 6:66–70 [b]Josh. 21:5
**63** [a]Josh. 21:7, 34–40
**64** [1]*open lands*
**66** [a]1 Chr. 6:61
**67** [a]Josh. 21:21
**68** [a]Josh. 21:22
**71** [1]*Beeshterah,* Josh. 21:27
**72** [1]*Kishon,* Josh. 21:28
**77** [1]Heb. *Rimmono,* an alternate spelling of Rimmon, 1 Chr. 4:32

*were given* from the tribe of Reuben: Bezer in the
wilderness with its common-lands, Jahzah with its
common-lands,
79 Kedemoth with its common-lands, and Mephaath with its common-lands.
80 And from the tribe of Gad: Ramoth in Gilead
with its common-lands, Mahanaim with its
common-lands,
81 Heshbon with its common-lands, and Jazer
with its common-lands.

### *The Families of Issachar, Benjamin, Naphtali, Manasseh (West), Ephraim, and Asher*

**7** The sons of Issachar *were* [a]Tola, [1]Puah, [2]Ja-
shub, and Shimron—four *in all.*
2 The sons of Tola *were* Uzzi, Rephaiah, Jeriel,
Jahmai, Jibsam, and Shemuel, heads of their
father's house. *The sons* of Tola *were* mighty men
of valor in their generations; [a]their number in the
days of David *was* twenty-two thousand six hundred.
3 The son of Uzzi *was* Izrahiah, and the sons of
Izrahiah *were* Michael, Obadiah, Joel, and Ishiah.
All five of them *were* chief men.
4 And with them, by their generations, according to their fathers' houses, *were* thirty-six thousand troops ready for war; for they had many
wives and sons.
5 Now their brethren among all the families of
Issachar *were* mighty men of valor, listed by their
genealogies, eighty-seven thousand in all.
**6** *The sons* of [a]Benjamin *were* Bela, Becher, and
Jediael—three *in all.*
7 The sons of Bela were Ezbon, Uzzi, Uzziel,
Jerimoth, and Iri—five *in all.* They *were* heads of
*their* fathers' houses, and they were listed by their
genealogies, twenty-two thousand and thirty-four
mighty men of valor.
8 The sons of Becher *were* Zemirah, Joash,
Eliezer, Elioenai, Omri, Jerimoth, Abijah, Anathoth, and Alemeth. All these *are* the sons of
Becher.
9 And they were recorded by genealogy according to their generations, heads of their fathers'
houses, twenty thousand two hundred mighty
men of valor.
10 The son of Jediael *was* Bilhan, and the sons of
Bilhan *were* Jeush, Benjamin, Ehud, Chenaanah,
Zethan, Tharshish, and Ahishahar.
11 All these sons of Jediael *were* heads of their
fathers' houses; *there were* seventeen thousand
two hundred mighty men of valor fit to go out for
war *and* battle.
12 [1]Shuppim and [2]Huppim *were* the sons of [3]Ir,
*and* Hushim *was* the son of [4]Aher.
**13** The [a]sons of Naphtali *were* [1]Jahziel, Guni,
Jezer, and [2]Shallum, the sons of Bilhah.
**14** The [a]descendants of Manasseh: his Syrian
concubine bore him [b]Machir the father of Gilead,
the father of Asriel.
15 Machir took as his wife *the sister* of [1]Huppim
and [2]Shuppim, whose name *was* Maachah. The
name of *Gilead's* [3]grandson *was* [a]Zelophehad, but
Zelophehad begot only daughters.
16 (Maachah the wife of Machir bore a son, and
she called his name Peresh. The name of his
brother *was* Sheresh, and his sons *were* Ulam and
Rakem.
17 The son of Ulam *was* [a]Bedan.) These *were* the
descendants of Gilead the son of Machir, the son
of Manasseh.
18 His sister Hammoleketh bore Ishhod, [1]Abiezer,
and Mahlah.
19 And the sons of Shemida were Ahian, Shechem, Likhi, and Aniam.
**20** [a]The sons of Ephraim *were* Shuthelah, Bered
his son, Tahath his son, Eladah his son, Tahath his
son,
21 Zabad his son, Shuthelah his son, and Ezer
and Elead. The men of Gath who were born in
*that* land killed *them* because they came down to
take away their cattle.
22 Then Ephraim their father mourned many
days, and his brethren came to comfort him.
**23** And when he went in to his wife, she conceived and bore a son; and he called his name
[1]Beriah, because tragedy had come upon his
house.
24 Now his daughter *was* Sheerah, who built
Lower and Upper [a]Beth Horon and Uzzen Sheerah;
25 and Rephah *was* his son, *as well* as Resheph,
and Telah his son, Tahan his son,
26 Laadan his son, Ammihud his son, [a]Elishama
his son,
27 [1]Nun his son, and [a]Joshua his son.
**28** Now their [a]possessions and dwelling places
*were* Bethel and its towns: to the east [1]Naaran, to
the west Gezer and its towns, and Shechem and
its towns, as far as [2]Ayyah and its towns;
29 and by the borders of the children of [a]Manas-
seh *were* Beth Shean and its towns, Taanach and
its towns, [b]Megiddo and its towns, Dor and its
towns. In these dwelt the children of Joseph, the
son of Israel.
**30** [a]The sons of Asher *were* Imnah, Ishvah, Ishvi,
Beriah, and their sister Serah.
31 The sons of Beriah *were* Heber and Malchiel,
who was the father of [1]Birzaith.
32 And Heber begot Japhlet, [1]Shomer, [2]Hotham,
and their sister Shua.
33 The sons of Japhlet *were* Pasach, Bimhal, and
Ashvath. These *were* the children of Japhlet.
34 The sons of [a]Shemer *were* Ahi, Rohgah, Je-
hubbah, and Aram.
35 And the sons of his brother Helem *were*
Zophah, Imna, Shelesh, and Amal.
36 The sons of Zophah *were* Suah, Harnepher,
Shual, Beri, Imrah,
37 Bezer, Hod, Shamma, Shilshah, [1]Jithran, and
Beera.
38 The sons of Jether *were* Jephunneh, Pispah,
and Ara.
39 The sons of Ulla *were* Arah, Haniel, and Rizia.
40 All these *were* the children of Asher, heads of
*their* fathers' houses, choice men, mighty men of
valor, chief leaders. And they were recorded by
genealogies among the army fit for battle; their
number *was* twenty-six thousand.

### *The Family Tree of King Saul of Benjamin*

**8** Now Benjamin begot [a]Bela his firstborn, Ashbel the second, [1]Aharah the third,
2 Nohah the fourth, and Rapha the fifth.
3 The sons of Bela *were* [1]Addar, Gera, Abihud,
4 Abishua, Naaman, Ahoah,
5 Gera, [1]Shephuphan, and Huram.
6 These *are* the sons of Ehud, who were the
heads of the fathers' *houses* of the inhabitants of
[a]Geba, and who forced them to move to [b]Mana-
hath:

CHAPTER 7
1 [a]Num. 26:23–25 [1]*Puvah,* Gen. 46:13 [2]*Job,* Gen. 46:13
2 [a]2 Sam. 24:1–9; 1 Chr. 27:1
6 [a]Gen. 46:21; Num. 26:38–41; 1 Chr. 8:1
12 [1]*Shupham,* Num. 26:39 [2]*Hupham,* Num. 26:39 [3]*Iri,* v. 7 [4]*Ahiram,* Num. 26:38
13 [a]Num. 26:48–50 [1]*Jahzeel,* Gen. 46:24 [2]*Shillem,* Gen. 46:24
14 [a]Num. 26:29–34 [b]1 Chr. 2:21
15 [a]Num. 26:30–33; 27:1 [1]*Hupham,* v. 12; Num. 26:39 [2]*Shupham,* v. 12; Num. 26:39 [3]Lit. *the second*
17 [a]1 Sam. 12:11
18 [1]*Jeezer,* Num. 26:30
20 [a]Num. 26:35–37
23 [1]Lit. *In Tragedy*
24 [a]Josh. 16:3, 5; 2 Chr. 8:5
26 [a]Num. 10:22
27 [a]Ex. 17:9, 14; 24:13; 33:11 [1]Heb. *Non*
28 [a]Josh. 16:1–10 [1]*Naarath,* Josh. 16:7 [2]Or *Azzah* or *Gazza*
29 [a]Gen. 41:51; Josh. 17:7 [b]Josh. 17:11
30 [a]Gen. 46:17; Num. 26:44–47
31 [1]Or *Birzavith* or *Birzoth*
32 [1]*Shemer,* 1 Chr. 7:34 [2]*Helem,* 1 Chr. 7:35
34 [a]1 Chr. 7:32
37 [1]*Jether,* v. 38

CHAPTER 8
1 [a]Gen. 46:21; Num. 26:38; 1 Chr. 7:6 [1]*Ahiram,* Num. 26:38
3 [1]*Ard,* Num. 26:40
5 [1]*Shupham,* Num. 26:39, or *Shuppim,* 1 Chr. 7:12
6 [a]1 Chr. 6:60 [b]1 Chr. 2:52

7 Naaman, Ahijah, and Gera who forced them to move. He begot Uzza and Ahihud.
8 Also Shaharaim had children in the country of Moab, after he had sent away Hushim and Baara his wives.
9 By Hodesh his wife he begot Jobab, Zibia, Mesha, Malcam,
10 Jeuz, Sachiah, and Mirmah. These *were* his sons, heads of their fathers' *houses.*
11 And by Hushim he begot Abitub and Elpaal.
12 The sons of Elpaal *were* Eber, Misham, and Shemed, who built Ono and Lod with its towns;
13 and Beriah and [a]Shema, who *were* heads of their fathers' *houses* of the inhabitants of Aijalon, who drove out the inhabitants of Gath.
14 Ahio, Shashak, Jeremoth,
15 Zebadiah, Arad, Eder,
16 Michael, Ispah, and Joha *were* the sons of Beriah.
17 Zebadiah, Meshullam, Hizki, Heber,
18 Ishmerai, Jizliah, and Jobab *were* the sons of Elpaal.
19 Jakim, Zichri, Zabdi,
20 Elienai, Zillethai, Eliel,
21 Adaiah, Beraiah, and Shimrath *were* the sons of [1]Shimei.
22 Ishpan, Eber, Eliel,
23 Abdon, Zichri, Hanan,
24 Hananiah, Elam, Antothijah,
25 Iphdeiah, and Penuel *were* the sons of Shashak.
26 Shamsherai, Shehariah, Athaliah,
27 Jaareshiah, Elijah, and Zichri *were* the sons of Jeroham.
28 These *were* heads of the fathers' *houses* by their generations, chief men. These dwelt in Jerusalem.
**29** Now [1]the father of Gibeon, whose [a]wife's name *was* Maacah, dwelt at Gibeon.
30 And his firstborn son *was* Abdon, then Zur, Kish, Baal, Nadab,
31 Gedor, Ahio, [1]Zecher,
32 and Mikloth, *who* begot [1]Shimeah. They also dwelt [2]alongside their [3]relatives in Jerusalem, with their brethren.
33 [a]Ner[1] begot Kish, Kish begot Saul, and Saul begot Jonathan, Malchishua, [2]Abinadab, and [3]Esh-Baal.
34 The son of Jonathan *was* [1]Merib-Baal, and Merib-Baal begot [a]Micah.
35 The sons of Micah *were* Pithon, Melech, [1]Tarea, and Ahaz.
36 And Ahaz begot [1]Jehoaddah; Jehoaddah begot Alemeth, Azmaveth, and Zimri; and Zimri begot Moza.
37 Moza begot Binea, [1]Raphah his son, Eleasah his son, *and* Azel his son.
38 Azel had six sons whose names *were* these: Azrikam, Bocheru, Ishmael, Sheariah, Obadiah, and Hanan. All these *were* the sons of Azel.
39 And the sons of Eshek his brother *were* Ulam his firstborn, Jeush the second, and Eliphelet the third.
40 The sons of Ulam were mighty men of valor—archers. *They* had many sons and grandsons, one hundred and fifty *in all.* These *were* all sons of Benjamin.

### *Priests and Levites in Jerusalem*

**9** So [a]all Israel was [1]recorded by genealogies, and indeed, they *were* inscribed in the book of the kings of Israel. But Judah was carried away captive to Babylon because of their unfaithfulness.
2 [a]And the first inhabitants who *dwelt* in their possessions in their cities *were* Israelites, priests, Levites, and [b]the Nethinim.
**3** Now in [a]Jerusalem the children of Judah dwelt, and some of the children of Benjamin, and of the children of Ephraim and Manasseh:
4 Uthai the son of Ammihud, the son of Omri, the son of Imri, the son of Bani, of the descendants of Perez, the son of Judah.
5 Of the Shilonites: Asaiah the firstborn and his sons.
6 Of the sons of Zerah: Jeuel, and their brethren—six hundred and ninety.
7 Of the sons of Benjamin: Sallu the son of Meshullam, the son of Hodaviah, the son of Hassenuah;
8 Ibneiah the son of Jeroham; Elah the son of Uzzi, the son of Michri; Meshullam the son of Shephatiah, the son of Reuel, the son of Ibnijah;
9 and their brethren, according to their generations—nine hundred and fifty-six. All these men *were* heads of a father's *house* in their fathers' houses.
**10** [a]Of the priests: Jedaiah, Jehoiarib, and Jachin;
11 [1]Azariah the son of Hilkiah, the son of Meshullam, the son of Zadok, the son of Meraioth, the son of Ahitub, the [a]officer over the house of God;
12 Adaiah the son of Jeroham, the son of Pashur, the son of Malchijah; Maasai the son of Adiel, the son of Jahzerah, the son of Meshullam, the son of Meshillemith, the son of Immer;
13 and their brethren, heads of their fathers' *houses*—one thousand seven hundred and sixty. *They were* [1]very able men for the work of the service of the house of God.
**14** Of the Levites: Shemaiah the son of Hasshub, the son of Azrikam, the son of Hashabiah, of the sons of Merari;
15 Bakbakkar, Heresh, Galal, and Mattaniah the son of Micah, the son of [a]Zichri, the son of Asaph;
16 [a]Obadiah the son of [b]Shemaiah, the son of Galal, the son of Jeduthun; and Berechiah the son of Asa, the son of Elkanah, who lived in the villages of the Netophathites.
**17** And the gatekeepers *were* Shallum, Akkub, Talmon, Ahiman, and their brethren. Shallum *was* the chief.
18 Until then *they had been* gatekeepers for the camps of the children of Levi at the King's Gate on the east.
19 Shallum the son of Kore, the son of Ebiasaph, the son of Korah, and his brethren, from his father's house, the Korahites, *were* in charge of the work of the service, [1]gatekeepers of the tabernacle. Their fathers had been keepers of the entrance to the camp of the LORD.
20 And [a]Phinehas the son of Eleazar had been the officer over them in time past; the LORD *was* with him.
21 [a]Zechariah the son of Meshelemiah *was* [1]keeper of the door of the tabernacle of meeting.
22 All those chosen as gatekeepers *were* two hundred and twelve. [a]They were recorded by their genealogy, in their villages. David and Samuel [b]the seer had appointed them to their trusted office.

---

**13** [a]1 Chr. 8:21
**21** [1]*Shema,* 1 Chr. 7:13
**29** [a]1 Chr. 9:35–38 [1]*Jeiel,* 1 Chr. 9:35
**31** [1]*Zechariah,* 1 Chr. 9:37
**32** [1]Or *Shimeam,* 1 Chr. 9:38 [2]Lit. *opposite* [3]*brethren*
**33** [a]1 Sam. 14:51 [1]Also the son of Gibeon, 1 Chr. 9:36, 39 [2]*Jishui,* 1 Sam. 14:49 [3]*Ishbosheth,* 2 Sam. 2:8
**34** [a]2 Sam. 9:12 [1]*Mephibosheth,* 2 Sam. 4:4
**35** [1]*Tahrea,* 1 Chr. 9:41
**36** [1]*Jarah,* 1 Chr. 9:42
**37** [1]*Raphaiah,* 1 Chr. 9:43

CHAPTER 9
**1** [a]Ezra 2:59 [1]*enrolled*
**2** [a]Ezra 2:70; Neh. 7:73 [b]Ezra 2:43; 8:20
**3** [a]Neh. 11:1, 2
**10** [a]Neh. 11:10–14
**11** [a]2 Chr. 31:13; Jer. 20:1 [1]*Seraiah,* Neh. 11:11
**13** [1]Lit. *mighty men of strength*
**15** [a]Neh. 11:17
**16** [a]Neh. 11:17 [b]Neh. 11:17
**19** [1]Lit. *thresholds*
**20** [a]Num. 25:6–13; 31:6
**21** [a]1 Chr. 26:2, 14 [1]*gatekeeper*
**22** [a]1 Chr. 26:1, 2 [b]1 Sam. 9:9

23 So they and their children *were* in charge of
the gates of the house of the LORD, the house of
the tabernacle, by assignment.
24 The gatekeepers were assigned to the four
directions: the east, west, north, and south.
25 And their brethren in their villages *had* to
come with them from time to time [a]for seven days.
26 For in this trusted office *were* four chief gatekeepers; they were Levites. And they had charge
over the chambers and treasuries of the house of
God.
27 And they lodged *all* around the house of God
because [1]they *had* the [a]responsibility, and they
*were* in charge of opening *it* every morning.
**28** Now *some* of them were in charge of the
serving vessels, for they brought them in and took
them out by count.
29 *Some* of them *were* appointed over the furnishings and over all the implements of the sanctuary, and over the [a]fine flour and the wine and
the oil and the incense and the spices.
30 And *some* of the sons of the priests made [a]the
ointment of the spices.
31 Mattithiah of the Levites, the firstborn of
Shallum the Korahite, had the trusted office [a]over
the things that were baked in the pans.
32 And some of their brethren of the sons of the
Kohathites [a]*were* in charge of preparing the showbread for every Sabbath.
**33** These are [a]the singers, heads of the fathers'
*houses* of the Levites, *who lodged* in the chambers, *and were* free *from other duties;* for they
were employed in *that* work day and night.
34 These heads of the fathers' *houses* of the
Levites *were* heads throughout their generations.
They dwelt at Jerusalem.
**35** Jeiel the father of Gibeon, whose wife's name
*was* [a]Maacah, dwelt at Gibeon.
36 His firstborn son *was* Abdon, then Zur, Kish,
Baal, Ner, Nadab,
37 Gedor, Ahio, [1]Zechariah, and Mikloth.
38 And Mikloth begot [1]Shimeam. They also dwelt
alongside their relatives in Jerusalem, with their
brethren.
39 [a]Ner begot Kish, Kish begot Saul, and Saul
begot Jonathan, Malchishua, Abinadab, and Esh-
Baal.
40 The son of Jonathan *was* Merib-Baal, and
Merib-Baal begot Micah.
41 The sons of Micah *were* Pithon, Melech, [1]Tah-
rea, [a]*and*[2] *Ahaz.*
42 And Ahaz begot [1]Jarah; Jarah begot Alemeth,
Azmaveth, and Zimri; and Zimri begot Moza;
43 Moza begot Binea, [1]Rephaiah his son, Eleasah
his son, and Azel his son.
44 And Azel had six sons whose names *were*
these: Azrikam, Bocheru, Ishmael, Sheariah, Obadiah, and Hanan; these *were* the sons of Azel.

### *The Death of Saul and His Sons*

**10** Now [a]the Philistines fought against Israel;
and the men of Israel fled from before the
Philistines, and fell slain on Mount Gilboa.
2 Then the Philistines followed hard after Saul
and his sons. And the Philistines killed Jonathan,
[1]Abinadab, and Malchishua, Saul's sons.
3 The battle became fierce against Saul. The
archers hit him, and he was wounded by the
archers.
4 Then Saul said to his armorbearer, "Draw
your sword, and thrust me through with it, lest
these uncircumcised men come and abuse me."
But his armorbearer would not, for he was greatly
afraid. Therefore Saul took a sword and fell on it.
5 And when his armorbearer saw that Saul was
dead, he also fell on his sword and died.
6 So Saul and his three sons died, and all his
house died together.
7 And when all the men of Israel who *were* in
the valley saw that they had fled and that Saul
and his sons were dead, they forsook their cities
and fled; then the Philistines came and dwelt in
them.
**8** So it happened the next day, when the Philistines came to [1]strip the slain, that they found Saul
and his sons fallen on Mount Gilboa.
9 And they stripped him and took his head and
his armor, and sent word *throughout* the land of
the Philistines to proclaim the news *in the temple*
of their idols and among the people.
10 [a]Then they put his armor in the [1]temple of
their gods, and fastened his head in the temple of
Dagon.
**11** And when all Jabesh Gilead heard all that the
Philistines had done to Saul,
12 all the [a]valiant men arose and took the body of
Saul and the bodies of his sons; and they brought
them to [b]Jabesh, and buried their bones under the
tamarisk tree at Jabesh, and fasted seven days.
**13** So Saul died for his unfaithfulness which he
had [1]committed against the LORD, [a]because he did
not keep the word of the LORD, and also because
[b]he consulted a medium for guidance.
14 But *he* did not inquire of the LORD; therefore
He killed him, and [a]turned the kingdom over to
David the son of Jesse.

### *David Made King over All Israel*

**11** Then [a]all Israel came together to David at
Hebron, saying, "Indeed we *are* your bone
and your flesh.
2 "Also, in time past, even when Saul was king,
you *were* the one who led Israel out and brought
them in; and the LORD your [a]God said to you, 'You
shall [b]shepherd My people Israel, and be ruler over
My people Israel.' "
3 Therefore all the elders of Israel came to the
king at Hebron, and David made a covenant with
them at Hebron before the LORD. And [a]they
anointed David king over Israel, according to the
word of the LORD [1]by [b]Samuel.
**4** And David and all Israel [a]went to Jerusalem,
which is Jebus, [b]where the Jebusites *were,* the
inhabitants of the land.
5 But the inhabitants of Jebus said to David,
"You shall not come in here!" Nevertheless David
took the stronghold of Zion (that is, the City of
David).
6 Now David said, "Whoever attacks the Jebusites first shall be [1]chief and captain." And Joab
the son of Zeruiah went up first, and became
chief.
7 Then David dwelt in the stronghold; therefore
they called it [1]the City of David.
8 And he built the city around it, from [1]the Millo
to the surrounding area. Joab [2]repaired the rest of
the city.
9 So David [a]went on and became great, and the
LORD of hosts *was* with [b]him.
**10** Now [a]these *were* the heads of the mighty men
whom David had, who strengthened themselves
with him in his kingdom, with all Israel, to make

**25** [a]2 Kin. 11:4–7; 2 Chr. 23:8
**27** [a]1 Chr. 23:30–32 [1]*the watch was committed to them*
**29** [a]1 Chr. 23:29
**30** [a]Ex. 30:22–25
**31** [a]Lev. 2:5; 6:21
**32** [a]Lev. 24:5–8
**33** [a]1 Chr. 6:31; 25:1
**35** [a]1 Chr. 8:29–32
**37** [1]*Zecher,* 1 Chr. 8:31
**38** [1]*Shimeah,* 1 Chr. 8:32
**39** [a]1 Chr. 8:33–38
**41** [a]1 Chr. 8:35 [1]*Tarea,* 1 Chr. 8:35 [2]So with Arab., Syr., Tg., Vg. (cf. 8:35); MT, LXX omit *and Ahaz*
**42** [1]*Jehoaddah,* 1 Chr. 8:36
**43** [1]*Raphah,* 1 Chr. 8:37

CHAPTER 10

**1** [a]1 Sam. 31:1, 2
**2** [1]*Jishui,* 1 Sam. 14:49
**8** [1]*plunder*
**10** [a]1 Sam. 31:10 [1]Lit. *house*
**12** [a]1 Sam. 14:52 [b]2 Sam. 21:12
**13** [a]1 Sam. 13:13, 14; 15:22–26 [b][Lev. 19:31; 20:6]; 1 Sam. 28:7 [1]Lit. *transgressed*
**14** [a]1 Sam. 15:28; 2 Sam. 3:9, 10; 5:3; 1 Chr. 12:23

CHAPTER 11

**1** [a]2 Sam. 5:1
**2** [a]1 Sam. 16:1–3; Ps. 78:70–72 [b]2 Sam. 7:7
**3** [a]2 Sam. 5:3 [b]1 Sam. 16:1, 4, 12, 13 [1]Lit. *by the hand of Samuel*
**4** [a]2 Sam. 5:6 [b]Josh. 15:8, 63; Judg. 1:21; 19:10, 11
**6** [1]Lit. *head*
**7** [1]*Zion,* 2 Sam. 5:7
**8** [1]Lit. *The Landfill* [2]Lit. *revived*
**9** [a]2 Sam. 3:1 [b]1 Sam. 16:18
**10** [a]2 Sam. 23:8

him king, according to [b]the word of the LORD
concerning Israel.
11 And this *is* the number of the mighty men
whom David had: [a]Jashobeam the son of a Hachmonite, [b]chief of [1]the captains; he had lifted up his
spear against three hundred, killed *by him* at one
time.
**12** After him *was* Eleazar the son of [a]Dodo, the
Ahohite, who *was one* of the three mighty men.
13 He was with David at [1]Pasdammim. Now there
the Philistines were gathered for battle, and there
was a piece of ground full of barley. So the people
fled from the Philistines.
14 But they [1]stationed themselves in the middle
of *that* field, defended it, and killed the Philistines.
So the LORD brought about a great victory.
**15** Now three of the thirty chief men [a]went down
to the rock to David, into the cave of Adullam;
and the army of the Philistines encamped [b]in the
Valley of [1]Rephaim.
16 David *was* then in the stronghold, and the
garrison of the Philistines *was* then in Bethlehem.
17 And David said with longing, "Oh, that someone would give me a drink of water from the well
of Bethlehem, which is by the gate!"
18 So the three broke through the camp of the
Philistines, drew water from the well of Bethlehem that *was* by the gate, and took *it* and brought
*it* to David. Nevertheless David would not drink it,
but poured it out to the LORD.
19 And he said, "Far be it from me, O my God,
that I should do this! Shall I drink the blood of
these men *who have put* their lives *in jeopardy?*
For at the risk of their lives they brought it."
Therefore he would not drink it. These things
were done by the three mighty men.
**20** [a]Abishai the brother of Joab was chief of
*another* [1]three. He had lifted up his spear against
three hundred *men,* killed *them,* and won a name
among *these* three.
21 [a]Of the three he was more honored than the
other two men. Therefore he became their captain. However he did not attain to the *first* three.
**22** Benaiah was the son of Jehoiada, the son of a
valiant man from Kabzeel, who [1]had done many
deeds. [a]He had killed two lion-like heroes of Moab.
He also had gone down and killed a lion in the
midst of a pit on a snowy day.
23 And he killed an Egyptian, a man of *great*
height, [1]five cubits tall. In the Egyptian's hand
*there was* a spear like a weaver's beam; and he
went down to him with a staff, wrested the spear
out of the Egyptian's hand, and killed him with his
own spear.
24 These *things* Benaiah the son of Jehoiada did,
and won a name among three mighty men.
25 Indeed he was more honored than the thirty,
but he did not attain to the *first* three. And David
appointed him over his guard.
**26** Also the mighty warriors *were* [a]Asahel the
brother of Joab, Elhanan the son of Dodo of
Bethlehem,
27 [1]Shammoth the Harorite, [a]Helez the [2]Pelonite,
28 [a]Ira the son of Ikkesh the Tekoite, [b]Abiezer
the Anathothite,
29 [1]Sibbechai the Hushathite, [2]Ilai the Ahohite,
30 [a]Maharai the Netophathite, [1]Heled the son of
Baanah the Netophathite,
31 [1]Ithai the son of Ribai of Gibeah, of the sons of
Benjamin, [a]Benaiah the Pirathonite,
32 [1]Hurai of the brooks of Gaash, [2]Abiel the
Arbathite,
33 Azmaveth the [1]Baharumite, Eliahba the Shaalbonite,
34 the sons of [1]Hashem the Gizonite, Jonathan
the son of Shageh the Hararite,
35 Ahiam the son of [1]Sacar the Hararite, [2]Eliphal
the son of [3]Ur,
36 Hepher the Mecherathite, Ahijah the Pelonite,
37 [1]Hezro the Carmelite, [2]Naarai the son of Ezbai,
38 Joel the brother of Nathan, Mibhar the son of
Hagri,
39 Zelek the Ammonite, Naharai the [1]Berothite
(the armorbearer of Joab the son of Zeruiah),
40 Ira the Ithrite, Gareb the Ithrite,
41 [a]Uriah the Hittite, [1]Zabad the son of Ahlai,
42 Adina the son of Shiza the Reubenite (a chief
of the Reubenites) and thirty with him,
43 Hanan the son of Maachah, Joshaphat the
Mithnite,
44 Uzzia the Ashterathite, Shama and Jeiel the
sons of Hotham the Aroerite,
45 Jediael the son of Shimri, and Joha his
brother, the Tizite,
46 Eliel the Mahavite, Jeribai and Joshaviah the
sons of Elnaam, Ithmah the Moabite,
47 Eliel, Obed, and Jaasiel the Mezobaite.

### *The Army of David*

**12** Now [a]these *were* the men who came to
David at [b]Ziklag while he was still a fugitive
from Saul the son of Kish; and they *were* among
the mighty men, helpers in the war,
2 armed with bows, using both the right hand
and [a]the left in *hurling* stones and *shooting* arrows
with the bow. *They were* of Benjamin, Saul's
brethren.
3 The chief *was* Ahiezer, then Joash, the sons of
[1]Shemaah the Gibeathite; Jeziel and Pelet the sons
of Azmaveth; Berachah, and Jehu the Anathothite;
4 Ishmaiah the Gibeonite, a mighty man among
the thirty, and over the thirty; Jeremiah, Jahaziel,
Johanan, and Jozabad the Gederathite;
5 Eluzai, Jerimoth, Bealiah, Shemariah, and
Shephatiah the Haruphite;
6 Elkanah, Jisshiah, Azarel, Joezer, and Jashobeam, the Korahites;
7 and Joelah and Zebadiah the sons of Jeroham
of Gedor.
**8** *Some* Gadites [1]joined David at the stronghold
in the wilderness, mighty men of valor, men
trained for battle, who could handle shield and
spear, whose faces *were like* the faces of lions, and
*were* [a]as swift as gazelles on the mountains:
9 Ezer the first, Obadiah the second, Eliab the
third,
10 Mishmannah the fourth, Jeremiah the fifth,
11 Attai the sixth, Eliel the seventh,
12 Johanan the eighth, Elzabad the ninth,
13 Jeremiah the tenth, and Machbanai the eleventh.
14 These *were* from the sons of Gad, captains of
the army; the least was over a hundred, and the
greatest was over a [a]thousand.
15 These *are* the ones who crossed the Jordan in
the first month, when it had overflowed all its
[a]banks; and they put to flight all *those* in the
valleys, to the east and to the west.
**16** Then some of the sons of Benjamin and Judah
came to David at the stronghold.

**10** [b]1 Sam. 16:1, 12
**11** [a]1 Chr. 27:2 [b]1 Chr. 12:18 [1]So with Qr.; Kt., LXX, Vg. *the thirty* (cf. 2 Sam. 23:8)
**12** [a]1 Chr. 27:4
**13** [1]*Ephes Dammim,* 1 Sam. 17:1
**14** [1]Lit. *took their stand*
**15** [a]2 Sam. 23:13 [b]2 Sam. 5:18; 1 Chr. 14:9 [1]Lit. *Giants*
**20** [a]2 Sam. 23:18; 1 Chr. 18:12 [1]So with MT, LXX, Vg.; Syr. *thirty*
**21** [a]2 Sam. 23:19
**22** [a]2 Sam. 23:20 [1]*was great in deeds*
**23** [1]About 7½ feet
**26** [a]2 Sam. 23:24
**27** [a]2 Sam. 23:26; 1 Chr. 27:10 [1]*Shammah the Harodite,* 2 Sam. 23:25 [2]*Paltite,* 2 Sam. 23:26
**28** [a]1 Chr. 27:9 [b]1 Chr. 27:12
**29** [1]*Mebunnai,* 2 Sam. 23:27 [2]*Zalmon,* 2 Sam. 23:28
**30** [a]1 Chr. 27:13 [1]*Heleb,* 2 Sam. 23:29, or *Heldai,* 1 Chr. 27:15
**31** [a]1 Chr. 27:14 [1]*Ittai,* 2 Sam. 23:29
**32** [1]*Hiddai,* 2 Sam. 23:30 [2]*Abi-Albon,* 2 Sam. 23:31
**33** [1]*Barhumite,* 2 Sam. 23:31
**34** [1]*Jashen,* 2 Sam. 23:32
**35** [1]*Sharar,* 2 Sam. 23:33 [2]*Eliphelet,* 2 Sam. 23:34 [3]*Ahasbai,* 2 Sam. 23:34
**37** [1]*Hezrai,* 2 Sam. 23:38 [2]*Paarai the Arbite,* 2 Sam. 23:35
**39** [1]*Beerothite,* 2 Sam. 23:37
**41** [a]2 Sam. 11 [1]The last sixteen are not added in 2 Sam. 23.

CHAPTER 12
**1** [a]1 Sam. 27:2 [b]1 Sam. 27:6
**2** [a]Judg. 3:15; 20:16
**3** [1]Or *Hasmaah*
**8** [a]2 Sam. 2:18 [1]Lit. *separated themselves to*
**14** [a]1 Sam. 18:13
**15** [a]Josh. 3:15; 4:18, 19

17 And David went out [1]to meet them, and answered and said to them, "If you have come
peaceably to me to help me, my heart will be
united with you; but if to betray me to my enemies, since *there is* no [2]wrong in my hands, may
the God of our fathers look and bring judgment."
18 Then the Spirit [1]came upon [a]Amasai, chief of
the captains, *and he said:*

"*We are* yours, O David;
We *are* on your side, O son of Jesse!
Peace, peace to you,
And peace to your helpers!
For your God helps you."

So David received them, and made them captains
of the troop.
**19** And *some* from Manasseh defected to David
[a]when he was going with the Philistines to battle
against Saul; but they did not help them, for the
lords of the Philistines sent him away by agreement, saying, [b]"He may defect to his master Saul
*and endanger* our heads."
20 When he went to Ziklag, those of Manasseh
who defected to him were Adnah, Jozabad, Jediael, Michael, Jozabad, Elihu, and Zillethai, captains of the thousands who *were* from Manasseh.
21 And they helped David against [a]the bands *of*
*raiders,* for they *were* all mighty men of valor, and
they were captains in the army.
22 For at *that* time they came to David day by
day to help him, until *it was* a great army, [a]like the
army of God.
**23** Now these *were* the numbers of the [1]divisions
*that were* equipped for *the* war, *and* [a]came to
David at [b]Hebron to [c]turn *over* the kingdom of
Saul to him, [d]according to the word of the LORD:
24 of the sons of Judah bearing shield and spear,
six thousand eight hundred [1]armed for war;
25 of the sons of Simeon, mighty men of valor fit
for war, seven thousand one hundred;
26 of the sons of Levi four thousand six hundred;
27 Jehoiada, the leader of the Aaronites, and with
him three thousand seven hundred;
28 [a]Zadok, a young man, a valiant warrior, and
from his father's house twenty-two captains;
29 of the sons of Benjamin, relatives of Saul,
three thousand (until then [a]the greatest part of
them had remained loyal to the house of Saul);
30 of the sons of Ephraim twenty thousand eight
hundred, mighty men of valor, [1]famous men
throughout their father's house;
31 of the half-tribe of Manasseh eighteen thousand, who were designated by name to come and
make David king;
32 of the sons of Issachar [a]who had understanding of the times, to know what Israel ought to do,
their chiefs were two hundred; and all their brethren were at their command;
33 of Zebulun there were fifty thousand who
went out to battle, expert in war with all weapons
of war, [a]stouthearted men who could keep ranks;
34 of Naphtali one thousand captains, and with
them thirty-seven thousand with shield and spear;
35 of the Danites who could keep battle formation, twenty-eight thousand six hundred;
36 of Asher, those who could go out to war, able
to keep battle formation, forty thousand;
37 of the Reubenites and the Gadites and the
half-tribe of Manasseh, from the other side of the
Jordan, one hundred and twenty thousand armed
for battle with every *kind* of weapon of war.
**38** All these men of war, who could keep ranks,
came to Hebron with a loyal heart, to make David
king over all Israel; and all the rest of Israel *were*
of [a]one mind to make David king.
39 And they were there with David three days,
eating and drinking, for their brethren had prepared for them.
40 Moreover those who were near to them, from
as far away as Issachar and Zebulun and Naphtali,
were bringing food on donkeys and camels, on
mules and oxen—provisions of flour and cakes of
figs and cakes of raisins, wine and oil and oxen
and sheep abundantly, for *there was* joy in Israel.

### *David's Desire to Remove the Ark*

**13** Then David consulted with the [a]captains of
thousands and hundreds, *and* with every
leader.
2 And David said to all the assembly of Israel,
"If *it seems* good to you, and if it is of the LORD
our God, let us send out to our brethren everywhere *who are* [a]left in all the land of Israel, and
with them to the priests and Levites *who are* in
their cities *and* their common-lands, that they
may gather together to us;
3 "and let us bring the ark of our God back to
us, [a]for we have not inquired at it since the days of
Saul."
4 Then all the assembly said that they would do
so, for the thing was right in the eyes of all the
people.
**5** So [a]David gathered all Israel together, from
[b]Shihor in Egypt to as far as the entrance of
Hamath, to bring the ark of God [c]from Kirjath
Jearim.
6 And David and all Israel went up to [a]Baalah,[1]
to Kirjath Jearim, which belonged to Judah, to
bring up from there the ark of God the LORD, [b]who
dwells *between* the cherubim, where *His* name is
proclaimed.
7 So they [1]carried the ark of God [a]on a new cart
[b]from the house of Abinadab, and Uzza and Ahio
drove the cart.
8 Then [a]David and all Israel played *music* before
God with all *their* might, with [1]singing, on harps,
on stringed instruments, on tambourines, on cymbals, and with trumpets.
**9** And when they came to [1]Chidon's threshing
floor, Uzza put out his hand to hold the ark, for
the oxen [2]stumbled.
10 Then the anger of the LORD was aroused
against Uzza, and He struck him [a]because he put
his hand to the ark; and he [b]died there before God.
11 And David became angry because of the
LORD's outbreak against Uzza; therefore that
place is called [1]Perez Uzza to this day.
12 David was afraid of God that day, saying,
"How can I bring the ark of God to me?"
**13** So David would not move the ark with him
into the City of David, but took it aside into the
house of Obed-Edom the Gittite.
14 [a]The ark of God remained with the family of
Obed-Edom in his house three months. And the
LORD blessed [b]the house of Obed-Edom and all
that he had.

### *David's Victories over the Philistines*

**14** Now [a]Hiram king of Tyre sent messengers
to David, and cedar trees, with masons and
carpenters, to build him a house.
2 So David knew that the LORD had established

17 [1]Lit. *before them* [2]Lit. *violence*
18 [a]2 Sam. 17:25 [1]Lit. *clothed*
19 [a]1 Sam. 29:2 [b]1 Sam. 29:4
21 [a]1 Sam. 30:1, 9, 10
22 [a]Gen. 32:2; Josh. 5:13–15
23 [a]2 Sam. 2:1–4 [b]1 Chr. 11:1 [c]1 Chr. 10:14 [d]1 Sam. 16:1–4 [1]Lit. *heads of those*
24 [1]*equipped*
28 [a]2 Sam. 8:17; 1 Chr. 6:8, 53
29 [a]2 Sam. 2:8, 9
30 [1]Lit. *men of names*
32 [a]Esth. 1:13
33 [a]Ps. 12:2; [James 1:8]
38 [a]2 Chr. 30:12

CHAPTER 13
1 [a]1 Chr. 11:15; 12:34
2 [a]1 Sam. 31:1; Is. 37:4
3 [a]1 Sam. 7:1, 2
5 [a]1 Sam. 7:5 [b]Josh. 13:3 [c]1 Sam. 6:21; 7:1, 2
6 [a]Josh. 15:9, 60 [b]Ex. 25:22; 1 Sam. 4:4; 2 Kin. 19:15 [1]*Baale Judah,* 2 Sam. 6:2
7 [a]Num. 4:15; 1 Sam. 6:7 [b]1 Sam. 7:1 [1]Lit. *caused the ark of God to ride*
8 [a]2 Sam. 6:5 [1]*songs*
9 [1]*Nachon,* 2 Sam. 6:6 [2]Or *let it go off*
10 [a][Num. 4:15]; 1 Chr. 15:13, 15 [b]Lev. 10:2
11 [1]Lit. *Outburst Against Uzza*
14 [a]2 Sam. 6:11 [b][Gen. 30:27]; 1 Chr. 26:4–8

CHAPTER 14
1 [a]2 Sam. 5:11; 1 Kin. 5:1

him as king over Israel, for his kingdom was
[a]highly exalted for the sake of His people Israel.
**3** Then David took more wives in Jerusalem,
and David begot more sons and daughters.
4 And [a]these are the names of his children
whom he had in Jerusalem: [1]Shammua, Shobab,
Nathan, Solomon,
5 Ibhar, [1]Elishua, [2]Elpelet,
6 Nogah, Nepheg, Japhia,
7 Elishama, [1]Beeliada, and Eliphelet.
**8** Now when the Philistines heard that [a]David
had been anointed king over all Israel, all the
Philistines went up to search for David. And
David heard *of it* and went out against them.
9 Then the Philistines went and made a raid [a]on
the Valley of [1]Rephaim.
10 And David [a]inquired of God, saying, "Shall I
go up against the Philistines? Will You deliver
them into my hand?" The LORD said to him, "Go
up, for I will deliver them into your hand."
11 So they went up to Baal Perazim, and David
defeated them there. Then David said, "God has
broken through my enemies by my hand like a
breakthrough of water." Therefore they called the
name of that place [1]Baal Perazim.
12 And when they left their gods there, David
gave a commandment, and they were burned with
fire.
**13** [a]Then the Philistines once again made a raid
on the valley.
14 Therefore David inquired again of God, and
God said to him, "You shall not go up after them;
circle around them, [a]and come upon them in front
of the mulberry trees.
15 "And it shall be, when you hear a sound of
marching in the tops of the mulberry trees, then
you shall go out to battle, for God has gone out
before you to strike the camp of the Philistines."
16 So David did as God commanded him, and
they drove back the army of the Philistines from
[1]Gibeon as far as Gezer.
17 Then [a]the fame of David went out into all
lands, and the LORD [b]brought the fear of him upon
all nations.

### *David Brings the Ark to Jerusalem*

**15** *David* built houses for himself in the City of
David; and he prepared a place for the ark
of God, [a]and pitched a tent for it.
2 Then David said, "No one may carry the [a]ark
of God but the Levites, for [b]the LORD has chosen
them to carry the ark of God and to minister
before Him forever."
3 And David [a]gathered all Israel together at
Jerusalem, to bring up the ark of the LORD to its
place, which he had prepared for it.
4 Then David assembled the children of Aaron
and the Levites:
5 of the sons of Kohath, Uriel the chief, and one
hundred and twenty of his [1]brethren;
6 of the sons of Merari, Asaiah the chief, and
two hundred and twenty of his brethren;
7 of the sons of Gershom, Joel the chief, and one
hundred and thirty of his brethren;
8 of the sons of [a]Elizaphan, Shemaiah the chief,
and two hundred of his brethren;
9 of the sons of [a]Hebron, Eliel the chief, and
eighty of his brethren;
10 of the sons of Uzziel, Amminadab the chief,
and one hundred and twelve of his brethren.
11 And David called for [a]Zadok and [b]Abiathar the
priests, and for the Levites: for Uriel, Asaiah, Joel,
Shemaiah, Eliel, and Amminadab.
12 He said to them, "You *are* the heads of the
fathers' *houses* of the Levites; [1]sanctify yourselves, you and your brethren, that you may bring
up the ark of the LORD God of Israel to *the place* I
have prepared for it.
13 "For [a]because you *did* not *do it* the first *time,*
[b]the LORD our God broke out against us, because
we did not consult Him [1]about the proper order."
14 So the priests and the Levites [1]sanctified
themselves to bring up the ark of the LORD God of
Israel.
15 And the children of the Levites bore the ark of
God on their shoulders, by its poles, as [a]Moses had
commanded according to the word of the LORD.
**16** Then David spoke to the leaders of the Levites
to appoint their brethren *to be* the singers accompanied by instruments of music, stringed instruments, harps, and cymbals, by raising the voice
with resounding joy.
17 So the Levites appointed [a]Heman the son of
Joel; and of his brethren, [b]Asaph the son
of Berechiah; and of their brethren, the sons
of Merari, [c]Ethan the son of Kushaiah;
18 and with them their brethren of the second
*rank:* Zechariah, [1]Ben, Jaaziel, Shemiramoth,
Jehiel, Unni, Eliab, Benaiah, Maaseiah, Mattithiah,
Elipheleh, Mikneiah, Obed-Edom, and Jeiel, the
gatekeepers;
19 the singers, Heman, Asaph, and Ethan, *were*
to sound the cymbals of bronze;
20 Zechariah, [1]Aziel, Shemiramoth, Jehiel, Unni,
Eliab, Maaseiah, and Benaiah, with strings according to [a]Alamoth;
21 Mattithiah, Elipheleh, Mikneiah, Obed-Edom,
Jeiel, and Azaziah, to direct with harps on the
[a]Sheminith;
22 Chenaniah, leader of the Levites, was instructor *in charge of* the music, because he *was* skillful;
23 Berechiah and Elkanah *were* doorkeepers for
the ark;
24 Shebaniah, Joshaphat, Nethanel, Amasai,
Zechariah, Benaiah, and Eliezer, the priests, [a]were
to blow the trumpets before the ark of God; and
[b]Obed-Edom and Jehiah, doorkeepers for the ark.
**25** So [a]David, the elders of Israel, and the captains over thousands went to bring up the ark of
the covenant of the LORD from the house of Obed-
Edom with joy.
26 And so it was, when God helped the Levites
who bore the ark of the covenant of the LORD,
that they offered seven bulls and seven rams.
27 David was clothed with a robe of fine [a]linen, as
were all the Levites who bore the ark, the singers,
and Chenaniah the music master *with* the singers.
David also wore a linen ephod.
28 [a]Thus all Israel brought up the ark of the
covenant of the LORD with shouting and with the
sound of the horn, with trumpets and with cymbals, making music with stringed instruments and
harps.
**29** And it happened, [a]*as* the ark of the covenant
of the LORD came to the City of David, that
Michal, Saul's daughter, looked through a window
and saw King David whirling and playing music;
and she despised him in her heart.

### *David's Song of Thanksgiving*

**16** So [a]they brought the ark of God, and set it
in the midst of the tabernacle that David
had erected for it. Then they offered burnt offerings and peace offerings before God.

---

2 [a]Num. 24:7
4 [a]1 Chr. 3:5–8 [1]*Shimea,* 1 Chr. 3:5
5 [1]*Elishama,* 1 Chr. 3:6 [2]*Eliphelet,* 1 Chr. 3:6
7 [1]*Eliada,* 2 Sam. 5:6; 1 Chr. 3:8
8 [a]2 Sam. 5:17–21
9 [a]1 Chr. 11:15; 14:13 [1]Lit. *Giants*
10 [a]1 Sam. 23:2, 4; 30:8
11 [1]Lit. *Master of Breakthroughs*
13 [a]2 Sam. 5:22–25
14 [a]2 Sam. 5:23
16 [1]*Geba,* 2 Sam. 5:25
17 [a]Josh. 6:27 [b][Deut. 2:25; 11:25]

CHAPTER 15

1 [a]1 Chr. 16:1
2 [a][Num. 4:15] [b]Deut. 10:8; 31:9
3 [a]1 Kin. 8:1
5 [1]*kinsmen*
8 [a]Ex. 6:22
9 [a]Ex. 6:18
11 [a]1 Chr. 12:28 [b]1 Kin. 2:22, 26, 27
12 [1]*consecrate*
13 [a]2 Sam. 6:3 [b]1 Chr. 13:7–11 [1]*regarding the ordinance*
14 [1]*consecrated*
15 [a]Ex. 25:14
17 [a]1 Chr. 6:33; 25:1 [b]1 Chr. 6:39 [c]1 Chr. 6:44
18 [1]So with MT, Vg.; LXX omits *Ben*
20 [a]Ps. 46:title [1]*Jaaziel,* v. 18
21 [a]Ps. 6:title
24 [a][Num. 10:8] [b]1 Chr. 13:13, 14
25 [a]1 Kin. 8:1
27 [a]1 Sam. 2:18, 28
28 [a]1 Chr. 13:8
29 [a]2 Sam. 3:13, 14; 6:16, 20–23

CHAPTER 16

1 [a]2 Sam. 6:17

2 And when David had finished offering the
burnt offerings and the peace offerings, [a]he
blessed the people in the name of the LORD.
3 Then he distributed to everyone of Israel, both
man and woman, to everyone a loaf of bread, a
piece *of meat,* and a cake of raisins.
**4** And he appointed some of the Levites to
minister before the ark of the LORD, to [a]com-
memorate, to thank, and to praise the LORD God
of Israel:
5 Asaph the chief, and next to him Zechariah,
*then* [a]Jeiel, Shemiramoth, Jehiel, Mattithiah,
Eliab, Benaiah, and Obed-Edom: Jeiel with
stringed instruments and harps, but Asaph made
music with cymbals;
6 Benaiah and Jahaziel the priests regularly
*blew* the trumpets before the ark of the covenant
of God.
**7** On that day [a]David [b]first delivered *this psalm*
into the hand of Asaph and his brethren, to thank
the LORD:

8 [a]Oh, give thanks to the LORD!
Call upon His name;
Make known His deeds among the peoples!
9 Sing to Him, sing psalms to Him;
Talk of all His wondrous works!
10 Glory in His holy name;
Let the hearts of those rejoice
who seek the LORD!
11 Seek the LORD and His strength;
Seek His face evermore!
12 Remember His marvelous works
which He has done,
His wonders, and the judgments
of His mouth,
13 O seed of Israel His servant,
You children of Jacob, His chosen ones!

**14** He *is* the LORD our God;
His [a]judgments *are* in all the earth.
15 Remember His covenant forever,
The word which He commanded,
for a thousand generations,
16 *The* [a]*covenant which* He made
with Abraham,
And His oath to Isaac,
17 And [a]confirmed it to [b]Jacob for a statute,
To Israel *for* an everlasting covenant,
18 Saying, "To you I will give
the land of Canaan
As the allotment of your inheritance,"
19 When you were [a]few in number,
Indeed very few, and strangers in it.

20 When they went from one nation to another,
And from *one* kingdom to another people,
21 He permitted no man to do them wrong;
Yes, He [a]rebuked kings for their sakes,
22 *Saying,* [a]"Do not touch My anointed ones,
And do My prophets no harm."

**23** [a]Sing to the LORD, all the earth;
Proclaim the good news of His salvation from
day to day.
24 Declare His glory among the nations,
His wonders among all peoples.

25 For the LORD *is* great
and greatly to be praised;
He *is* also to be feared above all gods.
26 For all the gods [a]of the peoples *are* [1]idols,
But the LORD made the heavens.
27 Honor and majesty *are* before Him;
Strength and gladness are in His place.

28 Give to the LORD, O families of the peoples,
Give to the LORD glory and strength.
29 Give to the LORD the glory *due* His name;
Bring an offering, and come before Him.
Oh, worship the LORD
in the beauty of holiness!
30 Tremble before Him, all the earth.
The world also is firmly established,
It shall not be moved.

31 Let the heavens rejoice,
and let the earth be glad;
And let them say among the nations, "The
LORD reigns."
32 Let the sea roar, and all its fullness;
Let the field rejoice, and all that *is* in it.
33 Then the [a]trees of the woods shall rejoice
before the LORD,
For He is [b]coming to judge the earth.

34 [a]Oh, give thanks to the LORD, for *He is* good!
For His mercy *endures* forever.
35 [a]And say, "Save us, O God of our salvation;
Gather us together,
and deliver us from the Gentiles,
To give thanks to Your holy name,
To triumph in Your praise."

36 [a]Blessed *be* the LORD God of Israel
From everlasting to everlasting!

And all [b]the people said, "Amen!" and praised the
LORD.
**37** So he left [a]Asaph and his brothers there before
the ark of the covenant of the LORD to minister
before the ark regularly, as every day's work
[b]required;
38 and [a]Obed-Edom with his sixty-eight brethren,
including Obed-Edom the son of Jeduthun, and
Hosah, *to be* gatekeepers;
39 and Zadok the priest and his brethren the
priests, [a]before the tabernacle of the LORD [b]at the
[1]high place that *was* at Gibeon,
40 to offer burnt offerings to the LORD on the
altar of burnt offering regularly [a]morning and
evening, and *to do* according to all that is written
in the Law of the LORD which He commanded
Israel;
41 and with them Heman and Jeduthun and the
rest who were chosen, who were designated by
name, to give thanks to the LORD, [a]because His
mercy *endures* forever;
42 and with them Heman and Jeduthun, to sound
aloud with trumpets and cymbals and the musical
instruments of God. Now the sons of Jeduthun
*were* gatekeepers.
43 [a]Then all the people departed, every man to
his house; and David returned to bless his house.

### *God's Promise to David*

**17** Now [a]it came to pass, when David was
dwelling in his house, that David said to
Nathan the prophet, "See now, I dwell in a house
of cedar, but the ark of the covenant of the LORD
*is* under tent curtains."
2 Then Nathan said to David, "Do all that *is* in
your heart, for God *is* with you."
**3** But it happened that night that the word of
God came to Nathan, saying,
4 "Go and tell My servant David, 'Thus says

**2** [a]1 Kin. 8:14
**4** [a]Ps. 38:title; 70:title
**5** [a]1 Chr. 15:18
**7** [a]2 Sam. 22:1; 23:1 [b]Ps. 105:1–15
**8** [a]1 Chr. 17:19, 20; Ps. 105:1–15
**14** [a]Ps. 48:10; [Is. 26:9]
**16** [a]Gen. 17:2; 26:3; 28:13; 35:11
**17** [a]Gen. 35:11, 12 [b]Gen. 28:10–15
**19** [a]Gen. 34:30; Deut. 7:7
**21** [a]Gen. 12:17; 20:3; Ex. 7:15–18
**22** [a]Gen. 20:7; Ps. 105:15
**23** [a]Ps. 96:1–13
**26** [a]Lev. 19:4; [1 Cor. 8:5, 6] [1]*worthless things*
**33** [a]Is. 55:12, 13 [b][Joel 3:1–14]; Zech. 14:1–14; [Matt. 25:31–46]
**34** [a]2 Chr. 5:13; 7:3; Ezra 3:11; Ps. 106:1; 107:1; 118:1; 136:1; Jer. 33:11
**35** [a]Ps. 106:47, 48
**36** [a]1 Kin. 8:15, 56; Ps. 72:18 [b]Deut. 27:15; Neh. 8:6
**37** [a]1 Chr. 16:4, 5 [b]2 Chr. 8:14; Ezra 3:4
**38** [a]1 Chr. 13:14
**39** [a]1 Chr. 21:29; 2 Chr. 1:3 [b]1 Kin. 3:4 [1]Place for pagan worship
**40** [a][Ex. 29:38–42; Num. 28:3, 4]
**41** [a]1 Chr. 25:1–6; 2 Chr. 5:13; 7:3; Ezra 3:11; Jer. 33:11
**43** [a]2 Sam. 6:18–20

CHAPTER 17

**1** [a]2 Sam. 7:1; 1 Chr. 14:1

the LORD: "You shall [a]not build Me a house to
dwell in.
5 "For I have not dwelt in a house since the
time that I brought up Israel, even to this day, but
have gone from tent to tent, and from *one* tabernacle *to another.*
6 "Wherever I have moved about with all Israel,
have I ever spoken a word to any of the judges of
Israel, whom I commanded to shepherd My people, saying, 'Why have you not built Me a house of
cedar?' " '
7 "Now therefore, thus shall you say to My
servant David, 'Thus says the LORD of hosts: "I
took you [a]from the sheepfold, from following the
sheep, to be [1]ruler over My people Israel.
8 "And I have been with you wherever you have
gone, and have cut off all your enemies from
before you, and have [1]made you a name like the
name of the great men who *are* on the earth.
9 "Moreover I will appoint a place for My people
Israel, and will [a]plant them, that they may dwell in
a place of their own and move no more; nor shall
the sons of wickedness oppress them anymore, as
previously,
10 "since the time that I commanded judges *to be*
over My people Israel. Also I will subdue all your
enemies. Furthermore I tell you that the LORD will
build you a [1]house.
11 "And it shall be, when your days are [a]fulfilled,
when you must [1]go *to be* with your fathers, that I
will set up your [b]seed after you, who will be of
your sons; and I will establish his kingdom.
12 [a]"He shall build Me a house, and I will establish his throne forever.
13 [a]"I will be his Father, and he shall be My son;
and I will not take My mercy away from him, [b]as
I took *it* from *him* who was before you.
14 "And [a]I will establish him in My house and in
My kingdom forever; and his throne shall be
established forever." ' "
15 According to all these words and according to
all this vision, so Nathan spoke to David.
**16** [a]Then King David went in and sat before the
LORD; and he said: "Who *am* I, O LORD God? And
what is my house, that You have brought me this
far?
17 "And *yet* this was a small thing in Your sight,
O God; and You have *also* spoken of Your servant's house for a great while to come, and have
regarded me according to the rank of a man of
high degree, O LORD God.
18 "What more can David *say* to You for the
honor of Your servant? For You know Your
servant.
19 "O LORD, for Your servant's sake, and according to Your own heart, You have done all this
greatness, in making known all these great things.
20 "O LORD, *there is* none like You, nor *is there
any* God besides You, according to all that we
have heard with our ears.
21 [a]"And who *is* like Your people Israel, the one
nation on the earth whom God went to redeem for
Himself *as* a people—to make for Yourself a name
by great and awesome deeds, by driving out
nations from before Your people whom You redeemed from Egypt?
22 "For You have made Your people Israel Your
very own people forever; and You, LORD, have
become their God.
**23** "And now, O LORD, the word which You have
spoken concerning Your servant and concerning
his house, *let it* be established forever, and do as
You have said.
24 "So let it be established, that Your name may
be magnified forever, saying, 'The LORD of hosts,
the God of Israel, *is* Israel's God.' And let the
house of Your servant David be established before
You.
25 "For You, O my God, [1]have revealed to Your
servant that You will build him a house. Therefore
Your servant has found it *in his heart* to pray
before You.
26 "And now, LORD, [1]You are God, and have
promised this goodness to Your servant.
27 "Now You have been pleased to bless the
house of Your servant, that it may continue
before You forever; for You have blessed it, O
LORD, and *it shall be* blessed forever."

## *David Extends His Kingdom*

**18** After this [a]it came to pass that David [1]at-
tacked the Philistines, subdued them, and
took Gath and its towns from the hand of the
Philistines.
2 Then he [1]defeated [a]Moab, and the Moabites
became David's [b]servants, *and* brought tribute.
**3** And [a]David [1]defeated [2]Hadadezer king of Zobah *as far as* Hamath, as he went to establish his
power by the River Euphrates.
4 David took from him one thousand chariots,
[1]seven thousand horsemen, and twenty thousand
foot soldiers. Also David [2]hamstrung all the
chariot *horses,* except that he spared enough of
them for one hundred chariots.
**5** When the [a]Syrians of Damascus came to help
Hadadezer king of Zobah, David killed twenty-
two thousand of the Syrians.
6 Then David put *garrisons* in Syria of Damascus; and the Syrians became David's servants, *and*
brought tribute. So the LORD preserved David
wherever he went.
7 And David took the shields of gold that were
on the servants of Hadadezer, and brought them
to Jerusalem.
8 Also from [1]Tibhath and from [2]Chun, cities of
[3]Hadadezer, David brought a large amount of
[a]bronze, with which [b]Solomon made the bronze
[4]Sea, the pillars, and the articles of bronze.
**9** Now when [1]Tou king of Hamath heard that
David had [2]defeated all the army of Hadadezer
king of Zobah,
10 he sent [1]Hadoram his son to King David, to
greet him and bless him, because he had fought
against Hadadezer and [2]defeated him (for Hadadezer had been at war with Tou); and *Hadoram
brought with him* all kinds of [a]articles of gold,
silver, and bronze.
11 King David also dedicated these to the LORD,
along with the silver and gold that he had brought
from all *these* nations—from Edom, from Moab,
from the [a]people of Ammon, from the [b]Philistines,
and from [c]Amalek.
**12** Moreover [a]Abishai the son of Zeruiah killed
[b]eighteen thousand [1]Edomites in the Valley of
Salt.
13 [a]He also put garrisons in Edom, and all the
Edomites became David's servants. And the LORD
preserved David wherever he went.
**14** So David reigned over all Israel, and administered judgment and justice to all his people.
15 Joab the son of Zeruiah *was* over the army;
Jehoshaphat the son of Ahilud *was* recorder;

**4** [a][1 Chr. 28:2, 3]
**7** [a]1 Sam. 16:11–13 [1]*leader*
**8** [1]*given you prestige*
**9** [a][Deut. 30:1–9; Jer. 16:14–16; 23:5–8; 24:6; Ezek. 37:21–27]; Amos 9:14
**10** [1]Royal dynasty
**11** [a]1 Kin. 2:10; 1 Chr. 29:28 [b]1 Kin. 5:5; 6:12; 8:19–21; [1 Chr. 22:9–13; 28:20]; Matt. 1:6; Luke 3:31 [1]Die and join your ancestors
**12** [a]1 Kin. 6:38; 2 Chr. 6:2; [Ps. 89:20–37]
**13** [a]2 Sam. 7:14, 15; Matt. 3:17; Mark 1:11; Luke 3:22; 2 Cor. 6:18; Heb. 1:5 [b][1 Sam. 15:23–28]; 1 Chr. 10:14
**14** [a]Ps. 89:3, 4; Matt. 19:28; 25:31; [Luke 1:31–33]
**16** [a]2 Sam. 7:18
**21** [a][Deut. 4:6–8, 33–38]; Ps. 147:20
**25** [1]Lit. *have uncovered the ear of*
**26** [1]Or *You alone are*

CHAPTER 18
**1** [a]2 Sam. 8:1–18 [1]Lit. *struck*
**2** [a]2 Sam. 8:2; Zeph. 2:9 [b]Ps. 60:8 [1]Lit. *struck*
**3** [a]2 Sam. 8:3 [1]Lit. *struck* [2]Heb. *Hadarezer*
**4** [1]*seven hundred,* 2 Sam. 8:4 [2]*crippled*
**5** [a]2 Sam. 8:5, 6; 1 Kin. 11:23–25
**8** [a]2 Sam. 8:8 [b]1 Kin. 7:15, 23; 2 Chr. 4:12, 15, 16 [1]*Betah,* 2 Sam. 8:8 [2]*Berothai,* 2 Sam. 8:8 [3]Heb. *Hadarezer* [4]Great laver or basin
**9** [1]*Toi,* 2 Sam. 8:9, 10 [2]Lit. *struck*
**10** [a]2 Sam. 8:10–12 [1]*Joram,* 2 Sam. 8:10 [2]Lit. *struck*
**11** [a]2 Sam. 10:12 [b]2 Sam. 5:17–25 [c]2 Sam. 1:1
**12** [a]2 Sam. 23:18; 1 Chr. 2:16 [b]2 Sam. 8:13 [1]*Syrians,* 2 Sam. 8:13
**13** [a]Gen. 27:29–40; Num. 24:18; 2 Sam. 8:14

16 Zadok the son of Ahitub and [1]Abimelech the
son of Abiathar *were* the priests; [2]Shavsha *was*
the scribe;
17 [a]Benaiah the son of Jehoiada *was* over the
Cherethites and the Pelethites; and David's sons
*were* [1]chief ministers at the king's side.

### *David Defeats Ammon and the Syrians*

**19** [a]It happened after this that Nahash the king
of the people of Ammon died, and his son
reigned in his place.
2 Then David said, "I will show kindness to
Hanun the son of Nahash, because his father
showed kindness to me." So David sent messengers to comfort him concerning his father. And
David's servants came to Hanun in the land of the
people of Ammon to comfort him.
3 And the princes of the people of Ammon said
to Hanun, [1]"Do you think that David really honors your father because he has sent comforters to
you? Did his servants not come to you to search
and to overthrow and to spy out the land?"
4 Therefore Hanun took David's servants,
shaved them, and cut off their garments [1]in the
middle, at their [a]buttocks, and sent them away.
5 Then *some* went and told David about the
men; and he sent to meet them, because the men
were greatly ashamed. And the king said, "Wait at
Jericho until your beards have grown, and *then*
return."
**6** When the people of Ammon saw that they had
made themselves repulsive to David, Hanun and
the people of Ammon sent a thousand talents of
silver to hire for themselves chariots and horsemen from [1]Mesopotamia, from Syrian Maacah,
[a]and from [2]Zobah.
7 So they hired for themselves thirty-two thousand chariots, with the king of Maacah and his
people, who came and encamped before Medeba.
Also the people of Ammon gathered together from
their cities, and came to battle.
8 Now when David heard *of it,* he sent Joab and
all the army of the mighty men.
9 Then the people of Ammon came out and put
themselves in battle array before the gate of the
city, and the kings who had come *were* by themselves in the field.
**10** When Joab saw that the battle line was
against him before and behind, he chose some of
Israel's best and put *them* in battle array against
the Syrians.
11 And the rest of the people he put under the
command of Abishai his brother, and they set
*themselves* in battle array against the people of
Ammon.
12 Then he said, "If the Syrians are too strong for
me, then you shall help me; but if the people of
Ammon are too strong for you, then I will help
you.
13 "Be of good courage, and let us be strong for
our people and for the cities of our God. And may
the LORD do *what is* good in His sight."
14 So Joab and the people who *were* with him
drew near for the battle against the Syrians, and
they fled before him.
15 When the people of Ammon saw that the
Syrians were fleeing, they also fled before Abishai
his brother, and entered the city. So Joab went to
Jerusalem.
**16** Now when the Syrians saw that they had been
defeated by Israel, they sent messengers and
brought the Syrians who were beyond [1]the River,
and [2]Shophach the commander of Hadadezer's
army *went* before them.
17 When it was told David, he gathered all Israel,
crossed over the Jordan and came upon them, and
set up in battle array against them. So when
David had set up in *battle* array against the
Syrians, they fought with him.
18 Then the Syrians fled before Israel; and David
killed [1]seven thousand charioteers and forty thousand [2]foot soldiers of the Syrians, and killed
Shophach the commander of the army.
19 And when the servants of Hadadezer saw that
they were defeated by Israel, they made peace
with David and became his servants. So the
Syrians were not willing to help the people of
Ammon anymore.

### *The Philistine Giants Slain*

**20** [a]It happened [1]in the spring of the year, at
the time kings go out *to battle,* that Joab led
out the armed forces and ravaged the country of
the people of Ammon, and came and besieged
Rabbah. But [b]David stayed at Jerusalem. And
[c]Joab defeated Rabbah and overthrew it.
2 Then David [a]took their king's crown from his
head, and found it to weigh a talent of gold, and
*there were* precious stones in it. And it was set on
David's head. Also he brought out the [1]spoil of the
city in great abundance.
3 And he brought out the people who *were* in it,
and [1]put *them* to work with saws, with iron picks,
and with axes. So David did to all the cities of the
people of Ammon. Then David and all the people
returned *to* Jerusalem.
4 Now it happened afterward [a]that war broke
out at [1]Gezer with the Philistines, at which time
[b]Sibbechai the Hushathite killed [2]Sippai, *who was
one* of the sons of [3]the giant. And they were
subdued.
5 Again there was war with the Philistines, and
Elhanan the son of [1]Jair killed Lahmi the brother
of Goliath the Gittite, the shaft of whose spear
*was* like a weaver's [a]beam.
6 Yet again [a]there was war at Gath, where there
was a man of *great* stature, with twenty-four
fingers and toes, six *on each hand* and six *on each
foot;* and he also was born to [1]the giant.
7 So when he defied Israel, Jonathan the son of
[1]Shimea, David's brother, killed him.
8 These were born to the giant in Gath, and they
fell by the hand of David and by the hand of his
servants.

### *David Builds an Altar*

**21** Now [a]Satan stood up against Israel, and
moved David to [1]number Israel.
2 So David said to Joab and to the leaders of the
people, "Go, number Israel from Beersheba to
Dan, [a]and bring the number of them to me that I
may know *it.*"
3 And Joab answered, "May the LORD make His
people a hundred times more than they are. But,
my lord the king, *are* they not all my lord's
servants? Why then does my lord require this
thing? Why should he be a cause of guilt in
Israel?"
4 Nevertheless the king's word prevailed against
Joab. Therefore Joab departed and went throughout all Israel and came to Jerusalem.
5 Then Joab gave the sum of the number of the

**16** [1]*Ahimelech,* 2 Sam. 8:17 [2]*Seraiah,* 2 Sam. 8:17, or *Shisha,* 1 Kin. 4:3
**17** [a]2 Sam. 8:18 [1]Lit. *at the hand of the king*

CHAPTER 19
**1** [a]1 Sam. 11:1; 2 Sam. 10:1–19
**3** [1]Lit. *In your eyes is David honoring your father because*
**4** [a]Is. 20:4 [1]*in half*
**6** [a]1 Chr. 18:5, 9 [1]Heb. *Aram Naharaim* [2]*Zoba,* 2 Sam. 10:6
**16** [1]The Euphrates [2]*Zoba,* 2 Sam. 10:6, or *Shobach,* 2 Sam. 10:16
**18** [1]*seven hundred,* 2 Sam. 10:18 [2]*horsemen,* 2 Sam. 10:18

CHAPTER 20
**1** [a]2 Sam. 11:1 [b]2 Sam. 11:2–12:25 [c]2 Sam. 12:26 [1]Lit. *at the return of the year*
**2** [a]2 Sam. 12:30, 31 [1]*plunder*
**3** [1]LXX *cut them with*
**4** [a]2 Sam. 21:18 [b]1 Chr. 11:29 [1]*Gob,* 2 Sam. 21:18 [2]*Saph,* 2 Sam. 21:18 [3]Or *Raphah*
**5** [a]1 Sam. 17:7; 1 Chr. 11:23 [1]*Jaare-Oregim,* 2 Sam. 21:19
**6** [a]1 Sam. 5:8; 2 Sam. 21:20 [1]Or *Raphah*
**7** [1]*Shammah,* 1 Sam. 16:9 or *Shimeah,* 2 Sam. 21:21

CHAPTER 21
**1** [a]2 Sam. 24:1–25; Job 1:6 [1]*take a census of*
**2** [a]1 Chr. 27:23, 24

people to David. All Israel *had* one million one
hundred thousand men who drew the sword, and
Judah *had* four hundred and seventy thousand
men who drew the sword.
6 [a]But he did not count Levi and Benjamin
among them, for the king's [1]word was abominable
to Joab.
7 And [1]God was displeased with this thing;
therefore He struck Israel.
8 So David said to God, [a]"I have sinned greatly,
because I have done this thing; [b]but now, I pray,
take away the iniquity of Your servant, for I have
done very foolishly."
**9** Then the LORD spoke to Gad, David's [a]seer,
saying,
10 "Go and tell David, [a]saying, 'Thus says the
LORD: "I offer you three *things;* choose one of
them for yourself, that I may do *it* to you." ' "
11 So Gad came to David and said to him, "Thus
says the LORD: 'Choose for yourself,
12 [a]'either [1]three years of famine, or three
months to be defeated by your foes with the
sword of your enemies overtaking *you,* or else for
three days the sword of the LORD—the plague in
the land, with the [2]angel of the LORD destroying
throughout all the territory of Israel.' Now consider what answer I should take back to Him who
sent me."
13 And David said to Gad, "I am in great distress.
Please let me fall into the hand of the LORD, for
His [a]mercies *are* very great; but do not let me fall
into the hand of man."
**14** So the LORD sent a [a]plague upon Israel, and
seventy thousand men of Israel fell.
15 And God sent [1]an [a]angel to Jerusalem to
destroy it. As [2]he was destroying, the LORD looked
and [b]relented of the disaster, and said to the angel
who was destroying, "It is enough; now restrain
[3]your hand." And the angel of the LORD stood by
the [c]threshing floor of [4]Ornan the Jebusite.
16 Then David lifted his eyes and [a]saw the angel
of the LORD standing between earth and heaven,
having in his hand a drawn sword stretched out
over Jerusalem. So David and the elders, clothed
in sackcloth, fell on their faces.
17 And David said to God, "Was it not I who
commanded the people to be numbered? I am the
one who has sinned and done evil indeed; but
these [a]sheep, what have they done? Let Your
hand, I pray, O LORD my God, be against me and
my father's house, but not against Your people
that they should be plagued."
**18** Therefore, the [a]angel of the LORD commanded
Gad to say to David that David should go and
erect an altar to the LORD on the threshing floor of
Ornan the Jebusite.
19 So David went up at the word of Gad, which
he had spoken in the name of the LORD.
20 Now Ornan turned and saw the angel; and his
four sons *who were* with him hid themselves, but
Ornan continued threshing wheat.
21 So David came to Ornan, and Ornan looked
and saw David. And he went out from the threshing floor, and bowed before David with *his* face to
the ground.
22 Then David said to Ornan, [1]"Grant me the
place of *this* threshing floor, that I may build an
altar on it to the LORD. You shall grant it to me at
the full price, that the plague may be withdrawn
from the people."
23 But Ornan said to David, "Take *it* to yourself,
and let my lord the king do *what is* good in his
eyes. Look, I *also* give *you* the oxen for burnt
offerings, the threshing implements for wood, and
the wheat for the grain offering; I give *it* all."
24 Then King David said to Ornan, "No, but I will
surely buy *it* for the full price, for I will not take
what is yours for the LORD, nor offer burnt offerings with *that which* costs *me* nothing."
25 So [a]David gave Ornan six hundred shekels of
gold by weight for the place.
26 And David built there an altar to the LORD,
and offered burnt offerings and peace offerings,
and called on the LORD; and [a]He answered him
from heaven by fire on the altar of burnt offering.
27 So the LORD commanded the angel, and he
returned his sword to its sheath.
**28** At that time, when David saw that the LORD
had answered him on the threshing floor of Ornan
the Jebusite, he sacrificed there.
29 [a]For the tabernacle of the LORD and the altar
of the burnt offering, which Moses had made in
the wilderness, *were* at that time at the high place
in [b]Gibeon.
30 But David could not go before it to inquire of
God, for he was afraid of the sword of the angel of
the LORD.

### *David Prepares to Build the Temple*

**22** Then David said, [a]"This *is* the house of the
LORD God, and this *is* the altar of burnt
offering for Israel."
2 So David commanded to gather the [a]aliens
who *were* in the land of Israel; and he appointed
masons to [b]cut hewn stones to build the house of
God.
3 And David prepared iron in abundance for the
nails of the doors of the gates and for the joints,
and bronze in abundance [a]beyond measure,
4 and cedar trees in abundance; for the [a]Sidoni-
ans and those from Tyre brought much cedar
wood to David.
5 Now David said, [a]"Solomon my son *is* young
and inexperienced, and the house to be built for
the LORD *must be* exceedingly magnificent, famous and glorious throughout all countries. I will
now make preparation for it." So David made
abundant preparations before his death.
**6** Then he called for his son Solomon, and
[1]charged him to build a house for the LORD God of
Israel.
7 And David said to Solomon: "My son, as for
me, [a]it was in my mind to build a house [b]to the
name of the LORD my God;
8 "but the word of the LORD came to me, saying,
[a]'You have shed much blood and have made great
wars; you shall not build a house for My name,
because you have shed much blood on the earth
in My sight.
9 [a]'Behold, a son shall be born to you, who shall
be a man of rest; and I will give him [b]rest from all
his enemies all around. His name shall be [1]Solo-
mon, for I will give peace and quietness to Israel
in his days.
10 [a]'He shall build a house for My name, and [b]he
shall be My son, and I *will be* his Father; and I will
establish the throne of his kingdom over Israel
forever.'
11 "Now, my son, may [a]the LORD be with you;
and may you prosper, and build the house of the
LORD your God, as He has said to you.
12 "Only may the LORD [a]give you wisdom and

**6** [a]1 Chr. 27:24 [1]*command*
**7** [1]Lit. *it was evil in the eyes of God*
**8** [a]2 Sam. 24:10 [b]2 Sam. 12:13
**9** [a]1 Sam. 9:9; 2 Kin. 17:13; 1 Chr. 29:29; 2 Chr. 16:7, 10; Is. 30:9, 10; Amos 7:12, 13
**10** [a]2 Sam. 24:12–14
**12** [a]2 Sam. 24:13 [1]*seven,* 2 Sam. 24:13 [2]Or *Angel,* and so throughout the chapter
**13** [a]Ps. 51:1; 130:4, 7
**14** [a]1 Chr. 27:24
**15** [a]2 Sam. 24:16 [b]Gen. 6:6 [c]2 Chr. 3:1 [1]Or *the Angel* [2]Or *He* [3]Or *Your* [4]*Araunah,* 2 Sam. 24:16, 18–24
**16** [a]Josh. 5:13; 2 Chr. 3:1
**17** [a]2 Sam. 7:8; Ps. 74:1
**18** [a]1 Chr. 21:11, 12; 2 Chr. 3:1
**22** [1]Lit. *Give*
**25** [a]2 Sam. 24:24
**26** [a]Lev. 9:24; Judg. 6:21; 1 Kin. 18:36–38; 2 Chr. 3:1; 7:1
**29** [a]1 Kin. 3:4; 2 Chr. 1:3 [b]1 Chr. 16:39

CHAPTER 22
**1** [a]Deut. 12:5; 2 Sam. 24:18; 1 Chr. 21:18, 19, 26, 28; 2 Chr. 3:1
**2** [a]1 Kin. 9:20, 21; 2 Chr. 2:17, 18 [b]1 Kin. 5:17, 18
**3** [a]1 Kin. 7:47; 1 Chr. 22:14
**4** [a]1 Kin. 5:6–10
**5** [a]1 Kin. 3:7; 1 Chr. 29:1, 2
**6** [1]*commanded*
**7** [a]2 Sam. 7:1, 2; 1 Kin. 8:17; 1 Chr. 17:1; 28:2 [b]Deut. 12:5, 11
**8** [a]2 Sam. 7:5–13; 1 Kin. 5:3; 1 Chr. 28:3
**9** [a]1 Chr. 28:5 [b]1 Kin. 4:20, 25; 5:4 [1]Lit. *Peaceful*
**10** [a]2 Sam. 7:13; 1 Kin. 5:5; 6:38; 1 Chr. 17:12, 13; 28:6; 2 Chr. 6:2 [b]Heb. 1:5
**11** [a]1 Chr. 22:16
**12** [a]1 Kin. 3:9–12; 2 Chr. 1:10

understanding, and give you charge concerning
Israel, that you may keep the law of the LORD
your God.
13 [a]"Then you will prosper, if you take care to
fulfill the statutes and judgments with which the
LORD [1]charged Moses concerning Israel. [b]Be
strong and of good courage; do not fear nor be
dismayed.
14 "Indeed I have taken much trouble to prepare
for the house of the LORD one hundred thousand
talents of gold and one million talents of silver,
and bronze and iron [a]beyond measure, for it is so
abundant. I have prepared timber and stone also,
and you may add to them.
15 "Moreover *there are* workmen with you in
abundance: woodsmen and stonecutters, and all
types of skillful men for every kind of work.
16 "Of gold and silver and bronze and iron *there
is* no limit. Arise and begin working, and [a]the
LORD be with you."
17 David also commanded all the [a]leaders of
Israel to help Solomon his son, *saying,*
18 "*Is* not the LORD your God with you? [a]And has
He *not* given you rest on every side? For He has
given the inhabitants of the land into my hand,
and the land is subdued before the LORD and
before His people.
19 "Now set your heart and your soul to seek the
LORD your God. Therefore arise and build the
sanctuary of the LORD God, to [a]bring the ark of
the covenant of the LORD and the holy articles of
God into the house that is to be built [b]for the
name of the LORD."

## *Divisions and Duties of the Levites*

**23** So when David was old and full of days, he
made his son [a]Solomon king over Israel.
2 And he gathered together all the leaders of
Israel, with the priests and the Levites.
3 Now the Levites were numbered from the age
of [a]thirty years and above; and the number of
individual males was thirty-eight thousand.
4 Of these, twenty-four thousand *were* to [a]look
after the work of the house of the LORD, six
thousand *were* [b]officers and judges,
5 four thousand *were* gatekeepers, and four
thousand [a]praised the LORD with *musical* instruments, [b]"which I made," *said David,* "for giving
praise."
6 Also [a]David separated them into [1]divisions
among the sons of Levi: Gershon, Kohath, and
Merari.
7 Of the [a]Gershonites: [1]Laadan and Shimei.
8 The sons of Laadan: the first Jehiel, then
Zetham and Joel—three *in all.*
9 The sons of Shimei: Shelomith, Haziel, and
Haran—three *in all.* These were the heads of the
fathers' *houses* of Laadan.
10 And the sons of Shimei: Jahath, [1]Zina, Jeush,
and Beriah. These *were* the four sons of Shimei.
11 Jahath was the first and Zizah the second. But
Jeush and Beriah did not have many sons; therefore they were assigned as one father's house.
12 [a]The sons of Kohath: Amram, Izhar, Hebron,
and Uzziel—four *in all.*
13 The sons of [a]Amram: Aaron and Moses; and
[b]Aaron was set apart, he and his sons forever, that
he should [1]sanctify the most holy things, [c]to burn
incense before the LORD, [d]to minister to Him, and
[e]to give the blessing in His name forever.
14 Now [a]the sons of Moses the man of God were
reckoned to the tribe of Levi.
15 [a]The sons of Moses *were* [1]Gershon and Eliezer.
16 Of the sons of Gershon, [a]Shebuel[1] *was* the
first.
17 Of the descendants of Eliezer, [a]Rehabiah was
the first. And Eliezer had no other sons, but the
sons of Rehabiah were very many.
18 Of the sons of Izhar, [a]Shelomith *was* the first.
19 [a]Of the sons of Hebron, Jeriah *was* the first,
Amariah the second, Jahaziel the third, and Jeka-
meam the fourth.
20 Of the sons of Uzziel, Michah *was* the first and
Jesshiah the second.
21 [a]The sons of Merari *were* Mahli and Mushi.
The sons of Mahli *were* Eleazar and [b]Kish.
22 And Eleazar died, and [a]had no sons, but only
daughters; and their [1]brethren, the sons of Kish,
[b]took them *as wives.*
23 [a]The sons of Mushi *were* Mahli, Eder, and
Jeremoth—three *in all.*
24 These *were* the sons of [a]Levi by their fathers'
houses—the heads of the fathers' *houses* as they
were counted individually by the number of their
names, who did the work for the service of the
house of the LORD, from the age of [b]twenty years
and above.
25 For David said, "The LORD God of Israel [a]has
given rest to His people, that they may dwell in
Jerusalem forever";
26 and also to the Levites, "They shall no longer
[a]carry the tabernacle, or any of the articles for its
service."
27 For by the [a]last words of David the Levites
*were* numbered from twenty years old and above;
28 because their duty *was* to help the sons of
Aaron in the service of the house of the LORD, in
the courts and in the chambers, in the purifying of
all holy things and the work of the service of the
house of God,
29 both with [a]the showbread and [b]the fine flour
for the grain offering, with [c]the unleavened cakes
and [d]*what is baked in* the pan, with what is mixed
and with all kinds of [e]measures and sizes;
30 to stand every morning to thank and praise
the LORD, and likewise at evening;
31 and at every presentation of a burnt offering
to the LORD [a]on the Sabbaths and on the New
Moons and on the [b]set[1] feasts, by number according to the ordinance governing them, regularly
before the LORD;
32 and that they should [a]attend to the [b]needs of
the tabernacle of meeting, the needs of the holy
*place,* and the [c]needs of the sons of Aaron their
brethren in the work of the house of the LORD.

## *The Divisions of the Priests*

**24** Now *these are* the divisions of the sons of
Aaron. [a]The sons of Aaron *were* Nadab,
Abihu, Eleazar, and Ithamar.
2 And [a]Nadab and Abihu died before their father, and had no children; therefore Eleazar and
Ithamar ministered as priests.
3 Then David with Zadok of the sons of Eleazar,
and [a]Ahimelech of the sons of Ithamar, divided
them according to the schedule of their service.
4 There were more leaders found of the sons of
Eleazar than of the sons of Ithamar, and *thus* they
were divided. Among the sons of Eleazar *were*
sixteen heads of *their* fathers' houses, and eight

13 [a]1 Chr. 28:7 [b][Josh. 1:6, 7, 9] [1]*commanded*
14 [a]1 Chr. 22:3
16 [a]1 Chr. 22:11
17 [a]1 Chr. 28:1–6
18 [a]Josh. 22:4
19 [a]2 Chr. 5:2–14 [b]1 Kin. 5:3

CHAPTER 23
1 [a]1 Kin. 1:33–40
3 [a]Num. 4:1–3
4 [a]Ezra 3:8, 9 [b]Deut. 16:18–20
5 [a]1 Chr. 15:16 [b]2 Chr. 29:25–27
6 [a]Ex. 6:16 [1]*groups*
7 [a]1 Chr. 26:21 [1]*Libni,* Ex. 6:17
10 [1]LXX, Vg. *Zizah* and v. 11
12 [a]Ex. 6:18
13 [a]Ex. 6:20 [b]Heb. 5:4 [c]1 Sam. 2:28 [d][Deut. 21:5] [e]Num. 6:23 [1]*consecrate*
14 [a]1 Chr. 26:20–24
15 [a]Ex. 18:3, 4 [1]Heb. *Gershom,* 1 Chr. 6:16
16 [a]1 Chr. 26:24 [1]*Shubael,* 1 Chr. 24:20
17 [a]1 Chr. 26:25
18 [a]1 Chr. 24:22
19 [a]1 Chr. 24:23
21 [a]1 Chr. 24:26 [b]1 Chr. 24:29
22 [a]1 Chr. 24:28 [b]Num. 36:6 [1]*kinsmen*
23 [a]1 Chr. 24:30
24 [a]Num. 10:17, 21 [b]Ezra 3:8
25 [a]1 Chr. 22:18
26 [a]Num. 4:5, 15; 7:9
27 [a]2 Sam. 23:1
29 [a]Ex. 25:30 [b]Lev. 6:20 [c]Lev. 2:1, 4 [d]Lev. 2:5, 7 [e]Lev. 19:35
31 [a]Num. 10:10 [b]Lev. 23:2–4 [1]*appointed feasts*
32 [a]2 Chr. 13:10, 11 [b][Num. 1:53] [c]Num. 3:6–9, 38

CHAPTER 24
1 [a]Lev. 10:1–6
2 [a]Num. 3:1–4; 26:61
3 [a]1 Chr. 18:16

heads of their fathers' houses among the sons of
Ithamar.
5 Thus they were divided by lot, one group as
another, for there were officials of the sanctuary
and officials *of the house* of God, from the sons of
Eleazar and from the sons of Ithamar.
6 And the scribe, Shemaiah the son of Nethanel,
*one of* the Levites, wrote them down before the
king, the leaders, Zadok the priest, Ahimelech the
son of Abiathar, and the heads of the fathers'
*houses* of the priests and Levites, one father's
house taken for Eleazar and *one* for Ithamar.
**7** Now the first lot fell to Jehoiarib, the second
to Jedaiah,
8 the third to Harim, the fourth to Seorim,
9 the fifth to Malchijah, the sixth to Mijamin,
10 the seventh to Hakkoz, the eighth to [a]Abijah,
11 the ninth to Jeshua, the tenth to Shecaniah,
12 the eleventh to Eliashib, the twelfth to Jakim,
13 the thirteenth to Huppah, the fourteenth to
Jeshebeab,
14 the fifteenth to Bilgah, the sixteenth to Immer,
15 the seventeenth to Hezir, the eighteenth to
[1]Happizzez,
16 the nineteenth to Pethahiah, the twentieth to
[1]Jehezekel,
17 the twenty-first to Jachin, the twenty-second
to Gamul,
18 the twenty-third to Delaiah, the twenty-fourth
to Maaziah.
19 This *was* the schedule of their service [a]for
coming into the house of the LORD according to
their ordinance by the hand of Aaron their father,
as the LORD God of Israel had commanded him.
**20** And the rest of the sons of Levi: of the sons of
Amram, [1]Shubael; of the sons of Shubael, Jehdeiah.
21 Concerning [a]Rehabiah, of the sons of Rehabiah, the first *was* Isshiah.
22 Of the Izharites, [1]Shelomoth; of the sons of
Shelomoth, Jahath.
23 Of the sons [1]*of* [a]*Hebron,* Jeriah [2]*was the first,*
Amariah the second, Jahaziel the third, *and* Jeka-
meam the fourth.
24 *Of* the sons of Uzziel, Michah; of the sons of
Michah, Shamir.
25 The brother of Michah, Isshiah; of the sons of
Isshiah, Zechariah.
26 [a]The sons of Merari *were* Mahli and Mushi;
the son of Jaaziah, Beno.
27 The sons of Merari by Jaaziah *were* Beno,
Shoham, Zaccur, and Ibri.
28 Of Mahli: Eleazar, [a]who had no sons.
29 Of Kish: the son of Kish, Jerahmeel.
30 Also [a]the sons of Mushi *were* Mahli, Eder, and
Jerimoth. These *were* the sons of the Levites
according to their fathers' houses.
31 These also cast lots just as their brothers the
sons of Aaron did, in the presence of King David,
Zadok, Ahimelech, and the heads of the fathers'
*houses* of the priests and Levites. The chief fathers *did* just as their younger brethren.

### *The Divisions of the Musicians*

**25** Moreover David and the captains of the
army separated for the service *some* of the
sons of [a]Asaph, of Heman, and of Jeduthun, who
*should* prophesy with harps, stringed instruments,
and cymbals. And the number of the skilled men
performing their service was:
2 Of the sons of Asaph: Zaccur, Joseph, Nethaniah, and [1]Asharelah; the sons of Asaph *were*
[2]under the direction of Asaph, who prophesied
according to the order of the king.
3 Of [a]Jeduthun, the sons of Jeduthun: Gedaliah,
[1]Zeri, Jeshaiah, [2]Shimei, Hashabiah, and Mattithiah, [3]six, under the direction of their father
Jeduthun, who prophesied with a harp to give
thanks and to praise the LORD.
4 Of Heman, the sons of Heman: Bukkiah, Mattaniah, [1]Uzziel, [2]Shebuel, [3]Jerimoth, Hananiah,
Hanani, Eliathah, Giddalti, Romamti-Ezer, Joshbekashah, Mallothi, Hothir, *and* Mahazioth.
5 All these *were* the sons of Heman the king's
seer in the words of God, to [1]exalt his [a]horn. For
God gave Heman fourteen sons and three daughters.
6 All these *were* under the direction of their
father for the music *in* the house of the LORD, with
cymbals, stringed instruments, and [a]harps, for the
service of the house of God. Asaph, Jeduthun, and
Heman *were* [b]under the authority of the king.
7 So the [a]number of them, with their brethren
who were instructed in the songs of the LORD, all
who were skillful, *was* two hundred and eighty-
eight.
8 And they cast lots for their duty, the small as
well as the great, [a]the teacher with the student.
**9** Now the first lot for Asaph came out for
Joseph; the second for Gedaliah, him with his
brethren and sons, twelve;
10 the third for Zaccur, his sons and his brethren,
twelve;
11 the fourth for [1]Jizri, his sons and his brethren,
twelve;
12 the fifth for Nethaniah, his sons and his brethren, twelve;
13 the sixth for Bukkiah, his sons and his brethren, twelve;
14 the seventh for [1]Jesharelah, his sons and his
brethren, twelve;
15 the eighth for Jeshaiah, his sons and his brethren, twelve;
16 the ninth for Mattaniah, his sons and his
brethren, twelve;
17 the tenth for Shimei, his sons and his brethren,
twelve;
18 the eleventh for [1]Azarel, his sons and his
brethren, twelve;
19 the twelfth for Hashabiah, his sons and his
brethren, twelve;
20 the thirteenth for [1]Shubael, his sons and his
brethren, twelve;
21 the fourteenth for Mattithiah, his sons and his
brethren, twelve;
22 the fifteenth for [1]Jeremoth, his sons and his
brethren, twelve;
23 the sixteenth for Hananiah, his sons and his
brethren, twelve;
24 the seventeenth for Joshbekashah, his sons
and his brethren, twelve;
25 the eighteenth for Hanani, his sons and his
brethren, twelve;
26 the nineteenth for Mallothi, his sons and his
brethren, twelve;
27 the twentieth for Eliathah, his sons and his
brethren, twelve;
28 the twenty-first for Hothir, his sons and his
brethren, twelve;
29 the twenty-second for Giddalti, his sons and
his brethren, twelve;

**10** [a]Neh. 12:4, 17; Luke 1:5
**15** [1]LXX, Vg. *Aphses*
**16** [1]MT *Jehezkel*
**19** [a]1 Chr. 9:25
**20** [1]*Shebuel,* 1 Chr. 23:16
**21** [a]1 Chr. 23:17
**22** [1]*Shelomith,* 1 Chr. 23:18
**23** [a]1 Chr. 23:19; 26:31 [1]Supplied from 23:19 (following some Heb. mss. and LXX mss.) [2]See previous note
**26** [a]Ex. 6:19; 1 Chr. 23:21
**28** [a]1 Chr. 23:22
**30** [a]1 Chr. 23:23

CHAPTER 25
**1** [a]1 Chr. 6:30, 33, 39, 44; 2 Chr. 5:12
**2** [1]*Jesharelah,* v. 14 [2]Lit. *at the hands of*
**3** [a]1 Chr. 16:41, 42 [1]*Jizri,* v. 11 [2]So with 1 Heb. ms., LXX mss. [3]Shimei is the sixth, v. 17
**4** [1]*Azarel,* v. 18 [2]*Shubael,* v. 20 [3]*Jeremoth,* v. 22
**5** [a]1 Chr. 16:42 [1]Increase his power or influence
**6** [a]1 Chr. 15:16 [b]1 Chr. 15:19; 25:2
**7** [a]1 Chr. 23:5
**8** [a]2 Chr. 23:13
**11** [1]*Zeri,* v. 3
**14** [1]*Asharelah,* v. 2
**18** [1]*Uzziel,* v. 4
**20** [1]*Shebuel,* v. 4
**22** [1]*Jerimoth,* v. 4

30 the twenty-third for Mahazioth, his sons and
his brethren, twelve;
31 the twenty-fourth for Romamti-Ezer, his sons
and his brethren, twelve.

## *The Gatekeepers and Overseers*

**26** Concerning the divisions of the gatekeepers: of the Korahites, [1]Meshelemiah the son
of [a]Kore, of the sons of [2]Asaph.
2 And the sons of Meshelemiah *were* [a]Zechariah
the firstborn, Jediael the second, Zebadiah the
third, Jathniel the fourth,
3 Elam the fifth, Jehohanan the sixth, Eliehoenai the seventh.
4 Moreover the sons of [a]Obed-Edom *were*
Shemaiah the firstborn, Jehozabad the second,
Joah the third, Sacar the fourth, Nethanel the
fifth,
5 Ammiel the sixth, Issachar the seventh, Peul-
thai the eighth; for God blessed him.
6 Also to Shemaiah his son were sons born who
governed their fathers' houses, because they *were*
men of great ability.
7 The sons of Shemaiah *were* Othni, Rephael,
Obed, and Elzabad, whose brothers Elihu and
Semachiah *were* able men.
8 All these *were* of the sons of Obed-Edom, they
and their sons and their brethren, [a]able men with
strength for the work: sixty-two of Obed-Edom.
9 And Meshelemiah had sons and brethren,
eighteen able men.
10 Also [a]Hosah, of the children of Merari, had
sons: Shimri the first (for *though* he was not the
firstborn, his father made him the first),
11 Hilkiah the second, Tebaliah the third, Zechariah the fourth; all the sons and brethren of Hosah
*were* thirteen.
12 Among these *were* the divisions of the gatekeepers, among the chief men, *having* duties just
like their brethren, to serve in the house of the
LORD.
13 And they [a]cast lots for each gate, the small as
well as the great, according to their father's
house.
14 The lot for the East *Gate* fell to [1]Shelemiah.
Then they cast lots *for* his son Zechariah, a wise
counselor, and his lot came out for the North
Gate;
15 to Obed-Edom the South Gate, and to his sons
the [1]storehouse.
16 To Shuppim and Hosah *the lot came out* for
the West Gate, with the Shallecheth Gate on the
[a]ascending highway—watchman opposite watchman.
17 On the east were *six* Levites, on the north four
each day, on the south four each day, and for the
[1]storehouse two by two.
18 As for the [1]Parbar on the west, *there were* four
on the highway *and* two at the Parbar.
19 These were the divisions of the gatekeepers
among the sons of Korah and among the sons of
Merari.
20 Of the Levites, Ahijah *was* [a]over the treasuries
of the house of God and over the treasuries of the
[b]dedicated[1] things.
21 The sons of [1]Laadan, the descendants of the
Gershonites of Laadan, heads of their fathers'
*houses,* of Laadan the Gershonite: [2]Jehieli.
22 The sons of Jehieli, Zetham and Joel his
brother, *were* over the treasuries of the house of
the LORD.
23 Of the [a]Amramites, the Izharites, the Hebronites, and the Uzzielites:
24 [a]Shebuel the son of Gershom, the son of Moses, *was* overseer of the treasuries.
25 And his brethren by Eliezer *were* Rehabiah his
son, Jeshaiah his son, Joram his son, Zichri his
son, and [a]Shelomith his son.
26 This Shelomith and his brethren *were* over all
the treasuries of the dedicated things [a]which King
David and the heads of fathers' *houses,* the captains over thousands and hundreds, and the captains of the army, had dedicated.
27 Some of the [1]spoils won in battles they dedicated to maintain the house of the LORD.
28 And all that Samuel [a]the seer, Saul the son of
Kish, Abner the son of Ner, and Joab the son of
Zeruiah had dedicated, every dedicated *thing,* was
under the hand of Shelomith and his brethren.
29 Of the Izharites, Chenaniah and his sons
[a]*performed* duties as [b]officials and judges over
Israel outside Jerusalem.
30 Of the Hebronites, [a]Hashabiah and his brethren, one thousand seven hundred able men, had
the oversight of Israel on the west side of the
Jordan for all the business of the LORD, and in the
service of the king.
31 Among the Hebronites, [a]Jerijah *was* head of
the Hebronites according to his genealogy of the
fathers. In the fortieth year of the reign of David
they were sought, and there were found among
them capable men [b]at Jazer of Gilead.
32 And his brethren *were* two thousand seven
hundred able men, heads of fathers' *houses,* whom
King David made officials over the Reubenites,
the Gadites, and the half-tribe of Manasseh, for
every matter pertaining to God and the [a]affairs of
the king.

## *The Officers of the Kingdom*

**27** And the children of Israel, according to
their number, the heads of fathers' *houses,*
the captains of thousands and hundreds and their
officers, served the king in every matter of the
*military* divisions. *These divisions* came in and
went out month by month throughout all the
months of the year, each division *having* twenty-
four thousand.
2 Over the first division for the first month *was*
[a]Jashobeam the son of Zabdiel, and in his division
*were* twenty-four thousand;
3 *he was* of the children of Perez, and the chief
of all the captains of the army for the first month.
4 Over the division of the second month *was*
[1]Dodai an Ahohite, and of his division Mikloth
also *was* the leader; in his division *were* twenty-
four thousand.
5 The third captain of the army for the third
month *was* [a]Benaiah, the son of Jehoiada the
priest, who was chief; in his division *were* twenty-
four thousand.
6 This was the Benaiah *who was* [a]mighty *among*
the thirty, and was over the thirty; in his division
*was* Ammizabad his son.
7 The fourth *captain* for the fourth month *was*
[a]Asahel the brother of Joab, and Zebadiah his son
after him; in his division *were* twenty-four thousand.
8 The fifth *captain* for the fifth month *was*
[1]Shamhuth the Izrahite; in his division were
twenty-four thousand.
9 The sixth *captain* for the sixth month *was* [a]Ira

CHAPTER 26

**1** [a]Ps. 42:title [1]*Shelemiah,* v. 14 [2]*Ebiasaph,* 1 Chr. 6:37; 9:19
**2** [a]1 Chr. 9:21
**4** [a]1 Chr. 15:18, 21
**8** [a]1 Chr. 9:13
**10** [a]1 Chr. 16:38
**13** [a]1 Chr. 24:5, 31; 25:8
**14** [1]*Meshelemiah,* v. 1
**15** [1]Heb. *asuppim*
**16** [a]1 Kin. 10:5; 2 Chr. 9:4
**17** [1]Heb. *asuppim*
**18** [1]Probably a court or colonnade extending west of the temple
**20** [a]1 Chr. 9:26 [b]2 Sam. 8:11; 1 Chr. 26:22, 24, 26; 28:12; Ezra 2:69 [1]*holy things*
**21** [1]*Libni,* 1 Chr. 6:17 [2]*Jehiel,* 1 Chr. 23:8; 29:8
**23** [a]Ex. 6:18; Num. 3:19
**24** [a]1 Chr. 23:16
**25** [a]1 Chr. 23:18
**26** [a]2 Sam. 8:11
**27** [1]*plunder*
**28** [a]1 Sam. 9:9
**29** [a]Neh. 11:16 [b]1 Chr. 23:4
**30** [a]1 Chr. 27:17
**31** [a]1 Chr. 23:19 [b]Josh. 21:39
**32** [a]2 Chr. 19:11

CHAPTER 27

**2** [a]1 Chr. 11:11
**4** [1]Heb. *Dodai,* usually spelled *Dodo,* 2 Sam. 23:9
**5** [a]1 Chr. 18:17
**6** [a]2 Sam. 23:20–23
**7** [a]2 Sam. 23:24; 1 Chr. 11:26
**8** [1]*Shammah,* 2 Sam. 23:11, or *Shammoth,* 1 Chr. 11:27
**9** [a]1 Chr. 11:28

the son of Ikkesh the Tekoite; in his division *were*
twenty-four thousand.
10 The seventh *captain* for the seventh month
*was* [a]Helez the Pelonite, of the children of
Ephraim; in his division *were* twenty-four thousand.
11 The eighth *captain* for the eighth month *was*
[a]Sibbechai the Hushathite, of the Zarhites; in his
division *were* twenty-four thousand.
12 The ninth *captain* for the ninth month *was*
[a]Abiezer the Anathothite, of the Benjamites; in his
division *were* twenty-four thousand.
13 The tenth *captain* for the tenth month *was*
[a]Maharai the Netophathite, of the Zarhites; in his
division *were* twenty-four thousand.
14 The eleventh *captain* for the eleventh month
*was* [a]Benaiah the Pirathonite, of the children of
Ephraim; in his division *were* twenty-four thousand.
15 The twelfth *captain* for the twelfth month *was*
[1]Heldai the Netophathite, of Othniel; in his division *were* twenty-four thousand.
**16** Furthermore, over the tribes of Israel: the
officer over the Reubenites *was* Eliezer the son of
Zichri; over the Simeonites, Shephatiah the son of
Maachah;
17 *over* the Levites, [a]Hashabiah the son of Kemuel; over the Aaronites, Zadok;
18 *over* Judah, [a]Elihu, *one* of David's brothers;
*over* Issachar, Omri the son of Michael;
19 *over* Zebulun, Ishmaiah the son of Obadiah;
*over* Naphtali, Jerimoth the son of Azriel;
20 *over* the children of Ephraim, Hoshea the son
of Azaziah; *over* the half-tribe of Manasseh, Joel
the son of Pedaiah;
21 *over* the half-*tribe* of Manasseh in Gilead, Iddo
the son of Zechariah; *over* Benjamin, Jaasiel the
son of Abner;
22 *over* Dan, Azarel the son of Jeroham. These
*were* the leaders of the tribes of Israel.
**23** But David did not take the number of those
twenty years old and under, because [a]the LORD
had said He would multiply Israel like the [b]stars of
the heavens.
24 Joab the son of Zeruiah began a census, but he
did not finish, for [a]wrath came upon Israel because of this census; nor was the number recorded
in the account of the chronicles of King David.
**25** And Azmaveth the son of Adiel *was* over the
king's treasuries; and Jehonathan the son of
Uzziah was over the storehouses in the field, in
the cities, in the villages, and in the fortresses.
26 Ezri the son of Chelub was over those who did
the work of the field for tilling the ground.
27 And Shimei the Ramathite *was* over the vineyards, and Zabdi the Shiphmite was over the
produce of the vineyards for the supply of wine.
28 Baal-Hanan the Gederite was over the olive
trees and the sycamore trees that *were* in the
lowlands, and Joash *was* over the store of oil.
29 And Shitrai the Sharonite *was* over the herds
that fed in Sharon, and Shaphat the son of Adlai
was over the herds *that were* in the valleys.
30 Obil the Ishmaelite *was* over the camels,
Jehdeiah the Meronothite *was* over the donkeys,
31 and Jaziz the [a]Hagrite *was* over the flocks. All
these *were* the officials over King David's property.
32 Also Jehonathan, David's uncle, *was* a counselor, a wise man, and a [1]scribe; and Jehiel the
[2]son of Hachmoni *was* with the king's sons.
33 [a]Ahithophel *was* the king's counselor, and
[b]Hushai the Archite *was* the king's companion.
34 After Ahithophel *was* Jehoiada the son of
Benaiah, then [a]Abiathar. And the general of the
king's army *was* [b]Joab.

### *Solomon Instructed to Build the Temple*

**28** Now David assembled at Jerusalem all [a]the
leaders of Israel: the officers of the tribes
and [b]the captains of the divisions who served the
king, the captains over thousands and captains
over hundreds, and [c]the stewards over all the
substance and [1]possessions of the king and of his
sons, with the officials, the valiant men, and all
[d]the mighty men of valor.
2 Then King David rose to his feet and said,
"Hear me, my brethren and my people: [a]I *had* it in
my heart to build a house of rest for the ark of the
covenant of the LORD, and for [b]the footstool of our
God, and had made preparations to build it.
3 "But God said to me, [a]'You shall not build a
house for My name, because you *have been* a man
of war and have shed [b]blood.'
4 "However the LORD God of Israel [a]chose me
above all the house of my father to be king over
Israel forever, for He has chosen [b]Judah *to be* the
ruler. And of the house of Judah, [c]the house of my
father, and [d]among the sons of my father, He was
pleased with me to make *me* king over all Israel.
5 [a]"And of all my sons (for the LORD has given
me many sons) [b]He has chosen my son Solomon
to sit on the throne of the kingdom of the LORD
over Israel.
6 "Now He said to me, 'It is [a]your son Solomon
*who* shall build My house and My courts; for I
have chosen him *to be* My son, and I will be his
Father.
7 'Moreover I will establish his kingdom forever,
[a]if he is steadfast to observe My commandments
and My judgments, as it is this day.'
8 "Now therefore, in the sight of all Israel, the
assembly of the LORD, and in the hearing of our
God, be careful to seek out all the commandments
of the LORD your God, that you may possess this
good land, and leave *it* as an inheritance for your
children after you forever.
**9** "As for you, my son Solomon, [a]know the God
of your father, and serve Him [b]with a loyal heart
and with a willing mind; for [c]the LORD searches all
hearts and understands all the intent of the
thoughts. [d]If you seek Him, He will be found by
you; but if you forsake Him, He will [e]cast you off
forever.
10 "Consider now, [a]for the LORD has chosen you
to build a house for the sanctuary; be strong, and
do it."
**11** Then David gave his son Solomon [a]the plans
for the vestibule, its houses, its treasuries, its
upper chambers, its inner chambers, and the place
of the mercy seat;
12 and the [a]plans for all that he had by the Spirit,
of the courts of the house of the LORD, of all the
chambers all around, [b]of the treasuries of the
house of God, and of the treasuries for the dedicated things;
13 also for the division of the priests and the
[a]Levites, for all the work of the service of the
house of the LORD, and for all the articles of
service in the house of the LORD.
14 *He gave* gold by weight for *things* of gold, for
all articles used in every kind of service; also *silver*

**10** [a]1 Chr. 11:27
**11** [a]2 Sam. 21:18; 1 Chr. 11:29; 20:4
**12** [a]1 Chr. 11:28
**13** [a]2 Sam. 23:28; 1 Chr. 11:30
**14** [a]1 Chr. 11:31
**15** [1]*Heleb,* 2 Sam. 23:29, or *Heled,* 1 Chr. 11:30
**17** [a]1 Chr. 26:30
**18** [a]1 Sam. 16:6
**23** [a][Deut. 6:3] [b]Gen. 15:5; 22:17; 26:4; Ex. 32:13; Deut. 1:10
**24** [a]2 Sam. 24:12–15; 1 Chr. 21:1–7
**31** [a]1 Chr. 5:10
**32** [1]*secretary* [2]Or *Hachmonite*
**33** [a]2 Sam. 15:12 [b]2 Sam. 15:32–37
**34** [a]1 Kin. 1:7 [b]1 Chr. 11:6

CHAPTER 28

**1** [a]1 Chr. 27:16 [b]1 Chr. 27:1, 2 [c]1 Chr. 27:25 [d]2 Sam. 23:8–39; 1 Chr. 11:10–47 [1]Or *livestock*
**2** [a]2 Sam. 7:2 [b]Ps. 99:5; 132:7; [Is. 66:1]
**3** [a]2 Sam. 7:5, 13; 1 Kin. 5:3 [b][1 Chr. 17:4; 22:8]
**4** [a]1 Sam. 16:6–13 [b]Gen. 49:8–10; 1 Chr. 5:2; Ps. 60:7 [c]1 Sam. 16:1 [d]1 Sam. 13:14; 16:12, 13; Acts 13:22
**5** [a]1 Chr. 3:1–9; 14:3–7; 23:1 [b]1 Chr. 22:9; 29:1
**6** [a]2 Sam. 7:13, 14; 1 Kin. 6:38; 1 Chr. 22:9, 10; 2 Chr. 1:9; 6:2
**7** [a]1 Chr. 22:13
**9** [a][1 Sam. 12:24]; Jer. 9:24; Hos. 4:1; [John 17:3] [b]2 Kin. 20:3 [c][1 Sam. 16:7; 1 Kin. 8:39; 1 Chr. 29:17]; Jer. 11:20; 17:10; 20:12; Rev. 2:23 [d]2 Chr. 15:2; [Jer. 29:13] [e]Deut. 31:17
**10** [a]1 Chr. 22:13; 28:6
**11** [a]1 Kin. 6:3; 1 Chr. 28:19
**12** [a]Ex. 25:40; Heb. 8:5 [b]1 Chr. 26:20, 28
**13** [a]1 Chr. 23:6

for all articles of silver by weight, for all articles
used in every kind of service;
15 the weight for the [a]lampstands of gold, and
their lamps of gold, by weight for each lampstand
and its lamps; for the lampstands of silver by
weight, for the lampstand and its lamps, according
to the use of each lampstand.
16 And by weight *he gave* gold for the tables of
the showbread, for each [a]table, and silver for the
tables of silver;
17 also pure gold for the forks, the basins, the
pitchers of pure gold, and the golden bowls—*he
gave gold* by weight for every bowl; and for the
silver bowls, *silver* by weight for every bowl;
18 and refined gold by weight for the [a]altar of
incense, and for the construction of the chariot,
that is, the gold [b]cherubim that spread *their wings*
and overshadowed the ark of the covenant of the
LORD.
19 "All *this,*" *said David,* [a]"the LORD made me
understand in writing, by *His* hand upon me, all
the [1]works of these plans."
**20** And David said to his son Solomon, [a]"Be
strong and of good courage, and do *it;* do not fear
nor be dismayed, for the LORD God—my God—
*will be* with you. [b]He will not leave you nor
forsake you, until you have finished all the work
for the service of the house of the LORD.
21 "*Here are* [a]the divisions of the priests and the
Levites for all the service of the house of God; and
[b]every willing craftsman *will be* with you for all
manner of workmanship, for every kind of service; also the leaders and all the people *will be*
completely at your command."

### *Offerings for Building the Temple*

**29** Furthermore King David said to all the
assembly: "My son Solomon, whom alone
God has [a]chosen, *is* [b]young and inexperienced;
and the work *is* great, because the [1]temple *is* not
for man but for the LORD God.
2 "Now for the house of my God I have prepared with all my might: gold for *things to be
made of* gold, silver for *things of* silver, bronze for
*things of* bronze, iron for *things of* iron, wood for
*things of* wood, [a]onyx stones, *stones* to be set,
glistening stones of various colors, all kinds of
precious stones, and marble slabs in abundance.
3 "Moreover, because I have set my affection on
the house of my God, I have given to the house of
my God, over and above all that I have prepared
for the holy house, my own special treasure of
gold and silver:
4 "three thousand talents of gold, of the gold of
[a]Ophir, and seven thousand talents of refined
silver, to overlay the walls of the houses;
5 "the gold for *things of* gold and the silver for
*things of* silver, and for all kinds of work *to be
done* by the hands of craftsmen. Who *then* is
[a]willing to [1]consecrate himself this day to the
LORD?"
**6** Then [a]the leaders of the fathers' *houses,* leaders of the tribes of Israel, the captains of thousands and of hundreds, with [b]the officers over the
king's work, [c]offered willingly.
7 They gave for the work of the house of God
five thousand talents and ten thousand darics of
gold, ten thousand talents of silver, eighteen
thousand talents of bronze, and one hundred
thousand talents of iron.
8 And whoever had *precious* stones gave *them*
to the treasury of the house of the LORD, into the
hand of [a]Jehiel[1] the Gershonite.
9 Then the people rejoiced, for they had offered
willingly, because with a loyal heart they had
[a]offered willingly to the LORD; and King David
also rejoiced greatly.
**10** Therefore David blessed the LORD before all
the assembly; and David said:

"Blessed are You, LORD God of Israel, our
Father, forever and ever.
11 [a]Yours, O LORD, *is* the greatness,
The power and the glory,
The victory and the majesty;
For all *that is* in heaven
and in earth *is Yours;*
Yours *is* the kingdom, O LORD,
And You are exalted as head over all.
12 [a]Both riches and honor *come* from You,
And You reign over all.
In Your hand *is* power and might;
In Your hand *it is* to make great
And to give strength to all.

**13** "Now therefore, our God,
We thank You
And praise Your glorious name.
14 But who *am* I, and who *are* my people,
That we should be able to offer
so willingly as this?
For all things *come* from You,
And [1]of Your own we have given You.
15 For [a]we *are* [1]aliens and [2]pilgrims before You,
As *were* all our fathers;
[b]Our days on earth *are* as a shadow,
And without hope.

**16** "O LORD our God, all this abundance that we
have prepared to build You a house for Your holy
name is from Your hand, and *is* all Your own.
17 "I know also, my God, that You [a]test the heart
and [b]have pleasure in uprightness. As for me, in
the uprightness of my heart I have willingly
offered all these *things;* and now with joy I have
seen Your people, who are present here to offer
willingly to You.
18 "O LORD God of Abraham, Isaac, and Israel,
our fathers, keep this forever in the intent of the
thoughts of the heart of Your people, and fix their
heart toward You.
19 "And [a]give my son Solomon a loyal heart to
keep Your commandments and Your testimonies
and Your statutes, to do all *these things,* and to
build the [1]temple for which [b]I have made provision."
20 Then David said to all the assembly, "Now
bless the LORD your God." So all the assembly
blessed the LORD God of their fathers, and bowed
their heads and prostrated themselves before the
LORD and the king.
**21** And they made sacrifices to the LORD and
offered burnt offerings to the LORD on the next
day: a thousand bulls, a thousand rams, a thousand lambs, with their drink offerings, and [a]sacri-
fices in abundance for all Israel.
22 So they ate and drank before the LORD with
great gladness on that day. And they made Solomon the son of David king the second time, and
[a]anointed *him* before the LORD *to be* the leader,
and Zadok *to be* priest.
23 Then Solomon sat on the throne of the LORD
as king instead of David his father, and prospered;
and all Israel obeyed him.

---

**15** [a]Ex. 25:31–39; 1 Kin. 7:49
**16** [a]1 Kin. 7:48
**18** [a]Ex. 30:1–10 [b]Ex. 25:18–22; 1 Sam. 4:4; 1 Kin. 6:23
**19** [a]Ex. 25:40; 1 Chr. 28:11, 12 [1]*details*
**20** [a]Deut. 31:6, 7; [Josh. 1:6–9]; 1 Chr. 22:13 [b]Josh. 1:5; Heb. 13:5
**21** [a]1 Chr. 24—26 [b]Ex. 35:25–35; 36:1, 2; 2 Chr. 2:13, 14

CHAPTER 29

**1** [a]1 Chr. 28:5 [b]1 Kin. 3:7; 1 Chr. 22:5; Prov. 4:3 [1]Lit. *palace*
**2** [a]Is. 54:11, 12; Rev. 21:18
**4** [a]1 Kin. 9:28
**5** [a]2 Chr. 29:31; [2 Cor. 8:5, 12] [1]Lit. *fill his hand*
**6** [a]1 Chr. 27:1; 28:1 [b]1 Chr. 27:25–31 [c]Ex. 35:21–35
**8** [a]1 Chr. 23:8 [1]Possibly the same as *Jehieli,* 1 Chr. 26:21, 22
**9** [a]Ex. 25:2; 1 Kin. 8:61; 2 Cor. 9:7
**11** [a]Matt. 6:13; 1 Tim. 1:17; Rev. 5:13
**12** [a]Rom. 11:36
**14** [1]Lit. *of your hand*
**15** [a]Lev. 25:23; Ps. 39:12; Heb. 11:13, 14; 1 Pet. 2:11 [b]Job 14:2; Ps. 90:9 [1]*sojourners,* temporary residents [2]*transients,* temporary residents in an even more temporary sense
**17** [a][1 Sam. 16:7; 1 Chr. 28:9] [b]Prov. 11:20
**19** [a][1 Chr. 28:9]; Ps. 72:1 [b]1 Chr. 29:1, 2 [1]Lit. *palace*
**21** [a]1 Kin. 8:62, 63
**22** [a]1 Kin. 1:32–35, 39; 1 Chr. 23:1

24 All the leaders and the mighty men, and also
all the sons of King David, [a]submitted[1] themselves
to King Solomon.
25 So the LORD exalted Solomon exceedingly in
the sight of all Israel, and [a]bestowed on him *such*
royal majesty as had not been on any king before
him in Israel.
**26** Thus David the son of Jesse reigned over all
Israel.
27 [a]And the period that he reigned over Israel
*was* forty years; [b]seven years he reigned in Hebron, and thirty-three *years* he reigned in Jerusalem.
28 So he [a]died in a good old age, [b]full of days and
riches and honor; and Solomon his son reigned in
his place.
29 Now the acts of King David, first and last,
indeed they *are* written in the [1]book of Samuel the
seer, in the book of Nathan the prophet, and in the
book of Gad the seer,
30 with all his reign and his might, [a]and the
events that happened to him, to Israel, and to all
the kingdoms of the lands.

**24** [a]Eccl. 8:2 [1]Lit. *gave the hand*
**25** [a]1 Kin. 3:13; 2 Chr. 1:12; Eccl. 2:9
**27** [a]2 Sam. 5:4; 1 Kin. 2:11 [b]2 Sam. 5:5
**28** [a]Gen. 25:8 [b]1 Chr. 23:1
**29** [1]Lit. *words*
**30** [a]Dan. 2:21; 4:23, 25

*The Second Book of the*

# CHRONICLES

## *Solomon's Prayer for Wisdom*

**N**OW [a]Solomon the son of David was
strengthened in his kingdom, and [b]the
LORD his God *was* with him and [c]exalted
him exceedingly.
2 And Solomon spoke to all Israel, to [a]the captains of thousands and of hundreds, to the judges,
and to every leader in all Israel, the heads of the
fathers' *houses.*
3 Then Solomon, and all the assembly with him,
went to [1]the high place that *was* at [a]Gibeon; for
the tabernacle of meeting with God was there,
which Moses the servant of the LORD had [b]made
in the wilderness.
4 [a]But David had brought up the ark of God
from Kirjath Jearim to *the place* David had prepared for it, for he had pitched a tent for it at
Jerusalem.
5 Now [a]the bronze altar that [b]Bezalel the son of
Uri, the son of Hur, had made, [1]he put before the
tabernacle of the LORD; Solomon and the assembly sought Him *there.*
6 And Solomon went up there to the bronze
altar before the LORD, which *was* at the tabernacle of meeting, and [a]offered a thousand burnt
offerings on it.
**7** [a]On that night God appeared to Solomon, and
said to him, "Ask! What shall I give you?"
8 And Solomon said to God: "You have shown
great [a]mercy to David my father, and have made
me [b]king in his place.
9 "Now, O LORD God, let Your promise to David
my father be established, [a]for You have made me
king over a people like the [b]dust of the earth in
multitude.
10 [a]"Now give me wisdom and knowledge, that I
may [b]go out and come in before this people; for
who can judge this great people of Yours?"
11 [a]Then God said to Solomon: "Because this was
in your heart, and you have not asked riches or
wealth or honor or the life of your enemies, nor
have you asked long life—but have asked wisdom
and knowledge for yourself, that you may judge
My people over whom I have made you king—
12 "wisdom and knowledge *are* granted to you;
and I will give you riches and wealth and honor,
such as [a]none of the kings have had who *were*
before you, nor shall any after you have the like."
13 So Solomon came to Jerusalem from [1]the high
place that *was* at Gibeon, from before the tabernacle of meeting, and reigned over Israel.
14 [a]And Solomon gathered chariots and horsemen; he had one thousand four hundred chariots
and twelve thousand horsemen, whom he stationed in the chariot cities and with the king in
Jerusalem.
15 [a]Also the king made silver and gold as common in Jerusalem as stones, and he made cedars
as abundant as the sycamores which *are* in the
lowland.
16 [a]And Solomon had horses imported from
Egypt and Keveh; the king's merchants bought
them in Keveh at the *current* price.
17 They also acquired and imported from Egypt a
chariot for six hundred *shekels* of silver, and a
horse for one hundred and fifty; thus, [1]through
their agents, they exported them to all the kings
of the Hittites and the kings of Syria.

## *Solomon Prepares to Build the Temple*

**2** Then Solomon [a]determined to build a temple
for the name of the LORD, and a royal house
for himself.
2 [a]Solomon selected seventy thousand men to
bear burdens, eighty thousand to quarry *stone* in
the mountains, and three thousand six hundred to
oversee them.
**3** Then Solomon sent to [1]Hiram king of Tyre,
saying:

[a]As you have dealt with David my father,
and sent him cedars to build himself a house
to dwell in, *so deal with me.*
4 Behold, [a]I am building a temple for the name
of the LORD my God, to dedicate *it* to Him,
[b]to burn before Him [1]sweet incense, for [c]the
continual showbread, for [d]the burnt offerings
morning and evening, on the [e]Sabbaths, on
the New Moons, and on the [2]set feasts of the
LORD our God. This *is an ordinance* forever
to Israel.
5 And the temple which I build *will be* great,
for [a]our God is greater than all gods.
6 [a]But who is able to build Him a temple, since
heaven and the heaven of heavens cannot
contain Him? Who *am* I then, that I should

CHAPTER 1
**1** [a]1 Kin. 2:46 [b]Gen. 39:2 [c]1 Chr. 29:25
**2** [a]1 Chr. 27:1–34
**3** [a]1 Kin. 3:4 [b]Ex. 25—27; 35:4—36:38 [1]Place for worship
**4** [a]2 Sam. 6:2–17
**5** [a]Ex. 27:1, 2; 38:1, 2 [b]Ex. 31:2 [1]Some authorities *it was there*
**6** [a]1 Kin. 3:4
**7** [a]1 Kin. 3:5–14; 9:2
**8** [a]Ps. 18:50 [b]1 Chr. 28:5
**9** [a]2 Sam. 7:8–16 [b]Gen. 13:16
**10** [a]1 Kin. 3:9 [b]Deut. 31:2
**11** [a]1 Kin. 3:11–13
**12** [a]2 Chr. 9:22
**13** [1]Place for worship
**14** [a]1 Kin. 10:26
**15** [a]2 Chr. 9:27
**16** [a]1 Kin. 10:28; 22:36
**17** [1]Lit. *by their hands*

CHAPTER 2
**1** [a]1 Kin. 5:5
**2** [a]2 Chr. 2:18
**3** [a]1 Chr. 14:1 [1]Heb. *Huram;* cf. 1 Kin. 5:1
**4** [a]2 Chr. 2:1 [b]Ex. 30:7 [c]Ex. 25:30 [d]Ex. 29:38–42 [e]Num. 28:3, 9–11 [1]Lit. *incense of spices* [2]*appointed*
**5** [a]Ps. 135:5
**6** [a]1 Kin. 8:27

build Him a temple, except to burn sacrifice
before Him?
7 Therefore send me at once a man skillful to
work in gold and silver, in bronze and iron,
in purple and crimson and blue, who has skill
to engrave with the skillful men who are
with me in Judah and Jerusalem, [a]whom
David my father provided.
8 [a]Also send me cedar and cypress and algum
logs from Lebanon, for I know that your
servants have skill to cut timber in Lebanon;
and indeed my servants *will be* with your
servants,
9 to prepare timber for me in abundance, for
the [1]temple which I am about to build *shall
be* great and wonderful.
10 [a]And indeed I will give to your servants, the
woodsmen who cut timber, twenty thousand
kors of ground wheat, twenty thousand kors
of barley, twenty thousand baths of wine,
and twenty thousand baths of oil.

**11** Then Hiram king of Tyre answered in writing,
which he sent to Solomon:

[a]Because the LORD loves His people, He has
made you king over them.

12 [1]Hiram also said:

[a]Blessed *be* the LORD God of Israel, [b]who
made heaven and earth, for He has given
King David a wise son, endowed with
prudence and understanding, who will build a
temple for the LORD and a royal house for
himself!
13 And now I have sent a skillful man, endowed
with understanding, [1]Huram my [2]master
*craftsman*
14 [a](the son of a woman of the daughters of
Dan, and his father was a man of Tyre),
skilled to work in gold and silver, bronze and
iron, stone and wood, purple and blue, fine
linen and crimson, and to make any
engraving and to accomplish any plan which
may be given to him, with your skillful men
and with the skillful men of my lord David
your father.
15 Now therefore, the wheat, the barley, the oil,
and the wine which [a]my lord has spoken of,
let him send to his servants.
16 [a]And we will cut wood from Lebanon, as
much as you need; we will bring it to you in
rafts by sea to [1]Joppa, and you will carry it
up to Jerusalem.

**17** [a]Then Solomon numbered all the aliens who
*were* in the land of Israel, after the census in
which [b]David his father had numbered them; and
there were found to be one hundred and fifty-
three thousand six hundred.
18 And he made [a]seventy thousand of them bearers of burdens, eighty thousand stonecutters in
the mountain, and three thousand six hundred
overseers to make the people work.

## *Dimensions and Materials of the Temple*

**3** Now [a]Solomon began to build the house of the
LORD at [b]Jerusalem on Mount Moriah, where
[1]*the LORD* had appeared to his father David, at the
place that David had prepared on the threshing
floor of [c]Ornan[2] the Jebusite.
2 And he began to build on the second *day* of
the second month in the fourth year of his reign.
**3** This is the foundation [a]which Solomon laid for
building the house of God: The length *was* sixty
cubits (by cubits according to the former measure) and the width twenty cubits.
4 And the [a]vestibule that *was* in front *of* [1]*the
sanctuary* was twenty cubits long across the
width of the house, and the height *was* [2]one
hundred and twenty. He overlaid the inside with
pure gold.
5 [a]The larger [1]room he [b]paneled with cypress
which he overlaid with fine gold, and he carved
palm trees and chainwork on it.
6 And he decorated the house with precious
stones for beauty, and the gold *was* gold from
Parvaim.
7 He also overlaid the house—the beams and
doorposts, its walls and doors—with gold; and he
carved cherubim on the walls.
**8** And he made the [a]Most Holy Place. Its length
was according to the width of the house, twenty
cubits, and its width twenty cubits. He overlaid it
with six hundred talents of fine gold.
9 The weight of the nails *was* fifty shekels of
gold; and he overlaid the upper [a]area with gold.
10 [a]In the Most Holy Place he made two cherubim, fashioned by carving, and overlaid them with
gold.
11 The wings of the cherubim *were* twenty cubits
in *overall* length: one wing *of the one cherub was*
five cubits, touching the wall of the room, and the
other wing *was* five cubits, touching the wing of
the other cherub;
12 *one* wing of the other cherub *was* five cubits,
touching the wall of the room, and the other wing
*also was* five cubits, touching the wing of the
other cherub.
13 The wings of these cherubim spanned twenty
cubits overall. They stood on their feet, and they
faced inward.
14 And he made the [a]veil of blue, purple, crimson,
and fine linen, and wove cherubim into it.
**15** Also he made in front of the [1]temple [a]two
pillars [2]thirty-five cubits [3]high, and the capital that
*was* on the top of each of *them* was five cubits.
16 He made wreaths of chainwork, as in the inner
sanctuary, and put *them* on top of the pillars; and
he made [a]one hundred pomegranates, and put
*them* on the wreaths of chainwork.
17 Then he [a]set up the pillars before the temple,
one on the right hand and the other on the left; he
called the name of the one on the right hand
[1]Jachin, and the name of the one on the left [2]Boaz.

## *The Construction and Furniture of the Temple*

**4** Moreover he made [a]a bronze altar: twenty
cubits was its length, twenty cubits its width,
and ten cubits its height.
**2** [a]Then he made the [1]Sea of cast *bronze,* ten
cubits from one brim to the other; *it was* completely round. Its height *was* five cubits, and a line
of thirty cubits measured its circumference.
3 [a]And under it *was* the likeness of oxen encircling it all around, ten to a cubit, all the way
around the Sea. The oxen *were* cast in two rows,
when it was cast.
4 It stood on twelve [a]oxen: three looking toward
the north, three looking toward the west, three
looking toward the south, and three looking

**7** [a] 1 Chr. 22:15
**8** [a] 1 Kin. 5:6
**9** [1] Lit. *house*
**10** [a] 1 Kin. 5:11
**11** [a] 1 Kin. 10:9; 2 Chr. 9:8
**12** [a] 1 Kin. 5:7 [b] Gen. 1; 2; Acts 4:24; 14:15; Rev. 10:6 [1] Heb. *Huram;* cf. 1 Kin. 5:1
**13** [1] *Hiram,* 1 Kin. 7:13 [2] Lit. *father,* 1 Kin. 7:13, 14
**14** [a] 1 Kin. 7:13, 14
**15** [a] 2 Chr. 2:10
**16** [a] 1 Kin. 5:8, 9 [1] Heb. *Japho*
**17** [a] 1 Kin. 5:13; 2 Chr. 8:7, 8 [b] 1 Chr. 22:2
**18** [a] 2 Chr. 2:2

CHAPTER 3
**1** [a] 1 Kin. 6:1 [b] Gen. 22:2–14 [c] 1 Chr. 21:18; 22:1 [1] Lit. *He,* following MT, Vg.; LXX *the LORD;* Tg. *the Angel of the LORD* [2] *Araunah,* 2 Sam. 24:16
**3** [a] 1 Kin. 6:2; 1 Chr. 28:11–19
**4** [a] 1 Kin. 6:3; 1 Chr. 28:11 [1] *the holy place,* the main room of the temple, 1 Kin. 6:3 [2] So with MT, LXX, Vg.; Arab., some LXX mss., Syr. *twenty*
**5** [a] 1 Kin. 6:17 [b] 1 Kin. 6:15; Jer. 22:14 [1] Lit. *house*
**8** [a] Ex. 26:33; 1 Kin. 6:16
**9** [a] 1 Chr. 28:11
**10** [a] Ex. 25:18–20; 1 Kin. 6:23–28
**14** [a] Ex. 26:31; Matt. 27:51; Heb. 9:3
**15** [a] 1 Kin. 7:15–20; Jer. 52:21 [1] Lit. *house* [2] *eighteen,* 1 Kin. 7:15; 2 Kin. 25:17; Jer. 52:21 [3] Lit. *long*
**16** [a] 1 Kin. 7:20
**17** [a] 1 Kin. 7:21 [1] Lit. *He Shall Establish* [2] Lit. *In It Is Strength*

CHAPTER 4
**1** [a] Ex. 27:1, 2; 2 Kin. 16:14; Ezek. 43:13, 16
**2** [a] Ex. 30:17–21; 1 Kin. 7:23–26 [1] Great laver or basin
**3** [a] 1 Kin. 7:24–26
**4** [a] 1 Kin. 7:25

toward the east; the Sea *was set* upon them, and
all their back parts *pointed* inward.
5 It *was* a handbreadth thick; and its brim was
shaped like the brim of a cup, *like* a lily blossom. It
contained [1]three thousand baths.
**6** He also made [a]ten lavers, and put five on the
right side and five on the left, to wash in them;
such things as they offered for the burnt offering
they would wash in them, but the [1]Sea *was* for the
[b]priests to wash in.
7 [a]And he made ten lampstands of gold [b]accord-
ing to their design, and set *them* in the temple,
five on the right side and five on the left.
8 [a]He also made ten tables, and placed *them* in
the temple, five on the right side and five on the
left. And he made one hundred [b]bowls of gold.
**9** Furthermore [a]he made the court of the priests,
and the [b]great court and doors for the court; and
he overlaid these doors with bronze.
10 [a]He set the Sea on the right side, toward the
southeast.
**11** Then [a]Huram made the pots and the shovels
and the bowls. So Huram finished doing the work
that he was to do for King Solomon for the house
of God:
12 the two pillars and [a]the bowl-shaped capitals
*that were* on top of the two pillars; the two
networks covering the two bowl-shaped capitals
which *were* on top of the pillars;
13 [a]four hundred pomegranates for the two networks (two rows of pomegranates for each network, to cover the two bowl-shaped capitals that
*were* on the pillars);
14 he also made [a]carts and the lavers on the
carts;
15 one Sea and twelve oxen under it;
16 also the pots, the shovels, the forks—and all
their articles [a]Huram his [1]master *craftsman* made
of burnished bronze for King Solomon for the
house of the LORD.
17 In the plain of Jordan the king had them cast
in clay molds, between Succoth and [1]Zeredah.
18 [a]And Solomon had all these articles made in
such great abundance that the weight of the
bronze was not determined.
**19** Thus [a]Solomon had all the furnishings made
for the house of God: the altar of gold and the
tables on which *was* [b]the showbread;
20 the lampstands with their lamps of pure gold,
to burn [a]in the prescribed manner in front of the
inner sanctuary,
21 with [a]the flowers and the lamps and the wick-
trimmers of gold, of purest gold;
22 the trimmers, the bowls, the ladles, and the
censers of pure gold. As for the entry of the
[1]sanctuary, its inner doors to the Most Holy *Place*,
and the doors of the main hall of the temple, *were*
gold.

### *The Ark Brought into the Temple*

**5** So [a]all the work that Solomon had done for
the house of the LORD was finished; and Solomon brought in the things which his father David
had dedicated: the silver and the gold and all the
furnishings. And he put *them* in the treasuries of
the house of God.
**2** [a]Now Solomon assembled the elders of Israel
and all the heads of the tribes, the chief fathers of
the children of Israel, in Jerusalem, that they
might bring the ark of the covenant of the LORD
up [b]from the City of David, which *is* Zion.

**5** [1]About 8,000 gallons; *two thousand*, 1 Kin. 7:26
**6** [a]1 Kin. 7:38, 40 [b]Ex. 30:19–21 [1]Great basin
**7** [a]1 Kin. 7:49 [b]Ex. 25:31; 1 Chr. 28:12, 19
**8** [a]1 Kin. 7:48 [b]1 Chr. 28:17
**9** [a]1 Kin. 6:36 [b]2 Kin. 21:5
**10** [a]1 Kin. 7:39
**11** [a]1 Kin. 7:40–51
**12** [a]1 Kin. 7:41
**13** [a]1 Kin. 7:20
**14** [a]1 Kin. 7:27, 43
**16** [a]1 Kin. 7:45; 2 Chr. 2:13 [1]Lit. *father*
**17** [1]*Zaretan*, 1 Kin. 7:46
**18** [a]1 Kin. 7:47
**19** [a]1 Kin. 7:48–50 [b]Ex. 25:30
**20** [a]Ex. 27:20, 21
**21** [a]Ex. 25:31
**22** [1]Lit. *house*

CHAPTER 5
**1** [a]1 Kin. 7:51
**2** [a]1 Kin. 8:1–9; Ps. 47:9 [b]2 Sam. 6:12
**3** [a]1 Kin. 8:2 [b]Lev. 23:34; 2 Chr. 7:8–10
**4** [a]1 Chr. 15:2, 15
**7** [a]2 Chr. 4:20 [1]Lit. *house*
**9** [a]Ex. 25:13–15 [1]Lit. *it is*
**10** [a]Ex. 25:16; Deut. 10:2, 5; 2 Chr. 6:11; Heb. 9:4 [1]Or *where*
**11** [a]1 Chr. 24:1–5 [1]*consecrated*
**12** [a]Ex. 32:26; 1 Chr. 25:1–7 [b]1 Chr. 13:8; 15:16, 24
**13** [a]1 Chr. 16:34, 41; 2 Chr. 7:3; Ezra 3:11; Ps. 100:5; 106:1; 136; Jer. 33:11
**14** [a]Ex. 40:35; 1 Kin. 8:11; 2 Chr. 7:2; Ezek. 43:5 [1]Lit. *stand to minister*

CHAPTER 6
**1** [a]Ex. 19:9; 20:21; 1 Kin. 8:12–21 [b][Lev. 16:2]; Ps. 97:2
**2** [a]2 Sam. 7:13; 1 Chr. 17:12; 2 Chr. 7:12
**3** [a]2 Sam. 6:18
**4** [a]1 Chr. 17:5

3 [a]Therefore all the men of Israel assembled
with the king [b]at the feast, which *was* in the
seventh month.
4 So all the elders of Israel came, and the [a]Le-
vites took up the ark.
5 Then they brought up the ark, the tabernacle
of meeting, and all the holy furnishings that *were*
in the tabernacle. The priests and the Levites
brought them up.
6 Also King Solomon, and all the congregation
of Israel who were assembled with him before the
ark, were sacrificing sheep and oxen that could
not be counted or numbered for multitude.
7 Then the priests brought in the ark of the
covenant of the LORD to its place, into the [a]inner
sanctuary of the [1]temple, to the Most Holy *Place*,
under the wings of the cherubim.
8 For the cherubim spread *their* wings over the
place of the ark, and the cherubim overshadowed
the ark and its poles.
9 The poles extended so that the ends of the
[a]poles of the ark could be seen from *the holy
place*, in front of the inner sanctuary; but they
could not be seen from outside. And [1]they are
there to this day.
10 Nothing was in the ark except the two tablets
which Moses [a]put *there* at Horeb, [1]when the LORD
made *a covenant* with the children of Israel, when
they had come out of Egypt.
**11** And it came to pass when the priests came out
of the *Most* Holy *Place* (for all the priests who
*were* present had [1]sanctified themselves, without
keeping to their [a]divisions),
12 [a]and the Levites *who were* the singers, all
those of Asaph and Heman and Jeduthun, with
their sons and their brethren, stood at the east end
of the altar, clothed in white linen, having cymbals, stringed instruments and harps, [b]and with
them one hundred and twenty priests sounding
with trumpets—
13 indeed it came to pass, when the trumpeters
and singers *were* as one, to make one sound to be
heard in praising and thanking the LORD, and
when they lifted up their voice with the trumpets
and cymbals and instruments of music, and
praised the LORD, *saying:*

[a]"*For He is* good,
For His mercy *endures* forever,"

that the house, the house of the LORD, was filled
with a cloud,
14 so that the priests could not [1]continue ministering because of the cloud; [a]for the glory of the
LORD filled the house of God.

### *Solomon's Prayer of Dedication*

**6** Then [a]Solomon spoke:
"The LORD said He would dwell in the [b]dark
cloud.
2 I have surely built You an exalted house,
And [a]a place for You to dwell in forever."

**3** Then the king turned around and [a]blessed the
whole assembly of Israel, while all the assembly of
Israel was standing.
4 And he said: "Blessed *be* the LORD God of
Israel, who has fulfilled with His hands *what* He
spoke with His mouth to my father David, [a]saying,
5 'Since the day that I brought My people out of
the land of Egypt, I have chosen no city from any
tribe of Israel *in which* to build a house, that My

name might be there, nor did I choose any man to
be a ruler over My people Israel.
6 [a]'Yet I have chosen Jerusalem, that My name
may be there, and I [b]have chosen David to be over
My people Israel.'
7 "Now [a]it was in the heart of my father David
to build a [1]temple for the name of the LORD God of
Israel.
8 "But the LORD said to my father David,
'Whereas it was in your heart to build a temple for
My name, you did well in that it was in your heart.
9 'Nevertheless you shall not build the temple,
but your son who will come from your body, he
shall build the temple for My [a]name.'
10 "So the LORD has fulfilled His word which He
spoke, and I have filled the position of my father
David, and [a]sit on the throne of Israel, as the LORD
promised; and I have built the temple for the
name of the LORD God of Israel.
11 "And there I have put the ark, [a]in which *is* the
covenant of the LORD which He made with the
children of Israel."
**12** [a]Then [1]*Solomon* stood before the altar of the
LORD in the presence of all the assembly of Israel,
and spread out his hands
13 (for Solomon had made a bronze platform five
cubits long, five cubits wide, and three cubits
high, and had set it in the midst of the court; and
he stood on it, knelt down on his knees before all
the assembly of Israel, and spread out his hands
toward heaven);
14 and he said: "LORD God of Israel, [a]*there is* no
God in heaven or on earth like You, who keep
*Your* [b]covenant and mercy with Your servants
who walk before You with all their hearts.
15 [a]"You have kept what You promised Your
servant David my father; You have both spoken
with Your mouth and fulfilled *it* with Your hand,
as *it is* this day.
16 "Therefore, LORD God of Israel, now keep
what You promised Your servant David my father, saying, [a]'You shall not fail to have a man sit
before Me on the throne of Israel, [b]only if your
sons take heed to their way, that they walk in My
law as you have walked before Me.'
17 "And now, O LORD God of Israel, let Your
word come true, which You have spoken to Your
servant David.
**18** "But will God indeed dwell with men on the
earth? [a]Behold, heaven and the heaven of heavens
cannot contain You. How much less this [1]temple
which I have built!
19 "Yet regard the prayer of Your servant and his
supplication, O LORD my God, and listen to the cry
and the prayer which Your servant is praying
before You:
20 "that Your eyes may be [a]open toward this
temple day and night, toward the place where *You*
said *You would* put Your name, that You may
hear the prayer which Your servant makes
[b]toward this place.
21 "And may You hear the supplications of Your
servant and of Your people Israel, when they pray
toward this place. Hear from heaven Your dwelling place, and when You hear, [a]forgive.
**22** "If anyone sins against his neighbor, and is
forced to take an [a]oath, and comes *and* takes an
oath before Your altar in this temple,
23 "then hear from heaven, and act, and judge
Your servants, bringing retribution on the wicked
by bringing his way on his own head, and justifying the righteous by giving him according to his
[a]righteousness.
**24** "Or if Your people Israel are defeated before
an [a]enemy because they have sinned against You,
and return and confess Your name, and pray and
make supplication before You in this temple,
25 "then hear from heaven and forgive the sin of
Your people Israel, and bring them back to the
land which You gave to them and their fathers.
**26** "When the [a]heavens are shut up and there is
no rain because they have sinned against You,
when they pray toward this place and confess
Your name, and turn from their sin because You
afflict them,
27 "then hear *in* heaven, and forgive the sin of
Your servants, Your people Israel, that You may
teach them the good way in which they should
walk; and send rain on Your land which You have
given to Your people as an inheritance.
**28** "When there [a]is famine in the land, pestilence
or blight or mildew, locusts or grasshoppers; when
their enemies besiege them in the land of their
cities; whatever plague or whatever [b]sickness
*there is;*
29 "whatever prayer, whatever supplication is
*made* by anyone, or by all Your people Israel,
when each one knows his own burden and his
own grief, and spreads out his hands to this
temple:
30 "then hear from heaven Your dwelling place,
and forgive, and give to everyone according to all
his ways, whose heart You know (for You alone
[a]know the [b]hearts of the sons of men),
31 "that they may fear You, to walk in Your
ways as long as they live in the land which You
gave to our fathers.
**32** "Moreover, concerning a foreigner, [a]who is
not of Your people Israel, but has come from a far
country for the sake of Your great name and Your
mighty hand and Your outstretched arm, when
they come and pray in this temple;
33 "then hear from heaven Your dwelling place,
and do according to all for which the foreigner
calls to You, that all peoples of the earth may
know Your name and fear You, as *do* Your people
Israel, and that they may know that [1]this temple
which I have built is called by Your name.
**34** "When Your people go out to battle against
their enemies, wherever You send them, and
when they pray to You toward this city which
You have chosen and the temple which I have
built for Your name,
35 "then hear from heaven their prayer and their
supplication, and maintain their cause.
**36** "When they sin against You (for *there is* [a]no
one who does not sin), and You become angry
with them and deliver them to the enemy, and
they take them [b]captive to a land far or near;
37 "*yet* when they [1]come to themselves in the
land where they were carried captive, and repent,
and make supplication to You in the land of their
captivity, saying, 'We have sinned, we have done
wrong, and have committed wickedness';
38 "and *when* they return to You with all their
heart and with all their soul in the land of their
captivity, where they have been carried captive,
and pray toward their land which You gave to
their fathers, the [a]city which You have chosen,
and toward the temple which I have built for Your
name:
39 "then hear from heaven Your dwelling place

**6** [a]Deut. 12:5–7; 2 Chr. 12:13; Zech. 2:12 [b]1 Sam. 16:7–13; 1 Chr. 28:4
**7** [a]2 Sam. 7:2; 1 Chr. 17:1; 28:2; Ps. 132:1–5 [1]Lit. *house,* and so in vv. 8–10
**9** [a]1 Chr. 28:3–6
**10** [a]1 Kin. 2:12; 10:9
**11** [a]2 Chr. 5:7–10
**12** [a]1 Kin. 8:22; 2 Chr. 7:7–9 [1]Lit. *he*
**14** [a][Ex. 15:11; Deut. 4:39] [b][Deut. 7:9]
**15** [a]1 Chr. 22:9, 10
**16** [a]2 Sam. 7:12, 16; 1 Kin. 2:4; 6:12; 2 Chr. 7:18 [b]Ps. 132:12
**18** [a][2 Chr. 2:6; Is. 66:1; Acts 7:49] [1]Lit. *house*
**20** [a]2 Chr. 7:15 [b]Ps. 5:7; Dan. 6:10
**21** [a][Is. 43:25; 44:22; Mic. 7:18]
**22** [a]Ex. 22:8–11
**23** [a][Job 34:11]
**24** [a]2 Kin. 21:14, 15
**26** [a]Deut. 28:23, 24; 1 Kin. 17:1
**28** [a]2 Chr. 20:9 [b][Mic. 6:13]
**30** [a][1 Chr. 28:9; Prov. 21:2; 24:12] [b][1 Sam. 16:7]
**32** [a]John 12:20; Acts 8:27
**33** [1]Lit. *Your name is called upon this house*
**36** [a]Prov. 20:9; Eccl. 7:20; [Rom. 3:9, 19; 5:12; Gal. 3:10]; James 3:2; 1 John 1:8 [b]Deut. 28:63–68
**37** [1]Lit. *bring back to their hearts*
**38** [a]Dan. 6:10

their prayer and their supplications, and maintain
their cause, and forgive Your people who have
sinned against You.
40 "Now, my God, I pray, let Your eyes be [a]open
and *let* Your ears *be* attentive to the prayer *made*
in this place.

**41** "Now[a] therefore,
Arise, O LORD God, to Your [b]resting place,
You and the ark of Your strength.
Let Your priests, O LORD God,
be clothed with salvation,
And let Your saints [c]rejoice in goodness.

42 "O LORD God, do not turn away
the face of Your Anointed;
[a]Remember the mercies
of Your servant David."

## *God's Promise to Solomon*

**7** When [a]Solomon had finished praying, [b]fire
came down from heaven and consumed the
burnt offering and the sacrifices; and [c]the glory of
the LORD filled the [1]temple.
2 [a]And the priests could not enter the house of
the LORD, because the glory of the LORD had filled
the LORD's house.
3 When all the children of Israel saw how the
fire came down, and the glory of the LORD on the
temple, they bowed their faces to the ground on
the pavement, and worshiped and praised the
LORD, *saying:*

[a]"For *He is* good,
[b]For His mercy *endures* forever."

**4** [a]Then the king and all the people offered
sacrifices before the LORD.
5 King Solomon offered a sacrifice of twenty-
two thousand bulls and one hundred and twenty
thousand sheep. So the king and all the people
dedicated the house of God.
6 [a]And the priests attended to their services; the
Levites also with instruments of the music of
the LORD, which King David had made to praise
the LORD, saying, [b]"For His mercy *endures* forever," whenever David offered praise by their
[1]ministry. The priests sounded trumpets opposite
them, while all Israel stood.
7 Furthermore [a]Solomon consecrated the middle of the court that *was* in front of the house of
the LORD; for there he offered burnt offerings and
the fat of the peace offerings, because the bronze
altar which Solomon had made was not able to
receive the burnt offerings, the grain offerings,
and the fat.
**8** [a]At that time Solomon kept the feast seven
days, and all Israel with him, a very great assembly [b]from the entrance of Hamath to [c]the[1] Brook
of Egypt.
9 And on the eighth day they held a [a]sacred
assembly, for they observed the dedication of the
altar seven days, and the feast seven days.
10 [a]On the twenty-third day of the seventh
month he sent the people away to their tents,
joyful and glad of heart for the good that the
LORD had done for David, for Solomon, and for
His people Israel.
11 Thus [a]Solomon finished the house of the LORD
and the king's house; and Solomon successfully
accomplished all that came into his heart to make
in the house of the LORD and in his own house.
**12** Then the LORD [a]appeared to Solomon by
night, and said to him: "I have heard your prayer,
[b]and have chosen this [c]place for Myself as a house
of sacrifice.
13 [a]"When I shut up heaven and there is no rain,
or command the locusts to devour the land, or
send pestilence among My people,
14 "if My people who are [a]called by My name will
[b]humble themselves, and pray and seek My face,
and turn from their wicked ways, [c]then I will hear
from heaven, and will forgive their sin and heal
their land.
15 "Now [a]My eyes will be open and My ears
attentive to prayer *made* in this place.
16 "For now [a]I have chosen and [1]sanctified this
house, that My name may be there forever; and
[2]My eyes and [3]My heart will be there perpetually.
17 [a]"As for you, if you walk before Me as your
father David walked, and do according to all that I
have commanded you, and if you keep My statutes and My judgments,
18 "then I will establish the throne of your kingdom, as I covenanted with David your father,
saying, [a]'You shall not fail *to have* a man as ruler
in Israel.'
**19** [a]"But if you turn away and forsake My statutes and My commandments which I have set
before you, and go and serve other gods, and
worship them,
20 [a]"then I will uproot them from My land which
I have given them; and this house which I have
[1]sanctified for My name I will cast out of My sight,
and will make it a proverb and a [b]byword among
all peoples.
21 "And *as for* [a]this [1]house, which [2]is exalted,
everyone who passes by it will be [b]astonished and
say, [c]'Why has the LORD done thus to this land
and this house?'
22 "Then they will answer, 'Because they forsook
the LORD God of their fathers, who brought them
out of the land of Egypt, and embraced other
gods, and worshiped them and served them; therefore He has brought all this calamity on them.' "

## *Solomon's Activities and Fame*

**8** It [a]came to pass at the end of [b]twenty years,
when Solomon had built the house of the
LORD and his own house,
2 that the cities which [1]Hiram had given to
Solomon, Solomon built them; and he settled the
children of Israel there.
3 And Solomon went to Hamath Zobah and
seized it.
4 [a]He also built Tadmor in the wilderness, and
all the storage cities which he built in [b]Hamath.
5 He built Upper Beth Horon and [a]Lower Beth
Horon, fortified cities *with* walls, gates, and bars,
6 also Baalath and all the storage cities that
Solomon had, and all the chariot cities and the
cities of the cavalry, and all that Solomon [a]desired
to build in Jerusalem, in Lebanon, and in all the
land of his dominion.
**7** [a]All the people *who were* left of the Hittites,
Amorites, Perizzites, Hivites, and Jebusites, who
*were* not of Israel—
8 that is, their descendants who were left in the
land after them, whom the children of Israel did
not destroy—from these Solomon raised forced
labor, as it is to this day.
9 But Solomon did not make the children of
Israel [1]servants for his work. Some *were* men of

**40** [a]2 Chr. 6:20
**41** [a]Ps. 132:8–10, 16 [b]1 Chr. 28:2 [c]Neh. 9:25
**42** [a]2 Sam. 7:15; Ps. 89:49; 132:1, 8–10; Is. 55:3

CHAPTER 7
**1** [a]1 Kin. 8:54 [b]Lev. 9:24; Judg. 6:21; 1 Kin. 18:38; 1 Chr. 21:26 [c]1 Kin. 8:10, 11 [1]Lit. *house*
**2** [a]2 Chr. 5:14
**3** [a]2 Chr. 5:13; Ps. 106:1; 136:1 [b]1 Chr. 16:41; 2 Chr. 20:21
**4** [a]1 Kin. 8:62, 63
**6** [a]1 Chr. 15:16 [b]2 Chr. 5:12 [1]Lit. *hand*
**7** [a]1 Kin. 8:64–66; 9:3
**8** [a]1 Kin. 8:65 [b]1 Kin. 4:21, 24; 2 Kin. 14:25 [c]Josh. 13:3 [1]The *Shihor,* 1 Chr. 13:5
**9** [a]Lev. 23:36
**10** [a]1 Kin. 8:66
**11** [a]1 Kin. 9:1
**12** [a]1 Kin. 3:5; 11:9 [b]Deut. 12:5, 11 [c]2 Chr. 6:20
**13** [a]Deut. 28:23, 24; 1 Kin. 17:1; 2 Chr. 6:26–28
**14** [a]Deut. 28:10; [Is. 43:7] [b]2 Chr. 12:6, 7; [James 4:10] [c]2 Chr. 6:27, 30
**15** [a]2 Chr. 6:20, 40
**16** [a]1 Kin. 9:3; 2 Chr. 6:6 [1]*set apart* [2]My attention [3]My concern
**17** [a]1 Kin. 9:4
**18** [a]2 Sam. 7:12–16; 1 Kin. 2:4; 2 Chr. 6:16
**19** [a]Lev. 26:14, 33; [Deut. 28:15, 36]
**20** [a]Deut. 28:63–68; 2 Kin. 25:1–7 [b]Ps. 44:14 [1]*set apart*
**21** [a]2 Kin. 25:9 [b]2 Chr. 29:8 [c][Deut. 29:24, 25; Jer. 22:8, 9] [1]Temple [2]Or *was*

CHAPTER 8
**1** [a]1 Kin. 9:10–14 [b]1 Kin. 6:38—7:1
**2** [1]Heb. *Huram,* 2 Chr. 2:3
**4** [a]1 Kin. 9:17, 18 [b]1 Chr. 18:3, 9
**5** [a]1 Chr. 7:24
**6** [a]2 Chr. 7:11
**7** [a]Gen. 15:18–21; 1 Kin. 9:20
**9** [1]*slaves*

war, captains of his officers, captains of his chariots, and his cavalry.
10 And others *were* chiefs of the officials of King
Solomon: [a]two hundred and fifty, who ruled over
the people.
11 Now Solomon [a]brought the daughter of Pharaoh up from the City of David to the house he
had built for her, for he said, "My wife shall not
dwell in the house of David king of Israel, because
*the places* to which the ark of the LORD has come
are holy."
12 Then Solomon offered burnt offerings to the
LORD on the altar of the LORD which he had built
before the vestibule,
13 according to the [a]daily rate, offering according
to the commandment of Moses, for the Sabbaths,
the New Moons, and the [b]three appointed yearly
[c]feasts—the Feast of Unleavened Bread, the Feast
of Weeks, and the Feast of Tabernacles.
14 And, according to the [1]order of David his
father, he appointed the [a]divisions of the priests
for their service, [b]the Levites for their duties (to
praise and serve before the priests) as the duty of
each day required, and the [c]gatekeepers by their
divisions at each gate; for so David the man of
God had commanded.
15 They did not depart from the command of the
king to the priests and Levites concerning any
matter or concerning the [a]treasuries.
16 Now all the work of Solomon was well-
ordered [1]from the day of the foundation of the
house of the LORD until it was finished. So the
house of the LORD was completed.
17 Then Solomon went to [a]Ezion Geber and
[1]Elath on the seacoast, in the land of Edom.
18 [a]And Hiram sent him ships by the hand of his
servants, and servants who knew the sea. They
went with the servants of Solomon to [b]Ophir, and
acquired four hundred and fifty talents of gold
from there, and brought it to King Solomon.

### *The Queen of Sheba Visits Solomon*

**9** Now [a]when the queen of Sheba heard of the
fame of Solomon, she came to Jerusalem to
test Solomon with hard questions, *having* a very
great retinue, camels that bore spices, gold in
abundance, and precious stones; and when she
came to Solomon, she spoke with him about all
that was in her heart.
2 So Solomon answered all her questions; there
was nothing so difficult for Solomon that he could
not explain it to her.
3 And when the queen of Sheba had seen the
wisdom of Solomon, the house that he had built,
4 the food on his table, the seating of his servants, the service of his waiters and their apparel,
his [a]cupbearers and their apparel, and his entryway by which he went up to the house of the
LORD, there was no more spirit in her.
5 Then she said to the king: "*It was* a true
report which I heard in my own land about your
words and your wisdom.
6 "However I did not believe their words until I
came and saw with my own eyes; and indeed the
half of the greatness of your wisdom was not told
me. You exceed the fame of which I heard.
7 "Happy *are* your men and happy *are* these
your servants, who stand continually before you
and hear your wisdom!
8 "Blessed be the LORD your God, who delighted
in you, setting you on His throne *to be* king for
the LORD your God! Because your God has [a]loved
Israel, to establish them forever, therefore He
made you king over them, to do justice and
righteousness."
9 And she gave the king one hundred and
twenty talents of gold, spices in great abundance,
and precious stones; there never were any spices
such as those the queen of Sheba gave to King
Solomon.
10 Also, the servants of Hiram and the servants
of Solomon, [a]who brought gold from Ophir,
brought [1]algum wood and precious stones.
11 And the king made walkways *of* the [1]algum
wood for the house of the LORD and for the king's
house, also harps and stringed instruments for
singers; and there were none such *as these* seen
before in the land of Judah.
12 Now King Solomon gave to the queen of
Sheba all she desired, whatever she asked, *much
more* than she had brought to the king. So she
turned and went to her own country, she and her
servants.
13 [a]The weight of gold that came to Solomon
yearly was six hundred and sixty-six talents of
gold,
14 besides *what* the traveling merchants and
traders brought. And all the kings of Arabia and
governors of the country brought gold and silver
to Solomon.
15 And King Solomon made two hundred large
shields of hammered gold; six hundred *shekels* of
hammered gold went into each shield.
16 *He* also *made* three hundred shields of hammered gold; [1]three hundred *shekels* of gold went
into each shield. The king put them in the [a]House
of the Forest of Lebanon.
17 Moreover the king made a great throne of
ivory, and overlaid it with pure gold.
18 The throne *had* six steps, with a footstool of
gold, *which were* fastened to the throne; there
were [1]armrests on either side of the place of the
seat, and two lions stood beside the armrests.
19 Twelve lions stood there, one on each side of
the six steps; nothing like *this* had been made for
any *other* kingdom.
20 All King Solomon's drinking vessels *were*
gold, and all the vessels of the House of the Forest
of Lebanon *were* pure gold. Not *one was* silver, for
this was accounted as nothing in the days of
Solomon.
21 For the king's ships went to [a]Tarshish with the
servants of [1]Hiram. Once every three years the
[2]merchant ships came, bringing gold, silver, ivory,
apes, and [3]monkeys.
22 So King Solomon surpassed all the kings of
the earth in riches and wisdom.
23 And all the kings of the earth sought the
presence of Solomon to hear his wisdom, which
God had put in his heart.
24 Each man brought his present: articles of
silver and gold, garments, [a]armor, spices, horses,
and mules, at a set rate year by year.
25 Solomon [a]had four thousand stalls for horses
and chariots, and twelve thousand horsemen
whom he stationed in the chariot cities and with
the king at Jerusalem.
26 [a]So he reigned over all the kings [b]from [1]the
River to the land of the Philistines, as far as the
border of Egypt.
27 [a]The king made silver *as common* in Jerusa-

**10** [a]1 Kin. 9:23
**11** [a]1 Kin. 3:1; 7:8; 9:24; 11:1
**13** [a]Ex. 29:38–42; Num. 28:3, 9, 11, 26; 29:1 [b]Ex. 23:14–17; 34:22, 23; Deut. 16:16 [c]Lev. 23:1–44
**14** [a]1 Chr. 24:3 [b]1 Chr. 25:1 [c]1 Chr. 9:17; 26:1 [1]*ordinance*
**15** [a]1 Chr. 26:20–28
**16** [1]So with LXX, Syr., Vg.; MT *as far as*
**17** [a]1 Kin. 9:26; 2 Chr. 20:36 [1]Heb. *Eloth,* 2 Kin. 14:22
**18** [a]1 Kin. 9:27; 2 Chr. 9:10, 13 [b]1 Chr. 29:4

CHAPTER 9

**1** [a]1 Kin. 10:1; Ps. 72:10; [Matt. 12:42; Luke 11:31]
**4** [a]Neh. 1:11
**8** [a]Deut. 7:8; 2 Chr. 2:11; [Ps. 44:3]
**10** [a]2 Chr. 8:18 [1]*almug,* 1 Kin. 10:11, 12
**11** [1]*almug,* 1 Kin. 10:11, 12
**13** [a]1 Kin. 10:14–29
**16** [a]1 Kin. 7:2 [1]*three minas,* 1 Kin. 10:17
**18** [1]Lit. *hands*
**21** [a]2 Chr. 20:36, 37; Ps. 72:10 [1]Heb. *Huram;* cf. 1 Kin. 10:22 [2]Lit. *ships of Tarshish,* deep-sea vessels [3]Or *peacocks*
**24** [a]1 Kin. 20:11
**25** [a]Deut. 17:16; 1 Kin. 4:26; 10:26; 2 Chr. 1:14; Is. 2:7
**26** [a]1 Kin. 4:21 [b]Gen. 15:18; Ps. 72:8 [1]The Euphrates
**27** [a]1 Kin. 10:27

lem as stones, and he made cedar trees [b]as abundant as the sycamores which *are* in the lowland.
28 [a]And they brought horses to Solomon from
Egypt and from all lands.
**29** [a]Now the rest of the acts of Solomon, first and
last, *are* they not written in the book of Nathan
the prophet, in the prophecy of [b]Ahijah the Shilonite, and in the visions of [c]Iddo the seer concerning Jeroboam the son of Nebat?
30 [a]Solomon reigned in Jerusalem over all Israel
forty years.
31 Then Solomon [1]rested with his fathers, and
was buried in the City of David his father. And
Rehoboam his son reigned in his place.

### *Rehoboam Succeeds Solomon*

**10** And [a]Rehoboam went to Shechem, for all
Israel had gone to Shechem to make him
king.
2 So it happened, when Jeroboam the son of
Nebat heard *it* (he was in Egypt, [a]where he had
fled from the presence of King Solomon), that
Jeroboam returned from Egypt.
3 Then they sent for him and called him. And
Jeroboam and all Israel came and spoke to Rehoboam, saying,
4 "Your father made our yoke heavy; now
therefore, lighten the burdensome service of your
father and his heavy yoke which he put on us, and
we will serve you."
5 So he said to them, "Come back to me after
three days." And the people departed.
**6** Then King Rehoboam consulted the elders
who stood before his father Solomon while he still
lived, saying, "How do you advise *me* to answer
these people?"
7 And they spoke to him, saying, "If you are
kind to these people, and please them, and speak
good words to them, they will be your servants
forever."
8 [a]But he rejected the advice which the elders
had given him, and consulted the young men who
had grown up with him, who stood before him.
9 And he said to them, "What advice do you
give? How should we answer this people who
have spoken to me, saying, 'Lighten the yoke
which your father put on us'?"
10 Then the young men who had grown up with
him spoke to him, saying, "Thus you should speak
to the people who have spoken to you, saying,
'Your father made our yoke heavy, but you make
*it* lighter on us'—thus you shall say to them: 'My
little *finger* shall be thicker than my father's waist!
11 'And now, whereas my father put a heavy
yoke on you, I will add to your yoke; my father
chastised you with whips, but I *will chastise you*
with [1]scourges!' "
**12** So [a]Jeroboam and all the people came to
Rehoboam on the third day, as the king had
directed, saying, "Come back to me the third
day."
13 Then the king answered them roughly. King
Rehoboam rejected the advice of the elders,
14 and he spoke to them according to the advice
of the young men, saying, [1]"My father made your
yoke heavy, but I will add to it; my father chastised you with whips, but I *will chastise you* with
[2]scourges!"
15 So the king did not listen to the people; [a]for
the turn *of events* was from God, that the LORD
might fulfill His [b]word, which He had spoken by

**27** [b]2 Chr. 1:15–17
**28** [a]1 Kin. 10:28; 2 Chr. 1:16
**29** [a]1 Kin. 11:41 [b]1 Kin. 11:29 [c]2 Chr. 12:15; 13:22
**30** [a]1 Kin. 4:21; 11:42, 43; 1 Chr. 29:28
**31** [1]Died and joined his ancestors

CHAPTER 10
**1** [a]1 Kin. 12:1–20
**2** [a]1 Kin. 11:40
**8** [a]1 Kin. 12:8–11
**11** [1]Scourges with points or barbs, lit. *scorpions*
**12** [a]1 Kin. 12:12–14
**14** [1]So with many Heb. mss., LXX, Syr., Vg. (cf. v. 10, 1 Kin. 12:14); MT *I* [2]Lit. *scorpions*
**15** [a]Judg. 14:4; 1 Chr. 5:22; 2 Chr. 11:4; 22:7 [b]1 Kin. 11:29–39
**19** [a]1 Kin. 12:19

CHAPTER 11
**1** [a]1 Kin. 12:21–24
**2** [a]1 Chr. 12:5; 2 Chr. 12:15
**14** [a]Num. 35:2–5 [b]1 Kin. 12:28–33; 2 Chr. 13:9
**15** [a]1 Kin. 12:31; 13:33; 14:9; [Hos. 13:2] [b][Lev. 17:7; 1 Cor. 10:20] [c]1 Kin. 12:28 [1]Places for pagan worship
**16** [a]2 Chr. 14:7 [b]2 Chr. 15:9, 10; 30:11, 18 [1]Lit. *them*
**17** [a]2 Chr. 12:1, 13

the hand of Ahijah the Shilonite to Jeroboam the
son of Nebat.
**16** Now when all Israel *saw* that the king did not
listen to them, the people answered the king,
saying:

> "What share have we in David?
> *We have* no inheritance in the son of Jesse.
> Every man to your tents, O Israel!
> Now see to your own house, O David!"

So all Israel departed to their tents.
17 But Rehoboam reigned over the children of
Israel who dwelt in the cities of Judah.
18 Then King Rehoboam sent Hadoram, who *was*
in charge of revenue; but the children of Israel
stoned him with stones, and he died. Therefore
King Rehoboam mounted *his* chariot in haste to
flee to Jerusalem.
19 [a]So Israel has been in rebellion against the
house of David to this day.

### *Rehoboam's Reign in Judah*

**11** Now [a]when Rehoboam came to Jerusalem,
he assembled from the house of Judah and
Benjamin one hundred and eighty thousand chosen *men* who were warriors, to fight against
Israel, that he might restore the kingdom to
Rehoboam.
**2** But the word of the LORD came [a]to Shemaiah
the man of God, saying,
3 "Speak to Rehoboam the son of Solomon, king
of Judah, and to all Israel in Judah and Benjamin,
saying,
4 'Thus says the LORD: "You shall not go up or
fight against your brethren! Let every man return
to his house, for this thing is from Me." ' " Therefore they obeyed the words of the LORD, and
turned back from attacking Jeroboam.
**5** So Rehoboam dwelt in Jerusalem, and built
cities for defense in Judah.
6 And he built Bethlehem, Etam, Tekoa,
7 Beth Zur, Sochoh, Adullam,
8 Gath, Mareshah, Ziph,
9 Adoraim, Lachish, Azekah,
10 Zorah, Aijalon, and Hebron, which are in
Judah and Benjamin, fortified cities.
11 And he fortified the strongholds, and put
captains in them, and stores of food, oil, and wine.
12 Also in every city *he put* shields and spears,
and made them very strong, having Judah and
Benjamin on his side.
**13** And from all their territories the priests and
the Levites who *were* in all Israel took their stand
with him.
14 For the Levites left [a]their common-lands and
their possessions and came to Judah and Jerusalem, for [b]Jeroboam and his sons had rejected them
from serving as priests to the LORD.
15 [a]Then he appointed for himself priests for the
[1]high places, for [b]the demons, and [c]the calf idols
which he had made.
16 [a]And after [1]*the Levites left*, those from all the
tribes of Israel, such as set their heart to seek the
LORD God of Israel, [b]came to Jerusalem to sacrifice to the LORD God of their fathers.
17 So they [a]strengthened the kingdom of Judah,
and made Rehoboam the son of Solomon strong
for three years, because they walked in the way of
David and Solomon for three years.
**18** Then Rehoboam took for himself as wife
Mahalath the daughter of Jerimoth the son of

David, *and of* Abihail the daughter of [a]Eliah the
son of Jesse.
19 And she bore him children: Jeush, Shamariah,
and Zaham.
20 After her he took [a]Maachah the [1]granddaugh-
ter of [b]Absalom; and she bore him [c]Abijah, Attai,
Ziza, and Shelomith.
21 Now Rehoboam loved Maachah the granddaughter of Absalom more than all his [a]wives and
his concubines; for he took eighteen wives and
sixty concubines, and begot twenty-eight sons
and sixty daughters.
22 And Rehoboam [a]appointed [b]Abijah the son of
Maachah as chief, *to be* leader among his brothers; for he *intended* to make him king.
23 He dealt wisely, and [1]dispersed some of his
sons throughout all the territories of Judah and
Benjamin, to every [a]fortified city; and he gave
them provisions in abundance. He also sought
many wives *for them.*

## *Egypt Invades Judah*

**12** Now [a]it came to pass, when Rehoboam
had established the kingdom and had
strengthened himself, that [b]he forsook the law of
the LORD, and all Israel along with him.
2 [a]And it happened in the fifth year of King
Rehoboam *that* Shishak king of Egypt came up
against Jerusalem, because they had transgressed
against the LORD,
3 with twelve hundred chariots, sixty thousand
horsemen, and people without number who came
with him out of Egypt—[a]the Lubim and the Suk-
kiim and the Ethiopians.
4 And he took the fortified cities of Judah and
came to Jerusalem.
5 Then [a]Shemaiah the prophet came to Rehoboam and the leaders of Judah, who were gathered together in Jerusalem because of Shishak,
and said to them, "Thus says the LORD: 'You have
forsaken Me, and therefore I also have left you in
the hand of Shishak.' "
6 So the leaders of Israel and the king [a]humbled
themselves; and they said, [b]"The LORD *is* righteous."
7 Now when the LORD saw that they humbled
themselves, [a]the word of the LORD came to
Shemaiah, saying, "They have humbled themselves; *therefore* I will not destroy them, but I will
grant them some deliverance. My wrath shall not
be poured out on Jerusalem by the hand of Shishak.
8 "Nevertheless [a]they will be his servants, that
they may distinguish [b]My service from the service
of the kingdoms of the nations."
9 [a]So Shishak king of Egypt came up against
Jerusalem, and took away the treasures of the
house of the LORD and the treasures of the king's
house; he took everything. He also carried away
the gold shields which Solomon had [b]made.
10 Then King Rehoboam made bronze shields in
their place, and committed *them* [a]to the hands of
the captains of the guard, who guarded the doorway of the king's house.
11 And whenever the king entered the house of
the LORD, the guard would go and bring them out;
then they would take them back into the guardroom.
12 When he humbled himself, the wrath of the
LORD turned from him, so as not to destroy *him*
completely; and things also went well in Judah.

18 [a]1 Sam. 16:6
20 [a]2 Chr. 13:2 [b]1 Kin. 15:2 [c]1 Kin. 14:31 [1]Lit. *daughter*, but in the broader sense of granddaughter
21 [a]Deut. 17:17
22 [a]Deut. 21:15–17 [b]2 Chr. 13:1
23 [a]2 Chr. 11:5 [1]*distributed*

CHAPTER 12
1 [a]2 Chr. 11:17 [b]1 Kin. 14:22–24
2 [a]1 Kin. 11:40; 14:25
3 [a]2 Chr. 16:8; Nah. 3:9
5 [a]2 Chr. 11:2
6 [a][James 4:10] [b]Ex. 9:27; [Dan. 9:14]
7 [a]1 Kin. 21:28, 29
8 [a]Is. 26:13 [b][Deut. 28:47, 48]
9 [a]1 Kin. 14:25, 26 [b]1 Kin. 10:16, 17; 2 Chr. 9:15, 16
10 [a]1 Kin. 14:27
13 [a]1 Kin. 14:21 [b]2 Chr. 6:6 [c]1 Kin. 11:1, 5
15 [a]2 Chr. 9:29; 13:22 [b]1 Kin. 14:30
16 [a]2 Chr. 11:20–22 [1]Died and joined his ancestors [2]*Abijam,* 1 Kin. 14:31

CHAPTER 13
1 [a]1 Kin. 15:1 [b]1 Kin. 12:17
2 [1]*Maacah,* 1 Kin. 15:2; 2 Chr. 11:20, 21
4 [a]Josh. 18:22
5 [a]2 Sam. 7:8–16 [b]Lev. 2:13; Num. 18:19
6 [a]1 Kin. 11:28; 12:20
7 [a]Judg. 9:4 [b]2 Chr. 12:13
8 [a]1 Kin. 12:28; 14:9; 2 Chr. 11:15; [Hos. 8:4–6]
9 [a]2 Chr. 11:13–15 [b]Ex. 29:29–33 [c]Jer. 2:11; 5:7
10 [a]Josh. 24:15
11 [a]Ex. 29:38; 2 Chr. 2:4 [b]Ex. 25:30; Lev. 24:5–9 [c]Ex. 27:20, 21; Lev. 24:2, 3
12 [a]Josh. 5:13–15; [Heb. 2:10] [b][Num. 10:8–10]

13 Thus King Rehoboam strengthened himself in
Jerusalem and reigned. Now [a]Rehoboam *was*
forty-one years old when he became king; and he
reigned seventeen years in Jerusalem, [b]the city
which the LORD had chosen out of all the tribes of
Israel, to put His name there. His mother's name
*was* Naamah, an [c]Ammonitess.
14 And he did evil, because he did not prepare his
heart to seek the LORD.
15 The acts of Rehoboam, first and last, *are* they
not written in the book of Shemaiah the prophet,
[a]and of Iddo the seer concerning genealogies?
[b]And *there were* wars between Rehoboam and
Jeroboam all their days.
16 So Rehoboam [1]rested with his fathers, and was
buried in the City of David. Then [a]Abijah[2] his son
reigned in his place.

## *The War Between Abijah and Jeroboam*

**13** In [a]the eighteenth year of King Jeroboam,
Abijah became king over [b]Judah.
2 He reigned three years in Jerusalem. His
mother's name *was* [1]Michaiah the daughter of
Uriel of Gibeah. And there was war between
Abijah and Jeroboam.
3 Abijah set the battle in order with an army of
valiant warriors, four hundred thousand choice
men. Jeroboam also drew up in battle formation
against him with eight hundred thousand choice
men, mighty men of valor.
4 Then Abijah stood on Mount [a]Zemaraim,
which *is* in the mountains of Ephraim, and said,
"Hear me, Jeroboam and all Israel:
5 "Should you not know that the LORD God of
Israel [a]gave the dominion over Israel to David
forever, to him and his sons, [b]by a covenant of
salt?
6 "Yet Jeroboam the son of Nebat, the servant
of Solomon the son of David, rose up and [a]rebelled
against his lord.
7 "Then [a]worthless rogues gathered to him, and
strengthened themselves against Rehoboam the
son of Solomon, when Rehoboam was [b]young and
inexperienced and could not withstand them.
8 "And now you think to withstand the kingdom of the LORD, which is in the hand of the sons
of David; and you *are* a great multitude, and with
you are the gold calves which Jeroboam [a]made for
you as gods.
9 [a]"Have you not cast out the priests of the
LORD, the sons of Aaron, and the Levites, and
made for yourselves priests, like the peoples of
*other* lands, [b]so that whoever comes to consecrate
himself with a young bull and seven rams may be
a priest of [c]*things that are* not gods?
10 "But as for us, the LORD *is* our [a]God, and we
have not forsaken Him; and the priests who
minister to the LORD *are* the sons of Aaron, and
the Levites *attend* to *their* duties.
11 [a]"And they burn to the LORD every morning
and every evening burnt sacrifices and sweet
incense; *they* also *set* the [b]showbread *in order on*
the pure *gold* table, and the lampstand of gold
with its lamps [c]to burn every evening; for we keep
the command of the LORD our God, but you have
forsaken Him.
12 "Now look, God Himself is with us as *our*
[a]head, [b]and His priests with sounding trumpets to
sound the alarm against you. O children of Israel,
do not fight against the LORD God of your fathers,
for you shall not prosper!"

**13** But Jeroboam caused an ambush to go around
behind them; so they were in front of Judah, and
the ambush *was* behind them.
14 And when Judah looked around, to their surprise the battle line *was* at both front and rear;
and they [a]cried out to the LORD, and the priests
sounded the trumpets.
15 Then the men of Judah gave a shout; and as
the men of Judah shouted, it happened that God
[a]struck Jeroboam and all Israel before Abijah and
Judah.
16 And the children of Israel fled before Judah,
and God delivered them into their hand.
17 Then Abijah and his people struck them with
a great slaughter; so five hundred thousand choice
men of Israel fell slain.
18 Thus the children of Israel were subdued at
that time; and the children of Judah prevailed,
[a]because they relied on the LORD God of their
fathers.
19 And Abijah pursued Jeroboam and took cities
from him: Bethel with its villages, Jeshanah with
its villages, and [a]Ephrain[1] with its villages.
20 So Jeroboam did not recover strength again in
the days of Abijah; and the LORD [a]struck him, and
[b]he died.
**21** But Abijah grew mighty, married fourteen
wives, and begot twenty-two sons and sixteen
daughters.
22 Now the rest of the acts of Abijah, his ways,
and his sayings *are* written in [a]the [1]annals of the
prophet Iddo.

## *Asa Reigns over Judah*

**14** So Abijah rested with his fathers, and they
buried him in the City of David. Then [a]Asa
his son reigned in his place. In his days the land
was quiet for ten years.
2 Asa did *what was* good and right in the eyes
of the LORD his God,
3 for he removed the altars of the foreign *gods*
and [a]the [1]high places, and [b]broke down the *sacred*
pillars [c]and cut down the wooden images.
4 He commanded Judah to [a]seek the LORD God
of their fathers, and to observe the law and the
commandment.
5 He also removed the [1]high places and the
incense altars from all the cities of Judah, and the
kingdom was quiet under him.
6 And he built fortified cities in Judah, for the
land had rest; he had no war in those years,
because the LORD had given him [a]rest.
7 Therefore he said to Judah, "Let us build these
cities and make walls around *them,* and towers,
gates, and bars, *while* the land *is* yet before us,
because we have sought the LORD our God; we
have sought *Him,* and He has given us rest on
every side." So they built and prospered.
8 And Asa had an army of three hundred thousand from Judah who carried [1]shields and spears,
and from Benjamin two hundred and eighty thousand men who carried shields and drew [a]bows; all
these *were* mighty men of [b]valor.
**9** [a]Then Zerah the Ethiopian came out against
them with an army of a million men and three
hundred chariots, and he came to [b]Mareshah.
10 So Asa went out against him, and they set the
troops in battle array in the Valley of Zephathah
at Mareshah.
11 And Asa [a]cried out to the LORD his God, and
said, "LORD, *it is* [b]nothing for You to help, whether
with many or with those who have no power; help
us, O LORD our God, for we rest on You, and [c]in
Your name we go against this multitude. O LORD,
You *are* our God; do not let man prevail against
You!"
**12** So the LORD [a]struck the Ethiopians before Asa
and Judah, and the Ethiopians fled.
13 And Asa and the people who *were* with him
pursued them to [a]Gerar. So the Ethiopians were
overthrown, and they could not recover, for they
were broken before the LORD and His army. And
they carried away very much [1]spoil.
14 Then they defeated all the cities around Gerar,
for [a]the fear of the LORD came upon them; and
they plundered all the cities, for there was exceedingly much [1]spoil in them.
15 They also [1]attacked the livestock enclosures,
and carried off sheep and camels in abundance,
and returned to Jerusalem.

## *The Reforms of Asa*

**15** Now [a]the Spirit of God came upon Azariah
the son of Oded.
2 And he went out [1]to meet Asa, and said to
him: "Hear me, Asa, and all Judah and Benjamin.
[a]The LORD *is* with you while you are with Him. [b]If
you seek Him, He will be found by you; but [c]if you
forsake Him, He will forsake you.
3 [a]"For a long time Israel *has been* without the
true God, without a [b]teaching priest, and without
[c]law;
4 "but [a]when in their trouble they turned to the
LORD God of Israel, and sought Him, He was
found by them.
5 "And in those times *there was* no peace to the
one who went out, nor to the one who came in,
but great turmoil *was* on all the inhabitants of the
lands.
6 [a]"So nation was [1]destroyed by nation, and city
by city, for God troubled them with every adversity.
7 "But you, be strong and do not let your hands
be weak, for your work shall be rewarded!"
**8** And when Asa heard these words and the
prophecy of [1]Oded the prophet, he took courage,
and removed the abominable idols from all the
land of Judah and Benjamin and from the cities
[a]which he had taken in the mountains of Ephraim;
and he restored the altar of the LORD that *was*
before the vestibule of the LORD.
9 Then he gathered all Judah and Benjamin, and
[a]those who dwelt with them from Ephraim, Manasseh, and Simeon, for they came over to him in
great numbers from Israel when they saw that the
LORD his God was with him.
**10** So they gathered together at Jerusalem in the
third month, in the fifteenth year of the reign of
Asa.
11 [a]And they offered to the LORD [1]at that time
seven hundred bulls and seven thousand sheep
from the [2]spoil they had brought.
12 Then they [a]entered into a covenant to seek
the LORD God of their fathers with all their heart
and with all their soul;
13 [a]and whoever would not seek the LORD God of
Israel [b]was to be put to death, whether small or
great, whether man or woman.
14 Then they took an oath before the LORD with
a loud voice, with shouting and trumpets and
rams' horns.
15 And all Judah rejoiced at the oath, for they

**14** [a]Josh. 24:7; 2 Chr. 6:34, 35; 14:11
**15** [a]1 Kin. 14:14; 2 Chr. 14:12
**18** [a]1 Chr. 5:20; 2 Chr. 14:11; [Ps. 22:5]
**19** [a]Josh. 15:9 [1]Or *Ephron*
**20** [a]1 Sam. 2:6; 25:38; Acts 12:23 [b]1 Kin. 14:20
**22** [a]2 Chr. 9:29 [1]Or *commentary,* Heb. *midrash*

CHAPTER 14
**1** [a]1 Kin. 15:8
**3** [a]1 Kin. 15:14; 2 Chr. 15:17 [b][Ex. 34:13] [c]1 Kin. 11:7 [1]Places for pagan worship
**4** [a][2 Chr. 7:14]
**5** [1]Places for pagan worship
**6** [a]2 Chr. 15:15
**8** [a]1 Chr. 12:2 [b]2 Chr. 13:3 [1]*large shields*
**9** [a]2 Chr. 12:2, 3; 16:8 [b]Josh. 15:44
**11** [a]Ex. 14:10; 2 Chr. 13:14; [Ps. 22:5] [b][1 Sam. 14:6] [c]1 Sam. 17:45; [Prov. 18:10]
**12** [a]2 Chr. 13:15
**13** [a]Gen. 10:19; 20:1 [1]*plunder*
**14** [a]Gen. 35:5; Deut. 11:25; Josh. 2:9; 2 Chr. 17:10 [1]*plunder*
**15** [1]Lit. *struck*

CHAPTER 15
**1** [a]Num. 24:2; Judg. 3:10; 2 Chr. 20:14; 24:20
**2** [a][James 4:8] [b][1 Chr. 28:9]; 2 Chr. 14:4; 33:12, 13; [Jer. 29:13; Matt. 7:7] [c]2 Chr. 24:20 [1]Lit. *before*
**3** [a]Hos. 3:4 [b]2 Kin. 12:2 [c]Lev. 10:11; 2 Chr. 17:8, 9
**4** [a][Deut. 4:29]
**6** [a]Matt. 24:7 [1]Lit. *beaten in pieces*
**8** [a]2 Chr. 13:19 [1]So with MT, LXX; Syr., Vg. *Azariah the son of Oded* (cf. v. 1)
**9** [a]2 Chr. 11:16
**11** [a]2 Chr. 14:13–15 [1]Lit. *in that day* [2]*plunder*
**12** [a]2 Kin. 23:3; 2 Chr. 23:16; 34:31; Neh. 10:29
**13** [a]Ex. 22:20 [b]Deut. 13:5–15

had sworn with all their heart and [a]sought Him
with all their soul; and He was found by them, and
the LORD gave them [b]rest all around.
16 Also he removed [a]Maachah, the [1]mother of
Asa the king, from *being* queen mother, because
she had made an obscene image of [2]Asherah; and
Asa cut down her obscene image, then crushed
and burned *it* by the Brook Kidron.
17 But [a]the [1]high places were not removed from
Israel. Nevertheless the heart of Asa was loyal all
his days.
18 He also brought into the house of God the
things that his father had dedicated and that he
himself had dedicated: silver and gold and utensils.
19 And there was no war until the thirty-fifth
year of the reign of Asa.

### *Asa's Treaty with Syria*

**16** In the thirty-sixth year of the reign of Asa,
[a]Baasha king of Israel came up against
Judah and built Ramah, [b]that he might let none go
out or come in to Asa king of Judah.
2 Then Asa brought silver and gold from the
treasuries of the house of the LORD and of the
king's house, and sent to Ben-Hadad king of Syria,
who dwelt in Damascus, saying,
3 "*Let there be* a treaty between you and me, as
there was between my father and your father. See,
I have sent you silver and gold; come, break your
treaty with Baasha king of Israel, so that he will
withdraw from me."
4 So Ben-Hadad heeded King Asa, and sent the
captains of his armies against the cities of Israel.
They attacked Ijon, Dan, Abel Maim, and all the
storage cities of Naphtali.
5 Now it happened, when Baasha heard *it,* that
he stopped building Ramah and ceased his work.
6 Then King Asa took all Judah, and they carried away the stones and timber of Ramah, which
Baasha had used for building; and with them he
built Geba and Mizpah.
7 And at that time [a]Hanani the seer came to Asa
king of Judah, and said to him: [b]"Because you
have relied on the king of Syria, and have not
relied on the LORD your God, therefore the army
of the king of Syria has escaped from your hand.
8 "Were [a]the Ethiopians and [b]the Lubim not a
huge army with very many chariots and horsemen? Yet, because you relied on the LORD, He
delivered them into your [c]hand.
9 [a]"For the eyes of the LORD run to and fro
throughout the whole earth, to show Himself
strong on behalf of *those* whose heart *is* loyal to
Him. In this [b]you have done foolishly; therefore
from now on [c]you shall have wars."
10 Then Asa was angry with the seer, and [a]put
him in prison, for *he was* enraged at him because
of this. And Asa oppressed *some* of the people at
that time.
11 [a]Note that the acts of Asa, first and last, are
indeed written in the book of the kings of Judah
and Israel.
12 And in the thirty-ninth year of his reign, Asa
became diseased in his feet, and his malady was
severe; yet in his disease he [a]did not seek the
LORD, but the physicians.
13 [a]So Asa [1]rested with his fathers; he died in the
forty-first year of his reign.
14 They buried him in his own tomb, which he
had [1]made for himself in the City of David; and
they laid him in the bed which was filled [a]with
spices and various ingredients prepared in a mixture of ointments. They made [b]a very great burning for him.

### *Jehoshaphat Reigns in Judah*

**17** Then [a]Jehoshaphat his son reigned in his
place, and strengthened himself against
Israel.
2 And he placed troops in all the fortified cities
of Judah, and set garrisons in the land of [a]Judah
and in the cities of Ephraim [b]which Asa his father
had taken.
3 Now the LORD was with Jehoshaphat, because
he walked in the former ways of his father David;
he did not seek the Baals,
4 but sought [1]the God of his father, and walked
in His commandments and not according to [a]the
acts of Israel.
5 Therefore the LORD established the kingdom
in his hand; and all Judah [a]gave presents to
Jehoshaphat, [b]and he had riches and honor in
abundance.
6 And his heart took delight in the ways of the
LORD; moreover [a]he removed the [1]high places and
wooden images from Judah.
7 Also in the third year of his reign he sent his
leaders, Ben-Hail, Obadiah, Zechariah, Nethanel,
and Michaiah, [a]to teach in the cities of Judah.
8 And with them *he sent* Levites: Shemaiah,
Nethaniah, Zebadiah, Asahel, Shemiramoth, Jehonathan, Adonijah, Tobijah, and Tobadonijah—
the Levites; and with them Elishama and Jehoram, the priests.
9 [a]So they taught in Judah, and *had* the Book of
the Law of the LORD with them; they went
throughout all the cities of Judah and taught the
people.
10 And [a]the fear of the LORD fell on all the
kingdoms of the lands that *were* around Judah, so
that they did not make war against Jehoshaphat.
11 Also *some* of the Philistines [a]brought Jehoshaphat presents and silver as tribute; and the Arabians brought him flocks, seven thousand seven
hundred rams and seven thousand seven hundred
male goats.
12 So Jehoshaphat became increasingly powerful, and he built fortresses and storage cities in
Judah.
13 He had much property in the cities of Judah;
and the men of war, mighty men of valor, *were* in
Jerusalem.
14 These *are* their numbers, according to their
fathers' houses. Of Judah, the captains of thousands: Adnah the captain, and with him three
hundred thousand mighty men of valor;
15 and next to him *was* Jehohanan the captain,
and with him two hundred and eighty thousand;
16 and next to him *was* Amasiah the son of
Zichri, [a]who willingly offered himself to the LORD,
and with him two hundred thousand mighty men
of valor.
17 Of Benjamin: Eliada a mighty man of valor,
and with him two hundred thousand men armed
with bow and shield;
18 and next to him *was* Jehozabad, and with him
one hundred and eighty thousand prepared for
war.

---

15 [a]2 Chr. 15:2 [b]2 Chr. 14:7
16 [a]1 Kin. 15:2, 10, 13 [1]Or *grandmother* [2]A Canaanite deity
17 [a]1 Kin. 15:14; 2 Chr. 14:3, 5 [1]Places for pagan worship

CHAPTER 16

1 [a]1 Kin. 15:17–22 [b]2 Chr. 15:9
7 [a]1 Kin. 16:1; 2 Chr. 19:2 [b]2 Chr. 32:8–10; Ps. 118:9; [Is. 31:1; Jer. 17:5]
8 [a]2 Chr. 14:9 [b]2 Chr. 12:3 [c]2 Chr. 13:16, 18
9 [a]Job 34:21; [Prov. 5:21; 15:3; Jer. 16:17; 32:19]; Zech. 4:10 [b]1 Sam. 13:13 [c]1 Kin. 15:32
10 [a]2 Chr. 18:26; Jer. 20:2; Matt. 14:3
11 [a]1 Kin. 15:23, 24; 2 Chr. 14:2
12 [a][Jer. 17:5]
13 [a]1 Kin. 15:24 [1]Died and joined his ancestors
14 [a]Gen. 50:2; Mark 16:1; John 19:39, 40 [b]2 Chr. 21:19; Jer. 34:5 [1]Lit. *dug*

CHAPTER 17

1 [a]1 Kin. 15:24; 2 Chr. 20:31
2 [a]2 Chr. 11:5 [b]2 Chr. 15:8
4 [a]1 Kin. 12:28 [1]LXX *the LORD God*
5 [a]1 Sam. 10:27; 1 Kin. 10:25 [b]2 Chr. 18:1
6 [a]1 Kin. 22:43; 2 Chr. 15:17; 19:3; 20:33 [1]Places for pagan worship
7 [a]2 Chr. 15:3; 35:3
9 [a]Deut. 6:4–9; 2 Chr. 35:3; Neh. 8:3, 7
10 [a]Gen. 35:5; 2 Chr. 14:14
11 [a]2 Sam. 8:2; 2 Chr. 9:14; 26:8
16 [a]Judg. 5:2, 9; 1 Chr. 29:9

19 These served the king, besides [a]those the king
put in the fortified cities throughout all Judah.

## *Micaiah's True Prophecy*

**18** Jehoshaphat [a]had riches and honor in abundance; and by marriage he [b]allied himself
with [c]Ahab.
2 [a]After some years he went down to *visit* Ahab
in Samaria; and Ahab killed sheep and oxen in
abundance for him and the people who were with
him, and persuaded him to go up *with him* to
Ramoth Gilead.
3 So Ahab king of Israel said to Jehoshaphat
king of Judah, "Will you go with me *against*
Ramoth Gilead?" And he answered him, "I *am* as
you *are*, and my people as your people; *we will be*
with you in the war."
**4** Also Jehoshaphat said to the king of Israel,
[a]"Please inquire for the word of the LORD today."
5 Then the king of Israel gathered the prophets
together, four hundred men, and said to them,
"Shall we go to war against Ramoth Gilead, or
shall I refrain?" So they said, "Go up, for God will
deliver it into the king's hand."
**6** But Jehoshaphat said, "*Is there* not still a
prophet of the LORD here, that we may inquire of
[a]Him?"[1]
7 So the king of Israel said to Jehoshaphat,
"*There is* still one man by whom we may inquire
of the LORD; but I hate him, because he never
prophesies good concerning me, but always evil.
He *is* Micaiah the son of Imla." And Jehoshaphat
said, "Let not the king say such things!"
8 Then the king of Israel called one *of his*
officers and said, "Bring Micaiah the son of Imla
quickly!"
9 The king of Israel and Jehoshaphat king of
Judah, clothed in *their* robes, sat each on his
throne; and they sat at a threshing floor at the
entrance of the gate of Samaria; and all the
prophets prophesied before them.
10 Now Zedekiah the son of Chenaanah had
made [a]horns of iron for himself; and he said,
"Thus says the LORD: 'With these you shall gore
the Syrians until they are destroyed.' "
11 And all the prophets prophesied so, saying,
"Go up to Ramoth Gilead and prosper, for the
LORD will deliver *it* into the king's hand."
**12** Then the messenger who had gone to call
Micaiah spoke to him, saying, "Now listen, the
words of the prophets with one accord encourage
the king. Therefore please let your word be like
*the word of* one of them, and speak encouragement."
13 And Micaiah said, "*As* the LORD lives, [a]what-
ever my God says, that I will speak."
14 Then he came to the king; and the king said to
him, "Micaiah, shall we go to war against Ramoth
Gilead, or shall I refrain?" And he said, "Go and
prosper, and they shall be delivered into your
hand!"
15 So the king said to him, "How many times
shall I make you swear that you tell me nothing
but the truth in the name of the LORD?"
16 Then he said, "I saw all Israel [a]scattered on
the mountains, as sheep that have no [b]shepherd.
And the LORD said, 'These have no master. Let
each return to his house in peace.' "
17 And the king of Israel said to Jehoshaphat,
"Did I not tell you he would not prophesy good
concerning me, but evil?"
**18** Then *Micaiah* said, "Therefore hear the word
of the LORD: I saw the LORD sitting on His [a]throne,
and all the host of heaven standing on His right
hand and His left.
19 "And the LORD said, 'Who will persuade Ahab
king of Israel to go up, that he may fall at Ramoth
Gilead?' So one spoke in this manner, and another
spoke in that manner.
20 "Then a [a]spirit came forward and stood before
the LORD, and said, 'I will persuade him.' The
LORD said to him, 'In what way?'
21 "So he said, 'I will go out and be a lying spirit
in the mouth of all his prophets.' And *the LORD*
said, 'You shall persuade *him* and also prevail; go
out and do so.'
22 "Therefore look! [a]The LORD has put a lying
spirit in the mouth of these prophets of yours, and
the LORD has declared disaster against you."
**23** Then Zedekiah the son of Chenaanah went
near and [a]struck Micaiah on the cheek, and said,
"Which way did the spirit from the LORD go from
me to speak to you?"
24 And Micaiah said, "Indeed you shall see on
that day when you go into an inner chamber to
hide!"
25 Then the king of Israel said, "Take Micaiah,
and return him to Amon the governor of the city
and to Joash the king's son;
26 "and say, 'Thus says the king: [a]"Put this *fellow*
in prison, and feed him with bread of affliction and
water of affliction, until I return in peace." ' "
27 But Micaiah said, "If you ever return in peace,
the LORD has not spoken by [a]me." And he said,
"Take heed, all you people!"
**28** So the king of Israel and Jehoshaphat the king
of Judah went up to Ramoth Gilead.
29 And the king of Israel said to Jehoshaphat, "I
will [a]disguise myself and go into battle; but you
put on your robes." So the king of Israel disguised
himself, and they went into battle.
30 Now the king of Syria had commanded the
captains of the chariots who *were* with him,
saying, "Fight with no one small or great, but only
with the king of Israel."
31 So it was, when the captains of the chariots
saw Jehoshaphat, that they said, "It *is* the king of
Israel!" Therefore they surrounded him to attack;
but Jehoshaphat [a]cried out, and the LORD helped
him, and God diverted them from him.
32 For so it was, when the captains of the chariots saw that it was not the king of Israel, that
they turned back from pursuing him.
33 Now a certain man drew a bow at random,
and struck the king of Israel between the [1]joints
of his armor. So he said to the driver of his
chariot, "Turn around and take me out of the
battle, for I am wounded."
34 The battle increased that day, and the king of
Israel propped *himself* up in *his* chariot facing the
Syrians until evening; and about the time of
sunset he died.

## *Jehoshaphat's Additional Reforms*

**19** Then Jehoshaphat the king of Judah returned safely to his house in Jerusalem.
2 And Jehu the son of Hanani [a]the seer went out
to meet him, and said to King Jehoshaphat,
"Should you help the wicked and [b]love those who
hate the LORD? Therefore the [c]wrath of the LORD
*is* upon you.
3 "Nevertheless [a]good things are found in you,

**19** [a]2 Chr. 17:2

CHAPTER 18
**1** [a]2 Chr. 17:5 [b]1 Kin. 22:44; 2 Kin. 8:18 [c]1 Kin. 22:40
**2** [a][Ex. 23:2]; 1 Kin. 22:2
**4** [a]1 Sam. 23:2, 4, 9; 2 Sam. 2:1
**6** [a]2 Kin. 3:11 [1]Or *him*
**10** [a]Zech. 1:18–21
**13** [a]Num. 22:18–20, 35; 23:12, 26; 1 Kin. 22:14
**16** [a][Jer. 23:1–8; 31:10] [b]Num. 27:17; 1 Kin. 22:17; [Ezek. 34:5–8]; Matt. 9:36; Mark 6:34
**18** [a]Is. 6:1–5; Dan. 7:9, 10
**20** [a]Job 1:6; 2 Thess. 2:9
**22** [a]Job 12:16, 17; Is. 19:12–14; Ezek. 14:9
**23** [a]Jer. 20:2; Mark 14:65; Acts 23:2
**26** [a]2 Chr. 16:10
**27** [a]Deut. 18:22
**29** [a]2 Chr. 35:22
**31** [a]2 Chr. 13:14, 15
**33** [1]Or *scale armor and the breastplate*

CHAPTER 19
**2** [a]1 Sam. 9:9; 1 Kin. 16:1; 2 Chr. 20:34 [b]Ps. 139:21 [c]2 Chr. 32:25
**3** [a]2 Chr. 17:4, 6

in that you have removed the [1]wooden images
from the land, and have [b]prepared your heart to
seek God."
**4** So Jehoshaphat dwelt at Jerusalem; and he
went out again among the people from Beersheba
to the mountains of Ephraim, and brought them
back to the LORD God of their [a]fathers.
5 Then he set [a]judges in the land throughout all
the fortified cities of Judah, city by city,
6 and said to the judges, "Take heed to what
you are doing, for [a]you do not judge for man but
for the LORD, [b]who *is* with you [1]in the judgment.
7 "Now therefore, let the fear of the LORD be
upon you; take care and do *it*, for [a]*there is* no
iniquity with the LORD our God, no [b]partiality, nor
taking of bribes."
**8** Moreover in Jerusalem, for the judgment of
the LORD and for controversies, Jehoshaphat
[a]appointed some of the Levites and priests, and
some of the chief fathers of Israel, [1]when they
returned to Jerusalem.
9 And he commanded them, saying, "Thus you
shall act [a]in the fear of the LORD, faithfully and
with a loyal heart:
10 [a]"Whatever case comes to you from your
brethren who dwell in their cities, whether of
bloodshed or offenses against law or commandment, against statutes or ordinances, you shall
warn them, lest they trespass against the LORD
and [b]wrath come upon [c]you and your brethren. Do
this, and you will not be guilty.
11 "And take notice: [a]Amariah the chief priest *is*
over you [b]in all matters of the LORD; and Zebadiah
the son of Ishmael, the ruler of the house of
Judah, for all the king's matters; also the Levites
*will be* officials before you. Behave courageously,
and the LORD will be [c]with the good."

### *Jehaziel Promises a Great Deliverance*

**20** It happened after this *that* the people of
[a]Moab with the people of [b]Ammon, and
*others* with them besides the [c]Ammonites,[1] came
to battle against Jehoshaphat.
2 Then some came and told Jehoshaphat, saying, "A great multitude is coming against you
from beyond the sea, from [1]Syria; and they are [a]in
Hazazon Tamar" (which *is* [b]En Gedi).
3 And Jehoshaphat feared, and set [1]himself to
[a]seek the LORD, and [b]proclaimed a fast throughout
all Judah.
4 So Judah gathered together to ask [a]*help* from
the LORD; and from all the cities of Judah they
came to seek the LORD.
**5** Then Jehoshaphat stood in the assembly of
Judah and Jerusalem, in the house of the LORD,
before the new court,
6 and said: "O LORD God of our fathers, *are* You
not [a]God in heaven, and [b]do You *not* rule over all
the kingdoms of the nations, and [c]in Your hand *is*
*there not* power and might, so that no one is able
to withstand You?
7 "*Are* You not [a]our God, *who* [b]drove out the
inhabitants of this land before Your people Israel,
and gave it to the descendants of Abraham [c]Your
friend forever?
8 "And they dwell in it, and have built You a
sanctuary in it for Your name, saying,
9 [a]'If disaster comes upon us—sword, judgment,
pestilence, or famine—we will stand before this
temple and in Your presence (for Your [b]name *is* in
this temple), and cry out to You in our affliction,
and You will hear and save.'
10 "And now, here are the people of Ammon,
Moab, and Mount Seir—whom You [a]would not let
Israel invade when they came out of the land of
Egypt, but [b]they turned from them and did not
destroy them—
11 "here they are, rewarding us [a]by coming to
throw us out of Your possession which You have
given us to inherit.
12 "O our God, will You not [a]judge them? For we
have no power against this great multitude that is
coming against us; nor do we know what to do,
but [b]our eyes *are* upon You."
13 Now all Judah, with their little ones, their
wives, and their children, stood before the LORD.
**14** Then [a]the Spirit of the LORD came upon Jahaziel the son of Zechariah, the son of Benaiah, the
son of Jeiel, the son of Mattaniah, a Levite of the
sons of Asaph, in the midst of the assembly.
15 And he said, "Listen, all you of Judah and you
inhabitants of Jerusalem, and you, King Jehoshaphat! Thus says the LORD to you: [a]'Do not be
afraid nor dismayed because of this great multitude, [b]for the battle *is* not yours, but God's.
16 'Tomorrow go down against them. They will
surely come up by the Ascent of Ziz, and you will
find them at the end of the [1]brook before the
Wilderness of Jeruel.
17 [a]'You will not *need* to fight in this *battle*.
Position yourselves, stand still and see the salvation of the LORD, who is with you, O Judah and
Jerusalem!' Do not fear or be dismayed; tomorrow
go out against them, [b]for the LORD *is* with you."
18 And Jehoshaphat [a]bowed his head with *his*
face to the ground, and all Judah and the inhabitants of Jerusalem bowed before the LORD, worshiping the LORD.
19 Then the Levites of the children of the Kohathites and of the children of the Korahites stood
up to praise the LORD God of Israel with voices
loud and high.
**20** So they rose early in the morning and went
out into the Wilderness of Tekoa; and as they
went out, Jehoshaphat stood and said, "Hear me,
O Judah and you inhabitants of Jerusalem: [a]Be-
lieve in the LORD your God, and you shall be
established; believe His prophets, and you shall
prosper."
21 And when he had consulted with the people,
he appointed those who should sing to the LORD,
[a]and who should praise the beauty of holiness, as
they went out before the army and were saying:

> [b]"Praise the LORD,
> [c]For His mercy *endures* forever."

**22** Now when they began to sing and to praise,
[a]the LORD set ambushes against the people of
Ammon, Moab, and Mount Seir, who had come
against Judah; and they were defeated.
23 For the people of Ammon and Moab stood up
against the inhabitants of Mount Seir to utterly
kill and destroy *them*. And when they [1]had made
an end of the inhabitants of Seir, [a]they helped to
destroy one another.
**24** So when Judah came to a place overlooking
the wilderness, they looked toward the multitude;
and there *were* their dead bodies, fallen on the
earth. No one had escaped.
25 When Jehoshaphat and his people came to
take away their spoil, they found among them an

---

**3** [b]2 Chr. 30:19 [1]Or *Asherim*, Heb. *Asheroth*
**4** [a]2 Chr. 15:8–13
**5** [a][Deut. 16:18–20]
**6** [a][Deut. 1:17] [b]Ps. 82:1 [1]Lit. *in the matter of the judgment*
**7** [a][Deut. 32:4] [b][Deut. 10:17, 18]
**8** [a]2 Chr. 17:8 [1]LXX, [Syr.], [Vg.] *for the inhabitants of Jerusalem*
**9** [a][2 Sam. 23:3]
**10** [a]Deut. 17:8 [b]Num. 16:46 [c][Ezek. 3:18]
**11** [a]Ezra 7:3 [b]1 Chr. 26:30 [c][2 Chr. 15:2; 20:17]

CHAPTER 20

**1** [a]1 Chr. 18:2 [b]1 Chr. 19:15 [c]2 Chr. 26:7 [1]So with MT, Vg.; LXX *Meunites*, 2 Chr. 26:7
**2** [a]Gen. 14:7 [b]Josh. 15:62 [1]So with MT, LXX, Vg.; Heb. mss., Old Lat. *Edom*
**3** [a]2 Chr. 19:3 [b]Ezra 8:21 [1]Lit. *his face*
**4** [a]2 Chr. 14:11
**6** [a]Deut. 4:39 [b]Dan. 4:17, 25, 32 [c]1 Chr. 29:12
**7** [a]Ex. 6:7 [b]Ps. 44:2 [c]Is. 41:8
**9** [a]2 Chr. 6:28–30 [b]2 Chr. 6:20
**10** [a]Deut. 2:4, 9, 19 [b]Num. 20:21
**11** [a]Ps. 83:1–18
**12** [a]Judg. 11:27 [b]Ps. 25:15; 121:1, 2; 123:1, 2; 141:8
**14** [a]2 Chr. 15:1; 24:20
**15** [a][Deut. 1:29, 30; 31:6, 8] [b]1 Sam. 17:47
**16** [1]*stream bed* or *wadi*
**17** [a]Ex. 14:13, 14 [b]Num. 14:9
**18** [a]Ex. 4:31
**20** [a]Is. 7:9
**21** [a]1 Chr. 16:29 [b]Ps. 106:1; 136:1 [c]2 Chr. 5:13
**22** [a]Judg. 7:22
**23** [a]1 Sam. 14:20 [1]*had finished*

abundance of valuables on the [1]dead bodies, and
precious jewelry, which they stripped off for
themselves, more than they could carry away; and
they were three days gathering the spoil because
there was so much.
26 And on the fourth day they assembled in the
Valley of [1]Berachah, for there they blessed the
LORD; therefore the name of that place was called
The Valley of Berachah until this day.
27 Then they returned, every man of Judah and
Jerusalem, with Jehoshaphat in front of them, to
go back to Jerusalem with joy, for the LORD had
[a]made them rejoice over their enemies.
28 So they came to Jerusalem, with stringed
instruments and harps and trumpets, to the house
of the LORD.
29 And [a]the fear of God was on all the kingdoms
of *those* countries when they heard that the LORD
had fought against the enemies of Israel.
30 Then the realm of Jehoshaphat was quiet, for
his [a]God gave him rest all around.
**31** [a]So Jehoshaphat was king over Judah. *He was*
thirty-five years old when he became king, and he
reigned twenty-five years in Jerusalem. His mother's name *was* Azubah the daughter of Shilhi.
32 And he walked in the way of his father [a]Asa,
and did not turn aside from it, doing *what was*
right in the sight of the LORD.
33 Nevertheless [a]the [1]high places were not taken
away, for as yet the people had not [b]directed their
hearts to the God of their fathers.
34 Now the rest of the acts of Jehoshaphat, first
and last, indeed they *are* written in the book of
Jehu the son of Hanani, [a]which *is* mentioned in
the book of the kings of Israel.
**35** After this [a]Jehoshaphat king of Judah allied
himself with Ahaziah king of Israel, [b]who acted
very [c]wickedly.
36 And he allied himself with him [a]to make ships
to go to Tarshish, and they made the ships in
Ezion Geber.
37 But Eliezer the son of Dodavah of Mareshah
prophesied against Jehoshaphat, saying, "Because
you have allied yourself with Ahaziah, the LORD
has destroyed your works." [a]Then the ships were
wrecked, so that they were not able to go [b]to
Tarshish.

### *Jehoram Reigns in Judah*

**21** And [a]Jehoshaphat [1]rested with his fathers,
and was buried with his fathers in the City
of David. Then Jehoram his son reigned in his
place.
2 He had brothers, the sons of Jehoshaphat:
Azariah, Jehiel, Zechariah, Azaryahu, Michael,
and Shephatiah; all these *were* the sons of Jehoshaphat king of Israel.
3 Their father gave them great gifts of silver and
gold and precious things, with fortified cities in
Judah; but he gave the kingdom to Jehoram,
because he *was* the firstborn.
**4** Now when Jehoram [1]was established over the
kingdom of his father, he strengthened himself
and killed all his brothers with the sword, and also
*others* of the princes of Israel.
5 [a]Jehoram *was* thirty-two years old when he
became king, and he reigned eight years in Jerusalem.
6 And he walked in the way of the kings of
Israel, just as the house of Ahab had done, for he
had the daughter of [a]Ahab as a wife; and he did
evil in the sight of the LORD.
7 Yet the LORD would not destroy the house of
David, because of the [a]covenant that He had made
with David, and since He had promised to give a
lamp to him and to his [b]sons forever.
**8** [a]In his days Edom revolted against Judah's
authority, and made a king over themselves.
9 So Jehoram went out with his officers, and all
his chariots with him. And he rose by night and
attacked the Edomites who had surrounded him
and the captains of the chariots.
10 Thus Edom has been in revolt against Judah's
authority to this day. At that time Libnah revolted
against his rule, because he had forsaken the
LORD God of his fathers.
11 Moreover he made [1]high places in the mountains of Judah, and caused the inhabitants of
Jerusalem to [a]commit harlotry, and led Judah
astray.
**12** And a letter came to him from Elijah the
prophet, saying,

> Thus says the LORD God of your father
> David:
> Because you have not walked in the ways of
> Jehoshaphat your father, or in the ways of
> Asa king of Judah,
> 13 but have walked in the way of the kings of
> Israel, and have [a]made Judah and the
> inhabitants of Jerusalem to [b]play the harlot
> like the [c]harlotry of the house of Ahab, and
> also have [d]killed your brothers, those of your
> father's household, *who were* better than
> yourself,
> 14 behold, the LORD will strike your people with
> a serious affliction—your children, your
> wives, and all your possessions;
> 15 and you *will become* very sick with a
> [a]disease of your intestines, until your
> intestines come out by reason of the
> sickness, day by day.

**16** Moreover the [a]LORD [b]stirred up against Jehoram the spirit of the Philistines and the [c]Arabians
who *were* near the Ethiopians.
17 And they came up into Judah and invaded it,
and carried away all the possessions that were
found in the king's house, and also [a]his sons and
his wives, so that there was not a son left to him
except [1]Jehoahaz, the youngest of his sons.
**18** After all this the LORD struck him [a]in his
intestines with an incurable disease.
19 Then it happened in the course of time, after
the end of two years, that his intestines came out
because of his sickness; so he died in severe pain.
And his people made no [1]burning for him, like [a]the
burning for his fathers.
20 He was thirty-two years old when he became
king. He reigned in Jerusalem eight years and, to
no one's sorrow, departed. However they buried
him in the City of David, but not in the tombs of
the kings.

### *Ahaziah Reigns in Judah*

**22** Then the inhabitants of Jerusalem made
[a]Ahaziah his youngest son king in his place,
for the raiders who came with the [b]Arabians into
the camp had killed all the [c]older *sons*. So Ahaziah
the son of Jehoram, king of Judah, reigned.
2 Ahaziah *was* [1]forty-two years old when he
became king, and he reigned one year in Jerusa-

---

**25** [1]A few mss., Lat., Vg. *garments;* LXX *armor*
**26** [1]Lit. *Blessing*
**27** [a]Neh. 12:43
**29** [a]2 Chr. 14:14; 17:10
**30** [a]1 Kin. 22:41–43; 2 Chr. 14:6, 7; 15:15; Job 34:29
**31** [a][1 Kin. 22:41–43]
**32** [a]2 Chr. 14:2
**33** [a]2 Chr. 15:17; 17:6 [b]2 Chr. 12:14; 19:3 [1]Places for pagan worship
**34** [a]1 Kin. 16:1, 7
**35** [a]2 Chr. 18:1 [b]1 Kin. 22:48–53 [c][2 Chr. 19:2]
**36** [a]1 Kin. 9:26; 10:22
**37** [a]1 Kin. 22:48 [b]2 Chr. 9:21

CHAPTER 21
**1** [a]1 Kin. 22:50 [1]Died and joined his ancestors
**4** [1]Lit. *arose*
**5** [a]2 Kin. 8:17–22
**6** [a]2 Chr. 18:1
**7** [a]2 Sam. 7:8–17 [b]1 Kin. 11:36; 2 Kin. 8:19; Ps. 132:11
**8** [a]2 Kin. 8:20; 14:7, 10; 2 Chr. 25:14, 19
**11** [a][Lev. 20:5] [1]Places for pagan worship
**13** [a]2 Chr. 21:11 [b][Ex. 34:15]; Deut. 31:16 [c]1 Kin. 16:31–33; 2 Kin. 9:22 [d]1 Kin. 2:32; 2 Chr. 21:4
**15** [a]2 Chr. 21:18, 19
**16** [a]2 Chr. 33:11; [Jer. 51:11] [b]1 Kin. 11:14, 23 [c]2 Chr. 17:11
**17** [a]2 Chr. 24:7 [1]*Ahaziah* or *Azariah,* 2 Chr. 22:1
**18** [a]2 Chr. 13:20; 21:15; Acts 12:23
**19** [a]2 Chr. 16:14 [1]Burning of spices

CHAPTER 22
**1** [a]2 Chr. 21:17; 22:6 [b]2 Chr. 21:16 [c]2 Chr. 21:17
**2** [1]*twenty-two,* 2 Kin. 8:26

lem. His mother's name *was* [a]Athaliah the [2]grand-
daughter of Omri.
3 He also walked in the ways of the house of
Ahab, for his mother advised him to do wickedly.
4 Therefore he did evil in the sight of the LORD,
like the house of Ahab; for they were his counselors after the death of his father, to his destruction.
5 He also followed their advice, and went with
[1]Jehoram the son of Ahab king of Israel to war
against Hazael king of Syria at Ramoth Gilead;
and the Syrians wounded Joram.
6 [a]Then he returned to Jezreel to recover from
the wounds which he had received at Ramah,
when he fought against Hazael king of Syria. And
[1]Azariah the son of Jehoram, king of Judah, went
down to see Jehoram the son of Ahab in Jezreel,
because he was sick.
**7** His going to Joram [a]was God's occasion for
Ahaziah's [1]downfall; for when he arrived, [b]he
went out with [2]Jehoram against Jehu the son of
Nimshi, [c]whom the LORD had anointed to [3]cut off
the house of Ahab.
8 And it happened, when Jehu was [a]executing
judgment on the house of Ahab, and [b]found the
princes of Judah and the sons of Ahaziah's brothers who served Ahaziah, that he killed them.
9 [a]Then he searched for Ahaziah; and they
caught him (he was hiding in Samaria), and
brought him to Jehu. When they had killed him,
they buried him, "because," they said, "he is the
son of [b]Jehoshaphat, who [c]sought the LORD with
all his heart." So the house of Ahaziah had no one
to assume power over the kingdom.
**10** [a]Now when Athaliah the mother of Ahaziah
saw that her son was dead, she arose and destroyed all the royal heirs of the house of Judah.
11 But [1]Jehoshabeath, the daughter of the king,
took [a]Joash the son of Ahaziah, and stole him
away from among the king's sons who were being
murdered, and put him and his nurse in a bedroom. So Jehoshabeath, the daughter of King
Jehoram, the wife of Jehoiada the priest (for she
was the sister of Ahaziah), hid him from Athaliah
so that she did not kill him.
12 And he was hidden with them in the house of
God for six years, while Athaliah reigned over the
land.

### *Joash Reigns in Judah*

**23** In [a]the seventh year [b]Jehoiada strengthened
himself, *and made a* covenant with the
captains of hundreds: Azariah the son of Jeroham,
Ishmael the son of Jehohanan, Azariah the son of
[c]Obed, Maaseiah the son of Adaiah, and Elisha-
phat the son of Zichri.
2 And they went throughout Judah and gathered the Levites from all the cities of Judah, and
the [a]chief fathers of Israel, and they came to
Jerusalem.
3 Then all the assembly made a covenant with
the king in the house of God. And he said to them,
"Behold, the king's son shall reign, as the LORD
has [a]said of the sons of David.
4 "This *is* what you shall do: One-third of you
[a]entering on the Sabbath, of the priests and the
Levites, *shall be* keeping watch over the doors;
5 "one-third *shall be* at the king's house; and
one-third at the Gate of the Foundation. All the
people *shall be* in the courts of the house of the
LORD.

**2** [a]2 Chr. 21:6 [2]Lit. *daughter*
**5** [1]*Joram,* v. 7; 2 Kin. 8:28
**6** [a]2 Kin. 9:15 [1]Heb. mss., LXX, Syr., Vg. *Ahaziah* and 2 Kin. 8:29
**7** [a]Judg. 14:4; 1 Kin. 12:15; 2 Chr. 10:15 [b]2 Kin. 9:21–24 [c]2 Kin. 9:6, 7 [1]Lit. *crushing* [2]*Joram,* vv. 5, 7; 2 Kin. 8:28 [3]*destroy*
**8** [a]2 Kin. 9:22–24 [b]2 Kin. 10:10–14; Hos. 1:4
**9** [a][2 Kin. 9:27] [b]1 Kin. 15:24 [c]2 Chr. 17:4; 20:3, 4
**10** [a]2 Kin. 11:1–3
**11** [a]2 Kin. 12:18 [1]*Jehosheba,* 2 Kin. 11:2

CHAPTER 23

**1** [a]2 Kin. 11:4 [b]2 Kin. 12:2 [c]1 Chr. 2:37, 38
**2** [a]Ezra 1:5
**3** [a]2 Sam. 7:12; 1 Kin. 2:4; 9:5; 2 Chr. 6:16; 7:18; 21:7
**4** [a]1 Chr. 9:25
**6** [a]1 Chr. 23:28–32
**8** [a]1 Chr. 24:1–31
**9** [a]2 Sam. 8:7
**11** [a]Deut. 17:18 [1]Law, Ex. 25:16, 21; 31:18; Deut. 11:9
**12** [a]2 Chr. 22:10
**13** [a]1 Chr. 25:8 [b]2 Kin. 9:23
**15** [a]Neh. 3:28; Jer. 31:40
**16** [a]Josh. 24:24, 25; 2 Chr. 15:12–15
**17** [a]Deut. 13:6–9; 1 Kin. 18:40 [1]Lit. *house*
**18** [a]1 Chr. 23:6, 30, 31; 24:1 [b]Num. 28:2
**19** [a]1 Chr. 26:1–19
**20** [a]1 Kin. 9:22; 2 Kin. 11:19

6 "But let no one come into the house of the
LORD except the priests and [a]those of the Levites
who serve. They may go in, for they *are* holy; but
all the people shall keep the watch of the LORD.
7 "And the Levites shall surround the king on
all sides, every man with his weapons in his hand;
and whoever comes into the house, let him be put
to death. You are to be with the king when he
comes in and when he goes out."
**8** So the Levites and all Judah did according to
all that Jehoiada the priest commanded. And each
man took his men who were to be on duty on the
Sabbath, with those who were going *off duty* on
the Sabbath; for Jehoiada the priest had not
dismissed [a]the divisions.
9 And Jehoiada the priest gave to the captains
of hundreds the spears and the large and small
[a]shields which *had belonged* to King David, that
*were* in the temple of God.
10 Then he set all the people, every man with his
weapon in his hand, from the right side of the
temple to the left side of the temple, along by the
altar and by the temple, all around the king.
11 And they brought out the king's son, put the
crown on him, [a]*gave him* the [1]Testimony, and
made him king. Then Jehoiada and his sons
anointed him, and said, "*Long* live the king!"
**12** Now when [a]Athaliah heard the noise of the
people running and praising the king, she came to
the people *in* the temple of the LORD.
13 When she looked, there was the king standing
by his pillar at the entrance; and the leaders and
the trumpeters *were* by the king. All the people of
the land were rejoicing and blowing trumpets,
also the singers with musical instruments, and
[a]those who led in praise. So Athaliah tore her
clothes and said, [b]"Treason! Treason!"
**14** And Jehoiada the priest brought out the captains of hundreds who were set over the army,
and said to them, "Take her outside under guard,
and slay with the sword whoever follows her." For
the priest had said, "Do not kill her in the house of
the LORD."
15 So they seized her; and she went by way of the
entrance [a]of the Horse Gate *into* the king's house,
and they killed her there.
**16** Then Jehoiada made a [a]covenant between
himself, the people, and the king, that they should
be the LORD's people.
17 And all the people went to the [1]temple of Baal,
and tore it down. They broke in pieces its altars
and images, and [a]killed Mattan the priest of Baal
before the altars.
18 Also Jehoiada appointed the oversight of the
house of the LORD to the hand of the priests, the
Levites, whom David had [a]assigned in the house
of the LORD, to offer the burnt offerings of the
LORD, as *it is* written in the [b]Law of Moses, with
rejoicing and with singing, *as it was established*
by David.
19 And he set the [a]gatekeepers at the gates of the
house of the LORD, so that no one *who was* in any
way unclean should enter.
20 [a]Then he took the captains of hundreds, the
nobles, the governors of the people, and all the
people of the land, and brought the king down
from the house of the LORD; and they went
through the Upper Gate to the king's house, and
set the king on the throne of the kingdom.
21 So all the people of the land rejoiced; and the

city was quiet, for they had slain Athaliah with
the sword.

### *Joash Repairs the Temple*

**24** Joash [a]*was* seven years old when he became
king, and he reigned forty years in Jerusalem. His mother's name *was* Zibiah of Beersheba.
2 Joash [a]did *what was* right in the sight of the
LORD all the days of Jehoiada the priest.
3 And Jehoiada took two wives for him, and he
had sons and daughters.
**4** Now it happened after this *that* Joash set his
heart on repairing the house of the LORD.
5 Then he gathered the priests and the Levites,
and said to them, "Go out to the cities of Judah,
and [a]gather from all Israel money to repair the
house of your God from year to year, and see that
you do it quickly." However the Levites did not do
it quickly.
6 [a]So the king called Jehoiada the chief *priest,*
and said to him, "Why have you not required the
Levites to bring in from Judah and from Jerusalem the collection, *according to the command-*
*ment* of [b]Moses the servant of the LORD and of the
assembly of Israel, for the [c]tabernacle of witness?"
7 For [a]the sons of Athaliah, that wicked woman,
had broken into the house of God, and had also
presented all the [b]dedicated things of the house of
the LORD to the Baals.
**8** Then at the king's command [a]they made a
chest, and set it outside at the gate of the house of
the LORD.
9 And they made a proclamation throughout
Judah and Jerusalem to bring to the LORD [a]the
collection *that* Moses the servant of God *had*
*imposed* on Israel in the wilderness.
10 Then all the leaders and all the people rejoiced, brought their contributions, and put *them*
into the chest until all had given.
11 So it was, at that time, when the chest was
brought to the king's official by the hand of the
Levites, and [a]when they saw that *there was* much
money, that the king's scribe and the high priest's
officer came and emptied the chest, and took it
and returned it to its place. Thus they did day by
day, and gathered money in abundance.
12 The king and Jehoiada gave it to those who
did the work of the service of the house of the
LORD; and they hired masons and carpenters to
[a]repair the house of the LORD, and also those who
worked in iron and bronze to restore the house of
the LORD.
13 So the workmen labored, and the work was
completed by them; they restored the house of
God to its original condition and reinforced it.
14 When they had finished, they brought the rest
of the money before the king and Jehoiada; [a]they
made from it articles for the house of the LORD,
articles for serving and offering, spoons and vessels of gold and silver. And they offered burnt
offerings in the house of the LORD continually all
the days of Jehoiada.
**15** But Jehoiada grew old and was full of days,
and he died; *he was* one hundred and thirty years
old when he died.
16 And they buried him in the City of David
among the kings, because he had done good in
Israel, both toward God and His house.
**17** Now after the death of Jehoiada the leaders of
Judah came and bowed down to the king. And the
king listened to them.
18 Therefore they left the house of the LORD God
of their fathers, and served [a]wooden images and
idols; and [b]wrath came upon Judah and Jerusalem
because of their trespass.
19 Yet He [a]sent prophets to them, to bring them
back to the LORD; and they testified against them,
but they would not listen.
20 Then the Spirit of God [1]came upon [a]Zechariah
the son of Jehoiada the priest, who stood above
the people, and said to them, "Thus says God:
[b]'Why do you transgress the commandments of
the LORD, so that you cannot prosper? [c]Because
you have forsaken the LORD, He also has forsaken
you.' "
21 So they conspired against him, and at the
command of the king they [a]stoned him with
stones in the court of the house of the LORD.
22 Thus Joash the king did not remember the
kindness which Jehoiada his [1]father had done to
him, but killed his son; and as he died, he said,
"The LORD look on *it,* and [a]repay!"
**23** So it happened in the spring of the year *that*
[a]the army of Syria came up against him; and they
came to Judah and Jerusalem, and destroyed all
the leaders of the people from among the people,
and sent all their [1]spoil to the king of Damascus.
24 For the army of the Syrians [a]came with a
small company of men; but the LORD [b]delivered a
very great army into their hand, because they had
forsaken the LORD God of their fathers. So they
[c]executed judgment against Joash.
25 And when they had withdrawn from him (for
they left him severely wounded), [a]his own servants conspired against him because of the blood
of the [1]sons of Jehoiada the priest, and killed him
on his bed. So he died. And they buried him in the
City of David, but they did not bury him in the
tombs of the kings.
**26** These are the ones who conspired against him:
[1]Zabad the son of Shimeath the Ammonitess, and
Jehozabad the son of [2]Shimrith the Moabitess.
27 Now *concerning* his sons, and [a]the many oracles about him, and the repairing of the house of
God, indeed they *are* written in the [1]annals of the
book of the kings. [b]Then Amaziah his son reigned
in his place.

### *War Between Judah and Israel*

**25** Amaziah [a]*was* twenty-five years old *when*
he became king, and he reigned twenty-
nine years in Jerusalem. His mother's name *was*
Jehoaddan of Jerusalem.
2 And he did *what was* right in the sight of the
LORD, [a]but not with a loyal heart.
**3** [a]Now it happened, as soon as the kingdom was
established for him, that he executed his servants
who had murdered his father the king.
4 However he did not execute their children, but
*did* as *it is* written in the Law in the Book of
Moses, where the LORD commanded, saying,
[a]"The fathers shall not be put to death for their
children, nor shall the children be put to death for
their fathers; but a person shall die for his own
sin."
**5** Moreover Amaziah gathered Judah together
and set over them captains of thousands and
captains of hundreds, according to *their* fathers'
houses, throughout all Judah and Benjamin; and
he numbered them [a]from twenty years old and
above, and found them to be three hundred thou-

CHAPTER 24

1 [a]2 Kin. 11:21; 12:1–15
2 [a]2 Chr. 26:4, 5
5 [a]2 Kin. 12:4
6 [a]2 Kin. 12:7 [b]Ex. 30:12–16 [c]Num. 1:50; Acts 7:44
7 [a]2 Chr. 21:17 [b]2 Kin. 12:4
8 [a]2 Kin. 12:9
9 [a]2 Chr. 24:6
11 [a]2 Kin. 12:10
12 [a]2 Chr. 30:12
14 [a]2 Kin. 12:13
18 [a]1 Kin. 14:23 [b][Ex. 34:12–14]; Judg. 5:8; 2 Chr. 19:2; 28:13; 29:8; 32:25
19 [a]2 Kin. 17:13; 21:10–15; 2 Chr. 36:15, 16; Jer. 7:25, 26; 25:4
20 [a]Judg. 6:34; Matt. 23:35 [b]Num. 14:41; [Prov. 28:13] [c][2 Chr. 15:2] [1]Lit. *clothed*
21 [a][Neh. 9:26]; Matt. 23:35; Acts 7:58, 59
22 [a][Gen. 9:5] [1]Foster father
23 [a]2 Kin. 12:17; Is. 7:2 [1]*plunder*
24 [a]Lev. 26:8; [Deut. 32:30]; Is. 30:17 [b]Lev. 26:25; [Deut. 28:25] [c]2 Chr. 22:8; Is. 10:5
25 [a]2 Kin. 12:20, 21; 2 Chr. 25:3 [1]LXX, Vg. *son* and vv. 20–22
26 [1]*Jozachar,* 2 Kin. 12:21 [2]*Shomer,* 2 Kin. 12:21
27 [a]2 Kin. 12:18 [b]2 Kin. 12:21 [1]Or *commentary,* Heb. *midrash*

CHAPTER 25

1 [a]2 Kin. 14:1–6
2 [a]2 Kin. 14:4; 2 Chr. 25:14
3 [a]2 Kin. 14:5; 2 Chr. 24:25
4 [a]Deut. 24:16; 2 Kin. 14:6; Jer. 31:30; [Ezek. 18:20]
5 [a]Num. 1:3

sand choice *men, able* to go to war, who could
handle spear and shield.
6 He also hired one hundred thousand mighty
men of valor from Israel for one hundred talents
of silver.
7 But a [a]man of God came to him, saying, "O
king, do not let the army of Israel go with you, for
the LORD *is* not with Israel—*not with* any of the
children of Ephraim.
8 "But if you go, be gone! Be strong in battle!
*Even so,* God shall make you fall before the
enemy; for God has [a]power to help and to overthrow."
9 Then Amaziah said to the man of God, "But
what *shall we* do about the hundred talents which
I have given to the troops of Israel?" And the man
of God answered, [a]"The LORD is able to give you
much more than this."
10 So Amaziah discharged the troops that had
come to him from Ephraim, to go back home.
Therefore their anger was greatly aroused against
Judah, and they returned home in great anger.
**11** Then Amaziah strengthened himself, and leading his people, he went to [a]the Valley of Salt and
killed ten thousand of the people of Seir.
12 Also the children of Judah took captive ten
thousand alive, brought them to the top of the
rock, and cast them down from the top of the
rock, so that they all were dashed in pieces.
**13** But as for the soldiers of the army which
Amaziah had discharged, so that they would not
go with him to battle, they raided the cities of
Judah from Samaria to Beth Horon, killed three
thousand in them, and took much [1]spoil.
**14** Now it was so, after Amaziah came from the
slaughter of the Edomites, that [a]he brought the
gods of the people of Seir, set them up *to be* [b]his
gods, and bowed down before them and burned
incense to them.
15 Therefore the anger of the LORD was aroused
against Amaziah, and He sent him a prophet who
said to him, "Why have you sought [a]the gods of
the people, which [b]could not rescue their own
people from your hand?"
16 So it was, as he talked with him, that *the king*
said to him, "Have we made you the king's counselor? Cease! Why should you be killed?" Then the
prophet ceased, and said, "I know that God has
[a]determined to destroy you, because you have
done this and have not heeded my advice."
**17** Now [a]Amaziah king of Judah asked advice
and sent to [1]Joash the son of Jehoahaz, the son of
Jehu, king of Israel, saying, "Come, let us face one
another *in battle.*"
18 And Joash king of Israel sent to Amaziah king
of Judah, saying, "The thistle that *was* in Lebanon
sent to the cedar that was in Lebanon, saying,
'Give your daughter to my son as wife'; and a wild
beast that *was* in Lebanon passed by and trampled
the thistle.
19 "Indeed you say that you have defeated the
Edomites, and your heart is lifted up to [a]boast.
Stay at home now; why should you meddle with
trouble, that you should fall—you and Judah with
you?"
20 But Amaziah would not heed, for [a]it *came*
from God, that He might give them into the hand
*of their enemies,* because they [b]sought the gods of
Edom.
21 So Joash king of Israel went out; and he and
Amaziah king of Judah faced one another at [a]Beth
Shemesh, which *belongs* to Judah.
22 And Judah was defeated by Israel, and every
man fled to his tent.
23 Then Joash the king of Israel captured Amaziah king of Judah, the son of Joash, the son of
[a]Jehoahaz, at Beth Shemesh; and he brought him
to Jerusalem, and broke down the wall of Jerusalem from the Gate of Ephraim to the Corner
Gate—four hundred cubits.
24 And *he took* all the gold and silver, all the
articles that were found in the house of God with
[a]Obed-Edom, the treasures of the king's house,
and hostages, and returned to Samaria.
**25** [a]Amaziah the son of Joash, king of Judah,
lived fifteen years after the death of Joash the son
of Jehoahaz, king of Israel.
26 Now the rest of the acts of Amaziah, from first
to last, indeed *are* they not written in the book of
the kings of Judah and Israel?
27 After the time that Amaziah turned away
from following the LORD, they made a conspiracy
against him in Jerusalem, and he fled to Lachish;
but they sent after him to Lachish and killed him
there.
28 Then they brought him on horses and buried
him with his fathers in [1]the City of Judah.

### *Uzziah Reigns in Judah*

**26** Now all the people of Judah took [1]Uzziah,
who *was* sixteen years old, and made him
king instead of his father Amaziah.
2 He built [1]Elath and restored it to Judah, after
the king rested with his fathers.
3 Uzziah *was* sixteen years old when he became
king, and he reigned fifty-two years in Jerusalem.
His mother's name was Jecholiah of Jerusalem.
4 And he did *what was* [a]right in the sight of the
LORD, according to all that his father Amaziah had
done.
5 [a]He sought God in the days of Zechariah, who
[b]had understanding in the [1]visions of God; and as
long as he sought the LORD, God made him [c]pros-
per.
**6** Now he went out and [a]made war against the
Philistines, and broke down the wall of Gath, the
wall of Jabneh, and the wall of Ashdod; and he
built cities *around* Ashdod and among the Philistines.
7 God helped him against [a]the Philistines,
against the Arabians who lived in Gur Baal, and
against the Meunites.
8 Also the Ammonites [a]brought tribute to Uzziah. His fame spread as far as the entrance of
Egypt, for he became exceedingly strong.
9 And Uzziah built towers in Jerusalem at the
[a]Corner Gate, at the Valley Gate, and at the
corner buttress of the wall; then he fortified them.
10 Also he built towers in the desert. He dug
many wells, for he had much livestock, both in the
lowlands and in the plains; *he also had* farmers
and vinedressers in the mountains and in [1]Carmel,
for he loved the soil.
**11** Moreover Uzziah had an army of fighting men
who went out to war by companies, according to
the number on their roll as prepared by Jeiel the
scribe and Maaseiah the officer, under the hand of
Hananiah, *one* of the king's captains.
12 The total number of [1]chief officers of the
mighty men of valor *was* two thousand six hundred.

7 [a]2 Chr. 11:2
8 [a]2 Chr. 14:11; 20:6
9 [a][Deut. 8:18]; Prov. 10:22
11 [a]2 Kin. 14:7
13 [1]*plunder*
14 [a]2 Chr. 28:23 [b][Ex. 20:3, 5]
15 [a][Ps. 96:5] [b]2 Chr. 25:11
16 [a][1 Sam. 2:25]
17 [a]2 Kin. 14:8–14 [1]*Jehoash,* 2 Kin. 14:8ff.
19 [a]2 Chr. 26:16; 32:25; [Prov. 16:18]
20 [a]1 Kin. 12:15; 2 Chr. 22:7 [b]2 Chr. 25:14
21 [a]Josh. 19:38
23 [a]2 Chr. 21:17; 22:1, 6
24 [a]1 Chr. 26:15
25 [a]2 Kin. 14:17–22
28 [1]The City of David

CHAPTER 26
1 [1]*Azariah,* 2 Kin. 14:21ff.
2 [1]Heb. *Eloth*
4 [a]2 Chr. 24:2
5 [a]2 Chr. 24:2 [b]Gen. 41:15; Dan. 1:17; 10:1 [c][2 Chr. 15:2; 20:20; 31:21] [1]Heb. mss., LXX, Syr., Tg., Arab. *fear*
6 [a]Is. 14:29
7 [a]2 Chr. 21:16
8 [a]2 Sam. 8:2; 2 Chr. 17:11
9 [a]2 Kin. 14:13; 2 Chr. 25:23; Neh. 3:13, 19, 32; Zech. 14:10
10 [1]Or *the fertile fields*
12 [1]Lit. *chief fathers*

13 And under their authority *was* an army of
three hundred and seven thousand five hundred,
that made war with mighty power, to help the
king against the enemy.
14 Then Uzziah prepared for them, for the entire
army, shields, spears, helmets, body armor, bows,
and slings *to cast* stones.
15 And he made devices in Jerusalem, invented
by [a]skillful men, to be on the towers and the
corners, to shoot arrows and large stones. So his
fame spread far and wide, for he was marvelously
helped till he became strong.
**16** But [a]when he was strong his heart was [b]lifted
up, to *his* destruction, for he transgressed against
the LORD his God [c]by entering the temple of the
LORD to burn incense on the altar of incense.
17 So [a]Azariah the priest went in after him, and
with him were eighty priests of the LORD—valiant
men.
18 And they withstood King Uzziah, and said to
him, "*It* [a]*is* not for you, Uzziah, to burn incense to
the LORD, but for the [b]priests, the sons of Aaron,
who are consecrated to burn incense. Get out of
the sanctuary, for you have trespassed! You *shall
have* no honor from the LORD God."
19 Then Uzziah became furious; and he *had* a
censer in his hand to burn incense. And while he
was angry with the priests, [a]leprosy broke out on
his forehead, before the priests in the house of the
LORD, beside the incense altar.
20 And Azariah the chief priest and all the priests
looked at him, and there, on his forehead, he *was*
leprous; so they thrust him out of that place.
Indeed he also [a]hurried to get out, because the
LORD had struck him.
21 [a]King Uzziah was a leper until the day of his
death. He dwelt in an [b]isolated house, because he
was a leper; for he was cut off from the house of
the LORD. Then Jotham his son *was* over the
king's house, judging the people of the land.
**22** Now the rest of the acts of Uzziah, from first
to last, the prophet [a]Isaiah the son of Amoz wrote.
23 [a]So Uzziah [1]rested with his fathers, and they
buried him with his fathers in the field of burial
which *belonged* to the kings, for they said, "He is
a leper." Then Jotham his son reigned in his place.

## *Jotham Reigns in Judah*

**27** Jotham [a]*was* twenty-five years old when he
became king, and he reigned sixteen years
in Jerusalem. His mother's name *was* [1]Jerushah
the daughter of Zadok.
2 And he did *what was* right in the sight of the
LORD, according to all that his father Uzziah had
done (although he did not enter the temple of the
LORD). But still [a]the people acted corruptly.
3 He built the Upper Gate of the house of the
LORD, and he built extensively on the wall of
[a]Ophel.
4 Moreover he built cities in the mountains of
Judah, and in the forests he built fortresses and
towers.
5 He also fought with the king of the [a]Ammon-
ites and defeated them. And the people of Ammon
gave him in that year one hundred talents of
silver, ten thousand kors of wheat, and ten thousand of barley. The people of Ammon paid this to
him in the second and third years also.
6 So Jotham became mighty, [a]because he prepared his ways before the LORD his God.
**7** Now the rest of the acts of Jotham, and all his
wars and his ways, indeed they *are* written in the
book of the kings of Israel and Judah.
8 He was twenty-five years old when he became
king, and he reigned sixteen years in Jerusalem.
9 [a]So Jotham [1]rested with his fathers, and they
buried him in the City of David. Then [b]Ahaz his
son reigned in his place.

## *War Between Ahaz and Pekah*

**28** Ahaz [a]*was* twenty years old when he became king, and he reigned sixteen years in
Jerusalem; and he did not do *what was* right in
the sight of the LORD, as his father David *had
done.*
2 For he walked in the ways of the kings of
Israel, and made [a]molded images for [b]the Baals.
3 He burned incense in [a]the Valley of the Son of
Hinnom, and burned [b]his children in the [c]fire,
according to the abominations of the nations
whom the LORD had [d]cast out before the children
of Israel.
4 And he sacrificed and burned incense on the
[1]high places, on the hills, and under every green
tree.
**5** Therefore [a]the LORD his God delivered him
into the hand of the king of Syria. They [b]defeated
him, and carried away a great multitude of them
as captives, and brought *them* to Damascus. Then
he was also delivered into the hand of the king of
Israel, who defeated him with a great slaughter.
6 For [a]Pekah the son of Remaliah killed one
hundred and twenty thousand in Judah in one
day, all valiant men, [b]because they had forsaken
the LORD God of their fathers.
7 Zichri, a mighty man of Ephraim, killed Maaseiah the king's son, Azrikam the officer over the
house, and Elkanah *who was* second to the king.
8 And the children of Israel carried away captive of their [a]brethren two hundred thousand
women, sons, and daughters; and they also took
away much [1]spoil from them, and brought the
spoil to Samaria.
**9** But a [a]prophet of the LORD was there, whose
name *was* Oded; and he went out before the army
that came to Samaria, and said to them: "Look,
[b]because the LORD God of your fathers was angry
with Judah, He has delivered them into your
hand; but you have killed them in a rage *that*
[c]reaches up to heaven.
10 "And now you propose to force the children of
Judah and Jerusalem to be your [a]male and female
slaves; *but are* you not also guilty before the LORD
your God?
11 "Now hear me, therefore, and return the
captives, whom you have taken captive from your
brethren, [a]for the fierce wrath of the LORD *is* upon
you."
12 Then some of the heads of the children of
Ephraim, Azariah the son of Johanan, Berechiah
the son of Meshillemoth, Jehizkiah the son of
Shallum, and Amasa the son of Hadlai, stood up
against those who came from the war,
13 and said to them, "You shall not bring the
captives here, for we *already* have offended the
LORD. You intend to add to our sins and to our
guilt; for our guilt is great, and *there is* fierce
wrath against Israel."
14 So the armed men left the captives and the
[1]spoil before the leaders and all the assembly.
15 Then the men [a]who were designated by name
rose up and took the captives, and from the [1]spoil

**15** [a]Ex. 39:3, 8
**16** [a][Deut. 32:15] [b]Deut. 8:14; 2 Chr. 25:19 [c]1 Kin. 13:1–4; 2 Kin. 16:12, 13
**17** [a]1 Chr. 6:10
**18** [a][Num. 3:10; 16:39, 40; 18:7] [b]Ex. 30:7, 8; Heb. 7:14
**19** [a]Lev. 13:42; Num. 12:10; 2 Kin. 5:25–27
**20** [a]Esth. 6:12
**21** [a]2 Kin. 15:5 [b][Lev. 13:46; Num. 5:2]
**22** [a]2 Kin. 20:1; 2 Chr. 32:20, 32; Is. 1:1
**23** [a]2 Kin. 15:7; 2 Chr. 21:20; 28:27; Is. 6:1 [1]Died and joined his ancestors

CHAPTER 27
**1** [a]2 Kin. 15:32–35 [1]*Jerusha,* 2 Kin. 15:33
**2** [a]2 Kin. 15:35; Ezek. 20:44; 30:13
**3** [a]2 Chr. 33:14; Neh. 3:26
**5** [a]2 Chr. 26:8
**6** [a]2 Chr. 26:5
**9** [a]2 Kin. 15:38 [b]Is. 1:1; Hos. 1:1; Mic. 1:1 [1]Died and joined his ancestors

CHAPTER 28
**1** [a]2 Kin. 16:2–4
**2** [a]Ex. 34:17; Lev. 19:4 [b]Judg. 2:11
**3** [a]Josh. 15:8 [b]2 Kin. 23:10 [c][Lev. 18:21]; 2 Kin. 16:3; 2 Chr. 33:6 [d][Lev. 18:24–30]
**4** [1]Places for pagan worship
**5** [a][Is. 10:5] [b]2 Kin. 16:5, 6; [2 Chr. 24:24]; Is. 7:1, 17
**6** [a]2 Kin. 15:27 [b][2 Chr. 29:8]
**8** [a]Deut. 28:25, 41; 2 Chr. 11:4 [1]*plunder*
**9** [a]2 Chr. 25:15 [b]Ps. 69:26; [Is. 10:5; 47:6]; Ezek. 25:12, 15; 26:2; Obad. 10; [Zech. 1:15] [c]Ezra 9:6; Rev. 18:5
**10** [a][Lev. 25:39, 42, 43, 46]
**11** [a]Ps. 78:49; James 2:13
**14** [1]*plunder*
**15** [a]2 Chr. 28:12 [1]*plunder*

they clothed all who were naked among them, dressed them and gave them sandals, [b]gave them food and drink, and anointed them; and they let all the feeble ones ride on donkeys. So they brought them to their brethren at Jericho, [c]the city of palm trees. Then they returned to Samaria.

**16** [a]At the same time King Ahaz sent to the [1]kings of Assyria to help him.

17 For again the [a]Edomites had come, attacked Judah, and carried away captives.

18 [a]The Philistines also had invaded the cities of the lowland and of the South of Judah, and had taken Beth Shemesh, Aijalon, Gederoth, Sochoh with its villages, Timnah with its villages, and Gimzo with its villages; and they dwelt there.

19 For the LORD [1]brought Judah low because of Ahaz king of [a]Israel, for he had [b]encouraged moral decline in Judah and had been continually unfaithful to the LORD.

20 Also [a]Tiglath-Pileser[1] king of Assyria came to him and distressed him, and did not assist him.

21 For Ahaz took part *of the treasures* from the house of the LORD, from the house of the king, and from the leaders, and he gave *it* to the king of Assyria; but he did not help him.

**22** Now in the time of his distress King Ahaz became increasingly unfaithful to the LORD. This *is that* King Ahaz.

23 For [a]he sacrificed to the gods of Damascus which had defeated him, saying, "Because the gods of the kings of Syria help them, I will sacrifice to them [b]that they may help me." But they were the ruin of him and of all Israel.

24 So Ahaz gathered the articles of the house of God, cut in pieces the articles of the house of God, [a]shut up the doors of the house of the LORD, and made for himself altars in every corner of Jerusalem.

25 And in every single city of Judah he made [1]high places to burn incense to other gods, and provoked to anger the LORD God of his fathers.

**26** [a]Now the rest of his acts and all his ways, from first to last, indeed they *are* written in the book of the kings of Judah and Israel.

27 So Ahaz [1]rested with his fathers, and they buried him in the city, in Jerusalem; but they [a]did not bring him into the tombs of the kings of Israel. Then Hezekiah his son reigned in his place.

### *Temple Worship Restored*

**29** Hezekiah [a]became king *when he was* twenty-five years old, and he reigned twenty-nine years in Jerusalem. His mother's name *was* [1]Abijah the daughter [b]of Zechariah.

2 And he did *what was* right in the sight of the LORD, according to all that his father David had done.

**3** In the first year of his reign, in the first month, he [a]opened the doors of the house of the LORD and repaired them.

4 Then he brought in the priests and the Levites, and gathered them in the East Square,

5 and said to them: "Hear me, Levites! Now [1]sanctify yourselves, [a]sanctify the house of the LORD God of your fathers, and carry out the rubbish from the holy *place*.

6 "For our fathers have trespassed and done evil in the eyes of the LORD our God; they have forsaken Him, have [a]turned their faces away from the [1]dwelling place of the LORD, and turned *their* backs *on Him*.

7 [a]"They have also shut up the doors of the vestibule, put out the lamps, and have not burned incense or offered burnt offerings in the holy *place* to the God of Israel.

8 "Therefore the [a]wrath of the LORD fell upon Judah and Jerusalem, and He has [b]given them up to trouble, to astonishment, and to [c]jeering, as you see with your [d]eyes.

9 "For indeed, because of this [a]our fathers have fallen by the sword; and our sons, our daughters, and our wives *are* in captivity.

10 "Now *it is* in my heart to make [a]a covenant with the LORD God of Israel, that His fierce wrath may turn away from us.

11 "My sons, do not be negligent now, for the LORD has [a]chosen you to stand before Him, to serve Him, and that you should minister to Him and burn incense."

**12** Then these Levites arose: [a]Mahath the son of Amasai and Joel the son of Azariah, of the sons of the [b]Kohathites; of the sons of Merari, Kish the son of Abdi and Azariah the son of Jehallelel; of the Gershonites, Joah the son of Zimmah and Eden the son of Joah;

13 of the sons of Elizaphan, Shimri and Jeiel; of the sons of Asaph, Zechariah and Mattaniah;

14 of the sons of Heman, Jehiel and Shimei; and of the sons of Jeduthun, Shemaiah and Uzziel.

15 And they gathered their brethren, [a]sanctified[1] themselves, and went according to the commandment of the king, at the words of the LORD, [b]to cleanse the house of the LORD.

16 Then the priests went into the inner part of the house of the LORD to cleanse *it*, and brought out all the debris that they found in the temple of the LORD to the court of the house of the LORD. And the Levites took *it* out and carried *it* to the Brook [a]Kidron.

17 Now they began to [1]sanctify on the first *day* of the first month, and on the eighth day of the month they came to the vestibule of the LORD. So they sanctified the house of the LORD in eight days, and on the sixteenth day of the first month they finished.

18 So they went in to King Hezekiah and said, "We have cleansed all the house of the LORD, the altar of burnt offerings with all its articles, and the table of the showbread with all its articles.

19 "Moreover all the articles which King Ahaz in his reign had [a]cast aside in his transgression we have prepared and [1]sanctified; and there they *are*, before the altar of the LORD."

**20** Then King Hezekiah rose early, gathered the rulers of the city, and went up to the house of the LORD.

21 And they brought seven bulls, seven rams, seven lambs, and seven male goats for a [a]sin offering for the kingdom, for the sanctuary, and for Judah. Then he commanded the priests, the sons of Aaron, to offer *them* on the altar of the LORD.

22 So they killed the bulls, and the priests received the blood and [a]sprinkled *it* on the altar. Likewise they killed the rams and sprinkled the blood on the altar. They also killed the lambs and sprinkled the blood on the altar.

23 Then they brought out the male goats *for* the sin offering before the king and the assembly, and they laid their [a]hands on them.

24 And the priests killed them; and they presented their blood on the altar as a sin offering [a]to

**15** [b][Prov. 25:21, 22; Luke 6:27; Rom. 12:20] [c]Deut. 34:3; Judg. 1:16
**16** [a]2 Kin. 16:7 [1]LXX, [Syr.], Vg. *king* (cf. v. 20)
**17** [a]2 Chr. 21:10; Obad. 10–14
**18** [a]2 Chr. 21:16, 17; Ezek. 16:27, 57
**19** [a]2 Kin. 16:2; 2 Chr. 21:2 [b]Ex. 32:25 [1]*humbled Judah*
**20** [a]2 Kin. 15:29; 16:7–9; 1 Chr. 5:26 [1]Heb. *Tilgath Pilneser*
**23** [a]2 Chr. 25:14 [b]Jer. 44:17, 18
**24** [a]2 Chr. 29:3, 7
**25** [1]Places for pagan worship
**26** [a]2 Kin. 16:19, 20
**27** [a]2 Chr. 21:20; 24:25 [1]Died and joined his ancestors

CHAPTER 29
**1** [a]2 Kin. 18:1; 2 Chr. 32:22, 33 [b]2 Chr. 26:5 [1]*Abi*, 2 Kin. 18:2
**3** [a]2 Chr. 28:24; 29:7
**5** [a]1 Chr. 15:12; 2 Chr. 29:15, 34; 35:6 [1]*consecrate*
**6** [a][Is. 1:4]; Jer. 2:27; Ezek. 8:16 [1]Temple
**7** [a]2 Chr. 28:24
**8** [a]2 Chr. 24:18 [b]2 Chr. 28:5 [c]1 Kin. 9:8; Jer. 18:16; 19:8; 25:9, 18; 29:18 [d]Deut. 28:32
**9** [a]Deut. 28:25; 2 Chr. 28:5–8, 17
**10** [a]2 Chr. 15:12; 23:16
**11** [a]Num. 3:6; 8:14; 18:2, 6; 2 Chr. 30:16, 17
**12** [a]2 Chr. 31:13 [b]Num. 3:19, 20
**15** [a]2 Chr. 29:5 [b]1 Chr. 23:28 [1]*consecrated*
**16** [a]2 Chr. 15:16; 30:14
**17** [1]*consecrate*
**19** [a]2 Chr. 28:24 [1]*consecrated*
**21** [a]Lev. 4:3–14
**22** [a]Lev. 8:14, 15, 19, 24; Heb. 9:21
**23** [a]Lev. 4:15, 24; 8:14
**24** [a]Lev. 14:20

make an atonement for all Israel, for the king
commanded *that* the burnt offering and the sin
offering *be made* for all Israel.
**25** [a]And he stationed the Levites in the house of
the LORD with cymbals, with stringed instruments, and with harps, [b]according to the commandment of David, of [c]Gad the king's seer, and
of Nathan the prophet; [d]for thus *was* the commandment of the LORD by his prophets.
26 The Levites stood with the instruments [a]of
David, and the priests with [b]the trumpets.
27 Then Hezekiah commanded *them* to offer the
burnt offering on the altar. And when the burnt
offering began, [a]the song of the LORD *also* began,
with the trumpets and with the instruments of
David king of Israel.
28 So all the assembly worshiped, the singers
sang, and the trumpeters sounded; all *this continued* until the burnt offering was finished.
29 And when they had finished offering, [a]the king
and all who were present with him bowed and
worshiped.
30 Moreover King Hezekiah and the leaders commanded the Levites to sing praise to the LORD
with the words of David and of Asaph the seer. So
they sang praises with gladness, and they bowed
their heads and worshiped.
**31** Then Hezekiah answered and said, "Now *that*
you have consecrated yourselves to the LORD,
come near, and bring sacrifices and [a]thank offerings into the house of the LORD." So the assembly
brought in sacrifices and thank offerings, and as
many as were of a [b]willing heart *brought* burnt
offerings.
32 And the number of the burnt offerings which
the assembly brought was seventy bulls, one
hundred rams, *and* two hundred lambs; all these
*were* for a burnt offering to the LORD.
33 The consecrated things *were* six hundred bulls
and three thousand sheep.
34 But the priests were too few, so that they
could not skin all the burnt offerings; therefore
[a]their brethren the Levites helped them until the
work was ended and until the *other* priests had
[1]sanctified themselves, [b]for the Levites were [c]more
diligent in [d]sanctifying themselves than the
priests.
35 Also the burnt offerings *were* in abundance,
with [a]the fat of the peace offerings and *with* [b]the
drink offerings for *every* burnt offering. So the
service of the house of the LORD was set in order.
36 Then Hezekiah and all the people rejoiced that
God had prepared the people, since the events
took place so suddenly.

### *Hezekiah Keeps the Passover*

**30** And Hezekiah sent to all Israel and Judah,
and also wrote letters to Ephraim and Manasseh, that they should come to the house of the
LORD at Jerusalem, to keep the Passover to the
LORD God of Israel.
2 For the king and his leaders and all the assembly in Jerusalem had agreed to keep the Passover
in the second [a]month.
3 For they could not keep it [a]at [1]the regular
time, [b]because a sufficient number of priests had
not consecrated themselves, nor had the people
gathered together at Jerusalem.
4 And the matter pleased the king and all the
assembly.
5 So they [1]resolved to make a proclamation
throughout all Israel, from Beersheba to Dan, that
they should come to keep the Passover to the
LORD God of Israel at Jerusalem, since they had
not done *it* for a long *time* in the *prescribed*
manner.
6 Then the [a]runners went throughout all Israel
and Judah with the letters from the king and his
leaders, and spoke according to the command of
the king: "Children of Israel, [b]return to the LORD
God of Abraham, Isaac, and Israel; then He will
return to the remnant of you who have escaped
from the hand of [c]the kings of [d]Assyria.
7 "And do not be [a]like your fathers and your
brethren, who trespassed against the LORD God of
their fathers, so that He [b]gave them up to [c]desola-
tion, as you see.
8 "Now do not be [a]stiff-necked,[1] as your fathers
*were, but* yield yourselves to the LORD; and enter
His sanctuary, which He has sanctified forever,
and serve the LORD your God, [b]that the fierceness
of His wrath may turn away from you.
9 "For if you return to the LORD, your brethren
and your children *will be treated* with [a]compas-
sion by those who lead them captive, so that they
may come back to this land; for the LORD your
God *is* [b]gracious and merciful, and will not turn
*His* face from you if you [c]return to Him."
**10** So the runners passed from city to city
through the country of Ephraim and Manasseh, as
far as Zebulun; but [a]they laughed at them and
mocked them.
11 Nevertheless [a]some from Asher, Manasseh,
and Zebulun humbled themselves and came to
Jerusalem.
12 Also [a]the hand of God was on Judah to give
them singleness of heart to obey the command of
the king and the leaders, [b]at the word of the LORD.
**13** Now many people, a very great assembly,
gathered at Jerusalem to keep the Feast of [a]Un-
leavened Bread in the second month.
14 They arose and took away the [a]altars that
*were* in Jerusalem, and they took away all the
incense altars and cast *them* into the Brook
[b]Kidron.
15 Then they slaughtered the Passover *lambs* on
the fourteenth *day* of the second month. The
priests and the Levites [1]were [a]ashamed, and [2]sanc-
tified themselves, and brought the burnt offerings
to the house of the LORD.
16 They stood in their [a]place [1]according to their
custom, according to the Law of Moses the man of
God; the priests sprinkled the blood *received* from
the hand of the Levites.
17 For *there were* many in the assembly who had
not [1]sanctified themselves; [a]therefore the Levites
had charge of the slaughter of the Passover *lambs*
for everyone *who was* not clean, to sanctify *them*
to the LORD.
18 For a multitude of the people, [a]many from
Ephraim, Manasseh, Issachar, and Zebulun, had
not cleansed themselves, [b]yet they ate the Passover contrary to what was written. But Hezekiah
prayed for them, saying, "May the good LORD
provide atonement for everyone
19 "*who* [a]prepares his heart to seek God, the
LORD God of his fathers, though *he is* not *cleansed*
according to the purification of the sanctuary."
20 And the LORD listened to Hezekiah and healed
the people.
**21** So the children of Israel who were present at
Jerusalem kept [a]the Feast of Unleavened Bread

**25** [a]1 Chr. 16:4; 25:6 [b]1 Chr. 23:5; 25:1; 2 Chr. 8:14 [c]2 Sam. 24:11 [d]2 Chr. 30:12
**26** [a]1 Chr. 23:5; Amos 6:5 [b]Num. 10:8, 10; 1 Chr. 15:24; 16:6; 2 Chr. 5:12
**27** [a]2 Chr. 23:18
**29** [a]2 Chr. 20:18
**31** [a]Lev. 7:12 [b]Ex. 35:5, 22
**34** [a]2 Chr. 35:11 [b]2 Chr. 30:3 [c]Ps. 7:10 [d]2 Chr. 29:5 [1]*consecrated*
**35** [a]Lev. 3:16 [b]Num. 15:5–10

CHAPTER 30
**2** [a]Num. 9:10, 11; 2 Chr. 30:13, 15
**3** [a]Ex. 12:6, 18 [b]2 Chr. 19:17, 34 [1]The first month, Lev. 23:5; lit. *that time*
**5** [1]*established a decree to*
**6** [a]Esth. 8:14; Job 9:25; Jer. 51:31 [b][Jer. 4:1; Joel 2:13] [c]2 Kin. 15:19, 29 [d]2 Chr. 28:20
**7** [a]Ezek. 20:18 [b]Is. 1:9 [c]2 Chr. 29:8
**8** [a]Ex. 32:9; Deut. 10:16; Acts 7:51 [b]2 Chr. 29:10 [1]Rebellious
**9** [a]Ps. 106:46 [b][Ex. 34:6; Mic. 7:18] [c][Is. 55:7]
**10** [a]2 Chr. 36:16
**11** [a]2 Chr. 11:16; 30:18, 21
**12** [a][2 Cor. 3:5; Phil. 2:13; Heb. 13:20, 21] [b]2 Chr. 29:25
**13** [a]Lev. 23:6; Num. 9:11
**14** [a]2 Chr. 28:24 [b]2 Chr. 29:16
**15** [a]2 Chr. 29:34 [1]*humbled themselves* [2]*set themselves apart*
**16** [a]2 Chr. 35:10, 15 [1]Or *in their proper order*
**17** [a]2 Chr. 29:34 [1]*consecrated*
**18** [a]2 Chr. 30:1, 11, 25 [b]Ex. 12:43–49; [Num. 9:10]
**19** [a]2 Chr. 19:3
**21** [a]Ex. 12:15; 13:6; 1 Kin. 8:65

seven days with great gladness; and the Levites and the priests praised the LORD day by day, *singing* to the LORD, accompanied by loud instruments.
22 And Hezekiah gave encouragement to all the Levites [a]who taught the good knowledge of the LORD; and they ate throughout the feast seven days, offering peace offerings and [b]making confession to the LORD God of their fathers.
**23** Then the whole assembly agreed to keep *the feast* [a]another seven days, and they kept it *another* seven days with gladness.
24 For Hezekiah king of Judah [a]gave to the assembly a thousand bulls and seven thousand sheep, and the leaders gave to the assembly a thousand bulls and ten thousand sheep; and a great number of priests [b]sanctified[1] themselves.
25 The whole assembly of Judah rejoiced, also the priests and Levites, all the assembly that came from Israel, the sojourners [a]who came from the land of Israel, and those who dwelt in Judah.
26 So there was great joy in Jerusalem, for since the time of [a]Solomon the son of David, king of Israel, *there had* been nothing like this in Jerusalem.
27 Then the priests, the Levites, arose and [a]blessed the people, and their voice was heard; and their prayer came *up* to [b]His holy dwelling place, to heaven.

## *Hezekiah's Provision for Priests and Levites*

**31** Now when all this was finished, all Israel who were present went out to the cities of Judah and [a]broke the sacred pillars in pieces, cut down the wooden images, and threw down the [1]high places and the altars—from all Judah, Benjamin, Ephraim, and Manasseh—until they had utterly destroyed them all. Then all the children of Israel returned to their own cities, every man to his possession.
**2** And Hezekiah appointed [a]the divisions of the priests and the Levites according to their divisions, each man according to his service, the priests and Levites [b]for burnt offerings and peace offerings, to serve, to give thanks, and to praise in the gates of the [1]camp of the LORD.
3 The king also *appointed* a [1]portion of his [a]possessions[2] for the burnt offerings: for the morning and evening burnt offerings, the burnt offerings for the Sabbaths and the New Moons and the set feasts, as *it is* written in the [b]Law of the LORD.
4 Moreover he commanded the people who dwelt in Jerusalem to contribute [a]support[1] for the priests and the Levites, that they might devote themselves to [b]the Law of the LORD.
**5** As soon as the commandment was circulated, the children of Israel brought in abundance [a]the firstfruits of grain and wine, oil and honey, and of all the produce of the field; and they brought in abundantly the [b]tithe of everything.
6 And the children of Israel and Judah, who dwelt in the cities of Judah, brought the tithe of oxen and sheep; also the [a]tithe of holy things which were consecrated to the LORD their God they laid in heaps.
**7** In the third month they began laying them in heaps, and they finished in the seventh month.
8 And when Hezekiah and the leaders came and saw the heaps, they blessed the LORD and His people Israel.

**22** [a][Deut. 33:10]; 2 Chr. 17:9; 35:3 [b]Ezra 10:11
**23** [a]1 Kin. 8:65; 2 Chr. 35:17, 18
**24** [a]2 Chr. 35:7, 8 [b]2 Chr. 29:34 [1]*consecrated*
**25** [a]2 Chr. 30:11, 18
**26** [a]2 Chr. 7:8–10
**27** [a]Num. 6:23 [b]Deut. 26:15; Ps. 68:5

CHAPTER 31

**1** [a]2 Kin. 18:4 [1]Places for pagan worship
**2** [a]1 Chr. 23:6; 24:1 [b]1 Chr. 23:30, 31 [1]Temple
**3** [a]2 Chr. 35:7 [b]Num. 28:1—29:40 [1]*share* [2]*property*
**4** [a]Num. 18:8; 2 Kin. 12:16; Neh. 13:10; Ezek. 44:29 [b]Mal. 2:7 [1]*the portion due*
**5** [a]Ex. 22:29; Neh. 13:12 [b][Lev. 27:30]; Deut. 14:28; 26:12, 13
**6** [a][Lev. 27:30]; Deut. 14:28
**10** [a]1 Chr. 6:8, 9 [b][Mal. 3:10] [c]Ex. 36:5
**11** [a]1 Kin. 6:5–8 [1]*storerooms*
**12** [a]2 Chr. 35:9; Neh. 13:13
**13** [a]1 Chr. 9:11; Jer. 20:1
**14** [a]Deut. 23:23; 2 Chr. 35:8
**15** [a]2 Chr. 29:12 [b]Josh. 21:1–3, 9 [c]1 Chr. 9:26
**17** [a]1 Chr. 23:24, 27
**18** [1]*consecrated*
**19** [a]Lev. 25:34; Num. 35:1–4 [b]2 Chr. 31:12–15
**20** [a]2 Kin. 20:3; 22:2
**21** [a]2 Chr. 26:5; 32:30; Ps. 1:3

CHAPTER 32

**1** [a]2 Kin. 18:13—19:37; Is. 36:1—37:38
**3** [1]Lit. *mighty men*
**4** [a]2 Kin. 20:20

9 Then Hezekiah questioned the priests and the Levites concerning the heaps.
10 And Azariah the chief priest, from the [a]house of Zadok, answered him and said, [b]"Since *the people* began to bring the offerings into the house of the LORD, we have had enough to eat and have plenty left, for the LORD has blessed His people; and what is left *is* this great [c]abundance."
**11** Now Hezekiah commanded *them* to prepare [a]rooms[1] in the house of the LORD, and they prepared them.
12 Then they faithfully brought in the offerings, the tithes, and the dedicated things; [a]Cononiah the Levite had charge of them, and Shimei his brother *was* the next.
13 Jehiel, Azaziah, Nahath, Asahel, Jerimoth, Jozabad, Eliel, Ismachiah, Mahath, and Benaiah *were* overseers under the hand of Cononiah and Shimei his brother, at the commandment of Hezekiah the king and Azariah the [a]ruler of the house of God.
14 Kore the son of Imnah the Levite, the keeper of the East Gate, *was* over the [a]freewill offerings to God, to distribute the offerings of the LORD and the most holy things.
15 And under him *were* [a]Eden, Miniamin, Jeshua, Shemaiah, Amariah, and Shecaniah, *his* faithful assistants in [b]the cities of the priests, to distribute [c]allotments to their brethren by divisions, to the great as well as the small.
16 Besides those males from three years old and up who were written in the genealogy, they distributed to everyone who entered the house of the LORD his daily portion for the work of his service, by his division,
17 and to the priests who were written in the genealogy according to their father's house, and to the Levites [a]from twenty years old and up according to their work, by their divisions,
18 and to all who were written in the genealogy—their little ones and their wives, their sons and daughters, the whole company of them—for in their faithfulness they [1]sanctified themselves in holiness.
19 Also for the sons of Aaron the priests, *who were* in [a]the fields of the common-lands of their cities, in every single city, *there were* men who were [b]designated by name to distribute portions to all the males among the priests and to all who were listed by genealogies among the Levites.
**20** Thus Hezekiah did throughout all Judah, and he [a]did what *was* good and right and true before the LORD his God.
21 And in every work that he began in the service of the house of God, in the law and in the commandment, to seek his God, he did *it* with all his heart. So he [a]prospered.

## *Sennacherib Invades Judah*

**32** After [a]these deeds of faithfulness, Sennacherib king of Assyria came and entered Judah; he encamped against the fortified cities, thinking to win them over to himself.
2 And when Hezekiah saw that Sennacherib had come, and that his purpose was to make war against Jerusalem,
3 he consulted with his leaders and [1]commanders to stop the water from the springs which *were* outside the city; and they helped him.
4 Thus many people gathered together who stopped all the [a]springs and the brook that ran

through the land, saying, "Why should the [1]kings
of Assyria come and find much water?"
5 And [a]he strengthened himself, [b]built up all the
wall that was broken, raised *it* up to the towers,
and *built* another wall outside; also he repaired
[1]the [c]Millo *in* the City of David, and made [2]weap-
ons and shields in abundance.
6 Then he set military captains over the people,
gathered them together to him in the open square
of the city gate, and [a]gave them encouragement,
saying,
7 [a]"Be strong and courageous; [b]do not be afraid
nor dismayed before the king of Assyria, nor
before all the multitude that *is* with him; for [c]*there*
*are* more with us than with him.
8 "With him *is* an [a]arm of flesh; but [b]with us *is*
the LORD our God, to help us and to fight our
battles." And the people were strengthened by the
words of Hezekiah king of Judah.
**9** [a]After this Sennacherib king of Assyria sent
his servants to Jerusalem (but he and all the
forces with him *laid siege* against Lachish), to
Hezekiah king of Judah, and to all Judah who
*were* in Jerusalem, saying,
10 [a]"Thus says Sennacherib king of Assyria: 'In
what do you trust, that you remain under siege in
Jerusalem?
11 'Does not Hezekiah persuade you to give
yourselves over to die by famine and by thirst,
saying, [a]"The LORD our God will deliver us from
the hand of the king of Assyria"?
12 [a]'Has not the same Hezekiah taken away His
high places and His altars, and commanded Judah
and Jerusalem, saying, "You shall worship before
one altar and burn incense on [b]it"?
13 'Do you not know what I and my fathers have
done to all the peoples of *other* lands? [a]Were the
gods of the nations of those lands in any way able
to deliver their lands out of my hand?
14 'Who *was there* among all the gods of those
nations that my fathers utterly destroyed that
could deliver his people from my hand, that your
God should be able to deliver you from my [a]hand?
15 'Now therefore, [a]do not let Hezekiah deceive
you or persuade you like this, and do not believe
him; for no god of any nation or kingdom was able
to deliver his people from my hand or the hand of
my fathers. How much less will your God deliver
you from my hand?' "
**16** Furthermore, his servants spoke against the
LORD God and against His servant Hezekiah.
17 He also wrote letters to revile the LORD God of
Israel, and to speak against Him, saying, [a]"As the
gods of the nations of *other* lands have not delivered their people from my hand, so the God of
Hezekiah will not deliver His people from my
[b]hand."
18 [a]Then they called out with a loud voice in
[1]Hebrew to the people of Jerusalem who *were* on
the wall, to frighten them and trouble them, that
they might take the city.
19 And they spoke against the God of Jerusalem,
as against the gods of the people of the earth—
[a]the work of men's hands.
**20** [a]Now because of this King Hezekiah and [b]the
prophet Isaiah, the son of Amoz, prayed and cried
out to heaven.
21 [a]Then the LORD sent an angel who cut down
every mighty man of valor, leader, and captain in
the camp of the king of Assyria. So he returned
[b]shamefaced to his own land. And when he had
gone into the temple of his god, some of his own
offspring struck him down with the sword there.
22 Thus the LORD saved Hezekiah and the
inhabitants of Jerusalem from the hand of Sennacherib the king of Assyria, and from the hand of
all *others*, and [1]guided them on every side.
23 And many brought gifts to the LORD at Jerusalem, and [a]presents[1] to Hezekiah king of Judah, so
that he was [b]exalted in the sight of all nations
thereafter.
**24** [a]In those days Hezekiah was sick and near
death, and he prayed to the LORD; and He spoke to
him and gave him a sign.
25 But Hezekiah [a]did not repay according to the
favor *shown* him, for [b]his heart was lifted up;
[c]therefore wrath was looming over him and over
Judah and Jerusalem.
26 [a]Then Hezekiah humbled himself for the pride
of his heart, he and the inhabitants of Jerusalem,
so that the wrath of the LORD did not come upon
them [b]in the days of Hezekiah.
**27** Hezekiah had very great riches and honor.
And he made himself treasuries for silver, for gold,
for precious stones, for spices, for shields, and for
all kinds of desirable items;
28 storehouses for the harvest of grain, wine, and
oil; and stalls for all kinds of livestock, and [1]folds
for flocks.
29 Moreover he provided cities for himself, and
possessions of flocks and herds in abundance; for
[a]God had given him very much property.
30 [a]This same Hezekiah also stopped the water
outlet of Upper Gihon, and [1]brought the water by
tunnel to the west side of the City of David.
Hezekiah [b]prospered in all his works.
**31** However, *regarding* the ambassadors of the
princes of Babylon, whom they [a]sent to him to
inquire about the wonder that was *done* in the
land, God withdrew from him, in order to [b]test
him, that He might know all *that was* in his heart.
**32** Now the rest of the acts of Hezekiah, and his
goodness, indeed they *are* written in [a]the vision of
Isaiah the prophet, the son of Amoz, *and* in the
[b]book of the kings of Judah and Israel.
33 [a]So Hezekiah [1]rested with his fathers, and they
buried him in the upper tombs of the sons of
David; and all Judah and the inhabitants of Jerusalem [b]honored him at his death. Then Manasseh
his son reigned in his place.

### *Manasseh Reigns over Judah*

**33** Manasseh [a]*was* twelve years old when he
became king, and he reigned fifty-five years
in Jerusalem.
2 But he did evil in the sight of the LORD,
according to the [a]abominations of the nations
whom the LORD had cast out before the children
of Israel.
3 For he rebuilt the [1]high places which Hezekiah
his father had [a]broken down; he raised up altars
for the Baals, and [b]made wooden images; and he
worshiped [c]all [2]the host of heaven and served
them.
4 He also built altars in the house of the LORD,
of which the LORD had said, [a]"In Jerusalem shall
My name be forever."
5 And he built altars for all the host of heaven
[a]in the two courts of the house of the LORD.
6 [a]Also he caused his sons to pass through the
fire in the Valley of the Son of Hinnom; he practiced [b]soothsaying, used witchcraft and sorcery,

**4** [1]So with MT, Vg.; Arab., LXX, Syr. *king*
**5** [a]Is. 22:9, 10 [b]2 Chr. 25:23 [c]2 Sam. 5:9 [1]Lit. *The Landfill* [2]*javelins*
**6** [a]2 Chr. 30:22
**7** [a][Deut. 31:6] [b]2 Chr. 20:15 [c]2 Kin. 6:16
**8** [a][Jer. 17:5] [b][Rom. 8:31]
**9** [a]2 Kin. 18:17
**10** [a]2 Kin. 18:19
**11** [a]2 Kin. 18:30
**12** [a]2 Kin. 18:22 [b]2 Chr. 31:1, 2
**13** [a]2 Kin. 18:33–35
**14** [a][Is. 10:5–12]
**15** [a]2 Kin. 18:29
**17** [a]2 Kin. 19:9 [b]2 Kin. 19:12
**18** [a]2 Kin. 18:28 [1]Lit. *Judean*
**19** [a][Ps. 96:5; 115:4–8]
**20** [a]2 Kin. 19:15 [b]2 Kin. 19:2
**21** [a]Zech. 14:3 [b]Ps. 44:7
**22** [1]LXX gave them rest; Vg. *gave them treasures*
**23** [a]2 Sam. 8:10 [b]2 Chr. 1:1 [1]Lit. *precious things*
**24** [a]Is. 38:1–8
**25** [a]Ps. 116:12 [b][Hab. 2:4] [c]2 Chr. 24:18
**26** [a]Jer. 26:18, 19 [b]2 Kin. 20:19
**28** [1]So with LXX, Vg.; Arab., Syr. omit *folds for flocks;* MT *flocks for sheepfolds*
**29** [a]1 Chr. 29:12
**30** [a]Is. 22:9–11 [b]2 Chr. 31:21 [1]Lit. *brought it straight to* (cf. 2 Kin. 20:20)
**31** [a]Is. 39:1 [b][Deut. 8:2, 16]
**32** [a]Is. 36—39 [b]2 Kin. 18—20
**33** [a]2 Kin. 20:21 [b]Prov. 10:7 [1]Died and joined his ancestors

CHAPTER 33
**1** [a]2 Kin. 21:1–9
**2** [a]2 Chr. 28:3
**3** [a]2 Kin. 18:4 [b]Deut. 16:21 [c]Deut. 17:3 [1]Places for pagan worship [2]The gods of the Assyrians
**4** [a]2 Chr. 6:6; 7:16
**5** [a]2 Chr. 4:9
**6** [a][Lev. 18:21] [b]Deut. 18:11

and [c]consulted mediums and spiritists. He did
much evil in the sight of the LORD, to provoke
Him to anger.
7 [a]He even set a carved image, the idol which he
had made, in the [1]house of God, of which God had
said to David and to Solomon his son, [b]"In this
house and in Jerusalem, which I have chosen out
of all the tribes of Israel, I will put My name
forever;
8 [a]"and I will not again remove the foot of Israel
from the land which I have appointed for your
fathers—only if they are careful to do all that I
have commanded them, according to the whole
law and the statutes and the ordinances by the
hand of Moses."
9 So Manasseh seduced Judah and the inhabitants of Jerusalem to do more evil than the nations
whom the LORD had destroyed before the children
of Israel.
**10** And the LORD spoke to Manasseh and his
people, but they would not [1]listen.
11 [a]Therefore the LORD brought upon them the
captains of the army of the king of Assyria, who
took Manasseh with [1]hooks, [b]bound him with
[2]bronze *fetters,* and carried him off to Babylon.
12 Now when he was in affliction, he implored
the LORD his God, and [a]humbled himself greatly
before the God of his fathers,
13 and prayed to Him; and He [a]received his
entreaty, heard his supplication, and brought him
back to Jerusalem into his kingdom. Then Manasseh [b]knew that the LORD *was* God.
**14** After this he built a wall outside the City of
David on the west side of [a]Gihon, in the valley, as
far as the entrance of the Fish Gate; and *it*
[b]enclosed Ophel, and he raised it to a very great
height. Then he put military captains in all the
fortified cities of Judah.
15 He took away [a]the foreign gods and the idol
from the house of the LORD, and all the altars that
he had built in the mount of the house of the LORD
and in Jerusalem; and he cast *them* out of the city.
16 He also repaired the altar of the LORD, sacrificed peace offerings and [a]thank offerings on it,
and commanded Judah to serve the LORD God of
Israel.
17 [a]Nevertheless the people still sacrificed on the
[1]high places, *but* only to the LORD their God.
**18** Now the rest of the acts of Manasseh, his
prayer to his God, and the words of [a]the seers who
spoke to him in the name of the LORD God of
Israel, indeed they *are written* in the [1]book of the
kings of Israel.
19 Also his prayer and *how God* received his
entreaty, and all his sin and trespass, and the sites
where he built [1]high places and set up wooden
images and carved images, before he was humbled, indeed they *are* written among the sayings
of [2]Hozai.
20 [a]So Manasseh rested with his fathers, and they
buried him in his own house. Then his son Amon
reigned in his place.
**21** [a]Amon *was* twenty-two years old when he
became king, and he reigned two years in Jerusalem.
22 But he did evil in the sight of the LORD, as his
father Manasseh had done; for Amon sacrificed to
all the carved images which his father Manasseh
had made, and served them.
23 And he did not humble himself before the
LORD, [a]as his father Manasseh had humbled himself; but Amon trespassed more and more.
24 [a]Then his servants conspired against him, and
[b]killed him in his own house.
25 But the people of the land executed all those
who had conspired against King Amon. Then the
people of the land made his son Josiah king in his
place.

### *Hilkiah Finds the Book of the Law*

**34** Josiah [a]*was* eight years old when he became
king, and he reigned thirty-one years in
Jerusalem.
2 And he did *what was* right in the sight of the
LORD, and walked in the ways of his father David;
*he* did *not* turn aside to the right hand or to the
left.
3 For in the eighth year of his reign, while he
was still [a]young, he began to [b]seek the God of his
father David; and in the twelfth year he began [c]to
purge Judah and Jerusalem [d]of the [1]high places,
the wooden images, the carved images, and the
molded images.
4 [a]They broke down the altars of the Baals in his
presence, and the incense altars which *were* above
them he cut down; and the wooden images, the
carved images, and the molded images he broke in
pieces, and made dust of them [b]and scattered *it* on
the graves of those who had sacrificed to them.
5 He also [a]burned the bones of the priests on
their [b]altars, and cleansed Judah and Jerusalem.
6 And *so he did* in the cities of Manasseh,
Ephraim, and Simeon, as far as Naphtali and all
around, with [1]axes.
7 When he had broken down the altars and the
wooden images, had [a]beaten the carved images
into powder, and cut down all the incense altars
throughout all the land of Israel, he returned to
Jerusalem.
**8** [a]In the eighteenth year of his reign, when he
had purged the land and the [1]temple, he sent
[b]Shaphan the son of Azaliah, Maaseiah the [c]gover-
nor of the city, and Joah the son of Joahaz the
recorder, to repair the house of the LORD his God.
9 When they came to Hilkiah the high priest,
they delivered [a]the money that was brought into
the house of God, which the Levites who kept the
doors had gathered from the hand of Manasseh
and Ephraim, from all the [b]remnant of Israel, from
all Judah and Benjamin, and *which* they had
brought back to Jerusalem.
10 Then they put *it* in the hand of the foremen
who had the oversight of the house of the LORD;
and they gave it to the workmen who worked in
the house of the LORD, to repair and restore the
house.
11 They gave *it* to the craftsmen and builders to
buy hewn stone and timber for beams, and to floor
the houses which the kings of Judah had destroyed.
12 And the men did the work faithfully. Their
overseers *were* Jahath and Obadiah the Levites, of
the sons of Merari, and Zechariah and Meshullam,
of the sons of the Kohathites, to supervise. *Others
of* the Levites, all of whom were skillful with
instruments of music,
13 *were* [a]over the burden bearers and *were* overseers of all who did work in any kind of service.
[b]And *some* of the Levites *were* scribes, officers,
and gatekeepers.
**14** Now when they brought out the money that

**6** [c][Lev. 19:31; 20:27]; 2 Kin. 21:6
**7** [a]2 Kin. 21:7; 2 Chr. 25:14 [b]Ps. 132:14 [1]Temple
**8** [a]2 Sam. 7:10
**10** [1]*obey*
**11** [a]Deut. 28:36 [b]2 Chr. 36:6; Job 36:8; Ps. 107:10, 11 [1]Nose hooks, 2 Kin. 19:28 [2]*chains*
**12** [a]2 Chr. 7:14; 32:26; [1 Pet. 5:6]
**13** [a]1 Chr. 5:20; Ezra 8:23 [b]1 Kin. 20:13; Ps. 9:16; Dan. 4:25
**14** [a]1 Kin. 1:33 [b]2 Chr. 27:3
**15** [a]2 Chr. 33:3, 5, 7
**16** [a]Lev. 7:12
**17** [a]2 Chr. 32:12 [1]Places for pagan worship
**18** [a]1 Sam. 9:9 [1]Lit. *words*
**19** [1]Places for pagan worship [2]LXX *the seers*
**20** [a]1 Kin. 1:21; 2 Kin. 21:18
**21** [a]2 Kin. 21:19–24; 1 Chr. 3:14
**23** [a]2 Chr. 33:12, 19
**24** [a]2 Kin. 21:23, 24; 2 Chr. 24:25 [b]2 Chr. 25:27

CHAPTER 34

**1** [a]2 Kin. 22:1, 2; Jer. 1:2; 3:6
**3** [a]Eccl. 12:1 [b]2 Chr. 15:2; [Prov. 8:17] [c]1 Kin. 13:2 [d]2 Chr. 33:17–19, 22 [1]Places for pagan worship
**4** [a]Lev. 26:30; 2 Kin. 23:4 [b]2 Kin. 23:6
**5** [a]1 Kin. 13:2 [b]2 Kin. 23:20
**6** [1]Lit. *swords*
**7** [a]Deut. 9:21
**8** [a]2 Kin. 22:3–20 [b]2 Kin. 25:22 [c]2 Chr. 18:25 [1]Lit. *house*
**9** [a]2 Kin. 12:4 [b]2 Chr. 30:6
**13** [a]2 Chr. 8:10 [b]1 Chr. 23:4, 5

was brought into the house of the LORD, Hilkiah
the priest [a]found the Book of the Law of the LORD
*given* by Moses.
15 Then Hilkiah answered and said to Shaphan
the scribe, "I have found the Book of the Law in
the house of the LORD." And Hilkiah gave the
[a]book to Shaphan.
16 So Shaphan carried the book to the king,
bringing the king word, saying, "All that was
committed to your servants they are doing.
17 "And they have [1]gathered the money that was
found in the house of the LORD, and have delivered it into the hand of the overseers and the
workmen."
18 Then Shaphan the scribe told the king, saying,
"Hilkiah the priest has given me a book." And
Shaphan read it before the king.
**19** Thus it happened, when the king heard the
words of the Law, that he tore his clothes.
20 Then the king commanded Hilkiah, [a]Ahikam
the son of Shaphan, [1]Abdon the son of Micah,
Shaphan the scribe, and Asaiah a servant of the
king, saying,
21 "Go, inquire of the LORD for me, and for those
who are left in Israel and Judah, concerning the
words of the book that is found; for great *is* the
wrath of the LORD that is poured out on us,
because our fathers have not [a]kept the word of
the LORD, to do according to all that is written in
this book."
**22** So Hilkiah and those the king *had appointed*
went to Huldah the prophetess, the wife of Shallum the son of [1]Tokhath, the son of [2]Hasrah,
keeper of the wardrobe. (She dwelt in Jerusalem
in the Second Quarter.) And they spoke to her to
that *effect*.
23 Then she answered them, "Thus says the
LORD God of Israel, 'Tell the man who sent you to
Me,
24 "Thus says the LORD: 'Behold, I will [a]bring
calamity on this place and on its inhabitants, all
the curses that are written in the [b]book which
they have read before the king of Judah,
25 'because they have forsaken Me and burned
incense to other gods, that they might provoke
Me to anger with all the works of their hands.
Therefore My wrath will be poured out on this
place, and not be quenched.' " '
26 "But as for the king of Judah, who sent you to
inquire of the LORD, in this manner you shall
speak to him, 'Thus says the LORD God of Israel:
"*Concerning* the words which you have heard—
27 "because your heart was tender, and you
humbled yourself before God when you heard His
words against this place and against its inhabitants, and you humbled yourself before Me, and
you tore your clothes and wept before Me, I also
have heard *you*," says the [a]LORD.
28 "Surely I will gather you to your fathers, and
you shall be gathered to your grave in peace; and
your eyes shall not see all the calamity which I
will bring on this place and its inhabitants." ' " So
they brought back word to the king.
**29** [a]Then the king sent and gathered all the elders
of Judah and Jerusalem.
30 The king went up to the house of the LORD,
with all the men of Judah and the inhabitants of
Jerusalem—the priests and the Levites, and all the
people, great and small. And he [a]read in their
hearing all the words of the Book of the Covenant
which had been found in the house of the LORD.
31 Then the king [a]stood in [b]his place and made a
[c]covenant before the LORD, to follow the LORD,
and to keep His commandments and His testimonies and His statutes with all his heart and all his
soul, to perform the words of the covenant that
were written in this book.
32 And he made all who were present in Jerusalem and Benjamin take a stand. So the inhabitants
of Jerusalem did according to the covenant of
God, the God of their fathers.
33 Thus Josiah removed all the [a]abominations
from all the country that *belonged* to the children
of Israel, and made all who were present in Israel
[1]diligently serve the LORD their God. [b]All his days
they did not depart from following the LORD God
of their fathers.

### *Josiah Keeps the Passover*

**35** Now [a]Josiah kept a Passover to the LORD in
Jerusalem, and they slaughtered the Passover *lambs* on the [b]fourteenth *day* of the first
month.
2 And he set the priests in their [a]duties and
[b]encouraged them for the service of the house of
the LORD.
3 Then he said to the Levites [a]who taught all
Israel, who were holy to the LORD: [b]"Put the holy
ark [c]in the house which Solomon the son of
David, king of Israel, built. [d]*It shall* no longer *be* a
burden on *your* shoulders. Now serve the LORD
your God and His people Israel.
4 "Prepare *yourselves* [a]according to your fathers' [1]houses, according to your divisions, following the [b]written instruction of David king of Israel
and the [c]written instruction of Solomon his son.
5 "And [a]stand in the holy *place* according to the
divisions of the fathers' houses of your brethren
the *lay* people, and *according to* the division of the
father's house of the Levites.
6 "So slaughter the Passover *offerings*, [a]conse-
crate yourselves, and prepare *them* for your brethren, that *they* may do according to the word of
the LORD by the hand of Moses."
**7** Then Josiah [a]gave the *lay* people lambs and
young goats from the flock, all for Passover
*offerings* for all who were present, to the number
of thirty thousand, as well as three thousand
cattle; these *were* from the king's [b]possessions.
8 And his [a]leaders gave willingly to the people,
to the priests, and to the Levites. Hilkiah, Zechariah, and Jehiel, rulers of the house of God, gave
to the priests for the Passover *offerings* two
thousand six hundred *from the flock*, and three
hundred cattle.
9 Also [a]Conaniah, his brothers Shemaiah and
Nethanel, and Hashabiah and Jeiel and Jozabad,
chief of the Levites, gave to the Levites for Passover *offerings* five thousand *from the flock* and
five hundred cattle.
**10** So the service was prepared, and the priests
[a]stood in their places, and the [b]Levites in their
divisions, according to the king's command.
11 And they slaughtered the Passover *offerings*;
and the priests [a]sprinkled *the blood* with their
hands, while the Levites [b]skinned *the animals*.
12 Then they removed the burnt offerings that
*they* might give them to the divisions of the
fathers' houses of the *lay* people, to offer to the
LORD, as *it is* written [a]in the Book of Moses. And
so *they did* with the cattle.
13 Also they [a]roasted the Passover *offerings* with

14 [a]2 Kin. 22:8
15 [a]Deut. 31:24, 26
17 [1]Lit. *poured out*
20 [a]Jer. 26:24 [1]*Achbor, the son of Michaiah,* 2 Kin. 22:12
21 [a]2 Kin. 17:15–19
22 [1]*Tikvah,* 2 Kin. 22:14 [2]*Harhas,* 2 Kin. 22:14
24 [a]2 Chr. 36:14–20 [b]Deut. 28:15–68
27 [a]2 Kin. 22:19; 2 Chr. 12:7; 30:6; 33:12, 13
29 [a]2 Kin. 23:1–3
30 [a]Neh. 8:1–3
31 [a]2 Chr. 6:13 [b]2 Kin. 11:14; 23:3; 2 Chr. 30:16 [c]2 Chr. 23:16; 29:10
33 [a]1 Kin. 11:5; 2 Chr. 33:2 [b]Jer. 3:10 [1]Lit. *serve to serve*

CHAPTER 35

1 [a]2 Kin. 23:21, 22 [b]Ex. 12:6; Num. 9:3; Ezra 6:19
2 [a]2 Chr. 23:18; Ezra 6:18 [b]2 Chr. 29:5–15
3 [a]Deut. 33:10; 2 Chr. 17:8, 9; Neh. 8:7 [b]2 Chr. 34:14 [c]Ex. 40:21; 2 Chr. 5:7 [d]1 Chr. 23:26
4 [a]1 Chr. 9:10–13 [b]1 Chr. 23—26 [c]2 Chr. 8:14 [1]*households*
5 [a]Ps. 134:1
6 [a]2 Chr. 29:5, 15
7 [a]2 Chr. 30:24 [b]2 Chr. 31:3
8 [a]Num. 7:2
9 [a]2 Chr. 31:12
10 [a]Ezra 6:18; Heb. 9:6 [b]2 Chr. 5:12; 7:6; 8:14, 15; 13:10; 29:25–34
11 [a]Ex. 12:22; 2 Chr. 29:22 [b]2 Chr. 29:34
12 [a]Lev. 3:3; Ezra 6:18
13 [a]Ex. 12:8, 9; Deut. 16:7

fire according to the ordinance; but the *other* holy
*offerings* they [b]boiled in pots, in caldrons, and in
pans, and divided *them* quickly among all the *lay*
people.
14 Then afterward they prepared portions for
themselves and for the priests, because the priests,
the sons of Aaron, *were busy* in offering burnt
offerings and fat until night; therefore the Levites
prepared portions for themselves and for the
priests, the sons of Aaron.
15 And the singers, the sons of Asaph, *were* in
their places, according to the [a]command of David,
Asaph, Heman, and Jeduthun the king's seer. Also
the gatekeepers [b]were at each gate; they did not
have to leave their position, because their brethren the Levites prepared portions for them.
16 So all the service of the LORD was prepared
the same day, to keep the Passover and to offer
burnt offerings on the altar of the LORD, according
to the command of King Josiah.
17 And the children of Israel who were present
kept the Passover at that time, and the Feast of
[a]Unleavened Bread for seven days.
18 [a]There had been no Passover kept in Israel
like that since the days of Samuel the prophet;
and none of the kings of Israel had kept such a
Passover as Josiah kept, with the priests and the
Levites, all Judah and Israel who were present,
and the inhabitants of Jerusalem.
19 In the eighteenth year of the reign of Josiah
this Passover was kept.
**20** [a]After all this, when Josiah had prepared the
temple, Necho king of Egypt came up to fight
against [b]Carchemish by the Euphrates; and Josiah
went out against him.
21 But he sent messengers to him, saying, "What
have I to do with you, king of Judah? *I have* not
*come* against you this day, but against the house
with which I have war; for God commanded me to
make haste. Refrain *from meddling with* God,
who *is* with me, lest He destroy you."
22 Nevertheless Josiah would not turn his face
from him, but [a]disguised himself so that he might
fight with him, and did not heed the words of
Necho from the mouth of God. So he came to
fight in the Valley of Megiddo.
23 And the archers shot King Josiah; and the
king said to his servants, "Take me away, for I am
severely wounded."
24 [a]His servants therefore took him out of that
chariot and put him in the second chariot that he
had, and they brought him to Jerusalem. So he
died, and was buried in *one of* the tombs of his
fathers. And [b]all Judah and Jerusalem mourned
for Josiah.
25 Jeremiah also [a]lamented for [b]Josiah. And to
this day [c]all the singing men and the singing
women speak of Josiah in their lamentations.
[d]They made it a custom in Israel; and indeed they
*are* written in the Laments.
**26** Now the rest of the acts of Josiah and his
goodness, according to *what was* written in the
Law of the LORD,
27 and his deeds from first to last, indeed they *are*
written in the book of the kings of Israel and
Judah.

### *Jehoiakim Reigns in Judah*

**36** Then [a]the people of the land took Jehoahaz
the son of Josiah, and made him king in his
father's place in Jerusalem.
2 [1]Jehoahaz *was* twenty-three years old when
he became king, and he reigned three months in
Jerusalem.
3 Now the king of Egypt deposed him at Jerusalem; and he imposed on the land a tribute of one
hundred talents of silver and a talent of gold.
4 Then the king of Egypt made [1]*Jehoahaz's*
brother Eliakim king over Judah and Jerusalem,
and changed his name to Jehoiakim. And Necho
took [2]Jehoahaz his brother and carried him off to
Egypt.
**5** [a]Jehoiakim *was* twenty-five years old when he
became king, and he reigned eleven years in
Jerusalem. And he did [b]evil in the sight of the
LORD his God.
6 [a]Nebuchadnezzar king of Babylon came up
against him, and bound him in [1]bronze *fetters* to
[b]carry him off to Babylon.
7 [a]Nebuchadnezzar also carried off *some* of the
articles from the house of the LORD to Babylon,
and put them in his temple at Babylon.
8 Now the rest of the acts of Jehoiakim, the
abominations which he did, and what was found
against him, indeed they *are* written in the book
of the kings of Israel and Judah. Then [1]Jehoiachin
his son reigned in his place.
**9** [a]Jehoiachin *was* [1]eight years old when he
became king, and he reigned in Jerusalem three
months and ten days. And he did evil in the sight
of the LORD.
10 At the turn of the year [a]King Nebuchadnezzar
summoned *him* and took him to Babylon, [b]with
the costly articles from the house of the LORD, and
made [c]Zedekiah,[1] [2]*Jehoiakim's* brother, king over
Judah and Jerusalem.
**11** [a]Zedekiah *was* twenty-one years old when he
became king, and he reigned eleven years in
Jerusalem.
12 He did evil in the sight of the LORD his God,
*and* [a]did not humble himself before Jeremiah the
prophet, *who spoke* from the mouth of the LORD.
13 And he also [a]rebelled against King Nebuchadnezzar, who had made him swear *an oath* by God;
but he [b]stiffened his neck and hardened his heart
against turning to the LORD God of Israel.
14 Moreover all the leaders of the priests and the
people transgressed more and more, *according* to
all the abominations of the nations, and defiled
the house of the LORD which He had consecrated
in Jerusalem.
**15** [a]And the LORD God of their fathers sent *warn-
ings* to them by His messengers, rising up early
and sending *them*, because He had compassion on
His people and on His dwelling place.
16 But [a]they mocked the messengers of God,
[b]despised His words, and [c]scoffed at His prophets,
until the [d]wrath of the LORD arose against His
people, till *there was* no remedy.
**17** [a]Therefore He brought against them the king
of the Chaldeans, who [b]killed their young men
with the sword in the house of their sanctuary,
and had no compassion on young man or virgin,
on the aged or the weak; He gave *them* all into his
hand.
18 [a]And all the articles from the house of God,
great and small, the treasures of the house of the
LORD, and the treasures of the king and of his
leaders, all *these* he took to Babylon.
19 [a]Then they burned the house of God, broke
down the wall of Jerusalem, burned all its palaces

**13** [b]1 Sam. 2:13–15
**15** [a]1 Chr. 25:1–6 [b]1 Chr. 9:17, 18
**17** [a]Ex. 12:15; 13:6; 2 Chr. 30:21
**18** [a]2 Kin. 23:22, 23
**20** [a]2 Kin. 23:29 [b]Is. 10:9; Jer. 46:2
**22** [a]1 Kin. 22:30; 2 Chr. 18:29
**24** [a]2 Kin. 23:30 [b]1 Kin. 14:18; Zech. 12:11
**25** [a]Lam. 4:20 [b]Jer. 22:10, 11 [c]Matt. 9:23 [d]Jer. 22:20

CHAPTER 36

**1** [a]2 Kin. 23:30–34
**2** [1]MT *Joahaz*
**4** [1]Lit. *his* [2]MT *Joahaz*
**5** [a]2 Kin. 23:36, 37; 1 Chr. 3:15 [b][Jer. 22:13–19]
**6** [a]2 Kin. 24:1; Hab. 1:6 [b][Deut. 29:22–29]; 2 Chr. 33:11; Jer. 36:30 [1]*chains*
**7** [a]2 Kin. 24:13; Dan. 1:1, 2
**8** [1]Or *Jeconiah*
**9** [a]2 Kin. 24:8–17 [1]Heb. mss., LXX, Syr. *eighteen* and 2 Kin. 24:8
**10** [a]2 Kin. 24:10–17 [b]Dan. 1:1, 2 [c]Jer. 37:1 [1]Or *Mattaniah* [2]Lit. *his brother,* 2 Kin. 24:17
**11** [a]2 Kin. 24:18–20; Jer. 52:1
**12** [a]Jer. 21:3–7; 44:10
**13** [a]Jer. 52:3; Ezek. 17:15 [b]2 Kin. 17:14; [2 Chr. 30:8]
**15** [a]Jer. 7:13; 25:3, 4
**16** [a]2 Chr. 30:10; Jer. 5:12, 13 [b][Prov. 1:24–32] [c]Jer. 38:6; Matt. 23:34 [d]2 Chr. 34:25; Ps. 79:5
**17** [a]Num. 33:56; Deut. 4:26; 28:49; 2 Kin. 25:1; Ezra 9:7; Is. 3:8 [b]Ps. 74:20
**18** [a]2 Kin. 25:13–15; 2 Chr. 36:7, 10
**19** [a]2 Kin. 25:9; Ps. 79:1, 7; Is. 1:7, 8; Jer. 52:13

with fire, and destroyed all its precious possessions.
20 And [a]those who escaped from the sword he
carried away to Babylon, [b]where they became
servants to him and his sons until the rule of the
kingdom of Persia,
21 to fulfill the word of the LORD by the mouth of
[a]Jeremiah, until the land [b]had enjoyed her Sabbaths. As long as she lay desolate [c]she kept
Sabbath, to fulfill seventy years.
22 [a]Now in the first year of Cyrus king of Persia,
that the word of the LORD by the mouth of [b]Jere-
miah might be fulfilled, the LORD stirred up the
spirit of [c]Cyrus king of Persia, so that he made a
proclamation throughout all his kingdom, and
also *put it* in writing, saying,

23 [a]Thus says Cyrus king of Persia: All the
kingdoms of the earth the LORD God of
heaven has given me. And He has
commanded me to build Him a [1]house at
Jerusalem which is in Judah. Who *is* among
you of all His people? May the LORD his God
*be* with him, and let him go up!

**20** [a]2 Kin. 25:11 [b]Jer. 17:4; 27:7
**21** [a]Jer. 25:9–12; 27:6–8; 29:10 [b]Lev. 26:34–43 [c]Lev. 25:4, 5
**22** [a]Ezra 1:1–3 [b]Jer. 29:10 [c]Is. 44:28; 45:1
**23** [a]Ezra 1:2, 3 [1]Temple

*The Book of*

# EZRA

## *The Return of the Captives to Jerusalem*

NOW in the first year of Cyrus king of Persia,
that the word of the LORD [a]by the mouth of
Jeremiah might be fulfilled, the LORD
stirred up the spirit of Cyrus king of Persia, [b]so
that he made a proclamation throughout all his
kingdom, and also *put it* in writing, saying,

2 Thus says Cyrus king of Persia: All the
kingdoms of the earth the LORD God of
heaven has given me. And He has
[a]commanded me to build Him a [1]house at
Jerusalem which *is* in Judah.
3 Who *is* among you of all His people? May his
God be with him, and let him go up to
Jerusalem which *is* in Judah, and build the
house of the LORD God of Israel [a](He *is* God),
which *is* in Jerusalem.
4 And whoever is left in any place where he
dwells, let the men of his place help him with
silver and gold, with goods and livestock,
besides the freewill offerings for the house of
God which *is* in Jerusalem.

5 Then the heads of the fathers' *houses* of Judah
and Benjamin, and the priests and the Levites,
with all whose spirits [a]God [1]had moved, arose to
go up and build the house of the LORD which *is* in
Jerusalem.
6 And all those who *were* around them [1]encour-
aged them with articles of silver and gold, with
goods and livestock, and with precious things,
besides all *that* was [a]willingly offered.
7 [a]King Cyrus also brought out the articles of
the house of the LORD, [b]which Nebuchadnezzar
had taken from Jerusalem and put in the [1]temple
of his gods;
8 and Cyrus king of Persia brought them out by
the hand of Mithredath the treasurer, and counted
them out to [a]Sheshbazzar the prince of Judah.
9 This *is* the number of them: thirty gold platters, one thousand silver platters, twenty-nine
knives,
10 thirty gold basins, four hundred and ten silver
basins of a similar *kind, and* one thousand other
articles.
11 All the articles of gold and silver *were* five
thousand four hundred. All *these* Sheshbazzar
took with the captives who were brought from
Babylon to Jerusalem.

CHAPTER 1

**1** [a]2 Chr. 36:22, 23; Jer. 25:12; 29:10 [b]Ezra 5:13, 14; Is. 44:28—45:13
**2** [a]Is. 44:28; 45:1, 13 [1]Temple
**3** [a]1 Kin. 8:23; 18:39; Is. 37:16; Dan. 6:26
**5** [a][Phil. 2:13] [1]*stirred up*
**6** [a]Ezra 2:68 [1]Lit. *strengthened their hands*
**7** [a]Ezra 5:14; 6:5; Dan. 1:2; 5:2, 3 [b]2 Kin. 24:13; 2 Chr. 36:7, 18 [1]Lit. *house*
**8** [a]Ezra 5:14, 16

CHAPTER 2

**1** [a]Neh. 7:6–73; Jer. 32:15; 50:5; Ezek. 14:22 [b]2 Kin. 24:14–16; 25:11; 2 Chr. 36:20
**2** [1]*Azariah,* Neh. 7:7 [2]*Raamiah,* Neh. 7:7 [3]*Mispereth,* Neh. 7:7 [4]*Nehum,* Neh. 7:7
**5** [a]Neh. 7:10
**6** [a]Neh. 7:11
**10** [1]*Binnui,* Neh. 7:15
**18** [1]*Hariph,* Neh. 7:24
**20** [1]*Gibeon,* Neh. 7:25

## *Those Who Returned from Captivity*

2 Now [a]these *are* the people of the province who
came back from the captivity, of those who
had been carried away, [b]whom Nebuchadnezzar
the king of Babylon had carried away to Babylon,
and who returned to Jerusalem and Judah, everyone to his *own* city.
2 *Those* who came with Zerubbabel *were*
Jeshua, Nehemiah, [1]Seraiah, [2]Reelaiah, Mordecai,
Bilshan, [3]Mispar, Bigvai, [4]Rehum, *and* Baanah.
The number of the men of the people of Israel:
3 the people of Parosh, two thousand one hundred and seventy-two;
4 the people of Shephatiah, three hundred and
seventy-two;
5 the people of Arah, [a]seven hundred and seventy-five;
6 the people of [a]Pahath-Moab, of the people of
Jeshua *and* Joab, two thousand eight hundred and
twelve;
7 the people of Elam, one thousand two hundred
and fifty-four;
8 the people of Zattu, nine hundred and forty-
five;
9 the people of Zaccai, seven hundred and sixty;
10 the people of [1]Bani, six hundred and forty-two;
11 the people of Bebai, six hundred and twenty-
three;
12 the people of Azgad, one thousand two hundred and twenty-two;
13 the people of Adonikam, six hundred and
sixty-six;
14 the people of Bigvai, two thousand and fifty-
six;
15 the people of Adin, four hundred and fifty-
four;
16 the people of Ater of Hezekiah, ninety-eight;
17 the people of Bezai, three hundred and
twenty-three;
18 the people of [1]Jorah, one hundred and twelve;
19 the people of Hashum, two hundred and
twenty-three;
20 the people of [1]Gibbar, ninety-five;
21 the people of Bethlehem, one hundred and
twenty-three;
22 the men of Netophah, fifty-six;
23 the men of Anathoth, one hundred and
twenty-eight;

24 the people of [1]Azmaveth, forty-two;
25 the people of [1]Kirjath Arim, Chephirah, and
Beeroth, seven hundred and forty-three;
26 the people of Ramah and Geba, six hundred
and twenty-one;
27 the men of Michmas, one hundred and
twenty-two;
28 the men of Bethel and Ai, two hundred and
twenty-three;
29 the people of Nebo, fifty-two;
30 the people of Magbish, one hundred and fifty-
six;
31 the people of the other [a]Elam, one thousand
two hundred and fifty-four;
32 the people of Harim, three hundred and
twenty;
33 the people of Lod, Hadid, and Ono, seven
hundred and twenty-five;
34 the people of Jericho, three hundred and forty-
five;
35 the people of Senaah, three thousand six
hundred and thirty.
**36** The priests: the sons of [a]Jedaiah, of the house
of Jeshua, nine hundred and seventy-three;
37 the sons of [a]Immer, one thousand and fifty-
two;
38 the sons of [a]Pashhur, one thousand two hundred and forty-seven;
39 the sons of [a]Harim, one thousand and seventeen.
**40** The Levites: the sons of Jeshua and Kadmiel,
of the sons of [1]Hodaviah, seventy-four.
**41** The singers: the sons of Asaph, one hundred
and twenty-eight.
**42** The sons of the gatekeepers: the sons of
Shallum, the sons of Ater, the sons of Talmon, the
sons of Akkub, the sons of Hatita, and the sons of
Shobai, one hundred and thirty-nine *in* all.
**43** [a]The Nethinim: the sons of Ziha, the sons of
Hasupha, the sons of Tabbaoth,
44 the sons of Keros, the sons of [1]Siaha, the sons
of Padon,
45 the sons of Lebanah, the sons of Hagabah, the
sons of Akkub,
46 the sons of Hagab, the sons of Shalmai, the
sons of Hanan,
47 the sons of Giddel, the sons of Gahar, the sons
of Reaiah,
48 the sons of Rezin, the sons of Nekoda, the
sons of Gazzam,
49 the sons of Uzza, the sons of Paseah, the sons
of Besai,
50 the sons of Asnah, the sons of Meunim, the
sons of [1]Nephusim,
51 the sons of Bakbuk, the sons of Hakupha, the
sons of Harhur,
52 the sons of [1]Bazluth, the sons of Mehida, the
sons of Harsha,
53 the sons of Barkos, the sons of Sisera, the sons
of Tamah,
54 the sons of Neziah, and the sons of Hatipha.
**55** The sons of [a]Solomon's servants: the sons of
Sotai, the sons of [b]Sophereth, the sons of [1]Peruda,
56 the sons of Jaala, the sons of Darkon, the sons
of Giddel,
57 the sons of Shephatiah, the sons of Hattil, the
sons of Pochereth of Zebaim, and the sons of
[1]Ami.
58 All the [a]Nethinim and the children of [b]Solo-
mon's servants were three hundred and ninety-
two.

**59** And these *were* the ones who came up from
Tel Melah, Tel Harsha, Cherub, [1]Addan, and Immer; but they could not [2]identify their father's
house or their [3]genealogy, whether they *were* of
Israel:
60 the sons of Delaiah, the sons of Tobiah, and
the sons of Nekoda, six hundred and fifty-two;
61 and of the sons of the priests: the sons of
[a]Habaiah, the sons of [1]Koz, and the sons of [b]Barzil-
lai, who took a wife of the daughters of Barzillai
the Gileadite, and was called by their name.
62 These sought their listing *among* those who
were registered by genealogy, but they were not
found; [a]therefore they *were excluded* from the
priesthood as defiled.
63 And the [1]governor said to them that they
[a]should not eat of the most holy things till a priest
could consult with the [b]Urim and Thummim.
**64** [a]The whole assembly together *was* forty-two
thousand three hundred *and* sixty,
65 besides their male and female servants, of
whom *there were* seven thousand three hundred
and thirty-seven; and they had two hundred men
and women singers.
66 Their horses *were* seven hundred and thirty-
six, their mules two hundred and forty-five,
67 their camels four hundred and thirty-five, and
*their* donkeys six thousand seven hundred and
twenty.
**68** [a]*Some* of the heads of the fathers' *houses,*
when they came to the house of the LORD which *is*
in Jerusalem, offered freely for the house of God,
to erect it in its place:
69 According to their ability, they gave to the
[a]treasury for the work sixty-one thousand gold
drachmas, five thousand minas of silver, and one
hundred priestly garments.
70 [a]So the priests and the Levites, *some* of the
people, the singers, the gatekeepers, and the
Nethinim, dwelt in their cities, and all Israel in
their cities.

### *The Restoration of Worship*

**3** And when the [a]seventh month had come, and
the children of Israel *were* in the cities, the
people gathered together as one man to Jerusalem.
2 Then [1]Jeshua the son of [a]Jozadak[2] and his
brethren the priests, [b]and Zerubbabel the son of
[c]Shealtiel and his brethren, arose and built the
altar of the God of Israel, to offer burnt offerings
on it, as *it is* [d]written in the Law of Moses the man
of God.
3 Though fear *had come* upon them because of
the people of those countries, they set the altar on
its [1]bases; and they offered [a]burnt offerings on it to
the LORD, *both* the morning and evening burnt
offerings.
4 [a]They also kept the Feast of Tabernacles, [b]as *it
is* written, and [c]*offered* the daily burnt offerings in
the number required by ordinance for each day.
5 Afterwards *they offered* the [a]regular burnt
offering, and *those* for New Moons and for all the
appointed feasts of the LORD that were consecrated, and *those* of everyone who willingly offered a freewill offering to the LORD.
6 From the first day of the seventh month they
began to offer burnt offerings to the LORD, although the foundation of the temple of the LORD
had not been laid.
7 They also gave money to the masons and the

**24** [1]*Beth Azmaveth,* Neh. 7:28
**25** [1]*Kiriath Jearim,* Neh. 7:29
**31** [a]Ezra 2:7
**36** [a]1 Chr. 24:7–18
**37** [a]1 Chr. 24:14
**38** [a]1 Chr. 9:12
**39** [a]1 Chr. 24:8
**40** [1]*Judah,* Ezra 3:9, or *Hodevah,* Neh. 7:43
**43** [a]1 Chr. 9:2; Ezra 7:7
**44** [1]*Sia,* Neh. 7:47
**50** [1]*Nephishesim,* Neh. 7:52
**52** [1]*Bazlith,* Neh. 7:54
**55** [a]1 Kin. 9:21 [b]Neh. 7:57–60 [1]*Perida,* Neh. 7:57
**57** [1]*Amon,* Neh. 7:59
**58** [a]Josh. 9:21, 27; 1 Chr. 9:2 [b]1 Kin. 9:21
**59** [1]Or *Addon,* Neh. 7:61 [2]Lit. *tell* [3]Lit. *seed*
**61** [a]Neh. 7:63 [b]2 Sam. 17:27; 1 Kin. 2:7 [1]Or *Hakkoz*
**62** [a]Num. 3:10
**63** [a]Lev. 22:2, 10, 15, 16 [b]Ex. 28:30; Num. 27:21 [1]Or *Tirshatha*
**64** [a]Neh. 7:66; Is. 10:22
**68** [a]Ezra 1:6; 3:5; Neh. 7:70
**69** [a]1 Chr. 26:20; Ezra 8:25–35
**70** [a]Ezra 6:16, 17; Neh. 7:73

CHAPTER 3

**1** [a]Neh. 7:73; 8:1, 2
**2** [a]1 Chr. 6:14, 15; Ezra 4:3; Neh. 12:1, 8; Hag. 1:1; 2:2 [b]Ezra 2:2; 4:2, 3; 5:2 [c]1 Chr. 3:17 [d]Deut. 12:5, 6 [1]Or *Joshua* [2]*Jehozadak,* 1 Chr. 6:14
**3** [a]Num. 28:3 [1]*foundations*
**4** [a]Lev. 23:33–43; Neh. 8:14–18; Zech. 14:16 [b]Ex. 23:16 [c]Num. 29:12, 13
**5** [a]Ex. 29:38; Num. 28:3, 11, 19, 26; Ezra 1:4; 2:68; 7:15, 16; 8:28

carpenters, and [a]food, drink, and oil to the people of Sidon and Tyre to bring cedar logs from Lebanon to the sea, to [b]Joppa, [c]according to the permission which they had from Cyrus king of Persia.

**8** Now in the second month of the second year of their coming to the house of God at Jerusalem, [a]Zerubbabel the son of Shealtiel, Jeshua the son of [1]Jozadak, and the rest of their brethren the priests and the Levites, and all those who had come out of the captivity to Jerusalem, began *work* [b]and appointed the Levites from twenty years old and above to oversee the work of the house of the LORD.

9 Then Jeshua *with* his sons and brothers, Kadmiel *with* his sons, and the sons of [1]Judah, arose as one to oversee those working on the house of God: the sons of Henadad *with* their sons and their brethren the Levites.

10 When the builders laid the foundation of the temple of the LORD, [a]the[1] priests stood in their apparel with trumpets, and the Levites, the sons of Asaph, with cymbals, to praise the LORD, according to the [b]ordinance[2] of David king of Israel.

11 [a]And they sang responsively, praising and giving thanks to the LORD:

[b]"For He *is* good,
[c]For His mercy *endures* forever
toward Israel."

Then all the people shouted with a great shout, when they praised the LORD, because the foundation of the house of the LORD was laid.

**12** But many of the priests and Levites and [a]heads of the fathers' *houses,* old men who had seen the first temple, wept with a loud voice when the foundation of this temple was laid before their eyes. Yet many shouted aloud for joy,

13 so that the people could not discern the noise of the shout of joy from the noise of the weeping of the people, for the people shouted with a loud shout, and the sound was heard afar off.

## *Enemies Try to Stop the Temple Work*

**4** Now when [a]the [1]adversaries of Judah and Benjamin heard that the descendants of the captivity were building the temple of the LORD God of Israel,

2 they came to Zerubbabel and the heads of the fathers' *houses,* and said to them, "Let us build with you, for we seek your God as you *do;* and we have sacrificed to Him [a]since the days of Esarhaddon king of Assyria, who brought us here."

3 But Zerubbabel and Jeshua and the rest of the heads of the fathers' *houses* of Israel said to them, [a]"You may do nothing with us to build a [1]house for our God; but we alone will build to the LORD God of Israel, as [b]King Cyrus the king of Persia has commanded us."

4 Then [a]the people of the land tried to discourage the people of Judah. They troubled them in building,

5 and hired counselors against them to frustrate their purpose all the days of Cyrus king of Persia, even until the reign of [a]Darius king of Persia.

**6** In the reign of Ahasuerus, in the beginning of his reign, they wrote an accusation against the inhabitants of Judah and Jerusalem.

**7** In the days of [a]Artaxerxes also, [1]Bishlam, Mithredath, Tabel, and the rest of their companions wrote to Artaxerxes king of Persia; and the letter *was* written in [b]Aramaic script, and translated into the Aramaic language.

8 [1]Rehum the commander and Shimshai the scribe wrote a letter against Jerusalem to King Artaxerxes in this fashion:

9 [1]From Rehum the commander, Shimshai the scribe, and the rest of their companions—*representatives* of [a]the Dinaites, the Apharsathchites, the Tarpelites, the people of Persia and Erech and Babylon and [2]Shushan, the Dehavites, the Elamites,

10 [a]and the rest of the nations whom the great and noble Osnapper took captive and settled in the cities of Samaria and the remainder beyond [1]the River—[b]and[2] so forth.

11 (This *is* a copy of the letter that they sent him)

To King Artaxerxes from your servants, the men *of the region* beyond the River, [1]and so forth:

12 Let it be known to the king that the Jews who came up from you have come to us at Jerusalem, and are building the [a]rebellious and evil city, and are finishing *its* [b]walls and repairing the foundations.

13 Let it now be known to the king that, if this city is built and the walls completed, they will not pay [a]tax, tribute, or custom, and the king's treasury will be diminished.

14 Now because we receive support from the palace, it was not proper for us to see the king's dishonor; therefore we have sent and informed the king,

15 that search may be made in the book of the records of your fathers. And you will find in the book of the records and know that this city *is* a rebellious city, harmful to kings and provinces, and that they have incited sedition within the city in former times, for which cause this city was destroyed.

16 We inform the king that if this city is rebuilt and its walls are completed, the result will be that you will have no dominion beyond the River.

**17** The king sent an answer:

To Rehum the commander, *to* Shimshai the scribe, *to* the rest of their companions who dwell in Samaria, and *to* the remainder beyond the River:

Peace, [1]and so forth.

18 The letter which you sent to us has been clearly read before me.

19 And [1]I gave the command, and a search has been made, and it was found that this city in former times has revolted against kings, and rebellion and sedition have been fostered in it.

20 There have also been mighty kings over Jerusalem, who have [a]ruled over all *the region* [b]beyond the River; and tax, tribute, and custom were paid to them.

21 Now [1]give the command to make these men cease, that this city may not be built until the command is given by me.

22 Take heed now that you do not fail to do this. Why should damage increase to the hurt of the kings?

**7** [a]1 Kin. 5:6, 9; 2 Chr. 2:10; Acts 12:20 [b]2 Chr. 2:16; Acts 9:36 [c]Ezra 1:2; 6:3
**8** [a]Ezra 3:2; 4:3 [b]1 Chr. 23:4, 24 [1]*Jehozadak,* 1 Chr. 6:14
**9** [1]*Hodaviah,* Ezra 2:40
**10** [a]1 Chr. 16:5, 6 [b]1 Chr. 6:31; 16:4; 25:1 [1]So with LXX, Syr., Vg.; MT *they stationed the priests* [2]Lit. *hands*
**11** [a]Ex. 15:21; 2 Chr. 7:3; Neh. 12:24 [b]1 Chr. 16:34; Ps. 136:1 [c]1 Chr. 16:41; Jer. 33:11
**12** [a]Ezra 2:68

CHAPTER 4

**1** [a]Ezra 4:7–9 [1]*enemies*
**2** [a]2 Kin. 17:24; 19:37; Ezra 4:10
**3** [a]Neh. 2:20 [b]Ezra 1:1–4 [1]Temple
**4** [a]Ezra 3:3
**5** [a]Ezra 5:5; 6:1
**7** [a]Ezra 7:1, 7, 21 [b]2 Kin. 18:26 [1]Or *in peace*
**8** [1]The original language of Ezra 4:8 through 6:18 is Aramaic.
**9** [a]2 Kin. 17:30, 31 [1]Lit. *Then* [2]Or *Susa*
**10** [a]2 Kin. 17:24; Ezra 4:1 [b]Ezra 4:11, 17; 7:12 [1]The Euphrates [2]Lit. *and now*
**11** [1]Lit. *and now*
**12** [a]2 Chr. 36:13 [b]Ezra 5:3, 9
**13** [a]Ezra 4:20; 7:24
**17** [1]Lit. *and now*
**19** [1]Lit. *by me a decree has been put forth*
**20** [a]1 Kin. 4:21; 1 Chr. 18:3; Ps. 72:8 [b]Gen. 15:18; Josh. 1:4
**21** [1]*put forth a decree*

**23** Now when the copy of King Artaxerxes' letter
*was* read before Rehum, Shimshai the scribe, and
their companions, they went up in haste to Jerusalem against the Jews, and by force of arms made
them cease.
**24** Thus the work of the house of God which *is* at
Jerusalem ceased, and it was discontinued until
the second year of the reign of Darius king of
Persia.

### *The Temple Rebuilt*

**5** Then the prophet [a]Haggai and [b]Zechariah the
son of Iddo, prophets, prophesied to the Jews
who *were* in Judah and Jerusalem, in the name of
the God of Israel, *who was* over them.
2 So [a]Zerubbabel the son of Shealtiel and Jeshua
the son of [1]Jozadak rose up and began to build the
house of God which *is* in Jerusalem; and [b]the
prophets of God *were* with them, helping them.
**3** At the same time [a]Tattenai the governor of *the*
*region* beyond [1]the River and Shethar-Boznai and
their companions came to them and spoke thus to
them: [b]"Who has commanded you to build this
[2]temple and finish this wall?"
4 [a]Then, accordingly, we told them the names of
the men who were constructing this building.
5 But [a]the eye of their God was upon the elders
of the Jews, so that they could not make them
cease till a report could go to Darius. Then a
[b]written answer was returned concerning this
*matter.*
**6** This is a copy of the letter that Tattenai sent:

The governor of *the region* beyond the River,
and Shethar-Boznai, [a]and his companions,
the Persians who *were in the region* beyond
the River, to Darius the king.

7 (They sent a letter to him, in which was
written thus)

To Darius the king:

All peace.

8 Let it be known to the king that we went
into the province of Judea, to the [1]temple of
the great God, which is being built with
[2]heavy stones, and timber is being laid in the
walls; and this work goes on diligently and
prospers in their hands.
9 Then we asked those elders, *and* spoke thus
to them: [a]"Who commanded you to build this
temple and to finish these walls?"
10 We also asked them their names to inform
you, that we might write the names of the
men who *were* chief among them.
11 And thus they returned us an answer, saying:
"We are the servants of the God of heaven
and earth, and we are rebuilding the [1]temple
that was built many years ago, which a great
king of Israel built [a]and completed.
12 "But [a]because our fathers provoked the God
of heaven to wrath, He gave them into the
hand of [b]Nebuchadnezzar king of Babylon,
the Chaldean, *who* destroyed this temple and
[c]carried the people away to Babylon.
13 "However, in the first year of [a]Cyrus king of
Babylon, King Cyrus issued a decree to build
this [1]house of God.
14 "Also, [a]the gold and silver articles of the
house of God, which Nebuchadnezzar had
taken from the temple that *was* in Jerusalem
and carried into the temple of Babylon—
those King Cyrus took from the temple of
Babylon, and they were given to [b]one named
Sheshbazzar, whom he had made governor.
15 "And he said to him, 'Take these articles; go,
carry them to the temple *site* that *is* in
Jerusalem, and let the house of God be
rebuilt on its former site.'
16 "Then the same Sheshbazzar came *and* [a]laid
the foundation of the house of God which *is*
in Jerusalem; but from that time even until
now it has been under construction, and [b]it is
not finished."
17 Now therefore, if *it seems* good to the king,
[a]let a search be made in the king's treasure
house, which *is* there in Babylon, whether it
is *so* that a decree was issued by King Cyrus
to build this house of God at Jerusalem, and
let the king send us his pleasure concerning
this *matter.*

### *Darius Confirms the Decree of Cyrus*

**6** Then King Darius issued a decree, [a]and a
search was made in the [1]archives, where the
treasures were stored in Babylon.
2 And at [1]Achmetha, in the palace that *is* in the
province of [a]Media, a scroll was found, and in it a
record *was* written thus:

3 In the first year of King Cyrus, King Cyrus
issued a [a]decree *concerning* the house of God
at Jerusalem: "Let the house be rebuilt, the
place where they offered sacrifices; and let
the foundations of it be firmly laid, its height
sixty cubits *and* its width sixty cubits,
4 [a]*with* three rows of heavy stones and one
row of new timber. Let the [b]expenses be paid
from the king's treasury.
5 Also let [a]the gold and silver articles of the
house of God, which Nebuchadnezzar took
from the temple which *is* in Jerusalem and
brought to Babylon, be restored and taken
back to the temple which *is* in Jerusalem,
*each* to its place; and deposit *them* in the
house of God"—
**6** [a]Now *therefore,* Tattenai, governor of *the*
*region* beyond the River, and Shethar-Boznai,
and your companions the Persians who *are*
beyond the River, keep yourselves far from
there.
7 Let the work of this house of God alone; let
the governor of the Jews and the elders of
the Jews build this house of God on its site.
8 Moreover I issue a decree *as to* what you
shall do for the elders of these Jews, for the
building of this house of God: Let the cost be
paid at the king's expense from taxes *on the*
*region* beyond the River; this is to be given
immediately to these men, so that they are
not hindered.
9 And whatever they need—young bulls, rams,
and lambs for the burnt offerings of the God
of heaven, wheat, salt, wine, and oil,
according to the request of the priests who
*are* in Jerusalem—let it be given them day by
day without fail,
10 [a]that they may offer sacrifices of sweet
aroma to the God of heaven, and pray for
the life of the king and his sons.
11 Also I issue a decree that whoever alters this
edict, let a timber be pulled from his house

CHAPTER 5
**1** [a]Hag. 1:1 [b]Zech. 1:1
**2** [a]Ezra 3:2; Hag. 1:12 [b]Ezra 6:14; Hag. 2:4 [1]*Jehozadak,* 1 Chr. 6:14
**3** [a]Ezra 5:6; 6:6 [b]Ezra 1:3; 5:9 [1]The Euphrates [2]Lit. *house*
**4** [a]Ezra 5:10
**5** [a]2 Chr. 16:9; Ezra 7:6, 28; Ps. 33:18 [b]Ezra 6:6
**6** [a]Ezra 4:7–10
**8** [1]Lit. *house* [2]Lit. *stones of rolling,* stones too heavy to be carried
**9** [a]Ezra 5:3, 4
**11** [a]1 Kin. 6:1, 38 [1]Lit. *house*
**12** [a]2 Chr. 34:25; 36:16, 17 [b]2 Kin. 24:2; 25:8–11; 2 Chr. 36:17; Jer. 52:12–15 [c]Jer. 13:19
**13** [a]Ezra 1:1 [1]Temple
**14** [a]Ezra 1:7, 8; 6:5; Dan. 5:2 [b]Hag. 1:14; 2:2, 21
**16** [a]Ezra 3:8–10; Hag. 2:18 [b]Ezra 6:15
**17** [a]Ezra 6:1, 2

CHAPTER 6
**1** [a]Ezra 5:17 [1]Lit. *house of the books*
**2** [a]2 Kin. 17:6 [1]Probably *Ecbatana,* the ancient capital of Media
**3** [a]Ezra 1:1; 5:13
**4** [a]1 Kin. 6:36 [b]Ezra 3:7
**5** [a]Ezra 1:7, 8; 5:14
**6** [a]Ezra 5:3, 6
**8** [1]Temple
**10** [a]Ezra 7:23; [Jer. 29:7; 1 Tim. 2:1, 2]

and erected, and let him be hanged on it;
[a]and let his house be made a refuse heap
because of this.
12 And may the God who causes His [a]name to
dwell there destroy any king or people who
put their hand to alter it, or to destroy this
[1]house of God which is in Jerusalem. I Darius
issue a decree; let it be done diligently.

**13** Then Tattenai, governor of *the region* beyond
the River, Shethar-Boznai, and their companions
diligently did according to what King Darius had
sent.
14 [a]So the elders of the Jews built, and they
prospered through the prophesying of Haggai the
prophet and Zechariah the son of Iddo. And they
built and finished *it,* according to the commandment of the God of Israel, and according to the
[1]command of [b]Cyrus, [c]Darius, and [d]Artaxerxes
king of Persia.
15 Now the temple was finished on the third day
of the month of Adar, which was in the sixth year
of the reign of King Darius.
16 Then the children of Israel, the priests and the
Levites and the rest of the descendants of the
captivity, celebrated [a]the dedication of this [1]house
of God with joy.
17 And they [a]offered sacrifices at the dedication
of this house of God, one hundred bulls, two
hundred rams, four hundred lambs, and as a sin
offering for all Israel twelve male goats, according
to the number of the tribes of Israel.
18 They assigned the priests to their [a]divisions
and the Levites to their [b]divisions, over the service
of God in Jerusalem, [c]as it is written in the Book
of Moses.
**19** [1]And the descendants of the captivity kept the
Passover [a]on the fourteenth *day* of the first
month.
20 For the priests and the Levites had [a]purified
themselves; all of them *were ritually* clean. And
they [b]slaughtered the Passover *lambs* for all the
descendants of the captivity, for their brethren
the priests, and for themselves.
21 Then the children of Israel who had returned
from the captivity ate together with all who had
separated themselves from the [a]filth[1] of the nations of the land in order to seek the LORD God of
Israel.
22 And they kept the [a]Feast of Unleavened Bread
seven days with joy; for the LORD made them
joyful, and [b]turned the heart [c]of the king of
Assyria toward them, to strengthen their hands in
the work of the house of God, the God of Israel.

## *Ezra Goes to Jerusalem*

**7** Now after these things, in the reign of [a]Artax-
erxes king of Persia, Ezra the [b]son of Seraiah,
[c]the son of Azariah, the son of [d]Hilkiah,
2 the son of Shallum, the son of Zadok, the son
of Ahitub,
3 the son of Amariah, the son of Azariah, the
son of Meraioth,
4 the son of Zerahiah, the son of Uzzi, the son of
Bukki,
5 the son of Abishua, the son of Phinehas, the
son of Eleazar, the son of Aaron the chief priest—
6 this Ezra came up from Babylon; and he *was*
[a]a skilled scribe in the Law of Moses, which the
LORD God of Israel had given. The king granted
him all his request, [b]according to the hand of the
LORD his God upon him.
7 [a]*Some* of the children of Israel, the priests,
[b]the Levites, the singers, the gatekeepers, and [c]the
Nethinim came up to Jerusalem in the seventh
year of King Artaxerxes.
8 And Ezra came to Jerusalem in the fifth
month, which *was* in the seventh year of the king.
9 On the first *day* of the first month he began
*his* journey from Babylon, and on the first *day* of
the fifth month he came to Jerusalem, [a]according
to the good hand of his God upon him.
10 For Ezra had prepared his heart to [a]seek[1] the
Law of the LORD, and to do *it,* and to [b]teach
statutes and ordinances in Israel.
**11** This *is* a copy of the letter that King Artaxerxes gave Ezra the priest, the scribe, expert in the
words of the commandments of the LORD, and of
His statutes to Israel:

12 [1]Artaxerxes, [a]king of kings,
To Ezra the priest, a scribe of the Law of the
God of heaven:

Perfect *peace,* [b]and[2] so forth.

13 I issue a decree that all those of the people
of Israel and the priests and Levites in my
realm, who volunteer to go up to Jerusalem,
may go with you.
14 And whereas you are being sent [1]by the king
and his [a]seven counselors to inquire
concerning Judah and Jerusalem, with regard
to the Law of your God which *is* in your
hand;
15 and *whereas you are* to carry the silver and
gold which the king and his counselors have
freely offered to the God of Israel, [a]whose
dwelling *is* in Jerusalem;
16 [a]and *whereas* all the silver and gold that you
may find in all the province of Babylon,
along with the freewill offering of the people
and the priests, *are to be* [b]freely offered for
the [1]house of their God in Jerusalem—
17 now therefore, be careful to buy with this
money bulls, rams, and lambs, with their
[a]grain offerings and their drink offerings, and
[b]offer them on the altar of the house of your
God in Jerusalem.
18 And whatever seems good to you and your
brethren to do with the rest of the silver and
the gold, do it according to the will of your
God.
19 Also the articles that are given to you for the
service of the house of your God, deliver in
full before the God of Jerusalem.
20 And whatever more may be needed for the
house of your God, which you may have
occasion to provide, pay *for it* from the
king's treasury.
21 And I, *even* I, Artaxerxes the king, issue a
decree to all the treasurers who *are in the
region* beyond the River, that whatever Ezra
the priest, the scribe of the Law of the God
of heaven, may require of you, let it be done
diligently,
22 up to one hundred talents of silver, one
hundred kors of wheat, one hundred baths of
wine, one hundred baths of oil, and salt
without prescribed limit.
23 Whatever [1]is commanded by the God of
heaven, let it diligently be done for the
[2]house of the God of heaven. For why should

**11** [a]Dan. 2:5; 3:29
**12** [a]Deut. 12:5, 11; 1 Kin. 9:3 [1]Temple
**14** [a]Ezra 5:1, 2 [b]Ezra 1:1; 5:13; 6:3 [c]Ezra 4:24; 6:12 [d]Ezra 7:1, 11; Neh. 2:1 [1]*decree*
**16** [a]1 Kin. 8:63; 2 Chr. 7:5 [1]Temple
**17** [a]Ezra 8:35
**18** [a]1 Chr. 24:1; 2 Chr. 35:5 [b]1 Chr. 23:6 [c]Num. 3:6; 8:9
**19** [a]Ex. 12:6 [1]The Hebrew language resumes in Ezra 6:19 and continues through 7:11.
**20** [a]2 Chr. 29:34; 30:15 [b]2 Chr. 35:11
**21** [a]Ezra 9:11 [1]*uncleanness*
**22** [a]Ex. 12:15; 13:6, 7; 2 Chr. 30:21; 35:17 [b]Ezra 7:27; [Prov. 21:1] [c]2 Kin. 23:29; 2 Chr. 33:11; Ezra 1:1; 6:1

CHAPTER 7

**1** [a]Neh. 2:1 [b]1 Chr. 6:14 [c]Jer. 52:24 [d]2 Chr. 35:8
**6** [a]Ezra 7:11, 12, 21 [b]Ezra 7:9, 28; 8:22
**7** [a]Ezra 8:1–14 [b]Ezra 8:15 [c]Ezra 2:43; 8:20
**9** [a]Ezra 7:6; Neh. 2:8, 18
**10** [a]Ps. 119:45 [b]Deut. 33:10; Ezra 7:6, 25; Neh. 8:1–8; [Mal. 2:7] [1]Study
**12** [a]Ezek. 26:7; Dan. 2:37 [b]Ezra 4:10 [1]The original language of Ezra 7:12–26 is Aramaic. [2]Lit. *and now*
**14** [a]Esth. 1:14 [1]*from before*
**15** [a]2 Chr. 6:2; Ezra 6:12; Ps. 135:21
**16** [a]Ezra 8:25 [b]1 Chr. 29:6, 9 [1]Temple
**17** [a]Num. 15:4–13 [b]Deut. 12:5–11
**23** [1]Lit. *is from the decree* [2]Temple

there be wrath against the realm of the king and his sons?
24 Also we inform you that it shall not be lawful to impose tax, tribute, or custom *on* any of the priests, Levites, singers, gatekeepers, Nethinim, or servants of this house of God.
25 And you, Ezra, according to your God-given wisdom, [a]set magistrates and judges who may judge all the people who *are in the region* beyond the River, all such as know the laws of your God; and [b]teach those who do not know *them*.
26 Whoever will not observe the law of your God and the law of the king, let judgment be executed speedily on him, whether *it be* death, or [1]banishment, or confiscation of goods, or imprisonment.

27 [a]Blessed[1] *be* the LORD God of our fathers, [b]who has put *such a thing* as this in the king's heart, to beautify the house of the LORD which *is* in Jerusalem,
28 and [a]has extended mercy to me before the king and his counselors, and before all the king's mighty princes.
So I was encouraged, as [b]the hand of the LORD my God *was* upon me; and I gathered leading men of Israel to go up with me.

### *List of Ezra's Companions*

**8** These *are* the heads of their fathers' *houses*, and *this is* the genealogy of those who went up with me from Babylon, in the reign of King Artaxerxes:
2 of the sons of Phinehas, Gershom; of the sons of Ithamar, Daniel; of the sons of David, [a]Hattush;
3 of the sons of Shecaniah, of the sons of [a]Parosh, Zechariah; and registered with him *were* one hundred and fifty males;
4 of the sons of [a]Pahath-Moab, Eliehoenai the son of Zerahiah, and with him two hundred males;
5 of [1]the sons of Shechaniah, Ben-Jahaziel, and with him three hundred males;
6 of the sons of Adin, Ebed the son of Jonathan, and with him fifty males;
7 of the sons of Elam, Jeshaiah the son of Athaliah, and with him seventy males;
8 of the sons of Shephatiah, Zebadiah the son of Michael, and with him eighty males;
9 of the sons of Joab, Obadiah the son of Jehiel, and with him two hundred and eighteen males;
10 of [1]the sons of Shelomith, Ben-Josiphiah, and with him one hundred and sixty males;
11 of the sons of [a]Bebai, Zechariah the son of Bebai, and with him twenty-eight males;
12 of the sons of Azgad, Johanan [1]the son of Hakkatan, and with him one hundred and ten males;
13 of the last sons of Adonikam, whose names *are* these—Eliphelet, Jeiel, and Shemaiah—and with them sixty males;
14 also of the sons of Bigvai, Uthai and [1]Zabbud, and with them seventy males.
**15** Now I gathered them by the river that flows to Ahava, and we camped there three days. And I looked among the people and the priests, and found none of the [a]sons of Levi there.
16 Then I sent for Eliezer, Ariel, Shemaiah, Elnathan, Jarib, Elnathan, Nathan, Zechariah, and [a]Meshullam, leaders; also for Joiarib and Elnathan, men of understanding.
17 And I gave them a command for Iddo the chief man at the place Casiphia, and [1]I told them what they should say to [2]Iddo *and* his brethren the Nethinim at the place Casiphia—that they should bring us servants for the house of our God.
18 Then, by the good hand of our God upon us, they [a]brought us a man of understanding, of the sons of Mahli the son of Levi, the son of Israel, namely Sherebiah, with his sons and brothers, eighteen men;
19 and [a]Hashabiah, and with him Jeshaiah of the sons of Merari, his brothers and their sons, twenty men;
20 [a]also of the Nethinim, whom David and the leaders had appointed for the service of the Levites, two hundred and twenty Nethinim. All of them were designated by name.
**21** Then I [a]proclaimed a fast there at the river of Ahava, that we might [b]humble ourselves before our God, to seek from Him the [c]right way for us and our little ones and all our possessions.
22 For [a]I was ashamed to request of the king an escort of soldiers and horsemen to help us against the enemy on the road, because we had spoken to the king, saying, [b]"The hand of our God *is* upon all those for [c]good who seek Him, but His power and His wrath *are* [d]against all those who [e]forsake Him."
23 So we fasted and entreated our God for this, and He [a]answered our prayer.
**24** And I separated twelve of the leaders of the priests—Sherebiah, Hashabiah, and ten of their brethren with them—
25 and weighed out to them [a]the silver, the gold, and the articles, the offering for the house of our God which the king and his counselors and his princes, and all Israel *who were* present, had offered.
26 I weighed into their hand six hundred and fifty talents of silver, silver articles *weighing* one hundred talents, one hundred talents of gold,
27 twenty gold basins *worth* a thousand drachmas, and two vessels of fine polished bronze, precious as gold.
28 And I said to them, "You *are* [a]holy[1] to the LORD; the articles *are* [b]holy also; and the silver and the gold *are* a freewill offering to the LORD God of your fathers.
29 "Watch and keep *them* until you weigh *them* before the leaders of the priests and the Levites and [a]heads of the fathers' *houses* of Israel in Jerusalem, *in* the chambers of the house of the LORD."
30 So the priests and the Levites received the silver and the gold and the articles by weight, to bring *them* to Jerusalem to the house of our God.
**31** Then we departed from the river of Ahava on the twelfth *day* of the first month, to go to Jerusalem. And [a]the hand of our God was upon us, and He delivered us from the hand of the enemy and from ambush along the road.
32 So we [a]came to Jerusalem, and stayed there three days.
**33** Now on the fourth day the silver and the gold and the articles were [a]weighed in the house of our God by the hand of Meremoth the son of Uriah the priest, and with him *was* Eleazar the son of Phinehas; with them *were* the Levites, [b]Jozabad the son of Jeshua and Noadiah the son of Binnui,
34 with the number *and* weight of everything. All the weight was written down at that time.

**25** [a]Ex. 18:21, 22; Deut. 16:18 [b]2 Chr. 17:7; Ezra 7:10; [Mal. 2:7; Col. 1:28]
**26** [1]Lit. *rooting out*
**27** [a]1 Chr. 29:10 [b]Ezra 6:22; [Prov. 21:1] [1]The Hebrew language resumes in Ezra 7:27.
**28** [a]Ezra 9:9 [b]Ezra 5:5; 7:6, 9; 8:18

CHAPTER 8

**2** [a]1 Chr. 3:22; Ezra 2:68
**3** [a]Ezra 2:3
**4** [a]Ezra 10:30
**5** [1]So with MT, Vg.; LXX *the sons of Zatho, Shechaniah*
**10** [1]So with MT, Vg.; LXX *the sons of Banni, Shelomith*
**11** [a]Ezra 10:28
**12** [1]Or *the youngest son,*
**14** [1]Or *Zakkur*
**15** [a]Ezra 7:7; 8:2
**16** [a]Ezra 10:15
**17** [1]Lit. *I put words in their mouths to say* [2]So with Vg.; MT reads *Iddo his brother;* LXX *to their brethren*
**18** [a]2 Chr. 30:22; Neh. 8:7
**19** [a]Neh. 12:24
**20** [a]Ezra 2:43; 7:7
**21** [a]1 Sam. 7:6; 2 Chr. 20:3 [b]Lev. 16:29; 23:29; Is. 58:3, 5 [c]Ps. 5:8
**22** [a]1 Cor. 9:15 [b]Ezra 7:6, 9, 28 [c][Ps. 33:18, 19; 34:15, 22; Rom. 8:28] [d][Ps. 34:16] [e][2 Chr. 15:2]
**23** [a][1 Chr. 5:20]; 2 Chr. 33:13; Is. 19:22
**25** [a]Ezra 7:15, 16
**28** [a]Lev. 21:6–9; Deut. 33:8 [b]Lev. 22:2, 3; Num. 4:4, 15, 19, 20 [1]*consecrated*
**29** [a]Ezra 4:3
**31** [a]Ezra 7:6, 9, 28
**32** [a]Neh. 2:11
**33** [a]Ezra 8:26, 30 [b]Neh. 11:16

35 The children of those who had been [a]carried away captive, who had come from the captivity, [b]offered burnt offerings to the God of Israel: twelve bulls for all Israel, ninety-six rams, seventy-seven lambs, and twelve male goats *as* a sin offering. All *this was* a burnt offering to the LORD.

**36** And they delivered the king's [a]orders to the king's satraps and the governors *in the region* beyond [1]the River. So they gave support to the people and the [2]house of God.

## *Ezra's Prayer of Confession*

**9** When these things were done, the leaders came to me, saying, "The people of Israel and the priests and the Levites have not [a]separated themselves from the peoples of the lands, [b]with respect to the abominations of the Canaanites, the Hittites, the Perizzites, the Jebusites, the Ammonites, the Moabites, the Egyptians, and the Amorites.

2 "For they have [a]taken some of their daughters *as wives* for themselves and their sons, so that the [b]holy seed is [c]mixed with the peoples of *those* lands. Indeed, the hand of the leaders and rulers has been foremost in this [1]trespass."

3 So when I heard this thing, [a]I tore my garment and my robe, and plucked out some of the hair of my head and beard, and sat down [b]astonished.

4 Then everyone who [a]trembled at the words of the God of Israel assembled to me, because of the transgression of those who had been carried away captive, and I sat astonished until the [b]evening sacrifice.

**5** At the evening sacrifice I arose from my fasting; and having torn my garment and my robe, I fell on my knees and [a]spread out my hands to the LORD my God.

6 And I said: "O my God, I am too [a]ashamed and humiliated to lift up my face to You, my God; for [b]our iniquities have risen higher than *our* heads, and our guilt has [c]grown up to the heavens.

7 "Since the days of our fathers to this day [a]we *have been* very guilty, and for our iniquities [b]we, our kings, *and* our priests have been delivered into the hand of the kings of the lands, to the [c]sword, to captivity, to plunder, and to [d]humiliation,[1] as *it is* this day.

8 "And now for a little while grace has been *shown* from the LORD our God, to leave us a remnant to escape, and to give us a peg in His holy place, that our God may [a]enlighten our eyes and give us a measure of revival in our bondage.

9 [a]"For we *were* slaves. [b]Yet our God did not forsake us in our bondage; but [c]He extended mercy to us in the sight of the kings of Persia, to revive us, to repair the house of our God, to rebuild its ruins, and to give us [d]a wall in Judah and Jerusalem.

10 "And now, O our God, what shall we say after this? For we have forsaken Your commandments,

11 "which You commanded by Your servants the prophets, saying, 'The land which you are entering to possess is an unclean land, with the [a]uncleanness of the peoples of the lands, with their abominations which have filled it from one end to another with their impurity.

12 'Now therefore, [a]do not give your daughters as wives for their sons, nor take their daughters to your sons; and [b]never seek their peace or prosperity, that you may be strong and eat the good of the land, and [c]leave *it* as an inheritance to your children forever.'

13 "And after all that has come upon us for our evil deeds and for our great guilt, since You our God [a]have punished us less than our iniquities *deserve,* and have given us *such* deliverance as this,

14 "should we [a]again break Your commandments, and [b]join in marriage with the people committing these abominations? Would You not be [c]angry with us until You had [1]consumed *us,* so that *there would be* no remnant or survivor?

15 "O LORD God of Israel, [a]You *are* righteous, for we are left as a remnant, as *it is* this day. [b]Here we *are* before You, [c]in our guilt, though no one can stand before You because of this!"

## *Pagan Marriages Annulled*

**10** Now [a]while Ezra was praying, and while he was confessing, weeping, and bowing down [b]before the house of God, a very large assembly of men, women, and children gathered to him from Israel; for the people wept very [c]bitterly.

2 And Shechaniah the son of Jehiel, *one* of the sons of Elam, spoke up and said to Ezra, "We have [a]trespassed[1] against our God, and have taken pagan wives from the peoples of the land; yet now there is hope in Israel in spite of this.

3 "Now therefore, let us make [a]a covenant with our God to put away all these wives and those who have been born to them, according to the advice of my master and of those who [b]tremble at [c]the commandment of our God; and let it be done according to the [d]law.

4 "Arise, for *this* matter *is* your *responsibility.* We also *are* with you. [a]Be of good courage, and do *it.*"

**5** Then Ezra arose, and made the leaders of the priests, the Levites, and all Israel [a]swear an oath that they would do according to this word. So they swore an oath.

6 Then Ezra rose up from before the house of God, and went into the chamber of Jehohanan the son of Eliashib; and *when* he came there, he [a]ate no bread and drank no water, for he mourned because of the guilt of those from the captivity.

7 And they issued a proclamation throughout Judah and Jerusalem to all the descendants of the captivity, that they must gather at Jerusalem,

8 and that whoever would not come within three days, according to the instructions of the leaders and elders, all his property would be confiscated, and he himself would be separated from the assembly of those from the captivity.

**9** So all the men of Judah and Benjamin gathered at Jerusalem within three days. It *was* the ninth month, on the twentieth of the month; and [a]all the people sat in the open square of the house of God, trembling because of *this* matter and because of heavy rain.

10 Then Ezra the priest stood up and said to them, "You have [1]transgressed and [2]have taken pagan wives, adding to the guilt of Israel.

11 "Now therefore, [a]make confession to the LORD God of your fathers, and do His will; [b]separate yourselves from the peoples of the land, and from the pagan wives."

12 Then all the assembly answered and said with a loud voice, "Yes! As you have said, so we must do.

13 "But *there are* many people; *it is* the season

---

**35** [a]Ezra 2:1 [b]Ezra 6:17
**36** [a]Ezra 7:21–24 [1]The Euphrates [2]Temple

CHAPTER 9
**1** [a]Ezra 6:21; Neh. 9:2 [b]Deut. 12:30, 31
**2** [a]Ex. 34:16; [Deut. 7:3]; Ezra 10:2; Neh. 13:23 [b]Ex. 22:31; [Deut. 7:6] [c][2 Cor. 6:14] [1]*unfaithfulness*
**3** [a]Job 1:20 [b]Ps. 143:4
**4** [a]Ezra 10:3; Is. 66:2 [b]Ex. 29:39
**5** [a]Ex. 9:29
**6** [a]Dan. 9:7, 8 [b]Ps. 38:4 [c]2 Chr. 28:9; [Ezra 9:13, 15]; Rev. 18:5
**7** [a]2 Chr. 36:14–17; Ps. 106:6; Dan. 9:5, 6 [b]Deut. 28:36; Neh. 9:30 [c]Deut. 32:25 [d]Dan. 9:7, 8 [1]Lit. *shame of faces*
**8** [a]Ps. 34:5
**9** [a]Neh. 9:36; Esth. 7:4 [b]Neh. 9:17; Ps. 136:23 [c]Ezra 7:28 [d]Is. 5:2
**11** [a]Ezra 6:21
**12** [a][Ex. 23:32; 34:15, 16; Deut. 7:3, 4]; Ezra 9:2 [b]Deut. 23:6 [c][Prov. 13:22; 20:7]
**13** [a][Ps. 103:10]
**14** [a][John 5:14; 2 Pet. 2:20] [b]Neh. 13:23 [c]Deut. 9:8 [1]*destroyed*
**15** [a]Neh. 9:33; Dan. 9:14 [b][Rom. 3:19] [c]1 Cor. 15:17

CHAPTER 10
**1** [a]Dan. 9:4, 20 [b]2 Chr. 20:9 [c]Neh. 8:1–9
**2** [a]Ezra 10:10, 13, 14, 17, 18; Neh. 13:23–27 [1]*been unfaithful to*
**3** [a]2 Chr. 34:31 [b]Ezra 9:4 [c]Deut. 7:2, 3 [d]Deut. 24:1, 2
**4** [a]1 Chr. 28:10
**5** [a]Ezra 10:12, 19; Neh. 5:12; 13:25
**6** [a]Deut. 9:18
**9** [a]1 Sam. 12:18; Ezra 9:4; 10:3
**10** [1]*acted unfaithfully* [2]Heb. *have caused to dwell* or *have brought back*
**11** [a][Lev. 26:40–42]; Josh. 7:19; [Prov. 28:13] [b]Ezra 10:3

for heavy rain, and we are not able to stand
outside. Nor *is this* the work of one or two days,
for *there are* many of us who have transgressed in
this matter.
14 "Please, let the leaders of our entire assembly
stand; and let all those in our cities who have
taken pagan wives come at appointed times,
together with the elders and judges of their cities,
until [a]the fierce wrath of our God is turned away
from us in this matter."
15 Only Jonathan the son of Asahel and Jahaziah
the son of Tikvah opposed this, and [a]Meshullam
and Shabbethai the Levite gave them support.
**16** Then the descendants of the captivity did so.
And Ezra the priest, *with* certain [a]heads of the
fathers' *households,* were set apart by the fathers'
*households,* each of them by name; and they sat
down on the first day of the tenth month to
examine the matter.
17 By the first day of the first month they finished *questioning* all the men who had taken
pagan wives.
**18** And among the sons of the priests who had
taken pagan wives *the following* were found of
the sons of [a]Jeshua the son of [1]Jozadak, and his
brothers: Maaseiah, Eliezer, Jarib, and Gedaliah.
19 And they [a]gave their promise that they would
put away their wives; and *being* [b]guilty, *they*
*presented* a ram of the flock as their [c]trespass
offering.
20 Also of the sons of Immer: Hanani and Zebadiah;
21 of the sons of Harim: Maaseiah, Elijah,
Shemaiah, Jehiel, and Uzziah;
22 of the sons of Pashhur: Elioenai, Maaseiah,
Ishmael, Nethanel, Jozabad, and Elasah.
23 Also of the Levites: Jozabad, Shimei, Kelaiah
(the same *is* Kelita), Pethahiah, Judah, and Eliezer.
24 Also of the singers: Eliashib; and of the gatekeepers: Shallum, Telem, and Uri.
25 And others of Israel: of the [a]sons of Parosh:
Ramiah, Jeziah, Malchiah, Mijamin, Eleazar, Malchijah, and Benaiah;
26 of the sons of Elam: Mattaniah, Zechariah,
Jehiel, Abdi, Jeremoth, and Eliah;
27 of the sons of Zattu: Elioenai, Eliashib, Mattaniah, Jeremoth, Zabad, and Aziza;
28 of the [a]sons of Bebai: Jehohanan, Hananiah,
Zabbai, *and* Athlai;
29 of the sons of Bani: Meshullam, Malluch,
Adaiah, Jashub, Sheal, *and* [1]Ramoth;
30 of the [a]sons of Pahath-Moab: Adna, Chelal,
Benaiah, Maaseiah, Mattaniah, Bezalel, Binnui,
and Manasseh;
31 *of* the sons of Harim: Eliezer, Ishijah, Malchijah, Shemaiah, Shimeon,
32 Benjamin, Malluch, *and* Shemariah;
33 of the sons of Hashum: Mattenai, Mattattah,
Zabad, Eliphelet, Jeremai, Manasseh, *and* Shimei;
34 of the sons of Bani: Maadai, Amram, Uel,
35 Benaiah, Bedeiah, [1]Cheluh,
36 Vaniah, Meremoth, Eliashib,
37 Mattaniah, Mattenai, [1]Jaasai,
38 Bani, Binnui, Shimei,
39 Shelemiah, Nathan, Adaiah,
40 Machnadebai, Shashai, Sharai,
41 Azarel, Shelemiah, Shemariah,
42 Shallum, Amariah, *and* Joseph;
43 of the sons of Nebo: Jeiel, Mattithiah, Zabad,
Zebina, [1]Jaddai, Joel, *and* Benaiah.
44 All these had taken pagan wives, and *some* of
them had wives *by whom* they had children.

**14** [a]2 Kin. 23:26; 2 Chr. 28:11–13; 29:10; 30:8
**15** [a]Ezra 8:16; Neh. 3:4
**16** [a]Ezra 4:3
**18** [a]Ezra 5:2; Hag. 1:1, 12; 2:4; Zech. 3:1; 6:11 [1]*Jehozadak,* 1 Chr. 6:14
**19** [a]2 Kin. 10:15 [b]Lev. 6:4, 6 [c]Lev. 5:6, 15
**25** [a]Ezra 2:3; 8:3; Neh. 7:8
**28** [a]Ezra 8:11
**29** [1]Or *Jeremoth*
**30** [a]Ezra 8:4
**35** [1]Or *Cheluhi* or *Cheluhu*
**37** [1]Or *Jaasu*
**43** [1]Or *Jaddu*

*The Book of*

# NEHEMIAH

### *Nehemiah's Prayer for Jerusalem*

THE words of [a]Nehemiah the son of Hacha-
liah.
It came to pass in the month of Chislev, *in*
the [b]twentieth year, as I was in [c]Shushan[1] the
[2]citadel,
2 that [a]Hanani one of my brethren came with
men from Judah; and I asked them concerning the
Jews who had escaped, who had survived the
captivity, and concerning Jerusalem.
3 And they said to me, "The survivors who are
left from the captivity in the [a]province *are* there in
great distress and [b]reproach. [c]The wall of Jerusalem [d]*is* also broken down, and its gates *are* burned
with fire."
**4** So it was, when I heard these words, that I sat
down and wept, and mourned *for many* days; I
was fasting and praying before the God of heaven.
5 And I said: "I pray, [a]LORD God of heaven, O
great and [b]awesome God, [c]*You* who keep *Your*
covenant and mercy with those who love [1]You
and observe [2]Your commandments,
6 "please let Your ear be attentive and [a]Your
eyes open, that You may hear the prayer of Your
servant which I pray before You now, day and
night, for the children of Israel Your servants, and
[b]confess the sins of the children of Israel which we
have sinned against You. Both my father's house
and I have sinned.
7 [a]"We have acted very corruptly against You,
and have [b]not kept the commandments, the statutes, nor the ordinances which You commanded
Your servant Moses.
8 "Remember, I pray, the word that You commanded Your servant Moses, saying, [a]'*If* you [1]are
unfaithful, I will scatter you among the nations;
9 [a]'but *if* you return to Me, and keep My commandments and do them, [b]though some of you
were cast out to the farthest part of the heavens,
*yet* I will gather them from there, and bring them
to the place which I have chosen as a dwelling for
My name.'
10 [a]"Now these *are* Your servants and Your
people, whom You have redeemed by Your great
power, and by Your strong hand.
11 "O Lord, I pray, please [a]let Your ear be attentive to the prayer of Your servant, and to the
prayer of Your servants who [b]desire to fear Your

CHAPTER 1
**1** [a]Neh. 10:1 [b]Neh. 2:1 [c]Esth. 1:1, 2, 5 [1]Or *Susa* [2]Or *fortified palace,* and so elsewhere in the book
**2** [a]Neh. 7:2
**3** [a]Neh. 7:6 [b]Neh. 2:17 [c]Neh. 2:17 [d]2 Kin. 25:10
**5** [a]Dan. 9:4 [b]Neh. 4:14 [c][Ex. 20:6; 34:6, 7] [1]Lit. *Him* [2]Lit. *His*
**6** [a]2 Chr. 6:40 [b]Dan. 9:20
**7** [a]Dan. 9:5 [b]Deut. 28:15
**8** [a]Lev. 26:33 [1]*act treacherously*
**9** [a][Deut. 4:29–31; 30:2–5] [b]Deut. 30:4
**10** [a]Deut. 9:29
**11** [a]Neh. 1:6 [b]Is. 26:8

name; and let Your servant prosper this day, I
pray, and grant him mercy in the sight of this
man." For I was the king's [c]cupbearer.

### *Nehemiah Sent to Jerusalem*

**2** And it came to pass in the month of Nisan, in
the twentieth year of [a]King [1]Artaxerxes, *when*
wine *was* before him, that [b]I took the wine and
gave it to the king. Now I had never been sad in
his presence before.
2 Therefore the king said to me, "Why *is* your
face sad, since you *are* not sick? This *is* nothing
but [a]sorrow of heart." So I became [1]dreadfully
afraid,
3 and said to the king, [a]"May the king live
forever! Why should my face not be sad, when
[b]the city, the place of my fathers' tombs, *lies*
waste, and its gates are burned with [c]fire?"
4 Then the king said to me, "What do you
request?" So I [a]prayed to the God of heaven.
5 And I said to the king, "If it pleases the king,
and if your servant has found favor in your sight,
I ask that you send me to Judah, to the city of my
fathers' tombs, that I may rebuild it."
6 Then the king said to me (the queen also
sitting beside him), "How long will your journey
be? And when will you return?" So it pleased the
king to send me; and I set him [a]a time.
7 Furthermore I said to the king, "If it pleases
the king, let letters be given to me for the [a]gover-
nors *of the region* beyond [1]the River, that they
must permit me to pass through till I come to
Judah,
8 "and a letter to Asaph the keeper of the king's
forest, that he must give me timber to make
beams for the gates of the [1]citadel which *pertains*
[a]to the [2]temple, for the city wall, and for the house
that I will occupy." And the king granted *them* to
me [b]according to the good hand of my God upon
me.
**9** Then I went to the governors *in the region*
beyond the River, and gave them the king's letters. Now the king had sent captains of the army
and horsemen with me.
10 When [a]Sanballat the Horonite and Tobiah the
Ammonite [1]official heard *of it,* they were deeply
disturbed that a man had come to seek the well-
being of the children of Israel.
**11** So I [a]came to Jerusalem and was there three
days.
12 Then I arose in the night, I and a few men
with me; I told no one what my God had put in
my heart to do at Jerusalem; nor was there any
animal with me, except the one on which I rode.
13 And I went out by night [a]through the Valley
Gate to the Serpent Well and the [1]Refuse Gate,
and [2]viewed the walls of Jerusalem which were
[b]broken down and its gates which were burned
with fire.
14 Then I went on to the [a]Fountain Gate and to
the [b]King's Pool, but *there was* no room for the
animal under me to pass.
15 So I went up in the night by the [a]valley,[1] and
[2]viewed the wall; then I turned back and entered
by the Valley Gate, and so returned.
16 And the officials did not know where I had
gone or what I had done; I had not yet told the
Jews, the priests, the nobles, the officials, or the
others who did the work.
**17** Then I said to them, "You see the distress that
we *are* in, how Jerusalem *lies* [1]waste, and its gates
are burned with fire. Come and let us build the
wall of Jerusalem, that we may no longer be [a]a
reproach."
18 And I told them of [a]the hand of my God which
had been good upon me, and also of the king's
words that he had spoken to me. So they said,
"Let us rise up and build." Then they [b]set[1] their
hands to *this* good *work.*
19 But when Sanballat the Horonite, Tobiah the
Ammonite official, and Geshem the Arab heard *of
it,* they laughed at us and despised us, and said,
"What *is* this thing that you are doing? [a]Will you
rebel against the king?"
20 So I answered them, and said to them, "The
God of heaven Himself will prosper us; therefore
we His servants will arise and build, [a]but you have
no heritage or right or memorial in Jerusalem."

### *The Builders of the Wall*

**3** Then [a]Eliashib the high priest rose up with his
brethren the priests [b]and built the Sheep Gate;
they consecrated it and hung its doors. They built
[c]as far as the Tower of [1]the Hundred, *and* consecrated it, then as far as the Tower of [d]Hananel.
2 [1]Next to *Eliashib* [a]the men of Jericho built.
And next to them Zaccur the son of Imri built.
**3** Also the sons of Hassenaah built [a]the Fish
Gate; they laid its beams and [b]hung its doors with
its bolts and bars.
4 And next to them [a]Meremoth the son of Urijah, the son of [1]Koz, made repairs. Next to them
[b]Meshullam the son of Berechiah, the son of
Meshezabel, made repairs. Next to them Zadok
the son of Baana made repairs.
5 Next to them the Tekoites made repairs; but
their nobles did not put their [1]shoulders to [a]the
work of their Lord.
**6** Moreover Jehoiada the son of Paseah and
Meshullam the son of Besodeiah repaired [a]the Old
Gate; they laid its beams and hung its doors, with
its bolts and bars.
7 And next to them Melatiah the Gibeonite,
Jadon the Meronothite, the [a]men of Gibeon and
Mizpah, repaired the [b]residence[1] of the governor
*of the region* [2]beyond the River.
8 Next to him Uzziel the son of Harhaiah, one of
the goldsmiths, made repairs. Also next to him
Hananiah, [1]one of the perfumers, made repairs;
and they [2]fortified Jerusalem as far as the [a]Broad
Wall.
9 And next to them Rephaiah the son of Hur,
leader of half the district of Jerusalem, made
repairs.
10 Next to them Jedaiah the son of Harumaph
made repairs in front of his house. And next to
him Hattush the son of Hashabniah made repairs.
11 Malchijah the son of Harim and Hashub the
son of Pahath-Moab repaired another section, [a]as
well as the Tower of the Ovens.
12 And next to him was Shallum the son of
Hallohesh, leader of half the district of Jerusalem;
he and his daughters made repairs.
**13** Hanun and the inhabitants of Zanoah repaired
[a]the Valley Gate. They built it, hung its doors with
its bolts and bars, and *repaired* a thousand cubits
of the wall as far as [b]the Refuse Gate.
**14** Malchijah the son of Rechab, leader of the
district of [a]Beth Haccerem, repaired the Refuse
Gate; he built it and hung its doors with its bolts
and bars.
**15** Shallun the son of Col-Hozeh, leader of the

---

11 [c]Gen. 40:21; Neh. 2:1

CHAPTER 2
1 [a]Ezra 7:1 [b]Neh. 1:11 [1]Artaxerxes Longimanus
2 [a]Prov. 15:13 [1]Lit. *very much*
3 [a]1 Kin. 1:31; Dan. 2:4; 5:10; 6:6, 21 [b]2 Kin. 25:8–10; 2 Chr. 36:19; Jer. 52:12–14 [c]2 Kin. 24:10; Neh. 1:3
4 [a]Neh. 1:4
6 [a]Neh. 5:14; 13:6
7 [a]Ezra 7:21; 8:36 [1]The Euphrates
8 [a]Neh. 3:7 [b]Ezra 5:5; 7:6, 9, 28; Neh. 2:18 [1]*palace* [2]Lit. *house*
10 [a]Neh. 2:19; 4:1 [1]Lit. *servant*
11 [a]Ezra 8:32
13 [a]2 Chr. 26:9; Neh. 3:13 [b]Neh. 1:3; 2:17 [1]*Dung* [2]*examined*
14 [a]Neh. 3:15 [b]2 Kin. 20:20
15 [a]2 Sam. 15:23; Jer. 31:40 [1]*torrent valley, wadi* [2]*examined*
17 [a]Neh. 1:3; Ps. 44:13; 79:4; Jer. 24:9; Ezek. 5:14, 15; 22:4 [1]*desolate*
18 [a]Neh. 2:8 [b]2 Sam. 2:7 [1]Lit. *strengthened*
19 [a]Neh. 6:6
20 [a]Ezra 4:3; Neh. 6:16

CHAPTER 3
1 [a]Neh. 3:20; 12:10; 13:4, 7, 28 [b]John 5:2 [c]Neh. 12:39 [d]Jer. 31:38; Zech. 14:10 [1]Heb. *Hammeah*
2 [a]Ezra 2:34; Neh. 7:36 [1]Lit. *On his hand*
3 [a]2 Chr. 33:14; Neh. 12:39; Zeph. 1:10 [b]Neh. 6:1; 7:1
4 [a]Ezra 8:33 [b]Ezra 10:15 [1]Or *Hakkoz*
5 [a][Judg. 5:23] [1]Lit. *necks*
6 [a]Neh. 12:39
7 [a]Neh. 7:25 [b]Ezra 8:36; Neh. 2:7–9 [1]Lit. *throne* [2]West of the Euphrates
8 [a]Neh. 12:38 [1]Lit. *the son* [2]*restored*
11 [a]Neh. 12:38
13 [a]Neh. 2:13, 15 [b]Neh. 2:13
14 [a]Jer. 6:1

district of Mizpah, repaired [a]the Fountain Gate; he
built it, covered it, hung its doors with its bolts
and bars, and repaired the wall of the Pool of
[b]Shelah[1] by the [c]King's Garden, as far as the stairs
that go down from the City of David.
16 After him Nehemiah the son of Azbuk, leader
of half the district of Beth Zur, made repairs as far
as the front of the [1]tombs of David, to the [a]man-
made pool, and as far as the House of the Mighty.
17 After him the Levites, *under* Rehum the son of
Bani, made repairs. Next to him Hashabiah, leader
of half the district of Keilah, made repairs for his
district.
18 After him their brethren, *under* [1]Bavai the son
of Henadad, leader of the *other* half of the district
of Keilah, made repairs.
19 And next to him Ezer the son of Jeshua, the
leader of Mizpah, repaired another section in front
of the Ascent to the Armory at the [a]buttress.[1]
20 After him Baruch the son of [1]Zabbai carefully
repaired the other section, from the [2]buttress to
the door of the house of Eliashib the high priest.
21 After him Meremoth the son of Urijah, the son
of [1]Koz, repaired another section, from the door of
the house of Eliashib to the end of the house of
Eliashib.
22 And after him the priests, the men of the plain,
made repairs.
23 After him Benjamin and Hasshub made repairs opposite their house. After them Azariah the
son of Maaseiah, the son of Ananiah, made repairs
by his house.
24 After him [a]Binnui the son of Henadad repaired
another section, from the house of Azariah to [b]the
[1]buttress, even as far as the corner.
25 Palal the son of Uzai *made repairs* opposite
the [1]buttress, and on the tower which projects
from the king's upper house that *was* by the
[a]court of the prison. After him Pedaiah the son of
Parosh *made repairs*.
26 Moreover [a]the Nethinim who dwelt in [b]Ophel
*made repairs* as far as *the place* in front of [c]the
Water Gate toward the east, and on the projecting
tower.
27 After them the Tekoites repaired another
section, next to the great projecting tower, and as
far as the wall of Ophel.
**28** Beyond the [a]Horse Gate the priests made
repairs, each in front of his *own* house.
29 After them Zadok the son of Immer made
repairs in front of his *own* house. After him
Shemaiah the son of Shechaniah, the keeper of
the East Gate, made repairs.
30 After him Hananiah the son of Shelemiah, and
Hanun, the sixth son of Zalaph, repaired another
section. After him Meshullam the son of Berechiah made repairs in front of his [1]dwelling.
31 After him Malchijah, [1]one of the goldsmiths,
made repairs as far as the house of the Nethinim
and of the merchants, in front of the [2]Miphkad
Gate, and as far as the upper room at the corner.
32 And between the upper room at the corner, as
far as the [a]Sheep Gate, the goldsmiths and the
merchants made repairs.

### *Nehemiah Opposed and Ridiculed*

**4** But it so happened, [a]when Sanballat heard
that we were rebuilding the wall, that he was
furious and very indignant, and mocked the Jews.
2 And he spoke before his brethren and the
army of Samaria, and said, "What are these feeble
Jews doing? Will they fortify themselves? Will
they offer sacrifices? Will they complete it in a
day? Will they revive the stones from the heaps of
rubbish—*stones* that are burned?"
3 Now [a]Tobiah the Ammonite *was* beside him,
and he said, "Whatever they build, if even a fox
goes up *on it*, he will break down their stone
wall."
4 [a]Hear, O our God, for we are despised; [b]turn
their reproach on their own heads, and give them
as plunder to a land of captivity!
5 [a]Do not cover their iniquity, and do not let
their sin be blotted out from before You; for they
have provoked *You* to anger before the builders.
**6** So we built the wall, and the entire wall was
joined together up to half its *height*, for the people
had a mind to work.
**7** Now it happened, [a]when Sanballat, Tobiah,
[b]the Arabs, the Ammonites, and the Ashdodites
heard that the walls of Jerusalem were being
restored and the [1]gaps were beginning to be
closed, that they became very angry,
8 and all of them [a]conspired together to come
*and* attack Jerusalem and create confusion.
9 Nevertheless [a]we made our prayer to our God,
and because of them we set a watch against them
day and night.
**10** Then Judah said, "The strength of the laborers
is failing, and *there is* so much rubbish that we are
not able to build the wall."
11 And our adversaries said, "They will neither
know nor see anything, till we come into their
midst and kill them and cause the work to cease."
12 So it was, when the Jews who dwelt near them
came, that they told us ten times, "From whatever
place you turn, *they will be* upon us."
**13** Therefore I positioned *men* behind the lower
parts of the wall, at the openings; and I set the
people according to their families, with their
swords, their spears, and their bows.
14 And I looked, and arose and said to the nobles,
to the leaders, and to the rest of the people, [a]"Do
not be afraid of them. Remember the Lord, [b]great
and awesome, and [c]fight for your brethren, your
sons, your daughters, your wives, and your
houses."
**15** And it happened, when our enemies heard
that it was known to us, and [a]*that* God had
brought their plot to nothing, that all of us returned to the wall, everyone to his work.
16 So it was, from that time on, *that* half of my
servants worked at construction, while the other
half held the spears, the shields, the bows, and
*wore* armor; and the leaders [1]*were* behind all the
house of Judah.
17 Those who built on the wall, and those who
carried burdens, loaded themselves so that with
one hand they worked at construction, and with
the other held a weapon.
18 Every one of the builders had his sword girded
at his side as he built. And the one who sounded
the trumpet *was* beside me.
**19** Then I said to the nobles, the rulers, and the
rest of the people, "The work *is* great and extensive, and we are separated far from one another
on the wall.
20 "Wherever you hear the sound of the trumpet,
rally to us there. [a]Our God will fight for us."
**21** So we labored in the work, and half of [1]*the
men* held the spears from daybreak until the stars
appeared.

**15** [a]Neh. 2:14 [b]Is. 8:6; John 9:7 [c]2 Kin. 25:4 [1]Or *Shiloah*
**16** [a]2 Kin. 20:20; Is. 7:3; 22:11 [1]LXX, Syr., Vg. *tomb*
**18** [1]So with MT, Vg.; some Heb. mss., LXX, Syr. *Binnui* (cf. v. 24)
**19** [a]2 Chr. 26:9 [1]Lit. *turning*
**20** [1]A few Heb. mss., Syr., Vg. *Zaccai* [2]Lit. *turning*
**21** [1]Or *Hakkoz*
**24** [a]Ezra 8:33 [b]Neh. 3:19 [1]Lit. *turning*
**25** [a]Jer. 32:2; 33:1; 37:21 [1]Lit. *turning*
**26** [a]Ezra 2:43; Neh. 11:21 [b]2 Chr. 27:3 [c]Neh. 8:1, 3; 12:37
**28** [a]2 Kin. 11:16; 2 Chr. 23:15; Jer. 31:40
**30** [1]Lit. *room*
**31** [1]Lit. *a son of the goldsmiths* [2]Lit. *Inspection* or *Recruiting*
**32** [a]Neh. 3:1; 12:39

CHAPTER 4

**1** [a]Neh. 2:10, 19
**3** [a]Neh. 2:10, 19
**4** [a]Ps. 123:3, 4 [b]Ps. 79:12; Prov. 3:34
**5** [a]Ps. 69:27, 28; 109:14, 15; Jer. 18:23
**7** [a]Neh. 4:1 [b]Neh. 2:19 [1]Lit. *breaks*
**8** [a]Ps. 83:3–5
**9** [a][Ps. 50:15]
**14** [a][Num. 14:9]; Deut. 1:29 [b][Deut. 10:17] [c]2 Sam. 10:12
**15** [a]Job 5:12
**16** [1]Supported
**20** [a]Ex. 14:14, 25; Deut. 1:30; 3:22; 20:4; Josh. 23:10; 2 Chr. 20:29
**21** [1]Lit. *them*

22 At the same time I also said to the people, "Let
each man and his servant stay at night in Jerusalem, that they may be our guard by night and a
working party by day."
23 So neither I, my brethren, my servants, nor
the men of the guard who followed me took off
our clothes, *except* that everyone took them off
for washing.

### *Nehemiah Opposes Injustice*

**5** And there was a great [a]outcry of the people
and their wives against their [b]Jewish brethren.
2 For there were those who said, "We, our sons,
and our daughters *are* many; therefore let us get
grain, that we may eat and live."
3 There were also *some* who said, "We have
mortgaged our lands and vineyards and houses,
that we might buy grain because of the famine."
4 There were also those who said, "We have
borrowed money for the king's tax *on* our lands
and vineyards.
5 "Yet now [a]our flesh *is* as the flesh of our
brethren, our children as their children; and indeed we [b]are forcing our sons and our daughters
to be slaves, and *some* of our daughters have been
brought into slavery. *It is* not in our power *to
redeem them*, for other men have our lands and
vineyards."
**6** And I became very angry when I heard their
outcry and these words.
7 After serious thought, I rebuked the nobles
and rulers, and said to them, [a]"Each of you is
[1]exacting usury from his brother." So I [2]called a
great assembly against them.
8 And I said to them, "According to our ability
we have [a]redeemed our Jewish brethren who were
sold to the nations. Now indeed, will you even sell
your brethren? Or should they be sold to us?"
Then they were silenced and found nothing *to
say*.
9 Then I said, "What you are doing *is* not good.
Should you not walk [a]in the fear of our God
[b]because of the reproach of the nations, our
enemies?"
10 "I also, *with* my brethren and my servants, am
lending them money and grain. Please, let us stop
this [1]usury!
11 "Restore now to them, even this day, their
lands, their vineyards, their olive groves, and their
houses, also a hundredth of the money and the
grain, the new wine and the oil, that you have
charged them."
12 So they said, "We will restore *it*, and will
require nothing from them; we will do as you
say." Then I called the priests, [a]and required an
oath from them that they would do according to
this promise.
13 Then [a]I shook out [1]the fold of my garment and
said, "So may God shake out each man from his
house, and from his property, who does not perform this promise. Even thus may he be shaken
out and emptied." And all the assembly said,
"Amen!" and praised the LORD. [b]Then the people
did according to this promise.
**14** Moreover, from the time that I was appointed
to be their governor in the land of Judah, from the
twentieth year [a]until the thirty-second year of
King Artaxerxes, twelve years, neither I nor my
brothers [b]ate the governor's provisions.
15 But the former governors who *were* before me
laid burdens on the people, and took from them

CHAPTER 5
1 [a]Lev. 25:35–37; Neh. 5:7, 8 [b]Deut. 15:7
5 [a]Is. 58:7 [b]Ex. 21:7; [Lev. 25:39]
7 [a][Ex. 22:25; Lev. 25:36; Deut. 23:19, 20]; Ezek. 22:12 [1]*charging interest* [2]Lit. *held*
8 [a]Lev. 25:48
9 [a]Lev. 25:36 [b]2 Sam. 12:14; Rom. 2:24; [1 Pet. 2:12]
10 [1]*interest*
12 [a]Ezra 10:5; Jer. 34:8, 9
13 [a]Matt. 10:14; Acts 13:51; 18:6 [b]2 Kin. 23:3 [1]Lit. *my lap*
14 [a]Neh. 2:1; 13:6 [b][1 Cor. 9:4–15]
15 [a]2 Cor. 11:9; 12:13 [b]Neh. 5:9
16 [a]Neh. 4:1; 6:1 [1]So with MT; LXX, Syr., Vg. *I*
17 [a]2 Sam. 9:7; 1 Kin. 18:19
18 [a]1 Kin. 4:22 [b]Neh. 5:14, 15
19 [a]2 Kin. 20:3; Neh. 13:14, 22, 31

CHAPTER 6
1 [a]Neh. 2:10, 19; 4:1, 7; 13:28 [b]Neh. 3:1, 3 [1]Or *Gashmu*
2 [a]Prov. 26:24, 25 [b]1 Chr. 8:12; Neh. 11:35 [c]Ps. 37:12, 32 [1]Or *Gashmu* [2]Or *in Kephirim*, exact location unknown
6 [a]Neh. 2:19 [1]Heb. *Gashmu*
10 [1]Lit. *house*
12 [a]Ezek. 13:22

bread and wine, besides forty shekels of silver.
Yes, even their servants bore rule over the people,
but [a]I did not do so, because of the [b]fear of God.
16 Indeed, I also continued the [a]work on this
wall, and [1]we did not buy any land. All my servants *were* gathered there for the work.
17 And [a]at my table *were* one hundred and fifty
Jews and rulers, besides those who came to us
from the nations around us.
18 Now *that* [a]which was prepared daily *was* one
ox *and* six choice sheep. Also fowl were prepared
for me, and once every ten days an abundance of
all kinds of wine. Yet in spite of this [b]I did not
demand the governor's provisions, because the
bondage was heavy on this people.
**19** [a]Remember me, my God, for good, *according
to* all that I have done for this people.

### *The Plot Against Nehemiah*

**6** Now it happened [a]when Sanballat, Tobiah,
[1]Geshem the Arab, and the rest of our enemies
heard that I had rebuilt the wall, and *that* there
were no breaks left in it [b](though at that time I
had not hung the doors in the gates),
2 that Sanballat and [1]Geshem [a]sent to me, saying, "Come, let us meet together among the
villages in the plain of [b]Ono." But they [c]thought to
do me harm.
3 So I sent messengers to them, saying, "I *am*
doing a great work, so that I cannot come down.
Why should the work cease while I leave it and go
down to you?"
4 But they sent me this message four times, and
I answered them in the same manner.
5 Then Sanballat sent his servant to me as
before, the fifth time, with an open letter in his
hand.
6 In it *was* written:

It is reported among the nations, and
[1]Geshem says, *that* you and the Jews plan to
rebel; therefore, according to these rumors,
you are rebuilding the wall, [a]that you may be
their king.
7 And you have also appointed prophets to
proclaim concerning you at Jerusalem,
saying, "*There is* a king in Judah!" Now
these matters will be reported to the king. So
come, therefore, and let us consult together.

8 Then I sent to him, saying, "No such things as
you say are being done, but you invent them in
your own heart."
9 For they all *were trying to* make us afraid,
saying, "Their hands will be weakened in the
work, and it will not be done."
Now therefore, *O God*, strengthen my hands.
**10** Afterward I came to the house of Shemaiah
the son of Delaiah, the son of Mehetabel, who *was*
a secret informer; and he said, "Let us meet
together in the house of God, within the [1]temple,
and let us close the doors of the temple, for they
are coming to kill you; indeed, at night they will
come to kill you."
11 And I said, "Should such a man as I flee? And
who *is there* such as I who would go into the
temple to save his life? I will not go in!"
12 Then I perceived that God had not sent him at
all, but that [a]he pronounced *this* prophecy against
me because Tobiah and Sanballat had hired him.
13 For this reason he *was* hired, that I should be

afraid and act that way and sin, so *that* they
might have *cause* for an evil report, that they
might reproach me.
**14** [a]My God, remember Tobiah and Sanballat,
according to these their works, and the [b]prophet-
ess Noadiah and the rest of the prophets who
would have made me afraid.
**15** So the wall was finished on the twenty-fifth
*day* of Elul, in fifty-two days.
16 And it happened, [a]when all our enemies heard
*of it,* and all the nations around us saw *these*
*things,* that they were very disheartened in their
own eyes; for [b]they perceived that this work was
done by our God.
**17** Also in those days the nobles of Judah sent
many letters to Tobiah, and *the letters of* Tobiah
came to them.
18 For many in Judah were pledged to him,
because he was the [a]son-in-law of Shechaniah the
son of Arah, and his son Jehohanan had married
the daughter of [b]Meshullam the son of Berechiah.
19 Also they reported his good deeds before me,
and reported my [1]words to him. Tobiah sent
letters to frighten me.

### *List of Returning Exiles*

**7** Then it was, when the wall was built and I had
[a]hung the doors, when the gatekeepers, the
singers, and the Levites had been appointed,
2 that I gave the charge of Jerusalem to my
brother [a]Hanani, and Hananiah the leader [b]of the
[1]citadel, for he *was* a faithful man and [c]feared God
more than many.
3 And I said to them, "Do not let the gates of
Jerusalem be opened until the sun is hot; and
while they stand *guard,* let them shut and bar the
doors; and appoint guards from among the
inhabitants of Jerusalem, one at his watch station
and another in front of his own house."
**4** Now the city *was* large and spacious, but the
people in it *were* [a]few, and the houses *were* not
rebuilt.
5 Then my God put it into my heart to gather
the nobles, the rulers, and the people, that they
might be registered by genealogy. And I found a
register of the genealogy of those who had come
up in the first *return,* and found written in it:

6 [a]These *are* the people of the province who
came back from the captivity, of those who
had been carried away, whom
Nebuchadnezzar the king of Babylon had
carried away, and who returned to Jerusalem
and Judah, everyone to his city.
7 Those who came with [a]Zerubbabel *were*
Jeshua, Nehemiah, [1]Azariah, Raamiah,
Nahamani, Mordecai, Bilshan, [2]Mispereth,
Bigvai, Nehum, and Baanah.
The number of the men of the people of
Israel:
8 the sons of Parosh, two thousand one
hundred and seventy-two;
9 the sons of Shephatiah, three hundred and
seventy-two;
10 the sons of Arah, six hundred and fifty-two;
11 the sons of Pahath-Moab, of the sons of
Jeshua and Joab, two thousand eight
hundred and eighteen;
12 the sons of Elam, one thousand two hundred
and fifty-four;
13 the sons of Zattu, eight hundred and forty-
five;
14 the sons of Zaccai, seven hundred and sixty;
15 the sons of [1]Binnui, six hundred and forty-
eight;
16 the sons of Bebai, six hundred and twenty-
eight;
17 the sons of Azgad, two thousand three
hundred and twenty-two;
18 the sons of Adonikam, six hundred and sixty-
seven;
19 the sons of Bigvai, two thousand and sixty-
seven;
20 the sons of Adin, six hundred and fifty-five;
21 the sons of Ater of Hezekiah, ninety-eight;
22 the sons of Hashum, three hundred and
twenty-eight;
23 the sons of Bezai, three hundred and twenty-
four;
24 the sons of [1]Hariph, one hundred and twelve;
25 the sons of [1]Gibeon, ninety-five;
26 the men of Bethlehem and Netophah, one
hundred and eighty-eight;
27 the men of Anathoth, one hundred and
twenty-eight;
28 the men of [1]Beth Azmaveth, forty-two;
29 the men of [1]Kirjath Jearim, Chephirah, and
Beeroth, seven hundred and forty-three;
30 the men of Ramah and Geba, six hundred
and twenty-one;
31 the men of Michmas, one hundred and
twenty-two;
32 the men of Bethel and Ai, one hundred and
twenty-three;
33 the men of the other Nebo, fifty-two;
34 the sons of the other [a]Elam, one thousand
two hundred and fifty-four;
35 the sons of Harim, three hundred and
twenty;
36 the sons of Jericho, three hundred and forty-
five;
37 the sons of Lod, Hadid, and Ono, seven
hundred and twenty-one;
38 the sons of Senaah, three thousand nine
hundred and thirty.
**39** The priests: the sons of [a]Jedaiah, of the
house of Jeshua, nine hundred and seventy-
three;
40 the sons of [a]Immer, one thousand and fifty-
two;
41 the sons of [a]Pashhur, one thousand two
hundred and forty-seven;
42 the sons of [a]Harim, one thousand and
seventeen.
**43** The Levites: the sons of Jeshua, of Kadmiel,
*and* of the sons of [1]Hodevah, seventy-four.
44 The singers: the sons of Asaph, one hundred
and forty-eight.
45 The gatekeepers: the sons of Shallum, the
sons of Ater, the sons of Talmon, the sons of
Akkub, the sons of Hatita, the sons of
Shobai, one hundred and thirty-eight.
**46** The Nethinim: the sons of Ziha, the sons of
Hasupha, the sons of Tabbaoth,
47 the sons of Keros, the sons of [1]Sia, the sons
of Padon,
48 the sons of [1]Lebana, the sons of [2]Hagaba, the
sons of [3]Salmai,
49 the sons of Hanan, the sons of Giddel, the
sons of Gahar,
50 the sons of Reaiah, the sons of Rezin, the
sons of Nekoda,
51 the sons of Gazzam, the sons of Uzza, the
sons of Paseah,

**14** [a]Neh. 13:29 [b]Ezek. 13:17
**16** [a]Neh. 2:10, 20; 4:1, 7; 6:1 [b]Ps. 126:2
**18** [a]Neh. 13:4, 28 [b]Ezra 10:15; Neh. 3:4
**19** [1]Or *affairs*

CHAPTER 7
**1** [a]Neh. 6:1, 15
**2** [a]Neh. 1:2 [b]Neh. 2:8; 10:23 [c]Ex. 18:21 [1]*palace*
**4** [a]Deut. 4:27
**6** [a]Ezra 2:1–70
**7** [a]Ezra 5:2; Neh. 12:1, 47; Matt. 1:12, 13 [1]*Seraiah,* Ezra 2:2 [2]*Mispar,* Ezra 2:2
**15** [1]*Bani,* Ezra 2:10
**24** [1]*Jorah,* Ezra 2:18
**25** [1]*Gibbar,* Ezra 2:20
**28** [1]*Azmaveth,* Ezra 2:24
**29** [1]*Kirjath Arim,* Ezra 2:25
**34** [a]Neh. 7:12
**39** [a]1 Chr. 24:7
**40** [a]1 Chr. 9:12
**41** [a]1 Chr. 9:12; 24:9
**42** [a]1 Chr. 24:8
**43** [1]*Hodaviah,* Ezra 2:40 or *Judah,* Ezra 3:9
**47** [1]*Siaha,* Ezra 2:44
**48** [1]MT *Lebanah* [2]MT *Hogabah* [3]*Shalmai,* Ezra 2:46; or *Shamlai*

52 the sons of Besai, the sons of Meunim, the
sons of [1]Nephishesim,
53 the sons of Bakbuk, the sons of Hakupha,
the sons of Harhur,
54 the sons of [1]Bazlith, the sons of Mehida, the
sons of Harsha,
55 the sons of Barkos, the sons of Sisera, the
sons of Tamah,
56 the sons of Neziah, and the sons of Hatipha.
**57** The sons of Solomon's servants: the sons of
Sotai, the sons of Sophereth, the sons of
[1]Perida,
58 the sons of Jaala, the sons of Darkon, the
sons of Giddel,
59 the sons of Shephatiah, the sons of Hattil,
the sons of Pochereth of Zebaim, and the
sons of [1]Amon.
60 All the Nethinim, and the sons of Solomon's
servants, *were* three hundred and ninety-two.
**61** And these *were* the ones who came up from
Tel Melah, Tel Harsha, Cherub, [1]Addon, and
Immer, but they could not identify their
father's house nor their lineage, whether
they *were* of Israel:
62 the sons of Delaiah, the sons of Tobiah, the
sons of Nekoda, six hundred and forty-two;
63 and of the priests: the sons of Habaiah, the
sons of [1]Koz, the sons of Barzillai, who took
a wife of the daughters of Barzillai the
Gileadite, and was called by their name.
64 These sought their listing *among* those who
were registered by genealogy, but it was not
found; therefore they were excluded from the
priesthood as defiled.
65 And the [1]governor said to them that they
should not eat of the most holy things till a
priest could consult with the Urim and
Thummim.
**66** Altogether the whole assembly *was* forty-two
thousand three hundred and sixty,
67 besides their male and female servants, of
whom *there were* seven thousand three
hundred and thirty-seven; and they had two
hundred and forty-five men and women
singers.
68 Their horses were seven hundred and thirty-
six, their mules two hundred and forty-five,
69 *their* camels four hundred and thirty-five,
*and* donkeys six thousand seven hundred and
twenty.
**70** And some of the heads of the fathers' houses
gave to the work. [a]The [1]governor gave to the
treasury one thousand gold drachmas, fifty
basins, and five hundred and thirty priestly
garments.
71 Some of the heads of the fathers' *houses*
gave to the treasury of the work [a]twenty
thousand gold drachmas, and two thousand
two hundred silver minas.
72 And *that* which the rest of the people gave
*was* twenty thousand gold drachmas, two
thousand silver minas, and sixty-seven
priestly garments.

73 So the priests, the Levites, the gatekeepers,
the singers, *some* of the people, the Nethinim, and
all Israel dwelt in their cities.
[a]When the seventh month came, the children
of Israel *were* in their cities.

## *Ezra Reads and Explains the Law*

**8** Now all [a]the people gathered together as one
man in the open square that *was* [b]in front of
the Water Gate; and they told Ezra the [c]scribe to
bring the Book of the Law of Moses, which the
LORD had commanded Israel.
2 So Ezra the priest brought [a]the Law before the
assembly, of men and women and all who *could*
hear with understanding, [b]on the first day of the
seventh month.
3 Then he [a]read from it in the open square that
*was* in front of the Water Gate [1]from morning
until midday, before the men and women and
those who could understand; and the ears of all
the people *were attentive* to the Book of the Law.
4 So Ezra the scribe stood on a platform of wood
which they had made for the purpose; and beside
him, at his right hand, stood Mattithiah, Shema,
Anaiah, Urijah, Hilkiah, and Maaseiah; and at his
left hand Pedaiah, Mishael, Malchijah, Hashum,
Hashbadana, Zechariah, *and* Meshullam.
5 And Ezra opened the book in the sight of all
the people, for he was *standing* above all the
people; and when he opened it, all the people
[a]stood up.
6 And Ezra blessed the LORD, the great God.
Then all the people [a]answered, "Amen, Amen!"
while [b]lifting up their hands. And they [c]bowed
their heads and worshiped the LORD with *their*
faces to the ground.
7 Also Jeshua, Bani, Sherebiah, Jamin, Akkub,
Shabbethai, Hodijah, Maaseiah, Kelita, Azariah,
Jozabad, Hanan, Pelaiah, and the Levites, [a]helped
the people to understand the Law; and the people
[b]*stood* in their place.
8 So they read distinctly from the book, in the
Law of God; and they gave the sense, and helped
*them* to understand the reading.
**9** [a]And Nehemiah, who *was* the [1]governor, Ezra
the priest *and* scribe, and the Levites who taught
the people said to all the people, [b]"This day *is* holy
to the LORD your God; [c]do not mourn nor weep."
For all the people wept, when they heard the
words of the Law.
10 Then he said to them, "Go your way, eat the
fat, drink the sweet, [a]and send portions to those
for whom nothing is prepared; for *this* day *is* holy
to our LORD. Do not sorrow, for the joy of the
LORD is your strength."
11 So the Levites quieted all the people, saying,
"Be still, for the day *is* holy; do not be grieved."
12 And all the people went their way to eat and
drink, to [a]send portions and rejoice greatly, because they [b]understood the words that were declared to them.
**13** Now on the second day the heads of the
fathers' *houses* of all the people, with the priests
and Levites, were gathered to Ezra the scribe, in
order to understand the words of the Law.
14 And they found written in the Law, which the
LORD had commanded by Moses, that the children
of Israel should dwell in [a]booths[1] during the feast
of the seventh month,
15 and [a]that they should announce and proclaim
in all their cities and [b]in Jerusalem, saying, "Go
out to the mountain, and [c]bring olive branches,
branches of oil trees, myrtle branches, palm
branches, and branches of leafy trees, to make
booths, as *it is* written."
16 Then the people went out and brought *them*
and made themselves booths, each one on the
[a]roof of his house, or in their courtyards or the
courts of the house of God, and in the open square
of the [b]Water Gate [c]and in the open square of the
Gate of Ephraim.

**52** [1]*Nephusim,* Ezra 2:50
**54** [1]*Bazluth,* Ezra 2:52
**57** [1]*Peruda,* Ezra 2:55
**59** [1]*Ami,* Ezra 2:57
**61** [1]*Addan,* Ezra 2:59
**63** [1]Or *Hakkoz*
**65** [1]Heb *Tirshathah*
**70** [a]Neh. 8:9 [1]Heb *Tirshathah*
**71** [a]Ezra 2:69
**73** [a]Ezra 3:1

CHAPTER 8

**1** [a]Ezra 3:1 [b]Neh. 3:26 [c]Ezra 7:6
**2** [a][Deut. 31:11, 12]; Neh. 8:9 [b]Lev. 23:24; Num. 29:1–6
**3** [a]Deut. 31:9–11; 2 Kin. 23:2 [1]Lit. *from the light*
**5** [a]Judg. 3:20; 1 Kin. 8:12–14
**6** [a]Neh. 5:13; [1 Cor. 14:16] [b]Ps. 28:2; Lam. 3:41; 1 Tim. 2:8 [c]Ex. 4:31; 12:27; 2 Chr. 20:18
**7** [a]Lev. 10:11; Deut. 33:10; 2 Chr. 17:7; [Mal. 2:7] [b]Neh. 9:3
**9** [a]Ezra 2:63; Neh. 7:65, 70; 10:1 [b]Lev. 23:24; Num. 29:1 [c]Deut. 16:14; Eccl. 3:4 [1]Heb *Tirshathah*
**10** [a][Deut. 26:11–13]; Esth. 9:19, 22; Rev. 11:10
**12** [a]Neh. 8:10 [b]Neh. 8:7, 8
**14** [a]Lev. 23:34, 40, 42; Deut. 16:13 [1]Temporary shelters
**15** [a]Lev. 23:4 [b]Deut. 16:16 [c]Lev. 23:40
**16** [a]Deut. 22:8 [b]Neh. 12:37 [c]2 Kin. 14:13; Neh. 12:39

17 So the whole assembly of those who had returned from the captivity made [1]booths and sat under the booths; for since the days of Joshua the son of Nun until that day the children of Israel had not done so. And there was very [a]great gladness.
18 Also [a]day by day, from the first day until the last day, he read from the Book of the Law of God. And they kept the feast [b]seven days; and on the [c]eighth day *there was* a sacred assembly, according to the *prescribed* manner.

### *The People Confess Their Sins*

**9** Now on the twenty-fourth day of [a]this month the children of Israel were assembled with fasting, in sackcloth, [b]and with [1]dust on their heads.
2 Then [a]those of Israelite lineage separated themselves from all foreigners; and they stood and [b]confessed their sins and the iniquities of their fathers.
3 And they stood up in their place and [a]read from the Book of the Law of the LORD their God *for one*-fourth of the day; and *for another* fourth they confessed and worshiped the LORD their God.
4 Then Jeshua, Bani, Kadmiel, Shebaniah, Bunni, Sherebiah, Bani, *and* Chenani stood on the [1]stairs of the Levites and cried out with a loud voice to the LORD their God.
5 And the Levites, Jeshua, Kadmiel, Bani, Hashabniah, Sherebiah, Hodijah, Shebaniah, *and* Pethahiah, said:

"Stand up *and* bless the LORD your God
Forever and ever!

"Blessed be [a]Your glorious name,
Which is exalted above all blessing
and praise!
6 [a]You alone *are* the LORD;
[b]You have made heaven,
[c]The heaven of heavens, with [d]all their host,
The earth and everything on it,
The seas and all that is in them,
And You [e]preserve them all.
The host of heaven worships You.

7 "You *are* the LORD God,
Who chose [a]Abram,
And brought him out of Ur of the Chaldeans,
And gave him the name [b]Abraham;
8 You found his heart [a]faithful before You,
And made a [b]covenant with him
To give the land of the Canaanites,
The Hittites, the Amorites,
The Perizzites, the Jebusites,
And the Girgashites—
To give *it* to his descendants.
You [c]have performed Your words,
For You *are* righteous.

9 "You[a] saw the affliction
of our fathers in Egypt,
And [b]heard their cry by the Red Sea.
10 You [a]showed signs and wonders
against Pharaoh,
Against all his servants,
And against all the people of his land.
For You knew that they [b]acted [1]proudly
against them.
So You [c]made a name for Yourself,
as *it is* this day.
11 [a]And You divided the sea before them,
So that they went through the midst
of the sea on the dry land;
And their persecutors You threw
into the deep,
[b]As a stone into the mighty waters.
12 Moreover You [a]led them by day
with a cloudy pillar,
And by night with a pillar of fire,
To give them light on the road
Which they should travel.

13 "You[a] came down also on Mount Sinai,
And spoke with them from heaven,
And gave them [b]just ordinances
and true laws,
Good statutes and commandments.
14 You made known to them
Your [a]holy Sabbath,
And commanded them precepts, statutes
and laws,
By the hand of Moses Your servant.
15 You [a]gave them bread from heaven
for their hunger,
And [b]brought them water out of the rock
for their thirst,
And told them to [c]go in to possess the land
Which You had [1]sworn to give them.

16 "But[a] they and our fathers acted [1]proudly,
[b]Hardened[2] their necks,
And did not heed Your commandments.
17 They refused to obey,
And [a]they were not mindful of Your wonders
That You did among them.
But they hardened their necks,
And [1]in their rebellion[1]
They appointed [b]a leader
To return to their bondage.
But You *are* God,
Ready to pardon,
[c]Gracious and merciful,
Slow to anger,
Abundant in kindness,
And did not forsake them.

18 "Even [a]when they made a molded calf for
themselves,
And said, 'This *is* your god
That brought you up out of Egypt,'
And worked great provocations,
19 Yet in Your [a]manifold mercies
You did not forsake them in the wilderness.
The [b]pillar of the cloud did not depart from
them by day,
To lead them on the road;
Nor the pillar of fire by night,
To show them light,
And the way they should go.
20 You also gave Your [a]good Spirit
to instruct them,
And did not withhold Your [b]manna from
their mouth,
And gave them [c]water for their thirst.
21 [a]Forty years You sustained them
in the wilderness;
They lacked nothing;
Their [b]clothes did not wear out
And their feet did not swell.

22 "Moreover You gave them kingdoms and
nations,
And divided them into [1]districts.

**17** [a]2 Chr. 30:21 [1]Temporary shelters
**18** [a]Deut. 31:11 [b]Lev. 23:36 [c]Num. 29:35

CHAPTER 9
**1** [a]Neh. 8:2 [b]Josh. 7:6; 1 Sam. 4:12; 2 Sam. 1:2; Job 2:12 [1]Lit. *earth on them*
**2** [a]Ezra 10:11; Neh. 13:3, 30 [b]Neh. 1:6
**3** [a]Neh. 8:7, 8
**4** [1]Lit. *ascent*
**5** [a]1 Chr. 29:13
**6** [a]Deut. 6:4; 2 Kin. 19:15, 19; [Ps. 86:10]; Is. 37:16, 20 [b]Gen. 1:1; Ex. 20:11; Rev. 14:7 [c][Deut. 10:14]; 1 Kin. 8:27 [d]Gen. 2:1 [e][Ps. 36:6]
**7** [a]Gen. 11:31 [b]Gen. 17:5
**8** [a]Gen. 15:6; 22:1–3; [James 2:21–23] [b]Gen. 15:18 [c]Josh. 23:14
**9** [a]Ex. 2:25; 3:7 [b]Ex. 14:10
**10** [a]Ex. 7—14 [b]Ex. 18:11 [c]Jer. 32:20 [1]*presumptuously* or *insolently*
**11** [a]Ex. 14:20–28 [b]Ex. 15:1, 5
**12** [a]Ex. 13:21, 22
**13** [a]Ex. 20:1–18 [b][Rom. 7:12]
**14** [a]Gen. 2:3; Ex. 16:23; 20:8; 23:12
**15** [a]Ex. 16:14–17; John 6:31 [b]Ex. 17:6; Num. 20:8; [1 Cor. 10:4] [c]Deut. 1:8 [1]Lit. *raised Your hand to*
**16** [a]Ps. 106:6 [b]Deut. 1:26–33; 31:27; Neh. 9:29 [1]*presumptuously* [2]*Stiffened their necks,* became stubborn
**17** [a]Ps. 78:11, 42–45 [b]Num. 14:4; Acts 7:39 [c]Joel 2:13 [1]So with MT, Vg.; LXX *in Egypt*
**18** [a]Ex. 32:4–8, 31
**19** [a]Ps. 106:45 [b]Ex. 13:20–22; 1 Cor. 10:1
**20** [a]Num. 11:17 [b]Ex. 16:14–16 [c]Ex. 17:6
**21** [a]Deut. 2:7 [b]Deut. 8:4; 29:5
**22** [1]Lit. *corners*

So they took possession of the land
of [a]Sihon,
[2]The land of the king of Heshbon,
And the land of Og king of Bashan.
23 You also multiplied [a]their children as the
stars of heaven,
And brought them into the land
Which You had told their fathers
To go in and possess.
24 So [a]the [1]people went in
And possessed the land;
[b]You subdued before them the inhabitants
of the land,
The Canaanites,
And gave them into their hands,
With their kings
And the people of the land,
That they might do with them as they would.
25 And they took strong cities and a [a]rich land,
And possessed [b]houses full of all goods,
Cisterns *already* dug, vineyards, olive groves,
And [1]fruit trees in abundance.
So they ate and were filled and [c]grew fat,
And delighted themselves
in Your great [d]goodness.

**26** "Nevertheless they [a]were disobedient
And rebelled against You,
[b]Cast Your law behind their backs
And killed Your [c]prophets,
who [1]testified against them
To turn them to Yourself;
And they worked great provocations.
27 [a]Therefore You delivered them into the hand
of their enemies,
Who oppressed them;
And in the time of their trouble,
When they cried to You,
You [b]heard from heaven;
And according to Your abundant mercies
[c]You gave them deliverers who saved them
From the hand of their enemies.

28 "But after they had rest,
[a]They again did evil before You.
Therefore You left them in the hand
of their enemies,
So that they had dominion over them;
Yet when they returned
and cried out to You,
You heard from heaven;
And [b]many times You delivered them
according to Your mercies,
29 And [1]testified against them,
That You might bring them back
to Your law.
Yet they acted [2]proudly,
And did not heed Your commandments,
But sinned against Your judgments,
[a]'Which if a man does, he shall live by them.'
And they shrugged their shoulders,
[3]Stiffened their necks,
And would not hear.
30 Yet for many years
You had patience with them,
And [1]testified [a]against them by Your Spirit
[b]in Your prophets.
Yet they would not listen;
[c]Therefore You gave them into the hand of
the peoples of the lands.
31 Nevertheless in Your great mercy
[a]You did not utterly consume them
nor forsake them;
For You *are* God, gracious and merciful.

**32** "Now therefore, our God,
The great, the [a]mighty, and awesome God,
Who keeps covenant and mercy:
Do not let all the [1]trouble seem small
before You
That has come upon us,
Our kings and our princes,
Our priests and our prophets,
Our fathers and on all Your people,
[b]From the days of the kings of Assyria
until this day.
33 However [a]You *are* just in all
that has befallen us;
For You have dealt faithfully,
But [b]we have done wickedly.
34 Neither our kings nor our princes,
Our priests nor our fathers,
Have kept Your law,
Nor heeded Your commandments
and Your testimonies,
With which You testified against them.
35 For they have [a]not served You
in their kingdom,
Or in the many good *things*
that You gave them,
Or in the large and rich land
which You set before them;
Nor did they turn from their wicked works.

36 "Here [a]we *are,* servants today!
And the land that You gave to our fathers,
To eat its fruit and its bounty,
Here we *are,* servants in it!
37 And [a]it yields much increase to the kings
You have set over us,
Because of our sins;
Also they have [b]dominion over our bodies
and our cattle
At their pleasure;
And we *are* in great distress.

**38** "And because of all this,
We [a]make a sure *covenant* and write *it;*
Our leaders, our Levites,
*and* our priests [b]seal *it.*"

### *The People Who Sealed the Covenant*

**10** Now those who placed *their* seal on *the* *document* were:
Nehemiah the [1]governor, [a]the son of Hacaliah,
and Zedekiah,
2 [a]Seraiah, Azariah, Jeremiah,
3 Pashhur, Amariah, Malchijah,
4 Hattush, Shebaniah, Malluch,
5 Harim, Meremoth, Obadiah,
6 Daniel, Ginnethon, Baruch,
7 Meshullam, Abijah, Mijamin,
8 Maaziah, Bilgai, *and* Shemaiah. These *were*
the priests.
9 The Levites: Jeshua the son of Azaniah, Binnui of the sons of Henadad, *and* Kadmiel.
10 Their brethren: Shebaniah, Hodijah, Kelita,
Pelaiah, Hanan,
11 Micha, Rehob, Hashabiah,
12 Zaccur, Sherebiah, Shebaniah,
13 Hodijah, Bani, *and* Beninu.
14 The leaders of the people: [a]Parosh, Pahath-
Moab, Elam, Zattu, Bani,
15 Bunni, Azgad, Bebai,
16 Adonijah, Bigvai, Adin,
17 Ater, Hezekiah, Azzur,

**22** [a]Num. 21:21–35 [2]So with MT, Vg.; LXX omits *The land of*
**23** [a]Gen. 15:5; 22:17; Heb. 11:12
**24** [a]Josh. 1:2–4 [b]Josh. 18:1; [Ps. 44:2, 3] [1]Lit. *sons*
**25** [a]Num. 13:27 [b]Deut. 6:11; Josh. 24:13 [c][Deut. 32:15] [d]Hos. 3:5 [1]Lit. *trees for eating*
**26** [a]Judg. 2:11 [b]1 Kin. 14:9; Ps. 50:17 [c]1 Kin. 18:4; 19:10; Matt. 23:37; Acts 7:52 [1]*admonished* or *warned them*
**27** [a]Judg. 2:14; Ps. 106:41 [b]Ps. 106:44 [c]Judg. 2:18
**28** [a]Judg. 3:12 [b]Ps. 106:43
**29** [a]Lev. 18:5; Rom. 10:5; [Gal. 3:12] [1]*admonished them* [2]*presumptuously* [3]Became stubborn
**30** [a]2 Kin. 17:13–18; 2 Chr. 36:11–20; Jer. 7:25 [b][Acts 7:51]; 1 Pet. 1:11 [c]Is. 5:5 [1]*admonished* or *warned them*
**31** [a]Jer. 4:27; [Rom. 11:2–5]
**32** [a][Ex. 34:6, 7] [b]2 Kin. 15:19; 17:3–6; Ezra 4:2, 10 [1]*hardship*
**33** [a]Ps. 119:137; [Dan. 9:14] [b]Ps. 106:6; [Dan. 9:5, 6, 8]
**35** [a]Deut. 28:47
**36** [a]Deut. 28:48; Ezra 9:9
**37** [a]Deut. 28:33, 51 [b]Deut. 28:48
**38** [a]2 Kin. 23:3; 2 Chr. 29:10; Ezra 10:3 [b]Neh. 10:1

CHAPTER 10

**1** [a]Neh. 1:1 [1]Or *Tirshatha*
**2** [a]Neh. 12:1–21
**14** [a]Ezra 2:3

18 Hodijah, Hashum, Bezai,
19 Hariph, Anathoth, Nebai,
20 Magpiash, Meshullam, Hezir,
21 Meshezabel, Zadok, Jaddua,
22 Pelatiah, Hanan, Anaiah,
23 Hoshea, Hananiah, Hasshub,
24 Hallohesh, Pilha, Shobek,
25 Rehum, Hashabnah, Maaseiah,
26 Ahijah, Hanan, Anan,
27 Malluch, Harim, *and* Baanah.
**28** [a]Now the rest of the people—the priests, the
Levites, the gatekeepers, the singers, the Nethinim, [b]and all those who had separated themselves
from the peoples of the lands to the Law of God,
their wives, their sons, and their daughters, everyone who had knowledge and understanding—
29 these joined with their brethren, their nobles,
[a]and entered into a curse and an oath [b]to walk in
God's Law, which was given by Moses the servant
of God, and to observe and do all the commandments of the LORD our Lord, and His ordinances
and His statutes:
30 We would not give [a]our daughters as wives to
the peoples of the land, nor take their daughters
for our sons;
31 [a]*if* the peoples of the land brought [1]wares or
any grain to sell on the Sabbath day, we would
not buy it from them on the Sabbath, or on a holy
day; and we would forego the [b]seventh year's
*produce* and the [c]exacting[2] of every debt.
**32** Also we made ordinances for ourselves, to
exact from ourselves yearly [a]one-third of a shekel
for the service of the house of our God:
33 for [a]the showbread, for the regular grain offering, for the [b]regular burnt offering of the Sabbaths, the New Moons, and the set feasts; for the
holy things, for the sin offerings to make atonement for Israel, and all the work of the house of
our God.
34 We cast lots among the priests, the Levites,
and the people, [a]for *bringing* the wood offering
into the house of our God, according to our
fathers' houses, at the appointed times year by
year, to burn on the altar of the LORD our God [b]as
*it is* written in the Law.
35 And *we made ordinances* [a]to bring the firstfruits of our ground and the firstfruits of all fruit
of all trees, year by year, to the house of the LORD;
36 to bring the [a]firstborn of our sons and our
cattle, as *it is* written in the Law, and the firstborn
of our herds and our flocks, to the house of our
God, to the priests who minister in the house of
our God;
37 [a]to bring the firstfruits of our dough, our
offerings, the fruit from all kinds of trees, *the* new
wine and oil, to the priests, to the storerooms of
the [1]house of our God; and to bring [b]the tithes of
our land to the Levites, for the Levites should
receive the tithes in all our farming communities.
38 And the priest, the descendant of Aaron, shall
be with the Levites [a]when the Levites receive
tithes; and the Levites shall bring up a tenth of the
tithes to the house of our God, to [b]the rooms of
the storehouse.
39 For the children of Israel and the children of
Levi [a]shall bring the offering of the grain, of the
new wine and the oil, to the storerooms where the
articles of the sanctuary *are, where* the priests
who minister and the gatekeepers [b]and the singers
*are;* and we will not [c]neglect the house of our God.

**28** [a]Ezra 2:36–43 [b]Ezra 9:1; Neh. 13:3
**29** [a]Deut. 29:12; Neh. 5:12; Ps. 119:106 [b]2 Kin. 23:3; 2 Chr. 34:31
**30** [a]Ex. 34:16; Deut. 7:3; [Ezra 9:12]
**31** [a]Ex. 20:10; Lev. 23:3; Deut. 5:12 [b]Ex. 23:10, 11; Lev. 25:4; Jer. 34:14 [c][Deut. 15:1, 2]; Neh. 5:12 [1]*merchandise* [2]*collection*
**32** [a]Ex. 30:11–16; 38:25, 26; 2 Chr. 24:6, 9; Matt. 17:24
**33** [a]Lev. 24:5; 2 Chr. 2:4 [b]Num. 28; 29
**34** [a]Neh. 13:31; [Is. 40:16] [b]Lev. 6:12
**35** [a]Ex. 23:19; 34:26; Lev. 19:23; Num. 18:12; Deut. 26:1, 2
**36** [a]Ex. 13:2, 12, 13; Lev. 27:26, 27; Num. 18:15, 16
**37** [a]Lev. 23:17; Num. 15:19; 18:12; Deut. 18:4; 26:2 [b]Lev. 27:30; Num. 18:21; Mal. 3:10 [1]Temple
**38** [a]Num. 18:26 [b]1 Chr. 9:26; 2 Chr. 31:11
**39** [a]Deut. 12:6, 11; 2 Chr. 31:12; Neh. 13:12 [b]Neh. 13:10, 11 [c][Heb. 10:25]

CHAPTER 11

**1** [a]Neh. 10:18; Matt. 4:5; 5:35; 27:53
**2** [a]Judg. 5:9; 2 Chr. 17:16
**3** [a]1 Chr. 9:2, 3 [b]Ezra 2:43 [c]Ezra 2:55
**4** [a]1 Chr. 9:3 [b]Gen. 38:29
**9** [1]Or *Hassenuah*
**10** [a]1 Chr. 9:10
**14** [1]Or *the son of Haggedolim*
**16** [a]Ezra 10:15 [b]Ezra 8:33 [c]1 Chr. 26:29 [1]Temple
**17** [1]Or *Michah*
**18** [a]Neh. 11:1

## *The People Dwelling in Jerusalem*

**11** Now the leaders of the people dwelt at
Jerusalem; the rest of the people cast lots to
bring one out of ten to dwell in Jerusalem, [a]the
holy city, and nine-tenths *were to dwell* in *other*
cities.
2 And the people blessed all the men who [a]will-
ingly offered themselves to dwell at Jerusalem.
**3** [a]These *are* the heads of the province who
dwelt in Jerusalem. (But in the cities of Judah
everyone dwelt in his own possession in their
cities—Israelites, priests, Levites, [b]Nethinim, and
[c]descendants of Solomon's servants.)
4 Also [a]in Jerusalem dwelt *some* of the children
of Judah and of the children of Benjamin.
The children of Judah: Athaiah the son of
Uzziah, the son of Zechariah, the son of Amariah,
the son of Shephatiah, the son of Mahalalel, of the
children of [b]Perez;
5 and Maaseiah the son of Baruch, the son of
Col-Hozeh, the son of Hazaiah, the son of Adaiah,
the son of Joiarib, the son of Zechariah, the son of
Shiloni.
6 All the sons of Perez who dwelt at Jerusalem
*were* four hundred and sixty-eight valiant men.
**7** And these are the sons of Benjamin: Sallu the
son of Meshullam, the son of Joed, the son of
Pedaiah, the son of Kolaiah, the son of Maaseiah,
the son of Ithiel, the son of Jeshaiah;
8 and after him Gabbai *and* Sallai, nine hundred
and twenty-eight.
9 Joel the son of Zichri *was* their overseer, and
Judah the son of [1]Senuah *was* second over the
city.
**10** [a]Of the priests: Jedaiah the son of Joiarib, and
Jachin;
11 Seraiah the son of Hilkiah, the son of Meshullam, the son of Zadok, the son of Meraioth, the
son of Ahitub, *was* the leader of the house of God.
12 Their brethren who did the work of the house
*were* eight hundred and twenty-two; and Adaiah
the son of Jeroham, the son of Pelaliah, the son of
Amzi, the son of Zechariah, the son of Pashhur,
the son of Malchijah,
13 and his brethren, heads of the fathers' *houses,*
*were* two hundred and forty-two; and Amashai
the son of Azarel, the son of Ahzai, the son of
Meshillemoth, the son of Immer,
14 and their brethren, mighty men of valor, *were*
one hundred and twenty-eight. Their overseer
*was* Zabdiel [1]the son of *one of* the great men.
**15** Also of the Levites: Shemaiah the son of
Hasshub, the son of Azrikam, the son of Hashabiah, the son of Bunni;
16 [a]Shabbethai and [b]Jozabad, of the heads of the
Levites, *had* the oversight of [c]the business outside
of the [1]house of God;
17 Mattaniah the son of [1]Micha, the son of Zabdi,
the son of Asaph, the leader *who* began the
thanksgiving with prayer; Bakbukiah, the second
among his brethren; and Abda the son of Shammua, the son of Galal, the son of Jeduthun.
18 All the Levites in [a]the holy city *were* two
hundred and eighty-four.
**19** Moreover the gatekeepers, Akkub, Talmon,
and their brethren who kept the gates, *were* one
hundred and seventy-two.
20 And the rest of Israel, of the priests *and*
Levites, *were* in all the cities of Judah, everyone in
his inheritance.

21 [a]But the Nethinim dwelt in Ophel. And Ziha
and Gishpa *were* over the Nethinim.
**22** Also the overseer of the Levites at Jerusalem
*was* Uzzi the son of Bani, the son of Hashabiah,
the son of Mattaniah, the son of Micha, of the
sons of Asaph, the singers in charge of the [1]service
of the [2]house of God.
23 For [a]*it was* the king's command concerning
them that a [1]certain portion should be for the
singers, a quota day by day.
24 Pethahiah the son of Meshezabel, of the children of [a]Zerah the son of Judah, *was* [b]the[1] king's
deputy in all matters concerning the people.
**25** And as for the villages with their fields, *some*
of the children of Judah dwelt in [a]Kirjath Arba
and its villages, Dibon and its villages, Jekabzeel
and its villages;
26 in Jeshua, Moladah, Beth Pelet,
27 Hazar Shual, and Beersheba and its villages;
28 in Ziklag and Meconah and its villages;
29 in En Rimmon, Zorah, Jarmuth,
30 Zanoah, Adullam, and their villages; in Lachish and its fields; in Azekah and its villages.
They dwelt from Beersheba to the Valley of Hinnom.
**31** Also the children of Benjamin from Geba
*dwelt* in Michmash, Aija, and Bethel, and their
villages;
32 in Anathoth, Nob, Ananiah;
33 in Hazor, Ramah, Gittaim;
34 in Hadid, Zeboim, Neballat;
35 in Lod, Ono, *and* [a]the Valley of Craftsmen.
36 Some of the Judean divisions of Levites *were*
in Benjamin.

### *Priests and Levites Who Came with Zerubbabel*

**12** Now these *are* the [a]priests and the Levites
who came up with [b]Zerubbabel the son of
Shealtiel, and Jeshua: [c]Seraiah, Jeremiah, Ezra,
2 Amariah, [1]Malluch, Hattush,
3 [1]Shechaniah, [2]Rehum, [3]Meremoth,
4 Iddo, [1]Ginnethoi, [a]Abijah,
5 [1]Mijamin, [2]Maadiah, Bilgah,
6 Shemaiah, Joiarib, Jedaiah,
7 [1]Sallu, Amok, Hilkiah, *and* Jedaiah.
These *were* the heads of the priests and their
brethren in the days of [a]Jeshua.
**8** Moreover the Levites *were* Jeshua, Binnui,
Kadmiel, Sherebiah, Judah, *and* Mattaniah [a]*who
led* the thanksgiving *psalms,* he and his brethren.
9 Also Bakbukiah and Unni, their brethren,
*stood* across from them in *their* duties.
**10** Jeshua begot Joiakim, Joiakim begot Eliashib,
Eliashib begot Joiada,
11 Joiada begot Jonathan, and Jonathan begot
Jaddua.
**12** Now in the days of Joiakim, the priests, the
[a]heads of the fathers' *houses were:* of Seraiah,
Meraiah; of Jeremiah, Hananiah;
13 of Ezra, Meshullam; of Amariah, Jehohanan;
14 of [1]Melichu, Jonathan; of [2]Shebaniah, Joseph;
15 of [1]Harim, Adna; of [2]Meraioth, Helkai;
16 of Iddo, Zechariah; of Ginnethon, Meshullam;
17 of Abijah, Zichri; *the son* of [1]Minjamin; of
[2]Moadiah, Piltai;
18 of Bilgah, Shammua; of Shemaiah, Jehonathan;
19 of Joiarib, Mattenai; of Jedaiah, Uzzi;
20 of [1]Sallai, Kallai; of Amok, Eber;
21 of Hilkiah, Hashabiah; *and* of Jedaiah, Nethanel.
**22** During the reign of Darius the Persian, a
record *was also kept* of the Levites and priests
*who had been* [a]heads of their fathers' *houses* in
the days of Eliashib, Joiada, Johanan, and Jaddua.
23 The sons of Levi, the heads of the fathers'
*houses* until the days of Johanan the son of
Eliashib, *were* written in the book of the [a]chron-
icles.
24 And the heads of the Levites *were* Hashabiah,
Sherebiah, and Jeshua the son of Kadmiel, with
their brothers across from them, to [a]praise *and*
give thanks, [b]group[1] alternating with group, [c]ac-
cording to the command of David the man of God.
25 Mattaniah, Bakbukiah, Obadiah, Meshullam,
Talmon, and Akkub *were* gatekeepers keeping the
watch at the storerooms of the gates.
26 These *lived* in the days of Joiakim the son of
Jeshua, the son of [1]Jozadak, and in the days of
Nehemiah [a]the governor, and of Ezra the priest,
[b]the scribe.
**27** Now at [a]the dedication of the wall of Jerusalem they sought out the Levites in all their places,
to bring them to Jerusalem to celebrate the dedication with gladness, [b]both with thanksgivings
and singing, *with* cymbals and stringed instruments and harps.
28 And the sons of the singers gathered together
from the countryside around Jerusalem, from the
[a]villages of the Netophathites,
29 from the house of Gilgal, and from the fields of
Geba and Azmaveth; for the singers had built
themselves villages all around Jerusalem.
30 Then the priests and Levites [a]purified themselves, and purified the people, the gates, and the
wall.
**31** So I brought the leaders of Judah up on the
wall, and appointed two large thanksgiving choirs.
[a]*One* went to the right hand on the wall [b]toward
the Refuse Gate.
32 After them went Hoshaiah and half of the
leaders of Judah,
33 and Azariah, Ezra, Meshullam,
34 Judah, Benjamin, Shemaiah, Jeremiah,
35 and some of the priests' sons [a]with trumpets—
Zechariah the son of Jonathan, the son of Shemaiah, the son of Mattaniah, the son of Michaiah, the
son of Zaccur, the son of Asaph,
36 and his brethren, Shemaiah, Azarel, Milalai,
Gilalai, Maai, Nethanel, Judah, *and* Hanani, with
[a]the musical [b]instruments of David the man of
God. And Ezra the scribe *went* before them.
37 [a]By the Fountain Gate, in front of them, they
went up [b]the stairs of the [c]City of David, on the
stairway of the wall, beyond the house of David,
as far as [d]the Water Gate eastward.
**38** [a]The other thanksgiving choir went the opposite *way,* and I *was* behind them with half of the
people on the wall, going past the [b]Tower of the
Ovens as far as [c]the Broad Wall,
39 [a]and above the Gate of Ephraim, above [b]the
Old Gate, above [c]the Fish Gate, [d]the Tower of
Hananel, the Tower of [1]the Hundred, as far as [e]the
Sheep Gate; and they stopped by [f]the Gate of the
Prison.
40 So the two thanksgiving choirs stood in the
house of God, likewise I and the half of the rulers
with me;
41 and the priests, Eliakim, Maaseiah, [1]Minjamin,
Michaiah, Elioenai, Zechariah, *and* Hananiah,
with trumpets;

**21** [a]2 Chr. 27:3; Neh. 3:26
**22** [1]*work* [2]Temple
**23** [a]Ezra 6:8, 9; 7:20 [1]*fixed share*
**24** [a]Gen. 38:30 [b]1 Chr. 18:17 [1]Lit. *at the king's hand*
**25** [a]Josh. 14:15
**35** [a]1 Chr. 4:14

CHAPTER 12
**1** [a]Ezra 2:1, 2; 7:7 [b]Neh. 7:7; Matt. 1:12, 13 [c]Neh. 10:2–8
**2** [1]*Melichu,* v. 14
**3** [1]*Shebaniah,* v. 14 [2]*Harim,* v. 15 [3]*Meraioth,* v. 15
**4** [a]Luke 1:5 [1]*Ginnethon,* v. 16
**5** [1]*Minjamin,* v. 17 [2]*Moadiah,* v. 17
**7** [a]Ezra 3:2; Hag. 1:1; Zech. 3:1 [1]*Sallai,* v. 20
**8** [a]Neh. 11:17
**12** [a]Neh. 7:70, 71; 8:13; 11:13
**14** [1]*Malluch,* v. 2 [2]*Shechaniah,* v. 3
**15** [1]*Rehum,* v. 3 [2]*Meremoth,* v. 3
**17** [1]*Mijamin,* v. 5 [2]*Maadiah,* v. 5
**20** [1]*Sallu,* v. 7
**22** [a]1 Chr. 24:6
**23** [a]1 Chr. 9:14–22
**24** [a]Neh. 11:17 [b]Ezra 3:11 [c]1 Chr. 23—26 [1]Lit. *watch by watch*
**26** [a]Neh. 8:9 [b]Ezra 7:6, 11 [1]*Jehozadak,* 1 Chr. 6:14
**27** [a]Deut. 20:5; Neh. 7:1; Ps. 30:title [b]1 Chr. 25:6; 2 Chr. 5:13; 7:6
**28** [a]1 Chr. 9:16
**30** [a]Ezra 6:20; Neh. 13:22, 30
**31** [a]Neh. 12:38 [b]Neh. 2:13; 3:13
**35** [a]Num. 10:2, 8
**36** [a]1 Chr. 23:5 [b]2 Chr. 29:26, 27
**37** [a]Neh. 2:14; 3:15 [b]Neh. 3:15 [c]2 Sam. 5:7–9 [d]Neh. 3:26; 8:1, 3, 16
**38** [a]Neh. 12:31 [b]Neh. 3:11 [c]Neh. 3:8
**39** [a]2 Kin. 14:13; Neh. 8:16 [b]Neh. 3:6 [c]Neh. 3:3 [d]Neh. 3:1 [e]Neh. 3:32 [f]Jer. 32:2 [1]Heb. *Hammeah*
**41** [1]Or *Mijamin,* v. 5

42 also Maaseiah, Shemaiah, Eleazar, Uzzi, Jehohanan, Malchijah, Elam, and Ezer. The singers
[1]sang loudly with Jezrahiah the director.
43 Also that day they offered great sacrifices, and
rejoiced, for God had made them rejoice with
great joy; the women and the children also rejoiced, so that the joy of Jerusalem was heard
[a]afar off.
**44** [a]And at the same time some were appointed
over the rooms of the storehouse for the offerings,
the firstfruits, and the [b]tithes, to gather into them
from the fields of the cities the portions specified
by the Law for the priests and Levites; for Judah
rejoiced over the priests and Levites who [1]minis-
tered.
45 Both the singers and the gatekeepers kept the
charge of their God and the charge of the purification, [a]according to the command of David *and*
Solomon his son.
46 For in the days of David [a]and Asaph of old
*there were* chiefs of the singers, and songs of
praise and thanksgiving to God.
47 In the days of Zerubbabel and in the days of
Nehemiah all Israel gave the portions for the
singers and the gatekeepers, a portion for [a]each
day. [b]They also [1]consecrated *holy things* for the
Levites, [c]and the Levites consecrated *them* for the
children of Aaron.

### *Nehemiah's Reforms*

**13** On that day [a]they read from the Book of
Moses in the hearing of the people, and in it
was found written [b]that no Ammonite or Moabite
should ever come into the assembly of God,
2 because they had not met the children of
Israel with bread and water, but [a]hired Balaam
against them to curse them. [b]However, our God
turned the curse into a blessing.
3 So it was, when they had heard the Law, [a]that
they separated all the mixed multitude from Israel.
**4** Now before this, [a]Eliashib the priest, having
authority over the storerooms of the house of our
God, *was* allied with [b]Tobiah.
5 And he had prepared for him a large room,
[a]where previously they had stored the grain offerings, the frankincense, the articles, the tithes of
grain, the new wine and oil, [b]which were commanded *to be given* to the Levites and singers and
gatekeepers, and the offerings for the priests.
6 But during all this I was not in Jerusalem, [a]for
in the thirty-second year of Artaxerxes king of
Babylon I had returned to the king. Then after
certain days I obtained leave from the king,
7 and I came to Jerusalem and discovered the
evil that Eliashib had done for Tobiah, in [a]prepar-
ing a room for him in the courts of the [1]house of
God.
8 And it grieved me bitterly; therefore I threw
all the household goods of Tobiah out of the room.
9 Then I commanded them to [a]cleanse the
rooms; and I brought back into them the articles
of the house of God, with the grain offering and
the frankincense.
**10** I also realized that the portions for the Levites
had [a]not been given *them;* for each of the Levites
and the singers who did the work had gone back
to [b]his field.
11 So [a]I contended with the rulers, and said,
[b]"Why is the house of God forsaken?" And I
gathered them together and set them in their
place.

**42** [1]Lit. *made their voice to be heard*
**43** [a]Ezra 3:13
**44** [a]2 Chr. 31:11, 12; Neh. 13:5, 12, 13 [b]Neh. 10:37–39 [1]Lit. *stood*
**45** [a]1 Chr. 25—26
**46** [a]1 Chr. 25:1; 2 Chr. 29:30
**47** [a]Neh. 11:23 [b]Num. 18:21, 24 [c]Num. 18:26 [1]*set apart*

CHAPTER 13

**1** [a][Deut. 31:11, 12]; 2 Kin. 23:2; Neh. 8:3, 8; 9:3; Is. 34:16 [b]Deut. 23:3, 4
**2** [a]Num. 22:5; Josh. 24:9, 10 [b]Num. 23:1; 24:10; Deut. 23:5
**3** [a]Neh. 9:2; 10:28
**4** [a]Neh. 12:10 [b]Neh. 2:10; 4:3; 6:1
**5** [a]Neh. 12:44 [b]Num. 18:21, 24
**6** [a]Neh. 5:14–16
**7** [a]Neh. 13:1, 5 [1]Temple
**9** [a]2 Chr. 29:5, 15, 16
**10** [a]Neh. 10:37; Mal. 3:8 [b]Num. 35:2
**11** [a]Neh. 13:17, 25 [b]Neh. 10:39
**12** [a]Neh. 10:38; 12:44
**13** [a]2 Chr. 31:12 [b]1 Cor. 4:2
**14** [a]Neh. 5:19; 13:22, 31
**15** [a][Ex. 20:10] [b]Neh. 10:31; [Jer. 17:21]
**18** [a]Ezra 9:13; [Jer. 17:21]
**19** [a]Lev. 23:32 [b]Jer. 17:21, 22
**20** [1]*merchandise* [2]*spent the night*
**21** [1]Lit. *before*
**22** [a]1 Chr. 15:12; Neh. 12:30
**23** [a][Ex. 34:16; Deut. 7:3, 4]; Ezra 9:2; Neh. 10:30 [b]Neh. 4:7
**25** [a]Prov. 28:4 [b]Ezra 10:5; Neh. 10:29, 30 [1]*pronounced them cursed*
**26** [a]1 Kin. 11:1, 2 [b]2 Sam. 12:24, 25 [c]1 Kin. 11:4–8
**27** [a][Ezra 10:2]; Neh. 13:23
**28** [a]Neh. 12:10, 12

12 [a]Then all Judah brought the tithe of the grain
and the new wine and the oil to the storehouse.
13 [a]And I appointed as treasurers over the storehouse Shelemiah the priest and Zadok the scribe,
and of the Levites, Pedaiah; and next to them *was*
Hanan the son of Zaccur, the son of Mattaniah;
for they were considered [b]faithful, and their task
*was* to distribute to their brethren.
**14** [a]Remember me, O my God, concerning this,
and do not wipe out my good deeds that I have
done for the house of my God, and for its services!
**15** In those days I saw in Judah *some people*
treading wine presses [a]on the Sabbath, and bringing in sheaves, and loading donkeys with wine,
grapes, figs, and all *kinds of* burdens, [b]which they
brought into Jerusalem on the Sabbath day. And I
warned *them* about the day on which they were
selling provisions.
16 Men of Tyre dwelt there also, who brought in
fish and all kinds of goods, and sold *them* on the
Sabbath to the children of Judah, and in Jerusalem.
17 Then I contended with the nobles of Judah,
and said to them, "What evil thing *is* this that you
do, by which you profane the Sabbath day?
18 [a]"Did not your fathers do thus, and did not our
God bring all this disaster on us and on this city?
Yet you bring added wrath on Israel by profaning
the Sabbath."
**19** So it was, at the gates of Jerusalem, as it
[a]began to be dark before the Sabbath, that I
commanded the gates to be shut, and charged
that they must not be opened till after the Sabbath. [b]Then I posted *some* of my servants at the
gates, *so that* no burdens would be brought in on
the Sabbath day.
20 Now the merchants and sellers of all kinds of
[1]wares [2]lodged outside Jerusalem once or twice.
21 Then I warned them, and said to them, "Why
do you spend the night [1]around the wall? If you do
*so* again, I will lay hands on you!" From that time
on they came no *more* on the Sabbath.
22 And I commanded the Levites that [a]they
should cleanse themselves, and that they should
go and guard the gates, to sanctify the Sabbath
day.
Remember me, O my God, *concerning* this
also, and spare me according to the greatness of
Your mercy!
**23** In those days I also saw Jews *who* [a]had married women of [b]Ashdod, Ammon, *and* Moab.
24 And half of their children spoke the language
of Ashdod, and could not speak the language of
Judah, but spoke according to the language of one
or the other people.
25 So I [a]contended with them and [1]cursed them,
struck some of them and pulled out their hair, and
made them [b]swear by God, *saying,* "You shall not
give your daughters as wives to their sons, nor
take their daughters for your sons or yourselves.
26 [a]"Did not Solomon king of Israel sin by these
things? Yet among many nations there was no
king like him, [b]who was beloved of his God; and
God made him king over all Israel. [c]Nevertheless
pagan women caused even him to sin.
27 "Should we then hear of your doing all this
great evil, [a]transgressing against our God by
marrying pagan women?"
**28** And *one* of the sons [a]of Joiada, the son of

Eliashib the high priest, *was* a son-in-law of
[b]Sanballat the Horonite; therefore I drove him
from me.
29 [a]Remember them, O my God, because they
have defiled the priesthood and [b]the covenant of
the priesthood and the Levites.
30 [a]Thus I cleansed them of everything pagan. I
also [b]assigned duties to the priests and the Levites,
each to his service,
31 and *to bringing* [a]the wood offering and the
firstfruits at appointed times.
[b]Remember me, O my God, for good!

28 [b]Neh. 4:1, 7; 6:1, 2
29 [a]Neh. 6:14 [b]Mal. 2:4, 11, 12
30 [a]Neh. 10:30 [b]Neh. 12:1
31 [a]Neh. 10:34 [b]Neh. 13:14, 22

*The Book of*

# Esther

## *The King Dethrones Queen Vashti*

NOW it came to pass in the days of [a]Ahasue-
rus[1] (this *was* the Ahasuerus who reigned
[b]over one hundred and twenty-seven provinces, [c]from India to Ethiopia),
2 in those days when King Ahasuerus [a]sat on
the throne of his kingdom, which *was* in [b]Shu-
shan[1] the [2]citadel,
3 *that* in the third year of his reign he [a]made a
feast for all his officials and servants—the powers
of Persia and Media, the nobles, and the princes of
the provinces *being* before him—
4 when he showed the riches of his glorious
kingdom and the splendor of his excellent majesty
for many days, one hundred and eighty days *in all.*
5 And when these days were completed, the
king made a feast lasting seven days for all the
people who were present in [1]Shushan the [2]citadel,
from great to small, in the court of the garden of
the king's palace.
6 *There were* white and blue linen *curtains*
fastened with cords of fine linen and purple on
silver rods and marble pillars; *and the* [a]couches
*were* of gold and silver on a *mosaic* pavement of
alabaster, turquoise, and white and black marble.
7 And they served drinks in golden vessels, each
vessel being different from the other, with royal
wine in abundance, [a]according to the [1]generosity
of the king.
8 In accordance with the law, the drinking was
not compulsory; for so the king had ordered all
the officers of his household, that they should do
according to each man's pleasure.
9 Queen Vashti also made a feast for the women
*in* the royal palace which *belonged* to King Ahasuerus.
10 On the seventh day, when the heart of the
king was merry with wine, he commanded Mehu-
man, Biztha, [a]Harbona, Bigtha, Abagtha, Zethar,
and Carcas, seven eunuchs who served in the
presence of King Ahasuerus,
11 to bring Queen Vashti before the king, *wearing* her royal crown, in order to show her beauty
to the people and the officials, for she *was* beautiful to behold.
12 But Queen Vashti refused to come at the
king's command *brought* by *his* eunuchs; therefore the king was furious, and his anger burned
within him.
13 Then the king said to the [a]wise men [b]who
understood the times (for this *was* the king's
manner toward all who knew law and justice,
14 those closest to him *being* Carshena, Shethar,
Admatha, Tarshish, Meres, Marsena, and Memucan, the [a]seven princes of Persia and Media, [b]who
had access to the king's presence, *and* who
[1]ranked highest in the kingdom):
15 "What *shall we* do to Queen Vashti, according
to law, because she did not obey the command of
King Ahasuerus *brought to her* by the eunuchs?"
16 And Memucan answered before the king and
the princes: "Queen Vashti has not only wronged
the king, but also all the princes, and all the
people who *are* in all the provinces of King Ahasuerus.
17 "For the queen's behavior will become known
to all women, so that they will [a]despise their
husbands in their eyes, when they report, 'King
Ahasuerus commanded Queen Vashti to be
brought in before him, but she did not come.'
18 "This very day the *noble* ladies of Persia and
Media will say to all the king's officials that they
have heard of the behavior of the queen. Thus
*there will be* excessive contempt and wrath.
19 "If it pleases the king, let a royal [1]decree go
out from him, and let it be recorded in the laws of
the Persians and the Medes, so that it will [a]not [2]be
altered, that Vashti shall come no more before
King Ahasuerus; and let the king give her royal
position to another who is better than she.
20 "When the king's decree which he will make is
proclaimed throughout all his empire (for it is
great), all wives will [a]honor their husbands, both
great and small."
21 And the reply pleased the king and the
princes, and the king did according to the word of
Memucan.
22 Then he sent letters to all the king's provinces,
[a]to each province in its own script, and to every
people in their own language, that each man
should [b]be master in his own house, and speak in
the language of his own people.

## *Esther Made Queen*

2 After these things, when the wrath of King
Ahasuerus subsided, he remembered Vashti,
[a]what she had done, and what had been decreed
against her.
2 Then the king's servants who attended him
said: "Let beautiful young virgins be sought for
the king;
3 "and let the king appoint officers in all the
provinces of his kingdom, that they may gather all
the beautiful young virgins to [1]Shushan the [2]cita-
del, into the women's quarters, under the custody
of [3]Hegai the king's eunuch, custodian of the
women. And let beauty preparations be given
*them.*

CHAPTER 1
1 [a]Ezra 4:6; Dan. 9:1 [b]Esth. 8:9 [c]Dan. 6:1 [1]Generally identified with Xerxes I (485–464 B.C.)
2 [a]1 Kin. 1:46 [b]Neh. 1:1; Dan. 8:2 [1]Or *Susa* [2]Or *fortified palace,* and so elsewhere in the book
3 [a]Gen. 40:20; Esth. 2:18
5 [1]Or *Susa* [2]*palace*
6 [a]Esth. 7:8; Ezek. 23:41; Amos 2:8; 6:4
7 [a]Esth. 2:18 [1]Lit. *hand*
10 [a]Esth. 7:9
13 [a]Jer. 10:7; Dan. 2:12; Matt. 2:1 [b]1 Chr. 12:32
14 [a]Ezra 7:14 [b]2 Kin. 25:19; [Matt. 18:10] [1]Lit. *sat in first place*
17 [a][Eph. 5:33]
19 [a]Esth. 8:8; Dan. 6:8 [1]Lit. *word* [2]*pass away*
20 [a][Eph. 5:33; Col. 3:18; 1 Pet. 3:1]
22 [a]Esth. 3:12; 8:9 [b][Eph. 5:22–24; 1 Tim. 2:12]

CHAPTER 2
1 [a]Esth. 1:19, 20
3 [1]Or *Susa* [2]*palace* [3]Heb. *Hege*

4 "Then let the young woman who pleases the
king be queen instead of Vashti." This thing
pleased the king, and he did so.
**5** In [1]Shushan the [2]citadel there was a certain
Jew whose name *was* Mordecai the son of Jair,
the son of Shimei, the son of [a]Kish, a Benjamite.
6 [a]*Kish*[1] had been carried away from Jerusalem
with the captives who had been captured with
[2]Jeconiah king of Judah, whom Nebuchadnezzar
the king of Babylon had carried away.
7 And *Mordecai* had brought up Hadassah, that
*is,* Esther, [a]his uncle's daughter, for she had
neither father nor mother. The young woman *was*
lovely and beautiful. When her father and mother
died, Mordecai took her as his own daughter.
**8** So it was, when the king's command and
decree were heard, and when many young women
were [a]gathered at [1]Shushan the [2]citadel, *under* the
custody of Hegai, that Esther also was taken to
the king's palace, into the care of Hegai the
custodian of the women.
9 Now the young woman pleased him, and she
obtained his favor; so he readily gave [a]beauty
preparations to her, besides [1]her allowance. Then
seven choice maidservants were provided for her
from the king's palace, and he moved her and her
maidservants to the best *place* in the house of the
women.
10 [a]Esther had not [1]revealed her people or family,
for Mordecai had charged her not to reveal *it.*
11 And every day Mordecai paced in front of the
court of the women's quarters, to learn of Esther's
welfare and what was happening to her.
**12** Each young woman's turn came to go in to
King Ahasuerus after she had completed twelve
months' preparation, according to the regulations
for the women, for thus were the days of their
preparation apportioned: six months with oil of
myrrh, and six months with perfumes and preparations for beautifying women.
13 Thus *prepared, each* young woman went to
the king, and she was given whatever she desired
to take with her from the women's quarters to the
king's palace.
14 In the evening she went, and in the morning
she returned to the second house of the women,
to the custody of Shaashgaz, the king's eunuch
who kept the concubines. She would not go in to
the king again unless the king delighted in her
and called for her by name.
**15** Now when the turn came for Esther [a]the
daughter of Abihail the uncle of Mordecai, who
had taken her as his daughter, to go in to the king,
she requested nothing but what Hegai the king's
eunuch, the custodian of the women, advised. And
Esther [b]obtained favor in the sight of all who saw
her.
16 So Esther was taken to King Ahasuerus, into
his royal palace, in the tenth month, which *is* the
month of Tebeth, in the seventh year of his reign.
17 The king loved Esther more than all the *other*
women, and she obtained grace and favor in his
sight more than all the virgins; so he set the royal
[a]crown upon her head and made her queen instead of Vashti.
18 Then the king [a]made a great feast, the Feast of
Esther, for all his officials and servants; and he
proclaimed a holiday in the provinces and gave
gifts according to the [1]generosity of a king.
**19** When virgins were gathered together a second
time, Mordecai sat within the king's gate.
20 [a]*Now* Esther had not revealed her family and
her people, just as Mordecai had charged her, for
Esther obeyed the command of Mordecai as when
she was brought up by him.
**21** In those days, while Mordecai sat within the
king's gate, two of the king's eunuchs, [1]Bigthan
and Teresh, doorkeepers, became furious and
sought to lay hands on King Ahasuerus.
22 So the matter became known to Mordecai,
[a]who told Queen Esther, and Esther informed the
king in Mordecai's name.
23 And when an inquiry was made into the matter, it was confirmed, and both were hanged on a
gallows; and it was written in [a]the book of the
chronicles in the presence of the king.

## *Haman's Plot to Destroy the Jews*

**3** After these things King Ahasuerus promoted
Haman, the son of Hammedatha the [a]Agagite,
and [b]advanced him and set his seat above all the
princes who *were* with him.
2 And all the king's servants who *were* [a]within
the king's gate bowed and paid homage to Haman, for so the king had commanded concerning
him. But Mordecai [b]would not bow or pay homage.
3 Then the king's servants who *were* within the
king's gate said to Mordecai, "Why do you transgress the [a]king's command?"
4 Now it happened, when they spoke to him
daily and he would not listen to them, that they
told *it* to Haman, to see whether Mordecai's words
would stand; for *Mordecai* had told them that he
*was* a Jew.
5 When Haman saw that Mordecai [a]did not bow
or pay him homage, Haman was [b]filled with
wrath.
6 But he disdained to lay hands on Mordecai
alone, for they had told him of the people of
Mordecai. Instead, Haman [a]sought to destroy all
the Jews who *were* throughout the whole kingdom of Ahasuerus—the people of Mordecai.
**7** In the first month, which is the month of
Nisan, in the twelfth year of King Ahasuerus,
[a]they cast Pur (that *is,* the lot), before Haman [1]to
determine the day and the [2]month, [3]until *it fell on
the* twelfth *month,* which *is* the month of Adar.
**8** Then Haman said to King Ahasuerus, "There
is a certain people scattered and dispersed among
the people in all the provinces of your kingdom;
[a]their laws *are* different from all *other* people's,
and they do not keep the king's laws. Therefore it
*is* not fitting for the king to let them remain.
9 "If it pleases the king, let *a decree* be written
that they be destroyed, and I will pay ten thousand talents of silver into the hands of those who
do the work, to bring *it* into the king's treasuries."
10 So the king [a]took [b]his signet ring from his
hand and gave it to Haman, the son of Hammedatha the Agagite, the [c]enemy of the Jews.
11 And the king said to Haman, "The money and
the people *are* given to you, to do with them as
seems good to you."
**12** [a]Then the king's scribes were called on the
thirteenth day of the first month, and *a decree*
was written according to all that Haman commanded—to the king's satraps, to the governors
who *were* over each province, to the officials of all
people, to every province [b]according to its script,
and to every people in their language. [c]In the
name of King Ahasuerus it was written, and
sealed with the king's signet ring.

**5** [a]1 Sam. 9:1 [1]Or *Susa* [2]*palace*
**6** [a]2 Kin. 24:14, 15; 2 Chr. 36:10, 20; Jer. 24:1 [1]Lit. *Who* [2]*Jehoiachin,* 2 Kin. 24:6
**7** [a]Esth. 2:15
**8** [a]Esth. 2:3 [1]Or *Susa* [2]*palace*
**9** [a]Esth. 2:3, 12 [1]Lit. *her portions*
**10** [a]Esth. 2:20 [1]Revealed the identity of
**15** [a]Esth. 2:7; 9:29 [b]Esth. 5:2, 8
**17** [a]Esth. 1:11
**18** [a]Esth. 1:3 [1]Lit. *hand*
**20** [a]Esth. 2:10; [Prov. 22:6]
**21** [1]*Bigthana,* Esth. 6:2
**22** [a]Esth. 6:1, 2
**23** [a]Esth. 6:1

CHAPTER 3

**1** [a]Num. 24:7; 1 Sam. 15:8 [b]Esth. 5:11
**2** [a]Esth. 2:19, 21; 5:9 [b]Esth. 3:5; Ps. 15:4
**3** [a]Esth. 3:2
**5** [a]Esth. 3:2; 5:9 [b]Dan. 3:19
**6** [a]Ps. 83:4; [Rev. 12:1–17]
**7** [a]Esth. 9:24–26 [1]Lit. *from day to day and month to month* [2]LXX adds *to destroy the people of Mordecai in one day;* Vg. adds *the nation of the Jews should be destroyed* [3]So with MT, Vg.; LXX *and the lot fell on the fourteenth of the month*
**8** [a]Ezra 4:12–15; Acts 16:20, 21
**10** [a]Gen. 41:42 [b]Esth. 8:2, 8 [c]Esth. 7:6
**12** [a]Esth. 8:9 [b]Esth. 1:22 [c]1 Kin. 21:8; Esth. 8:8–10

13 And the letters were [a]sent by couriers into all
the king's provinces, to destroy, to kill, and to
annihilate all the Jews, both young and old, little
children and women, [b]in one day, on the thirteenth *day* of the twelfth *month,* which *is* the
month of Adar, and [c]to plunder their [1]possessions.
14 [a]A copy of the document was to be issued as
law in every province, being published for all
people, that they should be ready for that day.
15 The couriers went out, hastened by the king's
command; and the decree was proclaimed in
[1]Shushan the [2]citadel. So the king and Haman sat
down to drink, but [a]the city of Shushan was
[3]perplexed.

### *Fasting Among the Jews*

4 When Mordecai learned all that had happened,
[1]he [a]tore his clothes and put on sackcloth [b]and
ashes, and went out into the midst of the city. He
[c]cried out with a loud and bitter cry.
2 He went as far as the front of the king's gate,
for no one *might* enter the king's gate clothed
with sackcloth.
3 And in every province where the king's command and decree arrived, *there was* great mourning among the Jews, with fasting, weeping, and
wailing; and many lay in sackcloth and ashes.
4 So Esther's maids and eunuchs came and told
her, and the queen was deeply distressed. Then
she sent garments to clothe Mordecai and take his
sackcloth away from him, but he would not accept *them.*
5 Then Esther called Hathach, *one* of the king's
eunuchs whom he had appointed to attend her,
and she gave him a command concerning Mordecai, to learn what and why this *was.*
6 So Hathach went out to Mordecai in the city
square that *was* in front of the king's gate.
7 And Mordecai told him all that had happened
to him, and [a]the sum of money that Haman had
promised to pay into the king's treasuries to
destroy the Jews.
8 He also gave him [a]a copy of the written decree
for their destruction, which was given at [1]Shu-
shan, that he might show it to Esther and explain
it to her, and that he might command her to go in
to the king to make supplication to him and plead
before him for her people.
9 So Hathach returned and told Esther the
words of Mordecai.
**10** Then Esther spoke to Hathach, and gave him
a command for Mordecai:
11 "All the king's servants and the people of the
king's provinces know that any man or woman
who goes into [a]the inner court to the king, who
has not been called, [b]*he has* but one law: put *all* to
death, except the one [c]to whom the king holds out
the golden scepter, that he may live. Yet I myself
have not been [d]called to go in to the king these
thirty days."
12 So they told Mordecai Esther's words.
**13** And Mordecai told *them* to answer Esther:
"Do not think in your heart that you will escape
in the king's palace any more than all the other
Jews.
14 "For if you remain completely silent at this
time, relief and deliverance will arise for the Jews
from another place, but you and your father's
house will perish. Yet who knows whether you
have come to the kingdom for *such* a time as
this?"
15 Then Esther told *them* to reply to Mordecai:
16 "Go, gather all the Jews who are present in
[1]Shushan, and fast for me; neither eat nor drink
for [a]three days, night or day. My maids and I will
fast likewise. And so I will go to the king, which *is*
against the law; [b]and if I perish, I perish!"
17 So Mordecai went his way and did according
to all that Esther commanded [1]him.

### *The Courage of Esther*

5 Now it happened [a]on the third day that Esther
put on *her* royal *robes* and stood in [b]the inner
court of the king's palace, across from the king's
house, while the king sat on his royal throne in
the royal house, facing the entrance of the [1]house.
2 So it was, when the king saw Queen Esther
standing in the court, *that* [a]she found favor in his
sight, and [b]the king held out to Esther the golden
scepter that *was* in his hand. Then Esther went
near and touched the top of the scepter.
3 And the king said to her, "What do you wish,
Queen Esther? What *is* your request? [a]It shall be
given to you—up to half the kingdom!"
4 So Esther answered, "If it pleases the king, let
the king and Haman come today to the banquet
that I have prepared for him."
5 Then the king said, "Bring Haman quickly,
that he may do as Esther has said." So the king
and Haman went to the banquet that Esther had
prepared.
**6** At the banquet of wine [a]the king said to
Esther, [b]"What *is* your petition? It shall be
granted you. What *is* your request, up to half the
kingdom? It shall be done!"
7 Then Esther answered and said, "My petition
and request *is this:*
8 "If I have found favor in the sight of the king,
and if it pleases the king to grant my petition and
[1]fulfill my request, then let the king and Haman
come to the [a]banquet which I will prepare for
them, and tomorrow I will do as the king has
said."
**9** So Haman went out that day [a]joyful and with
a glad heart; but when Haman saw Mordecai in
the king's gate, and [b]that he did not stand or
tremble before him, he was filled with indignation
against Mordecai.
10 Nevertheless Haman [a]restrained himself and
went home, and he sent and called for his friends
and his wife Zeresh.
11 Then Haman told them of his great riches, [a]the
multitude of his children, everything in which the
king had promoted him, and how he had [b]ad-
vanced him above the officials and servants of the
king.
12 Moreover Haman said, "Besides, Queen Esther
invited no one but me to come in with the king to
the banquet that she prepared; and tomorrow I
am again invited by her, along with the king.
13 "Yet all this avails me nothing, so long as I see
Mordecai the Jew sitting at the king's gate."
14 Then his wife Zeresh and all his friends said to
him, "Let a [a]gallows[1] be made, [2]fifty cubits high,
and in the morning [b]suggest to the king that
Mordecai be hanged on it; then go merrily with
the king to the banquet." And the thing pleased
Haman; so he had [c]the gallows made.

### *Haman Forced to Honor Mordecai*

6 That night [1]the king could not sleep. So one
was commanded to bring [a]the book of the
records of the chronicles; and they were read
before the king.

**13** [a]2 Chr. 30:6; Esth. 8:10, 14 [b]Esth. 8:12 [c]Esth. 8:11; 9:10 [1]LXX adds the text of the letter here.
**14** [a]Esth. 8:13, 14
**15** [a]Esth. 8:15; [Prov. 29:2] [1]Or *Susa* [2]*palace* [3]*in confusion*

CHAPTER 4
**1** [a]2 Sam. 1:11; Esth. 3:8–10; Jon. 3:5, 6 [b]Josh. 7:6; Ezek. 27:30 [c]Gen. 27:34 [1]Lit. *Mordecai*
**7** [a]Esth. 3:9
**8** [a]Esth. 3:14, 15 [1]Or *Susa*
**11** [a]Esth. 5:1; 6:4 [b]Dan. 2:9 [c]Esth. 5:2; 8:4 [d]Esth. 2:14
**16** [a]Esth. 5:1 [b]Gen. 43:14 [1]Or *Susa*
**17** [1]LXX adds a prayer of Mordecai here.

CHAPTER 5
**1** [a]Esth. 4:16 [b]Esth. 4:11; 6:4 [1]LXX adds many extra details in vv. 1, 2.
**2** [a][Prov. 21:1] [b]Esth. 4:11; 8:4
**3** [a]Esth. 7:2; Mark 6:23
**6** [a]Esth. 7:2 [b]Esth. 9:12
**8** [a]Esth. 6:14 [1]Lit. *to do*
**9** [a][Job 20:5; Luke 6:25] [b]Esth. 3:5
**10** [a]2 Sam. 13:22
**11** [a]Esth. 9:7–10 [b]Esth. 3:1
**14** [a]Esth. 7:9 [b]Esth. 6:4 [c]Esth. 7:10 [1]Lit. *tree* or *wood* [2]About 75 feet

CHAPTER 6
**1** [a]Esth. 2:23; 10:2 [1]Lit. *the king's sleep fled away*

2 And it was found written that Mordecai had
told of [1]Bigthana and Teresh, two of the king's
eunuchs, the doorkeepers who had sought to lay
hands on King Ahasuerus.
3 Then the king said, "What honor or dignity
has been bestowed on Mordecai for this?" And the
king's servants who attended him said, "Nothing
has been done for him."
4 So the king said, "Who *is* in the court?" Now
Haman had *just* entered [a]the outer court of the
king's palace [b]to suggest that the king hang
Mordecai on the gallows that he had prepared for
him.
5 The king's servants said to him, "Haman is
there, standing in the court." And the king said,
"Let him come in."
6 So Haman came in, and the king asked him,
"What shall be done for the man whom the king
delights to honor?" Now Haman thought in his
heart, "Whom would the king delight to honor
more than [a]me?"
7 And Haman answered the king, "*For* the man
whom the king delights to honor,
8 "let a royal robe be brought which the king
has worn, and [a]a horse on which the king has
ridden, which has a royal [1]crest placed on its head.
9 "Then let this robe and horse be delivered to
the hand of one of the king's most noble princes,
that he may array the man whom the king delights to honor. Then [1]parade him on horseback
through the city square, [a]and proclaim before him:
'Thus shall it be done to the man whom the king
delights to honor!' "
10 Then the king said to Haman, "Hurry, take the
robe and the horse, as you have suggested, and do
so for Mordecai the Jew who sits within the king's
gate! Leave nothing undone of all that you have
spoken."
11 So Haman took the robe and the horse, arrayed Mordecai and led him on horseback
through the city square, and proclaimed before
him, "Thus shall it be done to the man whom the
king delights to honor!"
12 Afterward Mordecai went back to the king's
gate. But Haman [a]hurried to his house, mourning
[b]and with his head covered.
13 When Haman told his wife Zeresh and all his
friends everything that had happened to him, his
wise men and his wife Zeresh said to him, "If
Mordecai, before whom you have begun to fall, is
of Jewish descent, you will not prevail against
[a]him but will surely fall before him."
14 While they *were* still talking with him, the
king's eunuchs came, and hastened to bring Haman to [a]the banquet which Esther had prepared.

### *Haman Hanged Instead of Mordecai*

**7** So the king and Haman went to dine with
Queen Esther.
2 And on the second day, [a]at the banquet of
wine, the king again said to Esther, "What *is* your
petition, Queen Esther? It shall be granted you.
And what *is* your request, up to half the kingdom?
It shall be done!"
3 Then Queen Esther answered and said, "If I
have found favor in your sight, O king, and if it
pleases the king, let my life be given me at my
petition, and my people at my request.
4 "For we have been [a]sold, my people and I, to
be destroyed, to be killed, and to be annihilated.
Had we been sold as [b]male and female slaves, I
would have held my tongue, although the enemy
could never compensate for the king's loss."
5 So King Ahasuerus answered and said to
Queen Esther, "Who is he, and where is he, who
would dare presume in his heart to do such a
thing?"
6 And Esther said, "The adversary and [a]enemy
*is* this wicked Haman!" So Haman was terrified
before the king and queen.
7 Then the king arose in his wrath from the
banquet of wine *and went* into the palace garden;
but Haman stood before Queen Esther, pleading
for his life, for he saw that evil was determined
against him by the king.
8 When the king returned from the palace garden to the place of the banquet of wine, Haman
had fallen across [a]the couch where Esther *was.*
Then the king said, "Will he also assault the queen
while I *am* in the house?" As the word left the
king's mouth, they [b]covered Haman's face.
9 Now [a]Harbonah, one of the eunuchs, said to
the king, "Look! [b]The [1]gallows, fifty cubits high,
which Haman made for Mordecai, who spoke
[c]good on the king's behalf, is standing at the
house of Haman." Then the king said, "Hang him
on it!"
10 So [a]they [b]hanged Haman on the gallows that
he had prepared for Mordecai. Then the king's
wrath subsided.

### *Esther Saves the Jews*

**8** On that day King Ahasuerus gave Queen
Esther the house of Haman, the [a]enemy of the
Jews. And Mordecai came before the king, for
Esther had told [b]how he *was related* to her.
2 So the king took off [a]his signet ring, which he
had taken from Haman, and gave it to Mordecai;
and Esther appointed Mordecai over the house of
Haman.
3 Now Esther spoke again to the king, fell down
at his feet, and implored him with tears to coun-
teract the evil of Haman the Agagite, and the
scheme which he had devised against the Jews.
4 And [a]the king held out the golden scepter
toward Esther. So Esther arose and stood before
the king,
5 and said, "If it pleases the king, and if I have
found favor in his sight and the thing *seems* right
to the king and I am pleasing in his eyes, let it be
written to revoke the [a]letters devised by Haman,
the son of Hammedatha the Agagite, which he
wrote to annihilate the Jews who *are* in all the
king's provinces.
6 "For how can I endure to see [a]the evil that will
come to my people? Or how can I endure to see
the destruction of my countrymen?"
7 Then King Ahasuerus said to Queen Esther
and Mordecai the Jew, "Indeed, [a]I have given
Esther the house of Haman, and they have hanged
him on the gallows because he *tried to* lay his
hand on the Jews.
8 "You yourselves write *a decree* concerning
the Jews, [1]as you please, in the king's name, and
seal *it* with the king's signet ring; for whatever is
written in the king's name and sealed with the
king's signet ring [a]no one can revoke."
9 [a]So the king's scribes were called at that time,
in the third month, which *is* the month of Sivan,
on the twenty-third *day;* and it was written,
according to all that Mordecai commanded, to the

2 [1]*Bigthan,* Esth. 2:21
4 [a]Esth. 5:1 [b]Esth. 5:14
6 [a][Prov. 16:18; 18:12]
8 [a]1 Kin. 1:33 [1]*crown*
9 [a]Gen. 41:43 [1]Lit. *cause him to ride*
12 [a]2 Chr. 26:20 [b]2 Sam. 15:30; Jer. 14:3, 4
13 [a][Gen. 12:3]; Zech. 2:8
14 [a]Esth. 5:8

CHAPTER 7

2 [a]Esth. 5:6
4 [a]Esth. 3:9; 4:7 [b]Deut. 28:68
6 [a]Esth. 3:10
8 [a]Esth. 1:6 [b]Job 9:24
9 [a]Esth. 1:10 [b]Esth. 5:14; [Ps. 7:16; Prov. 11:5, 6] [c]Esth. 6:2 [1]Lit. *tree* or *wood*
10 [a][Ps. 7:16; 94:23; Prov. 11:5, 6] [b]Ps. 37:35, 36; Dan. 6:24

CHAPTER 8

1 [a]Esth. 7:6 [b]Esth. 2:7, 15
2 [a]Esth. 3:10
4 [a]Esth. 4:11; 5:2
5 [a]Esth. 3:13
6 [a]Neh. 2:3; Esth. 7:4; 9:1
7 [a]Esth. 8:1; Prov. 13:22
8 [a]Esth. 1:19; Dan. 6:8, 12, 15 [1]Lit. *as is good in your eyes*
9 [a]Esth. 3:12

Jews, the satraps, the governors, and the princes
of the provinces [b]from India to Ethiopia, one
hundred and twenty-seven provinces *in all,* to
every province [c]in its own script, to every people
in their own language, and to the Jews in their
own script and language.
10 [a]And he wrote in the name of King Ahasuerus,
sealed *it* with the king's signet ring, and sent
letters by couriers on horseback, riding on royal
horses [1]bred from swift steeds.
11 By these letters the king permitted the Jews
who *were* in every city to [a]gather together and
protect their lives—to [b]destroy, kill, and annihilate
all the forces of any people or province that would
assault them, *both* little children and women, and
to plunder their possessions,
12 [a]on one day in all the provinces of King Ahasuerus, on the thirteenth *day* of the twelfth month,
which *is* the month of [1]Adar.
13 [a]A copy of the document was to be issued as a
decree in every province and published for all
people, so that the Jews would be ready on that
day to avenge themselves on their enemies.
14 The couriers who rode on royal horses went
out, hastened and pressed on by the king's command. And the decree was issued in [1]Shushan the
[2]citadel.
**15** So Mordecai went out from the presence of
the king in royal apparel of [1]blue and white, with a
great crown of gold and a garment of fine linen
and purple; and [a]the city of [2]Shushan rejoiced and
was glad.
16 The Jews had [a]light and gladness, joy and
honor.
17 And in every province and city, wherever the
king's command and decree came, the Jews had
joy and gladness, a feast [a]and a holiday. Then
many of the people of the land [b]became Jews,
because [c]fear of the Jews fell upon them.

### *The Jews Destroy Their Enemies*

**9** Now [a]in the twelfth month, that *is,* the month
of Adar, on the thirteenth day, [b]*the time* came
for the king's command and his decree to be
executed. On the day that the enemies of the Jews
had hoped to overpower them, the opposite occurred, in that the Jews themselves [c]overpowered
those who hated them.
2 The Jews [a]gathered together in their cities
throughout all the provinces of King Ahasuerus to
lay hands on those who [b]sought their harm. And
no one could withstand them, [c]because fear of
them fell upon all people.
3 And all the officials of the provinces, the
satraps, the governors, and all those doing the
king's work, helped the Jews, because the fear of
Mordecai fell upon them.
4 For Mordecai *was* great in the king's palace,
and his fame spread throughout all the provinces;
for this man Mordecai [a]became increasingly
prominent.
5 Thus the Jews defeated all their enemies with
the stroke of the sword, with slaughter and destruction, and did what they pleased with those
who hated them.
6 And in [a]Shushan[1] the [2]citadel the Jews killed
and destroyed five hundred men.
7 Also Parshandatha, Dalphon, Aspatha,
8 Poratha, Adalia, Aridatha,
9 Parmashta, Arisai, Aridai, and Vajezatha—
10 [a]the ten sons of Haman the son of Hammedatha, the enemy of the Jews—they killed; [b]but
they did not lay a hand on the [1]plunder.
**11** On that day the number of those who were
killed in [1]Shushan the [2]citadel [3]was brought to the
king.
12 And the king said to Queen Esther, "The Jews
have killed and destroyed five hundred men in
Shushan the citadel, and the ten sons of Haman.
What have they done in the rest of the king's
provinces? Now [a]what *is* your petition? It shall be
granted to you. Or what *is* your further request? It
shall be done."
13 Then Esther said, "If it pleases the king, let it
be granted to the Jews who *are* in Shushan to do
again tomorrow [a]according to today's decree, and
let Haman's ten sons [b]be hanged on the gallows."
14 So the king commanded this to be done; the
decree was issued in Shushan, and they hanged
Haman's ten sons.
**15** And the Jews who *were* in [1]Shushan [a]gathered
together again on the fourteenth day of the
month of Adar and killed three hundred men at
Shushan; [b]but they did not lay a hand on the
plunder.
**16** The remainder of the Jews in the king's provinces [a]gathered together and protected their lives,
had rest from their enemies, and killed seventy-
five thousand of their enemies; [b]but they did not
lay a hand on the plunder.
17 *This was* on the thirteenth day of the month
of Adar. And on the fourteenth of [1]*the month* they
rested and made it a day of feasting and gladness.
**18** But the Jews who *were* at [1]Shushan assembled
together [a]on the thirteenth *day,* as well as on the
fourteenth; and on the fifteenth of [2]*the month*
they rested, and made it a day of feasting and
gladness.
19 Therefore the Jews of the villages who dwelt
in the unwalled towns celebrated the fourteenth
day of the month of Adar [a]*with* gladness and
feasting, [b]as a holiday, and for [c]sending presents
to one another.
**20** And Mordecai wrote these things and sent
letters to all the Jews, near and far, who *were* in
all the provinces of King Ahasuerus,
21 to establish among them that they should
celebrate yearly the fourteenth and fifteenth days
of the month of Adar,
22 as the days on which the Jews had rest from
their enemies, as the month which was turned
from sorrow to joy for them, and from mourning
to a holiday; that they should make them days of
feasting and joy, of [a]sending presents to one
another and gifts to the [b]poor.
23 So the Jews accepted the custom which they
had begun, as Mordecai had written to them,
24 because Haman, the son of Hammedatha the
Agagite, the enemy of all the Jews, [a]had plotted
against the Jews to annihilate them, and had cast
Pur (that *is,* the lot), to consume them and destroy
them;
25 but [a]when [1]*Esther* came before the king, he
commanded by letter that [2]this wicked plot which
*Haman* had devised against the Jews should [b]re-
turn on his own head, and that he and his sons
should be hanged on the gallows.
**26** So they called these days Purim, after the
name [1]Pur. Therefore, because of all the words of
[a]this letter, what they had seen concerning this
matter, and what had happened to them,

**9** [b]Esth. 1:1 [c]Esth. 1:22; 3:12
**10** [a]1 Kin. 21:8; Esth. 3:12, 13 [1]Lit. *sons of the swift horses*
**11** [a]Esth. 9:2 [b]Esth. 9:10, 15, 16
**12** [a]Esth. 3:13; 9:1 [1]LXX adds the text of the letter here.
**13** [a]Esth. 3:14, 15
**14** [1]Or *Susa* [2]*palace*
**15** [a]Esth. 3:15; Prov. 29:2 [1]*violet* [2]Or *Susa*
**16** [a]Ps. 97:11; 112:4
**17** [a]1 Sam. 25:8; Esth. 9:19 [b]Ps. 18:43 [c]Gen. 35:5; Ex. 15:16; Deut. 2:25; 11:25; 1 Chr. 14:17; Esth. 9:2

CHAPTER 9

**1** [a]Esth. 8:12 [b]Esth. 3:13 [c]2 Sam. 22:41
**2** [a]Esth. 8:11; 9:15–18 [b]Ps. 71:13, 14 [c]Esth. 8:17
**4** [a]2 Sam. 3:1; 1 Chr. 11:9; [Prov. 4:18]
**6** [a]Esth. 1:2; 3:15; 4:16 [1]Or *Susa* [2]*palace*
**10** [a]Esth. 5:11; 9:7–10; Job 18:19; 27:13–15; Ps. 21:10 [b]Esth. 8:11 [1]*spoil*
**11** [1]Or *Susa* [2]*palace* [3]Lit. *came*
**12** [a]Esth. 5:6; 7:2
**13** [a]Esth. 8:11; 9:15 [b]2 Sam. 21:6, 9
**15** [a]Esth. 8:11; 9:2 [b]Esth. 9:10 [1]Or *Susa*
**16** [a]Esth. 9:2 [b]Esth. 8:11
**17** [1]Lit. *it*
**18** [a]Esth. 9:11, 15 [1]Or *Susa* [2]Lit. *it*
**19** [a]Deut. 16:11, 14 [b]Esth. 8:16, 17 [c]Neh. 8:10, 12; Esth. 9:22
**22** [a]Neh. 8:10; Esth. 9:19 [b][Deut. 15:7–11]; Job 29:16
**24** [a]Esth. 3:6, 7; 9:26
**25** [a]Esth. 7:4–10; 8:3; 9:13, 14 [b]Esth. 7:10 [1]Lit. *she* or *it* [2]Lit. *his*
**26** [a]Esth. 9:20 [1]Lit. *Lot*

27 the Jews established and imposed it upon
themselves and their descendants and all who
would [a]join them, that without fail they should
celebrate these two days every year, according to
the written *instructions* and according to the
*prescribed* time,
28 *that* these days *should be* remembered and
kept throughout every generation, every family,
every province, and every city, that these days of
Purim should not fail *to be observed* among the
Jews, and *that* the memory of them should not
perish among their descendants.
**29** Then Queen Esther, [a]the daughter of Abihail,
with Mordecai the Jew, wrote with full authority
to confirm this [b]second letter about Purim.
30 And *Mordecai* sent letters to all the Jews, to
[a]the one hundred and twenty-seven provinces of
the kingdom of Ahasuerus, *with* words of peace
and truth,
31 to confirm these days of Purim at their *appointed* time, as Mordecai the Jew and Queen
Esther had prescribed for them, and as they had
decreed for themselves and their descendants
concerning matters of their [a]fasting and lament-
ing.
32 So the decree of Esther confirmed these matters of Purim, and it was written in the book.

27 [a]Esth. 8:17
29 [a]Esth. 2:15 [b]Esth. 8:10; 9:20, 21
30 [a]Esth. 1:1
31 [a]Esth. 4:3, 16

CHAPTER 10
1 [a]Is. 11:11; 24:15
2 [a]Esth. 8:15; 9:4 [b]Esth. 6:1 [1]Lit. *made him great*
3 [a]Gen. 41:40, 43, 44 [b]Neh. 2:10 [1]Lit. *seed.* LXX, Vg. add a dream of Mordecai here; Vg. adds six more chapters.

### *Mordecai's Greatness*

**10** And King Ahasuerus imposed tribute on the
land and *on* [a]the islands of the sea.
2 Now all the acts of his power and his might,
and the account of the greatness of Mordecai, [a]to
which the king [1]advanced him, *are* they not
written in the book of the [b]chronicles of the kings
of Media and Persia?
3 For Mordecai the Jew *was* [a]second to King
Ahasuerus, and was great among the Jews and
well received by the multitude of his brethren,
[b]seeking the good of his people and speaking
peace to all his [1]countrymen.

# *The Book of* JOB

## *The Wealth and Faithfulness of Job*

THERE was a man [a]in the land of Uz, whose
name *was* [b]Job; and that man was [c]blameless
and upright, and one who [d]feared God and
[1]shunned evil.
2 And seven sons and three daughters were
born to him.
3 Also, his possessions were seven thousand
sheep, three thousand camels, five hundred yoke
of oxen, five hundred female donkeys, and a very
large household, so that this man was the greatest
of all the [1]people of the East.
4 And his sons would go and feast *in their*
houses, each on his *appointed* day, and would
send and invite their three sisters to eat and drink
with them.
5 So it was, when the days of feasting had run
their course, that Job would send and [1]sanctify
them, and he would rise early in the morning [a]and
offer burnt offerings *according to* the number of
them all. For Job said, "It may be that my sons
have sinned and [b]cursed[2] God in their hearts."
Thus Job did regularly.
**6** Now [a]there was a day when the sons of God
came to present themselves before the LORD, and
[1]Satan also came among them.
7 And the LORD said to [1]Satan, "From where do
you come?" So Satan answered the LORD and said,
"From [a]going to and fro on the earth, and from
walking back and forth on it."
8 Then the LORD said to Satan, "Have you
[1]considered My servant Job, that *there is* none like
him on the earth, a blameless and upright man,
one who fears God and [2]shuns evil?"
9 So Satan answered the LORD and said, "Does
Job fear God for nothing?
10 [a]"Have You not [1]made a hedge around him,
around his household, and around all that he has
on every side? [b]You have blessed the work of his
hands, and his possessions have increased in the
land.
11 [a]"But now, stretch out Your hand and touch
all that he has, and he will surely [b]curse[1] You to
Your face!"
12 And the LORD said to Satan, "Behold, all that
he has *is* in your [1]power; only do not lay a hand on
his *person.*" So Satan went out from the presence
of the LORD.
**13** Now there was a day [a]when his sons and
daughters *were* eating and drinking wine in their
oldest brother's house;
14 and a messenger came to Job and said, "The
oxen were plowing and the donkeys feeding beside them,
15 "when the [1]Sabeans [2]raided *them* and took
them away—indeed they have killed the servants
with the edge of the sword; and I alone have
escaped to tell you!"
16 While he *was* still speaking, another also came
and said, "The fire of God fell from heaven and
burned up the sheep and the servants, and [1]con-
sumed them; and I alone have escaped to tell
you!"
17 While he *was* still speaking, another also came
and said, "The Chaldeans formed three bands,
raided the camels and took them away, yes, and
killed the servants with the edge of the sword; and
I alone have escaped to tell you!"
18 While he *was* still speaking, another also came
and said, [a]"Your sons and daughters *were* eating
and drinking wine in their oldest brother's house,
19 "and suddenly a great wind came from [1]across
the wilderness and struck the four corners of the
house, and it fell on the young people, and they
are dead; and I alone have escaped to tell you!"
**20** Then Job arose, [a]tore his robe, and shaved his
head; and he [b]fell to the ground and worshiped.
21 And he said:

CHAPTER 1
1 [a]1 Chr. 1:17 [b]Ezek. 14:14, 20; James 5:11 [c]Gen. 6:9; 17:1; [Deut. 18:13] [d][Prov. 16:6] [1]Lit. *turned away from*
3 [1]Lit. *sons*
5 [a]Gen. 8:20; [Job 42:8] [b]1 Kin. 21:10, 13 [1]*consecrate* [2]Lit. *blessed,* but in an evil sense, Job 1:11; 2:5, 9
6 [a]Job 2:1 [1]Lit. *the Adversary*
7 [a][1 Pet. 5:8] [1]Lit. *the Adversary*
8 [1]Lit. *set your heart on* [2]Lit. *turns away from*
10 [a]Job 29:2–6; Ps. 34:7; Is. 5:2 [b][Ps. 128:1, 2; Prov. 10:22] [1]Protected him
11 [a]Job 2:5; 19:21 [b]Is. 8:21; Mal. 3:13, 14 [1]Lit. *bless,* but in an evil sense, Job 1:5
12 [1]Lit. *hand*
13 [a][Eccl. 9:12]
15 [1]Lit. *Sheba,* Job 6:19 [2]Lit. *fell upon*
16 [1]*destroyed*
18 [a]Job 1:4, 13
19 [1]LXX omits *across*
20 [a]Gen. 37:29, 34; Josh. 7:6; Ezra 9:3 [b][1 Pet. 5:6]

[a]"Naked I came from my mother's womb,
And naked shall I return there.
The LORD [b]gave, and the LORD
has [c]taken away;
[d]Blessed be the name of the LORD."

22 [a]In all this Job did not sin nor charge God with
wrong.

## *Satan Attacks Job's Health*

**2** Again [a]there was a day when the sons of God
came to present themselves before the LORD,
and Satan came also among them to present
himself before the LORD.
2 And the LORD said to Satan, "From where do
you come?" So [a]Satan answered the LORD and
said, "From going to and fro on the earth, and
from walking back and forth on it."
3 Then the LORD said to Satan, "Have you
considered My servant Job, that *there is* none like
him on the earth, [a]a blameless and upright man,
one who fears God and shuns evil? And still he
[b]holds fast to his integrity, although you incited
Me against him, [c]to [1]destroy him without cause."
4 So Satan answered the LORD and said, "Skin
for skin! Yes, all that a man has he will give for his
life.
5 [a]"But stretch out Your hand now, and touch
his [b]bone and his flesh, and he will surely [1]curse
You to Your face!"
6 [a]And the LORD said to Satan, "Behold, he *is* in
your hand, but spare his life."
7 So Satan went out from the presence of the
LORD, and struck Job with painful boils [a]from the
sole of his foot to the crown of his head.
8 And he took for himself a potsherd with which
to scrape himself [a]while he sat in the midst of the
ashes.
9 Then his wife said to him, "Do you still hold
fast to your integrity? [1]Curse God and die!"
10 But he said to her, "You speak as one of the
foolish women speaks. [a]Shall we indeed accept
good from God, and shall we not accept adversity?" [b]In all this Job did not [c]sin with his lips.
11 Now when Job's three friends heard of all this
adversity that had come upon him, each one came
from his own place—Eliphaz the [a]Temanite, Bildad the [b]Shuhite, and Zophar the Naamathite. For
they had made an appointment together to come
[c]and mourn with him, and to comfort him.
12 And when they raised their eyes from afar,
and did not recognize him, they lifted their voices
and wept; and each one tore his robe and [a]sprin-
kled dust on his head toward heaven.
13 So they sat down with him on the ground
[a]seven days and seven nights, and no one spoke a
word to him, for they saw that *his* grief was very
great.

## *Job Regrets His Birth*

**3** After this Job opened his mouth and cursed
the day of his *birth.*
2 And Job [1]spoke, and said:

3 "May[a] the day perish on which I was born,
And the night *in which* it was said,
'A male child is conceived.'
4 May that day be darkness;
May God above not seek it,
Nor the light shine upon it.
5 May darkness and [a]the shadow
of death claim it;
May a cloud settle on it;
May the blackness of the day terrify it.
6 *As for* that night, may darkness seize it;
May it not [1]rejoice among the days
of the year,
May it not come into the number
of the months.
7 Oh, may that night be barren!
May no joyful shout come into it!
8 May those curse it who curse the day,
Those [a]who are ready to arouse Leviathan.
9 May the stars of its morning be dark;
May it look for light, but *have* none,
And not see the [1]dawning of the day;
10 Because it did not shut up the doors
of my *mother's* womb,
Nor hide sorrow from my eyes.

11 "Why[a] did I not die at birth?
*Why* did I *not* [1]perish
when I came from the womb?
12 [a]Why did the knees receive me?
Or why the breasts, that I should nurse?
13 For now I would have lain still
and been quiet,
I would have been asleep;
Then I would have been at rest
14 With kings and counselors of the earth,
Who [a]built ruins for themselves,
15 Or with princes who had gold,
Who filled their houses *with* silver;
16 Or *why* was I not hidden
[a]like a stillborn child,
Like infants who never saw light?
17 There the wicked cease *from* troubling,
And there the [1]weary are at [a]rest.
18 *There* the prisoners [1]rest together;
[a]They do not hear the voice of the oppressor.
19 The small and great are there,
And the servant *is* free from his master.

20 "Why[a] is light given to him who is in misery,
And life to the [b]bitter of soul,
21 Who [a]long[1] for death, but it does not *come,*
And search for it more
than [b]hidden treasures;
22 Who rejoice exceedingly,
*And* are glad when they can find the [a]grave?
23 *Why is light given* to a man
whose way is hidden,
[a]And whom God has hedged in?
24 For my sighing comes before [1]I eat,
And my groanings pour out like water.
25 For the thing I greatly [a]feared
has come upon me,
And what I dreaded has happened to me.
26 I am not at ease, nor am I quiet;
I have no rest, for trouble comes."

## *Eliphaz Rebukes Job*

**4** Then Eliphaz the Temanite answered and said:

2 "If one attempts a word with you,
will you become weary?
But who can withhold himself
from speaking?
3 Surely you have instructed many,
And you [a]have strengthened weak hands.
4 Your words have upheld him
who was stumbling,
And you [a]have strengthened
the [1]feeble knees;

**21** [a][Ps. 49:17; Eccl. 5:15]; 1 Tim. 6:7 [b]Eccl. 5:19; [James 1:17] [c]Gen. 31:16; [1 Sam. 2:6] [d]Eph. 5:20; [1 Thess. 5:18]
**22** [a]Job 2:10

CHAPTER 2
**1** [a]Job 1:6–8
**2** [a]Job 1:7
**3** [a]Job 1:1, 8 [b]Job 27:5, 6 [c]Job 9:17 [1]Lit. *consume*
**5** [a]Job 1:11 [b]Job 19:20 [1]Lit. *bless,* but in an evil sense, Job 1:5
**6** [a]Job 1:12
**7** [a]Is. 1:6
**8** [a]Job 42:6; Jer. 6:26; Ezek. 27:30; Jon. 3:6; Matt. 11:21
**9** [1]Lit. *Bless,* but in an evil sense, Job 1:5
**10** [a]Job 1:21, 22; [Heb. 12:6; James 5:10, 11] [b]Job 1:22; [James 1:12] [c]Ps. 39:1
**11** [a]Gen. 36:11; 1 Chr. 1:36; Job 6:19; Jer. 49:7; Obad. 9 [b]Gen. 25:2; 1 Chr. 1:32 [c]Job 42:11; Rom. 12:15
**12** [a]Josh. 7:6; Neh. 9:1; Lam. 2:10; Ezek. 27:30
**13** [a]Gen. 50:10; Ezek. 3:15

CHAPTER 3
**2** [1]Lit. *answered*
**3** [a]Job 10:18, 19; Jer. 20:14–18
**5** [a]Job 10:21, 22; Jer. 13:16; Amos 5:8
**6** [1]LXX, Syr., Tg., Vg. *be joined*
**8** [a]Jer. 9:17
**9** [1]*eyelids of the dawn*
**11** [a]Job 10:18, 19 [1]*expire*
**12** [a]Gen. 30:3
**14** [a]Job 15:28; Is. 58:12
**16** [a]Ps. 58:8
**17** [a]Job 17:16 [1]Lit. *weary of strength*
**18** [a]Job 39:7 [1]*are at ease*
**20** [a]Jer. 20:18 [b]2 Kin. 4:27
**21** [a]Rev. 9:6 [b]Prov. 2:4 [1]Lit. *wait*
**22** [a]Job 7:15, 16
**23** [a]Job 19:8; Ps. 88:8; Lam. 3:7
**24** [1]Lit. *my bread*
**25** [a][Job 9:28; 30:15]

CHAPTER 4
**3** [a]Is. 35:3
**4** [a]Is. 35:3 [1]Lit. *bending*

5 But now it comes upon you,
and you are weary;
It touches you, and you are troubled.
6 *Is* not [a]your reverence [b]your confidence?
And the integrity of your ways your hope?

7 "Remember now, [a]who *ever* perished being
innocent?
Or where were the upright *ever* cut off?
8 Even as I have seen,
[a]Those who plow iniquity
And sow trouble reap the same.
9 By the blast of God they perish,
And by the breath of His anger
they are consumed.
10 The roaring of the lion,
The voice of the fierce lion,
And [a]the teeth of the young lions are broken.
11 [a]The old lion perishes for lack of prey,
And the cubs of the lioness are scattered.

**12** "Now a word was secretly brought to me,
And my ear received a whisper of it.
13 [a]In disquieting thoughts from the visions of
the night,
When deep sleep falls on men,
14 Fear came upon me, and [a]trembling,
Which made all my bones shake.
15 Then a spirit passed before my face;
The hair on my body stood up.
16 It stood still,
But I could not discern its appearance.
A form *was* before my eyes;
*There was* silence;
Then I heard a voice *saying:*
17 'Can a mortal be more righteous than God?
Can a man be more pure than his Maker?
18 If He [a]puts no trust in His servants,
*If* He charges His angels with error,
19 How much more those who dwell
in houses of clay,
Whose foundation is in the dust,
*Who* are crushed before a moth?
20 [a]They are broken in pieces from morning till
evening;
They perish forever, with no one regarding.
21 Does not their own excellence go away?
They die, even without wisdom.'

### *Eliphaz Continues to Rebuke Job*

**5** "Call out now;
Is there anyone who will answer you?
And to which of the holy ones will you turn?
2 For wrath kills a foolish man,
And envy slays a simple one.
3 [a]I have seen the foolish taking root,
But suddenly I cursed his dwelling place.
4 His sons are [a]far from safety,
They are crushed in the gate,
And [b]*there is* no deliverer.
5 Because the hungry eat up his harvest,
[1]Taking it even from the thorns,
[2]And a snare snatches their [3]substance.
6 For affliction does not come from the dust,
Nor does trouble spring from the ground;
7 Yet man is [a]born to [1]trouble,
As the sparks fly upward.

8 "But as for me, I would seek God,
And to God I would commit my cause—
9 Who does great things, and unsearchable,
Marvelous things without number.
10 [a]He gives rain on the earth,
And sends waters on the fields.
11 [a]He sets on high those who are lowly,
And those who mourn are lifted to safety.
12 [a]He frustrates the devices of the crafty,
So that their hands cannot carry out
their plans.
13 He catches the [a]wise in their own craftiness,
And the counsel of the cunning
comes quickly upon them.
14 They meet with darkness in the daytime,
And grope at noontime as in the night.
15 But [a]He saves the needy from the sword,
From the mouth of the mighty,
And from their hand.
16 [a]So the poor have hope,
And injustice shuts her mouth.

**17** "Behold,[a] happy *is* the man
whom God corrects;
Therefore do not despise the chastening
of the Almighty.
18 [a]For He bruises, but He binds up;
He wounds, but His hands make whole.
19 [a]He shall deliver you in six troubles,
Yes, in seven [b]no evil shall touch you.
20 [a]In famine He shall redeem you from death,
And in war from the [1]power of the sword.
21 [a]You shall be hidden from the scourge
of the tongue,
And you shall not be afraid of destruction
when it comes.
22 You shall laugh at destruction and famine,
And [a]you shall not be afraid of the [b]beasts
of the earth.
23 [a]For you shall have a covenant
with the stones of the field,
And the beasts of the field
shall be at peace with you.
24 You shall know that your tent *is* in peace;
You shall visit your dwelling
and find nothing amiss.
25 You shall also know that [a]your descendants
*shall be* many,
And your offspring [b]like the grass
of the earth.
26 [a]You shall come to the grave at a full age,
As a sheaf of grain ripens in its season.
27 Behold, this we have [a]searched out;
It *is* true.
Hear it, and know for yourself."

### *Job Pleads for Understanding*

**6** Then Job answered and said:

2 "Oh, that my grief were fully weighed,
And my calamity laid with it on the scales!
3 For then it would be heavier than the sand
of the sea—
Therefore my words have been rash.
4 [a]For the arrows of the Almighty *are*
within me;
My spirit drinks in their poison;
[b]The terrors of God are arrayed [c]against me.
5 Does the [a]wild donkey bray
when it has grass,
Or does the ox low over its fodder?
6 Can flavorless food be eaten without salt?
Or is there *any* taste in the white of an egg?
7 My soul refuses to touch them;
They *are* as loathsome food to me.

**6** [a]Job 1:1 [b]Prov. 3:26
**7** [a][Job 8:20; 36:6, 7; Ps. 37:25]
**8** [a][Job 15:31, 35; Prov. 22:8; Hos. 10:13; Gal. 6:7]
**10** [a]Job 5:15; Ps. 58:6
**11** [a]Job 29:17; Ps. 34:10
**13** [a]Job 33:15
**14** [a]Hab. 3:16
**18** [a]Job 15:15
**20** [a]Ps. 90:5, 6

CHAPTER 5
**3** [a][Ps. 37:35, 36]; Jer. 12:1–3
**4** [a]Ps. 119:155 [b]Ps. 109:12
**5** [1]LXX *They shall not be taken from evil men;* Vg. *And the armed men shall take him by violence* [2]LXX *The might shall draw them off;* Vg. *And the thirsty shall drink up their riches* [3]*wealth*
**7** [a]Job 14:1 [1]*labor*
**10** [a][Job 36:27–29; 37:6–11; 38:26]
**11** [a]Ps. 113:7
**12** [a]Neh. 4:15
**13** [a][Job 37:24; 1 Cor. 3:19]
**15** [a]Job 4:10, 11; Ps. 35:10
**16** [a]1 Sam. 2:8; Ps. 107:41, 42
**17** [a]Ps. 94:12; [Prov. 3:11, 12; Heb. 12:5, 6; Rev. 3:19]
**18** [a][Deut. 32:39; 1 Sam. 2:6, 7]; Is. 30:26; Hos. 6:1
**19** [a]Ps. 34:19; 91:3; [1 Cor. 10:13] [b]Ps. 91:10; [Prov. 24:16]
**20** [a]Ps. 33:19, 20; 37:19 [1]Lit. *hand*
**21** [a]Job 5:15; Ps. 31:20
**22** [a]Ps. 91:13; Is. 11:9; 35:9; 65:25; Ezek. 34:25 [b]Hos. 2:18
**23** [a]Ps. 91:12
**25** [a]Ps. 112:2 [b]Ps. 72:16
**26** [a][Prov. 9:11; 10:27]
**27** [a]Ps. 111:2

CHAPTER 6
**4** [a]Job 16:13; Ps. 38:2 [b]Ps. 88:15, 16 [c]Job 30:15
**5** [a]Job 39:5–8

8 "Oh, that I might have my request,
That God would grant *me* the thing that I long for!
9 That it would please God to crush me,
That He would loose His hand and [a]cut me off!
10 Then I would still have comfort;
Though in anguish I would exult,
He will not spare;
For [a]I have not concealed the words of [b]the Holy One.

11 "What strength do I have, that I should hope?
And what *is* my end, that I should prolong my life?
12 *Is* my strength the strength of stones?
Or is my flesh bronze?
13 *Is* my help not within me?
And is success driven from me?

14 "To[a] him who is [1]afflicted, kindness *should be shown* by his friend,
Even though he forsakes the fear of the Almighty.
15 [a]My brothers have dealt deceitfully like a brook,
[b]Like the streams of the brooks that pass away,
16 Which are dark because of the ice,
*And* into which the snow vanishes.
17 When it is warm, they cease to flow;
When it is hot, they vanish from their place.
18 The paths of their way turn aside,
They go nowhere and perish.
19 The caravans of [a]Tema look,
The travelers of [b]Sheba hope for them.
20 They are [a]disappointed[1] because they were confident;
They come there and are confused.
21 For now [a]you are nothing,
You see terror and [b]are afraid.
22 Did I ever say, 'Bring *something* to me'?
Or, 'Offer a bribe for me from your wealth'?
23 Or, 'Deliver me from the enemy's hand'?
Or, 'Redeem me from the hand of oppressors'?

24 "Teach me, and I will hold my tongue;
Cause me to understand wherein I have erred.
25 How forceful are right words!
But what does your arguing prove?
26 Do you intend to rebuke *my* words,
And the speeches of a desperate one, *which are* as wind?
27 Yes, you overwhelm the fatherless,
And you [a]undermine your friend.
28 Now therefore, be pleased to look at me;
For I would never lie to your face.
29 [a]Yield now, let there be no injustice!
Yes, concede, my [b]righteousness [1]still stands!
30 Is there injustice on my tongue?
Cannot my [1]taste discern the unsavory?

## *Job Pleads with God*

7 "*Is there* not [a]a time of hard service for man on earth?
*Are not* his days also like the days of a hired man?
2 Like a servant who [1]earnestly desires the shade,
And like a hired man who eagerly looks for his wages,
3 So I have been allotted [a]months of futility,
And wearisome nights have been appointed to me.
4 [a]When I lie down, I say, 'When shall I arise,
And the night be ended?'
For I have had my fill of tossing till dawn.
5 My flesh is [a]caked with worms and dust,
My skin is cracked and breaks out afresh.

6 "My[a] days are swifter than a weaver's shuttle,
And are spent without hope.
7 Oh, remember that [a]my life *is* a breath!
My eye will never again see good.
8 [a]The eye of him who sees me will see me no *more;*
*While* your *eyes* are upon me, I shall no longer *be.*
9 *As* the cloud disappears and vanishes away,
So [a]he who goes down to the grave does not come up.
10 He shall never return to his house,
[a]Nor shall his place know him anymore.

11 "Therefore I will [a]not restrain my mouth;
I will speak in the anguish of my spirit;
I will [b]complain in the bitterness of my soul.
12 *Am* I a sea, or a sea serpent,
That You set a guard over me?
13 [a]When I say, 'My bed will comfort me,
My couch will ease my complaint,'
14 Then You scare me with dreams
And terrify me with visions,
15 So that my soul chooses strangling
*And* death rather than [1]my body.
16 [a]I loathe *my life;*
I would not live forever.
[b]Let me alone,
For [c]my days *are but* [1]a breath.

17 "What[a] *is* man, that You should exalt him,
*That* You should set Your heart on him,
18 That You should [1]visit him every morning,
*And* test him every moment?
19 How long?
Will You not look away from me,
And let me alone till I swallow my saliva?
20 Have I sinned?
What have I done to You, [a]O watcher of men?
Why [b]have You set me as Your target,
So that I am a burden [1]to myself?
21 Why then do You not pardon my transgression,
And take away my iniquity?
For now I will lie down in the dust,
And You will seek me diligently,
But I *will* no longer *be.*"

## *Bildad Says Job Should Repent*

8 Then Bildad the Shuhite answered and said:
2 "How long will you speak these *things,*
And the words of your mouth *be like* a strong wind?
3 [a]Does God subvert judgment?
Or does the Almighty pervert justice?
4 If [a]your sons have sinned against Him,
He has cast them away [1]for their transgression.
5 [a]If you would earnestly seek God
And make your supplication to the Almighty,

**9** [a]Num. 11:15; 1 Kin. 19:4; Job 7:16; 9:21; 10:1
**10** [a]Acts 20:20 [b][Lev. 19:2; Is. 57:15]
**14** [a][Prov. 17:17] [1]Or *despairing*
**15** [a]Ps. 38:11 [b]Jer. 15:18
**19** [a]Gen. 25:15; Is. 21:14; Jer. 25:23 [b]1 Kin. 10:1; Ps. 72:10; Ezek. 27:22, 23
**20** [a]Jer. 14:3 [1]Lit. *ashamed*
**21** [a]Job 13:4 [b]Ps. 38:11
**27** [a]Ps. 57:6
**29** [a]Job 17:10 [b]Job 27:5, 6; 34:5 [1]Lit. *is in it*
**30** [1]*palate*

CHAPTER 7

**1** [a][Job 14:5, 13, 14]; Ps. 39:4
**2** [1]Lit. *pants for*
**3** [a][Job 15:31]
**4** [a]Deut. 28:67; Job 7:13, 14
**5** [a]Is. 14:11
**6** [a]Job 9:25; 16:22; 17:11; Is. 38:12; [James 4:14]
**7** [a]Job 7:16; Ps. 78:39; 89:47
**8** [a]Job 8:18; 20:9
**9** [a]2 Sam. 12:23
**10** [a]Ps. 103:16
**11** [a]Ps. 39:1, 9 [b]1 Sam. 1:10
**13** [a]Job 9:27
**15** [1]Lit. *my bones*
**16** [a]Job 10:1 [b]Job 14:6 [c]Ps. 62:9 [1]Without substance, futile
**17** [a]Job 22:2; Ps. 8:4; 144:3; Heb. 2:6
**18** [1]*attend to*
**20** [a]Ps. 36:6 [b]Ps. 21:12 [1]So with MT, Tg., Vg.; LXX, Jewish tradition *to You*

CHAPTER 8

**3** [a]Gen. 18:25; [Deut. 32:4; 2 Chr. 19:7; Job 34:10, 12; 36:23; 37:23]; Rom. 3:5
**4** [a]Job 1:5, 18, 19 [1]Lit. *into the hand of their transgression*
**5** [a][Job 5:17–27; 11:13]

6 If you *were* pure and upright,
Surely now He would [1]awake for you,
And prosper your rightful dwelling place.
7 Though your beginning was small,
Yet your latter end would [a]increase
abundantly.

8 "For[a] inquire, please, of the former age,
And consider the things discovered
by their fathers;
9 For [a]we *were born* yesterday,
and know [1]nothing,
Because our days on earth *are* a shadow.
10 Will they not teach you and tell you,
And utter words from their heart?

**11** "Can the papyrus grow up without a marsh?
Can the reeds flourish without water?
12 [a]While it *is* yet green *and* not cut down,
It withers before any *other* plant.
13 So *are* the paths of all who [a]forget God;
And the hope of the [b]hypocrite shall perish,
14 Whose confidence shall be cut off,
And whose trust *is* [1]a spider's web.
15 [a]He leans on his house, but it does not stand.
He holds it fast, but it does not endure.
16 He grows green in the sun,
And his branches spread out in his garden.
17 His roots wrap around the rock heap,
*And* look for a place in the stones.
18 [a]If he is destroyed from his place,
Then *it* will deny him, *saying,*
'I have not seen you.'

**19** "Behold, this is the joy of His way,
And [a]out of the earth others will grow.
20 Behold, [a]God will not [1]cast away the
blameless,
Nor will He uphold the evildoers.
21 He will yet fill your mouth with laughing,
And your lips with [1]rejoicing.
22 Those who hate you will be [a]clothed with
shame,
And the dwelling place of the wicked [1]will
come to nothing."

### *Job Finds No Comfort*

**9** Then Job answered and said:

2 "Truly I know *it is* so,
But how can a [a]man be [b]righteous
before God?
3 If one wished to [1]contend with Him,
He could not answer Him one time out of a
thousand.
4 [a]*God is* wise in heart and mighty in strength.
Who has hardened *himself* against Him
and prospered?
5 He removes the mountains, and they do not
know
When He overturns them in His anger;
6 He [a]shakes the earth out of its place,
And its [b]pillars tremble;
7 He commands the sun, and it does not rise;
He seals off the stars;
8 [a]He alone spreads out the heavens,
And [1]treads on the [2]waves of the sea;
9 [a]He made [1]the Bear, Orion, and the Pleiades,
And the chambers of the south;
10 [a]He does great things past finding out,
Yes, wonders without number.
11 [a]If He goes by me, I do not see *Him;*
If He moves past, I do not perceive Him;
12 [a]If He takes away, [1]who can hinder Him?
Who can say to Him, 'What are You doing?'
13 God will not withdraw His anger,
[a]The allies of [1]the proud lie prostrate
beneath Him.

**14** "How then can I answer Him,
*And* choose my words *to reason* with Him?
15 [a]For though I were righteous,
I could not answer Him;
I would beg mercy of my Judge.
16 If I called and He answered me,
I would not believe that He was listening
to my voice.
17 For He crushes me with a tempest,
And multiplies my wounds [a]without cause.
18 He will not allow me to catch my breath,
But fills me with bitterness.
19 If *it is a matter* of strength,
indeed *He is* strong;
And if of justice, who will appoint
my day *in court?*
20 Though I were righteous,
my own mouth would condemn me;
Though I *were* blameless,
it would prove me perverse.

21 "I am blameless, yet I do not know myself;
I despise my life.
22 It *is* all one *thing;*
Therefore I say, [a]'He destroys the
blameless and the wicked.'
23 If the scourge slays suddenly,
He laughs at the plight of the innocent.
24 The earth is given into the hand
of the wicked.
He covers the faces of its judges.
If it is not *He,* who else could it be?

25 "Now [a]my days are swifter than a runner;
They flee away, they see no good.
26 They pass by like [1]swift ships,
[a]Like an eagle swooping on its prey.
27 [a]If I say, 'I will forget my complaint,
I will put off my sad face and wear a smile,'
28 [a]I am afraid of all my sufferings;
I know that You [b]will not hold me innocent.
29 *If* I am condemned,
Why then do I labor in vain?
30 [a]If I wash myself with snow water,
And cleanse my hands with [1]soap,
31 Yet You will plunge me into the pit,
And my own clothes will [1]abhor me.

32 "For [a]*He is* not a man, as I *am*,
*That* I may answer Him,
*And that* we should go to court together.
33 [a]Nor is there any mediator between us,
*Who* may lay his hand on us both.
34 [a]Let Him take His rod away from me,
And do not let dread of Him terrify me.
35 *Then* I would speak and not fear Him,
But it is not so with me.

### *Job Pleads Further with God*

**10** "My [a]soul loathes my life;
I will [1]give free course to my complaint,
[b]I will speak in the bitterness of my soul.
2 I will say to God, 'Do not condemn me;
Show me why You contend with me.

**6** [1]*arise*
**7** [a]Job 42:12
**8** [a]Deut. 4:32; 32:7; Job 15:18; 20:4
**9** [a]Gen. 47:9; [1 Chr. 29:15]; Job 7:6; [Ps. 39:5; 102:11; 144:4] [1]Lit. *not*
**12** [a]Ps. 129:6
**13** [a]Ps. 9:17 [b]Job 11:20; 18:14; 27:8; Ps. 112:10; [Prov. 10:28]
**14** [1]Lit. *a spider's house*
**15** [a]Job 8:22; 27:18; Ps. 49:11
**18** [a]Job 7:10
**19** [a]Ps. 113:7
**20** [a]Job 4:7 [1]*reject*
**21** [1]Lit. *shouts of joy*
**22** [a]Ps. 35:26; 109:29 [1]Lit. *will not be*

CHAPTER 9
**2** [a][Job 4:17; 15:14–16; Ps. 143:2; Rom. 3:20] [b][Hab. 2:4; Rom. 1:17; Gal. 3:11; Heb. 10:38]
**3** [1]*argue*
**4** [a]Job 36:5
**6** [a]Is. 2:19, 21; Hag. 2:6; Heb. 12:26 [b]Job 26:11
**8** [a]Gen. 1:6; Job 37:18; Ps. 104:2, 3; Is. 40:22 [1]*walks* [2]Lit. *heights*
**9** [a]Gen. 1:16; Job 38:31; Amos 5:8 [1]Heb. *Ash, Kesil,* and *Kimah*
**10** [a]Job 5:9
**11** [a][Job 23:8, 9; 35:14]
**12** [a][Is. 45:9; Dan. 4:35; Rom. 9:20] [1]Lit. *who can turn Him back?*
**13** [a]Job 26:12 [1]Heb. *rahab*
**15** [a]Job 10:15; 23:1–7
**17** [a]Job 2:3
**22** [a][Eccl. 9:2, 3]; Ezek. 21:3
**25** [a]Job 7:6, 7
**26** [a]Job 39:29; Hab. 1:8 [1]Lit. *ships of reeds*
**27** [a]Job 7:13
**28** [a]Ps. 119:120 [b]Ex. 20:7
**30** [a][Jer. 2:22] [1]*lye*
**31** [1]*loathe*
**32** [a]Eccl. 6:10; [Is. 45:9; Jer. 49:19; Rom. 9:20]
**33** [a][1 Sam. 2:25]; Job 9:19; Is. 1:18
**34** [a]Job 13:20, 21; Ps. 39:10

CHAPTER 10
**1** [a]1 Kin. 19:4; Job 7:16; Jon. 4:3 [b]Job 7:11 [1]Lit. *leave on myself*

3 *Does it* seem good to You that You
should oppress,
That You should despise the work
of Your hands,
And smile on the counsel of the wicked?
4 Do You have eyes of flesh?
Or [a]do You see as man sees?
5 *Are* Your days like the days of a
mortal man?
*Are* Your years like the days of a
mighty man,
6 That You should seek for my iniquity
And search out my sin,
7 Although You know that I am not wicked,
And *there is* no one who can deliver from
Your hand?

8 'Your[a] hands have made me and
fashioned me,
An intricate unity;
Yet You would [b]destroy me.
9 Remember, I pray, [a]that You have
made me like clay.
And will You turn me into dust again?
10 [a]Did You not pour me out like milk,
And curdle me like cheese,
11 Clothe me with skin and flesh,
And knit me together with bones
and sinews?
12 You have granted me life and favor,
And Your care has preserved my spirit.

13 'And these *things* You have hidden
in Your heart;
I know that this *was* with You:
14 If I sin, then [a]You mark me,
And will not acquit me of my iniquity.
15 If I am wicked, [a]woe to me;
[b]Even *if* I am righteous,
I [1]cannot lift up my head.
*I am* full of disgrace;
[c]See my misery!
16 If *my head* is exalted,
[a]You hunt me like a fierce lion,
And again You show Yourself awesome
against me.
17 You renew Your witnesses against me,
And increase Your indignation toward me;
Changes and war are *ever* with me.

18 'Why[a] then have You brought me
out of the womb?
Oh, that I had perished
and no eye had seen me!
19 I would have been as though I had not been.
I would have been carried from the womb to
the grave.
20 [a]Are not my days few?
Cease! [b]Leave me alone,
that I may take a little comfort,
21 Before I go *to the place from which*
I shall not return,
[a]To the land of darkness
[b]and the shadow of death,
22 A land as dark as darkness *itself,*
As the shadow of death, without any order,
*Where* even the light *is* like darkness.' "

### *Zophar Urges Job to Repent*

**11** Then Zophar the Naamathite answered and said:

2 "Should not the multitude of words
be answered?
And should [1]a man full of talk be vindicated?
3 Should your empty talk make men [1]hold
their peace?
And when you mock,
should no one rebuke you?
4 For you have said,
[a]'My doctrine *is* pure,
And I am clean in your eyes.'
5 But oh, that God would speak,
And open His lips against you,
6 That He would show you the secrets
of wisdom!
For *they would* double *your* prudence.
Know therefore that [a]God [1]exacts from you
*Less* than your iniquity *deserves.*

7 "Can[a] you search out the deep things of God?
Can you find out the limits of the Almighty?
8 *They are* higher than heaven—
what can you do?
Deeper than [1]Sheol—what can you know?
9 Their measure *is* longer than the earth
And broader than the sea.

10 "If[a] He passes by, imprisons,
and gathers *to judgment,*
Then who can [1]hinder Him?
11 For [a]He knows deceitful men;
He sees wickedness also.
Will He not then consider *it?*
12 For an [a]empty-headed man will be wise,
When a wild donkey's colt is born a man.

13 "If you would [a]prepare your heart,
And [b]stretch out your hands toward Him;
14 If iniquity *were* in your hand,
*and you* put it far away,
And [a]would not let wickedness dwell
in your tents;
15 [a]Then surely you could lift up your face
without spot;
Yes, you could be steadfast, and not fear;
16 Because you would [a]forget *your* misery,
And remember *it* as waters *that have*
passed away,
17 And *your* life [a]would be brighter than
noonday.
*Though* you were dark,
you would be like the morning.
18 And you would be secure,
because there is hope;
Yes, you would dig *around you,*
*and* [a]take your rest in safety.
19 You would also lie down,
and no one would make *you* afraid;
*Yes,* many would court your favor.
20 But [a]the eyes of the wicked will fail,
And they shall not escape,
And [b]their hope—[1]loss of life!"

### *Job Answers His Critics*

**12** Then Job answered and said:

2 "No doubt you *are* the people,
And wisdom will die with you!
3 But I have [1]understanding as well as you;
I *am* not [a]inferior to you.
Indeed, who does not *know*
such things as these?

4 "I[a] am one mocked by his friends,
Who [b]called on God, and He answered him,
The just and blameless *who is* ridiculed.
5 A [1]lamp is despised in the thought
of one who is at ease;
*It is* made ready for [a]those whose feet slip.

**4** [a][1 Sam. 16:7; Job 28:24; 34:21]
**8** [a]Job 10:3; Ps. 119:73 [b][Job 9:22]
**9** [a]Gen. 2:7; Job 33:6
**10** [a][Ps. 139:14–16]
**14** [a]Job 7:20; Ps. 139:1
**15** [a]Job 10:7; Is. 3:11 [b][Job 9:12, 15] [c]Ps. 25:18 [1]Lit. *will not*
**16** [a]Is. 38:13; Lam. 3:10; Hos. 13:7
**18** [a]Job 3:11–13
**20** [a]Ps. 39:5 [b]Job 7:16, 19
**21** [a]Ps. 88:12 [b]Ps. 23:4

CHAPTER 11

**2** [1]Lit. *a man of lips*
**3** [1]*be silent*
**4** [a]Job 6:30
**6** [a][Ezra 9:13] [1]Lit. *forgets some of your iniquity for you*
**7** [a]Job 33:12, 13; 36:26; [Eccl. 3:11; Rom. 11:33]
**8** [1]The abode of the dead
**10** [a]Job 9:12; [Rev. 3:7] [1]*restrain*
**11** [a][Ps. 10:14]
**12** [a][Ps. 39:5]; Rom. 1:22
**13** [a][1 Sam. 7:3] [b]Ps. 88:9
**14** [a]Ps. 101:3
**15** [a]Job 22:26; Ps. 119:6; [1 John 3:21]
**16** [a]Is. 65:16
**17** [a]Ps. 37:6; Prov. 4:18; Is. 58:8, 10
**18** [a]Lev. 26:5, 6; Ps. 3:5; Prov. 3:24
**20** [a]Lev. 26:16; Deut. 28:65; Job 17:5 [b]Job 18:14; [Prov. 11:7] [1]Lit. *the breathing out of life*

CHAPTER 12

**3** [a]Job 13:2 [1]Lit. *a heart*
**4** [a]Job 21:3 [b]Ps. 91:15
**5** [a]Prov. 14:2 [1]Or *disaster*

6 [a]The tents of robbers prosper,
And those who provoke God are secure—
In what God provides by His hand.

7 "But now ask the beasts,
and they will teach you;
And the birds of the air,
and they will tell you;
8 Or speak to the earth, and it will teach you;
And the fish of the sea will explain to you.
9 Who among all these does not know
That the hand of the LORD has done this,
10 [a]In whose hand *is* the [1]life
of every living thing,
And the [b]breath of [2]all mankind?
11 Does not the ear test words
And the [1]mouth taste its food?
12 Wisdom *is* with aged men,
And with [1]length of days, understanding.

13 "With Him *are* [a]wisdom and strength,
He has counsel and understanding.
14 If [a]He breaks *a thing* down,
it cannot be rebuilt;
*If* He imprisons a man,
there can be no release.
15 If He [a]withholds the waters, they dry up;
*If* He [b]sends them out,
they overwhelm the earth.
16 With Him *are* strength and prudence.
The deceived and the deceiver *are* His.
17 He leads counselors away plundered,
And makes fools of the judges.
18 He loosens the bonds of kings,
And binds their waist with a belt.
19 He leads [1]princes away plundered,
And overthrows the mighty.
20 [a]He deprives the trusted ones of speech,
And takes away the discernment
of the elders.
21 [a]He pours contempt on princes,
And [1]disarms the mighty.
22 He [a]uncovers deep things out of darkness,
And brings the shadow of death to light.
23 [a]He makes nations great, and destroys them;
He [1]enlarges nations, and guides them.
24 He takes away the [1]understanding of the
chiefs of the people of the earth,
And [a]makes them wander in a pathless
wilderness.
25 [a]They grope in the dark without light,
And He makes them [b]stagger like a
drunken *man*.

### *Job Defends Himself*

**13** "Behold, my eye has seen all *this*,
My ear has heard and understood it.
2 [a]What you know, I also know;
I *am* not inferior to you.
3 [a]But I would speak to the Almighty,
And I desire to reason with God.
4 But you forgers of lies,
[a]You *are* all worthless physicians.
5 Oh, that you would be silent,
And [a]it would be your wisdom!
6 Now hear my reasoning,
And heed the pleadings of my lips.
7 [a]Will you speak [1]wickedly for God,
And talk deceitfully for Him?
8 Will you show partiality for Him?
Will you contend for God?
9 Will it be well when He searches you out?
Or can you mock Him as one mocks a man?
10 He will surely rebuke you
If you secretly show partiality.
11 Will not His [1]excellence make you afraid,
And the dread of Him fall upon you?
12 Your platitudes *are* proverbs of ashes,
Your defenses are defenses of clay.

13 "Hold[1] your peace with me, and let me speak,
Then let come on me what *may!*
14 Why [a]do I take my flesh in my teeth,
And put my life in my hands?
15 [a]Though He slay me, yet will I trust Him.
[b]Even so, I will defend my own ways
before Him.
16 He also *shall* be my salvation,
For a [a]hypocrite could not come before Him.
17 Listen carefully to my speech,
And to my declaration with your ears.
18 See now, I have prepared *my* case,
I know that I shall be [a]vindicated.
19 [a]Who *is* he *who* will contend with me?
If now I hold my tongue, I perish.

20 "Only[a] two *things* do not do to me,
Then I will not hide myself from You:
21 [a]Withdraw Your hand far from me,
And let not the dread of You
make me afraid.
22 Then call, and I will [a]answer;
Or let me speak, then You respond to me.
23 How many *are* my iniquities and sins?
Make me know my transgression and my sin.
24 [a]Why do You hide Your face,
And [b]regard me as Your enemy?
25 [a]Will You frighten a leaf driven to and fro?
And will You pursue dry stubble?
26 For You write bitter things against me,
And [a]make me inherit the iniquities
of my youth.
27 [a]You put my feet in the stocks,
And watch closely all my paths.
You [1]set a limit for the [2]soles of my feet.

28 "*Man*[1] decays like a rotten thing,
Like a garment that is moth-eaten.

### *Job Speaks of Life's Woes*

**14** "Man *who is* born of woman
Is of few days and [a]full of [1]trouble.
2 [a]He comes forth like a flower and fades away;
He flees like a shadow and does not
continue.
3 And [a]do You open Your eyes on [1]such a one,
And [b]bring me to judgment with Yourself?
4 Who [a]can bring a clean *thing*
out of an unclean?
No one!
5 [a]Since his days *are* determined,
The number of his months *is* with You;
You have appointed his limits,
so that he cannot pass.
6 [a]Look away from him that he may [1]rest,
Till [b]like a hired man he finishes his day.

7 "For there is hope for a tree,
If it is cut down, that it will sprout again,
And that its tender shoots will not cease.
8 Though its root may grow old in the earth,
And its stump may die in the ground,
9 *Yet* at the scent of water it will bud
And bring forth branches like a plant.

---

**6** [a][Job 9:24; 21:6–16]
**10** [a][Acts 17:28] [b]Job 27:3; 33:4 [1]Or *soul* [2]Lit. *all flesh of men*
**11** [1]*palate*
**12** [1]Long life
**13** [a]Job 9:4; 36:5
**14** [a]Job 11:10
**15** [a][1 Kin. 8:35, 36] [b]Gen. 7:11–24
**19** [1]Lit. *priests,* but not in a technical sense
**20** [a]Job 32:9
**21** [a]Ps. 107:40 [1]*loosens the belt of*
**22** [a][1 Cor. 4:5]
**23** [a]Is. 9:3; 26:15 [1]Lit. *spreads out*
**24** [a]Ps. 107:4 [1]Lit. *heart*
**25** [a]Job 5:14; 15:30; 18:18 [b]Ps. 107:27

CHAPTER 13

**2** [a]Job 12:3
**3** [a]Job 23:3; 31:35
**4** [a]Job 6:21
**5** [a]Prov. 17:28
**7** [a]Job 27:4; 36:4 [1]*unrighteously*
**11** [1]Lit. *exaltation*
**13** [1]*Be silent*
**14** [a]Job 18:4
**15** [a]Ps. 23:4 [b]Job 27:5
**16** [a]Job 8:13
**18** [a][Rom. 8:34]
**19** [a]Is. 50:8
**20** [a]Job 9:34
**21** [a]Ps. 39:10
**22** [a]Job 9:16; 14:15
**24** [a][Deut. 32:20] [b]Lam. 2:5
**25** [a]Is. 42:3
**26** [a]Job 20:11
**27** [a]Job 33:11 [1]Lit. *inscribe a print* [2]Lit. *roots*
**28** [1]Lit. *He*

CHAPTER 14

**1** [a]Eccl. 2:23 [1]*turmoil*
**2** [a]Job 8:9
**3** [a]Ps. 8:4; 144:3 [b][Ps. 143:2] [1]LXX, Syr., Vg. *him*
**4** [a][Ps. 51:2, 5, 10]
**5** [a]Job 7:1; 21:21
**6** [a]Ps. 39:13 [b]Job 7:1 [1]Lit. *cease*

10 But man dies and [1]is laid away;
Indeed he [2]breathes his last
And where *is* [a]he?
11 *As* water disappears from the sea,
And a river becomes parched and dries up,
12 So man lies down and does not rise.
[a]Till the heavens *are* no more,
They will not awake
Nor be roused from their sleep.

13 "Oh, that You would hide me in the grave,
That You would conceal me until Your
wrath is past,
That You would appoint me a set time, and
remember me!
14 If a man dies, shall he live *again?*
All the days of my hard service [a]I will wait,
Till my change comes.
15 [a]You shall call, and I will answer You;
You shall desire the work of Your hands.
16 For now [a]You number my steps,
But do not watch over my sin.
17 [a]My transgression *is* sealed up in a bag,
And You [1]cover my iniquity.

18 "But *as* a mountain falls *and* crumbles away,
And *as* a rock is moved from its place;
19 *As* water wears away stones,
*And as* torrents wash away the soil
of the earth;
So You destroy the hope of man.
20 You prevail forever against him,
and he passes on;
You change his countenance
and send him away.
21 His sons come to honor,
and [a]he does not know *it;*
They are brought low,
and he does not perceive *it.*
22 But his flesh will be in pain over it,
And his soul will mourn over it."

### *Eliphaz Accuses Job of Folly*

**15** Then [a]Eliphaz the Temanite answered and said:

2 "Should a wise man answer
with empty knowledge,
And fill [1]himself with the east wind?
3 Should he reason with unprofitable talk,
Or by speeches with which he
can do no good?
4 Yes, you cast off fear,
And restrain [1]prayer before God.
5 For your iniquity teaches your mouth,
And you choose the tongue of the crafty.
6 [a]Your own mouth condemns you, and not I;
Yes, your own lips testify against you.

7 "*Are* you the first man *who* was born?
[a]Or were you made before the hills?
8 [a]Have you heard the counsel of God?
Do you limit wisdom to yourself?
9 [a]What do you know that we do not know?
*What* do you understand that *is* not in us?
10 [a]Both the gray-haired and the aged
*are* among us,
Much older than your father.
11 *Are* the consolations of God
too small for you,
And the word *spoken* [1]gently with you?
12 Why does your heart carry you away,
And [1]what do your eyes wink at,

**10** [a]Job 10:21, 22 [1]*lies prostrate* [2]*expires*
**12** [a]Ps. 102:25, 26; [Is. 51:6; 65:17; 66:22]; Acts 3:21; [2 Pet. 3:7, 10, 11; Rev. 20:11; 21:1]
**14** [a]Job 13:15
**15** [a]Job 13:22
**16** [a]Job 10:6, 14; 13:27; 31:4; 34:21; Ps. 56:8; 139:1–3; Prov. 5:21; [Jer. 32:19]
**17** [a]Deut. 32:32–34 [1]Lit. *plaster over*
**21** [a]Eccl. 9:5; Is. 63:16

CHAPTER 15
**1** [a]Job 4:1
**2** [1]Lit. *his belly*
**4** [1]*meditation* or *complaint*
**6** [a]Job 9:20; [Luke 19:22]
**7** [a]Job 38:4, 21; Ps. 90:2; Prov. 8:25
**8** [a]Job 29:4; Rom. 11:34; [1 Cor. 2:11]
**9** [a]Job 12:3; 13:2
**10** [a]Job 8:8–10; 12:12; 32:6, 7
**11** [1]Or *a secret thing*
**12** [1]Or *why do your eyes flash*
**14** [a]Job 14:4; Prov. 20:9; [Eccl. 7:20; 1 John 1:8, 10]
**15** [a]Job 4:18; 25:5
**16** [a]Job 4:19; Ps. 14:3; 53:3 [b]Job 34:7; Prov. 19:28
**18** [a]Job 8:8; 20:4
**19** [a]Joel 3:17 [1]Or *earth*
**20** [a]Ps. 90:12
**21** [a]Job 20:21; 1 Thess. 5:3 [1]*Terrifying*
**22** [a]Job 14:10–12
**23** [a]Ps. 59:15; 109:10 [b]Job 18:12
**24** [1]*attack*
**27** [a]Ps. 17:10; 73:7; 119:70
**29** [a]Job 20:28; 27:16, 17
**30** [a]Job 4:9
**31** [a]Job 35:13; Is. 59:4
**32** [a]Job 22:16; Ps. 55:23; Eccl. 7:17
**35** [a]Ps. 7:14; Is. 59:4; [Hos. 10:13]

CHAPTER 16
**2** [a]Job 13:4; 21:34 [1]*Troublesome*

13 That you turn your spirit against God,
And let *such* words go out of your mouth?

14 "What[a] *is* man, that he could be pure?
And *he who is* born of a woman,
that he could be righteous?
15 [a]If *God* puts no trust in His saints,
And the heavens are not pure in His sight,
16 [a]How much less man,
*who is* abominable and filthy,
[b]Who drinks iniquity like water!

17 "I will tell you, hear me;
What I have seen I will declare,
18 What wise men have told,
Not hiding *anything received*
[a]from their fathers,
19 To whom alone the [1]land was given,
And [a]no alien passed among them:
20 The wicked man writhes with pain
all *his* days,
[a]And the number of years is hidden
from the oppressor.
21 [1]Dreadful sounds *are* in his ears;
[a]In prosperity the destroyer comes upon him.
22 He does not believe that he
will [a]return from darkness,
For a sword is waiting for him.
23 He [a]wanders about for bread, *saying,*
'Where *is it?*'
He knows [b]that a day of darkness is
ready at his hand.
24 Trouble and anguish make him afraid;
They overpower him,
like a king ready for [1]battle.
25 For he stretches out his hand against God,
And acts defiantly against the Almighty,
26 Running stubbornly against Him
With his strong, embossed shield.

27 "Though[a] he has covered his face
with his fatness,
And made *his* waist heavy with fat,
28 He dwells in desolate cities,
In houses which no one inhabits,
Which are destined to become ruins.
29 He will not be rich,
Nor will his wealth [a]continue,
Nor will his possessions overspread
the earth.
30 He will not depart from darkness;
The flame will dry out his branches,
And [a]by the breath of His mouth
he will go away.
31 Let him not [a]trust in futile *things,*
deceiving himself,
For futility will be his reward.
32 It will be accomplished [a]before his time,
And his branch will not be green.
33 He will shake off his unripe grape like a vine,
And cast off his blossom like an olive tree.
34 For the company of hypocrites
*will be* barren,
And fire will consume the tents of bribery.
35 [a]They conceive trouble
and bring forth futility;
Their womb prepares deceit."

### *Job Shames His Unsympathetic Friends*

**16** Then Job answered and said:

2 "I have heard many such things;
[a]Miserable[1] comforters *are* you all!

3 Shall [1]words of wind have an end?
Or what provokes you that you answer?
4 I also could speak as you *do,*
If your soul were in my soul's place.
I could heap up words against you,
And [a]shake my head at you;
5 *But* I would strengthen you with my mouth,
And the comfort of my lips would relieve
*your grief.*

6 "Though I speak, my grief is not relieved;
And *if* I remain silent, how am I eased?
7 But now He has [a]worn me out;
You [b]have made desolate all my company.
8 You have shriveled me up,
And it is a [a]witness *against me;*
My leanness rises up against me
*And* bears witness to my face.
9 [a]He tears *me* in His wrath, and hates me;
He gnashes at me with His teeth;
[b]My adversary sharpens His gaze on me.
10 They [a]gape at me with their mouth,
They [b]strike me reproachfully on the cheek,
They gather together against me.
11 God [a]has delivered me to the ungodly,
And turned me over to the hands
of the wicked.
12 I was at ease, but He has [a]shattered me;
He also has taken *me* by my neck,
and shaken me to pieces;
He has [b]set me up for His target,
13 His archers surround me.
He pierces my [1]heart and does not pity;
He pours out my gall on the ground.
14 He breaks me with wound upon wound;
He runs at me like a [1]warrior.

15 "I have sewn sackcloth over my skin,
And [a]laid my [1]head in the dust.
16 My face is [1]flushed from weeping,
And on my eyelids *is* the shadow of death;
17 Although no violence *is* in my hands,
And my prayer *is* pure.

18 "O earth, do not cover my blood,
And [a]let my cry have no *resting* place!
19 Surely even now [a]my witness *is* in heaven,
And my evidence *is* on high.
20 My friends scorn me;
My eyes pour out *tears* to God.
21 [a]Oh, that one might plead for a man with
God,
As a man *pleads* for his [1]neighbor!
22 For when a few years are finished,
I shall [a]go the way of no return.

## *Job Prays for Relief*

17 "My spirit is broken,
My days are extinguished,
[a]The grave *is ready* for me.
2 *Are* not mockers with me?
And does not my eye [1]dwell on their
[a]provocation?

3 "Now put down a pledge for me
with Yourself.
Who *is* he *who* [a]will shake hands with me?
4 For You have hidden their heart
from [a]understanding;
Therefore You will not exalt *them.*
5 He who speaks flattery to *his* friends,
Even the eyes of his children will [a]fail.

6 "But He has made me [a]a byword
of the people,
And I have become one in whose
face men spit.
7 [a]My eye has also grown dim because
of sorrow,
And all my members *are* like shadows.
8 Upright *men* are astonished at this,
And the innocent stirs himself up against the
hypocrite.
9 Yet the righteous will hold to his [a]way,
And he who has [b]clean hands will be
stronger and stronger.

10 "But please, [a]come back again, [1]all of you,
For I shall not find *one* wise *man*
among you.
11 [a]My days are past,
My purposes are broken off,
*Even* the [1]thoughts of my heart.
12 They change the night into day;
'The light *is* near,' *they say,*
in the face of darkness.
13 If I wait *for* the grave *as* my house,
If I make my bed in the darkness,
14 If I say to corruption, 'You *are* my father,'
And to the worm,
'You *are* my mother and my sister,'
15 Where then *is* my [a]hope?
As for my hope, who can see it?
16 *Will* they go down [a]to the gates of [1]Sheol?
Shall *we have* [b]rest together in the dust?"

## *Bildad Says the Wicked Are Punished*

18 Then [a]Bildad the Shuhite answered and
said:

2 "How long *till* you put an end to words?
Gain understanding,
and afterward we will speak.
3 Why are we counted [a]as beasts,
*And* regarded as stupid in your sight?
4 [a]You[1] who tear yourself in anger,
Shall the earth be forsaken for you?
Or shall the rock be removed from its place?

5 "The[a] light of the wicked indeed goes out,
And the flame of his fire does not shine.
6 The light is dark in his tent,
[a]And his lamp beside him is put out.
7 The steps of his strength are shortened,
And [a]his own counsel casts him down.
8 For [a]he is cast into a net by his own feet,
And he walks into a snare.
9 The net takes *him* by the heel,
*And* [a]a snare lays hold of him.
10 A noose *is* hidden for him on the ground,
And a trap for him in the road.
11 [a]Terrors frighten him on every side,
And drive him to his feet.
12 His strength is starved,
And [a]destruction *is* ready at his side.
13 It devours patches of his skin;
The firstborn of death devours his [1]limbs.
14 He is uprooted from [a]the shelter of his tent,
And they parade him before the king
of terrors.
15 They dwell in his tent *who are* none of his;
Brimstone is scattered on his dwelling.
16 [a]His roots are dried out below,
And his branch withers above.
17 [a]The memory of him perishes from the earth,
And he has no name [1]among the renowned.
18 [1]He is driven from light into darkness,
And chased out of the world.

**3** [1]Empty words
**4** [a]Ps. 22:7; 109:25
**7** [a]Job 7:3 [b]Job 16:20; 19:13–15
**8** [a]Job 10:17
**9** [a]Hos. 6:1 [b]Job 13:24; 33:10
**10** [a]Ps. 22:13; 35:21 [b]Lam. 3:30
**11** [a]Job 1:15, 17
**12** [a]Job 9:17 [b]Job 7:20
**13** [1]Lit. *kidneys*
**14** [1]Vg. *giant*
**15** [a]Ps. 7:5 [1]Lit. *horn*
**16** [1]Lit. *red*
**18** [a][Ps. 66:18]
**19** [a]Rom. 1:9
**21** [a]Job 31:35 [1]*friend*
**22** [a]Eccl. 12:5

CHAPTER 17
**1** [a]Ps. 88:3, 4
**2** [a]Job 12:4; 17:6; 30:1, 9; 34:7 [1]Lit. *lodge*
**3** [a]Prov. 6:1; 17:18; 22:26
**4** [a]Job 12:20; 32:9
**5** [a]Job 11:20
**6** [a]Job 30:9
**7** [a]Ps. 6:7; 31:9
**9** [a]Prov. 4:18 [b]Ps. 24:4
**10** [a]Job 6:29 [1]So with some Heb. mss., LXX, [Syr.], Vg.; MT, Tg. *all of them*
**11** [a]Job 7:6 [1]*desires*
**15** [a]Job 7:6; 13:15; 14:19; 19:10
**16** [a]Jon. 2:6 [b]Job 3:17–19; 21:33 [1]The abode of the dead

CHAPTER 18
**1** [a]Job 8:1
**3** [a]Ps. 73:22
**4** [a]Job 13:14 [1]Lit. *one who tears his soul*
**5** [a]Prov. 13:9; 20:20; 24:20
**6** [a]Job 21:17
**7** [a]Job 5:12, 13; 15:6
**8** [a]Job 22:10
**9** [a]Job 5:5
**11** [a]Jer. 6:25
**12** [a]Job 15:23
**13** [1]*parts*
**14** [a]Job 11:20
**16** [a]Job 29:19
**17** [a][Ps. 34:16] [1]Lit. *before the outside,* i.e., the distinguished or famous
**18** [1]Or *They drive him*

19 [a]He has neither son nor posterity among
his people,
Nor any remaining in his dwellings.
20 Those [1]in the west are astonished [a]at his day,
As those [2]in the east are frightened.
21 Surely such *are* the dwellings of the wicked,
And this *is* the place *of him*
*who* [a]does not know God."

## *Job Trusts in His Redeemer*

**19** Then Job answered and said:

2 "How long will you torment my soul,
And break me in pieces with words?
3 These ten times you have [1]reproached me;
You are not ashamed *that* you [2]have
wronged me.
4 And if indeed I have erred,
My error remains with me.
5 If indeed you [a]exalt *yourselves* against me,
And plead my disgrace against me,
6 Know then that [a]God has wronged me,
And has surrounded me with His net.

7 "If I cry out concerning [1]wrong,
I am not heard.
If I cry aloud, *there is* no justice.
8 [a]He has [1]fenced up my way,
so that I cannot pass;
And He has set darkness in my paths.
9 [a]He has stripped me of my glory,
And taken the crown *from* my head.
10 He breaks me down on every side,
And I am gone;
My [a]hope He has uprooted like a tree.
11 He has also kindled His wrath against me,
And [a]He counts me as *one of* His enemies.
12 His troops come together
And build up their road against me;
They encamp all around my tent.

**13** "He[a] has removed my brothers far from me,
And my acquaintances
are completely estranged from me.
14 My relatives have failed,
And my close friends have forgotten me.
15 Those who dwell in my house,
and my maidservants,
Count me as a stranger;
I am an alien in their sight.
16 I call my servant, but he gives no answer;
I beg him with my mouth.
17 My breath is offensive to my wife,
And I am [1]repulsive to the children
of my own body.
18 Even [a]young children despise me;
I arise, and they speak against me.
19 [a]All my close friends abhor me,
And those whom I love have turned
against me.
20 [a]My bone clings to my skin and to my flesh,
And I have escaped by the skin of my teeth.

**21** "Have pity on me, have pity on me,
O you my friends,
For the hand of God has struck me!
22 Why do you [a]persecute me as God *does*,
And are not satisfied with my flesh?

**23** "Oh, that my words were written!
Oh, that they were inscribed in a book!
24 That they were engraved on a rock
With an iron pen and lead, forever!
25 For I know *that* my Redeemer lives,
And He shall stand at last on the earth;
26 And after my skin is [1]destroyed, this *I know*,
That [a]in my flesh I shall see God,
27 Whom I shall see for myself,
And my eyes shall behold, and not another.
*How* my [1]heart yearns within me!
28 If you should say, 'How shall we persecute
him?'—
Since the root of the matter is found in me,
29 Be afraid of the sword for yourselves;
For wrath *brings* the punishment
of the sword,
That you may know *there is* a judgment."

## *Zophar's Sermon on the Wicked Man*

**20** Then [a]Zophar the Naamathite answered and said:

2 "Therefore my anxious thoughts make
me answer,
Because of the turmoil within me.
3 I have heard the rebuke [1]that reproaches me,
And the spirit of my understanding causes
me to answer.

4 "Do you *not* know this of [a]old,
Since man was placed on earth,
5 [a]That the triumphing of the wicked is short,
And the joy of the hypocrite is *but* for a
[b]moment?
6 [a]Though his haughtiness mounts up to the
heavens,
And his head reaches to the clouds,
7 *Yet* he will perish forever like his own refuse;
Those who have seen him will say,
'Where is he?'
8 He will fly away [a]like a dream,
and not be found;
Yes, he [b]will be chased away like a vision
of the night.
9 The eye *that* saw him will *see him* no more,
Nor will his place behold him anymore.
10 His children will seek the favor of the poor,
And his hands will restore his wealth.
11 His bones are full of [a]his youthful vigor,
[b]But it will lie down with him in the dust.

12 "Though evil is sweet in his mouth,
*And* he hides it under his tongue,
13 *Though* he spares it and does not forsake it,
But still keeps it in his [1]mouth,
14 *Yet* his food in his stomach turns sour;
It becomes cobra venom within him.
15 He swallows down riches
And vomits them up again;
God casts them out of his belly.
16 He will suck the poison of cobras;
The viper's tongue will slay him.
17 He will not see [a]the streams,
The rivers flowing with honey and cream.
18 He will restore that for which he labored,
And will not swallow *it* down;
From the proceeds of business
He will get no enjoyment.
19 For he has [1]oppressed *and* forsaken the poor,
He has violently seized a house
which he did not build.

20 "Because[a] he knows no quietness in his [1]heart,
He will not save anything he desires.
21 Nothing is left for him to eat;
Therefore his well-being will not last.

**19** [a]Job 27:14, 15; Is. 14:22
**20** [a]Ps. 37:13; Jer. 50:27; Obad. 12 [1]Lit. *who came after* [2]Lit. *who have gone before*
**21** [a]Jer. 9:3; 1 Thess. 4:5

CHAPTER 19

**3** [1]*shamed* or *disgraced* [2]A Jewish tradition *make yourselves strange to me*
**5** [a]Ps. 35:26; 38:16; 55:12, 13
**6** [a]Job 16:11
**7** [1]*violence*
**8** [a]Job 3:23; Ps. 88:8; Lam. 3:7, 9 [1]*walled off my way*
**9** [a]Job 12:17, 19; Ps. 89:44
**10** [a]Job 17:14, 16
**11** [a]Job 13:24; 33:10
**13** [a]Job 16:20; Ps. 31:11; 38:11; 69:8; 88:8, 18
**17** [1]Lit. *strange*
**18** [a]2 Kin. 2:23; Job 17:6
**19** [a]Ps. 38:11; 55:12, 13
**20** [a]Job 16:8; 33:21; Ps. 102:5; Lam. 4:8
**22** [a]Job 13:24, 25; 16:11; 19:6; Ps. 69:26
**26** [a][Ps. 17:15]; Matt. 5:8; 1 Cor. 13:12; [1 John 3:2] [1]Lit. *struck off*
**27** [1]Lit. *kidneys*

CHAPTER 20

**1** [a]Job 11:1
**3** [1]Lit. *of my insulting correction*
**4** [a]Job 8:8; 15:10
**5** [a]Ps. 37:35, 36 [b][Job 8:13; 13:16; 15:34; 27:8]
**6** [a]Is. 14:13, 14
**8** [a]Ps. 73:20; 90:5 [b]Job 18:18; 27:21–23
**11** [a]Job 13:26 [b]Job 21:26
**13** [1]Lit. *palate*
**17** [a]Ps. 36:8; Jer. 17:8
**19** [1]*crushed*
**20** [a]Eccl. 5:13–15 [1]Lit. *belly*

22 In his self-sufficiency he will be in distress;
Every hand of [1]misery will come against him.
23 *When* he is about to fill his stomach,
*God* will cast on him the fury of His wrath,
And will rain *it* on him while he is eating.
24 [a]He will flee from the iron weapon;
A bronze bow will pierce him through.
25 It is drawn, and comes out of the body;
Yes, [a]the glittering *point comes*
out of his [1]gall.
[b]Terrors *come* upon him;
26 Total darkness *is* reserved for his treasures.
[a]An unfanned fire will consume him;
It shall go ill with him who is left in his tent.
27 The heavens will reveal his iniquity,
And the earth will rise up against him.
28 The increase of his house will depart,
*And his goods* will flow away in
the day of His [a]wrath.
29 [a]This *is* the portion from God
for a wicked man,
The heritage appointed to him by God."

### *Job Complains About the Prosperity of the Wicked*

**21** Then Job answered and said:

2 "Listen carefully to my speech,
And let this be your [1]consolation.
3 Bear with me that I may speak,
And after I have spoken, keep [a]mocking.

4 "As for me, *is* my complaint against man?
And if *it were,* why should I not be
impatient?
5 Look at me and be astonished;
[a]Put *your* hand over *your* mouth.
6 Even when I remember I am terrified,
And trembling takes hold of my flesh.
7 [a]Why do the wicked live *and* become old,
Yes, become mighty in power?
8 Their descendants are established
with them in their sight,
And their offspring before their eyes.
9 Their houses *are* safe from fear,
[a]Neither *is* [1]the rod of God upon them.
10 Their bull breeds without failure;
Their cow calves [a]without miscarriage.
11 They send forth their little ones like a flock,
And their children dance.
12 They sing to the tambourine and harp,
And rejoice to the sound of the flute.
13 They [a]spend their days in wealth,
And [1]in a moment go down to the [2]grave.
14 [a]Yet they say to God, 'Depart from us,
For we do not desire the knowledge
of Your ways.
15 [a]Who *is* the Almighty, that we should
serve Him?
And [b]what profit do we have if we pray
to Him?'
16 Indeed [1]their prosperity *is* not in their hand;
[a]The counsel of the wicked is far from me.

**17** "How often is the lamp of the wicked
put out?
*How often* does their destruction come
upon them,
The sorrows *God* [a]distributes in His anger?
18 [a]They are like straw before the wind,
And like chaff that a storm [1]carries away.
19 *They say,* 'God [1]lays up [2]*one's* iniquity [a]for
his children';
Let Him recompense him,
that he may know *it.*
20 Let his eyes see his destruction,
And [a]let him drink of the wrath
of the Almighty.
21 For what does he care about his
household after him,
When the number of his months
is cut in half?

**22** "Can[a] *anyone* teach God knowledge,
Since He judges those on high?
23 One dies in his full strength,
Being wholly at ease and secure;
24 His [1]pails are full of milk,
And the marrow of his bones is moist.
25 Another man dies in the bitterness of
his soul,
Never having eaten with pleasure.
26 They [a]lie down alike in the dust,
And worms cover them.

27 "Look, I know your thoughts,
And the schemes *with which* you
would wrong me.
28 For you say,
'Where *is* the house of the prince?
And where *is* [1]the tent,
The dwelling place of the wicked?'
29 Have you not asked those who travel
the road?
And do you not know their signs?
30 [a]For the wicked are reserved
for the day of doom;
They shall be brought out
on the day of wrath.
31 Who condemns his way to his face?
And who repays him *for what* he has done?
32 Yet he shall be brought to the grave,
And a vigil kept over the tomb.
33 The clods of the valley shall be sweet to him;
[a]Everyone shall follow him,
As countless *have gone* before him.
34 How then can you comfort me with
empty words,
Since [1]falsehood remains in your answers?"

### *Eliphaz Accuses Job of Sin*

**22** Then [a]Eliphaz the Temanite answered and said:

2 "Can[a] a man be profitable to God,
Though he who is wise may be profitable
to himself?
3 *Is it* any pleasure to the Almighty
that you are righteous?
Or *is it* gain *to Him* that you make your
ways blameless?

4 "Is it because of your fear of Him
that He corrects you,
And enters into judgment with you?
5 *Is* not your wickedness great,
And your iniquity without end?
6 For you have [a]taken pledges from your
brother for no reason,
And stripped the naked of their clothing.
7 You have not given the weary water
to drink,
And you [a]have withheld bread from
the hungry.

**22** [1]Or *the wretched* or *sufferer*
**24** [a]Is. 24:18; Amos 5:19
**25** [a]Job 16:13 [b]Job 18:11, 14 [1]Gall bladder
**26** [a]Ps. 21:9
**28** [a]Job 20:15; 21:30
**29** [a]Job 27:13; 31:2, 3

CHAPTER 21
**2** [1]*comfort*
**3** [a]Job 16:10
**5** [a]Judg. 18:19; Job 13:5; 29:9; 40:4
**7** [a]Job 12:6; Ps. 17:10, 14; 73:3, 12; [Jer. 12:1]; Hab. 1:13, 16
**9** [a]Ps. 73:5 [1]The rod of God's chastisement
**10** [a]Ex. 23:26
**13** [a]Job 21:23; 36:11 [1]Without lingering [2]Or *sheol*
**14** [a]Job 22:17
**15** [a]Ex. 5:2; Job 22:17; 34:9 [b]Job 35:3; Mal. 3:14
**16** [a]Job 22:18; Ps. 1:1; Prov. 1:10 [1]Lit. *their goal*
**17** [a][Job 31:2, 3; Luke 12:46]
**18** [a]Ps. 1:4; 35:5; Is. 17:13; Hos. 13:3 [1]*steals away*
**19** [a][Ex. 20:5]; Jer. 31:29; Ezek. 18:2 [1]*stores up* [2]Lit. *his*
**20** [a]Ps. 75:8; Is. 51:17; Jer. 25:15; Rev. 14:10; 19:15
**22** [a]Job 35:11; 36:22; [Is. 40:13; 45:9; Rom. 11:34; 1 Cor. 2:16]
**24** [1]LXX, Vg. *bowels;* Syr. *sides;* Tg. *breasts*
**26** [a]Job 3:13; 20:11; Eccl. 9:2
**28** [1]Vg. omits *the tent*
**30** [a]Job 20:29; [Prov. 16:4; 2 Pet. 2:9]
**33** [a]Heb. 9:27
**34** [1]*faithlessness*

CHAPTER 22
**1** [a]Job 4:1; 15:1; 42:9
**2** [a]Job 35:7; [Ps. 16:2; Luke 17:10]
**6** [a][Ex. 22:26, 27]; Deut. 24:6, 10, 17; Job 24:3, 9; Ezek. 18:16
**7** [a]Deut. 15:7; Job 31:17; Is. 58:7; Ezek. 18:7; Matt. 25:42

8 But the [1]mighty man possessed the land,
And the honorable man dwelt in it.
9 You have sent widows away empty,
And the [1]strength of the fatherless
was crushed.
10 Therefore snares *are* all around you,
And sudden fear troubles you,
11 Or darkness *so that* you cannot see;
And an abundance of [a]water covers you.

12 "Is not God in the height of heaven?
And see the highest stars, how lofty they are!
13 And you say, [a]'What does God know?
Can He judge through the deep darkness?
14 [a]Thick clouds cover Him,
so that He cannot see,
And He walks above the circle of heaven.'
15 Will you keep to the old way
Which wicked men have trod,
16 Who [a]were cut down before their time,
Whose foundations were swept away
by a flood?
17 [a]They said to God, 'Depart from us!
What can the Almighty do to [1]them?'
18 Yet He filled their houses with good *things;*
But the counsel of the wicked is far from me.

19 "The[a] righteous see *it* and are glad,
And the innocent laugh at them:
20 'Surely our [1]adversaries are cut down,
And the fire consumes their remnant.'

**21** "Now acquaint yourself with Him,
and [a]be at peace;
Thereby good will come to you.
22 Receive, please, [a]instruction from His mouth,
And [b]lay up His words in your heart.
23 If you return to the Almighty,
you will be built up;
You will remove iniquity far from your tents.
24 Then you will [a]lay your gold in the dust,
And the *gold* of Ophir among the stones of
the brooks.
25 Yes, the Almighty will be your [1]gold
And your precious silver;
26 For then you will have your [a]delight
in the Almighty,
And lift up your face to God.
27 [a]You will make your prayer to Him,
He will hear you,
And you will pay your vows.
28 You will also declare a thing,
And it will be established for you;
So light will shine on your ways.
29 When they cast *you* down, and you say,
'Exaltation *will come!*'
Then [a]He will save the humble *person.*
30 He will *even* deliver one who is not innocent;
Yes, he will be delivered by the purity of
your hands."

## *God Knows Men's Ways*

**23** Then Job answered and said:

2 "Even today my [a]complaint is bitter;
[1]My hand is listless because of my groaning.
3 [a]Oh, that I knew where I might find Him,
*That* I might come to His seat!
4 I would present *my* case before Him,
And fill my mouth with arguments.
5 I would know the words *which* He would
answer me,
And understand what He would say to me.
6 [a]Would He contend with me in His great
power?
No! But He would take *note* of me.
7 There the upright could reason with Him,
And I would be delivered forever
from my Judge.

8 "Look,[a] I go forward, but He is not *there,*
And backward, but I cannot perceive Him;
9 When He works on the left hand,
I cannot behold *Him;*
When He turns to the right hand,
I cannot see *Him.*
10 But [a]He knows the way that I take;
*When* [b]He has tested me,
I shall come forth as gold.
11 [a]My foot has held fast to His steps;
I have kept His way and not turned aside.
12 I have not departed from the [a]commandment
of His lips;
[b]I have treasured the words of His mouth
More than my [1]necessary *food.*

13 "But He *is* unique,
and who can make Him change?
And *whatever* [a]His soul desires, *that* He does.
14 For He performs *what is* [a]appointed for me,
And many such *things are* with Him.
15 Therefore I am terrified at His presence;
When I consider *this,* I am afraid of Him.
16 For God [a]made my heart weak,
And the Almighty terrifies me;
17 Because I was not [a]cut off [1]from the
presence of darkness,
And He did *not* hide deep darkness
from my face.

## *Job Complains of the Violence on the Earth*

**24** "*Since* [a]times are not hidden from
the Almighty,
Why do those who know Him see
not His [b]days?

2 "*Some* remove [a]landmarks;
They seize flocks violently and feed
*on them;*
3 They drive away the donkey
of the fatherless;
They [a]take the widow's ox as a pledge.
4 They push the needy off the road;
All the [a]poor of the land are forced to hide.
5 Indeed, *like* wild donkeys in the desert,
They go out to their work,
searching for food.
The wilderness *yields* food for them *and* for
*their* children.
6 They gather their fodder in the field
And glean in the vineyard of the wicked.
7 They [a]spend the night naked,
without clothing,
And have no covering in the cold.
8 They are wet with the showers
of the mountains,
And [a]huddle around the rock
for want of shelter.

9 "*Some* snatch the fatherless from the breast,
And take a pledge from the poor.
10 They cause *the poor* to go naked,
without [a]clothing;
And they take away the sheaves
from the hungry.

**8** [1]Lit. *man of arm*
**9** [1]Lit. *arms*
**11** [a]Job 38:34; Ps. 69:1, 2; 124:5; Lam. 3:54
**13** [a]Ps. 73:11
**14** [a]Ps. 139:11, 12
**16** [a]Job 14:19; 15:32; Ps. 90:5; Is. 28:2; Matt. 7:26, 27
**17** [a]Job 21:14, 15 [1]LXX, Syr. *us*
**19** [a]Ps. 52:6; 58:10; 107:42
**20** [1]LXX *substance is*
**21** [a][Ps. 34:10]; Is. 27:5
**22** [a]Job 6:10; 23:12; Prov. 2:6 [b][Ps. 119:11]
**24** [a]2 Chr. 1:15
**25** [1]Ancient vss. suggest *defense;* MT *gold,* and v. 24
**26** [a]Job 27:10; Ps. 37:4; Is. 58:14
**27** [a]Job 11:13; 33:26; [Is. 58:9–11]
**29** [a]Job 5:11; [Matt. 23:12; James 4:6; 1 Pet. 5:5]

CHAPTER 23
**2** [a]Job 7:11 [1]So with MT, Tg., Vg.; LXX, Syr. *His*
**3** [a]Job 13:3, 18; 16:21; 31:35
**6** [a]Is. 57:16
**8** [a]Job 9:11; 35:14
**10** [a][Ps. 1:6; 139:1–3] [b][Ps. 17:3; 66:10; James 1:12]
**11** [a]Job 31:7; Ps. 17:5
**12** [a]Job 6:10; 22:22 [b]Ps. 44:18 [1]Lit. *appointed portion*
**13** [a][Ps. 115:3]
**14** [a][1 Thess. 3:2–4]
**16** [a]Ps. 22:14
**17** [a]Job 10:18, 19 [1]Or *by* or *before*

CHAPTER 24
**1** [a][Acts 1:7] [b][Is. 2:12]; Jer. 46:10; [Obad. 15]; Zeph. 1:7
**2** [a][Deut. 19:14; 27:17]; Prov. 22:28; 23:10; Hos. 5:10
**3** [a][Deut. 24:6, 10, 12, 17]; Job 22:6, 9
**4** [a]Job 29:16; Prov. 28:28
**7** [a]Ex. 22:26, 27; [Deut. 24:12, 13]; Job 22:6; [James 2:15, 16]
**8** [a]Lam. 4:5
**10** [a]Job 31:19

11 They press out oil within their walls,
And tread winepresses, yet suffer thirst.
12 The dying groan in the city,
And the souls of the wounded cry out;
Yet God does not charge *them* with wrong.

**13** "There are those who rebel against the light;
They do not know its ways
Nor abide in its paths.
14 [a]The murderer rises with the light;
He kills the poor and needy;
And in the night he is like a thief.
15 [a]The eye of the adulterer waits
for the twilight,
[b]Saying, 'No eye will see me';
And he [1]disguises *his* face.
16 In the dark they break into houses
Which they marked for themselves
in the daytime;
[a]They do not know the light.
17 For the morning is the same to them
as the shadow of death;
If *someone* recognizes *them,*
*They are in* the terrors of the shadow
of death.

18 "They *should be* swift on the face
of the waters,
Their portion *should be* cursed in the earth,
*So that* no *one would* turn into the way
of their vineyards.
19 As drought and heat [1]consume
the snow waters,
*So* [2]the grave *consumes those who* have
sinned.
20 The womb *should* forget him,
The worm *should* feed sweetly on him;
[a]He *should* be remembered no more,
And wickedness *should* be broken like a tree.
21 For he [1]preys on the barren *who* do not bear,
And does no good for the widow.

**22** "But *God* draws the mighty away
with His power;
He rises up, but no *man* is sure of life.
23 He gives them security, and they rely *on it;*
Yet [a]His eyes *are* on their ways.
24 They are exalted for a little while,
Then they are gone.
They are brought low;
They are [1]taken out of the way
like all *others;*
They dry out like the heads of grain.

**25** "Now if *it is* not *so,* who will prove me a liar,
And make my speech worth nothing?"

## *How Can Man Be Justified with God?*

**25** Then [a]Bildad the Shuhite answered and said:

2 "Dominion and fear *belong* to Him;
He makes peace in His high places.
3 [1]Is there any number to His armies?
Upon whom does [a]His light not rise?
4 [a]How then can man be righteous before God?
Or how can he be [b]pure *who is* born
of a woman?
5 If even the moon does not shine,
And the stars are not pure in His [a]sight,
6 How much less man, *who is* [a]a maggot,
And a son of man, *who is* a worm?"

## *Job Rebukes Bildad and Praises God*

**26** But Job answered and said:

2 "How have you helped *him who is* without
power?
*How* have you saved the arm *that has*
no strength?
3 How have you counseled *one who has*
no wisdom?
And *how* have you declared sound advice
to many?
4 To whom have you uttered words?
And whose spirit came from you?

5 "The dead tremble,
Those under the waters
and those inhabiting them.
6 [a]Sheol *is* naked before Him,
And Destruction has no covering.
7 [a]He stretches out the north over empty space;
*He* hangs the earth on nothing.
8 [a]He binds up the water in His thick clouds,
Yet the clouds [1]are not broken under it.
9 He covers the face of *His* throne,
*And* spreads His cloud over it.
10 [a]He drew a circular horizon on the face
of the waters,
At the boundary of light and darkness.
11 The pillars of heaven tremble,
And are [1]astonished at His rebuke.
12 [a]He stirs up the sea with His power,
And by His understanding He breaks up
[1]the storm.
13 [a]By His Spirit He adorned the heavens;
His hand pierced [b]the fleeing serpent.
14 Indeed these *are* the mere edges of His ways,
And how small a whisper we hear of Him!
But the thunder of His power
who can understand?"

## *The Hypocrite's Hopelessness*

**27** Moreover Job continued his discourse, and said:

2 "*As* God lives, [a]*who* has taken away
my justice,
And the Almighty, *who* has
made my soul bitter,
3 As long as my breath *is* in me,
And the breath of God in my nostrils,
4 My lips will not speak wickedness,
Nor my tongue utter deceit.
5 Far be it from me
That I should say you are right;
Till I die [a]I will not put away my
integrity from me.
6 My righteousness I [a]hold fast,
and will not let it go;
[b]My heart shall not [1]reproach *me*
as long as I live.

7 "May my enemy be like the wicked,
And he who rises up against me like the
unrighteous.
8 [a]For what is the hope of the hypocrite,
Though he may gain *much,*
If God takes away his life?
9 [a]Will God hear his cry
When trouble comes upon him?
10 [a]Will he delight himself in the Almighty?
Will he always call on God?

---

**14** [a]Ps. 10:8
**15** [a]Prov. 7:7–10 [b]Ps. 10:11 [1]Lit. *puts a covering on his face*
**16** [a][John 3:20]
**19** [1]Lit. *seize* [2]Or *sheol*
**20** [a]Job 18:17; Ps. 34:16; Prov. 10:7
**21** [1]Lit. *feeds on*
**23** [a]Ps. 11:4; [Prov. 15:3]
**24** [1]Lit. *gathered up*

CHAPTER 25

**1** [a]Job 8:1; 18:1
**3** [a]James 1:17 [1]Can His armies be counted?
**4** [a]Job 4:17; 15:14; Ps. 130:3; 143:2 [b][Job 14:4]
**5** [a]Job 15:15
**6** [a]Ps. 22:6

CHAPTER 26

**6** [a][Ps. 139:8]; Prov. 15:11; [Heb. 4:13]
**7** [a]Job 9:8; Ps. 24:2; 104:2
**8** [a]Job 37:11; Prov. 30:4 [1]*do not break*
**10** [a][Job 38:1–11]; Ps. 33:7; 104:9; Prov. 8:29; Jer. 5:22
**11** [1]*amazed*
**12** [a]Ex. 14:21; Job 9:13; Is. 51:15; [Jer. 31:35] [1]Lit. *rahab*
**13** [a][Job 9:8]; Ps. 33:6 [b]Is. 27:1

CHAPTER 27

**2** [a]Job 34:5
**5** [a]Job 2:9; 13:15
**6** [a]Job 2:3; 33:9 [b]Acts 24:16 [1]*reprove*
**8** [a]Matt. 16:26; Luke 12:20
**9** [a]Job 35:12, 13; Ps. 18:41; Prov. 1:28; 28:9; [Is. 1:15]; Jer. 14:12; Ezek. 8:18; [Mic. 3:4; John 9:31; James 4:3]
**10** [a]Job 22:26, 27; [Ps. 37:4; Is. 58:14]

11 "I will teach you [1]about the hand of God;
What *is* with the Almighty I will not conceal.
12 Surely all of you have seen *it;*
Why then do you behave with complete
nonsense?

**13** "This[a] is the portion of a wicked man
with God,
And the heritage of oppressors, received
from the Almighty:
14 [a]If his children are multiplied, *it is*
for the sword;
And his offspring shall not be satisfied
with bread.
15 Those who survive him shall be
buried in death,
And [a]their[1] widows shall not weep,
16 Though he heaps up silver like dust,
And piles up clothing like clay—
17 He may pile *it* up, but [a]the just will wear *it,*
And the innocent will divide the silver.
18 He builds his house like a [1]moth,
[a]Like a [2]booth *which* a watchman makes.
19 The rich man will lie down,
[1]But not be gathered *up;*
He opens his eyes,
And he *is* [a]no more.
20 [a]Terrors overtake him like a flood;
A tempest steals him away in the night.
21 The east wind carries him away,
and he is gone;
It sweeps him out of his place.
22 It hurls against him and does not [a]spare;
He flees desperately from its [1]power.
23 *Men* shall clap their hands at him,
And shall hiss him out of his place.

## *Wisdom Is God's Gift*

**28** "Surely there is a mine for silver,
And a place *where* gold is refined.
2 Iron is taken from the [1]earth,
And copper *is* smelted *from* ore.
3 *Man* puts an end to darkness,
And searches every recess
For ore in the darkness and the
shadow of death.
4 He breaks open a shaft away
from people;
*In places* forgotten by feet
They hang far away from men;
They swing to and fro.
5 *As for* the earth, from it comes bread,
But underneath it is turned up as by fire;
6 Its stones *are* the source of sapphires,
And it contains gold dust.
7 *That* path no bird knows,
Nor has the falcon's eye seen it.
8 The [1]proud lions have not trodden it,
Nor has the fierce lion passed over it.
9 He puts his hand on the flint;
He overturns the mountains [1]at the roots.
10 He cuts out channels in the rocks,
And his eye sees every precious thing.
11 He dams up the streams from trickling;
*What is* hidden he brings forth to light.

**12** "But[a] where can wisdom be found?
And where *is* the place of understanding?
13 Man does not know its [a]value,
Nor is it found in the land of the living.
14 [a]The deep says, '*It is* not in me';
And the sea says, '*It is* not with me.'
15 It [a]cannot be purchased for gold,
Nor can silver be weighed *for* its price.
16 It cannot be valued in the gold of Ophir,
In precious onyx or sapphire.
17 Neither [a]gold nor crystal can equal it,
Nor can it be exchanged for [1]jewelry
of fine gold.
18 No mention shall be made of [1]coral or quartz,
For the price of wisdom *is* above [a]rubies.
19 The topaz of Ethiopia cannot equal it,
Nor can it be valued in pure [a]gold.

**20** "From[a] where then does wisdom come?
And where *is* the place of understanding?
21 It is hidden from the eyes of all living,
And concealed from the birds of the [1]air.
22 [a]Destruction[1] and Death say,
'We have heard a report about it
with our ears.'
23 God understands its way,
And He knows its place.
24 For He looks to the ends of the earth,
*And* [a]sees under the whole heavens,
25 [a]To establish a weight for the wind,
And apportion the waters by measure.
26 When He [a]made a law for the rain,
And a path for the thunderbolt,
27 Then He saw [1]*wisdom* and declared it;
He prepared it, indeed, He searched it out.
28 And to man He said,
'Behold, [a]the fear of the Lord, that *is* wisdom,
And to depart from evil *is* understanding.' "

## *Job Speaks of Past Wealth*

**29** Job further continued his discourse, and
said:

2 "Oh, that I were as *in* months [a]past,
As *in* the days *when* God [b]watched over me;
3 [a]When His lamp shone upon my head,
*And when* by His light I walked *through*
darkness;
4 Just as I was in the days of my prime,
When [a]the friendly counsel of God *was*
over my tent;
5 When the Almighty *was* yet with me,
*When* my children *were* around me;
6 When [a]my steps were bathed with [1]cream,
And [b]the rock poured out rivers of oil for me!

7 "When I went out to the gate by the city,
*When* I took my seat in the open square,
8 The young men saw me and hid,
And the aged arose *and* stood;
9 The princes refrained from talking,
And [a]put *their* hand on their mouth;
10 The voice of nobles was hushed,
And their [a]tongue stuck to the roof
of their mouth.
11 When the ear heard, then it blessed me,
And when the eye saw, then it approved me;
12 Because [a]I delivered the poor who cried out,
The fatherless and *the one who* had
no helper.
13 The blessing of a perishing *man* came
upon me,
And I caused the widow's heart to sing
for joy.
14 [a]I put on righteousness, and it clothed me;
My justice *was* like a robe and a turban.

**11** [1]Or *by*
**13** [a]Job 20:29
**14** [a]Deut. 28:41; Esth. 9:10; Hos. 9:13
**15** [a]Ps. 78:64 [1]Lit. *his*
**17** [a]Prov. 28:8; [Eccl. 2:26]
**18** [a]Is. 1:8; Lam. 2:6 [1]So with MT, Vg.; LXX, Syr. *spider* (cf. 8:14); Tg. *decay* [2]Temporary shelter
**19** [a]Job 7:8, 21; 20:7 [1]So with MT, Tg.; LXX, Syr. *But shall not add* (i.e., do it again); Vg. *But take away nothing*
**20** [a]Job 18:11
**22** [a]Jer. 13:14; Ezek. 5:11; 24:14 [1]Lit. *hand*

CHAPTER 28
**2** [1]Lit. *dust*
**8** [1]Lit. *sons of pride,* figurative of the great lions
**9** [1]At the base
**12** [a]Eccl. 7:24
**13** [a]Prov. 3:15
**14** [a]Job 28:22
**15** [a]Prov. 3:13–15; 8:10, 11, 19
**17** [a]Prov. 8:10; 16:16 [1]*vessels*
**18** [a]Prov. 3:15; 8:11 [1]Heb. *ramoth*
**19** [a]Prov. 8:19
**20** [a]Job 28:12; [Ps. 111:10; Prov. 1:7; 9:10]
**21** [1]*heaven*
**22** [a]Job 28:14 [1]Heb. *Abaddon*
**24** [a][Ps. 11:4; 33:13, 14; 66:7; Prov. 15:3]
**25** [a]Ps. 135:7
**26** [a]Job 37:3; 38:25
**27** [1]Lit. *it*
**28** [a][Deut. 4:6; Ps. 111:10; Prov. 1:7; 9:10; Eccl. 12:13]

CHAPTER 29
**2** [a]Job 1:1–5 [b]Job 1:10
**3** [a]Job 18:6
**4** [a]Job 15:8; [Ps. 25:14; Prov. 3:32]
**6** [a]Gen. 49:11; Deut. 32:14; Job 20:17 [b]Deut. 32:13; Ps. 81:16 [1]MT *wrath;* ancient vss. and a few Heb. mss. *cream* and Job 20:17
**9** [a]Job 21:5
**10** [a]Ps. 137:6
**12** [a]Job 31:16–23; [Ps. 72:12; Prov. 21:13; 24:11]
**14** [a]Deut. 24:13; Job 27:5, 6; Ps. 132:9; [Is. 59:17; 61:10; Eph. 6:14]

15 I *was* [a]eyes to the blind,
And I *was* feet to the lame.
16 I *was* a father to the poor,
And [a]I searched out the case
*that* I did not know.
17 I broke [a]the fangs of the wicked,
And plucked the victim from his teeth.

18 "Then I said, [a]'I shall die in my nest,
And multiply *my* days as the sand.
19 [a]My root *is* spread out [b]to the waters,
And the dew lies all night on my branch.
20 My glory *is* fresh within me,
And my [a]bow is renewed in my hand.'

21 "*Men* listened to me and waited,
And kept silence for my counsel.
22 After my words they did not speak again,
And my speech settled on them *as dew.*
23 They waited for me *as* for the rain,
And they opened their mouth wide
*as* for [a]the spring rain.
24 *If* I mocked at them, they did not believe *it,*
And the light of my countenance
they did not cast down.
25 I chose the way for them, and sat as chief;
So I dwelt as a king in the army,
As one *who* comforts mourners.

### *Job's Wealth Now Poverty*

**30** "But now they mock at me,
*men* [1]younger than I,
Whose fathers I disdained to put with the
dogs of my flock.
2 Indeed, what *profit* is the strength
of their hands to me?
Their vigor has perished.
3 *They are* gaunt from want and famine,
Fleeing late to the wilderness,
desolate and waste,
4 Who pluck [1]mallow by the bushes,
And broom tree roots *for* their food.
5 They were driven out from among *men,*
They shouted at them as *at* a thief.
6 *They had* to live in the clefts of the [1]valleys,
*In* [2]caves of the earth and the rocks.
7 Among the bushes they brayed,
Under the nettles they nestled.
8 *They were* sons of fools,
Yes, sons of vile men;
They were scourged from the land.

9 "And[a] now I am their taunting song;
Yes, I am their byword.
10 They abhor me, they keep far from me;
They do not hesitate [a]to spit in my face.
11 Because [a]He has loosed [1]my bowstring and
afflicted me,
They have cast off restraint before me.
12 At *my* right *hand* the rabble arises;
They push away my feet,
And [a]they raise against me their ways of
destruction.
13 They break up my path,
They promote my calamity;
They have no helper.
14 They come as broad breakers;
Under the ruinous storm they roll along.
15 Terrors are turned upon me;
They pursue my honor as the wind,
And my prosperity has passed like a cloud.

16 "And[a] now my soul is [b]poured out because of
my *plight;*
The days of affliction take hold of me.
17 My bones are pierced in me at night,
And my gnawing pains take no rest.
18 By great force my garment is disfigured;
It binds me about as the collar of my coat.
19 He has cast me into the mire,
And I have become like dust and ashes.

**20** "I [a]cry out to You, but You do not
answer me;
I stand up, and You regard me.
21 *But* You have become cruel to me;
With the strength of Your hand
You [a]oppose me.
22 You lift me up to the wind
and cause me to ride *on it;*
You spoil my success.
23 For I know *that* You will bring me *to* death,
And *to* the house [a]appointed for all living.

**24** "Surely He would not stretch out *His* hand
against a heap of ruins,
If they cry out when He destroys *it.*
25 [a]Have I not wept for him who was in trouble?
Has *not* my soul grieved for the poor?
26 [a]But when I looked for good, evil came *to me;*
And when I waited for light,
then came darkness.
27 [1]My heart is in turmoil and cannot rest;
Days of affliction confront me.
28 [a]I go about mourning, but not in the sun;
I stand up in the assembly
*and* cry out for help.
29 [a]I am a brother of jackals,
And a companion of ostriches.
30 [a]My skin grows black and falls from me;
[b]My bones burn with fever.
31 My harp is *turned* to mourning,
And my flute to the voice of those
who weep.

### *Job Defends His Righteousness*

**31** "I have made a covenant with my eyes;
Why then should I [1]look upon a [a]young
woman?
2 For what *is* the [a]allotment of God
from above,
And the inheritance of the Almighty from
on high?
3 *Is* it not destruction for the wicked,
And disaster for the workers of iniquity?
4 [a]Does He not see my ways,
And count all my steps?

5 "If I have walked with falsehood,
Or if my foot has hastened to deceit,
6 [1]Let me be weighed on honest scales,
That God may know my [a]integrity.
7 If my step has turned from the way,
Or [a]my heart walked after my eyes,
Or if any spot adheres to my hands,
8 *Then* [a]let me sow, and another eat;
Yes, let my harvest be [1]rooted out.

9 "If my heart has been enticed by a woman,
Or *if* I have lurked at my neighbor's door,
10 *Then* let my wife grind for [a]another,
And let others bow down over her.
11 For that *would be* wickedness;

**15** [a]Num. 10:31
**16** [a]Prov. 29:7
**17** [a]Ps. 58:6; Prov. 30:14
**18** [a]Ps. 30:6
**19** [a]Job 18:16 [b]Ps. 1:3; [Jer. 17:7, 8]
**20** [a]Gen. 49:24; Ps. 18:34
**23** [a][Zech. 10:1]

CHAPTER 30

**1** [1]Lit. *of fewer days*
**4** [1]A plant of the salty marshes
**6** [1]*wadis* [2]Lit. *holes*
**9** [a]Job 17:6; Ps. 69:12; Lam. 3:14, 63
**10** [a]Num. 12:14; Deut. 25:9; Job 17:6; Is. 50:6; Matt. 26:67; 27:30
**11** [a]Job 12:18 [1]So with MT, Syr., Tg.; LXX, Vg. *His*
**12** [a]Job 19:12
**16** [a]Ps. 42:4 [b]Ps. 22:14; Is. 53:12
**20** [a]Job 19:7
**21** [a]Job 10:3; 16:9, 14; 19:6, 22
**23** [a][Heb. 9:27]
**25** [a]Ps. 35:13, 14; Rom. 12:15
**26** [a]Job 3:25, 26; Jer. 8:15
**27** [1]*I seethe inside*
**28** [a]Job 30:31; Ps. 38:6; 42:9; 43:2
**29** [a]Ps. 44:19; 102:6; Mic. 1:8
**30** [a]Ps. 119:83; Lam. 4:8; 5:10 [b]Ps. 102:3

CHAPTER 31

**1** [a][Matt. 5:28] [1]*look intently* or *gaze*
**2** [a]Job 20:29
**4** [a][2 Chr. 16:9]; Job 24:23; 28:24; 34:21; 36:7; [Prov. 5:21; 15:3; Jer. 32:19]
**6** [a]Job 23:10; 27:5, 6 [1]Lit. *Let Him weigh me*
**7** [a]Num. 15:39; [Eccl. 11:9]; Ezek. 6:9; [Matt. 5:29]
**8** [a]Lev. 26:16; Deut. 28:30, 38; Job 20:18; Mic. 6:15 [1]*uprooted*
**10** [a]Deut. 28:30; 2 Sam. 12:11; Jer. 8:10

Yes, [a]it *would be* iniquity *deserving of* judgment.
12 For that *would be* a fire *that* consumes to destruction,
And would root out all my increase.

13 "If I have [a]despised the cause of my male or female servant
When they complained against me,
14 What then shall I do when [a]God rises up?
When He punishes, how shall I answer Him?
15 [a]Did not He who made me in the womb make them?
Did not the same One fashion us in the womb?

16 "If I have kept the poor from *their* desire,
Or caused the eyes of the widow to [a]fail,
17 Or eaten my morsel by myself,
So that the fatherless could not eat of it
18 (But from my youth I reared him as a father,
And from my mother's womb
I guided [1]*the widow*);
19 If I have seen anyone perish for lack of clothing,
Or any poor *man* without covering;
20 If his [1]heart has not [a]blessed me,
And *if* he was *not* warmed with the fleece of my sheep;
21 If I have raised my hand [a]against the fatherless,
When I saw I had help in the gate;
22 *Then* let my arm fall from my shoulder,
Let my arm be torn from the socket.
23 For [a]destruction *from* God *is* a terror to me,
And because of His magnificence
I cannot endure.

24 "If[a] I have made gold my hope,
Or said to fine gold, '*You are* my confidence';
25 [a]If I have rejoiced because my wealth *was* great,
And because my hand had gained much;
26 [a]If I have observed the [1]sun when it shines,
Or the moon moving *in* brightness,
27 So that my heart has been secretly enticed,
And my mouth has kissed my hand;
28 This also *would be* an iniquity *deserving of* judgment,
For I would have denied God *who is* above.

29 "If[a] I have rejoiced at the destruction of him who hated me,
Or lifted myself up when evil found him
30 [a](Indeed I have not allowed my mouth to sin
By asking for a curse on his [1]soul);
31 If the men of my tent have not said,
'Who is there that has not been satisfied with his meat?'
32 [a](*But* no sojourner had to lodge in the street,
*For* I have opened my doors to the [1]traveler);
33 If I have covered my transgressions
[a]as[1] Adam,
By hiding my iniquity in my bosom,
34 Because I feared the great [a]multitude,
And dreaded the contempt of families,
So that I kept silence
*And* did not go out of the door—
35 [a]Oh, that I had one to hear me!
Here is my mark.
*Oh,* [b]*that* the Almighty would answer me,
*That* my [1]Prosecutor had written a book!
36 Surely I would carry it on my shoulder,
*And* bind it on me *like* a crown;
37 I would declare to Him the number of my steps;
Like a prince I would approach Him.

38 "If my land cries out against me,
And its furrows weep together;
39 If [a]I have eaten its [1]fruit without money,
Or [b]caused its owners to lose their lives;
40 *Then* let [a]thistles grow instead of wheat,
And weeds instead of barley."

The words of Job are ended.

### *Elihu Contradicts Job's Friends*

**32** So these three men ceased answering Job,
because he *was* [a]righteous in his own eyes.
2 Then the wrath of Elihu, the son of Barachel
the [a]Buzite, of the family of Ram, was aroused
against Job; his wrath was aroused because he
[b]justified himself rather than God.
3 Also against his three friends his wrath was
aroused, because they had found no answer, and
*yet* had condemned Job.
4 Now because they *were* years older than he,
Elihu had waited [1]to speak to Job.
5 When Elihu saw that *there was* no answer in
the mouth of these three men, his wrath was
aroused.
6 So Elihu, the son of Barachel the Buzite,
answered and said:

"I *am* [a]young in years, and you *are* very old;
Therefore I was afraid,
And dared not declare my opinion to you.
7 I said, [1]'Age should speak,
And multitude of years should teach wisdom.'
8 But *there is* a spirit in man,
And [a]the breath of the Almighty gives him understanding.
9 [a]Great[1] men are not *always* wise,
Nor do the aged *always* understand justice.

10 "Therefore I say, 'Listen to me,
I also will declare my opinion.'
11 Indeed I waited for your words,
I listened to your reasonings,
while you searched out what to say.
12 I paid close attention to you;
And surely not one of you convinced Job,
*Or* answered his words—
13 [a]Lest you say,
'We have found wisdom';
God will vanquish him, not man.
14 Now he has not [1]directed *his* words against me;
So I will not answer him with your words.

15 "They are dismayed and answer no more;
Words escape them.
16 And I have waited,
because they did not speak,
Because they stood still
*and* answered no more.
17 I also will answer my part,
I too will declare my opinion.
18 For I am full of words;
The spirit within me compels me.
19 Indeed my [1]belly *is* like wine *that* has no [2]vent;
It is ready to burst like new wineskins.
20 I will speak, that I may find relief;
I must open my lips and answer.

**11** [a]Gen. 38:24; [Lev. 20:10; Deut. 22:22]; Job 31:28
**13** [a][Deut. 24:14, 15]
**14** [a][Ps. 44:21]
**15** [a]Job 34:19; Prov. 14:31; 22:2; [Mal. 2:10]
**16** [a]Job 29:12
**18** [1]Lit. *her*
**20** [a][Deut. 24:13] [1]Lit. *loins*
**21** [a]Job 22:9
**23** [a]Is. 13:6
**24** [a][Matt. 6:19, 20; Mark 10:23–25]
**25** [a]Job 1:3, 10; Ps. 62:10
**26** [a][Deut. 4:19; 17:3]; Ezek. 8:16 [1]Lit. *light*
**29** [a][Prov. 17:5; 24:17]; Obad. 12
**30** [a][Matt. 5:44] [1]Or *life*
**32** [a]Gen. 19:2, 3 [1]So with LXX, Syr., Tg., Vg.; MT *road*
**33** [a]Gen. 3:10; [Prov. 28:13] [1]Or *as men do*
**34** [a]Ex. 23:2
**35** [a]Job 19:7; 30:20, 24, 28 [b]Job 13:22, 24; 33:10 [1]Lit. *Accuser*
**39** [a]Job 24:6, 10–12; [James 5:4] [b]1 Kin. 21:19 [1]Lit. *strength*
**40** [a]Gen. 3:18

CHAPTER 32
**1** [a]Job 6:29; 31:6; 33:9
**2** [a]Gen. 22:21 [b]Job 27:5, 6
**4** [1]Vg. *till Job had spoken*
**6** [a]Lev. 19:32
**7** [1]Lit. *Days,* years
**8** [a]1 Kin. 3:12; 4:29; [Job 35:11; 38:36; Prov. 2:6; Eccl. 2:26; Dan. 1:17; 2:21; Matt. 11:25; James 1:5]
**9** [a][1 Cor. 1:26] [1]Or *Men of many years*
**13** [a][Jer. 9:23; 1 Cor. 1:29]
**14** [1]*ordered*
**19** [1]*bosom* [2]*opening*

21 Let me not, I pray,
show partiality to anyone;
Nor let me flatter any man.
22 For I do not know how to flatter,
*Else* my Maker would soon take me [a]away.

### *Elihu Contradicts Job*

**33** "But please, Job, hear my speech,
And listen to all my words.
2 Now, I open my mouth;
My tongue speaks in my mouth.
3 My words *come* from my upright heart;
My lips utter pure knowledge.
4 [a]The Spirit of God has made me,
And the breath of the Almighty gives me life.
5 If you can answer me,
Set *your words* in order before me;
Take your stand.
6 [a]Truly I *am* [1]as your spokesman before God;
I also have been formed out of clay.
7 [a]Surely no fear of me will terrify you,
Nor will my hand be heavy on you.

8 "Surely you have spoken [1]in my hearing,
And I have heard the sound of *your* words,
*saying,*
9 'I[a] *am* pure, without transgression;
I *am* innocent, and *there is* no iniquity in me.
10 Yet He finds occasions against me,
[a]He counts me as His enemy;
11 [a]He puts my feet in the stocks,
He watches all my paths.'

12 "Look, *in* this you are not righteous.
I will answer you,
For God is greater than man.
13 Why do you [a]contend with Him?
For He does not give an accounting
of any of His words.
14 [a]For God may speak in one way,
or in another,
*Yet man* does not perceive it.
15 [a]In a dream, in a vision of the night,
When deep sleep falls upon men,
While slumbering on their beds,
16 [a]Then He opens the ears of men,
And seals their instruction.
17 In order to turn man *from his* deed,
And conceal pride from man,
18 He keeps back his soul from the Pit,
And his life from [1]perishing by the sword.

19 "*Man* is also chastened with pain on his [a]bed,
And with strong *pain* in many of his bones,
20 [a]So that his life abhors [b]bread,
And his soul [1]succulent food.
21 His flesh wastes away from sight,
And his bones stick out *which once*
were not seen.
22 Yes, his soul draws near the Pit,
And his life to the executioners.

23 "If there is a messenger for him,
A mediator, one among a thousand,
To show man His uprightness,
24 Then He is gracious to him, and says,
'Deliver him from going down to the Pit;
I have found [1]a ransom';
25 His flesh shall be young like a child's,
He shall return to the days of his youth.
26 He shall pray to God,
and He will delight in him,

22 [a]Job 27:8

CHAPTER 33

4 [a][Gen. 2:7]; Job 32:8
6 [a]Job 4:19 [1]Lit. *as your mouth*
7 [a]Job 9:34
8 [1]Lit. *in my ears*
9 [a]Job 10:7
10 [a]Job 13:24; 16:9
11 [a]Job 13:27; 19:8
13 [a]Job 40:2; [Is. 45:9]
14 [a]Job 33:29; 40:5; Ps. 62:11
15 [a][Num. 12:6]
16 [a][Job 36:10, 15]
18 [1]Lit. *passing*
19 [a]Job 30:17
20 [a]Ps. 107:18 [b]Job 3:24; 6:7 [1]*desirable*
24 [1]*an atonement*
27 [a][2 Sam. 12:13; Prov. 28:13; Luke 15:21; 1 John 1:9] [b][Rom. 6:21]
28 [a]Is. 38:17 [1]Kt. *my*
30 [a]Ps. 56:13
33 [a]Ps. 34:11 [1]*Keep silent*

CHAPTER 34

3 [a]Job 6:30; 12:11
5 [a]Job 13:18; 33:9 [b]Job 27:2
6 [a]Job 6:4; 9:17 [1]Lit. *arrow*
7 [a]Job 15:16 [1]*derision*
9 [a]Mal. 3:14
10 [a][Gen. 18:25; Deut. 32:4; 2 Chr. 19:7]; Job 8:3; 36:23; Ps. 92:15; Rom. 9:14 [1]*men of heart*
11 [a]Job 34:25; Ps. 62:12; [Prov. 24:12; Jer. 32:19]; Ezek. 33:20; [Matt. 16:27]; Rom. 2:6; [2 Cor. 5:10; Rev. 22:12]
12 [a]Job 8:3
14 [a]Job 12:10; Ps. 104:29; [Eccl. 12:7]
15 [a][Gen. 3:19]; Job 10:9; [Eccl. 12:7]
17 [a]2 Sam. 23:3; Job 34:30 [b]Job 40:8
18 [a]Ex. 22:28
19 [a][Deut. 10:17; Acts 10:34; Rom. 2:11, 12] [b]Job 31:15

He shall see His face with joy,
For He restores to man His righteousness.
27 Then he looks at men and [a]says,
'I have sinned, and perverted *what was* right,
And it [b]did not profit me.'
28 He will [a]redeem [1]his soul from going down
to the Pit,
And [1]his life shall see the light.

29 "Behold, God works all these *things,*
Twice, *in fact,* three *times* with a man,
30 [a]To bring back his soul from the Pit,
That he may be enlightened with the
light of life.

31 "Give ear, Job, listen to me;
Hold your peace, and I will speak.
32 If you have anything to say, answer me;
Speak, for I desire to justify you.
33 If not, [a]listen to me;
[1]Hold your peace, and I will teach you
wisdom."

### *God Cannot Be Unjust*

**34** Elihu further answered and said:

2 "Hear my words, you wise *men;*
Give ear to me, you who have knowledge.
3 [a]For the ear tests words
As the palate tastes food.
4 Let us choose justice for ourselves;
Let us know among ourselves what *is* good.

5 "For Job has said, [a]'I am righteous,
But [b]God has taken away my justice;
6 [a]Should I lie concerning my right?
My [1]wound *is* incurable,
*though I am* without transgression.'
7 What man *is* like Job,
[a]*Who* drinks [1]scorn like water,
8 Who goes in company
with the workers of iniquity,
And walks with wicked men?
9 For [a]he has said, 'It profits a man nothing
That he should delight in God.'

10 "Therefore listen to me,
you [1]men of understanding:
[a]Far be it from God *to do* wickedness,
And *from* the Almighty to *commit* iniquity.
11 [a]For He repays man *according to* his work,
And makes man to find a reward according
to *his* way.
12 Surely God will never do wickedly,
Nor will the Almighty [a]pervert justice.
13 Who gave Him charge over the earth?
Or who appointed *Him over* the whole world?
14 If He should set His heart on it,
*If* He should [a]gather to Himself His Spirit
and His breath,
15 [a]All flesh would perish together,
And man would return to dust.

16 "If *you have* understanding, hear this;
Listen to the sound of my words:
17 [a]Should one who hates justice govern?
Will you [b]condemn *Him who is* most just?
18 [a]*Is it fitting* to say to a king,
'*You are* worthless,'
*And* to nobles, '*You are* wicked'?
19 Yet He [a]is not partial to princes,
Nor does He regard the rich
more than the poor;
For [b]they *are* all the work of His hands.

20 In a moment they die,
[a]in the middle of the night;
The people are shaken and pass away;
The mighty are taken away without a hand.

21 "For[a] His eyes *are* on the ways of man,
And He sees all his steps.
22 [a]There is no darkness nor shadow of death
Where the workers of iniquity may hide themselves.
23 For He need not further consider a man,
That he should go before God in judgment.
24 [a]He breaks in pieces mighty men without inquiry,
And sets others in their place.
25 Therefore He knows their works;
He overthrows *them* in the night,
And they are crushed.
26 He strikes them as wicked *men*
In the open sight of others,
27 Because they [a]turned back from Him,
And [b]would not consider any of His ways,
28 So that they [a]caused the cry
of the poor to come to Him;
For He [b]hears the cry of the afflicted.
29 When He gives quietness,
who then can make trouble?
And when He hides *His* face,
who then can see Him,
Whether *it is* against a nation
or a man alone?—
30 That the hypocrite should not reign,
Lest the people be ensnared.

**31** "For has *anyone* said to God,
'I have borne *chastening;*
I will offend no more;
32 Teach me *what* I do not see;
If I have done iniquity, I will do no more'?
33 Should He repay *it* according to your *terms,*
*Just* because you disavow it?
You must choose, and not I;
Therefore speak what you know.

34 "Men of understanding say to me,
Wise men who listen to me:
35 'Job[a] speaks without knowledge,
His words *are* without wisdom.'
36 Oh, that Job were tried to the utmost,
Because *his* answers *are like* those
of wicked men!
37 For he adds [a]rebellion to his sin;
He claps *his hands* among us,
And multiplies his words against God."

## *Man Is Not Good*

**35** Moreover Elihu answered and said:

2 "Do you think this is right?
Do you say,
'My righteousness is more than God's'?
3 For [a]you say,
'What advantage will it be to You?
What profit shall I have,
more than *if* I had sinned?'

**4** "I will answer you,
And [a]your companions with you.
5 [a]Look to the heavens and see;
And behold the clouds—
They are higher than you.
6 If you sin, what do you accomplish
[a]against Him?
Or, *if* your transgressions are multiplied,
what do you do to Him?
7 [a]If you are righteous, what do you give Him?
Or what does He receive from your hand?
8 Your wickedness affects a man such as you,
And your righteousness a son of man.

9 "Because[a] of the multitude of oppressions
they cry out;
They cry out for help because of the arm
of the mighty.
10 But no one says, [a]'Where *is* God my Maker,
[b]Who gives songs in the night,
11 Who [a]teaches us more than the beasts
of the earth,
And makes us wiser than the birds of
heaven?'
12 [a]There they cry out, but He does not answer,
Because of the pride of evil men.
13 [a]Surely God will not listen to empty *talk,*
Nor will the Almighty regard it.
14 [a]Although you say you do not see Him,
*Yet* justice *is* before Him,
and [b]you must wait for Him.
15 And now, because He has not [a]punished
in His anger,
Nor taken much notice of folly,
16 [a]Therefore Job opens his mouth in vain;
He multiplies words without knowledge."

## *Results of Job's Sins*

**36** Elihu also proceeded and said:

2 "Bear with me a little, and I will show you
That *there are* yet words to speak
on God's behalf.
3 I will fetch my knowledge from afar;
I will ascribe righteousness to my Maker.
4 For truly my words *are* not false;
One who is perfect in knowledge *is* with you.

5 "Behold, God *is* mighty, but despises *no one;*
[a]*He is* mighty in strength [1]of understanding.
6 He does not preserve the life of the wicked,
But gives justice to the [a]oppressed.
7 [a]He does not withdraw His eyes from the
righteous;
But [b]*they are* on the throne with kings,
For He has seated them forever,
And they are exalted.
8 And [a]if *they are* bound in [1]fetters,
Held in the cords of affliction,
9 Then He tells them their work and their
transgressions—
That they have acted [1]defiantly.
10 [a]He also opens their ear to [1]instruction,
And commands that they turn from iniquity.
11 If they obey and serve *Him,*
They shall [a]spend their days in prosperity,
And their years in pleasures.
12 But if they do not obey,
They shall perish by the sword,
And they shall die [1]without [a]knowledge.

**13** "But the hypocrites in heart [a]store up wrath;
They do not cry for help
when He binds them.
14 [a]They[1] die in youth,
And their life *ends* among the [2]perverted
persons.

**20** [a]Ex. 12:29; Job 34:25; 36:20
**21** [a][2 Chr. 16:9]; Job 31:4; Ps. 34:15; [Prov. 5:21; 15:3; Jer. 16:17; 32:19]
**22** [a][Ps. 139:11, 12; Amos 9:2, 3]
**24** [a]Job 12:19; [Dan. 2:21]
**27** [a]1 Sam. 15:11 [b]Ps. 28:5; Is. 5:12
**28** [a]Job 35:9; James 5:4 [b][Ex. 22:23]; Job 22:27
**35** [a]Job 35:16; 38:2
**37** [a]Job 7:11; 10:1

CHAPTER 35
**3** [a]Job 21:15; 34:9
**4** [a]Job 34:8
**5** [a]Gen. 15:5; [Job 22:12; Ps. 8:3]
**6** [a]Job 7:20; [Prov. 8:36; Jer. 7:19]
**7** [a]Job 22:2; Ps. 16:2; Prov. 9:12; [Luke 17:10]; Rom. 11:35
**9** [a]Job 34:28
**10** [a]Is. 51:13 [b]Job 8:21; Ps. 42:8; 77:6; 149:5; Acts 16:25
**11** [a]Job 36:22; Ps. 94:12; [Is. 48:17]; Jer. 32:33; [1 Cor. 2:13]
**12** [a]Prov. 1:28
**13** [a]Job 27:9; [Prov. 15:29; Is. 1:15]; Jer. 11:11; [Mic. 3:4]
**14** [a]Job 9:11 [b][Ps. 37:5, 6]
**15** [a]Ps. 89:32
**16** [a]Job 34:35; 38:2

CHAPTER 36
**5** [a]Job 12:13, 16; 37:23; [Ps. 99:2–5] [1]*of heart*
**6** [a]Job 5:15
**7** [a][Ps. 33:18; 34:15] [b]Job 5:11; Ps. 113:8
**8** [a]Ps. 107:10 [1]*chains*
**9** [1]*proudly*
**10** [a]Job 33:16; 36:15 [1]*discipline*
**11** [a]Job 21:13; [Is. 1:19, 20]
**12** [a]Job 4:21 [1]MT *as one without knowledge*
**13** [a][Rom. 2:5]
**14** [a]Ps. 55:23 [1]Lit. *Their soul dies* [2]Heb. *qedeshim,* those practicing sodomy or prostitution in religious rituals

15 He delivers the poor in their affliction,
And opens their ears in oppression.

16 "Indeed He would have brought you
out of dire distress,
[a]*Into* a broad place where *there*
*is* no restraint;
And [b]what is set on your table
*would be* full of [c]richness.
17 But you are filled with the judgment
due the [a]wicked;
Judgment and justice take hold *of you.*
18 Because *there is* wrath, *beware* lest He take
you away with *one* blow;
For [a]a large ransom would not help
you avoid *it.*
19 [a]Will your riches,
Or all the mighty forces,
Keep you from distress?
20 Do not desire the night,
When people are cut off in their place.
21 Take heed, [a]do not turn to iniquity,
For [b]you have chosen this rather than
affliction.

**22** "Behold, God is exalted by His power;
Who teaches like Him?
23 [a]Who has assigned Him His way,
Or who has said, 'You have done [b]wrong'?

**24** "Remember to [a]magnify His work,
Of which men have sung.
25 Everyone has seen it;
Man looks on *it* from afar.

26 "Behold, God *is* great,
and we [a]do not know *Him;*
[b]Nor can the number of His years
*be* discovered.
27 For He [a]draws up drops of water,
Which distill as rain from the mist,
28 [a]Which the clouds drop down
*And* pour abundantly on man.
29 Indeed, can *anyone* understand the
spreading of clouds,
The thunder from His canopy?
30 Look, He [a]scatters His light upon it,
And covers the depths of the sea.
31 For [a]by these He judges the peoples;
He [b]gives food in abundance.
32 [a]He covers *His* hands with lightning,
And commands it to [1]strike.
33 [a]His thunder declares it,
The cattle also, concerning [1]the rising *storm.*

### *God's Works and Wisdom*

**37** "At this also my heart trembles,
And leaps from its place.
2 Hear attentively the thunder of His voice,
And the rumbling *that* comes
from His mouth.
3 He sends it forth under the whole heaven,
His [1]lightning to the ends of the earth.
4 After it [a]a voice roars;
He thunders with His majestic voice,
And He does not restrain them when His
voice is heard.
5 God thunders marvelously with His voice;
[a]He does great things which we cannot
comprehend.
6 For [a]He says to the snow, 'Fall *on* the earth';

**16** [a]Ps. 18:19; 31:8; 118:5 [b]Ps. 23:5 [c]Ps. 36:8
**17** [a]Job 22:5, 10, 11
**18** [a]Ps. 49:7
**19** [a][Prov. 11:4]
**21** [a][Ps. 31:6; 66:18] [b][Heb. 11:25]
**23** [a]Job 34:13; [Is. 40:13, 14] [b]Job 8:3
**24** [a][Rev. 15:3]
**26** [a][1 Cor. 13:12] [b]Heb. 1:12
**27** [a]Ps. 147:8
**28** [a][Prov. 3:20]
**30** [a]Job 37:3
**31** [a][Acts 14:17] [b]Ps. 104:14, 15
**32** [a]Ps. 147:8 [1]*strike the mark*
**33** [a]1 Kin. 18:41 [1]Lit. *what is rising*

CHAPTER 37
**3** [1]Or *light*
**4** [a]Ps. 29:3
**5** [a]Job 5:9; 9:10; 36:26
**6** [a]Ps. 147:16, 17 [1]Lit. *shower of rain*
**7** [a]Ps. 109:27 [b]Ps. 19:3, 4
**8** [a]Ps. 104:21, 22
**10** [a]Ps. 147:17, 18
**11** [1]*clouds of light*
**12** [a]Job 36:32 [1]Lit. *the world of the earth*
**13** [a]Ex. 9:18, 23 [b]Job 38:26, 27 [c]1 Kin. 18:41–46 [1]Lit. *a rod*
**14** [a]Ps. 111:2
**15** [1]*places them*
**16** [a]Job 36:29 [b]Job 36:4
**18** [a][Is. 44:24] [b]Ps. 104:2
**23** [a][1 Tim. 6:16] [b][Job 9:4; 36:5]
**24** [a][Matt. 10:28] [b][Matt. 11:25]

CHAPTER 38
**1** [a]Ex. 19:16
**2** [a]Job 34:35; 42:3 [b]1 Tim. 1:7
**3** [a]Job 40:7 [1]Lit. *gird up your loins like*
**4** [a]Ps. 104:5
**5** [1]*measuring line*

Likewise to the [1]gentle rain and the heavy
rain of His strength.
7 He seals the hand of every man,
[a]That [b]all men may know His work.
8 The beasts [a]go into dens,
And remain in their lairs.
9 From the chamber *of the south*
comes the whirlwind,
And cold from the scattering winds
*of the north.*
10 [a]By the breath of God ice is given,
And the broad waters are frozen.
11 Also with moisture He saturates
the thick clouds;
He scatters His [1]bright clouds.
12 And they swirl about, being turned
by His guidance,
That they may [a]do whatever He
commands them
On the face of [1]the whole earth.
13 [a]He causes it to come,
Whether for [1]correction,
Or [b]for His land,
Or [c]for mercy.

**14** "Listen to this, O Job;
Stand still and [a]consider the wondrous
works of God.
15 Do you know when God [1]dispatches them,
And causes the light of His cloud to shine?
16 [a]Do you know how the clouds are balanced,
Those wondrous works of [b]Him
who is perfect in knowledge?
17 Why *are* your garments hot,
When He quiets the earth by the south *wind?*
18 With Him, have you [a]spread out the [b]skies,
Strong as a cast metal mirror?

19 "Teach us what we should say to Him,
*For* we can prepare nothing because
of the darkness.
20 Should He be told that I *wish to* speak?
If a man were to speak,
surely he would be swallowed up.
21 Even now *men* cannot look at the light *when*
*it is* bright in the skies,
When the wind has passed and cleared them.
22 He comes from the north *as* golden *splendor;*
With God *is* awesome majesty.
23 *As for* the Almighty, [a]we cannot find Him;
[b]*He is* excellent in power,
*In* judgment and abundant justice;
He does not oppress.
24 Therefore men [a]fear Him;
He shows no partiality to any
*who are* [b]wise of heart."

### *God Shows Job's Ignorance*

**38** Then the LORD answered Job [a]out of the
whirlwind, and said:
2 "Who[a] *is* this who darkens counsel
By [b]words without knowledge?
3 [a]Now [1]prepare yourself like a man;
I will question you, and you shall answer Me.

4 "Where[a] were you when I laid the foundations
of the earth?
Tell *Me,* if you have understanding.
5 Who determined its measurements?
Surely you know!
Or who stretched the [1]line upon it?
6 To what were its foundations fastened?
Or who laid its cornerstone,

7 When the morning stars sang together,
And all [a]the sons of God shouted for joy?

8 "Or[a] *who* shut in the sea with doors,
When it burst forth
*and* issued from the womb;
9 When I made the clouds its garment,
And thick darkness its swaddling band;
10 When [a]I fixed My limit for it,
And set bars and doors;
11 When I said,
'This far you may come, but no farther,
And here your proud waves [a]must stop!'

12 "Have you [a]commanded the morning since
your days *began*,
*And* caused the dawn to know its place,
13 That it might take hold of the ends
of the earth,
And [a]the wicked be shaken out of it?
14 It takes on form like clay *under* a seal,
And stands out like a garment.
15 From the wicked their [a]light is withheld,
And [b]the [1]upraised arm is broken.

16 "Have you [a]entered the springs of the sea?
Or have you walked in search of the depths?
17 Have [a]the gates of death been [1]revealed
to you?
Or have you seen the doors of the
shadow of death?
18 Have you comprehended the breadth
of the earth?
Tell *Me*, if you know all this.

19 "Where *is* the way *to* the dwelling of light?
And darkness, where *is* its place,
20 That you may take it to its territory,
That you may know the paths *to* its home?
21 Do you know *it*,
because you were born then,
Or *because* the number of your days *is* great?

22 "Have you entered [a]the treasury of snow,
Or have you seen the treasury of hail,
23 [a]Which I have reserved for the time
of trouble,
For the day of battle and war?
24 By what way is light [1]diffused,
*Or* the east wind scattered over the earth?

25 "Who [a]has divided a channel
for the overflowing *water*,
Or a path for the thunderbolt,
26 To cause it to rain on a land *where*
*there is* no one,
A wilderness in which *there is* no man;
27 [a]To satisfy the desolate waste,
And cause to spring forth the growth of
tender grass?
28 [a]Has the rain a father?
Or who has begotten the drops of dew?
29 From whose womb comes the ice?
And the [a]frost of heaven, who gives it birth?
30 The waters harden like stone,
And the surface of the deep is [a]frozen.[1]

31 "Can you bind the cluster of the [a]Pleiades,[1]
Or loose the belt of Orion?
32 Can you bring out [1]Mazzaroth in its season?
Or can you guide [2]the Great Bear
with its cubs?
33 Do you know [a]the ordinances
of the heavens?
Can you set their dominion over the earth?

34 "Can you lift up your voice to the clouds,
That an abundance of water may cover you?
35 Can you send out lightnings,
that they may go,
And say to you, 'Here we *are!*'?
36 [a]Who has put wisdom in [1]the mind?
Or who has given understanding
to the heart?
37 Who can number the clouds by wisdom?
Or who can pour out the bottles of heaven,
38 When the dust hardens in clumps,
And the clods cling together?

39 "Can[a] you hunt the prey for the lion,
Or satisfy the appetite of the young lions,
40 When they crouch in *their* dens,
*Or* lurk in their lairs to lie in wait?
41 [a]Who provides food for the raven,
When its young ones cry to God,
And wander about for lack of food?

### *God Continues to Challenge Job*

**39** "Do you know the time when the wild
[a]mountain goats bear young?
*Or* can you mark when [b]the deer gives birth?
2 Can you number the months *that* they fulfill?
Or do you know the time
when they bear young?
3 They bow down,
They bring forth their young,
They deliver their [1]offspring.
4 Their young ones are healthy,
They grow strong with grain;
They depart and do not return to them.

5 "Who set the wild donkey free?
Who loosed the bonds of the [1]onager,
6 [a]Whose home I have made the wilderness,
And the [1]barren land his dwelling?
7 He scorns the tumult of the city;
He does not heed the shouts of the driver.
8 The range of the mountains *is* his pasture,
And he searches after [a]every green thing.

9 "Will the [a]wild ox be willing to serve you?
Will he bed by your manger?
10 Can you bind the wild ox in the furrow
with ropes?
Or will he plow the valleys behind you?
11 Will you trust him because his strength
*is* great?
Or will you leave your labor to him?
12 Will you trust him to bring home your [1]grain,
And gather it to your threshing floor?

13 "The wings of the ostrich wave proudly,
But are her wings and pinions *like the* kindly
stork's?
14 For she leaves her eggs on the ground,
And warms them in the dust;
15 She forgets that a foot may crush them,
Or that a wild beast may break them.
16 She [a]treats her young harshly,
as though *they were* not hers;
Her labor is in vain, without [1]concern,
17 Because God deprived her of wisdom,
And did not [a]endow her with understanding.
18 When she lifts herself on high,
She scorns the horse and its rider.

19 "Have you given the horse strength?
Have you clothed his neck with [1]thunder?

**7** [a]Job 1:6
**8** [a]Gen. 1:9; Ps. 33:7; 104:9; Prov. 8:29; [Jer. 5:22]
**10** [a]Job 26:10
**11** [a][Ps. 89:9; 93:4]
**12** [a][Ps. 74:16; 148:5]
**13** [a]Job 34:25; Ps. 104:35
**15** [a]Job 18:5; [Prov. 13:9] [b][Num. 15:30]; Ps. 10:15; 37:17 [1]Lit. *high*
**16** [a][Ps. 77:19]; Prov. 8:24
**17** [a]Ps. 9:13 [1]Lit. *opened*
**22** [a]Ps. 135:7
**23** [a]Ex. 9:18; Josh. 10:11; Is. 30:30; Ezek. 13:11, 13; Rev. 16:21
**24** [1]Lit. *divided*
**25** [a]Job 28:26
**27** [a]Ps. 104:13, 14; 107:35
**28** [a]Job 36:27, 28; [Ps. 147:8; Jer. 14:22]
**29** [a][Job 37:10]; Ps. 147:16, 17
**30** [a][Job 37:10] [1]Lit. *imprisoned*
**31** [a]Job 9:9; Amos 5:8 [1]Or *the Seven Stars*
**32** [1]Lit. *Constellations* [2]Or *Arcturus*
**33** [a][Ps. 148:6]; Jer. 31:35, 36
**36** [a][Job 9:4; 32:8; Ps. 51:6; Eccl. 2:26; James 1:5] [1]Lit. *the inward parts*
**39** [a]Ps. 104:21
**41** [a]Ps. 147:9; [Matt. 6:26; Luke 12:24]

CHAPTER 39

**1** [a]Deut. 14:5; 1 Sam. 24:2; Ps. 104:18 [b]Ps. 29:9
**3** [1]Lit. *pangs*
**5** [1]A species of wild donkey
**6** [a]Job 24:5; Jer. 2:24; Hos. 8:9 [1]Lit. *salt land*
**8** [a]Gen. 1:29
**9** [a]Num. 23:22; Deut. 33:17; Ps. 22:21; 29:6; 92:10; Is. 34:7
**12** [1]Lit. *seed*
**16** [a]Lam. 4:3 [1]Lit. *fear*
**17** [a]Job 35:11
**19** [1]Or *a mane*

20 Can you [1]frighten him like a locust?
His majestic snorting strikes terror.
21 He paws in the valley,
and rejoices in *his* strength;
[a]He gallops into the clash of arms.
22 He mocks at fear, and is not frightened;
Nor does he turn back from the sword.
23 The quiver rattles against him,
The glittering spear and javelin.
24 He devours the distance with fierceness
and rage;
Nor does he come to a halt
because the trumpet *has* sounded.
25 At *the blast of* the trumpet he says, 'Aha!'
He smells the battle from afar,
The thunder of captains and shouting.

26 "Does the hawk fly by your wisdom,
*And* spread its wings toward the south?
27 Does the [a]eagle mount up at your command,
And [b]make its nest on high?
28 On the rock it dwells and resides,
On the crag of the rock and the stronghold.
29 From there it spies out the prey;
Its eyes observe from afar.
30 Its young ones suck up blood;
And [a]where the slain *are,* there it *is.*"

## *God's Power and Wisdom*

40 Moreover the LORD [a]answered Job, and said:

2 "Shall [a]the one who contends with the
Almighty correct *Him?*
He who [b]rebukes God, let him answer it."

3 Then Job answered the LORD and said:

4 "Behold,[a] I am vile;
What shall I answer You?
[b]I lay my hand over my mouth.
5 Once I have spoken, but I will not answer;
Yes, twice, but I will proceed no further."

6 [a]Then the LORD answered Job out of the
whirlwind, and said:

7 "Now[a] [1]prepare yourself like a man;
[b]I will question you, and you shall answer Me:

8 "Would[a] you indeed [1]annul My judgment?
Would you condemn Me
that you may be justified?
9 Have you an arm like God?
Or can you thunder with [a]a voice like His?
10 [a]Then adorn yourself *with* majesty and
splendor,
And array yourself with glory and beauty.
11 Disperse the rage of your wrath;
Look on everyone *who is* proud,
and humble him.
12 Look on everyone *who is* [a]proud,
*and* bring him low;
Tread down the wicked in their place.
13 Hide them in the dust together,
Bind their faces in hidden *darkness.*
14 Then I will also confess to you
That your own right hand can save you.

15 "Look now at the [1]behemoth,
which I made *along* with you;
He eats grass like an ox.
16 See now, his strength *is* in his hips,
And his power *is* in his stomach muscles.
17 He moves his tail like a cedar;
The sinews of his thighs are tightly knit.
18 His bones *are like* beams of bronze,
His ribs like bars of iron.
19 He *is* the first of the [a]ways of God;
Only He who made him can bring near His
sword.
20 Surely the mountains [a]yield food for him,
And all the beasts of the field play there.
21 He lies under the lotus trees,
In a covert of reeds and marsh.
22 The lotus trees cover him *with* their shade;
The willows by the brook surround him.
23 Indeed the river may rage,
*Yet* he is not disturbed;
He is confident, though the Jordan gushes
into his mouth,
24 *Though* he takes it in his eyes,
*Or* one pierces *his* nose with a snare.

## *God's Power in the Leviathan*

41 "Can you draw out [a]Leviathan[1]
with a hook,
Or *snare* his tongue with a line
*which* you lower?
2 Can you [a]put a reed through his nose,
Or pierce his jaw with a [1]hook?
3 Will he make many supplications to you?
Will he speak softly to you?
4 Will he make a covenant with you?
Will you take him as a servant forever?
5 Will you play with him as *with* a bird,
Or will you leash him for your maidens?
6 Will *your* companions [1]make a banquet
of him?
Will they apportion him among the
merchants?
7 Can you fill his skin with harpoons,
Or his head with fishing spears?
8 Lay your hand on him;
Remember the battle—
Never do it again!
9 Indeed, *any* hope of *overcoming* him is false;
Shall *one not* be overwhelmed at the sight
of him?
10 No one *is so* fierce that he would dare stir
him up.
Who then is able to stand against Me?
11 [a]Who has preceded Me,
that I should pay *him?*
[b]Everything under heaven is Mine.

12 "I will not [1]conceal his limbs,
His mighty power,
or his graceful proportions.
13 Who can [1]remove his outer coat?
Who can approach *him* with a double bridle?
14 Who can open the doors of his face,
*With* his terrible teeth all around?
15 *His* rows of [1]scales *are his* pride,
Shut up tightly *as with* a seal;
16 One is so near another
That no air can come between them;
17 They are joined one to another,
They stick together and cannot be parted.
18 His sneezings flash forth light,
And his eyes *are* like the eyelids
of the morning.
19 Out of his mouth go burning lights;
Sparks of fire shoot out.
20 Smoke goes out of his nostrils,
As *from* a boiling pot and burning rushes.

**20** [1]*make him spring*
**21** [a]Jer. 8:6
**27** [a]Prov. 30:18, 19 [b]Jer. 49:16; Obad. 4
**30** [a]Matt. 24:28; Luke 17:37

CHAPTER 40

**1** [a]Job 38:1
**2** [a]Job 9:3; 10:2; 33:13 [b]Job 13:3; 23:4
**4** [a]Ezra 9:6; Job 42:6 [b]Job 29:9; Ps. 39:9
**6** [a]Job 38:1
**7** [a]Job 38:3 [b]Job 42:4 [1]Lit. *gird up your loins*
**8** [a]Job 16:11; 19:6; [Ps. 51:4; Rom. 3:4] [1]*nullify*
**9** [a]Job 37:4; [Ps. 29:3, 4]
**10** [a]Ps. 93:1; 104:1
**12** [a]1 Sam. 2:7; [Is. 2:12; 13:11]; Dan. 4:37
**15** [1]A large animal, exact identity unknown
**19** [a]Job 26:14
**20** [a]Ps. 104:14

CHAPTER 41

**1** [a]Ps. 74:14; 104:26; Is. 27:1 [1]A large sea creature, exact identity unknown
**2** [a]2 Kin. 19:38; Is. 37:29 [1]*thorn*
**6** [1]Or *bargain over him*
**11** [a][Rom. 11:35] [b]Ex. 19:5; [Deut. 10:14; Job 9:5–10; 26:6–14]; Ps. 24:1; 50:12; 1 Cor. 10:26, 28
**12** [1]Lit. *keep silent about*
**13** [1]Lit. *take off the face of his garment*
**15** [1]Lit. *shields*

21 His breath kindles coals,
And a flame goes out of his mouth.
22 Strength dwells in his neck,
And [1]sorrow dances before him.
23 The folds of his flesh are joined together;
They are firm on him and cannot be moved.
24 His heart is as hard as stone,
Even as hard as the lower *millstone.*
25 When he raises himself up,
the mighty are afraid;
Because of his crashings they [1]are
beside themselves.
26 *Though* the sword reaches him,
it cannot avail;
Nor does spear, dart, or javelin.
27 He regards iron as straw,
*And* bronze as rotten wood.
28 The arrow cannot make him flee;
Slingstones become like stubble to him.
29 Darts are regarded as straw;
He laughs at the threat of javelins.
30 His undersides *are* like sharp potsherds;
He spreads pointed *marks* in the mire.
31 He makes the deep boil like a pot;
He makes the sea like a pot of ointment.
32 He leaves a shining wake behind him;
*One* would think the deep had white hair.
33 On earth there is nothing like him,
Which is made without fear.
34 He beholds every high *thing;*
He *is* king over all the children of pride."

## *God Blesses Job*

**42** Then Job answered the LORD and said:

2 "I know that You [a]can do everything,
And that no purpose *of Yours* can be
withheld from You.
3 *You asked,* [a]'Who *is* this who hides counsel
without knowledge?'
Therefore I have uttered
what I did not understand,
[b]Things too wonderful for me,
which I did not know.
4 Listen, please, and let me speak;
*You said,* [a]'I will question you,
and you shall answer Me.'
5 "I have [a]heard of You by the hearing
of the ear,
But now my eye sees You.
6 Therefore I [a]abhor[1] *myself,*
And repent in dust and ashes."

7 And so it was, after the LORD had spoken
these words to Job, that the LORD said to Eliphaz
the Temanite, "My wrath is aroused against you
and your two friends, for you have not spoken of
Me *what is* right, as My servant Job *has.*
8 "Now therefore, take for yourselves [a]seven
bulls and seven rams, [b]go to My servant Job, and
offer up for yourselves a burnt offering; and My
servant Job shall [c]pray for you. For I will accept
[1]him, lest I deal with you *according to your* folly;
because you have not spoken of Me *what is* right,
as My servant Job *has.*"
9 So Eliphaz the Temanite and Bildad the Shuhite *and* Zophar the Naamathite went and did as
the LORD commanded them; for the LORD had
[1]accepted Job.
10 [a]And the LORD [1]restored Job's losses when he
prayed for his friends. Indeed the LORD gave Job
[b]twice as much as he had before.
11 Then [a]all his brothers, all his sisters, and all
those who had been his acquaintances before,
came to him and ate food with him in his house;
and they consoled him and comforted him for all
the adversity that the LORD had brought upon
him. Each one gave him a piece of silver and each
a ring of gold.
12 Now the LORD blessed [a]the latter *days* of Job
more than his beginning; for he had [b]fourteen
thousand sheep, six thousand camels, one thousand yoke of oxen, and one thousand female
donkeys.
13 [a]He also had seven sons and three daughters.
14 And he called the name of the first [1]Jemimah,
the name of the second [2]Keziah, and the name of
the third [3]Keren-Happuch.
15 In all the land were found no women *so*
beautiful as the daughters of Job; and their father
gave them an inheritance among their brothers.
16 After this Job [a]lived one hundred and forty
years, and saw his children and grandchildren *for*
four generations.
17 So Job died, old and [a]full of days.

**22** [1]*despair*
**25** [1]Or *purify themselves*

CHAPTER 42

**2** [a]Gen. 18:14; [Matt. 19:26; Mark 10:27; 14:36; Luke 18:27]
**3** [a]Job 38:2 [b]Ps. 40:5; 131:1; 139:6
**4** [a]Job 38:3; 40:7
**5** [a]Job 26:14; [Rom. 10:17]
**6** [a]Ezra 9:6; Job 40:4 [1]*despise*
**8** [a]Num. 23:1 [b][Matt. 5:24] [c]Gen. 20:17; [James 5:15, 16; 1 John 5:16] [1]Lit. *his face*
**9** [1]Lit. *lifted up the face of Job*
**10** [a]Deut. 30:3; Ps. 14:7; 85:1–3; 126:1 [b]Is. 40:2 [1]Lit. *turned the captivity of Job,* what was captured from Job
**11** [a]Job 19:13
**12** [a]Job 1:10; 8:7; James 5:11 [b]Job 1:3
**13** [a]Job 1:2
**14** [1]Lit. *Handsome as the Day* [2]*Cassia,* a fragrance [3]Lit. *The Horn of Color* or *The Colorful Ray*
**16** [a]Job 5:26; Prov. 3:16
**17** [a]Gen. 15:15; 25:8; Job 5:26

*The Book of*

# PSALMS

## BOOK ONE
## Psalms 1–41

### PSALM 1

BLESSED [a]*is* the man
Who walks not in the counsel
of the [1]ungodly,
Nor stands in the path of sinners,
[b]Nor sits in the seat of the scornful;
2 But [a]his delight *is* in the law of the LORD,
[b]And in His law he [1]meditates day and
night.
3 He shall be like a tree
[a]Planted by the [1]rivers of water,
That brings forth its fruit in its season,
Whose leaf also shall not wither;
And whatever he does shall [b]prosper.

4 The ungodly *are* not so,
But *are* [a]like the chaff which the wind drives
away.
5 Therefore the ungodly shall not stand in the
judgment,
Nor sinners in the congregation of the
righteous.

6 For [a]the LORD knows the way of the
righteous,
But the way of the ungodly shall perish.

### PSALM 2

WHY [a]do the [1]nations [2]rage,
And the people plot a [3]vain thing?
2 The kings of the earth set themselves,
And the [a]rulers take counsel together,
Against the LORD and against His [b]Anointed,[1]
*saying,*
3 "Let [a]us break Their bonds in pieces
And cast away Their cords from us."

4 He who sits in the heavens [a]shall laugh;
The LORD shall hold them in derision.
5 Then He shall speak to them in His wrath,
And distress them in His deep displeasure:
6 "Yet I have [1]set My King
[2]On My holy hill of Zion."

7 "I will declare the [1]decree:
The LORD has said to Me,
[a]'You *are* My Son,
Today I have begotten You.
8 Ask of Me, and I will give *You*
The nations *for* Your inheritance,
And the ends of the earth *for* Your
possession.
9 [a]You shall [1]break them with a rod of iron;
You shall dash them to pieces like a potter's
vessel.' "

10 Now therefore, be wise, O kings;
Be instructed, you judges of the earth.
11 Serve the LORD with fear,
And rejoice with trembling.
12 [1]Kiss the Son, lest [2]He be angry,
And you perish *in* the way,
When [a]His wrath is kindled but a little.
[b]Blessed *are* all those who put their trust in
Him.

### PSALM 3

A Psalm of David [a]when he fled from Absalom his son.

LORD, how they have increased who trouble
me!
Many *are* they who rise up against me.
2 Many *are* they who say of me,
"*There is* no help for him in God." Selah

3 But You, O LORD, *are* [a]a shield [1]for me,
My glory and [b]the One who lifts up my head.
4 I cried to the LORD with my voice,
And [a]He heard me from His [b]holy hill. Selah

5 [a]I lay down and slept;
I awoke, for the LORD sustained me.
6 [a]I will not be afraid of ten thousands
of people
Who have set *themselves* against me all
around.

7 Arise, O LORD;
Save me, O my God!
[a]For You have struck all my enemies on the
cheekbone;
You have broken the teeth of the ungodly.
8 [a]Salvation *belongs* to the LORD.
Your blessing *is* upon Your people. Selah

### PSALM 4

To the [1]Chief Musician. With stringed instruments. A
Psalm of David.

HEAR me when I call,
O God of my righteousness!
You have relieved me in *my* distress;
[1]Have mercy on me, and hear my prayer.

2 How long, O you sons of men,
*Will you turn* my glory to shame?
*How long* will you love worthlessness
*And* seek falsehood? Selah
3 But know that [a]the LORD has [1]set apart for
Himself him who is godly;
The LORD will hear when I call to Him.

4 [a]Be[1] angry, and do not sin.
[b]Meditate within your heart on your bed, and
be still. Selah
5 Offer [a]the sacrifices of righteousness,
And [b]put your trust in the LORD.

6 *There are* many who say,
"Who will show us *any* good?"
[a]LORD, lift up the light of Your countenance
upon us.
7 You have put [a]gladness in my heart,
More than in the season that their grain and
wine increased.
8 [a]I will both lie down in peace, and sleep;
[b]For You alone, O LORD, make me dwell in
safety.

### PSALM 5

To the Chief Musician. With [1]flutes. A Psalm of David.

GIVE [a]ear to my words, O LORD,
Consider my [1]meditation.
2 Give heed to the voice of my cry,
My King and my God,
For to You I will pray.

PSALM 1
**1** [a]Prov. 4:14 [b]Jer. 15:17 [1]*wicked*
**2** [a]Ps. 119:14, 16, 35 [b][Josh. 1:8] [1]*ponders* by talking to himself
**3** [a]Jer. 17:8 [b]Gen. 39:2, 3, 23 [1]*channels*
**4** [a]Job 21:18
**6** [a]Ps. 37:18

PSALM 2
**1** [a]Acts 4:25, 26 [1]*Gentiles* [2]*throng tumultuously* [3]*worthless* or *empty*
**2** [a][Mark 3:6; 11:18] [b][John 1:41] [1]Christ, Commissioned One, Heb. *Messiah*
**3** [a]Luke 19:14
**4** [a]Ps. 37:13
**6** [1]Lit. *installed* [2]Lit. *Upon Zion, the hill of My holiness*
**7** [a][Heb. 1:5; 5:5] [1]Or *decree of the LORD: He said to Me*
**9** [a]Ps. 89:23; 110:5, 6 [1]So with MT, Tg.; LXX, Syr., Vg. *rule* (cf. Rev. 2:27)
**12** [a][Rev. 6:16, 17] [b][Ps. 5:11; 34:22] [1]LXX, Vg. *Embrace discipline;* Tg. *Receive instruction* [2]LXX *the LORD*

PSALM 3
**title** [a]2 Sam. 15:13–17
**3** [a]Ps. 5:12; 28:7 [b]Ps. 9:13; 27:6 [1]Lit. *around*
**4** [a]Ps. 4:3; 34:4 [b]Ps. 2:6; 15:1; 43:3
**5** [a]Lev. 26:6
**6** [a]Ps. 23:4; 27:3
**7** [a]Job 16:10
**8** [a][Is. 43:11]

PSALM 4
**title** [1]*Choir Director*
**1** [1]*Be gracious to me*
**3** [a][2 Tim. 2:19] [1]Many Heb. mss., LXX, Tg., Vg. *made wonderful*
**4** [a][Eph. 4:26] [b]Ps. 77:6 [1]Lit. *Tremble* or *Be agitated*
**5** [a]Deut. 33:19 [b]Ps. 37:3, 5; 62:8
**6** [a]Num. 6:26
**7** [a]Is. 9:3
**8** [a]Ps. 3:5 [b][Lev. 25:18]

PSALM 5
**title** [1]Heb. *nehiloth*
**1** [a]Ps. 4:1 [1]Lit. *groaning*

3 My voice You shall hear in the morning, O LORD;
[a]In the morning I will direct *it* to You,
And I will look up.

4 For You *are* not a God who takes pleasure in wickedness,
Nor shall evil [1]dwell with You.
5 The [a]boastful shall not [b]stand in Your sight;
You hate all workers of iniquity.
6 You shall destroy those who speak falsehood;
The LORD abhors the [a]bloodthirsty and deceitful man.

7 But as for me, I will come into Your house in the multitude of Your mercy;
In fear of You I will worship toward [1]Your holy temple.
8 [a]Lead me, O LORD, in Your righteousness because of my enemies;
Make Your way straight before my face.

9 For *there is* no [1]faithfulness in their mouth;
Their inward part *is* destruction;
[a]Their throat *is* an open tomb;
They flatter with their tongue.
10 Pronounce them guilty, O God!
Let them fall by their own counsels;
Cast them out in the multitude of their transgressions,
For they have rebelled against You.

11 But let all those rejoice who put their trust in You;
Let them ever shout for joy, because You [1]defend them;
Let those also who love Your name
Be joyful in You.
12 For You, O LORD, will bless the righteous;
With favor You will surround him as *with* a shield.

## PSALM 6

To the Chief Musician. With stringed instruments. [a]On [1]an eight-stringed harp. A Psalm of David.

O LORD, [a]do not rebuke me in Your anger,
Nor chasten me in Your hot displeasure.
2 Have mercy on me, O LORD, for I *am* weak;
O LORD, [a]heal me, for my bones are troubled.
3 My soul also is greatly [a]troubled;
But You, O LORD—how long?

4 Return, O LORD, deliver me!
Oh, save me for Your mercies' sake!
5 [a]For in death *there is* no remembrance of You;
In the grave who will give You thanks?

6 I am weary with my groaning;
[1]All night I make my bed swim;
I drench my couch with my tears.
7 [a]My eye wastes away because of grief;
It grows old because of all my enemies.

8 [a]Depart from me, all you workers of iniquity;
For the LORD has [b]heard the voice of my weeping.
9 The LORD has heard my supplication;
The LORD will receive my prayer.
10 Let all my enemies be ashamed and greatly troubled;
Let them turn back *and* be ashamed suddenly.

## PSALM 7

A [a]Meditation[1] of David, which he sang to the LORD [b]concerning the words of Cush, a Benjamite.

O LORD my God, in You I put my trust;
[a]Save me from all those who persecute me;
And deliver me,
2 [a]Lest they tear me like a lion,
[b]Rending *me* in pieces, while *there is* none to deliver.

3 O LORD my God, [a]if I have done this:
If there is [b]iniquity in my hands,
4 If I have repaid evil to him who was at peace with me,
Or [a]have plundered my enemy without cause,
5 Let the enemy pursue me and overtake *me;*
Yes, let him trample my life to the earth,
And lay my honor in the dust. Selah

6 Arise, O LORD, in Your anger;
[a]Lift Yourself up because of the rage of my enemies;
[b]Rise up [1]for me *to* the judgment You have commanded!
7 So the congregation of the peoples shall surround You;
For their sakes, therefore, return on high.
8 The LORD shall judge the peoples;
[a]Judge me, O LORD, [b]according to my righteousness,
And according to my integrity within me.

9 Oh, let the wickedness of the wicked come to an end,
But establish the just;
[a]For the righteous God tests the hearts and [1]minds.
10 [1]My defense *is* of God,
Who saves the [a]upright in heart.

11 God *is* a just judge,
And God is angry *with the wicked* every day.
12 If he does not turn back,
He will [a]sharpen His sword;
He bends His bow and makes it ready.
13 He also prepares for Himself instruments of death;
He makes His arrows into fiery shafts.

14 [a]Behold, *the wicked* brings forth iniquity;
Yes, he conceives trouble and brings forth falsehood.
15 He made a pit and dug it out,
[a]And has fallen into the ditch *which* he made.
16 [a]His trouble shall return upon his own head,
And his violent dealing shall come down on [1]his own crown.

17 I will praise the LORD according to His righteousness,
And will sing praise to the name of the LORD Most High.

## PSALM 8

To the Chief Musician. [1]On the instrument of Gath. A Psalm of David.

O LORD, our Lord,
How [a]excellent *is* Your name in all the earth,

---

**3** [a]Ps. 55:17; 88:13
**4** [1]Lit. *sojourn*
**5** [a][Hab. 1:13] [b]Ps. 1:5
**6** [a]Ps. 55:23
**7** [1]Lit. *the temple of Your holiness*
**8** [a]Ps. 25:4, 5; 27:11; 31:3
**9** [a]Rom. 3:13 [1]*uprightness*
**11** [1]*protect,* lit. *cover*

PSALM 6
**title** [a]Ps. 12:title [1]Heb. *sheminith*
**1** [a]Ps. 38:1; 118:18; [Jer. 10:24]
**2** [a]Ps. 41:4; 147:3; [Hos. 6:1]
**3** [a]Ps. 88:3; John 12:27
**5** [a]Ps. 30:9; 88:10–12; 115:17; [Eccl. 9:10]; Is. 38:18
**6** [1]Or *Every night*
**7** [a]Job 17:7; Ps. 31:9
**8** [a][Matt. 25:41] [b]Ps. 3:4; 28:6

PSALM 7
**title** [a]Hab. 3:1 [b]2 Sam. 16 [1]Heb. *Shiggaion*
**1** [a]Ps. 31:15
**2** [a]Ps. 57:4; Is. 38:13 [b]Ps. 50:22
**3** [a]2 Sam. 16:7 [b]1 Sam. 24:11
**4** [a]1 Sam. 24:7; 26:9
**6** [a]Ps. 94:2 [b]Ps. 35:23; 44:23 [1]So with MT, Tg., Vg.; LXX *O LORD my God*
**8** [a]Ps. 26:1; 35:24; 43:1 [b]Ps. 18:20; 35:24
**9** [a][1 Sam. 16:7] [1]Lit. *kidneys,* the most secret part of man
**10** [a]Ps. 97:10, 11; 125:4 [1]Lit. *My shield is upon God*
**12** [a]Deut. 32:41
**14** [a]Job 15:35; Is. 59:4; [James 1:15]
**15** [a][Job 4:8]; Ps. 57:6
**16** [a]Esth. 9:25; Ps. 140:9 [1]The crown of his own head

PSALM 8
**title** [1]Heb. *Al Gittith*
**1** [a]Ps. 148:13

Who have [b]set Your glory above the
heavens!

2 [a]Out of the mouth of babes and nursing
infants
You have [1]ordained strength,
Because of Your enemies,
That You may silence [b]the enemy and the
avenger.

3 When I [a]consider Your heavens,
the work of Your fingers,
The moon and the stars,
which You have ordained,
4 [a]What is man that You are mindful of him,
And the son of man that You [b]visit[1] him?
5 For You have made him a little lower than
[1]the angels,
And You have crowned him with glory and
honor.

6 [a]You have made him to have dominion over
the works of Your hands;
[b]You have put all *things* under his feet,
7 All sheep and oxen—
Even the beasts of the field,
8 The birds of the air,
And the fish of the sea
That pass through the paths of the seas.

9 [a]O LORD, our Lord,
How excellent *is* Your name in all the earth!

## PSALM 9

To the Chief Musician. To *the tune of* [1]"Death of the Son." A Psalm of David.

I WILL praise *You,* O LORD, with my whole
heart;
I will tell of all Your marvelous works.
2 I will be glad and [a]rejoice in You;
I will sing praise to Your name,
[b]O Most High.

3 When my enemies turn back,
They shall fall and perish at Your presence.
4 For You have maintained my right and my
cause;
You sat on the throne judging in
righteousness.
5 You have rebuked the [1]nations,
You have destroyed the wicked;
You have [a]blotted out their name forever and
ever.

6 O enemy, destructions are finished forever!
And you have destroyed cities;
Even their memory has [a]perished.
7 [a]But the LORD shall endure forever;
He has prepared His throne for judgment.
8 [a]He shall judge the world in righteousness,
And He shall administer judgment for the
peoples in uprightness.

9 The LORD also will be a [a]refuge[1] for the
oppressed,
A refuge in times of trouble.
10 And those who [a]know Your name will put
their trust in You;
For You, LORD, have not forsaken those who
seek You.

11 Sing praises to the LORD, who dwells in Zion!
[a]Declare His deeds among the people.
12 [a]When He avenges blood,
He remembers them;
He does not forget the cry of the [1]humble.

13 Have mercy on me, O LORD!
Consider my trouble from those who hate
me,
You who lift me up from the gates of death,
14 That I may tell of all Your praise
In the gates of [1]the daughter of Zion.
I will [a]rejoice in Your salvation.

15 [a]The [1]nations have sunk down in the pit
*which* they made;
In the net which they hid,
their own foot is caught.
16 The LORD is [a]known *by* the judgment He
executes;
The wicked is snared in the work of his own
hands.
[b]Meditation.[1] Selah

17 The wicked shall be turned into hell,
*And* all the [1]nations [a]that forget God.
18 [a]For the needy shall not always be forgotten;
[b]The expectation of the poor shall *not* perish
forever.

19 Arise, O LORD,
Do not let man prevail;
Let the [1]nations be judged in Your sight.
20 Put them in fear, O LORD,
*That* the [1]nations may know themselves *to
be but* men. Selah

## PSALM 10

WHY do You stand afar off, O LORD?
*Why* do You hide in times of trouble?
2 The wicked in *his* pride [1]persecutes the poor;
[a]Let them be caught in the plots which they
have devised.

3 For the wicked [a]boasts of his heart's desire;
[1]He [b]blesses the greedy
*and* renounces the LORD.
4 The wicked in his proud countenance does
not seek *God;*
[1]God *is* in none of his [a]thoughts.

5 His ways [1]are always prospering;
Your judgments *are* far above,
out of his sight;
*As for* all his enemies, he sneers at them.
6 [a]He has said in his heart,
"I shall not be moved;
[b]I shall never be in adversity."
7 [a]His mouth is full of cursing and [b]deceit and
oppression;
Under his tongue *is* trouble and iniquity.

8 He sits in the lurking places of the villages;
In the secret places he murders the innocent;
His eyes are secretly fixed on the helpless.
9 He lies in wait secretly, as a lion in his den;
He lies in wait to catch the poor;
He catches the poor when he draws him into
his net.
10 So [1]he crouches, he lies low,
That the helpless may fall by his [2]strength.
11 He has said in his heart,
"God has forgotten;
He hides His face;
He will never see."

12 Arise, O LORD!
O God, [a]lift up Your hand!
Do not forget the [b]humble.

**1** [b]Ps. 113:4
**2** [a]Matt. 21:16; [1 Cor. 1:27] [b]Ps. 44:16 [1]*established*
**3** [a]Ps. 111:2
**4** [a]Job 7:17, 18; [Heb. 2:6–8] [b][Job 10:12] [1]*give attention to* or *care for*
**5** [1]Heb. *Elohim, God;* LXX, Syr., Tg., Jewish tradition *angels*
**6** [a][Gen. 1:26, 28] [b][1 Cor. 15:27; Eph. 1:22; Heb. 2:8]
**9** [a]Ps. 8:1

PSALM 9

**title** [1]Heb. *Muth Labben*
**2** [a]Ps. 5:11; 104:34 [b][Ps. 83:18; 92:1]
**5** [a]Prov. 10:7 [1]*Gentiles*
**6** [a][Ps. 34:16]
**7** [a]Ps. 102:12, 26; Heb. 1:11
**8** [a][Ps. 96:13; 98:9; Acts 17:31]
**9** [a]Ps. 32:7; 46:1; 91:2 [1]Lit. *secure height*
**10** [a]Ps. 91:14
**11** [a]Ps. 66:16; 107:22
**12** [a][Gen. 9:5; Ps. 72:14] [1]*afflicted*
**14** [a]Ps. 13:5; 20:5; 35:9 [1]Jerusalem
**15** [a]Ps. 7:15, 16 [1]*Gentiles*
**16** [a]Ex. 7:5 [b]Ps. 92:3 [1]Heb. *Higgaion*
**17** [a]Job 8:13; Ps. 50:22 [1]*Gentiles*
**18** [a]Ps. 9:12; 12:5 [b][Ps. 62:5; 71:5]; Prov. 23:18
**19** [1]*Gentiles*
**20** [1]*Gentiles*

PSALM 10

**2** [a]Ps. 7:16; 9:16 [1]*hotly pursues*
**3** [a]Ps. 49:6; 94:3, 4 [b]Prov. 28:4 [1]Or *The greedy man curses and spurns the LORD*
**4** [a]Ps. 14:1; 36:1 [1]Or *All his thoughts are, "There is no God"*
**5** [1]Lit. *are strong*
**6** [a]Ps. 49:11; [Eccl. 8:11] [b]Rev. 18:7
**7** [a][Rom. 3:14] [b]Ps. 55:10, 11
**10** [1]Or *he is crushed, is bowed* [2]Or *mighty ones*
**12** [a]Ps. 17:7; 94:2; Mic. 5:9 [b]Ps. 9:12

13 Why do the wicked renounce God?
He has said in his heart,
"You will not require *an account.*"

14 But You have [a]seen,
for You observe trouble and grief,
To repay *it* by Your hand.
The helpless [b]commits[1] himself to You;
[c]You are the helper of the fatherless.
15 Break the arm of the wicked
and the evil *man;*
Seek out his wickedness *until* You find none.

16 [a]The LORD *is* King forever and ever;
The nations have perished out of His land.
17 LORD, You have heard the desire of the humble;
You will prepare their heart;
You will cause Your ear to hear,
18 To [1]do justice to the fatherless and the oppressed,
That the man of the earth may [2]oppress no more.

## PSALM 11

To the Chief Musician. A Psalm of David.

IN [a]the LORD I put my trust;
How can you say to my soul,
"Flee *as* a bird to your mountain"?
2 For look! [a]The wicked bend *their* bow,
They make ready their arrow on the string,
That they may shoot [1]secretly at the upright in heart.
3 [a]If the foundations are destroyed,
What can the righteous do?

4 The LORD *is* in His holy temple,
The LORD's [a]throne *is* in heaven;
[b]His eyes behold,
His eyelids test the sons of men.
5 The LORD [a]tests the righteous,
But the wicked and the one who loves violence His soul hates.
6 Upon the wicked He will rain coals;
Fire and brimstone and a burning wind
[a]*Shall be* [1]the portion of their cup.

7 For the LORD *is* righteous,
He [a]loves righteousness;
[1]His countenance beholds the upright.

## PSALM 12

To the Chief Musician. [a]On [1]an eight-stringed harp. A Psalm of David.

HELP,[1] LORD, for the godly man [a]ceases!
For the faithful disappear from among the sons of men.
2 [a]They speak idly everyone with his neighbor;
*With* flattering lips *and* [1]a double heart they speak.

3 May the LORD [1]cut off all flattering lips,
*And* the tongue that speaks [2]proud things,
4 Who have said,
"With our tongue we will prevail;
Our lips *are* our own;
Who *is* lord over us?"

5 "For the oppression of the poor,
for the sighing of the needy,
Now I will arise," says the LORD;
"I will set *him* in the safety for which he yearns."

6 The words of the LORD *are* [a]pure words,
*Like* silver tried in a furnace of earth,
Purified seven times.
7 You shall keep them, O LORD,
You shall preserve them from this generation forever.

8 The wicked prowl on every side,
When vileness is exalted among the sons of men.

## PSALM 13

To the Chief Musician. A Psalm of David.

HOW long, O LORD?
Will You forget me forever?
[a]How long will You hide Your face from me?
2 How long shall I take counsel in my soul,
*Having* sorrow in my heart daily?
How long will my enemy be exalted over me?

3 Consider *and* hear me, O LORD my God;
[a]Enlighten my eyes,
[b]Lest I sleep the *sleep of* death;
4 Lest my enemy say,
"I have prevailed against him";
*Lest* those who trouble me rejoice when I am moved.

5 But I have trusted in Your mercy;
My heart shall rejoice in Your salvation.
6 I will sing to the LORD,
Because He has dealt bountifully with me.

## PSALM 14

To the Chief Musician. A Psalm of David.

THE [a]fool has said in his heart,
"*There is* no God."
They are corrupt,
They have done abominable works,
There is none who does good.

2 [a]The LORD looks down from heaven upon the children of men,
To see if there are any who understand, who seek God.
3 [a]They have all turned aside,
They have together become corrupt;
*There is* none who does good,
No, not one.

4 Have all the workers of iniquity no knowledge,
Who eat up my people *as* they eat bread,
And [a]do not call on the LORD?
5 There they are in great fear,
For God *is* with the generation of the righteous.
6 You shame the counsel of the poor,
But the LORD *is* his [a]refuge.

7 [a]Oh,[1] that the salvation of Israel *would come* out of Zion!
[b]When the LORD brings back [2]the captivity of His people,
Let Jacob rejoice *and* Israel be glad.

## PSALM 15

A Psalm of David.

LORD, [a]who may [1]abide in Your tabernacle?
Who may dwell in Your holy hill?

2 He who walks uprightly,
And works righteousness,
And speaks the [a]truth in his heart;

---

**14** [a][Ps. 11:4] [b][2 Tim. 1:12] [c]Ps. 68:5; Hos. 14:3 [1]Lit. *leaves,* entrusts
**16** [a]Ps. 29:10
**18** [1]*vindicate* [2]*terrify*

PSALM 11
**1** [a]Ps. 56:11
**2** [a]Ps. 64:3, 4 [1]Lit. *in darkness*
**3** [a]Ps. 82:5; 87:1; 119:152
**4** [a]Ps. 2:4; [Is. 66:1]; Matt. 5:34; 23:22; [Acts 7:49]; Rev. 4:2 [b][Ps. 33:18; 34:15, 16]
**5** [a]Gen. 22:1; [James 1:12]
**6** [a]1 Sam. 1:4; Ps. 75:8; Ezek. 38:22 [1]Their allotted portion or serving
**7** [a]Ps. 33:5; 45:7 [1]Or *The upright beholds His countenance*

PSALM 12
**title** [a]Ps. 6:title [1]Heb. *sheminith*
**1** [a][Is. 57:1]; Mic. 7:2 [1]*Save*
**2** [a]Ps. 10:7; 41:6 [1]An inconsistent mind
**3** [1]*destroy* [2]*great*
**6** [a]2 Sam. 22:31; Ps. 18:30; 119:140; Prov. 30:5

PSALM 13
**1** [a]Job 13:24; Ps. 89:46
**3** [a]1 Sam. 14:29; Ezra 9:8; Job 33:30; Ps. 18:28 [b]Jer. 51:39

PSALM 14
**1** [a]Ps. 10:4; 53:1
**2** [a]Ps. 33:13, 14; 102:19; Rom. 3:11
**3** [a]Rom. 3:12
**4** [a]Ps. 79:6; Is. 64:7; Jer. 10:25; Amos 8:4; Mic. 3:3
**6** [a]Ps. 9:9; 40:17; 46:1; 142:5
**7** [a]Ps. 53:6; [Rom. 11:25–27] [b]Deut. 30:3; Job 42:10 [1]Lit. *Who will give out of Zion the salvation of Israel?* [2]Or *His captive people*

PSALM 15
**1** [a]Ps. 24:3–5 [1]*sojourn*
**2** [a]Zech. 8:16; [Eph. 4:25]

3 He *who* [a]does not backbite with his tongue,
Nor does evil to his neighbor,
[b]Nor does he [1]take up a reproach against
his friend;
4 [a]In whose eyes a vile person is despised,
But he honors those who fear the LORD;
He *who* [b]swears to his own hurt and does not
change;
5 He *who* does not put out his money at usury,
Nor does he take a bribe against the
innocent.

He who does these *things* [a]shall never be
moved.

## PSALM 16

A [a]Michtam of David.

PRESERVE[1] me, O God,
for in You I put my trust.
2 *O my soul,* you have said to the LORD,
"You *are* my Lord,
[a]My goodness is nothing apart from You.
3 As for the saints who *are* on the earth,
"They are the excellent ones,
in [a]whom is all my delight."

4 Their sorrows shall be multiplied who hasten
*after* another *god;*
Their drink offerings of [a]blood I will not
offer,
[b]Nor take up their names on my lips.

5 O LORD, *You are* the portion of my
inheritance and my cup;
You [1]maintain my lot.
6 The lines have fallen to me in pleasant
*places;*
Yes, I have a good inheritance.

7 I will bless the LORD who has given me
counsel;
My [1]heart also instructs me in the night
seasons.
8 [a]I have set the LORD always before me;
Because *He is* at my right hand I shall not be
moved.

9 Therefore my heart is glad,
and my glory rejoices;
My flesh also will [1]rest in hope.
10 [a]For You will not leave my soul in [1]Sheol,
Nor will You allow Your Holy One
to [2]see corruption.
11 You will show me the [a]path of life;
In Your presence *is* fullness of joy;
At Your right hand *are* pleasures
forevermore.

## PSALM 17

A Prayer of David.

HEAR a just cause, O LORD,
Attend to my cry;
Give ear to my prayer *which is* not from
deceitful lips.
2 Let my vindication come from Your
presence;
Let Your eyes look on the things that are
upright.

3 You have tested my heart;
You have visited *me* in the night;
[a]You have [1]tried me and have found [2]nothing;
I have purposed that my mouth shall not
[b]transgress.
4 Concerning the works of men,
By the word of Your lips,
I have kept away from the paths of the
destroyer.
5 [a]Uphold my steps in Your paths,
*That* my footsteps may not slip.

6 [a]I have called upon You,
for You will hear me, O God;
Incline Your ear to me, *and* hear my speech.
7 Show Your marvelous lovingkindness by
Your right hand,
O You who [1]save those who trust *in You*
From those who rise up *against them.*
8 Keep me as the [1]apple of Your eye;
Hide me under the shadow of Your wings,
9 From the wicked who oppress me,
*From* my deadly enemies who surround me.

10 They have closed up their [a]fat *hearts;*
With their mouths they [b]speak proudly.
11 They have now surrounded us in our steps;
They have set their eyes,
crouching down to the earth,
12 As a lion is eager to tear his prey,
And like a young lion lurking in secret
places.

13 Arise, O LORD,
Confront him, cast him down;
Deliver my life from the wicked with Your
sword,
14 With Your hand from men, O LORD,
From men of the world *who have* their
portion in *this* life,
And whose belly You fill with Your hidden
treasure.
They are satisfied with children,
And leave the rest of their *possession* for
their babes.

15 As for me, [a]I will see Your face in
righteousness;
[b]I shall be satisfied when I [c]awake in Your
likeness.

## PSALM 18

To the Chief Musician. A Psalm of David [a]the servant of the LORD, who spoke to the LORD the words of [b]this song on the day that the LORD delivered him from the hand of all his enemies and from the hand of Saul. And he said:

I [a]WILL love You, O LORD, my strength.
2 The LORD is my rock and
my fortress and my deliverer;
My God, my [1]strength, [a]in whom I will trust;
My shield and the [2]horn of my salvation, my
stronghold.
3 I will call upon the LORD,
[a]*who is worthy* to be praised;
So shall I be saved from my enemies.

4 [a]The pangs of death
surrounded me,
And the floods of [1]ungodliness
made me afraid.
5 The sorrows of Sheol surrounded me;
The snares of death confronted me.
6 In my distress I called upon the LORD,
And cried out to my God;
He heard my voice from His temple,

3 [a][Lev. 19:16–18] [b]Ex. 23:1 [1]*receive*
4 [a]Esth. 3:2 [b]Lev. 5:4
5 [a]2 Pet. 1:10

PSALM 16
title [a]Ps. 56—60
1 [1]*Watch over*
2 [a]Job 35:7
3 [a]Ps. 119:63
4 [a]Ps. 106:37, 38 [b][Ex. 23:13]; Josh. 23:7
5 [1]Lit. *uphold*
7 [1]Mind, lit. *kidneys*
8 [a][Acts 2:25–28]
9 [1]Or *dwell securely*
10 [a]Ps. 49:15; 86:13; Acts 2:31, 32; Heb. 13:20 [1]The abode of the dead [2]*undergo*
11 [a]Ps. 139:24; [Matt. 7:14]

PSALM 17
3 [a]Job 23:10; Ps. 66:10; Zech. 13:9; [1 Pet. 1:7] [b]Ps. 39:1 [1]*examined* [2]Nothing evil
5 [a]Job 23:11; Ps. 44:18; 119:133
6 [a]Ps. 86:7; 116:2
7 [1]*deliver*
8 [1]*pupil*
10 [a]Ezek. 16:49 [b][1 Sam. 2:3]
15 [a][1 John 3:2] [b]Ps. 4:6, 7; 16:11 [c][Is. 26:19]

PSALM 18
title [a]Ps. 36:title [b]2 Sam. 22
1 [a]Ps. 144:1
2 [a]Heb. 2:13 [1]Lit. *rock* [2]Strength
3 [a]Ps. 76:4; Rev. 5:12
4 [a]Ps. 116:3 [1]Lit. *Belial*

And my cry came before Him,
*even* to His ears.

7 [a]Then the earth shook and trembled;
The foundations of the hills also
quaked and were shaken,
Because He was angry.
8 Smoke went up from His nostrils,
And devouring fire from His mouth;
Coals were kindled by it.
9 [a]He bowed the heavens also, and came down
With darkness under His feet.
10 [a]And He rode upon a cherub, and flew;
[b]He flew upon the wings
of the wind.
11 He made darkness His secret place;
[a]His canopy around Him *was* dark waters
*And* thick clouds of the skies.
12 [a]From the brightness before Him,
His thick clouds passed with hailstones and
coals of fire.

13 The LORD thundered from heaven,
And the Most High uttered [a]His voice,
[1]Hailstones and coals of fire.
14 [a]He sent out His arrows
and scattered [1]the foe,
Lightnings in abundance,
and He vanquished them.
15 Then the channels of the sea were seen,
The foundations of the world
were uncovered
At Your rebuke, O LORD,
At the blast of the breath of Your nostrils.

16 [a]He sent from above, He took me;
He drew me out of many waters.
17 He delivered me
from my strong enemy,
From those who hated me,
For they were too strong for me.
18 They confronted me in the day
of my calamity,
But the LORD was my support.
19 [a]He also brought me out
into a broad place;
He delivered me
because He delighted in me.

20 [a]The LORD rewarded me
according to my righteousness;
According to the cleanness of my hands
He has recompensed me.
21 For I have kept the ways of the LORD,
And have not wickedly departed
from my God.
22 For all His judgments *were* before me,
And I did not put away His statutes from me.
23 I was also blameless [1]before Him,
And I kept myself from my iniquity.
24 [a]Therefore the LORD has recompensed me
according to my righteousness,
According to the cleanness
of my hands in His sight.

25 [a]With the merciful
You will show Yourself merciful;
With a blameless man
You will show Yourself blameless;
26 With the pure
You will show Yourself pure;
And [a]with the devious
You will show Yourself shrewd.
27 For You will save the humble people,
But will bring down [a]haughty looks.

28 [a]For You will light my lamp;
The LORD my God will enlighten my
darkness.
29 For by You I can [1]run against a troop,
By my God I can leap over a wall.
30 *As for* God, [a]His way *is* perfect;
[b]The word of the LORD is [1]proven;
He *is* a shield [c]to all who trust in Him.

31 [a]For who *is* God, except the LORD?
And who *is* a rock, except our God?
32 *It is* God who [a]arms me with strength,
And makes my way perfect.
33 [a]He makes my feet like the *feet of* deer,
And [b]sets me on my high places.
34 [a]He teaches my hands to make war,
So that my arms
can bend a bow of bronze.

35 You have also given me
the shield of Your salvation;
Your right hand has held me up,
Your gentleness has made me great.
36 You enlarged my path under me,
[a]So my feet did not slip.

37 I have pursued my enemies
and overtaken them;
Neither did I turn back again
till they were destroyed.
38 I have wounded them,
So that they could not rise;
They have fallen under my feet.
39 For You have armed me with strength for
the battle;
You have [1]subdued under me those
who rose up against me.
40 You have also given me
the necks of my enemies,
So that I destroyed those who hated me.
41 They cried out,
but *there was* none to save;
[a]*Even* to the LORD,
but He did not answer them.
42 Then I beat them as fine as the dust before
the wind;
I [a]cast them out like dirt in the streets.

43 You have delivered me
from the strivings of the people;
[a]You have made me the head of the [1]nations;
[b]A people I have not known
shall serve me.
44 As soon as they hear of me they obey me;
The foreigners [1]submit to me.
45 [a]The foreigners fade away,
And come frightened from their hideouts.

46 The LORD lives!
Blessed *be* my Rock!
Let the God of my salvation be exalted.
47 *It is* God who avenges me,
[a]And subdues the peoples under me;
48 He delivers me from my enemies.
[a]You also lift me up
above those who rise against me;
You have delivered me from the violent man.
49 [a]Therefore I will give thanks to You,
O LORD, among the [1]Gentiles,
And sing praises to Your name.

50 [a]Great deliverance He gives to His king,
And shows mercy to His anointed,
To David and his [1]descendants forevermore.

**7** [a]Acts 4:31
**9** [a]Ps. 144:5
**10** [a]Ps. 80:1; 99:1 [b][Ps. 104:3]
**11** [a]Ps. 97:2
**12** [a]Ps. 97:3; 140:10; Hab. 3:11
**13** [a][Ps. 29:3–9; 104:7] [1]So with MT, Tg., Vg.; a few Heb. mss., LXX omit *Hailstones and coals of fire*
**14** [a]Josh. 10:10; Ps. 144:6; Is. 30:30; Hab. 3:11 [1]Lit. *them*
**16** [a]Ps. 144:7
**19** [a]Ps. 4:1; 31:8; 118:5
**20** [a]1 Sam. 24:19; [Job 33:26]; Ps. 7:8
**23** [1]*with*
**24** [a]1 Sam. 26:23; Ps. 18:20
**25** [a][1 Kin. 8:32; Ps. 62:12]; Matt. 5:7
**26** [a][Lev. 26:23–28]; Prov. 3:34
**27** [a][Ps. 101:5]; Prov. 6:17
**28** [a]1 Kin. 15:4; Job 18:6; [Ps. 119:105]
**29** [1]Or *run through*
**30** [a][Deut. 32:4]; Rev. 15:3 [b]Ps. 12:6; 119:140; [Prov. 30:5] [c][Ps. 17:7] [1]Lit. *refined*
**31** [a][Deut. 32:31, 39; 1 Sam. 2:2; Ps. 86:8–10; Is. 45:5]
**32** [a][Ps. 91:2]
**33** [a]2 Sam. 2:18; Hab. 3:19 [b]Deut. 32:13; 33:29
**34** [a]Ps. 144:1
**36** [a]Ps. 66:9; Prov. 4:12
**39** [1]Lit. *caused to bow*
**41** [a]Job 27:9; Prov. 1:28; Is. 1:15; Ezek. 8:18; Zech. 7:13
**42** [a]Zech. 10:5
**43** [a]2 Sam. 8; Ps. 89:27 [b]Is. 52:15 [1]*Gentiles*
**44** [1]*feign submission*
**45** [a]Mic. 7:17
**47** [a]Ps. 47:3
**48** [a]Ps. 27:6; 59:1
**49** [a]2 Sam. 22:50; Rom. 15:9 [1]*nations*
**50** [a]2 Sam. 7:12; Ps. 21:1; 144:10 [1]Lit. *seed*

## PSALM 19

To the Chief Musician. A Psalm of David.

THE [a]heavens declare the glory of God;
And the [b]firmament[1] shows [2]His handiwork.
2 Day unto day utters speech,
And night unto night reveals knowledge.
3 *There is* no speech nor language
*Where* their voice is not heard.
4 [a]Their [1]line has gone out through all the earth,
And their words to the end of the world.

In them He has set a [2]tabernacle for the sun,
5 Which *is* like a bridegroom coming out of his chamber,
[a]*And* rejoices like a strong man to run its race.
6 Its rising *is* from one end of heaven,
And its circuit to the other end;
And there is nothing hidden from its heat.

7 [a]The law of the LORD *is* perfect, [1]converting the soul;
The testimony of the LORD *is* sure, making [b]wise the simple;
8 The statutes of the LORD *are* right, rejoicing the heart;
The commandment of the LORD *is* pure, enlightening the eyes;
9 The fear of the LORD *is* clean, enduring forever;
The judgments of the LORD *are* true *and* righteous altogether.
10 More to be desired *are they* than [a]gold,
Yea, than much fine gold;
Sweeter also than honey and the [1]honeycomb.
11 Moreover by them Your servant is warned,
*And* in keeping them *there is* great reward.

12 Who can understand *his* errors?
[a]Cleanse me from secret *faults.*
13 Keep back Your servant also from [a]presumptuous *sins;*
Let them not have [b]dominion over me.
Then I shall be blameless,
And I shall be innocent of [1]great transgression.

14 [a]Let the words of my mouth
and the meditation of my heart
Be acceptable in Your sight,
O LORD, my [1]strength and my [b]Redeemer.

## PSALM 20

To the Chief Musician. A Psalm of David.

MAY the LORD answer you in the day of trouble;
May the name of the God of Jacob [1]defend you;
2 May He send you help from the sanctuary,
And strengthen you out of Zion;
3 May He remember all your offerings,
And accept your burnt sacrifice. Selah

4 May He grant you according to your heart's *desire,*
And [a]fulfill all your [1]purpose.
5 We will rejoice in your salvation,
And in the name of our God we will set up *our* banners!
May the LORD fulfill all your petitions.

6 Now I know that the LORD saves His [1]anointed;
He will answer him from His holy heaven
With the saving strength of His right hand.

7 Some *trust* in chariots, and some in [a]horses;
But we will remember the name of the LORD our God.
8 They have bowed down and fallen;
But we have risen and stand upright.

9 Save, LORD!
May the King answer us when we call.

## PSALM 21

To the Chief Musician. A Psalm of David.

THE king shall have joy in Your strength, O LORD;
And in Your salvation how greatly shall he rejoice!
2 You have given him his heart's desire,
And have not withheld the [a]request of his lips. Selah

3 For You meet him with the blessings of goodness;
You set a crown of pure gold upon his head.
4 [a]He asked life from You,
*and* You gave *it* to him—
Length of days forever and ever.
5 His glory *is* great in Your salvation;
Honor and majesty You have placed upon him.
6 For You have made him most blessed forever;
[a]You have made him [1]exceedingly glad with Your presence.
7 For the king trusts in the LORD,
And through the mercy of the Most High he shall not be [1]moved.

8 Your hand will find all Your enemies;
Your right hand will find those who hate You.
9 You shall make them as a fiery oven
in the time of Your anger;
The LORD shall swallow them up
in His wrath,
And the fire shall devour them.
10 Their offspring You shall destroy from the earth,
And their [1]descendants from among the sons of men.
11 For they intended evil against You;
They devised a plot *which* they are not able to [a]*perform.*
12 Therefore You will make them turn their back;
You will make ready *Your arrows* on Your string toward their faces.

13 Be exalted, O LORD, in Your own strength!
We will sing and praise Your power.

## PSALM 22

To the Chief Musician. Set to [1]"The Deer of the Dawn." A Psalm of David.

MY [a]God, My God, why have You forsaken Me?
*Why are You* so far from helping Me,
*And from* the words of My groaning?

PSALM 19
1 [a]Is. 40:22; [Rom. 1:19, 20] [b]Gen. 1:6, 7 [1]*expanse* of heaven [2]*the work of His hands*
4 [a]Rom. 10:18 [1]LXX, [Syr.], Vg. *sound;* Tg. *business* [2]*tent*
5 [a]Eccl. 1:5
7 [a]Ps. 111:7; [Rom. 7:12] [b]Ps. 119:130 [1]*restoring*
10 [a]Ps. 119:72, 127; Prov. 8:10, 11, 19 [1]*honey in the combs*
12 [a][Ps. 51:1, 2]
13 [a]Num. 15:30 [b]Ps. 119:133; [Rom. 6:12–14] [1]Or *much*
14 [a]Ps. 51:15 [b]Ps. 31:5; Is. 47:4 [1]Lit. *rock*

PSALM 20
1 [1]Lit. *set you on high*
4 [a]Ps. 21:2 [1]*counsel*
6 [1]Commissioned one, Heb. *messiah*
7 [a]Deut. 20:1; Ps. 33:16, 17; Prov. 21:31; Is. 31:1

PSALM 21
2 [a]2 Sam. 7:26–29
4 [a]Ps. 61:5, 6; 133:3
6 [a]Ps. 16:11; 45:7 [1]Lit. *joyful with gladness*
7 [1]*shaken*
10 [1]Lit. *seed*
11 [a]Ps. 2:1–4

PSALM 22
title [1]Heb. *Aijeleth Hashahar*
1 [a][Matt. 27:46; Mark 15:34]

2 O My God, I cry in the daytime,
but You do not hear;
And in the night season, and am not silent.

3 But You *are* holy,
Enthroned in the [a]praises of Israel.
4 Our fathers trusted in You;
They trusted, and You delivered them.
5 They cried to You, and were delivered;
[a]They trusted in You, and were not ashamed.

6 But I *am* [a]a worm, and no man;
[b]A reproach of men, and despised by the
people.
7 [a]All those who see Me ridicule Me;
They [1]shoot out the lip,
they shake the head, *saying,*
8 "He[a] [1]trusted in the LORD, let Him rescue Him;
[b]Let Him deliver Him,
since He delights in Him!"

9 [a]But You *are* He who took Me out of the
womb;
You made Me trust *while* on My mother's
breasts.
10 I was cast upon You from birth.
From My mother's womb
[a]You *have been* My God.
11 Be not far from Me,
For trouble *is* near;
For *there is* none to help.

12 [a]Many bulls have surrounded Me;
Strong *bulls* of [b]Bashan have encircled Me.
13 [a]They [1]gape at Me *with* their mouths,
*Like* a raging and roaring lion.

14 I am poured out like water,
[a]And all My bones are out of joint;
My heart is like wax;
It has melted [1]within Me.
15 [a]My strength is dried up like a potsherd,
And [b]My tongue clings to My jaws;
You have brought Me to the dust of death.

16 For dogs have surrounded Me;
The congregation of the wicked has enclosed
Me.
[a]They[1] pierced My hands and My feet;
17 I can count all My bones.
[a]They look *and* stare at Me.
18 [a]They divide My garments among them,
And for My clothing they cast lots.

19 But You, O LORD, do not be far from Me;
O My Strength, hasten to help Me!
20 Deliver Me from the sword,
[a]My[1] precious *life* from the power of the dog.
21 [a]Save Me from the lion's mouth
And from the horns of the wild oxen!

[b]You have answered Me.

22 [a]I will declare Your name to [b]My brethren;
In the midst of the assembly I will praise
You.
23 [a]You who fear the LORD, praise Him!
All you [1]descendants of Jacob, glorify Him,
And fear Him, all you offspring of Israel!
24 For He has not despised nor abhorred the
affliction of the afflicted;
Nor has He hidden His face from Him;
But [a]when He cried to Him, He heard.

25 [a]My praise *shall be* of You in the great
assembly;
[b]I will pay My vows before those who fear
Him.
26 The poor shall eat and be satisfied;
Those who seek Him will praise the LORD.
Let your heart live forever!

27 All the ends of the world
Shall remember and turn to the LORD,
And all the families of the [1]nations
Shall worship before [2]You.
28 [a]For the kingdom *is* the LORD's,
And He rules over the nations.

29 [a]All the prosperous of the earth
Shall eat and worship;
[b]All those who go down to [1]the dust
Shall bow before Him,
Even he who cannot keep himself alive.

30 A posterity shall serve Him.
It will be recounted of the Lord
to the *next* generation,
31 They will come and declare His righteousness
to a people who will be born,
That He has done *this.*

## PSALM 23

A Psalm of David.

THE LORD *is* [a]my shepherd;
[b]I shall not [1]want.
2 [a]He makes me to lie down in [1]green pastures;
[b]He leads me beside the [2]still waters.
3 He restores my soul;
[a]He leads me in the paths of righteousness
For His name's sake.

4 Yea, though I walk through the valley of
[a]the shadow of death,
[b]I will fear no evil;
[c]For You *are* with me;
Your rod and Your staff, they comfort me.

5 You [a]prepare a table before me in the
presence of my enemies;
You [b]anoint my head with oil;
My cup runs over.
6 Surely goodness and mercy shall follow me
All the days of my life;
And I will [1]dwell in the house of the LORD
[2]Forever.

## PSALM 24

A Psalm of David.

THE [a]earth *is* the LORD's, and all its fullness,
The world and those who dwell therein.
2 For He has [a]founded it upon the seas,
And established it upon the [1]waters.

3 [a]Who may ascend into the hill of the LORD?
Or who may stand in His holy place?
4 He who has [a]clean hands and [b]a pure heart,
Who has not lifted up his soul to an idol,
Nor [c]sworn deceitfully.
5 He shall receive blessing from the LORD,
And righteousness from the God of his
salvation.
6 This *is* Jacob, the generation of those who
[a]seek Him,
Who seek Your face. Selah

7 [a]Lift up your heads, O you gates!
And be lifted up, you everlasting doors!
[b]And the King of glory shall come in.
8 Who *is* this King of glory?

---

3 [a]Deut. 10:21
5 [a]Is. 49:23
6 [a]Is. 41:14 [b][Is. 53:3]
7 [a]Matt. 27:39 [1]Show contempt with their mouth
8 [a]Matt. 27:43 [b]Ps. 91:14 [1]LXX, [Syr.], Vg. *hoped;* Tg. *praised*
9 [a][Ps. 71:5, 6]
10 [a][Is. 46:3; 49:1]
12 [a]Ps. 22:21; 68:30 [b]Deut. 32:14
13 [a]Job 16:10 [1]Lit. *have opened their mouths at me*
14 [a]Dan. 5:6 [1]Lit. *in the midst of my bowels*
15 [a]Prov. 17:22 [b]John 19:28
16 [a]Matt. 27:35 [1]So with some Heb. mss., LXX, Syr., Vg.; MT *Like a lion* instead of *They pierced*
17 [a]Luke 23:27, 35
18 [a]Matt. 27:35
20 [a]Ps. 35:17 [1]Lit. *My only one*
21 [a]2 Tim. 4:17 [b]Is. 34:7
22 [a]Heb. 2:12 [b][Rom. 8:29]
23 [a]Ps. 135:19, 20 [1]Lit. *seed*
24 [a]Heb. 5:7
25 [a]Ps. 35:18; 40:9, 10 [b]Eccl. 5:4
27 [1]*Gentiles* [2]So with MT, LXX, Tg.; Arab., Syr., Vg. *Him*
28 [a]Matt. 6:13
29 [a]Ps. 17:10; 45:12 [b][Is. 26:19] [1]Death

PSALM 23
1 [a][Is. 40:11] [b][Phil. 4:19] [1]*lack*
2 [a]Ezek. 34:14 [b][Rev. 7:17] [1]Lit. *pastures of tender grass* [2]Lit. *waters of rest*
3 [a]Ps. 5:8; 31:3
4 [a]Job 3:5; 10:21, 22; 24:17 [b][Ps. 3:6; 27:1] [c][Is. 43:2]
5 [a]Ps. 104:15 [b]Ps. 92:10
6 [1]So with LXX, [Syr.], Tg., Vg.; MT *return* [2]Or *To the end of my days,* lit. *For length of days*

PSALM 24
1 [a]1 Cor. 10:26, 28
2 [a]Ps. 89:11 [1]Lit. *rivers*
3 [a]Ps. 15:1–5
4 [a][Job 17:9] [b][Matt. 5:8] [c]Ps. 15:4
6 [a]Ps. 27:4, 8
7 [a]Is. 26:2 [b]Ps. 29:2, 9; 97:6

The LORD strong and mighty,
The LORD mighty in [a]battle.
9 Lift up your heads, O you gates!
Lift up, you everlasting doors!
And the King of glory shall come in.
10 Who is this King of glory?
The LORD of hosts,
He *is* the King of glory. Selah

## PSALM 25

A Psalm of David.

TO [a]You, O LORD, I lift up my soul.
2 O my God, I [a]trust in You;
Let me not be ashamed;
[b]Let not my enemies triumph over me.
3 Indeed, let no one who [1]waits on You be ashamed;
Let those be ashamed who deal treacherously without cause.

4 [a]Show me Your ways, O LORD;
Teach me Your paths.
5 Lead me in Your truth and teach me,
For You *are* the God of my salvation;
On You I wait all the day.

6 Remember, O LORD, [a]Your tender mercies and Your lovingkindnesses,
For they *are* from of old.
7 Do not remember [a]the sins of my youth, nor my transgressions;
[b]According to Your mercy remember me,
For Your goodness' sake, O LORD.

8 Good and upright *is* the LORD;
Therefore He teaches sinners in the way.
9 The humble He guides in justice,
And the humble He teaches His way.
10 All the paths of the LORD *are* mercy and truth,
To such as keep His covenant and His testimonies.
11 [a]For Your name's sake, O LORD,
Pardon my iniquity, for it *is* great.

12 Who *is* the man that fears the LORD?
[a]Him shall [1]He teach in the way [2]He chooses.
13 [a]He himself shall dwell in [1]prosperity,
And [b]his descendants shall inherit the earth.
14 [a]The secret of the LORD *is* with those who fear Him,
And He will show them His covenant.
15 [a]My eyes *are* ever toward the LORD,
For He shall [1]pluck my feet out of the net.

16 [a]Turn Yourself to me, and have mercy on me,
For I *am* [1]desolate and afflicted.
17 The troubles of my heart have enlarged;
Bring me out of my distresses!
18 [a]Look on my affliction and my pain,
And forgive all my sins.
19 Consider my enemies, for they are many;
And they hate me with [1]cruel hatred.
20 Keep my soul, and deliver me;
Let me not be ashamed,
for I put my trust in You.
21 Let integrity and uprightness preserve me,
For I wait for You.

22 [a]Redeem Israel, O God,
Out of all their troubles!

## PSALM 26

A Psalm of David.

VINDICATE [a]me, O LORD,
For I have [b]walked in my integrity.
[c]I have also trusted in the LORD;
I shall not slip.
2 [a]Examine me, O LORD, and [1]prove me;
Try my mind and my heart.
3 For Your lovingkindness *is* before my eyes,
And [a]I have walked in Your truth.
4 I have not [a]sat with idolatrous mortals,
Nor will I go in with hypocrites.
5 I have [a]hated the assembly of evildoers,
And will not sit with the wicked.

6 I will wash my hands in innocence;
So I will go about Your altar, O LORD,
7 That I may proclaim with the voice of thanksgiving,
And tell of all Your wondrous works.
8 LORD, [a]I have loved the habitation of Your house,
And the place [1]where Your glory dwells.

9 [a]Do[1] not gather my soul with sinners,
Nor my life with bloodthirsty men,
10 In whose hands *is* a sinister scheme,
And whose right hand is full of [a]bribes.
11 But as for me, I will walk in my integrity;
Redeem me and be merciful to me.
12 [a]My foot stands in an even place;
In the congregations I will bless the LORD.

## PSALM 27

A Psalm of David.

THE LORD *is* my [a]light and my salvation;
Whom shall I fear?
The [b]LORD *is* the strength of my life;
Of whom shall I be afraid?
2 When the wicked came against me
To [a]eat[1] up my flesh,
My enemies and foes,
They stumbled and fell.
3 [a]Though an army may encamp against me,
My heart shall not fear;
Though war may rise against me,
In this I *will be* confident.

4 [a]One *thing* I have desired of the LORD,
That will I seek:
That I may [b]dwell in the house of the LORD
All the days of my life,
To behold the [1]beauty of the LORD,
And to inquire in His temple.
5 For [a]in the time of trouble
He shall hide me in His pavilion;
In the secret place of His tabernacle
He shall hide me;
He shall [b]set me high upon a rock.

6 And now [a]my head shall be [1]lifted up above my enemies all around me;
Therefore I will offer sacrifices of [2]joy in His tabernacle;
I will sing, yes, I will sing praises to the LORD.

7 Hear, O LORD, *when* I cry with my voice!
Have mercy also upon me, and answer me.
8 *When You said,* "Seek My face,"
My heart said to You,
"Your face, LORD, I will seek."
9 [a]Do not hide Your face from me;
Do not turn Your servant away in anger;
You have been my help;
Do not leave me nor forsake me,
O God of my salvation.
10 [a]When my father and my mother forsake me,
Then the LORD will take care of me.

---

24:8 [a]Rev. 19:13–16

PSALM 25
1 [a]Ps. 86:4; 143:8
2 [a]Ps. 34:8 [b]Ps. 13:4; 41:11
3 [1]Waits for You in faith
4 [a]Ex. 33:13; Ps. 5:8; 27:11; 86:11; 119:27; 143:8
6 [a]Ps. 103:17; 106:1
7 [a]Job 13:26; [Jer. 3:25] [b]Ps. 51:1
11 [a]Ps. 31:3; 79:9; 109:21; 143:11
12 [a][Ps. 25:8; 37:23] [1]Or *he* [2]Or *he*
13 [a][Prov. 19:23] [b]Ps. 37:11; 69:36; Matt. 5:5 [1]Lit. *goodness*
14 [a][Prov. 3:32; John 7:17]
15 [a][Ps. 123:2; 141:8] [1]Lit. *bring out*
16 [a]Ps. 69:16 [1]*lonely*
18 [a]2 Sam. 16:12; Ps. 31:7
19 [1]*violent hatred*
22 [a][Ps. 130:8]

PSALM 26
1 [a]Ps. 7:8 [b]2 Kin. 20:3; [Prov. 20:7] [c][Ps. 13:5; 28:7]
2 [a]Ps. 17:3; 139:23 [1]*test me*
3 [a]2 Kin. 20:3; Ps. 86:11
4 [a]Ps. 1:1; Jer. 15:17
5 [a]Ps. 31:6; 139:21
8 [a]Ps. 27:4; 84:1–4, 10 [1]Lit. *of the tabernacle of Your glory*
9 [a]Ps. 28:3 [1]*Do not take away*
10 [a]1 Sam. 8:3
12 [a]Ps. 40:2

PSALM 27
1 [a]Ps. 18:28; 84:11; [Is. 60:19, 20; Mic. 7:8] [b]Ex. 15:2; Ps. 62:7; 118:14; Is. 12:2; 33:2
2 [a]Ps. 14:4 [1]*devour*
3 [a]Ps. 3:6
4 [a]Ps. 26:8; 65:4 [b]Luke 2:37 [1]*delightfulness*
5 [a]Ps. 31:20; 91:1 [b]Ps. 40:2
6 [a]Ps. 3:3 [1]Lifted up in honor [2]*joyous shouts*
9 [a]Ps. 69:17; 143:7
10 [a]Is. 49:15

11 [a]Teach me Your way, O LORD,
And lead me in a smooth path,
because of my enemies.
12 Do not deliver me to the will of my adversaries;
For [a]false witnesses have risen against me,
And such as breathe out violence.
13 *I would have lost heart,* unless I had believed
That I would see the goodness of the LORD
[a]In the land of the living.

14 [a]Wait[1] on the LORD;
Be of good courage,
And He shall strengthen your heart;
Wait, I say, on the LORD!

## PSALM 28

A Psalm of David.

TO You I will cry, O LORD my Rock:
[a]Do not be silent to me,
[b]Lest, if You *are* silent to me,
I become like those who go down to the pit.
2 Hear the voice of my supplications
When I cry to You,
[a]When I lift up my hands [b]toward Your holy sanctuary.

3 Do not [1]take me away with the wicked
And with the workers of iniquity,
[a]Who speak peace to their neighbors,
But evil *is* in their hearts.
4 [a]Give them according to their deeds,
And according to the wickedness of their endeavors;
Give them according to the work of their hands;
Render to them what they deserve.
5 Because [a]they do not regard the works of the LORD,
Nor the operation of His hands,
He shall destroy them
And not build them up.

6 Blessed *be* the LORD,
Because He has heard the voice of my supplications!
7 The LORD *is* [a]my strength and my shield;
My heart [b]trusted in Him, and I am helped;
Therefore my heart greatly rejoices,
And with my song I will praise Him.

8 The LORD *is* [1]their strength,
And He *is* the [a]saving refuge of His [2]anointed.
9 Save Your people,
And bless [a]Your inheritance;
Shepherd them also,
[b]And bear them up forever.

## PSALM 29

A Psalm of David.

GIVE[1] [a]unto the LORD, O you mighty ones,
Give unto the LORD glory and strength.
2 [1]Give unto the LORD
the glory [2]due to His name;
Worship the LORD in [a]the [3]beauty of holiness.

3 The voice of the LORD *is* over the waters;
[a]The God of glory thunders;
The LORD *is* over many waters.
4 The voice of the LORD *is* powerful;
The voice of the LORD *is* full of majesty.
5 The voice of the LORD breaks [a]the cedars,
Yes, the LORD splinters the cedars of Lebanon.
6 [a]He makes them also skip like a calf,
Lebanon and [b]Sirion like a young wild ox.
7 The voice of the LORD [1]divides the flames of fire.

8 The voice of the LORD shakes the wilderness;
The LORD shakes the Wilderness of [a]Kadesh.
9 The voice of the LORD makes the [a]deer give birth,
And strips the forests bare;
And in His temple everyone says, "Glory!"

10 The [a]LORD sat *enthroned* at the Flood,
And [b]the LORD sits as King forever.
11 [a]The LORD will give strength to His people;
The LORD will bless His people with peace.

## PSALM 30

A Psalm. A Song [a]at the dedication of the house of David.

I WILL extol You, O LORD,
for You have [a]lifted me up,
And have not let my foes [b]rejoice over me.
2 O LORD my God, I cried out to You,
And You [a]healed me.
3 O LORD, [a]You brought my soul up from the grave;
You have kept me alive, [1]that I should not go down to the pit.

4 [a]Sing praise to the LORD, you saints of His,
And give thanks at the remembrance of [1]His holy name.
5 For [a]His anger *is but for* a moment,
[b]His favor *is for* life;
Weeping may endure for a night,
But [1]joy *comes* in the morning.

6 Now in my prosperity I said,
"I shall never be [1]moved."
7 LORD, by Your favor You have made my mountain stand strong;
[a]You hid Your face, *and* I was troubled.

8 I cried out to You, O LORD;
And to the LORD I made supplication:
9 "What profit *is there* in my blood,
When I go down to the pit?
[a]Will the dust praise You?
Will it declare Your truth?
10 Hear, O LORD, and have mercy on me;
LORD, be my helper!"

11 [a]You have turned for me my mourning into dancing;
You have put off [1]my sackcloth and clothed me with gladness,
12 To the end that *my* [1]glory may sing praise to You and not be silent.
O LORD my God,
I will give thanks to You forever.

## PSALM 31

To the Chief Musician. A Psalm of David.

IN [a]You, O LORD, I [1]put my trust;
Let me never be ashamed;
Deliver me in Your righteousness.
2 [a]Bow down Your ear to me,
Deliver me speedily;

---

**11** [a]Ps. 25:4; 86:11; 119:33
**12** [a]Ps. 35:11
**13** [a]Ezek. 26:20
**14** [a]Is. 25:9 [1]Wait in faith

PSALM 28
**1** [a]Ps. 35:22; 39:12; 83:1 [b]Ps. 88:4; 143:7
**2** [a]Ps. 5:7 [b]Ps. 138:2
**3** [a]Ps. 12:2; 52:21; 62:4 [1]*drag*
**4** [a][Rev. 18:6; 22:12]
**5** [a]Is. 5:12
**7** [a]Ps. 18:2; 59:17 [b]Ps. 13:5; 112:7
**8** [a]Ps. 20:6 [1]So with MT, Tg.; LXX, Syr., Vg. *the strength of His people* [2]Commissioned one, Heb. *messiah*
**9** [a][Deut. 9:29; 32:9] [b]Deut. 1:31

PSALM 29
**1** [a]1 Chr. 16:28, 29 [1]*Ascribe*
**2** [a]2 Chr. 20:21 [1]*Ascribe* [2]Lit. *of His name* [3]*majesty*
**3** [a][Job 37:4, 5]
**5** [a]Is. 2:13; 14:8
**6** [a]Ps. 114:4 [b]Deut. 3:9
**7** [1]*stirs up,* lit. *hews out*
**8** [a]Num. 13:26
**9** [a]Job 39:1
**10** [a]Gen. 6:17 [b]Ps. 10:16
**11** [a]Ps. 28:8; 68:35

PSALM 30
**title** [a]Deut. 20:5
**1** [a]Ps. 28:9 [b]Ps. 25:2
**2** [a]Ps. 6:2; 103:3
**3** [a]Ps. 86:13 [1]So with Qr., Tg.; Kt., LXX, Syr., Vg. *from those who descend to the pit*
**4** [a]Ps. 97:12 [1]Or *His holiness*
**5** [a]Ps. 103:9 [b]Ps. 63:3 [1]*a shout of joy*
**6** [1]*shaken*
**7** [a][Ps. 104:29; 143:7]
**9** [a][Ps. 6:5]
**11** [a]Jer. 31:4 [1]The sackcloth of my mourning
**12** [1]*soul*

PSALM 31
**1** [a]Ps. 22:5 [1]*have taken refuge*
**2** [a]Ps. 17:6; 71:2; 86:1; 102:2

Be my rock of [1]refuge,
A [2]fortress of defense to save me.
3 [a]For You *are* my rock and my fortress;
Therefore, [b]for Your name's sake,
Lead me and guide me.
4 Pull me out of the net which they have
secretly laid for me,
For You *are* my strength.
5 [a]Into Your hand I commit my spirit;
You have redeemed me,
O LORD God of [b]truth.

6 I have hated those [a]who regard useless idols;
But I trust in the LORD.
7 I will be glad and rejoice in Your mercy,
For You have considered my trouble;
You have [a]known my soul in [1]adversities,
8 And have not [a]shut[1] me up into the hand of
the enemy;
[b]You have set my feet in a wide place.

9 Have mercy on me, O LORD,
for I am in trouble;
[a]My eye wastes away with grief,
*Yes,* my soul and my [1]body!
10 For my life is spent with grief,
And my years with sighing;
My strength fails because of my iniquity,
And my bones waste away.
11 [a]I am a [1]reproach among all my enemies,
But [b]especially among my neighbors,
And *am* repulsive to my acquaintances;
[c]Those who see me outside flee from me.
12 [a]I am forgotten like a dead man, out of mind;
I am like a [1]broken vessel.
13 [a]For I hear the slander of many;
[b]Fear *is* on every side;
While they [c]take counsel together against
me,
They scheme to take away my life.

14 But as for me, I trust in You, O LORD;
I say, "You *are* my God."
15 My times *are* in Your [a]hand;
Deliver me from the hand of my enemies,
And from those who persecute me.
16 [a]Make Your face shine upon Your servant;
Save me for Your mercies' sake.
17 [a]Do not let me be ashamed, O LORD, for I
have called upon You;
Let the wicked be ashamed;
[b]Let them be silent in the grave.
18 [a]Let the lying lips be put to silence,
Which [b]speak insolent things proudly and
contemptuously against the righteous.

19 [a]Oh, how great *is* Your goodness,
Which You have laid up for those who fear
You,
*Which* You have prepared for those who
trust in You
In the presence of the sons of men!
20 [a]You shall hide them in the secret place of
Your presence
From the plots of man;
[b]You shall keep them secretly in a [1]pavilion
From the strife of tongues.

21 Blessed *be* the LORD,
For [a]He has shown me His marvelous
kindness in a [1]strong city!
22 For I said in my haste,
"I am cut off from before Your eyes";
Nevertheless You heard the voice of my
supplications
When I cried out to You.

23 Oh, love the LORD, all you His saints!
*For* the LORD preserves the faithful,
And fully repays the proud person.
24 [a]Be of good courage,
And He shall strengthen your heart,
All you who hope in the LORD.

## PSALM 32

A Psalm of David. A [1]Contemplation.

BLESSED *is he whose* [a]transgression *is*
forgiven,
*Whose* sin *is* covered.
2 Blessed *is* the man to whom the LORD [a]does
not [1]impute iniquity,
And [b]in whose spirit *there is* no deceit.

3 When I kept silent, my bones grew old
Through my groaning all the day long.
4 For day and night Your [a]hand was heavy
upon me;
My vitality was turned into the drought of
summer. Selah
5 I acknowledged my sin to You,
And my iniquity I have not hidden.
[a]I said, "I will confess my transgressions to
the LORD,"
And You forgave the iniquity of my sin.
Selah

6 [a]For this cause everyone who is godly shall
[b]pray to You
In a time when You may be found;
Surely in a flood of great waters
They shall not come near him.
7 [a]You *are* my hiding place;
You shall preserve me from trouble;
You shall surround me with [b]songs of
deliverance. Selah

8 I will instruct you and teach you in the way
you should go;
I will guide you with My eye.
9 Do not be like the [a]horse *or* like the mule,
*Which* have no understanding,
Which must be harnessed with bit and bridle,
Else they will not come near you.

10 [a]Many sorrows *shall be* to the wicked;
But [b]he who trusts in the LORD,
mercy shall surround him.
11 [a]Be glad in the LORD and rejoice,
you righteous;
And shout for joy, all *you* upright in heart!

## PSALM 33

REJOICE [a]in the LORD, O you righteous!
*For* praise from the upright is beautiful.
2 Praise the LORD with the harp;
[1]Make melody to Him with an instrument of
ten strings.
3 Sing to Him a new song;
Play skillfully with a shout of joy.

4 For the word of the LORD *is* right,
And all His work *is done* in truth.
5 He loves righteousness and justice;
The earth is full of the goodness of the LORD.

6 [a]By the word of the LORD
the heavens were made,

---

2 [1]*strength* [2]Lit. *house of fortresses*
3 [a][Ps. 18:2] [b]Ps. 23:3; 25:11
5 [a]Luke 23:46 [b][Deut. 32:4]; Ps. 71:22
6 [a]Jon. 2:8
7 [a][John 10:27] [1]*troubles*
8 [a][Deut. 32:30]; Ps. 37:33 [b][Ps. 4:1; 18:19] [1]*given me over*
9 [a]Ps. 6:7 [1]Lit. *belly*
11 [a][Is. 53:4] [b]Job 19:13; Ps. 38:11; 88:8, 18 [c]Ps. 64:8 [1]*despised thing*
12 [a]Ps. 88:4, 5 [1]Lit. *perishing*
13 [a]Ps. 50:20; Jer. 20:10 [b]Lam. 2:22 [c]Ps. 62:4; Matt. 27:1
15 [a][Job 14:5; 24:1]
16 [a]Ps. 4:6; 80:3
17 [a]Ps. 25:2, 20 [b][1 Sam. 2:9]; Ps. 94:17; 115:17
18 [a]Ps. 109:2; 120:2 [b][1 Sam. 2:3]; Ps. 94:4; [Jude 15]
19 [a]Ps. 145:7; [Rom. 2:4; 11:22]
20 [a][Ps. 27:5; 32:7] [b]Job 5:21 [1]*shelter*
21 [a][Ps. 17:7] [1]*fortified*
24 [a][Ps. 27:14]

PSALM 32
title [1]Heb. *Maschil*
1 [a][Ps. 85:2; 103:3]; Rom. 4:7, 8
2 [a][2 Cor. 5:19] [b]John 1:47 [1]*charge his account with*
4 [a]1 Sam. 5:6; Ps. 38:2; 39:10
5 [a]2 Sam. 12:13; Ps. 38:18; [Prov. 28:13; 1 John 1:9]
6 [a][1 Tim. 1:16] [b]Ps. 69:13; Is. 55:6
7 [a]Ps. 9:9 [b]Ex. 15:1; Judg. 5:1; [Ps. 40:3]
9 [a]Prov. 26:3
10 [a]Ps. 16:4; [Prov. 13:21; Rom. 2:9] [b][Ps. 5:11, 12]; Prov. 16:20
11 [a]Ps. 64:10; 68:3; 97:12

PSALM 33
1 [a]Ps. 32:11; 97:12; Phil. 3:1; 4:4
2 [1]Lit. *Sing to Him*
6 [a]Gen. 1:6, 7; Ps. 148:5; [Heb. 11:3; 2 Pet. 3:5]

And all the [b]host of them
[c]by the breath of His mouth.
7 [a]He gathers the waters of the sea together [1]as a heap;
He lays up the deep in storehouses.

8 Let all the earth fear the LORD;
Let all the inhabitants of the world stand in awe of Him.
9 For [a]He spoke, and it was *done;*
He commanded, and it stood fast.

10 [a]The LORD brings the counsel of the nations to nothing;
He makes the plans of the peoples
of no effect.
11 [a]The counsel of the LORD stands forever,
The plans of His heart to all generations.
12 Blessed *is* the nation whose God *is* the LORD,
The people He has [a]chosen
as His own inheritance.

13 [a]The LORD looks from heaven;
He sees all the sons of men.
14 From the place of His dwelling He looks
On all the inhabitants of the earth;
15 He fashions their hearts individually;
[a]He [1]considers all their works.

16 [a]No king *is* saved
by the multitude of an army;
A mighty man is not delivered
by great strength.
17 [a]A horse *is* a [1]vain hope for safety;
Neither shall it deliver *any*
by its great strength.

18 [a]Behold, the eye of the LORD *is* on those who fear Him,
On those who hope in His mercy,
19 To deliver their soul from death,
And [a]to keep them alive in famine.

20 Our soul waits for the LORD;
He *is* our help and our shield.
21 For our heart shall rejoice in Him,
Because we have trusted in His holy name.
22 Let Your mercy, O LORD, be upon us,
Just as we hope in You.

## PSALM 34

A Psalm of David when he pretended madness before Abimelech, who drove him away, and he departed.

I WILL [a]bless the LORD at all times;
His praise *shall* continually *be* in my mouth.
2 My soul shall make its boast in the LORD;
The humble shall hear *of it* and be glad.
3 Oh, magnify the LORD with me,
And let us exalt His name together.

4 I [a]sought the LORD, and He heard me,
And delivered me from all my fears.
5 They looked to Him and were radiant,
And their faces were not ashamed.
6 This poor man cried out,
and the LORD heard *him,*
And saved him out of all his troubles.
7 [a]The [1]angel of the LORD [b]encamps all around
those who fear Him,
And delivers them.

8 Oh, [a]taste and see that the LORD *is* good;
[b]Blessed *is* the man *who* trusts in Him!
9 Oh, fear the LORD, you His saints!
*There is* no [1]want to those who fear Him.

10 The young lions lack and suffer hunger;
[a]But those who seek the LORD shall not lack any good *thing.*

11 Come, you children, listen to me;
[a]I will teach you the fear of the LORD.
12 [a]Who *is* the man *who* desires life,
And loves *many* days, that he may see good?
13 Keep your tongue from evil,
And your lips from speaking [a]deceit.
14 [a]Depart from evil and do good;
[b]Seek peace and pursue it.

15 [a]The eyes of the LORD *are* on the righteous,
And His ears *are open* to their cry.
16 [a]The face of the LORD *is* against those who do evil,
[b]To [1]cut off the remembrance of them from the earth.

17 *The righteous* cry out, and [a]the LORD hears,
And delivers them out of all their troubles.
18 [a]The LORD *is* near [b]to those who have a broken heart,
And saves such as [1]have a contrite spirit.

19 [a]Many *are* the afflictions of the righteous,
[b]But the LORD delivers him out of them all.
20 He guards all his bones;
[a]Not one of them is broken.
21 [a]Evil shall slay the wicked,
And those who hate the righteous shall be [1]condemned.
22 The LORD [a]redeems the soul of His servants,
And none of those who trust in Him shall be condemned.

## PSALM 35

A Psalm of David.

PLEAD[1] *my cause,* O LORD, with those who strive with me;
Fight against those who fight against me.
2 Take hold of shield and [1]buckler,
And stand up for my help.
3 Also draw out the spear,
And stop those who pursue me.
Say to my soul,
"I *am* your salvation."

4 [a]Let those be put to shame
and brought to dishonor
Who seek after my life;
Let those be [b]turned back
and brought to confusion
Who plot my hurt.
5 [a]Let them be like chaff before the wind,
And let the [1]angel of the LORD chase *them.*
6 Let their way be [a]dark and slippery,
And let the angel of the LORD pursue them.
7 For without cause they have [a]hidden their net for me *in* a pit,
*Which* they have dug without cause for my life.
8 [1]Let [a]destruction come upon him unexpectedly,
And let his net that he has hidden catch himself;
Into that very destruction let him fall.

9 And my soul shall be joyful in the LORD;
It shall rejoice in His salvation.
10 [a]All my bones shall say,
"LORD, [b]who *is* like You,

---

6 [b]Gen. 2:1 [c][Job 26:13]
7 [a]Job 26:10; 38:8 [1]LXX, Tg., Vg. *in a vessel*
9 [a]Gen. 1:3
10 [a]Is. 8:10; 19:3
11 [a][Job 23:13]
12 [a][Ex. 19:5]
13 [a]Job 28:24
15 [a][Jer. 32:19] [1]*understands*
16 [a]Ps. 44:6; 60:11
17 [a][Prov. 21:31] [1]*false*
18 [a][Job 36:7]
19 [a]Job 5:20

PSALM 34
1 [a][Eph. 5:20]
4 [a][Matt. 7:7]
7 [a]Dan. 6:22 [b]2 Kin. 6:17 [1]Or *Angel*
8 [a]1 Pet. 2:3 [b]Ps. 2:12
9 [1]*lack*
10 [a][Ps. 84:11]
11 [a]Ps. 32:8
12 [a][1 Pet. 3:10–12]
13 [a][Eph. 4:25]
14 [a]Ps. 37:27 [b][Rom. 14:19]
15 [a]Job 36:7
16 [a]Lev. 17:10 [b][Prov. 10:7] [1]*destroy*
17 [a]Ps. 34:6; 145:19
18 [a][Ps. 145:18] [b][Is. 57:15] [1]*are crushed in spirit*
19 [a]Prov. 24:16 [b]Ps. 34:4, 6, 17
20 [a]John 19:33, 36
21 [a]Ps. 94:23; 140:11 [1]*held guilty*
22 [a]1 Kin. 1:29

PSALM 35
1 [1]*Contend for me*
2 [1]A small shield
4 [a]Ps. 40:14, 15; 70:2, 3 [b]Ps. 129:5
5 [a]Job 21:18 [1]Or *Angel*
6 [a]Ps. 73:18
7 [a]Ps. 9:15
8 [a][1 Thess. 5:3] [1]Lit. *Let destruction he does not know come upon him,*
10 [a]Ps. 51:8 [b][Ex. 15:11]

Delivering the poor from him who is too
strong for him,
Yes, the poor and the needy from him who
plunders him?"
11 Fierce witnesses rise up;
They ask me *things* that I do not know.
12 [a]They reward me evil for good,
*To* the sorrow of my soul.
13 But as for me, [a]when they were sick,
My clothing *was* sackcloth;
I humbled myself with fasting;
And my prayer would return to my own
[1]heart.
14 I paced about as though *he were* my friend
*or* brother;
I bowed down [1]heavily, as one who mourns
*for his* mother.
15 But in my [1]adversity they rejoiced
And gathered together;
Attackers gathered against me,
And I did not know *it;*
They tore *at me* and did not cease;
16 With ungodly mockers at feasts
They gnashed at me with their teeth.
17 Lord, how long will You [a]look on?
Rescue me from their destructions,
My precious *life* from the lions.
18 I will give You thanks in the great assembly;
I will praise You among [1]many people.
19 [a]Let them not rejoice over me
who are wrongfully my enemies;
Nor let them wink with the eye
who hate me without a cause.
20 For they do not speak peace,
But they devise deceitful matters
Against *the* quiet ones in the land.
21 They also opened their mouth wide against
me,
*And* said, "Aha, aha!
Our eyes have seen *it.*"
22 *This* You have seen, O LORD;
Do not keep silence.
O Lord, do not be far from me.
23 Stir up Yourself,
and awake to my vindication,
To my cause, my God and my Lord.
24 Vindicate me, O LORD my God, according to
Your righteousness;
And let them not rejoice over me.
25 Let them not say in their hearts,
"Ah, so we would have it!"
Let them not say,
"We have swallowed him up."
26 Let them be ashamed
and brought to mutual confusion
Who rejoice at my hurt;
Let them be [a]clothed with shame and
dishonor
Who exalt themselves against me.
27 [a]Let them shout for joy and be glad,
Who favor my righteous cause;
And let them say continually,
"Let the LORD be magnified,
Who has pleasure in the prosperity of His
servant."
28 And my tongue shall speak of Your
righteousness
*And* of Your praise all the day long.

## PSALM 36

To the Chief Musician. A Psalm of David the servant of the LORD.

AN oracle within my heart concerning the
transgression of the wicked:
[a]*There is* no fear of God before his eyes.
2 For he flatters himself in his own eyes,
When he finds out his iniquity *and* when he
hates.
3 The words of his mouth *are* wickedness and
deceit;
[a]He has ceased to be wise *and* to do good.
4 [a]He devises wickedness on his bed;
He sets himself [b]in a way *that is* not good;
He does not [1]abhor [c]evil.
5 Your mercy, O LORD, *is* in the heavens;
Your faithfulness *reaches* to the clouds.
6 Your righteousness *is* like the [1]great
mountains;
[a]Your judgments *are* a great deep;
O LORD, You preserve man and beast.
7 How precious *is* Your lovingkindness, O God!
Therefore the children of men [a]put their trust
under the shadow of Your wings.
8 [a]They are abundantly satisfied with the
fullness of Your house,
And You give them drink from [b]the river of
Your pleasures.
9 [a]For with You *is* the fountain of life;
[b]In Your light we see light.
10 Oh, continue Your lovingkindness
to those who know You,
And Your righteousness
to the upright in heart.
11 Let not the foot of pride come against me,
And let not the hand of the wicked drive me
away.
12 There the workers of iniquity have fallen;
They have been cast down
and are not able to rise.

## PSALM 37

A Psalm of David.

DO[a] not fret because of evildoers,
Nor be envious of the workers of iniquity.
2 For they shall soon be cut down [a]like the
grass,
And wither as the green herb.
3 Trust in the LORD, and do good;
Dwell in the land, and feed on His
faithfulness.
4 [a]Delight yourself also in the LORD,
And He shall give you the desires of your
[b]heart.
5 [a]Commit[1] your way to the LORD,
Trust also in Him,
And He shall bring *it* to pass.
6 [a]He shall bring forth your righteousness as
the light,
And your justice as the noonday.
7 Rest in the LORD,
[a]and wait patiently for Him;
Do not fret because of him who [b]prospers in
his way,
Because of the man who brings wicked
schemes to pass.

**12** [a]Ps. 38:20; 109:5; Jer. 18:20; John 10:32
**13** [a]Job 30:25 [1]Lit. *bosom*
**14** [1]*in mourning*
**15** [1]*limping, stumbling*
**17** [a]Ps. 13:1; [Hab. 1:13]
**18** [1]*a mighty*
**19** [a]Ps. 69:4; 109:3; Lam. 3:52; [John 15:25]
**26** [a]Ps. 109:29
**27** [a]Rom. 12:15

PSALM 36
**1** [a]Rom. 3:18
**3** [a]Ps. 94:8; Jer. 4:22
**4** [a]Prov. 4:16; [Mic. 2:1] [b]Is. 65:2 [c][Ps. 52:3; Rom. 12:9] [1]*reject, loathe*
**6** [a]Job 11:8; Ps. 77:19; [Rom. 11:33] [1]Lit. *mountains of God*
**7** [a]Ruth 2:12; Ps. 17:8; 57:1; 91:4
**8** [a]Ps. 63:5; 65:4; Is. 25:6; Jer. 31:12–14 [b]Ps. 46:4; Rev. 22:1
**9** [a][Jer. 2:13; John 4:10, 14] [b][1 Pet. 2:9]

PSALM 37
**1** [a]Ps. 73:3; [Prov. 23:17; 24:19]
**2** [a]Job 14:2; Ps. 90:5, 6; 92:7; James 1:11
**4** [a]Job 22:26; Ps. 94:19; Is. 58:14 [b]Ps. 21:2; 145:19; [Matt. 7:7, 8]
**5** [a][Ps. 55:22; Prov. 16:3; 1 Pet. 5:7] [1]Lit. *Roll off onto*
**6** [a]Job 11:17; [Is. 58:8, 10]
**7** [a]Ps. 40:1; 62:5; [Lam. 3:26] [b][Ps. 73:3–12]

8 [a]Cease from anger, and forsake wrath;
[b]Do not fret—*it* only *causes* harm.

9 For evildoers shall be [1]cut off;
But those who wait on the LORD,
They shall [a]inherit the earth.
10 For [a]yet a little while
and the wicked *shall be* no *more;*
Indeed, [b]you will look carefully for his place,
But it *shall be* no *more.*
11 [a]But the meek shall inherit the earth,
And shall delight themselves
in the abundance of peace.

12 The wicked plots against the just,
[a]And gnashes at him with his teeth.
13 [a]The Lord laughs at him,
For He sees that [b]his day is coming.
14 The wicked have drawn the sword
And have bent their bow,
To cast down the poor and needy,
To slay those who are of upright conduct.
15 Their sword shall enter their own heart,
And their bows shall be broken.

16 [a]A little that a righteous man has
*Is* better than the riches of many wicked.
17 For the arms of the wicked shall be broken,
But the LORD upholds the righteous.

18 The LORD knows the days of the upright,
And their inheritance shall be forever.
19 They shall not be ashamed in the evil time,
And in the days of famine they shall be
satisfied.
20 But the wicked shall perish;
And the enemies of the LORD,
Like the splendor of the meadows, shall
vanish.
Into smoke they shall vanish away.

21 The wicked borrows and does not repay,
But [a]the righteous shows mercy and gives.
22 [a]For *those* blessed by Him
shall inherit the earth,
But *those* cursed by Him shall be [1]cut off.

23 [a]The steps of a *good* man are [1]ordered by the
LORD,
And He delights in his way.
24 [a]Though he fall,
he shall not be utterly cast down;
For the LORD upholds *him with* His hand.

25 I have been young, and *now* am old;
Yet I have not seen the righteous forsaken,
Nor his descendants begging bread.
26 [a]*He is* [1]ever merciful, and lends;
And his descendants *are* blessed.

27 Depart from evil, and do good;
And dwell forevermore.
28 For the LORD loves justice,
And does not forsake His saints;
They are preserved forever,
But the descendants of the wicked shall be
cut off.
29 [a]The righteous shall inherit the land,
And dwell in it forever.

30 [a]The mouth of the righteous speaks wisdom,
And his tongue talks of justice.
31 The law of his God *is* in his heart;
None of his steps shall [1]slide.

32 The wicked [a]watches the righteous,
And seeks to slay him.
33 The LORD [a]will not leave him in his hand,
Nor condemn him when he is judged.

34 [a]Wait on the LORD,
And keep His way,
And He shall exalt you to inherit the land;
When the wicked are cut off, you shall see *it.*
35 I have seen the wicked in great power,
And spreading himself like a native green
tree.
36 Yet [1]he passed away, and behold,
he *was* no *more;*
Indeed I sought him,
but he could not be found.

37 Mark the blameless *man,*
and observe the upright;
For the future of *that* man *is* peace.
38 [a]But the transgressors shall be destroyed
together;
The future of the wicked shall be cut off.

39 But the salvation of the righteous *is* from the
LORD;
*He is* their strength [a]in the time of trouble.
40 And [a]the LORD shall help them
and deliver them;
He shall deliver them from the wicked,
And save them,
[b]Because they trust in Him.

## PSALM 38

A Psalm of David. [a]To bring to remembrance.

O LORD, do not [a]rebuke me in Your wrath,
Nor chasten me in Your hot displeasure!
2 For Your arrows pierce me deeply,
And Your hand presses me down.

3 *There is* no soundness in my flesh
Because of Your anger,
Nor *any* health in my bones
Because of my sin.
4 For my iniquities have gone over my head;
Like a heavy burden they are too heavy for
me.
5 My wounds are foul *and* festering
Because of my foolishness.

6 I am [1]troubled, I am bowed down greatly;
I go mourning all the day long.
7 For my loins are full of inflammation,
And *there is* no soundness in my flesh.
8 I am feeble and severely broken;
I groan because of the turmoil of my heart.

9 Lord, all my desire *is* before You;
And my sighing is not hidden from You.
10 My heart pants, my strength fails me;
As for the light of my eyes,
it also has gone from me.

11 My loved ones and my friends [a]stand aloof
from my plague,
And my relatives stand afar off.
12 Those also who seek my life lay snares *for
me;*
Those who seek my hurt speak of
destruction,
And plan deception all the day long.

13 But I, like a deaf *man,* do not hear;
And *I am* like a mute *who* does not open his
mouth.
14 Thus I am like a man who does not hear,
And in whose mouth *is* no response.

**8** [a][Eph. 4:26] [b]Ps. 73:3
**9** [a]Ps. 25:13; Prov. 2:21; [Is. 57:13; 60:21; Matt. 5:5] [1]*destroyed*
**10** [a][Heb. 10:36] [b]Job 7:10; Ps. 37:35, 36
**11** [a][Matt. 5:5]
**12** [a]Ps. 35:16
**13** [a]Ps. 2:4; 59:8 [b]1 Sam. 26:10; Job 18:20
**16** [a]Prov. 15:16; 16:8; [1 Tim. 6:6]
**21** [a]Ps. 112:5, 9
**22** [a][Prov. 3:33] [1]*destroyed*
**23** [a][1 Sam. 2:9]; Ps. 40:2; 66:9; 119:5 [1]*established*
**24** [a]Prov. 24:16
**26** [a][Deut. 15:8]; Ps. 37:21 [1]Lit. *all the day*
**29** [a]Ps. 37:9; Prov. 2:21
**30** [a][Matt. 12:35]
**31** [1]*slip*
**32** [a]Ps. 10:8; 17:11
**33** [a]Ps. 31:8; [2 Pet. 2:9]
**34** [a]Ps. 27:14; 37:9
**36** [1]So with MT, LXX, Tg.; Syr., Vg. *I passed by*
**38** [a][Ps. 1:4–6; 37:20, 28]
**39** [a]Ps. 9:9; 37:19
**40** [a]Ps. 22:4; Is. 31:5; Dan. 3:17; 6:23 [b]1 Chr. 5:20; Ps. 34:22

PSALM 38
**title** [a]Ps. 70:title
**1** [a]Ps. 6:1
**6** [1]Lit. *bent down*
**11** [a]Ps. 31:11; 88:18

15 For [1]in You, O LORD, [a]I hope;
You will [2]hear, O Lord my God.
16 For I said, "*Hear me,*
lest they rejoice over me,
Lest, when my foot slips,
they exalt *themselves* against me."

17 [a]For I *am* ready to fall,
And my sorrow *is* continually before me.
18 For I will [a]declare my iniquity;
I will be [b]in [1]anguish over my sin.
19 But my enemies *are* vigorous,
*and* they are strong;
And those who hate me wrongfully have
multiplied.
20 Those also [a]who render evil for good,
They are my adversaries,
because I follow *what is* good.

21 Do not forsake me, O LORD;
O my God, [a]be not far from me!
22 Make haste to help me,
O Lord, my salvation!

## PSALM 39

To the Chief Musician. To Jeduthun. A Psalm of David.

I SAID, "I will guard my ways,
Lest I sin with my [a]tongue;
I will restrain my mouth with a muzzle,
While the wicked are before me."
2 [a]I was mute with silence,
I held my peace *even* from good;
And my sorrow was stirred up.
3 My heart was hot within me;
While I was [1]musing, the fire burned.
*Then* I spoke with my tongue:

4 "LORD, [a]make me to know my end,
And what *is* the measure of my days,
*That* I may know how frail I *am.*
5 Indeed, You have made my days *as*
handbreadths,
And my age *is* as nothing before You;
Certainly every man at his best state *is* but
[a]vapor. Selah
6 Surely every man walks about like a shadow;
Surely they [1]busy themselves in vain;
He heaps up *riches,*
And does not know who will gather them.

7 "And now, Lord, what do I wait for?
My [a]hope *is* in You.
8 Deliver me from all my transgressions;
Do not make me [a]the reproach of the foolish.
9 [a]I was mute, I did not open my mouth,
Because it was [b]You who did *it.*
10 [a]Remove Your plague from me;
I am consumed by the blow of Your hand.
11 When with rebukes You correct man for
iniquity,
You make his beauty [a]melt away like a
moth;
Surely every man *is* vapor. Selah

12 "Hear my prayer, O LORD,
And give ear to my cry;
Do not be silent at my tears;
For I *am* a stranger with You,
A sojourner, [a]as all my fathers *were.*
13 [a]Remove Your gaze from me,
that I may regain strength,
Before I go away and [b]am no more."

15 [a][Ps. 39:7] [1]*I wait for You, O LORD* [2]*answer*
17 [a]Ps. 51:3
18 [a]Ps. 32:5 [b][2 Cor. 7:9, 10] [1]*anxiety*
20 [a]Ps. 35:12
21 [a]Ps. 22:19; 35:22

PSALM 39

1 [a]Job 2:10; Ps. 34:13; [James 3:5–12]
2 [a]Ps. 38:13
3 [1]*meditating*
4 [a]Ps. 90:12; 119:84
5 [a]Ps. 62:9; [Eccl. 6:12]
6 [1]*make an uproar for nothing*
7 [a]Ps. 38:15
8 [a]Ps. 44:13; 79:4; 119:22
9 [a]Ps. 39:2 [b]2 Sam. 16:10; Job 2:10
10 [a]Job 9:34; 13:21
11 [a]Job 13:28; [Ps. 90:7]; Is. 50:9
12 [a]Gen. 47:9; Lev. 25:23; 1 Chr. 29:15; Ps. 119:19; Heb. 11:13; 1 Pet. 2:11
13 [a]Job 7:19; 10:20, 21; 14:6; Ps. 102:24 [b][Job 14:10]

PSALM 40

1 [a]Ps. 25:5; 27:14; 37:7
2 [a]Ps. 69:2, 14; Jer. 38:6 [b]Ps. 27:5
3 [a]Ps. 32:7; 33:3
4 [a]Ps. 34:8; 84:12
5 [a]Job 9:10 [b]Ps. 139:17; [Is. 55:8]
6 [a][1 Sam. 15:22]; Ps. 51:16; Is. 1:11; [Jer. 6:20; 7:22, 23]; Amos 5:22; [Mic. 6:6–8; Heb. 10:5–9]
8 [a][Matt. 26:39; John 4:34; 6:38]; Heb. 10:7 [b][Ps. 37:31; Jer. 31:33; 2 Cor. 3:3]
9 [a]Ps. 22:22, 25 [b]Ps. 119:13
10 [a]Acts 20:20, 27
11 [a]Ps. 61:7; Prov. 20:28
12 [a]Ps. 38:4; 65:3
13 [a]Ps. 70:1
14 [a]Ps. 35:4, 26; 70:2; 71:13 [1]Lit. *soul*
15 [a]Ps. 73:19
16 [a]Ps. 70:4

## PSALM 40

To the Chief Musician. A Psalm of David.

I [a]WAITED patiently for the LORD;
And He inclined to me,
And heard my cry.
2 He also brought me up out of a horrible pit,
Out of [a]the miry clay,
And [b]set my feet upon a rock,
*And* established my steps.
3 [a]He has put a new song in my mouth—
Praise to our God;
Many will see *it* and fear,
And will trust in the LORD.

4 [a]Blessed *is* that man who makes the LORD his
trust,
And does not respect the proud,
nor such as turn aside to lies.
5 [a]Many, O LORD my God,
*are* Your wonderful works
*Which* You have done;
[b]And Your thoughts toward us
Cannot be recounted to You in order;
*If* I would declare and speak *of them,*
They are more than can be numbered.

6 [a]Sacrifice and offering You did not desire;
My ears You have opened.
Burnt offering and sin offering
You did not require.
7 Then I said, "Behold, I come;
In the scroll of the book *it is* written of me.
8 [a]I delight to do Your will, O my God,
And Your law *is* [b]within my heart."

9 [a]I have proclaimed the good news of
righteousness
In the great assembly;
Indeed, [b]I do not restrain my lips,
O LORD, You Yourself know.
10 [a]I have not hidden Your righteousness within
my heart;
I have declared Your faithfulness and Your
salvation;
I have not concealed Your lovingkindness
and Your truth
From the great assembly.

11 Do not withhold Your tender mercies from
me, O LORD;
[a]Let Your lovingkindness and Your truth
continually preserve me.
12 For innumerable evils have surrounded me;
[a]My iniquities have overtaken me,
so that I am not able to look up;
They are more than the hairs of my head;
Therefore my heart fails me.

13 [a]Be pleased, O LORD, to deliver me;
O LORD, make haste to help me!
14 [a]Let them be ashamed
and brought to mutual confusion
Who seek to destroy my [1]life;
Let them be driven backward
and brought to dishonor
Who wish me evil.
15 Let them be [a]confounded because of their
shame,
Who say to me, "Aha, aha!"
16 [a]Let all those who seek You
rejoice and be glad in You;

Let such as love Your salvation
[b]say continually,
"The LORD be magnified!"
17 [a]But I *am* poor and needy;
*Yet* the LORD thinks upon me.
You *are* my help and my deliverer;
[b]Do not delay, O my God.

## PSALM 41

To the Chief Musician. A Psalm of David.

BLESSED *is* he who considers the [1]poor;
The LORD will deliver him in time of trouble.
2 The LORD will preserve him
and keep him alive,
*And* he will be blessed on the earth;
[a]You will not deliver him to the will of his
enemies.
3 The LORD will strengthen him on his bed of
illness;
You will [1]sustain him on his sickbed.

4 I said, "LORD, be merciful to me;
[a]Heal my soul, for I have sinned against You."
5 My enemies speak evil of me:
"When will he die, and his name perish?"
6 And if he comes to see *me,* he speaks [1]lies;
His heart gathers iniquity to itself;
*When* he goes out, he tells *it.*

7 All who hate me whisper together against
me;
Against me they [1]devise my hurt.
8 "An[1] evil disease," *they say,* "clings to him.
And *now* that he lies down,
he will rise up no more."
9 [a]Even my own familiar friend in whom I
trusted,
[b]Who ate my bread,
Has [1]lifted up *his* heel against me.

10 But You, O LORD, be merciful to me, and
raise me up,
That I may repay them.
11 By this I know that You are well pleased
with me,
Because my enemy does not triumph over
me.
12 As for me, You uphold me in my integrity,
And [a]set me before Your face forever.

13 [a]Blessed *be* the LORD God of Israel
From everlasting to everlasting!
Amen and Amen.

# BOOK TWO
# Psalms 42–72

## PSALM 42

To the Chief Musician. A [1]Contemplation of the sons of Korah.

AS the deer [1]pants for the water brooks,
So pants my soul for You, O God.
2 [a]My soul thirsts for God, for the [b]living God.
When shall I come and [1]appear before God?
3 [a]My tears have been my food day and night,
While they continually say to me,
[b]"Where *is* your God?"

4 When I remember these *things,*
[a]I pour out my soul within me.
For I used to go with the multitude;
[b]I went with them to the house of God,
With the voice of joy and praise,
With a multitude that kept a pilgrim feast.

5 [a]Why are you [1]cast down, O my soul?
And *why* are you disquieted within me?
[b]Hope in God, for I shall yet praise Him
[2]*For* the help of His countenance.

6 [1]O my God, my soul is cast down within me;
Therefore I will remember You from the land
of the Jordan,
And from the heights of Hermon,
From [2]the Hill Mizar.
7 Deep calls unto deep at the noise of Your
waterfalls;
[a]All Your waves and billows have gone over
me.
8 The LORD will [a]command His lovingkindness
in the daytime,
And [b]in the night His song *shall be* with
me—
A prayer to the God of my life.

9 I will say to God my Rock,
[a]"Why have You forgotten me?
Why do I go mourning because of the
oppression of the enemy?"
10 *As* with a [1]breaking of my bones,
My enemies [2]reproach me,
[a]While they say to me all day long,
"Where *is* your God?"

11 [a]Why are you cast down, O my soul?
And why are you disquieted within me?
Hope in God;
For I shall yet praise Him,
The [1]help of my countenance and my God.

## PSALM 43

VINDICATE [a]me, O God,
And [b]plead my cause against an ungodly
nation;
Oh, deliver me from the deceitful and unjust
man!
2 For You *are* the God of my strength;
Why do You cast me off?
[a]Why do I go mourning because of
the oppression of the enemy?

3 [a]Oh, send out Your light and Your truth!
Let them lead me;
Let them bring me to [b]Your holy hill
And to Your [1]tabernacle.
4 Then I will go to the altar of God,
To God my exceeding joy;
And on the harp I will praise You,
O God, my God.

5 [a]Why are you cast down, O my soul?
And why are you disquieted within me?
Hope in God;
For I shall yet praise Him,
The [1]help of my countenance and my God.

## PSALM 44

To the Chief Musician. A [a]Contemplation[1] of the sons of Korah.

WE have heard with our ears, O God,
[a]Our fathers have told us,
The deeds You did in their days,
In days of old:
2 [a]You drove out the [1]nations with Your hand,
But them You planted;
You afflicted the peoples, and cast them out.

---

**16** [b]Ps. 35:27 **17** [a]Ps. 70:5; 86:1; 109:22 [b]1 Pet. 5:7

PSALM 41
**1** [1]*helpless* or *powerless* **2** [a]Ps. 27:12 **3** [1]*restore* **4** [a]Ps. 6:2; 103:3; 147:3 **6** [1]*empty words* **7** [1]*plot* **8** [1]Lit. *A thing of Belial* **9** [a]2 Sam. 15:12 [b]John 13:18, 21–30 [1]Acted as a traitor **12** [a][Job 36:7] **13** [a]Ps. 72:18, 19; 89:52; 106:48; 150:6

PSALM 42
**title** [1]Heb. *Maschil* **1** [1]Lit. *longs for* **2** [a]Ps. 63:1; 84:2; 143:6 [b]1 Thess. 1:9 [1]So with MT, Vg.; some Heb. mss., LXX, Syr., Tg. *I see the face of God* **3** [a]Ps. 80:5; 102:9 [b]Ps. 79:10; 115:2 **4** [a]Job 30:16 [b]Is. 30:29 **5** [a]Ps. 42:11; 43:5 [b]Lam. 3:24 [1]Lit. *bowed down* [2]So with MT, Tg.; a few Heb. mss., LXX, Syr., [Vg.] *The help of my countenance, my God* **6** [1]So with MT, Tg.; a few Heb. mss., LXX, Syr., [Vg.] put *my God* at the end of v. 5 [2]Or *Mount* **7** [a]Ps. 69:1, 2; 88:7 **8** [a]Deut. 28:8 [b]Job 35:10 **9** [a]Ps. 38:6 **10** [a]Joel 2:17 [1]Lit. *shattering* [2]*revile* **11** [a]Ps. 43:5 [1]Lit. *salvation*

PSALM 43
**1** [a][Ps. 26:1; 35:24] [b]Ps. 35:1 **2** [a]Ps. 42:9 **3** [a][Ps. 40:11] [b]Ps. 3:4 [1]*dwelling places* **5** [a]Ps. 42:5, 11 [1]Lit. *salvation*

PSALM 44
**title** [a]Ps. 42:title [1]Heb. *Maschil* **1** [a][Ex. 12:26, 27] **2** [a]Ex. 15:17 [1]*Gentiles, heathen*

3 For [a]they did not gain possession of the land
by their own sword,
Nor did their own arm save them;
But it was Your right hand, Your arm, and
the light of Your countenance,
[b]Because You favored them.

4 [a]You are my King, [1]O God;
[2]Command victories for Jacob.
5 Through You [a]we will push down our
enemies;
Through Your name we will trample those
who rise up against us.
6 For [a]I will not trust in my bow,
Nor shall my sword save me.
7 But You have saved us from our enemies,
And have put to shame those who hated us.
8 [a]In God we boast all day long,
And praise Your name forever. Selah
9 But [a]You have cast *us* off and put us to
shame,
And You do not go out with our armies.
10 You make us [a]turn back from the enemy,
And those who hate us have taken [1]spoil for
themselves.
11 [a]You have given us up like sheep *intended* for
food,
And have [b]scattered us among the nations.
12 [a]You sell Your people for *next to* nothing,
And are not enriched by selling them.

13 [a]You make us a reproach to our neighbors,
A scorn and a derision to those all around us.
14 [a]You make us a byword among the nations,
[b]A shaking of the head among the peoples.
15 My dishonor *is* continually before me,
And the shame of my face has covered me,
16 Because of the voice of him who reproaches
and reviles,
[a]Because of the enemy and the avenger.

17 [a]All this has come upon us;
But we have not forgotten You,
Nor have we dealt falsely with Your
covenant.
18 Our heart has not turned back,
[a]Nor have our steps departed from Your way;
19 But You have severely broken us
in [a]the place of jackals,
And covered us [b]with the shadow of death.

20 If we had forgotten the name of our God,
Or [a]stretched[1] out our hands to a foreign god,
21 [a]Would not God search this out?
For He knows the secrets of the heart.
22 [a]Yet for Your sake we are killed all day long;
We are accounted as sheep for the slaughter.

23 [a]Awake! Why do You sleep, O Lord?
Arise! Do not cast *us* off forever.
24 [a]Why do You hide Your face,
*And* forget our affliction and our oppression?
25 For [a]our soul is bowed down to the [1]dust;
Our body clings to the ground.
26 Arise for our help,
And redeem us for Your mercies' sake.

## PSALM 45

To the Chief Musician. [a]Set to [1]"The Lilies." A [2]Contemplation of the sons of Korah. A Song of Love.

MY heart is overflowing with a good theme;
I recite my composition concerning
the King;
My tongue *is* the pen of a [1]ready writer.

2 You are fairer than the sons of men;
[a]Grace is poured upon Your lips;
Therefore God has blessed You forever.
3 [1]Gird Your [a]sword upon *Your* thigh,
[b]O Mighty One,
With Your [c]glory and Your majesty.
4 [a]And in Your majesty ride prosperously
because of truth, humility, *and*
righteousness;
And Your right hand shall teach You
awesome things.
5 Your arrows *are* sharp in the heart of the
King's enemies;
The peoples fall under You.

6 [a]Your throne, O God, *is* forever and ever;
A [b]scepter of righteousness *is* the scepter of
Your kingdom.
7 You love righteousness and hate wickedness;
Therefore God, Your God, has [a]anointed You
With the oil of [b]gladness more than Your
companions.
8 All Your garments are [a]scented with myrrh
and aloes *and* cassia,
Out of the ivory palaces,
by which they have made You glad.
9 [a]Kings' daughters *are* among Your honorable
women;
[b]At Your right hand stands the queen
in gold from Ophir.

10 Listen, O daughter,
Consider and incline your ear;
[a]Forget your own people also,
and your father's house;
11 So the King will greatly desire your beauty;
[a]Because He *is* your Lord, worship Him.
12 And the daughter of Tyre *will come* with a
gift;
[a]The rich among the people will seek your
favor.

13 The royal daughter *is* all glorious within *the
palace;*
Her clothing *is* woven with gold.
14 [a]She shall be brought to the King
in robes of many colors;
The virgins, her companions who follow her,
shall be brought to You.
15 With gladness and rejoicing they shall be
brought;
They shall enter the King's palace.

16 Instead of Your fathers shall be Your sons,
[a]Whom You shall make princes in all the
earth.
17 [a]I will make Your name to be remembered in
all generations;
Therefore the people shall praise You forever
and ever.

## PSALM 46

To the Chief Musician. A Psalm of the sons of Korah. A Song [a]for Alamoth.

GOD *is* our [a]refuge and strength,
[b]A[1] very present help in trouble.
2 Therefore we will not fear,
Even though the earth be removed,
And though the mountains be carried into
the [1]midst of the sea;
3 [a]*Though* its waters roar *and* be troubled,

---

**3** [a][Deut. 8:17, 18]; Josh. 24:12 [b][Deut. 4:37; 7:7, 8]
**4** [a][Ps. 74:12] [1]So with MT, Tg.; LXX, Vg. *and my God* [2]So with MT, Tg.; LXX, Syr., Vg. *who commands*
**5** [a]Deut. 33:17; [Dan. 8:4]
**6** [a][1 Sam. 17:47]; Ps. 33:16; [Hos. 1:7]
**8** [a]Ps. 34:2; [Jer. 9:24]
**9** [a]Ps. 60:1
**10** [a]Lev. 26:17; Josh. 7:8, 12; Ps. 89:43 [1]*plunder*
**11** [a]Ps. 44:22; Rom. 8:36 [b]Lev. 26:33; Deut. 4:27; 28:64; Ps. 106:27; Ezek. 20:23
**12** [a]Is. 52:3, 4; Jer. 15:13
**13** [a]Deut. 28:37; Ps. 79:4; 80:6
**14** [a]Jer. 24:9 [b]Job 16:4
**16** [a]Ps. 8:2
**17** [a]Dan. 9:13
**18** [a]Job 23:11
**19** [a]Is. 34:13 [b][Ps. 23:4]
**20** [a][Deut. 6:14] [1]Worshiped
**21** [a]Job 31:14; [Ps. 139:1, 2; Jer. 17:10]
**22** [a]Rom. 8:36
**23** [a]Ps. 7:6
**24** [a]Job 13:24
**25** [a]Ps. 119:25 [1]Ground, in humiliation

PSALM 45

**title** [a]Ps. 69:title [1]Heb. *Shoshannim* [2]Heb. *Maschil*
**1** [1]*skillful*
**2** [a]Luke 4:22
**3** [a][Is. 49:2; Heb. 4:12]; Rev. 1:16 [b][Is. 9:6] [c]Jude 25 [1]*Belt on*
**4** [a]Rev. 6:2
**6** [a][Ps. 93:2]; Heb. 1:8, 9 [b][Num. 24:17]
**7** [a]Ps. 2:2 [b]Ps. 21:6; Heb. 1:8, 9
**8** [a]Song 1:12, 13
**9** [a]Song 6:8 [b]1 Kin. 2:19
**10** [a]Deut. 21:13; Ruth 1:16, 17
**11** [a]Ps. 95:6; [Is. 54:5]
**12** [a]Is. 49:23
**14** [a]Song 1:4
**16** [a][1 Pet. 2:9; Rev. 1:6; 20:6]
**17** [a]Mal. 1:11

PSALM 46

**title** [a]1 Chr. 15:20
**1** [a]Ps. 62:7, 8 [b][Deut. 4:7; Ps. 145:18] [1]*An abundantly available help*
**2** [1]Lit. *heart*
**3** [a][Ps. 93:3, 4]

*Though* the mountains shake with its
swelling. Selah

4 *There is* a [a]river whose streams shall make
glad the [b]city of God,
The holy *place* of the [1]tabernacle of the Most
High.
5 God *is* [a]in the midst of her,
she shall not be [1]moved;
God shall help her,
just [2]at the break of dawn.
6 [a]The nations raged, the kingdoms were
moved;
He uttered His voice, the earth melted.

7 The [a]LORD of hosts *is* with us;
The God of Jacob *is* our refuge. Selah

8 Come, behold the works of the LORD,
Who has made desolations in the earth.
9 [a]He makes wars cease to the end of the earth;
[b]He breaks the bow and cuts the spear in two;
[c]He burns the chariot in the fire.

10 Be still, and know that I *am* God;
[a]I will be exalted among the nations,
I will be exalted in the earth!

11 The LORD of hosts *is* with us;
The God of Jacob *is* our refuge. Selah

## PSALM 47

To the Chief Musician. A Psalm of the sons of Korah.

OH, clap your hands, all you peoples!
Shout to God with the voice of triumph!
2 For the LORD Most High *is* awesome;
*He is* a great [a]King over all the earth.
3 [a]He will subdue the peoples under us,
And the nations under our feet.
4 He will choose our [a]inheritance for us,
The excellence of Jacob whom He loves.
Selah

5 [a]God has gone up with a shout,
The LORD with the sound of a trumpet.
6 Sing praises to God, sing praises!
Sing praises to our King, sing praises!
7 [a]For God *is* the King of all the earth;
[b]Sing praises with understanding.

8 [a]God reigns over the nations;
God [b]sits on His [c]holy throne.
9 The princes of the people have gathered
together,
[a]The people of the God of Abraham.
[b]For the shields of the earth *belong* to God;
He is greatly exalted.

## PSALM 48

A Song. A Psalm of the sons of Korah.

GREAT *is* the LORD, and greatly to be praised
In the [a]city of our God,
*In* His holy mountain.
2 [a]Beautiful in [1]elevation,
The joy of the whole earth,
*Is* Mount Zion *on* the sides of the north,
The city of the great King.
3 God *is* in her palaces;
He is known as her refuge.

4 For behold, [a]the kings assembled,
They passed by together.
5 They saw *it, and* so they marveled;
They were troubled, they hastened away.
6 Fear [a]took hold of them there,
*And* pain, as of a woman in birth pangs,
7 *As when* You break the [a]ships of Tarshish
With an east wind.

8 As we have heard,
So we have seen
In the city of the LORD of hosts,
In the city of our God:
God will [a]establish it forever. Selah

9 We have thought, O God, on [a]Your
lovingkindness,
In the midst of Your temple.
10 According to [a]Your name, O God,
So *is* Your praise to the ends of the earth;
Your right hand is full of righteousness.
11 Let Mount Zion rejoice,
Let the daughters of Judah be glad,
Because of Your judgments.

12 Walk about Zion,
And go all around her.
Count her towers;
13 Mark well her bulwarks;
Consider her palaces;
That you may [a]tell *it*
to the generation following.
14 For this *is* God,
Our God forever and ever;
[a]He will be our guide
[1]*Even* to death.

## PSALM 49

To the Chief Musician. A Psalm of the sons of Korah.

HEAR this, all peoples;
Give ear, all inhabitants of the world,
2 Both low and high,
Rich and poor together.
3 My mouth shall speak wisdom,
And the meditation of my heart *shall give*
understanding.
4 I will incline my ear to a proverb;
I will disclose my [1]dark saying on the harp.

5 Why should I fear in the days of evil,
*When* the iniquity at my heels surrounds me?
6 Those who [a]trust in their wealth
And boast in the multitude of their riches,
7 None *of them* can by any means redeem *his*
brother,
Nor [a]give to God a ransom for him—
8 For [a]the redemption of their souls *is* costly,
And it shall cease forever—
9 That he should continue to live eternally,
*And* [a]not [1]see the Pit.

10 For he sees wise men die;
Likewise the fool and the senseless person
perish,
And leave their wealth to others.
11 [1]Their inner thought *is that* their houses *will
last* forever,
Their dwelling places to all generations;
They [a]call *their* lands after their own names.
12 Nevertheless man, *though* in honor, does not
[1]remain;
He is like the beasts *that* perish.

13 This is the way of those who *are* [a]foolish,
And of their posterity who approve their
sayings. Selah
14 Like sheep they are laid in the grave;
Death shall feed on them;

---

4 [a][Ezek. 47:1–12] [b]Ps. 48:1, 8; Is. 60:14 [1]*dwelling places*
5 [a][Deut. 23:14; Is. 12:6]; Ezek. 43:7; Hos. 11:9; [Joel 2:27; Zeph. 3:15; Zech. 2:5, 10, 11; 8:3] [1]*shaken* [2]Lit. *at the turning of the morning*
6 [a]Ps. 2:1, 2
7 [a]Num. 14:9; 2 Chr. 13:12
9 [a]Is. 2:4 [b]Ps. 76:3 [c]Ezek. 39:9
10 [a][Is. 2:11, 17]

PSALM 47
2 [a]Deut. 7:21; Neh. 1:5; Ps. 76:12
3 [a]Ps. 18:47
4 [a][1 Pet. 1:4]
5 [a]Ps. 68:24, 25
7 [a]Zech. 14:9 [b]1 Cor. 14:15
8 [a]1 Chr. 16:31 [b]Ps. 97:2 [c]Ps. 48:1
9 [a][Rom. 4:11, 12] [b][Ps. 89:18]

PSALM 48
1 [a]Ps. 46:4; 87:3; Matt. 5:35
2 [a]Ps. 50:2 [1]*height*
4 [a]2 Sam. 10:6, 14
6 [a]Ex. 15:15
7 [a]1 Kin. 10:22; Ezek. 27:25
8 [a][Ps. 87:5; Is. 2:2]; Mic. 4:1
9 [a]Ps. 26:3
10 [a][Deut. 28:58]; Josh. 7:9; Mal. 1:11
13 [a][Ps. 78:5–7]
14 [a]Is. 58:11 [1]So with MT, Syr.; LXX, Vg. *Forever*

PSALM 49
4 [1]*riddle*
6 [a]Job 31:24; Ps. 52:7; [Prov. 11:28; Mark 10:24]
7 [a]Job 36:18, 19
8 [a][Matt. 16:26]
9 [a]Ps. 89:48 [1]*experience corruption*
11 [a]Gen. 4:17; Deut. 3:14 [1]LXX, Syr., Tg., Vg. *Their graves shall be their houses forever*
12 [1]So with MT, Tg.; LXX, [Syr.], Vg. *understand* (cf. v. 20)
13 [a][Luke 12:20]

[a]The upright shall have dominion over them
in the morning;
[b]And their beauty shall be consumed
in [1]the grave, far from their dwelling.
15 But God [a]will redeem my soul
from the power of [1]the grave,
For He shall [b]receive me. Selah

16 Do not be afraid when one becomes rich,
When the glory of his house is increased;
17 For when he dies he shall carry nothing
away;
His glory shall not descend after him.
18 Though while he lives [a]he blesses himself
(For *men* will praise you when you do well
for yourself),
19 He shall go to the generation of his fathers;
They shall never see [a]light.[1]
20 A man *who is* in honor,
yet does not understand,
[a]Is like the beasts *that* perish.

## PSALM 50

A Psalm of Asaph.

THE [a]Mighty One, God the LORD,
Has spoken and called the earth
From the rising of the sun to its going down.
2 Out of Zion, the perfection of beauty,
[a]God will shine forth.
3 Our God shall come,
and shall not keep silent;
[a]A fire shall devour before Him,
And it shall be very tempestuous all around
Him.

4 [a]He shall call to the heavens from above,
And to the earth,
that He may judge His people:
5 "Gather [a]My saints together to Me,
[b]Those who have [1]made a covenant with Me
by sacrifice."
6 Let the [a]heavens declare His righteousness,
For [b]God Himself *is* Judge. Selah

7 "Hear, O My people, and I will speak,
O Israel, and I will testify against you;
[a]I *am* God, your God!
8 [a]I will not [1]rebuke you [b]for your sacrifices
Or your burnt offerings,
*Which are* continually before Me.
9 [a]I will not take a bull from your house,
*Nor* goats out of your folds.
10 For every beast of the forest *is* Mine,
*And* the cattle on a thousand hills.
11 I know all the birds of the mountains,
And the wild beasts of the field *are* Mine.

12 "If I were hungry, I would not tell you;
[a]For the world *is* Mine, and all its fullness.
13 [a]Will I eat the flesh of bulls,
Or drink the blood of goats?
14 [a]Offer to God thanksgiving,
And [b]pay your vows to the Most High.
15 [a]Call upon Me in the day of trouble;
I will deliver you, and you shall glorify Me."

16 But to the wicked God says:
"What *right* have you to declare My statutes,
Or take My covenant in your mouth,
17 [a]Seeing you hate instruction
And cast My words behind you?
18 When you saw a thief,
you [a]consented[1] with him,
And have been a [b]partaker with adulterers.

14 [a]Ps. 47:3; [Dan. 7:18; 1 Cor. 6:2; Rev. 2:26] [b]Job 4:21 [1]Or *Sheol*
15 [a][Hos. 13:4]; Mark 16:6, 7; Acts 2:31, 32 [b]Ps. 73:24 [1]Or *Sheol*
18 [a]Deut. 29:19; Luke 12:19
19 [a]Job 33:30 [1]The light of life
20 [a]Eccl. 3:19

PSALM 50
1 [a]Is. 9:6
2 [a]Deut. 33:2; Ps. 80:1
3 [a]Lev. 10:2; Num. 16:35; [Ps. 97:3]
4 [a]Deut. 4:26; 31:28; 32:1; Is. 1:2
5 [a]Deut. 33:3 [b]Ex. 24:7 [1]Lit. *cut*
6 [a][Ps. 97:6] [b]Ps. 75:7
7 [a]Ex. 20:2
8 [a]Jer. 7:22 [b]Is. 1:11; [Hos. 6:6] [1]*rebuke*
9 [a]Ps. 69:31
12 [a]Ex. 19:5; [Deut. 10:14; Job 41:11]; 1 Cor. 10:26
13 [a][Ps. 51:15–17]
14 [a]Hos. 14:2; Heb. 13:15 [b]Num. 30:2; Deut. 23:21
15 [a]Job 22:27; [Zech. 13:9]
17 [a]Neh. 9:26; Rom. 2:21
18 [a][Rom. 1:32] [b]1 Tim. 5:22 [1]LXX, [Syr.], [Tg.], Vg. *run*
19 [a]Ps. 52:2
21 [a][Rom. 2:4] [b][Ps. 90:8]
22 [a][Job 8:13]
23 [a]Gal. 6:16

PSALM 51
title [a]2 Sam. 12:1
1 [a][Is. 43:25; 44:22; Acts 3:19; Col. 2:14]
2 [a]Jer. 33:8; Ezek. 36:33; [Heb. 9:14; 1 John 1:7, 9]
4 [a]2 Sam. 12:13 [b][Luke 5:21] [c]Rom. 3:4 [1]LXX, Tg., Vg. *in Your words*
5 [a][Job 14:4; Ps. 58:3; John 3:6; Rom. 5:12]
7 [a]Ex. 12:22; Lev. 14:4; Num. 19:18; Heb. 9:19 [b][Is. 1:18]
8 [a][Matt. 5:4]
10 [a][Ezek. 18:31; Eph. 2:10]
11 [a][Luke 11:13]
12 [a][2 Cor. 3:17]
16 [a][1 Sam. 15:22]; Ps. 50:8–14; [Mic. 6:6–8]
17 [a]Ps. 34:18; [Is. 57:15]; 66:2

19 You give your mouth to evil,
And [a]your tongue frames deceit.
20 You sit *and* speak against your brother;
You slander your own mother's son.
21 These *things* you have done,
and I kept silent;
[a]You thought that I was altogether like you;
*But* I will rebuke you,
And [b]set *them* in order before your eyes.

22 "Now consider this, you who [a]forget God,
Lest I tear *you* in pieces,
And *there be* none to deliver:
23 Whoever offers praise glorifies Me;
And [a]to him who orders *his* conduct *aright*
I will show the salvation of God."

## PSALM 51

To the Chief Musician. A Psalm of David [a]when Nathan the prophet went to him, after he had gone in to Bathsheba.

HAVE mercy upon me, O God,
According to Your lovingkindness;
According to the multitude of Your tender
mercies,
[a]Blot out my transgressions.
2 [a]Wash me thoroughly from my iniquity,
And cleanse me from my sin.

3 For I acknowledge my transgressions,
And my sin *is* always before me.
4 [a]Against You, You only, have I sinned,
And done *this* evil [b]in Your sight—
[c]That You may be found just [1]when
You speak,
*And* blameless when You judge.

5 [a]Behold, I was brought forth in iniquity,
And in sin my mother conceived me.
6 Behold, You desire truth in the inward parts,
And in the hidden *part* You will make me to
know wisdom.

7 [a]Purge me with hyssop, and I shall be clean;
Wash me, and I shall be [b]whiter than snow.
8 Make me hear joy and gladness,
*That* the bones You have broken [a]may
rejoice.
9 Hide Your face from my sins,
And blot out all my iniquities.

10 [a]Create in me a clean heart, O God,
And renew a steadfast spirit within me.
11 Do not cast me away from Your presence,
And do not take Your [a]Holy Spirit from me.

12 Restore to me the joy of Your salvation,
And uphold me *by Your* [a]generous Spirit.
13 *Then* I will teach transgressors Your ways,
And sinners shall be converted to You.

14 Deliver me from the guilt of bloodshed,
O God,
The God of my salvation,
*And* my tongue shall sing aloud of Your
righteousness.
15 O Lord, open my lips,
And my mouth shall show forth Your praise.
16 For [a]You do not desire sacrifice,
or else I would give *it;*
You do not delight in burnt offering.
17 [a]The sacrifices of God *are* a broken spirit,
A broken and a contrite heart—
These, O God, You will not despise.

18 Do good in Your good pleasure to Zion;
Build the walls of Jerusalem.
19 Then You shall be pleased with [a]the sacrifices of righteousness,
With burnt offering and whole burnt offering;
Then they shall offer bulls on Your altar.

## PSALM 52

To the Chief Musician. A [1]Contemplation of David [a]when Doeg the Edomite went and [b]told Saul, and said to him, "David has gone to the house of Ahimelech."

WHY do you boast in evil, O mighty man?
The goodness of God *endures* continually.
2 Your tongue devises destruction,
Like a sharp razor, working deceitfully.
3 You love evil more than good,
Lying rather than speaking righteousness. Selah
4 You love all devouring words,
*You* deceitful tongue.

5 God shall likewise destroy you forever;
He shall take you away, and pluck you out of *your* dwelling place,
And uproot you from the land of the living. Selah
6 The righteous also shall see and fear,
And shall laugh at him, *saying,*
7 "Here is the man *who* did not make God his strength,
But trusted in the abundance of his riches,
*And* strengthened himself in his [1]wickedness."

8 But I *am* [a]like a green olive tree in the house of God;
I trust in the mercy of God forever and ever.
9 I will praise You forever,
Because You have done *it;*
And in the presence of Your saints
I will wait on Your name, for *it is* good.

## PSALM 53

To the Chief Musician. Set to "Mahalath." A [1]Contemplation of David.

THE [a]fool has said in his heart,
"*There is* no God."
They are corrupt,
and have done abominable iniquity;
[b]*There is* none who does good.

2 God looks down from heaven upon the children of men,
To see if there are *any* who understand, who [a]seek God.
3 Every one of them has turned aside;
They have together become corrupt;
*There is* none who does good,
No, not one.

4 Have the workers of iniquity [a]no knowledge,
Who eat up my people *as* they eat bread,
And do not call upon God?
5 [a]There they are in great fear
*Where* no fear was,
For God has scattered the bones of him who encamps against you;
You have put *them* to shame,
Because God has despised them.

6 [a]Oh, that the salvation of Israel would come out of Zion!
When God brings back [1]the captivity of His people,
Let Jacob rejoice *and* Israel be glad.

## PSALM 54

To the Chief Musician. With [1]stringed instruments. A [2]Contemplation of David [a]when the Ziphites went and said to Saul, "Is David not hiding with us?"

SAVE me, O God, by Your name,
And vindicate me by Your strength.
2 Hear my prayer, O God;
Give ear to the words of my mouth.
3 For strangers have risen up against me,
And oppressors have sought after my life;
They have not set God before them. Selah

4 Behold, God *is* my helper;
The Lord *is* with those who [1]uphold my life.
5 He will repay my enemies for their evil.
[1]Cut them off in Your [2]truth.

6 I will freely sacrifice to You;
I will praise Your name, O LORD,
for *it is* good.
7 For He has delivered me out of all trouble;
[a]And my eye has seen *its desire* upon my enemies.

## PSALM 55

To the Chief Musician. With [1]stringed instruments. A [2]Contemplation of David.

GIVE ear to my prayer, O God,
And do not hide Yourself from my supplication.
2 Attend to me, and hear me;
I [a]am[1] restless in my complaint,
and moan noisily,
3 Because of the voice of the enemy,
Because of the oppression of the wicked;
[a]For they bring down trouble upon me,
And in wrath they hate me.

4 [a]My heart is severely pained within me,
And the terrors of death have fallen upon me.
5 Fearfulness and trembling have come upon me,
And horror has overwhelmed me.
6 So I said, "Oh, that I had wings like a dove!
I would fly away and be at rest.
7 Indeed, I would wander far off,
*And* remain in the wilderness. Selah
8 I would hasten my escape
From the windy storm *and* tempest."

9 Destroy, O Lord, *and* divide their [1]tongues,
For I have seen [a]violence and strife in the city.
10 Day and night they go around it on its walls;
[a]Iniquity and trouble *are* also in the midst of it.
11 Destruction *is* in its midst;
[a]Oppression and deceit do not depart from its streets.

12 [a]For *it is* not an enemy *who* reproaches me;
Then I could bear *it.*
Nor *is it* one *who* hates me who has [b]exalted *himself* against me;
Then I could hide from him.
13 But *it was* you, a man my equal,
[a]My companion and my acquaintance.

---

**19** [a]Ps. 4:5

PSALM 52
**title** [a]1 Sam. 22:9 [b]Ezek. 22:9 [1]Heb. *Maschil*
**7** [1]Lit. *desire,* in evil sense
**8** [a]Jer. 11:16
**9** [1]Or *has a good reputation*

PSALM 53
**title** [1]Heb. *Maschil*
**1** [a]Ps. 10:4 [b]Rom. 3:10–12
**2** [a][2 Chr. 15:2]
**4** [a]Jer. 4:22
**5** [a]Lev. 26:17, 36; Prov. 28:1
**6** [a]Ps. 14:7 [1]Or *His captive people*

PSALM 54
**title** [a]1 Sam. 23:19 [1]Heb. *neginoth* [2]Heb. *Maschil*
**4** [1]*sustain my soul*
**5** [1]*Destroy them* [2]Or *faithfulness*
**7** [a]Ps. 59:10

PSALM 55
**title** [1]Heb. *neginoth* [2]Heb. *Maschil*
**2** [a]Is. 38:14; 59:11; Ezek. 7:16 [1]*wander*
**3** [a]2 Sam. 16:7, 8
**4** [a]Ps. 116:3
**9** [a]Jer. 6:7 [1]*speech,* their counsel
**10** [a]Ps. 10:7
**11** [a]Ps. 10:7
**12** [a]Ps. 41:9 [b]Ps. 35:26; 38:16
**13** [a]2 Sam. 15:12

14 We took sweet counsel together,
*And* [a]walked to the house of God
in the throng.

15 Let death seize them;
Let them [a]go down alive into [1]hell,
For wickedness *is* in their dwellings *and*
among them.

16 As for me, I will call upon God,
And the LORD shall save me.
17 [a]Evening and morning and at noon
I will pray, and cry aloud,
And He shall hear my voice.
18 He has redeemed my soul in peace
from the battle *that was* against me,
For [a]there were many against me.
19 God will hear, and afflict them,
[a]Even He who abides from of old. Selah
Because they do not change,
Therefore they do not fear God.

20 He has [a]put forth his hands against those
who [b]were at peace with him;
He has broken his [1]covenant.
21 [a]*The words* of his mouth were smoother than
butter,
But war *was* in his heart;
His words were softer than oil,
Yet they *were* drawn swords.

22 [a]Cast your burden on the LORD,
And [b]He shall sustain you;
He shall never permit the righteous
to be [1]moved.

23 But You, O God, shall bring them down to
the pit of destruction;
[a]Bloodthirsty and deceitful men [b]shall not live
out half their days;
But I will trust in You.

## PSALM 56

To the Chief Musician. Set to [1]"The Silent Dove in Distant Lands." A Michtam of David when the [a]Philistines captured him in Gath.

BE [a]merciful to me, O God,
for man would swallow me up;
Fighting all day he oppresses me.
2 My enemies would [a]hound *me* all day,
For *there are* many who fight against me, O
Most High.

3 Whenever I am afraid,
I will trust in You.
4 In God (I will praise His word),
In God I have put my trust;
[a]I will not fear.
What can flesh do to me?

5 All day they twist my words;
All their thoughts *are* against me for evil.
6 They gather together,
They hide, they mark my steps,
When they lie in wait for my life.
7 Shall they escape by iniquity?
In anger cast down the peoples, O God!

8 You number my wanderings;
Put my tears into Your bottle;
[a]*Are they* not in Your book?
9 When I cry out *to You,*
Then my enemies will turn back;
This I know, because [a]God *is* for me.

10 In God (I will praise *His* word),
In the LORD (I will praise *His* word),
11 In God I have put my trust;
I will not be afraid.
What can man do to me?

12 Vows *made* to You *are binding* upon me,
O God;
I will render praises to You,
13 [a]For You have delivered my soul from death.
*Have You* not *kept* my feet from falling,
That I may walk before God
In the [b]light of the living?

## PSALM 57

To the Chief Musician. Set to [1]"Do Not Destroy." A Michtam of David [a]when he fled from Saul into the cave.

BE merciful to me, O God, be merciful to me!
For my soul trusts in You;
[a]And in the shadow of Your wings
I will make my refuge,
[b]Until *these* calamities have passed by.

2 I will cry out to God Most High,
To God [a]who performs *all things* for me.
3 [a]He shall send from heaven and save me;
He reproaches the one who [1]would swallow
me up. Selah
God [b]shall send forth His mercy and His
truth.

4 My soul *is* among lions;
I lie *among* the sons of men
Who are set on fire,
[a]Whose teeth *are* spears and arrows,
And their tongue a sharp sword.
5 [a]Be exalted, O God, above the heavens;
*Let* Your glory *be* above all the earth.

6 [a]They have prepared a net for my steps;
My soul is bowed down;
They have dug a pit before me;
Into the midst of it they *themselves* have
fallen. Selah

7 [a]My heart is steadfast, O God,
my heart is steadfast;
I will sing and give praise.
8 Awake, [a]my glory!
Awake, lute and harp!
I will awaken the dawn.

9 [a]I will praise You, O Lord, among the peoples;
I will sing to You among the [1]nations.
10 [a]For Your mercy reaches unto the heavens,
And Your truth unto the clouds.

11 [a]Be exalted, O God, above the heavens;
*Let* Your glory *be* above all the earth.

## PSALM 58

To the Chief Musician. Set to [1]"Do Not Destroy." A Michtam of David.

DO you indeed speak righteousness,
you silent ones?
Do you judge uprightly, you sons of men?
2 No, in heart you work wickedness;
You weigh out the violence of your hands in
the earth.

3 [a]The wicked are estranged from the womb;
They go astray as soon as they are born,
speaking lies.
4 [a]Their poison *is* like the poison of a serpent;

---

**14** [a]Ps. 42:4
**15** [a]Num. 16:30, 33 [1]Or *Sheol*
**17** [a]Dan. 6:10; Luke 18:1; Acts 3:1; 10:3, 30
**18** [a]2 Chr. 32:7, 8
**19** [a][Deut. 33:27]
**20** [a]Acts 12:1 [b]Ps. 7:4 [1]*treaty*
**21** [a]Ps. 28:3; 57:4; [Prov. 5:3, 4; 12:18]
**22** [a][Ps. 37:5; Matt. 6:25–34; Luke 12:22–31; 1 Pet. 5:7] [b]Ps. 37:24 [1]*shaken*
**23** [a]Ps. 5:6 [b]Prov. 10:27

PSALM 56
**title** [a]1 Sam. 21:11 [1]Heb. *Jonath Elem Rechokim*
**1** [a]Ps. 57:1
**2** [a]Ps. 57:3
**4** [a]Ps. 118:6; Is. 31:3; [Heb. 13:6]
**8** [a][Mal. 3:16]
**9** [a][Ps. 118:6; Rom. 8:31]
**13** [a]Ps. 116:8, 9 [b]Job 33:30

PSALM 57
**title** [a]1 Sam. 22:1 [1]Heb. *Al Tashcheth*
**1** [a]Ruth 2:12; Ps. 17:8; 63:7 [b]Is. 26:20
**2** [a][Ps. 138:8]
**3** [a]Ps. 144:5, 7 [b]Ps. 43:3 [1]*snaps at* or *hounds me,* or *crushes me*
**4** [a]Prov. 30:14
**5** [a]Ps. 108:5
**6** [a]Ps. 9:15
**7** [a]Ps. 108:1–5
**8** [a]Ps. 16:9
**9** [a]Ps. 108:3 [1]*Gentiles*
**10** [a]Ps. 103:11
**11** [a]Ps. 57:5

PSALM 58
**title** [1]Heb. *Al Tashcheth*
**3** [a][Ps. 53:3; Is. 48:8]
**4** [a]Eccl. 10:11

*They are* like the deaf cobra *that* stops its
ear,
5 Which will not [a]heed the voice of charmers,
Charming ever so skillfully.

6 [a]Break[1] their teeth in their mouth, O God!
Break out the fangs of the young lions,
O LORD!
7 [a]Let them flow away as waters *which* run
continually;
*When* he bends *his bow,*
Let his arrows be as if cut in pieces.
8 *Let them be* like a snail which melts away as
it goes,
[a]*Like* a stillborn child of a woman,
that they may not see the sun.

9 Before your [a]pots can feel *the burning*
thorns,
He shall take them away [b]as with a
whirlwind,
As in His living and burning wrath.
10 The righteous shall rejoice when he sees the
[a]vengeance;
[b]He shall wash his feet in the blood of the
wicked,
11 [a]So that men will say,
"Surely *there is* a reward for the righteous;
Surely He is God who [b]judges in the earth."

## PSALM 59

To the Chief Musician. Set to [1]"Do Not Destroy." A Michtam of David [a]when Saul sent men, and they watched the house in order to kill him.

DELIVER me from my enemies, O my God;
Defend me from those who rise up against
me.
2 Deliver me from the workers of iniquity,
And save me from bloodthirsty men.

3 For look, they lie in wait for my life;
[a]The mighty gather against me,
Not *for* my transgression nor *for* my sin,
O LORD.
4 They run and prepare themselves through no
fault *of mine.*

[a]Awake to help me, and behold!
5 You therefore, O LORD God of hosts, the God
of Israel,
Awake to punish all the [1]nations;
Do not be merciful to any wicked
transgressors. Selah

6 [a]At evening they return,
They growl like a dog,
And go all around the city.
7 Indeed, they belch with their mouth;
[a]Swords *are* in their lips;
For *they say,* [b]"Who hears?"

8 But [a]You, O LORD, shall laugh at them;
You shall have all the [1]nations in derision.
9 I will wait for You, O You [1]his Strength;
[a]For God *is* my [2]defense.
10 [1]My God of mercy shall [a]come to meet me;
God shall let [b]me see *my desire* on my
enemies.

11 Do not slay them, lest my people forget;
Scatter them by Your power,
And bring them down,
O Lord our shield.
12 [a]*For* the sin of their mouth *and* the words of
their lips,

**5** [a]Jer. 8:17
**6** [a]Job 4:10 [1]*Break away*
**7** [a]Josh. 2:11; 7:5
**8** [a]Job 3:16
**9** [a]Eccl. 7:6 [b]Prov. 10:25
**10** [a]Jer. 11:20 [b]Ps. 68:23
**11** [a]Ps. 92:15 [b]Ps. 50:6; 75:7

PSALM 59
**title** [a]1 Sam. 19:11 [1]Heb. *Al Tashcheth*
**1** [1]Lit. *Set me on high*
**3** [a]Ps. 56:6
**4** [a]Ps. 35:23
**5** [1]*Gentiles*
**6** [a]Ps. 59:14
**7** [a]Prov. 12:18 [b]Ps. 10:11
**8** [a]Prov. 1:26 [1]*Gentiles*
**9** [a][Ps. 62:2] [1]So with MT, [Syr.]; some Heb. mss., LXX, Tg., Vg. *my Strength* [2]Lit. *fortress*
**10** [a]Ps. 21:3 [b]Ps. 54:7 [1]So with Qr.; some Heb. mss., LXX, Vg. *My God, His mercy;* Kt., some Heb. mss., Tg. *O God, my mercy;* Syr. *O God, Your mercy*
**12** [a]Prov. 12:13
**13** [a]Ps. 104:35 [b]Ps. 83:18
**14** [a]Ps. 59:6
**15** [a]Job 15:23 [1]So with LXX, Vg.; MT, Syr., Tg. *spend the night*
**17** [a]Ps. 18:1

PSALM 60
**title** [a]Ps. 80 [b]2 Sam. 8:3, 13 [1]Heb. *Shushan Eduth*
**1** [a]Ps. 44:9
**2** [a][2 Chr. 7:14]
**3** [a]Ps. 71:20 [b]Jer. 25:15 [1]*staggering*
**4** [a]Ps. 20:5
**5** [a]Ps. 108:6–13
**6** [a]Ps. 89:35 [b]Josh. 1:6 [c]Gen. 12:6 [d]Josh. 13:27
**7** [a]Deut. 33:17 [b][Gen. 49:10] [1]Lit. *protection*
**8** [a]2 Sam. 8:2 [b]2 Sam. 8:14 [c]2 Sam. 8:1
**10** [a]Ps. 108:11 [b]Josh. 7:12
**11** [a]Ps. 118:8; 146:3
**12** [a]Num. 24:18

PSALM 61
**title** [1]Heb. *neginah*

Let them even be taken in their pride,
And for the cursing and lying *which* they
speak.
13 [a]Consume *them* in wrath, consume *them,*
That they *may* not *be;*
And [b]let them know that God rules in Jacob
To the ends of the earth. Selah

14 And [a]at evening they return,
They growl like a dog,
And go all around the city.
15 They [a]wander up and down for food,
And [1]howl if they are not satisfied.

16 But I will sing of Your power;
Yes, I will sing aloud of Your mercy in the
morning;
For You have been my defense
And refuge in the day of my trouble.
17 To You, [a]O my Strength, I will sing praises;
For God *is* my defense,
My God of mercy.

## PSALM 60

To the Chief Musician. [a]Set to [1]"Lily of the Testimony." A Michtam of David. For teaching. [b]When he fought against Mesopotamia and Syria of Zobah, and Joab returned and killed twelve thousand Edomites in the Valley of Salt.

O GOD, [a]You have cast us off;
You have broken us down;
You have been displeased;
Oh, restore us again!
2 You have made the earth tremble;
You have broken it;
[a]Heal its breaches, for it is shaking.
3 [a]You have shown Your people hard things;
[b]You have made us drink the wine of
[1]confusion.

4 [a]You have given a banner to those who fear
You,
That it may be displayed because of the
truth. Selah
5 [a]That Your beloved may be delivered,
Save *with* Your right hand, and hear me.

6 God has [a]spoken in His holiness:
"I will rejoice;
I will [b]divide [c]Shechem
And measure out [d]the Valley of Succoth.
7 Gilead *is* Mine, and Manasseh *is* Mine;
[a]Ephraim also *is* the [1]helmet for My head;
[b]Judah *is* My lawgiver.
8 [a]Moab *is* My washpot;
[b]Over Edom I will cast My shoe;
[c]Philistia, shout in triumph because of Me."

9 Who will bring me *to* the strong city?
Who will lead me to Edom?
10 *Is it* not You, O God, [a]*who* cast us off?
And You, O God, *who* did [b]not go out with
our armies?
11 Give us help from trouble,
[a]For the help of man *is* useless.
12 Through God [a]we will do valiantly,
For *it is* He *who* shall tread down our
enemies.

## PSALM 61

To the Chief Musician. On [1]a stringed instrument. A Psalm of David.

HEAR my cry, O God;
Attend to my prayer.

2 From the end of the earth I will cry to You,
When my heart is overwhelmed;
Lead me to the rock that is higher than I.

3 For You have been a shelter for me,
[a]A strong tower from the enemy.
4 I will abide in Your [1]tabernacle forever;
[a]I will trust in the shelter of Your wings. Selah

5 For You, O God, have heard my vows;
You have given *me* the heritage of those who fear Your name.
6 You will prolong the king's life,
His years as many generations.
7 He shall abide before God forever.
Oh, prepare mercy [a]and truth, *which* may [1]preserve him!

8 So I will sing praise to Your name forever,
That I may daily perform my vows.

## PSALM 62

To the Chief Musician. To [a]Jeduthun. A Psalm of David.

TRULY [a]my soul silently *waits* for God;
From Him *comes* my salvation.
2 He alone *is* my rock and my salvation;
*He is* my [1]defense;
I shall not be greatly [a]moved.[2]

3 How long will you attack a man?
You shall be slain, all of you,
[a]Like a leaning wall and a tottering fence.
4 They only consult to cast *him* down from his high position;
They [a]delight in lies;
They bless with their mouth,
But they curse inwardly. Selah

5 My soul, wait silently for God alone,
For my [1]expectation *is* from Him.
6 He only *is* my rock and my salvation;
*He is* my defense;
I shall not be [1]moved.
7 [a]In God *is* my salvation and my glory;
The rock of my strength,
*And* my refuge, *is* in God.

8 Trust in Him at all times, you people;
[a]Pour out your heart before Him;
God *is* a refuge for us. Selah

9 [a]Surely men of low degree *are* [1]a vapor,
Men of high degree *are* a lie;
If they are weighed on the scales,
They *are* altogether *lighter* than vapor.
10 Do not trust in oppression,
Nor vainly hope in robbery;
[a]If riches increase,
Do not set *your* heart *on them.*

11 God has spoken once,
Twice I have heard this:
That power *belongs* to God.
12 Also to You, O Lord, *belongs* mercy;
For [a]You [1]render to each one according to his work.

## PSALM 63

A Psalm of David [a]when he was in the wilderness of Judah.

O GOD, You *are* my God;
Early will I seek You;
[a]My soul thirsts for You;
My flesh longs for You

3 [a]Prov. 18:10
4 [a]Ps. 91:4 [1]*tent*
7 [a]Ps. 40:11 [1]Lit. *guard* or *keep*

PSALM 62
title [a]1 Chr. 25:1
1 [a]Ps. 33:20
2 [a]Ps. 55:22 [1]*strong tower* [2]*shaken*
3 [a]Is. 30:13
4 [a]Ps. 28:3
5 [1]*hope*
6 [1]*shaken*
7 [a][Jer. 3:23]
8 [a]1 Sam. 1:15; Ps. 42:4; Lam. 2:19
9 [a]Job 7:16; Ps. 39:5; Is. 40:17 [1]*vanity*
10 [a]Job 31:25; [Mark 10:24; Luke 12:15; 1 Tim. 6:10]
12 [a][Matt. 16:27]; Rom. 2:6; 1 Cor. 3:8 [1]*reward*

PSALM 63
title [a]1 Sam. 22:5
1 [a]Ps. 42:2; [Matt. 5:6]
2 [a]Ps. 27:4
3 [a]Ps. 138:2
4 [a]Ps. 28:2; 143:6
5 [1]Lit. *fat* [2]Abundance
6 [a]Ps. 42:8
10 [1]Lit. *pour him out by the hand of the sword* [2]Prey
11 [a]Deut. 6:13; [Is. 45:23; 65:16]

PSALM 64
1 [1]*complaint*
3 [a]Ps. 58:7
5 [a]Ps. 10:11; 59:7
8 [a]Ps. 31:11
9 [a]Jer. 50:28; 51:10
10 [a]Job 22:19; Ps. 32:11

PSALM 65
1 [1]A promised deed
2 [a][Is. 66:23]

In a dry and thirsty land
Where there is no water.
2 So I have looked for You in the sanctuary,
To see [a]Your power and Your glory.

3 [a]Because Your lovingkindness *is* better than life,
My lips shall praise You.
4 Thus I will bless You while I live;
I will [a]lift up my hands in Your name.
5 My soul shall be satisfied as with [1]marrow and [2]fatness,
And my mouth shall praise You with joyful lips.

6 When [a]I remember You on my bed,
I meditate on You in the *night* watches.
7 Because You have been my help,
Therefore in the shadow of Your wings I will rejoice.
8 My soul follows close behind You;
Your right hand upholds me.

9 But those *who* seek my life, to destroy *it,*
Shall go into the lower parts of the earth.
10 They shall [1]fall by the sword;
They shall be [2]a portion for jackals.

11 But the king shall rejoice in God;
[a]Everyone who swears by Him shall glory;
But the mouth of those who speak lies shall be stopped.

## PSALM 64

To the Chief Musician. A Psalm of David.

HEAR my voice, O God, in my [1]meditation;
Preserve my life from fear of the enemy.
2 Hide me from the secret plots of the wicked,
From the rebellion of the workers of iniquity,
3 Who sharpen their tongue like a sword,
[a]And bend *their bows to shoot* their arrows—bitter words,
4 That they may shoot in secret at the blameless;
Suddenly they shoot at him and do not fear.

5 They encourage themselves *in* an evil matter;
They talk of laying snares secretly;
[a]They say, "Who will see them?"
6 They devise iniquities:
"We have perfected a shrewd scheme."
Both the inward thought and the heart of man are deep.

7 But God shall shoot at them *with* an arrow;
Suddenly they shall be wounded.
8 So He will make them stumble over their own tongue;
[a]All who see them shall flee away.
9 All men shall fear,
And shall [a]declare the work of God;
For they shall wisely consider His doing.

10 [a]The righteous shall be glad in the LORD, and trust in Him.
And all the upright in heart shall glory.

## PSALM 65

To the Chief Musician. A Psalm of David. A Song.

PRAISE is awaiting You, O God, in Zion;
And to You the [1]vow shall be performed.
2 O You who hear prayer,
[a]To You all flesh will come.
3 Iniquities prevail against me;

*As for* our transgressions,
You will [a]provide atonement for them.

4 [a]Blessed *is the man* You [b]choose,
And cause to approach *You,*
*That* he may dwell in Your courts.
[c]We shall be satisfied with the goodness of Your house,
Of Your holy temple.

5 *By* awesome deeds in righteousness You will answer us,
O God of our salvation,
*You who are* the confidence of all the ends of the earth,
And of the far-off seas;
6 Who established the mountains by His strength,
[a]*Being* clothed with power;
7 [a]You who still the noise of the seas,
The noise of their waves,
[b]And the tumult of the peoples.
8 They also who dwell in the farthest parts are afraid of Your signs;
You make the outgoings of the morning and evening [1]rejoice.

9 You [1]visit the earth and [a]water it,
You greatly enrich it;
[b]The river of God is full of water;
You provide their grain,
For so You have prepared it.
10 You water its ridges abundantly,
You settle its furrows;
You make it soft with showers,
You bless its growth.

11 You crown the year with Your goodness,
And Your paths drip *with* abundance.
12 They drop *on* the pastures of the wilderness,
And the little hills rejoice on every side.
13 The pastures are clothed with flocks;
[a]The valleys also are covered with grain;
They shout for joy, they also sing.

## PSALM 66

To the Chief Musician. A Song. A Psalm.

MAKE [a]a joyful shout to God, all the earth!
2 Sing out the honor of His name;
Make His praise glorious.
3 Say to God,
"How [a]awesome are Your works!
[b]Through the greatness of Your power
Your enemies shall submit themselves to You.
4 [a]All the earth shall worship You
And sing praises to You;
They shall sing praises *to* Your name." Selah

5 Come and see the works of God;
*He is* awesome *in His* doing toward the sons of men.
6 [a]He turned the sea into dry *land;*
[b]They went through the river on foot.
There we will rejoice in Him.
7 He rules by His power forever;
His eyes observe the nations;
Do not let the rebellious exalt themselves. Selah

8 Oh, bless our God, you peoples!
And make the voice of His praise to be heard,
9 Who keeps our soul among the living,
And does not allow our feet to [1]be moved.
10 For [a]You, O God, have tested us;
[b]You have refined us as silver is refined.
11 [a]You brought us into the net;
You laid affliction on our backs.
12 [a]You have caused men to ride over our heads;
[b]We went through fire and through water;
But You brought us out to [1]rich *fulfillment.*

13 [a]I will go into Your house with burnt offerings;
[b]I will pay You my [1]vows,
14 Which my lips have uttered
And my mouth has spoken when I was in trouble.
15 I will offer You burnt sacrifices of fat animals,
With the sweet aroma of rams;
I will offer bulls with goats. Selah

16 Come *and* hear, all you who fear God,
And I will declare what He has done for my soul.
17 I cried to Him with my mouth,
And He was [1]extolled with my tongue.
18 [a]If I regard iniquity in my heart,
The Lord will not hear.
19 *But* certainly God [a]has heard *me;*
He has attended to the voice of my prayer.

20 Blessed *be* God,
Who has not turned away my prayer,
Nor His mercy from me!

## PSALM 67

To the Chief Musician. On [1]stringed instruments. A Psalm. A Song.

GOD be merciful to us and bless us,
*And* [a]cause His face to shine upon us, Selah
2 That [a]Your way may be known on earth,
[b]Your salvation among all nations.

3 Let the peoples praise You, O God;
Let all the peoples praise You.
4 Oh, let the nations be glad and sing for joy!
For [a]You shall judge the people righteously,
And govern the nations on earth. Selah

5 Let the peoples praise You, O God;
Let all the peoples praise You.
6 [a]*Then* the earth shall [1]yield her increase;
God, our own God, shall bless us.
7 God shall bless us,
And all the ends of the earth shall fear Him.

## PSALM 68

To the Chief Musician. A Psalm of David. A Song.

LET [a]God arise,
Let His enemies be scattered;
Let those also who hate Him flee before Him.
2 [a]As smoke is driven away,
So drive *them* away;
[b]As wax melts before the fire,
*So* let the wicked perish at the presence of God.
3 But [a]let the righteous be glad;
Let them rejoice before God;
Yes, let them rejoice exceedingly.

4 Sing to God, sing praises to His name;
[a]Extol[1] Him who rides on the [2]clouds,
[b]By His name [3]YAH,
And rejoice before Him.

---

**3** [a]Ps. 51:2; 79:9; Is. 6:7; [Heb. 9:14; 1 John 1:7, 9]
**4** [a]Ps. 33:12 [b]Ps. 4:3 [c]Ps. 36:8
**6** [a]Ps. 93:1
**7** [a]Matt. 8:26 [b]Is. 17:12, 13
**8** [1]*shout for joy*
**9** [a][Deut. 11:12]; Jer. 5:24 [b]Ps. 46:4; 104:13; 147:8 [1]*give attention to*
**13** [a]Is. 44:23; 55:12

PSALM 66
**1** [a]Ps. 100:1
**3** [a]Ps. 65:5 [b]Ps. 18:44
**4** [a]Ps. 117:1; Zech. 14:16
**6** [a]Ex. 14:21 [b]Josh. 3:14–16
**9** [1]*slip*
**10** [a]Job 23:10; Ps. 17:3 [b][Is. 48:10; Zech. 13:9; Mal. 3:3; 1 Pet. 1:7]
**11** [a]Lam. 1:13; Ezek. 12:13
**12** [a]Is. 51:23 [b]Is. 43:2 [1]*abundance*
**13** [a]Ps. 100:4; 116:14, 17–19 [b][Eccl. 5:4] [1]Promised deeds
**17** [1]*praised*
**18** [a]Job 27:9; [Prov. 15:29; 28:9]; Is. 1:15; [John 9:31; James 4:3]
**19** [a]Ps. 116:1, 2

PSALM 67
**title** [1]Heb. *neginoth*
**1** [a]Num. 6:25
**2** [a]Acts 18:25 [b]Is. 52:10; Titus 2:11
**4** [a][Ps. 96:10, 13; 98:9]
**6** [a]Lev. 26:4; Ps. 85:12; [Ezek. 34:27]; Zech. 8:12 [1]*give her produce*

PSALM 68
**1** [a]Num. 10:35
**2** [a][Is. 9:18]; Hos. 13:3 [b]Ps. 97:5; Mic. 1:4
**3** [a]Ps. 32:11
**4** [a]Deut. 33:26 [b][Ex. 6:3] [1]*Praise* [2]MT *deserts;* Tg. *heavens,* cf. v. 34 and Is. 19:1 [3]Lit. *LORD,* a shortened Heb. form

5 [a]A father of the fatherless,
a defender of widows,
*Is* God in His holy habitation.
6 [a]God sets the solitary in families;
[b]He brings out those who are bound into prosperity;
But [c]the rebellious dwell in a dry *land.*

7 O God, [a]when You went out before Your people,
When You marched through the wilderness, Selah
8 The earth shook;
The heavens also dropped *rain* at the presence of God;
Sinai itself *was moved* at the presence of God, the God of Israel.
9 [a]You, O God, sent a plentiful rain,
Whereby You confirmed Your inheritance,
When it was weary.
10 Your congregation dwelt in it;
[a]You, O God, provided from Your goodness for the poor.

11 The Lord gave the word;
Great *was* the [1]company of those who proclaimed *it:*
12 "Kings[a] of armies flee, they flee,
And she who remains at home divides the [1]spoil.
13 [a]Though you lie down among the [1]sheepfolds,
[b]*You will be* like the wings of a dove covered with silver,
And her feathers with yellow gold."
14 [a]When the Almighty scattered kings in it,
It was *white* as snow in Zalmon.

15 A mountain of God *is* the mountain of Bashan;
A mountain *of many* peaks
*is* the mountain of Bashan.
16 Why do you [1]fume with envy,
you mountains of *many* peaks?
[a]*This is* the mountain *which* God desires to dwell in;
Yes, the LORD will dwell *in it* forever.

17 [a]The chariots of God *are* twenty thousand,
*Even* thousands of thousands;
The Lord is among them *as in* Sinai,
in the Holy *Place.*
18 [a]You have ascended on high,
[b]You have led captivity captive;
[c]You have received gifts among men,
Even *from* [d]the rebellious,
[e]That the LORD God might dwell *there.*

19 Blessed *be* the Lord,
*Who* daily loads us *with benefits,*
The God of our salvation! Selah
20 Our God *is* the God of salvation;
And [a]to GOD the Lord *belong* escapes from death.

21 But [a]God will wound the head of His enemies,
[b]The hairy scalp of the one who still goes on in his trespasses.
22 The Lord said, "I will bring [a]back from Bashan,
I will bring *them* back [b]from the depths of the sea,
23 [a]That [1]your foot may crush *them* in blood,
[b]And the tongues of your dogs *may have* their portion from *your* enemies."

24 They have seen Your [1]procession, O God,
The procession of my God, my King, into the sanctuary.
25 [a]The singers went before, the players on instruments *followed* after;
Among *them were* the maidens playing timbrels.
26 Bless God in the congregations,
The Lord, from [a]the fountain of Israel.
27 [a]There *is* little Benjamin, their leader,
The princes of Judah *and* their [1]company,
The princes of Zebulun *and* the princes of Naphtali.

28 [1]Your God has [a]commanded your strength;
Strengthen, O God, what You have done for us.
29 Because of Your temple at Jerusalem,
[a]Kings will bring presents to You.
30 Rebuke the beasts of the reeds,
[a]The herd of bulls with the calves of the peoples,
*Till everyone* [b]submits himself with pieces of silver.
Scatter the peoples *who* delight in war.
31 [a]Envoys will come out of Egypt;
[b]Ethiopia will quickly [c]stretch out her hands to God.

32 Sing to God, you [a]kingdoms of the earth;
Oh, sing praises to the Lord, Selah
33 To Him [a]who rides on the heaven of heavens, *which were* of old!
Indeed, He sends out His voice,
a [b]mighty voice.
34 [a]Ascribe strength to God;
His excellence *is* over Israel,
And His strength *is* in the clouds.
35 O God, [a]*You are* more awesome than Your holy places.
The God of Israel *is* He who gives strength and power to *His* people.

Blessed *be* God!

## PSALM 69

To the Chief Musician. Set to [1]"The Lilies." A Psalm of David.

SAVE me, O God!
For [a]the waters have come up to *my* [1]neck.
2 [a]I sink in deep mire,
Where *there is* no standing;
I have come into deep waters,
Where the floods overflow me.
3 [a]I am weary with my crying;
My throat is dry;
[b]My eyes fail while I wait for my God.

4 Those who [a]hate me without a cause
Are more than the hairs of my head;
They are mighty who would destroy me,
*Being* my enemies wrongfully;
Though I have stolen nothing,
I *still* must restore *it.*

5 O God, You know my foolishness;
And my sins are not hidden from You.
6 Let not those who [1]wait for You,
O Lord GOD of hosts, be ashamed because of me;

**5** [a][Ps. 10:14, 18; 146:9] **6** [a]Ps. 107:4–7 [b]Acts 12:6 [c]Ps. 107:34 **7** [a]Ex. 13:21; [Hab. 3:13] **9** [a]Lev. 26:4; Deut. 11:11; Job 5:10; Ezek. 34:26 **10** [a]Deut. 26:5; Ps. 74:19 **11** [1]*host* **12** [a]Num. 31:8; Josh. 10:16; Judg. 5:19 [1]*plunder* **13** [a]Ps. 81:6 [b]Ps. 105:37 [1]Or *saddle-bags* **14** [a]Josh. 10:10 **16** [a][Deut. 12:5]; 1 Kin. 9:3 [1]Lit. *stare* **17** [a]Deut. 33:2; Dan. 7:10 **18** [a]Mark 16:19; Acts 1:9; Eph. 4:8; Phil. 2:9; Col. 3:1; Heb. 1:3 [b]Judg. 5:12 [c]Acts 2:4, 33; 10:44–46; [1 Cor. 12:4–11; Eph. 4:7–12] [d][1 Tim. 1:13] [e]Ps. 78:60 **20** [a][Deut. 32:39] **21** [a]Hab. 3:13 [b]Ps. 55:23 **22** [a]Num. 21:33; Deut. 30:1–9; Amos 9:1–3 [b]Ex. 14:22 **23** [a]Ps. 58:10 [b]1 Kin. 21:19; Jer. 15:3 [1]LXX, [Syr.], Tg., Vg. *you may dip your foot* **24** [1]Lit. *goings* **25** [a]1 Chr. 13:8 **26** [a]Deut. 33:28; Is. 48:1 **27** [a]Judg. 5:14; 1 Sam. 9:21 [1]*throng* **28** [a]Ps. 42:8; Is. 26:12 [1]LXX, [Syr.], Tg., Vg. *Command, O God* **29** [a]1 Kin. 10:10, 25; 2 Chr. 32:23; Ps. 45:12; 72:10; Is. 18:7 **30** [a]Ps. 22:12 [b]2 Sam. 8:2 **31** [a]Is. 19:19–23 [b]Is. 45:14; Zeph. 3:10 [c]Ps. 44:20 **32** [a][Ps. 67:3, 4] **33** [a]Deut. 33:26; Ps. 18:10 [b]Ps. 46:6; Is. 30:30 **34** [a]Ps. 29:1 **35** [a]Ps. 76:12

PSALM 69

**title** [1]Heb. *Shoshannim* **1** [a]Job 22:11; Jon. 2:5 [1]Lit. *soul* **2** [a]Ps. 40:2 **3** [a]Ps. 6:6 [b]Deut. 28:32; Ps. 119:82, 123; Is. 38:14 **4** [a]Ps. 35:19; John 15:25 **6** [1]Wait in faith

Let not those who seek You be [2]confounded
because of me, O God of Israel.
7 Because for Your sake I have borne
reproach;
Shame has covered my face.
8 [a]I have become a stranger to my brothers,
And an alien to my mother's children;
9 [a]Because zeal for Your house has eaten me
up,
[b]And the reproaches of those who reproach
You have fallen on me.
10 When I wept *and chastened* my soul with
fasting,
That became my reproach.
11 I also [1]made sackcloth my garment;
I became a byword to them.
12 Those who [1]sit in the gate speak against me,
And I *am* the song of the [a]drunkards.

13 But as for me, my prayer *is* to You,
O LORD, *in* the acceptable time;
O God, in the multitude of Your mercy,
Hear me in the truth of Your salvation.
14 Deliver me out of the mire,
And let me not sink;
Let me be delivered from those who hate me,
And out of the deep waters.
15 Let not the floodwater overflow me,
Nor let the deep swallow me up;
And let not the pit shut its mouth on me.

16 Hear me, O LORD,
for Your lovingkindness *is* good;
Turn to me according to the multitude of
Your tender mercies.
17 And do not hide Your face from Your
servant,
For I am in trouble;
Hear me speedily.
18 Draw near to my soul, *and* redeem it;
Deliver me because of my enemies.

19 You know [a]my reproach, my shame, and my
dishonor;
My adversaries *are* all before You.
20 Reproach has broken my heart,
And I am full of [1]heaviness;
[a]I looked *for someone* to take pity,
but *there was* none;
And for [b]comforters, but I found none.
21 They also gave me gall for my food,
[a]And for my thirst they gave me vinegar to
drink.

22 [a]Let their table become a snare before them,
And their well-being a trap.
23 [a]Let their eyes be darkened,
so that they do not see;
And make their loins shake continually.
24 [a]Pour out Your indignation upon them,
And let Your wrathful anger take hold of
them.
25 [a]Let their dwelling place be desolate;
Let no one live in their tents.
26 For they persecute the *ones* [a]You have
struck,
And talk of the grief of those You have
wounded.
27 [a]Add iniquity to their iniquity,
[b]And let them not come into Your
righteousness.
28 Let them [a]be blotted out of the book of the
living,
[b]And not be written with the righteous.

29 But I *am* poor and sorrowful;
Let Your salvation, O God, set me up on
high.
30 [a]I will praise the name of God with a song,
And will magnify Him with thanksgiving.
31 [a]*This* also shall please the LORD better than an
ox *or* bull,
Which has horns and hooves.
32 [a]The humble shall see *this and* be glad;
And you who seek God,
[b]your hearts shall live.
33 For the LORD hears the poor,
And does not despise [a]His prisoners.

34 [a]Let heaven and earth praise Him,
The seas [b]and everything that moves in
them.
35 [a]For God will save Zion
And build the cities of Judah,
That they may dwell there and possess it.
36 Also, [a]the [1]descendants of His servants shall
inherit it,
And those who love His name shall dwell in
it.

## PSALM 70

To the Chief Musician. *A Psalm* of David. [a]To bring to remembrance.

MAKE *haste,* [a]O God, to deliver me!
Make haste to help me, O LORD!

2 [a]Let them be ashamed and confounded
Who seek my life;
Let them be [1]turned back and confused
Who desire my hurt.
3 [a]Let them be turned back because of their
shame,
Who say, [1]"Aha, aha!"

4 Let all those who seek You
rejoice and be glad in You;
And let those who love Your salvation say
continually,
"Let God be magnified!"

5 [a]But I *am* poor and needy;
[b]Make haste to me, O God!
You *are* my help and my deliverer;
O LORD, do not delay.

## PSALM 71

IN [a]You, O LORD, I put my trust;
Let me never be put to shame.
2 [a]Deliver me in Your righteousness,
and cause me to escape;
[b]Incline Your ear to me, and save me.
3 [a]Be my [1]strong refuge,
To which I may resort continually;
You have given the [b]commandment to save
me,
For You *are* my rock and my fortress.

4 [a]Deliver me, O my God, out of the hand of the
wicked,
Out of the hand of the unrighteous and cruel
man.
5 For You are [a]my hope, O Lord GOD;
*You are* my trust from my youth.
6 [a]By You I have been [1]upheld from birth;
You are He who took me out of my mother's
womb.
My praise *shall be* continually of You.

**6** [2]*dishonored*
**8** [a]Is. 53:3; Mark 3:21; Luke 8:19; John 7:3–5
**9** [a]John 2:17 [b]Rom. 15:3
**11** [1]Symbolic of sorrow
**12** [a]Job 30:9 [1]Sit as judges
**19** [a]Ps. 22:6, 7; Heb. 12:2
**20** [a]Is. 63:5 [b]Job 16:2 [1]Lit. *sickness*
**21** [a]Matt. 27:34, 48; Mark 15:23, 36; Luke 23:36; John 19:28–30
**22** [a]Rom. 11:9, 10
**23** [a]Is. 6:9, 10
**24** [a][1 Thess. 2:16; Jer. 10:25]
**25** [a]Matt. 23:38; Luke 13:35; Acts 1:20
**26** [a][Is. 53:4; 1 Pet. 2:24]
**27** [a]Neh. 4:5; [Rom. 1:28] [b][Is. 26:10]
**28** [a][Ex. 32:32]; Phil. 4:3; [Rev. 3:5; 13:8] [b]Ezek. 13:9; Luke 10:20; Heb. 12:23
**30** [a][Ps. 28:7]
**31** [a]Ps. 50:13, 14, 23; 51:16
**32** [a]Ps. 34:2 [b]Ps. 22:26
**33** [a][Ps. 68:6]; Eph. 3:1
**34** [a]Ps. 96:11; Is. 44:23; 49:13 [b]Is. 55:12
**35** [a]Ps. 51:18; Is. 44:26
**36** [a]Ps. 102:28 [1]Lit. *seed*

PSALM 70

**title** [a]Ps. 38:title
**1** [a]Ps. 40:13–17
**2** [a]Ps. 35:4, 26 [1]So with MT, LXX, Tg., Vg.; some Heb. mss., Syr. *appalled* (cf. 40:15)
**3** [a]Ps. 40:15 [1]An expression of scorn
**5** [a]Ps. 72:12, 13 [b]Ps. 141:1

PSALM 71

**1** [a]Ps. 25:2, 3
**2** [a]Ps. 31:1 [b]Ps. 17:6
**3** [a]Ps. 31:2, 3 [b]Ps. 44:4 [1]Lit. *rock of refuge* or *rock of habitation*
**4** [a]Ps. 140:1, 3
**5** [a]Jer. 14:8; 17:7, 13, 17; 50:7
**6** [a]Ps. 22:9, 10; Is. 46:3 [1]*sustained from the womb*

7 [a]I have become as a wonder to many,
But You *are* my strong refuge.
8 Let [a]my mouth be filled *with* Your praise
*And with* Your glory all the day.

9 Do not cast me off in the time of old age;
Do not forsake me when my strength fails.
10 For my enemies speak against me;
And those who lie in wait for my life [a]take counsel together,
11 Saying, "God has forsaken him;
Pursue and take him,
for *there is* none to deliver *him*."

12 [a]O God, do not be far from me;
O my God, [b]make haste to help me!
13 Let them be [1]confounded *and* consumed
Who are adversaries of my life;
Let them be covered *with* reproach and dishonor
Who seek my hurt.

14 But I will hope continually,
And will praise You yet more and more.
15 My mouth shall tell of Your righteousness
*And* Your salvation all the day,
For I do not know *their* limits.
16 I will go in the strength of the Lord GOD;
I will make mention of Your righteousness, of Yours only.

17 O God, You have taught me from my [a]youth;
And to this *day* I declare Your wondrous works.
18 Now also [a]when *I am* old and grayheaded,
O God, do not forsake me,
Until I declare Your strength to *this* generation,
Your power to everyone *who* is to come.
19 Also [a]Your righteousness, O God,
*is* [1]very high,
You who have done great things;
[b]O God, who *is* like You?
20 [a]*You,* who have shown me great and severe troubles,
[b]Shall revive me again,
And bring me up again from the depths of the earth.
21 You shall increase my greatness,
And comfort me on every side.

22 Also [a]with the lute I will praise You—
*And* Your faithfulness, O my God!
To You I will sing with the harp,
O [b]Holy One of Israel.
23 My lips shall greatly rejoice when I sing to You,
And [a]my soul, which You have redeemed.
24 My tongue also shall talk of Your righteousness all the day long;
For they are confounded,
For they are brought to shame
Who seek my hurt.

## PSALM 72

A Psalm [a]of Solomon.

GIVE the king Your judgments, O God,
And Your righteousness to the king's Son.
2 [a]He will judge Your people with righteousness,
And Your poor with justice.
3 [a]The mountains will bring peace to the people,
And the little hills, by righteousness.
4 [a]He will bring justice to the poor of the people;
He will save the children of the needy,
And will [1]break in pieces the oppressor.

5 [1]They shall fear You
[a]As long as the sun and moon endure,
Throughout all generations.
6 [a]He shall come down like rain upon the grass before mowing,
Like showers *that* water the earth.
7 In His days the righteous shall flourish,
[a]And abundance of peace,
Until the moon is no more.

8 [a]He shall have dominion also from sea to sea,
And from the River to the ends of the earth.
9 [a]Those who dwell in the wilderness will bow before Him,
[b]And His enemies will lick the dust.
10 [a]The kings of Tarshish and of the isles
Will bring presents;
The kings of Sheba and Seba
Will offer gifts.
11 [a]Yes, all kings shall fall down before Him;
All nations shall serve Him.

12 For He [a]will deliver the needy when he cries,
The poor also, and *him* who has no helper.
13 He will spare the poor and needy,
And will save the souls of the needy.
14 He will redeem their life from oppression and violence;
And [a]precious shall be their blood in His sight.

15 And He shall live;
And the gold of [a]Sheba will be given to Him;
Prayer also will be made for Him continually,
*And* daily He shall be praised.

16 There will be an abundance of grain in the earth,
On the top of the mountains;
Its fruit shall wave like Lebanon;
[a]And *those* of the city shall flourish like grass of the earth.

17 [a]His name shall endure forever;
His name shall continue as long as the sun.
And [b]*men* shall be blessed in Him;
[c]All nations shall call Him blessed.

18 [a]Blessed *be* the LORD God, the God of Israel,
[b]Who only does wondrous things!
19 And [a]blessed *be* His glorious name forever!
[b]And let the whole earth be filled *with* His glory.
Amen and Amen.

20 The prayers of David the son of Jesse are ended.

# BOOK THREE
# Psalms 73–89

## PSALM 73

A Psalm of [a]Asaph.

TRULY God *is* good to Israel,
To such as are pure in heart.
2 But as for me, my feet had almost stumbled;
My steps had nearly [a]slipped.

**7** [a]Is. 8:18; Zech. 3:8; 1 Cor. 4:9
**8** [a]Ps. 35:28
**10** [a]2 Sam. 17:1
**12** [a]Ps. 35:22 [b]Ps. 70:1
**13** [1]*ashamed*
**17** [a]Deut. 4:5; 6:7
**18** [a][Is. 46:4]
**19** [a]Deut. 3:24; Ps. 57:10 [b]Ps. 35:10 [1]*great,* lit. *to the height* of heaven
**20** [a]Ps. 60:3 [b]Hos. 6:1, 2
**22** [a]Ps. 92:1–3 [b]2 Kin. 19:22; Is. 1:4
**23** [a]Ps. 103:4

PSALM 72
**title** [a]Ps. 127:title
**2** [a][Is. 9:7; 11:2–5; 32:1]
**3** [a]Ps. 85:10
**4** [a]Is. 11:4 [1]*crush*
**5** [a]Ps. 72:7, 17; 89:36 [1]So with MT, Tg.; LXX, Vg. *They shall continue*
**6** [a]Deut. 32:2; 2 Sam. 23:4; Hos. 6:3
**7** [a]Is. 2:4
**8** [a]Ex. 23:31; [Is. 9:6; Zech. 9:10]
**9** [a]Ps. 74:14; Is. 23:13 [b]Is. 49:23; Mic. 7:17
**10** [a]1 Kin. 10:2; 2 Chr. 9:21
**11** [a]Is. 49:23
**12** [a]Job 29:12
**14** [a]1 Sam. 26:21; [Ps. 116:15]
**15** [a]Is. 60:6
**16** [a]1 Kin. 4:20
**17** [a][Ps. 89:36] [b][Gen. 12:3] [c]Luke 1:48
**18** [a]1 Chr. 29:10 [b]Ex. 15:11; Job 5:9
**19** [a][Neh. 9:5] [b]Num. 14:21; Hab. 2:14

PSALM 73
**title** [a]Ps. 50:title
**2** [a]Job 12:5

3 [a]For I *was* envious of the boastful,
When I saw the prosperity of the [b]wicked.
4 For *there are* no [1]pangs in their death,
But their strength *is* firm.
5 [a]They *are* not in trouble *as other* men,
Nor are they plagued like *other* men.
6 Therefore pride serves as their necklace;
Violence covers them [a]*like* a garment.
7 [a]Their [1]eyes bulge with abundance;
They have more than heart could wish.
8 [a]They scoff and speak wickedly *concerning* oppression;
They [b]speak [1]loftily.
9 They set their mouth [a]against the heavens,
And their tongue walks through the earth.
10 Therefore his people return here,
[a]And waters of a full *cup* are drained by them.
11 And they say, [a]"How does God know?
And is there knowledge in the Most High?"
12 Behold, these *are* the ungodly,
Who are always at ease;
They increase *in* riches.
13 Surely I have [1]cleansed my heart *in* [a]vain,
And washed my hands in innocence.
14 For all day long I have been plagued,
And chastened every morning.
15 If I had said, "I will speak thus,"
Behold, I would have been untrue to the generation of Your children.
16 When I thought *how* to understand this,
It *was* [1]too painful for me—
17 Until I went into the sanctuary of God;
*Then* I understood their [a]end.
18 Surely [a]You set them in slippery places;
You cast them down to destruction.
19 Oh, how they are *brought* to desolation, as in a moment!
They are utterly consumed with terrors.
20 As a dream when *one* awakes,
*So,* Lord, when You awake,
You shall despise their image.
21 Thus my heart was grieved,
And I was [1]vexed in my mind.
22 [a]I *was* so foolish and ignorant;
I was *like* a beast before You.
23 Nevertheless I *am* continually with You;
You hold *me* by my right hand.
24 [a]You will guide me with Your counsel,
And afterward receive me *to* glory.
25 [a]Whom have I in heaven *but You?*
And *there is* none upon earth *that* I desire besides You.
26 [a]My flesh and my heart fail;
*But* God *is* the [1]strength of my heart and my [b]portion forever.
27 For indeed, [a]those who are far from You shall perish;
You have destroyed all those who [1]desert You for harlotry.
28 But *it is* good for me to [a]draw near to God;
I have put my trust in the Lord GOD,
That I may [b]declare all Your works.

## PSALM 74

A [1]Contemplation of Asaph.

O GOD, why have You cast *us* off forever?
*Why* does Your anger smoke against the sheep of Your pasture?
2 Remember Your congregation,
*which* You have purchased of old,
The tribe of Your inheritance,
*which* You have redeemed—
This Mount Zion where You have dwelt.
3 Lift up Your feet to the perpetual desolations.
The enemy has damaged everything in the sanctuary.
4 [a]Your enemies roar in the midst of Your meeting place;
[b]They set up their banners *for* signs.
5 They seem like men who lift up
Axes among the thick trees.
6 And now they break down its carved work, all at once,
With axes and hammers.
7 They have set fire to Your sanctuary;
They have defiled the dwelling place of Your name to the ground.
8 [a]They said in their hearts,
"Let us [1]destroy them altogether."
They have burned up all the meeting places of God in the land.
9 We do not see our signs;
[a]*There is* no longer any prophet;
Nor *is there* any among us who knows how long.
10 O God, how long will the adversary [1]reproach?
Will the enemy blaspheme Your name forever?
11 [a]Why do You withdraw Your hand, even Your right hand?
*Take it* out of Your bosom and destroy *them.*
12 For [a]God *is* my King from of old,
Working salvation in the midst of the earth.
13 [a]You divided the sea by Your strength;
You broke the heads of the [1]sea serpents in the waters.
14 You broke the heads of [1]Leviathan in pieces,
*And* gave him *as* food to the people inhabiting the wilderness.
15 [a]You broke open the fountain and the flood;
[b]You dried up mighty rivers.
16 The day *is* Yours, the night also *is* [a]Yours;
[b]You have prepared the light and the sun.
17 You have [a]set all the borders of the earth;
[b]You have made summer and winter.
18 Remember this, *that* the enemy has reproached, O LORD,
And *that* a foolish people has blasphemed Your name.
19 Oh, do not deliver the life of Your turtledove to the wild beast!
Do not forget the life of Your poor forever.
20 [a]Have respect to the covenant;
For the [1]dark places of the earth are full of the [2]haunts of [3]cruelty.
21 Oh, do not let the oppressed return ashamed!
Let the poor and needy praise Your name.
22 Arise, O God, plead Your own cause;
Remember how the foolish man [1]reproaches You daily.
23 Do not forget the voice of Your enemies;
The tumult of those who rise up against You increases continually.

## PSALM 75

To the Chief Musician. Set to [a]"Do[1] Not Destroy." A Psalm of Asaph. A Song.

WE give thanks to You, O God,
we give thanks!

**3** [a]Ps. 37:1, 7; [Prov. 23:17] [b]Job 21:5–16; Jer. 12:1
**4** [1]*pains*
**5** [a]Job 21:9
**6** [a]Ps. 109:18
**7** [a]Job 15:27; Jer. 5:28 [1]Tg. *face bulges;* LXX, Syr., Vg. *iniquity bulges*
**8** [a]Ps. 53:1 [b]2 Pet. 2:18; Jude 16 [1]Proudly
**9** [a]Rev. 13:6
**10** [a][Ps. 75:8]
**11** [a]Job 22:13
**13** [a]Job 21:15; 35:3; Mal. 3:14 [1]*kept my heart pure in vain*
**16** [1]*trouble-some in my eyes*
**17** [a][Ps. 37:38; 55:23]
**18** [a]Ps. 35:6
**21** [1]Lit. *pierced in my kidneys*
**22** [a]Ps. 92:6
**24** [a]Ps. 32:8; 48:14; Is. 58:11
**25** [a][Phil. 3:8]
**26** [a]Ps. 84:2 [b]Ps. 16:5 [1]Lit. *rock*
**27** [a][Ps. 119:155] [1]Are unfaithful to You
**28** [a][Heb. 10:22; James 4:8] [b]Ps. 116:10; 2 Cor. 4:13

PSALM 74
**title** [1]Heb. *Maschil*
**4** [a]Lam. 2:7 [b]Num. 2:2
**8** [a]Ps. 83:4 [1]*oppress*
**9** [a]1 Sam. 3:1; Lam. 2:9; Ezek. 7:26; Amos 8:11
**10** [1]*revile*
**11** [a]Lam. 2:3
**12** [a]Ps. 44:4
**13** [a]Ex. 14:21 [1]*sea monsters*
**14** [1]A large sea creature of unknown identity
**15** [a]Ex. 17:5, 6; Num. 20:11; Ps. 105:41; Is. 48:21 [b]Ex. 14:21, 22; Josh. 2:10; 3:13
**16** [a]Job 38:12 [b]Gen. 1:14–18
**17** [a]Deut. 32:8; Acts 17:26 [b]Gen. 8:22
**20** [a]Gen. 17:7, 8; Lev. 26:44, 45 [1]*hiding places* [2]*homes* [3]*violence*
**22** [1]*reviles* or *taunts*

PSALM 75
**title** [a]Ps. 57:title [1]Heb. *Al Tashcheth*

For Your wondrous works declare *that* Your
name is near.
2 "When I choose the [1]proper time,
I will judge uprightly.
3 The earth and all its inhabitants are
dissolved;
I set up its pillars firmly. Selah

4 "I said to the boastful,
'Do not deal boastfully,'
And to the wicked, [a]'Do not [1]lift up the horn.
5 Do not lift up your horn on high;
Do *not* speak with [1]a stiff neck.' "

6 For exaltation *comes* neither from the east
Nor from the west nor from the south.
7 But [a]God *is* the Judge:
[b]He puts down one,
And exalts another.
8 For [a]in the hand of the LORD *there is* a cup,
And the wine is red;
It is fully mixed, and He pours it out;
Surely its dregs shall all the wicked of the
earth
Drain *and* drink down.

9 But I will declare forever,
I will sing praises to the God of Jacob.

10 "All[a] the [1]horns of the wicked
I will also cut off,
*But* [b]the horns of the righteous
shall be [c]exalted."

## PSALM 76

To the Chief Musician. On [1]stringed instruments. A Psalm of Asaph. A Song.

IN [a]Judah God *is* known;
His name *is* great in Israel.
2 In [1]Salem also is His tabernacle,
And His dwelling place in Zion.
3 There He broke the arrows of the bow,
The shield and sword of battle. Selah

4 You *are* more glorious and excellent
[a]*Than* the mountains of prey.
5 [a]The stouthearted were plundered;
[b]They [1]have sunk into their sleep;
And none of the mighty men have found the
use of their hands.
6 [a]At Your rebuke, O God of Jacob,
Both the chariot and horse were cast into a
dead sleep.

7 You, Yourself, *are* to be feared;
And [a]who may stand in Your presence
When once You are angry?
8 [a]You caused judgment to be heard from
heaven;
[b]The earth feared and was still,
9 When God [a]arose to judgment,
To deliver all the oppressed of the earth.
Selah

10 [a]Surely the wrath of man shall praise You;
With the remainder of wrath You shall gird
Yourself.

11 [a]Make vows to the LORD your God,
and pay *them;*
[b]Let all who are around Him bring presents to
Him who ought to be feared.
12 He shall cut off the spirit of princes;
[a]*He is* awesome to the kings of the earth.

## PSALM 77

To the Chief Musician. [a]To Jeduthun. A Psalm of Asaph.

I CRIED out to God with my voice—
To God with my voice;
And He gave ear to me.
2 In the day of my trouble I sought the Lord;
My hand was stretched out in the night
without ceasing;
My soul refused to be comforted.
3 I remembered God, and was troubled;
I complained, and my spirit was
overwhelmed. Selah

4 You hold my eyelids *open;*
I am so troubled that I cannot speak.
5 I have considered the days of old,
The years of ancient times.
6 I call to remembrance my song in the night;
I meditate within my heart,
And my spirit [1]makes diligent search.

7 Will the Lord cast off forever?
And will He be favorable no more?
8 Has His mercy ceased forever?
Has *His* [a]promise failed [1]forevermore?
9 Has God forgotten to be gracious?
Has He in anger shut up His tender mercies?
Selah

10 And I said, "This *is* my [1]anguish;
*But I will remember* the years of the right
hand of the Most High."
11 I will remember the works of the LORD;
Surely I will remember Your wonders of old.
12 I will also meditate on all Your work,
And talk of Your deeds.
13 Your way, O God, *is* in [1]the [a]sanctuary;
Who *is* so great a God as *our* God?
14 You *are* the God who does wonders;
You have declared Your strength among the
peoples.
15 You have with *Your* arm redeemed Your
people,
The sons of Jacob and Joseph. Selah

16 The waters saw You, O God;
The waters saw You, they were [a]afraid;
The depths also trembled.
17 The clouds poured out water;
The skies sent out a sound;
Your arrows also flashed about.
18 The voice of Your thunder *was* in the
whirlwind;
The lightnings lit up the world;
The earth trembled and shook.
19 Your way *was* in the sea,
Your path in the great waters,
And Your footsteps were not known.
20 You led Your people like a flock
By the hand of Moses and Aaron.

## PSALM 78

A [a]Contemplation[1] of Asaph.

GIVE ear, O my people, *to* my law;
Incline your ears to the words of my mouth.
2 I will open my mouth in a [a]parable;
I will utter [1]dark sayings of old,
3 Which we have heard and known,
And our fathers have told us.
4 [a]We will not hide *them* from their children,

---

**2** [1]*appointed*
**4** [a][1 Sam. 2:3]; Ps. 94:4 [1]Raise the head proudly like a horned animal
**5** [1]Insolent pride
**7** [a]Ps. 50:6 [b]1 Sam. 2:7; Ps. 147:6; Dan. 2:21
**8** [a]Job 21:20; Ps. 60:3; Jer. 25:15; Rev. 14:10; 16:19
**10** [a]Ps. 101:8; Jer. 48:25 [b]Ps. 89:17; 148:14 [c]1 Sam. 2:1 [1]Strength

PSALM 76

**title** [1]Heb. *neginoth*
**1** [a]Ps. 48:1, 3
**2** [1]Jerusalem
**4** [a]Ezek. 38:12
**5** [a]Is. 10:12; 46:12 [b]Ps. 13:3 [1]Lit. *have slumbered their sleep*
**6** [a]Ex. 15:1–21; Ezek. 39:20; Nah. 2:13; Zech. 12:4
**7** [a][Ezra 9:15; Nah. 1:6; Mal. 3:2; Rev. 6:17]
**8** [a]Ex. 19:9 [b]1 Chr. 16:30; 2 Chr. 20:29
**9** [a][Ps. 9:7–9]
**10** [a]Ex. 9:16; Rom. 9:17
**11** [a][Eccl. 5:4–6] [b]2 Chr. 32:22, 23
**12** [a]Ps. 68:35

PSALM 77

**title** [a]Ps. 39:title
**6** [1]*ponders diligently*
**8** [a][2 Pet. 2:8, 9] [1]Lit. *unto generation and generation*
**10** [1]Lit. *infirmity*
**13** [a]Ps. 73:17 [1]Or *holiness*
**16** [a]Ex. 14:21; Hab. 3:8, 10

PSALM 78

**title** [a]Ps. 74:title [1]Heb. *Maschil*
**2** [a]Matt. 13:34, 35 [1]*obscure sayings* or *riddles*
**4** [a]Ex. 12:26, 27; Deut. 4:9; 6:7; Job 15:18; Is. 38:19; Joel 1:3

[b]Telling to the generation to come the praises
of the LORD,
And His strength and His wonderful works
that He has done.

5 For [a]He established a testimony in Jacob,
And appointed a law in Israel,
Which He commanded our fathers,
That [b]they should make them known to their
children;
6 [a]That the generation to come might know
*them,*
The children *who* would be born,
*That* they may arise and declare *them* to
their children,
7 That they may set their hope in God,
And not forget the works of God,
But keep His commandments;
8 And [a]may not be like their fathers,
[b]A stubborn and rebellious generation,
A generation [c]*that* did not [1]set its heart
aright,
And whose spirit was not faithful to God.

9 The children of Ephraim,
*being* armed *and* [1]carrying bows,
Turned back in the day of battle.
10 [a]They did not keep the covenant of God;
They refused to walk in His law,
11 And [a]forgot His works
And His wonders that He had shown them.

12 [a]Marvelous things He did
in the sight of their fathers,
In the land of Egypt, [b]*in* the field of Zoan.
13 [a]He divided the sea
and caused them to pass through;
And [b]He made the waters stand up like a
heap.
14 [a]In the daytime also He led them with the
cloud,
And all the night with a light of fire.
15 [a]He split the rocks in the wilderness,
And gave *them* drink in abundance like the
depths.
16 He also brought [a]streams out of the rock,
And caused waters to run down like rivers.

17 But they sinned even more against Him
By [a]rebelling against the Most High in the
wilderness.
18 And [a]they tested God in their heart
By asking for the food of their fancy.
19 [a]Yes, they spoke against God:
They said, "Can God prepare a table in the
wilderness?
20 [a]Behold, He struck the rock,
So that the waters gushed out,
And the streams overflowed.
Can He give bread also?
Can He provide meat for His people?"

21 Therefore the LORD heard *this*
and [a]was furious;
So a fire was kindled against Jacob,
And anger also came up against Israel,
22 Because they [a]did not believe in God,
And did not trust in His salvation.
23 Yet He had commanded the clouds above,
[a]And opened the doors of heaven,
24 [a]Had rained down manna on them to eat,
And given them of the [1]bread of [b]heaven.
25 Men ate angels' food;
He sent them food to [1]the full.

26 [a]He caused an east wind to blow in the
heavens;
And by His power He brought in the south
wind.
27 He also rained meat on them like the dust,
Feathered fowl like the sand of the seas;
28 And He let *them* fall in the midst of their
camp,
All around their dwellings.
29 [a]So they ate and were well filled,
For He gave them their own desire.
30 They were not [1]deprived of their craving;
But [a]while their food *was* still in their
mouths,
31 The wrath of God came against them,
And slew the stoutest of them,
And struck down the choice *men* of Israel.

32 In spite of this [a]they still sinned,
And [b]did not believe in His wondrous works.
33 [a]Therefore their days He consumed in futility,
And their years in fear.

34 [a]When He slew them, then they sought Him;
And they returned
and sought earnestly for God.
35 Then they remembered that [a]God *was* their
rock,
And the Most High God [b]their Redeemer.
36 Nevertheless they [a]flattered Him with their
mouth,
And they lied to Him with their tongue;
37 For their heart was not steadfast with Him,
Nor were they faithful in His covenant.
38 [a]But He, *being* full of [b]compassion, forgave
*their* iniquity,
And did not destroy *them.*
Yes, many a time [c]He turned His anger away,
And [d]did not stir up all His wrath;
39 For [a]He remembered [b]that they *were but*
flesh,
[c]A breath that passes away
and does not come again.

40 How often they [a]provoked[1] Him in the
wilderness,
*And* grieved Him in the desert!
41 Yes, [a]again and again they tempted God,
And limited the Holy One of Israel.
42 They did not remember His [1]power:
The day when He redeemed them from the
enemy,
43 When He worked His signs in Egypt,
And His wonders in the field of Zoan;
44 [a]Turned their rivers into blood,
And their streams, that they could not drink.
45 [a]He sent swarms of flies among them, which
devoured them,
And [b]frogs, which destroyed them.
46 He also gave their crops to the caterpillar,
And their labor to the [a]locust.
47 [a]He destroyed their vines with hail,
And their sycamore trees with frost.
48 He also gave up their [a]cattle to the hail,
And their flocks to fiery [1]lightning.
49 He cast on them the fierceness of His anger,
Wrath, indignation, and trouble,
By sending angels of destruction *among*
*them.*
50 He made a path for His anger;
He did not spare their soul from death,
But gave [1]their life over to the plague,

**4** [b]Ex. 13:8, 14
**5** [a]Ps. 147:19 [b]Deut. 4:9; 11:19
**6** [a]Ps. 102:18
**8** [a]2 Kin. 17:14 [b]Ex. 32:9 [c]Ps. 78:37 [1]Lit. *prepare its heart*
**9** [1]Lit. *bow shooters*
**10** [a]2 Kin. 17:15
**11** [a]Ps. 106:13
**12** [a]Ex. 7—12 [b]Num. 13:22
**13** [a]Ex. 14:21 [b]Ex. 15:8
**14** [a]Ex. 13:21
**15** [a]Num. 20:11
**16** [a]Num. 20:8, 10, 11
**17** [a]Heb. 3:16
**18** [a]Ex. 16:2
**19** [a]Num. 11:4; 20:3; 21:5
**20** [a]Num. 20:11
**21** [a]Num. 11:1
**22** [a][Heb. 3:18]
**23** [a][Mal. 3:10]
**24** [a]Ex. 16:4 [b]John 6:31 [1]Lit. *grain*
**25** [1]*satiation*
**26** [a]Num. 11:31
**29** [a]Num. 11:19, 20
**30** [a]Num. 11:33 [1]Lit. *separated*
**32** [a]Num. 14:16, 17 [b]Num. 14:11
**33** [a]Num. 14:29, 35
**34** [a][Hos. 5:15]
**35** [a][Deut. 32:4, 15] [b]Is. 41:14; 44:6; 63:9
**36** [a]Ezek. 33:31
**38** [a][Num. 14:18–20] [b]Ex. 34:6 [c][Is. 48:9] [d]1 Kin. 21:29
**39** [a]Job 10:9 [b]John 3:6 [c][Job 7:7, 16]
**40** [a]Heb. 3:16 [1]*rebelled against Him*
**41** [a]Num. 14:22
**42** [1]Lit. *hand*
**44** [a]Ex. 7:20
**45** [a]Ex. 8:24 [b]Ex. 8:6
**46** [a]Ex. 10:14
**47** [a]Ex. 9:23–25
**48** [a]Ex. 9:19 [1]*lightning bolts*
**50** [1]Or *their beasts*

51 And destroyed all the [a]firstborn in Egypt,
The first of *their* strength in the tents of Ham.
52 But He [a]made His own people go forth like sheep,
And guided them in the wilderness like a flock;
53 And He [a]led them on safely,
so that they did not fear;
But the sea [b]overwhelmed their enemies.
54 And He brought them to His [a]holy border,
This mountain [b]*which* His right hand had acquired.
55 [a]He also drove out the nations before them,
[b]Allotted them an inheritance by [1]survey,
And made the tribes of Israel dwell in their tents.

56 [a]Yet they tested and provoked the Most High God,
And did not keep His testimonies,
57 But [a]turned back and acted unfaithfully like their fathers;
They were turned aside [b]like a deceitful bow.
58 [a]For they provoked Him to anger with their [b]high places,
And moved Him to jealousy with their carved images.
59 When God heard *this,* He was furious,
And greatly abhorred Israel,
60 [a]So that He forsook the tabernacle of Shiloh,
The tent He had placed among men,
61 [a]And delivered His strength into captivity,
And His glory into the enemy's hand.
62 [a]He also gave His people over to the sword,
And was furious with His inheritance.
63 The fire consumed their young men,
And [a]their maidens were not given in marriage.
64 [a]Their priests fell by the sword,
And [b]their widows made no lamentation.

65 Then the Lord awoke as *from* sleep,
[a]Like a mighty man who shouts because of wine.
66 And [a]He beat back His enemies;
He put them to a perpetual reproach.

67 Moreover He rejected the tent of Joseph,
And did not choose the tribe of Ephraim,
68 But chose the tribe of Judah,
Mount Zion [a]which He loved.
69 And He built His [a]sanctuary like the heights,
Like the earth which He has established forever.
70 [a]He also chose David His servant,
And took him from the sheepfolds;
71 From following [a]the ewes that had young He brought him,
[b]To shepherd Jacob His people,
And Israel His inheritance.
72 So he shepherded them according to the [a]integrity of his heart,
And guided them by the skillfulness of his hands.

## PSALM 79

A Psalm of Asaph.

O GOD, the [1]nations have come into [a]Your inheritance;
Your holy temple they have defiled;
[b]They have laid Jerusalem [2]in heaps.
2 [a]The dead bodies of Your servants
They have given *as* food
for the birds of the heavens,
The flesh of Your saints
to the beasts of the earth.
3 Their blood they have shed like water all around Jerusalem,
And *there was* no one to bury *them.*
4 We have become a reproach to our [a]neighbors,
A scorn and derision to those who are around us.

5 [a]How long, LORD?
Will You be angry forever?
Will Your [b]jealousy burn like fire?
6 [a]Pour out Your wrath on the [1]nations that [b]do not know You,
And on the kingdoms that [c]do not call on Your name.
7 For they have devoured Jacob,
And laid waste his dwelling place.

8 [a]Oh, do not remember [1]former iniquities against us!
Let Your tender mercies come speedily to meet us,
For we have been brought very low.
9 Help us, O God of our salvation,
For the glory of Your name;
And deliver us,
and provide atonement for our sins,
[a]For Your name's sake!
10 [a]Why should the [1]nations say,
"Where *is* their God?"
Let there be known among the nations in our sight
The avenging of the blood of Your servants
*which has been* shed.

11 Let [a]the groaning of the prisoner come before You;
According to the greatness of Your [1]power
Preserve those who are appointed to die;
12 And return to our neighbors [a]sevenfold into their bosom
[b]Their reproach with which they have reproached You, O Lord.

13 So [a]we, Your people and sheep of Your pasture,
Will give You thanks forever;
[b]We will show forth Your praise to all generations.

## PSALM 80

To the Chief Musician. [a]Set to [1]"The Lilies." A [2]Testimony of Asaph. A Psalm.

GIVE ear, O Shepherd of Israel,
[a]You who lead Joseph [b]like a flock;
You who dwell *between* the cherubim, [c]shine forth!
2 Before [a]Ephraim, Benjamin, and Manasseh,
Stir up Your strength,
And come *and* save us!

3 [a]Restore us, O God;
[b]Cause Your face to shine,
And we shall be saved!

4 O LORD God of hosts,
[a]How long will You be angry
Against the prayer of Your people?

---

**51** [a]Ex. 12:29, 30
**52** [a]Ps. 77:20
**53** [a]Ex. 14:19, 20 [b]Ex. 14:27, 28
**54** [a]Ex. 15:17 [b]Ps. 44:3
**55** [a]Ps. 44:2 [b]Josh. 13:7; 19:51; 23:4 [1]*surveyed measurement,* lit. *measuring cord*
**56** [a]Judg. 2:11–13
**57** [a]Ezek. 20:27, 28 [b]Hos. 7:16
**58** [a]Judg. 2:12 [b]Deut. 12:2
**60** [a]1 Sam. 4:11
**61** [a]Judg. 18:30
**62** [a]1 Sam. 4:10
**63** [a]Jer. 7:34; 16:9; 25:10
**64** [a]1 Sam. 4:17; 22:18 [b]Job 27:15; Ezek. 24:23
**65** [a]Is. 42:13
**66** [a]1 Sam. 5:6
**68** [a][Ps. 87:2]
**69** [a]1 Kin. 6:1–38
**70** [a]1 Sam. 16:11, 12
**71** [a][Is. 40:11] [b]2 Sam. 5:2
**72** [a]1 Kin. 9:4

PSALM 79

**1** [a]Ps. 74:2 [b]Mic. 3:12 [1]*Gentiles* [2]*in ruins*
**2** [a]Jer. 7:33; 19:7; 34:20
**4** [a]Ps. 44:13
**5** [a]Ps. 74:1, 9 [b][Zeph. 3:8]
**6** [a]Jer. 10:25 [b]Is. 45:4, 5 [c]Ps. 53:4 [1]*Gentiles*
**8** [a]Is. 64:9 [1]Or *against us the iniquities of those who were before us*
**9** [a]Jer. 14:7, 21
**10** [a]Ps. 42:10 [1]*Gentiles*
**11** [a]Ps. 102:20 [1]Lit. *arm*
**12** [a]Gen. 4:15 [b]Ps. 74:10, 18, 22
**13** [a]Ps. 74:1; 95:7 [b]Is. 43:21

PSALM 80

**title** [a]Ps. 45:title [1]Heb. *Shoshannim* [2]Heb. *Eduth*
**1** [a][Ex. 25:20–22] [b]Ps. 77:20 [c]Deut. 33:2
**2** [a]Ps. 78:9, 67
**3** [a]Lam. 5:21 [b]Num. 6:25
**4** [a]Ps. 79:5

5 [a]You have fed them with the bread of tears,
And given them tears to drink in great measure.
6 You have made us a strife to our neighbors,
And our enemies laugh among themselves.

7 Restore us, O God of hosts;
Cause Your face to shine,
And we shall be saved!

8 You have brought [a]a vine out of Egypt;
[b]You have cast out the [1]nations, and planted it.
9 You prepared *room* for it,
And caused it to take deep root,
And it filled the land.
10 The hills were covered with its shadow,
And the [1]mighty cedars with its [a]boughs.
11 She sent out her boughs to [1]the Sea,
And her branches to [2]the River.

12 Why have You [a]broken down her [1]hedges,
So that all who pass by the way pluck her *fruit?*
13 The boar out of the woods uproots it,
And the wild beast of the field devours it.

14 Return, we beseech You, O God of hosts;
[a]Look down from heaven and see,
And visit this vine
15 And the vineyard which Your right hand has planted,
And the branch *that* You made strong [a]for Yourself.
16 *It is* burned with fire, *it is* cut down;
[a]They perish at the rebuke of Your countenance.
17 [a]Let Your hand be upon the man of Your right hand,
Upon the son of man *whom* You made strong for Yourself.
18 Then we will not turn back from You;
Revive us, and we will call upon Your name.

19 Restore us, O LORD God of hosts;
Cause Your face to shine,
And we shall be saved!

## PSALM 81

To the Chief Musician. [a]On[1] an instrument of Gath. A Psalm of Asaph.

SING aloud to God our strength;
Make a joyful shout to the God of Jacob.
2 Raise a song and strike the timbrel,
The pleasant harp with the lute.

3 Blow the trumpet at the time of the New Moon,
At the full moon, on our solemn feast day.
4 For [a]this *is* a statute for Israel,
A law of the God of Jacob.
5 This He established in Joseph *as* a testimony,
When He went throughout the land of Egypt,
[a]*Where* I heard a language I did not understand.

6 "I removed his shoulder from the burden;
His hands were freed from the baskets.
7 [a]You called in trouble, and I delivered you;
[b]I answered you in the secret place of thunder;
I [c]tested you at the waters of [1]Meribah. Selah

8 "Hear,[a] O My people, and I will admonish you!
O Israel, if you will listen to Me!
9 There shall be no [a]foreign god among you;
Nor shall you worship any foreign god.
10 [a]I *am* the LORD your God,
Who brought you out of the land of Egypt;
[b]Open your mouth wide, and I will fill it.

11 "But My people would not heed My voice,
And Israel would *have* [a]none of Me.
12 [a]So I gave them over to [1]their own stubborn heart,
To walk in their own counsels.

13 "Oh,[a] that My people would listen to Me,
That Israel would walk in My ways!
14 I would soon subdue their enemies,
And turn My hand against their adversaries.
15 [a]The haters of the LORD would pretend submission to Him,
But their [1]fate would endure forever.
16 He would [a]have fed them also with [1]the finest of wheat;
And with honey [b]from the rock
I would have satisfied you."

## PSALM 82

A Psalm of Asaph.

GOD [a]stands in the congregation of [1]the mighty;
He judges among [b]the [2]gods.
2 How long will you judge unjustly,
And [a]show partiality to the wicked? Selah
3 [1]Defend the poor and fatherless;
Do justice to the afflicted and [a]needy.
4 Deliver the poor and needy;
Free *them* from the hand of the wicked.

5 They do not know, nor do they understand;
They walk about in darkness;
All the [a]foundations of the earth are [1]unstable.

6 I said, [a]"You *are* [1]gods,
And all of you *are* children of the Most High.
7 But you shall die like men,
And fall like one of the princes."

8 Arise, O God, judge the earth;
[a]For You shall inherit all nations.

## PSALM 83

A Song. A Psalm of Asaph.

DO[a] not keep silent, O God!
Do not hold Your peace,
And do not be still, O God!
2 For behold, [a]Your enemies make a [1]tumult;
And those who hate You have [2]lifted up their head.
3 They have taken crafty counsel against Your people,
And consulted together [a]against Your sheltered ones.
4 They have said, "Come, and [a]let us cut them off from *being* a nation,
That the name of Israel may be remembered no more."

5 For they have consulted together with one [1]consent;
They [2]form a confederacy against You:
6 [a]The tents of Edom and the Ishmaelites;
Moab and the Hagrites;
7 Gebal, Ammon, and Amalek;
Philistia with the inhabitants of Tyre;

---

5 [a]Is. 30:20
8 [a][Is. 5:1, 7] [b]Ps. 44:2 [1]*Gentiles*
10 [a]Lev. 23:40 [1]Lit. *cedars of God*
11 [1]The Mediterranean [2]The Euphrates
12 [a]Is. 5:5 [1]*walls* or *fences*
14 [a]Is. 63:15
15 [a][Is. 49:5]
16 [a][Ps. 39:11]
17 [a]Ps. 89:21

PSALM 81
title [a]Ps. 8:title [1]Heb. *Al Gittith*
4 [a]Num. 10:10
5 [a]Ps. 114:1
7 [a]Ex. 2:23; 14:10 [b]Ex. 19:19; 20:18 [c]Ex. 17:6, 7 [1]Lit. *Strife* or *Contention*
8 [a][Ps. 50:7]
9 [a][Is. 43:12]
10 [a]Ex. 20:2 [b]Ps. 103:5
11 [a]Deut. 32:15
12 [a][Acts 7:42] [1]*the dictates of their heart*
13 [a][Is. 48:18]
15 [a]Rom. 1:30 [1]Lit. *time*
16 [a]Deut. 32:14 [b]Job 29:6 [1]Lit. *fat of wheat*

PSALM 82
1 [a][2 Chr. 19:6] [b]Ps. 82:6 [1]Heb. *El*, Lit. *God* [2]*Judges;* Heb. *elohim*, lit. *mighty ones* or *gods*
2 [a][Deut. 1:17]
3 [a][Deut. 24:17] [1]*Vindicate*
5 [a]Ps. 11:3 [1]*moved*
6 [a]John 10:34 [1]*Judges;* Heb. *elohim*, lit. *mighty ones* or *gods*
8 [a][Rev. 11:15]

PSALM 83
1 [a]Ps. 28:1
2 [a]Ps. 81:15 [1]*uproar* [2]Exalted themselves
3 [a][Ps. 27:5]
4 [a]Jer. 11:19; 31:36
5 [1]Lit. *heart* [2]Lit. *cut a covenant*
6 [a]2 Chr. 20:1, 10, 11

8 Assyria also has joined with them;
They have helped the children of Lot. Selah

9 Deal with them as *with* [a]Midian,
As *with* [b]Sisera,
As *with* Jabin at the Brook Kishon,
10 Who perished at En Dor,
[a]*Who* became *as* refuse on the earth.
11 Make their nobles like Oreb and like [a]Zeeb,
Yes, all their princes like [b]Zebah and
Zalmunna,
12 Who said, "Let us take for ourselves
The pastures of God for a possession."

13 [a]O my God, make them like the whirling dust,
[b]Like the chaff before the wind!
14 As the fire burns the woods,
And as the flame [a]sets the mountains on fire,
15 So pursue them with Your tempest,
And frighten them with Your storm.
16 Fill their faces with shame,
That they may seek Your name, O LORD.
17 Let them be [1]confounded
and dismayed forever;
Yes, let them be put to shame and perish,
18 [a]That they may know that You,
whose [b]name alone *is* the LORD,
*Are* [c]the Most High over all the earth.

## PSALM 84

To the Chief Musician. [a]On[1] an instrument of Gath. A Psalm of the sons of Korah.

HOW [a]lovely [1]*is* Your tabernacle,
O LORD of hosts!
2 [a]My soul longs, yes, even faints
For the courts of the LORD;
My heart and my flesh cry out for the living
God.

3 Even the sparrow has found a home,
And the swallow a nest for herself,
Where she may lay her young—
*Even* Your altars, O LORD of hosts,
My King and my God.
4 Blessed *are* those who dwell in Your [a]house;
They will still be praising You. Selah

5 Blessed *is* the man whose strength *is* in You,
Whose heart *is* set on pilgrimage.
6 *As they* pass through the Valley [a]of [1]Baca,
They make it a spring;
The rain also covers it with [2]pools.
7 They go [a]from strength to strength;
[1]*Each one* [b]appears before God in Zion.

8 O LORD God of hosts, hear my prayer;
Give ear, O God of Jacob! Selah
9 [a]O God, behold our shield,
And look upon the face of Your [1]anointed.

10 For a day in Your courts *is* better than a
thousand.
I would rather [1]be a doorkeeper in the house
of my God
Than dwell in the tents of wickedness.
11 For the LORD God *is* [a]a sun and [b]shield;
The LORD will give grace and glory;
[c]No good *thing* will He withhold
From those who walk uprightly.

12 O LORD of hosts,
[a]Blessed *is* the man who trusts in You!

9 [a]Num. 31:7; Judg. 7:22 [b]Judg. 4:15–24; 5:20, 21
10 [a]Zeph. 1:17
11 [a]Judg. 7:25 [b]Judg. 8:12–21
13 [a]Is. 17:13 [b]Job 21:18; Ps. 35:5; Is. 40:24; Jer. 13:24
14 [a]Ex. 19:18; Deut. 32:22
17 [1]*ashamed*
18 [a]Ps. 59:13 [b]Ex. 6:3 [c][Ps. 92:8]

PSALM 84
title [a]Ps. 8:title [1]Heb. *Al Gittith*
1 [a]Ps. 27:4; 46:4, 5 [1]*are your dwellings*
2 [a]Ps. 42:1, 2
4 [a][Ps. 65:4]
6 [a]2 Sam. 5:22–25 [1]Lit. *Weeping* [2]Or *blessings*
7 [a]Prov. 4:18; Is. 40:31; John 1:16; 2 Cor. 3:18 [b]Ex. 34:23; Deut. 16:16 [1]LXX, Syr., Vg. *The God of gods shall be seen*
9 [a]Gen. 15:1 [1]Commissioned one, Heb. *messiah*
10 [1]*stand at the threshold*
11 [a]Is. 60:19, 20; Mal. 4:2; Rev. 21:23 [b]Gen. 15:1 [c]Ps. 34:9, 10
12 [a][Ps. 2:12; 40:4]

PSALM 85
title [a]Ps. 42:title
1 [a]Ezra 1:11—2:1; Ps. 14:7; Jer. 30:18; 31:23; Ezek. 39:25; Hos. 6:11; Joel 3:1
4 [a]Ps. 80:3, 7
5 [a]Ps. 79:5
6 [a]Hab. 3:2
8 [1]*foolishness*
9 [a]Is. 46:13 [b]Hag. 2:7; Zech. 2:5; [John 1:14]
10 [a]Ps. 72:3; [Is. 32:17]; Luke 2:14
12 [a][Ps. 84:11; James 1:17]

PSALM 86
2 [1]Lit. *soul*
4 [a]Ps. 25:1; 143:8 [1]*Make glad*
5 [a]Ps. 130:7; 145:9; [Joel 2:13]
8 [a][Ex. 15:11]; 2 Sam. 7:22; 1 Kin. 8:23; Ps. 89:6; Jer. 10:6
10 [a][Ex. 15:11] [b]Deut. 6:4; Is. 37:16; Mark 12:29; 1 Cor. 8:4

## PSALM 85

To the Chief Musician. A Psalm [a]of the sons of Korah.

LORD, You have been favorable to Your land;
You have [a]brought back the captivity of
Jacob.
2 You have forgiven the iniquity of Your
people;
You have covered all their sin. Selah
3 You have taken away all Your wrath;
You have turned from the fierceness of Your
anger.

4 [a]Restore us, O God of our salvation,
And cause Your anger toward us to cease.
5 [a]Will You be angry with us forever?
Will You prolong Your anger to all
generations?
6 Will You not [a]revive us again,
That Your people may rejoice in You?
7 Show us Your mercy, LORD,
And grant us Your salvation.

8 I will hear what God the LORD will speak,
For He will speak peace
To His people and to His saints;
But let them not turn back to [1]folly.
9 Surely [a]His salvation *is* near to those who
fear Him,
[b]That glory may dwell in our land.

10 Mercy and truth have met together;
[a]Righteousness and peace have kissed.
11 Truth shall spring out of the earth,
And righteousness shall look down from
heaven.
12 [a]Yes, the LORD will give *what is* good;
And our land will yield its increase.
13 Righteousness will go before Him,
And shall make His footsteps *our* pathway.

## PSALM 86

A Prayer of David.

BOW down Your ear, O LORD, hear me;
For I *am* poor and needy.
2 Preserve my [1]life, for I *am* holy;
You are my God;
Save Your servant who trusts in You!
3 Be merciful to me, O Lord,
For I cry to You all day long.
4 [1]Rejoice the soul of Your servant,
[a]For to You, O Lord, I lift up my soul.
5 For [a]You, Lord, *are* good,
and ready to forgive,
And abundant in mercy to all those who call
upon You.

6 Give ear, O LORD, to my prayer;
And attend to the voice of my supplications.
7 In the day of my trouble I will call upon
You,
For You will answer me.

8 [a]Among the gods *there is* none like You,
O Lord;
Nor *are there any works* like Your works.
9 All nations whom You have made
Shall come and worship before You, O Lord,
And shall glorify Your name.
10 For You *are* great, and [a]do wondrous things;
[b]You alone *are* God.

11 [a]Teach me Your way, O LORD;
I will walk in Your truth;
[1]Unite my heart to fear Your name.
12 I will praise You, O Lord my God, with all my heart,
And I will glorify Your name forevermore.
13 For great *is* Your mercy toward me,
And You have delivered my soul from the depths of [1]Sheol.

14 O God, the proud have risen against me,
And a mob of violent *men* have sought my life,
And have not set You before them.
15 But [a]You, O Lord, *are* a God full of compassion, and gracious,
Longsuffering and abundant in mercy and truth.

16 Oh, turn to me, and have mercy on me!
Give Your strength to Your servant,
And save the son of Your maidservant.
17 Show me a sign for good,
That those who hate me may see *it* and be ashamed,
Because You, LORD, have helped me and comforted me.

## PSALM 87

A Psalm of the sons of Korah. A Song.

HIS foundation *is* in the holy mountains.
2 [a]The LORD loves the gates of Zion
More than all the dwellings of Jacob.
3 [a]Glorious things are spoken of you,
O city of God! Selah

4 "I will make mention of [1]Rahab and Babylon to those who know Me;
Behold, O Philistia and Tyre, with Ethiopia:
'This *one* was born there.' "

5 And of Zion it will be said,
"This *one* and that *one* were born in her;
And the Most High Himself shall establish her."
6 The LORD will record,
When He [a]registers the peoples:
"This *one* was born there." Selah

7 Both the singers and the players on instruments *say,*
"All my springs *are* in you."

## PSALM 88

A Song. A Psalm of the sons of Korah. To the Chief Musician. Set to "Mahalath Leannoth." A [1]Contemplation of [a]Heman the Ezrahite.

O LORD, [a]God of my salvation,
I have cried out day and night before You.
2 Let my prayer come before You;
[1]Incline Your ear to my cry.

3 For my soul is full of troubles,
And my life [a]draws near to the grave.
4 I am counted with those who [a]go[1] down to the pit;
[b]I am like a man *who has* no strength,
5 [1]Adrift among the dead,
Like the slain who lie in the grave,
Whom You remember no more,
And who are cut off from Your hand.

6 You have laid me in the lowest pit,
In darkness, in the depths.
7 Your wrath lies heavy upon me,
And You have afflicted *me* with all [a]Your waves. Selah
8 [a]You have [1]put away my acquaintances far from me;
You have made me an abomination to them;
[b]*I am* shut up, and I cannot get out;
9 My eye wastes away because of affliction.

[a]LORD, I have called daily upon You;
I have stretched out my hands to You.
10 Will You work wonders for the dead?
Shall [1]the dead arise *and* praise You? Selah
11 Shall Your lovingkindness be declared in the grave?
*Or* Your faithfulness
in the place of destruction?
12 Shall Your wonders be known in the dark?
And Your righteousness
in the land of forgetfulness?

13 But to You I have cried out, O LORD,
And in the morning my prayer comes before You.
14 LORD, why do You cast off my soul?
*Why* do You hide Your face from me?
15 I *have been* afflicted and ready to die from *my* youth;
I suffer Your terrors;
I am distraught.
16 Your fierce wrath has gone over me;
Your terrors have [1]cut me off.
17 They came around me all day long like water;
They engulfed me altogether.
18 [a]Loved one and friend You have put far from me,
*And* my acquaintances into darkness.

## PSALM 89

A [1]Contemplation of [a]Ethan the Ezrahite.

I WILL sing of the mercies of the LORD forever;
With my mouth will I make known Your faithfulness to all generations.
2 For I have said, "Mercy shall be built up forever;
[a]Your faithfulness You shall establish in the very heavens."

3 "I[a] have made a covenant with My chosen,
I have [b]sworn to My servant David:
4 'Your seed I will establish forever,
And build up your throne [a]to all generations.' " Selah

5 And [a]the heavens will praise Your wonders, O LORD;
Your faithfulness also in the assembly of the saints.
6 [a]For who in the heavens can be compared to the LORD?
*Who* among the sons of the mighty can be likened to the LORD?
7 [a]God is greatly to be feared in the assembly of the saints,
And to be held in reverence by all *those* around Him.
8 O LORD God of hosts,
Who *is* mighty like You, O LORD?
Your faithfulness also surrounds You.
9 [a]You rule the raging of the sea;
When its waves rise, You still them.

---

**11** [a]Ps. 27:11; 143:8 [1]Give me singleness of heart
**13** [1]The abode of the dead
**15** [a]Ex. 34:6; [Ps. 86:5]

PSALM 87
**2** [a]Ps. 78:67, 68
**3** [a]Is. 60:1
**4** [1]Egypt
**6** [a]Is. 4:3

PSALM 88
**title** [a]1 Kin. 4:31; 1 Chr. 2:6 [1]Heb. *Maschil*
**1** [a]Ps. 27:9; [Luke 18:7]
**2** [1]Listen to
**3** [a]Ps. 107:18
**4** [a][Ps. 28:1] [b]Ps. 31:12 [1]Die
**5** [1]Lit. *Free*
**7** [a]Ps. 42:7
**8** [a]Job 19:13, 19; Ps. 31:11; 142:4 [b]Lam. 3:7 [1]*taken away my friends*
**9** [a]Ps. 86:3
**10** [1]*shades, ghosts*
**16** [1]*destroyed me*
**18** [a]Job 19:13; Ps. 31:11; 38:11

PSALM 89
**title** [a]1 Kin. 4:31 [1]Heb. *Maschil*
**2** [a][Ps. 119:89, 90]
**3** [a]1 Kin. 8:16 [b]2 Sam. 7:11; 1 Chr. 17:10–12
**4** [a][2 Sam. 7:13; Is. 9:7; Luke 1:33]
**5** [a][Ps. 19:1]
**6** [a]Ps. 86:8; 113:5
**7** [a]Ps. 76:7, 11
**9** [a]Ps. 65:7; 93:3, 4; 107:29

10 [a]You have broken [1]Rahab in pieces,
as one who is slain;
You have scattered Your enemies with Your
mighty arm.
11 [a]The heavens *are* Yours,
the earth also *is* Yours;
The world and all its fullness,
You have founded them.
12 The north and the south,
You have created them;
[a]Tabor and [b]Hermon rejoice in Your name.
13 You have a mighty arm;
Strong is Your hand,
*and* high is Your right hand.
14 Righteousness and justice *are* the foundation
of Your throne;
Mercy and truth go before Your face.
15 Blessed *are* the people who know the [a]joyful
sound!
They walk, O LORD, in the light of Your
countenance.
16 In Your name they rejoice all day long,
And in Your righteousness they are exalted.
17 For You *are* the glory of their strength,
And in Your favor our [1]horn is [a]exalted.
18 For our shield *belongs* to the LORD,
And our king to the Holy One of Israel.

19 Then You spoke in a vision to Your [1]holy
one,
And said: "I have given help to *one who is*
mighty;
I have exalted one [a]chosen from the people.
20 [a]I have found My servant David;
With My holy oil I have anointed him,
21 [a]With whom My hand shall be established;
Also My arm shall strengthen him.
22 The enemy shall not [1]outwit him,
Nor the son of wickedness afflict him.
23 I will beat down his foes before his face,
And plague those who hate him.

24 "But My faithfulness and My mercy *shall be*
with him,
And in My name his horn shall be exalted.
25 Also I will [a]set his hand over the sea,
And his right hand over the rivers.
26 He shall cry to Me,'You *are* [a]my Father,
My God, and [b]the rock of my salvation.'
27 Also I will make him [a]*My* firstborn,
[b]The highest of the kings of the earth.
28 [a]My mercy I will keep for him forever,
And My covenant shall stand firm with him.
29 His seed also I will make *to endure* forever,
[a]And his throne [b]as the days of heaven.

30 "If[a] his sons [b]forsake My law
And do not walk in My judgments,
31 If they [1]break My statutes
And do not keep My commandments,
32 Then I will punish their transgression with
the rod,
And their iniquity with stripes.
33 [a]Nevertheless My lovingkindness I will not
[1]utterly take from him,
Nor [2]allow My faithfulness to fail.
34 My covenant I will not break,
Nor [a]alter the word that has gone out of My
lips.
35 Once I have sworn [a]by My holiness;
I will not lie to David:
36 [a]His seed shall endure forever,
And his throne [b]as the sun before Me;
37 It shall be established forever like the moon,
Even *like* the faithful witness in the sky."
Selah

38 But You have [a]cast off and [b]abhorred,[1]
You have been furious with Your [2]anointed.
39 You have renounced the covenant of Your
servant;
[a]You have [1]profaned his crown *by casting it*
to the ground.
40 You have broken down all his hedges;
You have brought his [1]strongholds to ruin.
41 All who pass by the way [a]plunder him;
He is a reproach to his neighbors.
42 You have exalted the right hand of his
adversaries;
You have made all his enemies rejoice.
43 You have also turned back the edge of his
sword,
And have not sustained him in the battle.
44 You have made his [1]glory cease,
And cast his throne down to the ground.
45 The days of his youth You have shortened;
You have covered him with shame. Selah

46 How long, LORD?
Will You hide Yourself forever?
Will Your wrath burn like fire?
47 Remember how short my time [a]is;
For what [b]futility have You created all the
children of men?
48 What man can live and not [1]see [a]death?
Can he deliver his life from the power of [2]the
grave? Selah

49 Lord, where *are* Your former
lovingkindnesses,
*Which* You [a]swore to David [b]in Your truth?
50 Remember, Lord, the reproach of Your
servants—
[a]*How* I bear in my bosom *the reproach of* all
the many peoples,
51 [a]With which Your enemies have reproached,
O LORD,
With which they have reproached the
footsteps of Your [1]anointed.

52 [a]Blessed *be* the LORD forevermore!
Amen and Amen.

## BOOK FOUR
## Psalms 90–106

### PSALM 90

A Prayer [a]of Moses the man of God.

LORD, [a]You have been our [1]dwelling place in all
generations.
2 [a]Before the mountains were brought forth,
Or ever You [1]had formed the earth and the
world,
Even from everlasting to everlasting, You *are*
God.

3 You turn man to destruction,
And say, [a]"Return, O children of men."
4 [a]For a thousand years in Your sight
*Are* like yesterday when it is past,
And *like* a watch in the night.
5 You carry them away *like* a flood;
[a]*They are* like a sleep.
In the morning [b]they are like grass *which*
grows up:

10 [a]Ps. 87:4 [1]Egypt
11 [a][Gen. 1:1]
12 [a]Josh. 19:22 [b]Josh. 11:17; 12:1
15 [a]Ps. 98:6
17 [a]Ps. 75:10; 92:10; 132:17 [1]Strength
19 [a]1 Kin. 11:34 [1]So with many Heb. mss.; MT, LXX, Tg., Vg. *holy ones*
20 [a]1 Sam. 13:14; 16:1–12
21 [a]Ps. 80:17
22 [1]Or *exact usury from him*
25 [a]Ps. 72:8
26 [a][1 Chr. 22:10] [b]2 Sam. 22:47
27 [a][Col. 1:15, 18] [b]Rev. 19:16
28 [a]Is. 55:3
29 [a]Jer. 33:17 [b]Deut. 11:21
30 [a][2 Sam. 7:14] [b]Ps. 119:53
31 [1]*profane*
32 [1]*attend to*
33 [a]2 Sam. 7:14, 15 [1]Lit. *break off* [2]Lit. *deal falsely with My faithfulness*
34 [a]Jer. 33:20–22
35 [a]Amos 4:2
36 [a][Luke 1:33] [b]Ps. 72:17
38 [a][1 Chr. 28:9] [b]Deut. 32:19 [1]*rejected* [2]Commissioned one, Heb. *messiah*
39 [a]Lam. 5:16 [1]*defiled*
40 [1]*fortresses*
41 [a]Ps. 80:12
44 [1]*splendor* or *brightness*
47 [a]Ps. 90:9 [b]Ps. 62:9
48 [a][Eccl. 3:19] [1]*experience death* [2]Or *Sheol*
49 [a][2 Sam. 7:15] [b]Ps. 54:5
50 [a]Ps. 69:9, 19
51 [a]Ps. 74:10, 18, 22 [1]Commissioned one, Heb. *messiah*
52 [a]Ps. 41:13

PSALM 90

title [a]Deut. 33:1
1 [a][Ezek. 11:16] [1]LXX, [Tg.], Vg. *refuge*
2 [a][Prov. 8:25, 26] [1]Lit. *gave birth to*
3 [a]Gen. 3:19
4 [a]2 Pet. 3:8
5 [a]Ps. 73:20 [b]Is. 40:6

6 In the morning it flourishes and grows up;
In the evening it is cut down and withers.

7 For we have been consumed by Your anger,
And by Your wrath we are terrified.
8 [a]You have set our iniquities before You,
Our [b]secret *sins* in the light of Your countenance.
9 For all our days have passed away in Your wrath;
We finish our years like a sigh.
10 The days of our lives *are* seventy years;
And if by reason of strength *they are* eighty years,
Yet their boast *is* only labor and sorrow;
For it is soon cut off, and we fly away.
11 Who knows the power of Your anger?
For as the fear of You, *so is* Your wrath.
12 [a]So teach *us* to number our days,
That we may gain a heart of wisdom.

13 Return, O LORD!
How long?
And [a]have compassion on Your servants.
14 Oh, satisfy us early with Your mercy,
[a]That we may rejoice and be glad all our days!
15 Make us glad according to the days *in which* You have afflicted us,
The years *in which* we have seen evil.
16 Let [a]Your work appear to Your servants,
And Your glory to their children.
17 [a]And let the beauty of the LORD our God be upon us,
And [b]establish the work of our hands for us;
Yes, establish the work of our hands.

## PSALM 91

HE [a]who dwells in the secret place of the Most High
Shall abide [b]under the shadow of the Almighty.
2 [a]I will say of the LORD, "*He is* my refuge and my fortress;
My God, in Him I will trust."

3 Surely [a]He shall deliver you from the snare of the [1]fowler
*And* from the perilous pestilence.
4 [a]He shall cover you with His feathers,
And under His wings you shall take refuge;
His truth *shall be your* shield and [1]buckler.
5 [a]You shall not be afraid of the terror by night,
*Nor* of the arrow *that* flies by day,
6 *Nor* of the pestilence *that* walks in darkness,
*Nor* of the destruction *that* lays waste at noonday.

7 A thousand may fall at your side,
And ten thousand at your right hand;
*But* it shall not come near you.
8 Only [a]with your eyes shall you look,
And see the reward of the wicked.

9 Because you have made the LORD,
*who is* [a]my refuge,
*Even* the Most High, [b]your dwelling place,
10 [a]No evil shall befall you,
Nor shall any plague come near your dwelling;
11 [a]For He shall give His angels charge over you,
To keep you in all your ways.
12 In *their* hands they shall [1]bear you up,
[a]Lest you [2]dash your foot against a stone.
13 You shall tread upon the lion and the cobra,
The young lion and the serpent you shall trample underfoot.

14 "Because he has set his love upon Me,
therefore I will deliver him;
I will [1]set him on high,
because he has [a]known My name.
15 He shall [a]call upon Me,
and I will answer him;
I *will be* [b]with him in trouble;
I will deliver him and honor him.
16 With [1]long life I will satisfy him,
And show him My salvation."

## PSALM 92

A Psalm. A Song for the Sabbath day.

*IT is* [a]good to give thanks to the LORD,
And to sing praises to Your name,
O Most High;
2 To [a]declare Your lovingkindness in the morning,
And Your faithfulness every night,
3 [a]On an instrument of ten strings,
On the lute,
And on the harp,
With [1]harmonious sound.
4 For You, LORD, have made me glad through Your work;
I will triumph in the works of Your hands.

5 [a]O LORD, how great are Your works!
[b]Your thoughts are very deep.
6 [a]A senseless man does not know,
Nor does a fool understand this.
7 When [a]the wicked [1]spring up like grass,
And when all the workers of iniquity flourish,
*It is* that they may be destroyed forever.

8 [a]But You, LORD, *are* on high forevermore.
9 For behold, Your enemies, O LORD,
For behold, Your enemies shall perish;
All the workers of iniquity shall [a]be scattered.

10 But [a]my [1]horn You have exalted like a wild ox;
I have been [b]anointed with fresh oil.
11 [a]My eye also has seen *my desire* on my enemies;
My ears hear *my desire* on the wicked
Who rise up against me.

12 [a]The righteous shall flourish like a palm tree,
He shall grow like a cedar in Lebanon.
13 Those who are planted in the house of the LORD
Shall flourish in the courts of our God.
14 They shall still bear fruit in old age;
They shall be [1]fresh and [2]flourishing,
15 To declare that the LORD is upright;
[a]*He is* my rock, and [b]*there is* no unrighteousness in Him.

## PSALM 93

THE [a]LORD reigns, He is clothed with majesty;
The LORD is clothed,
[b]He has girded Himself with strength.
Surely the world is established,
so that it cannot be [1]moved.
2 [a]Your throne *is* established from of old;
You *are* from everlasting.

---

**8** [a]Ps. 50:21; [Jer. 16:17] [b]Ps. 19:12; [Eccl. 12:14]
**12** [a]Deut. 32:29; Ps. 39:4
**13** [a]Ex. 32:12; Deut. 32:36
**14** [a]Ps. 85:6
**16** [a][Deut. 32:4]; Hab. 3:2
**17** [a]Ps. 27:4 [b]Is. 26:12

PSALM 91
**1** [a]Ps. 27:5; 31:20; 32:7 [b]Ps. 17:8; Is. 25:4; 32:2
**2** [a]Ps. 142:5
**3** [a]Ps. 124:7; Prov. 6:5 [1]One who catches birds in a trap or snare
**4** [a]Ps. 17:8 [1]A small shield
**5** [a][Job 5:19; Ps. 112:7; Is. 43:2]
**8** [a]Ps. 37:34; Mal. 1:5
**9** [a]Ps. 91:2 [b]Ps. 90:1
**10** [a][Prov. 12:21]
**11** [a]Ps. 34:7; Matt. 4:6; Luke 4:10; [Heb. 1:14]
**12** [a]Matt. 4:6; Luke 4:11 [1]*lift* [2]*strike*
**14** [a][Ps. 9:10] [1]*exalt him*
**15** [a]Job 12:4; Ps. 50:15 [b]Is. 43:2
**16** [1]Lit. *length of days*

PSALM 92
**1** [a]Ps. 147:1
**2** [a]Ps. 89:1
**3** [a]1 Chr. 23:5 [1]*melodic*
**5** [a]Ps. 40:5; [Rev. 15:3] [b]Ps. 139:17, 18; [Is. 28:29; Rom. 11:33, 34]
**6** [a]Ps. 73:22
**7** [a]Job 12:6; Ps. 37:1, 2; Jer. 12:1, 2; [Mal. 3:15] [1]*sprout*
**8** [a][Ps. 83:18]
**9** [a]Ps. 68:1
**10** [a]Ps. 89:17 [b]Ps. 23:5 [1]Strength
**11** [a]Ps. 54:7
**12** [a]Num. 24:6; Ps. 52:8; Jer. 17:8; Hos. 14:5, 6
**14** [1]Full of oil or sap, lit. *fat* [2]*green*
**15** [a][Deut. 32:4] [b][Rom. 9:14]

PSALM 93
**1** [a]Ps. 96:10 [b]Ps. 65:6 [1]*shaken*
**2** [a]Ps. 45:6; [Lam. 5:19]

3 The floods have [1]lifted up, O LORD,
The floods have lifted up their voice;
The floods lift up their waves.
4 [a]The LORD on high *is* mightier
Than the noise of many waters,
*Than* the mighty waves of the sea.

5 Your testimonies are very sure;
Holiness adorns Your house,
O LORD, [1]forever.

## PSALM 94

O LORD God, [a]to whom vengeance belongs—
O God, to whom vengeance belongs, shine forth!
2 Rise up, O [a]Judge of the earth;
[1]Render punishment to the proud.
3 LORD, [a]how long will the wicked,
How long will the wicked triumph?

4 They [a]utter speech, *and* speak insolent things;
All the workers of iniquity boast in themselves.
5 They break in pieces Your people, O LORD,
And afflict Your heritage.
6 They slay the widow and the stranger,
And murder the fatherless.
7 [a]Yet they say, "The LORD does not see,
Nor does the God of Jacob [1]understand."

8 Understand, you senseless among the people;
And *you* fools, when will you be wise?
9 [a]He who planted the ear, shall He not hear?
He who formed the eye, shall He not see?
10 He who [1]instructs the [2]nations, shall He not correct,
He who teaches man knowledge?
11 The LORD [a]knows the thoughts of man,
That they *are* futile.

12 Blessed *is* the man whom You [a]instruct, O LORD,
And teach out of Your law,
13 That You may give him [1]rest from the days of adversity,
Until the pit is dug for the wicked.
14 For the LORD will not [1]cast off His people,
Nor will He forsake His inheritance.
15 But judgment will return to righteousness,
And all the upright in heart will follow it.

16 Who will rise up for me against the evildoers?
Who will stand up for me against the workers of iniquity?
17 Unless the LORD *had been* my help,
My soul would soon have settled in silence.
18 If I say, "My foot slips,"
Your mercy, O LORD, will hold me up.
19 In the multitude of my anxieties within me,
Your comforts delight my soul.

20 Shall [a]the throne of iniquity, which devises evil by law,
Have fellowship with You?
21 They gather together against the life of the righteous,
And condemn [a]innocent blood.
22 But the LORD has been my defense,
And my God the rock of my refuge.
23 He has brought on them their own iniquity,
And shall [1]cut them off in their own wickedness;
The LORD our God shall cut them off.

## PSALM 95

OH come, let us sing to the LORD!
Let us shout joyfully to the Rock of our salvation.
2 Let us come before His presence with thanksgiving;
Let us shout joyfully to Him with [a]psalms.
3 For [a]the LORD *is* the great God,
And the great King above all gods.
4 [1]In His hand *are* the deep places of the earth;
The heights of the hills *are* His also.
5 [a]The sea *is* His, for He made it;
And His hands formed the dry *land.*

6 Oh come, let us worship and bow down;
Let [a]us kneel before the LORD our Maker.
7 For He *is* our God,
And [a]we *are* the people of His pasture,
And the sheep [1]of His hand.

[b]Today, if you will hear His voice:
8 "Do not harden your hearts, as in the [1]rebellion,
[a]As *in* the day of [2]trial in the wilderness,
9 When [a]your fathers tested Me;
They tried Me, though they [b]saw My work.
10 For [a]forty years I was [1]grieved with *that* generation,
And said, 'It *is* a people who go astray in their hearts,
And they do not know My ways.'
11 So [a]I swore in My wrath,
'They shall not enter My rest.' "

## PSALM 96

OH, [a]sing to the LORD a new song!
Sing to the LORD, all the earth.
2 Sing to the LORD, bless His name;
Proclaim the good news of His salvation from day to day.
3 Declare His glory among the [1]nations,
His wonders among all peoples.

4 For [a]the LORD *is* great and [b]greatly to be praised;
[c]He *is* to be feared above all gods.
5 For [a]all the gods of the peoples *are* idols,
[b]But the LORD made the heavens.
6 Honor and majesty *are* before Him;
Strength and [a]beauty *are* in His sanctuary.

7 [a]Give[1] to the LORD, O families of the peoples,
Give to the LORD glory and strength.
8 [1]Give to the LORD the glory *due* His name;
Bring an offering, and come into His courts.
9 Oh, worship the LORD [a]in the beauty of holiness!
Tremble before Him, all the earth.

10 Say among the [1]nations, [a]"The LORD reigns;
The world also is firmly established,
It shall not be [2]moved;
[b]He shall judge the peoples righteously."

11 [a]Let the heavens rejoice, and let the earth be glad;
[b]Let the sea roar, and [1]all its fullness;
12 Let the field be joyful, and all that *is* in it.
Then all the trees of the woods will rejoice before the LORD.
13 For He is coming, for He is coming to judge the earth.

---

3 [1] *raised up*
4 [a] Ps. 65:7
5 [1] Lit. *for length of days*

PSALM 94
1 [a] [Nah. 1:2]
2 [a] [Gen. 18:25] [1] *Repay with*
3 [a] [Job 20:5]
4 [a] Ps. 31:18
7 [a] Ps. 10:11 [1] *pay attention*
9 [a] [Ex. 4:11]
10 [1] *disciplines* [2] *Gentiles*
11 [a] 1 Cor. 3:20
12 [a] [Heb. 12:5, 6]
13 [1] *relief*
14 [1] *abandon*
20 [a] Amos 6:3
21 [a] [Ex. 23:7]
23 [1] *destroy them*

PSALM 95
2 [a] James 5:13
3 [a] [Ps. 96:4]
4 [1] In His possession
5 [a] Gen. 1:9, 10
6 [a] [Phil. 2:10]
7 [a] Ps. 79:13 [b] Heb. 3:7–11, 15; 4:7 [1] Under His care
8 [a] Ex. 17:2–7 [1] Or *Meribah,* lit. *Strife, Contention* [2] Or *Massah,* lit. *Trial, Testing*
9 [a] Ps. 78:18 [b] Num. 14:22
10 [a] Heb. 3:10, 17 [1] *disgusted*
11 [a] Heb. 4:3, 5

PSALM 96
1 [a] 1 Chr. 16:23–33
3 [1] *Gentiles*
4 [a] Ps. 145:3 [b] Ps. 18:3 [c] Ps. 95:3
5 [a] [Jer. 10:11] [b] Is. 42:5
6 [a] Ps. 29:2
7 [a] Ps. 29:1, 2 [1] *Ascribe*
8 [1] *Ascribe*
9 [a] Ps. 29:2
10 [a] Ps. 93:1; 97:1 [b] Ps. 67:4 [1] *Gentiles* [2] *shaken*
11 [a] Ps. 69:34 [b] Ps. 98:7 [1] *all that is in it*

[a]He shall judge the world with righteousness,
And the peoples with His truth.

## PSALM 97

THE LORD [a]reigns;
Let the earth rejoice;
Let the multitude of [1]isles be glad!

2 [a]Clouds and darkness surround Him;
[b]Righteousness and justice *are* the foundation of His throne.
3 [a]A fire goes before Him,
And burns up His enemies round about.
4 [a]His lightnings light the world;
The earth sees and trembles.
5 [a]The mountains melt like wax at the presence of the LORD,
At the presence of the Lord of the whole earth.
6 [a]The heavens declare His righteousness,
And all the peoples see His glory.

7 [a]Let all be put to shame who serve carved images,
Who boast of idols.
[b]Worship Him, all *you* gods.
8 Zion hears and is glad,
And the daughters of Judah rejoice
Because of Your judgments, O LORD.
9 For You, LORD, *are* [a]most high above all the earth;
[b]You are exalted far above all gods.

10 You who love the LORD, [a]hate evil!
[b]He preserves the souls of His saints;
[c]He delivers them out of the hand of the wicked.
11 [a]Light is sown for the righteous,
And gladness for the upright in heart.
12 [a]Rejoice in the LORD, you righteous,
[b]And give thanks [1]at the remembrance of [2]His holy name.

## PSALM 98

A Psalm.

OH, [a]sing to the LORD a new song!
For He has [b]done marvelous things;
His right hand and His holy arm have gained Him the victory.
2 [a]The LORD has made known His salvation;
[b]His righteousness He has revealed in the sight of the [1]nations.
3 He has remembered His mercy and His faithfulness to the house of Israel;
[a]All the ends of the earth have seen the salvation of our God.

4 Shout joyfully to the LORD, all the earth;
Break forth in song, rejoice, and sing praises.
5 Sing to the LORD with the harp,
With the harp and the sound of a psalm,
6 With trumpets and the sound of a horn;
Shout joyfully before the LORD, the King.

7 Let the sea roar, and all its fullness,
The world and those who dwell in it;
8 Let the rivers clap *their* hands;
Let the hills be joyful together before the LORD,
9 [a]For He is coming to judge the earth.
With righteousness He shall judge the world,
And the peoples with [1]equity.

## PSALM 99

THE LORD reigns;
Let the peoples tremble!
[a]He dwells *between* the cherubim;
Let the earth be [1]moved!
2 The LORD *is* great in Zion,
And He *is* high above all the peoples.
3 Let them praise Your great and awesome name—
[1]He *is* holy.

4 The King's strength also loves justice;
You have established equity;
You have executed justice and righteousness in Jacob.
5 Exalt the LORD our God,
And worship at His footstool—
He *is* holy.

6 Moses and Aaron were among His priests,
And Samuel was among those who [a]called upon His name;
They called upon the LORD, and He answered them.
7 He spoke to them in the cloudy pillar;
They kept His testimonies and the [1]ordinance He gave them.

8 You answered them, O LORD our God;
You were to them God-Who-Forgives,
Though You took vengeance on their deeds.
9 Exalt the LORD our God,
And worship at His holy hill;
For the LORD our God *is* holy.

## PSALM 100

[a]A Psalm of Thanksgiving.

MAKE [a]a joyful shout to the LORD, [1]all you lands!
2 Serve the LORD with gladness;
Come before His presence with singing.
3 Know that the LORD, He *is* God;
[a]*It is* He *who* has made us, and [1]not we ourselves;
[b]*We are* His people and the sheep of His pasture.

4 [a]Enter into His gates with thanksgiving,
*And* into His courts with praise.
Be thankful to Him, *and* bless His name.
5 For the LORD *is* good;
[a]His mercy *is* everlasting,
And His truth *endures* to all generations.

## PSALM 101

A Psalm of David.

I WILL sing of mercy and justice;
To You, O LORD, I will sing praises.

2 I will behave wisely in a [1]perfect way.
Oh, when will You come to me?
I will [a]walk within my house with a perfect heart.

3 I will set nothing [1]wicked before my eyes;
[a]I hate the work of those [b]who fall away;
It shall not cling to me.
4 A perverse heart shall depart from me;
I will not [a]know wickedness.

5 Whoever secretly slanders his neighbor,
Him I will destroy;

---

13 [a][Rev. 19:11]

PSALM 97
1 [a][Ps. 96:10] [1]Or *coastlands*
2 [a]Ex. 19:9; Deut. 4:11; 1 Kin. 8:12; Ps. 18:11 [b][Ps. 89:14]
3 [a]Ps. 18:8; Dan. 7:10; Hab. 3:5
4 [a]Ex. 19:18
5 [a]Ps. 46:6; Amos 9:5; Mic. 1:4; Nah. 1:5
6 [a]Ps. 19:1
7 [a][Ex. 20:4] [b][Heb. 1:6]
9 [a]Ps. 83:18 [b]Ex. 18:11; Ps. 95:3; 96:4
10 [a][Ps. 34:14; Prov. 8:13; Amos 5:15; Rom. 12:9] [b]Ps. 31:23; 145:20; Prov. 2:8 [c]Ps. 37:40; Jer. 15:21; Dan. 3:28
11 [a]Job 22:28; Ps. 112:4; Prov. 4:18
12 [a]Ps. 33:1 [b]Ps. 30:4 [1]Or *for the memory* [2]Or *His holiness*

PSALM 98
1 [a]Ps. 33:3; Is. 42:10 [b]Ex. 15:11; Ps. 77:14
2 [a]Is. 52:10; [Luke 1:77; 2:30, 31] [b]Is. 62:2; Rom. 3:25 [1]*Gentiles*
3 [a][Is. 49:6]; Luke 3:6; [Acts 13:47; 28:28]
9 [a][Ps. 96:10, 13] [1]*uprightness*

PSALM 99
1 [a]Ex. 25:22; 1 Sam. 4:4; Ps. 80:1 [1]*shaken*
3 [1]Or *It*
6 [a]1 Sam. 7:9; 12:18
7 [1]*statute*

PSALM 100
title [a]Ps. 145:title
1 [a]Ps. 95:1 [1]Lit. *all the earth*
3 [a]Job 10:3, 8; Ps. 119:73; 139:13, 14; [Eph. 2:10] [b]Ps. 95:7; [Is. 40:11]; Ezek. 34:30, 31 [1]So with Kt., LXX, Vg.; Qr., many Heb. mss., Tg. *we are His*
4 [a]Ps. 66:13; 116:17–19
5 [a]Ps. 136:1

PSALM 101
2 [a]1 Kin. 11:4 [1]*blameless*
3 [a]Ps. 97:10 [b]Josh. 23:6 [1]*worthless*
4 [a][Ps. 119:115]

[a]The one who has a haughty look and a proud heart,
Him I will not endure.

6 My eyes *shall be* on the faithful of the land,
That they may dwell with me;
He who walks in a [1]perfect way,
He shall serve me.
7 He who works deceit shall not dwell within my house;
He who tells lies shall not [1]continue in my presence.
8 [a]Early I will destroy all the wicked of the land,
That I may cut off all the evildoers [b]from the city of the LORD.

## PSALM 102

A Prayer of the afflicted, [a]when he is overwhelmed and pours out his complaint before the LORD.

HEAR my prayer, O LORD,
And let my cry come to You.
2 [a]Do not hide Your face from me
in the day of my trouble;
Incline Your ear to me;
In the day that I call, answer me speedily.

3 For my days [1]are [a]consumed like smoke,
And my bones are burned like a hearth.
4 My heart is stricken and withered like grass,
So that I forget to eat my bread.
5 Because of the sound of my groaning
My bones cling to my [1]skin.
6 I am like a pelican of the wilderness;
I am like an owl of the desert.
7 I lie awake,
And am like a sparrow alone on the housetop.

8 My enemies reproach me all day long;
Those who deride me swear an oath against me.
9 For I have eaten ashes like bread,
And mingled my drink with weeping,
10 Because of Your indignation and Your wrath;
For You have lifted me up and cast me away.
11 My days *are* like a shadow that lengthens,
And I wither away like grass.

12 But You, O LORD, shall endure forever,
And the remembrance of Your name to all generations.
13 You will arise *and* have mercy on Zion;
For the time to favor her,
Yes, the set time, has come.
14 For Your servants take pleasure in her stones,
And show favor to her dust.
15 So the [1]nations shall [a]fear
the name of the LORD,
And all the kings of the earth Your glory.
16 For the LORD shall build up Zion;
[a]He shall appear in His glory.
17 [a]He shall regard the prayer of the destitute,
And shall not despise their prayer.

18 This will be [a]written for the generation to come,
That [b]a people yet to be created may praise the LORD.
19 For He [a]looked down from the height of His sanctuary;
From heaven the LORD viewed the earth,
20 [a]To hear the groaning of the prisoner,
To release those appointed to death,
21 To [a]declare the name of the LORD in Zion,
And His praise in Jerusalem,
22 [a]When the peoples are gathered together,
And the kingdoms, to serve the LORD.

23 He weakened my strength in the way;
He [a]shortened my days.
24 [a]I said, "O my God,
Do not take me away in the midst of my days;
[b]Your years *are* throughout all generations.
25 [a]Of old You laid the foundation of the earth,
And the heavens *are* the work of Your hands.
26 [a]They will perish, but You will [1]endure;
Yes, they will all grow old like a garment;
Like a cloak You will change them,
And they will be changed.
27 But [a]You *are* the same,
And Your years will have no end.
28 [a]The children of Your servants will continue,
And their descendants will be established before You."

## PSALM 103

*A Psalm* of David.

BLESS [a]the LORD, O my soul;
And all that is within me,
*bless* His holy name!
2 Bless the LORD, O my soul,
And forget not all His benefits:
3 [a]Who forgives all your iniquities,
Who [b]heals all your diseases,
4 Who redeems your life from destruction,
[a]Who crowns you with lovingkindness and tender mercies,
5 Who satisfies your mouth with good *things*,
*So that* [a]your youth is renewed like the eagle's.

6 The LORD executes righteousness
And justice for all who are oppressed.
7 [a]He made known His ways to Moses,
His acts to the children of Israel.
8 [a]The LORD *is* merciful and gracious,
Slow to anger, and abounding in mercy.
9 [a]He will not always strive *with us*,
Nor will He keep *His anger* forever.
10 [a]He has not dealt with us according to our sins,
Nor punished us according to our iniquities.

11 For as the heavens are high above the earth,
*So* great is His mercy toward those who fear Him;
12 As far as the east is from the west,
*So* far has He [a]removed our transgressions from us.
13 [a]As a father pities *his* children,
*So* the LORD pities those who fear Him.
14 For He [1]knows our frame;
He remembers that we *are* dust.

15 *As for* man, [a]his days *are* like grass;
As a flower of the field, so he flourishes.
16 [a]For the wind passes over it, and it is [1]gone,
And [b]its place remembers it no more.
17 But the mercy of the LORD *is* from everlasting to everlasting
On those who fear Him,
And His righteousness to children's children,

---

**5** [a]Prov. 6:17
**6** [1]*blameless*
**7** [1]Lit. *be established*
**8** [a][Ps. 75:10]; Jer. 21:12 [b]Ps. 48:2, 8

PSALM 102

**title** [a]Ps. 61:2
**2** [a]Ps. 27:9; 69:17
**3** [a]James 4:14 [1]Lit. *end in*
**5** [1]*flesh*
**15** [a]1 Kin. 8:43 [1]*Gentiles*
**16** [a][Is. 60:1, 2]
**17** [a]Neh. 1:6; Ps. 22:24
**18** [a]Deut. 31:19; [Rom. 15:4; 1 Cor. 10:11] [b]Ps. 22:31
**19** [a]Deut. 26:15; Ps. 14:2
**20** [a]Ps. 79:11
**21** [a]Ps. 22:22
**22** [a][Is. 2:2, 3; 49:22, 23; 60:3]; Zech. 8:20–23
**23** [a]Job 21:21
**24** [a][Ps. 39:13]; Is. 38:10 [b]Job 36:26; [Ps. 90:2]; Hab. 1:12
**25** [a][Gen. 1:1; Neh. 9:6; Heb. 1:10–12]
**26** [a]Is. 34:4; 51:6; Matt. 24:35; [2 Pet. 3:7, 10–12]; Rev. 20:11 [1]*continue*
**27** [a][Is. 41:4; 43:10; Mal. 3:6; Heb. 13:8]; James 1:17
**28** [a]Ps. 69:36

PSALM 103

**1** [a]Ps. 104:1, 35
**3** [a]Ps. 130:8; Is. 33:24 [b][Ex. 15:26]; Ps. 147:3; [Is. 53:5]; Jer. 17:14
**4** [a][Ps. 5:12]
**5** [a][Is. 40:31]
**7** [a]Ex. 33:12–17; Ps. 147:19
**8** [a][Ex. 34:6, 7; Num. 14:18]; Deut. 5:10; Neh. 9:17; Ps. 86:15; Jer. 32:18; Jon. 4:2; James 5:11
**9** [a][Ps. 30:5; Is. 57:16]; Jer. 3:5; [Mic. 7:18]
**10** [a][Ezra 9:13; Lam. 3:22]
**12** [a][2 Sam. 12:13; Is. 38:17; 43:25; Zech. 3:9; Heb. 9:26]
**13** [a]Mal. 3:17
**14** [1]Understands our constitution
**15** [a]Is. 40:6–8; James 1:10, 11; 1 Pet. 1:24
**16** [a][Is. 40:7] [b]Job 7:10 [1]*not*

18 [a]To such as keep His covenant,
And to those who remember His
commandments to do them.

19 The LORD has established His throne in
heaven,
And [a]His kingdom rules over all.

20 [a]Bless the LORD, you His angels,
Who excel in strength, who [b]do His word,
Heeding the voice of His word.
21 Bless the LORD, all *you* His hosts,
[a]*You* [1]ministers of His, who do His pleasure.
22 Bless the LORD, all His works,
In all places of His dominion.

Bless the LORD, O my soul!

## PSALM 104

BLESS [a]the LORD, O my soul!

O LORD my God, You are very great:
You are clothed with honor and majesty,
2 Who cover *Yourself* with light as *with* a
garment,
Who stretch out the heavens like a curtain.

3 [a]He lays the beams of His upper chambers in
the waters,
Who makes the clouds His chariot,
Who walks on the wings of the wind,
4 Who makes His angels spirits,
His [1]ministers a flame of fire.

5 *You who* [1]laid the foundations of the earth,
So *that* it should not be moved forever,
6 You [a]covered it with the deep as *with* a
garment;
The waters stood above the mountains.
7 At Your rebuke they fled;
At the voice of Your thunder they hastened
away.
8 [1]They went up over the mountains;
They went down into the valleys,
To the place which You founded for them.
9 You have [a]set a boundary that they may not
pass over,
[b]That they may not return to cover the earth.

10 He sends the springs into the valleys;
They flow among the hills.
11 They give drink to every beast of the field;
The wild donkeys quench their thirst.
12 By them the birds of the heavens have their
home;
They sing among the branches.
13 [a]He waters the hills from His upper chambers;
The earth is satisfied with [b]the fruit of Your
works.

14 [a]He causes the grass to grow for the cattle,
And vegetation for the service of man,
That he may bring forth [b]food from the
earth,
15 And [a]wine *that* makes glad the heart of man,
Oil to make *his* face shine,
And bread *which* strengthens man's heart.
16 The trees of the LORD are full *of sap,*
The cedars of Lebanon which He planted,
17 Where the birds make their nests;
The stork has her home in the fir trees.
18 The high hills *are* for the wild goats;
The cliffs are a refuge for the [a]rock[1] badgers.

19 [a]He appointed the moon for seasons;
The [b]sun knows its going down.
20 [a]You make darkness, and it is night,
In which all the beasts of the forest creep
about.
21 [a]The young lions roar after their prey,
And seek their food from God.
22 *When* the sun rises, they gather together
And lie down in their dens.
23 Man goes out to [a]his work
And to his labor until the evening.

24 [a]O LORD, how manifold are Your works!
In wisdom You have made them all.
The earth is full of Your [b]possessions—
25 This great and wide sea,
In which *are* innumerable teeming things,
Living things both small and great.
26 There the ships sail about;
*There is* that [a]Leviathan[1]
Which You have [2]made to play there.

27 [a]These all wait for You,
That You may give *them* their food in due
season.
28 *What* You give them they gather in;
You open Your hand,
they are filled with good.
29 You hide Your face, they are troubled;
[a]You take away their breath, they die and
return to their dust.
30 [a]You send forth Your Spirit, they are created;
And You renew the face of the earth.

31 May the glory of the LORD endure forever;
May the LORD [a]rejoice in His works.
32 He looks on the earth, and it [a]trembles;
[b]He touches the hills, and they smoke.

33 [a]I will sing to the LORD as long as I live;
I will sing praise to my God while I have my
being.
34 May my [a]meditation be sweet to Him;
I will be glad in the LORD.
35 May [a]sinners be consumed from the earth,
And the wicked be no more.

Bless the LORD, O my soul!
[1]Praise the LORD!

## PSALM 105

OH, [a]give thanks to the LORD!
Call upon His name;
[b]Make known His deeds among the peoples!
2 Sing to Him, sing psalms to Him;
[a]Talk of all His wondrous works!
3 Glory in His holy name;
Let the hearts of those rejoice who seek the
LORD!
4 Seek the LORD and His strength;
[a]Seek His face evermore!
5 [a]Remember His marvelous works which He
has done,
His wonders, and the judgments of His
mouth,
6 O seed of Abraham His servant,
You children of Jacob, His chosen ones!

7 He *is* the LORD our God;
[a]His judgments *are* in all the earth.
8 He [a]remembers His covenant forever,
The word *which* He commanded,
for a thousand generations,
9 [a]*The covenant* which He made with Abraham,
And His oath to Isaac,
10 And confirmed it to Jacob for a statute,
To Israel *as* an everlasting covenant,

---

**18** [a][Deut. 7:9]; Ps. 25:10
**19** [a][Ps. 47:2; Dan. 4:17, 25]
**20** [a]Ps. 148:2 [b][Matt. 6:10]
**21** [a][Heb. 1:14] [1]*servants*

PSALM 104
**1** [a]Ps. 103:1
**3** [a][Amos 9:6]
**4** [1]*servants*
**5** [1]Lit. *founded the earth upon her bases*
**6** [a]Gen. 1:6
**8** [1]Or *The mountains rose up; The valleys sank down*
**9** [a]Job 26:10; Ps. 33:7; [Jer. 5:22] [b]Gen. 9:11–15
**13** [a]Ps. 147:8 [b]Jer. 10:13
**14** [a]Gen. 1:29 [b]Job 28:5
**15** [a]Judg. 9:13; Ps. 23:5; Prov. 31:6; Eccl. 10:19
**18** [a]Lev. 11:5 [1]*rock hyraxes*
**19** [a]Gen. 1:14 [b]Job 38:12; Ps. 19:6
**20** [a][Ps. 74:16; Is. 45:7]
**21** [a]Job 38:39
**23** [a]Gen. 3:19
**24** [a]Ps. 40:5; Prov. 3:19; [Jer. 10:12]; 51:15 [b]Ps. 65:9
**26** [a]Job 41:1; Is. 27:1 [1]A large sea creature of unknown identity [2]Lit. *formed*
**27** [a]Job 36:31; Ps. 136:25
**29** [a]Job 34:15; [Eccl. 12:7]
**30** [a]Is. 32:15
**31** [a]Gen. 1:31; Prov. 8:31
**32** [a]Hab. 3:10 [b]Ex. 19:18; Ps. 144:5
**33** [a]Ps. 63:4
**34** [a]Ps. 19:14
**35** [a]Ps. 37:38 [1]Heb. *Hallelujah*

PSALM 105
**1** [a]1 Chr. 16:8–22, 34; Ps. 106:1; Is. 12:4 [b]Ps. 145:12
**2** [a]Ps. 119:27
**4** [a]Ps. 27:8
**5** [a]Ps. 77:11
**7** [a][Is. 26:9]
**8** [a]Luke 1:72
**9** [a]Gen. 17:2; Luke 1:73; [Gal. 3:17]; Heb. 6:17

11 Saying, [a]"To you I will give the land of
Canaan
As the allotment of your inheritance,"
12 [a]When they were few in number,
Indeed very few, [b]and strangers in it.
13 When they went from one nation to another,
From *one* kingdom to another people,
14 [a]He permitted no one to do them wrong;
Yes, [b]He rebuked kings for their sakes,
15 *Saying,* "Do not touch My anointed ones,
And do My prophets no harm."

16 Moreover [a]He called for a famine in the land;
He destroyed all the [b]provision of bread.
17 [a]He sent a man before them—
Joseph—*who* [b]was sold as a slave.
18 [a]They hurt his feet with fetters,
[1]He was laid in irons.
19 Until the time that his word came to pass,
[a]The word of the LORD tested him.
20 [a]The king sent and released him,
The ruler of the people let him go free.
21 [a]He made him lord of his house,
And ruler of all his possessions,
22 To [1]bind his princes at his pleasure,
And teach his elders wisdom.

23 [a]Israel also came into Egypt,
And Jacob dwelt [b]in the land of Ham.
24 [a]He increased His people greatly,
And made them stronger than their enemies.
25 [a]He turned their heart to hate His people,
To deal craftily with His servants.

26 [a]He sent Moses His servant,
*And* Aaron whom He had chosen.
27 They [a]performed His signs among them,
And wonders in the land of Ham.
28 He sent darkness, and made *it* dark;
And they did not rebel against His word.
29 [a]He turned their waters into blood,
And killed their fish.
30 [a]Their land abounded with frogs,
*Even* in the chambers of their kings.
31 [a]He spoke, and there came swarms of flies,
*And* lice in all their territory.
32 [a]He gave them hail for rain,
*And* flaming fire in their land.
33 [a]He struck their vines also, and their fig trees,
And splintered the trees of their territory.
34 [a]He spoke, and locusts came,
Young locusts without number,
35 And ate up all the vegetation in their land,
And devoured the fruit of their ground.
36 [a]He also [1]destroyed all the firstborn in their
land,
[b]The first of all their strength.

37 [a]He also brought them out with silver and
gold,
And *there was* none feeble among His tribes.
38 [a]Egypt was glad when they departed,
For the fear of them had fallen upon them.
39 [a]He spread a cloud for a covering,
And fire to give light in the night.
40 [a]*The people* asked, and He brought quail,
And [b]satisfied them with the bread of
heaven.
41 [a]He opened the rock, and water gushed out;
It ran in the dry places *like* a river.

42 For He remembered [a]His holy promise,
*And* Abraham His servant.

**11** [a]Gen. 13:15; 15:18
**12** [a][Deut. 7:7] [b]Heb. 11:9
**14** [a]Gen. 35:5 [b]Gen. 12:17
**16** [a]Gen. 41:54 [b]Lev. 26:26
**17** [a][Gen. 45:5] [b]Gen. 37:28, 36
**18** [a]Gen. 40:15 [1]*His soul came into iron*
**19** [a]Gen. 39:11–21; 41:25, 42, 43
**20** [a]Gen. 41:14
**21** [a]Gen. 41:40–44
**22** [1]Bind as prisoners
**23** [a]Gen. 46:6 [b]Ps. 78:51
**24** [a]Ex. 1:7, 9
**25** [a]Ex. 1:8–10; 4:21
**26** [a]Ex. 3:10; 4:12–15
**27** [a]Ps. 78:43
**29** [a]Ex. 7:20, 21
**30** [a]Ex. 8:6
**31** [a]Ex. 8:16, 17
**32** [a]Ex. 9:23–25
**33** [a]Ps. 78:47
**34** [a]Ex. 10:4
**36** [a]Ex. 12:29; 13:15 [b]Gen. 49:3 [1]Lit. *struck down*
**37** [a]Ex. 12:35, 36
**38** [a]Ex. 12:33
**39** [a]Ex. 13:21
**40** [a]Ex. 16:12 [b]Ps. 78:24
**41** [a]Ex. 17:6
**42** [a]Gen. 15:13, 14
**43** [1]*a joyful shout*
**44** [a]Josh. 11:16–23; 13:7 [1]*nations*
**45** [a][Deut. 4:1, 40] [1]Heb. *Hallelujah*

PSALM 106
**1** [a]1 Chr. 16:34, 41 [1]Heb. *Hallelujah*
**2** [1]*express*
**3** [a]Ps. 15:2 [b][Gal. 6:9] [1]LXX, [Syr.], Tg., Vg. *those who do*
**4** [a]Ps. 119:132
**5** [1]The people of Your inheritance
**6** [a][Dan. 9:5]
**7** [a]Ex. 14:11, 12
**8** [a]Ex. 9:16
**9** [a]Ex. 14:21 [b]Is. 63:11–13
**10** [a]Ex. 14:30
**11** [a]Ex. 14:27, 28; 15:5
**12** [a]Ex. 15:1–21
**13** [a]Ex. 15:24; 16:2; 17:2
**14** [a]1 Cor. 10:6
**15** [a]Num. 11:31 [b]Is. 10:16
**16** [a]Num. 16:1–3
**17** [a]Deut. 11:6
**18** [a]Num. 16:35, 46
**19** [a]Ex. 32:1–4
**20** [a]Rom. 1:23

43 He brought out His people with joy,
His chosen ones with [1]gladness.
44 [a]He gave them the lands of the [1]Gentiles,
And they inherited the labor of the nations,
45 [a]That they might observe His statutes
And keep His laws.

[1]Praise the LORD!

## PSALM 106

PRAISE[1] the LORD!
[a]Oh, give thanks to the LORD, for *He is* good!
For His mercy *endures* forever.

2 Who can [1]utter the mighty acts of the LORD?
Who can declare all His praise?
3 Blessed *are* those who keep justice,
*And* [1]he who [a]does righteousness at [b]all
times!

4 [a]Remember me, O LORD, with the favor *You
have toward* Your people.
Oh, visit me with Your salvation,
5 That I may see the benefit of Your chosen
ones,
That I may rejoice in the gladness of Your
nation,
That I may glory with [1]Your inheritance.

6 [a]We have sinned with our fathers,
We have committed iniquity,
We have done wickedly.
7 Our fathers in Egypt did not understand
Your wonders;
They did not remember the multitude of
Your mercies,
[a]But rebelled by the sea—the Red Sea.
8 Nevertheless He saved them for His name's
sake,
[a]That He might make His mighty power
known.
9 [a]He rebuked the Red Sea also, and it dried up;
So [b]He led them through the depths,
As through the wilderness.
10 He [a]saved them from the hand of him who
hated *them,*
And redeemed them from the hand of the
enemy.
11 [a]The waters covered their enemies;
There was not one of them left.
12 [a]Then they believed His words;
They sang His praise.

13 [a]They soon forgot His works;
They did not wait for His counsel,
14 [a]But lusted exceedingly in the wilderness,
And tested God in the desert.
15 [a]And He gave them their request,
But [b]sent leanness into their soul.

16 When [a]they envied Moses in the camp,
*And* Aaron the saint of the LORD,
17 [a]The earth opened up and swallowed Dathan,
And covered the faction of Abiram.
18 [a]A fire was kindled in their company;
The flame burned up the wicked.

19 [a]They made a calf in Horeb,
And worshiped the molded image.
20 Thus [a]they changed their glory
Into the image of an ox that eats grass.
21 They forgot God their Savior,
Who had done great things in Egypt,

22 Wondrous works in the land of Ham,
Awesome things by the Red Sea.
23 [a]Therefore He said that He would destroy them,
Had not Moses His chosen one [b]stood before Him in the breach,
To turn away His wrath,
lest He destroy *them.*

24 Then they despised [a]the pleasant land;
They [b]did not believe His word,
25 [a]But complained in their tents,
*And* did not heed the voice of the LORD.
26 [a]Therefore He raised up His hand *in an oath* against them,
[b]To [1]overthrow them in the wilderness,
27 [a]To [1]overthrow their descendants among the [2]nations,
And to scatter them in the lands.

28 [a]They joined themselves also to Baal of Peor,
And ate sacrifices [1]made to the dead.
29 Thus they provoked *Him* to anger with their deeds,
And the plague broke out among them.
30 [a]Then Phinehas stood up and intervened,
And the plague was stopped.
31 And that was accounted to him [a]for righteousness
To all generations forevermore.

32 [a]They angered *Him* also at the waters of [1]strife,
[b]So that it went ill with Moses on account of them;
33 [a]Because they rebelled against His Spirit,
So that he spoke rashly with his lips.

34 [a]They did not destroy the peoples,
[b]Concerning whom the LORD had commanded them,
35 [a]But they mingled with the Gentiles
And learned their works;
36 [a]They served their idols,
[b]Which became a snare to them.
37 [a]They even sacrificed their sons
And their daughters to [b]demons,
38 And shed innocent blood,
The blood of their sons and daughters,
Whom they sacrificed to the idols of Canaan;
And [a]the land was polluted with blood.
39 Thus they [1]were [a]defiled by their own works,
And [b]played[2] the harlot by their own deeds.

40 Therefore [a]the wrath of the LORD was kindled against His people,
So that He abhorred [b]His own inheritance.
41 And [a]He gave them into the hand of the Gentiles,
And those who hated them ruled over them.
42 Their enemies also oppressed them,
And they were brought into subjection under their hand.
43 [a]Many times He delivered them;
But they rebelled in their counsel,
And were brought low for their iniquity.

44 Nevertheless He regarded their affliction,
When [a]He heard their cry;
45 [a]And for their sake He remembered His covenant,
And [b]relented [c]according to the multitude of His mercies.
46 [a]He also made them to be pitied
By all those who carried them away captive.

47 [a]Save us, O LORD our God,
And gather us from among the Gentiles,
To give thanks to Your holy name,
To triumph in Your praise.

48 [a]Blessed *be* the LORD God of Israel
From everlasting to everlasting!
And let all the people say, "Amen!"

[1]Praise the LORD!

## BOOK FIVE
## Psalms 107–150

### PSALM 107

OH, [a]give thanks to the LORD, for *He is* good!
For His [1]mercy *endures* forever.
2 Let the redeemed of the LORD say *so,*
Whom He has redeemed from the hand of the enemy,
3 And [a]gathered out of the lands,
From the east and from the west,
From the north and from the south.

4 They wandered in [a]the wilderness in a desolate way;
They found no city to dwell in.
5 Hungry and thirsty,
Their soul fainted in them.
6 [a]Then they cried out to the LORD in their trouble,
*And* He delivered them out of their distresses.
7 And He led them forth by the [a]right way,
That they might go to a city for a dwelling place.
8 [a]Oh, that *men* would give thanks to the LORD *for* His goodness,
And *for* His wonderful works to the children of men!
9 For [a]He satisfies the longing soul,
And fills the hungry soul with goodness.

10 Those who [a]sat in darkness and in the shadow of death,
[b]Bound[1] in affliction and irons—
11 Because they [a]rebelled against the words of God,
And [1]despised [b]the counsel of the Most High,
12 Therefore He brought down their heart with labor;
They fell down, and *there was* [a]none to help.
13 Then they cried out to the LORD in their trouble,
*And* He saved them out of their distresses.
14 [a]He brought them out of darkness and the shadow of death,
And broke their chains in pieces.
15 Oh, that *men* would give thanks to the LORD *for* His goodness,
And *for* His wonderful works to the children of men!
16 For He has [a]broken the gates of bronze,
And cut the bars of iron in two.

17 Fools, [a]because of their transgression,
And because of their iniquities, were afflicted.
18 [a]Their soul abhorred all manner of food,
And they [b]drew near to the gates of death.
19 Then they cried out to the LORD in their trouble,
*And* He saved them out of their distresses.

**23** [a]Ex. 32:10 [b]Ezek. 22:30
**24** [a]Deut. 8:7 [b][Heb. 3:18, 19]
**25** [a]Num. 14:2, 27
**26** [a]Ezek. 20:15, 16 [b]Num. 14:28–30 [1]*make them fall*
**27** [a]Lev. 26:33 [1]*make their descendants fall also* [2]*Gentiles*
**28** [a]Hos. 9:10 [1]*offered*
**30** [a]Num. 25:7, 8
**31** [a]Num. 25:11–13
**32** [a]Num. 20:3–13 [b]Deut. 1:37; 3:26 [1]Or *Meribah*
**33** [a]Num. 20:3, 10
**34** [a]Judg. 1:21 [b][Deut. 7:2, 16]
**35** [a]Judg. 3:5, 6
**36** [a]Judg. 2:12 [b]Deut. 7:16
**37** [a]2 Kin. 16:3; 17:17 [b][Lev. 17:7]
**38** [a][Num. 35:33]
**39** [a]Ezek. 20:18 [b][Lev. 17:7] [1]*became unclean* [2]Were unfaithful
**40** [a]Judg. 2:14 [b][Deut. 9:29; 32:9]
**41** [a]Judg. 2:14
**43** [a]Judg. 2:16
**44** [a]Judg. 3:9; 6:7; 10:10
**45** [a][Lev. 26:41, 42] [b]Judg. 2:18 [c]Ps. 69:16
**46** [a]Ezra 9:9
**47** [a]1 Chr. 16:35, 36
**48** [a]Ps. 41:13 [1]Heb. *Hallelujah*

PSALM 107
**1** [a]Ps. 106:1 [1]Heb. same as *goodness,* vv. 8, 15, 21, 31, and *lovingkindness,* v. 43
**3** [a]Is. 43:5, 6
**4** [a][Deut. 2:7; 32:10]
**6** [a]Ps. 50:15
**7** [a]Ezra 8:21
**8** [a]Ps. 107:15, 21
**9** [a][Ps. 34:10]
**10** [a][Luke 1:79] [b]Job 36:8 [1]*Prisoners*
**11** [a]Lam. 3:42 [b][Ps. 73:24] [1]*scorned*
**12** [a]Ps. 22:11
**14** [a]Ps. 68:6
**16** [a]Is. 45:1, 2
**17** [a]Lam. 3:39
**18** [a]Job 33:20 [b]Job 33:22

20 [a]He sent His word and [b]healed them,
And [c]delivered *them* from their destructions.
21 Oh, that *men* would give thanks to the LORD *for* His goodness,
And *for* His wonderful works to the children of men!
22 [a]Let them sacrifice the sacrifices of thanksgiving,
And [b]declare His works with [1]rejoicing.

23 Those who go down to the sea in ships,
Who do business on great waters,
24 They see the works of the LORD,
And His wonders in the deep.
25 For He commands and [a]raises the stormy wind,
Which lifts up the waves of the sea.
26 They mount up to the heavens,
They go down again to the depths;
[a]Their soul melts because of trouble.
27 They reel to and fro,
and stagger like a drunken man,
And [1]are at their wits' end.
28 Then they cry out to the LORD in their trouble,
And He brings them out of their distresses.
29 [a]He calms the storm,
So that its waves are still.
30 Then they are glad because they are quiet;
So He guides them to their desired haven.
31 [a]Oh, that *men* would give thanks to the LORD *for* His goodness,
And *for* His wonderful works to the children of men!
32 Let them exalt Him also [a]in the assembly of the people,
And praise Him in the company of the elders.

33 He [a]turns rivers into a wilderness,
And the watersprings into dry ground;
34 A [a]fruitful land into [1]barrenness,
For the wickedness of those who dwell in it.
35 [a]He turns a wilderness into pools of water,
And dry land into watersprings.
36 There He makes the hungry dwell,
That they may establish a city for a dwelling place,
37 And sow fields and plant vineyards,
That they may yield a fruitful harvest.
38 [a]He also blesses them,
and they multiply greatly;
And He does not let their cattle [b]decrease.

39 When they are [a]diminished and brought low
Through oppression, affliction and sorrow,
40 [a]He pours contempt on princes,
And causes them to wander in the wilderness *where there is* no way;
41 [a]Yet He sets the poor on high,
far from affliction,
And [b]makes *their* families like a flock.
42 [a]The righteous see *it* and rejoice,
And all [b]iniquity stops its mouth.

43 [a]Whoever *is* wise will observe these *things*,
And they will understand the lovingkindness of the LORD.

## PSALM 108

A Song. A Psalm of David.

O [a]GOD, my heart is steadfast;
I will sing and give praise,
even with my glory.
2 [a]Awake, lute and harp!
I will awaken the dawn.
3 I will praise You, O LORD, among the peoples,
And I will sing praises to You among the nations.
4 For Your mercy *is* great above the [1]heavens,
And Your truth *reaches* to the clouds.

5 [a]Be exalted, O God, above the heavens,
And Your glory above all the earth;
6 [a]That Your beloved may be delivered,
Save *with* Your right hand, and [1]hear me.

7 God has spoken in His holiness:
"I will rejoice;
I will divide Shechem
And measure out the Valley of Succoth.
8 Gilead *is* Mine; Manasseh *is* Mine;
Ephraim also *is* the [1]helmet for My head;
[a]Judah *is* My lawgiver.
9 Moab *is* My washpot;
Over Edom I will cast My shoe;
Over Philistia I will triumph."

10 [a]Who will bring me *into* the strong city?
Who will lead me to Edom?
11 *Is it* not *You*, O God, *who* cast us off?
And *You*, O God, *who* did not go out with our armies?
12 Give us help from trouble,
For the help of man is useless.
13 [a]Through God we will do valiantly,
For *it is* He *who* shall tread down our enemies.

## PSALM 109

To the Chief Musician. A Psalm of David.

DO[a] not keep silent,
O God of my praise!
2 For the mouth of the wicked and the mouth of the deceitful
Have opened against me;
They have spoken against me with a [a]lying tongue.
3 They have also surrounded me with words of hatred,
And fought against me [a]without a cause.
4 In return for my love they are my accusers,
But I *give myself to* prayer.
5 Thus [a]they have rewarded me evil for good,
And hatred for my love.

6 Set a wicked man over him,
And let [a]an [1]accuser stand at his right hand.
7 When he is judged, let him be found guilty,
And [a]let his prayer become sin.
8 Let his days be [a]few,
*And* [b]let another take his office.
9 [a]Let his children be fatherless,
And his wife a widow.
10 Let his children [1]continually be vagabonds, and beg;
Let them [2]seek *their bread* also from their desolate places.
11 [a]Let the creditor seize all that he has,
And let strangers plunder his labor.
12 Let there be none to extend mercy to him,
Nor let there be any to favor his fatherless children.
13 [a]Let his posterity be [1]cut off,

**20** [a]Matt. 8:8 [b]2 Kin. 20:5; Ps. 30:2 [c]Job 33:28, 30
**22** [a]Lev. 7:12; Ps. 50:14; Heb. 13:15 [b]Ps. 9:11 [1]*joyful singing*
**25** [a]Jon. 1:4
**26** [a]Ps. 22:14
**27** [1]Lit. *all their wisdom is swallowed up*
**29** [a]Ps. 89:9; Matt. 8:26; Luke 8:24
**31** [a]Ps. 107:8, 15, 21
**32** [a]Ps. 22:22, 25
**33** [a]1 Kin. 17:1, 7; Is. 50:2
**34** [a]Gen. 13:10; Deut. 29:23 [1]Lit. *a salty waste*
**35** [a]Ps. 114:8; [Is. 41:17, 18]
**38** [a]Gen. 12:2; 17:16, 20 [b]Ex. 1:7; [Deut. 7:14]
**39** [a]2 Kin. 10:32
**40** [a]Job 12:21, 24
**41** [a]1 Sam. 2:8; [Ps. 113:7, 8] [b]Ps. 78:52
**42** [a]Job 5:15, 16 [b]Job 5:16; Ps. 63:11; [Rom. 3:19]
**43** [a]Ps. 64:9; Jer. 9:12; [Hos. 14:9]

PSALM 108

**1** [a]Ps. 57:7–11
**2** [a]Ps. 57:8–11
**4** [1]*skies*
**5** [a]Ps. 57:5, 11
**6** [a]Ps. 60:5–12 [1]Lit. *answer*
**8** [a][Gen. 49:10] [1]Lit. *protection*
**10** [a]Ps. 60:9
**13** [a]Ps. 60:12

PSALM 109

**1** [a]Ps. 83:1
**2** [a]Ps. 27:12
**3** [a]Ps. 35:7; 69:4; John 15:25
**5** [a]Ps. 35:7, 12; 38:20; Prov. 17:13
**6** [a]Zech. 3:1 [1]Heb. *satan*
**7** [a][Prov. 28:9]
**8** [a][Ps. 55:23]; John 17:12 [b]Ps. 69:25; Acts 1:20
**9** [a]Ex. 22:24
**10** [1]*wander continuously* [2]So with MT, Tg.; LXX, Vg. *be cast out*
**11** [a]Neh. 5:7; Job 5:5; 18:9
**13** [a]Job 18:19; Ps. 37:28 [1]*descendants be destroyed*

*And* in the generation following let their
[b]name be blotted out.

14 [a]Let the iniquity of his fathers be remembered
before the LORD,
And let not the sin of his mother [b]be blotted
out.
15 Let them be continually before the LORD,
That He may [a]cut off the memory of them
from the earth;
16 Because he did not remember to show mercy,
But persecuted the poor and needy man,
That he might even slay the [a]broken in heart.
17 [a]As he loved cursing, so let it come to him;
As he did not delight in blessing,
so let it be far from him.
18 As he clothed himself with cursing as with
his garment,
So let it [a]enter his body like water,
And like oil into his bones.
19 Let it be to him like the garment which
covers him,
And for a belt with which he girds himself
continually.
20 *Let* this *be* the LORD's reward to my
accusers,
And to those who speak evil against my
person.

21 But You, O GOD the Lord,
Deal with me for Your name's sake;
Because Your mercy *is* good, deliver me.
22 For I *am* poor and needy,
And my heart is wounded within me.
23 I am gone [a]like a shadow when it lengthens;
I am shaken off like a locust.
24 My [a]knees are weak through fasting,
And my flesh is feeble from lack of fatness.
25 I also have become [a]a reproach to them;
*When* they look at me,
[b]they shake their heads.

26 Help me, O LORD my God!
Oh, save me according to Your mercy,
27 [a]That they may know that this *is* Your
hand—
*That* You, LORD, have done it!
28 [a]Let them curse, but You bless;
When they arise, let them be ashamed,
But let [b]Your servant rejoice.
29 [a]Let my accusers be clothed with shame,
And let them cover themselves with their
own disgrace as with a mantle.

30 I will greatly praise the LORD with my
mouth;
Yes, [a]I will praise Him among the multitude.
31 For [a]He shall stand at the right hand of the
poor,
To save *him* from those [1]who condemn him.

## PSALM 110

A Psalm of David.

THE [a]LORD said to my Lord,
"Sit at My right hand,
Till I make Your enemies Your [b]footstool."
2 The LORD shall send the rod of Your strength
[a]out of Zion.
[b]Rule in the midst of Your enemies!

3 [a]Your people *shall be* volunteers
In the day of Your power;

**13** [b]Prov. 10:7
**14** [a][Ex. 20:5; Num. 14:18]; Is. 65:6; [Jer. 32:18] [b]Neh. 4:5; Jer. 18:23
**15** [a]Job 18:17; [Ps. 34:16]
**16** [a][Ps. 34:18]
**17** [a]Prov. 14:14; [Matt. 7:2]
**18** [a]Num. 5:22
**23** [a]Ps. 102:11
**24** [a]Heb. 12:12
**25** [a]Ps. 22:7; Jer. 18:16; Lam. 2:15 [b]Matt. 27:39; Mark 15:29
**27** [a]Job 37:7
**28** [a]2 Sam. 6:11, 12 [b]Is. 65:14
**29** [a]Job 8:22; Ps. 35:26
**30** [a]Ps. 35:18; 111:1
**31** [a][Ps. 16:8] [1]Lit. *judging his soul*

PSALM 110
**1** [a]Matt. 22:44; Mark 12:36; 16:19; Luke 20:42, 43; Acts 2:34, 35; Col. 3:1; Heb. 1:13 [b][1 Cor. 15:25; Eph. 1:22]
**2** [a][Rom. 11:26, 27] [b][Ps. 2:9; Dan. 7:13, 14]
**3** [a]Judg. 5:2; Neh. 11:2 [b]1 Chr. 16:29; Ps. 96:9
**4** [a][Num. 23:19] [b][Zech. 6:13] [c][Heb. 5:6, 10; 6:20]
**5** [a][Ps. 16:8] [b]Ps. 2:5, 12; [Rom. 2:5; Rev. 6:17] [1]Lit. *break kings in pieces*
**6** [a]Ps. 68:21 [1]Lit. *break in pieces*
**7** [a][Is. 53:12]

PSALM 111
**1** [a]Ps. 35:18 [1]Heb. *Hallelujah*
**2** [a]Ps. 92:5 [b]Ps. 143:5
**3** [a]Ps. 145:4, 5
**4** [a][Ps. 86:5]
**6** [1]*inheritance*
**7** [a][Rev. 15:3] [1]*truth*
**8** [a]Is. 40:8; Matt. 5:18 [b][Rev. 15:3]
**9** [a]Luke 1:68 [b]Luke 1:49
**10** [a]Job 28:28; [Prov. 1:7; 9:10]; Eccl. 12:13

PSALM 112
**1** [a]Ps. 128:1 [1]Heb. *Hallelujah*
**2** [a][Ps. 102:28]
**3** [a]Prov. 3:16; 8:18; [Matt. 6:33] [1]*stands*
**4** [a]Job 11:17; Ps. 97:11
**5** [a]Ps. 37:26; [Luke 6:35] [b][Eph. 5:15; Col. 4:5]
**6** [a]Prov. 10:7
**7** [a][Prov. 1:33]

[b]In the beauties of holiness, from the womb of the morning,
You have the dew of Your youth.
4 The LORD has sworn
And [a]will not relent,
"You *are* a [b]priest forever
According to the order of [c]Melchizedek."

5 The Lord *is* [a]at Your right hand;
He shall [1]execute kings [b]in the day of His
wrath.
6 He shall judge among the nations,
He shall fill *the places* with dead bodies,
[a]He shall [1]execute the heads of many
countries.
7 He shall drink of the brook by the wayside;
[a]Therefore He shall lift up the head.

## PSALM 111

PRAISE[1] the LORD!

[a]I will praise the LORD with *my* whole heart,
In the assembly of the upright and *in* the
congregation.

2 [a]The works of the LORD *are* great,
[b]Studied by all who have pleasure in them.
3 His work *is* [a]honorable and glorious,
And His righteousness endures forever.
4 He has made His wonderful works to be
remembered;
[a]The LORD *is* gracious and full of compassion.
5 He has given food to those who fear Him;
He will ever be mindful of His covenant.
6 He has declared to His people the power of
His works,
In giving them the [1]heritage of the nations.

7 The works of His hands
*are* [a]verity[1] and justice;
All His precepts *are* sure.
8 [a]They stand fast forever and ever,
*And are* [b]done in truth and uprightness.
9 [a]He has sent redemption to His people;
He has commanded His covenant forever:
[b]Holy and awesome *is* His name.

10 [a]The fear of the LORD
*is* the beginning of wisdom;
A good understanding have all those who do
*His commandments.*
His praise endures forever.

## PSALM 112

PRAISE[1] the LORD!

Blessed *is* the man *who* fears the LORD,
*Who* [a]delights greatly in His commandments.

2 [a]His descendants will be mighty on earth;
The generation of the upright will be blessed.
3 [a]Wealth and riches *will be* in his house,
And his righteousness [1]endures forever.
4 [a]Unto the upright there arises light in the
darkness;
*He is* gracious, and full of compassion, and
righteous.
5 [a]A good man deals graciously and lends;
He will guide his affairs [b]with discretion.
6 Surely he will never be shaken;
[a]The righteous will be in everlasting
remembrance.
7 [a]He will not be afraid of evil tidings;
His heart is steadfast, trusting in the LORD.

8 His [a]heart *is* established;
[b]He will not be afraid,
Until he [c]sees *his desire* upon his enemies.

9 He has dispersed abroad,
He has given to the poor;
His righteousness endures forever;
His [1]horn will be exalted with honor.
10 The wicked will see *it* and be grieved;
He will gnash his teeth and melt away;
The desire of the wicked shall perish.

## PSALM 113

PRAISE[1] the LORD!

[a]Praise, O servants of the LORD,
Praise the name of the LORD!
2 [a]Blessed be the name of the LORD
From this time forth and forevermore!
3 [a]From the rising of the sun to its going down
The LORD's name *is* to be praised.

4 The LORD *is* [a]high above all nations,
[b]His glory above the heavens.
5 [a]Who *is* like the LORD our God,
Who dwells on high,
6 [a]Who humbles Himself to behold
*The things that are* in the heavens and in the earth?

7 [a]He raises the poor out of the dust,
*And* lifts the [b]needy out of the ash heap,
8 That He may [a]seat *him* with princes—
With the princes of His people.
9 [a]He grants the [1]barren woman a home,
Like a joyful mother of children.

Praise the LORD!

## PSALM 114

WHEN [a]Israel went out of Egypt,
The house of Jacob [b]from a people [1]of strange language,
2 [a]Judah became His sanctuary,
*And* Israel His dominion.

3 [a]The sea saw *it* and fled;
[b]Jordan turned back.
4 [a]The mountains skipped like rams,
The little hills like lambs.
5 [a]What ails you, O sea, that you fled?
O Jordan, *that* you turned back?
6 O mountains, *that* you skipped like rams?
O little hills, like lambs?

7 Tremble, O earth, at the presence of the Lord,
At the presence of the God of Jacob,
8 [a]Who turned the rock *into* a pool of water,
The flint into a fountain of waters.

## PSALM 115

NOT [a]unto us, O LORD, not unto us,
But to Your name give glory,
Because of Your mercy,
Because of Your truth.
2 Why should the [1]Gentiles say,
[a]"So where *is* their God?"

3 [a]But our God *is* in heaven;
He does whatever He pleases.
4 [a]Their idols *are* silver and gold,
The work of men's hands.
5 They have mouths, but they do not speak;
Eyes they have, but they do not see;

**8** [a]Heb. 13:9 [b][Ps. 27:1; 56:11]; Prov. 1:33; 3:24; [Is. 12:2] [c]Ps. 59:10
**9** [1]Strength

PSALM 113
**1** [a]Ps. 135:1 [1]Heb. *Halle-lujah*
**2** [a][Dan. 2:20]
**3** [a]Is. 59:19; Mal. 1:11
**4** [a]Ps. 97:9; 99:2 [b][Ps. 8:1]
**5** [a]Ps. 89:6; [Is. 57:15]
**6** [a][Ps. 11:4; Is. 57:15]
**7** [a]1 Sam. 2:8; Ps. 107:41 [b]Ps. 72:12
**8** [a][Job 36:7]
**9** [a]1 Sam. 2:5; Is. 54:1 [1]*childless*

PSALM 114
**1** [a]Ex. 12:51; 13:3 [b]Ps. 81:5 [1]*who spoke unintelligibly*
**2** [a]Ex. 6:7; 19:6; 25:8; 29:45, 46; Deut. 27:9
**3** [a]Ex. 14:21; Ps. 77:16 [b]Josh. 3:13–16
**4** [a]Ex. 19:18; Judg. 5:5; Ps. 29:6; Hab. 3:6
**5** [a]Hab. 3:8
**8** [a]Ex. 17:6; Num. 20:11; Ps. 107:35

PSALM 115
**1** [a][Is. 48:11]; Ezek. 36:32
**2** [a]Ps. 42:3, 10 [1]*nations*
**3** [a][1 Chr. 16:26]
**4** [a]Deut. 4:28; 2 Kin. 19:18; Is. 37:19; 44:10, 20; Jer. 10:3
**8** [a]Ps. 135:18; Is. 44:9–11
**9** [a]Ps. 118:2, 3 [b]Ps. 33:20
**12** [1]*has remembered us*
**13** [a]Ps. 128:1, 4
**15** [a][Gen. 14:19] [b]Gen. 1:1; Acts 14:15; Rev. 14:7
**17** [a]Ps. 6:5; 88:10–12; [Is. 38:18]
**18** [a]Ps. 113:2; Dan. 2:20

PSALM 116
**1** [a]Ps. 18:1
**3** [a]Ps. 18:4–6 [1]Lit. *cords* [2]*distresses* [3]Lit. *found me*
**5** [a][Ps. 103:8] [b][Ezra 9:15]; Neh. 9:8; [Ps. 119:137; 145:17; Jer. 12:1; Dan. 9:14]
**7** [a][Jer. 6:16; Matt. 11:29] [b]Ps. 13:6
**8** [a]Ps. 56:13
**9** [a]Ps. 27:13
**10** [a]2 Cor. 4:13
**11** [a]Ps. 31:22 [b]Rom. 3:4
**14** [a]Ps. 116:18

6 They have ears, but they do not hear;
Noses they have, but they do not smell;
7 They have hands, but they do not handle;
Feet they have, but they do not walk;
Nor do they mutter through their throat.
8 [a]Those who make them are like them;
*So is* everyone who trusts in them.

9 [a]O Israel, trust in the LORD;
[b]He *is* their help and their shield.
10 O house of Aaron, trust in the LORD;
He *is* their help and their shield.
11 You who fear the LORD, trust in the LORD;
He *is* their help and their shield.

12 The LORD [1]has been mindful of *us;*
He will bless *us;*
He will bless the house of Israel;
He will bless the house of Aaron.
13 [a]He will bless those who fear the LORD,
*Both* small and great.

14 May the LORD give you increase more and more,
You and your children.
15 *May* you *be* [a]blessed by the LORD,
[b]Who made heaven and earth.

16 The heaven, *even* the heavens, *are* the LORD's;
But the earth He has given to the children of men.
17 [a]The dead do not praise the LORD,
Nor any who go down into silence.
18 [a]But we will bless the LORD
From this time forth and forevermore.

Praise the LORD!

## PSALM 116

I [a]LOVE the LORD, because He has heard
My voice *and* my supplications.
2 Because He has inclined His ear to me,
Therefore I will call *upon Him* as long as I live.

3 [a]The [1]pains of death surrounded me,
And the [2]pangs of Sheol [3]laid hold of me;
I found trouble and sorrow.
4 Then I called upon the name of the LORD:
"O LORD, I implore You, deliver my soul!"

5 [a]Gracious *is* the LORD, and [b]righteous;
Yes, our God *is* merciful.
6 The LORD preserves the simple;
I was brought low, and He saved me.
7 Return to your [a]rest, O my soul,
For [b]the LORD has dealt bountifully with you.

8 [a]For You have delivered my soul from death,
My eyes from tears,
*And* my feet from falling.
9 I will walk before the LORD
[a]In the land of the living.
10 [a]I believed, therefore I spoke,
"I am greatly afflicted."
11 [a]I said in my haste,
[b]"All men *are* liars."

12 What shall I render to the LORD
*For* all His benefits toward me?
13 I will take up the cup of salvation,
And call upon the name of the LORD.
14 [a]I will pay my vows to the LORD
Now in the presence of all His people.

15 [a]Precious in the sight of the LORD
*Is* the death of His saints.

16 O LORD, truly [a]I *am* Your servant;
I *am* Your servant,
[b]the son of Your maidservant;
You have loosed my bonds.
17 I will offer to You [a]the sacrifice of thanksgiving,
And will call upon the name of the LORD.

18 I will pay my vows to the LORD
Now in the presence of all His people,
19 In the [a]courts of the LORD's house,
In the midst of you, O Jerusalem.

[1]Praise the LORD!

## PSALM 117

PRAISE [a]the LORD, all you Gentiles!
[1]Laud Him, all you peoples!
2 For His merciful kindness is great toward us,
And [a]the truth of the LORD *endures* forever.

Praise the LORD!

## PSALM 118

OH, [a]give thanks to the LORD, for *He is* good!
[b]For His mercy *endures* forever.

2 [a]Let Israel now say,
"His mercy *endures* forever."
3 Let the house of Aaron now say,
"His mercy *endures* forever."
4 Let those who fear the LORD now say,
"His mercy *endures* forever."

5 [a]I called on the LORD in distress;
The LORD answered me
*and* [b]*set me* in a broad place.
6 [a]The LORD *is* on my side;
I will not fear.
What can man do to me?
7 [a]The LORD is for me among those who help me;
Therefore [b]I shall see *my desire* on those who hate me.
8 [a]*It is* better to trust in the LORD
Than to put confidence in man.
9 [a]*It is* better to trust in the LORD
Than to put confidence in princes.

10 All nations surrounded me,
But in the name of the LORD I will destroy them.
11 They [a]surrounded me,
Yes, they surrounded me;
But in the name of the LORD I will destroy them.
12 They surrounded me [a]like bees;
They were quenched [b]like a fire of thorns;
For in the name of the LORD I will [1]destroy them.
13 You pushed me violently, that I might fall,
But the LORD helped me.
14 [a]The LORD *is* my strength and song,
And He has become my salvation.

15 The voice of rejoicing and salvation
*Is* in the tents of the righteous;
The right hand of the LORD does valiantly.
16 [a]The right hand of the LORD is exalted;
The right hand of the LORD does valiantly.
17 [a]I shall not die, but live,
And [b]declare the works of the LORD.
18 The LORD has [a]chastened[1] me severely,
But He has not given me over to death.

19 [a]Open to me the gates of righteousness;
I will go through them,
*And* I will praise the LORD.
20 [a]This is the gate of the LORD,
[b]Through which the righteous shall enter.

21 I will praise You,
For You have [a]answered me,
And have become my salvation.

22 [a]The stone *which* the builders rejected
Has become the chief cornerstone.
23 [1]This was the LORD's doing;
It *is* marvelous in our eyes.
24 This *is* the day the LORD has made;
We will rejoice and be glad in it.

25 Save now, I pray, O LORD;
O LORD, I pray, send now prosperity.
26 [a]Blessed *is* he who comes in the name of the LORD!
We have blessed you from the house of the LORD.
27 God *is* the LORD,
And He has given us [a]light;
Bind the sacrifice with cords to the horns of the altar.
28 You *are* my God, and I will praise You;
[a]*You are* my God, I will exalt You.

29 Oh, give thanks to the LORD, for *He is* good!
For His mercy *endures* forever.

## PSALM 119

### א ALEPH

BLESSED *are* the [1]undefiled in the way,
[a]Who walk in the law of the LORD!
2 Blessed *are* those who keep His testimonies,
Who seek Him with the [a]whole heart!
3 [a]They also do no iniquity;
They walk in His ways.
4 You have commanded *us*
To keep Your precepts diligently.
5 Oh, that my ways were directed
To keep Your statutes!
6 [a]Then I would not be ashamed,
When I look into all Your commandments.
7 I will praise You with uprightness of heart,
When I learn Your righteous judgments.
8 I will keep Your statutes;
Oh, do not forsake me utterly!

### ב BETH

9 How can a young man cleanse his way?
By taking heed according to Your word.
10 With my whole heart I have [a]sought You;
Oh, let me not wander from Your commandments!
11 [a]Your word I have hidden in my heart,
That I might not sin against You.
12 Blessed *are* You, O LORD!
Teach me Your statutes.
13 With my lips I have [a]declared
All the judgments of Your mouth.
14 I have rejoiced in the way of Your testimonies,
As *much as* in all riches.
15 I will meditate on Your precepts,
And [1]contemplate Your ways.

---

**15** [a]Ps. 72:14; [Rev. 14:13] **16** [a]Ps. 119:125; 143:12 [b]Ps. 86:16 **17** [a]Lev. 7:12; Ps. 50:14; 107:22 **19** [a]Ps. 96:8 [1]Heb. *Hallelujah*

PSALM 117
**1** [a]Rom. 15:11 [1]*Praise* **2** [a][Ps. 100:5]

PSALM 118
**1** [a]1 Chr. 16:8, 34; Jer. 33:11 [b]2 Chr. 5:13; 7:3; Ezra 3:11; [Ps. 136:1–26] **2** [a][Ps. 115:9] **5** [a]Ps. 120:1 [b]Ps. 18:19 **6** [a]Ps. 27:1; 56:9; [Rom. 8:31; Heb. 13:6] **7** [a]Ps. 54:4 [b]Ps. 59:10 **8** [a]2 Chr. 32:7, 8; Ps. 40:4; Is. 31:1, 3; 57:13; Jer. 17:5 **9** [a]Ps. 146:3 **11** [a]Ps. 88:17 **12** [a]Deut. 1:44 [b]Eccl. 7:6; Nah. 1:10 [1]*cut them off* **14** [a]Ex. 15:2; Is. 12:2 **16** [a]Ex. 15:6 **17** [a][Ps. 6:5]; Hab. 1:12 [b]Ps. 73:28 **18** [a]Ps. 73:14; Jer. 31:18; [1 Cor. 11:32]; 2 Cor. 6:9 [1]*disciplined* **19** [a]Is. 26:2 **20** [a]Ps. 24:7 [b]Is. 35:8; [Rev. 21:27; 22:14, 15] **21** [a]Ps. 116:1 **22** [a]Matt. 21:42; Mark 12:10, 11; Luke 20:17; Acts 4:11; [Eph. 2:20; 1 Pet. 2:7, 8] **23** [1]Lit. *This is from the LORD* **26** [a]Matt. 21:9; 23:39; Mark 11:9; Luke 13:35; 19:38 **27** [a]Esth. 8:16; [1 Pet. 2:9] **28** [a]Ex. 15:2; Is. 25:1

PSALM 119
**1** [a]Ps. 128:1; [Ezek. 11:20; 18:17]; Mic. 4:2 [1]*blameless* **2** [a]Deut. 6:5; 10:12; 11:13; 13:3 **3** [a][1 John 3:9; 5:18] **6** [a]Job 22:26 **10** [a]2 Chr. 15:15 **11** [a]Ps. 37:31; Luke 2:19 **13** [a]Ps. 34:11 **15** [1]*look into*

16 I will [a]delight myself in Your statutes;
I will not forget Your word.

### ג GIMEL

17 [a]Deal bountifully with Your servant,
*That* I may live and keep Your word.
18 Open my eyes, that I may see
Wondrous things from Your law.
19 [a]I *am* a stranger in the earth;
Do not hide Your commandments from me.
20 [a]My soul [1]breaks with longing
For Your judgments at all times.
21 You rebuke the proud—the cursed,
Who stray from Your commandments.
22 [a]Remove from me reproach and contempt,
For I have kept Your testimonies.
23 Princes also sit *and* speak against me,
*But* Your servant meditates on Your statutes.
24 Your testimonies also *are* my delight
*And* my counselors.

### ד DALETH

25 [a]My soul clings to the dust;
[b]Revive me according to Your word.
26 I have declared my ways,
and You answered me;
[a]Teach me Your statutes.
27 Make me understand the way of Your
precepts;
So [a]shall I meditate on Your wonderful
works.
28 [a]My soul [1]melts from [2]heaviness;
Strengthen me according to Your word.
29 Remove from me the way of lying,
And grant me Your law graciously.
30 I have chosen the way of truth;
Your judgments I have laid *before me.*
31 I cling to Your testimonies;
O LORD, do not put me to shame!
32 I will run the course of Your
commandments,
For You shall [a]enlarge my heart.

### ה HE

33 [a]Teach me, O LORD, the way of Your statutes,
And I shall keep it *to* the end.
34 [a]Give me understanding,
and I shall keep Your law;
Indeed, I shall observe it with *my* whole
heart.
35 Make me walk in the path of Your
commandments,
For I delight in it.
36 [1]Incline my heart to Your testimonies,
And not to [a]covetousness.
37 [a]Turn[1] away my eyes from [b]looking at
worthless things,
*And* revive me in [2]Your way.
38 [a]Establish Your word to Your servant,
Who *is devoted* to fearing You.
39 Turn away my reproach which I dread,
For Your judgments *are* good.
40 Behold, I long for Your precepts;
Revive me in Your righteousness.

### ו WAW

41 Let Your mercies come also to me, O LORD—
Your salvation according to Your word.
42 So shall I have an answer for him who
[1]reproaches me,
For I trust in Your word.
43 And take not the word of truth utterly out of
my mouth,
For I have hoped in Your ordinances.
44 So shall I keep Your law continually,
Forever and ever.
45 And I will walk [1]at [a]liberty,
For I seek Your precepts.
46 [a]I will speak of Your testimonies also before
kings,
And will not be ashamed.
47 And I will delight myself in Your
commandments,
Which I love.
48 My hands also I will lift up to Your
commandments,
Which I love,
And I will meditate on Your statutes.

### ז ZAYIN

49 Remember the word to Your servant,
Upon which You have caused me to hope.
50 This *is* my [a]comfort in my affliction,
For Your word has given me life.
51 The proud have me in great derision,
*Yet* I do not turn aside from Your law.
52 I remembered Your judgments of old,
O LORD,
And have comforted myself.
53 [a]Indignation has taken hold of me
Because of the wicked,
who forsake Your law.
54 Your statutes have been my songs
In the house of my pilgrimage.
55 [a]I remember Your name in the night, O LORD,
And I keep Your law.
56 This has become mine,
Because I kept Your precepts.

### ח HETH

57 [a]*You are* my portion, O LORD;
I have said that I would keep Your words.
58 I entreated Your favor with *my* whole heart;
Be merciful to me according to Your word.
59 I [a]thought about my ways,
And turned my feet to Your testimonies.
60 I made haste, and did not delay
To keep Your commandments.
61 The cords of the wicked have bound me,
*But* I have not forgotten Your law.
62 [a]At midnight I will rise to give thanks to You,
Because of Your righteous judgments.
63 I *am* a companion of all who fear You,
And of those who keep Your precepts.
64 [a]The earth, O LORD, is full of Your mercy;
Teach me Your statutes.

### ט TETH

65 You have dealt well with Your servant,
O LORD, according to Your word.
66 Teach me good judgment and [a]knowledge,
For I believe Your commandments.
67 Before I was [a]afflicted I went astray,
But now I keep Your word.
68 You *are* [a]good, and do good;
Teach me Your statutes.
69 The proud have [a]forged[1] a lie against me,

**16** [a]Ps. 1:2
**17** [a]Ps. 116:7
**19** [a]Gen. 47:9; Lev. 25:23; 1 Chr. 29:15; Ps. 39:12; Heb. 11:13
**20** [a]Ps. 42:1, 2; 63:1; 84:2 [1]*is crushed*
**22** [a]Ps. 39:8
**25** [a]Ps. 44:25 [b]Ps. 143:11
**26** [a]Ps. 25:4; 27:11; 86:11
**27** [a]Ps. 145:5, 6
**28** [a]Ps. 107:26 [1]Lit. *drops* [2]*grief*
**32** [a]1 Kin. 4:29; Is. 60:5; 2 Cor. 6:11, 13
**33** [a][Matt. 10:22; Rev. 2:26]
**34** [a][Prov. 2:6; James 1:5]
**36** [a]Ezek. 33:31; [Mark 7:20–23]; Luke 12:15; [Heb. 13:5] [1]Cause me to long for
**37** [a]Is. 33:15 [b]Prov. 23:5 [1]Lit. *Cause my eyes to pass away from* [2]So with MT, LXX, Vg.; [DSS], Tg. *Your words*
**38** [a]2 Sam. 7:25
**42** [1]*taunts*
**45** [a]Prov. 4:12 [1]Lit. *in a wide place*
**46** [a]Ps. 138:1; Matt. 10:18; Acts 26
**50** [a]Job 6:10; [Rom. 15:4]
**53** [a]Ex. 32:19; Ezra 9:3; Neh. 13:25
**55** [a]Ps. 63:6
**57** [a]Num. 18:20; Ps. 16:5; Jer. 10:16; Lam. 3:24
**59** [a]Mark 14:72; Luke 15:17
**62** [a]Acts 16:25
**64** [a]Ps. 33:5
**66** [a]Phil. 1:9
**67** [a]Prov. 3:11; Jer. 31:18, 19; [Heb. 12:5–11]
**68** [a]Ps. 106:1; 107:1; [Matt. 19:17]
**69** [a]Job 13:4; Ps. 109:2 [1]Lit. *smeared me with a lie*

*But* I will keep Your precepts with *my* whole
heart.
70 [a]Their heart is [1]as fat as grease,
*But* I delight in Your law.
71 *It is* good for me that I have been afflicted,
That I may learn Your statutes.
72 [a]The law of Your mouth *is* better to me
Than thousands of *coins of* gold and silver.

י YOD

73 [a]Your hands have made me and fashioned me;
Give me understanding, that I may learn
Your commandments.
74 [a]Those who fear You will be glad when they
see me,
Because I have hoped in Your word.
75 I know, O LORD, [a]that Your judgments *are*
[1]right,
And *that* in faithfulness You have afflicted
me.
76 Let, I pray, Your merciful kindness be for my
comfort,
According to Your word to Your servant.
77 Let Your tender mercies come to me, that I
may live;
For Your law *is* my delight.
78 Let the proud [a]be ashamed,
For they treated me wrongfully with
falsehood;
*But* I will meditate on Your precepts.
79 Let those who fear You turn to me,
Those who know Your testimonies.
80 Let my heart be blameless regarding Your
statutes,
That I may not be ashamed.

כ KAPH

81 [a]My soul faints for Your salvation,
But I hope in Your word.
82 My eyes fail *from searching* Your word,
Saying, "When will You comfort me?"
83 For [a]I have become like a wineskin in smoke,
*Yet* I do not forget Your statutes.
84 [a]How many *are* the days of Your servant?
[b]When will You execute judgment on those
who persecute me?
85 [a]The proud have dug pits for me,
Which *is* not according to Your law.
86 All Your commandments *are* faithful;
They persecute me [a]wrongfully;
Help me!
87 They almost made an end of me on earth,
But I did not forsake Your precepts.
88 Revive me according to Your lovingkindness,
So that I may keep the testimony of Your
mouth.

ל LAMED

89 [a]Forever, O LORD,
Your word [1]is settled in heaven.
90 Your faithfulness *endures* to all generations;
You established the earth, and it [1]abides.
91 They continue this day according to [a]Your
ordinances,
For all *are* Your servants.
92 Unless Your law *had been* my delight,
I would then have perished in my affliction.
93 I will never forget Your precepts,
For by them You have given me life.
94 I *am* Yours, save me;
For I have sought Your precepts.
95 The wicked wait for me to destroy me,
*But* I will [1]consider Your testimonies.
96 [a]I have seen the consummation of all
perfection,
*But* Your commandment *is* exceedingly
broad.

מ MEM

97 Oh, how I love Your law!
[a]It *is* my meditation all the day.
98 You, through Your commandments,
make me [a]wiser than my enemies;
For they *are* ever with me.
99 I have more understanding than all my
teachers,
[a]For Your testimonies *are* my meditation.
100 [a]I understand more than the [1]ancients,
Because I keep Your precepts.
101 I have restrained my feet from every evil
way,
That I may keep Your word.
102 I have not departed from Your judgments,
For You Yourself have taught me.
103 [a]How sweet are Your words to my taste,
*Sweeter* than honey to my mouth!
104 Through Your precepts I get understanding;
Therefore I hate every false way.

נ NUN

105 [a]Your word *is* a lamp to my feet
And a light to my path.
106 [a]I have sworn and confirmed
That I will keep Your righteous judgments.
107 I am afflicted very much;
Revive me, O LORD, according to Your
word.
108 Accept, I pray, [a]the freewill offerings of my
mouth, O LORD,
And teach me Your judgments.
109 [a]My life *is* continually [1]in my hand,
Yet I do not forget Your law.
110 [a]The wicked have laid a snare for me,
Yet I have not strayed from Your precepts.
111 [a]Your testimonies I have taken as a [1]heritage
forever,
For they *are* the rejoicing of my heart.
112 I have inclined my heart to perform Your
statutes
Forever, to the very end.

ס SAMEK

113 I hate the [1]double-minded,
But I love Your law.
114 [a]You *are* my hiding place and my shield;
I hope in Your word.
115 [a]Depart from me, you evildoers,
For I will keep the commandments of my
God!
116 Uphold me according to Your word, that I
may live;
And do not let me [a]be ashamed of my hope.
117 [1]Hold me up, and I shall be safe,
And I shall observe Your statutes
continually.
118 You reject all those who stray from Your
statutes,
For their deceit *is* falsehood.
119 You [1]put away all the wicked of the earth
[a]*like* [2]dross;
Therefore I love Your testimonies.

**70** [a]Deut. 32:15; Job 15:27; Ps. 17:10; Is. 6:10; Jer. 5:28; Acts 28:27 [1]Insensible
**72** [a]Ps. 19:10; Prov. 8:10, 11, 19
**73** [a]Job 10:8; 31:15; [Ps. 139:15, 16]
**74** [a]Ps. 34:2
**75** [a][Heb. 12:10] [1]Lit. *righteous*
**78** [a]Ps. 25:3
**81** [a]Ps. 73:26; 84:2
**83** [a]Job 30:30
**84** [a]Ps. 39:4 [b]Rev. 6:10
**85** [a]Ps. 35:7; Prov. 16:27; Jer. 18:22
**86** [a]Ps. 35:19
**89** [a]Ps. 89:2; Is. 40:8; Matt. 24:35; [1 Pet. 1:25] [1]Lit. *stands firm*
**90** [1]Lit. *stands*
**91** [a]Jer. 33:25
**95** [1]*give attention to*
**96** [a]Matt. 5:18
**97** [a]Ps. 1:2
**98** [a]Deut. 4:6
**99** [a][2 Tim. 3:15]
**100** [a][Job 32:7–9] [1]*aged*
**103** [a]Ps. 19:10; Prov. 8:11
**105** [a]Prov. 6:23
**106** [a]Neh. 10:29
**108** [a]Hos. 14:2; Heb. 13:15
**109** [a]Judg. 12:3; Job 13:14 [1]In danger
**110** [a]Ps. 140:5
**111** [a]Deut. 33:4 [1]*inheritance*
**113** [1]Lit. *divided* in heart or mind
**114** [a][Ps. 32:7]
**115** [a]Ps. 6:8; Matt. 7:23
**116** [a]Ps. 25:2; [Rom. 5:5; 9:33; 10:11; Phil. 1:20]
**117** [1]*Uphold me*
**119** [a]Is. 1:22, 25; Ezek. 22:18, 19 [1]*destroy*, lit. *cause to cease* [2]*slag* or *refuse*

120 [a]My flesh trembles for fear of You,
And I am afraid of Your judgments.

### ע AYIN

121 I have done justice and righteousness;
Do not leave me to my oppressors.
122 Be [a]surety[1] for Your servant for good;
Do not let the proud oppress me.
123 My eyes fail *from seeking* Your salvation
And Your righteous word.
124 Deal with Your servant according to Your mercy,
And teach me Your statutes.
125 [a]I *am* Your servant;
Give me understanding,
That I may know Your testimonies.
126 *It is* time for *You* to act, O LORD,
*For* they have [1]regarded Your law as void.
127 [a]Therefore I love Your commandments
More than gold, yes, than fine gold!
128 Therefore all *Your* precepts *concerning* all *things*
I consider *to be* right;
I hate every false way.

### פ PE

129 Your testimonies are wonderful;
Therefore my soul keeps them.
130 The entrance of Your words gives light;
[a]It gives understanding to the [b]simple.
131 I opened my mouth and [a]panted,
For I longed for Your commandments.
132 [a]Look upon me and be merciful to me,
[b]As Your custom *is* toward those who love Your name.
133 [a]Direct my steps by Your word,
And [b]let no iniquity have dominion over me.
134 [a]Redeem me from the oppression of man,
That I may keep Your precepts.
135 [a]Make Your face shine upon Your servant,
And teach me Your statutes.
136 [a]Rivers of water run down from my eyes,
Because *men* do not keep Your law.

### צ TSADDE

137 [a]Righteous *are* You, O LORD,
And upright *are* Your judgments.
138 [a]Your testimonies, *which* You have commanded,
*Are* righteous and very faithful.
139 [a]My zeal has [1]consumed me,
Because my enemies have forgotten Your words.
140 [a]Your word *is* very [1]pure;
Therefore Your servant loves it.
141 I *am* small and despised,
*Yet* I do not forget Your precepts.
142 Your righteousness *is* an everlasting righteousness,
And Your law *is* [a]truth.
143 Trouble and anguish have [1]overtaken me,
*Yet* Your commandments *are* my delights.
144 The righteousness of Your testimonies *is* everlasting;
Give me understanding, and I shall live.

### ק QOPH

145 I cry out with *my* whole heart;
Hear me, O LORD!
I will keep Your statutes.
146 I cry out to You;
Save me, and I will keep Your testimonies.
147 [a]I rise before the dawning of the morning,
And cry for help;
I hope in Your word.
148 [a]My eyes are awake through the *night* watches,
That I may meditate on Your word.
149 Hear my voice according to Your lovingkindness;
O LORD, revive me according to Your justice.
150 They draw near who follow after wickedness;
They are far from Your law.
151 You *are* [a]near, O LORD,
And all Your commandments *are* truth.
152 Concerning Your testimonies,
I have known of old that You have founded them [a]forever.

### ר RESH

153 [a]Consider my affliction and deliver me,
For I do not forget Your law.
154 [a]Plead my cause and redeem me;
Revive me according to Your word.
155 Salvation *is* far from the wicked,
For they do not seek Your statutes.
156 [1]Great *are* Your tender mercies, O LORD;
Revive me according to Your judgments.
157 Many *are* my persecutors and my enemies,
*Yet* I do not [a]turn from Your testimonies.
158 I see the treacherous, and [a]am disgusted,
Because they do not keep Your word.
159 Consider how I love Your precepts;
Revive me, O LORD, according to Your lovingkindness.
160 The entirety of Your word *is* truth,
And every one of Your righteous judgments *endures* forever.

### ש SHIN

161 [a]Princes persecute me without a cause,
But my heart stands in awe of Your word.
162 I rejoice at Your word
As one who finds great treasure.
163 I hate and abhor lying,
*But* I love Your law.
164 Seven times a day I praise You,
Because of Your righteous judgments.
165 [a]Great peace have those who love Your law,
And [1]nothing causes them to stumble.
166 [a]LORD, I hope for Your salvation,
And I do Your commandments.
167 My soul keeps Your testimonies,
And I love them exceedingly.
168 I keep Your precepts and Your testimonies,
[a]For all my ways *are* before You.

### ת TAU

169 Let my cry come before You, O LORD;
[a]Give me understanding according to Your word.
170 Let my [1]supplication come before You;
Deliver me according to Your word.
171 [a]My lips shall utter praise,
For You teach me Your statutes.
172 My tongue shall speak of Your word,

**120** [a]Job 4:14; Hab. 3:16
**122** [a]Job 17:3; Heb. 7:22 [1]*guaranty*
**125** [a]Ps. 116:16
**126** [1]*broken Your law*
**127** [a]Ps. 19:10
**130** [a]Prov. 6:23 [b][Ps. 19:7]; Prov. 1:4
**131** [a]Ps. 42:1
**132** [a]Ps. 106:4 [b]Ps. 51:1; [2 Thess. 1:6]
**133** [a]Ps. 17:5 [b][Ps. 19:13; Rom. 6:12]
**134** [a]Luke 1:74
**135** [a]Num. 6:25; Ps. 4:6
**136** [a]Jer. 9:1, 18; 14:17; Lam. 3:48; Ezek. 9:4
**137** [a]Ezra 9:15; Neh. 9:33; Jer. 12:1; Lam. 1:18; Dan. 9:7, 14
**138** [a][Ps. 19:7–9]
**139** [a]Ps. 69:9; John 2:17 [1]*put an end to*
**140** [a]Ps. 12:6 [1]Lit. *refined* or *tried*
**142** [a][Ps. 19:9; John 17:17]
**143** [1]Lit. *found*
**147** [a]Ps. 5:3
**148** [a]Ps. 63:1, 6
**151** [a][Ps. 145:18]; Is. 50:8
**152** [a]Luke 21:33
**153** [a]Lam. 5:1
**154** [a]1 Sam. 24:15; Mic. 7:9
**156** [1]Or *Many*
**157** [a]Ps. 44:18
**158** [a]Ezek. 9:4
**161** [a]1 Sam. 24:11; 26:18
**165** [a]Prov. 3:2; [Is. 26:3; 32:17] [1]Lit. *they have no stumbling block*
**166** [a]Gen. 49:18
**168** [a]Job 24:23; Prov. 5:21
**169** [a]Ps. 119:27, 144
**170** [1]Prayer of supplication
**171** [a]Ps. 119:7

For all Your commandments *are*
righteousness.
173 Let Your hand become my help,
For [a]I have chosen Your precepts.
174 [a]I long for Your salvation, O LORD,
And [b]Your law *is* my delight.
175 Let my soul live, and it shall praise You;
And let Your judgments help me.
176 [a]I have gone astray like a lost sheep;
Seek Your servant,
For I do not forget Your commandments.

## PSALM 120

A Song of Ascents.

1 IN [a]my distress I cried to the LORD,
And He heard me.
2 Deliver my soul, O LORD, from lying lips
*And* from a deceitful tongue.

3 What shall be given to you,
Or what shall be done to you,
You false tongue?
4 Sharp arrows of the [1]warrior,
With coals of the broom tree!

5 Woe is me, that I dwell in [a]Meshech,
[b]*That* I dwell among the tents of Kedar!
6 My soul has dwelt too long
With one who hates peace.
7 I *am for* peace;
But when I speak, they *are* for war.

## PSALM 121

A Song of Ascents.

1 I [a]WILL lift up my eyes to the hills—
From whence comes my help?
2 [a]My help *comes* from the LORD,
Who made heaven and earth.

3 [a]He will not allow your foot to [1]be moved;
[b]He who keeps you will not slumber.
4 Behold, He who keeps Israel
Shall neither slumber nor sleep.

5 The LORD *is* your [1]keeper;
The LORD *is* [a]your shade [b]at your right hand.
6 [a]The sun shall not strike you by day,
Nor the moon by night.

7 The LORD shall [1]preserve you from all evil;
He shall [a]preserve your soul.
8 The LORD shall [a]preserve[1] your going out and
your coming in
From this time forth, and even forevermore.

## PSALM 122

A Song of Ascents. Of David.

1 I WAS glad when they said to me,
[a]"Let us go into the house of the LORD."
2 Our feet have been standing
Within your gates, O Jerusalem!

3 Jerusalem is built
As a city that is [a]compact together,
4 [a]Where the tribes go up,
The tribes of the LORD,
[1]To [b]the Testimony of Israel,
To give thanks to the name of the LORD.
5 [a]For thrones are set there for judgment,
The thrones of the house of David.

6 [a]Pray for the peace of Jerusalem:
"May they prosper who love you.
7 Peace be within your walls,
Prosperity within your palaces."
8 For the sake of my brethren and
companions,
I will now say, "Peace *be* within you."
9 Because of the house of the LORD our God
I will [a]seek your good.

## PSALM 123

A Song of Ascents.

1 UNTO You [a]I lift up my eyes,
O You [b]who dwell in the heavens.
2 Behold, as the eyes of servants *look* to the
hand of their masters,
As the eyes of a maid to the hand of her
mistress,
[a]So our eyes *look* to the LORD our God,
Until He has mercy on us.

3 Have mercy on us, O LORD,
have mercy on us!
For we are exceedingly filled with contempt.
4 Our soul is exceedingly filled
With the scorn of those who are at ease,
With the contempt of the proud.

## PSALM 124

A Song of Ascents. Of David.

1 "IF it had not been the LORD who was on our
[a]side,"
[b]Let Israel now say—
2 "If it had not been the LORD who was on our
side,
When men rose up against us,
3 Then they would have [a]swallowed us alive,
When their wrath was kindled against us;
4 Then the waters would have overwhelmed
us,
The stream would have [1]gone over our soul;
5 Then the swollen waters
Would have [1]gone over our soul."

6 Blessed *be* the LORD,
Who has not given us *as* prey to their teeth.
7 [a]Our soul has escaped [b]as a bird from the
snare of the [1]fowlers;
The snare is broken, and we have escaped.
8 [a]Our help *is* in the name of the LORD,
[b]Who made heaven and earth.

## PSALM 125

A Song of Ascents.

1 THOSE who trust in the LORD
*Are* like Mount Zion,
*Which* cannot be moved, *but* abides forever.
2 As the mountains surround Jerusalem,
So the LORD surrounds His people
From this time forth and forever.

3 For [a]the scepter of wickedness shall not rest
On the land allotted to the righteous,
Lest the righteous reach out their hands to
iniquity.

4 Do good, O LORD, to *those who are* good,
And to *those who are* upright in their hearts.

5 As for such as turn aside to their [a]crooked
ways,
The LORD shall lead them away
With the workers of iniquity.

[b]Peace *be* upon Israel!

---

**173** [a]Josh. 24:22; Luke 10:42
**174** [a]Ps. 119:166 [b]Ps. 119:16, 24
**176** [a][Is. 53:6]; Jer. 50:6; Matt. 18:12; Luke 15:4; [1 Pet. 2:25]

PSALM 120
**1** [a]Jon. 2:2
**4** [1]*mighty one*
**5** [a]Gen. 10:2; 1 Chr. 1:5; Ezek. 27:13; 38:2, 3; 39:1 [b]Gen. 25:13; Is. 21:16; 60:7; Jer. 2:10; 49:28; Ezek. 27:21

PSALM 121
**1** [a][Jer. 3:23]
**2** [a][Ps. 124:8]
**3** [a]1 Sam. 2:9; Prov. 3:23, 26 [b][Ps. 127:1; Prov. 24:12]; Is. 27:3 [1]*slip*
**5** [a]Is. 25:4 [b]Ps. 16:8 [1]*protector*
**6** [a]Ps. 91:5; Is. 49:10; Jon. 4:8; Rev. 7:16
**7** [a]Ps. 41:2 [1]*keep*
**8** [a]Deut. 28:6; [Prov. 2:8; 3:6] [1]*keep*

PSALM 122
**1** [a][Is. 2:3; Mic. 4:2]; Zech. 8:21
**3** [a]2 Sam. 5:9
**4** [a]Ex. 23:17; Deut. 16:16 [b]Ex. 16:34 [1]Or *As a testimony to*
**5** [a]Deut. 17:8; 2 Chr. 19:8
**6** [a]Ps. 51:18
**9** [a]Neh. 2:10; Esth. 10:3

PSALM 123
**1** [a]Ps. 121:1; 141:8 [b]Ps. 2:4; 11:4; 115:3
**2** [a]Ps. 25:15

PSALM 124
**1** [a]Ps. 118:6; [Rom. 8:31] [b]Ps. 129:1
**3** [a]Num. 16:30; Ps. 56:1, 2; 57:3; Prov. 1:12
**4** [1]*swept over*
**5** [1]*swept over*
**7** [a]Ps. 91:3 [b]Prov. 6:5; Hos. 9:8 [1]Persons who catch birds in a trap or snare
**8** [a][Ps. 121:2] [b]Gen. 1:1; Ps. 134:3

PSALM 125
**3** [a]Prov. 22:8; Is. 14:5
**5** [a]Prov. 2:15; Is. 59:8 [b]Ps. 128:6; [Gal. 6:16]

# CHILDREN'S ILLUSTRATED BIBLE STORIES

The best way to introduce the young reader to the Bible is through its stories. The Bible contains many kinds of literature. There are epic narratives as well as simple stories. There are passages of history and theology, poetry and songs, parables and sermons. Taken altogether it is a record of man's relationship with God, of man's sins and his redemption through Jesus Christ. Man has never found a better way of coming to terms with life than by the teachings of the Holy Scripture.

But some of the Bible is not easy to read. Theologians have struggled with and argued about difficult passages for centuries. Wisdom and truth are there, sometimes as readily understandable as the Sermon on the Mount. Other passages, such as the visions of Zechariah, may seem hard to understand. Once a youngster begins reading the Bible, he can read it the rest of his life without exhausting its substance for the mind and the spirit.

A good beginning is the group of fifteen stories contained in this section, each with its own full-color illustration painted by Charles McBarron. These stories were especially written for this Nelson family Bible to help parents introduce the Scriptures to their children. They are written in simple language and with the child's attention span in mind. The illustrations also are unique, painted to capture young imaginations.

These stories inspire interest in reading others directly from the Bible text. An index to a number of favorite Bible stories will be found on the last page of this section.

# ADAM AND EVE

Forever and ever, before He created anything, God had always been alone. Then—before the beginning of time—God decided to create all things. So God made everything. God was very pleased on the day when He had finished making the heavens, the earth, the sea, and all the plants and animals.

But when God had completed His work of creating all these things, there was still one important part missing from the plan. In all the world God had made, there was still no one like Himself that God could have as a friend!

Not that God needed a friend—God is perfect and complete. God doesn't *need* anyone to love Him the way we need to be loved. But God *is love.* Therefore He wanted to *give* His love to you and me. That is why He created people. Isn't that just like God?

So God made the very first man. His name was Adam. This man was very much like God, because he could think and love the way God does.

But the man Adam was lonely because there was no one else like him in the whole world. Of course Adam loved the trees and the animals. But who ever could have a real good talk with an oak tree?—or a porcupine? So God was very kind to Adam, and God created the first woman. She became Adam's wife, and her name was Eve. So Adam and Eve were our very first parents. Adam wasn't lonely any more.

Now God gave Adam and Eve a home in a beautiful garden in a place called Eden. "Be sure to have children," God commanded them, "and take good care of My garden. Make the whole earth grow food and many other good things." So Adam and Eve enjoyed working in God's garden every day, and in the cool of the evenings God would walk and talk with them. Adam and Eve became the very special friends of God.

In those days there was a disobedient angel, named Satan, who hated God and all the wonderful things God had made. Satan especially hated Adam and Eve because God loved them so much. Therefore Satan disguised himself as a beautiful serpent-like animal. Then he tricked Eve into eating some fruit from a special tree that God had forbidden. In fact, God had warned Adam and Eve, "You will die if you eat that fruit." But Satan falsely promised Eve that she wouldn't die. "God is only afraid you will become as great as He is," Satan lied.

Poor Eve! She fell for Satan's trick. And even her husband Adam ate the forbidden fruit. So their friendship with God was broken. When God came to walk with them that evening, Adam and Eve were foolishly trying to hide among the trees from God.

Of course God knew what had happened. So Adam and Eve did die, just as God warned. Yes, because of what they did—we all die.

But God still loved Adam and Eve. The Lord promised them that one day He would send a Savior who would destroy Satan and death. Then God would forgive Adam and Eve's disobedience. Once again the Lord would walk and talk with us as His friends forever.

Have you asked the Lord Jesus to come in and give you an obedient heart? God wants to be your friend, too.

Now memorize Genesis 3:15

# NOAH AND THE ARK

There have been times of very great evil in the world. But the world has never been more evil than it was in the days when Noah lived. In fact, things were so bad in Noah's time that God was even sorry He had created people! They only thought about evil things all the time. Ask yourself, "What do I spend my time thinking about?"

So God decided there was only one thing to do—He would have to destroy His favorite and best-loved creation. Yes, man would have to be destroyed from the earth. God truly loved His people, but the people did not love God any more. The sad truth is that nearly everyone hated God, even though God has given them life. So the people had to die before they completely ruined everything God had planned.

But there was *one man,* named Noah, who still loved and obeyed God. True friends like to walk together. So Noah enjoyed walking with God. This meant that Noah loved to do the things that pleased God. People who walk with God like this are the happiest people in the world.

As time went by, during Noah's lifetime, the world got worse and worse. The planet earth became a very violent place. Murder and the breaking of all God's laws were happening everywhere. The time was coming soon when God was going to take everyone away with a terrible flood.

So God said to Noah one day, "I want you to build a very large house that will float on water. The house will have to be big enough for your family and a great many animals to live in." You see, God wasn't going to destroy everything, really. God was planning to save enough people and animals to start the world all over again, after the flood was gone.

Of course the fish didn't have to worry. They would be very happy swimming around in the great flood that was coming.

The big, floating house that Noah built is called an "ark" in the Bible. It had to be waterproof on top, sides, and bottom. Then it wouldn't sink in the terrible flood that was coming.

There was enough space in the ark for seven of every kind of clean animal and two of every unclean animal. Of course, Noah and his family had to have room to live in the ark, too.

Can't you see all the animals marching into the ark two by two?—There were lions and tigers, giraffes and monkeys, dogs and cats, goats and cows and sheep. There were tall ones, short ones, skinny ones, and fat ones. There were red ones, black ones, brown ones, and yellow ones. They all waddled and trotted and hopped into the ark.

After Noah and his family and all the animals were safely settled down in the ark, God closed the door. Then came the terrible flood. Not only did it rain harder than it had ever rained before, but it rained forty whole days and nights! The water even gushed up from the bottom of the ocean, and all the mountains were covered up by the water.

After 150 days Noah's ark finally sat on the top of Mount Ararat in a country called Turkey. You can find Turkey on a map. The flood had stopped, but it took another six whole months for the land to get dry.

Then God told Noah and his family and all the animals to leave the ark. They must start life over again on earth. Everything in the world had died except Noah and those who were with him in the ark. It was a very sad thing that so many had died. But aren't you glad that God saved Noah, along with his family and the animals?

Because of Noah's ark, you and I are here today. Now we too can walk with God the way Noah did.

Now memorize Genesis 8:22

# THE TOWER OF BABEL

A very long time ago, after Noah and the flood, everybody in the world spoke the same language. Just think of it! No one had to go to school to learn how to speak the languages of other nations. Yes, learning another language is hard work. So God was very wise when He made people in the beginning. He gave them all the same speech and writing.

After the flood everybody lived as one nation in a land called Shinar. But even though people there enjoyed having one language, there was still a lot of unhappiness.

Wherever there is sin, there is going to be unhappiness. Sin, or disobeying God, had long ago entered people's hearts at the time of Adam and Eve. The flood of Noah's time couldn't wash sin away from human hearts. Only God can cleanse our hearts and make us love to obey Him. The people of Shinar were unhappy *in their hearts* because they didn't love God. They didn't walk with God the way Noah did before the flood.

Later, these people at Shinar had a very strange idea. They believed that if they built a city and a very high tower, then they would be happy. Silly as it seems to you and me, the people actually planned to build their tower all the way up to heaven!

Now there are some very high towers in the world, like the Eiffel Tower in Paris, France. The tallest tower in the world is the CN Tower in Toronto, Canada. It's so high you can even see the airplanes flying down below you. But no matter how high we may get in the world, we can never get any closer to God. Why? Because the only way we ever get close to God is when God comes down and lives in the hearts of people who truly love Him.

Just the same, the people of Shinar belived they could get to heaven by building a tower! That was their greatest sin—*believing their own works could possibly get them to heaven.* But you might be surprised to know how many people today—even people who know a lot about outer space—still believe they can work their way to heaven.

Well, God simply had to show the people of Shinar how foolish they were. "I'm just going to come down and chase them away," said God. Then the people would have more important things to do than building a tower! They would have to learn to earn their living in strange, new countries. So God scattered the people of Shinar over the whole earth.

Not only that, but the Lord gave them all different languages. No longer could people clearly understand what their neighbors were saying. Every new country's speech sounded like nonsense to all the others. It still takes a lot of study to learn the languages of other nations. Missionaries must spend a lot of time just learning a new language, even before they can work as missionaries.

So the people of Shinar never did finish building their city or their tower. But God changed the name of Shinar to "Babel." The word sounds like "babble," doesn't it? And "babbling" is really all we can do when we don't learn to think God's thoughts in the Bible. We only waste our time babbling and doing nothing that pleases God.

Aren't you glad you don't have to learn the hard lesson God taught the people of Babel? Even now God wants to give you a new heart. He wants to live with you every day, so that you can please Him in everything you do.

Now memorize Genesis 11:9

# JOSEPH AND HIS BROTHERS

Abraham was the great father of the Hebrew people. Abraham's grandson was Jacob. There were twelve sons born to Jacob, who were going to be the great leaders of the Hebrews. Joseph was Jacob's eleventh son.

Brothers are often jealous of one another, and there was jealousy among the sons of Jacob. Young Joseph was seeing visions from God. When Joseph told this to his older brothers, they were angry. "Our little brother is only showing off," they laughed.

But God really was visiting Joseph in dreams. In some of his dreams, Joseph saw that one day he would rule over his older brothers—and even over his own parents! Can't you just imagine what Joseph's family must have thought?—"Just who does this young know-it-all think he is, spouting off like that?"

So, when his older brothers got fed up with Joseph's dreams, they at first decided to kill him. *That will keep his talky mouth shut for good!* they thought.

It was a very good thing for Joseph that his oldest brother, Reuben, had more sense than the others. Reuben got his brothers to agree to putting Joseph down a deep hole. *Later,* Reuben thought, *I'll rescue Joseph and bring him back to his dad.*

Joseph was wearing a many-colored coat that his father Jacob had given him. Jacob loved his young son very much. The father's special love for Joseph made his brothers even more jealous. So they took off his colored coat. Then they hid him in the deep hole.

But Reuben's brothers did a terrible thing. When Reuben was gone, his brothers sold the boy Joseph to some traders going down to Egypt. Reuben was very upset when he found out what they had done. But they all agreed to dip Joseph's colored coat in a goat's blood. Then they showed their father Jacob the coat, saying, "Look, Joseph's blood is on the coat!"

Poor Jacob! For many years the father mourned for Joseph, his best-loved son. Jacob believed his young son was truly dead.

But unknown to his family, Joseph became a very important person in Egypt. The king of Egypt had a dream. Joseph told him that the dream meant the farmers' crops were going to fail everywhere, and food would become very scarce. So the king of Egypt put Joseph in charge of all the food in the land. Then Joseph taught the Egyptians how to store their grain before the farm crops failed. So there was plenty to eat during the time when the farmers' crops didn't grow.

Now at last the day was coming near when Joseph's dreams about ruling over his family would actually come true. Jacob and his sons were hungry, too, and the whole family had to move to Egypt for food. Can you imagine how surprised they were when they found out who was in charge in Egypt?—It was their very own little brother, Joseph!

At first Joseph played a good-natured trick on his brothers. Of course they couldn't recognize Joseph, who was older now and all dressed up in his royal robes. And Joseph kept it a secret that he was really the young boy they had so cruelly sold as a slave. In his heart Joseph truly forgave his brothers' bad deed, but Joseph also wanted to teach them a lesson. So when he was convinced they were sorry for what they had done—only then did Joseph tell his brothers who he really was.

How ashamed Joseph's older brothers were! But how relieved they were that Joseph was not angry with them! So Joseph and his brothers cried with joy, because they were together again and because Joseph had forgiven them.

That certainly was a great day for Joseph. And what a happy day for Jacob when he at last found his long-lost son!

The Egyptians were also glad, because God had planned everything so that good came to them, too. Without Joseph they would all have died when the crops failed. But God had saved everybody—by using a young slave-boy.

Now memorize Genesis 45:5

# MOSES AND PHARAOH'S DAUGHTER

Israel is the name of the great people that came from Jacob. They are also called "Hebrews." The Hebrews were happy and welcome in Egypt for a very long time. The Egyptians had loved Joseph, the Hebrew leader who saved them from starving. Therefore they loved Joseph's people, too.

But after Joseph died, Israel grew into a large nation. The Egyptians began to be afraid that the Hebrews might become rebels against Egypt. So the Egyptians took away Israel's freedom and made them slaves.

Not only that but Pharaoh, the king of Egypt, decided to kill all the boy babies of Israel. He wanted to make sure the Hebrews didn't grow into an even larger nation. Pharaoh was really trying to destroy the nation of Israel. But first he wanted to use them as slaves to build his cities.

Now Moses was born at this time to a family of Israel. In order to save Moses from being killed, his parents hid the baby for three months. After that, the infant's mother realized she could hide him no longer.

Whatever could they do to save the baby Moses? His mother thought of a bold but dangerous plan. She would make a little waterproof box, like a baby's crib, and place the infant Moses inside it. She would then set the crib-like box afloat in the tall grass at the edge of the river Nile. Moses' big sister Miriam would watch to see what happened to the baby.

While Miriam watched over the little crib, one of the great moments in Moses' life happened. None other than Pharaoh's daughter—a princess—came with her ladies to bathe in the Nile, right where Moses was floating in his crib! So the princess spotted the strange little box and sent a maid to fetch it.

As soon as they opened the box, little Moses began to cry. The lovely princess cried softly, too. "Why, he's a beautiful little Hebrew boy!" she exclaimed. And right then she fell in love with the helpless baby in the box. Can't you just see the princess picking up little Moses in her arms?

Meanwhile, Moses' sister Miriam had joined the group, while also trying not to be noticed among the other girls. But now she spoke up: "Why don't you ask one of the Hebrew women to keep the baby for you?" Wasn't Miriam a clever little girl?

Till that moment the daughter of Pharaoh had no idea of what to do with her new treasure. Whatever would she say to her father about the baby? Worse still, what would her father say to *her?* No, she must not tell Pharaoh about the child. Moses must be saved from the sad fate of the other Hebrew boys.

Well, the Egyptian princess didn't know it then, but the Hebrew lady who came to take the baby home was really Moses' own mother.

Later, before Moses became a teenager, he went to live in the king's palace with the lovely princess. At last her dream came true—the king's daughter could keep Moses as her very own son!

And what a marvelous adventure for young Moses—to grow up in the king's palace! Hundreds of rooms to play in, servants to grant his every wish, and such a very wonderful lady for a mother! Moses' parents would always be grateful to the kind princess who had saved their little son.

Moses also went to school in Pharaoh's palace. In fact, his new mother made sure he had the best tutors in the land. Moses learned to read and write, and he struggled with some of those hard problems in mathematics we study in school today. The young man was taught Egyptian science and medicine. He read all about geography and history. He probably studied the history of his own Hebrew people. Yes, Moses became one of the wisest men in Egypt—perhaps the very wisest of them all.

So we see how well God plans everything He does. Nobody knew just yet what great things God would call Moses to do. But God was preparing Moses to perform one of the greatest acts of all time. Moses would save the Hebrew people from their slavery in Egypt.

Now memorize Exodus 2:10

# MOSES AT THE RED SEA

After Jacob came from Canaan to stay in Egypt, his family lived there for over four hundred years. They were called Hebrews, and were very special people to God. But the Egyptians had made the Hebrews into slaves.

Then the day finally came when God was going to save His people, the Hebrews, from their slavery. Moses the Hebrew, who had grown up as a prince in Egypt, was chosen by God to lead His people to freedom.

Now the king of Egypt had broken his promise to let the Hebrews leave. So God finally had to send terrible punishments on the Egyptians.

By the time God was through punishing the Egyptians, the king was more than happy to let the Hebrews leave. In fact, as the Hebrews were planning to leave the country, the Egyptians even gave them expensive gifts. So you can see how glad the Egyptians were to let the Hebrews go.

In order to leave Egypt, the Hebrews would have to cross the Red Sea. They they would all march to Mount Sinai. There God was planning to meet with them and teach them His laws. Look for the Red Sea and Mount Sinai on a map.

Can't you just see Moses leading the thousands and thousands of Hebrews to the Red Sea? They marched in line, rank after rank, like a very big army.

By the time the Hebrew people arrived at the Red Sea, the king of Egypt was angry because he had let the people go. So he quickly gathered his soldiers and horses, and they chased after the Hebrews. Finally, the Egyptians caught up with the thousands of Hebrew slaves who were standing helpless at the edge of the Red Sea.

Whatever could Moses do now? The people were very frightened. There was the sea in front of them—and behind them the Egyptians! The Hebrews were also angry at Moses for bringing them out of Egypt. They even wished they had stayed back there and died as slaves!

But Moses calmly said to the people, "Stand still, and see the salvation of the Lord! God is going to fight for you!" Just then the Angel of God took the form of a dark cloud standing between the Hebrews and the Egyptians. So the king's soldiers got lost in the cloud. But that same cloud gave light to the Hebrews.

Meanwhile, God commanded Moses, "Tell the people of Israel to go forward." Well! What could God possibly mean by an order like that? "Go forward"!—How in the world could the people walk into the sea without drowning?

It was really quite simple for God. He just ordered Moses to raise his walking stick up over the Red Sea. When Moses did that, a wonderful thing happened. A big east wind blew the water back, and the people were able to walk across to the other side. They didn't even get their feet wet!

Not only the men and the women, the boys and the girls, but also the cows and the sheep, the goats and the chickens—everything the Hebrews owned—marched safely across the Red Sea.

But the king of Egypt was furious. So he sent his army charging across the sea to catch the Hebrews. Then the Lord gave the order, and Moses lifted up his arm once more. Can you imagine what happened?

By this time the Eygptian army was right in the middle of the way through the sea. So when Moses raised his arm, the water came down like thunder over the heads of the soldiers. They were all drowned.

But God's people were saved from their enemies. God always leads us in victory when we trust and obey Him the way the Hebrews did.

Now memorize Exodus 14:13

# MOSES AND THE TEN COMMANDMENTS

For hundreds of years the Hebrews had been slaves in Egypt. Now at last God had led them out of slavery, and Moses was God's chosen leader of the people. Then God met with Moses and the Hebrews at Mount Sinai. There the Lord showed them that He must be their God forever and ever. Also, God wanted to teach the Hebrews His laws. Obedience to God's laws would prove the Hebrews were truly His people.

So, when God commanded him, Moses climbed up Mount Sinai. There God spoke with Moses in a thick cloud that looked like fire. Moses stayed on the mountain forty days and forty nights, and there God gave Moses the Ten Commandments of His law. The Ten Commandments were cut in two stone tablets by the very finger of God!

But while Moses was listening to God's words on the mountain, a terrible thing was happening. At the bottom of the mountain the Hebrew people were already breaking God's law. With the help of Aaron, the brother of Moses, the people had made a gold calf—and they were worshiping it!

So God said to Moses, "Get down there at once! The people are worshiping a gold calf. They are even shouting, 'The gold calf is the god that brought us out of Egypt!' "

God was very angry. He wanted to burn the people up right then and there! But Moses prayed for the people: "Please don't let Your enemies say You only wanted to destroy Your people. Please forgive Your people for the sake of Your promise to them."

Yes, hundreds of years before Mount Sinai, God had made great promises to Abraham, Isaac, and Jacob. They were the fathers of the Hebrew nation. He had promised to make the Hebrews His people forever, and to give them the land where Moses was now leading them. So Moses was praying and asking God to keep His promises.

Of course God already knew He would forgive the sin of the people. He remembered His promises, and He granted Moses' request. God did not destroy the people.

Now as Moses came down from Mount Sinai, he saw for himself what the people had done. Then Moses was very angry, and he smashed the tablets of the law against the mountain. He also burned the gold calf, and made the people drink the powder from the burnt metal. That must have been a bitter drink!

Worse than that, Moses ordered the priests to put 3,000 people to death that day. Moses had saved the whole nation from God's anger. But Moses also realized that the guilty must be punished. Other Hebrews might do what the guilty ones had done, and the whole nation would be ruined. Moses wanted to save the nation from its sins. The lesson is that sin leads to death, but obedience leads to life.

After this, the Lord promised to go with Moses and the Hebrews to the land which God had promised them before. Also, God commanded Moses again, "Cut two stone tablets like the first ones, and I will write on the new tablets the same commandments as before." So God forgave the people, and He made peace with them. They would be His people, and He would be their God.

God wants to make peace with you, too—Jesus died on the cross so you wouldn't have to die for your sins. Jesus is the way of God's peace for you. Have you received the peace that Jesus brings when He comes to live in your heart?

Now memorize Exodus 20:1-17

# DAVID AND GOLIATH

David was only a shepherd-boy when Saul became king of the Hebrews.

Some day David would be Israel's greatest king. But King Saul didn't know that when he asked young David to be his full-time armorbearer. This meant that David would carry King Saul's weapons in battle. What a great honor for a shepherd-boy!

One day David proved what a very great soldier he was going to be. The Hebrews were at war with the Philistines. One of the Philistine soldiers, named Goliath, wanted to fight one of the Hebrew soldiers. Goliath dared the Hebrews to send him a man. "If he is able to fight me and kill me," he shouted, "then we will be your slaves!"

Now Goliath was nearly ten feet tall! He carried a huge spear over his shoulder, too heavy for any ordinary man to carry. A great sword swung at Goliath's side. On his head he wore a big bronze helmet. Another soldier carried a large shield in front of Goliath to protect him. So this giant of a man stood on the side of a mountain, shouting and screaming at the Hebrew soldiers on the other side. The Hebrews were terrified. Who wouldn't be afraid of such a monster?

Well—David wasn't afraid. David was only a shepherd-boy. But he had fought many times to save his father's sheep from wild animals. David knew how to use a heavy staff to drive off bears and even lions. "I caught the lion by its beard and killed it," he told King Saul.

But David's favorite weapon was the sling. His sling was made of two long leather strings fastened to a leather pocket in the middle. You had to put a stone in the pocket of the sling. Then you swung the stone round and round your head by the strings. When the sling was spinning around your head very fast, you let go of one string. Then the stone would shoot out like a bullet!

So David decided to use his sling against Goliath.

Goliath laughed when he saw the boy David with no armor and not even a sword. The giant laughed so hard, even the mountain seemed to shake. "Come on!" he dared David, "I'll feed you to the birds!"

But David answered Goliath calmly: "Today the Lord will give you to me. The Lord does not need spears and swords to win His battles."

Just as Goliath started forward, young David surprised him. Instead of running away, David ran toward Goliath! Then the shepherd-boy quickly dropped a stone in his sling. The sling whizzed round and round so fast you couldn't see it any more. Suddenly the stone shot out of the sling—straight at the giant's head! Like a huge tree, Goliath crashed to the ground with all of his armor and his weapons.

Losing no time, David ran forward and picked up Goliath's great sword and cut off his head. That was enough for Goliath's fellow-soldiers. They ran for the hills.

What a great day for Israel and for David! But this was only the beginning of David's adventures for God.

The Lord will probably never ask you to fight any real giants. But when you are on the Lord's side, you can never lose the battle of life.

Now memorize 1 Samuel 17:47

# THE BIRTH OF JESUS

For a very long time God's people had been expecting a Savior. They kept asking one another, "Where is the Messiah, the One who is to be King of the Jews?"

Then one day God spoke in a dream to a man named Joseph. The Lord told him, "Your wife, Mary, is going to have a Son. You must call Him Jesus, because He will save His people from their sins." The name "Jesus" means "Savior."

Joseph was amazed, because the Lord told him that the true Father of Jesus would be God. In fact, Jesus would really be God Himself living with us!

But these things were no surprise to Mary, Joseph's wife. The angel Gabriel had earlier told Mary that her baby would be the Son of God.

In those days the king of the land wanted to have everybody's name written down in a book. So he commanded all the people to go back to their hometowns and write their names in the king's book. Joseph and Mary had to go to Bethlehem, a town in Judea. Ever since King David's time their family had always lived in that town.

While Joseph and Mary were in Bethlehem, there was no room for them in the local hotel. The only place for them was in a stable.

You and I have never lived in a stable. But it was under the roof of that rough building that Jesus, the Son of God, came into the world. The only crib Mary had for her Baby was a manger. This was just a wooden box from which the cows ate their food. So the King of heaven chose a manger to be born in. Just think of that!

The birth of Jesus was not first announced to kings or other important people. But an angel of the Lord told it to poor shepherds living out with their sheep in the fields. "I am bringing you very good news for everyone," the angel said. "Christ the Lord was born today in Bethlehem, the city where David was born. You will find Him, all wrapped up, in a manger."

Suddenly, the heavens were blazing brightly with the glory of God. At the same time a very great choir of angels appeared, and they sang the praises of God:

"Glory to God in the highest,
And on earth peace,
goodwill toward men!"

So the shepherds hurried away to Bethlehem. There they found the baby Jesus, just as the angel had told them.

While all these wonderful things were happening, there were wise men studying the stars. They lived far away to the east of Judea, the country where Jesus was born. But one night they saw a very special, bright star. They knew that this star was a sign that a great king was going to be born.

As the wise men watched the star, it moved toward the country of Judea. So they followed the star. At last they came to the town of Bethlehem, and the star stopped right over the place where Jesus was.

So the wise men went into the poor home of Mary and Joseph. Then they knelt down and worshiped the Lord Jesus. They gave Him beautiful gifts fit for a king—gifts of gold, frankincense, and myrrh. We all know how expensive gold is. Frankincense and myrrh were very costly perfumes, too.

At that time there was a very bad king in Judea, named Herod. This king asked the wise men, "Where is the Baby? I would like to worship Him, too." But the wise men were warned in a dream not to fall for Herod's trick. Herod only meant to kill Jesus. So Joseph and Mary took the Baby and escaped to the land of Egypt.

After King Herod was dead, Jesus and His family came back to their own land. They lived in Nazareth, a town not far from the Sea of Galilee. There Jesus grew up helping Joseph in his carpenter's shop.

Now memorize Luke 2:11

# THE BOY JESUS IN THE TEMPLE

Every year Mary and Joseph took Jesus to Jerusalem. There they enjoyed the great Feast of the Passover together. "Passover" was the time of year when the Jews remembered how God had saved them from slavery in Egypt long ago.

When Jesus was twelve, His family went up to the Passover as they always did. It was a long journey by donkey from Nazareth, where they lived.

After the Feast, Joseph and Mary were returning home from Jerusalem. But Jesus was not with them.

"Oh, well! He is probably with some of His aunts and uncles," they said. "Or maybe He decided to travel with some of His friends."

But nobody had seen the young Jesus.

Then Mary and Joseph were very upset. "Wherever could that Boy be?" His mother thought. So they turned around and went all the way back to Jerusalem. For three whole days Joseph and Mary looked everywhere for Jesus.

Finally Mary said, "We haven't looked in the temple yet. Maybe Jesus is there."

"Oh, no!" laughed Joseph. "Whatever in the world would a young boy find to do in the temple?"

"Well, we have nowhere else to look!" Mary replied firmly. "We just have to go and see. Besides, I've noticed lately that Jesus is reading His Bible more. He may have gone to see the temple He was reading about."

God's temple was the most beautiful building in the whole land. It was also very large, and there were a great many rooms in it. Mary and Joseph looked all through the temple. At last they came to a room where a lot of important teachers were sitting in a kind of circle.

But what really surprised Mary and Joseph was who they saw sitting in the middle of the circle. It was Jesus, their very own Son! As young Jesus listened to the great teachers, He was also asking them questions. (He probably asked some questions you would like to ask, too.) And Jesus seemed to understand all of their answers about God and the Bible.

But the great men were also asking Jesus hard questions. They were amazed at how much Jesus knew. In fact, the longer they talked with Him, the more it seemed that Jesus was their Teacher!

At that point Mary decided she must stop Jesus from talking any more. Jesus' mother was afraid her Son might make the great teachers angry. So Mary broke into the meeting: "Son! What are You saying to these gentlemen? And what are You doing here? Don't You know Your father and I have been worried about You?"

But Jesus answered His mother in a strange way: "Why were you worried? Didn't you know I have to take care of My Father's business?"

"Your father's business!" snorted Joseph. "Your father's business is in my carpenter's shop in Nazareth, not here in the temple!"

But Mary and Joseph really didn't understand that Jesus was talking about His true Father in heaven. As the Boy grew, they must have asked a lot more questions about the wonderful Son that God had given them.

But the answers to His parents' questions would have to wait until much later. First, there was a cross for Jesus to be nailed to—there was a world for Jesus to die for.

Now memorize Luke 2:49

# JESUS FEEDS THE CROWDS

## Matthew 14:13–21; John 6:4–14

Jesus and His disciples were tired, because they had been teaching and healing people for a long time. Besides, John the Baptist had been killed by the wicked King Herod. This made Jesus very sad, because John the Baptist was His friend. Jesus loved John like His own brother.

At that time Jesus decided to rest with His disciples for a while. So they got into a boat and sailed away to a quiet place on the shore of the Sea of Galilee. You can find the Sea of Galilee on a map.

But the crowds who were following Jesus saw Him leaving. They also knew where He was going. So the people hurried on foot to catch up to Jesus and the disciples. There were 5,000 men and their families who came to Jesus from all the cities around Galilee.

Jesus didn't want to turn the crowd away. They were so very poor, and many of them were sick. They needed Jesus to heal them and teach them about the kingdom of His Father in heaven. They were like sheep with no shepherd to take care of them. Jesus wanted to be their shepherd who would lead them in the truth. He told them, "I am the Way, the Truth, and the Life."

Jesus wants you to know Him as your shepherd, too. *He is* the true Way that leads to heaven.

The Lord Jesus had been teaching and healing the crowds of people all day long. The day was almost over, and it would soon be night. So the disciples reminded Jesus that they were in a place where there was no food. "Send the people away," they said. "Then they can find food somewhere else."

But Jesus gave His disciples a very strange answer: *"You* give them something to eat." Now what could Jesus mean by that? Wherever would the disciples find enough food for this big crowd?

So the disciples replied to Jesus, "We'll just have to go into the next town and buy some food."

Now Jesus knew there was someone in the crowd who had a small amount of food. So He told the disciples to go and see how much they could find. They went and looked. But one of them said to the others, "What difference does it make? This crowd will starve on the few scraps of food these people have!"

When they looked, they found a young boy who had brought a lunch for himself and his family. So the disciples came back and told Jesus what they had found—"Five loaves of bread and two fish. That's all there is!"

But Jesus quietly commanded His disciples to tell all of the people to sit down on the ground. After that, Jesus did a very important thing. He looked up to heaven and said, "Thank You, Father, for all that You give us. Thank You for our food." Do you always remember to thank your heavenly Father for your food? He supplies all your needs.

When Jesus had prayed, He divided the five loaves of bread and two fish among His disciples. The disciples didn't question Jesus any more. They just started passing out the food to the hungry people.

Well, what a surprise! There was actually enough food for everybody! Every single one of those thousands of people got filled up. Not only that—but there were twelve baskets of food left over!

Now how do you suppose Jesus did that? It was a miracle! You see, Jesus is the Son of God. Jesus was there in the very beginning when His Father in heaven made everything. So it was not hard for Jesus to make five loaves and two fish become enough for 5,000 men and their families.

Just remember that it is very easy for God to supply all your needs. He made everything you need. God wants you to come and tell Him what your needs are. But it is even more important to thank Him for all things—the way Jesus did.

Now memorize Matthew 14:20

# JESUS WALKS ON THE SEA

## Matthew 14:22–33

Jesus had just fed 5,000 men and their families with only five loaves of bread and two fish! Then, after sending everybody home, Jesus climbed up a mountain alone to pray.

By that evening the disciples were crossing the Sea of Galilee in their fishing boat. You can find the Sea of Galilee on a map. Sometimes terrible storms happen on that sea.

Just as they reached the middle of the sea, one of those frightening storms arose. The wind was howling, and the waves washed over the sides of the boat. In fact, the little boat was filling up with water. The disciples' lives were in danger from the storm.

Between three and six o'clock in the morning the disciples were losing hope that they could save themselves. It was very dark. The wind was roaring so loudly the men could hardly hear what they were shouting to each other. There was water everywhere. Now they thought the boat was really sinking.

Suddenly, a bright light appeared across the stormy sea. The light was coming toward the boat! The disciples were terrified: "It's a ghost!" one of them yelled. Then they all began screaming with fear. The men held on to each other for safety.

But just when the disciples were sure they were going to drown, they heard a loud voice coming through the storm. It was the voice of Jesus: "It is I! Don't be afraid!" So it was no ghost the disciples had seen. It was Jesus Himself they saw striding over the heaving waves. Now they would be safe.

Peter and John were good sailors. When the storm was at its worst, the two were in the back of the boat trying to steer. But now that Jesus had come, Peter ran forward to the front. He jumped so fast he even stepped on the other men as he went. Then Peter shouted, "Lord, *if it is really You,* command me to walk on the water, too!" You see, Peter wasn't really sure that it was Jesus. He didn't believe Jesus' voice.

"Come on, then!" Jesus replied.

So Peter jumped out of the boat and started to walk on the sea toward Jesus. Then Peter suddenly realized where he was. When he saw the raging waves and felt the gusting wind, he was very frightened. Peter began to sink in the water. Just as the waves nearly closed over his head, Peter called out to Jesus, "Lord, save me!"

The Lord Jesus at once reached out and took hold of Peter's hand. Peter was safe. But Jesus taught Peter a lesson: "Why did you doubt Me, Peter? Your faith is really very small."

Now didn't Peter look foolish jumping out of the boat like that? It should have been enough that Jesus came to them, and they were all safe. But Peter was often in a hurry to do things he wasn't ready to do. Then he would get into trouble. It took Jesus a long time to teach Peter to ask God first about things a young disciple ought to do.

Like Peter, we're sure to fail unless Jesus holds us up. That is the lesson all of us need to learn.

Now memorize Matthew 14:27

# JESUS BRINGS A YOUNG GIRL BACK TO LIFE

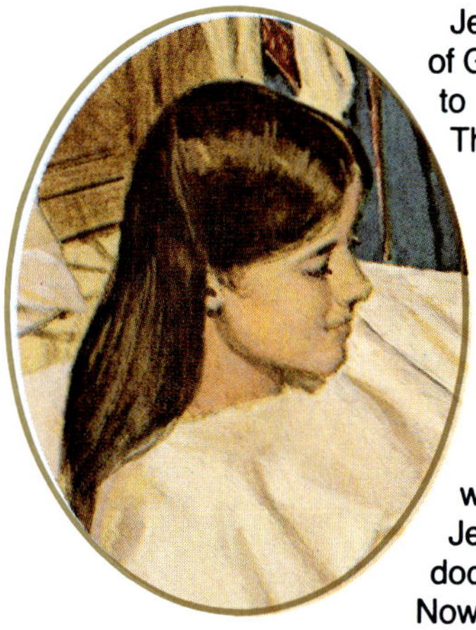

Jesus was teaching and healing people all around the Sea of Galilee. At that time Jesus crossed over the sea and came to His own town. The name of the town was Capernaum. There Jesus was teaching the crowds on the seashore.

While He was teaching, a very important man came and knelt down at Jesus' feet. His name was Jairus, and he was a leader in the synagogue. That was the place where the Jews worshiped God. As Jairus was kneeling, he begged Jesus to come to his house: "My little daughter is dying," he said. "Please come and lay Your hands on her. Then she will live."

So Jesus was following Jairus to his house. Just then, a woman who had been sick for a long time came up behind Jesus. She had been bleeding for twelve long years. Many doctors had treated this lady, but none of them could help her. Now she just reached out and touched Jesus' clothes—and right away she was healed!

As Jesus was talking to the woman, somebody came up and spoke to Jairus, the father of the little girl: "Your daughter has died, Jairus. No need to bother Jesus any longer."

But Jesus said to Jairus, "Don't be afraid. Only believe in the power of God." Then Jairus led Jesus to his home, where the little girl lay dead.

When Jesus went into the house of Jairus, there was a terrible noise of people crying and sobbing and wailing like this: "Oh, our poor little Anna! How could the good daughter of Jairus die so young? Oh, our Anna is dead!" They had cried like this for hours.

This was the way people tried to show how sorry they were when someone died in that country. Strange as it seems, their crying and wailing were really make-believe. In those days people were even paid money to cry and make a lot of noise at funerals. In fact, people do this in some parts of the world even today.

So Jesus was angry with the people who only pretended to be crying. He put them all out of the house. "You crying experts, get out of here!" He said. "Besides, this little girl is not dead. She is only sleeping."

Everybody laughed at Jesus when He said that. But Jesus knew He had total power over death. After all, He was the great Creator of life. For Jesus, death was no more a problem than sleeping.

Then Jesus took the father and mother, and they went into the little dead girl's room. Three of the disciples of Jesus—Peter, James, and John—also went in with Jesus.

Jesus didn't make a big fuss. He only took hold of the little girl's hand. Then He quietly spoke these words, "Little girl, I say to you—wake up!" Well, what do you think happened? Jairus' daughter opened her eyes and got up at once! In fact, she walked around the room and spoke to Jesus and her parents. What a wonderful way to meet Jesus!

If you love Him, some day you, too, will meet Jesus in the same way Jairus' daughter did. Yes, we can lie down and sleep with no fear, because the angels watch over us.

We can also lie down and die in the arms of the Lord Jesus. In the morning we will wake up in His heavenly kingdom. Then we will be with Jesus forever.

Now memorize Mark 5:36

# JESUS CARRIES THE CROSS

Jesus was arrested because He said He was the Son of God. He had taught the people about the kingdom of God, and He had healed a lot of men, women, and children. Some of them had even been brought back from the dead. Jesus truly was the Son of God.

But many of the leaders of the people in that time hated Jesus. Some of the leaders were angry because Jesus taught with more authority than the priests and the Pharisees did. "After all, He is only a carpenter!" they said. "He has no right to teach the people about God. Who does this Jesus think He is, anyway?"

Of course, Jesus was not "only a carpenter," although He had helped in a carpenter's shop when He was growing up. No, Jesus really was God's Son. That is why He was such a great Teacher.

So the leaders arrested Jesus. They sent soldiers to bring Him to trial before the high priest at Jerusalem. Then the high priest asked Jesus, "What are You teaching our people?"

But Jesus knew that the high priest hated Him. So Jesus replied to the high priest, "Ask those who heard Me teaching. They know what I taught." When Jesus said that, one of the soldiers slapped Him on the face.

Later, they brought Jesus to the Roman governor. In those days Rome ruled the whole world. Everybody had to obey the governor from Rome. The governor's name was Pilate. So Pilate asked Jesus, "Are You really the King of the Jews? What have You done wrong?"

Jesus answered him, "My kingdom is not of this world. My kingdom is a heavenly one. I have come into this world to tell people the truth."

Pilate shrugged his shoulders and said, "What is the truth, anyway?" Now Pilate was beginning to doubt what the leaders said against Jesus. So he told the Jewish leaders who arrested Jesus, "I find no fault in Him at all."

Just the same, Pilate thought he should do something to please those evil men who hated Jesus. So Pilate whipped the Son of God. The soldiers also made a cruel crown of thorn branches. Then they pressed the ugly crown over Jesus' head until the blood ran down over His face. After that, they pretended to worship Jesus, saying, "King of the Jews! We salute You!" And they laughed and beat Him with their hands.

Then the priests started demanding that Pilate must put Jesus to death: "Crucify Him, crucify Him!" they shouted.

But Pilate tried to have Jesus released. He even brought Jesus out to the crowd that was gathered there. And Pilate said in a loud voice: "Look, here is your King!" The whole body of Jesus, from head to foot, was drenched in blood. *Surely now they will let this poor Man go,* Pilate thought.

The mob was not satisfied. They only shouted louder than before, "Crucify Him!" So Pilate let the crowd drag Jesus away to be crucified. They laid a heavy wooden cross on Jesus' shoulders. Then they made Him carry it out to where they used to put criminals to death. It was a lonely place outside the walls of Jerusalem. They called it the "Place of a Skull."

There they crucified our Lord Jesus. They nailed His hands and His feet to a rough wooden cross. Jesus hung on the nails of that cross for nine hours. At last He said, "It is finished!" And He bent His bleeding head and died.

What did Jesus mean by those words, "It is finished"? He meant that He had paid the full cost of your sins and mine. He was the Lord Himself from heaven. We all disobey God, which is sin. Therefore, Jesus had to die in our place. Because Jesus died for you, His heavenly Father will forgive your sins—if you truly ask Him.

Now memorize John 19:30

# JESUS RISES FROM THE DEAD

Before He was crucified, Jesus promised, "I will rise again on the third day." But His disciples did not believe Him.

Jesus was put to death on a Friday, and was placed in the tomb of a rich friend. So the third day was Sunday, the first day of the week.

At sunrise on Sunday morning a young woman came to visit the tomb. Her name was Mary Magdalene. Jesus once had driven evil spirits out of her life. "Now I will go and weep for Jesus," she said.

But when Mary got there, the tomb was empty. The heavy stone that covered the doorway of the tomb was gone—and so was Jesus! So Mary ran to tell the disciples Peter and John what she had seen: "They have stolen Jesus away, and I don't know where they have taken Him."

Now Peter and John also ran to the tomb of Jesus, and they found it just as Mary had told them. Jesus' graveclothes were there, but not Jesus. So Peter and John left, wondering where the body of Jesus was.

But Mary was still standing outside the tomb, crying. Then she turned and looked inside the tomb, hoping she might see her dead Lord Jesus. Instead, she saw two angels. One of the angels asked her, "Why are you crying?"

And she answered, "Because they have stolen away my Lord, and I don't know where they have taken Him."

Just then she turned around. Now there was a beautiful garden where the tomb of Jesus was. As she looked, through her tears she saw a strange Man. So she thought He was probably the gardenkeeper. As she wiped the tears from her eyes, the Man in the garden spoke to her: "Why are you crying, young lady?" He asked. "Are you looking for someone?"

"Oh, sir!" sobbed Mary. "Please tell me where You have carried Jesus. Tell me, and I will take Him away from here."

Suddenly, it was very quiet in the garden. Even the birds seemed to stop singing. Then the Man spoke one word to the young woman—"Mary!"

At once she knew who it was. Her heart leaped up, as she cried out, "My Teacher!" Yes, it really was Jesus, and He was alive! Mary fell to her knees. Her Teacher somehow seemed even more alive now than ever before. Mary was holding on to Jesus' feet, sobbing and crying with thankfulness that Jesus was alive.

But Jesus said, "Don't hold Me back, Mary! I must go up to heaven and speak with My Father. Now please go and tell My other friends that I am going up to My Father, who is also your Father. He is My God, and He is also your God."

So Mary went and told the others all that she had seen and heard.

That same evening the disciples of Jesus were gathered together in a locked room, because they were afraid of the enemies of Jesus. Suddenly—Jesus was standing right there with them! Then He spoke quietly to them, "Peace be with you." And He showed them the wounds made by the nails in His hands and feet when He was crucified. There was also a large wound in His side. Jesus really was alive! How very glad the disciples were to see their Friend. Now they believed Him. Jesus was alive and glowing with health.

But one of the disciples, Thomas, was not there when Jesus came. "I won't believe it," Thomas said. "Unless I see the nail-wounds for myself, I will not believe it!" So several days later all the disciples were gathered in the same room. Again the doors were locked. And again, suddenly, Jesus was standing right there with them! So what do you think He said to Thomas? Jesus just quietly told Thomas, "Now you can see and touch My wounds for yourself."

Poor Thomas was so ashamed! He just hung his head, and the tears ran down his cheeks, his voice choking with sobs. Thomas exclaimed, "My Lord and my God!"

So Jesus reminded Thomas of the great privilege he had been given: "You have seen Me, and you believe. There will be many others who cannot see Me, yet they also will believe."

You and I are those "others" who can't see Jesus now. He asks us to believe that He truly did die and rise again from the dead for our sins. When we believe this, Jesus comes to live in us. But one day we, too, will see Him as He really is. Won't it be worth everything in the world to see Jesus?

Now memorize John 20:27

## STORIES OF GOD AND MAN

| | |
|---|---|
| Creation | Genesis 1—3 |
| Abraham and Isaac | Genesis 22:1—18 |
| Jacob and Esau | Genesis 27:1–46 |
| Jericho Falls | Joshua 5:10—6:26 |
| The Day the Sun Stood Still | Joshua 10 |
| Deborah to the Rescue | Judges 4 |
| Gideon's Strange Army | Judges 6, 7 |
| Ruth and Boaz | Ruth |
| The Call of Samuel | 1 Samuel 3 |
| David's Call to Destiny | 1 Samuel 16:1–13 |
| David and Jonathan | 1 Samuel 20 |
| David and Saul | 1 Samuel 23, 24 |
| David and Bathsheba | 2 Samuel 11, 12 |
| David and Absalom | 2 Samuel 15—18 |
| The Queen of Sheba | 1 Kings 10 |
| Elijah's God Outdoes the False Gods | 1 Kings 18 |
| Elisha and the General | 2 Kings 5 |
| Josiah's Great Discovery | 2 Kings 22 |
| Nehemiah's Dream Comes True | Nehemiah |
| Esther's Finest Hour | Esther |
| Job's Problems | Job 1—3 |
| The Fiery Furnace | Daniel 3 |
| Philip and the Ethiopian | Acts 8 |
| Conversion of Saul | Acts 9 |
| The Philippian Jailer | Acts 16 |
| Paul's Shipwreck | Acts 27, 28 |

## STORIES OF JESUS

| | |
|---|---|
| Baptism and Temptation | Matthew 3, 4 |
| Nicodemus in the Night | John 3 |
| Early Miracles in Galilee | Mark 1:14—2:28 |
| Trouble in His Hometown | Luke 4:16–30 |
| Choosing the Twelve Apostles | Mark 3:13–19 |
| Sermon on the Mount | Matthew 5—7 |
| The Lord's Prayer | Matthew 6:9–13 |
| Invitation to Rest | Matthew 11:28–30 |
| Parables of the Kingdom | Matthew 13 |
| The Good Shepherd | John 10 |
| Foretelling His Death | John 3:14–16<br>Matthew 16:21–27; 20:17–19<br>Luke 18:31–34 |
| Judging the Religious Leaders | Matthew 23;<br>Luke 11:39–54 |
| Raising of Lazarus | John 11:1–45 |
| Triumphal Entry | Matthew 21:1–11<br>Mark 11:1–11 |
| Prediction of the Future | Matthew 24, 25 |

## LIFE IN BIBLE TIMES

| | |
|---|---|
| Abraham and Lot | Genesis 13 |
| The Twelve Spies | Numbers 13, 14 |
| Be Kind to Animals | Exodus 23:1–12 |
| Ruth the Gleaner | Ruth 2 |
| David the Musician | 1 Samuel 16:14–23;<br>18:6–8 |
| Living in the Wilderness | 1 Samuel 24 |
| Solomon's Riches | 1 Kings 4:21;<br>5:10, 18 |
| Elijah Predicts a Famine | 1 Kings 17 |
| How a Wall Was Built | Nehemiah 4—6 |
| A Time for Everything | Ecclesiastes 3:1–9 |
| The Potter's Wheel | Jeremiah 18:1–6 |
| Farming with Problems | Joel 1 |
| Parable of the Talents | Matthew 25:14–30 |
| Render to Caesar | Mark 12:13–17 |
| Parable of the Fig Tree | Luke 13:6–9 |
| Riot in Jerusalem | Acts 22:22–29 |
| Paul's Persecutions | 2 Corinthians<br>11:24–27 |

## PSALM 126

A Song of Ascents.

WHEN [a]the LORD brought back [1]the captivity of Zion,
[b]We were like those who dream.
2 Then [a]our mouth was filled with laughter,
And our tongue with singing.
Then they said among the [1]nations,
"The LORD has done great things for them."
3 The LORD has done great things for us,
*And* we are glad.

4 Bring back our captivity, O LORD,
As the streams in the South.

5 [a]Those who sow in tears
Shall reap in joy.
6 He who continually goes [1]forth weeping,
Bearing [2]seed for sowing,
Shall doubtless come again [3]with [a]rejoicing,
Bringing his sheaves *with him.*

## PSALM 127

A Song of Ascents. Of Solomon.

UNLESS the LORD builds the house,
They labor in vain who build it;
Unless [a]the LORD guards the city,
The watchman stays awake in vain.
2 *It is* vain for you to rise up early,
To sit up late,
To [a]eat the bread of sorrows;
*For* so He gives His beloved sleep.

3 Behold, [a]children *are* a heritage from the LORD,
[b]The fruit of the womb *is* a [c]reward.
4 Like arrows in the hand of a warrior,
So *are* the children of one's youth.
5 [a]Happy *is* the man who has his quiver full of them;
[b]They shall not be ashamed,
But shall speak with their enemies in the gate.

## PSALM 128

A Song of Ascents.

BLESSED [a]*is* every one who fears the LORD,
Who walks in His ways.

2 [a]When you eat the [1]labor of your hands,
You *shall be* happy,
and *it shall be* [b]well with you.
3 Your wife *shall be* [a]like a fruitful vine
In the very heart of your house,
Your [b]children [c]like olive plants
All around your table.
4 Behold, thus shall the man be blessed
Who fears the LORD.

5 [a]The LORD bless you out of Zion,
And may you see the good of Jerusalem
All the days of your life.
6 Yes, may you [a]see your children's children.

[b]Peace *be* upon Israel!

## PSALM 129

A Song of Ascents.

"MANY a time they have [a]afflicted[1] me from [b]my youth,"
[c]Let Israel now say—
2 "Many a time they have afflicted me from my youth;
Yet they have not prevailed against me.
3 The plowers plowed on my back;
They made their furrows long."
4 The LORD *is* righteous;
He has cut in pieces the cords of the wicked.

5 Let all those who hate Zion
Be put to shame and turned back.
6 Let them be as the [a]grass *on* the housetops,
Which withers before it grows up,
7 With which the reaper does not fill his hand,
Nor he who binds sheaves, his [1]arms.
8 Neither let those who pass by them say,
[a]"The blessing of the LORD *be* upon you;
We bless you in the name of the LORD!"

## PSALM 130

A Song of Ascents.

OUT [a]of the depths I have cried to You, O LORD;
2 Lord, hear my voice!
Let Your ears be attentive
To the voice of my supplications.

3 [a]If You, LORD, should [1]mark iniquities,
O Lord, who could [b]stand?
4 But *there is* [a]forgiveness with You,
That [b]You may be feared.

5 [a]I wait for the LORD, my soul waits,
And [b]in His word I do hope.
6 [a]My soul *waits* for the Lord
More than those who watch for the morning—
*Yes, more than* those who watch for the morning.

7 [a]O Israel, hope in the LORD;
For [b]with the LORD *there is* mercy,
And with Him *is* abundant redemption.
8 And [a]He shall redeem Israel
From all his iniquities.

## PSALM 131

A Song of Ascents. Of David.

LORD, my heart is not [1]haughty,
Nor my eyes [2]lofty.
[a]Neither do I [3]concern myself with great matters,
Nor with things too [4]profound for me.

2 Surely I have calmed and quieted my soul,
[a]Like a weaned child with his mother;
Like a weaned child *is* my soul within me.

3 [a]O Israel, hope in the LORD
From this time forth and forever.

## PSALM 132

A Song of Ascents.

LORD, remember David
*And* all his afflictions;
2 How he swore to the LORD,
[a]*And* vowed to [b]the Mighty One of Jacob:
3 "Surely I will not go into the chamber of my house,
Or go up to the comfort of my bed;
4 I will [a]not give sleep to my eyes
*Or* slumber to my eyelids,
5 Until I [a]find a place for the LORD,

PSALM 126
1 [a]Hos. 6:11 [b]Acts 12:9 [1]Those of the captivity
2 [a]Job 8:21 [1]*Gentiles*
5 [a]Jer. 31:9
6 [a]Is. 61:3 [1]*to and fro* [2]Lit. *a bag of seed for sowing* [3]*with shouts of joy*

PSALM 127
1 [a][Ps. 121:3–5]
2 [a][Gen. 3:17, 19]
3 [a][Josh. 24:3, 4] [b]Deut. 7:13; 28:4 [c][Ps. 113:9]
5 [a]Ps. 128:2, 3 [b]Prov. 27:11

PSALM 128
1 [a]Ps. 119:1
2 [a]Is. 3:10 [b]Deut. 4:40 [1]Fruit of the labor
3 [a]Ezek. 19:10 [b]Ps. 127:3–5 [c]Ps. 52:8; 144:12
5 [a]Ps. 134:3
6 [a]Job 42:16 [b]Ps. 125:5

PSALM 129
1 [a][Jer. 1:19; 15:20] [b]Ezek. 23:3; [c]Ps. 124:1 [1]*persecuted*
6 [a]Ps. 37:2
7 [1]*arms full,* lit. *bosom*
8 [a]Ruth 2:4

PSALM 130
1 [a]Lam. 3:55
3 [a][Ps. 143:2] [b][Nah. 1:6] [1]*take note of*
4 [a][Ex. 34:7] [b][1 Kin. 8:39, 40]
5 [a][Ps. 27:14] [b]Ps. 119:81
6 [a]Ps. 119:147
7 [a]Ps. 131:3 [b][Is. 55:7]
8 [a][Ps. 103:3, 4]

PSALM 131
1 [a][Rom. 12:16] [1]Proud [2]Arrogant [3]Lit. *walk in* [4]*difficult*
2 [a][Matt. 18:3]
3 [a][Ps. 130:7]

PSALM 132
2 [a]Ps. 65:1 [b]Gen. 49:24
4 [a]Prov. 6:4
5 [a]Acts 7:46

A dwelling place for the Mighty One of
Jacob."

6 Behold, we heard of it [a]in Ephrathah;
[b]We found it [c]in the fields of [1]the woods.
7 Let us go into His tabernacle;
[a]Let us worship at His footstool.
8 [a]Arise, O LORD, to Your resting place,
You and [b]the ark of Your strength.
9 Let Your priests [a]be clothed with
righteousness,
And let Your saints shout for joy.

10 For Your servant David's sake,
Do not turn away the face of Your
[1]Anointed.

11 [a]The LORD has sworn *in* truth to David;
He will not turn from it:
"I will set upon your throne [b]the [1]fruit of your
body.
12 If your sons will keep My covenant
And My testimony which I shall teach them,
Their sons also shall sit upon your throne
forevermore."

13 [a]For the LORD has chosen Zion;
He has desired *it* for His [1]dwelling place:
14 "This[a] *is* My resting place forever;
Here I will dwell, for I have desired it.
15 [a]I will abundantly bless her [1]provision;
I will satisfy her poor with bread.
16 [a]I will also clothe her priests with salvation,
[b]And her saints shall shout aloud for joy.
17 [a]There I will make the [1]horn of David grow;
[b]I will prepare a lamp for My [2]Anointed.
18 His enemies I will [a]clothe with shame,
But upon Himself His crown shall flourish."

## PSALM 133

A Song of Ascents. Of David.

BEHOLD, how good and how pleasant *it is*
For [a]brethren to dwell together in unity!

2 *It is* like the precious oil upon the head,
Running down on the beard,
The beard of Aaron,
Running down on the edge of his garments.
3 *It is* like the dew of [a]Hermon,
Descending upon the mountains of Zion;
For [b]there the LORD commanded the
blessing—
Life forevermore.

## PSALM 134

A Song of Ascents.

BEHOLD, bless the LORD,
All *you* servants of the LORD,
Who by night stand in the house of the
LORD!
2 [a]Lift up your hands *in* the sanctuary,
And bless the LORD.

3 The LORD who made heaven and earth
Bless you from Zion!

## PSALM 135

PRAISE the LORD!

Praise the name of the LORD;
[a]Praise *Him*, O you servants of the LORD!
2 [a]You who stand in the house of the LORD,
In [b]the courts of the house of our God,
3 Praise the LORD, for [a]the LORD *is* good;
Sing praises to His name, [b]for *it is* pleasant.

6 [a]1 Sam. 17:12 [b]1 Sam. 7:1 [c]1 Chr. 13:5 [1]Or *Jaar*, lit. *Woods*
7 [a]Ps. 5:7; 99:5
8 [a]Num. 10:35 [b]Ps. 78:61
9 [a]Job 29:14
10 [1]Commissioned One, Heb. *Messiah*
11 [a][Ps. 89:3, 4, 33; 110:4] [b]2 Sam. 7:12 [1]*offspring*
13 [a][Ps. 48:1, 2] [1]*home*
14 [a]Ps. 68:16
15 [a]Ps. 147:14 [1]*supply of food*
16 [a]2 Chr. 6:41 [b]1 Sam. 4:5
17 [a]Ezek. 29:21 [b]1 Kin. 11:36; 15:4 [1]Government [2]Heb. *Messiah*
18 [a]Ps. 35:26

PSALM 133
1 [a]Gen. 13:8
3 [a]Deut. 4:48 [b]Lev. 25:21

PSALM 134
2 [a][1 Tim. 2:8]

PSALM 135
1 [a]Ps. 113:1
2 [a]Luke 2:37 [b]Ps. 116:19
3 [a][Ps. 119:68] [b]Ps. 147:1
4 [a][Ex. 19:5] [1]*precious possession*
5 [a]Ps. 95:3; 97:9
6 [a]Ps. 115:3
7 [a]Jer. 10:13 [b]Job 28:25, 26; 38:24–28 [c]Jer. 51:16 [1]Water vapor
8 [a]Ex. 12:12 [1]Lit. *struck down* [2]Lit. *From man to beast*
9 [a]Ex. 7:10 [b]Ps. 136:15
10 [a]Num. 21:24
11 [a]Josh. 12:7–24
12 [a]Ps. 78:55; 136:21, 22 [1]*inheritance*
13 [a][Ex. 3:15]
14 [a]Deut. 32:36
15 [a][Ps. 115:4–8]
19 [a][Ps. 115:9]
21 [a]Ps. 134:3

PSALM 136
1 [a]Ps. 106:1 [b]1 Chr. 16:34
2 [a][Deut. 10:17]
4 [a]Ps. 72:18
5 [a]Jer. 51:15
6 [a]Jer. 10:12
7 [a]Gen. 1:14–18
8 [a]Gen. 1:16

4 For [a]the LORD has chosen Jacob for Himself,
Israel for His [1]special treasure.

5 For I know that [a]the LORD *is* great,
And our Lord *is* above all gods.
6 [a]Whatever the LORD pleases He does,
In heaven and in earth,
In the seas and in all deep places.
7 [a]He causes the [1]vapors to ascend from the
ends of the earth;
[b]He makes lightning for the rain;
He brings the wind out of His [c]treasuries.

8 [a]He [1]destroyed the firstborn of Egypt,
[2]Both of man and beast.
9 [a]He sent signs and wonders into the midst of
you, O Egypt,
[b]Upon Pharaoh and all his servants.
10 [a]He defeated many nations
And slew mighty kings—
11 Sihon king of the Amorites,
Og king of Bashan,
And [a]all the kingdoms of Canaan—
12 [a]And gave their land *as* a [1]heritage,
A heritage to Israel His people.

13 [a]Your name, O LORD, *endures* forever,
Your fame, O LORD, throughout all
generations.
14 [a]For the LORD will judge His people,
And He will have compassion on His
servants.

15 [a]The idols of the nations *are* silver and gold,
The work of men's hands.
16 They have mouths, but they do not speak;
Eyes they have, but they do not see;
17 They have ears, but they do not hear;
Nor is there *any* breath in their mouths.
18 Those who make them are like them;
*So is* everyone who trusts in them.

19 [a]Bless the LORD, O house of Israel!
Bless the LORD, O house of Aaron!
20 Bless the LORD, O house of Levi!
You who fear the LORD, bless the LORD!
21 Blessed be the LORD [a]out of Zion,
Who dwells in Jerusalem!

Praise the LORD!

## PSALM 136

OH, [a]give thanks to the LORD, for *He is* good!
[b]For His mercy *endures* forever.
2 Oh, give thanks to [a]the God of gods!
For His mercy *endures* forever.
3 Oh, give thanks to the Lord of lords!
For His mercy *endures* forever:

4 To Him [a]who alone does great wonders,
For His mercy *endures* forever;
5 [a]To Him who by wisdom made the heavens,
For His mercy *endures* forever;
6 [a]To Him who laid out the earth above the
waters,
For His mercy *endures* forever;
7 [a]To Him who made great lights,
For His mercy *endures* forever—
8 [a]The sun to rule by day,
For His mercy *endures* forever;
9 The moon and stars to rule by night,
For His mercy *endures* forever.

10 [a]To Him who struck Egypt in their firstborn,
For His mercy *endures* forever;
11 [a]And brought out Israel from among them,
For His mercy *endures* forever;
12 [a]With a strong hand,
and with [1]an outstretched arm,
For His mercy *endures* forever;
13 [a]To Him who divided the Red Sea in two,
For His mercy *endures* forever;
14 And made Israel pass through the midst of it,
For His mercy *endures* forever;
15 [a]But overthrew Pharaoh and his army in the Red Sea,
For His mercy *endures* forever;
16 [a]To Him who led His people through the wilderness,
For His mercy *endures* forever;
17 [a]To Him who struck down great kings,
For His mercy *endures* forever;
18 [a]And slew famous kings,
For His mercy *endures* forever—
19 [a]Sihon king of the Amorites,
For His mercy *endures* forever;
20 [a]And Og king of Bashan,
For His mercy *endures* forever—
21 [a]And gave their land as a [1]heritage,
For His mercy *endures* forever;
22 A heritage to Israel His servant,
For His mercy *endures* forever.

23 Who [a]remembered us in our lowly state,
For His mercy *endures* forever;
24 And [a]rescued us from our enemies,
For His mercy *endures* forever;
25 [a]Who gives food to all flesh,
For His mercy *endures* forever.

26 Oh, give thanks to the God of heaven!
For His mercy *endures* forever.

## PSALM 137

BY the rivers of Babylon,
There we sat down, yea, we wept
When we remembered Zion.
2 We hung our harps
Upon the willows in the midst of it.
3 For there those who carried us away captive asked of us a song,
And those who [a]plundered us *requested* mirth,
*Saying,* "Sing us *one* of the songs of Zion!"

4 How shall we sing the LORD's song
In a foreign land?
5 If I forget you, O Jerusalem,
Let my right hand forget *its skill!*
6 If I do not remember you,
Let my [a]tongue cling to the roof of my mouth—
If I do not exalt Jerusalem
Above my chief joy.

7 Remember, O LORD, against [a]the sons of Edom
The day of Jerusalem,
Who said, [1]"Raze *it,* raze *it,*
To its very foundation!"

8 O daughter of Babylon,
[a]who are to be destroyed,
Happy the one [b]who repays you as you have served us!
9 Happy the one who takes and [a]dashes
Your little ones against the rock!

10 [a]Ex. 12:29
11 [a]Ex. 12:51; 13:3, 16
12 [a]Ex. 6:6 [1]Mighty power
13 [a]Ex. 14:21
15 [a]Ex. 14:27
16 [a]Ex. 13:18; 15:22
17 [a]Ps. 135:10–12
18 [a]Deut. 29:7
19 [a]Num. 21:21
20 [a]Num. 21:33
21 [a]Josh. 12:1 [1]*inheritance*
23 [a]Gen. 8:1
24 [a]Ps. 44:7
25 [a]Ps. 104:27; 145:15

PSALM 137
3 [a]Ps. 79:1
6 [a]Ezek. 3:26
7 [a]Jer. 49:7–22 [1]Lit. *Make it bare*
8 [a]Is. 13:1–6; 47:1 [b]Jer. 50:15
9 [a]Is. 13:16

PSALM 138
1 [a]Ps. 119:46
2 [a]Ps. 28:2 [b]1 Kin. 8:29 [c]Is. 42:21
4 [a]Ps. 102:15
6 [a][Ps. 113:4–7] [b][James 4:6]
7 [a][Ps. 23:3, 4]
8 [a]Ps. 57:2 [b]Job 10:3, 8 [1]*complete*

PSALM 139
1 [a]Ps. 17:3
2 [a]2 Kin. 19:27 [b]Matt. 9:4
3 [a]Job 14:16; 31:4 [1]Lit. *winnow*
4 [a][Heb. 4:13]
5 [1]*enclosed*
6 [a]Job 42:3
7 [a][Jer. 23:24]
8 [a][Amos 9:2–4] [b][Job 26:6] [1]Or *Sheol*
11 [1]Vg., Symmachus *cover*
12 [a]Job 26:6; 34:22 [1]Lit. *is not dark*
13 [1]*wove*
14 [1]So with MT, Tg.; LXX, Syr., Vg. *You are fearfully wonderful*

## PSALM 138

*A Psalm* of David.

I WILL praise You with my whole heart;
[a]Before the gods I will sing praises to You.
2 [a]I will worship [b]toward Your holy temple,
And praise Your name
For Your lovingkindness and Your truth;
For You have [c]magnified Your word above all Your name.
3 In the day when I cried out,
You answered me,
*And* made me bold *with* strength in my soul.

4 [a]All the kings of the earth shall praise You, O LORD,
When they hear the words of Your mouth.
5 Yes, they shall sing of the ways of the LORD,
For great *is* the glory of the LORD.
6 [a]Though the LORD *is* on high,
Yet [b]He regards the lowly;
But the proud He knows from afar.

7 [a]Though I walk in the midst of trouble, You will revive me;
You will stretch out Your hand
Against the wrath of my enemies,
And Your right hand will save me.
8 [a]The LORD will [1]perfect *that which* concerns me;
Your mercy, O LORD, *endures* forever;
[b]Do not forsake the works of Your hands.

## PSALM 139

For the Chief Musician. A Psalm of David.

O LORD, [a]You have searched me
and known *me.*
2 [a]You know my sitting down and my rising up;
You [b]understand my thought afar off.
3 [a]You [1]comprehend my path
and my lying down,
And are acquainted with all my ways.
4 For *there is* not a word on my tongue,
*But* behold, O LORD, [a]You know it altogether.
5 You have [1]hedged me behind and before,
And laid Your hand upon me.
6 [a]*Such* knowledge *is* too wonderful for me;
It is high, I cannot *attain* it.

7 [a]Where can I go from Your Spirit?
Or where can I flee from Your presence?
8 [a]If I ascend into heaven, You *are* there;
[b]If I make my bed in [1]hell, behold,
You *are there.*
9 *If* I take the wings of the morning,
*And* dwell in the uttermost parts of the sea,
10 Even there Your hand shall lead me,
And Your right hand shall hold me.
11 If I say, "Surely the darkness shall [1]fall on me,"
Even the night shall be light about me;
12 Indeed, [a]the darkness [1]shall not hide from You,
But the night shines as the day;
The darkness and the light *are* both alike *to* You.

13 For You formed my inward parts;
You [1]covered me in my mother's womb.
14 I will praise You, for [1]I am fearfully *and* wonderfully made;

Marvelous are Your works,
And *that* my soul knows very well.
15 [a]My [1]frame was not hidden from You,
When I was made in secret,
*And* skillfully wrought in the lowest parts of the earth.
16 Your eyes saw my substance, being yet unformed.
And in Your book they all were written,
The days fashioned for me,
When *as yet there were* none of them.

17 [a]How precious also are Your thoughts to me, O God!
How great is the sum of them!
18 *If* I should count them, they would be more in number than the sand;
When I awake, I am still with You.

19 Oh, that You would [a]slay the wicked, O God!
[b]Depart from me, therefore, you [1]bloodthirsty men.
20 For they [a]speak against You wickedly;
[1]Your enemies take *Your name* in vain.
21 [a]Do I not hate them, O LORD, who hate You?
And do I not loathe those who rise up against You?
22 I hate them with [1]perfect hatred;
I count them my enemies.

23 [a]Search me, O God, and know my heart;
Try me, and know my anxieties;
24 And see if *there is any* wicked way in me,
And [a]lead me in the way everlasting.

## PSALM 140

To the Chief Musician. A Psalm of David.

DELIVER me, O LORD, from evil men;
Preserve me from violent men,
2 Who plan evil things in *their* hearts;
[a]They continually gather together *for* war.
3 They sharpen their tongues like a serpent;
The [a]poison of asps *is* under their lips. Selah

4 [a]Keep me, O LORD, from the hands of the wicked;
Preserve me from violent men,
Who have purposed to make my steps stumble.
5 The proud have hidden a [a]snare for me, and cords;
They have spread a net by the wayside;
They have set traps for me. Selah

6 I said to the LORD: "You *are* my God;
Hear the voice of my supplications, O LORD.
7 O GOD the Lord, the strength of my salvation,
You have [1]covered my head in the day of battle.
8 Do not grant, O LORD, the desires of the wicked;
Do not further his *wicked* scheme,
[a]*Lest* they be exalted. Selah

9 "*As for* the head of those who surround me,
Let the evil of their lips cover them;
10 [a]Let burning coals fall upon them;
Let them be cast into the fire,
Into deep pits, that they rise not up again.
11 Let not a slanderer be established in the earth;
Let evil hunt the violent man to overthrow *him*."

12 I know that the LORD will [a]maintain
The cause of the afflicted,
*And* justice for the poor.
13 Surely the righteous shall give thanks to Your name;
The upright shall dwell in Your presence.

## PSALM 141

A Psalm of David.

LORD, I cry out to You;
Make haste to me!
Give ear to my voice when I cry out to You.
2 Let my prayer be set before You [a]*as* incense,
[b]The lifting up of my hands *as* [c]the evening sacrifice.

3 Set a guard, O LORD, over my [a]mouth;
Keep watch over the door of my lips.
4 Do not incline my heart to any evil thing,
To practice wicked works
With men who work iniquity;
[a]And do not let me eat of their delicacies.

5 [a]Let the righteous strike me;
*It shall be* a kindness.
And let him rebuke me;
*It shall be* as excellent oil;
Let my head not refuse it.

For still my prayer *is* against the deeds of the wicked.
6 Their judges are overthrown by the sides of the [1]cliff,
And they hear my words, for they are sweet.
7 Our bones are scattered at the mouth of the grave,
As when one plows and breaks up the earth.

8 But [a]my eyes *are* upon You, O GOD the Lord;
In You I take refuge;
[1]Do not leave my soul destitute.
9 Keep me from [a]the snares they have laid for me,
And from the traps of the workers of iniquity.
10 [a]Let the wicked fall into their own nets,
While I escape safely.

## PSALM 142

A [a]Contemplation[1] of David. A Prayer [b]when he was in the cave.

I CRY out to the LORD with my voice;
With my voice to the LORD I make my supplication.
2 I pour out my complaint before Him;
I declare before Him my trouble.

3 When my spirit [1]was [a]overwhelmed within me,
Then You knew my path.
In the way in which I walk
They have secretly [b]set a snare for me.
4 Look on *my* right hand and see,
For *there is* no one who acknowledges me;
Refuge has failed me;
No one cares for my soul.

5 I cried out to You, O LORD:
I said, "You *are* my refuge,
My portion in the land of the living.
6 [1]Attend to my cry,

15 [a]Job 10:8, 9; Eccl. 11:5 [1]Lit. *bones were*
17 [a][Ps. 40:5; Rom. 11:33]
19 [a][Is. 11:4] [b]Ps. 119:115 [1]Lit. *men of bloodshed*
20 [a]Jude 15 [1]LXX, Vg. *they take your cities in vain*
21 [a]2 Chr. 19:2
22 [1]*complete*
23 [a]Job 31:6; Ps. 26:2
24 [a]Ps. 5:8; 143:10

PSALM 140
2 [a]Ps. 56:6
3 [a]Ps. 58:4; Rom. 3:13; James 3:8
4 [a]Ps. 71:4
5 [a]Ps. 35:7; Jer. 18:22
7 [1]*sheltered*
8 [a]Deut. 32:27
10 [a]Ps. 11:6
12 [a]1 Kin. 8:45; Ps. 9:4

PSALM 141
2 [a][Ex. 30:8]; Luke 1:10; [Rev. 5:8; 8:3, 4] [b]Ps. 134:2; [1 Tim. 2:8] [c]Ex. 29:39, 41; 1 Kin. 18:29, 36; Dan. 9:21
3 [a][Prov. 13:3; 21:23]
4 [a]Prov. 23:6
5 [a][Prov. 9:8; Eccl. 7:5; Gal. 6:1]
6 [1]*rock*
8 [a]2 Chr. 20:12; Ps. 25:15 [1]Lit. *Do not make my soul bare*
9 [a]Ps. 119:110
10 [a]Ps. 35:8

PSALM 142
title [a]Ps. 32:title [b]1 Sam. 22:1; Ps. 57:title [1]Heb. *Maschil*
3 [a]Ps. 77:3 [b]Ps. 141:9 [1]Lit. *fainted*
6 [1]*Give heed*

For I am brought very low;
Deliver me from my persecutors,
For they are stronger than I.
7 Bring my soul out of prison,
That I may [a]praise Your name;
The righteous shall surround me,
For You shall deal bountifully with me."

## PSALM 143

A Psalm of David.

HEAR my prayer, O LORD,
Give ear to my supplications!
In Your faithfulness answer me,
*And* in Your righteousness.
2 Do not enter into judgment with Your servant,
[a]For in Your sight no one living is righteous.

3 For the enemy has persecuted my soul;
He has crushed my life to the ground;
He has made me dwell in [1]darkness,
Like those who have long been dead.
4 [a]Therefore my spirit is overwhelmed within me;
My heart within me is distressed.

5 [a]I remember the days of old;
I meditate on all Your works;
I [1]muse on the work of Your hands.
6 I spread out my hands to You;
[a]My soul *longs* for You like a thirsty land. Selah

7 Answer me speedily, O LORD;
My spirit fails!
Do not hide Your face from me,
[a]Lest I [1]be like those who [2]go down into the pit.
8 Cause me to hear Your lovingkindness [a]in the morning,
For in You do I trust;
[b]Cause me to know the way in which I should walk,
For [c]I lift up my soul to You.

9 Deliver me, O LORD, from my enemies;
[1]In You I take shelter.
10 [a]Teach me to do Your will,
For You *are* my God;
[b]Your Spirit *is* good.
Lead me in [c]the land of uprightness.

11 [a]Revive me, O LORD, for Your name's sake!
For Your righteousness' sake bring my soul out of trouble.
12 In Your mercy [a]cut[1] off my enemies,
And destroy all those who afflict my soul;
For I *am* Your servant.

## PSALM 144

A Psalm of David.

BLESSED *be* the LORD my Rock,
[a]Who trains my hands for war,
*And* my fingers for battle—
2 My lovingkindness and my fortress,
My high tower and my deliverer,
My shield and *the One* in whom I take refuge,
Who subdues [1]my people under me.

3 [a]LORD, what *is* man,
that You take knowledge of him?
*Or* the son of man,
that You are mindful of him?
4 [a]Man is like a breath;
[b]His days *are* like a passing shadow.

5 [a]Bow down Your heavens, O LORD,
and come down;
[b]Touch the mountains, and they shall smoke.
6 [a]Flash forth lightning and scatter them;
Shoot out Your arrows and destroy them.
7 Stretch out Your hand from above;
Rescue me and deliver me out of great waters,
From the hand of foreigners,
8 Whose mouth [a]speaks [1]lying words,
And whose right hand *is* a right hand of falsehood.

9 I will [a]sing a new song to You, O God;
On a harp of ten strings I will sing praises to You,
10 *The One* who gives [1]salvation to kings,
[a]Who delivers David His servant
From the deadly sword.

11 Rescue me and deliver me from the hand of foreigners,
Whose mouth speaks lying words,
And whose right hand *is* a right hand of falsehood—
12 That our sons *may be* [a]as plants grown up in their youth;
*That* our daughters *may be* as [1]pillars,
Sculptured in palace style;
13 *That* our barns *may be* full,
Supplying all kinds of produce;
*That* our sheep may bring forth thousands
And ten thousands in our fields;
14 *That* our oxen *may be* well-laden;
*That there be* no [1]breaking in or going out;
*That there be* no outcry in our streets.
15 [a]Happy *are* the people
who are in such a state;
Happy *are* the people
whose God *is* the LORD!

## PSALM 145

[a]A Praise of David.

I WILL [1]extol You, my God, O King;
And I will bless Your name forever and ever.
2 Every day I will bless You,
And I will praise Your name
forever and ever.
3 [a]Great *is* the LORD, and greatly to be praised;
And [b]His greatness *is* [1]unsearchable.

4 [a]One generation shall praise Your works to another,
And shall declare Your mighty acts.
5 [1]I will meditate on the glorious splendor of Your majesty,
And [2]on Your wondrous works.
6 *Men* shall speak of the might of Your awesome acts,
And I will declare Your greatness.
7 They shall [1]utter the memory of Your great goodness,
And shall sing of Your righteousness.

8 [a]The LORD *is* gracious and full of compassion,
Slow to anger and great in mercy.
9 [a]The LORD *is* good to all,

**7** [a]Ps. 34:1, 2

PSALM 143
**2** [a][Ex. 34:7]; Job 4:17; 9:2; 25:4; Ps. 130:3; Eccl. 7:20; [Rom. 3:20–23; Gal. 2:16]
**3** [1]*dark places*
**4** [a]Ps. 77:3
**5** [a]Ps. 77:5, 10, 11 [1]*ponder*
**6** [a]Ps. 63:1
**7** [a]Ps. 28:1 [1]*become* [2]Die
**8** [a]Ps. 46:5 [b]Ps. 5:8 [c]Ps. 25:1
**9** [1]LXX, Vg. *To You I flee*
**10** [a]Ps. 25:4, 5 [b]Neh. 9:20 [c]Is. 26:10
**11** [a]Ps. 119:25
**12** [a]Ps. 54:5 [1]*put an end to*

PSALM 144
**1** [a]2 Sam. 22:35; Ps. 18:34
**2** [1]So with MT, LXX, Vg.; Syr., Tg. *the peoples* (cf. 18:47)
**3** [a]Job 7:17; Ps. 8:4; Heb. 2:6
**4** [a]Ps. 39:11 [b]Job 8:9; 14:2; Ps. 102:11
**5** [a]Ps. 18:9; Is. 64:1 [b]Ps. 104:32
**6** [a]Ps. 18:13, 14
**8** [a]Ps. 12:2 [1]*empty* or *worthless*
**9** [a]Ps. 33:2, 3; 40:3
**10** [a]Ps. 18:50 [1]*deliverance*
**12** [a]Ps. 128:3 [1]*corner pillars*
**14** [1]Lit. *breach*
**15** [a]Deut. 33:29; [Ps. 33:12; Jer. 17:7]

PSALM 145
**title** [a]Ps. 100:title
**1** [1]*praise*
**3** [a][Ps. 147:5] [b]Job 5:9; 9:10; 11:7; Is. 40:28; [Rom. 11:33] [1]Beyond our understanding
**4** [a]Is. 38:19
**5** [1]So with MT, Tg.; DSS, LXX, Syr., Vg. *they* [2]Lit. *on the words of Your wondrous works*
**7** [1]*eagerly utter,* lit. *bubble forth*
**8** [a][Ex. 34:6, 7; Num. 14:18]; Ps. 86:5, 15
**9** [a][Ps. 100:5]; Jer. 33:11; Nah. 1:7; [Matt. 19:17; Mark 10:18]

And His tender mercies *are* over all His
works.

10 [a]All Your works shall praise You, O LORD,
And Your saints shall bless You.
11 They shall speak of the glory of Your
kingdom,
And talk of Your power,
12 To make known to the sons of men His
mighty acts,
And the glorious majesty of His kingdom.
13 [a]Your kingdom *is* an everlasting kingdom,
And Your dominion *endures* throughout all
[1]generations.

14 The LORD upholds all who fall,
And [a]raises up all *who are* bowed down.
15 [a]The eyes of all look expectantly to You,
And [b]You give them their food in due season.
16 You open Your hand
[a]And satisfy the desire of every living thing.

17 The LORD *is* righteous in all His ways,
Gracious in all His works.
18 [a]The LORD *is* near to all who call upon Him,
To all who call upon Him [b]in truth.
19 He will fulfill the desire of those who fear
Him;
He also will hear their cry and save them.
20 [a]The LORD preserves all who love Him,
But all the wicked He will destroy.
21 My mouth shall speak the praise of the LORD,
And all flesh shall bless His holy name
Forever and ever.

## PSALM 146

PRAISE[1] the LORD!
Praise the LORD, O my soul!
2 [a]While I live I will praise the LORD;
I will sing praises to my God while I have
my being.

3 [a]Do not put your trust in princes,
*Nor* in [1]a son of man,
in whom *there is* no [2]help.
4 [a]His spirit departs, he returns to his earth;
In that very day [b]his plans perish.

5 [a]Happy *is he* who *has* the God of Jacob for
his help,
Whose hope *is* in the LORD his God,
6 [a]Who made heaven and earth,
The sea, and all that *is* in them;
Who keeps truth forever,
7 [a]Who executes justice for the oppressed,
[b]Who gives food to the hungry.
[c]The LORD gives freedom to the prisoners.

8 [a]The LORD opens *the eyes of* the blind;
[b]The LORD raises those who are bowed down;
The LORD loves the righteous.
9 [a]The LORD watches over the strangers;
He relieves the fatherless and widow;
[b]But the way of the wicked He [1]turns upside
down.

10 [a]The LORD shall reign forever—
Your God, O Zion, to all generations.

Praise the LORD!

## PSALM 147

PRAISE[1] the LORD!
For [a]*it is* good to sing praises to our God;
[b]For *it is* pleasant, *and* [c]praise is beautiful.

2 The LORD [a]builds up Jerusalem;
[b]He gathers together the outcasts of Israel.
3 [a]He heals the brokenhearted
And binds up their [1]wounds.
4 [a]He counts the number of the stars;
He calls them all by name.
5 [a]Great *is* our Lord, and [b]mighty in power;
[c]His understanding *is* infinite.
6 [a]The LORD lifts up the humble;
He casts the wicked down to the ground.

7 Sing to the LORD with thanksgiving;
Sing praises on the harp to our God,
8 [a]Who covers the heavens with clouds,
Who prepares rain for the earth,
Who makes grass to grow on the mountains.
9 [a]He gives to the beast its food,
*And* [b]to the young ravens that cry.

10 [a]He does not delight
in the strength of the horse;
He takes no pleasure in the legs of a man.
11 The LORD takes pleasure
in those who fear Him,
In those who hope in His mercy.

12 Praise the LORD, O Jerusalem!
Praise your God, O Zion!
13 For He has strengthened the bars of your
gates;
He has blessed your children within you.
14 [a]He makes peace *in* your borders,
*And* [b]fills you with [1]the finest wheat.

15 [a]He sends out His command *to the* earth;
His word runs very swiftly.
16 [a]He gives snow like wool;
He scatters the frost like ashes;
17 He casts out His hail like [1]morsels;
Who can stand before His cold?
18 [a]He sends out His word and melts them;
He causes His wind to blow,
*and* the waters flow.

19 [a]He declares His word to Jacob,
[b]His statutes and His judgments to Israel.
20 [a]He has not dealt thus with any nation;
And *as for His* judgments,
they have not known them.

[1]Praise the LORD!

## PSALM 148

PRAISE[1] the LORD!
Praise the LORD from the heavens;
Praise Him in the heights!
2 Praise Him, all His angels;
Praise Him, all His hosts!
3 Praise Him, sun and moon;
Praise Him, all you stars of light!
4 Praise Him, [a]you heavens of heavens,
And [b]you waters above the heavens!

5 Let them praise the name of the LORD,
For [a]He commanded and they were created.
6 [a]He also established them forever and ever;
He made a decree which shall not pass away.

7 Praise the LORD from the earth,
[a]You great sea creatures and all the depths;
8 Fire and hail, snow and clouds;
Stormy wind, fulfilling His word;
9 [a]Mountains and all hills;
Fruitful trees and all cedars;

**10** [a]Ps. 19:1
**13** [a][1 Tim. 1:17] [1]So with MT, Tg.; DSS, LXX, Syr., Vg. add *The LORD is faithful in all His words, and holy in all His works*
**14** [a]Ps. 146:8
**15** [a]Ps. 104:27 [b]Ps. 136:25
**16** [a]Ps. 104:21, 28
**18** [a][Deut. 4:7] [b][John 4:24]
**20** [a][Ps. 31:23]

PSALM 146
**1** [a]Ps. 103:1 [1]Heb. *Hallelujah*
**2** [a]Ps. 104:33
**3** [a][Is. 2:22] [1]A human being [2]*salvation*
**4** [a][Eccl. 12:7] [b][1 Cor. 2:6]
**5** [a]Jer. 17:7
**6** [a]Rev. 14:7
**7** [a]Ps. 103:6 [b]Ps. 107:9 [c]Ps. 107:10
**8** [a]Matt. 9:30 [b]Luke 13:13
**9** [a]Deut. 10:18 [b]Ps. 147:6 [1]Lit. *makes crooked*
**10** [a]Ex. 15:18

PSALM 147
**1** [a]Ps. 92:1 [b]Ps. 135:3 [c]Ps. 33:1 [1]Heb. *Hallelujah*
**2** [a]Ps. 102:16 [b]Deut. 30:3
**3** [a][Ps. 51:17] [1]Lit. *sorrows*
**4** [a]Is. 40:26
**5** [a]Ps. 48:1 [b]Nah. 1:3 [c]Is. 40:28
**6** [a]Ps. 146:8, 9
**8** [a]Job 38:26
**9** [a]Job 38:41 [b][Matt. 6:26]
**10** [a]Ps. 33:16, 17
**14** [a]Is. 54:13; 60:17, 18 [b]Ps. 132:15 [1]Lit. *fat of wheat*
**15** [a][Ps. 107:20]
**16** [a]Job 37:6
**17** [1]*fragments* of food
**18** [a]Job 37:10
**19** [a]Deut. 33:4 [b]Mal. 4:4
**20** [a][Rom. 3:1, 2] [1]Heb. *Hallelujah*

PSALM 148
**1** [1]Heb. *Hallelujah*
**4** [a]1 Kin. 8:27 [b]Gen. 1:7
**5** [a]Gen. 1:1, 6
**6** [a]Ps. 89:37
**7** [a]Is. 43:20
**9** [a]Is. 44:23; 49:13

10 Beasts and all cattle;
Creeping things and flying fowl;
11 Kings of the earth and all peoples;
Princes and all judges of the earth;
12 Both young men and maidens;
Old men and children.

13 Let them praise the name of the LORD,
For His [a]name alone is exalted;
His glory *is* above the earth and heaven.
14 And He [a]has exalted the [1]horn of His people,
The praise of [b]all His saints—
Of the children of Israel,
[c]A people near to Him.

[2]Praise the LORD!

## PSALM 149

PRAISE[1] the LORD!

[a]Sing to the LORD a new song,
*And* His praise in the assembly of saints.

2 Let Israel rejoice in their Maker;
Let the children of Zion be joyful in their [a]King.
3 [a]Let them praise His name with the dance;
Let them sing praises to Him with the timbrel and harp.
4 For [a]the LORD takes pleasure in His people;
[b]He will beautify the [1]humble with salvation.

5 Let the saints be joyful in glory;
Let them [a]sing aloud on their beds.
6 *Let* the high praises of God *be* in their mouth,
And [a]a two-edged sword in their hand,
7 To execute vengeance on the nations,
And punishments on the peoples;
8 To bind their kings with chains,
And their nobles with fetters of iron;
9 [a]To execute on them the written judgment—
[b]This honor have all His saints.

[1]Praise the LORD!

## PSALM 150

PRAISE[a1] the LORD!

Praise God in His sanctuary;
Praise Him in His mighty [2]firmament!

2 Praise Him for His mighty acts;
Praise Him according to His excellent [a]greatness!

3 Praise Him with the sound of the [1]trumpet;
Praise Him with the lute and harp!
4 Praise Him with the timbrel and dance;
Praise Him with stringed instruments and flutes!
5 Praise Him with loud cymbals;
Praise Him with clashing cymbals!

6 Let everything that has breath praise the LORD.

[1]Praise the LORD!

13 [a]Ps. 8:1
14 [a]1 Sam. 2:1; Ps. 75:10 [b]Ps. 149:9 [c]Lev. 10:3; Eph. 2:17 [1]Strength or dominion [2]Heb. *Hallelujah*

PSALM 149
1 [a]Ps. 33:3 [1]Heb. *Hallelujah*
2 [a]Judg. 8:23; Zech. 9:9; Matt. 21:5
3 [a]Ex. 15:20; Ps. 81:2
4 [a]Ps. 35:27 [b]Ps. 132:16; Is. 61:3 [1]*meek*
5 [a]Job 35:10
6 [a]Heb. 4:12; Rev. 1:16
9 [a]Deut. 7:1, 2; Ezek. 28:26 [b]Ps. 148:14; 1 Cor. 6:2 [1]Heb. *Hallelujah*

PSALM 150
1 [a]Ps. 145:5, 6 [1]Heb. *Hallelujah* [2]*expanse* of heaven
2 [a]Deut. 3:24
3 [1]*cornet*
6 [1]Heb. *Hallelujah*

# *The Book of* PROVERBS

### *The Beginning of Knowledge*

THE [a]proverbs of Solomon the son of David, king of Israel:

2 To know wisdom and instruction,
To [1]perceive the words of understanding,
3 To receive the instruction of wisdom,
Justice, judgment, and equity;
4 To give prudence to the [a]simple,
To the young man knowledge and discretion—
5 [a]A wise *man* will hear and increase learning,
And a man of understanding will [1]attain wise counsel,
6 To understand a proverb and an enigma,
The words of the wise and their [a]riddles.

7 [a]The fear of the LORD *is* the beginning of knowledge,
*But* fools despise wisdom and instruction.

8 [a]My son, hear the instruction of your father,
And do not forsake the law of your mother;
9 For they *will be* a [a]graceful ornament on your head,
And chains about your neck.

10 My son, if sinners entice you,
[a]Do not consent.
11 If they say, "Come with us,
Let us [a]lie in wait to *shed* blood;
Let us lurk secretly for the innocent without cause;
12 Let us swallow them alive like [1]Sheol,
And whole, [a]like those who go down to the Pit;
13 We shall find all *kinds* of precious [1]possessions,
We shall fill our houses with [2]spoil;
14 Cast in your lot among us,
Let us all have one purse"—
15 My son, [a]do not walk in the way with them,
[b]Keep your foot from their path;
16 [a]For their feet run to evil,
And they make haste to shed blood.
17 Surely, in [1]vain the net is spread
In the sight of any [2]bird;
18 But they lie in wait for their *own* blood,
They lurk secretly for their *own* lives.
19 [a]So *are* the ways of everyone who is greedy for gain;
It takes away the life of its owners.

20 [a]Wisdom calls aloud [1]outside;
She raises her voice in the open squares.
21 She cries out in the [1]chief concourses,
At the openings of the gates in the city
She speaks her words:
22 "How long, you [1]simple ones, will you love [2]simplicity?
For scorners delight in their scorning,
And fools hate knowledge.

CHAPTER 1
1 [a]1 Kin. 4:32
2 [1]*understand* or *discern*
4 [a]Prov. 9:4
5 [a]Prov. 9:9 [1]*acquire*
6 [a]Ps. 78:2
7 [a]Job 28:28
8 [a]Prov. 4:1
9 [a]Prov. 3:22
10 [a]Gen. 39:7–10
11 [a]Jer. 5:26
12 [a]Ps. 28:1 [1]Or *the grave*
13 [1]Lit. *wealth* [2]*plunder*
15 [a]Ps. 1:1 [b]Ps. 119:101
16 [a][Is. 59:7]
17 [1]*futility* [2]Lit. *lord of the wing*
19 [a][1 Tim. 6:10]
20 [a][John 7:37] [1]*in the street*
21 [1]LXX, [Syr.], [Tg.] *top of the walls;* Vg. *the head of the multitudes*
22 [1]*naive* [2]*naivete*

23 Turn at my rebuke;
Surely [a]I will pour out my spirit on you;
I will make my words known to you.
24 [a]Because I have called and you refused,
I have stretched out my hand
and no one regarded,
25 Because you [a]disdained all my counsel,
And would have none of my rebuke,
26 [a]I also will laugh at your calamity;
I will mock when your terror comes,
27 When [a]your terror comes like a storm,
And your destruction comes like a whirlwind,
When distress and anguish come upon you.

28 "Then[a] they will call on me,
but I will not answer;
They will seek me diligently,
but they will not find me.
29 Because they [a]hated knowledge
And did not [b]choose the fear of the LORD,
30 [a]They would have none of my counsel
*And* despised my every rebuke.
31 Therefore [a]they shall eat the fruit of their
own way,
And be filled to the full with their own
fancies.
32 For the [1]turning away of the simple
will slay them,
And the complacency of fools
will destroy them;
33 But whoever listens to me will dwell [a]safely,
And [b]will be [1]secure, without fear of evil."

## *The Value of Wisdom*

**2** My son, if you receive my words,
And [a]treasure my commands within you,
2 So that you incline your ear to wisdom,
*And* apply your heart to understanding;
3 Yes, if you cry out for discernment,
*And* lift up your voice for understanding,
4 [a]If you seek her as silver,
And search for her as *for* hidden treasures;
5 [a]Then you will understand the fear
of the LORD,
And find the knowledge of God.
6 [a]For the LORD gives wisdom;
From His mouth *come* knowledge and
understanding;
7 He stores up sound wisdom for the upright;
[a]*He is* a shield to those who walk uprightly;
8 He guards the paths of justice,
And [a]preserves the way of His saints.
9 Then you will understand righteousness and
justice,
Equity *and* every good path.

10 When wisdom enters your heart,
And knowledge is pleasant to your soul,
11 Discretion will preserve you;
[a]Understanding will keep you,
12 To deliver you from the way of evil,
From the man who speaks perverse things,
13 From those who leave the paths
of uprightness
To [a]walk in the ways of darkness;
14 [a]Who rejoice in doing evil,
*And* delight in the perversity of the wicked;
15 [a]Whose ways *are* crooked,
And *who are* devious in their paths;
16 To deliver you from [a]the immoral woman,
[b]From the seductress *who* flatters with her
words,
17 Who forsakes the companion of her youth,
And forgets the covenant of her God.
18 For [a]her house [1]leads down to death,
And her paths to the dead;
19 None who go to her return,
Nor do they [1]regain the paths of life—
20 So you may walk in the way of goodness,
And keep *to* the paths of righteousness.
21 For the upright will dwell in the [a]land,
And the blameless will remain in it;
22 But the wicked will be [1]cut off from the
[2]earth,
And the unfaithful will be uprooted from it.

## *Guidance for the Young*

**3** My son, do not forget my law,
[a]But let your heart keep my commands;
2 For length of days and long life
And [a]peace they will add to you.

3 Let not mercy and truth forsake you;
[a]Bind them around your neck,
[b]Write them on the tablet of your heart,
4 [a]*And* so find favor and [1]high esteem
In the sight of God and man.

5 [a]Trust in the LORD with all your heart,
[b]And lean not on your own understanding;
6 [a]In all your ways acknowledge Him,
And He shall [1]direct your paths.

7 Do not be wise in your own [a]eyes;
Fear the LORD and depart from evil.
8 It will be health to your [1]flesh,
And [a]strength[2] to your bones.

9 [a]Honor the LORD with your possessions,
And with the firstfruits of all your increase;
10 [a]So your barns will be filled with plenty,
And your vats will overflow with new wine.

11 [a]My son, do not despise the chastening of the
LORD,
Nor detest His correction;
12 For whom the LORD loves He corrects,
[a]Just as a father the son *in whom* he delights.

13 [a]Happy *is* the man *who* finds wisdom,
And the man *who* gains understanding;
14 [a]For her proceeds *are* better than the profits
of silver,
And her gain than fine gold.
15 She *is* more precious than rubies,
And [a]all the things you may desire cannot
compare with her.
16 [a]Length of days *is* in her right hand,
In her left hand riches and honor.
17 [a]Her ways *are* ways of pleasantness,
And all her paths *are* peace.
18 She *is* [a]a tree of life to those who take hold
of her,
And happy *are all* who [1]retain her.

19 [a]The LORD by wisdom founded the earth;
By understanding
He established the heavens;
20 By His knowledge
the depths were [a]broken up,
And clouds drop down the dew.

21 My son, let them not depart from your
eyes—
Keep sound wisdom and discretion;
22 So they will be life to your soul
And grace to your neck.

**23** [a]Joel 2:28
**24** [a]Jer. 7:13
**25** [a]Luke 7:30
**26** [a]Ps. 2:4
**27** [a][Prov. 10:24, 25]
**28** [a]Is. 1:15
**29** [a]Job 21:14 [b]Ps. 119:173
**30** [a]Ps. 81:11
**31** [a]Job 4:8
**32** [1]*waywardness*
**33** [a]Prov. 3:24–26 [b]Ps. 112:7 [1]*at ease*

CHAPTER 2
**1** [a][Prov. 4:21]
**4** [a][Prov. 3:14]
**5** [a][James 1:5, 6]
**6** [a]1 Kin. 3:9, 12
**7** [a][Ps. 84:11]
**8** [a][1 Sam. 2:9]
**11** [a]Prov. 4:6; 6:22
**13** [a][John 3:19, 20]
**14** [a][Rom. 1:32]
**15** [a]Ps. 125:5
**16** [a]Prov. 5:20; 6:24; 7:5 [b]Prov. 5:3
**18** [a]Prov. 7:27 [1]*sinks*
**19** [1]Lit. *reach*
**21** [a]Ps. 37:3
**22** [1]*destroyed* [2]*land*

CHAPTER 3
**1** [a]Deut. 8:1
**2** [a]Ps. 119:165
**3** [a]Prov. 6:21 [b][2 Cor. 3:3]
**4** [a]Rom. 14:18 [1]Lit. *good understanding*
**5** [a][Ps. 37:3, 5] [b][Jer. 9:23, 24]
**6** [a][1 Chr. 28:9] [1]Or *make smooth* or *straight*
**7** [a]Rom. 12:16
**8** [a]Job 21:24 [1]Body, lit. *navel* [2]Lit. *drink*
**9** [a]Ex. 22:29
**10** [a]Deut. 28:8
**11** [a]Job 5:17
**12** [a]Deut. 8:5
**13** [a]Prov. 8:32, 34, 35
**14** [a]Job 28:13
**15** [a]Matt. 13:44
**16** [a][1 Tim. 4:8]
**17** [a][Matt. 11:29]
**18** [a]Gen. 2:9 [1]*hold her fast*
**19** [a]Ps. 104:24
**20** [a]Gen. 7:11

23 [a]Then you will walk safely in your way,
And your foot will not stumble.
24 When you lie down, you will not be afraid;
Yes, you will lie down
and your sleep will be sweet.
25 [a]Do not be afraid of sudden terror,
Nor of trouble from the wicked when it comes;
26 For the LORD will be your confidence,
And will keep your foot from being caught.

**27** [a]Do not withhold good from [1]those to whom it is due,
When it is in the power of your hand to do *so.*
28 [a]Do not say to your neighbor,
"Go, and come back,
And tomorrow I will give *it,*"
When *you have* it with you.
29 Do not devise evil against your neighbor,
For he dwells by you for safety's sake.
30 [a]Do not strive with a man without cause,
If he has done you no harm.

**31** [a]Do not envy the oppressor,
And choose none of his ways;
32 For the perverse *person*
*is* an abomination to the LORD,
[a]But His secret *counsel is* with the upright.
33 [a]The curse of the LORD *is* on the house of the wicked,
But [b]He blesses the home of the just.
34 [a]Surely He scorns the scornful,
But gives grace to the humble.
35 The wise shall inherit glory,
But shame shall be the legacy of fools.

## *Security in Wisdom*

**4** Hear, [a]*my* children,
the instruction of a father,
And give attention to know understanding;
2 For I give you good doctrine:
Do not forsake my law.
3 When I was my father's son,
[a]Tender and the only one in the sight of my mother,
4 [a]He also taught me, and said to me:
"Let your heart retain my words;
[b]Keep my commands, and live.
5 [a]Get wisdom! Get understanding!
Do not forget, nor turn away from the words of my mouth.
6 Do not forsake her,
and she will preserve you;
[a]Love her, and she will keep you.
7 [a]Wisdom *is* the principal thing;
*Therefore* get wisdom.
And in all your getting, get understanding.
8 [a]Exalt her, and she will promote you;
She will bring you honor,
when you embrace her.
9 She will place on your head [a]an ornament of grace;
A crown of glory she will deliver to you."

10 Hear, my son, and receive my sayings,
[a]And the years of your life will be many.
11 I have [a]taught you in the way of wisdom;
I have led you in right paths.
12 When you walk,
[a]your steps will not be hindered,
[b]And when you run, you will not stumble.
13 Take firm hold of instruction, do not let go;
Keep her, for she *is* your life.

**14** [a]Do not enter the path of the wicked,
And do not walk in the way of evil.
15 Avoid it, do not travel on it;
Turn away from it and pass on.
16 [a]For they do not sleep
unless they have done evil;
And their sleep is [1]taken away
unless they make *someone* fall.
17 For they eat the bread of wickedness,
And drink the wine of violence.

18 [a]But the path of the just [b]*is* like the shining [1]sun,
That shines ever brighter unto the perfect day.
19 [a]The way of the wicked *is* like darkness;
They do not know what makes them stumble.

**20** My son, give attention to my words;
Incline your ear to my sayings.
21 Do not let them depart from your eyes;
Keep them in the midst of your heart;
22 For they *are* life to those who find them,
And health to all their flesh.
23 Keep your heart with all diligence,
For out of it *spring* the issues of [a]life.
24 Put away from you a [1]deceitful mouth,
And put perverse lips far from you.
25 Let your eyes look straight ahead,
And your eyelids look right before you.
26 Ponder the path of your [a]feet,
And let all your ways be established.
27 Do not turn to the right or the left;
Remove your foot from evil.

## *Warning Against Immorality*

**5** My son, pay attention to my wisdom;
[1]Lend your ear to my understanding,
2 That you may [1]preserve discretion,
And your lips [a]may keep knowledge.
3 [a]For the lips of [1]an immoral woman
drip honey,
And her mouth *is* [b]smoother than oil;
4 But in the end she is bitter as wormwood,
Sharp as a two-edged sword.
5 Her feet go down to death,
[a]Her steps lay hold of [1]hell.
6 Lest you ponder *her* path of life—
Her ways are unstable;
You do not know *them.*

**7** Therefore hear me now, *my* children,
And do not depart from the words of my mouth.
8 Remove your way far from her,
And do not go near the door of her house,
9 Lest you give your [1]honor to others,
And your years to the cruel *one;*
10 Lest aliens be filled with your [1]wealth,
And your labors *go* to the house of a foreigner;
11 And you mourn at last,
When your flesh and your body
are consumed,
12 And say:
"How I have hated instruction,
And my heart despised correction!

---

**23** [a][Ps. 37:24; 91:11, 12]; Prov. 10:9
**25** [a]Ps. 91:5; 1 Pet. 3:14
**27** [a]Rom. 13:7; [Gal. 6:10] [1]Lit. *its owners*
**28** [a]Lev. 19:13; Deut. 24:15
**30** [a]Prov. 26:17; [Rom. 12:18]
**31** [a]Ps. 37:1; Prov. 24:1
**32** [a]Ps. 25:14
**33** [a]Lev. 26:14, 16; Deut. 11:28; Zech. 5:3, 4; Mal. 2:2 [b]Job 8:6; Ps. 1:3
**34** [a]James 4:6; 1 Pet. 5:5

CHAPTER 4

**1** [a]Ps. 34:11; Prov. 1:8
**3** [a]1 Chr. 29:1
**4** [a]1 Chr. 28:9; Eph. 6:4 [b]Prov. 7:2
**5** [a]Prov. 2:2, 3
**6** [a]2 Thess. 2:10
**7** [a]Prov. 3:13, 14; Matt. 13:44
**8** [a]1 Sam. 2:30
**9** [a]Prov. 3:22
**10** [a]Prov. 3:2
**11** [a]1 Sam. 12:23
**12** [a]Job 18:7; Ps. 18:36 [b][Ps. 91:11]; Prov. 3:23
**14** [a]Ps. 1:1; Prov. 1:15
**16** [a]Ps. 36:4; Mic. 2:1 [1]Lit. *robbed*
**18** [a]Is. 26:7; Matt. 5:14, 45; Phil. 2:15 [b]2 Sam. 23:4 [1]Lit. *light*
**19** [a]1 Sam. 2:9; [Job 18:5, 6]; Prov. 2:13; [Is. 59:9, 10; Jer. 23:12]; John 12:35
**23** [a][Matt. 12:34; 15:18, 19; Mark 7:21; Luke 6:45]
**24** [1]*devious*
**26** [a]Prov. 5:21; Heb. 12:13

CHAPTER 5

**1** [1]Lit. *Bow*
**2** [a]Mal. 2:7 [1]*appreciate good judgment*
**3** [a]Prov. 2:16 [b]Ps. 55:21 [1]Lit. *a strange*
**5** [a]Prov. 7:27 [1]Or *Sheol*
**9** [1]*vigor*
**10** [1]Lit. *strength*

13 I have not obeyed the voice of my teachers,
Nor inclined my ear to those who instructed me!
14 I was on the verge of total ruin,
In the midst of the assembly and congregation."

**15** Drink water from your own cistern,
And running water from your own well.
16 Should your fountains be dispersed abroad,
[1]Streams of water in the streets?
17 Let them be only your own,
And not for strangers with you.
18 Let your fountain be blessed,
And rejoice with [a]the wife of your youth.
19 [a]*As a* loving deer and a graceful doe,
Let her breasts satisfy you at all times;
And always be [1]enraptured with her love.
20 For why should you, my son,
be enraptured by [a]an immoral woman,
And be embraced in the arms of a seductress?

21 [a]For the ways of man *are* before the eyes of the LORD,
And He [1]ponders all his paths.
22 [a]His own iniquities entrap the wicked *man*,
And he is caught in the cords of his sin.
23 [a]He shall die for lack of instruction,
And in the greatness of his folly
he shall go astray.

## *Seven Deadly Sins*

**6** My son, [a]if you become [1]surety
for your friend,
*If* you have [2]shaken hands in pledge
for a stranger,
2 You are snared by the words of your mouth;
You are taken by the words of your mouth.
3 So do this, my son, and deliver yourself;
For you have come into the hand
of your friend:
Go and humble yourself;
Plead with your friend.
4 [a]Give no sleep to your eyes,
Nor slumber to your eyelids.
5 Deliver yourself like a gazelle from the hand
*of the hunter*,
And like a bird from the hand of the [1]fowler.

**6** [a]Go to the ant, you sluggard!
Consider her ways and be wise,
7 Which, having no [1]captain,
Overseer or ruler,
8 Provides her [1]supplies in the summer,
*And* gathers her food in the harvest.
9 [a]How long will you [1]slumber, O sluggard?
When will you rise from your sleep?
10 A little sleep, a little slumber,
A little folding of the hands to sleep—
11 [a]So shall your poverty come on you like a prowler,
And your need like an armed man.

**12** A worthless person, a wicked man,
Walks with a perverse mouth;
13 [a]He winks with his eyes,
He [1]shuffles his feet,
He points with his fingers;
14 Perversity *is* in his heart,
[a]He devises evil continually,
[b]He sows discord.
15 Therefore his calamity shall come [a]suddenly;
Suddenly he shall [b]be broken [c]without remedy.

**16** These six *things* the LORD hates,
Yes, seven *are* an abomination to [1]Him:
17 [a]A[1] proud look,
[b]A lying tongue,
[c]Hands that shed innocent blood,
18 [a]A heart that devises wicked plans,
[b]Feet that are swift in running to evil,
19 [a]A false witness *who* speaks lies,
And one who [b]sows discord among brethren.

**20** [a]My son, keep your father's command,
And do not forsake the law of your mother.
21 [a]Bind them continually upon your heart;
Tie them around your neck.
22 [a]When you roam, [1]they will lead you;
When you sleep, [b]they will keep you;
And *when* you awake, they will speak with you.
23 [a]For the commandment *is* a lamp,
And the law a light;
Reproofs of instruction *are* the way of life,
24 [a]To keep you from the evil woman,
From the flattering tongue of a seductress.
25 [a]Do not lust after her beauty in your heart,
Nor let her allure you with her eyelids.
26 For [a]by means of a harlot
*A man is reduced* to a crust of bread;
[b]And [1]an adulteress will [c]prey upon his precious life.
27 Can a man take fire to his bosom,
And his clothes not be burned?
28 Can one walk on hot coals,
And his feet not be seared?
29 So *is* he who goes in to his neighbor's wife;
Whoever touches her shall not be innocent.

30 *People* do not despise a thief
If he steals to satisfy himself when he is starving.
31 Yet *when* he is found,
[a]he must restore sevenfold;
He may have to give up all the substance of his house.
32 Whoever commits adultery with a woman
[a]lacks understanding;
He *who* does so destroys his own soul.
33 Wounds and dishonor he will get,
And his reproach will not be wiped away.
34 For [a]jealousy *is* a husband's fury;
Therefore he will not spare in the day of vengeance.
35 He will [1]accept no recompense,
Nor will he be appeased
though you give many gifts.

## *The Wiles of a Harlot*

**7** My son, keep my words,
And [a]treasure my commands within you.
2 [a]Keep my commands and live,
[b]And my law as the apple of your eye.
3 [a]Bind them on your fingers;
Write them on the tablet of your heart.
4 Say to wisdom, "You *are* my sister,"
And call understanding *your* nearest kin,
5 [a]That they may keep you from the immoral woman,
From the seductress
*who* flatters with her words.

**6** For at the window of my house
I looked through my lattice,

**16** [1]*Channels*
**18** [a]Mal. 2:14
**19** [a]Song 2:9 [1]Lit. *intoxicated*
**20** [a]Prov. 2:16
**21** [a]Hos. 7:2 [1]*observes*, lit. *weighs*
**22** [a]Num. 32:23
**23** [a]Job 4:21

CHAPTER 6
**1** [a]Prov. 11:15 [1]*guaranty* or *collateral* [2]Lit. *struck*
**4** [a]Ps. 132:4
**5** [1]One who catches birds in a trap or snare
**6** [a]Job 12:7
**7** [1]Lit. *leader*
**8** [1]Lit. *bread*
**9** [a]Prov. 24:33, 34 [1]Lit. *lie down*
**11** [a]Prov. 10:4
**13** [a]Job 15:12 [1]*gives signals*, lit. *scrapes*
**14** [a]Mic. 2:1 [b]Prov. 6:19
**15** [a]Is. 30:13 [b]Jer. 19:11 [c]2 Chr. 36:16
**16** [1]Lit. *His soul*
**17** [a]Ps. 101:5 [b]Ps. 120:2 [c]Is. 1:15 [1]Lit. *Haughty eyes*
**18** [a]Gen. 6:5 [b]Is. 59:7
**19** [a]Ps. 27:12 [b]Prov. 6:14
**20** [a]Eph. 6:1
**21** [a]Prov. 3:3
**22** [a][Prov. 3:23] [b]Prov. 2:11 [1]Lit. *it*
**23** [a]Ps. 19:8
**24** [a]Prov. 2:16
**25** [a]Matt. 5:28
**26** [a]Prov. 29:3 [b]Gen. 39:14 [c]Ezek. 13:18 [1]Wife of another, lit. *a man's wife*
**31** [a]Ex. 22:1–4
**32** [a]Prov. 7:7
**34** [a]Song 8:6
**35** [1]Lit. *lift up the face of any*

CHAPTER 7
**1** [a]Prov. 2:1
**2** [a]Lev. 18:5 [b]Deut. 32:10
**3** [a]Deut. 6:8
**5** [a]Prov. 2:16; 5:3

7 And saw among the simple,
I perceived among the [1]youths,
A young man [a]devoid[2] of understanding,
8 Passing along the street near her corner;
And he took the path to her house
9 [a]In the twilight, in the evening,
In the black and dark night.

10 And there a woman met him,
*With* the attire of a harlot,
and a crafty heart.
11 [a]She *was* loud and rebellious,
[b]Her feet would not stay at home.
12 At times *she was* outside,
at times in the open square,
Lurking at every corner.
13 So she caught him and kissed him;
With an [1]impudent face she said to him:
14 "*I have* peace offerings with me;
Today I have paid my vows.
15 So I came out to meet you,
Diligently to seek your face,
And I have found you.
16 I have spread my bed with tapestry,
Colored coverings of [a]Egyptian linen.
17 I have perfumed my bed
With myrrh, aloes, and cinnamon.
18 Come, let us take our fill of love until
morning;
Let us delight ourselves with love.
19 For [1]my husband *is* not at home;
He has gone on a long journey;
20 He has taken a bag of money [1]with him,
*And* will come home [2]on the appointed day."

21 [1]With [a]her enticing speech
she caused him to yield,
[b]With her flattering lips she [2]seduced him.
22 Immediately he went after her,
as an ox goes to the slaughter,
Or [1]as a fool to the correction of the [2]stocks,
23 Till an arrow struck his liver.
[a]As a bird hastens to the snare,
He did not know it [1]*would cost* his life.

**24** Now therefore, listen to me, *my* children;
Pay attention to the words of my mouth:
25 Do not let your heart turn aside to her ways,
Do not stray into her paths;
26 For she has cast down many wounded,
And [a]all who were slain by her were strong
*men.*
27 [a]Her house *is* the way to [1]hell,
Descending to the chambers of death.

### *Wisdom Is Everlasting*

**8** Does not [a]wisdom cry out,
And understanding lift up her voice?
2 She takes her stand on the top of the [1]high
hill,
Beside the way, where the paths meet.
3 She cries out by the gates,
at the entry of the city,
At the entrance of the doors:
4 "To you, O men, I call,
And my voice *is* to the sons of men.
5 O you [1]simple ones, understand prudence,
And you fools, be of an understanding heart.
6 Listen, for I will speak of [a]excellent things,
And from the opening of my lips
*will come* right things;
7 For my mouth will speak truth;
Wickedness *is* an abomination to my lips.
8 All the words of my mouth *are* with
righteousness;
Nothing crooked or perverse *is* in them.
9 They *are* all plain to him who understands,
And right to those who find knowledge.
10 Receive my instruction, and not silver,
And knowledge rather than choice gold;
11 [a]For wisdom *is* better than rubies,
And all the things one may desire cannot be
compared with her.

**12** "I, wisdom, dwell with prudence,
And find out knowledge *and* discretion.
13 [a]The fear of the LORD *is* to hate evil;
[b]Pride and arrogance and the evil way
And [c]the perverse mouth I hate.
14 Counsel *is* mine, and sound wisdom;
I *am* understanding, [a]I have strength.
15 [a]By me kings reign,
And rulers decree justice.
16 By me princes rule, and nobles,
All the judges of [1]the earth.
17 [a]I love those who love me,
And [b]those who seek me diligently
will find me.
18 [a]Riches and honor *are* with me,
Enduring riches and righteousness.
19 My fruit *is* better than gold,
yes, than fine gold,
And my revenue than choice silver.
20 I [1]traverse the way of righteousness,
In the midst of the paths of justice,
21 That I may cause those who love me
to inherit wealth,
That I may fill their treasuries.

**22** "The[a] LORD possessed me at the beginning of
His way,
Before His works of old.
23 [a]I have been established from everlasting,
From the beginning,
before there was ever an earth.
24 When *there were* no depths
I was brought forth,
When *there were* no fountains abounding
with water.
25 [a]Before the mountains were settled,
Before the hills, I was brought forth;
26 While as yet He had not made the earth or
the [1]fields,
Or the [2]primal dust of the world.
27 When He prepared the heavens, I *was* there,
When He drew a circle on the face
of the deep,
28 When He established the clouds above,
When He strengthened the fountains of the
deep,
29 [a]When He assigned to the sea its limit,
So that the waters would not transgress His
command,
When [b]He marked out the foundations of the
earth,
30 [a]Then I was beside Him
*as* [1]a master craftsman;
[b]And I was daily *His* delight,
Rejoicing always before Him,
31 Rejoicing in His inhabited world,
And [a]my delight *was* with the sons of men.

**32** "Now therefore, listen to me, *my* children,
For [a]blessed *are those who* keep my ways.

**7** [a][Prov. 6:32; 9:4, 16] [1]Lit. *sons* [2]*lacking*
**9** [a]Job 24:15
**11** [a]Prov. 9:13 [b]Titus 2:5
**13** [1]*shameless*
**16** [a]Is. 19:9
**19** [1]Lit. *the man*
**20** [1]Lit. *in his hand* [2]*at the full moon*
**21** [a]Prov. 5:3 [b]Ps. 12:2 [1]*By the greatness of her words* [2]*compelled*
**22** [1]LXX, Syr., Tg. *as a dog to bonds;* Vg. *as a lamb . . . to bonds* [2]*shackles*
**23** [a]Eccl. 9:12 [1]Lit. *is for*
**26** [a]Neh. 13:26
**27** [a]Prov. 2:18; 5:5; 9:18 [1]Or *Sheol*

CHAPTER 8
**1** [a]Prov. 1:20, 21; 9:3
**2** [1]Lit. *heights*
**5** [1]*naive*
**6** [a]Prov. 22:20
**11** [a]Job 28:15
**13** [a]Prov. 3:7; 16:6 [b][Prov. 16:17, 18] [c]Prov. 4:24
**14** [a]Eccl. 7:19; 9:16
**15** [a]Rom. 13:1
**16** [1]MT, Syr., Tg., Vg. *righteousness;* LXX, Bg., some mss. and editions *earth*
**17** [a][John 14:21] [b]James 1:5
**18** [a]Prov. 3:16
**20** [1]*walk about on*
**22** [a]Prov. 3:19
**23** [a][Ps. 2:6]
**25** [a]Job 15:7, 8
**26** [1]*outer places* [2]Lit. *beginning of the dust*
**29** [a]Gen. 1:9, 10 [b]Job 28:4, 6
**30** [a][John 1:1–3, 18] [b][Matt. 3:17] [1]A Jewish tradition *one brought up*
**31** [a]Ps. 16:3
**32** [a]Luke 11:28

33 Hear instruction and be wise,
And do not disdain *it.*
34 [a]Blessed is the man who listens to me,
Watching daily at my gates,
Waiting at the posts of my doors.
35 For whoever finds me finds life,
And [a]obtains favor from the LORD;
36 But he who sins against me
[a]wrongs his own soul;
All those who hate me love death."

### *Wisdom's Invitation*

**9** Wisdom has [a]built her house,
She has hewn out her seven pillars;
2 [a]She has slaughtered her meat,
[b]She has mixed her wine,
She has also [1]furnished her table.
3 She has sent out her maidens,
She cries out from the highest places
of the city,
4 "Whoever[a] *is* simple, let him turn in here!"
*As for* him who lacks understanding, she
says to him,
5 "Come,[a] eat of my bread
And drink of the wine I have mixed.
6 Forsake foolishness and live,
And go in the way of understanding.

**7** "He who corrects a scoffer
gets shame for himself,
And he who rebukes a wicked *man*
*only* harms himself.
8 [a]Do not correct a scoffer, lest he hate you;
[b]Rebuke a wise *man,* and he will love you.
9 Give *instruction* to a wise *man,*
and he will be still wiser;
Teach a just *man,*
[a]and he will increase in learning.

10 "The[a] fear of the LORD
*is* the beginning of wisdom,
And the knowledge of the Holy One
*is* understanding.
11 [a]For by me your days will be multiplied,
And years of life will be added to you.
12 [a]If you are wise, you are wise for yourself,
And *if* you scoff, you will bear *it* alone."

**13** [a]A foolish woman is [1]clamorous;
*She is* simple, and knows nothing.
14 For she sits at the door of her house,
On a seat [a]*by* the highest places of the city,
15 To call to those who pass by,
Who go straight on their way:
16 "Whoever[a] *is* [1]simple, let him turn in here";
And *as for* him who lacks understanding, she
says to him,
17 "Stolen[a] water is sweet,
And bread *eaten* in secret is pleasant."
18 But he does not know that [a]the dead *are*
there,
*That* her guests *are* in the depths of [1]hell.

### *A Wise Son and a Foolish Son*

**10** The proverbs of [a]Solomon:

[b]A wise son makes a glad father,
But a foolish son *is* the grief of his mother.
2 [a]Treasures of wickedness profit nothing,
[b]But righteousness delivers from death.
3 [a]The LORD will not allow the righteous soul to
famish,
But He casts away the desire of the wicked.
4 [a]He who has a slack hand becomes poor,
But [b]the hand of the diligent makes rich.
5 He who gathers in [a]summer *is* a wise son;
He who sleeps in harvest
*is* [b]a son who causes shame.

6 Blessings *are* on the head of the righteous,
But violence covers the mouth of the wicked.
7 [a]The memory of the righteous *is* blessed,
But the name of the wicked will rot.

8 The wise in heart will receive commands,
[a]But [1]a prating fool will [2]fall.

9 [a]He who walks with integrity walks securely,
But he who perverts his ways
will become known.

10 He who winks with the eye causes trouble,
But a prating fool will fall.

11 The mouth of the righteous *is* a well of life,
But violence covers the mouth of the wicked.

12 Hatred stirs up strife,
But [a]love covers all sins.

13 Wisdom is found on the lips of him who has
understanding,
But [a]a rod *is* for the back of him
who [1]is devoid of understanding.

14 Wise *people* store up knowledge,
But [a]the mouth of the foolish *is* near
destruction.

15 The [a]rich man's wealth *is* his strong city;
The destruction of the poor *is* their poverty.

16 The labor of the righteous *leads* to [a]life,
The wages of the wicked to sin.

17 He who keeps instruction *is in* the way of
life,
But he who refuses correction [1]goes astray.

**18** Whoever [a]hides hatred *has* lying lips,
And [b]whoever spreads slander *is* a fool.

19 [a]In the multitude of words sin is not lacking,
But [b]he who restrains his lips *is* wise.
20 The tongue of the righteous *is* choice silver;
The heart of the wicked *is worth* little.
21 The lips of the righteous feed many,
But fools die for lack of [1]wisdom.

22 [a]The blessing of the LORD makes *one* rich,
And He adds no sorrow with it.

**23** [a]To do evil *is* like sport to a fool,
But a man of understanding has wisdom.
24 [a]The fear of the wicked will come upon him,
And [b]the desire of the righteous
will be granted.
25 When the whirlwind passes by,
[a]the wicked *is* no *more,*
But [b]the righteous
*has* an everlasting foundation.

26 As vinegar to the teeth
and smoke to the eyes,
So *is* the lazy *man* to those who send him.

**27** [a]The fear of the LORD prolongs days,
But [b]the years of the wicked
will be shortened.
28 The hope of the righteous *will be* gladness,
But the [a]expectation of the wicked
will perish.
29 The way of the LORD *is* strength
for the upright,

**34** [a]Prov. 3:13, 18
**35** [a][John 17:3]
**36** [a]Prov. 20:2

CHAPTER 9
**1** [a][Matt. 16:18]
**2** [a]Matt. 22:4 [b]Prov. 23:30 [1]*arranged*
**4** [a]Ps. 19:7
**5** [a]Is. 55:1
**8** [a]Matt. 7:6 [b]Ps. 141:5
**9** [a][Matt. 13:12]
**10** [a]Job 28:28
**11** [a]Prov. 3:2, 16
**12** [a]Job 35:6, 7
**13** [a]Prov. 7:11 [1]*boisterous*
**14** [a]Prov. 9:3
**16** [a]Prov. 7:7, 8 [1]*naive*
**17** [a]Prov. 20:17
**18** [a]Prov. 2:18; 7:27 [1]Or *Sheol*

CHAPTER 10
**1** [a]Prov. 1:1; 25:1 [b]Prov. 15:20; 17:21, 25; 19:13; 29:3, 15
**2** [a][Luke 12:19, 20] [b]Dan. 4:27
**3** [a]Ps. 34:9, 10; 37:25
**4** [a]Prov. 19:15 [b]Prov. 12:24; 13:4; 21:5
**5** [a]Prov. 6:8 [b]Prov. 19:26
**7** [a]Eccl. 8:10
**8** [a]Prov. 10:10 [1]Lit. *the foolish of lips* [2]*be thrust down* or *ruined*
**9** [a][Ps. 23:4]
**12** [a][1 Cor. 13:4–7]
**13** [a]Prov. 26:3 [1]Lit. *lacks heart*
**14** [a]Prov. 18:7
**15** [a]Job 31:24
**16** [a]Prov. 6:23
**17** [1]*leads*
**18** [a]Prov. 26:24 [b]Ps. 15:3; 101:5
**19** [a]Eccl. 5:3 [b][James 1:19; 3:2]
**21** [1]Lit. *heart*
**22** [a]Gen. 24:35; 26:12
**23** [a]Prov. 2:14; 15:21
**24** [a]Job 15:21 [b]Ps. 145:19
**25** [a]Ps. 37:9, 10 [b]Ps. 15:5
**27** [a]Prov. 9:11 [b]Job 15:32
**28** [a]Job 8:13

But [a]destruction *will come*
to the workers of iniquity.

30 [a]The righteous will never be removed,
But the wicked will not inhabit the [1]earth.
31 [a]The mouth of the righteous brings forth
wisdom,
But the perverse tongue will be cut out.
32 The lips of the righteous know
what is acceptable,
But the mouth of the wicked
*what is* perverse.

### *The Folly of Wickedness*

**11** [a]Dishonest[1] scales *are* an abomination to
the LORD,
But a [2]just weight *is* His delight.

2 When pride comes, then comes [a]shame;
But with the humble *is* wisdom.

3 The integrity of the upright will guide [a]them,
But the perversity of the unfaithful
will destroy them.
4 [a]Riches do not profit in the day of wrath,
But [b]righteousness delivers from death.
5 The righteousness of the blameless
will [1]direct his way aright,
But the wicked will fall
by his own [a]wickedness.
6 The righteousness of the upright
will deliver them,
But the unfaithful will be caught
by *their* lust.

**7** When a wicked man dies,
*his* expectation will [a]perish,
And the hope of the unjust perishes.
8 [a]The righteous is delivered from trouble,
And it comes to the wicked instead.
9 The hypocrite with *his* mouth destroys his
neighbor,
But through knowledge the righteous will be
delivered.
10 [a]When it goes well with the righteous, the
city rejoices;
And when the wicked perish,
*there is* jubilation.
11 By the blessing of the upright
the city is [a]exalted,
But it is overthrown
by the mouth of the wicked.

12 He who [1]is devoid of wisdom despises his
neighbor,
But a man of understanding holds his peace.

13 [a]A talebearer reveals secrets,
But he who is of a faithful spirit [b]conceals a
matter.

14 [a]Where *there is* no counsel, the people fall;
But in the multitude of counselors *there is*
safety.

15 He who is [a]surety[1] for a stranger will suffer,
But one who hates [2]being surety is secure.

**16** A gracious woman retains honor,
But ruthless *men* retain riches.
17 [a]The merciful man
does good for his own soul,
But *he who is* cruel troubles his own flesh.
18 The wicked *man* does deceptive work,
But [a]he who sows righteousness
*will have* a sure reward.

19 As righteousness *leads* to [a]life,
So he who pursues evil *pursues it* to his own
[b]death.
20 Those who are of a perverse heart
*are* an abomination to the LORD,
But *the* blameless in their ways *are* His
delight.
21 [a]*Though they join* [1]forces,
the wicked will not go unpunished;
But [b]the posterity of the righteous will be
delivered.

22 *As* a ring of gold in a swine's snout,
*So is* a lovely woman who lacks [1]discretion.

23 The desire of the righteous *is* only good,
*But* the expectation of the wicked [a]*is* wrath.

**24** There is *one* who [a]scatters,
yet increases more;
And there is *one* who withholds more than is
right,
But it *leads* to poverty.
25 [a]The generous soul will be made rich,
[b]And he who waters will also be watered
himself.
26 The people will curse [a]him who withholds
grain,
But [b]blessing *will be* on the head
of him who sells *it.*

27 He who earnestly seeks good [1]finds favor,
[a]But trouble will come to him who seeks *evil.*
28 [a]He who trusts in his riches will fall,
But [b]the righteous will flourish like foliage.

29 He who troubles his own house [a]will inherit
the wind,
And the fool *will be* [b]servant to the wise of
heart.

30 The fruit of the righteous *is a* tree of life,
And [a]he who [1]wins souls *is* wise.

31 [a]If the righteous will be [1]recompensed
on the earth,
How much more the ungodly and the sinner.

### *The House of the Righteous Shall Stand*

**12** Whoever loves instruction loves
knowledge,
But he who hates correction *is* stupid.

2 A good *man* obtains favor from the LORD,
But a man of wicked intentions He will
condemn.

3 A man is not established by wickedness,
But the [a]root of the righteous
cannot be moved.

4 [a]An[1] excellent wife *is* the crown of her
husband,
But she who causes shame *is* [b]like rottenness
in his bones.

**5** The thoughts of the righteous *are* right,
*But* the counsels of the wicked *are* deceitful.
6 [a]The words of the wicked *are,*
"Lie in wait for blood,"
[b]But the mouth of the upright
will deliver them.

7 [a]The wicked are overthrown and *are* no more,
But the house of the righteous will stand.

---

**29** [a]Ps. 1:6
**30** [a]Ps. 37:22 [1]*land*
**31** [a]Ps. 37:30

CHAPTER 11
**1** [a]Lev. 19:35, 36 [1]*deceptive* [2]Lit. *perfect stone*
**2** [a]Prov. 16:18; 18:12; 29:23
**3** [a]Prov. 13:6
**4** [a]Ezek. 7:19 [b]Gen. 7:1
**5** [a]Prov. 5:22 [1]Or *make smooth* or *straight*
**7** [a]Prov. 10:28
**8** [a]Prov. 21:18
**10** [a]Prov. 28:12
**11** [a]Prov. 14:34
**12** [1]Lit. *lacks heart*
**13** [a]Lev. 19:16 [b]Prov. 19:11
**14** [a]1 Kin. 12:1
**15** [a]Prov. 6:1, 2 [1]*guaranty* [2]*those pledging guaranty,* lit. *those who strike hands*
**17** [a][Matt. 5:7; 25:34–36]
**18** [a]Hos. 10:12
**19** [a]Prov. 10:16; 12:28 [b][Rom. 6:23]
**21** [a]Prov. 16:5 [b]Ps. 112:2 [1]Lit. *hand to hand*
**22** [1]*taste*
**23** [a]Rom. 2:8, 9
**24** [a]Ps. 112:9
**25** [a][2 Cor. 9:6, 7] [b][Matt. 5:7]
**26** [a]Amos 8:5, 6 [b]Job 29:13
**27** [a]Esth. 7:10 [1]Lit. *seeks*
**28** [a]Job 31:24 [b]Ps. 1:3
**29** [a]Eccl. 5:16 [b]Prov. 14:19
**30** [a][Dan. 12:3] [1]Lit. *takes,* in the sense of *brings,* cf. 1 Sam. 16:11
**31** [a]Jer. 25:29 [1]*rewarded*

CHAPTER 12
**3** [a][Prov. 10:25]
**4** [a]1 Cor. 11:7 [b]Prov. 14:30 [1]Lit. *A woman of valor*
**6** [a]Prov. 1:11, 18 [b]Prov. 14:3
**7** [a]Matt. 7:24–27

8 A man will be commended according to his
wisdom,
[a]But he who is of a perverse heart will be
despised.

9 [a]Better *is the one* who is [1]slighted
but has a servant,
Than he who honors himself but lacks bread.

10 [a]A righteous *man* regards the life of his
animal,
But the tender mercies of the wicked *are*
cruel.

11 [a]He who [1]tills his land will be satisfied with
[b]bread,
But he who follows [2]frivolity [c]*is* devoid of
[3]understanding.

**12** The wicked covet the catch of evil *men,*
But the root of the righteous yields *fruit.*
13 [a]The wicked is ensnared by the transgression
of *his* lips,
[b]But the righteous will come through trouble.
14 [a]A man will be satisfied with good by the fruit
of *his* mouth,
[b]And the recompense of a man's hands will be
rendered to him.

15 [a]The way of a fool *is* right in his own eyes,
But he who heeds counsel *is* wise.
16 [a]A fool's wrath is known at once,
But a prudent *man* covers shame.

**17** [a]He *who* speaks truth declares righteousness,
But a false witness, deceit.
18 [a]There is one who speaks like the piercings of
a sword,
But the tongue of the wise *promotes* health.
19 The truthful lip shall be established forever,
[a]But a lying tongue *is* but for a moment.
20 Deceit is in the heart of those who devise
evil,
But counselors of peace have joy.
21 [a]No grave [1]trouble will overtake the righteous,
But the wicked shall be filled with evil.
22 [a]Lying lips *are* an abomination to the LORD,
But those who deal truthfully *are* His delight.

23 [a]A prudent man conceals knowledge,
But the heart of fools proclaims foolishness.

24 [a]The hand of the diligent will rule,
But the lazy *man* will be put to forced labor.

25 [a]Anxiety in the heart of man causes
depression,
But [b]a good word makes it glad.

26 The righteous should choose his friends
carefully,
For the way of the wicked leads them astray.

27 The lazy *man* does not roast
what he took in hunting,
But diligence *is* man's precious possession.

28 In the way of righteousness *is* life,
And in *its* pathway *there is* no death.

## *Wisdom Loves Righteousness*

**13** A wise son *heeds* his father's instruction,
[a]But a scoffer does not listen to rebuke.

2 [a]A man shall eat well
by the fruit of *his* mouth,
But the soul of the unfaithful
feeds on violence.

3 [a]He who guards his mouth preserves his life,
*But* he who opens wide his lips
shall have destruction.

4 [a]The soul of a lazy *man* desires,
and *has* nothing;
But the soul of the diligent
shall be made rich.

5 A righteous *man* hates lying,
But a wicked *man* is loathsome
and comes to shame.
6 [a]Righteousness guards *him whose* way is
blameless,
But wickedness overthrows the sinner.

7 [a]There is one who makes himself rich, yet *has*
nothing;
*And* one who makes himself poor,
yet *has* great riches.

8 The ransom of a man's life *is* his riches,
But the poor does not hear rebuke.

9 The light of the righteous rejoices,
[a]But the lamp of the wicked will be put out.

10 By pride comes nothing but [a]strife,
But with the well-advised *is* wisdom.

11 [a]Wealth *gained by* dishonesty
will be diminished,
But he who gathers by labor will increase.

12 Hope deferred makes the heart sick,
But [a]*when* the desire comes,
*it is* a tree of life.

**13** He who [a]despises the word will be destroyed,
But he who fears the commandment will be
rewarded.
14 [a]The law of the wise *is* a fountain of life,
To turn *one* away from [b]the snares of death.

15 Good understanding [1]gains [a]favor,
But the way of the unfaithful *is* hard.
16 [a]Every prudent *man* acts with knowledge,
But a fool lays open *his* folly.

17 A wicked messenger falls into trouble,
But [a]a faithful ambassador *brings* health.

18 Poverty and shame *will come* to him who
[1]disdains correction,
But [a]he who regards a rebuke will be
honored.

19 A desire accomplished is sweet to the soul,
But *it is* an abomination to fools to depart
from evil.

20 He who walks with wise *men* will be wise,
But the companion of fools will be destroyed.

21 [a]Evil pursues sinners,
But to the righteous, good shall be repaid.

22 A good *man* leaves an inheritance to his
children's children,
But [a]the wealth of the sinner is stored up for
the righteous.

23 [a]Much food *is in* the [1]fallow *ground* of the
poor,
And for lack of justice there is [2]waste.

24 [a]He who spares his rod hates his son,
But he who loves him disciplines him
[1]promptly.

**8** [a]1 Sam. 25:17; Prov. 18:3
**9** [a]Prov. 13:7 [1]*lightly esteemed*
**10** [a]Deut. 25:4
**11** [a]Gen. 3:19 [b]Prov. 28:19 [c]Prov. 6:32 [1]*works* or *cultivates* [2]Lit. *vain things* [3]Lit. *heart*
**13** [a]Prov. 18:7 [b][2 Pet. 2:9]
**14** [a]Prov. 13:2; 15:23; 18:20 [b]Job 34:11; Prov. 1:31; 24:12; [Is. 3:10, 11]; Hos. 4:9
**15** [a]Prov. 3:7; Luke 18:11
**16** [a]Prov. 11:13; 29:11
**17** [a]Prov. 14:5
**18** [a]Ps. 57:4; Prov. 4:22; 15:4
**19** [a][Ps. 52:4, 5]; Prov. 19:9
**21** [a]Ps. 91:10; Prov. 1:33; 1 Pet. 3:13 [1]*harm*
**22** [a]Prov. 6:17; 11:20; Rev. 22:15
**23** [a]Prov. 13:16
**24** [a]Prov. 10:4
**25** [a]Prov. 15:13 [b]Is. 50:4

CHAPTER 13
**1** [a]Is. 28:14, 15
**2** [a]Prov. 12:14
**3** [a]Ps. 39:1; Prov. 21:23; [James 3:2]
**4** [a]Prov. 10:4
**6** [a]Prov. 11:3, 5, 6
**7** [a][Prov. 11:24; 12:9; Luke 12:20, 21]
**9** [a]Job 18:5, 6; 21:17; Prov. 24:20
**10** [a]Prov. 10:12
**11** [a]Prov. 10:2; 20:21
**12** [a]Prov. 13:19
**13** [a]Num. 15:31; 2 Chr. 36:16; Is. 5:24
**14** [a]Prov. 6:22; 10:11; 14:27 [b]2 Sam. 22:6
**15** [a]Ps. 111:10; Prov. 3:4 [1]*gives*
**16** [a]Prov. 12:23
**17** [a]Prov. 25:13
**18** [a]Prov. 15:5, 31, 32 [1]Lit. *ignores*
**21** [a]Prov. 32:10; Is. 47:11
**22** [a]Job 27:16, 17; Prov. 28:8; [Eccl. 2:26]
**23** [a]Prov. 12:11 [1]*uncultivated* [2]Lit. *what is swept away*
**24** [a]Prov. 19:18 [1]*early*

25 [a]The righteous eats to the satisfying of his soul,
But the stomach of the wicked shall be in want.

### *The Ways of Life and Death*

**14** The wise woman builds her house,
But the foolish pulls it down with her hands.

2 He who walks in his uprightness
fears the LORD,
[a]But *he who is* perverse in his ways despises Him.

3 In the mouth of a fool *is* a rod of pride,
[a]But the lips of the wise will preserve them.

4 Where no oxen *are,* the [1]trough *is* clean;
But much increase *comes* by the strength of an ox.

5 A [a]faithful witness does not lie,
But a false witness will utter [b]lies.

6 A scoffer seeks wisdom and does not *find it,*
But [a]knowledge
*is* easy to him who understands.
7 Go from the presence of a foolish man,
When you do not perceive *in him* the lips of [a]knowledge.
8 The wisdom of the prudent
*is* to understand his way,
But the folly of fools *is* deceit.

9 [a]Fools mock at [1]sin,
But among the upright *there is* favor.

10 The heart knows its own bitterness,
And a stranger does not share its joy.

11 [a]The house of the wicked will be overthrown,
But the tent of the upright will flourish.

12 [a]There is a way *that seems* right to a man,
But [b]its end *is* the way of [c]death.

13 Even in laughter the heart may sorrow,
And [a]the end of mirth *may be* grief.

14 The backslider in heart will be [a]filled with his own ways,
But a good man *will be satisfied* [1]from [b]above.

15 The simple believes every word,
But the prudent considers well his steps.
16 [a]A wise *man* fears and departs from evil,
But a fool rages and is self-confident.
17 A quick-tempered *man* acts foolishly,
And a man of wicked intentions is hated.
18 The simple inherit folly,
But the prudent are crowned with knowledge.
19 The evil will bow before the good,
And the wicked at the gates of the righteous.

20 [a]The poor *man* is hated
even by his own neighbor,
But [1]the rich *has* many [b]friends.
21 He who despises his neighbor sins;
[a]But he who has mercy on the poor, happy *is* he.

22 Do they not go astray who devise evil?
But mercy and truth *belong* to those who devise good.

25 [a]Ps. 34:10; Prov. 10:3

CHAPTER 14
2 [a][Rom. 2:4]
3 [a]Prov. 12:6
4 [1]*manger* or *feed trough*
5 [a]Rev. 1:5; 3:14 [b]Ex. 23:1; Deut. 19:16; Prov. 6:19; 12:17
6 [a]Prov. 8:9; 17:24
7 [a]Prov. 23:9
9 [a]Prov. 10:23 [1]Lit. *guilt*
11 [a]Job 8:15
12 [a]Prov. 16:25 [b]Rom. 6:21 [c]Prov. 12:15
13 [a]Prov. 5:4; Eccl. 2:1, 2
14 [a]Prov. 1:31; 12:15 [b]Prov. 13:2; 18:20 [1]Lit. *from above himself*
16 [a]Job 28:28; Ps. 34:14; Prov. 22:3
20 [a]Prov. 19:7 [b]Prov. 19:4 [1]Lit. *many are the lovers of the rich*
21 [a]Ps. 112:9; [Prov. 19:17]
23 [1]Lit. *talk of the lips*
25 [a][Ezek. 3:18–21] [1]*saves lives*
27 [a]Prov. 13:14
29 [a]Prov. 16:32; 19:11; Eccl. 7:9; James 1:19 [1]Lit. *short of spirit*
30 [a]Ps. 112:10 [b]Prov. 12:4; Hab. 3:16
31 [a]Prov. 17:5; Matt. 25:40; 1 John 3:17 [b][Job 31:15; Prov. 22:2]
32 [a]Gen. 49:18; Job 13:15; [Ps. 16:11; 73:24]; 2 Cor. 1:9; 5:8; [2 Tim. 4:18]
33 [a]Prov. 12:16
34 [a]Prov. 11:11 [1]*shame* or *disgrace*
35 [a]Matt. 24:45–47

CHAPTER 15
1 [a]Prov. 25:15 [b]1 Sam. 25:10
2 [a]Prov. 12:23
3 [a]2 Chr. 16:9; Job 34:21; Prov. 5:21; Jer. 16:17; 32:19; Zech. 4:10; Heb. 4:13
4 [1]Lit. *healing*
5 [a]Prov. 10:1 [b]Prov. 13:18 [1]Lit. *keeps*
7 [1]*spread*
8 [a]Prov. 21:27; Eccl. 5:1; Is. 1:11; Jer. 6:20; Mic. 6:7
9 [a]Prov. 21:21
10 [a]1 Kin. 22:8 [b]Prov. 5:12

23 In all labor there is profit,
But [1]idle chatter *leads* only to poverty.
24 The crown of the wise is their riches,
*But* the foolishness of fools *is* folly.
25 A true witness [1]delivers [a]souls,
But a deceitful *witness* speaks lies.
26 In the fear of the LORD
*there is* strong confidence,
And His children will have a place of refuge.
27 [a]The fear of the LORD *is* a fountain of life,
To turn *one* away from the snares of death.
28 In a multitude of people *is* a king's honor,
But in the lack of people
*is* the downfall of a prince.

29 [a]*He who is* slow to wrath
has great understanding,
But *he who is* [1]impulsive exalts folly.
30 A sound heart *is* life to the body,
But [a]envy *is* [b]rottenness to the bones.
31 [a]He who oppresses the poor
reproaches [b]his Maker,
But he who honors Him
has mercy on the needy.
32 The wicked is banished in his wickedness,
But [a]the righteous has a refuge in his death.
33 Wisdom rests in the heart of him who has understanding,
But [a]*what is* in the heart of fools is made known.
34 Righteousness exalts a [a]nation,
But sin *is* a [1]reproach to *any* people.
35 [a]The king's favor *is* toward a wise servant,
But his wrath *is against* him who causes shame.

### *A Soft Answer Turns Away Wrath*

**15** A [a]soft answer turns away wrath,
But [b]a harsh word stirs up anger.
2 The tongue of the wise uses knowledge rightly,
[a]But the mouth of fools pours forth foolishness.

3 [a]The eyes of the LORD *are* in every place,
Keeping watch on the evil and the good.

4 A [1]wholesome tongue *is* a tree of life,
But perverseness in it breaks the spirit.

5 [a]A fool despises his father's instruction,
[b]But he who [1]receives correction is prudent.

6 *In* the house of the righteous
*there is* much treasure,
But in the revenue of the wicked is trouble.

7 The lips of the wise [1]disperse knowledge,
But the heart of the fool *does* not *do* so.

8 [a]The sacrifice of the wicked
*is* an abomination to the LORD,
But the prayer of the upright *is* His delight.
9 The way of the wicked
*is* an abomination to the LORD,
But He loves him who [a]follows righteousness.

10 [a]Harsh discipline *is* for him who forsakes the way,
*And* [b]he who hates correction will die.

11 [a]Hell[1] and [2]Destruction *are* before the LORD;
So how much more [b]the hearts of the sons of men.

12 [a]A scoffer does not love one who corrects him,
Nor will he go to the wise.

13 [a]A merry heart
makes a cheerful [1]countenance,
But [b]by sorrow of the heart
the spirit is broken.

14 The heart of him who has understanding
seeks knowledge,
But the mouth of fools feeds on foolishness.

15 All the days of the afflicted *are* evil,
[a]But he who is of a merry heart *has* a continual feast.

16 [a]Better *is* a little with the fear of the LORD,
Than great treasure with trouble.
17 [a]Better *is* a dinner of [1]herbs where love is,
Than a fatted calf with hatred.

18 [a]A wrathful man stirs up strife,
But *he who is* slow to anger allays contention.

19 [a]The way of the lazy *man*
*is* like a hedge of thorns,
But the way of the upright *is* a highway.

20 [a]A wise son makes a father glad,
But a foolish man despises his mother.

21 [a]Folly *is* joy *to him who is* destitute of [1]discernment,
[b]But a man of understanding walks uprightly.

22 [a]Without counsel, plans go awry,
But in the multitude of counselors
they are established.

23 A man has joy by the answer of his mouth,
And [a]a word *spoken* [1]in due season,
how good *it is!*

24 [a]The way of life *winds* upward for the wise,
That he may [b]turn away from [1]hell below.

25 [a]The LORD will destroy the house of the proud,
But [b]He will establish the boundary of the widow.

26 [a]The thoughts of the wicked
*are* an abomination to the LORD,
[b]But *the words* of the pure *are* pleasant.

27 [a]He who is greedy for gain troubles his own house,
But he who hates bribes will live.

28 The heart of the righteous
[a]studies how to answer,
But the mouth of the wicked pours forth evil.

29 [a]The LORD *is* far from the wicked,
But [b]He hears the prayer of the righteous.

30 The light of the eyes rejoices the heart,
*And* a good report makes the bones [1]healthy.

31 The ear that hears the rebukes of life
Will abide among the wise.
32 He who disdains instruction
despises his own soul,
But he who heeds rebuke gets understanding.

33 [a]The fear of the LORD *is* the instruction of wisdom,
And [b]before honor *is* humility.

### *Wisdom Is Better than Gold*

16 The [a]preparations[1] of the heart *belong* to man,
[b]But the answer of the tongue *is* from the LORD.

2 All the ways of a man *are* pure in his own [a]eyes,
But the LORD weighs the spirits.

3 [a]Commit[1] your works to the LORD,
And your thoughts will be established.

4 The [a]LORD has made all for Himself,
[b]Yes, even the wicked for the day of [1]doom.

5 [a]Everyone proud in heart *is* an abomination to the LORD;
*Though they join* [1]forces,
none will go unpunished.

6 [a]In mercy and truth
Atonement is provided for iniquity;
And [b]by the fear of the LORD
*one* departs from evil.

7 When a man's ways please the LORD,
He makes even his enemies to be at peace with him.

8 [a]Better *is* a little with righteousness,
Than vast revenues without justice.

9 [a]A man's heart plans his way,
[b]But the LORD directs his steps.

**10** Divination *is* on the lips of the king;
His mouth must not transgress in judgment.
11 [a]Honest weights and scales *are* the LORD's;
All the weights in the bag *are* His [1]work.
12 *It is* an abomination for kings to commit wickedness,
For [a]a throne is established by righteousness.
13 [a]Righteous lips *are* the delight of kings,
And they love him who speaks *what is* right.
14 As messengers of death *is* the king's wrath,
But a wise man will [a]appease it.
15 In the light of the king's face *is* life,
And his favor *is* like a [a]cloud of the latter rain.

16 [a]How much better to get wisdom than gold!
And to get understanding is to be chosen
rather than silver.

17 The highway of the upright *is* to depart from evil;
He who keeps his way preserves his soul.

18 Pride *goes* before destruction,
And a haughty spirit before [1]a fall.
19 Better *to be* of a humble spirit
with the lowly,
Than to divide the [1]spoil with the proud.

20 He who heeds the word wisely will find good,
And whoever [a]trusts in the LORD, happy *is* he.

21 The wise in heart will be called prudent,
And sweetness of the lips increases learning.

22 Understanding *is* a wellspring of life
to him who has it.
But the correction of fools *is* folly.

**11** [a]Job 26:6; Ps. 139:8 [b]1 Sam. 16:7; 2 Chr. 6:30; Ps. 44:21; Acts 1:24 [1]Or *Sheol* [2]Heb. *Abaddon*
**12** [a]Prov. 13:1; Amos 5:10; 2 Tim. 4:3
**13** [a]Prov. 12:25 [b]Prov. 17:22 [1]*face*
**15** [a]Prov. 17:22
**16** [a]Ps. 37:16; Prov. 16:8; Eccl. 4:6; 1 Tim. 6:6
**17** [a]Prov. 17:1 [1]Or *vegetables*
**18** [a]Prov. 26:21
**19** [a]Prov. 22:5
**20** [a]Prov. 10:1
**21** [a]Prov. 10:23 [b]Eph. 5:15 [1]Lit. *heart*
**22** [a]Prov. 11:14
**23** [a]Prov. 25:11; Is. 50:4 [1]Lit. *in its time*
**24** [a]Phil. 3:20; [Col. 3:1, 2] [b]Prov. 14:16 [1]Or *Sheol*
**25** [a]Prov. 12:7; Is. 2:11 [b]Ps. 68:5, 6
**26** [a]Prov. 6:16, 18 [b]Ps. 37:30
**27** [a]Is. 5:8; [Jer. 17:11]
**28** [a]1 Pet. 3:15
**29** [a]Ps. 10:1; 34:16 [b]Ps. 145:18; [James 5:16]
**30** [1]Lit. *fat*
**33** [a]Prov. 1:7 [b]Prov. 18:12

CHAPTER 16
**1** [a]Jer. 10:23 [b]Matt. 10:19 [1]*plans*
**2** [a]Prov. 21:2
**3** [a]Ps. 37:5; Prov. 3:6; [1 Pet. 5:7] [1]Lit. *Roll*
**4** [a]Is. 43:7; Rom. 11:36 [b]Job 21:30; [Rom. 9:22] [1]Lit. *evil*
**5** [a]Prov. 6:17; 8:13 [1]Lit. *hand to hand*
**6** [a]Dan. 4:27; Luke 11:41 [b]Prov. 8:13; 14:16
**8** [a]Ps. 37:16; Prov. 15:16
**9** [a]Prov. 19:21 [b]Ps. 37:23; Prov. 20:24; Jer. 10:23
**11** [a]Lev. 19:36 [1]*concern*
**12** [a]Prov. 25:5
**13** [a]Prov. 14:35
**14** [a]Prov. 25:15
**15** [a]Zech. 10:1
**16** [a]Prov. 8:10, 11, 19
**18** [1]*stumbling*
**19** [1]*plunder*
**20** [a]Ps. 34:8; Jer. 17:7

23 The heart of the wise teaches his mouth,
And adds learning to his lips.

24 Pleasant words *are like* a honeycomb,
Sweetness to the soul
and health to the bones.

25 There is a way *that seems* right to a man,
But its end *is* the way of [a]death.

26 The person who labors, labors for himself,
For his *hungry* mouth drives [a]him *on.*

27 [1]An ungodly man digs up evil,
And *it is* on his lips like a burning [a]fire.
28 A perverse man sows strife,
And [a]a whisperer separates the best of friends.
29 A violent man entices his neighbor,
And leads him in a way *that is* not good.
30 He winks his eye to devise perverse things;
He [1]purses his lips *and* brings about evil.

31 [a]The silver-haired head *is* a crown of glory,
*If* it is found in the way of righteousness.

32 [a]*He who is* slow to anger *is* better than the mighty,
And he who rules his spirit than he who takes a city.

33 The lot is cast into the lap,
But its every decision *is* from the LORD.

### *The LORD Tests Hearts*

17 Better *is* [a]a dry morsel with quietness,
Than a house full of [1]feasting *with* strife.

2 A wise servant will rule over [a]a son who causes shame,
And will share an inheritance among the brothers.

3 The refining pot *is* for silver
and the furnace for gold,
[a]But the LORD tests the hearts.

4 An evildoer gives heed to false lips;
A liar listens eagerly to a [1]spiteful tongue.

5 [a]He who mocks the poor
reproaches his Maker;
[b]He who is glad at calamity
will not go unpunished.

6 [a]Children's children *are* the crown of old men,
And the glory of children *is* their father.

7 Excellent speech is not becoming to a fool,
Much less lying lips to a prince.

8 A present *is* a precious stone in the eyes of its possessor;
Wherever he turns, he prospers.

9 [a]He who covers a transgression seeks love,
But [b]he who repeats a matter
separates friends.

10 [a]Rebuke is more effective for a wise *man*
Than a hundred blows on a fool.

11 An evil *man* seeks only rebellion;
Therefore a cruel messenger will be sent against him.

12 Let a man meet [a]a bear robbed of her cubs,
Rather than a fool in his folly.

13 Whoever [a]rewards evil for good,
Evil will not depart from his house.

14 The beginning of strife *is like* releasing water;
Therefore [a]stop contention before a quarrel starts.

15 [a]He who justifies the wicked,
and he who condemns the just,
Both of them alike *are* an abomination to the LORD.

16 Why *is there* in the hand of a fool the purchase price of wisdom,
Since *he has* no heart *for it?*

17 [a]A friend loves at all times,
And a brother is born for adversity.

18 [a]A man devoid of [1]understanding [2]shakes hands in a pledge,
*And* becomes [3]surety for his friend.

19 He who loves transgression loves strife,
And [a]he who exalts his gate seeks destruction.

20 He who has a [1]deceitful heart finds no good,
And he who has [a]a perverse tongue
falls into evil.

21 He who begets a scoffer *does so* to his sorrow,
And the father of a fool has no joy.

22 A [a]merry heart [1]does good, *like* medicine,
But a broken spirit dries the bones.

23 A wicked *man* accepts a bribe [1]behind the back
To pervert the ways of justice.

24 [a]Wisdom *is* in the sight of him who has understanding,
But the eyes of a fool *are* on the ends of the earth.

25 A [a]foolish son *is* a grief to his father,
And bitterness to her who bore him.

26 Also, to punish the righteous *is* not good,
*Nor* to strike princes for *their* uprightness.

27 [a]He who has knowledge spares his words,
*And* a man of understanding
is of a calm spirit.
28 [a]Even a fool is counted wise
when he holds his peace;
*When* he shuts his lips,
*he is considered* perceptive.

### *The Name of the LORD Is a Strong Tower*

18 A man who isolates himself seeks his own desire;
He rages against all [1]wise judgment.

2 A fool has no delight in understanding,
But in expressing his [a]own heart.

3 When the wicked comes,
contempt comes also;
And with dishonor *comes* reproach.

4 [a]The words of a man's mouth
*are* deep waters;
[b]The wellspring of wisdom *is* a flowing brook.

5 *It is* not good to show partiality
to the wicked,
*Or* to overthrow the righteous in [a]judgment.

---

**25** [a]Prov. 14:12 **26** [a][Eccl. 6:7; John 6:35] **27** [a][James 3:6] [1]Lit. *A man of Belial* **28** [a]Prov. 17:9 **30** [1]Lit. *compresses* **31** [a]Prov. 20:29 **32** [a]Prov. 14:29; 19:11

CHAPTER 17

**1** [a]Prov. 15:17 [1]Or *sacrificial meals* **2** [a]Prov. 10:5 **3** [a]1 Chr. 29:17; Ps. 26:2; Prov. 15:11; Jer. 17:10; [Mal. 3:3] **4** [1]Lit. *destructive* **5** [a]Prov. 14:31 [b]Job 31:29; Prov. 24:17; Obad. 12; 1 Cor. 13:6 **6** [a][Ps. 127:3; 128:3] **9** [a][Prov. 10:12; 1 Cor. 13:5–7; James 5:20] [b]Prov. 16:28 **10** [a]Prov. 10:17; [Mic. 7:9] **12** [a]2 Sam. 17:8; Hos. 13:8 **13** [a]Ps. 109:4, 5; Jer. 18:20; Rom. 12:17; 1 Thess. 5:15; [1 Pet. 3:9] **14** [a][Prov. 20:3; 1 Thess. 4:11] **15** [a]Ex. 23:7; Prov. 24:24; Is. 5:23 **17** [a]Ruth 1:16; Prov. 18:24 **18** [a]Prov. 6:1 [1]Lit. *heart* [2]Lit. *strikes the hands* [3]*guaranty* or *collateral* **19** [a]Prov. 16:18 **20** [a]James 3:8 [1]*crooked* **22** [a]Prov. 12:25; 15:13, 15 [1]Or *makes medicine even better* **23** [1]Under cover, lit. *from the bosom* **24** [a]Eccl. 2:14 **25** [a]Prov. 10:1; 15:20; 19:13 **27** [a]Prov. 10:19; James 1:19 **28** [a]Job 13:5

CHAPTER 18

**1** [1]*sound wisdom* **2** [a]Eccl. 10:3 **4** [a]Prov. 10:11 [b][James 3:17] **5** [a]Lev. 19:15; Deut. 1:17; 16:19; Ps. 82:2; Prov. 17:15

6 A fool's lips enter into contention,
And his mouth calls for blows.
7 [a]A fool's mouth *is* his destruction,
And his lips *are* the snare of his [b]soul.
8 [a]The words of a [1]talebearer *are* like [2]tasty trifles,
And they go down into the [3]inmost body.

9 He who is slothful in his work
Is a brother to him who is a great destroyer.

10 The name of the LORD *is* a strong [a]tower;
The righteous run to it and are [1]safe.
11 The rich man's wealth *is* his strong city,
And like a high wall in his own esteem.

12 [a]Before destruction the heart of a man is haughty,
And before honor *is* humility.

13 He who answers a matter before he hears *it,*
It *is* folly and shame to him.

14 The spirit of a man will sustain him in sickness,
But who can bear a broken spirit?

15 The heart of the prudent acquires knowledge,
And the ear of the wise seeks knowledge.

16 [a]A man's gift makes room for him,
And brings him before great men.

17 The first *one* to plead his cause *seems* right,
Until his neighbor comes and examines him.

18 Casting [a]lots causes contentions to cease,
And keeps the mighty apart.

19 A brother offended *is harder to win* than a strong city,
And contentions *are* like the bars of a castle.

20 [a]A man's stomach shall be satisfied from the fruit of his mouth;
*From* the produce of his lips he shall be filled.

21 [a]Death and life *are* in the power of the tongue,
And those who love it will eat its fruit.

22 [a]*He who* finds a wife finds a good *thing,*
And obtains favor from the LORD.

23 The poor *man* uses entreaties,
But the rich answers [a]roughly.

24 A man *who has* friends [1]must himself be friendly,
[a]But there is a friend *who* sticks closer than a brother.

## *The Fear of the LORD Leads to Life*

**19** Better [a]*is* the poor
who walks in his integrity
Than *one who is* perverse in his lips, and is a fool.

2 Also it is not good *for* a soul *to be* without knowledge,
And he sins who hastens with *his* feet.

3 The foolishness of a man twists his way,
And his heart frets against the LORD.

4 [a]Wealth makes many friends,
But the poor is separated from his friend.

5 A [a]false witness will not go unpunished,
And *he who* speaks lies will not escape.

6 Many entreat the favor of the nobility,
And every man *is* a friend to one who gives gifts.
7 [a]All the brothers of the poor hate him;
How much more do his friends go [b]far from him!
He may pursue *them with* words,
*yet* they [1]abandon *him.*

8 He who gets [1]wisdom loves his own soul;
He who keeps understanding [a]will find good.

9 A false witness will not go unpunished,
And *he who* speaks lies shall perish.

10 Luxury is not fitting for a fool,
Much less [a]for a servant to rule over princes.

11 [a]The discretion of a man makes him slow to anger,
[b]And his glory *is* to overlook a transgression.

12 [a]The king's wrath *is* like the roaring of a lion,
But his favor *is* [b]like dew on the grass.

13 [a]A foolish son *is* the ruin of his father,
[b]And the contentions of a wife *are* a continual [1]dripping.

14 [a]Houses and riches *are* an inheritance from fathers,
But [b]a prudent wife *is* from the LORD.

15 [a]Laziness casts *one* into a deep sleep,
And an idle person will [b]suffer hunger.

16 [a]He who keeps the commandment keeps his soul,
*But* he who [1]is careless of his ways will die.

17 [a]He who has pity on the poor lends to the LORD,
And He will pay back what he has given.

18 [a]Chasten your son while there is hope,
And do not set your heart [1]on his destruction.

19 *A man of* great wrath will suffer punishment;
For if you rescue *him,*
you will have to do it again.

20 Listen to counsel and receive instruction,
That you may be wise [a]in your latter days.

21 There are many plans in a man's heart,
[a]Nevertheless the LORD's counsel—
that will stand.

22 What is desired in a man is [1]kindness,
And a poor man is better than a liar.

23 [a]The fear of the LORD *leads* to life,
And *he who has it* will abide in satisfaction;
He will not be visited with evil.

24 [a]A lazy *man* buries his hand in the [1]bowl,
And will not so much as bring it to his mouth again.

25 Strike a scoffer,
and the simple [a]will become wary;
[b]Rebuke one who has understanding, *and* he will discern knowledge.

26 He who mistreats *his* father
*and* chases away *his* mother
*Is* [a]a son who causes shame
and brings reproach.

27 Cease listening to instruction, my son,
And you will stray from the words of knowledge.

---

**7** [a]Prov. 10:14 [b]Eccl. 10:12
**8** [a]Prov. 12:18 [1]*gossip* or *slanderer* [2]A Jewish tradition *wounds* [3]Lit. *rooms of the belly*
**10** [a]2 Sam. 22:2, 3, 33 [1]*secure,* lit. *set on high*
**12** [a]Prov. 15:33; 16:18
**16** [a]Gen. 32:20, 21
**18** [a][Prov. 16:33]
**20** [a]Prov. 12:14; 14:14
**21** [a]Matt. 12:37
**22** [a][Prov. 12:4; 19:14]
**23** [a]James 2:3, 6
**24** [a]Prov. 17:17 [1]Or *may come to ruin*

CHAPTER 19
**1** [a]Prov. 28:6
**4** [a]Prov. 14:20
**5** [a]Ex. 23:1
**7** [a]Prov. 14:20 [b]Ps. 38:11 [1]Lit. *are not*
**8** [a]Prov. 16:20 [1]Lit. *heart*
**10** [a]Prov. 30:21, 22
**11** [a]James 1:19 [b]Eph. 4:32
**12** [a]Prov. 16:14 [b]Hos. 14:5
**13** [a]Prov. 10:1 [b]Prov. 21:9, 19 [1]Irritation
**14** [a]2 Cor. 12:14 [b]Prov. 18:22
**15** [a]Prov. 6:9 [b]Prov. 10:4
**16** [a]Luke 10:28; 11:28 [1]Is reckless, lit. *despises*
**17** [a][2 Cor. 9:6–8]
**18** [a]Prov. 13:24 [1]Lit. *to put him to death,* a Jewish tradition *on his crying*
**20** [a]Ps. 37:37
**21** [a]Heb. 6:17
**22** [1]Lit. *lovingkindness*
**23** [a][1 Tim. 4:8]
**24** [a]Prov. 15:19 [1]LXX, Syr. *bosom;* Tg., Vg. *armpit*
**25** [a]Deut. 13:11 [b]Prov. 9:8
**26** [a]Prov. 17:2

28 A [1]disreputable witness scorns justice,
And [a]the mouth of the wicked devours
iniquity.

29 Judgments are prepared for scoffers,
[a]And beatings for the backs of fools.

## *Wine Is a Mocker*

**20** Wine [a]*is* a mocker,
Strong drink *is* a brawler,
And whoever is led astray by it is not wise.

2 The [1]wrath of a king *is* like the roaring of a
lion;
*Whoever* provokes him to anger sins *against*
his own life.

3 [a]*It is* honorable for a man to stop striving,
Since any fool can start a quarrel.

4 [a]The lazy *man* will not plow because of
winter;
[b]He will beg during harvest and *have* nothing.

5 Counsel in the heart of man *is like* deep
water,
But a man of understanding will draw it out.

6 Most men will proclaim each his own
[1]goodness,
But who can find a faithful man?

7 [a]The righteous *man* walks in his integrity;
[b]His children *are* blessed after him.

8 A king who sits on the throne of judgment
Scatters all evil with his eyes.

9 [a]Who can say, "I have made my heart clean,
I am pure from my sin"?

10 [a]Diverse weights *and* diverse measures,
They *are* both alike,
an abomination to the LORD.

11 Even a child is [a]known by his deeds,
Whether what he does *is* pure and right.

12 [a]The hearing ear and the seeing eye,
The LORD has made them both.

13 [a]Do not love sleep, lest you come to poverty;
Open your eyes, *and* you will be satisfied
with bread.

14 "*It is* [1]good for nothing," cries the buyer;
But when he has gone his way,
then he boasts.

15 There is gold and a multitude of rubies,
But [a]the lips of knowledge *are* a precious
jewel.

16 [a]Take the garment of one who is surety *for* a
stranger,
And hold it as a pledge *when it* is for a
seductress.

17 [a]Bread gained by deceit *is* sweet to a man,
But afterward his mouth will be filled with
gravel.

18 [a]Plans are established by counsel;
[b]By wise counsel wage war.

19 [a]He who goes about *as* a talebearer reveals
secrets;
Therefore do not associate with one [b]who
flatters with his lips.

20 [a]Whoever curses his father or his mother,
[b]His lamp will be put out in deep darkness.

21 [a]An inheritance gained hastily at the
beginning
[b]Will not be blessed at the end.

22 [a]Do not say, "I will [1]recompense evil";
[b]Wait for the LORD, and He will save you.

23 Diverse weights *are* an abomination
to the LORD,
And dishonest scales *are* not good.

24 A man's steps *are* of the LORD;
How then can a man understand his own
way?

25 *It is* a snare for a man to devote rashly
*something as* holy,
And afterward to reconsider *his* vows.

26 [a]A wise king sifts out the wicked,
And brings the threshing wheel over them.

27 [a]The spirit of a man *is* the lamp of the LORD,
Searching all the [1]inner depths of his heart.

28 [a]Mercy and truth preserve the king,
And by [1]lovingkindness he upholds his
throne.

29 The glory of young men *is* their strength,
And [a]the splendor of old men
*is* their gray head.

30 Blows that hurt cleanse away evil,
As *do* stripes the [1]inner depths of the heart.

## *The LORD Considers the Heart*

**21** The king's heart *is* in the hand of the
LORD,
*Like* the [1]rivers of water;
He turns it wherever He wishes.

2 [a]Every way of a man *is* right in his own eyes,
[b]But the LORD weighs the hearts.

3 [a]To do righteousness and justice
*Is* more acceptable to the LORD than
sacrifice.

4 [a]A haughty look, a proud heart,
*And* the [1]plowing of the wicked *are* sin.

5 [a]The plans of the diligent *lead* surely to
plenty,
But *those of* everyone *who is* hasty, surely to
poverty.

6 [a]Getting treasures by a lying tongue
[1]*Is* the fleeting fantasy of those who seek
death.

7 The violence of the wicked will [1]destroy
them,
Because they refuse to do justice.

8 The way of [1]a guilty man *is* perverse;
But *as for* the pure, his work *is* right.

9 Better to dwell in a corner of a housetop,
Than in a house shared with [a]a contentious
woman.

10 [a]The soul of the wicked desires evil;
His neighbor finds no favor in his eyes.

11 When the scoffer is punished,
the simple is made wise;
But when the [a]wise is instructed,
he receives knowledge.

**28** [a]Job 15:16 [1]Lit. *witness of Belial, worthless witness*
**29** [a]Prov. 26:3

CHAPTER 20

**1** [a]Gen. 9:21
**2** [1]Lit. *fear* or *terror,* produced by the king's wrath
**3** [a]Prov. 17:14
**4** [a]Prov. 10:4 [b]Prov. 19:15
**6** [1]Lit. *mercy*
**7** [a]2 Cor. 1:12 [b]Ps. 37:26
**9** [a][1 Kin. 8:46]
**10** [a]Deut. 25:13
**11** [a]Matt. 7:16
**12** [a]Ex. 4:11
**13** [a]Rom. 12:11
**14** [1]Lit. *evil, evil*
**15** [a][Prov. 3:13–15]
**16** [a]Prov. 22:26
**17** [a]Prov. 9:17
**18** [a]Prov. 24:6 [b]Luke 14:31
**19** [a]Prov. 11:13 [b]Rom. 16:18
**20** [a]Matt. 15:4 [b]Job 18:5, 6
**21** [a]Prov. 28:20 [b]Hab. 2:6
**22** [a][Rom. 12:17–19] [b]2 Sam. 16:12 [1]*repay*
**26** [a]Ps. 101:8
**27** [a]1 Cor. 2:11 [1]Lit. *rooms of the belly*
**28** [a]Prov. 21:21 [1]*mercy*
**29** [a]Prov. 16:31
**30** [1]Lit. *rooms of the belly*

CHAPTER 21

**1** [1]*channels*
**2** [a]Prov. 16:2 [b]Prov. 24:12
**3** [a]1 Sam. 15:22
**4** [a]Prov. 6:17 [1]Or *lamp*
**5** [a]Prov. 10:4
**6** [a]2 Pet. 2:3 [1]LXX *Pursue vanity on the snares of death;* Vg. *Is vain and foolish, and shall stumble on the snares of death;* Tg. *They shall be destroyed, and they shall fall who seek death*
**7** [1]Lit. *drag them away*
**8** [1]Or *The way of a man is perverse and strange;*
**9** [a]Prov. 19:13
**10** [a]James 4:5
**11** [a]Prov. 19:25

12 The righteous *God* wisely considers the
house of the wicked,
Overthrowing the wicked for *their*
wickedness.

13 [a]Whoever shuts his ears to the cry of the poor
Will also cry himself and not be heard.

14 A gift in secret pacifies anger,
And a bribe [1]behind the back, strong wrath.

15 *It is* a joy for the just to do justice,
But destruction *will come* to the workers of
iniquity.

16 A man who wanders from the way of
understanding
Will rest in the assembly of the [a]dead.

17 He who loves pleasure *will be* a poor man;
He who loves wine and oil will not be rich.

18 The wicked *shall be* a ransom for the
righteous,
And the unfaithful for the upright.

19 Better to dwell [1]in the wilderness,
Than with a contentious and angry woman.

20 [a]*There is* desirable treasure,
And oil in the dwelling of the wise,
But a foolish man squanders it.

21 [a]He who follows righteousness and mercy
Finds life, righteousness and honor.

22 A [a]wise *man* [1]scales the city of the mighty,
And brings down the trusted stronghold.

23 [a]Whoever guards his mouth and tongue
Keeps his soul from troubles.

24 A proud *and* haughty *man*—
"Scoffer" *is* his name;
He acts with arrogant pride.

25 The [a]desire of the lazy *man* kills him,
For his hands refuse to labor.
26 He covets greedily all day long,
But the righteous [a]gives and does not spare.

27 [a]The sacrifice of the wicked *is* an
abomination;
How much more *when* he brings it with
wicked intent!

28 A false witness shall perish,
But the man who hears *him* will speak
endlessly.

29 A wicked man hardens his face,
But *as for* the upright,
he [1]establishes his way.

30 [a]*There is* no wisdom or understanding
Or counsel against the LORD.

31 The horse *is* prepared for the day of battle,
But [a]deliverance *is* of the LORD.

## *The Value of a Good Name*

**22** A [a]*good* name is to be chosen rather than
great riches,
Loving favor rather than silver and gold.

2 The [a]rich and the poor have this in common,
The [b]LORD *is* the maker of them all.

3 A prudent *man* foresees evil
and hides himself,
But the simple pass on and are [a]punished.

4 By humility *and* the fear of the LORD
*Are* riches and honor and life.

5 Thorns *and* snares *are* in the way of the
perverse;
He who guards his soul will be far from
them.

6 [a]Train up a child in the way he should go,
[1]And when he is old
he will not depart from it.

7 The [a]rich rules over the poor,
And the borrower *is* servant to the lender.

8 He who sows iniquity will reap [a]sorrow,[1]
And the rod of his anger will fail.

9 [a]He who has a [1]generous eye will be [b]blessed,
For he gives of his bread to the poor.

10 [a]Cast out the scoffer,
and contention will leave;
Yes, strife and reproach will cease.

11 [a]He who loves purity of heart
*And has* grace on his lips,
The king *will be* his friend.

12 The eyes of the LORD preserve knowledge,
But He overthrows the words of the faithless.

13 [a]The lazy *man* says, "*There is* a lion outside!
I shall be slain in the streets!"

14 [a]The mouth of an immoral woman *is* a deep
pit;
[b]He who is abhorred by the LORD will fall
there.

15 Foolishness *is* bound up in the heart of a
child;
[a]The rod of correction will drive it far from
him.

16 He who oppresses the poor to increase his
*riches,*
*And* he who gives to the rich,
*will* surely *come* to poverty.

**17** Incline your ear
and hear the words of the wise,
And apply your heart to my knowledge;
18 For *it is* a pleasant thing if you keep them
within you;
Let them all be fixed upon your lips,
19 So that your trust may be in the LORD;
I have instructed you today, even you.
20 Have I not written to you excellent things
Of counsels and knowledge,
21 [a]That I may make you know
the certainty of the words of truth,
[b]That you may answer words of truth
To those who [1]send to you?

**22** Do not rob the [a]poor because he *is* poor,
Nor oppress the afflicted at the gate;
23 [a]For the LORD will plead their cause,
And plunder the soul of those who plunder
them.

24 Make no friendship with an angry man,
And with a [a]furious man do not go,
25 Lest you learn his ways
And set a snare for your soul.

26 [a]Do not be one of those
who [1]shakes hands in a pledge,
One of those who is [2]surety for debts;

**13** [a][Matt. 7:2; 18:30–34]; James 2:13; 1 John 3:17
**14** [1]Under cover, lit. *in the bosom*
**16** [a]Ps. 49:14
**19** [1]Lit. *in the land of the desert*
**20** [a]Ps. 112:3; Prov. 8:21
**21** [a]Prov. 15:9; Matt. 5:6; [Rom. 2:7]; 1 Cor. 15:58
**22** [a]2 Sam. 5:6–9; Prov. 24:5; Eccl. 7:19; 9:15, 16 [1]Climbs over the walls of
**23** [a]Prov. 12:13; 13:3; 18:21; [James 3:2]
**25** [a]Prov. 13:4
**26** [a][Prov. 22:9; Eph. 4:28]
**27** [a]Prov. 15:8; Is. 66:3; Jer. 6:20; Amos 5:22
**29** [1]Qr., LXX *understands*
**30** [a]Is. 8:9, 10; [Jer. 9:23, 24]; Acts 5:39; 1 Cor. 3:19, 20
**31** [a]Ps. 3:8; Jer. 3:23; [1 Cor. 15:57]

CHAPTER 22
**1** [a][Prov. 10:7]; Eccl. 7:1
**2** [a]Prov. 29:13 [b]Job 31:15; [Prov. 14:31]
**3** [a]Prov. 27:12; Is. 26:20
**6** [a]Eph. 6:4; 2 Tim. 3:15 [1]*Even*
**7** [a]Prov. 18:23; James 2:6
**8** [a]Job 4:8 [1]*trouble*
**9** [a]2 Cor. 9:6 [b][Prov. 19:17] [1]Lit. *good*
**10** [a]Ps. 101:5
**11** [a]Ps. 101:6
**13** [a]Prov. 26:13
**14** [a]Prov. 2:16; 5:3; 7:5 [b]Eccl. 7:26
**15** [a]Prov. 13:24; 23:13, 14
**21** [a]Luke 1:3, 4 [b]Prov. 25:13; 1 Pet. 3:15 [1]Or *send you*
**22** [a]Ex. 23:6; Job 31:16–21; Zech. 7:10
**23** [a]1 Sam. 24:12; Ps. 12:5; 140:12
**24** [a]Prov. 29:22
**26** [a]Prov. 11:15 [1]Lit. *strikes* [2]*guaranty*

27 If you have nothing *with which* to pay,
Why should he take away your bed from under you?

28 [a]Do not remove the ancient [1]landmark
Which your fathers have set.

29 Do you see a man *who* [1]excels in his work?
He will stand before kings;
He will not stand before [2]unknown *men.*

## *Listen to Your Father*

**23** When you sit down to eat with a ruler,
Consider carefully what *is* before you;
2 And put a knife to your throat
If you *are* a man given to appetite.
3 Do not desire his delicacies,
For they *are* deceptive food.

4 [a]Do not overwork to be rich;
[b]Because of your own understanding, cease!
5 [1]Will you set your eyes on that which is not?
For *riches* certainly make themselves wings;
They fly away like an eagle *toward* heaven.

6 Do not eat the bread of [a]a[1] miser,
Nor desire his delicacies;
7 For as he thinks in his heart, so *is* he.
"Eat and drink!" [a]he says to you,
But his heart is not with you.
8 The morsel you have eaten,
you will vomit up,
And waste your pleasant words.

9 [a]Do not speak in the hearing of a fool,
For he will despise the wisdom of your words.

10 Do not remove the ancient [1]landmark,
Nor enter the fields of the fatherless;
11 [a]For their Redeemer *is* mighty;
He will plead their cause against you.

12 Apply your heart to instruction,
And your ears to words of knowledge.

13 [a]Do not withhold correction from a child,
For *if* you beat him with a rod,
he will not die.
14 You shall beat him with a rod,
And deliver his soul from [1]hell.

15 My son, if your heart is wise,
My heart will rejoice—indeed, I myself;
16 Yes, my [1]inmost being will rejoice
When your lips speak right things.

17 [a]Do not let your heart envy sinners,
But [b]*be zealous* for the fear of the LORD
all the day;
18 [a]For surely there is a [1]hereafter,
And your hope will not be cut off.

19 Hear, my son, and be wise;
And guide your heart in the way.
20 [a]Do not mix with winebibbers,
*Or* with gluttonous eaters of meat;
21 For the drunkard and the glutton
will come to poverty,
And drowsiness will clothe *a man* with rags.

22 [a]Listen to your father who begot you,
And do not despise your mother when she is old.

23 [a]Buy the truth, and do not sell *it,*
*Also* wisdom and instruction
and understanding.

24 [a]The father of the righteous
will greatly rejoice,
And he who begets a wise *child*
will delight in him.
25 Let your father and your mother be glad,
And let her who bore you rejoice.

26 My son, give me your heart,
And let your eyes observe my ways.
27 [a]For a harlot *is* a deep pit,
And a seductress *is* a narrow well.
28 [a]She also lies in wait as *for* a victim,
And increases the unfaithful among men.

**29** [a]Who has woe?
Who has sorrow?
Who has contentions?
Who has complaints?
Who has wounds without cause?
Who [b]has redness of eyes?
30 [a]Those who linger long at the wine,
Those who go in search of [b]mixed wine.
31 Do not look on the wine when it is red,
When it sparkles in the cup,
*When* it [1]swirls around smoothly;
32 At the last it bites like a serpent,
And stings like a viper.
33 Your eyes will see strange things,
And your heart will utter perverse things.
34 Yes, you will be like one who lies down in the [1]midst of the sea,
Or like one who lies at the top of the mast,
*saying:*
35 "They[a] have struck me, *but* I was not hurt;
They have beaten me, but I did not feel *it.*
When shall [b]I awake,
that I may seek another *drink?*"

## *Do Not Envy Evil Men*

**24** Do not be [a]envious of evil men,
Nor desire to be with them;
2 For their heart devises violence,
And their lips talk of troublemaking.

3 Through wisdom a house is built,
And by understanding it is established;
4 By knowledge the rooms are filled
With all precious and pleasant riches.

5 [a]A wise man *is* strong,
Yes, a man of knowledge increases strength;
6 [a]For by wise counsel
you will wage your own war,
And in a multitude of counselors
*there is* safety.

7 [a]Wisdom *is* too lofty for a fool;
He does not open his mouth in the gate.

8 He who [a]plots to do evil
Will be called a [1]schemer.
9 The devising of foolishness *is* sin,
And the scoffer *is* an abomination to men.

10 *If* you [a]faint in the day of adversity,
Your strength *is* small.

11 [a]Deliver *those who* are drawn toward death,
And hold back *those* stumbling to the slaughter.
12 If you say, "Surely we did not know this,"
Does not [a]He who weighs the hearts consider *it?*
He who keeps your soul,
does He *not* know *it?*

---

**28** [a]Deut. 19:14; 27:17; Job 24:2; Prov. 23:10 [1]*boundary*
**29** [1]*is prompt in his business* [2]*obscure*

CHAPTER 23
**4** [a][Prov. 28:20; Matt. 6:19; 1 Tim. 6:9, 10; Heb. 13:5] [b]Rom. 12:16
**5** [1]Lit. *Will you cause your eyes to fly upon it and it is not?*
**6** [a]Deut. 15:9; Prov. 28:22 [1]Lit. *one who has an evil eye*
**7** [a]Prov. 12:2
**9** [a]Prov. 9:8; Matt. 7:6
**10** [1]*boundary*
**11** [a]Prov. 22:23
**13** [a]Prov. 13:24
**14** [1]Or *Sheol*
**16** [1]Lit. *kidneys*
**17** [a]Ps. 37:1; Prov. 24:1, 19 [b]Prov. 28:14
**18** [a][Ps. 37:37] [1]Future, lit. *latter end*
**20** [a]Prov. 20:1; 23:29, 30; Is. 5:22; Matt. 24:49; [Luke 21:34]; Rom. 13:13; [Eph. 5:18]
**22** [a]Prov. 1:8; Eph. 6:1
**23** [a]Prov. 4:7; 18:15; [Matt. 13:44]
**24** [a]Prov. 10:1
**27** [a]Prov. 22:14
**28** [a]Prov. 7:12; Eccl. 7:26
**29** [a]Is. 5:11, 22 [b]Gen. 49:12
**30** [a]1 Sam. 25:36; Prov. 20:1; 21:17; Is. 5:11; 28:7; [Eph. 5:18] [b]Ps. 75:8
**31** [1]*goes around*
**34** [1]Lit. *heart*
**35** [a]Prov. 27:22; Jer. 5:3 [b]Eph. 4:19

CHAPTER 24
**1** [a]Ps. 1:1; 37:1; Prov. 23:17
**5** [a]Prov. 21:22; Eccl. 9:16
**6** [a]Luke 14:31
**7** [a]Ps. 10:5; Prov. 14:6
**8** [a]Prov. 6:14; 14:22; Rom. 1:30 [1]Lit. *master of evil plots*
**10** [a]Deut. 20:8; Job 4:5; Jer. 51:46; Heb. 12:3
**11** [a]Ps. 82:4; Is. 58:6, 7; 1 John 3:16
**12** [a]1 Sam. 16:7; Prov. 21:2

And will He *not* render to *each* man
[b]according to his deeds?

13 My son, [a]eat honey because *it is* good,
And the honeycomb *which is* sweet to your taste;
14 [a]So *shall* the knowledge of wisdom
*be* to your soul;
If you have found *it,* there is a [1]prospect,
And your hope will not be cut off.

15 Do not lie in wait, O wicked *man,* against the dwelling of the righteous;
Do not plunder his resting place;
16 [a]For a righteous *man* may fall seven times
And rise again,
[b]But the wicked shall fall by calamity.

17 [a]Do not rejoice when your enemy falls,
And do not let your heart be glad when he stumbles;
18 Lest the LORD see *it,* and [1]it displease Him,
And He turn away His wrath from him.

19 [a]Do not fret because of evildoers,
Nor be envious of the wicked;
20 For there will be no prospect
for the evil *man;*
The lamp of the wicked will be put out.

21 My son, [a]fear the LORD and the king;
Do not associate with those given to change;
22 For their calamity will rise suddenly,
And who knows the ruin those two can bring?

**23** These *things* also *belong* to the wise:

[a]*It is* not good to [1]show partiality in judgment.
24 [a]He who says to the wicked,
"You *are* righteous,"
Him the people will curse;
Nations will abhor him.
25 But those who rebuke *the wicked*
will have [a]delight,
And a good blessing will come upon them.

26 He who gives a right answer kisses the lips.

27 [a]Prepare your outside work,
Make it fit for yourself in the field;
And afterward build your house.

28 [a]Do not be a witness against your neighbor without cause,
[1]For would you deceive with your lips?
29 [a]Do not say, "I will do to him
just as he has done to me;
I will render to the man
according to his work."

**30** I went by the field of the lazy *man,*
And by the vineyard of the man devoid of understanding;
31 And there it was, [a]all overgrown with thorns;
Its surface was covered with nettles;
Its stone wall was broken down.
32 When I saw *it,* I considered *it* well;
I looked on *it and* received instruction:
33 [a]A little sleep, a little slumber,
A little folding of the hands to rest;
34 [a]So shall your poverty come *like* [1]a prowler,
And your need like [2]an armed man.

## *Rule Your Spirit*

**25** These[a] also *are* proverbs of Solomon which the men of Hezekiah king of Judah copied:

2 [a]*It is* the glory of God to conceal a matter,
But the glory of kings
*is* to search out a matter.

3 *As* the heavens for height
and the earth for depth,
So the heart of kings *is* unsearchable.

4 [a]Take away the dross from silver,
And it will go to the silversmith *for* jewelry.
5 Take away the wicked from before the king,
And his throne will be established in
[a]righteousness.

6 Do not exalt yourself in the presence of the king,
And do not stand in the place of the great;
7 [a]For *it is* better that he say to you,
"Come up here,"
Than that you should be put lower in the presence of the prince,
Whom your eyes have seen.

8 [a]Do not go hastily to [1]court;
For what will you do in the end,
When your neighbor has put you to shame?
9 [a]Debate your case with your neighbor,
And do not disclose the secret to another;
10 Lest he who hears *it* expose your shame,
And [1]your reputation be ruined.

11 A word fitly [a]spoken *is like* apples of gold
In settings of silver.
12 *Like* an earring of gold
and an ornament of fine gold
*Is* a wise rebuker to an obedient ear.

13 [a]Like the cold of snow in time of harvest
*Is* a faithful messenger to those who send him,
For he refreshes the soul of his masters.

14 [a]Whoever falsely boasts of giving
*Is like* [b]clouds and wind without rain.

15 [a]By long forbearance a ruler is persuaded,
And a gentle tongue breaks a bone.

16 Have you found honey?
Eat only as much as you need,
Lest you be filled with it and vomit.

17 Seldom set foot in your neighbor's house,
Lest he become weary of you and hate you.

18 [a]A man who bears false witness against his neighbor
*Is like* a club, a sword, and a sharp arrow.

19 Confidence in an unfaithful *man* in time of trouble
*Is like* a bad tooth and a foot out of joint.

20 *Like* one who takes away a garment
in cold weather,
*And like* vinegar on soda,
*Is* one who [a]sings songs to a heavy heart.

21 [a]If your enemy is hungry,
give him bread to eat;
And if he is thirsty, give him water to drink;
22 For *so* you will heap coals of fire on his head,
[a]And the LORD will reward you.

23 The north wind brings forth rain,
And [a]a backbiting tongue an angry countenance.

**12** [b]Job 34:11; Ps. 62:12; Rev. 2:23; 22:12
**13** [a]Ps. 19:10; 119:103; Prov. 25:16; Song 5:1
**14** [a]Ps. 19:10; 58:11; Prov. 23:18 [1]Lit. *latter end*
**16** [a]Job 5:19; [Ps. 34:19; 37:24; Mic. 7:8] [b]Esth. 7:10; Amos 5:2
**17** [a]Job 31:29; Ps. 35:15, 19; [Prov. 17:5]; Obad. 12
**18** [1]Lit. *it be evil in His eyes*
**19** [a]Ps. 37:1
**21** [a][Rom. 13:7; 1 Pet. 2:17]
**23** [a]Lev. 19:15; Deut. 1:17; 16:19; [John 7:24] [1]Lit. *recognize faces*
**24** [a]Prov. 17:15; Is. 5:23
**25** [a]Prov. 28:23
**27** [a]1 Kin. 5:17; Prov. 27:23–27
**28** [a]Lev. 6:2, 3; 19:11; Eph. 4:25 [1]LXX, Vg. *Do not deceive*
**29** [a][Prov. 20:22; Matt. 5:39–44; Rom. 12:17–19]
**31** [a]Gen. 3:18
**33** [a]Prov. 6:9, 10
**34** [a]Prov. 6:9–11 [1]Lit. *one who walks about* [2]Lit. *a man with a shield*

CHAPTER 25
**1** [a]1 Kin. 4:32
**2** [a]Deut. 29:29; Rom. 11:33
**4** [a]2 Tim. 2:21
**5** [a]Prov. 16:12; 20:8
**7** [a]Luke 14:7–11
**8** [a]Prov. 17:14; Matt. 5:25 [1]Lit. *contend* or *bring a lawsuit*
**9** [a][Matt. 18:15]
**10** [1]*the evil report concerning you not pass away*
**11** [a]Prov. 15:23; Is. 50:4
**13** [a]Prov. 13:17
**14** [a]Prov. 20:6 [b]Jude 12
**15** [a]Prov. 15:1
**18** [a]Ps. 57:4; Prov. 12:18
**20** [a]Dan. 6:18
**21** [a]Ex. 23:4, 5; 2 Kin. 6:22; 2 Chr. 28:15; Matt. 5:44; Rom. 12:20
**22** [a]2 Sam. 16:12; [Matt. 6:4, 6]
**23** [a]Ps. 101:5

24 [a]*It is* better to dwell in a corner of a housetop,
Than in a house shared with a contentious woman.
25 *As* cold water to a weary soul,
So *is* [a]good news from a far country.
26 A righteous *man* who falters before the wicked
*Is like* a murky spring and a [1]polluted well.
27 *It is* not good to eat much honey;
So [a]to seek one's own glory *is not* glory.
28 [a]Whoever *has* no rule over his own spirit
*Is like* a city broken down, without walls.

## *Honor Is Not Fitting for a Fool*

**26** As snow in summer [a]and rain in harvest,
So honor is not fitting for a fool.
2 Like a flitting sparrow, like a flying swallow,
So [a]a curse without cause shall not alight.
3 [a]A whip for the horse,
A bridle for the donkey,
And a rod for the fool's back.
4 Do not answer a fool according to his folly,
Lest you also be like him.
5 [a]Answer a fool according to his folly,
Lest he be wise in his own eyes.
6 He who sends a message by the hand of a fool
Cuts off *his own* feet *and* drinks violence.
7 *Like* the legs of the lame that hang limp
*Is* a proverb in the mouth of fools.
8 Like one who binds a stone in a sling
*Is* he who gives honor to a fool.
9 *Like* a thorn *that* goes into the hand of a drunkard
*Is* a proverb in the mouth of fools.
10 [1]The great *God* who formed everything
Gives the fool *his* hire
and the transgressor *his* wages.
11 [a]As a dog returns to his own vomit,
[b]So a fool repeats his folly.
12 [a]Do you see a man wise in his own eyes?
*There is* more hope for a fool than for him.
13 The lazy *man* says,
"*There is* a lion in the road!
A fierce lion *is* in the [1]streets!"
14 *As* a door turns on its hinges,
So *does* the lazy *man* on his bed.
15 The [a]lazy *man* buries his hand in the [1]bowl;
It wearies him to bring it back to his mouth.
16 The lazy *man is* wiser in his own eyes
Than seven men who can answer sensibly.
17 He who passes by *and* meddles in a quarrel not his own
*Is like* one who takes a dog by the ears.
18 Like a madman who throws firebrands,
arrows, and death,
19 *Is* the man *who* deceives his neighbor,
And says, [a]"I was only joking!"
20 Where *there is* no wood, the fire goes out;
And where *there is* no [1]talebearer,
strife ceases.
21 [a]*As* charcoal *is* to burning coals,
and wood to fire,
So *is* a contentious man to kindle strife.
22 The words of a [1]talebearer *are* like [2]tasty trifles,
And they go down into the [3]inmost body.
23 Fervent lips with a wicked heart
*Are like* earthenware covered with silver dross.
24 He who hates, disguises *it* with his lips,
And lays up deceit within himself;
25 [a]When [1]he speaks kindly, do not believe him,
For *there are* seven abominations in his heart;
26 *Though his* hatred is covered by deceit,
His wickedness will be revealed before the assembly.
27 [a]Whoever digs a pit will fall into it,
And he who rolls a stone
will have it roll back on him.
28 A lying tongue hates *those who are* crushed by it,
And a flattering mouth works [a]ruin.

## *My Son, Be Wise*

**27** Do[a] not boast about tomorrow,
For you do not know what a day may bring forth.
2 [a]Let another man praise you,
and not your own mouth;
A stranger, and not your own lips.
3 A stone *is* heavy and sand *is* weighty,
But a fool's wrath *is* heavier than both of them.
4 Wrath *is* cruel and anger a torrent,
But [a]who *is* able to stand before jealousy?
5 [a]Open rebuke *is* better
Than love carefully concealed.
6 Faithful *are* the wounds of a friend,
But the kisses of an enemy *are* [a]deceitful.
7 A satisfied soul [1]loathes the honeycomb,
But to a hungry soul every bitter thing *is* sweet.
8 Like a bird that wanders from its nest
*Is* a man who wanders from his place.
9 Ointment and perfume delight the heart,
And the sweetness of a man's friend *gives delight* by [1]hearty counsel.
10 Do not forsake your own friend
or your father's friend,
Nor go to your brother's house in the day of your calamity;
[a]Better *is* a neighbor nearby than a brother far away.
11 My son, be wise, and make my heart glad,
[a]That I may answer him who reproaches me.
12 A prudent *man* foresees evil
*and* hides himself;
The simple pass on *and* are [a]punished.
13 Take the garment of him who is surety for a stranger,
And hold it in pledge *when* he is surety for a seductress.
14 He who blesses his friend with a loud voice,
rising early in the morning,
It will be counted a curse to him.
15 A [a]continual dripping on a very rainy day
And a contentious woman are alike;
16 Whoever [1]restrains her restrains the wind,
And grasps oil with his right hand.

**24** [a]Prov. 19:13
**25** [a]Prov. 15:30
**26** [1]*ruined*
**27** [a]Prov. 27:2; [Luke 14:11]
**28** [a]Prov. 16:32

CHAPTER 26
**1** [a]1 Sam. 12:17
**2** [a]Num. 23:8; Deut. 23:5; 2 Sam. 16:12
**3** [a]Ps. 32:9; Prov. 19:29
**5** [a]Matt. 16:1–4; Rom. 12:16
**10** [1]Heb. difficult in v. 10; ancient and modern translators differ greatly
**11** [a]2 Pet. 2:22 [b]Ex. 8:15
**12** [a]Prov. 29:20; Luke 18:11, 12; [Rev. 3:17]
**13** [1]Or *plazas, squares*
**15** [a]Prov. 19:24 [1]LXX, Syr. *bosom;* Tg., Vg. *armpit*
**19** [a]Eph. 5:4
**20** [1]*gossip* or *slanderer,* lit. *whisperer*
**21** [a]Prov. 15:18
**22** [1]*gossip* or *slanderer* [2]A Jewish tradition *wounds* [3]Lit. *rooms of the belly*
**25** [a]Ps. 28:3; Prov. 26:23; Jer. 9:8 [1]Lit. *his voice is gracious*
**27** [a]Esth. 7:10; Ps. 7:15; Prov. 28:10; Eccl. 10:8
**28** [a]Prov. 29:5

CHAPTER 27
**1** [a]Luke 12:19–21; James 4:13–16
**2** [a]Prov. 25:27; 2 Cor. 10:12, 18; 12:11
**4** [a]Prov. 6:34; 1 John 3:12
**5** [a][Prov. 28:23]; Gal. 2:14
**6** [a]Matt. 26:49
**7** [1]*tramples on*
**9** [1]Lit. *counsel of the soul*
**10** [a]Prov. 17:17; 18:24
**11** [a]Prov. 10:1; 23:15–26
**12** [a]Prov. 22:3
**15** [a]Prov. 19:13
**16** [1]Lit. *hides*

17 *As* iron sharpens iron,
So a man sharpens the countenance of his friend.

18 [a]Whoever [1]keeps the fig tree will eat its fruit;
So he who waits on his master
will be honored.

19 As in water face *reflects* face,
So a man's heart *reveals* the man.

20 [a]Hell[1] and [2]Destruction are never full;
So [b]the eyes of man are never satisfied.

21 [a]The refining pot *is* for silver
and the furnace for gold,
And a man *is valued* by what others say of him.

22 [a]Though you grind a fool in a mortar with a pestle along with crushed grain,
*Yet* his foolishness will not depart from him.

**23** Be diligent to know the state of your [a]flocks,
*And* attend to your herds;
24 For riches *are* not forever,
Nor does a crown *endure* to all generations.
25 [a]*When* the hay is removed,
and the tender grass shows itself,
And the herbs of the mountains are gathered in,
26 The lambs *will provide* your clothing,
And the goats the price of a field;
27 *You shall have* enough goats' milk for your food,
For the food of your household,
And the nourishment of your maidservants.

## *The Righteous Are Bold as a Lion*

**28** The [a]wicked flee when no one pursues,
But the righteous are bold as a lion.

2 Because of the transgression of a land, many *are* its princes;
But by a man of understanding
*and* knowledge
Right will be prolonged.

3 [a]A poor man who oppresses the poor
*Is like* a driving rain [1]which leaves no food.

4 [a]Those who forsake the law praise the wicked,
[b]But such as keep the law contend with them.

5 [a]Evil men do not understand justice,
But [b]those who seek the LORD understand all.

6 Better *is* the poor who walks in his integrity
Than one perverse *in his* ways,
though he *be* rich.

7 Whoever keeps the law *is* a discerning son,
But a companion of gluttons
shames his father.

8 One who increases his possessions by usury
and extortion
Gathers it for him who will pity the poor.

9 One who turns away his ear from hearing the law,
[a]Even his prayer *is* an abomination.

10 [a]Whoever causes the upright to go astray in an evil way,
He himself will fall into his own pit;
[b]But the blameless will inherit good.

11 The rich man *is* wise in his own eyes,
But the poor who has understanding
searches him out.

12 When the righteous rejoice,
*there is* great [a]glory;
But when the wicked arise,
men [1]hide themselves.

13 [a]He who covers his sins will not prosper,
But whoever confesses and forsakes *them*
will have mercy.

14 Happy *is* the man who is always reverent,
But he who hardens his heart
will fall into calamity.

15 [a]*Like* a roaring lion and a charging bear
[b]*Is* a wicked ruler over poor people.

16 A ruler who lacks understanding
*is* a great [a]oppressor,
*But* he who hates covetousness
will prolong *his* days.

17 [a]A man burdened with bloodshed
will flee into a pit;
Let no one help him.

18 Whoever walks blamelessly will be [1]saved,
But *he who is* perverse *in his* ways
will suddenly fall.

19 [a]He who tills his land
will have plenty of bread,
But he who follows frivolity
will have poverty enough!

20 A faithful man will abound with blessings,
[a]But he who hastens to be rich
will not go unpunished.

21 [a]To [1]show partiality *is* not good,
[b]Because for a piece of bread a man will transgress.

22 A man with an evil eye hastens after riches,
And does not consider that [a]poverty will come upon him.

23 [a]He who rebukes a man will find more favor afterward
Than he who flatters with the tongue.

24 Whoever robs his father or his mother,
And says, "*It is* no transgression,"
The same [a]*is* companion to a destroyer.

25 [a]He who is of a proud heart stirs up strife,
[b]But he who trusts in the LORD
will be prospered.

26 He who [a]trusts in his own heart is a fool,
But whoever walks wisely will be delivered.

27 [a]He who gives to the poor will not lack,
But he who hides his eyes will have many curses.

28 When the wicked arise,
[a]men hide themselves;
But when they perish, the righteous increase.

## *Happy Is He Who Keeps the Law*

**29** He[a] who is often rebuked,
*and* hardens *his* neck,
Will suddenly be destroyed,
and that without remedy.

**18** [a]2 Kin. 18:31; Song 8:12; Is. 36:16; [1 Cor. 3:8; 9:7–13]; 2 Tim. 2:6 [1]*protects* or *tends*
**20** [a]Prov. 30:15, 16; Hab. 2:5 [b]Eccl. 1:8; 4:8 [1]Or *Sheol* [2]Heb. *Abaddon*
**21** [a]Prov. 17:3
**22** [a]Prov. 23:35; 26:11; Jer. 5:3
**23** [a]Prov. 24:27
**25** [a]Ps. 104:14

CHAPTER 28
**1** [a]Lev. 26:17, 36; Ps. 53:5
**3** [a]Matt. 18:28 [1]Lit. *and there is no bread*
**4** [a]Ps. 49:18; Rom. 1:32 [b]1 Kin. 18:18; Neh. 13:11, 15; Matt. 3:7; 14:4; Eph. 5:11
**5** [a]Ps. 92:6; Is. 6:9; 44:18 [b]Ps. 119:100; Prov. 2:9; John 17:17; 1 Cor. 2:15; [1 John 2:20, 27]
**9** [a]Ps. 66:18; 109:7; Prov. 15:8
**10** [a]Ps. 7:15; Prov. 26:27 [b][Matt. 6:33; Heb. 6:12; 1 Pet. 3:9]
**12** [a]Prov. 11:10; 29:2 [1]Lit. *will be searched for*
**13** [a]Ps. 32:3–5; 1 John 1:8–10
**15** [a]Prov. 19:12; 1 Pet. 5:8 [b]Ex. 1:14; Prov. 29:2; Matt. 2:16
**16** [a]Eccl. 10:16; Is. 3:12
**17** [a]Gen. 9:6
**18** [1]*delivered*
**19** [a]Prov. 12:11; 20:13
**20** [a]Prov. 13:11; 20:21; 23:4; 1 Tim. 6:9
**21** [a]Prov. 18:5 [b]Ezek. 13:19 [1]Lit. *recognize faces*
**22** [a]Prov. 21:5
**23** [a]Prov. 27:5, 6
**24** [a]Prov. 18:9
**25** [a]Prov. 13:10 [b]Prov. 29:25; 1 Tim. 6:6
**26** [a]Prov. 3:5
**27** [a]Deut. 15:7; Prov. 19:17; 22:9
**28** [a]Job 24:4

CHAPTER 29
**1** [a]2 Chr. 36:16; Prov. 6:15

2 When the righteous [1]are in authority, the
[a]people rejoice;
But when a wicked *man* rules,
[b]the people groan.

3 Whoever loves wisdom makes his father
rejoice,
But a companion of harlots wastes *his*
wealth.

4 The king establishes the land by justice,
But he who receives bribes overthrows it.

5 A man who [a]flatters his neighbor
Spreads a net for his feet.

6 By transgression an evil man is snared,
But the righteous sings and rejoices.

7 The righteous [a]considers the cause of the
poor,
*But* the wicked does not understand *such*
knowledge.

8 Scoffers [a]set a city aflame,
But wise *men* turn away wrath.

9 *If* a wise man contends with a foolish man,
[a]Whether *the fool* rages or laughs, *there is* no
peace.

10 [a]The bloodthirsty hate the blameless,
But the upright seek his [1]well-being.

11 A fool vents all his [a]feelings,[1]
But a wise *man* holds them back.

12 If a ruler pays attention to lies,
All his servants *become* wicked.

13 The poor *man* and the oppressor
have this in common:
[a]The LORD gives light to the eyes of both.

14 The king who judges the [a]poor with truth,
His throne will be established forever.

15 The rod and rebuke give [a]wisdom,
But a child left *to himself* brings shame to his
mother.

16 When the wicked are multiplied,
transgression increases;
But the righteous will see their [a]fall.

17 Correct your son, and he will give you rest;
Yes, he will give delight to your soul.

18 [a]Where *there is* no [1]revelation,
the people cast off restraint;
But [b]happy *is* he who keeps the law.

19 A servant will not be corrected by mere
words;
For though he understands,
he will not respond.

20 Do you see a man hasty in his words?
[a]*There is* more hope for a fool than for him.

21 He who pampers his servant from childhood
Will have him as a son in the end.

22 [a]An angry man stirs up strife,
And a furious man abounds in transgression.

23 [a]A man's pride will bring him low,
But the humble in spirit will retain honor.

24 Whoever is a partner with a thief
hates his own life;
[a]He [1]swears to tell the truth,
but reveals nothing.

25 [a]The fear of man brings a snare,
But whoever trusts in the LORD shall be [1]safe.

26 [a]Many seek the ruler's [1]favor,
But justice for man *comes* from the LORD.

27 An unjust man *is* an abomination to the
righteous,
And *he who is* upright in the way *is* an
abomination to the wicked.

## *The Wisdom of Agur*

**30** The words of Agur the son of Jakeh, *his*
utterance. This man declared to Ithiel—to
Ithiel and Ucal:

2 [a]Surely I *am* more stupid than *any* man,
And do not have the understanding of a
man.
3 I neither learned wisdom
Nor have [a]knowledge of the Holy One.

4 [a]Who has ascended into heaven,
or descended?
[b]Who has gathered the wind in His fists?
Who has bound the waters in a garment?
Who has established all the ends of the
earth?
What *is* His name,
and what *is* His Son's name,
If you know?

5 [a]Every word of God *is* [1]pure;
[b]He *is* a shield to those who put their trust in
Him.
6 [a]Do not add to His words,
Lest He rebuke you, and you be found a liar.

7 Two *things* I request of You
(Deprive me not before I die):
8 Remove falsehood and lies far from me;
Give me neither poverty nor riches—
[a]Feed me with the food allotted to me;
9 [a]Lest I be full and deny *You*,
And say, "Who *is* the LORD?"
Or lest I be poor and steal,
And profane the name of my God.

10 Do not malign a servant to his master,
Lest he curse you, and you be found guilty.

11 *There is* a generation *that* curses its [a]father,
And does not bless its mother.
12 *There is* a generation
[a]*that is* pure in its own eyes,
*Yet* is not washed from its filthiness.
13 *There is* a generation—
oh, how [a]lofty are their eyes!
And their eyelids are [1]lifted up.
14 [a]*There is* a generation whose teeth *are like*
swords,
And whose fangs *are like* knives,
[b]To devour the poor from off the earth,
And the needy from *among* men.

15 The leech has two daughters—
Give *and* Give!

There are three *things that* are never
satisfied,
Four never say, "Enough!":
16 [a]The[1] grave,
The barren womb,
The earth *that* is not satisfied with water—
And the fire never says, "Enough!"

17 [a]The eye *that* mocks *his* father,
And scorns obedience to *his* mother,

**2** [a]Prov. 28:12 [b]Esth. 4:3 [1]*become great*
**5** [a]Prov. 26:28
**7** [a]Job 29:16
**8** [a]Prov. 11:11
**9** [a]Matt. 11:17
**10** [a]1 John 3:12 [1]Lit. *soul* or *life*
**11** [a]Prov. 14:33 [1]Lit. *spirit*
**13** [a][Matt. 5:45]
**14** [a]Is. 11:4
**15** [a]Prov. 22:15
**16** [a]Ps. 37:34
**18** [a]1 Sam. 3:1 [b]John 13:17 [1]*prophetic vision*
**20** [a]Prov. 26:12
**22** [a]Prov. 26:21
**23** [a]Is. 66:2
**24** [a]Lev. 5:1 [1]Lit. *hears the adjuration* or *oath*
**25** [a]Gen. 12:12; 20:2 [1]*secure,* lit. *set on high*
**26** [a]Ps. 20:9 [1]Lit. *face*

CHAPTER 30
**2** [a]Ps. 73:22
**3** [a][Prov. 9:10]
**4** [a][John 3:13] [b]Job 38:4
**5** [a]Ps. 12:6; 19:8; 119:140 [b]Ps. 18:30; 84:11; 115:9–11 [1]*tested, refined, found pure*
**6** [a]Deut. 4:2; 12:32
**8** [a]Matt. 6:11
**9** [a]Deut. 8:12–14
**11** [a]Ex. 21:17
**12** [a]Luke 18:11
**13** [a]Prov. 6:17 [1]In arrogance
**14** [a]Job 29:17 [b]Amos 8:4
**16** [a]Prov. 27:20 [1]Or *Sheol*
**17** [a]Gen. 9:22

The ravens of the valley will pick it out,
And the young eagles will eat it.

**18** There are three *things which* are too wonderful for me,
Yes, four *which* I do not understand:
19 The way of an eagle in the air,
The way of a serpent on a rock,
The way of a ship in the [1]midst of the sea,
And the way of a man with a virgin.

**20** This *is* the way of an adulterous woman:
She eats and wipes her mouth,
And says, "I have done no wickedness."

21 For three *things* the earth is perturbed,
Yes, for four it cannot bear up:
22 [a]For a servant when he reigns,
A fool when he is filled with food,
23 A [1]hateful *woman* when she is married,
And a maidservant who succeeds her mistress.

**24** There are four *things which* are little on the earth,
But they *are* exceedingly wise:
25 [a]The ants *are* a people not strong,
Yet they prepare their food in the summer;
26 [a]The [1]rock badgers are a feeble folk,
Yet they make their homes in the crags;
27 The locusts have no king,
Yet they all advance in ranks;
28 The [1]spider skillfully grasps with its hands,
And it is in kings' palaces.

**29** There are three *things which* are majestic in pace,
Yes, four *which* are stately in walk:
30 A lion, *which is* mighty among beasts
And does not turn away from any;
31 A [1]greyhound,
A male goat also,
And [2]a king *whose* troops *are* with him.

**32** If you have been foolish in exalting yourself,
Or if you have devised evil,
[a]*put your* hand on *your* mouth.
33 For *as* the churning of milk produces butter,
And wringing the nose produces blood,
So the forcing of wrath produces strife.

## *The Words of King Lemuel's Mother*

**31** The words of King Lemuel, the utterance which his mother taught him:

2 What, my son?
And what, son of my womb?
And what, [a]son of my vows?
3 [a]Do not give your strength to women,
Nor your ways [b]to that which destroys kings.

**4** [a]*It is* not for kings, O Lemuel,
*It is* not for kings to drink wine,
Nor for princes intoxicating drink;

**19** [1]Lit. *heart*
**22** [a]Prov. 19:10; Eccl. 10:7
**23** [1]Or *hated*
**25** [a]Prov. 6:6
**26** [a]Lev. 11:5; Ps. 104:18 [1]*rock hyraxes*
**28** [1]Or *lizard*
**31** [1]Or perhaps *strutting rooster,* lit. *girded of waist* [2]A Jewish tradition *a king against whom there is no uprising*
**32** [a]Job 21:5; 40:4; Mic. 7:16

CHAPTER 31

**2** [a]Is. 49:15
**3** [a]Prov. 5:9 [b]Deut. 17:17; 1 Kin. 11:1; Neh. 13:26; Prov. 7:26; Hos. 4:11
**4** [a]Eccl. 10:17
**5** [a]Hos. 4:11 [1]Lit. *sons of affliction*
**6** [a]Ps. 104:15
**8** [a]Job 29:15, 16; Ps. 82 [1]Lit. *sons of passing away*
**9** [a]Lev. 19:15; Deut. 1:16 [b]Job 29:12; Is. 1:17; Jer. 22:16
**10** [a]Ruth 3:11; Prov. 12:4; 19:14 [1]Vv. 10–31 are an alphabetic acrostic in Hebrew; cf. Ps. 119 [2]Lit. *a wife of valor,* in the sense of all forms of excellence
**15** [a]Prov. 20:13; Rom. 12:11 [b]Luke 12:42
**16** [1]Lit. *the fruit of her hands*
**20** [a]Deut. 15:11; Job 31:16–20; Prov. 22:9; Rom. 12:13; Eph. 4:28; Heb. 13:16
**23** [a]Prov. 12:4

5 [a]Lest they drink and forget the law,
And pervert the justice of all [1]the afflicted.
6 [a]Give strong drink to him who is perishing,
And wine to those who are bitter of heart.
7 Let him drink and forget his poverty,
And remember his misery no more.

**8** [a]Open your mouth for the speechless,
In the cause of all *who are* [1]appointed to die.
9 Open your mouth, [a]judge righteously,
And [b]plead the cause of the poor and needy.

**10** [a]Who[1] can find a [2]virtuous wife?
For her worth *is* far above rubies.
11 The heart of her husband safely trusts her;
So he will have no lack of gain.
12 She does him good and not evil
All the days of her life.
13 She seeks wool and flax,
And willingly works with her hands.
14 She is like the merchant ships,
She brings her food from afar.
15 [a]She also rises while it is yet night,
And [b]provides food for her household,
And a portion for her maidservants.
16 She considers a field and buys it;
From [1]her profits she plants a vineyard.
17 She girds herself with strength,
And strengthens her arms.
18 She perceives that her merchandise *is* good,
And her lamp does not go out by night.
19 She stretches out her hands to the distaff,
And her hand holds the spindle.
20 [a]She extends her hand to the poor,
Yes, she reaches out her hands to the needy.
21 She is not afraid of snow for her household,
For all her household *is* clothed with scarlet.
22 She makes tapestry for herself;
Her clothing *is* fine linen and purple.
23 [a]Her husband is known in the gates,
When he sits among the elders of the land.
24 She makes linen garments and sells *them,*
And supplies sashes for the merchants.
25 Strength and honor *are* her clothing;
She shall rejoice in time to come.
26 She opens her mouth with wisdom,
And on her tongue *is* the law of kindness.
27 She watches over the ways of her household,
And does not eat the bread of idleness.
28 Her children rise up and call her blessed;
Her husband *also,* and he praises her:
29 "Many daughters have done well,
But you excel them all."
30 Charm *is* deceitful and beauty *is* passing,
But a woman *who* fears the LORD, she shall be praised.
31 Give her of the fruit of her hands,
And let her own works praise her in the gates.

*The Book of*

# ECCLESIASTES

## *The Problem of Wisdom*

THE words of the Preacher, the son of David, [a]king in Jerusalem.

2 "Vanity[a1] of vanities," says the Preacher;
"Vanity of vanities, [b]all *is* vanity."

3 [a]What profit has a man from all his labor
In which he [1]toils under the sun?
4 *One* generation passes away,
and *another* generation comes;
[a]But the earth abides forever.
5 [a]The sun also rises, and the sun goes down,
And [1]hastens to the place where it arose.
6 [a]The wind goes toward the south,
And turns around to the north;
The wind whirls about continually,
And comes again on its circuit.
7 [a]All the rivers run into the sea,
Yet the sea *is* not full;
To the place from which the rivers come,
There they return again.
8 All things *are* [1]full of labor;
Man cannot express *it*.
[a]The eye is not satisfied with seeing,
Nor the ear filled with hearing.

9 [a]That which has been *is* what will be,
That which *is* done is what will be done,
And *there is* nothing new under the sun.
10 Is there anything of which it may be said,
"See, this *is* new"?
It has already been in ancient times before
us.
11 *There is* [a]no remembrance of former *things*,
Nor will there be any remembrance
of *things* that are to come
By *those* who will come after.

12 I, the Preacher, was king over Israel in Jerusalem.
13 And I set my heart to seek and [a]search out by
wisdom concerning all that is done under heaven;
[b]this burdensome task God has given to the sons
of man, by which they may be [1]exercised.
14 I have seen all the works that are done under
the sun; and indeed, all *is* vanity and grasping for
the wind.

15 [a]*What is* crooked cannot be made straight,
And what is lacking cannot be numbered.

16 I communed with my heart, saying, "Look, I
have attained greatness, and have gained [a]more
wisdom than all who were before me in Jerusalem.
My heart has [1]understood great wisdom and
knowledge."
17 [a]And I set my heart to know wisdom and to
know madness and folly. I perceived that this also
is grasping for the wind.

18 For [a]in much wisdom *is* much grief,
And he who increases knowledge increases
sorrow.

## *Pleasure Is Vain*

2 I said [a]in my heart, "Come now, I will test you
with [b]mirth;[1] therefore enjoy pleasure"; but
surely, [c]this also *was* vanity.
2 I said of laughter—"Madness!"; and of mirth,
"What does it accomplish?"
3 [a]I searched in my heart *how* [1]to gratify my
flesh with wine, while guiding my heart with
wisdom, and how to lay hold on folly, till I might
see what *was* [b]good for the sons of men to do
under heaven all the days of their lives.
4 I made my works great, I built myself [a]houses,
and planted myself vineyards.
5 I made myself gardens and orchards, and I
planted all *kinds* of fruit trees in them.
6 I made myself water pools from which to
[1]water the growing trees of the grove.
7 I acquired male and female servants, and had
[1]servants born in my house. Yes, I had greater
possessions of herds and flocks than all who were
in Jerusalem before me.
8 [a]I also gathered for myself silver and gold and
the special treasures of kings and of the provinces.
I acquired male and female singers, the delights of
the sons of men, *and* [1]musical instruments of all
kinds.
9 [a]So I became great and [1]excelled [b]more than
all who were before me in Jerusalem. Also my
wisdom remained with me.

10 Whatever my eyes desired
I did not keep from them.
I did not withhold my heart
from any pleasure,
For my heart rejoiced in all my labor;
And [a]this was my [1]reward from all my labor.
11 Then I looked on all the works that my
hands had done
And on the labor in which I had toiled;
And indeed all *was* [a]vanity
and grasping for the wind.
*There was* no profit under the sun.

12 Then I turned myself to consider wisdom
[a]and madness and folly;
For what *can* the man *do* who succeeds the
king?—
*Only* what he has already [b]done.
13 Then I saw that wisdom [a]excels folly
As light excels darkness.
14 [a]The wise man's eyes *are* in his head,
But the fool walks in darkness.
Yet I myself perceived
That [b]the same event happens to them all.

15 So I said in my heart,
"As it happens to the fool,
It also happens to me,
And why was I then more wise?"
Then I said in my heart,
"This also *is* vanity."
16 For *there is* [a]no more remembrance of the
wise than of the fool forever,
Since all that now *is* will be forgotten in the
days to come.
And how does a wise *man* die?
As the fool!

17 Therefore I hated life because the work that
was done under the sun *was* distressing to me, for
all *is* vanity and grasping for the wind.
18 Then I hated all my labor in which I had toiled

CHAPTER 1
1 [a]Prov. 1:1
2 [a]Ps. 39:5, 6; 62:9; 144:4; Eccl. 12:8 [b][Rom. 8:20, 21] [1]Or *Absurdity, Frustration, Futility, Nonsense;* and so throughout the book
3 [a]Eccl. 2:22; 3:9 [1]*labors*
4 [a]Ps. 104:5; 119:90
5 [a]Ps. 19:4–6 [1]Is eager for, lit. *panting*
6 [a]Eccl. 11:5; John 3:8
7 [a][Ps. 104:8, 9; Jer. 5:22]
8 [a]Prov. 27:20; Eccl. 4:8 [1]*wearisome*
9 [a]Eccl. 3:15
11 [a]Eccl. 2:16
13 [a][Eccl. 7:25; 8:16, 17] [b]Gen. 3:19; Eccl. 3:10 [1]Or *afflicted*
15 [a]Eccl. 7:13
16 [a]1 Kin. 3:12, 13; Eccl. 2:9 [1]Lit. *seen*
17 [a]Eccl. 2:3, 12; 7:23, 25; [1 Thess. 5:21]
18 [a]Eccl. 12:12

CHAPTER 2
1 [a]Luke 12:19 [b]Prov. 14:13; [Eccl. 7:4; 8:15] [c]Eccl. 1:2 [1]*gladness*
3 [a]Eccl. 1:17 [b][Eccl. 3:12, 13; 5:18; 6:12] [1]Lit. *to draw my flesh*
4 [a]1 Kin. 7:1–12
6 [1]*irrigate*
7 [1]Lit. *sons of my house*
8 [a]1 Kin. 9:28; 10:10, 14, 21 [1]Exact meaning unknown
9 [a]Eccl. 1:16 [b]2 Chr. 9:22 [1]Lit. *increased*
10 [a]Eccl. 3:22; 5:18; 9:9 [1]Lit. *portion*
11 [a]Eccl. 1:3, 14
12 [a]Eccl. 1:17; 7:25 [b]Eccl. 1:9
13 [a]Eccl. 7:11, 14, 19; 9:18; 10:10
14 [a]Prov. 17:24; Eccl. 8:1 [b]Ps. 49:10; Eccl. 9:2, 3, 11
16 [a]Eccl. 1:11; 4:16

under the sun, because [a]I must leave it to the man
who will come after me.
19 And who knows whether he will be wise or a
fool? Yet he will rule over all my labor in which I
toiled and in which I have shown myself wise
under the sun. This also *is* vanity.
20 Therefore I turned my heart and despaired of
all the labor in which I had toiled under the sun.
21 For there is a man whose labor *is* with wisdom, knowledge, and skill; yet he must leave his
[1]heritage to a man who has not labored for it. This
also *is* vanity and a great evil.
22 [a]For what has man for all his labor, and for the
striving of his heart with which he has toiled
under the sun?
23 For all his days *are* [a]sorrowful, and his work
burdensome; even in the night his heart takes no
rest. This also is vanity.
**24** [a]Nothing *is* better for a man *than* that he
should eat and drink, and *that* his soul should
enjoy good in his labor. This also, I saw, was from
the hand of God.
25 For who can eat, or who can have enjoyment,
[1]more than I?
26 For *God* gives [a]wisdom and knowledge and joy
to a man who *is* good in His sight; but to the
sinner He gives the work of gathering and collecting, that [b]he may give to *him who is* good before
God. This also *is* vanity and grasping for the wind.

### *Everything Has Its Time*

**3** To everything *there is* a season,
A [a]time for every purpose under heaven:

2 A time [1]to be born,
And [a]a time to die;
A time to plant,
And a time to pluck *what is* planted;
3 A time to kill,
And a time to heal;
A time to break down,
And a time to build up;
4 A time to [a]weep,
And a time to laugh;
A time to mourn,
And a time to dance;
5 A time to cast away stones,
And a time to gather stones;
[a]A time to embrace,
And a time to refrain from embracing;
6 A time to gain,
And a time to lose;
A time to keep,
And a time to throw away;
7 A time to tear,
And a time to sew;
[a]A time to keep silence,
And a time to [b]speak;
8 A time to love,
And a time to [a]hate;
A time of war,
And a time of peace.

**9** [a]What profit has the worker from that in
which he labors?
10 [a]I have seen the God-given task with which
the sons of men are to be occupied.
11 He has made everything beautiful in its time.
Also He has put eternity in their hearts, except
that [a]no one can find out the work that God does
from beginning to end.
**12** I know that nothing *is* [a]better for them than to
rejoice, and to do good in their lives,
13 and also that [a]every man should eat and drink
and enjoy the good of all his labor—it *is* the gift of
God.

14 I know that whatever God does,
It shall be forever.
[a]Nothing can be added to it,
And nothing taken from it.
God does *it*, that men should fear before
Him.
15 [a]That which is has already been,
And what is to be has already been;
And God [1]requires an account of [2]what is
past.

**16** Moreover [a]I saw under the sun:

*In* the place of [1]judgment,
Wickedness *was* there;
And *in* the place of righteousness,
[2]Iniquity *was* there.

17 I said in my heart,

[a]"God shall judge the righteous
and the wicked,
For *there is* a time there for
every [1]purpose and for every work."

18 I said in my heart, "Concerning the condition
of the sons of men, God tests them, that they may
see that they themselves are *like* animals."
19 [a]For what happens to the sons of men also
happens to animals; one thing befalls them: as one
dies, so dies the other. Surely, they all have one
breath; man has no advantage over animals, for
all *is* vanity.
20 All go to one place: [a]all are from the dust, and
all return to dust.
21 [a]Who[1] knows the spirit of the sons of men,
which goes upward, and the spirit of the animal,
which goes down to the earth?
22 [a]So I perceived that nothing *is* better than that
a man should rejoice in his own works, for [b]that *is*
his [1]heritage. [c]For who can bring him to see what
will happen after him?

### *The Uselessness of Selfish Toil*

**4** Then I returned and considered all the [a]op-
pression that is done under the sun:

And look! The tears of the oppressed,
But they have no comforter—
[1]On the side of their oppressors *there is*
power,
But they have no comforter.
2 [a]Therefore I praised the dead who were
already dead,
More than the living who are still alive.
3 [a]Yet, better than both *is he* who has never
existed,
Who has not seen the evil work that is done
under the sun.

**4** Again, I saw that for all toil and every skillful
work a man is envied by his neighbor. This also *is*
vanity and grasping for the wind.

5 [a]The fool folds his hands
And consumes his own flesh.
6 [a]Better a handful *with* quietness
Than both hands full, *together with* toil and
grasping for the wind.

---

**18** [a]Ps. 49:10 **21** [1]Lit. *portion* **22** [a]Eccl. 1:3; 3:9 **23** [a]Job 5:7; 14:1 **24** [a]Eccl. 3:12, 13, 22; Is. 56:12; Luke 12:19; 1 Cor. 15:32; [1 Tim. 6:17] **25** [1]So with MT, Tg., Vg.; some Heb. mss., LXX, Syr. *without Him* **26** [a]Job 32:8; Prov. 2:6; James 1:5 [b]Job 27:16, 17; Prov. 28:8

CHAPTER 3

**1** [a]Eccl. 3:17; 8:6 **2** [a]Job 14:5; Heb. 9:27 [1]Lit. *to bear* **4** [a]Rom. 12:15 **5** [a]Joel 2:16; 1 Cor. 7:5 **7** [a]Amos 5:13 [b]Prov. 25:11 **8** [a]Prov. 13:5; Luke 14:26 **9** [a]Eccl. 1:3 **10** [a]Eccl. 1:13 **11** [a]Job 5:9; Eccl. 7:23; 8:17; Rom. 11:33 **12** [a]Eccl. 2:3, 24 **13** [a]Eccl. 2:24 **14** [a]James 1:17 **15** [a]Eccl. 1:9 [1]Lit. *seeks* [2]*what is pursued* **16** [a]Eccl. 5:8 [1]*justice* [2]*Wickedness* **17** [a]Gen. 18:25; Ps. 96:13; Eccl. 11:9; [Matt. 16:27; Rom. 2:6–10; 2 Cor. 5:10; 2 Thess. 1:6–9] [1]*desire* **19** [a]Ps. 49:12, 20; 73:22; [Eccl. 2:16] **20** [a]Gen. 3:19; Ps. 103:14 **21** [a]Eccl. 12:7 [1]LXX, Syr., Tg., Vg. *Who knows whether the spirit . . . goes upward, and whether . . . goes downward to the earth?* **22** [a]Eccl. 2:24; 5:18 [b]Eccl. 2:10 [c]Eccl. 6:12; 8:7 [1]*portion* or *lot*

CHAPTER 4

**1** [a]Job 35:9; Ps. 12:5; Eccl. 3:16; 5:8; Is. 5:7 [1]Lit. *At the hand* **2** [a]Job 3:17, 18 **3** [a]Job 3:11–22; Eccl. 6:3; Luke 23:29 **5** [a]Prov. 6:10; 24:33 **6** [a]Prov. 15:16, 17; 16:8

**7** Then I returned, and I saw vanity under the sun:

8 There is one alone, without [1]companion:
He has neither son nor brother.
Yet *there is* no end to all his labors,
Nor is his [a]eye satisfied with riches.
*But* [b]*he never asks,*
"For whom do I toil and deprive myself of [c]good?"
This also *is* vanity and a [2]grave misfortune.

**9** Two *are* better than one,
Because they have a good reward for their labor.
10 For if they fall,
one will lift up his companion.
But woe to him *who is* alone when he falls,
For *he has* no one to help him up.
11 Again, if two lie down together,
they will keep warm;
But how can one be warm *alone?*
12 Though one may be overpowered by another,
two can withstand him.
And a threefold cord is not quickly broken.

**13** Better a poor and wise youth
Than an old and foolish king who will be admonished no more.
14 For he comes out of prison to be king,
Although [1]he was born poor in his kingdom.
15 I saw all the living who walk under the sun;
They were with the second youth who stands in his place.
16 *There was* no end of all the people [1]over
whom he was made king;
Yet those who come afterward will not
rejoice in him.
Surely this also *is* vanity
and grasping for the wind.

## *Fear God and Keep Your Word*

**5** Walk [a]prudently when you go to the house of God; and draw near to hear rather [b]than to give the sacrifice of fools, for they do not know that they do evil.

2 Do not be [a]rash with your mouth,
And let not your heart utter anything hastily before God.
For God *is* in heaven, and you on earth;
Therefore let your words [b]be few.
3 For a dream comes through much activity,
And [a]a fool's voice *is known* by *his* many words.

**4** [a]When you make a vow to God,
do not delay to [b]pay it;
For *He has* no pleasure in fools.
Pay what you have vowed—
5 [a]Better not to vow than to vow and not pay.

6 Do not let your [a]mouth cause your flesh to sin,
[b]nor say before the messenger *of God* that it *was*
an error. Why should God be angry at your
[1]excuse and destroy the work of your hands?
7 For in the multitude of dreams and many
words *there is* also vanity. But [a]fear God.
**8** If you [a]see the oppression of the poor, and the
violent [1]perversion of justice and righteousness in
a province, do not marvel at the matter; for [b]high
official watches over high official, and higher
officials are over them.

**8** [a]Prov. 27:20; Eccl. 5:10; [1 John 2:16] [b]Ps. 39:6 [c]Eccl. 2:18–21 [1]Lit. *a second* [2]Lit. *evil task*
**14** [1]The youth
**16** [1]Lit. *to all before whom he was to be*

CHAPTER 5
**1** [a]Ex. 3:5; Is. 1:12 [b][1 Sam. 15:22]; Ps. 50:8; Prov. 15:8; 21:27; [Hos. 6:6]
**2** [a]Prov. 20:25 [b]Prov. 10:19; Matt. 6:7
**3** [a]Prov. 10:19
**4** [a]Num. 30:2; Deut. 23:21–23; Ps. 50:14; 76:11 [b]Ps. 66:13, 14
**5** [a]Prov. 20:25; Acts 5:4
**6** [a]Prov. 6:2 [b]1 Cor. 11:10 [1]Lit. *voice*
**7** [a][Eccl. 12:13]
**8** [a]Eccl. 3:16 [b][Ps. 12:5; 58:11; 82:1] [1]*wresting*
**13** [a]Eccl. 6:1, 2
**14** [1]Lit. *bad business*
**15** [a]Job 1:21; Ps. 49:17; 1 Tim. 6:7
**16** [a]Eccl. 1:3 [b]Prov. 11:29
**17** [a]Ps. 127:2
**18** [a]Eccl. 2:24; 3:12, 13; [1 Tim. 6:17] [b]Eccl. 2:10; 3:22 [1]Lit. *portion*
**19** [a][Eccl. 6:2] [b]Eccl. 2:24; 3:13 [1]Lit. *portion*

CHAPTER 6
**1** [a]Eccl. 5:13
**2** [a]Job 21:10; Ps. 17:14; 73:7 [b]Luke 12:20 [1]*disease*
**3** [a]2 Kin. 9:35; Is. 14:19, 20; Jer. 22:19 [b]Job 3:16; Ps. 58:8; Eccl. 4:3 [1]Or *miscarriage*
**6** [a]Eccl. 2:14, 15
**7** [a]Prov. 16:26

9 Moreover the profit of the land is for all; *even*
the king is served from the field.

**10** He who loves silver will not be satisfied with silver;
Nor he who loves abundance, with increase.
This also *is* vanity.

11 When goods increase,
They increase who eat them;
So what profit have the owners
Except to see *them* with their eyes?

12 The sleep of a laboring man *is* sweet,
Whether he eats little or much;
But the abundance of the rich
will not permit him to sleep.

**13** [a]There is a severe evil *which* I have seen
under the sun:
Riches kept for their owner to his hurt.
14 But those riches perish through [1]misfortune;
When he begets a son,
*there is* nothing in his hand.
15 [a]As he came from his mother's womb, naked
shall he return,
To go as he came;
And he shall take nothing from his labor
Which he may carry away in his hand.

16 And this also *is* a severe evil—
Just exactly as he came, so shall he go.
And [a]what profit has he
[b]who has labored for the wind?
17 All his days [a]he also eats in darkness,
And *he has* much sorrow and sickness and
anger.

**18** Here is what I have seen: [a]*It is* good and fitting
*for one* to eat and drink, and to enjoy the good of
all his labor in which he toils under the sun all the
days of his life which God gives him; [b]for it *is* his
[1]heritage.
19 As for [a]every man to whom God has given
riches and wealth, and given him power to eat of
it, to receive his [1]heritage and rejoice in his
labor—this *is* the [b]gift of God.
20 For he will not dwell unduly on the days of his
life, because God keeps *him* busy with the joy of
his heart.

## *Wealth Is Not the Goal of Life*

**6** There[a] is an evil which I have seen under the
sun, and it *is* common among men:
2 A man to whom God has given riches and
wealth and honor, [a]so that he lacks nothing for
himself of all he desires; [b]yet God does not give
him power to eat of it, but a foreigner consumes it.
This *is* vanity, and it *is* an evil [1]affliction.
**3** If a man begets a hundred *children* and lives
many years, so that the days of his years are
many, but his soul is not satisfied with goodness,
or [a]indeed he has no burial, I say *that* [b]a [1]stillborn
child *is* better than he—
4 for it comes in vanity and departs in darkness,
and its name is covered with darkness.
5 Though it has not seen the sun or known
*anything,* this has more rest than that man,
6 even if he lives a thousand years twice—but
has not seen goodness. Do not all go to one [a]place?

**7** [a]All the labor of man *is* for his mouth,
And yet the soul is not satisfied.
8 For what more has the wise *man* than the
fool?

What does the poor man have,
Who knows *how* to walk before the living?
9 Better *is* [1]the [a]sight of the eyes than the
wandering of [2]desire.
This also *is* vanity and grasping for the wind.

10 Whatever one is,
he has been named [a]already,
For it is known that he *is* man;
[b]And he cannot contend with Him
who is mightier than he.
11 Since there are many things that increase
vanity,
How *is* man the better?

12 For who knows what *is* good for man in life,
[1]all the days of his [2]vain life which he passes like
[a]a shadow? [b]Who can tell a man what will happen
after him under the sun?

### *The Value of Practical Wisdom*

**7** A good[a] name *is* better than precious
ointment,
And the day of death than the day of one's
[b]birth;
2 Better to go to the house of mourning
Than to go to the house of feasting,
For that *is* the end of all men;
And the living will take *it* to [a]heart.
3 [1]Sorrow *is* better than laughter,
[a]For by a sad countenance the heart is made
[2]better.
4 The heart of the wise *is* in the house
of mourning,
But the heart of fools *is* in the house
of mirth.

5 [a]*It is* better to [1]hear the rebuke of the wise
Than for a man to hear the song of fools.
6 [a]For like the [1]crackling of thorns under a pot,
So *is* the laughter of the fool.
This also is vanity.
7 Surely oppression destroys a wise *man's*
reason,
[a]And a bribe [1]debases the heart.

8 The end of a thing *is* better
than its beginning;
[a]The patient in spirit *is* better
than the proud in spirit.
9 [a]Do not hasten in your spirit to be angry,
For anger rests in the bosom of fools.
10 Do not say,
"Why were the former days better than
these?"
For you do not inquire wisely concerning
this.

11 Wisdom *is* good with an inheritance,
And profitable [a]to those who see the sun.
12 For wisdom *is* [1]a [a]defense *as* money *is* a
defense,
But the [2]excellence of knowledge
*is that* wisdom gives [b]life
to those who have it.

**13** Consider the work of God;
For [a]who can make straight what He has
made crooked?
14 [a]In the day of prosperity be joyful,
But in the day of adversity consider:
Surely God has appointed the one [1]as well as
the other,
So that man can find out nothing *that will
come* after him.

**15** I have seen everything in my days of vanity:

[a]There is a just *man* who perishes
in his righteousness,
And there is a wicked *man* who prolongs *life*
in his wickedness.

16 [a]Do not be overly righteous,
[b]Nor be overly wise:
Why should you destroy yourself?
17 Do not be overly wicked,
Nor be foolish:
[a]Why should you die before your time?
18 *It is* good that you grasp this,
And also not remove your hand
from the other;
For he who [a]fears God will [1]escape them all.

19 [a]Wisdom strengthens the wise
More than ten rulers of the city.

20 [a]For *there is* not a just man on earth who
does good
And does not sin.

**21** Also do not take to heart everything people
say,
Lest you hear your servant cursing you.
22 For many times, also, your own heart has
known
That even you have cursed others.

**23** All this I have [1]proved by wisdom.
[a]I said, "I will be wise";
But it *was* far from me.
24 [a]As for that which is far off
and [b]exceedingly deep,
Who can find it out?
25 [a]I applied my heart to know,
To search and seek out wisdom
and the reason *of things,*
To know the wickedness of folly,
Even of foolishness *and* madness.
26 [a]And I find more bitter than death
The woman whose heart *is* snares and nets,
Whose hands *are* fetters.
[1]He who pleases God shall escape from her,
But the sinner shall be trapped by her.

**27** "Here is what I have found,"
says [a]the Preacher,
"*Adding* one thing to the other to find out the
reason,
28 Which my soul still seeks but I cannot find:
[a]One man among a thousand I have found,
But a woman among all these
I have not found.
29 Truly, this only I have found:
[a]That God made man upright,
But [b]they have sought out many schemes."

### *Obey Authorities for God's Sake*

**8** Who *is* like a wise *man?*
And who knows the interpretation of a
thing?
[a]A man's wisdom makes his face shine,
And [b]the [1]sternness of his face is changed.

**2** I *say,* "Keep the king's commandment [a]for the
sake of your oath to God.
3 [a]"Do not be hasty to go from his presence. Do
not take your stand for an evil thing, for he does
whatever pleases him."

4 Where the word of a king *is, there is* power;
And [a]who may say to him,
"What are you doing?"

---

**9** [a]Eccl. 11:9 [1]What the eyes see [2]Lit. *soul*
**10** [a]Eccl. 1:9; 3:15 [b]Job 9:32; Is. 45:9; Jer. 49:19
**12** [a]Ps. 102:11; James 4:14 [b]Ps. 39:6; Eccl. 3:22 [1]Lit. *the number of the days* [2]*futile*

CHAPTER 7
**1** [a]Prov. 15:30; 22:1 [b]Eccl. 4:2
**2** [a][Ps. 90:12]
**3** [a][2 Cor. 7:10] [1]*Vexation* or *Grief* [2]*well* or *pleasing*
**5** [a]Ps. 141:5; [Prov. 13:18; 15:31, 32] [1]*listen to*
**6** [a]Eccl. 2:2 [1]Lit. *sound*
**7** [a]Ex. 23:8; Deut. 16:19; [Prov. 17:8, 23] [1]*destroys*
**8** [a]Prov. 14:29; Gal. 5:22; Eph. 4:2
**9** [a]Prov. 14:17; James 1:19
**11** [a]Eccl. 11:7
**12** [a]Eccl. 9:18 [b]Prov. 3:18 [1]A protective shade, lit. *shadow* [2]*advantage* or *profit*
**13** [a]Job 12:14
**14** [a]Deut. 28:47 [1]*alongside*
**15** [a]Eccl. 8:12–14
**16** [a]Prov. 25:16; Phil. 3:6 [b]Rom. 12:3
**17** [a]Job 15:32; Ps. 55:23
**18** [a]Eccl. 3:14; 5:7; 8:12, 13 [1]Lit. *come forth from all of them*
**19** [a]Prov. 21:22; Eccl. 9:13–18
**20** [a]1 Kin. 8:46; 2 Chr. 6:36; Prov. 20:9; Rom. 3:23; 1 John 1:8
**23** [a]Rom. 1:22 [1]*tested*
**24** [a]Job 28:12; 1 Tim. 6:16 [b]Rom. 11:33
**25** [a]Eccl. 1:17
**26** [a]Prov. 5:3, 4 [1]Lit. *He who is good before God*
**27** [a]Eccl. 1:1, 2
**28** [a]Job 33:23
**29** [a]Gen. 1:27 [b]Gen. 3:6, 7

CHAPTER 8
**1** [a]Prov. 4:8, 9; Acts 6:15 [b]Deut. 28:50 [1]Lit. *strength*
**2** [a]Ex. 22:11; 2 Sam. 21:7; 1 Chr. 29:24; Ezek. 17:18; [Rom. 13:5]
**3** [a]Eccl. 10:4
**4** [a]1 Sam. 13:11, 13; Job 34:18

5 He who keeps his command will experience
nothing harmful;
And a wise man's heart [1]discerns both time
and judgment,
6 Because [a]for every matter there is a time and
judgment,
Though the misery of man [1]increases greatly.
7 [a]For he does not know what will happen;
So who can tell him when it will occur?
8 [a]No one has power over the spirit to retain
the spirit,
And no one has power in the day of death.
*There is* [b]no release from that war,
And wickedness will not deliver those who
are given to it.

9 All this I have seen, and applied my heart to
every work that is done under the sun: *There is* a
time in which one man rules over another to his
own hurt.
**10** Then I saw the wicked buried, who had come
and gone from the place of holiness, and they
were [a]forgotten[1] in the city where they had so
done. This also *is* vanity.
11 [a]Because the sentence against an evil work is
not executed speedily, therefore the heart of the
sons of men is fully set in them to do evil.
12 [a]Though a sinner does evil a hundred *times,*
and his *days* are prolonged, yet I surely know that
[b]it will be well with those who fear God, who fear
before Him.
13 But it will not be well with the wicked; nor will
he prolong *his* days, *which are* as a shadow,
because he does not fear before God.
**14** There is a vanity which occurs on earth, that
there are just *men* to whom it [a]happens according
to the work of the wicked; again, there are wicked
*men* to whom it happens according to the work of
the [b]righteous. I said that this also *is* vanity.
15 [a]So I commended enjoyment, because a man
has nothing better under the sun than to eat,
drink, and be merry; for this will remain with him
in his labor *all* the days of his life which God gives
him under the sun.
**16** When I applied my heart to know wisdom and
to see the business that is done on earth, even
though one sees no sleep day or night,
17 then I saw all the work of God, that [a]a man
cannot find out the work that is done under the
sun. For though a man labors to discover *it,* yet he
will not find *it;* moreover, though a wise *man*
attempts to know *it,* he will not be able to find *it.*

## *Death Comes to All*

**9** For I [1]considered all this in my heart, so that I
could declare it all: [a]that the righteous and the
wise and their works *are* in the hand of God.
People know neither love nor hatred *by* anything
*they see* before them.
2 [a]All things *come* alike to all:

One event *happens* to the righteous
and the wicked;
To the [1]good, the clean, and the unclean;
To him who sacrifices
and him who does not sacrifice.
As is the good, so *is* the sinner;
He who takes an oath
as *he* who fears an oath.

3 This *is* an evil in all that is done under the sun:
that one thing *happens* to all. Truly the hearts of
the sons of men are full of evil; madness *is* in their
hearts while they live, and after that *they go* to
the dead.
4 But for him who is joined to all the living there
is hope, for a living dog is better than a dead lion.

5 For the living know that they will die;
But [a]the dead know nothing,
And they have no more reward,
For [b]the memory of them is forgotten.
6 Also their love, their hatred,
and their envy have now perished;
Nevermore will they have a share
In anything done under the sun.

7 Go, [a]eat your bread with joy,
And drink your wine with a merry heart;
For God has already accepted your works.
8 Let your garments always be white,
And let your head lack no oil.

**9** [1]Live joyfully with the wife whom you love all
the days of your vain life which He has given you
under the sun, all your days of vanity; [a]for that *is*
your portion in life, and in the labor which you
perform under the sun.
10 [a]Whatever your hand finds to do, do *it* with
your [b]might; for *there is* no work or device or
knowledge or wisdom in the grave where you are
going.
11 I returned [a]and saw under the sun that—

The race *is* not to the swift,
Nor the battle to the strong,
Nor bread to the wise,
Nor riches to men of understanding,
Nor favor to men of skill;
But time and [b]chance happen to them all.
12 For [a]man also does not know his time:
Like fish taken in a cruel net,
Like birds caught in a snare,
So the sons of men *are* [b]snared in an evil
time,
When it falls suddenly upon them.

**13** This wisdom I have also seen under the sun,
and it *seemed* great to me:
14 [a]*There was* a little city with few men in it; and
a great king came against it, besieged it, and built
great [1]snares around it.
15 Now there was found in it a poor wise man,
and he by his wisdom delivered the city. Yet no
one remembered that same poor man.
16 Then I said:

"Wisdom *is* better than [a]strength.
Nevertheless [b]the poor man's wisdom *is*
despised,
And his words are not heard.
17 Words of the wise, *spoken* quietly, *should be*
heard
Rather than the shout of a ruler of fools.
18 Wisdom *is* better than weapons of war;
But [a]one sinner destroys much good."

## *Wisdom and Folly*

**10** [1]Dead flies [2]putrefy the perfumer's
ointment,
And cause it to give off a foul odor;
*So does* a little folly to one respected for
wisdom *and* honor.
2 A wise man's heart *is* at his right hand,
But a fool's heart at his left.

---

**8:5** [1]Lit. *knows*
**6** [a]Eccl. 3:1, 17 [1]*is great upon him*
**7** [a]Prov. 24:22; Eccl. 6:12
**8** [a]Ps. 49:6, 7; Job 14:5 [b]Deut. 20:5–8
**10** [a]Eccl. 2:16; 9:5 [1]Some Heb. mss., LXX, Vg. *praised*
**11** [a]Ps. 10:6; 50:21; Is. 26:10
**12** [a]Is. 65:20; [Rom. 2:5–7] [b][Deut. 4:40; Ps. 37:11, 18, 19; Prov. 1:32, 33; Is. 3:10; Matt. 25:34, 41]
**14** [a]Ps. 73:14 [b]Eccl. 2:14; 7:15; 9:1–3
**15** [a]Eccl. 2:24
**17** [a]Job 5:9; Ps. 73:16; Eccl. 3:11; Rom. 11:33

CHAPTER 9
**1** [a]Deut. 33:3; Job 12:10; Eccl. 8:14 [1]Lit. *put*
**2** [a]Gen. 3:17–19; Job 21:7; Ps. 73:3, 12, 13; Mal. 3:15 [1]LXX, Syr., Vg. *good and bad,*
**5** [a]Job 14:21; Is. 63:16 [b]Job 7:8–10; Eccl. 1:11; 2:16; 8:10; Is. 26:14
**7** [a]Eccl. 8:15
**9** [a]Eccl. 2:10 [1]Lit. *See life*
**10** [a][Col. 3:17] [b]Rom. 12:11; Col. 3:23
**11** [a]Jer. 9:23; Amos 2:14, 15 [b]1 Sam. 6:9
**12** [a]Eccl. 8:7 [b]Prov. 29:6; Luke 12:20, 39; 17:26; 1 Thess. 5:3
**14** [a]2 Sam. 20:16–22 [1]LXX, Syr., Vg. *bulwarks*
**16** [a]Eccl. 7:12, 19 [b]Mark 6:2, 3
**18** [a]Josh. 7:1–26; 2 Kin. 21:2–17

CHAPTER 10
**1** [1]Lit. *Flies of death* [2]Tg., Vg. omit *putrefy*

3 Even when a fool walks along the way,
He lacks wisdom,
[a]And he shows everyone *that* he *is* a fool.
4 If the spirit of the ruler rises against you,
[a]Do not leave your post;
For [b]conciliation[1] pacifies great offenses.

**5** There is an evil I have seen under the sun,
As an error proceeding from the ruler:
6 [a]Folly is set in [1]great dignity,
While the rich sit in a lowly place.
7 I have seen servants [a]on horses,
While princes walk on the ground like
servants.

**8** [a]He who digs a pit will fall into it,
And whoever breaks through a wall will be
bitten by a serpent.
9 He who quarries stones
may be hurt by them,
*And* he who splits wood
may be endangered by it.
10 If the ax is dull,
And one does not sharpen the edge,
Then he must use more strength;
But wisdom [1]brings success.

**11** A serpent may bite [a]when *it is* not charmed;
The [1]babbler is no different.
12 [a]The words of a wise man's mouth
*are* gracious,
But [b]the lips of a fool shall swallow him up;
13 The words of his mouth
begin with foolishness,
And the end of his talk *is* raving madness.
14 [a]A fool also multiplies words.
No man knows what is to be;
Who can tell him [b]what will be after him?
15 The labor of fools wearies them,
For they do not even know how to go to the
city!

**16** [a]Woe to you, O land,
when your king *is* a child,
And your princes feast in the morning!
17 Blessed *are* you, O land,
when your king *is* the son of nobles,
And your [a]princes feast at the proper time—
For strength and not for drunkenness!
18 Because of laziness the [1]building decays,
And [a]through idleness of hands the house
leaks.
19 A feast is made for laughter,
And [a]wine makes merry;
But money answers everything.

20 [a]Do not curse the king, even in your thought;
Do not curse the rich, even in your bedroom;
For a bird of the air may carry your voice,
And a bird in flight may tell the matter.

### *The Value of Diligence*

**11** Cast your bread [a]upon the waters,
[b]For you will find it after many days.
2 [a]Give a serving [b]to seven, and also to eight,
[c]For you do not know what evil
will be on the earth.

3 If the clouds are full of rain,
They empty *themselves* upon the earth;
And if a tree falls to the south or the north,
In the place where the tree falls,
there it shall lie.
4 He who observes the wind will not sow,
And he who regards the clouds will not reap.
5 As [a]you do not know what *is* the way
of the [1]wind,
[b]*Or* how the bones *grow* in the womb
of her who is with child,
So you do not know the works of God who
makes everything.
6 In the morning sow your seed,
And in the evening do not withhold your
hand;
For you do not know which will prosper,
Either this or that,
Or whether both alike *will be* good.

7 Truly the light is sweet,
And *it is* pleasant for the eyes
[a]to behold the sun;
8 But if a man lives many years
*And* [a]rejoices in them all,
Yet let him [b]remember the days of darkness,
For they will be many.
All that is coming *is* vanity.

**9** Rejoice, O young man, in your youth,
And let your heart cheer you in the days of
your youth;
[a]Walk in the [1]ways of your heart,
And [2]in the sight of your eyes;
But know that for all these
[b]God will bring you into judgment.
10 Therefore remove [1]sorrow from your heart,
And [a]put away evil from your flesh,
[b]For childhood and [2]youth *are* vanity.

### *Seek God in Early Life*

**12** Remember[a] now your Creator
in the days of your youth,
Before the [1]difficult days come,
And the years draw near [b]when you say,
"I have no pleasure in them":
2 While the sun and the light,
The moon and the stars,
Are not darkened,
And the clouds do not return after the rain;
3 In the day when the keepers of the house
tremble,
And the strong men bow down;
When the grinders cease because they are
few,
And those that look through the windows
grow dim;
4 When the doors are shut in the streets,
And the sound of grinding is low;
When one rises up at the sound of a bird,
And all [a]the daughters of music
are brought low.
5 Also they are afraid of height,
And of terrors in the way;
When the almond tree blossoms,
The grasshopper is a burden,
And desire fails.
For man goes to [a]his eternal home,
And [b]the mourners go about the streets.

6 *Remember your Creator* before the silver
cord is [1]loosed,
Or the golden bowl is broken,
Or the pitcher shattered at the fountain,
Or the wheel broken at the well.
7 [a]Then the dust will return to the earth as it
was,
[b]And the spirit will return to God
[c]who gave it.

**3** [a]Prov. 13:16; 18:2
**4** [a]Eccl. 8:3 [b]1 Sam. 25:24–33; Prov. 25:15 [1]Lit. *healing, health*
**6** [a]Esth. 3:1 [1]*exalted positions*
**7** [a]Prov. 19:10; 30:22
**8** [a]Ps. 7:15; Prov. 26:27
**10** [1]Lit. *is a successful advantage*
**11** [a]Ps. 58:4, 5; Jer. 8:17 [1]Lit. *master of the tongue*
**12** [a]Prov. 10:32; Luke 4:22 [b]Prov. 10:14; Eccl. 4:5
**14** [a][Prov. 15:2]; Eccl. 5:3 [b]Eccl. 3:22; 8:7
**16** [a]Is. 3:4, 5; 5:11
**17** [a]Prov. 31:4; Is. 5:11
**18** [a]Prov. 24:30–34 [1]Lit. *rafters sink*
**19** [a]Judg. 9:13; Ps. 104:15; Eccl. 2:3
**20** [a]Ex. 22:28; Acts 23:5

CHAPTER 11
**1** [a]Is. 32:20 [b][Deut. 15:10; Prov. 19:17; Matt. 10:42; 2 Cor. 9:8; Gal. 6:9, 10; Heb. 6:10]
**2** [a]Ps. 112:9; Matt. 5:42; Luke 6:30; [1 Tim. 6:18, 19] [b]Mic. 5:5 [c]Eph. 5:16
**5** [a]John 3:8 [b]Ps. 139:14 [1]Or *spirit*
**7** [a]Eccl. 7:11
**8** [a]Eccl. 9:7 [b]Eccl. 12:1
**9** [a]Num. 15:39; Job 31:7; Eccl. 2:10 [b]Eccl. 3:17; 12:14; [Rom. 14:10] [1]Impulses [2]As you see to be best
**10** [a]2 Cor. 7:1; 2 Tim. 2:22 [b]Ps. 39:5 [1]*vexation* [2]Prime of life

CHAPTER 12
**1** [a]2 Chr. 34:3; Prov. 22:6; Lam. 3:27 [b]2 Sam. 19:35 [1]Lit. *evil*
**4** [a]2 Sam. 19:35
**5** [a]Job 17:13 [b]Gen. 50:10; Jer. 9:17
**6** [1]So with Qr., Tg.; Kt. *removed;* LXX, Vg. *broken*
**7** [a]Gen. 3:19; Job 34:15; Ps. 90:3 [b]Eccl. 3:21 [c]Num. 16:22; 27:16; Job 34:14; Is. 57:16; Zech. 12:1

8 "Vanity[a] of vanities," says the Preacher,
"All *is* vanity."

**9** And moreover, because the Preacher was
wise, he still taught the people knowledge; yes, he
pondered and sought out *and* [a]set[1] in order many
proverbs.
10 The Preacher sought to find [1]acceptable
words; and *what was* written *was* upright—words
of truth.
**11** The words of the wise are like goads, and the
words of [1]scholars are like well-driven nails, given
by one Shepherd.

**8** [a]Ps. 62:9
**9** [a]1 Kin. 4:32 [1]*arranged*
**10** [1]Lit. *delightful*
**11** [1]Lit. *masters of assemblies*
**12** [a]Eccl. 1:18
**13** [a][Deut. 6:2; 10:12]
**14** [a]Matt. 12:36

12 And further, my son, be admonished by these.
Of making many books *there is* no end, and [a]much
study *is* wearisome to the flesh.
**13** Let us hear the conclusion of the whole matter:

[a]Fear God and keep His commandments,
For this is man's all.
14 For [a]God will bring every work into
judgment,
Including every secret thing,
Whether good or evil.

*The*
# SONG OF SOLOMON

## *Solomon's Love for a Shulamite Girl*

THE [a]song of songs, which *is* Solomon's.

THE [1]SHULAMITE

2 Let him kiss me with the kisses of his
mouth—
[a]For [1]your love *is* better than wine.
3 Because of the fragrance of your good
ointments,
Your name *is* ointment poured forth;
Therefore the virgins love you.
4 [a]Draw me away!

THE DAUGHTERS OF JERUSALEM

[b]We will run after [1]you.

THE SHULAMITE

The king [c]has brought me into his chambers.

THE DAUGHTERS OF JERUSALEM

We will be glad and rejoice in [2]you.
We will remember [1]your love
more than wine.

THE SHULAMITE

Rightly do they love [1]you.

5 I *am* dark, but lovely,
O daughters of Jerusalem,
Like the tents of Kedar,
Like the curtains of Solomon.
6 Do not look upon me, because I *am* dark,
Because the sun has [1]tanned me.
My mother's sons were angry with me;
They made me the keeper of the vineyards,
*But* my own [a]vineyard I have not kept.

(TO HER BELOVED)

**7** Tell me, O you whom I love,
Where you feed *your flock,*
Where you make *it* rest at noon.
For why should I be as one
who [1]veils herself
By the flocks of your companions?

THE BELOVED

8 If you do not know,
[a]O fairest among women,

CHAPTER 1
**1** [a]1 Kin. 4:32 [1]A Palestinian young woman, Song 6:13. The speaker and audience are identified according to the number, gender, and person of the Hebrew words. Occasionally the identity is not certain.
**2** [a]Song 4:10 [1]The Beloved
**4** [a]Hos. 11:4; John 6:44; 12:32 [b]Phil. 3:12–14 [c]Ps. 45:14, 15; John 14:2; Eph. 2:6 [1]The Beloved [2]The Shulamite
**6** [a]Song 8:11, 12 [1]Lit. *looked upon me*
**7** [1]LXX, Syr., Vg. *wanders*
**8** [a]Song 5:9 [1]Lit. *Go out*
**9** [a]Song 2:2, 10, 13; 4:1, 7; John 15:14 [b]2 Chr. 1:16
**10** [a]Ezek. 16:11
**11** [1]The Shulamite
**12** [1]*perfume*
**15** [a]Song 4:1; 5:12 [1]*my companion, friend*
**16** [a]Song 5:10–16 [1]*couch*
CHAPTER 2
**3** [a]Song 4:16; Rev. 22:1, 2

[1]Follow in the footsteps of the flock,
And feed your little goats
Beside the shepherds' tents.
9 I have compared you, [a]my love,
[b]To my filly among Pharaoh's chariots.
10 [a]Your cheeks are lovely with ornaments,
Your neck with chains *of gold.*

THE DAUGHTERS OF JERUSALEM

11 We will make [1]you ornaments of gold
With studs of silver.

THE SHULAMITE

**12** While the king *is* at his table,
My [1]spikenard sends forth its fragrance.
13 A bundle of myrrh *is* my beloved to me,
That lies all night between my breasts.
14 My beloved *is* to me
a cluster of henna *blooms*
In the vineyards of En Gedi.

THE BELOVED

15 [a]Behold, you *are* fair, [1]my love!
Behold, you *are* fair!
You *have* dove's eyes.

THE SHULAMITE

16 Behold, you *are* [a]handsome, my beloved!
Yes, pleasant!
Also our [1]bed *is* green.
17 The beams of our houses *are* cedar,
*And* our rafters of fir.

## *A Country Girl in a Palace*

**2** I *am* the rose of Sharon,
*And* the lily of the valleys.

THE BELOVED

2 Like a lily among thorns,
So is my love among the daughters.

THE SHULAMITE

3 Like an apple tree among the trees
of the woods,
So *is* my beloved among the sons.
I sat down in his shade with great delight,
And [a]his fruit *was* sweet to my taste.

THE SHULAMITE TO THE DAUGHTERS OF JERUSALEM

4 He brought me to the [1]banqueting house,
And his banner over me *was* love.
5 Sustain me with cakes of raisins,
Refresh me with apples,
For I *am* lovesick.

6 [a]His left hand *is* under my head,
And his right hand embraces me.
7 [a]I [1]charge you, O daughters of Jerusalem,
By the gazelles or by the does of the field,
Do not stir up nor awaken love
Until it pleases.

THE SHULAMITE

8 The voice of my beloved!
Behold, he comes
Leaping upon the mountains,
Skipping upon the hills.
9 [a]My beloved is like a gazelle or a young stag.
Behold, he stands behind our wall;
He is looking through the windows,
Gazing through the lattice.

10 My beloved spoke, and said to me:
"Rise up, my love, my fair one,
And come away.
11 For lo, the winter is past,
The rain is over *and* gone.
12 The flowers appear on the earth;
The time of singing has come,
And the voice of the turtledove
Is heard in our land.
13 The fig tree puts forth her green figs,
And the vines *with* the tender grapes
Give a good smell.
Rise up, my love, my fair one,
And come away!

14 "O my [a]dove, in the clefts of the rock,
In the secret *places* of the cliff,
Let me see your [1]face,
[b]Let me hear your voice;
For your voice *is* sweet,
And your face *is* lovely."

HER BROTHERS

15 Catch us [a]the foxes,
The little foxes that spoil the vines,
For our vines *have* tender grapes.

THE SHULAMITE

16 [a]My beloved *is* mine, and I *am* his.
He feeds *his flock* among the lilies.

(TO HER BELOVED)

17 [a]Until the day breaks
And the shadows flee away,
Turn, my beloved,
And be [b]like a gazelle
Or a young stag
Upon the mountains of [1]Bether.

## *The Shulamite Seeks Her True Love*

THE SHULAMITE

3 By [a]night on my bed I sought the one I love;
I sought him, but I did not find him.
2 "I will rise now," *I said,*
"And go about the city;
In the streets and in the squares
I will seek the one I love."
I sought him, but I did not find him.
3 [a]The watchmen who go about the city
found me;
*I said,*
"Have you seen the one I love?"

4 Scarcely had I passed by them,
When I found the one I love.
I held him and would not let him go,
Until I had brought him to the [a]house of my
mother,
And into the [1]chamber of her who conceived
me.

5 [a]I [1]charge you, O daughters of Jerusalem,
By the gazelles or by the does of the field,
Do not stir up nor awaken love
Until it pleases.

THE SHULAMITE

6 [a]Who *is* this coming out of the wilderness
Like pillars of smoke,
Perfumed with myrrh and frankincense,
With all the merchant's fragrant powders?
7 Behold, it *is* Solomon's [1]couch,
*With* sixty valiant men around it,
Of the valiant of Israel.
8 They all hold swords,
*Being* expert in war.
Every man *has* his sword on his thigh
Because of fear in the night.

9 Of the wood of Lebanon
Solomon the King
Made himself a [1]palanquin:
10 He made its pillars *of* silver,
Its support *of* gold,
Its seat *of* purple,
Its interior paved *with* love
By the daughters of Jerusalem.
11 Go forth, O daughters of Zion,
And see King Solomon with the crown
With which his mother crowned him
On the day of his wedding,
The day of the gladness of his heart.

## *The Bridegroom Praises the Bride*

THE BELOVED

4 Behold, [a]you *are* fair, my love!
Behold, you *are* fair!
You *have* dove's eyes behind your veil.
Your hair *is* like a [b]flock of goats,
Going down from Mount Gilead.
2 [a]Your teeth *are* like a flock of shorn *sheep*
Which have come up from the washing,
Every one of which bears twins,
And none *is* [1]barren among them.
3 Your lips *are* like a strand of scarlet,
And your mouth is lovely.
[a]Your temples behind your veil
*Are* like a piece of pomegranate.
4 [a]Your neck *is* like the tower of David,
Built [b]for an armory,
On which hang a thousand [1]bucklers,
All shields of mighty men.
5 [a]Your two breasts *are* like two fawns,
Twins of a gazelle,
Which feed among the lilies.

6 [a]Until the day breaks
And the shadows flee away,

---

4 [1]Lit. *house of wine*
6 [a]Song 8:3
7 [a]Song 3:5; 8:4 [1]*adjure*
9 [a]Prov. 6:5; Song 2:17
14 [a]Song 5:2 [b]Song 8:13 [1]Lit. *appearance*
15 [a]Ps. 80:13; Ezek. 13:4; Luke 13:32
16 [a]Song 6:3
17 [a]Song 4:6 [b]Song 8:14 [1]Lit. *Separation*

CHAPTER 3
1 [a]Is. 26:9
3 [a]Song 5:7; Is. 21:6–8, 11, 12
4 [a]Song 8:2 [1]*room*
5 [a]Song 2:7; 8:4 [1]*adjure*
6 [a]Song 8:5
7 [1]*portable enclosed chair*
9 [1]A portable enclosed chair

CHAPTER 4
1 [a]Song 1:15; 5:12 [b]Song 6:5
2 [a]Song 6:6 [1]*bereaved*
3 [a]Song 6:7
4 [a]Song 7:4 [b]Neh. 3:19 [1]Small shields
5 [a]Prov. 5:19; Song 7:3
6 [a]Song 2:17

I will go my way to the mountain of myrrh
And to the hill of frankincense.

**7** [a]You *are* all fair, my love,
And *there is* no spot in you.
8 Come with me from Lebanon, *my* spouse,
With me from Lebanon.
Look from the top of Amana,
From the top of Senir [a]and Hermon,
From the lions' dens,
From the mountains of the leopards.

9 You have ravished my heart,
My sister, *my* spouse;
You have ravished my heart
With one *look* of your eyes,
With one link of your necklace.
10 How fair is your love,
My sister, *my* spouse!
[a]How much better than wine is your love,
And the [1]scent of your perfumes
Than all spices!
11 Your lips, O *my* spouse,
Drip as the honeycomb;
[a]Honey and milk *are* under your tongue;
And the fragrance of your garments
*Is* [b]like the fragrance of Lebanon.

12 A garden [1]enclosed
*Is* my sister, *my* spouse,
A spring shut up,
A fountain sealed.
13 Your plants *are* an orchard of pomegranates
With pleasant fruits,
Fragrant henna with spikenard,
14 Spikenard and saffron,
Calamus and cinnamon,
With all trees of frankincense,
Myrrh and aloes,
With all the chief spices—
15 A fountain of gardens,
A well of [a]living waters,
And streams from Lebanon.

THE SHULAMITE

**16** Awake, O north *wind*,
And come, O south!
Blow upon my garden,
*That* its spices may flow out.
[a]Let my beloved come to his garden
And eat its pleasant [b]fruits.

## *The Bride Praises the Bridegroom*

THE BELOVED

**5** I [a]have come to my garden,
my [b]sister, *my* spouse;
I have gathered my myrrh with my spice;
[c]I have eaten my honeycomb with my honey;
I have drunk my wine with my milk.

(TO HIS FRIENDS)

Eat, O [d]friends!
Drink, yes, drink deeply,
O beloved ones!

THE SHULAMITE

2 I sleep, but my heart is awake;
*It is* the voice of my beloved!
[a]He knocks, *saying*,
"Open for me, my sister, [1]my love,
My dove, my perfect one;
For my head is covered with dew,
My [2]locks with the drops of the night."
3 I have taken off my robe;
How can I put it on *again?*
I have washed my feet;
How can I [1]defile them?
4 My beloved put his hand
By the [1]latch *of the door*,
And my heart yearned for him.
5 I arose to open for my beloved,
And my hands dripped *with* myrrh,
My fingers with liquid myrrh,
On the handles of the lock.

**6** I opened for my beloved,
But my beloved had turned away
*and* was gone.
My [1]heart leaped up when he spoke.
[a]I sought him, but I could not find him;
I called him, but he gave me no answer.
7 [a]The watchmen who went about the city
found me.
They struck me, they wounded me;
The keepers of the walls
Took my veil away from me.
8 I charge you, O daughters of Jerusalem,
If you find my beloved,
That you tell him I *am* lovesick!

THE DAUGHTERS OF JERUSALEM

**9** What *is* your beloved
More than *another* beloved,
[a]O fairest among women?
What *is* your beloved
More than *another* beloved,
That you so [1]charge us?

THE SHULAMITE

10 My beloved *is* white and ruddy,
[1]Chief among ten thousand.
11 His head *is like* the finest gold;
His locks *are* wavy,
*And* black as a raven.
12 [a]His eyes *are* like doves
By the rivers of waters,
Washed with milk,
*And* [1]fitly set.
13 His cheeks *are* like a bed of spices,
Banks of scented herbs.
His lips *are* lilies,
Dripping liquid myrrh.

14 His hands *are* rods of gold
Set with beryl.
His body *is* carved ivory
Inlaid *with* sapphires.
15 His legs *are* pillars of marble
Set on bases of fine gold.
His countenance *is* like Lebanon,
Excellent as the cedars.
16 His mouth *is* most sweet,
Yes, he *is* altogether lovely.
This *is* my beloved,
And this *is* my friend,
O daughters of Jerusalem!

## *I Am My Beloved's*

THE DAUGHTERS OF JERUSALEM

**6** Where has your beloved gone,
[a]O fairest among women?
Where has your beloved turned aside,
That we may seek him with you?

**7** [a]Song 1:15; Eph. 5:27
**8** [a]Deut. 3:9; 1 Chr. 5:23; Ezek. 27:5
**10** [a]Song 1:2, 4 [1]*fragrance*
**11** [a]Prov. 24:13, 14; Song 5:1 [b]Gen. 27:27; Hos. 14:6, 7
**12** [1]*locked* or *barred*
**15** [a]Zech. 14:8; John 4:10; 7:38
**16** [a]Song 5:1 [b]Song 7:13

CHAPTER 5
**1** [a]Song 4:16 [b]Song 4:9 [c]Song 4:11 [d]Luke 15:7, 10; John 3:29
**2** [a]Rev. 3:20 [1]*my companion, friend* [2]*curls* or *hair*
**3** [1]*dirty*
**4** [1]*opening*
**6** [a]Song 3:1 [1]Lit. *soul*
**7** [a]Song 3:3
**9** [a]Song 1:8; 6:1 [1]*adjure*
**10** [1]*Distinguished*
**12** [a]Song 1:15; 4:1 [1]*sitting in a setting*

CHAPTER 6
**1** [a]Song 1:8; 5:9

THE SHULAMITE

2 My beloved has gone to his [a]garden,
To the beds of spices,
To feed *his flock* in the gardens,
And to gather lilies.
3 [a]I *am* my beloved's,
And my beloved *is* mine.
He feeds *his flock* among the lilies.

THE BELOVED

4 O my love, you *are as* beautiful as Tirzah,
Lovely as Jerusalem,
Awesome as *an army* with banners!
5 Turn your eyes away from me,
For they have [1]overcome me.
Your hair *is* [a]like a flock of goats
Going down from Gilead.
6 [a]Your teeth *are* like a flock of sheep
Which have come up from the washing;
Every one bears twins,
And none *is* [1]barren among them.
7 [a]Like a piece of pomegranate
*Are* your temples behind your veil.

8 There are sixty queens
And eighty concubines,
And [a]virgins without number.
9 My dove, my [a]perfect one,
Is the only one,
The only one of her mother,
The favorite of the one who bore her.
The daughters saw her
And called her blessed,
The queens and the concubines,
And they praised her.

10 Who is she who looks forth as the morning,
Fair as the moon,
Clear as the sun,
[a]Awesome as *an army* with banners?

THE SHULAMITE

11 I went down to the garden of nuts
To see the verdure of the valley,
[a]To see whether the vine had budded
*And* the pomegranates had bloomed.
12 Before I was even aware,
My soul had made me
*As* the chariots of [1]my noble people.

THE BELOVED AND HIS FRIENDS

13 Return, return, O Shulamite;
Return, return, that we may look upon you!

THE SHULAMITE

What would you see in the Shulamite—
As it were, the dance of [1]the two camps?

## *The Beauty of the Shulamite Girl*

THE BELOVED

7 How beautiful are your feet in sandals,
[a]O prince's daughter!
The curves of your thighs *are* like jewels,
The work of the hands of a skillful workman.
2 Your navel *is* a rounded goblet;
It lacks no [1]blended beverage.
Your waist *is* a heap of wheat
Set about with lilies.
3 [a]Your two breasts *are* like two fawns,
Twins of a gazelle.
4 [a]Your neck *is* like an ivory tower,
Your eyes *like* the pools in Heshbon
By the gate of Bath Rabbim.
Your nose *is* like the tower of Lebanon
Which looks toward Damascus.
5 Your head *crowns* you like *Mount* Carmel,
And the hair of your head *is* like purple;
A king *is* held captive by *your* tresses.

6 How fair and how pleasant you are,
O love, with your delights!
7 This stature of yours is like a palm tree,
And your breasts *like* its clusters.
8 I said, "I will go up to the palm tree,
I will take hold of its branches."
Let now your breasts be like clusters
of the vine,
The fragrance of your [1]breath like apples,
9 And the roof of your mouth
like the best wine.

THE SHULAMITE

*The wine* goes *down* smoothly for my
beloved,
[1]Moving gently the [2]lips of sleepers.
10 [a]I *am* my beloved's,
And [b]his desire *is* toward me.

11 Come, my beloved,
Let us go forth to the field;
Let us lodge in the villages.
12 Let us get up early to the vineyards;
Let us [a]see if the vine has budded,
*Whether* the grape blossoms are open,
*And* the pomegranates are in bloom.
There I will give you my love.
13 The [a]mandrakes give off a fragrance,
And at our gates [b]*are* pleasant *fruits,*
All manner, new and old,
Which I have laid up for you, my beloved.

## *Lovers Reunited at Their Country Home*

8 Oh, that you were like my brother,
Who nursed at my mother's breasts!
*If* I should find you outside,
I would kiss you;
I would not be despised.
2 I would lead you *and* bring you
Into the [a]house of my mother,
She *who* used to instruct me.
I would cause you to drink of [b]spiced wine,
Of the juice of my pomegranate.

(TO THE DAUGHTERS OF JERUSALEM)

3 [a]His left hand *is* under my head,
And his right hand embraces me.
4 [a]I charge you, O daughters of Jerusalem,
Do not stir up nor awaken love
Until it pleases.

A RELATIVE

5 [a]Who *is* this coming up from the wilderness,
Leaning upon her beloved?

I awakened you under the apple tree.
There your mother brought you forth;
There she *who* bore you brought *you* forth.

THE SHULAMITE TO HER BELOVED

6 [a]Set me as a seal upon your heart,
As a seal upon your arm;
For love *is as* strong as death,
[b]Jealousy *as* [1]cruel as [2]the grave;

---

2 [a]Song 4:16; 5:1
3 [a]Song 2:16; 7:10
5 [a]Song 4:1 [1]*overwhelmed*
6 [a]Song 4:2 [1]*bereaved*
7 [a]Song 4:3
8 [a]Song 1:3
9 [a]Song 2:14; 5:2
10 [a]Song 6:4
11 [a]Song 7:12
12 [1]Or *Ammi Nadib*
13 [1]Or *Mahanaim*

CHAPTER 7
1 [a]Ps. 45:13
2 [1]Lit. *mixed* or *spiced drink*
3 [a]Song 4:5
4 [a]Song 4:4
8 [1]Lit. *nose*
9 [1]*Gliding over* [2]LXX, Syr., Vg. *lips and teeth.*
10 [a]Song 2:16; 6:3 [b]Ps. 45:11
12 [a]Song 6:11
13 [a]Gen. 30:14 [b]Song 2:3; 4:13, 16; Matt. 13:52

CHAPTER 8
2 [a]Song 3:4 [b]Prov. 9:2
3 [a]Song 2:6
4 [a]Song 2:7; 3:5
5 [a]Song 3:6
6 [a]Is. 49:16; Jer. 22:24; Hag. 2:23 [b]Prov. 6:34, 35 [1]*severe,* lit. *hard* [2]Or *Sheol*

Its flames *are* flames of fire,
[3]A most vehement flame.
7 Many waters cannot quench love,
Nor can the floods drown it.
[a]If a man would give for love
All the wealth of his house,
It would be utterly despised.

THE SHULAMITE'S BROTHERS

**8** [a]We have a little sister,
And she has no breasts.
What shall we do for our sister
In the day when she is spoken for?
9 If she *is* a wall,
We will build upon her
A battlement of silver;
And if she *is* a door,
We will enclose her
With boards of cedar.

THE SHULAMITE

10 I *am* a wall,
And my breasts like towers;
Then I became in his eyes
As one who found peace.
11 Solomon had a vineyard at Baal Hamon;
[a]He leased the vineyard to keepers;
Everyone was to bring for its fruit
A thousand silver coins.

(TO SOLOMON)

12 My own vineyard *is* before me.
You, O Solomon, *may have* a thousand,
And those who tend its fruit two hundred.

THE BELOVED

**13** You who dwell in the gardens,
The companions listen for your voice—
[a]Let me hear it!

THE SHULAMITE

14 [a]Make[1] haste, my beloved,
And [b]be like a gazelle
Or a young stag
On the mountains of spices.

**6** [3]Lit. *A flame of YAH,* poetic form of *YHWH, the* LORD
**7** [a]Prov. 6:35
**8** [a]Ezek. 23:33
**11** [a]Matt. 21:33
**13** [a]Song 2:14
**14** [a]Rev. 22:17, 20 [b]Song 2:7, 9, 17 [1]*Hurry,* lit. *Flee*

*The Book of*

# ISAIAH

## *Judah Called to Repentance*

THE [a]vision of Isaiah the son of Amoz, which he saw concerning Judah and Jerusalem in the [b]days of Uzziah, Jotham, Ahaz, *and* Hezekiah, kings of Judah.

**2** [a]Hear, O heavens, and give ear, O earth!
For the LORD has spoken:
"I have nourished and brought up children,
And they have rebelled against Me;
3 [a]The ox knows its owner
And the donkey its master's [1]crib;
*But* Israel [b]does not know,
My people do not [2]consider."

4 Alas, sinful nation,
A people [1]laden with iniquity,
[a]A [2]brood of evildoers,
Children who are corrupters!
They have forsaken the LORD,
They have provoked to anger
The Holy One of Israel,
They have turned away backward.

**5** [a]Why should you be stricken again?
You will revolt more and more.
The whole head is sick,
And the whole heart faints.
6 From the sole of the foot even to the head,
*There is* no soundness in it,
*But* wounds and bruises and putrefying sores;
They have not been closed or bound up,
Or soothed with ointment.

7 [a]Your country *is* desolate,
Your cities *are* burned with fire;
Strangers devour your land in your presence;
And *it is* desolate,
as overthrown by strangers.
8 So the daughter of Zion is left [a]as a [1]booth in
a vineyard,
As a hut in a garden of cucumbers,
[b]As a besieged city.
9 [a]Unless the LORD of hosts
Had left to us a very small remnant,
We would have become like [b]Sodom,
We would have been made like Gomorrah.

**10** Hear the word of the LORD,
You rulers [a]of Sodom;
Give ear to the law of our God,
You people of Gomorrah:
11 "To what purpose *is* the multitude of your
[a]sacrifices to Me?"
Says the LORD.
"I have had enough of burnt offerings of rams
And the fat of fed cattle.
I do not delight in the blood of bulls,
Or of lambs or goats.

12 "When you come [a]to appear before Me,
Who has required this from your hand,
To trample My courts?
13 Bring no more [a]futile[1] sacrifices;
Incense is an abomination to Me.
The New Moons, the Sabbaths,
and [b]the calling of assemblies—
I cannot endure iniquity
and the sacred meeting.
14 Your [a]New Moons and your [b]appointed feasts
My soul hates;
They are a trouble to Me,
I am weary of bearing *them.*
15 [a]When you [1]spread out your hands,
I will hide My eyes from you;
[b]Even though you make many prayers,
I will not hear.
Your hands are full of [2]blood.

CHAPTER 1
**1** [a]Num. 12:6 [b]2 Chr. 26—32
**2** [a]Jer. 2:12
**3** [a]Jer. 8:7 [b]Jer. 9:3, 6 [1]*manger* or *feed trough* [2]*understand*
**4** [a]Is. 57:3, 4; Matt. 3:7 [1]Lit. *heavy, weighed down* [2]*offspring, seed*
**5** [a]Jer. 5:3
**7** [a]Deut. 28:51, 52; 2 Chr. 36:19
**8** [a]Job 27:18 [b]Jer. 4:17 [1]*shelter*
**9** [a]2 Kin. 25:11, 22; Lam. 3:22 [b]Gen. 19:24; Rom. 9:29
**10** [a]Deut. 32:32
**11** [a][1 Sam. 15:22]
**12** [a]Ex. 23:17
**13** [a]Matt. 15:9 [b]Joel 1:14 [1]*worthless*
**14** [a]Num. 28:11 [b]Lam. 2:6
**15** [a]Prov. 1:28 [b]Ps. 66:18; Is. 59:1–3; Mic. 3:4 [1]Pray [2]*bloodshed*

16 "Wash[a] yourselves, make yourselves clean;
Put away the evil of your doings
from before My eyes.
[b]Cease to do evil,
17 Learn to do good;
Seek justice,
Rebuke [1]the oppressor;
[2]Defend the fatherless,
Plead for the widow.

**18** "Come now, and let us [a]reason together,"
Says the LORD,
"Though your sins are like scarlet,
[b]They shall be as white as snow;
Though they are red like crimson,
They shall be as wool.
19 If you are willing and obedient,
You shall eat the good of the land;
20 But if you refuse and rebel,
You shall be devoured by the sword";
[a]For the mouth of the LORD has spoken.

**21** [a]How the faithful city has become a [1]harlot!
It was full of justice;
Righteousness lodged in it,
But now [b]murderers.
22 [a]Your silver has become dross,
Your wine mixed with water.
23 [a]Your princes *are* rebellious,
And [b]companions of thieves;
[c]Everyone loves bribes,
And follows after rewards.
They [d]do not defend the fatherless,
Nor does the cause of the widow
come before them.

**24** Therefore the Lord says,
The LORD of hosts, the Mighty One of Israel,
"Ah, [a]I will [1]rid Myself of My adversaries,
And [2]take vengeance on My enemies.
25 I will turn My hand against you,
And [a]thoroughly[1] purge away your dross,
And take away all your alloy.
26 I will restore your judges [a]as at the first,
And your counselors as at the beginning.
Afterward [b]you shall be called the city of
righteousness, the faithful city."

27 Zion shall be redeemed with justice,
And her [1]penitents with righteousness.
28 The [a]destruction of transgressors
and of sinners *shall be* together,
And those who forsake the LORD
shall be consumed.
29 For [1]they shall be ashamed of the [2]terebinth
trees
Which you have desired;
And you shall be embarrassed
because of the gardens
Which you have chosen.
30 For you shall be as a terebinth whose leaf
fades,
And as a garden that has no water.
31 [a]The strong shall be as tinder,
And the work of it as a spark;
Both will burn together,
And no one shall [b]quench *them.*

## *Judgment on the Proud*

**2** The word that Isaiah the son of Amoz saw concerning Judah and Jerusalem.

2 Now [a]it shall come to pass [b]in the latter days
[c]*That* the mountain of the LORD's house
Shall be established on the top of the
mountains,
And shall be exalted above the hills;
And all nations shall flow to it.
3 Many people shall come and say,
[a]"Come, and let us go up to the mountain of
the LORD,
To the house of the God of Jacob;
He will teach us His ways,
And we shall walk in His paths."
[b]For out of Zion shall go forth the law,
And the word of the LORD from Jerusalem.
4 He shall judge between the nations,
And rebuke many people;
They shall beat their swords into plowshares,
And their spears into pruning [1]hooks;
Nation shall not lift up sword against nation,
Neither shall they learn war anymore.

**5** O house of Jacob, come and let us [a]walk
In the light of the LORD.

6 For You have forsaken Your people, the
house of Jacob,
Because they are filled [a]with eastern ways;
They *are* [b]soothsayers like the Philistines,
[c]And they [1]are pleased with the children of
foreigners.
7 [a]Their land is also full of silver and gold,
And there is no end to their treasures;
Their land is also full of horses,
And there is no end to their chariots.
8 [a]Their land is also full of idols;
They worship the work of their own hands,
That which their own fingers have made.
9 People bow down,
And each man humbles himself;
Therefore do not forgive them.

**10** [a]Enter into the rock, and hide in the dust,
From the terror of the LORD
And the glory of His majesty.
11 The [1]lofty looks of man shall be [a]humbled,
The haughtiness of men
shall be bowed down,
And the LORD alone
shall be exalted [b]in that day.

**12** For the day of the LORD of hosts
*Shall come* upon everything proud and lofty,
Upon everything lifted up—
And it shall be brought low—
13 Upon all [a]the cedars of Lebanon
*that are* high and lifted up,
And upon all the oaks of Bashan;
14 [a]Upon all the high mountains,
And upon all the hills *that are* lifted up;
15 Upon every high tower,
And upon every fortified wall;
16 [a]Upon all the ships of Tarshish,
And upon all the beautiful sloops.
17 The [1]loftiness of man shall be bowed down,
And the haughtiness of men
shall be brought low;
The LORD alone will be exalted in that day,
18 But the idols [1]He shall utterly abolish.

19 They shall go into the [a]holes of the rocks,
And into the caves of the [1]earth,
[b]From the terror of the LORD
And the glory of His majesty,
When He arises [c]to shake the earth mightily.

20 In that day a man will cast away
his idols of silver
And his idols of gold,

**16** [a]Jer. 4:14 [b]Rom. 12:9
**17** [1]Some ancient vss. *the oppressed* [2]*Vindicate*
**18** [a]Is. 43:26 [b]Ps. 51:7
**20** [a][Titus 1:2]
**21** [a]Jer. 2:20 [b]Mic. 3:1–3 [1]Unfaithful
**22** [a]Jer. 6:28
**23** [a]Hos. 9:15 [b]Prov. 29:24 [c]Jer. 22:17 [d]Jer. 5:28
**24** [a]Deut. 28:63 [1]*be relieved of* [2]*avenge Myself*
**25** [a]Mal. 3:3 [1]*refine with lye*
**26** [a]Jer. 33:7–11 [b]Zech. 8:3
**27** [1]Lit. *returners*
**28** [a][2 Thess. 1:8, 9]
**29** [1]So with MT, LXX, Vg.; some Heb. mss., Tg. *you* [2]Sites of pagan worship
**31** [a]Ezek. 32:21 [b]Mark 9:43

CHAPTER 2
**2** [a]Mic. 4:1 [b]Gen. 49:1 [c]Ps. 68:15
**3** [a]Jer. 50:5 [b]Luke 24:47
**4** [1]*knives*
**5** [a]Eph. 5:8
**6** [a]Num. 23:7 [b]Deut. 18:14 [c]Ps. 106:35 [1]Or *clap, shake hands to make bargains with the children*
**7** [a]Deut. 17:16
**8** [a]Jer. 2:28
**10** [a]Rev. 6:15, 16
**11** [a]Prov. 16:5 [b]Hos. 2:16 [1]*proud*
**13** [a]Zech. 11:1, 2
**14** [a]Is. 30:25
**16** [a]1 Kin. 10:22
**17** [1]*pride*
**18** [1]Or *shall utterly vanish*
**19** [a]Hos. 10:8 [b][2 Thess. 1:9] [c]Hag. 2:6, 7 [1]Lit. *dust*

Which they made,
*each* for himself to worship,
To the moles and bats,
21 To go into the clefts of the rocks,
And into the crags of the rugged rocks,
From the terror of the LORD
And the glory of His majesty,
When He arises to shake the earth mightily.

22 [a]Sever[1] yourselves from such a man,
Whose [b]breath *is* in his nostrils;
For [2]of what account is he?

## *Judgment on Judah*

**3** For behold, the Lord, the LORD of hosts,
[a]Takes away from Jerusalem and from Judah
[b]The[1] stock and the store,
The whole supply of bread
and the whole supply of water;
2 [a]The mighty man and the man of war,
The judge and the prophet,
And the diviner and the elder;
3 The captain of fifty and the [1]honorable man,
The counselor and the skillful artisan,
And the expert enchanter.

4 "I will give [a]children[1] *to be* their princes,
And [2]babes shall rule over them.
5 The people will be oppressed,
Every one by another and every one
by his neighbor;
The child will be insolent toward the [1]elder,
And the [2]base toward the honorable."

6 When a man takes hold of his brother
In the house of his father, *saying,*
"You have clothing;
You be our ruler,
And *let* these ruins *be* under your
[1]power,"
7 In that day he will protest, saying,
"I cannot cure *your* ills,
For in my house *is* neither food nor clothing;
Do not make me a ruler of the people."

8 For [a]Jerusalem stumbled,
And Judah is fallen,
Because their tongue and their doings
*Are* against the LORD,
To provoke the eyes of His glory.
9 The look on their countenance witnesses
against them,
And they declare their sin as [a]Sodom;
They do not hide *it.*
Woe to their soul!
For they have brought evil upon themselves.

**10** "Say to the righteous
[a]that *it shall be* well *with them,*
[b]For they shall eat the fruit of their doings.
11 Woe to the wicked! [a]*It shall be* ill *with him,*
For the reward of his hands shall be [1]given
him.
12 *As for* My people,
children *are* their oppressors,
And women rule over them.
O My people! [a]Those who lead you [1]cause
*you* to err,
And destroy the way of your paths."

**13** The LORD stands up [a]to [1]plead,
And stands to judge the people.
14 The LORD will enter into judgment
With the elders of His people
And His princes:
"For you have [1]eaten up [a]the vineyard;
The plunder of the poor *is* in your houses.
15 What do you mean by [a]crushing My people
And grinding the faces of the poor?"
Says the Lord GOD of hosts.

**16** Moreover the LORD says:
"Because the daughters of Zion are haughty,
And walk with [1]outstretched necks
And [2]wanton eyes,
Walking and [3]mincing *as* they go,
Making a jingling with their feet,
17 Therefore the Lord will strike with [a]a scab
The crown of the head
of the daughters of Zion,
And the LORD will [b]uncover
their secret parts."

**18** In that day the Lord will take away the
finery:
The jingling anklets, the [1]scarves, and the
[a]crescents;
19 The pendants, the bracelets, and the veils;
20 The headdresses, the leg ornaments, and the
headbands;
The perfume boxes, the charms,
21 and the rings;
The nose jewels,
22 the festal apparel, and the mantles;
The outer garments, the purses,
23 and the mirrors;
The fine linen, the turbans, and the robes.

**24** And so it shall be:

Instead of a sweet smell
there will be a stench;
Instead of a sash, a rope;
Instead of well-set hair, [a]baldness;
Instead of a rich robe, a girding of sackcloth;
And [1]branding instead of beauty.
25 Your men shall fall by the sword,
And your [1]mighty in the war.

26 [a]Her gates shall lament and mourn,
And she *being* desolate
[b]shall sit on the ground.

## *Jerusalem's Glorious Future*

**4** And [a]in that day seven women shall take
hold of one man, saying,
"We will [b]eat our own food
and wear our own apparel;
Only let us be called by your name,
To take away [c]our reproach."

2 In that day [a]the Branch of the LORD shall be
beautiful and glorious;
And the fruit of the earth *shall be* excellent
and appealing
For those of Israel who have escaped.

3 And it shall come to pass that *he who is* left in
Zion and remains in Jerusalem [a]will be called
holy—everyone who is [b]recorded among the living
in Jerusalem.
4 When [a]the Lord has washed away the filth of
the daughters of Zion, and purged the [1]blood of
Jerusalem from her midst, by the spirit of judgment and by the spirit of burning,
5 then the LORD will create above every dwelling place of Mount Zion, and above her assemblies, [a]a cloud and smoke by day and [b]the shining
of a flaming fire by night. For over all the glory
there *will be* a [1]covering.

---

**22** [a]Ps. 146:3; Jer. 17:5 [b]Job 27:3 [1]Lit. *Cease yourselves from the man* [2]Lit. *in what is he to be esteemed*

CHAPTER 3

**1** [a]2 Kin. 25:3; Is. 5:13; Jer. 37:21 [b]Lev. 26:26 [1]Every support
**2** [a]2 Kin. 24:14; Is. 9:14, 15; Ezek. 17:12, 13
**3** [1]Eminent looking men
**4** [a]Eccl. 10:16 [1]*boys* [2]Or *capricious ones*
**5** [1]*aged* [2]*despised, lightly esteemed*
**6** [1]Lit. *hand*
**8** [a]2 Chr. 36:16, 17; Mic. 3:12
**9** [a]Gen. 13:13; Is. 1:10–15
**10** [a][Deut. 28:1–14; Eccl. 8:12; Is. 54:17] [b]Ps. 128:2
**11** [a][Ps. 11:6; Eccl. 8:12, 13] [1]*done to him*
**12** [a]Is. 9:16 [1]*lead you astray*
**13** [a]Is. 66:16; Hos. 4:1; Mic. 6:2 [1]*contend, plead His case*
**14** [a]Matt. 21:33 [1]*burned*
**15** [a]Mic. 3:2, 3
**16** [1]Head held high [2]*seductive, ogling* [3]*tripping* or *skipping*
**17** [a]Deut. 28:27 [b]Jer. 13:22
**18** [a]Judg. 8:21, 26 [1]*headbands*
**24** [a]Is. 22:12; Ezek. 27:31; Amos 8:10 [1]*burning scar*
**25** [1]Lit. *strength*
**26** [a]Jer. 14:2; Lam. 1:4 [b]Lam. 2:10

CHAPTER 4

**1** [a]Is. 2:11, 17 [b]2 Thess. 3:12 [c]Luke 1:25
**2** [a]Is. 12:1–6; [Jer. 23:5]; Zech. 3:8
**3** [a]Is. 60:21 [b]Phil. 4:3
**4** [a]Mal. 3:2, 3 [1]*bloodshed*
**5** [a]Ex. 13:21, 22; Num. 9:15–23 [b]Zech. 2:5 [1]*canopy*

6 And there will be a tabernacle for shade in the daytime from the heat, [a]for a place of refuge, and for a shelter from storm and rain.

### *Woes Pronounced on the Faithless*

5 Now let me sing to my Well-beloved
A song of my Beloved [a]regarding His
vineyard:

My Well-beloved has a vineyard
[1]On a very fruitful hill.
2 He dug it up and cleared out its stones,
And planted it with the choicest vine.
He built a tower in its midst,
And also [1]made a winepress in it;
[a]So He expected *it* to bring forth *good* grapes,
But it brought forth wild grapes.

3 "And now, O inhabitants of Jerusalem and
men of Judah,
[a]Judge, please, between Me and My vineyard.
4 What more could have been done to My
vineyard
That I have not done in [a]it?
Why then, when I expected *it* to bring forth
*good* grapes,
Did it bring forth wild grapes?
5 And now, please let Me tell you
what I will do to My vineyard:
[a]I will take away its hedge,
and it shall be burned;
*And* break down its wall,
and it shall be trampled down.
6 I will lay it [a]waste;
It shall not be pruned or [1]dug,
But there shall come up briers and [b]thorns.
I will also command the clouds
That they rain no rain on it."

7 For the vineyard of the LORD of hosts *is* the
house of Israel,
And the men of Judah are His pleasant plant.
He looked for justice, but behold, oppression;
For righteousness, but behold, [1]a cry *for help.*

8 Woe to those who [1]join [a]house to house;
They add field to field,
Till *there is* no place
Where they may dwell alone
in the midst of the land!
9 [a]In my hearing the LORD of hosts *said,*
"Truly, many houses shall be desolate,
Great and beautiful ones, without inhabitant.
10 For ten acres of vineyard shall yield one
[a]bath,[1]
And a [2]homer of seed shall yield one ephah."

11 [a]Woe to those who rise early in the morning,
*That* they may [1]follow intoxicating drink;
Who continue until night,
*till* wine inflames them!
12 [a]The harp and the strings,
The tambourine and flute,
And wine are in their feasts;
But [b]they do not regard the work
of the LORD,
Nor consider the operation of His hands.

13 [a]Therefore my people have gone
into captivity,
Because *they have* no [b]knowledge;
Their honorable men *are* famished,
And their multitude dried up with thirst.
14 Therefore Sheol has enlarged itself
And opened its mouth beyond measure;
Their glory and their multitude
and their pomp,
And he who is jubilant, shall descend into it.
15 People shall be brought down,
[a]Each man shall be humbled,
And the eyes of the lofty shall be humbled.
16 But the LORD of hosts
shall be [a]exalted in judgment,
And God who is holy shall be hallowed in
righteousness.
17 Then the lambs shall feed in their pasture,
And in the waste places of [a]the [1]fat ones
strangers shall eat.

18 Woe to those who [1]draw iniquity
with cords of [2]vanity,
And sin as if with a cart rope;
19 [a]That say, "Let Him make speed
*and* hasten His work,
That we may see *it;*
And let the counsel of the Holy One
of Israel draw near and come,
That we may know *it.*"

20 Woe to those who call evil good,
and good evil;
Who put darkness for light,
and light for darkness;
Who put bitter for sweet,
and sweet for bitter!

21 Woe to *those who are* [a]wise
in their own eyes,
And prudent in their own sight!

22 Woe to men mighty at drinking wine,
Woe to men valiant for mixing intoxicating
drink,
23 Who [a]justify the wicked for a bribe,
And take away justice from the righteous
man!

24 Therefore, [a]as the [1]fire devours the stubble,
And the flame consumes the chaff,
*So* [b]their root will be as rottenness,
And their blossom will ascend like dust;
Because they have rejected the law of the
LORD of hosts,
And despised the word of the Holy One of
Israel.
25 [a]Therefore the anger of the LORD is aroused
against His people;
He has stretched out His hand against them
And stricken them,
And [b]the hills trembled.
Their carcasses *were* as refuse
in the midst of the streets.

[c]For all this His anger is not turned away,
But His hand *is* stretched out still.

26 [a]He will lift up a banner to the nations from
afar,
And will [b]whistle to them from [c]the end of
the earth;
Surely [d]they shall come with speed, swiftly.
27 No one will be weary or stumble among
them,
No one will slumber or sleep;
Nor [a]will the belt on their loins be loosed,
Nor the strap of their sandals be broken;
28 [a]Whose arrows *are* sharp,
And all their bows bent;
Their horses' hooves will [1]seem like flint,
And their wheels like a whirlwind.

---

6 [a]Ps. 27:5; Is. 25:4

CHAPTER 5

1 [a]Ps. 80:8; Jer. 2:21; Matt. 21:33; Mark 12:1; Luke 20:9 [1]Lit. *In a horn, the son of fatness*
2 [a]Deut. 32:6 [1]Lit. *hewed out*
3 [a][Rom. 3:4]
4 [a]2 Chr. 36:15, 16; Jer. 2:5; 7:25, 26; Mic. 6:3; Matt. 23:37
5 [a]2 Chr. 36:19; Ps. 80:12; 89:40, 41
6 [a]2 Chr. 36:19–21 [b]Is. 7:19–25; Jer. 25:11 [1]*hoed*
7 [1]*wailing*
8 [a]Jer. 22:13–17; Mic. 2:2; Hab. 2:9–12 [1]Accumulate houses
9 [a]Is. 22:14
10 [a]Ezek. 45:11 [1]1 bath = 1/10 homer [2]1 homer = 1/10 ephah
11 [a]Prov. 23:29, 30; Eccl. 10:16, 17; Is. 5:22 [1]*pursue*
12 [a]Amos 6:5 [b]Job 34:27; Ps. 28:5
13 [a]2 Kin. 24:14–16 [b]Is. 1:3; 27:11; Hos. 4:6
15 [a]Is. 2:9, 11
16 [a]Is. 2:11
17 [a]Is. 10:16 [1]Lit. *fatlings,* rich ones
18 [1]*drag* [2]*emptiness* or *falsehood*
19 [a]Jer. 17:15; Amos 5:18
21 [a]Prov. 3:7; Rom. 1:22; 12:16; [1 Cor. 3:18–20]
23 [a]Ex. 23:8; Prov. 17:15; Is. 1:23; Mic. 3:11; 7:3
24 [a]Ex. 15:7 [b]Job 18:16 [1]Lit. *tongue of fire*
25 [a]2 Kin. 22:13, 17; Is. 66:15 [b]Ps. 18:7; Is. 64:3; Jer. 4:24; Nah. 1:5 [c]Is. 9:12, 17; Jer. 4:8; Dan. 9:16
26 [a]Is. 11:10, 12 [b]Is. 7:18; Zech. 10:8 [c]Mal. 1:11 [d]Joel 2:7
27 [a]Dan. 5:6
28 [a]Jer. 5:16 [1]Lit. *be regarded as*

29 Their roaring *will be* like a lion,
They will roar like young lions;
Yes, they will roar
And lay hold of the prey;
They will carry *it* away safely,
And no one will deliver.
30 In that day they will roar against them
Like the roaring of the sea.
And if *one* [a]looks to the land,
Behold, darkness *and* [1]sorrow;
And the light is darkened by the clouds.

## *Isaiah's Vision and Commission*

**6** In the year that [a]King Uzziah died, I [b]saw the Lord sitting on a throne, high and lifted up, and the train of His *robe* filled the temple.
2 Above it stood seraphim; each one had six wings: with two he covered his face, [a]with two he covered his feet, and with two he flew.
3 And one cried to another and said:

[a]"Holy, holy, holy *is* the LORD of hosts;
[b]The whole earth *is* full of His glory!"

4 And the posts of the door were shaken by the voice of him who cried out, and the house was filled with smoke.
5 So I said:

"Woe *is* me, for I am [1]undone!
Because I *am* a man of [a]unclean lips,
And I dwell in the midst of a people
of unclean lips;
For my eyes have seen the King,
The LORD of hosts."

**6** Then one of the seraphim flew to me, having in his hand a live coal *which* he had taken with the tongs from [a]the altar.
7 And he [a]touched my mouth *with it,* and said:

"Behold, this has touched your lips;
Your iniquity is taken away,
And your sin [1]purged."

**8** Also I heard the voice of the Lord, saying:

"Whom shall I send,
And who will go for [a]Us?"

Then I said, "Here *am* I! Send me."

**9** And He said, "Go, and [a]tell this people:

'Keep on hearing, but do not understand;
Keep on seeing, but do not perceive.'

10 "Make [a]the heart of this people dull,
And their ears heavy,
And shut their eyes;
[b]Lest they see with their eyes,
And hear with their ears,
And understand with their heart,
And return and be healed."

**11** Then I said, "Lord, how long?" And He answered:

[a]"Until the cities are laid waste
and without inhabitant,
The houses are without a man,
The land is utterly desolate,
12 [a]The LORD has removed men far away,
And the forsaken places *are* many in the
midst of the land.
13 But yet a tenth *will be* in it,
And will return and be for consuming,
As a terebinth tree or as an oak,
Whose stump *remains* when it is cut down.
So [a]the holy seed *shall be* its stump."

## *Isaiah Predicts the Messiah*

**7** Now it came to pass in the days of [a]Ahaz the son of Jotham, the son of Uzziah, king of Judah, *that* Rezin king of Syria and Pekah the son of Remaliah, king of Israel, went up to Jerusalem to *make* war against [b]it, but could not [1]prevail against it.
2 And it was told to the house of David, saying, "Syria's forces are [1]deployed in Ephraim." So his heart and the heart of his people were moved as the trees of the woods are moved with the wind.
**3** Then the LORD said to Isaiah, "Go out now to meet Ahaz, you and [1]Shear-Jashub your son, at the end of the aqueduct from the upper pool, on the highway to the Fuller's Field,
4 "and say to him: [1]'Take heed, and [2]be [a]quiet; do not fear or be fainthearted for these two stubs of smoking firebrands, for the fierce anger of Rezin and Syria, and the son of Remaliah.
5 'Because Syria, Ephraim, and the son of Remaliah have plotted evil against you, saying,
6 "Let us go up against Judah and [1]trouble it, and let us make a gap in its wall for ourselves, and set a king over them, the son of Tabel"—
7 'thus says the Lord GOD:

[a]"It shall not stand,
Nor shall it come to pass.
8 [a]For the head of Syria *is* Damascus,
And the head of Damascus *is* Rezin.
Within sixty-five years
Ephraim will be [1]broken,
*So that it will* not *be* a people.
9 The head of Ephraim *is* Samaria,
And the head of Samaria *is* Remaliah's son.
[a]If you will not believe,
Surely you shall not be established." ' "

**10** Moreover the LORD spoke again to Ahaz, saying,
11 [a]"Ask a sign for yourself from the LORD your God; [1]ask it either in the depth or in the height above."
12 But Ahaz said, "I will not ask, nor will I test the LORD!"
13 Then he said, "Hear now, O house of David! *Is it* a small thing for you to weary men, but will you weary my God also?
14 "Therefore the Lord Himself will give you a sign: [a]Behold, the virgin shall conceive and bear [b]a Son, and shall call His name [c]Immanuel.[1]
15 "Curds and honey He shall eat, that He may know to refuse the evil and choose the good.
16 [a]"For before the Child shall know to refuse the evil and choose the good, the land that you dread will be forsaken by [b]both her kings.
17 [a]"The LORD will bring the king of Assyria upon you and your people and your father's house—days that have not come since the day that [b]Ephraim departed from Judah."

**18** And it shall come to pass in that day
*That* the LORD [a]will whistle for the fly
That *is* in the farthest part of the rivers of
Egypt,
And for the bee that *is* in the land of Assyria.
19 They will come, and all of them will rest
In the desolate valleys
and in [a]the clefts of the rocks,
And on all thorns and in all pastures.

**30** [a]Is. 8:22; Jer. 4:23–28; Joel 2:10; Luke 21:25, 26 [1]*distress*

CHAPTER 6

**1** [a]2 Kin. 15:7; 2 Chr. 26:23; Is. 1:1 [b]John 12:41; Rev. 4:2, 3; 20:11
**2** [a]Ezek. 1:11
**3** [a]Rev. 4:8 [b]Num. 14:21; Ps. 72:19
**5** [a]Ex. 6:12, 30 [1]*destroyed, cut off*
**6** [a]Rev. 8:3
**7** [a]Jer. 1:9; Dan. 10:16 [1]*atoned for*
**8** [a]Gen. 1:26
**9** [a]Is. 43:8; Matt. 13:14; Mark 4:12; Luke 8:10; John 12:40; Acts 28:26; Rom. 11:8
**10** [a]Ps. 119:70; Mark 6:1–6; Acts 7:51; Rom. 10:1–4 [b]Jer. 5:21
**11** [a]Mic. 3:12
**12** [a]2 Kin. 25:21; Is. 5:9
**13** [a]Deut. 7:6; Ezra 9:2

CHAPTER 7

**1** [a]2 Chr. 28 [b]2 Kin. 16:5, 9 [1]*conquer it*
**2** [1]Lit. *settled upon*
**3** [1]Lit. *A Remnant Shall Return*
**4** [a]Ex. 14:13; Is. 30:15; Lam. 3:26 [1]*Be careful* [2]*be calm*
**6** [1]*cause a sickening dread*
**7** [a]2 Kin. 16:5; Is. 8:10; Acts 4:25, 26
**8** [a]2 Sam. 8:6; 2 Kin. 17:6 [1]Lit. *shattered*
**9** [a]2 Chr. 20:20; Is. 5:24
**11** [a]Matt. 12:38 [1]Lit. *make the request deep or make it high above*
**14** [a]Matt. 1:23; Luke 1:31; John 1:45; Rev. 12:5 [b][Is. 9:6] [c]Is. 8:8, 10 [1]Lit. *God With Us*
**16** [a]Is. 8:4 [b]2 Kin. 15:30
**17** [a]2 Chr. 28:19, 20; Is. 8:7, 8; 10:5, 6 [b]1 Kin. 12:16
**18** [a]Is. 5:26
**19** [a]Is. 2:19; Jer. 16:16

20 In the same day the Lord will shave with a
[a]hired [b]razor,
With those from beyond [1]the River, with the
king of Assyria,
The head and the hair of the legs,
And will also remove the beard.

21 It shall be in that day
*That* a man will keep alive
a young cow and two sheep;
22 So it shall be, from the abundance of milk
they give,
That he will eat curds;
For curds and honey everyone will eat who is
left in the land.

**23** It shall happen in that day,
*That* wherever there could be a thousand
vines
*Worth* a thousand *shekels* of silver,
[a]It will be for briers and thorns.
24 With arrows and bows men will come there,
Because all the land will become briers and
thorns.

25 And to any hill which could be dug with the
hoe,
You will not go there for fear of briers and
thorns;
But it will become a range for oxen
And a place for sheep to roam.

### *Assyria Will Invade the Land*

**8** Moreover the LORD said to me, "Take a large
scroll, and [a]write on it with a man's pen
concerning [1]Maher-Shalal-Hash-Baz.
2 "And I will take for Myself faithful witnesses
to record, [a]Uriah the priest and Zechariah the son
of Jeberechiah."
3 Then I went to the prophetess, and she conceived and bore a son. Then the LORD said to me,
"Call his name Maher-Shalal-Hash-Baz;
4 [a]"for before the child [1]shall have knowledge to
cry 'My father' and 'My mother,' [b]the riches of
Damascus and the [2]spoil of Samaria will be taken
away before the king of Assyria."
**5** The LORD also spoke to me again, saying:

6 "Inasmuch as these people refused
The waters of [a]Shiloah that flow softly,
And rejoice [b]in Rezin and in Remaliah's son;
7 Now therefore, behold,
the Lord brings up over them
The waters of [1]the River,
strong and mighty—
The king of Assyria and all his glory;
He will [2]go up over all his channels
And go over all his banks.
8 He will pass through Judah,
He will overflow and pass over,
[a]He will reach up to the neck;
And the stretching out of his wings
Will [1]fill the breadth of Your land,
O [b]Immanuel.[2]

**9** "Be[a] shattered, O you peoples,
and be broken in pieces!
Give ear, all you from far countries.
Gird yourselves, but be broken in pieces;
Gird yourselves, but be broken in pieces.
10 [a]Take counsel together,
but it will come to nothing;
Speak the word, [b]but it will not stand,
[c]For [1]God *is* with us."

**11** For the LORD spoke thus to me with [1]a strong
hand, and instructed me that I should not walk in
the way of this people, saying:

12 "Do not say, 'A conspiracy,'
Concerning all that this people
call a conspiracy,
Nor be afraid of their [1]threats,
nor be [2]troubled.
13 The LORD of hosts, Him you shall hallow;
*Let* Him *be* your fear,
And *let* Him *be* your dread.
14 [a]He will be as a [1]sanctuary,
But [b]a stone of stumbling
and a rock of [2]offense
To both the houses of Israel,
As a trap and a snare to the inhabitants of
Jerusalem.
15 And many among them shall [a]stumble;
They shall fall and be broken,
Be snared and [1]taken."

**16** Bind up the testimony,
Seal the law among my disciples.
17 And I will wait on the LORD,
Who [a]hides His face from the house of Jacob;
And I [b]will hope in Him.
18 [a]Here am I and the children whom the LORD
has given me!
*We* [b]*are* for signs and wonders in Israel
From the LORD of hosts,
Who dwells in Mount Zion.

**19** And when they say to you, [a]"Seek those who
are mediums and wizards, [b]who whisper and
mutter," should not a people seek their God?
*Should they* [c]*seek* the dead on behalf of the living?
20 [a]To the law and to the testimony! If they do
not speak according to this word, *it is* because
[b]*there*[1] *is* no light in them.
21 They will pass through it hard pressed and
hungry; and it shall happen, when they are hungry, that they will be enraged and [a]curse [1]their
king and their God, and look upward.
22 Then they will look to the earth, and see
trouble and darkness, gloom of anguish; and *they
will be* driven into darkness.

### *The Birth of the Prince of Peace*

**9** Nevertheless [a]the gloom *will* not *be* upon her
who *is* distressed,
As when at [b]first He lightly esteemed
The land of Zebulun and the land of
Naphtali,
And [c]afterward more heavily oppressed *her,*
*By* the way of the sea, beyond the Jordan,
In Galilee of the Gentiles.
2 [a]The people who walked in darkness
Have seen a great light;
Those who dwelt in the land of the shadow
of death,
Upon them a light has shined.

3 You have multiplied the nation
*And* [1]increased its joy;
They rejoice before You
According to the joy of harvest,
As *men* rejoice [a]when they divide the spoil.
4 For You have broken the yoke of his burden
And the staff of his shoulder,
The rod of his oppressor,
As in the day of [a]Midian.
5 For every warrior's [1]sandal from the noisy
battle,

**20** [a]Is. 10:5, 15 [b]2 Kin. 16:7; 2 Chr. 28:20 [1]The Euphrates
**23** [a]Is. 5:6

CHAPTER 8
**1** [a]Is. 30:8; Hab. 2:2 [1]Lit. *Speed the Spoil, Hasten the Booty*
**2** [a]2 Kin. 16:10
**4** [a]2 Kin. 17:6; Is. 7:16 [b]2 Kin. 15:29 [1]*knows how* [2]*plunder*
**6** [a]John 9:7 [b]Is. 7:1, 2
**7** [1]The Euphrates [2]Overflow
**8** [a]Is. 30:28 [b]Is. 7:14; Matt. 1:23 [1]Lit. *be the fullness of* [2]Lit. *God With Us*
**9** [a]Joel 3:9
**10** [a]Is. 7:7; Acts 5:38 [b]Is. 7:14 [c]Rom. 8:31 [1]Heb. *Immanuel*
**11** [1]Mighty power
**12** [1]Lit. *fear or terror* [2]Lit. *in dread*
**14** [a]Is. 4:6; 25:4; Ezek. 11:16 [b]Luke 2:34; 20:17; Rom. 9:33; 1 Pet. 2:8 [1]*holy abode* [2]*stumbling over*
**15** [a]Matt. 21:44 [1]*captured*
**17** [a]Deut. 31:17; Is. 54:8 [b]Hab. 2:3
**18** [a]Heb. 2:13 [b]Ps. 71:7
**19** [a]1 Sam. 28:8 [b]Is. 29:4 [c]Ps. 106:28
**20** [a]Is. 1:10; 8:16; Luke 16:29 [b]Is. 8:22; Mic. 3:6 [1]Or *they have no dawn*
**21** [a]Rev. 16:11 [1]Or *by their king and by their God*

CHAPTER 9
**1** [a]Is. 8:22 [b]2 Kin. 15:29; 2 Chr. 16:4 [c]Matt. 4:13–16
**2** [a]Matt. 4:16; Luke 1:79; 2 Cor. 4:6; Eph. 5:8
**3** [a]Judg. 5:30 [1]So with Qr., Tg.; Kt., Vg. *not increased joy;* LXX *most of the people You brought down in Your joy*
**4** [a]Judg. 7:22
**5** [1]*boot*

And garments rolled in blood,
[a]Will be used for burning *and* fuel [2]of fire.

6 [a]For unto us a Child is born,
Unto us a [b]Son is given;
And [c]the government will be upon His
shoulder.
And His name will be called
[d]Wonderful, Counselor, [e]Mighty God,
Everlasting Father, [f]Prince of Peace.
7 Of the increase of *His* government and peace
[a]*There will be* no end,
Upon the throne of David
and over His kingdom,
To order it and establish it with judgment
and justice
From that time forward, even forever.
The [b]zeal of the LORD of hosts will perform
this.

**8** The LORD sent a word against [a]Jacob,
And it has fallen on Israel.
9 All the people will know—
Ephraim and the inhabitant of Samaria—
Who say in pride and arrogance of heart:
10 "The bricks have fallen down,
But we will rebuild with hewn stones;
The sycamores are cut down,
But we will replace *them* with cedars."
11 Therefore the LORD shall set up
The adversaries of Rezin against him,
And spur his enemies on,
12 The Syrians before
and the Philistines behind;
And they shall devour Israel with an open
mouth.

For all this His anger is not turned away,
But His hand *is* [1]stretched out still.

**13** For the people do not turn to Him who
strikes them,
Nor do they seek the LORD of hosts.
14 Therefore the LORD will cut off
head and tail from Israel,
Palm branch and bulrush [a]in one day.
15 The elder and honorable, he *is* the head;
The prophet who teaches lies, he *is* the tail.
16 For [a]the leaders of this people cause *them* to
err,
And *those who are* led by them are
destroyed.
17 Therefore the LORD [a]will have no joy in their
young men,
Nor have mercy on their fatherless and
widows;
For everyone *is* a hypocrite and an evildoer,
And every mouth speaks [1]folly.

[b]For all this His anger is not turned away,
But His hand *is* stretched out still.

**18** For wickedness [a]burns as the fire;
It shall devour the briers and thorns,
And kindle in the thickets of the forest;
They shall mount up *like* rising smoke.
19 Through the wrath of the LORD of hosts
[a]The land is burned up,
And the people shall be as fuel for the fire;
[b]No man shall spare his brother.
20 And he shall [1]snatch on the right hand
And be hungry;
He shall devour on the left hand
[a]And not be satisfied;
[b]Every man shall eat the flesh of his own arm.
21 Manasseh *shall devour* Ephraim,
and Ephraim Manasseh,
Together they *shall be* [a]against Judah.

[b]For all this His anger is not turned away,
But His hand *is* stretched out still.

## *Assyria Shall Be Broken*

**10** "Woe to those who [a]decree unrighteous
decrees,
Who write misfortune,
*Which* they have prescribed
2 To rob the needy of justice,
And to take what is right from the poor of
My people,
That widows may be their prey,
And *that* they may rob the fatherless.
3 [a]What will you do in [b]the day of punishment,
And in the desolation *which* will come from
[c]afar?
To whom will you flee for help?
And where will you leave your glory?
4 Without Me they shall bow down among the
[a]prisoners,
And they shall fall [1]among the slain."

[b]For all this His anger is not turned away,
But His hand *is* stretched out still.

**5** "Woe to Assyria, [a]the rod of My anger
And the staff in whose hand is My
indignation.
6 I will send him against [a]an ungodly nation,
And against the people of My wrath
I will [b]give him charge,
To seize the spoil, to take the prey,
And to tread them down like the mire of the
streets.
7 [a]Yet he does not mean so,
Nor does his heart think so;
But *it is* in his heart to destroy,
And cut off not a few nations.
8 [a]For he says,
'*Are* not my princes altogether kings?
9 *Is* not [a]Calno [b]like Carchemish?
*Is* not Hamath like Arpad?
*Is* not Samaria [c]like Damascus?
10 As my hand has found the kingdoms of the
idols,
Whose carved images excelled those
of Jerusalem and Samaria,
11 As I have done to Samaria and her idols,
Shall I not do also to Jerusalem
and her idols?' "

**12** Therefore it shall come to pass, when the
LORD has [1]performed all His work [a]on Mount Zion
and on Jerusalem, *that He will say,* [b]"I will punish
the fruit of the arrogant heart of the king of
Assyria, and the glory of his haughty looks."
13 [a]For he says:

"By the strength of my hand I have done *it,*
And by my wisdom, for I am prudent;
Also I have removed the boundaries
of the people,
And have robbed their treasuries;
So I have put down the inhabitants
like a [1]valiant *man.*
14 [a]My hand has found like a nest the riches of
the people,
And as one gathers eggs *that are* left,
I have gathered all the earth;
And there was no one who moved *his* wing,
Nor opened *his* mouth with even a peep."

**5** [a]Is. 66:15 [2]*for the fire*
**6** [a][Is. 7:14; Luke 2:11]; John 1:45 [b]Luke 2:7; [John 3:16; 1 John 4:9] [c][Matt. 28:18; 1 Cor. 15:25]; Rev. 12:5 [d]Judg. 13:18 [e]Titus 2:13 [f]Eph. 2:14
**7** [a]Dan. 2:44; Matt. 1:1, 6; Luke 1:32, 33; John 7:42 [b]Is. 37:32
**8** [a]Gen. 32:28
**12** [1]In judgment
**14** [a]Rev. 18:8
**16** [a]Is. 3:12; Mic. 3:1, 5, 9; Matt. 15:14
**17** [a]Ps. 147:10 [b]Is. 5:25 [1]*foolishness*
**18** [a]Ps. 83:14; [Is. 1:7; 10:17]; Nah. 1:10; Mal. 4:1
**19** [a]Is. 8:22 [b]Mic. 7:2, 6
**20** [a]Lev. 26:26 [b]Jer. 19:9 [1]*slice off* or *tear*
**21** [a]2 Chr. 28:6, 8; Is. 11:13 [b]Is. 9:12, 17

CHAPTER 10
**1** [a]Ps. 58:2
**3** [a]Job 31:14 [b]Is. 13:6; Jer. 9:9; Hos. 9:7; Luke 19:44 [c]Is. 5:26
**4** [a]Is. 24:22 [b]Is. 5:25 [1]Lit. *under*
**5** [a]Jer. 51:20
**6** [a]Is. 9:17 [b]2 Kin. 17:6; Jer. 34:22
**7** [a]Gen. 50:20; Mic. 4:11, 12; Acts 2:23, 24
**8** [a]2 Kin. 19:10
**9** [a]Gen. 10:10; Amos 6:2 [b]2 Chr. 35:20 [c]2 Kin. 16:9
**12** [a]2 Kin. 19:31; Is. 28:21 [b]2 Kin. 19:35; 2 Chr. 32:21; Jer. 50:18 [1]*completed*
**13** [a][2 Kin. 19:22–24]; Is. 37:24–27; Ezek. 28:4; Dan. 4:30 [1]*mighty*
**14** [a]Job 31:25

**15** Shall [a]the ax boast itself against
him who chops with it?
*Or* shall the saw exalt itself against him who
saws with it?
As if a rod could wield *itself* against those
who lift it up,
*Or* as if a staff could lift up,
*as if it were* not wood!
16 Therefore the Lord, the [1]Lord of hosts,
Will send leanness among his fat ones;
And under his glory
He will kindle a burning
Like the burning of a fire.
17 So the Light of Israel will be for a fire,
And his Holy One for a flame;
[a]It will burn and devour
His thorns and his briers in one day.
18 And it will consume the glory of his forest
and of [a]his fruitful field,
Both soul and body;
And they will be as when a sick man wastes
away.
19 Then the rest of the trees of his forest
Will be so few in number
That a child may write them.

**20** And it shall come to pass in that day
*That* the remnant of Israel,
And such as have escaped of the house of
Jacob,
[a]Will never again depend on him who
[1]defeated them,
But will depend on the LORD,
the Holy One of Israel, in truth.
21 The remnant will return,
the remnant of Jacob,
To the [a]Mighty God.
22 [a]For though your people, O Israel,
be as the sand of the sea,
[b]A remnant of them will return;
The destruction decreed shall overflow with
righteousness.
23 [a]For the Lord GOD of hosts
Will make a determined end
In the midst of all the land.

**24** Therefore thus says the Lord GOD of hosts: "O
My people, who dwell in Zion, [a]do not be afraid of
the Assyrian. He shall strike you with a rod and
lift up his staff against you, in the manner of
[b]Egypt.
25 "For yet a very little while [a]and the indignation will cease, as will My anger in their destruction."
26 And the LORD of hosts will [1]stir up [a]a scourge
for him like the slaughter of [b]Midian at the rock of
Oreb; [c]*as* His rod was on the sea, so will He lift it
up in the manner of Egypt.

27 It shall come to pass in that day
*That* his burden will be taken away from
your shoulder,
And his yoke from your neck,
And the yoke will be destroyed because of
[a]the anointing oil.

**28** He has come to Aiath,
He has passed Migron;
At Michmash he has attended to his
equipment.
29 They have gone [1]along [a]the ridge,
They have taken up lodging at Geba.
Ramah is afraid,
[b]Gibeah of Saul has fled.
30 [1]Lift up your voice,
O daughter [a]of Gallim!
Cause it to be heard as far as [b]Laish—
[2]O poor Anathoth!
31 [a]Madmenah has fled,
The inhabitants of Gebim seek refuge.
32 As yet he will remain [a]at Nob that day;
He will [b]shake his fist at the mount of [c]the
daughter of Zion,
The hill of Jerusalem.

**33** Behold, the Lord,
The LORD of hosts,
Will lop off the bough with terror;
[a]Those of high stature *will be* hewn down,
And the haughty will be humbled.
34 He will cut down the thickets of the forest
with iron,
And Lebanon will fall by the Mighty One.

### *The Righteous Reign of the Messiah*

**11** There [a]shall come forth a [1]Rod
from the [2]stem of [b]Jesse,
And [c]a Branch shall [3]grow out of his roots.
2 [a]The Spirit of the LORD shall rest upon Him,
The Spirit of wisdom and understanding,
The Spirit of counsel and might,
The Spirit of knowledge
and of the fear of the LORD.

3 His delight *is* in the fear of the LORD,
And He shall not judge by the sight of His
eyes,
Nor decide by the hearing of His ears;
4 But [a]with righteousness He shall judge the
poor,
And decide with equity for the meek of the
earth;
He shall [b]strike the earth with the rod of His
mouth,
And with the breath of His lips He shall slay
the wicked.
5 Righteousness shall be the belt of His loins,
And faithfulness the belt of His waist.

**6** "The[a] wolf also shall dwell with the lamb,
The leopard shall lie down
with the young goat,
The calf and the young lion
and the fatling together;
And a little child shall lead them.
7 The cow and the bear shall graze;
Their young ones shall lie down together;
And the lion shall eat straw like the ox.
8 The nursing child shall play
by the cobra's hole,
And the weaned child shall put his hand in
the viper's den.
9 [a]They shall not hurt nor destroy in all My
holy mountain,
For [b]the earth shall be full of the knowledge
of the LORD
As the waters cover the sea.

**10** "And[a] in that day [b]there shall be a Root of
Jesse,
Who shall stand as a [c]banner to the people;
For the [d]Gentiles shall seek Him,
And His resting place shall be glorious."

**11** It shall come to pass in that day
*That* the LORD shall set His hand again the
second time
To recover the remnant of His people who
are left,

---

**15** [a]Jer. 51:20
**16** [1]So with Bg.; MT, DSS *YHWH, the LORD*
**17** [a]Is. 9:18
**18** [a]2 Kin. 19:23
**20** [a]2 Kin. 16:7 [1]Lit. *struck*
**21** [a][Is. 9:6]
**22** [a]Rom. 9:27, 28 [b]Is. 6:13
**23** [a]Is. 28:22; Dan. 9:27; Rom. 9:28
**24** [a]Is. 7:4; 12:2 [b]Ex. 14
**25** [a]Is. 10:5; 26:20; Dan. 11:36
**26** [a]2 Kin. 19:35 [b]Judg. 7:25; Is. 9:4 [c]Ex. 14:26, 27 [1]*arouse*
**27** [a]Ps. 105:15; [1 John 2:20]
**29** [a]1 Sam. 13:23 [b]1 Sam. 11:4 [1]Or *over the pass*
**30** [a]1 Sam. 25:44 [b]Judg. 18:7 [1]Or *Cry shrilly* [2]So with MT, Tg., Vg.; LXX, Syr. *Listen to her, O Anathoth*
**31** [a]Josh. 15:31
**32** [a]1 Sam. 21:1; Neh. 11:32 [b]Is. 13:2 [c]Is. 37:22
**33** [a]Is. 37:24, 36–38; Ezek. 31:3; Amos 2:9

CHAPTER 11
**1** [a][Zech. 6:12]; Rev. 5:5 [b][Is. 9:7; 11:10]; Matt. 1:5; [Acts 13:23] [c]Is. 4:2 [1]*Shoot* [2]*stock* or *trunk* [3]*be fruitful*
**2** [a][Is. 42:1; 48:16; 61:1; Matt. 3:16]; Mark 1:10; Luke 3:22; [John 1:32]
**4** [a]Rev. 19:11 [b]Job 4:9; Is. 30:28, 33; Mal. 4:6; 2 Thess. 2:8
**6** [a]Hos. 2:18
**9** [a]Job 5:23; Is. 65:25; Ezek. 34:25; Hos. 2:18 [b]Ps. 98:2, 3; Is. 45:6; Hab. 2:14
**10** [a]Is. 2:11 [b]Is. 11:1; Rom. 15:12 [c]Is. 27:12, 13 [d]Rom. 15:10

[a]From Assyria and Egypt,
From Pathros and Cush,
From Elam and Shinar,
From Hamath and the [1]islands of the sea.
12 He will set up a banner for the nations,
And will [1]assemble the outcasts of Israel,
And gather together [a]the dispersed of Judah
From the four [2]corners of the earth.
13 Also [a]the envy of Ephraim shall depart,
And the adversaries of Judah shall be cut off;
Ephraim shall not envy Judah,
And Judah shall not harass Ephraim.
14 But they shall fly down upon the shoulder of
the Philistines toward the west;
Together they shall plunder the [1]people of
the East;
[a]They shall lay their hand on Edom and
Moab;
And the people of Ammon shall obey them.
15 The LORD [a]will utterly [1]destroy the tongue of
the Sea of Egypt;
With His mighty wind He will shake His fist
over [2]the River,
And strike it in the seven streams,
And make *men* cross over [3]dryshod.
16 [a]There will be a highway for the remnant of
His people
Who will be left from Assyria,
[b]As it was for Israel
In the day that he came up
from the land of Egypt.

## *Thanksgiving for God's Mercies*

**12** And [a]in that day you will say:

"O LORD, I will praise You;
Though You were angry with me,
Your anger is turned away,
and You comfort me.
2 Behold, God *is* my salvation,
I will trust and not be afraid;
[a]'For [b]YAH, the LORD, *is* my strength and song;
He also has become my salvation.' "
3 Therefore with joy you will draw [a]water
From the wells of salvation.
4 And in that day you will say:

[a]"Praise the LORD, call upon His name;
[b]Declare His deeds among the peoples,
Make mention that His [c]name is exalted.
5 [a]Sing to the LORD,
For He has done excellent things;
This *is* known in all the earth.
6 [a]Cry out and shout, O inhabitant of Zion,
For great *is* [b]the Holy One of Israel
in your midst!"

## *The Doom of Babylon Predicted*

**13** The [a]burden[1] against Babylon which Isaiah the son of Amoz saw.

2 "Lift[a] up a banner [b]on the high mountain,
Raise your voice to them;
[c]Wave your hand, that they may enter the
gates of the nobles.
3 I have commanded My [1]sanctified ones;
I have also called [a]My mighty ones for My
anger—
Those who [b]rejoice in My exaltation."
4 The [a]noise of a multitude in the mountains,
Like that of many people!
A tumultuous noise of the kingdoms
of nations gathered together!
The LORD of hosts musters
The army for battle.
5 They come from a far country,
From the end of heaven—
The [a]LORD and His [1]weapons of indignation,
To destroy the whole [b]land.
6 Wail, [a]for the day of the LORD *is* at hand!
[b]It will come as destruction from the
Almighty.
7 Therefore all hands will be limp,
Every man's heart will melt,
8 And they will be afraid.
[a]Pangs[1] and sorrows will take hold of *them;*
They will be in pain
as a woman in childbirth;
They will be amazed at one another;
Their faces *will be like* flames.
9 Behold, [a]the day of the LORD comes,
Cruel, with both wrath and fierce anger,
To lay the land desolate;
And He will destroy [b]its sinners from it.
10 For the stars of heaven and their
constellations
Will not give their light;
The sun will be [a]darkened in its going forth,
And the moon will not cause its light to
shine.
11 "I will [a]punish the world for *its* evil,
And the wicked for their iniquity;
[b]I will halt the arrogance of the proud,
And will lay low the haughtiness of the
[1]terrible.
12 I will make a mortal more rare than fine
gold,
A man more than the golden wedge of Ophir.
13 [a]Therefore I will shake the heavens,
And the earth will move out of her place,
In the wrath of the LORD of hosts
And in [b]the day of His fierce anger.
14 It shall be as the hunted gazelle,
And as a sheep that no man [1]takes up;
[a]Every man will turn to his own people,
And everyone will flee to his own land.
15 Everyone who is found
will be thrust through,
And everyone who is captured
will fall by the sword.
16 Their children also will be [a]dashed
to pieces before their eyes;
Their houses will be plundered
And their wives [b]ravished.
17 "Behold,[a] I will stir up the Medes
against them,
Who will not [1]regard silver;
And *as for* gold, they will not delight in it.
18 Also *their* bows will dash
the young men to pieces,
And they will have no pity
on the fruit of the womb;
Their eye will not spare children.
19 [a]And Babylon, the glory of kingdoms,
The beauty of the Chaldeans' pride,
Will be as when God overthrew [b]Sodom and
Gomorrah.
20 [a]It will never be inhabited,
Nor will it be settled
from generation to generation;
Nor will the Arabian pitch tents there,

11 [a]Zech. 10:10 [1]Or *coastlands*
12 [a]John 7:35 [1]*gather* [2]Lit. *wings*
13 [a]Jer. 3:18
14 [a]Dan. 11:41 [1]Lit. *sons*
15 [a]Zech. 10:10, 11 [1]So with MT, Vg.; LXX, [Syr.], Tg. *dry up* [2]The Euphrates [3]Lit. *in sandals*
16 [a]Is. 19:23 [b]Ex. 14:29

CHAPTER 12
1 [a]Is. 2:11
2 [a]Ps. 83:18 [b]Ex. 15:2
3 [a][John 4:10, 14; 7:37, 38]
4 [a]1 Chr. 16:8 [b]Ps. 145:4–6 [c]Ps. 34:3
5 [a]Ex. 15:1
6 [a]Zeph. 3:14, 15 [b]Ps. 89:18

CHAPTER 13
1 [a]Jer. 50; 51 [1]*oracle, prophecy*
2 [a]Is. 18:3 [b]Jer. 51:25 [c]Is. 10:32
3 [a]Joel 3:11 [b]Ps. 149:2 [1]*consecrated* or *set apart*
4 [a]Is. 17:12
5 [a]Is. 42:13 [b]Is. 24:1; 34:2 [1]Or *instruments*
6 [a]Zeph. 1:7 [b]Joel 1:15
8 [a]Ps. 48:6 [1]*Sharp pains*
9 [a]Mal. 4:1 [b]Prov. 2:22
10 [a]Joel 2:31
11 [a]Is. 26:21 [b][Is. 2:17] [1]Or *tyrants*
13 [a]Hag. 2:6 [b]Lam. 1:12
14 [a]Jer. 50:16; 51:9 [1]*gathers*
16 [a]Nah. 3:10 [b]Zech. 14:2
17 [a]Dan. 5:28, 31 [1]*esteem*
19 [a]Is. 14:4 [b]Gen. 19:24
20 [a]Jer. 50:3

Nor will the shepherds make their sheepfolds
there.
21 [a]But wild beasts of the desert will lie there,
And their houses will be full of [1]owls;
Ostriches will dwell there,
And wild goats will caper there.
22 The hyenas will howl in their citadels,
And jackals in their pleasant palaces.
[a]Her time *is* near to come,
And her days will not be prolonged."

### *The Proverbs Against the King of Babylon*

**14** For the LORD [a]will have mercy on Jacob,
and [b]will still choose Israel, and settle them
in their own land. [c]The strangers will be joined
with them, and they will cling to the house of
Jacob.
2 Then people will take them [a]and bring them to
their place, and the house of Israel will possess
them for servants and maids in the land of the
LORD; they will take them captive whose captives
they were, [b]and rule over their oppressors.
**3** It shall come to pass in the day the LORD gives
you rest from your sorrow, and from your fear and
the hard bondage in which you were made to
serve,
4 that you [a]will take up this proverb against the
king of Babylon, and say:

"How the oppressor has ceased,
The [b]golden[1] city ceased!
5 The LORD has broken [a]the staff
of the wicked,
The scepter of the rulers;
6 He who struck the people in wrath with a
continual stroke,
He who ruled the nations in anger,
Is persecuted *and* no one hinders.
7 The whole earth is at rest *and* quiet;
They break forth into singing.
8 [a]Indeed the cypress trees rejoice over you,
*And* the cedars of Lebanon,
*Saying,* 'Since you [1]were cut down,
No woodsman has come up against us.'

9 "Hell[a1] from beneath is excited about you,
To meet *you* at your coming;
It stirs up the dead for you,
All the chief ones of the earth;
It has raised up from their thrones
All the kings of the nations.
10 They all shall [a]speak and say to you:
'Have you also become as weak as we?
Have you become like us?
11 Your pomp is brought down to Sheol,
*And* the sound of your stringed instruments;
The maggot is spread under you,
And worms cover you.'

**12** "How[a] you are fallen from heaven,
O [1]Lucifer, son of the morning!
*How* you are cut down to the ground,
You who weakened the nations!
13 For you have said in your heart:
[a]'I will ascend into heaven,
[b]I will exalt my throne above the stars of
God;
I will also sit on the [c]mount of the
congregation
[d]On the farthest sides of the north;
14 I will ascend above the heights of the clouds,
[a]I will be like the Most High.'

**21** [a]Is. 34:11–15; Zeph. 2:14; Rev. 18:2 [1]Or *howling creatures*
**22** [a]Jer. 51:33

CHAPTER 14

**1** [a]Ps. 102:13; Is. 49:13, 15; 54:7, 8 [b]Is. 41:8, 9; Zech. 1:17; 2:12 [c]Is. 60:4, 5, 10
**2** [a]Is. 49:22; 60:9; 66:20 [b]Is. 60:14
**4** [a]Is. 13:19; Hab. 2:6 [b]Rev. 18:16 [1]Or *insolent*
**5** [a]Ps. 125:3
**8** [a]Is. 55:12; Ezek. 31:16 [1]*have lain down*
**9** [a]Ezek. 32:21 [1]Or *Sheol*
**10** [a]Ezek. 32:21
**12** [a]Is. 34:4; Luke 10:18; [Rev. 12:7–9] [1]Lit. *Day Star*
**13** [a]Ezek. 28:2; Matt. 11:23 [b]Dan. 8:10; 2 Thess. 2:4 [c]Ezek. 28:14 [d]Ps. 48:2
**14** [a]Is. 47:8; 2 Thess. 2:4
**15** [a]Ezek. 28:8; Matt. 11:23; Luke 10:15 [1]Lit. *recesses*
**17** [1]Would not release
**19** [1]*despised* [2]*Pierced*
**20** [a]Job 18:19; Ps. 21:10; 109:13; Is. 1:4; 31:2
**21** [a]Ex. 20:5; Lev. 26:39; Is. 13:16; Matt. 23:35
**22** [a]Prov. 10:7; Is. 26:14; Jer. 51:62 [b]1 Kin. 14:10 [c]Job 18:19; Is. 47:9
**23** [a]Is. 34:11; Zeph. 2:14
**24** [a]Is. 43:13
**25** [a]Mic. 5:5, 6; Zeph. 2:13 [b]Is. 10:27; Nah. 1:13
**26** [a]Is. 23:9; Zeph. 3:6, 8
**27** [a]2 Chr. 20:6; Job 9:12; 23:13; Ps. 33:11; Prov. 19:21; 21:30; Is. 43:13; Dan. 4:31, 35
**28** [a]2 Kin. 16:20; 2 Chr. 28:27 [1]*oracle, prophecy*
**29** [a]2 Chr. 26:6 [b]2 Kin. 18:8

15 Yet you [a]shall be brought down to Sheol,
To the [1]lowest depths of the Pit.

16 "Those who see you will gaze at you,
*And* consider you, *saying:*
'*Is* this the man who made the earth tremble,
Who shook kingdoms,
17 Who made the world as a wilderness
And destroyed its cities,
*Who* [1]did not open the house of his
prisoners?'

18 "All the kings of the nations,
All of them, sleep in glory,
Everyone in his own house;
19 But you are cast out of your grave
Like an [1]abominable branch,
*Like* the garment of those who are slain,
[2]Thrust through with a sword,
Who go down to the stones of the pit,
Like a corpse trodden underfoot.
20 You will not be joined with them in burial,
Because you have destroyed your land
*And* slain your people.
[a]The brood of evildoers shall never be named.
21 Prepare slaughter for his children
[a]Because of the iniquity of their fathers,
Lest they rise up and possess the land,
And fill the face of the world with cities."

**22** "For I will rise up against them,"
says the LORD of hosts,
"And cut off from Babylon
[a]the name and [b]remnant,
[c]And offspring and posterity," says the LORD.
23 "I will also make it a possession
for the [a]porcupine,
And marshes of muddy water;
I will sweep it with the broom of
destruction," says the LORD of hosts.

**24** The LORD of hosts has sworn, saying,
"Surely, as I have thought,
so it shall come to pass,
And as I have purposed, *so* it shall [a]stand:
25 That I will break the [a]Assyrian in My land,
And on My mountains tread him underfoot.
Then [b]his yoke shall be removed from them,
And his burden removed from their
shoulders.
26 This *is* the [a]purpose that is purposed against
the whole earth,
And this *is* the hand that is stretched out
over all the nations.
27 For the LORD of hosts has [a]purposed,
And who will annul *it?*
His hand *is* stretched out,
And who will turn it back?"

**28** This is the [1]burden which came in the year
that [a]King Ahaz died.

29 "Do not rejoice, all you of Philistia,
[a]Because the rod that struck you is broken;
For out of the serpent's roots
will come forth a viper,
[b]And its offspring *will be*
a fiery flying serpent.
30 The firstborn of the poor will feed,
And the needy will lie down in safety;
I will kill your roots with famine,
And it will slay your remnant.
31 Wail, O gate! Cry, O city!
All you of Philistia *are* dissolved;
For smoke will come from the north,

And no one *will be* alone in his [1]appointed
times."
32 What will they answer the messengers of the
nation?
That [a]the LORD has founded Zion,
And [b]the poor of His people shall take refuge
in it.

## *Prophecy Against Moab*

15 The [a]burden[1] against Moab.

Because in the night
[b]Ar of [c]Moab is laid waste
*And* destroyed,
Because in the night
Kir of Moab is laid waste
*And* destroyed,
2 He has gone up to the [1]temple and Dibon,
To the high places to weep.
Moab will wail over Nebo and over Medeba;
[a]On all their heads *will be* baldness,
*And* every beard cut off.
3 In their streets they will clothe themselves
with sackcloth;
On the tops of their houses
And in their streets
Everyone will wail, [a]weeping bitterly.
4 Heshbon and Elealeh will cry out,
Their voice shall be heard as far as [a]Jahaz;
Therefore the [1]armed soldiers of Moab will
cry out;
His life will be burdensome to him.

5 "My[a] heart will cry out for Moab;
His fugitives *shall flee* to Zoar,
*Like* [1]a three-year-old heifer.
For [b]by the Ascent of Luhith
They will go up with weeping;
For in the way of Horonaim
They will raise up a cry of destruction,
6 For the waters [a]of Nimrim will be desolate,
For the green grass has withered away;
The grass fails, there is nothing green.
7 Therefore the abundance they have gained,
And what they have laid up,
They will carry away to the Brook of the
Willows.
8 For the cry has gone all around the borders
of Moab,
Its wailing to Eglaim
And its wailing to Beer Elim.
9 For the waters of [1]Dimon
will be full of blood;
Because I will bring more upon [2]Dimon,
[a]Lions upon him who escapes from Moab,
And on the remnant of the land."

## *Moab Will Be Destroyed*

16 Send [a]the lamb to the ruler of the land,
[b]From [1]Sela to the wilderness,
To the mount of the daughter of Zion.
2 For it shall be as a [a]wandering bird thrown
out of the nest;
*So* shall be the daughters of Moab at the
fords of the [b]Arnon.

3 "Take counsel, execute judgment;
Make your shadow like the night
in the middle of the day;
Hide the outcasts,
Do not betray him who escapes.
4 Let My outcasts dwell with you, O Moab;
Be a shelter to them from the face
of the [1]spoiler.
For the extortioner is at an end,
Devastation ceases,
The oppressors are consumed out of the land.
5 In mercy [a]the throne will be established;
And One will sit on it in truth,
in the tabernacle of David,
[b]Judging and seeking justice
and hastening [c]righteousness."

6 We have heard of the [a]pride of Moab—
*He is* very proud—
Of his haughtiness and his pride
and his wrath;
[b]*But* his [1]lies *shall* not *be* so.
7 Therefore Moab shall [a]wail for Moab;
Everyone shall wail.
For the foundations [b]of Kir Hareseth you
shall mourn;
Surely *they are* stricken.

8 For [a]the fields of Heshbon languish,
*And* [b]the vine of Sibmah;
The lords of the nations have broken down
its choice plants,
Which have reached to Jazer
And wandered through the wilderness.
Her branches are stretched out,
They are gone over the [c]sea.
9 Therefore I will bewail the vine of Sibmah,
With the weeping of Jazer;
I will drench you with my tears,
[a]O Heshbon and Elealeh;
For [1]battle cries have fallen
Over your summer fruits and your harvest.

10 [a]Gladness is taken away,
And joy from the plentiful field;
In the vineyards there will be no singing,
Nor will there be shouting;
No treaders will tread out wine
in the presses;
I have made their shouting cease.
11 Therefore [a]my [1]heart shall resound
like a harp for Moab,
And my inner being for [2]Kir Heres.

12 And it shall come to pass,
When it is seen that Moab is weary
on [a]the high place,
That he will come to his sanctuary to pray;
But he will not prevail.

13 This *is* the word which the LORD has spoken
concerning Moab since that time.
14 But now the LORD has spoken, saying, "Within
three years, [a]as the years of a hired man, the glory
of Moab will be despised with all that great
multitude, and the remnant *will be* very small *and*
feeble."

## *Prophecy Against Damascus*

17 The [a]burden[1] against Damascus.

"Behold, Damascus will cease from *being* a
city,
And it will be a ruinous heap.
2 [1]The cities of [a]Aroer *are* forsaken;
They will be for flocks
Which lie down,
and [b]no one will make *them* afraid.

31 [1]Or *ranks*
32 [a]Ps. 87:1, 5 [b]Zech. 11:11

CHAPTER 15
1 [a]2 Kin. 3:4 [b]Deut. 2:9 [c]Amos 2:1–3 [1]*oracle, prophecy*
2 [a]Lev. 21:5 [1]Heb. *bayith, house*
3 [a]Jer. 48:38
4 [a]Jer. 48:34 [1]So with MT, Tg., Vg.; LXX, Syr. *loins*
5 [a]Jer. 48:31 [b]Jer. 48:5 [1]Or *The Third Eglath,* an unknown city, Jer. 48:34
6 [a]Num. 32:36
9 [a]2 Kin. 17:25 [1]So with MT, Tg.; DSS, Vg. *Dibon;* LXX *Rimon* [2]See preceding note

CHAPTER 16
1 [a]2 Kin. 3:4 [b]2 Kin. 14:7 [1]Lit. *Rock*
2 [a]Prov. 27:8 [b]Num. 21:13
4 [1]*devastator*
5 [a][Dan. 7:14] [b]Ps. 72:2 [c]Is. 9:7
6 [a]Jer. 48:29 [b]Is. 28:15 [1]Lit. *vain talk*
7 [a]Jer. 48:20 [b]2 Kin. 3:25
8 [a]Is. 24:7 [b]Is. 16:9 [c]Jer. 48:32
9 [a]Is. 15:4 [1]Or *shouting has*
10 [a]Is. 24:8
11 [a]Jer. 48:36 [1]Lit. *belly* [2]*Kir Hareseth,* v. 7
12 [a]Is. 15:2
14 [a]Is. 21:16

CHAPTER 17
1 [a]Zech. 9:1 [1]*oracle, prophecy*
2 [a]Num. 32:34 [b]Jer. 7:33 [1]So with MT, Vg.; LXX *It shall be forsaken forever;* Tg. *Its cities shall be forsaken and desolate*

3 [a]The fortress also will cease from Ephraim,
The kingdom from Damascus,
And the remnant of Syria;
They will be as the glory of the children of
Israel,"
Says the LORD of hosts.

4 "In that day it shall come to pass
*That* the glory of Jacob will [1]wane,
And [a]the fatness of his flesh grow lean.
5 [a]It shall be as when the harvester gathers the
grain,
And reaps the heads with his arm;
It shall be as he who gathers heads of grain
In the Valley of Rephaim.
6 [a]Yet gleaning grapes will be left in it,
Like the shaking of an olive tree,
Two *or* three olives at the top of the
uppermost bough,
Four *or* five in its most fruitful branches,"
Says the LORD God of Israel.

7 In that day a man will [a]look to his Maker,
And his eyes will have respect
for the Holy One of Israel.
8 He will not look to the altars,
The work of his hands;
He will not respect what his [a]fingers have
made,
Nor the [1]wooden images
nor the incense altars.

9 In that day his strong cities
will be as a forsaken [1]bough
And [2]an uppermost branch,
Which they left because of
the children of Israel;
And there will be desolation.

10 Because you have forgotten
[a]the God of your salvation,
And have not been mindful of the Rock of
your [1]stronghold,
Therefore you will plant pleasant plants
And set out foreign seedlings;
11 In the day you will make your plant to grow,
And in the morning you will make your seed
to flourish;
*But* the harvest *will be* a heap of ruins
In the day of grief and desperate sorrow.

12 Woe to the multitude of many people
*Who* make a noise [a]like the roar of the seas,
And to the rushing of nations
*That* make a rushing like the rushing
of mighty waters!
13 The nations will rush like the rushing of
many waters;
But *God* will [a]rebuke them
and they will flee far away,
And [b]be chased like the chaff of the
mountains before the wind,
Like a rolling thing before the whirlwind.
14 Then behold, at eventide, trouble!
*And* before the morning, he *is* no more.
This *is* the portion of those who plunder us,
And the lot of those who rob us.

## *Prophecy Against Ethiopia*

**18** Woe [a]to the land shadowed with buzzing
wings,
Which *is* beyond the rivers of [1]Ethiopia,
2 Which sends ambassadors by sea,
Even in vessels of reed on the waters, *saying,*
"Go, swift messengers,
to a nation tall and smooth *of skin,*
To a people terrible
from their beginning onward,
A nation powerful and treading down,
Whose land the rivers divide."

3 All inhabitants of the world and dwellers on
the earth:
[a]When he lifts up a banner on the mountains,
you see *it;*
And when he blows a trumpet, you hear *it.*
4 For so the LORD said to me,
"I will take My rest,
And I will [1]look from My dwelling place
Like clear heat in sunshine,
Like a cloud of dew in the heat of harvest."
5 For before the harvest,
when the bud is perfect
And the sour grape is ripening in the flower,
He will both cut off the sprigs with pruning
hooks
And take away *and* cut down the branches.
6 They will be left together for the mountain
birds of prey
And for the beasts of the earth;
The birds of prey will summer on them,
And all the beasts of the earth will winter on
them.

7 In that time [a]a present will be brought to the
LORD of hosts
[1]From a people tall and smooth *of skin,*
And from a people terrible from their
beginning onward,
A nation powerful and treading down,
Whose land the rivers divide—
To the place of the name of the LORD of
hosts,
To Mount Zion.

## *Prophecy Against Egypt*

**19** The [a]burden[1] against Egypt.

Behold, the LORD [b]rides on a swift cloud,
And will come into Egypt;
[c]The idols of Egypt will [2]totter
at His presence,
And the heart of Egypt will melt in its midst.

2 "I will [a]set Egyptians against Egyptians;
Everyone will fight against his brother,
And everyone against his neighbor,
City against city, kingdom against kingdom.
3 The spirit of Egypt will fail in its midst;
I will destroy their counsel,
And they will [a]consult the idols
and the charmers,
The mediums and the sorcerers.
4 And the Egyptians I will give
[a]Into the hand of a cruel master,
And a fierce king will rule over them,"
Says the Lord, the LORD of hosts.

5 [a]The waters will fail from the sea,
And the river will be wasted and dried up.
6 The rivers will turn foul;
The brooks [a]of defense will be emptied and
dried up;
The reeds and rushes will wither.
7 The papyrus reeds by [1]the River,
by the mouth of the River,
And everything sown by the River,
Will wither, be driven away, and be no more.

**3** [a]Is. 7:16; 8:4
**4** [a]Is. 10:16 [1]*fade*
**5** [a]Is. 17:11; Jer. 51:33; Joel 3:13; Matt. 13:30
**6** [a]Deut. 4:27; Is. 24:13; Obad. 5
**7** [a]Is. 10:20; Hos. 3:5; Mic. 7:7
**8** [a]Is. 2:8; 31:7 [1]Or *Asherim,* Canaanite deities
**9** [1]LXX *Hivites;* Tg. *laid waste;* Vg. *as the ploughs* [2]LXX *Amorites;* Tg. *in ruins;* Vg. *corn*
**10** [a]Ps. 68:19; Is. 51:13 [1]*refuge*
**12** [a]Is. 5:30; Jer. 6:23; Ezek. 43:2; Luke 21:25
**13** [a]Ps. 9:5; Is. 41:11 [b]Ps. 83:13; Hos. 13:3

CHAPTER 18
**1** [a]2 Kin. 19:9; Is. 20:4, 5; Ezek. 30:4, 5, 9; Zeph. 2:12; 3:10 [1]Heb. *Cush*
**3** [a]Is. 5:26
**4** [1]*watch*
**7** [a]Ps. 68:31; 72:10; Is. 16:1; Zeph. 3:10; Mal. 1:11; Acts 8:27–38 [1]So with DSS, LXX, Vg.; MT omits *From;* Tg. *To*

CHAPTER 19
**1** [a]Jer. 9:25, 26; Ezek. 29:1—30:19; Joel 3:19 [b]Ps. 18:10; 104:3; Matt. 26:64; Rev. 1:7 [c]Ex. 12:12; Jer. 43:12 [1]*oracle, prophecy* [2]Lit. *shake*
**2** [a]Judg. 7:22; 1 Sam. 14:16, 20; 2 Chr. 20:23; Matt. 10:21, 36
**3** [a]1 Chr. 10:13; Is. 8:19; 47:12; Dan. 2:2
**4** [a]Is. 20:4; Jer. 46:26; Ezek. 29:19
**5** [a]Is. 50:2; Jer. 51:36; Ezek. 30:12
**6** [a]2 Kin. 19:24
**7** [1]The Nile

8 The fishermen also will mourn;
All those will lament who cast hooks into the River,
And they will languish who spread nets on the waters.
9 Moreover those who work in [a]fine flax
And those who weave fine fabric will be ashamed;
10 And its foundations will be broken.
All who make wages *will be* troubled of soul.

11 Surely the princes of [a]Zoan *are* fools;
Pharaoh's wise counselors give foolish counsel.
[b]How do you say to Pharaoh,
"I *am* the son of the wise,
The son of ancient kings?"
12 [a]Where *are* they?
Where are your wise men?
Let them tell you now,
And let them know what the LORD of hosts has [b]purposed against Egypt.
13 The princes of Zoan have become fools;
[a]The princes of [1]Noph are deceived;
They have also [2]deluded Egypt,
*Those who are* the [3]mainstay of its tribes.
14 The LORD has mingled
[a]a perverse spirit in her midst;
And they have caused Egypt
to err in all her work,
As a drunken man staggers in his vomit.
15 Neither will there be *any* work for Egypt,
Which [a]the head or tail,
Palm branch or bulrush, may do.

16 In that day Egypt will [a]be like women, and will
be afraid and fear because of the waving of the
hand of the LORD of hosts, [b]which He waves over
it.
17 And the land of Judah will be a terror to
Egypt; everyone who makes mention of it will be
afraid in himself, because of the counsel of the
LORD of hosts which He has [a]determined against
it.
18 In that day five cities in the land of Egypt will
[a]speak the language of Canaan and [b]swear by the
LORD of hosts; one will be called the City of
[1]Destruction.
19 In that day [a]there will be an altar to the LORD
in the midst of the land of Egypt, and a pillar to
the [b]LORD at its border.
20 And [a]it will be for a sign and for a witness to
the LORD of hosts in the land of Egypt; for they
will cry to the LORD because of the oppressors,
and He will send them a [b]Savior and a Mighty
One, and He will deliver them.
21 Then the LORD will be known to Egypt, and
the Egyptians will [a]know the LORD in that day,
and [b]will make sacrifice and offering; yes, they will
make a vow to the LORD and perform *it*.
22 And the LORD will strike Egypt, He will strike
and [a]heal *it;* they will return to the LORD, and He
will be entreated by them and heal them.
23 In that day [a]there will be a highway from
Egypt to Assyria, and the Assyrian will come into
Egypt and the Egyptian into Assyria, and the
Egyptians will [b]serve with the Assyrians.
24 In that day Israel will be one of three with
Egypt and Assyria—a blessing in the midst of the
land,
25 whom the LORD of hosts shall bless, saying,
"Blessed *is* Egypt My people, and Assyria [a]the
work of My hands, and Israel My inheritance."

### *Assyria Will Conquer Egypt and Ethiopia*

**20** In the year that [a]Tartan[1] came to Ashdod,
when Sargon the king of Assyria sent him,
and he fought against Ashdod and took it,
2 at the same time the LORD spoke by Isaiah the
son of Amoz, saying, "Go, and remove [a]the sackcloth from your [1]body, and take your sandals off
your feet." And he did so, [b]walking naked and
barefoot.
3 Then the LORD said, "Just as My servant
Isaiah has walked naked and barefoot three years
[a]*for* a sign and a wonder against Egypt and Ethiopia,
4 "so shall the [a]king of Assyria lead away the
Egyptians as prisoners and the Ethiopians as
captives, young and old, naked and barefoot,
[b]with their buttocks uncovered, to the shame of
Egypt.
5 [a]"Then they shall be afraid and ashamed of
Ethiopia their expectation and Egypt their glory.
6 "And the inhabitant of this territory will say in
that day, 'Surely such *is* our expectation, wherever we flee for [a]help to be delivered from the king
of Assyria; and how shall we escape?' "

### *The Fall of Babylon Predicted*

**21** The [1]burden against the Wilderness of the Sea.

As [a]whirlwinds in the South pass through,
*So* it comes from the desert,
from a terrible land.
2 A distressing vision is declared to me;
[a]The treacherous dealer deals treacherously,
And the plunderer plunders.
[b]Go up, O Elam!
Besiege, O Media!
All its sighing I have made to cease.

3 Therefore [a]my loins are filled with pain;
[b]Pangs have taken hold of me,
like the pangs of a woman in labor.
I was [1]distressed when *I* heard *it;*
I was dismayed when *I* saw *it*.
4 My heart wavered, fearfulness frightened me;
[a]The night for which I longed
He turned into fear for me.
5 [a]Prepare the table,
Set a watchman in the tower,
Eat and drink.
Arise, you princes,
Anoint the shield!

6 For thus has the Lord said to me:
"Go, set a watchman,
Let him declare what he sees."
7 And he saw a chariot
*with* a pair of horsemen,
A chariot of donkeys,
*and* a chariot of camels,
And he listened earnestly with great care.
8 [1]Then he cried, "A lion, my Lord!
I stand continually on the [a]watchtower in the daytime;
I have sat at my post every night.
9 And look, here comes a chariot of men *with* a pair of horsemen!"
Then he answered and said,
[a]"Babylon is fallen, is fallen!
And [b]all the carved images of her gods
He has broken to the ground."

9 [a]Prov. 7:16
11 [a]Num. 13:22 [b]1 Kin. 4:29, 30
12 [a]1 Cor. 1:20 [b]Ps. 33:11
13 [a]Jer. 2:16 [1]Ancient Memphis [2]Lit. *caused to stagger* [3]*cornerstone*
14 [a]Is. 29:10
15 [a]Is. 9:14–16
16 [a]Nah. 3:13 [b]Is. 11:15
17 [a]Dan. 4:35
18 [a]Zeph. 3:9 [b]Is. 45:23 [1]Some Heb. mss., Arab., DSS, Tg., Vg. *Sun;* LXX *Asedek*, lit. *Righteousness*
19 [a]Ex. 24:4 [b]Ps. 68:31
20 [a]Josh. 4:20; 22:27 [b]Is. 43:11
21 [a][Is. 2:3, 4; 11:9] [b]Mal. 1:11
22 [a]Deut. 32:39
23 [a]Is. 11:16; 35:8; 49:11; 62:10 [b]Is. 27:13
25 [a]Is. 29:23

CHAPTER 20
1 [a]2 Kin. 18:17 [1]Or *the Commander in Chief*
2 [a]Zech. 13:4 [b]1 Sam. 19:24 [1]Lit. *loins*
3 [a]Is. 8:18
4 [a]Is. 19:4 [b]Jer. 13:22
5 [a]2 Kin. 18:21
6 [a]Is. 30:5, 7

CHAPTER 21
1 [a]Zech. 9:14 [1]*oracle, prophecy*
2 [a]Is. 33:1 [b]Jer. 49:34
3 [a]Is. 15:5; 16:11 [b]Is. 13:8 [1]Lit. *bowed*
4 [a]Deut. 28:67
5 [a]Dan. 5:5
8 [a]Hab. 2:1 [1]DSS *Then the observer cried, "My Lord!*
9 [a]Jer. 51:8 [b]Is. 46:1

10 [a]Oh, my threshing and the grain of my floor!
That which I have heard
from the LORD of hosts,
The God of Israel,
I have declared to you.

11 [a]The [1]burden against Dumah.

He calls to me out of [b]Seir,
"Watchman, what of the night?
Watchman, what of the night?"
12 The watchman said,
"The morning comes, and also the night.
If you will inquire, inquire;
Return! Come back!"

13 [a]The [1]burden against Arabia.

In the forest in Arabia you will lodge,
O you traveling companies [b]of Dedanites.
14 O inhabitants of the land of Tema,
Bring water to him who is thirsty;
With their bread they met him who fled.
15 For they fled from the swords,
from the drawn sword,
From the bent bow,
and from the distress of war.

16 For thus the LORD has said to me: "Within a
year, [a]according to the year of a hired man, all the
glory of [b]Kedar will fail;
17 "and the remainder of the number of archers,
the mighty men of the people of Kedar, will
be diminished; for the LORD God of Israel has
spoken *it*."

### *Prophecy Against Jerusalem*

**22** The [1]burden against the Valley of Vision.

What ails you now, that you have
all gone up to the housetops,
2 You who are full of noise,
A [1]tumultuous city, [a]a joyous city?
Your slain *men are* not slain with the sword,
Nor dead in battle.
3 All your rulers have fled together;
They are captured by the archers.
All who are found in you are bound together;
They have fled from afar.
4 Therefore I said, "Look away from me,
[a]I will weep bitterly;
Do not labor to comfort me
Because of the plundering of the daughter of
my people."

5 [a]For *it is* a day of trouble
and treading down and perplexity
[b]By the Lord GOD of hosts
In the Valley of Vision—
Breaking down the walls
And of crying to the mountain.
6 [a]Elam bore the quiver
With chariots of men *and* horsemen,
And [b]Kir uncovered the shield.
7 It shall come to pass *that* your choicest
valleys
Shall be full of chariots,
And the horsemen shall set themselves in
array at the gate.

8 [a]He removed the [1]protection of Judah.
You looked in that day to the armor
[b]of the House of the Forest;
9 [a]You also saw the [1]damage to the city
of David,
That it was great;
And you gathered together the waters of the
lower pool.
10 You numbered the houses of Jerusalem,
And the houses you broke down
To fortify the wall.
11 [a]You also made a reservoir
between the two walls
For the water of the old [b]pool.
But you did not look to its Maker,
Nor did you have respect for Him who
fashioned it long ago.

12 And in that day the Lord GOD of hosts
[a]Called for weeping and for mourning,
[b]For baldness and for girding with sackcloth.
13 But instead, joy and gladness,
Slaying oxen and killing sheep,
Eating meat and [a]drinking wine:
[b]"Let us eat and drink, for tomorrow we die!"

14 [a]Then it was revealed in my hearing
by the LORD of hosts,
"Surely for this iniquity there [b]will be no
atonement for you,
Even to your death,"
says the Lord GOD of hosts.

15 Thus says the Lord GOD of hosts:

"Go, proceed to this steward,
To [a]Shebna, who *is* over the house, *and say:*
16 'What have you here,
and whom have you here,
That you have hewn a sepulcher here,
*As* he [a]who hews himself a sepulcher on
high,
Who carves a tomb for himself in a rock?
17 Indeed, the LORD will throw you away
violently,
O mighty man,
[a]And will surely seize you.
18 He will surely turn violently
and toss you like a ball
Into a large country;
There you shall die,
and there [a]your glorious chariots
*Shall be* the shame of your master's house.
19 So I will drive you out of your office,
And from your position [1]he will pull you
down.

20 'Then it shall be in that day,
That I will call My servant [a]Eliakim
the son of Hilkiah;
21 I will clothe him with your robe
And strengthen him with your belt;
I will commit your responsibility into his
hand.
He shall be a father to the inhabitants of
Jerusalem
And to the house of Judah.
22 The key of the house of David
I will lay on his [a]shoulder;
So he shall [b]open, and no one shall shut;
And he shall shut, and no one shall open.
23 I will fasten him *as* [a]a peg in a secure place,
And he will become a glorious throne to his
father's house.

10 [a]Jer. 51:33; Mic. 4:13
11 [a]Gen. 25:14; 1 Chr. 1:30; Josh. 15:52 [b]Gen. 32:3; Jer. 49:7; Ezek. 35:2; Obad. 1 [1]*oracle, prophecy*
13 [a]Jer. 25:24; 49:28 [b]Gen. 10:7; 1 Chr. 1:9, 32; Jer. 25:23; Ezek. 27:15 [1]*oracle, prophecy*
16 [a]Is. 16:14 [b]Ps. 120:5; Song 1:5; Is. 42:11; 60:7; Ezek. 27:21

CHAPTER 22
1 [1]*oracle, prophecy*
2 [a]Is. 32:13 [1]*boisterous*
4 [a]Jer. 4:19
5 [a]Is. 37:3 [b]Lam. 1:5; 2:2
6 [a]Jer. 49:35 [b]Is. 15:1
8 [a]2 Kin. 18:15, 16 [b]1 Kin. 7:2; 10:17 [1]Lit. *covering*
9 [a]2 Kin. 20:20; 2 Chr. 32:4; Neh. 3:16 [1]Lit. *breaches* in the city walls
11 [a]Neh. 3:16 [b]2 Kin. 20:20; 2 Chr. 32:3, 4
12 [a]Is. 32:11; Joel 1:13; 2:17 [b]Ezra 9:3; Is. 15:2; Mic. 1:16
13 [a]Is. 5:11, 22; 28:7, 8; Luke 17:26–29 [b]Is. 56:12; 1 Cor. 15:32
14 [a]Is. 5:9 [b]1 Sam. 3:14; Ezek. 24:13
15 [a]2 Kin. 18:37; Is. 36:3
16 [a]2 Sam. 18:18; 2 Chr. 16:14; Matt. 27:60
17 [a]Esth. 7:8
18 [a]Is. 2:7
19 [1]LXX omits *he will pull you down;* Syr., Tg., Vg. *I will pull you down*
20 [a]2 Kin. 18:18; Is. 36:3, 22; 37:2
22 [a]Is. 9:6 [b]Job 12:14; Rev. 3:7
23 [a]Ezra 9:8; Zech. 10:4

24 'They will hang on him all the glory of his father's house, the offspring and the posterity, all vessels of small quantity, from the cups to all the pitchers.
25 'In that day,' says the LORD of hosts, 'the peg that is fastened in the secure place will be removed and be cut down and fall, and the burden that *was* on it will be cut off; for the LORD has spoken.' "

### *Prophecy Against Tyre*

**23** The [a]burden[1] against Tyre.

Wail, you ships of Tarshish!
For it is laid waste,
So that there is no house, no harbor;
From the land of [2]Cyprus it is revealed to them.

2 Be still, you inhabitants of the coastland,
You merchants of Sidon,
[1]Whom those who cross the sea have filled.
3 And on great waters the grain of Shihor,
The harvest of [1]the River, *is* her revenue;
And [a]she is a marketplace for the nations.

4 Be ashamed, O Sidon;
For the sea has spoken,
The strength of the sea, saying,
"I do not labor, nor bring forth children;
Neither do I rear young men,
*Nor* bring up virgins."
5 [a]When the report *reaches* Egypt,
They also will be in agony at the report of Tyre.

6 Cross over to Tarshish;
Wail, you inhabitants of the coastland!
7 *Is* this your [a]joyous *city,*
Whose antiquity *is* from ancient days,
Whose feet carried her far off to dwell?
8 Who has taken this counsel against Tyre,
[a]the crowning *city,*
Whose merchants *are* princes,
Whose traders *are* the honorable of the earth?
9 The LORD of hosts has [a]purposed it,
To [1]bring to dishonor the [b]pride of all glory,
To bring into contempt all the honorable of the earth.

10 Overflow through your land like [1]the River,
O daughter of Tarshish;
*There is* no more [2]strength.
11 He stretched out His hand over the sea,
He shook the kingdoms;
The LORD has given a commandment
[a]against Canaan
To destroy its strongholds.
12 And He said, "You will rejoice no more,
O you oppressed virgin daughter of Sidon.
Arise, [a]cross over to Cyprus;
There also you will have no rest."

13 Behold, the land of the [a]Chaldeans,
This people *which* was not;
Assyria founded it for [b]wild beasts of the desert.
They set up its towers,
They raised up its palaces,
*And* brought it to ruin.

14 [a]Wail, you ships of Tarshish!
For your strength is laid waste.

15 Now it shall come to pass in that day that Tyre
will be forgotten seventy years, according to the
days of one king. At the end of seventy years it
will happen to Tyre as *in* the song of the harlot:

16 "Take a harp, go about the city,
You forgotten harlot;
Make sweet melody, sing many songs,
That you may be remembered."

17 And it shall be, at the end of seventy years,
that the LORD will deal with Tyre. She will return
to her hire, and [a]commit fornication with all the
kingdoms of the world on the face of the earth.
18 Her gain and her pay [a]will be set apart for the
LORD; it will not be treasured nor laid up, for her
gain will be for those who dwell before the LORD,
to eat sufficiently, and for [1]fine clothing.

### *The Coming Judgment on the Earth*

**24** Behold, the LORD makes the earth empty and makes it waste,
Distorts its surface
And scatters abroad its inhabitants.
2 And it shall be:
As with the people, so with the [a]priest;
As with the servant, so with his master;
As with the maid, so with her mistress;
[b]As with the buyer, so with the seller;
As with the lender, so with the borrower;
As with the creditor, so with the debtor.
3 The land shall be entirely emptied and utterly plundered,
For the LORD has spoken this word.

4 The earth mourns *and* fades away,
The world languishes *and* fades away;
The [a]haughty[1] people of the earth languish.
5 [a]The earth is also defiled under its inhabitants,
Because they have [b]transgressed the laws,
Changed the ordinance,
Broken the [c]everlasting covenant.
6 Therefore [a]the curse has devoured the earth,
And those who dwell in it are [1]desolate.
Therefore the inhabitants of the earth are [b]burned,
And few men *are* left.

7 [a]The new wine fails, the vine languishes,
All the merry-hearted sigh.
8 The mirth [a]of the tambourine ceases,
The noise of the jubilant ends,
The joy of the harp ceases.
9 They shall not drink wine with a song;
Strong drink is bitter to those who drink it.
10 The city of confusion is broken down;
Every house is shut up,
so that none may go in.
11 *There is* a cry for wine in the streets,
All joy is darkened,
The mirth of the land is gone.
12 In the city desolation is left,
And the gate is stricken with destruction.
13 When it shall be thus in the midst of the land among the people,
[a]*It shall be* like the shaking of an olive tree,
Like the gleaning of grapes when the vintage is done.

14 They shall lift up their voice, they shall sing;
For the majesty of the LORD
They shall cry aloud from the sea.
15 Therefore [a]glorify the LORD in the dawning light,

CHAPTER 23
**1** [a]Jer. 25:22; 47:4; Ezek. 26—28; Amos 1:9; Zech. 9:2, 4 [1]*oracle, prophecy* [2]Heb. *Kittim,* western lands, especially Cyprus
**2** [1]So with MT, Vg.; LXX, Tg. *passing over the water;* DSS *your messengers passing over the sea*
**3** [a]Ezek. 27:3–23 [1]The Nile
**5** [a]Is. 19:16
**7** [a]Is. 22:2; 32:13
**8** [a]Ezek. 28:2, 12
**9** [a]Is. 14:26 [b]Job 40:11, 12; Is. 13:11; 24:4; Dan. 4:37 [1]*pollute*
**10** [1]The Nile [2]*restraint,* lit. *belt*
**11** [a]Zech. 9:2–4
**12** [a]Ezek. 26:13, 14; Rev. 18:22
**13** [a]Is. 47:1 [b]Ps. 72:9
**14** [a]Ezek. 27:25–30
**17** [a]Rev. 17:2
**18** [a]Ex. 28:36; Zech. 14:20, 21 [1]*choice*

CHAPTER 24
**2** [a]Hos. 4:9 [b]Ezek. 7:12, 13
**4** [a]Is. 25:11 [1]*proud*
**5** [a]Gen. 3:17; Num. 35:33; Is. 9:17; 10:6 [b]Is. 59:12 [c]1 Chr. 16:14–19; Ps. 105:7–12
**6** [a]Mal. 4:6 [b]Is. 9:19 [1]Or *held guilty*
**7** [a]Is. 16:8–10; Joel 1:10, 12
**8** [a]Is. 5:12, 14; Jer. 7:34; 16:9; 25:10; Ezek. 26:13; Hos. 2:11; Rev. 18:22
**13** [a][Is. 17:5, 6; 27:12]
**15** [a]Is. 25:3

[b]The name of the LORD God of Israel in the
coastlands of the sea.
16 From the ends of the earth we have heard
songs:
"Glory to the righteous!"
But I said, [1]"I am ruined, ruined!
Woe to me!
[a]The treacherous dealers have dealt
treacherously,
Indeed, the treacherous dealers have dealt
very treacherously."

17 [a]Fear and the pit and the snare
*Are* upon you, O inhabitant of the earth.
18 And it shall be
*That* he who flees from the noise of the fear
Shall fall into the pit,
And he who comes up from the midst of the
pit
Shall be [1]caught in the snare;
For [a]the windows from on high are open,
And [b]the foundations of the earth
are shaken.

19 [a]The earth is violently broken,
The earth is split open,
The earth is shaken exceedingly.
20 The earth shall [a]reel[1] to and fro
like a drunkard,
And shall totter like a hut;
Its transgression shall be heavy upon it,
And it will fall, and not rise again.

21 It shall come to pass in that day
*That* the LORD will punish on high
the host of exalted ones,
And on the earth [a]the kings of the earth.
22 They will be gathered together,
*As* prisoners are gathered in the [1]pit,
And will be shut up in the prison;
After many days they will be punished.
23 Then the [a]moon will be disgraced
And the sun ashamed;
For the LORD of hosts will [b]reign
On [c]Mount Zion and in Jerusalem
And before His elders, gloriously.

## *The Song of Praise by the Redeemed*

**25** O LORD, You *are* my God.
[a]I will exalt You,
I will praise Your name,
[b]For You have done wonderful *things;*
[c]*Your* counsels of old *are* faithfulness *and*
truth.
2 For You have made [a]a city a ruin,
A fortified city a ruin,
A palace of foreigners to be a city no more;
It will never be rebuilt.
3 Therefore the strong people will [a]glorify You;
The city of the [1]terrible nations will fear You.
4 For You have been a strength to the poor,
A strength to the needy in his distress,
[a]A refuge from the storm,
A shade from the heat;
For the blast of the terrible ones *is* as a
storm *against* the wall.
5 You will reduce the noise of aliens,
As heat in a dry place;
*As* heat in the shadow of a cloud,
The song of the terrible ones
will be [1]diminished.

6 And in [a]this mountain
[b]The LORD of hosts will make for [c]all people
A feast of [1]choice pieces,
A feast of [2]wines on the lees,
Of fat things full of marrow,
Of well-refined wines on the lees.
7 And He will destroy on this mountain
The surface of the covering cast over all
people,
And [a]the veil that is spread over all nations.
8 He will [a]swallow up death forever,
And the Lord GOD will [b]wipe away tears
from all faces;
The rebuke of His people
He will take away from all the earth;
For the LORD has spoken.

9 And it will be said in that day:
"Behold, this *is* our God;
[a]We have waited for Him,
and He will save us.
This *is* the LORD;
We have waited for Him;
[b]We will be glad and rejoice in His salvation."

10 For on this mountain the hand
of the LORD will rest,
And [a]Moab shall be trampled down under
Him,
As straw is trampled down for the refuse
heap.
11 And He will spread out His hands
in their midst
As a swimmer reaches out to swim,
And He will bring down their [a]pride
Together with the trickery of their hands.
12 The [a]fortress of the high fort of your walls
He will bring down, lay low,
*And* bring to the ground, down to the dust.

## *A Hymn of Praise*

**26** In [a]that day this song will be sung in the
land of Judah:

"We have a strong city;
[b]*God* will appoint salvation *for* walls and
bulwarks.
2 [a]Open the gates,
That the righteous nation which [1]keeps the
truth may enter in.
3 You will keep *him* in perfect [a]peace,
*Whose* mind *is* stayed *on You,*
Because he trusts in You.
4 Trust in the LORD forever,
[a]For in YAH, the LORD,
*is* [1]everlasting strength.
5 For He brings [1]down those
who dwell on high,
[a]The lofty city;
He lays it low,
He lays it low to the ground,
He brings it down to the dust.
6 The foot shall [1]tread it down—
The feet of the poor
*And* the steps of the needy."

7 The way of the just *is* uprightness;
[a]O Most Upright,
You [1]weigh the path of the just.
8 Yes, [a]in the way of Your judgments,
O LORD, we have [b]waited for You;
The desire of *our* soul *is* for Your name
And for the remembrance of You.

**15** [b]Mal. 1:11
**16** [a]Is. 21:2; 33:1; Jer. 3:20; 5:11 [1]Lit. *Leanness to me, leanness to me*
**17** [a]Jer. 48:43; Amos 5:19
**18** [a]Gen. 7:11 [b]Ps. 18:7; 46:2; Is. 2:19, 21; 13:13 [1]Lit. *taken*
**19** [a]Jer. 4:23
**20** [a]Is. 19:14; 24:1; 28:7 [1]*stagger*
**21** [a]Ps. 76:12
**22** [1]*dungeon*
**23** [a]Is. 13:10; 60:19; Ezek. 32:7; Joel 2:31; 3:15 [b]Rev. 19:4, 6 [c][Heb. 12:22]

CHAPTER 25
**1** [a]Ex. 15:2 [b]Ps. 98:1 [c]Num. 23:19
**2** [a]Is. 21:9; 23:13; Jer. 51:37
**3** [a]Is. 24:15; Rev. 11:13 [1]*terrifying*
**4** [a]Is. 4:6
**5** [1]*humbled*
**6** [a][Is. 2:2–4; 56:7] [b]Prov. 9:2; Matt. 22:4 [c][Dan. 7:14; Matt. 8:11] [1]Lit. *fat things* [2]*wines matured on the sediment*
**7** [a]2 Cor. 3:15; [Eph. 4:18]
**8** [a][Hos. 13:14; 1 Cor. 15:54; Rev. 20:14] [b]Is. 30:19; Rev. 7:17; 21:4
**9** [a]Gen. 49:18; Is. 8:17; 26:8; [Titus 2:13] [b]Ps. 20:5
**10** [a]Is. 16:14; Jer. 48:1–47; Ezek. 25:8–11; Amos 2:1–3; Zeph. 2:9
**11** [a]Is. 24:4; 26:5
**12** [a]Is. 26:5

CHAPTER 26
**1** [a]Is. 2:11; 12:1 [b]Is. 60:18
**2** [a]Ps. 118:19, 20 [1]Or *remains faithful*
**3** [a]Is. 57:19; [Phil. 4:6, 7]
**4** [a]Is. 12:2; 45:17 [1]Or *Rock of Ages*
**5** [a]Is. 25:11, 12 [1]*low*
**6** [1]*trample*
**7** [a]Ps. 37:23 [1]Or *make level*
**8** [a]Is. 64:5 [b]Is. 25:9; 33:2

9 [a]With my soul I have desired You in the
night,
Yes, by my spirit within me
I will seek You early;
For when Your judgments *are* in the earth,
The inhabitants of the world
will learn righteousness.

10 [a]Let grace be shown to the wicked,
*Yet* he will not learn righteousness;
In [b]the land of uprightness
he will deal unjustly,
And will not behold the majesty of the LORD.
11 LORD, *when* Your hand is lifted up, [a]they will
not see.
But they will see and be ashamed
For [1]*their* envy of people;
Yes, the fire of Your enemies
shall devour them.

**12** LORD, You will establish peace for us,
For You have also done all our works [1]in us.
13 O LORD our God, [a]masters besides You
Have had dominion over us;
*But* by You only we make mention
of Your name.
14 *They are* dead, they will not live;
*They are* deceased, they will not rise.
Therefore You have punished
and destroyed them,
And made all their memory to [a]perish.
15 You have increased the nation, O LORD,
You have [a]increased the nation;
You are glorified;
You have expanded all the [1]borders
of the land.

16 LORD, [a]in trouble they have visited You,
They poured out a prayer *when* Your
chastening *was* upon them.
17 As [a]a woman with child
Is in pain and cries out in her [1]pangs,
*When* she draws near the time
of her delivery,
So have we been in Your sight, O LORD.
18 We have been with child,
we have been in pain;
We have, as it were, [1]brought forth wind;
We have not accomplished any deliverance
in the earth,
Nor have [a]the inhabitants of the world fallen.

19 [a]Your dead shall live;
*Together with* [1]my dead body they shall arise.
[b]Awake and sing, you who dwell in dust;
For your dew *is like* the dew of herbs,
And the earth shall cast out the dead.

**20** Come, my people, [a]enter your chambers,
And shut your doors behind you;
Hide yourself, as it were, [b]for a little moment,
Until the indignation is past.
21 For behold, the LORD [a]comes out of His place
To punish the inhabitants of the earth for
their iniquity;
The earth will also disclose her [1]blood,
And will no more cover her slain.

### *Israel Will Be Restored*

**27** In that day the LORD with His severe
sword, great and strong,
Will punish Leviathan the fleeing serpent,
[a]Leviathan that twisted serpent;
And He will slay [b]the reptile
that *is* in the sea.

2 In that day [a]sing to her,
[b]"A vineyard of [1]red wine!
3 [a]I, the LORD, keep it,
I water it every moment;
Lest any hurt it,
I keep it night and day.
4 Fury *is* not in Me.
Who would set [a]briers *and* thorns
Against Me in battle?
I would go through them,
I would burn them together.
5 Or let him take hold [a]of My strength,
*That* he may [b]make peace with Me;
*And* he shall make peace with Me."

6 Those who come He shall cause
[a]to take root in Jacob;
Israel shall blossom and bud,
And fill the face of the world with fruit.

**7** [a]Has He struck [1]Israel as He struck those who
struck him?
Or has He been slain according to the
slaughter of those who were slain by Him?
8 [a]In measure, by sending it away,
You contended with it.
[b]He removes *it* by His rough wind
In the day of the east wind.
9 Therefore by this the iniquity of Jacob will
be covered;
And this *is* all the fruit of taking away his
sin:
When he makes all the stones of the altar
Like chalkstones that are beaten to dust,
[1]Wooden images and incense altars shall not
stand.

10 Yet the fortified city *will be* [a]desolate,
The habitation forsaken
and left like a wilderness;
There the calf will feed,
and there it will lie down
And consume its branches.
11 When its boughs are withered,
they will be broken off;
The women come *and* set them on fire.
For [a]it *is* a people of no understanding;
Therefore He who made them will [b]not have
mercy on them,
And [c]He who formed them will show them
no favor.

**12** And it shall come to pass in that day
*That* the LORD will thresh,
From the channel of [1]the River
to the Brook of Egypt;
And you will be [a]gathered one by one,
O you children of Israel.

13 [a]So it shall be in that day:
[b]The great trumpet will be blown;
They will come, who are about to perish in
the land of Assyria,
And they who are outcasts in the land of
[c]Egypt,
And shall [d]worship the LORD in the holy
mount at Jerusalem.

### *Jerusalem Warned*

**28** Woe to the crown of pride,
to the drunkards of Ephraim,
Whose glorious beauty *is* a fading flower
Which *is* at the head of the [1]verdant valleys,
To those who are overcome with wine!

**9** [a]Ps. 63:6
**10** [a][Rom. 2:4] [b]Ps. 143:10
**11** [a]Is. 5:12 [1]Or *Your zeal for the people*
**12** [1]Or *for us*
**13** [a]2 Chr. 12:8
**14** [a]Eccl. 9:5
**15** [a]Is. 9:3 [1]Or *ends*
**16** [a]Hos. 5:15
**17** [a][John 16:21] [1]*sharp pains*
**18** [a]Ps. 17:14 [1]*given birth to*
**19** [a][Ezek. 37:1–14] [b][Dan. 12:2] [1]So with MT, Vg.; Syr., Tg. *their dead bodies;* LXX *those in the tombs*
**20** [a]Ex. 12:22, 23 [b][Ps. 30:5]
**21** [a]Mic. 1:3 [1]Or *bloodshed*

CHAPTER 27
**1** [a]Ps. 74:13, 14 [b]Is. 51:9
**2** [a]Is. 5:1 [b]Is. 5:7 [1]So with MT (Kittel's *Biblia Hebraica*), Bg., Vg.; MT (*Biblia Hebraica Stuttgartensia*), some Heb. mss., LXX *delight;* Tg. *choice vineyard*
**3** [a]Is. 31:5
**4** [a]2 Sam. 23:6
**5** [a]Is. 25:4 [b]Job 22:21
**6** [a]Is. 37:31
**7** [a]Is. 10:12, 17; 30:30–33 [1]Lit. *him*
**8** [a]Job 23:6 [b][Ps. 78:38]
**9** [1]Or *Asherim,* Canaanite deities
**10** [a]Is. 5:6, 17; 32:14
**11** [a]Deut. 32:28 [b]Is. 9:17 [c]Deut. 32:18
**12** [a][Is. 11:11; 56:8] [1]The Euphrates
**13** [a]Is. 2:11 [b]Rev. 11:15 [c]Is. 19:21, 22 [d]Zech. 14:16

CHAPTER 28
**1** [1]Lit. *valleys of fatness*

2 Behold, the Lord has a mighty and strong
one,
[a]Like a tempest of hail
and a destroying storm,
Like a flood of mighty waters overflowing,
Who will bring *them* down
to the earth with *His* hand.
3 The crown of pride, the drunkards
of Ephraim,
Will be trampled underfoot;
4 And the glorious beauty is a fading flower
Which *is* at the head of the [1]verdant valley,
Like the first fruit before the summer,
Which an observer sees;
He eats it up while it is still in his hand.

**5** In that day the LORD of hosts will be
For a crown of glory and a diadem of beauty
To the remnant of His people,
6 For a spirit of justice to him
who sits in judgment,
And for strength to those who turn back the
battle at the gate.

**7** But they also [a]have erred through wine,
And through intoxicating drink are out of
the way;
[b]The priest and the prophet have erred
through intoxicating drink,
They are swallowed up by wine,
They are out of the way through intoxicating
drink;
They err in vision, they stumble *in* judgment.
8 For all tables are full of vomit *and* filth;
No place *is clean.*

**9** "Whom[a] will he teach knowledge?
And whom will he make to understand the
message?
Those *just* weaned from milk?
Those *just* drawn from the breasts?
10 [a]For precept *must be* upon precept, precept
upon precept,
Line upon line, line upon line,
Here a little, there a little."

**11** For with [a]stammering lips
and another tongue
He will speak to this people,
12 To whom He said,
"This *is* the [a]rest *with which*
You may cause the weary to rest,"
And, "This *is* the refreshing";
Yet they would not hear.
13 But the word of the LORD was to them,
"Precept upon precept, precept upon precept,
Line upon line, line upon line,
Here a little, there a little,"
That they might go and fall backward, and
be broken
And snared and caught.

**14** Therefore hear the word of the LORD, you
scornful men,
Who rule this people who *are* in Jerusalem,
15 Because you have said,
"We have made a covenant with death,
And with Sheol we are in agreement.
When the overflowing scourge passes
through,
It will not come to us,
[a]For we have made lies our refuge,
And under falsehood we have hidden
ourselves."

**16** Therefore thus says the Lord GOD:
"Behold, I lay in Zion [a]a stone for a
foundation,
A tried stone, a precious cornerstone,
a sure foundation;
Whoever believes will not act hastily.
17 Also I will make justice the measuring line,
And righteousness the plummet;
The hail will sweep away the refuge of lies,
And the waters will overflow
the hiding place.
18 Your covenant with death will be annulled,
And your agreement with Sheol
will not stand;
When the overflowing scourge passes
through,
Then you will be trampled down by it.
19 As often as it goes out it will take you;
For morning by morning it will pass over,
And by day and by night;
It will be a terror just to understand the
report."

**20** For the bed is too short to stretch out *on,*
And the covering so narrow that one cannot
wrap himself *in it.*
21 For the LORD will rise up as *at* Mount
[a]Perazim,
He will be angry as in the Valley of
[b]Gibeon—
That He may do His work,
[c]His awesome work,
And bring to pass His act, His [1]unusual act.
22 Now therefore, do not be mockers,
Lest your bonds be made strong;
For I have heard from the Lord GOD of hosts,
[a]A [1]destruction determined even upon the
whole earth.

**23** Give ear and hear my voice,
Listen and hear my speech.
24 Does the plowman keep plowing all day to
sow?
Does he keep turning his soil
and breaking the clods?
25 When he has leveled its surface,
Does he not sow the black cummin
And scatter the cummin,
Plant the wheat in rows,
The barley in the appointed place,
And the [1]spelt in its place?
26 For He instructs him in right judgment,
His God teaches him.

27 For the black cummin is not threshed with a
threshing sledge,
Nor is a cartwheel rolled over the cummin;
But the black cummin is beaten out with a
stick,
And the cummin with a rod.
28 Bread *flour* must be ground;
Therefore he does not thresh it forever,
Break *it with* his cartwheel,
Or crush it *with* his horsemen.
29 This also comes from the LORD of hosts,
[a]*Who* is wonderful in counsel
*and* excellent in [1]guidance.

## *The Blindness of Israel*

**29** "Woe [a]to [1]Ariel, to Ariel,
the city [b]*where* David dwelt!
Add year to year;
Let feasts come around.

**2** [a]Is. 30:30; Ezek. 13:11
**4** [1]Lit. *valley of fatness*
**7** [a]Prov. 20:1; Is. 5:11, 22; Hos. 4:11 [b]Is. 56:10, 12
**9** [a]Jer. 6:10
**10** [a][2 Chr. 36:15; Neh. 9:30; Jer. 25:3, 4; 35:15; 44:4]
**11** [a]Is. 33:19; 1 Cor. 14:21
**12** [a]Is. 30:15; Jer. 6:16; [Matt. 11:28, 29]
**15** [a]Is. 9:15; Ezek. 13:22; Amos 2:4
**16** [a]Gen. 49:24; Ps. 118:22; Is. 8:14, 15; Matt. 21:42; Mark 12:10; Luke 20:17; Acts 4:11; Rom. 9:33; 10:11; Eph. 2:20; 1 Pet. 2:6–8
**21** [a]2 Sam. 5:20; 1 Chr. 14:11 [b]Josh. 10:10, 12; 2 Sam. 5:25; 1 Chr. 14:16 [c][Lam. 3:33; Luke 19:41–44] [1]Lit. *foreign*
**22** [a]Is. 10:22; Dan. 9:27 [1]Lit. *complete end*
**25** [1]*rye*
**29** [a]Ps. 92:5; Is. 9:6; Jer. 32:19 [1]*sound wisdom*

CHAPTER 29
**1** [a]Ezek. 24:6, 9 [b]2 Sam. 5:9 [1]Jerusalem, Lit. *Lion of God*

2 Yet I will distress Ariel;
There shall be heaviness and sorrow,
And it shall be to Me as Ariel.
3 I will encamp against you all around,
I will lay siege against you with a mound,
And I will raise siegeworks against you.
4 You shall be brought down,
You shall speak out of the ground;
Your speech shall be low, out of the dust;
Your voice shall be like a medium's, [a]out of the ground;
And your speech shall whisper out of the dust.

**5** "Moreover the multitude of your [a]foes
Shall be like fine dust,
And the multitude of the terrible ones
Like [b]chaff that passes away;
Yes, it shall be [c]in an instant, suddenly.
6 [a]You will be punished by the LORD of hosts
With thunder and [b]earthquake and great noise,
*With* storm and tempest
And the flame of devouring fire.
7 [a]The multitude of all the nations who fight against [1]Ariel,
Even all who fight against her and her fortress,
And distress her,
Shall be [b]as a dream of a night vision.
8 [a]It shall even be as when a hungry man dreams,
And look—he eats;
But he awakes, and his soul is still empty;
Or as when a thirsty man dreams,
And look—he drinks;
But he awakes, and indeed *he is* faint,
And his soul still craves:
So the multitude of all the nations shall be,
Who fight against Mount Zion."

**9** Pause and wonder!
Blind yourselves and be blind!
[a]They are drunk, [b]but not with wine;
They stagger, but not with intoxicating drink.
10 For [a]the LORD has poured out on you
The spirit of deep sleep,
And has [b]closed your eyes, namely, the prophets;
And He has covered your heads, *namely,* [c]the seers.

**11** The whole vision has become to you like the
words of a [1]book [a]that is sealed, which *men* deliver
to one who is literate, saying, "Read this, please."
[b]And he says, "I cannot, for it *is* sealed."
12 Then the book is delivered to one who [1]is
illiterate, saying, "Read this, please." And he says,
"I am not literate."
**13** Therefore the LORD said:

[a]"Inasmuch as these people draw near with their mouths
And honor Me [b]with their lips,
But have removed their hearts far from Me,
And their fear toward Me is taught by the commandment of men,
14 [a]Therefore, behold, I will again do a marvelous work
Among this people,
A marvelous work and a wonder;
[b]For the wisdom of their wise *men* shall perish,
And the understanding of their prudent *men* shall be hidden."

**15** [a]Woe to those who seek deep to hide their counsel far from the LORD,
And their works are in the dark;
[b]They say, "Who sees us?" and, "Who knows us?"
16 Surely you have things turned around!
Shall the potter be esteemed as the clay;
For shall the [a]thing made say of him who made it,
"He did not make me"?
Or shall the thing formed say of him who formed it,
"He has no understanding"?

**17** *Is* it not yet a very little while
Till [a]Lebanon shall be turned into a fruitful field,
And the fruitful field be esteemed as a forest?
18 [a]In that day the deaf shall hear the words of the book,
And the eyes of the blind shall see out of obscurity and out of darkness.
19 [a]The humble also shall increase *their* joy in the LORD,
And [b]the poor among men shall rejoice
In the Holy One of Israel.
20 For the [1]terrible one is brought to nothing,
[a]The scornful one is consumed,
And all who [b]watch for iniquity are cut off—
21 Who make a man an offender by a word,
And [a]lay a snare for him who reproves in the gate,
And turn aside the just [b]by empty words.

**22** Therefore thus says the LORD, [a]who redeemed
Abraham, concerning the house of Jacob:

"Jacob shall not now be [b]ashamed,
Nor shall his face now grow pale;
23 But when he sees his children,
[a]The work of My hands, in his midst,
They will hallow My name,
And hallow the Holy One of Jacob,
And fear the God of Israel.
24 These also [a]who erred in spirit will come to understanding,
And those who complained will learn doctrine."

### *The Futility of Relying on Egypt*

**30** "Woe to the rebellious children," says the LORD,
[a]"Who take counsel, but not of Me,
And who [1]devise plans, but not of My Spirit,
[b]That they may add sin to sin;
2 [a]Who walk to go down to Egypt,
And [b]have not asked My advice,
To strengthen themselves in the strength of Pharaoh,
And to trust in the shadow of Egypt!
3 [a]Therefore the strength of Pharaoh
Shall be your shame,
And trust in the shadow of Egypt
Shall be *your* humiliation.
4 For his princes were at [a]Zoan,
And his ambassadors came to Hanes.
5 [a]They were all ashamed of a people *who* could not benefit them,
Or be help or benefit,
But a shame and also a reproach."

**4** [a]Is. 8:19
**5** [a]Is. 25:5 [b]Job 21:18; Is. 17:13 [c]Is. 30:13; 47:11; 1 Thess. 5:3
**6** [a]Is. 28:2; 30:30 [b]1 Sam. 2:10; Zech. 14:4; Matt. 24:7; Mark 13:8; Luke 21:11; Rev. 16:18, 19
**7** [a]Is. 37:36; Mic. 4:11, 12; Zech. 12:9 [b]Job 20:8 [1]Jerusalem
**8** [a]Ps. 73:20
**9** [a]Is. 28:7, 8 [b]Is. 51:21
**10** [a]Ps. 69:23; Is. 6:9, 10; Mic. 3:6; Rom. 11:8 [b]Ps. 69:23; Is. 6:10 [c]1 Sam. 9:9; Is. 44:18; Mic. 3:6; [2 Thess. 2:9–12]
**11** [a]Is. 8:16 [b]Dan. 12:4, 9; [Matt. 13:11–16]; Rev. 5:1–5, 9 [1]*scroll*
**12** [1]Lit. *does not know books*
**13** [a]Ps. 78:36; Ezek. 33:31; Matt. 15:8, 9; Mark 7:6, 7 [b]Col. 2:22
**14** [a]Is. 6:9, 10; 28:21; Hab. 1:5 [b]Is. 44:25; Jer. 49:7; Obad 8; 1 Cor. 1:19
**15** [a]Is. 30:1 [b]Ps. 10:11; 94:7; Is. 47:10; Ezek. 8:12; Mal. 2:17
**16** [a]Is. 45:9; Jer. 18:1–6; [Rom. 9:19–21]
**17** [a]Is. 32:15
**18** [a]Is. 35:5; Matt. 11:5; Mark 7:37
**19** [a][Ps. 25:9; 37:11; Is. 11:4; 61:1; Matt. 5:5; 11:29] [b]Is. 14:30; [Matt. 5:3; 11:5; James 2:5]
**20** [a]Is. 28:14 [b]Is. 59:4; Mic. 2:1 [1]*terrifying*
**21** [a]Amos 5:10, 12 [b]Prov. 28:21
**22** [a]Josh. 24:3 [b]Is. 45:17
**23** [a][Is. 45:11; 49:20–26; Eph. 2:10]
**24** [a]Is. 28:7

CHAPTER 30
**1** [a]Is. 29:15 [b]Deut. 29:19 [1]Lit. *weave a web*
**2** [a]Is. 31:1; Jer. 43:7 [b]Num. 27:21; Josh. 9:14; 1 Kin. 22:7; Jer. 21:2; 42:2, 20
**3** [a]Is. 20:5; Jer. 37:5, 7
**4** [a]Is. 19:11
**5** [a]Jer. 2:36

**6** [a]The [1]burden against the beasts of the South.

Through a land of trouble and anguish,
From which *came* the lioness and lion,
[b]The viper and fiery flying serpent,
They will carry their riches on the backs of young donkeys,
And their treasures on the humps of camels,
To a people *who* shall not profit;
7 [a]For the Egyptians shall help in vain and to no purpose.
Therefore I have called her
[1]Rahab-Hem-Shebeth.

**8** Now go, [a]write it before them on a tablet,
And note it on a scroll,
That it may be for time to come,
Forever and ever:
9 That [a]this *is* a rebellious people,
Lying children,
Children *who* will not hear the law of the LORD;
10 [a]Who say to the seers, "Do not see,"
And to the prophets,
"Do not prophesy to us right things;
[b]Speak to us smooth things, prophesy deceits.
11 Get out of the way,
Turn aside from the path,
Cause the Holy One of Israel
To cease from before us."

**12** Therefore thus says the Holy One of Israel:

"Because you [a]despise this word,
And trust in oppression and perversity,
And rely on them,
13 Therefore this iniquity shall be to you
[a]Like a breach ready to fall,
A bulge in a high wall,
Whose breaking [b]comes suddenly, in an instant.
14 And [a]He shall break it like the breaking of the potter's vessel,
Which is broken in pieces;
He shall not spare.
So there shall not be found among its fragments
[1]A shard to take fire from the hearth,
Or to take water from the cistern."

**15** For thus says the Lord GOD, the Holy One of Israel:

[a]"In returning and rest you shall be saved;
In quietness and confidence shall be your strength."
[b]But you would not,
16 And you said,
"No, for we will flee on horses"—
Therefore you shall flee!
And, "We will ride on swift *horses*"—
Therefore those who pursue you shall be swift!

17 [a]One thousand *shall flee* at the threat of one,
At the threat of five you shall flee,
Till you are left as a [1]pole on top of a mountain
And as a banner on a hill.

**18** Therefore the LORD will wait, that He may be [a]gracious to you;
And therefore He will be exalted, that He may have mercy on you.
For the LORD *is* a God of justice;
[b]Blessed *are* all those who [c]wait for Him.

19 For the people [a]shall dwell in Zion at Jerusalem;
You shall [b]weep no more.
He will be very gracious to you at the sound of your cry;
When He hears it, He will [c]answer you.
20 And *though* the Lord gives you
[a]The bread of adversity and the water of [1]affliction,
Yet [b]your teachers will not be moved into a corner anymore,
But your eyes shall see your teachers.
21 Your ears shall hear a word behind you, saying,
"This *is* the way, walk in it,"
Whenever you [a]turn to the right hand
Or whenever you turn to the left.
22 [a]You will also defile the covering of your images of silver,
And the ornament of your molded images of gold.
You will throw them away as an unclean thing;
[b]You will say to them, "Get away!"

**23** [a]Then He will give the rain for your seed
With which you sow the ground,
And bread of the increase of the earth;
It will be [1]fat and plentiful.
In that day your cattle will feed
In large pastures.
24 Likewise the oxen and the young donkeys that work the ground
Will eat cured fodder,
Which has been winnowed with the shovel and fan.
25 There will be [a]on every high mountain
And on every high hill
Rivers *and* streams of waters,
In the day of the [b]great slaughter,
When the towers fall.
26 Moreover [a]the light of the moon will be as the light of the sun,
And the light of the sun will be sevenfold,
As the light of seven days,
In the day that the LORD binds up the bruise of His people
And heals the stroke of their wound.

**27** Behold, the name of the LORD comes from afar,
Burning *with* His anger,
And *His* burden *is* heavy;
His lips are full of indignation,
And His tongue like a devouring fire.
28 [a]His breath is like an overflowing stream,
[b]Which reaches up to the neck,
To sift the nations with the sieve of futility;
And *there shall be* [c]a bridle in the jaws of the people,
Causing *them* to err.
29 You shall have a song
As in the night *when* a holy festival is kept,
And gladness of heart as when one goes with a flute,
To come into [a]the mountain of the LORD,
To [1]the Mighty One of Israel.
30 [a]The LORD will cause His glorious voice to be heard,
And show the descent of His arm,
With the indignation of *His* anger
And the flame of a devouring fire,
*With* scattering, tempest, [b]and hailstones.

**6** [a]Is. 57:9; Hos. 8:9; 12:1 [b]Deut. 8:15; Is. 14:29 [1]*oracle, prophecy*
**7** [a]Jer. 37:7 [1]Lit. *Rahab Sits Idle*
**8** [a]Hab. 2:2
**9** [a]Deut. 32:20; Is. 1:2, 4; 65:2
**10** [a]Is. 5:20; Jer. 11:21; Amos 2:12; Mic. 2:6 [b]1 Kin. 22:8, 13; Jer. 6:14; 23:17, 26; Ezek. 13:7; Mic. 2:11; Rom. 16:18; 2 Tim. 4:3, 4
**12** [a]Lev. 26:43; Num. 15:31; Prov. 1:30; 13:13; Is. 5:24; Ezek. 20:13, 16, 24; Amos 2:4
**13** [a]1 Kin. 20:30; Ps. 62:3, 4; Is. 58:12 [b]Is. 29:5
**14** [a]Ps. 2:9; Jer. 19:11 [1]A piece of broken pottery
**15** [a]Ps. 116:7; Is. 7:4; 28:12 [b]Matt. 23:37
**17** [a]Lev. 26:36; Deut. 28:25; 32:30; Josh. 23:10; [Prov. 28:1] [1]A tree stripped of branches
**18** [a]Is. 33:2 [b]Ps. 2:12; 34:8; Prov. 16:20; Jer. 17:7 [c]Is. 26:8
**19** [a]Is. 65:9; [Ezek. 37:25, 28] [b]Is. 25:8 [c]Ps. 50:15; Is. 65:24; [Matt. 7:7–11]
**20** [a]1 Kin. 22:27; Ps. 127:2 [b]Ps. 74:9; Amos 8:11 [1]*oppression*
**21** [a]Josh. 1:7
**22** [a]2 Chr. 31:1; Is. 2:20; 31:7 [b]Hos. 14:8
**23** [a][Matt. 6:33]; 1 Tim. 6:8 [1]*rich*
**25** [a]Is. 2:14, 15 [b]Is. 2:10–21; 34:2
**26** [a][Is. 60:19, 20; Rev. 21:23; 22:5]
**28** [a]Is. 11:4; 2 Thess. 2:8 [b]Is. 8:8 [c]2 Kin. 19:28; Is. 37:29
**29** [a][Is. 2:3] [1]Lit. *the Rock*
**30** [a]Is. 29:6 [b]Is. 28:2

31 For [a]through the voice of the LORD
Assyria will be [1]beaten down,
*As* He strikes with the [b]rod.
32 And *in* every place where the staff of
punishment passes,
Which the LORD lays on him,
*It* will be with tambourines and harps;
And in battles of [a]brandishing He will fight
with it.
33 [a]For Tophet *was* established of old,
Yes, for the king it is prepared.
He has made *it* deep and large;
Its pyre *is* fire with much wood;
The breath of the LORD,
like a stream of brimstone,
Kindles it.

## *God, Not Egypt, Will Defend Judah*

**31** Woe to those [a]who go down to Egypt for
help,
*And* [b]rely on horses,
Who trust in chariots
because *they are* many,
And in horsemen
because they are very strong,
But who do not look to the Holy One of
Israel,
[c]Nor seek the LORD!
2 Yet He also *is* wise and will bring disaster,
And [a]will not [1]call back His words,
But will arise against the house of evildoers,
And against the help of those who work
iniquity.
3 Now the Egyptians *are* men, and not God;
And their horses are flesh, and not spirit.
When the LORD stretches out His hand,
Both he who helps will fall,
And he who is helped will fall down;
They all will perish [a]together.

4 For thus the LORD has spoken to me:

[a]"As a lion roars,
And a young lion over his prey
(When a multitude of shepherds is
summoned against him,
*He* will not be afraid of their voice
Nor be disturbed by their noise),
So the LORD of hosts will come down
To fight for Mount Zion and for its hill.
5 [a]Like birds flying about,
So will the LORD of hosts defend Jerusalem.
Defending, He will also deliver *it;*
Passing over, He will preserve *it.*"

**6** Return *to Him* against whom the children of
Israel have [a]deeply revolted.
7 For in that day every man shall [a]throw away
his idols of silver and his idols of gold—[b]sin, which
your own hands have made for yourselves.

8 "Then Assyria shall [a]fall
by a sword not of man,
And a sword not of mankind shall [b]devour
him.
But he shall flee from the sword,
And his young men shall become forced
labor.
9 [a]He shall cross over to his stronghold for fear,
And his princes shall be afraid of the
banner,"
Says the LORD,
Whose fire *is* in Zion
And whose furnace *is* in Jerusalem.

30:31 [a]Is. 14:25; 37:36 [b]Is. 10:5, 24 [1]Lit. *shattered*
32 [a]Is. 11:15
33 [a]2 Kin. 23:10; Jer. 7:31

CHAPTER 31
1 [a]Is. 30:1, 2 [b]Deut. 17:16; Ps. 20:7; Is. 2:7; 30:16 [c]Is. 9:13; Dan. 9:13; Amos 5:4–8
2 [a]Num. 23:19; Jer. 44:29 [1]*retract*
3 [a]Is. 20:6
4 [a]Num. 24:9; Hos. 11:10; Amos 3:8
5 [a]Deut. 32:11; Ps. 91:4
6 [a]Hos. 9:9
7 [a]Is. 2:20; 30:22 [b]1 Kin. 12:30
8 [a]2 Kin. 19:35, 36 [b]Is. 37:36
9 [a]Is. 37:37

CHAPTER 32
1 [a]Ps. 45:1
2 [a]Is. 4:6 [1]*shelter*
3 [a]Is. 29:18; 35:5
4 [a]Is. 29:24 [1]*hasty*
5 [1]*noble*
6 [a]Prov. 24:7–9
7 [a]Jer. 5:26–28; Mic. 7:3
8 [1]*noble*
9 [a]Is. 47:8; Amos 6:1; Zeph. 2:15
13 [a]Is. 7:23–25; Hos. 9:6 [b]Is. 22:2
14 [a]Is. 27:10
15 [a][Is. 11:2]; Ezek. 39:29; [Joel 2:28] [b]Ps. 107:35; Is. 29:17
17 [a]Ps. 119:165; Is. 2:4; Rom. 14:17; James 3:18
18 [a]Is. 11:10; 14:3; 30:15; [Hos. 2:18–23; Zech. 2:5; 3:10]
19 [a]Is. 30:30 [b]Zech. 11:2

## *Women of Jerusalem Warned*

**32** Behold, [a]a king will reign in righteousness,
And princes will rule with justice.
2 A man will be as a hiding place from the
wind,
And [a]a [1]cover from the tempest,
As rivers of water in a dry place,
As the shadow of a great rock in a weary
land.
3 [a]The eyes of those who see will not be dim,
And the ears of those who hear will listen.
4 Also the heart of the [1]rash
will [a]understand knowledge,
And the tongue of the stammerers
will be ready to speak plainly.

5 The foolish person will no longer
be called [1]generous,
Nor the miser said *to be* bountiful;
6 For the foolish person will speak foolishness,
And his heart will work [a]iniquity:
To practice ungodliness,
To utter error against the LORD,
To keep the hungry unsatisfied,
And he will cause the drink of the thirsty to
fail.
7 Also the schemes of the schemer *are* evil;
He devises wicked plans
To destroy the poor with [a]lying words,
Even when the needy speaks justice.
8 But a [1]generous man devises generous things,
And by generosity he shall stand.

**9** Rise up, you women [a]who are at ease,
Hear my voice;
You complacent daughters,
Give ear to my speech.
10 In a year and *some* days
You will be troubled,
you complacent women;
For the vintage will fail,
The gathering will not come.
11 Tremble, you *women* who are at ease;
Be troubled, you complacent ones;
Strip yourselves, make yourselves bare,
And gird *sackcloth* on *your* waists.

12 People shall mourn upon their breasts
For the pleasant fields, for the fruitful vine.
13 [a]On the land of my people will come up
thorns *and* briers,
Yes, on all the happy homes *in* [b]the joyous
city;
14 [a]Because the palaces will be forsaken,
The bustling city will be deserted.
The forts and towers
will become lairs forever,
A joy of wild donkeys, a pasture of flocks—
15 Until [a]the Spirit is poured upon us
from on high,
And [b]the wilderness becomes a fruitful field,
And the fruitful field is counted as a forest.

**16** Then justice will dwell in the wilderness,
And righteousness remain in the fruitful field.
17 [a]The work of righteousness will be peace,
And the effect of righteousness, quietness
and assurance forever.
18 My people will dwell in a peaceful habitation,
In secure dwellings,
and in quiet [a]resting places,
19 [a]Though hail comes down [b]on the forest,
And the city is brought low in humiliation.

20 Blessed *are* you who sow beside all waters,
Who send out freely the feet of [a]the ox and
the donkey.

### *Salvation for Those Who Trust in God*

**33** Woe to you [a]who plunder,
though you *have* not *been* plundered;
And you who deal treacherously, though
they have not dealt treacherously with
you!
[b]When you cease plundering,
You will be [c]plundered;
When you make an end
of dealing treacherously,
They will deal treacherously with you.

2 O LORD, be gracious to us;
[a]We have waited for You.
Be [1]their arm every morning,
Our salvation also in the time of trouble.
3 At the noise of the tumult
the people [a]shall flee;
When You lift Yourself up,
the nations shall be scattered;
4 And Your plunder shall be gathered
*Like* the gathering of the caterpillar;
As the running to and fro of locusts,
He shall run upon them.

5 [a]The LORD is exalted, for He dwells on high;
He has filled Zion with justice
and righteousness.
6 Wisdom and knowledge
will be the stability of your times,
*And* the strength of salvation;
The fear of the LORD *is* His treasure.

7 Surely their valiant ones shall cry outside,
[a]The ambassadors of peace shall weep bitterly.
8 [a]The highways lie waste,
The traveling man ceases.
[b]He has broken the covenant,
[1]He has despised the [2]cities,
He regards no man.
9 [a]The earth mourns *and* languishes,
Lebanon is shamed *and* shriveled;
Sharon is like a wilderness,
And Bashan and Carmel
shake off *their fruits.*

10 "Now[a] I will rise," says the LORD;
"Now I will be exalted,
Now I will lift Myself up.
11 [a]You shall conceive chaff,
You shall bring forth stubble;
Your breath, *as* fire, shall devour you.
12 And the people shall be *like* the burnings of
lime;
[a]*Like* thorns cut up they shall be burned in
the fire.
13 Hear, [a]you *who are* afar off,
what I have done;
And you *who are* near,
acknowledge My might."

14 The sinners in Zion are afraid;
Fearfulness has seized the hypocrites:
"Who among us shall dwell with the
devouring [a]fire?
Who among us shall dwell with everlasting
burnings?"
15 He who [a]walks righteously
and speaks uprightly,
He who despises the gain of oppressions,
Who gestures with his hands, refusing bribes,
Who stops his ears from hearing
of bloodshed,
And [b]shuts his eyes from seeing evil:
16 He will dwell on [1]high;
His place of defense *will be* the fortress of
rocks;
Bread will be given him,
His water *will be* sure.

17 Your eyes will see the King in His [a]beauty;
They will see the land that is very far off.
18 Your heart will meditate on terror:
[a]"Where *is* the scribe?
Where *is* he who weighs?
Where *is* he who counts the towers?"
19 [a]You will not see a fierce people,
[b]A people of obscure speech,
beyond perception,
Of a [1]stammering tongue *that you* cannot
understand.

20 [a]Look upon Zion,
the city of our appointed feasts;
Your eyes will see [b]Jerusalem, a quiet home,
A tabernacle *that* will not be taken down;
[c]Not one of [d]its stakes will ever be removed,
Nor will any of its cords be broken.
21 But there the majestic LORD *will be* for us
A place of broad rivers *and* streams,
In which no [1]galley with oars will sail,
Nor majestic ships pass by
22 (For the LORD *is* our [a]Judge,
The LORD *is* our [b]Lawgiver,
[c]The LORD *is* our King;
He will save us);
23 Your tackle is loosed,
They could not strengthen their mast,
They could not spread the sail.

Then the prey of great plunder is divided;
The lame take the prey.
24 And the inhabitant will not say, "I am sick";
[a]The people who dwell in it *will be* forgiven
*their* iniquity.

### *The LORD's Wrath upon the Nations*

**34** Come [a]near, you nations, to hear;
And heed, you people!
[b]Let the earth hear, and all that is in it,
The world and all things that come forth
from it.
2 For the indignation of the LORD
*is* against all nations,
And *His* fury against all their armies;
He has utterly destroyed them,
He has given them over to the [a]slaughter.
3 Also their slain shall be thrown out;
[a]Their stench shall rise from their corpses,
And the mountains shall be melted with their
blood.
4 [a]All the host of heaven shall be dissolved,
And the heavens shall be rolled up
like a scroll;
[b]All their host shall fall down
As the leaf falls from the vine,
And as [c]*fruit* falling from a fig tree.

5 "For [a]My sword shall be bathed in heaven;
Indeed it [b]shall come down on Edom,
And on the people of My curse,
for judgment.
6 The [a]sword of the LORD is filled with blood,
It is made [1]overflowing with fatness,

**20** [a][Eccl. 11:1]; Is. 30:23, 24

CHAPTER 33

**1** [a]Is. 21:2; Hab. 2:8 [b]Rev. 13:10 [c]Is. 10:12; 14:25; 31:8
**2** [a]Is. 25:9; 26:8 [1]LXX omits *their;* Syr., Tg., Vg. *our*
**3** [a]Is. 17:13
**5** [a]Ps. 97:9
**7** [a]2 Kin. 18:18, 37
**8** [a]Judg. 5:6 [b]2 Kin. 18:13–17 [1]Tg. *They have been removed from their cities* [2]So with MT, Vg.; DSS *witnesses;* LXX omits *cities*
**9** [a]Is. 24:4
**10** [a]Ps. 12:5; Is. 2:19, 21
**11** [a][Ps. 7:14; Is. 26:18; 59:4; James 1:15]
**12** [a]Is. 9:18
**13** [a]Ps. 48:10; Is. 49:1
**14** [a]Is. 30:27, 30; Heb. 12:29
**15** [a]Ps. 15:2; 24:3, 4; Is. 58:6–11 [b]Ps. 119:37
**16** [1]Lit. *heights*
**17** [a]Ps. 27:4
**18** [a]1 Cor. 1:20
**19** [a]2 Kin. 19:32 [b]Deut. 28:49, 50; Is. 28:11; Jer. 5:15 [1]Unintelligible speech
**20** [a]Ps. 48:12 [b]Ps. 46:5; 125:1; Is. 32:18 [c]Is. 37:33 [d]Is. 54:2
**21** [1]*ship*
**22** [a][Acts 10:42] [b]Is. 1:10; 51:4, 7; James 4:12 [c]Ps. 89:18; Is. 25:9; 35:4; Zech. 9:9
**24** [a]Is. 40:2; Jer. 50:20; Mic. 7:18, 19; 1 John 1:7–9

CHAPTER 34

**1** [a]Ps. 49:1; Is. 41:1; 43:9 [b]Deut. 32:1; Is. 1:2
**2** [a]Is. 13:5
**3** [a]Joel 2:20; Amos 4:10
**4** [a]Ps. 102:26; Is. 13:13; Ezek. 32:7, 8; Joel 2:31; Matt. 24:29; 2 Pet. 3:10 [b]Is. 14:12 [c]Rev. 6:12–14
**5** [a]Deut. 32:41, 42; Jer. 46:10; Ezek. 21:3–5 [b]Is. 63:1; Jer. 49:7, 8, 20; Ezek. 25:12–14; 35:1–15; Amos 1:11, 12; Obad. 1–14; Mal. 1:4
**6** [a]Is. 66:16 [1]Lit. *fat*

With the blood of lambs and goats,
With the fat of the kidneys of rams.
For [b]the LORD has a sacrifice in Bozrah,
And a great slaughter in the land of Edom.
7 The wild oxen shall come down with them,
And the young bulls with the mighty bulls;
Their land shall be soaked with blood,
And their dust [1]saturated with fatness."

8 For *it is* the day of the LORD's [a]vengeance,
The year of recompense for the cause of Zion.
9 [a]Its streams shall be turned into pitch,
And its dust into brimstone;
Its land shall become burning pitch.
10 It shall not be quenched night or day;
[a]Its smoke shall ascend forever.
[b]From generation to generation
it shall lie waste;
No one shall pass through it forever and ever.
11 [a]But the [1]pelican and the [2]porcupine
shall possess it,
Also the owl and the raven shall dwell in it.
And [b]He shall stretch out over it
The line of confusion
and the stones of emptiness.
12 They shall call its nobles to the kingdom,
But none *shall be* there,
and all its princes shall be nothing.

13 And [a]thorns shall come up in its palaces,
Nettles and brambles in its fortresses;
[b]It shall be a habitation of jackals,
A courtyard for ostriches.
14 The wild beasts of the desert
shall also meet with the [1]jackals,
And the wild goat shall bleat
to its companion;
Also [2]the night creature shall rest there,
And find for herself a place of rest.
15 There the arrow snake shall make her nest
and lay *eggs*
And hatch, and gather *them* under her shadow;
There also shall the hawks be gathered,
Every one with her mate.

16 "Search from [a]the book of the LORD, and read:
Not one of these shall fail;
Not one shall lack her mate.
For My mouth has commanded it,
and His Spirit has gathered them.
17 He has cast the lot for them,
And His hand has divided it among them
with a measuring line.
They shall possess it forever;
From generation to generation they shall
dwell in it."

### *The Future Glory of Zion*

**35** The [a]wilderness and the [1]wasteland shall
be glad for them,
And the [b]desert[2] shall rejoice
and blossom as the rose;
2 [a]It shall blossom abundantly and rejoice,
Even with joy and singing.
The glory of Lebanon shall be given to it,
The excellence of Carmel and Sharon.
They shall see the [b]glory of the LORD,
The excellency of our God.

3 [a]Strengthen the [1]weak hands,
And make firm the [2]feeble knees.
4 Say to those *who are* fearful-hearted,
"Be strong, do not fear!
Behold, your God will come *with* [a]vengeance,
*With* the recompense of God;
He will come and [b]save you."
5 Then the [a]eyes of the blind shall be opened,
And [b]the ears of the deaf shall be unstopped.
6 Then the [a]lame shall leap like a deer,
And the [b]tongue of the dumb sing.
For [c]waters shall burst forth in the
wilderness,
And streams in the desert.
7 The parched ground shall become a pool,
And the thirsty land springs of water;
In [a]the habitation of jackals, where each lay,
*There shall be* grass with reeds and rushes.

8 A [a]highway shall be there, and a road,
And it shall be called
the Highway of Holiness.
[b]The unclean shall not pass over it,
But it *shall be* for others.
Whoever walks the road, although a fool,
Shall not go astray.
9 [a]No lion shall be there,
Nor shall *any* ravenous beast go up on it;
It shall not be found there.
But the redeemed shall walk *there,*
10 And the [a]ransomed of the LORD shall return,
And come to Zion with singing,
With everlasting joy on their heads.
They shall obtain joy and gladness,
And [b]sorrow and sighing shall flee away.

### *Sennacherib Invades Judah*

**36** Now [a]it came to pass in the fourteenth year
of King Hezekiah *that* Sennacherib king of
Assyria came up against all the fortified cities of
Judah and took them.
2 Then the king of Assyria sent *the* [1]Rabshakeh
with a great army from Lachish to King Hezekiah
at Jerusalem. And he stood by the aqueduct from
the upper pool, on the highway to the Fuller's
Field.
3 And [a]Eliakim the son of Hilkiah, who was over
the household, [b]Shebna the scribe, and Joah the
son of Asaph, the recorder, came out to him.
4 [a]Then *the* Rabshakeh said to them, "Say now
to Hezekiah, 'Thus says the great king, the king of
Assyria: "What confidence is this in which you
trust?
5 "I say you speak of having plans and power
for war; but *they are* [1]mere words. Now in whom
do you trust, that you rebel against me?
6 "Look! You are trusting in the [a]staff of this
broken reed, Egypt, on which if a man leans, it
will go into his hand and pierce it. So *is* Pharaoh
king of Egypt to all who [b]trust in him.
7 "But if you say to me, 'We trust in the LORD
our God,' *is it* not He whose high places and
whose altars Hezekiah has taken away, and said
to Judah and Jerusalem, 'You shall worship before
this altar'?" '
8 "Now therefore, I urge you, give a pledge to
my master the king of Assyria, and I will give you
two thousand horses—if you are able on your part
to put riders on them!
9 "How then will you repel one captain of the
least of my master's servants, and put your trust
in Egypt for chariots and horsemen?
10 "Have I now come up without the LORD

**6** [b]Zeph. 1:7
**7** [1]Lit. *made fat*
**8** [a]Is. 63:4
**9** [a]Deut. 29:23; Ps. 11:6; Is. 30:33
**10** [a]Rev. 14:11; 18:18; 19:3 [b]Is. 13:20–22; 24:1; 34:10–15; Mal. 1:3, 4
**11** [a]Is. 14:23; Zeph. 2:14; Rev. 18:2 [b]2 Kin. 21:13; Lam. 2:8 [1]Or *owl* [2]Or *hedgehog*
**13** [a]Is. 32:13; Hos. 9:6 [b]Is. 13:21
**14** [1]Lit. *howling creatures* [2]Heb. *lilith*
**16** [a][Mal. 3:16]

CHAPTER 35
**1** [a]Is. 32:15; 55:12 [b]Is. 41:19; 51:3 [1]*desert* [2]Heb. *arabah*
**2** [a]Is. 32:15 [b]Is. 40:5
**3** [a]Job 4:3, 4; Heb. 12:12 [1]Lit. *sinking* [2]*tottering* or *stumbling*
**4** [a]Is. 34:8 [b]Ps. 145:19; Is. 33:22
**5** [a]Is. 29:18; Matt. 9:27; John 9:6, 7 [b][Matt. 11:5]
**6** [a]Matt. 11:5; 15:30; John 5:8, 9; Acts 8:7 [b]Is. 32:4; Matt. 9:32; 12:22 [c]Is. 41:18; [John 7:38]
**7** [a]Is. 34:13
**8** [a]Is. 19:23 [b]Is. 52:1; Joel 3:17; [Matt. 7:13, 14]; 1 Pet. 1:15, 16; Rev. 21:27
**9** [a]Lev. 26:6; [Is. 11:7, 9]; Ezek. 34:25
**10** [a]Is. 51:11 [b]Is. 25:8; 30:19; 65:19; [Rev. 7:17; 21:4]

CHAPTER 36
**1** [a]2 Kin. 18:13, 17; 2 Chr. 32:1
**2** [1]A title, probably *Chief of Staff* or *Governor*
**3** [a]Is. 22:20 [b]Is. 22:15
**4** [a]2 Kin. 18:19
**5** [1]Lit. *a word of the lips*
**6** [a]Ezek. 29:6 [b]Ps. 146:3; Is. 30:3, 5, 7

against this land to destroy it? The LORD said to
me, 'Go up against this land, and destroy it.' "
11 Then Eliakim, Shebna, and Joah said to *the*
Rabshakeh, "Please speak to your servants in
Aramaic, for we understand *it;* and do not speak
to us in [1]Hebrew in the hearing of the people who
*are* on the wall."
12 But *the* Rabshakeh said, "Has my master sent
me to your master and to you to speak these
words, and not to the men who sit on the wall,
who will eat and drink their own waste with
you?"
13 Then *the* Rabshakeh stood and called out with
a loud voice in Hebrew, and said, "Hear the words
of the great king, the king of Assyria!
14 "Thus says the king: 'Do not let Hezekiah
deceive you, for he will not be able to deliver you;
15 'nor let Hezekiah make you trust in the LORD,
saying, "The LORD will surely deliver us; this city
will not be given into the hand of the king of
Assyria." '
16 "Do not listen to Hezekiah; for thus says the
king of Assyria: 'Make *peace* with me *by a* present
and come out to me; [a]and every one of you eat
from his own vine and every one from his own fig
tree, and every one of you drink the waters of his
own cistern;
17 'until I come and take you away to a land like
your own land, a land of grain and new wine, a
land of bread and vineyards.
18 '*Beware* lest Hezekiah persuade you, saying,
"The LORD will deliver us." Has any one of the
[a]gods of the nations delivered its land from the
hand of the king of Assyria?
19 'Where *are* the gods of Hamath and Arpad?
Where *are* the gods of Sepharvaim? Indeed, have
they delivered [a]Samaria from my hand?
20 'Who among all the gods of these lands have
delivered their countries from my hand, that the
LORD should deliver Jerusalem from my hand?' "
21 But they [1]held their peace and answered him
not a word; for the king's commandment was,
"Do not answer him."
22 Then Eliakim the son of Hilkiah, who *was*
over the household, Shebna the scribe, and Joah
the son of Asaph, the recorder, came to Hezekiah
with *their* clothes torn, and told him the words of
*the* Rabshakeh.

### *Judah Rescued from Sennacherib*

**37** And [a]so it was, when King Hezekiah heard
*it,* that he tore his clothes, covered himself
with sackcloth, and went into the house of the
LORD.
2 Then he sent Eliakim, who *was* over the
household, Shebna the scribe, and the elders of
the priests, covered with sackcloth, to Isaiah the
prophet, the son of Amoz.
3 And they said to him, "Thus says Hezekiah:
'This day *is* a day of [a]trouble and rebuke and
[1]blasphemy; for the children have come to birth,
but *there is* no strength to bring them forth.
4 'It may be that the LORD your God will hear
the words of *the* Rabshakeh, whom his master the
king of Assyria has sent to [a]reproach the living
God, and will rebuke the words which the LORD
your God has heard. Therefore lift up *your* prayer
for the remnant that is left.' "
5 So the servants of King Hezekiah came to
Isaiah.
6 And Isaiah said to them, "Thus you shall say
to your master, 'Thus says the LORD: "Do not be
afraid of the words which you have heard, with
which the servants of the king of Assyria have
blasphemed Me.
7 "Surely I will send a spirit upon him, and he
shall hear a rumor and return to his own land; and
I will cause him to fall by the sword in his own
land." ' "
8 Then *the* Rabshakeh returned, and found the
king of Assyria warring against Libnah, for he
heard that he had departed from Lachish.
9 And the king heard concerning Tirhakah king
of Ethiopia, "He has come out to make war with
you." So when he heard *it,* he sent messengers to
Hezekiah, saying,
10 "Thus you shall speak to Hezekiah king of
Judah, saying: 'Do not let your God in whom you
trust deceive you, saying, "Jerusalem shall not be
given into the hand of the king of Assyria."
11 'Look! You have heard what the kings of
Assyria have done to all lands by utterly destroying them; and shall you be delivered?
12 'Have the [a]gods of the nations delivered those
whom my fathers have destroyed, Gozan and
Haran and Rezeph, and the people of Eden who
*were* in Telassar?
13 'Where *is* the king of [a]Hamath, the king of
Arpad, and the king of the city of Sepharvaim,
Hena, and Ivah?' "
14 And Hezekiah received the letter from the
hand of the messengers, and read it; and Hezekiah
went up to the house of the LORD, and spread it
before the LORD.
15 Then Hezekiah prayed to the LORD, saying:
16 "O LORD of hosts, God of Israel, *the One* who
dwells *between* the cherubim, You *are* God, You
[a]alone, of all the kingdoms of the earth. You have
made heaven and earth.
17 [a]"Incline Your ear, O LORD, and hear; open
Your eyes, O LORD, and see; and [b]hear all the
words of Sennacherib, which he has sent to reproach the living God.
18 "Truly, LORD, the kings of Assyria have laid
waste all the nations and their [a]lands,
19 "and have cast their gods into the fire; for they
*were* [a]not gods, but the work of men's hands—
wood and stone. Therefore they destroyed them.
20 "Now therefore, O LORD our God, [a]save us
from his hand, that all the kingdoms of the earth
may [b]know that You *are* the LORD, You alone."
21 Then Isaiah the son of Amoz sent to Hezekiah, saying, "Thus says the LORD God of Israel,
'Because you have prayed to Me against Sennacherib king of Assyria,
22 'this *is* the word which the LORD has spoken
concerning him:

"The virgin, the daughter of Zion,
Has despised you, laughed you to scorn;
The daughter of Jerusalem
Has shaken *her* head behind your back!

23 "Whom have you reproached and
blasphemed?
Against whom have you raised *your* voice,
And lifted up your eyes on high?
Against the Holy One of Israel.
24 By your servants you have reproached the
Lord,
And said, 'By the multitude of my chariots
I have come up to the height of the
mountains,
To the limits of Lebanon;
I will cut down its tall cedars

---

11 [1]Lit. *Judean*
16 [a]1 Kin. 4:25; Mic. 4:4; Zech. 3:10
18 [a]2 Kin. 19:12; Is. 37:12
19 [a]2 Kin. 17:6
21 [1]*were silent*
CHAPTER 37
1 [a]2 Kin. 19:1–37; Is. 37:1–38
3 [a]Is. 22:5; 26:16; 33:2 [1]*contempt*
4 [a]Is. 36:15, 18, 20
12 [a]Is. 36:18, 19
13 [a]Is. 49:23
16 [a]Is. 43:10, 11
17 [a]2 Chr. 6:40; Ps. 17:6; Dan. 9:18 [b]Ps. 74:22
18 [a]2 Kin. 15:29; 16:9; 17:6, 24; 1 Chr. 5:26
19 [a]Is. 40:19, 20
20 [a]Is. 33:22 [b]Ps. 83:18

*And* its choice cypress trees;
I will enter its farthest height,
To its fruitful forest.
25 I have dug and drunk water,
And with the soles of my feet I have dried up
All the brooks of [1]defense.'

26 "Did you not hear [a]long ago
*How* I made it,
From ancient times that I formed it?
Now I have brought it to pass,
That you should be
For crushing fortified cities
*into* heaps of ruins.
27 Therefore their inhabitants *had* little power;
They were dismayed and confounded;
They were *as* the grass of the field
And the green herb,
*As* the grass on the housetops
And *grain* blighted before it is grown.

28 "But I know your dwelling place,
Your going out and your coming in,
And your rage against Me.
29 Because your rage against Me
and your tumult
Have come up to My ears,
Therefore [a]I will put My hook in your nose
And My bridle in your lips,
And I will [b]turn you back
By the way which you came." '

**30** "This *shall be* a sign to you:

You shall eat this year
such as grows of itself,
And the second year
what springs from the same;
Also in the third year sow and reap,
Plant vineyards and eat the fruit of them.
31 And the remnant who have escaped
of the house of Judah
Shall again take root downward,
And bear fruit upward.
32 For out of Jerusalem shall go a remnant,
And those who escape from Mount Zion.
The [a]zeal of the LORD of hosts will do this.

**33** "Therefore thus says the LORD
concerning the king of Assyria:

'He shall not come into this city,
Nor shoot an arrow there,
Nor come before it with shield,
Nor build a siege mound against it.
34 By the way that he came,
By the same shall he return;
And he shall not come into this city,'
Says the LORD.
35 'For I will [a]defend this city, to save it
For My own sake
and for My servant [b]David's sake.' "

**36** Then the [a]angel[1] of the LORD went out, and
[2]killed in the camp of the Assyrians one hundred
and eighty-five thousand; and when *people* arose
early in the morning, there were the corpses—all
dead.
37 So Sennacherib king of Assyria departed and
went away, returned *home,* and remained at
Nineveh.
38 Now it came to pass, as he was worshiping in
the house of Nisroch his god, that his sons Adrammelech and Sharezer struck him down with the
sword; and they escaped into the land of Ararat.
Then [a]Esarhaddon his son reigned in his place.

## *Hezekiah's Sickness and Healing*

**38** In [a]those days Hezekiah was sick and near
death. And Isaiah the prophet, the son of
Amoz, went to him and said to him, "Thus says
the LORD: [b]'Set your house in order, for you shall
die and not live.' "
2 Then Hezekiah turned his face toward the
wall, and prayed to the LORD,
3 and said, [a]"Remember now, O LORD, I pray,
how I have walked before You in truth and with a
[1]loyal heart, and have done *what is* good in Your
[b]sight." And Hezekiah wept bitterly.
**4** And the word of the LORD came to Isaiah,
saying,
5 "Go and tell Hezekiah, 'Thus says the LORD,
the God of David your father: "I have heard your
prayer, I have seen your tears; surely I will add to
your days fifteen years.
6 "I will deliver you and this city from the hand
of the king of Assyria, and [a]I will defend this
city." '
7 "And this *is* [a]the sign to you from the LORD,
that the LORD will do this thing which He has
spoken:
8 "Behold, I will bring the shadow on the sundial, which has gone down with the sun on the
sundial of Ahaz, ten degrees backward." So the
sun returned ten degrees on the dial by which it
had gone down.
**9** This is the writing of Hezekiah king of Judah,
when he had been sick and had recovered from
his sickness:

10 I said,
"In the prime of my life
I shall go to the gates of Sheol;
I am deprived of the remainder of my years."
11 I said,
"I shall not see [1]YAH,
The LORD [a]in the land of the living;
I shall observe man no more [2]among the
inhabitants of [3]the world.
12 [a]My life span is gone,
Taken from me like a shepherd's tent;
I have cut off my life like a weaver.
He cuts me off from the loom;
From day until night
You make an end of me.
13 I have considered until morning—
Like a lion,
So He breaks all my bones;
From day until night
You make an end of me.
14 Like a crane *or* a swallow, so I chattered;
[a]I mourned like a dove;
My eyes fail *from looking* upward.
O [1]LORD, I am oppressed;
[2]Undertake for me!

**15** "What shall I say?
[1]He has both spoken to me,
And He Himself has done *it.*
I shall walk carefully all my years
[a]In the bitterness of my soul.
16 O LORD, by these *things men* live;
And in all these *things is* the life of my spirit;
So You will restore me and make me live.
17 Indeed *it was* for *my own* peace
*That* I had great bitterness;
But You have lovingly *delivered* my soul
from the pit of corruption,
For You have cast all my sins behind Your
back.

**25** [1]Or perhaps *Egypt*
**26** [a]Is. 25:1; 40:21; 45:21
**29** [a]2 Kin. 19:35–37; 2 Chr. 32:21; Is. 30:28; Ezek. 38:4 [b]Ezek. 38:4; 39:2
**32** [a]2 Kin. 19:31; Is. 9:7; 59:17; Joel 2:18; Zech. 1:14
**35** [a]2 Kin. 20:6; Is. 31:5; 38:6 [b]1 Kin. 11:13
**36** [a]2 Kin. 19:35; Is. 10:12, 33, 34 [1]Or *Angel* [2]Lit. *struck*
**38** [a]Ezra 4:2

CHAPTER 38
**1** [a]2 Kin. 20:1–6, 9–11; 2 Chr. 32:24; Is. 38:1–8 [b]2 Sam. 17:23
**3** [a]Neh. 13:14 [b]2 Kin. 18:5, 6; Ps. 26:3 [1]*whole* or *peaceful*
**6** [a]2 Kin. 19:35–37; 2 Chr. 32:21; Is. 31:5; 37:35
**7** [a]Judg. 6:17, 21, 36–40; 2 Kin. 20:8; Is. 7:11
**11** [a]Ps. 27:13; 116:9 [1]Heb. *YAH, YAH* [2]LXX omits *among the inhabitants of the world* [3]So with some Heb. mss.; MT, Vg. *rest;* Tg. *land*
**12** [a]Job 7:6
**14** [a]Is. 59:11; Ezek. 7:16; Nah. 2:7 [1]So with Bg.; MT, DSS *Lord* [2]*Be my surety*
**15** [a]Job 7:11; 10:1; Is. 38:17 [1]So with MT, Vg.; DSS, Tg. *And shall I say to Him;* LXX omits first half of this verse

18 For [a]Sheol cannot thank You,
Death cannot praise You;
Those who go down to the pit cannot hope
for Your truth.
19 The living, the living man,
he shall praise You,
As I *do* this day;
[a]The father shall make known Your truth to
the children.

20 "The LORD *was ready* to save me;
Therefore we will sing my songs with
stringed instruments
All the days of our life,
in the house of the LORD."

**21** Now [a]Isaiah had said, "Let them take a lump
of figs, and apply *it* as a poultice on the boil, and
he shall recover."
22 And [a]Hezekiah had said, "What *is* the sign
that I shall go up to the house of the LORD?"

## *Babylonian Captivity of Judah Foretold*

**39** At [a]that time [1]Merodach-Baladan the son of
Baladan, king of Babylon, sent letters and a
present to Hezekiah, for he heard that he had
been sick and had recovered.
2 [a]And Hezekiah was pleased with them, and
showed them the house of his treasures—the
silver and gold, the spices and precious ointment,
and all his armory—all that was found among his
treasures. There was nothing in his house or in all
his dominion that Hezekiah did not show them.
**3** Then Isaiah the prophet went to King Hezekiah, and said to him, "What did these men say,
and from where did they come to you?" So Hezekiah said, "They came to me from a [a]far country,
from Babylon."
4 And he said, "What have they seen in your
house?" So Hezekiah answered, "They have seen
all that *is* in my house; there is nothing among my
treasures that I have not shown them."
5 Then Isaiah said to Hezekiah, "Hear the word
of the LORD of hosts:
6 'Behold, the days are coming [a]when all that *is*
in your house, and what your fathers have accu-
mulated until this day, shall be carried to Babylon;
nothing shall be left,' says the LORD.
7 'And they shall take away *some* of your [a]sons
who will descend from you, whom you will beget;
and they shall be eunuchs in the palace of the
king of Babylon.' "
8 So Hezekiah said to Isaiah, [a]"The word of the
LORD which you have spoken *is* good!" For he
said, "At least there will be peace and truth in my
days."

## *The Majesty of the LORD*

**40** "Comfort, yes, comfort My people!"
Says your God.
2 "Speak [1]comfort to Jerusalem,
and cry out to her,
That her warfare is ended,
That her iniquity is pardoned;
[a]For she has received from the LORD's hand
Double for all her sins."

**3** [a]The voice of one crying in the wilderness:
[b]"Prepare the way of the LORD;
[c]Make straight [1]in the desert
A highway for our God.
4 Every valley shall be exalted
And every mountain and hill brought low;
[a]The crooked places shall be made [1]straight
And the rough places smooth;
5 The [a]glory of the LORD shall be revealed,
And all flesh shall see *it* together;
For the mouth of the LORD has spoken."

**6** The voice said, "Cry out!"
And [1]he said, "What shall I cry?"

[a]"All flesh *is* grass,
And all its loveliness *is* like the flower of the
field.
7 The grass withers, the flower fades,
Because the breath of the LORD blows upon
it;
Surely the people *are* grass.
8 The grass withers, the flower fades,
But [a]the word of our God stands forever."

**9** O Zion,
You who bring good tidings,
Get up into the high mountain;
O Jerusalem,
You who bring good tidings,
Lift up your voice with strength,
Lift *it* up, be not afraid;
Say to the cities of Judah,
"Behold your God!"

10 Behold, the Lord GOD shall come
[1]with a strong *hand,*
And [a]His arm shall rule for Him;
Behold, [b]His reward *is* with Him,
And His [2]work before Him.
11 He will [a]feed His flock like a shepherd;
He will gather the lambs with His arm,
And carry *them* in His bosom,
*And* gently lead those who are with young.

**12** [a]Who has measured the [1]waters
in the hollow of His hand,
Measured heaven with a [2]span
And calculated the dust of the earth
in a measure?
Weighed the mountains in scales
And the hills in a balance?
13 [a]Who has directed the Spirit of the LORD,
Or *as* His counselor has taught Him?
14 With whom did He take counsel,
and *who* instructed Him,
And [a]taught Him in the path of justice?
Who taught Him knowledge,
And showed Him the way of understanding?

15 Behold, the nations *are* as a drop in a bucket,
And are counted as the small dust
on the scales;
Look, He lifts up the isles as a very little
thing.
16 And Lebanon *is* not sufficient to burn,
Nor its beasts sufficient for a burnt offering.
17 All nations before Him *are* as [a]nothing,
And [b]they are counted by Him less than
nothing and worthless.

**18** To whom then will you [a]liken God?
Or what likeness will you compare to Him?
19 [a]The workman molds an image,
The goldsmith overspreads it with gold,
And the silversmith casts silver chains.
20 Whoever *is* too impoverished for *such* [1]a
contribution
Chooses a tree *that* will not rot;
He seeks for himself a skillful workman
[a]To prepare a carved image *that* will not
totter.

**18** [a]Ps. 6:5; 30:9; 88:11; 115:17; [Eccl. 9:10]
**19** [a]Deut. 4:9; 6:7; Ps. 78:3, 4
**21** [a]2 Kin. 20:7
**22** [a]2 Kin. 20:8

CHAPTER 39
**1** [a]2 Kin. 20:12–19; 2 Chr. 32:31; Is. 39:1–8 [1]*Berodach-Baladan,* 2 Kin. 20:12
**2** [a]2 Chr. 32:25, 31; Job 31:25
**3** [a]Deut. 28:49; Jer. 5:15
**6** [a]2 Kin. 24:13; 25:13–15; Jer. 20:5
**7** [a]Dan. 1:1–7
**8** [a]1 Sam. 3:18

CHAPTER 40
**2** [a]Is. 61:7 [1]Lit. *to the heart of*
**3** [a]Matt. 3:3; Mark 1:3; Luke 3:4–6; John 1:23 [b][Mal. 3:1; 4:5, 6] [c]Ps. 68:4 [1]So with MT, Tg., Vg.; LXX omits *in the desert*
**4** [a]Is. 45:2 [1]Or *a plain*
**5** [a]Is. 35:2
**6** [a]Job 14:2; James 1:10; 1 Pet. 1:24, 25 [1]So with MT, Tg.; DSS, LXX, Vg. *I*
**8** [a][John 12:34]
**10** [a]Is. 59:16, 18 [b]Is. 62:11; Rev. 22:12 [1]*in strength* [2]*recompense*
**11** [a]Jer. 31:10; [Ezek. 34:23, 31]; Mic. 5:4; [John 10:11, 14–16; Heb. 13:20; 1 Pet. 2:25]
**12** [a]Prov. 30:4 [1]So with MT, LXX, Vg.; DSS adds *of the sea;* Tg. adds *of the world* [2]A span = ½ cubit, 9 inches; or, the width of His hand
**13** [a]Job 21:22; Rom. 11:34; [1 Cor. 2:16]
**14** [a]Job 36:22, 23
**17** [a]Dan. 4:35 [b]Ps. 62:9
**18** [a]Ex. 8:10; 15:11; 1 Sam. 2:2; Is. 46:5; [Mic. 7:18]; Acts 17:29
**19** [a]Ps. 115:4–8; Is. 41:7; 44:10; Hab. 2:18, 19
**20** [a]1 Sam. 5:3, 4; Is. 41:7; 46:7; Jer. 10:3 [1]*an offering*

**21** [a]Have you not known?
Have you not heard?
Has it not been told you from the beginning?
Have you not understood
from the foundations of the earth?
22 *It is* He who sits above the circle
of the earth,
And its inhabitants *are* like grasshoppers,
Who [a]stretches out the heavens
like a curtain,
And spreads them out like a [b]tent to dwell in.
23 He [1]brings the [a]princes to nothing;
He makes the judges of the earth useless.

24 Scarcely shall they be planted,
Scarcely shall they be sown,
Scarcely shall their stock take root
in the earth,
When He will also blow on them,
And they will wither,
And the whirlwind will take them away like
stubble.

**25** "To[a] whom then will you liken Me,
Or *to whom* shall I be equal?"
says the Holy One.
26 Lift up your eyes on high,
And see who has created these *things,*
Who brings out their host by number;
[a]He calls them all by name,
By the greatness of His might
And the strength of *His* power;
Not one is missing.

**27** [a]Why do you say, O Jacob,
And speak, O Israel:
"My way is hidden from the LORD,
And my just claim is passed over
by my God"?
28 Have you not known?
Have you not heard?
The everlasting God, the LORD,
The Creator of the ends of the earth,
Neither faints nor is weary.
[a]His understanding is unsearchable.
29 He gives power to the weak,
And to *those who have* no might
He increases strength.
30 Even the youths shall faint and be weary,
And the young men shall utterly fall,
31 But those who [a]wait on the LORD
[b]Shall renew *their* strength;
They shall mount up with wings like eagles,
They shall run and not be weary,
They shall walk and not faint.

## *The Final Restoration of Israel*

**41** "Keep [a]silence before Me, O coastlands,
And let the people renew *their* strength!
Let them come near, then let them speak;
Let us [b]come near together for judgment.

2 "Who raised up one [a]from the east?
Who in righteousness called him to His feet?
Who [b]gave the nations before him,
And made *him* rule over kings?
Who gave *them* as the dust *to* his sword,
As driven stubble to his bow?
3 Who pursued them, *and* passed [1]safely
By the way *that* he had not gone with his
feet?
4 [a]Who has performed and done *it,*
Calling the generations from the beginning?
'I, the LORD, am [b]the first;
And with the last I *am* [c]He.' "

**5** The coastlands saw *it* and feared,
The ends of the earth were afraid;
They drew near and came.
6 [a]Everyone helped his neighbor,
And said to his brother,
[1]Be of good courage!"
7 [a]So the craftsman encouraged the [b]goldsmith;[1]
He who smooths *with* the hammer *inspired*
him who strikes the anvil,
Saying, [2]"It *is* ready for the soldering";
Then he fastened it with pegs,
[c]*That* it might not totter.

**8** "But you, Israel, *are* My servant,
Jacob whom I have [a]chosen,
The descendants of Abraham My [b]friend.
9 *You* whom I have taken from the ends of the
earth,
And called from its farthest regions,
And said to you,
'You *are* My servant,
I have chosen you
and have not cast you away:
10 [a]Fear not, [b]for I *am* with you;
Be not dismayed, for I *am* your God.
I will strengthen you,
Yes, I will help you,
I will uphold you with My righteous right
hand.'
11 "Behold, all those who were incensed against
you
Shall be [a]ashamed and disgraced;
They shall be as nothing,
And those who strive with you shall perish.
12 You shall seek them and not find them—
[1]Those who contended with you.
Those who war against you
Shall be as nothing,
As a nonexistent thing.
13 For I, the LORD your God,
will hold your right hand,
Saying to you, 'Fear not, I will help you.'

**14** "Fear not, you [a]worm Jacob,
You men of Israel!
I will help you," says the LORD
And your Redeemer, the Holy One of Israel.
15 "Behold, [a]I will make you into a new
threshing sledge with sharp teeth;
You shall thresh the mountains
and beat *them* small,
And make the hills like chaff.
16 You shall [a]winnow them,
the wind shall carry them away,
And the whirlwind shall scatter them;
You shall rejoice in the LORD,
*And* [b]glory in the Holy One of Israel.

**17** "The poor and needy seek water, but *there is*
none,
Their tongues fail for thirst.
I, the LORD, will hear them;
*I,* the God of Israel, will not [a]forsake them.
18 I will open [a]rivers in desolate heights,
And fountains in the midst of the valleys;
I will make the [b]wilderness a pool of water,
And the dry land springs of water.
19 I will plant in the wilderness the cedar and
the acacia tree,
The myrtle and the oil tree;

**21** [a]Ps. 19:1; Is. 37:26; Acts 14:17; Rom. 1:19
**22** [a]Job 9:8; Ps. 104:2; Is. 42:5; 44:24; Jer. 10:12 [b]Job 36:29; Ps. 19:4
**23** [a]Job 12:21; Ps. 107:40; Is. 34:12; [1 Cor. 1:26–29] [1]*reduces*
**25** [a][Deut. 4:15]; Is. 40:18; [John 14:9; Col. 1:15]
**26** [a]Ps. 147:4
**27** [a]Is. 54:7, 8
**28** [a]Ps. 147:5; Eccl. 11:5; Rom. 11:33
**31** [a]Is. 30:15; 49:23 [b][Job 17:9]; Ps. 103:5; [2 Cor. 4:8–10, 16]

CHAPTER 41
**1** [a]Hab. 2:20; Zech. 2:13 [b]Is. 1:18
**2** [a]Is. 46:11 [b]Gen. 14:14; Is. 45:1, 13
**3** [1]Lit. *in peace*
**4** [a]Is. 41:26 [b]Rev. 1:8, 17; 22:13 [c]Is. 43:10; 44:6
**6** [a]Is. 40:19 [1]Lit. *Be strong*
**7** [a]Is. 44:13 [b]Is. 40:19 [c]Is. 40:20 [1]*refiner* [2]Or *The soldering is good*
**8** [a]Deut. 7:6; 10:15; Ps. 135:4; [Is. 43:1] [b]2 Chr. 20:7; James 2:23
**10** [a]Is. 41:13, 14; 43:5 [b][Deut. 31:6]
**11** [a]Ex. 23:22; Is. 45:24; 60:12; Zech. 12:3
**12** [1]Lit. *Men of your strife*
**14** [a]Job 25:6; Ps. 22:6
**15** [a]Mic. 4:13; Hab. 3:12; [2 Cor. 10:4]
**16** [a]Jer. 51:2 [b]Is. 45:25
**17** [a]Ps. 94:14; Rom. 11:2
**18** [a]Is. 35:6, 7; 43:19; 44:3 [b]Ps. 107:35

I will set in the [a]desert the cypress tree *and*
the pine
And the box tree together,
20 [a]That they may see and know,
And consider and understand together,
That the hand of the LORD has done this,
And the Holy One of Israel has created it.

**21** "Present your case," says the LORD.
"Bring forth your strong *reasons,*" says the
[a]King of Jacob.
22 "Let[a] them bring forth and show us
what will happen;
Let them show the [b]former things,
what they *were,*
That we may [1]consider them,
And know the latter end of them;
Or declare to us things to come.
23 [a]Show the things that are to come hereafter,
That we may know that you *are* gods;
Yes, [b]do good or do evil,
That we may be dismayed
and see *it* together.
24 Indeed [a]you *are* nothing,
And your work *is* nothing;
*He who* chooses you *is* an abomination.

**25** "I have raised up one from the north,
And he shall come;
From the [1]rising of the sun [a]he shall call on
My name;
[b]And he shall come against princes as *though*
mortar,
As the potter treads clay.
26 [a]Who has declared from the beginning, that
we may know?
And former times, that we may say, '*He is*
righteous'?
Surely *there is* no one who shows,
Surely *there is* no one who declares,
Surely *there is* no one who hears your words.
27 [a]The first time [b]*I said* to Zion,
'Look, there they are!'
And I will give to Jerusalem one who brings
good tidings.
28 [a]For I looked, and *there was* no man;
I looked among them,
but *there was* no counselor,
Who, when I asked of them,
could answer a word.
29 [a]Indeed they *are* all [1]worthless;
Their works *are* nothing;
Their molded images *are* wind and confusion.

### *The Servant Comes to Glorify the LORD*

**42** "Behold! [a]My Servant whom I uphold,
My [1]Elect One *in whom* My soul [b]delights!
[c]I have put My Spirit upon Him;
He will bring forth justice to the Gentiles.
2 He will not cry out, nor raise *His voice,*
Nor cause His voice to be heard in the street.
3 A bruised reed He will not break,
And [1]smoking flax He will not [2]quench;
He will bring forth justice for truth.
4 He will not fail nor be discouraged,
Till He has established justice in the earth;
[a]And the coastlands shall wait for His law."

**5** Thus says God the LORD,
[a]Who created the heavens
and stretched them out,
Who spread forth the earth
and that which comes from it,
[b]Who gives breath to the people on it,
And spirit to those who walk on it:
6 "I,[a] the LORD, have called You in
righteousness,
And will hold Your hand;
I will keep You [b]and give You as a covenant
to the people,
As [c]a light to the Gentiles,
7 [a]To open blind eyes,
To [b]bring out prisoners from the prison,
Those who sit in [c]darkness from the prison
house.
8 I *am* the LORD, that *is* My name;
And My [a]glory I will not give to another,
Nor My praise to carved images.
9 Behold, the former things have come to pass,
And new things I declare;
Before they spring forth I tell you of them."

**10** [a]Sing to the LORD a new song,
*And* His praise from the ends of the earth,
[b]You who go down to the sea,
and [1]all that is in it,
You coastlands and you inhabitants of them!
11 Let the wilderness and its cities
lift up *their voice,*
The villages *that* Kedar inhabits.
Let the inhabitants of Sela sing,
Let them shout from the top of the
mountains.
12 Let them give glory to the LORD,
And declare His praise in the coastlands.
13 The LORD shall go forth like a mighty man;
He shall stir up *His* zeal like a man of war.
He shall cry out, [a]yes, shout aloud;
He shall prevail against His enemies.

**14** "I have held My peace a long time,
I have been still and restrained Myself.
*Now* I will cry like a woman in [1]labor,
I will pant and gasp at once.
15 I will lay waste the mountains and hills,
And dry up all their vegetation;
I will make the rivers coastlands,
And I will dry up the pools.
16 I will bring the blind by a way
they did not know;
I will lead them in paths
they have not known.
I will make darkness light before them,
And crooked places straight.
These things I will do for them,
And not forsake them.
17 They shall be [a]turned back,
They shall be greatly ashamed,
Who trust in carved images,
Who say to the molded images,
'You *are* our gods.'

**18** "Hear, you deaf;
And look, you blind, that you may see.
19 [a]Who *is* blind but My servant,
Or deaf as My messenger *whom* I send?
Who *is* blind as *he who is* perfect,
And blind as the LORD's servant?
20 Seeing many things, [a]but you do not observe;
Opening the ears, but he does not hear."

**21** The LORD is well pleased for His
righteousness' sake;
He will exalt the law and make *it* honorable.

**19** [a]Is. 35:1
**20** [a]Job 12:9; Is. 66:14
**21** [a]Is. 43:15
**22** [a]Is. 45:21 [b]Is. 43:9 [1]Lit. *set our heart on them*
**23** [a]Is. 42:9; 44:7, 8; 45:3; [John 13:19] [b]Jer. 10:5
**24** [a]Ps. 115:8; Is. 44:9; [Rom. 3:10–20; 1 Cor. 8:4]
**25** [a]Ezra 1:2 [b]Is. 41:2; Jer. 50:3 [1]East
**26** [a]Is. 43:9
**27** [a]Is. 41:4 [b]Is. 40:9; Nah. 1:15
**28** [a]Is. 63:5
**29** [a]Is. 41:24 [1]So with MT, Vg.; DSS, Syr., Tg. *nothing;* LXX omits first line

CHAPTER 42

**1** [a]Is. 43:10; 49:3, 6; Matt. 12:18; [Phil. 2:7] [b]Matt. 3:17; 17:5; Mark 1:11; Luke 3:22; Eph. 1:6 [c][Is. 11:2]; Matt. 3:16; [Luke 4:18, 19, 21]; John 3:34 [1]*Chosen*
**3** [1]*dimly burning* [2]*extinguish*
**4** [a][Gen. 49:10]
**5** [a]Is. 44:24; Zech. 12:1 [b]Job 12:10; 33:4; Is. 57:16; Dan. 5:23; Acts 17:25
**6** [a]Is. 43:1 [b]Is. 49:8 [c]Is. 49:6; Luke 2:32; [Acts 10:45; 13:47; Gal. 3:14]
**7** [a]Is. 35:5 [b]Is. 61:1; Luke 4:18; [2 Tim. 2:26; Heb. 2:14] [c]Is. 9:2
**8** [a]Ex. 20:3–5; Is. 48:11
**10** [a]Ps. 33:3; 40:3; 98:1 [b]Ps. 107:23 [1]Lit. *its fullness*
**13** [a]Is. 31:4
**14** [1]*childbirth*
**17** [a]Ps. 97:7; Is. 1:29; 44:11; 45:16
**19** [a]Is. 43:8; Ezek. 12:2; [John 9:39, 41]
**20** [a]Rom. 2:21

22 But this *is* a people robbed and plundered;
All of them are [1]snared in holes,
And they are hidden in prison houses;
They are for prey, and no one delivers;
For plunder, and no one says, "Restore!"

**23** Who among you will give ear to this?
*Who* will listen and hear for the time to come?
24 Who gave Jacob for plunder,
and Israel to the robbers?
Was it not the LORD,
He against whom we have sinned?
[a]For they would not walk in His ways,
Nor were they obedient to His law.
25 Therefore He has poured on him the fury of His anger
And the strength of battle;
[a]It has set him on fire all around,
[b]Yet he did not know;
And it burned him,
Yet he did not take *it* to [c]heart.

### *The LORD the Only Redeemer*

**43** But now, thus says the LORD, who created you, O Jacob,
And He who formed you, O Israel:
"Fear not, [a]for I have redeemed you;
[b]I have called *you* by your name;
You *are* Mine.
2 [a]When you pass through the waters,
[b]I *will be* with you;
And through the rivers,
they shall not overflow you.
When you [c]walk through the fire,
you shall not be burned,
Nor shall the flame scorch you.
3 For I *am* the LORD your God,
The Holy One of Israel, your Savior;
[a]I gave Egypt for your ransom,
Ethiopia and Seba in your place.
4 Since you were precious in My sight,
You have been honored,
And I have [a]loved you;
Therefore I will give men for you,
And people for your life.
5 [a]Fear not, for I *am* with you;
I will bring your descendants from the east,
And [b]gather you from the west;
6 I will say to the [a]north, 'Give them up!'
And to the south, 'Do not keep them back!'
Bring My sons from afar,
And My daughters from the ends
of the earth—
7 Everyone who is [a]called by My name,
Whom [b]I have created for My glory;
I have formed him, yes, I have made him."

**8** [a]Bring out the blind people who have eyes,
And the [b]deaf who have ears.
9 Let all the nations be gathered together,
And let the people be assembled.
[a]Who among them can declare this,
And show us former things?
Let them bring out their witnesses,
that they may be justified;
Or let them hear and say, "*It is* truth."
10 "You[a] *are* My witnesses," says the LORD,
[b]"And My servant whom I have chosen,
That you may know and [c]believe Me,
And understand that I *am* He.
Before Me there was no God formed,
Nor shall there be after Me.
11 I, *even* I, [a]*am* the LORD,
And besides Me *there is* no savior.
12 I have declared and saved,
I have proclaimed,
And *there was* no [a]foreign *god* among you;
[b]Therefore you *are* My witnesses,"
Says the LORD, "that I *am* God.
13 [a]Indeed before the day *was*, I *am* He;
And *there is* no one who can deliver out of My hand;
I work, and who will [b]reverse it?"

**14** Thus says the LORD, your Redeemer,
The Holy One of Israel:
"For your sake I will send to Babylon,
And bring them all down as fugitives—
The Chaldeans, who rejoice in their ships.
15 I *am* the LORD, your Holy One,
The Creator of Israel, your [a]King."

**16** Thus says the LORD,
who [a]makes a way in the sea
And a [b]path through the mighty waters,
17 Who [a]brings forth the chariot and horse,
The army and the power
(They shall lie down together,
they shall not rise;
They are extinguished,
they are quenched like a wick):
18 "Do[a] not remember the former things,
Nor consider the things of old.
19 Behold, I will do a [a]new thing,
Now it shall spring forth;
Shall you not know it?
[b]I will even make a road in the wilderness
*And* rivers in the desert.
20 The beast of the field will honor Me,
The jackals and the ostriches,
Because [a]I give waters in the wilderness
*And* rivers in the desert,
To give drink to My people, My chosen.
21 [a]This people I have formed for Myself;
They shall declare My [b]praise.

**22** "But you have not called upon Me, O Jacob;
And you [a]have been weary of Me, O Israel.
23 [a]You have not brought Me the sheep for your burnt offerings,
Nor have you honored Me
with your sacrifices.
I have not caused you to serve
with grain offerings,
Nor wearied you with incense.
24 You have bought Me no sweet cane with money,
Nor have you satisfied Me
with the fat of your sacrifices;
But you have burdened Me with your sins,
You have [a]wearied Me with your iniquities.

**25** "I, *even* I, *am* He who [a]blots out your
transgressions [b]for My own sake;
[c]And I will not remember your sins.
26 Put Me in remembrance;
Let us contend together;
State your *case*, that you may be [1]acquitted.
27 Your first father sinned,
And your [1]mediators have transgressed
against Me.
28 Therefore I will profane the princes
of the sanctuary;
[a]I will give Jacob to the curse,
And Israel to reproaches.

**22** [1]Or *trapped in caves*
**24** [a]Is. 65:2
**25** [a]2 Kin. 25:9 [b]Is. 1:3; 5:13; Hos. 7:9 [c]Is. 29:13

CHAPTER 43
**1** [a]Is. 43:5; 44:6 [b]Is. 42:6; 45:4
**2** [a][Ps. 66:12; 91:3] [b][Deut. 31:6]; Jer. 30:11 [c]Dan. 3:25
**3** [a][Prov. 11:8; 21:18]
**4** [a]Is. 63:9
**5** [a]Is. 41:10; 44:2; Jer. 30:10; 46:27, 28 [b]Is. 54:7
**6** [a]Is. 49:12
**7** [a]Is. 63:19; James 2:7 [b]Ps. 100:3; Is. 29:23; [John 3:2, 3; 2 Cor. 5:17; Eph. 2:10]
**8** [a]Is. 6:9; 42:19; Ezek. 12:2 [b]Is. 29:18
**9** [a]Is. 41:21, 22, 26
**10** [a]Is. 44:8 [b]Is. 55:4 [c]Is. 41:4; 44:6
**11** [a]Is. 45:21; Hos. 13:4
**12** [a]Deut. 32:16; Ps. 81:9 [b]Is. 44:8
**13** [a]Ps. 90:2; Is. 48:16 [b]Job 9:12; Is. 14:27
**15** [a]Is. 41:20, 21
**16** [a]Ex. 14:16, 21, 22; Ps. 77:19; Is. 51:10 [b]Josh. 3:13
**17** [a]Ex. 14:4–9, 25
**18** [a]Jer. 16:14
**19** [a]Is. 42:9; 48:6; [2 Cor. 5:17; Rev. 21:5] [b]Ex. 17:6; Num. 20:11; Deut. 8:15; Ps. 78:16; Is. 35:1, 6
**20** [a]Is. 48:21
**21** [a]Ps. 102:18; Is. 42:12; [Luke 1:74, 75; Eph. 1:5, 6; 1 Pet. 2:9] [b]Jer. 13:11
**22** [a]Mic. 6:3; Mal. 1:13; 3:14
**23** [a]Amos 5:25
**24** [a]Ps. 95:10; Is. 1:14; 7:13; Ezek. 6:9; Mal. 2:17
**25** [a]Is. 44:22; Jer. 50:20; [Acts 3:19] [b]Ezek. 36:22 [c]Is. 1:18; Jer. 31:34
**26** [1]*justified*
**27** [1]*interpreters*
**28** [a]Ps. 79:4; Jer. 24:9; Dan. 9:11; Zech. 8:13

### *The Folly of Idolatry*

44 "Yet hear now, O Jacob My servant,
And Israel whom I have chosen.
2 Thus says the LORD who made you
And formed you from the womb, *who* will help you:
'Fear not, O Jacob My servant;
And you, Jeshurun, whom I have chosen.
3 For I will pour water on him who is thirsty,
And floods on the dry ground;
I will pour My Spirit on your descendants,
And My blessing on your offspring;
4 They will spring up among the grass
Like willows by the watercourses.'
5 One will say, 'I *am* the LORD's';
Another will call *himself* by the name of Jacob;
Another will write *with* his hand, 'The LORD's,'
And name *himself* by the name of Israel.

6 "Thus says the LORD, the King of Israel,
And his Redeemer, the LORD of hosts:
[a]'I *am* the First and I *am* the Last;
Besides Me *there is* no God.
7 And [a]who can proclaim as I do?
Then let him declare it and set it in order for Me,
Since I appointed the ancient people.
And the things that are coming and shall come,
Let them show these to them.
8 Do not fear, nor be afraid;
[a]Have I not told you from that time, and declared *it?*
[b]You *are* My witnesses.
Is there a God besides Me?
Indeed [c]*there is* no other Rock;
I know not *one.*' "

9 [a]Those who make an image, all of them *are* useless,
And their precious things shall not profit;
They *are* their own witnesses;
[b]They neither see nor know, that they may be ashamed.
10 Who would form a god or mold an image
[a]*That* profits him nothing?
11 Surely all his companions would be [a]ashamed;
And the workmen, they *are* mere men.
Let them all be gathered together,
Let them stand up;
Yet they shall fear,
They shall be ashamed together.

12 [a]The blacksmith with the tongs works one in the coals,
Fashions it with hammers,
And works it with the strength of his arms.
Even so, he is hungry, and his strength fails;
He drinks no water and is faint.

13 The craftsman stretches out *his* rule,
He marks one out with chalk;
He fashions it with a plane,
He marks it out with the compass,
And makes it like the figure of a man,
According to the beauty of a man, that it may remain in the house.
14 He cuts down cedars for himself,
And takes the cypress and the oak;
He [1]secures *it* for himself among the trees of the forest.
He plants a pine, and the rain nourishes *it.*
15 Then it shall be for a man to burn,
For he will take some of it and warm himself;
Yes, he kindles *it* and bakes bread;
Indeed he makes a god and worships *it;*
He makes it a carved image, and falls down to it.
16 He burns half of it in the fire;
With this half he eats meat;
He roasts a roast, and is satisfied.
He even warms *himself* and says,
"Ah! I am warm,
I have seen the fire."
17 And the rest of it he makes into a god,
His carved image.
He falls down before it and worships *it,*
Prays to it and says,
"Deliver me, for you *are* my god!"

18 [a]They do not know nor understand;
For [b]He has [1]shut their eyes, so that they cannot see,
*And* their hearts, so that they cannot [c]understand.
19 And no one [a]considers in his heart,
Nor *is there* knowledge nor understanding to say,
"I have burned half of it in the fire,
Yes, I have also baked bread on its coals;
I have roasted meat and eaten *it;*
And shall I make the rest of it an abomination?
Shall I fall down before a block of wood?"
20 He feeds on ashes;
[a]A deceived heart has turned him aside;
And he cannot deliver his soul,
Nor say, "*Is there* not a [b]lie in my right hand?"

21 "Remember these, O Jacob,
And Israel, for you *are* My servant;
I have formed you, you *are* My servant;
O Israel, you will not be [a]forgotten by Me!
22 [a]I have blotted out, like a thick cloud, your transgressions,
And like a cloud, your sins.
Return to Me, for [b]I have redeemed you."

23 [a]Sing, O heavens, for the LORD has done *it!*
Shout, you lower parts of the earth;
Break forth into singing, you mountains,
O forest, and every tree in it!
For the LORD has redeemed Jacob,
And [b]glorified Himself in Israel.

24 Thus says the LORD, [a]your Redeemer,
And [b]He who formed you from the womb:
"I *am* the LORD, who makes all *things,*
[c]Who stretches out the heavens [1]all alone,
Who spreads abroad the earth by Myself;
25 Who [a]frustrates the signs [b]of the babblers,
And drives diviners mad;
Who turns wise men backward,
[c]And makes their knowledge foolishness;
26 [a]Who confirms the word of His servant,
And performs the counsel of His messengers;
Who says to Jerusalem,
'You shall be inhabited,'
To the cities of Judah, 'You shall be built,'
And I will raise up her waste places;

CHAPTER 44
6 [a]Is. 41:4; [Rev. 1:8, 17; 22:13]
7 [a]Is. 41:4, 22, 26
8 [a]Is. 41:22 [b]Is. 43:10, 12 [c]Deut. 4:35; 32:39; 1 Sam. 2:2; 2 Sam. 22:32; Is. 45:5; Joel 2:27
9 [a]Is. 41:24 [b]Ps. 115:4
10 [a]Is. 41:29; Jer. 10:5; Hab. 2:18; Acts 19:26
11 [a]Ps. 97:7; Is. 1:29; 42:17
12 [a]Is. 40:19; Jer. 10:3–5
14 [1]Lit. *appropriates*
18 [a]Is. 45:20 [b][Ps. 81:12]; Is. 6:9, 10; 29:10; 2 Thess. 2:11 [c]Jer. 10:14 [1]Lit. *smeared over*
19 [a]Is. 46:8
20 [a]Job 15:31; Hos. 4:12; Rom. 1:21, 22; 2 Thess. 2:11; 2 Tim. 3:13 [b]Is. 57:11; 59:3, 4, 13; Rom. 1:25
21 [a]Is. 49:15
22 [a]Is. 43:25 [b]Is. 43:1; 1 Cor. 6:20; [1 Pet. 1:18, 19]
23 [a]Ps. 69:34; Is. 42:10; 49:13; Jer. 51:48; Rev. 18:20 [b]Is. 49:3; 60:21
24 [a]Is. 43:14 [b]Is. 43:1 [c]Job 9:8 [1]By Himself
25 [a]Is. 47:13 [b]Jer. 50:36 [c]2 Sam. 15:31; Job 5:12–14; Ps. 33:10; Is. 29:14; Jer. 51:57; 1 Cor. 1:20, 27
26 [a]Zech. 1:6; Matt. 5:18

27 [a]Who says to the deep, 'Be dry!
And I will dry up your rivers';
28 Who says of [a]Cyrus, '*He is* My shepherd,
And he shall perform all My pleasure,
Saying to Jerusalem, [b]"You shall be built,"
And to the temple,
"Your foundation shall be laid." '

### *Salvation Will Come Only by the LORD*

45 "Thus says the LORD to His anointed,
To [a]Cyrus, whose [b]right hand I have [1]held—
[c]To subdue nations before him
And [d]loose the armor of kings,
To open before him the double doors,
So that the gates will not be shut:
2 'I will go before you
[a]And[1] make the [2]crooked places straight;
[b]I will break in pieces the gates of bronze
And cut the bars of iron.
3 I will give you the treasures of darkness
And hidden riches of secret places,
[a]That you may know that I, the LORD,
Who [b]call *you* by your name,
*Am* the God of Israel.
4 For [a]Jacob My servant's sake,
And Israel My elect,
I have even called you by your name;
I have named you,
though you have not known Me.
5 I [a]*am* the LORD, and [b]*there is* no other;
*There is* no God besides Me.
[c]I will gird you,
though you have not known Me,
6 [a]That they may [b]know from the rising
of the sun to its setting
That *there is* none besides Me.
I *am* the LORD, and *there is* no other;
7 I form the light and create darkness,
I make peace and [a]create calamity;
I, the LORD, do all these *things*.'

8 "Rain[a] down, you heavens, from above,
And let the skies pour down righteousness;
Let the earth open,
let them bring forth salvation,
And let righteousness spring up together.
I, the LORD, have created it.

9 "Woe to him who strives with [a]his Maker!
*Let* the potsherd *strive*
with the potsherds of the earth!
[b]Shall the clay say to him who forms it, 'What are you making?'
Or shall your handiwork *say*,
'He has no hands'?
10 Woe to him who says to *his* father, 'What are you begetting?'
Or to the woman,
'What have you brought forth?' "

11 Thus says the LORD,
The Holy One of Israel, and his Maker:
[a]"Ask Me of things to come concerning [b]My sons;
And concerning [c]the work of My hands, you command Me.
12 [a]I have made the earth,
And [b]created man on it.
I—My hands—stretched out the heavens,
And [c]all their host I have commanded.
13 [a]I have raised him up in righteousness,
And I will [1]direct all his ways;
He shall [b]build My city
And let My exiles go free,
[c]Not for price nor reward,"
Says the LORD of hosts.

14 Thus says the LORD:
[a]"The labor of Egypt and merchandise of Cush
And of the Sabeans, men of stature,
Shall come over to you,
and they shall be yours;
They shall walk behind you,
They shall come over [b]in chains;
And they shall bow down to you.
They will make supplication to you, *saying*,
[c]'Surely God *is* in you,
And *there is* no other;
[d]*There is* no other God.' "
15 Truly You *are* God, [a]who hide Yourself,
O God of Israel, the Savior!
16 They shall be [a]ashamed
And also disgraced, all of them;
They shall go in confusion together,
*Who are* makers of idols.
17 [a]*But* Israel shall be saved by the LORD
With an [b]everlasting salvation;
You shall not be ashamed or [c]disgraced
Forever and ever.

18 For thus says the LORD,
[a]Who created the heavens,
Who is God,
Who formed the earth and made it,
Who has established it,
Who did not create it [1]in vain,
Who formed it to be [b]inhabited:
[c]"I *am* the LORD, and *there is* no other.
19 I have not spoken in [a]secret,
In a dark place of the earth;
I did not say to the seed of Jacob,
'Seek Me [1]in vain';
[b]I, the LORD, speak righteousness,
I declare things that are right.

20 "Assemble yourselves and come;
Draw near together,
You *who have* escaped from the nations.
[a]They have no knowledge,
Who carry the wood of their carved image,
And pray to a god *that* cannot save.
21 Tell and bring forth *your case;*
Yes, let them take counsel together.
[a]Who has declared this from ancient time?
*Who* has told it from that time?
*Have* not I, the LORD?
[b]And *there is* no other God besides Me,
A just God and a Savior;
*There is* none besides Me.

22 "Look to Me, and be saved,
[a]All you ends of the earth!
For I *am* God, and *there is* no other.
23 [a]I have sworn by Myself;
The word has gone out of My mouth *in* righteousness,
And shall not return,
That to Me every [b]knee shall bow,
[c]Every tongue shall take an oath.
24 He shall say,
[1]'Surely in the LORD I have [a]righteousness and strength.
To Him *men* shall come,
And [b]all shall be ashamed
Who are incensed against Him.

**27** [a]Jer. 50:38; 51:36
**28** [a]Ezra 1:1 [b]Ezra 6:7
CHAPTER 45
**1** [a]Is. 44:28 [b]Is. 41:13 [c]Dan. 5:30 [d]Job 12:21 [1]*strengthened* or *sustained*
**2** [a]Is. 40:4 [b]Ps. 107:16 [1]Tg. *I will trample down the walls;* Vg. *I will humble the great ones of the earth* [2]DSS, LXX *mountains*
**3** [a]Is. 41:23 [b]Ex. 33:12
**4** [a]Is. 44:1
**5** [a]Deut. 4:35; 32:39 [b]Is. 45:14, 18 [c]Ps. 18:32
**6** [a]Mal. 1:11 [b][Is. 11:9; 52:10]
**7** [a]Amos 3:6
**8** [a]Ps. 85:11
**9** [a]Is. 64:8 [b]Jer. 18:6
**11** [a]Is. 8:19 [b]Jer. 31:9 [c]Is. 29:23; 60:21; 64:8
**12** [a]Is. 42:5 [b]Gen. 1:26 [c]Gen. 2:1
**13** [a]Is. 41:2 [b]2 Chr. 36:22 [c][Rom. 3:24] [1]Or *make all his ways straight*
**14** [a]Zech. 8:22, 23 [b]Ps. 149:8 [c]1 Cor. 14:25 [d]Is. 45:5
**15** [a]Ps. 44:24
**16** [a]Is. 44:11
**17** [a]Is. 26:4 [b]Is. 51:6 [c]Is. 29:22
**18** [a]Is. 42:5 [b]Ps. 115:16 [c]Is. 45:5 [1]Or *empty, a waste*
**19** [a]Deut. 30:11 [b]Ps. 19:8 [1]Or *in a waste place*
**20** [a]Is. 44:9; 46:7
**21** [a]Is. 41:22; 43:9 [b]Is. 44:8
**22** [a]Ps. 22:27; 65:5
**23** [a][Heb. 6:13] [b]Rom. 14:11 [c]Deut. 6:13
**24** [a][1 Cor. 1:30] [b]Is. 41:11 [1]Or *Only in the LORD are all righteousness and strength*

25 [a]In the LORD all the descendants of Israel
Shall be justified, and [b]shall glory.' "

## *The Power of the LORD and the Weakness of Idols*

46 Bel [a]bows down, Nebo stoops;
Their idols were on the beasts
and on the cattle.
Your carriages *were* heavily loaded,
[b]A burden to the weary *beast.*
2 They stoop, they bow down together;
They could not deliver the burden,
[a]But have themselves gone into captivity.

3 "Listen to Me, O house of Jacob,
And all the remnant of the house of Israel,
[a]Who have been upheld *by Me* from [1]birth,
Who have been carried from the womb:
4 Even to *your* old age, [a]I *am* He,
And *even* to gray hairs [b]I will carry *you!*
I have made, and I will bear;
Even I will carry, and will deliver *you.*

5 "To[a] whom will you liken Me,
and make *Me* equal
And compare Me, that we should be alike?
6 [a]They lavish gold out of the bag,
And weigh silver on the scales;
They hire a [b]goldsmith,
and he makes it a god;
They prostrate themselves, yes, they worship.
7 [a]They bear it on the shoulder, they carry it
And set it in its place, and it stands;
From its place it shall not move.
Though [b]*one* cries out to it,
yet it cannot answer
Nor save him out of his trouble.

8 "Remember this, and [1]show yourselves men;
[a]Recall to mind, O you transgressors.
9 [a]Remember the former things of old,
For I *am* God, and [b]*there is* no other;
*I am* God, and *there is* none like Me,
10 [a]Declaring the end from the beginning,
And from ancient times *things* that are not
*yet* done,
Saying, [b]'My counsel shall stand,
And I will do all My pleasure,'
11 Calling a bird of prey [a]from the east,
The man [b]who executes My counsel, from a
far country.
Indeed [c]I have spoken *it;*
I will also bring it to pass.
I have purposed *it;*
I will also do it.

12 "Listen to Me, you [a]stubborn-hearted,
[b]Who *are* far from righteousness:
13 [a]I bring My righteousness near,
it shall not be far off;
My salvation [b]shall not [1]linger.
And I will place [c]salvation in Zion,
For Israel My glory.

## *Judgment on Babylon*

47 "Come [a]down and [b]sit in the dust,
O virgin daughter of [c]Babylon;
Sit on the ground without a throne,
O daughter of the Chaldeans!
For you shall no more be called
Tender and [1]delicate.
2 [a]Take the millstones and grind meal.
Remove your veil,
Take off the skirt,
Uncover the thigh,
Pass through the rivers.
3 [a]Your nakedness shall be uncovered,
Yes, your shame will be seen;
[b]I will take vengeance,
And I will not arbitrate with a man."

4 *As for* [a]our Redeemer,
the LORD of hosts *is* His name,
The Holy One of Israel.

5 "Sit in [a]silence, and go into darkness,
O daughter of the Chaldeans;
[b]For you shall no longer be called
The Lady of Kingdoms.
6 [a]I was angry with My people;
[b]I have profaned My inheritance,
And given them into your hand.
You showed them no mercy;
[c]On the elderly you laid your yoke very
heavily.
7 And you said, 'I shall be [a]a lady forever,'
*So* that you did not [b]take these *things* to
heart,
[c]Nor remember the latter end of them.

8 "Therefore hear this now,
*you who are* given to pleasures,
Who dwell securely,
Who say in your heart,
'I *am,* and *there is* no one else besides me;
I shall not sit *as* a widow,
Nor shall I know the loss of children';
9 But these two *things* shall come to you
[a]In a moment, in one day:
The loss of children, and widowhood.
They shall come upon you in their fullness
Because of the multitude of your sorceries,
For the great abundance of your
enchantments.

10 "For you have trusted in your wickedness;
You have said, 'No one [a]sees me';
Your wisdom and your knowledge have
[1]warped you;
And you have said in your heart,
'I *am,* and *there is* no one else besides me.'
11 Therefore evil shall come upon you;
You shall not know from where it arises.
And trouble shall fall upon you;
You will not be able [1]to put it off.
And [a]desolation shall come upon you
[b]suddenly,
*Which* you shall not know.

12 "Stand now with your enchantments
And the multitude of your sorceries,
In which you have labored from your
youth—
Perhaps you will be able to profit,
Perhaps you will prevail.
13 [a]You are wearied in the multitude of your
counsels;
Let now [b]the[1] astrologers, the stargazers,
*And* [2]the monthly prognosticators
Stand up and save you
From what shall come upon you.
14 Behold, they shall be [a]as stubble,
The fire shall [b]burn them;
They shall not deliver themselves
From the power of the flame;
*It shall* not *be* a coal to be warmed by,
*Nor* a fire to sit before!

**25** [a]Is. 45:17 [b]1 Cor. 1:31

CHAPTER 46
**1** [a]Jer. 50:2 [b]Jer. 10:5
**2** [a]Jer. 48:7
**3** [a]Ps. 71:6 [1]Lit. *the belly*
**4** [a]Mal. 3:6 [b]Ps. 48:14
**5** [a]Is. 40:18, 25
**6** [a]Is. 40:19; 41:6 [b]Is. 44:12
**7** [a]Jer. 10:5 [b]Is. 45:20
**8** [a]Is. 44:19 [1]*be men,* take courage
**9** [a]Deut. 32:7 [b]Is. 45:5, 21
**10** [a]Is. 45:21; 48:3 [b]Ps. 33:11
**11** [a]Is. 41:2, 25 [b]Is. 44:28 [c]Num. 23:19
**12** [a]Ps. 76:5 [b][Rom. 10:3]
**13** [a][Rom. 1:17] [b]Hab. 2:3 [c]Is. 62:11 [1]*delay*

CHAPTER 47
**1** [a]Jer. 48:18 [b]Is. 3:26 [c]Jer. 25:12; 50:1—51:64 [1]*dainty*
**2** [a]Ex. 11:5
**3** [a]Is. 3:17; 20:4 [b][Rom. 12:19]
**4** [a]Jer. 50:34
**5** [a]1 Sam. 2:9 [b][Dan. 2:37]
**6** [a]2 Sam. 24:14 [b]Is. 43:28 [c]Deut. 28:49, 50
**7** [a]Rev. 18:7 [b]Is. 42:25; 46:8 [c]Deut. 32:29
**9** [a]1 Thess. 5:3
**10** [a]Is. 29:15 [1]*led you astray*
**11** [a]1 Thess. 5:3 [b]Is. 29:5 [1]Lit. *to cover it* or *atone for it*
**13** [a]Is. 57:10 [b]Dan. 2:2, 10 [1]Lit. *viewers of the heavens* [2]Lit. *those giving knowledge for new moons*
**14** [a]Nah. 1:10 [b]Jer. 51:58

15 Thus shall they be to you
With whom you have labored,
[a]Your merchants from your youth;
They shall wander each one to his [1]quarter.
No one shall save you.

### *Israel's Unfaithfulness Rebuked*

**48** "Hear this, O house of Jacob,
Who are called by the name of Israel,
And have come forth from
the wellsprings of Judah;
Who swear by the name of the LORD,
And make mention of the God of Israel,
*But* [a]not in truth or in righteousness;
2 For they call themselves [a]after the holy city,
And [b]lean on the God of Israel;
The LORD of hosts *is* His name:

**3** "I have [a]declared the former things
from the beginning;
They went forth from My mouth,
and I caused them to hear it.
Suddenly I did *them,* [b]and they came to pass.
4 Because I knew that you *were* [1]obstinate,
And [a]your neck *was* an iron sinew,
And your brow bronze,
5 Even from the beginning
I have declared *it* to you;
Before it came to pass I proclaimed *it* to you,
Lest you should say, 'My idol has done them,
And my carved image and my molded image
Have commanded them.'

6 "You have heard;
See all this.
And will you not declare *it?*
I have made you hear new things
from this time,
Even hidden things,
and you did not know them.
7 They are created now
and not from the beginning;
And before this day you have not heard
them,
Lest you should say,
'Of course I knew them.'
8 Surely you did not hear,
Surely you did not know;
Surely from long ago your ear was not
opened.
For I knew that you would deal very
treacherously,
And were called [a]a transgressor from the
womb.

9 "For[a] My name's sake [b]I will [1]defer My anger,
And *for* My praise I will restrain it from you,
So that I do not cut you off.
10 Behold, [a]I have refined you, but not as silver;
I have tested you in the [b]furnace of affliction.
11 For My own sake, for My own sake,
I will do *it;*
For [a]how should *My name* be profaned?
And [b]I will not give My glory to another.

**12** "Listen to Me, O Jacob,
And Israel, My called:
I *am* He, [a]I *am* the [b]First,
I *am* also the Last.
13 Indeed [a]My hand has laid the foundation of
the earth,
And My right hand has stretched out the
heavens;
*When* [b]I call to them,
They stand up together.

14 "All of you, assemble yourselves, and hear!
Who among them has declared these *things?*
[a]The LORD loves him;
[b]He shall do His pleasure on Babylon,
And His arm *shall be against* the Chaldeans.
15 I, *even* I, have spoken;
Yes, [a]I have called him,
I have brought him, and his way will prosper.

16 "Come near to Me, hear this:
[a]I have not spoken in secret from the
beginning;
From the time that it was, I *was* there.
And now [b]the Lord GOD and His Spirit
[1]Have sent Me."

**17** Thus says [a]the LORD, your Redeemer,
The Holy One of Israel:
"I *am* the LORD your God,
Who teaches you to profit,
[b]Who leads you by the way you should go.
18 [a]Oh, that you had heeded My commandments!
[b]Then your peace would have been
like a river,
And your righteousness like the waves of the
sea.
19 [a]Your descendants also would have been like
the sand,
And the offspring of your body
like the grains of sand;
His name would not have been cut off
Nor destroyed from before Me."

**20** [a]Go forth from Babylon!
Flee from the Chaldeans!
With a voice of singing,
Declare, proclaim this,
Utter it to the end of the earth;
Say, "The LORD has [b]redeemed
His servant Jacob!"
21 And they [a]did not thirst
When He led them through the deserts;
He [b]caused the waters to flow from the rock
for them;
He also split the rock,
and the waters gushed out.

22 "*There*[a] *is* no peace," says the LORD,
"for the wicked."

### *The Messiah Is the Light to the Gentiles*

**49** "Listen, [a]O coastlands, to Me,
And take heed, you peoples from afar!
[b]The LORD has called Me from the womb;
From the [1]matrix of My mother
He has made mention of My name.
2 And He has made [a]My mouth like a sharp
sword;
[b]In the shadow of His hand He has hidden
Me,
And made Me [c]a polished shaft;
In His quiver He has hidden Me."

3 "And He said to me,
[a]'You *are* My servant, O Israel,
[b]In whom I will be glorified.'
4 [a]Then I said, 'I have labored in vain,
I have spent my strength for nothing and in
vain;
Yet surely my [1]just reward *is* with the LORD,
And my [2]work with my God.'"

**15** [a]Rev. 18:11 [1]*own side* or *way*

CHAPTER 48

**1** [a]Jer. 4:2; 5:2
**2** [a]Is. 52:1; 64:10 [b]Mic. 3:11
**3** [a]Is. 44:7, 8; 46:10 [b]Josh. 21:45
**4** [a]Deut. 31:27 [1]Heb. *hard*
**8** [a]Ps. 58:3
**9** [a]Ezek. 20:9, 14, 22, 44 [b]Ps. 78:38 [1]*delay*
**10** [a]Ps. 66:10 [b]Deut. 4:20
**11** [a]Ezek. 20:9 [b]Is. 42:8
**12** [a]Deut. 32:39 [b][Rev. 22:13]
**13** [a]Ps. 102:25 [b]Is. 40:26
**14** [a]Is. 45:1 [b]Is. 44:28; 47:1–15
**15** [a]Is. 45:1, 2
**16** [a]Is. 45:19 [b]Zech. 2:8, 9, 11 [1]Heb. verb is sing.; or *Has sent Me and His Spirit*
**17** [a]Is. 43:14 [b]Ps. 32:8
**18** [a]Ps. 81:13 [b]Ps. 119:165
**19** [a]Gen. 22:17
**20** [a]Zech. 2:6, 7 [b][Ex. 19:4–6]
**21** [a][Is. 41:17, 18] [b]Ex. 17:6
**22** [a][Is. 57:21]

CHAPTER 49

**1** [a]Is. 41:1 [b]Jer. 1:5 [1]Lit. *inward parts*
**2** [a]Rev. 1:16; 2:12 [b]Is. 51:16 [c]Ps. 45:5
**3** [a][Zech. 3:8] [b]Is. 44:23
**4** [a][Ezek. 3:19] [1]*justice* [2]*recompense*

5 "And now the LORD says,
Who formed Me from the womb
*to be* His Servant,
To bring Jacob back to Him,
So that Israel [a]is [1]gathered to Him
(For I shall be glorious in the eyes of the
LORD,
And My God shall be My strength),
6 Indeed He says,
'It is too small a thing that You should be My
Servant
To raise up the tribes of Jacob,
And to restore the preserved ones of Israel;
I will also give You as a [a]light
to the Gentiles,
That You should be My salvation
to the ends of the earth.' "

7 Thus says the LORD,
The Redeemer of Israel, [1]their Holy One,
[a]To Him [2]whom man despises,
To Him whom the nation abhors,
To the Servant of rulers:
[b]"Kings shall see and arise,
Princes also shall worship,
Because of the LORD who is faithful,
The Holy One of Israel;
And He has chosen You."

8 Thus says the LORD:

"In an [a]acceptable[1] time I have heard You,
And in the day of salvation I have helped You;
I will [2]preserve You [b]and give You
As a covenant to the people,
To restore the earth,
To cause them to inherit
the desolate [3]heritages;
9 That You may say [a]to the prisoners, 'Go
forth,'
To those who *are* in darkness,
'Show yourselves.'

"They shall feed along the roads,
And their pastures *shall be* on all desolate
heights.
10 They shall neither [a]hunger nor thirst,
[b]Neither heat nor sun shall strike them;
For He who has mercy on them [c]will lead
them,
Even by the springs of water He will guide
them.
11 [a]I will make each of My mountains a road,
And My highways shall be elevated.
12 Surely [a]these shall come from afar;
Look! Those from the north and the west,
And these from the land of Sinim."

13 [a]Sing, O heavens!
Be joyful, O earth!
And break out in singing, O mountains!
For the LORD has comforted His people,
And will have mercy on His afflicted.

14 [a]But Zion said, "The LORD has forsaken me,
And my Lord has forgotten me."

15 "Can[a] a woman forget her nursing child,
[1]And not have compassion on the son of her
womb?
Surely they may forget,
[b]Yet I will not forget you.
16 See, [a]I have inscribed you on the palms *of
My hands;*
Your walls *are* continually before Me.

17 Your [1]sons shall make haste;
Your destroyers and those who laid you
waste
Shall go away from you.
18 [a]Lift up your eyes, look around and see;
All these gather together *and* come to you.
*As* I live," says the LORD,
"You shall surely clothe yourselves with them
all [b]as an ornament,
And bind them *on you* as a bride *does.*

19 "For your waste and desolate places,
And the land of your destruction,
[a]Will even now be too small for the
inhabitants;
And those who swallowed you up
will be far away.
20 [a]The children you will have,
[b]After you have lost the others,
Will say again in your ears,
'The place *is* too small for me;
Give me a place where I may dwell.'
21 Then you will say in your heart,
'Who has begotten these for me,
Since I have lost my children
and am desolate,
A captive, and wandering to and fro?
And who has brought these up?
There I was, left alone;
But these, where *were* they?' "

22 [a]Thus says the Lord GOD:

"Behold, I will lift My hand
in an oath to the nations,
And set up My [1]standard for the peoples;
They shall bring your sons in *their* [2]arms,
And your daughters shall be carried
on *their* shoulders;
23 [a]Kings shall be your foster fathers,
And their queens your nursing mothers;
They shall bow down to you
with *their* faces to the earth,
And [b]lick up the dust of your feet.
Then you will know that I *am* the LORD,
[c]For they shall not be ashamed
who wait for Me."

24 [a]Shall the prey be taken from the mighty,
Or the captives [1]of the righteous
be delivered?

25 But thus says the LORD:

"Even the captives of the mighty
shall be taken away,
And the prey of the terrible be delivered;
For I will contend with him who contends
with you,
And I will save your children.
26 I will [a]feed those who oppress you
with their own flesh,
And they shall be drunk with their own
[b]blood as with sweet wine.
All flesh [c]shall know
That I, the LORD, *am* your Savior,
And your Redeemer,
the Mighty One of Jacob."

### *The Messiah Is Israel's Hope*

**50** Thus says the LORD:

"Where *is* [a]the certificate of your mother's
divorce,

**5** [a]Matt. 23:37; [Rom. 11:25–29] [1]Qr., DSS, LXX *gathered to Him;* Kt. *not gathered*
**6** [a]Is. 42:6; 51:4; [Luke 2:32]; Acts 13:47; [Gal. 3:14]
**7** [a][Ps. 22:6; Is. 53:3; Matt. 26:67; 27:41]; Mark 15:29; Luke 23:35 [b][Is. 52:15] [1]Lit. *his* or *its* [2]Lit. *who is despised of soul*
**8** [a]Ps. 69:13; 2 Cor. 6:2 [b]Is. 42:6 [1]*favorable* [2]*keep* [3]*inheritances*
**9** [a]Is. 61:1; Zech. 9:12; Luke 4:18
**10** [a]Is. 33:16; 48:21; Rev. 7:16 [b]Ps. 121:6 [c]Ps. 23:2; Is. 40:11; 48:17
**11** [a]Is. 40:4
**12** [a]Is. 43:5, 6
**13** [a]Is. 44:23
**14** [a]Is. 40:27
**15** [a]Ps. 103:13; Mal. 3:17 [b]Rom. 11:29 [1]Lit. *From having compassion*
**16** [a]Ex. 13:9; Song 8:6; Hag. 2:23
**17** [1]DSS, LXX, Tg., Vg. *builders*
**18** [a]Is. 60:4; John 4:35 [b]Prov. 17:6
**19** [a]Is. 54:1, 2; Zech. 10:10
**20** [a]Is. 60:4 [b][Matt. 3:9; Rom. 11:11]
**22** [a]Is. 60:4 [1]*banner* [2]Lit. *bosom*
**23** [a]Ps. 72:11; Is. 52:15 [b]Ps. 72:9; Mic. 7:17 [c]Ps. 34:22; [Rom. 5:5]
**24** [a]Matt. 12:29; Luke 11:21, 22 [1]So with MT, Tg.; DSS, Syr., Vg. *of the mighty;* LXX *unjustly*
**26** [a]Is. 9:20 [b]Rev. 14:20 [c]Ps. 9:16; Is. 60:16

CHAPTER 50
**1** [a]Deut. 24:1; Jer. 3:8

Whom I have put away?
Or which of My [b]creditors *is it*
to whom I have sold you?
For your iniquities [c]you have sold yourselves,
And for your transgressions your mother has
been put away.
2 Why, when I came, *was there* no man?
*Why,* when I called,
*was there* none to answer?
Is My hand shortened at all that it cannot
redeem?
Or have I no power to deliver?
Indeed with My [a]rebuke I dry up the sea,
I make the rivers a wilderness;
Their fish stink because *there is* no water,
And die of thirst.
3 [a]I clothe the heavens with blackness,
[b]And I make sackcloth their covering."

4 "The[a] Lord GOD has given Me
The tongue of the learned,
That I should know how to speak
A word in season to *him who is* [b]weary.
He awakens Me morning by morning,
He awakens My ear
To hear as the learned.
5 The Lord GOD [a]has opened My ear;
And I was not [b]rebellious,
Nor did I turn away.
6 [a]I gave My back to those who struck *Me,*
And [b]My cheeks to those
who plucked out the beard;
I did not hide My face from shame and
[c]spitting.

7 "For the Lord GOD will help Me;
Therefore I will not be disgraced;
Therefore [a]I have set My face like a flint,
And I know that I will not be ashamed.
8 [a]*He is* near who justifies Me;
Who will contend with Me?
Let us stand together.
Who *is* [1]My adversary?
Let him come near Me.
9 Surely the Lord GOD will help Me;
Who *is* he *who* will condemn Me?
[a]Indeed they will all grow old like a garment;
[b]The moth will eat them up.

10 "Who among you fears the LORD?
Who obeys the voice of His Servant?
Who [a]walks in darkness
And has no light?
[b]Let him trust in the name of the LORD
And rely upon his God.
11 Look, all you who kindle a fire,
Who encircle *yourselves* with sparks:
Walk in the light of your fire and in the
sparks you have kindled—
[a]This you shall have from My hand:
You shall lie down [b]in torment.

### *The Faithful Are Called to Courage*

**51** "Listen to Me, [a]you who [1]follow after
righteousness,
You who seek the LORD:
Look to the rock *from which* you were hewn,
And to the hole of the pit
*from which* you were dug.
2 [a]Look to Abraham your father,
And to Sarah *who* bore you;
[b]For I called him alone,
And [c]blessed him and increased him."

1 [b]Deut. 32:30; 2 Kin. 4:1 [c]Is. 52:3
2 [a]Nah. 1:4
3 [a]Ex. 10:21 [b]Rev. 6:12
4 [a]Ex. 4:11 [b]Matt. 11:28
5 [a]Ps. 40:6 [b]Matt. 26:39
6 [a]Matt. 27:26 [b]Matt. 26:67; 27:30 [c]Lam. 3:30
7 [a]Ezek. 3:8, 9
8 [a][Rom. 8:32–34] [1]Lit. *master of My judgment*
9 [a]Job 13:28 [b]Is. 51:6, 8
10 [a]Ps. 23:4 [b]2 Chr. 20:20
11 [a][John 9:39] [b]Ps. 16:4

CHAPTER 51
1 [a][Rom. 9:30–32] [1]*pursue*
2 [a]Heb. 11:11 [b]Gen. 12:1 [c]Gen. 24:35
3 [a]Is. 40:1; 52:9 [b]Gen. 13:10
4 [a]Is. 2:3 [b]Is. 42:6
5 [a]Is. 46:13 [b]Ps. 67:4 [c]Is. 60:9 [d][Rom. 1:16]
6 [a]Is. 40:26 [b]Matt. 24:35 [c]Is. 24:19, 20; 50:9 [d]Is. 45:17 [1]*broken*
7 [a]Ps. 37:31 [b][Matt. 5:11, 12; 10:28]
8 [a]Is. 50:9
9 [a]Ps. 44:23 [b]Ps. 93:1 [c]Ps. 44:1 [d]Job 26:12 [e]Ps. 87:4 [f]Ps. 74:13
10 [a]Ex. 14:21
11 [a]Is. 35:10
12 [a]2 Cor. 1:3 [b]Ps. 118:6 [c]Is. 40:6, 7
13 [a]Is. 17:10 [b]Ps. 104:2 [c]Job 20:7
14 [a]Zech. 9:11
15 [a]Job 26:12

3 For the LORD will [a]comfort Zion,
He will comfort all her waste places;
He will make her wilderness like Eden,
And her desert [b]like the garden of the LORD;
Joy and gladness will be found in it,
Thanksgiving and the voice of melody.

4 "Listen to Me, My people;
And give ear to Me, O My nation:
[a]For law will proceed from Me,
And I will make My justice rest
[b]As a light of the peoples.
5 [a]My righteousness *is* near,
My salvation has gone forth,
[b]And My arms will judge the peoples;
[c]The coastlands will wait upon Me,
And [d]on My arm they will trust.
6 [a]Lift up your eyes to the heavens,
And look on the earth beneath.
For [b]the heavens will vanish away like
smoke,
[c]The earth will grow old like a garment,
And those who dwell in it will die in like
manner;
But My salvation will be [d]forever,
And My righteousness will not be [1]abolished.

7 "Listen to Me, you who know righteousness,
You people [a]in whose heart *is* My law:
[b]Do not fear the reproach of men,
Nor be afraid of their insults.
8 For [a]the moth will eat them up like a
garment,
And the worm will eat them like wool;
But My righteousness will be forever,
And My salvation from generation to
generation."

9 [a]Awake, awake, [b]put on strength,
O arm of the LORD!
Awake [c]as in the ancient days,
In the generations of old.
[d]*Are* You not *the arm* that cut [e]Rahab apart,
*And* wounded the [f]serpent?
10 *Are* You not *the One* who [a]dried up the sea,
The waters of the great deep;
That made the depths of the sea a road
For the redeemed to cross over?
11 So [a]the ransomed of the LORD shall return,
And come to Zion with singing,
With everlasting joy on their heads.
They shall obtain joy and gladness;
Sorrow and sighing shall flee away.

12 "I, *even* I, *am* He [a]who comforts you.
Who *are* you that you should be afraid
[b]Of a man *who* will die,
And of the son of a man *who* will be made
[c]like grass?
13 And [a]you forget the LORD your Maker,
[b]Who stretched out the heavens
And laid the foundations of the earth;
You have feared continually every day
Because of the fury of the oppressor,
When *he has* prepared to destroy.
[c]And where *is* the fury of the oppressor?
14 The captive exile hastens,
that he may be loosed,
[a]That he should not die in the pit,
And that his bread should not fail.
15 But I *am* the LORD your God,
Who [a]divided the sea whose waves roared—
The LORD of hosts *is* His name.

16 And [a]I have put My words in your mouth;
[b]I have covered you with the shadow
of My hand,
[c]That I may [1]plant the heavens,
Lay the foundations of the earth,
And say to Zion, 'You *are* My people.' "

17 [a]Awake, awake!
Stand up, O Jerusalem,
You who [b]have drunk at the hand
of the LORD
The cup of His fury;
You have drunk the dregs of the cup
of trembling,
*And* drained *it* out.
18 *There is* no one to guide her
Among all the sons she has brought forth;
Nor *is there any* who takes her by the hand
Among all the sons she has brought up.
19 [a]These two *things* have come to you;
Who will be sorry for you?—
Desolation and destruction,
famine and sword—
[b]By whom will I comfort you?
20 [a]Your sons have fainted,
They lie at the head of all the streets,
Like an antelope in a net;
They are full of the fury of the LORD,
The rebuke of your God.

21 Therefore please hear this, you afflicted,
And drunk [a]but not with wine.
22 Thus says your Lord,
The LORD and your God,
*Who* [a]pleads the cause of His people:
"See, I have taken out of your hand
The cup of trembling,
The dregs of the cup of My fury;
You shall no longer drink it.
23 [a]But I will put it into the hand
of those who afflict you,
Who have said to [1]you,
'Lie down, that we may walk over you.'
And you have laid your body like the ground,
And as the street, for those who walk over."

## *God Will Restore Jerusalem*

**52** Awake, awake!
Put on your strength, O Zion;
Put on your beautiful garments,
O Jerusalem, the holy city!
For the uncircumcised [a]and the unclean
Shall no longer come to you.
2 [a]Shake yourself from the dust, arise;
Sit down, O Jerusalem!
[b]Loose yourself from the bonds of your neck,
O captive daughter of Zion!

3 For thus says the LORD:

[a]"You have sold yourselves for nothing,
And you shall be redeemed [b]without money."

4 For thus says the Lord GOD:

"My people went down at first
Into [a]Egypt to [1]dwell there;
Then the Assyrian oppressed them without
cause.
5 Now therefore, what have I here,"
says the LORD,
"That My people are taken away for nothing?
Those who rule over them
[1]Make them wail," says the LORD,
"And My name *is* [a]blasphemed continually
every day.
6 Therefore My people shall know My name;
Therefore *they shall know* in that day
That I *am* He who speaks:
'Behold, *it is* I.' "

7 [a]How beautiful upon the mountains
Are the feet of him who brings good news,
Who proclaims peace,
Who brings glad tidings of good *things*,
Who proclaims salvation,
Who says to Zion,
[b]"Your God reigns!"
8 Your watchmen shall lift up *their* voices,
With their voices they shall sing together;
For they shall see eye to eye
When the LORD brings back Zion.
9 Break forth into joy, sing together,
You waste places of Jerusalem!
For the LORD has comforted His people,
He has redeemed Jerusalem.
10 [a]The LORD has [1]made bare His holy arm
In the eyes of [b]all the nations;
And all the ends of the earth shall see
The salvation of our God.

11 [a]Depart! Depart! Go out from there,
Touch no unclean *thing;*
Go out from the midst of her,
[b]Be clean,
You who bear the vessels of the LORD.
12 For [a]you shall not go out with haste,
Nor go by flight;
[b]For the LORD will go before you,
[c]And the God of Israel *will be* your rear
guard.

13 Behold, [a]My Servant shall [1]deal prudently;
[b]He shall be exalted and [2]extolled
and be very high.
14 Just as many were astonished at you,
So His [a]visage[1] was marred more than any
man,
And His form more than the sons of men;
15 [a]So shall He [1]sprinkle many nations.
Kings shall shut their mouths at Him;
For [b]what had not been told them
they shall see,
And what they had not heard
they shall consider.

## *The Sin-Bearing Messiah*

**53** Who [a]has believed our report?
And to whom has the arm of the LORD
been revealed?
2 For He shall grow up before Him
as a tender plant,
And as a root out of dry ground.
He has no [1]form or [2]comeliness;
And when we see Him,
*There is* no [3]beauty
that we should desire Him.
3 [a]He is despised and [1]rejected by men,
A Man of [2]sorrows
and [b]acquainted with [3]grief.
And we hid, as it were, *our* faces from Him;
He was despised,
and [c]we did not esteem Him.

4 Surely [a]He has borne our [1]griefs
And carried our [2]sorrows;

**16** [a]Deut. 18:18 [b]Is. 49:2 [c]Is. 65:17 [1]*establish*
**17** [a]Is. 52:1 [b]Job 21:20
**19** [a]Is. 47:9 [b]Amos 7:2
**20** [a]Lam. 2:11
**21** [a]Lam. 3:15
**22** [a]Jer. 50:34
**23** [a]Zech. 12:2 [1]Lit. *your soul*

CHAPTER 52
**1** [a][Rev. 21:2–27]
**2** [a]Is. 3:26 [b]Zech. 2:7
**3** [a]Ps. 44:12 [b]Is. 45:13
**4** [a]Gen. 46:6 [1]As resident aliens
**5** [a]Ezek. 36:20, 23 [1]DSS *Mock;* LXX *Marvel and wail;* Tg. *Boast themselves;* Vg. *Treat them unjustly*
**7** [a]Rom. 10:15 [b]Ps. 93:1
**10** [a]Ps. 98:1–3 [b]Luke 3:6 [1]Revealed His power
**11** [a]Is. 48:20 [b]Lev. 22:2
**12** [a]Ex. 12:11, 33 [b]Mic. 2:13 [c]Ex. 14:19, 20
**13** [a]Is. 42:1 [b]Phil. 2:9 [1]*prosper* [2]Lit. *be lifted up*
**14** [a]Ps. 22:6, 7 [1]*appearance*
**15** [a]Ezek. 36:25 [b]Rom. 15:21 [1]Or *startle*

CHAPTER 53
**1** [a]John 12:38
**2** [1]Stately form [2]*splendor* [3]Lit. *appearance*
**3** [a]Ps. 22:6 [b][Heb. 4:15] [c][John 1:10, 11] [1]Or *forsaken* [2]Lit. *pains* [3]Lit. *sickness*
**4** [a][Matt. 8:17] [1]Lit. *sicknesses* [2]Lit. *pains*

Yet we [3]esteemed Him stricken,
[4]Smitten by God, and afflicted.
5 But He *was* [a]wounded[1] for our transgressions,
*He was* [2]bruised for our iniquities;
The chastisement for our peace *was* upon Him,
And by His [b]stripes[3] we are healed.
6 All we like sheep have gone astray;
We have turned, every one, to his own way;
And the LORD [1]has laid on Him the iniquity of us all.

7 He was oppressed and He was afflicted,
Yet [a]He opened not His mouth;
[b]He was led as a lamb to the slaughter,
And as a sheep before its shearers is silent,
So He opened not His mouth.
8 He was [a]taken from [1]prison and from judgment,
And who will declare His generation?
For [b]He was cut off from the land of the living;
For the transgressions of My people He was stricken.
9 [a]And [1]they made His grave with the wicked—
But with the rich at His death,
Because He had done no violence,
Nor *was any* [b]deceit in His mouth.

10 Yet it pleased the LORD to [1]bruise Him;
He has put *Him* to grief.
When You make His soul [a]an offering for sin,
He shall see *His* seed,
He shall prolong *His* days,
And the pleasure of the LORD shall prosper in His hand.
11 [1]He shall see the labor of His soul, *and* be satisfied.
By His knowledge [a]My righteous [b]Servant shall [c]justify many,
For He shall bear their iniquities.
12 [a]Therefore I will divide Him a portion with the great,
[b]And He shall divide the [1]spoil with the strong,
Because He [c]poured out His soul unto death,
And He was [d]numbered with the transgressors,
And He bore the sin of many,
And [e]made intercession for the transgressors.

## *A Promise of Everlasting Kindness*

**54** "Sing, O [a]barren,
You *who* have not borne!
Break forth into singing, and cry aloud,
You *who* have not labored with child!
For more *are* the children of the desolate
Than the children of the married woman,"
says the LORD.
2 "Enlarge[a] the place of your tent,
And let them stretch out the curtains of your dwellings;
Do not spare;
Lengthen your cords,
And strengthen your stakes.
3 For you shall expand to the right and to the left,
And your descendants will [a]inherit the nations,
And make the desolate cities inhabited.

4 "Do[a] not fear, for you will not be ashamed;
Neither be disgraced, for you will not be put to shame;
For you will forget the shame of your youth,
And will not remember the reproach of your widowhood anymore.
5 [a]For your Maker *is* your husband,
The LORD of hosts *is* His name;
And your Redeemer *is* the Holy One of Israel;
He is called [b]the God of the whole earth.
6 For the LORD [a]has called you
Like a woman forsaken and grieved in spirit,
Like a youthful wife when you were refused,"
Says your God.
7 "For[a] a mere moment I have forsaken you,
But with great mercies [b]I will gather you.
8 With a little wrath I hid My face from you for a moment;
[a]But with everlasting kindness I will have mercy on you,"
Says the LORD, your Redeemer.

9 "For this *is* like the waters of [a]Noah to Me;
For as I have sworn
That the waters of Noah would no longer cover the earth,
So have I sworn
That I would not be angry with [b]you, nor rebuke you.
10 For [a]the mountains shall depart
And the hills be removed,
[b]But My kindness shall not depart from you,
Nor shall My covenant of peace be removed,"
Says the LORD, who has mercy on you.

11 "O you afflicted one,
Tossed with tempest, *and* not comforted,
Behold, I will lay your stones with [a]colorful gems,
And lay your foundations with sapphires.
12 I will make your pinnacles of rubies,
Your gates of crystal,
And all your walls of precious stones.
13 All your children *shall be* [a]taught by the LORD,
And [b]great *shall be* the peace of your children.
14 In righteousness you shall be established;
You shall be far from oppression, for you shall not fear;
And from terror, for it shall not come near you.
15 Indeed they shall surely assemble, *but* not because of Me.
Whoever assembles against you shall [a]fall for your sake.

16 "Behold, I have created the blacksmith
Who blows the coals in the fire,
Who brings forth an [1]instrument for his work;
And I have created the [2]spoiler to destroy.
17 No weapon formed against you shall [a]prosper,
And every tongue *which* rises against you in judgment
You shall condemn.
This *is* the heritage of the servants of the LORD,
[b]And their righteousness *is* from Me,"
Says the LORD.

**4** [3]*reckoned* [4]*Struck down*
**5** [a][Rom. 4:25] [b][1 Pet. 2:24, 25] [1]Or *pierced through* [2]*crushed* [3]Blows that cut in
**6** [1]Lit. *has caused to land on Him*
**7** [a]Matt. 26:63; 27:12–14 [b]Acts 8:32, 33
**8** [a]Luke 23:1–25 [b][Dan. 9:26] [1]*confinement*
**9** [a]Matt. 27:57–60 [b]1 Pet. 2:22 [1]Lit. *he* or *He*
**10** [a][2 Cor. 5:21] [1]*crush*
**11** [a][1 John 2:1] [b]Is. 42:1 [c][Rom. 5:15–18] [1]So with MT, Tg., Vg.; DSS, LXX *From the labor of His soul He shall see light,*
**12** [a]Ps. 2:8 [b]Col. 2:15 [c]Is. 50:6 [d]Matt. 27:38 [e]Luke 23:34 [1]*plunder*

CHAPTER 54
**1** [a]Gal. 4:27
**2** [a]Is. 49:19, 20
**3** [a]Is. 14:2; 49:22, 23; 60:9
**4** [a]Is. 41:10
**5** [a]Jer. 3:14 [b]Zech. 14:9
**6** [a]Is. 62:4
**7** [a]Is. 26:20; 60:10 [b][Is. 43:5; 56:8]
**8** [a]Jer. 31:3
**9** [a]Gen. 8:21; 9:11 [b]Ezek. 39:29
**10** [a]Is. 51:6 [b]Ps. 89:33, 34
**11** [a]Rev. 21:18, 19
**13** [a][John 6:45] [b]Ps. 119:165
**15** [a]Is. 41:11–16
**16** [1]Or *weapon* [2]*destroyer*
**17** [a]Is. 17:12–14; 29:8 [b]Is. 45:24, 25; 54:14

### *A Free Offer of Mercy to All*

**55** "Ho! [a]Everyone who thirsts,
Come to the waters;
And you who have no money,
[b]Come, buy and eat.
Yes, come, buy wine and milk
Without money and without price.
2 Why do you [1]spend money
for *what is* not bread,
And your wages for *what* does not satisfy?
Listen carefully to Me, and eat *what is* good,
And let your soul delight itself in abundance.
3 Incline your ear, and [a]come to Me.
Hear, and your soul shall live;
[b]And I will make an everlasting covenant
with you—
The [c]sure mercies of David.
4 Indeed I have given him *as* [a]a witness
to the people,
[b]A leader and commander for the people.
5 [a]Surely you shall call a nation
you do not know,
[b]And nations *who* do not know you shall run
to you,
Because of the LORD your God,
And the Holy One of Israel;
[c]For He has glorified you."

**6** [a]Seek the LORD while He may be [b]found,
Call upon Him while He is near.
7 [a]Let the [1]wicked forsake his way,
And the unrighteous man [b]his thoughts;
Let him return to the LORD,
[c]And He will have mercy on him;
And to our God,
For He will abundantly pardon.

**8** "For[a] My thoughts *are* not your thoughts,
Nor *are* your ways My ways," says the LORD.
9 "For[a] *as* the heavens are higher than the
earth,
So are My ways higher than your ways,
And My thoughts than your thoughts.

10 "For [a]as the rain comes down,
and the snow from heaven,
And do not return there,
But water the earth,
And make it bring forth and bud,
That it may give seed to the sower
And bread to the eater,
11 [a]So shall My word be that goes forth from My
mouth;
It shall not return to Me [1]void,
But it shall accomplish what I please,
And it shall [b]prosper *in the thing* for which I
sent it.

12 "For[a] you shall go out with joy,
And be led out with peace;
The mountains and the hills
Shall [b]break forth into singing before you,
And [c]all the trees of the field shall clap *their*
hands.
13 [a]Instead of [b]the thorn shall come up the
cypress tree,
And instead of the brier shall come up the
myrtle tree;
And it shall be to the LORD [c]for a name,
For an everlasting sign *that* shall not be cut
off."

### *Salvation for the Gentiles*

**56** Thus says the LORD:
"Keep justice, and do righteousness,
[a]For My salvation *is* about to come,
And My righteousness to be revealed.
2 Blessed *is* the man *who* does this,
And the son of man *who* lays hold on it;
[a]Who keeps from defiling the Sabbath,
And keeps his hand from doing any evil."

**3** Do not let [a]the son of the foreigner
Who has joined himself to the LORD
Speak, saying,
"The LORD has utterly separated me from His
people";
Nor let the [b]eunuch say,
"Here I am, a dry tree."
4 For thus says the LORD:
"To the eunuchs who keep My Sabbaths,
And choose what pleases Me,
And hold fast My covenant,
5 Even to them I will give in [a]My house
And within My walls a place [b]and a name
Better than that of sons and daughters;
I will give [1]them an everlasting name
That shall not be cut off.

**6** "Also the sons of the foreigner
Who join themselves to the LORD,
to serve Him,
And to love the name of the LORD,
to be His servants—
Everyone who keeps from defiling the
Sabbath,
And holds fast My covenant—
7 Even them I will [a]bring to My holy
mountain,
And make them joyful in My [b]house
of prayer.
[c]Their burnt offerings and their sacrifices
*Will be* [d]accepted on My altar;
For [e]My house shall be called a house of
prayer [f]for all nations."
8 The Lord GOD, [a]who gathers the outcasts of
Israel, says,
[b]"Yet I will gather to him
*Others* besides those who are gathered to
him."

**9** [a]All you beasts of the field, come to devour,
All you beasts in the forest.
10 His watchmen *are* [a]blind,
They are all ignorant;
[b]They *are* all dumb dogs,
They cannot bark;
[1]Sleeping, lying down, loving to slumber.
11 Yes, *they are* [a]greedy[1] dogs
*Which* [b]never[2] have enough.
And they *are* shepherds
Who cannot understand;
They all look to their own way,
Every one for his own gain,
From his *own* territory.
12 "Come," *one says,* "I will bring wine,
And we will fill ourselves with intoxicating
[a]drink;
[b]Tomorrow will be [c]as today,
*And* much more abundant."

CHAPTER 55
**1** [a][John 4:14; 7:37] [b][Rev. 3:18]
**2** [1]Lit. *weigh out silver*
**3** [a]Matt. 11:28 [b]Jer. 32:40 [c]2 Sam. 7:8
**4** [a][Rev. 1:5] [b][Dan. 9:25]
**5** [a]Eph. 2:11, 12 [b]Is. 60:5 [c]Is. 60:9
**6** [a][Heb. 3:13] [b]Ps. 32:6
**7** [a]Is. 1:16 [b]Zech. 8:17 [c]Jer. 3:12 [1]Lit. *man of iniquity*
**8** [a]2 Sam. 7:19
**9** [a]Ps. 103:11
**10** [a]Deut. 32:2
**11** [a]Is. 45:23 [b]Is. 46:9–11 [1]*empty,* without fruit
**12** [a]Is. 35:10 [b]Ps. 98:8 [c]1 Chr. 16:33
**13** [a]Is. 41:19 [b]Mic. 7:4 [c]Jer. 13:11

CHAPTER 56
**1** [a]Matt. 3:2; 4:17
**2** [a]Is. 58:13
**3** [a][Eph. 2:12–19] [b]Acts 8:27
**5** [a]1 Tim. 3:15 [b][1 John 3:1, 2] [1]Lit. *him*
**7** [a][Is. 2:2, 3; 60:11] [b]Mark 11:17 [c][Rom. 12:1] [d]Is. 60:7 [e]Matt. 21:13 [f][Mal. 1:11]
**8** [a]Is. 11:12; 27:12; 54:7 [b][John 10:16]
**9** [a]Jer. 12:9
**10** [a]Matt. 15:14 [b]Phil. 3:2 [1]Or *Dreaming*
**11** [a][Mic. 3:5, 11] [b]Ezek. 34:2–10 [1]Lit. *strong of soul* [2]Lit. *do not know satisfaction*
**12** [a]Is. 28:7 [b]Luke 12:19 [c]2 Pet. 3:4

## *Condemnation of Israel's Idolatry*

**57** The righteous perishes,
And no man takes *it* to heart;
[a]Merciful men *are* taken away,
[b]While no one considers
That the righteous is taken away from [1]evil.
2 He shall enter into peace;
They shall rest in [a]their beds,
*Each one* walking *in* his uprightness.

3 "But come here,
[a]You sons of the sorceress,
You offspring of the adulterer and the harlot!
4 Whom do you ridicule?
Against whom do you make a wide mouth
*And* stick out the tongue?
*Are* you not children of transgression,
Offspring of falsehood,
5 Inflaming yourselves with gods [a]under every
green tree,
[b]Slaying the children in the valleys,
Under the clefts of the rocks?
6 Among the smooth [a]*stones* of the stream
*Is* your portion;
They, they, *are* your lot!
Even to them you have poured a drink
offering,
You have offered a grain offering.
Should I receive comfort in [b]these?

7 "On[a] a lofty and high mountain
You have set [b]your bed;
Even there you went up
To offer sacrifice.
8 Also behind the doors and their posts
You have set up your remembrance;
For you have uncovered yourself *to those
other* than Me,
And have gone up to them;
You have enlarged your bed
And [1]made *a covenant* with them;
[a]You have loved their bed,
Where you saw *their* [2]nudity.
9 [a]You went to the king with ointment,
And increased your perfumes;
You sent your [b]messengers far off,
And *even* descended to Sheol.
10 You are wearied in the length of your way;
[a]*Yet* you did not say, 'There is no hope.'
You have found the life of your hand;
Therefore you were not grieved.

11 "And [a]of whom have you been afraid,
or feared,
That you have lied
And not remembered Me,
Nor taken *it* to your heart?
Is it not because [b]I have [1]held My peace from
of old
That you do not fear Me?
12 I will declare your righteousness
And your works,
For they will not profit you.
13 When you cry out,
Let your collection *of idols* deliver you.
But the wind will carry them all away,
A breath will take *them*.
But he who puts his trust in Me shall possess
the land,
And shall inherit My holy mountain."

14 And one shall say,
[a]"Heap it up! Heap it up!
Prepare the way,
Take the stumbling block
out of the way of My people."
15 For thus says the High and Lofty One
Who inhabits eternity, [a]whose name *is* Holy:
[b]"I dwell in the high and holy *place*,
[c]With him *who* has
a contrite and humble spirit,
[d]To revive the spirit of the humble,
And to revive the heart of the contrite ones.
16 [a]For I will not contend forever,
Nor will I always be angry;
For the spirit would fail before Me,
And the souls [b]*which* I have made.
17 For the iniquity of [a]his covetousness
I was angry and struck him;
[b]I hid and was angry,
[c]And he went on [1]backsliding
in the way of his heart.
18 I have seen his ways, and [a]will heal him;
I will also lead him,
And restore comforts to him
And to [b]his mourners.
19 "I create [a]the fruit of the lips:
Peace, peace [b]to *him who is* far off
and to *him who is* near,"
Says the LORD,
"And I will heal him."
20 [a]But the wicked *are* like the troubled sea,
When it cannot rest,
Whose waters cast up mire and dirt.

21 "*There*[a] *is* no peace,"
Says my God, "for the wicked."

## *A Description of True Religion*

**58** "Cry aloud, [1]spare not;
Lift up your voice like a trumpet;
[a]Tell My people their transgression,
And the house of Jacob their sins.
2 Yet they seek Me daily,
And delight to know My ways,
As a nation that did righteousness,
And did not forsake the ordinance
of their God.
They ask of Me the ordinances of justice;
They take delight in approaching God.
3 'Why[a] have we fasted,' *they say*,
'and You have not seen?
*Why* have we [b]afflicted our souls,
and You take no notice?'

"In fact, in the day of your fast
you find pleasure,
And [1]exploit all your laborers.
4 [a]Indeed you fast for strife and debate,
And to strike with the fist of wickedness.
You will not fast as *you do* this day,
To make your voice heard on high.
5 Is [a]it a fast that I have chosen,
[b]A day for a man to afflict his soul?
*Is it* to bow down his head like a bulrush,
And [c]to spread out sackcloth and ashes?
Would you call this a fast,
And an acceptable day to the LORD?

6 "*Is* this not the fast that I have chosen:
To [a]loose the bonds of wickedness,
[b]To undo the [1]heavy burdens,
[c]To let the oppressed go free,
And that you break every yoke?

CHAPTER 57
**1** [a]Ps. 12:1 [b]1 Kin. 14:13 [1]Lit. *the face of evil*
**2** [a]2 Chr. 16:14
**3** [a]Is. 1:4; Matt. 16:4
**5** [a]2 Kin. 16:4 [b]2 Kin. 23:10; Ps. 106:37, 38; Jer. 7:31; Ezek. 16:20
**6** [a]Jer. 3:9; Hab. 2:19 [b]Jer. 5:9, 29; 9:9
**7** [a]Jer. 3:6; Ezek. 16:16 [b]Ezek. 23:41
**8** [a]Ezek. 16:26 [1]Lit. *cut* [2]Lit. *hand,* a euphemism
**9** [a]Hos. 7:11 [b]Ezek. 23:16, 40
**10** [a]Jer. 2:25; 18:12
**11** [a]Prov. 29:25; Is. 51:12, 13 [b]Ps. 50:21; Eccl. 8:11; Is. 42:14 [1]*remained silent*
**14** [a]Is. 40:3; 62:10; Jer. 18:15
**15** [a]Job 6:10; Luke 1:49 [b]Ps. 68:35; Zech. 2:13 [c]Ps. 34:18; 51:17; Is. 66:2 [d]Ps. 147:3; Is. 61:1–3
**16** [a]Ps. 85:5; 103:9; [Mic. 7:18] [b]Num. 16:22; Job 34:14; Heb. 12:9
**17** [a]Is. 2:7; 56:11; Jer. 6:13 [b]Is. 8:17; 45:15; 59:2 [c]Is. 9:13 [1]Or *turning back*
**18** [a]Jer. 3:22 [b]Is. 61:2
**19** [a]Is. 6:7; 51:16; 59:21; Heb. 13:15 [b]Acts 2:39; Eph. 2:17
**20** [a]Job 15:20; Prov. 4:16; Jude 13
**21** [a]Is. 48:22

CHAPTER 58
**1** [a]Mic. 3:8 [1]*do not hold back*
**3** [a]Mal. 3:13–18; Luke 18:12 [b]Lev. 16:29; 23:27 [1]Lit. *drive hard*
**4** [a]1 Kin. 21:9
**5** [a]Zech. 7:5 [b]Lev. 16:29 [c]Esth. 4:3; Job 2:8; Dan. 9:3
**6** [a]Luke 4:18, 19 [b]Neh. 5:10–12 [c]Jer. 34:9 [1]Lit. *bonds of the yoke*

7 *Is it* not [a]to share your bread with the
hungry,
And that you bring to your house the poor
who are [1]cast out;
[b]When you see the naked,
that you cover him,
And not hide yourself from [c]your own flesh?
8 [a]Then your light shall break forth like the
morning,
Your healing shall spring forth speedily,
And your righteousness shall go before you;
[b]The glory of the LORD shall be your rear
guard.
9 Then you shall call,
and the LORD will answer;
You shall cry, and He will say, 'Here I *am.*'

"If you take away the yoke from your midst,
The [1]pointing of the finger,
and [a]speaking wickedness,
10 *If* you extend your soul to the hungry
And satisfy the afflicted soul,
Then your light shall dawn in the darkness,
And your [1]darkness shall *be* as the noonday.
11 The LORD will guide you continually,
And satisfy your soul in drought,
And strengthen your bones;
You shall be like a watered garden,
And like a spring of water,
whose waters do not fail.
12 Those from among you
[a]Shall build the old waste places;
You shall raise up the foundations
of many generations;
And you shall be called
the Repairer of the Breach,
The Restorer of [1]Streets to Dwell In.

**13** "If [a]you turn away your foot
from the Sabbath,
*From* doing your pleasure on My holy day,
And call the Sabbath a delight,
The holy *day* of the LORD honorable,
And shall honor Him,
not doing your own ways,
Nor finding your own pleasure,
Nor speaking *your own* words,
14 [a]Then you shall delight yourself in the LORD;
And I will cause you to [b]ride on the high hills
of the earth,
And feed you with the heritage of Jacob your
father.
[c]The mouth of the LORD has spoken."

### *Corruption Separates the Nation from God*

**59** Behold, the LORD's hand is not [a]shortened,
That it cannot save;
Nor His ear heavy,
That it cannot hear.
2 But your iniquities have separated
you from your God;
And your sins have hidden
*His* face from you,
So that He will [a]not hear.
3 For [a]your hands are defiled with [1]blood,
And your fingers with iniquity;
Your lips have spoken lies,
Your tongue has muttered perversity.

4 No one calls for justice,
Nor does *any* plead for truth.
They trust in [a]empty words and speak lies;
[b]They conceive [1]evil and bring forth iniquity.
5 They hatch vipers' eggs
and weave the spider's web;
He who eats of their eggs dies,
And *from* that which is crushed
a viper breaks out.

6 [a]Their webs will not become garments,
Nor will they cover themselves with their
works;
Their works *are* works of iniquity,
And the act of violence *is* in their hands.
7 [a]Their feet run to evil,
And they make haste to shed [b]innocent
blood;
[c]Their thoughts *are* thoughts of iniquity;
Wasting and [d]destruction *are* in their paths.
8 The way of [a]peace they have not known,
And *there is* no justice in their ways;
[b]They have made themselves crooked paths;
Whoever takes that way
shall not know peace.

**9** Therefore justice is far from us,
Nor does righteousness overtake us;
[a]We look for light, but there is darkness!
For brightness, *but* we walk in blackness!
10 [a]We grope for the wall like the blind,
And we grope as if *we had* no eyes;
We stumble at noonday as at twilight;
*We are* as dead *men* in desolate places.
11 We all growl like bears,
And [a]moan sadly like doves;
We look for justice, but *there is* none;
For salvation, *but* it is far from us.
12 For our [a]transgressions are multiplied before
You,
And our sins testify against us;
For our transgressions *are* with us,
And *as for* our iniquities, we know them:
13 In transgressing and lying against the LORD,
And departing from our God,
Speaking oppression and revolt,
Conceiving and uttering [a]from the heart
words of falsehood.
14 Justice is turned back,
And righteousness stands afar off;
For truth is fallen in the street,
And equity cannot enter.
15 So truth fails,
And he *who* departs from evil makes himself
a [a]prey.

Then the LORD saw *it,* and [1]it displeased Him
That *there was* no justice.
16 [a]He saw that *there was* no man,
And [b]wondered that *there was* no
intercessor;
[c]Therefore His own arm brought salvation for
Him;
And His own righteousness, it sustained Him.
17 [a]For He put on righteousness as a breastplate,
And a helmet of salvation on His head;
He put on the garments of vengeance for
clothing,
And was clad with zeal as a cloak.
18 [a]According to *their* deeds,
accordingly He will repay,
Fury to His adversaries,
Recompense to His enemies;
The coastlands He will fully repay.
19 [a]So shall they fear
The name of the LORD from the west,
And His glory from the rising of the sun;

**7** [a]Ezek. 18:7; Matt. 25:35 [b]Job 31:19–22; James 2:14–17 [c]Gen. 29:14; Neh. 5:5 [1]*wandering*
**8** [a]Job 11:17 [b]Ex. 14:19; Is. 52:12
**9** [a]Ps. 12:2; Is. 59:13 [1]Lit. *sending out of*
**10** [1]Or *gloom*
**12** [a]Is. 61:4 [1]Lit. *Paths*
**13** [a]Ex. 31:16, 17; 35:2, 3; Is. 56:2, 4, 6; Jer. 17:21–27
**14** [a]Job 22:26; Is. 61:10 [b]Deut. 32:13; 33:29; Is. 33:16; Hab. 3:19 [c]Is. 1:20; 40:5; Mic. 4:4

CHAPTER 59
**1** [a]Num. 11:23; Is. 50:2; Jer. 32:17
**2** [a]Is. 1:15
**3** [a]Is. 1:15, 21; Jer. 2:30, 34; Ezek. 7:23; Hos. 4:2 [1]*bloodshed*
**4** [a]Is. 30:12; Jer. 7:4 [b]Job 15:35; Ps. 7:14; Is. 33:11 [1]*trouble*
**6** [a]Job 8:14
**7** [a]Prov. 1:16; Rom. 3:15 [b]Prov. 6:17 [c]Is. 55:7 [d]Rom. 3:16, 17
**8** [a]Is. 57:20, 21 [b]Ps. 125:5; Prov. 2:15
**9** [a]Jer. 8:15
**10** [a]Deut. 28:29; Job 5:14; Amos 8:9
**11** [a]Is. 38:14; Ezek. 7:16
**12** [a]Is. 24:5; 58:1
**13** [a]Matt. 12:34
**15** [a]Is. 5:23; 10:2; 29:21; 32:7 [1]Lit. *it was evil in His eyes*
**16** [a]Is. 41:28; 63:5; 64:7; Ezek. 22:30 [b]Mark 6:6 [c]Ps. 98:1; Is. 63:5
**17** [a]Eph. 6:14, 17; 1 Thess. 5:8
**18** [a]Is. 63:6; Rom. 2:6
**19** [a]Ps. 113:3; Mal. 1:11

When the enemy comes in [b]like a flood,
The Spirit of the LORD will lift up a standard
against him.

20 "The[a] Redeemer will come to Zion,
And to those who turn from transgression in
Jacob,"
Says the LORD.

21 "As[a] for Me," says the LORD, "this *is* My
covenant with them: My Spirit who *is* upon you,
and My words which I have put in your mouth,
shall not depart from your mouth, nor from the
mouth of your descendants, nor from the mouth
of your descendants' descendants," says the LORD,
"from this time and forevermore."

### *The Future Glory of Zion*

60 Arise, [a]shine;
For your light has come!
And [b]the glory of the LORD is risen upon you.
2 For behold, the darkness shall cover the
earth,
And deep darkness the people;
But the LORD will arise over you,
And His glory will be seen upon you.
3 The [a]Gentiles shall come to your light,
And kings to the brightness of your rising.

4 "Lift[a] up your eyes all around, and see:
They all gather together, [b]they come to you;
Your sons shall come from afar,
And your daughters shall be nursed at *your*
side.
5 Then you shall see and become radiant,
And your heart shall swell with joy;
Because [a]the abundance of the sea shall be
turned to you,
The wealth of the Gentiles shall come to you.
6 The multitude of camels shall cover your
*land,*
The dromedaries of Midian and [a]Ephah;
All those from [b]Sheba shall come;
They shall bring [c]gold and incense,
And they shall proclaim the praises
of the LORD.
7 All the flocks of [a]Kedar shall be gathered
together to you,
The rams of Nebaioth shall minister to you;
They shall ascend with [b]acceptance on My
altar,
And [c]I will glorify the house of My glory.

8 "Who *are* these *who* fly like a cloud,
And like doves to their roosts?
9 [a]Surely the coastlands shall wait for Me;
And the ships of Tarshish *will come* first,
[b]To bring your sons from afar,
[c]Their silver and their gold with them,
To the name of the LORD your God,
And to the Holy One of Israel,
[d]Because He has glorified you.

10 "The[a] sons of foreigners shall build up your
walls,
[b]And their kings shall minister to you;
For [c]in My wrath I struck you,
[d]But in My favor I have had mercy on you.
11 Therefore your gates [a]shall be open
continually;
They shall not be shut day or night,
That *men* may bring to you the wealth of the
Gentiles,
And their kings in procession.
12 [a]For the nation and kingdom
which will not serve you shall perish,
And *those* nations shall be utterly ruined.

13 "The[a] glory of Lebanon shall come to you,
The cypress, the pine,
and the box tree together,
To beautify the place of My sanctuary;
And I will make [b]the place of My feet
glorious.
14 Also the sons of those who afflicted you
Shall come [a]bowing to you,
And all those who despised you
shall [b]fall prostrate at the soles of your
feet;
And they shall call you The City of the LORD,
[c]Zion of the Holy One of Israel.

15 "Whereas you have been forsaken and hated,
So that no one went through *you,*
I will make you an eternal excellence,
A joy of many generations.
16 You shall drink the milk of the Gentiles,
[a]And milk the breast of kings;
You shall know that [b]I, the LORD,
*am* your Savior
And your Redeemer,
the Mighty One of Jacob.

17 "Instead of bronze I will bring gold,
Instead of iron I will bring silver,
Instead of wood, bronze,
And instead of stones, iron.
I will also make your officers peace,
And your magistrates righteousness.
18 Violence shall no longer be heard
in your land,
Neither [1]wasting nor destruction
within your borders;
But you shall call [a]your walls Salvation,
And your gates Praise.

19 "The [a]sun shall no longer be your light by
day,
Nor for brightness shall the moon
give light to you;
But the LORD will be to you an everlasting
light,
And [b]your God your glory.
20 [a]Your sun shall no longer go down,
Nor shall your moon withdraw itself;
For the LORD will be your everlasting light,
And the days of your mourning shall be
ended.
21 [a]Also your people *shall* all *be* righteous;
[b]They shall inherit the land forever,
[c]The branch of My planting,
[d]The work of My hands,
That I may be glorified.
22 [a]A little one shall become a thousand,
And a small one a strong nation.
I, the LORD, will hasten it in its time."

### *The Good News of Salvation*

61 "The [a]Spirit of the Lord GOD *is* upon Me,
Because the LORD [b]has anointed Me
To preach good tidings to the poor;
He has sent Me [c]to [1]heal the brokenhearted,
To proclaim [d]liberty to the captives,
And the opening of the prison to *those who*
*are* bound;
2 [a]To proclaim the acceptable year of the LORD,

19 [b]Rev. 12:15
20 [a]Rom. 11:26
21 [a][Heb. 8:10; 10:16]

CHAPTER 60
1 [a]Eph. 5:14 [b]Mal. 4:2
3 [a]Is. 49:6, 23; Rev. 21:24
4 [a]Is. 49:18 [b]Is. 49:20–22
5 [a][Rom. 11:25–27]
6 [a]Gen. 25:4 [b]Gen. 25:3; Ps. 72:10 [c]Is. 61:6; Matt. 2:11
7 [a]Gen. 25:13 [b]Is. 56:7 [c]Is. 60:13; Hag. 2:7, 9
9 [a]Ps. 72:10 [b][Gal. 4:26] [c]Jer. 3:17 [d]Is. 55:5
10 [a]Is. 14:1, 2; 61:5; Zech. 6:15 [b]Is. 49:23; Rev. 21:24 [c]Is. 57:17 [d]Is. 54:7, 8
11 [a]Is. 26:2; 60:18; 62:10; Rev. 21:25, 26
12 [a]Is. 14:2; Zech. 14:17; Matt. 21:44
13 [a]Is. 35:2 [b]1 Chr. 28:2; Ps. 132:7
14 [a]Is. 45:14 [b]Is. 49:23; Rev. 3:9 [c][Heb. 12:22; Rev. 14:1]
16 [a]Is. 49:23 [b]Is. 43:3
18 [a]Is. 26:1 [1]*devastation*
19 [a]Rev. 21:23; 22:5 [b]Is. 41:16; 45:25; Zech. 2:5
20 [a]Amos 8:9
21 [a]Is. 52:1; Rev. 21:27 [b]Ps. 37:11; Matt. 5:5 [c]Is. 61:3; [Matt. 15:13; John 15:2] [d]Is. 29:23; [Eph. 2:10]
22 [a]Matt. 13:31, 32

CHAPTER 61
1 [a]Is. 11:2; Matt. 3:17; Luke 4:18, 19; John 1:32; 3:34 [b]Ps. 45:7; Matt. 11:5; Luke 7:22 [c]Ps. 147:3 [d]Is. 42:7; [Acts 10:43] [1]Lit. *bind up*
2 [a]Lev. 25:9

And [b]the day of vengeance of our God;
[c]To comfort all who mourn,
3 To [1]console those who mourn in Zion,
[a]To give them beauty for ashes,
The oil of joy for mourning,
The garment of praise for the spirit
of heaviness;
That they may be called trees of
righteousness,
[b]The planting of the LORD,
[c]that He may be glorified."

4 And they shall [a]rebuild the old ruins,
They shall raise up the former desolations,
And they shall repair the ruined cities,
The desolations of many generations.
5 [a]Strangers shall stand and feed your flocks,
And the sons of the foreigner
*Shall be* your plowmen
and your vinedressers.
6 [a]But you shall be named
the priests of the LORD,
They shall call you the servants of our God.
[b]You shall eat the riches of the Gentiles,
And in their glory you shall boast.
7 [a]Instead of your shame
*you shall have* double *honor,*
And *instead of* confusion
they shall rejoice in their portion.
Therefore in their land
they shall possess double;
Everlasting joy shall be theirs.

8 "For [a]I, the LORD, love justice;
[b]I hate robbery [1]for burnt offering;
I will direct their work in truth,
[c]And will make with them an everlasting
covenant.
9 Their descendants shall be known among the
Gentiles,
And their offspring among the people.
All who see them shall acknowledge them,
[a]That they *are* the posterity
*whom* the LORD has blessed."

10 [a]I will greatly rejoice in the LORD,
My soul shall be joyful in my God;
For [b]He has clothed me
with the garments of salvation,
He has covered me
with the robe of righteousness,
[c]As a bridegroom decks *himself*
with ornaments,
And as a bride adorns *herself*
with her jewels.
11 For as the earth brings forth its bud,
As the garden causes the things that are
sown in it to spring forth,
So the Lord GOD will cause [a]righteousness
and [b]praise to spring forth before all the
nations.

### *Assurance of Jerusalem's Deliverance*

**62** For Zion's sake I will not [1]hold My peace,
And for Jerusalem's sake I will not rest,
Until her righteousness goes forth
as brightness,
And her salvation as a lamp *that* burns.
2 [a]The Gentiles shall see your righteousness,
And all [b]kings your glory.
[c]You shall be called by a new name,
Which the mouth of the LORD will name.
3 You shall also be [a]a crown of glory
In the hand of the LORD,
And a royal diadem
In the hand of your God.
4 [a]You shall no longer be termed [b]Forsaken,[1]
Nor shall your land any more be termed
[c]Desolate;[2]
But you shall be called [3]Hephzibah, and your
land [4]Beulah;
For the LORD delights in you,
And your land shall be married.
5 For *as* a young man marries a virgin,
*So* shall your sons marry you;
And *as* the bridegroom rejoices over the
bride,
[a]*So* shall your God rejoice over you.

6 [a]I have set watchmen on your walls,
O Jerusalem;
They shall [1]never hold their peace
day or night.
You who [2]make mention of the LORD, do not
keep silent,
7 And give Him no rest till He establishes
And till He makes Jerusalem
[a]a praise in the earth.

8 The LORD has sworn by His right hand
And by the arm of His strength:
"Surely I will no longer [a]give your grain
*As* food for your enemies;
And the sons of the foreigner
shall not drink your new wine,
For which you have labored.
9 But those who have gathered it shall eat it,
And praise the LORD;
Those who have brought it together shall
drink it [a]in My holy courts."

10 Go through,
Go through the gates!
[a]Prepare the way for the people;
Build up,
Build up the highway!
Take out the stones,
[b]Lift up a banner for the peoples!

11 Indeed the LORD has proclaimed
To the end of the world:
[a]"Say to the daughter of Zion,
'Surely your salvation is coming;
Behold, His [b]reward *is* with Him,
And His [1]work before Him.' "
12 And they shall call them The Holy People,
The Redeemed of the LORD;
And you shall be called Sought Out,
A City Not Forsaken.

### *God's Mercy Remembered*

**63** Who *is* this who comes from Edom,
With dyed garments from Bozrah,
This *One who is* [1]glorious in His apparel,
Traveling in the greatness of His strength?—

"I who speak in righteousness,
mighty to save."

2 Why [a]*is* Your apparel red,
And Your garments like one who treads in
the winepress?

3 "I have [a]trodden the winepress alone,
And from the peoples no one *was* with Me.
For I have trodden them in My anger,
And trampled them in My fury;

2 [b]Is. 34:8; Mal. 4:1, 3; [2 Thess. 1:7] [c]Is. 57:18; Jer. 31:13; Matt. 5:4
3 [a]Ps. 30:11 [b]Is. 60:21; [Jer. 17:7, 8] [c][John 15:8] [1]Lit. *appoint*
4 [a]Is. 49:8; 58:12; Ezek. 36:33; Amos 9:14
5 [a][Eph. 2:12]
6 [a]Ex. 19:6 [b]Is. 60:5, 11
7 [a]Is. 40:2; Zech. 9:12
8 [a]Ps. 11:7 [b]Is. 1:11, 13 [c]Gen. 17:7; Ps. 105:10; Is. 55:3; Jer. 32:40 [1]Or *in*
9 [a]Is. 65:23
10 [a]Hab. 3:18 [b]Ps. 132:9, 16 [c]Is. 49:18; Rev. 21:2
11 [a]Ps. 72:3; 85:11 [b]Is. 60:18; 62:7

CHAPTER 62
1 [1]*keep silent*
2 [a]Is. 60:3 [b]Ps. 102:15, 16; 138:4, 5; 148:11, 13 [c]Is. 62:4, 12; 65:15
3 [a]Is. 28:5; Zech. 9:16; 1 Thess. 2:19
4 [a]Hos. 1:10; 1 Pet. 2:10 [b]Is. 49:14; 54:6, 7 [c]Is. 54:1 [1]Heb. *Azubah* [2]Heb. *Shemamah* [3]Lit. *My Delight Is in Her* [4]Lit. *Married*
5 [a]Is. 65:19
6 [a]Is. 52:8; Jer. 6:17; Ezek. 3:17; 33:7 [1]*not be silent* [2]*remember*
7 [a]Is. 60:18; 61:11; Jer. 33:9; Zeph. 3:19, 20
8 [a]Lev. 26:16; Deut. 28:31, 33; Judg. 6:3–6; Is. 1:7; Jer. 5:17
9 [a]Deut. 12:12; 14:23, 26
10 [a]Is. 40:3; 57:14 [b]Is. 11:12
11 [a]Zech. 9:9; Matt. 21:5; John 12:15 [b]Is. 40:10; [Rev. 22:12] [1]*recompense*

CHAPTER 63
1 [1]Or *adorned*
2 [a][Rev. 19:13, 15]
3 [a]Lam. 1:15; Rev. 14:19, 20; 19:15

Their blood is sprinkled upon My garments,
And I have stained all My robes.
4 For the [a]day of vengeance *is* in My heart,
And the year of My redeemed has come.
5 [a]I looked, but [b]*there was* no one to help,
And I wondered
That *there was* no one to uphold;
Therefore My own [c]arm brought salvation for Me;
And My own fury, it sustained Me.
6 I have trodden down the peoples
in My anger,
Made them drunk in My fury,
And brought down their strength
to the earth."

7 I will mention the lovingkindnesses
of the LORD
*And* the praises of the LORD,
According to all that the LORD has bestowed
on us,
And the great goodness toward the house of
Israel,
Which He has bestowed on them according
to His mercies,
According to the multitude of His
lovingkindnesses.
8 For He said, "Surely they *are* My people,
Children *who* will not lie."
So He became their Savior.
9 [a]In all their affliction He was [1]afflicted,
[b]And the Angel of His Presence saved them;
[c]In His love and in His pity
He redeemed them;
And [d]He bore them and carried them
All the days of old.
10 But they [a]rebelled and [b]grieved
His Holy Spirit;
[c]So He turned Himself against them
as an enemy,
*And* He fought against them.

11 Then he [a]remembered the days of old,
Moses *and* his people, *saying:*
"Where *is* He who [b]brought them up out of
the sea
With the [1]shepherd of His flock?
[c]Where *is* He who put His Holy Spirit within
them,
12 Who led *them* by the right hand of Moses,
[a]With His glorious arm,
[b]Dividing the water before them
To make for Himself an everlasting name,
13 [a]Who led them through the deep,
As a horse in the wilderness,
*That* they might not stumble?"

14 As a beast goes down into the valley,
*And* the Spirit of the LORD causes him to
rest,
So You lead Your people,
[a]To make Yourself a glorious name.

15 [a]Look down from heaven,
And see [b]from Your habitation,
holy and glorious.
Where *are* Your zeal and Your strength,
The yearning [c]of Your heart
and Your mercies toward me?
Are they restrained?
16 [a]Doubtless You *are* our Father,
Though Abraham [b]was ignorant of us,
And Israel does not acknowledge us.
You, O LORD, *are* our Father;
Our Redeemer from Everlasting
*is* Your name.
17 O LORD, why have You [a]made us stray from
Your ways,
*And* hardened our heart from Your fear?
Return for Your servants' sake,
The tribes of Your inheritance.
18 [a]Your holy people have possessed *it*
but a little while;
[b]Our adversaries have trodden down Your
sanctuary.
19 We have become *like* those of old,
over whom You never ruled,
Those who were never called by Your name.

## *A Prayer for Help*

**64** Oh, that You would [1]rend the heavens!
That You would come down!
That the mountains might shake
at Your [a]presence—
2 As fire burns brushwood,
As fire causes water to boil—
To make Your name known
to Your adversaries,
*That* the nations may tremble
at Your presence!
3 When [a]You did awesome things *for which*
we did not look,
You came down,
The mountains shook at Your presence.
4 For since the beginning of the world
[a]*Men* have not heard
nor perceived by the ear,
Nor has the eye seen any God besides You,
Who acts for the one who waits for Him.
5 You meet him who rejoices and does
righteousness,
*Who* remembers You in Your ways.
You are indeed angry, for we have sinned—
[a]In these ways we continue;
And we need to be saved.

6 But we are all like an unclean *thing,*
And all [a]our righteousnesses *are* like [1]filthy
rags;
We all [b]fade as a leaf,
And our iniquities, like the wind,
Have taken us away.
7 And *there is* no one who calls on Your name,
Who stirs himself up to take hold of You;
For You have hidden Your face from us,
And have [1]consumed us
because of our iniquities.

8 But now, O LORD,
You *are* our Father;
We *are* the clay, and You our [a]potter;
And all we *are* the work of Your hand.
9 Do not be furious, O LORD,
Nor remember iniquity forever;
Indeed, please look—we all *are* Your people!
10 Your holy cities are a wilderness,
Zion is a wilderness,
Jerusalem a desolation.
11 Our holy and beautiful [1]temple,
Where our fathers praised You,
Is burned up with fire;
And all [a]our pleasant things [2]are laid waste.
12 [a]Will You restrain Yourself
because of these *things,* O LORD?
[b]Will You [1]hold Your peace,
and afflict us very severely?

**4** [a]Is. 34:8; 35:4; 61:2; Jer. 51:6
**5** [a]Is. 41:28; 59:16 [b][John 16:32] [c]Ps. 98:1; Is. 59:16
**9** [a]Judg. 10:16 [b]Ex. 14:19 [c]Deut. 7:7 [d]Ex. 19:4 [1]Kt., LXX, Syr. *not afflicted*
**10** [a]Ex. 15:24 [b]Num. 14:11; Ps. 78:40; Acts 7:51; 1 Cor. 10:1–11 [c]Ex. 23:21; Ps. 106:40
**11** [a]Ps. 106:44, 45 [b]Ex. 14:30 [c]Num. 11:17, 25, 29; Hag. 2:5 [1]MT, Vg. *shepherds*
**12** [a]Ex. 15:6 [b]Ex. 14:21, 22; Josh. 3:16; Is. 11:15; 51:10
**13** [a]Ps. 106:9
**14** [a]2 Sam. 7:23
**15** [a]Deut. 26:15; Ps. 80:14 [b]Ps. 33:14 [c]Jer. 31:20; Hos. 11:8
**16** [a]Deut. 32:6 [b]Job 14:21
**17** [a]Is. 6:9, 10; John 12:40
**18** [a]Deut. 7:6 [b]Ps. 74:3–7; Is. 64:11

CHAPTER 64
**1** [a]Ex. 19:18; Ps. 18:9; 144:5; Mic. 1:3, 4; [Hab. 3:13] [1]*tear open*
**3** [a]Ex. 34:10
**4** [a]Ps. 31:19
**5** [a]Mal. 3:6
**6** [a][Phil. 3:9] [b]Ps. 90:5, 6; Is. 1:30 [1]Lit. *a filthy garment*
**7** [1]Lit. *caused us to melt*
**8** [a]Is. 29:16; 45:9; Jer. 18:6; [Rom. 9:20, 21]
**11** [a]Ezek. 24:21 [1]Lit. *house* [2]*have become a ruin*
**12** [a]Is. 42:14 [b]Ps. 83:1 [1]*keep silent*

### *The Rebellious Will Be Punished*

65 "I was [a]sought by *those who* did not ask *for Me;*
I was found by *those who* did not seek Me.
I said, 'Here I am, here I am,'
To a nation *that* [b]was not called
by My name.
2 [a]I have stretched out My hands
all day long to a [b]rebellious people,
Who [c]walk in a way *that is* not good,
According to their own thoughts;
3 A people [a]who provoke Me to anger
continually to My face;
[b]Who sacrifice in gardens,
And burn incense on altars of brick;
4 [a]Who sit among the graves,
And spend the night in the tombs;
[b]Who eat swine's flesh,
And the broth of [1]abominable things
is *in* their vessels;
5 [a]Who say, 'Keep to yourself,
Do not come near me,
For I am holier than you!'
These [1]*are* smoke in My nostrils,
A fire that burns all the day.

6 "Behold, [a]*it is* written before Me:
[b]I will not keep silence, [c]but will repay—
Even repay into their bosom—
7 Your iniquities and [a]the iniquities
of your fathers together,"
Says the LORD,
[b]"Who have burned incense on the mountains
[c]And blasphemed Me on the hills;
Therefore I will measure their former work
into their bosom."

8 Thus says the LORD:

"As the new wine is found in the cluster,
And *one* says, 'Do not destroy it,
For [a]a blessing *is* in it,'
So will I do for My servants' sake,
That I may not destroy them [b]all.
9 I will bring forth descendants from Jacob,
And from Judah an heir of My mountains;
My [a]elect shall inherit it,
And My servants shall dwell there.
10 [a]Sharon shall be a fold of flocks,
And [b]the Valley of Achor a place for herds to
lie down,
For My people who have [c]sought Me.

11 "But you *are* those who forsake the LORD,
Who forget [a]My holy mountain,
Who prepare [b]a table for [1]Gad,
And who furnish a drink offering for [2]Meni.
12 Therefore I will number you for the sword,
And you shall all bow down to the slaughter;
[a]Because, when I called, you did not answer;
When I spoke, you did not hear,
But did evil before My eyes,
And chose *that* in which I do not delight."

13 Therefore thus says the Lord GOD:

"Behold, My servants shall eat,
But you shall be hungry;
Behold, My servants shall drink,
But you shall be thirsty;
Behold, My servants shall rejoice,
But you shall be ashamed;
14 Behold, My servants shall sing
for joy of heart,
But you shall cry for sorrow of heart,
And [a]wail for [1]grief of spirit.
15 You shall leave your name [a]as a curse to [b]My
chosen;
For the Lord GOD will slay you,
And [c]call His servants by another name;
16 [a]So that he who blesses himself in the earth
Shall bless himself in the God of truth;
And [b]he who swears in the earth
Shall swear by the God of truth;
Because the former troubles are forgotten,
And because they are hidden from My eyes.

17 "For behold, I create [a]new heavens
and a new earth;
And the former shall not be remembered or
[1]come to mind.
18 But be glad and rejoice forever in what I
create;
For behold, I create Jerusalem *as* a rejoicing,
And her people a joy.
19 [a]I will rejoice in Jerusalem,
And joy in My people;
The [b]voice of weeping shall no longer be
heard in her,
Nor the voice of crying.

20 "No more shall an infant from there
*live but a few* days,
Nor an old man who has not fulfilled his
days;
For the child shall die one hundred years old,
[a]But the sinner *being* one hundred years old
shall be accursed.
21 [a]They shall build houses and inhabit *them;*
They shall plant vineyards and eat their fruit.
22 They shall not build and another inhabit;
They shall not plant and [a]another eat;
For [b]as the days of a tree,
*so shall be* the days of My people,
And [c]My elect shall long enjoy the work of
their hands.
23 They shall not labor in vain,
[a]Nor bring forth children for trouble;
For [b]they *shall be* the descendants of the
blessed of the LORD,
And their offspring with them.

24 "It shall come to pass
That [a]before they call, I will answer;
And while they are still speaking, I will [b]hear.
25 The [a]wolf and the lamb shall feed together,
The lion shall eat straw like the ox,
[b]And dust *shall be* the serpent's food.
They shall not hurt nor destroy in all My
holy mountain,"
Says the LORD.

### *Zion's Future Hope*

66 Thus says the LORD:

[a]"Heaven *is* My throne,
And earth *is* My footstool.
Where *is* the house that you will build Me?
And where *is* the place of My rest?
2 For all those *things* My hand has made,
And all those *things* exist,"
Says the LORD.
[a]"But on this *one* will I look:
[b]On *him who is* poor and of a contrite spirit,
And who trembles at My word.

CHAPTER 65
1 [a]Rom. 9:24; 10:20 [b]Is. 63:19
2 [a]Rom. 10:21 [b]Is. 1:2, 23 [c]Is. 42:24
3 [a]Deut. 32:21 [b]Is. 1:29
4 [a]Deut. 18:11 [b]Lev. 11:7; Is. 66:17 [1]Unclean meats, Lev. 7:18; 19:7
5 [a]Matt. 9:11; Luke 7:39; 18:9–12 [1]Cause My wrath to smoke
6 [a]Deut. 32:34 [b]Ps. 50:3 [c]Ps. 79:12
7 [a]Ex. 20:5 [b]Ezek. 18:6 [c]Is. 57:7; Ezek. 20:27, 28
8 [a]Joel 2:14 [b]Is. 1:9; Amos 9:8, 9
9 [a]Matt. 24:22
10 [a]Is. 33:9 [b]Josh. 7:24; Hos. 2:15 [c]Is. 55:6
11 [a]Is. 56:7 [b]Ezek. 23:41; [1 Cor. 10:21] [1]Lit. *Troop* or *Fortune;* a pagan deity [2]Lit. *Number* or *Destiny;* a pagan deity
12 [a]2 Chr. 36:15, 16; Prov. 1:24; Is. 41:28; 50:2; 66:4; Jer. 7:13
14 [a]Matt. 8:12; Luke 13:28 [1]Or *a broken spirit*
15 [a]Jer. 29:22; Zech. 8:13 [b]Is. 65:9, 22 [c][Acts 11:26]
16 [a]Ps. 72:17; Jer. 4:2 [b]Deut. 6:13; Zeph. 1:5
17 [a]Is. 51:16; 66:22; [2 Pet. 3:13]; Rev. 21:1 [1]Lit. *come upon the heart*
19 [a]Is. 62:4, 5 [b]Is. 35:10; 51:11; Rev. 7:17; 21:4
20 [a]Eccl. 8:12, 13; Is. 3:11; 22:14
21 [a]Ezek. 28:26; 45:4; Hos. 11:11; Amos 9:14
22 [a]Is. 62:8, 9 [b]Ps. 92:12 [c]Is. 65:9, 15
23 [a]Hos. 9:12 [b]Is. 61:9; [Jer. 32:38, 39; Acts 2:39]
24 [a]Ps. 91:15; Is. 58:9 [b]Is. 30:19; Dan. 9:20–23
25 [a]Is. 11:6–9 [b]Gen. 3:14; Mic. 7:17

CHAPTER 66
1 [a]1 Kin. 8:27; 2 Chr. 6:18; Ps. 11:4; Matt. 5:34; Acts 17:24
2 [a]Ps. 34:18; [Is. 57:15; 61:1; Matt. 5:3, 4; Luke 18:13, 14] [b]Ps. 34:18; 51:17

3 "He[a] who kills a bull *is as if* he slays a man;
He who sacrifices a lamb,
*as if* he [b]breaks a dog's neck;
He who offers a grain offering,
*as if he offers* swine's blood;
He who burns incense,
*as if* he blesses an idol.
Just as they have chosen their own ways,
And their soul delights in their abominations,
4 So will I choose their delusions,
And bring their fears on them;
[a]Because, when I called, no one answered,
When I spoke they did not hear;
But they did evil before My eyes,
And chose *that* in which I do not delight."

5 Hear the word of the LORD,
You who tremble at His word:
"Your brethren who [a]hated you,
Who cast you out for My name's sake, said,
[b]'Let the LORD be glorified,
That [c]we may see your joy.'
But they shall be ashamed."

6 The sound of noise from the city!
A voice from the temple!
The voice of the LORD,
Who fully repays His enemies!

7 "Before she was in labor, she gave birth;
Before her pain came,
She delivered a male child.
8 Who has heard such a thing?
Who has seen such things?
Shall the earth be made to give birth
in one day?
*Or* shall a nation be born at once?
For as soon as Zion was in labor,
She gave birth to her children.
9 Shall I bring to the time of birth, and not
cause delivery?" says the LORD.
"Shall I who cause delivery shut up *the*
*womb?*" says your God.
10 "Rejoice with Jerusalem,
And be glad with her, all you who love her;
Rejoice for joy with her,
all you who mourn for her;
11 That you may feed and be satisfied
With the consolation of her bosom,
That you may drink deeply and be delighted
With the abundance of her glory."

12 For thus says the LORD:

"Behold, [a]I will extend peace to her
like a river,
And the glory of the Gentiles
like a flowing stream.
Then you shall [b]feed;
On *her* sides shall you be [c]carried,
And be dandled on *her* knees.

13 As one whom his mother comforts,
So I will [a]comfort you;
And you shall be comforted in Jerusalem."

14 When you see *this*, your heart shall rejoice,
And [a]your bones shall flourish like grass;
The hand of the LORD shall be known to His
servants,
And *His* indignation to His enemies.
15 [a]For behold, the LORD will come with fire
And with His chariots, like a whirlwind,
To render His anger with fury,
And His rebuke with flames of fire.
16 For by fire and by [a]His sword
The LORD will judge all flesh;
And the slain of the LORD shall be [b]many.

17 "Those[a] who sanctify themselves
and purify themselves,
*To go* to the gardens
[1]After an *idol* in the midst,
Eating swine's flesh and the abomination and
the mouse,
Shall [2]be consumed together," says the LORD.

18 "For I *know* their works and their [a]thoughts.
It shall be that I will [b]gather all nations and
tongues; and they shall come and see My glory.
19 [a]"I will set a sign among them; and those
among them who escape I will send to the nations: *to* Tarshish and [1]Pul and Lud, who draw the
bow, and Tubal and Javan, *to* the coastlands afar
off who have not heard My fame nor seen My
glory. [b]And they shall declare My glory among the
Gentiles.
20 "Then they shall [a]bring all your brethren [b]for
an offering to the LORD out of all nations, on
horses and in chariots and in litters, on mules and
on camels, to My holy mountain Jerusalem," says
the LORD, "as the children of Israel bring an
offering in a clean vessel into the house of the
LORD.
21 "And I will also take some of them for [a]priests
*and* Levites," says the LORD.

22 "For as [a]the new heavens and the new earth
Which I will make shall remain before Me,"
says the LORD,
"So shall your descendants
and your name remain.
23 And [a]it shall come to pass
*That* from one New Moon to another,
And from one Sabbath to another,
[b]All flesh shall come to worship before Me,"
says the LORD.

24 "And they shall go forth and look
Upon the corpses of the men
Who have transgressed against Me.
For their [a]worm does not die,
And their fire is not quenched.
They shall be an abhorrence to all flesh."

**3** [a][Is. 1:10–17; 58:1–7; Mic. 6:7, 8] [b]Deut. 23:18
**4** [a]Prov. 1:24; Is. 65:12; Jer. 7:13
**5** [a]Ps. 38:20; Is. 60:15; [Luke 6:22, 23] [b]Is. 5:19 [c][2 Thess. 1:10; Titus 2:13]
**12** [a]Is. 48:18; 60:5 [b]Is. 60:16 [c]Is. 49:22; 60:4
**13** [a]Is. 51:3; [2 Cor. 1:3, 4]
**14** [a]Ezek. 37:1
**15** [a]Is. 9:5; [2 Thess. 1:8]
**16** [a]Is. 27:1 [b]Is. 34:6
**17** [a]Is. 65:3–8 [1]Lit. *After one* [2]*come to an end*
**18** [a]Is. 59:7 [b]Is. 45:22–25; Jer. 3:17
**19** [a]Luke 2:34 [b]Mal. 1:11 [1]So with MT, Tg., [Vg.]; LXX *Put* (cf. Jer. 46:9)
**20** [a]Is. 49:22 [b]Is. 18:7; [Rom. 15:16]
**21** [a]Ex. 19:6; Is. 61:6; 1 Pet. 2:9; Rev. 1:6
**22** [a]Is. 65:17; Heb. 12:26, 27; 2 Pet. 3:13; Rev. 21:1
**23** [a]Zech. 14:16 [b]Zech. 14:17–21
**24** [a]Is. 14:11; Mark 9:44, 46, 48

The Book of

# JEREMIAH

### *Jeremiah Called to Be a Priest*

**1** THE words of Jeremiah the son of Hilkiah, of
the priests who *were* [a]in Anathoth in the
land of Benjamin,
2 to whom the word of the LORD came in the
days of [a]Josiah the son of Amon, king of Judah, [b]in
the thirteenth year of his reign.
3 It came also in the days of [a]Jehoiakim the son
of Josiah, king of Judah, [b]until the end of the
eleventh year of Zedekiah the son of Josiah, king
of Judah, [c]until the carrying away of Jerusalem
captive [d]in the fifth month.
**4** Then the word of the LORD came to me,
saying:

5 "Before I [a]formed you in the womb
[b]I knew you;
Before you were born I [c]sanctified[1] you;
I [2]ordained you a prophet to the nations."

6 Then said I:

[a]"Ah, Lord GOD!
Behold, I cannot speak, for I *am* a youth."

7 But the LORD said to me:

"Do not say, 'I *am* a youth,'
For you shall go to all to whom I send you,
And [a]whatever I command you,
you shall speak.
8 [a]Do not be afraid of their faces,
For [b]I *am* with you to deliver you,"
says the LORD.

**9** Then the LORD put forth His hand and
[a]touched my mouth, and the LORD said to me:

"Behold, I have [b]put My words in your mouth.
**10** [a]See, I have this day set you over the nations
and over the kingdoms,
To [b]root out and to pull down,
To destroy and to throw down,
To build and to plant."

**11** Moreover the word of the LORD came to me,
saying, "Jeremiah, what do you see?" And I said,
"I see a [1]branch of an almond tree."
12 Then the LORD said to me, "You have seen
well, for I am [1]ready to perform My word."
**13** And the word of the LORD came to me the
second time, saying, "What do you see?" And I
said, "I see [a]a boiling pot, and it is facing away
from the north."
14 Then the LORD said to me:

"Out of the [a]north calamity shall break forth
On all the inhabitants of the land.
15 For behold, I am [a]calling
All the families of the kingdoms of the
north," says the LORD;
"They shall come and [b]each one set his throne
At the entrance of the gates of Jerusalem,
Against all its walls all around,
And against all the cities of Judah.
16 I will utter My judgments
Against them concerning all their
wickedness,
Because [a]they have forsaken Me,
Burned [b]incense to other gods,
And worshiped the works of their
own [c]hands.
**17** "Therefore [a]prepare yourself and arise,
And speak to them all that I command you.
[b]Do not be dismayed before their faces,
Lest I dismay you before them.
18 For behold, I have made you this day
[a]A fortified city and an iron pillar,
And bronze walls against the whole land—
Against the kings of Judah,
Against its princes,
Against its priests,
And against the people of the land.
19 They will fight against you,
But they shall not prevail against you.
For I *am* with you," says the LORD, "to
deliver you."

### *Israel's Sufferings the Result of Sin*

**2** Moreover the word of the LORD came to me,
saying,
2 "Go and cry in the hearing of Jerusalem, saying,
'Thus says the LORD:

"I remember you,
The kindness of your [a]youth,
The love of your betrothal,
[b]When you [1]went after Me in the wilderness,
In a land not sown.
3 [a]Israel *was* holiness to the LORD,
[b]The firstfruits of His increase.
[c]All that devour him will offend;
Disaster will [d]come upon them,"
says the LORD.' "

**4** Hear the word of the LORD, O house of Jacob
and all the families of the house of Israel.
5 Thus says the LORD:

[a]"What injustice have your fathers
found in Me,
That they have gone far from Me,
[b]Have followed [1]idols,
And have become idolaters?
6 Neither did they say, 'Where *is* the LORD,
Who [a]brought us up out of the land of Egypt,
Who led us through [b]the wilderness,
Through a land of deserts and pits,
Through a land of drought
and the shadow of death,
Through a land that no one crossed
And where no one dwelt?'
7 I brought you into [a]a bountiful country,
To eat its fruit and its goodness.
But when you entered, you [b]defiled My land
And made My heritage an abomination.
8 The priests did not say, 'Where *is* the LORD?'
And those who handle the [a]law
did not know Me;
The rulers also transgressed against Me;
[b]The prophets prophesied by Baal,
And walked after *things that* do not profit.
**9** "Therefore [a]I will yet [1]bring charges against
you," says the LORD,
"And against your children's children I will
bring charges.

CHAPTER 1
**1** [a]Josh. 21:18
**2** [a]2 Kin. 21:24 [b]Jer. 25:3
**3** [a]2 Kin. 23:34 [b]Jer. 39:2 [c]Jer. 52:12 [d]2 Kin. 25:8
**5** [a]Is. 49:1, 5 [b]Ex. 33:12 [c][Luke 1:15] [1]*set you apart* [2]*appointed*
**6** [a]Ex. 4:10; 6:12, 30
**7** [a]Num. 22:20, 38
**8** [a]Ezek. 2:6; 3:9 [b]Ex. 3:12
**9** [a]Is. 6:7 [b]Is. 51:16
**10** [a]1 Kin. 19:17 [b][2 Cor. 10:4, 5]
**11** [1]Lit. *rod*
**12** [1]Lit. *watching*
**13** [a]Ezek. 11:3; 24:3
**14** [a]Jer. 6:1
**15** [a]Jer. 6:22; 25:9 [b]Jer. 39:3
**16** [a]Deut. 28:20 [b]Jer. 7:9 [c]Is. 37:19
**17** [a]Job 38:3 [b]Ezek. 2:6
**18** [a]Is. 50:7

CHAPTER 2
**2** [a]Ezek. 16:8 [b]Deut. 2:7 [1]*followed*
**3** [a][Ex. 19:5, 6] [b]Rev. 14:4 [c]Jer. 12:14 [d]Is. 41:11
**5** [a]Is. 5:4 [b]2 Kin. 17:15 [1]*vanities* or *futilities*
**6** [a]Is. 63:11 [b]Deut. 8:15; 32:10
**7** [a]Num. 13:27 [b]Num. 35:33
**8** [a]Rom. 2:20 [b]Jer. 23:13
**9** [a]Mic. 6:2 [1]*contend with*

10 For pass beyond the coasts of [1]Cyprus
and see,
Send to [2]Kedar and consider diligently,
And see if there has been such *a* [a]*thing.*
11 [a]Has a nation changed *its* gods,
Which *are* [b]not gods?
[c]But My people have changed their Glory
For *what* does not profit.
12 Be astonished, O heavens, at this,
And be horribly afraid;
Be very desolate," says the LORD.
13 "For My people have committed two evils:
They have forsaken Me,
the [a]fountain of living waters,
*And* hewn themselves cisterns—broken
cisterns that can hold no water.

**14** "*Is* Israel [a]a servant?
*Is* he a homeborn *slave?*
Why is he plundered?
15 [a]The young lions roared at him, *and* growled;
They made his land waste;
His cities are burned, without inhabitant.
16 Also the people of [1]Noph and [a]Tahpanhes
Have [2]broken the crown of your head.
17 [a]Have you not brought this on yourself,
In that you have forsaken the LORD your
God
When [b]He led you in the way?
18 And now why take [a]the road to Egypt,
To drink the waters of [b]Sihor?
Or why take the road to [c]Assyria,
To drink the waters of [1]the River?
19 Your own wickedness will [a]correct you,
And your backslidings will rebuke you.
Know therefore and see that *it is* an evil and
bitter *thing*
That you have forsaken the LORD your God,
And the [1]fear of Me *is* not in you,"
Says the Lord GOD of hosts.

**20** "For of old I have [a]broken your yoke *and*
burst your bonds;
And [b]you said, 'I will not [1]transgress,'
When [c]on every high hill
and under every green tree
You lay down, [d]playing the harlot.
21 Yet I had [a]planted you a noble vine,
a seed of highest quality.
How then have you turned before Me
Into [b]the degenerate plant of an alien vine?
22 For though you wash yourself with lye, and
use much soap,
*Yet* your iniquity is [a]marked[1] before Me,"
says the Lord GOD.

23 "How[a] can you say, 'I am not [1]polluted,
I have not gone after the Baals'?
See your way in the valley;
Know what you have done:
*You are* a swift dromedary
breaking loose in her ways,
24 A wild donkey used to the wilderness,
*That* sniffs at the wind in her desire;
In her time of mating,
who can turn her away?
All those who seek her will not weary
themselves;
In her month they will find her.
25 Withhold your foot from being unshod, and
your throat from thirst.
But you said, [a]'There is no hope.
No! For I have loved [b]aliens,
and after them I will go.'

**26** "As the thief is ashamed
when he is found out,
So is the house of Israel ashamed;
They and their kings and their princes, and
their priests and their [a]prophets,
27 Saying to a tree, 'You *are* my father,'
And to a [a]stone, 'You gave birth to me.'
For they have turned *their* back to Me, and
not *their* face.
But in the time of their [b]trouble
They will say, 'Arise and save us.'
28 But [a]where *are* your gods
that you have made for yourselves?
Let them arise,
If they [b]can save you in the time of your
[1]trouble;
For [c]*according to* the number of your cities
Are your gods, O Judah.

**29** "Why will you plead with Me?
You all have transgressed against Me," says
the LORD.
30 "In vain I have [a]chastened your children;
They [b]received no correction.
Your sword has [c]devoured your prophets
Like a destroying lion.

31 "O generation, see the word of the LORD!
Have I been a wilderness to Israel,
Or a land of darkness?
Why do My people say, 'We [1]are lords;
[a]We will come no more to You'?
32 Can a virgin forget her ornaments,
*Or* a bride her attire?
Yet My people [a]have forgotten Me
days without number.

33 "Why do you beautify your way to seek love?
Therefore you have also taught
The wicked women your ways.
34 Also on your skirts is found
[a]The blood of the lives of the poor innocents.
I have not found it by [1]secret search,
But plainly on all these things.
35 [a]Yet you say, 'Because I am innocent,
Surely His anger shall turn from me.'
Behold, [b]I will plead My case against you,
[c]Because you say, 'I have not sinned.'
36 [a]Why do you gad about so much
to change your way?
Also [b]you shall be ashamed of Egypt
[c]as you were ashamed of Assyria.
37 Indeed you will go forth from him
With your hands on [a]your head;
For the LORD has rejected your trusted allies,
And you will [b]not prosper by them.

### *Israel and Judah Urged to Repent*

**3** "They say, 'If a man divorces his wife,
And she goes from him
And becomes another man's,
[a]May he return to her again?'
Would not that [b]land be greatly polluted?
But you have [c]played the harlot with many
lovers;
[d]Yet return to Me," says the LORD.
2 "Lift up your eyes to [a]the desolate heights and
see:

10 [a]Jer. 18:13 [1]Heb. *Kittim,* representative of western cultures [2]In northern Arabian desert, representative of eastern cultures
11 [a]Mic. 4:5 [b]Is. 37:19 [c]Rom. 1:23
13 [a]Ps. 36:9
14 [a][Ex. 4:22]
15 [a]Is. 1:7
16 [a]Jer. 43:7–9 [1]Memphis in ancient Egypt [2]Or *grazed*
17 [a]Jer. 4:18 [b]Deut. 32:10
18 [a]Is. 30:1–3 [b]Josh. 13:3 [c]Hos. 5:13 [1]The Euphrates
19 [a]Jer. 4:18 [1]*dread*
20 [a]Lev. 26:13 [b]Judg. 10:16 [c]Deut. 12:2 [d]Ex. 34:15 [1]Kt. *serve*
21 [a]Ex. 15:17 [b]Is. 5:4
22 [a]Job 14:16, 17 [1]*stained*
23 [a]Prov. 30:12 [1]*defiled*
25 [a]Jer. 18:12 [b]Jer. 3:13
26 [a]Is. 28:7
27 [a]Jer. 3:9 [b]Is. 26:16
28 [a]Judg. 10:14 [b]Is. 45:20 [c]Jer. 11:13 [1]Or *evil*
30 [a]Is. 9:13 [b]Jer. 5:3; 7:28 [c]Neh. 9:26
31 [a]Deut. 32:15 [1]*have dominion*
32 [a]Ps. 106:21
34 [a]Ps. 106:38 [1]*digging*
35 [a]Jer. 2:23, 29 [b]Jer. 2:9 [c][Prov. 28:13]
36 [a]Hos. 5:13; 12:1 [b]Is. 30:3 [c]2 Chr. 28:16
37 [a]2 Sam. 13:19 [b]Jer. 37:7–10

CHAPTER 3
1 [a]Deut. 24:1–4 [b]Jer. 2:7 [c]Ezek. 16:26 [d][Zech. 1:3]
2 [a]Deut. 12:2

Where have you not [1]lain *with men?*
[b]By the road you have sat for them
Like an Arabian in the wilderness;
[c]And you have polluted the land
With your harlotries and your wickedness.
3 Therefore the [a]showers have been withheld,
And there has been no latter rain.
You have had a [b]harlot's forehead;
You refuse to be ashamed.
4 Will you not from this time cry to Me,
'My Father, You *are* [a]the guide of [b]my youth?
5 [a]Will He remain angry forever?
Will He keep it to the end?'
Behold, you have spoken
and done evil things,
As you were able."

**6** The LORD said also to me in the days of Josiah
the king: "Have you seen what [a]backsliding Israel
has done? She has [b]gone up on every high mountain and under every green tree, and there played
the harlot.
7 [a]"And I said, after she had done all these
*things,* 'Return to Me.' But she did not return. And
her treacherous [b]sister Judah saw it.
8 "Then I saw that [a]for all the causes for which
backsliding Israel had committed adultery, I had
[b]put her away and given her a certificate of
divorce; [c]yet her treacherous sister Judah did not
fear, but went and played the harlot also.
9 "So it came to pass, through her casual harlotry, that she [a]defiled the land and committed
adultery with [b]stones and trees.
10 "And yet for all this her treacherous sister
Judah has not turned to Me [a]with her whole heart,
but in pretense," says the LORD.
**11** Then the LORD said to me, [a]"Backsliding Israel
has shown herself more righteous than treacherous Judah.
12 "Go and proclaim these words toward [a]the
north, and say:

'Return, backsliding Israel,' says the LORD;
'I will not cause My anger to fall on you.
For I *am* [b]merciful,' says the LORD;
'I will not remain angry forever.
13 [a]Only acknowledge your iniquity,
That you have transgressed against the LORD
your God,
And have [b]scattered your [1]charms
To [c]alien deities [d]under every green tree,
And you have not obeyed My voice,' says the
LORD.

14 "Return, O backsliding children," says the
LORD; [a]"for I am married to you. I will take you,
[b]one from a city and two from a family, and I will
bring you to [c]Zion.
15 "And I will give you [a]shepherds according to
My heart, who will [b]feed you with knowledge and
understanding.
16 "Then it shall come to pass, when you are
multiplied and [a]increased in the land in those
days," says the LORD, "that they will say no more,
'The ark of the covenant of the LORD.' [b]It shall not
come to mind, nor shall they remember it, nor
shall they visit *it,* nor shall it be made anymore.
17 "At that time Jerusalem shall be called The
Throne of the LORD, and all the nations shall be
gathered to it, [a]to the name of the LORD, to
Jerusalem. No more shall they [b]follow[1] the dictates of their evil hearts.
18 "In those days [a]the house of Judah shall walk
with the house of Israel, and they shall come
together out of the land of [b]the north to [c]the land
that I have given as an inheritance to your fathers.
**19** "But I said:

'How can I put you among the children
And give you [a]a pleasant land,
A beautiful heritage of the hosts of nations?'

"And I said:

'You shall call Me, [b]"My Father,"
And not turn away from Me.'
20 Surely, *as* a wife treacherously departs from
her [1]husband,
So [a]have you dealt treacherously with Me,
O house of Israel," says the LORD.

**21** A voice was heard on [a]the desolate heights,
Weeping *and* supplications of the children of
Israel.
For they have perverted their way;
They have forgotten the LORD their God.

22 "Return, you backsliding children,
*And* I will [a]heal your backslidings."

"Indeed we do come to You,
For You are the LORD our God.
23 [a]Truly, in vain *is salvation hoped for* from the
hills,
*And from* the multitude of mountains;
[b]Truly, in the LORD our God
*Is* the salvation of Israel.
24 [a]For shame has devoured
The labor of our fathers from our youth—
Their flocks and their herds,
Their sons and their daughters.
25 We lie down in our shame,
And our [1]reproach covers us.
[a]For we have sinned against the LORD our
God,
We and our fathers,
From our youth even to this day,
And [b]have not obeyed the voice of the LORD
our God."

## *Jeremiah Laments over Judah*

**4** "If you will return, O Israel,"
says the LORD,
[a]"Return to Me;
And if you will put away your abominations
out of My sight,
Then you shall not be moved.
2 [a]And you shall swear, 'The LORD lives,'
[b]In truth, in [1]judgment, and in righteousness;
[c]The nations shall bless themselves in Him,
And in Him they shall [d]glory."

**3** For thus says the LORD to the men of Judah
and Jerusalem:

[a]"Break up your [1]fallow ground,
And [b]do not sow among thorns.
4 [a]Circumcise yourselves to the LORD,
And take away the foreskins of your hearts,
You men of Judah
and inhabitants of Jerusalem,
Lest My fury come forth like fire,
And burn so that no one can quench *it,*
Because of the evil of your doings."

2 [b]Prov. 23:28 [c]Jer. 2:7 [1]Kt. *been violated*
3 [a]Lev. 26:19 [b]Zeph. 3:5
4 [a]Prov. 2:17 [b]Jer. 2:2
5 [a][Is. 57:16]
6 [a]Jer. 7:24 [b]Jer. 2:20
7 [a]2 Kin. 17:13 [b]Ezek. 16:47, 48
8 [a]Ezek. 23:9 [b]2 Kin. 17:6 [c]Ezek. 23:11
9 [a]Jer. 2:7 [b]Jer. 2:27
10 [a]Jer. 12:2
11 [a]Ezek. 16:51, 52
12 [a]2 Kin. 17:6 [b]Ps. 86:15
13 [a]Deut. 30:1, 2 [b]Ezek. 16:15 [c]Jer. 2:25 [d]Deut. 12:2 [1]Lit. *ways*
14 [a]Hos. 2:19, 20 [b]Jer. 31:6 [c][Rom. 11:5]
15 [a]Eph. 4:11 [b]Acts 20:28
16 [a]Is. 49:19 [b]Is. 65:17
17 [a]Is. 60:9 [b]Deut. 29:19 [1]*walk after the stubbornness* or *imagination*
18 [a]Is. 11:13 [b]Jer. 31:8 [c]Amos 9:15
19 [a]Ps. 106:24 [b]Is. 63:16
20 [a]Is. 48:8 [1]Lit. *companion*
21 [a]Is. 15:2
22 [a]Hos. 6:1; 14:4
23 [a]Ps. 121:1, 2 [b]Ps. 3:8
24 [a]Hos. 9:10
25 [a]Ezra 9:6, 7 [b]Jer. 22:21 [1]*disgrace*

CHAPTER 4
1 [a]Joel 2:12
2 [a]Deut. 10:20 [b]Zech. 8:8 [c][Gen. 22:18] [d]1 Cor. 1:31 [1]*justice*
3 [a]Hos. 10:12 [b]Matt. 13:7 [1]*untilled*
4 [a]Deut. 10:16; 30:6

**5** Declare in Judah and proclaim in Jerusalem, and say:

[a]"Blow the trumpet in the land;
Cry, 'Gather together,'
And say, [b]'Assemble yourselves,
And let us go into the fortified cities.'
6 Set up the [1]standard toward Zion.
Take refuge! Do not delay!
For I will bring disaster from the [a]north,
And great destruction."

7 [a]The lion has come up from his thicket,
And [b]the destroyer of nations is on his way.
He has gone forth from his place
[c]To make your land desolate.
Your cities will be laid waste,
Without inhabitant.
8 For this, [a]clothe yourself with sackcloth,
Lament and wail.
For the fierce anger of the LORD
Has not turned back from us.

9 "And it shall come to pass in that day," says the LORD,
"*That* the heart of the king shall perish,
And the heart of the princes;
The priests shall be astonished,
And the prophets shall wonder."

**10** Then I said, "Ah, Lord GOD!
[a]Surely You have greatly deceived
this people and Jerusalem,
[b]Saying, 'You shall have peace,'
Whereas the sword reaches to the [1]heart."

**11** At that time it will be said
To this people and to Jerusalem,
[a]"A dry wind of the desolate heights *blows* in the wilderness
Toward the daughter of My people—
Not to fan or to cleanse—
12 A wind too strong for these will come for Me;
Now [a]I will also speak judgment against them."

13 "Behold, he shall come up like clouds,
And [a]his chariots like a whirlwind.
[b]His horses are swifter than eagles.
Woe to us, for we are plundered!"

14 O Jerusalem, [a]wash your heart from
wickedness,
That you may be saved.
How long shall your evil thoughts lodge
within you?
15 For a voice declares [a]from Dan
And proclaims [1]affliction
from Mount Ephraim:
16 "Make mention to the nations,
Yes, proclaim against Jerusalem,
*That* watchers come from a [a]far country
And raise their voice against the cities of Judah.
17 [a]Like keepers of a field
they are against her all around,
Because she has been rebellious against Me,"
says the LORD.
18 "Your[a] ways and your doings
Have procured these *things* for you.
This *is* your wickedness,
Because it is bitter,
Because it reaches to your heart."

**19** O my [a]soul, my soul!
I am pained in my very heart!
My heart makes a noise in me;
I cannot hold my peace,
Because you have heard, O my soul,
The sound of the trumpet,
The alarm of war.
20 [a]Destruction upon destruction is cried,
For the whole land is plundered.
Suddenly [b]my tents are plundered,
*And* my curtains in a moment.
21 How long will I see the [1]standard,
*And* hear the sound of the trumpet?

22 "For My people *are* foolish,
They have not known Me.
They *are* [1]silly children,
And they have no understanding.
[a]They *are* wise to do evil,
But to do good they have no knowledge."

**23** [a]I beheld the earth, and indeed
*it was* [b]without form, and void;
And the heavens, they *had* no light.
24 [a]I beheld the mountains,
and indeed they trembled,
And all the hills moved back and forth.
25 I beheld, and indeed *there was* no man,
And [a]all the birds of the heavens had fled.
26 I beheld, and indeed the fruitful land *was* a [a]wilderness,
And all its cities were broken down
At the presence of the LORD,
By His fierce anger.

**27** For thus says the LORD:

"The whole land shall be desolate;
[a]Yet I will not make a full end.
28 For this [a]shall the earth mourn,
And [b]the heavens above be black,
Because I have spoken.
I have [c]purposed and [d]will not relent,
Nor will I turn back from it.
29 The whole city shall flee from the noise of
the horsemen and bowmen.
They shall go into thickets
and climb up on the rocks.
Every city *shall be* forsaken,
And not a man shall dwell in it.

30 "And *when* you *are* plundered,
What will you do?
Though you clothe yourself with crimson,
Though you adorn *yourself*
with ornaments of gold,
[a]Though you enlarge your eyes with paint,
In vain you will make yourself fair;
[b]*Your* lovers will despise you;
They will seek your life.

31 "For I have heard a voice
as of a woman in [1]labor,
The anguish as of her
who brings forth her first child,
The voice of the daughter of Zion bewailing herself;
She [a]spreads her hands, *saying*,
'Woe *is* me now, for my soul is [2]weary
Because of murderers!'

*The Sins of Judah Outlined*

**5** "Run to and fro through the streets
of Jerusalem;
See now and know;

**5** [a]Jer. 6:1; Hos. 8:1 [b]Josh. 10:20; Jer. 8:14
**6** [a]Jer. 1:13–15; 6:1, 22; 50:17 [1]*banner*
**7** [a]2 Kin. 24:1; Dan. 7:4 [b]Jer. 25:9; Ezek. 26:7–10 [c]Is. 1:7; 6:11; Jer. 2:15
**8** [a]Is. 22:12; Jer. 6:26
**10** [a]2 Kin. 25:10–12; Ezek. 14:9; 2 Thess. 2:11 [b]Jer. 5:12; 14:13 [1]Lit. *soul*
**11** [a]Jer. 51:1; Ezek. 17:10; Hos. 13:15
**12** [a]Jer. 1:16
**13** [a]Is. 5:28 [b]Deut. 28:49; Lam. 4:19; Hos. 8:1; Hab. 1:8
**14** [a]Prov. 1:22; Is. 1:16; Jer. 13:27; James 4:8
**15** [a]Jer. 8:16; 50:17 [1]Or *wickedness*
**16** [a]Is. 39:3; Jer. 5:15
**17** [a]2 Kin. 25:1, 4
**18** [a]Ps. 107:17; Is. 50:1; Jer. 2:17, 19
**19** [a]2 Kin. 25:11; 2 Chr. 36:20; Is. 15:5; 16:11; 21:3; 22:4; Jer. 9:1, 10; 20:9
**20** [a]Ps. 42:7; Ezek. 7:26 [b]Jer. 10:20
**21** [1]*banner*
**22** [a]Jer. 9:3; 13:23; Rom. 16:19; 1 Cor. 14:20 [1]*foolish*
**23** [a]Is. 24:19 [b]Gen. 1:2
**24** [a]Is. 5:25; Jer. 10:10; Ezek. 38:20
**25** [a]Jer. 9:10; 12:4; Zeph. 1:3
**26** [a]Jer. 9:10
**27** [a]Jer. 5:10, 18; 30:11; 46:28
**28** [a]Jer. 12:4, 11; 14:2; Hos. 4:3 [b]Is. 5:30; 50:3; Joel 2:30, 31 [c]Is. 46:10, 11; [Dan. 4:35] [d][Num. 23:19]; Jer. 7:16; 23:30; 30:24
**30** [a]2 Kin. 9:30; Ezek. 23:40 [b]Jer. 22:20, 22; Lam. 1:2, 19; Ezek. 23:9, 10, 22
**31** [a]Is. 1:15; Lam. 1:17 [1]*childbirth* [2]*faint*

And seek in her open places
[a]If you can find a man,
[b]If there is *anyone* who executes [1]judgment,
Who seeks the truth,
[c]And I will pardon her.
2 [a]Though they say, '*As* [b]the LORD lives,'
Surely they [c]swear falsely."

3 O LORD, *are* not [a]Your eyes on the truth?
You have [b]stricken them,
But they have not grieved;
You have consumed them,
But [c]they have refused to receive correction.
They have made their faces harder
than rock;
They have refused to return.

4 Therefore I said, "Surely these *are* poor.
They are foolish;
For [a]they do not know the way of the LORD,
The judgment of their God.
5 I will go to the great men and speak to them,
For [a]they have known the way of the LORD,
The judgment of their God."

But these have altogether [b]broken the yoke
*And* burst the bonds.
6 Therefore [a]a lion from the forest
shall slay them,
[b]A wolf of the deserts shall destroy them;
[c]A leopard will watch over their cities.
Everyone who goes out from there shall be
torn in pieces,
Because their transgressions are many;
Their backslidings have increased.

7 "How shall I pardon you for this?
Your children have forsaken Me
And [a]sworn by *those* [b]*that are* not gods.
[c]When I had fed them to the full,
Then they committed adultery
And assembled themselves by troops
in the harlots' houses.
8 [a]They were *like* well-fed lusty stallions;
Every one neighed after his neighbor's wife.
9 Shall I not punish *them* for these *things?*"
says the LORD.
"And shall I not [a]avenge Myself
on such a nation as this?

10 "Go up on her walls and destroy,
But do not [1]make a [a]complete end.
Take away her branches,
For they *are* not the LORD's.
11 For [a]the house of Israel
and the house of Judah
Have dealt very treacherously with Me," says
the LORD.

12 [a]They have lied about the LORD,
And said, [b]"*It is* not He.
[c]Neither will [1]evil come upon us,
Nor shall we see sword or famine.
13 And the prophets become wind,
For the word *is* not in them.
Thus shall it be done to them."

14 Therefore thus says the LORD God of hosts:

"Because you speak this word,
[a]Behold, I will make My words in your mouth
fire,
And this people wood,
And it shall devour them.
15 Behold, I will bring a [a]nation against you
[b]from afar,
O house of Israel," says the LORD.
"It *is* a mighty nation,
It *is* an ancient nation,
A nation whose language you do not know,
Nor can you understand what they say.
16 Their quiver *is* like an open tomb;
They *are* all mighty men.
17 And they shall eat up your [a]harvest
and your bread,
*Which* your sons and daughters should eat.
They shall eat up your flocks and your herds;
They shall eat up your vines
and your fig trees;
They shall destroy your fortified cities,
In which you trust, with the sword.

18 "Nevertheless in those days," says the LORD,
"I [a]will not [1]make a complete end of you.
19 "And it will be when you say, [a]'Why does the
LORD our God do all these *things* to us?' then you
shall answer them, 'Just as you have [b]forsaken Me
and served foreign gods in your land, so [c]you shall
serve aliens in a land *that is* not yours.'

20 "Declare this in the house of Jacob
And proclaim it in Judah, saying,
21 'Hear this now, O [a]foolish people,
Without [1]understanding,
Who have eyes and see not,
And who have ears and hear not:
22 [a]Do you not fear Me?' says the LORD.
'Will you not tremble at My presence,
Who have placed the sand
as the [b]bound of the sea,
By a perpetual decree,
that it cannot pass beyond it?
And though its waves toss to and fro,
Yet they cannot prevail;
Though they roar,
yet they cannot pass over it.
23 But this people has a defiant and rebellious
heart;
They have revolted and departed.
24 They do not say in their heart,
"Let us now fear the LORD our God,
[a]Who gives rain, both the [b]former
and the latter, in its season.
[c]He reserves for us the appointed weeks of
the harvest."
25 [a]Your iniquities have turned these *things*
away,
And your sins have withheld good from you.

26 'For among My people are found wicked *men;*
They [a]lie in wait as one who sets snares;
They set a trap;
They catch men.
27 As a cage is full of birds,
So their houses *are* full of deceit.
Therefore they have become great
and grown rich.
28 They have grown [a]fat, they are sleek;
Yes, they [1]surpass the deeds of the wicked;
They do not plead [b]the cause,
The cause of the fatherless;
[c]Yet they prosper,
And the right of the needy
they do not defend.
29 [a]Shall I not punish *them* for these *things?*'
says the LORD.

CHAPTER 5
**1** [a]Ezek. 22:30 [b]Gen. 18:23–32 [c]Gen. 18:26 [1]*justice*
**2** [a]Titus 1:16 [b]Jer. 4:2 [c]Jer. 7:9
**3** [a][2 Chr. 16:9] [b]Is. 1:5; 9:13 [c]Zeph. 3:2
**4** [a]Jer. 8:7
**5** [a]Mic. 3:1 [b]Ps. 2:3
**6** [a]Jer. 4:7 [b]Zeph. 3:3 [c]Hos. 13:7
**7** [a]Zeph. 1:5 [b]Deut. 32:21 [c]Deut. 32:15
**8** [a]Ezek. 22:11
**9** [a]Jer. 9:9
**10** [a]Jer. 4:27 [1]*completely destroy*
**11** [a]Jer. 3:6, 7, 20
**12** [a]2 Chr. 36:16 [b]Jer. 23:17 [c]Jer. 14:13 [1]*disaster*
**14** [a]Jer. 1:9; 23:29
**15** [a]Deut. 28:49 [b]Jer. 4:16
**17** [a]Lev. 26:16
**18** [a]Jer. 30:11 [1]*completely destroy*
**19** [a]Deut. 29:24–29 [b]Jer. 1:16; 2:13 [c]Deut. 28:48
**21** [a]Matt. 13:14 [1]Lit. *heart*
**22** [a][Rev. 15:4] [b]Job 26:10
**24** [a]Acts 14:17 [b]Joel 2:23 [c][Gen. 8:22]
**25** [a]Jer. 3:3
**26** [a]Hab. 1:15
**28** [a]Deut. 32:15 [b]Zech. 7:10 [c]Job 12:6 [1]Or *pass over* or *overlook*
**29** [a]Mal. 3:5

'Shall I not avenge Myself
on such a nation as this?'

30 "An astonishing and [a]horrible thing
Has been committed in the land:
31 The prophets prophesy [a]falsely,
And the priests rule by their *own* power;
And My people [b]love *to have it* so.
But what will you do in the end?

## *The Destruction of Judah*

6 "O you children of Benjamin,
Gather yourselves to flee from the midst of
Jerusalem!
Blow the trumpet in Tekoa,
And set up a signal-fire in [a]Beth Haccerem;
[b]For disaster appears out of the north,
And great destruction.
2 I have likened the daughter of Zion
To a lovely and delicate woman.
3 The [a]shepherds with their flocks shall come
to her.
They shall pitch *their* tents against her all
around.
Each one shall pasture in his own place."

4 "Prepare[a] war against her;
Arise, and let us go up [b]at noon.
Woe to us, for the day goes away,
For the shadows of the evening
are lengthening.
5 Arise, and let us go by night,
And let us destroy her palaces."

6 For thus has the LORD of hosts said:

"Cut down trees,
And build a mound against Jerusalem.
This *is* the city to be punished.
She *is* full of oppression in her midst.
7 [a]As a fountain [1]wells up with water,
So she wells up with her wickedness.
[b]Violence and plundering are heard in her.
Before Me continually *are* [2]grief and wounds.
8 Be instructed, O Jerusalem,
Lest [a]My soul depart from you;
Lest I make you desolate,
A land not inhabited."

9 Thus says the LORD of hosts:

"They shall thoroughly glean as a vine the
remnant of Israel;
As a grape-gatherer,
put your hand back into the branches."

10 To whom shall I speak and give warning,
That they may hear?
Indeed their [a]ear *is* uncircumcised,
And they cannot give heed.
Behold, [b]the word of the LORD is a reproach
to them;
They have no delight in it.
11 Therefore I am full of the fury of the LORD.
[a]I am weary of holding *it* in.
"I will pour it out [b]on the children outside,
And on the assembly of young men together;
For even the husband shall be taken with the
wife,
The aged with *him who is* full of days.
12 And [a]their houses shall be turned over to
others,
Fields and wives together;
For I will stretch out My hand
Against the inhabitants of the land," says the
LORD.
13 "Because from the least of them
even to the greatest of them,
Everyone *is* given to [a]covetousness;
And from the prophet even to the [b]priest,
Everyone deals falsely.
14 They have also [a]healed the [1]hurt
of My people [2]slightly,
[b]Saying, 'Peace, peace!'
When *there is* no peace.
15 Were they [a]ashamed when they had
committed abomination?
No! They were not at all ashamed;
Nor did they know how to blush.
Therefore they shall fall among those who
fall;
At the time I punish them,
They shall be cast down," says the LORD.

16 Thus says the LORD:

"Stand in the ways and see,
And ask for the [a]old paths,
where the good way *is*,
And walk in it;
Then you will find [b]rest for your souls.
But they said, 'We will not walk *in it*.'
17 Also, I set [a]watchmen over you, *saying*,
[b]'Listen to the sound of the trumpet!'
But they said, 'We will not listen.'
18 Therefore hear, you nations,
And know, O congregation,
what *is* among them.
19 [a]Hear, O earth!
Behold, I will certainly bring [b]calamity on
this people—
[c]The fruit of their thoughts,
Because they have not heeded My words
Nor My law, but rejected it.
20 [a]For what purpose to Me
Comes frankincense [b]from Sheba,
And [c]sweet cane from a far country?
[d]Your burnt offerings *are* not acceptable,
Nor your sacrifices sweet to Me."

21 Therefore thus says the LORD:

"Behold, I will lay stumbling blocks before
this people,
And the fathers and the sons together shall
fall on them.
The neighbor and his friend shall perish."

22 Thus says the LORD:

"Behold, a people comes from the [a]north
country,
And a great nation will be raised from the
farthest parts of the earth.
23 They will lay hold on bow and spear;
They *are* cruel and have no mercy;
Their voice [a]roars like the sea;
And they ride on horses,
As men of war set in array against you, O
daughter of Zion."

24 We have heard the report of it;
Our hands grow feeble.
[a]Anguish has taken hold of us,
Pain as of a woman in [1]labor.
25 Do not go out into the field,
Nor walk by the way.
Because of the sword of the enemy,
Fear *is* on every side.

30 [a]Jer. 23:14; Hos. 6:10; 2 Tim. 4:3
31 [a]Jer. 14:14; Ezek. 13:6 [b]Mic. 2:11

CHAPTER 6
1 [a]Neh. 3:14 [b]Jer. 4:6
3 [a]2 Kin. 25:1–4; Jer. 4:17; 12:10
4 [a]Jer. 51:27; Joel 3:9 [b]Jer. 15:8; Zeph. 2:4
7 [a]Is. 57:20 [b]Ps. 55:9 [1]*gushes* [2]*sickness*
8 [a]Ezek. 23:18; Hos. 9:12
10 [a]Ex. 6:12; Jer. 5:21; 7:26; [Acts 7:51] [b]Jer. 8:9; 20:8
11 [a]Jer. 20:9 [b]Jer. 9:21
12 [a]Deut. 28:30; Jer. 8:10; 38:22
13 [a]Is. 56:11; Jer. 8:10; 22:17 [b]Jer. 5:31; 23:11; Mic. 3:5, 11
14 [a]Jer. 8:11–15; Ezek. 13:10 [b]Jer. 4:10; 23:17 [1]Lit. *crushing* [2]Superficially
15 [a]Jer. 3:3; 8:12
16 [a]Is. 8:20; Jer. 18:15; Mal. 4:4; Luke 16:29 [b]Matt. 11:29
17 [a]Is. 21:11; 58:1; Jer. 25:4; Ezek. 3:17; Hab. 2:1 [b]Deut. 4:1
19 [a]Is. 1:2 [b]Jer. 19:3, 15 [c]Prov. 1:31
20 [a]Ps. 40:6; 50:7–9; Is. 1:11; 66:3; Amos 5:21; Mic. 6:6, 7 [b]Is. 60:6 [c]Is. 43:24 [d]Jer. 7:21–23
22 [a]Jer. 1:15; 10:22; 50:41–43
23 [a]Is. 5:30
24 [a]Jer. 4:31; 13:21; 49:24 [1]*childbirth*

26 O daughter of my people,
[a]Dress in sackcloth
[b]And roll about in ashes!
[c]Make mourning *as for* an only son, most bitter lamentation;
For the plunderer will suddenly come upon us.

**27** "I have set you *as* an assayer
*and* [a]a fortress among My people,
That you may know and test their way.
28 [a]They *are* all stubborn rebels,
[b]walking as slanderers.
*They are* [c]bronze and iron,
They *are* all corrupters;
29 The bellows blow fiercely,
The lead is consumed by the fire;
The smelter refines in vain,
For the wicked are not drawn off.
30 *People* will call them [a]rejected silver,
Because the LORD has rejected them."

### *Jeremiah Calls for Repentance*

**7** The word that came to Jeremiah from the
LORD, saying,
2 [a]"Stand in the gate of the LORD's house, and
proclaim there this word, and say, 'Hear the word
of the LORD, all *you of* Judah who enter in at these
gates to worship the LORD!' "
3 Thus says the LORD of hosts, the God of Israel:
[a]"Amend your ways and your doings, and I will
cause you to dwell in this place.
4 [a]"Do not trust in these lying words, saying,
'The temple of the LORD, the temple of the LORD,
the temple of the LORD *are* these.'
5 "For if you thoroughly amend your ways and
your doings, if you thoroughly [a]execute [1]judgment
between a man and his neighbor,
6 "*if* you do not oppress the stranger, the fatherless, and the widow, and do not shed innocent
blood in this place, [a]or walk after other gods to
your hurt,
7 [a]"then I will cause you to dwell in this place,
in [b]the land that I gave to your fathers forever and
ever.
**8** "Behold, you trust in [a]lying words that cannot
profit.
9 [a]"Will you steal, murder, commit adultery,
swear falsely, burn incense to Baal, and [b]walk
after other gods whom you do not know,
10 [a]"and *then* come and stand before Me in this
house [b]which is called by My name, and say, 'We
are delivered to do all these abominations'?
11 "Has [a]this house, which is called by My name,
become a [b]den of thieves in your eyes? Behold, I,
even I, have seen *it*," says the LORD.
**12** "But go now to [a]My place which *was* in Shiloh, [b]where I set My name at the first, and see
[c]what I did to it because of the wickedness of My
people Israel.
13 "And now, because you have done all these
works," says the LORD, "and I spoke to you,
[a]rising up early and speaking, but you did not
hear, and I [b]called you, but you did not answer,
14 "therefore I will do to the house which is
called by My name, in which you trust, and to this
place which I gave to you and your fathers, as I
have done to [a]Shiloh.
15 "And I will cast you out of My sight, [a]as I have
cast out all your brethren—[b]the whole posterity of
Ephraim.

**26** [a]Jer. 4:8 [b]Mic. 1:10 [c][Zech. 12:10]
**27** [a]Jer. 1:18
**28** [a]Jer. 5:23 [b]Jer. 9:4 [c]Ezek. 22:18
**30** [a]Is. 1:22

CHAPTER 7
**2** [a]Jer. 17:19; 26:2
**3** [a]Jer. 4:1; 18:11; 26:13
**4** [a]Mic. 3:11
**5** [a]Jer. 21:12; 22:3 [1]*justice*
**6** [a]Deut. 6:14, 15
**7** [a]Deut. 4:40 [b]Jer. 3:18
**8** [a]Jer. 5:31; 14:13, 14
**9** [a]1 Kin. 18:21 [b]Ex. 20:3
**10** [a]Ezek. 23:39 [b]Jer. 7:11, 14; 32:34; 34:15
**11** [a]Is. 56:7 [b]Matt. 21:13
**12** [a]Josh. 18:1 [b]Deut. 12:11 [c]1 Sam. 4:10
**13** [a]2 Chr. 36:15 [b]Prov. 1:24
**14** [a]1 Sam. 4:10, 11
**15** [a]2 Kin. 17:23 [b]Ps. 78:67
**16** [a]Ex. 32:10; Jer. 11:14 [b]Jer. 15:1
**18** [a]Jer. 44:17 [b]Jer. 19:13
**19** [a]Deut. 32:16, 21
**21** [a]Jer. 6:20
**22** [a][Hos. 6:6]
**23** [a]Deut. 6:3 [b][Ex. 19:5, 6]
**24** [a]Ps. 81:11 [b]Deut. 29:19 [c]Jer. 32:33 [1]*walked in* [2]*stubbornness,* or *imagination* [3]Lit. *they were*
**25** [a]2 Chr. 36:15
**26** [a]Jer. 11:8 [b]Neh. 9:17 [c]Jer. 16:12
**27** [a]Ezek. 2:7
**28** [a]Jer. 5:3 [b]Jer. 9:3
**29** [a]Mic. 1:16
**30** [a]Dan. 9:27; 11:31 [1]*defile*
**31** [a]2 Kin. 23:10 [b]Ps. 106:38 [c]Deut. 17:3
**32** [a]Jer. 19:6 [b]2 Kin. 23:10
**33** [a]Jer. 9:22; 19:11
**34** [a]Is. 24:7, 8

**16** "Therefore [a]do not pray for this people, nor lift
up a cry or prayer for them, nor make intercession
to Me; [b]for I will not hear you.
17 "Do you not see what they do in the cities of
Judah and in the streets of Jerusalem?
18 [a]"The children gather wood, the fathers kindle
the fire, and the women knead dough, to make
cakes for the queen of heaven; and *they* [b]pour out
drink offerings to other gods, that they may
provoke Me to anger.
19 [a]"Do they provoke Me to anger?" says the
LORD. "*Do they* not *provoke* themselves, to the
shame of their own faces?"
20 Therefore thus says the Lord GOD: "Behold,
My anger and My fury will be poured out on this
place—on man and on beast, on the trees of the
field and on the fruit of the ground. And it will
burn and not be quenched."
**21** Thus says the LORD of hosts, the God of Israel:
[a]"Add your burnt offerings to your sacrifices and
eat meat.
22 [a]"For I did not speak to your fathers, or
command them in the day that I brought them
out of the land of Egypt, concerning burnt offerings or sacrifices.
23 "But this is what I commanded them, saying,
[a]'Obey My voice, and [b]I will be your God, and you
shall be My people. And walk in all the ways that
I have commanded you, that it may be well with
you.'
24 [a]"Yet they did not obey or incline their ear,
but [b]followed[1] the counsels *and* the [2]dictates of
their evil hearts, and [c]went[3] backward and not
forward.
25 "Since the day that your fathers came out of
the land of Egypt until this day, I have even [a]sent
to you all My servants the prophets, daily rising
up early and sending *them*.
26 [a]"Yet they did not obey Me or incline their ear,
but [b]stiffened their neck. [c]They did worse than
their fathers.
**27** "Therefore [a]you shall speak all these words to
them, but they will not obey you. You shall also
call to them, but they will not answer you.
**28** "So you shall say to them, 'This *is* a nation
that does not obey the voice of the LORD their God
[a]nor receive correction. [b]Truth has perished and
has been cut off from their mouth.
29 [a]'Cut off your hair and cast *it* away, and take
up a lamentation on the desolate heights; for the
LORD has rejected and forsaken the generation of
His wrath.'
30 "For the children of Judah have done evil in
My sight," says the LORD. [a]"They have set their
abominations in the house which is called by My
name, to [1]pollute it.
31 "And they have built the [a]high places of
Tophet, which *is* in the Valley of the Son of
Hinnom, to [b]burn their sons and their daughters in
the fire, [c]which I did not command, nor did it
come into My heart.
**32** "Therefore behold, [a]the days are coming,"
says the LORD, "when it will no more be called
Tophet, or the Valley of the Son of Hinnom, but
the Valley of Slaughter; [b]for they will bury in
Tophet until there is no room.
33 "The [a]corpses of this people will be food for
the birds of the heaven and for the beasts of the
earth. And no one will frighten *them away*.
34 "Then I will cause to [a]cease from the cities of
Judah and from the streets of Jerusalem the voice

of mirth and the voice of gladness, the voice of the
bridegroom and the voice of the bride. For [b]the
land shall be desolate.

*Jeremiah Mourns for His People*

**8** "At that time," says the LORD, "they shall
bring out the bones of the kings of Judah, and
the bones of its princes, and the bones of the
priests, and the bones of the prophets, and the
bones of the inhabitants of Jerusalem, out of their
graves.
2 "They shall spread them before the sun and
the moon and all the host of heaven, which they
have loved and which they have served and after
which they have walked, which they have sought
and [a]which they have worshiped. They shall not
be gathered [b]nor buried; they shall be like refuse
on the face of the earth.
3 "Then [a]death shall be chosen rather than life
by all the [1]residue of those who remain of this evil
family, who remain in all the places where I have
driven them," says the LORD of hosts.
**4** "Moreover you shall say to them, 'Thus says
the LORD:

"Will they fall and not rise?
Will one turn away and not return?
5 Why has this people [a]slidden back,
Jerusalem, in a perpetual backsliding?
[b]They hold fast to deceit,
[c]They refuse to return.
6 [a]I listened and heard,
*But* they do not speak aright.
[b]No man repented of his wickedness,
Saying, 'What have I done?'
Everyone turned to his own course,
As the horse rushes into the battle.

7 "Even [a]the stork in the heavens
Knows her appointed times;
And the turtledove, the swift,
and the swallow
Observe the time of their coming.
But [b]My people do not know the judgment of
the LORD.

**8** "How can you say, 'We *are* wise,
[a]And the law of the LORD *is* with us'?
Look, the false pen of the scribe certainly
works falsehood.
9 [a]The wise men are ashamed,
They are dismayed and taken.
Behold, they have rejected the word
of the LORD;
So [b]what wisdom do they have?
10 Therefore [a]I will give their wives to others,
*And* their fields to those who will inherit
*them;*
Because from the least even to the greatest
Everyone is given to [b]covetousness;
From the prophet even to the priest
Everyone deals falsely.
11 For they have [a]healed the hurt of the
daughter of My people [1]slightly,
Saying, [b]'Peace, peace!'
When *there is* no peace.
12 Were they [a]ashamed when they had
committed abomination?
No! They were not at all ashamed,
Nor did they know how to blush.
Therefore they shall fall among those who
fall;

**34** [b]Lev. 26:33; Is. 1:7; Jer. 4:27

CHAPTER 8

**2** [a]2 Kin. 23:5; Jer. 19:13; Ezek. 8:16; Zeph. 1:5; Acts 7:42 [b]Jer. 22:19

**3** [a]Job 3:21, 22; 7:15, 16; Jon. 4:3; Rev. 9:6 [1]*remnant*

**5** [a]Jer. 7:24 [b]Jer. 9:6 [c]Jer. 5:3

**6** [a]Ps. 14:2; [Is. 30:18; Mal. 3:16; 2 Pet. 3:9] [b]Ezek. 22:30; Mic. 7:2; Rev. 9:20

**7** [a]Prov. 6:6–8; Song 2:12; Is. 1:3; Matt. 16:2, 3 [b]Jer. 5:4; 9:3

**8** [a]Rom. 2:17

**9** [a]Is. 19:11; Jer. 6:15; [1 Cor. 1:27] [b]Is. 44:25; Jer. 4:22

**10** [a]Deut. 28:30; Amos 5:11; Zeph. 1:13 [b]Is. 56:11; 57:17; Jer. 6:13

**11** [a]Jer. 6:14 [b]Ezek. 13:10 [1]Superficially

**12** [a]Ps. 52:1, 7; Is. 3:9; Jer. 3:3; 6:15; Zeph. 3:5

**13** [a]Jer. 5:17; 7:20; Joel 1:17 [b]Matt. 21:19; Luke 13:6 [c]Deut. 28:39, 40 [1]Or *take them away*

**14** [a]Jer. 4:5 [b]Deut. 29:18; Ps. 69:21; Jer. 9:15; Lam. 3:19; Matt. 27:34 [1]Bitter or poisonous water

**15** [a]Jer. 14:19

**16** [a]Judg. 18:29; Jer. 4:15 [b]Jer. 47:3

**17** [a]Ps. 58:4, 5

**19** [a]Is. 39:3; Jer. 5:15

**21** [a]Jer. 9:1 [b]Jer. 14:2; Joel 2:6; Nah. 2:10

**22** [a]Gen. 37:25; Jer. 46:11

CHAPTER 9

**1** [a]Is. 22:4; Jer. 10:19; Lam. 2:18

**2** [a]Jer. 5:7, 8; 23:10; Hos. 4:2

**3** [a]Ps. 64:3; Is. 59:4; Jer. 9:8; Hos. 4:1, 2

In the time of their punishment
They shall be cast down," says the LORD.

**13** "I will surely [1]consume them," says the LORD.
"No grapes *shall be* [a]on the vine,
Nor figs on the [b]fig tree,
And the leaf shall fade;
And *the things* I have given them
shall [c]pass away from them."'"

14 "Why do we sit still?
[a]Assemble yourselves,
And let us enter the fortified cities,
And let us be silent there.
For the LORD our God has put us to silence
And given us [b]water[1] of gall to drink,
Because we have sinned against the LORD.

15 "*We* [a]looked for peace, but no good *came;*
And for a time of health,
and there was trouble!
16 The snorting of His horses
was heard from [a]Dan.
The whole land trembled at the sound of the
neighing of His [b]strong ones;
For they have come and devoured the land
and all that is in it,
The city and those who dwell in it."

17 "For behold, I will send serpents among you,
Vipers which cannot be [a]charmed,
And they shall bite you," says the LORD.

**18** I would comfort myself in sorrow;
My heart *is* faint in me.
19 Listen! The voice,
The cry of the daughter of my people
From [a]a far country:
"*Is* not the LORD in Zion?
*Is* not her King in her?"

"Why have they provoked Me to anger
With their carved images—
With foreign idols?"

20 "The harvest is past,
The summer is ended,
And we are not saved!"

21 [a]For the hurt of the daughter of my people I
am hurt.
I am [b]mourning;
Astonishment has taken hold of me.
22 *Is there* no [a]balm in Gilead,
*Is there* no physician there?
Why then is there no recovery
For the health of the daughter of my people?

*Disobedience Brings God's Judgment*

**9** Oh, [a]that my head were waters,
And my eyes a fountain of tears,
That I might weep day and night
For the slain of the daughter of my people!
2 Oh, that I had in the wilderness
A lodging place for travelers;
That I might leave my people,
And go from them!
For [a]they *are* all adulterers,
An assembly of treacherous men.

3 "And *like* their bow
[a]they have bent their tongues *for* lies.
They are not valiant for the truth on the
earth.

For they proceed from [b]evil to evil,
And they [c]do not know Me," says the LORD.
4 "Everyone[a] take heed to his [1]neighbor,
And do not trust any brother;
For every brother will utterly supplant,
And every neighbor will [b]walk with
slanderers.
5 Everyone will [a]deceive his neighbor,
And will not speak the truth;
They have taught their tongue to speak lies;
Weary themselves to commit iniquity.
6 Your dwelling place *is* in the midst of deceit;
Through deceit they refuse to know Me,"
says the LORD.

**7** Therefore thus says the LORD of hosts:

"Behold, [a]I will refine them and [1]try them;
[b]For how shall I deal with the daughter of My
people?
8 Their tongue *is* an arrow shot out;
It speaks [a]deceit;
*One* speaks [b]peaceably to his neighbor with
his mouth,
But [1]in his heart he [2]lies in wait.
9 [a]Shall I not punish them for these *things?"*
says the LORD.
"Shall I not avenge Myself
on such a nation as this?"

10 I will take up a weeping and wailing for the
mountains,
And [a]for the [1]dwelling places of the
wilderness a lamentation,
Because they are burned up,
So that no one can pass through;
Nor can *men* hear the voice of the cattle.
[b]Both the birds of the heavens
and the beasts have fled;
They are gone.

11 "I will make Jerusalem [a]a heap of ruins, [b]a
den of jackals.
I will make the cities of Judah desolate,
without an inhabitant."

**12** [a]Who *is* the wise man who may understand
this? And *who is he* to whom the mouth of the
LORD has spoken, that he may declare it? Why
does the land perish *and* burn up like a wilderness,
so that no one can pass through?
13 And the LORD said, "Because they have forsaken My law which I set before them, and have
[a]not obeyed My voice, nor walked according to it,
14 "but they have [a]walked according to the [1]dic-
tates of their own hearts and after the Baals,
[b]which their fathers taught them,"
15 therefore thus says the LORD of hosts, the God
of Israel: "Behold, I will [a]feed them, this people,
[b]with wormwood, and give them [1]water of gall to
drink.
16 "I will [a]scatter them also among the Gentiles,
whom neither they nor their fathers have known.
[b]And I will send a sword after them until I have
consumed them."

**17** Thus says the LORD of hosts:

"Consider and call for [a]the mourning women,
That they may come;
And send for skillful wailing women,
That they may come.
18 Let them make haste
And take up a wailing for us,
That [a]our eyes may run with tears,
And our eyelids gush with water.

19 For a voice of wailing is heard from Zion:
'How we are plundered!
We are greatly ashamed,
Because we have forsaken the land,
Because we have been cast out of [a]our
dwellings.'"

20 Yet hear the word of the LORD, O women,
And let your ear receive the word of His
mouth;
Teach your daughters wailing,
And everyone her neighbor a lamentation.
21 For death has come through our windows,
Has entered our palaces,
To kill off [a]the children—
[1]*no longer to be* outside!
*And* the young men—
[2]*no longer* on the streets!

22 Speak, "Thus says the LORD:

'Even the carcasses of men shall fall [a]as
refuse on the open field,
Like cuttings after the harvester,
And no one shall gather *them.'* "

**23** Thus says the LORD:

[a]"Let not the wise *man* glory in his wisdom,
Let not the mighty *man* glory in his [b]might,
Nor let the rich *man* glory in his riches;
24 But [a]let him who glories glory in this,
That he understands and knows Me,
That I *am* the LORD, exercising
lovingkindness, [1]judgment, and
righteousness in the earth.
[b]For in these I delight," says the LORD.

**25** "Behold, the days are coming," says the LORD,
"that [a]I will punish all *who are* circumcised with
the uncircumcised—
26 "Egypt, Judah, Edom, the people of Ammon,
Moab, and all *who are* in the [a]farthest corners,
who dwell in the wilderness. For all *these* nations
*are* uncircumcised, and all the house of Israel *are*
[b]uncircumcised in the heart."

## *God and the Idol*

**10** Hear the word which the LORD speaks to
you, O house of Israel.
2 Thus says the LORD:

[a]"Do not learn the way of the Gentiles;
Do not be dismayed at the signs of heaven,
For the Gentiles are dismayed at them.
3 For the customs of the peoples *are* [1]futile;
For [a]*one* cuts a tree from the forest,
The work of the hands of the workman, with
the ax.
4 They decorate it with silver and gold;
They [a]fasten it with nails and hammers
So that it will not topple.
5 They *are* upright, like a palm tree,
And [a]they cannot speak;
They must be [b]carried,
Because they cannot go *by themselves.*
Do not be afraid of them,
For [c]they cannot do evil,
Nor can they do any good."

**6** Inasmuch as *there is* none [a]like You, O LORD
(You *are* great,
and Your name *is* great in might),
7 [a]Who would not fear You,
O King of the nations?

**3** [b]Jer. 4:22; 13:23 [c]1 Sam. 2:12
**4** [a]Mic. 7:5, 6 [b]Jer. 6:28 [1]*friend*
**5** [a]Is. 59:4
**7** [a]Is. 1:25 [b]Hos. 11:8 [1]*test*
**8** [a]Ps. 12:2 [b]Ps. 55:21 [1]Inwardly he [2]*sets his ambush*
**9** [a]Jer. 5:9, 29
**10** [a]Hos. 4:3 [b]Jer. 4:25 [1]Or *pastures*
**11** [a]Is. 25:2 [b]Is. 13:22; 34:13
**12** [a]Hos. 14:9
**13** [a]Jer. 3:25; 7:24
**14** [a]Jer. 7:24; 11:8 [b]Gal. 1:14
**15** [a]Ps. 80:5 [b]Lam. 3:15 [1]Bitter or poisonous water
**16** [a]Lev. 26:33 [b]Ezek. 5:2
**17** [a]2 Chr. 35:25
**18** [a]Jer. 9:1; 14:17
**19** [a]Lev. 18:28
**21** [a]Jer. 6:11; 18:21 [1]Lit. *from outside* [2]Lit. *from the square*
**22** [a]Jer. 8:1, 2
**23** [a][Eccl. 9:11] [b]Ps. 33:16–18
**24** [a]1 Cor. 1:31 [b]Mic. 7:18 [1]*justice*
**25** [a][Rom. 2:28, 29]
**26** [a]Jer. 25:23 [b][Rom. 2:28]

CHAPTER 10
**2** [a][Lev. 18:3; 20:23]
**3** [a]Is. 40:19; 45:20 [1]Lit. *vanity*
**4** [a]Is. 41:7
**5** [a]Ps. 115:5 [b]Ps. 115:7 [c]Is. 41:23, 24
**6** [a]Ex. 15:11
**7** [a]Rev. 15:4

For this is Your rightful due,
For [b]among all the wise *men* of the nations,
And in all their kingdoms,
*There is* none like You.
8 But they are altogether [a]dull-hearted and foolish;
A wooden idol *is* a [1]worthless doctrine.
9 Silver is beaten into plates;
It is brought from Tarshish,
And [a]gold from Uphaz,
The work of the craftsman
And of the hands of the metalsmith;
Blue and purple *are* their clothing;
They *are* all [b]the work of skillful *men.*
10 But the LORD *is* the true God;
He *is* [a]the living God
and the [b]everlasting King.
At His wrath the earth will tremble,
And the nations will not be able to endure
His indignation.

**11** Thus you shall say to them: [a]"The gods that
have not made the heavens and the earth [b]shall
perish from the earth and from under these heavens."

**12** He [a]has made the earth by His power,
He has [b]established the world by His wisdom,
And [c]has stretched out the heavens
at His discretion.
13 [a]When He utters His voice,
*There is* a [1]multitude of waters
in the heavens:
[b]"And He causes the vapors to ascend from the
ends of the earth.
He makes lightning for the rain,
He brings the wind out of His treasuries."

14 [a]Everyone is [b]dull-hearted,
without knowledge;
[c]Every metalsmith is put to shame by an image;
[d]For his molded image *is* falsehood,
And *there is* no breath in them.
15 They *are* futile, a work of errors;
In the time of their punishment they shall perish.
16 [a]The Portion of Jacob *is* not like them,
For He *is* the Maker of all *things,*
And [b]Israel *is* the tribe of His inheritance;
[c]The LORD of hosts *is* His name.

**17** [a]Gather up your wares from the land,
O [1]inhabitant of the fortress!
18 For thus says the LORD:

"Behold, I will [a]throw out at this time
The inhabitants of the land,
And will distress them,
[b]That they may find *it so.*"

**19** [a]Woe is me for my hurt!
My wound is severe.
But I say, [b]"Truly this *is* an infirmity,
And [c]I must bear it."
20 [a]My tent is plundered,
And all my cords are broken;
My children have gone from me,
And they *are* [b]no more.
*There is* no one to pitch my tent anymore,
Or set up my curtains.
21 For the shepherds have become dull-hearted,
And have not sought the LORD;
Therefore they shall not prosper,
And all their flocks shall be [a]scattered.
22 Behold, the noise of the report has come,
And a great commotion out of the [a]north country,
To make the cities of Judah desolate,
a [b]den of jackals.

**23** O LORD, I know the [a]way of man *is* not in himself;
*It is* not in man who walks to direct his own steps.
24 O LORD, [a]correct me, but with justice;
Not in Your anger,
lest You bring me to nothing.
25 [a]Pour out Your fury on the Gentiles, [b]who do not know You,
And on the families who do not call on Your name;
For they have eaten up Jacob,
[c]Devoured him and consumed him,
And made his dwelling place desolate.

## *The Broken Covenant*

**11** The word that came to Jeremiah from the
LORD, saying,
2 "Hear the words of this covenant, and speak
to the men of Judah and to the inhabitants of
Jerusalem;
3 "and say to them, 'Thus says the LORD God of
Israel: [a]"Cursed *is* the man who does not obey the
words of this covenant
4 "which I commanded your fathers in the day I
brought them out of the land of Egypt, [a]from the
iron furnace, saying, [b]'Obey My voice, and do
according to all that I command you; so shall you
be My people, and I will be your God,'
5 "that I may establish the [a]oath which I have
sworn to your fathers, to give them [b]'a land
flowing with milk and honey,' as *it is* this day." ' "
And I answered and said, [1]"So be it, LORD."
**6** Then the LORD said to me, "Proclaim all these
words in the cities of Judah and in the streets of
Jerusalem, saying: 'Hear the words of this covenant [a]and do them.
7 'For I earnestly exhorted your fathers in the
day I brought them up out of the land of Egypt,
until this day, [a]rising early and exhorting, saying,
"Obey My voice."
8 [a]'Yet they did not obey or incline their ear, but
[b]everyone [1]followed the dictates of his evil heart;
therefore I will bring upon them all the words of
this covenant, which I commanded *them* to do,
but *which* they have not done.' "
**9** And the LORD said to me, [a]"A conspiracy has
been found among the men of Judah and among
the inhabitants of Jerusalem.
10 "They have turned back to [a]the iniquities of
their forefathers who refused to hear My words,
and they have gone after other gods to serve
them; the house of Israel and the house of Judah
have broken My covenant which I made with
their fathers."
**11** Therefore thus says the LORD: "Behold, I will
surely bring calamity on them which they will not
be able to [1]escape; and [a]though they cry out to
Me, I will not listen to them.
12 "Then the cities of Judah and the inhabitants
of Jerusalem will go and [a]cry out to the gods to
whom they offer incense, but they will not save
them at all in the time of their trouble.

**7** [b]Ps. 89:6
**8** [a]Ps. 115:8; Hab. 2:18 [1]*vain teaching*
**9** [a]Dan. 10:5 [b]Ps. 115:4
**10** [a]1 Tim. 6:17 [b]Ps. 10:16
**11** [a]Ps. 96:5 [b]Is. 2:18; Zeph. 2:11
**12** [a]Gen. 1:1, 6, 7; Jer. 51:15 [b]Ps. 93:1 [c]Job 9:8; Ps. 104:2; Is. 40:22
**13** [a]Job 38:34 [b]Ps. 135:7 [1]Or *noise*
**14** [a]Jer. 51:17 [b]Prov. 30:2 [c]Is. 42:17; 44:11 [d]Hab. 2:18
**16** [a]Ps. 16:5; Jer. 51:19; Lam. 3:24 [b]Deut. 32:9; Ps. 74:2 [c]Is. 47:4
**17** [a]Jer. 6:1 [1]Or *you who dwell under siege*
**18** [a]1 Sam. 25:29; 2 Chr. 36:20 [b]Ezek. 6:10
**19** [a]Jer. 8:21 [b]Ps. 77:10 [c]Mic. 7:9
**20** [a]Jer. 4:20; Lam. 2:4 [b]Jer. 31:15; Lam. 1:5
**21** [a]Jer. 23:2
**22** [a]Jer. 5:15 [b]Jer. 9:11
**23** [a]Prov. 16:1; 20:24
**24** [a]Ps. 6:1; 38:1; Jer. 30:11
**25** [a]Ps. 79:6, 7; Zeph. 3:8 [b]Job 18:21; 1 Thess. 4:5; [2 Thess. 1:8] [c]Jer. 8:16

CHAPTER 11
**3** [a]Deut. 27:26; [Jer. 17:5]; Gal. 3:10
**4** [a]Deut. 4:20; 1 Kin. 8:51 [b]Lev. 26:3; Deut. 11:27; Jer. 7:23
**5** [a]Ex. 13:5; Deut. 7:12; Ps. 105:9; Jer. 32:22 [b]Ex. 3:8 [1]Heb. *Amen*
**6** [a]Deut. 17:19; [Rom. 2:13]; James 1:22
**7** [a]Jer. 35:15
**8** [a]Jer. 7:26 [b]Jer. 13:10 [1]*walked in the stubbornness* or *imagination*
**9** [a]Ezek. 22:25; Hos. 6:9
**10** [a]1 Sam. 15:11; Jer. 3:10, 11; Ezek. 20:18
**11** [a]Ps. 18:41; Prov. 1:28; Is. 1:15; Jer. 14:12; Ezek. 8:18; Mic. 3:4; Zech. 7:13 [1]Lit. *go out*
**12** [a]Deut. 32:37; Jer. 44:17

13 "For *according to* the number of your [a]cities
were your gods, O Judah; and *according to* the
number of the streets of Jerusalem you have set
up altars to *that* shameful thing, altars to burn
incense to Baal.
**14** "So [a]do not pray for this people, or lift up a cry
or prayer for them; for I will not hear *them* in the
time that they cry out to Me because of their
trouble.

15 "What[a] has My beloved to do in My house,
Having [b]done lewd deeds with many?
And [c]the holy flesh has passed from you.
When you do evil, then you [d]rejoice.
16 The LORD called your name,
[a]Green Olive Tree, Lovely *and* of Good Fruit.
With the noise of a great tumult
He has kindled fire on it,
And its branches are broken.

17 "For the LORD of hosts, [a]who planted you, has
pronounced doom against you for the evil of the
house of Israel and of the house of Judah, which
they have done against themselves to provoke Me
to anger in offering incense to Baal."
**18** Now the LORD gave me knowledge *of it,* and I
know *it;* for You showed me their doings.
19 But I *was* like a docile lamb brought to the
slaughter; and I did not know that they had
devised schemes against me, *saying,* "Let us
destroy the tree with its fruit, [a]and let us cut him
off from [b]the land of the living, that his name may
be remembered no more."

20 But, O LORD of hosts,
You who judge righteously,
[a]Testing the [1]mind and the heart,
Let me see Your [b]vengeance on them,
For to You I have revealed my cause.

**21** "Therefore thus says the LORD concerning the
men of [a]Anathoth who seek your life, saying, [b]'Do
not prophesy in the name of the LORD, lest you die
by our hand'—
22 "therefore thus says the LORD of hosts: 'Behold, I will punish them. The young men shall die
by the sword, their sons and their daughters shall
[a]die by famine;
23 'and there shall be no remnant of them, for I
will bring catastrophe on the men of Anathoth,
*even* [a]the year of their punishment.' "

## *Jeremiah's Complaint and God's Answer*

**12** Righteous [a]*are* You, O LORD,
when I plead with You;
Yet let me talk with You about *Your*
judgments.
[b]Why does the way of the wicked prosper?
*Why* are those happy who deal so
treacherously?
2 You have planted them,
yes, they have taken root;
They grow, yes, they bear fruit.
[a]You *are* near in their mouth
But far from their [1]mind.

3 But You, O LORD, [a]know me;
You have seen me,
And You have [b]tested my heart toward You.
Pull them out like sheep for the slaughter,
And prepare them for [c]the day of slaughter.
4 How long will [a]the land mourn,
And the herbs of every field wither?
[b]The beasts and birds are consumed,
[c]For the wickedness of those who dwell there,
Because they said,
"He will not see our final end."

**5** "If you have run with the footmen,
and they have wearied you,
Then how can you contend with horses?
And *if* in the land of peace,
*In which* you trusted, *they wearied you,*
Then how will you do in [a]the [1]flood plain of
the Jordan?
6 For even [a]your brothers,
the house of your father,
Even they have dealt treacherously with you;
Yes, they have called [1]a multitude after you.
[b]Do not believe them,
Even though they speak [2]smooth words to
you.

**7** "I have forsaken My house,
I have left My heritage;
I have given the dearly beloved of My soul
into the hand of her enemies.
8 My heritage is to Me like a lion in the forest;
It cries out against Me;
Therefore I have [a]hated it.
9 My [1]heritage *is* to Me *like* a speckled vulture;
The vultures all around *are* against her.
Come, assemble all the beasts of the field,
[a]Bring them to devour!

10 "Many [a]rulers[1] have destroyed [b]My vineyard,
They have [c]trodden My portion underfoot;
They have made My [2]pleasant portion
a desolate wilderness.
11 They have made it [a]desolate;
Desolate, it mourns to Me;
The whole land is made desolate,
Because [b]no one takes *it* to heart.
12 The plunderers have come
On all the desolate heights in the wilderness,
For the sword of the LORD shall devour
From *one* end of the land to the *other* end of
the land;
No flesh shall have peace.
13 [a]They have sown wheat but reaped thorns;
They have [1]put themselves to pain
*but* do not profit.
But be ashamed of your harvest
Because of the fierce anger of the LORD."

**14** Thus says the LORD: "Against all My evil
neighbors who [a]touch the inheritance which I
have caused My people Israel to inherit—behold, I
will [b]pluck them out of their land and pluck out
the house of Judah from among them.
15 [a]"Then it shall be, after I have plucked them
out, that I will return and have compassion on
them [b]and bring them back, everyone to his
heritage and everyone to his land.
16 "And it shall be, if they will learn carefully the
ways of My people, [a]to swear by My name, 'As the
LORD lives,' as they taught My people to swear by
Baal, then they shall be [b]established in the midst
of My people.
17 "But if they do not [a]obey, I will utterly pluck
up and destroy that nation," says the LORD.

## *The Symbol of the Linen Sash*

**13** Thus the LORD said to me: "Go and get
yourself a linen sash, and put it [1]around
your waist, but do not put it in water."

---

**13** [a]Jer. 2:28
**14** [a]Ex. 32:10
**15** [a]Ps. 50:16 [b]Ezek. 16:25 [c][Titus 1:15] [d]Prov. 2:14
**16** [a]Ps. 52:8
**17** [a]Is. 5:2
**19** [a]Ps. 83:4 [b]Ps. 27:13
**20** [a]Ps. 7:9 [b]Jer. 15:15 [1]Most secret parts, lit. *kidneys*
**21** [a]Jer. 1:1; 12:5, 6 [b]Mic. 2:6
**22** [a]Jer. 9:21
**23** [a]Jer. 23:12

CHAPTER 12
**1** [a]Ps. 51:14 [b]Mal. 3:15
**2** [a]Matt. 15:8 [1]Most secret parts, lit. *kidneys*
**3** [a]Ps. 17:3 [b]Jer. 11:20 [c]James 5:5
**4** [a]Hos. 4:3 [b]Jer. 9:10 [c]Ps. 107:34
**5** [a]Josh. 3:15 [1]Or *thicket*
**6** [a]Jer. 9:4, 5 [b]Prov. 26:25 [1]Or *abundantly* [2]Lit. *good*
**8** [a]Hos. 9:15
**9** [a]Lev. 26:22 [1]*inheritance*
**10** [a]Jer. 6:3; 23:1 [b]Is. 5:1–7 [c]Is. 63:18 [1]Lit. *shepherds* or *pastors* [2]*desired portion* of land
**11** [a]Jer. 10:22; 22:6 [b]Is. 42:25
**13** [a]Hag. 1:6 [1]Or *strained*
**14** [a]Zech. 2:8 [b]Deut. 30:3
**15** [a]Ezek. 28:25 [b]Amos 9:14
**16** [a][Jer. 4:2] [b][1 Pet. 2:5]
**17** [a]Is. 60:12

CHAPTER 13
**1** [1]Lit. *upon your loins*

2 So I got a [1]sash according to the word of the
LORD, and put *it* around my waist.
**3** And the word of the LORD came to me the
second time, saying,
4 "Take the [1]sash that you acquired, which *is*
[2]around your waist, and arise, go to the [3]Euphra-
tes, and hide it there in a hole in the rock."
5 So I went and hid it by the Euphrates, as the
LORD commanded me.
6 Now it came to pass after many days that the
LORD said to me, "Arise, go to the Euphrates, and
take from there the sash which I commanded you
to hide there."
7 Then I went to the Euphrates and dug, and I
took the [1]sash from the place where I had hidden
it; and there was the sash, ruined. It was profitable
for nothing.
**8** Then the word of the LORD came to me,
saying,
9 "Thus says the LORD: 'In this manner [a]I will
ruin the pride of Judah and the great [b]pride of
Jerusalem.
10 'This evil people, who [a]refuse to hear My
words, who [b]follow[1] the dictates of their hearts,
and walk after other gods to serve them and
worship them, shall be just like this sash which is
profitable for nothing.
11 'For as the sash clings to the waist of a man,
so I have caused the whole house of Israel and the
whole house of Judah to cling to Me,' says the
LORD, 'that [a]they may become My people, [b]for
renown, for praise, and for [c]glory; but they would
[d]not hear.'
**12** "Therefore you shall speak to them this word:
'Thus says the LORD God of Israel: "Every bottle
shall be filled with wine." ' And they will say to
you, 'Do we not certainly know that every bottle
will be filled with wine?'
13 "Then you shall say to them, 'Thus says the
LORD: "Behold, I will fill all the inhabitants of this
land—even the kings who sit on David's throne,
the priests, the prophets, and all the inhabitants of
Jerusalem—[a]with drunkenness!
14 "And [a]I will dash them [1]one against another,
even the fathers and the sons together," says the
LORD. "I will not pity nor spare nor have mercy,
but will destroy them." ' "

**15** Hear and give ear:
Do not be proud,
For the LORD has spoken.
16 [a]Give glory to the LORD your God
Before He causes [b]darkness,
And before your feet stumble
On the dark mountains,
And while you are [c]looking for light,
He turns it into [d]the shadow of death
*And* makes *it* dense darkness.
17 But if you will not hear it,
My soul will [a]weep in secret for *your* pride;
My eyes will weep bitterly
And run down with tears,
Because the LORD's flock has been taken
captive.

**18** Say to [a]the king and to the queen mother,
"Humble yourselves;
Sit down,
For your rule shall collapse,
the crown of your glory."
19 The cities of the South shall be shut up,
And no one shall open *them;*
Judah shall be carried away captive, all of it;
It shall be wholly carried away captive.

**20** Lift up your eyes and see
Those who come from the [a]north.
Where *is* the flock *that* was given to you,
Your beautiful sheep?
21 What will you say when He punishes you?
For you have taught them
*To be* chieftains, to be head over you.
Will not [a]pangs seize you,
Like a woman in [1]labor?
22 And if you say in your heart,
[a]"Why have these things come upon me?"
For the greatness of your iniquity
[b]Your skirts have been uncovered,
Your heels [1]made bare.
23 Can the Ethiopian change his skin
or the leopard its spots?
*Then* may you also do good
who are accustomed to do evil.

**24** "Therefore I will [a]scatter them [b]like stubble
That passes away by the wind of the
wilderness.
25 [a]This is your lot,
The portion of your measures from Me,"
says the LORD,
"Because you have forgotten Me
And trusted in [b]falsehood.
26 Therefore [a]I will uncover your skirts over
your face,
That your shame may appear.
27 I have seen your adulteries
And your *lustful* [a]neighings,
The lewdness of your harlotry,
Your abominations [b]on the hills in the fields.
Woe to you, O Jerusalem!
Will you still not be made clean?"

## *The Message of Famine*

**14** The word of the LORD that came to Jeremiah concerning the droughts.

2 "Judah mourns,
And [a]her gates languish;
They [b]mourn for the land,
And [c]the cry of Jerusalem has gone up.
3 Their nobles have sent their lads for water;
They went to the cisterns
*and* found no water.
They returned with their vessels empty;
They were [a]ashamed and confounded
[b]And covered their heads.
4 Because the ground is parched,
For there was [a]no rain in the land,
The plowmen were ashamed;
They covered their heads.
5 Yes, the deer also gave birth in the field,
But [1]left because there was no grass.
6 And [a]the wild donkeys stood in the desolate
heights;
They sniffed at the wind like jackals;
Their eyes failed because *there was* no
grass."

**7** O LORD, though our iniquities testify
against us,
Do it [a]for Your name's sake;
For our backslidings are many,
We have sinned against You.
8 [a]O the Hope of Israel,
his Savior in time of trouble,

**2** [1]*waistband*
**4** [1]*waistband* [2]Lit. *upon your loins* [3]Heb. *Perath*
**7** [1]*waistband*
**9** [a]Lev. 26:19 [b][Is. 2:10–17; 23:9]; Zeph. 3:11
**10** [a]Jer. 16:12 [b]Jer. 7:24; 16:12 [1]*walk in the stubbornness* or *imagination*
**11** [a][Ex. 19:5, 6; Deut. 32:10, 11] [b]Jer. 33:9 [c]Is. 43:21 [d]Ps. 81:11; Jer. 7:13, 24, 26
**13** [a]Ps. 60:3; 75:8; Is. 51:17; 63:6; Jer. 25:27; 51:7, 57
**14** [a]2 Chr. 36:17; Ps. 2:9; Is. 9:20, 21; Jer. 19:9–11 [1]Lit. *a man against his brother*
**16** [a]Josh. 7:19; Ps. 96:8; Mal. 2:2 [b]Is. 5:30; 8:22; Amos 8:9 [c]Is. 59:9 [d]Ps. 44:19; Jer. 2:6
**17** [a]Ps. 119:136; Jer. 9:1; 14:17; Luke 19:41, 42
**18** [a]2 Kin. 24:12; Jer. 22:26
**20** [a]Jer. 10:22; 46:20
**21** [a]Jer. 6:24 [1]*childbirth*
**22** [a]Jer. 16:10 [b]Is. 47:2; Ezek. 16:37; Nah. 3:5 [1]Lit. *suffer violence*
**24** [a]Lev. 26:33; Jer. 9:16; Ezek. 5:2, 12 [b]Ps. 1:4; Hos. 13:3
**25** [a]Job 20:29; Ps. 11:6; Matt. 24:51 [b]Jer. 10:14
**26** [a]Lam. 1:8; Ezek. 16:37; Hos. 2:10
**27** [a]Jer. 5:7, 8 [b]Is. 65:7; Jer. 2:20; Ezek. 6:13

CHAPTER 14
**2** [a]2 Kin. 25:3; Is. 3:26 [b]Jer. 8:21 [c]1 Sam. 5:12; Jer. 11:11; 46:12; Zech. 7:13
**3** [a]Job 6:20; Ps. 40:14 [b]2 Sam. 15:30
**4** [a]Jer. 3:3; Ezek. 22:24
**5** [1]*abandoned* her young
**6** [a]Job 39:5, 6; Jer. 2:24
**7** [a]Ps. 25:11; Jer. 14:21
**8** [a]Jer. 17:13

Why should You be like a stranger in the land,
And like a traveler *who* turns aside to tarry for a night?
9 Why should You be like a man astonished,
Like a mighty one [a]*who* cannot save?
Yet You, O LORD, [b]*are* in our midst,
And we are called by Your name;
Do not leave us!

**10** Thus says the LORD to this people:

[a]"Thus they have loved to wander;
They have not restrained their feet.
Therefore the LORD does not accept them;
[b]He will remember their iniquity now,
And punish their sins."

**11** Then the LORD said to me, [a]"Do not pray for
this people, for *their* good.
12 [a]"When they fast, I will not hear their cry; and
[b]when they offer burnt offering and grain offering,
I will not accept them. But [c]I will consume them
by the sword, by the famine, and by the pestilence."
**13** [a]Then I said, "Ah, Lord GOD! Behold, the
prophets say to them, 'You shall not see the
sword, nor shall you have famine, but I will give
you [1]assured [b]peace in this place.' "
14 And the LORD said to me, [a]"The prophets
prophesy lies in My name. [b]I have not sent them,
commanded them, nor spoken to them; they
prophesy to you a false vision, [1]divination, a
worthless thing, and the [c]deceit of their heart.
15 "Therefore thus says the LORD concerning the
prophets who prophesy in My name, whom I did
not send, [a]and who say, 'Sword and famine shall
not be in this land'—'By sword and famine those
prophets shall be consumed!
16 'And the people to whom they prophesy shall
be cast out in the streets of Jerusalem because of
the famine and the sword; [a]they will have no one
to bury them—them nor their wives, their sons
nor their daughters—for I will pour their wickedness on them.'
**17** "Therefore you shall say this word to them:

[a]'Let my eyes flow with tears night and day,
And let them not cease;
[b]For the virgin daughter of my people
Has been broken with a mighty stroke, with a very severe blow.
18 If I go out to [a]the field,
Then behold, those slain with the sword!
And if I enter the city,
Then behold, those sick from famine!
Yes, both prophet and [b]priest go about in a land they do not know.' "

**19** [a]Have You utterly rejected Judah?
Has Your soul loathed Zion?
Why have You stricken us
so that [b]*there is* no healing for us?
[c]We looked for peace, but *there was* no good;
And for the time of healing,
and there was trouble.
20 We acknowledge, O LORD, our wickedness
*And* the iniquity of our [a]fathers,
For [b]we have sinned against You.
21 Do not abhor *us,* for Your name's sake;
Do not disgrace the throne of Your glory.
[a]Remember, do not break Your covenant with us.
22 [a]Are there any among [b]the idols of the nations that can cause [c]rain?
Or can the heavens give showers?
[d]*Are* You not He, O LORD our God?
Therefore we will wait for You,
Since You have made all these.

### *The LORD's Anger with Judah*

**15** Then the LORD said to me, [a]"*Even* if [b]Moses
and [c]Samuel stood before Me, My [1]mind
*would* not *be* favorable toward this people. Cast
*them* out of My sight, and let them go forth.
2 "And it shall be, if they say to you, 'Where
should we go?' then you shall tell them, 'Thus says
the LORD:

[a]"Such as *are* for death, to death;
And such as *are* for the sword, to the sword;
And such as *are* for the famine,
to the famine;
And such as *are* for the [b]captivity,
to the captivity." '

3 "And I will [a]appoint over them four forms *of
destruction,*" says the LORD: "the sword to slay,
the dogs to drag, [b]the birds of the heavens and the
beasts of the earth to devour and destroy.
4 "I will hand them over to [a]trouble, to all
kingdoms of the earth, because of [b]Manasseh the
son of Hezekiah, king of Judah, for what he did in
Jerusalem.

**5** "For who will have pity on you, O Jerusalem?
Or who will bemoan you?
Or who will turn aside to ask
how you are doing?
6 [a]You have forsaken Me," says the LORD,
"You have [b]gone backward.
Therefore I will stretch out My hand against you and destroy you;
[c]I am [1]weary of relenting!
7 And I will winnow them with a winnowing fan in the gates of the land;
I will [a]bereave *them* of children;
I will destroy My people,
*Since* they [b]do not return from their ways.
8 Their widows will be increased to Me more than the sand of the seas;
I will bring against them,
Against the mother of the young men,
A plunderer at noonday;
I will cause anguish and terror to fall on them [a]suddenly.

**9** "She[a] languishes who has borne seven;
She has breathed her last;
[b]Her sun has gone down
While *it was* yet day;
She has been ashamed and confounded.
And the remnant of them
I will deliver to the sword
Before their enemies," says the LORD.

**10** [a]Woe is me, my mother,
That you have borne me,
A man of strife and a man of contention to the whole [1]earth!
I have neither lent for interest,
Nor have men lent to me for interest.
Every one of them curses me.
11 The LORD said:

"Surely it will be well with your remnant;
Surely I will cause [a]the enemy to intercede with you

**9** [a]Is. 59:1 [b]Ex. 29:45; Lev. 26:11; Ps. 46:5; Jer. 8:19
**10** [a]Jer. 2:23–25 [b][Jer. 44:21–23]; Hos. 8:13
**11** [a]Ex. 32:10; Jer. 7:16; 11:14
**12** [a]Prov. 1:28; [Is. 1:15; 58:3–6]; Ezek. 8:18; Mic. 3:4; Zech. 7:13 [b]Jer. 6:20 [c]Jer. 9:16
**13** [a]Jer. 4:10 [b]Jer. 8:11; 23:17 [1]*true*
**14** [a]Jer. 27:10 [b]Jer. 29:8, 9 [c]Jer. 23:16; Ezek. 12:24 [1]Telling the future by signs and omens
**15** [a]Jer. 5:12; Ezek. 14:10
**16** [a]Ps. 79:2, 3; Jer. 7:32; 15:2, 3
**17** [a]Jer. 9:1; 13:17; Lam. 1:16 [b]Is. 37:22; Jer. 8:21; Lam. 1:15; 2:13
**18** [a]Jer. 6:25; Lam. 1:20; Ezek. 7:15 [b]Jer. 23:11
**19** [a]Jer. 6:30; 7:29; 12:7; Lam. 5:22 [b]Jer. 15:18 [c]Job 30:26; Jer. 8:15; 1 Thess. 5:3
**20** [a]Neh. 9:2; Ps. 32:5; Jer. 3:25 [b]Ps. 106:6; Jer. 8:14; 14:7; Dan. 9:8
**21** [a]Ps. 106:45
**22** [a]Zech. 10:1 [b]Deut. 32:21 [c]1 Kin. 17:1; Jer. 5:24 [d]Ps. 135:7

CHAPTER 15
**1** [a]Ps. 99:6; Ezek. 14:14 [b]Ex. 32:11–14; Num. 14:13–20; Ps. 99:6 [c]1 Sam. 7:9 [1]Lit. *soul was not toward*
**2** [a]Jer. 43:11; Ezek. 5:2, 12; Zech. 11:9; [Rev. 13:10] [b]Jer. 9:16; 16:13
**3** [a]Lev. 26:16, 21, 25; Jer. 12:3; Ezek. 14:21 [b]Jer. 7:33
**4** [a]Deut. 28:25 [b]2 Kin. 24:3, 4
**6** [a]Jer. 2:13 [b]Is. 1:4; Jer. 7:24 [c]Jer. 20:16; Zech. 8:14 [1]*tired*
**7** [a]Jer. 18:21; Hos. 9:12–16 [b]Is. 9:13; Jer. 5:3; Amos 4:10, 11
**8** [a]Is. 29:5
**9** [a]1 Sam. 2:5; Is. 47:9 [b]Jer. 6:4; Amos 8:9
**10** [a]Job 3:1; Jer. 20:14 [1]Or *land*
**11** [a]Jer. 40:4, 5

In the time of adversity
and in the time of affliction.
12 Can anyone break iron,
The northern iron and the bronze?
13 Your wealth and your treasures
I will give as [a]plunder without price,
Because of all your sins,
Throughout your territories.
14 And I will [1]make *you* cross over with your
enemies
[a]Into a land *which* you do not know;
For a [b]fire is kindled in My anger,
*Which* shall burn upon you."

**15** O LORD, [a]You know;
Remember me and [1]visit me,
And [b]take vengeance for me on my
persecutors.
In Your enduring patience, do not take me
away.
Know that [c]for Your sake
I have suffered rebuke.
16 Your words were found, and I [a]ate them,
And [b]Your word was to me
the joy and rejoicing of my heart;
For I am called by Your name,
O LORD God of hosts.
17 [a]I did not sit in the assembly of the mockers,
Nor did I rejoice;
I sat alone because of Your hand,
For You have filled me with indignation.
18 Why is my [a]pain perpetual
And my wound incurable,
*Which* refuses to be healed?
Will You surely be to me [b]like an unreliable
stream,
*As* waters *that* [1]fail?

**19** Therefore thus says the LORD:

[a]"If you return,
Then I will bring you back;
You shall [b]stand before Me;
If you [c]take out the precious from the vile,
You shall be as My mouth.
Let them return to you,
But you must not return to them.
20 And I will make you to this people
a fortified bronze [a]wall;
And they will fight against you,
But [b]they shall not prevail against you;
For I *am* with you to save you
And deliver you," says the LORD.
21 "I will deliver you from the hand
of the wicked,
And I will redeem you from the grip
of the terrible."

### *The Signs of Coming Captivity*

**16** The word of the LORD also came to me,
saying,
2 "You shall not take a wife, nor shall you have
sons or daughters in this place."
3 For thus says the LORD concerning the sons
and daughters who are born in this place, and
concerning their mothers who bore them and
their fathers who begot them in this land:
4 "They shall die [a]gruesome deaths; they shall
not be [b]lamented nor shall they be [c]buried, *but*
they shall be [d]like refuse on the face of the earth.
They shall be consumed by the sword and by
famine, and their [e]corpses shall be meat for the
birds of heaven and for the beasts of the earth."

**5** For thus says the LORD: [a]"Do not enter the
house of mourning, nor go to lament or bemoan
them; for I have taken away My peace from this
people," says the LORD, "lovingkindness and mercies.
6 "Both the great and the small shall die in this
land. They shall not be buried; [a]neither shall men
lament for them, [b]cut themselves, nor [c]make
themselves bald for them.
7 "Nor shall *men* break *bread* in mourning for
them, to comfort them for the dead; nor shall *men*
give them the cup of consolation to [a]drink for
their father or their mother.
8 "Also you shall not go into the house of
feasting to sit with them, to eat and drink."
9 For thus says the LORD of hosts, the God of
Israel: "Behold, [a]I will cause to cease from this
place, before your eyes and in your days, the voice
of [1]mirth and the voice of gladness, the voice of
the bridegroom and the voice of the bride.
**10** "And it shall be, when you show this people all
these words, and they say to you, [a]'Why has the
LORD pronounced all this great disaster against
us? Or what *is* our iniquity? Or what *is* our sin
that we have committed against the LORD our
God?'
11 "then you shall say to them, [a]'Because your
fathers have forsaken Me,' says the LORD; 'they
have walked after other gods and have served
them and worshiped them, and have forsaken Me
and not kept My law.
12 'And you have done [a]worse than your fathers,
for behold, [b]each one [1]follows the dictates of his
own evil heart, so that no one listens to Me.
13 [a]'Therefore I will cast you out of this land [b]into
a land that you do not know, neither you nor your
fathers; and there you shall serve other gods day
and night, where I will not show you favor.'
**14** "Therefore behold, the [a]days are coming,"
says the LORD, "that it shall no more be said, 'The
LORD lives who brought up the children of Israel
from the land of Egypt,'
15 "but, 'The LORD lives who brought up the
children of Israel from the land of the [a]north and
from all the lands where He had driven them.' For
[b]I will bring them back into their land which I
gave to their fathers.
**16** "Behold, I will send for many [a]fishermen,"
says the LORD, "and they shall fish them; and
afterward I will send for many hunters, and they
shall hunt them from every mountain and every
hill, and out of the holes of the rocks.
17 "For My [a]eyes *are* on all their ways; they are
not hidden from My face, nor is their iniquity
hidden from My eyes.
18 "And first I will repay [a]double for their iniquity and their sin, because [b]they have defiled My
land; they have filled My inheritance with the
carcasses of their detestable and abominable
idols."

**19** O LORD, [a]my strength and my fortress,
[b]My refuge in the day of affliction,
The Gentiles shall come to You
From the ends of the earth and say,
"Surely our fathers have inherited lies,
Worthlessness and [c]unprofitable *things*."
20 Will a man make gods for himself,
[a]Which *are* not gods?

**21** "Therefore behold, I will this once
cause them to know,

13 [a]Ps. 44:12
14 [a]Jer. 16:13 [b]Deut. 32:22 [1]So with MT, Vg.; LXX, Syr., Tg. *cause you to serve* (cf. 17:4)
15 [a]Jer. 12:3 [b]Jer. 20:12 [c]Ps. 69:7–9 [1]*attend to*
16 [a]Ezek. 3:1, 3 [b][Job 23:12]
17 [a]Ps. 26:4, 5
18 [a]Jer. 10:19; 30:15 [b]Job 6:15 [1]Or *cannot be trusted*
19 [a]Zech. 3:7 [b]Jer. 15:1 [c]Ezek. 22:26; 44:23
20 [a]Ezek. 3:9 [b]Jer. 1:8, 19; 20:11; 37:21; 38:13; 39:11, 12

CHAPTER 16
4 [a]Jer. 15:2 [b]Jer. 22:18; 25:33 [c]Jer. 14:16; 19:11 [d]Ps. 83:10 [e]Ps. 79:2
5 [a]Ezek. 24:17, 22, 23
6 [a]Jer. 22:18 [b]Deut. 14:1 [c]Is. 22:12
7 [a]Prov. 31:6
9 [a]Rev. 18:23 [1]*rejoicing*
10 [a]Deut. 29:24
11 [a]Jer. 22:9
12 [a]Jer. 7:26 [b]Jer. 3:17; 18:12 [1]*walks after the stubbornness* or *imagination*
13 [a]Deut. 4:26; 28:36, 63 [b]Jer. 15:14
14 [a]Jer. 23:7, 8
15 [a]Jer. 3:18 [b]Jer. 24:6; 30:3; 32:37
16 [a]Amos 4:2
17 [a]Heb. 4:13
18 [a]Jer. 17:18 [b][Ezek. 43:7]
19 [a]Ps. 18:1, 2 [b]Jer. 17:17 [c]Is. 44:10
20 [a]Gal. 4:8

I will cause them to know
My hand and My might;
And they shall know that [a]My name
is the LORD.

### *Judah's Sin and Punishment*

**17** "The sin of Judah *is* [a]written
with a [b]pen of iron;
With the point of a diamond *it is* [c]engraved
On the tablet of their heart,
And on the horns of your altars,
2 While their children remember
Their altars and their [a]wooden[1] images
By the green trees on the high hills.
3 O My mountain in the field,
I will give as plunder your wealth,
all your treasures,
*And* your high places of sin
within all your borders.
4 And you, even yourself,
Shall let go of your heritage which I gave
you;
And I will cause you to serve your enemies
In [a]the land which you do not know;
For [b]you have kindled a fire in My anger
*which* shall burn forever."

**5** Thus says the LORD:

[a]"Cursed *is* the man who trusts in man
And makes [b]flesh his [1]strength,
Whose heart departs from the LORD.
6 For he shall be [a]like a shrub in the desert,
And [b]shall not see when good comes,
But shall inhabit the parched places in the
wilderness,
[c]*In* a salt land *which is* not inhabited.

7 "Blessed[a] *is* the man who trusts in the LORD,
And whose hope is the LORD.
8 For he shall be [a]like a tree
planted by the waters,
Which spreads out its roots by the river,
And will not [1]fear when heat comes;
But its leaf will be green,
And will not be anxious in the year
of drought,
Nor will cease from yielding fruit.

**9** "The [a]heart *is* deceitful above all *things*,
And [1]desperately wicked;
Who can know it?
10 I, the LORD, [a]search the heart,
*I* test the [1]mind,
[b]Even to give every man according to his
ways,
According to the fruit of his doings.

**11** "*As* a partridge that [1]broods
but does not hatch,
*So is* he who gets riches, but not by right;
It [a]will leave him in the midst of his days,
And at his end he will be [b]a fool."

12 A glorious high throne from the beginning
*Is* the place of our sanctuary.
13 O LORD, [a]the hope of Israel,
[b]All who forsake You shall be ashamed.

"Those who depart from Me
Shall be [c]written in the earth,
Because they have forsaken the LORD,
The [d]fountain of living waters."

**14** Heal me, O LORD, and I shall be healed;
Save me, and I shall be saved,
For [a]You *are* my praise.
15 Indeed they say to me,
[a]"Where *is* the word of the LORD?
Let it come now!"
16 As for me, [a]I have not hurried away from
*being* a shepherd *who* follows You,
Nor have I desired the woeful day;
You know what came out of my lips;
It was right there before You.
17 Do not be a terror to me;
[a]You *are* my hope in the day of doom.
18 [a]Let them be ashamed who persecute me,
But [b]do not let me be put to shame;
Let them be dismayed,
But do not let me be dismayed.
Bring on them the day of doom,
And [c]destroy[1] them with double destruction!

**19** Thus the LORD said to me: "Go and stand in
the gate of the children of the people, by which
the kings of Judah come in and by which they go
out, and in all the gates of Jerusalem;
20 "and say to them, [a]'Hear the word of the LORD,
you kings of Judah, and all Judah, and all the
inhabitants of Jerusalem, who enter by these
gates.
21 'Thus says the LORD: [a]"Take heed to yourselves, and bear no burden on the Sabbath day,
nor bring *it* in by the gates of Jerusalem;
22 "nor carry a burden out of your houses on the
Sabbath day, nor do any work, but hallow the
Sabbath day, as I [a]commanded your fathers.
23 [a]"But they did not obey nor incline their ear,
but [1]made their neck stiff, that they might not
hear nor receive instruction.
**24** "And it shall be, [a]if you heed Me carefully,"
says the LORD, "to bring no burden through the
gates of this city on the [b]Sabbath day, but hallow
the Sabbath day, to do no work in it,
25 [a]"then shall enter the gates of this city kings
and princes sitting on the throne of David, riding
in chariots and on horses, they and their princes,
accompanied by the men of Judah and the
inhabitants of Jerusalem; and this city shall remain forever.
26 "And they shall come from the cities of Judah
and from [a]the places around Jerusalem, from the
land of Benjamin and from [b]the [1]lowland, from the
mountains and from [c]the [2]South, bringing burnt
offerings and sacrifices, grain offerings and incense, bringing [d]sacrifices of praise to the house of
the LORD.
27 "But if you will not heed Me to hallow the
Sabbath day, such as not carrying a burden when
entering the gates of Jerusalem on the Sabbath
day, then [a]I will kindle a fire in its gates, [b]and it
shall devour the palaces of Jerusalem, and it shall
not be [c]quenched." ' "

### *The Lesson from the Potter*

**18** The word which came to Jeremiah from the
LORD, saying:
2 "Arise and go down to the potter's house, and
there I will cause you to hear My words."
3 Then I went down to the potter's house, and
there he was, making something at the [1]wheel.
4 And the vessel that he [1]made of clay was
[2]marred in the hand of the potter; so he made it

**21** [a]Amos 5:8

CHAPTER 17
**1** [a]Jer. 2:22 [b]Job 19:24 [c]2 Cor. 3:3
**2** [a]Judg. 3:7 [1]Or *Asherim*, Canaanite deities
**4** [a]Jer. 16:13 [b]Jer. 15:14
**5** [a]Is. 30:1, 2; 31:1 [b]Is. 31:3 [1]Lit. *arm*
**6** [a]Jer. 48:6 [b]Job 20:17 [c]Deut. 29:23
**7** [a][Is. 30:18]
**8** [a][Ps. 1:3] [1]Qr., Tg. *see*
**9** [a][Eccl. 9:3] [1]Or *incurably sick*
**10** [a]Rev. 2:23 [b]Rom. 2:6 [1]Most secret parts, lit. *kidneys*
**11** [a]Ps. 55:23 [b]Luke 12:20 [1]Sits on eggs
**13** [a]Jer. 14:8 [b][Is. 1:28] [c]Luke 10:20 [d]Jer. 2:13
**14** [a]Deut. 10:21
**15** [a]Is. 5:19
**16** [a]Jer. 1:4–12
**17** [a]Jer. 16:19
**18** [a]Ps. 35:4; 70:2 [b]Ps. 25:2 [c]Jer. 11:20 [1]Lit. *crush*
**20** [a]Jer. 19:3, 4
**21** [a]Neh. 13:19
**22** [a]Ex. 20:8; 31:13
**23** [a]Jer. 7:24, 26 [1]Were stubborn
**24** [a]Jer. 11:4; 26:3 [b]Ex. 16:23–30; 20:8–10
**25** [a]Jer. 22:4
**26** [a]Jer. 33:13 [b]Zech. 7:7 [c]Judg. 1:9 [d]Ps. 107:22; 116:17 [1]Heb. *shephelah* [2]Heb. *Negev*
**27** [a]Lam. 4:11 [b]2 Kin. 25:9 [c]Jer. 7:20

CHAPTER 18
**3** [1]Potter's wheel
**4** [1]*was making* [2]*ruined*

again into another vessel, as it seemed good to the
potter to make.
**5** Then the word of the LORD came to me,
saying:
6 "O house of Israel, [a]can I not do with you as
this potter?" says the LORD. "Look, [b]as the clay *is*
in the potter's hand, so *are* you in My hand, O
house of Israel!
7 "The instant I speak concerning a nation and
concerning a kingdom, to [a]pluck up, to pull down,
and to destroy *it*,
8 [a]"if that nation against whom I have spoken
turns from its evil, [b]I will relent of the disaster
that I thought to bring upon it.
9 "And the instant I speak concerning a nation
and concerning a kingdom, to build and to
plant *it*,
10 "if it does evil in My sight so that it does not
obey My voice, then I will relent concerning the
good with which I said I would benefit it.
**11** "Now therefore, speak to the men of Judah
and to the inhabitants of Jerusalem, saying, 'Thus
says the LORD: "Behold, I am fashioning a disaster
and devising a plan against you. [a]Return now
every one from his evil way, and make your ways
and your doings [b]good." ' "
12 And they said, [a]"That is hopeless! So we will
walk according to our own plans, and we will
every one [1]obey the [b]dictates[2] of his evil heart."
**13** Therefore thus says the LORD:

[a]"Ask now among the Gentiles,
Who has heard such things?
The virgin of Israel has done [b]a very horrible
thing.
14 Will *a man* [1]leave the snow-water of
Lebanon,
*Which comes* from the rock of the field?
Will the cold flowing waters be forsaken for
strange waters?

15 "Because My people have forgotten [a]Me,
They have burned incense to worthless idols.
And they have caused themselves to stumble
in their ways,
*From* the [b]ancient paths,
To walk in pathways and not on a highway,
16 To make their land [a]desolate
*and* a perpetual [b]hissing;
Everyone who passes by it will be astonished
And shake his head.
17 [a]I will scatter them [b]as with an east wind
before the enemy;
[c]I will [1]show them the back and not the face
In the day of their calamity."

**18** Then they said, [a]"Come and let us devise plans
against Jeremiah; [b]for the law shall not perish
from the priest, nor counsel from the wise, nor the
word from the prophet. Come and let us attack
him with the tongue, and let us not give heed to
any of his words."

**19** Give heed to me, O LORD,
And listen to the voice of those who contend
with me!
20 [a]Shall evil be repaid for good?
For they have [b]dug a pit for my life.
Remember that I [c]stood before You
To speak good [1]for them,
To turn away Your wrath from them.
21 Therefore [a]deliver up their children to the
famine,
And pour out their *blood*
By the force of the sword;
Let their wives *become* widows
And [b]bereaved of their children.
Let their men be put to death,
Their young men *be* slain
By the sword in battle.
22 Let a cry be heard from their houses,
When You bring a troop suddenly upon
them;
For they have dug a pit to take me,
And hidden snares for my feet.
23 Yet, LORD, You know all their counsel
Which is against me, to slay *me*.
[a]Provide no atonement for their iniquity,
Nor blot out their sin from Your sight;
But let them be overthrown before You.
Deal *thus* with them
In the time of Your [b]anger.

### *The Lesson from the Broken Pottery*

**19** Thus says the LORD: "Go and get a potter's
earthen flask, and *take* some of the elders of
the people and some of the elders of the priests.
2 "And go out to [a]the Valley of the Son of
Hinnom, which *is* by the entry of the Potsherd
Gate; and proclaim there the words that I will tell
you,
3 [a]"and say, 'Hear the word of the LORD, O kings
of Judah and inhabitants of Jerusalem. Thus says
the LORD of hosts, the God of Israel: "Behold, I
will bring such a catastrophe on this place, that
whoever hears of it, his ears will [b]tingle.
**4** "Because they [a]have forsaken Me and made
this an alien place, because they have burned
incense in it to other gods whom neither they,
their fathers, nor the kings of Judah have known,
and have filled this place with [b]the blood of the
innocents
5 [a]"(they have also built the high places of Baal,
to burn their sons with fire *for* burnt offerings to
Baal, [b]which I did not command or speak, nor did
it come into My mind),
6 "therefore behold, the days are coming," says
the LORD, "that this place shall no more be called
Tophet or [a]the Valley of the Son of Hinnom, but
the Valley of Slaughter.
7 "And I will make void the counsel of Judah
and Jerusalem in this place, [a]and I will cause them
to fall by the sword before their enemies and by
the hands of those who seek their lives; their
[b]corpses I will give as meat for the birds of the
heaven and for the beasts of the earth.
8 "I will make this city [a]desolate and a hissing;
everyone who passes by it will be astonished and
hiss because of all its plagues.
9 "And I will cause them to eat the [a]flesh of
their sons and the flesh of their daughters, and
everyone shall eat the flesh of his friend in the
siege and in the desperation with which their
enemies and those who seek their lives shall drive
them to despair." '
**10** [a]"Then you shall break the flask in the sight of
the men who go with you,
11 "and say to them, 'Thus says the LORD of
hosts: [a]"Even so I will break this people and this
city, as *one* breaks a potter's vessel, which cannot
be [1]made whole again; and they shall [b]bury *them*
in Tophet till *there is* no place to bury.
12 "Thus I will do to this place," says the LORD,

**6** [a]Is. 45:9; Rom. 9:20, 21 [b]Is. 64:8
**7** [a]Jer. 1:10
**8** [a]Jer. 7:3–7; 12:16; [Ezek. 18:21; 33:11] [b][Ps. 106:45]; Jer. 26:3; [Hos. 11:8; Joel 2:13]; Jon. 3:10
**11** [a]2 Kin. 17:13; Is. 1:16–19; Jer. 4:1; Acts 26:20 [b]Jer. 7:3–7
**12** [a]Is. 57:10; Jer. 2:25 [b]Jer. 3:17; 23:17 [1]Lit. *do* [2]*stubbornness*, or *imagination*
**13** [a]Is. 66:8; Jer. 2:10, 11; 1 Cor. 5:1 [b]Jer. 5:30; Hos. 6:10
**14** [1]*forsake*
**15** [a]Jer. 2:13, 32 [b]Jer. 6:16
**16** [a]Jer. 19:8 [b]1 Kin. 9:8; Lam. 2:15; Mic. 6:16
**17** [a]Jer. 13:24 [b]Ps. 48:7 [c]Jer. 2:27 [1]So with LXX, Syr., Tg., Vg.; MT *look them in*
**18** [a]Jer. 11:19 [b]Lev. 10:11; Mal. 2:7; [John 7:48]
**20** [a]Ps. 109:4 [b]Ps. 35:7; 57:6; Jer. 5:26 [c]Jer. 14:7—15:1 [1]*concerning*
**21** [a]Ps. 109:9–20; Jer. 11:22; 14:16 [b]Jer. 15:7, 8; Ezek. 22:25
**23** [a]Neh. 4:5; Ps. 35:14; 109:14; Is. 2:9; Jer. 11:20 [b]Jer. 7:20

CHAPTER 19
**2** [a]Josh. 15:8; 2 Kin. 23:10; Jer. 7:31; 32:35
**3** [a]Jer. 17:20 [b]1 Sam. 3:11; 2 Kin. 21:12
**4** [a]Deut. 28:20; Is. 65:11; Jer. 2:13, 17, 19; 15:6; 17:13 [b]2 Kin. 21:12; Jer. 2:34; 7:6
**5** [a]Num. 22:41; Jer. 7:31; 32:35 [b]Lev. 18:21; 2 Kin. 17:17; Ps. 106:37, 38
**6** [a]Josh. 15:8; Jer. 7:32
**7** [a]Lev. 26:17; Deut. 28:25; Jer. 15:2, 9 [b]Ps. 79:2; Jer. 7:33; 16:4; 34:20
**8** [a]Jer. 18:16; 49:13; 50:13
**9** [a]Lev. 26:29; Deut. 28:53, 55; Is. 9:20; Lam. 4:10; Ezek. 5:10
**10** [a]Jer. 51:63, 64
**11** [a]Ps. 2:9; Is. 30:14; Jer. 13:14; Lam. 4:2; Rev. 2:27 [b]Jer. 7:32 [1]*restored*

"and to its inhabitants, and make this city like
Tophet.
13 "And the houses of Jerusalem and the houses
of the kings of Judah shall be defiled [a]like the
place of Tophet, because of all the houses on
whose [b]roofs they have burned incense to all the
host of heaven, and [c]poured out drink offerings to
other gods." ' "
**14** Then Jeremiah came from Tophet, where the
LORD had sent him to prophesy; and he stood in
[a]the court of the Lord's house and said to all the
people,
15 "Thus says the LORD of hosts, the God of
Israel: 'Behold, I will bring on this city and on all
her towns all the doom that I have pronounced
against it, because [a]they have stiffened their necks
that they might not hear My words.' "

### *Jeremiah Imprisoned*

**20** Now [a]Pashhur the son of [b]Immer, the priest
who *was* also chief governor in the house of
the LORD, heard that Jeremiah prophesied these
things.
2 Then Pashhur struck Jeremiah the prophet,
and put him in the stocks that *were* in the high
[a]gate of Benjamin, which *was* by the house of the
LORD.
3 And it happened on the next day that Pashhur
brought Jeremiah out of the stocks. Then Jeremiah said to him, "The LORD has not called your
name Pashhur, but [1]Magor-Missabib.
4 "For thus says the LORD: 'Behold, I will make
you a terror to yourself and to all your friends;
and they shall fall by the sword of their enemies,
and your eyes shall see *it.* I will [a]give all Judah
into the hand of the king of Babylon, and he shall
carry them captive to Babylon and slay them with
the sword.
5 'Moreover I [a]will deliver all the wealth of this
city, all its produce, and all its precious things; all
the treasures of the kings of Judah I will give into
the hand of their enemies, who will plunder them,
seize them, and [b]carry them to Babylon.
6 'And you, Pashhur, and all who dwell in your
house, shall go into captivity. You shall go to
Babylon, and there you shall die, and be buried
there, you and all your friends, to whom you have
[a]prophesied lies.' "

**7** O LORD, You [1]induced me,
and I was persuaded;
[a]You are stronger than I, and have prevailed.
[b]I am [2]in derision daily;
Everyone mocks me.
8 For when I spoke, I cried out;
[a]I shouted, "Violence and plunder!"
Because the word of the LORD was made to
me
A reproach and a derision daily.
9 Then I said, "I will not make mention of
Him,
Nor speak anymore in His name."
But *His word* was in my heart
like a [a]burning fire
Shut up in my bones;
I was weary of holding *it* back,
And [b]I could not.
10 [a]For I heard many [1]mocking:
"Fear on every side!"
"Report," *they say,* "and we will report it!"
[b]All my acquaintances watched for my
stumbling, *saying,*
"Perhaps he can be induced;
Then we will prevail against him,
And we will take our revenge on him."

**11** But the LORD *is* [a]with me as a mighty,
awesome One.
Therefore my persecutors will stumble, and
will not [b]prevail.
They will be greatly ashamed,
for they will not prosper.
*Their* [c]everlasting confusion will never be
forgotten.
12 But, O LORD of hosts,
You who [a]test the righteous,
*And* see the [1]mind and heart,
[b]Let me see Your vengeance on them;
For I have pleaded my cause before You.

**13** Sing to the LORD! Praise the LORD!
For [a]He has delivered the life of the poor
From the hand of evildoers.

**14** [a]Cursed *be* the day in which I was born!
Let the day not be blessed
in which my mother bore me!
15 Let the man *be* cursed
Who brought news to my father, saying,
"A male child has been born to you!"
Making him very glad.
16 And let that man be like the cities
Which the LORD [a]overthrew,
and did not relent;
Let him [b]hear the cry in the morning
And the shouting at noon,
17 [a]Because he did not kill me from the womb,
That my mother might have been my grave,
And her womb always enlarged *with me.*
18 [a]Why did I come forth from the womb to [b]see
[1]labor and sorrow,
That my days should be consumed with
shame?

### *The Destruction of Jerusalem Foretold*

**21** The word which came to Jeremiah from the
LORD when [a]King Zedekiah sent to him
[b]Pashhur the son of Melchiah, and [c]Zephaniah the
son of Maaseiah, the priest, saying,
2 [a]"Please inquire of the LORD for us, for [1]Nebu-
chadnezzar king of Babylon makes war against
us. Perhaps the LORD will deal with us according
to all His wonderful works, that *the king* may go
away from us."
**3** Then Jeremiah said to them, "Thus you shall
say to Zedekiah,
4 'Thus says the LORD God of Israel: "Behold, I
will turn back the weapons of war that *are* in your
hands, with which you fight against the king of
Babylon and the [1]Chaldeans who besiege you
outside the walls; and [a]I will assemble them in the
midst of this city.
5 "I [a]Myself will fight against you with an
[b]outstretched hand and with a strong arm, even in
anger and fury and great wrath.
6 "I will strike the inhabitants of this city, both
man and beast; they shall die of a great pestilence.
7 "And afterward," says the LORD, [a]"I will deliver Zedekiah king of Judah, his servants and
the people, and such as are left in this city
from the pestilence and the sword and the famine,
into the hand of Nebuchadnezzar king of

---

13 [a]2 Kin. 23:10 [b]Zeph. 1:5 [c]Jer. 7:18
14 [a]2 Chr. 20:5
15 [a]Neh. 9:17, 29

CHAPTER 20
1 [a]Ezra 2:37, 38 [b]1 Chr. 24:14
2 [a]Jer. 37:13
3 [1]Lit. *Fear on Every Side*
4 [a]Jer. 21:4–10
5 [a]2 Kin. 20:17 [b]Is. 39:6
6 [a]Jer. 14:13–15
7 [a]Jer. 1:6, 7 [b]Lam. 3:14 [1]*enticed* or *persuaded* [2]Lit. *a laughingstock all the day*
8 [a]Jer. 6:7
9 [a]Ps. 39:3 [b]Job 32:18
10 [a]Ps. 31:13 [b]Ps. 41:9; 55:13, 14 [1]*slandering*
11 [a]Jer. 1:18, 19 [b]Jer. 15:20; 17:18 [c]Jer. 23:40
12 [a][Jer. 11:20; 17:10] [b]Ps. 54:7; 59:10 [1]Most secret parts, lit. *kidneys*
13 [a]Ps. 35:9, 10; 109:30, 31
14 [a]Job 3:3
16 [a]Gen. 19:25 [b]Jer. 18:22
17 [a]Job 3:10, 11
18 [a]Job 3:20 [b]Lam. 3:1 [1]*toil*

CHAPTER 21
1 [a]2 Kin. 24:17, 18 [b]Jer. 38:1 [c]2 Kin. 25:18
2 [a]Jer. 37:3, 7 [1]Heb. *Nebuchadrezzar,* and so elsewhere in the book
4 [a]Is. 13:4 [1]Or *Babylonians,* and so elsewhere in the book
5 [a]Is. 63:10 [b]Ex. 6:6
7 [a]Jer. 37:17; 39:5; 52:9

Babylon, into the hand of their enemies, and into
the hand of those who seek their life; and he shall
strike them with the edge of the sword. [b]He shall
not spare them, or have pity or mercy." '
8 "Now you shall say to this people, 'Thus says
the LORD: "Behold, [a]I set before you the way of life
and the way of death.
9 "He who [a]remains in this city shall die by the
sword, by famine, and by pestilence; but he who
goes out and [1]defects to the Chaldeans who besiege you, he shall [b]live, and his life shall be as a
prize to him.
10 "For I have [a]set My face against this city for
adversity and not for good," says the LORD. [b]"It
shall be given into the hand of the king of Babylon, and he shall [c]burn it with fire." '
11 "And concerning the house of the king of
Judah, *say*, 'Hear the word of the LORD,
12 'O house of David! Thus says the LORD:

[a]"Execute[1] judgment [b]in the morning;
And deliver *him who is* plundered
Out of the hand of the oppressor,
Lest My fury go forth like fire
And burn so that no one can quench *it*,
Because of the evil of your doings.

13 "Behold, [a]I *am* against you,
O [1]inhabitant of the valley,
*And* rock of the plain," says the LORD,
"Who say, [b]'Who shall come down against us?
Or who shall enter our dwellings?'
14 But I will punish you according to the [a]fruit
of your [1]doings," says the LORD;
"I will kindle a fire in its forest,
And [b]it shall devour all things around it." ' "

## *Prophecies Against the Kings of Judah*

**22** Thus says the LORD: "Go down to the house
of the king of Judah, and there speak this
word,
2 "and say, [a]'Hear the word of the LORD, O king
of Judah, you who sit on the throne of David, you
and your servants and your people who enter
these gates!
3 'Thus says the LORD: [a]"Execute[1] judgment and
righteousness, and deliver the plundered out of
the hand of the oppressor. Do no wrong and do no
violence to the stranger, the [b]fatherless, or the
widow, nor shed innocent blood in this place.
4 "For if you indeed do this thing, [a]then shall
enter the gates of this house, riding on horses and
in chariots, accompanied by servants and people,
kings who sit on the throne of David.
5 "But if you will not [1]hear these words, [a]I swear
by Myself," says the LORD, "that this house shall
become a desolation." ' "
6 For thus says the LORD to the house of the
king of Judah:

"You *are* [a]Gilead to Me,
The head of Lebanon;
*Yet* I surely will make you a wilderness,
Cities *which* are not inhabited.
7 I will prepare destroyers against you,
Everyone with his weapons;
They shall cut down [a]your choice cedars
[b]And cast *them* into the fire.

8 "And many nations will pass by this city; and
everyone will say to his neighbor, [a]'Why has the
LORD done so to this great city?'

9 "Then they will answer, [a]'Because they have
forsaken the covenant of the LORD their God, and
worshiped other gods and served them.' "
10 Weep not for [a]the dead, nor bemoan him;
Weep bitterly for him [b]who goes away,
For he shall return no more,
Nor see his native country.

11 For thus says the LORD concerning [a]Shallum[1]
the son of Josiah, king of Judah, who reigned
instead of Josiah his father, [b]who went from this
place: "He shall not return here anymore,
12 "but he shall die in the place where they have
led him captive, and shall see this land no more.

13 "Woe[a] to him who builds his house by
unrighteousness
And his [1]chambers by injustice,
[b]*Who* uses his neighbor's service without
wages
And gives him nothing for his work,
14 Who says, 'I will build myself a wide house
with spacious [1]chambers,
And cut out windows for it,
Paneling *it* with cedar
And painting *it* with vermilion.'
15 "Shall you reign because you enclose *yourself*
in cedar?
Did not your father eat and drink,
And do justice and righteousness?
Then [a]*it was* well with him.
16 He [1]judged the cause of the poor and needy;
Then *it was* well.
*Was* not this knowing Me?" says the LORD.
17 "Yet[a] your eyes and your heart *are* for
nothing but your covetousness,
For shedding innocent blood,
And practicing oppression and violence."

18 Therefore thus says the LORD concerning
Jehoiakim the son of Josiah, king of Judah:

[a]"They shall not lament for him,
*Saying*, [b]'Alas, my brother!'
or 'Alas, my sister!'
They shall not lament for him,
*Saying*, 'Alas, master!' or 'Alas, his glory!'
19 [a]He shall be buried with the burial
of a donkey,
Dragged and cast out beyond the gates of
Jerusalem.

20 "Go up to Lebanon, and cry out,
And lift up your voice in Bashan;
Cry from Abarim,
For all your lovers are destroyed.
21 I spoke to you in your prosperity,
*But* you said, 'I will not hear.'
[a]This *has been* your manner from your youth,
That you did not obey My voice.
22 The wind shall eat up all [a]your [1]rulers,
And your lovers shall go into captivity;
Surely then you will be ashamed and
humiliated
For all your wickedness.
23 O inhabitant of Lebanon,
Making your nest in the cedars,
How gracious will you be when pangs come
upon you,
Like [a]the pain of a woman in [1]labor?

24 "*As* I live," says the LORD, [a]"though [1]Coniah
the son of Jehoiakim, king of Judah, [b]were the

---

7 [b]2 Chr. 36:17
8 [a]Deut. 30:15, 19
9 [a]Jer. 38:2 [b]Jer. 39:18 [1]Lit. *falls away to*
10 [a]Amos 9:4 [b]Jer. 38:3 [c]Jer. 34:2, 22; 37:10
12 [a]Zech. 7:9 [b]Ps. 101:8 [1]*Dispense justice*
13 [a][Ezek. 13:8] [b]Jer. 49:4 [1]*dweller*
14 [a]Is. 3:10, 11; [b]2 Chr. 36:19 [1]*deeds*

CHAPTER 22
2 [a]Jer. 17:20
3 [a]Jer. 21:12 [b]Jer. 7:6 [1]*Dispense justice*
4 [a]Jer. 17:25
5 [a]Heb. 6:13, 17 [1]Obey
6 [a]Song 4:1
7 [a]Is. 37:24 [b]Jer. 21:14
8 [a]Deut. 29:24–26
9 [a]2 Chr. 34:25
10 [a]2 Kin. 22:20 [b]Jer. 14:17; 22:11
11 [a]1 Chr. 3:15 [b]2 Kin. 23:34 [1]Or *Jehoahaz*
13 [a]2 Kin. 23:35 [b]James 5:4 [1]Lit. *roof chambers, upper chambers*
14 [1]Lit. *roof chambers, upper chambers*
15 [a]Ps. 128:2
16 [1]Defended
17 [a]Ezek. 19:6
18 [a]Jer. 16:4, 6 [b]1 Kin. 13:30
19 [a]Jer. 36:30
21 [a]Jer. 3:24, 25; 32:30
22 [a]Jer. 23:1 [1]Lit. *shepherds*
23 [a]Jer. 6:24 [1]*childbirth*
24 [a]2 Kin. 24:6, 8 [b]Hag. 2:23 [1]Or *Jeconiah* or *Jehoiachin*

[2]signet on My right hand, yet I would pluck you
off;
25 [a]"and I will give you into the hand of those
who seek your life, and into the hand *of those*
whose face you fear—the hand of Nebuchadnezzar king of Babylon and the hand of the [1]Chalde-
ans.
26 [a]"So I will cast you out, and your mother who
bore you, into another country where you were
not born; and there you shall die.
27 "But to the land to which they desire to
return, there they shall not return.

28 "Is this man [1]Coniah a despised, broken idol—
[a]A vessel in which *is* no pleasure?
Why are they cast out,
he and his descendants,
And cast into a land which they
do not know?
**29** [a]O earth, earth, earth,
Hear the word of the LORD!
30 Thus says the LORD:
'Write this man down as [a]childless,
A man *who* shall not prosper in his days;
For [b]none of his descendants shall prosper,
Sitting on the throne of David,
And ruling anymore in Judah.' "

## *False Prophets*

**23** "Woe [a]to the shepherds who destroy and
scatter the sheep of My pasture!" says the
LORD.
2 Therefore thus says the LORD God of Israel
against the shepherds who feed My people: "You
have scattered My flock, driven them away, and
not attended to them. [a]Behold, I will attend to you
for the evil of your doings," says the LORD.
3 "But [a]I will gather the remnant of My flock
out of all countries where I have driven them, and
bring them back to their folds; and they shall be
fruitful and increase.
4 "I will set up [a]shepherds over them who will
feed them; and they shall fear no more, nor be
dismayed, nor shall they be lacking," says the
LORD.

**5** "Behold, [a]*the* days are coming,"
says the LORD,
"That I will raise to David
a Branch of righteousness;
A King shall reign and [1]prosper,
[b]And execute [2]judgment and righteousness in
the [3]earth.
6 [a]In His days Judah will be saved,
And Israel [b]will dwell safely;
Now [c]this *is* His name by which He will be
called:

[1]THE LORD OUR RIGHTEOUSNESS.

**7** "Therefore, behold, [a]*the* days are coming,"
says the LORD, "that they shall no longer say, 'As
the LORD lives who brought up the children of
Israel from the land of Egypt,'
8 but, 'As the LORD lives who brought up and
led the descendants of the house of Israel from the
north country [a]and from all the countries where I
had driven them.' And they shall dwell in their
own [b]land."

**9** My heart within me is broken
Because of the prophets;
[a]All my bones shake.
I am like a drunken man,
And like a man whom wine has overcome,
Because of the LORD,
And because of His holy words.
10 For [a]the land is full of adulterers;
For [b]because of a curse the land mourns.
[c]The pleasant places of the wilderness are
dried up.
Their course of life is evil,
And their might *is* not right.

**11** "For [a]both prophet and priest are profane;
Yes, [b]in My house I have found their
wickedness," says the LORD.
12 "Therefore[a] their way shall be to them
Like slippery *ways;*
In the darkness they shall be driven on
And fall in them;
For I [b]will bring disaster on them,
The year of their punishment,"
says the LORD.
13 "And I have seen [1]folly in the prophets of
Samaria:
[a]They prophesied by Baal
And [b]caused My people Israel to err.
14 Also I have seen a horrible thing in the
prophets of Jerusalem:
[a]They commit adultery and walk in lies;
They also [b]strengthen the hands of evildoers,
So that no one turns back from his
wickedness.
All of them are like [c]Sodom to Me,
And her inhabitants like Gomorrah.

15 "Therefore thus says the LORD of hosts
concerning the prophets:
'Behold, I will feed them with [a]wormwood,
And make them drink the water of gall;
For from the prophets of Jerusalem
[1]Profaneness has gone out into all the land.' "

**16** Thus says the LORD of hosts:

"Do not listen to the words of the prophets
who prophesy to you.
They make you worthless;
[a]They speak a vision of their own heart,
Not from the mouth of the LORD.
17 They continually say to those who despise
Me,
'The LORD has said, [a]"You shall have peace" ';
And to everyone who [b]walks according to
the [1]dictates of his own heart,
[c]'No evil shall come upon you.' "

**18** For [a]who has stood in the counsel of the
LORD,
And has perceived and heard His word?
Who has marked His word and heard *it?*
19 Behold, a [a]whirlwind of the LORD has gone
forth in fury—
A violent whirlwind!
It will fall violently on the head of the
wicked.
20 The [a]anger of the LORD will not turn back
Until He has executed and performed the
thoughts of His heart.
[b]In the latter days you will understand it
perfectly.

**21** "I[a] have not sent these prophets, yet they ran.
I have not spoken to them,
yet they prophesied.
22 But if they had stood in My counsel,
And had caused My people to hear My
words,

**24** [2]*signet ring*
**25** [a]Jer. 34:20 [1]Or *Babylonians*
**26** [a]2 Kin. 24:15
**28** [a]Hos. 8:8 [1]See note at v. 24
**29** [a]Deut. 32:1
**30** [a]Matt. 1:12 [b]Jer. 36:30

CHAPTER 23
**1** [a]Jer. 10:21
**2** [a]Ex. 32:34
**3** [a]Jer. 32:37
**4** [a]Jer. 3:15
**5** [a]Jer. 33:14 [b]Ps. 72:2 [1]*act wisely* [2]*justice* [3]*land*
**6** [a]Zech. 14:11 [b]Jer. 32:37 [c][1 Cor. 1:30] [1]Heb. *YHWH Tsidkenu*
**7** [a]Jer. 16:14
**8** [a]Is. 43:5, 6 [b]Gen. 12:7
**9** [a]Hab. 3:16
**10** [a]Jer. 9:2 [b]Hos. 4:2 [c]Jer. 9:10
**11** [a]Zeph. 3:4 [b]Jer. 7:30; 32:34
**12** [a][Prov. 4:19] [b]Jer. 11:23
**13** [a]Jer. 2:8 [b]Is. 9:16 [1]Lit. *distastefulness*
**14** [a]Jer. 29:23 [b]Ezek. 13:22, 23 [c]Is. 1:9, 10
**15** [a]Jer. 9:15 [1]Or *Pollution*
**16** [a]Jer. 14:14
**17** [a]Ezek. 13:10 [b]Deut. 29:19; Jer. 3:17 [c]Mic. 3:11 [1]*stubbornness,* or *imagination*
**18** [a][1 Cor. 2:16]
**19** [a]Amos 1:14
**20** [a]Jer. 30:24 [b]Gen. 49:1
**21** [a]Jer. 14:14; 23:32; 27:15

Then they would have [a]turned them from
their evil way
And from the evil of their doings.

**23** "*Am* I a God near at hand," says the LORD,
"And not a God afar off?
24 Can anyone [a]hide himself in secret places,
So I shall not see him?" says the LORD;
[b]"Do I not fill heaven and earth?"
says the LORD.

25 "I have heard what the prophets have said
who prophesy lies in My name, saying, 'I have
dreamed, I have dreamed!'
26 "How long will *this* be in the heart of the
prophets who prophesy lies? Indeed *they are*
prophets of the deceit of their own heart,
27 "who try to make My people forget My name
by their dreams which everyone tells his neighbor,
[a]as their fathers forgot My name for Baal.

28 "The prophet who has a dream,
let him tell a dream;
And he who has My word,
let him speak My word faithfully.
What *is* the chaff to the wheat?"
says the LORD.
29 "*Is* not My word like a [a]fire?" says the LORD,
"And like a hammer *that* breaks the rock in
pieces?

**30** "Therefore behold, [a]I *am* against the prophets," says the LORD, "who steal My words every
one from his neighbor.
31 "Behold, I *am* [a]against the prophets," says the
LORD, "who use their tongues and say, 'He says.'
32 "Behold, I *am* against those who prophesy
false dreams," says the LORD, "and tell them, and
cause My people to err by their [a]lies and by [b]their
recklessness. Yet I did not send them or command
them; therefore they shall not [c]profit this people at
all," says the LORD.
**33** "So when these people or the prophet or the
priest ask you, saying, 'What is [a]the [1]oracle of the
LORD?' you shall then say to them, [2]'What oracle?'
I will even forsake you," says the LORD.
34 "And *as for* the prophet and the priest and the
people who say, 'The [1]oracle of the LORD!' I will
even punish that man and his house.
35 "Thus every one of you shall say to his neighbor, and every one to his brother, 'What has the
LORD answered?' and, 'What has the LORD spoken?'
36 "And the [1]oracle of the LORD you shall mention no more. For every man's word will be his
oracle, for you have [a]perverted the words of the
living God, the LORD of hosts, our God.
37 "Thus you shall say to the prophet, 'What has
the LORD answered you?' and, 'What has the LORD
spoken?'
38 "But since you say, 'The [1]oracle of the LORD!'
therefore thus says the LORD: 'Because you say
this word, "The oracle of the LORD!" and I have
sent to you, saying, "Do not say, 'The oracle of the
LORD!' "
39 'therefore behold, I, even I, [a]will utterly forget
you and forsake you, and the city that I gave you
and your fathers, and *will cast you* out of My
presence.
40 'And I will bring [a]an everlasting reproach
upon you, and a perpetual [b]shame, which shall not
be forgotten.' "

**22** [a]Jer. 25:5
**24** [a][Ps. 139:7]; Amos 9:2, 3 [b][1 Kin. 8:27]; Ps. 139:7
**27** [a]Judg. 3:7
**29** [a]Jer. 5:14
**30** [a]Deut. 18:20; Ps. 34:16; Jer. 14:14, 15; Ezek. 13:8, 9
**31** [a]Ezek. 13:9
**32** [a]Jer. 20:6; 27:10; Lam. 2:14; 3:37 [b]Zeph. 3:4 [c]Jer. 7:8; Lam. 2:14
**33** [a]Is. 13:1; Nah. 1:1; Hab. 1:1; Zech. 9:1; Mal. 1:1 [1]*burden, prophecy* [2]LXX, Tg., Vg. *'You are the burden'*
**34** [1]*burden, prophecy*
**36** [a]Deut. 4:2 [1]*burden, prophecy*
**38** [1]*burden, prophecy*
**39** [a]Hos. 4:6
**40** [a]Jer. 20:11; Ezek. 5:14, 15 [b]Mic. 3:5–7

CHAPTER 24
**1** [a]Amos 7:1, 4; 8:1 [b]2 Kin. 24:12–16; 2 Chr. 36:10 [c]Jer. 22:24–28; 29:2
**2** [a]Is. 5:4, 7; Jer. 29:17
**5** [1]*regard*
**6** [a]Jer. 12:15; 29:10; Ezek. 11:17 [b]Jer. 32:41; 33:7; 42:10
**7** [a][Deut. 30:6; Jer. 32:39; Ezek. 11:19; 36:26, 27] [b]Is. 51:16; Jer. 30:22; 31:33; 32:38; Ezek. 14:11; Zech. 8:8; [Heb. 8:10] [c]1 Sam. 7:3; Ps. 119:2; Jer. 29:13
**8** [a]Jer. 29:17 [b]Jer. 39:9 [c]Jer. 44:1, 26–30
**9** [a]Deut. 28:25, 37; 1 Kin. 9:7; 2 Chr. 7:20; Jer. 15:4; 29:18; 34:17 [b]Ps. 44:13, 14
**10** [1]*destroyed*

CHAPTER 25
**1** [a]Jer. 36:1 [b]2 Kin. 24:1, 2; 2 Chr. 36:4–6; Dan. 1:1, 2
**3** [a]Jer. 1:2 [b]Jer. 7:13; 11:7, 8, 10
**4** [a]Jer. 7:13, 25
**5** [a]2 Kin. 17:13; [Is. 55:6, 7]; Jer. 18:11; Ezek. 18:30; [Jon. 3:8–10]

### *The Lesson from the Good and Bad Figs*

**24** The [a]LORD showed me, and there were two
baskets of figs set before the temple of the
LORD, after Nebuchadnezzar [b]king of Babylon had
carried away captive [c]Jeconiah the son of Jehoiakim, king of Judah, and the princes of Judah with
the craftsmen and smiths, from Jerusalem, and
had brought them to Babylon.
2 One basket *had* very good figs, like the figs
*that are* first ripe; and the other basket *had* very
bad figs which could not be eaten, they were so
[a]bad.
3 Then the LORD said to me, "What do you see,
Jeremiah?" And I said, "Figs, the good figs, very
good; and the bad, very bad, which cannot be
eaten, they are so bad."
**4** Again the word of the LORD came to me,
saying,
5 "Thus says the LORD, the God of Israel: 'Like
these good figs, so will I [1]acknowledge those who
are carried away captive from Judah, whom I
have sent out of this place for *their own* good, into
the land of the Chaldeans.
6 'For I will set My eyes on them for good, and
[a]I will bring them back to this land; [b]I will build
them and not pull *them* down, and I will plant
them and not pluck *them* up.
7 'Then I will give them [a]a heart to know Me,
that I *am* the LORD; and they shall be [b]My people,
and I will be their God, for they shall return to Me
[c]with their whole heart.
**8** 'And as the bad [a]figs which cannot be eaten,
they are so bad'—surely thus says the LORD—'so
will I give up Zedekiah the king of Judah, his
princes, the [b]residue of Jerusalem who remain in
this land, and [c]those who dwell in the land of
Egypt.
9 'I will deliver them to [a]trouble into all the
kingdoms of the earth, for *their* harm, [b]*to be* a
reproach and a byword, a taunt and a curse, in all
places where I shall drive them.
10 'And I will send the sword, the famine, and the
pestilence among them, till they are [1]consumed
from the land that I gave to them and their
fathers.' "

### *Seventy Years of Suffering*

**25** The word that came to Jeremiah concerning all the people of Judah, [a]in the fourth
year of [b]Jehoiakim the son of Josiah, king of
Judah (which *was* the first year of Nebuchadnezzar king of Babylon),
2 which Jeremiah the prophet spoke to all the
people of Judah and to all the inhabitants of
Jerusalem, saying:
3 [a]"From the thirteenth year of Josiah the son of
Amon, king of Judah, even to this day, this *is* the
twenty-third year in which the word of the LORD
has come to me; and I have spoken to you, rising
early and speaking, [b]but you have not listened.
4 "And the LORD has sent to you all His servants
the prophets, [a]rising early and sending *them,* but
you have not listened nor inclined your ear to
hear.
5 "They said, [a]'Repent now everyone of his evil
way and his evil doings, and dwell in the land that
the LORD has given to you and your fathers
forever and ever.
6 'Do not go after other gods to serve them and
worship them, and do not provoke Me to anger

with the works of your hands; and I will not harm
you.'
7 "Yet you have not listened to Me," says the
LORD, "that you might [a]provoke Me to anger with
the works of your hands to your own hurt.
**8** "Therefore thus says the LORD of hosts: 'Because you have not heard My words,
9 'behold, I will send and take [a]all the families of
the north,' says the LORD, 'and Nebuchadnezzar
the king of Babylon, [b]My servant, and will bring
them against this land, against its inhabitants, and
against these nations all around, and will utterly
destroy them, and [c]make them an astonishment, a
hissing, and perpetual desolations.
10 'Moreover I will [1]take from them the [a]voice of
mirth and the voice of gladness, the voice of the
bridegroom and the voice of the bride, [b]the sound
of the millstones and the light of the lamp.
11 'And this whole land shall be a desolation *and*
an astonishment, and these nations shall serve the
king of Babylon seventy [a]years.
**12** 'Then it will come to pass, [a]when [1]seventy
years are completed, *that* I will punish the king of
Babylon and that nation, the land of the Chaldeans, for their iniquity,' says the LORD; [b]'and I will
make it a perpetual desolation.
13 'So I will bring on that land all My words
which I have pronounced against it, all that is
written in this book, which Jeremiah has prophesied concerning all the nations.
14 [a]'(For many nations [b]and great kings shall [c]be
served by them also; [d]and I will repay them
according to their deeds and according to the
works of their own hands.)' "
**15** For thus says the LORD God of Israel to me:
"Take this [a]wine cup of [1]fury from My hand, and
cause all the nations, to whom I send you, to
drink it.
16 "And [a]they will drink and stagger and go mad
because of the sword that I will send among
them."
17 Then I took the cup from the LORD's hand,
and made all the nations drink, to whom the LORD
had sent me:
18 Jerusalem and the cities of Judah, its kings
and its princes, to make them [a]a desolation, an
astonishment, a hissing, and [b]a curse, as *it is* this
day;
19 Pharaoh king of Egypt, his servants, his
princes, and all his people;
20 all the mixed multitude, all the kings of [a]the
land of Uz, all the kings of the land of the [b]Philis-
tines (namely, Ashkelon, Gaza, Ekron, and [c]the
remnant of Ashdod);
21 [a]Edom, Moab, and the people of Ammon;
22 all the kings of [a]Tyre, all the kings of Sidon,
and the kings of the coastlands which *are* across
the [b]sea;
23 [a]Dedan, Tema, Buz, and all *who are* in the
farthest corners;
24 all the kings of Arabia and all the kings of the
[a]mixed multitude who dwell in the desert;
25 all the kings of Zimri, all the kings of [a]Elam,
and all the kings of the [b]Medes;
26 [a]all the kings of the north, far and near, one
with another; and all the kingdoms of the world
which *are* on the face of the earth. Also the king
of [1]Sheshach shall drink after them.
**27** "Therefore you shall say to them, 'Thus says
the LORD of hosts, the God of Israel: [a]"Drink, [b]be
drunk, and vomit! Fall and rise no more, because
of the sword which I will send among you." '
28 "And it shall be, if they refuse to take the cup
from your hand to drink, then you shall say to
them, 'Thus says the LORD of hosts: "You shall
certainly drink!
29 "For behold, [a]I begin to bring calamity on the
city [b]which is called by My name, and should you
be utterly unpunished? You shall not be unpunished, for [c]I will call for a sword on all the inhabitants of the earth," says the LORD of hosts.'
**30** "Therefore prophesy against them all these
words, and say to them:

'The LORD will [a]roar from on high,
And utter His voice from [b]His holy
habitation;
He will roar mightily against [c]His fold.
He will give [d]a shout,
as those who tread *the grapes,*
Against all the inhabitants of the earth.
31 A noise will come to the ends of the earth—
For the LORD has [a]a controversy with the
nations;
[b]He will plead His case with all flesh.
He will give those *who are* wicked
to the sword,' says the LORD."

**32** Thus says the LORD of hosts:

"Behold, disaster shall go forth
From nation to nation,
And [a]a great whirlwind shall be raised up
From the farthest parts of the earth.

33 [a]"And at that day the slain of the LORD shall
be from *one* end of the earth even to the *other* end
of the earth. They shall not be [b]lamented, [c]or
gathered, or buried; they shall become refuse on
the ground.

**34** "Wail,[a] shepherds, and cry!
Roll about *in the ashes,*
You leaders of the flock!
For the days of your slaughter and your
dispersions are fulfilled;
You shall fall like a precious vessel.
35 And the shepherds will have no [1]way to flee,
Nor the leaders of the flock to escape.
36 A voice of the cry of the shepherds,
And a wailing of the leaders to the flock *will
be heard.*
For the LORD has plundered their pasture,
37 And the peaceful dwellings are cut down
Because of the fierce anger of the LORD.
38 He has left His lair like the lion;
For their land is desolate
Because of the fierceness of the Oppressor,
And because of His fierce anger."

### *Jeremiah Saved from Death*

**26** In the beginning of the reign of Jehoiakim
the son of Josiah, king of Judah, this word
came from the LORD, saying,
2 "Thus says the LORD: 'Stand in [a]the court of
the LORD's house, and speak to all the cities of
Judah, which come to worship *in* the LORD's
house, [b]all the words that I command you to
speak to them. [c]Do not diminish a word.
3 [a]'Perhaps everyone will listen and turn from
his evil way, that I may [b]relent concerning the
calamity which I purpose to bring on them because of the evil of their doings.'

---

7 [a]Deut. 32:21
9 [a]Jer. 1:15 [b]Is. 45:1 [c]Jer. 18:16
10 [a]Rev. 18:23 [b]Eccl. 12:4 [1]Lit. *cause to perish from them*
11 [a]Jer. 29:10
12 [a]Ezra 1:1 [b]Is. 13:20 [1]Beginning circa 605 B.C. (2 Kin. 24:1) and ending circa 536 B.C. (Ezra 1:1)
14 [a]Jer. 50:9; 51:27, 28 [b]Jer. 51:27 [c]Jer. 27:7 [d]Jer. 50:29; 51:6, 24
15 [a]Rev. 14:10 [1]*wrath*
16 [a]Nah. 3:11
18 [a]Jer. 25:9, 11 [b]Jer. 24:9
20 [a]Job 1:1 [b]Jer. 47:1–7 [c]Is. 20:1
21 [a]Jer. 49:7
22 [a]Jer. 47:4 [b]Jer. 49:23
23 [a]Jer. 49:7, 8
24 [a]Ezek. 30:5
25 [a]Jer. 49:34 [b]Jer. 51:11, 28
26 [a]Jer. 50:9 [1]A code word for *Babylon,* Jer. 51:41
27 [a]Hab. 2:16 [b]Is. 63:6
29 [a]Ezek. 9:6 [b]Dan. 9:18 [c]Ezek. 38:21
30 [a]Amos 1:2 [b]Ps. 11:4 [c]1 Kin. 9:3 [d]Is. 16:9
31 [a]Mic. 6:2 [b]Is. 66:16
32 [a]Jer. 23:19; 30:23
33 [a]Is. 34:2, 3; 66:16 [b]Jer. 16:4, 6 [c]Ps. 79:3
34 [a]Jer. 4:8; 6:26
35 [1]Or *refuge,*
CHAPTER 26
2 [a]Jer. 19:14 [b]Matt. 28:20 [c]Acts 20:27
3 [a]Jer. 36:3–7 [b]Jer. 18:8

4 "And you shall say to them, 'Thus says the LORD: [a]"If you will not listen to Me, to walk in My law which I have set before you,

5 "to heed the words of My servants the prophets [a]whom I sent to you, both rising up early and sending *them* (but you have not heeded),

6 "then I will make this house like [a]Shiloh, and will make this city [b]a curse to all the nations of the earth." ' "

**7** So the priests and the prophets and all the people heard Jeremiah speaking these words in the house of the LORD.

8 Now it happened, when Jeremiah had made an end of speaking all that the LORD had commanded *him* to speak to all the people, that the priests and the prophets and all the people seized him, saying, "You will surely die!

9 "Why have you prophesied in the name of the LORD, saying, 'This house shall be like Shiloh, and this city shall be [a]desolate, without an inhabitant'?" And all the people were gathered against Jeremiah in the house of the LORD.

**10** When the princes of Judah heard these things, they came up from the king's house to the house of the LORD and sat down in the entry of the New Gate of the LORD's *house.*

11 And the priests and the prophets spoke to the princes and all the people, saying, [1]"This man deserves to [a]die! For he has prophesied against this city, as you have heard with your ears."

**12** Then Jeremiah spoke to all the princes and all the people, saying: "The LORD sent me to prophesy against this house and against this city with all the words that you have heard.

13 "Now therefore, [a]amend your ways and your doings, and obey the voice of the LORD your God; then the LORD will relent concerning the doom that He has pronounced against you.

14 "As for me, here [a]I am, in your hand; do with me as seems good and [1]proper to you.

15 "But know for certain that if you put me to death, you will surely bring innocent blood on yourselves, on this city, and on its inhabitants; for truly the LORD has sent me to you to speak all these words in your hearing."

**16** So the princes and all the people said to the priests and the prophets, "This man does not deserve to die. For he has spoken to us in the name of the LORD our God."

17 [a]Then certain of the elders of the land rose up and spoke to all the assembly of the people, saying:

18 [a]"Micah of Moresheth prophesied in the days of Hezekiah king of Judah, and spoke to all the people of Judah, saying, 'Thus says the LORD of hosts:

[b]"Zion shall be plowed *like* a field,
Jerusalem shall become [c]heaps of ruins,
And the mountain of the [1]temple
Like the [2]bare hills of the forest." '

19 "Did Hezekiah king of Judah and all Judah ever put him to death? [a]Did he not fear the LORD and [b]seek the LORD's favor? And the Lord [c]relented concerning the doom which He had pronounced against them. [d]But we are doing great evil against ourselves."

**20** Now there was also a man who prophesied in the name of the LORD, Urijah the son of Shemaiah of Kirjath Jearim, who prophesied against this city and against this land according to all the words of Jeremiah.

21 And when Jehoiakim the king, with all his mighty men and all the princes, heard his words, the king sought to put him to death; but when Urijah heard *it,* he was afraid and fled, and went to Egypt.

22 Then Jehoiakim the king sent men to Egypt: Elnathan the son of Achbor, and *other* men *who went* with him to Egypt.

23 And they brought Urijah from Egypt and brought him to Jehoiakim the king, who killed him with the sword and cast his dead body into the graves of the [1]common people.

24 Nevertheless [a]the hand of Ahikam the son of Shaphan was with Jeremiah, so that they should not give him into the hand of the people to put him to death.

## *Symbol of the Bonds and Yokes*

**27** In[1] the beginning of the reign of [2]Jehoiakim the son of Josiah, [a]king of Judah, this word came to Jeremiah from the LORD, saying,

2 "Thus says the LORD to me: 'Make for yourselves bonds and yokes, [a]and put them on your neck,

3 'and send them to the king of Edom, the king of Moab, the king of the Ammonites, the king of Tyre, and the king of Sidon, by the hand of the messengers who come to Jerusalem to Zedekiah king of Judah.

4 'And command them to say to their masters, "Thus says the LORD of hosts, the God of Israel—thus you shall say to your masters:

5 [a]'I have made the earth, the man and the beast that *are* on the ground, by My great power and by My outstretched arm, and [b]have given it to whom it seemed proper to Me.

6 [a]'And now I have given all these lands into the hand of Nebuchadnezzar the king of Babylon, [b]My servant; and [c]the beasts of the field I have also given him to serve him.

7 [a]'So all nations shall serve him and his son and his son's son, [b]until the time of his land comes; [c]and then many nations and great kings shall make him serve them.

8 'And it shall be, *that* the nation and kingdom which will not serve Nebuchadnezzar the king of Babylon, and which will not put its neck under the yoke of the king of Babylon, that nation I will punish,' says the LORD, 'with the sword, the famine, and the pestilence, until I have consumed them by his hand.

9 'Therefore do not listen to your prophets, your diviners, your [1]dreamers, your soothsayers, or your sorcerers, who speak to you, saying, "You shall not serve the king of Babylon."

10 'For they prophesy a [a]lie to you, to remove you far from your land; and I will drive you out, and you will perish.

11 'But the nations that bring their necks under the yoke of the king of Babylon and serve him, I will let them remain in their own land,' says the LORD, 'and they shall till it and dwell in it.' " ' "

**12** I also spoke to [a]Zedekiah king of Judah according to all these words, saying, "Bring your necks under the yoke of the king of Babylon, and serve him and his people, and live!

13 [a]"Why will you die, you and your people, by the sword, by the famine, and by the pestilence, as

**4** [a]Lev. 26:14, 15; Deut. 28:15; 1 Kin. 9:6; Is. 1:20; Jer. 17:27; 22:5
**5** [a]Jer. 25:4; 29:19
**6** [a]1 Sam. 4:10, 11; Ps. 78:60; Jer. 7:12, 14 [b]2 Kin. 22:19; Is. 65:15; Jer. 24:9
**9** [a]Jer. 9:11
**11** [a]Jer. 38:4 [1]Lit. *A judgment of death to this man*
**13** [a]Jer. 7:3; [Joel 2:13]; Jon. 3:8
**14** [a]Jer. 38:5 [1]*right*
**17** [a]Acts 5:34
**18** [a]Mic. 1:1 [b]Mic. 3:12 [c]Neh. 4:2; Ps. 79:1; Jer. 9:11 [1]Lit. *house* [2]Lit. *high places*
**19** [a]2 Chr. 32:26; Is. 37:1, 4, 15–20 [b]2 Kin. 20:1–19 [c]Ex. 32:14; 2 Sam. 24:16; Jer. 18:8 [d][Acts 5:39]
**23** [1]Lit. *sons of the people*
**24** [a]2 Kin. 22:12–14; Jer. 39:14; 40:5–7

CHAPTER 27
**1** [a]Jer. 27:3, 12, 20; 28:1 [1]LXX omits v. 1 [2]So with MT, Tg., Vg.; some Heb. mss., Arab., Syr. *Zedekiah* (cf. 27:3, 12; 28:1)
**2** [a]Jer. 28:10, 12; Ezek. 4:1; 12:3; 24:3
**5** [a]Ps. 115:15; 146:6; Is. 45:12 [b]Deut. 9:29; Ps. 115:16; Jer. 32:17; Dan. 4:17, 25, 32
**6** [a]Jer. 28:14 [b]Jer. 25:9; 43:10; Ezek. 29:18, 20 [c]Jer. 28:14; Dan. 2:38
**7** [a]2 Chr. 36:20 [b]Jer. 25:12; 50:27; [Dan. 5:26]; Zech. 2:8, 9 [c]Jer. 25:14
**9** [1]Lit. *dreams*
**10** [a]Jer. 23:16, 32; 28:15
**12** [a]Jer. 28:1; 38:17
**13** [a][Prov. 8:36]; Jer. 27:8; 38:23; [Ezek. 18:31]

the LORD has spoken against the nation that will not serve the king of Babylon?

14 "Therefore [a]do not listen to the words of the prophets who speak to you, saying, 'You shall not serve the king of Babylon,' for they prophesy [b]a lie to you;

15 "for I have [a]not sent them," says the LORD, "yet they prophesy a lie in My name, that I may drive you out, and that you may perish, you and the prophets who prophesy to you."

**16** Also I spoke to the priests and to all this people, saying, "Thus says the LORD: 'Do not listen to the words of your prophets who prophesy to you, saying, "Behold, [a]the vessels of the LORD's house will now shortly be brought back from Babylon"; for they prophesy a lie to you.

17 'Do not listen to them; serve the king of Babylon, and live! Why should this city be laid waste?

18 'But if they *are* prophets, and if the word of the LORD is with them, let them now make intercession to the LORD of hosts, that the vessels which are left in the house of the LORD, *in* the house of the king of Judah, and at Jerusalem, do not go to Babylon.'

**19** "For thus says the LORD of hosts [a]concerning the pillars, concerning the Sea, concerning the carts, and concerning the remainder of the vessels that remain in this city,

20 "which Nebuchadnezzar king of Babylon did not take, when he carried away [a]captive Jeconiah the son of Jehoiakim, king of Judah, from Jerusalem to Babylon, and all the nobles of Judah and Jerusalem—

21 "yes, thus says the LORD of hosts, the God of Israel, concerning the [a]vessels that remain in the house of the LORD, and in the house of the king of Judah and of Jerusalem:

22 'They shall be [a]carried to Babylon, and there they shall be until the day that I [b]visit them,' says the LORD. 'Then [c]I will bring them up and restore them to this place.' "

### *The False Prophecy of Hananiah*

**28** And [a]it happened in the same year, at the beginning of the reign of Zedekiah king of Judah, in the [b]fourth year *and* in the fifth month, *that* Hananiah the son of [c]Azur the prophet, who *was* from Gibeon, spoke to me in the house of the LORD in the presence of the priests and of all the people, saying,

2 "Thus speaks the LORD of hosts, the God of Israel, saying: 'I have broken [a]the yoke of the king of Babylon.

3 [a]'Within two full years I will bring back to this place all the vessels of the LORD's house, that Nebuchadnezzar king of Babylon [b]took away from this place and carried to Babylon.

4 'And I will bring back to this place [1]Jeconiah the son of Jehoiakim, king of Judah, with all the captives of Judah who went to Babylon,' says the LORD, 'for I will break the yoke of the king of Babylon.' "

**5** Then the prophet Jeremiah spoke to the prophet Hananiah in the presence of the priests and in the presence of all the people who stood in the house of the LORD,

6 and the prophet Jeremiah said, [a]"Amen! The LORD do so; the LORD perform your words which you have prophesied, to bring back the vessels of the LORD's house and all who were carried away captive, from Babylon to this place.

7 "Nevertheless hear now this word that I speak in your hearing and in the hearing of all the people:

8 "The prophets who have been before me and before you of old prophesied against many countries and great kingdoms—of war and disaster and pestilence.

9 "As for [a]the prophet who prophesies of [b]peace, when the word of the prophet comes to pass, the prophet will be known *as* one whom the LORD has truly sent."

**10** Then Hananiah the prophet took the [a]yoke off the prophet Jeremiah's neck and broke it.

11 And Hananiah spoke in the presence of all the people, saying, "Thus says the LORD: 'Even so I will break the yoke of Nebuchadnezzar king of Babylon [a]from the neck of all nations within the space of two full years.' " And the prophet Jeremiah went his way.

**12** Now the word of the LORD came to Jeremiah, after Hananiah the prophet had broken the yoke from the neck of the prophet Jeremiah, saying,

13 "Go and tell Hananiah, saying, 'Thus says the LORD: "You have broken the yokes of wood, but you have made in their place yokes of iron."

14 'For thus says the LORD of hosts, the God of Israel: [a]"I have put a yoke of iron on the neck of all these nations, that they may serve Nebuchadnezzar king of Babylon; and they shall serve him. [b]I have given him the beasts of the field also." ' "

15 Then the prophet Jeremiah said to Hananiah the prophet, "Hear now, Hananiah, the LORD has not sent you, but [a]you make this people trust in a [b]lie.

16 "Therefore thus says the LORD: 'Behold, I will cast you from the face of the earth. This year you shall [a]die, because you have taught [b]rebellion against the LORD.' "

17 So Hananiah the prophet died the same year in the seventh month.

### *Jeremiah's Letter to the Captives*

**29** Now these *are* the words of the letter that Jeremiah the prophet sent from Jerusalem to the remainder of the elders who were [a]carried away captive—to the priests, the prophets, and all the people whom Nebuchadnezzar had carried away captive from Jerusalem to Babylon.

2 (This happened after [a]Jeconiah[1] the king, the [b]queen mother, the [2]eunuchs, the princes of Judah and Jerusalem, the craftsmen, and the smiths had departed from Jerusalem.)

3 *The letter was sent* by the hand of Elasah the son of [a]Shaphan, and Gemariah the son of Hilkiah, whom Zedekiah king of Judah sent to Babylon, to Nebuchadnezzar king of Babylon, saying,

4 Thus says the LORD of hosts, the God of
Israel, to all who were carried away captive,
whom I have caused to be carried away from
Jerusalem to Babylon:
5 Build houses and dwell *in them;* plant
gardens and eat their fruit.
6 Take wives and beget sons and daughters;
and take wives for your sons and give your
daughters to husbands, so that they may
bear sons and daughters—that you may be
increased there, and not diminished.

---

**14** [a]Jer. 23:16 [b]Jer. 14:14; 23:21; 29:8, 9; Ezek. 13:22
**15** [a]Jer. 23:21; 29:9
**16** [a]2 Kin. 24:13; 2 Chr. 36:7, 10; Jer. 28:3; Dan. 1:2
**19** [a]1 Kin. 7:15; 2 Kin. 25:13–17; Jer. 52:17, 20, 21
**20** [a]2 Kin. 24:14, 15; 2 Chr. 36:10, 18; Jer. 24:1
**21** [a]Jer. 20:5
**22** [a]2 Kin. 25:13; 2 Chr. 36:18 [b]2 Chr. 36:21; Jer. 29:10; 32:5 [c]Ezra 1:7; 7:19

CHAPTER 28
**1** [a]Jer. 27:1 [b]Jer. 51:59 [c]Ezek. 11:1
**2** [a]Jer. 27:12
**3** [a]Jer. 27:16 [b]2 Kin. 24:13; Dan. 1:2
**4** [1]*Jehoiachin,* 2 Kin. 24:12
**6** [a]1 Kin. 1:36; Ps. 41:13; Jer. 11:5
**9** [a]Deut. 18:22 [b]Jer. 23:17; Ezek. 13:10, 16
**10** [a]Jer. 27:2
**11** [a]Jer. 27:7
**14** [a]Deut. 28:48; Jer. 27:7, 8 [b]Jer. 27:6
**15** [a]Jer. 20:6; 29:31; Lam. 2:14; Ezek. 13:22; Zech. 13:3 [b]Jer. 27:10; 29:9
**16** [a]Jer. 20:6 [b]Deut. 13:5; Jer. 29:32

CHAPTER 29
**1** [a]Jer. 27:20
**2** [a]2 Kin. 24:12–16; 2 Chr. 36:9, 10; Jer. 22:24–28 [b]2 Kin. 24:12, 15; Jer. 13:18 [1]*Jehoiachin,* 2 Kin. 24:12; 2 Chr. 36:10 [2]Or *officers*
**3** [a]2 Chr. 34:8

7 And seek the peace of the city where I have
caused you to be carried away captive, [a]and
pray to the LORD for it; for in its peace you
will have peace.
**8** For thus says the LORD of hosts, the God of
Israel: Do not let your prophets and your
diviners who are in your midst [a]deceive you,
nor listen to your dreams which you cause to
be dreamed.
9 For they prophesy [a]falsely to you in My
name; I have not sent them, says the LORD.
**10** For thus says the LORD: After [a]seventy years
are completed at Babylon, I will visit you and
perform My good word toward you, and
cause you to [b]return to this place.
11 For I know the thoughts that I think toward
you, says the LORD, thoughts of peace and
not of evil, to give you a future and a hope.
12 Then you will [a]call upon Me and go and pray
to Me, and I will [b]listen to you.
13 And [a]you will seek Me and find *Me,* when
you search for Me [b]with all your heart.
14 [a]I will be found by you, says the LORD, and I
will bring you back from your captivity; [b]I
will gather you from all the nations and from
all the places where I have driven you, says
the LORD, and I will bring you to the place
from which I cause you to be carried away
captive.
**15** Because you have said, "The LORD has raised
up prophets for us in Babylon"—
16 [a]therefore thus says the LORD concerning the
king who sits on the throne of David,
concerning all the people who dwell in this
city, and concerning your brethren who have
not gone out with you into captivity—
17 thus says the LORD of hosts: Behold, I will
send on them the sword, the famine, and the
pestilence, and will make them like [a]rotten
figs that cannot be eaten, they are so bad.
18 And I will pursue them with the sword, with
famine, and with pestilence; and I [a]will
deliver them to trouble among all the
kingdoms of the earth—to be [b]a curse, an
astonishment, a hissing, and a reproach
among all the nations where I have driven
them,
19 because they have not heeded My words,
says the LORD, which [a]I sent to them by My
servants the prophets, rising up early and
sending *them;* neither would you heed, says
the LORD.
20 Therefore hear the word of the LORD, all you
of the captivity, whom I have sent from
Jerusalem to Babylon.
**21** Thus says the LORD of hosts, the God of
Israel, concerning Ahab the son of Kolaiah,
and Zedekiah the son of Maaseiah, who
prophesy a [a]lie to you in My name: Behold, I
will deliver them into the hand of
Nebuchadnezzar king of Babylon, and he
shall slay them before your eyes.
22 [a]And because of them a curse shall be taken
up by all the captivity of Judah who *are* in
Babylon, saying, "The LORD make you like
Zedekiah and Ahab, [b]whom the king of
Babylon roasted in the fire";
23 because [a]they have done disgraceful things in
Israel, have committed adultery with their
neighbors' wives, and have spoken lying
words in My name, which I have not
commanded them. Indeed I [b]know, and *am* a
witness, says the LORD.
**24** You shall also speak to Shemaiah the
Nehelamite, saying,
25 Thus speaks the LORD of hosts, the God of
Israel, saying: You have sent letters in your
name to all the people who *are* at Jerusalem,
[a]to Zephaniah the son of Maaseiah the priest,
and to all the priests, saying,
26 "The LORD has made you priest instead of
Jehoiada the priest, so that there should be
[a]officers *in* the house of the LORD over every
man *who* is [b]demented and considers himself
a prophet, that you should [c]put him in prison
and in the stocks.
27 Now therefore, why have you not rebuked
Jeremiah of Anathoth who makes himself a
prophet to you?
28 For he has sent to us *in* Babylon, saying,
'This *captivity is* long; build houses and dwell
*in them,* and plant gardens and eat their
fruit.' "
**29** Now Zephaniah the priest read this letter in
the hearing of Jeremiah the prophet.
30 Then the word of the LORD came to
Jeremiah, saying:
31 Send to all those in captivity, saying,
Thus says the LORD concerning Shemaiah
the Nehelamite: Because Shemaiah has
prophesied to you, [a]and I have not sent him,
and he has caused you to trust in a [b]lie—
32 therefore thus says the LORD: Behold, I will
punish Shemaiah the Nehelamite and his
[1]family: he shall not have anyone to dwell
among this people, nor shall he see the good
that I will do for My people, says the LORD,
[a]because he has taught rebellion against the
LORD.

## *The Promised Return of the Captives*

**30** The word that came to Jeremiah from the
LORD, saying,
2 "Thus speaks the LORD God of Israel, saying:
'Write in a book for yourself all the words that I
have spoken to you.
3 'For behold, the days are coming,' says the
LORD, 'that [a]I will bring back from captivity My
people Israel and Judah,' says the LORD. [b]'And I
will cause them to return to the land that I gave
to their fathers, and they shall possess it.' "
4 Now these *are* the words that the LORD spoke
concerning Israel and Judah.
5 "For thus says the LORD:

'We have heard a voice of trembling,
Of [1]fear, and not of peace.
6 Ask now, and see,
Whether a [1]man is ever in [2]labor with child?
So why do I see every man
*with* his hands on his loins
[a]Like a woman in labor,
And all faces turned pale?
7 [a]Alas! For that day *is* great,
[b]So that none *is* like it;
And it *is* the time of Jacob's trouble,
But he shall be saved out of it.

**7** [a]Ezra 6:10; Neh. 1:4–11; Dan. 9:16; 1 Tim. 2:2
**8** [a]Jer. 14:14; 23:21; 27:14, 15; Eph. 5:6
**9** [a]Jer. 28:15; 37:19
**10** [a]2 Chr. 36:21–23; Ezra 1:1–4; Jer. 25:12; 27:22; Dan. 9:2; Zech. 7:5 [b][Jer. 24:6, 7]; Zeph. 2:7
**12** [a]Ps. 50:15; Jer. 33:3; Dan. 9:3 [b]Ps. 145:19
**13** [a]Lev. 26:39–42; Deut. 30:1–3 [b]1 Chr. 22:19; 2 Chr. 22:9; Jer. 24:7
**14** [a][Deut. 4:7]; Ps. 32:6; 46:1; [Is. 55:6, 7]; Jer. 24:7 [b]Is. 43:5, 6; Jer. 23:8; 32:37
**16** [a]Jer. 38:2, 3, 17–23
**17** [a]Jer. 24:3, 8–10
**18** [a]Deut. 28:25; 2 Chr. 29:8; Jer. 15:4; 24:9; 34:17; Ezek. 12:15 [b]Jer. 26:6; 42:18
**19** [a]Jer. 25:4; 26:5; 35:15
**21** [a]Jer. 14:14, 15; Lam. 2:14; 2 Pet. 2:1
**22** [a]Gen. 48:20; Is. 65:15 [b]Dan. 3:6, 21
**23** [a]Jer. 23:14 [b][Prov. 5:21; Jer. 16:17]; Mal. 3:5; [Heb. 4:13]
**25** [a]2 Kin. 25:18; Jer. 21:1
**26** [a]Jer. 20:1 [b]2 Kin. 9:11; Hos. 9:7; Mark 3:21; John 10:20; Acts 26:24; [2 Cor. 5:13] [c]Jer. 20:1, 2; Acts 16:24
**31** [a]Jer. 28:15 [b]Ezek. 13:8–16, 22, 23
**32** [a]Jer. 28:16 [1]*descendants,* lit. *seed*

CHAPTER 30
**3** [a]Ps. 53:6; Jer. 29:14; 30:18; 32:44; Ezek. 39:25; Amos 9:14; Zeph. 3:20 [b]Jer. 16:15; Ezek. 20:42; 36:24
**5** [1]*dread*
**6** [a]Jer. 4:31; 6:24 [1]Lit. *male can give birth* [2]*childbirth*
**7** [a][Is. 2:12]; Hos. 1:11; Joel 2:11; Amos 5:18; Zeph. 1:14 [b]Lam. 1:12; Dan. 9:12; 12:1

8 'For it shall come to pass in that day,'
Says the LORD of hosts,
'*That* I will break his yoke from your neck,
And will burst your bonds;
Foreigners shall no more enslave them.
9 But they shall serve the LORD their God,
And [a]David their king,
Whom I will [b]raise up for them.

**10** 'Therefore [a]do not fear, O My servant Jacob,'
says the LORD,
'Nor be dismayed, O Israel;
For behold, I will save you from afar,
And your seed [b]from the land of their
captivity.
Jacob shall return, have rest and be quiet,
And no one shall make *him* afraid.
11 For I *am* with [a]you,' says the LORD,
'to save you;
[b]Though I make a full end of all nations
where I have scattered you,
[c]Yet I will not make a complete end of you.
But I will correct you [d]in justice,
And will not let you go altogether
unpunished.'

**12** "For thus says the LORD:

[a]'Your affliction *is* incurable,
Your wound *is* severe.
13 *There is* no one to plead your cause,
That you may be bound up;
[a]You have no healing medicines.
14 [a]All your lovers have forgotten you;
They do not seek you;
For I have wounded you with the wound [b]of
an enemy,
With the chastisement [c]of a cruel one,
For the multitude of your iniquities,
[d]*Because* your sins have increased.
15 Why [a]do you cry about your affliction?
Your sorrow *is* incurable.
Because of the multitude of your iniquities,
*Because* your sins have increased,
I have done these things to you.

16 'Therefore all those who devour
you [a]shall be devoured;
And all your adversaries, every one of them,
shall go into [b]captivity;
Those who plunder you
shall become [c]plunder,
And all who prey upon you
I will make a [d]prey.
17 [a]For I will restore health to you
And heal you of your wounds,'
says the LORD,
'Because they called you an outcast *saying:*
"This *is* Zion;
No one seeks her." '

**18** "Thus says the LORD:

'Behold, I will bring back the captivity of
Jacob's tents,
And [a]have mercy on his dwelling places;
The city shall be built upon its own [1]mound,
And the palace shall remain according to its
own plan.
19 Then [a]out of them shall proceed thanksgiving
And the voice of those who make merry;
[b]I will multiply them,
and they shall not diminish;
I will also glorify them,
and they shall not be small.
20 Their children also shall be [a]as before,
And their congregation shall be established
before Me;
And I will punish all who oppress them.
21 Their nobles shall be from among them,
[a]And their governor shall come from their
midst;
Then I will [b]cause him to draw near,
And he shall approach Me;
For who *is* this who pledged his heart to
approach Me?' says the LORD.
22 'You shall be [a]My people,
And I will be your God.' "

**23** Behold, the [a]whirlwind of the LORD
Goes forth with fury,
A [1]continuing whirlwind;
It will fall violently on the head
of the wicked.
24 The fierce anger of the LORD
will not return until He has done it,
And until He has performed
the intents of His heart.

[a]In the latter days you will consider it.

### *Judah Will Be Restored*

**31** "At [a]the same time," says the LORD, [b]"I will
be the God of all the families of Israel, and
they shall be My people."
**2** Thus says the LORD:

"The people who survived the sword
Found grace in the wilderness—
Israel, when [a]I went to give him rest."

3 The LORD has appeared [1]of old to me, *saying:*
"Yes, [a]I have loved you
with [b]an everlasting love;
Therefore with lovingkindness
I have [c]drawn you.
4 Again [a]I will build you,
and you shall be rebuilt,
O virgin of Israel!
You shall again be adorned
with your [b]tambourines,
And shall go forth in the dances
of those who rejoice.
5 [a]You shall yet plant vines
on the mountains of Samaria;
The planters shall plant
and [1]eat *them* as ordinary food.
6 For there shall be a day
*When* the watchmen will cry on Mount
Ephraim,
[a]'Arise, and let us go up *to* Zion,
To the LORD our God.' "

**7** For thus says the LORD:

[a]"Sing with gladness for Jacob,
And shout among the chief of the nations;
Proclaim, give praise, and say,
'O LORD, save Your people,
The remnant of Israel!'
8 Behold, I will bring them [a]from the north
country,
And [b]gather them from the ends of the earth,
*Among* them the blind and the lame,

**9** [a]Is. 55:3; Ezek. 34:23; 37:24; Hos. 3:5 [b][Luke 1:69; Acts 2:30; 13:23]
**10** [a]Is. 41:13; 43:5; 44:2; Jer. 46:27, 28 [b]Jer. 3:18
**11** [a][Is. 43:2–5] [b]Amos 9:8 [c]Jer. 4:27; 46:27, 28 [d]Ps. 6:1; Is. 27:8; Jer. 10:24; 46:28
**12** [a]2 Chr. 36:16; Jer. 15:18
**13** [a]Jer. 8:22
**14** [a]Jer. 22:20, 22; Lam. 1:2 [b]Job 13:24; 16:9; 19:11 [c]Job 30:21 [d]Jer. 5:6
**15** [a]Jer. 15:18
**16** [a]Ex. 23:22; Is. 41:11; Jer. 10:25 [b]Is. 14:2; Joel 3:8 [c]Is. 33:1; Ezek. 39:10 [d]Jer. 2:3
**17** [a]Ex. 15:26; Ps. 107:20; Is. 30:26; Jer. 33:6
**18** [a]Ps. 102:13 [1]*ruins*
**19** [a]Ps. 126:1, 2; Is. 51:11; Jer. 31:4; Zeph. 3:14 [b]Is. 49:19–21; Jer. 23:3; 33:22; Zech. 10:8
**20** [a]Is. 1:26
**21** [a]Gen. 49:10 [b]Num. 16:5; Ps. 65:4
**22** [a]Ex. 6:7; Jer. 32:38; Ezek. 36:28; Hos. 2:23; Zech. 13:9
**23** [a]Jer. 23:19, 20; 25:32 [1]Or *sweeping*
**24** [a]Gen. 49:1

CHAPTER 31
**1** [a]Jer. 30:24 [b]Jer. 30:22
**2** [a]Ex. 33:14; Num. 10:33; Deut. 1:33; Josh. 1:13; Ps. 95:11; Is. 63:14
**3** [a]Deut. 4:37; 7:8; Mal. 1:2 [b]Is. 43:4; Rom. 11:28 [c]Hos. 11:4 [1]Lit. *from afar*
**4** [a]Jer. 33:7 [b]Ex. 15:20; Judg. 11:34; Ps. 149:3
**5** [a]Ps. 107:37; Is. 65:21; Ezek. 28:26; Amos 9:14 [1]Lit. *treat them as common*
**6** [a][Is. 2:3; Jer. 31:12; 50:4, 5; Mic. 4:2]
**7** [a]Is. 12:5, 6
**8** [a]Jer. 3:12, 18; 23:8 [b]Deut. 30:4; Is. 43:6; Ezek. 20:34, 41; 34:13

The woman with child
And the one who labors with child, together;
A great throng shall return there.
9 [a]They shall come with weeping,
And with supplications I will lead them.
I will cause them to walk [b]by the rivers of
waters,
In a straight way in which they shall not
stumble;
For I am a Father to Israel,
And Ephraim *is* My [c]firstborn.

**10** "Hear the word of the LORD, O nations,
And declare *it* in the [1]isles afar off, and say,
'He who scattered Israel [a]will gather him,
And keep him as a shepherd *does* his flock.'
11 For [a]the LORD has redeemed Jacob,
And ransomed him [b]from the hand of one
stronger than he.
12 Therefore they shall come
and sing in [a]the height of Zion,
Streaming to [b]the goodness of the LORD—
For wheat and new wine and oil,
For the young of the flock and the herd;
Their souls shall be like a [c]well-watered
garden,
[d]And they shall sorrow no more at all.

13 "Then shall the virgin rejoice in the dance,
And the young men and the old, together;
For I will turn their mourning to joy,
Will comfort them,
And make them rejoice rather than sorrow.
14 I will [1]satiate the soul of the priests with
abundance,
And My people shall be satisfied with My
goodness, says the LORD."

**15** Thus says the LORD:

[a]"A voice was heard in [b]Ramah,
Lamentation *and* bitter [c]weeping,
Rachel weeping for her children,
Refusing to be comforted for her children,
Because [d]they *are* no more."

**16** Thus says the LORD:

"Refrain your voice from [a]weeping,
And your eyes from tears;
For your work shall be rewarded,
says the LORD,
And they shall come back
from the land of the enemy.
17 There is [a]hope in your future, says the LORD,
That *your* children shall come back
to their own border.

**18** "I have surely heard Ephraim bemoaning
himself:
'You have [a]chastised me, and I was chastised,
Like an untrained bull;
[b]Restore me, and I will return,
For You *are* the LORD my God.
19 Surely, [a]after my turning, I repented;
And after I was instructed,
I struck myself on the thigh;
I was [b]ashamed, yes, even humiliated,
Because I bore the reproach of my youth.'
20 *Is* Ephraim My dear son?
*Is he* a pleasant child?
For though I spoke against him,
I earnestly remember him still;
[a]Therefore My [1]heart yearns for him;
[b]I will surely have mercy on him,
says the LORD.

**21** "Set up signposts,
Make landmarks;
[a]Set your heart toward the highway,
The way in *which* you went.
[1]Turn back, O virgin of Israel,
Turn back to these your cities.
22 How long will you [a]gad about,
O you [b]backsliding daughter?
For the LORD has created a new thing in the
earth—
A woman shall encompass a man."

**23** Thus says the LORD of hosts, the God of Israel:
"They shall again use this speech in the land of
Judah and in its cities, when I bring back their
captivity: [a]'The LORD bless you, O home of justice,
*and* [b]mountain of holiness!'
24 "And there shall dwell in Judah itself, and [a]in
all its cities together, farmers and those going out
with flocks.
25 "For I have [1]satiated the weary soul, and I
have replenished every sorrowful soul."
26 After this I awoke and looked around, and my
sleep was [a]sweet to me.
**27** "Behold, the days are coming, says the LORD,
that [a]I will sow the house of Israel and the house
of Judah with the seed of man and the seed of
beast.
28 "And it shall come to pass, *that* as I have
[a]watched over them [b]to pluck up, to break down,
to throw down, to destroy, and to afflict, so I will
watch over them [c]to build and to plant, says the
LORD.
29 [a]"In those days they shall say no more:

'The fathers have eaten sour grapes,
And the children's teeth are set on edge.'

30 [a]"But every one shall die for his own iniquity;
every man who eats the sour grapes, his teeth
shall be set on edge.
**31** "Behold, the [a]days are coming, says the LORD,
when I will make a new covenant with the house
of Israel and with the house of Judah—
32 "not according to the covenant that I made
with their fathers in the day *that* [a]I took them by
the hand to lead them out of the land of Egypt,
My covenant which they broke, [1]though I was a
husband to them, says the LORD.
33 [a]"But this *is* the covenant that I will make
with the house of Israel after those days, says the
LORD: [b]I will put My law in their minds, and write
it on their [1]hearts; [c]and I will be their God, and
they shall be My people.
34 "No more shall every man teach his neighbor,
and every man his brother, saying, 'Know the
LORD,' for [a]they all shall know Me, from the least
of them to the greatest of them, says the LORD.
For [b]I will forgive their iniquity, and their sin I will
remember no more."

**35** Thus says the LORD,
[a]Who gives the sun for a light by day,
The ordinances of the moon and the stars for
a light by night,
Who disturbs [b]the sea,
And its waves roar
[c](The LORD of hosts *is* His name):

36 "If [a]those ordinances depart
From before Me, says the LORD,
*Then* the seed of Israel shall also cease
From being a nation before Me forever."

**9** [a][Jer. 50:4] [b]Is. 35:8; 43:19; 49:10, 11 [c]Ex. 4:22
**10** [a]Is. 40:11 [1]Or *coastlands*
**11** [a]Is. 44:23; 48:20 [b]Is. 49:24
**12** [a]Ezek. 17:23 [b]Hos. 3:5 [c]Is. 58:11 [d]Is. 35:10; 65:19
**14** [1]Fill to the full
**15** [a]Matt. 2:17, 18 [b]Josh. 18:25 [c]Gen. 37:35 [d]Jer. 10:20
**16** [a][Is. 25:8; 30:19]
**17** [a]Jer. 29:11
**18** [a]Ps. 94:12 [b]Lam. 5:21
**19** [a]Deut. 30:2 [b]Ezek. 36:31
**20** [a]Is. 63:15 [b][Hos. 14:4] [1]Lit. *inward parts*
**21** [a]Jer. 50:5 [1]Or *Return*
**22** [a]Jer. 2:18, 23, 36 [b]Jer. 3:6, 8, 11, 12, 14, 22
**23** [a]Is. 1:26 [b][Zech. 8:3]
**24** [a]Jer. 33:12
**25** [1]*fully satisfied*
**26** [a]Prov. 3:24
**27** [a]Ezek. 36:9–11
**28** [a]Jer. 44:27 [b]Jer. 1:10; 18:7 [c]Jer. 24:6
**29** [a]Ezek. 18:2, 3
**30** [a][Gal. 6:5, 7]
**31** [a]Heb. 8:8–12; 10:16, 17
**32** [a]Deut. 1:31 [1]So with MT, Tg., Vg.; LXX, Syr. *and I turned away from them*
**33** [a]Jer. 32:40 [b]Ps. 40:8 [c]Jer. 24:7; 30:22; 32:38 [1]Lit. *inward parts*
**34** [a][John 6:45] [b][Rom. 11:27]
**35** [a]Gen. 1:14–18 [b]Is. 51:15 [c]Jer. 10:16
**36** [a]Ps. 148:6

37 Thus says the LORD:

[a]"If heaven above can be measured,
And the foundations of the earth searched
out beneath,
I will also [b]cast off all the seed of Israel
For all that they have done, says the LORD.

**38** "Behold, the days are coming, says the LORD,
that the city shall be built for the LORD [a]from the
Tower of Hananel to the Corner Gate.
39 [a]"The surveyor's line shall again extend
straight forward over the hill Gareb; then it shall
turn toward Goath.
40 "And the whole valley of the dead bodies and
of the ashes, and all the fields as far as the Brook
Kidron, [a]to the corner of the Horse Gate toward
the east, [b]*shall be* holy to the LORD. It shall not be
plucked up or thrown down anymore forever."

## *Jerusalem Will Be Destroyed and Restored*

**32** The word that came to Jeremiah from the
LORD [a]in the tenth year of Zedekiah king of
Judah, which was the eighteenth year of Nebuchadnezzar.
2 For then the king of Babylon's army besieged
Jerusalem, and Jeremiah the prophet was shut up
[a]in the court of the prison, which *was in* the king
of Judah's house.
3 For Zedekiah king of Judah had shut him up,
saying, "Why do you [a]prophesy and say, 'Thus
says the LORD: [b]"Behold, I will give this city into
the hand of the king of Babylon, and he shall
take it;
4 "and Zedekiah king of Judah [a]shall not escape
from the hand of the Chaldeans, but shall surely
be delivered into the hand of the king of Babylon,
and shall speak with him [1]face to face, and see
him [b]eye to eye;
5 "then he shall [a]lead Zedekiah to Babylon, and
there he shall be [b]until I visit him," says the LORD;
[c]"though you fight with the Chaldeans, you shall
not succeed" '?"
**6** And Jeremiah said, "The word of the LORD
came to me, saying,
7 'Behold, Hanamel the son of Shallum your
uncle will come to you, saying, "Buy my field
which *is* in Anathoth, for the [a]right of redemption
*is* yours to buy *it*." '
8 "Then Hanamel my uncle's son came to me in
the court of the prison according to the word of
the LORD, and said to me, 'Please buy my field that
*is* in Anathoth, which *is* in the country of Benjamin; for the right of inheritance *is* yours, and the
redemption yours; buy *it* for yourself.' Then I
knew that this was the word of the LORD.
9 "So I bought the field from Hanamel, the son
of my uncle who *was* in Anathoth, and [a]weighed
*out to* him the money—seventeen shekels of
silver.
10 "And I signed the [1]deed and sealed *it,* took
witnesses, and weighed the money on the scales.
11 "So I took the purchase deed, *both* that which
was sealed *according* to the law and custom, and
that which was open;
12 "and I gave the purchase deed to [a]Baruch the
son of Neriah, son of Mahseiah, in the presence of
Hanamel my uncle's *son,* and in the presence of
the [b]witnesses who signed the purchase deed,
before all the Jews who sat in the court of the
prison.
**13** "Then I charged [a]Baruch before them, saying,
14 'Thus says the LORD of hosts, the God of
Israel: "Take these deeds, both this purchase deed
which is sealed and this deed which is open, and
put them in an earthen vessel, that they may last
many days."
15 'For thus says the LORD of hosts, the God of
Israel: "Houses and fields and vineyards shall be
[a]possessed again in this land." '
**16** "Now when I had delivered the purchase deed
to Baruch the son of Neriah, I prayed to the LORD,
saying:
17 'Ah, Lord GOD! Behold, [a]You have made the
heavens and the earth by Your great power and
outstretched arm. [b]There is nothing too [1]hard for
You.
18 '*You* show [a]lovingkindness to thousands, and
repay the iniquity of the fathers into the bosom of
their children after them—the Great, [b]the Mighty
God, whose name *is* [c]the LORD of hosts.
19 '*You are* [a]great in counsel and mighty in
[1]work, for your [b]eyes *are* open to all the ways of
the sons of men, [c]to give everyone according to
his ways and according to the fruit of his doings.
20 'You have set signs and wonders in the land of
Egypt, to this day, and in Israel and among *other*
men; and You have made Yourself [a]a name, as it is
this day.
21 'You [a]have brought Your people Israel out of
the land of Egypt with signs and wonders, with a
strong hand and an outstretched arm, and with
great terror;
22 'You have given them this land, of which You
swore to their fathers to give them—[a]"a land
flowing with milk and honey."
23 'And they came in and took possession of it,
but [a]they have not obeyed Your voice or walked
in Your law. They have done nothing of all that
You commanded them to do; therefore You have
caused all this calamity to come upon them.
24 'Look, the siege mounds! They have come to
the city to take it; and the city has been given into
the hand of the Chaldeans who fight against it,
because of [a]the sword and famine and pestilence.
What You have spoken has happened; there You
see *it!*
25 'And You have said to me, O Lord GOD, "Buy
the field for money, and take witnesses"!—yet the
city has been given into the hand of the Chaldeans.' "
**26** Then the word of the LORD came to Jeremiah,
saying,
27 "Behold, I *am* the LORD, the [a]God of all flesh.
Is there anything too hard for Me?
28 "Therefore thus says the LORD: 'Behold, I will
give this city into the hand of the Chaldeans, into
the hand of Nebuchadnezzar king of Babylon, and
he shall take it.
29 'And the Chaldeans who fight against this city
shall come and [a]set fire to this city and burn it,
with the houses [b]on whose roofs they have offered
incense to Baal and poured out drink offerings to
other gods, to provoke Me to anger;
30 'because the children of Israel and the children of Judah [a]have done only evil before Me from
their youth. For the children of Israel have provoked Me only to anger with the work of their
hands,' says the LORD.
31 'For this city has been to Me *a provocation of*
My anger and My fury from the day that they

**37** [a]Jer. 33:22 [b][Rom. 11:2–5, 26, 27]
**38** [a]Zech. 14:10
**39** [a]Zech. 2:1, 2
**40** [a]Neh. 3:28 [b][Joel 3:17]
CHAPTER 32
**1** [a]Jer. 39:1, 2
**2** [a]Jer. 33:1; 37:21; 39:14
**3** [a]Jer. 26:8, 9 [b]Jer. 21:3–7; 34:2
**4** [a]Jer. 34:3; 38:18, 23; 39:5; 52:9 [b]Jer. 39:5 [1]Lit. *mouth to mouth*
**5** [a]Ezek. 12:12, 13 [b]Jer. 27:22 [c]Jer. 21:4; 33:5
**7** [a]Ruth 4:4
**9** [a]Zech. 11:12
**10** [1]Lit. *book*
**12** [a]Jer. 36:4 [b]Is. 8:2
**13** [a]Jer. 36:4
**15** [a][Jer. 31:5, 12, 14]
**17** [a]2 Kin. 19:15 [b]Luke 18:27 [1]*difficult*
**18** [a]Deut. 5:9, 10 [b][Is. 9:6] [c]Jer. 10:16
**19** [a]Is. 28:29 [b]Prov. 5:21 [c]Jer. 17:10 [1]*deed*
**20** [a]Is. 63:12
**21** [a]Ex. 6:6
**22** [a]Ex. 3:8, 17
**23** [a][Neh. 9:26]
**24** [a]Jer. 14:12
**27** [a][Num. 16:22]
**29** [a]2 Chr. 36:19 [b]Jer. 19:13
**30** [a]Jer. 2:7; 3:25; 7:22–26

built it, even to this day; [a]so I will remove it from
before My face
32 'because of all the evil of the children of Israel
and the children of Judah, which they have done
to provoke Me to anger—[a]they, their kings, their
princes, their priests, [b]their prophets, the men of
Judah, and the inhabitants of Jerusalem.
33 'And they have turned to Me the [a]back, and
not the face; though I taught them, [b]rising up
early and teaching *them,* yet they have not listened to receive instruction.
34 'But they [a]set their abominations in [1]the house
which is called by My name, to defile it.
35 'And they built the high places of Baal which
*are* in the Valley of the Son of Hinnom, to [a]cause
their sons and their daughters to pass through *the
fire* to [b]Molech, [c]which I did not command them,
nor did it come into My mind that they should do
this abomination, to cause Judah to sin.'
**36** "Now therefore, thus says the LORD, the God
of Israel, concerning this city of which you say, 'It
shall be delivered into the hand of the king of
Babylon by the sword, by the famine, and by the
pestilence':
37 'Behold, I will [a]gather them out of all countries
where I have driven them in My anger, in My
fury, and in great wrath; I will bring them back to
this place, and I will cause them [b]to dwell safely.
38 'They shall be [a]My people, and I will be their
God;
39 'then I will [a]give them one heart and one way,
that they may fear Me forever, for the good of
them and their children after them.
40 'And [a]I will make an everlasting covenant
with them, that I will not turn away from doing
them good; but [b]I will put My fear in their hearts
so that they will not depart from Me.
41 'Yes, [a]I will rejoice over them to do them
good, and [b]I will [1]assuredly plant them in this
land, with all My heart and with all My soul.'
**42** "For thus says the LORD: [a]'Just as I have
brought all this great calamity on this people, so I
will bring on them all the good that I have promised them.
43 'And fields will be bought in this land [a]of
which you say, "*It is* desolate, without man or
beast; it has been given into the hand of the
Chaldeans."
44 'Men will buy fields for money, sign deeds and
seal *them,* and take witnesses, in [a]the land of
Benjamin, in the places around Jerusalem, in the
cities of Judah, in the cities of the mountains, in
the cities of the [1]lowland, and in the cities of the
[2]South; for [b]I will cause their captives to return,'
says the LORD."

### *A Glorious Return Promised to the Captives*

**33** Moreover the word of the LORD came to
Jeremiah a second time, while he was still
[a]shut up in the court of the prison, saying,
2 "Thus says the LORD [a]who made it, the LORD
who formed it to establish it [b](the[1] LORD *is* His
name):
3 [a]'Call to Me, and I will answer you, and show
you great and [1]mighty things, which you do not
know.'
**4** "For thus says the LORD, the God of Israel,
concerning the houses of this city and the houses
of the kings of Judah, which have been pulled
down *to fortify* against [a]the siege mounds and the
sword:
5 'They come to fight with the Chaldeans, but
*only* to [a]fill their places with the dead bodies of
men whom I will slay in My anger and My fury, all
for whose wickedness I have hidden My face from
this city.
6 'Behold, [a]I will bring it health and healing; I
will heal them and reveal to them the abundance
of peace and truth.
7 'And [a]I will cause the captives of Judah and
the captives of Israel to return, and will rebuild
those places [b]as at the first.
8 'I will [a]cleanse them from all their iniquity by
which they have sinned against Me, and I will
pardon all their iniquities by which they have
sinned and by which they have transgressed
against Me.
9 [a]'Then it shall be to Me a name of joy, a praise,
and an honor before all nations of the earth, who
shall hear all the good that I do to them; they shall
[b]fear and tremble for all the goodness and all the
prosperity that I provide for it.'
**10** "Thus says the LORD: 'Again there shall be
heard in this place—[a]of which you say, "It *is*
desolate, without man and without beast"—in the
cities of Judah, in the streets of Jerusalem that are
desolate, without man and without inhabitant and
without beast,
11 'the [a]voice of joy and the voice of gladness, the
voice of the bridegroom and the voice of the bride,
the voice of those who will say:

[b]"Praise the LORD of hosts,
For the LORD *is* good,
For His mercy *endures* forever"—

*and* of those *who will* bring [c]the sacrifice of praise
into the house of the LORD. For I will cause the
captives of the land to return as at the first,' says
the LORD.
**12** "Thus says the LORD of hosts: [a]'In this place
which is desolate, without man and without beast,
and in all its cities, there shall again be a dwelling
place of shepherds causing *their* flocks to lie
down.
13 [a]'In the cities of the mountains, in the cities of
the lowland, in the cities of the South, in the land
of Benjamin, in the places around Jerusalem, and
in the cities of Judah, the flocks shall again [b]pass
under the hands of him who counts *them,*' says
the LORD.
**14** [a]'Behold, the days are coming,' says the LORD,
'that [b]I will perform that good thing which I have
promised to the house of Israel and to the house
of Judah:

15 'In those days and at that time
I will cause to grow up to David
A [a]Branch of righteousness;
He shall execute judgment and righteousness
in the earth.
16 In those days Judah will be saved,
And Jerusalem will dwell safely.
And this *is the name* by which she will be
called:

[1]THE LORD OUR RIGHTEOUSNESS.'

17 "For thus says the LORD: 'David shall never
[a]lack a man to sit on the throne of the house of
Israel;
18 'nor shall the [a]priests, the Levites, lack a man
to [b]offer burnt offerings before Me, to [1]kindle
grain offerings, and to sacrifice continually.' "

31 [a]2 Kin. 23:27; 24:3
32 [a]Dan. 9:8 [b]Jer. 23:14
33 [a]Jer. 2:27; 7:24 [b]Jer. 7:13
34 [a]Jer. 7:10–12, 30; 23:11 [1]The temple
35 [a]Jer. 7:31; 19:5 [b]Lev. 18:21 [c]Jer. 7:31
37 [a]Deut. 30:3 [b]Jer. 33:16
38 [a][Jer. 24:7; 30:22; 31:33]
39 [a][Ezek. 11:19]
40 [a]Is. 55:3 [b][Jer. 31:33]
41 [a]Deut. 30:9 [b]Amos 9:15 [1]*truly*
42 [a]Jer. 31:28
43 [a]Jer. 33:10
44 [a]Jer. 17:26 [b]Jer. 33:7, 11 [1]Heb. *shephelah* [2]Heb. *Negev*

CHAPTER 33
1 [a]Jer. 32:2, 3
2 [a]Is. 37:26 [b]Ex. 15:3 [1]Heb. *YHWH*
3 [a]Jer. 29:12 [1]*inaccessible*
4 [a]Is. 22:10
5 [a]2 Kin. 23:14
6 [a]Jer. 30:17
7 [a]Jer. 30:3; 32:44 [b]Is. 1:26
8 [a]Zech. 13:1
9 [a]Is. 62:7 [b]Is. 60:5
10 [a]Jer. 32:43
11 [a]Rev. 18:23 [b]Is. 12:4 [c]Lev. 7:12
12 [a]Is. 65:10
13 [a]Jer. 17:26; 32:44 [b]Lev. 27:33
14 [a]Jer. 23:5; 31:27, 31 [b]Jer. 29:10; 32:42
15 [a]Jer. 23:5
16 [1]Heb. *YHWH Tsidkenu;* cf. Jer. 23:5, 6
17 [a]2 Sam. 7:16
18 [a]Ezek. 44:15 [b][1 Pet. 2:5, 9] [1]*burn*

**19** And the word of the LORD came to Jeremiah,
saying,
20 "Thus says the LORD: 'If you can break My
covenant with the day and My covenant with the
night, so that there will not be day and night in
their season,
21 'then [a]My covenant may also be broken with
David My servant, so that he shall not have a son
to reign on his throne, and with the Levites, the
priests, My ministers.
22 'As [a]the host of heaven cannot be numbered,
nor the sand of the sea measured, so will I [b]multi-
ply the descendants of David My servant and the
[c]Levites who minister to Me.' "
**23** Moreover the word of the LORD came to Jeremiah, saying,
24 "Have you not considered what these people
have spoken, saying, 'The two families which the
LORD has chosen, He has also cast them off'?
Thus they have [a]despised My people, as if they
should no more be a nation before them.
**25** "Thus says the LORD: 'If [a]My covenant *is* not
with day and night, *and if* I have not [b]appointed
the ordinances of heaven and earth,
26 [a]'then I will [b]cast away the descendants of
Jacob and David My servant, *so* that I will not
take *any* of his descendants *to be* rulers over the
descendants of Abraham, Isaac, and Jacob. For I
will cause their captives to return, and will have
mercy on them.' "

## *King Zedekiah Warned by God*

**34** The word which came to Jeremiah from the
LORD, [a]when Nebuchadnezzar king of Babylon and all his army, [b]all the kingdoms of the earth
under his dominion, and all the people, fought
against Jerusalem and all its cities, saying,
2 "Thus says the LORD, the God of Israel: 'Go
and [a]speak to Zedekiah king of Judah and tell
him, "Thus says the LORD: 'Behold, [b]I will give this
city into the hand of the king of Babylon, and he
shall burn it with fire.
3 'And [a]you shall not escape from his hand, but
shall surely be taken and delivered into his hand;
your eyes shall see the eyes of the king of Babylon, he shall speak with you [b]face[1] to face, and you
shall go to Babylon.' " '
4 "Yet hear the word of the LORD, O Zedekiah
king of Judah! Thus says the LORD concerning
you: 'You shall not die by the sword.
5 'You shall die in peace; as in [a]the ceremonies
of your fathers, the former kings who were before
you, [b]so they shall burn incense for you and
[c]lament for you, *saying,* "Alas, lord!" For I have
pronounced the word, says the LORD.' "
**6** Then Jeremiah the prophet spoke all these
words to Zedekiah king of Judah in Jerusalem,
7 when the king of Babylon's army fought
against Jerusalem and all the cities of Judah that
were left, against Lachish and Azekah; for *only*
[a]these fortified cities remained of the cities of
Judah.
**8** *This is* the word that came to Jeremiah from
the LORD, after King Zedekiah had made a covenant with all the people who *were* at Jerusalem
to proclaim [a]liberty to them:
9 [a]that every man should set free his male and
female slave—a Hebrew man or woman—[b]that no
one should keep a Jewish brother in bondage.
10 Now when all the princes and all the people,
who had entered into the covenant, heard that

**21** [a]2 Sam. 23:5; Ps. 89:34
**22** [a]Gen. 15:5; 22:17 [b]Jer. 30:19 [c]Is. 66:21
**24** [a]Esth. 3:6–8
**25** [a]Gen. 8:22 [b]Ps. 74:16; 104:19
**26** [a]Jer. 31:37 [b]Rom. 11:1, 2

CHAPTER 34
**1** [a]2 Kin. 25:1 [b]Jer. 1:15; 25:9
**2** [a]2 Chr. 36:11, 12 [b]Jer. 21:10; 32:3, 28
**3** [a]2 Kin. 25:4, 5 [b]Jer. 32:4; 39:5, 6 [1]Lit. *mouth to mouth*
**5** [a]2 Chr. 16:14; 21:19 [b]Dan. 2:46 [c]Jer. 22:18
**7** [a]2 Kin. 18:13; 19:8
**8** [a]Ex. 21:2
**9** [a]Neh. 5:11 [b]Lev. 25:39–46
**13** [a]Ex. 24:3, 7, 8
**14** [a]Deut. 15:12 [1]Or *sold himself*
**15** [a]Neh. 10:29 [b]Jer. 7:10 [1]Lit. *today*
**16** [a]Ex. 20:7
**17** [a][Matt. 7:2] [b]Jer. 32:24, 36 [c]Deut. 28:25, 64
**18** [a]Gen. 15:10, 17
**19** [1]Or *officers*
**20** [a]Jer. 22:25 [b]Jer. 7:33; 16:4; 19:7
**21** [a]Jer. 37:5–11; 39:4–7
**22** [a]Jer. 37:8, 10 [b]Jer. 38:3; 39:1, 2, 8; 52:7, 13 [c]Jer. 9:11; 44:2, 6

CHAPTER 35
**2** [a]1 Chr. 2:55 [b]1 Kin. 6:5, 8

everyone should set free his male and female
slaves, that no one should keep them in bondage
anymore, they obeyed and let *them* go.
11 But afterward they changed their minds and
made the male and female slaves return, whom
they had set free, and brought them into subjection as male and female slaves.
**12** Therefore the word of the LORD came to
Jeremiah from the LORD, saying,
13 "Thus says the LORD, the God of Israel: 'I
made a [a]covenant with your fathers in the day
that I brought them out of the land of Egypt, out
of the house of bondage, saying,
14 "At the end of [a]seven years let every man set
free his Hebrew brother, who [1]has been sold to
him; and when he has served you six years, you
shall let him go free from you." But your fathers
did not obey Me nor incline their ear.
15 'Then you [1]recently turned and did what was
right in My sight—every man proclaiming liberty
to his neighbor; and you [a]made a covenant before
Me [b]in the house which is called by My name.
16 'Then you turned around and [a]profaned My
name, and every one of you brought back his male
and female slaves, whom he had set at liberty, at
their pleasure, and brought them back into subjection, to be your male and female slaves.'
**17** "Therefore thus says the LORD: 'You have not
obeyed Me in proclaiming liberty, every one to his
brother and every one to his neighbor. [a]Behold, I
proclaim liberty to you,' says the LORD—[b]'to the
sword, to pestilence, and to famine! And I will
deliver you to [c]trouble among all the kingdoms of
the earth.
18 'And I will give the men who have transgressed My covenant, who have not performed
the words of the covenant which they made
before Me, when [a]they cut the calf in two and
passed between the parts of it—
19 'the princes of Judah, the princes of Jerusalem, the [1]eunuchs, the priests, and all the people of
the land who passed between the parts of the
calf—
20 'I will [a]give them into the hand of their enemies and into the hand of those who seek their
life. Their [b]dead bodies shall be for meat for the
birds of the heaven and the beasts of the earth.
21 'And I will give Zedekiah king of Judah and
his princes into the hand of their enemies, into the
hand of those who seek their life, and into the
hand of the king of Babylon's army [a]which has
gone back from you.
22 [a]'Behold, I will command,' says the LORD, 'and
cause them to return to this city. They will fight
against it [b]and take it and burn it with fire; and [c]I
will make the cities of Judah a desolation without
inhabitant.' "

## *The Obedient Rechabites*

**35** The word which came to Jeremiah from the
LORD in the days of Jehoiakim the son of
Josiah, king of Judah, saying,
2 "Go to the house of the [a]Rechabites, speak to
them, and bring them into the house of the LORD,
into one of [b]the chambers, and give them wine to
drink."
3 Then I took Jaazaniah the son of Jeremiah,
the son of Habazziniah, his brothers and all his
sons, and the whole house of the Rechabites,

4 and I brought them into the house of
the LORD, into the chamber of the sons of
Hanan the son of Igdaliah, a man of God, which
*was* by the chamber of the princes, above the
chamber of Maaseiah the son of Shallum, [a]the
keeper of the [1]door.
5 Then I set before the sons of the house of the
Rechabites bowls full of wine, and cups; and I said
to them, "Drink wine."
6 But they said, "We will drink no wine, for
[a]Jonadab the son of Rechab, our father, commanded us, saying, 'You shall drink [b]no wine, you
nor your sons, forever.
7 'You shall not build a house, sow seed, plant a
vineyard, nor have *any of these;* but all your days
you shall dwell in tents, [a]that you may live many
days in the land where you are sojourners.'
8 "Thus we have [a]obeyed the voice of Jonadab
the son of Rechab, our father, in all that he
charged us, to drink no wine all our days, we, our
wives, our sons, or our daughters,
9 "nor to build ourselves houses to dwell in; nor
do we have vineyard, field, or seed.
10 "But we have dwelt in tents, and have obeyed
and done according to all that Jonadab our father
commanded us.
11 "But it came to pass, when Nebuchadnezzar
king of Babylon came up into the land, that we
said, 'Come, let us [a]go to Jerusalem for fear of the
army of the Chaldeans and for fear of the army of
the Syrians.' So we dwell at Jerusalem."
**12** Then came the word of the LORD to Jeremiah,
saying,
13 "Thus says the LORD of hosts, the God of
Israel: 'Go and tell the men of Judah and the
inhabitants of Jerusalem, "Will you not [a]receive
instruction to [1]obey My words?" says the LORD.
14 "The words of Jonadab the son of Rechab,
which he commanded his sons, not to drink wine,
are performed; for to this day they drink none,
and obey their father's commandment. [a]But although I have spoken to you, [b]rising early and
speaking, you did not [1]obey Me.
15 "I have also sent to you all My [a]servants the
prophets, rising up early and sending *them,* saying, [b]'Turn now everyone from his evil way,
amend your doings, and do not go after other gods
to serve them; then you will [c]dwell in the land
which I have given you and your fathers.' But you
have not inclined your ear, nor obeyed Me.
16 "Surely the sons of Jonadab the son of Rechab
have performed the commandment of their [a]fa-
ther, which he commanded them, but this people
has not obeyed Me." '
17 "Therefore thus says the LORD God of hosts,
the God of Israel: 'Behold, I will bring on Judah
and on all the inhabitants of Jerusalem all the
doom that I have pronounced against them; [a]be-
cause I have spoken to them but they have not
heard, and I have called to them but they have not
answered.' "
**18** And Jeremiah said to the house of the Rechabites, "Thus says the LORD of hosts, the God of
Israel: 'Because you have obeyed the commandment of Jonadab your father, and kept all his
precepts and done according to all that he commanded you,
19 'therefore thus says the LORD of hosts, the
God of Israel: "Jonadab the son of Rechab shall
not lack a man to [a]stand before Me forever." ' "

## *The Burning of the Scroll*

**36** Now it came to pass in the [a]fourth year of
Jehoiakim the son of Josiah, king of Judah,
*that* this word came to Jeremiah from the LORD,
saying:
2 "Take a [a]scroll of a book and [b]write on it all
the words that I have spoken to you against
Israel, against Judah, and against [c]all the nations,
from the day I spoke to you, from the days of
[d]Josiah even to this day.
3 "It [a]may be that the house of Judah will hear
all the adversities which I purpose to bring upon
them, that everyone may [b]turn from his evil way,
that I may forgive their iniquity and their sin."
**4** Then Jeremiah [a]called Baruch the son of Neriah; and [b]Baruch wrote on a scroll of a book, [1]at
the instruction of Jeremiah, all the words of the
LORD which He had spoken to him.
5 And Jeremiah commanded Baruch, saying, "I
*am* confined, I cannot go into the house of the
LORD.
6 "You go, therefore, and read from the scroll
which you have written [1]at my instruction, the
words of the LORD, in the hearing of the people in
the LORD's house on [a]the day of fasting. And you
shall also read them in the hearing of all Judah
who come from their cities.
7 "It may be that they will present their supplication before the LORD, and everyone will turn
from his evil way. For great *is* the anger and the
fury that the LORD has pronounced against this
people."
8 And Baruch the son of Neriah did according to
all that Jeremiah the prophet commanded him,
reading from the book the words of the LORD in
the LORD's house.
**9** Now it came to pass in the fifth year of Jehoiakim the son of Josiah, king of Judah, in the ninth
month, *that* they proclaimed a fast before the
LORD to all the people in Jerusalem, and to all the
people who came from the cities of Judah to
Jerusalem.
10 Then Baruch read from the book the words of
Jeremiah in the house of the LORD, in the chamber
of Gemariah the son of Shaphan the scribe, in the
upper court at the [a]entry of the New Gate of the
LORD's house, in the [1]hearing of all the people.
**11** When Michaiah the son of Gemariah, the son
of Shaphan, heard all the words of the LORD from
the book,
12 he then went down to the king's house, into
the scribe's chamber; and there all the princes
were sitting—[a]Elishama the scribe, Delaiah the
son of Shemaiah, [b]Elnathan the son of Achbor,
Gemariah the son of Shaphan, Zedekiah the son
of Hananiah, and all the princes.
13 Then Michaiah declared to them all the words
that he had heard when Baruch read the book in
the hearing of the people.
14 Therefore all the princes sent Jehudi the son
of Nethaniah, the son of Shelemiah, the son of
Cushi, to Baruch, saying, "Take in your hand the
scroll from which you have read in the hearing of
the people, and come." So Baruch the son of
Neriah took the scroll in his hand and came to
them.
15 And they said to him, "Sit down now, and read
it in our hearing." So Baruch read *it* in their
hearing.

**4** [a]2 Kin. 12:9; 25:18; 1 Chr. 9:18, 19 [1]Lit. *threshold*
**6** [a]2 Kin. 10:15, 23 [b]Lev. 10:9; Num. 6:2–4; Judg. 13:7, 14; Prov. 31:4; Ezek. 44:21; Luke 1:15
**7** [a]Ex. 20:12; Eph. 6:2, 3
**8** [a][Prov. 1:8, 9; 4:1, 2, 10; 6:20; Eph. 6:1; Col. 3:20]
**11** [a]Jer. 4:5–7; 8:14
**13** [a][Is. 28:9–12]; Jer. 6:10; 17:23; 32:33 [1]*listen to*
**14** [a]2 Chr. 36:15 [b]Jer. 7:13; 25:3 [1]*listen to*
**15** [a]Jer. 26:4, 5; 29:19 [b][Is. 1:16, 17]; Jer. 18:11; 25:5, 6; [Ezek. 18:30–32]; Acts 26:20 [c]Jer. 7:7; 25:5, 6
**16** [a][Heb. 12:9]
**17** [a]Prov. 1:24; Is. 65:12; 66:4; Jer. 7:13
**19** [a][Ex. 20:12]; Jer. 15:19; [Luke 21:36; Eph. 6:2, 3]

CHAPTER 36
**1** [a]2 Kin. 24:1; 2 Chr. 36:5–7; Jer. 25:1, 3; 45:1; Dan. 1:1
**2** [a]Is. 8:1; Ezek. 2:9; Zech. 5:1 [b]Jer. 30:2; Hab. 2:2 [c]Jer. 25:15 [d]Jer. 25:3
**3** [a]Jer. 26:3; Ezek. 12:3 [b][Deut. 30:2, 8; 1 Sam. 7:3]; Is. 55:7; Jer. 18:8; Jon. 3:8
**4** [a]Jer. 32:12 [b]Jer. 45:1 [1]Lit. *from Jeremiah's mouth*
**6** [a]Lev. 16:29; 23:27–32; Acts 27:9 [1]Lit. *from my mouth*
**10** [a]Jer. 26:10 [1]Lit. *ears*
**12** [a]Jer. 41:1 [b]Jer. 26:22

16 Now it happened, when they had heard all the words, that they looked in fear from one to another, and said to Baruch, "We will surely tell the king of all these words."

17 And they asked Baruch, saying, "Tell us now, how did you write all these words—[1]at his instruction?"

18 So Baruch answered them, "He proclaimed with his mouth all these words to me, and I wrote *them* with ink in the book."

19 Then the princes said to Baruch, "Go and hide, you and Jeremiah; and let no one know where you are."

**20** And they went to the king, into the court; but they stored the scroll in the chamber of Elishama the scribe, and told all the words in the hearing of the king.

21 So the king sent Jehudi to bring the scroll, and he took it from Elishama the scribe's chamber. And Jehudi read it in the hearing of the king and in the hearing of all the princes who stood beside the king.

22 Now the king was sitting in [a]the winter house in the ninth month, with *a fire* burning on the hearth before him.

23 And it happened, when Jehudi had read three or four columns, *that the king* cut it with the scribe's knife and cast *it* into the fire that *was* on the hearth, until all the scroll was consumed in the fire that *was* on the hearth.

24 Yet they were [a]not afraid, nor did they [b]tear their garments, the king nor any of his servants who heard all these words.

25 Nevertheless Elnathan, Delaiah, and Gemariah implored the king not to burn the scroll; but he would not listen to them.

26 And the king commanded Jerahmeel [1]the king's son, Seraiah the son of Azriel, and Shelemiah the son of Abdeel, to seize Baruch the scribe and Jeremiah the prophet, but the LORD hid them.

**27** Now after the king had burned the scroll with the words which Baruch had written [1]at the instruction of Jeremiah, the word of the LORD came to Jeremiah, saying:

28 "Take yet another scroll, and write on it all the former words that were in the first scroll which Jehoiakim the king of Judah has burned.

29 "And you shall say to Jehoiakim king of Judah, 'Thus says the LORD: "You have burned this scroll, saying, [a]'Why have you written in it that the king of Babylon will certainly come and destroy this land, and cause man and beast to [b]cease from here?' "

30 'Therefore thus says the LORD concerning Jehoiakim king of Judah: [a]"He shall have no one to sit on the throne of David, and his dead body shall be [b]cast out to the heat of the day and the frost of the night.

31 "I will punish him, his [1]family, and his servants for their iniquity; and I will bring on them, on the inhabitants of Jerusalem, and on the men of Judah all the doom that I have pronounced against them; but they did not heed." ' "

**32** Then Jeremiah took another scroll and gave it to Baruch the scribe, the son of Neriah, who wrote on it [1]at the instruction of Jeremiah all the words of the book which Jehoiakim king of Judah had burned in the fire. And besides, there were added to them many similar words.

**17** [1]Lit. *with his mouth*
**22** [a]Judg. 3:20; Amos 3:15
**24** [a][Ps. 36:1]; Jer. 36:16 [b]Gen. 37:29, 34; 2 Sam. 1:11; 1 Kin. 21:27; 2 Kin. 19:1, 2; 22:11; Is. 36:22; 37:1; Jon. 3:6
**26** [1]Or *son of Hammelech*
**27** [1]Lit. *from Jeremiah's mouth*
**29** [a]Jer. 32:3 [b]Jer. 25:9–11; 26:9
**30** [a]Jer. 22:30 [b]Jer. 22:19
**31** [1]Lit. *seed*
**32** [1]Lit. *from Jeremiah's mouth*

CHAPTER 37
**1** [a]2 Kin. 24:17; 1 Chr. 3:15; 2 Chr. 36:10; Jer. 22:24
**2** [a]2 Kin. 24:19, 20; 2 Chr. 36:12–16; [Prov. 29:12]
**3** [a]Jer. 21:1, 2; 29:25; 52:24 [b]1 Kin. 13:6; Jer. 42:2; Acts 8:24
**5** [a]2 Kin. 24:7; Jer. 37:7; Ezek. 17:15
**7** [a]Is. 36:6; Jer. 21:2; Ezek. 17:17
**8** [a]2 Chr. 36:19; Jer. 34:22
**10** [a]Lev. 26:36–38; Is. 30:17; Jer. 21:4, 5
**14** [1]*a lie*
**15** [a]Jer. 20:2; [Matt. 21:35] [b]Gen. 39:20; 2 Chr. 16:10; 18:26; Jer. 38:26; Acts 5:18
**16** [a]Jer. 38:6
**17** [a]2 Kin. 25:4–7; Jer. 21:7; Ezek. 12:12, 13; 17:19–21

## *Jeremiah Imprisoned*

**37** Now King [a]Zedekiah the son of Josiah reigned instead of Coniah the son of Jehoiakim, whom Nebuchadnezzar king of Babylon made king in the land of Judah.

2 [a]But neither he nor his servants nor the people of the land gave heed to the words of the LORD which He spoke by the prophet Jeremiah.

**3** And Zedekiah the king sent Jehucal the son of Shelemiah, and [a]Zephaniah the son of Maaseiah, the priest, to the prophet Jeremiah, saying, [b]"Pray now to the LORD our God for us."

4 Now Jeremiah was coming and going among the people, for they had not *yet* put him in prison.

5 Then [a]Pharaoh's army came up from Egypt; and when the Chaldeans who were besieging Jerusalem heard news of them, they departed from Jerusalem.

**6** Then the word of the LORD came to the prophet Jeremiah, saying,

7 "Thus says the LORD, the God of Israel, 'Thus you shall say to the king of Judah, [a]who sent you to Me to inquire of Me: "Behold, Pharaoh's army which has come up to help you will return to Egypt, to their own land.

8 [a]"And the Chaldeans shall come back and fight against this city, and take it and burn it with fire." '

9 "Thus says the LORD: 'Do not deceive yourselves, saying, "The Chaldeans will surely depart from us," for they will not depart.

10 [a]'For though you had defeated the whole army of the Chaldeans who fight against you, and there remained *only* wounded men among them, they would rise up, every man in his tent, and burn the city with fire.' "

**11** And it happened, when the army of the Chaldeans left *the siege* of Jerusalem for fear of Pharaoh's army,

12 that Jeremiah went out of Jerusalem to go into the land of Benjamin to claim his property there among the people.

13 And when he was in the Gate of Benjamin, a captain of the guard *was* there whose name *was* Irijah the son of Shelemiah, the son of Hananiah; and he seized Jeremiah the prophet, saying, "You are defecting to the Chaldeans!"

14 Then Jeremiah said, [1]"False! I am not defecting to the Chaldeans." But he did not listen to him. So Irijah seized Jeremiah and brought him to the princes.

15 Therefore the princes were angry with Jeremiah, and they struck him [a]and put him in prison in the [b]house of Jonathan the scribe. For they had made that the prison.

**16** When Jeremiah entered [a]the dungeon and the cells, and Jeremiah had remained there many days,

17 then Zedekiah the king sent and took him *out*. The king asked him secretly in his house, and said, "Is there *any* word from the LORD?" And Jeremiah said, "There is." Then he said, "You shall be [a]delivered into the hand of the king of Babylon!"

18 Moreover Jeremiah said to King Zedekiah, "What offense have I committed against you, against your servants, or against this people, that you have put me in prison?

19 "Where now *are* your prophets who prophesied to you, saying, 'The king of Babylon will not come against you or against this land?'

20 "Therefore please hear now, O my lord the
king. Please, let my petition be accepted before
you, and do not make me return to the house of
Jonathan the scribe, lest I die there."
21 Then Zedekiah the king commanded that they
should commit Jeremiah [a]to the court of the
prison, and that they should give him daily a piece
of bread from the bakers' street, [b]until all the
bread in the city was gone. Thus Jeremiah remained in the court of the prison.

### *Zedekiah Seeks Advice from Jeremiah*

**38** Now Shephatiah the son of Mattan, Gedaliah the son of Pashhur, [a]Jucal[1] the son of
Shelemiah, and [b]Pashhur the son of Malchiah
[c]heard the words that Jeremiah had spoken to all
the people, saying,
2 "Thus says the LORD: [a]'He who remains in this
city shall die by the sword, by famine, and by
pestilence; but he who goes over to the Chaldeans
shall live; his life shall be as a prize to him, and he
shall live.'
3 "Thus says the LORD: [a]'This city shall surely be
[b]given into the hand of the king of Babylon's
army, which shall take it.' "
4 Therefore the princes said to the king, "Please,
[a]let this man be put to death, for thus he [1]weakens
the hands of the men of war who remain in this
city, and the hands of all the people, by speaking
such words to them. For this man does not seek
the [2]welfare of this people, but their harm."
5 Then Zedekiah the king said, "Look, he *is* in
your hand. For the king can *do* nothing against
you."
6 [a]So they took Jeremiah and cast him into the
dungeon of Malchiah [1]the king's son, which *was*
in the court of the prison, and they let Jeremiah
down with ropes. And in the dungeon *there was*
no water, but mire. So Jeremiah sank in the mire.
7 [a]Now Ebed-Melech the Ethiopian, one of the
[1]eunuchs, who was in the king's house, heard that
they had put Jeremiah in the dungeon. When the
king was sitting at the Gate of Benjamin,
8 Ebed-Melech went out of the king's house and
spoke to the king, saying:
9 "My lord the king, these men have done evil in
all that they have done to Jeremiah the prophet,
whom they have cast into the dungeon, and he is
likely to die from hunger in the place where he is.
For *there is* [a]no more bread in the city."
10 Then the king commanded Ebed-Melech the
Ethiopian, saying, "Take from here thirty men
with you, and lift Jeremiah the prophet out of the
dungeon before he dies."
11 So Ebed-Melech took the men with him and
went into the house of the king under the treasury, and took from there old clothes and old rags,
and let them down by ropes into the dungeon to
Jeremiah.
12 Then Ebed-Melech the Ethiopian said to Jeremiah, "Please put these old clothes and rags
under your armpits, under the ropes." And Jeremiah did so.
13 So they pulled Jeremiah up with ropes and
lifted him out of the dungeon. And Jeremiah
remained [a]in the court of the prison.
**14** Then Zedekiah the king sent and had Jeremiah the prophet brought to him at the third
entrance of the house of the LORD. And the king
said to Jeremiah, "I will [a]ask you something. Hide
nothing from me."
15 Jeremiah said to Zedekiah, "If I declare *it* to
you, will you not surely put me to death? And if I
give you advice, you will not listen to me."
16 So Zedekiah the king swore secretly to Jeremiah, saying, "*As* the LORD lives, [a]who made our
very souls, I will not put you to death, nor will I
give you into the hand of these men who seek
your life."
**17** Then Jeremiah said to Zedekiah, "Thus says
the LORD, the God of hosts, the God of Israel: 'If
you surely [a]surrender[1] [b]to the king of Babylon's
princes, then your soul shall live; this city shall
not be burned with fire, and you and your house
shall live.
18 'But if you do not [1]surrender to the king of
Babylon's princes, then this city shall be given
into the hand of the Chaldeans; they shall burn it
with fire, and [a]you shall not escape from their
hand.' "
19 And Zedekiah the king said to Jeremiah, "I am
afraid of the Jews who have [a]defected to the
Chaldeans, lest they deliver me into their hand,
and they [b]abuse me."
20 But Jeremiah said, "They shall not deliver *you*.
Please, obey the voice of the LORD which I speak
to you. So it shall be [a]well with you, and your soul
shall live.
21 "But if you refuse to [1]surrender, this *is* the
word that the LORD has shown me:
22 'Now behold, all the [a]women who are left in
the king of Judah's house *shall be* surrendered to
the king of Babylon's princes, and those *women*
shall say:

"Your close friends have [1]set upon you
And prevailed against you;
Your feet have sunk in the mire,
*And* they have [2]turned away again."

23 'So they shall surrender all your wives and
[a]children to the Chaldeans. [b]You shall not escape
from their hand, but shall be taken by the hand of
the king of Babylon. And you shall cause this city
to be burned with fire.' "
**24** Then Zedekiah said to Jeremiah, "Let no one
know of these words, and you shall not die.
25 "But if the princes hear that I have talked
with you, and they come to you and say to you,
'Declare to us now what you have said to the
king, and also what the king said to you; do not
hide *it* from us, and we will not put you to death,'
26 "then you shall say to them, [a]'I presented my
request before the king, that he would not make
me return [b]to Jonathan's house to die there.' "
27 Then all the princes came to Jeremiah and
asked him. And he told them according to all
these words that the king had commanded. So
they stopped speaking with him, for the conversation had not been heard.
28 Now [a]Jeremiah remained in the court of the
prison until the day that Jerusalem was taken.
And he was *there* when Jerusalem was taken.

### *The Fall of Jerusalem*

**39** In the [a]ninth year of Zedekiah king of
Judah, in the tenth month, Nebuchadnezzar
king of Babylon and all his army came against
Jerusalem, and besieged it.
2 In the [a]eleventh year of Zedekiah, in the
fourth month, on the ninth *day* of the month, the
[1]city was penetrated.

**21** [a]Jer. 32:2; 38:13, 28 [b]2 Kin. 25:3; Jer. 38:9; 52:6

CHAPTER 38

**1** [a]Jer. 37:3 [b]Jer. 21:1 [c]Jer. 21:8 [1]*Jehucal*, Jer. 37:3
**2** [a]Jer. 21:9
**3** [a]Jer. 21:10; 32:3 [b]Jer. 34:2
**4** [a]Jer. 26:11 [1]Is discouraging [2]Well-being; lit. *peace*
**6** [a]Jer. 37:21; Lam. 3:55 [1]Or *son of Hammelech*
**7** [a]Jer. 39:16 [1]Or *officers*
**9** [a]Jer. 37:21
**13** [a]Neh. 3:25; Jer. 37:21; Acts 23:35; 24:27; 28:16, 30
**14** [a]Jer. 21:1, 2; 37:17
**16** [a]Num. 16:22; Is. 57:16; Zech. 12:1; [Acts 17:25, 28]
**17** [a]2 Kin. 24:12 [b]Jer. 39:3 [1]Lit. *go out*
**18** [a]Jer. 32:4; 34:3 [1]Lit. *go out*
**19** [a]Jer. 39:9 [b]1 Sam. 31:4
**20** [a]Jer. 40:9
**21** [1]Lit. *go out*
**22** [a]Jer. 8:10 [1]Or *misled* [2]Deserted you
**23** [a]Jer. 39:6; 41:10 [b]Jer. 39:5
**26** [a]Jer. 37:20 [b]Jer. 37:15
**28** [a][Ps. 23:4]; Jer. 37:21; 39:14

CHAPTER 39

**1** [a]2 Kin. 25:1–12; Jer. 52:4; Ezek. 24:1, 2
**2** [a]Jer. 1:3 [1]*city wall was breached*

3 [a]Then all the princes of the king of Babylon came in and sat in the Middle Gate: Nergal-Sharezer, Samgar-Nebo, Sarsechim, [1]Rabsaris, Nergal-Sarezer, [2]Rabmag, with the rest of the princes of the king of Babylon.

4 [a]So it was, when Zedekiah the king of Judah and all the men of war saw them, that they fled and went out of the city by night, by way of the king's garden, by the gate between the two walls. And he went out by way of the [1]plain.

5 But the Chaldean army pursued them and [a]overtook Zedekiah in the plains of Jericho. And when they had captured him, they brought him up to Nebuchadnezzar king of Babylon, to [b]Riblah in the land of Hamath, where he pronounced judgment on him.

6 Then the king of Babylon killed the sons of Zedekiah before his [a]eyes in Riblah; the king of Babylon also killed all the [b]nobles of Judah.

7 Moreover [a]he put out Zedekiah's eyes, and bound him with bronze [1]fetters to carry him off to Babylon.

8 [a]And the Chaldeans burned the king's house and the houses of the people with [b]fire, and broke down the [c]walls of Jerusalem.

9 [a]Then Nebuzaradan the captain of the guard carried away captive to Babylon the remnant of the people who remained in the city and those who [b]defected to him, with the rest of the people who remained.

10 But Nebuzaradan the captain of the guard left in the land of Judah the [a]poor people, who had nothing, and gave them vineyards and fields [1]at the same time.

**11** Now Nebuchadnezzar king of Babylon gave charge concerning Jeremiah to Nebuzaradan the captain of the guard, saying,

12 "Take him and look after him, and do him no [a]harm; but do to him just as he says to you."

13 So Nebuzaradan the captain of the guard sent Nebushasban, Rabsaris, Nergal-Sharezer, Rabmag, and all the king of Babylon's chief officers;

14 then they sent *someone* [a]to take Jeremiah from the court of the prison, and committed him [b]to Gedaliah the son of [c]Ahikam, the son of Shaphan, that he should take him home. So he dwelt among the people.

**15** Meanwhile the word of the LORD had come to Jeremiah while he was shut up in the court of the prison, saying,

16 "Go and speak to [a]Ebed-Melech the Ethiopian, saying, 'Thus says the LORD of hosts, the God of Israel: "Behold, [b]I will bring My words upon this city for adversity and not for good, and they shall be *performed* in that day before you.

17 "But I will deliver you in that day," says the LORD, "and you shall not be given into the hand of the men of whom you *are* afraid.

18 "For I will surely deliver you, and you shall not fall by the sword; but [a]your life shall be as a prize to you, [b]because you have put your trust in Me," says the LORD.' "

### *Jeremiah Lives with Gedaliah*

**40** The word that came to Jeremiah from the LORD [a]after Nebuzaradan the captain of the guard had let him go from Ramah, when he had taken him bound in chains among all who were carried away captive from Jerusalem and Judah, who were carried away captive to Babylon.

2 And the captain of the guard took Jeremiah and [a]said to him: "The LORD your God has pronounced this doom on this place.

3 "Now the LORD has brought *it*, and has done just as He said. [a]Because you *people* have sinned against the LORD, and not obeyed His voice, therefore this thing has come upon you.

4 "And now look, I free you this day from the chains that [1]*were* on your hand. [a]If it seems good to you to come with me to Babylon, come, and I will look after you. But if it seems wrong for you to come with me to Babylon, remain here. See, [b]all the land *is* before you; wherever it seems good and convenient for you to go, go there."

5 Now while Jeremiah had not yet gone back, *Nebuzaradan said,* "Go back to [a]Gedaliah the son of Ahikam, the son of Shaphan, [b]whom the king of Babylon has made governor over the cities of Judah, and dwell with him among the people. Or go wherever it seems convenient for you to go." So the captain of the guard gave him rations and a gift and let him go.

6 [a]Then Jeremiah went to Gedaliah the son of Ahikam, to [b]Mizpah, and dwelt with him among the people who were left in the land.

**7** [a]And when all the captains of the armies who *were* in the fields, they and their men, heard that the king of Babylon had made Gedaliah the son of Ahikam governor in the land, and had committed to him men, women, children, and [b]the poorest of the land who had not been carried away captive to Babylon,

8 then they came to Gedaliah at Mizpah—[a]Ishmael the son of Nethaniah, [b]Johanan and Jonathan the sons of Kareah, Seraiah the son of Tanhumeth, the sons of Ephai the Netophathite, and [c]Jezaniah[1] the son of a [d]Maachathite, they and their men.

9 And Gedaliah the son of Ahikam, the son of Shaphan, took an oath before them and their men, saying, "Do not be afraid to serve the Chaldeans. Dwell in the land and serve the king of Babylon, and it shall be [a]well with you.

10 "As for me, I will indeed dwell at Mizpah and serve the Chaldeans who come to us. But you, gather wine and summer fruit and oil, put *them* in your vessels, and dwell in your cities that you have taken."

11 Likewise, when all the Jews who *were* in Moab, among the Ammonites, in Edom, and who *were* in all the countries, heard that the king of Babylon had left a remnant of Judah, and that he had set over them Gedaliah the son of Ahikam, the son of Shaphan,

12 then all the Jews [a]returned out of all places where they had been driven, and came to the land of Judah, to Gedaliah at Mizpah, and gathered wine and summer fruit in abundance.

**13** Moreover Johanan the son of Kareah and all the captains of the forces that *were* in the fields came to Gedaliah at Mizpah,

14 and said to him, [1]"Do you certainly know that [a]Baalis the king of the Ammonites has sent Ishmael the son of Nethaniah to murder you?" But Gedaliah the son of Ahikam did not believe them.

15 Then Johanan the son of Kareah spoke secretly to Gedaliah in Mizpah, saying, "Let me go, please, and I will kill Ishmael the son of Nethaniah, and no one will know *it*. Why should he murder you, so that all the Jews who are gathered to you would be scattered, and the [a]remnant in Judah perish?"

**3** [a]Jer. 1:15; 38:17 [1]A title, probably *Chief Officer;* also v. 13 [2]A title, probably *Troop Commander;* also v. 13
**4** [a]2 Kin. 25:4; Is. 30:16; Jer. 52:7; Amos 2:14 [1]Or *Arabah;* the Jordan Valley
**5** [a]Jer. 21:7; 32:4; 38:18, 23 [b]2 Kin. 23:33; Jer. 52:9, 26, 27
**6** [a]Deut. 28:34 [b]Jer. 34:19–21
**7** [a]2 Kin. 25:7; Jer. 52:11; Ezek. 12:13 [1]*chains*
**8** [a]2 Kin. 25:9; Jer. 38:18; 52:13 [b]Jer. 21:10 [c]2 Kin. 25:10; Neh. 1:3; Jer. 52:14
**9** [a]2 Kin. 25:8, 11, 12, 20 [b]Jer. 38:19
**10** [a]Jer. 40:7 [1]Lit. *on that day*
**12** [a]Jer. 1:18, 19; 15:20, 21
**14** [a]Jer. 38:28 [b]Jer. 40:5 [c]2 Kin. 22:12, 14; 2 Chr. 34:20; Jer. 26:24
**16** [a]Jer. 38:7, 12 [b]Jer. 21:10; [Dan. 9:12; Zech. 1:6]
**18** [a]Jer. 21:9; 45:5 [b]1 Chr. 5:20; Ps. 37:40; [Jer. 17:7, 8]

CHAPTER 40
**1** [a]Jer. 39:9, 11
**2** [a]Jer. 50:7
**3** [a]Deut. 29:24, 25; Jer. 50:7; Dan. 9:11; [Rom. 2:5]
**4** [a]Jer. 39:12 [b]Gen. 20:15 [1]Or *are*
**5** [a]Jer. 39:14 [b]2 Kin. 25:22; Jer. 41:10
**6** [a]Jer. 39:14 [b]Judg. 20:1; 1 Sam. 7:5; 2 Chr. 16:6
**7** [a]2 Kin. 25:23, 24 [b]Jer. 39:10
**8** [a]Jer. 41:1–10 [b]Jer. 41:11; 43:2 [c]Jer. 42:1 [d]Deut. 3:14; Josh. 12:5; 2 Sam. 10:6 [1]*Jaazaniah,* 2 Kin. 25:23
**9** [a]Jer. 27:11; 38:17–20
**12** [a]Jer. 43:5
**14** [a]Jer. 41:10 [1]Or *Certainly you know that*
**15** [a]Jer. 42:2

16 But Gedaliah the son of Ahikam said to Johanan the son of Kareah, "You shall not do this
thing, for you speak falsely concerning Ishmael."

### *Ishmael Murders Gedaliah*

**41** Now it came to pass in the seventh month
[a]*that* Ishmael the son of Nethaniah, the son
of Elishama, of the royal [1]family and of the officers
of the king, came with ten men to Gedaliah the
son of Ahikam, at [b]Mizpah. And there they ate
bread together in Mizpah.
2 Then Ishmael the son of Nethaniah, and the
ten men who were with him, arose and [a]struck
Gedaliah the son of [b]Ahikam, the son of Shaphan,
with the sword, and killed him whom the king of
Babylon had made [c]governor over the land.
3 Ishmael also struck down all the Jews who
were with him, *that is,* with Gedaliah at Mizpah,
and the Chaldeans who were found there, the men
of war.
4 And it happened, on the second day after he
had killed Gedaliah, when as yet no one knew *it,*
5 that certain men came from Shechem, from
Shiloh, and from Samaria, eighty men [a]with their
beards shaved and their clothes torn, having cut
themselves, with offerings and incense in their
hand, to bring *them* to [b]the house of the LORD.
6 Now Ishmael the son of Nethaniah went out
from Mizpah to meet them, weeping as he went
along; and it happened as he met them that he
said to them, "Come to Gedaliah the son of
Ahikam!"
7 So it was, when they came into the midst of
the city, that Ishmael the son of Nethaniah [a]killed
them *and cast them* into the midst of a [1]pit, he and
the men who were with him.
8 But ten men were found among them who
said to Ishmael, "Do not kill us, for we have
treasures of wheat, barley, oil, and honey in the
field." So he desisted and did not kill them among
their brethren.
9 Now the [1]pit into which Ishmael had cast all
the dead bodies of the men whom he had slain,
because of Gedaliah, *was* [a]the same one Asa the
king had made for fear of Baasha king of Israel.
Ishmael the son of Nethaniah filled it with *the*
slain.
10 Then Ishmael carried away captive all the
[a]rest of the people who *were* in Mizpah, [b]the
king's daughters and all the people who remained
in Mizpah, [c]whom Nebuzaradan the captain of the
guard had committed to Gedaliah the son of
Ahikam. And Ishmael the son of Nethaniah carried them away captive and departed to go over to
[d]the Ammonites.
11 But when [a]Johanan the son of Kareah and all
the captains of the forces that *were* with him
heard of all the evil that Ishmael the son of
Nethaniah had done,
12 they took all the men and went to fight with
Ishmael the son of Nethaniah; and they found him
by [a]the great pool that *is* in Gibeon.
13 So it was, when all the people who *were* with
Ishmael saw Johanan the son of Kareah, and all
the captains of the forces who *were* with him, that
they were glad.
14 Then all the people whom Ishmael had carried
away captive from Mizpah turned around and
came back, and went to Johanan the son of
Kareah.
15 But Ishmael the son of Nethaniah escaped
from Johanan with eight men and went to the
Ammonites.
16 Then Johanan the son of Kareah, and all the
captains of the forces that were with him, took
from Mizpah all the [a]rest of the people whom he
had recovered from Ishmael the son of Nethaniah
after he had murdered Gedaliah the son of Ahikam—the mighty men of war and the women and
the children and the eunuchs, whom he had
brought back from Gibeon.
17 And they departed and dwelt in the habitation
of [a]Chimham, which is near Bethlehem, as they
went on their way to [b]Egypt,
18 because of the Chaldeans; for they were afraid
of them, because Ishmael the son of Nethaniah
had murdered Gedaliah the son of Ahikam,
[a]whom the king of Babylon had made governor in
the land.

### *Escape to Egypt Is Forbidden*

**42** Now all the captains of the forces, [a]Johanan
the son of Kareah, Jezaniah the son of
Hoshaiah, and all the people, from the least to the
greatest, came near
2 and said to Jeremiah the prophet, [a]"Please, let
our petition be acceptable to you, and [b]pray for us
to the LORD your God, for all this remnant (since
we are left *but* [c]a few of many, as you can see),
3 "that the LORD your God may show us [a]the
way in which we should walk and the thing we
should do."
4 Then Jeremiah the prophet said to them, "I
have heard. Indeed, I will pray to the LORD your
God according to your words, and it shall be, *that*
[a]whatever the LORD answers you, I will declare *it*
to you. I will [b]keep nothing back from you."
5 So they said to Jeremiah, [a]"Let the LORD be a
true and faithful witness between us, if we do not
do according to everything which the LORD your
God sends us by you.
6 "Whether *it is* [1]pleasing or [2]displeasing, we
will [a]obey the voice of the LORD our God to whom
we send you, [b]that it may be well with us when we
obey the voice of the LORD our God."
7 And it happened after ten days that the word
of the LORD came to Jeremiah.
8 Then he called Johanan the son of Kareah, all
the captains of the forces which *were* with him,
and all the people from the least even to the
greatest,
9 and said to them, "Thus says the LORD, the
God of Israel, to whom you sent me to present
your petition before Him:
10 'If you will still remain in this land, then [a]I will
build you and not pull *you* down, and I will plant
you and not pluck *you* up. For I [b]relent concerning the disaster that I have brought upon you.
11 'Do not be afraid of the king of Babylon, of
whom you are afraid; do not be afraid of him,'
says the LORD, [a]'for I *am* with you, to save you
and deliver you from his hand.
12 'And [a]I will show you mercy, that he may have
mercy on you and cause you to return to your
own land.'
13 "But if [a]you say, 'We will not dwell in this
land,' disobeying the voice of the LORD your God,
14 "saying, 'No, but we will go to the land of
[a]Egypt where we shall see no war, nor hear the
sound of the trumpet, nor be hungry for bread,
and there we will dwell'—

CHAPTER 41
1 [a]2 Kin. 25:25 [b]Jer. 40:6, 10 [1]Lit. *seed*
2 [a]2 Sam. 3:27; 20:9, 10; 2 Kin. 25:25; Ps. 41:9; 109:5; John 13:18 [b]Jer. 26:24 [c]Jer. 40:5
5 [a]Lev. 19:27, 28; Deut. 14:1; Is. 15:2 [b]1 Sam. 1:7; 2 Kin. 25:9; Neh. 10:34, 35
7 [a]Ps. 55:23; Is. 59:7; Ezek. 22:27; 33:24, 26 [1]Or *cistern*
9 [a]1 Kin. 15:22; 2 Chr. 16:6 [1]Or *cistern*
10 [a]Jer. 40:11, 12 [b]Jer. 43:6 [c]Jer. 40:7 [d]Jer. 40:14
11 [a]Jer. 40:7, 8, 13–16
12 [a]2 Sam. 2:13
16 [a]Jer. 40:11, 12; 43:4–7
17 [a]2 Sam. 19:37, 38 [b]Jer. 43:7
18 [a]Jer. 40:5

CHAPTER 42
1 [a]Jer. 40:8, 13; 41:11
2 [a]Jer. 15:11 [b]Ex. 8:28; 1 Sam. 7:8; 12:19; 1 Kin. 13:6; Is. 37:4; Jer. 37:3; Acts 8:24; [James 5:16] [c]Lev. 26:22; Deut. 28:62; Is. 1:9; Lam. 1:1
3 [a]Ezra 8:21
4 [a]1 Kin. 22:14; Jer. 23:28 [b]1 Sam. 3:17, 18; Ps. 40:10; Acts 20:20
5 [a]Gen. 31:50; Judg. 11:10; Jer. 43:2; Mic. 1:2; Mal. 2:14; 3:5
6 [a]Ex. 24:7; Deut. 5:27; Josh. 24:24 [b]Deut. 5:29, 33; 6:3; Jer. 7:23 [1]Lit. *good* [2]Lit. *evil*
10 [a]Jer. 24:6; 31:28; 33:7; Ezek. 36:36 [b]Deut. 32:36; [Jer. 18:8]
11 [a]Num. 14:9; 2 Chr. 32:7, 8; Is. 8:9, 10; 43:2, 5; Jer. 1:19; 15:20; Rom. 8:31
12 [a]Neh. 1:11; Ps. 106:46; Prov. 16:7
13 [a]Jer. 44:16
14 [a]Is. 31:1; Jer. 41:17; 43:7

15 "Then hear now the word of the LORD, O
remnant of Judah! Thus says the LORD of hosts,
the God of Israel: 'If you [a]wholly[1] set [b]your faces
to enter Egypt, and go to dwell there,
16 'then it shall be *that* the [a]sword which you
feared shall overtake you there in the land of
Egypt; the famine of which you were afraid shall
follow close after you there *in* Egypt; and there
you shall die.
17 'So shall it be with all the men who set their
faces to go to Egypt to dwell there. They shall die
by the sword, by famine, and by pestilence. And
[a]none of them shall remain or escape from the
disaster that I will bring upon them.'
18 "For thus says the LORD of hosts, the God of
Israel: 'As My anger and My fury have been
[a]poured out on the inhabitants of Jerusalem, so
will My fury be poured out on you when you enter
Egypt. And [b]you shall be an oath, an astonishment, a curse, and a reproach; and you shall see
this place no more.'
19 "The LORD has said concerning you, O remnant of Judah, [a]'Do not go to Egypt!' Know
certainly that I have [1]admonished you this day.
20 "For you [1]were hypocrites in your hearts
when you sent me to the LORD your God, saying,
'Pray for us to the LORD our God, and according to
all that the LORD your God says, so declare to us
and we will do *it*.'
21 "And I have this day declared *it* to you, but
you have [a]not obeyed the voice of the LORD your
God, or anything which He has sent you by me.
22 "Now therefore, know certainly that you
[a]shall die by the sword, by famine, and by pestilence in the place where you desire to go to
dwell."

## *Jeremiah Taken to Egypt*

**43** Now it happened, when Jeremiah had
stopped speaking to all the people all the
[a]words of the LORD their God, for which the LORD
their God had sent him to them, all these words,
2 [a]that Azariah the son of Hoshaiah, Johanan
the son of Kareah, and all the proud men spoke,
saying to Jeremiah, "You speak falsely! The LORD
our God has not sent you to say, 'Do not go to
Egypt to dwell there.'
3 "But [a]Baruch the son of Neriah has [1]set you
against us, to deliver us into the hand of the
Chaldeans, that they may put us to death or carry
us away captive to Babylon."
4 So Johanan the son of Kareah, all the captains
of the forces, and all the people would [a]not obey
the voice of the LORD, to remain in the land of
Judah.
5 But Johanan the son of Kareah and all the
captains of the forces took [a]all the remnant of
Judah who had returned to dwell in the land of
Judah, from all nations where they had been
driven—
6 men, women, children, [a]the king's daughters,
[b]and every person whom Nebuzaradan the captain of the guard had left with Gedaliah the son of
Ahikam, the son of Shaphan, and Jeremiah the
prophet and Baruch the son of Neriah.
7 [a]So they went to the land of Egypt, for they
did not obey the voice of the LORD. And they went
as far as [b]Tahpanhes.
8 Then the [a]word of the LORD came to Jeremiah
in Tahpanhes, saying,
9 "Take large stones in your hand, and hide
them in the sight of the men of Judah, in the [1]clay
in the brick courtyard which *is* at the entrance to
Pharaoh's house in Tahpanhes;
10 "and say to them, 'Thus says the LORD of
hosts, the God of Israel: "Behold, I will send and
bring Nebuchadnezzar the king of Babylon, [a]My
servant, and will set his throne above these stones
that I have hidden. And he will spread his royal
pavilion over them.
11 [a]"When he comes, he shall strike the land of
Egypt *and deliver* to death [b]*those appointed* for
death, and to captivity *those appointed* for captivity, and to the sword *those appointed* for the
sword.
12 [1]"I will kindle a fire in the houses of [a]the gods
of Egypt, and he shall burn them and carry them
away captive. And he shall array himself with the
land of Egypt, as a shepherd puts on his garment,
and he shall go out from there in peace.
13 "He shall also break the sacred pillars of [1]Beth
Shemesh that *are* in the land of Egypt; and the
houses of the gods of the Egyptians he shall burn
with fire." ' "

## *Jeremiah Prophesies to the Jews in Egypt*

**44** The word that came to Jeremiah concerning all the Jews who dwell in the land of
Egypt, who dwell at [a]Migdol, at [b]Tahpanhes, at
[c]Noph,[1] and in the country of [d]Pathros, saying,
2 "Thus says the LORD of hosts, the God of
Israel: 'You have seen all the calamity that I have
brought on Jerusalem and on all the cities of
Judah; and behold, this day they *are* [a]a desolation,
and no one dwells in them,
3 'because of their wickedness which they have
committed to provoke Me to anger, in that they
went [a]to burn incense *and* to [b]serve other gods
whom they did not know, they nor you nor your
fathers.
4 'However [a]I have sent to you all My servants
the prophets, rising early and sending *them*, saying, "Oh, do not do this abominable thing that I
hate!"
5 'But they did not listen or incline their ear to
turn from their wickedness, to burn no incense to
other gods.
6 'So My fury and My anger were poured out
and kindled in the cities of Judah and in the
streets of Jerusalem; and they [1]are wasted *and*
desolate, as it is this day.'
7 "Now therefore, thus says the LORD, the God
of hosts, the God of Israel: 'Why do you commit
*this* great evil [a]against yourselves, to cut off from
you man and woman, child and infant, out of
Judah, leaving none to remain,
8 'in that you [a]provoke Me to wrath with the
works of your hands, burning incense to other
gods in the land of Egypt where you have gone to
dwell, that you may cut yourselves off and be [b]a
curse and a reproach among all the nations of the
earth?
9 'Have you forgotten the wickedness of your
fathers, the wickedness of the kings of Judah, the
wickedness of their wives, your own wickedness,
and the wickedness of your wives, which they
committed in the land of Judah and in the streets
of Jerusalem?
10 'They have not been [a]humbled,[1] to this day,
nor have they [b]feared; they have not walked in

15 [a]Deut. 17:16 [b]Luke 9:51 [1]Or *surely*
16 [a]Ezek. 11:8
17 [a]Jer. 44:14, 28
18 [a]Jer. 7:20 [b]Is. 65:15
19 [a]Deut. 17:16 [1]*warned*
20 [1]Lit. *used deceit against your souls*
21 [a]Is. 30:1–7
22 [a]Ezek. 6:11

CHAPTER 43
1 [a]Jer. 42:9–18
2 [a]Jer. 42:1
3 [a]Jer. 36:4; 45:1 [1]Or *incited*
4 [a]2 Kin. 25:26
5 [a]Jer. 40:11, 12
6 [a]Jer. 41:10 [b]Jer. 39:10; 40:7
7 [a]Jer. 42:19 [b]Jer. 2:16; 44:1
8 [a]Jer. 44:1–30
9 [1]Or *mortar*
10 [a]Jer. 25:9; 27:6
11 [a]Jer. 25:15–19; 44:13; 46:1, 2, 13–26 [b]Jer. 15:2
12 [a]Jer. 46:25 [1]So with MT, Tg.; LXX, Syr., Vg. *He*
13 [1]Lit. *House of the Sun*, ancient On, later called Heliopolis

CHAPTER 44
1 [a]Jer. 46:14 [b]Jer. 43:7 [c]Is. 19:13 [d]Ezek. 29:14; 30:14 [1]Ancient Memphis
2 [a]Jer. 4:7; 9:11; 34:22
3 [a]Jer. 19:4 [b]Deut. 13:6; 32:17
4 [a]Jer. 7:25; 25:4; 26:5; 29:19
6 [1]Or *became a ruin*
7 [a]Num. 16:38
8 [a]Jer. 25:6, 7; 44:3 [b]Jer. 42:18
10 [a]Jer. 6:15; 8:12 [b][Prov. 28:14] [1]Lit. *crushed*

My law or in My statutes that I set before you and your fathers.'

11 "Therefore thus says the LORD of hosts, the God of Israel: 'Behold, [a]I will set My face against you for catastrophe and for [1]cutting off all Judah.

12 'And I will take the remnant of Judah who have set their faces to go into the land of Egypt to dwell there, and [a]they shall all be consumed *and* fall in the land of Egypt. They shall be consumed by the sword *and* by famine. They shall die, from the least to the greatest, by the sword and by famine; and [b]they shall be an oath, an astonishment, a curse and a reproach!

13 [a]'For I will punish those who dwell in the land of Egypt, as I have punished Jerusalem, by the sword, by famine, and by pestilence,

14 'so that none of the remnant of Judah who have gone into the land of Egypt to dwell there shall escape or survive, lest they return to the land of Judah, to which they [a]desire[1] to return and dwell. For [b]none shall return except those who escape.' "

15 Then all the men who knew that their wives had burned incense to other gods, with all the women who stood by, a great multitude, and all the people who dwelt in the land of Egypt, in Pathros, answered Jeremiah, saying:

16 "*As for* the word that you have spoken to us in the name of the LORD, [a]we will not listen to you!

17 "But we will certainly do [a]whatever has gone out of our own mouth, to burn incense to the [b]queen of heaven and pour out drink offerings to her, as we have done, we and our fathers, our kings and our princes, in the cities of Judah and in the streets of Jerusalem. For *then* we had plenty of [1]food, were well-off, and saw no trouble.

18 "But since we stopped burning incense to the queen of heaven and pouring out drink offerings to her, we have lacked everything and have been consumed by the sword and by famine."

19 *The women also said,* [a]"And when we burned incense to the queen of heaven and poured out drink offerings to her, did we make cakes for her, to worship her, and pour out drink offerings to her without our husbands' *permission?*"

20 Then Jeremiah spoke to all the people—the men, the women, and all the people who had given him *that* answer—saying:

21 "The incense that you burned in the cities of Judah and in the streets of Jerusalem, you and your fathers, your kings and your princes, and the people of the land, did not the LORD remember them, and did it *not* come into His mind?

22 "So the LORD could no longer bear *it,* because of the evil of your doings *and* because of the abominations which you committed. Therefore your land is a desolation, an astonishment, a curse, and without an inhabitant, [a]as *it is* this day.

23 "Because you have burned incense and because you have sinned against the LORD, and have not obeyed the voice of the LORD or walked in His law, in His statutes or in His testimonies, [a]therefore this calamity has happened to you, as *at* this day."

24 Moreover Jeremiah said to all the people and to all the women, "Hear the word of the LORD, all Judah who *are* in the land of Egypt!

25 "Thus says the LORD of hosts, the God of Israel, saying: 'You and your wives have spoken with your mouths and fulfilled with your hands, saying, "We will surely keep our vows that we have made, to burn incense to the queen of heaven and pour out drink offerings to her." You will surely keep your vows and perform your vows!'

26 "Therefore hear the word of the LORD, all Judah who dwell in the land of Egypt: 'Behold, [a]I have sworn by My [b]great name,' says the LORD, 'that [c]My name shall no more be named in the mouth of any man of Judah in all the land of Egypt, saying, "The Lord GOD lives."

27 'Behold, I will watch over them for adversity and not for good. And all the men of Judah who *are* in the land of Egypt [a]shall be consumed by the sword and by famine, until there is an end to them.

28 'Yet [a]a small number who escape the sword shall return from the land of Egypt to the land of Judah; and all the remnant of Judah, who have gone to the land of Egypt to dwell there, shall know whose words will stand, Mine or theirs.

29 'And this *shall be* a sign to you,' says the LORD, 'that I will punish you in this place, that you may know that My words will surely [a]stand against you for adversity.'

30 "Thus says the LORD: 'Behold, [a]I will give Pharaoh Hophra king of Egypt into the hand of his enemies and into the hand of those who seek his life, as I gave [b]Zedekiah king of Judah into the hand of Nebuchadnezzar king of Babylon, his enemy who sought his life.' "

### *Jeremiah's Message to Baruch*

**45** The [a]word that Jeremiah the prophet spoke to [b]Baruch the son of Neriah, when he had written these words in a book [1]at the instruction of Jeremiah, in the [c]fourth year of Jehoiakim the son of Josiah, king of Judah, saying,

2 "Thus says the LORD, the God of Israel, to you, O Baruch:

3 'You said, "Woe is me now! For the LORD has added grief to my sorrow. I [a]fainted in my sighing, and I find no rest." '

4 "Thus you shall say to him, 'Thus says the LORD: "Behold, [a]what I have built I will break down, and what I have planted I will pluck up, that is, this whole land.

5 "And do you seek great things for yourself? Do not seek *them;* for behold, [a]I will bring adversity on all flesh," says the LORD. "But I will give your [b]life to you as a prize in all places, wherever you go." ' "

### *Prophecy Against Egypt*

**46** The word of the LORD which came to Jeremiah the prophet against [a]the nations.

2 Against [a]Egypt.

[b]Concerning the army of Pharaoh Necho, king of Egypt, which was by the River Euphrates in Carchemish, and which Nebuchadnezzar king of Babylon [c]defeated in the [d]fourth year of Jehoiakim the son of Josiah, king of Judah:

3 "Order[1] the [2]buckler and shield,
And draw near to battle!
4 Harness the horses,
And mount up, you horsemen!
Stand forth with *your* helmets,
Polish the spears,
[a]Put on the armor!
5 Why have I seen them dismayed *and* turned
back?

11 [a]Lev. 17:10; 20:5, 6; Jer. 21:10; Amos 9:4 [1]*destroying*
12 [a]Jer. 42:15–17, 22 [b]Is. 65:15; Jer. 42:18
13 [a]Jer. 43:11
14 [a]Jer. 22:26, 27 [b][Is. 4:2; 10:20]; Jer. 44:28; [Rom. 9:27] [1]Lit. *lift up their soul*
16 [a]Jer. 6:16
17 [a]Num. 30:12; Deut. 23:23; Judg. 11:36 [b]2 Kin. 17:16; Jer. 7:18 [1]Lit. *bread*
19 [a]Jer. 7:18
22 [a]Jer. 25:11, 18, 38
23 [a]1 Kin. 9:9; Neh. 13:18; Jer. 44:2; Dan. 9:11, 12
26 [a]Gen. 22:16; Deut. 32:40, 41; Jer. 22:5; Amos 6:8; Heb. 6:13 [b]Jer. 10:6 [c]Neh. 9:5; Ps. 50:16; Ezek. 20:39
27 [a]Jer. 1:10; 31:28; Ezek. 7:6
28 [a]Is. 10:19; 27:12, 13
29 [a][Ps. 33:11]
30 [a]Jer. 46:25, 26; Ezek. 29:3; 30:21 [b]2 Kin. 25:4–7; Jer. 39:5

CHAPTER 45
1 [a]Jer. 36:1, 4, 32 [b]Jer. 32:12, 16; 43:3 [c]Jer. 25:1; 36:1; 46:2 [1]Lit. *from Jeremiah's mouth*
3 [a]Ps. 6:6; 69:3; [2 Cor. 4:1, 16; Gal. 6:9]
4 [a]Is. 5:5; Jer. 1:10; 11:17; 18:7–10; 31:28
5 [a]Jer. 25:26 [b]Jer. 21:9; 38:2; 39:18

CHAPTER 46
1 [a]Jer. 25:15
2 [a]Jer. 25:17–19; Ezek. 29:2—32:32 [b]2 Kin. 23:33–35 [c]2 Kin. 23:29; 24:7; 2 Chr. 35:20 [d]Jer. 45:1
3 [1]*Set in order* [2]A small shield
4 [a]Is. 21:5; Jer. 51:11, 12; Joel 3:9; Nah. 2:1; 3:14

Their mighty ones are beaten down;
They have speedily fled,
And did not look back,
*For* [a]fear *was* all around," says the LORD.
6 "Do not let the swift flee away,
Nor the mighty man escape;
They will [a]stumble and fall
Toward the north, by the River Euphrates.

7 "Who *is* this coming up [a]like a flood,
Whose waters move like the rivers?
8 Egypt rises up like a flood,
And *its* waters move like the rivers;
And he says, 'I will go up
*and* cover the earth,
I will destroy the city and its inhabitants.'
9 Come up, O horses, and rage, O chariots!
And let the mighty men come forth:
[1]The Ethiopians and [2]the Libyans
who handle the shield,
And the Lydians [a]who handle
*and* bend the bow.
10 For this *is* [a]the day of the Lord GOD of hosts,
A day of vengeance,
That He may avenge Himself on His
adversaries.
[b]The sword shall devour;
It shall be [1]satiated
and made drunk with their blood;
For the Lord GOD of hosts [c]has a sacrifice
In the north country by the River Euphrates.

11 "Go[a] up to Gilead and take balm,
[b]O virgin, the daughter of Egypt;
In vain you will use many medicines;
[c]You shall not be cured.
12 The nations have heard of your [a]shame,
And your cry has filled the land;
For the mighty man has stumbled against
the mighty;
They both have fallen together."

**13** The word that the LORD spoke to Jeremiah the
prophet, how Nebuchadnezzar king of Babylon
would come *and* [a]strike the land of Egypt.

14 "Declare in Egypt, and proclaim in [a]Migdol;
Proclaim in [1]Noph and in [b]Tahpanhes;
Say, 'Stand fast and prepare yourselves,
For the sword devours all around you.'
15 Why are your valiant *men* swept away?
They did not stand
Because the LORD drove them away.
16 He made many fall;
Yes, [a]one fell upon another.
And they said, 'Arise!
[b]Let us go back to our own people
And to the land of our nativity
From the oppressing sword.'
17 They cried there,
'Pharaoh, king of Egypt, *is but* a noise.
He has passed by the appointed time!'

18 "*As* I live," says the King,
[a]Whose name *is* the LORD of hosts,
"Surely as Tabor *is* among the mountains
And as Carmel by the sea, *so* he shall come.
19 O [a]you daughter dwelling in Egypt,
Prepare yourself [b]to go into captivity!
For [1]Noph shall be waste
and desolate, without inhabitant.

**20** "Egypt *is* a very pretty [a]heifer,
*But* destruction comes,
it comes [b]from the north.
21 Also her mercenaries are in her midst like
[1]fat bulls,
For they also are turned back,
They have fled away together.
They did not stand,
For [a]the day of their calamity
had come upon them,
The time of their punishment.
22 [a]Her noise shall go like a serpent,
For they shall march with an army
And come against her with axes,
Like those who chop wood.

23 "They shall [a]cut down her forest,"
says the LORD,
"Though it cannot be searched,
Because they *are* innumerable,
And more numerous than [b]grasshoppers.
24 The daughter of Egypt shall be ashamed;
She shall be delivered into the hand
Of [a]the people of the north."

25 The LORD of hosts, the God of Israel, says:
"Behold, I will bring punishment on [1]Amon of
[a]No,[2] and Pharaoh and Egypt, [b]with their gods and
their kings—Pharaoh and those who [c]trust in him.
26 [a]"And I will deliver them into the hand
of those who seek their lives, into the hand of
Nebuchadnezzar king of Babylon and the hand of
his servants. [b]Afterward it shall be inhabited as in
the days of old," says the LORD.

**27** "But[a] do not fear, O My servant Jacob,
And do not be dismayed, O Israel!
For behold, I will [b]save you from afar,
And your offspring from the land of their
captivity;
Jacob shall return, have rest and be at ease;
No one shall make *him* afraid.
28 Do not fear, O Jacob My servant," says the
LORD,
"For I *am* with you;
For I will make a complete end
of all the nations
To which I have driven you,
But I will not make [a]a complete end of you.
I will rightly [b]correct you,
For I will not leave you wholly unpunished."

## *Prophecy Against the Philistines*

**47** The word of the LORD that came to Jeremiah the prophet [a]against the Philistines,
[b]before Pharaoh attacked Gaza.
2 Thus says the LORD:

"Behold, [a]waters rise [b]out of the north,
And shall be an overflowing flood;
They shall overflow the land and all that is in
it,
The city and those who dwell within;
Then the men shall cry,
And all the inhabitants of the land shall wail.
3 At the [a]noise of the stamping hooves
of his strong horses,
At the rushing of his chariots,
*At* the rumbling of his wheels,
The fathers will not look back
for *their* children,
[1]Lacking courage,

**5** [a]Jer. 49:29
**6** [a]Jer. 46:12, 16; Dan. 11:19
**7** [a]Is. 8:7, 8; Jer. 47:2; Dan. 11:22
**9** [a]Is. 66:19 [1]Heb. *Cush* [2]Heb. *Put*
**10** [a]Is. 13:6; Joel 1:15 [b]Deut. 32:42; Is. 31:8; Jer. 12:12 [c]Is. 34:6; Zeph. 1:7; Ezek. 39:17 [1]Filled to the full
**11** [a]Jer. 8:22 [b]Is. 47:1; Jer. 31:4, 21 [c]Ezek. 30:21
**12** [a]Jer. 2:36; Nah. 3:8–10
**13** [a]Is. 19:1; Jer. 43:10, 11; Ezek. 29:1–21
**14** [a]Jer. 44:1 [b]Ezek. 30:18 [1]Ancient Memphis
**16** [a]Lev. 26:36, 37; Jer. 46:6 [b]Jer. 51:9
**18** [a]Is. 47:4; Jer. 48:15; Mal. 1:14
**19** [a]Jer. 48:18 [b]Is. 20:4 [1]Ancient Memphis
**20** [a]Hos. 10:11 [b]Jer. 1:14
**21** [a][Ps. 37:13]; Jer. 50:27 [1]Lit. *calves of the stall*
**22** [a][Is. 29:4]
**23** [a]Is. 10:34 [b]Judg. 6:5; 7:12; Joel 2:25
**24** [a]Jer. 1:15
**25** [a]Ezek. 30:14–16; Nah. 3:8 [b]Ex. 12:12; Jer. 43:12, 13; Ezek. 30:13; Zeph. 2:11 [c]Is. 30:1–5; 31:1–3 [1]A sun god [2]Ancient Thebes
**26** [a]Jer. 44:30; Ezek. 32:11 [b]Ezek. 29:8–14
**27** [a]Is. 41:13, 14; 43:5; 44:2; Jer. 30:10, 11 [b]Is. 11:11; Jer. 23:3, 4; Mic. 7:12
**28** [a]Jer. 10:24; Amos 9:8, 9 [b]Jer. 30:11

CHAPTER 47
**1** [a]Is. 14:29–31; Ezek. 25:15–17; Zeph. 2:4, 5; Zech. 9:6 [b]Amos 1:6
**2** [a]Is. 8:7, 8; Jer. 46:7, 8 [b]Jer. 1:14
**3** [a]Judg. 5:22; Jer. 8:16; Nah. 3:2 [1]Lit. *From sinking hands*

4 Because of the day that comes
to plunder all the [a]Philistines,
To cut off from [b]Tyre and Sidon
every helper who remains;
For the LORD shall plunder the Philistines,
[c]The remnant of the country of [d]Caphtor.[1]
5 [a]Baldness has come upon Gaza,
[b]Ashkelon is cut off
*With* the remnant of their valley.
How long will you cut yourself?

6 "O you [a]sword of the LORD,
How long until you are quiet?
Put yourself up into your scabbard,
Rest and be still!
7 How can [1]it be quiet,
Seeing the LORD has [a]given it a charge
Against Ashkelon and against the seashore?
There He has [b]appointed it."

## *Prophecy Against Moab*

**48** Against [a]Moab.
Thus says the LORD of hosts, the God of Israel:

"Woe to [b]Nebo!
For it is plundered,
[c]Kirjathaim is shamed *and* taken;
[1]The high stronghold is shamed
and dismayed—
2 [a]No more praise of Moab.
In [b]Heshbon they have devised evil against
her:
'Come, and let us cut her off as a nation.'
You also shall be cut down, O [c]Madmen![1]
The sword shall pursue you;
3 A voice of crying *shall be* from [a]Horonaim:
'Plundering and great destruction!'

4 "Moab is destroyed;
[1]Her little ones have caused a cry to be heard;
5 [a]For in the Ascent of Luhith
they ascend with continual weeping;
For in the descent of Horonaim
the enemies have heard a cry of
destruction.

6 "Flee, save your lives!
And be like [1]the [a]juniper in the wilderness.
7 For because you have trusted in your works
and your [a]treasures,
You also shall be taken.
And [b]Chemosh shall go forth into captivity,
His [c]priests and his princes together.
8 And [a]the plunderer shall come against every
city;
No one shall escape.
The valley also shall perish,
And the plain shall be destroyed,
As the LORD has spoken.

9 "Give[a] wings to Moab,
That she may flee and get away;
For her cities shall be desolate,
Without any to dwell in them.
10 [a]Cursed *is* he who does
the work of the LORD deceitfully,
And cursed *is* he who keeps back
his sword from blood.

11 "Moab has been at ease from [1]his youth;
He [a]has settled on his dregs,
And has not been emptied from vessel to
vessel,
Nor has he gone into captivity.
Therefore his taste remained in him,
And his scent has not changed.

12 "Therefore behold, the days are coming," says
the LORD,
"That I shall send him [1]wine-workers
Who will tip him over
And empty his vessels
And break the bottles.
13 Moab shall be ashamed of [a]Chemosh,
As the house of Israel [b]was ashamed
of [c]Bethel, their confidence.

14 "How can you say, [a]'We *are* mighty
And strong men for the war'?
15 Moab is plundered and gone up *from* her
cities;
Her chosen young men have [a]gone down to
the slaughter," says [b]the King,
Whose name *is* the LORD of hosts.

16 "The calamity of Moab *is* near at hand,
And his affliction comes quickly.
17 Bemoan him, all you who are around him;
And all you who know his name,
Say, [a]'How the strong staff is broken,
The beautiful rod!'

18 "O [a]daughter inhabiting [b]Dibon,
Come down from *your* glory,
And sit in thirst;
For the plunderer of Moab has come against
you,
He has destroyed your strongholds.
19 O inhabitant of [a]Aroer,
[b]Stand by the way and watch;
Ask him who flees
And her who escapes;
Say, 'What has happened?'
20 Moab is shamed, for he is broken down.
[a]Wail and cry!
Tell it in [b]Arnon, that Moab is plundered.

21 "And judgment has come
on the plain country:
On Holon and Jahzah and Mephaath,
22 On Dibon and Nebo and Beth Diblathaim,
23 On Kirjathaim and Beth Gamul
and Beth Meon,
24 On [a]Kerioth and Bozrah,
On all the cities of the land of Moab,
Far or near.
25 [a]The [1]horn of Moab is cut off,
And his [b]arm is broken," says the LORD.

26 "Make[a] him drunk,
Because he exalted *himself* against the LORD.
Moab shall wallow in his vomit,
And he shall also be in derision.
27 For [a]was not Israel a derision to you?
[b]Was he found among thieves?
For whenever you speak of him,
You shake *your head in* [c]*scorn*.
28 You who dwell in Moab,
Leave the cities and [a]dwell in the rock,
And be like [b]the dove *which* makes her nest
In the sides of the cave's mouth.

29 "We have heard the [a]pride of Moab
(He *is* exceedingly proud),
Of his loftiness and arrogance and [b]pride,
And of the haughtiness of his heart."

**4** [a]Is. 14:29–31 [b]Jer. 25:22 [c]Ezek. 25:16 [d]Gen. 10:14 [1]Cappadocia in Asia Minor
**5** [a]Mic. 1:16 [b]Jer. 25:20
**6** [a]Ezek. 21:3–5
**7** [a]Ezek. 14:17 [b]Mic. 6:9 [1]Lit. *you*

CHAPTER 48
**1** [a]Is. 15:1—16:14; 25:10 [b]Is. 15:2 [c]Num. 32:37 [1]Or *Misgab*
**2** [a]Is. 16:14 [b]Jer. 49:3 [c]Is. 10:31 [1]A city of Moab
**3** [a]Is. 15:5
**4** [1]So with MT, Tg., Vg.; LXX *Proclaim it in Zoar*
**5** [a]Is. 15:5
**6** [a]Jer. 17:6 [1]Or *Aroer*, a city of Moab
**7** [a]Jer. 9:23 [b]Jer. 48:7 [c]Jer. 49:3
**8** [a]Jer. 6:26
**9** [a]Ps. 55:6
**10** [a]1 Sam. 15:3
**11** [a]Zeph. 1:12 [1]Heb. uses masc. and fem. pronouns interchangeably in this chapter.
**12** [1]Lit. *tippers* of wine bottles
**13** [a]1 Kin. 11:7 [b]Hos. 10:6 [c]1 Kin. 12:29; 13:32–34
**14** [a]Is. 16:6
**15** [a]Jer. 50:27 [b]Jer. 46:18; 51:57
**17** [a]Is. 9:4; 14:4, 5
**18** [a]Is. 47:1 [b]Is. 15:2
**19** [a]Deut. 2:36 [b]1 Sam. 4:13, 14, 16
**20** [a]Is. 16:7 [b]Num. 21:13
**24** [a]Amos 2:2
**25** [a]Ps. 75:10 [b]Ezek. 30:21 [1]Strength
**26** [a]Jer. 25:15
**27** [a]Zeph. 2:8 [b]Jer. 2:26 [c]Lam. 2:15
**28** [a]Ps. 55:6, 7 [b]Song 2:14
**29** [a]Is. 16:6 [b]Jer. 49:16

30 "I know his wrath," says the LORD,
"But it *is* not right;
[a]His [1]lies have made nothing right.
31 Therefore [a]I will wail for Moab,
And I will cry out for all Moab;
[1]I will mourn for the men of Kir Heres.
32 [a]O vine of Sibmah! I will weep for you with the weeping of [b]Jazer.
Your plants have gone over the sea,
They reach to the sea of Jazer.
The plunderer has fallen on your summer fruit and your vintage.
33 [a]Joy and gladness are taken
From the plentiful field
And from the land of Moab;
I have caused wine to [1]fail from the winepresses;
No one will tread with joyous shouting—
Not joyous shouting!

**34** "From[a] the cry of Heshbon to [b]Elealeh and to Jahaz
They have uttered their voice,
[c]From Zoar to Horonaim,
*Like* [1]a three-year-old heifer;
For the waters of Nimrim also shall be desolate.

35 "Moreover," says the LORD,
"I will cause to cease in Moab
[a]The one who offers *sacrifices* in the [1]high places
And burns incense to his gods.
36 Therefore [a]My heart shall wail like flutes for Moab,
And like flutes My heart shall wail
For the men of Kir Heres.
Therefore [b]the riches they have acquired have perished.

37 "For [a]every head *shall be* bald,
and every beard clipped;
On all the hands *shall be* cuts,
and [b]on the loins sackcloth—
38 A general lamentation
On all the [a]housetops of Moab,
And in its streets;
For I have [b]broken Moab like a vessel in which *is* no pleasure," says the LORD.
39 "They shall wail:
'How she is broken down!
How Moab has turned her back with shame!'
So Moab shall be a derision
And a dismay to all those about her."

**40** For thus says the LORD:

"Behold, [a]one shall fly like an eagle,
And [b]spread his wings over Moab.
41 Kerioth is taken,
And the strongholds are surprised;
[a]The mighty men's hearts in Moab on that day shall be
Like the heart of a woman in birth pangs.
42 And Moab shall be destroyed [a]as a people,
Because he exalted *himself* against the LORD.
43 [a]Fear and the pit and the snare *shall be* upon you,
O inhabitant of Moab," says the LORD.
44 "He who flees from the fear shall fall into the pit,
And he who gets out of the pit shall be caught in the [a]snare.
For upon Moab, upon it [b]I will bring
The year of their punishment,"
says the LORD.

**45** "Those who fled stood under the shadow of Heshbon
Because of exhaustion.
But [a]a fire shall come out of Heshbon,
A flame from the midst of [b]Sihon,
And [c]shall devour the brow of Moab,
The crown of the head of the sons of tumult.
46 [a]Woe to you, O Moab!
The people of Chemosh perish;
For your sons have been taken captive,
And your daughters captive.

47 "Yet I will bring back the captives of Moab
[a]In the latter days," says the LORD.

Thus far *is* the judgment of Moab.

## *Prophecies Against Ammon, Edom, Damascus, Elam, Kedar, and Hazor*

**49** Against the [a]Ammonites.
Thus says the LORD:

"Has Israel no sons?
Has he no heir?
Why *then* does [1]Milcom inherit [b]Gad,
And his people dwell in its cities?
2 [a]Therefore behold, the days are coming," says the LORD,
"That I will cause to be heard an alarm of war
In [b]Rabbah of the Ammonites;
It shall be a desolate mound,
And her [1]villages shall be burned with fire.
Then Israel shall take possession of his inheritance," says the LORD.

3 "Wail, O [a]Heshbon, for Ai is plundered!
Cry, you daughters of Rabbah,
[b]Gird yourselves with sackcloth!
Lament and run to and fro by the walls;
For [1]Milcom shall go into captivity
With his [c]priests and his princes together.
4 Why [a]do you boast in the valleys,
[1]Your flowing valley, O [b]backsliding daughter?
Who trusted in her [c]treasures, [d]*saying,*
'Who will come against me?'
5 Behold, I will bring fear upon you,"
Says the Lord GOD of hosts,
"From all those who are around you;
You shall be driven out, everyone headlong,
And no one will gather those who wander off.
6 But [a]afterward I will bring back
The captives of the people of Ammon," says the LORD.

**7** [a]Against Edom.
Thus says the LORD of hosts:

[b]"*Is* wisdom no more in Teman?
[c]Has counsel perished from the prudent?
Has their wisdom [d]vanished?
8 Flee, turn back, dwell in the depths,
O inhabitants of [a]Dedan!
For I will bring the calamity of Esau upon him,
The time *that* I will punish him.
9 [a]If grape-gatherers came to you,
Would they not leave *some* gleaning grapes?

**30** [a]Jer. 50:36 [1]*idle talk*
**31** [a]Is. 15:5; 16:7, 11 [1]So with DSS, LXX, Vg.; MT *He*
**32** [a]Is. 16:8, 9 [b]Num. 21:32
**33** [a]Joel 1:12 [1]*cease*
**34** [a]Is. 15:4–6 [b]Num. 32:3, 37 [c]Is. 15:5, 6 [1]Or *The Third Eglath,* an unknown city, Is. 15:5
**35** [a]Is. 15:2; 16:12 [1]Places for pagan worship
**36** [a]Is. 15:5; 16:11 [b]Is. 15:7
**37** [a]Is. 15:2, 3 [b]Gen. 37:34
**38** [a]Is. 15:3 [b]Jer. 22:28
**40** [a]Deut. 28:49 [b]Is. 8:8
**41** [a]Is. 13:8; 21:3
**42** [a]Ps. 83:4
**43** [a]Is. 24:17, 18
**44** [a]Is. 24:18 [b]Jer. 11:23
**45** [a]Num. 21:28, 29 [b]Ps. 135:11 [c]Num. 24:17
**46** [a]Num. 21:29
**47** [a]Jer. 49:6, 39

CHAPTER 49
**1** [a]Ezek. 21:28–32; 25:1–7 [b]Amos 1:13–15 [1]Heb. *Malcam,* lit. *their king;* an Ammonite god, 1 Kin. 11:5; *Molech,* Lev. 18:21
**2** [a]Amos 1:13–15 [b]Ezek. 25:5 [1]Lit. *daughters*
**3** [a]Jer. 48:2 [b]Is. 32:11 [c]Jer. 48:7 [1]See v. 1
**4** [a]Jer. 9:23 [b]Jer. 3:14 [c]Jer. 48:7 [d]Jer. 21:13 [1]Lit. *Your valley is flowing*
**6** [a]Jer. 48:47
**7** [a]Ezek. 25:12–14; 35:1–15 [b]Gen. 36:11 [c]Is. 19:11 [d]Jer. 8:9
**8** [a]Jer. 25:23
**9** [a]Obad. 5, 6

If thieves by night,
Would they not destroy
until they have enough?
10 [a]But I have made Esau bare;
I have uncovered his secret places,
And he shall not be able to hide himself.
His descendants are plundered,
His brethren and his neighbors,
And [b]he *is* no more.
11 Leave your fatherless children,
I will preserve *them* alive;
And let your widows trust in Me."

**12** For thus says the LORD: "Behold, [a]those whose
judgment *was* not to drink of the cup have assuredly drunk. And *are* you the one who will
altogether go unpunished? You shall not go unpunished, but you shall surely drink *of it.*
13 "For [a]I have sworn by Myself," says the LORD,
"that [b]Bozrah shall become a desolation, a reproach, a [1]waste, and a curse. And all its cities
shall be perpetual [2]wastes."

**14** [a]I have heard a message from the LORD,
And an ambassador has been sent
to the nations:
"Gather together, come against her,
And rise up to battle!

**15** "For indeed, I will make you small among
nations,
Despised among men.
16 Your fierceness has deceived you,
The [a]pride of your heart,
O you who dwell in the clefts of the rock,
Who hold the height of the hill!
[b]Though you make your [c]nest
as high as the eagle,
[d]I will bring you down from there,"
says the LORD.

17 "Edom also shall be an astonishment;
[a]Everyone who goes by it will be astonished
And will hiss at all its plagues.
18 [a]As in the overthrow of Sodom and Gomorrah
And their neighbors," says the LORD,
"No one shall remain there,
Nor shall a son of man dwell in it.

19 "Behold,[a] he shall come up like a lion from
[b]the [1]flood plain of the Jordan
Against the dwelling place of the strong;
But I will suddenly make him run away from
her.
And who *is* a chosen *man*
*that* I may appoint over her?
For [c]who *is* like Me?
Who will arraign Me?
And [d]who *is* that shepherd
Who will withstand Me?"

**20** [a]Therefore hear the counsel of the LORD that
He has taken against Edom,
And His purposes that He has proposed
against the inhabitants of Teman:
Surely the least of the flock shall [1]draw them
out;
Surely He shall make their dwelling places
desolate with them.
21 [a]The earth shakes at the noise of their fall;
At the cry its noise is heard at the Red Sea.
22 Behold, [a]He shall come up
and fly like the eagle,
And spread His wings over Bozrah;

**10** [a]Obad. 5, 6; Mal. 1:3 [b]Is. 17:14
**12** [a]Jer. 25:29; Obad. 16
**13** [a]Gen. 22:16; Is. 45:23; Jer. 44:26; Amos 6:8 [b]Gen. 36:33; 1 Chr. 1:44; Is. 34:6; 63:1; Amos 1:12 [1]*ruin* [2]*ruins*
**14** [a]Obad. 1–4
**16** [a]Jer. 48:29 [b]Obad. 3, 4 [c]Job 39:27; Is. 14:13–15 [d]Amos 9:2
**17** [a]Jer. 18:16; 49:13; 50:13; Ezek. 35:7
**18** [a]Gen. 19:24, 25; Deut. 29:23; Jer. 50:40; Amos 4:11; Zeph. 2:9
**19** [a]Jer. 50:44 [b]Josh. 3:15; Jer. 12:5 [c]Ex. 15:11; Is. 46:9 [d]Job 41:10 [1]Or *thicket*
**20** [a]Is. 14:24, 27; Jer. 50:45 [1]Or *drag them away*
**21** [a]Jer. 50:46; Ezek. 26:15, 18
**22** [a]Jer. 48:40, 41
**23** [a]Is. 17:1–3; Amos 1:3, 5; Zech. 9:1, 2 [b]Jer. 39:5; Zech. 9:2 [c][Is. 57:20] [1]*anxiety*
**24** [a]Is. 13:8; Jer. 4:31; 6:24; 48:21 [1]*childbirth*
**25** [a]Jer. 33:9
**26** [a]Jer. 50:30; Amos 4:10
**27** [a]Amos 1:4
**28** [a]Gen. 25:13; Ps. 120:5; Is. 21:16, 17; Jer. 2:10; Ezek. 27:21 [b]Judg. 6:3; Job 1:3
**29** [a]Ps. 120:5 [b]Jer. 46:5
**31** [a]Ezek. 38:11 [b]Num. 23:9; Deut. 33:28; Mic. 7:16
**32** [a]Ezek. 5:10 [1]Lit. *cut off at the corner,* Jer. 9:26; 25:23
**33** [a]Jer. 9:11; 10:22; Zeph. 2:9, 12–15; Mal. 1:3
**34** [a]Gen. 10:22; Jer. 25:25; Ezek. 32:24; Dan. 8:2 [b]2 Kin. 24:17, 18; Jer. 28:1
**35** [a]Ps. 46:9; Is. 22:6 [1]Power

The heart of the mighty men of Edom in that
day shall be
Like the heart of a woman in birth pangs.

**23** [a]Against Damascus.

[b]"Hamath and Arpad are shamed,
For they have heard bad news.
They are fainthearted;
[c]*There is* [1]trouble on the sea;
It cannot be quiet.
24 Damascus has grown feeble;
She turns to flee,
And fear has seized *her.*
[a]Anguish and sorrows have taken her like a
woman in [1]labor.
25 Why is [a]the city of praise not deserted, the
city of My joy?
26 [a]Therefore her young men shall fall in her
streets,
And all the men of war shall be cut off in
that day," says the LORD of hosts.
27 "I[a] will kindle a fire in the wall of Damascus,
And it shall consume the palaces of Ben-
Hadad."

**28** [a]Against Kedar and against the kingdoms of
Hazor, which Nebuchadnezzar king of Babylon
shall strike.
Thus says the LORD:

"Arise, go up to Kedar,
And devastate [b]the men of the East!
29 Their [a]tents and their flocks
they shall take away.
They shall take for themselves their curtains,
All their vessels and their camels;
And they shall cry out to them,
[b]'Fear *is* on every side!'

30 "Flee, get far away! Dwell in the depths,
O inhabitants of Hazor!" says the LORD.
"For Nebuchadnezzar king of Babylon has
taken counsel against you,
And has conceived a plan against you.

31 "Arise, go up to [a]the wealthy nation
that dwells securely," says the LORD,
"Which has neither gates nor bars,
[b]Dwelling alone.
32 Their camels shall be for booty,
And the multitude of their cattle for plunder.
I will [a]scatter to all winds those [1]in the
farthest corners,
And I will bring their calamity from all its
sides," says the LORD.
33 "Hazor [a]shall be a dwelling for jackals,
a desolation forever;
No one shall reside there,
Nor son of man dwell in it."

**34** The word of the LORD that came to Jeremiah
the prophet against [a]Elam, in the [b]beginning of the
reign of Zedekiah king of Judah, saying,
35 "Thus says the LORD of hosts:

'Behold, I will break [a]the [1]bow of Elam,
The foremost of their might.
36 Against Elam I will bring the four winds
From the four quarters of heaven,
And scatter them toward all those winds;
There shall be no nations where the outcasts
of Elam will not go.
37 For I will cause Elam to be dismayed before
their enemies
And before those who seek their life.

[a]I will bring disaster upon them,
My fierce anger,' says the LORD;
'And I will send the sword after them
Until I have consumed them.
38 I will [a]set My throne in Elam,
And will destroy from there the king and the princes,' says the LORD.

39 'But it shall come to pass [a]in the latter days:
I will bring back the captives of Elam,' says the LORD."

### *Prophecy Against Babylon and Babylonia*

**50** The word that the LORD spoke [a]against Babylon *and* against the land of the Chaldeans by Jeremiah the prophet.

2 "Declare among the nations,
Proclaim, and [1]set up a standard;
Proclaim—do not conceal *it*—
Say, 'Babylon is [a]taken, [b]Bel is shamed.
[2]Merodach is broken in pieces;
[c]Her idols are humiliated,
Her images are broken in pieces.'
3 [a]For out of the north [b]a nation comes up against her,
Which shall make her land desolate,
And no one shall dwell therein.
They shall [1]move, they shall depart,
Both man and beast.

4 "In those days and in that time,"
says the LORD,
"The children of Israel shall come,
[a]They and the children of Judah together;
[b]With continual weeping they shall come,
[c]And seek the LORD their God.
5 They shall ask the way to Zion,
With their faces toward it, *saying,*
'Come and let us join ourselves to the LORD
*In* [a]a perpetual covenant
*That* will not be forgotten.'

6 "My people have been [a]lost sheep.
Their shepherds have led them [b]astray;
They have turned them away *on* [c]the mountains.
They have gone from mountain to hill;
They have forgotten their resting place.
7 All who found them have [a]devoured them;
And [b]their adversaries said,
[c]'We have not offended,
Because they have sinned against the LORD,
[d]the habitation of justice,
The LORD, [e]the hope of their fathers.'

8 "Move[a] from the midst of Babylon,
Go out of the land of the Chaldeans;
And be like the [1]rams before the flocks.
9 [a]For behold, I will raise and cause to come up against Babylon
An assembly of great nations
from the north country,
And they shall array themselves against her;
From there she shall be captured.
Their arrows *shall be* like *those* of [1]an expert warrior;
[b]None shall return in vain.
10 And Chaldea shall become plunder;
[a]All who plunder her shall be satisfied," says the LORD.

11 "Because[a] you were glad,
because you rejoiced,
You destroyers of My heritage,
Because you have grown fat
[b]like a heifer threshing grain,
And you [1]bellow like bulls,
12 Your mother shall be deeply ashamed;
She who bore you shall be ashamed.
Behold, the least of the nations
*shall be* a [a]wilderness,
A dry land and a desert.
13 Because of the wrath of the LORD
She shall not be inhabited,
[a]But she shall be wholly desolate.
[b]Everyone who goes by Babylon
shall be horrified
And hiss at all her plagues.

14 "Put[a] yourselves in array
against Babylon all around,
All you who bend the bow;
Shoot at her, spare no arrows,
For she has sinned against the LORD.
15 Shout against her all around;
She has [a]given her hand,
Her foundations have fallen,
[b]Her walls are thrown down;
For [c]it *is* the vengeance of the LORD.
Take vengeance on her.
As she has done, so do to her.
16 Cut off the sower from Babylon,
And him who handles the sickle at harvest time.
For fear of the oppressing sword
[a]Everyone shall turn to his own people,
And everyone shall flee to his own land.

17 "Israel *is* like [a]scattered sheep;
[b]The lions have driven *him* away.
First [c]the king of Assyria devoured him;
Now at last this [d]Nebuchadnezzar king of Babylon has broken his bones."

18 Therefore thus says the LORD of hosts, the God of Israel:

"Behold, I will punish the king of Babylon and his land,
As I have punished the king of [a]Assyria.
19 [a]But I will bring back Israel to his home,
And he shall feed on Carmel and Bashan;
His soul shall be satisfied on Mount Ephraim and Gilead.
20 In those days and in that time,"
says the LORD,
[a]"The iniquity of Israel shall be sought, but *there shall be* none;
And the sins of Judah,
but they shall not be found;
For I will pardon those [b]whom I preserve.

21 "Go up against the land of Merathaim, against it,
And against the inhabitants of [a]Pekod.
[1]Waste and utterly destroy them,"
says the LORD,
"And do [b]according to all that I have commanded you.
22 [a]A sound of battle *is* in the land,
And of great destruction.
23 How [a]the hammer of the whole earth has been cut apart and broken!
How Babylon has become a desolation
among the nations!
I have laid a snare for you;

**37** [a]Jer. 9:16
**38** [a]Jer. 43:10
**39** [a]Jer. 48:47

CHAPTER 50
**1** [a]Is. 13:1; 47:1
**2** [a]Is. 21:9 [b]Is. 46:1 [c]Jer. 43:12, 13 [1]*lift* [2]Or *Marduk;* a Babylonian god
**3** [a]Jer. 51:48 [b]Is. 13:17, 18, 20 [1]Or *wander*
**4** [a]Hos. 1:11 [b]Ezra 3:12, 13 [c]Hos. 3:5
**5** [a]Jer. 31:31
**6** [a]Is. 53:6 [b]Jer. 23:1 [c][Jer. 2:20; 3:6, 23]
**7** [a]Ps. 79:7 [b]Zech. 11:5 [c]Jer. 2:3 [d][Ps. 90:1; 91:1] [e]Ps. 22:4
**8** [a]Is. 48:20 [1]*male goats*
**9** [a]Jer. 15:14; 51:27 [b]2 Sam. 1:22 [1]So with some Heb. mss., LXX, Syr.; MT, Tg., Vg. *a warrior who makes childless*
**10** [a][Rev. 17:16]
**11** [a]Is. 47:6 [b]Hos. 10:11 [1]Or *neigh like steeds*
**12** [a]Jer. 51:43
**13** [a]Jer. 25:12 [b]Jer. 49:17
**14** [a]Jer. 51:2
**15** [a]Lam. 5:6 [b]Jer. 51:58 [c]Jer. 51:6, 11
**16** [a]Is. 13:14
**17** [a]2 Kin. 24:10, 14 [b]Jer. 2:15 [c]2 Kin. 15:29; 17:6; 18:9–13 [d]2 Kin. 24:10–14; 25:1–7
**18** [a]Ezek. 31:3, 11, 12
**19** [a]Is. 65:10
**20** [a][Jer. 31:34] [b]Is. 1:9
**21** [a]Ezek. 23:23 [b]2 Sam. 16:11 [1]Or *Attack* with the sword
**22** [a]Jer. 51:54
**23** [a]Jer. 51:20–24

24 You have indeed been [a]trapped, O Babylon,
And you were not aware;
You have been found and also caught,
Because you have [b]contended against the
Lord.
25 The LORD has opened His armory,
And has brought out [a]the weapons of His
indignation;
For this *is* the work of the Lord GOD of hosts
In the land of the Chaldeans.
26 Come against her from the farthest border;
Open her storehouses;
Cast her up as heaps of ruins,
And destroy her utterly;
Let nothing of her be left.
27 Slay all her [a]bulls,
Let them go down to the slaughter.
Woe to them!
For their day has come,
the time of [b]their punishment.
28 The voice of those who flee
and escape from the land of Babylon
[a]Declares in Zion the vengeance of the LORD
our God,
The vengeance of His temple.

**29** "Call together the archers against Babylon.
All you who bend the bow,
encamp against it all around;
Let none of them [1]escape.
[a]Repay her according to her work;
According to all she has done, do to her;
[b]For she has been proud against the LORD,
Against the Holy One of Israel.
30 [a]Therefore her young men shall fall in the
streets,
And all her men of war shall be cut off in
that day," says the LORD.
31 "Behold, I *am* against you,
O most haughty one!"
says the Lord GOD of hosts;
"For your day has come,
[1]The time *that* I will punish you.
32 The most [a]proud shall stumble and fall,
And no one will raise him up;
[b]I will kindle a fire in his cities,
And it will devour all around him."

**33** Thus says the LORD of hosts:

"The children of Israel *were* oppressed,
Along with the children of Judah;
All who took them captive have held them
fast;
They have refused to let them go.
34 [a]Their Redeemer *is* strong;
[b]The LORD of hosts *is* His name.
He will thoroughly plead their [c]case,
That He may give rest to the land,
And disquiet the inhabitants of Babylon.

**35** "A sword *is* against the Chaldeans," says the
LORD,
"Against the inhabitants of Babylon,
And [a]against her princes and [b]her wise men.
36 A sword *is* [a]against the soothsayers,
and they will be fools.
A sword *is* against her mighty men, and they
will be dismayed.
37 A sword *is* against their horses,
Against their chariots,
And against all [a]the mixed peoples who *are*
in her midst;
And [b]they will become like women.
A sword *is* against her treasures,
and they will be robbed.
38 [a]A [1]drought *is* against her waters,
and they will be dried up.
For it *is* the land of carved images,
And they are insane with *their* idols.

39 "Therefore[a] the wild desert beasts
shall dwell *there* with the jackals,
And the ostriches shall dwell in it.
[b]It shall be inhabited no more forever,
Nor shall it be dwelt in from generation to
generation.
40 [a]As God overthrew Sodom and Gomorrah
And their neighbors," says the LORD,
"*So* no one shall reside there,
Nor son of man [b]dwell in it.

**41** "Behold,[a] a people shall come from the north,
And a great nation and many kings
Shall be raised up from the ends of the earth.
42 [a]They shall hold the bow and the lance;
[b]They *are* cruel and shall not show mercy.
[c]Their voice shall roar like the sea;
They shall ride on horses,
Set in array, like a man for the battle,
Against you, O daughter of Babylon.

43 "The king of Babylon has [a]heard
the report about them,
And his hands grow feeble;
Anguish has taken hold of him,
Pangs as of a woman in [b]childbirth.

44 "Behold,[a] he shall come up like a lion from the
[1]flood plain of the Jordan
Against the dwelling place of the strong;
But I will make them suddenly run away
from her.
And who *is* a chosen *man*
*that* I may appoint over her?
For who *is* like Me?
Who will arraign Me?
And [b]who *is* that shepherd
Who will withstand Me?"

45 Therefore hear [a]the counsel of the LORD that
He has taken against Babylon,
And His [b]purposes that He has proposed
against the land of the Chaldeans:
[c]Surely the least of the flock shall draw them
out;
Surely He will make their dwelling place
desolate with them.
46 [a]At the noise of the taking of Babylon
The earth trembles,
And the cry is heard among the nations.

## *The LORD's Judgment on Babylon*

**51** Thus says the LORD:

"Behold, I will raise up against [a]Babylon,
Against those who dwell in [1]Leb Kamai,
[b]A destroying wind.
2 And I will send [a]winnowers to Babylon,
Who shall winnow her and empty her land.
[b]For in the day of doom
They shall be against her all around.
3 Against *her* [a]let the archer bend his bow,
And lift himself up against *her* in his armor.
Do not spare her young men;
[b]Utterly destroy all her army.

**24** [a]Dan. 5:30 [b][Is. 45:9]
**25** [a]Is. 13:5
**27** [a]Is. 34:7 [b]Jer. 48:44
**28** [a]Jer. 51:10
**29** [a]Jer. 51:56 [b][Is. 47:10] [1]Qr., some Heb. mss., LXX, Tg. add *to her*
**30** [a]Jer. 49:26; 51:4
**31** [1]So with MT, [Tg.]; LXX, Vg. *The time of your punishment*
**32** [a]Mal. 4:1 [b]Jer. 21:14
**34** [a]Rev. 18:8 [b]Is. 47:4 [c]Jer. 32:18; 51:19–22
**35** [a]Dan. 5:30 [b]Is. 47:13
**36** [a]Is. 44:25
**37** [a]Jer. 25:20 [b]Jer. 51:30
**38** [a]Rev. 16:12 [1]So with MT, Tg., Vg.; Syr. *sword;* LXX omits *A drought is*
**39** [a]Rev. 18:2 [b]Is. 13:20
**40** [a]Is. 13:19 [b]Is. 13:20
**41** [a]Jer. 6:22; 25:14; 51:27
**42** [a]Jer. 6:23 [b]Is. 13:18 [c]Is. 5:30
**43** [a]Jer. 51:31 [b]Jer. 6:24
**44** [a]Jer. 49:19–21 [b]Job 41:10 [1]Or *thicket*
**45** [a]Jer. 51:10, 11 [b]Jer. 51:29 [c]Jer. 49:19, 20
**46** [a]Rev. 18:9

CHAPTER 51
**1** [a]Is. 47:1 [b]Jer. 4:11 [1]Lit. *The Midst of Those Who Rise Up Against Me;* a code word for Chaldea, Babylonia
**2** [a]Jer. 15:7 [b]Jer. 50:14
**3** [a]Jer. 50:14, 29 [b]Jer. 50:21

4 Thus the slain shall fall
in the land of the Chaldeans,
[a]And *those* thrust through in her streets.
5 For Israel is [a]not forsaken, nor Judah,
By his God, the LORD of hosts,
Though their land was filled with sin against
the Holy One of Israel."

**6** [a]Flee from the midst of Babylon,
And every one save his life!
Do not be cut off in her iniquity,
For [b]this *is* the time of the LORD's vengeance;
[c]He shall recompense her.
7 [a]Babylon *was* a golden cup in the LORD's
hand,
That made all the earth drunk.
[b]The nations drank her wine;
Therefore the nations [c]are deranged.
8 Babylon has suddenly [a]fallen
and been destroyed.
[b]Wail for her!
[c]Take balm for her pain;
Perhaps she may be healed.

9 We would have healed Babylon,
But she is not healed.
Forsake her, and [a]let us go
everyone to his own country;
[b]For her judgment reaches to heaven and is
lifted up to the skies.
10 The LORD has [a]revealed our righteousness.
Come and let us [b]declare in Zion
the work of the LORD our God.

**11** [a]Make[1] the arrows bright!
Gather the shields!
[b]The LORD has raised up the spirit
of the kings of the Medes.
[c]For His plan *is* against Babylon to destroy it,
Because it *is* [d]the vengeance of the LORD,
The vengeance for His temple.
12 [a]Set up the standard on the walls of Babylon;
Make the guard strong,
Set up the watchmen,
Prepare the ambushes.
For the LORD has both devised and done
What He spoke against the inhabitants of
Babylon.
13 [a]O you who dwell by many waters,
Abundant in treasures,
Your end has come,
The measure of your covetousness.
14 [a]The LORD of hosts has sworn by Himself:
"Surely I will fill you with men,
[b]as with locusts,
And they shall lift [c]up a shout against you."

**15** [a]He has made the earth by His power;
He has established the world by His wisdom,
And [b]stretched out the heaven
by His understanding.
16 When He utters *His* voice—
*There is* a multitude of waters in the
heavens:
[a]"He causes the vapors to ascend from the
ends of the earth;
He makes lightnings for the rain;
He brings the wind out of His treasuries."

17 [a]Everyone is dull-hearted, without knowledge;
Every metalsmith is put to shame by the
carved image;
[b]For his molded image *is* falsehood,
And *there is* no breath in them.
18 They *are* futile, a work of errors;
In the time of their punishment
they shall perish.
19 The Portion of Jacob *is* not like them,
For He *is* the Maker of all things;
And *Israel is* the tribe of His inheritance.
The LORD of hosts *is* His name.

**20** "You[a] *are* My battle-ax *and* weapons of war:
For with you I will break the nation in
pieces;
With you I will destroy kingdoms;
21 With you I will break in pieces
the horse and its rider;
With you I will break in pieces
the chariot and its rider;
22 With you also I will break in pieces man and
woman;
With you I will break in pieces
[a]old and young;
With you I will break in pieces
the young man and the maiden;
23 With you also I will break in pieces
the shepherd and his flock;
With you I will break in pieces
the farmer and his yoke of oxen;
And with you I will break in pieces
governors and rulers.

**24** "And[a] I will repay Babylon
And all the inhabitants of Chaldea
For all the evil they have done
In Zion in your sight," says the LORD.

25 "Behold, I *am* against you,
[a]O destroying mountain,
Who destroys all the earth," says the LORD.
"And I will stretch out My hand against you,
Roll you down from the rocks,
[b]And make you a burnt mountain.
26 They shall not take from you a stone for a
corner
Nor a stone for a foundation,
[a]But you shall be desolate forever,"
says the LORD.

**27** [a]Set up a banner in the land,
Blow the trumpet among the nations!
[b]Prepare the nations against her,
Call [c]the kingdoms together against her:
Ararat, Minni, and Ashkenaz.
Appoint a general against her;
Cause the horses to come up like the
bristling locusts.
28 Prepare against her the nations,
With the kings of the Medes,
Its governors and all its rulers,
All the land of his dominion.
29 And the land will tremble and sorrow;
For every [a]purpose of the LORD
shall be performed against Babylon,
[b]To make the land of Babylon
a desolation without inhabitant.
30 The mighty men of Babylon have ceased
fighting,
They have remained in their strongholds;
Their might has failed,
[a]They became *like* women;
They have burned her dwelling places,
[b]The bars of her *gate* are broken.
31 [a]One runner will run to meet another,
And one messenger to meet another,
To show the king of Babylon
that his city is taken on *all* sides;

**4** [a]Jer. 49:26; 50:30, 37
**5** [a][Is. 54:7, 8; Jer. 33:24–26; 46:28]
**6** [a]Jer. 50:8; Rev. 18:4 [b]Jer. 50:15 [c]Jer. 25:14
**7** [a]Jer. 25:15; Hab. 2:16; Rev. 17:4 [b]Rev. 14:8 [c]Jer. 25:16
**8** [a]Is. 21:9; Jer. 50:2; Rev. 14:8; 18:2 [b][Is. 48:20]; Rev. 18:9, 11, 19 [c]Jer. 46:11
**9** [a]Is. 13:14; Jer. 46:16; 50:16 [b]Ezra 9:6; Rev. 18:5
**10** [a]Ps. 37:6; Mic. 7:9 [b][Is. 40:2]; Jer. 50:28
**11** [a]Jer. 46:4, 9; Joel 3:9, 10 [b]Is. 13:17 [c]Jer. 50:45 [d]Jer. 50:28 [1]*Polish the arrows!*
**12** [a]Nah. 2:1; 3:14
**13** [a]Rev. 17:1, 15
**14** [a]Jer. 49:13; Amos 6:8 [b]Jer. 51:27; Nah. 3:15 [c]Jer. 50:15
**15** [a]Gen. 1:1, 6; Jer. 10:12–16 [b]Job 9:8; Ps. 104:2; Is. 40:22
**16** [a]Ps. 135:7; Jer. 10:13
**17** [a][Is. 44:18–20]; Jer. 10:14 [b]Jer. 50:2
**20** [a]Is. 10:5, 15; Jer. 50:23
**22** [a]2 Chr. 36:17; Is. 13:15, 16
**24** [a]Jer. 50:15, 29
**25** [a]Is. 13:2; Zech. 4:7 [b]Rev. 8:8
**26** [a]Jer. 50:26, 40
**27** [a]Is. 13:2; Jer. 50:2; 51:12 [b]Jer. 25:14 [c]Jer. 50:41, 42
**29** [a]Jer. 50:45 [b]Is. 13:19, 20; 47:11; Jer. 50:13; 51:26, 43
**30** [a]Is. 19:16; Jer. 48:41 [b]Is. 45:1, 2; Lam. 2:9; Amos 1:5; Nah. 3:13
**31** [a]Jer. 50:24

32 [a]The passages are blocked,
The reeds they have burned with fire,
And the men of war are terrified.

**33** For thus says the LORD of hosts, the God of Israel:

"The daughter of Babylon
*is* [a]like a threshing floor
*When* [b]*it is* time to thresh her;
Yet a little while
[c]And the time of her harvest will come."

**34** "Nebuchadnezzar the king of Babylon
Has [a]devoured me, he has crushed me;
He has made me an [b]empty vessel,
He has swallowed me up like a monster;
He has filled his stomach with my delicacies,
He has spit me out.
35 Let the violence *done* to me and my flesh *be*
upon Babylon,"
The inhabitant of Zion will say;
"And my blood be upon the inhabitants of
Chaldea!"
Jerusalem will say.

36 Therefore thus says the LORD:

"Behold, [a]I will plead your case
and take vengeance for you.
[b]I will dry up her sea
and make her springs dry.
37 [a]Babylon shall become a heap,
A dwelling place for jackals,
[b]An astonishment and a hissing,
Without an inhabitant.
38 They shall roar together like lions,
They shall growl like lions' whelps.
39 In their excitement I will prepare their feasts;
[a]I will make them drunk,
That they may rejoice,
And sleep a perpetual sleep
And not awake," says the LORD.
40 "I will bring them down
Like lambs to the slaughter,
Like rams with male goats.

**41** "Oh, how [a]Sheshach[1] is taken!
Oh, how [b]the praise of the whole earth is
seized!
How Babylon has become
desolate among the nations!
42 [a]The sea has come up over Babylon;
She is covered with the multitude
of its waves.
43 [a]Her cities are a desolation,
A dry land and a wilderness,
A land where [b]no one dwells,
Through which no son of man passes.
44 I will punish [a]Bel[1] in Babylon,
And I will bring out of his mouth
what he has swallowed;
And the nations shall not stream
to him anymore.
Yes, [b]the wall of Babylon shall fall.

**45** "My[a] people, go out of the midst of her!
And let everyone deliver [1]himself
from the fierce anger of the LORD.
46 And lest your heart faint,
And you fear [a]for the rumor
that *will be* heard in the land
(A rumor will come *one* year,
And after that, in *another* year
A rumor *will come,*
And violence in the land,
Ruler against ruler),
47 Therefore behold, the days are coming
That I will bring judgment on the carved
images of Babylon;
Her whole land shall be ashamed,
And all her slain shall fall in her midst.
48 Then [a]the heavens and the earth
and all that *is* in them
Shall sing joyously over Babylon;
[b]For the plunderers shall come to her from
the north," says the LORD.

**49** As Babylon *has caused* the slain of Israel to
fall,
So at Babylon the slain of all the earth shall
fall.
50 [a]You who have escaped the sword,
Get away! Do not stand still!
[b]Remember the LORD afar off,
And let Jerusalem come to your mind.

**51** [a]We are ashamed because we have heard
reproach.
Shame has covered our faces,
For strangers [b]have come into the
[1]sanctuaries of the LORD's house.

**52** "Therefore behold, the days are coming," says
the LORD,
"That I will bring judgment on her carved
images,
And throughout all her land the wounded
shall groan.
53 [a]Though Babylon were to [1]mount up to
heaven,
And though she were to fortify the height of
her strength,
*Yet* from Me plunderers would come
to her," says the LORD.

**54** [a]The sound of a cry *comes* from Babylon,
And great destruction
from the land of the Chaldeans,
55 Because the LORD is plundering Babylon
And silencing her loud voice,
Though her waves roar like great waters,
And the noise of their voice is uttered,
56 Because the plunderer comes against her,
against Babylon,
And her mighty men are taken.
Every one of their bows is broken;
[a]For the LORD *is* the God of recompense,
He will surely repay.

57 "And I will make drunk
Her princes and [a]wise men,
Her governors, her deputies,
and her mighty men.
And they shall sleep a perpetual sleep
And not awake," says [b]the King,
Whose name *is* the LORD of hosts.

**58** Thus says the LORD of hosts:

"The broad walls of Babylon
shall be utterly [a]broken,[1]
And her high gates shall be burned with fire;
[b]The people will labor in vain,
And the nations, because of the fire;
And they shall be weary."

**59** The word which Jeremiah the prophet commanded Seraiah the son of [a]Neriah, the son of Mahseiah, when he went with Zedekiah the king

---

**32** [a]Jer. 50:38
**33** [a]Is. 21:10; Dan. 2:35; Amos 1:3; Mic. 4:13 [b]Is. 41:15; Hab. 3:12 [c]Is. 17:15; Hos. 6:11; Joel 3:13; Rev. 14:15
**34** [a]Jer. 50:17 [b]Is. 24:1–3
**36** [a][Ps. 140:12]; Jer. 50:34 [b]Jer. 50:38
**37** [a]Is. 13:22; Jer. 50:39; [Rev. 18:2] [b]Jer. 25:9, 11
**39** [a]Jer. 51:57
**41** [a]Jer. 25:26 [b]Is. 13:19; Jer. 49:25; [Dan. 4:30] [1]A code word for *Babylon,* Jer. 25:26
**42** [a]Is. 8:7, 8; Jer. 51:55; Dan. 9:26
**43** [a]Jer. 50:39, 40 [b]Is. 13:20
**44** [a]Jer. 50:2; Is. 46:1 [b]Jer. 50:15 [1]A Babylonian god
**45** [a]Is. 48:20; [Jer. 50:8, 28; 51:6; Rev. 18:4] [1]Lit. *his soul*
**46** [a]2 Kin. 19:7; Is. 13:3–5
**48** [a]Is. 44:23; 48:20; 49:13; Rev. 18:20 [b]Jer. 50:3, 41
**50** [a]Jer. 44:28 [b][Deut. 4:29–31]; Ezek. 6:9
**51** [a]Ps. 44:15; 79:4 [b]Ps. 74:3–8; Jer. 52:13; Lam. 1:10 [1]*holy places*
**53** [a]Gen. 11:4; Job 20:6; [Ps. 139:8–10; Is. 14:12–14]; Jer. 49:16; Amos 9:2; Obad. 4 [1]*ascend*
**54** [a]Jer. 50:22
**56** [a]Ps. 94:1; Jer. 50:29
**57** [a]Jer. 50:35 [b]Jer. 46:18; 48:15
**58** [a]Jer. 50:15 [b]Hab. 2:13 [1]Lit. *laid utterly bare*
**59** [a]Jer. 32:12

of Judah to Babylon in the fourth year of his
reign. And Seraiah *was* the quartermaster.
60 So Jeremiah [a]wrote in a book all the evil that
would come upon Babylon, all these words that
are written against Babylon.
61 And Jeremiah said to Seraiah, "When you
arrive in Babylon and see it, and read all these
words,
62 "then you shall say, 'O LORD, You have spoken
against this place to cut it off, so that [a]none shall
remain in it, neither man nor beast, but it shall be
desolate forever.'
63 "Now it shall be, when you have finished
reading this book, [a]*that* you shall tie a stone to it
and throw it out into the Euphrates.
64 "Then you shall say, 'Thus Babylon shall sink
and not rise from the catastrophe that I will bring
upon her. And they shall be weary.' " Thus far *are*
the words of Jeremiah.

## *The Fall of Jerusalem Reviewed*

**52** Zedekiah *was* [a]twenty-one years old when
he became king, and he reigned eleven
years in Jerusalem. His mother's name *was* Ha-
mutal the daughter of Jeremiah of [b]Libnah.
2 He also did evil in the sight of the LORD,
according to all that Jehoiakim had done.
3 For because of the anger of the LORD *this*
happened in Jerusalem and Judah, till He finally
cast them out from His presence. Then Zedekiah
[a]rebelled against the king of Babylon.
**4** Now it came to pass in the [a]ninth year of his
reign, in the tenth month, on the tenth *day* of the
month, *that* Nebuchadnezzar king of Babylon and
all his army came against Jerusalem and encamped against it; and *they* built a siege wall
against it all around.
5 So the city was besieged until the eleventh
year of King Zedekiah.
6 By the fourth month, on the ninth day of
the month, the famine had become so severe
in the city that there was no food for the people
of the land.
7 Then the city wall was broken through, and all
the men of war fled and went out of the city at
night by way of the gate between the two walls,
which *was* by the king's garden, even though the
Chaldeans *were* near the city all around. And they
went by way of the [1]plain.
**8** But the army of the Chaldeans pursued the
king, and they overtook Zedekiah in the plains of
Jericho. All his army was scattered from him.
9 [a]So they took the king and brought him up to
the king of Babylon at Riblah in the land of
Hamath, and he pronounced judgment on him.
10 [a]Then the king of Babylon killed the sons of
Zedekiah before his eyes. And he killed all the
princes of Judah in Riblah.
11 He also [a]put out the eyes of Zedekiah; and the
king of Babylon bound him in [1]bronze fetters,
took him to Babylon, and put him in prison till the
day of his death.
**12** [a]Now in the fifth month, on the tenth *day* of
the month ([b]which *was* the nineteenth year of
King Nebuchadnezzar king of Babylon), [c]Nebu-
zaradan, the captain of the guard, *who* served the
king of Babylon, came to Jerusalem.
13 He burned the house of the LORD and the
king's house; all the houses of Jerusalem, that is,
all the houses of the great, he burned with fire.
14 And all the army of the Chaldeans who *were*
with the captain of the guard broke down all the
walls of Jerusalem all around.
15 [a]Then Nebuzaradan the captain of the guard
carried away captive *some* of the poor people, the
rest of the people who remained in the city, the
defectors who had deserted to the king of Babylon, and the rest of the craftsmen.
16 But Nebuzaradan the captain of the guard left
*some* of the poor of the land as vinedressers and
farmers.
**17** [a]The [b]bronze pillars that *were* in the house of
the LORD, and the carts and the bronze Sea that
*were* in the house of the LORD, the Chaldeans
broke in pieces, and carried all their bronze to
Babylon.
18 They also took away [a]the pots, the shovels,
the trimmers, the [1]bowls, the spoons, and all the
bronze utensils with which the priests ministered.
19 The basins, the firepans, the bowls, the pots,
the lampstands, the spoons, and the cups, whatever *was* solid gold and whatever *was* solid silver,
the captain of the guard took away.
20 The two pillars, one Sea, the twelve bronze
bulls which *were* under *it, and* the carts, which
King Solomon had made for the house of the
LORD—[a]the bronze of all these articles was beyond
measure.
21 Now *concerning* the [a]pillars: the height of one
pillar *was* eighteen [1]cubits, a measuring line of
twelve cubits could measure its circumference,
and its thickness *was* [2]four fingers; *it was* hollow.
22 A capital of bronze *was* on it; and the height
of one capital *was* five cubits, with a network and
pomegranates all around the capital, all of bronze.
The second pillar, with pomegranates was the
same.
23 There were ninety-six pomegranates on the
sides; [a]all the pomegranates, all around on the
network, *were* one hundred.
**24** [a]The captain of the guard took Seraiah the
chief priest, [b]Zephaniah the second priest, and the
three doorkeepers.
25 He also took out of the city an [1]officer who
had charge of the men of war, seven men of the
king's close associates who were found in the city,
the principal scribe of the army who mustered the
people of the land, and sixty men of the people of
the land who were found in the midst of the city.
26 And Nebuzaradan the captain of the guard
took these and brought them to the king of
Babylon at Riblah.
27 Then the king of Babylon struck them and put
them to death at Riblah in the land of Hamath.
Thus Judah was carried away captive from its
own land.
**28** [a]These *are* the people whom Nebuchadnezzar
carried away captive: [b]in the seventh year, [c]three
thousand and twenty-three Jews;
29 [a]in the eighteenth year of Nebuchadnezzar he
carried away captive from Jerusalem eight hundred and thirty-two persons;
30 in the twenty-third year of Nebuchadnezzar,
Nebuzaradan the captain of the guard carried
away captive of the Jews seven hundred and
forty-five persons. All the persons *were* four
thousand six hundred.
**31** [a]Now it came to pass in the thirty-seventh
year of the captivity of Jehoiachin king of Judah,
in the twelfth month, on the twenty-fifth *day* of
the month, *that* [1]Evil-Merodach king of Babylon,
in the first *year* of his reign, [b]lifted[2] up the head of

**60** [a]Is. 30:8; Jer. 36:2
**62** [a]Is. 13:20; 14:22, 23; Jer. 50:3, 39
**63** [a]Jer. 19:10, 11; Rev. 18:21

CHAPTER 52
**1** [a]2 Kin. 24:18; 2 Chr. 36:11 [b]Josh. 10:29; 2 Kin. 8:22; Is. 37:8
**3** [a]2 Chr. 36:13
**4** [a]2 Kin. 25:1; Jer. 39:1; Ezek. 24:1, 2; Zech. 8:19
**7** [1]Or *Arabah;* the Jordan Valley
**9** [a]2 Kin. 25:6; Jer. 32:4; 39:5
**10** [a]Ezek. 12:13
**11** [a]Ezek. 12:13 [1]*shackles*
**12** [a]2 Kin. 25:8–21 [b]Jer. 52:29 [c]Jer. 39:9
**15** [a]Jer. 39:9
**17** [a]Jer. 27:19 [b]1 Kin. 7:15, 23, 27, 50
**18** [a]Ex. 27:3; 1 Kin. 7:40, 45; 2 Kin. 25:14 [1]*basins*
**20** [a]1 Kin. 7:47; 2 Kin. 25:16
**21** [a]1 Kin. 7:15; 2 Kin. 25:17; 2 Chr. 3:15 [1]18 inches each [2]3 inches
**23** [a]1 Kin. 7:20
**24** [a]2 Kin. 25:18; 1 Chr. 6:14; Ezra 7:1 [b]Jer. 21:1; 29:25
**25** [1]Lit. *eunuch*
**28** [a]2 Kin. 24:2 [b]2 Kin. 24:12 [c]2 Kin. 24:14
**29** [a]2 Kin. 25:11; Jer. 39:9
**31** [a]2 Kin. 25:27–30 [b]Gen. 40:13, 20; Ps. 3:3; 27:6 [1]Or *Awil Marduk;* lit. *The Man of Marduk* [2]Showed favor to

Jehoiachin king of Judah and brought him out of prison.
32 And he spoke kindly to him and gave him a more prominent seat than those of the kings who *were* with him in Babylon.
33 So [1]Jehoiachin changed from his prison garments, [a]and he ate bread regularly before the king all the days of his life.
34 And as for his provisions, there was a regular ration given him by the king of Babylon, a portion for each day until the day of his death, all the days of his life.

**33** [a]2 Sam. 9:7, 13; 1 Kin. 2:7 [1]Lit. *he*

*The Book of*

# LAMENTATIONS

## *The Sorrows of Captive Zion*

HOW lonely sits the city
*That was* full of people!
[a]*How* like a widow is she,
Who *was* great among the nations!
The [b]princess among the provinces
Has become a [1]slave!

2 She [a]weeps bitterly in the [b]night,
Her tears *are* on her cheeks;
Among all her lovers
She has none to comfort *her.*
All her friends have dealt treacherously with her;
They have become her enemies.

3 [a]Judah has gone into captivity,
Under affliction and hard servitude;
[b]She dwells among the [1]nations,
She finds no [c]rest;
All her persecutors overtake her
in dire straits.

4 The roads to Zion mourn
Because no one comes to the [1]set feasts.
All her gates are [a]desolate;
Her priests sigh,
Her virgins are afflicted,
And she *is* in bitterness.

5 Her adversaries [a]have become [1]the master,
Her enemies prosper;
For the LORD has afflicted her
[b]Because of the multitude of her
transgressions.
Her [c]children have gone into captivity before
the enemy.

6 And from the daughter of Zion
All her splendor has departed.
Her princes have become like deer
*That* find no pasture,
That [1]flee without strength
Before the pursuer.

7 In the days of her affliction and roaming,
Jerusalem [a]remembers all her pleasant things
That she had in the days of old.
When her people fell into the hand
of the enemy,
With no one to help her,
The adversaries saw her
*And* mocked at her [1]downfall.

8 [a]Jerusalem has sinned gravely,
Therefore she has become [1]vile.
All who honored her despise her
Because [b]they have seen her nakedness;
Yes, she sighs and turns away.

9 Her uncleanness *is* in her skirts;
She [a]did not consider her destiny;
Therefore her collapse was awesome;
She had no comforter.
"O LORD, behold my affliction,
For *the* enemy is exalted!"

10 The adversary has spread his hand
Over all her [1]pleasant things;
For she has seen [a]the nations enter
her [2]sanctuary,
Those whom You commanded
[b]Not to enter Your assembly.

11 All her people sigh,
[a]They [1]seek bread;
They have given their [2]valuables for food to
restore life.
"See, O LORD, and consider,
For I am scorned."

12 "*Is it* nothing to you, all you who [1]pass by?
Behold and see
[a]If there is any sorrow like my sorrow,
Which has been brought on me,
Which the LORD has inflicted
In the day of His fierce anger.

13 "From above He has sent fire into my bones,
And it overpowered them;
He has [a]spread a net for my feet
And turned me back;
He has made me desolate
*And* faint all the day.

14 "The[a] yoke of my transgressions was [1]bound;
They were woven together by His hands,
*And* thrust upon my neck.
He made my strength fail;
The Lord delivered me into the hands of
*those whom* I am not able to withstand.

15 "The Lord has trampled underfoot
all my mighty *men* in my midst;
He has called an assembly against me
To crush my young men;
[a]The Lord trampled *as* in a winepress
The virgin daughter of Judah.

16 "For these *things* I weep;
My eye, [a]my eye overflows with water;
Because the comforter, who should restore
my life,
Is far from me.
My children are desolate
Because the enemy prevailed."

CHAPTER 1
**1** [a]Is. 47:7–9 [b]1 Kin. 4:21; Ezra 4:20; Jer. 31:7 [1]Lit. *forced laborer*
**2** [a]Jer. 13:17 [b]Job 7:3
**3** [a]Jer. 52:27 [b]Lam. 2:9 [c]Deut. 28:65 [1]*Gentiles*
**4** [a]Is. 27:10 [1]*appointed*
**5** [a]Deut. 28:43 [b]Jer. 30:14, 15; Dan. 9:7, 16 [c]Jer. 52:28 [1]Lit. *her head*
**6** [1]Lit. *are gone*
**7** [a]Ps. 137:1 [1]Vg. *Sabbaths*
**8** [a][1 Kin. 8:46] [b]Jer. 13:22; Ezek. 16:37; Hos. 2:10 [1]LXX, Vg. *moved* or *removed*
**9** [a]Deut. 32:29; Is. 47:7; Jer. 5:31
**10** [a]Ps. 74:4–8; Is. 64:10, 11; Jer. 51:51 [b]Deut. 23:3; Neh. 13:1 [1]*desirable* [2]*holy place,* the temple
**11** [a]Jer. 38:9; 52:6 [1]*hunt food* [2]*desirable things*
**12** [a]Dan. 9:12 [1]Lit. *pass by this way*
**13** [a]Ezek. 12:13; 17:20
**14** [a]Deut. 28:48 [1]So with MT, Tg.; LXX, Syr., Vg. *watched over*
**15** [a]Is. 63:3; [Rev. 14:19]
**16** [a]Ps. 69:20; Eccl. 4:1; Jer. 13:17; Lam. 2:18

17 [a]Zion [1]spreads out her hands,
*But* no one comforts her;
The LORD has commanded concerning Jacob
*That* those [b]around him *become* his
adversaries;
Jerusalem has become an unclean thing
among them.

18 "The LORD is [a]righteous,
For I [b]rebelled against His [1]commandment.
Hear now, all peoples,
And behold my sorrow;
My virgins and my young men
Have gone into captivity.

19 "I called for my lovers,
*But* they deceived me;
My priests and my elders
Breathed their last in the city,
While they sought food
To restore their life.

20 "See, O LORD, that I *am* in distress;
My [a]soul[1] is troubled;
My heart is overturned within me,
For I have been very rebellious.
[b]Outside the sword bereaves,
At home *it is* like death.

21 "They have heard that I sigh,
*But* no one comforts me.
All my enemies have heard of my trouble;
They are [a]glad that You have done *it*.
Bring on [b]the day You have [1]announced,
That they may become like me.

22 "Let[a] all their wickedness come before You,
And do to them as You have done to me
For all my transgressions;
For my sighs *are* many,
And my heart *is* faint."

## *God's Anger with Jerusalem*

**2** How the Lord has covered the daughter of
Zion
With a [a]cloud in His anger!
[b]He cast down from heaven to the earth
[c]The beauty of Israel,
And did not remember [d]His footstool
In the day of His anger.

2 The Lord has swallowed up
and has [a]not pitied
All the dwelling places of Jacob.
He has thrown down in His wrath
The strongholds of the daughter of Judah;
He has brought *them* down to the ground;
[b]He has profaned the kingdom and its princes.

3 He has cut off in fierce anger
Every [1]horn of Israel;
[a]He has drawn back His right hand
From before the enemy.
[b]He has blazed against Jacob
like a flaming fire
Devouring all around.

4 [a]Standing like an enemy,
He has bent His bow;
With His right hand, like an adversary,
He has slain [b]all *who were* pleasing
to His eye;
On the tent of the daughter of Zion,
He has poured out His fury like fire.

5 [a]The Lord was like an enemy.
He has swallowed up Israel,
He has swallowed up all her palaces;
[b]He has destroyed her strongholds,
And has increased mourning and lamentation
In the daughter of Judah.

6 He has done violence [a]to His [1]tabernacle,
[b]*As if it were* a garden;
He has destroyed His place of assembly;
The LORD has caused
The appointed feasts and Sabbaths
to be forgotten in Zion.
In His burning indignation He has [c]spurned
the king and the priest.

7 The Lord has spurned His altar,
He has [a]abandoned His sanctuary;
He has [1]given up the walls of her palaces
Into the hand of the enemy.
[b]They have made a noise in the house of the
LORD
As on the day of a set feast.

8 The LORD has [1]purposed to destroy
The [a]wall of the daughter of Zion.
[b]He has stretched out a line;
He has not withdrawn His hand
from destroying;
Therefore He has caused the rampart and
wall to lament;
They languished together.

9 Her gates have sunk into the ground;
He has destroyed and [a]broken her bars.
[b]Her king and her princes *are* among the
[1]nations;
[c]The Law *is* no *more*,
And her [d]prophets find no [2]vision
from the LORD.

10 The elders of the daughter of Zion
[a]Sit on the ground *and* keep silence;
[1]They [b]throw dust on their heads
And [c]gird themselves with sackcloth.
The virgins of Jerusalem
Bow their heads to the ground.

11 [a]My eyes fail with tears,
My [1]heart is troubled;
[b]My [2]bile is poured on the ground
Because of the destruction of the daughter of
my people,
Because [c]the children and the infants
Faint in the streets of the city.

12 They say to their mothers,
"Where *is* grain and wine?"
As they swoon like the wounded
In the streets of the city,
As their life is poured out
In their mothers' bosom.

13 How shall I [a]console[1] you?
To what shall I liken you,
O daughter of Jerusalem?
What shall I compare with you,
that I may comfort you,
O virgin daughter of Zion?
For your ruin *is* spread wide as the sea;
Who can heal you?

14 Your [a]prophets have seen for you
False and deceptive visions;
They have not [b]uncovered your iniquity,

**17** [a][Is. 1:15]; Jer. 4:31 [b]2 Kin. 24:2–4; Jer. 12:9 [1]Prays
**18** [a]Neh. 9:33; Ps. 119:75; Dan. 9:7, 14 [b]1 Sam. 12:14, 15; Jer. 4:17 [1]Lit. *mouth*
**20** [a]Job 30:27; Is. 16:11; Jer. 4:19; Lam. 2:11; Hos. 11:8 [b]Deut. 32:25; Ezek. 7:15 [1]Lit. *inward parts*
**21** [a]Ps. 35:15; Jer. 48:27; 50:11; Lam. 2:15; Obad. 12 [b]Is. 13; [Jer. 46] [1]*proclaimed*
**22** [a]Neh. 4:4, 5; Ps. 109:15; 137:7, 8; Jer. 30:16

CHAPTER 2

**1** [a][Lam. 3:44] [b]Matt. 11:23 [c]2 Sam. 1:19 [d]1 Chr. 28:2; Ps. 99:5; Ezek. 43:7
**2** [a]Ps. 21:9; Lam. 3:43 [b]Ps. 89:39, 40; Is. 43:28
**3** [a]Ps. 74:11; Jer. 21:4, 5 [b]Ps. 89:46 [1]Strength
**4** [a]Is. 63:10 [b]Ezek. 24:25
**5** [a]Jer. 30:14 [b]2 Kin. 25:9; Jer. 52:13; Lam. 2:2
**6** [a]Ps. 80:12; 89:40; Is. 5:5; Jer. 7:14 [b]Is. 1:8; Jer. 52:13 [c]Is. 43:28 [1]Lit. *booth*
**7** [a]Ezek. 24:21 [b]Ps. 74:3–8 [1]*delivered*
**8** [a]Jer. 52:14 [b][2 Kin. 21:13; Is. 34:11; Amos 7:7–9] [1]*determined*
**9** [a]Jer. 51:30 [b]Deut. 28:36; 2 Kin. 24:15; 25:7; Lam. 1:3; 4:20 [c]2 Chr. 15:3 [d]Ps. 74:9; Mic. 3:6 [1]*Gentiles* [2]Prophetic revelation
**10** [a]Job 2:13; Is. 3:26 [b]Job 2:12; Ezek. 27:30 [c]Is. 15:3; Jon. 3:6–8 [1]A sign of mourning
**11** [a]Ps. 6:7; Lam. 3:48 [b]Job 16:13; Ps. 22:14 [c]Lam. 4:4 [1]Lit. *inward parts* [2]Lit. *liver*
**13** [a]Lam. 1:12; Dan. 9:12 [1]Or *bear witness to*
**14** [a]Jer. 2:8; 23:25–29; 29:8, 9; 37:19; Ezek. 13:2 [b]Is. 58:1; Ezek. 23:36; Mic. 3:8

To bring back your captives,
But have envisioned for you
false [c]prophecies and delusions.

15 All who [1]pass by [a]clap *their* hands at you;
They hiss [b]and shake their heads
At the daughter of Jerusalem:
"*Is* this the city that is called
[c]'The perfection of beauty,
The joy of the whole earth'?"

16 [a]All your enemies have opened their mouth
against you;
They hiss and gnash *their* teeth.
They say, [b]"We have swallowed *her* up!
Surely this *is* the [c]day we have waited for;
We have found *it,* [d]we have seen *it!*"

17 The LORD has done what He [a]purposed;
He has fulfilled His word
Which He commanded in days of old.
He has thrown down and has not pitied,
And He has caused an enemy to [b]rejoice over
you;
He has exalted the [1]horn of your adversaries.

**18** Their heart cried out to the Lord,
"O wall of the daughter of Zion,
[a]Let tears run down like a river
day and night;
Give yourself no relief;
Give [1]your eyes no rest.

19 "Arise, [a]cry out in the night,
At the beginning of the watches;
[b]Pour out your heart like water
before the face of the Lord.
Lift your hands toward Him
For the life of your young children,
Who faint from hunger
[c]at the head of every street."

**20** "See, O LORD, and consider!
To whom have You done this?
[a]Should the women eat their offspring,
The children [1]they have cuddled?
Should the priest and prophet be slain
In the sanctuary of the Lord?

21 "Young[a] and old lie
On the ground in the streets;
My virgins and my young men
Have fallen by the [b]sword;
You have slain *them* in the day of Your
anger,
You have slaughtered *and* not pitied.

22 "You have invited as to a feast day
[a]The terrors that surround me.
In the day of the LORD's anger
There was no refugee or survivor.
[b]Those whom I have borne and brought up
My enemies have [c]destroyed."

### *Hope and Relief Through God's Mercy*

**3** I *am* the man *who* has seen affliction
by the rod of His wrath.
2 He has led me and made *me* walk
*In* darkness and not *in* light.
3 Surely He has turned His hand against me
Time and time again throughout the day.

4 He has aged [a]my flesh and my skin,
And [b]broken my bones.
5 He has besieged me
And surrounded *me* with bitterness and [1]woe.

**14** [c]Jer. 23:33–36
**15** [a]Ezek. 25:6 [b]Ps. 44:14 [c][Ps. 48:2; 50:2] [1]Lit. *pass by this way*
**16** [a]Job 16:9, 10 [b]Ps. 56:2; 124:3 [c]Lam. 1:21 [d]Ps. 35:21
**17** [a]Lev. 26:16 [b]Ps. 38:16 [1]Strength
**18** [a]Jer. 14:17 [1]Lit. *the daughter of your eye*
**19** [a]Ps. 119:147 [b]Ps. 42:4; 62:8 [c]Is. 51:20
**20** [a]Lev. 26:29 [1]Vg. *a span long*
**21** [a]2 Chr. 36:17 [b]Jer. 18:21
**22** [a]Ps. 31:13 [b]Hos. 9:12 [c]Jer. 16:2–4; 44:7

CHAPTER 3
**4** [a]Job 16:8 [b]Ps. 51:8
**5** [1]*hardship* or *weariness*
**6** [a][Ps. 88:5, 6; 143:3]
**7** [a]Hos. 2:6
**8** [a]Job 30:20
**10** [a]Is. 38:13 [1]Lit. *secret places*
**11** [a]Hos. 6:1
**12** [a]Job 7:20; 16:12
**13** [a]Job 6:4 [1]Lit. *sons of* [2]Lit. *kidneys*
**14** [a]Jer. 20:7 [b]Job 30:9
**15** [a]Jer. 9:15
**16** [a][Prov. 20:17] [1]Lit. *bent me down in*
**17** [1]Lit. *good*
**18** [a]Ps. 31:22
**19** [a]Jer. 9:15 [1]*bitterness*
**20** [1]Lit. *bowed down*
**21** [a]Ps. 130:7
**22** [a][Mal. 3:6] [b]Ps. 78:38
**23** [a]Is. 33:2
**24** [a]Ps. 16:5; 73:26; 119:57 [b]Mic. 7:7
**25** [a]Is. 30:18
**26** [a][Rom. 4:16–18] [b]Ps. 37:7
**27** [a]Ps. 94:12
**28** [a]Jer. 15:17
**29** [a]Job 42:6
**30** [a]Is. 50:6
**31** [a]Ps. 77:7; 94:14
**33** [a][Ezek. 33:11] [1]Lit. *from his heart*

6 [a]He has set me in dark places
Like the dead of long ago.

7 [a]He has hedged me in so that
I cannot get out;
He has made my chain heavy.
8 Even [a]when I cry and shout,
He shuts out my prayer.
9 He has blocked my ways with hewn stone;
He has made my paths crooked.

10 [a]He *has been* to me a bear lying in wait,
*Like* a lion in [1]ambush.
11 He has turned aside my ways
and [a]torn me in pieces;
He has made me desolate.
12 He has bent His bow
And [a]set me up as a target for the arrow.

13 He has caused [a]the [1]arrows of His quiver
To pierce my [2]loins.
14 I have become the [a]ridicule of all
my people—
[b]Their taunting song all the day.
15 [a]He has filled me with bitterness,
He has made me drink wormwood.

16 He has also broken my teeth [a]with gravel,
And [1]covered me with ashes.
17 You have moved my soul far from peace;
I have forgotten [1]prosperity.
18 [a]And I said, "My strength and my hope
Have perished from the LORD."

**19** Remember my affliction and roaming,
[a]The wormwood and the [1]gall.
20 My soul still remembers
And [1]sinks within me.
21 This I recall to my mind,
Therefore I have [a]hope.

22 [a]*Through* the LORD's mercies
we are not consumed,
Because His compassions [b]fail not.
23 *They are* new [a]every morning;
Great *is* Your faithfulness.
24 "The LORD *is* my [a]portion," says my soul,
"Therefore I [b]hope in Him!"

25 The LORD *is* good to those
who [a]wait for Him,
To the soul *who* seeks Him.
26 *It is* good that *one* should [a]hope
[b]and wait quietly
For the salvation of the LORD.
27 [a]*It is* good for a man to bear
The yoke in his youth.

28 [a]Let him sit alone and keep silent,
Because *God* has laid *it* on him;
29 [a]Let him put his mouth in the dust—
There may yet be hope.
30 [a]Let him give *his* cheek to the one
who strikes him,
*And* be full of reproach.

31 [a]For the Lord will not cast off forever.
32 Though He causes grief,
Yet He will show compassion
According to the multitude of His mercies.
33 For [a]He does not afflict [1]willingly,
Nor grieve the children of men.

34 To crush under one's feet
All the prisoners of the earth,

35 To turn aside the justice *due* a man
Before the face of the Most High,
36 Or subvert a man in his cause—
[a]The Lord does not approve.

37 Who *is* he [a]*who* speaks and it comes to pass,
*When* the Lord has not commanded *it?*
38 *Is it* not from the mouth of the Most High
That [a]woe and well-being proceed?
39 [a]Why should a living man [1]complain,
[b]A man for the punishment of his sins?

40 Let us search out and examine our ways,
And turn back to the LORD;
41 [a]Let us lift our hearts and hands
To God in heaven.
42 [a]We have transgressed and rebelled;
You have not pardoned.

**43** You have covered *Yourself* with anger
And pursued us;
You have slain *and* not pitied.
44 You have covered Yourself with a cloud,
That prayer should not pass through.
45 You have made us an [a]offscouring and refuse
In the midst of the peoples.

46 [a]All our enemies
Have opened their mouths against us.
47 [a]Fear and a snare have come upon us,
[b]Desolation and destruction.
48 [a]My eyes overflow with rivers of water
For the destruction of the daughter of my
people.

49 [a]My eyes flow and do not cease,
Without interruption,
50 Till the LORD from heaven
[a]Looks down and sees.
51 My eyes bring suffering to my soul
Because of all the daughters of my city.

52 My enemies [a]without cause
Hunted me down like a bird.
53 They [1]silenced my life [a]in the pit
And [b]threw [2]stones at me.
54 [a]The waters flowed over my head;
[b]I said, "I am cut off!"

**55** [a]I called on Your name, O LORD,
From the lowest [b]pit.
56 [a]You have heard my voice:
"Do not hide Your ear
From my sighing, from my cry for help."
57 You [a]drew near on the day I called on You,
And said, [b]"Do not fear!"

58 O Lord, You have [a]pleaded
the case for my soul;
[b]You have redeemed my life.
59 O LORD, You have seen [1]*how* I am wronged;
[a]Judge my case.
60 You have seen all their vengeance,
All their [a]schemes against me.

61 You have heard their reproach, O LORD,
All their schemes against me,
62 The lips of my enemies
And their whispering against me all the day.
63 Look at their [a]sitting down
and their rising up;
I *am* their taunting song.

64 [a]Repay them, O LORD,
According to the work of their hands.
65 Give them [1]a veiled heart;
Your curse *be* upon them!
66 In Your anger,
Pursue and destroy them
[a]From under the heavens of the [b]LORD.

## *Zion Degraded*

4 How the gold has become dim!
*How* changed the fine gold!
The stones of the sanctuary are [1]scattered
At the head of every street.

2 The precious sons of Zion,
[1]Valuable as fine gold,
How they are [2]regarded [a]as clay pots,
The work of the hands of the potter!

3 Even the jackals present their breasts
To nurse their young;
*But* the daughter of my people *is* cruel,
[a]Like ostriches in the wilderness.

4 The tongue of the infant clings
To the roof of its mouth for thirst;
[a]The young children ask for bread,
*But* no one breaks *it* for them.

5 Those who ate delicacies
Are desolate in the streets;
Those who were brought up in scarlet
[a]Embrace ash heaps.

6 The punishment of the iniquity
of the daughter of my people
Is greater than the punishment
of the [a]sin of Sodom,
Which was [b]overthrown in a moment,
With no hand to help her!

7 Her [1]Nazirites were [2]brighter than snow
And whiter than milk;
They were more ruddy in body than rubies,
*Like* sapphire in their [3]appearance.

8 *Now* their appearance is blacker than soot;
They go unrecognized in the streets;
[a]Their skin clings to their bones,
It has become as dry as wood.

9 *Those* slain by the sword are better off
Than *those* who die of hunger;
For these [a]pine away,
Stricken *for lack* of the fruits of the [b]field.

10 The hands of the [a]compassionate women
Have [1]cooked their [b]own children;
They became [c]food for them
In the destruction of the daughter
of my people.

11 The LORD has fulfilled His fury,
[a]He has poured out His fierce anger.
[b]He kindled a fire in Zion,
And it has devoured its foundations.

12 The kings of the earth,
And all inhabitants of the world,
Would not have believed
That the adversary and the enemy
Could [a]enter the gates of Jerusalem—

**13** [a]Because of the sins of her prophets
*And* the iniquities of her priests,
[b]Who shed in her midst
The blood of the just.

14 They wandered blind in the streets;
[a]They have defiled themselves with blood,
[b]So that no one would touch their garments.

**36** [a][Hab. 1:13]
**37** [a][Ps. 33:9–11]
**38** [a]Job 2:10
**39** [a]Prov. 19:3 [b]Mic. 7:9 [1]Or *murmur*
**41** [a]Ps. 86:4
**42** [a]Dan. 9:5
**45** [a]1 Cor. 4:13
**46** [a]Lam. 2:16
**47** [a]Is. 24:17, 18 [b]Is. 51:19
**48** [a]Jer. 4:19; 14:17
**49** [a]Jer. 14:17
**50** [a]Is. 63:15
**52** [a]Ps. 35:7, 19
**53** [a]Jer. 37:16 [b]Dan. 6:17 [1]LXX *put to death* [2]Lit. *a stone on*
**54** [a]Ps. 69:2 [b]Is. 38:10
**55** [a]Ps. 130:1 [b]Jer. 38:6–13
**56** [a]Ps. 3:4
**57** [a]James 4:8 [b]Is. 41:10, 14
**58** [a]Jer. 51:36 [b]Ps. 71:23
**59** [a]Ps. 9:4 [1]Lit. *my wrong*
**60** [a]Jer. 11:19
**63** [a]Ps. 139:2
**64** [a]Ps. 28:4
**65** [1]A Jewish tradition *sorrow of*
**66** [a]Deut. 25:19 [b]Ps. 8:3

CHAPTER 4
**1** [1]Lit. *poured out*
**2** [a]Is. 30:14 [1]Lit. *Weighed against* [2]*reckoned*
**3** [a]Job 39:14–17
**4** [a]Ps. 22:15
**5** [a]Job 24:8
**6** [a]Ezek. 16:48 [b]Gen. 19:25
**7** [1]Or *nobles* [2]Or *purer* [3]Lit. *polishing*
**8** [a]Ps. 102:5
**9** [a]Lev. 26:39 [b]Jer. 16:4
**10** [a]Lam. 2:20 [b]Is. 49:15 [c]Deut. 28:57 [1]*boiled*
**11** [a]Jer. 7:20 [b]Deut. 32:22
**12** [a]Jer. 21:13
**13** [a]Jer. 5:31 [b]Matt. 23:31
**14** [a]Jer. 2:34 [b]Num. 19:16

15 They cried out to them,
"Go away, [a]unclean!
Go away, go away,
Do not touch us!"
When they fled and wandered,
*Those* among the nations said,
"They shall no longer dwell *here.*"
16 The [1]face of the LORD scattered them;
He no longer regards them.
[a]*The people* do not respect the priests
Nor show favor to the elders.
17 Still [a]our eyes failed us,
*Watching* vainly for our help;
In our watching we watched
For a nation *that* could not save *us.*
18 [a]They [1]tracked our steps
So that we could not walk in our streets.
[b]Our end was near;
Our days were over,
For our end had come.
19 Our pursuers were [a]swifter
Than the eagles of the heavens.
They pursued us on the mountains
And lay in wait for us in the wilderness.
20 The [a]breath of our nostrils,
the anointed of the LORD,
[b]Was caught in their pits,
Of whom we said, "Under his shadow
We shall live among the nations."
**21** Rejoice and be glad, O daughter of [a]Edom,
*You* who dwell in the land of Uz!
[b]The cup shall also pass over to you
And you shall become drunk
and make yourself naked.
22 [a]*The punishment of* your iniquity
[1]is accomplished,
O daughter of Zion;
He will no longer send you into captivity.
[b]He will punish your iniquity,
O daughter of Edom;
He will uncover your sins!

### *Prayer for Restoration*

**5** Remember, [a]O LORD,
what has come upon us;
Look, and behold [b]our reproach!
2 [a]Our inheritance has been turned over to
aliens,
And our houses to foreigners.
3 We have become orphans and waifs,
Our mothers *are* like [a]widows.
4 We pay for the water we drink,
And our wood comes at a price.
5 [a]*They* pursue at our [1]heels;
We labor *and* have no rest.
6 [a]We have given our hand [b]*to* the Egyptians
*And* the [c]Assyrians,
to be satisfied with bread.
7 [a]Our fathers sinned *and are* no more,
But we bear their iniquities.
8 Servants rule over us;
*There is* none to deliver *us* from their hand.
9 We get our bread *at the risk* of our lives,
Because of the sword in the wilderness.
**10** Our skin is hot as an oven,
Because of the fever of famine.
11 They [a]ravished the women in Zion,
The maidens in the cities of Judah.
12 Princes were hung up by their hands,
And elders were not respected.
13 Young men [a]ground at the millstones;
Boys staggered under *loads of* wood.
14 The elders have ceased *gathering at* the gate,
And the young men from their [a]music.
15 The joy of our heart has ceased;
Our dance has turned into [a]mourning.
16 [a]The crown has fallen *from* our head.
Woe to us, for we have sinned!
17 Because of this our heart is faint;
[a]Because of these *things* our eyes grow dim;
18 Because of Mount Zion which is [a]desolate,
With foxes walking about on it.
**19** You, O LORD, [a]remain forever;
[b]Your throne from generation to generation.
20 [a]Why do You forget us forever,
*And* forsake us for so long a time?
21 [a]Turn us back to You, O LORD,
and we will be [1]restored;
Renew our days as of old,
22 Unless You have utterly rejected us,
*And* are very angry with us!

**15** [a]Lev. 13:45, 46
**16** [a]Lam. 5:12 [1]Tg. *anger*
**17** [a]2 Kin. 24:7
**18** [a]2 Kin. 25:4 [b]Ezek. 7:2, 3, 6; Amos 8:2 [1]Lit. *hunted*
**19** [a]Deut. 28:49
**20** [a]Gen. 2:7 [b]Jer. 52:9; Ezek. 12:13
**21** [a]Ps. 83:3–6 [b]Jer. 25:15; Obad. 10
**22** [a][Is. 40:2; Jer. 33:7, 8] [b]Ps. 137:7 [1]*has been completed*

CHAPTER 5
**1** [a]Ps. 89:50 [b]Ps. 79:4; Lam. 2:15
**2** [a]Ps. 79:1
**3** [a]Ex. 22:24; Jer. 15:8; 18:21
**5** [a]Deut. 28:48; Jer. 28:14 [1]Lit. *necks*
**6** [a]Gen. 24:2 [b]Hos. 9:3; 12:1 [c]Jer. 2:18; Hos. 5:13
**7** [a]Jer. 31:29
**11** [a]Is. 13:16; Zech. 14:2
**13** [a]Judg. 16:21
**14** [a]Is. 24:8; Jer. 7:34
**15** [a]Jer. 25:10; Amos 8:10
**16** [a]Job 19:9; Ps. 89:39; Jer. 13:18
**17** [a]Ps. 6:7
**18** [a]Is. 27:10
**19** [a]Ps. 9:7; Hab. 1:12 [b]Ps. 45:6
**20** [a]Ps. 13:1; 44:24
**21** [a]Ps. 80:3, 7, 19; Jer. 31:18 [1]*returned*

# *The Book of* EZEKIEL

### *Ezekiel's Vision of God's Glory*

NOW it came to pass in the thirtieth year, in
the fourth *month,* on the fifth *day* of the
month, as I *was* among the captives by
[a]the River Chebar, *that* [b]the heavens were opened
and I saw [c]visions[1] of God.
2 On the fifth *day* of the month, which *was* in
the fifth year of King Jehoiachin's captivity,
3 the word of the LORD came expressly to Ezekiel the priest, the son of Buzi, in the land of the
[1]Chaldeans by the River Chebar; and [a]the hand of
the LORD was upon him there.
4 Then I looked, and behold, [a]a whirlwind was
coming [b]out of the north, a great cloud with
raging fire engulfing itself; and brightness *was* all
around it and radiating out of its midst like the
color of amber, out of the midst of the fire.
5 [a]Also from within it *came* the likeness of four
living creatures. And [b]this *was* their appearance:
they had [c]the likeness of a man.
6 Each one had four faces, and each one had
four wings.

CHAPTER 1
**1** [a]Ezek. 3:15, 23; 10:15 [b]Rev. 4:1; 19:11 [c]Ezek. 8:3 [1]So with MT, LXX, Vg.; Syr., Tg. *a vision*
**3** [a]Ezek. 3:14, 22 [1]Or *Babylonians,* and so elsewhere in the book
**4** [a]Jer. 23:19; 25:32 [b]Jer. 1:14

**5** [a]Rev. 4:6–8 [b]Ezek. 10:8 [c]Ezek. 10:14

7 Their [1]legs *were* straight, and the soles of their
feet *were* like the soles of calves' feet. They
sparkled [a]like the color of burnished bronze.
8 [a]The hands of a man *were* under their wings
on their four sides; and each of the four had faces
and wings.
9 Their wings touched one another. *The creatures* did not turn when they went, but each one
went straight [a]forward.
10 As for [a]the likeness of their faces, *each* [b]had
the face of a man; each of the four had [c]the face of
a lion on the right side, [d]each of the four had the
face of an ox on the left side, [e]and each of the four
had the face of an eagle.
11 Thus *were* their faces. Their wings stretched
upward; two *wings* of each one touched one
another, and [a]two covered their bodies.
12 And [a]each one went straight forward; they
went wherever the spirit wanted to go, and they
did not turn when they went.
13 As for the likeness of the living creatures,
their appearance *was* like burning coals of fire,
[a]like the appearance of torches going back and
forth among the living creatures. The fire was
bright, and out of the fire went lightning.
14 And the living creatures ran back and forth,
[a]in appearance like a flash of lightning.
**15** Now as I looked at the living creatures, behold, [a]a wheel *was* on the earth beside each living
creature with its four faces.
16 [a]The appearance of the wheels and their work-
ings *was* [b]like the color of beryl, and all four had
the same likeness. The appearance of their work-
ings *was*, as it were, a wheel in the middle of a
wheel.
17 When they moved, they went toward any one
of four directions; they did not turn aside when
they went.
18 As for their rims, they were so high they were
awesome; and their rims *were* [a]full of eyes, all
around the four of them.
19 [a]When the living creatures went, the wheels
went beside them; and when the living creatures
were lifted up from the earth, the wheels were
lifted up.
20 Wherever the spirit wanted to go, they went,
*because* there the spirit went; and the wheels
were lifted together with them, [a]for the spirit of
the [1]living creatures *was* in the wheels.
21 When those went, *these* went; when those
stood, *these* stood; and when those were lifted up
from the earth, the wheels were lifted up together
with them, for the spirit of the [1]living creatures
*was* in the wheels.
**22** [a]The likeness of the [1]firmament above the
heads of the [2]living creatures *was* like the color of
an awesome [b]crystal, stretched out [c]over their
heads.
23 And under the firmament their wings *spread
out* straight, one toward another. Each one had
two which covered one side, and each one had
two which covered the other side of the body.
24 [a]When they went, I heard the noise of their
wings, [b]like the noise of many waters, like [c]the
voice of the Almighty, a tumult like the noise of
an army; and when they stood still, they let down
their wings.
25 A voice came from above the firmament that
*was* over their heads; whenever they stood, they
let down their wings.
**26** [a]And above the firmament over their heads
*was* the likeness of a throne, [b]in appearance like a
sapphire stone; on the likeness of the throne *was*
a likeness with the appearance of a man high
above [c]it.
27 Also from the appearance of His waist and
upward [a]I saw, as it were, the color of amber with
the appearance of fire all around within it; and
from the appearance of His waist and downward I
saw, as it were, the appearance of fire with brightness all around.
28 [a]Like the appearance of a rainbow in a cloud
on a rainy day, so *was* the appearance of the
brightness all around it. [b]This *was* the appearance
of the likeness of the glory of the LORD.
So when I saw *it*, [c]I fell on my face, and I
heard a voice of One speaking.

### *Ezekiel Called to Be a Prophet*

**2** And He said to me, "Son of man, [a]stand on
your feet, and I will speak to you."
2 Then [a]the Spirit entered me when He spoke to
me, and set me on my feet; and I heard Him who
spoke to me.
3 And He said to me: "Son of man, I am sending
you to the children of Israel, to a rebellious nation
that has [a]rebelled against Me; [b]they and their
fathers have transgressed against Me to this very
day.
4 [a]"For *they are* [1]impudent and stubborn children. I am sending you to them, and you shall say
to them, 'Thus says the Lord GOD.'
5 [a]"As for them, whether they hear or whether
they refuse—for they *are* a [b]rebellious house—yet
they [c]will know that a prophet has been among
them.
**6** "And you, son of man, [a]do not be afraid of
them nor be afraid of their words, though [b]briers
and thorns *are* with you and you dwell among
scorpions; [c]do not be afraid of their words or
dismayed by their looks, [d]though they *are* a
rebellious house.
7 [a]"You shall speak My words to them, whether
they hear or whether they refuse, for they *are*
rebellious.
8 "But you, son of man, hear what I say to you.
Do not be rebellious like that rebellious house;
open your mouth and [a]eat what I give you."
**9** Now when I looked, there was [a]a hand
stretched out to me; and behold, [b]a scroll of a
book *was* in it.
10 Then He spread it before me; and *there was*
writing on the inside and on the outside, and
written on it *were* lamentations and mourning
and woe.

### *The Responsibility of the Prophet*

**3** Moreover He said to me, "Son of man, eat
what you find; [a]eat this scroll, and go, speak to
the house of Israel."
2 So I opened my mouth, and He caused me to
eat that scroll.
3 And He said to me, "Son of man, feed your
belly, and fill your stomach with this scroll that I
give you." So I [a]ate, and it was in my mouth [b]like
honey in sweetness.
4 Then He said to me: "Son of man, go to the
house of Israel and speak with My words to them.
5 "For you *are* not sent to a people of unfamiliar
speech and of hard language, *but* to the house of
Israel,
6 "not to many people of unfamiliar speech and
of hard language, whose words you cannot under-

**7** [a]Dan. 10:6 [1]Lit. *feet*
**8** [a]Ezek. 10:8, 21
**9** [a]Ezek. 1:12; 10:20–22
**10** [a]Rev. 4:7 [b]Num. 2:10 [c]Num. 2:3 [d]Num. 2:18 [e]Num. 2:25
**11** [a]Is. 6:2
**12** [a]Ezek. 10:11, 22
**13** [a]Rev. 4:5
**14** [a][Matt. 24:27]
**15** [a]Ezek. 10:9
**16** [a]Ezek. 10:9, 10 [b]Dan. 10:6
**18** [a]Ezek. 10:12
**19** [a]Ezek. 10:16, 17
**20** [a]Ezek. 10:17 [1]Lit. *living creature;* LXX, Vg. *spirit of life;* Tg. *creatures*
**21** [1]See note at v. 20
**22** [a]Ezek. 10:1 [b]Rev. 4:6 [c]Ezek. 10:1 [1]Or *expanse* [2]So with LXX, Tg., Vg.; MT reads *living creature*
**24** [a]Ezek. 3:13; 10:5 [b]Rev. 1:15 [c]Job 37:4, 5
**26** [a]Ezek. 10:1 [b]Ex. 24:10, 16 [c]Ezek. 8:2
**27** [a]Ezek. 8:2
**28** [a]Rev. 4:3; 10:1 [b]Ezek. 3:23; 8:4 [c]Dan. 8:17

CHAPTER 2
**1** [a]Dan. 10:11
**2** [a]Ezek. 3:24
**3** [a]Ezek. 5:6; 20:8, 13, 18 [b]Jer. 3:25
**4** [a]Ezek. 3:7 [1]Lit. *stiff-faced and hard-hearted sons*
**5** [a]Ezek. 3:11, 26, 27 [b]Ezek. 3:26 [c]Ezek. 33:33
**6** [a]Jer. 1:8, 17 [b]Mic. 7:4 [c][1 Pet. 3:14] [d]Ezek. 3:9, 26, 27
**7** [a]Jer. 1:7, 17
**8** [a]Rev. 10:9
**9** [a][Ezek. 8:3] [b]Ezek. 3:1

CHAPTER 3
**1** [a]Ezek. 2:8, 9
**3** [a]Rev. 10:9 [b]Ps. 19:10; 119:103

stand. Surely, [a]had I sent you to them, they would
have listened to you.
7 "But the house of Israel will not listen to you,
[a]because they will not listen to Me; [b]for all the
house of Israel *are* [1]impudent and hard-hearted.
8 "Behold, I have made your face strong against
their faces, and your forehead strong against their
foreheads.
9 [a]"Like adamant stone, harder than flint, I have
made your forehead; [b]do not be afraid of them,
nor be dismayed at their looks, though they *are* a
rebellious house."
10 Moreover He said to me: "Son of man, receive
into your heart all My words that I speak to you,
and hear with your ears.
11 "And go, get to the captives, to the children of
your people, and speak to them and tell them,
[a]'Thus says the Lord GOD,' whether they hear, or
whether they refuse."
**12** Then [a]the Spirit lifted me up, and I heard
behind me a great thunderous voice: "Blessed *is*
the [b]glory of the LORD from His place!"
13 *I* also *heard* the [a]noise of the wings of the
living creatures that touched one another, and the
noise of the wheels beside them, and a great
thunderous noise.
14 So the Spirit lifted me up and took me away,
and I went in bitterness, in the [1]heat of my spirit;
but [a]the hand of the LORD was strong upon me.
15 Then I came to the captives at Tel Abib, who
dwelt by the River Chebar; and [a]I sat where they
sat, and remained there astonished among them
seven days.
**16** Now it [a]came to pass at the end of seven days
that the word of the LORD came to me, saying,
17 [a]"Son of man, I have made you [b]a watchman
for the house of Israel; therefore hear a word from
My mouth, and give them [c]warning from Me:
18 "When I say to the wicked, 'You shall surely
die,' and you give him no warning, nor speak to
warn the wicked from his wicked way, to save his
life, that same wicked *man* [a]shall die in his iniquity; but his blood I will require at your hand.
19 "Yet, if you warn the wicked, and he does not
turn from his wickedness, nor from his wicked
way, he shall die in his iniquity; [a]but you have
delivered your soul.
20 "Again, when a [a]righteous *man* turns from his
righteousness and commits iniquity, and I lay a
stumbling block before him, he shall die; because
you did not give him warning, he shall die in his
sin, and his righteousness which he has done shall
not be remembered; but his blood I will require at
your hand.
21 "Nevertheless if you warn the righteous *man*
that the righteous should not sin, and he does not
sin, he shall surely live because he took warning;
also you will have delivered your soul."
**22** [a]Then the hand of the LORD was upon me
there, and He said to me, "Arise, go out [b]into the
plain, and there I shall talk with you."
23 So I arose and went out into the plain, and
behold, [a]the glory of the LORD stood there, like the
glory which I [b]saw by the River Chebar; [c]and I fell
on my face.
24 Then [a]the Spirit entered me and set me on my
feet, and spoke with me and said to me: "Go, shut
yourself inside your house.
25 "And you, O son of man, surely [a]they will put
ropes on you and bind you with them, so that you
cannot go out among them.
26 [a]"I will make your tongue cling to the roof of
your mouth, so that you shall be mute and [b]not be
[1]one to rebuke them, [c]for they *are* a rebellious
house.
27 [a]"But when I speak with you, I will open your
mouth, and you shall say to them, [b]'Thus says the
Lord GOD.' He who hears, let him hear; and he
who refuses, let him refuse; for they *are* a rebellious house.

### *The Siege of Jerusalem Illustrated*

**4** "You also, son of man, take a clay tablet and
lay it before you, and portray on it a city,
Jerusalem.
2 [a]"Lay siege against it, build a siege wall
against it, and heap up a [b]mound against it; set
camps against it also, and place battering rams
against it all around.
3 "Moreover take for yourself an iron plate, and
set it *as* an iron wall between you and the city. Set
your face against it, and it shall be [a]besieged, and
you shall lay siege against it. [b]This *will be* a sign to
the house of Israel.
4 "Lie also on your left side, and lay the iniquity
of the house of Israel upon it. *According* to the
number of the days that you lie on it, you shall
bear their iniquity.
5 "For I have laid on you the years of their
iniquity, according to the number of the days,
three hundred and ninety days; [a]so you shall bear
the iniquity of the house of Israel.
6 "And when you have completed them, lie
again on your right side; then you shall bear the
iniquity of the house of Judah forty days. I have
laid on you a day for each year.
7 "Therefore you shall set your face toward the
siege of Jerusalem; your arm *shall be* uncovered,
and you shall prophesy against it.
8 [a]"And surely I will [1]restrain you so that you
cannot turn from one side to another till you have
ended the days of your siege.
**9** "Also take for yourself wheat, barley, beans,
lentils, millet, and spelt; put them into one vessel,
and make bread of them for yourself. *During* the
number of days that you lie on your side, three
hundred and ninety days, you shall eat it.
10 "And your food which you eat *shall be* by
weight, twenty shekels a day; from time to time
you shall eat it.
11 "You shall also drink water by measure, one-
sixth of a hin; from time to time you shall drink.
12 "And you shall eat it *as* barley cakes; and bake
it using fuel of human waste in their sight."
13 Then the LORD said, "So [a]shall the children of
Israel eat their defiled bread among the Gentiles,
where I will drive them."
14 So I said, [a]"Ah, Lord GOD! Indeed I have never
defiled myself from my youth till now; I have
never eaten [b]what died of itself or was torn by
beasts, nor has [c]abominable[1] flesh ever come into
my mouth."
15 Then He said to me, "See, I am giving you cow
dung instead of human waste, and you shall
prepare your bread over it."
16 Moreover He said to me, "Son of man, surely I
will cut off the [a]supply of bread in Jerusalem; they
shall [b]eat bread by weight and with anxiety, and
shall [c]drink water by measure and with dread,
17 "that they may lack bread and water, and be
dismayed with one another, and [a]waste away
because of their iniquity.

**6** [a]Matt. 11:21
**7** [a]John 15:20, 21 [b]Ezek. 2:4 [1]Lit. *strong of forehead*
**9** [a]Mic. 3:8 [b]Jer. 1:8, 17
**11** [a]Ezek. 2:5, 7
**12** [a]Acts 8:39 [b]Ezek. 1:28; 8:4
**13** [a]Ezek. 1:24; 10:5
**14** [a]2 Kin. 3:15 [1]Or *anger*
**15** [a]Job 2:13
**16** [a]Jer. 42:7
**17** [a]Ezek. 33:7–9 [b]Jer. 6:17 [c][Lev. 19:17]
**18** [a][John 8:21, 24]
**19** [a]Acts 18:6; 20:26
**20** [a]Ezek. 18:24; 33:18
**22** [a]Ezek. 1:3 [b]Ezek. 8:4
**23** [a]Ezek. 1:28 [b]Ezek. 1:1 [c]Ezek. 1:28
**24** [a]Ezek. 2:2
**25** [a]Ezek. 4:8
**26** [a]Luke 1:20, 22 [b]Hos. 4:17 [c]Ezek. 2:5–7 [1]Lit. *one who rebukes*
**27** [a]Ezek. 24:27; 33:22 [b]Ezek. 3:11

CHAPTER 4
**2** [a]Jer. 6:6 [b]2 Kin. 25:1
**3** [a]Jer. 39:1, 2 [b]Ezek. 12:6, 11; 24:24, 27
**5** [a]Num. 14:34
**8** [a]Ezek. 3:25 [1]Lit. *put ropes on*
**13** [a]Hos. 9:3
**14** [a]Acts 10:14 [b]Lev. 17:15; 22:8 [c]Deut. 14:3 [1]Ritually unclean flesh, Lev. 7:18
**16** [a]Is. 3:1 [b]Ezek. 4:10, 11; 12:19 [c]Ezek. 4:11
**17** [a]Lev. 26:39

### *A Sword Against Jerusalem*

**5** "And you, son of man, take a sharp sword,
take it as a barber's razor, [a]and pass *it* over
your head and your beard; then take scales to
weigh and divide the hair.
2 [a]"You shall burn with fire one-third in the
midst of [b]the city, when [c]the days of the siege are
finished; then you shall take one-third and strike
around *it* with the sword, and one-third you shall
scatter in the wind: I will draw out a sword after
[d]them.
3 [a]"You shall also take a small number of them
and bind them in the edge of your *garment.*
4 "Then take some of them again and [a]throw
them into the midst of the fire, and burn them in
the fire. From there a fire will go out into all the
house of Israel.
5 "Thus says the Lord GOD: 'This *is* Jerusalem; I
have set her in the midst of the nations and the
countries all around her.
6 'She has rebelled against My judgments by
doing wickedness more than the nations, and
against My statutes more than the countries that
*are* all around her; for they have refused My
judgments, and they have not walked in My
statutes.'
7 "Therefore thus says the Lord GOD: 'Because
you have [1]multiplied *disobedience* more than the
nations that *are* all around you, have not walked
in My statutes [a]nor kept My judgments, [2]nor even
done according to the judgments of the nations
that *are* all around you'—
8 "therefore thus says the Lord GOD: 'Indeed I,
even I, *am* against you and will execute judgments in your midst in the sight of the nations.
9 [a]'And I will do among you what I have never
done, and the like of which I will never do again,
because of all your abominations.
10 'Therefore fathers [a]shall eat *their* sons in your
midst, and sons shall eat their fathers; and I will
execute judgments among you, and all of you who
remain I will [b]scatter to all the winds.
11 'Therefore, *as* I live,' says the Lord GOD,
'surely, because you have [a]defiled My sanctuary
with all your [b]detestable things and with all your
abominations, therefore I will also diminish *you;*
[c]My eye will not spare, nor will I have any pity.
12 [a]'One-third of you shall die of the pestilence,
and be consumed with famine in your midst; and
one-third shall fall by the sword all around you;
and [b]I will scatter another third to all the winds,
and I will draw out a sword after [c]them.
13 'Thus shall My anger [a]be spent, and I will
[b]cause My fury to rest upon them, [c]and I will be
avenged; [d]and they shall know that I, the LORD,
have spoken *it* in My zeal, when I have spent My
fury upon them.
14 'Moreover [a]I will make you a waste and a
reproach among the nations that *are* all around
you, in the sight of all who pass by.
15 'So [1]it shall be a [a]reproach, a taunt, a [b]lesson,
and an astonishment to the nations that *are* all
around you, when I execute judgments among
you in anger and in fury and in [c]furious rebukes. I,
the LORD, have spoken.
16 'When I [a]send against them the terrible arrows
of famine which shall be for destruction, which I
will send to destroy you, I will increase the famine
upon you and cut off your [b]supply of bread.
17 'So I will send against you famine and [a]wild
beasts, and they will bereave you. [b]Pestilence and
blood shall pass through you, and I will bring the
sword against you. I, the LORD, have spoken.' "

### *Judgment on Israel's Idolatry*

**6** Now the word of the LORD came to me, saying:
2 "Son of man, [a]set your face toward the
[b]mountains of Israel, and prophesy against them,
3 "and say, 'O mountains of Israel, hear the
word of the Lord GOD! Thus says the Lord GOD to
the mountains, to the hills, to the ravines, and to
the valleys: "Indeed I, *even* I, will bring a sword
against you, and [a]I will destroy your [1]high places.
4 "Then your altars shall be desolate, your
incense altars shall be broken, and [a]I will cast
down your slain *men* before your idols.
5 "And I will lay the corpses of the children of
Israel before their idols, and I will scatter your
bones all around your altars.
6 "In all your dwelling places the cities shall be
laid waste, and the [1]high places shall be desolate,
so that your altars may be laid waste and made
desolate, your idols may be broken and made to
cease, your incense altars may be cut down, and
your works may be abolished.
7 "The slain shall fall in your midst, and [a]you
shall know that I *am* the LORD.
8 [a]"Yet I will leave a remnant, so that you may
have *some* who escape the sword among the
nations, when you are [b]scattered through the
countries.
9 "Then those of you who escape will [a]remem-
ber Me among the nations where they are carried
captive, because [b]I was crushed by their adulterous heart which has departed from Me, and [c]by
their eyes which play the harlot after their idols;
[d]they will loathe themselves for the evils which
they committed in all their abominations.
10 "And they shall know that I *am* the LORD; I
have not said in vain that I would bring this
calamity upon them."
11 'Thus says the Lord GOD: [a]"Pound[1] your fists
and stamp your feet, and say, 'Alas, for all the evil
abominations of the house of Israel! [b]For they
shall fall by the sword, by famine, and by pestilence.
12 'He who is far off shall die by the pestilence, he
who is near shall fall by the sword, and he who
remains and is besieged shall die by the famine.
[a]Thus will I spend My fury upon them.
13 'Then you shall know that I *am* the LORD,
when their slain are among their idols all around
their altars, [a]on every high hill, [b]on all the mountaintops, [c]under every green tree, and under every
thick oak, wherever they offered sweet incense to
all their idols.
14 'So I will [a]stretch out My hand against them
and make the land desolate, yes, more desolate
than the wilderness toward [b]Diblah, in all their
dwelling places. Then they shall know that I *am*
the LORD.' " ' "

### *Judgment on Israel Is Near*

**7** Moreover the word of the LORD came to me,
saying,
2 "And you, son of man, thus says the Lord GOD
to the land of Israel:

[a]'An end! The end has come
upon the four corners of the land.
3 Now the end *has come* upon you,
And I will send My anger against you;

CHAPTER 5
1 [a]Is. 7:20
2 [a]Ezek. 5:12 [b]Ezek. 4:1 [c]Ezek. 4:8, 9 [d]Lev. 26:25
3 [a]Jer. 40:6; 52:16
4 [a]Jer. 41:1, 2; 44:14
7 [a]Jer. 2:10, 11 [1]Or *raged* [2]So with MT, LXX, Tg., Vg.; many Heb. mss., Syr. *but have done* (cf. 11:12)
9 [a][Amos 3:2]
10 [a]Jer. 19:9 [b]Zech. 2:6; 7:14
11 [a][Jer. 7:9–11] [b]Ezek. 11:21 [c]Ezek. 7:4, 9; 8:18; 9:10
12 [a]Ezek. 6:12 [b]Jer. 9:16 [c]Jer. 43:10, 11; 44:27
13 [a]Lam. 4:11 [b]Ezek. 21:17 [c]Is. 1:24 [d]Ezek. 36:6; 38:19
14 [a]Lev. 26:31
15 [a]Jer. 24:9 [b][Is. 26:9] [c]Ezek. 5:8; 25:17 [1]LXX, [Syr.], Tg., Vg. *you*
16 [a]Deut. 32:23 [b]Lev. 26:26
17 [a]Lev. 26:22 [b]Ezek. 38:22

CHAPTER 6
2 [a]Ezek. 20:46; 21:2; 25:2 [b]Ezek. 36:1
3 [a]Lev. 26:30 [1]Places for pagan worship
4 [a]Lev. 26:30
6 [1]Places for pagan worship
7 [a]Ezek. 7:4, 9
8 [a]Jer. 44:28 [b]Ezek. 5:12
9 [a][Deut. 4:29] [b]Ps. 78:40 [c]Ezek. 20:7, 24 [d]Ezek. 20:43; 36:31
11 [a]Ezek. 21:14 [b]Ezek. 5:12 [1]Lit. *Strike your hands*
12 [a]Ezek. 5:13
13 [a]Jer. 2:20; 3:6 [b]Hos. 4:13 [c]Is. 57:5
14 [a]Is. 5:25 [b]Num. 33:46

CHAPTER 7
2 [a]Amos 8:2, 10

I will judge you [a]according to your ways,
And I will repay you
for all your abominations.
4 [a]My eye will not spare you,
Nor will I have pity;
But I will repay your ways,
And your abominations will be in your midst;
[b]Then you shall know that I *am* the LORD!'

5 "Thus says the Lord GOD:

'A disaster, a singular [a]disaster;
Behold, it has come!
6 An end has come,
The end has come;
It has dawned for you;
Behold, it has come!
7 [a]Doom has come to you,
you who dwell in the land;
[b]The time has come,
A day of trouble *is* near,
And not of rejoicing in the mountains.
8 Now upon you I will soon [a]pour out My fury,
And spend My anger upon you;
I will judge you according to your ways,
And I will repay you
for all your abominations.

9 'My eye shall not spare,
Nor will I have pity;
I will [1]repay you according to your ways,
And your abominations will be in your midst.
Then you shall know
that I *am* the LORD who strikes.

10 'Behold, the day!
Behold, it has come!
[a]Doom has gone out;
The rod has blossomed,
Pride has budded.
11 [a]Violence has risen up
into a rod of wickedness;
None of them *shall remain,*
None of their multitude,
None of [1]them;
[b]Nor *shall there be* wailing for them.
12 The time has come,
The day draws near.

'Let not the buyer [a]rejoice,
Nor the seller [b]mourn,
For wrath *is* on their whole multitude.
13 For the seller shall not return
to what has been sold,
Though he may still be alive;
For the vision concerns the whole multitude,
And it shall not turn back;
No one will strengthen himself
Who lives in iniquity.

14 'They have blown the trumpet
and made everyone ready,
But no one goes to battle;
For My wrath *is* on all their multitude.
15 [a]The sword *is* outside,
And the pestilence and famine within.
Whoever *is* in the field
Will die by the sword;
And whoever *is* in the city,
Famine and pestilence will devour him.

16 'Those who [a]survive will escape
and be on the mountains
Like doves of the valleys,
All of them mourning,
Each for his iniquity.
17 Every [a]hand will be feeble,
And every knee will be *as* weak *as* water.
18 They will also [a]be girded with sackcloth;
Horror will cover them;
Shame *will be* on every face,
Baldness on all their heads.

19 'They will throw their silver into the streets,
And their gold will be like refuse;
Their [a]silver and their gold
will not be able to deliver them
In the day of the wrath of the LORD;
They will not satisfy their souls,
Nor fill their stomachs,
Because it became their stumbling block of
iniquity.

20 'As for the beauty of his ornaments,
He set it in majesty;
[a]But they made from it
The images of their abominations—
Their detestable things;
Therefore I have made it
Like refuse to them.
21 I will give it as [a]plunder
Into the hands of strangers,
And to the wicked of the earth as spoil;
And they shall defile it.
22 I will turn My face from them,
And they will defile My secret place;
For robbers shall enter it and defile it.

23 'Make a chain,
For [a]the land is filled with crimes of blood,
And the city is full of violence.
24 Therefore I will bring the [a]worst of the
Gentiles,
And they will possess their houses;
I will cause the pomp of the strong to cease,
And their holy places shall be [b]defiled.
25 [1]Destruction comes;
They will seek peace,
but *there shall be* none.
26 [a]Disaster will come upon disaster,
And rumor will be upon rumor.
[b]Then they will seek a vision from a prophet;
But the law will perish from the priest,
And counsel from the elders.

27 'The king will mourn,
The prince will be clothed with desolation,
And the hands of the common people will
tremble.
I will do to them according to their way,
And according to what they deserve
I will judge them;
Then they shall know that I *am* the LORD!' "

### *A Vision of Evil in the Temple*

8 And it came to pass in the sixth year, in the
sixth *month,* on the fifth *day* of the month, as
I sat in my house with [a]the elders of Judah sitting
before me, that [b]the hand of the Lord GOD fell
upon me there.
2 [a]Then I looked, and there was a likeness, like
the appearance of fire—from the appearance of
His waist and downward, fire; and from His waist
and upward, like the appearance of brightness,
[b]like the color of amber.
3 He [a]stretched out the form of a hand, and took
me by a lock of my hair; and [b]the Spirit lifted me

3 [a][Rom. 2:6]
4 [a]Ezek. 5:11 [b]Ezek. 12:20
5 [a]2 Kin. 21:12, 13; Nah. 1:9
7 [a]Ezek. 7:10 [b]Zeph. 1:14, 15
8 [a]Ezek. 20:8, 21
9 [1]Lit. *give*
10 [a]Ezek. 7:7
11 [a]Jer. 6:7 [b]Jer. 16:5, 6; Ezek. 24:16, 22 [1]Or *their wealth*
12 [a]Prov. 20:14; 1 Cor. 7:30 [b]Is. 24:2
15 [a]Deut. 32:25; Jer. 14:18; Lam. 1:20; Ezek. 5:12
16 [a]Ezra 9:15; Is. 37:31; Ezek. 6:8; 14:22
17 [a]Is. 13:7; Jer. 6:24; Ezek. 21:7; Heb. 12:12
18 [a]Is. 3:24; 15:2, 3; Jer. 48:37; Ezek. 27:31; Amos 8:10
19 [a]Prov. 11:4; Jer. 15:13; Zeph. 1:18
20 [a]Jer. 7:30
21 [a]2 Kin. 24:13; Jer. 20:5
23 [a]2 Kin. 21:16
24 [a]Ezek. 21:31; 28:7 [b]2 Chr. 7:20; Ezek. 24:21
25 [1]Lit. *Shuddering*
26 [a]Deut. 32:23; Is. 47:11; Jer. 4:20 [b]Ps. 74:9; Lam. 2:9; Ezek. 20:1, 3; Mic. 3:6

CHAPTER 8
1 [a]Ezek. 14:1; 20:1; 33:31 [b]Ezek. 1:3; 3:22
2 [a]Ezek. 1:26, 27 [b]Ezek. 1:4, 27
3 [a]Dan. 5:5 [b]Ezek. 3:14; Acts 8:39

up between earth and heaven, and [c]brought me in
visions of God to Jerusalem, to the door of the
north gate of the inner *court,* [d]where the seat of
the image of jealousy *was,* which [e]provokes[1] to
jealousy.
4 And behold, the [a]glory of the God of Israel
*was* there, like the vision that I [b]saw in the plain.
**5** Then He said to me, "Son of man, lift your
eyes now toward the north." So I lifted my eyes
toward the north, and there, north of the altar
gate, was this image of jealousy in the entrance.
6 Furthermore He said to me, "Son of man, do
you see what they are doing, the great [a]abomina-
tions that the house of Israel commits here, to
make Me go far away from My sanctuary? Now
turn again, you will see greater abominations."
**7** So He brought me to the door of the court;
and when I looked, there was a hole in the wall.
8 Then He said to me, "Son of man, dig into the
wall"; and when I dug into the wall, there was a
door.
9 And He said to me, "Go in, and see the wicked
abominations which they are doing there."
10 So I went in and saw, and there—every [a]sort
of [b]creeping thing, abominable beasts, and all the
idols of the house of Israel, [1]portrayed all around
on the walls.
11 And there stood before them [a]seventy men of
the elders of the house of Israel, and in their midst
stood Jaazaniah the son of Shaphan. Each man
had a censer in his hand, and a thick cloud of
incense went up.
12 Then He said to me, "Son of man, have you
seen what the elders of the house of Israel do in
the dark, every man in the room of his idols? For
they say, [a]'The LORD does not see us, the LORD has
forsaken the land.' "
**13** And He said to me, "Turn again, *and* you will
see greater abominations that they are doing."
14 So He brought me to the door of the north
gate of the LORD's house; and to my dismay,
women were sitting there weeping for [1]Tammuz.
**15** Then He said to me, "Have you seen *this,* O
son of man? Turn again, you will see greater
abominations than these."
16 So He brought me into the inner court of the
LORD's house; and there, at the door of the temple
of the LORD, [a]between the porch and the altar,
[b]*were* about twenty-five men [c]with their backs
toward the temple of the LORD and their faces
toward the east, and they were worshiping [d]the
sun toward the east.
**17** And He said to me, "Have you seen *this,* O son
of man? Is it a trivial thing to the house of Judah
to commit the abominations which they commit
here? For they have [a]filled the land with violence;
then they have returned to provoke Me to anger.
Indeed they put the branch to their nose.
18 [a]"Therefore I also will act in fury. My [b]eye will
not spare nor will I have pity; and though they
[c]cry in My ears with a loud voice, I will not hear
them."

### *Vision of the Slaughter of the Guilty*

**9** Then He called out in my hearing with a loud
voice, saying, "Let those who have charge
over the city draw near, each *with* a [1]deadly
weapon in his hand."
2 And suddenly six men came from the direction
of the upper gate, which faces north, each with his
[1]battle-ax in his hand. [a]One man among them *was*
clothed with linen and had a writer's inkhorn [2]at
his side. They went in and stood beside the bronze
altar.
**3** Now [a]the glory of the God of Israel had gone
up from the cherub, where it had been, to the
threshold of the [1]temple. And He called to the man
clothed with linen, who *had* the writer's inkhorn
at his side;
4 and the LORD said to him, "Go through the
midst of the city, through the midst of Jerusalem,
and put [a]a mark on the foreheads of the men [b]who
sigh and cry over all the abominations that are
done within it."
5 To the others He said in my [1]hearing, "Go
after him through the city and [a]kill;[2] [b]do not let
your eye spare, nor have any pity.
6 [a]"Utterly[1] slay old *and* young men, maidens
and little children and women; but [b]do not come
near anyone on whom *is* the mark; and [c]begin at
My sanctuary." [d]So they began with the elders
who *were* before the [2]temple.
7 Then He said to them, "Defile the [1]temple, and
fill the courts with the slain. Go out!" And they
went out and killed in the city.
**8** So it was, that while they were killing them, I
was left *alone;* and I [a]fell on my face and cried out,
and said, [b]"Ah, Lord GOD! Will You destroy all the
remnant of Israel in pouring out Your fury on
Jerusalem?"
9 Then He said to me, "The iniquity of the house
of Israel and Judah *is* exceedingly great, and [a]the
land is full of bloodshed, and the city full of
perversity; for they say, [b]'The LORD has forsaken
the land, and [c]the LORD does not see!'
10 "And as for Me also, My [a]eye will neither
spare, nor will I have pity, *but* [b]I will recompense
their deeds on their own head."
11 Just then, the man clothed with linen, who
*had* the inkhorn at his side, reported back and
said, "I have done as You commanded me."

### *God's Glory Departs from the Temple*

**10** And I looked, and there in the [a]firmament[1]
that was above the head of the cherubim,
there appeared something like a sapphire stone,
having the appearance of the likeness of a throne.
2 [a]Then He spoke to the man clothed with linen,
and said, "Go in among the wheels, under the
cherub, fill your hands with [b]coals of fire from
among the cherubim, and [c]scatter *them* over the
city." And he went in as I watched.
**3** Now the cherubim were standing on the
[1]south side of the [2]temple when the man went in,
and the [a]cloud filled the inner court.
4 [a]Then the glory of the LORD went up from the
cherub, *and paused* over the threshold of the
[1]temple; and [b]the house was filled with the cloud,
and the court was full of the brightness of the
LORD's [c]glory.
5 And the [a]sound of the wings of the cherubim
was heard *even* in the outer court, like [b]the voice
of Almighty God when He speaks.
**6** Then it happened, when He commanded the
man clothed in linen, saying, "Take fire from
among the wheels, from among the cherubim,"
that he went in and stood beside the wheels.
7 And the cherub stretched out his hand from
among the cherubim to the fire that *was* among
the cherubim, and took *some of it* and put *it* into

---

3 [c]Ezek. 11:1, 24; 40:2 [d]Ezek. 5:11 [e]Deut. 32:16, 21 [1]Arouses the LORD's jealousy
4 [a]Ezek. 3:12; 9:3 [b]Ezek. 1:28; 3:22, 23
6 [a]2 Kin. 23:4, 5
10 [a]Ex. 20:4 [b]Rom. 1:23 [1]Or *carved*
11 [a]Num. 11:16, 25
12 [a]Ezek. 9:9
14 [1]A Sumerian fertility god similar to the Gr. god Adonis
16 [a]Joel 2:17 [b]Ezek. 11:1 [c]Jer. 2:27; 32:33 [d]Deut. 4:19
17 [a]Ezek. 9:9
18 [a]Ezek. 5:13; 16:42; 24:13 [b]Ezek. 5:11; 7:4, 9; 9:5, 10 [c]Mic. 3:4

CHAPTER 9
1 [1]Or *destroying*
2 [a]Lev. 16:4 [1]Lit. *shattering weapon* [2]Lit. *upon his loins*
3 [a]Ezek. 3:23; 8:4; 10:4, 18; 11:22, 23 [1]Lit. *house*
4 [a]Rev. 7:2, 3; 9:4; 14:1 [b]Jer. 13:17
5 [a]Ezek. 7:9 [b]Ezek. 5:11 [1]Lit. *ears* [2]Lit. *strike*
6 [a]2 Chr. 36:17 [b]Rev. 9:4 [c]Jer. 25:29 [d]Ezek. 8:11, 12, 16 [1]Lit. *Slay to destruction* [2]Lit. *house*
7 [1]Lit. *house*
8 [a]Josh. 7:6 [b]Ezek. 11:13
9 [a]2 Kin. 21:16 [b]Ezek. 8:12 [c]Is. 29:15
10 [a]Ezek. 5:11; 7:4; 8:18 [b]Ezek. 11:21

CHAPTER 10
1 [a]Ezek. 1:22, 26 [1]*expanse*
2 [a]Dan. 10:5 [b]Ezek. 1:13 [c]Rev. 8:5
3 [a]1 Kin. 8:10, 11 [1]Lit. *right* [2]Lit. *house*
4 [a]Ezek. 1:28 [b]Ezek. 43:5 [c]Ezek. 11:22, 23 [1]Lit. *house*
5 [a]Ezek. 1:24 [b][Ps. 29:3]

the hands of the *man* clothed with linen, who took
*it* and went out.
8 [a]The cherubim appeared to have the form of a
man's hand under their wings.
**9** [a]And when I looked, there were four wheels
by the cherubim, one wheel by one cherub and
another wheel by each other cherub; the wheels
appeared *to have* the color of a [b]beryl stone.
10 *As for* their appearance, all four looked alike—
as it were, a wheel in the middle of a wheel.
11 [a]When they went, they went toward *any of*
their four directions; they did not turn aside when
they went, but followed in the direction the head
was facing. They did not turn aside when they
went.
12 And their whole body, with their back, their
hands, their wings, and the wheels that the four
had, *were* [a]full of eyes all around.
13 As for the wheels, they were called in my
[1]hearing, "Wheel."
14 [a]Each one had four faces: the first face *was*
the face of a cherub, the second face the face of a
man, the third the face of a lion, and the fourth
the face of an eagle.
**15** And the cherubim were lifted up. This *was*
[a]the living creature I saw by the River Chebar.
16 [a]When the cherubim went, the wheels went
beside them; and when the cherubim lifted their
wings to mount up from the earth, the same
wheels also did not turn from beside them.
17 [a]When [1]*the cherubim* stood still, *the wheels*
stood still, and when *one* was lifted up, *the other*
lifted itself up, for the spirit of the living creature
*was* in them.
**18** Then [a]the glory of the LORD [b]departed from
the threshold of the [1]temple and stood over the
cherubim.
19 And [a]the cherubim lifted their wings and
mounted up from the earth in my sight. When
they went out, the wheels *were* beside them; and
they stood at the door of the [b]east gate of the
LORD's house, and the glory of the God of Israel
*was* above them.
**20** [a]This *is* the living creature I saw under the
God of Israel [b]by the River Chebar, and I knew
they *were* cherubim.
21 [a]Each one had four faces and each one four
wings, and the likeness of the hands of a man *was*
under their wings.
22 And [a]the likeness of their faces *was* the same
*as* the faces which I had seen by the River Chebar,
their appearance and their persons. [b]They each
went straight forward.

### *God Will Restore Israel*

**11** Then [a]the Spirit lifted me up and brought
me to [b]the East Gate of the LORD's house,
which faces eastward; and there [c]at the door of
the gate were twenty-five men, among whom I
saw Jaazaniah the son of Azzur, and Pelatiah the
son of Benaiah, princes of the people.
2 And He said to me: "Son of man, these *are* the
men who devise iniquity and give wicked [1]counsel
in this city,
3 "who say, '*The time is* not [a]near to build
houses; [b]this *city is* the [1]caldron, and we *are* the
meat.'
4 "Therefore prophesy against them, prophesy,
O son of man!"
**5** Then [a]the Spirit of the LORD fell upon me, and
said to me, "Speak! 'Thus says the LORD: "Thus
you have said, O house of Israel; for [b]I know the
things that come into your mind.
6 [a]"You have multiplied your slain in this city,
and you have filled its streets with the slain."
7 'Therefore thus says the Lord GOD: [a]"Your
slain whom you have laid in its midst, they *are* the
meat, and this *city is* the caldron; [b]but I shall bring
you out of the midst of it.
8 "You have [a]feared the sword; and I will bring
a sword upon you," says the Lord GOD.
9 "And I will bring you out of its midst, and
deliver you into the hands of strangers, and
[a]execute judgments on you.
10 [a]"You shall fall by the sword. I will judge you
at [b]the border of Israel. [c]Then you shall know that
I *am* the LORD.
11 [a]"This *city* shall not be your [1]caldron, nor shall
you be the meat in its midst. I will judge you at
the border of Israel.
12 "And you shall know that I *am* the LORD; for
you have not walked in My statutes nor executed
My judgments, but [a]have done according to the
customs of the Gentiles which *are* all around
you." ' "
**13** Now it happened, while I was prophesying,
that [a]Pelatiah the son of Benaiah died. Then [b]I fell
on my face and cried with a loud voice, and said,
"Ah, Lord GOD! Will You make a complete end of
the remnant of Israel?"
**14** Again the word of the LORD came to me,
saying,
15 "Son of man, your brethren, your relatives,
your countrymen, and all the house of Israel in its
entirety, *are* those about whom the inhabitants of
Jerusalem have said, 'Get far away from the LORD;
this land has been given to us as a possession.'
16 "Therefore say, 'Thus says the Lord GOD:
"Although I have cast them far off among the
Gentiles, and although I have scattered them
among the countries, [a]yet I shall be a little [1]sanc-
tuary for them in the countries where they have
gone." '
17 "Therefore say, 'Thus says the Lord GOD: [a]"I
will gather you from the peoples, assemble you
from the countries where you have been scattered, and I will give you the land of Israel." '
18 "And they will go there, and they will take
away all its [a]detestable things and all its abominations from there.
19 "Then [a]I will give them one heart, and I will
put [b]a new spirit within [1]them, and take [c]the stony
heart out of their flesh, and give them a heart of
flesh,
20 [a]"that they may walk in My statutes and keep
My judgments and do them; [b]and they shall be My
people, and I will be their God.
21 "But *as for those* whose hearts follow the
desire for their detestable things and their abominations, [a]I will recompense their deeds on their
own heads," says the Lord GOD.
**22** So the cherubim [a]lifted up their wings, with
the wheels beside them, and the glory of the God
of Israel *was* high above them.
23 And [a]the glory of the LORD went up from the
midst of the city and stood [b]on the mountain,
[c]which *is* on the east side of the city.
**24** Then [a]the Spirit took me up and brought me in
a vision by the Spirit of God into [1]Chaldea, to
those in captivity. And the vision that I had seen
went up from me.
25 So I spoke to those in captivity of all the
things the LORD had shown me.

8 [a]Ezek. 1:8; 10:21
9 [a]Ezek. 1:15 [b]Ezek. 1:16
11 [a]Ezek. 1:17
12 [a]Rev. 4:6, 8
13 [1]Lit. *ears*
14 [a]Ezek. 1:6, 10, 11
15 [a]Ezek. 1:3, 5
16 [a]Ezek. 1:19
17 [a]Ezek. 1:12, 20, 21 [1]Lit. *they* [2]Lit. *they were* [3]Lit. *they lifted them*
18 [a]Ezek. 10:4 [b]Hos. 9:12 [1]Lit. *house*
19 [a]Ezek. 11:22 [b]Ezek. 11:1
20 [a]Ezek. 1:22 [b]Ezek. 1:1
21 [a]Ezek. 1:6, 8; 10:14; 41:18, 19
22 [a]Ezek. 1:10 [b]Ezek. 1:9, 12

CHAPTER 11
1 [a]Ezek. 3:12, 14 [b]Ezek. 10:19 [c]Ezek. 8:16
2 [1]Advice
3 [a]2 Pet. 3:4 [b]Jer. 1:13 [1]Pot
5 [a]Ezek. 2:2; 3:24 [b][Jer. 16:17; 17:10]
6 [a]Ezek. 7:23; 22:2–6, 9, 12, 27
7 [a]Mic. 3:2, 3 [b]Ezek. 11:9
8 [a]Jer. 42:16
9 [a]Ezek. 5:8
10 [a]Jer. 39:6; 52:10 [b]2 Kin. 14:25 [c]Ps. 9:16
11 [a]Ezek. 11:3, 7 [1]Pot
12 [a]Deut. 12:30, 31
13 [a]Acts 5:5 [b]Ezek. 9:8
16 [a]Is. 8:14 [1]*holy place*
17 [a]Jer. 3:12, 18; 24:5
18 [a]Ezek. 37:23
19 [a]Jer. 32:39 [b]Ezek. 18:31 [c]Zech. 7:12 [1]Lit. *you* (pl.)
20 [a]Ps. 105:45 [b]Jer. 24:7
21 [a]Ezek. 9:10
22 [a]Ezek. 1:19
23 [a]Ezek. 8:4; 9:3 [b]Zech. 14:4 [c]Ezek. 43:2
24 [a]Ezek. 8:3 [1]Or *Babylon*, and so elsewhere in the book

### *Judah's Captivity Illustrated*

**12** Now the word of the LORD came to me,
saying:
2 "Son of man, you dwell in the midst of [a]a
rebellious house, which [b]has eyes to see but does
not see, and ears to hear but does not hear; [c]for
they *are* a rebellious house.
3 "Therefore, son of man, prepare your belongings for captivity, and go into captivity by day in
their sight. You shall go from your place into
captivity to another place in their sight. It may be
that they will consider, though they *are* a rebellious house.
4 "By day you shall bring out your belongings in
their sight, as though going into captivity; and at
evening you shall go in their sight, like those who
go into captivity.
5 "Dig through the wall in their sight, and carry
your belongings out through it.
6 "In their sight you shall bear *them* on *your*
shoulders *and* carry *them* out at twilight; you
shall cover your face, so that you cannot see the
ground, [a]for I have made you a sign to the house
of Israel."
**7** So I did as I was commanded. I brought out
my belongings by day, as though going into
captivity, and at evening I dug through the wall
with my hand. I brought *them* out at twilight, *and*
I bore *them* on *my* shoulder in their sight.
**8** And in the morning the word of the LORD
came to me, saying,
9 "Son of man, has not the house of Israel, [a]the
rebellious house, said to you, [b]'What are you
doing?'
10 "Say to them, 'Thus says the Lord GOD: "This
[a]burden[1] *concerns* the prince in Jerusalem and all
the house of Israel who are among them." '
11 "Say, [a]'I *am* a sign to you. As I have done, so
shall it be done to them; [b]they shall be carried
away into captivity.'
12 "And [a]the prince who *is* among them shall
bear *his belongings* on *his* shoulder at twilight and
go out. They shall dig through the wall to carry
*them* out through it. He shall cover his face, so
that he cannot see the ground with *his* eyes.
13 "I will also spread My [a]net over him, and he
shall be caught in My snare. [b]I will bring him to
Babylon, *to* the land of the Chaldeans; yet he shall
not see it, though he shall die there.
14 [a]"I will scatter to every wind all who *are*
around him to help him, and all his troops; and [b]I
will draw out the sword after them.
15 [a]"Then they shall know that I *am* the LORD,
when I scatter them among the nations and
disperse them throughout the countries.
16 [a]"But I will spare a few of their men from the
sword, from famine, and from pestilence, that
they may declare all their abominations among
the Gentiles wherever they go. Then they shall
know that I *am* the LORD."
**17** Moreover the word of the LORD came to me,
saying,
18 "Son of man, [a]eat your bread with [1]quaking,
and drink your water with trembling and anxiety.
19 "And say to the people of the land, 'Thus says
the Lord GOD to the inhabitants of Jerusalem *and*
to the land of Israel: "They shall eat their bread
with anxiety, and drink their water with dread, so
that her land may [a]be emptied of all who are in it,
[b]because of the violence of all those who dwell
in it.
20 "Then the cities that are inhabited shall be laid
waste, and the land shall become desolate; and
you shall know that I *am* the LORD." ' "
**21** And the word of the LORD came to me, saying,
22 "Son of man, what *is* this proverb *that* you
*people* have about the land of Israel, which says,
[a]'The days are prolonged, and every vision fails'?
23 "Tell them therefore, 'Thus says the Lord GOD:
"I will lay this proverb to rest, and they shall no
more use it as a proverb in Israel." But say to
them, [a]"The days are at hand, and the [1]fulfillment
of every vision.
24 "For [a]no more shall there be any [b]false[1] vision
or flattering divination within the house of Israel.
25 "For I *am* the LORD. I speak, and [a]the word
which I speak will come to pass; it will no more be
postponed; for in your days, O rebellious house, I
will say the word and [b]perform it," says the Lord
GOD.' "
**26** Again the word of the LORD came to me,
saying,
27 [a]"Son of man, look, the house of Israel is
saying, 'The vision that he sees *is* [b]for many days
*from now,* and he prophesies of times far off.'
28 [a]"Therefore say to them, 'Thus says the Lord
GOD: "None of My words will be postponed any
more, but the word which I speak [b]will be done,"
says the Lord GOD.' "

### *False Prophets Condemned*

**13** And the word of the LORD came to me,
saying,
2 "Son of man, prophesy [a]against the prophets of
Israel who prophesy, and say to [b]those who
prophesy out of their own [c]heart,[1] 'Hear the word
of the LORD!' "
3 Thus says the Lord GOD: "Woe to the foolish
prophets, who follow their own spirit and have
seen [1]nothing!
4 "O Israel, your prophets are [a]like foxes in the
deserts.
5 "You [a]have not gone up into the [1]gaps to build
a wall for the house of Israel to stand in battle on
the day of the LORD.
6 [a]"They have envisioned futility and false divination, saying, 'Thus says the LORD!' But the LORD
has [b]not sent them; yet they hope that the word
may [1]be confirmed.
7 "Have you not seen a futile vision, and have
you not spoken false divination? You say, 'The
LORD says,' but I have not spoken."
**8** Therefore thus says the Lord GOD: "Because
you have spoken nonsense and envisioned lies,
therefore I *am* indeed against you," says the Lord
GOD.
9 "My hand will be [a]against the prophets who
envision futility and who [b]divine lies; they shall
not be in the assembly of My people, [c]nor be
written in the record of the house of Israel, [d]nor
shall they enter into the land of Israel. [e]Then you
shall know that I *am* the Lord GOD.
10 "Because, indeed, because they have seduced
My people, saying, [a]'Peace!' when *there is* no
peace—and one builds a wall, and they [b]plaster[1] it
with untempered *mortar*—
11 "say to those who plaster *it* with untempered
*mortar,* that it will fall. [a]There will be flooding
rain, and you, O great hailstones, shall fall; and a
stormy wind shall tear *it* down.
12 "Surely, when the wall has fallen, will it not be

CHAPTER 12
2 [a]Ezek. 2:3, 6–8 [b]Jer. 5:21 [c]Ezek. 2:5
6 [a]Ezek. 4:3; 24:24
9 [a]Ezek. 2:5 [b]Ezek. 17:12; 24:19
10 [a]Mal. 1:1 [1]*oracle, prophecy*
11 [a]Ezek. 12:6 [b]2 Kin. 25:4, 5, 7
12 [a]Jer. 39:4; 52:7
13 [a]Jer. 52:9 [b]Jer. 52:11
14 [a]Ezek. 5:10 [b]Ezek. 5:2, 12
15 [a]Ezek. 6:7, 14; 12:16, 20
16 [a]Ezek. 6:8–10
18 [a]Ezek. 4:16 [1]*shaking*
19 [a]Zech. 7:14 [b]Ps. 107:34
22 [a]Ezek. 11:3; 12:27
23 [a]Zeph. 1:14 [1]Lit. *word*
24 [a]Ezek. 13:6 [b]Lam. 2:14 [1]Lit. *vain*
25 [a][Luke 21:33] [b][Is. 14:24]
27 [a]Ezek. 12:22 [b]Dan. 10:14
28 [a]Ezek. 12:23, 25 [b]Jer. 4:7

CHAPTER 13
2 [a]Ezek. 22:25–28 [b]Ezek. 13:17 [c]Jer. 14:14; 23:16, 26 [1]Inspiration
3 [1]No vision
4 [a]Song 2:15
5 [a]Ps. 106:23 [1]*breaches*
6 [a]Ezek. 22:28 [b]Jer. 27:8–15 [1]Come true
9 [a]Jer. 23:30 [b]Jer. 20:3–6 [c]Ezra 2:59, 62 [d]Jer. 20:3–6 [e]Ezek. 11:10, 12
10 [a]Jer. 6:14; 8:11 [b]Ezek. 22:28 [1]Or *whitewash*
11 [a]Ezek. 38:22

said to you, 'Where *is* the mortar with which you
plastered *it?*' "
13 Therefore thus says the Lord GOD: "I will
cause a stormy wind to break forth in My fury;
and there shall be a flooding rain in My anger, and
great hailstones in fury to consume *it.*
14 "So I will break down the wall you have
plastered with untempered *mortar,* and bring it
down to the ground, so that its foundation will be
uncovered; it will fall, and you shall be consumed
in the midst of it. [a]Then you shall know that I *am*
the LORD.
15 "Thus will I accomplish My wrath on the wall
and on those who have plastered it with untempered *mortar;* and I will say to you, 'The wall *is* no
*more,* nor those who plastered it,
16 '*that is,* the prophets of Israel who prophesy
concerning Jerusalem, and who [a]see visions of
peace for her when *there is* no peace,' " says the
Lord GOD.
**17** "Likewise, son of man, [a]set your face against
the daughters of your people, [b]who prophesy out
of their own [1]heart; prophesy against them,
18 "and say, 'Thus says the Lord GOD: "Woe to
the *women* who sew *magic* charms [1]on their
sleeves and make veils for the heads of people of
every height to hunt souls! Will you [a]hunt the
souls of My people, and keep yourselves alive?
19 "And will you profane Me among My people
[a]for handfuls of barley and for pieces of bread,
killing people who should not die, and keeping
people alive who should not live, by your lying to
My people who listen to lies?"
**20** 'Therefore thus says the Lord GOD: "Behold, I
*am* against your *magic* charms by which you hunt
souls there like [1]birds. I will tear them from your
arms, and let the souls go, the souls you hunt like
birds.
21 "I will also tear off your veils and deliver My
people out of your hand, and they shall no longer
be as prey in your hand. [a]Then you shall know
that I *am* the LORD.
22 "Because with [a]lies you have made the heart
of the righteous sad, whom I have not made sad;
and you have [b]strengthened the hands of the
wicked, so that he does not turn from his wicked
way to save his life.
23 "Therefore [a]you shall no longer envision futility nor practice divination; for I will deliver My
people out of your hand, and you shall know that
I *am* the LORD." ' "

### *Judgments on Jerusalem*

**14** Now [a]some of the elders of Israel came to
me and sat before me.
2 And the word of the LORD came to me, saying,
3 "Son of man, these men have set up their idols
in their hearts, and put before them [a]that which
causes them to stumble into iniquity. [b]Should I let
Myself be inquired of at all by them?
4 "Therefore speak to them, and say to them,
'Thus says the Lord GOD: "Everyone of the house
of Israel who sets up his idols in his heart, and
puts before him what causes him to stumble into
iniquity, and then comes to the prophet, I the
LORD will answer him who comes, according to
the multitude of his idols,
5 "that I may seize the house of Israel by their
heart, because they are all estranged from Me by
their idols." '
**6** "Therefore say to the house of Israel, 'Thus
says the Lord GOD: "Repent, turn away from your
idols, and [a]turn your faces away from all your
abominations.
7 "For anyone of the house of Israel, or of the
strangers who dwell in Israel, who separates
himself from Me and sets up his idols in his heart
and puts before him what causes him to stumble
into iniquity, then comes to a prophet to inquire of
him concerning Me, I the LORD will answer him by
Myself.
8 [a]"I will set My face against that man and
make him a [b]sign and a proverb, and I will cut him
off from the midst of My people. [c]Then you shall
know that I *am* the LORD.
9 "And if the prophet is induced to speak anything, I the LORD [a]have induced that prophet, and
I will stretch out My hand against him and destroy him from among My people Israel.
10 "And they shall bear their iniquity; the punishment of the prophet shall be the same as the
punishment of the one who inquired,
11 "that the house of Israel may [a]no longer stray
from Me, nor be profaned anymore with all their
transgressions, [b]but that they may be My people
and I may be their God," says the Lord GOD.' "
**12** The word of the LORD came again to me,
saying:
13 "Son of man, when a land sins against Me by
persistent unfaithfulness, I will stretch out My
hand against it; I will cut off its [a]supply of bread,
send famine on it, and cut off man and beast
from it.
14 [a]"Even *if* these three men, Noah, Daniel, and
Job, were in it, they would deliver *only* themselves
[b]by their righteousness," says the Lord GOD.
**15** "If I cause [a]wild beasts to pass through the
land, and they [1]empty it, and make it so desolate
that no man may pass through because of the
beasts,
16 "*even* [a]*though* these three men *were* [1]in it, *as* I
live," says the Lord GOD, "they would deliver
neither sons nor daughters; only they would be
delivered, and the land would be [b]desolate.
**17** "Or *if* [a]I bring a sword on that land, and say,
'Sword, go through the land,' and I [b]cut off man
and beast from it,
18 "even [a]*though* these three men *were* in it, *as* I
live," says the Lord GOD, "they would deliver
neither sons nor daughters, but only they themselves would be delivered.
**19** "Or *if* I send [a]a pestilence into that land and
[b]pour out My fury on it in blood, and cut off from
it man and beast,
20 "even [a]*though* Noah, Daniel, and Job *were* in
it, *as* I live," says the Lord GOD, "they would
deliver neither son nor daughter; they would
deliver *only* themselves by their righteousness."
**21** For thus says the Lord GOD: "How much more
it shall be when [a]I send My four [1]severe judgments on Jerusalem—the sword and famine and
wild beasts and pestilence—to cut off man and
beast from it?
22 [a]"Yet behold, there shall be left in it a remnant
who will be [b]brought out, *both* sons and daughters; surely they will come out to you, and [c]you
will see their ways and their doings. Then you will
be comforted concerning the disaster that I have
brought upon Jerusalem, all that I have brought
upon it.
23 "And they will comfort you, when you see

14 [a]Ezek. 13:9, 21, 23; 14:8
16 [a]Jer. 6:14; 8:11; 28:9
17 [a]Ezek. 20:46; 21:2 [b]Ezek. 13:2 [1]Inspiration
18 [a][2 Pet. 2:14] [1]Lit. *over all the joints of My hands;* Vg. *under every elbow;* LXX, Tg. *on all elbows of the hands*
19 [a]Mic. 3:5
20 [1]Lit. *flying ones*
21 [a]Ezek. 13:9
22 [a]Jer. 28:15 [b]Jer. 23:14
23 [a]Mic. 3:5, 6

CHAPTER 14
1 [a]Ezek. 8:1; 20:1; 33:31
3 [a]Ezek. 7:19 [b]Ezek. 20:3, 31
6 [a]Is. 2:20; 30:22; 55:6, 7
8 [a]Jer. 44:11 [b]Num. 26:10 [c]Ezek. 6:7; 13:14
9 [a]2 Thess. 2:11
11 [a]2 Pet. 2:15 [b]Ezek. 11:20; 37:27
13 [a]Is. 3:1
14 [a]Jer. 15:1 [b][Prov. 11:4]
15 [a]Lev. 26:22 [1]Lit. *bereave it* of children
16 [a]Ezek. 14:14, 18, 20 [b]Ezek. 15:8; 33:28, 29 [1]Lit. *in the midst of it*
17 [a]Lev. 26:25 [b]Zeph. 1:3
18 [a]Ezek. 14:14
19 [a]2 Sam. 24:15 [b]Ezek. 7:8
20 [a]Ezek. 14:14
21 [a]Ezek. 5:17; 33:27 [1]Lit. *evil*
22 [a]Ezek. 12:16; 36:20 [b]Ezek. 6:8 [c]Ezek. 20:43

their ways and their doings; and you shall know
that I have done nothing [a]without cause that I
have done in it," says the Lord GOD.

### *Jerusalem Like a Useless Vine*

**15** Then the word of the LORD came to me,
saying:
2 "Son of man, how is the wood of the vine *better*
than any other wood, the vine branch which is
among the trees of the forest?
3 "Is wood taken from it to make any object?
Or can *men* make a peg from it to hang any
vessel on?
4 "Instead, [a]it is thrown into the fire for fuel; the
fire devours both ends of it, and its middle is
burned. Is it useful for *any* work?
5 "Indeed, when it was whole, no object could
be made from it. How much less will it be useful
for *any* work when the fire has devoured it, and it
is burned?
**6** "Therefore thus says the Lord GOD: 'Like the
wood of the vine among the trees of the forest,
which I have given to the fire for fuel, so I will
give up the inhabitants of Jerusalem;
7 'and [a]I will set My face against them. [b]They
will go out from *one* fire, but *another* fire shall
devour them. [c]Then you shall know that I *am* the
LORD, when I set My face against them.
8 'Thus I will make the land desolate, because
they have persisted in unfaithfulness,' says the
Lord GOD."

### *Jerusalem's Unfaithfulness*

**16** Again the word of the LORD came to me,
saying,
2 "Son of man, [a]cause Jerusalem to know her
abominations,
3 "and say, 'Thus says the Lord GOD to Jerusalem: "Your [1]birth [a]and your nativity *are* from the
land of Canaan; [b]your father *was* an Amorite and
your mother a Hittite.
4 "*As for* your nativity, [a]on the day you were
born your navel cord was not cut, nor were you
washed in water to cleanse *you;* you were not
rubbed with salt nor wrapped in swaddling cloths.
5 "No eye pitied you, to do any of these things
for you, to have compassion on you; but you were
thrown out into the open field, when you yourself
were [1]loathed on the day you were born.
**6** "And when I passed by you and saw you
struggling in your own blood, I said to you in your
blood, 'Live!' Yes, I said to you in your blood,
'Live!'
7 [a]"I made you [1]thrive like a plant in the field;
and you grew, matured, and became very beautiful. *Your* breasts were formed, your hair grew, but
you *were* naked and bare.
8 "When I passed by you again and looked upon
you, indeed your time *was* the time of love; [a]so I
spread [1]My wing over you and covered your
nakedness. Yes, I [b]swore an oath to you and
entered into a [c]covenant with you, and [d]you
became Mine," says the Lord GOD.
9 "Then I washed you in water; yes, I thoroughly washed off your blood, and I anointed you
with oil.
10 "I clothed you in embroidered cloth and gave
you sandals of [1]badger skin; I clothed you with
fine linen and covered you with silk.
11 "I adorned you with ornaments, [a]put bracelets
on your wrists, [b]and a chain on your neck.
12 "And I put a [1]jewel in your nose, earrings in
your ears, and a beautiful crown on your head.
13 "Thus you were adorned with gold and silver,
and your clothing *was of* fine linen, silk, and
embroidered cloth. [a]You ate *pastry of* fine flour,
honey, and oil. You were exceedingly [b]beautiful,
and succeeded to royalty.
14 [a]"Your fame went out among the nations
because of your beauty, for it *was* perfect through
My splendor which I had bestowed on you," says
the Lord GOD.
**15** [a]"But you trusted in your own beauty, [b]played
the harlot because of your fame, and poured out
your harlotry on everyone passing by who *would
have* it.
16 [a]"You took some of your garments and
adorned multicolored [1]high places for yourself,
and played the harlot on them. *Such* things should
not happen, nor be.
17 "You have also taken your beautiful jewelry
from My gold and My silver, which I had given
you, and made for yourself male images and
played the harlot with them.
18 "You took your embroidered garments and
covered them, and you set My oil and My incense
before them.
19 "Also [a]My food which I gave you—the pastry
of fine flour, oil, and honey *which* I fed you—you
set it before them as [1]sweet incense; and *so* it
was," says the Lord GOD.
20 [a]"Moreover you took your sons and your
daughters, whom you bore to Me, and these you
sacrificed to them to be devoured. *Were* your *acts*
of harlotry a small matter,
21 "that you have slain My children and offered
them up to them by causing them to pass through
*the* [a]*fire?*
22 "And in all your abominations and acts of
harlotry you did not remember the days of your
[a]youth, [b]when you were naked and bare, struggling in your blood.
**23** "Then it was so, after all your wickedness—
'Woe, woe to you!' says the Lord GOD—
24 "*that* [a]you also built for yourself a shrine, and
[b]made a [1]high place for yourself in every street.
25 "You built your high places [a]at the head of
every road, and made your beauty to be abhorred.
You offered yourself to everyone who passed by,
and multiplied your acts of harlotry.
26 "You also committed harlotry with [a]the Egyptians, your very fleshly neighbors, and increased
your acts of harlotry to [b]provoke Me to anger.
27 "Behold, therefore, I stretched out My hand
against you, diminished your [1]allotment, and gave
you up to the will of those who hate you, [a]the
daughters of the Philistines, who were ashamed of
your lewd behavior.
28 "You also played the harlot with the [a]Assyr-
ians, because you were insatiable; indeed you
played the harlot with them and still were not
satisfied.
29 "Moreover you multiplied your acts of harlotry as far as the land of the trader, [a]Chaldea; and
even then you were not satisfied.
30 "How degenerate is your heart!" says the Lord
GOD, "seeing you do all these *things,* the deeds of
a brazen harlot.
**31** [a]"You erected your shrine at the head of every
road, and built your [1]high place in every street.
Yet you were not like a harlot, because you
scorned [b]payment.

**23** [a]Jer. 22:8, 9

CHAPTER 15
**4** [a][John 15:6]
**7** [a]Ezek. 14:8 [b]Is. 24:18 [c]Ezek. 7:4

CHAPTER 16
**2** [a]Ezek. 20:4; 22:2
**3** [a]Ezek. 21:30 [b]Ezek. 16:45 [1]*origin and your birth*
**4** [a]Hos. 2:3
**5** [1]*abhorred*
**7** [a]Ex. 1:7 [1]Lit. *a myriad*
**8** [a]Ruth 3:9 [b]Gen. 22:16–18 [c]Ex. 24:6–8 [d][Ex. 19:5] [1]Or *the corner of My garment*
**10** [1]Or *dolphin* or *dugong*
**11** [a]Gen. 24:22, 47 [b]Prov. 1:9
**12** [1]Lit. *ring*
**13** [a]Deut. 32:13, 14 [b]Ps. 48:2
**14** [a]Lam. 2:15
**15** [a]Mic. 3:11 [b]Is. 1:21; 57:8
**16** [a]Ezek. 7:20 [1]Places for pagan worship
**19** [a]Hos. 2:8 [1]Or *a sweet aroma*
**20** [a]Jer. 7:31
**21** [a]Jer. 19:5
**22** [a]Jer. 2:2 [b]Ezek. 16:4–6
**24** [a]Jer. 11:13 [b]Jer. 2:20; 3:2 [1]Place for pagan worship
**25** [a]Prov. 9:14
**26** [a]Ezek. 16:26; 20:7, 8 [b]Deut. 31:20
**27** [a]Ezek. 16:57 [1]Allowance of food
**28** [a]Jer. 2:18, 36
**29** [a]Ezek. 23:14–17
**31** [a]Ezek. 16:24, 39 [b]Is. 52:3 [1]Place for pagan worship

32 "*You are* an adulterous wife, *who* takes
strangers instead of her husband.
33 "Men make payment to all harlots, but [a]you
made your payments to all your lovers, and [1]hired
them to come to you from all around for your
harlotry.
34 "You are the opposite of *other* women in your
harlotry, because no one solicited you to be a
harlot. In that you gave payment but no payment
was given you, therefore you are the opposite."
**35** 'Now then, O harlot, hear the word of the
LORD!
36 'Thus says the Lord GOD: "Because your filthiness was poured out and your nakedness uncovered in your harlotry with your lovers, and with
all your abominable idols, and because of [a]the
blood of your children which you gave to them,
37 "surely, therefore, [a]I will gather all your lovers
with whom you took pleasure, all those you loved,
*and* all those you hated; I will gather them from
all around against you and will uncover your
nakedness to them, that they may see all your
nakedness.
38 "And I will judge you as [a]women who break
wedlock or [b]shed blood are judged; I will bring
blood upon you in fury and jealousy.
39 "I will also give you into their hand, and they
shall throw down your shrines and break down
[a]your [1]high places. [b]They shall also strip you of
your clothes, take your beautiful jewelry, and
leave you naked and bare.
40 [a]"They shall also bring up an assembly against
you, [b]and they shall stone you with stones and
thrust you through with their swords.
41 "They shall [a]burn your houses with fire, and
[b]execute judgments on you in the sight of many
women; and I will make you [c]cease playing the
harlot, and you shall no longer hire lovers.
42 "So [a]I will lay to rest My fury toward you, and
My jealousy shall depart from you. I will be quiet,
and be angry no more.
43 "Because [a]you did not remember the days of
your youth, but [1]agitated Me with all these *things*,
surely [b]I will also recompense your [2]deeds on *your
own* head," says the Lord GOD. "And you shall not
commit lewdness in addition to all your abominations.
**44** "Indeed everyone who quotes proverbs will
use *this* proverb against you: 'Like mother, like
daughter!'
45 "You *are* your mother's daughter, [1]loathing
husband and children; and you *are* the [a]sister of
your sisters, who loathed their husbands and
children; [b]your mother *was* a Hittite and your
father an Amorite.
46 "Your elder sister *is* Samaria, who dwells with
her daughters to the north of you; and [a]your
younger sister, who dwells to the south of you, *is*
Sodom and her daughters.
47 "You did not walk in their ways nor act
according to their abominations; but, as *if that
were* too little, [a]you became more corrupt than
they in all your ways.
48 "*As* I live," says the Lord GOD, "neither [a]your
sister Sodom nor her daughters have done as you
and your daughters have done.
49 "Look, this was the iniquity of your sister
Sodom: She and her daughter had pride, [a]fullness
of food, and abundance of idleness; neither did she
strengthen the hand of the poor and needy.
50 "And they were haughty and [a]committed
abomination before Me; therefore [b]I took them
away as [1]I saw *fit*.
51 "Samaria did not commit [a]half of your sins;
but you have multiplied your abominations more
than they, and [b]have justified your sisters by all
the abominations which you have done.
52 "You who judged your sisters, bear your own
shame also, because the sins which you committed were more abominable than theirs; they
are more righteous than you. Yes, be disgraced
also, and bear your own shame, because you
justified your sisters.
**53** [a]"When I bring back their captives, the captives of Sodom and her daughters, and the captives of Samaria and her daughters, then *I will
also bring back* [b]the captives of your captivity
among them,
54 "that you may bear your own shame and be
disgraced by all that you did when [a]you comforted
them.
55 "When your sisters, Sodom and her daughters,
return to their former state, and Samaria and her
daughters return to their former state, then you
and your daughters will return to your former
state.
56 "For your sister Sodom was not a byword in
your mouth in the days of your pride,
57 "before your wickedness was uncovered. It
was like the time of the [a]reproach of the daughters of [1]Syria and all *those* around her, and of [b]the
daughters of the Philistines, who despise you
everywhere.
58 [a]"You have paid for your lewdness and your
abominations," says the LORD.
59 'For thus says the Lord GOD: "I will deal with
you as you have done, who [a]despised [b]the oath by
breaking the covenant.
**60** "Nevertheless I will [a]remember My covenant
with you in the days of your youth, and I will
establish [b]an everlasting covenant with you.
61 "Then [a]you will remember your ways and be
ashamed, when you receive your older and your
younger sisters; for I will give them to you for
[b]daughters, [c]but not because of My covenant with
you.
62 [a]"And I will establish My covenant with you.
Then you shall know that I *am* the LORD,
63 "that you may [a]remember and be ashamed,
[b]and never open your mouth anymore because of
your shame, when I provide you an atonement for
all you have done," says the Lord GOD.' "

### *The Parable of the Eagles and the Vine*

**17** And the word of the LORD came to me,
saying,
2 "Son of man, pose a riddle, and speak a [a]parable
to the house of Israel,
3 "and say, 'Thus says the Lord GOD:

[a]"A great eagle with large wings
and long pinions,
Full of feathers of various colors,
Came to Lebanon
And [b]took from the cedar the highest branch.
4 He cropped off its topmost young twig
And carried it to a land of trade;
He set it in a city of merchants.
5 Then he took some of the seed of the land
And planted it in [a]a fertile field;
He placed *it* by abundant waters
*And* set it [b]like a willow tree.

**33** [a]Hos. 8:9, 10 [1]Or *bribed*
**36** [a]Jer. 2:34
**37** [a]Lam. 1:8
**38** [a]Lev. 20:10 [b]Gen. 9:6
**39** [a]Ezek. 16:24, 31 [b]Hos. 2:3 [1]Places for pagan worship
**40** [a]Ezek. 23:45–47 [b]John 8:5, 7
**41** [a]Deut. 13:16 [b]Ezek. 5:8; 23:10, 48 [c]Ezek. 23:27
**42** [a]Ezek. 5:13; 21:17
**43** [a]Ps. 78:42 [b]Ezek. 9:10; 11:21; 22:31 [1]So with LXX, Syr., Tg., Vg.; MT *were agitated with Me* [2]Lit. *way*
**45** [a]Ezek. 23:2–4 [b]Ezek. 16:3 [1]Or *despising*
**46** [a]Is. 1:10
**47** [a]Ezek. 5:6, 7
**48** [a]Matt. 10:15; 11:24
**49** [a]Gen. 13:10
**50** [a]Gen. 13:13; 18:20; 19:5 [b]Gen. 19:24 [1]Vg. *you saw;* LXX *he saw;* Tg. *as was revealed to Me*
**51** [a]Ezek. 23:11 [b]Jer. 3:8–11
**53** [a]Is. 1:9 [b]Jer. 20:16
**54** [a]Ezek. 14:22
**57** [a]2 Kin. 16:5 [b]Ezek. 16:27 [1]Heb. *Aram;* so with MT, LXX, Tg., Vg.; many Heb. mss., Syr. *Edom*
**58** [a]Ezek. 23:49
**59** [a]Ezek. 17:13 [b]Deut. 29:12
**60** [a]Ps. 106:45 [b]Is. 55:3
**61** [a]Ezek. 20:43; 36:31 [b][Gal. 4:26] [c]Jer. 31:31
**62** [a]Hos. 2:19, 20
**63** [a]Ezek. 36:31, 32 [b][Rom. 3:19]

CHAPTER 17
**2** [a]Ezek. 20:49; 24:3
**3** [a]Ezek. 17:12 [b]2 Kin. 24:12
**5** [a]Deut. 8:7–9 [b]Is. 44:4

6 And it grew and became a spreading vine [a]of low stature;
Its branches turned toward him,
But its roots were under it.
So it became a vine,
Brought forth branches,
And put forth shoots.

7 "But there was [1]another great eagle
with large wings and many feathers;
And behold, [a]this vine bent its roots toward him,
And stretched its branches toward him,
From the garden terrace where it had been planted,
That he might water it.
8 It was planted in [1]good soil by many waters,
To bring forth branches, bear fruit,
*And* become a majestic vine." '

9 "Say, 'Thus says the Lord GOD:

"Will it thrive?
[a]Will he not pull up its roots,
Cut off its fruit,
And leave it to wither?
All of its spring leaves will wither,
And no great power or many people
Will be needed to pluck it up by its roots.
10 Behold, *it is* planted,
Will it thrive?
[a]Will it not utterly wither
when the east wind touches it?
It will wither in the garden terrace where it grew." ' "

11 Moreover the word of the LORD came to me,
saying,
12 "Say now to [a]the rebellious house: 'Do you not
know what these *things mean?*' Tell *them,* 'Indeed [b]the king of Babylon went to Jerusalem and
took its king and princes, and led them with him
to Babylon.
13 [a]'And he took the king's offspring, made a
covenant with him, [b]and put him under oath. He
also took away the mighty of the land,
14 'that the kingdom might be [a]brought low and
not lift itself up, *but* that by keeping his covenant
it might stand.
15 'But [a]he rebelled against him by sending his
ambassadors to Egypt, [b]that they might give him
horses and many people. [c]Will he prosper? Will he
who does such *things* escape? Can he break a
covenant and still be delivered?
16 '*As* I live,' says the Lord GOD, 'surely [a]in the
place *where* the king *dwells* who made him king,
whose oath he despised and whose covenant he
broke—with him in the midst of Babylon he shall
die.
17 [a]'Nor will Pharaoh with *his* mighty army and
great company do anything in the war, [b]when
they heap up a siege mound and build a [1]wall to
cut off many persons.
18 'Since he despised the oath by breaking the
covenant, and in fact [a]gave[1] his hand and still did
all these *things,* he shall not escape.' "
19 Therefore thus says the Lord GOD: "*As* I live,
surely My oath which he despised, and My covenant which he broke, I will recompense on his
own head.
20 "I will [a]spread My net over him, and he shall
be taken in My snare. I will bring him to Babylon
and [b]try him there for the [1]treason which he
committed against Me.

6 [a]Ezek. 17:14
7 [a]Ezek. 17:15 [1]So with LXX, Syr., Vg.; MT, Tg. *one*
8 [1]Lit. *a good field*
9 [a]2 Kin. 25:7
10 [a]Hos. 13:15
12 [a]Ezek. 2:3–5; 12:9 [b]2 Kin. 24:11–16
13 [a]2 Kin. 24:17 [b]2 Chr. 36:13
14 [a]Ezek. 29:14
15 [a]2 Kin. 24:20 [b]Deut. 17:16 [c]Ezek. 17:9
16 [a]Ezek. 12:13
17 [a]Jer. 37:7 [b]Jer. 52:4 [1]Or *siege wall*
18 [a]1 Chr. 29:24 [1]Took an oath
20 [a]Ezek. 12:13 [b]Ezek. 20:36 [1]Lit. *unfaithful act*
21 [a]Ezek. 12:14 [b]Ezek. 12:15; 22:15 [1]So with MT, Vg.; many Heb. mss., Syr. *choice men;* Tg. *mighty men;* LXX omits *All his fugitives*
22 [a][Zech. 3:8] [b]Is. 53:2 [c][Ps. 2:6]
23 [a][Is. 2:2, 3] [b]Dan. 4:12
24 [a]Amos 9:11 [b]Ezek. 22:14

CHAPTER 18
2 [a]Lam. 5:7
4 [a]Num. 16:22; 27:16 [b][Rom. 6:23]
6 [a]Ezek. 22:9 [b]Lev. 18:20; 20:10 [c]Lev. 18:19; 20:18 [1]At the mountain shrines
7 [a]Ex. 22:21 [b]Deut. 24:12 [c]Deut. 15:7, 11 [d]Is. 58:7
8 [a]Ex. 22:25 [b]Zech. 8:16 [1]Lent money at interest [2]*justice*
9 [a]Amos 5:4
10 [a]Num. 35:31
11 [1]At the mountain shrines
12 [a]Ezek. 8:6, 17

21 [a]"All his [1]fugitives with all his troops shall fall
by the sword, and those who remain shall be
[b]scattered to every wind; and you shall know that
I, the LORD, have spoken."
22 Thus says the Lord GOD: "I will take also *one*
of the highest [a]branches of the high cedar and set
*it* out. I will crop off from the topmost of its young
twigs [b]a tender one, and will [c]plant *it* on a high
and prominent mountain.
23 [a]"On the mountain height of Israel I will plant
it; and it will bring forth boughs, and bear fruit,
and be a majestic cedar. [b]Under it will dwell birds
of every sort; in the shadow of its branches they
will dwell.
24 "And all the trees of the field shall know that
I, the LORD, [a]have brought down the high tree and
exalted the low tree, dried up the green tree and
made the dry tree flourish; [b]I, the LORD, have
spoken and have done *it.*"

## *The Soul That Sins Shall Die*

**18** The word of the LORD came to me again,
saying,
2 "What do you mean when you use this proverb
concerning the land of Israel, saying:

'The [a]fathers have eaten sour grapes,
And the children's teeth are set on edge'?

3 "*As* I live," says the Lord GOD, "you shall no
longer use this proverb in Israel.

4 "Behold, all souls are [a]Mine;
The soul of the father
As well as the soul of the son is Mine;
[b]The soul who sins shall die.
5 But if a man is just
And does what is lawful and right;
6 [a]If he has not eaten [1]on the mountains,
Nor lifted up his eyes
to the idols of the house of Israel,
Nor [b]defiled his neighbor's wife,
Nor approached [c]a woman during her
impurity;
7 If he has not [a]oppressed anyone,
*But* has restored to the debtor his [b]pledge;
Has robbed no one by violence,
*But* has [c]given his bread to the hungry
And covered the naked with [d]clothing;
8 If he has not [1]exacted [a]usury
Nor taken any increase,
*But* has withdrawn his hand from iniquity
*And* [b]executed true [2]judgment
between man and man;
9 *If* he has walked in My statutes
And kept My judgments faithfully—
He *is* just;
He shall surely [a]live!"
Says the Lord GOD.

10 "If he begets a son *who is* a robber
Or [a]a shedder of blood,
*Who* does any of these *things*
11 And does none of those *duties,*
But has eaten [1]on the mountains
Or defiled his neighbor's wife;
12 If he has oppressed the poor and needy,
Robbed by violence,
Not restored the pledge,
Lifted his eyes to the idols,
*Or* [a]committed abomination;
13 If he has exacted usury
Or taken increase—

Shall he then live?
He shall not live!
If he has done any of these abominations,
He shall surely die;
[a]His blood shall be upon him.

14 "*If*, however, he begets a son
Who sees all the sins which his father has
done,
And considers but does not do likewise;
15 [a]*Who* has not eaten [1]on the mountains,
Nor lifted his eyes
to the idols of the house of Israel,
Nor defiled his neighbor's wife;
16 Has not oppressed anyone,
Nor withheld a pledge,
Nor robbed by violence,
*But* has given his bread to the hungry
And covered the naked with clothing;
17 *Who* has withdrawn his hand from [1]the poor
*And* not received usury or increase,
But has executed My judgments
And walked in My statutes—
He shall not die for the iniquity of his father;
He shall surely live!

18 "*As for* his father,
Because he cruelly oppressed,
Robbed his brother by violence,
And did what *is* not good among his people,
Behold, [a]he shall die for his iniquity.

19 "Yet you say, 'Why [a]should the son not bear
the guilt of the father?' Because the son has done
what is lawful and right, and has kept all My
statutes and observed them, he shall surely live.
20 [a]"The soul who sins shall die. [b]The son shall
not bear the guilt of the father, nor the father bear
the guilt of the son. [c]The righteousness of the
righteous shall be upon himself, [d]and the wickedness of the wicked shall be upon himself.
21 "But [a]if a wicked man turns from all his sins
which he has committed, keeps all My statutes,
and does what is lawful and right, he shall surely
live; he shall not die.
22 [a]"None of the transgressions which he has
committed shall be remembered against him;
because of the righteousness which he has done,
he shall [b]live.
23 [a]"Do I have any pleasure at all that the wicked
should die?" says the Lord GOD, "*and* not that he
should turn from his ways and live?
24 "But [a]when a righteous man turns away from
his righteousness and commits iniquity, and does
according to all the abominations that the wicked
*man* does, shall he live? [b]All the righteousness
which he has done shall not be remembered;
because of the unfaithfulness of which he is guilty
and the sin which he has committed, because of
them he shall die.
25 "Yet you say, [a]'The way of the Lord is not
fair.' Hear now, O house of Israel, is it not My way
which is fair, and your ways which are not fair?
26 [a]"When a righteous *man* turns away from his
righteousness, commits iniquity, and dies in it, it is
because of the iniquity which he has done that he
dies.
27 "Again, [a]when a wicked *man* turns away from
the wickedness which he committed, and does
what is lawful and right, he preserves himself
alive.
28 "Because he [a]considers and turns away from
all the transgressions which he committed, he
shall surely live; he shall not die.
29 [a]"Yet the house of Israel says, 'The way of the
Lord is not fair.' O house of Israel, is it not My
ways which are fair, and your ways which are not
fair?
30 [a]"Therefore I will judge you, O house of Israel,
every one according to his ways," says the Lord
GOD. [b]"Repent, and turn from all your transgressions, so that iniquity will not be your ruin.
31 [a]"Cast away from you all the transgressions
which you have committed, and get yourselves a
[b]new heart and a new spirit. For why should you
die, O house of Israel?
32 "For [a]I have no pleasure in the death of one
who dies," says the Lord GOD. "Therefore turn
and [b]live!"

### *Mourning for Degraded Israel*

**19** "Moreover [a]take up a lamentation for the
princes of Israel,
2 "and say:

'What *is* your mother? A lioness:
She lay down among the lions;
Among the young lions
she nourished her cubs.
3 She brought up one of her cubs,
And [a]he became a young lion;
He learned to catch prey,
And he devoured men.
4 The nations also heard of him;
He was trapped in their pit,
And they brought him with chains
to the land of [a]Egypt.

5 'When she saw that she waited,
*that* her hope was lost,
She took [a]another of her cubs
*and* made him a young lion.
6 [a]He roved among the lions,
And [b]became a young lion;
He learned to catch prey;
He devoured men.
7 [1]He knew their desolate places,
And laid waste their cities;
The land with its fullness was desolated
By the noise of his roaring.
8 [a]Then the nations set against him
from the provinces on every side,
And spread their net over him;
[b]He was trapped in their pit.
9 [a]They put him in a cage with [1]chains,
And brought him to the king of Babylon;
They brought him in nets,
That his voice should no longer be heard on
[b]the mountains of Israel.

10 'Your mother *was* [a]like a vine
in your [1]bloodline,
Planted by the waters,
[b]Fruitful and full of branches
Because of many waters.
11 She had strong branches for scepters of
rulers.
[a]She towered in stature above the thick
branches,
And was seen in her height amid the [1]dense
foliage.
12 But she was [a]plucked up in fury,
She was cast down to the ground,
And the [b]east wind dried her fruit.

13 [a]Lev. 20:9, 11–13, 16, 27
15 [a]Ezek. 18:6 [1]At the mountain shrines
17 [1]So with MT, Tg., Vg.; LXX *iniquity* (cf. v. 8)
18 [a]Ezek. 3:18
19 [a]Ex. 20:5
20 [a]Ezek. 18:4 [b]Deut. 24:16 [c]Is. 3:10, 11 [d]Rom. 2:6–9
21 [a]Ezek. 18:27; 33:12, 19
22 [a]Ezek. 18:24; 33:16 [b][Ps. 18:20–24]
23 [a][Ezek. 18:32; 33:11]
24 [a]Ezek. 3:20; 18:26; 33:18 [b][2 Pet. 2:20]
25 [a]Ezek. 18:29; 33:17, 20
26 [a]Ezek. 18:24
27 [a]Ezek. 18:21
28 [a]Ezek. 18:14
29 [a]Ezek. 18:25
30 [a]Ezek. 7:3; 33:20 [b]Matt. 3:2
31 [a]Ezek. 4:22, 23 [b]Jer. 32:39
32 [a]Lam. 3:33 [b][Prov. 4:2, 5, 6]

CHAPTER 19
1 [a]Ezek. 26:17; 27:2
3 [a]2 Kin. 23:31, 32
4 [a]2 Kin. 23:33, 34
5 [a]2 Kin. 23:34
6 [a]Jer. 22:13–17 [b]Ezek. 19:3
7 [1]LXX *He stood in insolence;* Tg. *He destroyed its palaces;* Vg. *He learned to make widows*
8 [a]2 Kin. 24:2, 11 [b]Ezek. 19:4
9 [a]2 Chr. 36:6 [b]Ezek. 6:2 [1]Or *hooks*
10 [a]Ezek. 17:6 [b]Deut. 8:7–9 [1]Lit. *blood.* So with MT, Syr., Vg.; LXX *like a flower on a pomegranate tree;* Tg. *in your likeness*
11 [a]Dan. 4:11 [1]Or *many branches*
12 [a]Jer. 31:27, 28 [b]Hos. 13:5

Her strong branches were broken
and withered;
The fire consumed them.
13 And now she *is* planted in the wilderness,
In a dry and thirsty land.
14 [a]Fire has come out from a rod of her branches
*And* devoured her fruit,
So that she has no strong branch—
a scepter for ruling.' "

[b]This *is* a lamentation, and has become a lamentation.

## *The History of Rebellious Israel*

**20** It came to pass in the seventh year, in the
fifth *month,* on the tenth *day* of the month,
*that* [a]certain of the elders of Israel came to inquire
of the LORD, and sat before me.
2 Then the word of the LORD came to me,
saying,
3 "Son of man, speak to the elders of Israel, and
say to them, 'Thus says the Lord GOD: "Have you
come to inquire of Me? *As* I live," says the Lord
GOD, [a]"I will not be inquired of by you." '
4 "Will you judge them, son of man, will you
judge *them?* Then [a]make known to them the
abominations of their fathers.
**5** "Say to them, 'Thus says the Lord GOD: "On
the day when [a]I chose Israel and raised My hand
in an oath to the descendants of the house of
Jacob, and made Myself [b]known to them in the
land of Egypt, I raised My hand in an oath to
them, saying, [c]'I *am* the LORD your God.'
6 "On that day I raised My hand in an oath to
them, [a]to bring them out of the land of Egypt into
a land that I had searched out for them, [b]'flowing
with milk and honey,' [c]the glory of all lands.
7 "Then I said to them, 'Each of you, [a]throw
away [b]the abominations which are before his eyes,
and do not defile yourselves with [c]the idols of
Egypt. I *am* the LORD your God.'
8 "But they rebelled against Me and would not
[1]obey Me. They did not all cast away the abominations which were before their eyes, nor did they
forsake the idols of Egypt. Then I said, 'I will
[a]pour out My fury on them and fulfill My anger
against them in the midst of the land of Egypt.'
9 [a]"But I acted for My name's sake, that it
should not be profaned before the Gentiles among
whom they *were,* in whose sight I had made
Myself [b]known to them, to bring them out of the
land of Egypt.
**10** "Therefore I [a]made them go out of the land of
Egypt and brought them into the wilderness.
11 [a]"And I gave them My statutes and [1]showed
them My judgments, [b]'which, *if* a man does, he
shall live by them.'
12 "Moreover I also gave them My [a]Sabbaths, to
be a sign between them and Me, that they might
know that I *am* the LORD who sanctifies them.
13 "Yet the house of Israel [a]rebelled against Me
in the wilderness; they did not walk in My statutes; they [b]despised My judgments, 'which, *if* a
man does, he shall live by them'; and they greatly
[c]defiled My Sabbaths. Then I said I would pour
out My fury on them in the [d]wilderness, to consume them.
14 [a]"But I acted for My name's sake, that it
should not be profaned before the Gentiles, in
whose sight I had brought them out.
15 "So [a]I also raised My hand in an oath to them
in the wilderness, that I would not bring them into
the land which I had given *them,* [b]'flowing with
milk and honey,' [c]the glory of all lands,
16 [a]"because they despised My judgments and
did not walk in My statutes, but profaned My
Sabbaths; for [b]their heart went after their idols.
17 [a]"Nevertheless My eye spared them from destruction. I did not make an end of them in the
wilderness.
**18** "But I said to their children in the wilderness,
'Do not walk in the statutes of your fathers, nor
observe their judgments, nor defile yourselves
with their idols.
19 'I *am* the LORD your God: [a]Walk in My statutes, keep My judgments, and do them;
20 [a]'hallow My Sabbaths, and they will be a sign
between Me and you, that you may know that I
*am* the LORD your God.'
21 "Notwithstanding, [a]the children rebelled
against Me; they did not walk in My statutes, and
were not careful to observe My judgments,
[b]'which, *if* a man does, he shall live by them'; but
they profaned My Sabbaths. Then I said I would
pour out My fury on them and fulfill My anger
against them in the wilderness.
22 "Nevertheless I [1]withdrew My hand and acted
for My name's sake, that it should not be profaned
in the sight of the Gentiles, in whose sight I had
brought them out.
23 "Also I raised My hand in an oath to those in
the wilderness, that [a]I would scatter them among
the Gentiles and disperse them throughout the
countries,
24 [a]"because they had not executed My judgments, but had despised My statutes, profaned My
Sabbaths, and [b]their eyes were fixed on their
fathers' idols.
25 "Therefore [a]I also gave them up to statutes
*that were* not good, and judgments by which they
could not live;
26 "and I pronounced them unclean because of
their ritual gifts, in that they caused all [1]their
firstborn to pass [a]through *the fire,* that I might
make them desolate and that they [b]might know
that I am the LORD." '
**27** "Therefore, son of man, speak to the house of
Israel, and say to them, 'Thus says the Lord GOD:
"In this too your fathers have [a]blasphemed Me, by
being unfaithful to Me.
28 "When I brought them into the land *concerning* which I had raised My hand in an oath to give
them, and [a]they saw all the high hills and all the
thick trees, there they offered their sacrifices and
provoked Me with their offerings. There they also
sent up their [b]sweet aroma and poured out their
drink offerings.
29 "Then I said to them, 'What *is* this [1]high place
to which you go?' So its name is called [2]Bamah to
this day." '
30 "Therefore say to the house of Israel, 'Thus
says the Lord GOD: "Are you defiling yourselves in
the manner of your [a]fathers, and committing
harlotry according to their [b]abominations?
31 "For when you offer [a]your gifts and make
your sons pass through the fire, you defile yourselves with all your idols, even to this day. So shall
I be inquired of by you, O house of Israel? *As* I
live," says the Lord GOD, "I will [b]not be inquired of
by you.
32 [a]"What you have in your mind shall never be,
when you say, 'We will be like the Gentiles, like
the families in other countries, serving wood and
stone.'

**14** [a]Judg. 9:15 [b]Lam. 2:5

CHAPTER 20
**1** [a]Ezek. 8:1, 11, 12; 14:1
**3** [a]Ezek. 7:26; 14:3
**4** [a]Ezek. 16:2; 22:2
**5** [a]Ex. 6:6–8 [b]Deut. 4:34 [c]Ex. 20:2
**6** [a]Jer. 32:22 [b]Ex. 3:8 [c]Jer. 11:5; 32:22
**7** [a]Ezek. 18:31 [b]2 Chr. 15:8 [c]Lev. 18:3
**8** [a]Ezek. 7:8 [1]Lit. *listen to*
**9** [a]Num. 14:13 [b]Josh. 2:10; 9:9, 10
**10** [a]Ex. 13:18
**11** [a]Neh. 9:13 [b]Lev. 18:5 [1]Lit. *made known to*
**12** [a]Deut. 5:12
**13** [a]Num. 14:22 [b]Prov. 1:25 [c]Ex. 16:27 [d]Num. 14:29
**14** [a]Ezek. 20:9, 20
**15** [a]Num. 14:28 [b]Ex. 3:8 [c]Ezek. 20:6
**16** [a]Ezek. 20:13, 24 [b]Amos 5:25
**17** [a][Ps. 78:38]
**19** [a]Deut. 5:32
**20** [a]Jer. 17:22
**21** [a]Num. 25:1 [b]Lev. 18:5
**22** [1]Refrained from judgment
**23** [a]Lev. 26:33
**24** [a]Ezek. 20:13, 16 [b]Ezek. 6:9
**25** [a]Rom. 1:24
**26** [a]Jer. 32:35 [b]Ezek. 6:7; 20:12, 20 [1]Lit. *that open the womb*
**27** [a]Rom. 2:24
**28** [a]Ezek. 6:13 [b]Ezek. 16:19
**29** [1]Place for pagan worship [2]Lit. *High Place*
**30** [a]Judg. 2:19 [b]Jer. 7:26; 16:12
**31** [a]Ezek. 16:20; 20:26 [b]Ezek. 20:3
**32** [a]Ezek. 11:5

**33** "*As* I live," says the Lord GOD, "surely with a
mighty hand, [a]with an outstretched arm, and with
fury poured out, I will rule over you.
34 "I will bring you out from the peoples and
gather you out of the countries where you are
scattered, with a mighty hand, with an outstretched arm, and with fury poured out.
35 "And I will bring you into the wilderness of
the peoples, and there [a]I will plead My case with
you face to face.
36 [a]"Just as I pleaded My case with your fathers
in the wilderness of the land of Egypt, so I will
plead My case with you," says the Lord GOD.
37 "I will make you [a]pass under the rod, and I
will bring you into the bond of the [b]covenant;
38 [a]"I will purge the rebels from among you, and
those who transgress against Me; I will bring
them out of the country where they dwell, but
[b]they shall not enter the land of Israel. Then you
will know that I *am* the LORD.
**39** "As for you, O house of Israel," thus says the
Lord GOD: [a]"Go, serve every one of you his idols—
and hereafter—if you will not obey Me; [b]but
profane My holy name no more with your gifts
and your idols.
40 "For [a]on My holy mountain, on the mountain
height of Israel," says the Lord GOD, "there [b]all
the house of Israel, all of them in the land, shall
serve Me; there [c]I will accept them, and there I
will require your offerings and the firstfruits of
your [1]sacrifices, together with all your holy things.
41 "I will accept you as a [a]sweet aroma when I
bring you out from the peoples and gather you out
of the countries where you have been scattered;
and I will be hallowed in you before the Gentiles.
42 [a]"Then you shall know that I *am* the LORD,
[b]when I bring you into the land of Israel, into the
country *for* which I raised My hand in an oath to
give to your fathers.
43 "And [a]there you shall remember your ways
and all your doings with which you were defiled;
and [b]you shall [1]loathe yourselves in your own
sight because of all the evils that you have committed.
44 [a]"Then you shall know that I *am* the LORD,
when I have dealt with you [b]for My name's sake,
not according to your wicked ways nor according
to your corrupt doings, O house of Israel," says
the Lord GOD.' "
**45** Furthermore the word of the LORD came to
me, saying,
46 [a]"Son of man, set your face toward the south;
[1]preach against the south and prophesy against
the forest land, the [2]South,
47 "and say to the forest of the South, 'Hear the
word of the LORD! Thus says the Lord GOD:
"Behold, [a]I will kindle a fire in you, and it shall
devour [b]every green tree and every dry tree in
you; the blazing flame shall not be quenched, and
all faces [c]from the south to the north shall be
scorched by it.
48 "All flesh shall see that I, the LORD, have
kindled it; it shall not be quenched." ' "
49 Then I said, "Ah, Lord GOD! They say of me,
'Does he not speak [a]parables?' "

## *The Sword of the LORD*

**21** And the word of the LORD came to me,
saying,
2 [a]"Son of man, set your face toward Jerusalem,
[b]preach[1] against the holy places, and prophesy
against the land of Israel;
3 "and say to the land of Israel, 'Thus says the
LORD: "Behold, I *am* [a]against you, and I will draw
My sword out of its sheath and cut off both
[b]righteous and wicked from you.
4 "Because I will cut off both righteous and
wicked from you, therefore My sword shall go out
of its sheath against all flesh [a]from south *to* north,
5 "that all flesh may know that I, the LORD,
have drawn My sword out of its sheath; it [a]shall
not return anymore." '
6 [a]"Sigh therefore, son of man, with [1]a breaking
heart, and sigh with bitterness before their eyes.
7 "And it shall be when they say to you, 'Why
are you sighing?' that you shall answer, 'Because
of the news; when it comes, every heart will melt,
[a]all hands will be feeble, every spirit will faint, and
all knees will be weak *as* water. Behold, it is
coming and shall be brought to pass,' says the
Lord GOD."
**8** Again the word of the LORD came to me,
saying,
9 "Son of man, prophesy and say, 'Thus says the
LORD!' Say:

[a]'A sword, a sword is sharpened
And also polished!
10 Sharpened to make a dreadful slaughter,
Polished to flash like lightning!
Should we then make mirth?
It despises the scepter of My son,
*As it does* all wood.
11 And He has given it to be polished,
That it may be handled;
This sword is sharpened, and it is polished
To be given into the hand of [a]the slayer.'

12 "Cry and wail, son of man;
For it will be against My people,
Against all the princes of Israel.
Terrors including the sword
will be against My people;
Therefore [a]strike *your* thigh.

13 "Because *it is* [a]a testing,
And what if *the sword* despises
even the scepter?
[b]*The scepter* shall be no *more*,"

says the Lord GOD.

**14** "You therefore, son of man, prophesy,
And [a]strike *your* hands together.
The third time let the sword
do double *damage*.
It *is* the sword *that* slays,
The sword that slays the great *men*,
That enters their [b]private chambers.
15 I have set the point of the sword against all
their gates,
That the heart may melt
and many may stumble.
Ah! [a]*It is* made bright;
*It is* grasped for slaughter:

16 "Swords[a1] at the ready!
Thrust right!
Set your blade!
Thrust left—
Wherever your [2]edge is ordered!

17 "I also will [a]beat My fists together,
And [b]I will cause My fury to rest;
I, the LORD, have spoken."

**33** [a]Jer. 21:5
**35** [a]Jer. 2:9, 35; Ezek. 17:20
**36** [a]Num. 14:21–23, 28
**37** [a]Lev. 27:32 [b]Ps. 89:30–34
**38** [a]Ezek. 34:17 [b]Jer. 44:14
**39** [a]Amos 4:4 [b]Is. 1:13–15
**40** [a]Is. 2:2, 3 [b]Ezek. 37:22 [c]Zech. 8:20–22 [1]*offerings*
**41** [a]Phil. 4:18
**42** [a]Ezek. 36:23; 38:23 [b]Ezek. 11:17; 34:13; 36:24
**43** [a]Ezek. 16:61 [b]Lev. 26:39 [1]Or *despise*
**44** [a]Ezek. 24:24 [b]Ezek. 36:22
**46** [a]Ezek. 21:2 [1]*proclaim*, lit. *drop* [2]Heb. *Negev*
**47** [a]Jer. 21:14 [b]Luke 23:31 [c]Ezek. 21:4
**49** [a]Ezek. 12:9; 17:2

CHAPTER 21
**2** [a]Ezek. 20:46 [b]Amos 7:16 [1]*proclaim*, lit. *drop*
**3** [a]Ezek. 5:8 [b]Job 9:22
**4** [a]Ezek. 20:47
**5** [a][Is. 45:23; 55:11]
**6** [a]Is. 22:4 [1]Emotional distress, lit. *the breaking of your loins*
**7** [a]Ezek. 7:17
**9** [a]Deut. 32:41
**11** [a]Ezek. 21:19
**12** [a]Jer. 31:19
**13** [a]Job 9:23 [b]Ezek. 21:27
**14** [a]Num. 24:10 [b]1 Kin. 20:30
**15** [a]Ezek. 21:10, 28
**16** [a]Ezek. 14:17 [1]Lit. *Sharpen yourself!* or *Unite yourself!* [2]Lit. *face*
**17** [a]Ezek. 22:13 [b]Ezek. 5:13; 16:42; 24:13

**18** The word of the LORD came to me again,
saying:
19 "And son of man, appoint for yourself two
ways for the sword of the king of Babylon to go;
both of them shall go from the same land. Make a
sign; put *it* at the head of the road to the city.
20 "Appoint a road for the sword to go to [a]Rab-
bah of the Ammonites, and to Judah, into fortified
Jerusalem.
21 "For the king of Babylon stands at the parting
of the road, at the fork of the two roads, to use
divination: he shakes the arrows, he consults the
[1]images, he looks at the liver.
22 "In his right hand is the divination for Jerusalem: to set up battering rams, to call for a slaughter, to [a]lift the voice with shouting, [b]to set battering rams against the gates, to heap up a *siege*
mound, and to build a wall.
23 "And it will be to them like a false divination
in the eyes of those who [a]have sworn oaths with
them; but he will bring their iniquity to remembrance, that they may be taken.
**24** "Therefore thus says the Lord GOD: 'Because
you have made your iniquity to be remembered, in
that your transgressions are uncovered, so that in
all your doings your sins appear—because you
have come to remembrance, you shall be taken in
hand.
25 'Now to you, O [a]profane, wicked prince of
Israel, [b]whose day has come, whose iniquity *shall*
end,
26 'thus says the Lord GOD:

"Remove the turban, and take off the crown;
Nothing *shall remain* the same.
[a]Exalt the humble, and humble the exalted.
27 [1]Overthrown, overthrown,
I will make it overthrown!
[a]It shall be no *longer,*
Until He comes whose right it is,
And I will give it *to* [b]*Him.*" '

**28** "And you, son of man, prophesy and say,
'Thus says the Lord GOD [a]concerning the Ammonites and concerning their reproach,' and say:

'A sword, a sword *is* drawn,
Polished for slaughter,
For consuming, for flashing—
29 While they [a]see false visions for you,
While they divine a lie to you,
To bring you on the necks of the wicked, the
slain
[b]Whose day has come,
Whose iniquity *shall* end.

30 'Return[a] *it* to its sheath.
[b]I will judge you
In the place where you were created,
[c]In the land of your [1]nativity.
31 I will [a]pour out My indignation on you;
I will [b]blow against you with the fire of My
wrath,
And deliver you into the hands
of brutal men *who are* skillful to [c]destroy.
32 You shall be fuel for the fire;
Your blood shall be in the midst of the land.
[a]You shall not be remembered,
For I the LORD have spoken.' "

### *The Sins of Jerusalem*

**22** Moreover the word of the LORD came to me,
saying,
2 "Now, son of man, [a]will you judge, will you
judge [b]the bloody city? Yes, show her all her
abominations!
3 "Then say, 'Thus says the Lord GOD: "The city
sheds [a]blood in her own midst, that her time may
come; and she makes idols within herself to defile
herself.
4 "You have become guilty by the blood which
you have [a]shed, and have defiled yourself with the
idols which you have made. You have caused your
days to draw near, and have come to *the end of*
your years; [b]therefore I have made you a reproach
to the nations, and a mockery to all countries.
5 "*Those* near and *those* far from you will mock
you as [1]infamous *and* full of tumult.
**6** "Look, [a]the princes of Israel: each one has
used his [1]power to shed blood in you.
7 "In you they have [a]made light of father and
mother; in your midst they have [b]oppressed the
stranger; in you they have mistreated the [1]father-
less and the widow.
8 "You have despised My holy things and [a]pro-
faned My Sabbaths.
9 "In you are [a]men who slander to cause bloodshed; [b]in you are those who eat on the mountains;
in your midst they commit lewdness.
10 "In you men [a]uncover their fathers' nakedness; in you they violate women who are [b]set
apart during their impurity.
11 "One commits abomination [a]with his neighbor's wife; [b]another lewdly defiles his daughter-in-
law; and another in you violates his sister, his
father's [c]daughter.
12 "In you [a]they take bribes to shed blood; [b]you
take usury and increase; you have made profit
from your neighbors by extortion, and [c]have
forgotten Me," says the Lord GOD.
**13** "Behold, therefore, I [a]beat My fists at the
dishonest profit which you have made, and at the
bloodshed which has been in your midst.
14 [a]"Can your heart endure, or can your hands
remain strong, in the days when I shall deal with
you? [b]I, the LORD, have spoken, and will do *it.*
15 [a]"I will scatter you among the nations, disperse you throughout the countries, and [b]remove
your filthiness completely from you.
16 "You shall defile yourself in the sight of the
nations; then [a]you shall know that I *am* the
LORD." ' "
**17** The word of the LORD came to me, saying,
18 "Son of man, [a]the house of Israel has become
dross to Me; they *are* all bronze, tin, iron, and
lead, in the midst of a [b]furnace; they have become
dross from silver.
19 "Therefore thus says the Lord GOD: 'Because
you have all become dross, therefore behold, I will
gather you into the midst of Jerusalem.
20 '*As men* gather silver, bronze, iron, lead, and
tin into the midst of a furnace, to blow fire on it,
to [a]melt *it;* so I will gather *you* in My anger and in
My fury, and I will leave *you there* and melt you.
21 'Yes, I will gather you and blow on you with
the fire of My wrath, and you shall be melted in its
midst.
22 'As silver is melted in the midst of a furnace,
so shall you be melted in its midst; then you shall
know that I, the LORD, have [a]poured out My fury
on you.' "
**23** And the word of the LORD came to me, saying,
24 "Son of man, say to her: 'You *are* a land that is
[a]not [1]cleansed or rained on in the day of indignation.'

**20** [a]Jer. 49:2
**21** [1]Heb. *teraphim*
**22** [a]Jer. 51:14 [b]Ezek. 4:2
**23** [a]Ezek. 17:16, 18
**25** [a]Jer. 52:2 [b]Ezek. 21:29
**26** [a]Luke 1:52
**27** [a][Luke 1:32, 33] [b][Jer. 23:5, 6] [1]Or *Distortion, Ruin*
**28** [a]Ezek. 25:1–7
**29** [a]Ezek. 12:24; 13:6–9; 22:28 [b]Job 18:20
**30** [a]Jer. 47:6, 7 [b]Gen. 15:14 [c]Ezek. 16:3 [1]Or *origin*
**31** [a]Ezek. 7:8 [b]Ezek. 22:20, 21 [c]Hab. 1:6–10
**32** [a]Ezek. 25:10

CHAPTER 22
**2** [a]Ezek. 20:4 [b]Nah. 3:1
**3** [a]Ezek. 24:6, 7
**4** [a]2 Kin. 21:16 [b]Deut. 28:37
**5** [1]Lit. *defiled of name*
**6** [a]Is. 1:23 [1]Lit. *arm*
**7** [a]Lev. 20:9 [b]Ex. 22:22 [1]Lit. *orphan*
**8** [a]Lev. 19:30
**9** [a]Lev. 19:16 [b]Ezek. 18:6, 11
**10** [a]Lev. 18:7, 8 [b]Lev. 18:19; 20:18
**11** [a]Ezek. 18:11 [b]Lev. 18:15 [c]Lev. 18:9
**12** [a]Ex. 23:8 [b]Ex. 22:25 [c]Ezek. 23:35
**13** [a]Ezek. 21:17
**14** [a]Ezek. 21:7 [b]Ezek. 17:24
**15** [a]Deut. 4:27 [b]Ezek. 23:27, 48
**16** [a]Ps. 9:16
**18** [a]Is. 1:22 [b]Prov. 17:3
**20** [a]Is. 1:25
**22** [a]Ezek. 20:8, 33
**24** [a]Ezek. 24:13 [1]So with MT, Syr., Vg.; LXX *showered upon*

25 [a]"The conspiracy of her [1]prophets in her midst
is like a roaring lion tearing the prey; they [b]have
devoured [2]people; [c]they have taken treasure and
precious things; they have made many widows in
her midst.
26 [a]"Her priests have [1]violated My law and [b]pro-
faned My holy things; they have not [c]distin-
guished between the holy and unholy, nor have
they made known *the difference* between the
unclean and the clean; and they have hidden their
eyes from My Sabbaths, so that I am profaned
among them.
27 "Her [a]princes in her midst *are* like wolves
tearing the prey, to shed blood, to destroy [1]people,
and to get dishonest gain.
28 [a]"Her prophets plastered them with untempered *mortar,* [b]seeing false visions, and divining
[c]lies for them, saying, 'Thus says the Lord GOD,'
when the LORD had not spoken.
29 "The people of the land have used oppressions,
committed robbery, and mistreated the poor and
needy; and they wrongfully [a]oppress the stranger.
30 [a]"So I sought for a man among them who
would [b]make a wall, and [c]stand in the gap before
Me on behalf of the land, that I should not destroy
it; but I found no one.
31 "Therefore I have [a]poured out My indignation
on them; I have consumed them with the fire of
My wrath; and I have recompensed [b]their deeds
on their own heads," says the Lord GOD.

### *The Parable of the Two Sisters*

**23** The word of the LORD came again to me, saying:

2 "Son of man, there were [a]two women,
The daughters of one mother.
3 [a]They committed harlotry in Egypt,
They committed harlotry in [b]their youth;
Their breasts were there embraced,
Their virgin bosom was there pressed.
4 Their names: [1]Oholah the elder
and [2]Oholibah [a]her sister;
[b]They were Mine,
And they bore sons and daughters.
*As for* their names,
Samaria *is* Oholah,
and Jerusalem *is* Oholibah.

5 "Oholah played the harlot
even though she was Mine;
And she lusted for her lovers,
the neighboring [a]Assyrians,
6 *Who were* clothed in purple,
Captains and rulers,
All of them desirable young men,
Horsemen riding on horses.
7 Thus she committed her harlotry with them,
All of them choice men of Assyria;
And with all for whom she lusted,
With all their idols, she defiled herself.
8 She has never given up her harlotry *brought*
[a]from Egypt,
For in her youth they had lain with her,
Pressed her virgin bosom,
And poured out their immorality upon her.

9 "Therefore I have delivered her
Into the hand of her lovers,
Into the hand of the [a]Assyrians,
For whom she lusted.
10 They uncovered her nakedness,
Took away her sons and daughters,
And slew her with the sword;
She became a byword among women,
For they had executed judgment on her.

11 "Now [a]although her sister Oholibah saw *this,*
[b]she became more corrupt in her lust than she,
and in her harlotry more corrupt than her sister's
harlotry.

12 "She lusted for the neighboring [a]Assyrians,
[b]Captains and rulers,
Clothed most gorgeously,
Horsemen riding on horses,
All of them desirable young men.
13 Then I saw that she was defiled;
Both *took* the same way.
14 But she increased her harlotry;
She looked at men portrayed on the wall,
Images of [a]Chaldeans portrayed in vermilion,
15 Girded with belts around their waists,
Flowing turbans on their heads,
All of them looking like captains,
In the manner of the Babylonians of
Chaldea,
The land of their nativity.
16 [a]As soon as her eyes saw them,
She lusted for them
And sent [b]messengers to them in Chaldea.

17 "Then the [1]Babylonians came to her,
into the bed of love,
And they defiled her with their immorality;
So she was defiled by them,
[a]and alienated herself from them.
18 She revealed her harlotry
and uncovered her nakedness.
Then [a]I [b]alienated Myself from her,
As I had alienated Myself from her sister.

19 "Yet she multiplied her harlotry
In calling to remembrance the days of her
youth,
[a]When she had played the harlot
in the land of Egypt.
20 For she lusted for her [1]paramours,
Whose flesh *is like* the flesh of donkeys,
And whose issue *is like* the issue of horses.
21 Thus you called to remembrance
the lewdness of your youth,
When the [a]Egyptians pressed your bosom
Because of your youthful breasts.

**22** "Therefore, Oholibah, thus says the Lord GOD:

[a]'Behold, I will stir up your lovers against you,
From whom you have alienated yourself,
And I will bring them against you
from every side:
23 The Babylonians,
All the Chaldeans,
[a]Pekod, Shoa, Koa,
[b]All the Assyrians with them,
All of them desirable young men,
Governors and rulers,
Captains and men of renown,
All of them riding on horses.
24 And they shall come against you
With chariots, wagons, and war-horses,
With a horde of people.
They shall array against you
Buckler, shield, and helmet all around.

**25** [a]Jer. 11:9; Hos. 6:9 [b]Matt. 23:14 [c]Mic. 3:11; Zeph. 3:3, 4 [1]So with MT, Vg.; LXX *princes;* Tg. *scribes* [2]Lit. *souls*
**26** [a]Jer. 32:32; Lam. 4:3; Mal. 2:8 [b]1 Sam. 2:29 [c]Lev. 10:10 [1]Lit. *done violence to*
**27** [a]Is. 1:23; Ezek. 22:6; Mic. 3:1–3, 9–11; Zeph. 3:3 [1]Lit. *souls*
**28** [a]Ezek. 13:10 [b]Ezek. 13:6, 7 [c]Jer. 23:25–32; Ezek. 21:29
**29** [a]Ex. 23:9; Lev. 19:33
**30** [a]Is. 59:16; 63:5; Jer. 5:1 [b]Ezek. 13:5 [c]Ps. 106:23; Jer. 15:1
**31** [a]Ezek. 22:22 [b]Ezek. 9:10; [Rom 2:8, 9]
CHAPTER 23
**2** [a]Jer. 3:7, 8; Ezek. 16:44–46
**3** [a]Lev. 17:7; Josh. 24:14; Jer. 3:9 [b]Ezek. 16:22
**4** [a]Jer. 3:6, 7 [b]Ezek. 16:8, 20 [1]Lit. *Her Own Tabernacle* [2]Lit. *My Tabernacle Is in Her*
**5** [a]2 Kin. 15:19; 16:7; 17:3; Ezek. 16:28; Hos. 5:13; 8:9, 10
**8** [a]Ex. 32:4; 1 Kin. 12:28; 2 Kin. 10:29; 17:16; Ezek. 23:3, 19
**9** [a]2 Kin. 17:3
**11** [a]Jer. 3:8 [b]Jer. 3:8–11; Ezek. 16:51, 52
**12** [a]2 Kin. 16:27, 28; Ezek. 16:28 [b]Ezek. 23:6, 23
**14** [a]Jer. 50:2; Ezek. 8:10; 16:29
**16** [a]2 Kin. 24:1 [b]Is. 57:9
**17** [a]Ezek. 23:22, 28 [1]Lit. *sons of Babel*
**18** [a]Jer. 6:8 [b]Ps. 78:59; 106:40; Jer. 12:8
**19** [a]Lev. 18:3; Ezek. 23:2
**20** [1]Illicit lovers
**21** [a]Ezek. 16:26
**22** [a]Ezek. 16:37–41; 23:28
**23** [a]Jer. 50:21 [b]Ezek. 23:12

'I will delegate judgment to them,
And they shall judge you
according to their judgments.
25 I will set My [a]jealousy against you,
And they shall deal furiously with you;
They shall remove your nose and your ears,
And your remnant shall fall by the sword;
They shall take your sons
and your daughters,
And your remnant shall be devoured by fire.
26 [a]They shall also strip you of your clothes
And take away your beautiful jewelry.

27 'Thus [a]I will make you cease
your lewdness and your [b]harlotry
*Brought* from the land of Egypt,
So that you will not lift your eyes to them,
Nor remember Egypt anymore.'

28 "For thus says the Lord GOD: 'Surely I will
deliver you into the hand of [a]those you hate, into
the hand *of those* [b]from whom you alienated
yourself.
29 [a]'They will deal hatefully with you, take away
all you have worked for, and [b]leave you naked and
bare. The nakedness of your harlotry shall be
uncovered, both your lewdness and your harlotry.
30 'I will do these *things* to you because you have
[a]gone as a harlot after the Gentiles, because you
have become defiled by their idols.
31 'You have walked in the way of your sister;
therefore I will put her [a]cup in your hand.'
**32** "Thus says the Lord GOD:

'You shall drink of your sister's cup,
The deep and wide one;
[a]You shall be laughed to scorn
And held in derision;
It contains much.
33 You will be filled with drunkenness and
sorrow,
The cup of horror and desolation,
The cup of your sister Samaria.
34 You shall [a]drink and drain it,
You shall break its [1]shards,
And tear at your own breasts;
For I have spoken,'
Says the Lord GOD.

35 "Therefore thus says the Lord GOD:

'Because you [a]have forgotten Me
and [b]cast Me behind your back,
Therefore you shall bear the *penalty*
*Of* your lewdness and your harlotry.' "

**36** The LORD also said to me: "Son of man, will
you [a]judge Oholah and Oholibah? Then [b]declare to
them their abominations.
37 "For they have committed adultery, and
[a]blood *is* on their hands. They have committed
adultery with their idols, and even sacrificed their
sons [b]whom they bore to Me, passing them
through *the fire,* to devour *them.*
38 "Moreover they have done this to Me: They
have [a]defiled My sanctuary on the same day and
[b]profaned My Sabbaths.
39 "For after they had slain their children for
their idols, on the same day they came into My
sanctuary to profane it; and indeed [a]thus they
have done in the midst of My house.
40 "Furthermore you sent for men to come from
afar, [a]to whom a messenger *was* sent; and there
they came. And you [b]washed yourself for them,
[c]painted your eyes, and adorned yourself with
ornaments.
41 "You sat on a stately [a]couch, with a table
prepared before it, [b]on which you had set My
incense and My oil.
42 "The sound of a carefree multitude *was* with
her, and [1]Sabeans *were* brought from the wilderness with men of the common sort, who put
bracelets on their [2]wrists and beautiful crowns on
their heads.
43 "Then I said concerning *her who had grown*
old in adulteries, 'Will they commit harlotry with
her now, and she *with them?*'
44 "Yet they went in to her, as men go in to a
woman who plays the harlot; thus they went in to
Oholah and Oholibah, the lewd women.
45 "But righteous men will [a]judge them after the
manner of adulteresses, and after the manner of
women who shed blood, because they *are* adulteresses, and [b]blood *is* on their hands.
**46** "For thus says the Lord GOD: [a]'Bring up an
assembly against them, give them up to trouble
and plunder.
47 [a]'The assembly shall stone them with stones
and [1]execute them with their swords; [b]they shall
slay their sons and their daughters, and burn their
houses with fire.
48 'Thus [a]I will cause lewdness to cease from the
land, [b]that all women may be taught not to practice your lewdness.
49 'They shall repay you for your lewdness, and
you shall [a]pay for your idolatrous sins. [b]Then you
shall know that I *am* the Lord GOD.' "

## *The Parable of the Boiling Pot*

**24** Again, in the ninth year, in the tenth
month, on the tenth *day* of the month, the
word of the LORD came to me, saying,
2 "Son of man, write down the name of the day,
this very day—the king of Babylon started his
siege against Jerusalem [a]this very day.
3 [a]"And utter a parable to the rebellious house,
and say to them, 'Thus says the Lord GOD:

[b]"Put on a pot, set *it* on,
And also pour water into it.
4 Gather pieces *of meat* in it,
Every good piece,
The thigh and the shoulder.
Fill *it* with choice [1]cuts;
5 Take the choice of the flock.
Also pile *fuel* bones under it,
Make it boil well,
And let the cuts simmer in it."

**6** 'Therefore thus says the Lord GOD:

"Woe to [a]the bloody city,
To the pot whose scum *is* in it,
And whose scum is not gone from it!
Bring it out piece by piece,
On which no [b]lot has fallen.
7 For her blood is in her midst;
She set it on top of a rock;
[a]She did not pour it on the ground,
To cover it with dust.
8 That it may raise up fury
and take vengeance,
[a]I have set her blood on top of a rock,
That it may not be covered."

**25** [a]Ex. 34:14
**26** [a]Is. 3:18–23
**27** [a]Ezek. 16:41; 22:15 [b]Ezek. 23:3, 19
**28** [a]Ezek. 16:37–41 [b]Ezek. 23:17
**29** [a]Deut. 28:48 [b]Ezek. 16:39
**30** [a]Ezek. 6:9
**31** [a]Jer. 7:14, 15; 25:15
**32** [a]Ezek. 22:4, 5
**34** [a]Is. 51:17 [1]Earthenware fragments
**35** [a]Jer. 3:21 [b]1 Kin. 14:9
**36** [a]Ezek. 20:4; 22:2 [b]Is. 58:1
**37** [a]Ezek. 16:38 [b]Ezek. 16:20, 21, 36, 45; 20:26, 31
**38** [a]2 Kin. 21:4, 7 [b]Ezek. 22:8
**39** [a]2 Kin. 21:2–8
**40** [a]Is. 57:9 [b]Ruth 3:3 [c]Jer. 4:30
**41** [a]Is. 57:7 [b]Prov. 7:17
**42** [1]Or *drunkards* [2]Lit. *hands*
**45** [a]Ezek. 16:38 [b]Ezek. 23:37
**46** [a]Ezek. 16:40
**47** [a]Ezek. 16:40 [b]Ezek. 24:21 [1]Lit. *cut down*
**48** [a]Ezek. 22:15 [b]Deut. 13:11
**49** [a]Ezek. 23:35 [b]Ezek. 20:38, 42, 44; 25:5

CHAPTER 24
**2** [a]2 Kin. 25:1
**3** [a]Ezek. 17:12 [b]Jer. 1:13
**4** [1]Lit. *bones*
**6** [a]Ezek. 22:2, 3, 27 [b]Nah. 3:10
**7** [a]Lev. 17:13
**8** [a][Matt. 7:2]

9 'Therefore thus says the Lord GOD:

[a]"Woe to the bloody city!
I too will make the pyre great.
10 Heap on the wood,
Kindle the fire;
Cook the meat well,
Mix in the spices,
And let the [1]cuts be burned up.

11 "Then set the pot empty on the coals,
That it may become hot
and its bronze may burn,
*That* [a]its filthiness may be melted in it,
*That* its scum may be consumed.
12 She has [1]grown weary with [2]lies,
And her great scum has not gone from her.
*Let* her scum *be* in the fire!
13 In your [a]filthiness *is* lewdness.
Because I have cleansed you,
and you were not cleansed,
You will [b]not be cleansed of your filthiness
anymore,
[c]Till I have caused My fury to rest upon you.
14 [a]I, the LORD, have spoken *it;*
[b]It shall come to pass, and I will do *it;*
I will not hold back,
[c]Nor will I spare,
Nor will I relent;
According to your ways
And according to your deeds
[1]They will judge you,"
Says the Lord GOD.' "

**15** Also the word of the LORD came to me, saying,
16 "Son of man, behold, I take away from you
the desire of your eyes with one stroke; yet you
shall [a]neither mourn nor weep, nor shall your
tears run down.
17 "Sigh in silence, [a]make no mourning for the
dead; [b]bind your turban on your head, and [c]put
your sandals on your feet; [d]do not cover *your* [1]lips,
and do not eat man's bread *of sorrow.*"
18 So I spoke to the people in the morning, and at
evening my wife died; and the next morning I did
as I was commanded.
**19** And the people said to me, [a]"Will you not tell
us what these *things signify* to us, that you
behave so?"
20 Then I answered them, "The word of the LORD
came to me, saying,
21 'Speak to the house of Israel, "Thus says the
Lord GOD: 'Behold, [a]I will profane My sanctuary,
[1]your arrogant boast, the desire of your eyes, the
[2]delight of your soul; [b]and your sons and daughters whom you left behind shall fall by the sword.
22 'And you shall do as I have done; [a]you shall
not cover *your* [1]lips nor eat man's bread *of sorrow.*
23 'Your turbans shall be on your heads and your
sandals on your feet; [a]you shall neither mourn nor
weep, but [b]you shall pine away in your iniquities
and mourn with one another.
24 'Thus [a]Ezekiel is a sign to you; according to all
that he has done you shall do; [b]and when this
comes, [c]you shall know that I *am* the Lord GOD.' "
**25** 'And you, son of man—*will it* not *be* in the day
when I take from them [a]their stronghold, their joy
and their glory, the desire of their eyes, and [1]that
on which they set their minds, their sons and their
daughters:
26 'on that day [a]one who escapes will come to
you to let *you* hear *it* with *your* ears;
27 [a]'on that day your mouth will be opened to
him who has escaped; you shall speak and no
longer be mute. Thus you will be a sign to them,
and they shall know that I *am* the LORD.' "

## *Prophecies Against Ammon, Moab, Edom, and the Philistines*

**25** The word of the LORD came to me, saying,
2 "Son of man, [a]set your face [b]against the
Ammonites, and prophesy against them.
3 "Say to the Ammonites, 'Hear the word of the
Lord GOD! Thus says the Lord GOD: [a]"Because you
said, 'Aha!' against My sanctuary when it was
profaned, and against the land of Israel when it
was desolate, and against the house of Judah
when they went into captivity,
4 "indeed, therefore, I will deliver you as a
possession to the [1]men of the East, and they shall
set their encampments among you and make their
dwellings among you; they shall eat your fruit,
and they shall drink your milk.
5 "And I will make [a]Rabbah [b]a stable for camels
and Ammon a resting place for flocks. [c]Then you
shall know that I *am* the LORD."
6 'For thus says the Lord GOD: "Because you
[a]clapped *your* hands, stamped your feet, and
[b]rejoiced in heart with all your disdain for the land
of Israel,
7 "indeed, therefore, I will [a]stretch out My hand
against you, and give you as plunder to the
nations; I will cut you off from the peoples, and I
will cause you to perish from the countries; I will
destroy you, and you shall know that I *am* the
LORD."
**8** 'Thus says the Lord GOD: "Because [a]Moab and
[b]Seir say, 'Look! The house of Judah *is* like all the
nations,'
9 "therefore, behold, I will clear the territory of
Moab of cities, of the cities on its frontier, the
glory of the country, Beth Jeshimoth, Baal Meon,
and [a]Kirjathaim.
10 [a]"To the men of the East I will give it as a
possession, together with the Ammonites, that the
Ammonites [b]may not be remembered among the
nations.
11 "And I will execute judgments upon Moab,
and they shall know that I *am* the LORD."
**12** 'Thus says the Lord GOD: [a]"Because of what
Edom did against the house of Judah by taking
vengeance, and has greatly offended by avenging
itself on them,"
13 'therefore thus says the Lord GOD: "I will also
stretch out My hand against Edom, cut off man
and beast from it, and make it desolate from
Teman; [1]Dedan shall fall by the sword.
14 [a]"I will lay My vengeance on Edom by the
hand of My people Israel, that they may do in
Edom according to My anger and according to My
fury; and they shall know My vengeance," says
the Lord GOD.
**15** 'Thus says the Lord GOD: [a]"Because [b]the Philistines dealt vengefully and took vengeance with
[1]a spiteful heart, to destroy because of the [2]old
hatred,"
16 'therefore thus says the Lord GOD: [a]"I will
stretch out My hand against the Philistines, and I
will cut off the [b]Cherethites [c]and destroy the
remnant of the seacoast.
17 "I will [a]execute great vengeance on them with
furious rebukes; [b]and they shall know that I *am*

**9** [a]Hab. 2:12
**10** [1]Lit. *bones*
**11** [a]Ezek. 22:15
**12** [1]Or *wearied Me* [2]Or *toil*
**13** [a]Ezek. 23:36–48 [b]Jer. 6:28–30 [c]Ezek. 5:13; 8:18; 16:42
**14** [a][1 Sam. 15:29] [b]Is. 55:11 [c]Ezek. 5:11 [1]LXX, [Syr.], Tg., Vg. *I*
**16** [a]Jer. 16:5
**17** [a]Jer. 16:5 [b]Lev. 10:6; 21:10 [c]2 Sam. 15:30 [d]Mic. 3:7 [1]Lit. *moustache*
**19** [a]Ezek. 12:9; 37:18
**21** [a]Jer. 7:14 [b]Ezek. 23:25, 47 [1]Lit. *the pride of your strength* [2]Lit. *compassion*
**22** [a]Jer. 16:6, 7 [1]Lit. *moustache*
**23** [a]Job 27:15 [b]Lev. 26:39
**24** [a]Is. 20:3 [b]Jer. 17:15 [c]Ezek. 6:7; 25:5
**25** [a]Ezek. 24:21 [1]Lit. *the lifting up of their soul*
**26** [a]Ezek. 33:21
**27** [a]Ezek. 3:26; 33:22

CHAPTER 25
**2** [a]Ezek. 35:2 [b]Jer. 49:1
**3** [a]Ezek. 26:2
**4** [1]Lit. *sons*
**5** [a]Ezek. 21:20 [b]Is. 17:2 [c]Ezek. 24:24
**6** [a]Job 27:23 [b]Ezek. 36:5
**7** [a]Ezek. 35:3
**8** [a]Amos 2:1, 2 [b]Ezek. 35:2, 5
**9** [a]Jer. 48:23
**10** [a]Ezek. 25:4 [b]Ezek. 21:32
**12** [a]Obad. 10–14
**13** [1]Or *even to Dedan they shall fall*
**14** [a]Is. 11:14
**15** [a]Jer. 25:20 [b]2 Chr. 28:18 [1]Lit. *spite in soul* [2]Or *perpetual*
**16** [a]Zeph. 2:4 [b]1 Sam. 30:14 [c]Jer. 47:4
**17** [a]Ezek. 5:15 [b]Ps. 9:16

the LORD, when I lay My vengeance upon
them." ' "

### *Prophecy Against Tyre*

**26** And it came to pass in the eleventh year, on
the first *day* of the month, *that* the word of
the LORD came to me, saying,
2 "Son of man, [a]because Tyre has said against
Jerusalem, [b]'Aha! She is broken who *was* the
gateway of the peoples; now she is turned over to
me; I shall be filled; she is laid waste.'
3 "Therefore thus says the Lord GOD: 'Behold, I
*am* against you, O Tyre, and will cause many
nations to come up against you, as the sea causes
its waves to come up.
4 'And they shall destroy the walls of Tyre and
break down her towers; I will also scrape her dust
from her, and [a]make her like the top of a rock.
5 'It shall be *a place for* spreading nets [a]in the
midst of the sea, for I have spoken,' says the Lord
GOD; 'it shall become plunder for the nations.
6 'Also her daughter *villages* which *are* in the
fields shall be slain by the sword. [a]Then they shall
know that I am the LORD.'
**7** "For thus says the Lord GOD: 'Behold, I will
bring against Tyre from the north [a]Nebuchadnez-
zar[1] king of Babylon, [b]king of kings, with horses,
with chariots, and with horsemen, and an army
with many people.
8 'He will slay with the sword your daughter
*villages* in the fields; he will [a]heap up a siege
mound against you, build a wall against you, and
raise a [1]defense against you.
9 'He will direct his battering rams against your
walls, and with his axes he will break down your
towers.
10 'Because of the abundance of his horses, their
dust will cover you; your walls will shake at the
noise of the horsemen, the wagons, and the chariots, when he enters your gates, as men enter a
city that has been breached.
11 'With the hooves of his [a]horses he will trample
all your streets; he will slay your people by the
sword, and your strong pillars will fall to the
ground.
12 'They will plunder your riches and pillage your
merchandise; they will break down your walls and
destroy your pleasant houses; they will lay your
stones, your timber, and your soil in the [a]midst of
the water.
13 [a]'I will put an end to the sound of [b]your songs,
and the sound of your harps shall be heard no
more.
14 [a]'I will make you like the top of a rock; you
shall be *a place for* spreading nets, and you shall
never be rebuilt, for I the LORD have spoken,' says
the Lord GOD.
**15** "Thus says the Lord GOD to Tyre: 'Will the
coastlands not [a]shake at the sound of your fall,
when the wounded cry, when slaughter is made in
the midst of you?
16 'Then all the [a]princes of the sea will [b]come
down from their thrones, lay aside their robes, and
take off their embroidered garments; they will
clothe themselves with trembling; [c]they will sit on
the ground, [d]tremble *every* moment, and [e]be
astonished at you.
17 'And they will take up a [a]lamentation for you,
and say to you:

"How you have perished,
O one inhabited by seafaring men,
O renowned city,
Who was [b]strong at sea,
She and her inhabitants,
Who caused their terror
*to be* on all her inhabitants!
18 Now [a]the coastlands tremble
on the day of your fall;
Yes, the coastlands by the sea
are troubled at your departure." '

**19** "For thus says the Lord GOD: 'When I make
you a desolate city, like cities that are not inhabited, when I bring the deep upon you, and great
waters cover you,
20 'then I will bring you down [a]with those who
descend into the Pit, to the people of old, and I
will make you dwell in the lowest part of the
earth, in places desolate from antiquity, with
those who go down to the Pit, so that you may
never be inhabited; and I shall establish glory [b]in
the land of the living.
21 [a]'I will make you a terror, and you *shall be* no
*more;* [b]though you are sought for, you will never
be found again,' says the Lord GOD."

### *Mourning for Tyre*

**27** The word of the LORD came again to me,
saying,
2 "Now, son of man, [a]take up a lamentation for
Tyre,
3 "and say to Tyre, [a]'You who [1]are situated at
the entrance of the sea, [b]merchant of the peoples
on many coastlands, thus says the Lord GOD:

"O Tyre, you have said,
[c]'I *am* perfect in beauty.'
4 Your borders *are* in the midst of the seas.
Your builders have perfected your beauty.
5 They [1]made all *your* planks
of fir trees from [a]Senir;
They took a cedar from Lebanon
to make you a mast.
6 *Of* [a]oaks from Bashan they made your oars;
The company of Ashurites
have inlaid your planks
*With* ivory from [b]the coasts of [1]Cyprus.
7 Fine embroidered linen from Egypt was what
you spread for your sail;
Blue and purple from the coasts of Elishah
was what covered you.

8 "Inhabitants of Sidon and Arvad
were your oarsmen;
Your wise men, O Tyre, were in you;
They became your pilots.
9 Elders of [a]Gebal and its wise men
Were in you to caulk your seams;
All the ships of the sea
And their oarsmen were in you
To market your merchandise.

**10** "Those from Persia, [1]Lydia, and [2]Libya
Were in your army as men of war;
They hung shield and helmet in you;
They gave splendor to you.
11 Men of Arvad with your army
*were* on your walls *all* around,
And the men of Gammad
were in your towers;
They hung their shields
on your walls *all* around;
They made [a]your beauty perfect.

CHAPTER 26
**2** [a]2 Sam. 5:11; Is. 23:1; Jer. 25:22; Amos 1:9; Zech. 9:2 [b]Ezek. 25:3
**4** [a]Ezek. 26:14
**5** [a]Ezek. 27:32
**6** [a]Ezek. 25:5
**7** [a]Jer. 27:3–6; Ezek. 29:18 [b]Ezra 7:12; Is. 10:8; Jer. 52:32; Dan. 2:37, 47 [1]Heb. *Nebuchadrezzar,* and so elsewhere in the book
**8** [a]Jer. 52:4; Ezek. 21:22 [1]Lit. *a large shield*
**11** [a]Hab. 1:8
**12** [a]Ezek. 27:27, 32
**13** [a]Is. 14:11; 24:8; Jer. 7:34; 25:10; Amos 6:5 [b]Is. 23:16; Ezek. 28:13; Rev. 18:22
**14** [a]Ezek. 26:4, 5
**15** [a]Jer. 49:21; Ezek. 27:28
**16** [a]Is. 23:8 [b]Jon. 3:6 [c]Job 2:13 [d]Ezek. 32:10; Hos. 11:10 [e]Ezek. 27:35
**17** [a]Ezek. 27:2–36; Rev. 18:9 [b]Josh. 19:29; Is. 23:4
**18** [a]Ezek. 26:15
**20** [a]Ezek. 32:18 [b]Ezek. 32:23
**21** [a]Ezek. 27:36; 28:19 [b]Ps. 37:10, 36; Ezek. 28:19

CHAPTER 27
**2** [a]Ezek. 26:17
**3** [a]Ezek. 26:17; 28:2 [b]Is. 23:3 [c]Ezek. 28:12 [1]Lit. *sit* or *dwell*
**5** [a]Deut. 3:9; 1 Chr. 5:23; Song 4:8 [1]*built*
**6** [a]Is. 2:12, 13; Zech. 11:2 [b]Gen. 10:4; Is. 23:1, 12; Jer. 2:10 [1]Heb. *Kittim,* western lands, especially Cyprus
**9** [a]Josh. 13:5; 1 Kin. 5:18; Ps. 83:7
**10** [1]Heb. *Lud* [2]Heb. *Put*
**11** [a]Ezek. 27:3

12 [a]"Tarshish *was* your merchant because of
your many luxury goods. They gave you silver,
iron, tin, and lead for your goods.
13 [a]"Javan, Tubal, and Meshech *were* your traders. They bartered [b]human lives and vessels of
bronze for your merchandise.
14 "Those from the house of [a]Togarmah traded
for your wares with horses, steeds, and mules.
15 "The men of [a]Dedan *were* your traders; many
isles *were* the market of your hand. They brought
you ivory tusks and ebony as payment.
16 "Syria *was* your merchant because of the
abundance of goods you made. They gave you for
your wares emeralds, purple, embroidery, fine
linen, corals, and rubies.
17 "Judah and the land of Israel *were* your traders. They traded for your merchandise wheat of
[a]Minnith, millet, honey, oil, and [b]balm.
18 "Damascus *was* your merchant because of the
abundance of goods you made, because of your
many luxury items, with the wine of Helbon and
with white wool.
19 "Dan and Javan paid for your wares, [1]travers-
ing back and forth. Wrought iron, cassia, and cane
were among your merchandise.
20 [a]"Dedan *was* your merchant in saddlecloths
for riding.
21 "Arabia and all the princes of [a]Kedar *were*
your regular merchants. They traded with you in
lambs, rams, and goats.
22 "The merchants of [a]Sheba and Raamah *were*
your merchants. They traded for your wares the
choicest spices, all kinds of precious stones, and
gold.
23 [a]"Haran, Canneh, Eden, the merchants of
[b]Sheba, Assyria, *and* Chilmad *were* your merchants.
24 "These *were* your merchants in choice items—
in purple clothes, in embroidered garments, in
chests of multicolored apparel, in sturdy woven
cords, which were in your marketplace.

25 "The [a]ships of Tarshish were carriers
of your merchandise.
You were filled and very glorious
[b]in the midst of the seas.
26 Your oarsmen brought you
into many waters,
But [a]the east wind broke you
in the midst of the seas.

27 "Your [a]riches, wares, and merchandise,
Your mariners and pilots,
Your caulkers and merchandisers,
All your men of war who *are* in you,
And the entire company which *is* in your
midst,
Will fall into the midst of the seas
on the day of your ruin.
28 The [a]common-land[1] will shake at the sound
of the cry of your pilots.

29 "All [a]who handle the oar,
The mariners,
All the pilots of the sea
Will come down from their ships
*and* stand on the [1]shore.
30 They will make their voice heard because of
you;
They will cry bitterly
and [a]cast dust on their heads;
They [b]will roll about in ashes;

12 [a]Gen. 10:4; 2 Chr. 20:36; Ezek. 38:13
13 [a]Gen. 10:2; Is. 66:19; Ezek. 27:19 [b]Joel 3:3–6; Rev. 18:13
14 [a]Gen. 10:3; Ezek. 38:6
15 [a]Gen. 10:7; Is. 21:13
17 [a]Judg. 11:33; 1 Kin. 5:9, 11; Ezra 3:7; Acts 12:20 [b]Jer. 8:22
19 [1]LXX, Syr. *from Uzal*
20 [a]Gen. 25:3
21 [a]Gen. 25:13; Jer. 49:28; Is. 60:7
22 [a]Gen. 10:7; 1 Kin. 10:1, 2; Ps. 72:10; Is. 60:6; Ezek. 38:13
23 [a]Gen. 11:31; 2 Kin. 19:12; Is. 37:12 [b]Gen. 25:3
25 [a]Ps. 48:7; Is. 2:16 [b]Ezek. 27:4
26 [a]Ps. 48:7; Jer. 18:17; Acts 27:14
27 [a][Prov. 11:4]
28 [a]Ezek. 26:15 [1]*open lands* or *pasture lands*
29 [a]Rev. 18:17 [1]Lit. *land*
30 [a]1 Sam. 4:12; 2 Sam. 1:2; Job 2:12; Lam. 2:10; Rev. 18:19 [b]Esth. 4:1, 3; Jer. 6:26; Jon. 3:6
31 [a]Is. 15:2; Jer. 16:6; Ezek. 29:18
32 [a]Ezek. 26:17 [b]Ezek. 26:4, 5; Rev. 18:18
33 [a]Rev. 18:19
34 [a]Ezek. 26:19 [b]Ezek. 27:27
35 [a]Is. 23:6; Ezek. 26:15, 16
36 [a]Jer. 18:16; Zeph. 2:15 [b]Ezek. 26:2 [c]Ps. 37:10, 36; Ezek. 28:19

CHAPTER 28

2 [a]Jer. 49:16; Ezek. 31:10 [b]Is. 14:14; 47:8; Ezek. 28:9; 2 Thess. 2:4 [c]Ezek. 27:3, 4 [d]Is. 31:3; Ezek. 28:9 [1]Proud
3 [a]Ezek. 14:14; Dan. 1:20; 2:20–23, 28; 5:11, 12; Zech. 9:3
4 [a]Ezek. 27:33; Zech. 9:1–3
5 [a]Ps. 62:10; Zech. 9:3
7 [a]Ezek. 26:7 [b]Ezek. 7:24; 21:31; 30:11; Hab. 1:6–8
8 [a]Is. 14:15
9 [a]Ezek. 28:2

31 They will [a]shave themselves completely bald
because of you,
Gird themselves with sackcloth,
And weep for you
With bitterness of heart *and* bitter wailing.
32 In their wailing for you
They will [a]take up a lamentation,
And lament for you:
[b]'What *city is* like Tyre,
Destroyed in the midst of the sea?

33 'When[a] your wares went out by sea,
You satisfied many people;
You enriched the kings of the earth
With your many luxury goods
and your merchandise.
34 But [a]you are broken by the seas
in the depths of the waters;
[b]Your merchandise and the entire company
will fall in your midst.
35 [a]All the inhabitants of the isles
will be astonished at you;
Their kings will be greatly afraid,
And *their* countenance will be troubled.
36 The merchants among the peoples
[a]will hiss at you;
[b]You will become a horror,
and *be* no [c]more forever.' " ' "

### *The Prince of Tyre Rebuked*

**28** The word of the LORD came to me again,
saying,
2 "Son of man, say to the prince of Tyre, 'Thus
says the Lord GOD:

"Because your heart *is* [a]lifted[1] up,
And [b]you say, 'I *am* a god,
I sit *in* the seat of gods,
[c]In the midst of the seas,'
[d]Yet you *are* a man, and not a god,
Though you set your heart
as the heart of a god
3 (Behold, [a]you *are* wiser than Daniel!
There is no secret that can be hidden from
you!
4 With your wisdom and your understanding
You have gained [a]riches for yourself,
And gathered gold and silver
into your treasuries;
5 [a]By your great wisdom in trade
you have increased your riches,
And your heart is lifted up
because of your riches),"
6 'Therefore thus says the Lord GOD:

"Because you have set your heart
as the heart of a god,
7 Behold, therefore, I will bring [a]strangers
against you,
[b]The most terrible of the nations;
And they shall draw their swords against the
beauty of your wisdom,
And defile your splendor.
8 They shall throw you down into the [a]Pit,
And you shall die the death of the slain
In the midst of the seas.
9 "Will you still [a]say before him who slays you,
'I *am* a god'?
But you *shall be* a man, and not a god,
In the hand of him who slays you.

10 You shall die the death of [a]the uncircumcised
By the hand of aliens;
For I have spoken," says the Lord GOD.' "

11 Moreover the word of the LORD came to me,
saying,
12 "Son of man, [a]take up a lamentation for the
king of Tyre, and say to him, 'Thus says the Lord
GOD:

[b]"You *were* the seal of perfection,
Full of wisdom and perfect in beauty.
13 You were in [a]Eden, the garden of God;
Every precious stone *was* your covering:
The sardius, topaz, and diamond,
Beryl, onyx, and jasper,
Sapphire, turquoise, and emerald with gold.
The workmanship of [b]your timbrels and pipes
Was prepared for you
on the day you were created.

14 "You *were* the anointed [a]cherub who covers;
I established you;
You were on [b]the holy mountain of God;
You walked back and forth
in the midst of fiery stones.
15 You *were* perfect in your ways
from the day you were created,
Till [a]iniquity was found in you.

16 "By the abundance of your trading
You became filled with violence within,
And you sinned;
Therefore I cast you as a profane thing
Out of the mountain of God;
And I destroyed you, [a]O covering cherub,
From the midst of the fiery stones.

17 "Your [a]heart was [1]lifted up
because of your beauty;
You corrupted your wisdom
for the sake of your splendor;
I cast you to the ground,
I laid you before kings,
That they might gaze at you.

18 "You defiled your sanctuaries
By the multitude of your iniquities,
By the iniquity of your trading;
Therefore I brought fire from your midst;
It devoured you,
And I turned you to ashes upon the earth
In the sight of all who saw you.
19 All who knew you among the peoples are
astonished at you;
[a]You have become a horror,
And *shall be* no [b]more forever." ' "

20 Then the word of the LORD came to me,
saying,
21 "Son of man, [a]set your face [b]toward Sidon, and
prophesy against her,
22 "and say, 'Thus says the Lord GOD:

[a]"Behold, I *am* against you, O Sidon;
I will be glorified in your midst;
And [b]they shall know that I *am* the LORD,
When I execute judgments in her
and am [c]hallowed in her.
23 [a]For I will send pestilence upon her,
And blood in her streets;
The wounded shall be judged in her midst
By the sword against her on every side;
Then they shall know that I *am* the LORD.

24 "And there shall no longer be a pricking brier
or [a]a painful thorn for the house of Israel from
among all *who are* around them, who [b]despise
them. Then they shall know that I *am* the Lord
GOD."
25 'Thus says the Lord GOD: "When I have [a]gath-
ered the house of Israel from the peoples among
whom they are scattered, and am [b]hallowed in
them in the sight of the Gentiles, then they will
dwell in their own land which I gave to My
servant Jacob.
26 "And they will [a]dwell [1]safely there, [b]build
houses, and [c]plant vineyards; yes, they will dwell
securely, when I execute judgments on all those
around them who despise them. Then they shall
know that I *am* the LORD their God." ' "

## *Prophecy Against Egypt*

**29** In the tenth year, in the tenth *month,* on
the twelfth *day* of the month, the word of
the LORD came to me, saying,
2 "Son of man, [a]set your face against Pharaoh
king of Egypt, and prophesy against him, and
[b]against all Egypt.
3 "Speak, and say, 'Thus says the Lord GOD:

[a]"Behold, I *am* against you,
O Pharaoh king of Egypt,
O great [b]monster who lies in the midst of his
rivers,
[c]Who has said, 'My [1]River *is* my own;
I have made *it* for myself.'
4 But [a]I will put hooks in your jaws,
And cause the fish of your rivers
to stick to your scales;
I will bring you up out of the midst
of your rivers,
And all the fish in your rivers
will stick to your scales.
5 I will leave you in the wilderness,
You and all the fish of your rivers;
You shall fall on the [1]open [a]field;
[b]You shall not be picked up or [2]gathered.
[c]I have given you as food
To the beasts of the field
And to the birds of the heavens.

6 "Then all the inhabitants of Egypt
Shall know that I *am* the LORD,
Because they have been a [a]staff of reed to
the house of Israel.
7 [a]When they took hold of you with the hand,
You broke and tore all their [1]shoulders;
When they leaned on you,
You broke and made all their backs quiver."

8 'Therefore thus says the Lord GOD: "Surely I
will bring [a]a sword upon you and cut off from you
man and beast.
9 "And the land of Egypt shall become [a]desolate
and waste; then they will know that I *am* the
LORD, because he said, 'The River *is* mine, and I
have made *it.*'
10 "Indeed, therefore, I *am* against you and
against your rivers, [a]and I will make the land of
Egypt utterly waste and desolate, [b]from [1]Migdol
*to* Syene, as far as the border of Ethiopia.
11 [a]"Neither foot of man shall pass through it nor
foot of beast pass through it, and it shall be
uninhabited forty years.
12 [a]"I will make the land of Egypt desolate in the
midst of the countries *that are* desolate; and

**10** [a]Ezek. 31:18; 32:19, 21, 25, 27
**12** [a]Ezek. 27:2 [b]Ezek. 27:3; 28:3
**13** [a]Ezek. 31:8, 9; 36:35 [b]Ezek. 26:13
**14** [a]Ex. 25:20 [b]Ezek. 20:40
**15** [a][Is. 14:12]
**16** [a]Ezek. 28:14
**17** [a]Ezek. 28:2, 5 [1]Proud
**19** [a]Ezek. 26:21 [b]Ezek. 27:36
**21** [a]Ezek. 6:2; 25:2; 29:2 [b]Is. 23:2, 4, 12
**22** [a]Ex. 14:4, 17 [b]Ps. 9:16 [c]Ezek. 28:25
**23** [a]Ezek. 38:22
**24** [a]Josh. 23:13 [b]Ezek. 16:57; 25:6, 7
**25** [a]Is. 11:12, 13 [b]Ezek. 28:22
**26** [a]Jer. 23:6 [b]Amos 9:13, 14 [c]Jer. 31:5 [1]*securely*

CHAPTER 29
**2** [a]Ezek. 28:21 [b]Is. 19:1
**3** [a]Jer. 44:30 [b]Ps. 74:13, 14 [c]Ezek. 28:2 [1]The Nile
**4** [a]Ezek. 38:4
**5** [a]Ezek. 32:4–6 [b]Jer. 8:2; 16:4; 25:33 [c]Jer. 7:33; 34:20 [1]Lit. *face of the field* [2]So with MT, LXX, Vg.; some Heb. mss., Tg. *buried*
**6** [a]Is. 36:6
**7** [a]Ezek. 17:17 [1]So with MT, Vg.; LXX, [Syr.] *hand*
**8** [a]Ezek. 14:17; 32:11–13
**9** [a]Ezek. 30:7, 8
**10** [a]Ezek. 30:12 [b]Ezek. 30:6 [1]Or *the tower*
**11** [a]Ezek. 32:13
**12** [a]Ezek. 30:7, 26 [b]Ezek.

among the cities *that are* laid waste, her cities
shall be desolate forty years; and I will [b]scatter the
Egyptians among the nations and disperse them
throughout the countries."
**13** 'Yet, thus says the Lord GOD: "At the [a]end of
forty years I will gather the Egyptians from the
peoples among whom they were scattered.
14 "I will bring back the captives of Egypt and
cause them to return to the land of Pathros, to the
land of their origin, and there they shall be a
[a]lowly kingdom.
15 "It shall be the lowliest of kingdoms; it shall
never again exalt itself above the nations, for I
will diminish them so that they will not rule over
the nations anymore.
16 "No longer shall it be [a]the confidence of the
house of Israel, but will remind them of *their*
iniquity when they turned to follow them. Then
they shall know that I *am* the Lord GOD." ' "
**17** And it came to pass in the twenty-seventh
year, in the first *month,* on the first *day* of the
month, that the word of the LORD came to me,
saying,
18 "Son of man, [a]Nebuchadnezzar king of Babylon caused his army to labor strenuously against
Tyre; every head *was* made [b]bald, and every
shoulder rubbed raw; yet neither he nor his army
received wages from Tyre, for the labor which
they expended on it.
19 "Therefore thus says the Lord GOD: 'Surely I
will give the land of Egypt to [a]Nebuchadnezzar
king of Babylon; he shall take away her wealth,
carry off her spoil, and remove her pillage; and
that will be the wages for his army.
20 'I have given him the land of Egypt *for* his
labor, because they [a]worked for Me,' says the Lord
GOD.
**21** 'In that day [a]I will cause the [1]horn of the
house of Israel to spring forth, and I will [b]open
your mouth to speak in their midst. Then they
shall know that I *am* the LORD.' "

## *The Fall of Egypt*

**30** The word of the LORD came to me again, saying,
2 "Son of man, prophesy and say, 'Thus says the
Lord GOD:

[a]"Wail, 'Woe to the day!'
3 For [a]the day *is* near,
Even the day of the LORD *is* near;
It will be a day of clouds,
the time of the Gentiles.
4 The sword shall come upon Egypt,
And great anguish shall be in [1]Ethiopia,
When the slain fall in Egypt,
And they [a]take away her wealth,
And [b]her foundations are broken down.

5 "Ethiopia, [1]Libya, [2]Lydia, [a]all the mingled
people, Chub, and the men of the lands who are
allied, shall fall with them by the sword."
**6** 'Thus says the LORD:

"Those who uphold Egypt shall fall,
And the pride of her power shall come down.
[a]From [1]Migdol *to* Syene
Those within her shall fall by the sword,"
Says the Lord GOD.

7 "They[a] shall be desolate in the midst
of the desolate countries,
And her cities shall be in the midst
of the cities *that are* laid waste.
8 Then they will know that I *am* the LORD,
When I have set a fire in Egypt
And all her helpers are destroyed.
9 On that day [a]messengers shall go forth from
Me in ships
To make the [1]careless Ethiopians afraid,
And great anguish shall come upon them,
As on the day of Egypt;
For indeed it is coming!"

**10** 'Thus says the Lord GOD:

[a]"I will also make a multitude of Egypt to
cease
By the hand of Nebuchadnezzar
king of Babylon.
11 He and his people with him,
[a]the most terrible of the nations,
Shall be brought to destroy the land;
They shall draw their swords against Egypt,
And fill the land with the slain.
12 [a]I will make the rivers dry,
And [b]sell the land into the hand of the
wicked;
I will make the land waste,
and all that is in it,
By the hand of aliens.
I, the LORD, have spoken."

**13** 'Thus says the Lord GOD:

"I will also [a]destroy the idols,
And cause the images to cease from [1]Noph;
[b]There shall no longer be princes
from the land of Egypt;
[c]I will put fear in the land of Egypt.
14 I will make [a]Pathros desolate,
Set fire to [b]Zoan,
[c]And execute judgments in [1]No.
15 I will pour My fury on [1]Sin,
the strength of Egypt;
[a]I will cut off the multitude of [2]No,
16 And [a]set a fire in Egypt;
Sin shall have great pain,
No shall be split open,
And Noph *shall be in* distress daily.
17 The young men of [1]Aven
and Pi Beseth shall fall by the sword,
And these *cities* shall go into captivity.
18 [a]At [1]Tehaphnehes the day shall also be
[2]darkened,
When I break the yokes of Egypt there.
And her arrogant strength shall cease in her;
As for her, a cloud shall cover her,
And her daughters shall go into captivity.
19 Thus I will [a]execute judgments on Egypt,
Then they shall know
that I *am* the LORD." ' "

**20** And it came to pass in the eleventh year, in
the first *month,* on the seventh *day* of the month,
*that* the word of the LORD came to me, saying,
21 "Son of man, I have [a]broken the arm of Pharaoh king of Egypt; and see, [b]it has not been
bandaged for healing, nor a [1]splint put on to bind
it, to make it strong enough to hold a sword.
22 "Therefore thus says the Lord GOD: 'Surely I
*am* [a]against Pharaoh king of Egypt, and will
[b]break his arms, both the strong one and the one
that was broken; and I will make the sword fall
out of his hand.

12 [b]Jer. 46:19; Ezek. 30:23, 26
13 [a]Is. 19:23; Jer. 46:26
14 [a]Ezek. 17:6, 14
16 [a]Is. 30:2, 3; 36:4, 6; Lam. 4:17; Ezek. 17:15; 29:6
18 [a]Jer. 25:9; 27:6; Ezek. 26:7–12 [b]Jer. 48:37; Ezek. 27:31
19 [a]Jer. 43:10–13; Ezek. 30:10
20 [a]Is. 10:6, 7; 45:1–3; Jer. 25:9
21 [a]1 Sam. 2:10; Ps. 92:10; 132:17 [b]Ezek. 24:27; Amos 3:7, 8; [Luke 21:15] [1]Strength

CHAPTER 30
2 [a]Is. 13:6; 15:2; Ezek. 21:12; Joel 1:5, 11, 13
3 [a]Ezek. 7:7, 12; Joel 2:1; Obad. 15; Zeph. 1:7
4 [a]Ezek. 29:19 [b]Jer. 50:15 [1]Heb. *Cush*
5 [a]Jer. 25:20, 24 [1]Heb. *Put* [2]Heb. *Lud*
6 [a]Ezek. 29:10 [1]Or *the tower*
7 [a]Jer. 25:18–26; Ezek. 29:12
9 [a]Is. 18:1, 2 [1]Or *secure*
10 [a]Ezek. 29:19
11 [a]Ezek. 28:7; 31:12
12 [a]Is. 19:5, 6 [b]Is. 19:4
13 [a]Is. 19:1; Jer. 43:12; 46:25; Zech. 13:2 [b]Zech. 10:11 [c]Is. 19:16 [1]Ancient Memphis
14 [a]Is. 11:11; Jer. 44:1, 15; Ezek. 29:14 [b]Ps. 78:12, 43; Is. 19:11, 13 [c]Jer. 46:25; Ezek. 30:15, 16; Nah. 3:8–10 [1]Ancient Thebes
15 [a]Jer. 46:25 [1]Ancient Pelusium [2]Ancient Thebes
16 [a]Ezek. 30:8
17 [1]Ancient On, Heliopolis
18 [a]Jer. 2:16 [1]*Tahpanhes,* Jer. 43:7 [2]So with many Heb. mss., Bg., LXX, [Syr.], Tg., Vg.; MT *refrained*
19 [a][Ps. 9:16]; Ezek. 5:8; 25:11
21 [a]Jer. 48:25 [b]Jer. 46:11 [1]Lit. *bandage*
22 [a]Jer. 46:25; Ezek. 29:3 [b]Ps. 37:17

23 [a]'I will scatter the Egyptians among the nations, and disperse them throughout the countries.
24 'I will strengthen the arms of the king of
Babylon and put My sword in his hand; but I will
break Pharaoh's arms, and he will groan before
him with the groanings of a mortally wounded
*man.*
25 'Thus I will strengthen the arms of the king of
Babylon, but the arms of Pharaoh shall fall down;
[a]they shall know that I *am* the LORD, when I put
My sword into the hand of the king of Babylon
and he stretches it out against the land of Egypt.
26 [a]'I will scatter the Egyptians among the nations and disperse them throughout the countries.
Then they shall know that I *am* the LORD.' "

### *Prophecy Against Pharaoh*

**31** Now it came to pass in the [a]eleventh year,
in the third *month,* on the first *day* of the
month, *that* the word of the LORD came to me,
saying,
2 "Son of man, say to Pharaoh king of Egypt
and to his multitude:

[a]'Whom are you like in your greatness?
3 [a]Indeed Assyria *was* a cedar in Lebanon,
With fine branches that shaded the forest,
And of high stature;
And its top was among the thick boughs.
4 [a]The waters made it grow;
Underground waters gave it height,
With their rivers running around
the place where it was planted,
And sent out [1]rivulets
to all the trees of the field.

5 'Therefore [a]its height was exalted
above all the trees of the field;
Its boughs were multiplied,
And its branches became long
because of the abundance of water,
As it sent them out.
6 All the [a]birds of the heavens
made their nests in its boughs;
Under its branches all the beasts of the field
brought forth their young;
And in its shadow all great nations [1]made
their home.

7 'Thus it was beautiful in greatness
and in the length of its branches,
Because its roots reached to abundant
waters.
8 The cedars in the [a]garden of God
could not hide it;
The fir trees were not like its boughs,
And the [1]chestnut trees were not like its
branches;
No tree in the garden of God
was like it in beauty.
9 I made it beautiful with a multitude of
branches,
So that all the trees of Eden envied it,
That *were* in the garden of God.'

**10** "Therefore thus says the Lord GOD: 'Because
you have increased in height, and it set its top
among the thick boughs, and [a]its heart was [1]lifted
up in its height,
11 'therefore I will deliver it into the hand of the
[a]mighty one of the nations, and he shall surely
deal with it; I have driven it out for its wickedness.
12 'And aliens, [a]the most terrible of the nations,
have cut it down and left it; its branches have
fallen [b]on the mountains and in all the valleys; its
boughs lie [c]broken by all the rivers of the land;
and all the peoples of the earth have gone from
under its shadow and left it.

13 'On [a]its ruin will remain
all the birds of the heavens,
And all the beasts of the field
will come to its branches—

14 'So that no trees by the waters may ever again
exalt themselves for their height, nor set their
tops among the thick boughs, that no tree which
drinks water may ever be high enough to reach up
to them.

'For [a]they have all been delivered to death,
[b]To the depths of the earth,
Among the children of men who go down to
the Pit.'

**15** "Thus says the Lord GOD: 'In the day when it
[a]went down to [1]hell, I caused mourning. I covered
the deep because of it. I restrained its rivers, and
the great waters were held back. I caused Lebanon to [2]mourn for it, and all the trees of the field
wilted because of it.
16 'I made the nations [a]shake at the sound of its
fall, when I [b]cast it down to [1]hell together with
those who descend into the Pit; and [c]all the trees
of Eden, the choice and best of Lebanon, all that
drink water, [d]were comforted in the depths of the
earth.
17 'They also went down to hell with it, with
those *slain* by the sword; and *those who were* its
*strong* arm [a]dwelt in its shadows among the
nations.
18 [a]'To which of the trees in Eden will you then
be likened in glory and greatness? Yet you shall be
brought down with the trees of Eden to the depths
of the earth; [b]you shall lie in the midst of the
uncircumcised, with *those* slain by the sword. This
*is* Pharaoh and all his multitude,' says the Lord
GOD."

### *Mourning for Pharaoh and Egypt*

**32** And it came to pass in the twelfth year, in
the [a]twelfth *month,* on the first *day* of the
month, *that* the word of the LORD came to me,
saying,
2 "Son of man, [a]take up a lamentation for Pharaoh king of Egypt, and say to him:

[b]'You are like a young lion among the nations,
And [c]you *are* like a monster in the seas,
[d]Bursting forth in your rivers,
Troubling the waters with your feet,
And [e]fouling their rivers.'

3 "Thus says the Lord GOD:

'I will therefore [a]spread My net over you with
a company of many people,
And they will draw you up in My net.
4 Then [a]I will leave you on the land;
I will cast you out on the open fields,
[b]And cause to [1]settle on you all the birds of
the heavens.
And with you I will fill the beasts of the
whole earth.

---

23 [a]Ezek. 29:12; 30:17, 18, 26
25 [a]Ps. 9:16
26 [a]Ezek. 29:12

CHAPTER 31
1 [a]Jer. 52:5, 6; Ezek. 30:20; 32:1
2 [a]Ezek. 31:18
3 [a]Is. 10:33, 34; Ezek. 17:3, 4, 22; 31:16; Dan. 4:10, 20–23
4 [a]Jer. 51:36; Ezek. 29:3–9 [1]Or *channels*
5 [a]Dan. 4:11
6 [a]Ezek. 17:23; 31:13; Dan. 4:12, 21; Matt. 13:32 [1]Lit. *dwelled*
8 [a]Gen. 2:8, 9; 13:10; Is. 51:3; Ezek. 28:13; 31:16, 18 [1]Or *plane,* Heb. *armon*
10 [a]2 Chr. 32:25; Is. 10:12; 14:13, 14; Ezek. 28:17; Dan. 5:20 [1]Proud
11 [a]Ezek. 30:10; Dan. 5:18, 19
12 [a]Ezek. 28:7; 30:11; 32:12 [b]Ezek. 32:5; 35:8 [c]Ezek. 30:24, 25
13 [a]Is. 18:6; Ezek. 32:4
14 [a]Ps. 82:7 [b]Ezek. 32:18
15 [a]Ezek. 32:22, 23 [1]Or *Sheol* [2]Lit. *be darkened*
16 [a]Ezek. 26:15; Hag. 2:7 [b]Is. 14:15; Ezek. 32:18 [c]Is. 14:8; Hab. 2:17 [d]Ezek. 32:31 [1]Or *Sheol*
17 [a]Lam. 4:20
18 [a]Ezek. 32:19 [b]Jer. 9:25, 26; Ezek. 28:10; 32:19, 21

CHAPTER 32
1 [a]Ezek. 31:1; 33:21
2 [a]Ezek. 27:2 [b]Jer. 4:7; Ezek. 19:2–6; Nah. 2:11–13 [c]Is. 27:1; Ezek. 29:3 [d]Jer. 46:7, 8 [e]Ezek. 34:18
3 [a]Ezek. 12:13; 17:20
4 [a]Ezek. 29:5 [b]Is. 18:6; Ezek. 31:13 [1]Lit. *sit* or *dwell*

5 I will lay your flesh [a]on the mountains,
And fill the valleys with your carcass.

6 'I will also water the land
with the flow of your blood,
*Even* to the mountains;
And the riverbeds will be full of you.
7 When *I* put out your light,
[a]I will cover the heavens,
and make its stars dark;
I will cover the sun with a cloud,
And the moon shall not give her light.
8 All the [1]bright lights of the heavens
I will make dark over you,
And bring darkness upon your land,'
Says the Lord GOD.

9 'I will also trouble the hearts of many peoples,
when I bring your destruction among the nations,
into the countries which you have not known.
10 'Yes, I will make many peoples astonished at
you, and their kings shall be horribly afraid of you
when I brandish My sword before them; and [a]they
shall tremble *every* moment, every man for his
own life, in the day of your fall.'
**11** [a]"For thus says the Lord GOD: 'The sword of
the king of Babylon shall come upon you.
12 'By the swords of the mighty warriors, all of
them [a]the most terrible of the nations, I will cause
your multitude to fall.

[b]'They shall plunder the pomp of Egypt,
And all its multitude shall be destroyed.
13 Also I will destroy all its animals
From beside its great waters;
[a]The foot of man shall muddy them no more,
Nor shall the hooves of animals muddy them.
14 Then I will make their waters [1]clear,
And make their rivers run like oil,'
Says the Lord GOD.

15 'When I make the land of Egypt desolate,
And the country is destitute of all that once
filled it,
When I strike all who dwell in it,
[a]Then they shall know that I *am* the LORD.

16 'This *is* the [a]lamentation
With which they shall lament her;
The daughters of the nations shall lament
her;
They shall lament for her, for Egypt,
And for all her multitude,'
Says the Lord GOD."

**17** It came to pass also in the twelfth year, on the
fifteenth *day* of the month, [a]that the word of the
LORD came to me, saying:

18 "Son of man,
wail over the multitude of Egypt,
And [a]cast them down to the depths of the
earth,
Her and the daughters of the famous nations,
With those who go down to the Pit:
19 'Whom [a]do you surpass in beauty?
[b]Go down, be placed with the uncircumcised.'

20 "They shall fall in the midst
of *those* slain by the sword;
She is delivered to the sword,
[a]Drawing her and all her multitudes.
21 [a]The strong among the mighty
Shall speak to him out of the midst of hell
With those who help him:

'They have [b]gone down,
They lie with the uncircumcised,
slain by the sword.'

**22** "Assyria[a] *is* there, and all her company,
With their graves all around her,
All of them slain, fallen by the sword.
23 [a]Her graves are set in the recesses of the Pit,
And her company is all around her grave,
All of them slain, fallen by the sword,
Who [b]caused terror in the land of the living.

**24** "There *is* [a]Elam and all her multitude,
All around her grave,
All of them slain, fallen by the sword,
Who have [b]gone down uncircumcised
to the lower parts of the earth,
[c]Who caused their terror in the land of the
living;
Now they bear their shame with those who
go down to the Pit.
25 They have set her [a]bed
in the midst of the slain,
With all her multitude,
With her graves all around it,
All of them uncircumcised,
slain by the sword;
Though their terror was caused
In the land of the living,
Yet they bear their shame
With those who go down to the Pit;
It was put in the midst of the slain.

**26** "There *are* [a]Meshech and Tubal
and all their multitudes,
With all their graves around it,
All of them [b]uncircumcised,
slain by the sword,
Though they caused their terror in the land
of the living.
27 [a]They do not lie with the mighty
*Who are* fallen of the uncircumcised,
Who have gone down to hell
with their weapons of war;
They have laid their swords
under their heads,
But their iniquities will be on their bones,
Because of the terror of the mighty
in the land of the living.
28 Yes, you shall be broken in the midst of the
uncircumcised,
And lie with *those* slain by the sword.

**29** "There *is* [a]Edom,
Her kings and all her princes,
Who despite their might
Are laid beside *those* slain by the sword;
They shall lie with the uncircumcised,
And with those who go down to the Pit.
30 [a]There *are* the princes of the north,
All of them, and all the [b]Sidonians,
Who have gone down with the slain
In shame at the terror which they caused by
their might;
They lie uncircumcised
with *those* slain by the sword,
And bear their shame
with those who go down to the Pit.

**31** "Pharaoh will see them
And be [a]comforted over all his multitude,
Pharaoh and all his army,
Slain by the sword,"
Says the Lord GOD.

5 [a]Ezek. 31:12
7 [a]Is. 13:10; Joel 2:31; 3:15; Amos 8:9; Matt. 24:29; Mark 13:24; Luke 21:25; Rev. 6:12, 13; 8:12
8 [1]Or *shining*
10 [a]Ezek. 26:16
11 [a]Jer. 46:26; Ezek. 30:4
12 [a]Ezek. 28:7; 30:11; 31:12 [b]Ezek. 29:19
13 [a]Ezek. 29:11
14 [1]Lit. *sink; settle, grow clear*
15 [a]Ex. 7:5; 14:4, 18; Ps. 9:16; Ezek. 6:7
16 [a]2 Sam. 1:17; 2 Chr. 35:25; Jer. 9:17; Ezek. 26:17
17 [a]Ezek. 32:1; 33:21
18 [a]Ezek. 26:20; 31:14
19 [a]Jer. 9:25, 26; Ezek. 31:2, 18 [b]Ezek. 28:10
20 [a]Ps. 28:3
21 [a]Is. 1:31; 14:9, 10; Ezek. 32:27 [b]Ezek. 32:19, 25
22 [a]Ezek. 31:3, 16
23 [a]Is. 14:15 [b]Ezek. 32:24–27, 32
24 [a]Gen. 10:22; 14:1; Is. 11:11; Jer. 25:25; 49:34–39 [b]Ezek. 32:21 [c]Ezek. 32:23
25 [a]Ps. 139:8
26 [a]Gen. 10:2; Ezek. 27:13; 38:2, 3; 39:1 [b]Ezek. 32:19
27 [a]Is. 14:18, 19
29 [a]Is. 9:25, 26; 34:5, 6; Jer. 49:7–22; Ezek. 25:12–14
30 [a]Jer. 1:15; 25:26; Ezek. 38:6, 15; 39:2 [b]Jer. 25:22; Ezek. 28:21–23
31 [a]Ezek. 14:22; 31:16

32 "For I have caused My terror
in the land of the living;
And he shall be placed in the midst of the
uncircumcised
With *those* slain by the sword,
Pharaoh and all his multitude,"
Says the Lord GOD.

### *God's Dealings Are Just*

**33** Again the word of the LORD came to me,
saying,
2 "Son of man, speak to [a]the children of your
people, and say to them: [b]'When I bring the sword
upon a land, and the people of the land take a man
from their territory and make him their [c]watch-
man,
3 'when he sees the sword coming upon the
land, if he blows the trumpet and warns the
people,
4 'then whoever hears the sound of the trumpet
and does [a]not take warning, if the sword comes
and takes him away, [b]his blood shall be on his *own*
head.
5 'He heard the sound of the trumpet, but did
not take warning; his blood shall be upon himself.
But he who takes warning will [1]save his life.
6 'But if the watchman sees the sword coming
and does not blow the trumpet, and the people are
not warned, and the sword comes and takes *any*
person from among them, [a]he is taken away in his
iniquity; but his blood I will require at the watchman's hand.'
**7** [a]"So you, son of man: I have made you a
watchman for the house of Israel; therefore you
shall hear a word from My mouth and warn them
for Me.
8 "When I say to the wicked, 'O wicked *man*,
you shall surely die!' and you do not speak to
warn the wicked from his way, that wicked *man*
shall die in his iniquity; but his blood I will require
at your hand.
9 "Nevertheless if you warn the wicked to turn
from his way, and he does not turn from his way,
he shall die in his iniquity; but you have [1]delivered
your soul.
**10** "Therefore you, O son of man, say to the
house of Israel: 'Thus you say, "If our transgressions and our sins *lie* upon us, and we [a]pine[1] away
in them, [b]how can we then live?"'
11 "Say to them: '*As* I live,' says the Lord GOD, [a]'I
have no pleasure in the death of the wicked, but
that the wicked [b]turn from his way and live. Turn,
turn from your evil ways! For [c]why should you
die, O house of Israel?'
**12** "Therefore you, O son of man, say to the
children of your people: 'The [a]righteousness of the
righteous man shall not deliver him in the day of
his transgression; as for the wickedness of the
wicked, [b]he shall not fall because of it in the day
that he turns from his wickedness; nor shall the
righteous be able to live because of *his righteousness* in the day that he sins.'
13 "When I say to the righteous *that* he shall
surely live, [a]but he trusts in his own righteousness
and commits iniquity, none of his righteous works
shall be remembered; but because of the iniquity
that he has committed, he shall die.
14 "Again, [a]when I say to the wicked, 'You shall
surely die,' if he turns from his sin and does [1]what
is lawful and [2]right,
15 "*if* the wicked [a]restores the pledge, [b]gives back
what he has stolen, and walks in [c]the statutes of
life without committing iniquity, he shall surely
live; he shall not die.
16 [a]"None of his sins which he has committed
shall be remembered against him; he has done
what is lawful and right; he shall surely live.
**17** [a]"Yet the children of your people say, 'The
way of the LORD is not [1]fair.' But it is their way
which is not fair!
18 [a]"When the righteous turns from his righteousness and commits iniquity, he shall die because of it.
19 "But when the wicked turns from his wickedness and does what is lawful and right, he shall
live because of it.
20 "Yet you say, [a]'The way of the LORD is not
[1]fair.' O house of Israel, I will judge every one of
you according to his own ways."
**21** And it came to pass in the twelfth year [a]of our
captivity, in the tenth *month*, on the fifth *day* of
the month, [b]*that* one who had escaped from
Jerusalem came to me and said, [c]"The city has
been [1]captured!"
22 Now [a]the hand of the LORD had been upon me
the evening before the man came who had escaped. And He had [b]opened my mouth; so when
he came to me in the morning, my mouth was
opened, and I was no longer mute.
**23** Then the word of the LORD came to me,
saying:
24 "Son of man, [a]they who inhabit those [b]ruins in
the land of Israel are saying, [c]'Abraham was only
one, and he inherited the land. [d]But we *are* many;
the land has been given to us as a [e]possession.'
25 "Therefore say to them, 'Thus says the Lord
GOD: [a]"You eat *meat* with blood, you [b]lift up your
eyes toward your idols, and [c]shed blood. Should
you then possess the [d]land?
26 "You rely on your sword, you commit abominations, and you [a]defile one another's wives.
Should you then possess the land?"'
27 "Say thus to them, 'Thus says the Lord GOD:
"*As* I live, surely [a]those who *are* in the ruins shall
fall by the sword, and the one who *is* in the open
field [b]I will give to the beasts to be devoured, and
those who *are* in the strongholds and [c]caves shall
die of the pestilence.
28 [a]"For I will make the land most desolate, [1]her
[b]arrogant strength shall cease, and [c]the mountains
of Israel shall be so desolate that no one will pass
through.
29 "Then they shall know that I *am* the LORD,
when I have made the land most desolate because
of all their abominations which they have committed."'
**30** "As for you, son of man, the children of your
people are talking about you beside the walls and
in the doors of the houses; and they [a]speak to one
another, everyone saying to his brother, 'Please
come and hear what the word is that comes from
the LORD.'
31 "So [a]they come to you as people do, they [b]sit
before you *as* My people, and they [c]hear your
words, but they do not do them; [d]for with their
mouth they show much love, *but* [e]their hearts
pursue their *own* gain.
32 "Indeed you *are* to them as a very lovely song
of one who has a pleasant voice and can play well
on an instrument; for they hear your words, but
they do [a]not do them.

CHAPTER 33
**2** [a]Ezek. 3:11 [b]Ezek. 14:17 [c]2 Sam. 18:24, 25
**4** [a]Zech. 1:4 [b][Acts 18:6]
**5** [1]Or *deliver his soul*
**6** [a]Ezek. 33:8
**7** [a]Is. 62:6
**9** [1]Or *saved your life*
**10** [a]Ezek. 24:23 [b]Is. 49:14 [1]Or *waste away*
**11** [a][2 Sam. 14:14] [b][Acts 3:19] [c]Ezek. 18:30, 31
**12** [a]Ezek. 3:20; 18:24, 26 [b][2 Chr. 7:14]
**13** [a]Ezek. 3:20; 18:24
**14** [a]Ezek. 3:18, 19; 18:27 [1]*justice* [2]*righteousness*
**15** [a]Ezek. 18:7 [b]Lev. 6:2, 4, 5 [c]Ezek. 20:11, 13, 21
**16** [a][Is. 1:18; 43:25]
**17** [a]Ezek. 18:25, 29 [1]Or *equitable*
**18** [a]Ezek. 18:26
**20** [a]Ezek. 18:25, 29 [1]Or *equitable*
**21** [a]Ezek. 1:2 [b]Ezek. 24:26 [c]2 Kin. 25:4 [1]Lit. *struck down*
**22** [a]Ezek. 1:3; 8:1; 37:1 [b]Ezek. 24:27
**24** [a]Ezek. 34:2 [b]Ezek. 36:4 [c]Is. 51:2 [d][Matt. 3:9] [e]Ezek. 11:15
**25** [a]Lev. 3:17; 7:26; 17:10–14; 19:26 [b]Ezek. 18:6 [c]Ezek. 22:6, 9 [d]Deut. 29:28
**26** [a]Ezek. 18:6; 22:11
**27** [a]Ezek. 33:24 [b]Ezek. 39:4 [c]1 Sam. 13:6
**28** [a]Jer. 44:2, 6, 22 [b]Ezek. 7:24; 24:21 [c]Ezek. 6:2, 3, 6 [1]Lit. *pride of her strength*
**30** [a]Is. 29:13
**31** [a]Ezek. 14:1 [b]Ezek. 8:1 [c]Is. 58:2 [d]Ps. 78:36, 37 [e][Matt. 13:22]
**32** [a][Matt. 7:21–28]

33 [a]"And when this comes to pass—surely it will
come—then [b]they will know that a prophet has
been among them."

### *God the True Shepherd*

**34** And the word of the LORD came to me,
saying,
2 "Son of man, prophesy against the shepherds of
Israel, prophesy and say to them, 'Thus says the
Lord GOD to the shepherds: [a]"Woe to the shepherds of Israel who feed themselves! Should not
the shepherds feed the flocks?
3 [a]"You eat the fat and clothe yourselves with
the wool; you [b]slaughter the fatlings, *but* you do
not feed the flock.
4 [a]"The weak you have not strengthened, nor
have you healed those who were sick, nor bound
up the broken, nor brought back what was driven
away, nor [b]sought what was lost; but with [c]force
and [1]cruelty you have ruled them.
5 [a]"So they were [b]scattered because *there was*
no shepherd; [c]and they became food for all the
beasts of the field when they were scattered.
6 "My sheep [a]wandered through all the mountains, and on every high hill; yes, My flock was
scattered over the whole face of the earth, and no
one was seeking or searching *for them.*"
7 'Therefore, you shepherds, hear the word of
the LORD:
8 "*as* I live," says the Lord GOD, "surely because
My flock became a prey, and My flock [a]became
food for every beast of the field, because *there
was* no shepherd, nor did My shepherds search for
My flock, [b]but the shepherds fed themselves and
did not feed My flock"—
9 'therefore, O shepherds, hear the word of the
LORD!
10 'Thus says the Lord GOD: "Behold, I *am*
[a]against the shepherds, and [b]I will require My
flock at their hand; I will cause them to cease
feeding the sheep, and the shepherds shall [c]feed
themselves no more; for I will [d]deliver My flock
from their mouths, that they may no longer be
food for them."
11 'For thus says the Lord GOD: "Indeed I Myself
will search for My sheep and seek them out.
12 "As a [a]shepherd seeks out his flock on the day
he is among his scattered sheep, so will I seek out
My sheep and deliver them from all the places
where they were scattered on [b]a cloudy and dark
day.
13 "And [a]I will bring them out from the peoples
and gather them from the countries, and will
bring them to their own land; I will feed them on
the mountains of Israel, [1]in the valleys and in all
the inhabited places of the country.
14 [a]"I will feed them in good pasture, and their
fold shall be on the high mountains of Israel.
[b]There they shall lie down in a good fold and feed
in rich pasture on the mountains of Israel.
15 "I will feed My flock, and I will make them lie
down," says the Lord GOD.
16 [a]"I will seek what was lost and bring back
what was driven away, bind up the broken and
strengthen what was sick; but I will destroy [b]the
fat and the strong, and feed them [c]in judgment."
17 'And *as for* you, O My flock, thus says the
Lord GOD: [a]"Behold, I shall judge between sheep
and sheep, between rams and goats.
18 "*Is it* too little for you to have eaten up the
good pasture, that you must tread down with your
feet the [1]residue of your pasture—and to have
drunk of the clear waters, that you must foul the
residue with your feet?
19 "And *as for* My flock, they eat what you have
trampled with your feet, and they drink what you
have fouled with your feet."
20 'Therefore thus says the Lord GOD to them:
[a]"Behold, I Myself will judge between the fat and
the lean sheep.
21 "Because you have pushed with side and
shoulder, butted all the weak ones with your
horns, and scattered them abroad,
22 "therefore I will save My flock, and they shall
no longer be a prey; and I will judge between
sheep and sheep.
23 "I will establish one [a]shepherd over them, and
he shall feed them—[b]My servant David. He shall
feed them and be their shepherd.
24 "And [a]I, the LORD, will be their God, and My
servant David [b]a prince among them; I, the LORD,
have spoken.
25 [a]"I will make a covenant of peace with them,
and [b]cause wild beasts to cease from the land; and
they [c]will dwell safely in the wilderness and sleep
in the woods.
26 "I will make them and the places all around
[a]My hill [b]a blessing; and I will [c]cause showers to
come down in their season; there shall be [d]show-
ers of blessing.
27 "Then [a]the trees of the field shall yield their
fruit, and the earth shall yield her increase. They
shall be safe in their land; and they shall know
that I *am* the LORD, when I have [b]broken the
bands of their yoke and delivered them from the
hand of those who [c]enslaved them.
28 "And they shall no longer be a prey for the
nations, nor shall beasts of the land devour them;
but [a]they shall dwell safely, and no one shall make
*them* afraid.
29 "I will raise up for them a [a]garden[1] of renown,
and they shall [b]no longer be consumed with
hunger in the land, [c]nor bear the shame of the
Gentiles anymore.
30 "Thus they shall know that [a]I, the LORD their
God, *am* with them, and they, the house of Israel,
*are* [b]My people," says the Lord GOD.' "
31 "You are My [a]flock, the flock of My pasture;
you *are* men, *and* I *am* your God," says the Lord
GOD.

### *Prophecy Against Mount Seir*

**35** Moreover the word of the LORD came to me,
saying,
2 "Son of man, set your face against [a]Mount
Seir and [b]prophesy against it,
3 "and say to it, 'Thus says the Lord GOD:

"Behold, O Mount Seir, I *am* against you;
[a]I will stretch out My hand against you,
And make you [1]most desolate;
4 I shall lay your cities waste,
And you shall be desolate.
Then you shall know that I *am* the LORD.

5 [a]"Because you have had an [1]ancient hatred,
and have shed *the blood of* the children of Israel
by the power of the sword at the time of their
calamity, [b]*when* their iniquity *came to an* end,
6 "therefore, *as* I live," says the Lord GOD, "I
will prepare you for [a]blood, and blood shall pursue
you; [b]since you have not hated [1]blood, therefore
blood shall pursue you.

---

33 [a]1 Sam. 3:20 [b]Ezek. 2:5

CHAPTER 34
2 [a]Zech. 11:17
3 [a]Zech. 11:16 [b]Ezek. 33:25, 26
4 [a]Zech. 11:16 [b]Luke 15:4 [c][1 Pet. 5:3] [1]*harshness* or *rigor*
5 [a]Ezek. 33:21 [b]Matt. 9:36 [c]Is. 56:9
6 [a]1 Pet. 2:25
8 [a]Ezek. 34:5, 6 [b]Ezek. 34:2, 10
10 [a]Jer. 21:13; 52:24–27 [b]Heb. 13:17 [c]Ezek. 34:2, 8 [d]Ezek. 13:23
12 [a]Jer. 31:10 [b]Ezek. 30:3
13 [a]Jer. 23:3 [1]Or *by the streams*
14 [a][John 10:9] [b]Jer. 33:12
16 [a]Mic. 4:6 [b]Is. 10:16 [c]Jer. 10:24
17 [a][Matt. 25:32]
18 [1]*remainder*
20 [a]Ezek. 34:17
23 [a][Is. 40:11] [b]Jer. 30:9
24 [a]Ex. 29:45 [b]Ezek. 37:24, 25
25 [a]Ezek. 37:26 [b]Is. 11:6–9 [c]Jer. 23:6
26 [a]Is. 56:7 [b]Zech. 8:13 [c]Lev. 26:4 [d]Ps. 68:9
27 [a]Is. 4:2 [b]Jer. 2:20 [c]Jer. 25:14
28 [a]Jer. 30:10
29 [a][Is. 11:1] [b]Ezek. 36:29 [c]Ezek. 36:3, 6, 15 [1]Lit. *planting place*
30 [a]Ezek. 34:24 [b]Ezek. 14:11; 36:28
31 [a]Ps. 100:3

CHAPTER 35
2 [a]Ezek. 25:12–14 [b]Amos 1:11
3 [a]Ezek. 6:14 [1]Lit. *a desolation and a waste*
5 [a]Ezek. 25:12 [b]Ps. 137:7 [1]Or *everlasting*
6 [a]Is. 63:1–6 [b]Ps. 109:17 [1]Or *bloodshed*

7 "Thus I will make Mount Seir [1]most desolate,
and cut off from it the [a]one who leaves and the
one who returns.
8 "And I will fill its mountains with the slain; on
your hills and in your valleys and in all your
ravines those who are slain by the sword shall fall.
9 [a]"I will make you [1]perpetually desolate, and
your cities shall be uninhabited; [b]then you shall
know that I *am* the LORD.
**10** "Because you have said, 'These two nations
and these two countries shall be mine, and we will
[a]possess them,' although [b]the LORD was there,
11 "therefore, *as* I live," says the Lord GOD, "I
will do [a]according to your anger and according to
the envy which you showed in your hatred
against them; and I will make Myself known
among them when I judge you.
12 [a]"Then you shall know that I *am* the LORD. I
have [b]heard all your [c]blasphemies which you have
spoken against the mountains of Israel, saying,
'They are desolate; they are given to us to consume.'
13 "Thus [a]with your mouth you have [1]boasted
against Me and multiplied your [b]words against
Me; I have heard *them.*"
14 'Thus says the Lord GOD: [a]"The whole earth
will rejoice when I make you desolate.
15 [a]"As you rejoiced because the inheritance of
the house of Israel was desolate, [b]so I will do to
you; you shall be desolate, O Mount Seir, as well
as all of Edom—all of it! Then they shall know
that I *am* the LORD." '

### *A New Heart and a New Spirit*

**36** "And you, son of man, prophesy to the
[a]mountains of Israel, and say, 'O mountains
of Israel, hear the word of the LORD!
2 'Thus says the Lord GOD: "Because [a]the
enemy has said of you, 'Aha! [b]The [1]ancient heights
[c]have become our possession,' " '
3 "therefore prophesy, and say, 'Thus says the
Lord GOD: "Because they made *you* desolate and
swallowed you up on every side, so that you
became the possession of the rest of the nations,
[a]and you are taken up by the lips of [b]talkers and
slandered by the people"—
4 'therefore, O mountains of Israel, hear the
word of the Lord GOD! Thus says the Lord GOD to
the mountains, the hills, the [1]rivers, the valleys,
the desolate wastes, and the cities that have been
forsaken, which [a]became plunder and [b]mockery to
the rest of the nations all around—
5 'therefore thus says the Lord GOD: [a]"Surely I
have spoken in My burning jealousy against the
rest of the nations and against all Edom, [b]who
gave My land to themselves as a possession, with
whole-hearted joy *and* [1]spiteful minds, in order to
plunder its open country." '
6 "Therefore prophesy concerning the land of
Israel, and say to the mountains, the hills, the
rivers, and the valleys, 'Thus says the Lord GOD:
"Behold, I have spoken in My jealousy and My
fury, because you have [a]borne the shame of the
nations."
7 'Therefore thus says the Lord GOD: "I have
[a]raised My hand in an oath that surely the nations
that *are* around you shall [b]bear their own shame.
**8** "But you, O mountains of Israel, you shall
shoot forth your branches and yield your fruit to
My people Israel, for they are about to come.
9 "For indeed I *am* for you, and I will turn to
you, and you shall be tilled and sown.
10 "I will multiply men upon you, all the house of
Israel, all of it; and the cities shall be inhabited
and [a]the ruins rebuilt.
11 [a]"I will multiply upon you man and beast; and
they shall increase and [1]bear young; I will make
you inhabited as in former times, and do [b]better
*for you* than at your beginnings. [c]Then you shall
know that I *am* the LORD.
12 "Yes, I will cause men to walk on you, My
people Israel; [a]they shall take possession of you,
and you shall be their inheritance; no more shall
you [b]bereave them *of children.*"
13 'Thus says the Lord GOD: "Because they say to
you, [a]'You devour men and bereave your nation *of
children,*'
14 "therefore you shall devour men no more, nor
bereave your nation anymore," says the Lord
GOD.
15 [a]"Nor will I let you hear the taunts of the
nations anymore, nor bear the reproach of the
peoples anymore, nor shall you cause your nation
to stumble anymore," says the Lord GOD.' "
**16** Moreover the word of the LORD came to me,
saying:
17 "Son of man, when the house of Israel dwelt
in their own land, [a]they defiled it by their own
ways and deeds; to Me their way was like [b]the
uncleanness of a woman in her customary impurity.
18 "Therefore I poured out My fury on them [a]for
the blood they had shed on the land, and for their
idols *with which* they had defiled it.
19 "So I [a]scattered them among the nations, and
they were dispersed throughout the countries; I
judged them [b]according to their ways and their
deeds.
20 "When they came to the nations, wherever
they went, they [a]profaned My holy name—when
they said of them, 'These *are* the people of the
LORD, *and* yet they have gone out of His land.'
21 "But I had concern [a]for My holy name, which
the house of Israel had profaned among the
nations wherever they went.
**22** "Therefore say to the house of Israel, 'Thus
says the Lord GOD: "I do not do *this* for your sake,
O house of Israel, [a]but for My holy name's sake,
which you have profaned among the nations
wherever you went.
23 "And I will sanctify My great name, which has
been profaned among the nations, which you
have profaned in their midst; and the nations shall
know that I *am* the LORD," says the Lord GOD,
"when I am [a]hallowed in you before their eyes.
24 "For [a]I will take you from among the nations,
gather you out of all countries, and bring you into
your own land.
25 [a]"Then I will sprinkle clean water on you, and
you shall be clean; I will cleanse you [b]from all
your filthiness and from all your idols.
26 "I will give you a [a]new heart and put a new
spirit within you; I will take the heart of stone out
of your flesh and give you a heart of flesh.
27 "I will put My [a]Spirit within you and cause
you to walk in My statutes, and you will keep My
judgments and do *them.*
28 [a]"Then you shall dwell in the land that I gave
to your fathers; [b]you shall be My people, and I will
be your God.
29 "I will [a]deliver you from all your unclean-

7 [a]Judg. 5:6 [1]Lit. *a waste and a desolation*
9 [a]Jer. 49:13 [b]Ezek. 36:11 [1]Lit. *desolated forever*
10 [a]Ps. 83:4–12 [b][Ps. 48:1–3; 132:13, 14]
11 [a][James 2:13]
12 [a]Ps. 9:16 [b]Zeph. 2:8 [c]Is. 52:5
13 [a][1 Sam. 2:3] [b]Ezek. 36:3 [1]Lit. *made yourself great*
14 [a]Is. 65:13, 14
15 [a]Obad. 12, 15 [b]Lam. 4:21

CHAPTER 36
1 [a]Ezek. 6:2, 3
2 [a]Ezek. 25:3; 26:2 [b]Deut. 32:13 [c]Ezek. 35:10 [1]Or *everlasting*
3 [a]Deut. 28:37 [b]Ezek. 35:13
4 [a]Ezek. 34:8, 28 [b]Ps. 79:4 [1]Or *ravines*
5 [a]Deut. 4:24 [b]Ezek. 35:10, 12 [1]Lit. *scorning souls*
6 [a]Ps. 74:10; 123:3, 4
7 [a]Ezek. 20:5 [b]Jer. 25:9, 15, 29
10 [a]Amos 9:14
11 [a]Jer. 31:27; 33:12 [b]Is. 51:3 [c]Ezek. 35:9; 37:6, 13 [1]Lit. *be fruitful*
12 [a]Obad. 17 [b]Jer. 15:7
13 [a]Num. 13:32
15 [a]Ezek. 34:29
17 [a]Jer. 2:7 [b]Lev. 15:19
18 [a]Ezek. 16:36, 38; 23:37
19 [a]Deut. 28:64 [b][Rom. 2:6]
20 [a]Rom. 2:24
21 [a]Ezek. 20:9, 14
22 [a]Ps. 106:8
23 [a]Ezek. 20:41; 28:22
24 [a]Ezek. 34:13; 37:21
25 [a]Heb. 9:13, 19; 10:22 [b]Jer. 33:8
26 [a]Ezek. 11:19
27 [a]Ezek. 11:19; 37:14
28 [a]Ezek. 28:25; 37:25 [b]Jer. 30:22
29 [a][Rom. 11:26]

nesses. [b]I will call for the grain and multiply it,
and [c]bring no famine upon you.
30 [a]"And I will multiply the fruit of your trees
and the increase of your fields, so that you need
never again bear the reproach of famine among
the nations.
31 "Then [a]you will remember your evil ways and
your deeds that *were* not good; and you [b]will
[1]loathe yourselves in your own sight, for your
iniquities and your abominations.
32 [a]"Not for your sake do I do *this,*" says the
Lord GOD, "let it be known to you. Be ashamed
and confounded for your own ways, O house of
Israel!"
**33** 'Thus says the Lord GOD: "On the day that I
cleanse you from all your iniquities, I will also
enable *you* to dwell in the cities, [a]and the ruins
shall be rebuilt.
34 "The desolate land shall be tilled instead of
lying desolate in the sight of all who pass by.
35 "So they will say, 'This land that was desolate
has become like the garden of [a]Eden; and the
wasted, desolate, and ruined cities *are now* fortified *and* inhabited.'
36 "Then the nations which are left all around
you shall know that I, the LORD, have rebuilt the
ruined places *and* planted what was desolate. [a]I,
the LORD, have spoken *it,* and I will do *it.*"
**37** 'Thus says the Lord GOD: [a]"I will also let the
house of Israel inquire of Me to do this for them: I
will [b]increase their men like a flock.
38 "Like a [1]flock *offered as* holy *sacrifices,* like
the flock at Jerusalem on its [2]feast days, so shall
the ruined cities be filled with flocks of men. Then
they shall know that I *am* the LORD."'"

### *The Valley of Dry Bones*

**37** The [a]hand of the LORD came upon me and
brought me out [b]in the Spirit of the LORD,
and set me down in the midst of the valley; and it
*was* full of bones.
2 Then He caused me to pass by them all
around, and behold, *there were* very many in the
open valley; and indeed *they were* very dry.
3 And He said to me, "Son of man, can these
bones live?" So I answered, "O Lord GOD, [a]You
know."
4 Again He said to me, "Prophesy to these
bones, and say to them, 'O dry bones, hear the
word of the LORD!
5 'Thus says the Lord GOD to these bones:
"Surely I will [a]cause breath to enter into you, and
you shall live.
6 "I will put sinews on you and bring flesh upon
you, cover you with skin and put breath in you;
and you shall live. [a]Then you shall know that I *am*
the LORD."'"
**7** So I prophesied as I was commanded; and as I
prophesied, there was a noise, and suddenly a
rattling; and the bones came together, bone to
bone.
8 Indeed, as I looked, the sinews and the flesh
came upon them, and the skin covered them over;
but *there was* no breath in them.
9 Also He said to me, "Prophesy to the breath,
prophesy, son of man, and say to the [1]breath,
'Thus says the Lord GOD: [a]"Come from the four
winds, O breath, and breathe on these slain, that
they may live."'"
10 So I prophesied as He commanded me, [a]and

**29** [b]Ps. 105:16 [c]Ezek. 34:27, 29
**30** [a]Ezek. 34:27
**31** [a]Ezek. 16:61, 63 [b]Ezek. 6:9; 20:43 [1]*despise*
**32** [a]Deut. 9:5
**33** [a]Ezek. 36:10
**35** [a]Joel 2:3
**36** [a]Ezek. 17:24; 22:14; 37:14
**37** [a]Ezek. 14:3; 20:3, 31 [b]Ezek. 36:10
**38** [1]Lit. *holy flock* [2]*appointed feasts*

CHAPTER 37
**1** [a]Ezek. 1:3 [b]Ezek. 3:14; 8:3; 11:24
**3** [a][1 Sam. 2:6]
**5** [a]Ps. 104:29, 30
**6** [a]Joel 2:27; 3:17
**9** [a][Ps. 104:30] [1]Breath of life
**10** [a]Rev. 11:11 [1]Breath of life
**11** [a]Ezek. 36:10 [b]Ps. 141:7
**12** [a]Is. 26:19; 66:14 [b]Ezek. 36:24
**14** [a]Ezek. 36:27
**16** [a]Num. 17:2, 3 [b]2 Chr. 11:12, 13, 16; 15:9; 30:11, 18
**17** [a]Hos. 1:11
**18** [a]Ezek. 12:9; 24:19
**19** [a]Zech. 10:6 [b]Ezek. 37:16, 17
**20** [a]Ezek. 12:3
**21** [a]Ezek. 36:24
**22** [a]Jer. 3:18 [b]Ezek. 34:23
**23** [a]Ezek. 36:25 [b]Ezek. 36:28, 29
**24** [a]Is. 40:11 [b][John 10:16] [c]Ezek. 36:27
**25** [a]Ezek. 36:28 [b]Is. 60:21 [c]John 12:34
**26** [a]Is. 55:3 [b]Ezek. 36:10 [c][2 Cor. 6:16] [1]Lit. *cut*

[1]breath came into them, and they lived, and stood
upon their feet, an exceedingly great army.
**11** Then He said to me, "Son of man, these bones
are the [a]whole house of Israel. They indeed say,
[b]'Our bones are dry, our hope is lost, and we
ourselves are cut off!'
12 "Therefore prophesy and say to them, 'Thus
says the Lord GOD: "Behold, [a]O My people, I will
open your graves and cause you to come up from
your graves, and [b]bring you into the land of Israel.
13 "Then you shall know that I *am* the LORD,
when I have opened your graves, O My people,
and brought you up from your graves.
14 "I [a]will put My Spirit in you, and you shall live,
and I will place you in your own land. Then you
shall know that I, the LORD, have spoken *it* and
performed *it,*" says the LORD.'"
**15** Again the word of the LORD came to me,
saying,
16 "As for you, son of man, [a]take a stick for
yourself and write on it: 'For Judah and for [b]the
children of Israel, his companions.' Then take
another stick and write on it, 'For Joseph, the
stick of Ephraim, and *for* all the house of Israel,
his companions.'
17 "Then [a]join them one to another for yourself
into one stick, and they will become one in your
hand.
**18** "And when the children of your people speak
to you, saying, [a]'Will you not show us what you
*mean* by these?'—
19 [a]"say to them, 'Thus says the Lord GOD:
"Surely I will take [b]the stick of Joseph, which *is* in
the hand of Ephraim, and the tribes of Israel, his
companions; and I will join them with it, with the
stick of Judah, and make them one stick, and they
will be one in My hand."'
20 "And the sticks on which you write will be in
your hand [a]before their eyes.
21 "Then say to them, 'Thus says the Lord GOD:
"Surely [a]I will take the children of Israel from
among the nations, wherever they have gone, and
will gather them from every side and bring them
into their own land;
22 "and [a]I will make them one nation in the land,
on the mountains of Israel; and [b]one king shall be
king over them all; they shall no longer be two
nations, nor shall they ever be divided into two
kingdoms again.
23 [a]"They shall not defile themselves anymore
with their idols, nor with their detestable things,
nor with any of their transgressions; but [b]I will
deliver them from all their dwelling places in
which they have sinned, and will cleanse them.
Then they shall be My people, and I will be their
God.
**24** [a]"David My servant *shall be* king over them,
and [b]they shall all have one shepherd; [c]they shall
also walk in My judgments and observe My statutes, and do them.
25 [a]"Then they shall dwell in the land that I have
given to Jacob My servant, where your fathers
dwelt; and they shall dwell there, they, their
children, and their children's children, [b]forever;
and [c]My servant David *shall be* their prince forever.
26 "Moreover I will [1]make [a]a covenant of peace
with them, and it shall be an everlasting covenant
with them; I will establish them and [b]multiply
them, and I will set My [c]sanctuary in their midst
forevermore.

27 [a]"My tabernacle also shall be with them;
indeed I will be [b]their God, and they shall be My
people.
28 [a]"The nations also will know that I, the LORD,
[b]sanctify Israel, when My sanctuary is in their
midst forevermore." ' "

## *Prophecy Against Gog*

38 Now the word of the LORD came to me,
saying,
2 [a]"Son of man, [b]set your face against [c]Gog, of the
land of [d]Magog, [1]the prince of Rosh, [e]Meshech,
and Tubal, and prophesy against him,
3 "and say, 'Thus says the Lord GOD: "Behold, I
*am* against you, O Gog, the prince of Rosh, Meshech, and Tubal.
4 [a]"I will turn you around, put hooks into your
jaws, and [b]lead you out, with all your army,
horses, and horsemen, [c]all splendidly clothed, a
great company *with* bucklers and shields, all of
them handling swords.
5 "Persia, [1]Ethiopia, and [2]Libya are with them,
all of them *with* shield and helmet;
6 [a]"Gomer and all its troops; the house of [b]To-
garmah *from* the far north and all its troops—
many people *are* with you.
7 [a]"Prepare yourself and be ready, you and all
your companies that are gathered about you; and
be a guard for them.
8 [a]"After many days [b]you will be visited. In the
latter years you will come into the land of those
brought back from the sword [c]*and* gathered from
many people on [d]the mountains of Israel, which
had long been desolate; they were brought out of
the nations, and now all of them [e]dwell safely.
9 "You will ascend, coming [a]like a storm, covering the [b]land like a cloud, you and all your troops
and many peoples with you."
10 'Thus says the Lord GOD: "On that day it shall
come to pass *that* thoughts will arise in your
mind, and you will make an evil plan:
11 "You will say, 'I will go up against a land of
[a]unwalled villages; I will [b]go to a peaceful people,
[c]who dwell [1]safely, all of them dwelling without
walls, and having neither bars nor gates'—
12 "to take plunder and to take booty, to stretch
out your hand against the waste places *that are
again* inhabited, [a]and against a people gathered
from the nations, who have acquired livestock
and goods, who dwell in the midst of the land.
13 [a]"Sheba, [b]Dedan, the merchants [c]of Tarshish,
and all [d]their young lions will say to you, 'Have
you come to take plunder? Have you gathered
your army to take booty, to carry away silver and
gold, to take away livestock and goods, to take
great plunder?' " '
14 "Therefore, son of man, prophesy and say to
Gog, 'Thus says the Lord GOD: [a]"On that day
when My people Israel [b]dwell safely, will you not
know *it?*
15 [a]"Then you will come from your place out of
the far north, you and many peoples with you, all
of them riding on horses, a great company and a
mighty army.
16 "You will come up against My people Israel
like a cloud, to cover the land. It will be in the
latter days that I will bring you against My land,
so that the nations may [a]know Me, when I am
[b]hallowed in you, O Gog, before their eyes."
17 'Thus says the Lord GOD: "Are *you* he of
whom I have spoken in former days by My servants the prophets of Israel, who prophesied for
years in those days that I would bring you against
them?
18 "And it will come to pass at the same time,
when Gog comes against the land of Israel," says
the Lord GOD, "*that* My fury will show in My face.
19 "For [a]in My jealousy [b]*and* in the fire of My
wrath I have spoken: [c]'Surely in that day there
shall be a great [1]earthquake in the land of Israel,
20 'so that [a]the fish of the sea, the birds of the
heavens, the beasts of the field, all creeping things
that creep on the earth, and all men who *are* on
the face of the earth shall shake at My presence.
[b]The mountains shall be thrown down, the steep
places shall fall, and every wall shall fall to the
ground.'
21 "I will [a]call for [b]a sword against Gog throughout all My mountains," says the Lord GOD. [c]"Every man's sword will be against his brother.
22 "And I will [a]bring him to judgment with
[b]pestilence and bloodshed; [c]I will rain down on
him, on his troops, and on the many peoples who
*are* with him, flooding rain, [d]great hailstones, fire,
and brimstone.
23 "Thus I will magnify Myself and [a]sanctify
Myself, [b]and I will be known in the eyes of many
nations. Then they shall know that I *am* the
LORD." '

## *Gog's Armies Destroyed*

39 "And [a]you, son of man, prophesy against
Gog, and say, 'Thus says the Lord GOD:
"Behold, I *am* against you, O Gog, [1]the prince of
Rosh, Meshech, and Tubal;
2 "and I will [a]turn you around and lead you on,
[b]bringing you up from the far north, and bring you
against the mountains of Israel.
3 "Then I will knock the bow out of your left
hand, and cause the arrows to fall out of your
right hand.
4 [a]"You shall [1]fall upon the mountains of Israel,
you and all your troops and the peoples who *are*
with you; [b]I will give you to birds of prey of every
sort and *to* the beasts of the field to be devoured.
5 "You shall [1]fall on [2]the open field; for I have
spoken," says the Lord GOD.
6 [a]"And I will send fire on Magog and on those
who live [1]in security in [b]the coastlands. Then they
shall know that I *am* the LORD.
7 [a]"So I will make My holy name known in the
midst of My people Israel, and I will not *let them*
[b]profane My holy name anymore. [c]Then the nations shall know that *I am* the LORD, the Holy One
in Israel.
8 [a]"Surely it is coming, and it shall be done,"
says the Lord GOD. "This *is* the day [b]of which I
have spoken.
9 "Then those who dwell in the cities of Israel
will go out and set on fire and burn the weapons,
both the shields and bucklers, the bows and
arrows, the [1]javelins and spears; and they will
make fires with them for seven years.
10 "They will not take wood from the field nor
cut down *any* from the forests, because they will
make fires with the weapons; [a]and they will
plunder those who plundered them, and pillage
those who pillaged them," says the Lord GOD.
11 "It will come to pass in that day *that* I will
give Gog a burial place there in Israel, the valley
of those who pass by east of the sea; and it will

27 [a][John 1:14] [b]Ezek. 11:20
28 [a]Ezek. 36:23 [b]Ezek. 20:12

CHAPTER 38
2 [a]Ezek. 39:1 [b]Ezek. 35:2, 3 [c]Rev. 20:8 [d]Gen. 10:2 [e]Ezek. 32:26 [1]Tg., Vg., Aquila *the chief prince of Meshech,* also v. 3
4 [a]2 Kin. 19:28 [b]Is. 43:17 [c]Ezek. 23:12
5 [1]Heb. *Cush* [2]Heb. *Put*
6 [a]Gen. 10:2 [b]Ezek. 27:14
7 [a]Is. 8:9, 10
8 [a]Is. 24:22 [b]Is. 29:6 [c]Ezek. 34:13 [d]Ezek. 36:1, 4 [e]Ezek. 34:25; 39:26
9 [a]Is. 28:2 [b]Jer. 4:13
11 [a]Zech. 2:4 [b]Jer. 49:31 [c]Ezek. 38:8 [1]*securely*
12 [a]Ezek. 38:8
13 [a]Ezek. 27:22 [b]Ezek. 27:15, 20 [c]Ezek. 27:12 [d]Ezek. 19:3, 5
14 [a]Is. 4:1 [b]Ezek. 38:8, 11
15 [a]Ezek. 39:2
16 [a]Ezek. 35:11 [b]Ezek. 28:22
19 [a]Ezek. 36:5, 6 [b]Ps. 89:46 [c]Rev. 16:8 [1]Lit. *shaking*
20 [a]Hos. 4:3 [b]Jer. 4:24
21 [a]Ps. 105:16 [b]Ezek. 14:17 [c]1 Sam. 14:20
22 [a]Is. 66:16 [b]Ezek. 5:17 [c]Ps. 11:6 [d]Rev. 16:21
23 [a]Ezek. 36:23 [b]Ezek. 37:28; 38:16

CHAPTER 39
1 [a]Ezek. 38:2, 3 [1]Tg., Vg., Aquila *the chief prince of Meshech*
2 [a]Ezek. 38:8 [b]Ezek. 38:15
4 [a]Ezek. 38:4, 21 [b]Ezek. 33:27 [1]Be slain
5 [1]Be slain [2]Lit. *the face of the field*
6 [a]Amos 1:4, 7, 10 [b]Ps. 72:10 [1]*securely* or *confidently*
7 [a]Ezek. 39:25 [b]Lev. 18:21 [c]Ezek. 38:16
8 [a]Rev. 16:17; 21:6 [b]Ezek. 38:17
9 [1]Lit. *hand staffs*
10 [a]Is. 14:2; 33:1

obstruct travelers, because there they will bury
Gog and all his multitude. Therefore they will call
*it* the Valley of [1]Hamon Gog.
12 "For seven months the house of Israel will be
burying them, [a]in order to cleanse the land.
13 "Indeed all the people of the land will be
burying, and they will gain [a]renown for it on the
day that [b]I am glorified," says the Lord GOD.
14 "They will set apart men regularly employed,
with the help of [1]a search party, to pass through
the land and bury those bodies remaining on the
ground, in order [a]to cleanse it. At the end of seven
months they will make a search.
15 "The search party will pass through the land;
and *when anyone* sees a man's bone, he shall [1]set
up a marker by it, till the buriers have buried it in
the Valley of Hamon Gog.
16 "*The* name of *the* city *will* also *be* [1]Hamonah.
Thus they shall [a]cleanse the land." '
**17** "And as for you, son of man, thus says the
Lord GOD, [a]'Speak to every sort of bird and to
every beast of the field:

[b]"Assemble yourselves and come;
Gather together from all sides
to My [c]sacrificial meal
Which I am sacrificing for you,
A great sacrificial meal
[d]on the mountains of Israel,
That you may eat flesh and drink blood.
18 [a]You shall eat the flesh of the mighty,
Drink the blood of the princes of the earth,
Of rams and lambs,
Of goats and bulls,
All of them [b]fatlings of Bashan.
19 You shall eat fat till you are full,
And drink blood till you are drunk,
At My sacrificial meal
Which I am sacrificing for you.
20 [a]You shall be filled at My table
With horses and riders,
[b]With mighty men
And with all the men of war,"
says the Lord GOD.

**21** [a]"I will set My glory among the nations; all the
nations shall see My judgment which I have
executed, and [b]My hand which I have laid on
them.
22 [a]"So the house of Israel shall know that I *am*
the LORD their God from that day forward.
23 [a]"The Gentiles shall know that the house of
Israel went into captivity for their iniquity; because they were unfaithful to Me, therefore [b]I hid
My face from them. I [c]gave them into the hand of
their enemies, and they all fell by the sword.
24 [a]"According to their uncleanness and according to their transgressions I have dealt with them,
and hidden My face from them." '
**25** "Therefore thus says the Lord GOD: [a]'Now I
will bring back the captives of Jacob, and have
mercy on the [b]whole house of Israel; and I will be
jealous for My holy name—
26 [a]'after they have borne their shame, and all
their unfaithfulness in which they were unfaithful
to Me, when they [b]dwelt safely in their *own* land
and no one made *them* afraid.
27 [a]'When I have brought them back from the
peoples and gathered them out of their enemies'
lands, and I [b]am hallowed in them in the sight of
many nations,
28 [a]'then they shall know that I *am* the LORD
their God, who sent them into captivity among
the nations, but also brought them back to their
land, and left none of them [1]captive any longer.
29 [a]'And I will not hide My face from them
anymore; for I shall have [b]poured out My Spirit on
the house of Israel,' says the Lord GOD."

### *The Vision of the Temple*

**40** In the twenty-fifth year of our captivity, at
the beginning of the year, on the tenth *day*
of the month, in the fourteenth year after [a]the city
was [1]captured, on the very same day [b]the hand of
the LORD was upon me; and He took me there.
2 [a]In the visions of God He took me into the
land of Israel and [b]set me on a very high mountain; on it toward the south *was* something like
the structure of a city.
3 He took me there, and behold, *there was* a
man whose appearance *was* [a]like the appearance
of bronze. [b]He had a line of flax [c]and a measuring
rod in his hand, and he stood in the gateway.
4 And the man said to me, [a]"Son of man, look
with your eyes and hear with your ears, and [1]fix
your mind on everything I show you; for you *were*
brought here so that I might show *them* to you.
[b]Declare to the house of Israel everything you
see."
5 Now there was [a]a wall all around the outside
of the [1]temple. In the man's hand was a measuring
rod six [2]cubits *long, each being a* cubit and a
handbreadth; and he measured the width of the
wall structure, one rod; and the height, one rod.
**6** Then he went to the gateway which faced
[a]east; and he went up its stairs and measured the
threshold of the gateway, *which was* one rod
wide, and the other threshold *was* one rod wide.
7 Each gate chamber *was* one rod long and one
rod wide; between the gate chambers *was a space*
*of* five cubits; and the threshold of the gateway by
the vestibule of the inside gate *was* one rod.
8 He also measured the vestibule of the inside
gate, one rod.
9 Then he measured the vestibule of the gateway, eight cubits; and the gateposts, two cubits.
The vestibule of the gate *was* on the inside.
10 In the eastern gateway *were* three gate chambers on one side and three on the other; the three
*were* all the same size; also the gateposts were of
the same size on this side and that side.
11 He measured the width of the entrance to the
gateway, ten cubits; *and* the length of the gate,
thirteen cubits.
12 *There was* a [1]space in front of the gate chambers, one cubit *on this side* and one cubit on that
side; the gate chambers *were* six cubits on this
side and six cubits on that side.
13 Then he measured the gateway from the roof
of *one* gate chamber to the roof of the other; the
width *was* twenty-five cubits, as door faces door.
14 He measured the gateposts, sixty cubits high,
and the court all around the gateway *extended* to
the gatepost.
15 *From* the front of the entrance gate to the
front of the vestibule of the inner gate *was* fifty
cubits.
16 *There were* [a]beveled window *frames* in the
gate chambers and in their intervening archways
on the inside of the gateway all around, and
likewise in the vestibules. *There were* windows all
around on the inside. And on each gatepost *were*
[b]palm trees.

---

11 [1]Lit. *The Multitude of Gog*
12 [a]Deut. 21:23
13 [a]Zeph. 3:19, 20 [b]Ezek. 28:22
14 [a]Ezek. 39:12 [1]Lit. *those who pass through*
15 [1]*build*
16 [a]Ezek. 39:12 [1]Lit. *Multitude*
17 [a]Rev. 19:17, 18 [b]Is. 18:6 [c]Zeph. 1:7 [d]Ezek. 39:4
18 [a]Rev. 19:18 [b]Deut. 32:14
20 [a]Ps. 76:5, 6 [b]Rev. 19:18
21 [a]Ezek. 36:23; 38:23 [b]Ex. 7:4
22 [a]Ex. 39:7, 28
23 [a]Ezek. 36:18–20, 23 [b]Is. 1:15; 59:2 [c]Lev. 26:25
24 [a]Ezek. 36:19
25 [a]Ezek. 34:13; 36:24 [b]Hos. 1:11
26 [a]Dan. 9:16 [b]Lev. 26:5, 6
27 [a]Ezek. 28:25, 26 [b]Ezek. 36:23, 24; 38:16
28 [a]Ezek. 34:30 [1]Lit. *there*
29 [a]Is. 54:8, 9 [b][Joel 2:28]

CHAPTER 40
1 [a]Ezek. 33:21 [b]Ezek. 1:3; 3:14, 22; 37:1 [1]Lit. *struck*
2 [a]Ezek. 1:1; 3:14; 8:3; 37:1 [b]Rev. 21:10
3 [a]Dan. 10:6 [b]Ezek. 47:3 [c]Rev. 11:1; 21:15
4 [a]Ezek. 44:5 [b]Ezek. 43:10 [1]Lit. *set your heart*
5 [a]Ezek. 42:20 [1]Lit. *house* [2]A royal cubit of about 21 inches
6 [a]Ezek. 43:1
12 [1]Lit. *border*
16 [a]1 Kin. 6:4 [b]1 Kin. 6:29, 32, 35

**17** Then he brought me into [a]the outer court; and
*there were* [b]chambers and a pavement made all
around the court; [c]thirty chambers faced the
pavement.
18 The pavement was by the side of the gate-
ways, corresponding to the length of the gate-
ways; *this was* the lower pavement.
19 Then he measured the width from the front of
the lower gateway to the front of the inner court
exterior, one hundred cubits toward the east and
the north.
**20** On the outer court was also a gateway facing
north, and he measured its length and its width.
21 Its gate chambers, three on this side and three
on that side, its gateposts and its archways, had
the same measurements as the first gate; its
length *was* fifty cubits and its width twenty-five
cubits.
22 Its windows and those of its archways, and
also its palm trees, *had* the same measurements as
the gateway facing east; it was ascended by seven
steps, and its archway *was* in front of it.
23 A gate of the inner court was opposite the
northern gateway, just as the eastern *gateway;*
and he measured from gateway to gateway, one
hundred cubits.
**24** After that he brought me toward the south,
and there a gateway was facing south; and he
measured its gateposts and archways according to
these same measurements.
25 *There were* windows in it and in its archways
all around like those windows; its length *was* fifty
cubits and its width twenty-five cubits.
26 Seven steps led up to it, and its archway *was*
in front of them; and it had palm trees on its
gateposts, one on this side and one on that side.
27 *There was* also a gateway on the inner court,
facing south; and he measured from gateway to
gateway toward the south, one hundred cubits.
**28** Then he brought me to the inner court
through the southern gateway; he measured the
southern gateway according to these same measurements.
29 Also its gate chambers, its gateposts, and its
archways *were* according to these same measurements; *there were* windows in it and in its archways all around; *it was* fifty cubits long and
twenty-five cubits wide.
30 *There were* archways all around, [a]twenty-five
cubits long and five cubits wide.
31 Its archways faced the outer court, palm trees
*were* on its gateposts, and going up to it *were*
eight steps.
**32** And he brought me into the inner court facing
east; he measured the gateway according to these
same measurements.
33 Also its gate chambers, its gateposts, and its
archways *were* according to these same measurements; and *there were* windows in it and in its
archways all around; *it was* fifty cubits long and
twenty-five cubits wide.
34 Its archways faced the outer court, and palm
trees *were* on its gateposts on this side and on that
side; and going up to it *were* eight steps.
**35** Then he brought me to the north gateway and
measured *it* according to these same measurements—
36 also its gate chambers, its gateposts, and its
archways. It had windows all around; its length
*was* fifty cubits and its width twenty-five cubits.
37 Its gateposts faced the outer court, palm trees
*were* on its gateposts on this side and on that side,
and going up to it *were* eight steps.
**38** *There was* a chamber and its entrance by the
gateposts of the gateway, where they [a]washed the
burnt offering.
39 In the vestibule of the gateway *were* two
tables on this side and two tables on that side, on
which to slay the burnt offering, [a]the sin offering,
and [b]the trespass offering.
40 At the outer side of the vestibule, as one goes
up to the entrance of the northern gateway, *were*
two tables; and on the other side of the vestibule
of the gateway *were* two tables.
41 Four tables *were* on this side and four tables
on that side, by the side of the gateway, eight
tables on which they slaughtered *the sacrifices.*
42 *There were* also four tables of hewn stone for
the burnt offering, one cubit and a half long, one
cubit and a half wide, and one cubit high; on these
they laid the instruments with which they slaughtered the burnt offering and the sacrifice.
43 Inside *were* hooks, a handbreadth wide, fastened all around; and the flesh of the sacrifices
*was* on the tables.
**44** Outside the inner gate *were* the chambers for
[a]the singers in the inner court, one facing south at
the side of the northern gateway, and the other
facing north at the side of the southern gateway.
45 Then he said to me, "This chamber which
faces south *is* for [a]the priests who have charge of
the temple.
46 "The chamber which faces north *is* for the
priests [a]who have charge of the altar; these *are*
the sons of [b]Zadok, from the sons of Levi, who
come near the LORD to minister to Him."
**47** And he measured the court, one hundred
cubits long and one hundred cubits wide, four-
square. The altar *was* in front of the temple.
48 Then he brought me to the [a]vestibule of the
temple and measured the doorposts of the vestibule, five cubits on this side and five cubits on that
side; and the width of the gateway was three
cubits on this side and three cubits on that side.
49 [a]The length of the vestibule *was* twenty cubits, and the width eleven cubits; and by the steps
which led up to it *there were* [b]pillars by the
doorposts, one on this side and another on that
side.

### *Measurements and Design of the Temple Area*

**41** Then he [a]brought me into the [1]sanctuary
and measured the doorposts, six cubits wide
on one side and six cubits wide on the other side—
the width of the tabernacle.
2 The width of the entryway *was* ten cubits, and
the side walls of the entrance *were* five cubits on
this side and five cubits on the other side; and he
measured its length, forty cubits, and its width,
twenty cubits.
3 Also he went inside and measured the doorposts, two cubits; and the entrance, six cubits
*high;* and the width of the entrance, seven cubits.
4 [a]He measured the length, twenty cubits; and
the width, twenty cubits, beyond the sanctuary;
and he said to me, "This *is* the Most Holy *Place.*"
**5** Next, he measured the wall of the [1]temple, six
cubits. The width of each side chamber all around
the temple *was* four cubits on every side.

**17** [a]Ezek. 10:5; 42:1; 46:21; Rev. 11:2 [b]1 Kin. 6:5; 2 Chr. 31:11; Ezek. 40:38 [c]Ezek. 45:5
**30** [a]Ezek. 40:21, 25, 33, 36
**38** [a]2 Chr. 4:6
**39** [a]Lev. 4:2, 3 [b]Lev. 5:6; 6:6; 7:1
**44** [a]1 Chr. 6:31, 32; 16:41–43; 25:1–7
**45** [a]Lev. 8:35; Num. 3:27, 28, 32, 38; 18:5; 1 Chr. 9:23; 2 Chr. 13:11; Ps. 134:1
**46** [a]Lev. 6:12, 13; Num. 18:5; Ezek. 44:15 [b]1 Kin. 2:35; Ezek. 43:19; 44:15, 16
**48** [a]1 Kin. 6:3; 2 Chr. 3:4
**49** [a]1 Kin. 6:3 [b]1 Kin. 7:15–22; 2 Chr. 3:17; Jer. 52:17–23; [Rev. 3:12]

CHAPTER 41
**1** [a]Ezek. 40:2, 3, 17 [1]Heb. *heykal;* the main room in the temple, the holy place, Ex. 26:33
**4** [a]1 Kin. 6:20; 2 Chr. 3:8
**5** [1]Lit. *house*

6 [a]The side chambers *were* in three stories, one
above the other, thirty chambers in each story;
they rested on [1]ledges which *were* for the side
chambers all around, that they might be supported, but [b]not fastened to the wall of the temple.
7 As one went up from story to story, the side
chambers [a]became wider all around, because their
supporting ledges in the wall of the temple ascended like steps; therefore the width of the
structure increased as one went up *from* the
lowest *story* to the highest by way of the middle
one.
8 I also saw an elevation all around the temple;
it was the foundation of the side chambers, [a]a full
rod, *that is,* six cubits *high.*
9 The thickness of the outer wall of the side
chambers *was* five cubits, and so also the remaining terrace by the place of the side chambers of
the [1]temple.
10 And between *it and* the *wall* chambers was a
width of twenty cubits all around the temple on
every side.
11 The doors of the side chambers opened on the
terrace, one door toward the north and another
toward the south; and the width of the terrace
*was* five cubits all around.
**12** The building that faced the separating courtyard at its western end *was* seventy cubits wide;
the wall of the building *was* five cubits thick all
around, and its length ninety cubits.
**13** So he measured the temple, one [a]hundred
cubits long; and the separating courtyard with the
building and its walls *was* one hundred cubits
long;
14 also the width of the eastern face of the
temple, including the separating courtyard, *was*
one hundred cubits.
15 He measured the length of the building behind
it, facing the separating courtyard, with its [a]gal-
leries on the one side and on the other side, one
hundred cubits, as well as the inner [1]temple and
the porches of the court,
16 their doorposts and [a]the beveled window
frames. And the galleries all around their three
stories opposite the threshold were paneled with
[b]wood from the ground to the windows—the
windows were covered—
17 from the space above the door, even to the
inner [1]room, as well as outside, and on every wall
all around, inside and outside, by measure.
**18** And *it was* made [a]with cherubim and [b]palm
trees, a palm tree between cherub and cherub.
*Each* cherub had two faces,
19 [a]so that the face of a man *was* toward a palm
tree on one side, and the face of a young lion
toward a palm tree on the other side; thus *it was*
made throughout the temple all around.
20 From the floor to the space above the door,
and on the wall of the sanctuary, cherubim and
palm trees *were* carved.
**21** The [a]doorposts of the temple *were* square, *as*
*was* the front of the sanctuary; their appearance
was similar.
22 [a]The altar *was* of wood, three cubits high, and
its length two cubits. Its corners, its length, and
its sides *were* of wood; and he said to me, "This *is*
[b]the table that *is* [c]before the LORD."
23 [a]The temple and the sanctuary had two doors.
24 The doors had two [a]panels *apiece,* two folding
panels: two *panels* for one door and two panels for
the other *door.*
25 Cherubim and palm trees *were* carved on the
doors of the temple just as they *were* carved on
the walls. A wooden canopy *was* on the front of
the vestibule outside.
26 *There were* [a]beveled window *frames* and palm
trees on one side and on the other, on the sides of
the vestibule—also on the side chambers of the
temple and on the canopies.

### *The Priests' Rooms and the Outer Measurements*

**42** Then he [a]brought me out into the outer
court, by the way toward the [b]north; and he
brought me into [c]the chamber which *was* opposite
the separating courtyard, and which *was* opposite
the building toward the north.
2 Facing the length, *which was* one hundred
cubits (the width was fifty cubits), was the north
door.
3 Opposite the inner court of twenty *cubits,* and
opposite the [a]pavement of the outer court, *was*
[b]gallery against gallery in three *stories.*
4 In front of the chambers, toward the inside,
*was* a walk ten cubits wide, at a distance of one
cubit; and their doors faced north.
5 Now the upper chambers *were* shorter, because the galleries took away *space* from them
more than from the lower and middle stories of
the building.
6 For they *were* in three *stories* and did not have
pillars like the pillars of the courts; therefore *the*
*upper level* was [1]shortened more than the lower
and middle levels from the ground up.
7 And a wall which *was* outside ran parallel to
the chambers, at the front of the chambers,
toward the outer court; its length *was* fifty cubits.
8 The length of the chambers toward the outer
court *was* fifty cubits, whereas that facing the
temple *was* one [a]hundred cubits.
9 At the lower chambers *was* the entrance on
the east side, as one goes into them from the outer
court.
**10** Also *there were* chambers in the thickness of
the wall of the court toward the east, opposite the
separating courtyard and opposite the building.
11 [a]*There was* a walk in front of them also, and
their appearance *was* like the chambers which
*were* toward the north; they *were* as long and as
wide as the others, and all their exits and entrances *were* according to plan.
12 And corresponding to the doors of the chambers that *were* facing south, as one enters them,
*there was* a door in front of the walk, the way
directly in front of the wall toward the east.
**13** Then he said to me, "The north chambers *and*
the south chambers, which *are* opposite the separating courtyard, *are* the holy chambers where the
priests who approach the LORD [a]shall eat the most
holy offerings. There they shall lay the most holy
offerings—[b]the grain offering, the sin offering, and
the trespass offering—for the place *is* holy.
14 [a]"When the priests enter them, they shall not
go out of the holy *chamber* into the outer court;
but there they shall leave their garments in which
they minister, for they *are* holy. They shall put on
other garments; then they may approach *that*
which *is* for the people."
**15** Now when he had finished measuring the
inner [1]temple, he brought me out through the
gateway that faces toward the [a]east, and measured it all around.

**6** [a]1 Kin. 6:5–10 [b]1 Kin. 6:6, 10 [1]Lit. *the wall*
**7** [a]1 Kin. 6:8
**8** [a]Ezek. 40:5
**9** [1]Lit. *house*
**13** [a]Ezek. 40:47
**15** [a]Ezek. 42:3, 5 [1]Or *sanctuary*
**16** [a]1 Kin. 6:4; Ezek. 40:16, 25 [b]1 Kin. 6:15
**17** [1]Lit. *house;* the Most Holy Place
**18** [a]1 Kin. 6:29; 2 Chr. 3:7 [b]2 Chr. 3:5; Ezek. 40:16
**19** [a]Ezek. 1:10; 10:14
**21** [a]1 Kin. 6:33; Ezek. 40:9, 14, 16; 41:1
**22** [a]Ex. 30:1–3; 1 Kin. 6:20; Rev. 8:3 [b]Ex. 25:23, 30; Lev. 24:6; Ezek. 23:41; 44:16; Mal. 1:7, 12 [c]Ex. 30:8
**23** [a]1 Kin. 6:31–35
**24** [a]1 Kin. 6:34
**26** [a]Ezek. 40:16

CHAPTER 42
**1** [a]Ezek. 41:1 [b]Ezek. 40:20 [c]Ezek. 41:12, 15
**3** [a]Ezek. 40:17 [b]Ezek. 41:15, 16; 42:5
**6** [1]Or *narrowed*
**8** [a]Ezek. 41:13, 14
**11** [a]Ezek. 42:4
**13** [a]Lev. 6:16, 26; 24:9; Ezek. 43:19 [b]Lev. 2:3, 10; 6:14, 17, 25
**14** [a]Ezek. 44:19
**15** [a]Ezek. 40:6; 43:1 [1]Lit. *house*

16 He measured the east side with the [1]measuring
rod, five hundred rods by the measuring rod all
around.
17 He measured the north side, five hundred rods
by the measuring rod all around.
18 He measured the south side, five hundred rods
by the measuring rod.
19 He came around to the west side *and* measured five hundred rods by the measuring rod.
20 He measured it on the four sides; [a]it had a wall
all around, [b]five hundred *cubits* long and five
hundred wide, to separate the holy areas from the
[1]common.

## *The Laws of the Temple*

**43** Afterward he brought me to the gate, the
gate [a]that faces toward the east.
2 [a]And behold, the glory of the God of Israel
came from the way of the east. [b]His voice *was* like
the sound of many waters; [c]and the earth shone
with His glory.
3 *It was* [a]like the appearance of the vision which
I saw—like the vision which I saw when [1]I came
[b]to destroy the city. The visions *were* like the
vision which I saw [c]by the River Chebar; and I fell
on my face.
4 [a]And the glory of the LORD came into the
[1]temple by way of the gate which faces toward the
east.
5 [a]The Spirit lifted me up and brought me into
the inner court; and behold, [b]the glory of the LORD
filled the [1]temple.
**6** Then I heard *Him* speaking to me from the
temple, while [a]a man stood beside me.
7 And He said to me, "Son of man, *this is* [a]the
place of My throne and [b]the place of the soles of
My feet, [c]where I will dwell in the midst of the
children of Israel forever. [d]No more shall the
house of Israel defile My holy name, they nor their
kings, by their [1]harlotry or with [e]the carcasses of
their kings on their high places.
8 [a]"When they set their threshold by My threshold, and their doorpost by My doorpost, with a
wall between them and Me, they defiled My holy
name by the abominations which they committed;
therefore I have consumed them in My anger.
9 "Now let them put their harlotry and the
carcasses of their kings far away from Me, and I
will dwell in their midst forever.
**10** "Son of man, [a]describe the [1]temple to the
house of Israel, that they may be ashamed of their
iniquities; and let them measure the pattern.
11 "And if they are ashamed of all that they have
done, make known to them the design of the
[1]temple and its arrangement, its exits and its
entrances, its entire design and all its [a]ordinances,
all its forms and all its laws. Write *it* down in their
sight, so that they may keep its whole design and
all its ordinances, and [b]perform them.
12 "This *is* the law of the [1]temple: The whole area
surrounding [a]the mountaintop *is* most holy. Behold, this *is* the law of the temple.
**13** "These are the measurements of the [a]altar in
cubits [b](the [1]*cubit is* one cubit and a handbreadth): the base one cubit high and one cubit
wide, with a rim all around its edge of one span.
This *is* the height of the altar:
14 "from the base on the ground to the lower
ledge, two cubits; the width of the ledge, one
cubit; from the smaller ledge to the larger ledge,
four cubits; and the width of the ledge, *one* cubit.

**16** [1]About 10.5 feet, Ezek. 40:5
**20** [a]Ezek. 40:5 [b]Ezek. 45:2 [1]Or *profane*

CHAPTER 43

**1** [a]Ezek. 10:19; 46:1
**2** [a]Ezek. 11:23 [b]Rev. 1:15; 14:2 [c]Rev. 18:1
**3** [a]Ezek. 1:4–28 [b]Jer. 1:10 [c]Ezek. 1:28; 3:23 [1]Some mss., Vg. *He*
**4** [a]Ezek. 10:19; 11:23 [1]Lit. *house*
**5** [a]Ezek. 3:12, 14; 8:3 [b]1 Kin. 8:10, 11 [1]Lit. *house*
**6** [a]Ezek. 1:26; 40:3
**7** [a]Ps. 99:1 [b]1 Chr. 28:2 [c]Joel 3:17 [d]Ezek. 39:7 [e]Lev. 26:30 [1]Unfaithful idolatry
**8** [a]Ezek. 8:3; 23:39; 44:7
**10** [a]Ezek. 40:4 [1]Lit. *house*
**11** [a]Ezek. 44:5 [b]Ezek. 11:20 [1]Lit. *house*
**12** [a]Ezek. 40:2 [1]Lit. *house*
**13** [a]Ex. 27:1–8 [b]Ezek. 41:8 [1]A royal cubit of about 21 inches
**15** [a]Ex. 27:2 [1]Heb. *ariel*
**16** [a]Ex. 27:1
**17** [a]Ex. 20:26
**18** [a]Ex. 40:29 [b]Lev. 1:5, 11
**19** [a]Lev. 8:14 [b]Ezek. 44:15, 16 [c]Ezek. 40:46
**21** [a]Ex. 29:14 [b]Heb. 13:11 [1]Lit. *house*
**24** [a]Lev. 2:13
**25** [a]Ex. 29:35
**26** [1]Lit. *fill its hands* [2]LXX, Syr. *themselves*
**27** [a]Lev. 9:1–4 [b]Ezek. 20:40, 41

CHAPTER 44

**1** [a]Ezek. 43:1
**2** [a]Ezek. 43:2–4
**3** [a]Gen. 31:54 [b]Ezek. 46:2, 8
**4** [a]Ezek. 3:23; 43:5 [b]Ezek. 1:28; 43:3 [1]Lit. *house*
**5** [a]Ezek. 40:4 [b]Ezek. 43:10, 11 [1]Lit. *set your heart*
**6** [a]Ezek. 2:5 [b]1 Pet. 4:3

15 "The altar hearth *is* four cubits high, with four
[a]horns extending upward from the [1]hearth.
16 "The altar hearth *is* twelve cubits long, twelve
wide, [a]square at its four corners;
17 "the ledge, fourteen *cubits* long and fourteen
wide on its four sides, with a rim of half a cubit
around it; its base, one cubit all around; and [a]its
steps face toward the east."
**18** And He said to me, "Son of man, thus says the
Lord GOD: 'These *are* the ordinances for the altar
on the day when it is made, for sacrificing [a]burnt
offerings on it, and for [b]sprinkling blood on it.
19 'You shall give [a]a young bull for a sin offering
to [b]the priests, the Levites, who are of the seed of
[c]Zadok, who approach Me to minister to Me,' says
the Lord GOD.
20 'You shall take some of its blood and put *it* on
the four horns of the altar, on the four corners of
the ledge, and on the rim around it; thus you shall
cleanse it and make atonement for it.
21 'Then you shall also take the bull of the sin
offering, and [a]burn it in the appointed place of the
[1]temple, [b]outside the sanctuary.
22 'On the second day you shall offer a kid of the
goats without blemish for a sin offering; and they
shall cleanse the altar, as they cleansed *it* with the
bull.
23 'When you have finished cleansing *it,* you
shall offer a young bull without blemish, and a
ram from the flock without blemish.
24 'When you offer them before the LORD, [a]the
priests shall throw salt on them, and they will
offer them up *as* a burnt offering to the LORD.
25 'Every day for [a]seven days you shall prepare a
goat *for* a sin offering; they shall also prepare a
young bull and a ram from the flock, both without
blemish.
26 'Seven days they shall make atonement for
the altar and purify it, and so [1]consecrate [2]*it.*
27 [a]'When these days are over it shall be, on the
eighth day and thereafter, that the priests shall
offer your burnt offerings and your peace offerings on the altar; and I will [b]accept you,' says the
Lord GOD."

## *Instructions for the Priests*

**44** Then He brought me back to the outer gate
of the sanctuary [a]which faces toward the
east, but it *was* shut.
2 And the LORD said to me, "This gate shall be
shut; it shall not be opened, and no man shall
enter by it, [a]because the LORD God of Israel has
entered by it; therefore it shall be shut.
3 "*As for* the [a]prince, *because* he *is* the prince,
he may sit in it to [b]eat bread before the LORD; he
shall enter by way of the vestibule of the gateway,
and go out the same way."
**4** Also He brought me by way of the north gate
to the front of the [1]temple; so I looked, and
[a]behold, the glory of the LORD filled the house of
the LORD; [b]and I fell on my face.
5 And the LORD said to me, [a]"Son of man, [1]mark
well, see with your eyes and hear with your ears,
all that I say to you concerning all the [b]ordinances
of the house of the LORD and all its laws. Mark
well who may enter the house and all who go out
from the sanctuary.
6 "Now say to the [a]rebellious, to the house of
Israel, 'Thus says the Lord GOD: "O house of
Israel, [b]let Us have no more of all your abominations.

7 [a]“When you brought in [b]foreigners, [c]uncir-
cumcised in heart and uncircumcised in flesh, to
be in My sanctuary to defile it—My house—and
when you offered [d]My food, [e]the fat and the blood,
then they broke My covenant because of all your
abominations.
8 “And you have not [a]kept charge of My holy
things, but you have set *others* to keep charge of
My sanctuary for you.”
9 ‘Thus says the Lord GOD: [a]“No foreigner,
uncircumcised in heart or uncircumcised in flesh,
shall enter My sanctuary, including any foreigner
who *is* among the children of Israel.
**10** [a]“And the Levites who went far from Me,
when Israel went astray, who strayed away from
Me after their idols, they shall bear their iniquity.
11 “Yet they shall be ministers in My sanctuary,
[a]*as* gatekeepers of the house and ministers of the
house; [b]they shall slay the burnt offering and the
sacrifice for the people, and [c]they shall stand
before them to minister to them.
12 “Because they ministered to them before their
idols and [a]caused[1] the house of Israel to fall into
iniquity, therefore I have [b]raised My hand in an
oath against them,” says the Lord GOD, “that they
shall bear their iniquity.
13 [a]“And they shall not come near Me to minister
to Me as priest, nor come near any of My holy
things, nor into the Most Holy *Place;* but they
shall [b]bear their shame and their abominations
which they have committed.
14 “Nevertheless I will make them [a]keep charge
of the temple, for all its work, and for all that has
to be done in it.
**15** [a]“But the priests, the Levites, [b]the sons of
Zadok, who kept charge of My sanctuary [c]when
the children of Israel went astray from Me, they
shall come near Me to minister to Me; and they
[d]shall stand before Me to offer to Me the [e]fat and
the blood,” says the Lord GOD.
16 “They shall [a]enter My sanctuary, and they
shall come near [b]My table to minister to Me, and
they shall keep My charge.
17 “And it shall be, whenever they enter the
gates of the inner court, that [a]they shall put on
linen garments; no wool shall come upon them
while they minister within the gates of the inner
court or within the house.
18 [a]“They shall have linen turbans on their heads
and linen trousers on their bodies; they shall not
clothe themselves with *anything that causes*
sweat.
19 “When they go out to the outer court, to the
*outer* court to the people, [a]they shall take off their
garments in which they have ministered, leave
them in the holy chambers, and put on other
garments; and in their holy garments they shall
[b]not sanctify the people.
20 [a]“They shall neither shave their heads, nor let
their hair grow [b]long; but they shall keep their
hair well trimmed.
21 [a]“No priest shall drink wine when he enters
the inner court.
22 “They shall not take as wife a [a]widow or a
divorced woman, but take virgins of the descendants of the house of Israel, or widows of priests.
23 “And [a]they shall teach My people *the difference* between the holy and the unholy, and cause
them to [b]discern between the unclean and the
clean.
24 [a]“In controversy they shall stand as judges,
*and* judge it according to My judgments. They
shall keep My laws and My statutes in all My
appointed meetings, [b]and they shall hallow My
Sabbaths.
25 “They shall not defile *themselves* by coming
near a dead person. Only for father or mother, for
son or daughter, for brother or unmarried sister
may they defile themselves.
26 [a]“After he is cleansed, they shall count seven
days for him.
27 “And on the day that he goes to the sanctuary
to minister in the sanctuary, [a]he must offer his sin
offering [b]in the inner court,” says the Lord GOD.
**28** “It shall be, in regard to their inheritance, *that*
I [a]*am* their inheritance. You shall give them no
[b]possession in Israel, for I *am* their possession.
29 [a]“They shall eat the grain offering, the sin
offering, and the trespass offering; [b]every dedicated thing in Israel shall be theirs.
30 “The [a]best[1] of all firstfruits of any kind, and
every sacrifice of any kind from all your sacrifices,
shall be the priest’s; also you [b]shall give to the
priest the first of your ground meal, [c]to cause a
blessing to rest on your house.
31 “The priests shall not eat anything, bird or
beast, that [a]died naturally or was torn *by wild
beasts.*

### *The Prince and the Land*

**45** “Moreover, when you [a]divide the land by lot
into inheritance, you shall [b]set apart a district for the LORD, a holy section of the land; its
length *shall be* twenty-five thousand *cubits,* and
the width ten thousand. It *shall be* holy throughout its territory all around.
2 “Of this there shall be a square plot for the
sanctuary, [a]five hundred by five hundred *rods,*
with fifty cubits around it for an open space.
3 “So this is the district you shall measure:
twenty-five thousand *cubits* long and ten thousand wide; [a]in it shall be the sanctuary, the Most
Holy *Place.*
4 “It shall be [a]a holy *section* of the land, belonging to the priests, the ministers of the sanctuary,
who come near to minister to the LORD; it shall be
a place for their houses and a holy place for the
sanctuary.
5 [a]“*An area* twenty-five thousand *cubits* long
and ten thousand wide shall belong to the Levites,
the ministers of the [1]temple; they shall have
[b]twenty[2] chambers as a possession.
**6** [a]“You shall appoint as the property of the city
*an area* five thousand *cubits* wide and twenty-five
thousand long, adjacent to the district of the holy
*section;* it shall belong to the whole house of
Israel.
**7** [a]“The prince shall have *a section* on one side
and the other of the holy district and the city’s
property; and bordering on the holy district and
the city’s property, extending westward on the
west side and eastward on the east side, the length
*shall be* side by side with one of the *tribal* portions, from the west border to the east border.
8 “The land shall be his possession in Israel; and
[a]My princes shall no more oppress My people, but
they shall give *the rest of* the land to the house of
Israel, according to their tribes.”
**9** ‘Thus says the Lord GOD: [a]“Enough, O princes
of Israel! [b]Remove violence and plundering,

**7** [a]Acts 21:28 [b]Lev. 22:25 [c]Lev. 26:41 [d]Lev. 21:17 [e]Lev. 3:16
**8** [a]Lev. 22:2
**9** [a]Ezek. 44:7
**10** [a]2 Kin. 23:8
**11** [a]1 Chr. 26:1–19 [b]2 Chr. 29:34; 30:17 [c]Num. 16:9
**12** [a]Is. 9:16 [b]Ps. 106:26 [1]Lit. *became a stumbling block of iniquity to the house of Israel*
**13** [a]2 Kin. 23:9 [b]Ezek. 32:30
**14** [a]Num. 18:4
**15** [a]Ezek. 40:46 [b][1 Sam. 2:35] [c]Ezek. 44:10 [d]Deut. 10:8 [e]Ezek. 44:7
**16** [a]Num. 18:5, 7, 8 [b]Ezek. 41:22
**17** [a]Ex. 28:39–43; 39:27–29
**18** [a]Ex. 28:40; 39:28
**19** [a]Ezek. 42:14 [b]Lev. 6:27
**20** [a]Lev. 21:5 [b]Num. 6:5
**21** [a]Lev. 10:9
**22** [a]Lev. 21:7, 13, 14
**23** [a]Mal. 2:6–8 [b]Lev. 20:25
**24** [a]Deut. 17:8, 9 [b]Ezek. 22:26
**26** [a]Num. 6:10; 19:11, 13–19
**27** [a]Lev. 5:3, 6 [b]Ezek. 44:17
**28** [a]Num. 18:20 [b]Ezek. 45:4
**29** [a]Lev. 7:6 [b]Lev. 27:21, 28
**30** [a]Num. 3:13; 18:12 [b]Neh. 10:37 [c][Mal. 3:10] [1]Lit. *first*
**31** [a]Lev. 22:8

CHAPTER 45
**1** [a]Ezek. 47:22 [b]Ezek. 48:8, 9
**2** [a]Ezek. 42:20
**3** [a]Ezek. 48:10
**4** [a]Ezek. 48:10, 11
**5** [a]Ezek. 48:13 [b]Ezek. 40:17 [1]Lit. *house* [2]So with MT, Tg., Vg.; LXX *a possession, cities of dwelling*
**6** [a]Ezek. 48:15
**7** [a]Ezek. 48:21
**8** [a]Ezek. 22:27
**9** [a]Ezek. 44:6 [b]Jer. 22:3

execute justice and righteousness, and stop dis-
possessing My people," says the Lord GOD.
10 "You shall have honest[a] scales, an honest
ephah, and an honest bath.
11 "The ephah and the bath shall be of the same
measure, so that the bath contains one-tenth of a
homer, and the ephah one-tenth of a homer; their
measure shall be according to the homer.
12 "The [a]shekel *shall be* twenty gerahs; twenty
shekels, twenty-five shekels, *and* fifteen shekels
shall be your mina.
13 "This *is* the offering which you shall offer: you
shall give one-sixth of an ephah from a homer of
wheat, and one-sixth of an ephah from a homer of
barley.
14 "The ordinance concerning oil, the bath of oil,
*is* one-tenth of a bath from a kor. A kor *is* a homer
or ten baths, for ten baths *are* a homer.
15 "And one lamb shall be given from a flock of
two hundred, from the rich pastures of Israel.
These shall be for grain offerings, burnt offerings,
and peace offerings, [a]to make atonement for
them," says the Lord GOD.
16 "All the people of the land shall give this
offering for the prince in Israel.
17 "Then it shall be the [a]prince's part *to give*
burnt offerings, grain offerings, and drink offerings, at the feasts, the New Moons, the Sabbaths,
and at all the appointed seasons of the house of
Israel. He shall prepare the sin offering, the grain
offering, the burnt offering, and the peace offerings to make atonement for the house of Israel."
**18** 'Thus says the Lord GOD: "In the first *month,*
on the first *day* of the month, you shall take a
young bull without blemish and [a]cleanse the
sanctuary.
19 [a]"The priest shall take some of the blood of
the sin offering and put *it* on the doorposts of the
[1]temple, on the four corners of the ledge of the
altar, and on the gateposts of the gate of the inner
court.
20 "And so you shall do on the seventh *day* of the
month [a]for everyone who has sinned unintentionally or in ignorance. Thus you shall make atonement for the temple.
**21** [a]"In the first *month,* on the fourteenth day of
the month, you shall observe the Passover, a feast
of seven days; unleavened bread shall be eaten.
22 "And on that day the prince shall prepare for
himself and for all the people of the land [a]a bull *for*
a sin offering.
23 "On the [a]seven days of the feast he shall
prepare a burnt offering to the LORD, seven bulls
and seven rams without blemish, daily for seven
days, [b]and a kid of the goats daily *for* a sin
offering.
24 [a]"And he shall prepare a grain offering of one
ephah for each bull and one ephah for each ram,
together with a hin of oil for each ephah.
25 "In the seventh *month,* on the fifteenth day of
the month, at the [a]feast, he shall do likewise for
seven days, according to the sin offering, the
burnt offering, the grain offering, and the oil."

### *The Worshiping Prince*

**46** 'Thus says the Lord GOD: "The gateway of
the inner court that faces toward the east
shall be shut the six [a]working days; but on the
Sabbath it shall be opened, and on the day of the
New Moon it shall be opened.
2 [a]"The prince shall enter by way of the vestibule of the gateway from the outside, and stand
by the gatepost. The priests shall prepare his
burnt offering and his peace offerings. He shall
worship at the threshold of the gate. Then he shall
go out, but the gate shall not be shut until evening.
3 "Likewise the people of the land shall worship
at the entrance to this gateway before the LORD
on the Sabbaths and the New Moons.
4 "The burnt offering that [a]the prince offers to
the LORD on the [b]Sabbath day *shall be* six lambs
without blemish, and a ram without blemish;
5 [a]"and the grain offering *shall be one* ephah for
a ram, and the grain offering for the lambs, [1]as
much as he wants to give, as well as a hin of oil
with every ephah.
6 "On the day of the New Moon *it shall be* a
young bull without blemish, six lambs, and a ram;
they shall be without blemish.
7 "He shall prepare a grain offering of an ephah
for a bull, an ephah for a ram, [1]as much as he
wants to give for the lambs, and a hin of oil with
every ephah.
8 [a]"When the prince enters, he shall go in by
way of the vestibule of the gateway, and go out
the same way.
**9** "But when the people of the land [a]come before
the LORD on the appointed feast days, whoever
enters by way of the north [b]gate to worship shall
go out by way of the south gate; and whoever
enters by way of the south gate shall go out by
way of the north gate. He shall not return by way
of the gate through which he came, but shall go
out through the opposite gate.
10 "The prince shall then be in their midst. When
they go in, he shall go in; and when they go out,
he shall go out.
11 "At the festivals and the appointed feast days
[a]the grain offering shall be an ephah for a bull, an
ephah for a ram, as much as he wants to give for
the lambs, and a hin of oil with every ephah.
**12** "Now when the prince makes a voluntary
burnt offering or voluntary peace offering to the
LORD, the gate that faces toward the east [a]shall
then be opened for him; and he shall prepare his
burnt offering and his peace offerings as he did on
the Sabbath day. Then he shall go out, and after
he goes out the gate shall be shut.
13 [a]"You shall daily make a burnt offering to the
LORD *of* a lamb of the first year without blemish;
you shall prepare it [1]every morning.
14 "And you shall prepare a grain offering with it
every morning, a sixth of an ephah, and a third of
a hin of oil to moisten the fine flour. This grain
offering is a perpetual ordinance, to be made
regularly to the LORD.
15 "Thus they shall prepare the lamb, the grain
offering, and the oil, *as* a [a]regular burnt offering
every morning."
**16** 'Thus says the Lord GOD: "If the prince gives a
gift *of some* of his inheritance to any of his sons, it
shall belong to his sons; it is their possession by
inheritance.
17 "But if he gives a gift of some of his inheritance to one of his servants, it shall be his until
[a]the year of liberty, after which it shall return to
the prince. But his inheritance shall belong to his
sons; it shall become theirs.
18 "Moreover [a]the prince shall not take any of
the people's inheritance by evicting them from

**10** [a]Lev. 19:36; Deut. 25:15; Prov. 16:11; Amos 8:4–6; Mic. 6:10, 11
**12** [a]Ex. 30:13; Lev. 27:25; Num. 3:47
**15** [a]Lev. 1:4; 6:30
**17** [a]Ezek. 46:4–12
**18** [a]Lev. 16:16, 33; Ezek. 43:22, 26
**19** [a]Lev. 16:18–20; Ezek. 43:20 [1]Lit. *house*
**20** [a]Lev. 4:27; Ps. 19:12
**21** [a]Ex. 12:18; Lev. 23:5, 6; Num. 9:2, 3; 28:16, 17; Deut. 16:1
**22** [a]Lev. 4:14
**23** [a]Lev. 23:8 [b]Num. 28:15, 22, 30; 29:5, 11, 16, 19
**24** [a]Num. 28:12–15; Ezek. 46:5, 7
**25** [a]Lev. 23:34; Num. 29:12; Deut. 16:13; 2 Chr. 5:3; 7:8, 10

CHAPTER 46
**1** [a]Ex. 20:9
**2** [a]Ezek. 44:3
**4** [a]Ezek. 45:17 [b]Num. 28:9, 10
**5** [a]Num. 28:12; Ezek. 45:24; 46:7, 11 [1]Lit. *the gift of his hand*
**7** [1]Lit. *as much as his hand can reach*
**8** [a]Ezek. 44:3; 46:2
**9** [a]Ex. 23:14–17; 34:23; Deut. 16:16, 17; Ps. 84:7; Mic. 6:6 [b]Ezek. 48:31, 33
**11** [a]Ezek. 46:5, 7
**12** [a]Ezek. 44:3; 46:1, 2, 8
**13** [a]Ex. 29:38; Num. 28:3–5 [1]Lit. *morning by morning*
**15** [a]Ex. 29:42; Num. 28:6
**17** [a]Lev. 25:10
**18** [a]Ezek. 45:8

their property; he shall provide an inheritance for
his sons from his own property, so that none of
My people may be scattered from his property." ' "
**19** Now he brought me through the entrance,
which *was* at the side of the gate, into the holy
[a]chambers of the priests which face toward the
north; and there a place *was* situated at their
extreme western end.
20 And he said to me, "This *is* the place where
the priests shall [a]boil the trespass offering and the
sin offering, *and* where they shall [b]bake the grain
offering, so that they do not bring *them* out into
the outer court [c]to sanctify the people."
21 Then he brought me out into the outer court
and caused me to pass by the four corners of the
court; and in fact, in every corner of the court
*there was another* court.
22 In the four corners of the court *were* enclosed
courts, forty *cubits* long and thirty wide; all four
corners *were* the same size.
23 *There was* a row *of building stones* all around
in them, all around the four of them; and [1]cooking
hearths were made under the rows of stones all
around.
24 And he said to me, "These *are* the [1]kitchens
where the ministers of the [2]temple shall [a]boil the
sacrifices of the people."

## *The River Flowing from the Temple*

**47** Then he brought me back to the door of the
[1]temple; and there was [a]water, flowing from
under the threshold of the temple toward the east,
for the front of the temple faced east; the water
was flowing from under the right side of the
temple, south of the altar.
2 He brought me out by way of the north gate,
and led me around on the outside to the outer
gateway that faces [a]east; and there was water,
running out on the right side.
**3** And when [a]the man went out to the east with
the line in his hand, he measured one thousand
cubits, and he brought me through the waters; the
water *came up to my* ankles.
4 Again he measured one thousand and brought
me through the waters; the water *came up to my*
knees. Again he measured one thousand and
brought me through; the water *came up to my*
waist.
5 Again he measured one thousand, *and it was* a
river that I could not cross; for the water was too
deep, water in which one must swim, a river that
could not be crossed.
**6** He said to me, "Son of man, have you seen
*this?*" Then he brought me and returned me to
the bank of the river.
7 When I returned, there, along the bank of the
river, *were* very many [a]trees on one side and the
other.
8 Then he said to me: "This water flows toward
the eastern region, goes down into the [1]valley, and
enters the sea. *When it* reaches the sea, *its* waters
are healed.
9 "And it shall be *that* every living thing that
moves, wherever [1]the rivers go, will live. There
will be a very great multitude of fish, because
these waters go there; for they will be healed, and
everything will live wherever the river goes.
10 "It shall be *that* fishermen will stand by it
from En Gedi to En Eglaim; they will be *places* for
spreading their nets. Their fish will be of the same
kinds as the fish [a]of the Great Sea, exceedingly
many.
11 "But its swamps and marshes will not be
healed; they will be given over to salt.
12 [a]"Along the bank of the river, on this side and
that, will grow all *kinds of* trees used for food;
[b]their leaves will not wither, and their fruit will
not fail. They will bear fruit every month, because
their water flows from the sanctuary. Their fruit
will be for food, and their leaves for [c]medicine."[1]
**13** Thus says the Lord GOD: "These *are* the [a]bor-
ders by which you shall divide the land as an
inheritance among the twelve tribes of Israel.
[b]Joseph *shall have two* portions.
14 "You shall inherit it equally with one another;
for I [a]raised My hand in an oath to give it to your
fathers, and this land shall [b]fall to you as your
inheritance.
15 "This *shall be* the border of the land on the
north: from the Great Sea, *by* [a]the road to Hethlon, as one goes to [b]Zedad,
16 [a]"Hamath, [b]Berothah, Sibraim (which *is* between the border of Damascus and the border of
Hamath), to Hazar Hatticon (which *is* on the
border of Hauran).
17 "Thus the boundary shall be from the Sea to
[a]Hazar Enan, the border of Damascus; and as for
the north, northward, it is the border of Hamath.
*This is* the north side.
18 "On the east side you shall mark out the
border from between Hauran and Damascus, and
between Gilead and the land of Israel, along the
Jordan, and along the eastern side of the sea. *This*
*is* the east side.
19 "The south side, toward the [1]South, *shall be*
from Tamar to [a]the waters of [2]Meribah by Kadesh,
along the brook to the Great Sea. *This is* the south
side, toward the South.
20 "The west side *shall be* the Great Sea, from
the *southern* boundary until one comes to a point
opposite Hamath. This *is* the west side.
**21** "Thus you shall [a]divide this land among yourselves according to the tribes of Israel.
22 "It shall be that you will divide it by [a]lot as an
inheritance for yourselves, [b]and for the strangers
who dwell among you and who bear children
among you. [c]They shall be to you as native-born
among the children of Israel; they shall have an
inheritance with you among the tribes of Israel.
23 "And it shall be *that* in whatever tribe the
stranger dwells, there you shall give *him* his
inheritance," says the Lord GOD.

## *The Boundaries and Divisions of the Land*

**48** "Now these *are* the names of the tribes:
[a]From the northern border along the road to
Hethlon at the entrance of Hamath, to Hazar
Enan, the border of Damascus northward, in the
direction of Hamath, *there shall be* one *section for*
[b]Dan from its east to its west side;
2 "by the border of Dan, from the east side to
the west, one *section for* [a]Asher;
3 "by the border of Asher, from the east side to
the west, one *section for* [a]Naphtali;
4 "by the border of Naphtali, from the east side
to the west, one *section for* [a]Manasseh;
5 "by the border of Manasseh, from the east side
to the west, one *section for* [a]Ephraim;
6 "by the border of Ephraim, from the east side
to the west, one *section for* [a]Reuben;

**19** [a]Ezek. 42:13
**20** [a]2 Chr. 35:13 [b]Lev. 2:4, 5, 7 [c]Ezek. 44:19
**23** [1]Lit. *boiling places*
**24** [a]Ezek. 46:20 [1]Lit. *house of those who boil* [2]Lit. *house*

CHAPTER 47
**1** [a]Ps. 46:4; Is. 30:25; 55:1; [Jer. 2:13]; Joel 3:18; Zech. 13:1; 14:8; [Rev. 22:1, 17] [1]Lit. *house*
**2** [a]Ezek. 44:1, 2
**3** [a]Ezek. 40:3
**7** [a][Is. 60:13, 21; 61:3; Ezek. 47:12; Rev. 22:2]
**8** [1]Or *Arabah,* The Jordan Valley
**9** [1]Lit. *two rivers*
**10** [a]Num. 34:3; Josh. 23:4; Ezek. 48:28
**12** [a]Ezek. 47:7; [Rev. 22:2] [b]Job 18:16; [Ps. 1:3; Jer. 17:8] [c][Rev. 22:2] [1]Or *healing*
**13** [a]Num. 34:1–29 [b]Gen. 48:5; 1 Chr. 5:1; Ezek. 48:4, 5
**14** [a]Gen. 12:7; 13:15; 15:7; 17:8; 26:3; 28:13; Deut. 1:8; Ezek. 20:5, 6, 28, 42 [b]Ezek. 48:29
**15** [a]Ezek. 48:1 [b]Num. 34:7, 8
**16** [a]Num. 34:8 [b]2 Sam. 8:8
**17** [a]Num. 34:9; Ezek. 48:1
**19** [a]Num. 20:13; Deut. 32:51; Ps. 81:7; Ezek. 48:28 [1]Heb. *Negev* [2]Lit. *Strife*
**21** [a]Ezek. 45:1
**22** [a]Num. 26:55, 56 [b][Eph. 3:6; Rev. 7:9, 10] [c][Acts 11:18; 15:9; Gal. 3:28; Eph. 2:12–14; Col. 3:11]

CHAPTER 48
**1** [a]Ezek. 47:15 [b]Josh. 19:40–48
**2** [a]Josh. 19:24–31
**3** [a]Josh. 19:32–39
**4** [a]Josh. 13:29–31; 17:1–11, 17, 18
**5** [a]Josh. 16:5–10; 17:8–10, 14–18
**6** [a]Josh. 13:15–23

7 "by the border of Reuben, from the east side
to the west, one *section for* [a]Judah;
**8** "by the border of Judah, from the east side to
the west, shall be [a]the district which you shall set
apart, twenty-five thousand *cubits* in width, and
*in* length the same as one of the *other* portions,
from the east side to the west, with the [b]sanctuary
in the center.
**9** "The district that you shall set apart for the
LORD *shall be* twenty-five thousand *cubits* in
length and ten thousand in width.
10 "To these—to the priests—the holy district
shall belong: on the north twenty-five thousand
*cubits in length,* on the west ten thousand in
width, on the east ten thousand in width, and on
the south twenty-five thousand in length. The
sanctuary of the LORD shall be in the center.
11 [a]"*It shall be* for the priests of the sons of
Zadok, who are sanctified, who have kept My
charge, who did not go astray when the children
of Israel went astray, [b]as the Levites went astray.
12 "And *this* district of land that is set apart shall
be to them a thing most [a]holy by the border of the
Levites.
**13** "Opposite the border of the priests, the [a]Le-
vites *shall have an area* twenty-five thousand
*cubits* in length and ten thousand in width; its
entire length *shall be* twenty-five thousand and its
width ten thousand.
14 [a]"And they shall not sell or exchange any of it;
they may not alienate this best *part* of the land,
for *it is* holy to the LORD.
**15** [a]"The five thousand *cubits* in width that remain, along the edge of the twenty-five thousand,
shall be [b]for general use by the city, for dwellings
and common-land; and the city shall be in the
center.
16 "These *shall be* its measurements: the north
side four thousand five hundred *cubits,* the south
side four thousand five hundred, the east side four
thousand five hundred, and the west side four
thousand five hundred.
17 "The common-land of the city shall be: to the
north two hundred and fifty *cubits,* to the south
two hundred and fifty, to the east two hundred
and fifty, and to the west two hundred and fifty.
18 "The rest of the length, alongside the district
of the holy *section, shall be* ten thousand *cubits* to
the east and ten thousand to the west. It shall be
adjacent to the district of the holy *section,* and its
produce shall be food for the workers of the city.
19 [a]"The workers of the city, from all the tribes of
Israel, shall cultivate it.
20 "The entire district *shall be* twenty-five thousand *cubits* by twenty-five thousand *cubits,* four-
square. You shall set apart the holy district with
the property of the city.
**21** [a]"The rest *shall belong* to the prince, on one
side and on the other of the holy district and of
the city's property, next to the twenty-five thousand *cubits* of the *holy* district as far as the
eastern border, and westward next to the twenty-
five thousand as far as the western border, adjacent to the *tribal* portions; *it shall belong* to the
prince. It shall be the holy district, [b]and the
sanctuary of the [1]temple *shall be* in the center.
22 "Moreover, apart from the possession of the
Levites and the possession of the city *which are* in
the midst of what *belongs* to the prince, *the area*
between the border of Judah and the border of
[a]Benjamin shall belong to the prince.
23 "As for the rest of the tribes, from the east side
to the west, Benjamin *shall have* one *section;*
24 "by the border of Benjamin, from the east side
to the west, [a]Simeon *shall have* one *section;*
25 "by the border of Simeon, from the east side to
the west, [a]Issachar *shall have* one *section;*
26 "by the border of Issachar, from the east side
to the west, [a]Zebulun *shall have* one *section;*
27 "by the border of Zebulun, from the east side
to the west, [a]Gad *shall have* one *section;*
28 "by the border of Gad, on the south side,
toward the [1]South, the border shall be from Tamar
*to* [a]the waters of [2]Meribah *by* Kadesh, along the
brook to the [b]Great Sea.
29 [a]"This *is* the land which you shall divide by lot
as an inheritance among the tribes of Israel, and
these *are* their portions," says the Lord GOD.
**30** "These *are* the exits of the city. On the north
side, measuring four thousand five hundred *cubits*
31 [a]"(the gates of the city *shall be* named after
the tribes of Israel), the three gates northward:
one gate for Reuben, one gate for Judah, and one
gate for Levi;
32 "on the east side, four thousand five hundred
*cubits,* three gates: one gate for Joseph, one gate
for Benjamin, and one gate for Dan;
33 "on the south side, measuring four thousand
five hundred *cubits,* three gates: one gate for
Simeon, one gate for Issachar, and one gate for
Zebulun;
34 "on the west side, four thousand five hundred
*cubits* with their three gates: one gate for Gad,
one gate for Asher, and one gate for Naphtali.
35 "All the way around *shall be* eighteen thousand cubits; [a]and the name of the city from *that*
day *shall be:* [b]THE[1] LORD *IS* THERE."

**7** [a]Josh. 15:1–63; 19:9
**8** [a]Ezek. 45:1–6 [b][Is. 12:6; 33:20–22]; Ezek. 45:3, 4
**11** [a]Ezek. 40:46; 44:15 [b]Ezek. 44:10, 12
**12** [a]Ezek. 45:4
**13** [a]Ezek. 45:5
**14** [a]Ex. 22:29; Lev. 27:10, 28, 33; Ezek. 44:30
**15** [a]Ezek. 45:6 [b]Ezek. 42:20
**19** [a]Ezek. 45:6
**21** [a]Ezek. 34:24; 45:7; 48:22 [b]Ezek. 48:8, 10 [1]Lit. *house*
**22** [a]Josh. 18:21–28
**24** [a]Josh. 19:1–9
**25** [a]Josh. 19:17–23
**26** [a]Josh. 19:10–16
**27** [a]Josh. 13:24–28
**28** [a]Gen. 14:7; 2 Chr. 20:2; Ezek. 47:19 [b]Ezek. 47:10, 15, 19, 20 [1]Heb. *Negev* [2]Lit. *Strife*
**29** [a]Ezek. 47:14, 21, 22
**31** [a][Rev. 21:10–14]
**35** [a]Jer. 23:6; 33:16 [b]Is. 12:6; 14:32; 24:23; Jer. 3:17; 8:19; 14:9; Ezek. 35:10; Joel 3:21; Zech. 2:10; Rev. 21:3; 22:3 [1]Heb. *YHWH Shammah*

*The Book of*

# DANIEL

### *Daniel and His Friends Obey God*

IN the third year of the reign of [a]Jehoiakim king
of Judah, Nebuchadnezzar king of Babylon
came to Jerusalem and besieged it.
2 And the Lord gave Jehoiakim king of Judah
into his hand, with [a]some of the articles of [1]the
house of God, which he carried [b]into the land of
Shinar to the house of his god; [c]and he brought
the articles into the treasure house of his god.
**3** Then the king instructed Ashpenaz, the master of his eunuchs, to bring [a]some of the children
of Israel and some of the king's descendants and
some of the nobles,
4 young men [a]in whom *there was* no blemish,
but good-looking, gifted in all wisdom, possessing

CHAPTER 1
**1** [a]2 Kin. 24:1, 2
**2** [a]Jer. 27:19, 20 [b]Zech. 5:11 [c]2 Chr. 36:7 [1]The temple
**3** [a]Is. 39:7
**4** [a]Lev. 24:19, 20

knowledge and quick to understand, who *had*
ability to serve in the king's palace, and [b]whom
they might teach the language and [1]literature of
the Chaldeans.
5 And the king appointed for them a daily
provision of the king's delicacies and of the wine
which he drank, and three years of training for
them, so that at the end of *that time* they might
[a]serve before the king.
6 Now from among those of the sons of Judah
were Daniel, Hananiah, Mishael, and Azariah.
7 [a]To them the chief of the eunuchs gave
names: [b]he gave Daniel *the name* Belteshazzar; to
Hananiah, Shadrach; to Mishael, Meshach; and to
Azariah, Abed-Nego.
**8** But Daniel purposed in his heart that he would
not defile himself [a]with the portion of the king's
delicacies, nor with the wine which he drank;
therefore he requested of the chief of the eunuchs
that he might not defile himself.
9 Now [a]God had brought Daniel into the favor
and [1]goodwill of the chief of the eunuchs.
10 And the chief of the eunuchs said to Daniel, "I
fear my lord the king, who has appointed your
food and drink. For why should he see your faces
looking worse than the young men who *are* your
age? Then you would endanger my head before
the king."
**11** So Daniel said to [1]the steward whom the chief
of the eunuchs had set over Daniel, Hananiah,
Mishael, and Azariah,
12 "Please test your servants for ten days, and let
them give us vegetables to eat and water to drink.
13 "Then let our appearance be examined before
you, and the appearance of the young men who
eat the portion of the king's delicacies; and as you
see fit, *so* deal with your servants."
**14** So he consented with them in this matter, and
tested them ten days.
15 And at the end of ten days their features
appeared better and fatter in flesh than all the
young men who ate the portion of the king's
delicacies.
16 Thus [1]the steward took away their portion of
delicacies and the wine that they were to drink,
and gave them vegetables.
**17** As for these four young men, [a]God gave them
[b]knowledge and skill in all literature and wisdom;
and Daniel had [c]understanding in all visions and
dreams.
18 Now at the end of the days, when the king had
said that they should be brought in, the chief of
the eunuchs brought them in before Nebuchadnezzar.
19 Then the king [1]interviewed them, and among
them all none was found like Daniel, Hananiah,
Mishael, and Azariah; therefore [a]they served
before the king.
20 [a]And in all matters of wisdom *and* understanding about which the king examined them, he
found them ten times better than all the magicians *and* astrologers who *were* in all his realm.
21 [a]Thus Daniel continued until the first year of
King Cyrus.

### *Daniel Explains the King's Dream*

**2** Now in the second year of Nebuchadnezzar's
reign, Nebuchadnezzar had dreams; [a]and his
spirit was *so* troubled that [b]his sleep left him.
2 [a]Then the king gave the command to call the
magicians, the astrologers, the sorcerers, and the
Chaldeans to tell the king his dreams. So they
came and stood before the king.
3 And the king said to them, "I have had a
dream, and my spirit is anxious to [1]know the
dream."
4 Then the Chaldeans spoke to the king in
Aramaic, [a]"O[1] king, live forever! Tell your servants the dream, and we will give the interpretation."
5 The king answered and said to the Chaldeans,
"My [1]decision is firm: if you do not make known
the dream to me, and its interpretation, you shall
be [a]cut in pieces, and your houses shall be made
an ash heap.
6 [a]"However, if you tell the dream and its interpretation, you shall receive from me gifts, rewards, and great honor. Therefore tell me the
dream and its interpretation."
7 They answered again and said, "Let the king
tell his servants the dream, and we will give its
interpretation."
8 The king answered and said, "I know for
certain that you would gain time, because you see
that my decision is firm:
9 "if you do not make known the dream to me,
*there is only* one decree for you! For you have
agreed to speak lying and corrupt words before
me till the [1]time has changed. Therefore tell me
the dream, and I shall know that you can [2]give me
its interpretation."
10 The Chaldeans answered the king, and said,
"There is not a man on earth who can tell the
king's matter; therefore no king, lord, or ruler has
*ever* asked such things of any magician, astrolo-
ger, or Chaldean.
11 "*It is* a [1]difficult thing that the king requests,
and there is no other who can tell it to the king
[a]except the gods, whose dwelling is not with
flesh."
12 For this reason the king was angry and very
furious, and gave the command to destroy all the
wise *men* of Babylon.
13 So the decree went out, and they began killing
the wise *men;* and they sought [a]Daniel and his
companions, to kill *them.*
**14** Then with counsel and wisdom Daniel answered Arioch, the captain of the king's guard,
who had gone out to kill the wise *men* of Babylon;
15 he answered and said to Arioch the king's
captain, "Why is the decree from the king so
[1]urgent?" Then Arioch made the decision known
to Daniel.
16 So Daniel went in and asked the king to give
him time, that he might tell the king the interpretation.
**17** Then Daniel went to his house, and made the
decision known to Hananiah, Mishael, and Azariah, his companions,
18 [a]that they might seek mercies from the God of
heaven concerning this secret, so that Daniel and
his companions might not perish with the rest of
the wise *men* of Babylon.
19 Then the secret was revealed to Daniel [a]in a
night vision. So Daniel blessed the God of heaven.
20 Daniel answered and said:

[a]"Blessed be the name of God forever and ever,
[b]For wisdom and might are His.
21 And He changes [a]the times and the seasons;
[b]He removes kings and raises up kings;

4 [b]Acts 7:22 [1]Lit. *writing* or *book*
5 [a]Dan. 1:19
7 [a]2 Kin. 24:17 [b]Dan. 2:26; 4:8; 5:12
8 [a]Hos. 9:3
9 [a]Gen. 39:21 [1]*kindness*
11 [1]Or *Melzar*
16 [1]Or *Melzar*
17 [a][James 1:5–7] [b]Acts 7:22 [c]2 Chr. 26:5
19 [a]Gen. 41:46 [1]Lit. *talked with them*
20 [a]1 Kin. 10:1
21 [a]Dan. 6:28; 10:1

CHAPTER 2
1 [a]Gen. 40:5–8; 41:1, 8 [b]Esth. 6:1
2 [a]Ex. 7:11
3 [1]Or *understand*
4 [a]Dan. 3:9; 5:10; 6:6, 21 [1]The original language of Daniel 2:4b through 7:28 is Aramaic.
5 [a]Ezra 6:11 [1]The command
6 [a]Dan. 5:16
9 [1]Situation [2]Or *declare to me*
11 [a]Dan. 5:11 [1]Or *rare*
13 [a]Dan. 1:19, 20
15 [1]Or *harsh*
18 [a][Matt. 18:19]
19 [a]Job 33:15
20 [a]Ps. 113:2 [b][Jer. 32:19]
21 [a]Esth. 1:13 [b][Ps. 75:6, 7]

[c]He gives wisdom to the wise
And knowledge to those who have
understanding.
22 [a]He reveals deep and secret things;
[b]He knows what *is* in the darkness,
And [c]light dwells with Him.

23 "I thank You and praise You,
O God of my fathers;
You have given me wisdom and might,
And have now made known to me what we
[a]asked of You,
For You have made known to us
the king's [1]demand."

24 Therefore Daniel went to Arioch, whom the
king had appointed to destroy the wise *men* of
Babylon. He went and said thus to him: "Do not
destroy the wise *men* of Babylon; take me before
the king, and I will tell the king the interpretation."
25 Then Arioch quickly brought Daniel before
the king, and said thus to him, "I have found a
man of the [1]captives of Judah, who will make
known to the king the interpretation."
26 The king answered and said to Daniel, whose
name *was* Belteshazzar, "Are you able to make
known to me the dream which I have seen, and its
interpretation?"
27 Daniel answered in the presence of the king,
and said, "The secret which the king has demanded, the wise *men*, the astrologers, the magicians, and the soothsayers cannot declare to the
king.
28 [a]"But there is a God in heaven who reveals
secrets, and He has made known to King Nebuchadnezzar [b]what will be in the latter days. Your
dream, and the visions of your head upon your
bed, were these:
29 "As for you, O king, thoughts came *to* your
*mind while* on your bed, *about* what would come
to pass after this; [a]and He who reveals secrets has
made known to you what will be.
30 [a]"But as for me, this secret has not been
revealed to me because I have more wisdom than
anyone living, but for *our* sakes who make known
the interpretation to the king, [b]and that you may
[1]know the thoughts of your heart.
**31** "You, O king, were watching; and behold, a
great image! This great image, whose splendor
*was* excellent, stood before you; and its form *was*
awesome.
32 [a]"This image's head *was* of fine gold, its chest
and arms of silver, its belly and [1]thighs of bronze,
33 "its legs of iron, its feet partly of iron and
partly of [1]clay.
34 "You watched while a stone was cut out
[a]without hands, which struck the image on its feet
of iron and clay, and broke them in pieces.
35 [a]"Then the iron, the clay, the bronze, the
silver, and the gold were crushed together, and
became [b]like chaff from the summer threshing
floors; the wind carried them away so that [c]no
trace of them was found. And the stone that
struck the image [d]became a great mountain [e]and
filled the whole earth.
**36** "This *is* the dream. Now we will tell the
interpretation of it before the king.
37 [a]"You, O king, *are* a king of kings. [b]For the
God of heaven has given you a kingdom, power,
strength, and glory;
38 [a]"and wherever the children of men dwell, or
the beasts of the field and the birds of the heaven,
He has given *them* into your hand, and has made
you ruler over them all—[b]you *are* this head of
gold.
39 "But after you shall arise [a]another kingdom
[b]inferior to yours; then another, a third kingdom
of bronze, which shall rule over all the earth.
40 "And [a]the fourth kingdom shall be as strong as
iron, inasmuch as iron breaks in pieces and shat-
ters everything; and like iron that crushes, *that*
*kingdom* will break in pieces and crush all the
others.
41 "Whereas you saw the feet and toes, partly of
potter's clay and partly of iron, the kingdom shall
be divided; yet the strength of the iron shall be in
it, just as you saw the iron mixed with ceramic
clay.
42 "And *as* the toes of the feet *were* partly of iron
and partly of clay, [a]so the kingdom shall be partly
strong and partly [1]fragile.
43 "As you saw iron mixed with ceramic clay,
they will mingle with the seed of men; but they
will not adhere to one another, just as iron does
not mix with clay.
44 "And in the days of these kings [a]the God of
heaven will set up a kingdom [b]which shall never
be destroyed; and the kingdom shall not be left to
other people; [c]it shall [1]break in pieces and [2]con-
sume all these kingdoms, and it shall stand forever.
45 [a]"Inasmuch as you saw that the stone was cut
out of the mountain without hands, and that it
broke in pieces the iron, the bronze, the clay, the
silver, and the gold—the great God has made
known to the king what will come to pass after
this. The dream is certain, and its interpretation is
sure."
**46** [a]Then King Nebuchadnezzar fell on his face,
prostrate before Daniel, and commanded that
they should present an offering [b]and incense to
him.
47 The king answered Daniel, and said, "Truly
[a]your God *is* the God of [b]gods, the Lord of kings,
and a revealer of secrets, since you could reveal
this secret."
48 [a]Then the king promoted Daniel [b]and gave
him many great gifts; and he made him ruler over
the whole province of Babylon, and [c]chief admin-
istrator over all the wise *men* of Babylon.
49 Also Daniel petitioned the king, [a]and he set
Shadrach, Meshach, and Abed-Nego over the
affairs of the province of Babylon; but Daniel [b]*sat*
in [1]the gate of the king.

## *Daniel's Friends Saved in the Fire*

**3** Nebuchadnezzar the king made an image of
gold, whose height *was* [1]sixty cubits *and* its
width six cubits. He set it up in the plain of Dura,
in the province of Babylon.
2 And King Nebuchadnezzar sent *word* to
gather together the satraps, the administrators,
the governors, the counselors, the treasurers, the
judges, the magistrates, and all the officials of the
provinces, to come to the dedication of the image
which King Nebuchadnezzar had set up.
3 So the satraps, the administrators, the governors, the counselors, the treasurers, the judges,
the magistrates, and all the officials of the provinces gathered together for the dedication of the
image that King Nebuchadnezzar had set up; and
they stood before the image that Nebuchadnezzar
had set up.

**21** [c]1 Kin. 3:9, 10; 4:29; [James 1:5]
**22** [a]Job 12:22; Ps. 25:14; [Prov. 3:22] [b]Job 26:6; Ps. 139:12; [Is. 45:7; Jer. 23:24; Heb. 4:13] [c][Ps. 36:9]; Dan. 5:11, 14; [1 Tim. 6:16; James 1:17; 1 John 1:5]
**23** [a]Ps. 21:2, 4; Dan. 2:18, 29, 30 [1]Lit. *word*
**25** [1]Lit. *sons of the captivity*
**28** [a]Gen. 40:8; Amos 4:13 [b]Gen. 49:1; Is. 2:2; Dan. 10:14; Mic. 4:1
**29** [a][Dan. 2:22, 28]
**30** [a]Acts 3:12 [b]Dan. 2:47 [1]Understand
**32** [a]Dan. 2:38, 45 [1]Or *sides*
**33** [1]Or *baked clay,* also vv. 34, 35, 42
**34** [a]Dan. 8:25; [Zech. 4:6]; 2 Cor. 5:1; Heb. 9:24
**35** [a]Dan. 7:23–27; [Rev. 16:14] [b]Ps. 1:4; Is. 17:13; 41:15, 16; Hos. 13:3 [c]Ps. 37:10, 36 [d][Is. 2:2, 3]; Mic. 4:1 [e]Ps. 80:9
**37** [a]Ezra 7:12; Is. 47:5; Jer. 27:6, 7; Ezek. 26:7; Hos. 8:10 [b]Ezra 1:2
**38** [a]Ps. 50:10, 11; Jer. 27:6; Dan. 4:21, 22 [b]Dan. 2:32
**39** [a]Dan. 5:28, 31 [b]Dan. 2:32
**40** [a]Dan. 7:7, 23
**42** [a]Dan. 7:24 [1]Or *brittle*
**44** [a]Dan. 2:28, 37 [b]Is. 9:6, 7; Ezek. 37:25; Dan. 4:3, 34; 6:26; 7:14, 27; Mic. 4:7; [Luke 1:32, 33] [c]Ps. 2:9; Is. 60:12; Dan. 2:34, 35; [1 Cor. 15:24] [1]Or *crush* [2]Lit. *put an end to*
**45** [a]Dan. 2:35; Is. 28:16
**46** [a]Dan. 3:5, 7; Acts 10:25; 14:13; Rev. 19:10; 22:8 [b]Lev. 26:31; Ezra 6:10
**47** [a]Dan. 3:28, 29; 4:34–37 [b][Deut. 10:17]
**48** [a][Prov. 14:35; 21:1] [b]Dan. 2:6 [c]Dan. 4:9; 5:11
**49** [a]Dan. 1:7; 3:12 [b]Esth. 2:19, 21; 3:2; Amos 5:15 [1]The king's court

CHAPTER 3
**1** [1]About 90 feet

4 Then a herald cried [1]aloud: "To you it is commanded, [a]O peoples, nations, and languages,
5 "*that* at the time you hear the sound of the horn, flute, harp, lyre, *and* psaltery, in symphony with all kinds of music, you shall fall down and worship the gold image that King Nebuchadnezzar has set up;
6 "and whoever does not fall down and worship shall [a]be cast immediately into the midst of a burning fiery furnace."
**7** So at that time, when all the people heard the sound of the horn, flute, harp, *and* lyre, in symphony with all kinds of music, all the people, nations, and languages fell down *and* worshiped the gold image which King Nebuchadnezzar had set up.
**8** Therefore at that time certain Chaldeans [a]came forward and accused the Jews.
9 They spoke and said to King Nebuchadnezzar, [a]"O king, live forever!
10 "You, O king, have made a decree that everyone who hears the sound of the horn, flute, harp, lyre, *and* psaltery, in symphony with all kinds of music, shall fall down and worship the gold image;
11 "and whoever does not fall down and worship shall be cast into the midst of a burning fiery furnace.
12 [a]"There are certain Jews whom you have set over the affairs of the province of Babylon: Shadrach, Meshach, and Abed-Nego; these men, O king, have [b]not paid due regard to you. They do not serve your gods or worship the gold image which you have set up."
**13** Then Nebuchadnezzar, in [a]rage and fury, gave the command to bring Shadrach, Meshach, and Abed-Nego. So they brought these men before the king.
14 Nebuchadnezzar spoke, saying to them, "*Is it* true, Shadrach, Meshach, and Abed-Nego, *that* you do not serve my gods or worship the gold image which I have set up?
15 "Now if you are ready at the time you hear the sound of the horn, flute, harp, lyre, *and* psaltery, in symphony with all kinds of music, and you fall down and worship the image which I have made, [a]*good!* But if you do not worship, you shall be cast immediately into the midst of a burning fiery furnace. [b]And who *is* the god who will deliver you from my hands?"
**16** Shadrach, Meshach, and Abed-Nego answered and said to the king, "O Nebuchadnezzar, [a]we have no need to answer you in this matter.
17 "If that *is the case,* our [a]God whom we serve is able to [b]deliver us from the burning fiery furnace, and He will deliver *us* from your hand, O king.
18 "But if not, let it be known to you, O king, that we do not serve your gods, nor will we [a]worship the gold image which you have set up."
**19** Then Nebuchadnezzar was full of fury, and the expression on his face changed toward Shadrach, Meshach, and Abed-Nego. He spoke and commanded that they heat the furnace seven times more than it was usually heated.
20 And he commanded certain mighty men of valor who *were* in his army to bind Shadrach, Meshach, and Abed-Nego, *and* cast *them* into the burning fiery furnace.
21 Then these men were bound in their coats, their trousers, their turbans, and their *other* garments, and were cast into the midst of the burning fiery furnace.
22 Therefore, because the king's command was [1]urgent, and the furnace exceedingly hot, the flame of the fire killed those men who took up Shadrach, Meshach, and Abed-Nego.
23 And these three men, Shadrach, Meshach, and Abed-Nego, fell down bound into the midst of the burning fiery furnace.
**24** Then King Nebuchadnezzar was astonished; and he rose in haste *and* spoke, saying to his [1]counselors, "Did we not cast three men bound into the midst of the fire?" They answered and said to the king, "True, O king."
25 "Look!" he answered, "I see four men loose, [a]walking in the midst of the fire; and they are not hurt, and the form of the fourth is like [b]the[1] Son of God."
**26** Then Nebuchadnezzar went near the [1]mouth of the burning fiery furnace *and* spoke, saying, "Shadrach, Meshach, and Abed-Nego, servants of the [a]Most High God, come out, and come *here.*" Then Shadrach, Meshach, and Abed-Nego came from the midst of the fire.
27 And the satraps, administrators, governors, and the king's counselors gathered together, and they saw these men [a]on whose bodies the fire had no power; the hair of their head was not singed nor were their garments affected, and the smell of fire was not on them.
28 Nebuchadnezzar spoke, saying, "Blessed be the God of Shadrach, Meshach, and Abed-Nego, who sent His [a]Angel[1] and delivered His servants who trusted in Him, and they have frustrated the king's word, and yielded their bodies, that they should not serve nor worship any god except their own God!
29 [a]"Therefore I make a decree that any people, nation, or language which speaks anything amiss against the [b]God of Shadrach, Meshach, and Abed-Nego shall be [c]cut in pieces, and their houses shall be made an ash heap; [d]because there is no other God who can deliver like this."
30 Then the king [1]promoted Shadrach, Meshach, and Abed-Nego in the province of Babylon.

### *The King's Second Dream Explained*

**4** Nebuchadnezzar the king,
[a]To all peoples, nations, and
languages that dwell in all the earth:
Peace be multiplied to you.

2 I thought it good to declare the signs and
wonders [a]that the Most High God has
worked for me.

3 [a]How great *are* His signs,
And how mighty His wonders!
His kingdom *is* [b]an everlasting kingdom,
And His dominion *is* from generation to
generation.

4 I, Nebuchadnezzar, was at rest in my house,
and flourishing in my palace.
5 I saw a dream which made me afraid, [a]and
the thoughts on my bed and the visions of
my head [b]troubled me.
6 Therefore I issued a decree to bring in all the
wise *men* of Babylon before me, that they
might make known to me the interpretation
of the dream.
7 [a]Then the magicians, the astrologers, the
Chaldeans, and the soothsayers came in, and
I told them the dream; but they did not
make known to me its interpretation.

**4** [a]Dan. 4:1; 6:25 [1]Lit. *with strength*
**6** [a]Jer. 29:22; Ezek. 22:18–22; Matt. 13:42, 50; Rev. 9:2; 13:15; 14:11
**8** [a]Ezra 4:12–16; Esth. 3:8, 9; Dan. 6:12, 13
**9** [a]Dan. 2:4; 5:10; 6:6, 21
**12** [a]Dan. 2:49 [b]Dan. 1:8; 6:12, 13
**13** [a]Dan. 2:12; 3:19
**15** [a]Ex. 32:32; Luke 13:9 [b]Ex. 5:2; 2 Kin. 18:35; Is. 36:18–20; Dan. 2:47
**16** [a][Matt. 10:19]
**17** [a]Job 5:19; [Ps. 27:1, 2; Is. 26:3, 4]; Jer. 1:8; 15:20, 21; Dan. 6:19–22 [b]1 Sam. 17:37; Jer. 1:8; 15:20, 21; 42:11; Dan. 6:16, 19–22; Mic. 7:7; 2 Cor. 1:10
**18** [a]Job 13:15
**22** [1]Or *harsh*
**24** [1]High officials
**25** [a][Ps. 91:3–9]; Is. 43:2 [b]Job 1:6; 38:7; [Ps. 34:7]; Dan. 3:28 [1]Or *a son of the gods*
**26** [a][Dan. 4:2, 3, 17, 34, 35] [1]Lit. *door*
**27** [a][Is. 43:2]; Heb. 11:34
**28** [a][Ps. 34:7, 8]; Is. 37:36; [Jer. 17:7]; Dan. 6:22, 23; Acts 5:19; 12:7 [1]Or *angel*
**29** [a]Dan. 6:26 [b]Dan. 2:46, 47; 4:34–37 [c]Ezra 6:11; Dan. 2:5 [d]Dan. 6:27
**30** [1]Lit. *caused to prosper*

CHAPTER 4
**1** [a]Ezra 4:17; Dan. 3:4; 6:25
**2** [a]Dan. 3:26
**3** [a]2 Sam. 7:16; Ps. 89:35–37; Dan. 6:27; 7:13, 14; [Luke 1:31–33] [b][Dan. 2:44; 4:34; 6:26]
**5** [a]Dan. 2:28, 29 [b]Dan. 2:1
**7** [a]Dan. 2:2

8 But at last Daniel came before me [a](his name *is* Belteshazzar, according to the name of my god; [b]in him *is* the Spirit of the Holy God), and I told the dream before him, *saying:*

9 "Belteshazzar, [a]chief of the magicians, because I know that the Spirit of the Holy God *is* in you, and no secret troubles you, explain to me the visions of my dream that I have seen, and its interpretation.

10 "These *were* the visions of my head *while* on my bed:

I was looking, and behold,
[a]A tree in the midst of the earth,
And its height was great.
11 The tree grew and became strong;
Its height reached to the heavens,
And it could be seen to the ends
of all the earth.
12 Its leaves *were* lovely,
Its fruit abundant,
And in it *was* food for all.
[a]The beasts of the field found shade under it,
The birds of the heavens dwelt
in its branches,
And all flesh was fed from it.

**13** "I saw in the visions of my head *while* on my bed, and there was [a]a watcher, [b]a holy one, coming down from heaven.

14 He cried [1]aloud and said thus:

[a]'Chop down the tree and cut off its branches,
Strip off its leaves and scatter its fruit.
[b]Let the beasts get out from under it,
And the birds from its branches.
15 Nevertheless leave the stump and roots in
the earth,
*Bound* with a band of iron and bronze,
In the tender grass of the field.
Let it be wet with the dew of heaven,
And *let* him graze with the beasts
On the grass of the earth.
16 Let his heart be changed from *that of* a man,
Let him be given the heart of a beast,
And let seven [a]times[1] pass over him.

17 'This decision *is* by the decree
of the watchers,
And the sentence by the word
of the holy ones,
In order [a]that the living may know
[b]That the Most High rules in the kingdom of
men,
[c]Gives it to whomever He will,
And sets over it the [d]lowest of men.'

18 "This dream I, King Nebuchadnezzar, have seen. Now you, Belteshazzar, declare its interpretation, [a]since all the wise *men* of my kingdom are not able to make known to me the interpretation; but you *are* able, [b]for the Spirit of the Holy God *is* in you."

**19** Then Daniel, [a]whose name was Belteshazzar, was astonished for a time, and his thoughts [b]troubled him. *So* the king spoke, and said, "Belteshazzar, do not let the dream or its interpretation trouble you." Belteshazzar answered and said,

"My lord, *may* [c]the dream [1]concern those who hate you, and its interpretation [2]concern your enemies!

**8** [a]Dan. 1:7 [b]Is. 63:11; Dan. 2:11; 4:18; 5:11, 14
**9** [a]Dan. 2:48; 5:11
**10** [a]Ezek. 31:3; Dan. 4:20
**12** [a]Jer. 27:6; Ezek. 17:23; 31:6; Lam. 4:20
**13** [a][Dan. 4:17, 23] [b]Deut. 33:2; Ps. 89:7; Dan. 8:13; Zech. 14:5; Jude 14
**14** [a]Ezek. 31:10–14; Dan. 4:23; [Matt. 3:10; 7:19; Luke 13:7–9] [b]Ezek. 31:12, 13; Dan. 4:12 [1]Lit. *with strength*
**16** [a]Dan. 11:13; 12:7 [1]Possibly *years*
**17** [a]Ps. 9:16; 83:18 [b]Dan. 2:21; 4:25, 32; 5:21 [c]Jer. 27:5–7; Ezek. 29:18–20; Dan. 2:37; 5:18 [d]1 Sam. 2:8; Dan. 11:21
**18** [a]Gen. 41:8, 15; Dan. 5:8, 15 [b]Dan. 4:8, 9; 5:11, 14
**19** [a]Dan. 4:8 [b]Jer. 4:19; Dan. 7:15, 28; 8:27 [c]2 Sam. 18:32; Jer. 29:7; Dan. 4:24; 10:16 [1]*be for* [2]*for*
**20** [a]Dan. 4:10–12
**22** [a]Dan. 2:37, 38 [b]Jer. 27:6–8
**23** [a]Dan. 4:13–15 [b]Dan. 5:21 [1]Possibly *years*
**25** [a]Dan. 4:32; 5:21 [b]Ps. 106:20 [c]Ps. 83:18; Dan. 4:2; 17:32 [d]Jer. 27:5 [1]Possibly *years*
**26** [a]Matt. 21:25; Luke 15:18 [1]God
**27** [a][Prov. 28:13]; Is. 55:7; Ezek. 18:21, 22; [Rom. 2:9–11; 1 Pet. 4:8] [b][Ps. 41:1–3]; Is. 58:6, 7, 10 [c]1 Kin. 21:29 [1]*prolonging*
**29** [1]Or *upon*
**30** [a]Prov. 16:18; Is. 13:19; Dan. 5:20
**31** [a]Dan. 5:5; Luke 12:20 [b]Dan. 4:24
**32** [a][Dan. 4:25] [1]Possibly *years*
**34** [a]Dan. 4:26 [b]Ps. 102:24–27; Dan. 6:26; 12:7; [Rev. 4:10] [1]Lit. *days*

20 [a]The tree that you saw, which grew and became strong, whose height reached to the heavens and which *could be seen* by all the earth,

21 whose leaves *were* lovely and its fruit abundant, in which *was* food for all, under which the beasts of the field dwelt, and in whose branches the birds of the heaven had their home—

22 [a]it *is* you, O king, who have grown and become strong; for your greatness has grown and reaches to the heavens, [b]and your dominion to the end of the earth.

**23** [a]And inasmuch as the king saw a watcher, a holy one, coming down from heaven and saying, 'Chop down the tree and destroy it, but leave its stump and roots in the earth, *bound* with a band of iron and bronze in the tender grass of the field; let it be wet with the dew of heaven, [b]and let him graze with the beasts of the field, till seven [1]times pass over him';

24 this is the interpretation, O king, and this is the decree of the Most High, which has come upon my lord the king:

25 They shall [a]drive you from men, your dwelling shall be with the beasts of the field, and they shall make you [b]eat grass like oxen. They shall wet you with the dew of heaven, and seven [1]times shall pass over you, [c]till you know that the Most High rules in the kingdom of men, and [d]gives it to whomever He chooses.

**26** And inasmuch as they gave the command to leave the stump *and* roots of the tree, your kingdom shall be assured to you, after you come to know that [a]Heaven[1] rules.

27 Therefore, O king, let my advice be acceptable to you; [a]break off your sins by *being* righteous, and your iniquities by showing mercy to *the* poor. [b]Perhaps there may be [c]a [1]lengthening of your prosperity."

**28** All *this* came upon King Nebuchadnezzar.

29 At the end of the twelve months he was walking [1]about the royal palace of Babylon.

30 The king [a]spoke, saying, "Is not this great Babylon, that I have built for a royal dwelling by my mighty power and for the honor of my majesty?"

**31** [a]While the word *was still* in the king's mouth, [b]a voice fell from heaven: "King Nebuchadnezzar, to you it is spoken: the kingdom has departed from you!

32 And [a]they shall drive you from men, and your dwelling *shall be* with the beasts of the field. They shall make you eat grass like oxen; and seven [1]times shall pass over you, until you know that the Most High rules in the kingdom of men, and gives it to whomever He chooses."

33 That very hour the word was fulfilled concerning Nebuchadnezzar; he was driven from men and ate grass like oxen; his body was wet with the dew of heaven till his hair had grown like eagles' *feathers* and his nails like birds' *claws.*

**34** And [a]at the end of the [1]time I, Nebuchadnezzar, lifted my eyes to heaven, and my understanding returned to me; and I blessed the Most High and praised and honored Him [b]who lives forever:

For His dominion *is* [c]an everlasting dominion,
And His kingdom *is* from generation
to generation.
35 [a]All the inhabitants of the earth *are* reputed
as nothing;
[b]He does according to His will in the army of
heaven
And *among* the inhabitants of the earth.
[c]No one can restrain His hand
Or say to Him, [d]"What have You done?"

**36** At the same time my reason returned to me,
[a]and for the glory of my kingdom, my honor
and splendor returned to me. My counselors
and nobles resorted to me, I was [b]restored to
my kingdom, and excellent majesty was
[c]added to me.
37 Now I, Nebuchadnezzar, [a]praise and extol
and honor the King of heaven, [b]all of whose
works *are* truth, and His ways justice. [c]And
those who walk in pride He is able to put
down.

### *The Handwriting on the Wall*

**5** Belshazzar the king [a]made a great feast for a
thousand of his lords, and drank wine in the
presence of the thousand.
2 While he tasted the wine, Belshazzar gave the
command to bring the gold and silver vessels
[a]which his [1]father Nebuchadnezzar had taken
from the temple which *had been* in Jerusalem,
that the king and his lords, his wives, and his
concubines might drink from them.
3 Then they brought the gold [a]vessels that had
been taken from the temple of the house of God
which *had been* in Jerusalem; and the king and
his lords, his wives, and his concubines drank
from them.
4 They drank wine, [a]and praised the gods of gold
and silver, bronze and iron, wood and stone.
**5** [a]In the same hour the fingers of a man's hand
appeared and wrote opposite the lampstand on
the plaster of the wall of the king's palace; and the
king saw the part of the hand that wrote.
6 Then the king's countenance changed, and his
thoughts troubled him, so that the joints of his
hips were loosened and his [a]knees knocked
against each other.
7 [a]The king cried [1]aloud to bring in [b]the astrologers, the Chaldeans, and the soothsayers. The
king spoke, saying to the wise *men* of Babylon,
"Whoever reads this writing, and tells me its
interpretation, shall be clothed with purple and
*have* a chain of gold around his neck; [c]and he shall
be the third ruler in the kingdom."
8 Now all the king's wise *men* came, [a]but they
could not read the writing, or make known to the
king its interpretation.
9 Then King Belshazzar was greatly [a]troubled,
his countenance was changed, and his lords were
[1]astonished.
**10** The queen, because of the words of the king
and his lords, came to the banquet hall. The queen
spoke, saying, "O king, live forever! Do not let
your thoughts trouble you, nor let your countenance change.
11 [a]"There is a man in your kingdom in whom *is*
the Spirit of the Holy God. And in the days of your
[1]father, light and understanding and wisdom, like
the wisdom of the gods, were found in him; and
King Nebuchadnezzar your [1]father—your father
the king—made him chief of the magicians, astrologers, Chaldeans, *and* soothsayers.
12 "Inasmuch as an excellent spirit, knowledge,
understanding, interpreting dreams, solving riddles, and [1]explaining enigmas were found in this
Daniel, [a]whom the king named Belteshazzar, now
let Daniel be called, and he will give the interpretation."
**13** Then Daniel was brought in before the king.
The king spoke, and said to Daniel, "*Are* you that
Daniel [1]who is one of the captives from Judah,
whom my [2]father the king brought from Judah?
14 "I have heard of you, that [a]the [1]Spirit of God *is*
in you, and *that* light and understanding and
excellent wisdom are found in you.
15 Now [a]the wise *men*, the astrologers, have been
brought in before me, that they should read this
writing and make known to me its interpretation,
but they could not give the interpretation of the
thing.
16 "And I have heard of you, that you can give
interpretations and [1]explain enigmas. [a]Now if you
can read the writing and make known to me its
interpretation, you shall be clothed with purple
and *have* a chain of gold around your neck, and
shall be the third ruler in the kingdom."
**17** Then Daniel answered, and said before the
king, "Let your gifts be for yourself, and give your
rewards to another; yet I will read the writing to
the king, and make known to him the interpretation.
18 "O king, [a]the Most High God gave Nebuchadnezzar your [1]father a kingdom and majesty, glory
and honor.
19 "And because of the majesty that He gave
him, [a]all peoples, nations, and languages trembled
and feared before him. Whomever he wished, he
[b]executed; whomever he wished, he kept alive;
whomever he wished, he set up; and whomever he
wished, he put down.
20 [a]"But when his heart was lifted up, and his
spirit was hardened in pride, he was deposed from
his kingly throne, and they took his glory from
him.
21 "Then he was [a]driven from the sons of men,
his heart was made like the beasts, and his dwelling *was* with the wild donkeys. They fed him with
grass like oxen, and his body was wet with the
dew of heaven, [b]till he [1]knew that the Most High
God rules in the kingdom of men, and appoints
over it whomever He chooses.
22 "But you his son, Belshazzar, [a]have not humbled your heart, although you knew all this.
23 [a]"And you have [1]lifted yourself up against the
Lord of heaven. They have brought the [b]vessels of
[2]His house before you, and you and your lords,
your wives and your concubines, have drunk wine
from them. And you have praised the gods of
silver and gold, bronze and iron, wood and stone,
[c]which do not see or hear or know; and the God
who *holds* your breath in His hand [d]and owns all
your ways, you have not glorified.
24 "Then the [1]fingers of the hand were sent from
Him, and this writing was written.
**25** "And this is the inscription that was written:

[1]MENE, MENE, [2]TEKEL, [3]UPHARSIN.

26 "This *is* the interpretation of *each* word.
MENE: God has numbered your kingdom, and
finished it;
27 "TEKEL: [a]You have been weighed in the balances, and found wanting;

**34** [c][Luke 1:33]
**35** [a]Is. 40:15, 17 [b]Ps. 115:3; 135:6 [c]Job 34:29 [d]Rom. 9:20
**36** [a]Dan. 4:26 [b]2 Chr. 20:20 [c][Prov. 22:4]
**37** [a]Dan. 2:46, 47; 3:28, 29 [b][Ps. 33:4] [c]Ex. 18:11

CHAPTER 5
**1** [a]Esth. 1:3
**2** [a]Dan. 1:2 [1]Or *ancestor*
**3** [a]2 Chr. 36:10
**4** [a]Rev. 9:20
**5** [a]Dan. 4:31
**6** [a]Dan. 4:6
**7** [a]Dan. 4:6, 7; 5:11, 15 [b]Is. 47:13 [c]Dan. 6:2, 3 [1]Lit. *with strength*
**8** [a]Dan. 2:27; 4:7; 5:15
**9** [a]Dan. 2:1; 5:6 [1]*perplexed*
**11** [a]Dan. 2:48; 4:8, 9, 18 [1]Or *ancestor*
**12** [a]Dan. 1:7; 4:8 [1]Lit. *untying knots*
**13** [1]Lit. *who is of the sons of the captivity* [2]Or *ancestor*
**14** [a]Dan. 4:8, 9, 18; 5:11, 12 [1]Or *spirit of the gods*
**15** [a]Dan. 5:7, 8
**16** [a]Dan. 5:7, 29 [1]Lit. *untie knots*
**18** [a]Dan. 2:37, 38; 4:17, 22, 25 [1]Or *ancestor*
**19** [a]Jer. 27:7 [b]Dan. 2:12, 13; 3:6
**20** [a]Dan. 4:30, 37
**21** [a]Dan. 4:32, 33 [b]Ezek. 17:24 [1]Recognized
**22** [a]2 Chr. 33:23; 36:12
**23** [a]Dan. 5:3, 4 [b]Ex. 40:9 [c]Ps. 115:5, 6 [d][Jer. 10:23] [1]Exalted [2]The temple
**24** [1]Lit. *palm*
**25** [1]Lit. *a mina* (50 shekels) from the verb "to number" [2]Lit. *a shekel* from the verb "to weigh" [3]Lit. *and half-shekels* from the verb "to divide"; pl. of *Peres*, v. 28
**27** [a]Ps. 62:9

28 "PERES: Your kingdom has been divided, and
given to the [a]Medes and [b]Persians."[1]
29 Then Belshazzar gave the command, and they
clothed Daniel with purple and *put* a chain of gold
around his neck, and made a proclamation concerning him [a]that he should be the third ruler in
the kingdom.
**30** [a]That very night Belshazzar, king of the Chaldeans, was slain.
31 [a]And Darius the Mede received the kingdom,
*being* about sixty-two years old.

## *The Plot Against Daniel*

**6** It pleased Darius to set over the kingdom one
hundred and twenty satraps, to be over the
whole kingdom;
2 and over these, three governors, of whom
Daniel *was* one, that the satraps might give
account to them, so that the king would suffer no
loss.
3 Then this Daniel distinguished himself above
the governors and satraps, [a]because an excellent
spirit *was* in him; and the king gave thought to
setting him over the whole realm.
4 [a]So the governors and satraps sought to find
*some* charge against Daniel concerning the kingdom; but they could find no charge or fault,
because he *was* faithful; nor was there any error
or fault found in him.
5 Then these men said, "We shall not find any
charge against this Daniel unless we find *it*
against him concerning the law of his God."
**6** So these governors and satraps thronged before the king, and said thus to him: [a]"King Darius,
live forever!
7 "All the governors of the kingdom, the administrators and satraps, the counselors and advisors,
have [a]consulted together to establish a royal
statute and to make a firm decree, that whoever
petitions any god or man for thirty days, except
you, O king, shall be cast into the den of lions.
8 "Now, O king, establish the decree and sign
the writing, so that it cannot be changed, according to the [a]law of the Medes and Persians, which
[1]does not alter."
9 Therefore King Darius signed the written
decree.
**10** Now when Daniel knew that the writing was
signed, he went home. And in his upper room,
with his windows open [a]toward Jerusalem, he
knelt down on his knees [b]three times that day,
and prayed and gave thanks before his God, as
was his custom since early days.
11 Then these men assembled and found Daniel
praying and making supplication before his God.
12 [a]And they went before the king, and spoke
concerning the king's decree: "Have you not
signed a decree that every man who petitions any
god or man within thirty days, except you, O king,
shall be cast into the den of lions?" The king
answered and said, "The thing *is* true, [b]according
to the law of the Medes and Persians, which [1]does
not alter."
13 So they answered and said before the king,
"That Daniel, [a]who is [1]one of the captives from
Judah, [b]does not show due regard for you, O king,
or for the decree that you have signed, but makes
his petition three times a day."
14 And the king, when he heard *these* words,
[a]was greatly displeased with himself, and set *his*
heart on Daniel to deliver him; and he [1]labored till
the going down of the sun to deliver him.
15 Then these men [1]approached the king, and
said to the king, "Know, O king, that *it is* [a]the law
of the Medes and Persians that no decree or
statute which the king establishes may be
changed."
16 So the king gave the command, and they
brought Daniel and cast *him* into the den of lions.
*But* the king spoke, saying to Daniel, "Your God,
whom you serve continually, He will deliver you."
17 [a]Then a stone was brought and laid on the
mouth of the den, [b]and the king sealed it with his
own signet ring and with the signets of his lords,
that the purpose concerning Daniel might not be
changed.
**18** Now the king went to his palace and spent the
night fasting; and no [1]musicians were brought
before him. [a]Also his sleep [2]went from him.
19 Then the [a]king arose very early in the morning
and went in haste to the den of lions.
20 And when he came to the den, he cried out
with a [1]lamenting voice to Daniel. The king spoke,
saying to Daniel, "Daniel, servant of the living
God, [a]has your God, whom you serve continually,
been able to deliver you from the lions?"
21 Then Daniel said to the king, [a]"O king, live
forever!
22 [a]"My God sent His angel and [b]shut the lions'
mouths, so that they have not hurt me, because I
was found innocent before Him; and also, O king,
I have done no wrong before you."
23 Now the king was exceedingly glad for him,
and commanded that they should take Daniel up
out of the den. So Daniel was taken up out of the
den, and no injury whatever was found on him,
[a]because he believed in his God.
**24** And the king gave the command, [a]and they
brought those men who had accused Daniel, and
they cast *them* into the den of lions—them, [b]their
children, and their wives; and the lions overpowered them, and broke all their bones in pieces
before they ever came to the bottom of the den.
**25** [a]Then King Darius wrote:

To all peoples, nations, and languages that
dwell in all the earth:
Peace be multiplied to you.
26 [a]I make a decree that in every dominion of
my kingdom *men must* [b]tremble and fear
before the God of Daniel.

[c]For He *is* the living God,
And steadfast forever;
His kingdom *is the one* which
shall not be [d]destroyed,
And His dominion *shall endure* to the end.
27 He delivers and rescues,
[a]And He works signs and wonders
In heaven and on earth,
Who has delivered Daniel from the [1]power of
the lions.

**28** So this Daniel prospered in the reign of Darius
[a]and in the reign of [b]Cyrus the Persian.

## *Daniel's Vision of the Four Beasts*

**7** In the first year of Belshazzar king of Babylon,
[a]Daniel [1]had a dream and [b]visions of his head
*while* on his bed. Then he wrote down the dream,
telling [2]the main facts.
2 Daniel spoke, saying, "I saw in my vision by

**28** [a]Dan. 5:31; 9:1 [b]Dan. 6:28 [1]Aram. *Paras,* consonant with *Peres*
**29** [a]Dan. 5:7, 16
**30** [a]Jer. 51:31, 39, 57
**31** [a]Dan. 2:39; 9:1

CHAPTER 6
**3** [a]Dan. 5:12
**4** [a]Eccl. 4:4
**6** [a]Neh. 2:3
**7** [a]Ps. 59:3; 62:4; 64:2–6
**8** [a]Esth. 1:19; 8:8 [1]Lit. *does not pass away*
**10** [a]Jon. 2:4 [b]Ps. 55:17
**12** [a]Dan. 3:8–12 [b]Dan. 6:8, 15 [1]Lit. *does not pass away*
**13** [a]Dan. 1:6; 5:13 [b]Dan. 3:12 [1]Lit. *who is of the sons of the captivity*
**14** [a]Mark 6:26 [1]*strove*
**15** [a]Dan. 6:8, 12 [1]Lit. *thronged before*
**17** [a]Lam. 3:53 [b]Matt. 27:66
**18** [a]Dan. 2:1 [1]Exact meaning unknown [2]Or *fled*
**19** [a]Dan. 3:24
**20** [a]Dan. 3:17 [1]Or *grieved*
**21** [a]Dan. 2:4; 6:6
**22** [a]Dan. 3:28 [b]Heb. 11:33
**23** [a]Heb. 11:33
**24** [a]Deut. 19:18, 19 [b]Deut. 24:16
**25** [a]Dan. 4:1
**26** [a]Dan. 3:29 [b]Ps. 99:1 [c]Dan. 4:34; 6:20 [d]Dan. 2:44; 4:3; 7:14, 27
**27** [a]Dan. 4:2, 3 [1]Lit. *hand*
**28** [a]Dan. 1:21 [b]Ezra 1:1, 2

CHAPTER 7
**1** [a][Amos 3:7] [b][Dan. 2:28] [1]Lit. *saw* [2]Lit. *the head* or *chief of the words*

night, and behold, the four winds of heaven were
stirring up the Great Sea.
3 "And four great beasts [a]came up from the sea,
each different from the other.
4 "The first *was* [a]like a lion, and had eagle's
wings. I watched till its wings were plucked off;
and it was lifted up from the earth and made to
stand on two feet like a man, and a [b]man's heart
was given to it.
5 [a]"And suddenly another beast, a second, like a
bear. It was raised up on one side, and *had* three
ribs in its mouth between its teeth. And they said
thus to it: 'Arise, devour much flesh!'
6 "After this I looked, and there was another,
like a leopard, which had on its back four wings of
a bird. The beast also had [a]four heads, and dominion was given to it.
7 "After this I saw in the night visions, and
behold, [a]a fourth beast, dreadful and terrible,
exceedingly strong. It had huge iron teeth; it was
devouring, breaking in pieces, and trampling the
residue with its feet. It *was* different from all the
beasts that *were* before it, [b]and it had ten horns.
8 "I was considering the horns, and [a]there was
another horn, a little one, coming up among them,
before whom three of the first horns were plucked
out by the roots. And there, in this horn, *were*
eyes like the eyes [b]of a man, [c]and a mouth speaking [1]pompous words.

**9** "I[a] watched till thrones were [1]put in place,
And [b]the Ancient of Days was seated;
[c]His garment *was* white as snow,
And the hair of His head *was* like pure wool.
His throne *was* a fiery flame,
[d]Its wheels a burning fire;
10 [a]A fiery stream issued
And came forth from before Him.
[b]A thousand thousands ministered to Him;
Ten thousand times ten thousand
stood before Him.
[c]The [1]court was seated,
And the books were opened.

11 "I watched then because of the sound of the
[1]pompous words which the horn was speaking; [a]I
watched till the beast was slain, and its body
destroyed and given to the burning flame.
12 "As for the rest of the beasts, they had their
dominion taken away, yet their lives were prolonged for a season and a time.

**13** "I was watching in the night visions,
And behold, [a]*One* like the Son of Man,
Coming with the clouds of heaven!
He came to the Ancient of Days,
And they brought Him near before Him.
14 [a]Then to Him was given dominion and glory
and a kingdom,
That all [b]peoples, nations, and languages
should serve Him.
His dominion *is* [c]an everlasting dominion,
Which shall not pass away,
And His kingdom *the one*
Which shall not be destroyed.

**15** "I, Daniel, was grieved in my spirit [1]within *my*
body, and the visions of my head troubled me.
16 "I came near to one of those who stood by,
and asked him the truth of all this. So he told me
and made known to me the interpretation of these
things:
17 'Those great beasts, which are four, *are* four
[1]kings *which* arise out of the earth.
18 'But [a]the saints of the Most High shall receive
the kingdom, and possess the kingdom forever,
even forever and ever.'
19 "Then I wished to know the truth about the
fourth beast, which was different from all the
others, exceedingly dreadful, *with* its teeth of iron
and its nails of bronze, *which* devoured, broke in
pieces, and trampled the residue with its feet;
20 "and the ten horns that *were* on its head, and
the other *horn* which came up, before which three
fell, namely, that horn which had eyes and a
mouth which spoke [1]pompous words, whose appearance *was* greater than his fellows.
21 "I was watching; [a]and the same horn was
making war against the saints, and prevailing
against them,
22 "until the Ancient of Days came, [a]and a judgment was made *in favor* of the saints of the Most
High, and the time came for the saints to possess
the kingdom.
**23** "Thus he said:

'The fourth beast shall be
[a]A fourth kingdom on earth,
Which shall be different from all *other*
kingdoms,
And shall devour the whole earth,
Trample it and break it in pieces.
24 [a]The ten horns *are* ten kings
*Who* shall arise from this kingdom.
And another shall rise after them;
He shall be different from the first *ones*,
And shall subdue three kings.
25 [a]He shall speak *pompous* words
against the Most High,
Shall [b]persecute[1] the saints of the Most High,
And shall [c]intend to change times and law.
Then [d]*the saints* shall be given into his hand
[e]For a time and times and half a time.

**26** 'But[a] the court shall be seated,
And they shall [b]take away his dominion,
To consume and destroy *it* forever.
27 Then the [a]kingdom and dominion,
And the greatness of the kingdoms under the
whole heaven,
Shall be given to the people,
the saints of the Most High.
[b]His kingdom *is* an everlasting kingdom,
[c]And all dominions shall serve and obey Him.'

28 "This *is* the end of the [1]account. As for me,
Daniel, [a]my thoughts greatly troubled me, and my
countenance changed; but I [b]kept the matter in
my heart."

## *Daniel's Vision of the Ram and Goat*

**8** In[1] the third year of the reign of King Belshazzar a vision appeared *to* me—to me, Daniel—
after the one that appeared to me [a]the first time.
2 I saw in the vision, and it so happened while I
was looking, that I *was* in [a]Shushan,[1] the [2]citadel,
which *is* in the province of Elam; and I saw in the
vision that I was by the River Ulai.
3 Then I lifted my eyes and saw, and there,
standing beside the river, was a ram which had
two horns, and the two horns *were* high; but one
*was* [a]higher than the other, and the higher *one*
came up last.
4 I saw the ram pushing westward, northward,

3 [a]Rev. 13:1; 17:8
4 [a]Deut. 28:49 [b]Dan. 4:16, 34
5 [a]Dan. 2:39
6 [a]Dan. 8:8, 22
7 [a]Dan. 2:40 [b]Rev. 12:3; 13:1
8 [a]Dan. 8:9 [b]Rev. 9:7 [c]Rev. 13:5, 6 [1]Lit. *great things*
9 [a][Rev. 20:4] [b]Ps. 90:2 [c]Rev. 1:14 [d]Ezek. 1:15 [1]Or *set up*
10 [a]Is. 30:33; 66:15 [b]Rev. 5:11 [c][Rev. 20:11–15] [1]Or *judgment*
11 [a][Rev. 19:20; 20:10] [1]Lit. *great*
13 [a][Matt. 24:30; 26:64]
14 [a][John 3:35, 36] [b]Dan. 3:4 [c]Mic. 4:7
15 [1]Lit. *in the midst of its sheath*
17 [1]Representing their kingdoms, v. 23
18 [a]Is. 60:12–14
20 [1]Lit. *great things*
21 [a]Rev. 11:7; 13:7; 17:14
22 [a][Rev. 1:6]
23 [a]Dan. 2:40
24 [a]Rev. 13:1; 17:12
25 [a]Rev. 13:1–6 [b]Rev. 17:6 [c]Dan. 2:21 [d]Rev. 13:7; 18:24 [e]Rev. 12:14 [1]Lit. *wear out*
26 [a][Dan. 2:35; 7:10, 22] [b]Rev. 19:20
27 [a]Dan. 7:14, 18, 22 [b][Luke 1:33, 34] [c]Is. 60:12
28 [a]Dan. 8:27 [b]Luke 2:19, 51 [1]Lit. *word*

CHAPTER 8
1 [a]Dan. 7:1 [1]The Hebrew language resumes in Dan. 8:1.
2 [a]Esth. 1:2; 2:8 [1]Or *Susa* [2]Or *fortified palace*
3 [a]Dan. 7:5

and southward, so that no animal could [1]with-
stand him; nor *was there any* that could deliver
from his hand, [a]but he did according to his will
and became great.
5 And as I was considering, suddenly a male
goat came from the west, across the surface of the
whole earth, without touching the ground; and
the goat *had* a notable [a]horn between his eyes.
6 Then he came to the ram that had two horns,
which I had seen standing beside the river, and
ran at him with furious power.
7 And I saw him confronting the ram; he was
moved with rage against him, [1]attacked the ram,
and broke his two horns. There was no power in
the ram to withstand him, but he cast him down
to the ground and trampled him; and there was no
one that could deliver the ram from his hand.
8 Therefore the male goat grew very great; but
when he became strong, the large horn was broken, and in place of it [a]four notable ones came up
toward the four winds of heaven.
9 [a]And out of one of them came a little horn
which grew exceedingly great toward the south,
[b]toward the east, and toward the [c]Glorious *Land.*
10 [a]And it grew up to [b]the host of heaven; and [c]it
cast down *some* of the host and *some* of the stars
to the ground, and trampled them.
11 [a]He even exalted *himself* as high as [b]the Prince
of the host; [c]and by him [d]the daily *sacrifices* were
taken away, and the place of [1]His sanctuary was
cast down.
12 Because of transgression, [a]an army was given
over *to the horn* to oppose the daily *sacrifices;* and
he cast [b]truth down to the ground. He [c]did *all this*
and prospered.
13 Then I heard [a]a holy one speaking; and *another* holy one said to that certain *one* who was
speaking, "How long *will* the vision *be, concerning* the daily *sacrifices* and the transgression [1]of
desolation, the giving of both the sanctuary and
the host to be trampled underfoot?"
14 And he said to me, "For two thousand three
hundred [1]days; then the sanctuary shall be
cleansed."
15 Then it happened, when I, Daniel, had seen
the vision and [a]was seeking the meaning, that
suddenly there stood before me [b]one having the
appearance of a man.
16 And I heard a man's voice [a]between *the banks
of* the Ulai, who called, and said, [b]"Gabriel, make
this *man* understand the vision."
17 So he came near where I stood, and when he
came I was afraid and [a]fell on my face; but he said
to me, "Understand, son of man, that the vision
*refers* to the time of the end."
18 [a]Now, as he was speaking with me, I was in a
deep sleep with my face to the ground; [b]but he
touched me, and stood me upright.
19 And he said, "Look, I am making known to
you what shall happen in the latter time of the
indignation; [a]for at the appointed time the end
*shall be.*
20 "The ram which you saw, having the two
horns—*they are* the kings of Media and Persia.
21 "And the [1]male goat *is* the [2]kingdom of
Greece. The large horn that *is* between its eyes [a]*is*
the first king.
22 [a]"As for the broken *horn* and the four that
stood up in its place, four kingdoms shall arise out
of that nation, but not with its power.

23 "And in the latter time of their kingdom,
When the transgressors have
reached their fullness,
A king shall arise,
[a]Having fierce [1]features,
Who understands sinister schemes.
24 His power shall be mighty,
[a]but not by his own power;
He shall destroy [1]fearfully,
[b]And shall prosper and thrive;
[c]He shall destroy the mighty,
and *also* the holy people.

25 "Through[a] his cunning
He shall cause deceit to prosper
under his [1]rule;
[b]And he shall exalt *himself* in his heart.
He shall destroy many in *their* prosperity.
[c]He shall even rise against
the Prince of princes;
But he shall be [d]broken without
*human* [2]means.

26 "And the vision of the evenings and mornings
Which was told is true;
[a]Therefore seal up the vision,
For *it refers* to many days *in the future.*"

27 [a]And I, Daniel, fainted and was sick for days;
afterward I arose and went about the king's
business. I was [1]astonished by the vision, but no
one understood it.

## *Daniel's Prayer for His People*

9 In the first year [a]of Darius the son of Ahasuerus, of the lineage of the Medes, who was
made king over the realm of the Chaldeans—
2 in the first year of his reign I, Daniel, understood by the books the number of the years
*specified* by the word of the LORD through [a]Jere-
miah the prophet, that He would accomplish
seventy years in the desolations of Jerusalem.
3 [a]Then I set my face toward the Lord God to
make request by prayer and supplications, with
fasting, sackcloth, and ashes.
4 And I prayed to the LORD my God, and made
confession, and said, "O [a]Lord, great and awesome
God, who keeps His covenant and mercy with
those who love Him, and with those who keep His
commandments,
5 [a]"we have sinned and committed iniquity, we
have done wickedly and rebelled, even by departing from Your precepts and Your judgments.
6 [a]"Neither have we heeded Your servants the
prophets, who spoke in Your name to our kings
and our princes, to our fathers and all the people
of the land.
7 "O Lord, [a]righteousness *belongs* to You, but to
us shame of face, as *it is* this day—to the men of
Judah, to the inhabitants of Jerusalem and all
Israel, those near and those far off in all the
countries to which You have driven them, because of the unfaithfulness which they have
committed against You.
8 "O Lord, to us *belongs* shame of face, to our
kings, our princes, and our fathers, because we
have sinned against You.
9 [a]"To the Lord our God *belong* mercy and
forgiveness, though we have rebelled against Him.
10 "We have not obeyed the voice of the LORD
our God, to walk in His laws, which He set before
us by His servants the prophets.

4 [a]Dan. 5:19 [1]Lit. *stand before him*
5 [a]Dan. 8:8, 21; 11:3
7 [1]Lit. *struck*
8 [a]Dan. 7:6; 8:22; 11:4
9 [a]Dan. 11:21 [b]Dan. 11:25 [c]Ps. 48:2
10 [a]Dan. 11:28 [b]Is. 14:13 [c]Rev. 12:4
11 [a]Dan. 8:25; 11:36, 37 [b]Josh. 5:14 [c]Dan. 11:31; 12:11 [d]Ex. 29:38 [1]The temple
12 [a]Dan. 11:31 [b]Is. 59:14 [c]Dan. 8:4; 11:36
13 [a]Dan. 4:13, 23 [1]Or *making desolate*
14 [1]Lit. *evening-mornings*
15 [a]1 Pet. 1:10 [b]Ezek. 1:26
16 [a]Dan. 12:6, 7 [b]Luke 1:19, 26
17 [a]Rev. 1:17
18 [a]Luke 9:32 [b]Ezek. 2:2
19 [a]Hab. 2:3
21 [a]Dan. 11:3 [1]*shaggy male* [2]Lit. *king,* representing his kingdom, Dan. 7:17, 23
22 [a]Dan. 11:4
23 [a]Deut. 28:50 [1]Lit. *countenance*
24 [a]Rev. 17:13 [b]Dan. 11:36 [c]Dan. 7:25 [1]Or *extraordinarily*
25 [a]Dan. 11:21 [b]Dan. 8:11–13; 11:36; 12:7 [c]Rev. 19:19, 20 [d]Job 34:20 [1]Lit. *hand* [2]Lit. *hand*
26 [a]Ezek. 12:27
27 [a]Dan. 7:28; 8:17 [1]*amazed*

CHAPTER 9
1 [a]Dan. 1:21
2 [a]2 Chr. 36:21
3 [a]Neh. 1:4
4 [a]Ex. 20:6
5 [a]1 Kin. 8:47, 48
6 [a]2 Chr. 36:15
7 [a]Neh. 9:33
9 [a][Ps. 130:4, 7]

11 "Yes, [a]all Israel has transgressed Your law,
and has departed so as not to obey Your voice;
therefore the curse and the oath written in the
[b]Law of Moses the servant of God have been
poured out on us, because we have sinned against
Him.
12 "And He has [a]confirmed His words, which He
spoke against us and against our judges who
judged us, by bringing upon us a great disaster;
[b]for under the whole heaven such has never been
done as what has been done to Jerusalem.
13 [a]"As *it is* written in the Law of Moses, all this
disaster has come upon us; [b]yet we have not made
our prayer before the LORD our God, that we
might turn from our iniquities and understand
Your truth.
14 "Therefore the LORD has [a]kept the disaster in
mind, and brought it upon us; for [b]the LORD our
God *is* righteous in all the works which He does,
though we have not obeyed His voice.
15 "And now, O Lord our God, [a]who brought
Your people out of the land of Egypt with a
mighty hand, and made Yourself [b]a name, as *it is*
this day—we have sinned, we have done wickedly!
**16** "O Lord, [a]according to all Your righteousness,
I pray, let Your anger and Your fury be turned
away from Your city Jerusalem, [b]Your holy mountain; because for our sins, [c]and for the iniquities of
our fathers, [d]Jerusalem and Your people [e]*are* a
reproach to all *those* around us.
17 "Now therefore, our God, hear the prayer of
Your servant, and his supplications, [a]and [b]for the
Lord's sake [1]cause Your face to shine on [2]Your
sanctuary, [c]which is desolate.
18 [a]"O my God, incline Your ear and hear; open
Your eyes [b]and see our desolations, and the city
[c]which is called by Your name; for we do not
present our supplications before You because of
our righteous deeds, but because of Your great
mercies.
19 "O Lord, hear! O Lord, forgive! O Lord, listen
and act! Do not delay for Your own sake, my God,
for Your city and Your people are called by Your
name."
**20** Now while I *was* speaking, praying, and confessing my sin and the sin of my people Israel, and
presenting my supplication before the LORD my
God for the holy mountain of my God,
21 yes, while I *was* speaking in prayer, the man
[a]Gabriel, whom I had seen in the vision at the
beginning, being caused to [1]fly swiftly, reached me
about the time of the evening offering.
22 And he informed *me,* and talked with me, and
said, "O Daniel, I have now come forth to give you
skill to understand.
23 "At the beginning of your supplications the
[1]command went out, and I have come to tell *you,*
for you *are* greatly [a]beloved; therefore [b]consider
the matter, and understand the vision:

**24** "Seventy [1]weeks are determined
For your people and for your holy city,
To finish the transgression,
[2]To make an end of sins,
[a]To make reconciliation for iniquity,
[b]To bring in everlasting righteousness,
To seal up vision and prophecy,
[c]And to anoint [3]the Most Holy.

25 "Know therefore and understand,
*That* from the going forth of the command
To restore and build Jerusalem
Until [a]Messiah [b]the Prince,
*There shall be* seven weeks
and sixty-two weeks;
The [1]street shall be built again, and the [2]wall,
Even in troublesome times.

26 "And after the sixty-two weeks
[a]Messiah shall [1]be cut off,
[b]but not for Himself;
And [c]the people of the prince who is to come
[d]Shall destroy the city and the sanctuary.
The end of it *shall be* with a flood,
And till the end of the war
desolations are determined.
27 Then he shall confirm [a]a [1]covenant with
[b]many for one week;
But in the middle of the week
He shall bring an end to sacrifice
and offering.
And on the wing of abominations shall be
one who makes desolate,
[c]Even until the consummation,
which is determined,
Is poured out on the [2]desolate."

### *Daniel's Vision by the Great River*

**10** In the third year of Cyrus king of Persia a
message was revealed to Daniel, whose
[a]name was called Belteshazzar. The message *was*
true, [1]but the appointed time *was* long; and he
understood the message, and had understanding
of the vision.
2 In those days I, Daniel, was mourning three
full weeks.
3 I ate no [1]pleasant food, no meat or wine came
into my mouth, nor did I anoint myself at all, till
three whole weeks were fulfilled.
4 Now on the twenty-fourth day of the first
month, as I was by the side of the great river, that
*is,* the [1]Tigris,
5 I lifted my eyes and looked, and behold, a
certain man clothed in [a]linen, whose waist *was*
[b]girded with gold of Uphaz!
6 His body *was* like beryl, his face like the
appearance of lightning, his eyes like torches of
fire, his arms and feet like burnished bronze in
color, [a]and the sound of his words like the voice of
a multitude.
7 And I, Daniel, alone saw the vision, for the
men who were with me did not see the vision; but
a great terror fell upon them, so that they fled to
hide themselves.
8 Therefore I was left alone when I saw this
great vision, and no strength remained in me; for
my [1]vigor was turned to [2]frailty in me, and I
retained no strength.
9 Yet I heard the sound of his words; and while
I heard the sound of his words I was in a deep
sleep on my face, with my face to the ground.
**10** [a]Suddenly, a hand touched me, which made
me tremble on my knees and *on* the palms of my
hands.
11 And he said to me, "O Daniel, [a]man greatly
beloved, understand the words that I speak to
you, and stand upright, for I have now been sent
to you." While he was speaking this word to me, I
stood trembling.
12 Then he said to me, [a]"Do not fear, Daniel, for
from the first day that you set your heart to
understand, and to humble yourself before your

**11** [a]Is. 1:3–6 [b]Lev. 26:14
**12** [a]Zech. 1:6 [b]Lam. 1:12; 2:13
**13** [a]Deut. 28:15–68 [b]Is. 9:13
**14** [a]Jer. 31:28; 44:27 [b]Neh. 9:33
**15** [a]Neh. 1:10 [b]Neh. 9:10
**16** [a]1 Sam. 12:7 [b]Zech. 8:3 [c]Ex. 20:5 [d]Lam. 2:16 [e]Ps. 79:4
**17** [a]Num. 6:24–26 [b]Lam. 5:18 [c][John 16:24] [1]Be gracious [2]The temple
**18** [a]Is. 37:17 [b]Ex. 3:7 [c]Jer. 25:29
**21** [a]Dan. 8:16 [1]Or *being weary with weariness*
**23** [a]Dan. 10:11, 19 [b]Matt. 24:15 [1]Lit. *word*
**24** [a][Is. 53:10] [b]Rev. 14:6 [c]Ps. 45:7 [1]Lit. *sevens,* and so throughout the chapter [2]So with Qr., LXX, Syr., Vg.; Kt., Theodotion *To seal up* [3]The Most Holy Place
**25** [a]John 1:41; 4:25 [b]Is. 55:4 [1]Or *open square* [2]Or *moat*
**26** [a][Is. 53:8] [b][1 Pet. 2:21] [c]Matt. 22:7 [d]Luke 19:43, 44 [1]Suffer the death penalty
**27** [a]Is. 42:6 [b][Matt. 26:28] [c]Dan. 11:36 [1]Or *treaty* [2]Or *desolator*

CHAPTER 10
**1** [a]Dan. 1:7 [1]Or *and of great conflict;*
**3** [1]*desirable*
**4** [1]Heb. *Hiddekel*
**5** [a]Ezek. 9:2; 10:2 [b]Rev. 1:13; 15:6
**6** [a][Rev. 1:15]
**8** [1]Lit. *splendor* [2]Lit. *ruin*
**10** [a]Dan. 9:21
**11** [a]Dan. 9:23
**12** [a]Rev. 1:17

God, [b]your words were heard; and I have come
because of your words.
13 [a]"But the prince of the kingdom of Persia
withstood me twenty-one days; and behold, [b]Mi-
chael, one of the chief princes, came to help me,
for I had been left alone there with the kings of
Persia.
14 "Now I have come to make you understand
what will happen to your people [a]in the latter
days, [b]for the vision *refers* to *many* days yet *to
come.*"
**15** When he had spoken such words to me, [a]I
[1]turned my face toward the ground and became
speechless.
16 And suddenly, [a]*one* having the likeness of the
[1]sons of men [b]touched my lips; then I opened my
mouth and spoke, saying to him who stood before
me, "My lord, because of the vision [c]my sorrows
have [2]overwhelmed me, and I have retained no
strength.
17 "For how can this servant of my lord talk with
you, my lord? As for me, no strength remains in
me now, nor is any breath left in me."
**18** Then again, *the one* having the likeness of a
man touched me and strengthened me.
19 [a]And he said, "O man greatly beloved, [b]fear
not! Peace *be* to you; be strong, yes, be strong!"
So when he spoke to me I was strengthened, and
said, "Let my lord speak, for you have
strengthened me."
20 Then he said, "Do you know why I have come
to you? And now I must return to fight [a]with the
prince of Persia; and when I have gone forth,
indeed the prince of Greece will come.
21 "But I will tell you what is noted in the
Scripture of Truth. (No one upholds me against
these, [a]except Michael your prince.

## *Warring Kings of North and South*

**11** "Also [a]in the first year of [b]Darius the
Mede, I, *even* I, stood up to confirm and
strengthen him.)
2 "And now I will tell you the truth: Behold,
three more kings will arise in Persia, and the
fourth shall be far richer than *them* all; by his
strength, through his riches, he shall stir up all
against the realm of Greece.
3 "Then [a]a mighty king shall arise, who shall
rule with great dominion, and [b]do according to his
will.
4 "And when he has arisen, [a]his kingdom shall
be broken up and divided toward the four winds of
heaven, but not among his posterity [b]nor according to his dominion with which he ruled; for his
kingdom shall be uprooted, even for others besides these.
**5** "Also the king of the South shall become
strong, as well as *one* of his princes; and he shall
gain power over him and have dominion. His
dominion *shall be* a great dominion.
6 "And at the end of *some* years they shall join
forces, for the daughter of the king of the South
shall go to the king of the North to make an
agreement; but she shall not retain the power of
her [1]authority, and neither he nor his [1]authority
shall stand; but she shall be given up, with those
who brought her, and with him who begot her,
and with him who strengthened her in *those*
times.
7 "But from a branch of her roots *one* shall arise
in his place, who shall come with an army, enter
the fortress of the king of the North, and deal with
them and prevail.
8 "And he shall also carry their gods captive to
Egypt, with their [1]princes *and* their precious
articles of silver and gold; and he shall continue
*more* years than the king of the North.
9 "Also *the king of the North* shall come to the
kingdom of the king of the South, but shall return
to his own land.
10 "However his sons shall stir up strife, and
assemble a multitude of great forces; and *one* shall
certainly come [a]and overwhelm and pass through;
then he shall return [b]to his fortress and stir up
strife.
**11** "And the king of the South shall be [a]moved
with rage, and go out and fight with him, with the
king of the North, who shall muster a great
multitude; but the [b]multitude shall be given into
the hand of his *enemy.*
12 "When he has taken away the multitude, his
heart will be [1]lifted up; and he will cast down tens
of thousands, but he will not prevail.
13 "For the king of the North will return and
muster a multitude greater than the former, and
shall certainly come at the end of some years with
a great army and much equipment.
**14** "Now in those times many shall rise up
against the king of the South. Also, [1]violent men
of your people shall exalt themselves [2]in fulfillment of the vision, but they shall [a]fall.
15 "So the king of the North shall come and
[a]build a siege mound, and take a fortified city; and
the [1]forces of the South shall not withstand *him.*
Even his choice troops *shall have* no strength to
resist.
16 "But he who comes against him [a]shall do
according to his own will, and [b]no one shall stand
against him. He shall stand in the Glorious Land
with destruction in his [1]power.
17 "He shall also [a]set his face to enter with the
strength of his whole kingdom, and [1]upright ones
with him; thus shall he do. And he shall give him
the daughter of women to destroy it; but she shall
not stand *with him,* [b]or be for him.
18 "After this he shall turn his face to the coastlands, and shall take many. But a ruler shall bring
the reproach against them to an end; and with the
reproach removed, he shall turn back on him.
19 "Then he shall turn his face toward the fortress of his own land; but he shall [a]stumble and
fall, [b]and not be found.
**20** "There shall arise in his place one who imposes taxes *on* the glorious kingdom; but within a
few days he shall be destroyed, but not in anger or
in battle.
21 "And in his place [a]shall arise a vile person, to
whom they will not give the honor of royalty; but
he shall come in peaceably, and seize the kingdom
by intrigue.
22 "With the [1]force of a [a]flood they shall be
swept away from before him and be broken, [b]and
also the prince of the covenant.
23 "And after the league *is made* with him [a]he
shall act deceitfully, for he shall come up and
become strong with a small *number of* people.
24 "He shall enter peaceably, even into the rich-
est places of the province; and he shall do *what*
his fathers have not done, nor his forefathers: he
shall disperse among them the plunder, [1]spoil, and
riches; and he shall devise his plans against the
strongholds, but *only* for a time.

**12** [b]Dan. 9:3, 4, 22, 23; Acts 10:4
**13** [a]Dan. 10:20 [b]Dan. 10:21; 12:1; Jude 9; [Rev. 12:7]
**14** [a]Gen. 49:1; Deut. 31:29; Dan. 2:28 [b]Dan. 8:26; 10:1
**15** [a]Dan. 8:18; 10:9 [1]Lit. *set*
**16** [a]Dan. 8:15 [b]Jer. 1:9; Dan. 10:10 [c]Dan. 10:8, 9 [1]Theodotion, Vg. *the son;* LXX *a hand* [2]Or *turned upon*
**19** [a]Dan. 10:11 [b]Judg. 6:23; Is. 43:1; Dan. 10:12
**20** [a]Dan. 10:13
**21** [a]Dan. 10:13; Jude 9; [Rev. 12:7]

CHAPTER 11
**1** [a]Dan. 9:1 [b]Dan. 5:31
**3** [a]Dan. 7:6; 8:5 [b]Dan. 8:4; 10:16, 36
**4** [a]Jer. 49:36; Ezek. 37:9; Dan. 7:2; 8:8; Zech. 2:6; Rev. 7:1 [b]Dan. 8:22
**6** [1]Lit. *arm*
**8** [1]Or *molded images*
**10** [a]Is. 8:8; Jer. 46:7, 8; 51:42; Dan. 9:26; 11:26, 40 [b]Dan. 11:7
**11** [a]Prov. 16:14 [b][Ps. 33:10, 16]
**12** [1]Proud
**14** [a]Job 9:13 [1]Or *robbers,* lit. *sons of breakage* [2]Lit. *to establish*
**15** [a]Jer. 6:6; Ezek. 4:2; 17:17 [1]Lit. *arms*
**16** [a]Dan. 8:4, 7 [b]Josh. 1:5 [1]Lit. *hand*
**17** [a]2 Kin. 12:17; 2 Chr. 20:3; Ezek. 4:3, 7 [b]Dan. 9:26 [1]Or *bring equitable terms*
**19** [a]Ps. 27:2; Jer. 46:6 [b]Job 20:8; Ps. 37:36; Ezek. 26:21
**21** [a]Dan. 7:8
**22** [a]Dan. 9:26 [b]Dan. 8:10, 11 [1]Lit. *arms*
**23** [a]Dan. 8:25
**24** [1]*booty*

25 "He shall stir up his power and his courage against the king of the South with a great army. And the king of the South shall be stirred up to battle with a very great and mighty army; but he shall not stand, for they shall devise plans against him.

26 "Yes, those who eat of the portion of his delicacies shall destroy him; his army shall [1]be swept away, and many shall fall down slain.

27 "Both these kings' hearts *shall be* bent on evil, and they shall speak lies at the same table; but it shall not prosper, for the end *will* still *be* at the [a]appointed time.

28 "While returning to his land with great riches, his heart shall be *moved* against the holy covenant; so he shall do *damage* and return to his own land.

**29** "At the appointed time he shall return and go toward the south; but it shall not be like the former or the latter.

30 [a]"For ships from [1]Cyprus shall come against him; therefore he shall be grieved, and return in rage against the holy covenant, and do *damage*. So he shall return and show regard for those who forsake the holy covenant.

31 "And [1]forces shall be mustered by him, [a]and they shall defile the sanctuary fortress; then they shall take away the daily *sacrifices*, and place *there* the abomination of desolation.

32 "Those who do wickedly against the covenant he shall [1]corrupt with flattery; but the people who know their God shall be strong, and carry out *great exploits*.

33 "And those of the people who understand shall instruct many; yet *for many* days they shall fall by sword and flame, by captivity and plundering.

34 "Now when they fall, they shall be aided with a little help; but many shall join with them by [1]intrigue.

35 "And *some* of those of understanding shall fall, [a]to refine them, purify *them*, and make *them* white, *until* the time of the end; because *it is* still for the appointed time.

**36** "Then the king shall do according to his own will: he shall [a]exalt and magnify himself above every god, shall speak blasphemies against the God of gods, and shall prosper till the wrath has been accomplished; for what has been determined shall be done.

37 "He shall regard neither the [1]God of his fathers nor the desire of women, [a]nor regard any god; for he shall exalt himself above *them* all.

38 "But in their place he shall honor a god of fortresses; and a god which his fathers did not know he shall honor with gold and silver, with precious stones and pleasant things.

39 "Thus he shall act against the strongest fortresses with a foreign god, which he shall acknowledge, *and* advance *its* glory; and he shall cause them to rule over many, and divide the land for [1]gain.

**40** "At the [a]time of the end the king of the South shall attack him; and the king of the North shall come against him [b]like a whirlwind, with chariots, [c]horsemen, and with many ships; and he shall enter the countries, overwhelm *them*, and pass through.

41 "He shall also enter the Glorious Land, and many *countries* shall be overthrown; but these shall escape from his hand: [a]Edom, Moab, and the [1]prominent people of Ammon.

42 "He shall stretch out his hand against the countries, and the land of [a]Egypt shall not escape.

43 "He shall have power over the treasures of gold and silver, and over all the precious things of Egypt; also the Libyans and Ethiopians *shall follow* [a]at his heels.

44 "But news from the east and the north shall trouble him; therefore he shall go out with great fury to destroy and annihilate many.

45 "And he shall plant the tents of his palace between the seas and [a]the glorious holy mountain; [b]yet he shall come to his end, and no one will help him.

### *The Time of the End*

**12** "At that time Michael shall stand up,
The great prince who stands *watch* over
the sons of your people;
[a]And there shall be a time of trouble,
Such as never was since there was a nation,
*Even* to that time.
And at that time your people [b]shall be
delivered,
Every one who is found [c]written in the book.
2 And many of those who sleep in the dust of
the earth shall awake,
[a]Some to everlasting life,
Some to shame [b]*and* everlasting [1]contempt.
3 Those who are wise shall [a]shine
Like the brightness of the firmament,
[b]And those who turn many to righteousness
[c]Like the stars forever and ever.

4 "But you, Daniel, [a]shut up the words, and seal the book until the time of the end; many shall [b]run to and fro, and knowledge shall increase."

**5** Then I, Daniel, looked; and there stood two others, one on this riverbank and the other on that [a]riverbank.

6 And *one* said to the man clothed in [a]linen, who *was* above the waters of the river, [b]"How long shall the fulfillment of these wonders *be?*"

7 Then I heard the man clothed in linen, who *was* above the waters of the river, when he [a]held up his right hand and his left hand to heaven, and swore by Him [b]who lives forever, [c]that *it shall be* for a time, times, and half *a time;* [d]and when the power of [e]the holy people has been completely shattered, all these *things* shall be finished.

8 Although I heard, I did not understand. Then I said, "My lord, what *shall be* the end of these *things?*"

9 And he said, "Go *your way*, Daniel, for the words *are* closed up and sealed till the time of the end.

10 [a]"Many shall be purified, made white, and refined, [b]but the wicked shall do wickedly; and none of the wicked shall understand, but [c]the wise shall understand.

11 "And from the time *that* the daily *sacrifice* is taken away, and the abomination of desolation is set up, *there shall be* one thousand two hundred and ninety days.

12 "Blessed *is* he who waits, and comes to the one thousand three hundred and thirty-five days.

13 "But you, go *your way* till the end; [a]for you shall rest, [b]and will arise to your inheritance at the end of the days."

**26** [1]Or *overflow*
**27** [a]Dan. 8:19; Hab. 2:3
**30** [a]Gen. 10:4; Num. 24:24; Is. 23:1, 12; Jer. 2:10 [1]Heb. *Kittim*, western lands, especially Cyprus
**31** [a]Dan. 8:11–13; 12:11 [1]Lit. *arms*
**32** [1]*pollute*
**34** [1]Or *slipperiness, flattery*
**35** [a][Deut. 8:16; Prov. 17:3]; Dan. 12:10; Zech. 13:9; Mal. 3:2, 3
**36** [a]Dan. 7:8, 25
**37** [a]Is. 14:13; 2 Thess. 2:4 [1]Or *gods*
**39** [1]*profit*
**40** [a]Dan. 11:27, 35; 12:4, 9 [b]Is. 21:1 [c]Ezek. 38:4; Rev. 9:16
**41** [a]Is. 11:14 [1]Lit. *chief of the sons of Ammon*
**42** [a]Joel 3:19
**43** [a]Ex. 11:8
**45** [a]Ps. 48:2 [b]Rev. 19:20

CHAPTER 12
**1** [a]Is. 26:20; Jer. 30:7; Ezek. 5:9; Dan. 9:12; Matt. 24:21; Mark 13:19 [b]Rom. 11:26 [c]Ex. 32:32; Ps. 56:8
**2** [a][Matt. 25:46; John 5:28, 29; Acts 24:15] [b][Is. 66:24; Rom. 9:21] [1]Lit. *abhorrence*
**3** [a]Prov. 3:35; Dan. 11:33, 35; Matt. 13:43 [b]Prov. 11:30; [James 5:19, 20] [c]1 Cor. 15:41
**4** [a]Is. 8:16; Dan. 12:9; Rev. 22:10 [b]Amos 8:12
**5** [a]Dan. 10:4
**6** [a]Ezek. 9:2; Dan. 10:5 [b]Dan. 8:13; 12:8; Matt. 24:3; Mark 13:4
**7** [a]Deut. 32:40 [b]Dan. 4:34 [c]Dan. 7:25; Rev. 12:14 [d]Luke 21:24 [e]Dan. 8:24
**10** [a]Zech. 13:9 [b]Is. 32:6, 7; Rev. 22:11 [c]Dan. 12:3; Hos. 14:9; John 7:17; 8:47
**13** [a]Is. 57:2; Rev. 14:13 [b]Ps. 1:5

*The Book of*

# HOSEA

## *Hosea's Unfaithful Wife*

1 THE word of the LORD that came to Hosea the son of Beeri, in the days of [a]Uzziah, [b]Jotham, [c]Ahaz, *and* [d]Hezekiah, kings of Judah, and in the days of [e]Jeroboam the son of Joash, king of Israel.

**2** When the LORD began to speak by Hosea, the LORD said to Hosea:

[a]"Go, take yourself a wife of harlotry
And children of harlotry,
For [b]the land has committed great [1]harlotry
*By departing* from the LORD."

3 So he went and took Gomer the daughter of Diblaim, and she conceived and bore him a son.
**4** Then the LORD said to him:

"Call his name Jezreel,
For in a little *while*
[a]I will avenge the bloodshed of Jezreel
on the house of Jehu,
[b]And bring an end to the kingdom of the
house of Israel.
5 [a]It shall come to pass in that day
That I will break the bow of Israel in the
Valley of Jezreel."

**6** And she conceived again and bore a daughter. Then *God* said to him:

"Call her name [1]Lo-Ruhamah,
[a]For I will no longer have mercy
on the house of Israel,
[2]But I will utterly take them away.
7 [a]Yet I will have mercy on the house of Judah,
Will save them by the LORD their God,
And [b]will not save them by bow,
Nor by sword or battle,
By horses or horsemen."

**8** Now when she had weaned Lo-Ruhamah, she conceived and bore a son.
9 Then *God* said:

"Call his name [1]Lo-Ammi,
For you *are* not My people,
And I will not be your *God.*

**10** "Yet [a]the number of the children of Israel
Shall be as the sand of the sea,
Which cannot be measured or numbered.
[b]And it shall come to pass
In the place where it was said to them,
'You *are* [1]not My [c]people,'
*There* it shall be said to them,
'*You are* [d]sons of the living God.'
11 [a]Then the children of Judah
and the children of Israel
Shall be gathered together,
And appoint for themselves one head;
And they shall come up out of the land,
For great *will be* the day of Jezreel!

## *The LORD's Love for His Unfaithful People*

**2** Say to your brethren, [1]'My people,'
And to your sisters, [2]'Mercy *is shown.*'

**2** "Bring[1] charges against your mother, [2]bring
charges;
For [a]she *is* not My wife,
nor *am* I her Husband!
Let her put away her [b]harlotries
from her sight,
And her adulteries from between her breasts;
3 Lest [a]I strip her naked
And expose her, as in the day she was [b]born,
And make her like a wilderness,
And set her like a dry land,
And slay her with [c]thirst.

4 "I will not have mercy on her children,
For they *are* the [a]children of harlotry.
5 For their mother has played the harlot;
She who conceived them has behaved
shamefully.
For she said, 'I will go after my lovers,
[a]Who give *me* my bread and my water,
My wool and my linen,
My oil and my drink.'

**6** "Therefore, behold,
[a]I will hedge up your way with thorns,
And [1]wall her in,
So that she cannot find her paths.
7 She will [1]chase her lovers,
But not overtake them;
Yes, she will seek them, but not find *them.*
Then she will say,
[a]'I will go and return to my [b]first husband,
For then *it was* better for me than now.'
8 For she did not [a]know
That I gave her grain, new wine, and oil,
And multiplied her silver and gold—
*Which* they prepared for Baal.

**9** "Therefore I will return and take away
My grain in its time
And My new wine in its season,
And will take back My wool and My linen,
*Given* to cover her nakedness.
10 Now [a]I will uncover her lewdness in the sight
of her lovers,
And no one shall deliver her from My hand.
11 [a]I will also cause all her mirth to cease,
Her feast days,
Her New Moons,
Her Sabbaths—
All her appointed feasts.

12 "And I will destroy her vines and her fig trees,
Of which she has said,
'These *are* my wages that my lovers have
given me.'
So I will make them a forest,
And the beasts of the field shall eat them.
13 I will punish her
For the days of the Baals to which she
burned incense.
She decked herself with her earrings and
jewelry,
And went after her lovers;
But Me she forgot," says the LORD.

**14** "Therefore, behold, I will allure her,
Will bring her into the wilderness,
And speak [1]comfort to her.
15 I will give her her vineyards from there,
And [a]the Valley of Achor as a door of hope;

---

CHAPTER 1
**1** [a]2 Chr. 26; Is. 1:1; Amos 1:1 [b]2 Kin. 15:5, 7, 32–38; 2 Chr. 27; Mic. 1:1 [c]2 Kin. 16:1–20; 2 Chr. 28 [d]2 Kin. 18—20; 2 Chr. 29:1—32:33; Mic. 1:1 [e]2 Kin. 13:13; 14:23–29; Amos 1:1
**2** [a]Hos. 3:1 [b]Deut. 31:16; Judg. 2:17; Ps. 73:27; Jer. 2:13; Ezek. 16:1–59; 23:1–49 [1]Spiritual adultery
**4** [a]2 Kin. 10:11 [b]2 Kin. 15:8–10; 17:6, 23; 18:11
**5** [a]2 Kin. 15:29
**6** [a]2 Kin. 17:6 [1]Lit. *No Mercy* [2]Or *That I may forgive them at all*
**7** [a]2 Kin. 19:29–35; Is. 30:18; 37:36, 37 [b]Ps. 44:3–7; [Zech. 4:6]
**9** [1]Lit. *Not My People*
**10** [a]Gen. 22:17; 32:12; Jer. 33:22 [b]1 Pet. 2:10 [c]Rom. 9:26 [d]Is. 63:16; 64:8; [John 1:12] [1]Heb. *lo-ammi,* v. 9
**11** [a]Is. 11:11–13; Jer. 3:18; 50:4; [Ezek. 34:23; 37:15–28]

CHAPTER 2
**1** [1]Heb. *Ammi,* Hos. 1:9, 10 [2]Heb. *Ruhamah,* Hos. 1:6
**2** [a]Is. 50:1 [b]Ezek. 16:25 [1]Or *Contend with* [2]Or *contend*
**3** [a]Jer. 13:22, 26; Ezek. 16:37–39 [b]Ezek. 16:4–7, 22 [c]Jer. 14:3; Amos 8:11–13
**4** [a]John 8:41
**5** [a]Ezek. 23:5; Hos. 2:8, 12
**6** [a]Job 19:8; Lam. 3:7, 9 [1]Lit. *wall up her wall*
**7** [a]Luke 15:17, 18 [b]Is. 54:5–8; Jer. 2:2; 3:1; Ezek. 16:8; 23:4 [1]Or *pursue*
**8** [a]Is. 1:3; Ezek. 16:19
**10** [a]Ezek. 16:37
**11** [a]Jer. 7:34; 16:9; Hos. 3:4; Amos 5:21; 8:10
**14** [1]Lit. *to her heart*
**15** [a]Josh. 7:26

She shall sing there,
As in [b]the days of her youth,
[c]As in the day when she came up
from the land of Egypt.

16 "And it shall be, in that day,"
Says the LORD,
"*That* you will call Me [1]'My Husband,'
And no longer call Me [2]'My Master,'
17 For [a]I will take from her mouth the names of
the Baals,
And they shall be remembered by their name
no more.
18 In that day I will make a [a]covenant for them
With the beasts of the field,
With the birds of the air,
And *with* the creeping things of the ground.
Bow and sword of battle
[b]I will shatter from the earth,
To make them [c]lie down safely.

19 "I will betroth you to Me forever;
Yes, I will betroth you to Me
In righteousness and justice,
In lovingkindness and mercy;
20 I will betroth you to Me in faithfulness,
And [a]you shall know the LORD.

**21** "It shall come to pass in that day
*That* [a]I will answer," says the LORD;
"I will answer the heavens,
And they shall answer the earth.
22 The earth shall answer
With grain,
With new wine,
And with oil;
They shall answer [1]Jezreel.
23 Then [a]I will sow her for Myself in the earth,
[b]And I will have mercy on *her who had* [1]not
obtained mercy;
Then [c]I will say to *those who were* [2]not My
people,
'You *are* [3]My people!'
And they shall say, *'You are* my God!' "

### *Hosea and the Adulteress*

**3** Then the LORD said to me, "Go again, love a
woman *who is* loved by a [a]lover[1] and is committing adultery, just like the love of the LORD for
the children of Israel, who look to other gods and
love *the* raisin cakes *of the pagans.*"
2 So I bought her for myself for fifteen *shekels*
of silver, and one and one-half homers of barley.
3 And I said to her, "You shall [a]stay with me
many days; you shall not play the harlot, nor shall
you have a man—so, too, *will* I *be* toward you."
4 For the children of Israel shall abide many
days [a]without king or prince, without sacrifice or
sacred pillar, without [b]ephod or [c]teraphim.
5 Afterward the children of Israel shall return
and [a]seek the LORD their God and [b]David their
king. They shall fear the LORD and His goodness in
the [c]latter days.

### *The LORD's Controversy with Israel*

**4** Hear the word of the LORD,
You children of Israel,
For the LORD *brings* a [a]charge[1]
against the inhabitants of the land:

"There is no truth or mercy
Or [b]knowledge of God in the land.
2 *By* swearing and lying,
Killing and stealing and committing adultery,
They break all restraint,
With bloodshed [1]upon bloodshed.
3 Therefore [a]the land will mourn;
And [b]everyone who dwells there will waste
away
With the beasts of the field
And the birds of the air;
Even the fish of the sea will be taken away.

4 "Now let no man contend, or rebuke another;
For your people *are* like those [a]who contend
with the priest.
5 Therefore you shall stumble [a]in the day;
The prophet also shall stumble with you in
the night;
And I will destroy your mother.
6 [a]My people are destroyed for lack of
knowledge.
Because you have rejected knowledge,
I also will reject you from being priest for
Me;
[b]Because you have forgotten the law of your
God,
I also will forget your children.

**7** "The more they increased,
The more they sinned against Me;
[a]I[1] will change [2]their glory into shame.
8 They eat up the sin of My people;
They set their [1]heart on their iniquity.
9 And it shall be: [a]like people, like priest.
So I will punish them for their ways,
And [1]reward them for their deeds.
10 For [a]they shall eat, but not have enough;
They shall commit harlotry, but not increase;
Because they have ceased obeying the LORD.

**11** "Harlotry, wine, and new wine
[a]enslave the heart.
12 My people ask counsel from their [a]wooden
*idols,*
And their [1]staff informs them.
For [b]the spirit of harlotry has caused *them* to
stray,
And they have played the harlot against their
God.
13 [a]They offer sacrifices on the mountaintops,
And burn incense on the hills,
Under oaks, poplars, and terebinths,
Because their shade *is* good.
[b]Therefore your daughters commit harlotry,
And your brides commit adultery.

14 "I will not punish your daughters when they
commit harlotry,
Nor your brides when they commit adultery;
For *the men* themselves go apart with
harlots,
And offer sacrifices with a
[a]ritual harlot.
Therefore people *who* do not understand will
be trampled.

**15** "Though you, Israel, play the harlot,
Let not Judah offend.
[a]Do not come up to Gilgal,
Nor go up to [b]Beth[1] Aven,
[c]Nor swear an oath, *saying,*
'As the LORD lives'—

16 "For Israel [a]is stubborn
Like a stubborn calf;

---

**15** [b]Ezek. 16:8–14 [c]Ex. 15:1
**16** [1]Heb. *Ishi* [2]Heb. *Baali*
**17** [a]Ex. 23:13
**18** [a]Job 5:23 [b]Is. 2:4 [c]Lev. 26:5
**20** [a][Jer. 31:33, 34]
**21** [a]Zech. 8:12
**22** [1]Lit. *God Will Sow*
**23** [a]Jer. 31:27 [b]Hos. 1:6 [c]Hos. 1:10 [1]Heb. *lo-ruhamah* [2]Heb. *lo-ammi* [3]Heb. *ammi*

CHAPTER 3
**1** [a]Jer. 3:20 [1]Lit. *friend* or *husband*
**3** [a]Deut. 21:13
**4** [a]Hos. 10:3 [b]Ex. 28:4–12 [c]Judg. 17:5; 18:14, 17
**5** [a]Jer. 50:4 [b]Jer. 30:9 [c][Is. 2:2, 3]

CHAPTER 4
**1** [a]Is. 1:18 [b]Jer. 4:22 [1]A legal complaint
**2** [1]Lit. *touching*
**3** [a]Amos 5:16; 8:8 [b]Zeph. 1:3
**4** [a]Deut. 17:12
**5** [a]Jer. 15:8
**6** [a]Is. 5:13 [b]Ezek. 22:26
**7** [a]1 Sam. 2:30 [1]So with MT, LXX, Vg.; scribal tradition, Syr., Tg. *They will change* [2]So with MT, LXX, Syr., Tg., Vg.; scribal tradition *My glory*
**8** [1]Desires
**9** [a]Is. 24:2 [1]*repay*
**10** [a]Lev. 26:26
**11** [a]Is. 5:12; 28:7
**12** [a]Jer. 2:27 [b]Is. 44:19, 20 [1]Diviner's rod
**13** [a]Is. 1:29; 57:5, 7 [b]Amos 7:17
**14** [a]Deut. 23:18
**15** [a]Hos. 9:15; 12:11 [b]1 Kin. 12:29 [c]Amos 8:14 [1]Lit. *House of Idolatry* or *Wickedness*
**16** [a]Jer. 3:6; 7:24; 8:5

Now the LORD will let them forage
Like a lamb in [1]open country.

17 "Ephraim *is* joined to idols,
[a]Let him alone.
18 Their drink [1]is rebellion,
They commit harlotry continually.
[a]Her [2]rulers [3]dearly love dishonor.
19 [a]The wind has wrapped her up in its wings,
And [b]they shall be ashamed
because of their sacrifices.

### *God's Displeasure with Israel*

5 "Hear this, O priests!
Take heed, O house of Israel!
Give ear, O house of the king!
For [1]yours *is* the judgment,
Because [a]you have been a snare to Mizpah
And a net spread on Tabor.
2 The revolters are [a]deeply involved in
slaughter,
Though I rebuke them all.
3 [a]I know Ephraim,
And Israel is not hidden from Me;
For now, O Ephraim, [b]you commit harlotry;
Israel is defiled.

4 "They[1] do not direct their deeds
Toward turning to their God,
For [a]the spirit of harlotry is in their midst,
And they do not know the LORD.
5 The [a]pride of Israel testifies to his face;
Therefore Israel and Ephraim stumble in
their iniquity;
Judah also stumbles with them.

6 "With their flocks and herds
[a]They shall go to seek the LORD,
But they will not find *Him;*
He has withdrawn Himself from them.
7 They have [a]dealt treacherously with the
LORD,
For they have begotten [1]pagan children.
Now a New Moon shall devour them and
their heritage.

8 "Blow[a] the ram's horn in Gibeah,
The trumpet in Ramah!
[b]Cry aloud *at* [c]Beth Aven,
'*Look* behind you, O Benjamin!'
9 Ephraim shall be desolate
in the day of rebuke;
Among the tribes of Israel
I make known what is sure.

10 "The princes of Judah are like those who
[a]remove a landmark;
I will pour out my wrath on them like water.
11 Ephraim is [a]oppressed
*and* broken in judgment,
Because he willingly walked by [b]*human*
precept.
12 Therefore I *will be* to Ephraim like a moth,
And to the house of Judah [a]like rottenness.

13 "When Ephraim saw his sickness,
And Judah *saw* his [a]wound,
Then Ephraim went [b]to Assyria
And sent to King Jareb;
Yet he cannot cure you,
Nor heal you of your wound.
14 For [a]I *will be* like a lion to Ephraim,
And like a young lion to the house of Judah.
[b]I, *even* I, will tear *them* and go away;
I will take *them* away,
and no one shall rescue.
15 I will return again to My place
Till they [1]acknowledge their offense.
Then they will seek My face;
In their affliction
they will earnestly seek Me."

### *Israel's Insincere Repentance*

6 Come,[a] and let us return to the LORD;
For [b]He has torn, but [c]He will heal us;
He has stricken, but He will [1]bind us up.
2 [a]After two days He will revive us;
On the third day He will raise us up,
That we may live in His sight.
3 [a]Let us know,
Let us pursue the knowledge of the LORD.
His going forth is established [b]as the
morning;
[c]He will come to us [d]like the rain,
Like the latter *and* former rain to the earth.

4 "O Ephraim, what shall I do to you?
O Judah, what shall I do to you?
For your faithfulness is like a morning cloud,
And like the early dew it goes away.
5 Therefore I have hewn *them* by the prophets,
I have slain them by [a]the words
of My mouth;
And [1]your judgments *are like* light
*that* goes forth.
6 For I desire [a]mercy[1] and [b]not sacrifice,
And the [c]knowledge of God
more than burnt offerings.

7 "But like [1]men they transgressed the
covenant;
There they dealt treacherously with Me.
8 [a]Gilead *is* a city of evildoers
*And* [1]defiled with blood.
9 As bands of robbers lie in wait for a man,
*So* the company of [a]priests [b]murder on the
way to Shechem;
Surely they commit [c]lewdness.
10 I have seen a horrible thing in the house of
Israel:
There *is* the [1]harlotry of Ephraim;
Israel is defiled.
11 Also, O Judah, a harvest is appointed for you,
When I return the captives of My people.

### *Israel Has Rebelled Against God*

7 "When I would have healed Israel,
Then the iniquity of Ephraim was uncovered,
And the wickedness of Samaria.
For [a]they have committed fraud;
A thief comes in;
A band of robbers [1]takes spoil outside.
2 They [1]do not consider in their hearts
*That* [a]I remember all their wickedness;
Now their own deeds have surrounded them;
They are before My face.
3 They make a [a]king glad with their
wickedness,
And princes [b]with their lies.

4 "They[a] *are* all adulterers.
Like an oven heated by a baker—
He ceases stirring *the fire*
after kneading the dough,
Until it is leavened.

**16** [1]Lit. *a large place*
**17** [a]Matt. 15:14
**18** [a]Mic. 3:11 [1]Or *has turned aside* [2]Lit. *shields* [3]Heb. difficult; a Jewish tradition *shamefully love, 'Give!'*
**19** [a]Jer. 51:1 [b]Is. 1:29

CHAPTER 5
**1** [a]Hos. 6:9 [1]Or *to you*
**2** [a]Is. 29:15
**3** [a]Amos 3:2; 5:12 [b]Hos. 4:17
**4** [a]Hos. 4:12 [1]Or *Their deeds will not allow them to turn*
**5** [a]Hos. 7:10
**6** [a]Prov. 1:28
**7** [a]Jer. 3:20 [1]Lit. *strange*
**8** [a]Joel 2:1 [b]Is. 10:30 [c]Josh. 7:2
**10** [a]Deut. 19:14; 27:17
**11** [a]Deut. 28:33 [b]Mic. 6:16
**12** [a]Prov. 12:4
**13** [a]Jer. 30:12–15 [b]2 Kin. 15:19
**14** [a]Lam. 3:10 [b]Ps. 50:22
**15** [1]Lit. *become guilty* or *bear punishment*

CHAPTER 6
**1** [a]Is. 1:18 [b]Deut. 32:39 [c]Jer. 30:17 [1]Bandage
**2** [a][1 Cor. 15:4]
**3** [a]Is. 54:13 [b]2 Sam. 23:4 [c]Ps. 72:6 [d]Job 29:23
**5** [a][Jer. 23:29] [1]Or *the judgments on you*
**6** [a]Matt. 9:13; 12:7 [b][Mic. 6:6–8] [c][John 17:3] [1]Or *faithfulness* or *loyalty*
**7** [1]Or *Adam*
**8** [a]Hos. 12:11 [1]Lit. *foot-tracked*
**9** [a]Hos. 5:1 [b]Jer. 7:9, 10 [c]Ezek. 22:9; 23:27
**10** [1]Spiritual adultery

CHAPTER 7
**1** [a]Hos. 5:1 [1]*plunders*
**2** [a]Jer. 14:10; 17:1 [1]Lit. *do not say to*
**3** [a]Hos. 1:1 [b][Rom. 1:32]
**4** [a]Jer. 9:2; 23:10

5 In the day of our king
Princes have made *him* sick,
[1]inflamed with [a]wine;
He stretched out his hand with scoffers.
6 They prepare their heart like an oven,
While they lie in wait;
[1]Their baker sleeps all night;
In the morning it burns like a flaming fire.
7 They are all hot, like an oven,
And have devoured their judges;
All their kings have fallen.
[a]None among them calls upon Me.

8 "Ephraim [a]has mixed himself
among the peoples;
Ephraim is a cake unturned.
9 [a]Aliens have devoured his strength,
But he does not know *it;*
Yes, gray hairs are here and there on him,
Yet he does not know *it.*
10 And the [a]pride of Israel testifies to his face,
But [b]they do not return to the LORD their
God,
Nor seek Him for all this.

11 "Ephraim[a] also is like a silly dove, without
[1]sense—
[b]They call to Egypt,
They go to [c]Assyria.
12 Wherever they go, I will [a]spread My net on
them;
I will bring them down like birds of the air;
I will chastise them
[b]According to what their congregation has
heard.

13 "Woe to them, for they have fled from Me!
Destruction to them,
Because they have transgressed against Me!
Though [a]I redeemed them,
Yet they have spoken lies against Me.
14 [a]They did not cry out to Me with their heart
When they wailed upon their beds.

"They [1]assemble together for grain
and new [b]wine,
[2]They rebel against Me;
15 Though I disciplined *and* strengthened their
arms,
Yet they devise evil against Me;
16 They return, *but* not [1]to the Most High;
[a]They are like a treacherous bow.
Their princes shall fall by the sword
For the [b]cursings of their tongue.
This *shall be* their derision [c]in the land of
Egypt.

## *Sow the Wind and Reap the Whirlwind*

8 "*Set* the [1]trumpet to your mouth!
*He shall come* [a]like an eagle against the
house of the LORD,
Because they have transgressed My covenant
And rebelled against My law.
2 [a]Israel will cry to Me,
'My God, [b]we know You!'
3 Israel has rejected the good;
The enemy will pursue him.

4 "They[a] set up kings, but not by Me;
They made princes,
but I did not acknowledge *them.*
From their silver and gold
They made idols for themselves—
That they might be cut off.

5 Your [1]calf [2]is rejected, O Samaria!
My anger is aroused against them—
[a]How long until they attain to innocence?
6 For from Israel *is* even this:
A [a]workman made it, and it *is* not God;
But the calf of Samaria shall be broken to
pieces.

7 "They[a] sow the wind,
And reap the whirlwind.
The stalk has no bud;
It shall never produce meal.
If it should produce,
[b]Aliens would swallow it up.
8 [a]Israel is swallowed up;
Now they are among the Gentiles
[b]Like a vessel in which *is* no pleasure.
9 For they have gone up to Assyria,
*Like* [a]a wild donkey alone by itself;
Ephraim [b]has hired lovers.
10 Yes, though they have hired among the
nations,
Now [a]I will gather them;
And they shall [1]sorrow a little,
Because of the [2]burden of [b]the king of
princes.

11 "Because Ephraim has made
many altars for sin,
They have become for him altars for sinning.
12 I have written for him
[a]the great things of My law,
*But* they were considered a strange thing.
13 *For* the sacrifices of My offerings [a]they
sacrifice flesh and eat *it,*
[b]*But* the LORD does not accept them.
[c]Now He will remember their iniquity and
punish their sins.
They shall return to Egypt.

14 "For[a] Israel has forgotten [b]his Maker,
And has built [1]temples;
Judah also has multiplied [c]fortified cities;
But [d]I will send fire upon his cities,
And it shall devour his [2]palaces."

## *The Days of Judgment Have Come*

9 Do[a] not rejoice, O Israel, with joy like *other*
peoples,
For you have played the harlot against your
God.
You have made love *for* [b]hire on every
threshing floor.
2 The threshing floor and the winepress
Shall not feed them,
And the new wine shall fail in her.

3 They shall not dwell in [a]the LORD's land,
[b]But Ephraim shall return to Egypt,
And [c]shall eat unclean *things* in Assyria.
4 They shall not offer wine *offerings*
to the LORD,
Nor [a]shall their [b]sacrifices be pleasing to Him.
*It shall be* like bread of mourners to them;
All who eat it shall be defiled.
For their bread *shall be* for their *own* life;
It shall not come into the house of the LORD.

5 What will you do in the appointed day,
And in the day of the feast of the LORD?
6 For indeed they are gone because
of destruction.
Egypt shall gather them up;
Memphis shall bury them.

**5** [a]Is. 28:1, 7 [1]Lit. *with the heat of*
**6** [1]So with MT, Vg.; Syr., Tg. *Their anger;* LXX *Ephraim*
**7** [a]Is. 64:7
**8** [a]Ps. 106:35
**9** [a]Hos. 8:7
**10** [a]Hos. 5:5 [b]Is. 9:13
**11** [a]Hos. 11:11 [b]Is. 30:3 [c]Hos. 5:13; 8:9 [1]Lit. *heart*
**12** [a]Ezek. 12:13 [b]Lev. 26:14
**13** [a]Mic. 6:4
**14** [a]Job 35:9, 10 [b]Amos 2:8 [1]So with MT, Tg.; Vg. *thought upon;* LXX *slashed themselves for* (cf. 1 Kin. 18:28) [2]So with MT, [Syr.], Tg.; LXX omits *They rebel against Me;* Vg. *They departed from Me*
**16** [a]Ps. 78:57 [b]Ps. 73:9 [c]Hos. 8:13; 9:3 [1]Or *upward*

CHAPTER 8
**1** [a]Deut. 28:49 [1]*ram's horn,* Heb. *shophar*
**2** [a]Ps. 78:34 [b]Titus 1:16
**4** [a]2 Kin. 15:23, 25
**5** [a]Jer. 13:27 [1]Golden calf image [2]Or *has rejected you*
**6** [a]Is. 40:19
**7** [a]Prov. 22:8 [b]Hos. 7:9
**8** [a]2 Kin. 17:6 [b]Jer. 22:28; 25:34
**9** [a]Jer. 2:24 [b]Ezek. 16:33, 34
**10** [a]Ezek. 16:37; 22:20 [b]Is. 10:8 [1]Or *begin to diminish* [2]Or *oracle* or *proclamation*
**12** [a][Deut. 4:6–8]
**13** [a]Zech. 7:6 [b]Jer. 14:10 [c]Amos 8:7
**14** [a]Deut. 32:18 [b]Is. 29:23 [c]Num. 32:17 [d]Jer. 17:27 [1]Or *palaces* [2]Or *citadels*

CHAPTER 9
**1** [a]Is. 22:12, 13 [b]Jer. 44:17
**3** [a][Lev. 25:23] [b]Hos. 7:16; 8:13 [c]Ezek. 4:13
**4** [a]Jer. 6:20 [b]Hos. 8:13

[a]Nettles shall possess their valuables of silver;
Thorns *shall be* in their tents.

**7** The days of punishment have come;
The days of recompense have come.
Israel [a]knows!
The prophet *is* a [b]fool,
[c]The spiritual man *is* insane,
Because of the greatness of your iniquity and great enmity.
8 The [a]watchman of Ephraim *is* with my God;
But the prophet *is* a [1]fowler's snare in all his ways—
Enmity in the house of his God.
9 [a]They are deeply corrupted,
As in the days of [b]Gibeah.
He will remember their iniquity;
He will punish their sins.

**10** "I found Israel
Like grapes in the [a]wilderness;
I saw your fathers
As the [b]firstfruits on the fig tree in its first season.
*But* they went to [c]Baal Peor,
And [1]separated themselves *to that* shame;
[d]They became an abomination like the thing they loved.
11 *As for* Ephraim, their glory shall fly away like a bird—
No birth, no pregnancy, and no conception!
12 Though they bring up their children,
Yet I will bereave them to the last man.
Yes, [a]woe to them when I depart from them!
13 Just [a]as I saw Ephraim like Tyre, planted in a pleasant place,
So Ephraim will bring out his children to the murderer."

14 Give them, O LORD—
What will You give?
Give them [a]a miscarrying womb
And dry breasts!

15 "All their wickedness *is* in [a]Gilgal,
For there I hated them.
Because of the evil of their deeds
I will drive them from My house;
I will love them no more.
[b]All their princes *are* rebellious.
16 Ephraim is [a]stricken,
Their root is dried up;
They shall bear no fruit.
Yes, were they to bear children,
I would kill the darlings of their womb."

**17** My God will [a]cast them away,
Because they did not obey Him;
And they shall be [b]wanderers among the nations.

## *The Punishment of Israel*

**10** Israel [a]empties *his* vine;
He brings forth fruit for himself.
According to the multitude of his fruit
[b]He has increased the altars;
According to the bounty of his land
They have embellished *his* sacred pillars.
2 Their heart is [a]divided;[1]
Now they are held guilty.
He will break down their altars;
He will ruin their sacred pillars.

**3** For now they say,
"We have no king,
Because we did not fear the LORD.
And as for a king, what would he do for us?"
4 They have spoken words,
Swearing falsely in making a covenant.
Thus judgment springs up [a]like hemlock in the furrows of the field.

5 The inhabitants of Samaria fear
Because of the [a]calf[1] of Beth Aven.
For its people mourn for it,
And [2]its priests shriek for it—
Because its [b]glory has departed from it.
6 *The idol* also shall be carried to Assyria
*As* a present for King [a]Jareb.
Ephraim shall receive shame,
And Israel shall be ashamed of his own counsel.

7 *As for* Samaria, her king is cut off
Like a twig on the water.
8 Also the [a]high places of [1]Aven,
[b]the sin of Israel,
Shall be destroyed.
The thorn and thistle shall grow on their altars;
[c]They shall say to the mountains, "Cover us!"
And to the hills, "Fall on us!"

**9** "O Israel, you have sinned from the days of [a]Gibeah;
There they stood.
The [b]battle in Gibeah against the children of [1]iniquity
Did not [2]overtake them.
10 When *it is* My desire, I will chasten them.
[a]Peoples shall be gathered against them
When I bind them [1]for their two transgressions.
11 Ephraim *is* [a]a trained heifer
That loves to thresh *grain;*
But I harnessed her fair neck,
I will make Ephraim [1]pull *a plow.*
Judah shall plow;
Jacob shall break his clods."

**12** Sow for yourselves righteousness;
Reap in mercy;
[a]Break up your fallow ground,
For *it is* time to seek the LORD,
Till He [b]comes and rains righteousness on you.

13 [a]You have plowed wickedness;
You have reaped iniquity.
You have eaten the fruit of lies,
Because you trusted in your own way,
In the multitude of your mighty men.
14 Therefore tumult shall arise among your people,
And all your fortresses shall be plundered
As Shalman plundered Beth Arbel in the day of battle—
A mother dashed in pieces upon *her* children.
15 Thus it shall be done to you, O Bethel,
Because of your great wickedness.
At dawn the king of Israel
Shall be cut off utterly.

## *God's Love for Faithless Israel*

**11** "When Israel *was* a [1]child, I loved him,
And out of Egypt [a]I called My [b]son.
2 [1]*As* they called them,

---

**6** [a]Is. 5:6; 7:23
**7** [a]Is. 10:3 [b]Lam. 2:14 [c]Mic. 2:11
**8** [a]Ezek. 3:17; 33:7 [1]One who catches birds in a trap or snare
**9** [a]Hos. 10:9 [b]Judg. 19:22
**10** [a]Jer. 2:2 [b]Is. 28:4 [c]Num. 25:3 [d]Ps. 81:12 [1]Or *dedicated*
**12** [a]Deut. 31:17
**13** [a]Ezek. 26—28
**14** [a]Luke 23:29
**15** [a]Hos. 4:15; 12:11 [b]Is. 1:23
**16** [a]Hos. 5:11
**17** [a][Zech. 10:6] [b]Lev. 26:33

CHAPTER 10
**1** [a]Nah. 2:2 [b]Jer. 2:28
**2** [a]1 Kin. 18:21 [1]Divided in loyalty
**4** [a]Amos 5:7
**5** [a]Hos. 8:5, 6; 13:2 [b]Hos. 9:11 [1]Lit. *calves,* images [2]*idolatrous priests*
**6** [a]Hos. 5:13
**8** [a]Hos. 4:15 [b]1 Kin. 13:34 [c]Luke 23:30 [1]Lit. *Idolatry* or *Wickedness*
**9** [a]Hos. 9:9 [b]Judg. 20 [1]So with many Heb. mss., LXX, Vg.; MT *unruliness* [2]Or *overcome*
**10** [a]Jer. 16:16 [1]Or *in their two habitations*
**11** [a][Mic. 4:13] [1]Lit. *to ride*
**12** [a]Jer. 4:3 [b]Hos. 6:3
**13** [a][Prov. 22:8]

CHAPTER 11
**1** [a]Matt. 2:15 [b]Ex. 4:22, 23 [1]Or *youth*
**2** [1]So with MT, Vg.; LXX *Just as I called them;* Tg. interpreted as *I sent prophets to a thousand of them*

So they [a]went [2]from them;
They sacrificed to the Baals,
And burned incense to carved images.

3 "I[a] taught Ephraim to walk,
Taking them by [1]their arms;
But they did not know that [b]I healed them.
4 I drew them with [1]gentle cords,
With bands of love,
And [a]I was to them as those who take the yoke from their [2]neck.
[b]I stooped *and* fed them.

**5** "He shall not return to the land of Egypt;
But the Assyrian shall be his king,
Because they refused to repent.
6 And the sword shall slash in his cities,
Devour his districts,
And consume *them,*
Because of their own counsels.
7 My people are bent on [a]backsliding from Me.
Though [1]they call [2]to the Most High,
None at all exalt *Him.*

**8** "How[a] can I give you up, Ephraim?
*How* can I hand you over, Israel?
How can I make you like [b]Admah?
*How* can I set you like Zeboiim?
My heart [1]churns within Me;
My sympathy is stirred.
9 I will not execute the fierceness of My anger;
I will not again destroy Ephraim.
[a]For I *am* God, and not man,
The Holy One in your midst;
And I will not [1]come with terror.

10 "They shall walk after the LORD.
[a]He will roar like a lion.
When He roars,
Then *His* sons shall come trembling from the west;
11 They shall come trembling like a bird from Egypt,
[a]Like a dove from the land of Assyria.
[b]And I will let them dwell in their houses,"
Says the LORD.

**12** "Ephraim has encircled Me with lies,
And the house of Israel with deceit;
But Judah still walks with God,
Even with the [1]Holy One *who is* faithful.

### *Ephraim's Sins Rebuked by God*

**12** "Ephraim [a]feeds on the wind,
And pursues the east wind;
He daily increases lies and [1]desolation.
[b]Also they make a [2]covenant with the Assyrians,
And [c]oil is carried to Egypt.

2 "The[a] LORD also *brings* a [1]charge against Judah,
And will punish Jacob according to his ways;
According to his deeds
He will recompense him.
3 He took his brother [a]by the heel in the womb,
And in his strength he [b]struggled with God.
4 Yes, he struggled with the Angel and prevailed;
He wept, and sought favor from Him.
He found Him *in* [a]Bethel,
And there He spoke to us—

**2** [a]2 Kin. 17:13–15 [2]So with MT, Tg., Vg.; LXX *from My face*
**3** [a]Deut. 1:31; 32:10, 11 [b]Ex. 15:26 [1]Some Heb. mss., LXX, Syr., Vg. *My arms*
**4** [a]Lev. 26:13 [b]Ps. 78:25 [1]Lit. *cords of a man* [2]Lit. *jaws*
**7** [a]Jer. 3:6, 7; 8:5 [1]The prophets [2]Or *upward*
**8** [a]Jer. 9:7 [b]Gen. 14:8; 19:24, 25 [1]Lit. *turns over*
**9** [a]Num. 23:19 [1]Or *enter a city*
**10** [a][Joel 3:16]
**11** [a]Is. 11:11; 60:8 [b]Ezek. 28:25, 26; 34:27, 28
**12** [1]Or *holy ones*

CHAPTER 12
**1** [a]Job 15:2, 3 [b]2 Kin. 17:4 [c]Is. 30:6 [1]*ruin* [2]Or *treaty*
**2** [a]Mic. 6:2 [1]A legal complaint
**3** [a]Gen. 25:26 [b]Gen. 32:24–28
**4** [a][Gen. 28:12–19; 35:9–15]
**5** [a]Ex. 3:15
**6** [a]Mic. 6:8
**7** [a]Amos 8:5 [1]Or *merchant*
**8** [a]Rev. 3:17
**9** [a]Lev. 23:42
**10** [a]2 Kin. 17:13 [1]Or *parables* [2]Lit. *by the hand*
**11** [a]Hos. 6:8 [b]Hos. 9:15 [1]*worthless*
**12** [a]Gen. 28:5 [b]Gen. 29:20, 28
**13** [a]Ex. 12:50, 51; 13:3
**14** [a]Ezek. 18:10–13 [b]Dan. 11:18

CHAPTER 13
**2** [1]Or *those who offer human sacrifice* [2]Worship with kisses
**3** [a]Dan. 2:35
**4** [a]Is. 43:11 [b]Is. 43:11; 45:21, 22
**5** [a]Deut. 2:7; 32:10 [b]Deut. 8:15 [1]Cared for you [2]Lit. *droughts*
**6** [a]Deut. 8:12, 14; 32:13–15
**7** [a]Lam. 3:10 [b]Jer. 5:6

5 That is, the LORD God of hosts.
The LORD *is* His [a]memorable name.
6 [a]So you, by *the help of* your God, return;
Observe mercy and justice,
And wait on your God continually.

**7** "A cunning [1]Canaanite!
[a]Deceitful scales *are* in his hand;
He loves to oppress.
8 And Ephraim said,
[a]'Surely I have become rich,
I have found wealth for myself;
*In* all my labors
They shall find in me no iniquity that *is* sin.'

**9** "But I *am* the LORD your God,
Ever since the land of Egypt;
[a]I will again make you dwell in tents,
As in the days of the appointed feast.
10 [a]I have also spoken by the prophets,
And have multiplied visions;
I have given [1]symbols [2]through the witness of the prophets."

11 Though [a]Gilead *has* idols—
Surely they are [1]vanity—
Though they sacrifice bulls in [b]Gilgal,
Indeed their altars *shall be* heaps in the furrows of the field.

12 Jacob [a]fled to the country of Syria;
[b]Israel served for a spouse,
And for a wife he tended *sheep.*
13 [a]By a prophet the LORD brought Israel out of Egypt,
And by a prophet he was preserved.
14 Ephraim [a]provoked *Him* to anger most bitterly;
Therefore his Lord will leave the guilt of his bloodshed upon him,
[b]And return his reproach upon him.

### *Ephraim's Destruction Foretold*

**13** When Ephraim spoke, trembling,
He exalted *himself* in Israel;
But when he offended through Baal *worship,* he died.
2 Now they sin more and more,
And have made for themselves molded images,
Idols of their silver, according to their skill;
All of it *is* the work of craftsmen.
They say of them,
"Let [1]the men who sacrifice [2]kiss the calves!"
3 Therefore they shall be like the morning cloud
And like the early dew that passes away,
[a]Like chaff blown off from a threshing floor
And like smoke from a chimney.

4 "Yet [a]I *am* the LORD your God
Ever since the land of Egypt,
And you shall know no God but Me;
For [b]*there is* no savior besides Me.
5 [a]I [1]knew you in the wilderness,
[b]In the land of [2]great drought.
6 [a]When they had pasture, they were filled;
They were filled and their heart was exalted;
Therefore they forgot Me.

7 "So [a]I will be to them like a lion;
Like [b]a leopard by the road I will lurk;

8 I will meet them [a]like a bear deprived *of her* cubs;
I will tear open their rib cage,
And there I will devour them like a lion.
The [1]wild beast shall tear them.

**9** "O Israel, [1]you are destroyed,
But [2]your help *is* from Me.
10 [1]I will be your King;
[a]Where *is any other,*
That he may save you in all your cities?
And your judges to whom [b]you said,
'Give me a king and princes'?
11 [a]I gave you a king in My anger,
And took *him* away in My wrath.

**12** "The[a] iniquity of Ephraim *is* bound up;
His sin *is* stored up.
13 [a]The sorrows of a woman in childbirth shall come upon him.
He *is* an unwise son,
For he should not stay long
where children are born.

14 "I will ransom them from the [1]power
of [2]the grave;
I will redeem them from death.
[a]O Death, [3]I will be your plagues!
O [4]Grave, [5]I will be your destruction!
[b]Pity is hidden from My eyes.

**15** Though he is fruitful among *his* brethren,
[a]An east wind shall come;
The wind of the LORD shall come up from the wilderness.
Then his spring shall become dry,
And his fountain shall be dried up.
He shall plunder the treasury of every desirable prize.
16 Samaria [1]is held guilty,
For she has [a]rebelled against her God.
They shall fall by the sword,
Their infants shall be dashed in pieces,
And their women with child [b]ripped open.

**8** [a]2 Sam. 17:8 [1]Lit. *beast of the field*
**9** [1]Lit. *it* or *he destroyed you* [2]Lit. *in your help*
**10** [a]Deut. 32:38 [b]1 Sam. 8:5, 6 [1]LXX, Syr., Tg., Vg. *Where is your king?*
**11** [a]1 Sam. 8:7; 10:17–24
**12** [a]Deut. 32:34, 35
**13** [a]Is. 13:8
**14** [a][1 Cor. 15:54, 55] [b]Jer. 15:6 [1]Lit. *hand* [2]Or *Sheol* [3]LXX *Where is your punishment?* [4]Or *Sheol* [5]LXX *Where is your sting?*
**15** [a]Jer. 4:11, 12
**16** [a]2 Kin. 8:12 [b]2 Kin. 15:16 [1]LXX *shall be disfigured*

CHAPTER 14
**1** [a][Joel 2:13]
**2** [a][Heb. 13:15] [1]Lit. *bull calves;* LXX *fruit*
**3** [a]Hos. 7:11; 10:13; 12:1 [b][Ps. 33:17] [c]Ps. 10:14; 68:5
**4** [a]Jer. 14:7 [b][Eph. 1:6]
**5** [a]Prov. 19:12 [1]Lit. *bud* or *sprout* [2]Lit. *strike*
**6** [a]Ps. 52:8; 128:3 [b]Gen. 27:27 [1]Lit. *go*
**7** [a]Dan. 4:12 [1]Lit. *bud* or *sprout* [2]Lit. *remembrance*
**8** [a][John 15:4]
**9** [a][Prov. 10:29]

### *Israel Restored at Last*

**14** O Israel, [a]return to the LORD your God,
For you have stumbled because of your iniquity;
2 Take words with you,
And return to the LORD.
Say to Him,
"Take away all iniquity;
Receive *us* graciously,
For we will offer the [a]sacrifices[1] of our lips.
3 Assyria shall [a]not save us,
[b]We will not ride on horses,
Nor will we say anymore to the work of our hands,
*'You are* our gods.'
[c]For in You the fatherless finds mercy."

4 "I will heal their [a]backsliding,
I will [b]love them freely,
For My anger has turned away from him.
5 I will be like the [a]dew to Israel;
He shall [1]grow like the lily,
And [2]lengthen his roots like Lebanon.
6 His branches shall [1]spread;
[a]His beauty shall be like an olive tree,
And [b]his fragrance like Lebanon.
7 [a]Those who dwell under his shadow shall return;
They shall be revived *like* grain,
And [1]grow like a vine.
Their [2]scent *shall be* like the wine of Lebanon.

**8** "Ephraim *shall say,*
'What have I to do anymore with idols?'
I have heard and observed him.
I *am* like a green cypress tree;
[a]Your fruit is found in Me."

**9** Who *is* wise?
Let him understand these things.
*Who is* prudent?
Let him know them.
For [a]the ways of the LORD *are* right;
The righteous walk in them,
But transgressors stumble in them.

*The Book of*

# JOEL

### *The Locust Plague in Judah*

THE word of the LORD that came to [a]Joel the son of Pethuel.

**2** Hear this, you elders,
And give ear, all you inhabitants of the land!
[a]Has *anything like* this happened in your days,
Or even in the days of your fathers?
3 [a]Tell your children about it,
*Let* your children *tell* their children,
And their children another generation.

**4** [a]What the chewing [1]locust left,
the [b]swarming locust has eaten;
What the swarming locust left,
the crawling locust has eaten;

CHAPTER 1
**1** [a]Acts 2:16
**2** [a]Joel 2:2
**3** [a]Ps. 78:4
**4** [a]Deut. 28:38 [b]Is. 33:4 [1]Exact identity of these locusts unknown
**5** [a]Is. 5:11; 28:1 [b]Is. 32:10
**6** [a]Joel 2:2, 11, 25 [b]Rev. 9:8 [1]Or *lioness*
**7** [a]Is. 5:6 [1]Or *splintered*
**8** [a]Is. 22:12 [b]Jer. 3:4

And what the crawling locust left,
the consuming locust has eaten.

**5** Awake, you [a]drunkards, and weep;
And wail, all you drinkers of wine,
Because of the new wine,
[b]For it has been cut off from your mouth.
6 For [a]a nation has come up against My land,
Strong, and without number;
[b]His teeth *are* the teeth of a lion,
And he has the fangs of a [1]fierce lion.
7 He has [a]laid waste My vine,
And [1]ruined My fig tree;
He has stripped it bare and thrown *it* away;
Its branches are made white.

**8** [a]Lament like a virgin girded with sackcloth
For [b]the husband of her youth.

9 [a]The grain offering and the drink offering
Have been cut off from the house of the
LORD;
The priests [b]mourn,
who minister to the LORD.
10 The field is wasted,
[a]The land mourns;
For the grain is ruined,
[b]The new wine is dried up,
The oil fails.

11 [a]Be ashamed, you farmers,
Wail, you vinedressers,
For the wheat and the barley;
Because the harvest of the field has perished.
12 [a]The vine has dried up,
And the fig tree has withered;
The pomegranate tree,
The palm tree also,
And the apple tree—
All the trees of the field are withered;
Surely [b]joy has withered away from the sons
of men.

**13** [a]Gird yourselves and lament, you priests;
Wail, you who minister before the altar;
Come, lie all night in sackcloth,
You who minister to my God;
For the grain offering and the drink offering
Are withheld from the house of your God.
14 [a]Consecrate a fast,
Call [b]a sacred assembly;
Gather the elders
*And* [c]all the inhabitants of the land
*Into* the house of the LORD your God,
And cry out to the LORD.

15 [a]Alas for the day!
For [b]the day of the LORD *is* at hand;
It shall come as destruction from the
Almighty.
16 Is not the food [a]cut off before our eyes,
[b]Joy and gladness from the house of our God?
17 The seed shrivels under the clods,
Storehouses are in shambles;
Barns are broken down,
For the grain has withered.
18 How [a]the animals groan!
The herds of cattle are restless,
Because they have no pasture;
Even the flocks of sheep [1]suffer punishment.

19 O LORD, [a]to You I cry out;
For [b]fire has devoured the [1]open pastures,
And a flame has burned all the trees
of the field.
20 The beasts of the field also [a]cry out to You,
For [b]the water brooks are dried up,
And fire has devoured the [1]open pastures.

### *Judgment on Judah and Israel*

**2** Blow [a]the [1]trumpet in Zion,
And [b]sound an alarm in My holy mountain!
Let all the inhabitants of the land tremble;
For [c]the day of the LORD is coming,
For it is at hand:
2 [a]A day of darkness and gloominess,
A day of clouds and thick darkness,
Like the morning *clouds* spread over the
mountains.
[b]A people *come,* great and strong,
[c]The like of whom has never been;
Nor will there ever be any *such* after them,
Even for many successive generations.

3 A fire devours before them,
And behind them a flame burns;
The land *is* like [a]the Garden of Eden before
them,
[b]And behind them a desolate wilderness;
Surely nothing shall escape them.
4 [a]Their appearance is like the appearance of
horses;
And like [1]swift steeds, so they run.
5 [a]With a noise like chariots
Over mountaintops they leap,
Like the noise of a flaming fire
that devours the stubble,
Like a strong people set in battle array.

6 Before them the people writhe in pain;
[a]All faces [1]are drained of color.
7 They run like mighty men,
They climb the wall like men of war;
Every one marches in formation,
And they do not break [a]ranks.
8 They do not push one another;
Every one marches in his own [1]column.
Though they lunge between the weapons,
They are not [2]cut down.
9 They run to and fro in the city,
They run on the wall;
They climb into the houses,
They [a]enter at the windows [b]like a thief.

10 [a]The earth quakes before them,
The heavens tremble;
[b]The sun and moon grow dark,
And the stars diminish their brightness.
11 [a]The LORD gives voice before His army,
For His camp is very great;
[b]For strong *is the One* who executes His
word.
For the [c]day of the LORD *is* great
and very terrible;
[d]Who can endure it?

**12** "Now, therefore," says the LORD,
[a]"Turn to Me with all your heart,
With fasting, with weeping,
and with mourning."
13 So [a]rend your heart, and not [b]your garments;
Return to the LORD your God,
For He *is* [c]gracious and merciful,
Slow to anger, and of great kindness;
And He relents from doing harm.
14 [a]Who knows *if* He will turn and relent,
And leave [b]a blessing behind Him—
[c]A grain offering and a drink offering
For the LORD your God?

**15** [a]Blow the [1]trumpet in Zion,
[b]Consecrate a fast,
Call a sacred assembly;
16 Gather the people,
[a]Sanctify the congregation,
Assemble the elders,
Gather the children and nursing babes;
[b]Let the bridegroom go out from his chamber,
And the bride from her dressing room.
17 Let the priests, who minister to the LORD,
Weep [a]between the porch and the altar;
Let them say, [b]"Spare Your people, O LORD,
And do not give Your heritage to reproach,
That the nations should [1]rule over them.

**9** [a]Joel 1:13; 2:14 [b]Joel 2:17
**10** [a]Jer. 12:11 [b]Is. 24:7
**11** [a]Jer. 14:3, 4
**12** [a]Joel 1:10 [b]Jer. 48:33
**13** [a]Jer. 4:8
**14** [a]Joel 2:15, 16 [b]Lev. 23:36 [c]2 Chr. 20:13
**15** [a][Jer. 30:7] [b]Is. 13:6
**16** [a]Is. 3:1 [b]Deut. 12:7
**18** [a]Hos. 4:3 [1]LXX, Vg. *are made desolate*
**19** [a][Ps. 50:15] [b]Jer. 9:10 [1]Lit. *pastures of the wilderness*
**20** [a]Ps. 104:21; 147:9 [b]1 Kin. 17:7; 18:5 [1]Lit. *pastures of the wilderness*

CHAPTER 2
**1** [a]Jer. 4:5 [b]Num. 10:5 [c][Obad. 15] [1]*ram's horn*
**2** [a]Amos 5:18 [b]Joel 1:6; 2:11, 25 [c]Dan. 9:12; 12:1
**3** [a]Is. 51:3 [b]Zech. 7:14
**4** [a]Rev. 9:7 [1]Or *horsemen*
**5** [a]Rev. 9:9
**6** [a]Nah. 2:10 [1]LXX, Tg., Vg. *gather blackness*
**7** [a]Prov. 30:27
**8** [1]Lit. *highway* [2]Halted by losses
**9** [a]Jer. 9:21 [b]John 10:1
**10** [a]Ps. 18:7 [b]Is. 13:10; 34:4
**11** [a]Jer. 25:30 [b]Rev. 18:8 [c]Amos 5:18 [d][Mal. 3:2]
**12** [a]Jer. 4:1
**13** [a][Ps. 34:18; 51:17] [b]Gen. 37:34 [c][Ex. 34:6]
**14** [a]Jer. 26:3 [b]Hag. 2:19 [c]Joel 1:9, 13
**15** [a]Num. 10:3 [b]Joel 1:14 [1]*ram's horn*
**16** [a]Ex. 19:10 [b]Ps. 19:5
**17** [a]Matt. 23:35 [b]Ex. 32:11, 12 [1]Or *speak a proverb against them*

[c]Why should they say among the peoples,
'Where *is* their God?' "

18 Then the LORD will [a]be zealous for His land,
And pity His people.
19 The LORD will answer and say to His people,
"Behold, I will send you [a]grain and
new wine and oil,
And you will be satisfied by them;
I will no longer make you a reproach among
the nations.

20 "But [a]I will remove far from you [b]the northern
*army,*
And will drive him away into a barren and
desolate land,
With his face toward the eastern sea
And his back [c]toward the western sea;
His stench will come up,
And his foul odor will rise,
Because he has done [1]monstrous things."

21 Fear not, O land;
Be glad and rejoice,
For the LORD has done [1]marvelous things!
22 Do not be afraid, you beasts of the field;
For [a]the open pastures are springing up,
And the tree bears its fruit;
The fig tree and the vine yield their strength.
23 Be glad then, you children of Zion,
And [a]rejoice in the LORD your God;
For He has given you the [1]former rain
faithfully,
And He [b]will cause the rain to come down
for you—
The former rain,
And the latter rain in the first *month.*
24 The threshing floors shall be full of wheat,
And the vats shall overflow with
new wine and oil.

25 "So I will restore to you the years [a]that the
swarming [1]locust has eaten,
The crawling locust,
The consuming locust,
And the chewing locust,
My great army which I sent among you.
26 You shall [a]eat in plenty and be satisfied,
And praise the name of the LORD your God,
Who has dealt wondrously with you;
And My people shall never be put to [b]shame.
27 Then you shall know that I *am* [a]in the midst
of Israel:
[b]I *am* the LORD your God
And there is no other.
My people shall never be put to shame.

28 "And[a] it shall come to pass afterward
That [b]I will pour out My Spirit on all flesh;
[c]Your sons and your [d]daughters shall
prophesy,
Your old men shall dream dreams,
Your young men shall see visions.
29 And also on *My* [a]menservants
and on *My* maidservants
I will pour out My Spirit in those days.

30 "And [a]I will show wonders
in the heavens and in the earth:
Blood and fire and pillars of smoke.
31 [a]The sun shall be turned into darkness,
And the moon into blood,
[b]Before the coming of the great and awesome
day of the LORD.
32 And it shall come to pass
*That* [a]whoever calls on the name of the LORD
Shall be [1]saved.
For [b]in Mount Zion and in Jerusalem there
shall be [2]deliverance,
As the LORD has said,
Among [c]the remnant whom the LORD calls.

## *Judgment on the Nations*

3 "For behold, [a]in those days and at that time,
When I bring back the captives of Judah and
Jerusalem,
2 [a]I will also gather all nations,
And bring them down to the Valley of
Jehoshaphat;
And I [b]will enter into judgment with them
there
On account of My people, My heritage Israel,
Whom they have scattered among the
nations;
They have also divided up My land.
3 They have [a]cast lots for My people,
Have given a boy *as payment* for a harlot,
And sold a girl for wine, that they may drink.

4 "Indeed, what have you to do with Me,
[a]O Tyre and Sidon,
and all the coasts of Philistia?
Will you [1]retaliate against Me?
But if you [2]retaliate against Me,
Swiftly and speedily I will return your
[3]retaliation upon your own head;
5 Because you have taken My silver
and My gold,
And have carried into your temples
My [1]prized possessions.
6 Also the people of Judah
and the people of Jerusalem
You have sold to the Greeks,
That you may remove them far from their
borders.

7 "Behold, [a]I will raise them
Out of the place to which you have sold
them,
And will return your [1]retaliation upon your
own head.
8 I will sell your sons and your daughters
Into the hand of the people of Judah,
And they will sell them to the [a]Sabeans,[1]
To a people [b]far off;
For the LORD has spoken."

9 [a]Proclaim this among the nations:
"Prepare for war!
Wake up the mighty men,
Let all the men of war draw near,
Let them come up.
10 [a]Beat your plowshares into swords
And your [1]pruning hooks into spears;
[b]Let the weak say, 'I *am* strong.' "
11 Assemble and come, all you nations,
And gather together all around.
Cause [a]Your mighty ones to go down there,
O LORD.

12 "Let the nations be wakened,
and come up to the Valley of Jehoshaphat;
For there I will sit to [a]judge
all the surrounding nations.
13 [a]Put in the sickle, for [b]the harvest is ripe.
Come, go down;
For the [c]winepress is full,

**17** [c]Ps. 42:10
**18** [a][Is. 60:10; 63:9, 15]
**19** [a][Mal. 3:10]
**20** [a]Ex. 10:19 [b]Jer. 1:14, 15 [c]Deut. 11:24 [1]Lit. *great*
**21** [1]Lit. *great*
**22** [a]Joel 1:19
**23** [a]Is. 41:16 [b]Lev. 26:4 [1]Or *teacher of righteousness*
**25** [a]Joel 1:4–7; 2:2–11 [1]Exact identity of these locusts unknown
**26** [a]Lev. 26:5 [b]Is. 45:17
**27** [a]Lev. 26:11, 12 [b][Is. 45:5, 6]
**28** [a]Ezek. 39:29 [b]Zech. 12:10 [c]Is. 54:13 [d]Acts 21:9
**29** [a][Gal. 3:28]
**30** [a]Matt. 24:29
**31** [a]Is. 13:9, 10; 34:4 [b][Mal. 4:1, 5, 6]
**32** [a]Rom. 10:13 [b]Is. 46:13 [c][Mic. 4:7] [1]Or *delivered* [2]Or *salvation*

CHAPTER 3
**1** [a]Jer. 30:3
**2** [a]Zech. 14:2 [b]Is. 66:16
**3** [a]Nah. 3:10
**4** [a]Amos 1:6–8 [1]Or *render me repayment* [2]Or *repay me* [3]Or *repayment*
**5** [1]Lit. *precious good things*
**7** [a]Jer. 23:8 [1]Or *repayment*
**8** [a]Ezek. 23:42 [b]Jer. 6:20 [1]Lit. *Shebaites,* Is. 60:6; Ezek. 27:22
**9** [a]Ezek. 38:7
**10** [a][Is. 2:4] [b]Zech. 12:8 [1]*pruning knives*
**11** [a]Is. 13:3
**12** [a]Is. 2:4
**13** [a]Rev. 14:15 [b]Jer. 51:33 [c][Is. 63:3]

The vats overflow—
For their wickedness *is* great."

14 Multitudes, multitudes in the valley of
decision!
For [a]the day of the LORD *is* near in the valley
of decision.
15 The sun and moon will grow dark,
And the stars will diminish their brightness.
16 The LORD also will roar from Zion,
And utter His voice from Jerusalem;
The heavens and earth will shake;
[a]But the LORD will be a shelter for His people,
And the strength of the children of Israel.

17 "So you shall know that I *am* the LORD your
God,
Dwelling in Zion My [a]holy mountain.
Then Jerusalem shall be holy,
And no aliens shall ever pass through her
again."

14 [a]Joel 2:1
16 [a][Is. 51:5, 6]
17 [a]Obad. 16; Zech. 8:3
18 [a]Ps. 46:4; Ezek. 47:1; Zech. 14:8; [Rev. 22:1] [1]Heb. *Shittim*
21 [a]Is. 4:4

18 And it will come to pass in that day
*That* the mountains shall drip with new wine,
The hills shall flow with milk,
And all the brooks of Judah shall be flooded
with water;
A [a]fountain shall flow from the house of the
LORD
And water the Valley of [1]Acacias.

19 "Egypt shall be a desolation,
And Edom a desolate wilderness,
Because of violence *against* the people of
Judah,
For they have shed innocent blood in their
land.
20 But Judah shall abide forever,
And Jerusalem from generation to
generation.
21 "For I will [a]acquit them of the guilt of
bloodshed, whom I had not acquitted;
For the LORD dwells in Zion."

*The Book of*

# AMOS

## *Judgments on Israel's Neighbors*

THE words of Amos, who was among the
[a]sheepbreeders of [b]Tekoa, which he saw
concerning Israel in the days of [c]Uzziah king
of Judah, and in the days of [d]Jeroboam the son of
Joash, king of Israel, two years before the [e]earth-
quake.
2 And he said:

"The LORD [a]roars from Zion,
And utters His voice from Jerusalem;
The pastures of the shepherds mourn,
And the top of [b]Carmel withers."

**3** Thus says the LORD:

"For three transgressions of [a]Damascus, and
for four,
I will not turn away its *punishment*,
Because they have [b]threshed Gilead with
implements of iron.
4 [a]But I will send a fire into the house of
Hazael,
Which shall devour the palaces
of [b]Ben-Hadad.
5 I will also break the *gate* [a]bar of Damascus,
And cut off the inhabitant from the Valley of
Aven,
And the one who [1]holds the scepter from
[2]Beth Eden.
The people of Syria shall go captive to Kir,"
Says the LORD.

**6** Thus says the LORD:

"For three transgressions of [a]Gaza,
and for four,
I will not turn away its *punishment*,
Because they took captive the whole
captivity
To deliver *them* up to Edom.
7 [a]But I will send a fire upon the wall of Gaza,
Which shall devour its palaces.

CHAPTER 1
1 [a]2 Kin. 3:4; Amos 7:14 [b]2 Sam. 14:2 [c]2 Chr. 26:1–23 [d]Amos 7:10 [e]Zech. 14:5
2 [a]Joel 3:16 [b]1 Sam. 25:2
3 [a]Is. 8:4; 17:1–3 [b]2 Kin. 10:32, 33
4 [a]Jer. 49:27; 51:30 [b]2 Kin. 6:24
5 [a]Jer. 51:30 [1]Rules [2]Lit. *House of Eden*
6 [a]Jer. 47:1, 5
7 [a]Jer. 47:1
8 [a]Zeph. 2:4 [b]Ps. 81:14 [c]Ezek. 25:16
9 [a]Is. 23:1–18
11 [a]Is. 21:11 [b]Obad. 10–12
12 [a]Obad. 9, 10
13 [a]Ezek. 25:2
14 [a]Deut. 3:11

8 I will cut off the inhabitant [a]from Ashdod,
And the one who holds the scepter from
Ashkelon;
I will [b]turn My hand against Ekron,
And [c]the remnant of the Philistines shall
perish,"
Says the Lord GOD.

**9** Thus says the LORD:

"For three transgressions of [a]Tyre,
and for four,
I will not turn away its *punishment*,
Because they delivered up the whole
captivity to Edom,
And did not remember the covenant of
brotherhood.
10 But I will send a fire upon the wall of Tyre,
Which shall devour its palaces."

**11** Thus says the LORD:

"For three transgressions of [a]Edom,
and for four,
I will not turn away its *punishment*,
Because he pursued his [b]brother with the
sword,
And cast off all pity;
His anger tore perpetually,
And he kept his wrath forever.
12 But [a]I will send a fire upon Teman,
Which shall devour the palaces of Bozrah."

**13** Thus says the LORD:

"For three transgressions of [a]the people of
Ammon, and for four,
I will not turn away its *punishment*,
Because they ripped open the women with
child in Gilead,
That they might enlarge their territory.
14 But I will kindle a fire in the wall of [a]Rabbah,
And it shall devour its palaces,

[b]Amid shouting in the day of battle,
And a tempest in the day of the whirlwind.
15 [a]Their king shall go into captivity,
He and his princes together,"
Says the LORD.

### *Judgment on Israel*

2 Thus says the LORD:

[a]"For three transgressions of Moab,
and for four,
I will not turn away its *punishment,*
Because he [b]burned the bones of the king of
Edom to lime.
2 But I will send a fire upon Moab,
And it shall devour the palaces of [a]Kerioth;
Moab shall die with tumult,
With shouting *and* trumpet sound.
3 And I will cut off [a]the judge from its midst,
And slay all its princes with him,"
Says the LORD.

4 Thus says the LORD:

"For three transgressions of [a]Judah,
and for four,
I will not turn away its *punishment,*
[b]Because they have despised
the law of the LORD,
And have not kept His commandments.
[c]Their lies lead them astray,
*Lies* [d]which their fathers followed.
5 [a]But I will send a fire upon Judah,
And it shall devour the palaces of
Jerusalem."

6 Thus says the LORD:

"For three transgressions of [a]Israel,
and for four,
I will not turn away its *punishment,*
Because [b]they sell the righteous for silver,
And the [c]poor for a pair of sandals.
7 They [1]pant after the dust of the earth *which*
*is* on the head of the poor,
And [a]pervert the way of the humble.
[b]A man and his father go in to the *same* girl,
[c]To defile My holy name.
8 They lie down [a]by every altar on clothes
[b]taken in pledge,
And drink the wine of [1]the condemned *in* the
house of their god.

9 "Yet *it was* I *who* destroyed the [a]Amorite
before them,
Whose height *was* like the [b]height of the
cedars,
And he *was as* strong as the oaks;
Yet I [c]destroyed his fruit above
And his roots beneath.
10 Also *it was* [a]I *who* brought you up from the
land of Egypt,
And [b]led you forty years through the
wilderness,
To possess the land of the Amorite.
11 I raised up some of your sons as [a]prophets,
And some of your young men as [b]Nazirites.
*Is it* not so, O you children of Israel?"
Says the LORD.
12 "But you gave the Nazirites wine to drink,
And commanded the prophets [a]saying,
'Do not prophesy!'

13 "Behold,[a] I am [1]weighed down by you,
As a cart full of sheaves [2]is weighed down.
14 [a]Therefore [1]flight shall perish from the swift,
The strong shall not strengthen his power,
[b]Nor shall the mighty [2]deliver himself;
15 He shall not stand who handles the bow,
The swift of foot shall not [1]escape,
Nor shall he who rides a horse deliver
himself.
16 The most [1]courageous men of might
Shall flee naked in that day,"
Says the LORD.

### *The Condemnation of Samaria*

3 Hear this word that the LORD has spoken
against you, O children of Israel, against the
whole family which I brought up from the land of
Egypt, saying:

2 "You[a] only have I known of all the families of
the earth;
[b]Therefore I will punish you for all your
iniquities."

3 Can two walk together,
unless they are agreed?
4 Will a lion roar in the forest,
when he has no prey?
Will a young lion [1]cry out of his den,
if he has caught nothing?
5 Will a bird fall into a snare on the earth,
where there is no [1]trap for it?
Will a snare spring up from the earth, if it
has caught nothing at all?
6 If a [1]trumpet is blown in a city,
will not the people be afraid?
[a]If there is calamity in a city,
will not the LORD have done *it?*

7 Surely the Lord GOD does nothing,
Unless [a]He reveals His secret
to His servants the prophets.
8 A lion has roared!
Who will not fear?
The Lord GOD has spoken!
[a]Who can but prophesy?

9 "Proclaim in the palaces at Ashdod,
And in the palaces in the land of Egypt, and
say:
'Assemble on the mountains of Samaria;
See great tumults in her midst,
And the [1]oppressed within her.
10 For they [a]do not know to do right,'
Says the LORD,
'Who store up violence and [1]robbery in their
palaces.' "

11 Therefore thus says the Lord GOD:

"An adversary *shall be* all around the land;
He shall sap your strength from you,
And your palaces shall be plundered."

12 Thus says the LORD:

"As a shepherd [1]takes from the mouth of a
lion
Two legs or a piece of an ear,
So shall the children of Israel be taken out
Who dwell in Samaria—
In the corner of a bed
and [2]on the edge of a couch!
13 Hear and testify against the house of Jacob,"
Says the Lord GOD, the God of hosts,

---

**14** [b]Amos 2:2
**15** [a]Jer. 49:3

CHAPTER 2
**1** [a]Zeph. 2:8–11 [b]2 Kin. 3:26, 27
**2** [a]Jer. 48:24, 41
**3** [a]Num. 24:17
**4** [a]Hos. 12:2 [b]Lev. 26:14 [c]Jer. 16:19 [d]Ezek. 20:13, 16, 18
**5** [a]Hos. 8:14
**6** [a]2 Kin. 17:7–18; 18:12 [b]Is. 29:21 [c]Amos 4:1; 5:11; 8:6
**7** [a]Amos 5:12 [b]Ezek. 22:11 [c]Lev. 20:3 [1]Or *trample on*
**8** [a]1 Cor. 8:10 [b]Ex. 22:26 [1]Or *those punished by fines*
**9** [a]Num. 21:25 [b]Ezek. 31:3 [c][Mal. 4:1]
**10** [a]Ex. 12:51 [b]Deut. 2:7
**11** [a]Num. 12:6 [b]Num. 6:2, 3
**12** [a]Is. 30:10
**13** [a]Is. 1:14 [1]Or *tottering under* [2]Or *totters*
**14** [a]Jer. 46:6 [b]Ps. 33:16 [1]Or *the place of refuge* [2]Lit. *save his soul* or *life*
**15** [1]Or *save*
**16** [1]Lit. *strong of his heart among the mighty*

CHAPTER 3
**2** [a][Deut. 7:6] [b][Rom. 2:9]
**4** [1]Lit. *give his voice*
**5** [1]Or *bait* or *lure*
**6** [a]Is. 45:7 [1]*ram's horn*
**7** [a][John 15:15]
**8** [a]Acts 4:20
**9** [1]Or *oppression*
**10** [a]Jer. 4:22 [1]Or *devastation*
**12** [1]Or *snatches* [2]Heb. uncertain, possibly *on the cover*

14 "That in the day I punish Israel for their
transgressions,
I will also visit *destruction* on the altars of
[a]Bethel;
And the horns of the altar shall be cut off
And fall to the ground.
15 I will [1]destroy [a]the winter house along with
[b]the summer house;
The [c]houses of ivory shall perish,
And the great houses shall have an end,"
Says the LORD.

## *God's Punishments Have Not Reformed Israel*

4 Hear this word, you [a]cows of Bashan, who
*are* on the mountain of Samaria,
Who oppress the [b]poor,
Who crush the needy,
Who say to [1]your husbands,
"Bring *wine,* let us [c]drink!"
2 [a]The Lord GOD has sworn by His holiness:
"Behold, the days shall come upon you
When He will take you away [b]with
fishhooks,
And your posterity with fishhooks.
3 [a]You will go out *through* broken *walls,*
Each one straight ahead of her,
And you will [1]be cast into Harmon,"
Says the LORD.
4 "Come[a] to Bethel and transgress,
At [b]Gilgal multiply transgression;
[c]Bring your sacrifices every morning,
[d]Your tithes every three [1]days.
5 [a]Offer a sacrifice of thanksgiving with leaven,
Proclaim *and* announce [b]the freewill
offerings;
For this you love,
*You* children of Israel!"
Says the Lord GOD.

6 "Also I gave you [1]cleanness of teeth in all
your cities.
And lack of bread in all your places;
[a]Yet you have not returned to Me,"
Says the LORD.
7 "I also withheld rain from you,
When *there were* still three months
to the harvest.
I made it rain on one city,
I withheld rain from another city.
One part was rained upon,
And where it did not rain the part withered.
8 So two *or* three cities wandered to another
city to drink water,
But they were not satisfied;
Yet you have not returned to Me,"
Says the LORD.

9 "I[a] blasted you with blight and mildew.
When your gardens increased,
Your vineyards,
Your fig trees,
And your olive trees,
[b]The locust devoured *them;*
Yet you have not returned to Me,"
Says the LORD.

10 "I sent among you a plague [a]after the manner
of Egypt;
Your young men I killed with a sword,
Along with your captive horses;
I made the stench of your camps come up
into your nostrils;
Yet you have not returned to Me,"
Says the LORD.

11 "I overthrew *some* of you,
As God overthrew [a]Sodom and Gomorrah,
And you were like a firebrand plucked from
the burning;
Yet you have not returned to Me,"
Says the LORD.

12 "Therefore thus will I do to you, O Israel;
Because I will do this to you,
[a]Prepare to meet your God, O Israel!"

13 For behold,
He who forms mountains,
And creates the [1]wind,
[a]Who declares to man what [2]his thought *is,*
And makes the morning darkness,
[b]Who treads the high places of the earth—
[c]The LORD God of hosts *is* His name.

## *A Call to Repentance*

5 Hear this word which I [a]take up against you, a
lamentation, O house of Israel:

2 The virgin of Israel has fallen;
She will rise no more.
She lies forsaken on her land;
*There is* no one to raise her up.

3 For thus says the Lord GOD:

"The city that goes out by a thousand
Shall have a hundred left,
And that which goes out by a hundred
Shall have ten left to the house of Israel."

4 For thus says the LORD to the house of Israel:

[a]"Seek Me [b]and live;
5 But do not seek [a]Bethel,
Nor enter Gilgal,
Nor pass over to [b]Beersheba;
For Gilgal shall surely go into captivity,
And [c]Bethel shall come to nothing.
6 [a]Seek the LORD and live,
Lest He break out like fire *in* the house of
Joseph,
And devour *it,*
With no one to quench *it* in Bethel—
7 You who [a]turn justice to wormwood,
And lay righteousness to rest in the earth!"

8 He made the [a]Pleiades and Orion;
He turns the shadow of death into morning
[b]And makes the day dark as night;
He [c]calls for the waters of the sea
And pours them out on the face of the earth;
[d]The LORD *is* His name.
9 He [1]rains ruin upon the strong,
So that fury comes upon the fortress.

10 [a]They hate the one who rebukes in the gate,
And they [b]abhor the one who speaks
uprightly.
11 [a]Therefore, because you [1]tread down the poor
And take grain [2]taxes from him,
Though [b]you have built houses of hewn
stone,
Yet you shall not dwell in them;
You have planted [3]pleasant vineyards,
But you shall not drink wine from them.

14 [a]2 Kin. 23:15; Hos. 10:5–8, 14, 15; Amos 4:4
15 [a]Jer. 36:22 [b]Judg. 3:20 [c]1 Kin. 22:39; Ps. 45:8 [1]Lit. *strike*

CHAPTER 4
1 [a]Ps. 22:12; Ezek. 39:18 [b]Amos 2:6 [c]Prov. 23:20 [1]Lit. *their masters* or *lords*
2 [a]Ps. 89:35 [b]Jer. 16:16; Ezek. 29:4; Hab. 1:15
3 [a]Ezek. 12:5 [1]Or *cast them*
4 [a]Ezek. 20:39; Amos 3:14 [b]Hos. 4:15 [c]Num. 28:3; Amos 5:21, 22 [d]Deut. 14:28 [1]Or *years,* Deut. 14:28
5 [a]Lev. 7:13 [b]Lev. 22:18; Deut. 12:6
6 [a]2 Chr. 28:22; Is. 26:11; Jer. 5:3; Hag. 2:17 [1]Hunger
9 [a]Deut. 28:22; Hag. 2:17 [b]Joel 1:4, 7; Amos 7:1, 2
10 [a]Ex. 9:3, 6; Lev. 26:25; Deut. 28:27, 60; Ps. 78:50
11 [a]Gen. 19:24, 25; Deut. 29:23; Is. 13:19; Jer. 49:18; Lam. 4:6
12 [a]Amos 4:12
13 [a]Ps. 139:2; Dan. 2:28 [b]Mic. 1:3 [c]Is. 47:4; Jer. 10:16 [1]Or *spirit* [2]Or *His*

CHAPTER 5
1 [a]Jer. 7:29; 9:10, 17; Ezek. 19:1
4 [a][Deut. 4:29; 2 Chr. 15:2; Jer. 29:13] [b][Is. 55:3]
5 [a]1 Kin. 12:28, 29; Amos 4:4 [b]Gen. 21:31–33; Amos 8:14 [c]Hos. 4:15
6 [a][Is. 55:3, 6, 7; Amos 5:14]
7 [a]Amos 6:12
8 [a]Job 9:9; 38:31 [b]Ps. 104:20 [c]Job 38:34 [d][Amos 4:13]
9 [1]Or *flashes forth destruction*
10 [a]Is. 29:21; 66:5; Amos 5:15 [b]1 Kin. 22:8; Is. 59:15; Jer. 17:16–18
11 [a]Amos 2:6 [b]Deut. 28:30, 38, 39; Mic. 6:15; Zeph. 1:13; Hag. 1:6 [1]*trample* [2]Or *tribute* [3]*desirable*

12 For I [a]know your manifold transgressions
And your mighty sins:
[b]Afflicting the just *and* taking bribes;
[c]Diverting the poor *from justice* at the gate.
13 Therefore [a]the prudent keep silent at that time,
For it *is* an evil time.

**14** Seek good and not evil,
That you may live;
So the LORD God of hosts will be with you,
[a]As you have spoken.
15 [a]Hate evil, love good;
Establish justice in the gate.
[b]It may be that the LORD God of hosts
Will be gracious to the remnant of Joseph.

**16** Therefore the LORD God of hosts, the Lord,
says this:

"*There shall be* wailing in all streets,
And they shall say in all the highways,
'Alas! Alas!'
They shall call the farmer to mourning,
[a]And skillful lamenters to wailing.
17 In all vineyards *there shall be* wailing,
For [a]I will pass through you,"
Says the LORD.

**18** [a]Woe to you who desire the day of the LORD!
For what good *is* [b]the day of the LORD to you?
It *will be* darkness, and not light.
19 It *will be* [a]as though a man fled from a lion,
And a bear met him!
Or *as though* he went into the house,
Leaned his hand on the wall,
And a serpent bit him!
20 *Is* not the day of the LORD darkness, and not light?
*Is it not* very dark, with no brightness in it?

**21** "I[a] hate, I despise your feast days,
And [b]I do not savor your sacred assemblies.
22 [a]Though you offer Me burnt offerings and your grain offerings,
I will not accept *them*,
Nor will I regard your fattened peace offerings.
23 Take away from Me the noise of your songs,
For I will not hear the melody of your stringed instruments.
24 [a]But let justice run down like water,
And righteousness like a mighty stream.

**25** "Did[a] you offer Me sacrifices and offerings
In the wilderness forty years,
O house of Israel?
26 You also carried [1]Sikkuth[2] [a]your king
And [2]Chiun, your idols,
The star of your gods,
Which you made for yourselves.
27 Therefore I will send you into captivity
[a]beyond Damascus,"
Says the LORD,
[b]whose name *is* the God of hosts.

### *Warnings to Zion and Samaria*

**6** Woe [a]to you *who are* at [b]ease in Zion,
And [c]trust in Mount Samaria,
Notable persons in the [d]chief nation,
To whom the house of Israel comes!
2 [a]Go over to [b]Calneh and see;
And from there go to [c]Hamath the great;
Then go down to Gath of the Philistines.
[d]*Are you* better than these kingdoms?
Or is their territory greater than your territory?

**3** *Woe to* you who [a]put far off the day of [b]doom,
[c]Who cause [d]the seat of violence to come near;
4 Who lie on beds of ivory,
Stretch out on your couches,
Eat lambs from the flock
And calves from the midst of the stall;
5 [a]Who sing idly to the sound of stringed instruments,
*And* invent for yourselves [b]musical instruments [c]like David;
6 Who [a]drink wine from bowls,
And anoint yourselves with the best ointments,
[b]But are not grieved for the affliction of Joseph.
7 Therefore they shall now go [a]captive as the first of the captives,
And those who recline at banquets shall be removed.

**8** [a]The Lord GOD has sworn by Himself,
The LORD God of hosts says:
"I abhor [b]the pride of Jacob,
And hate his palaces;
Therefore I will deliver up *the* city
And all that is in it."

9 Then it shall come to pass, that if ten men
remain in one house, they shall die.
10 And when [1]a relative *of the dead,* with one
who will burn *the bodies,* picks up the [2]bodies to
take them out of the house, he will say to one
inside the house, "*Are there* any more with you?"
Then someone will say, "None." And he will say,
[a]"Hold your tongue! [b]For we dare not mention the
name of the LORD."

11 For behold, [a]the LORD gives a command:
[b]He will break the great house into bits,
And the little house into pieces.

**12** Do horses run on rocks?
Does *one* plow *there* with oxen?
Yet [a]you have turned justice into gall,
And the fruit of righteousness into wormwood,
13 You who rejoice over [1]Lo Debar,
Who say, "Have we not taken [2]Karnaim for ourselves
By our own strength?"

14 "But, behold, [a]I will raise up a nation against you,
O house of Israel,"
Says the LORD God of hosts;
"And they will afflict you from the [b]entrance of Hamath
To the Valley of the Arabah."

### *Amos and Amaziah*

**7** Thus the Lord GOD showed me: Behold, He
formed locust swarms at the [1]beginning of the
late crop; indeed *it was* the late crop after the
king's mowings.
2 And so it was, when they had finished eating
the grass of the land, that I said:

---

**5:12** [a]Hos. 5:3 [b]Amos 2:6 [c]Is. 29:21
**13** [a]Amos 6:10
**14** [a]Mic. 3:11
**15** [a]Rom. 12:9 [b]Joel 2:14
**16** [a]Jer. 9:17
**17** [a]Ex. 12:12
**18** [a]Is. 5:19 [b]Joel 2:2
**19** [a]Jer. 48:44
**21** [a]Is. 1:11–16 [b]Lev. 26:31
**22** [a]Mic. 6:6, 7
**24** [a]Mic. 6:8
**25** [a]Deut. 32:17
**26** [a]1 Kin. 11:33 [1]LXX, Vg. *tabernacle of Moloch* [2]A pagan deity
**27** [a]2 Kin. 17:6 [b]Amos 4:13

CHAPTER 6
**1** [a]Luke 6:24 [b]Zeph. 1:12 [c]Is. 31:1 [d]Ex. 19:5
**2** [a]Jer. 2:10 [b]Is. 10:9 [c]2 Kin. 18:34 [d]Nah. 3:8
**3** [a]Is. 56:12 [b]Amos 5:18 [c]Amos 5:12 [d]Ps. 94:20
**5** [a]Is. 5:12 [b]Amos 5:23; 3:10 [c]1 Chr. 23:5
**6** [a]Amos 2:8; 4:1 [b]Gen. 37:25
**7** [a]Amos 5:27
**8** [a]Jer. 51:14 [b]Amos 8:7
**10** [a]Amos 5:13 [b]Amos 8:3 [1]Lit. *his loved one* or *uncle* [2]Lit. *bones*
**11** [a]Is. 55:11 [b]Amos 3:15
**12** [a]Hos. 10:4
**13** [1]Lit. *Nothing* [2]Lit. *Horns,* a symbol of strength
**14** [a]Jer. 5:15 [b]1 Kin. 8:65

CHAPTER 7
**1** [1]Lit. *beginning of the sprouting of*

“O Lord GOD, forgive, I pray!
[a]Oh,[1] that Jacob may stand,
For he *is* small!”
3 *So* [a]the LORD relented concerning this.
“It shall not be,” said the LORD.

4 Thus the Lord GOD showed me: Behold, the
Lord GOD called [1]for conflict by fire, and it consumed the great deep and devoured the [2]territory.
5 Then I said:

“O Lord GOD, cease, I pray!
[a]Oh, that Jacob may stand,
For he *is* small!”
6 *So* the LORD relented concerning this.
“This also shall not be,” said the Lord GOD.

7 Thus He showed me: Behold, the Lord stood
on a wall *made* with a plumb line, with a plumb
line in His hand.
8 And the LORD said to me, “Amos, what do you
see?” And I said, “A plumb line.” Then the Lord
said:

“Behold, [a]I am setting a plumb line
In the midst of My people Israel;
[b]I will not pass by them anymore.
9 [a]The [1]high places of Isaac shall be desolate,
And the [2]sanctuaries of Israel shall be laid
waste.
[b]I will rise with the sword against the house
of Jeroboam.”

10 Then Amaziah the [a]priest of [b]Bethel sent to
[c]Jeroboam king of Israel, saying, “Amos has
conspired against you in the midst of the house of
Israel. The land is not able to [1]bear all his words.
11 “For thus Amos has said:

‘Jeroboam shall die by the sword,
And Israel shall surely be led away [a]captive
From their own land.’ ”

12 Then Amaziah said to Amos:

“Go, you seer!
Flee to the land of Judah.
There eat bread,
And there prophesy.
13 But [a]never again prophesy at Bethel,
[b]For it *is* the king’s [1]sanctuary,
And it *is* the royal [2]residence.”

14 Then Amos answered, and said to Amaziah:

“I *was* no prophet,
Nor *was* I [a]a son of a prophet,
But I *was* a [b]sheepbreeder
And a tender of sycamore fruit.
15 Then the LORD took me [1]as I followed the
flock,
And the LORD said to me,
‘Go, [a]prophesy to My people Israel.’
16 Now therefore, hear the word of the LORD:
You say, ‘Do not prophesy against Israel,
And [a]do not [1]spout against the house of
Isaac.’

17 “Therefore[a] thus says the LORD:

[b]‘Your wife shall be a harlot in the city;
Your sons and daughters shall fall by the
sword;
Your land shall be divided by *survey* line;
You shall die in a [c]defiled land;
And Israel shall surely be led away captive
From his own land.’ ”

2 [a]Is. 51:19 [1]Or *How shall Jacob stand*
3 [a]Jon. 3:10
4 [1]*to contend* [2]Lit. *portion*
5 [a]Amos 7:2, 3
8 [a]2 Kin. 21:13 [b]Mic. 7:18
9 [a]Gen. 46:1 [b]2 Kin. 15:8–10 [1]Places of pagan worship [2]Or *holy places*
10 [a]1 Kin. 12:31, 32; 13:33 [b]Amos 4:4 [c]2 Kin. 14:23 [1]Or *endure*
11 [a]Amos 5:27; 6:7
13 [a]Amos 2:12 [b]1 Kin. 12:29, 32 [1]Or *holy place* [2]Lit. *house*
14 [a]1 Kin. 20:35 [b]Zech. 13:5
15 [a]Amos 3:8 [1]Lit. *from behind*
16 [a]Ezek. 21:2 [1]Lit. *drip*
17 [a]Jer. 28:12; 29:21, 32 [b]Zech. 14:2 [c]Hos. 9:3

CHAPTER 8
2 [a]Ezek. 7:2 [b]Amos 7:8
3 [a]Amos 5:23 [b]Amos 6:9, 10
4 [1]Or *trample on,* Amos 2:7
5 [a]Neh. 13:15 [b]Mic. 6:10, 11 [c]Lev. 19:35, 36 [1]Lit. *open*
6 [a]Amos 2:6
7 [a]Amos 6:8 [b]Hos. 7:2; 8:13
8 [a]Hos. 4:3 [b]Amos 9:5 [1]The Nile; some Heb. mss., LXX, Tg., Syr., Vg. *River* (cf. 9:5); MT *the light*
9 [a]Job 5:14 [1]Lit. *a day of light*
10 [a]Ezek. 7:18 [b]Ezek. 27:31 [c][Zech. 12:10]
11 [a]Ezek. 7:26
12 [a]Hos. 5:6
14 [a]Hos. 4:15 [b]Deut. 9:21 [c]Amos 5:5 [1]Or *Ashima,* a Syrian goddess

### *Vision of the Summer Fruit*

8 Thus the Lord GOD showed me: Behold, a
basket of summer fruit.
2 And He said, “Amos, what do you see?” So I
said, “A basket of summer fruit.” Then the LORD
said to me:

[a]“The end has come upon My people Israel;
[b]I will not pass by them anymore.
3 And [a]the songs of the temple
Shall be wailing in that day,”
Says the Lord GOD—
“Many dead bodies everywhere,
[b]They shall be thrown out in silence.”

4 Hear this, you who [1]swallow up the needy,
And make the poor of the land fail,

5 Saying:

“When will the New Moon be past,
That we may sell grain?
And [a]the Sabbath,
That we may [1]trade wheat?
[b]Making the ephah small and the shekel large,
Falsifying the scales by [c]deceit,
6 That we may buy the poor for [a]silver,
And the needy for a pair of sandals—
Even sell the bad wheat?”

7 The LORD has sworn by [a]the pride of Jacob:
“Surely [b]I will never forget any of their works.
8 [a]Shall the land not tremble for this,
And everyone mourn who dwells in it?
All of it shall swell like [1]the River,
Heave and subside
[b]Like the River of Egypt.

9 “And it shall come to pass in that day,”
says the Lord GOD,
[a]“That I will make the sun go down at noon,
And I will darken the earth in [1]broad
daylight;
10 I will turn your feasts into [a]mourning,
[b]And all your songs into lamentation;
[c]I will bring sackcloth on every waist,
And baldness on every head;
I will make it like mourning for an only *son,*
And its end like a bitter day.

11 “Behold, the days are coming,”
says the Lord GOD,
“That I will send a famine on the land,
Not a famine of bread,
Nor a thirst for water,
But [a]of hearing the words of the LORD.
12 They shall wander from sea to sea,
And from north to east;
They shall run to and fro,
seeking the word of the LORD,
But shall [a]not find *it.*

13 “In that day the fair virgins
And strong young men
Shall faint from thirst.
14 Those who [a]swear by [b]the [1]sin of Samaria,
Who say,
‘As your god lives, O Dan!’
And, ‘As the way of [c]Beersheba lives!’
They shall fall and never rise again.”

### *The LORD’s Judgments Inescapable*

9 I saw the Lord standing by the altar, and He
said:

"Strike the [1]doorposts,
that the thresholds may shake,
And [a]break them on the heads of them all.
I will slay the last of them with the sword.
[b]He who flees from them shall not get away,
And he who escapes from them shall not be delivered.

2 "Though[a] they dig into [1]hell,
From there My hand shall take them;
[b]Though they climb up to heaven,
From there I will bring them down;
3 And though they [a]hide themselves on top of Carmel,
From there I will search and take them;
Though they hide from My sight at the bottom of the sea,
From there I will command the serpent, and it shall bite them;
4 Though they go into captivity before their enemies,
From there [a]I will command the sword,
And it shall slay them.
[b]I will set My eyes on them for harm and not for good."

5 The Lord GOD of hosts,
He who touches the earth and it [a]melts,
[b]And all who dwell there mourn;
All of it shall swell like [1]the River,
And subside like the River of Egypt.
6 He who builds His [a]layers[1] in the sky,
And has founded His strata in the earth;
Who [b]calls for the waters of the sea,
And pours them out on the face of the earth—
[c]The LORD *is* His name.

7 "*Are* you not like the [1]people of Ethiopia to Me,
O children of Israel?" says the LORD.
"Did I not bring up Israel from the land of Egypt,
The [a]Philistines from [b]Caphtor,[2]
And the Syrians from [c]Kir?

8 "Behold, [a]the eyes of the Lord GOD *are* on the sinful kingdom,
And I [b]will destroy it from the face of the earth;
Yet I will not utterly destroy the house of Jacob,"
Says the LORD.
9 "For surely I will command,
And will [1]sift the house of Israel among all nations,
As *grain* is sifted in a sieve;
[a]Yet not the smallest [2]grain shall fall to the ground.
10 All the sinners of My people shall die by the sword,
[a]Who say, 'The calamity shall not overtake nor confront us.'

11 "On[a] that day I will raise up
The [1]tabernacle of David,
which has fallen down,
And [2]repair its damages;
I will raise up its ruins,
And rebuild it as in the days of old;
12 [a]That they may possess the remnant of [b]Edom,[1]
And all the Gentiles who are called by My name,"
Says the LORD who does this thing.

13 "Behold, [a]the days are coming,"
says the LORD,
"When the plowman shall overtake the reaper,
And the treader of grapes him who sows seed;
[b]The mountains shall drip with sweet wine,
And all the hills shall flow *with it.*
14 [a]I will bring back the captives of My people Israel;
[b]They shall build the waste cities
and inhabit *them;*
They shall plant vineyards
and drink wine from them;
They shall also make gardens
and eat fruit from them.
15 I will plant them in their land,
[a]And no longer shall they be pulled up
From the land I have given them,"
Says the LORD your God.

CHAPTER 9
1 [a]Hab. 3:13 [b]Amos 2:14 [1]Capitals of the pillars
2 [a]Ps. 139:8 [b]Jer. 51:53 [1]Or *Sheol*
3 [a]Jer. 23:24
4 [a]Lev. 26:33 [b]Jer. 21:10; 39:16; 44:11
5 [a]Mic. 1:4 [b]Amos 8:8 [1]The Nile
6 [a]Ps. 104:3, 13 [b]Amos 5:8 [c]Amos 4:13; 5:27 [1]Or *stairs*
7 [a]Jer. 47:4 [b]Deut. 2:23 [c]Amos 1:5 [1]Lit. *sons of the Ethiopians* [2]Crete
8 [a]Amos 9:4 [b]Jer. 5:10; 30:11
9 [a][Is. 65:8–16] [1]*shake* [2]Lit. *pebble*
10 [a]Amos 6:3
11 [a]Acts 15:16–18 [1]Lit. *booth;* a figure of a deposed dynasty [2]Lit. *wall up its breaches*
12 [a]Obad. 19 [b]Num. 24:18 [1]LXX *mankind*
13 [a]Lev. 26:5 [b]Joel 3:18
14 [a]Jer. 30:3, 18 [b]Is. 61:4
15 [a]Ezek. 34:28; 37:25

*The Book of*

# OBADIAH

### *Coming Judgment on Edom and Israel's Triumph*

THE vision of Obadiah.

Thus says the Lord GOD [a]concerning Edom
[b](We have heard a report from the LORD,
And a messenger has been sent among the nations, *saying,*
"Arise, and let us rise up against her for battle"):

2 "Behold, I will make you small among the nations;
You shall be greatly despised.
3 The [a]pride of your heart has deceived you,
*You* who dwell in the clefts of the rock,
Whose habitation is high;
[b]*You* who say in your heart,
'Who will bring me down to the ground?'
4 [a]Though you ascend *as* high as the eagle,
And though you [b]set your nest among the stars,
From there I will bring you down," says the LORD.

5 "If [a]thieves had come to you,
If robbers by night—
Oh, how you will be cut off!—

CHAPTER
1 [a]Is. 21:11; Ezek. 25:12; Joel 3:19; Mal. 1:3 [b]Jer. 49:14–16; Obad. 1–4
3 [a]Is. 16:6; Jer. 49:16 [b]Is. 14:13–15; Rev. 18:7
4 [a]Job 20:6 [b]Hab. 2:9; Mal. 1:4
5 [a]Jer. 49:9

Would they not have stolen till they had
  enough?
If grape-gatherers had come to you,
[b]Would they not have left *some* gleanings?

6 "Oh, how Esau shall be searched out!
*How* his hidden treasures shall be sought
  after!
7 All the men in your confederacy
Shall force you to the border;
[a]The men at peace with you
Shall deceive you *and* prevail against you.
*Those who eat* your bread shall lay a [1]trap
  for you.
[b]No[2] one is aware of it.
8 "Will[a] I not in that day," says the LORD,
"Even destroy the wise *men* from Edom,
And understanding from the mountains of
  Esau?
9 Then your [a]mighty men, O [b]Teman,
  shall be dismayed,
To the end that everyone from the
  mountains of Esau
May be cut off by slaughter.

**10** "For [a]violence against your brother Jacob,
Shame shall cover you,
And [b]you shall be cut off forever.
11 In the day that you [a]stood on the other
  side—
In the day that strangers carried captive his
  forces,
When foreigners entered his gates
And [b]cast lots for Jerusalem—
Even you *were* as one of them.

12 But you should not have [a]gazed[1] on the day
  of your brother
[2]In the day of his captivity;
Nor should you have [b]rejoiced over the
  children of Judah
In the day of their destruction;
Nor should you have spoken proudly
In the day of distress.
13 You should not have entered the gate of My
  people
In the day of their calamity.
Indeed, you should not have [1]gazed on their
  affliction
In the day of their calamity,
Nor laid *hands* on their substance
In the day of their calamity.
14 You should not have stood at the crossroads
To cut off those among them who escaped;
Nor should you have [1]delivered up those
  among them who remained
In the day of distress.

**15** "For[a] the day of the LORD upon all the nations
  *is* near;
[b]As you have done, it shall be done to you;
Your [1]reprisal shall return upon your own
  head.
16 [a]For as you drank on my holy mountain,
*So* shall all the nations drink continually;
Yes, they shall drink, and swallow,
And they shall be as though they had never
  been.

17 "But on Mount Zion there [a]shall be
  [1]deliverance,
And there shall be holiness;
The house of Jacob shall possess their
  possessions.
18 The house of Jacob shall be a fire,
And the house of Joseph [a]a flame;
But the house of Esau *shall be* stubble;
They shall kindle them and devour them,
And no survivor shall *remain* of the house of
  Esau,"
For the LORD has spoken.

**19** The [1]South [a]shall possess the mountains of
  Esau,
[b]And the Lowland shall possess Philistia.
They shall possess the fields of Ephraim
And the fields of Samaria.
Benjamin *shall possess* Gilead.
20 And the captives of this host of the children
  of Israel
*Shall possess the land* of the Canaanites
As [a]far as Zarephath.
The captives of Jerusalem who are in
  Sepharad
[b]Shall possess the cities of the [1]South.
21 Then [a]saviors[1] shall come to Mount Zion
To judge the mountains of Esau,
And the [b]kingdom shall be the LORD's.

**5** [b]Deut. 24:21
**7** [a]Jer. 38:22 [b]Is. 19:11; Jer. 49:7 [1]Or *wound* or *plot* [2]Or *There is no understanding in him*
**8** [a][Job 5:12–14]; Is. 29:14
**9** [a]Ps. 76:5 [b]Gen. 36:11; 1 Chr. 1:45; Job 2:11; Jer. 49:7
**10** [a]Gen. 27:41; Ezek. 25:12; Amos 1:11 [b]Ezek. 35:9; Joel 3:19
**11** [a]Ps. 83:5–8; Amos 1:6, 9 [b]Joel 3:3; Nah. 3:10
**12** [a]Mic. 4:11; 7:10 [b][Prov. 17:5]; Ezek. 35:15; 36:5 [1]Gloated over [2]Lit. *On the day he became a foreigner*
**13** [1]Gloated over
**14** [1]Handed over to the enemy
**15** [a]Ezek. 30:3; [Joel 1:15; 2:1, 11, 31; Amos 5:18, 20] [b]Jer. 50:29; 51:56; Hab. 2:8 [1]Or *reward*
**16** [a]Joel 3:17
**17** [a]Is. 14:1, 2; Joel 2:32; Amos 9:8 [1]Or *salvation*
**18** [a]Is. 5:24; 9:18, 19; Zech. 12:6
**19** [a]Is. 11:14; Amos 9:12 [b]Zeph. 2:7 [1]Heb. *Negev*
**20** [a]1 Kin. 17:9; Luke 4:26 [b]Jer. 32:44 [1]Heb. *Negev*
**21** [a][James 5:20] [b]Ps. 22:28; [Dan. 2:44; 7:14; Zech. 14:9; Rev. 11:15] [1]*deliverers*

# *The Book of* JONAH

## *Jonah's Disobedience and Punishment*

NOW the word of the LORD came to [a]Jonah
the son of Amittai, saying,
2 "Arise, go to [a]Nineveh, that [b]great city,
and cry out against it; for [c]their wickedness has
come up before Me."
3 But Jonah arose to flee to Tarshish from the
presence of the LORD. He went down to [a]Joppa,
and found a ship going to Tarshish; so he paid the
fare, and went down into it, to go with them to
[b]Tarshish [c]from the presence of the LORD.
**4** But [a]the LORD [1]sent out a great wind on the
sea, and there was a mighty tempest on the sea, so
that the ship was about to be broken up.
5 Then the mariners were afraid; and every man
cried out to his god, and threw the cargo that *was*
in the ship into the sea, to lighten [1]the load. But
Jonah had gone down [a]into the lowest parts of the
ship, had lain down, and was fast asleep.
6 So the captain came to him, and said to him,
"What do you mean, sleeper? Arise, [a]call on your
God; [b]perhaps your God will consider us, so that
we may not perish."
7 And they said to one another, "Come, let us
[a]cast lots, that we may know for whose cause this

CHAPTER 1
**1** [a]2 Kin. 14:25
**2** [a]Is. 37:37 [b]Gen. 10:11, 12 [c]Gen. 18:20
**3** [a]Josh. 19:46 [b]Is. 23:1 [c]Gen. 4:16
**4** [a]Ps. 107:25 [1]Lit. *hurled*
**5** [a]1 Sam. 24:3 [1]Lit. *from upon them*
**6** [a]Ps. 107:28 [b]Joel 2:14
**7** [a]Josh. 7:14

trouble *has come* upon us." So they cast lots, and
the lot fell on Jonah.
8 Then they said to him, [a]"Please tell us! For
whose cause *is* this trouble upon us? What is your
occupation? And where do you come from? What
is your country? And of what people are you?"
9 So he said to them, "I *am* a Hebrew; and I fear
[1]the LORD, the God of heaven, [a]who made the sea
and the dry *land.*"
**10** Then the men were exceedingly afraid, and
said to him, "Why have you done this?" For the
men knew that he fled from the presence of the
LORD, because he had told them.
11 Then they said to him, "What shall we do to
you that the sea may be calm for us?"—for the sea
was growing more tempestuous.
12 And he said to them, [a]"Pick me up and [1]throw
me into the sea; then the sea will become calm for
you. For I know that this great tempest *is* because
of me."
13 Nevertheless the men rowed hard to return to
land, [a]but they could not, for the sea continued to
grow more tempestuous against them.
14 Therefore they cried out to the LORD and said,
"We pray, O LORD, please do not let us perish for
this man's life, and [a]do not charge us with innocent blood; for You, O LORD, [b]have done as it
pleased You."
15 So they picked up Jonah and threw him into
the sea, [a]and the sea ceased from its raging.
16 Then the men [a]feared the LORD exceedingly,
and offered a sacrifice to the LORD and took vows.
**17** Now the LORD had prepared a great fish to
swallow Jonah. And [a]Jonah was in the belly of the
fish three days and three nights.

### *Jonah's Prayer and God's Answer*

**2** Then Jonah prayed to the LORD his God from
the fish's belly.
2 And he said:

"I [a]cried out to the LORD because of my
affliction,
[b]And He answered me.

"Out of the belly of Sheol I cried,
*And* You heard my voice.
3 [a]For You cast me into the deep,
Into the heart of the seas,
And the floods surrounded me;
[b]All Your billows and Your waves passed over
me.
4 [a]Then I said, 'I have been cast out of Your
sight;
Yet I will look again [b]toward Your holy
temple.'
5 The [a]waters surrounded me, *even* to my soul;
The deep closed around me;
Weeds were wrapped around my head.
6 I went down to the [1]moorings of the
mountains;
The earth with its bars *closed* behind me
forever;
Yet You have brought up my [a]life from the
pit,
O LORD, my God.

7 "When my soul fainted within me,
I remembered the LORD;
[a]And my prayer went *up* to You,
Into Your holy temple.

8 "Those who regard [a]worthless idols
Forsake their own [1]Mercy.

**8** [a]Josh. 7:19; 1 Sam. 14:43
**9** [a][Neh. 9:6]; Ps. 146:6; Acts 17:24 [1]Heb. *YHWH*
**12** [a]John 11:50 [1]Lit. *hurl*
**13** [a][Prov. 21:30]
**14** [a]Deut. 21:8 [b]Ps. 115:3; [Dan. 4:35]
**15** [a][Ps. 89:9; 107:29]; Luke 8:24
**16** [a]Mark 4:41; Acts 5:11
**17** [a][Matt. 12:40; Luke 11:30]

CHAPTER 2
**2** [a]1 Sam. 30:6; Ps. 120:1; Lam. 3:55 [b]Ps. 65:2
**3** [a]Ps. 88:6 [b]Ps. 42:7
**4** [a]Ps. 31:22; Jer. 7:15 [b]1 Kin. 8:38; 2 Chr. 6:38; Ps. 5:7
**5** [a]Ps. 69:1; Lam. 3:54
**6** [a]Job 33:28; [Ps. 16:10; Is. 38:17] [1]*foundations* or *bases*
**7** [a]2 Chr. 30:27; Ps. 18:6
**8** [a]2 Kin. 17:15; Ps. 31:6; Jer. 10:8 [1]Or *Lovingkindness*
**9** [a]Ps. 50:14, 23; Jer. 33:11; Hos. 14:2 [b]Job 22:27; [Eccl. 5:4, 5] [c]Ps. 3:8; [Is. 45:17] [d][Jer. 3:23]

CHAPTER 3
**3** [1]Exact meaning unknown
**4** [a][Deut. 18:22]
**5** [a][Matt. 12:41; Luke 11:32]
**6** [a]Job 2:8
**7** [a]2 Chr. 20:3; Dan. 3:29; Joel 2:15 [1]Lit. *great ones*
**8** [a]Is. 58:6 [b]Is. 59:6
**9** [a]2 Sam. 12:22; Joel 2:14; Amos 5:15
**10** [a]Ex. 32:14; Jer. 18:8; Amos 7:3, 6

CHAPTER 4
**2** [a]Jon. 1:3 [b]Ex. 34:6; Num. 14:18; Ps. 86:5, 15; Joel 2:13
**3** [a]1 Kin. 19:4; Job 6:8, 9 [b]Jon. 4:8
**6** [1]Heb. *kikayon,* exact identity unknown [2]Lit. *rejoiced with great joy*

9 But I will [a]sacrifice to You
With the voice of thanksgiving;
I will pay what I have [b]vowed.
[c]Salvation *is* of the [d]LORD."

**10** So the LORD spoke to the fish, and it vomited
Jonah onto dry *land.*

### *Nineveh Repents*

**3** Now the word of the LORD came to Jonah the
second time, saying,
2 "Arise, go to Nineveh, that great city, and
preach to it the message that I tell you."
3 So Jonah arose and went to Nineveh, according to the word of the LORD. Now Nineveh was an
exceedingly great city, [1]a three-day journey *in*
*extent.*
4 And Jonah began to enter the city on the first
day's walk. Then [a]he cried out and said, "Yet forty
days, and Nineveh shall be overthrown!"
**5** So the [a]people of Nineveh believed God, proclaimed a fast, and put on sackcloth, from the
greatest to the least of them.
6 Then word came to the king of Nineveh; and
he arose from his throne and laid aside his robe,
covered *himself* with sackcloth [a]and sat in ashes.
7 [a]And he caused *it* to be proclaimed and published throughout Nineveh by the decree of the
king and his [1]nobles, saying,

Let neither man nor beast, herd nor flock,
taste anything; do not let them eat, or drink
water.
8 But let man and beast be covered with
sackcloth, and cry mightily to God; yes, [a]let
every one turn from his evil way and from
[b]the violence that is in his hands.
9 [a]Who can tell *if* God will turn and relent, and
turn away from His fierce anger, so that we
may not perish?

**10** [a]Then God saw their works, that they turned
from their evil way; and God relented from the
disaster that He had said He would bring upon
them, and He did not do it.

### *God's Lesson to Jonah*

**4** But it displeased Jonah exceedingly, and he
became angry.
2 So he prayed to the LORD, and said, "Ah, LORD,
was not this what I said when I was still in my
country? Therefore I [a]fled previously to Tarshish;
for I know that You *are* a [b]gracious and merciful
God, slow to anger and abundant in lovingkindness, One who relents from doing harm.
3 [a]"Therefore now, O LORD, please take my life
from me, for [b]*it is* better for me to die than to
live!"
4 Then the LORD said, "*Is it* right for you to be
angry?"
**5** So Jonah went out of the city and sat on the
east side of the city. There he made himself a
shelter and sat under it in the shade, till he might
see what would become of the city.
6 And the LORD God prepared a [1]plant and made
it come up over Jonah, that it might be shade for
his head to deliver him from his misery. So Jonah
[2]was very grateful for the plant.
7 But as morning dawned the next day God
prepared a worm, and it *so* damaged the plant that
it withered.
8 And it happened, when the sun arose, that

God prepared a vehement east wind; and the sun
beat on Jonah's head, so that he grew faint. Then
he wished death for himself, and said, [a]"*It is* better
for me to die than to live."
9 Then God said to Jonah, "*Is it* right for you to
be angry about the plant?" And he said, "*It is* right
for me to be angry, even to death!"
10 But the LORD said, "You have had pity on the
plant for which you have not labored, nor made it
grow, which [1]came up in a night and perished in a
night.
11 "And should I not pity Nineveh, [a]that great
city, in which are more than one hundred and
twenty thousand persons [b]who cannot discern
between their right hand and their left—and
much livestock?"

8 [a]Jon. 4:3
10 [1]Lit. *was a son of a night*
11 [a]Jon. 1:2; 3:2, 3 [b]Deut. 1:39; Is. 7:16

*The Book of*

# MICAH

## *Judgment on Israel and Judah*

THE word of the LORD that came to [a]Micah of
Moresheth in the days of [b]Jotham, Ahaz, *and*
Hezekiah, kings of Judah, which he saw
concerning Samaria and Jerusalem.

2 Hear, all you peoples!
Listen, O earth, and all that is in it!
Let the Lord GOD be a witness against you,
The Lord from [a]His holy temple.

3 For behold, the LORD is coming out of His
place;
He will come down
And tread on the high places of the earth.
4 [a]The mountains will melt under Him,
And the valleys will split
Like wax before the fire,
Like waters poured down a steep place.
5 All this is for the transgression of Jacob
And for the sins of the house of Israel.
What *is* the transgression of Jacob?
*Is it* not Samaria?
And what *are* the [a]high places of Judah?
*Are they* not Jerusalem?

6 "Therefore I will make Samaria [a]a heap of
ruins in the field,
Places for planting a vineyard;
I will pour down her stones into the valley,
And I will [b]uncover her foundations.
7 All her carved images shall be beaten to
pieces,
And all her [a]pay as a harlot shall be burned
with the fire;
All her idols I will lay desolate,
For she gathered *it* from the pay of a harlot,
And they shall return to the [b]pay of a
harlot."

8 Therefore I will wail and howl,
I will go stripped and naked;
[a]I will make a wailing like the jackals
And a mourning like the ostriches,
9 For her wounds *are* incurable.
For [a]it has come to Judah;
It has come to the gate of My people—
To Jerusalem.

10 [a]Tell *it* not in Gath,
Weep not at all in [1]Beth Aphrah,
Roll yourself in the dust.
11 Pass by in naked shame,
you inhabitant of [1]Shaphir;
The inhabitant of [2]Zaanan does not go out.
Beth Ezel mourns;
Its place to stand is taken away from you.
12 For the inhabitant of [1]Maroth
[2]pined for good,
But [a]disaster came down from the LORD
To the gate of Jerusalem.
13 O inhabitant of [a]Lachish,
Harness the chariot to the swift steeds
(She *was* the beginning of sin to the
daughter of Zion),
For the transgressions of Israel were [b]found
in you.

14 Therefore you shall [a]give presents to
[1]Moresheth Gath;
The houses of [b]Achzib[2] *shall be* a lie
to the kings of Israel.
15 I will yet bring an heir to you,
O inhabitant of [a]Mareshah;[1]
The glory of Israel shall come to [b]Adullam.[2]
16 Make yourself [a]bald and cut off your hair,
Because of your [b]precious children;
Enlarge your baldness like an eagle,
For they shall go from you into [c]captivity.

## *Woe to the Oppressor of the Poor*

2 Woe to those who devise iniquity,
And [1]work out evil on their beds!
At [a]morning light they practice it,
Because it is in the power of their hand.
2 They [a]covet fields and take *them* by violence,
Also houses, and seize *them*.
So they oppress a man and his house,
A man and his inheritance.

3 Therefore thus says the LORD:

"Behold, against this [a]family I am devising
[b]disaster,
From which you cannot remove your necks;
Nor shall you walk haughtily,
For this *is* an evil time.
4 In that day *one* shall take up a proverb
against you,
And [a]lament with a bitter lamentation,
saying:
'We are utterly destroyed!
He has changed the [1]heritage of my people;
How He has removed *it* from me!
To [2]a turncoat He has divided our fields.'"
5 Therefore you will have no [1]one to determine
boundaries by lot
In the assembly of the LORD.

CHAPTER 1
1 [a][2 Pet. 1:21]; Jer. 26:18 [b]2 Kin. 15:5, 7, 32–38; 2 Chr. 27:1–9; Is. 1:1; Hos. 1:1
2 [a][Ps. 11:4]
4 [a]Amos 9:5
5 [a]Deut. 32:13; 33:29; Amos 4:13
6 [a]2 Kin. 19:25; Mic. 3:12 [b]Ezek. 13:14
7 [a]Hos. 2:5 [b]Deut. 23:18; Is. 23:17
8 [a]Ps. 102:6
9 [a]2 Kin. 18:13; Is. 8:7, 8
10 [a]2 Sam. 1:20 [1]Lit. *House of Dust*
11 [1]Lit. *Beautiful* [2]Lit. *Going Out*
12 [a]Is. 59:9–11; Jer. 14:19; Amos 3:6 [1]Lit. *Bitterness* [2]Lit. *was sick*
13 [a]Josh. 10:3; 2 Kin. 14:19; 18:14; Is. 36:2 [b]Ezek. 23:11
14 [a]2 Sam. 8:2 [b]Josh. 15:44 [1]Lit. *Possession of Gath* [2]Lit. *Lie*
15 [a]Josh. 15:44 [b]2 Chr. 11:7 [1]Lit. *Inheritance* [2]Lit. *Refuge*
16 [a]Job 1:20 [b]Lam. 4:5 [c]2 Kin. 17:6; Amos 7:11, 17; [Mic. 4:10]

CHAPTER 2
1 [a]Hos. 7:6, 7 [1]Plan
2 [a]Is. 5:8
3 [a]Ex. 20:5; Jer. 8:3; Amos 3:1, 2 [b]Amos 5:13
4 [a]2 Sam. 1:17 [1]Lit. *portion* [2]Lit. *one turning back,* an apostate
5 [1]Lit. *one casting a surveyor's line*

**6** "Do not prattle," *you say to those* who
[1]prophesy.
So they shall not prophesy [2]to you;
[3]They shall not return insult for insult.
7 *You who are* named the house of Jacob:
"Is the Spirit of the LORD restricted?
*Are* these His doings?
Do not My words do good
To him who walks uprightly?

8 "Lately My people have risen up as an
enemy—
You pull off the robe with the garment
From those who trust *you,* as they pass by,
Like men returned from war.
9 The women of My people you cast out
From their pleasant houses;
From their children
You have taken away My glory forever.

10 "Arise and depart,
For this *is* not *your* [a]rest;
Because it is [b]defiled, it shall destroy,
Yes, with utter destruction.
11 If a man should walk in a false spirit
And speak a lie, *saying,*
'I will [1]prophesy to you [2]of wine and drink,'
Even he would be the [a]prattler of this people.

**12** "I[a] will surely assemble all of you, O Jacob,
I will surely gather the remnant of Israel;
I will put them together [b]like sheep of [1]the
fold,
Like a flock in the midst of their pasture;
[c]They shall make a loud noise because of *so
many* people.
13 The one who breaks open will come up
before them;
They will break out,
Pass through the gate,
And go out by it;
[a]Their king will pass before them,
[b]With the LORD at their head."

## *Wicked Rulers and Prophets*

**3** And I said:
"Hear now, O heads of Jacob,
And you [a]rulers of the house of Israel:
[b]*Is it* not for you to know justice?
2 You who hate good and love evil;
Who strip the skin from [1]*My* people,
And the flesh from their bones;
3 Who also [a]eat the flesh of My people,
Flay their skin from them,
Break their bones,
And chop *them* in pieces
Like *meat* for the pot,
[b]Like flesh in the caldron."

4 Then [a]they will cry to the LORD,
But He will not hear them;
He will even hide His face from them at that
time,
Because they have been evil in their deeds.

**5** Thus says the LORD [a]concerning the prophets
Who make my people stray;
Who chant [1]"Peace"
[2]While they [b]chew with their teeth,
But who prepare war against him
[c]Who puts nothing into their mouths:
6 "Therefore[a] you shall have night
without [1]vision,
And you shall have darkness
without divination;
The sun shall go down on the prophets,
And the day shall be dark for [b]them.
7 So the seers shall be ashamed,
And the diviners abashed;
Indeed they shall all cover their lips;
[a]For *there is* no answer from God."

**8** But truly I am full of power
by the Spirit of the LORD,
And of justice and might,
[a]To declare to Jacob his transgression
And to Israel his sin.
9 Now hear this,
You heads of the house of Jacob
And rulers of the house of Israel,
Who abhor justice
And [1]pervert all equity,
10 [a]Who build up Zion with [b]bloodshed
And Jerusalem with iniquity:
11 [a]Her heads judge for a bribe,
[b]Her priests teach for pay,
And her prophets divine for [1]money.
[c]Yet they lean on the LORD, and say,
"Is not the LORD among us?
No harm can come upon us."
12 Therefore because of you
Zion shall be [a]plowed *like* a field,
[b]Jerusalem shall become heaps of ruins,
And [c]the mountain of the [1]temple
Like the bare hills of the forest.

## *Swords into Plowshares*

**4** Now [a]it shall come to pass in the latter days
*That* the mountain of the LORD's house
Shall be established on the top of the
mountains,
And shall be exalted above the hills;
And peoples shall flow to it.
2 Many nations shall come and say,
"Come, and let us go up to the mountain of
the LORD,
To the house of the God of Jacob;
He will teach us His ways,
And we shall walk in His paths."
For out of Zion the law shall go forth,
And the word of the LORD from Jerusalem.
3 He shall judge between many peoples,
And rebuke strong nations afar off;
They shall beat their swords
into [a]plowshares,
And their spears into [1]pruning hooks;
Nation shall not lift up sword against nation,
[b]Neither shall they learn war anymore.

4 [a]But everyone shall sit under his vine
and under his fig tree,
And no one shall make *them* afraid;
For the mouth of the LORD of hosts has
spoken.
5 For all people walk
each in the name of his god,
But [a]we will walk
in the name of the LORD our God
Forever and ever.

**6** "In that day," says the LORD,
[a]"I will assemble the lame,
[b]I will gather the outcast
And those whom I have afflicted;

**6** [1]Or *preach,* lit. *drip* words [2]Lit. *to these* [3]Vg. *He shall not take shame*
**10** [a]Deut. 12:9 [b]Lev. 18:25
**11** [a]Is. 30:10; Jer. 5:30, 31; 2 Tim. 4:3, 4 [1]Or *preach,* lit. *drip* [2]*concerning*
**12** [a][Mic. 4:6, 7] [b]Jer. 31:10 [c]Ezek. 33:22; 36:37 [1]Heb. *Bozrah*
**13** [a][Hos. 3:5] [b]Is. 52:12

CHAPTER 3
**1** [a]Ezek. 22:27 [b]Ps. 82:1–5; Jer. 5:4, 5
**2** [1]Lit. *them*
**3** [a]Ps. 14:4; 27:2; Zeph. 3:3 [b]Ezek. 11:3, 6, 7
**4** [a]Ps. 18:41; Prov. 1:28; Is. 1:15; Jer. 11:11
**5** [a]Is. 56:10, 11; Jer. 6:13; Ezek. 13:10, 19 [b]Matt. 7:15 [c]Ezek. 13:18 [1]All is well [2]For those who feed them
**6** [a]Is. 8:20–22; 29:10–12 [b]Is. 29:10; [Jer. 23:33–40]; Ezek. 13:23 [1]Prophetic revelation
**7** [a]Amos 8:11
**8** [a]Is. 58:1
**9** [1]Lit. *twist*
**10** [a]Jer. 22:13, 17 [b]Ezek. 22:27; Hab. 2:12
**11** [a]Is. 1:23; Mic. 7:3 [b]Jer. 6:13 [c]Is. 48:2; Jer. 7:4 [1]Lit. *silver*
**12** [a]Jer. 26:18 [b]Ps. 79:1; Jer. 9:11 [c]Mic. 4:1, 2 [1]Lit. *house*

CHAPTER 4
**1** [a]Is. 2:2–4; Ezek. 17:22; Dan. 2:28; 10:14; Hos. 3:5
**3** [a]Is. 2:4; Joel 3:10 [b]Ps. 72:7 [1]*pruning knives*
**4** [a]1 Kin. 4:25; Zech. 3:10
**5** [a]Zech. 10:12
**6** [a]Ezek. 34:16 [b]Ps. 147:2

7 I will make the lame [a]a remnant,
And the outcast a strong nation;
So the LORD [b]will reign over them in Mount Zion
From now on, even forever.
8 And you, O tower of the flock,
The stronghold of the daughter of Zion,
To you shall it come,
Even the former dominion shall come,
The kingdom of the daughter of Jerusalem."

**9** Now why do you cry aloud?
[a]*Is there* no king in your midst?
Has your counselor perished?
For [b]pangs have seized you like a woman in [1]labor.
10 Be in pain, and labor to bring forth,
O daughter of Zion,
Like a woman in birth pangs.
For now you shall go forth from the city,
You shall dwell in the field,
And to [a]Babylon you shall go.
There you shall be delivered;
There the [b]LORD will [c]redeem you
From the hand of your enemies.

11 [a]Now also many nations have gathered against you,
Who say, "Let her be defiled,
And let our eye [b]look upon Zion."
12 But they do not know [a]the thoughts of the LORD,
Nor do they understand His counsel;
For He will gather them [b]like sheaves to the threshing floor.

13 "Arise[a] and [b]thresh, O daughter of Zion;
For I will make your horn iron,
And I will make your hooves bronze;
You shall [c]beat in pieces many peoples;
[d]I will consecrate their gain to the LORD,
And their substance to [e]the Lord of the whole earth."

## *The Messiah Will Be Born at Bethlehem*

**5** Now gather yourself in troops,
O daughter of troops;
He has laid siege against us;
They will [a]strike the judge of Israel with a rod on the cheek.

**2** "But you, [a]Bethlehem [b]Ephrathah,
*Though* you are little [c]among the [d]thousands of Judah,
*Yet* out of you shall come forth to Me
The One to be [e]Ruler in Israel,
[f]Whose goings forth *are* from of old,
From [1]everlasting."

3 Therefore He shall give them up,
Until the time *that* [a]she who is in labor has given birth;
Then [b]the remnant of His brethren
Shall return to the children of Israel.
4 And He shall stand and [a]feed[1] *His flock*
In the strength of the LORD,
In the majesty of the name of the LORD His God;
And they shall abide,
For now He [b]shall be great
To the ends of the earth;
5 And this *One* [a]shall be peace.

When the Assyrian comes into our land,
And when he treads in our palaces,
Then we will raise against him
Seven shepherds and eight princely men.
6 They shall [1]waste with the sword the land of Assyria,
And the land of [a]Nimrod at its entrances;
Thus He shall [b]deliver *us* from the Assyrian,
When he comes into our land
And when he treads within our borders.

7 Then [a]the remnant of Jacob
Shall be in the midst of many peoples,
[b]Like dew from the LORD,
Like showers on the grass,
That [1]tarry for no man
Nor [2]wait for the sons of men.
8 And the remnant of Jacob
Shall be among the Gentiles,
In the midst of many peoples,
Like a [a]lion among the beasts of the forest,
Like a young lion among flocks of sheep,
Who, if he passes through,
Both treads down and tears in pieces,
And none can deliver.
9 Your hand shall be lifted against your adversaries,
And all your enemies shall be [1]cut off.

**10** "And it shall be in that day," says the LORD,
"That I will [a]cut[1] off your [b]horses from your midst
And destroy your [c]chariots.
11 I will cut off the cities of your land
And throw down all your strongholds.
12 I will cut off sorceries from your hand,
And you shall have no [a]soothsayers.
13 [a]Your carved images I will also cut off,
And your sacred pillars from your midst;
You shall [b]no more worship
the work of your hands;
14 I will pluck your [1]wooden images from your midst;
Thus I will destroy your cities.
15 And I will [a]execute vengeance in anger and fury
On the nations that have not [1]heard."

## *God Pleads with Israel*

**6** Hear now what the LORD says:
"Arise, plead your case before the mountains,
And let the hills hear your voice.
2 [a]Hear, O you mountains, [b]the LORD's complaint,
And you strong foundations of the earth;
For [c]the LORD has a complaint against His people,
And He will [1]contend with Israel.

3 "O My people, what [a]have I done to you?
And how have I [b]wearied you?
Testify against Me.
4 [a]For I brought you up from the land of Egypt,
I redeemed you from the house of bondage;
And I sent before you Moses, Aaron, and Miriam.
5 O My people, remember now
What [a]Balak king of Moab counseled,
And what Balaam the son of Beor answered him,
From [1]Acacia Grove to Gilgal,
That you may know [b]the righteousness of the LORD."

---

**7** [a]Mic. 2:12 [b][Is. 9:6; 24:23]
**9** [a]Jer. 8:19 [b]Is. 13:8 [1]*childbirth*
**10** [a]Amos 5:27 [b][Is. 45:13] [c]Ps. 18:17
**11** [a]Lam. 2:16 [b]Obad. 12
**12** [a][Is. 55:8, 9] [b]Is. 21:10
**13** [a]Jer. 51:33 [b]Is. 41:15 [c]Dan. 2:44 [d]Is. 18:7 [e]Zech. 4:14

CHAPTER 5
**1** [a]Lam. 3:30
**2** [a]John 7:42 [b]Gen. 35:19; 48:7 [c]1 Sam. 23:23 [d]Ex. 18:25 [e][Is. 9:6] [f]Ps. 90:2 [1]Lit. *the days of eternity*
**3** [a]Mic. 4:10 [b]Mic. 4:7; 7:18
**4** [a][Is. 40:11; 49:9] [b]Ps. 72:8 [1]*shepherd*
**5** [a][Is. 9:6]
**6** [a]Gen. 10:8–11 [b]Is. 14:25 [1]*devastate*
**7** [a]Mic. 5:3 [b]Deut. 32:2 [1]*wait* [2]*delay*
**8** [a]Num. 24:9
**9** [1]*destroyed*
**10** [a]Zech. 9:10 [b]Deut. 17:16 [c]Is. 2:7; 22:18 [1]*destroy*
**12** [a]Is. 2:6
**13** [a]Zech. 13:2 [b]Is. 2:8
**14** [1]Or *Asherim,* Canaanite deities
**15** [a][2 Thess. 1:8] [1]*obeyed*

CHAPTER 6
**2** [a]Ps. 50:1, 4 [b]Hos. 12:2 [c][Is. 1:18] [1]*bring charges against*
**3** [a]Jer. 2:5, 31 [b]Is. 43:22, 23
**4** [a][Deut. 4:20]
**5** [a]Num. 22:5, 6 [b]Judg. 5:11 [1]Heb. *Shittim,* Num. 25:1; Josh. 2:1; 3:1

**6** With what shall I come before the LORD,
*And* bow myself before the High God?
Shall I come before Him with burnt offerings,
With calves a year old?
7 [a]Will the LORD be pleased with thousands of rams,
Ten thousand [b]rivers of oil?
[c]Shall I give my firstborn *for* my transgression,
[1]The fruit of my body *for* the sin of my soul?

8 He has [a]shown you, O man, what *is* good;
And what does the LORD require of you
But [b]to do justly,
To love [1]mercy,
And to walk humbly with your God?

**9** The LORD's voice cries to the city—
Wisdom shall see Your name:

"Hear the rod!
Who has appointed it?
10 Are there yet the treasures of wickedness
In the house of the wicked,
And the short measure *that is* an abomination?
11 Shall I count pure
*those* with [a]the wicked scales,
And with the bag of deceitful weights?
12 For her rich men are full of [a]violence,
Her inhabitants have spoken lies,
And [b]their tongue is deceitful in their mouth.

13 "Therefore I will also [a]make *you* sick by striking you,
By making *you* desolate because of your sins.
14 [a]You shall eat, but not be satisfied;
[1]Hunger *shall be* in your midst.
[2]You may carry *some* away,
but shall not save *them;*
And what you do rescue I will give over to the sword.

15 "You shall [a]sow, but not reap;
You shall tread the olives,
but not anoint yourselves with oil;
And *make* sweet wine, but not drink wine.
16 For the statutes of [a]Omri are [b]kept;
All the works of Ahab's house *are done;*
And you walk in their counsels,
That I may make you a [1]desolation,
And your inhabitants a hissing.
Therefore you shall bear the [c]reproach of [2]My people."

## *God Will Forgive Israel*

**7** Woe is me!
For I am like those who gather summer fruits,
Like those who [a]glean vintage grapes;
*There is no* cluster to eat
Of the first-ripe fruit *which* [b]my soul desires.
2 The [a]faithful[1] *man* has perished from the earth,
And *there is* no one upright among men.
They all lie in wait for blood;
[b]Every man hunts his brother with a net.

3 That they may successfully do evil with both hands—
The prince asks *for gifts,*
The judge *seeks* a [a]bribe,
And the great *man* utters his evil desire;
So they scheme together.
4 The best of them *is* [a]like a brier;
The most upright *is sharper* than a thorn hedge;
The day of your watchman and your punishment comes;
Now shall be their perplexity.

5 [a]Do not trust in a friend;
Do not put your confidence in a companion;
Guard the doors of your mouth
From her who lies in your [b]bosom.
6 For [a]son dishonors father,
Daughter rises against her mother,
Daughter-in-law against her mother-in-law;
A man's enemies *are* the men of his own household.
7 Therefore I will look to the LORD;
I will [a]wait for the God of my salvation;
My God will hear me.

**8** [a]Do not rejoice over me, my enemy;
[b]When I fall, I will arise;
When I sit in darkness,
The LORD *will be* a light to me.
9 [a]I will bear the indignation of the LORD,
Because I have sinned against Him,
Until He pleads my [b]case
And executes justice for me.
He will bring me forth to the light;
I will see His righteousness.
10 Then *she who is* my enemy will see,
And [a]shame will cover her who said to me,
[b]"Where is the LORD your God?"
My eyes will see her;
Now she will be trampled down
Like mud in the streets.

11 *In* the day when your [a]walls are to be built,
*In* that day [1]the decree shall go far and wide.
12 *In* that day [a]they[1] shall come to you
From Assyria and the [2]fortified cities,
From the [3]fortress to [4]the River,
From sea to sea,
And mountain *to* mountain.
13 Yet the land shall be desolate
Because of those who dwell in it,
And [a]for the fruit of their deeds.

**14** Shepherd Your people with Your staff,
The flock of Your heritage,
Who dwell [1]solitarily *in* a [a]woodland,
In the midst of Carmel;
Let them feed *in* Bashan and Gilead,
As in days of old.

15 "As[a] in the days when you came out of the land of Egypt,
I will show [1]them [b]wonders."

**16** The nations [a]shall see and be ashamed
of all their might;
[b]They shall put *their* hand over *their* mouth;
Their ears shall be deaf.
17 They shall lick the [a]dust like a serpent;
[b]They shall crawl from their holes like [1]snakes of the earth.
[c]They shall be afraid of the LORD our God,
And shall fear because of You.
18 [a]Who *is* a God like You,
[b]Pardoning iniquity

**7** [a]Is. 1:11 [b]Job 29:6 [c]2 Kin. 16:3 [1]My own child
**8** [a][Deut. 10:12] [b]Gen. 18:19 [1]Or *lovingkindness*
**11** [a]Hos. 12:7
**12** [a]Mic. 2:1, 2 [b]Jer. 9:2–6, 8
**13** [a]Lev. 26:16
**14** [a]Lev. 26:26 [1]Or *Emptiness* or *Humiliation* [2]Tg., Vg. *You shall take hold*
**15** [a]Amos 5:11
**16** [a]1 Kin. 16:25, 26 [b]Hos. 5:11 [c]Is. 25:8 [1]Or *object of horror* [2]So with MT, Tg., Vg.; LXX *nations*

CHAPTER 7
**1** [a]Is. 17:6 [b]Is. 28:4
**2** [a]Is. 57:1 [b]Hab. 1:15 [1]Or *loyal*
**3** [a]Mic. 3:11
**4** [a]Ezek. 2:6
**5** [a]Jer. 9:4 [b]Deut. 28:56
**6** [a]Matt. 10:36
**7** [a]Is. 25:9
**8** [a]Prov. 24:17 [b][Prov. 24:16]
**9** [a]Lam. 3:39, 40 [b]Jer. 50:34
**10** [a]Ps. 35:26 [b]Ps. 42:3
**11** [a][Amos 9:11] [1]Or *the boundary shall be extended*
**12** [a][Is. 11:16; 19:23–25] [1]Lit. *he,* collective of the captives [2]Heb. *arey mazor,* possibly *cities of Egypt* [3]Heb. *mazor,* possibly *Egypt* [4]The Euphrates
**13** [a]Jer. 21:14
**14** [a]Is. 37:24 [1]Alone
**15** [a]Ps. 68:22; 78:12 [b]Ex. 34:10 [1]Lit. *him,* collective for the captives
**16** [a]Is. 26:11 [b]Job 21:5
**17** [a][Is. 49:23] [b]Ps. 18:45 [c]Jer. 33:9 [1]Lit. *crawlers*
**18** [a]Ex. 15:11 [b]Ex. 34:6, 7, 9

And passing over the transgression of [c]the
remnant of His heritage?
[d]He does not retain His anger forever,
Because He delights *in* [e]mercy.[1]
19 He will again have compassion on us,
And will subdue our iniquities.
You will cast all [1]our sins
Into the depths of the sea.
20 [a]You will give truth to Jacob
*And* [1]mercy to Abraham,
[b]Which You have sworn to our fathers
From days of old.

18 [c]Mic. 4:7 [d]Ps. 103:8, 9, 13 [e][Ezek. 33:11] [1]Or *lovingkindness*
19 [1]Lit. *their*
20 [a]Luke 1:72, 73 [b]Ps. 105:9 [1]Or *lovingkindness*

*The Book of*

# NAHUM

### *God's Mercy and Judgment*

THE [1]burden [a]against Nineveh. The book of the vision of Nahum the Elkoshite.

2 God *is* [a]jealous, and the LORD avenges;
The LORD avenges and *is* furious.
The LORD will take vengeance on His
adversaries,
And He reserves *wrath* for His enemies;
3 The LORD *is* [a]slow to anger
and [b]great in power,
And will not at all acquit *the wicked.*
[c]The LORD has His way
In the whirlwind and in the storm,
And the clouds *are* the dust of His feet.
4 [a]He rebukes the sea and makes it dry,
And dries up all the rivers.
[b]Bashan and Carmel wither,
And the flower of Lebanon wilts.
5 The mountains quake before Him,
The hills melt,
And the earth [1]heaves at His presence,
Yes, the world and all who dwell in it.
6 Who can stand before His indignation?
And [a]who can endure the fierceness of His
anger?
His fury is poured out like fire,
And the rocks are thrown down by Him.
7 [a]The LORD *is* good,
A stronghold in the day of trouble;
And [b]He knows those who trust in Him.
8 But with an overflowing flood
He will make an utter end of its place,
And darkness will pursue His enemies.
9 [a]What do you [1]conspire against the LORD?
[b]He will make an utter end *of it.*
Affliction will not rise up a second time.
10 For while tangled [a]*like* thorns,
[b]And while drunken *like* drunkards,
[c]They shall be devoured like stubble fully
dried.
11 From you comes forth *one*
Who plots evil against the LORD,
A [1]wicked counselor.
12 Thus says the LORD:
"Though *they are* [1]safe, and likewise many,
Yet in this manner they will be [a]cut down
When he passes through.
Though I have afflicted you,
I will afflict you no more;
13 For now I will break off his yoke from you,
And burst your bonds apart."
14 The LORD has given a command concerning
you:
[1]"Your name shall be perpetuated no longer.
Out of the house of your gods
I will cut off the carved image
and the molded image.
I will dig your [a]grave,
For you are [b]vile."[2]
15 Behold, on the mountains
The [a]feet of him who brings good tidings,
Who proclaims peace!
O Judah, keep your appointed feasts,
Perform your vows.
For the [1]wicked one shall no more pass
through you;
He is [b]utterly cut off.

### *The Destruction of Nineveh*

2 He[1] who scatters has come up before your
face.
Man the fort!
Watch the road!
Strengthen *your* flanks!
Fortify *your* power mightily.
2 For the LORD will restore the excellence of
Jacob
Like the excellence of Israel,
For the emptiers have emptied them out
And ruined their vine branches.
3 The shields of his mighty men *are* made red,
The valiant men *are* in scarlet.
The chariots *come* with flaming torches
In the day of his preparation,
And [1]the spears are brandished.
4 The chariots rage in the streets,
They jostle one another in the broad roads;
They seem like torches,
They run like lightning.
5 He remembers his nobles;
They stumble in their walk;
They make haste to her walls,
And the defense is prepared.
6 The gates of the rivers are opened,
And the palace is dissolved.
7 [1]It is decreed:
She shall be led away captive,
She shall be brought up;
And her maidservants shall lead *her*
as with the voice of doves,
Beating their breasts.

CHAPTER 1
1 [a]2 Kin. 19:36; Jon. 1:2; Nah. 2:8; Zeph. 2:13 [1]*oracle, prophecy*
2 [a]Ex. 20:5; Josh. 24:19
3 [a]Ex. 34:6, 7; Neh. 9:17; Ps. 103:8 [b][Job 9:4] [c]Ps. 18:17
4 [a]Josh. 3:15, 16; Ps. 106:9; Is. 50:2; Matt. 8:26 [b]Is. 33:9
5 [1]Tg. *burns*
6 [a]Jer. 10:10; [Mal. 3:2]
7 [a]Ps. 25:8; 37:39, 40; 100:5; [Jer. 33:11]; Lam. 3:25 [b]Ps. 1:6; John 10:14; 2 Tim. 2:19
9 [a]Ps. 2:1; Nah. 1:11 [b]1 Sam. 3:12 [1]Or *devise*
10 [a]2 Sam. 23:6; Mic. 7:4 [b]Is. 56:12; Nah. 3:11 [c]Is. 5:24; 10:17; Mal. 4:1
11 [1]Lit. *counselor of Belial*
12 [a][Is. 10:16–19, 33, 34] [1]Or *at peace* or *complete*
14 [a]Ezek. 32:22, 23 [b]Nah. 3:6 [1]Lit. *No more of your name shall be fruitful* [2]Or *contemptible*
15 [a]Is. 40:9; 52:7; Rom. 10:15 [b]Is. 29:7, 8 [1]Lit. *one of Belial*

CHAPTER 2
1 [1]Vg. *He who destroys*
3 [1]Lit. *the cypresses are shaken;* LXX, Syr. *the horses rush about;* Vg. *the drivers are stupefied*
7 [1]Heb. *Huzzab*

8 Though Nineveh of old *was* like a pool of
water,
Now they flee away.
[1]"Halt! Halt!" *they cry;*
But no one turns back.
9 [1]Take spoil of silver!
Take spoil of [a]gold!
*There is* no end of treasure,
Or wealth of every desirable prize.
10 She is empty, desolate, and waste!
The heart melts, and the knees shake;
Much pain *is* in every side,
And all their faces [1]are drained of color.

11 Where *is* the dwelling of the [a]lions,
And the feeding place of the young lions,
Where the lion walked,
the lioness *and* lion's cub,
And no one made *them* afraid?
12 The lion tore in pieces enough for his cubs,
[1]Killed for his lionesses,
[a]Filled his caves with prey,
And his dens with [2]flesh.

13 "Behold, [a]I *am* against you," says the LORD of
hosts, "I will burn [1]your chariots in smoke, and
the sword shall devour your young lions; I will cut
off your prey from the earth, and the voice of your
[b]messengers shall be heard no more."

### *Judgment for Nineveh's Sins*

**3** Woe to the [a]bloody city!
It *is* all full of lies *and* robbery.
*Its* [1]victim never departs.
2 The noise of a whip
And the noise of rattling wheels,
Of galloping horses,
Of [1]clattering chariots!
3 Horsemen charge with bright sword and
glittering spear.
*There is* a multitude of slain,
A great number of bodies,
Countless corpses—
They stumble over the corpses—
4 Because of the multitude of [1]harlotries of the
[2]seductive harlot,
[a]The mistress of sorceries,
Who sells nations through her harlotries,
And families through her sorceries.

5 "Behold, I *am* [a]against you,"
says the LORD of hosts;
[b]"I will lift your skirts over your face,
I will show the nations your nakedness,
And the kingdoms your shame.
6 I will cast abominable filth upon you,
Make you [a]vile,[1]
And make you [b]a spectacle.
7 It shall come to pass *that* all who look upon
you
[a]Will flee from you, and say,
[b]'Nineveh is laid waste!
[c]Who will bemoan her?'
Where shall I seek comforters for you?"

8 [a]Are you better than [b]No[1] Amon
*That was* situated by the [2]River,
That had the waters around her,
Whose rampart *was* the sea,
Whose wall *was* the sea?
9 Ethiopia and Egypt *were* her strength,
And *it was* boundless;
[a]Put and Lubim were [1]your helpers.
10 Yet she *was* carried away,
She went into captivity;
[a]Her young children also were dashed to
pieces
[b]At the head of every street;
They [c]cast lots for her honorable men,
And all her great men were bound in chains.
11 You also will be [a]drunk;
You will be hidden;
You also will seek refuge from the enemy.

12 All your strongholds *are* [a]fig trees with
ripened figs:
If they are shaken,
They fall into the mouth of the eater.
13 Surely, [a]your people in your midst *are*
women!
The gates of your land are wide open for
your enemies;
Fire shall devour the [b]bars of your *gates.*

14 Draw your water for the siege!
[a]Fortify your strongholds!
Go into the clay and tread the mortar!
Make strong the brick kiln!
15 There the fire will devour you,
The sword will cut you off;
It will eat you up like a [a]locust.

Make yourself many—like the locust!
Make yourself many—
like the *swarming* locusts!
16 You have multiplied your [a]merchants more
than the stars of heaven.
The locust plunders and flies away.
17 [a]Your commanders *are* like *swarming* locusts,
And your generals like great grasshoppers,
Which camp in the hedges on a cold day;
When the sun rises they flee away,
And the place where they *are* is not known.

18 [a]Your shepherds slumber, O [b]king of Assyria;
Your nobles rest *in the dust.*
Your people are [c]scattered on the mountains,
And no one gathers them.
19 Your injury *has* no healing,
[a]Your wound is severe.
[b]All who hear news of you
Will clap *their* hands over you,
For upon whom has not your wickedness
passed continually?

---

8 [1]Lit. *Stand*
9 [a]Zeph. 1:18 [1]*Plunder*
10 [1]LXX, Tg., Vg. *gather blackness;* Joel 2:6
11 [a]Job 4:10, 11
12 [a]Jer. 51:34 [1]Lit. *Strangled* [2]Torn flesh
13 [a]Nah. 3:5 [b]2 Kin. 18:17–25; 19:9–13, 23 [1]Lit. *her*

CHAPTER 3
1 [a]Hab. 2:12 [1]Lit. *prey*
2 [1]*bounding* or *jolting*
4 [a]Is. 47:9–12 [1]Spiritual unfaithfulness [2]Lit. *goodly charm,* in a bad sense
5 [a]Nah. 2:13 [b]Is. 47:2, 3
6 [a]Nah. 1:14 [b]Heb. 10:33 [1]*despicable*
7 [a]Rev. 18:10 [b]Jon. 3:3; 4:11 [c]Jer. 15:5
8 [a]Amos 6:2 [b]Jer. 46:25 [1]Ancient Thebes; Tg., Vg. *populous Alexandria* [2]Lit. *rivers,* the Nile and the surrounding canals
9 [a]Ezek. 27:10 [1]LXX *her*
10 [a]Hos. 13:16 [b]Lam. 2:19 [c]Joel 3:3
11 [a]Nah. 1:10
12 [a]Rev. 6:12, 13
13 [a]Is. 19:16 [b]Jer. 51:30
14 [a]Nah. 2:1
15 [a]Joel 1:4
16 [a]Rev. 18:3, 11–19
17 [a]Rev. 9:7
18 [a]Ps. 76:5, 6 [b]Jer. 50:18 [c]1 Kin. 22:17
19 [a]Mic. 1:9 [b]Lam. 2:15

The Book of

# Habakkuk

### The Prophet Questions God's Judgments

THE [1]burden which the prophet Habakkuk saw.

2 O LORD, how long shall I cry,
[a]And You will not hear?
Even cry out to You, [b]"Violence!"
And You will [c]not save.
3 Why do You show me iniquity,
And cause *me* to see [1]trouble?
For plundering and violence *are* before me;
There is strife, and contention arises.
4 Therefore the law is powerless,
And justice never goes forth.
For the [a]wicked surround the righteous;
Therefore perverse judgment proceeds.

5 "Look[a] among the nations and watch—
Be utterly astounded!
For *I will* work a work in your days
*Which* you would not believe,
though it were told *you*.
6 For indeed I am [a]raising up the Chaldeans,
A bitter and hasty [b]nation
Which marches through the breadth of the earth,
To possess dwelling places *that are* not theirs.
7 They are terrible and dreadful;
Their judgment and their dignity proceed from themselves.
8 Their horses also are [a]swifter than leopards,
And more fierce than evening wolves.
Their [1]chargers [2]charge ahead;
Their cavalry comes from afar;
They fly as the [b]eagle *that* hastens to eat.

9 "They all come for violence;
Their faces are set *like* the east wind.
They gather captives like sand.
10 They scoff at kings,
And princes are scorned by them.
They deride every stronghold,
For they heap up earthen *mounds*
and seize it.
11 Then *his* [1]mind changes, and he transgresses;
He commits offense,
[a]*Ascribing* this power to his god."

12 Are You not [a]from everlasting,
O LORD my God, my Holy One?
We shall not die.
O LORD, [b]You have appointed them
for judgment;
O Rock, You have marked them
for [c]correction.
13 *You are* of purer eyes than to behold evil,
And cannot look on wickedness.
Why do You look on those who deal treacherously,
*And* hold Your tongue when the wicked devours
A *person* more righteous than he?
14 *Why* do You make men like fish of the sea,
Like creeping things *that have* no ruler over them?

15 They take up all of them with a hook,
They catch them in their net,
And gather them in their dragnet.
Therefore they rejoice and are glad.
16 Therefore [a]they sacrifice to their net,
And burn incense to their dragnet;
Because by them their share *is* [1]sumptuous
And their food plentiful.
17 Shall they therefore empty their net,
And continue to slay nations without pity?

### The Just Shall Live By Faith

2 I will [a]stand my watch
And set myself on the rampart,
And watch to see what He will say to me,
And what I will answer when I am corrected.

2 Then the LORD answered me and said:
[a]"Write the vision
And make *it* plain on tablets,
That he may run who reads it.
3 For [a]the vision *is* yet for an appointed time;
But at the end it will speak,
and it will [b]not lie.
Though it tarries, [c]wait for it;
Because it will [d]surely come,
It will not tarry.

4 "Behold the proud,
His soul is not upright in him;
But the [a]just shall live by his faith.

5 "Indeed, because he transgresses by wine,
*He is* a proud man,
And he does not stay at home.
Because he [a]enlarges his desire as [1]hell,
And he *is* like death, and cannot be satisfied,
He gathers to himself all nations
And heaps up for himself all peoples.

6 "Will not all these [a]take up a proverb against him,
And a taunting riddle against him, and say,
'Woe to him who increases
*What* is not his—how long?
And to him who loads himself with [1]many pledges'?
7 Will not [1]your creditors rise up suddenly?
Will they not awaken who oppress you?
And you will become their booty.
8 [a]Because you have plundered many nations,
All the remnant of the people shall plunder you,
Because of men's [1]blood
And the violence of the land *and* the city,
And of all who dwell in it.

9 "Woe to him who covets evil gain for his house,
That he may [a]set his nest on high,
That he may be delivered from the [1]power of disaster!
10 You give shameful counsel to your house,
Cutting off many peoples,
And sin *against* your soul.
11 For the stone will cry out from the wall,
And the beam from the timbers will
answer it.

CHAPTER 1
1 [1]*oracle, prophecy*
2 [a]Lam. 3:8 [b]Mic. 2:1, 2; 3:1–3 [c][Job 21:5–16]
3 [1]Or *toil*
4 [a]Jer. 12:1
5 [a]Is. 29:14; Ezek. 12:22–28
6 [a]Deut. 28:49, 50; 2 Kin. 24:2; 2 Chr. 36:17; Jer. 4:11–13; Mic. 4:10 [b]Ezek. 7:24; 21:31
8 [a]Jer. 4:13 [b]Job 9:26; 39:29, 30; Lam. 4:19; Ezek. 17:3; Hos. 8:1; Matt. 24:28; Luke 17:37 [1]Lit. *horsemen* [2]Lit. *spring about*
11 [a]Dan. 5:4 [1]Lit. *spirit* or *wind*
12 [a]Deut. 33:27; Ps. 90:2; 93:2; Mal. 3:6 [b]Is. 10:5–7; Mal. 3:5 [c]Jer. 25:9
16 [a]Deut. 8:17 [1]Lit. *fat*

CHAPTER 2
1 [a]Is. 21:8, 11
2 [a]Is. 8:1
3 [a]Dan. 8:17, 19; 10:14 [b]Ezek. 12:24, 25 [c][Heb. 10:37, 38] [d]Ps. 27:13, 14; [James 5:7, 8; 2 Pet. 3:9]
4 [a][John 3:36]
5 [a]Prov. 27:20; 30:16; Is. 5:11–15 [1]Or *Sheol*
6 [a]Mic. 2:4 [1]Syr., Vg. *thick clay*
7 [1]Lit. *those who bite you*
8 [a]Is. 33:1; Jer. 27:7; Ezek. 39:10; Zech. 2:8 [1]Or *bloodshed*
9 [a]Jer. 49:16; Obad. 4 [1]Lit. *hand of evil*

**12** "Woe to him who builds a town with
bloodshed,
Who establishes a city by iniquity!
13 Behold, *is it* not of the LORD of hosts
That the peoples labor [1]to feed the fire,
And nations weary themselves in vain?
14 For the earth will be filled
With the knowledge of the glory of the LORD,
As the waters cover the sea.

**15** "Woe to him who gives drink to his neighbor,
[1]Pressing *him to* your [a]bottle,
Even to make *him* drunk,
That you may look on [2]his nakedness!
16 You are filled with shame instead of glory.
You also—drink!
And [1]be exposed as uncircumcised!
The cup of the LORD's right hand *will be*
turned against you,
And utter shame will be on your glory.
17 For the violence *done to* Lebanon will cover
you,
And the plunder of beasts *which* made them
afraid,
Because of men's blood
And the violence of the land *and* the city,
And of all who dwell in it.

**18** "What profit is the image,
that its maker should carve it,
The molded image, a teacher of lies,
That the maker of its mold should trust in it,
To make mute idols?
19 Woe to him who says to wood, 'Awake!'
To silent stone, 'Arise! It shall teach!'
Behold, it is overlaid with gold and silver,
Yet in it there is no breath at all.

20 "But[a] the LORD is in His holy temple.
Let all the earth keep silence before Him."

## *The Prophet's Prayer*

**3** A prayer of Habakkuk the prophet, on [1]Shigionoth.

**2** O LORD, I have heard your speech
*and* was afraid;
O LORD, revive Your work
in the midst of the years!
In the midst of the years make *it* known;
In wrath remember mercy.

**3** God came from Teman,
The Holy One from Mount Paran. Selah

His glory covered the heavens,
And the earth was full of His praise.
4 *His* brightness was like the light;
He had rays *flashing* from His hand,
And there His power *was* hidden.
5 Before Him went pestilence,
And fever followed at His feet.

6 He stood and measured the earth;
He looked and startled the nations.
[a]And the everlasting mountains were
scattered,
The perpetual hills bowed.
His ways *are* everlasting.
7 I saw the tents of Cushan in affliction;
The curtains of the land of Midian trembled.

**8** O LORD, were *You* displeased with the rivers,
*Was* Your anger against the rivers,
*Was* Your wrath against the sea,
That You rode on Your horses,
Your chariots of salvation?
9 Your bow was made quite ready;
Oaths were sworn over *Your* [1]arrows. Selah

You divided the earth with rivers.
10 The mountains saw You *and* trembled;
The overflowing of the water passed by.
The deep uttered its voice,
*And* [a]lifted its hands on high.
11 The [a]sun and moon stood still in their
habitation;
At the light of Your arrows they went,
At the shining of Your glittering spear.

12 You marched through the land in
indignation;
You [1]trampled the nations in anger.
13 You went forth for the salvation of Your
people,
For salvation with Your Anointed.
You struck the head from the house of the
wicked,
By laying bare from foundation to neck. Selah

14 You thrust through with his own arrows
The head of his villages.
They came out like a whirlwind to scatter
me;
Their rejoicing was like feasting on the poor
in secret.
15 [a]You walked through the sea with Your
horses,
Through the heap of great waters.

**16** When I heard, [a]my body trembled;
My lips quivered at *the* voice;
Rottenness entered my bones;
And I trembled in myself,
That I might rest in the day of trouble.
When he comes up to the people,
He will invade them with his troops.

**17** Though the fig tree may not blossom,
Nor fruit be on the vines;
Though the labor of the olive may fail,
And the fields yield no food;
Though the flock may be cut off from the
fold,
And there be no herd in the stalls—
18 Yet I will [a]rejoice in the LORD,
I will joy in the God of my salvation.

19 [1]The LORD God is my strength;
He will make my feet like [a]deer's *feet*,
And He will make me [b]walk on my high hills.

To the Chief Musician. With my stringed instruments.

---

**13** [1]Lit. *for what satisfies fire,* for what is of no lasting value
**15** [a]Hos. 7:5 [1]Lit. *Attaching* or *Joining* [2]Lit. *their*
**16** [1]DSS, LXX *reel;* [Syr.], Vg. *fall fast asleep*
**20** [a]Zeph. 1:7; Zech. 2:13

CHAPTER 3
**1** [1]Exact meaning unknown
**6** [a]Nah. 1:5
**9** [1]Lit. *tribes* or *rods,* cf. v. 14
**10** [a]Ex. 14:22
**11** [a]Josh. 10:12–14
**12** [1]Or *threshed*
**15** [a]Ps. 77:19; Hab. 3:8
**16** [a]Ps. 119:120
**18** [a]Is. 41:16; 61:10
**19** [a]2 Sam. 22:34; Ps. 18:33 [b]Deut. 32:13; 33:29 [1]Heb. *YHWH Adonai*

# The Book of ZEPHANIAH

*The Great Day of the Lord*

THE word of the LORD which came to Zephaniah the son of Cushi, the son of Gedaliah, the son of Amariah, the son of Hezekiah, in the days of ªJosiah the son of Amon, king of Judah.

2 "I will ¹utterly consume everything
    From the face of the land,"
    Says the LORD;
3 "Iª will consume man and beast;
    I will consume the birds of the heavens,
    The fish of the sea,
    And the ¹stumbling blocks along with the wicked.
    I will cut off man from the face of the ²land,"
    Says the LORD.
4 "I will stretch out My hand against Judah,
    And against all the inhabitants of Jerusalem.
    ¹I will cut off every trace of Baal from this place,
    The names of the ªidolatrous² priests with the *pagan* priests—
5 Those ªwho worship the host of heaven on the housetops;
    Those who worship and swear *oaths* by the LORD,
    But who also swear ᵇby ¹Milcom;
6 ªThose who have turned back from *following* the LORD,
    And ᵇhave not sought the LORD, nor inquired of Him."
7 ªBe silent in the presence of the Lord GOD;
    ᵇFor the day of the LORD *is* at hand,
    For ᶜthe LORD has prepared a sacrifice;
    He has ¹invited His guests.
8 "And it shall be,
    In the day of the LORD'S sacrifice,
    That I will punish ªthe princes and the king's children,
    And all such as are clothed with foreign apparel.
9 In the same day I will punish
    All those who ªleap over the threshold,
    Who fill their masters' houses with violence and deceit.
10 "And there shall be on that day,"
    says the LORD,
    "The sound of a mournful cry from ªthe Fish Gate,
    A wailing from the Second Quarter,
    And a loud crashing from the hills.
11 ªWail, you inhabitants of ¹Maktesh!
    For all the merchant people are cut down;
    All those who handle money are cut off.
12 "And it shall come to pass at that time
    *That* I will search Jerusalem with lamps,
    And punish the men
    Who are ªsettled ¹in complacency,
    ᵇWho say in their heart,
    'The LORD will not do good,
    Nor will He do evil.'
13 Therefore their goods shall become booty,
    And their houses a desolation;
    They shall build houses,
    but not inhabit *them;*
    They shall plant vineyards,
    but ªnot drink their wine."
14 Theª great day of the LORD *is* near;
    *It is* near and hastens quickly.
    The noise of the day of the LORD is bitter;
    There the mighty men shall cry out.
15 ªThat day *is* a day of wrath,
    A day of trouble and distress,
    A day of devastation and desolation,
    A day of darkness and gloominess,
    A day of clouds and thick darkness,
16 A day of ªtrumpet and alarm
    Against the fortified cities
    And against the high towers.
17 "I will bring distress upon men,
    And they shall ªwalk like blind men,
    Because they have sinned against the LORD;
    Their blood shall be poured out like dust,
    And their flesh like refuse."
18 ªNeither their silver nor their gold
    Shall be able to deliver them
    In the day of the LORD'S wrath;
    But the whole land shall be devoured
    By the fire of His jealousy,
    For He will make speedy riddance
    Of all those who dwell in the land.

*Warning to the Nations*

2 Gatherª yourselves together,
    yes, gather together,
    O ¹undesirable nation,
2 Before the decree is issued,
    *Or* the day passes like chaff,
    Before the LORD'S fierce anger comes upon you,
    Before the day of the LORD'S anger comes upon you!
3 ªSeek the LORD, ᵇall you meek of the earth,
    Who have upheld His justice.
    Seek righteousness, seek humility.
    ᶜIt may be that you will be hidden
    In the day of the LORD'S anger.
4 For ªGaza shall be forsaken,
    And Ashkelon desolate;
    They shall drive out Ashdod ᵇat noonday,
    And Ekron shall be uprooted.
5 Woe to the inhabitants of ªthe seacoast,
    The nation of the Cherethites!
    The word of the LORD *is* against you,
    O ᵇCanaan, land of the Philistines:
    "I will destroy you;
    So there shall be no inhabitant."
6 The seacoast shall be pastures,
    With ¹shelters for shepherds
    ªand folds for flocks.
7 The coast shall be for ªthe remnant of the house of Judah;
    They shall feed *their* flocks there;
    In the houses of Ashkelon they shall lie down at evening.

---

**CHAPTER 1**
1 ª2 Kin. 22:1, 2; 2 Chr. 34:1–33; Jer. 1:2; 22:11
2 ¹Lit. *make a complete end of,* Jer. 8:13
3 ªHos. 4:3 ¹Idols ²*ground*
4 ª2 Kin. 23:5; Hos. 10:5 ¹Fulfilled in 2 Kin. 23:4, 5 ²Heb. *chemarim*
5 ª2 Kin. 23:12; Jer. 19:13 ᵇJosh. 23:7 ¹Or *Malcam,* An Ammonite god, 1 Kin. 11:5; Jer. 49:1; *Molech,* Lev. 18:21
6 ªIs. 1:4; Jer. 2:13 ᵇHos. 7:7
7 ªHab. 2:20; Zech. 2:13 ᵇIs. 13:6 ᶜDeut. 28:26; Is. 34:6; Jer. 46:10; Ezek. 39:17–19 ¹Lit. *set apart, consecrated*
8 ªJer. 39:6
9 ª1 Sam. 5:5
10 ª2 Chr. 33:14; Neh. 3:3; 12:39
11 ªJames 5:1 ¹A market district of Jerusalem, lit. *Mortar*
12 ªJer. 48:11; Amos 6:1 ᵇPs. 94:7 ¹Lit. *on their lees;* like the dregs of wine
13 ªDeut. 28:39
14 ªJer. 30:7; Joel 2:1, 11
15 ªIs. 22:5
16 ªIs. 27:13; Jer. 4:19
17 ªDeut. 28:29
18 ªEzek. 7:19

**CHAPTER 2**
1 ª2 Chr. 20:4; Joel 1:14; 2:16 ¹Or *shameless*
3 ªPs. 105:4; Amos 5:6 ᵇPs. 76:9 ᶜJoel 2:14; Amos 5:14, 15
4 ªJer. 47:1, 5; Amos 1:7, 8; Zech. 9:5 ᵇJer. 6:4
5 ªEzek. 25:15–17 ᵇJosh. 13:3
6 ªIs. 17:2 ¹Underground huts or cisterns, lit. *excavations*
7 ª[Mic. 5:7, 8]

For the LORD their God will [b]intervene[1] for them,
And [c]return their captives.

8 "I[a] have heard the reproach of Moab,
And [b]the insults of the people of Ammon,
With which they have reproached My people,
And [c]made arrogant threats against their borders.
9 Therefore, as I live,"
Says the LORD of hosts, the God of Israel,
"Surely [a]Moab shall be like Sodom,
And [b]the people of Ammon like Gomorrah—
[c]Overrun[1] with weeds and saltpits,
And a [2]perpetual desolation.
The residue of My people shall plunder them,
And the remnant of My people shall possess them."

10 This they shall have [a]for their pride,
Because they have reproached and made arrogant threats
Against the people of the LORD of hosts.
11 The LORD *will be* awesome to them,
For He will reduce to nothing all the gods of the earth;
[a]*People* shall worship Him,
Each one from his place,
Indeed all [b]the shores of the nations.

12 "You[a] Ethiopians also,
You shall be slain by [b]My sword."

13 And He will stretch out His hand against the north,
[a]Destroy Assyria,
And make Nineveh a desolation,
As dry as the wilderness.
14 The herds shall lie down in her midst,
[a]Every beast of the nation.
Both the [b]pelican and the bittern
Shall lodge on the capitals *of* her *pillars;*
Their voice shall sing in the windows;
Desolation *shall be* at the threshold;
For He will lay bare the [c]cedar work.
15 This is the rejoicing city
[a]That dwelt securely,
[b]That said in her heart,
"I *am it,* and *there is* none besides me."
How has she become a desolation,
A place for beasts to lie down!
Everyone who passes by her
[c]Shall hiss and [d]shake his fist.

### *Jerusalem's Sin and Redemption*

3 Woe to her who is rebellious and polluted,
To the oppressing city!
2 She has not obeyed *His* voice,
She has not received correction;
She has not trusted in the LORD,
She has not drawn near to her God.

3 [a]Her princes in her midst *are* roaring lions;
Her judges *are* [b]evening wolves
That leave not a bone till morning.
4 Her [a]prophets are insolent, treacherous people;
Her priests have [1]polluted the sanctuary,
They have done [b]violence to the law.
5 The LORD *is* righteous in her midst,
He will do no unrighteousness.
[1]Every morning He brings His justice to light;
He never fails,
But [a]the unjust knows no shame.

6 "I have cut off nations,
Their fortresses are devastated;
I have made their streets desolate,
With none passing by.
Their cities are destroyed;
*There is* no one, no inhabitant.
7 [a]I said, 'Surely you will fear Me,
You will receive instruction'—
So that her dwelling would not be cut off,
*Despite* everything for which I punished her.
But [1]they rose early
and [b]corrupted all their deeds.

8 "Therefore [a]wait for Me," says the LORD,
"Until the day I rise up [1]for plunder;
My determination *is* to [b]gather the nations
To My assembly of kingdoms,
To pour on them My indignation,
All my fierce anger;
All the earth [c]shall be devoured
With the fire of My jealousy.

9 "For then I will restore to the peoples
[a]a pure [1]language,
That they all may call on the name of the LORD,
To serve Him with one accord.
10 [a]From beyond the rivers of Ethiopia
My worshipers,
The daughter of My dispersed ones,
Shall bring My offering.
11 In that day you shall not be shamed for any of your deeds
In which you transgress against Me;
For then I will take away from your midst
Those who [a]rejoice in your pride,
And you shall no longer be haughty
In My holy mountain.
12 I will leave in your midst
[a]A meek and humble people,
And they shall trust in the name of the LORD.
13 [a]The remnant of Israel [b]shall do no unrighteousness
[c]And speak no lies,
Nor shall a deceitful tongue be found in their mouth;
For [d]they shall feed *their* flocks and lie down,
And no one shall make *them* afraid."

14 [a]Sing, O daughter of Zion!
Shout, O Israel!
Be glad and rejoice with all *your* heart,
O daughter of Jerusalem!
15 The LORD has taken away your judgments,
He has cast out your enemy.
[a]The King of Israel, the LORD,
[b]*is* in your midst;
You shall [1]see disaster no more.

16 In that day [a]it shall be said to Jerusalem:
"Do not fear;
Zion, [b]let not your hands be weak.
17 The LORD your God [a]in your midst,
The Mighty One, will save;
[b]He will rejoice over you with gladness,
He will quiet *you* with His love,
He will rejoice over you with singing."

18 "I will gather those who [a]sorrow over the appointed assembly,
Who are among you,
*To whom* its reproach *is* a burden.
19 Behold, at that time
I will deal with all who afflict you;
I will save the [a]lame,

7 [b]Luke 1:68 [c]Jer. 29:14 [1]Lit. *visit them*
8 [a]Jer. 48:27 [b]Ezek. 25:3 [c]Jer. 49:1
9 [a]Is. 15:1–9 [b]Amos 1:13 [c]Deut. 29:23 [1]Lit. *Possessed by nettles* [2]Or *permanent ruin*
10 [a]Is. 16:6
11 [a]Mal. 1:11 [b]Gen. 10:5
12 [a]Is. 18:1–7 [b]Ps. 17:13
13 [a]Is. 10:5–27; 14:24–27
14 [a]Is. 13:21 [b]Is. 14:23; 34:11 [c]Jer. 22:14
15 [a]Is. 47:8 [b]Rev. 18:7 [c]Lam. 2:15 [d]Nah. 3:19

CHAPTER 3
3 [a]Ezek. 22:27 [b]Hab. 1:8
4 [a]Hos. 9:7 [b]Ezek. 22:26 [1]Or *profaned*
5 [a]Jer. 3:3 [1]Lit. *Morning by morning*
7 [a]Jer. 8:6 [b]Gen. 6:12 [1]They were eager
8 [a]Hab. 2:3 [b]Joel 3:2 [c]Zeph. 1:18 [1]LXX, [Syr.] *for witness;* Tg. *for the day of My revelation for judgment;* Vg. *for the day of My resurrection that is to come*
9 [a]Is. 19:18; 57:19 [1]Lit. *lip*
10 [a]Ps. 68:31
11 [a]Is. 2:12; 5:15
12 [a]Is. 14:32
13 [a][Mic. 4:7] [b]Is. 60:21 [c]Rev. 14:5 [d]Ezek. 34:13–15, 28
14 [a]Is. 12:6
15 [a][John 1:49] [b]Ezek. 48:35 [1]So with Heb. mss., LXX, Bg.; MT, Vg. *fear*
16 [a]Is. 35:3, 4 [b]Heb. 12:12
17 [a]Zeph. 3:5, 15 [b]Is. 62:5; 65:19
18 [a]Lam. 2:6
19 [a][Mic. 4:6, 7]

And gather those who were driven out;
I will appoint them for praise and fame
In every land where they were put to shame.
20 At that time [a]I will bring you back,
Even at the time I gather you;
For I will give you [1]fame and praise
Among all the peoples of the earth,
When I return your captives before your eyes,"
Says the LORD.

20 [a]Is. 11:12; Ezek. 28:25; Amos 9:14 [1]Lit. *a name*

*The Book of*
# HAGGAI

## *The Command to Build God's House*

IN [a]the second year of King Darius, in the sixth
month, on the first day of the month, the
word of the LORD came by [b]Haggai the
prophet to [c]Zerubbabel the son of Shealtiel, governor of Judah, and to [d]Joshua the son of [e]Jehoza-
dak, the high priest, saying,
2 "Thus speaks the LORD of hosts, saying: 'This
people says, "The time has not come, the time
that the LORD's house should be built." ' "
3 Then the word of the LORD [a]came by Haggai
the prophet, saying,
4 "*Is it* [a]time for you yourselves to dwell in your
paneled houses, and this [1]temple *to lie* in ruins?"
5 Now therefore, thus says the LORD of hosts:
[a]"Consider your ways!

6 "You have [a]sown much, and bring in little;
You eat, but do not have enough;
You drink, but you are not filled with drink;
You clothe yourselves, but no one is warm;
And [b]he who earns wages,
Earns wages *to put* into a bag with holes."

7 Thus says the LORD of hosts: "Consider your
ways!
8 "Go up to the [a]mountains and bring wood and
build the [1]temple, that I may take pleasure in it
and be glorified," says the LORD.
9 [a]"*You* looked for much, but indeed *it came to*
little; and when you brought it home, [b]I blew it
away. Why?" says the LORD of hosts. "Because of
My house that *is in* ruins, while every one of you
runs to his own house.
10 "Therefore [a]the heavens above you withhold
the dew, and the earth withholds its fruit.
11 "For I [a]called for a drought on the land and
the mountains, on the grain and the new wine and
the oil, on whatever the ground brings forth, on
men and livestock, and on [b]all the labor of *your*
hands."
12 [a]Then Zerubbabel the son of Shealtiel, and
Joshua the son of Jehozadak, the high priest, with
all the remnant of the people, obeyed the voice of
the LORD their God, and the words of Haggai the
prophet, as the LORD their God had sent him; and
the people feared the presence of the LORD.
13 Then Haggai, the LORD's messenger, spoke the
LORD's message to the people, saying, [a]"I *am* with
you, says the LORD."
14 So [a]the LORD stirred up the spirit of Zerubbabel the son of Shealtiel, [b]governor of Judah, and
the spirit of Joshua the son of Jehozadak, the high
priest, and the spirit of all the remnant of the
people; [c]and they came and worked on the house
of the LORD of hosts, their God,
15 on the twenty-fourth day of the sixth month,
in the second year of King Darius.

## *The Glory of the New Temple*

2 In the seventh *month,* on the twenty-first of
the month, the word of the LORD came [1]by
Haggai the prophet, saying:
2 "Speak now to Zerubbabel the son of Shealtiel, governor of Judah, and to Joshua the son of
Jehozadak, the high priest, and to the remnant of
the people, saying:
3 [a]'Who is left among you who saw this [1]temple
in its former glory? And how do you see it now? In
comparison with it, [b]*is this* not in your eyes as
nothing?
4 'Yet now [a]be strong, Zerubbabel,' says the
LORD; 'and be strong, Joshua, son of Jehozadak,
the high priest; and be strong, all you people of
the land,' says the LORD, 'and work; for I *am* with
you,' says the LORD of hosts.
5 [a]'*According to* the word that I covenanted
with you when you came out of Egypt, so [b]My
Spirit remains among you; do not fear!'
6 "For thus says the LORD of hosts: [a]'Once more
(it *is* a little while) [b]I will shake heaven and earth,
the sea and dry land;
7 'and I will shake all nations, and they shall
come to [a]the [1]Desire of All Nations, and I will fill
this [2]temple with [b]glory,' says the LORD of hosts.
8 'The silver *is* Mine, and the gold *is* Mine,' says
the LORD of hosts.
9 [a]'The glory of this latter [1]temple shall be
greater than the former,' says the LORD of hosts.
'And in this place I will give [b]peace,' says the LORD
of hosts."
10 On the twenty-fourth *day* of the ninth *month,*
in the second year of Darius, the word of the LORD
came by Haggai the prophet, saying,
11 "Thus says the LORD of hosts: 'Now, [a]ask the
priests *concerning the* law, saying,
12 "If one carries holy meat in the fold of his
garment, and with the edge he touches bread or
stew, wine or oil, or any food, will it become
holy?" ' " Then the priests answered and said,
"No."
13 And Haggai said, "If *one who is* [a]unclean
*because* of a dead body touches any of these, will
it be unclean?" So the priests answered and said,
"It shall be unclean."
14 Then Haggai answered and said, [a]" 'So is this
people, and so is this nation before Me,' says the
LORD, 'and so is every work of their hands; and
what they offer there is unclean.
15 'And now, carefully [a]consider from this day

CHAPTER 1
1 [a]Ezra 4:24; Hag. 2:10; Zech. 1:1, 7 [b]Ezra 5:1; 6:14 [c]1 Chr. 3:19; Ezra 2:2; Neh. 7:7; Zech. 4:6; Matt. 1:12, 13 [d]Ezra 5:2, 3; Zech. 6:11 [e]1 Chr. 6:15
3 [a]Ezra 5:1
4 [a]2 Sam. 7:2 [1]Lit. *house*
5 [a]Lam. 3:40
6 [a]Deut. 28:38–40; Hos. 8:7; Hag. 1:9, 10; 2:16, 17 [b]Zech. 8:10
8 [a]Ezra 3:7 [1]Lit. *house*
9 [a]Hag. 2:16 [b]Hag. 2:17
10 [a]Lev. 26:19; Deut. 28:23; 1 Kin. 8:35; Joel 1:18–20
11 [a]1 Kin. 17:1; 2 Kin. 8:1 [b]Hag. 2:17
12 [a]Ezra 5:2
13 [a][Matt. 28:20; Rom. 8:31]
14 [a]2 Chr. 36:22; Ezra 1:1 [b]Hag. 2:21 [c]Ezra 5:2, 8; Neh. 4:6

CHAPTER 2
1 [1]Lit. *by the hand of*
3 [a]Ezra 3:12, 13 [b]Zech. 4:10 [1]Lit. *house*
4 [a]Deut. 31:23; 1 Chr. 22:13; 28:20; Zech. 8:9; Eph. 6:10
5 [a]Ex. 29:45, 46 [b][Neh. 9:20]; Is. 63:11, 14
6 [a]Heb. 12:26 [b][Joel 3:16]
7 [a]Gen. 49:10; Mal. 3:1 [b]1 Kin. 8:11; Is. 60:7; Zech. 2:5 [1]Or *desire of all nations* [2]Lit. *house*
9 [a][John 1:14] [b]Ps. 85:8, 9; Luke 2:14; [Eph. 2:14] [1]Lit. *house*
11 [a]Lev. 10:10, 11; Deut. 33:10; Mal. 2:7
13 [a]Lev. 22:4–6; Num. 19:11, 22
14 [a][Titus 1:15]
15 [a]Hag. 1:5, 7; 2:18

forward: from before stone was laid upon stone in
the temple of the LORD—
16 'since those *days,* [a]when *one* came to a heap of
twenty ephahs, there were *but* ten; when *one*
came to the wine vat to draw out fifty baths from
the press, there were *but* twenty.
17 [a]'I struck you with blight and mildew and hail
[b]in all the labors of your hands; [c]yet you did not
*turn* to Me,' says the LORD.
18 'Consider now from this day forward, from the
twenty-fourth day of the ninth month, from [a]the
day that the foundation of the LORD's temple was
laid—consider it:
19 [a]'Is the seed still in the barn? As yet the vine,
the fig tree, the pomegranate, and the olive tree
have not yielded *fruit. But* from this day I will
[b]bless *you.'* "
**20** And again the word of the LORD came to
Haggai on the twenty-fourth day of the month,
saying,
21 "Speak to Zerubbabel, [a]governor of Judah,
saying:

[b]'I will shake heaven and earth.
22 [a]I will overthrow the throne of kingdoms;
I will destroy the strength
of the Gentile kingdoms.
[b]I will overthrow the chariots
And those who ride in them;
The horses and their riders shall come down,
Every one by the sword of his brother.

23 'In that day,' says the LORD of hosts, 'I will
take you, Zerubbabel My servant, the son of
Shealtiel,' says the LORD, [a]'and will make you like
a signet *ring;* for [b]I have chosen you,' says the
LORD of hosts."

16 [a]Zech. 8:10
17 [a]Deut. 28:22 [b]Hag. 1:11 [c]Amos 4:6–11
18 [a]Zech. 8:9
19 [a]Zech. 8:12 [b][Mal. 3:10]
21 [a]Zech. 4:6–10 [b]Hag. 2:6, 7
22 [a][Dan. 2:44] [b]Mic. 5:10
23 [a]Song 8:6 [b]Is. 42:1; 43:10

*The Book of*

# ZECHARIAH

## *The Vision of the Horses*

IN the eighth month [a]of the second year of
Darius, the word of the LORD came [b]to Zechariah the son of Berechiah, the son of [c]Iddo the
prophet, saying,
2 "The LORD has been very angry with your
fathers.
3 "Therefore say to them, 'Thus says the LORD
of hosts: "Return [a]to Me," says the LORD of hosts,
"and I will return to you," says the LORD of hosts.
4 "Do not be like your fathers, [a]to whom the
former prophets preached, saying, 'Thus says the
LORD of hosts: [b]"Turn now from your evil ways
and your evil deeds." ' But they did not hear nor
heed Me," says the LORD.

5 "Your fathers, where *are* they?
And the prophets, do they live forever?
6 Yet surely [a]My words and My statutes,
Which I commanded My servants the
prophets,
Did they not overtake your fathers?

"So they returned and said:

[b]'Just as the LORD of hosts determined
to do to us,
According to our ways
and according to our deeds,
So He has dealt with us.' " ' "

7 On the twenty-fourth day of the eleventh
month, which is the month Shebat, in the second
year of Darius, the word of the LORD came to
Zechariah the son of Berechiah, the son of Iddo
the prophet:
8 I saw by night, and behold, [a]a man riding on a
red horse, and it stood among the myrtle trees in
the hollow; and behind him *were* [b]horses: red,
sorrel, and white.
9 Then I said, [a]"My lord, what *are* these?" So
the angel who talked with me said to me, "I will
show you what they *are.*"
10 And the man who stood among the myrtle
trees answered and said, [a]"These *are the ones*
whom the LORD has sent to walk to and fro
throughout the earth."
11 [a]So they answered the Angel of the LORD, who
stood among the myrtle trees, and said, "We have
walked to and fro throughout the earth, and
behold, all the earth is [1]resting quietly."
**12** Then the Angel of the LORD answered and
said, "O LORD of hosts, [a]how long will You not
have mercy on Jerusalem and on the cities of
Judah, against which You were angry [b]these
seventy years?"
13 And the LORD answered the angel who talked
to me, *with* [a]good *and* comforting words.
14 So the angel who spoke with me said to me,
[1]"Proclaim, saying, 'Thus says the LORD of hosts:

"I am [a]zealous[2] for Jerusalem
And for Zion with great [3]zeal.
15 I am exceedingly angry with the nations at
ease;
For [a]I was a little angry,
And they helped—*but* with evil *intent."*

16 'Therefore thus says the LORD:

[a]"I am returning to Jerusalem with mercy;
My [b]house [c]shall be built in it,"
says the LORD of hosts,
"And [d]a *surveyor's* line shall be stretched out
over Jerusalem." '

17 "Again proclaim, saying, 'Thus says the LORD
of hosts:

"My cities shall again [1]spread out through
prosperity;
[a]The LORD will again comfort Zion,
And [b]will again choose Jerusalem." ' "

**18** Then I raised my eyes and looked, and there
*were* four [a]horns.
19 And I said to the angel who talked with me,
"What *are* these?" So he answered me, [a]"These

CHAPTER 1
1 [a]Zech. 7:1 [b]Matt. 23:35 [c]Neh. 12:4, 16
3 [a][Mal. 3:7–10]
4 [a]2 Chr. 36:15, 16 [b]Is. 31:6
6 [a][Is. 55:11] [b]Lam. 1:18; 2:17
8 [a][Rev. 6:4] [b][Zech. 6:2–7]
9 [a]Zech. 4:4, 5, 13; 6:4
10 [a][Heb. 1:14]
11 [a][Ps. 103:20, 21] [1]Lit. *sitting and quiet*
12 [a]Ps. 74:10 [b]Jer. 25:11, 12; 29:10
13 [a]Jer. 29:10
14 [a]Zech. 8:2 [1]Lit. *Cry out* [2]Or *jealous* [3]Or *jealousy*
15 [a]Is. 47:6
16 [a][Zech. 2:10; 8:3] [b]Ezra 6:14, 15 [c]Is. 44:28 [d]Zech. 2:1–3
17 [a][Is. 40:1, 2; 51:3] [b]Zech. 2:12 [1]Or *overflow with good*
18 [a][Lam. 2:17]
19 [a]Ezra 4:1, 4, 7

*are* the [1]horns that have scattered Judah, Israel,
and Jerusalem."
20 Then the LORD showed me four craftsmen.
21 And I said, "What are these coming to do?" So
he said, "These *are* the [a]horns that scattered
Judah, so that no one could lift up his head; but
[1]*the craftsmen* are coming to terrify them, to cast
out the horns of the nations that [b]lifted up *their*
horn against the land of Judah to scatter it."

### *The Man with the Measuring Line*

2 Then I raised my eyes and looked, and behold,
[a]a man with a measuring line in his hand.
2 So I said, "Where are you going?" And he said
to me, [a]"To measure Jerusalem, to see what *is* its
width and what *is* its length."
3 And there *was* the angel who talked with me,
going out; and another angel was coming out to
meet him,
4 who said to him, "Run, speak to this young
man, saying: [a]'Jerusalem shall be inhabited *as*
towns without walls, because of the multitude of
men and livestock in it.
5 'For I,' says the LORD, 'will be [a]a wall of fire all
around her, [b]and I will be the glory in her midst.' "
6 "Up, up! Flee [a]from the land of the north,"
says the LORD; "for I have [b]spread you abroad like
the four winds of heaven," says the LORD.
7 "Up, Zion! [a]Escape, you who dwell with the
daughter of Babylon."
8 For thus says the LORD of hosts: "He sent Me
after glory, to the nations which plunder you; for
he who [a]touches you touches the [1]apple of His
eye.
9 "For surely I will [a]shake My hand against
them, and they shall become [1]spoil for their servants. Then [b]you will know that the LORD of hosts
has sent Me.
10 [a]"Sing and rejoice, O daughter of Zion! For
behold, I am coming and I [b]will dwell in your
midst," says the LORD.
11 [a]"Many nations shall be joined to the LORD [b]in
that day, and they shall become [c]My people. And I
will dwell in your midst. Then [d]you will know that
the LORD of hosts has sent Me to you.
12 "And the LORD will [a]take possession of Judah
as His inheritance in the Holy Land, and will again
choose Jerusalem.
13 [a]"Be silent, all flesh, before the LORD, for He is
aroused [b]from His holy habitation!"

### *Joshua Vindicated*

3 Then he showed me [a]Joshua the high priest
standing before the Angel of the LORD, and
[b]Satan[1] standing at his right hand to oppose him.
2 And the LORD said to Satan, [a]"The LORD
rebuke you, Satan! The LORD who [b]has chosen
Jerusalem rebuke you! [c]*Is* this not a brand plucked
from the fire?"
3 Now Joshua was clothed with [a]filthy garments, and was standing before the Angel.
4 Then He answered and spoke to those who
stood before Him, saying, "Take away the filthy
garments from him." And to him He said, "See, I
have removed your iniquity from you, [a]and I will
clothe you with rich robes."
5 And I said, "Let them put a clean [a]turban on
his head." So they put a clean turban on his head,
and they put the clothes on him. And the Angel of
the LORD stood by.
6 Then the Angel of the LORD admonished
Joshua, saying,
7 "Thus says the LORD of hosts:

'If you will walk in My ways,
And if you will [a]keep My command,
Then you shall also [b]judge My house,
And likewise have charge of My courts;
I will give you places to walk
Among these who [c]stand here.

8 'Hear, O Joshua, the high priest,
You and your companions who sit before
you,
For they are [a]a[1] wondrous sign;
For behold, I am bringing forth [b]My Servant
the [c]BRANCH.
9 For behold, the stone
That I have laid before Joshua:
[a]Upon the stone *are* [b]seven eyes.
Behold, I will engrave its inscription,'
Says the LORD of hosts,
'And [c]I will remove the iniquity of that land
in one day.
10 [a]In that day,' says the LORD of hosts,
'Everyone will invite his neighbor
[b]Under his vine and under his fig tree.' "

### *The Lampstand and the Olive Trees*

4 Now [a]the angel who talked with me came
back and wakened me, [b]as a man who is
wakened out of his sleep.
2 And he said to me, "What do you see?" So I
said, "I am looking, and there *is* [a]a lampstand of
solid gold with a bowl on top of it, [b]and on the
*stand* seven lamps with seven pipes to the seven
lamps.
3 [a]"Two olive trees *are* by it, one at the right of
the bowl and the other at its left."
4 So I answered and spoke to the angel who
talked with me, saying, "What *are* these, my
lord?"
5 Then the angel who talked with me answered
and said to me, "Do you not know what these
are?" And I said, "No, my lord."
6 So he answered and said to me:

"This *is* the word of the LORD to [a]Zerubbabel:
[b]'Not by might nor by power,
but by My Spirit,'
Says the LORD of hosts.
7 'Who *are* you, [a]O great mountain?
Before Zerubbabel *you shall become* a plain!
And he shall bring forth [b]the capstone
[c]With shouts of "Grace, grace to it!" ' "

8 Moreover the word of the LORD came to me,
saying:

9 "The hands of Zerubbabel
[a]Have laid the foundation of this [1]temple;
His hands [b]shall also finish *it*.
Then [c]you will know
That the [d]LORD of hosts has sent Me to you.
10 For who has despised the day of [a]small
things?
For these seven rejoice to see
The [1]plumb line in the hand of Zerubbabel.
[b]They are the eyes of the LORD,
Which scan to and fro throughout the whole
earth."
11 Then I answered and said to him, "What *are*

---

19 [1]Kingdoms or powers
21 [a][Ps. 75:10] [b]Ps. 75:4, 5 [1]Lit. *these*

CHAPTER 2
1 [a]Jer. 31:39
2 [a]Rev. 11:1
4 [a]Jer. 31:27
5 [a][Is. 26:1] [b][Is. 60:19]
6 [a]Is. 48:20 [b]Deut. 28:64
7 [a]Is. 48:20
8 [a]Deut. 32:10 [1]Lit. *pupil*
9 [a]Is. 19:16 [b]Zech. 4:9 [1]*booty* or *plunder*
10 [a]Is. 12:6 [b][Lev. 26:12]
11 [a][Is. 2:2, 3] [b]Zech. 3:10 [c]Ex. 12:49 [d]Ezek. 33:33
12 [a][Deut. 32:9]
13 [a]Hab. 2:20 [b]Ps. 68:5

CHAPTER 3
1 [a]Hag. 1:1 [b]Ps. 109:6 [1]Lit. *the Adversary*
2 [a][Jude 9] [b][Rom. 8:33] [c]Amos 4:11
3 [a]Is. 64:6
4 [a]Is. 61:10
5 [a]Ex. 29:6
7 [a]Lev. 8:35 [b]Deut. 17:9, 12 [c]Zech. 4:4
8 [a]Ps. 71:7 [b]Is. 42:1 [c]Is. 11:1; 53:2 [1]Lit. *men of a sign* or *wonder*
9 [a][Zech. 4:10] [b]Ps. 118:22 [c]Jer. 31:34; 50:20
10 [a]Zech. 2:11 [b]Is. 36:16

CHAPTER 4
1 [a]Zech. 1:9; 2:3 [b]Dan. 8:18
2 [a]Rev. 1:12 [b][Rev. 4:5]
3 [a]Rev. 11:3, 4
6 [a]Hag. 1:1 [b]Hos. 1:7
7 [a]Jer. 51:25 [b]Ps. 118:22 [c]Ezra 3:10, 11, 13
9 [a]Ezra 3:8–10; 5:16 [b]Ezra 6:14, 15 [c]Zech. 2:9, 11; 6:15 [d][Is. 43:16] [1]Lit. *house*
10 [a]Hag. 2:3 [b]2 Chr. 16:9 [1]Lit. *plummet stone*

these [a]two olive trees—at the right of the lampstand and at its left?"
12 And I further answered and said to him,
"What *are these* two olive branches that *drip* [1]into
the receptacles of the two gold pipes from which
the golden *oil* drains?"
13 Then he answered me and said, "Do you not
know what these *are?*" And I said, "No, my lord."
14 So he said, [a]"These *are* the two [1]anointed ones,
[b]who stand beside the Lord of the whole earth."

## *The Woman in a Basket*

**5** Then I turned and raised my eyes, and saw
there a flying [a]scroll.
2 And he said to me, "What do you see?" So I
answered, "I see a flying scroll. Its length *is*
twenty cubits and its width ten cubits."
3 Then he said to me, "This *is* the [a]curse that
goes out over the face of the whole earth: 'Every
thief shall be expelled,' according *to* this side of
*the scroll;* and, 'Every perjurer shall be expelled,'
according *to* that side of it."

4 "I will send out *the curse,*"
   says the LORD of hosts;
"It shall enter the house of the [a]thief
 And the house of [b]the one who swears falsely
   by My name.
 It shall remain in the midst of his house
 And consume [c]it, with its timber and stones."

5 Then the angel who talked with me came out
and said to me, "Lift your eyes now, and see what
this *is* that goes forth."
6 So I asked, "What *is* it?" And he said, "It *is* a
[1]basket that is going forth." He also said, "This *is*
their resemblance throughout the earth:
7 "Here *is* a lead disc lifted up, and this *is* a
woman sitting inside the basket";
8 then he said, "This *is* Wickedness!" And he
thrust her down into the basket, and threw the
lead [1]cover over its mouth.
9 Then I raised my eyes and looked, and there
*were* two women, coming with the wind in their
wings; for they had wings like the wings of a
[a]stork, and they lifted up the basket between
earth and heaven.
10 So I said to the [a]angel who talked with me,
"Where are they carrying the basket?"
11 And he said to me, "To [a]build a house for it in
[b]the land of [1]Shinar; when it is ready, *the basket*
will be set there on its base."

## *The Four Chariots*

**6** Then I turned and raised my eyes and looked,
and behold, four chariots *were* coming from
between two mountains, and the mountains *were*
mountains of bronze.
2 With the first chariot *were* [a]red horses, with
the second chariot [b]black horses,
3 with the third chariot white horses, and with
the fourth chariot dappled horses—strong *steeds.*
4 Then I answered [a]and said to the angel who
talked with me, "What *are* these, my lord?"
5 And the angel answered and said to me,
[a]"These *are* four spirits of heaven, who go out
from *their* [b]station before the Lord of all the earth.
6 [1]"The one with the black horses is going to
[a]the north country, the white are going after
them, and the dappled are going toward the south
country."
7 Then the strong *steeds* went out, eager to go,
that they might [a]walk to and fro throughout the
earth. And He said, "Go, walk to and fro throughout the earth." So they walked to and fro throughout the earth.
8 And He called to me, and spoke to me, saying,
"See, those who go toward the north country
have given rest to My [a]Spirit in the north country."
9 Then the word of the LORD came to me,
saying:
10 "Receive *the gift* from the captives—from
Heldai, Tobijah, and Jedaiah, who have come
from Babylon—and go the same day and enter the
house of Josiah the son of Zephaniah.
11 "Take the silver and gold, make [a]an[1] elaborate
crown, and set *it* on the head of [b]Joshua the son of
Jehozadak, the high priest.
12 "Then speak to him, saying, 'Thus says the
LORD of hosts, saying:

"Behold, [a]the Man whose name *is* the
   [b]BRANCH!
 From His place He shall [1]branch out,
 [c]And He shall build the temple of the LORD;
13 Yes, He shall build the temple of the LORD.
 He [a]shall bear the glory,
 And shall sit and rule on His throne;
 So [b]He shall be a priest on His throne,
 And the counsel of peace shall be between
   [1]them both." '

14 "Now the [1]elaborate crown shall be [a]for a
memorial in the temple of the LORD [2]for Helem,
Tobijah, Jedaiah, and Hen the son of Zephaniah.
15 "Even [a]those from afar shall come and build
the temple of the LORD. Then you shall know that
the LORD of hosts has sent Me to you. And *this*
shall come to pass if you diligently obey the voice
of the LORD your God."

## *Disobedience the Cause of Captivity*

**7** Now in the fourth year of King Darius it came
to pass *that* the word of the LORD came to
Zechariah, on the fourth day of the ninth month,
Chislev,
2 when [1]*the people* sent [2]Sherezer, with Regem-
Melech and his men, *to* [3]the house of God, [4]to pray
before the LORD,
3 *and* to [a]ask the priests who *were* in the house
of the LORD of hosts, and the prophets, saying,
"Should I weep in [b]the fifth month and [1]fast as I
have done for so many years?"
4 Then the word of the LORD of hosts came to
me, saying,
5 "Say to all the people of the land, and to the
priests: 'When you [a]fasted and mourned in the
fifth [b]and seventh *months* [c]during those seventy
years, did you really fast [d]for Me—for Me?
6 [a]'When you eat and when you drink, do you
not eat and drink *for yourselves?*
7 *'Should you* not *have obeyed* the words which
the LORD proclaimed through the [a]former prophets when Jerusalem and the cities around it were
inhabited and prosperous, and [b]the [1]South and the
Lowland were inhabited?' "
8 Then the word of the LORD came to Zechariah,
saying,
9 "Thus says the LORD of hosts:

[a]'Execute true justice,
 Show [1]mercy and compassion
 Everyone to his brother.

---

11 [a]Zech. 4:3
12 [1]Lit. *into the hands of*
14 [a]Rev. 11:4 [b]Zech. 3:1–7 [1]Lit. *sons of fresh oil*

CHAPTER 5
1 [a]Ezek. 2:9
3 [a]Mal. 4:6
4 [a]Ex. 20:15 [b]Lev. 19:12 [c]Lev. 14:34, 35
6 [1]Heb. *ephah,* a measuring container, and so elsewhere
8 [1]Lit. *stone*
9 [a]Lev. 11:13, 19
10 [a]Zech. 5:5
11 [a]Jer. 29:5, 28 [b]Gen. 10:10 [1]Babylon

CHAPTER 6
2 [a]Zech. 1:8 [b]Rev. 6:5
4 [a]Zech. 5:10
5 [a][Heb. 1:7, 14] [b]Dan. 7:10
6 [a]Jer. 1:14 [1]The chariot
7 [a]Gen. 1:10
8 [a]Eccl. 10:4
11 [a]Ex. 29:6 [b]Hag. 1:1 [1]Lit. *crowns*
12 [a]John 1:45 [b]Zech. 3:8 [c][Eph. 2:20] [1]Lit. *sprout up*
13 [a]Is. 22:24 [b]Ps. 110:4 [1]Both offices
14 [a]Ex. 12:14 [1]Lit. *crowns* [2]So with MT, Tg., Vg.; Syr. *for Heldai* (cf. v. 10); LXX *for the patient ones*
15 [a]Is. 57:19

CHAPTER 7
2 [1]Lit. *they,* cf. v. 5 [2]Or *Sar-Ezer* [3]Heb. *Bethel* [4]Or *to entreat the favor of*
3 [a]Mal. 2:7 [b]Zech. 8:19 [1]Lit. *consecrate myself*
5 [a][Is. 58:1–9] [b]Jer. 41:1 [c]Zech. 1:12 [d][Rom. 14:6]
6 [a]1 Chr. 29:22
7 [a]Zech. 1:4 [b]Jer. 17:26 [1]Heb. *Negev*
9 [a]Jer. 7:28 [1]Or *loving-kindness*

10 [a]Do not oppress the widow or the fatherless,
The alien or the poor.
[b]Let none of you plan evil in his heart
Against his brother.'

11 "But they refused to heed, [a]shrugged[1] their
shoulders, and [b]stopped[2] their ears so that they
could not hear.
12 "Yes, they made their [a]hearts like flint, [b]refus-
ing to hear the law and the words which the LORD
of hosts had sent by His Spirit through the former
prophets. [c]Thus great wrath came from the LORD
of hosts.
13 "Therefore it happened, *that* just as He proclaimed and they would not hear, so [a]they called
out and I would not listen," says the LORD of
hosts.
14 "But [a]I scattered them with a whirlwind
among all the nations which they had not known.
Thus the land became desolate after them, so that
no one passed through or returned; for they made
the pleasant land desolate."

### *Jerusalem, Holy City of the Future*

8 Again the word of the LORD of hosts came,
saying,
2 "Thus says the LORD of hosts:

[a]'I am [1]zealous for Zion with great [2]zeal;
With great [3]fervor I am zealous for her.'

3 "Thus says the LORD:

[a]'I will return to Zion,
And [b]dwell in the midst of Jerusalem.
Jerusalem [c]shall be called the City of Truth,
[d]The Mountain of the LORD of hosts,
[e]The Holy Mountain.'

4 "Thus says the LORD of hosts:

[a]'Old men and old women shall again sit
In the streets of Jerusalem,
Each one with his staff in his hand
Because of [1]great age.
5 The streets of the city
Shall be [a]full of boys and girls
Playing in its streets.'

6 "Thus says the LORD of hosts:

'If it is [1]marvelous in the eyes of the remnant
of this people in these days,
[a]Will it also be marvelous in My eyes?'
Says the LORD of hosts.

7 "Thus says the LORD of hosts:

'Behold, [a]I will save My people
from the land of the [1]east
And from the land of the [2]west;
8 I will [a]bring them *back*,
And they shall dwell in the midst of
Jerusalem.
[b]They shall be My people
And I will be their God,
[c]In truth and righteousness.'

9 "Thus says the LORD of hosts:

[a]'Let your hands be strong,
You who have been hearing in these days
These words by the mouth of [b]the prophets,
Who *spoke* in [c]the day the foundation was
laid
For the house of the LORD of hosts,
That the temple might be built.

10 [a]Ex. 22:22 [b]Mic. 2:1
11 [a]Neh. 9:29 [b]Jer. 17:23 [1]Lit. *gave a stubborn* or *rebellious shoulder* [2]Lit. *made their ears heavy*
12 [a]Ezek. 11:19 [b]Neh. 9:29, 30 [c]Dan. 9:11, 12
13 [a]Prov. 1:24–28
14 [a]Deut. 4:27; 28:64
CHAPTER 8
2 [a]Zech. 1:14 [1]Or *jealous* [2]Or *jealousy* [3]Lit. *heat* or *rage*
3 [a]Zech. 1:16 [b]Zech. 2:10, 11 [c]Is. 1:21 [d][Is. 2:2, 3] [e]Jer. 31:23
4 [a]Is. 65:20 [1]Lit. *many days*
5 [a]Jer. 30:19, 20
6 [a][Luke 1:37] [1]Or *wonderful*
7 [a]Is. 11:11 [1]Lit. *rising sun* [2]Lit. *setting sun*
8 [a]Zeph. 3:20 [b][Jer. 30:22; 31:1, 33] [c]Jer. 4:2
9 [a]Hag. 2:4 [b]Ezra 5:1, 2; 6:14 [c]Hag. 2:18
10 [a]Hag. 1:6, 9
11 [a]Hag. 2:15–19
12 [a]Joel 2:22 [b]Ps. 67:6 [c]Hag. 1:10 [1]Lit. *seed of peace*
13 [a]Jer. 42:18 [b]Gen. 12:2
14 [a]Jer. 31:28 [b][2 Chr. 36:16] [1]Lit. *bring calamity to you*
16 [a]Zech. 7:9, 10 [b][Eph. 4:25]
17 [a]Prov. 3:29 [1]Lit. *his*
19 [a]Jer. 52:6 [b]Jer. 52:12 [c]2 Kin. 25:25 [d]Jer. 52:4 [e]Esth. 8:17 [f]Zech. 8:16
21 [a][Is. 2:2, 3]
22 [a]Is. 60:3; 66:23

10 For before these days
*There were* no [a]wages for man
nor any hire for beast;
*There was* no peace from the enemy for
whoever went out or came in;
For I set all men, everyone, against his
neighbor.

11 [a]'But now I *will* not *treat* the remnant of this
people as in the former days,' says the LORD of
hosts.

12 'For[a] the [1]seed *shall be* prosperous,
The vine shall give its fruit,
[b]The ground shall give her increase,
And [c]the heavens shall give their dew—
I will cause the remnant of this people
To possess all these.
13 And it shall come to pass
*That* just as you were [a]a curse among the
nations,
O house of Judah and house of Israel,
So I will save you,
and [b]you shall be a blessing.
Do not fear,
Let your hands be strong.'

14 "For thus says the LORD of hosts:

[a]'Just as I determined to [1]punish you
When your fathers provoked Me to wrath,'
Says the LORD of hosts,
[b]'And I would not relent,
15 So again in these days
I am determined to do good
To Jerusalem and to the house of Judah.
Do not fear.
16 These *are* the things you shall [a]do:
[b]Speak each man the truth to his neighbor;
Give judgment in your gates for truth,
justice, and peace;
17 [a]Let none of you think evil in [1]your heart
against your neighbor;
And do not love a false oath.
For all these *are things* that I hate,'
Says the LORD."

18 Then the word of the LORD of hosts came to
me, saying,
19 "Thus says the LORD of hosts:

[a]'The fast of the fourth *month*,
[b]The fast of the fifth,
[c]The fast of the seventh,
[d]And the fast of the tenth,
Shall be [e]joy and gladness and cheerful feasts
For the house of Judah.
[f]Therefore love truth and peace.'

20 "Thus says the LORD of hosts:

'Peoples shall yet come,
Inhabitants of many cities;
21 The inhabitants of one *city* shall go to
another, saying,
[a]"Let us continue to go
and pray before the LORD,
And seek the LORD of hosts.
I myself will go also."
22 Yes, [a]many peoples and strong nations
Shall come to seek the LORD of hosts in
Jerusalem,
And to pray before the LORD.'

23 "Thus says the LORD of hosts: 'In those days ten men [a]from every language of the nations shall [b]grasp the [1]sleeve of a Jewish man, saying, "Let us go with you, for we have heard [c]*that* God *is* with you." ' "

## *Zion's Coming King*

9 The [1]burden of the word of the LORD
Against the land of Hadrach,
And [a]Damascus its resting place
(For [b]the eyes of men
And all the tribes of Israel
Are on the LORD);
2 Also *against* [a]Hamath, *which* borders on it,
And *against* [b]Tyre and [c]Sidon,
though they are very [d]wise.

3 For Tyre built herself a tower,
Heaped up silver like the dust,
And gold like the mire of the streets.
4 Behold, [a]the LORD will cast her out;
He will destroy [b]her power in the sea,
And she will be devoured by fire.

5 Ashkelon shall see *it* and fear;
Gaza also shall be very sorrowful;
And [a]Ekron, for He dried up her expectation.
The king shall perish from Gaza,
And Ashkelon shall not be inhabited.

6 "A[1] mixed race shall settle [a]in Ashdod,
And I will cut off the pride of the [b]Philistines.
7 I will take away the blood from his mouth,
And the abominations
from between his teeth.
But he who remains,
even he *shall be* for our God,
And shall be like a leader in Judah,
And Ekron like a Jebusite.
8 [a]I will camp around My house
Because of the army,
Because of him who passes by
and him who returns.
No more shall an oppressor pass through
them,
For now I have seen with My eyes.

9 "Rejoice [a]greatly, O daughter of Zion!
Shout, O daughter of Jerusalem!
Behold, [b]your King is coming to you;
He *is* just and having salvation,
Lowly and riding on a donkey,
A colt, the foal of a donkey.
10 I [a]will cut off the chariot from Ephraim
And the horse from Jerusalem;
The [b]battle bow shall be cut off.
He shall speak peace to the nations;
His dominion *shall be* [c]'from sea to sea,
And from the River to the ends of the earth.'

11 "As for you also,
Because of the blood of your covenant,
I will set your [a]prisoners free from the
waterless pit.
12 Return to the stronghold,
[a]You prisoners of hope.
Even today I declare
*That* I will restore [b]double to you.
13 For I have bent Judah, My *bow*,
Fitted the bow with Ephraim,
And raised up your sons, O Zion,
Against your sons, O Greece,
And made you like the sword of a mighty
man."

14 Then the LORD will be seen over them,
And [a]His arrow will go forth like lightning.
The Lord GOD will blow the trumpet,
And go [b]with whirlwinds from the south.
15 The LORD of hosts will [a]defend them;
They shall devour and subdue with
slingstones.
They shall drink *and* roar as if with wine;
They shall be filled *with blood* like [1]basins,
Like the corners of the altar.
16 The LORD their God will [a]save them in that
day,
As the flock of His people.
For [b]they *shall be like* the [1]jewels of a crown,
[c]Lifted like a banner over His land—
17 For [a]how great is [1]its goodness
And how great [1]its [b]beauty!
[c]Grain shall make the young men thrive,
And new wine the young women.

## *Judah and Israel Restored*

10 Ask [a]the LORD for [b]rain
In [c]the time of the [1]latter rain.
The LORD will make [2]flashing clouds;
He will give them showers of rain,
Grass in the field for everyone.

2 For the [a]idols[1] speak delusion;
The diviners envision [b]lies,
And tell false dreams;
They [c]comfort in vain.
Therefore *the people* wend their way like
[d]sheep;
They are [2]in trouble [e]because *there is* no
shepherd.

3 "My anger is kindled against the [a]shepherds,
[b]And I will punish the [1]goatherds.
For the LORD of hosts [c]will visit His flock,
The house of Judah,
And [d]will make them as His royal horse in
the battle.
4 From him comes [a]the cornerstone,
From him [b]the tent peg,
From him the battle bow,
From him every [1]ruler together.
5 They shall be like mighty men,
Who [a]tread down *their enemies*
In the mire of the streets in the battle.
They shall fight because the LORD is with
them,
And the riders on horses shall be put to
shame.

6 "I will strengthen the house of Judah,
And I will save the house of Joseph.
[a]I will bring them back,
Because I [b]have mercy on them.
They shall be as though I had not cast them
aside;
For I *am* the LORD their God,
And I [c]will hear them.
7 *Those of* Ephraim shall be like a mighty man,
And their [a]heart shall rejoice as if with wine.
Yes, their children shall see *it* and be glad;
Their heart shall rejoice in the LORD.
8 I will [a]whistle for them and gather them,
For I will redeem them;
[b]And they shall increase as they once
increased.

9 "I[a] will [1]sow them among the peoples,
And they shall [b]remember Me in far
countries;

**23** [a]Is. 3:6 [b][Is. 45:14] [c]1 Cor. 14:25 [1]Lit. *wing,* corner of a garment

CHAPTER 9
**1** [a]Is. 17:1 [b]Amos 1:3–5 [1]*oracle, prophecy*
**2** [a]Jer. 49:23 [b]Is. 23 [c]1 Kin. 17:9 [d]Ezek. 28:3
**4** [a]Is. 23:1 [b]Ezek. 26:17
**5** [a]Zeph. 2:4, 5
**6** [a]Amos 1:8 [b]Ezek. 25:15–17 [1]Lit. *An illegitimate one*
**8** [a][Ps. 34:7]
**9** [a]Zech. 2:10 [b][Jer. 23:5, 6]
**10** [a]Hos. 1:7 [b]Hos. 2:18 [c]Ps. 72:8
**11** [a]Is. 42:7
**12** [a]Is. 49:9 [b]Is. 61:7
**14** [a]Ps. 18:14 [b]Is. 21:1
**15** [a]Zech. 12:8 [1]Sacrificial basins
**16** [a]Jer. 31:10, 11 [b]Is. 62:3 [c]Is. 11:12 [1]Lit. *stones*
**17** [a][Ps. 31:19] [b][Ps. 45:1–16] [c]Joel 3:18 [1]Or *His*

CHAPTER 10
**1** [a][Jer. 14:22] [b][Deut. 11:13, 14] [c][Joel 2:23] [1]Spring rain [2]Or *lightning flashes*
**2** [a]Jer. 10:8 [b]Jer. 27:9 [c]Job 13:4 [d]Jer. 50:6, 17 [e]Ezek. 34:5–8 [1]Heb. *teraphim* [2]*afflicted*
**3** [a]Jer. 25:34–36 [b]Ezek. 34:17 [c]Luke 1:68 [d]Song 1:9 [1]Leaders
**4** [a]Is. 28:16 [b]Is. 22:23 [1]Or *despot*
**5** [a]Ps. 18:42
**6** [a]Jer. 3:18 [b]Hos. 1:7 [c]Zech. 13:9
**7** [a]Ps. 104:15
**8** [a]Is. 5:26 [b]Ezek. 36:37
**9** [a]Hos. 2:23 [b]Deut. 30:1 [1]Or *scatter*

They shall live, together with their children,
And they shall return.
10 [a]I will also bring them back from the land of
Egypt,
And gather them from Assyria.
I will bring them into the land of Gilead and
Lebanon,
[b]Until no *more room* is found for them.
11 [a]He shall pass through the sea with affliction,
And strike the waves of the sea:
All the depths of [1]the River shall dry up.
Then [b]the pride of Assyria shall be brought
down,
And [c]the scepter of Egypt shall depart.

12 "So I will strengthen them in the LORD,
And [a]they shall walk up and down in His
name,"
Says the LORD.

## *Prophecy About the Shepherds*

**11** Open [a]your doors, O Lebanon,
That fire may devour your cedars.
2 Wail, O cypress, for the [a]cedar has fallen,
Because the mighty *trees* are ruined.
Wail, O oaks of Bashan,
[b]For the thick forest has come down.
3 *There is* the sound of wailing [a]shepherds!
For their glory is in ruins.
*There is* the sound of roaring lions!
For the [1]pride of the Jordan is in ruins.

4 Thus says the LORD my God, "Feed the flock
for slaughter,
5 "whose owners slaughter them and [a]feel no
guilt; those who sell them [b]say, 'Blessed be the
LORD, for I am rich'; and their shepherds do [c]not
pity them.
6 "For I will no longer pity the inhabitants of
the land," says the LORD. "But indeed I will give
everyone into his neighbor's hand and into the
hand of his king. They shall [1]attack the land, and I
will not deliver *them* from their hand."
7 So I fed the flock for slaughter, [1]in particular
[a]the poor of the flock. I took for myself two staffs:
the one I called [2]Beauty, and the other I called
[3]Bonds; and I fed the flock.
8 I [1]dismissed the three shepherds [a]in one
month. My soul loathed them, and their soul also
abhorred me.
9 Then I said, "I will not feed you. [a]Let what is
dying die, and what is perishing perish. Let those
that are left eat each other's flesh."
10 And I took my staff, [1]Beauty, and cut it in two,
that I might break the covenant which I had
made with all the peoples.
11 So it was broken on that day. Thus [a]the[1] poor
of the flock, who were watching me, knew that it
*was* the word of the LORD.
12 Then I said to them, "If it is [1]agreeable to you,
give *me* my wages; and if not, refrain." So they
[a]weighed out for my wages thirty *pieces* of silver.
13 And the LORD said to me, "Throw it to the
[a]potter"—that princely price they set on me. So I
took the thirty *pieces* of silver and threw them
into the house of the LORD for the potter.
14 Then I cut in two my other staff, [1]Bonds, that
I might break the brotherhood between Judah
and Israel.
**15** And the LORD said to me, [a]"Next, take for
yourself the implements of a foolish shepherd.
16 "For indeed I will raise up a shepherd in the
land *who* will not care for those who are cut off,
nor seek the young, nor heal those that are
broken, nor feed those that still stand. But he will
eat the flesh of the fat and tear their hooves in
[a]pieces.

17 "Woe[a] to the worthless shepherd,
Who leaves the flock!
A sword *shall be* against his arm
And against his right eye;
His arm shall completely wither,
And his right eye shall be totally blinded."

## *Mourning for the Pierced Son*

**12** The [1]burden of the word of the LORD
against Israel. Thus says the LORD, [a]who
stretches out the heavens, lays the foundation of
the earth, and [b]forms the spirit of man within him:
2 "Behold, I will make Jerusalem [a]a cup of
[1]drunkenness to all the surrounding peoples, when
they lay siege against Judah and Jerusalem.
3 [a]"And it shall happen in that day that I will
make Jerusalem [b]a very heavy stone for all peoples; all who would heave it away will surely be
cut in pieces, though all nations of the earth are
gathered against it.
4 "In that day," says the LORD, [a]"I will strike
every horse with confusion, and its rider with
madness; I will open My eyes on the house of
Judah, and will strike every horse of the peoples
with blindness.
5 "And the governors of Judah shall say in their
heart, 'The inhabitants of Jerusalem *are* my
strength in the LORD of hosts, their God.'
6 "In that day I will make the governors of
Judah [a]like a firepan in the woodpile, and like a
fiery torch in the sheaves; they shall devour all the
surrounding peoples on the right hand and on the
left, but Jerusalem shall be inhabited again in her
own place—Jerusalem.
7 "The LORD will save the tents of Judah first, so
that the glory of the house of David and the glory
of the inhabitants of Jerusalem shall not become
greater than that of Judah.
8 "In that day the LORD will defend the inhabitants of Jerusalem; the one who is feeble among
them in that day shall be like David, and the
house of David *shall be* like God, like the Angel of
the LORD before them.
9 "It shall be in that day *that* I will seek to
[a]destroy all the nations that come against Jerusalem.
**10** [a]"And I will pour on the house of David and
on the inhabitants of Jerusalem the Spirit of grace
and supplication; then they will [b]look on Me
whom they pierced. Yes, they will mourn for Him
[c]as one mourns for *his* only *son,* and grieve for
Him as one grieves for a firstborn.
11 "In that day there shall be a great [a]mourning
in Jerusalem, [b]like the mourning at Hadad Rimmon in the plain of [1]Megiddo.
12 [a]"And the land shall mourn, every family by
itself: the family of the house of David by itself,
and their wives by themselves; the family of the
house of [b]Nathan by itself, and their wives by
themselves;
13 "the family of the house of Levi by itself, and
their wives by themselves; the family of Shimei by
itself, and their wives by themselves;
14 "all the families that remain, every family by
itself, and their wives by themselves.

**10** [a]Is. 11:11 [b]Is. 49:19, 20
**11** [a]Is. 11:15 [b]Zeph. 2:13 [c]Ezek. 30:13 [1]The Nile
**12** [a]Mic. 4:5

CHAPTER 11
**1** [a]Zech. 10:10
**2** [a]Ezek. 31:3 [b]Is. 32:19
**3** [a]Jer. 25:34–36 [1]Or *flood plain, thicket*
**5** [a][Jer. 2:3]; 50:7 [b]Hos. 12:8 [c]Ezek. 34:2, 3
**6** [1]Lit. *strike*
**7** [a]Zeph. 3:12 [1]So with MT, Tg., Vg.; LXX *for the Canaanites* [2]Or *Grace* [3]Or *Unity*
**8** [a]Hos. 5:7 [1]Or *destroyed,* lit. *cut off*
**9** [a]Jer. 15:2
**10** [1]Or *Grace*
**11** [a]Zeph. 3:12 [1]So with MT, Tg., Vg.; LXX *the Canaanites*
**12** [a]Ex. 21:32 [1]*good in your sight*
**13** [a]Matt. 27:3–10
**14** [1]Or *Unity*
**15** [a]Is. 56:11
**16** [a]Ezek. 34:1–10
**17** [a]Jer. 23:1

CHAPTER 12
**1** [a]Is. 42:5; 44:24 [b][Is. 57:16] [1]*oracle, prophecy*
**2** [a]Is. 51:17 [1]Lit. *reeling*
**3** [a]Zech. 12:4, 6, 8; 13:1 [b]Matt. 21:44
**4** [a]Ezek. 38:4
**6** [a]Obad. 18
**9** [a]Hag. 2:22
**10** [a][Joel 2:28, 29] [b]John 19:34, 37; 20:27 [c]Jer. 6:26
**11** [a][Rev. 1:7] [b]2 Kin. 23:39 [1]Heb. *Megiddon*
**12** [a][Matt. 24:30] [b]Luke 3:31

## The Shepherd Savior

13 "In that [a]day [b]a fountain shall be opened for
the house of David and for the inhabitants
of Jerusalem, for sin and for [c]uncleanness.
2 "It shall be in that day," says the LORD of
hosts, "*that* I will [a]cut off the names of the idols
from the land, and they shall no longer be remembered. I will also cause [b]the prophets and the
unclean spirit to depart from the land.
3 "It shall come to pass *that* if anyone still
prophesies, then his father and mother who begot
him will say to him, 'You shall [a]not live, because
you have spoken lies in the name of the LORD.'
And his father and mother who begot him [b]shall
thrust him through when he prophesies.
4 "And it shall be in that day *that* [a]every
prophet will be ashamed of his vision when he
prophesies; they will not wear [b]a robe of coarse
hair to deceive.
5 [a]"But he will say, 'I *am* no prophet, I *am* a
farmer; for a man taught me to keep cattle from
my youth.'
6 "And *one* will say to him, 'What are these
wounds between your [1]arms?' Then he will answer, '*Those* with which I was wounded in the
house of my friends.'

7 "Awake, O sword, against [a]My Shepherd,
Against the Man [b]who is My Companion,"
Says the LORD of hosts.
[c]"Strike the Shepherd,
And the sheep will be scattered;
Then I will turn My hand against [d]the little
ones.
8 And it shall come to pass in all the land,"
Says the LORD,
"*That* [a]two-thirds in it shall be cut off *and* die,
[b]But *one*-third shall be left in it:
9 I will bring the *one*-third [a]through the fire,
Will [b]refine them as silver is refined,
And test them as gold is tested.
[c]They will call on My name,
And I will answer them.
[d]I will say, 'This *is* My people';
And each one will say,
'The LORD *is* my God.' "

## The Coming Day of the LORD

14 Behold, [a]the day of the LORD is coming,
And your [1]spoil will be divided in your
midst.
2 For [a]I will gather all the nations to battle
against Jerusalem;
The city shall be taken,
The houses [1]rifled,
And the women ravished.
Half of the city shall go into captivity,
But the remnant of the people shall not be
cut off from the city.

3 Then the LORD will go forth
And fight against those nations,
As He fights in the day of battle.
4 And in that day His feet will stand [a]on the
Mount of Olives,
Which faces Jerusalem on the east.
And the Mount of Olives shall be split in two,
From east to west,
[b]*Making* a very large valley;
Half of the mountain shall move toward the
north
And half of it toward the south.

CHAPTER 13
1 [a][Rev. 21:6, 7] [b][Heb. 9:14] [c]Ezek. 36:25
2 [a]Ex. 23:13 [b]Jer. 23:14, 15
3 [a]Deut. 18:20 [b]Deut. 13:6–11
4 [a][Mic. 3:6, 7] [b]2 Kin. 1:8
5 [a]Amos 7:14
6 [1]Or *hands*
7 [a]Is. 40:11 [b][John 10:30] [c]Matt. 26:31, 56, 67 [d]Luke 12:32
8 [a]Ezek. 5:2, 4, 12 [b][Rom. 11:5]
9 [a]Is. 48:10 [b]1 Pet. 1:6 [c]Ps. 50:15 [d]Hos. 2:23

CHAPTER 14
1 [a][Is. 13:6, 9] [1]*plunder* or *booty*
2 [a]Zech. 12:2, 3 [1]Or *plundered*
4 [a]Ezek. 11:23 [b]Joel 3:12
5 [a]Amos 1:1 [b]Matt. 24:30, 31; 25:31 [c]Joel 3:11 [1]Or *you;* LXX, Tg., Vg. *Him*
6 [1]Lit. *glorious ones*
7 [a]Matt. 24:36 [b]Is. 30:26
8 [a]Ezek. 47:1–12 [1]The Dead Sea [2]The Mediterranean Sea
9 [a][Rev. 11:15] [b]Deut. 6:4
10 [a]Zech. 12:6 [b]Jer. 31:38 [1]Lit. *She*
11 [a]Jer. 31:40 [b]Jer. 23:6
12 [1]Lit. *decay*
13 [a]1 Sam. 14:15, 20 [b]Judg. 7:22
14 [a]Ezek. 39:10, 17
15 [a]Zech. 14:12
16 [a][Is. 2:2, 3; 60:6–9; 66:18–21] [b]Is. 27:13 [c]Lev. 23:34–44

5 Then you shall flee *through* My mountain
valley,
For the mountain valley shall reach to Azal.
Yes, you shall flee
As you fled from the [a]earthquake
In the days of Uzziah king of Judah.

[b]Thus the LORD my God will come,
*And* [c]all the saints with [1]You.

6 It shall come to pass in that day
*That* there will be no light;
The [1]lights will diminish.
7 It shall be one day
[a]Which is known to the LORD—
Neither day nor night.
But at [b]evening time it shall happen
*That* it will be light.

8 And in that day it shall be
*That* living [a]waters shall flow from
Jerusalem,
Half of them toward [1]the eastern sea
And half of them toward [2]the western sea;
In both summer and winter it shall occur.
9 And the LORD shall be [a]King over all the
earth.
In that day it shall be—
[b]"The LORD *is* one,"
And His name one.

10 All the land shall be turned into a plain from
Geba to Rimmon south of Jerusalem. [1]*Jerusalem*
shall be raised up and [a]inhabited in her place from
Benjamin's Gate to the place of the First Gate and
the Corner Gate, [b]and *from* the Tower of Hananel
to the king's winepresses.

11 *The people* shall dwell in it;
And [a]no longer shall there be utter
destruction,
[b]But Jerusalem shall be safely inhabited.

12 And this shall be the plague with which the
LORD will strike all the people who fought against
Jerusalem:

Their flesh shall [1]dissolve
while they stand on their feet,
Their eyes shall dissolve in their sockets,
And their tongues shall dissolve
in their mouths.

13 It shall come to pass in that day
*That* [a]a great panic from the LORD
will be among them.
Everyone will seize the hand of his neighbor,
And raise [b]his hand against his neighbor's
hand;
14 Judah also will fight at Jerusalem.
[a]And the wealth of all the surrounding
nations
Shall be gathered together:
Gold, silver, and apparel in great abundance.

15 [a]Such also shall be the plague
On the horse *and* the mule,
On the camel and the donkey,
And on all the cattle that will be in those
camps.
So *shall* this plague *be*.

16 And it shall come to pass *that* everyone who is
left of all the nations which came against Jerusalem shall [a]go up from year to year to [b]worship the
King, the LORD of hosts, and to keep [c]the Feast of
Tabernacles.

17 [a]And it shall be *that* whichever of the families
of the earth do not come up to Jerusalem to
worship the King, the LORD of hosts, on them
there will be no rain.
18 If the family of [a]Egypt will not come up and
enter in, [b]they *shall have* no *rain;* they shall
receive the plague with which the LORD strikes
the nations who do not come up to keep the Feast
of Tabernacles.
19 This shall be the [1]punishment of Egypt and the
punishment of all the nations that do not come up
to keep the Feast of Tabernacles.
**20** In that day [a]"HOLINESS TO THE LORD"
shall be *engraved* on the bells of the horses. The
[b]pots in the LORD's house shall be like the bowls
before the altar.
21 Yes, [1]every pot in Jerusalem and Judah shall
be holiness to the LORD of hosts. Everyone who
sacrifices shall come and take them and cook in
them. In that day there shall no longer be a
[a]Canaanite [b]in the house of the LORD of hosts.

**17** [a]Is. 60:12 **18** [a]Is. 19:21 [b]Deut. 11:10 **19** [1]Lit. *sin* **20** [a]Is. 23:18 [b]Ezek. 46:20 **21** [a]Is. 35:8 [b][Eph. 2:19–22] [1]Or *on every pot . . . shall be engraved "HOLINESS TO THE LORD OF HOSTS"*

*The Book of*

# MALACHI

### *Polluted Offerings to God*

THE [1]burden of the word of the LORD to Israel [2]by Malachi.

**2** "I[a] have loved you," says the LORD.
"Yet you say,
'In what way have You loved us?'
"*Was* not Esau Jacob's brother?"
Says the LORD.
"Yet [b]Jacob I have loved;
3 But Esau I have hated,
And [a]laid waste his mountains
and his heritage
For the jackals of the wilderness."

4 Even though Edom has said,
"We have been impoverished,
But we will return
and build the desolate places,"

Thus says the LORD of hosts:

"They may build, but I will [a]throw down;
They shall be called the Territory of
Wickedness,
And the people against whom the LORD will
have indignation forever.
5 Your eyes shall see,
And you shall say,
[a]'The LORD is magnified beyond the border of
Israel.'

**6** "A son [a]honors *his* father,
And a servant *his* master.
[b]If then I am the Father,
Where *is* My honor?
And if I *am* a Master,
Where *is* My reverence?
Says the LORD of hosts
To you priests who despise My name.
[c]Yet you say, 'In what way have we despised
Your name?'

7 "You offer [a]defiled food on My altar,
But say,
'In what way have we defiled You?'
By saying,
[b]'The table of the LORD is [1]contemptible.'
8 And [a]when you offer the blind as a sacrifice,
*Is it* not evil?
And when you offer the lame and sick,
*Is it* not evil?
Offer it then to your governor!
Would he be pleased with you?
Would he [b]accept[1] you favorably?"
Says the LORD of hosts.

9 "But now entreat God's favor,
That He may be gracious to us.
[a]*While* this is being *done* by your hands,
Will He accept you favorably?"
Says the LORD of hosts.
10 "Who *is there* even among you who would
shut the doors,
[a]So that you would not kindle fire *on* My altar
in vain?
I have no pleasure in you,"
Says the LORD of hosts,
[b]"Nor will I accept an offering from your
hands.
11 For [a]from the rising of the sun,
even to its going down,
My name *shall be* great [b]among the Gentiles;
[c]In every place [d]incense *shall be* offered to
My name,
And a pure offering;
[e]For My name shall be great among the
nations,"
Says the LORD of hosts.

12 "But you profane it,
In that you say,
[a]'The table of the [1]LORD is defiled;
And its fruit, its food, *is* contemptible.'
13 You also say,
'Oh, what a [a]weariness!'
And you sneer at it,"
Says the LORD of hosts.
"And you bring the stolen,
the lame, and the sick;
Thus you bring an offering!
[b]Should I accept this from your hand?"
Says the LORD.
14 "But cursed *be* [a]the deceiver
Who has in his flock a male,
And takes a vow,
But sacrifices to the Lord [b]what is
blemished—

CHAPTER 1
**1** [1]*oracle, prophecy* [2]Lit. *by the hand of*
**2** [a]Deut. 4:37; 7:8; 23:5; Is. 41:8, 9; [Jer. 31:3]; John 15:12 [b]Rom. 9:13
**3** [a]Jer. 49:18; Ezek. 35:9, 15
**4** [a]Jer. 49:16–18
**5** [a]Ps. 35:27; Mic. 5:4
**6** [a][Ex. 20:12]; Prov. 30:11, 17; [Matt. 15:4–8; Eph. 6:2, 3] [b][Is. 63:16; 64:8]; Jer. 31:9; Luke 6:46 [c]Mal. 2:14
**7** [a]Deut. 15:21 [b]Ezek. 41:22 [1]Or *to be despised*
**8** [a]Lev. 22:22; Deut. 15:19–23 [b][Job 42:8] [1]Lit. *lift up your face*
**9** [a]Hos. 13:9
**10** [a]1 Cor. 9:13 [b]Is. 1:11
**11** [a]Is. 59:19 [b]Is. 60:3, 5 [c]1 Tim. 2:8 [d]Rev. 8:3 [e]Is. 66:18, 19
**12** [a]Mal. 1:7 [1]So with Bg.; MT *Lord*
**13** [a]Is. 43:22 [b]Lev. 22:20
**14** [a]Mal. 1:8 [b]Lev. 22:18–20

For [c]I *am* a great King,"
Says the LORD of hosts,
"And My name *is to be* feared among the nations.

### Corrupt Priests

2 "And now, O [a]priests,
this commandment is for you.
2 [a]If you will not hear,
And if you will not take *it* to heart,
To give glory to My name,"
Says the LORD of hosts,
"I will send a curse upon you,
And I will curse your blessings.
Yes, I have cursed them [b]already,
Because you do not take *it* to heart.

3 "Behold, I will rebuke your descendants
And spread [a]refuse on your faces,
The refuse of your solemn feasts;
And *one* will [b]take you away [1]with it.
4 Then you shall know that I have sent
this commandment to you,
That My covenant with Levi may continue,"
Says the LORD of hosts.
5 "My[a] covenant was with him,
*one* of life and peace,
And I gave them to him [b]*that he might* fear *Me;*
So he feared Me
And was reverent before My name.
6 [a]The[1] law of truth was in his mouth,
And [2]injustice was not found on his lips.
He walked with Me in peace and equity,
And [b]turned many away from iniquity.

7 "For[a] the lips of a priest should keep knowledge,
And *people* should seek the law from his mouth;
[b]For he is the messenger of the LORD of hosts.
8 But you have departed from the way;
You [a]have caused many to stumble at the law.
[b]You have corrupted the covenant of Levi,"
Says the LORD of hosts.
9 "Therefore [a]I also have made you
contemptible and base
Before all the people,
Because you have not kept My ways
But have shown [b]partiality in the law."

**10** [a]Have we not all one Father?
[b]Has not one God created us?
Why do we deal treacherously with one another
By profaning the covenant of the fathers?
11 Judah has dealt treacherously,
And an abomination has been committed in Israel and in Jerusalem,
For Judah has [a]profaned
The LORD's holy *institution* which He loves:
He has married the daughter of a foreign god.
12 May the LORD cut off from the tents of Jacob
The man who does this,
being [1]awake and aware,
Yet [a]who brings an offering to the LORD of hosts!

**13** And this is the second thing you do:
You cover the altar of the LORD with tears,
With weeping and crying;
So He does not regard the offering anymore,
Nor receive *it* with goodwill from your hands.
14 Yet you say, "For what reason?"
Because the LORD has been witness
Between you and [a]the wife of your youth,
With whom you have dealt treacherously;
[b]Yet she is your companion
And your wife by covenant.
15 But [a]did He not make *them* one,
Having a remnant of the Spirit?
And why one?
He seeks [b]godly offspring.
Therefore take heed to your spirit,
And let none deal treacherously with the wife of his youth.

16 "For [a]the LORD God of Israel says
That He hates divorce,
For it covers one's garment with violence,"
Says the LORD of hosts.
"Therefore take heed to your spirit,
That you do not deal treacherously."

**17** [a]You have wearied the LORD with your words;
Yet you say,
"In what way have we wearied *Him?*"
In that you say,
[b]"Everyone who does evil
*Is* good in the sight of the LORD,
And He delights in them,"
Or, "Where *is* the God of justice?"

### The Coming Messenger of God

3 "Behold, [a]I send My messenger,
And he will [b]prepare the way before Me.
And the Lord, whom you seek,
Will suddenly come to His temple,
[c]Even the Messenger of the covenant,
In whom you delight.
Behold, [d]He is coming,"
Says the LORD of hosts.

2 "But who can endure [a]the day of His coming?
And [b]who can stand when He appears?
For [c]He *is* like a refiner's fire
And like launderers' soap.
3 [a]He will sit as a refiner and a purifier of silver;
He will purify the sons of Levi,
And [1]purge them as gold and silver,
That they may [b]offer to the LORD
An offering in righteousness.

4 "Then [a]the offering of Judah and Jerusalem
Will be [1]pleasant to the LORD,
As in the days of old,
As in former years.
5 And I will come near you for judgment;
I will be a swift witness
Against sorcerers,
Against adulterers,
[a]Against perjurers,
Against those who [b]exploit wage earners and [c]widows and orphans,
And against those who turn away an alien—
Because they do not fear Me,"
Says the LORD of hosts.

6 "For I *am* the LORD, [a]I do not change;
[b]Therefore you are not consumed,
O sons of Jacob.
7 Yet from the days of [a]your fathers
You have gone away from My ordinances
And have not kept *them.*

**14** [c]Ps. 47:2

CHAPTER 2
**1** [a]Mal. 1:6
**2** [a][Lev. 26:14, 15; Deut. 28:15] [b]Mal. 3:9
**3** [a]Ex. 29:14 [b]1 Kin. 14:10 [1]Lit. *to it*
**5** [a]Num. 25:12; Ezek. 34:25 [b]Deut. 33:9
**6** [a]Deut. 33:10 [b]Jer. 23:22; [James 5:20] [1]Or *True instruction* [2]Or *unrighteousness*
**7** [a]Num. 27:21; Deut. 17:8–11; Jer. 18:18 [b][Gal. 4:14]
**8** [a]Jer. 18:15 [b]Num. 25:12, 13; Neh. 13:29; Ezek. 44:10
**9** [a]1 Sam. 2:30 [b]Deut. 1:17; Mic. 3:11; 1 Tim. 5:21
**10** [a]Jer. 31:9; 1 Cor. 8:6; [Eph. 4:6] [b]Job 31:15
**11** [a]Ezra 9:1, 2; Neh. 13:23
**12** [a]Neh. 13:29 [1]Talmud, Vg. *teacher and student*
**14** [a]Prov. 5:18; Jer. 9:2; Mal. 3:5 [b]Prov. 2:17
**15** [a]Gen. 2:24; Matt. 19:4, 5 [b]Ezra 9:2; [1 Cor. 7:14]
**16** [a]Deut. 24:1; [Matt. 5:31; 19:6–8]
**17** [a]Is. 43:22, 24 [b]Is. 5:20; Zeph. 1:12

CHAPTER 3
**1** [a]Matt. 11:10; Mark 1:2; Luke 1:76; 7:27; John 1:23; 2:14, 15 [b][Is. 40:3] [c]Is. 63:9 [d]Hab. 2:7
**2** [a]Jer. 10:10; Joel 2:11; Nah. 1:6; [Mal. 4:1] [b]Is. 33:14; Ezek. 22:14; Rev. 6:17 [c]Is. 4:4; Zech. 13:9; [Matt. 3:10–12; 1 Cor. 3:13–15]
**3** [a]Is. 1:25; Dan. 12:10; Zech. 13:9 [b][1 Pet. 2:5] [1]Or *refine*
**4** [a]Mal. 1:11 [1]*pleasing*
**5** [a]Lev. 19:12; Zech. 5:4; [James 5:12] [b]Lev. 19:13; James 5:4 [c]Ex. 22:22
**6** [a][Num. 23:19; Rom. 11:29; James 1:17] [b][Lam. 3:22]
**7** [a]Acts 7:51

[b]Return to Me, and I will return to you,"
Says the LORD of hosts.
[c]"But you said,
'In what way shall we return?'

8 "Will a man rob God?
Yet you have robbed Me!
But you say,
'In what way have we robbed You?'
[a]In tithes and offerings.
9 You are cursed with a curse,
For you have robbed Me,
*Even* this whole nation.
10 [a]Bring all the tithes into the [b]storehouse,
That there may be food in My house,
And try Me now in this,"
Says the LORD of hosts,
"If I will not open for you the [c]windows of heaven
And [d]pour out for you *such* blessing
That *there will* not *be room* enough *to receive it.*

11 "And I will rebuke [a]the devourer for your sakes,
So that he will not destroy the fruit of your ground,
Nor shall the vine fail to bear fruit for you in the field,"
Says the LORD of hosts;
12 "And all nations will call you blessed,
For you will be [a]a delightful land,"
Says the LORD of hosts.

**13** "Your[a] words have been [1]harsh against Me,"
Says the LORD,
"Yet you say,
'What have we spoken against You?'
14 [a]You have said,
'It is useless to serve God;
What profit *is it* that we have kept His ordinance,
And that we have walked as mourners
Before the LORD of hosts?
15 So now [a]we call the proud blessed,
For those who do wickedness are [1]raised up;
They even [b]tempt God and go free.' "

**16** Then those [a]who feared the LORD
[b]spoke to one another,
And the LORD listened and heard *them;*
So [c]a book of remembrance was written before Him
For those who fear the LORD
And who [1]meditate on His name.

17 "They[a] shall be Mine," says the LORD of hosts,
"On the day that I make them My [b]jewels.[1]
And [c]I will spare them
As a man spares his own son who serves him."
18 [a]Then you shall again discern
Between the righteous and the wicked,
Between one who serves God
And one who does not serve Him.

## *The Coming Day of the LORD*

4 "For behold, [a]the day is coming,
Burning like an oven,
And all [b]the proud,
yes, all who do wickedly will be [c]stubble.
And the day which is coming shall burn them up,"
Says the LORD of hosts,
"That will [d]leave them neither root nor branch.
2 But to you who [a]fear My name
The [b]Sun of Righteousness shall arise
With healing in His wings;
And you shall go out
And grow fat like stall-fed calves.
3 [a]You shall trample the wicked,
For they shall be ashes under the soles of your feet
On the day that I do *this,*"
Says the LORD of hosts.

4 "Remember the [a]Law of Moses, My servant,
Which I commanded him in Horeb for all Israel,
*With* [b]*the* statutes and judgments.
5 Behold, I will send you [a]Elijah the prophet
[b]Before the coming of the great and dreadful day of the LORD.
6 And he will turn
The hearts of the fathers to the children,
And the hearts of the children to their fathers,
Lest I come and [a]strike the earth with [b]a curse."

---

**7** [b]Zech. 1:3 [c]Mal. 1:6
**8** [a]Neh. 13:10–12
**10** [a]Prov. 3:9, 10 [b]1 Chr. 26:20 [c]Gen. 7:11 [d]2 Chr. 31:10
**11** [a]Amos 4:9
**12** [a]Dan. 8:9
**13** [a]Mal. 2:17 [1]Lit. *strong*
**14** [a]Job 21:14
**15** [a]Ps. 73:12 [b]Ps. 95:9 [1]Lit. *built*
**16** [a]Ps. 66:16 [b]Heb. 3:13 [c]Ps. 56:8 [1]Or *esteem*
**17** [a]Ex. 19:5; Deut. 7:6; Is. 43:21; [1 Pet. 2:9] [b]Is. 62:3 [c]Ps. 103:13 [1]Lit. *special treasure*
**18** [a][Ps. 58:11]

CHAPTER 4
**1** [a]Ps. 21:9; [Nah. 1:5, 6; Mal. 3:2, 3; 2 Pet. 3:7] [b]Mal. 3:18 [c]Is. 5:24; Obad. 18 [d]Amos 2:9
**2** [a]Mal. 3:16 [b]Matt. 4:16; Luke 1:78; Acts 10:43; 2 Cor. 4:6; Eph. 5:14
**3** [a]Mic. 7:10
**4** [a]Ex. 20:3 [b]Deut. 4:10
**5** [a][Matt. 11:14; 17:10–13; Mark 9:11–13; Luke 1:17]; John 1:21 [b]Joel 2:31
**6** [a]Zech. 14:12 [b]Zech. 5:3

# HOW TO ESTABLISH YOUR FAMILY DEVOTIONAL TIME

**Why Family Worship?**

If we are to truly live as Christians, we must make our holy God the center of our lives. God must enter into all of our daily activities. And our family circle is the divinely made-to-order environment where we can nourish and foster this deep and powerful awareness of God. Certainly the greater Christian community will also provide us with vast mutual support—but only insofar as it reflects the spiritual strength of our basic family unit.

Yet our family's Christian spirituality cannot be automatically wished into existence. Having good intentions, setting a fine example, even praying for our family—none of these is enough. Haven't we all noticed the religiously active father whose own children grow up indifferent to God and to Christ? Too often such parents assume that getting the family to church or Sunday school on time is enough. After all, isn't the church supposed to be the leader in Christian training?

But recall in the Bible—God refers to His people as "families." Long before there was the larger community of believers, there was the essential *family*. Remember Abraham, whom God befriended "in order that he may command his children and his household after him" (Gen. 18:19). Fathers were later commanded to "teach [these words] diligently to your children" (Deut. 6:7). Overseers were required to control their children, prompting Paul to observe rather sharply: "if a man does not know how to rule his own house, how will he take care of the church of God?" (1 Tim. 3:5). So the family is truly the primary unit of the larger believing community (the church). Meeting God regularly within our family structure is thus an awesome, vital necessity.

Fortunately, the family is especially qualified in several ways to lead its members in a devotional life toward biblical goodness:

- Parents, with their natural bond to their children, are the best suited to understand and speak to the spiritual needs of their young ones.
- Family members, living as they normally do under the same roof for an extended time, share the same needs and problems. Such closeness is ideal for developing spiritual communion.
- Children habitually rely upon their parents, which opens a direct channel of communication. This in turn provides a ready-made open door to the hearts of their children.
- Family members have diverse needs which can lead to strife and division. But when they are shared at the family devotional time, they become a fertile ground for family solidarity.

Thus we violate the divine order of things if we suppose that devotional activity—the active worship of God—is either a private, personal matter, or else an exclusively church concern. Rather, it is *fathers* who are instructed: "Do not provoke your children to wrath, but bring them up in the training and admonition of the Lord" (Eph. 6:4). In this verse, two ideas are imparted to us parents in one breath: if we neglect our children's early spiritual training in the home, we will earn their later hostility. If we had daily meetings with God around the family table, there would be vital, overflowing churches and fewer jails, mental institutions, and less human suffering and failure of all kinds.

There is an even more urgent reason for regular family worship. It is not merely to prevent later negative experiences in the material world. It is to provide positive, spiritual conversion, or rebirth. The salvation of our children cannot be left to the random happenstance of "being in the right place at the right time." Our daily family meeting with God will afford the optimum setting for our young ones to constantly confront Christ and feel His claim upon their precious lives. Once His saving grace is lifted up in the family, and illuminated by the parents' leadership, spiritual birth in the children should follow in good time.

With this regular family concern for Bible study, prayer, and spiritual meditation, God Himself becomes the mainspring of family life—and in turn acts as the driving force behind each family member. The spiritual health of the whole community of Christ is enriched, and the wider world itself will be a saner place to live in.

**Repairing the Family Altar**

How shall we begin? In too many homes, the family altar is in grave disrepair. Consequently, the prayer life of the family members has become slipshod and intermittent. Elijah "repaired the altar of the LORD *that was* broken down" (1 Kin. 18:30). In this same spirit, let the father of the household rebuild the altar in his home.

The opportunity will soon arise—such as at a family cookout, or at the end of the evening meal. When everyone has finished eating, instead of letting people depart as usual, dad should say something like this:

"Ah, Mother, Jack, Mary, Mike—and little Louise. There's something I'd like to say to all of you. Let's all wait at the table a few minutes more.

"Well, it's hard to begin, but . . . when your mother and I first got married, we promised we'd always meet God as a couple, every day. For a while there, we *kept* that promise. We never went to sleep at night without spending a little time reading God's Word, and praying some [pause] but you know, everything got tougher and busier. My job got more involved, and you kids arrived one after the other. Before we knew it, God, well, He just got crowded out of our family life. Now it's really mostly my fault. For some time now, you've—*we've* all—been deprived of the greatest value in life—a living friendship with God in our family.

"But tonight I want to promise you that from here on out, I'm going to seriously try to spend time with you, every single day, in the worship of God. We'll seek ways *together* to enrich our lives from God's Word. [pause]

Now we've had our little differences lately. Let's face it, we've had some arguments that got pretty hot at times. Now instead of carrying on like that anymore, we're going to pray for one another's spiritual and material needs. And just like God shows in His Word, we'll also remember to pray for those outside our family circle. Not just our favorite friends, either. Some of those neighbors that we aren't the most fond of—some of those kids at school who aren't always nice—and maybe people down at work we aren't sure are always fair to us. [pause] We are no better than any of them, and we should pray for them. We'll ask God to forgive us anything we may have done even accidentally to hurt any of them. . . . And we'll pray for all the unfortunate folks, the ones who are sick or living in poverty. We are so lucky and blessed, and we'll share our prayers with those less fortunate.

"Now, that's a pretty big speech, but what d'you say? Wouldn't it it be nice after dinner to give a few minutes to God? Let me start it off, by asking God's forgiveness for letting so many years slip past without this kind of family prayer."

Naturally these remarks will vary with each family's situation. But we are not all that different, either. It may be the very first time in which we parents have resolved to pursue a devotional life together. The father's confession, supported by the mother, is sure to make an indelible impression on the hearts of the other family members.

At this point, mother might hand dad the Bible, that he could read from Ephesians 5:22—6:4, regarding conduct of the family. Then Dad should offer a prayer of confession, as well as ask by God's grace that all members of the family receive and begin to follow the directions in the passage.

### The Family Commitment

Now the whole family must commit itself to a set, daily period for the worship of God. This will be easier to regulate with younger children, but even with teenagers nearing the age of maturity, a full effort must be made to obtain each family member's cooperation. Adolescent rebellion is common enough, but love, patience, and prayer can do much to lessen it and bring the teenager into the family sphere of worship. The key to persuasion in such cases is consistency of purpose, and the steady, sincere practice of prayer at the family altar.

### Where Shall We Meet?

To secure unity of mind among your family, be as flexible as possible in adjusting the family worship to the varying schedules of all. With differing school and work hours, time conflicts are almost inevitable. What works Monday through Friday may not on Saturday, when son Jack and daughter Mary are working late in town. Perhaps not everyone can be present at every meeting, and compromises are part of life.

Generally, the best time is following the morning or evening meal. At least plan your mealtime so that time remains for family devotions, before other activities begin.

### How Long Should We Meet?

If the devotional quality is high, time will not drag. Less than twenty minutes will probably not leave a serious enough impression on all family members, with thirty minutes as the maximum. With younger children, there especially needs to be time to draw a lesson and drive home its point. But its duration must not exceed the attention span of the very young.

### Where Shall We Meet?

At the table is easiest, with everyone already gathered. But small children can become restless, since young bodies soon tire of sitting still, and "a change is as good as a rest." It may be more effective, then, for the family to move to the living room or family room to keep the interest fresh and alive.

### Who Leads Family Worship?

The biblical pattern for leadership in family worship is quite straightforward. In a Christian home, the father is the ultimately responsible head of the family. But this is easily misunderstood. The father is no absolute monarch—Christ Himself is King of all, and we meet our various responsibilities subject to His revealed will in Scripture. When the husband presides over family matters, he does so only as Christ's representative, recognizing his own great fallibility as well as his unique responsibility.

From both these perspectives, he acknowledges the dignity and special attributes of his wife, and is quick to consult her in family decisions. While the Bible says "Wives, submit to your own husbands" (Eph. 5:22), it urges also "Husbands, love your wives" (Eph. 5:25). These two principles are absolute, and to violate either breaks down family life as it is meant to be. For instance, the Greek verb for "love" in this context is *agapao,* meaning not merely affection but love in its fullest sense, embracing respect and reverence. In this sort of "love," then, the divine pattern for the family is maintained. No one is tyrannized; each cooperates in loving submission to the headship of Christ in the home. The father, as his family's priest at the family altar, performs his office in gentle consideration of his wife's worth as a person. He gives "honor to the wife, as to the weaker vessel, and as *being* heirs together of the grace of life, that your prayers may not be hindered" (1 Pet. 3:7).

We are speaking, of course, of the ideal family structure. There are increasing numbers of single-parent homes today. Sometimes a father has to be "mother" and vice versa, but such double roles can be fulfilled with the support Christ gives: "I can do all things through Christ who strengthens me" (Phil. 4:13). Susannah Wesley, mother of John and Charles Wesley, was not a single parent, but her husband's rigorous duties demanded that she educate her surviving eleven children.

Then there is the not uncommon spiritually divided home: one spouse is a believer, the other is not. The encouragement here is in 1 Corinthians 7:16: "For how do you know, O wife, whether you will save *your* husband? Or how do you know, O husband, whether you will save *your* wife?" By depending on God, as though the children's souls were at stake, with or without the support of the spouse, let the believer try to lead the family to the throne of grace. As much as possible, avoid all opportunity for strife—for a gracious, believing spirit is the most likely to prevail.

### Role of the Children

Family worship should not be a monologue. We are upbuilding the children spiritually, not training monkeys! Even immature or difficult children are susceptible to the nourishment of "the pure milk of the word" (1 Pet. 2:2), since they too, are created in God's image with immortal souls.

"Participation" is always the key word. If children are forced or allowed to be merely passive in worship, boredom will soon set in. Sitting through an exercise of meaningless, monotonous words will lead children to conclude that worship is a painful ordeal, something to avoid in later life.

However, public worship, though largely a passive experience, can still lead young people to sense the infinite greatness and majesty of God in a way that cannot be duplicated in the more active, but more modest, family worship program. They are two separate occasions—public worship reinforces the awe and majesty of God, and family worship emphasizes intimacy and dialogue. Instructional methods are especially needed to promote spiritual growth among the younger family members.

### A Model for Family Worship

Though interpersonal in form, family worship must have structure and in no way be chaotic. If everyone talks at once, if there is very little order, much time will be lost since there will be no clear goals. It's better to have fairly fixed *form* of family devotional time, and vary the *content*. Continuity from day to day will insure stability, which is all-important in instilling the habit of instinctive worship with young people.

### The Call to Worship

There are various ways in which the father might open the family devotions with a call to worship:

Oh come, let us worship and bow down;
Let us kneel before the
LORD our Maker (Ps. 95:6).
*or*
The LORD is in His holy temple.
Let all the earth keep silence
before Him (Hab. 2:20).
*or*
Come to Me, all *you* who labor and are
heavy laden, and I will give you rest.
Take My yoke upon you and learn from
Me, for I am gentle and lowly in heart,
and you will find rest for your souls
(Matt. 11:28, 29).

Such invitations to worship (or "opening sentences" before worship) occur throughout the Scriptures. They set a worshipful tone for what follows, preparing our hearts and minds for the devotional occasion. The book of Psalms is a treasury of such opening lines, and ideal for family worship. To avoid mere ceremonialism, which can suffocate all vitality, vary the use of such openings.

### Praise

Following your call to worship, try a hymn of praise which should be an uplifting way to begin. Even if you have no instrument to accompany your singing (piano, organ, guitar, etc.), attempt it *a capella* (without instrument). Hopefully your family has one member with a strong leading voice. Everyone else do their best to join right in!

Holy, Holy, Holy, Lord God Almighty!
Early in the morning our song shall rise to Thee;
Holy, Holy, Holy! Merciful and Mighty!
God in Three Persons, blessed Trinity!
(Rev. John B. Dykes, 1861)
*or*
Praise, my soul, the King of heaven,
To His feet Thy tribute bring;
Ransomed, healed, restored, forgiven,
Who, like me, His praise should sing?
Praise Him, praise Him, praise Him,
praise Him,
Praise the Everlasting King.
(Sir John Goss, 1869)

### Scripture Reading

Next, the day's Scripture lesson should be read by mother, or someone else, on a daily rotating schedule. To help apply the Scripture lesson emphatically, father should ask searching questions to underscore the message. In the parable of the Good Samaritan (Luke 10:25–37), he might ask:

Who is the hero of this story?
Why do we like the Good Samaritan?
Who were the men who passed by the injured man?
Why didn't they help him?
Should we be surprised it was the *Samaritan* who showed mercy? (Why, or why not?)

Such a line of inquiry leads to some profound conclusions:

The religious position of the priest and Levite did not result in love, which is what Christ looks for in a truly spiritual person.
Do we love, and show mercy as the Samaritan did?
Or are we merely outwardly religious, like the priest and the Levite?
What do we need from God to be like the Samaritan? (Answer: a new heart).

### Memory Verse

Then father can read a memory verse, either from the Scripture lesson or somewhere else. The whole family should recite it together. A good one to reinforce the lesson of the Samaritan would be 1 Corinthians 13:1: "Though I speak with the tongues of men and of angels, but have not love, I have become as a sounding brass or a clanging cymbal."

By next family meeting, everyone who is old enough should have this memorized!

### Prayer Time

As family members prepare for the indispensable prayer time, there is a fine opportunity for them to open up to one another and to share their inner joys and burdens. Family prayer should create a growing level of confidence and depth of caring among them. Family harmony will improve with the practice of earnest family prayer. So it is important that each family member, whether present or absent, should be prayed for by name.

Other prayer requests outside the family circle can be stressed—families in special distress, friends at school and work, national and world concerns, and the missionary needs of the church.

Jesus has given us a formula for prayer in the "Lord's Prayer" (Matt. 6:8–13):

> "Our Father in heaven,
> Hallowed be Your name"—

Notice that this prayer is God-centered. All genuine prayers open with praise and adoration for God.

> "Your kingdom come.
> Your will be done
> On earth as *it is* in heaven"—

True prayer is concerned with God's kingdom righteousness, fulfilling the divine will throughout all creation.

> "Give us this day our daily bread"—

As your family prays, you should think each day how you depend on God to provide all things. Without Him you have and can do nothing.

> "And forgive us our debts,
> As we forgive our debtors"—

Our Lord's prayer is so demanding that you have no room left to harbor resentments within your family. Confession and forgiveness at the throne of God are the healing medicines for family discord.

> "And do not lead us into
> temptation,
> But deliver us from the evil one"—

You will become confident that God will protect all of you from temptations that otherwise might destroy your souls. Family prayer instills healthy fearlessness, since God will defeat the enemy of your souls if you only trust in Him.

> "For Yours is the kingdom and the power and the
> glory forever. Amen."—

Acknowledging God's sovereignty and glory is the uppermost principle of your prayer life and language. As your family grows in awareness of God's attributes, it strengthens its own character as a true family of God.

Each family member should also learn to express his or her soul's unique desires by praying aloud. Although our Lord showed us the *pattern* of prayer, we also see in Scripture that God's people have always voiced their particular concerns in their own words to God. Urgency, hastened by the Holy Spirit, will trigger these vocal prayers, just as Jesus taught in His model prayer: "Your will be done," etc.

After all members have thus prayed aloud briefly, dad should close the family worship time with his own prayer. It may be introduced by one of the great, spiritually enriching prayers from the Bible, or perhaps by a prayer-hymn. Then he should pray for his family's perceived needs, thanking God for caring for the family, as well as praying for the church and for the world (and for anyone perhaps omitted by other family members in prayer).

### Activities for Family Worship

Within this basic structure, content can be quite varied, especially for younger children who need activity learning. Abstract ideas have little appeal for youngsters, and we adults enjoy learning by doing also. We must keep in mind, however, that it would be wrong to convey the message by fun and games that we merely worship God for our enjoyment. Permitting the *means* of worship to become the *end* is the ancient error of idolatry. God Himself is the One who preoccupies us in family worship—not the routines and activities we practice while worshiping Him.

Yet God condescends to our various weaknesses, revealing Himself to us in our everyday life. Common human experiences are transformed into the symbols and vivid pictures portraying the kingdom of heaven. In His teaching Jesus used familiar images from the world immediately around Him. Consider the image of a man sowing his field, a fisherman drawing his nets, or the storm beating on a house.

### The Bible

Have you thought about how important the Bible itself has become, as a visible symbol of God's revelation? Not only its *content,* but that wonderful leather-bound object *itself* has come to embody the magnificent truth of God and His plan of redemption through all the ages of time. This *symbolic* value of the Bible must not be lost! Otherwise, we will also lose much of our esteem for its *content.* This is why there is some danger in having so many translations. There is value in most of them, but if we lose a commonly *shared* translation, our children's respect for the Book itself will be lost amid their bewilderment over so many seemingly conflicting Bibles.

Of course our King James Version has blessed us for hundreds of years. It has united English-speaking believers everywhere. It is like a very old friend—and it is a most reliable reproduction of God's revelation to us.

So in family worship, the first symbol of importance is the Bible *itself.* Let all family members share a common Bible. You are holding a New King James Bible, the twentieth-century rendering of the most revered Bible of all time. If dad uses it during family devotions, it ought to be used by other family members for unity of worship. Other translations can be referred to for comparison. But in family worship, let us all read from the same text. Otherwise, there is chaos.

### The Hymnbook

Besides a commonly shared Bible, everyone should have a hymnbook—the same one you use at church. Sometimes opening sentences and spiritually illuminating prayers can be selected from it. Hymnbooks are also needed when your family sings in unison.

### Audiovisuals

Instead of always discussing a Scripture lesson, you will occasionally wish to portray a Bible story visually.

The slide projector is one traditional method—or you may wish to introduce Bible story books, flash-card stories, puppets—or to combine sound with pictures, you may play Bible stories and teaching on tape cassettes.

Today, instructional "software" is available in the form of video cassettes that can be projected on the television screen.

**Drama**

Children love to playact, and adults love to be their audiences. The parable of the Good Samaritan would be a good starting point for a hastily dramatized skit. The children can go to another room and pick their roles—the "certain man" who went down to Jericho, the priest, the Levite, the Samaritan himself. They can then return to the room and dramatize the action. Some may have to double as "the thieves." Everyone will have fun—and the story will never be forgotten!

**Daily Devotional Guides**

In every Christian bookstore is an abundance of daily devotional reading guides. They are not meant as regular family reading fare. But switching to such a book for a week would give a refreshing change to the content of your family prayer time.

**Prayer Bulletin Board**

One way to maintain meaningful family prayer is to keep an up-to-date bulletin board. Mounted on it can be snapshots, postcards, letters, and prayer requests from absent family members, friends, and missionaries. Its prayer emphasis should vary from day to day, keeping prayer from becoming generalized, since "general" prayers can easily degenerate into insincerity. *Specific* needs of the subjects prayed for should be highlighted.

**Maps**

In addition to the usual maps contained in the Bible, a globe and other maps will pinpoint the locations of missionaries, relatives, and friends, as well as geographical areas for Bible study and localities needing Christian work and prayer. *Seeing* the place fixes the concern in the minds of the praying family members, and helps prevent prayer from becoming nebulous and abstract.

**Topical Studies**

The ages and special needs of your family will indicate which Bible books you will require. Topical studies indexed by subject should direct you to specific Scriptures at your time of need. Family illness, financial distress, and death in your family are circumstances that cry out for particular emphasis. The great promises of God to His troubled people are mandatory at such moments of trial.

This is why the book of Psalms is so frequently turned to in periods of trouble. There we find the burdened individual baring his heart and gaining relief by drawing nearer to the Redeemer of his soul:

> I waited patiently for the LORD;
> And He inclined to me,
> And heard my cry (Ps. 40:1).

God has always been the sufficiency of His people. "Yea, though I walk through the valley of the shadow of death, I will fear no evil; for You *are* with me" (Ps. 23:4); "I *am* the LORD who heals you" (Ex. 15:26); "my God shall supply all your need according to His riches in glory by Christ Jesus" (Phil. 4:19); "I will never leave you nor forsake you" (Heb. 13:5). The Lord never abandons those who love Him.

**Biography**

We all learn by imitation. Children begin by imitating their parents, and perhaps their older brothers and sisters and then relatives. Later, movie and music stars may become objects of admiration, not always very good ones.

The Bible is rich in the portrayal of thrilling, inspiring lives that can still excite and stimulate the whole family. We all need assurance that the God who triumphed in the lives of His people in former times, is the identical God moving among us today: "Jesus Christ *is* the same yesterday, today, and forever" (Heb. 13:8).

See how God remained faithful to faithful Abraham. Read how God sustained David throughout his victories and failures. Revel in the triumph of God's grace in the life of that seemingly most hopeless of men, Saul the Pharisee—who became the most effective Christian missionary of all time, Paul the apostle.

**Study Helps**

In addition to the materials described above, your family should acquire several basic study helps. Among these a Bible concordance is needed for locating Bible texts and for word studies. A Bible dictionary will be useful in looking up the meanings of Bible terms, in following themes through the Bible, in checking spellings of places and names, and in understanding life in Bible times. A good single-volume commentary is helpful in preparing lesson plans. Other books of value include a Bible atlas, a book of Scripture quotations arranged by subject, and special subject studies. Consult your pastor, church librarian, or Christian bookstore for further ideas. As your library of biblical studies grows, family devotional life will be enriched for all members.

**Conclusion**

In our busy world there are always excuses for breaking a routine, especially with each of us pulled in many directions by school, work, friends, and various other things. It will be easy to miss a session of family worship and postpone our time at the family altar. *We can always "catch up next week" or start over,* we may be tempted to rationalize. While we must not condemn ourselves if we lapse, God wants us to persist with faith in Christ to enter a deepening family worship experience. We are frail and imperfect human beings; but by working as one body, in the family, we can become stronger Christians each day of our lives. The place to begin is not at church or Sunday school, or with a Christian magazine or book, or by watching a television ministry, fine as all these may be. The place to begin is with each other, in our own home, where God lives and wants us to live with Him.

# LIST OF SUGGESTED SCRIPTURE READINGS

| *Book* | *Reading* | *Day* |
|---|---|---|
| Genesis | 1:1—2:3 | 1 |
| | 3:1–24 | 2 |
| | 4:1–15 | 3 |
| | 6:1–13 | 4 |
| | 6:14–22 | 5 |
| | 7:1–24 | 6 |
| | 8:1–22 | 7 |
| | 9:18–29 | 8 |
| | 11:1–9 | 9 |
| | 11:31—12:9 | 10 |
| | 15:1–21 | 11 |
| | 17:1–22 | 12 |
| | 18:1–15 | 13 |
| | 19:1–11 | 14 |
| | 19:12–29 | 15 |
| | 22:1–19 | 16 |
| | 25:19–34 | 17 |
| | 27:1–29 | 18 |
| | 27:30–45 | 19 |
| | 28:10–22 | 20 |
| | 32:1, 2, 22–32 | 21 |
| | 37:1–11 | 22 |
| | 37:12–36 | 23 |
| | 45:1–28 | 24 |
| | 50:15–26 | 25 |
| Exodus | 3:1–18 | 26 |
| | 12:1–13 | 27 |
| | 14:10–27 | 28 |
| | 15:20–27 | 29 |
| | 20:1–17 | 30 |
| | 23:20–33 | 31 |
| Leviticus | 16:1–10 | 32 |
| Numbers | 9:15–23 | 33 |
| | 13:1, 2, 21–33 | 34 |
| | 14:26–38 | 35 |
| | 21:4–9 | 36 |
| | 22:21–35 | 37 |
| Deuteronomy | 6:1–9 | 38 |
| | 10:12–22 | 39 |
| | 30:11–20 | 40 |
| Joshua | 1:1–9 | 41 |
| | 4:1–10 | 42 |
| | 7:1, 10–21 | 43 |
| | 8:30–35 | 44 |
| Judges | 7:1–7 | 45 |
| | 16:23–31 | 46 |
| Ruth | 1:1–18 | 47 |
| 1 Samuel | 3:1–18 | 48 |
| | 16:1–13 | 49 |
| 2 Samuel | 1:17–27 | 50 |
| | 7:1–17 | 51 |
| | 12:1–14 | 52 |
| | 18:24–33 | 53 |
| | 22:1–51 | 54 |
| 1 Kings | 3:1–15 | 55 |
| | 8:22–40 | 56 |
| | 9:1–9 | 57 |
| | 11:1–11 | 58 |
| | 12:1–15 | 59 |
| | 17:1, 8, 9, 17–24 | 60 |
| | 18:20–39 | 61 |
| 2 Kings | 5:1–14 | 62 |
| | 20:12–19 | 63 |
| | 22:3–20 | 64 |
| 1 Chronicles | 29:10–20 | 65 |
| 2 Chronicles | 27:1–9 | 66 |
| | 32:9–22 | 67 |
| Job | 1:20—2:10 | 68 |
| Psalms | 1:1–6 | 69 |
| | 8:1–9 | 70 |
| | 16:1–11 | 71 |
| | 19:1–14 | 72 |
| | 20:1–9 | 73 |
| | 22:1–31 | 74 |
| | 23:1–6 | 75 |
| | 24:1–10 | 76 |
| | 27:1–14 | 77 |
| | 32:1–11 | 78 |
| | 40:1–17 | 79 |
| | 42:1–11 | 80 |
| | 45:1–17 | 81 |
| | 51:1–19 | 82 |
| | 63:1–11 | 83 |
| | 69:1–21 | 84 |
| | 72:1–20 | 85 |
| | 90:1–17 | 86 |
| | 91:1–16 | 87 |
| | 95:1–11 | 88 |
| | 110:1–7 | 89 |
| | 121:1–8 | 90 |
| Proverbs | 3:1–26 | 91 |
| | 16:1–33 | 92 |
| | 31:10–31 | 93 |
| Ecclesiastes | 3:1–8 | 94 |
| | 12:1–14 | 95 |
| Isaiah | 6:1–13 | 96 |
| | 9:1–7 | 97 |
| | 11:1–10 | 98 |
| | 26:1–9 | 99 |
| | 30:15–26 | 100 |
| | 40:1–11 | 101 |
| | 40:21–31 | 102 |
| | 41:1–20 | 103 |
| | 42:1–9 | 104 |
| | 43:1–21 | 105 |
| | 49:1–13 | 106 |
| | 50:1–11 | 107 |
| | 52:13—53:12 | 108 |
| | 54:1–17 | 109 |
| | 61:1–11 | 110 |
| | 65:17–25 | 111 |
| | 66:1–13 | 112 |
| Jeremiah | 17:5–18 | 113 |
| | 23:1–10 | 114 |
| | 33:12–26 | 115 |
| Lamentations | 3:1–27 | 116 |
| Ezekiel | 11:14–25 | 117 |
| | 18:1–18 | 118 |
| | 37:1–14 | 119 |
| Daniel | 2:24–45 | 120 |
| | 3:19–30 | 121 |
| Hosea | 6:1–11 | 122 |
| | 14:1–9 | 123 |
| Joel | 3:1–21 | 124 |
| Amos | 9:11–15 | 125 |

| *Book* | *Reading* | *Day* |
|---|---|---|
| Jonah | 3:1, 2, 10; 4:1–11 | 126 |
| Micah | 5:1–5 | 127 |
| Habakkuk | 1:12—2:4 | 128 |
| Zephaniah | 3:8–20 | 129 |
| Zechariah | 9:9–17 | 130 |
| Malachi | 3:16—4:6 | 131 |
| Matthew | 1:18—2:12 | 132 |
| | 3:1–12 | 133 |
| | 3:13—4:11 | 134 |
| | 5:1–26 | 135 |
| | 5:27–48 | 136 |
| | 6:1–18 | 137 |
| | 6:19–34 | 138 |
| | 7:1–20 | 139 |
| | 7:21–29 | 140 |
| | 9:1–17 | 141 |
| | 9:18–38 | 142 |
| | 10:5–26 | 143 |
| | 10:32–42 | 144 |
| | 11:11–30 | 145 |
| | 12:22–37 | 146 |
| | 13:1–23 | 147 |
| | 13:24–43 | 148 |
| | 13:44–52 | 149 |
| | 14:13–33 | 150 |
| | 15:1–20 | 151 |
| | 16:13–28 | 152 |
| | 17:1–13 | 153 |
| | 18:1–20 | 154 |
| | 19:1–9 | 155 |
| | 19:16–30 | 156 |
| | 20:1–16 | 157 |
| | 21:1–17 | 158 |
| | 21:33–46 | 159 |
| | 22:1–14 | 160 |
| | 22:15–46 | 161 |
| | 24:1–14 | 162 |
| | 25:1–13 | 163 |
| | 25:31–46 | 164 |
| | 26:1–16 | 165 |
| | 26:26–46 | 166 |
| | 26:47–75 | 167 |
| | 27:1–26 | 168 |
| | 27:45–66 | 169 |
| | 28:1–20 | 170 |
| Mark | 8:1–21 | 171 |
| | 16:12–20 | 172 |
| Luke | 1:5–25 | 173 |
| | 1:26–38 | 174 |
| | 1:39–56 | 175 |
| | 2:1–20 | 176 |
| | 4:16–30 | 177 |
| | 5:1–26 | 178 |
| | 6:1–19 | 179 |
| | 7:1–17 | 180 |
| | 7:18–35 | 181 |
| | 7:36–50 | 182 |
| | 10:1–20 | 183 |
| | 10:25–37 | 184 |
| | 12:1–21 | 185 |
| | 12:35–56 | 186 |
| | 13:22–35 | 187 |
| | 14:7–24 | 188 |
| | 15:11–32 | 189 |
| | 16:1–13 | 190 |
| | 16:19–31 | 191 |
| | 17:20–37 | 192 |
| | 18:1–14 | 193 |
| | 19:1–10 | 194 |
| | 24:13–35 | 195 |
| John | 1:1–18 | 196 |
| | 1:19–34 | 197 |
| | 2:1–12 | 198 |
| | 3:1–21 | 199 |
| | 3:22–26 | 200 |
| | 4:1–26 | 201 |
| | 5:1–15 | 202 |
| | 5:16–23, 39–47 | 203 |
| | 6:22–40 | 204 |
| | 7:10–24 | 205 |
| | 8:1–12 | 206 |
| | 8:21–36 | 207 |
| | 9:1–12, 35–41 | 208 |
| | 10:1–30 | 209 |
| | 11:11–27, 38–44 | 210 |
| | 13:1–20 | 211 |
| | 14:1–18 | 212 |
| | 14:19–31 | 213 |
| | 15:1–17 | 214 |
| | 16:1–15 | 215 |
| | 16:16–33 | 216 |
| | 17:1–26 | 217 |
| | 19:1–30 | 218 |
| | 21:1–25 | 219 |
| Acts | 1:4–14 | 220 |
| | 2:1–39 | 221 |
| | 3:1–10 | 222 |
| | 3:11–26 | 223 |
| | 4:5–22 | 224 |
| | 5:1–11 | 225 |
| | 5:17–42 | 226 |
| | 6:8–11; 7:1–16 | 227 |
| | 7:17–50 | 228 |
| | 7:51—8:3 | 229 |
| | 9:1–22 | 230 |
| | 10:1–16 | 231 |
| | 10:34–48 | 232 |
| | 12:1–17 | 233 |
| | 13:13–41 | 234 |
| | 15:1–21 | 235 |
| | 16:16–34 | 236 |
| | 17:16–34 | 237 |
| | 19:21–41 | 238 |
| | 23:1–10 | 239 |
| | 27:1, 13–38 | 240 |
| | 27:39—28:10 | 241 |
| | 28:16–31 | 242 |
| Romans | 1:16–32 | 243 |
| | 2:1–16 | 244 |
| | 3:9–31 | 245 |
| | 4:1–13 | 246 |
| | 5:1–21 | 247 |
| | 6:1–14 | 248 |
| | 7:1–25 | 249 |
| | 8:1–17 | 250 |
| | 8:18–39 | 251 |
| | 9:14–33 | 252 |
| | 10:6–17 | 253 |
| | 12:1–21 | 254 |
| | 15:1–13 | 255 |
| 1 Corinthians | 1:18–31 | 256 |
| | 2:1–16 | 257 |

| Book | Reading | Day |
|---|---|---|
| | 6:1–20 | 258 |
| | 7:1–16 | 259 |
| | 13:1–13 | 260 |
| | 15:1–19 | 261 |
| | 15:35–58 | 262 |
| 2 Corinthians | 5:1–21 | 263 |
| Galatians | 3:1–29 | 264 |
| | 5:1–26 | 265 |
| Ephesians | 1:1–23 | 266 |
| | 2:1–18 | 267 |
| | 5:15—6:9 | 268 |
| | 6:10–20 | 269 |
| Philippians | 1:1–26 | 270 |
| | 2:1–11 | 271 |
| | 3:7—4:1 | 272 |
| | 4:4–20 | 273 |
| Colossians | 1:9–29 | 274 |
| | 2:1–23 | 275 |
| | 3:1—4:1 | 276 |
| 1 Thessalonians | 4:13—5:11 | 277 |
| 2 Thessalonians | 2:1–17 | 278 |
| 1 Timothy | 4:1–16 | 279 |
| 2 Timothy | 2:1–26 | 280 |
| | 3:1–17 | 281 |
| | 4:1–18 | 282 |
| Titus | 1:5–16 | 283 |
| | 2:1–15 | 284 |
| | 3:1–11 | 285 |
| Philemon | 1:1–25 | 286 |
| Hebrews | 1:1–14 | 287 |
| | 2:1–9 | 288 |
| | 2:10–18 | 289 |
| | 3:1–19 | 290 |
| | 4:1–13 | 291 |
| | 4:14—5:11 | 292 |
| | 5:12—6:12 | 293 |
| | 6:13–20 | 294 |
| | 7:1–19 | 295 |
| | 8:1–13 | 296 |
| | 9:1–15 | 297 |
| | 10:1–18 | 298 |
| | 10:19–39 | 299 |
| | 11:1–16 | 300 |
| | 11:17–40 | 301 |
| | 12:1–11 | 302 |
| | 12:18–29 | 303 |
| | 13:1–17, 20, 21 | 304 |
| James | 1:1–27 | 305 |
| | 2:1–13 | 306 |
| | 2:14–26 | 307 |
| | 3:1–18 | 308 |
| | 4:1–17 | 309 |
| | 5:1–12 | 310 |
| | 5:13–20 | 311 |
| 1 Peter | 1:3–21 | 312 |
| | 1:22—2:3 | 313 |
| | 2:4–10 | 314 |
| | 2:11–25 | 315 |
| | 3:1–12 | 316 |
| | 3:13—4:6 | 317 |
| | 4:7–19 | 318 |
| | 5:1–11 | 319 |
| 2 Peter | 1:1–11 | 320 |
| | 2:1–22 | 321 |
| | 3:1–18 | 322 |
| 1 John | 1:1–10 | 323 |
| | 2:1–14 | 324 |
| | 2:15–23 | 325 |
| | 2:24—3:3 | 326 |
| | 3:10–23 | 327 |
| | 3:24—4:16 | 328 |
| | 4:17—5:5 | 329 |
| | 5:9–21 | 330 |
| 2 John | 1:1–13 | 331 |
| 3 John | 1:1–14 | 332 |
| Jude | 1:1–25 | 333 |
| Revelation | 1:1–8 | 334 |
| | 1:9–20 | 335 |
| | 2:1–7 | 336 |
| | 2:8–17 | 337 |
| | 2:18–29 | 338 |
| | 3:1–13 | 339 |
| | 3:14–22 | 340 |
| | 4:1–11 | 341 |
| | 5:1–14 | 342 |
| | 6:1–17 | 343 |
| | 7:1–17 | 344 |
| | 8:1–13 | 345 |
| | 9:1–12 | 346 |
| | 9:13–21 | 347 |
| | 10:1–11 | 348 |
| | 11:1–14 | 349 |
| | 11:15–19 | 350 |
| | 12:1–17 | 351 |
| | 13:1–10 | 352 |
| | 13:11–18 | 353 |
| | 14:1–13 | 354 |
| | 14:14–20 | 355 |
| | 15:1–8 | 356 |
| | 16:1–21 | 357 |
| | 17:1–18 | 358 |
| | 18:1–8, 21–24 | 359 |
| | 19:1–10 | 360 |
| | 19:11–21 | 361 |
| | 20:1–15 | 362 |
| | 21:1–8 | 363 |
| | 21:9–27 | 364 |
| | 22:1–21 | 365 |

## Additional or Alternate Readings for Christmas

| | |
|---|---|
| December 21 | Luke 1:5–25 (Birth of John) |
| December 22 | Luke 1:26–38 (Jesus' birth) |
| December 23 | Luke 1:39–56 (Mary's visit) |
| December 24 | Matthew 1:18—2:12 (Announcement and birth of Jesus) |
| December 25 | Luke 2:1–20 (Birth of Jesus) |

## Additional or Alternate Readings for Easter

(Crucifixion and Resurrection Texts)

| | |
|---|---|
| Mid-March to Mid-April | Matthew 26—28 |
| | Luke 24 |
| | John 19; 21 |

# Read Your Bible Through In a Year

A systematic division of the books of the Bible, primarily for reading.

## JANUARY

| Date | MORNING | EVENING |
|---|---|---|
| | MATT. | GEN. |
| 1 | 1 | 1, 2, 3 |
| 2 | 2 | 4, 5, 6 |
| 3 | 3 | 7, 8, 9 |
| 4 | 4 | 10, 11, 12 |
| 5 | 5: 1–26 | 13, 14, 15 |
| 6 | 5:27–48 | 16, 17 |
| 7 | 6: 1–18 | 18, 19 |
| 8 | 6:19–34 | 20, 21, 22 |
| 9 | 7 | 23, 24 |
| 10 | 8: 1–17 | 25, 26 |
| 11 | 8:18–34 | 27, 28 |
| 12 | 9: 1–17 | 29, 30 |
| 13 | 9:18–38 | 31, 32 |
| 14 | 10: 1–20 | 33, 34, 35 |
| 15 | 10:21–42 | 36, 37, 38 |
| 16 | 11 | 39, 40 |
| 17 | 12: 1–23 | 41, 42 |
| 18 | 12:24–50 | 43, 44, 45 |
| 19 | 13: 1–30 | 46, 47, 48 |
| 20 | 13:31–58 | 49, 50 |
| | | EX. |
| 21 | 14: 1–21 | 1, 2, 3 |
| 22 | 14:22–36 | 4, 5, 6 |
| 23 | 15: 1–20 | 7, 8 |
| 24 | 15:21–39 | 9, 10, 11 |
| 25 | 16 | 12, 13 |
| 26 | 17 | 14, 15 |
| 27 | 18: 1–20 | 16, 17, 18 |
| 28 | 18:21–35 | 19, 20 |
| 29 | 19 | 21, 22 |
| 30 | 20: 1–16 | 23, 24 |
| 31 | 20:17–34 | 25, 26 |

## FEBRUARY

| Date | MORNING | EVENING |
|---|---|---|
| | MATT. | EX. |
| 1 | 21: 1–22 | 27, 28 |
| 2 | 21:23–46 | 29, 30 |
| 3 | 22: 1–22 | 31, 32, 33 |
| 4 | 22:23–46 | 34, 35 |
| 5 | 23: 1–22 | 36, 37, 38 |
| 6 | 23:23–39 | 39, 40 |
| | | LEV. |
| 7 | 24: 1–28 | 1, 2, 3 |
| 8 | 24:29–51 | 4, 5 |
| 9 | 25: 1–30 | 6, 7 |
| 10 | 25:31–46 | 8, 9, 10 |
| 11 | 26: 1–25 | 11, 12 |
| 12 | 26:26–50 | 13 |
| 13 | 26:51–75 | 14 |
| 14 | 27: 1–26 | 15, 16 |
| 15 | 27:27–50 | 17, 18 |
| 16 | 27:51–66 | 19, 20 |
| 17 | 28 | 21, 22 |
| | MARK | |
| 18 | 1: 1–22 | 23, 24 |
| 19 | 1:23–45 | 25 |
| 20 | 2 | 26, 27 |
| | | NUM. |
| 21 | 3: 1–19 | 1, 2 |
| 22 | 3:20–35 | 3, 4 |
| 23 | 4: 1–20 | 5, 6 |
| 24 | 4:21–41 | 7, 8 |
| 25 | 5: 1–20 | 9, 10, 11 |
| 26 | 5:21–43 | 12, 13, 14 |
| 27 | 6: 1–29 | 15, 16 |
| 28 | 6:30–56 | 17, 18, 19 |
| 29 | 7: 1–13 | 20, 21, 22 |

## MARCH

| Date | MORNING | EVENING |
|---|---|---|
| | MARK | NUM. |
| 1 | 7:14–37 | 23, 24, 25 |
| 2 | 8: 1–21 | 26, 27 |
| 3 | 8:22–38 | 28, 29, 30 |
| 4 | 9: 1–29 | 31, 32, 33 |
| 5 | 9:30–50 | 34, 35, 36 |
| | | DEUT. |
| 6 | 10: 1–31 | 1, 2 |
| 7 | 10:32–52 | 3, 4 |
| 8 | 11: 1–18 | 5, 6, 7 |
| 9 | 11:19–33 | 8, 9, 10 |
| 10 | 12: 1–27 | 11, 12, 13 |
| 11 | 12:28–44 | 14, 15, 16 |
| 12 | 13: 1–20 | 17, 18, 19 |
| 13 | 13:21–37 | 20, 21, 22 |
| 14 | 14: 1–26 | 23, 24, 25 |
| 15 | 14:27–53 | 26, 27 |
| 16 | 14:54–72 | 28, 29 |
| 17 | 15: 1–25 | 30, 31 |
| 18 | 15:26–47 | 32, 33, 34 |
| | | JOSH. |
| 19 | 16 | 1, 2, 3 |
| | LUKE | |
| 20 | 1: 1–20 | 4, 5, 6 |
| 21 | 1:21–38 | 7, 8, 9 |
| 22 | 1:39–56 | 10, 11, 12 |
| 23 | 1:57–80 | 13, 14, 15 |
| 24 | 2: 1–24 | 16, 17, 18 |
| 25 | 2:25–52 | 19, 20, 21 |
| 26 | 3 | 22, 23, 24 |
| | | JUDG. |
| 27 | 4: 1–30 | 1, 2, 3 |
| 28 | 4:31–44 | 4, 5, 6 |
| 29 | 5: 1–16 | 7, 8 |
| 30 | 5:17–39 | 9, 10 |
| 31 | 6: 1–26 | 11, 12 |

## APRIL

| Date | MORNING | EVENING |
|---|---|---|
| | LUKE | JUDG. |
| 1 | 6:27–49 | 13, 14, 15 |
| 2 | 7: 1–30 | 16, 17, 18 |
| 3 | 7:31–50 | 19, 20, 21 |
| | | RUTH |
| 4 | 8: 1–25 | 1, 2, 3, 4 |
| | | 1 SAM. |
| 5 | 8:26–56 | 1, 2, 3 |
| 6 | 9: 1–17 | 4, 5, 6 |
| 7 | 9:18–36 | 7, 8, 9 |
| 8 | 9:37–62 | 10, 11, 12 |
| 9 | 10: 1–24 | 13, 14 |
| 10 | 10:25–42 | 15, 16 |
| 11 | 11: 1–28 | 17, 18 |
| 12 | 11:29–54 | 19, 20, 21 |
| 13 | 12: 1–31 | 22, 23, 24 |
| 14 | 12:32–59 | 25, 26 |
| 15 | 13: 1–22 | 27, 28, 29 |
| 16 | 13:23–35 | 30, 31 |
| | | 2 SAM. |
| 17 | 14: 1–24 | 1, 2 |
| 18 | 14:25–35 | 3, 4, 5 |
| 19 | 15: 1–10 | 6, 7, 8 |
| 20 | 15:11–32 | 9, 10, 11 |
| 21 | 16 | 12, 13 |
| 22 | 17: 1–19 | 14, 15 |
| 23 | 17:20–37 | 16, 17, 18 |
| 24 | 18: 1–23 | 19, 20 |
| 25 | 18:24–43 | 21, 22 |
| 26 | 19: 1–27 | 23, 24 |
| | | 1 KIN. |
| 27 | 19:28–48 | 1, 2 |
| 28 | 20: 1–26 | 3, 4, 5 |
| 29 | 20:27–47 | 6, 7 |
| 30 | 21: 1–19 | 8, 9 |

## MAY

| Date | MORNING | EVENING |
|---|---|---|
| | LUKE | 1 KIN. |
| 1 | 21:20–38 | 10, 11 |
| 2 | 22: 1–20 | 12, 13 |
| 3 | 22:21–46 | 14, 15 |
| 4 | 22:47–71 | 16, 17, 18 |
| 5 | 23: 1–25 | 19, 20 |
| 6 | 23:26–56 | 21, 22 |
| | | 2 KIN. |
| 7 | 24: 1–35 | 1, 2, 3 |
| 8 | 24:36–53 | 4, 5, 6 |
| | JOHN | |
| 9 | 1: 1–28 | 7, 8, 9 |
| 10 | 1:29–51 | 10, 11, 12 |
| 11 | 2 | 13, 14 |
| 12 | 3: 1–18 | 15, 16 |
| 13 | 3:19–38 | 17, 18 |
| 14 | 4: 1–30 | 19, 20, 21 |
| 15 | 4:31–54 | 22, 23 |
| 16 | 5: 1–24 | 24, 25 |
| | | 1 CHR. |
| 17 | 5:25–47 | 1, 2, 3 |
| 18 | 6: 1–21 | 4, 5, 6 |
| 19 | 6:22–44 | 7, 8, 9 |
| 20 | 6:45–71 | 10, 11, 12 |
| 21 | 7: 1–27 | 13, 14, 15 |
| 22 | 7:28–53 | 16, 17, 18 |
| 23 | 8: 1–27 | 19, 20, 21 |
| 24 | 8:28–59 | 22, 23, 24 |
| 25 | 9: 1–23 | 25, 26, 27 |
| 26 | 9:24–41 | 28, 29 |
| | | 2 CHR. |
| 27 | 10: 1–23 | 1, 2, 3 |
| 28 | 10:24–42 | 4, 5, 6 |
| 29 | 11: 1–29 | 7, 8, 9 |
| 30 | 11:30–57 | 10, 11, 12 |
| 31 | 12: 1–26 | 13, 14 |

## JUNE

| Date | MORNING | EVENING |
|---|---|---|
| | JOHN | 2 CHR. |
| 1 | 12:27–50 | 15, 16 |
| 2 | 13: 1–20 | 17, 18 |
| 3 | 13:21–38 | 19, 20 |
| 4 | 14 | 21, 22 |
| 5 | 15 | 23, 24 |
| 6 | 16 | 25, 26, 27 |
| 7 | 17 | 28, 29 |
| 8 | 18: 1–18 | 30, 31 |
| 9 | 18:19–40 | 32, 33 |
| 10 | 19: 1–22 | 34, 35, 36 |
| | | EZRA |
| 11 | 19:23–42 | 1, 2 |
| 12 | 20 | 3, 4, 5 |
| 13 | 21 | 6, 7, 8 |
| | ACTS | |
| 14 | 1 | 9, 10 |
| | | NEH. |
| 15 | 2: 1–21 | 1, 2, 3 |
| 16 | 2:22–47 | 4, 5, 6 |
| 17 | 3 | 7, 8, 9 |
| 18 | 4: 1–22 | 10, 11 |
| 19 | 4:23–37 | 12, 13 |
| | | ESTH. |
| 20 | 5: 1–21 | 1, 2 |
| 21 | 5:22–42 | 3, 4, 5 |
| 22 | 6 | 6, 7, 8 |
| 23 | 7: 1–21 | 9, 10 |
| | | JOB |
| 24 | 7:22–43 | 1, 2 |
| 25 | 7:44–60 | 3, 4 |
| 26 | 8: 1–25 | 5, 6, 7 |
| 27 | 8:26–40 | 8, 9, 10 |
| 28 | 9: 1–21 | 11, 12, 13 |
| 29 | 9:22–43 | 14, 15, 16 |
| 30 | 10: 1–23 | 17, 18, 19 |

## JULY

| Date | MORNING | EVENING |
|---|---|---|
| | **ACTS** | **JOB** |
| 1 | 10:24–48 | 20, 21 |
| 2 | 11 | 22, 23, 24 |
| 3 | 12 | 25, 26, 27 |
| 4 | 13: 1–25 | 28, 29 |
| 5 | 13:26–52 | 30, 31 |
| 6 | 14 | 32, 33 |
| 7 | 15: 1–21 | 34, 35 |
| 8 | 15:22–41 | 36, 37 |
| 9 | 16: 1–21 | 38, 39, 40 |
| 10 | 16:22–40 | 41, 42 |
| | | **PS.** |
| 11 | 17: 1–15 | 1, 2, 3 |
| 12 | 17:16–34 | 4, 5, 6 |
| 13 | 18 | 7, 8, 9 |
| 14 | 19: 1–20 | 10, 11, 12 |
| 15 | 19:21–41 | 13, 14, 15 |
| 16 | 20: 1–16 | 16, 17 |
| 17 | 20:17–38 | 18, 19 |
| 18 | 21: 1–17 | 20, 21, 22 |
| 19 | 21:18–40 | 23, 24, 25 |
| 20 | 22 | 26, 27, 28 |
| 21 | 23: 1–15 | 29, 30 |
| 22 | 23:16–35 | 31, 32 |
| 23 | 24 | 33, 34 |
| 24 | 25 | 35, 36 |
| 25 | 26 | 37, 38, 39 |
| 26 | 27: 1–26 | 40, 41, 42 |
| 27 | 27:27–44 | 43, 44, 45 |
| 28 | 28 | 46, 47, 48 |
| | **ROM.** | |
| 29 | 1 | 49, 50 |
| 30 | 2 | 51, 52, 53 |
| 31 | 3 | 54, 55, 56 |

## AUGUST

| Date | MORNING | EVENING |
|---|---|---|
| | **ROM.** | **PS.** |
| 1 | 4 | 57, 58, 59 |
| 2 | 5 | 60, 61, 62 |
| 3 | 6 | 63, 64, 65 |
| 4 | 7 | 66, 67 |
| 5 | 8: 1–21 | 68, 69 |
| 6 | 8:22–39 | 70, 71 |
| 7 | 9: 1–15 | 72, 73 |
| 8 | 9:16–33 | 74, 75, 76 |
| 9 | 10 | 77, 78 |
| 10 | 11: 1–18 | 79, 80 |
| 11 | 11:19–36 | 81, 82, 83 |
| 12 | 12 | 84, 85, 86 |
| 13 | 13 | 87, 88 |
| 14 | 14 | 89, 90 |
| 15 | 15: 1–13 | 91, 92, 93 |
| 16 | 15:14–33 | 94, 95, 96 |
| 17 | 16 | 97, 98, 99 |
| | **1 COR.** | |
| 18 | 1 | 100, 101, 102 |
| 19 | 2 | 103, 104 |
| 20 | 3 | 105, 106 |
| 21 | 4 | 107, 108, 109 |
| 22 | 5 | 110, 111, 112 |
| 23 | 6 | 113, 114, 115 |
| 24 | 7: 1–19 | 116, 117, 118 |
| 25 | 7:20–40 | 119: 1–88 |
| 26 | 8 | 119: 89–176 |
| 27 | 9 | 120, 121, 122 |
| 28 | 10: 1–18 | 123, 124, 125 |
| 29 | 10:19–33 | 126, 127, 128 |
| 30 | 11: 1–16 | 129, 130, 131 |
| 31 | 11:17–34 | 132, 133, 134 |

## SEPTEMBER

| Date | MORNING | EVENING |
|---|---|---|
| | **1 COR.** | **PS.** |
| 1 | 12 | 135, 136 |
| 2 | 13 | 137, 138, 139 |
| 3 | 14: 1–20 | 140, 141, 142 |
| 4 | 14:21–40 | 143, 144, 145 |
| 5 | 15: 1–28 | 146, 147 |
| 6 | 15:29–58 | 148, 149, 150 |
| | | **PROV.** |
| 7 | 16 | 1, 2 |
| | **2 COR.** | |
| 8 | 1 | 3, 4, 5 |
| 9 | 2 | 6, 7 |
| 10 | 3 | 8, 9 |
| 11 | 4 | 10, 11, 12 |
| 12 | 5 | 13, 14, 15 |
| 13 | 6 | 16, 17, 18 |
| 14 | 7 | 19, 20, 21 |
| 15 | 8 | 22, 23, 24 |
| 16 | 9 | 25, 26 |
| 17 | 10 | 27, 28, 29 |
| 18 | 11: 1–15 | 30, 31 |
| | | **ECCL.** |
| 19 | 11:16–33 | 1, 2, 3 |
| 20 | 12 | 4, 5, 6 |
| 21 | 13 | 7, 8, 9 |
| | **GAL.** | |
| 22 | 1 | 10, 11, 12 |
| | | **SONG** |
| 23 | 2 | 1, 2, 3 |
| 24 | 3 | 4, 5 |
| 25 | 4 | 6, 7, 8 |
| | | **IS.** |
| 26 | 5 | 1, 2 |
| 27 | 6 | 3, 4 |
| | **EPH.** | |
| 28 | 1 | 5, 6 |
| 29 | 2 | 7, 8 |
| 30 | 3 | 9, 10 |

## OCTOBER

| Date | MORNING | EVENING |
|---|---|---|
| | **EPH.** | **IS.** |
| 1 | 4 | 11, 12, 13 |
| 2 | 5: 1–16 | 14, 15, 16 |
| 3 | 5:17–33 | 17, 18, 19 |
| 4 | 6 | 20, 21, 22 |
| | **PHIL.** | |
| 5 | 1 | 23, 24, 25 |
| 6 | 2 | 26, 27 |
| 7 | 3 | 28, 29 |
| 8 | 4 | 30, 31 |
| | **COL.** | |
| 9 | 1 | 32, 33 |
| 10 | 2 | 34, 35, 36 |
| 11 | 3 | 37, 38 |
| 12 | 4 | 39, 40 |
| | **1 THESS.** | |
| 13 | 1 | 41, 42 |
| 14 | 2 | 43, 44 |
| 15 | 3 | 45, 46 |
| 16 | 4 | 47, 48, 49 |
| 17 | 5 | 50, 51, 52 |
| | **2 THESS.** | |
| 18 | 1 | 53, 54, 55 |
| 19 | 2 | 56, 57, 58 |
| 20 | 3 | 59, 60, 61 |
| | **1 TIM.** | |
| 21 | 1 | 62, 63, 64 |
| 22 | 2 | 65, 66 |
| | | **JER.** |
| 23 | 3 | 1, 2 |
| 24 | 4 | 3, 4, 5 |
| 25 | 5 | 6, 7, 8 |
| 26 | 6 | 9, 10, 11 |
| | **2 TIM.** | |
| 27 | 1 | 12, 13, 14 |
| 28 | 2 | 15, 16, 17 |
| 29 | 3 | 18, 19 |
| 30 | 4 | 20, 21 |
| | **TITUS** | |
| 31 | 1 | 22, 23 |

## NOVEMBER

| Date | MORNING | EVENING |
|---|---|---|
| | **TITUS** | **JER.** |
| 1 | 2 | 24, 25, 26 |
| 2 | 3 | 27, 28, 29 |
| 3 | **PHILEM.** | 30, 31 |
| | **HEB.** | |
| 4 | 1 | 32, 33 |
| 5 | 2 | 34, 35, 36 |
| 6 | 3 | 37, 38, 39 |
| 7 | 4 | 40, 41, 42 |
| 8 | 5 | 43, 44, 45 |
| 9 | 6 | 46, 47 |
| 10 | 7 | 48, 49 |
| 11 | 8 | 50 |
| 12 | 9 | 51, 52 |
| | | **LAM.** |
| 13 | 10: 1–18 | 1, 2 |
| 14 | 10:19–39 | 3, 4, 5 |
| | | **EZEK.** |
| 15 | 11: 1–19 | 1, 2 |
| 16 | 11:20–40 | 3, 4 |
| 17 | 12 | 5, 6, 7 |
| 18 | 13 | 8, 9, 10 |
| | **JAMES** | |
| 19 | 1 | 11, 12, 13 |
| 20 | 2 | 14, 15 |
| 21 | 3 | 16, 17 |
| 22 | 4 | 18, 19 |
| 23 | 5 | 20, 21 |
| | **1 PET.** | |
| 24 | 1 | 22, 23 |
| 25 | 2 | 24, 25, 26 |
| 26 | 3 | 27, 28, 29 |
| 27 | 4 | 30, 31, 32 |
| 28 | 5 | 33, 34 |
| | **2 PET.** | |
| 29 | 1 | 35, 36 |
| 30 | 2 | 37, 38, 39 |

## DECEMBER

| Date | MORNING | EVENING |
|---|---|---|
| | **2 PET.** | **EZEK.** |
| 1 | 3 | 40, 41 |
| | **1 JOHN** | |
| 2 | 1 | 42, 43, 44 |
| 3 | 2 | 45, 46 |
| 4 | 3 | 47, 48 |
| | | **DAN.** |
| 5 | 4 | 1, 2 |
| 6 | 5 | 3, 4 |
| 7 | **2 JOHN** | 5, 6, 7 |
| 8 | **3 JOHN** | 8, 9, 10 |
| 9 | **JUDE** | 11, 12 |
| | **REV.** | **HOS.** |
| 10 | 1 | 1, 2, 3, 4 |
| 11 | 2 | 5, 6, 7, 8 |
| 12 | 3 | 9, 10, 11 |
| 13 | 4 | 12, 13, 14 |
| 14 | 5 | **JOEL** |
| | | **AMOS** |
| 15 | 6 | 1, 2, 3 |
| 16 | 7 | 4, 5, 6 |
| 17 | 8 | 7, 8, 9 |
| 18 | 9 | **OBAD.** |
| 19 | 10 | **JON.** |
| | | **MIC.** |
| 20 | 11 | 1, 2, 3 |
| 21 | 12 | 4, 5 |
| 22 | 13 | 6, 7 |
| 23 | 14 | **NAH.** |
| 24 | 15 | **HAB.** |
| 25 | 16 | **ZEPH.** |
| 26 | 17 | **HAG.** |
| | | **ZECH.** |
| 27 | 18 | 1, 2, 3, 4 |
| 28 | 19 | 5, 6, 7, 8 |
| 29 | 20 | 9, 10, 11, 12 |
| 30 | 21 | 13, 14 |
| 31 | 22 | **MAL.** |

# THE NEW TESTAMENT

WORDS OF CHRIST
IN RED

*The Gospel According to*

# MATTHEW

### *The Birth of Jesus Christ*

THE book of the [a]genealogy[1] of Jesus Christ, [b]the Son of David, [c]the Son of Abraham:
2 [a]Abraham begot Isaac, [b]Isaac begot Jacob, and Jacob begot [c]Judah and his brothers.
3 [a]Judah begot Perez and Zerah by Tamar, [b]Perez begot Hezron, and Hezron begot Ram.
4 Ram begot Amminadab, Amminadab begot Nahshon, and Nahshon begot Salmon.
5 Salmon begot [a]Boaz by Rahab, Boaz begot Obed by Ruth, Obed begot Jesse,
6 and [a]Jesse begot David the king. [b]David the king begot Solomon by her [1]*who had been the wife* of Uriah.
7 [a]Solomon begot Rehoboam, Rehoboam begot [b]Abijah, and Abijah begot [1]Asa.
8 Asa begot [a]Jehoshaphat, Jehoshaphat begot Joram, and Joram begot [b]Uzziah.
9 Uzziah begot Jotham, Jotham begot [a]Ahaz, and Ahaz begot Hezekiah.
10 [a]Hezekiah begot Manasseh, Manasseh begot [1]Amon, and Amon begot [b]Josiah.
11 [a]Josiah begot [1]Jeconiah and his brothers about the time they were [b]carried away to Babylon.
**12** And after they were brought to Babylon, [a]Jeconiah begot Shealtiel, and Shealtiel begot [b]Zerubbabel.
13 Zerubbabel begot Abiud, Abiud begot Eliakim, and Eliakim begot Azor.
14 Azor begot Zadok, Zadok begot Achim, and Achim begot Eliud.
15 Eliud begot Eleazar, Eleazar begot Matthan, and Matthan begot Jacob.
16 And Jacob begot Joseph the husband of [a]Mary, of whom was born Jesus who is called Christ.
17 So all the generations from Abraham to David *are* fourteen generations, from David until the captivity in Babylon *are* fourteen generations, and from the captivity in Babylon until the Christ *are* fourteen generations.
**18** Now the [a]birth of Jesus Christ was as follows: After His mother Mary was betrothed to Joseph, before they came together, she was found with child [b]of the Holy Spirit.
19 Then Joseph her husband, being [1]a just *man*, and not wanting [a]to make her a public example, was minded to put her away secretly.
20 But while he thought about these things, behold, an angel of the Lord appeared to him in a dream, saying, "Joseph, son of David, do not be afraid to take to you Mary your wife, [a]for that which is [1]conceived in her is of the Holy Spirit.
21 [a]"And she will bring forth a Son, and you shall call His name [1]JESUS, [b]for He will save His people from their sins."
22 So all this was done that it might be fulfilled which was spoken by the Lord through the prophet, saying:
23 [a]*"Behold,*[1] *the virgin shall be with child, and bear a Son, and they shall call His name Immanuel,"* which is translated, "God with us."
24 Then Joseph, being aroused from sleep, did as the angel of the Lord commanded him and took to him his wife,
25 and [1]did not know her till she had brought forth [a]her[2] firstborn Son. And he called His name JESUS.

### *The Wise Men and Herod*

**2** Now after [a]Jesus was born in Bethlehem of Judea in the days of Herod the king, behold, [1]wise men [b]from the East came to Jerusalem,
2 saying, [a]"Where is He who has been born King of the Jews? For we have seen [b]His star in the East and have come to worship Him."
3 When Herod the king heard *this,* he was troubled, and all Jerusalem with him.
4 And when he had gathered all [a]the chief priests and [b]scribes of the people together, [c]he inquired of them where the Christ was to be born.
5 So they said to him, "In Bethlehem of Judea, for thus it is written by the prophet:

6 *'But*[a] *you, Bethlehem, in the land of Judah,*
*Are not the least among the rulers of Judah;*
*For out of you shall come a Ruler*
[b]*Who will shepherd My people Israel.'*"

7 Then Herod, when he had secretly called the [1]wise men, determined from them what time the [a]star appeared.
8 And he sent them to Bethlehem and said, "Go and search carefully for the young Child, and when you have found *Him,* bring back word to me, that I may come and worship Him also."
9 When they heard the king, they departed; and behold, the star which they had seen in the East went before them, till it came and stood over where the young Child was.
10 When they saw the star, they rejoiced with exceedingly great joy.
11 And when they had come into the house, they saw the young Child with Mary His mother, and fell down and worshiped Him. And when they had opened their treasures, [a]they presented gifts to Him: gold, frankincense, and myrrh.
12 Then, being divinely warned [a]in a dream that they should not return to Herod, they departed for their own country another way.
**13** Now when they had departed, behold, an angel of the Lord appeared to Joseph in a dream, saying, "Arise, take the young Child and His mother, flee to Egypt, and stay there until I bring you word; for Herod will seek the young Child to destroy Him."
14 When he arose, he took the young Child and His mother by night and departed for Egypt,
15 and was there until the death of Herod, that it might be fulfilled which was spoken by the Lord through the prophet, saying, [a]*"Out of Egypt I called My Son."*
**16** Then Herod, when he saw that he was deceived by the wise men, was exceedingly angry; and he sent forth and put to death all the male children who were in Bethlehem and in all its districts, from two years old and under, according to the time which he had determined from the wise men.
17 Then was fulfilled what was spoken by [a]Jeremiah the prophet, saying:

CHAPTER 1
**1** [a]Luke 3:23 [b]John 7:42 [c]Gen. 12:3; 22:18 [1]Lit. *generation*
**2** [a]Gen. 21:2, 12 [b]Gen. 25:26; 28:14 [c]Gen. 29:35
**3** [a]Gen. 38:27; 49:10 [b]Ruth 4:18–22
**5** [a]Ruth 2:1; 4:1–13
**6** [a]1 Sam. 16:1 [b]2 Sam. 7:12; 12:24 [1]Words in italic type have been added for clarity. They are not found in the original Greek.
**7** [a]1 Chr. 3:10 [b]2 Chr. 11:20 [1]NU *Asaph*
**8** [a]1 Chr. 3:10 [b]2 Kin. 15:13
**9** [a]2 Kin. 15:38
**10** [a]2 Kin. 20:21 [b]1 Kin. 13:2 [1]NU *Amos*
**11** [a]1 Chr. 3:15, 16 [b]2 Kin. 24:14–16 [1]Or *Coniah* or *Jehoiachin*
**12** [a]1 Chr. 3:17 [b]Ezra 3:2
**16** [a]Matt. 13:55
**18** [a]Luke 1:27 [b]Luke 1:35
**19** [a]Deut. 24:1 [1]*an upright*
**20** [a]Luke 1:35 [1]Lit. *begotten*
**21** [a]Luke 1:31; 2:21 [b]John 1:29 [1]Lit. *Savior*
**23** [a]Is. 7:14 [1]Words in oblique type in the New Testament are quoted from the Old Testament.
**25** [a]Luke 2:7, 21 [1]Kept her a virgin [2]NU *a Son*

CHAPTER 2
**1** [a]Luke 2:4–7 [b]Gen. 25:6 [1]Gr. *magoi*
**2** [a]Luke 2:11 [b][Num. 24:17]
**4** [a]2 Chr. 36:14 [b]2 Chr. 34:13 [c]Mal. 2:7
**6** [a]Mic. 5:2 [b][Rev. 2:27]
**7** [a]Num. 24:17 [1]Gr. *magoi*
**11** [a]Is. 60:6
**12** [a]Matt. 1:20
**15** [a]Hos. 11:1
**17** [a]Jer. 31:15

18 *"A voice was heard in Ramah,*
*Lamentation, weeping, and great mourning,*
*Rachel weeping for her children,*
*Refusing to be comforted,*
*Because they are no more."*

**19** Now when Herod was dead, behold, an angel of the Lord appeared in a dream to Joseph in Egypt,
20 [a]saying, "Arise, take the young Child and His mother, and go to the land of Israel, for those who [b]sought the young Child's life are dead."
21 Then he arose, took the young Child and His mother, and came into the land of Israel.
22 But when he heard that Archelaus was reigning over Judea instead of his father Herod, he was afraid to go there. And being warned by God in a [a]dream, he turned aside [b]into the region of Galilee.
23 And he came and dwelt in a city called [a]Nazareth, that it might be fulfilled [b]which was spoken by the prophets, "He shall be called a Nazarene."

## *John the Baptist Prepares the Way*

**3** In those days [a]John the Baptist came preaching [b]in the wilderness of Judea,
2 and saying, "Repent, for [a]the kingdom of heaven is at hand!"
3 For this is he who was spoken of by the prophet Isaiah, saying:

[a]*"The voice of one crying in the wilderness:*
[b]*'Prepare the way of the* LORD*;*
*Make His paths straight.' "*

4 Now [a]John himself was clothed in camel's hair, with a leather belt around his waist; and his food was [b]locusts and [c]wild honey.
5 [a]Then Jerusalem, all Judea, and all the region around the Jordan went out to him
6 [a]and were baptized by him in the Jordan, confessing their sins.
7 But when he saw many of the Pharisees and Sadducees coming to his baptism, he said to them, [a]"Brood of vipers! Who warned you to flee from [b]the wrath to come?
8 "Therefore bear fruits worthy of repentance,
9 "and do not think to say to yourselves, [a]'We have Abraham as *our* father.' For I say to you that God is able to raise up children to Abraham from these stones.
10 "And even now the ax is laid to the root of the trees. [a]Therefore every tree which does not bear good fruit is cut down and thrown into the fire.
11 [a]"I indeed baptize you with water unto repentance, but He who is coming after me is mightier than I, whose sandals I am not worthy to carry. [b]He will baptize you with the Holy Spirit [1]and fire.
12 [a]"His winnowing fan *is* in His hand, and He will thoroughly clean out His threshing floor, and gather His wheat into the barn; but He will [b]burn up the chaff with unquenchable fire."
**13** [a]Then Jesus came [b]from Galilee to John at the Jordan to be baptized by him.
14 And John *tried to* prevent Him, saying, "I need to be baptized by You, and are You coming to me?"
15 But Jesus answered and said to him, "Permit *it to be so* now, for thus it is fitting for us to fulfill all righteousness." Then he allowed Him.
16 [a]When He had been baptized, Jesus came up immediately from the water; and behold, the heavens were opened to Him, and He saw [b]the Spirit of God descending like a dove and alighting upon Him.
17 [a]And suddenly a voice *came* from heaven, saying, [b]"This is My beloved Son, in whom I am well pleased."

## *The Temptation of Jesus*

**4** Then [a]Jesus was led up by [b]the Spirit into the wilderness to be tempted by the devil.
2 And when He had fasted forty days and forty nights, afterward He was hungry.
3 Now when the tempter came to Him, he said, "If You are the Son of God, command that these stones become bread."
4 But He answered and said, "It is written, [a]*'Man shall not live by bread alone, but by every word that proceeds from the mouth of God.'* "
5 Then the devil took Him up [a]into the holy city, set Him on the pinnacle of the temple,
6 and said to Him, "If You are the Son of God, throw Yourself down. For it is written:

[a]*'He shall give His angels charge over you,'*

and,

[b]*'In their hands they shall bear you up,*
*Lest you dash your foot against a stone.'* "

7 Jesus said to him, "It is written again, [a]*'You shall not* [1]*tempt the* LORD *your God.'* "
8 Again, the devil took Him up on an exceedingly high mountain, and [a]showed Him all the kingdoms of the world and their glory.
9 And he said to Him, "All these things I will give You if You will fall down and worship me."
10 Then Jesus said to him, [1]"Away with you, Satan! For it is written, [a]*'You shall worship the* LORD *your God, and Him only you shall serve.'* "
11 Then the devil [a]left Him, and behold, [b]angels came and ministered to Him.
**12** [a]Now when Jesus heard that John had been put in prison, He departed to Galilee.
13 And leaving Nazareth, He came and dwelt in Capernaum, which is by the sea, in the regions of Zebulun and Naphtali,
14 that it might be fulfilled which was spoken by Isaiah the prophet, saying:

15 *"The*[a] *land of Zebulun and the land*
*of Naphtali,*
*By the way of the sea, beyond the Jordan,*
*Galilee of the Gentiles:*
16 [a]*The people who sat in darkness have seen*
*a great light,*
*And upon those who sat in the region*
*and shadow of death*
*Light has dawned."*

17 [a]From that time Jesus began to preach and to say, [b]"Repent, for the kingdom of heaven is [1]at hand."
**18** [a]And Jesus, walking by the Sea of Galilee, saw two brothers, Simon [b]called Peter, and Andrew his brother, casting a net into the sea; for they were fishermen.
19 Then He said to them, "Follow Me, and [a]I will make you fishers of men."
20 [a]They immediately left *their* nets and followed Him.
21 [a]Going on from there, He saw two other brothers, James *the son* of Zebedee, and John his brother, in the boat with Zebedee their father, mending their nets. He called them,

**20** [a]Luke 2:39 [b]Matt. 2:16
**22** [a]Matt. 2:12, 13, 19 [b]Luke 2:39
**23** [a]John 1:45, 46 [b]Judg. 13:5

CHAPTER 3
**1** [a]Mark 1:3–8 [b]Josh. 14:10
**2** [a]Dan. 2:44
**3** [a]Is. 40:3 [b]Luke 1:76
**4** [a]Mark 1:6 [b]Lev. 11:22 [c]1 Sam. 14:25, 26
**5** [a]Mark 1:5
**6** [a]Acts 19:4, 18
**7** [a]Matt. 12:34 [b][1 Thess. 1:10]
**9** [a]John 8:33
**10** [a]Matt. 7:19
**11** [a]Luke 3:16 [b][Acts 2:3, 4] [1]M omits *and fire*
**12** [a]Mal. 3:3 [b]Matt. 13:30
**13** [a]Mark 1:9–11 [b]Matt. 2:22
**16** [a]Mark 1:10 [b]John 1:32
**17** [a]John 12:28 [b]Ps. 2:7

CHAPTER 4
**1** [a]Mark 1:12 [b]Ezek. 3:14
**4** [a]Deut. 8:3
**5** [a]Neh. 11:1, 18
**6** [a]Ps. 91:11 [b]Ps. 91:12
**7** [a]Deut. 6:16 [1]*test*
**8** [a][1 John 2:15–17]
**10** [a]Deut. 6:13; 10:20 [1]M *Get behind Me*
**11** [a][James 4:7] [b][Heb. 1:14]
**12** [a]John 4:43
**15** [a]Is. 9:1, 2
**16** [a]Luke 2:32
**17** [a]Mark 1:14, 15 [b]Matt. 3:2; 10:7 [1]*has drawn near*
**18** [a]Mark 1:16–20 [b]John 1:40–42
**19** [a]Luke 5:10
**20** [a]Mark 10:28
**21** [a]Mark 1:19

22 and immediately they left the boat and their
father, and followed Him.
23 And Jesus went about all Galilee, [a]teaching in
their synagogues, preaching [b]the gospel of the
kingdom, [c]and healing all kinds of sickness and all
kinds of disease among the people.
24 Then [1]His fame went throughout all Syria; and
they [a]brought to Him all sick people who were
afflicted with various diseases and torments, and
those who were demon-possessed, epileptics, and
paralytics; and He healed them.
25 [a]Great multitudes followed Him—from Galilee, and *from* [1]Decapolis, Jerusalem, Judea, and
beyond the Jordan.

### *The Beatitudes*

**5** And seeing the multitudes, [a]He went up on a
mountain, and when He was seated His disciples came to Him.
2 Then He opened His mouth and [a]taught them,
saying:

3 "Blessed[a] *are* the poor in spirit,
For theirs is the kingdom of heaven.
4 [a]Blessed *are* those who mourn,
For they shall be comforted.
5 [a]Blessed *are* the meek,
For [b]they shall inherit the [1]earth.
6 Blessed *are* those who [a]hunger and thirst for
righteousness,
[b]For they shall be filled.
7 Blessed *are* the merciful,
[a]For they shall obtain mercy.
8 [a]Blessed *are* the pure in heart,
For [b]they shall see God.
9 Blessed *are* the peacemakers,
For they shall be called sons of God.
10 [a]Blessed are those who are persecuted for
righteousness' sake,
For theirs is the kingdom of heaven.

11 [a]"Blessed are you when they revile and persecute you, and say all kinds of [b]evil against you
falsely for My sake.
12 [a]"Rejoice and be exceedingly glad, for great *is*
your reward in heaven, for [b]so they persecuted the
prophets who were before you.
**13** "You are the salt of the earth; [a]but if the salt
loses its flavor, how shall it be seasoned? It is then
good for nothing but to be thrown out and trampled underfoot by men.
14 [a]"You are the light of the world. A city that is
set on a hill cannot be hidden.
15 "Nor do they [a]light a lamp and put it under a
basket, but on a lampstand, and it gives light to all
*who are* in the house.
16 "Let your light so shine before men, [a]that they
may see your good works and [b]glorify your Father
in heaven.
**17** [a]"Do not think that I came to destroy the Law
or the Prophets. I did not come to destroy but to
fulfill.
18 "For assuredly, I say to you, [a]till heaven and
earth pass away, one [1]jot or one [2]tittle will by no
means pass from the law till all is fulfilled.
19 [a]"Whoever therefore breaks one of the least of
these commandments, and teaches men so, shall
be called least in the kingdom of heaven; but
whoever does and teaches *them,* he shall be called
great in the kingdom of heaven.
20 "For I say to you, that unless your righteousness exceeds [a]*the righteousness* of the scribes and
Pharisees, you will by no means enter the kingdom of heaven.
**21** "You have heard that it was said to those [1]of
old, [a]*'You shall not murder,* and whoever murders
will be in danger of the judgment.'
22 "But I say to you that [a]whoever is angry with
his brother [1]without a cause shall be in danger of
the judgment. And whoever says to his brother,
[b]'Raca!'[2] shall be in danger of the council. But
whoever says, [3]'You fool!' shall be in danger of
[4]hell fire.
23 "Therefore [a]if you bring your gift to the altar,
and there remember that your brother has something against you,
24 [a]"leave your gift there before the altar, and go
your way. First be reconciled to your brother, and
then come and offer your gift.
25 [a]"Agree with your adversary quickly, [b]while
you are on the way with him, lest your adversary
deliver you to the judge, the judge hand you over
to the officer, and you be thrown into prison.
26 "Assuredly, I say to you, you will by no means
get out of there till you have paid the last penny.
**27** "You have heard that it was said [1]to those of
old, [a]*'You shall not commit adultery.'*
28 "But I say to you that whoever [a]looks at a
woman to lust for her has already committed
adultery with her in his heart.
29 [a]"If your right eye causes you to [1]sin, [b]pluck it
out and cast *it* from you; for it is more profitable
for you that one of your members perish, than for
your whole body to be cast into hell.
30 "And if your right hand causes you to [1]sin, cut
it off and cast *it* from you; for it is more profitable
for you that one of your members perish, than for
your whole body to be cast into hell.
**31** "Furthermore it has been said, [a]'Whoever
divorces his wife, let him give her a certificate of
divorce.'
32 "But I say to you that [a]whoever divorces his
wife for any reason except [1]sexual immorality
causes her to commit adultery; and whoever
marries a woman who is divorced commits adultery.
**33** "Again you have heard that [a]it was said to
those of [1]old, [b]'You shall not swear falsely, but
[c]shall perform your oaths to the Lord.'
34 "But I say to you, [a]do not swear at all: neither
by heaven, for it is [b]God's throne;
35 "nor by the earth, for it is His footstool; nor by
Jerusalem, for it is the city of [a]the great King.
36 "Nor shall you swear by your head, because
you cannot make one hair white or black.
37 [a]"But let [1]your 'Yes' be 'Yes,' and your 'No,'
'No.' For whatever is more than these is from the
evil one.
**38** "You have heard that it was said, [a]*'An eye for
an eye and a tooth for a tooth.'*
39 [a]"But I tell you not to resist an evil person.
[b]But whoever slaps you on your right cheek, turn
the other to him also.
40 "If anyone wants to sue you and take away
your tunic, let him have *your* cloak also.
41 "And whoever [a]compels you to go one mile, go
with him two.
42 "Give to him who asks you, and [a]from him
who wants to borrow from you do not turn away.
**43** "You have heard that it was said, [a]*'You shall
love your neighbor* [b]and hate your enemy.'

**23** [a]Matt. 9:35 [b][Matt. 24:14] [c]Mark 1:34
**24** [a]Luke 4:40 [1]Lit. *the report of Him*
**25** [a]Mark 3:7, 8 [1]Lit. *Ten Cities*

CHAPTER 5
**1** [a]Mark 3:13
**2** [a][Matt. 7:29]
**3** [a]Luke 6:20–23
**4** [a]Rev. 21:4
**5** [a]Ps. 37:11 [b][Rom. 4:13] [1]Or *land*
**6** [a]Luke 1:53 [b][Is. 55:1; 65:13]
**7** [a]Ps. 41:1
**8** [a]Ps. 15:2; 24:4 [b]1 Cor. 13:12
**10** [a]1 Pet. 3:14
**11** [a]Luke 6:22 [b]1 Pet. 4:14
**12** [a]1 Pet. 4:13, 14 [b]Acts 7:52
**13** [a]Luke 14:34
**14** [a][John 8:12]
**15** [a]Luke 8:16
**16** [a]1 Pet. 2:12 [b][John 15:8]
**17** [a]Rom. 10:4
**18** [a]Luke 16:17 [1]Gr. *iota,* Heb. *yod,* the smallest letter [2]The smallest stroke in a Heb. letter
**19** [a][James 2:10]
**20** [a][Rom. 10:3]
**21** [a]Ex. 20:13; Deut. 5:17 [1]*in ancient times*
**22** [a][1 John 3:15] [b][James 2:20; 3:6] [1]NU omits *without a cause* [2]Lit., in Aram., *Empty head* [3]Gr. *More* [4]Gr. *Gehenna*
**23** [a]Matt. 8:4
**24** [a][Job 42:8]
**25** [a]Luke 12:58, 59 [b][Is. 55:6]
**27** [a]Ex. 20:14; Deut. 5:18 [1]NU, M omit *to those of old*
**28** [a]Prov. 6:25
**29** [a]Mark 9:43 [b][Col. 3:5] [1]Lit. *stumble* or *offend*
**30** [1]Lit. *stumble* or *offend*
**31** [a]Deut. 24:1
**32** [a][Luke 16:18] [1]Or *fornication*
**33** [a]Matt. 23:16 [b]Lev. 19:12 [c]Deut. 23:23 [1]*ancient times*
**34** [a]James 5:12 [b]Is. 66:1
**35** [a]Ps. 48:2
**37** [a][Col. 4:6] [1]Lit. *your word be yes yes*
**38** [a]Ex. 21:24; Lev. 24:20; Deut. 19:21
**39** [a]Luke 6:29 [b]Is. 50:6
**41** [a]Matt. 27:32
**42** [a]Luke 6:30–34

**43** [a]Lev. 19:18 [b]Deut. 23:3–6; Ps. 41:10

44 [1]"But I say to you, [a]love your enemies, bless those who curse you, [b]do good to those who hate you, and pray [c]for those who spitefully use you and persecute you,
45 "that you may be sons of your Father in heaven; for [a]He makes His sun rise on the evil and on the good, and sends rain on the just and on the unjust.
46 [a]"For if you love those who love you, what reward have you? Do not even the tax collectors do the same?
47 "And if you greet your [1]brethren only, what do you do more *than others*? Do not even the [2]tax collectors do so?
48 [a]"Therefore you shall be perfect, just [b]as your Father in heaven is perfect.

## *The Sermon on the Mount*

6 "Take heed that you do not do your charitable deeds before men, to be seen by them. Otherwise you have no reward from your Father in heaven.
2 "Therefore, [a]when you do a charitable deed, do not sound a trumpet before you as the hypocrites do in the synagogues and in the streets, that they may have glory from men. Assuredly, I say to you, they have their reward.
3 "But when you do a charitable deed, do not let your left hand know what your right hand is doing,
4 "that your charitable deed may be in secret; and your Father who sees in secret [a]will Himself reward you [1]openly.
5 "And when you pray, you shall not be like the [1]hypocrites. For they love to pray standing in the synagogues and on the corners of the streets, that they may be seen by men. Assuredly, I say to you, they have their reward.
6 "But you, when you pray, [a]go into your room, and when you have shut your door, pray to your Father who *is* in the secret *place;* and your Father who sees in secret will reward you [1]openly.
7 "And when you pray, [a]do not use vain repetitions as the heathen *do*. [b]For they think that they will be heard for their many words.
8 "Therefore do not be like them. For your Father [a]knows the things you have need of before you ask Him.
9 "In this [a]manner, therefore, pray:

[b]Our Father in heaven,
Hallowed be Your [c]name.
10 Your kingdom come.
[a]Your will be done
On earth [b]as *it is* in heaven.
11 Give us this day our [a]daily bread.
12 And [a]forgive us our debts,
As we forgive our debtors.
13 [a]And do not lead us into temptation,
But [b]deliver us from the evil one.
[1]For Yours is the kingdom and the power and the glory forever. Amen.

14 [a]"For if you forgive men their trespasses, your heavenly Father will also forgive you.
15 "But [a]if you do not forgive men their trespasses, neither will your Father forgive your trespasses.
16 "Moreover, [a]when you fast, do not be like the [1]hypocrites, with a sad countenance. For they disfigure their faces that they may appear to men to be fasting. Assuredly, I say to you, they have their reward.
17 "But you, when you fast, [a]anoint your head and wash your face,
18 "so that you do not appear to men to be fasting, but to your Father who *is* in the secret *place;* and your Father who sees in secret will reward you [1]openly.
19 [a]"Do not lay up for yourselves treasures on earth, where moth and rust destroy and where thieves break in and steal;
20 [a]"but lay up for yourselves treasures in heaven, where neither moth nor rust destroys and where thieves do not break in and steal.
21 "For where your treasure is, there your heart will be also.
22 [a]"The lamp of the body is the eye. If therefore your eye is [1]good, your whole body will be full of light.
23 "But if your eye is [1]bad, your whole body will be full of darkness. If therefore the light that is in you is darkness, how great *is* that darkness!
24 [a]"No one can serve two masters; for either he will hate the one and love the other, or else he will be loyal to the one and despise the other. [b]You cannot serve God and [1]mammon.
25 "Therefore I say to you, [a]do not worry about your life, what you will eat or what you will drink; nor about your body, what you will put on. Is not life more than food and the body more than clothing?
26 [a]"Look at the birds of the air, for they neither sow nor reap nor gather into barns; yet your heavenly Father feeds them. Are you not of more value than they?
27 "Which of you by worrying can add one [1]cubit to his [2]stature?
28 "So why do you worry about clothing? Consider the lilies of the field, how they grow: they neither toil nor spin;
29 "and yet I say to you that even Solomon in all his glory was not [1]arrayed like one of these.
30 "Now if God so clothes the grass of the field, which today is, and tomorrow is thrown into the oven, *will He* not much more *clothe* you, O you of little faith?
31 "Therefore do not worry, saying, 'What shall we eat?' or 'What shall we drink?' or 'What shall we wear?'
32 "For after all these things the Gentiles seek. For your heavenly Father knows that you need all these things.
33 "But [a]seek first the kingdom of God and His righteousness, and all these things shall be added to you.
34 "Therefore do not worry about tomorrow, for tomorrow will worry about its own things. Sufficient for the day *is* its own trouble.

## *Things That Count with God*

7 "Judge[1] [a]not, that you be not judged.
2 "For with what [1]judgment you judge, you will be judged; [a]and with the measure you use, it will be measured back to you.
3 [a]"And why do you look at the speck in your brother's eye, but do not consider the plank in your own eye?
4 "Or how can you say to your brother, 'Let me remove the speck from your eye'; and look, a plank *is* in your own eye?
5 "Hypocrite! First remove the plank from your own eye, and then you will see clearly to remove the speck from your brother's eye.

44 [a]Luke 6:27 [b][Rom. 12:20] [c]Acts 7:60 [1]NU *But I say to you, love your enemies and pray for those who persecute you*
45 [a]Job 25:3
46 [a]Luke 6:32
47 [1]M *friends* [2]NU *Gentiles*
48 [a][Col. 1:28; 4:12] [b]Eph. 5:1

CHAPTER 6
2 [a]Rom. 12:8
4 [a]Luke 14:12–14 [1]NU omits *openly*
5 [1]*pretenders*
6 [a]2 Kin. 4:33 [1]NU omits *openly*
7 [a]Eccl. 5:2 [b]1 Kin. 18:26
8 [a][Rom. 8:26, 27]
9 [a]Luke 11:2–4 [b][Matt. 5:9, 16] [c]Mal. 1:11
10 [a]Matt. 26:42 [b]Ps. 103:20
11 [a]Prov. 30:8
12 [a][Matt. 18:21, 22]
13 [a][2 Pet. 2:9] [b]John 17:15 [1]NU omits the rest of v. 13.
14 [a]Mark 11:25
15 [a]Matt. 18:35
16 [a]Is. 58:3–7 [1]*pretenders*
17 [a]Ruth 3:3
18 [1]NU, M omit *openly*
19 [a]Prov. 23:4
20 [a]Matt. 19:21
22 [a]Luke 11:34, 35 [1]Clear, or healthy
23 [1]Evil, or unhealthy
24 [a]Luke 16:9, 11, 13 [b][Gal. 1:10] [1]Lit., in Aram., *riches*
25 [a]Luke 12:22
26 [a]Luke 12:24
27 [1]About 18 inches [2]*height*
29 [1]*dressed*
33 [a][1 Tim. 4:8]

CHAPTER 7
1 [a]Rom. 14:3 [1]Condemn
2 [a]Luke 6:38 [1]Condemnation
3 [a]Luke 6:41

6 [a]"Do not give what is holy to the dogs; nor
cast your pearls before swine, lest they trample
them under their feet, and turn and tear you in
pieces.
7 [a]"Ask, and it will be given to you; seek, and
you will find; knock, and it will be opened to you.
8 "For [a]everyone who asks receives, and he who
seeks finds, and to him who knocks it will be
opened.
9 [a]"Or what man is there among you who, if his
son asks for bread, will give him a stone?
10 "Or if he asks for a fish, will he give him a
serpent?
11 "If you then, [a]being evil, know how to give
good gifts to your children, how much more will
your Father who is in heaven give good things to
those who ask Him!
12 "Therefore, [a]whatever you want men to do to
you, do also to them, for [b]this is the Law and the
Prophets.
13 [a]"Enter by the narrow gate; for wide *is* the
gate and broad *is* the way that leads to destruction, and there are many who go in by it.
14 [1]"Because narrow *is* the gate and [2]difficult *is*
the way which leads to life, and there are few who
find it.
15 [a]"Beware of false prophets, [b]who come to you
in sheep's clothing, but inwardly they are ravenous wolves.
16 [a]"You will know them by their fruits. [b]Do men
gather grapes from thornbushes or figs from
thistles?
17 "Even so, [a]every good tree bears good fruit,
but a bad tree bears bad fruit.
18 "A good tree cannot bear bad fruit, nor *can* a
bad tree bear good fruit.
19 [a]"Every tree that does not bear good fruit is
cut down and thrown into the fire.
20 "Therefore by their fruits you will know them.
21 "Not everyone who says to Me, [a]'Lord, Lord,'
shall enter the kingdom of heaven, but he who
[b]does the will of My Father in heaven.
22 "Many will say to Me in that day, 'Lord, Lord,
have we [a]not prophesied in Your name, cast out
demons in Your name, and done many wonders in
Your name?'
23 "And [a]then I will declare to them, 'I never
knew you; [b]depart from Me, you who practice
lawlessness!'
24 "Therefore [a]whoever hears these sayings of
Mine, and does them, I will liken him to a wise
man who built his house on the rock:
25 "and the rain descended, the floods came, and
the winds blew and beat on that house; and it did
not fall, for it was founded on the rock.
26 "But everyone who hears these sayings of
Mine, and does not do them, will be like a foolish
man who built his house on the sand:
27 "and the rain descended, the floods came, and
the winds blew and beat on that house; and it fell.
And great was its fall."
28 And so it was, when Jesus had ended these
sayings, that [a]the people were astonished at His
teaching,
29 [a]for He taught them as one having authority,
and not as the scribes.

### *Jesus Lord of All*

8 When He had come down from the mountain,
great multitudes followed Him.
2 [a]And behold, a leper came and [b]worshiped
Him, saying, "Lord, if You are willing, You can
make me clean."
3 Then Jesus put out *His* hand and touched him,
saying, "I am willing; be cleansed." Immediately
his leprosy [a]was cleansed.
4 And Jesus said to him, [a]"See that you tell no
one; but go your way, show yourself to the priest,
and offer the gift that [b]Moses [c]commanded, as a
testimony to them."
5 [a]Now when Jesus had entered Capernaum, a
[b]centurion came to Him, pleading with Him,
6 saying, "Lord, my servant is lying at home
paralyzed, dreadfully tormented."
7 And Jesus said to him, "I will come and heal
him."
8 The centurion answered and said, "Lord, [a]I am
not worthy that You should come under my roof.
But only [b]speak a word, and my servant will be
healed.
9 "For I also am a man under authority, having
soldiers under me. And I say to this *one,* 'Go,' and
he goes; and to another, 'Come,' and he comes;
and to my servant, 'Do this,' and he does *it.*"
10 When Jesus heard *it,* He marveled, and said to
those who followed, "Assuredly, I say to you, I
have not found such great faith, not even in
Israel!
11 "And I say to you that [a]many will come from
east and west, and sit down with Abraham, Isaac,
and Jacob in the kingdom of heaven.
12 "But [a]the sons of the kingdom [b]will be cast out
into outer darkness. There will be weeping and
gnashing of teeth."
13 Then Jesus said to the centurion, "Go your
way; and as you have believed, so let it be done for
you." And his servant was healed that same hour.
14 [a]Now when Jesus had come into Peter's house,
He saw [b]his wife's mother lying sick with a fever.
15 So He touched her hand, and the fever left her.
And she arose and served [1]them.
16 [a]When evening had come, they brought to
Him many who were demon-possessed. And He
cast out the spirits with a word, and healed all
who were sick,
17 that it might be fulfilled which was spoken by
Isaiah the prophet, saying:

[a]*"He Himself took our infirmities*
*And bore our sicknesses."*

18 And when Jesus saw great multitudes about
Him, He gave a command to depart to the other
side.
19 [a]Then a certain scribe came and said to Him,
"Teacher, I will follow You wherever You go."
20 And Jesus said to him, "Foxes have holes and
birds of the air *have* nests, but the Son of Man has
nowhere to lay *His* head."
21 [a]Then another of His disciples said to Him,
"Lord, [b]let me first go and bury my father."
22 But Jesus said to him, "Follow Me, and let the
dead bury their own dead."
23 Now when He got into a boat, His disciples
followed Him.
24 [a]And suddenly a great tempest arose on the
sea, so that the boat was covered with the waves.
But He was asleep.
25 Then His disciples came to *Him* and awoke
Him, saying, "Lord, save us! We are perishing!"
26 But He said to them, "Why are you fearful, O
you of little faith?" Then [a]He arose and rebuked
the winds and the sea, and there was a great calm.

6 [a]Prov. 9:7, 8
7 [a][Mark 11:24]
8 [a]Prov. 8:17
9 [a]Luke 11:11
11 [a]Gen. 6:5; 8:21
12 [a]Luke 6:31 [b]Gal. 5:14
13 [a]Luke 13:24
14 [1]NU, M *How narrow . . . !* [2]*confined*
15 [a]Jer. 23:16 [b]Mic. 3:5
16 [a]Matt. 7:20; 12:33 [b]Luke 6:43
17 [a]Matt. 12:33
19 [a][John 15:2, 6]
21 [a]Luke 6:46 [b]Rom. 2:13
22 [a]Num. 24:4
23 [a][2 Tim. 2:19] [b]Ps. 5:5; 6:8
24 [a]Luke 6:47–49
28 [a]Matt. 13:54
29 [a][John 7:46]

CHAPTER 8
2 [a]Mark 1:40–45 [b]John 9:38
3 [a]Luke 4:27
4 [a]Mark 5:43 [b]Luke 5:14 [c]Deut. 24:8
5 [a]Luke 7:1–3 [b]Matt. 27:54
8 [a]Luke 15:19, 21 [b]Ps. 107:20
11 [a]Mal. 1:11
12 [a][Matt. 21:43] [b]Luke 13:28
14 [a]Mark 1:29–31 [b]1 Cor. 9:5
15 [1]NU, M *Him*
16 [a]Luke 4:40, 41
17 [a]Is. 53:4
19 [a]Luke 9:57, 58
21 [a]Luke 9:59, 60 [b]1 Kin. 19:20
24 [a]Mark 4:37
26 [a]Ps. 65:7; 89:9; 107:29

27 So the men marveled, saying, [1]"Who can this
be, that even the winds and the sea obey Him?"
**28** [a]When He had come to the other side, to the
country of the [1]Gergesenes, there met Him two
demon-possessed *men*, coming out of the tombs,
exceedingly fierce, so that no one could pass that
way.
29 And suddenly they cried out, saying, "What
have we to do with You, Jesus, You Son of God?
Have You come here to torment us before the
time?"
30 Now a good way off from them there was a
herd of many swine feeding.
31 So the demons begged Him, saying, "If You
cast us out, [1]permit us to go away into the herd of
swine."
32 And He said to them, "Go." So when they had
come out, they went into the herd of swine. And
suddenly the whole herd of swine ran violently
down the steep place into the sea, and perished in
the water.
33 Then those who kept *them* fled; and they went
away into the city and told everything, including
what *had happened* to the demon-possessed *men*.
34 And behold, the whole city came out to meet
Jesus. And when they saw Him, [a]they begged *Him*
to depart from their region.

### *Jesus' Ministry at Nazareth*

**9** So He got into a boat, crossed over, [a]and came
to His own city.
2 [a]Then behold, they brought to Him a paralytic
lying on a bed. [b]When Jesus saw their faith, He
said to the paralytic, "Son, be of good cheer; your
sins are forgiven you."
3 And at once some of the scribes said within
themselves, "This Man blasphemes!"
4 But Jesus, [a]knowing their thoughts, said,
"Why do you think evil in your hearts?
5 "For which is easier, to say, '*Your* sins are
forgiven you,' or to say, 'Arise and walk'?
6 "But that you may know that the Son of Man
has power on earth to forgive sins"—then He said
to the paralytic, "Arise, take up your bed, and go
to your house."
7 And he arose and departed to his house.
8 Now when the multitudes saw *it*, they [a]mar-
veled[1] and glorified God, who had given such
power to men.
**9** [a]As Jesus passed on from there, He saw a man
named Matthew sitting at the tax office. And He
said to him, "Follow Me." So he arose and followed Him.
10 [a]Now it happened, as Jesus sat at the table in
the house, *that* behold, many tax collectors and
sinners came and sat down with Him and His
disciples.
11 And when the Pharisees saw *it*, they said to
His disciples, "Why does your Teacher eat with
[a]tax collectors and [b]sinners?"
12 When Jesus heard *that*, He said to them,
"Those who are well have no need of a physician,
but those who are sick.
13 "But go and learn what *this* means: [a]'*I desire
mercy and not sacrifice.*' For I did not come to call
the righteous, [b]but sinners, [1]to repentance."
**14** Then the disciples of John came to Him, saying, [a]"Why do we and the Pharisees fast [1]often,
but Your disciples do not fast?"
15 And Jesus said to them, "Can [a]the [1]friends of
the bridegroom mourn as long as the bridegroom
is with them? But the days will come when the
bridegroom will be taken away from them, and
[b]then they will fast.
16 "No one puts a piece of unshrunk cloth on an
old garment; for [1]the patch pulls away from the
garment, and the tear is made worse.
17 "Nor do they put new wine into old wineskins,
or else the wineskins [1]break, the wine is spilled,
and the wineskins are ruined. But they put new
wine into new wineskins, and both are preserved."
**18** [a]While He spoke these things to them, behold,
a ruler came and worshiped Him, saying, "My
daughter has just died, but come and lay Your
hand on her and she will live."
19 So Jesus arose and followed him, and so *did*
His [a]disciples.
20 [a]And suddenly, a woman who had a flow of
blood for twelve years came from behind and
[b]touched the hem of His garment.
21 For she said to herself, "If only I may touch
His garment, I shall be made well."
22 But Jesus turned around, and when He saw
her He said, "Be of good cheer, daughter; [a]your
faith has made you well." And the woman was
made well from that hour.
23 [a]When Jesus came into the ruler's house, and
saw [b]the flute players and the noisy crowd wailing,
24 He said to them, [a]"Make room, for the girl is
not dead, but sleeping." And they ridiculed Him.
25 But when the crowd was put outside, He went
in and [a]took her by the hand, and the girl arose.
26 And the [a]report of this went out into all that
land.
**27** When Jesus departed from there, [a]two blind
men followed Him, crying out and saying, [b]"Son
of David, have mercy on us!"
28 And when He had come into the house, the
blind men came to Him. And Jesus said to them,
"Do you believe that I am able to do this?" They
said to Him, "Yes, Lord."
29 Then He touched their eyes, saying, "According to your faith let it be to you."
30 And their eyes were opened. And Jesus sternly
warned them, saying, [a]"See *that* no one knows *it*."
31 [a]But when they had departed, they [1]spread the
news about Him in all that [2]country.
**32** [a]As they went out, behold, they brought to
Him a man, mute and demon-possessed.
33 And when the demon was cast out, the mute
spoke. And the multitudes marveled, saying, "It
was never seen like this in Israel!"
34 But the Pharisees said, [a]"He casts out demons
by the ruler of the demons."
**35** Then Jesus went about all the cities and
villages, [a]teaching in their synagogues, preaching
the gospel of the kingdom, and healing every
sickness and every disease [1]among the people.
36 [a]But when He saw the multitudes, He was
moved with compassion for them, because they
were [1]weary and scattered, [b]like sheep having no
shepherd.
37 Then He said to His disciples, [a]"The harvest
truly *is* plentiful, but the laborers *are* few.
38 [a]"Therefore pray the Lord of the harvest to
send out laborers into His harvest."

### *Discipleship and Its Cost*

**10** And [a]when He had called His twelve disciples to *Him*, He gave them power *over*
unclean spirits, to cast them out, and to heal all
kinds of sickness and all kinds of disease.

**27** [1]Lit. *What sort of man is this*
**28** [a]Mark 5:1–4 [1]NU *Gadarenes*
**31** [1]NU *send us into*
**34** [a]Luke 5:8; Acts 16:39

CHAPTER 9
**1** [a]Matt. 4:13; 11:23
**2** [a]Luke 5:18–26 [b]Matt. 8:10
**4** [a]Matt. 12:25
**8** [a]John 7:15 [1]NU *were afraid*
**9** [a]Luke 5:27
**10** [a]Mark 2:15
**11** [a]Matt. 11:19 [b][Gal. 2:15]
**13** [a]Hos. 6:6 [b]1 Tim. 1:15 [1]NU omits *to repentance*
**14** [a]Luke 5:33–35; 18:12 [1]NU brackets *often* as disputed.
**15** [a]John 3:29 [b]Acts 13:2, 3; 14:23 [1]Lit. *sons of the bridechamber*
**16** [1]Lit. *that which is put on*
**17** [1]*burst*
**18** [a]Luke 8:41–56
**19** [a]Matt. 10:2–4
**20** [a]Luke 8:43 [b]Matt. 14:36; 23:5
**22** [a]Luke 7:50; 8:48; 17:19; 18:42
**23** [a]Mark 5:38 [b]2 Chr. 35:25
**24** [a]Acts 20:10
**25** [a]Mark 1:31
**26** [a]Matt. 4:24
**27** [a]Matt. 20:29–34 [b]Luke 18:38, 39
**30** [a]Matt. 8:4
**31** [a]Mark 7:36 [1]Lit. *made Him known* [2]Lit. *land*
**32** [a]Matt. 12:22, 24
**34** [a]Luke 11:15
**35** [a]Matt. 4:23 [1]NU omits *among the people*
**36** [a]Mark 6:34 [b]Num. 27:17 [1]NU, M *harassed*
**37** [a]Luke 10:2
**38** [a]2 Thess. 3:1

CHAPTER 10
**1** [a]Luke 6:13

2 Now the names of the twelve apostles are these: first, Simon, [a]who is called Peter, and Andrew his brother; James the *son* of Zebedee, and John his brother;
3 Philip and Bartholomew; Thomas and Matthew the tax collector; James the *son* of Alphaeus, and [1]Lebbaeus, whose surname was Thaddaeus;
4 [a]Simon the [1]Canaanite, and Judas [b]Iscariot, who also betrayed Him.
**5** These twelve Jesus sent out and commanded them, saying: [a]"Do not go into the way of the Gentiles, and do not enter a city of [b]the Samaritans.
6 [a]"But go rather to the [b]lost sheep of the house of Israel.
7 [a]"And as you go, preach, saying, [b]'The kingdom of heaven [1]is at hand.'
8 "Heal the sick, [1]cleanse the lepers, [2]raise the dead, cast out demons. [a]Freely you have received, freely give.
9 [a]"Provide neither gold nor silver nor [b]copper in your moneybelts,
10 "nor bag for *your* journey, nor two tunics, nor sandals, nor staffs; [a]for a worker is worthy of his food.
11 [a]"Now whatever city or town you enter, inquire who in it is worthy, and stay there till you go out.
12 "And when you go into a household, greet it.
13 [a]"If the household is worthy, let your peace come upon it. [b]But if it is not worthy, let your peace return to you.
14 [a]"And whoever will not receive you nor hear your words, when you depart from that house or city, [b]shake off the dust from your feet.
15 "Assuredly, I say to you, [a]it will be more tolerable for the land of Sodom and Gomorrah in the day of judgment than for that city!
**16** [a]"Behold, I send you out as sheep in the midst of wolves. [b]Therefore be wise as serpents and [c]harmless[1] as doves.
17 "But beware of men, for [a]they will deliver you up to councils and [b]scourge you in their synagogues.
18 [a]"You will be brought before governors and kings for My sake, as a testimony to them and to the Gentiles.
19 [a]"But when they deliver you up, do not worry about how or what you should speak. For [b]it will be given to you in that hour what you should speak;
20 [a]"for it is not you who speak, but the Spirit of your Father who speaks in you.
21 [a]"Now brother will deliver up brother to death, and a father *his* child; and children will rise up against parents and cause them to be put to death.
22 "And [a]you will be hated by all for My name's sake. [b]But he who endures to the end will be saved.
23 [a]"When they persecute you in this city, flee to another. For assuredly, I say to you, you will not have [b]gone through the cities of Israel [c]before the Son of Man comes.
24 [a]"A disciple is not above *his* teacher, nor a servant above his master.
25 "It is enough for a disciple that he be like his teacher, and a servant like his master. If [a]they have called the master of the house [1]Beelzebub, how much more *will they call* those of his household!
26 "Therefore do not fear them. [a]For there is nothing covered that will not be revealed, and hidden that will not be known.
**27** "Whatever I tell you in the dark, [a]speak in the light; and what you hear in the ear, preach on the housetops.
28 [a]"And do not fear those who kill the body but cannot kill the soul. But rather [b]fear Him who is able to destroy both soul and body in [1]hell.
29 "Are not two [a]sparrows sold for a [1]copper coin? And not one of them falls to the ground apart from your Father's will.
30 [a]"But the very hairs of your head are all numbered.
31 "Do not fear therefore; you are of more value than many sparrows.
**32** [a]"Therefore whoever confesses Me before men, [b]him I will also confess before My Father who is in heaven.
33 [a]"But whoever denies Me before men, him I will also deny before My Father who is in heaven.
**34** [a]"Do not think that I came to bring peace on earth. I did not come to bring peace but a sword.
35 "For I have come to [a]*'set[1] a man against his father, a daughter against her mother, and a daughter-in-law against her mother-in-law'*;
36 "and [a]*'a man's enemies will be those of his own household.'*
37 [a]"He who loves father or mother more than Me is not worthy of Me. And he who loves son or daughter more than Me is not worthy of Me.
38 [a]"And he who does not take his cross and follow after Me is not worthy of Me.
39 [a]"He who finds his life will lose it, and he who loses his life for My sake will find it.
**40** [a]"He who receives you receives Me, and he who receives Me receives Him who sent Me.
41 [a]"He who receives a prophet in the name of a prophet shall receive a prophet's reward. And he who receives a righteous man in the name of a righteous man shall receive a righteous man's reward.
42 [a]"And whoever gives one of these little ones only a cup of cold *water* in the name of a disciple, assuredly, I say to you, he shall by no means lose his reward."

### *Jesus Explains His Ministry*

**11** Now it came to pass, when Jesus finished commanding His twelve disciples, that He departed from there to [a]teach and to preach in their cities.
2 [a]And when John had heard [b]in prison about the works of Christ, he [1]sent two of his disciples
3 and said to Him, "Are You [a]the Coming One, or do we look for another?"
4 Jesus answered and said to them, "Go and tell John the things which you hear and see:
5 [a]"*The* blind see and *the* lame walk; *the* lepers are cleansed and *the* deaf hear; *the* dead are raised up and [b]*the* poor have the gospel preached to them.
6 "And blessed is he who is not [a]offended because of Me."
7 [a]As they departed, Jesus began to say to the multitudes concerning John: "What did you go out into the wilderness to see? [b]A reed shaken by the wind?
8 "But what did you go out to see? A man clothed in soft garments? Indeed, those who wear soft *clothing* are in kings' houses.

**2** [a]John 1:42
**3** [1]NU omits *Lebbaeus, whose surname was*
**4** [a]Acts 1:13 [b]John 13:2, 26 [1]NU *Canaanaean*
**5** [a]Matt. 4:15 [b]John 4:9
**6** [a]Matt. 15:24 [b]Jer. 50:6
**7** [a]Luke 9:2 [b]Matt. 3:2 [1]*has drawn near*
**8** [a][Acts 8:18] [1]NU *raise the dead, cleanse the lepers* [2]M omits *raise the dead*
**9** [a]1 Sam. 9:7 [b]Mark 6:8
**10** [a]1 Tim. 5:18
**11** [a]Luke 10:8
**13** [a]Luke 10:5 [b]Ps. 35:13
**14** [a]Mark 6:11 [b]Acts 13:51
**15** [a]Matt. 11:22, 24
**16** [a]Luke 10:3 [b]Eph. 5:15 [c][Phil. 2:14–16] [1]*innocent*
**17** [a]Mark 13:9 [b]Acts 5:40; 22:19; 26:11
**18** [a]2 Tim. 4:16
**19** [a]Luke 12:11, 12; 21:14, 15 [b]Ex. 4:12
**20** [a]2 Sam. 23:2
**21** [a]Mic. 7:6
**22** [a]Luke 21:17 [b]Mark 13:13
**23** [a]Acts 8:1 [b][Mark 13:10] [c]Matt. 16:28
**24** [a]John 15:20
**25** [a]John 8:48, 52 [1]NU, M *Beelzebul;* a Philistine deity, 2 Kin. 1:2, 3
**26** [a]Mark 4:22
**27** [a]Acts 5:20
**28** [a]Luke 12:4 [b]Luke 12:5 [1]Gr. *Gehenna*
**29** [a]Luke 12:6, 7 [1]Gr. *assarion,* a coin worth about 1/16 of a denarius
**30** [a]Luke 21:18
**32** [a]Luke 12:8 [b][Rev. 3:5]
**33** [a]2 Tim. 2:12
**34** [a][Luke 12:49]
**35** [a]Mic. 7:6 [1]*alienate a man from*
**36** [a]John 13:18
**37** [a]Luke 14:26
**38** [a][Mark 8:34]
**39** [a]John 12:25
**40** [a]Luke 9:48
**41** [a]1 Kin. 17:10
**42** [a]Mark 9:41

CHAPTER 11
**1** [a]Luke 23:5
**2** [a]Luke 7:18–35 [b]Matt. 4:12; 14:3 [1]NU *sent by his*
**3** [a]John 6:14
**5** [a]Is. 29:18; 35:4–6 [b]Is. 61:1
**6** [a]Is. 8:14, 15; [Rom. 9:32]; 1 Pet. 2:8
**7** [a]Luke 7:24 [b][Eph. 4:14]

9 "But what did you go out to see? A prophet?
Yes, I say to you, [a]and more than a prophet.
10 "For this is *he* of whom it is written:

[a]*'Behold, I send My messenger*
*before Your face,*
*Who will prepare Your way before You.'*

11 "Assuredly, I say to you, among those born of
women there has not risen one greater than John
the Baptist; but he who is least in the kingdom of
heaven is greater than he.
12 [a]"And from the days of John the Baptist until
now the kingdom of heaven suffers violence, and
the violent take it by force.
13 [a]"For all the prophets and the law prophesied
until John.
14 "And if you are willing to receive *it,* he is
[a]Elijah who is to come.
15 [a]"He who has ears to hear, let him hear!
16 [a]"But to what shall I liken this generation? It
is like children sitting in the marketplaces and
calling to their companions,
17 "and saying:

'We played the flute for you,
And you did not dance;
We mourned to you,
And you did not [1]lament.'

18 "For John came neither eating nor drinking,
and they say, 'He has a demon.'
19 "The Son of Man came eating and drinking,
and they say, 'Look, a glutton and a [1]winebibber,
[a]a friend of tax collectors and sinners!' [b]But wisdom is justified by her [2]children."
**20** [a]Then He began to rebuke the cities in which
most of His mighty works had been done, because
they did not repent:
21 "Woe to you, Chorazin! Woe to you, Bethsaida! For if the mighty works which were done in
you had been done in Tyre and Sidon, they would
have repented long ago [a]in sackcloth and ashes.
22 "But I say to you, [a]it will be more tolerable for
Tyre and Sidon in the day of judgment than for
you.
23 "And you, Capernaum, [a]who[1] are exalted to
heaven, will be brought down to Hades; for if the
mighty works which were done in you had been
done in Sodom, it would have remained until this
day.
24 "But I say to you [a]that it shall be more tolerable for the land of Sodom in the day of judgment
than for you."
**25** [a]At that time Jesus answered and said, "I
thank You, Father, Lord of heaven and earth, that
[b]You have hidden these things from *the* wise and
prudent [c]and have revealed them to babes.
26 "Even so, Father, for so it seemed good in
Your sight.
27 [a]"All things have been delivered to Me by My
Father, and no one knows the Son except the
Father. [b]Nor does anyone know the Father except
the Son, and *the one* to whom the Son wills to
reveal *Him.*
28 "Come to [a]Me, all *you* who labor and are
heavy laden, and I will give you rest.
29 "Take My yoke upon you [a]and learn from Me,
for I am [1]gentle and [b]lowly in heart, [c]and you will
find rest for your souls.
30 [a]"For My yoke *is* easy and My burden is light."

**9** [a]Luke 1:76; 20:6
**10** [a]Mal. 3:1
**12** [a]Luke 16:16
**13** [a]Mal. 4:4–6
**14** [a]Luke 1:17
**15** [a]Luke 8:8
**16** [a]Luke 7:31
**17** [1]Lit. *beat your breast*
**19** [a]Matt. 9:10 [b]Luke 7:35 [1]*wine drinker* [2]NU *works*
**20** [a]Luke 10:13–15, 18
**21** [a]Jon. 3:6–8
**22** [a]Matt. 10:15; 11:24
**23** [a]Is. 14:13 [1]NU *will you be exalted to heaven? No, you will be*
**24** [a]Matt. 10:15
**25** [a]Luke 10:21, 22 [b]Ps. 8:2 [c]Matt. 16:17
**27** [a]Matt. 28:18 [b]John 1:18; 6:46; 10:15
**28** [a][John 6:35–37]
**29** [a][Phil. 2:5] [b]Zech. 9:9 [c]Jer. 6:16 [1]*meek*
**30** [a][1 John 5:3]

CHAPTER 12
**1** [a]Luke 6:1–5 [b]Deut. 23:25
**3** [a]1 Sam. 21:6
**4** [a]Lev. 24:5 [b]Ex. 29:32
**5** [a]Num. 28:9 [1]*desecrate*
**6** [a][Is. 66:1, 2]
**7** [a][Hos. 6:6]
**8** [1]NU, M omit *even*
**9** [a]Mark 3:1–6
**10** [a]John 9:16
**14** [a]Mark 3:6
**15** [a]Mark 3:7 [b]Matt. 19:2 [1]NU brackets *multitudes* as disputed.
**16** [a]Matt. 8:4; 9:30; 17:9
**18** [a]Is. 42:1–4; 49:3 [b]Matt. 3:17; 17:5
**22** [a]Luke 11:14, 15 [1]NU omits *blind and*
**23** [a]Matt. 9:27; 21:9

### *Sabbath Works, Good Fruit, and Jesus' True Family*

**12** At that time [a]Jesus went through the grainfields on the Sabbath. And His disciples
were hungry, and began to [b]pluck heads of grain
and to eat.
2 And when the Pharisees saw *it,* they said to
Him, "Look, Your disciples are doing what is not
lawful to do on the Sabbath!"
3 But He said to them, "Have you not read
[a]what David did when he was hungry, he and
those who were with him:
4 "how he entered the house of God and ate [a]the
showbread which was not lawful for him to eat,
nor for those who were with him, [b]but only for the
priests?
5 "Or have you not read in the [a]law that on the
Sabbath the priests in the temple [1]profane the
Sabbath, and are blameless?
6 "Yet I say to you that in this place there is
[a]*One* greater than the temple.
7 "But if you had known what *this* means, [a]*'I
desire mercy and not sacrifice,'* you would not
have condemned the guiltless.
8 "For the Son of Man is Lord [1]even of the
Sabbath."
**9** [a]Now when He had departed from there, He
went into their synagogue.
10 And behold, there was a man who had a
withered hand. And they asked Him, saying, [a]"Is it
lawful to heal on the Sabbath?"—that they might
accuse Him.
11 Then He said to them, "What man is there
among you who has one sheep, and if it falls into a
pit on the Sabbath, will not lay hold of it and lift *it*
out?
12 "Of how much more value then is a man than
a sheep? Therefore it is lawful to do good on the
Sabbath."
13 Then He said to the man, "Stretch out your
hand." And he stretched *it* out, and it was restored
as whole as the other.
14 Then [a]the Pharisees went out and plotted
against Him, how they might destroy Him.
**15** But when Jesus knew *it,* [a]He withdrew from
there. [b]And great [1]multitudes followed Him, and
He healed them all.
16 Yet He [a]warned them not to make Him
known,
17 that it might be fulfilled which was spoken by
Isaiah the prophet, saying:

18 *"Behold!*[a] *My Servant whom I have chosen,*
*My Beloved* [b]*in whom My soul*
*is well pleased!*
*I will put My Spirit upon Him,*
*And He will declare justice to the Gentiles.*
19 *He will not quarrel nor cry out,*
*Nor will anyone hear His voice in the streets.*
20 *A bruised reed He will not break,*
*And smoking flax He will not quench,*
*Till He sends forth justice to victory;*
21 *And in His name Gentiles will trust."*

**22** [a]Then one was brought to Him who was
demon-possessed, blind and mute; and He healed
him, so that the [1]blind and mute man both spoke
and saw.
23 And all the multitudes were amazed and said,
"Could this be the [a]Son of David?"

24 [a]Now when the Pharisees heard *it* they said,
"This *fellow* does not cast out demons except by
[1]Beelzebub, the ruler of the demons."
25 But Jesus [a]knew their thoughts, and said to
them: "Every kingdom divided against itself is
brought to desolation, and every city or house
divided against itself will not stand.
26 "If Satan casts out Satan, he is divided against
himself. How then will his kingdom stand?
27 "And if I cast out demons by Beelzebub, by
whom do your sons cast *them* out? Therefore they
shall be your judges.
28 "But if I cast out demons by the Spirit of God,
[a]surely the kingdom of God has come upon you.
29 [a]"Or how can one enter a strong man's house
and plunder his goods, unless he first binds the
strong man? And then he will plunder his house.
30 "He who is not with Me is against Me, and he
who does not gather with Me scatters abroad.
**31** "Therefore I say to you, [a]every sin and blasphemy will be forgiven men, [b]but the blasphemy
*against* the Spirit will not be forgiven men.
32 "Anyone who [a]speaks a word against the Son
of Man, [b]it will be forgiven him; but whoever
speaks against the Holy Spirit, it will not be
forgiven him, either in this age or in the *age* to
come.
**33** "Either make the tree good and [a]its fruit good,
or else make the tree bad and its fruit bad; for a
tree is known by *its* fruit.
34 [a]"Brood[1] of vipers! How can you, being evil,
speak good things? [b]For out of the abundance of
the heart the mouth speaks.
35 "A good man out of the good treasure [1]of his
heart brings forth good things, and an evil man
out of the evil treasure brings forth evil things.
36 "But I say to you that for every idle word men
may speak, they will give account of it in the day
of judgment.
37 "For by your words you will be justified, and
by your words you will be condemned."
**38** [a]Then some of the scribes and Pharisees answered, saying, "Teacher, we want to see a sign
from You."
39 But He answered and said to them, "An evil
and [a]adulterous generation seeks after a sign, and
no sign will be given to it except the sign of the
prophet Jonah.
40 [a]"For as Jonah was three days and three
nights in the belly of the great fish, so will the Son
of Man be three days and three nights in the heart
of the earth.
41 [a]"The men of Nineveh will rise up in the
judgment with this generation and [b]condemn it,
[c]because they repented at the preaching of Jonah;
and indeed a greater than Jonah *is* here.
42 [a]"The queen of the South will rise up in the
judgment with this generation and condemn it,
for she came from the ends of the earth to hear
the wisdom of Solomon; and indeed a greater than
Solomon *is* here.
**43** [a]"When an unclean spirit goes out of a man,
[b]he goes through dry places, seeking rest, and
finds none.
44 "Then he says, 'I will return to my house from
which I came.' And when he comes, he finds *it*
empty, swept, and put in order.
45 "Then he goes and takes with him seven other
spirits more wicked than himself, and they enter
and dwell there; [a]and the last *state* of that man is
worse than the first. So shall it also be with this
wicked generation."
**46** While He was still talking to the multitudes,
[a]behold, His mother and [b]brothers stood outside,
seeking to speak with Him.
47 Then one said to Him, "Look, [a]Your mother
and Your brothers are standing outside, seeking
to speak with You."
48 But He answered and said to the one who told
Him, "Who is My mother and who are My brothers?"
49 And He stretched out His hand toward His
disciples and said, "Here are My mother and My
[a]brothers!
50 "For [a]whoever does the will of My Father in
heaven is My brother and sister and mother."

### *Parables About the Kingdom of Heaven*

**13** On the same day Jesus went out of the
house [a]and sat by the sea.
2 [a]And great multitudes were gathered together
to Him, so that [b]He got into a boat and sat; and
the whole multitude stood on the shore.
3 Then He spoke many things to them in parables, saying: [a]"Behold, a sower went out to sow.
4 "And as he sowed, some *seed* fell by the
wayside; and the birds came and devoured them.
5 "Some fell on stony places, where they did not
have much earth; and they immediately sprang up
because they had no depth of earth.
6 "But when the sun was up they were
scorched, and because they had no root they
withered away.
7 "And some fell among thorns, and the thorns
sprang up and choked them.
8 "But others fell on good ground and yielded a
crop: some [a]a hundredfold, some sixty, some
thirty.
9 [a]"He who has ears to hear, let him hear!"
**10** And the disciples came and said to Him, "Why
do You speak to them in parables?"
11 He answered and said to them, "Because [a]it
has been given to you to know the [1]mysteries of
the kingdom of heaven, but to them it has not
been given.
12 [a]"For whoever has, to him more will be given,
and he will have abundance; but whoever does
not have, even what he has will be taken away
from him.
13 "Therefore I speak to them in parables, because seeing they do not see, and hearing they do
not hear, nor do they understand.
14 "And in them the prophecy of Isaiah is fulfilled, which says:

[a]*'Hearing you will hear*
*and shall not understand,*
*And seeing you will see and not* [b]*perceive;*
15 *For the hearts of this people*
*have grown dull.*
*Their ears* [a]*are hard of hearing,*
*And their eyes they have* [b]*closed,*
*Lest they should see with their eyes*
*and hear with their ears,*
*Lest they should understand*
*with their hearts and turn,*
*So that I* [1]*should* [c]*heal them.'*

16 "But [a]blessed *are* your eyes for they see, and
your ears for they hear;
17 "for assuredly, I say to you [a]that many prophets and righteous *men* desired to see what you see,
and did not see *it*, and to hear what you hear, and
did not hear *it*.

**24** [a]Matt. 9:34 [1]NU, M *Beelzebul*, a Philistine deity
**25** [a]Matt. 9:4
**28** [a][Dan. 2:44; 7:14]
**29** [a]Is. 49:24
**31** [a]Mark 3:28–30 [b]Acts 7:51
**32** [a]John 7:12, 52 [b]1 Tim. 1:13
**33** [a]Matt. 7:16–18
**34** [a]Matt. 3:7; 23:33 [b]Luke 6:45 [1]*Offspring*
**35** [1]NU, M omit *of his heart*
**38** [a]Mark 8:11
**39** [a]Matt. 16:4
**40** [a]Jon. 1:17
**41** [a]Luke 11:32 [b]Jer. 3:11 [c]Jon. 3:5
**42** [a]1 Kin. 10:1–13
**43** [a]Luke 11:24–26 [b][1 Pet. 5:8]
**45** [a][2 Pet. 2:20–22]
**46** [a]Luke 8:19–21 [b]John 2:12; 7:3, 5
**47** [a]Matt. 13:55, 56
**49** [a]John 20:17
**50** [a]John 15:14

CHAPTER 13
**1** [a]Mark 4:1–12
**2** [a]Luke 8:4 [b]Luke 5:3
**3** [a]Luke 8:5
**8** [a]Gen. 26:12
**9** [a]Matt. 11:15
**11** [a]Mark 4:10, 11 [1]*secret* or *hidden truths*
**12** [a]Matt. 25:29
**14** [a]Is. 6:9, 10 [b][John 3:36]
**15** [a]Heb. 5:11 [b]Luke 19:42 [c]Acts 28:26, 27 [1]NU, M *would*
**16** [a]Luke 10:23, 24
**17** [a]Heb. 11:13

**18** [a]"Therefore hear the parable of the sower:
19 "When anyone hears the word [a]of the kingdom, and does not understand *it,* then the wicked *one* comes and snatches away what was sown in his heart. This is he who received seed by the wayside.
20 "But he who received the seed on stony places, this is he who hears the word and immediately [a]receives it with joy;
21 "yet he has no root in himself, but endures only for a while. For when [a]tribulation or persecution arises because of the word, immediately [b]he stumbles.
22 "Now [a]he who received seed [b]among the thorns is he who hears the word, and the cares of this world and the deceitfulness of riches choke the word, and he becomes unfruitful.
23 "But he who received seed on the good ground is he who hears the word and understands *it,* who indeed bears [a]fruit and produces: some a hundredfold, some sixty, some thirty."
**24** Another parable He put forth to them, saying: "The kingdom of heaven is like a man who sowed good seed in his field;
25 "but while men slept, his enemy came and sowed tares among the wheat and went his way.
26 "But when the grain had sprouted and produced a crop, then the tares also appeared.
27 "So the servants of the owner came and said to him, 'Sir, did you not sow good seed in your field? How then does it have tares?'
28 "He said to them, 'An enemy has done this.' The servants said to him, 'Do you want us then to go and gather them up?'
29 "But he said, 'No, lest while you gather up the tares you also uproot the wheat with them.
30 'Let both grow together until the harvest, and at the time of harvest I will say to the reapers, "First gather together the tares and bind them in bundles to burn them, but [a]gather the wheat into my barn." ' "
**31** Another parable He put forth to them, saying: [a]"The kingdom of heaven is like a mustard seed, which a man took and sowed in his field,
32 "which indeed is the least of all the seeds; but when it is grown it is greater than the herbs and becomes a [a]tree, so that the birds of the air come and nest in its branches."
**33** [a]Another parable He spoke to them: "The kingdom of heaven is like leaven, which a woman took and hid in three [1]measures of meal till [b]it was all leavened."
**34** [a]All these things Jesus spoke to the multitude in parables; and without a parable He did not speak to them,
35 that it might be fulfilled which was spoken by the prophet, saying:

[a]*"I will open My mouth in parables;*
[b]*I will utter things kept secret from the foundation of the world."*

**36** Then Jesus sent the multitude away and went into the house. And His disciples came to Him, saying, "Explain to us the parable of the tares of the field."
37 He answered and said to them: "He who sows the good seed is the Son of Man.
38 [a]"The field is the world, the good seeds are the sons of the kingdom, but the tares are [b]the sons of the wicked *one.*
39 "The enemy who sowed them is the devil, [a]the harvest is the end of the age, and the reapers are the angels.
40 "Therefore as the tares are gathered and burned in the fire, so it will be at the end of this age.
41 "The Son of Man will send out His angels, [a]and they will gather out of His kingdom all things that offend, and those who practice lawlessness,
42 [a]"and will cast them into the furnace of fire. [b]There will be wailing and gnashing of teeth.
43 [a]"Then the righteous will shine forth as the sun in the kingdom of their Father. [b]He who has ears to hear, let him hear!
**44** "Again, the kingdom of heaven is like treasure hidden in a field, which a man found and hid; and for joy over it he goes and [a]sells all that he has and [b]buys that field.
**45** "Again, the kingdom of heaven is like a merchant seeking beautiful pearls,
46 "who, when he had found [a]one pearl of great price, went and sold all that he had and bought it.
**47** "Again, the kingdom of heaven is like a dragnet that was cast into the sea and [a]gathered some of every kind,
48 "which, when it was full, they drew to shore; and they sat down and gathered the good into vessels, but threw the bad away.
49 "So it will be at the end of the age. The angels will come forth, [a]separate the wicked from among the just,
50 "and cast them into the furnace of fire. There will be wailing and gnashing of teeth."
51 [1]Jesus said to them, "Have you understood all these things?" They said to Him, "Yes, [2]Lord."
52 Then He said to them, "Therefore every [1]scribe instructed [2]concerning the kingdom of heaven is like a householder who brings out of his treasure [a]*things* new and old."
**53** Now it came to pass, when Jesus had finished these parables, that He departed from there.
54 [a]When He had come to His own country, He taught them in their synagogue, so that they were astonished and said, "Where did this *Man* get this wisdom and *these* mighty works?
55 [a]"Is this not the carpenter's son? Is not His mother called Mary? And [b]His brothers [c]James, [1]Joses, Simon, and Judas?
56 "And His sisters, are they not all with us? Where then did this *Man* get all these things?"
57 So they [a]were offended at Him. But Jesus said to them, [b]"A prophet is not without honor except in his own country and in his own house."
58 Now [a]He did not do many mighty works there because of their unbelief.

### *Five Thousand Fed*

# 14
At that time [a]Herod the tetrarch heard the report about Jesus
2 and said to his servants, "This is John the Baptist; he is risen from the dead, and therefore these powers are at work in him."
3 [a]For Herod had laid hold of John and bound him, and put *him* in prison for the sake of Herodias, his brother Philip's wife.
4 Because John had said to him, [a]"It is not lawful for you to have her."
5 And although he wanted to put him to death, he feared the multitude, [a]because they counted him as a prophet.

**18** [a]Mark 4:13–20
**19** [a]Matt. 4:23
**20** [a]Is. 58:2
**21** [a][Acts 14:22] [b]Matt. 11:6
**22** [a]1 Tim. 6:9 [b]Jer. 4:3
**23** [a]Col. 1:6
**30** [a]Matt. 3:12
**31** [a]Luke 13:18, 19
**32** [a]Ezek. 17:22–24; 31:3–9
**33** [a]Luke 13:20, 21 [b][1 Cor. 5:6] [1]Gr. *saton,* same as a Heb. *seah;* approximately 2 pecks in all
**34** [a]Mark 4:33, 34
**35** [a]Ps. 78:2 [b]Eph. 3:9
**38** [a]Rom. 10:18 [b]John 8:44
**39** [a]Rev. 14:15
**41** [a]Matt. 18:7
**42** [a]Rev. 19:20; 20:10 [b]Matt. 8:12; 13:50
**43** [a][Dan. 12:3] [b]Matt. 13:9
**44** [a]Phil. 3:7, 8 [b][Is. 55:1]
**46** [a]Prov. 2:4; 3:14, 15; 8:10, 19
**47** [a]Matt. 22:9, 10
**49** [a]Matt. 25:32
**51** [1]NU omits *Jesus said to them* [2]NU omits *Lord*
**52** [a]Song 7:13 [1]A scholar of the Old Testament [2]Or *for*
**54** [a]Luke 4:16
**55** [a]John 6:42 [b]Matt. 12:46 [c]Mark 15:40 [1]NU *Joseph*
**57** [a]Matt. 11:6 [b]Luke 4:24
**58** [a]Mark 6:5, 6

CHAPTER 14
**1** [a]Mark 6:14–29
**3** [a]Luke 3:19, 20
**4** [a]Lev. 18:16; 20:21
**5** [a]Luke 20:6

6 But when Herod's birthday was celebrated, the daughter of Herodias danced before them and pleased Herod.
7 Therefore he promised with an oath to give her whatever she might ask.
8 So she, having been prompted by her mother, said, "Give me John the Baptist's head here on a platter."
9 And the king was sorry; nevertheless, because of the oaths and because of those who sat with him, he commanded *it* to be given to *her*.
10 So he sent and had John beheaded in prison.
11 And his head was brought on a platter and given to the girl, and she brought *it* to her mother.
12 Then his disciples came and took away the body and buried it, and went and told Jesus.
**13** [a]When Jesus heard *it*, He departed from there by boat to a deserted place by Himself. But when the multitudes heard it, they followed Him on foot from the cities.
14 And when Jesus went out He saw a great multitude; and He [a]was moved with compassion for them, and healed their sick.
15 [a]When it was evening, His disciples came to Him, saying, "This is a deserted place, and the hour is already late. Send the multitudes away, that they may go into the villages and buy themselves food."
16 But Jesus said to them, "They do not need to go away. You give them something to eat."
17 And they said to Him, "We have here only five loaves and two fish."
18 He said, "Bring them here to Me."
19 Then He commanded the multitudes to sit down on the grass. And He took the five loaves and the two fish, and looking up to heaven, [a]He blessed and broke and gave the loaves to the disciples; and the disciples gave to the multitudes.
20 So they all ate and were filled, and they took up twelve baskets full of the fragments that remained.
21 Now those who had eaten were about five thousand men, besides women and children.
**22** Immediately Jesus [1]made His disciples get into the boat and go before Him to the other side, while He sent the multitudes away.
23 [a]And when He had sent the multitudes away, He went up on a mountain by Himself to pray. [b]Now when evening came, He was alone there.
24 But the boat was now [1]in the middle of the sea, tossed by the waves, for the wind was contrary.
25 Now in the fourth watch of the night Jesus went to them, walking on the sea.
26 And when the disciples saw Him [a]walking on the sea, they were troubled, saying, "It is a ghost!" And they cried out for fear.
27 But immediately Jesus spoke to them, saying, [1]"Be of good [a]cheer! [2]It is I; do not be afraid."
28 And Peter answered Him and said, "Lord, if it is You, command me to come to You on the water."
29 So He said, "Come." And when Peter had come down out of the boat, he walked on the water to go to Jesus.
30 But when he saw [1]that the wind *was* boisterous, he was afraid; and beginning to sink he cried out, saying, "Lord, save me!"
31 And immediately Jesus stretched out *His* hand and caught him, and said to him, "O you of [a]little faith, why did you doubt?"
32 And when they got into the boat, the wind ceased.
33 Then those who were in the boat [1]came and worshiped Him, saying, "Truly [a]You are the Son of God."
**34** [a]When they had crossed over, they came [1]to the land of Gennesaret.
35 And when the men of that place recognized Him, they sent out into all that surrounding region, brought to Him all who were sick,
36 and begged Him that they might only [a]touch the hem of His garment. And [b]as many as touched *it* were made perfectly well.

## *God's Commandments and Men's Traditions*

**15** Then [a]the scribes and Pharisees who were from Jerusalem came to Jesus, saying,
2 [a]"Why do Your disciples transgress the tradition of the elders? For they do not wash their hands when they eat bread."
3 He answered and said to them, "Why do you also transgress the commandment of God because of your tradition?
4 "For God commanded, saying, [a]*'Honor your father and your mother'*; and, [b]*'He who curses father or mother, let him be put to death.'*
5 "But you say, 'Whoever says to his father or mother, [a]"Whatever profit you might have received from me *is* a gift *to God*"—
6 'then he need not honor his father [1]or mother.' Thus you have made the [2]commandment of God of no effect by your tradition.
7 [a]"Hypocrites! Well did Isaiah prophesy about you, saying:

8 *'These[a] people [1]draw near to Me*
*with their mouth,*
*And honor Me with their lips,*
*But their heart is far from Me.*
9 *And in vain they worship Me,*
[a]*Teaching as doctrines the commandments of men.'"*

10 [a]When He had called the multitude to *Himself*, He said to them, "Hear and understand:
11 [a]"Not what goes into the mouth defiles a man; but what comes out of the mouth, this defiles a man."
12 Then His disciples came and said to Him, "Do You know that the Pharisees were offended when they heard this saying?"
13 But He answered and said, [a]"Every plant which My heavenly Father has not planted will be uprooted.
14 "Let them alone. [a]They are blind leaders of the blind. And if the blind leads the blind, both will fall into a ditch."
15 [a]Then Peter answered and said to Him, "Explain this parable to us."
16 So Jesus said, [a]"Are you also still without understanding?
17 "Do you not yet understand that [a]whatever enters the mouth goes into the stomach and is eliminated?
18 "But [a]those things which proceed out of the mouth come from the heart, and they defile a man.
19 [a]"For out of the heart proceed evil thoughts, murders, adulteries, fornications, thefts, false witness, blasphemies.

**13** [a]John 6:1, 2
**14** [a]Mark 6:34
**15** [a]Luke 9:12
**19** [a]Matt. 15:36; 26:26
**22** [1]*invited, strongly urged*
**23** [a]Mark 6:46 [b]John 6:16
**24** [1]NU *many furlongs away from the land*
**26** [a]Job 9:8
**27** [a]Acts 23:11; 27:22, 25, 36 [1]*Take courage* [2]Lit. *I am*
**30** [1]NU brackets *that* and *boisterous* as disputed.
**31** [a]Matt. 6:30; 8:26
**33** [a]Ps. 2:7 [1]NU omits *came and*
**34** [a]Mark 6:53 [1]NU *to land at*
**36** [a][Mark 5:24–34] [b][Luke 6:19]

CHAPTER 15
**1** [a]Mark 7:1
**2** [a]Mark 7:5
**4** [a][Deut. 5:16] [b]Ex. 21:17
**5** [a]Mark 7:11, 12
**6** [1]NU omits *or mother* [2]NU *word*
**7** [a]Mark 7:6
**8** [a]Is. 29:13 [1]NU omits *draw near to Me with their mouth, And*
**9** [a][Col. 2:18–22]
**10** [a]Mark 7:14
**11** [a][Acts 10:15]
**13** [a][John 15:2]
**14** [a]Luke 6:39
**15** [a]Mark 7:17
**16** [a]Matt. 16:9
**17** [a][1 Cor. 6:13]
**18** [a][James 3:6]
**19** [a]Prov. 6:14

20 "These are *the things* which defile a man, but
to eat with unwashed hands does not defile a
man."
21 [a]Then Jesus went out from there and departed
to the region of Tyre and Sidon.
22 And behold, a woman of Canaan came from
that region and cried out to Him, saying, "Have
mercy on me, O Lord, [a]Son of David! My daughter
is severely demon-possessed."
23 But He answered her not a word. And His
disciples came and urged Him, saying, "Send her
away, for she cries out after us."
24 But He answered and said, [a]"I was not sent
except to the lost sheep of the house of Israel."
25 Then she came and worshiped Him, saying,
"Lord, help me!"
26 But He answered and said, "It is not good to
take the children's bread and throw *it* to the little
[a]dogs."
27 And she said, "Yes, Lord, yet even the little
dogs eat the crumbs which fall from their masters'
table."
28 Then Jesus answered and said to her, "O
woman, [a]great *is* your faith! Let it be to you as you
desire." And her daughter was healed from that
very hour.
**29** [a]Jesus departed from there, [b]skirted the Sea of
Galilee, and went up on the mountain and sat
down there.
30 [a]Then great multitudes came to Him, having
with them *the* lame, blind, mute, [1]maimed, and
many others; and they laid them down at Jesus'
[b]feet, and He healed them.
31 So the multitude marveled when they saw *the*
mute speaking, *the* [1]maimed made whole, *the*
lame walking, and *the* blind seeing; and they
[a]glorified the God of Israel.
**32** [a]Now Jesus called His disciples to *Himself* and
said, "I have compassion on the multitude, because they have now continued with Me three
days and have nothing to eat. And I do not want
to send them away hungry, lest they faint on the
way."
33 [a]Then His disciples said to Him, "Where could
we get enough bread in the wilderness to fill such
a great multitude?"
34 Jesus said to them, "How many loaves do you
have?" And they said, "Seven, and a few little
fish."
35 So He commanded the multitude to sit down
on the ground.
36 And [a]He took the seven loaves and the fish
and [b]gave thanks, broke *them* and gave *them* to
His disciples; and the disciples *gave* to the multitude.
37 So they all ate and were filled, and they took
up seven large baskets full of the fragments that
were left.
38 Now those who ate were four thousand men,
besides women and children.
39 [a]And He sent away the multitude, got into the
boat, and came to the region of [1]Magdala.

### *Peter's Confession of Faith*

**16** Then the [a]Pharisees and Sadducees came,
and testing Him asked that He would show
them a sign from heaven.
2 He answered and said to them, "When it is
evening you say, '*It will be* fair weather, for the
sky is red';
3 "and in the morning, '*It will be* foul weather
today, for the sky is red and threatening.' [1]Hypo-
crites! You know how to discern the face of the
sky, but you cannot *discern* the signs of the times.
4 [a]"A wicked and adulterous generation seeks
after a sign, and no sign shall be given to it except
the sign of [1]the prophet Jonah." And He left them
and departed.
**5** Now [a]when His disciples had come to the
other side, they had forgotten to take bread.
6 Then Jesus said to them, [a]"Take heed and
beware of the [1]leaven of the Pharisees and the
Sadducees."
7 And they reasoned among themselves, saying,
"*It is* because we have taken no bread."
8 But Jesus, being aware of *it*, said to them, "O
you of little faith, why do you reason among
yourselves because you [1]have brought no bread?
9 [a]"Do you not yet understand, or remember the
five loaves of the five thousand and how many
baskets you took up?
10 [a]"Nor the seven loaves of the four thousand
and how many large baskets you took up?
11 "How is it you do not understand that I did
not speak to you concerning bread?—*but* to beware of the [1]leaven of the Pharisees and Sadducees."
12 Then they understood that He did not tell
*them* to beware of the leaven of bread, but of the
[1]doctrine of the Pharisees and Sadducees.
**13** When Jesus came into the region of Caesarea
Philippi, He asked His disciples, saying, [a]"Who do
men say that I, the Son of Man, am?"
14 So they said, [a]"Some *say* John the Baptist,
some Elijah, and others Jeremiah or [b]one of the
prophets."
15 He said to them, "But who do [a]you say that I
am?"
16 Simon Peter answered and said, [a]"You are the
Christ, the Son of the living God."
17 Jesus answered and said to him, "Blessed are
you, Simon Bar-Jonah, [a]for flesh and blood has
not revealed *this* to you, but [b]My Father who is in
heaven.
18 "And I also say to you that [a]you are Peter, and
[b]on this rock I will build My church, and [c]the
gates of Hades shall not [1]prevail against it.
19 [a]"And I will give you the keys of the kingdom
of heaven, and whatever you bind on earth [1]will
be bound in heaven, and whatever you loose on
earth will be loosed in heaven."
20 [a]Then He commanded His disciples that they
should tell no one that He was Jesus the Christ.
**21** From that time Jesus began [a]to show to His
disciples that He must go to Jerusalem, and suffer
many things from the elders and chief priests and
scribes, and be killed, and be raised the third day.
22 Then Peter took Him aside and began to
rebuke Him, saying, [1]"Far be it from You, Lord;
this shall not happen to You!"
23 But He turned and said to Peter, "Get behind
Me, [a]Satan! [b]You are [1]an offense to Me, for you
are not mindful of the things of God, but the
things of men."
**24** [a]Then Jesus said to His disciples, "If anyone
desires to come after Me, let him deny himself,
and take up his cross, and [b]follow Me.
25 "For [a]whoever desires to save his life will lose
it, but whoever loses his life for My sake will
find it.

**21** [a]Mark 7:24–30
**22** [a]Matt. 1:1; 22:41, 42
**24** [a]Matt. 10:5, 6
**26** [a]Matt. 7:6
**28** [a]Luke 7:9
**29** [a]Mark 7:31–37 [b]Matt. 4:18
**30** [a]Is. 35:5, 6 [b]Luke 7:38; 8:41; 10:39 [1]*crippled*
**31** [a]Luke 5:25, 26; 19:37, 38 [1]*crippled*
**32** [a]Mark 8:1–10
**33** [a]2 Kin. 4:43
**36** [a]Matt. 14:19; 26:27 [b]Luke 22:19
**39** [a]Mark 8:10 [1]NU *Magadan*

CHAPTER 16
**1** [a]Mark 8:11
**3** [1]NU omits *Hypocrites*
**4** [a]Matt. 12:39 [1]NU omits *the prophet*
**5** [a]Mark 8:14
**6** [a]Luke 12:1 [1]*yeast*
**8** [1]NU *have no bread*
**9** [a]Matt. 14:15–21
**10** [a]Matt. 15:32–38
**11** [1]*yeast*
**12** [1]*teaching*
**13** [a]Luke 9:18
**14** [a]Matt. 14:2 [b]Matt. 21:11
**15** [a]John 6:67
**16** [a]Acts 8:37; 9:20
**17** [a][Eph. 2:8] [b]Gal. 1:16
**18** [a]John 1:42 [b][Eph. 2:20] [c]Is. 38:10 [1]*be victorious*
**19** [a]Matt. 18:18 [1]Or *will have been bound . . . will have been loosed*
**20** [a]Luke 9:21
**21** [a]Luke 9:22; 18:31; 24:46
**22** [1]Lit. *Merciful to you,* May God be merciful
**23** [a]Matt. 4:10 [b][Rom. 8:7] [1]*a stumbling block*
**24** [a][2 Tim. 3:12] [b][1 Pet. 2:21]
**25** [a]John 12:25

26 "For what [a]profit is it to a man if he gains the whole world, and loses his own soul? Or [b]what will a man give in exchange for his soul?

27 "For [a]the Son of Man will come in the glory of His Father [b]with His angels, [c]and then He will reward each according to his works.

28 "Assuredly, I say to you, [a]there are some standing here who shall not taste death till they see the Son of Man coming in His kingdom."

### *The Transfiguration of Christ*

**17** Now [a]after six days Jesus took Peter, James, and John his brother, led them up on a high mountain by themselves;

2 and He was transfigured before them. His face shone like the sun, and His clothes became as white as the light.

3 And behold, Moses and Elijah appeared to them, talking with Him.

4 Then Peter answered and said to Jesus, "Lord, it is good for us to be here; if You wish, [1]let us make here three tabernacles: one for You, one for Moses, and one for Elijah."

5 [a]While he was still speaking, behold, a bright cloud overshadowed them; and suddenly a voice came out of the cloud, saying, [b]"This is My beloved Son, [c]in whom I am well pleased. [d]Hear Him!"

6 [a]And when the disciples heard *it,* they fell on their faces and were greatly afraid.

7 But Jesus came and [a]touched them and said, "Arise, and do not be afraid."

8 When they had lifted up their eyes, they saw no one but Jesus only.

9 Now as they came down from the mountain, Jesus commanded them, saying, "Tell the vision to no one until the Son of Man is risen from the dead."

10 And His disciples asked Him, saying, [a]"Why then do the scribes say that Elijah must come first?"

11 Jesus answered and said to them, "Indeed, Elijah is coming [1]first and will [a]restore all things.

12 [a]"But I say to you that Elijah has come already, and they [b]did not know him but did to him whatever they wished. Likewise [c]the Son of Man is also about to suffer at their hands."

13 [a]Then the disciples understood that He spoke to them of John the Baptist.

**14** [a]And when they had come to the multitude, a man came to Him, kneeling down to Him and saying,

15 "Lord, have mercy on my son, for he is [1]an epileptic and suffers severely; for he often falls into the fire and often into the water.

16 "So I brought him to Your disciples, but they could not cure him."

17 Then Jesus answered and said, "O [1]faithless and [a]perverse generation, how long shall I be with you? How long shall I bear with you? Bring him here to Me."

18 And Jesus [a]rebuked the demon, and it came out of him; and the child was cured from that very hour.

19 Then the disciples came to Jesus privately and said, "Why could we not cast it out?"

20 So Jesus said to them, "Because of your [1]unbelief; for assuredly, I say to you, [a]if you have faith as a mustard seed, you will say to this mountain, 'Move from here to there,' and it will move; and nothing will be impossible for you.

21 [1]"However, this kind does not go out except by prayer and fasting."

**22** [a]Now while they were [1]staying in Galilee, Jesus said to them, "The Son of Man is about to be betrayed into the hands of men,

23 "and they will kill Him, and the third day He will be raised up." And they were exceedingly [a]sorrowful.

**24** [a]When they had come to [1]Capernaum, those who received the [2]*temple* tax came to Peter and said, "Does your Teacher not pay the *temple* tax?"

25 He said, "Yes." And when he had come into the house, Jesus anticipated him, saying, "What do you think, Simon? From whom do the kings of the earth take customs or taxes, from their sons or from [a]strangers?"

26 Peter said to Him, "From strangers." Jesus said to him, "Then the sons are free.

27 "Nevertheless, lest we offend them, go to the sea, cast in a hook, and take the fish that comes up first. And when you have opened its mouth, you will find a [1]piece of money; take that and give it to them for Me and you."

### *Offenses and Forgiveness*

**18** At [a]that time the disciples came to Jesus, saying, "Who then is greatest in the kingdom of heaven?"

2 Then Jesus called a little [a]child to Him, set him in the midst of them,

3 and said, "Assuredly, I say to you, [a]unless you are converted and become as little children, you will by no means enter the kingdom of heaven.

4 [a]"Therefore whoever humbles himself as this little child is the greatest in the kingdom of heaven.

5 [a]"Whoever receives one little child like this in My name receives Me.

**6** [a]"But whoever causes one of these little ones who believe in Me to sin, it would be better for him if a millstone were hung around his neck, and he were drowned in the depth of the sea.

7 "Woe to the world because of [1]offenses! For [a]offenses must come, but [b]woe to that man by whom the offense comes!

8 [a]"If your hand or foot causes you to sin, cut it off and cast *it* from you. It is better for you to enter into life lame or maimed, rather than having two hands or two feet, to be cast into the everlasting fire.

9 "And if your eye causes you to sin, pluck it out and cast *it* from you. It is better for you to enter into life with one eye, rather than having two eyes, to be cast into [1]hell fire.

**10** "Take heed that you do not despise one of these little ones, for I say to you that in heaven [a]their angels always [b]see the face of My Father who is in heaven.

11 [a]"For[1] the Son of Man has come to save that which was lost.

12 [a]"What do you think? If a man has a hundred sheep, and one of them goes astray, does he not leave the ninety-nine and go to the mountains to seek the one that is straying?

13 "And if he should find it, assuredly, I say to you, he rejoices more over that *sheep* than over the ninety-nine that did not go astray.

14 "Even so it is not the [a]will of your Father who is in heaven that one of these little ones should perish.

**26** [a]Luke 12:20, 21 [b]Ps. 49:7, 8
**27** [a]Mark 8:38 [b][Dan. 7:10] [c]Rom. 2:6
**28** [a]Luke 9:27

CHAPTER 17
**1** [a]Mark 9:2–8
**4** [1]NU *I will make*
**5** [a]2 Pet. 1:17 [b]Mark 1:11 [c]Matt. 3:17; 12:18 [d][Deut. 18:15, 19]
**6** [a]2 Pet. 1:18
**7** [a]Dan. 8:18
**10** [a]Mal. 4:5
**11** [a][Mal. 4:6] [1]NU omits *first*
**12** [a]Mark 9:12, 13 [b]Matt. 14:3, 10 [c]Matt. 16:21
**13** [a]Matt. 11:14
**14** [a]Mark 9:14–28
**15** [1]Lit. *moonstruck*
**17** [a]Phil. 2:15 [1]*unbelieving*
**18** [a]Luke 4:41
**20** [a]Luke 17:6 [1]NU *little faith*
**21** [1]NU omits v. 21.
**22** [a]Mark 8:31 [1]NU *gathering together*
**23** [a]John 16:6; 19:30
**24** [a]Mark 9:33 [1]NU *Capharnaum,* here and elsewhere [2]Lit. *double drachma*
**25** [a][Is. 60:10–17]
**27** [1]Gr. *stater,* the exact temple tax for two

CHAPTER 18
**1** [a]Luke 9:46–48; 22:24–27
**2** [a]Matt. 19:14
**3** [a]Luke 18:16
**4** [a][Matt. 20:27; 23:11]
**5** [a][Matt. 10:42]
**6** [a]Mark 9:42
**7** [a][1 Cor. 11:19] [b]Matt. 26:24; 27:4, 5 [1]*enticements to sin*
**8** [a]Matt. 5:29, 30
**9** [1]Gr. *Gehenna*
**10** [a][Heb. 1:14] [b]Luke 1:19
**11** [a]Luke 9:56 [1]NU omits v. 11.
**12** [a]Luke 15:4–7
**14** [a][1 Tim. 2:4]

**15** "Moreover [a]if your brother sins against you,
go and tell him his fault between you and him
alone. If he hears you, [b]you have gained your
brother.
16 "But if he will not hear, take with you one or
two more, that [a]*'by the mouth of two or three
witnesses every word may be established.'*
17 "And if he refuses to hear them, tell *it* to the
church. But if he refuses even to hear the church,
let him be to you like a [a]heathen and a tax
collector.
18 "Assuredly, I say to you, [a]whatever you bind
on earth will be bound in heaven, and whatever
you loose on earth will be loosed in heaven.
19 [a]"Again[1] I say to you that if two of you agree
on earth concerning anything that they ask, [b]it
will be done for them by My Father in heaven.
20 "For where two or three are gathered [a]together in My name, I am there in the midst of
them."
**21** Then Peter came to Him and said, "Lord, how
often shall my brother sin against me, and I
forgive him? [a]Up to seven times?"
22 Jesus said to him, "I do not say to you, [a]up to
seven times, but up to seventy times seven.
23 "Therefore the kingdom of heaven is like a
certain king who wanted to settle accounts with
his servants.
24 "And when he had begun to settle accounts,
one was brought to him who owed him ten thousand talents.
25 "But as he was not able to pay, his master
commanded [a]that he be sold, with his wife and
children and all that he had, and that payment be
made.
26 "The servant therefore fell down before him,
saying, 'Master, have patience with me, and I will
pay you all.'
27 "Then the master of that servant was moved
with compassion, released him, and forgave him
the debt.
28 "But that servant went out and found one of
his fellow servants who owed him a hundred
denarii; and he laid hands on him and took *him* by
the throat, saying, 'Pay me what you owe!'
29 "So his fellow servant fell down [1]at his feet
and begged him, saying, 'Have patience with me,
and I will pay you [2]all.'
30 "And he would not, but went and threw him
into prison till he should pay the debt.
31 "So when his fellow servants saw what had
been done, they were very grieved, and came and
told their master all that had been done.
32 "Then his master, after he had called him, said
to him, 'You wicked servant! I forgave you [a]all
that debt because you begged me.
33 'Should you not also have had compassion on
your fellow servant, just as I had pity on you?'
34 "And his master was angry, and delivered him
to the torturers until he should pay all that was
due to him.
35 [a]"So My heavenly Father also will do to you if
each of you, from his heart, does not forgive his
brother [1]his trespasses."

## *Christ's Teaching on Divorce*

**19** Now it came to pass, [a]when Jesus had finished these sayings, *that* He departed from
Galilee and came to the region of Judea beyond
the Jordan.
2 [a]And great multitudes followed Him, and He
healed them there.
3 The Pharisees also came to Him, testing Him,
and saying to Him, "Is it lawful for a man to
divorce his wife for *just* any reason?"
4 And He answered and said to them, "Have you
not read that He who [1]made *them* at the beginning [a]*'made them male and female,'*
5 "and said, [a]*'For this reason a man shall leave
his father and mother and be joined to his wife,
and* [b]*the two shall become one flesh'*?
6 "So then, they are no longer two but one flesh.
Therefore what God has joined together, let not
man separate."
7 They said to Him, [a]"Why then did Moses
command to give a certificate of divorce, and to
put her away?"
8 He said to them, "Moses, because of the [a]hardness of your hearts, permitted you to divorce your
[b]wives, but from the beginning it was not so.
9 [a]"And I say to you, whoever divorces his wife,
except for [1]sexual immorality, and marries another, commits adultery; and whoever marries her
who is divorced commits adultery."
10 His disciples said to Him, [a]"If such is the case
of the man with *his* wife, it is better not to marry."
**11** But He said to them, [a]"All cannot accept this
saying, but only *those* to whom it has been given:
12 "For there are [1]eunuchs who were born thus
from *their* mother's womb, and [a]there are eunuchs
who were made eunuchs by men, and there are
eunuchs who have made themselves eunuchs for
the kingdom of heaven's sake. He who is able to
accept *it,* let him accept *it.*"
**13** [a]Then little children were brought to Him that
He might put *His* hands on them and pray, but the
disciples rebuked them.
14 But Jesus said, "Let the little children come to
Me, and do not forbid them; for [a]of such is the
kingdom of heaven."
15 And He laid *His* hands on them and departed
from there.
**16** [a]Now behold, one came and said to Him,
[b]"Good[1] Teacher, what good thing shall I do that I
may have eternal life?"
17 So He said to him, [1]"Why do you call Me
good? [2]No one *is* [a]good but One, *that is,* God. But
if you want to enter into life, [b]keep the commandments."
18 He said to Him, "Which ones?" Jesus said,
[a]"*'You shall not murder,' 'You shall not commit
adultery,' 'You shall not steal,' 'You shall not bear
false witness,'*
19 [a]*'Honor your father and your mother,'* and,
[b]*'You shall love your neighbor as yourself.'* "
20 The young man said to Him, "All these things
I have [a]kept [1]from my youth. What do I still
lack?"
21 Jesus said to him, "If you want to be perfect,
[a]go, sell what you have and give to the poor, and
you will have treasure in heaven; and come,
follow Me."
22 But when the young man heard that saying,
he went away sorrowful, for he had great possessions.
**23** Then Jesus said to His disciples, "Assuredly, I
say to you that [a]it is hard for a rich man to enter
the kingdom of heaven.
24 "And again I say to you, it is easier for a camel
to go through the eye of a needle than for a rich
man to enter the kingdom of God."

**15** [a]Lev. 19:17 [b][James 5:20]
**16** [a]Deut. 17:6; 19:15
**17** [a][2 Thess. 3:6, 14]
**18** [a][John 20:22, 23]
**19** [a][1 Cor. 1:10] [b][1 John 3:22; 5:14] [1]NU, M *Again, assuredly, I say*
**20** [a]Acts 20:7
**21** [a]Luke 17:4
**22** [a]Col. 3:13
**25** [a]2 Kin. 4:1
**29** [1]NU omits *at his feet* [2]NU, M omit *all*
**32** [a]Luke 7:41–43
**35** [a]James 2:13 [1]NU omits *his trespasses*

CHAPTER 19
**1** [a]Mark 10:1–12
**2** [a]Matt. 12:15
**4** [a]Gen. 1:27; 5:2 [1]NU *created*
**5** [a]Gen. 2:24 [b][1 Cor. 6:16; 7:2]
**7** [a]Deut. 24:1–4
**8** [a]Heb. 3:15 [b]Mal. 2:16
**9** [a][Matt. 5:32] [1]Or *fornication*
**10** [a][Prov. 21:19]
**11** [a][1 Cor. 7:2, 7, 9, 17]
**12** [a][1 Cor. 7:32] [1]Emasculated men
**13** [a]Luke 18:15
**14** [a]Matt. 18:3, 4
**16** [a]Mark 10:17–30 [b]Luke 10:25 [1]NU omits *Good*
**17** [a]Nah. 1:7 [b]Lev. 18:5 [1]NU *Why do you ask Me about what is good?* [2]NU *There is One who is good. But*
**18** [a]Ex. 20:13–16
**19** [a]Ex. 20:12–16; Deut. 5:16–20 [b]Lev. 19:18
**20** [a][Phil. 3:6, 7] [1]NU omits *from my youth*
**21** [a]Acts 2:45; 4:34, 35
**23** [a][1 Tim. 6:9]

25 When His disciples heard *it,* they were greatly astonished, saying, "Who then can be saved?"
26 But Jesus looked at *them* and said to them, "With men this is impossible, but [a]with God all things are possible."
27 Then Peter answered and said to Him, "See, [a]we have left all and followed You. Therefore what shall we have?"
28 So Jesus said to them, "Assuredly I say to you, that in the regeneration, when the Son of Man sits on the throne of His glory, [a]you who have followed Me will also sit on twelve thrones, judging the twelve tribes of Israel.
29 [a]"And everyone who has left houses or brothers or sisters or father or mother [1]or wife or children or [2]lands, for My name's sake, shall receive a hundredfold, and inherit eternal life.
30 [a]"But many *who are* first will be last, and the last first.

### *Christ Foretells His Sufferings*

**20** "For the kingdom of heaven is like a landowner who went out early in the morning to hire laborers for his vineyard.
2 "Now when he had agreed with the laborers for a denarius a day, he sent them into his vineyard.
3 "And he went out about the third hour and saw others standing idle in the marketplace,
4 "and said to them, 'You also go into the vineyard, and whatever is right I will give you.' So they went.
5 "Again he went out about the sixth and the ninth hour, and did likewise.
6 "And about the eleventh hour he went out and found others standing [1]idle, and said to them, 'Why have you been standing here idle all day?'
7 "They said to him, 'Because no one hired us.' He said to them, 'You also go into the vineyard, [1]and whatever is right you will receive.'
8 "So when evening had come, the owner of the vineyard said to his steward, 'Call the laborers and give them *their* wages, beginning with the last to the first.'
9 "And when those came who *were hired* about the eleventh hour, they each received a denarius.
10 "But when the first came, they supposed that they would receive more; and they likewise received each a denarius.
11 "And when they had received *it,* they [1]complained against the landowner,
12 "saying, 'These last *men* have worked *only* one hour, and you made them equal to us who have borne the burden and the heat of the day.'
13 "But he answered one of them and said, 'Friend, I am doing you no wrong. Did you not agree with me for a denarius?
14 'Take *what is* yours and go your way. I wish to give to this last man *the same* as to you.
15 [a]'Is it not lawful for me to do what I wish with my own things? Or [b]is your eye evil because I am good?'
16 [a]"So the last will be first, and the first last. [b]For[1] many are called, but few chosen."
**17** [a]Now Jesus, going up to Jerusalem, took the twelve disciples aside on the road and said to them,
18 [a]"Behold, we are going up to Jerusalem, and the Son of Man will be betrayed to the chief priests and to the scribes; and they will condemn Him to death,
19 [a]"and deliver Him to the Gentiles to [b]mock and to [c]scourge and to [d]crucify. And the third day He will [e]rise again."
**20** [a]Then the mother of [b]Zebedee's sons came to Him with her sons, kneeling down and asking something from Him.
21 And He said to her, "What do you wish?" She said to Him, "Grant that these two sons of mine [a]may sit, one on Your right hand and the other on the left, in Your kingdom."
22 But Jesus answered and said, "You do not know what you ask. Are you able to drink [a]the cup that I am about to drink, [1]and be baptized with [b]the baptism that I am baptized with?" They said to Him, "We are able."
23 So He said to them, [a]"You will indeed drink My cup, [1]and be baptized with the baptism that I am baptized with; but to sit on My right hand and on My left is not Mine to give, but *it is for those* for whom it is prepared by My Father."
24 [a]And when the ten heard *it,* they were greatly displeased against the two brothers.
25 But Jesus called them to *Himself* and said, "You know that the rulers of the Gentiles lord it over them, and those who are great exercise authority over them.
26 "Yet [a]it shall not be so among you; but [b]whoever desires to become great among you, let him be your servant.
27 [a]"And whoever desires to be first among you, let him be your slave—
28 [a]"just as the [b]Son of Man did not come to be served, [c]but to serve, and [d]to give His life a ransom [e]for many."
**29** [a]Now as they went out of Jericho, a great multitude followed Him.
30 And behold, [a]two blind men sitting by the road, when they heard that Jesus was passing by, cried out, saying, "Have mercy on us, O Lord, [b]Son of David!"
31 Then the multitude [a]warned them that they should be quiet; but they cried out all the more, saying, "Have mercy on us, O Lord, Son of David!"
32 So Jesus stood still and called them, and said, "What do you want Me to do for you?"
33 They said to Him, "Lord, that our eyes may be opened."
34 So Jesus had [a]compassion and touched their eyes. And immediately their eyes received sight, and they followed Him.

### *Jesus Rides into Jerusalem*

**21** Now [a]when they drew near Jerusalem, and came to [1]Bethphage, at [b]the Mount of Olives, then Jesus sent two disciples,
2 saying to them, "Go into the village opposite you, and immediately you will find a donkey tied, and a colt with her. Loose *them* and bring *them* to Me.
3 "And if anyone says anything to you, you shall say, 'The Lord has need of them,' and immediately he will send them."
4 [1]All this was done that it might be fulfilled which was spoken by the prophet, saying:

5 *"Tell[a] the daughter of Zion,*
*'Behold, your King is coming to you,*
*Lowly, and sitting on a donkey,*
*A colt, the foal of a donkey.'"*

**26** [a]Jer. 32:17
**27** [a]Deut. 33:9
**28** [a]Luke 22:28–30
**29** [a]Mark 10:29, 30 [1]NU omits *or wife* [2]Lit. *fields*
**30** [a]Luke 13:30

CHAPTER 20
**6** [1]NU omits *idle*
**7** [1]NU omits the rest of v. 7.
**11** [1]*grumbled*
**15** [a][Rom. 9:20, 21] [b]Deut. 15:9
**16** [a]Matt. 19:30 [b]Matt. 22:14 [1]NU omits the rest of v. 16.
**17** [a]Mark 10:32–34
**18** [a]Matt. 16:21; 26:47–57
**19** [a]Matt. 27:2 [b]Matt. 26:67, 68; 27:29, 41 [c]Matt. 27:26 [d]Acts 3:13–15 [e]Matt. 28:5, 6
**20** [a]Mark 10:35–45 [b]Matt. 4:21; 10:2
**21** [a][Matt. 19:28]
**22** [a]Luke 22:42 [b]Luke 12:50 [1]NU omits *and be baptized with the baptism that I am baptized with*
**23** [a][Acts 12:2] [1]NU omits *and be baptized with the baptism that I am baptized with*
**24** [a]Mark 10:41
**26** [a][1 Pet. 5:3] [b]Matt. 23:11
**27** [a][Matt. 18:4]
**28** [a]John 13:4 [b][Phil. 2:6, 7] [c]Luke 22:27 [d][Is. 53:10, 11] [e][Rom. 5:15, 19]
**29** [a]Mark 10:46–52
**30** [a]Matt. 9:27 [b][Ezek. 37:21–25]
**31** [a]Matt. 19:13
**34** [a]Matt. 9:36; 14:14; 15:32; 18:27

CHAPTER 21
**1** [a]Luke 19:29–38 [b][Zech. 14:4] [1]M *Bethsphage*
**4** [1]NU omits *All*
**5** [a]Zech. 9:9

6 [a]So the disciples went and did as Jesus commanded them.

7 They brought the donkey and the colt, [a]laid their clothes on them, [1]and set *Him* on them.

8 And a very great multitude spread their clothes on the road; [a]others cut down branches from the trees and spread *them* on the road.

9 Then the multitudes who went before and those who followed cried out, saying:

> "Hosanna to the Son of David!
> [a]*'Blessed is He who comes*
> *in the name of the* LORD*!'*
> Hosanna in the highest!"

10 [a]And when He had come into Jerusalem, all the city was moved, saying, "Who is this?"

11 So the multitudes said, "This is Jesus, [a]the prophet from Nazareth of Galilee."

**12** [a]Then Jesus went into the temple [1]of God and drove out all those who bought and sold in the temple, and overturned the tables of the [b]money-changers and the seats of those who sold doves.

13 And He said to them, "It is written, [a]*'My house shall be called a house of prayer,'* but you have made it a [b]*'den of thieves.'*"

14 Then *the* blind and *the* lame came to Him in the temple, and He healed them.

15 But when the chief priests and scribes saw the wonderful things that He did, and the children crying out in the temple and saying, "Hosanna to the [a]Son of David!" they were [1]indignant

16 and said to Him, "Do You hear what these are saying?" And Jesus said to them, "Yes. Have you never read,

> [a]*'Out of the mouth of babes and nursing*
> *infants*
> *You have perfected praise'*?"

17 Then He left them and [a]went out of the city to Bethany, and He lodged there.

**18** [a]Now in the morning, as He returned to the city, He was hungry.

19 [a]And seeing a fig tree by the road, He came to it and found nothing on it but leaves, and said to it, "Let no fruit grow on you ever again." Immediately the fig tree withered away.

**20** [a]And when the disciples saw *it,* they marveled, saying, "How did the fig tree wither away so soon?"

21 So Jesus answered and said to them, "Assuredly, I say to you, [a]if you have faith and [b]do not doubt, you will not only do what was done to the fig tree, [c]but also if you say to this mountain, 'Be removed and be cast into the sea,' it will be done.

22 "And [a]whatever things you ask in prayer, believing, you will receive."

**23** [a]Now when He came into the temple, the chief priests and the elders of the people confronted Him as He was teaching, and [b]said, "By what authority are You doing these things? And who gave You this authority?"

24 But Jesus answered and said to them, "I also will ask you one thing, which if you tell Me, I likewise will tell you by what authority I do these things:

25 "The [a]baptism of [b]John—where was it from? From heaven or from men?" And they reasoned among themselves, saying, "If we say, 'From heaven,' He will say to us, 'Why then did you not believe him?'

26 "But if we say, 'From men,' we [a]fear the multitude, [b]for all count John as a prophet."

27 So they answered Jesus and said, "We do not know." And He said to them, "Neither will I tell you by what authority I do these things.

**28** "But what do you think? A man had two sons, and he came to the first and said, 'Son, go, work today in my [a]vineyard.'

29 "He answered and said, 'I will not,' but afterward he regretted it and went.

30 "Then he came to the second and said likewise. And he answered and said, 'I *go,* sir,' but he did not go.

31 "Which of the two did the will of *his* father?" They said to Him, "The first." Jesus said to them, [a]"Assuredly, I say to you that tax collectors and harlots enter the kingdom of God before you.

32 "For [a]John came to you in the way of righteousness, and you did not believe him; [b]but tax collectors and harlots believed him; and when you saw *it,* you did not afterward [1]relent and believe him.

**33** "Hear another parable: There was a certain landowner [a]who planted a vineyard and set a hedge around it, dug a winepress in it and built a tower. And he leased it to vinedressers and [b]went into a far country.

34 "Now when vintage-time drew near, he sent his servants to the vinedressers, that they might receive its fruit.

35 [a]"And the vinedressers took his servants, beat one, killed one, and stoned another.

36 "Again he sent other servants, more than the first, and they did likewise to them.

37 "Then last of all he sent his [a]son to them, saying, 'They will respect my son.'

38 "But when the vinedressers saw the son, they said among themselves, [a]'This is the heir. [b]Come, let us kill him and seize his inheritance.'

39 [a]"So they took him and cast *him* out of the vineyard and killed *him.*

40 "Therefore, when the owner of the vineyard comes, what will he do to those vinedressers?"

41 [a]They said to Him, [b]"He will destroy those wicked men miserably, [c]and lease *his* vineyard to other vinedressers who will [1]render to him the fruits in their seasons."

42 Jesus said to them, "Have you never read in the Scriptures:

> [a]*'The stone which the builders rejected*
> *Has become the chief cornerstone.*
> *This was the* LORD*'s doing,*
> *And it is marvelous in our eyes'*?

43 "Therefore I say to you, [a]the kingdom of God will be taken from you and given to a nation bearing the fruits of it.

44 "And [a]whoever falls on this stone will be broken; but on whomever it falls, [b]it will grind him to powder."

45 Now when the chief priests and Pharisees heard His parables, they [1]perceived that He was speaking of them.

46 But when they sought to lay hands on Him, they [a]feared the multitudes, because [b]they took Him for a prophet.

### *The Marriage of the King's Son*

**22** And Jesus answered [a]and spoke to them again by parables and said:

2 "The kingdom of heaven is like a certain king who arranged a marriage for his son,

---

6 [a]Mark 11:4
7 [a]2 Kin. 9:13 [1]NU *and He sat*
8 [a]Lev. 23:40
9 [a]Ps. 118:25, 26 [b]Matt. 23:39
10 [a]John 2:13, 15
11 [a]John 6:14; 7:40; 9:17
12 [a]Mark 11:15–18 [b]Deut. 14:25 [1]NU omits *of God*
13 [a]Is. 56:7 [b]Jer. 7:11
15 [a]John 7:42 [1]*angry*
16 [a]Ps. 8:2
17 [a]John 11:1, 18; 12:1
18 [a]Mark 11:12–14, 20–24
19 [a]Mark 11:13
20 [a]Mark 11:20
21 [a]Matt. 17:20 [b]James 1:6 [c]1 Cor. 13:2
22 [a]Matt. 7:7–11
23 [a]Luke 20:1–8 [b]Ex. 2:14
25 [a][John 1:29–34] [b]John 1:15–28
26 [a]Matt. 14:5; 21:46 [b]Mark 6:20
28 [a]Matt. 20:1; 21:33
31 [a]Luke 7:29, 37–50
32 [a]Luke 3:1–12; 7:29 [b]Luke 3:12, 13 [1]*regret it*
33 [a]Luke 20:9–19 [b]Matt. 25:14
35 [a][1 Thess. 2:15]
37 [a][John 3:16]
38 [a][Heb. 1:2] [b]John 11:53
39 [a][Acts 2:23]
41 [a]Luke 20:16 [b][Luke 21:24] [c][Acts 13:46] [1]*give*
42 [a]Ps. 118:22, 23
43 [a][Matt. 8:12]
44 [a]Is. 8:14, 15 [b][Dan. 2:44]
45 [1]*knew*
46 [a]Matt. 21:26 [b]Matt. 21:11

CHAPTER 22
1 [a][Rev. 19:7–9]

3 "and sent out his servants to call those who
were invited to the wedding; and they were not
willing to come.
4 "Again, he sent out other servants, saying,
'Tell those who are invited, "See, I have prepared
my dinner; [a]my oxen and fatted cattle *are* killed,
and all things *are* ready. Come to the wedding." '
5 "But they made light of it and went their
ways, one to his own farm, another to his business.
6 "And the rest seized his servants, treated *them*
[1]spitefully, and killed *them*.
7 "But when the king heard *about it*, he was
furious. And he sent out [a]his armies, destroyed
those murderers, and burned up their city.
8 "Then he said to his servants, 'The wedding is
ready, but those who were invited were not [a]wor-
thy.
9 'Therefore go into the highways, and as many
as you find, invite to the wedding.'
10 "So those servants went out into the highways and [a]gathered together all whom they found,
both bad and good. And the wedding *hall* was
filled with guests.
11 "But when the king came in to see the guests,
he saw a man there [a]who did not have on a
wedding garment.
12 "So he said to him, 'Friend, how did you come
in here without a wedding garment?' And he was
[a]speechless.
13 "Then the king said to the servants, 'Bind him
hand and foot, [1]take him away, and cast *him* [a]into
outer darkness; there will be weeping and gnashing of teeth.'
14 [a]"For many are called, but few *are* chosen."
**15** [a]Then the Pharisees went and plotted how
they might entangle Him in *His* talk.
16 And they sent to Him their disciples with the
[a]Herodians, saying, "Teacher, we know that You
are true, and teach the way of God in truth; nor
do You care about anyone, for You do not [1]regard
the person of men.
17 "Tell us, therefore, what do You think? Is it
lawful to pay taxes to Caesar, or not?"
18 But Jesus [1]perceived their wickedness, and
said, "Why do you test Me, *you* hypocrites?
19 "Show Me the tax money." So they brought
Him a denarius.
20 And He said to them, "Whose image and
inscription *is* this?"
21 They said to Him, "Caesar's." And He said to
them, [a]"Render[1] therefore to Caesar the things
that are [b]Caesar's, and to God the things that are
[c]God's."
22 When they had heard *these words*, they marveled, and left Him and went their way.
**23** [a]The same day the Sadducees, [b]who say there
is no resurrection, came to Him and asked Him,
24 saying: "Teacher, [a]Moses said that if a man
dies, having no children, his brother shall marry
his wife and raise up offspring for his brother.
25 "Now there were with us seven brothers. The
first died after he had married, and having no
offspring, left his wife to his brother.
26 "Likewise the second also, and the third, even
to the seventh.
27 "Last of all the woman died also.
28 "Therefore, in the resurrection, whose wife of
the seven will she be? For they all had her."
29 Jesus answered and said to them, "You are
[1]mistaken, [a]not knowing the Scriptures nor the
power of God.

**4** [a]Prov. 9:2
**6** [1]*insolently*
**7** [a][Dan. 9:26]
**8** [a]Matt. 10:11
**10** [a]Matt. 13:38, 47, 48
**11** [a][Col. 3:10, 12]
**12** [a][Rom. 3:19]
**13** [a]Matt. 8:12; 25:30 [1]NU omits *take him away and*
**14** [a]Matt. 20:16
**15** [a]Mark 12:13–17
**16** [a]Mark 3:6; 8:15; 12:13 [1]Lit. *look at the face of*
**18** [1]*knew*
**21** [a]Matt. 17:25 [b][Rom. 13:1–7] [c][1 Cor. 3:23; 6:19, 20; 12:27] [1]*Pay*
**23** [a]Luke 20:27–40 [b]Acts 23:8
**24** [a]Deut. 25:5
**29** [a]John 20:9 [1]*deceived*
**30** [a][1 John 3:2] [1]NU omits *of God*
**32** [a]Ex. 3:6, 15
**33** [a]Matt. 7:28
**34** [a]Mark 12:28–31
**35** [a]Luke 7:30; 10:25; 11:45, 46, 52; 14:3
**37** [a]Deut. 6:5; 10:12; 30:6
**39** [a]Lev. 19:18
**40** [a][Matt. 7:12]
**41** [a]Luke 20:41–44
**42** [a]Matt. 1:1; 21:9
**44** [a]Ps. 110:1
**46** [a]Luke 14:6 [b]Mark 12:34

CHAPTER 23
**2** [a]Neh. 8:4, 8
**3** [a][Rom. 2:19] [1]NU omits *to observe*
**4** [a]Luke 11:46
**5** [a][Matt. 6:1–6, 16–18]
**6** [a]Luke 11:43; 20:46 [1]Or *place of honor*
**8** [a][James 3:1] [1]*Leader* [2]NU omits *the Christ*
**9** [a][Mal. 1:6]
**11** [a]Matt. 20:26, 27

30 "For in the resurrection they neither marry
nor are given in marriage, but [a]are like angels [1]of
God in heaven.
31 "But concerning the resurrection of the dead,
have you not read what was spoken to you by
God, saying,
32 [a]'*I am the God of Abraham, the God of Isaac,
and the God of Jacob*'? God is not the God of the
dead, but of the living."
33 And when the multitudes heard *this*, [a]they
were astonished at His teaching.
**34** [a]But when the Pharisees heard that He had
silenced the Sadducees, they gathered together.
35 Then one of them, [a]a lawyer, asked *Him a
question*, testing Him, and saying,
36 "Teacher, which *is* the great commandment in
the law?"
37 Jesus said to him, [a]" '*You shall love the* LORD
*your God with all your heart, with all your soul,
and with all your mind.*'
38 "This is *the* first and great commandment.
39 "And *the* second *is* like it: [a]'*You shall love
your neighbor as yourself.*'
40 [a]"On these two commandments hang all the
Law and the Prophets."
**41** [a]While the Pharisees were gathered together,
Jesus asked them,
42 saying, "What do you think about the Christ?
Whose Son is He?" They said to Him, "*The* [a]*Son* of
David."
43 He said to them, "How then does David in the
Spirit call Him '*Lord*,' saying:

44 '*The*[a] LORD *said to my Lord,
"Sit at My right hand,
Till I make Your enemies Your footstool*" '?

45 "If David then calls Him '*Lord*,' how is He his
Son?"
46 [a]And no one was able to answer Him a word,
[b]nor from that day on did anyone dare question
Him anymore.

## *Jesus Rebukes the Scribes and Pharisees*

**23** Then Jesus spoke to the multitudes and to
His disciples,
2 saying: [a]"The scribes and the Pharisees sit in
Moses' seat.
3 "Therefore whatever they tell you [1]to observe,
*that* observe and do, but do not do according to
their works; for [a]they say, and do not do.
4 [a]"For they bind heavy burdens, hard to bear,
and lay *them* on men's shoulders; but they *themselves* will not move them with one of their
fingers.
5 "But all their works they do to [a]be seen by
men. They make their phylacteries broad and
enlarge the borders of their garments.
6 [a]"They love the [1]best places at feasts, the best
seats in the synagogues,
7 "greetings in the marketplaces, and to be
called by men, 'Rabbi, Rabbi.'
8 [a]"But you, do not be called 'Rabbi'; for One is
your [1]Teacher, [2]the Christ, and you are all brethren.
9 "Do not call anyone on earth your father; [a]for
One is your Father, He who is in heaven.
10 "And do not be called teachers; for One is your
Teacher, the Christ.
11 "But [a]he who is greatest among you shall be
your servant.

12 [a]"And whoever exalts himself will be [1]hum-
bled, and he who humbles himself will be [2]exalted.
13 "But [a]woe to you, scribes and Pharisees, hypocrites! For you shut up the kingdom of heaven
against men; for you neither go in *yourselves,* nor
do you allow those who are entering to go in.
14 [1]"Woe to you, scribes and Pharisees, hypocrites! [a]For you devour widows' houses, and for a
pretense make long prayers. Therefore you will
receive greater condemnation.
15 "Woe to you, scribes and Pharisees, hypocrites! For you travel land and sea to win one
proselyte, and when he is won, you make him
twice as much a son of [1]hell as yourselves.
16 "Woe to you, [a]blind guides, who say, [b]'Whoever swears by the temple, it is nothing; but
whoever swears by the gold of the temple, he is
obliged *to perform it.*'
17 "Fools and blind! For which is greater, the
gold [a]or the temple that [1]sanctifies the gold?
18 "And, 'Whoever swears by the altar, it is
nothing; but whoever swears by the gift that is on
it, he is obliged *to perform it.*'
19 "Fools and blind! For which is greater, the gift
[a]or the altar that sanctifies the gift?
20 "Therefore he who [1]swears by the altar,
swears by it and by all things on it.
21 "He who swears by the temple, swears by it
and by [a]Him who [1]dwells in it.
22 "And he who swears by heaven, swears by
[a]the throne of God and by Him who sits on it.
23 "Woe to you, scribes and Pharisees, hypocrites! [a]For you pay tithe of mint and anise and
cummin, and [b]have neglected the weightier *matters* of the law: justice and mercy and faith. These
you ought to have done, without leaving the
others undone.
24 "Blind guides, who strain out a gnat and
swallow a camel!
25 "Woe to you, scribes and Pharisees, hypocrites! [a]For you cleanse the outside of the cup and
dish, but inside they are full of extortion and [1]self-
indulgence.
26 "Blind Pharisee, first cleanse the inside of the
cup and dish, that the outside of them may be
clean also.
27 "Woe to you, scribes and Pharisees, hypocrites! [a]For you are like whitewashed tombs which
indeed appear beautiful outwardly, but inside are
full of dead *men's* bones and all uncleanness.
28 "Even so you also outwardly appear righteous
to men, but inside you are full of hypocrisy and
lawlessness.
29 [a]"Woe to you, scribes and Pharisees, hypocrites! Because you build the tombs of the prophets and [1]adorn the monuments of the righteous,
30 "and say, 'If we had lived in the days of our
fathers, we would not have been partakers with
them in the blood of the prophets.'
31 "Therefore you are witnesses against yourselves that [a]you are sons of those who murdered
the prophets.
32 [a]"Fill up, then, the measure of your fathers'
*guilt.*
33 "Serpents, [a]brood[1] of vipers! How can you
escape the condemnation of hell?
34 [a]"Therefore, indeed, I send you prophets, wise
men, and scribes: [b]*some* of them you will kill and
crucify, and [c]*some* of them you will scourge in
your synagogues and persecute from city to city,
35 [a]"that on you may come all the righteous
blood shed on the earth, [b]from the blood of righteous Abel to [c]the blood of Zechariah, son of
Berechiah, whom you murdered between the
temple and the altar.
36 "Assuredly, I say to you, all these things will
come upon this generation.
**37** [a]"O Jerusalem, Jerusalem, the one who kills
the prophets [b]and stones those who are sent to
her! How often [c]I wanted to gather your children
together, as a hen gathers her chicks [d]under *her*
wings, but you were not willing!
38 "See! Your house is left to you desolate;
39 "for I say to you, you shall see Me no more till
you say, [a]*'Blessed is He who comes in the name of
the LORD!'*"

### *Destruction of the Temple Foretold*

**24** Then [a]Jesus went out and departed from the
temple, and His disciples came up to show
Him the buildings of the temple.
2 And Jesus said to them, "Do you not see all
these things? Assuredly, I say to you, [a]not *one*
stone shall be left here upon another, that shall
not be thrown down."
**3** Now as He sat on the Mount of Olives, [a]the
disciples came to Him privately, saying, [b]"Tell us,
when will these things be? And what *will be* the
sign of Your coming, and of the end of the age?"
4 And Jesus answered and said to them: [a]"Take
heed that no one deceives you.
5 "For [a]many will come in My name, saying, 'I
am the Christ,' [b]and will deceive many.
6 "And you will hear of [a]wars and rumors of
wars. See that you are not troubled; for [1]all *these
things* must come to pass, but the end is not yet.
7 "For [a]nation will rise against nation, and
kingdom against kingdom. And there will be
[b]famines, [1]pestilences, and earthquakes in various
places.
8 "All these *are* the beginning of sorrows.
9 [a]"Then they will deliver you up to tribulation
and kill you, and you will be hated by all nations
for My name's sake.
10 "And then many will be offended, will betray
one another, and will hate one another.
11 "Then [a]many false prophets will rise up and
[b]deceive many.
12 "And because lawlessness will abound, the
love of many will grow [a]cold.
13 [a]"But he who endures to the end shall be
saved.
14 "And this [a]gospel of the kingdom [b]will be
preached in all the world as a witness to all the
nations, and then the end will come.
**15** [a]"Therefore when you see the [b]*'abomination
of desolation,'* spoken of by Daniel the prophet,
standing in the holy place" [c](whoever reads, let
him understand),
16 "then let those who are in Judea flee to the
mountains.
17 "Let him who is on the housetop not go down
to take anything out of his house.
18 "And let him who is in the field not go back to
get his clothes.
19 "But [a]woe to those who are pregnant and to
those who are nursing babies in those days!
20 "And pray that your flight may not be in
winter or on the Sabbath.
21 "For [a]then there will be great tribulation, such

**12** [a]Luke 14:11; 18:14 [1]*put down* [2]*lifted up*
**13** [a]Luke 11:52
**14** [a]Mark 12:40 [1]NU omits v. 14.
**15** [1]Gr. *Gehenna*
**16** [a]Matt. 15:14; 23:24 [b][Matt. 5:33, 34]
**17** [a]Ex. 30:29 [1]NU *sanctified*
**19** [a]Ex. 29:37
**20** [1]Swears an oath
**21** [a]1 Kin. 8:13 [1]M *dwelt*
**22** [a]Matt. 5:34
**23** [a]Luke 11:42; 18:12 [b][Hos. 6:6]
**25** [a]Luke 11:39 [1]M *unrighteousness*
**27** [a]Acts 23:3
**29** [a]Luke 11:47, 48 [1]*decorate*
**31** [a][Acts 7:51, 52]
**32** [a][1 Thess. 2:16]
**33** [a]Matt. 3:7; 12:34 [1]*offspring*
**34** [a]Luke 11:49 [b]Acts 7:54–60; 22:19 [c]2 Cor. 11:24, 25
**35** [a]Rev. 18:24 [b]Gen. 4:8 [c]2 Chr. 24:20, 21
**37** [a]Luke 13:34, 35 [b]2 Chr. 24:20, 21; 36:15, 16 [c]Deut. 32:11, 12 [d]Ps. 17:8; 91:4
**39** [a]Ps. 118:26

CHAPTER 24
**1** [a]Mark 13:1
**2** [a]Luke 19:44
**3** [a]Mark 13:3 [b][1 Thess. 5:1–3]
**4** [a][Col. 2:8, 18]
**5** [a]John 5:43 [b]Matt. 24:11
**6** [a][Rev. 6:2–4] [1]NU omits *all*
**7** [a]Hag. 2:22 [b]Rev. 6:5, 6 [1]NU omits *pestilences*
**9** [a]Matt. 10:17
**11** [a]2 Pet. 2:1 [b][1 Tim. 4:1]
**12** [a][2 Thess. 2:3]
**13** [a]Matt. 10:22
**14** [a]Matt. 4:23 [b]Rom. 10:18
**15** [a]Mark 13:14 [b]Dan. 9:27; 11:31; 12:11 [c]Dan. 9:23
**19** [a]Luke 23:29
**21** [a]Dan. 9:26

as has not been since the beginning of the world until this time, no, nor ever shall be.
22 "And unless those days were shortened, no flesh would be saved; [a]but for the [1]elect's sake those days will be shortened.
23 [a]"Then if anyone says to you, 'Look, here *is* the Christ!' or 'There!' do not believe *it*.
24 "For [a]false christs and false prophets will rise and show great signs and wonders to deceive, [b]if possible, even the elect.
25 "See, I have told you beforehand.
26 "Therefore if they say to you, 'Look, He is in the desert!' do not go out; *or* 'Look, *He is* in the inner rooms!' do not believe *it*.
27 [a]"For as the lightning comes from the east and flashes to the west, so also will the coming of the Son of Man be.
28 [a]"For wherever the carcass is, there the eagles will be gathered together.
**29** [a]"Immediately after the tribulation of those days [b]the sun will be darkened, and the moon will not give its light; the stars will fall from heaven, and the powers of the heavens will be shaken.
30 [a]"Then the sign of the Son of Man will appear in heaven, [b]and then all the tribes of the earth will mourn, and they will see the Son of Man coming on the clouds of heaven with power and great glory.
31 [a]"And He will send His angels with a great sound of a trumpet, and they will gather together His [1]elect from the four winds, from one end of heaven to the other.
**32** "Now learn [a]this parable from the fig tree: When its branch has already become tender and puts forth leaves, you know that summer *is* near.
33 "So you also, when you see all these things, know [a]that [1]it is near—at the doors!
34 "Assuredly, I say to you, [a]this generation will by no means pass away till all these things take place.
35 [a]"Heaven and earth will pass away, but My words will by no means pass away.
**36** [a]"But of that day and hour no one knows, not even the angels of [1]heaven, [b]but My Father only.
37 "But as the days of Noah *were*, so also will the coming of the Son of Man be.
38 [a]"For as in the days before the flood, they were eating and drinking, marrying and giving in marriage, until the day that Noah entered the ark,
39 "and did not know until the flood came and took them all away, so also will the coming of the Son of Man be.
40 [a]"Then two *men* will be in the field: one will be taken and the other left.
41 "Two *women will be* grinding at the mill: one will be taken and the other left.
42 [a]"Watch therefore, for you do not know what [1]hour your Lord is coming.
43 [a]"But know this, that if the master of the house had known what [1]hour the thief would come, he would have watched and not allowed his house to be broken into.
44 [a]"Therefore you also be ready, for the Son of Man is coming at an hour you do not expect.
**45** [a]"Who then is a faithful and wise servant, whom his master made ruler over his household, to give them food [1]in due season?
46 [a]"Blessed *is* that servant whom his master, when he comes, will find so doing.
47 "Assuredly, I say to you that [a]he will make him ruler over all his goods.
48 "But if that evil servant says in his heart, 'My master [a]is delaying [1]his coming,'
49 "and begins to beat *his* fellow servants, and to eat and drink with the drunkards,
50 "the master of that servant will come on a day when he is not looking for *him* and at an hour that he is [a]not aware of,
51 "and will cut him in two and appoint *him* his portion with the hypocrites. [a]There shall be weeping and gnashing of teeth.

### *The Return of Christ in Judgment*

**25** "Then the kingdom of heaven shall be likened to ten virgins who took their lamps and went out to meet [a]the bridegroom.
2 [a]"Now five of them were wise, and five *were* foolish.
3 "Those who *were* foolish took their lamps and took no oil with them,
4 "but the wise took oil in their vessels with their lamps.
5 "But while the bridegroom was delayed, [a]they all slumbered and slept.
6 "And at midnight [a]a cry was *heard:* 'Behold, the bridegroom [1]is coming; go out to meet him!'
7 "Then all those virgins arose and [a]trimmed their lamps.
8 "And the foolish said to the wise, 'Give us *some* of your oil, for our lamps are going out.'
9 "But the wise answered, saying, '*No,* lest there should not be enough for us and you; but go rather to those who sell, and buy for yourselves.'
10 "And while they went to buy, the bridegroom came, and those who were ready went in with him to the wedding; and [a]the door was shut.
11 "Afterward the other virgins came also, saying, [a]'Lord, Lord, open to us!'
12 "But he answered and said, 'Assuredly, I say to you, [a]I do not know you.'
13 [a]"Watch therefore, for you [b]know neither the day nor the hour [1]in which the Son of Man is coming.
**14** [a]"For *the kingdom of heaven is* [b]like a man traveling to a far country, *who* called his own servants and delivered his goods to them.
15 "And to one he gave five talents, to another two, and to another one, [a]to each according to his own ability; and immediately he went on a journey.
16 "Then he who had received the five talents went and traded with them, and made another five talents.
17 "And likewise he who *had received* two gained two more also.
18 "But he who had received one went and dug in the ground, and hid his lord's money.
19 "After a long time the lord of those servants came and settled accounts with them.
20 "So he who had received five talents came and brought five other talents, saying, 'Lord, you delivered to me five talents; look, I have gained five more talents besides them.'
21 "His lord said to him, 'Well *done,* good and faithful servant; you were [a]faithful over a few things, [b]I will make you ruler over many things. Enter into [c]the joy of your lord.'
22 "He also who had received two talents came and said, 'Lord, you delivered to me two talents; look, I have gained two more talents besides them.'

**22** [a]Is. 65:8, 9 [1]*chosen ones'*
**23** [a]Luke 17:23
**24** [a][2 Thess. 2:9] [b][2 Tim. 2:19]
**27** [a]Luke 17:24
**28** [a]Luke 17:37
**29** [a][Dan. 7:11] [b]Ezek. 32:7
**30** [a][Dan. 7:13, 14] [b]Zech. 12:12
**31** [a][1 Cor. 15:52] [1]*chosen ones*
**32** [a]Luke 21:29
**33** [a][James 5:9] [1]Or *He*
**34** [a][Matt. 10:23; 16:28; 23:36]
**35** [a]Luke 21:33
**36** [a]Acts 1:7 [b]Zech. 14:7 [1]NU adds *nor the Son*
**38** [a][Gen. 6:3–5]
**40** [a]Luke 17:34
**42** [a]Matt. 25:13 [1]NU *day*
**43** [a]Luke 12:39 [1]Lit. *watch of the night*
**44** [a][1 Thess. 5:6]
**45** [a]Luke 12:42–46 [1]*at the right time*
**46** [a]Rev. 16:15
**47** [a]Matt. 25:21, 23
**48** [a][2 Pet. 3:4–9] [1]NU omits *his coming*
**50** [a]Mark 13:32
**51** [a]Matt. 8:12; 25:30

CHAPTER 25
**1** [a][Eph. 5:29, 30]
**2** [a]Matt. 13:47; 22:10
**5** [a]1 Thess. 5:6
**6** [a][1 Thess. 4:16] [1]NU omits *is coming*
**7** [a]Luke 12:35
**10** [a]Luke 13:25
**11** [a][Matt. 7:21–23]
**12** [a][Hab. 1:13]
**13** [a]Mark 13:35 [b]Matt. 24:36, 42 [1]NU omits the rest of v. 13.
**14** [a]Luke 19:12–27 [b]Matt. 21:33
**15** [a][Rom. 12:6]
**21** [a][1 Cor. 4:2] [b][Luke 12:44; 22:29, 30] [c][Heb. 12:2]

23 "His lord said to him, [a]'Well *done,* good and
faithful servant; you have been faithful over a few
things, I will make you ruler over many things.
Enter into [b]the joy of your lord.'
24 "Then he who had received the one talent
came and said, 'Lord, I knew you to be a hard
man, reaping where you have not sown, and
gathering where you have not scattered seed.
25 'And I was afraid, and went and hid your
talent in the ground. Look, *there* you have *what is*
yours.'
26 "But his lord answered and said to him, 'You
[a]wicked and lazy servant, you knew that I reap
where I have not sown, and gather where I have
not scattered seed.
27 'So you ought to have deposited my money
with the bankers, and at my coming I would have
received back my own with interest.
28 'Therefore take the talent from him, and give
*it* to him who has ten talents.
29 [a]'For to everyone who has, more will be given,
and he will have abundance; but from him who
does not have, even what he has will be taken
away.
30 'And cast the unprofitable servant [a]into the
outer darkness. [b]There will be weeping and
[c]gnashing of teeth.'
**31** [a]"When the Son of Man comes in His glory,
and all the [1]holy angels with Him, then He will sit
on the throne of His glory.
32 [a]"All the nations will be gathered before Him,
and [b]He will separate them one from another, as a
shepherd divides *his* sheep from the goats.
33 "And He will set the [a]sheep on His right hand,
but the goats on the left.
34 "Then the King will say to those on His right
hand, 'Come, you blessed of My Father, [a]inherit
the kingdom [b]prepared for you from the foundation of the world:
35 [a]'for I was hungry and you gave Me food; I
was thirsty and you gave Me drink; [b]I was a
stranger and you took Me in;
36 'I *was* [a]naked and you clothed Me; I was sick
and you visited Me; [b]I was in prison and you came
to Me.'
37 "Then the righteous will answer Him, saying,
'Lord, when did we see You hungry and feed *You,*
or thirsty and give *You* drink?
38 'When did we see You a stranger and take *You*
in, or naked and clothe *You?*
39 'Or when did we see You sick, or in prison, and
come to You?'
40 "And the King will answer and say to them,
'Assuredly, I say to you, [a]inasmuch as you did *it* to
one of the least of these My brethren, you did *it* to
Me.'
41 "Then He will also say to those on the left
hand, [a]'Depart from Me, you cursed, [b]into the
everlasting fire prepared for [c]the devil and his
angels:
42 'for I was hungry and you gave Me no food; I
was thirsty and you gave Me no drink;
43 'I was a stranger and you did not take Me in,
naked and you did not clothe Me, sick and in
prison and you did not visit Me.'
44 "Then they also will answer [1]Him, saying,
'Lord, when did we see You hungry or thirsty or a
stranger or naked or sick or in prison, and did not
minister to You?'
45 "Then He will answer them, saying, 'Assuredly, I say to you, [a]inasmuch as you did not do
*it* to one of the least of these, you did not do *it* to
Me.'
46 "And [a]these will go away into everlasting
punishment, but the righteous into eternal life."

### *The Beginning of the Lord's Supper*

**26** Now it came to pass, when Jesus had finished all these sayings, *that* He said to His
disciples,
2 [a]"You know that after two days is the Passover, and the Son of Man will be delivered up to
be crucified."
3 [a]Then the chief priests, [1]the scribes, and the
elders of the people assembled at the palace of the
high priest, who was called Caiaphas,
4 and [a]plotted to take Jesus by [1]trickery and kill
*Him.*
5 But they said, "Not during the feast, lest there
be an uproar among the [a]people."
**6** And when Jesus was in [a]Bethany at the house
of Simon the leper,
7 a woman came to Him having an alabaster
flask of very costly fragrant oil, and she poured *it*
on His head as He sat *at the table.*
8 [a]But when His disciples saw *it,* they were
indignant, saying, "Why this waste?
9 "For this fragrant oil might have been sold for
much and given to *the* poor."
10 But when Jesus was aware of *it,* He said to
them, "Why do you trouble the woman? For she
has done a good work for Me.
11 [a]"For you have the poor with you always, but
[b]Me you do not have always.
12 "For in pouring this fragrant oil on My body,
she did *it* for My [a]burial.
13 "Assuredly, I say to you, wherever this gospel
is preached in the whole world, what this woman
has done will also be told as a memorial to her."
**14** [a]Then one of the twelve, called [b]Judas Iscariot,
went to the chief priests
15 and said, [a]"What are you willing to give me if
I deliver Him to you?" And they counted out to
him thirty pieces of silver.
16 So from that time he sought opportunity to
betray Him.
**17** [a]Now on the first *day* of the *Feast* of the
Unleavened Bread the disciples came to Jesus,
saying to Him, "Where do You want us to prepare
for You to eat the Passover?"
18 And He said, "Go into the city to a certain
man, and say to him, 'The Teacher says, [a]"My
time is at hand; I will keep the Passover at your
house with My disciples." ' "
19 So the disciples did as Jesus had directed
them; and they prepared the Passover.
20 [a]When evening had come, He sat down with
the twelve.
21 Now as they were eating, He said, "Assuredly,
I say to you, one of you will [a]betray Me."
22 And they were exceedingly sorrowful, and
each of them began to say to Him, "Lord, is it I?"
23 He answered and said, [a]"He who dipped *his*
hand with Me in the dish will betray Me.
24 "The Son of Man indeed goes just as it is
written of Him, but [b]woe to that man by whom
the Son of Man is betrayed! [c]It would have been
good for that man if he had not been born."
25 Then Judas, who was betraying Him, answered and said, "Rabbi, is it I?" He said to him,
"You have said it."

**23** [a]Matt. 24:45, 47; 25:21 [b][Ps. 16:11]
**26** [a]Matt. 18:32
**29** [a]Matt. 13:12
**30** [a]Matt. 8:12; 22:13 [b]Matt. 7:23; 8:12; 24:51 [c]Ps. 112:10
**31** [a][1 Thess. 4:16] [1]NU omits *holy*
**32** [a][2 Cor. 5:10] [b]Ezek. 20:38
**33** [a][John 10:11, 27, 28]
**34** [a][Rom. 8:17] [b]Mark 10:40
**35** [a]Is. 58:7 [b][Heb. 13:2]
**36** [a][James 2:15, 16] [b]2 Tim. 1:16
**40** [a]Mark 9:41
**41** [a]Matt. 7:23 [b]Matt. 13:40, 42 [c][2 Pet. 2:4]
**44** [1]NU, M omit *Him*
**45** [a]Prov. 14:31
**46** [a][Dan. 12:2]

CHAPTER 26
**2** [a]Luke 22:1, 2
**3** [a]John 11:47 [1]NU omits *the scribes*
**4** [a]Acts 4:25–28 [1]*deception*
**5** [a]Matt. 21:26
**6** [a]Mark 14:3–9
**8** [a]John 12:4
**11** [a][Deut. 15:11] [b][John 13:33; 14:19; 16:5, 28; 17:11]
**12** [a]John 19:38–42
**14** [a]Mark 14:10, 11; Luke 22:3–6 [b]Matt. 10:4
**15** [a]Zech. 11:12
**17** [a]Ex. 12:6, 18–20
**18** [a]Luke 9:51
**20** [a]Mark 14:17–21
**21** [a]John 6:70, 71; 13:21
**23** [a]Ps. 41:9
**24** [a]1 Cor. 15:3 [b]Luke 17:1 [c]John 17:12

**26** [a]And as they were eating, [b]Jesus took bread, [1]blessed and broke *it,* and gave *it* to the disciples and said, "Take, eat; [c]this is My body."
27 Then He took the cup, and gave thanks, and gave *it* to them, saying, [a]"Drink from it, all of you.
28 "For [a]this is My blood [b]of the [1]new covenant, which is shed [c]for many for the [2]remission of sins.
29 "But [a]I say to you, I will not drink of this fruit of the vine from now on [b]until that day when I drink it new with you in My Father's kingdom."
30 [a]And when they had sung a hymn, they went out to the Mount of Olives.
**31** Then Jesus said to them, [a]"All of you will [b]be [1]made to stumble because of Me this night, for it is written:

[c]*'I will strike the Shepherd,*
*And the sheep of the flock will be scattered.'*

32 "But after I have been raised, [a]I will go before you to Galilee."
33 Peter answered and said to Him, "Even if all are [1]made to stumble because of You, I will never be made to stumble."
34 Jesus said to him, [a]"Assuredly, I say to you that this night, before the rooster crows, you will deny Me three times."
35 Peter said to Him, "Even if I have to die with You, I will not deny You!" And so said all the disciples.
**36** [a]Then Jesus came with them to a place called Gethsemane, and said to the disciples, "Sit here while I go and pray over there."
37 And He took with Him Peter and [a]the two sons of Zebedee, and He began to be sorrowful and deeply distressed.
38 Then He said to them, [a]"My soul is exceedingly sorrowful, even to death. Stay here and watch with Me."
39 He went a little farther and fell on His face, and [a]prayed, saying, [b]"O My Father, if it is possible, [c]let this cup pass from Me; nevertheless, [d]not as I will, but as You *will.*"
40 Then He came to the disciples and found them sleeping, and said to Peter, "What? Could you not watch with Me one hour?
41 [a]"Watch and pray, lest you enter into temptation. [b]The spirit indeed *is* willing, but the flesh *is* weak."
42 Again, a second time, He went away and prayed, saying, "O My Father, [1]if this cup cannot pass away from Me unless I drink it, Your will be done."
43 And He came and found them asleep again, for their eyes were heavy.
44 So He left them, went away again, and prayed the third time, saying the same words.
45 Then He came to His disciples and said to them, "Are *you* still sleeping and resting? Behold, the hour [1]is at hand, and the Son of Man is being [a]betrayed into the hands of sinners.
46 "Rise, let us be going. See, My betrayer is at hand."
**47** And [a]while He was still speaking, behold, Judas, one of the twelve, with a great multitude with swords and clubs, came from the chief priests and elders of the people.
48 Now His betrayer had given them a sign, saying, "Whomever I kiss, He is the One; seize Him."
49 Immediately he went up to Jesus and said, "Greetings, Rabbi!" [a]and kissed Him.

**26** [a]Mark 14:22–25 [b]1 Cor. 11:23–25 [c][1 Pet. 2:24] [1]M *gave thanks for*
**27** [a]Mark 14:23
**28** [a][Ex. 24:8] [b]Jer. 31:31 [c]Matt. 20:28 [1]NU omits *new* [2]*forgiveness*
**29** [a]Mark 14:25 [b]Acts 10:41
**30** [a]Mark 14:26–31
**31** [a]John 16:32 [b][Matt. 11:6] [c]Zech. 13:7 [1]*caused to take offense at Me*
**32** [a]Matt. 28:7, 10, 16
**33** [1]*caused to take offense at You*
**34** [a]John 13:38
**36** [a]Mark 14:32–35
**37** [a]Matt. 4:21; 17:1
**38** [a]John 12:27
**39** [a][Heb. 5:7–9] [b]John 12:27 [c]Matt. 20:22 [d]John 5:30; 6:38
**41** [a]Luke 22:40, 46 [b][Gal. 5:17]
**42** [1]NU *if this may not pass away unless*
**45** [a]Matt. 17:22, 23; 20:18, 19 [1]*has drawn near*
**47** [a]Acts 1:16
**49** [a]2 Sam. 20:9
**50** [a]Ps. 41:9; 55:13
**51** [a]John 18:10
**52** [a]Rev. 13:10 [1]M *die*
**53** [a]Dan. 7:10
**54** [a]Is. 50:6; 53:2–11
**56** [a]Lam. 4:20 [b]John 18:15
**57** [a]John 18:12, 19–24
**58** [a]John 18:15, 16
**59** [a]Ps. 35:11 [1]NU omits *the elders*
**60** [a]Mark 14:55 [b]Deut. 19:15 [1]NU *but found none, even though many false witnesses came forward.* [2]NU omits *false witnesses*
**61** [a]John 2:19
**62** [a]Mark 14:60
**63** [a]Is. 53:7 [b]Lev. 5:1
**64** [a]Dan. 7:13 [b][Acts 7:55]
**65** [a]2 Kin. 18:37 [b]John 10:30–36
**66** [a]Lev. 24:16
**67** [a]Is. 50:6; 53:3 [b]Luke 22:63–65 [1]Or *rods,*
**68** [a]Mark 14:65
**69** [a]John 18:16–18, 25–27

50 But Jesus said to him, [a]"Friend, why have you come?" Then they came and laid hands on Jesus and took Him.
51 And suddenly, [a]one of those *who were* with Jesus stretched out *his* hand and drew his sword, struck the servant of the high priest, and cut off his ear.
52 But Jesus said to him, "Put your sword in its place, [a]for all who take the sword will [1]perish by the sword.
53 "Or do you think that I cannot now pray to My Father, and He will provide Me with [a]more than twelve legions of angels?
54 "How then could the Scriptures be fulfilled, [a]that it must happen thus?"
55 In that hour Jesus said to the multitudes, "Have you come out, as against a robber, with swords and clubs to take Me? I sat daily with you, teaching in the temple, and you did not seize Me.
56 "But all this was done that the [a]Scriptures of the prophets might be fulfilled." Then [b]all the disciples forsook Him and fled.
**57** [a]And those who had laid hold of Jesus led *Him* away to Caiaphas the high priest, where the scribes and the elders were assembled.
58 But [a]Peter followed Him at a distance to the high priest's courtyard. And he went in and sat with the servants to see the end.
59 Now the chief priests, [1]the elders, and all the council sought [a]false testimony against Jesus to put Him to death,
60 [1]but found none. Even though [a]many false witnesses came forward, they found none. But at last [b]two [2]false witnesses came forward
61 and said, "This *fellow* said, [a]'I am able to destroy the temple of God and to build it in three days.' "
62 [a]And the high priest arose and said to Him, "Do You answer nothing? What *is it* these men testify against You?"
63 But [a]Jesus kept silent. And the high priest answered and said to Him, [b]"I put You under oath by the living God: Tell us if You are the Christ, the Son of God!"
64 Jesus said to him, "*It is as* you said. Nevertheless, I say to you, [a]hereafter you will see the Son of Man [b]sitting at the right hand of the Power, and coming on the clouds of heaven."
65 [a]Then the high priest tore his clothes, saying, "He has spoken blasphemy! What further need do we have of witnesses? Look, now you have heard His [b]blasphemy!
66 "What do you think?" They answered and said, [a]"He is deserving of death."
67 [a]Then they spat in His face and beat Him; and [b]others struck *Him* with [1]the palms of their hands,
68 saying, [a]"Prophesy to us, Christ! Who is the one who struck You?"
**69** [a]Now Peter sat outside in the courtyard. And a servant girl came to him, saying, "You also were with Jesus of Galilee."
70 But he denied it before *them* all, saying, "I do not know what you are saying."
71 And when he had gone out to the gateway, another *girl* saw him and said to those *who were* there, "This *fellow* also was with Jesus of Nazareth."
72 But again he denied with an oath, "I do not know the Man!"
73 And a little later those who stood by came up

and said to Peter, "Surely you also are *one* of
them, for your [a]speech betrays you."
74 Then [a]he began to [1]curse and [2]swear, *saying,*
"I do not know the Man!" Immediately a rooster
crowed.
75 And Peter remembered the word of Jesus who
had said to him, [a]"Before the rooster crows, you
will deny Me three times." So he went out and
wept bitterly.

### *Jesus Is Tried and Crucified*

**27** When morning came, [a]all the chief priests
and elders of the people plotted against
Jesus to put Him to death.
2 And when they had bound Him, they led Him
away and [a]delivered Him to [1]Pontius Pilate the
governor.
**3** [a]Then Judas, His betrayer, seeing that He had
been condemned, was remorseful and brought
back the thirty [b]pieces of silver to the chief priests
and elders,
4 saying, "I have sinned by betraying innocent
blood." And they said, "What *is that* to us? You
see *to it!*"
5 Then he threw down the pieces of silver in the
temple and [a]departed, and went and hanged himself.
6 But the chief priests took the silver pieces and
said, "It is not lawful to put them into the treasury, because they are the price of blood."
7 And they consulted together and bought with
them the potter's field, to bury strangers in.
8 Therefore that field has been called [a]the Field
of Blood to this day.
9 Then was fulfilled what was spoken by Jeremiah the prophet, saying, [a]*"And they took the
thirty pieces of silver, the value of Him who was
priced,* whom they of the children of Israel priced,
10 *"and [a]gave them for the potter's field, as the
LORD directed me."*
**11** Now Jesus stood before the governor. [a]And
the governor asked Him, saying, "Are You the
King of the Jews?" Jesus said to him, [b]*"It is as* you
say."
12 And while He was being accused by the chief
priests and elders, [a]He answered nothing.
13 Then Pilate said to Him, [a]"Do You not hear
how many things they testify against You?"
14 But He answered him not one word, so that
the governor marveled greatly.
**15** [a]Now at the feast the governor was accustomed to releasing to the multitude one prisoner
whom they wished.
16 And at that time they had a notorious prisoner
called [1]Barabbas.
17 Therefore, when they had gathered together,
Pilate said to them, "Whom do you want me to
release to you? Barabbas, or Jesus who is called
Christ?"
18 For he knew that they had handed Him over
because of [a]envy.
19 While he was sitting on the judgment seat, his
wife sent to him, saying, "Have nothing to do with
that just Man, for I have suffered many things
today in a dream because of Him."
20 [a]But the chief priests and elders persuaded the
multitudes that they should ask for Barabbas and
destroy Jesus.
21 The governor answered and said to them,
"Which of the two do you want me to release to
you?" They said, [a]"Barabbas!"
22 Pilate said to them, "What then shall I do with
Jesus who is called Christ?" *They* all said to him,
"Let Him be crucified!"
23 Then the governor said, [a]"Why, what evil has
He done?" But they cried out all the more, saying,
"Let Him be crucified!"
24 When Pilate saw that he could not prevail at
all, but rather *that* a [1]tumult was rising, he [a]took
water and washed *his* hands before the multitude,
saying, "I am innocent of the blood of this [2]just
Person. You see *to it.*"
25 And all the people answered and said, [a]"His
blood *be* on us and on our children."
26 Then he released Barabbas to them; and when
[a]he had [1]scourged Jesus, he delivered *Him* to be
crucified.
**27** [a]Then the soldiers of the governor took Jesus
into the [1]Praetorium and gathered the whole
[2]garrison around Him.
28 And they [a]stripped Him and [b]put a scarlet robe
on Him.
29 [a]When they had [1]twisted a crown of thorns,
they put *it* on His head, and a reed in His right
hand. And they bowed the knee before Him and
mocked Him, saying, "Hail, King of the Jews!"
30 Then [a]they spat on Him, and took the reed and
struck Him on the head.
31 And when they had mocked Him, they took
the robe off Him, put His *own* clothes on Him,
[a]and led Him away to be crucified.
**32** [a]Now as they came out, [b]they found a man of
Cyrene, Simon by name. Him they compelled to
bear His cross.
33 [a]And when they had come to a place called
Golgotha, that is to say, Place of a Skull,
34 [a]they gave Him [1]sour wine mingled with gall
to drink. But when He had tasted *it,* He would not
drink.
35 [a]Then they crucified Him, and divided His
garments, casting lots, [1]that it might be fulfilled
which was spoken by the prophet:

> [b]*"They divided My garments among them,*
> *And for My clothing they cast lots."*

36 [a]Sitting down, they kept watch over Him
there.
37 And they [a]put up over His head the accusation
written against Him:

THIS IS JESUS THE KING OF THE JEWS.

38 [a]Then two robbers were crucified with Him,
one on the right and another on the left.
39 And [a]those who passed by blasphemed Him,
wagging their heads
40 and saying, [a]"You who destroy the temple and
build *it* in three days, save Yourself! [b]If You are
the Son of God, come down from the cross."
41 Likewise the chief priests also, mocking with
the [1]scribes and elders, said,
42 "He [a]saved others; Himself He cannot save. [1]If
He is the King of Israel, let Him now come down
from the cross, and we will believe [2]Him.
43 [a]"He trusted in God; let Him deliver Him now
if He will have Him; for He said, 'I am the Son of
God.' "
44 [a]Even the robbers who were crucified with
Him reviled Him with the same thing.
**45** [a]Now from the sixth hour until the ninth hour
there was darkness over all the land.
46 And about the ninth hour [a]Jesus cried out
with a loud voice, saying, "Eli, Eli, lama sabach-

**73** [a]Luke 22:59
**74** [a]Mark 14:71 [1]*call down curses* [2]Swear oaths
**75** [a]Matt. 26:34

CHAPTER 27
**1** [a]John 18:28
**2** [a]Acts 3:13 [1]NU omits *Pontius*
**3** [a]Matt. 26:14 [b]Matt. 26:15
**5** [a]Acts 1:18
**8** [a]Acts 1:19
**9** [a]Zech. 11:12
**10** [a]Jer. 32:6–9; Zech. 11:12, 13
**11** [a]Mark 15:2–5 [b]John 18:37
**12** [a]John 19:9
**13** [a]Matt. 26:62
**15** [a]Luke 23:17–25
**16** [1]NU *Jesus Barabbas*
**18** [a]Matt. 21:38
**20** [a]Acts 3:14
**21** [a]Acts 3:14
**23** [a]Acts 3:13
**24** [a]Deut. 21:6–8 [1]*an uproar* [2]NU omits *just*
**25** [a]Josh. 2:19
**26** [a][Is. 50:6; 53:5] [1]*flogged* with a Roman scourge
**27** [a]Mark 15:16–20 [1]The governor's headquarters [2]*cohort*
**28** [a]John 19:2 [b]Luke 23:11
**29** [a]Is. 53:3 [1]Lit. *woven*
**30** [a]Matt. 26:67
**31** [a]Is. 53:7
**32** [a]Heb. 13:12 [b]Mark 15:21
**33** [a]John 19:17
**34** [a]Ps. 69:21 [1]NU omits *sour*
**35** [a]Luke 23:34 [b]Ps. 22:18 [1]NU, M omit the rest of v. 35.
**36** [a]Matt. 27:54
**37** [a]John 19:19
**38** [a]Is. 53:9, 12
**39** [a]Mark 15:29
**40** [a]John 2:19 [b]Matt. 26:63
**41** [1]M *scribes, the Pharisees, and the elders*
**42** [a][John 3:14, 15] [1]NU omits *If* [2]NU, M *in Him*
**43** [a]Ps. 22:8
**44** [a]Luke 23:39–43
**45** [a]Mark 15:33–41
**46** [a][Heb. 5:7]

thani?" that is, [b]*"My God, My God, why have You*
*forsaken Me?"*
47 Some of those who stood there, when they
heard *that,* said, "This Man is calling for Elijah!"
48 Immediately one of them ran and took a
sponge, [a]filled *it* with sour wine and put *it* on a
reed, and offered it to Him to drink.
49 The rest said, "Let Him alone; let us see if
Elijah will come to save Him."
50 And Jesus cried out again with a loud voice,
and [b]yielded up His spirit.
51 Then, behold, [a]the veil of the temple was torn
in two from top to bottom; and the earth quaked,
and the rocks were split,
52 and the graves were opened; and many bodies
of the saints who had fallen asleep were raised;
53 and coming out of the graves after His resurrection, they went into the holy city and appeared
to many.
54 [a]So when the centurion and those with him,
who were guarding Jesus, saw the earthquake and
the things that had happened, they feared greatly,
saying, [b]"Truly this was the Son of God!"
55 And many women [a]who followed Jesus from
Galilee, ministering to Him, were there looking on
from afar,
56 [a]among whom were Mary Magdalene, Mary
the mother of James and [1]Joses, and the mother of
Zebedee's sons.
**57** Now [a]when evening had come, there came a
rich man from Arimathea, named Joseph, who
himself had also become a disciple of Jesus.
58 This man went to Pilate and asked for the
body of Jesus. Then Pilate commanded the body
to be given to him.
59 When Joseph had taken the body, he wrapped
it in a clean linen cloth,
60 and [a]laid it in his new tomb which he had
hewn out of the rock; and he rolled a large stone
against the door of the tomb, and departed.
61 And Mary Magdalene was there, and the other
Mary, sitting [1]opposite the tomb.
**62** On the next day, which followed the Day of
Preparation, the chief priests and Pharisees gathered together to Pilate,
63 saying, "Sir, we remember, while He was still
alive, how that deceiver said, [a]'After three days I
will rise.'
64 "Therefore command that the tomb be made
secure until the third day, lest His disciples come
[1]by night and steal Him *away,* and say to the
people, 'He has risen from the dead.' So the last
deception will be worse than the first."
65 Pilate said to them, "You have a guard; go
your way, make *it* as secure as you know how."
66 So they went and made the tomb secure,
[a]sealing the stone and setting the guard.

## *The Risen Christ*

**28** Now [a]after the Sabbath, as the first *day* of
the week began to dawn, Mary Magdalene
[b]and the other Mary came to see the tomb.
2 And behold, there was a great earthquake; for
[a]an angel of the Lord descended from heaven, and
came and rolled back the stone [1]from the door,
and sat on it.
3 [a]His countenance was like lightning, and his
clothing as white as snow.
4 And the guards shook for fear of him, and
became like [a]dead *men.*
5 But the angel answered and said to the
women, "Do not be afraid, for I know that you
seek Jesus who was crucified.
6 "He is not here; for He is risen, [a]as He said.
Come, see the place where the Lord lay.
7 "And go quickly and tell His disciples that He
is risen from the dead, and indeed [a]He is going
before you into Galilee; there you will see Him.
Behold, I have told you."
8 So they went out quickly from the tomb with
fear and great joy, and ran to bring His disciples
word.
**9** And [1]as they went to tell His disciples, behold,
[a]Jesus met them, saying, "Rejoice!" So they came
and held Him by the feet and worshiped Him.
10 Then Jesus said to them, "Do not be afraid. Go
*and* tell [a]My brethren to go to Galilee, and there
they will see Me."
**11** Now while they were going, behold, some of
the guard came into the city and reported to the
chief priests all the things that had happened.
12 When they had assembled with the elders and
consulted together, they gave a large sum of
money to the soldiers,
13 saying, "Tell them, 'His disciples came at night
and stole Him *away* while we slept.'
14 "And if this comes to the governor's ears, we
will appease him and make you secure."
15 So they took the money and did as they were
instructed; and this saying is commonly reported
among the Jews until this day.
**16** Then the eleven disciples went away into
Galilee, to the mountain [a]which Jesus had appointed for them.
17 When they saw Him, they worshiped Him; but
some [a]doubted.
18 And Jesus came and spoke to them, saying,
[a]"All authority has been given to Me in heaven
and on earth.
19 [a]"Go [1]therefore and [b]make disciples of all the
nations, baptizing them in the name of the Father
and of the Son and of the Holy Spirit,
20 [a]"teaching them to observe all things that I
have commanded you; and lo, I am [b]with you
always, *even* to the end of the age." [1]Amen.

**46** [b]Ps. 22:1
**48** [a]Ps. 69:21
**50** [a]Luke 23:46 [b][John 10:18]
**51** [a]Ex. 26:31
**54** [a]Mark 15:39 [b]Matt. 14:33
**55** [a]Luke 8:2, 3
**56** [a]Mark 15:40, 47; 16:9 [1]NU *Joseph*
**57** [a]John 19:38–42
**60** [a]Is. 53:9
**61** [1]*in front of*
**63** [a]Mark 8:31; 10:34
**64** [1]NU omits *by night*
**66** [a]Dan. 6:17

CHAPTER 28
**1** [a]Luke 24:1–10 [b]Matt. 27:56, 61
**2** [a]Mark 16:5 [1]NU omits *from the door*
**3** [a]Dan. 7:9; 10:6
**4** [a]Rev. 1:17
**6** [a]Matt. 12:40; 16:21; 17:23; 20:19
**7** [a]Mark 16:7
**9** [a]John 20:14 [1]NU omits *as they went to tell His disciples*
**10** [a]John 20:17
**16** [a]Matt. 26:32; 28:7, 10
**17** [a]John 20:24–29
**18** [a][Dan. 7:13, 14]
**19** [a]Mark 16:15 [b]Luke 24:47 [1]M omits *therefore*
**20** [a][Acts 2:42] [b][Acts 4:31; 18:10; 23:11] [1]NU omits *Amen*

*The Gospel According to*

# MARK

### *John and Jesus Begin Their Ministry*

THE [a]beginning of the gospel of Jesus Christ,
[b]the Son of God.
2 As it is written in [1]the Prophets:

[a]*"Behold, I send My messenger*
*before Your face,*
*Who will prepare Your way before You."*
3 *"The[a] voice of one crying in the wilderness:*
*'Prepare the way of the LORD;*
*Make His paths straight.' "*

4 [a]John came baptizing in the wilderness and
preaching a baptism of repentance [1]for the remission of sins.
5 [a]Then all the land of Judea, and those from
Jerusalem, went out to him and were all baptized
by him in the Jordan River, confessing their sins.
6 Now John was [a]clothed with camel's hair and
with a leather belt around his waist, and he ate
locusts and wild honey.
7 And he preached, saying, [a]"There comes One
after me who is mightier than I, whose sandal
strap I am not worthy to stoop down and loose.
8 [a]"I indeed baptized you with water, but He
will baptize you [b]with the Holy Spirit."
**9** [a]It came to pass in those days *that* Jesus came
from Nazareth of Galilee, and was baptized by
John in the Jordan.
10 [a]And immediately, coming up [1]from the water,
He saw the heavens [2]parting and the Spirit [b]de-
scending upon Him like a dove.
11 Then a voice came from heaven, [a]"You are My
beloved Son, in whom I am well pleased."
**12** [a]Immediately the Spirit [1]drove Him into the
wilderness.
13 And He was there in the wilderness forty days,
tempted by Satan, and was with the wild beasts;
[a]and the angels ministered to Him.
**14** [a]Now after John was put in prison, Jesus came
to Galilee, [b]preaching the gospel [1]of the kingdom
of God,
15 and saying, [a]"The time is fulfilled, and [b]the
kingdom of God [1]is at hand. Repent, and believe in
the gospel."
**16** [a]And as He walked by the Sea of Galilee, He
saw Simon and Andrew his brother casting a net
into the sea; for they were fishermen.
17 Then Jesus said to them, "Follow Me, and I
will make you become [a]fishers of men."
18 [a]They immediately left their nets and followed
Him.
19 When He had gone a little farther from there,
He saw James the *son* of Zebedee, and John his
brother, who also *were* in the boat mending their
nets.
20 And immediately He called them, and they left
their father Zebedee in the boat with the hired
servants, and went after Him.
**21** [a]Then they went into Capernaum, and immediately on the Sabbath He entered the [b]synagogue
and taught.
22 [a]And they were astonished at His teaching, for
He taught them as one having authority, and not
as the scribes.
23 Now there was a man in their synagogue with
an [a]unclean spirit. And he cried out,
24 saying, "Let *us* alone! [a]What have we to do
with You, Jesus of Nazareth? Did You come to
destroy us? I [b]know who You are—the [c]Holy One
of God!"
25 But Jesus [a]rebuked him, saying, [1]"Be quiet,
and come out of him!"
26 And when the unclean spirit [a]had convulsed
him and cried out with a loud voice, he came out
of him.
27 Then they were all amazed, so that they
questioned among themselves, saying, [1]"What is
this? What new [2]doctrine *is* this? For with authority He commands even the unclean spirits, and
they obey Him."
28 And immediately His [a]fame spread throughout
all the region around Galilee.
**29** [a]Now as soon as they had come out of the
synagogue, they entered the house of Simon and
Andrew, with James and John.
30 But Simon's wife's mother lay sick with a
fever, and they told Him about her at once.
31 So He came and took her by the hand and
lifted her up, and immediately the fever left her.
And she served them.
**32** [a]At evening, when the sun had set, they
brought to Him all who were sick and those who
were demon-possessed.
33 And the whole city was gathered together at
the door.
34 Then He healed many who were sick with
various diseases, and [a]cast out many demons; and
He [b]did not allow the demons to speak, because
they knew Him.
**35** Now [a]in the morning, having risen a long
while before daylight, He went out and departed
to a [1]solitary place; and there He [b]prayed.
36 And Simon and those *who were* with Him
searched for Him.
37 When they found Him, they said to Him,
[a]"Everyone [b]is looking for You."
38 But He said to them, [a]"Let us go into the next
towns, that I may preach there also, because [b]for
this purpose I have come forth."
39 [a]And He was preaching in their synagogues
throughout all Galilee, and [b]casting out demons.
**40** [a]Now a leper came to Him, imploring Him,
kneeling down to Him and saying to Him, "If You
are willing, You can make me clean."
41 Then Jesus, moved with [a]compassion,
stretched out *His* hand and touched him, and said
to him, "I am willing; be cleansed."
42 As soon as He had spoken, [a]immediately the
leprosy left him, and he was cleansed.
43 And He strictly warned him and sent him
away at once,
44 and said to him, "See that you say nothing to
anyone; but go your way, show yourself to the
priest, and offer for your cleansing those things
[a]which Moses commanded, as a testimony to
them."
45 [a]However, he went out and began to proclaim
*it* freely, and to spread the matter, so that Jesus
could no longer openly enter the city, but was
outside in deserted places; [b]and they came to Him
from every direction.

CHAPTER 1
**1** [a]Luke 3:22 [b]Matt. 14:33
**2** [a]Mal. 3:1 [1]NU *Isaiah the prophet*
**3** [a]Is. 40:3
**4** [a]Matt. 3:1 [1]*because of forgiveness*
**5** [a]Matt. 3:5
**6** [a]Matt. 3:4
**7** [a]John 1:27
**8** [a]Acts 1:5; 11:16 [b]Is. 44:3
**9** [a]Matt. 3:13–17
**10** [a]Matt. 3:16 [b]Acts 10:38 [1]NU *out of* [2]*torn open*
**11** [a]Matt. 3:17; 12:18
**12** [a]Matt. 4:1–11 [1]*sent Him out*
**13** [a]Matt. 4:10, 11
**14** [a]Matt. 4:12 [b]Matt. 4:23 [1]NU omits *of the kingdom*
**15** [a][Gal. 4:4] [b]Matt. 3:2; 4:17 [1]*has drawn near*
**16** [a]Luke 5:2–11
**17** [a]Matt. 13:47, 48
**18** [a][Luke 14:26]
**21** [a]Luke 4:31–37 [b]Matt. 4:23
**22** [a]Matt. 7:28, 29; 13:54
**23** [a][Matt. 12:43]
**24** [a]Matt. 8:28, 29 [b]James 2:19 [c]Ps. 16:10
**25** [a][Luke 4:39] [1]Lit. *Be muzzled*
**26** [a]Mark 9:20
**27** [1]NU *What is this? A new doctrine with authority. He* [2]*teaching*
**28** [a]Matt. 4:24; 9:31
**29** [a]Luke 4:38, 39
**32** [a]Matt. 8:16, 17
**34** [a]Luke 13:32 [b]Acts 16:17, 18
**35** [a]Luke 4:42, 43 [b]Luke 5:16; 6:12; 9:28, 29 [1]*deserted*
**37** [a]John 3:26; 12:19 [b][Heb. 11:6]
**38** [a]Luke 4:43 [b][Is. 61:1, 2]
**39** [a]Matt. 4:23; 9:35 [b]Mark 5:8, 13; 7:29, 30
**40** [a]Luke 5:12–14
**41** [a]Luke 7:13
**42** [a]Matt. 15:28
**44** [a]Lev. 14:1–32
**45** [a]Luke 5:15 [b]Mark 2:2, 13; 3:7

### *Jesus Is Lord of Healing and the Sabbath*

**2** And again [a]He entered Capernaum after *some*
days, and it was heard that He was in the
house.
2 [1]Immediately many gathered together, so that
there was no longer room to receive *them,* not
even near the door. And He preached the word to
them.
3 Then they came to Him, bringing a [a]paralytic
who was carried by four *men.*
4 And when they could not come near Him
because of the crowd, they uncovered the roof
where He was. So when they had broken through,
they let down the bed on which the paralytic was
lying.
5 When Jesus saw their faith, He said to the
paralytic, "Son, your sins are forgiven you."
6 And some of the scribes were sitting there and
reasoning in their hearts,
7 "Why does this *Man* speak blasphemies like
this? [a]Who can forgive sins but God alone?"
8 But immediately, when Jesus perceived in His
spirit that they reasoned thus within themselves,
He said to them, "Why do you reason about these
things in your hearts?
9 [a]"Which is easier, to say to the paralytic, '*Your*
sins are forgiven you,' or to say, 'Arise, take up
your bed and walk'?
10 "But that you may know that the Son of Man
has [1]power on earth to forgive sins"—He said to
the paralytic,
11 "I say to you, arise, take up your bed, and go
to your house."
12 Immediately he arose, took up the bed, and
went out in the presence of them all, so that all
were amazed and [a]glorified God, saying, "We
never saw *anything* like this!"
**13** [a]Then He went out again by the sea; and all
the multitude came to Him, and He taught them.
14 [a]As He passed by, He saw Levi the *son* of
Alphaeus sitting at the tax office. And He said to
him, [b]"Follow Me." So he arose and [c]followed
Him.
15 [a]Now it happened, as He was dining in *Levi's*
house, that many tax collectors and sinners also
sat together with Jesus and His disciples; for there
were many, and they followed Him.
16 And when the scribes [1]and Pharisees saw Him
eating with the tax collectors and sinners, they
said to His disciples, "How *is it* that He eats and
drinks with tax collectors and sinners?"
17 When Jesus heard *it,* He said to them, [a]"Those
who are well have no need of a physician, but
those who are sick. I did not come to call *the*
righteous, but sinners, [1]to repentance."
**18** [a]The disciples of John and of the Pharisees
were fasting. Then they came and said to Him,
"Why do the disciples of John and of the Pharisees
fast, but Your disciples do not fast?"
19 And Jesus said to them, "Can the [1]friends of
the bridegroom fast while the bridegroom is with
them? As long as they have the bridegroom with
them they cannot fast.
20 "But the days will come when the bridegroom
will be [a]taken away from them, and then they will
fast in those days.
21 "No one sews a piece of unshrunk cloth on an
old garment; or else the new piece pulls away
from the old, and the tear is made worse.
22 "And no one puts new wine into old wineskins; or else the new wine bursts the wineskins,
the wine is spilled, and the wineskins are ruined.
But new wine must be put into new wineskins."
**23** [a]Now it happened that He went through the
grainfields on the Sabbath; and as they went His
disciples began [b]to pluck the heads of grain.
24 And the Pharisees said to Him, "Look, why do
they do what is [a]not lawful on the Sabbath?"
25 But He said to them, "Have you never read
[a]what David did when he was in need and hungry,
he and those with him:
26 "how he went into the house of God *in the*
*days* of Abiathar the high priest, and ate the
showbread, [a]which is not lawful to eat except for
the priests, and also gave some to those who were
with him?"
27 And He said to them, "The Sabbath was made
for man, and not man for the [a]Sabbath.
28 "Therefore [a]the Son of Man is also Lord of the
Sabbath."

### *Jesus' Apostles and His True Family*

**3** And [a]He entered the synagogue again, and a
man was there who had a withered hand.
2 So they [a]watched Him closely, whether He
would [b]heal him on the Sabbath, so that they
might [1]accuse Him.
3 And He said to the man who had the withered
hand, [1]"Step forward."
4 Then He said to them, "Is it lawful on the
Sabbath to do good or to do evil, to save life or to
kill?" But they kept silent.
5 And when He had looked around at them with
anger, being grieved by the [a]hardness of their
hearts, He said to the man, "Stretch out your
hand." And he stretched *it* out, and his hand was
restored [1]as whole as the other.
6 [a]Then the Pharisees went out and immediately
plotted with [b]the Herodians against Him, how
they might destroy Him.
**7** But Jesus withdrew with His disciples to the
sea. And a great multitude from Galilee followed
Him, [a]and from Judea
8 and Jerusalem and Idumea and beyond the
Jordan; and those from Tyre and Sidon, a great
multitude, when they heard how [a]many things He
was doing, came to Him.
9 So He told His disciples that a small boat
should be kept ready for Him because of the
multitude, lest they should crush Him.
10 For He healed [a]many, so that as many as had
afflictions pressed about Him to [b]touch Him.
11 [a]And the unclean spirits, whenever they saw
Him, fell down before Him and cried out, saying,
[b]"You are the Son of God."
12 But [a]He sternly warned them that they should
not make Him known.
**13** [a]And He went up on the mountain and called
to *Him* those He Himself wanted. And they came
to Him.
14 Then He appointed twelve, [1]that they might be
with Him and that He might send them out to
preach,
15 and to have [1]power [2]to heal sicknesses and to
cast out demons:
16 [1]Simon, [a]to whom He gave the name Peter;
17 James the *son* of Zebedee and John the
brother of James, to whom He gave the name
Boanerges, that is, "Sons of Thunder";

CHAPTER 2
1 [a]Matt. 9:1
2 [1]NU omits *Immediately*
3 [a]Matt. 4:24; 8:6
7 [a]Is. 43:25
9 [a]Matt. 9:5
10 [1]*authority*
12 [a][Phil. 2:11]
13 [a]Matt. 9:9
14 [a]Luke 5:27–32 [b]John 1:43; 12:26; 21:22 [c]Luke 18:28
15 [a]Matt. 9:10
16 [1]NU *of the*
17 [a]Matt. 9:12, 13; 18:11 [1]NU omits *to repentance*
18 [a]Luke 5:33–38
19 [1]Lit. *sons of the bridechamber*
20 [a]Acts 1:9; 13:2, 3; 14:23
23 [a]Luke 6:1–5 [b]Deut. 23:25
24 [a]Ex. 20:10; 31:15
25 [a]1 Sam. 21:1–6
26 [a]Lev. 24:5–9
27 [a]Deut. 5:14
28 [a]Matt. 12:8

CHAPTER 3
1 [a]Luke 6:6–11
2 [a]Luke 14:1; 20:20 [b]Luke 13:14 [1]*bring charges against*
3 [1]Lit. *Arise into the midst*
5 [a]Zech. 7:12 [1]NU omits *as whole as the other*
6 [a]Mark 12:13 [b]Matt. 22:16
7 [a]Luke 6:17
8 [a]Mark 5:19
10 [a]Luke 7:21 [b]Matt. 9:21; 14:36
11 [a]Luke 4:41 [b]Matt. 8:29; 14:33
12 [a]Mark 1:25, 34
13 [a]Luke 9:1
14 [1]NU adds *whom He also named apostles*
15 [1]*authority* [2]NU omits *to heal sicknesses and*
16 [a]John 1:42 [1]NU *and He appointed the twelve: Simon*

18 Andrew, Philip, Bartholomew, Matthew,
Thomas, James the *son* of Alphaeus, Thaddaeus,
Simon the Canaanite;
19 and Judas Iscariot, who also betrayed Him.
And they went into a house.
**20** Then the multitude came together again, [a]so
that they could not so much as eat bread.
21 But when His [a]own people heard *about this,*
they went out to lay hold of Him, [b]for they said,
"He is out of His mind."
22 And the scribes who came down from Jerusalem said, [a]"He has Beelzebub," and, "By the [b]ruler
of the demons He casts out demons."
23 [a]So He called them to *Himself* and said to
them in parables: "How can Satan cast out Satan?
24 "If a kingdom is divided against itself, that
kingdom cannot stand.
25 "And if a house is divided against itself, that
house cannot stand.
26 "And if Satan has risen up against himself, and
is divided, he cannot stand, but has an end.
27 [a]"No one can enter a strong man's house and
plunder his goods, unless he first binds the strong
man. And then he will plunder his house.
**28** [a]"Assuredly, I say to you, all sins will be
forgiven the sons of men, and whatever blasphemies they may utter;
29 "but he who blasphemes against the Holy
Spirit never has forgiveness, but is subject to
eternal condemnation"—
30 because they [a]said, "He has an unclean spirit."
**31** [a]Then His brothers and His mother came, and
standing outside they sent to Him, calling Him.
32 And a multitude was sitting around Him; and
they said to Him, "Look, Your mother and Your
brothers [1]are outside seeking You."
33 But He answered them, saying, "Who is My
mother, or My brothers?"
34 And He looked around in a circle at those who
sat about Him, and said, "Here are My mother and
My brothers!
35 "For whoever does the [a]will of God is My
brother and My sister and mother."

## *Parables of the Kingdom of God*

**4** And [a]again He began to teach by the sea. And
a great multitude was gathered to Him, so that
He got into a boat and sat *in it* on the sea; and the
whole multitude was on the land facing the sea.
2 Then He taught them many things by parables, [a]and said to them in His teaching:
3 "Listen! Behold, a sower went out to sow.
4 "And it happened, as he sowed, *that* some
*seed* fell by the wayside; and the birds [1]of the air
came and devoured it.
5 "Some fell on stony ground, where it did not
have much earth; and immediately it sprang up
because it had no depth of earth.
6 "But when the sun was up it was scorched,
and because it had no root it withered away.
7 "And some *seed* fell among thorns; and the
thorns grew up and choked it, and it yielded no
[1]crop.
8 "But other *seed* fell on good ground and
yielded a crop that sprang up, increased and
produced: some thirtyfold, some sixty, and some a
hundred."
9 And He said [1]to them, "He who has ears to
hear, let him hear!"
**10** [a]But when He was alone, those around Him
with the twelve asked Him about the parable.
11 And He said to them, "To you it has been
given to [a]know the [1]mystery of the kingdom of
God; but to [b]those who are outside, all things
come in parables,
12 "so that

[a]*'Seeing they may see and not perceive,*
*And hearing they may hear and not*
*understand;*
*Lest they should turn,*
*And their sins be forgiven them.'*"

**13** And He said to them, "Do you not understand
this parable? How then will you understand all the
parables?
14 [a]"The sower sows the word.
15 "And these are the ones by the wayside where
the word is sown. When they hear, Satan comes
immediately and takes away the word that was
sown in their hearts.
16 "These likewise are the ones sown on stony
ground who, when they hear the word, immediately receive it with gladness;
17 "and they have no root in themselves, and so
endure only for a time. Afterward, when tribulation or persecution arises for the word's sake,
immediately they stumble.
18 "Now these are the ones sown among thorns;
*they are* the ones who hear the word,
19 "and the [a]cares of this world, [b]the deceitfulness of riches, and the desires for other things
entering in choke the word, and it becomes unfruitful.
20 "But these are the ones sown on good ground,
those who hear the word, [1]accept *it,* and bear
[a]fruit: some thirtyfold, some sixty, and some a
hundred."
**21** [a]Also He said to them, "Is a lamp brought to
be put under a basket or under a bed? Is it not to
be set on a lampstand?
22 [a]"For there is nothing hidden which will not
be revealed, nor has anything been kept secret but
that it should come to light.
23 [a]"If anyone has ears to hear, let him hear."
24 Then He said to them, "Take heed what you
hear. [a]With the same measure you use, it will be
measured to you; and to you who hear, more will
be given.
25 [a]"For whoever has, to him more will be given;
but whoever does not have, even what he has will
be taken away from him."
**26** And He said, [a]"The kingdom of God is as if a
man should [1]scatter seed on the ground,
27 "and should sleep by night and rise by day,
and the seed should sprout and [a]grow, he himself
does not know how.
28 "For the earth [a]yields crops by itself: first the
blade, then the head, after that the full grain in
the head.
29 "But when the grain ripens, immediately [a]he
puts in the sickle, because the harvest has come."
**30** Then He said, [a]"To what shall we liken the
kingdom of God? Or with what parable shall we
picture it?
31 "*It is* like a mustard seed which, when it is
sown on the ground, is smaller than all the seeds
on earth;
32 "but when it is sown, it grows up and becomes
greater than all herbs, and shoots out large
branches, so that the birds of the air may nest
under its shade."

**20** [a]Mark 6:31
**21** [a]Mark 6:3 [b]John 7:5; 10:20
**22** [a]Matt. 9:34; 10:25 [b][John 12:31; 14:30; 16:11]
**23** [a]Matt. 12:25–29
**27** [a][Is. 49:24, 25]
**28** [a]Luke 12:10
**30** [a]Matt. 9:34
**31** [a]Matt. 12:46–50
**32** [1]NU, M add *and your sisters*
**35** [a]Eph. 6:6

CHAPTER 4
**1** [a]Luke 8:4–10
**2** [a]Mark 12:38
**4** [1]NU, M omit *of the air*
**7** [1]Lit. *fruit*
**9** [1]NU, M omit *to them*
**10** [a]Luke 8:9
**11** [a][1 Cor. 2:10–16] [b][Col. 4:5] [1]*secret* or *hidden truths*
**12** [a]Is. 6:9, 10; 43:8
**14** [a]Matt. 13:18–23
**19** [a]Luke 21:34 [b]1 Tim. 6:9, 10, 17
**20** [a][Rom. 7:4] [1]*receive*
**21** [a]Matt. 5:15
**22** [a]Matt. 10:26, 27
**23** [a]Matt. 11:15; 13:9, 43
**24** [a]Matt. 7:2
**25** [a]Luke 8:18; 19:26
**26** [a][Matt. 13:24–30, 36–43] [1]*sow*
**27** [a][2 Pet. 3:18]
**28** [a][John 12:24]
**29** [a]Rev. 14:15
**30** [a]Matt. 13:31, 32

# THE UNCHANGING LAND OF THE BIBLE

A fortunate few can travel to the Holy Land and walk where Jesus walked. It is indeed a thrill to stand where the Apostles preached. To retrace the steps of Jesus is an experience never to be forgotten. For those who have always desired to travel to the Holy Land, and gaze on the part of the world that was the cradle of Christianity, the actual photographs which follow will afford the opportunity.

Two photographers have trudged the length and breadth of the unchanging land of the Bible, to bring to the reader, through pictures, the story of God's redemptive plan. Although the pictures are recent, the story is ancient. Strangely, however, the story of the land of the Bible, though old, is ever new.

From Bethlehem to Golgotha, the steps of Jesus have been followed. His triumphal entry into Jerusalem stirred the same sands which now lie under the Golden Gate. Gethsemane remains unchanged. The upper room, now silent, once echoed the song of Jesus and His disciples, before they went out to face the madness of a mob.

If one picture is really worth a thousand words, volumes are written in the following pages. And pictures are only necessary, because the frailty of human speech cannot adequately describe what the heart knows to be true.

Hear the unchanging truths uttered by Jesus as He stood by the Sea of Galilee! Know that this land was chosen by God, to give birth to this Christ, who remains as unchanging as the land of His birth!

*THE SEA OF GALILEE. Matthew 8:24*

*GOLGOTHA, THE PLACE OF THE SKULL. THE SITE OF CHRIST'S CRUCIFIXION. John 19:16-19*

*THE TOMB OF CHRIST. John 19:41, 42*

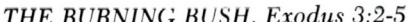

*MT. GERIZIM, ANCIENT SHECHEM AND MT. EBAL. Joshua 8:33*

*THE BURNING BUSH. Exodus 3:2-5*

*NAZARETH, SITE OF GABRIEL'S VISIT TO MARY; AND THE LOCALE OF CHRIST'S BOYHOOD. Matthew 2:23*

*CHURCH OF THE VISITATION, AIN KARIM, WHERE MARY VISITED ELIZABETH.* Luke 1:39-42

*ANCIENT OLIVE TREE IN THE GARDEN OF GETHSEMANE. Mark 14:32*

*TOMB OF THE VIRGIN MARY, Valley of Gethsemane*

*CHURCH OF GETHSEMANE, SITE OF THE GARDEN. Matthew 26:36*

*TODAY'S WALLED JERUSALEM. Beyond, the Mt. of Olives*

*THE UPPER ROOM ON MT. ZION. Luke 22:12*

*CHURCH OF THE DORMITION, SITE OF THE LAST SUPPER. Mark 14:22-26*

*CAMELS ARE USED TODAY as in the day of Jacob*

*TOMB OF LAZARUS. John 11:38-44*

*HEBRON, HOME OF ABRAHAM AND ISAAC. Genesis 13:18*

*THE DEAD SEA AT SUNRISE* ➧

*WHEAT HARVEST on Madaba threshing floor*

*THE FAMOUS CEDARS OF LEBANON. Psalm 92:12, 13*

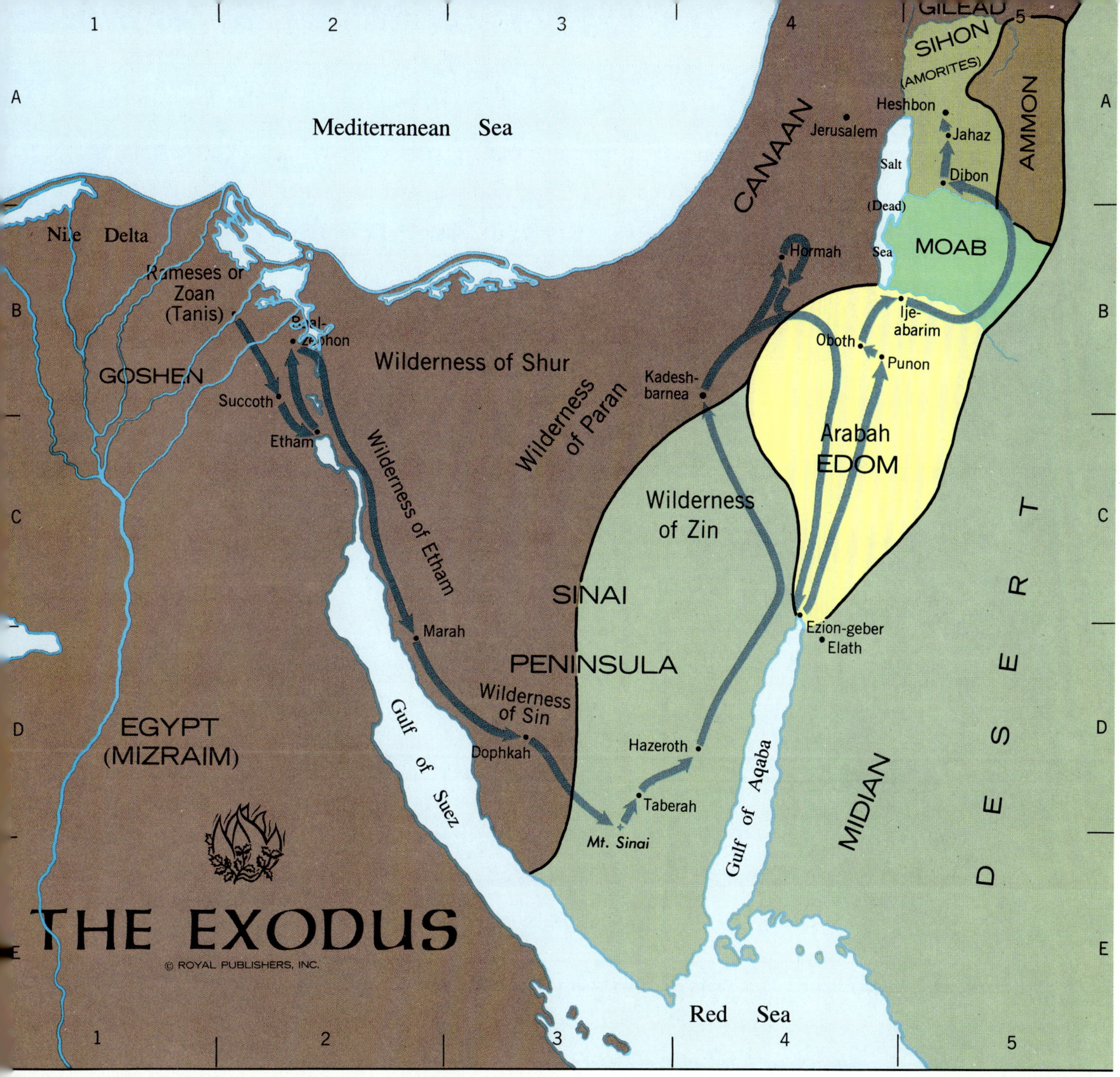
THE EXODUS
© ROYAL PUBLISHERS, INC.
Mediterranean Sea
Nile Delta
Rameses or Zoan (Tanis)
GOSHEN
Baal-zephon
Succoth
Etham
Wilderness of Shur
Wilderness of Etham
Wilderness of Paran
Kadesh-barnea
CANAAN
Jerusalem
Salt (Dead) Sea
GILEAD
SIHON (AMORITES)
Heshbon
Jahaz
Dibon
AMMON
MOAB
Hormah
Ije-abarim
Oboth
Punon
Arabah
EDOM
Wilderness of Zin
SINAI PENINSULA
Marah
Wilderness of Sin
Dophkah
Hazeroth
Taberah
Mt. Sinai
Ezion-geber
Elath
Gulf of Suez
Gulf of Aqaba
MIDIAN
DESERT
EGYPT (MIZRAIM)
Red Sea
1
2
3
4
5
A
B
C
D
E

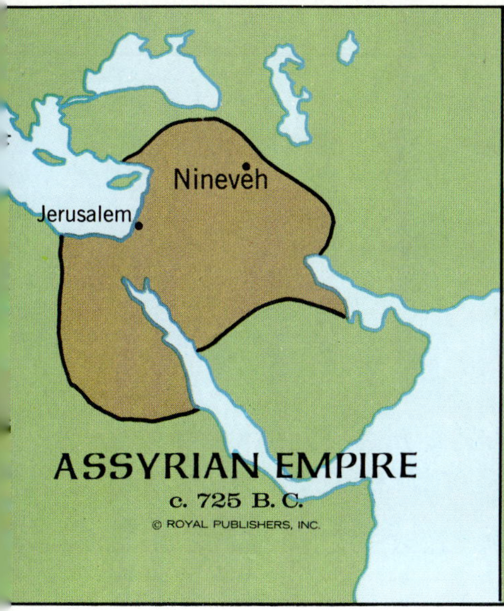
Nineveh
Jerusalem
ASSYRIAN EMPIRE
c. 725 B.C.
© ROYAL PUBLISHERS, INC.

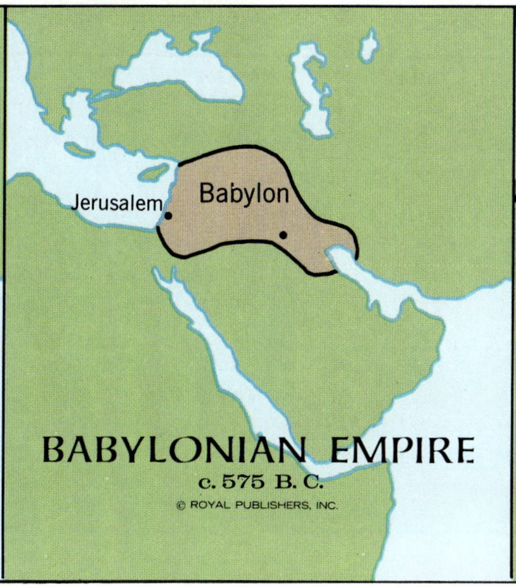
Jerusalem
Babylon
BABYLONIAN EMPIRE
c. 575 B.C.
© ROYAL PUBLISHERS, INC.

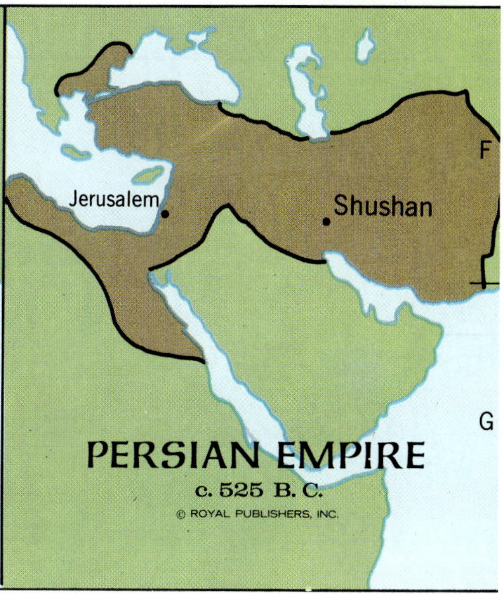
Jerusalem
Shushan
PERSIAN EMPIRE
c. 525 B.C.
© ROYAL PUBLISHERS, INC.
F
G

# PAUL'S JOURNEY TO ROME

## AND THE SEVEN CHURCHES OF ASIA

Revelation 1:19-3:22



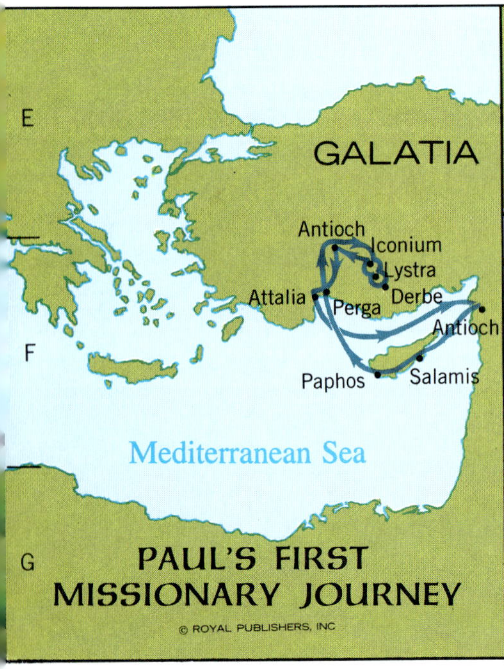


PAUL'S FIRST MISSIONARY JOURNEY

PAUL'S SECOND MISSIONARY JOURNEY

PAUL'S THIRD MISSIONARY JOURNEY

**33** [a]And with many such parables He spoke the
word to them as they were able to hear *it.*
34 But without a parable He did not speak to
them. And when they were alone, [a]He explained
all things to His disciples.
**35** [a]On the same day, when evening had come, He
said to them, "Let us cross over to the other side."
36 Now when they had left the multitude, they
took Him along in the boat as He was. And other
little boats were also with Him.
37 And a great windstorm arose, and the waves
beat into the boat, so that it was already filling.
38 But He was in the stern, asleep on a pillow.
And they awoke Him and said to Him, [a]"Teacher,
[b]do You not care that we are perishing?"
39 Then He arose and [a]rebuked the wind, and
said to the sea, [b]"Peace,[1] be still!" And the wind
ceased and there was a great calm.
40 But He said to them, "Why are you so fearful?
[a]How[1] *is it* that you have no faith?"
41 And they feared exceedingly, and said to one
another, "Who can this be, that even the wind and
the sea obey Him!"

### *Jesus Commands Demons, Death, and Disease*

**5** Then [a]they came to the other side of the sea,
to the country of the [1]Gadarenes.
2 And when He had come out of the boat,
immediately there met Him out of the tombs a
man with an [a]unclean spirit,
3 who had *his* dwelling among the tombs; and
no one could bind [1]him, not even with chains,
4 because he had often been bound with shackles and chains. And the chains had been pulled
apart by him, and the shackles broken in pieces;
neither could anyone tame him.
5 And always, night and day, he was in the
mountains and in the tombs, crying out and
cutting himself with stones.
6 When he saw Jesus from afar, he ran and
worshiped Him.
7 And he cried out with a loud voice and said,
"What have I to do with You, Jesus, Son of the
Most High God? I [a]implore[1] You by God that You
do not torment me."
8 For He said to him, [a]"Come out of the man,
unclean spirit!"
9 Then He asked him, "What *is* your name?"
And he answered, saying, "My name *is* Legion; for
we are many."
10 Also he begged Him earnestly that He would
not send them out of the country.
11 Now a large herd of [a]swine was feeding there
near the mountains.
12 So all the demons begged Him, saying, "Send
us to the swine, that we may enter them."
13 And [1]at once Jesus gave them permission.
Then the unclean spirits went out and entered
the swine (there were about two thousand);
and the herd ran violently down the steep place
into the sea, and drowned in the sea.
14 So those who fed the swine fled, and they told
*it* in the city and in the country. And they went
out to see what it was that had happened.
15 Then they came to Jesus, and saw the one
*who had been* [a]demon-possessed and had the
legion, [b]sitting and [c]clothed and in his right mind.
And they were afraid.
16 And those who saw it told them how it happened to him *who had been* demon-possessed, and
about the swine.
17 Then [a]they began to plead with Him to depart
from their region.
18 And when He got into the boat, [a]he who had
been demon-possessed begged Him that he might
be with Him.
19 However, Jesus did not permit him, but said to
him, "Go home to your friends, and tell them what
great things the Lord has done for you, and how
He has had compassion on you."
20 And he departed and began to [a]proclaim in
[1]Decapolis all that Jesus had done for him; and all
[b]marveled.
**21** [a]Now when Jesus had crossed over again by
boat to the other side, a great multitude gathered
to Him; and He was by the sea.
22 [a]And behold, one of the rulers of the synagogue came, Jairus by name. And when he saw
Him, he fell at His feet
23 and begged Him earnestly, saying, "My little
daughter lies at the point of death. Come and [a]lay
Your hands on her, that she may be healed, and
she will live."
24 So *Jesus* went with him, and a great multitude
followed Him and thronged Him.
25 Now a certain woman [a]had a flow of blood for
twelve years,
26 and had suffered many things from many
physicians. She had spent all that she had and was
no better, but rather grew worse.
27 When she heard about Jesus, she came behind
*Him* in the crowd and [a]touched His garment.
28 For she said, "If only I may touch His clothes,
I shall be made well."
29 Immediately the fountain of her blood was
dried up, and she felt in *her* body that she was
healed of the [1]affliction.
30 And Jesus, immediately knowing in Himself
that [a]power had gone out of Him, turned around
in the crowd and said, "Who touched My
clothes?"
31 But His disciples said to Him, "You see the
multitude thronging You, and You say, 'Who
touched Me?' "
32 And He looked around to see her who had
done this thing.
33 But the woman, [a]fearing and trembling, knowing what had happened to her, came and fell down
before Him and told Him the whole truth.
34 And He said to her, "Daughter, [a]your faith has
made you well. [b]Go in peace, and be healed of
your affliction."
35 [a]While He was still speaking, *some* came from
the ruler of the synagogue's *house* who said,
"Your daughter is dead. Why trouble the Teacher
any further?"
36 As soon as Jesus heard the word that was
spoken, He said to the ruler of the synagogue, "Do
not be afraid; only [a]believe."
37 And He permitted no one to follow Him except
Peter, James, and John the brother of James.
38 Then He came to the house of the ruler of the
synagogue, and saw [1]a tumult and those who
[a]wept and wailed loudly.
39 When He came in, He said to them, "Why
make this commotion and weep? The child is not
dead, but [a]sleeping."
40 And they ridiculed Him. [a]But when He had put
them all outside, He took the father and the

**33** [a]Matt. 13:34, 35; [John 16:12]
**34** [a]Luke 24:27, 45
**35** [a]Matt. 8:18, 23–27; Luke 8:22, 25
**38** [a][Matt. 23:8–10] [b]Ps. 44:23
**39** [a]Mark 9:25; Luke 4:39 [b]Ps. 65:7; 89:9; 93:4; 104:6, 7; Matt. 8:26; Luke 8:24 [1]Lit. *Be quiet*
**40** [a]Matt. 14:31, 32; Luke 8:25 [1]NU *Have you still no faith?*

CHAPTER 5
**1** [a]Matt. 8:28–34; Luke 8:26–37 [1]NU *Gerasenes*
**2** [a]Mark 1:23; 7:25; [Rev. 16:13, 14]
**3** [1]NU adds *anymore*
**7** [a]Matt. 26:63; Mark 1:24; Acts 19:13 [1]*adjure*
**8** [a]Mark 1:25; 9:25; [Acts 16:18]
**11** [a]Lev. 11:7, 8; Deut. 14:8; Luke 15:15, 16
**13** [1]NU *He gave*
**15** [a]Matt. 4:24; 8:16; Mark 1:32 [b]Luke 10:39 [c][Is. 61:10]
**17** [a]Matt. 8:34; Acts 16:39
**18** [a]Luke 8:38, 39
**20** [a]Ex. 15:2; Ps. 66:16 [b]Matt. 9:8, 33; John 5:20; 7:21; Acts 3:12; 4:13 [1]Lit. *Ten Cities*
**21** [a]Matt. 9:1; Luke 8:40
**22** [a]Matt. 9:18–26; Luke 8:41–56; Acts 13:15
**23** [a]Matt. 8:15; Mark 6:5; 7:32; 8:23, 25; 16:18; Luke 4:40; Acts 9:17; 28:8
**25** [a]Lev. 15:19, 25; Matt. 9:20
**27** [a]Matt. 14:35, 36; Mark 3:10; 6:56
**29** [1]*suffering*
**30** [a]Luke 6:19; 8:46
**33** [a][Ps. 89:7]
**34** [a]Matt. 9:22; Mark 10:52; Acts 14:9 [b]1 Sam. 1:17; 20:42; 2 Kin. 5:19; Luke 7:50; 8:48; Acts 16:36; [James 2:16]
**35** [a]Luke 8:49
**36** [a][Mark 9:23; John 11:40]
**38** [a]Mark 16:10; Acts 9:39 [1]*an uproar*
**39** [a]John 11:4, 11
**40** [a]Acts 9:40

mother of the child, and those *who were* with
Him, and entered where the child was lying.
41 Then He took the child by the hand, and said
to her, "Talitha, cumi," which is translated, "Little
girl, I say to you, arise."
42 Immediately the girl arose and walked, for she
was twelve years *of age.* And they were [a]over-
come with great amazement.
43 But [a]He commanded them strictly that no one
should know it, and said that *something* should be
given her to eat.

### *The Death of John the Baptist*

**6** Then [a]He went out from there and came to His
own country, and His disciples followed Him.
2 And when the Sabbath had come, He began to
teach in the synagogue. And many hearing *Him*
were [a]astonished, saying, [b]"Where *did* this Man
*get* these things? And what wisdom *is* this which
is given to Him, that such mighty works are
performed by His hands!
3 "Is this not the carpenter, the Son of Mary,
and [a]brother of James, Joses, Judas, and Simon?
And are not His sisters here with us?" So they
[b]were offended at Him.
4 But Jesus said to them, [a]"A prophet is not
without honor except in his own country, among
his own relatives, and in his own house."
5 [a]Now He could do no mighty work there,
except that He laid His hands on a few sick people
and healed *them.*
6 And [a]He marveled because of their unbelief.
[b]Then He went about the villages in a circuit,
teaching.
**7** [a]And He called the twelve to *Himself,* and
began to send them out [b]two *by* two, and gave
them power over unclean spirits.
8 He commanded them to take nothing for the
journey except a staff—no bag, no bread, no
copper in *their* money belts—
9 but [a]to wear sandals, and not to put on two
tunics.
10 [a]Also He said to them, "In whatever place you
enter a house, stay there till you depart from that
place.
11 [a]"And [1]whoever will not receive you nor hear
you, when you depart from there, [b]shake off the
dust under your feet as a testimony against them.
[2]Assuredly, I say to you, it will be more tolerable
for Sodom and Gomorrah in the day of judgment
than for that city!"
12 So they went out and preached that *people*
should repent.
13 And they cast out many demons, [a]and
anointed with oil many who were sick, and healed
*them.*
**14** [a]Now King Herod heard *of Him,* for His name
had become well known. And he said, "John the
Baptist is risen from the dead, and therefore [b]these
powers are at work in him."
15 [a]Others said, "It is Elijah." And others said, "It
is [1]the Prophet, [b]or like one of the prophets."
16 [a]But when Herod heard, he said, "This is John,
whom I beheaded; he has been raised from the
dead!"
17 For Herod himself had sent and laid hold of
John, and bound him in prison for the sake of
Herodias, his brother Philip's wife; for he had
married her.
18 Because John had said to Herod, [a]"It is not
lawful for you to have your brother's wife."
19 Therefore Herodias [1]held it against him and
wanted to kill him, but she could not;
20 for Herod [a]feared John, knowing that he *was* a
just and holy man, and he protected him. And
when he heard him, he did many things, and
heard him gladly.
21 [a]Then an opportune day came when Herod [b]on
his birthday gave a feast for his nobles, the high
officers, and the chief *men* of Galilee.
22 And when Herodias' daughter herself came in
and danced, and pleased Herod and those who sat
with him, the king said to the girl, "Ask me
whatever you want, and I will give *it* to you."
23 He also swore to her, [a]"Whatever you ask me,
I will give you, up to half my kingdom."
24 So she went out and said to her mother,
"What shall I ask?" And she said, "The head of
John the Baptist!"
25 Immediately she came in with haste to the
king and asked, saying, "I want you to give me at
once the head of John the Baptist on a platter."
26 [a]And the king was exceedingly sorry; *yet,*
because of the oaths and because of those who sat
with him, he did not want to refuse her.
27 Immediately the king sent an executioner and
commanded his head to be brought. And he went
and beheaded him in prison,
28 brought his head on a platter, and gave it to
the girl; and the girl gave it to her mother.
29 When his disciples heard *of it,* they came and
[a]took away his corpse and laid it in a tomb.
**30** [a]Then the apostles gathered to Jesus and told
Him all things, both what they had done and what
they had taught.
31 [a]And He said to them, "Come aside by yourselves to a deserted place and rest a while." For
[b]there were many coming and going, and they did
not even have time to eat.
32 [a]So they departed to a deserted place in the
boat by themselves.
33 But [1]the multitudes saw them departing, and
many [a]knew Him and ran there on foot from all
the cities. They arrived before them and came
together to Him.
34 [a]And Jesus, when He came out, saw a great
multitude and was moved with compassion for
them, because they were like [b]sheep not having a
shepherd. So [c]He began to teach them many
things.
35 [a]When the day was now far spent, His disciples came to Him and said, "This is a deserted
place, and already the hour *is* late.
36 "Send them away, that they may go into the
surrounding country and villages and buy themselves [1]bread; for they have nothing to eat."
37 But He answered and said to them, "You give
them something to eat." And they said to Him,
[a]"Shall we go and buy two hundred denarii worth
of bread and give them *something* to eat?"
38 But He said to them, "How many loaves do
you have? Go and see." And when they found out
they said, [a]"Five, and two fish."
39 Then He [a]commanded them to make them all
sit down in groups on the green grass.
40 So they sat down in ranks, in hundreds and in
fifties.
41 And when He had taken the five loaves and
the two fish, He [a]looked up to heaven, [b]blessed
and broke the loaves, and gave *them* to His
disciples to set before them; and the two fish He
divided among *them* all.

---

**42** [a]Mark 1:27; 7:37
**43** [a][Matt. 8:4; 12:16–19; 17:9]

CHAPTER 6
**1** [a]Matt. 13:54
**2** [a]Matt. 7:28 [b]John 6:42
**3** [a]Matt. 12:46 [b][Matt. 11:6]
**4** [a]John 4:44
**5** [a]Gen. 19:22; 32:25
**6** [a]Is. 59:16 [b]Matt. 9:35
**7** [a]Mark 3:13, 14 [b][Eccl. 4:9, 10]
**9** [a][Eph. 6:15]
**10** [a]Matt. 10:11
**11** [a]Matt. 10:14 [b]Acts 13:51; 18:6 [1]NU *whatever place* [2]NU omits the rest of v. 11.
**13** [a][James 5:14]
**14** [a]Luke 9:7–9 [b]Luke 19:37
**15** [a]Mark 8:28 [b]Matt. 21:11 [1]NU, M *a prophet, like one*
**16** [a]Luke 3:19
**18** [a]Lev. 18:16; 20:21
**19** [1]*held a grudge*
**20** [a]Matt. 14:5; 21:26
**21** [a]Matt. 14:6 [b]Gen. 40:20
**23** [a]Esth. 5:3, 6; 7:2
**26** [a]Matt. 14:9
**29** [a]1 Kin. 13:29, 30
**30** [a]Luke 9:10
**31** [a]Matt. 14:13 [b]Mark 3:20
**32** [a]Matt. 14:13–21
**33** [a][Col. 1:6] [1]NU, M *they*
**34** [a]Matt. 9:36; 14:14 [b]Num. 27:17 [c]Luke 9:11
**35** [a]Matt. 14:15
**36** [1]NU *something to eat* and omits the rest of v. 36.
**37** [a]2 Kin. 4:43
**38** [a]John 6:9
**39** [a]Matt. 15:35
**41** [a]John 11:41, 42 [b]Matt. 15:36; 26:26

42 So they all ate and were filled.
43 And they took up twelve baskets full of fragments and of the fish.
44 Now those who had eaten the loaves were [1]about five thousand men.
**45** [a]Immediately He [1]made His disciples get into the boat and go before Him to the other side, to Bethsaida, while He sent the multitude away.
46 And when He had sent them away, He [a]departed to the mountain to pray.
47 Now when evening came, the boat was in the middle of the sea; and He *was* alone on the land.
48 Then He saw them straining at rowing, for the wind was against them. Now about the fourth watch of the night He came to them, walking on the sea, and [a]would have passed them by.
49 And when they saw Him walking on the sea, they supposed it was a [a]ghost, and cried out;
50 for they all saw Him and were troubled. But immediately He talked with them and said to them, [a]"Be[1] of good cheer! It is I; do not be [b]afraid."
51 Then He went up into the boat to them, and the wind [a]ceased. And they were greatly [b]amazed in themselves beyond measure, and marveled.
52 For [a]they had not understood about the loaves, because their [b]heart was hardened.
**53** [a]When they had crossed over, they came to the land of Gennesaret and anchored there.
54 And when they came out of the boat, immediately [1]the people recognized Him,
55 ran through that whole surrounding region, and began to carry about on beds those who were sick to wherever they heard He was.
56 Wherever He entered, into villages, cities, or the country, they laid the sick in the marketplaces, and begged Him that [a]they might just touch the [b]hem of His garment. And as many as touched Him were made well.

### *Jesus Rebukes the Pharisees' Traditions*

**7** Then [a]the Pharisees and some of the scribes came together to Him, having come from Jerusalem.
2 Now [1]when they saw some of His disciples eat bread with defiled, that is, with [a]unwashed hands, [2]they found fault.
3 For the Pharisees and all the Jews do not eat unless they wash *their* hands [1]in a special way, holding the [a]tradition of the elders.
4 *When they come* from the marketplace, they do not eat unless they wash. And there are many other things which they have received and hold, *like* the washing of cups, pitchers, copper vessels, and couches.
5 [a]Then the Pharisees and scribes asked Him, "Why do Your disciples not walk according to the tradition of the elders, but eat bread with unwashed hands?"
6 He answered and said to them, "Well did Isaiah prophesy of you [a]hypocrites, as it is written:

[b]*'This people honors Me with their lips,*
*But their heart is far from Me.*
7 *And in vain they worship Me,*
*Teaching as doctrines the commandments of men.'*

8 "For laying aside the commandment of God, you hold the tradition of men—[1]the washing of pitchers and cups, and many other such things you do."
9 He said to them, "*All too* well [a]you [1]reject the commandment of God, that you may keep your tradition.
10 "For Moses said, [a]*'Honor your father and your mother'*; and, [b]*'He who curses father or mother, let him be put to death.'*
11 "But you say, 'If a man says to his father or mother, [a]"Whatever profit you might have received from me *is* Corban"—' (that is, a gift *to God*);
12 "and you no longer let him do anything for his father or his mother,
13 "making the word of God of no effect through your tradition which you have handed down. And many such things you do."
14 [a]When He had called all the multitude to *Himself*, He said to them, "Hear Me, everyone, and [b]understand:
15 "There is nothing that enters a man from outside which can defile him; but the things which come out of him, those are the things that [a]defile a man.
16 [a]"If[1] anyone has ears to hear, let him hear!"
17 [a]When He had entered a house away from the crowd, His disciples asked Him concerning the parable.
18 So He said to them, [a]"Are you thus without understanding also? Do you not perceive that whatever enters a man from outside cannot defile him,
19 "because it does not enter his heart but his stomach, and is eliminated, [1]*thus* purifying all foods?"
20 And He said, [a]"What comes out of a man, that defiles a man.
21 [a]"For from within, out of the heart of men, [b]proceed evil thoughts, [c]adulteries, [d]fornications, murders,
22 "thefts, [a]covetousness, wickedness, [b]deceit, [c]lewdness, an evil eye, [d]blasphemy, [e]pride, foolishness.
23 "All these evil things come from within and defile a man."
**24** [a]From there He arose and went to the region of Tyre [1]and Sidon. And He entered a house and wanted no one to know *it*, but He could not be [b]hidden.
25 For a woman whose young daughter had an unclean spirit heard about Him, and she came and [a]fell at His feet.
26 The woman was a [1]Greek, a [2]Syro-Phoenician by birth, and she kept [3]asking Him to cast the demon out of her daughter.
27 But Jesus said to her, "Let the children be filled first, for it is not good to take the children's bread and throw *it* to the little dogs."
28 And she answered and said to Him, "Yes, Lord, yet even the little dogs under the table eat from the children's crumbs."
29 Then He said to her, "For this saying go your way; the demon has gone out of your daughter."
30 And when she had come to her house, she found the demon gone out, and her daughter lying on the bed.
**31** [a]Again, departing from the region of Tyre and Sidon, He came through the midst of the region of Decapolis to the Sea of Galilee.
32 Then [a]they brought to Him one who was deaf and had an impediment in his speech, and they begged Him to put His hand on him.

**44** [1]NU, M omit *about*
**45** [a]John 6:15–21 [1]*invited, strongly urged*
**46** [a]Luke 5:16
**48** [a]Luke 24:28
**49** [a]Matt. 14:26
**50** [a]Matt. 9:2 [b]Is. 41:10 [1]*Take courage*
**51** [a]Ps. 107:29 [b]Mark 1:27; 2:12; 5:42; 7:37
**52** [a]Mark 8:17, 18 [b]Mark 3:5; 16:14
**53** [a]Matt. 14:34–36
**54** [1]Lit. *they*
**56** [a]Matt. 9:20 [b]Num. 15:38, 39

CHAPTER 7
**1** [a]Matt. 15:1–20
**2** [a]Matt. 15:20 [1]NU omits *when* [2]NU omits *they found fault*
**3** [a]Gal. 1:14 [1]Lit. *with the fist*
**5** [a]Matt. 15:2
**6** [a]Matt. 23:13–29 [b]Is. 29:13
**8** [1]NU omits the rest of v. 8.
**9** [a]Prov. 1:25 [1]*set aside*
**10** [a]Ex. 20:12; Deut. 5:16 [b]Ex. 21:17
**11** [a]Matt. 15:5; 23:18
**14** [a]Matt. 15:10 [b]Matt. 16:9, 11, 12
**15** [a]Is. 59:3
**16** [a]Matt. 11:15 [1]NU omits v. 16.
**17** [a]Matt. 15:15
**18** [a][Heb. 5:11–14]
**19** [1]NU sets off the final phrase as Mark's comment that Jesus has declared all foods clean.
**20** [a]Ps. 39:1
**21** [a]Gen. 6:5; 8:21 [b][Gal. 5:19–21] [c]2 Pet. 2:14 [d]1 Thess. 4:3
**22** [a]Luke 12:15 [b]Rom. 1:28, 29 [c]1 Pet. 4:3 [d]Rev. 2:9 [e]1 John 2:16
**24** [a]Matt. 15:29 [b]Mark 2:1, 2 [1]NU omits *and Sidon*
**25** [a]John 11:32
**26** [1]*Gentile* [2]*A Syrian of Phoenicia* [3]*begging*
**31** [a]Matt. 15:29
**32** [a]Luke 11:14

33 And He took him aside from the multitude,
and put His fingers in his ears, and [a]He spat and
touched his tongue.
34 Then, [a]looking up to heaven, [b]He sighed, and
said to him, "Ephphatha," that is, "Be opened."
35 [a]Immediately his ears were opened, and the
[1]impediment of his tongue was loosed, and he
spoke plainly.
36 Then [a]He commanded them that they should
tell no one; but the more He commanded them,
the more widely they proclaimed *it.*
37 And they were [a]astonished beyond measure,
saying, "He has done all things well. He [b]makes
both the deaf to hear and the mute to speak."

### *The Four Thousand Fed*

8 In those days, [a]the multitude being very great
and having nothing to eat, Jesus called His
disciples *to Him* and said to them,
2 "I have [a]compassion on the multitude, because they have now continued with Me three
days and have nothing to eat.
3 "And if I send them away hungry to their own
houses, they will faint on the way; for some of
them have come from afar."
4 Then His disciples answered Him, "How can
one satisfy these people with bread here in the
wilderness?"
5 [a]He asked them, "How many loaves do you
have?" And they said, "Seven."
6 So He commanded the multitude to sit down
on the ground. And He took the seven loaves and
gave thanks, broke *them* and gave *them* to His
disciples to set before *them;* and they set *them*
before the multitude.
7 They also had a few small fish; and [a]having
blessed them, He said to set them also before
*them.*
8 So they ate and were filled, and they took up
seven large baskets of leftover fragments.
9 Now those who had eaten were about four
thousand. And He sent them away,
10 [a]immediately got into the boat with His disciples, and came to the region of Dalmanutha.
**11** [a]Then the Pharisees came out and began to
dispute with Him, seeking from Him a sign from
heaven, testing Him.
12 But He [a]sighed deeply in His spirit, and said,
"Why does this generation seek a sign? Assuredly,
I say to you, [b]no sign shall be given to this
generation."
**13** And He left them, and getting into the boat
again, departed to the other side.
14 [a]Now [1]the disciples had forgotten to take
bread, and they did not have more than one loaf
with them in the boat.
15 [a]Then He charged them, saying, "Take heed,
beware of the [1]leaven of the Pharisees and the
leaven of Herod."
16 And they reasoned among themselves, saying,
"*It is* because we have no bread."
17 But Jesus, being aware of *it,* said to them,
"Why do you reason because you have no bread?
[a]Do you not yet perceive nor understand? Is your
heart [1]still hardened?
18 "Having eyes, do you not see? And having
ears, do you not hear? And do you not remember?
19 [a]"When I broke the five loaves for the five
thousand, how many baskets full of fragments did
you take up?" They said to Him, "Twelve."
20 "Also, [a]when I broke the seven for the four
thousand, how many large baskets full of fragments did you take up?" And they said, "Seven."
21 So He said to them, "How *is it* [a]you do not
understand?"
**22** Then He came to Bethsaida; and they brought
a [a]blind man to Him, and begged Him to [b]touch
him.
23 So He took the blind man by the hand and led
him out of the town. And when [a]He had spit on his
eyes and put His hands on him, He asked him if he
saw anything.
24 And he looked up and said, "I see men like
trees, walking."
25 Then He put *His* hands on his eyes again and
made him look up. And he was restored and saw
everyone clearly.
26 Then He sent him away to his house, saying,
[1]"Neither go into the town, [a]nor tell anyone in the
town."
**27** [a]Now Jesus and His disciples went out to the
towns of Caesarea Philippi; and on the road He
asked His disciples, saying to them, "Who do men
say that I am?"
28 So they answered, [a]"John the Baptist; but
some *say,* [b]Elijah; and others, one of the prophets."
29 He said to them, "But who do you say that I
am?" Peter answered and said to Him, [a]"You are
the Christ."
30 [a]Then He strictly warned them that they
should tell no one about Him.
**31** And [a]He began to teach them that the Son of
Man must suffer many things, and be [b]rejected by
the elders and chief priests and scribes, and be
[c]killed, and after three days rise again.
32 He spoke this word openly. Then Peter took
Him aside and began to rebuke Him.
33 But when He had turned around and looked at
His disciples, He [a]rebuked Peter, saying, "Get
behind Me, Satan! For you are not [1]mindful of the
things of God, but the things of men."
**34** When He had called the people to *Himself,*
with His disciples also, He said to them, [a]"Whoever desires to come after Me, let him deny
himself, and take up his cross, and follow Me.
35 "For [a]whoever desires to save his life will lose
it, but whoever loses his life for My sake and the
gospel's will save it.
36 "For what will it profit a man if he gains the
whole world, and loses his own soul?
37 "Or what will a man give in exchange for his
soul?
38 [a]"For whoever [b]is ashamed of Me and My
words in this adulterous and sinful generation, of
him the Son of Man also will be ashamed when He
comes in the glory of His Father with the holy
angels."

### *The Transfiguration of Christ*

9 And He said to them, [a]"Assuredly, I say to you
that there are some standing here who will not
taste death till they see [b]the kingdom of God
[1]present with power."
**2** [a]Now after six days Jesus took Peter, James,
and John, and led them up on a high mountain
apart by themselves; and He was transfigured
before them.
3 His clothes became shining, exceedingly
[a]white, like snow, such as no launderer on earth
can whiten them.

33 [a]Mark 8:23
34 [a]Mark 6:41 [b]John 11:33, 38
35 [a]Is. 35:5, 6 [1]Lit. *bond*
36 [a]Mark 5:43
37 [a]Mark 6:51; 10:26 [b]Matt. 12:22

CHAPTER 8
1 [a]Matt. 15:32–39
2 [a]Mark 1:41; 6:34
5 [a]Mark 6:38
7 [a]Matt. 14:19
10 [a]Matt. 15:39
11 [a]Matt. 12:38; 16:1
12 [a]Mark 7:34 [b]Matt. 12:39
14 [a]Matt. 16:5 [1]NU, M *they*
15 [a]Luke 12:1 [1]*yeast*
17 [a]Mark 6:52; 16:14 [1]NU omits *still*
19 [a]Matt. 14:20
20 [a]Matt. 15:37
21 [a][Mark 6:52]
22 [a]John 9:1 [b]Luke 18:15
23 [a]Mark 7:33
26 [a]Mark 5:43; 7:36 [1]NU *Do not even go into the town*
27 [a]Luke 9:18–20
28 [a]Matt. 14:2 [b]Luke 9:7, 8
29 [a]John 1:41; 4:42; 6:69; 11:27
30 [a]Matt. 8:4; 16:20
31 [a]Matt. 16:21; 20:19 [b]Mark 10:33 [c]Mark 9:31; 10:34
33 [a][Rev. 3:19] [1]*setting your mind on*
34 [a]Luke 14:27
35 [a]John 12:25
38 [a]Matt. 10:33 [b]2 Tim. 1:8, 9; 2:12

CHAPTER 9
1 [a]Luke 9:27 [b][Matt. 24:30] [1]*having come*
2 [a]Matt. 17:1–8
3 [a]Dan. 7:9

4 And Elijah appeared to them with Moses, and
they were talking with Jesus.
5 Then Peter answered and said to Jesus,
"Rabbi, it is good for us to be here; and let us
make three tabernacles: one for You, one for
Moses, and one for Elijah"—
6 because he did not know what to say, for they
were greatly afraid.
7 And a [a]cloud came and overshadowed them;
and a voice came out of the cloud, saying, "This is
[b]My beloved Son. [c]Hear Him!"
8 Suddenly, when they had looked around, they
saw no one anymore, but only Jesus with themselves.
9 [a]Now as they came down from the mountain,
He commanded them that they should tell no one
the things they had seen, till the Son of Man had
risen from the dead.
10 So they kept this word to themselves, questioning [a]what the rising from the dead meant.
11 And they asked Him, saying, "Why do the
scribes say [a]that Elijah must come first?"
12 Then He answered and told them, "Indeed,
Elijah is coming first and restores all things. And
[a]how is it written concerning the Son of Man, that
He must suffer many things and [b]be treated with
contempt?
13 "But I say to you that [a]Elijah has also come,
and they did to him whatever they wished, as it is
written of him."
**14** [a]And when He came to the disciples, He saw a
great multitude around them, and scribes disputing with them.
15 Immediately, when they saw Him, all the
people were greatly amazed, and running to *Him,*
greeted Him.
16 And He asked the scribes, "What are you
discussing with them?"
17 Then [a]one of the crowd answered and said,
"Teacher, I brought You my son, who has a mute
spirit.
18 "And wherever it seizes him, it throws him
down; he foams at the mouth, gnashes his teeth,
and becomes rigid. So I spoke to Your disciples,
that they should cast it out, but they could not."
19 He answered him and said, "O [a]faithless[1]
generation, how long shall I be with you? How
long shall I [2]bear with you? Bring him to Me."
20 Then they brought him to Him. And [a]when he
saw Him, immediately the spirit convulsed him,
and he fell on the ground and wallowed, foaming
at the mouth.
21 So He asked his father, "How long has this
been happening to him?" And he said, "From
childhood.
22 "And often he has thrown him both into the
fire and into the water to destroy him. But if You
can do anything, have compassion on us and help
us."
23 Jesus said to him, [a]"If[1] you can believe, all
things *are* possible to him who believes."
24 Immediately the father of the child cried out
and said with tears, "Lord, I believe; [a]help my
unbelief!"
25 When Jesus saw that the people came running
together, He [a]rebuked the unclean spirit, saying to
it: "Deaf and dumb spirit, I command you, come
out of him and enter him no more!"
26 Then *the spirit* cried out, convulsed him
greatly, and came out of him. And he became as
one dead, so that many said, "He is dead."
27 But Jesus took him by the hand and lifted him
up, and he arose.
28 [a]And when He had come into the house, His
disciples asked Him privately, "Why could we not
cast it out?"
29 So He said to them, "This kind can come out
by nothing but [a]prayer [1]and fasting."
**30** Then they departed from there and passed
through Galilee, and He did not want anyone to
know *it.*
31 [a]For He taught His disciples and said to them,
"The Son of Man is being betrayed into the hands
of men, and they will [b]kill Him. And after He is
killed, He will [c]rise the third day."
32 But they [a]did not understand this saying, and
were afraid to ask Him.
**33** [a]Then He came to Capernaum. And when He
was in the house He asked them, "What was it
you [1]disputed among yourselves on the road?"
34 But they kept silent, for on the road they had
[a]disputed among themselves who *would be the*
[b]greatest.
35 And He sat down, called the twelve, and said
to them, [a]"If anyone desires to be first, he shall be
last of all and servant of all."
36 Then [a]He took a little child and set him in the
midst of them. And when He had taken him in His
arms, He said to them,
37 "Whoever receives one of these little children
in My name receives Me; and [a]whoever receives
Me, receives not Me but Him who sent Me."
**38** [a]Now John answered Him, saying, "Teacher,
we saw someone who does not follow us casting
out demons in Your name, and we forbade him
because he does not follow us."
39 But Jesus said, "Do not forbid him, [a]for no one
who works a miracle in My name can soon afterward speak evil of Me.
40 "For [a]he who is not against [1]us is on [2]our side.
41 [a]"For whoever gives you a cup of water to
drink in My name, because you belong to Christ,
assuredly, I say to you, he will by no means lose
his reward.
**42** [a]"But whoever causes one of these little ones
who believe in Me [1]to stumble, it would be better
for him if a millstone were hung around his neck,
and he were thrown into the sea.
43 [a]"If your hand causes you to sin, cut it off. It is
better for you to enter into life [1]maimed, rather
than having two hands, to go to [2]hell, into the fire
that shall never be quenched—
44 [1]"where

[a]*'Their worm does not die,*
*And the fire is not quenched.'*

45 "And if your foot causes you to sin, cut it off.
It is better for you to enter life lame, rather than
having two feet, to be cast into [1]hell, [2]into the fire
that shall never be quenched—
46 "where

[a]*'Their worm does not die,*
*And the fire is not quenched.'*

47 "And if your eye causes you to sin, pluck it
out. It is better for you to enter the kingdom of
God with one eye, rather than having two eyes, to
be cast into [1]hell fire—
48 "where

[a]*'Their worm does not die,*
*And the [b]fire is not quenched.'*

---

**7** [a]Ex. 40:34 [b]Mark 1:11 [c]Acts 3:22
**9** [a]Matt. 17:9–13
**10** [a]John 2:19–22
**11** [a]Mal. 4:5
**12** [a]Is. 53:3 [b]Phil. 2:7
**13** [a]Luke 1:17
**14** [a]Matt. 17:14–19
**17** [a]Luke 9:38
**19** [a]John 4:48 [1]*unbelieving* [2]*put up with*
**20** [a]Mark 1:26
**23** [a]John 11:40 [1]NU *If you can! All things*
**24** [a]Luke 17:5
**25** [a]Mark 1:25
**28** [a]Matt. 17:19
**29** [a][James 5:16] [1]NU omits *and fasting*
**31** [a]Luke 9:44 [b]Matt. 16:21; 27:50 [c]1 Cor. 15:4
**32** [a]Luke 2:50; 18:34
**33** [a]Matt. 18:1–5 [1]*discussed*
**34** [a][Prov. 13:10] [b]Luke 22:24; 23:46; 24:46
**35** [a]Luke 22:26, 27
**36** [a]Mark 10:13–16
**37** [a]Matt. 10:40
**38** [a]Num. 11:27–29
**39** [a]1 Cor. 12:3
**40** [a][Matt. 12:30] [1]M *you* [2]M *your*
**41** [a]Matt. 10:42
**42** [a]Luke 17:1, 2 [1]To fall into sin
**43** [a]Matt. 5:29, 30; 18:8, 9 [1]*crippled* [2]Gr. *Gehenna*
**44** [a]Is. 66:24 [1]NU omits v. 44.
**45** [1]Gr. *Gehenna* [2]NU omits the rest of v. 45 and all of v. 46.
**46** [a]Is. 66:24
**47** [1]Gr. *Gehenna*
**48** [a]Is. 66:24 [b]Jer. 7:20

49 "For everyone will be [a]seasoned with fire,
[b]and[1] every sacrifice will be seasoned with salt.
50 [a]"Salt *is* good, but if the salt loses its flavor,
how will you season it? [b]Have salt in yourselves,
and [c]have peace with one another."

### *Divorce and the Danger of Riches*

**10** Then [a]He arose from there and came to the
region of Judea by the other side of the
Jordan. And multitudes gathered to Him again,
and as He was accustomed, He taught them again.
2 [a]The Pharisees came and asked Him, "Is it
lawful for a man to divorce *his* wife?" testing Him.
3 And He answered and said to them, "What did
Moses command you?"
4 They said, [a]"Moses permitted *a man* to write a
certificate of divorce, and to dismiss *her.*"
5 And Jesus answered and said to them, "Because of the hardness of your heart he wrote you
this [1]precept.
6 "But from the beginning of the creation, God
[a]*'made them male and female.'*
7 [a]*'For this reason a man shall leave his father
and mother and be joined to his wife,*
8 *'and the two shall become one flesh'*; so then
they are no longer two, but one flesh.
9 "Therefore what God has joined together, let
not man separate."
10 In the house His disciples also asked Him
again about the same *matter.*
11 So He said to them, [a]"Whoever divorces his
wife and marries another commits adultery
against her.
12 "And if a woman divorces her husband and
marries another, she commits adultery."
13 [a]Then they brought little children to Him, that
He might touch them; but the disciples rebuked
those who brought *them.*
14 But when Jesus saw *it,* He was greatly displeased and said to them, "Let the little children
come to Me, and do not forbid them; for [a]of such is
the kingdom of God.
15 "Assuredly, I say to you, [a]whoever does not
receive the kingdom of God as a little child will
[b]by no means enter it."
16 And He took them up in His arms, laid *His*
hands on them, and blessed them.
17 [a]Now as He was going out on the road, one
came running, knelt before Him, and asked Him,
"Good Teacher, what shall I [b]do that I may inherit
eternal life?"
18 So Jesus said to him, "Why do you call Me
good? No one *is* good but One, *that is,* [a]God.
19 "You know the commandments: [a]*'Do not
commit adultery,' 'Do not murder,' 'Do not steal,'
'Do not bear false witness,'* 'Do not defraud,'
*'Honor your father and your mother.'* "
20 And he answered and said to Him, "Teacher,
all these things I have [a]kept from my youth."
21 Then Jesus, looking at him, loved him, and
said to him, "One thing you lack: Go your way,
[a]sell whatever you have and give to the poor, and
you will have [b]treasure in heaven; and come, [c]take
up the cross, and follow Me."
22 But he was sad at this word, and went away
sorrowful, for he had great possessions.
23 [a]Then Jesus looked around and said to His
disciples, "How hard it is for those who have
riches to enter the kingdom of God!"
24 And the disciples were astonished at His
words. But Jesus answered again and said to
them, "Children, how hard it is [1]for those [a]who
trust in riches to enter the kingdom of God!
25 "It is easier for a camel to go through the eye
of a needle than for a [a]rich man to enter the
kingdom of God."
26 And they were greatly astonished, saying
among themselves, "Who then can be saved?"
27 But Jesus looked at them and said, "With men
*it is* impossible, but not [a]with God; for with God all
things are possible."
28 [a]Then Peter began to say to Him, "See, we
have left all and followed You."
29 So Jesus answered and said, "Assuredly, I say
to you, there is no one who has left house or
brothers or sisters or father or mother [1]or wife or
children or [2]lands, for My sake and the gospel's,
30 [a]"who shall not receive a hundredfold now in
this time—houses and brothers and sisters and
mothers and children and lands, with [b]persecu-
tions—and in the age to come, eternal life.
31 [a]"But many *who are* first will be last, and the
last first."
32 [a]Now they were on the road, going up to
Jerusalem, and Jesus was going before them; and
they were amazed. And as they followed they
were afraid. [b]Then He took the twelve aside again
and began to tell them the things that would
happen to Him:
33 "Behold, we are going up to Jerusalem, and
the Son of Man will be betrayed to the chief
priests and to the scribes; and they will condemn
Him to death and deliver Him to the Gentiles;
34 "and they will mock Him, and [1]scourge Him,
and spit on Him, and kill Him. And the third day
He will rise again."
35 [a]Then James and John, the sons of Zebedee,
came to Him, saying, "Teacher, we want You to
do for us whatever we ask."
36 And He said to them, "What do you want Me
to do for you?"
37 They said to Him, "Grant us that we may sit,
one on Your right hand and the other on Your
left, in Your glory."
38 But Jesus said to them, "You do not know
what you ask. Are you able to drink the [a]cup that
I drink, and be baptized with the [b]baptism that I
am baptized with?"
39 They said to Him, "We are able." So Jesus said
to them, [a]"You will indeed drink the cup that I
drink, and with the baptism I am baptized with
you will be baptized;
40 "but to sit on My right hand and on My left is
not Mine to give, but *it is for those* [a]for whom it is
prepared."
41 [a]And when the ten heard *it,* they began to be
greatly displeased with James and John.
42 But Jesus called them to *Himself* and said to
them, [a]"You know that those who are considered
rulers over the Gentiles lord it over them, and
their great ones exercise authority over them.
43 [a]"Yet it shall not be so among you; but whoever desires to become great among you shall be
your servant.
44 "And whoever of you desires to be first shall
be slave of all.
45 "For even [a]the Son of Man did not come to be
served, but to serve, and [b]to give His life a ransom
for many."
46 [a]Now they came to Jericho. As He went out of
Jericho with His disciples and a great multitude,

---

49 [a][Matt. 3:11] [b]Lev. 2:13 [1]NU omits the rest of v. 49.
50 [a]Matt. 5:13 [b]Col. 4:6 [c]Rom. 12:18; 14:19

CHAPTER 10
1 [a]Matt 19:1–9
2 [a]Matt. 19:3
4 [a]Deut. 24:1–4
5 [1]*command*
6 [a]Gen. 1:27; 5:2
7 [a]Gen. 2:24
11 [a][Matt. 5:32; 19:9]
13 [a]Luke 18:15–17
14 [a][1 Pet. 2:2]
15 [a]Matt. 18:3, 4; 19:14 [b]Luke 13:28
17 [a]Matt. 19:16–30 [b]John 6:28
18 [a]1 Sam. 2:2
19 [a]Ex. 20:12–16; Deut. 5:16–20
20 [a]Phil. 3:6
21 [a][Luke 12:33; 16:9] [b]Matt. 6:19, 20; 19:21 [c][Mark 8:34]
23 [a]Matt. 19:23
24 [a][1 Tim. 6:17] [1]NU omits *for those who trust in riches*
25 [a][Matt. 13:22; 19:24]
27 [a]Jer. 32:17
28 [a]Luke 18:28
29 [1]NU omits *or wife* [2]Lit. *fields*
30 [a]Luke 18:29, 30 [b][1 Pet. 4:12, 13]
31 [a]Luke 13:30
32 [a]Matt. 20:17–19 [b]Mark 8:31; 9:31
34 [1]*flog Him with a Roman scourge*
35 [a][James 4:3]
38 [a]John 18:11 [b]Luke 12:50
39 [a]Acts 12:2
40 [a][Heb. 11:16]
41 [a]Matt. 20:24
42 [a]Luke 22:25
43 [a]Mark 9:35
45 [a][Phil. 2:7, 8] [b][Titus 2:14]
46 [a]Luke 18:35–43

blind Bartimaeus, the son of Timaeus, sat by the road begging.

47 And when he heard that it was Jesus of Nazareth, he began to cry out and say, "Jesus, [a]Son of David, [b]have mercy on me!"

48 Then many warned him to be quiet; but he cried out all the more, "Son of David, have mercy on me!"

49 So Jesus stood still and commanded him to be called. Then they called the blind man, saying to him, "Be of good cheer. Rise, He is calling you."

50 And throwing aside his garment, he rose and came to Jesus.

51 So Jesus answered and said to him, "What do you want Me to do for you?" The blind man said to Him, [1]"Rabboni, that I may receive my sight."

52 Then Jesus said to him, "Go your way; [a]your faith has [1]made you well." And immediately he received his sight and followed Jesus on the road.

### *Jesus Rides into Jerusalem*

**11** Now [a]when they drew near Jerusalem, to [1]Bethphage and Bethany, at the Mount of Olives, He sent two of His disciples;

2 and He said to them, "Go into the village opposite you; and as soon as you have entered it you will find a colt tied, on which no one has sat. Loose it and bring *it*.

3 "And if anyone says to you, 'Why are you doing this?' say, 'The Lord has need of it,' and immediately he will send it here."

4 So they went their way, and found [1]the colt tied by the door outside on the street, and they loosed it.

5 But some of those who stood there said to them, "What are you doing, loosing the colt?"

6 And they spoke to them just as Jesus had commanded. So they let them go.

7 Then they brought the colt to Jesus and threw their clothes on it, and He sat on it.

8 [a]And many spread their clothes on the road, and others cut down leafy branches from the trees and spread *them* on the road.

9 Then those who went before and those who followed cried out, saying:

"Hosanna!
[a]'*Blessed is He who comes in the name of the* LORD!'
10 Blessed *is* the kingdom of our father David
That comes [1]in the name of the Lord!
[a]Hosanna in the highest!"

11 [a]And Jesus went into Jerusalem and into the temple. So when He had looked around at all things, as the hour was already late, He went out to Bethany with the twelve.

**12** [a]Now the next day, when they had come out from Bethany, He was hungry.

13 [a]And seeing from afar a fig tree having leaves, He went to see if perhaps He would find something on it. When He came to it, He found nothing but leaves, for it was not the season for figs.

14 In response Jesus said to it, "Let no one eat fruit from you ever again." And His disciples heard *it*.

**15** [a]So they came to Jerusalem. Then Jesus went into the temple and began to drive out those who bought and sold in the temple, and overturned the tables of the moneychangers and the seats of those who sold [b]doves.

16 And He would not allow anyone to carry wares through the temple.

17 Then He taught, saying to them, "Is it not written, [a]'*My house shall be called a house of prayer for all nations*'? But you have made it a [b]'*den of thieves*.'"

18 And [a]the scribes and chief priests heard it and sought how they might destroy Him; for they feared Him, because [b]all the people were astonished at His teaching.

19 When evening had come, He went out of the city.

**20** [a]Now in the morning, as they passed by, they saw the fig tree dried up from the roots.

21 And Peter, remembering, said to Him, "Rabbi, look! The fig tree which You cursed has withered away."

22 So Jesus answered and said to them, "Have faith in God.

23 "For [a]assuredly, I say to you, whoever says to this mountain, 'Be removed and be cast into the sea,' and does not doubt in his heart, but believes that those things he says will be done, he will have whatever he says.

24 "Therefore I say to you, [a]whatever things you ask when you pray, believe that you receive *them*, and you will have *them*.

**25** "And whenever you stand praying, [a]if you have anything against anyone, forgive him, that your Father in heaven may also forgive you your trespasses.

26 [1]"But [a]if you do not forgive, neither will your Father in heaven forgive your trespasses."

**27** Then they came again to Jerusalem. [a]And as He was walking in the temple, the chief priests, the scribes, and the elders came to Him.

28 And they said to Him, "By what [a]authority are You doing these things? And who gave You this authority to do these things?"

29 But Jesus answered and said to them, "I also will ask you one question; then answer Me, and I will tell you by what authority I do these things:

30 "The [a]baptism of John—was it from heaven or from men? Answer Me."

31 And they reasoned among themselves, saying, "If we say, 'From heaven,' He will say, 'Why then did you not believe him?'

32 "But if we say, 'From men' "—they feared the people, for [a]all counted John to have been a prophet indeed.

33 So they answered and said to Jesus, "We do not know." And Jesus answered and said to them, "Neither will I tell you by what authority I do these things."

### *Wicked Vinedressers*

**12** Then [a]He began to speak to them in parables: "A man planted a vineyard and set a hedge around *it*, dug *a place for* the wine vat and built a tower. And he leased it to [1]vinedressers and went into a far country.

2 "Now at vintage-time he sent a servant to the vinedressers, that he might receive some of the fruit of the vineyard from the vinedressers.

3 "And they took *him* and beat him and sent *him* away empty-handed.

4 "Again he sent them another servant, [1]and at him they threw stones, wounded *him* in the head, and sent *him* away shamefully treated.

5 "And again he sent another, and him they

**47** [a]Jer. 23:5; Matt. 22:42; Rom. 1:3, 4; Rev. 22:16 [b]Matt. 15:22; Luke 17:13
**51** [1]Lit. *My Great One*
**52** [a]Mark 9:22; Mark 5:34 [1]Lit. *saved you*

CHAPTER 11

**1** [a]Matt. 21:1–9; Luke 19:29; John 2:13 [1]M *Bethsphage*
**4** [1]NU, M *a*
**8** [a]Matt. 21:8
**9** [a]Ps. 118:25, 26; Matt. 21:9
**10** [a]Ps. 148:1 [1]NU omits *in the name of the Lord*
**11** [a]Matt. 21:12
**12** [a]Matt. 21:18–22
**13** [a]Matt. 21:19
**15** [a]Mal. 3:1; Matt. 21:12–16; Luke 19:45–47; John 2:13–16 [b]Lev. 14:22
**17** [a]Is. 56:7 [b]Jer. 7:11
**18** [a]Ps. 2:2; Matt. 21:45, 46; Luke 19:47 [b]Matt. 7:28; Mark 1:22; 6:2; Luke 4:32
**20** [a]Matt. 21:19–22
**23** [a]Matt. 17:20; 21:21; Luke 17:6
**24** [a]Matt. 7:7; Luke 11:9; [John 14:13; 15:7; 16:24; James 1:5, 6]
**25** [a]Matt. 6:14; 18:23–35; Eph. 4:32; [Col. 3:13]
**26** [a]Matt. 6:15; 18:35 [1]NU omits v. 26.
**27** [a]Matt. 21:23–27; Luke 20:1–8
**28** [a]John 5:27
**30** [a][Mark 1:4, 5, 8]; Luke 7:29, 30
**32** [a]Matt. 3:5; 14:5; Mark 6:20

CHAPTER 12

**1** [a]Matt. 21:33–46; Luke 20:9–19 [1]*tenant farmers*
**4** [1]NU omits *and at him they threw stones*

killed; and many others, [a]beating some and killing some.

6 "Therefore still having one son, his beloved, he also sent him to them last, saying, 'They will respect my son.'

7 "But those [1]vinedressers said among themselves, 'This is the heir. Come, let us kill him, and the inheritance will be ours.'

8 "So they took him and [a]killed *him* and cast *him* out of the vineyard.

9 "Therefore what will the owner of the vineyard do? He will come and destroy the vinedressers, and give the vineyard to others.

10 "Have you not even read this Scripture:

[a]*'The stone which the builders rejected*
*Has become the chief cornerstone.*
11 *This was the LORD's doing,*
*And it is marvelous in our eyes'?*"

12 [a]And they sought to lay hands on Him, but feared the multitude, for they knew He had spoken the parable against them. So they left Him and went away.

**13** [a]Then they sent to Him some of the Pharisees and the Herodians, to catch Him in *His* words.

14 When they had come, they said to Him, "Teacher, we know that You are true, and [1]care about no one; for You do not [2]regard the person of men, but teach the [a]way of God in truth. Is it lawful to pay taxes to Caesar, or not?

15 "Shall we pay, or shall we not pay?" But He, knowing their [a]hypocrisy, said to them, "Why do you test Me? Bring Me a denarius that I may see *it*."

16 So they brought *it*. And He said to them, "Whose image and inscription *is* this?" They said to Him, "Caesar's."

17 And Jesus answered and said to them, [1]"Render to Caesar the things that are Caesar's, and to [a]God the things that are God's." And they marveled at Him.

**18** [a]Then *some* Sadducees, [b]who say there is no resurrection, came to Him; and they asked Him, saying:

19 "Teacher, [a]Moses wrote to us that if a man's brother dies, and leaves *his* wife behind, and leaves no children, his brother should take his wife and raise up offspring for his brother.

20 "Now there were seven brothers. The first took a wife; and dying, he left no offspring.

21 "And the second took her, and he died; nor did he leave any offspring. And the third likewise.

22 "So the seven had her and left no offspring. Last of all the woman died also.

23 "Therefore, in the resurrection, when they rise, whose wife will she be? For all seven had her as wife."

24 Jesus answered and said to them, "Are you not therefore [1]mistaken, because you do not know the Scriptures nor the power of God?

25 "For when they rise from the dead, they neither marry nor are given in marriage, but [a]are like angels in heaven.

26 "But concerning the dead, that they [a]rise, have you not read in the book of Moses, in the *burning* bush *passage,* how God spoke to him, saying, [b]*'I am the God of Abraham, the God of Isaac, and the God of Jacob'*?

27 "He is not the God of the dead, but the God of the living. You are therefore greatly [1]mistaken."

**28** [a]Then one of the scribes came, and having heard them reasoning together, [1]perceiving that He had answered them well, asked Him, "Which is the [2]first commandment of all?"

29 Jesus answered him, "The [1]first of all the commandments *is:* [a]*'Hear, O Israel, the LORD our God, the LORD is one.*

30 *'And you shall* [a]*love the LORD your God with all your heart, with all your soul, with all your mind, and with all your strength.'* [1]This *is* the first commandment.

31 "And the second, like *it, is* this: [a]*'You shall love your neighbor as yourself.'* There is no other commandment greater than [b]these."

32 So the scribe said to Him, "Well *said,* Teacher. You have spoken the truth, for there is one God, [a]and there is no other but He.

33 "And to love Him with all the heart, with all the understanding, [1]with all the soul, and with all the strength, and to love one's neighbor as oneself, [a]is more than all the whole burnt offerings and sacrifices."

34 Now when Jesus saw that he answered wisely, He said to him, "You are not far from the kingdom of God." [a]But after that no one dared question Him.

**35** [a]Then Jesus answered and said, while He taught in the temple, "How *is it* that the scribes say that the Christ is the Son of David?

36 "For David himself said [a]by the Holy Spirit:

[b]*'The LORD said to my Lord,*
*"Sit at My right hand,*
*Till I make Your enemies Your footstool."'*

37 "Therefore David himself calls Him *'Lord'*; how is He *then* his [a]Son?" And the common people heard Him gladly.

**38** Then [a]He said to them in His teaching, [b]"Beware of the scribes, who desire to go around in long robes, [c]*love* greetings in the marketplaces,

39 "the [a]best seats in the synagogues, and the best places at feasts,

40 [a]"who devour widows' houses, and [1]for a pretense make long prayers. These will receive greater condemnation."

**41** [a]Now Jesus sat opposite the treasury and saw how the people put money [b]into the treasury. And many *who were* rich put in much.

42 Then one poor widow came and threw in two [1]mites, which make a [2]quadrans.

43 So He called His disciples to *Himself* and said to them, "Assuredly, I say to you that [a]this poor widow has put in more than all those who have given to the treasury;

44 "for they all put in out of their abundance, but she out of her poverty put in all that she had, [a]her whole livelihood."

### *Jesus Foretells the Destruction of the Temple*

**13** Then [a]as He went out of the temple, one of His disciples said to Him, "Teacher, see what manner of stones and what buildings *are here!*"

2 And Jesus answered and said to him, "Do you see these great buildings? [a]Not *one* stone shall be left upon another, that shall not be thrown down."

**3** Now as He sat on the Mount of Olives opposite the temple, [a]Peter, [b]James, [c]John, and [d]Andrew asked Him privately,

**5** [a]2 Chr. 36:16
**7** [1]*tenant farmers*
**8** [a][Acts 2:23]
**10** [a]Ps. 118:22, 23
**12** [a]John 7:25, 30, 44
**13** [a]Luke 20:20–26
**14** [a]Acts 18:26 [1]Court no man's favor [2]Lit. *look at the face of men*
**15** [a]Luke 12:1
**17** [a][Eccl. 5:4, 5] [1]*Pay*
**18** [a]Luke 20:27–38 [b]Acts 23:8
**19** [a]Deut. 25:5
**24** [1]Or *deceived*
**25** [a][1 Cor. 15:42, 49, 52]
**26** [a][Rev. 20:12, 13] [b]Ex. 3:6, 15
**27** [1]Or *deceived*
**28** [a]Matt. 22:34–40 [1]NU *seeing* [2]*foremost*
**29** [a]Deut. 6:4, 5 [1]*foremost*
**30** [a][Deut. 10:12; 30:6] [1]NU omits the rest of v. 30.
**31** [a]Lev. 19:18 [b][Rom. 13:9]
**32** [a]Deut. 4:39
**33** [a][Hos. 6:6] [1]NU omits *with all the soul*
**34** [a]Matt. 22:46
**35** [a]Luke 20:41–44
**36** [a]2 Sam. 23:2 [b]Ps. 110:1
**37** [a][Acts 2:29–31]
**38** [a]Mark 4:2 [b]Matt. 23:1–7 [c]Matt. 23:7
**39** [a]Luke 14:7
**40** [a]Matt. 23:14 [1]*For appearance' sake*
**41** [a]Luke 21:1–4 [b]2 Kin. 12:9
**42** [1]Gr. *lepta,* very small copper coins [2]A Roman coin
**43** [a][2 Cor. 8:12]
**44** [a]Deut. 24:6

CHAPTER 13
**1** [a]Luke 21:5–36
**2** [a]Luke 19:44
**3** [a]Matt. 16:18 [b]Mark 1:19 [c]Mark 1:19 [d]John 1:40

4 [a]"Tell us, when will these things be? And what
*will be* the sign when all these things will be
fulfilled?"
5 And Jesus, answering them, began to say:
[a]"Take heed that no one deceives you.
6 "For many will come in My name, saying, 'I
am *He,*' and will deceive many.
7 "But when you hear of wars and rumors of
wars, do not be troubled; for *such things* must
happen, but the end *is* not yet.
8 "For nation will rise against nation, and [a]king-
dom against kingdom. And there will be earthquakes in various places, and there will be famines
[1]and troubles. [b]These *are* the beginnings of [2]sor-
rows.
9 "But [a]watch out for yourselves, for they will
deliver you up to councils, and you will be beaten
in the synagogues. You will [1]be brought before
rulers and kings for My sake, for a testimony to
them.
10 "And [a]the gospel must first be preached to all
the nations.
11 [a]"But when they arrest *you* and deliver you
up, do not worry beforehand, [1]or premeditate
what you will speak. But whatever is given you in
that hour, speak that; for it is not you who speak,
[b]but the Holy Spirit.
12 "Now [a]brother will betray brother to death,
and a father *his* child; and children will rise up
against parents and cause them to be put to death.
13 [a]"And you will be hated by all for My name's
sake. But [b]he who [1]endures to the end shall be
saved.
**14** [a]"So when you see the [b]*'abomination of desolation,'* [1]spoken of by Daniel the prophet, standing
where it ought not" (let the reader understand),
"then [c]let those who are in Judea flee to the
mountains.
15 "Let him who is on the housetop not go down
into the house, nor enter to take anything out of
his house.
16 "And let him who is in the field not go back to
get his clothes.
17 [a]"But woe to those who are pregnant and to
those nursing babies in those days!
18 "And pray that your flight may not be in
winter.
19 [a]"For *in* those days there will be tribulation,
such as has not been since the beginning of the
creation which God created until this time, nor
ever shall be.
20 "And unless the Lord had shortened those
days, no flesh would be saved; but for the elect's
sake, whom He chose, He shortened the days.
21 [a]"Then if anyone says to you, 'Look, here *is*
the Christ!' or, 'Look, *He is* there!' do not
believe it.
22 "For false christs and false prophets will rise
and show signs and [a]wonders to deceive, if possible, even the [1]elect.
23 "But [a]take heed; see, I have told you all things
beforehand.
**24** [a]"But in those days, after that tribulation, the
sun will be darkened, and the moon will not give
its light;
25 "the stars of heaven will fall, and the powers
in the heavens will be [a]shaken.
26 [a]"Then they will see the Son of Man coming in
the clouds with great power and glory.
27 "And then He will send His angels, and gather
together His [1]elect from the four winds, from the
farthest part of earth to the farthest part of
heaven.
**28** [a]"Now learn this parable from the fig tree:
When its branch has already become tender, and
puts forth leaves, you know that summer is near.
29 "So you also, when you see these things
happening, know that [1]it is near—at the doors!
30 "Assuredly, I say to you, this generation will
by no means pass away till all these things take
place.
31 "Heaven and earth will pass away, but [a]My
words will by no means pass away.
**32** "But of that day and hour [a]no one knows, not
even the angels in heaven, nor the Son, but only
the [b]Father.
33 [a]"Take heed, watch and pray; for you do not
know when the time is.
34 [a]"*It is* like a man going to a far country, who
left his house and gave [b]authority to his servants,
and to each his work, and commanded the doorkeeper to watch.
35 [a]"Watch therefore, for you do not know when
the master of the house is coming—in the evening, at midnight, at the crowing of the rooster, or
in the morning—
36 "lest, coming suddenly, he find you sleeping.
37 "And what I say to you, I say to all: Watch!"

### *The Beginning of the Lord's Supper*

**14** After [a]two days it was the Passover and [b]*the
Feast* of Unleavened Bread. And the chief
priests and the scribes sought how they might
take Him by [1]trickery and put *Him* to death.
2 But they said, "Not during the feast, lest there
be an uproar of the people."
**3** [a]And being in Bethany at the house of Simon
the leper, as He sat at the table, a woman came
having an alabaster flask of very costly [1]oil of
spikenard. Then she broke the flask and poured *it*
on His head.
4 But there were some who were indignant
among themselves, and said, "Why was this fragrant oil wasted?
5 "For it might have been sold for more than
three hundred [a]denarii and given to the poor."
And they [b]criticized[1] her sharply.
6 But Jesus said, "Let her alone. Why do you
trouble her? She has done a good work for Me.
7 [a]"For you have the poor with you always, and
whenever you wish you may do them good; [b]but
Me you do not have always.
8 "She has done what she could. She has come
beforehand to anoint My body for burial.
9 "Assuredly, I say to you, wherever this gospel
is [a]preached in the whole world, what this woman
has done will also be told as a memorial to her."
**10** [a]Then Judas Iscariot, one of the twelve, went
to the chief priests to betray Him to them.
11 And when they heard *it,* they were glad, and
promised to give him money. So he sought how he
might conveniently betray Him.
**12** [a]Now on the first day of Unleavened Bread,
when they [1]killed the Passover *lamb,* His disciples
said to Him, "Where do You want us to go and
prepare, that You may eat the Passover?"
13 And He sent out two of His disciples and said
to them, "Go into the city, and a man will meet
you carrying a pitcher of water; follow him.
14 "Wherever he goes in, say to the master of the
house, 'The Teacher says, "Where is the guest

**4** [a]Matt. 24:3
**5** [a]Eph. 5:6
**8** [a]Hag. 2:22 [b]Matt. 24:8 [1]NU omits *and troubles* [2]Lit. *birth pangs*
**9** [a]Matt. 10:17, 18; 24:9 [1]NU, M *stand*
**10** [a]Matt. 24:14
**11** [a]Luke 12:11; 21:12–17 [b]Acts 2:4; 4:8, 31 [1]NU omits *or premeditate*
**12** [a]Mic. 7:6
**13** [a]Luke 21:17 [b]Matt. 10:22; 24:13 [1]*bears patiently*
**14** [a]Matt. 24:15 [b]Dan. 9:27; 11:31; 12:11 [c]Luke 21:21 [1]NU omits *spoken of by Daniel the prophet*
**17** [a]Luke 21:23
**19** [a]Dan. 9:26; 12:1
**21** [a]Luke 17:23; 21:8
**22** [a]Rev. 13:13, 14 [1]*chosen ones*
**23** [a][2 Pet. 3:17]
**24** [a]Zeph. 1:15
**25** [a]Is. 13:10; 34:4
**26** [a][Dan. 7:13, 14]
**27** [1]*chosen ones*
**28** [a]Luke 21:29
**29** [1]Or *He*
**31** [a]Is. 40:8
**32** [a]Matt. 25:13 [b]Acts 1:7
**33** [a]1 Thess. 5:6
**34** [a]Matt. 24:45; 25:14 [b][Matt. 16:19]
**35** [a]Matt. 24:42, 44

CHAPTER 14
**1** [a]Luke 22:1, 2 [b]Ex. 12:1–27 [1]*deception*
**3** [a]Luke 7:37 [1]Perfume of pure nard
**5** [a]Matt. 18:28 [b]John 6:61 [1]*scolded*
**7** [a]Deut. 15:11 [b][John 7:33; 8:21; 14:2, 12; 16:10, 17, 28]
**9** [a]Luke 24:47
**10** [a]Matt. 10:2–4
**12** [a]Matt. 26:17–19 [1]*sacrificed*

room in which I may eat the Passover with My disciples?" '

15 "Then he will show you a large upper room, furnished *and* prepared; there make ready for us."

16 So His disciples went out, and came into the city, and found it just as He had said to them; and they prepared the Passover.

17 [a]In the evening He came with the twelve.

18 Now as they sat and ate, Jesus said, "Assuredly, I say to you, [a]one of you who eats with Me will betray Me."

19 And they began to be sorrowful, and to say to Him one by one, "*Is* it I?" [1]And another *said,* "*Is* it I?"

20 He answered and said to them, "*It is* one of the twelve, who dips with Me in the dish.

21 [a]"The Son of Man indeed goes just as it is written of Him, but woe to that man by whom the Son of Man is betrayed! It would have been good for that man if he had never been born."

**22** [a]And as they were eating, Jesus took bread, blessed and broke *it,* and gave *it* to them and said, "Take, [1]eat; this is My [b]body."

23 Then He took the cup, and when He had given thanks He gave *it* to them, and they all drank from it.

24 And He said to them, "This is My blood of the [1]new covenant, which is shed for many.

25 "Assuredly, I say to you, I will no longer drink of the fruit of the vine until that day when I drink it new in the kingdom of God."

26 [a]And when they had sung [1]a hymn, they went out to the Mount of Olives.

**27** [a]Then Jesus said to them, "All of you will be made to stumble [1]because of Me this night, for it is written:

[b]*'I will strike the Shepherd,*
*And the sheep will be scattered.'*

28 "But [a]after I have been raised, I will go before you to Galilee."

29 [a]Peter said to Him, "Even if all are made to [1]stumble, yet I *will* not *be.*"

30 Jesus said to him, "Assuredly, I say to you that today, *even* this night, before the rooster crows twice, you will deny Me three times."

31 But he spoke more vehemently, "If I have to die with You, I will not deny You!" And they all said likewise.

**32** [a]Then they came to a place which was named Gethsemane; and He said to His disciples, "Sit here while I pray."

33 And He [a]took Peter, James, and John with Him, and He began to be troubled and deeply distressed.

34 Then He said to them, [a]"My soul is exceedingly sorrowful, *even* to death. Stay here and watch."

35 He went a little farther, and fell on the ground, and prayed that if it were possible, the hour might pass from Him.

36 And He said, [a]"Abba, Father, [b]all things *are* possible for You. Take this cup away from Me; [c]nevertheless, not what I will, but what You *will.*"

37 Then He came and found them sleeping, and said to Peter, "Simon, are you sleeping? Could you not watch one hour?

38 [a]"Watch and pray, lest you enter into temptation. [b]The spirit indeed *is* willing, but the flesh *is* weak."

39 Again He went away and prayed, and spoke the same words.

40 And when He returned, He found them asleep again, for their eyes were heavy; and they did not know what to answer Him.

41 Then He came the third time and said to them, "Are you still sleeping and resting? It is enough! [a]The hour has come; behold, the Son of Man is being betrayed into the hands of sinners.

42 [a]"Rise, let us be going. See, My betrayer is at hand."

**43** [a]And immediately, while He was still speaking, Judas, one of the twelve, with a great multitude with swords and clubs, came from the chief priests and the scribes and the elders.

44 Now His betrayer had given them a signal, saying, "Whomever I [a]kiss, He is the One; seize Him and lead *Him* away safely."

45 As soon as He had come, immediately he went up to Him and said to Him, "Rabbi, Rabbi!" and kissed Him.

46 Then they laid their hands on Him and took Him.

47 And one of those who stood by drew his sword and struck the servant of the high priest, and cut off his ear.

48 [a]Then Jesus answered and said to them, "Have you come out, as against a robber, with swords and clubs to take Me?

49 "I was daily with you in the temple [a]teaching, and you did not seize Me. But [b]the Scriptures must be fulfilled."

50 [a]Then they all forsook Him and fled.

**51** Now a certain young man followed Him, having a linen cloth thrown around *his* naked *body.* And the young men laid hold of him,

52 and he left the linen cloth and fled from them naked.

**53** [a]And they led Jesus away to the high priest; and with him were [b]assembled all the [c]chief priests, the elders, and the scribes.

54 But [a]Peter followed Him at a distance, right into the courtyard of the high priest. And he sat with the servants and warmed himself at the fire.

55 [a]Now the chief priests and all the council sought testimony against Jesus to put Him to death, but found none.

56 For many bore [a]false witness against Him, but their testimonies [1]did not agree.

57 Then some rose up and bore false witness against Him, saying,

58 "We heard Him say, [a]'I will destroy this temple made with hands, and within three days I will build another made without hands.' "

59 But not even then did their testimony agree.

60 [a]And the high priest stood up in the midst and asked Jesus, saying, "Do You answer nothing? What *is it* these men testify against You?"

61 But [a]He kept silent and answered nothing. [b]Again the high priest asked Him, saying to Him, "Are You the Christ, the Son of the Blessed?"

62 Jesus said, "I am. [a]And you will see the Son of Man sitting at the right hand of the Power, and coming with the clouds of heaven."

63 Then the high priest tore his clothes and said, "What further need do we have of witnesses?

64 "You have heard the [a]blasphemy! What do you think?" And they all condemned Him to be deserving of [b]death.

65 Then some began to [a]spit on Him, and to blindfold Him, and to beat Him, and to say to Him,

**17** [a]Matt. 26:20–24
**18** [a]John 6:70, 71; 13:18
**19** [1]NU omits the rest of v. 19.
**21** [a]Luke 22:22
**22** [a]1 Cor. 11:23–25 [b][1 Pet. 2:24] [1]NU omits *eat*
**24** [1]NU omits *new*
**26** [a]Matt. 26:30 [1]Or *hymns*
**27** [a]Matt. 26:31–35 [b]Zech. 13:7 [1]NU omits *because of Me this night*
**28** [a]Mark 16:7
**29** [a]John 13:37, 38 [1]*fall away*
**32** [a]Luke 22:40–46
**33** [a]Mark 5:37; 9:2; 13:3
**34** [a]John 12:27
**36** [a]Gal. 4:6 [b][Heb. 5:7] [c]John 5:30; 6:38
**38** [a]Luke 21:36 [b][Rom. 7:18, 21–24]
**41** [a]John 13:1; 17:1
**42** [a]John 13:21; 18:1, 2
**43** [a]Luke 22:47–53
**44** [a][Prov. 27:6]
**48** [a]Matt. 26:55
**49** [a]Matt. 21:23 [b]Is. 53:7
**50** [a]Ps. 88:8
**53** [a]Matt. 26:57–68 [b]Mark 15:1 [c]John 7:32; 18:3; 19:6
**54** [a]John 18:15
**55** [a]Matt. 26:59
**56** [a]Ex. 20:16 [1]*were not consistent*
**58** [a]John 2:19
**60** [a]Matt. 26:62
**61** [a]Is. 53:7 [b]Luke 22:67–71
**62** [a]Luke 22:69
**64** [a]John 10:33, 36 [b]John 19:7
**65** [a]Is. 50:6; 52:14

"Prophesy!" And the officers [1]struck Him with the
palms of their hands.
**66** [a]Now as Peter was below in the courtyard, one
of the servant girls of the high priest came.
67 And when she saw Peter warming himself, she
looked at him and said, "You also were with
[a]Jesus of Nazareth."
68 But he denied it, saying, "I neither know nor
understand what you are saying." And he went
out on the porch, and a rooster crowed.
69 [a]And the servant girl saw him again, and
began to say to those who stood by, "This is one
of them."
70 But he denied it again. [a]And a little later those
who stood by said to Peter again, "Surely you are
*one* of them; [b]for you are a Galilean, [1]and your
[2]speech shows *it*."
71 Then he began to curse and swear, "I do not
know this Man of whom you speak!"
72 [a]A second time *the* rooster crowed. Then Peter
called to mind the word that Jesus had said to
him, "Before the rooster crows twice, you will
deny Me three times." And when he thought
about it, he wept.

### *Jesus Is Tried and Crucified*

**15** Immediately, [a]in the morning, the chief
priests held a consultation with the elders
and scribes and the whole council; and they
bound Jesus, led *Him* away, and [b]delivered *Him* to
Pilate.
2 [a]Then Pilate asked Him, "Are You the King of
the Jews?" He answered and said to him, "*It is as
you say.*"
3 And the chief priests accused Him of many
things, but He [a]answered nothing.
4 [a]Then Pilate asked Him again, saying, "Do
You answer nothing? See how many things [1]they
testify against You!"
5 [a]But Jesus still answered nothing, so that
Pilate marveled.
**6** Now [a]at the feast he was accustomed to releasing one prisoner to them, whomever they
requested.
7 And there was one named Barabbas, *who was*
chained with his fellow rebels; they had committed murder in the rebellion.
8 Then the multitude, [1]crying aloud, began to
ask *him to do* just as he had always done for them.
9 But Pilate answered them, saying, "Do you
want me to release to you the King of the Jews?"
10 For he knew that the chief priests had handed
Him over because of envy.
11 But [a]the chief priests stirred up the crowd, so
that he should rather release Barabbas to them.
12 Pilate answered and said to them again,
"What then do you want me to do *with Him*
whom you call the [a]King of the Jews?"
13 So they cried out again, "Crucify Him!"
14 Then Pilate said to them, "Why, [a]what evil has
He done?" But they cried out all the more, "Crucify Him!"
15 [a]So Pilate, wanting to gratify the crowd, released Barabbas to them; and he delivered Jesus,
after he had scourged *Him*, to be [b]crucified.
**16** [a]Then the soldiers led Him away into the hall
called [1]Praetorium, and they called together the
whole garrison.
17 And they clothed Him with purple; and they
twisted a crown of thorns, put it on His *head*,
18 and began to salute Him, "Hail, King of the
Jews!"
19 Then they [a]struck Him on the head with a
reed and spat on Him; and bowing the knee, they
worshiped Him.
20 And when they had [a]mocked Him, they took
the purple off Him, put His own clothes on Him,
and led Him out to crucify Him.
**21** [a]Then they compelled a certain man, Simon a
Cyrenian, the father of Alexander and Rufus, as
he was coming out of the country and passing by,
to bear His cross.
22 [a]And they brought Him to the place Golgotha,
which is translated, Place of a Skull.
23 [a]Then they gave Him wine mingled with
myrrh to drink, but He did not take *it*.
24 And when they crucified Him, [a]they divided
His garments, casting lots for them to determine
what every man should take.
25 Now [a]it was the third hour, and they crucified
Him.
26 And [a]the inscription of His [1]accusation was
written above:

THE KING OF THE JEWS.

27 [a]With Him they also crucified two robbers, one
on His right and the other on His left.
28 [1]So the Scripture was fulfilled which says,
[a]*"And He was numbered with the transgressors."*
29 And [a]those who passed by blasphemed Him,
[b]wagging their heads and saying, "Aha! [c]*You* who
destroy the temple and build *it* in three days,
30 "save Yourself, and come down from the
cross!"
31 Likewise the chief priests also, [a]mocking
among themselves with the scribes, said, "He
saved [b]others; Himself He cannot save.
32 "Let the Christ, the King of Israel, descend
now from the cross, that we may see and [1]be-
lieve." Even [a]those who were crucified with Him
reviled Him.
**33** Now [a]when the sixth hour had come, there
was darkness over the whole land until the ninth
hour.
34 And at the ninth hour Jesus cried out with a
loud voice, saying, "Eloi, Eloi, lama sabachthani?"
which is translated, [a]*"My God, My God, why have
You forsaken Me?"*
35 Some of those who stood by, when they heard
*that*, said, "Look, He is calling for Elijah!"
36 Then [a]someone ran and filled a sponge full of
sour wine, put *it* on a reed, and [b]offered *it* to Him
to drink, saying, "Let Him alone; let us see if
Elijah will come to take Him down."
37 [a]And Jesus cried out with a loud voice, and
breathed His last.
38 Then [a]the veil of the temple was torn in two
from top to bottom.
39 So [a]when the centurion, who stood opposite
Him, saw that [1]He cried out like this and breathed
His last, he said, "Truly this Man was the Son of
God!"
40 [a]There were also women looking on [b]from
afar, among whom were Mary Magdalene, Mary
the mother of James the Less and of Joses, and
Salome,
41 who also [a]followed Him and ministered to Him
when He was in Galilee, and many other women
who came up with Him to Jerusalem.
**42** [a]Now when evening had come, because it was
the Preparation Day, that is, the day before the
Sabbath,
43 Joseph of Arimathea, a prominent council
member, who [a]was himself waiting for the

**65** [1]NU *received Him with slaps*
**66** [a]John 18:16–18, 25–27
**67** [a]John 1:45
**69** [a]Matt. 26:71
**70** [a]Luke 22:59 [b]Acts 2:7 [1]NU omits the rest of v. 70. [2]*accent*
**72** [a]Matt. 26:75

CHAPTER 15
**1** [a]Ps. 2:2 [b]Acts 3:13
**2** [a]Matt. 27:11–14
**3** [a]John 19:9
**4** [a]Matt. 27:13 [1]NU *of which they accuse You*
**5** [a]Is. 53:7
**6** [a]Matt. 27:15–26
**8** [1]NU *going up*
**11** [a]Acts 3:14
**12** [a]Mic. 5:2
**14** [a]1 Pet. 2:21–23
**15** [a]Matt. 27:26 [b][Is. 53:8]
**16** [a]Matt. 27:27–31 [1]The governor's headquarters
**19** [a][Is. 50:6; 52:14; 53:5]
**20** [a]Luke 22:63; 23:11
**21** [a]Matt. 27:32
**22** [a]John 19:17–24
**23** [a]Matt. 27:34
**24** [a]Ps. 22:18
**25** [a]John 19:14
**26** [a]Matt. 27:37 [1]*crime*
**27** [a]Luke 22:37
**28** [a]Is. 53:12 [1]NU omits v. 28.
**29** [a]Ps. 22:6, 7; 69:7 [b]Ps. 109:25 [c]John 2:19–21
**31** [a]Luke 18:32 [b]John 11:43, 44
**32** [a]Matt. 27:44 [1]M *believe Him*
**33** [a]Luke 23:44–49
**34** [a]Ps. 22:1
**36** [a]John 19:29 [b]Ps. 69:21
**37** [a]Matt. 27:50
**38** [a]Ex. 26:31–33
**39** [a]Luke 23:47 [1]NU *He thus breathed His last*
**40** [a]Matt. 27:55 [b]Ps. 38:11
**41** [a]Luke 8:2, 3
**42** [a]John 19:38–42
**43** [a]Luke 2:25, 38; 23:51

kingdom of God, coming and taking courage,
went in to Pilate and asked for the body of Jesus.
44 Pilate marveled that He was already dead; and
summoning the centurion, he asked him if He had
been dead for some time.
45 So when he found out from the centurion, he
granted the body to Joseph.
46 [a]Then he bought fine linen, took Him down,
and wrapped Him in the linen. And he laid Him in
a tomb which had been hewn out of the rock, and
rolled a stone against the door of the tomb.
47 And Mary Magdalene and Mary *the mother* of
Joses observed where He was laid.

### *The Risen and Ascended Christ*

**16** Now [a]when the Sabbath was past, Mary
Magdalene, Mary *the mother* of James, and
Salome [b]bought spices, that they might come and
anoint Him.
2 [a]Very early in the morning, on the first *day* of
the week, they came to the tomb when the sun
had risen.
3 And they said among themselves, "Who will
roll away the stone from the door of the tomb for
us?"
4 But when they looked up, they saw that the
stone had been rolled away—for it was very large.
5 [a]And entering the tomb, they saw a young
man clothed in a long white robe sitting on the
right side; and they were alarmed.
6 [a]But he said to them, "Do not be alarmed. You
seek Jesus of Nazareth, who was crucified. He is
risen! He is not here. See the place where they laid
Him.
7 "But go, tell His disciples—and Peter—that He
is going [1]before you into Galilee; there you will see
Him, [a]as He said to you."
8 So they went out [1]quickly and fled from the

**46** [a]Matt. 27:59, 60

CHAPTER 16
**1** [a]John 20:1–8 [b]Luke 23:56
**2** [a]Luke 24:1
**5** [a]John 20:11, 12
**6** [a]Matt. 28:6
**7** [a]Matt. 26:32; 28:16, 17 [1]*ahead of*
**8** [a]Matt. 28:8 [1]NU, M omit *quickly*
**9** [a]Luke 8:2 [1]Vv. 9–20 are bracketed in NU as not in the original text. They are lacking in Codex Sinaiticus and Codex Vaticanus, although nearly all other mss. of Mark contain them.
**10** [a]Luke 24:10
**11** [a]Luke 24:11, 41
**12** [a]Luke 24:13–35
**14** [a]1 Cor. 15:5
**15** [a]Matt. 28:19 [b][Col. 1:23]
**16** [a][John 3:18, 36] [b][John 12:48]
**17** [a]Acts 5:12 [b]Luke 10:17 [c][Acts 2:4] [1]*have believed*
**18** [a]Acts 28:3–6 [b]James 5:14 [1]NU *and in their hands they will*

tomb, for they trembled and were amazed. [a]And
they said nothing to anyone, for they were afraid.
**9** [1]Now when *He* rose early on the first *day* of
the week, He appeared first to Mary Magdalene,
[a]out of whom He had cast seven demons.
10 [a]She went and told those who had been with
Him, as they mourned and wept.
11 [a]And when they heard that He was alive and
had been seen by her, they did not believe.
**12** After that, He appeared in another form [a]to
two of them as they walked and went into the
country.
13 And they went and told *it* to the rest, *but* they
did not believe them either.
**14** [a]Later He appeared to the eleven as they sat at
the table; and He rebuked their unbelief and
hardness of heart, because they did not believe
those who had seen Him after He had risen.
15 [a]And He said to them, "Go into all the world
[b]and preach the gospel to every creature.
16 [a]"He who believes and is baptized will be
saved; [b]but he who does not believe will be condemned.
17 "And these [a]signs will follow those who [1]believe: [b]In My name they will cast out demons;
[c]they will speak with new tongues;
18 [a]"they[1] will take up serpents; and if they drink
anything deadly, it will by no means hurt them;
[b]they will lay hands on the sick, and they will
recover."
**19** So then, [a]after the Lord had spoken to them,
He was [b]received up into heaven, and [c]sat down at
the right hand of God.
20 And they went out and preached everywhere,
the Lord working with *them* [a]and confirming the
word through the accompanying signs. Amen.

**19** [a]Acts 1:2, 3 [b]Luke 9:51; 24:51 [c][Ps. 110:1]
**20** [a][Heb. 2:4]

*The Gospel According to*

# LUKE

### *John the Baptist Is Born*

**I**NASMUCH as many have taken in hand to set
in order a narrative of those [a]things which
[1]have been fulfilled among us,
2 just as those who [a]from the beginning were
[b]eyewitnesses and ministers of the word [c]delivered
them to us,
3 it seemed good to me also, having [1]had perfect
understanding of all things from the very first, to
write to you an orderly account, [a]most excellent
Theophilus,
4 [a]that you may know the certainty of those
things in which you were instructed.
**5** There was [a]in the days of Herod, the king of
Judea, a certain priest named Zacharias, [b]of the
division of [c]Abijah. His [d]wife *was* of the daughters
of Aaron, and her name *was* Elizabeth.
6 And they were both righteous before God,
walking in all the commandments and ordinances
of the Lord blameless.
7 But they had no child, because Elizabeth was
barren, and they were both well advanced in
years.

CHAPTER 1
**1** [a]John 20:31 [1]Or *are most surely believed*
**2** [a]Acts 1:21, 22 [b]Acts 1:2 [c]Heb. 2:3
**3** [a]Acts 1:1 [1]Lit. *accurately followed*
**4** [a][John 20:31]
**5** [a]Matt. 2:1 [b]1 Chr. 24:1, 10 [c]Neh. 12:4 [d]Lev. 21:13, 14
**9** [a]Ex. 30:7, 8 [1]*he was chosen by lot*
**10** [a]Lev. 16:17
**11** [a]Ex. 30:1
**12** [a]Luke 2:9
**13** [a]Luke 1:57, 60, 63
**14** [a]Luke 1:58
**15** [a][Luke 7:24–28] [b]Num. 6:3 [c]Jer. 1:5

8 So it was, that while he was serving as priest
before God in the order of his division,
9 according to the custom of the priesthood, [1]his
lot fell [a]to burn incense when he went into the
temple of the Lord.
10 [a]And the whole multitude of the people was
praying outside at the hour of incense.
11 Then an angel of the Lord appeared to him,
standing on the right side of [a]the altar of incense.
12 And when Zacharias saw *him*, [a]he was troubled, and fear fell upon him.
13 But the angel said to him, "Do not be afraid,
Zacharias, for your prayer is heard; and your wife
Elizabeth will bear you a son, and [a]you shall call
his name John.
14 "And you will have joy and gladness, and
[a]many will rejoice at his birth.
15 "For he will be [a]great in the sight of the Lord,
and [b]shall drink neither wine nor strong drink. He
will also be filled with the Holy Spirit, [c]even from
his mother's womb.
16 "And he will turn many of the children of
Israel to the Lord their God.

17 [a]"He will also go before Him in the spirit and
power of Elijah, [b]*'to turn the hearts of the fathers
to the children,'* and the disobedient to the wisdom of the just, to make ready a people prepared
for the Lord."
18 And Zacharias said to the angel, [a]"How shall I
know this? For I am an old man, and my wife is
well advanced in years."
19 And the angel answered and said to him, "I
am [a]Gabriel, who stands in the presence of God,
and was sent to speak to you and bring you [1]these
glad [b]tidings.
20 "But behold, [a]you will be mute and not able to
speak until the day these things take place, because you did not believe my words which will be
fulfilled in their own time."
21 And the people waited for Zacharias, and
marveled that he lingered so long in the temple.
22 But when he came out, he could not speak to
them; and they perceived that he had seen a
vision in the temple, for he beckoned to them and
remained speechless.
23 So it was, as soon as [a]the days of his service
were completed, that he departed to his own
house.
24 Now after those days his wife Elizabeth conceived; and she hid herself five months, saying,
25 "Thus the Lord has dealt with me, in the days
when He looked on *me,* to [a]take away my reproach among people."
**26** Now in the sixth month the angel Gabriel was
sent by God to a city of Galilee named Nazareth,
27 to a virgin [a]betrothed to a man whose name
was Joseph, of the house of David. The virgin's
name *was* Mary.
28 And having come in, the angel said to her,
[a]"Rejoice, highly favored *one,* [b]the Lord *is* with
you; [1]blessed *are* you among women!"
29 But [1]when she saw *him,* [a]she was troubled at
his saying, and considered what manner of greeting this was.
30 Then the angel said to her, "Do not be afraid,
Mary, for you have found [a]favor with God.
31 [a]"And behold, you will conceive in your womb
and bring forth a Son, and [b]shall call His name
JESUS.
32 "He will be great, [a]and will be called the Son of
the Highest; and [b]the Lord God will give Him the
[c]throne of His [d]father David.
33 [a]"And He will reign over the house of Jacob
forever, and of His kingdom there will be no end."
34 Then Mary said to the angel, "How can this
be, since I [1]do not know a man?"
35 And the angel answered and said to her, [a]"*The*
Holy Spirit will come upon you, and the power of
the Highest will overshadow you; therefore, also,
that Holy One who is to be born will be called [b]the
Son of God.
36 "Now indeed, Elizabeth your relative has also
conceived a son in her old age; and this is now the
sixth month for her who was called barren.
37 "For [a]with God nothing will be impossible."
38 Then Mary said, "Behold the maidservant of
the Lord! Let it be to me according to your word."
And the angel departed from her.
**39** Now Mary arose in those days and went into
the hill country with haste, [a]to a city of Judah,
40 and entered the house of Zacharias and
greeted Elizabeth.
41 And it happened, when Elizabeth heard the
greeting of Mary, that the babe leaped in her
womb; and Elizabeth was [a]filled with the Holy
Spirit.
42 Then she spoke out with a loud voice and said,
[a]"Blessed *are* you among women, and blessed *is*
the fruit of your womb!
43 "But why *is* this *granted* to me, that the
mother of my Lord should come to me?
44 "For indeed, as soon as the voice of your
greeting sounded in my ears, the babe leaped in
my womb for joy.
45 [a]"Blessed *is* she who [1]believed, for there will be
a fulfillment of those things which were told her
from the Lord."
**46** And Mary said:

[a]"My soul [1]magnifies the Lord,
47 And my spirit has [a]rejoiced
in [b]God my Savior.
48 For [a]He has regarded the lowly state
of His maidservant;
For behold, henceforth [b]all generations will
call me blessed.
49 For He who is mighty [a]has done
great things for me,
And [b]holy *is* His name.
50 And [a]His mercy *is* on those who fear Him
From generation to generation.
51 [a]He has shown strength with His arm;
[b]He has scattered *the* proud in the
imagination of their hearts.
52 [a]He has put down the mighty
from *their* thrones,
And exalted *the* lowly.
53 He has [a]filled *the* hungry with good things,
And *the* rich He has sent away empty.
54 He has helped His [a]servant Israel,
[b]In remembrance of *His* mercy,
55 [a]As He spoke to our [b]fathers,
To Abraham and to his [c]seed forever."

56 And Mary remained with her about three
months, and returned to her house.
**57** Now Elizabeth's full time came for her to be
delivered, and she brought forth a son.
58 When her neighbors and relatives heard how
the Lord had shown great mercy to her, they
[a]rejoiced with her.
**59** So it was, [a]on the eighth day, that they came
to circumcise the child; and they would have
called him by the name of his father, Zacharias.
60 His mother answered and said, [a]"No; he shall
be called John."
61 But they said to her, "There is no one among
your relatives who is called by this name."
62 So they made signs to his father—what he
would have him called.
63 And he asked for a writing tablet, and wrote,
saying, "His name is John." So they all marveled.
64 Immediately his mouth was opened and his
tongue *loosed,* and he spoke, praising God.
65 Then fear came on all who dwelt around them;
and all these sayings were discussed throughout
all the hill country of Judea.
66 And all those who heard *them* [a]kept *them* in
their hearts, saying, "What kind of child will this
be?" And [b]the hand of the Lord was with him.
**67** Now his father Zacharias [a]was filled with the
Holy Spirit, and prophesied, saying:

68 "Blessed[a] *is* the Lord God of Israel,
For [b]He has visited and redeemed His people,
69 [a]And has raised up a horn of salvation for us
In the house of His servant David,

**17** [a]Mal. 4:5, 6; Matt. 3:2; 11:14
**18** [a]Gen. 17:17
**19** [a]Dan. 8:16 [b]Luke 2:10 [1]*this good news*
**20** [a]Ezek. 3:26; 24:27
**23** [a]2 Kin. 11:5
**25** [a]Gen. 30:23
**27** [a]Matt. 1:18
**28** [a]Dan. 9:23 [b]Judg. 6:12 [1]NU omits *blessed are you among women*
**29** [a]Luke 1:12 [1]NU omits *when she saw him*
**30** [a]Luke 2:52
**31** [a]Is. 7:14 [b]Luke 2:21
**32** [a]Mark 5:7 [b]2 Sam. 7:12, 13, 16 [c]2 Sam. 7:14–17 [d]Matt. 1:1
**33** [a][Dan. 2:44]
**34** [1]Am a virgin
**35** [a]Matt. 1:20 [b][Heb. 1:2, 8]
**37** [a]Jer. 32:17
**39** [a]Josh. 21:9
**41** [a]Acts 6:3
**42** [a]Judg. 5:24
**45** [a]John 20:29 [1]Or *believed that there*
**46** [a]1 Sam. 2:1–10 [1]Declares the greatness of
**47** [a]Hab. 3:18 [b]1 Tim. 1:1; 2:3
**48** [a]Ps. 138:6 [b]Luke 11:27
**49** [a]Ps. 71:19; 126:2, 3 [b]Ps. 111:9
**50** [a]Ps. 103:17
**51** [a]Ps. 98:1; 118:15 [b][1 Pet. 5:5]
**52** [a]1 Sam. 2:7, 8
**53** [a][Matt. 5:6]
**54** [a]Is. 41:8 [b][Jer. 31:3]
**55** [a]Gen. 17:19 [b][Rom. 11:28] [c]Gen. 17:7
**58** [a][Rom. 12:15]
**59** [a]Gen. 17:12
**60** [a]Luke 1:13, 63
**66** [a]Luke 2:19 [b]Acts 11:21
**67** [a]Joel 2:28
**68** [a]1 Kin. 1:48 [b]Ex. 3:16
**69** [a]Ps. 132:17

70 [a]As He spoke by the mouth of His holy
prophets,
Who *have been* [b]since the world began,
71 That we should be saved from our enemies
And from the hand of all who hate us,
72 [a]To perform the mercy *promised* to our
fathers
And to remember His holy covenant,
73 [a]The oath which He swore to our father
Abraham:
74 To grant us that we,
Being delivered from the hand of our
enemies,
Might [a]serve Him without fear,
75 [a]In holiness and righteousness before Him all
the days of our life.

76 And you, child, will be called the [a]prophet of
the Highest;
For [b]you will go before the face of the Lord
to prepare His ways,
77 To give [a]knowledge of salvation to His people
By the remission of their sins,
78 Through the tender mercy of our God,
With which the [1]Dayspring from on high [2]has
visited us;
79 [a]To give light to those who sit in darkness
and the shadow of death,
To [b]guide our feet into the way of peace."

80 So [a]the child grew and became strong in spirit,
and [b]was in the deserts till the day of his manifestation to Israel.

### *The Birth and Childhood of Jesus*

**2** And it came to pass in those days *that* a
decree went out from Caesar Augustus that all
the world should be registered.
2 [a]This census first took place while Quirinius
was governing Syria.
3 So all went to be registered, everyone to his
own city.
4 Joseph also went up from Galilee, out of the
city of Nazareth, into Judea, to [a]the city of David,
which is called Bethlehem, [b]because he was of the
house and lineage of David,
5 to be registered with Mary, [a]his betrothed
[1]wife, who was with child.
6 So it was, that while they were there, the days
were completed for her to be delivered.
7 And [a]she brought forth her firstborn Son, and
wrapped Him in swaddling cloths, and laid Him in
a [1]manger, because there was no room for them in
the inn.
**8** Now there were in the same country shepherds living out in the fields, keeping watch over
their flock by night.
9 And [1]behold, an angel of the Lord stood before
them, and the glory of the Lord shone around
them, [a]and they were greatly afraid.
10 Then the angel said to them, [a]"Do not be
afraid, for behold, I bring you good tidings of
great joy [b]which will be to all people.
11 [a]"For there is born to you this day in the city
of David [b]a Savior, [c]who is Christ the Lord.
12 "And this *will be* the sign to you: You will find
a Babe wrapped in swaddling cloths, lying in a
[1]manger."
13 [a]And suddenly there was with the angel a
multitude of the heavenly host praising God and
saying:

14 "Glory[a] to God in the highest,
And on earth [b]peace,
[c]goodwill[1] toward men!"

15 So it was, when the angels had gone away
from them into heaven, that the shepherds said to
one another, "Let us now go to Bethlehem and see
this thing that has come to pass, which the Lord
has made known to us."
16 And they came with haste and found Mary
and Joseph, and the Babe lying in a manger.
17 Now when they had seen *Him*, they made
[1]widely known the saying which was told them
concerning this Child.
18 And all those who heard *it* marveled at those
things which were told them by the shepherds.
19 [a]But Mary kept all these things and pondered
*them* in her heart.
20 Then the shepherds returned, glorifying and
[a]praising God for all the things that they had
heard and seen, as it was told them.
**21** [a]And when eight days were completed [1]for the
circumcision of the Child, His name was called
[b]JESUS, the name given by the angel [c]before He
was conceived in the womb.
**22** Now when [a]the days of her purification according to the law of Moses were completed, they
brought Him to Jerusalem to present *Him* to the
Lord
23 [a](as it is written in the law of the Lord, [b]*"Every
male who opens the womb shall be called holy to
the LORD"*),
24 and to offer a sacrifice according to what is
said in the law of the Lord, [a]*"A pair of turtledoves
or two young pigeons."*
**25** And behold, there was a man in Jerusalem
whose name was Simeon, and this man was just
and devout, [a]waiting for the Consolation of Israel,
and the Holy Spirit was upon him.
26 And it had been revealed to him by the Holy
Spirit that he would not [a]see death before he had
seen the Lord's Christ.
27 So he came [a]by the Spirit into the temple. And
when the parents brought in the Child Jesus, to do
for Him according to the custom of the law,
28 he took Him up in his arms and blessed God
and said:

29 "Lord, [a]now You are letting Your servant
depart in peace,
According to Your word;
30 For my eyes [a]have seen Your salvation
31 Which You have prepared before the face of
all peoples,
32 [a]A light to *bring* revelation to the Gentiles,
And the glory of Your people Israel."

33 [1]And Joseph and His mother marveled at those
things which were spoken of Him.
34 Then Simeon blessed them, and said to Mary
His mother, "Behold, this *Child* is destined for the
[a]fall and rising of many in Israel, and for [b]a sign
which will be spoken against
35 (yes, [a]a sword will pierce through your own
soul also), that the thoughts of many hearts may
be revealed."
**36** Now there was one, Anna, a prophetess, the
daughter of Phanuel, of the tribe of [a]Asher. She
was of a great age, and had lived with a husband
seven years from her virginity;
37 and this woman *was* a widow [1]of about eighty-
four years, who did not depart from the temple,

**70** [a]Rom. 1:2 [b]Acts 3:21
**72** [a]Lev. 26:42
**73** [a]Gen. 12:3; 22:16–18
**74** [a][Heb. 9:14]
**75** [a][Eph. 4:24]
**76** [a]Matt. 3:3; 11:9 [b]Is. 40:3
**77** [a][Mark 1:4]
**78** [1]Lit. *Dawn;* the Messiah [2]NU *shall visit*
**79** [a]Is. 9:2 [b][John 10:4; 14:27; 16:33]
**80** [a]Luke 2:40 [b]Matt. 3:1

CHAPTER 2
**2** [a]Acts 5:37
**4** [a]1 Sam. 16:1 [b]Matt. 1:16
**5** [a][Matt. 1:18] [1]NU omits *wife*
**7** [a]Matt. 1:25 [1]*feed trough*
**9** [a]Luke 1:12 [1]NU omits *behold*
**10** [a]Luke 1:13, 30 [b]Gen. 12:3
**11** [a]Is. 9:6 [b]Matt. 1:21 [c]Acts 2:36
**12** [1]*feed trough*
**13** [a]Dan. 7:10
**14** [a]Luke 19:38 [b]Is. 57:19 [c][Eph. 2:4, 7] [1]NU *toward men of goodwill*
**17** [1]NU omits *widely*
**19** [a]Gen. 37:11
**20** [a]Luke 19:37
**21** [a]Lev. 12:3 [b][Matt. 1:21] [c]Luke 1:31 [1]NU *for His circumcision*
**22** [a]Lev. 12:2–8
**23** [a]Deut. 18:4 [b]Ex. 13:2, 12, 15
**24** [a]Lev. 12:2, 8
**25** [a]Mark 15:43
**26** [a][Heb. 11:5]
**27** [a]Matt. 4:1
**29** [a]Gen. 46:30
**30** [a][Is. 52:10]
**32** [a]Acts 10:45; 13:47; 28:28
**33** [1]NU *And His father and mother*
**34** [a][1 Pet. 2:7, 8] [b]Acts 4:2; 17:32; 28:22
**35** [a]Ps. 42:10
**36** [a]Josh. 19:24
**37** [1]NU *until she was eighty-four*

but served *God* with fastings and prayers [a]night
and day.
38 And coming in that instant she gave thanks to
[1]the Lord, and spoke of Him to all those who
[a]looked for redemption in Jerusalem.
**39** So when they had performed all things according to the law of the Lord, they returned to
Galilee, to their *own* city, Nazareth.
40 [a]And the Child grew and became strong [1]in
spirit, filled with wisdom; and the grace of God
was upon Him.
**41** His parents went to [a]Jerusalem [b]every year at
the Feast of the Passover.
42 And when He was twelve years old, they went
up to Jerusalem according to the [a]custom of the
feast.
43 When they had finished the [a]days, as they
returned, the Boy Jesus lingered behind in Jerusalem. And [1]Joseph and His mother did not know *it;*
44 but supposing Him to have been in the company, they went a day's journey, and sought Him
among *their* relatives and acquaintances.
45 So when they did not find Him, they returned
to Jerusalem, seeking Him.
46 Now so it was *that* after three days they found
Him in the temple, sitting in the midst of the
teachers, both listening to them and asking them
questions.
47 And [a]all who heard Him were astonished at
His understanding and answers.
48 So when they saw Him, they were amazed;
and His mother said to Him, "Son, why have You
done this to us? Look, Your father and I have
sought You anxiously."
49 And He said to them, "Why did you seek Me?
Did you not know that I must be [a]about [b]My
Father's business?"
50 But [a]they did not understand the statement
which He spoke to them.
**51** Then He went down with them and came to
Nazareth, and was [1]subject to them, but His
mother [a]kept all these things in her heart.
52 And Jesus [a]increased in wisdom and stature,
[b]and in favor with God and men.

### *John the Baptist Prepares the Way*

**3** Now in the fifteenth year of the reign of
Tiberius Caesar, [a]Pontius Pilate being governor of Judea, Herod being tetrarch of Galilee, his
brother Philip tetrarch of Iturea and the region of
Trachonitis, and Lysanias tetrarch of Abilene,
2 [1]while [a]Annas and Caiaphas were high priests,
the word of God came to [b]John the son of Zacharias in the wilderness.
3 [a]And he went into all the region around the
Jordan, preaching a baptism of repentance [b]for
the remission of sins,
4 as it is written in the book of the words of
Isaiah the prophet, saying:

[a]*"The voice of one crying in the wilderness:*
*'Prepare the way of the LORD;*
*Make His paths straight.*
5 *Every valley shall be filled*
*And every mountain and hill brought low;*
*The crooked places shall be made straight*
*And the rough ways smooth;*
6 *And [a]all flesh shall see the salvation*
*of God.'"*

**7** Then he said to the multitudes that came out
to be baptized by him, [a]"Brood[1] of vipers! Who
warned you to flee from the wrath to come?
8 "Therefore bear fruits [a]worthy of repentance,
and do not begin to say to yourselves, 'We have
Abraham as *our* father.' For I say to you that God
is able to raise up children to Abraham from these
stones.
9 "And even now the ax is laid to the root of the
trees. Therefore [a]every tree which does not bear
good fruit is cut down and thrown into the fire."
10 So the people asked him, saying, [a]"What shall
we do then?"
11 He answered and said to them, [a]"He who has
two tunics, let him give to him who has none; and
he who has food, [b]let him do likewise."
12 Then [a]tax collectors also came to be baptized,
and said to him, "Teacher, what shall we do?"
13 And he said to them, [a]"Collect no more than
what is appointed for you."
14 Likewise the soldiers asked him, saying, "And
what shall we do?" So he said to them, "Do not
[1]intimidate anyone [a]or accuse falsely, and be
content with your wages."
15 Now as the people were in expectation, and all
reasoned in their hearts about John, whether he
was the Christ *or* not,
16 John answered, saying to all, [a]"I indeed baptize you with water; but One mightier than I is
coming, whose sandal strap I am not worthy to
loose. He will [b]baptize you with the Holy Spirit
and fire.
17 "His winnowing fan *is* in His hand, and He will
thoroughly clean out His threshing floor, and
[a]gather the wheat into His barn; but the chaff He
will burn with unquenchable fire."
18 And with many other exhortations he
preached to the people.
19 [a]But Herod the tetrarch, being rebuked by him
concerning Herodias, his [1]brother Philip's wife,
and for all the evils which Herod had done,
20 also added this, above all, that he shut John up
in prison.
**21** When all the people were baptized, [a]it came to
pass that Jesus also was baptized; and while He
prayed, the heaven was opened.
22 And the Holy Spirit descended in bodily form
like a dove upon Him, and a voice came from
heaven which said, "You are My beloved Son; in
You I am [a]well pleased."
**23** Now Jesus Himself began *His ministry at*
[a]about thirty years of age, being (as was supposed) [b]*the* son of Joseph, *the son* of Heli,
24 *the son* of Matthat, *the son* of Levi, *the son* of
Melchi, *the son* of Janna, *the son* of Joseph,
25 *the son* of Mattathiah, *the son* of Amos, *the*
*son* of Nahum, *the son* of Esli, *the son* of Naggai,
26 *the son* of Maath, *the son* of Mattathiah, *the*
*son* of Semei, *the son* of Joseph, *the son* of Judah,
27 *the son* of Joannas, *the son* of Rhesa, *the son*
of [a]Zerubbabel, *the son* of Shealtiel, *the son* of
Neri,
28 *the son* of Melchi, *the son* of Addi, *the son* of
Cosam, *the son* of Elmodam, *the son* of Er,
29 *the son* of Jose, *the son* of Eliezer, *the son* of
Jorim, *the son* of Matthat, *the son* of Levi,
30 *the son* of Simeon, *the son* of Judah, *the son* of
Joseph, *the son* of Jonan, *the son* of Eliakim,
31 *the son* of Melea, *the son* of Menan, *the son* of
Mattathah, *the son* of [a]Nathan, [b]*the son* of David,
32 [a]*the son* of Jesse, *the son* of Obed, *the son* of
Boaz, *the son* of Salmon, *the son* of Nahshon,

**37** [a]1 Tim. 5:5
**38** [a]Mark 15:43 [1]NU *God*
**40** [a]Luke 1:80; 2:52 [1]NU omits *in spirit*
**41** [a]John 4:20 [b]Deut. 16:1, 16
**42** [a]Ex. 23:14, 15
**43** [a]Ex. 12:15 [1]NU *His parents*
**47** [a]Matt. 7:28; 13:54; 22:33
**49** [a]John 9:4 [b][Luke 4:22, 32]
**50** [a]John 7:15, 46
**51** [a]Dan. 7:28 [1]*obedient*
**52** [a][Col. 2:2, 3] [b]1 Sam. 2:26

CHAPTER 3
**1** [a]Matt. 27:2
**2** [a]Acts 4:6 [b]Luke 1:13 [1]NU, M *in the high priesthood of Annas and Caiaphas*
**3** [a]Mark 1:4 [b]Luke 1:77
**4** [a]Is. 40:3–5
**6** [a]Is. 52:10
**7** [a]Matt. 3:7; 12:34; 23:33 [1]*Offspring*
**8** [a][2 Cor. 7:9–11]
**9** [a]Matt. 7:19
**10** [a][Acts 2:37, 38; 16:30, 31]
**11** [a]2 Cor. 8:14 [b]Is. 58:7
**12** [a]Luke 7:29
**13** [a]Luke 19:8
**14** [a]Ex. 20:16; 23:1 [1]Lit. *shake down* for money
**16** [a]Matt. 3:11, 12 [b]John 7:39; 20:22
**17** [a]Matt. 13:24–30
**19** [a]Mark 6:17 [1]NU *brother's wife*
**21** [a]Matt. 3:13–17
**22** [a]2 Pet. 1:17
**23** [a][Num. 4:3, 35, 39, 43, 47] [b]John 6:42
**27** [a]Ezra 2:2; 3:8
**31** [a]Zech. 12:12 [b]2 Sam. 5:14; 7:12
**32** [a]Ruth 4:18–22

33 *the son* of Amminadab, *the son* of Ram, *the*
*son* of Hezron, *the son* of Perez, *the son* of Judah,
34 *the son* of Jacob, *the son* of Isaac, *the son* of
Abraham, [a]*the son* of Terah, *the son* of Nahor,
35 *the son* of Serug, *the son* of Reu, *the son* of
Peleg, *the son* of Eber, *the son* of Shelah,
36 [a]*the son* of Cainan, *the son* of [b]Arphaxad, [c]*the*
*son* of Shem, *the son* of Noah, *the son* of Lamech,
37 *the son* of Methuselah, *the son* of Enoch, *the*
*son* of Jared, *the son* of Mahalalel, *the son* of
Cainan,
38 *the son* of Enosh, *the son* of Seth, *the son* of
Adam, [a]*the son* of God.

### *The Temptation of Jesus*

**4** Then [a]Jesus, being filled with the Holy Spirit,
returned from the Jordan and [b]was led by the
Spirit [1]into the wilderness,
2 being [1]tempted for forty days by the devil. And
[a]in those days He ate nothing, and afterward,
when they had ended, He was hungry.
3 And the devil said to Him, "If You are [a]the Son
of God, command this stone to become bread."
4 But Jesus answered him, saying, "It is written,
[a]*'Man shall not live by bread alone, [1]but by every*
*word of God.'* "
5 [1]Then the devil, taking Him up on a high
mountain, showed Him all the kingdoms of the
world in a moment of time.
6 And the devil said to Him, "All this authority I
will give You, and their glory; for [a]*this* has been
delivered to me, and I give it to whomever I wish.
7 "Therefore, if You will worship before me, all
will be Yours."
8 And Jesus answered and said to him, [1]"Get
behind Me, Satan! [2]For it is written, [a]*'You shall*
*worship the* LORD *your God, and Him only you*
*shall serve.'* "
9 [a]Then he brought Him to Jerusalem, set Him
on the pinnacle of the temple, and said to Him, "If
You are the Son of God, throw Yourself down
from here.
10 "For it is written:

[a]*'He shall give His angels charge over you,*
*To keep you,'*

11 "and,

[a]*'In their hands they shall bear you up,*
*Lest you dash your foot against a stone.'* "

12 And Jesus answered and said to him, "It has
been said, [a]*'You shall not [1]tempt the* LORD *your*
*God.'* "
13 Now when the devil had ended every [1]tempta-
tion, he departed from Him [a]until an opportune
time.
**14** [a]Then Jesus returned [b]in the power of the
Spirit to [c]Galilee, and [d]news of Him went out
through all the surrounding region.
15 And He [a]taught in their synagogues, [b]being
glorified by all.
**16** So He came to [a]Nazareth, where He had been
brought up. And as His custom was, [b]He went into
the synagogue on the Sabbath day, and stood up
to read.
17 And He was handed the book of the prophet
Isaiah. And when He had opened the book, He
found the place where it was written:

18 *"The[a] Spirit of the* LORD *is upon Me,*
*Because He has anointed Me to preach the*
*gospel to the poor;*
*He has sent Me [1]to heal the brokenhearted,*
*To proclaim liberty to the captives*
*And recovery of sight to the blind,*
*To [b]set at liberty those who are [2]oppressed;*
19 *To proclaim the acceptable year of the*
LORD*."*

20 Then He closed the book, and gave *it* back to
the attendant and sat down. And the eyes of all
who were in the synagogue were fixed on Him.
21 And He began to say to them, "Today this
Scripture is [a]fulfilled in your hearing."
22 So all bore witness to Him, and [a]marveled at
the gracious words which proceeded out of His
mouth. And they said, [b]"Is this not Joseph's son?"
23 He said to them, "You will surely say this
proverb to Me, 'Physician, heal yourself! Whatever we have heard done in [a]Capernaum,[1] do also
here in [b]Your country.' "
24 Then He said, "Assuredly, I say to you, no
[a]prophet is accepted in his own country.
25 "But I tell you truly, [a]many widows were in
Israel in the days of Elijah, when the heaven was
shut up three years and six months, and there was
a great famine throughout all the land;
26 "but to none of them was Elijah sent except to
[1]Zarephath, *in the region* of Sidon, to a woman
*who was* a widow.
27 [a]"And many lepers were in Israel in the time
of Elisha the prophet, and none of them was
cleansed except Naaman the Syrian."
28 So all those in the synagogue, when they
heard these things, were [a]filled with [1]wrath,
29 [a]and rose up and thrust Him out of the city;
and they led Him to the brow of the hill on which
their city was built, that they might throw Him
down over the cliff.
30 Then [a]passing through the midst of them, He
went His way.
**31** Then [a]He went down to Capernaum, a city of
Galilee, and was teaching them on the Sabbaths.
32 And they were [a]astonished at His teaching,
[b]for His word was with authority.
33 [a]Now in the synagogue there was a man who
had a spirit of an unclean demon. And he cried out
with a loud voice,
34 saying, "Let *us* alone! What have we to do
with You, Jesus of Nazareth? Did You come to
destroy us? [a]I know who You are—[b]the Holy One
of God!"
35 But Jesus rebuked him, saying, [1]"Be quiet, and
come out of him!" And when the demon had
thrown him in *their* midst, it came out of him and
did not hurt him.
36 Then they were all amazed and spoke among
themselves, saying, "What a word this *is!* For with
authority and power He commands the unclean
spirits, and they come out."
37 And the report about Him went out into every
place in the surrounding region.
**38** [a]Now He arose from the synagogue and entered Simon's house. But Simon's wife's mother
was [1]sick with a high fever, and they [b]made
request of Him concerning her.
39 So He stood over her and [a]rebuked the fever,
and it left her. And immediately she arose and
served them.
**40** [a]When the sun was setting, all those who had
any that were sick with various diseases brought
them to Him; and He laid His hands on every one
of them and healed them.

**34** [a]Gen. 11:24, 26–30; 12:3
**36** [a]Gen. 11:12 [b]Gen. 10:22, 24; 11:10–13 [c]Gen. 5:6–32; 9:27; 11:10
**38** [a]Gen. 5:1, 2

CHAPTER 4
**1** [a]Matt. 4:1–11 [b]Luke 2:27 [1]NU *in*
**2** [a]Ex. 34:28 [1]*tested*
**3** [a]John 20:31
**4** [a]Deut. 8:3 [1]NU omits *but by every word of God*
**5** [1]NU *And taking Him up, he showed Him*
**6** [a][Rev. 13:2, 7]
**8** [a]Deut. 6:13; 10:20 [1]NU omits *Get behind Me, Satan* [2]NU, M omit *For*
**9** [a]Matt. 4:5–7
**10** [a]Ps. 91:11, 12
**12** [a]Deut. 6:16 [1]*test*
**13** [a][Heb. 4:15] [1]*testing*
**14** [a]Matt. 4:12 [b]John 4:43 [c]Acts 10:37 [d]Matt. 4:24
**15** [a]Matt. 4:23 [b]Is. 52:13
**16** [a]Mark 6:1 [b]Acts 13:14–16; 17:2
**18** [a]Is. 49:8, 9; 61:1, 2 [b][Dan. 9:24] [1]NU omits *to heal the brokenhearted* [2]*downtrodden*
**21** [a]Acts 13:29
**22** [a][Ps. 45:2] [b]John 6:42
**23** [a]Matt. 4:13; 11:23 [b]Matt. 13:54 [1]NU *Capharnaum,* here and elsewhere
**24** [a]John 4:44
**25** [a]1 Kin. 17:9
**26** [1]Gr. *Sarepta*
**27** [a]2 Kin. 5:1–14
**28** [a]Luke 6:11 [1]*rage*
**29** [a]John 8:37; 10:31
**30** [a]John 8:59; 10:39
**31** [a]Matt. 4:13
**32** [a]Matt. 7:28, 29 [b][John 6:63; 7:46; 8:26, 28, 38, 47; 12:49, 50]
**33** [a]Mark 1:23
**34** [a]Luke 4:41 [b]Ps. 16:10
**35** [1]Lit. *Be muzzled*
**38** [a]Mark 1:29–31 [b]Mark 5:23 [1]*afflicted with*
**39** [a]Luke 8:24
**40** [a]Matt. 8:16, 17

41 [a]And demons also came out of many, crying out and saying, [b]"You are [1]the Christ, the Son of God!" And He, [c]rebuking *them,* did not allow them to [2]speak, for they knew that He was the Christ.
42 [a]Now when it was day, He departed and went into a deserted place. And the crowd sought Him and came to Him, and tried to keep Him from leaving them;
43 but He said to them, "I must [a]preach the kingdom of God to the other cities also, because for this purpose I have been sent."
44 [a]And He was preaching in the synagogues of [1]Galilee.

### *Discipleship, Healing, and Forgiveness*

5 So [a]it was, as the multitude pressed about Him to [b]hear the word of God, that He stood by the Lake of Gennesaret,
2 and saw two boats standing by the lake; but the fishermen had gone from them and were washing *their* nets.
3 Then He got into one of the boats, which was Simon's, and asked him to put out a little from the land. And He [a]sat down and taught the multitudes from the boat.
4 When He had stopped speaking, He said to Simon, [a]"Launch out into the deep and let down your nets for a catch."
5 But Simon answered and said to Him, "Master, we have toiled all night and caught [a]nothing; nevertheless [b]at Your word I will let down the net."
6 And when they had done this, they caught a great number of fish, and their net was breaking.
7 So they signaled to *their* partners in the other boat to come and help them. And they came and filled both the boats, so that they began to sink.
8 When Simon Peter saw *it,* he fell down at Jesus' knees, saying, [a]"Depart from me, for I am a sinful man, O Lord!"
9 For he and all who were with him were [a]astonished at the catch of fish which they had taken;
10 and so also *were* James and John, the sons of Zebedee, who were partners with Simon. And Jesus said to Simon, "Do not be afraid. [a]From now on you will catch men."
11 So when they had brought their boats to land, [a]they [1]forsook all and followed Him.
12 [a]And it happened when He was in a certain city, that behold, a man who was full of [b]leprosy saw Jesus; and he fell on *his* face and [1]implored Him, saying, "Lord, if You are willing, You can make me clean."
13 Then He put out *His* hand and touched him, saying, "I am willing; be cleansed." [a]Immediately the leprosy left him.
14 [a]And He charged him to tell no one, "But go and show yourself to the priest, and make an offering for your cleansing, as a testimony to them, [b]just as Moses commanded."
15 However, [a]the report went around concerning Him all the more; and [b]great multitudes came together to hear, and to be healed by Him of their infirmities.
16 [a]So He Himself *often* withdrew into the wilderness and [b]prayed.
17 Now it happened on a certain day, as He was teaching, that there were Pharisees and teachers of the law sitting by, who had come out of every town of Galilee, Judea, and Jerusalem. And the power of the Lord was *present* [1]to heal them.
18 [a]Then behold, men brought on a bed a man who was paralyzed, whom they sought to bring in and lay before Him.
19 And when they could not find how they might bring him in, because of the crowd, they went up on the housetop and let him down with *his* bed through the tiling into the midst [a]before Jesus.
20 When He saw their faith, He said to him, "Man, your sins are forgiven you."
21 [a]And the scribes and the Pharisees began to reason, saying, "Who is this who speaks blasphemies? [b]Who can forgive sins but God alone?"
22 But when Jesus [a]perceived their thoughts, He answered and said to them, "Why are you reasoning in your hearts?
23 "Which is easier, to say, 'Your sins are forgiven you,' or to say, 'Rise up and walk'?
24 "But that you may know that the Son of Man has power on earth to forgive sins"—He said to the man who was paralyzed, [a]"I say to you, arise, take up your bed, and go to your house."
25 Immediately he rose up before them, took up what he had been lying on, and departed to his own house, [a]glorifying God.
26 And they were all amazed, and they [a]glorified God and were filled with fear, saying, "We have seen strange things today!"
27 [a]After these things He went out and saw a tax collector named Levi, sitting at the tax office. And He said to him, [b]"Follow Me."
28 So he left all, rose up, and [a]followed Him.
29 [a]Then Levi gave Him a great feast in his own house. And [b]there were a great number of tax collectors and others who sat down with them.
30 [1]And their scribes and the Pharisees [2]complained against His disciples, saying, [a]"Why do You eat and drink with tax collectors and sinners?"
31 Jesus answered and said to them, "Those who are well have no need of a physician, but those who are sick.
32 [a]"I have not come to call *the* righteous, but sinners, to repentance."
33 Then they said to Him, [a]"Why[1] do the disciples of John fast often and make prayers, and likewise those of the Pharisees, but Yours eat and drink?"
34 And He said to them, "Can you make the friends of the bridegroom fast while the [a]bridegroom is with them?
35 "But the days will come when the bridegroom will be taken away from them; then they will fast in those days."
36 [a]Then He spoke a parable to them: "No one [1]puts a piece from a new garment on an old one; otherwise the new makes a tear, and also the piece that was *taken* out of the new does not match the old.
37 "And no one puts new wine into old wineskins; or else the new wine will burst the wineskins and be spilled, and the wineskins will be ruined.
38 "But new wine must be put into new wineskins, [1]and both are preserved.
39 "And no one, having drunk old *wine,* [1]immediately desires new; for he says, 'The old is [2]better.' "

### *Jesus Chooses Twelve Disciples*

6 Now [a]it happened [1]on the second Sabbath after the first that He went through the grainfields. And His disciples plucked the heads of grain and ate *them,* rubbing *them* in *their* hands.

41 [a]Mark 1:34; 3:11 [b]Mark 8:29 [c]Mark 1:25, 34; 3:11 [1]NU omits *the Christ* [2]Or *say that they knew*
42 [a]Mark 1:35–38
43 [a][John 9:4]
44 [a]Matt. 4:23; 9:35 [1]NU *Judea*

CHAPTER 5
1 [a]Mark 1:16–20 [b]Acts 13:44
3 [a]John 8:2
4 [a]John 21:6
5 [a]John 21:3 [b]Ps. 33:9
8 [a]1 Kin. 17:18
9 [a]Mark 5:42; 10:24, 26
10 [a]Matt. 4:19
11 [a]Matt. 4:20; 19:27 [1]*left behind*
12 [a]Mark 1:40–44 [b]Lev. 13:14 [1]*begged*
13 [a]John 5:9
14 [a]Matt. 8:4 [b]Lev. 13:1–3; 14:2–32
15 [a]Mark 1:45 [b]John 6:2
16 [a]Luke 9:10 [b]Matt. 14:23
17 [1]NU *with Him to heal*
18 [a]Mark 2:3–12
19 [a]Matt. 15:30
21 [a]Mark 2:6, 7 [b]Is. 43:25
22 [a]John 2:25
24 [a]Luke 7:14
25 [a]Acts 3:8
26 [a]Luke 1:65; 7:16
27 [a]Matt. 9:9–17 [b]John 12:26; 21:19, 22
28 [a]Mark 10:28
29 [a]Matt. 9:9, 10 [b]Luke 15:1
30 [a]Luke 15:2 [1]NU *But the Pharisees and their scribes* [2]*grumbled*
32 [a]1 Tim. 1:15
33 [a]Matt. 9:14 [1]NU omits *Why do,* making the verse a statement
34 [a]John 3:29
36 [a]Mark 2:21, 22 [1]NU *tears a piece from a new garment and puts it on an old one*
38 [1]NU omits *and both are preserved*
39 [1]NU omits *immediately* [2]NU *good*

CHAPTER 6
1 [a]Matt. 12:1–8 [1]NU *on a Sabbath that He went*

2 And some of the Pharisees said to them, "Why
are you doing [a]what is not lawful to do on the
Sabbath?"
3 But Jesus answering them said, "Have you not
even read this, [a]what David did when he was
hungry, he and those who were with him:
4 "how he went into the house of God, took and
ate the showbread, and also gave some to those
with him, [a]which is not lawful for any but the
priests to eat?"
5 And He said to them, "The Son of Man is also
Lord of the Sabbath."
**6** [a]Now it happened on another Sabbath, also,
that He entered the synagogue and taught. And a
man was there whose right hand was withered.
7 So the scribes and Pharisees watched Him
closely, whether He would [a]heal on the Sabbath,
that they might find an [b]accusation against Him.
8 But He [a]knew their thoughts, and said to the
man who had the withered hand, "Arise and stand
here." And he arose and stood.
9 Then Jesus said to them, "I will ask you one
thing: [a]Is it lawful on the Sabbath to do good or to
do evil, to save life or [1]to destroy?"
10 And when He had looked around at them all,
He said to [1]the man, "Stretch out your hand." And
he did so, and his hand was restored [2]as whole as
the other.
11 But they were filled with rage, and discussed
with one another what they might do to Jesus.
**12** Now it came to pass in those days that He
went out to the mountain to pray, and continued
all night in [a]prayer to God.
13 And when it was day, He called His disciples to
*Himself;* [a]and from them He chose [b]twelve whom
He also named apostles:
14 Simon, [a]whom He also named Peter, and Andrew his brother; James and John; Philip and
Bartholomew;
15 Matthew and Thomas; James the *son* of Alphaeus, and Simon called the Zealot;
16 Judas [a]*the son* of James, and [b]Judas Iscariot
who also became a traitor.
**17** And He came down with them and stood on a
level place with a crowd of His disciples [a]and a
great multitude of people from all Judea and
Jerusalem, and from the seacoast of Tyre and
Sidon, who came to hear Him and be healed of
their diseases,
18 as well as those who were tormented with
unclean spirits. And they were healed.
19 And the whole multitude [a]sought to [b]touch
Him, for [c]power went out from Him and healed
*them* all.
**20** Then He lifted up His eyes toward His disciples, and said:

[a]"Blessed *are you* poor,
For yours is the kingdom of God.
21 [a]Blessed *are you* who hunger now,
For you shall be [b]filled.[1]
[c]Blessed *are you* who weep now,
For you shall [d]laugh.
22 [a]Blessed are you when men hate you,
And when they [b]exclude you,
And revile *you,* and cast out your name as
evil,
For the Son of Man's sake.
23 [a]Rejoice in that day and leap for joy!
For indeed your reward *is* great in heaven,
For [b]in like manner their fathers did to the
prophets.

**24** "But[a] woe to you [b]who are rich,
For [c]you have received your consolation.
25 [a]Woe to you who are full,
For you shall hunger.
[b]Woe to you who laugh now,
For you shall mourn and [c]weep.
26 [a]Woe [1]to you when [2]all men speak well of
you,
For so did their fathers
to the false prophets.

**27** [a]"But I say to you who hear: Love your enemies, do good to those who hate you,
28 [a]"bless those who curse you, and [b]pray for
those who spitefully use you.
29 [a]"To him who strikes you on the *one* cheek,
offer the other also. [b]And from him who takes
away your cloak, do not withhold *your* tunic
either.
30 [a]"Give to everyone who asks of you. And from
him who takes away your goods do not ask *them*
back.
31 [a]"And just as you want men to do to you, you
also do to them likewise.
32 [a]"But if you love those who love you, what
credit is that to you? For even sinners love those
who love them.
33 "And if you do good to those who do good to
you, what credit is that to you? For even sinners
do the same.
34 [a]"And if you lend *to those* from whom you
hope to receive back, what credit is that to you?
For even sinners lend to sinners to receive as
much back.
35 "But [a]love your enemies, [b]do good, and [c]lend,
[1]hoping for nothing in return; and your reward
will be great, and [d]you will be sons of the Most
High. For He is kind to the unthankful and evil.
36 [a]"Therefore be merciful, just as your Father
also is merciful.
**37** [a]"Judge not, and you shall not be judged.
Condemn not, and you shall not be condemned.
[b]Forgive, and you will be forgiven.
38 [a]"Give, and it will be given to you: good
measure, pressed down, shaken together, and
running over will be put into your [b]bosom. For
[c]with the same measure that you use, it will be
measured back to you."
39 And He spoke a parable to them: [a]"Can the
blind lead the blind? Will they not both fall into
the ditch?
40 [a]"A disciple is not above his teacher, but
everyone who is perfectly trained will be like his
teacher.
41 [a]"And why do you look at the speck in your
brother's eye, but do not perceive the plank in
your own eye?
42 "Or how can you say to your brother,
'Brother, let me remove the speck that *is* in your
eye,' when you yourself do not see the plank that
*is* in your own eye? Hypocrite! First remove the
plank from your own eye, and then you will see
clearly to remove the speck that is in your brother's eye.
**43** [a]"For a good tree does not bear bad fruit, nor
does a bad tree bear good fruit.
44 "For [a]every tree is known by its own fruit. For
*men* do not gather figs from thorns, nor do they
gather grapes from a bramble bush.
45 [a]"A good man out of the good treasure of his
heart brings forth good; and an evil man out of

2 [a]Ex. 20:10
3 [a]1 Sam. 21:6
4 [a]Lev. 24:9
6 [a]Mark 3:1–6
7 [a]Luke 13:14; 14:1–6 [b]Luke 20:20
8 [a]Matt. 9:4
9 [a]John 7:23 [1]M *to kill*
10 [1]NU, M *him,* [2]NU omits *as whole as the other*
12 [a]Mark 1:35
13 [a]John 6:70 [b]Matt. 10:1
14 [a]John 1:42
16 [a]Jude 1 [b]Luke 22:3–6
17 [a]Mark 3:7, 8
19 [a]Matt. 9:21; 14:36 [b]Mark 5:27, 28 [c]Luke 8:46
20 [a]Matt. 5:3–12; [11:5]
21 [a]Is. 55:1; 65:13 [b][Rev. 7:16] [c][Is. 61:3] [d]Ps. 126:5 [1]*satisfied*
22 [a]1 Pet. 2:19; 3:14; 4:14 [b][John 16:2]
23 [a]James 1:2 [b]Acts 7:51
24 [a]James 5:1–6 [b]Luke 12:21 [c]Luke 16:25
25 [a][Is. 65:13] [b][Prov. 14:13] [c]James 4:9
26 [a][John 15:19] [1]NU, M omit *to you* [2]M omits *all*
27 [a]Rom. 12:20
28 [a]Rom. 12:14 [b]Acts 7:60
29 [a]Matt. 5:39–42 [b][1 Cor. 6:7]
30 [a]Deut. 15:7, 8
31 [a]Matt. 7:12
32 [a]Matt. 5:45
34 [a]Matt. 5:42
35 [a][Rom. 13:10] [b]Heb. 13:16 [c]Ps. 37:26 [d]Matt. 5:46 [1]*expecting*
36 [a]Matt. 5:48
37 [a]Matt. 7:1–5 [b]Matt. 18:21–35
38 [a][Prov. 19:17; 28:27] [b]Ps. 79:12 [c]James 2:13
39 [a]Matt. 15:14; 23:16
40 [a][John 13:16; 15:20]
41 [a]Matt. 7:3
43 [a]Matt. 7:16–18, 20
44 [a]Matt. 12:33
45 [a]Matt. 12:35

the evil [1]treasure of his heart brings forth evil. For
out [b]of the abundance of the heart his mouth
speaks.
46 [a]"But why do you call Me 'Lord, Lord,' and not
do the things which I say?
47 [a]"Whoever comes to Me, and hears My sayings and does them, I will show you whom he is
like:
48 "He is like a man building a house, who dug
deep and laid the foundation on the rock. And
when the flood arose, the stream beat vehemently
against that house, and could not shake it, for it
was [1]founded on the rock.
49 "But he who heard and did nothing is like a
man who built a house on the earth without a
foundation, against which the stream beat vehemently; and immediately it [1]fell. And the ruin of
that house was great."

### *Jesus Heals and Teaches in Galilee*

7 Now when He concluded all His sayings in the
hearing of the people, He [a]entered Capernaum.
2 And a certain centurion's servant, who was
dear to him, was sick and ready to die.
3 So when he heard about Jesus, he sent elders
of the Jews to Him, pleading with Him to come
and heal his servant.
4 And when they came to Jesus, they begged
Him earnestly, saying that the one for whom He
should do this was deserving,
5 "for he loves our nation, and has built us a
synagogue."
6 Then Jesus went with them. And when He
was already not far from the house, the centurion
sent friends to Him, saying to Him, "Lord, do not
trouble Yourself, for I am not worthy that You
should enter under my roof.
7 "Therefore I did not even think myself worthy
to come to You. But [a]say the word, and my
servant will be healed.
8 "For I also am a man placed under [a]authority,
having soldiers under me. And I say to one, 'Go,'
and he goes; and to another, 'Come,' and he
comes; and to my servant, 'Do this,' and he
does *it*."
9 When Jesus heard these things, He marveled
at him, and turned around and said to the crowd
that followed Him, "I say to you, I have not found
such great faith, not even in Israel!"
10 And those who were sent, returning to the
house, found the servant well [1]who had been sick.
11 Now it happened, the day after, *that* He went
into a city called Nain; and many of His disciples
went with Him, and a large crowd.
12 And when He came near the gate of the city,
behold, a dead man was being carried out, the
only son of his mother; and she was a widow. And
a large crowd from the city was with her.
13 When the Lord saw her, He had [a]compassion
on her and said to her, [b]"Do not weep."
14 Then He came and touched the open coffin,
and those who carried *him* stood still. And He
said, "Young man, I say to you, [a]arise."
15 So he who was dead [a]sat up and began to
speak. And He [b]presented him to his mother.
16 [a]Then fear [1]came upon all, and they [b]glorified
God, saying, [c]"A great prophet has risen up
among us"; and, [d]"God has visited His people."
17 And this report about Him went throughout
all Judea and all the surrounding region.
18 [a]Then the disciples of John reported to him
concerning all these things.
19 And John, calling two of his disciples to *him*,
sent *them* to [1]Jesus, saying, "Are You [a]the Coming
One, or [2]do we look for another?"
20 When the men had come to Him, they said,
"John the Baptist has sent us to You, saying, 'Are
You the Coming One, or do we look for another?' "
21 And that very hour He cured many of [1]infirmi-
ties, afflictions, and evil spirits; and to many blind
He gave sight.
22 [a]Jesus answered and said to them, "Go and tell
John the things you have seen and heard: [b]that
*the* blind [c]see, *the* lame [d]walk, *the* lepers are
[e]cleansed, *the* deaf [f]hear, *the* dead are raised, [g]*the*
poor have the gospel preached to them.
23 "And blessed is *he* who is not [1]offended because of Me."
24 [a]When the messengers of John had departed,
He began to speak to the multitudes concerning
John: "What did you go out into the wilderness to
see? A reed shaken by the wind?
25 "But what did you go out to see? A man
clothed in soft garments? Indeed those who are
gorgeously appareled and live in luxury are in
kings' courts.
26 "But what did you go out to see? A prophet?
Yes, I say to you, and more than a prophet.
27 "This is *he* of whom it is written:

[a]*'Behold, I send My messenger*
*before Your face,*
*Who will prepare Your way before You.'*

28 "For I say to you, among those born of women
there is [1]not a [a]greater prophet than John the
Baptist; but he who is least in the kingdom of God
is greater than he."
29 And when all the people heard *Him*, even the
tax collectors [1]justified God, [a]having been baptized with the baptism of John.
30 But the Pharisees and [1]lawyers rejected [a]the
will of God for themselves, not having been baptized by him.
31 [1]And the Lord said, [a]"To what then shall I
liken the men of this generation, and what are
they like?
32 "They are like children sitting in the marketplace and calling to one another, saying:

'We played the flute for you,
And you did not dance;
We mourned to you,
And you did not weep.'

33 "For [a]John the Baptist came [b]neither eating
bread nor drinking wine, and you say, 'He has a
demon.'
34 "The Son of Man has come [a]eating and drinking, and you say, 'Look, a glutton and a [1]winebib-
ber, a friend of tax collectors and sinners!'
35 [a]"But wisdom is justified by all her children."
36 [a]Then one of the Pharisees asked Him to eat
with him. And He went to the Pharisee's house,
and sat down to eat.
37 And behold, a woman in the city who was a
sinner, when she knew that *Jesus* sat at the table
in the Pharisee's house, brought an alabaster flask
of fragrant oil,
38 and stood at His feet behind *Him* weeping; and
she began to wash His feet with her tears, and
wiped *them* with the hair of her head; and she

45 [b]Prov. 15:2, 28; 16:23; 18:21; Matt. 12:34 [1]NU omits *treasure of his heart*
46 [a]Mal. 1:6; Matt. 7:21; 25:11; Luke 13:25
47 [a]Matt. 7:24–27; [John 14:21]; James 1:22–25
48 [1]NU *well built.*
49 [1]NU *collapsed*

CHAPTER 7

1 [a]Matt. 8:5–13
7 [a]Ps. 33:9; 107:20
8 [a][Mark 13:34]
10 [1]NU omits *who had been sick*
13 [a]Lam. 3:32; John 11:35; [Heb. 4:15] [b]Luke 8:52
14 [a]Mark 5:41; Luke 8:54; John 11:43; Acts 9:40; [Rom. 4:17]
15 [a]Matt. 11:5; Luke 8:55; John 11:44 [b]1 Kin. 17:23; 2 Kin. 4:36
16 [a]Luke 1:65 [b]Luke 5:26 [c]Luke 24:19; John 4:19; 6:14; 9:17 [d]Luke 1:68 [1]*seized them all*
18 [a]Matt. 11:2–19
19 [a][Mic. 5:2; Zech. 9:9; Mal. 3:1–3] [1]NU *the Lord* [2]*should we expect*
21 [1]*illnesses*
22 [a]Matt. 11:4 [b]Is. 35:5 [c]John 9:7 [d]Matt. 15:31 [e]Luke 17:12–14 [f]Mark 7:37 [g][Is. 61:1–3; Luke 4:18]
23 [1]*caused to stumble*
24 [a]Matt. 11:7
27 [a]Is. 40:3; Mal. 3:1; Matt. 11:10; Mark 1:2
28 [a][Luke 1:15] [1]NU *none greater than John;*
29 [a]Matt. 3:5; Luke 3:12 [1]*declared the righteousness of*
30 [a]Acts 20:27 [1]*the experts in the law*
31 [a]Matt. 11:16 [1]NU, M omit *And the Lord said*
33 [a]Matt. 3:1 [b][Matt. 3:4]; Luke 1:15
34 [a]Luke 15:2 [1]An excessive drinker
35 [a]Matt. 11:19
36 [a]Matt. 26:6; Mark 14:3; John 11:2

kissed His feet and anointed *them* with the fragrant oil.
39 Now when the Pharisee who had invited Him
saw *this,* he spoke to himself, saying, [a]"This man,
if He were a prophet, would know who and what
manner of woman *this is* who is touching Him, for
she is a sinner."
40 And Jesus answered and said to him, "Simon,
I have something to say to you." So he said,
"Teacher, say it."
41 "There was a certain creditor who had two
debtors. One owed five hundred [a]denarii, and the
other fifty.
42 "And when they had nothing with which to
repay, he freely forgave them both. Tell Me,
therefore, which of them will love him more?"
43 Simon answered and said, "I suppose the *one*
whom he forgave more." And He said to him,
"You have rightly judged."
44 Then He turned to the woman and said to
Simon, "Do you see this woman? I entered your
house; you gave Me no [a]water for My feet, but she
has washed My feet with her tears and wiped
*them* with the hair of her head.
45 "You gave Me no [a]kiss, but this woman has
not ceased to kiss My feet since the time I
came in.
46 [a]"You did not anoint My head with oil, but
this woman has anointed My feet with fragrant
oil.
47 [a]"Therefore I say to you, her sins, *which are*
many, are forgiven, for she loved much. But to
whom little is forgiven, *the same* loves little."
48 Then He said to her, [a]"Your sins are forgiven."
49 And those who sat at the table with Him
began to say to themselves, [a]"Who is this who
even forgives sins?"
50 Then He said to the woman, [a]"Your faith has
saved you. Go in peace."

## *Parables and Their Meaning*

**8** Now it came to pass, afterward, that He went
through every city and village, preaching and
[1]bringing the glad tidings of the kingdom of God.
And the twelve *were* with Him,
2 and [a]certain women who had been healed of
evil spirits and [1]infirmities—Mary called Magdalene, [b]out of whom had come seven demons,
3 and Joanna the wife of Chuza, Herod's steward, and Susanna, and many others who provided
for [1]Him from their [2]substance.
4 [a]And when a great multitude had gathered,
and they had come to Him from every city, He
spoke by a parable:
5 "A sower went out to sow his seed. And as he
sowed, some fell by the wayside; and it was
trampled down, and the birds of the air
devoured it.
6 "Some fell on rock; and as soon as it sprang
up, it withered away because it lacked moisture.
7 "And some fell among thorns, and the thorns
sprang up with it and choked it.
8 "But others fell on good ground, sprang up,
and yielded [1]a crop a hundredfold." When He had
said these things He cried, [a]"He who has ears to
hear, let him hear!"
9 [a]Then His disciples asked Him, saying, "What
does this parable mean?"
10 And He said, "To you it has been given to
know the [1]mysteries of the kingdom of God, but
to the rest *it is given* in parables, that

[a]*'Seeing they may not see,*
*And hearing they may not understand.'*

11 [a]"Now the parable is this: The seed is the
[b]word of God.
12 "Those by the wayside are the ones who hear;
then the devil comes and takes away the word out
of their hearts, lest they should believe and be
saved.
13 "But the ones on the rock *are those* who,
when they hear, receive the word with joy; and
these have no root, who believe for a while and in
time of [1]temptation fall away.
14 "Now the ones *that* fell among thorns are
those who, when they have heard, go out and are
choked with cares, [a]riches, and pleasures of life,
and bring no fruit to maturity.
15 "But the ones *that* fell on the good ground are
those who, having heard the word with a noble
and good heart, keep *it* and bear fruit with [a]pa-
tience.[1]
16 [a]"No one, when he has lit a lamp, covers it
with a vessel or puts *it* under a bed, but sets *it* on
a lampstand, that those who enter may see the
[b]light.
17 [a]"For nothing is secret that will not be [b]re-
vealed, nor *anything* hidden that will not be
known and come to light.
18 "Therefore take heed how you hear. [a]For
whoever has, to him *more* will be given; and
whoever does not have, even what he [1]seems to
[b]have will be taken from him."
19 [a]Then His mother and brothers came to Him,
and could not approach Him because of the
crowd.
20 And it was told Him *by some,* who said, "Your
mother and Your brothers are standing outside,
desiring to see You."
21 But He answered and said to them, "My
mother and My brothers are these who hear the
word of God and do it."
22 [a]Now it happened, on a certain day, that He
got into a boat with His disciples. And He said to
them, "Let us cross over to the other side of the
lake." And they launched out.
23 But as they sailed He fell asleep. And a windstorm came down on the lake, and they were
filling *with water,* and were in [1]jeopardy.
24 And they came to Him and awoke Him, saying, "Master, Master, we are perishing!" Then He
arose and rebuked the wind and the raging of the
water. And they ceased, and there was a calm.
25 But He said to them, [a]"Where is your faith?"
And they were afraid, and marveled, saying to one
another, [b]"Who can this be? For He commands
even the winds and water, and they obey Him!"
26 [a]Then they sailed to the country of the [1]Gada-
renes, which is opposite Galilee.
27 And when He stepped out on the land, there
met Him a certain man from the city who had
demons [1]for a long time. And he wore no clothes,
nor did he live in a house but in the tombs.
28 When he saw Jesus, he [a]cried out, fell down
before Him, and with a loud voice said, [b]"What
have I to do with [c]You, Jesus, Son of the Most
High God? I beg You, do not torment me!"
29 For He had commanded the unclean spirit to
come out of the man. For it had often seized him,
and he was kept under guard, bound with chains
and shackles; and he broke the bonds and was
driven by the demon into the wilderness.

39 [a]Luke 15:2
41 [a]Matt. 18:28
44 [a]Gen. 18:4; 19:2; 43:24
45 [a]Rom. 16:16
46 [a]Ps. 23:5
47 [a][1 Tim. 1:14]
48 [a]Matt. 9:2
49 [a]Luke 5:21
50 [a]Matt. 9:22

CHAPTER 8
1 [1]*proclaiming the good news*
2 [a]Matt. 27:55 [b]Mark 16:9 [1]*sicknesses*
3 [1]NU, M *them* [2]*possessions*
4 [a]Mark 4:1–9
8 [a]Luke 14:35 [1]Lit. *fruit*
9 [a]Matt. 13:10–23
10 [a]Is. 6:9 [1]*secret* or *hidden truths*
11 [a][1 Pet. 1:23] [b]Luke 5:1; 11:28
13 [1]*testing*
14 [a]1 Tim. 6:9, 10
15 [a][Heb. 10:36–39] [1]*endurance*
16 [a]Luke 11:33 [b]Matt. 5:14
17 [a]Luke 12:2 [b][2 Cor. 5:10]
18 [a]Matt. 25:29 [b]Matt. 13:12 [1]*thinks that he has*
19 [a]Mark 3:31–35
22 [a]Matt. 8:23–27
23 [1]*danger*
25 [a]Luke 9:41 [b]Luke 4:36; 5:26
26 [a]Mark 5:1–17 [1]NU *Gerasenes*
27 [1]NU *and for a long time wore no clothes*
28 [a]Mark 1:26; 9:26 [b]Mark 1:23, 24 [c]Luke 4:41

30 Jesus asked him, saying, "What is your name?" And he said, "Legion," because many demons had entered him.
31 And they begged Him that He would not command them to go out [a]into the abyss.
32 Now a herd of many [a]swine was feeding there on the mountain. So they begged Him that He would permit them to enter them. And He permitted them.
33 Then the demons went out of the man and entered the swine, and the herd ran violently down the steep place into the lake and drowned.
34 When those who fed *them* saw what had happened, they fled and told *it* in the city and in the country.
35 Then they went out to see what had happened, and came to Jesus, and found the man from whom the demons had departed, [a]sitting at the [b]feet of Jesus, clothed and in his [c]right mind. And they were afraid.
36 They also who had seen *it* told them by what means he who had been demon-possessed was [1]healed.
37 [a]Then the whole multitude of the surrounding region of the [1]Gadarenes [b]asked Him to [c]depart from them, for they were seized with great [d]fear. And He got into the boat and returned.
38 Now [a]the man from whom the demons had departed begged Him that he might be with Him. But Jesus sent him away, saying,
39 "Return to your own house, and tell what great things God has done for you." And he went his way and proclaimed throughout the whole city what great things Jesus had done for him.
**40** So it was, when Jesus returned, that the multitude welcomed Him, for they were all waiting for Him.
41 [a]And behold, there came a man named Jairus, and he was a ruler of the synagogue. And he fell down at Jesus' feet and begged Him to come to his house,
42 for he had an only daughter about twelve years of age, and she [a]was dying. But as He went, the multitudes thronged Him.
43 [a]Now a woman, having a [b]flow of blood for twelve years, who had spent all her livelihood on physicians and could not be healed by any,
44 came from behind and [a]touched the border of His garment. And immediately her flow of blood stopped.
45 And Jesus said, "Who touched Me?" When all denied it, Peter [1]and those with him said, "Master, the multitudes throng and press You, [2]and You say, 'Who touched Me?' "
46 But Jesus said, "Somebody touched Me, for I perceived [a]power going out from Me."
47 Now when the woman saw that she was not hidden, she came trembling; and falling down before Him, she declared to Him in the presence of all the people the reason she had touched Him and how she was healed immediately.
48 And He said to her, "Daughter, [1]be of good cheer; [a]your faith has made you well. [b]Go in peace."
49 [a]While He was still speaking, someone came from the ruler of the synagogue's *house,* saying to him, "Your daughter is dead. Do not trouble the [1]Teacher."
50 But when Jesus heard *it,* He answered him, saying, "Do not be afraid; [a]only believe, and she will be made well."

**31** [a]Rom. 10:7; [Rev. 20:1, 3]
**32** [a]Lev. 11:7; Deut. 14:8
**35** [a][Matt. 11:28] [b]Matt. 28:9; Mark 7:25; Luke 10:39; 17:16; John 11:32 [c][2 Tim. 1:7]
**36** [1]*delivered*
**37** [a]Matt. 8:34 [b]Mark 1:24; Luke 4:34 [c]Job 21:14; Acts 16:39 [d]Luke 5:26 [1]NU *Gerasenes*
**38** [a]Mark 5:18–20
**41** [a]Matt. 9:18–26; Mark 5:22–43
**42** [a]Luke 7:2
**43** [a]Matt. 9:20 [b]Luke 15:19–22
**44** [a]Mark 6:56; Luke 5:13
**45** [1]NU omits *and those with him* [2]NU omits the rest of v. 45.
**46** [a]Mark 5:30; Luke 6:19
**48** [a]Mark 5:34; Luke 7:50 [b]John 8:11 [1]NU omits *be of good cheer*
**49** [a]Mark 5:35 [1]NU adds *anymore*
**50** [a][Mark 11:22–24]
**51** [1]NU adds *with Him* [2]NU, M *Peter, John, and James*
**52** [a]Luke 7:13 [b][John 11:11, 13]
**54** [a]Luke 7:14; John 11:43 [1]NU omits *put them all outside*
**56** [a]Matt. 8:4; 9:30; Mark 5:43

CHAPTER 9
**1** [a]Matt. 10:1, 2; Mark 3:13; 6:7 [b]Mark 16:17, 18; [John 14:12]
**2** [a]Matt. 10:7, 8; Mark 6:12; Luke 10:1, 9
**3** [a]Matt. 10:9–15; Mark 6:8–11; Luke 10:4–12; 22:35
**4** [a]Matt. 10:11; Mark 6:10
**5** [a]Matt. 10:14 [b]Luke 10:11; Acts 13:51
**6** [a]Mark 6:12; Luke 8:1
**7** [a]Matt. 14:1, 2; Mark 6:14
**9** [a]Luke 23:8
**10** [a]Mark 6:30 [b]Matt. 14:13
**12** [a]Matt. 14:15; Mark 6:35; John 6:1, 5
**16** [a]Luke 22:19; 24:30
**17** [1]*satisfied*

51 When He came into the house, He permitted no one to go [1]in except [2]Peter, James, and John, and the father and mother of the girl.
52 Now all wept and mourned for her; but He said, [a]"Do not weep; she is not dead, [b]but sleeping."
53 And they ridiculed Him, knowing that she was dead.
54 But He [1]put them all outside, took her by the hand and called, saying, "Little girl, [a]arise."
55 Then her spirit returned, and she arose immediately. And He commanded that she be given *something* to eat.
56 And her parents were astonished, but [a]He charged them to tell no one what had happened.

### *Jesus Feeds Five Thousand*

**9** Then [a]He called His twelve disciples together and [b]gave them power and authority over all demons, and to cure diseases.
2 [a]He sent them to preach the kingdom of God and to heal the sick.
3 [a]And He said to them, "Take nothing for the journey, neither staffs nor bag nor bread nor money; and do not have two tunics apiece.
4 [a]"Whatever house you enter, stay there, and from there depart.
5 [a]"And whoever will not receive you, when you go out of that city, [b]shake off the very dust from your feet as a testimony against them."
6 [a]So they departed and went through the towns, preaching the gospel and healing everywhere.
7 [a]Now Herod the tetrarch heard of all that was done by Him; and he was perplexed, because it was said by some that John had risen from the dead,
8 and by some that Elijah had appeared, and by others that one of the old prophets had risen again.
9 Herod said, "John I have beheaded, but who is this of whom I hear such things?" [a]So he sought to see Him.
**10** [a]And the apostles, when they had returned, told Him all that they had done. [b]Then He took them and went aside privately into a deserted place belonging to the city called Bethsaida.
11 But when the multitudes knew *it,* they followed Him; and He received them and spoke to them about the kingdom of God, and healed those who had need of healing.
12 [a]When the day began to wear away, the twelve came and said to Him, "Send the multitude away, that they may go into the surrounding towns and country, and lodge and get provisions; for we are in a deserted place here."
13 But He said to them, "You give them something to eat." And they said, "We have no more than five loaves and two fish, unless we go and buy food for all these people."
14 For there were about five thousand men. Then He said to His disciples, "Make them sit down in groups of fifty."
15 And they did so, and made them all sit down.
16 Then He took the five loaves and the two fish, and looking up to heaven, He [a]blessed and broke *them,* and gave *them* to the disciples to set before the multitude.
17 So they all ate and were [1]filled, and twelve baskets of the leftover fragments were taken up by them.

**18** [a]And it happened, as He was alone praying,
*that* His disciples joined Him, and He asked them,
saying, "Who do the crowds say that I am?"
19 So they answered and said, [a]"John the Baptist,
but some *say* Elijah; and others *say* that one of
the old prophets has risen again."
20 He said to them, "But who do you say that I
am?" [a]Peter answered and said, "The Christ of
God."
**21** [a]And He strictly warned and commanded
them to tell this to no one,
22 saying, [a]"The Son of Man must suffer many
things, and be rejected by the elders and chief
priests and scribes, and be killed, and be raised the
third day."
**23** [a]Then He said to *them* all, "If anyone desires
to come after Me, let him deny himself, and take
up his cross [1]daily, and follow Me.
24 [a]"For whoever desires to save his life will lose
it, but whoever loses his life for My sake will
save it.
25 [a]"For what profit is it to a man if he gains the
whole world, and is himself destroyed or lost?
26 [a]"For whoever is ashamed of Me and My
words, of him the Son of Man will be [b]ashamed
when He comes in His *own* glory, and *in His*
Father's, and of the holy angels.
**27** [a]"But I tell you truly, there are some standing
here who shall not taste death till they see the
kingdom of God."
28 [a]Now it came to pass, about eight days after
these sayings, that He took Peter, John, and
James and went up on the mountain to pray.
29 As He prayed, the appearance of His face was
altered, and His robe *became* white *and* glistening.
30 And behold, two men talked with Him, who
were [a]Moses and [b]Elijah,
31 who appeared in glory and spoke of His [1]de-
cease which He was about to accomplish at Jerusalem.
32 But Peter and those with him [a]were heavy
with sleep; and when they were fully awake, they
saw His glory and the two men who stood with
Him.
33 Then it happened, as they were parting from
Him, *that* Peter said to Jesus, "Master, it is good
for us to be here; and let us make three [1]taberna-
cles: one for You, one for Moses, and one for
Elijah"—not knowing what he said.
34 While he was saying this, a cloud came and
overshadowed them; and they were fearful as
they entered the [a]cloud.
35 And a voice came out of the cloud, saying,
[a]"This is [1]My beloved Son. [b]Hear Him!"
36 When the voice had ceased, Jesus was found
alone. [a]But they kept quiet, and told no one in
those days any of the things they had seen.
**37** [a]Now it happened on the next day, when they
had come down from the mountain, that a great
multitude met Him.
38 Suddenly a man from the multitude cried out,
saying, "Teacher, I implore You, look on my son,
for he is my only child.
39 "And behold, a spirit seizes him, and he suddenly cries out; it convulses him so that he foams
*at the mouth;* and it departs from him with great
difficulty, bruising him.
40 "So I implored Your disciples to cast it out,
but they could not."
41 Then Jesus answered and said, "O [1]faithless
and perverse generation, how long shall I be with
you and [2]bear with you? Bring your son here."

18 [a]Matt. 16:13–16
19 [a]Matt. 14:2
20 [a]John 6:68, 69
21 [a]Matt. 8:4; 16:20
22 [a]Matt. 16:21; 17:22
23 [a]Matt. 10:38; 16:24 [1]M omits *daily*
24 [a][John 12:25]
25 [a]Mark 8:36
26 [a][Rom. 1:16] [b]Matt. 10:33
27 [a]Matt. 16:28
28 [a]Mark 9:2–8
30 [a]Heb. 11:23–29 [b]2 Kin. 2:1–11
31 [1]Death, lit. *departure*
32 [a]Dan. 8:18; 10:9
33 [1]*tents*
34 [a]Ex. 13:21
35 [a][Matt. 3:17; 12:18] [b]Acts 3:22 [1]NU *My Son, My Chosen One*
36 [a]Matt. 17:9
37 [a]Mark 9:14–27
41 [1]*unbelieving* [2]*put up with*
44 [a]Matt. 17:22
45 [a]Mark 9:32
46 [a]Matt. 18:1–5
47 [a]Matt. 9:4 [b]Luke 18:17
48 [a]Matt. 18:5 [b]John 12:44 [c]John 13:20 [d]Eph. 3:8
49 [a]Mark 9:38–40
50 [a]Luke 11:23 [1]NU *you* [2]NU *your*
51 [a]Mark 16:19
53 [a]John 4:4, 9
54 [a]Mark 3:17 [b]2 Kin. 1:10, 12 [1]NU omits *just as Elijah did*
55 [a][2 Tim. 1:7] [1]NU omits the rest of v. 55.
56 [a]John 3:17; 12:47 [1]NU omits *For the Son of Man did not come to destroy men's lives but to save them.*
57 [a]Matt. 8:19–22
58 [a]Luke 2:7; 8:23
59 [a]Matt. 8:21, 22
61 [a]1 Kin. 19:20
62 [a]2 Tim. 4:10

CHAPTER 10
1 [a]Mark 6:7 [1]NU *seventy-two others*
2 [a]John 4:35 [b]2 Thess. 3:1

42 And as he was still coming, the demon threw
him down and convulsed *him.* Then Jesus rebuked
the unclean spirit, healed the child, and gave him
back to his father.
**43** And they were all amazed at the majesty of
God. But while everyone marveled at all the
things which Jesus did, He said to His disciples,
44 [a]"Let these words sink down into your ears,
for the Son of Man is about to be betrayed into the
hands of men."
45 [a]But they did not understand this saying, and
it was hidden from them so that they did not
perceive it; and they were afraid to ask Him about
this saying.
**46** [a]Then a dispute arose among them as to which
of them would be greatest.
47 And Jesus, [a]perceiving the thought of their
heart, took a [b]little child and set him by Him,
48 and said to them, [a]"Whoever receives this
little child in My name receives Me; and [b]whoever
receives Me [c]receives Him who sent Me. [d]For he
who is least among you all will be great."
**49** [a]Now John answered and said, "Master, we
saw someone casting out demons in Your name,
and we forbade him because he does not follow
with us."
50 But Jesus said to him, "Do not forbid *him,* for
[a]he who is not against [1]us is on [2]our side."
**51** Now it came to pass, when the time had come
for [a]Him to be received up, that He steadfastly set
His face to go to Jerusalem,
52 and sent messengers before His face. And as
they went, they entered a village of the Samaritans, to prepare for Him.
53 But [a]they did not receive Him, because His
face was *set* for the journey to Jerusalem.
54 And when His disciples [a]James and John saw
*this,* they said, "Lord, do You want us to command fire to come down from heaven and consume them, [1]just as [b]Elijah did?"
55 But He turned and rebuked them, [1]and said,
"You do not know what manner of [a]spirit you
are of.
56 [1]"For [a]the Son of Man did not come to destroy
men's lives but to save *them.*" And they went to
another village.
**57** [a]Now it happened as they journeyed on the
road, *that* someone said to Him, "Lord, I will
follow You wherever You go."
58 And Jesus said to him, "Foxes have holes and
birds of the air *have* nests, but the Son of Man
[a]has nowhere to lay *His* head."
59 [a]Then He said to another, "Follow Me." But he
said, "Lord, let me first go and bury my father."
60 Jesus said to him, "Let the dead bury their
own dead, but you go and preach the kingdom of
God."
61 And another also said, "Lord, [a]I will follow
You, but let me first go *and* bid them farewell who
are at my house."
62 But Jesus said to him, "No one, having put his
hand to the plow, and looking back, is [a]fit for the
kingdom of God."

### *Sending the Seventy; the Good Samaritan*

**10** After these things the Lord appointed [1]sev-
enty others also, and [a]sent them two by two
before His face into every city and place where He
Himself was about to go.
2 Then He said to them, [a]"The harvest truly *is*
great, but the laborers *are* few; therefore [b]pray the

Lord of the harvest to send out laborers into His
harvest.
3 "Go your way; [a]behold, I send you out as
lambs among wolves.
4 [a]"Carry neither money bag, knapsack, nor
sandals; and [b]greet no one along the road.
5 [a]"But whatever house you enter, first say,
'Peace to this house.'
6 "And if a son of peace is there, your peace will
rest on it; if not, it will return to you.
7 [a]"And remain in the same house, [b]eating and
drinking such things as they give, for [c]the laborer
is worthy of his wages. Do not go from house to
house.
8 "Whatever city you enter, and they receive
you, eat such things as are set before you.
9 [a]"And heal the sick there, and say to them,
[b]'The kingdom of God has come near to you.'
10 "But whatever city you enter, and they do not
receive you, go out into its streets and say,
11 [a]'The very dust of your city which clings to [1]us
we wipe off against you. Nevertheless know this,
that the kingdom of God has come near you.'
12 [1]"But I say to you that [a]it will be more tolerable in that Day for Sodom than for that city.
**13** [a]"Woe to you, Chorazin! Woe to you, Bethsaida! [b]For if the mighty works which were done in
you had been done in Tyre and Sidon, they would
have repented long ago, sitting in sackcloth and
ashes.
14 "But it will be more tolerable for Tyre and
Sidon at the judgment than for you.
15 [a]"And you, Capernaum, [1]who are [b]exalted to
heaven, [c]will be brought down to Hades.
16 [a]"He who hears you hears Me, [b]he who rejects
you rejects Me, and [c]he who rejects Me rejects
Him who sent Me."
**17** Then [a]the [1]seventy returned with joy, saying,
"Lord, even the demons are subject to us in Your
name."
18 And He said to them, [a]"I saw Satan fall like
lightning from heaven.
19 "Behold, [a]I give you the authority to trample
on serpents and scorpions, and over all the power
of the enemy, and nothing shall by any means
hurt you.
20 "Nevertheless do not rejoice in this, that the
spirits are subject to you, but [1]rather rejoice
because [a]your names are written in heaven."
**21** [a]In that hour Jesus rejoiced in the Spirit and
said, "I thank You, Father, Lord of heaven and
earth, that You have hidden these things from *the*
wise and prudent and revealed them to babes.
Even so, Father, for so it seemed good in Your
sight.
22 [a]"All[1] things have been delivered to Me by My
Father, and [b]no one knows who the Son is except
the Father, and who the Father is except the Son,
and *the one* to whom the Son wills to reveal *Him.*"
23 Then He turned to *His* disciples and said
privately, [a]"Blessed *are* the eyes which see the
things you see;
24 "for I tell you [a]that many prophets and kings
have desired to see what you see, and have not
seen *it,* and to hear what you hear, and have not
heard *it.*"
**25** And behold, a certain [1]lawyer stood up and
tested Him, saying, [a]"Teacher, what shall I do to
inherit eternal life?"
26 He said to him, "What is written in the law?
What is your reading *of it?*"
27 So he answered and said, [a]"*'You shall love the*
*LORD your God with all your heart, with all your*
*soul, with all your strength, and with all your*
*mind,'* and [b]*'your neighbor as yourself.'*"
28 And He said to him, "You have answered
rightly; do this and [a]you will live."
29 But he, wanting to [a]justify himself, said to
Jesus, "And who is my neighbor?"
30 Then Jesus answered and said: "A certain *man*
went down from Jerusalem to Jericho, and fell
among [1]thieves, who stripped him of his clothing,
wounded *him,* and departed, leaving *him* half
dead.
31 "Now by chance a certain priest came down
that road. And when he saw him, [a]he passed by on
the other side.
32 "Likewise a Levite, when he arrived at the
place, came and looked, and passed by on the
other side.
33 "But a certain [a]Samaritan, as he journeyed,
came where he was. And when he saw him, he
had [b]compassion.
34 "So he went to *him* and bandaged his wounds,
pouring on oil and wine; and he set him on his
own animal, brought him to an inn, and took care
of him.
35 "On the next day, [1]when he departed, he took
out two [a]denarii, gave *them* to the innkeeper, and
said to him, 'Take care of him; and whatever more
you spend, when I come again, I will repay you.'
36 "So which of these three do you think was
neighbor to him who fell among the thieves?"
37 And he said, "He who showed mercy on him."
Then Jesus said to him, [a]"Go and do likewise."
**38** Now it happened as they went that He entered
a certain village; and a certain woman named
[a]Martha welcomed Him into her house.
39 And she had a sister called Mary, [a]who also
[b]sat at [1]Jesus' feet and heard His word.
40 But Martha was distracted with much serving,
and she approached Him and said, "Lord, do You
not care that my sister has left me to serve alone?
Therefore tell her to help me."
41 And [1]Jesus answered and said to her, "Martha,
Martha, you are worried and troubled about many
things.
42 "But [a]one thing is needed, and Mary has
chosen that good part, which will not be taken
away from her."

### *Jesus Teaches How to Pray*

**11** Now it came to pass, as He was praying in a
certain place, when He ceased, *that* one of
His disciples said to Him, "Lord, teach us to pray,
as John also taught his disciples."
2 So He said to them, "When you pray, say:

[a]Our[1] Father [2]in heaven,
Hallowed be Your name.
Your kingdom come.
[3]Your will be done
On earth as *it is* in heaven.
3 Give us day by day our daily bread.
4 And [a]forgive us our sins,
For we also forgive everyone who is indebted
to us.
And do not lead us into temptation,
[1]But deliver us from the evil one."

**5** And He said to them, "Which of you shall
have a friend, and go to him at midnight and say
to him, 'Friend, lend me three loaves;

**3** [a]Matt. 10:16
**4** [a]Luke 9:3–5 [b]2 Kin. 4:29
**5** [a]Matt. 10:12
**7** [a]Matt. 10:11 [b]1 Cor. 10:27 [c]1 Tim. 5:18
**9** [a]Mark 3:15 [b]Matt. 3:2; 10:7
**11** [a]Acts 13:51 [1]NU *our feet*
**12** [a]Matt. 10:15; 11:24 [1]NU, M omit *But*
**13** [a]Matt. 11:21–23 [b]Ezek. 3:6
**15** [a]Matt. 11:23 [b]Is. 14:13–15 [c]Ezek. 26:20 [1]NU *will you be exalted to heaven? You will be thrust down to Hades!*
**16** [a]John 13:20 [b]1 Thess. 4:8 [c]John 5:23
**17** [a]Luke 10:1 [1]NU *seventy-two*
**18** [a]John 12:31
**19** [a]Mark 16:18
**20** [a]Is. 4:3 [1]NU, M omit *rather*
**21** [a]Matt. 11:25–27
**22** [a]John 3:35; 5:27; 17:2 [b][John 1:18; 6:44, 46] [1]M *And turning to the disciples He said, "All*
**23** [a]Matt. 13:16, 17
**24** [a]1 Pet. 1:10, 11
**25** [a]Matt. 19:16–19; 22:35 [1]*expert in the law*
**27** [a]Deut. 6:5 [b]Lev. 19:18
**28** [a]Ezek. 20:11, 13, 21
**29** [a]Luke 16:15
**30** [1]*robbers*
**31** [a]Ps. 38:11
**33** [a]John 4:9 [b]Luke 15:20
**35** [a]Matt. 20:2 [1]NU omits *when he departed*
**37** [a]Prov. 14:21
**38** [a]John 11:1; 12:2, 3
**39** [a][1 Cor. 7:32–40] [b]Acts 22:3 [1]NU *the Lord's*
**41** [1]NU *the Lord*
**42** [a][Ps. 27:4]

CHAPTER 11
**2** [a]Matt. 6:9–13 [1]NU omits *Our* [2]NU omits *in heaven* [3]NU omits the rest of v. 2.
**4** [a][Eph. 4:32] [1]NU omits *But deliver us from the evil one*

6 'for a friend of mine has come to me on his journey, and I have nothing to set before him';

7 "and he will answer from within and say, 'Do not trouble me; the door is now shut, and my children are with me in bed; I cannot rise and give to you'?

8 "I say to you, [a]though he will not rise and give to him because he is his friend, yet because of his persistence he will rise and give him as many as he needs.

**9** [a]"So I say to you, ask, and it will be given to you; [b]seek, and you will find; knock, and it will be opened to you.

10 "For everyone who asks receives, and he who seeks finds, and to him who knocks it will be opened.

11 [a]"If a son asks for [1]bread from any father among you, will he give him a stone? Or if *he asks* for a fish, will he give him a serpent instead of a fish?

12 "Or if he asks for an egg, will he offer him a scorpion?

13 "If you then, being evil, know how to give [a]good gifts to your children, how much more will *your* heavenly Father give the Holy Spirit to those who ask Him!"

**14** [a]And He was casting out a demon, and it was mute. So it was, when the demon had gone out, that the mute spoke; and the multitudes marveled.

15 But some of them said, [a]"He casts out demons by [1]Beelzebub, the ruler of the demons."

16 Others, testing *Him*, [a]sought from Him a sign from heaven.

17 [a]But [b]He, knowing their thoughts, said to them: "Every kingdom divided against itself is brought to desolation, and a house *divided* against a house falls.

18 "If Satan also is divided against himself, how will his kingdom stand? Because you say I cast out demons by Beelzebub.

19 "And if I cast out demons by Beelzebub, by whom do your sons cast *them* out? Therefore they will be your judges.

20 "But if I cast out demons [a]with the finger of God, surely the kingdom of God has come upon you.

21 [a]"When a strong man, fully armed, guards his own palace, his goods are in peace.

22 "But [a]when a stronger than he comes upon him and overcomes him, he takes from him all his armor in which he trusted, and divides his [1]spoils.

23 [a]"He who is not with Me is against Me, and he who does not gather with Me scatters.

**24** [a]"When an unclean spirit goes out of a man, he goes through dry places, seeking rest; and finding none, he says, 'I will return to my house from which I came.'

25 "And when he comes, he finds *it* swept and put in order.

26 "Then he goes and takes with *him* seven other spirits more wicked than himself, and they enter and dwell there; and [a]the last *state* of that man is worse than the first."

**27** And it happened, as He spoke these things, that a certain woman from the crowd raised her voice and said to Him, [a]"Blessed *is* the womb that bore You, and *the* breasts which nursed You!"

28 But He said, [a]"More than that, blessed *are* those who hear the word of God and keep it!"

**29** [a]And while the crowds were thickly gathered together, He began to say, "This is an evil generation. It seeks a [b]sign, and no sign will be given to it except the sign of Jonah [1]the prophet.

30 "For as [a]Jonah became a sign to the Ninevites, so also the Son of Man will be to this generation.

31 [a]"The queen of the South will rise up in the judgment with the men of this generation and condemn them, for she came from the ends of the earth to hear the wisdom of Solomon; and indeed a [b]greater than Solomon *is* here.

32 "The men of Nineveh will rise up in the judgment with this generation and condemn it, for [a]they repented at the preaching of Jonah; and indeed a greater than Jonah *is* here.

**33** [a]"No one, when he has lit a lamp, puts *it* in a secret place or under a [b]basket, but on a lampstand, that those who come in may see the light.

34 [a]"The lamp of the body is the eye. Therefore, when your eye is [1]good, your whole body also is full of light. But when *your eye* is [2]bad, your body also *is* full of darkness.

35 "Therefore take heed that the light which is in you is not darkness.

36 "If then your whole body *is* full of light, having no part dark, *the* whole *body* will be full of light, as when the bright shining of a lamp gives you light."

**37** And as He spoke, a certain Pharisee asked Him to dine with him. So He went in and sat down to eat.

38 [a]When the Pharisee saw *it,* he marveled that He had not first washed before dinner.

39 [a]Then the Lord said to him, "Now you Pharisees make the outside of the cup and dish clean, but [b]your inward part is full of [1]greed and wickedness.

40 "Foolish ones! Did not [a]He who made the outside make the inside also?

41 [a]"But rather give alms of [1]such things as you have; then indeed all things are clean to you.

42 [a]"But woe to you Pharisees! For you tithe the mint and rue and all manner of herbs, and [b]pass by justice and the [c]love of God. These you ought to have done, without leaving the others undone.

43 [a]"Woe to you Pharisees! For you love the [1]best seats in the synagogues and greetings in the marketplaces.

44 [a]"Woe to you, [1]scribes and Pharisees, hypocrites! [b]For you are like graves which are not seen, and the men who walk over *them* are not aware *of them.*"

45 Then one of the lawyers answered and said to Him, "Teacher, by saying these things You reproach us also."

46 And He said, "Woe to you also, lawyers! [a]For you load men with burdens hard to bear, and you yourselves do not touch the burdens with one of your fingers.

47 [a]"Woe to you! For you build the tombs of the prophets, and your fathers killed them.

48 "In fact, you bear witness that you approve the deeds of your fathers; for they indeed killed them, and you build their tombs.

49 "Therefore the wisdom of God also said, [a]'I will send them prophets and apostles, and *some* of them they will kill and persecute,'

50 "that the blood of all the prophets which was shed from the foundation of the world may be required of this generation,

51 [a]"from the blood of Abel to [b]the blood of Zechariah who perished between the altar and the temple. Yes, I say to you, it shall be required of this generation.

**8** [a][Luke 18:1–5]
**9** [a][John 15:7] [b]Is. 55:6
**11** [a]Matt. 7:9 [1]NU omits *bread from any father among you, will he give him a stone? Or if he asks for*
**13** [a]James 1:17
**14** [a]Matt. 9:32–34; 12:22, 24
**15** [a]Matt. 9:34; 12:24 [1]NU, M *Beelzebul*
**16** [a]Matt. 12:38; 16:1
**17** [a]Matt. 12:25–29 [b]John 2:25
**20** [a]Ex. 8:19
**21** [a]Mark 3:27
**22** [a][Is. 53:12] [1]*plunder*
**23** [a]Matt. 12:30
**24** [a]Matt. 12:43–45
**26** [a][2 Pet. 2:20]
**27** [a]Luke 1:28, 48
**28** [a][Luke 8:21]
**29** [a]Matt. 12:38–42 [b]1 Cor. 1:22 [1]NU omits *the prophet*
**30** [a]Jon. 1:17; 2:10; 3:3–10
**31** [a]1 Kin. 10:1–9 [b][Rom. 9:5]
**32** [a]Jon. 3:5
**33** [a]Mark 4:21 [b]Matt. 5:15
**34** [a]Matt. 6:22, 23 [1]Clear, or healthy [2]Evil, or unhealthy
**38** [a]Mark 7:2, 3
**39** [a]Matt. 23:25 [b]Titus 1:15 [1]Lit. *eager grasping* or *robbery*
**40** [a]Gen. 1:26, 27
**41** [a][Luke 12:33; 16:9] [1]Or *what is inside*
**42** [a]Matt. 23:23 [b][Mic. 6:7, 8] [c]John 5:42
**43** [a]Mark 12:38, 39 [1]Or *places of honor*
**44** [a]Matt. 23:27 [b]Ps. 5:9 [1]NU omits *scribes and Pharisees, hypocrites*
**46** [a]Matt. 23:4
**47** [a]Matt. 23:29
**49** [a]Matt. 23:34
**51** [a]Gen. 4:8 [b]2 Chr. 24:20, 21

52 [a]"Woe to you lawyers! For you have taken
away the key of knowledge. You did not enter in
yourselves, and those who were entering in you
hindered."
53 [1]And as He said these things to them, the
scribes and the Pharisees began to assail *Him*
vehemently, and to cross-examine Him about
many things,
54 lying in wait for Him, [1]and [a]seeking to catch
Him in something He might say, [2]that they might
accuse Him.

## *Jesus Preaches to the Multitude*

**12** In [a]the meantime, when an innumerable
multitude of people had gathered together,
so that they trampled one another, He began to
say to His disciples first *of all,* [b]"Beware of the
[1]leaven of the Pharisees, which is hypocrisy.
2 [a]"For there is nothing covered that will not be
revealed, nor hidden that will not be known.
3 "Therefore whatever you have spoken in the
dark will be heard in the light, and what you have
spoken in the ear in inner rooms will be proclaimed on the housetops.
4 [a]"And I say to you, [b]My friends, do not be
afraid of those who kill the body, and after that
have no more that they can do.
5 "But I will show you whom you should fear:
Fear Him who, after He has killed, has power to
cast into hell; yes, I say to you, [a]fear Him!
6 "Are not five sparrows sold for two [1]copper
coins? And [a]not one of them is forgotten before
God.
7 "But the very hairs of your head are all numbered. Do not fear therefore; you are of more
value than many sparrows.
**8** [a]"Also I say to you, whoever confesses Me
[b]before men, him the Son of Man also will confess
before the angels of God.
9 "But he who [a]denies Me before men will be
denied before the angels of God.
10 "And [a]anyone who speaks a word against the
Son of Man, it will be forgiven him; but to him
who blasphemes against the Holy Spirit, it will not
be forgiven.
11 [a]"Now when they bring you to the synagogues
and magistrates and authorities, do not worry
about how or what you should answer, or what
you should say.
12 "For the Holy Spirit will [a]teach you in that
very hour what you ought to say."
**13** Then one from the crowd said to Him,
"Teacher, tell my brother to divide the inheritance
with me."
14 But He said to him, [a]"Man, who made Me a
judge or an arbitrator over you?"
15 And He said to them, [a]"Take heed and beware
of [1]covetousness, for one's life does not consist in
the abundance of the things he possesses."
16 Then He spoke a parable to them, saying:
"The ground of a certain rich man yielded plenti-
fully.
17 "And he thought within himself, saying,
'What shall I do, since I have no room to store my
crops?'
18 "So he said, 'I will do this: I will pull down my
barns and build greater, and there I will store all
my crops and my goods.
19 'And I will say to my soul, [a]"Soul, you have
many goods laid up for many years; take your
ease; [b]eat, drink, *and* be merry."'

**11:52** [a]Matt. 23:13
**53** [1]NU *And when He left there*
**54** [a]Mark 12:13 [1]NU omits *and seeking* [2]NU omits *that they might accuse Him*

CHAPTER 12
**1** [a]Mark 8:15 [b]Matt. 16:12 [1]*yeast*
**2** [a]Matt. 10:26; [1 Cor. 4:5]
**4** [a]Is. 51:7, 8, 12, 13 [b][John 15:13–15]
**5** [a]Ps. 119:120
**6** [a]Matt. 6:26 [1]Gr. *assarion,* a coin worth about 1/16 of a denarius
**8** [a]Matt. 10:32 [b]Ps. 119:46
**9** [a]Matt. 10:33
**10** [a][Matt. 12:31, 32]
**11** [a]Mark 13:11
**12** [a][John 14:26]
**14** [a][John 18:36]
**15** [a][1 Tim. 6:6–10] [1]NU *all covetousness*
**19** [a]Eccl. 11:9 [b][Eccl. 2:24; 3:13; 5:18; 8:15]
**20** [a]Ps. 52:7 [b]Ps. 39:6
**21** [a][James 2:5; 5:1–5]
**22** [a]Matt. 6:25–33
**24** [a]Job 38:41
**26** [1]*do you worry*
**27** [a]1 Kin. 10:4–7 [1]*clothed*
**28** [a]Matt. 6:30; 8:26; 14:31; 16:8
**30** [a]Matt. 6:31, 32
**31** [a]Matt. 6:33 [1]NU *His kingdom, and these things*
**32** [a][Matt. 11:25, 26]
**33** [a]Matt. 19:21 [b]Luke 11:41 [c]Matt. 6:20
**35** [a][1 Pet. 1:13] [b][Matt. 25:1–13]
**37** [a]Matt. 24:46
**39** [a]Rev. 3:3; 16:15 [1]NU *not have allowed*
**40** [a]Mark 13:33
**42** [a]Matt. 24:45, 46; 25:21 [1]*at the right time*
**44** [a]Matt. 24:47; 25:21

20 "But God said to him, 'Fool! This night [a]your
soul will be required of you; [b]then whose will
those things be which you have provided?'
21 "So *is* he who lays up treasure for himself,
[a]and is not rich toward God."
**22** Then He said to His disciples, "Therefore I say
to you, [a]do not worry about your life, what you
will eat; nor about the body, what you will put on.
23 "Life is more than food, and the body *is more*
than clothing.
24 "Consider the ravens, for they neither sow nor
reap, which have neither storehouse nor barn; and
[a]God feeds them. Of how much more value are
you than the birds?
25 "And which of you by worrying can add one
cubit to his stature?
26 "If you then are not able to do *the* least, why
[1]are you anxious for the rest?
27 "Consider the lilies, how they grow: they
neither toil nor spin; and yet I say to you, even
[a]Solomon in all his glory was not [1]arrayed like one
of these.
28 "If then God so clothes the grass, which today
is in the field and tomorrow is thrown into the
oven, how much more *will He clothe* you, O *you*
of [a]little faith?
29 "And do not seek what you should eat or what
you should drink, nor have an anxious mind.
30 "For all these things the nations of the world
seek after, and your Father [a]knows that you need
these things.
31 [a]"But seek [1]the kingdom of God, and all these
things shall be added to you.
32 "Do not fear, little flock, for [a]it is your Father's
good pleasure to give you the kingdom.
33 [a]"Sell what you have and give [b]alms; [c]provide
yourselves money bags which do not grow old, a
treasure in the heavens that does not fail, where
no thief approaches nor moth destroys.
34 "For where your treasure is, there your heart
will be also.
**35** [a]"Let your waist be girded and [b]*your* lamps
burning;
36 "and you yourselves be like men who wait for
their master, when he will return from the wedding, that when he comes and knocks they may
open to him immediately.
37 [a]"Blessed *are* those servants whom the master,
when he comes, will find watching. Assuredly, I
say to you that he will gird himself and have them
sit down *to eat,* and will come and serve them.
38 "And if he should come in the second watch,
or come in the third watch, and find *them* so,
blessed are those servants.
39 [a]"But know this, that if the master of the
house had known what hour the thief would
come, he would [1]have watched and not allowed
his house to be broken into.
40 [a]"Therefore you also be ready, for the Son of
Man is coming at an hour you do not expect."
41 Then Peter said to Him, "Lord, do You speak
this parable *only* to us, or to all *people?*"
42 And the Lord said, [a]"Who then is that faithful
and wise steward, whom *his* master will make
ruler over his household, to give *them their* portion of food [1]in due season?
43 "Blessed *is* that servant whom his master will
find so doing when he comes.
44 [a]"Truly, I say to you that he will make him
ruler over all that he has.

45 [a]"But if that servant says in his heart, 'My
master is delaying his coming,' and begins to beat
the male and female servants, and to eat and
drink and be drunk,
46 "the master of that servant will come on a
[a]day when he is not looking for *him*, and at an
hour when he is not aware, and will cut him in
two and appoint *him* his portion with the unbelievers.
47 "And [a]that servant who [b]knew his master's
will, and did not prepare *himself* or do according
to his will, shall be beaten with many *stripes*.
48 [a]"But he who did not know, yet committed
things deserving of stripes, shall be beaten with
few. For everyone to whom much is given, from
him much will be required; and to whom much
has been committed, of him they will ask the
more.
**49** [a]"I came to send fire on the earth, and how I
wish it were already kindled!
50 "But [a]I have a baptism to be baptized with,
and how distressed I am till it is [b]accomplished!
51 [a]"Do *you* suppose that I came to give peace on
earth? I tell you, not at all, [b]but rather division.
52 [a]"For from now on five in one house will be
divided: three against two, and two against three.
53 [a]"Father will be divided against son and son
against father, mother against daughter and
daughter against mother, mother-in-law against
her daughter-in-law and daughter-in-law against
her mother-in-law."
**54** Then He also said to the multitudes, [a]"Whenever you see a cloud rising out of the west,
immediately you say, 'A shower is coming'; and so
it is.
55 "And when you see the [a]south wind blow, you
say, 'There will be hot weather'; and there is.
56 "Hypocrites! You can discern the face of the
sky and of the earth, but how *is it* you do not
discern [a]this time?
**57** "Yes, and why, even of yourselves, do you not
judge what is right?
58 [a]"When you go with your adversary to the
magistrate, make every effort [b]along the way to
settle with him, lest he drag you to the judge, the
judge deliver you to the officer, and the officer
throw you into prison.
59 "I tell you, you shall not depart from there till
you have paid the very last mite."

### *Parables of the Kingdom*

**13** There were present at that season some
who told Him about the Galileans whose
blood Pilate had [1]mingled with their sacrifices.
2 And Jesus answered and said to them, "Do
you suppose that these Galileans were worse
sinners than all *other* Galileans, because they
suffered such things?
3 "I tell you, no; but unless you repent you will
all likewise perish.
4 "Or those eighteen on whom the tower in
Siloam fell and killed them, do you think that they
were worse sinners than all *other* men who dwelt
in Jerusalem?
5 "I tell you, no; but unless you repent you will
all likewise perish."
**6** He also spoke this parable: [a]"A certain *man*
had a fig tree planted in his vineyard, and he came
seeking fruit on it and found none.
7 "Then he said to the keeper of his vineyard,
'Look, for three years I have come seeking fruit
on this fig tree and find none. Cut it down; why
does it [1]use up the ground?'
8 "But he answered and said to him, 'Sir, let it
alone this year also, until I dig around it and
fertilize *it*.
9 [1]'And if it bears fruit, *well*. But if not, after that
you can [a]cut it down.'"
**10** Now He was teaching in one of the synagogues on the Sabbath.
11 And behold, there was a woman who had a
spirit of infirmity eighteen years, and was bent
over and could in no way [1]raise *herself* up.
12 But when Jesus saw her, He called *her* to *Him*
and said to her, "Woman, you are loosed from
your [a]infirmity."
13 [a]And He laid *His* hands on her, and immediately she was made straight, and glorified God.
14 But the ruler of the synagogue answered with
indignation, because Jesus had [a]healed on the
Sabbath; and he said to the crowd, [b]"There are six
days on which men ought to work; therefore
come and be healed on them, and [c]not on the
Sabbath day."
15 The Lord then answered him and said, [1]"Hypocrite! [a]Does not each one of you on the Sabbath
loose his ox or donkey from the stall, and lead *it*
away to water it?
16 "So ought not this woman, [a]being a daughter
of Abraham, whom Satan has bound—think of
it—for eighteen years, be loosed from this bond on
the Sabbath?"
17 And when He said these things, all His adversaries were put to shame; and all the multitude
rejoiced for all the glorious things that were [a]done
by Him.
**18** [a]Then He said, "What is the kingdom of God
like? And to what shall I compare it?
19 "It is like a mustard seed, which a man took
and put in his garden; and it grew and became a
[1]large tree, and the birds of the air nested in its
branches."
**20** And again He said, "To what shall I liken the
kingdom of God?
21 "It is like [1]leaven, which a woman took and
hid in three [a]measures[2] of meal till it was all
leavened."
**22** [a]And He went through the cities and villages,
teaching, and journeying toward Jerusalem.
23 Then one said to Him, "Lord, are there [a]few
who are saved?" And He said to them,
24 [a]"Strive to enter through the narrow gate, for
[b]many, I say to you, will seek to enter and will not
be able.
25 [a]"When once the Master of the house has
risen up and [b]shut the door, and you begin to
stand outside and knock at the door, saying,
[c]'Lord, Lord, open for us,' and He will answer and
say to you, [d]'I do not know you, where you are
from,'
26 "then you will begin to say, 'We ate and drank
in Your presence, and You taught in our streets.'
27 [a]"But He will say, 'I tell you I do not know
you, where you are from. [b]Depart from Me, all you
workers of iniquity.'
28 [a]"There will be weeping and gnashing of teeth,
[b]when you see Abraham and Isaac and Jacob and
all the prophets in the kingdom of God, and
yourselves thrust out.
29 "They will come from the east and the west,
from the north and the south, and sit down in the
kingdom of God.

**45** [a]2 Pet. 3:3, 4
**46** [a]1 Thess. 5:3
**47** [a]Deut. 25:2 [b][James 4:17]
**48** [a][Lev. 5:17]
**49** [a]Luke 12:51
**50** [a]Mark 10:38 [b]John 12:27; 19:30
**51** [a]Matt. 10:34–36 [b]John 7:43; 9:16; 10:19
**52** [a]Mark 13:12
**53** [a]Matt. 10:21, 36
**54** [a]Matt. 16:2, 3
**55** [a]Job 37:17
**56** [a]Luke 19:41–44
**58** [a]Prov. 25:8 [b][Is. 55:6]

CHAPTER 13
**1** [1]*mixed*
**6** [a]Matt. 21:19
**7** [1]*waste*
**9** [a][John 15:2] [1]NU *And if it bears fruit after that, well. But if not, you can*
**11** [1]*straighten up*
**12** [a]Luke 7:21; 8:2
**13** [a]Acts 9:17
**14** [a][Luke 6:6–11; 14:1–6] [b]Ex. 20:9; 23:12 [c]Mark 3:2
**15** [a]Luke 14:5 [1]NU, M *Hypocrites*
**16** [a]Luke 19:9
**17** [a]Mark 5:19, 20
**18** [a]Mark 4:30–32
**19** [1]NU omits *large*
**21** [a]Matt. 13:33 [1]*yeast* [2]Gr. *saton,* same as Heb. *seah;* Approximately 2 pecks in all
**22** [a]Mark 6:6
**23** [a][Matt. 7:14; 20:16]
**24** [a][Matt. 7:13] [b][John 7:34; 8:21; 13:33]
**25** [a]Is. 55:6 [b]Matt. 25:10 [c]Luke 6:46 [d]Matt. 7:23; 25:12
**27** [a][Matt. 7:23; 25:41] [b]Ps. 6:8
**28** [a]Matt. 8:12; 13:42; 24:51 [b]Matt. 8:11

30 [a]"And indeed there are last who will be first, and there are first who will be last."
31 [1]On that very day some Pharisees came, saying to Him, "Get out and depart from here, for Herod wants to kill You."
32 And He said to them, "Go, tell that fox, 'Behold, I cast out demons and perform cures today and tomorrow, and the third *day* [a]I shall be [1]perfected.'
33 "Nevertheless I must journey today, tomorrow, and the *day* following; for it cannot be that a prophet should perish outside of Jerusalem.
**34** [a]"O Jerusalem, Jerusalem, the one who kills the prophets and stones those who are sent to her! How often I wanted to gather your children together, as a hen *gathers* her brood under *her* wings, but you were not willing!
35 "See! [a]Your house is left to you desolate; and [1]assuredly, I say to you, you shall not see Me until *the time* comes when you say, [b]*'Blessed is He who comes in the name of the LORD!'* "

### *The Parable of the Great Supper*

**14** Now it happened, as He went into the house of one of the rulers of the Pharisees to eat bread on the Sabbath, that they watched Him closely.
2 And behold, there was a certain man before Him who had dropsy.
3 And Jesus, answering, spoke to the lawyers and Pharisees, saying, [a]"Is it lawful to heal on the [1]Sabbath?"
4 But they kept silent. And He took *him* and healed him, and let him go.
5 Then He answered them, saying, [a]"Which of you, having a [1]donkey or an ox that has fallen into a pit, will not immediately pull him out on the Sabbath day?"
6 And they could not answer Him regarding these things.
**7** So He told a parable to those who were invited, when He noted how they chose the best places, saying to them:
8 "When you are invited by anyone to a wedding feast, do not sit down in the best place, lest one more honorable than you be invited by him;
9 "and he who invited you and him come and say to you, 'Give place to this man,' and then you begin with shame to take the lowest place.
10 [a]"But when you are invited, go and sit down in the lowest place, so that when he who invited you comes he may say to you, 'Friend, go up higher.' Then you will have glory in the presence of those who sit at the table with you.
11 [a]"For whoever exalts himself will be [1]humbled, and he who humbles himself will be exalted."
12 Then He also said to him who invited Him, "When you give a dinner or a supper, do not ask your friends, your brothers, your relatives, nor rich neighbors, lest they also invite you back, and you be repaid.
13 "But when you give a feast, invite [a]*the* poor, *the* [1]maimed, *the* lame, *the* blind.
14 "And you will be [a]blessed, because they cannot repay you; for you shall be repaid at the resurrection of the just."
**15** Now when one of those who sat at the table with Him heard these things, he said to Him, [a]"Blessed *is* he who shall eat [1]bread in the kingdom of God!"
16 [a]Then He said to him, "A certain man gave a great supper and invited many,
17 "and [a]sent his servant at supper time to say to those who were invited, 'Come, for all things are now ready.'
18 "But they all with one *accord* began to make excuses. The first said to him, 'I have bought a piece of ground, and I must go and see it. I ask you to have me excused.'
19 "And another said, 'I have bought five yoke of oxen, and I am going to test them. I ask you to have me excused.'
20 "Still another said, 'I have married a wife, and therefore I cannot come.'
21 "So that servant came and reported these things to his master. Then the master of the house, being angry, said to his servant, 'Go out quickly into the streets and lanes of the city, and bring in here *the* poor and *the* [1]maimed and *the* lame and *the* blind.'
22 "And the servant said, 'Master, it is done as you commanded, and still there is room.'
23 "Then the master said to the servant, 'Go out into the highways and hedges, and compel *them* to come in, that my house may be filled.
24 'For I say to you [a]that none of those men who were invited shall taste my supper.' "
**25** Now great multitudes went with Him. And He turned and said to them,
26 [a]"If anyone comes to Me [b]and does not hate his father and mother, wife and children, brothers and sisters, [c]yes, and his own life also, he cannot be My disciple.
27 "And [a]whoever does not bear his cross and come after Me cannot be My disciple.
28 "For [a]which of you, intending to build a tower, does not sit down first and count the cost, whether he has *enough* to finish *it*—
29 "lest, after he has laid the foundation, and is not able to finish, all who see *it* begin to mock him,
30 "saying, 'This man began to build and was not able to finish.'
31 "Or what king, going to make war against another king, does not sit down first and consider whether he is able with ten thousand to meet him who comes against him with twenty thousand?
32 "Or else, while the other is still a great way off, he sends a delegation and asks conditions of peace.
33 "So likewise, whoever of you [a]does not forsake all that he has cannot be My disciple.
**34** [a]"Salt *is* good; but if the salt has lost its flavor, how shall it be seasoned?
35 "It is neither fit for the land nor for the [1]dunghill, *but* men throw it out. He who has ears to hear, let him hear!"

### *The Lost Sheep, the Lost Coin, and the Lost Son*

**15** Then [a]all the tax collectors and the sinners drew near to Him to hear Him.
2 And the Pharisees and scribes complained, saying, "This Man [1]receives sinners [a]and eats with them."
3 So He spoke this parable to them, saying:
4 [a]"What man of you, having a hundred sheep, if he loses one of them, does not leave the ninety-nine in the wilderness, and go after the one which is lost until he finds it?

**30** [a][Matt. 19:30; 20:16]; Mark 10:31
**31** [1]NU *In that very hour*
**32** [a]Luke 24:46; Acts 10:40; 1 Cor. 15:4; [Heb. 2:10; 5:9; 7:28] [1]Resurrected
**34** [a]Matt. 23:37–39; 2 Chr. 24:20, 21; 36:15, 16
**35** [a]Lev. 26:31, 32; Ps. 69:25; Is. 1:7; Jer. 22:5; Dan. 9:27; Mic. 3:12 [b]Ps. 118:26; Matt. 21:9; Mark 11:10; Luke 19:38; John 12:13 [1]NU, M omit *assuredly*

CHAPTER 14
**3** [a]Matt. 12:10 [1]NU adds *or not*
**5** [a][Ex. 23:5; Deut. 22:4]; Luke 13:15 [1]NU, M *son*
**10** [a]Prov. 25:6, 7
**11** [a]Job 22:29; Ps. 18:27; Prov. 29:23; Matt. 23:12; Luke 18:14; James 4:6; [1 Pet. 5:5] [1]*put down*
**13** [a]Neh. 8:10, 12 [1]*crippled*
**14** [a][Matt. 25:34–40]
**15** [a]Rev. 19:9 [1]M *the best*
**16** [a]Matt. 22:2–14
**17** [a]Prov. 9:2, 5
**21** [1]*crippled*
**24** [a][Matt. 21:43; 22:8; Acts 13:46]
**26** [a]Deut. 13:6; 33:9; Matt. 10:37 [b]Rom. 9:13 [c]Rev. 12:11
**27** [a]Matt. 16:24; Mark 8:34; Luke 9:23; [2 Tim. 3:12]
**28** [a]Prov. 24:27
**33** [a]Matt. 19:27
**34** [a]Matt. 5:13; [Mark 9:50]
**35** [1]*rubbish heap*

CHAPTER 15
**1** [a][Matt. 9:10–15]
**2** [a]Acts 11:3; Gal. 2:12 [1]*welcomes*
**4** [a]Matt. 18:12–14; 1 Pet. 2:25

5 "And when he has found *it,* he lays *it* on his shoulders, rejoicing.

6 "And when he comes home, he calls together *his* friends and neighbors, saying to them, [a]'Rejoice with me, for I have found my sheep [b]which was lost!'

7 "I say to you that likewise there will be more joy in heaven over one sinner who repents [a]than over ninety-nine [1]just persons who [b]need no repentance.

8 "Or what woman, having ten silver [1]coins, if she loses one coin, does not light a lamp, sweep the house, and search carefully until she finds *it?*

9 "And when she has found *it,* she calls *her* friends and neighbors together, saying, 'Rejoice with me, for I have found the piece which I lost!'

10 "Likewise, I say to you, there is joy in the presence of the angels of God over one sinner who repents."

**11** Then He said: "A certain man had two sons.

12 "And the younger of them said to *his* father, 'Father, give me the portion of goods that falls *to me.*' So he divided to them [a]*his* livelihood.

13 "And not many days after, the younger son gathered all together, journeyed to a far country, and there wasted his possessions with [1]prodigal living.

14 "But when he had spent all, there arose a severe famine in that land, and he began to be in want.

15 "Then he went and joined himself to a citizen of that country, and he sent him into his fields to feed swine.

16 "And he would gladly have filled his stomach with the [1]pods that the swine ate, and no one gave him *anything.*

17 "But when he came to himself, he said, 'How many of my father's hired servants have bread enough and to spare, and I perish with hunger!

18 'I will arise and go to my father, and will say to him, "Father, [a]I have sinned against heaven and before you,

19 and I am no longer worthy to be called your son. Make me like one of your hired servants." '

20 "And he arose and came to his father. But [a]when he was still a great way off, his father saw him and had compassion, and ran and fell on his neck and kissed him.

21 "And the son said to him, 'Father, I have sinned against heaven [a]and in your sight, and am no longer worthy to be called your son.'

22 "But the father said to his servants, [1]'Bring out the best robe and put *it* on him, and put a ring on his hand and sandals on *his* feet.

23 'And bring the fatted calf here and kill *it,* and let us eat and be merry;

24 [a]'for this my son was dead and is alive again; he was lost and is found.' And they began to be merry.

25 "Now his older son was in the field. And as he came and drew near to the house, he heard music and dancing.

26 "So he called one of the servants and asked what these things meant.

27 "And he said to him, 'Your brother has come, and because he has received him safe and sound, your father has killed the fatted calf.'

28 "But he was angry and would not go in. Therefore his father came out and pleaded with him.

29 "So he answered and said to *his* father, 'Lo, these many years I have been serving you; I never transgressed your commandment at any time; and yet you never gave me a young goat, that I might make merry with my friends.

30 'But as soon as this son of yours came, who has devoured your livelihood with harlots, you killed the fatted calf for him.'

31 "And he said to him, 'Son, you are always with me, and all that I have is yours.

32 'It was right that we should make merry and be glad, [a]for your brother was dead and is alive again, and was lost and is found.' "

### *The Parable of the Dishonest Servant*

**16** He also said to His disciples: "There was a certain rich man who had a steward, and an accusation was brought to him that this man was [1]wasting his goods.

2 "So he called him and said to him, 'What is this I hear about you? Give an [a]account of your stewardship, for you can no longer be steward.'

3 "Then the steward said within himself, 'What shall I do? For my master is taking the stewardship away from me. I cannot dig; I am ashamed to beg.

4 'I have resolved what to do, that when I am put out of the stewardship, they may receive me into their houses.'

5 "So he called every one of his master's debtors to *him,* and said to the first, 'How much do you owe my master?'

6 "And he said, 'A hundred [1]measures of oil.' So he said to him, 'Take your bill, and sit down quickly and write fifty.'

7 "Then he said to another, 'And how much do you owe?' So he said, 'A hundred [1]measures of wheat.' And he said to him, 'Take your bill, and write eighty.'

8 "So the master commended the unjust steward because he had dealt shrewdly. For the sons of this world are more shrewd in their generation than [a]the sons of light.

9 "And I say to you, [a]make friends for yourselves by unrighteous [1]mammon, that when [2]you fail, they may receive you into an everlasting home.

10 [a]"He who *is* faithful in *what is* least is faithful also in much; and he who is unjust in *what is* least is unjust also in much.

11 "Therefore if you have not been faithful in the unrighteous mammon, who will commit to your trust the true *riches?*

12 "And if you have not been faithful in what is another man's, who will give you what is your [a]own?

13 [a]"No servant can serve two masters; for either he will hate the one and love the other, or else he will be loyal to the one and despise the other. You cannot serve God and mammon."

**14** Now the Pharisees, [a]who were lovers of money, also heard all these things, and they [1]derided Him.

15 And He said to them, "You are those who [a]justify yourselves [b]before men, but [c]God knows your hearts. For [d]what is highly esteemed among men is an abomination in the sight of God.

16 [a]"The law and the prophets *were* until John. Since that time the kingdom of God has been preached, and everyone is pressing into it.

17 [a]"And it is easier for heaven and earth to pass away than for one [1]tittle of the law to fail.

---

**6** [a][Rom. 12:15] [b][Luke 19:10; 1 Pet. 2:10, 25]
**7** [a][Luke 5:32] [b][Mark 2:17] [1]*upright*
**8** [1]Gr. *drachma,* a valuable coin often worn in a ten-piece garland by married women
**12** [a]Mark 12:44
**13** [1]*wasteful*
**16** [1]*carob pods*
**18** [a]Ex. 9:27; 10:16; Num. 22:34; Josh. 7:20; 1 Sam. 15:24, 30; 26:21; 2 Sam. 12:13; 24:10, 17; Ps. 51:4; Matt. 27:4
**20** [a][Jer. 3:12]; Matt. 9:36; [Acts 2:39; Eph. 2:13, 17]
**21** [a]Ps. 51:4
**22** [1]NU *Quickly bring*
**24** [a]Matt. 8:22; Luke 9:60; 15:32; Rom. 11:15; [Eph. 2:1, 5; 5:14; Col. 2:13; 1 Tim. 5:6]
**32** [a]Luke 15:24

CHAPTER 16
**1** [1]*squandering*
**2** [a][Rom. 14:12; 2 Cor. 5:10; 1 Pet. 4:5, 6]
**6** [1]Gr. *batos,* same as Heb. *bath;* 8 or 9 gallons each
**7** [1]Gr. *koros,* same as Heb. *kor;* 10 or 12 bushels each
**8** [a][John 12:36; Eph. 5:8]; 1 Thess. 5:5
**9** [a]Dan. 4:27; [Matt. 6:19; 19:21]; Luke 11:41; [1 Tim. 6:17–19] [1]Lit., in Aram., *wealth* [2]NU *it fails*
**10** [a]Matt. 25:21; Luke 19:17
**12** [a][1 Pet. 1:3, 4]
**13** [a]Matt. 6:24; Gal. 1:10
**14** [a]Matt. 23:14 [1]Lit. *turned up their nose at*
**15** [a]Luke 10:29 [b][Matt. 6:2, 5, 16] [c]1 Chr. 28:9; 2 Chr. 6:30; Ps. 7:9; Prov. 15:11; Jer. 17:10 [d]1 Sam. 16:7; Ps. 10:3; Prov. 6:16–19; 16:5
**16** [a]Matt. 3:1–12; 4:17; 11:12, 13; Luke 7:29
**17** [a]Ps. 102:26, 27; Is. 40:8; 51:6; Matt. 5:18; 1 Pet. 1:25 [1]The smallest stroke in a Heb. letter

18 [a]"Whoever divorces his wife and marries another commits adultery; and whoever marries her who is divorced from *her* husband commits adultery.

**19** "There was a certain rich man who was clothed in purple and fine linen and [1]fared sumptuously every day.

20 "But there was a certain beggar named Lazarus, full of sores, who was laid at his gate,

21 "desiring to be fed with [1]the crumbs which fell from the rich man's table. Moreover the dogs came and licked his sores.

22 "So it was that the beggar died, and was carried by the angels to [a]Abraham's bosom. The rich man also died and was buried.

23 "And being in torments in Hades, he lifted up his eyes and saw Abraham afar off, and Lazarus in his bosom.

24 "Then he cried and said, 'Father Abraham, have mercy on me, and send Lazarus that he may dip the tip of his finger in water and [a]cool my tongue; for I [b]am tormented in this flame.'

25 "But Abraham said, 'Son, [a]remember that in your lifetime you received your good things, and likewise Lazarus evil things; but now he is comforted and you are tormented.

26 'And besides all this, between us and you there is a great gulf fixed, so that those who want to pass from here to you cannot, nor can those from there pass to us.'

27 "Then he said, 'I beg you therefore, father, that you would send him to my father's house,

28 'for I have five brothers, that he may testify to them, lest they also come to this place of torment.'

29 "Abraham said to him, [a]'They have Moses and the prophets; let them hear them.'

30 "And he said, 'No, father Abraham; but if one goes to them from the dead, they will repent.'

31 "But he said to him, [a]'If they do not hear Moses and the prophets, [b]neither will they be persuaded though one rise from the dead.' "

### *The Coming of the Kingdom*

**17** Then He said to the disciples, [a]"It is impossible that no [1]offenses should come, but [b]woe *to him* through whom they do come!

2 "It would be better for him if a millstone were hung around his neck, and he were thrown into the sea, than that he should [1]offend one of these little ones.

3 "Take heed to yourselves. [a]If your brother sins [1]against you, [b]rebuke him; and if he repents, forgive him.

4 "And if he sins against you seven times in a day, and seven times in a day returns [1]to you, saying, 'I repent,' you shall forgive him."

**5** And the apostles said to the Lord, "Increase our faith."

6 [a]So the Lord said, "If you have faith as a mustard seed, you can say to this mulberry tree, 'Be pulled up by the roots and be planted in the sea,' and it would obey you.

7 "And which of you, having a servant plowing or tending sheep, will say to him when he has come in from the field, 'Come at once and sit down to eat'?

8 "But will he not rather say to him, 'Prepare something for my supper, and gird yourself [a]and serve me till I have eaten and drunk, and afterward you will eat and drink'?

9 "Does he thank that servant because he did the things that were commanded [1]him? I think not.

10 "So likewise you, when you have done all those things which you are commanded, say, 'We are [a]unprofitable servants. We have done what was our duty to do.' "

**11** Now it happened [a]as He went to Jerusalem that He passed through the midst of Samaria and Galilee.

12 Then as He entered a certain village, there met Him ten men who were lepers, [a]who stood afar off.

13 And they lifted up *their* voices and said, "Jesus, Master, have mercy on us!"

14 So when He saw *them,* He said to them, [a]"Go, show yourselves to the priests." And so it was that as they went, they were cleansed.

15 And one of them, when he saw that he was healed, returned, and with a loud voice [a]glorified God,

16 and fell down on *his* face at His feet, giving Him thanks. And he was a [a]Samaritan.

17 So Jesus answered and said, "Were there not ten cleansed? But where *are* the nine?

18 "Were there not any found who returned to give glory to God except this foreigner?"

19 [a]And He said to him, "Arise, go your way. Your faith has made you well."

**20** Now when He was asked by the Pharisees when the kingdom of God would come, He answered them and said, "The kingdom of God does not come with observation;

21 [a]"nor will they say, 'See here!' or 'See there!' For indeed, [b]the kingdom of God is [1]within you."

22 Then He said to the disciples, [a]"The days will come when you will desire to see one of the days of the Son of Man, and you will not see *it.*

23 [a]"And they will say to you, [1]'Look here!' or 'Look there!' Do not go after *them* or follow *them.*

24 [a]"For as the lightning that flashes out of one *part* under heaven shines to the other *part* under heaven, so also the Son of Man will be in His day.

25 [a]"But first He must suffer many things and be [b]rejected by this generation.

26 [a]"And as it [b]was in the [c]days of [d]Noah, so it will be also in the days of the Son of Man:

27 "They ate, they drank, they married wives, they were given in marriage, until the [a]day that Noah entered the ark, and the flood came and [b]destroyed them all.

28 [a]"Likewise as it was also in the days of Lot: They ate, they drank, they bought, they sold, they planted, they built;

29 "but on [a]the day that Lot went out of Sodom it rained fire and brimstone from heaven and destroyed *them* all.

30 "Even so will it be in the day when the Son of Man [a]is revealed.

31 "In that day, he [a]who is on the housetop, and his [1]goods *are* in the house, let him not come down to take them away. And likewise the one who is in the field, let him not turn back.

32 [a]"Remember Lot's wife.

33 [a]"Whoever seeks to save his life will lose it, and whoever loses his life will preserve it.

34 [a]"I tell you, in that night there will be two [1]*men* in one bed: the one will be taken and the other will be left.

35 [a]"Two *women* will be grinding together: the one will be taken and the other left.

36 [1]"Two *men* will be in the field: the one will be taken and the other left."

**18** [a]1 Cor. 7:10, 11
**19** [1]*lived in luxury*
**21** [1]NU *what fell*
**22** [a]Matt. 8:11
**24** [a]Zech. 14:12 [b][Mark 9:42–48]
**25** [a]Luke 6:24
**29** [a]Acts 15:21; 17:11
**31** [a][John 5:46] [b]John 12:10, 11

CHAPTER 17
**1** [a][1 Cor. 11:19] [b][2 Thess. 1:6] [1]*stumbling blocks*
**2** [1]*cause one of these little ones to stumble*
**3** [a][Matt. 18:15, 21] [b][Prov. 17:10] [1]NU omits *against you*
**4** [1]M omits *to you*
**6** [a][Mark 9:23; 11:23]
**8** [a][Luke 12:37]
**9** [1]NU omits the rest of v. 9; M omits *him*
**10** [a]Rom. 3:12; 11:35
**11** [a]Luke 9:51, 52
**12** [a]Lev. 13:46
**14** [a]Matt. 8:4
**15** [a]Luke 5:25; 18:43
**16** [a]2 Kin. 17:24
**19** [a]Matt. 9:22
**21** [a]Luke 17:23 [b][Rom. 14:17] [1]*in your midst*
**22** [a]Matt. 9:15
**23** [a]Matt. 24:23 [1]NU reverses *here* and *there*
**24** [a]Matt. 24:27
**25** [a]Mark 8:31; 9:31; 10:33 [b]Luke 9:22
**26** [a]Matt. 24:37–39 [b][Gen. 6:5–7] [c][Gen. 6:8–13] [d]1 Pet. 3:20
**27** [a]Gen. 7:1–16 [b]Gen. 7:19–23
**28** [a]Gen. 19
**29** [a]Gen. 19:16, 24, 29
**30** [a][2 Thess. 1:7]
**31** [a]Mark 13:15 [1]*possessions*
**32** [a]Gen. 19:26
**33** [a]Matt. 10:39; 16:25
**34** [a][1 Thess. 4:17] [1]Or *people*
**35** [a]Matt. 24:40, 41
**36** [1]NU, M omit v. 36.

37 And they answered and said to Him, [a]"Where,
Lord?" So He said to them, "Wherever the body is,
there the eagles will be gathered together."

### *The Parable of the Persistent Widow*

**18** Then He spoke a parable to them, that men
[a]always ought to pray and not lose heart,
2 saying: "There was in a certain city a judge
who did not fear God nor [1]regard man.
3 "Now there was a widow in that city; and she
came to him, saying, [1]'Get justice for me from my
adversary.'
4 "And he would not for a while; but afterward
he said within himself, 'Though I do not fear God
nor regard man,
5 [a]'yet because this widow troubles me I will
[1]avenge her, lest by her continual coming she
weary me.' "
6 Then the Lord said, "Hear what the unjust
judge said.
7 "And [a]shall God not avenge His own elect who
cry out day and night to Him, though He bears
long with them?
8 "I tell you [a]that He will avenge them speedily.
Nevertheless, when the Son of Man comes, will
He really find faith on the earth?"
**9** Also He spoke this parable to some [a]who
trusted in themselves that they were righteous,
and despised others:
10 "Two men went up to the temple to pray, one
a Pharisee and the other a tax collector.
11 "The Pharisee [a]stood and prayed thus with
himself, [b]'God, I thank You that I am not like
other men—extortioners, unjust, adulterers, or
even as this tax collector.
12 'I fast twice a week; I give tithes of all that I
possess.'
13 "And the tax collector, standing afar off,
would not so much as raise *his* eyes to heaven, but
beat his breast, saying, 'God be merciful to me a
sinner!'
14 "I tell you, this man went down to his house
justified *rather* than the other; [a]for everyone who
exalts himself will be [1]humbled, and he who
humbles himself will be exalted."
**15** [a]Then they also brought infants to Him that
He might touch them; but when the disciples saw
*it,* they rebuked them.
16 But Jesus called them to *Him* and said, "Let
the little children come to Me, and do not forbid
them; for [a]of such is the kingdom of God.
17 [a]"Assuredly, I say to you, whoever does not
receive the kingdom of God as a little child will by
no means enter it."
**18** [a]Now a certain ruler asked Him, saying, "Good
Teacher, what shall I do to inherit eternal life?"
19 So Jesus said to him, "Why do you call Me
good? No one *is* good but [a]One, *that is,* God.
20 "You know the commandments: [a]*'Do not
commit adultery,' 'Do not murder,' 'Do not steal,'
'Do not bear false witness,'* [b]*'Honor your father
and your mother.' "*
21 And he said, "All [a]these things I have kept
from my youth."
22 So when Jesus heard these things, He said to
him, "You still lack one thing. [a]Sell all that you
have and distribute to the poor, and you will have
treasure in heaven; and come, follow Me."
23 But when he heard this, he became very sorrowful, for he was very rich.
**24** And when Jesus saw that he became very
sorrowful, He said, [a]"How hard it is for those who
have riches to enter the kingdom of God!
25 "For it is easier for a camel to go through the
eye of a needle than for a rich man to enter the
kingdom of God."
26 And those who heard it said, "Who then can
be saved?"
27 But He said, [a]"The things which are impossible
with men are possible with God."
28 [a]Then Peter said, "See, we have left [1]all and
followed You."
29 So He said to them, "Assuredly, I say to you,
[a]there is no one who has left house or parents or
brothers or wife or children, for the sake of the
kingdom of God,
30 [a]"who shall not receive many times more in
this present time, and in the age to come eternal
life."
**31** [a]Then He took the twelve aside and said to
them, "Behold, we are going up to Jerusalem, and
all things [b]that are written by the prophets concerning the Son of Man will be [1]accomplished.
32 "For [a]He will be delivered to the Gentiles and
will be mocked and insulted and spit upon.
33 "They will scourge *Him* and kill Him. And the
third day He will rise again."
34 [a]But they understood none of these things;
this saying was hidden from them, and they did
not know the things which were spoken.
**35** [a]Then it happened, that as He was coming
near Jericho, that a certain blind man sat by the
road begging.
36 And hearing a multitude passing by, he asked
what it meant.
37 So they told him that Jesus of Nazareth was
passing by.
38 And he cried out, saying, "Jesus, [a]Son of
David, have mercy on me!"
39 Then those who went before warned him that
he should be quiet; but he cried out all the more,
"Son of David, have mercy on me!"
40 So Jesus stood still and commanded him to be
brought to Him. And when he had come near, He
asked him,
41 saying, "What do you want Me to do for you?"
He said, "Lord, that I may receive my sight."
42 Then Jesus said to him, "Receive your sight;
[a]your faith has made you well."
43 And immediately he received his sight, and
followed Him, [a]glorifying God. And all the people,
when they saw *it,* gave praise to God.

### *Jesus Rides into Jerusalem*

**19** Then *Jesus* entered and passed through
[a]Jericho.
2 Now behold, *there was* a man named Zacchaeus who was a chief tax collector, and he was
rich.
3 And he sought to [a]see who Jesus was, but
could not because of the crowd, for he was of
short stature.
4 So he ran ahead and climbed up into a sycamore tree to see Him, for He was going to pass
that *way.*
5 And when Jesus came to the place, He looked
up [1]and saw him, and said to him, "Zacchaeus,
[2]make haste and come down, for today I must
stay at your house."
6 So he [1]made haste and came down, and received Him joyfully.

**37** [a]Matt. 24:28

CHAPTER 18
**1** [a]Luke 11:5–10
**2** [1]*respect*
**3** [1]*Avenge me on*
**5** [a]Luke 11:8 [1]*vindicate*
**7** [a]Rev. 6:10
**8** [a]Heb. 10:37
**9** [a]Luke 10:29; 16:15
**11** [a]Ps. 135:2 [b]Is. 1:15; 58:2
**14** [a]Luke 14:11 [1]*put down*
**15** [a]Mark 10:13–16
**16** [a]1 Pet. 2:2
**17** [a]Mark 10:15
**18** [a]Matt. 19:16–29
**19** [a]Ps. 86:5; 119:68
**20** [a]Ex. 20:12–16; Deut. 5:16–20 [b]Eph. 6:2; Col. 3:20
**21** [a]Phil. 3:6
**22** [a]Matt. 6:19, 20; 19:21
**24** [a]Mark 10:23
**27** [a]Jer. 32:17
**28** [a]Matt. 19:27 [1]NU *our own*
**29** [a]Deut. 33:9
**30** [a]Job 42:10
**31** [a]Matt. 16:21; 17:22; 20:17 [b]Ps. 22 [1]*fulfilled*
**32** [a]Acts 3:13
**34** [a]Luke 2:50; 9:45
**35** [a]Matt. 20:29–34
**38** [a]Matt. 9:27
**42** [a]Luke 17:19
**43** [a]Luke 5:26

CHAPTER 19
**1** [a]Josh. 6:26
**3** [a]John 12:21
**5** [1]NU omits *and saw him* [2]*hurry*
**6** [1]*hurried*

7 But when they saw *it,* they all [1]complained,
saying, [a]"He has gone to be a guest with a man
who is a sinner."
8 Then Zacchaeus stood and said to the Lord,
"Look, Lord, I give half of my goods to the [a]poor;
and if I have taken anything from anyone by
[b]false accusation, [c]I restore fourfold."
9 And Jesus said to him, "Today salvation has
come to this house, because [a]he also is [b]a son of
Abraham;
10 [a]"for the Son of Man has come to seek and to
save that which was lost."
**11** Now as they heard these things, He spoke
another parable, because He was near Jerusalem
and because [a]they thought the kingdom of God
would appear immediately.
12 [a]Therefore He said: "A certain nobleman went
into a far country to receive for himself a kingdom
and to return.
13 "So he called ten of his servants, delivered to
them ten [1]minas, and said to them, 'Do business
till I come.'
14 [a]"But his citizens hated him, and sent a delegation after him, saying, 'We will not have this
*man* to reign over us.'
15 "And so it was that when he returned, having
received the kingdom, he then commanded these
servants, to whom he had given the money, to be
called to him, that he might know how much
every man had gained by trading.
16 "Then came the first, saying, 'Master, your
mina has earned ten minas.'
17 "And he said to him, [a]'Well *done,* good servant; because you were [b]faithful in a very little,
have authority over ten cities.'
18 "And the second came, saying, 'Master, your
mina has earned five minas.'
19 "Likewise he said to him, 'You also be over
five cities.'
20 "Then another came, saying, 'Master, here is
your mina, which I have kept put away in a
handkerchief.
21 [a]'For I feared you, because you are [1]an austere
man. You collect what you did not deposit, and
reap what you did not sow.'
22 "And he said to him, [a]'Out of your own mouth
I will judge you, *you* wicked servant. [b]You knew
that I was an austere man, collecting what I did
not deposit and reaping what I did not sow.
23 'Why then did you not put my money in the
bank, that at my coming I might have collected it
with interest?'
24 "And he said to those who stood by, 'Take the
mina from him, and give *it* to him who has ten
minas.'
25 ("But they said to him, 'Master, he has ten
minas.')
26 'For I say to you, [a]that to everyone who has
will be given; and from him who does not have,
even what he has will be taken away from him.
27 'But bring here those enemies of mine, who
did not want me to reign over them, and slay *them*
before me.' "
**28** When He had said this, [a]He went on ahead,
going up to Jerusalem.
29 [a]And it came to pass, when He drew near to
[1]Bethphage and [b]Bethany, at the mountain called
[c]Olivet, *that* He sent two of His disciples,
30 saying, "Go into the village opposite *you,*
where as you enter you will find a colt tied, on
which no one has ever sat. Loose it and bring *it*
*here.*
31 "And if anyone asks you, 'Why are you
loosing *it?*' thus you shall say to him, 'Because the
Lord has need of it.' "
32 So those who were sent went their way and
found *it* just [a]as He had said to them.
33 But as they were loosing the colt, the owners
of it said to them, "Why are you loosing the colt?"
34 And they said, "The Lord has need of him."
35 Then they brought him to Jesus. [a]And they
threw their own clothes on the colt, and they set
Jesus on him.
36 And as He went, *many* spread their clothes on
the road.
37 Then, as He was now drawing near the descent of the Mount of Olives, the whole multitude
of the disciples began to [a]rejoice and praise God
with a loud voice for all the mighty works they
had seen,
38 saying:

> [a]"*'Blessed is the King who comes*
> *in the name of the LORD!'*
> [b]Peace in heaven and glory in the highest!"

39 And some of the Pharisees called to Him from
the crowd, "Teacher, rebuke Your disciples."
40 But He answered and said to them, "I tell you
that if these should keep silent, [a]the stones would
immediately cry out."
**41** Now as He drew near, He saw the city and
[a]wept over it,
42 saying, "If you had known, even you, especially in this [a]your day, the things *that* [b]*make* for
your [c]peace! But now they are hidden from your
eyes.
43 "For days will come upon you when your
enemies will [a]build an embankment around you,
surround you and close you in on every side,
44 [a]"and level you, and your children within you,
to the ground; and [b]they will not leave in you one
stone upon another, [c]because you did not know
the time of your visitation."
**45** [a]Then He went into the temple and began to
drive out those who [1]bought and sold in it,
46 saying to them, "It is written, [a]*'My house* [1]*is a*
*house of prayer,'* but you have made it a [b]*'den of*
*thieves.'* "
47 And He [a]was teaching daily in the temple. But
[b]the chief priests, the scribes, and the leaders of
the people sought to destroy Him,
48 and were unable to do anything; for all the
people were very attentive to [a]hear Him.

### *Disputes in Jerusalem*

**20** Now [a]it happened on one of those days, as
He taught the people in the temple and
preached the gospel, *that* the chief priests and the
scribes, together with the elders, confronted *Him*
2 and spoke to Him, saying, "Tell us, [a]by what
authority are You doing these things? Or who is
he who gave You this authority?"
3 But He answered and said to them, "I also will
ask you one thing, and answer Me:
4 "The [a]baptism of John—was it from heaven or
from men?"
5 And they reasoned among themselves, saying,
"If we say, 'From heaven,' He will say, 'Why [1]then
did you not believe him?'
6 "But if we say, 'From men,' all the people will

**7** [a]Luke 5:30; 15:2 [1]*grumbled*
**8** [a][Ps. 41:1] [b]Luke 3:14 [c]Ex. 22:1
**9** [a][Gal. 3:7] [b][Luke 13:16]
**10** [a]Matt. 18:11
**11** [a]Acts 1:6
**12** [a]Matt. 25:14–30
**13** [1]Gr. *mna,* same as Heb. *minah,* each worth about three months' salary
**14** [a][John 1:11]
**17** [a]Matt. 25:21, 23 [b]Luke 16:10
**21** [a]Matt. 25:24 [1]*a severe*
**22** [a]Job 15:6 [b]Matt. 25:26
**26** [a]Luke 8:18
**28** [a]Mark 10:32
**29** [a]Matt. 21:1 [b]John 12:1 [c]Acts 1:12 [1]M *Bethsphage*
**32** [a]Luke 22:13
**35** [a]2 Kin. 9:13
**37** [a]Luke 13:17; 18:43
**38** [a]Ps. 118:26 [b][Eph. 2:14]
**40** [a]Hab. 2:11
**41** [a]John 11:35
**42** [a]Heb. 3:13 [b][Acts 10:36] [c][Rom. 5:1]
**43** [a]Jer. 6:3, 6
**44** [a]1 Kin. 9:7, 8 [b]Matt. 24:2 [c][1 Pet. 2:12]
**45** [a]Mark 11:11, 15–17 [1]NU *were selling, saying*
**46** [a]Is. 56:7 [b]Jer. 7:11 [1]NU *shall be*
**47** [a]Luke 21:37; 22:53 [b]John 7:19; 8:37
**48** [a]Luke 21:38

CHAPTER 20
**1** [a]Matt. 21:23–27
**2** [a]Acts 4:7; 7:27
**4** [a]John 1:26, 31
**5** [1]NU, M omit *then*

stone us, [a]for they are persuaded that John was a
prophet."
7 So they answered that they did not know
where *it was* from.
8 And Jesus said to them, "Neither will I tell you
by what authority I do these things."
**9** Then He began to tell the people this parable:
[a]"A certain man planted a vineyard, leased it to
[1]vinedressers, and went into a far country for a
long time.
10 "Now at [1]vintage-time he [a]sent a servant to
the vinedressers, that they might give him some of
the fruit of the vineyard. But the vinedressers beat
him and sent *him* away empty-handed.
11 "Again he sent another servant; and they beat
him also, treated *him* shamefully, and sent *him*
away empty-handed.
12 "And again he sent a third; and they wounded
him also and cast *him* out.
13 "Then the owner of the vineyard said, 'What
shall I do? I will send my beloved son. Probably
they will respect *him* when they see him.'
14 "But when the vinedressers saw him, they
reasoned among themselves, saying, 'This is the
[a]heir. Come, [b]let us kill him, that the inheritance
may be [c]ours.'
15 "So they cast him out of the vineyard and
[a]killed *him*. Therefore what will the owner of the
vineyard do to them?
16 "He will come and destroy those vinedressers
and give the vineyard to [a]others." And when they
heard *it* they said, "Certainly not!"
17 Then He looked at them and said, "What then
is this that is written:

> [a]*'The stone which the builders rejected*
> *Has become the chief cornerstone'*?

18 "Whoever falls on that stone will be [a]broken;
but [b]on whomever it falls, it will grind him to
powder."
19 And the chief priests and the scribes that very
hour sought to lay hands on Him, but they [1]feared
the people—for they knew He had spoken this
parable against them.
**20** [a]So they watched *Him*, and sent spies who
pretended to be righteous, that they might seize
on His words, in order to deliver Him to the power
and the authority of the governor.
21 Then they asked Him, saying, [a]"Teacher, we
know that You say and teach rightly, and You do
not show personal favoritism, but teach the way
of God in truth:
22 "Is it lawful for us to pay taxes to Caesar or
not?"
23 But He perceived their craftiness, and said to
them, [1]"Why do you test Me?
24 "Show Me a denarius. Whose image and inscription does it have?" They answered and said,
"Caesar's."
25 And He said to them, [a]"Render[1] therefore to
Caesar the things that are Caesar's, and to God
the things that are God's."
26 But they could not catch Him in His words in
the presence of the people. And they marveled at
His answer and kept silent.
**27** [a]Then some of the Sadducees, [b]who deny that
there is a resurrection, came to *Him* and asked
Him,
28 saying: "Teacher, Moses wrote to us *that* if a
man's brother dies, having a wife, and he dies
without children, his brother should take his wife
and raise up offspring for his brother.
29 "Now there were seven brothers. And the first
took a wife, and died without children.
30 "And the second [1]took her as wife, and he died
childless.
31 "Then the third took her, and in like manner
the seven [1]also; and they left no children, and
died.
32 "Last of all the woman died also.
33 "Therefore, in the resurrection, whose wife
does she become? For all seven had her as wife."
34 Jesus answered and said to them, "The sons of
this age marry and are given in marriage.
35 "But those who are [a]counted worthy to attain
that age, and the resurrection from the dead,
neither marry nor are given in marriage;
36 "nor can they die anymore, for [a]they are equal
to the angels and are sons of God, [b]being sons of
the resurrection.
37 "But even Moses showed in the *burning* bush
*passage* that the dead are raised, when he called
the Lord [a]*'the God of Abraham, the God of Isaac,*
*and the God of Jacob.'*
38 "For He is not the God of the dead but of the
living, for [a]all live to Him."
39 Then some of the scribes answered and said,
"Teacher, You have spoken well."
40 But after that they dared not question Him
anymore.
**41** And He said to them, [a]"How can they say that
the Christ is the Son of David?
42 "Now David himself said in the Book of
Psalms:

> [a]*'The LORD said to my Lord,*
> *"Sit at My right hand,*
> 43 *Till I make Your enemies Your footstool."'*

44 "Therefore David calls Him *'Lord'*; [a]how is He
then his Son?"
**45** [a]Then, in the hearing of all the people, He said
to His disciples,
46 [a]"Beware of the scribes, who desire to go
around in long robes, [b]love greetings in the marketplaces, the best seats in the synagogues, and
the best places at feasts,
47 [a]"who devour widows' houses, and for a [b]pre-
tense make long prayers. These will receive
greater condemnation."

## *The Return of Christ in Judgment*

**21** And He looked up [a]and saw the rich putting
their gifts into the treasury,
2 and He saw also a certain [a]poor widow putting
in two [b]mites.[1]
3 So He said, "Truly I say to you [a]that this poor
widow has put in more than all;
4 "for all these out of their abundance have put
in offerings [1]for God, but she out of her poverty
put in [a]all the livelihood that she had."
**5** [a]Then, as some spoke of the temple, how it
was [1]adorned with beautiful stones and donations,
He said,
6 "These things which you see—the days will
come in which [a]not *one* stone shall be left upon
another that shall not be thrown down."
**7** So they asked Him, saying, "Teacher, but
when will these things be? And what sign *will*
*there be* when these things are about to take
place?"
8 And He said: [a]"Take heed that you not be
deceived. For many will come in My name, saying,

**6** [a]Luke 7:24–30
**9** [a]Mark 12:1–12 [1]*tenant farmers*
**10** [a][1 Thess. 2:15] [1]Lit. *the season*
**14** [a][Heb. 1:1–3] [b]Matt. 27:21–23 [c]John 11:47, 48
**15** [a]Luke 23:33
**16** [a]Rom. 11:1, 11
**17** [a]Ps. 118:22
**18** [a]Is. 8:14, 15 [b][Dan. 2:34, 35, 44, 45]
**19** [1]M *were afraid—for*
**20** [a]Matt. 22:15
**21** [a]Mark 12:14
**23** [1]NU omits *Why do you test Me?*
**25** [a][1 Pet. 2:13–17] [1]*Pay*
**27** [a]Mark 12:18–27 [b]Acts 23:6, 8
**30** [1]NU omits the rest of v. 30.
**31** [1]NU, M *also left no children*
**35** [a]Phil. 3:11
**36** [a][1 John 3:2] [b]Rom. 8:23
**37** [a]Ex. 3:1–6, 15
**38** [a][Rom. 6:10, 11; 14:8, 9]
**41** [a]Matt. 22:41–46
**42** [a]Ps. 110:1
**44** [a]Rom. 1:3; 9:4, 5
**45** [a]Matt. 23:1–7
**46** [a]Matt. 23:5 [b]Luke 11:43; 14:7
**47** [a]Matt. 23:14 [b][Matt. 6:5, 6]

CHAPTER 21
**1** [a]Mark 12:41–44
**2** [a][2 Cor. 6:10] [b]Mark 12:42 [1]Gr. *lepta*, very small copper coins
**3** [a][2 Cor. 8:12]
**4** [a][2 Cor. 8:12] [1]NU omits *for God*
**5** [a]Mark 13:1 [1]*decorated*
**6** [a]Luke 19:41–44
**8** [a]Eph. 5:6

'I am *He*,' and, 'The time has drawn near.' [1]There-
fore do not [2]go after them.
9 "But when you hear of [a]wars and commotions,
do not be terrified; for these things must come to
pass first, but the end *will not come* immediately."
**10** [a]Then He said to them, "Nation will rise
against nation, and kingdom against kingdom.
11 "And there will be great [a]earthquakes in various places, and famines and pestilences; and
there will be fearful sights and great signs from
heaven.
12 [a]"But before all these things, they will lay their
hands on you and persecute *you*, delivering *you*
up to the synagogues and [b]prisons. [c]You will be
brought before kings and rulers [d]for My name's
sake.
13 "But [a]it will turn out for you as an occasion for
testimony.
14 [a]"Therefore settle *it* in your hearts not to
meditate beforehand on what you will [1]answer;
15 "for I will give you a mouth and wisdom
[a]which all your adversaries will not be able to
contradict or [1]resist.
16 [a]"You will be betrayed even by parents and
brothers, relatives and friends; and they will put
[b]*some* of you to death.
17 "And [a]you will be hated by all for My name's
sake.
18 [a]"But not a hair of your head shall be lost.
19 "By your patience possess your souls.
**20** [a]"But when you see Jerusalem surrounded by
armies, then know that its desolation is near.
21 "Then let those who are in Judea flee to the
mountains, let those who are in the midst of her
depart, and let not those who are in the country
enter her.
22 "For these are the days of vengeance, that [a]all
things which are written may be fulfilled.
23 [a]"But woe to those who are pregnant and to
those who are nursing babies in those days! For
there will be great distress in the land and wrath
upon this people.
24 "And they will fall by the edge of the sword,
and be led away captive into all nations. And
Jerusalem will be trampled by Gentiles [a]until the
times of the Gentiles are fulfilled.
**25** [a]"And there will be signs in the sun, in the
moon, and in the stars; and on the earth distress
of nations, with perplexity, the sea and the waves
roaring;
26 "men's hearts failing them from fear and the
expectation of those things which are coming on
the earth, [a]for the powers of the heavens will be
shaken.
27 "Then they will see the Son of Man [a]coming in
a cloud with power and great glory.
28 "Now when these things begin to happen,
look up and lift up your heads, because [a]your
redemption draws near."
**29** [a]Then He spoke to them a parable: "Look at
the fig tree, and all the trees.
30 "When they are already budding, you see and
know for yourselves that summer is now near.
31 "So you also, when you see these things
happening, know that the kingdom of God is near.
32 "Assuredly, I say to you, this generation will
by no means pass away till all things take place.
33 [a]"Heaven and earth will pass away, but My
[b]words will by no means pass away.
**34** "But [a]take heed to yourselves, lest your hearts
be weighed down with [1]carousing, drunkenness,
and [b]cares of this life, and that Day come on you
unexpectedly.
35 "For [a]it will come as a snare on all those who
dwell on the face of the whole earth.
36 [a]"Watch therefore, and [b]pray always that you
may [1]be counted [c]worthy to escape all these
things that will come to pass, and [d]to stand before
the Son of Man."
37 [a]And in the daytime He was teaching in the
temple, but [b]at night He went out and stayed on
the mountain called Olivet.
38 Then early in the morning all the people came
to Him in the temple to hear Him.

### *The Beginning of the Lord's Supper*

**22** Now [a]the Feast of Unleavened Bread drew
near, which is called Passover.
2 And [a]the chief priests and the scribes sought
how they might kill Him, for they feared the
people.
3 [a]Then Satan entered Judas, surnamed Iscariot,
who was numbered among the [b]twelve.
4 So he went his way and conferred with the
chief priests and captains, how he might betray
Him to them.
5 And they were glad, and [a]agreed to give him
money.
6 So he promised and sought opportunity to
[a]betray Him to them in the absence of the multitude.
**7** [a]Then came the Day of Unleavened Bread,
when the Passover must be [1]killed.
8 And He sent Peter and John, saying, "Go and
prepare the Passover for us, that we may eat."
9 So they said to Him, "Where do You want us
to prepare?"
10 And He said to them, "Behold, when you have
entered the city, a man will meet you carrying a
pitcher of water; follow him into the house which
he enters.
11 "Then you shall say to the master of the
house, 'The Teacher says to you, "Where is the
guest room where I may eat the Passover with My
disciples?" '
12 "Then he will show you a large, furnished
upper room; there make ready."
13 So they went and [a]found it just as He had said
to them, and they prepared the Passover.
**14** [a]When the hour had come, He sat down, and
the [1]twelve apostles with Him.
15 Then He said to them, "With *fervent* desire I
have desired to eat this Passover with you before I
suffer;
16 "for I say to you, I will no longer eat of it
[a]until it is fulfilled in the kingdom of God."
17 Then He took the cup, and gave thanks, and
said, "Take this and divide *it* among yourselves;
18 "for [a]I say to you, [1]I will not drink of the fruit
of the vine until the kingdom of God comes."
19 [a]And He took bread, gave thanks and broke *it*,
and gave *it* to them, saying, "This is My [b]body
which is given for you; [c]do this in remembrance of
Me."
20 Likewise He also *took* the cup after supper,
saying, [a]"This cup *is* the new covenant in My
blood, which is shed for you.
21 [a]"But behold, the hand of My betrayer *is* with
Me on the table.
22 [a]"And truly the Son of Man goes [b]as it has
been determined, but woe to that man by whom
He is betrayed!"

**8** [1]NU omits *Therefore* [2]*follow*
**9** [a]Rev. 6:4
**10** [a]Matt. 24:7
**11** [a]Rev. 6:12
**12** [a][Rev. 2:10] [b]Acts 4:3; 5:18; 12:4; 16:24 [c]Acts 25:23 [d]1 Pet. 2:13
**13** [a][Phil. 1:12–14, 28]
**14** [a]Luke 12:11 [1]*say in defense*
**15** [a]Acts 6:10 [1]*withstand*
**16** [a]Mic. 7:6 [b]Acts 7:59; 12:2
**17** [a]Matt. 10:22
**18** [a]Matt. 10:30
**20** [a]Mark 13:14
**22** [a][Dan. 9:24–27]
**23** [a]Matt. 24:19
**24** [a][Dan. 9:27; 12:7]
**25** [a][2 Pet. 3:10–12]
**26** [a]Matt. 24:29
**27** [a]Rev. 1:7; 14:14
**28** [a][Rom. 8:19, 23]
**29** [a]Mark 13:28
**33** [a]Matt. 24:35 [b]Is. 40:8
**34** [a]1 Thess. 5:6 [b]Luke 8:14 [1]*dissipation*
**35** [a]Rev. 3:3; 16:15
**36** [a]Matt. 24:42; 25:13 [b]Luke 18:1 [c]Luke 20:35 [d][Eph. 6:13] [1]NU *have strength to*
**37** [a]John 8:1, 2 [b]Luke 22:39

CHAPTER 22

**1** [a]Matt. 26:2–5
**2** [a]John 11:47
**3** [a]Mark 14:10, 11 [b]Matt. 10:2–4
**5** [a]Zech. 11:12
**6** [a]Ps. 41:9
**7** [a]Matt. 26:17–19 [1]Sacrificed
**13** [a]Luke 19:32
**14** [a]Mark 14:17 [1]NU omits *twelve*
**16** [a][Rev. 19:9]
**18** [a]Mark 14:25 [1]NU adds *from now on*
**19** [a]Matt. 26:26 [b][1 Pet. 2:24] [c]1 Cor. 11:23–26
**20** [a]1 Cor. 10:16
**21** [a]John 13:21, 26, 27
**22** [a]Matt. 26:24 [b]Acts 2:23

23 [a]Then they began to question among themselves, which of them it was who would do this
thing.
**24** [a]Now there was also a dispute among them, as
to which of them should be considered the greatest.
25 [a]And He said to them, "The kings of the
Gentiles exercise lordship over them, and those
who exercise authority over them are called
'benefactors.'
26 [a]"But not so *among* you; on the contrary, [b]he
who is greatest among you, let him be as the
younger, and he who governs as he who serves.
27 [a]"For who *is* greater, he who sits at the table,
or he who serves? *Is* it not he who sits at the
table? Yet [b]I am among you as the One who
serves.
28 "But you are those who have continued with
Me in [a]My trials.
29 "And [a]I bestow upon you a kingdom, just as
My Father bestowed *one* upon Me,
30 "that [a]you may eat and drink at My table [1]in
My kingdom, [b]and sit on thrones judging the
twelve tribes of Israel."
**31** [1]And the Lord said, "Simon, Simon! Indeed,
[a]Satan has asked for you, that he may [b]sift *you* as
wheat.
32 "But [a]I have prayed for you, that your faith
should not fail; and when you have returned to
*Me,* [b]strengthen your brethren."
33 But he said to Him, "Lord, I am ready to go
with You, both to prison and to death."
34 [a]Then He said, "I tell you, Peter, the rooster
shall not crow this day before you will deny three
times that you know Me."
**35** [a]And He said to them, "When I sent you
without money bag, knapsack, and sandals, did
you lack anything?" So they said, "Nothing."
36 Then He said to them, "But now, he who has a
money bag, let him take *it,* and likewise a knapsack; and he who has no sword, let him sell his
garment and buy one.
37 "For I say to you that this which is written
must still be [1]accomplished in Me: [a]*'And He was
numbered with the transgressors.'* For the things
concerning Me have an end."
38 So they said, "Lord, look, here *are* two
swords." And He said to them, "It is enough."
**39** [a]Coming out, [b]He went to the Mount of Olives,
as He was accustomed, and His disciples also
followed Him.
40 [a]When He came to the place, He said to them,
"Pray that you may not enter into temptation."
41 [a]And He was withdrawn from them about a
stone's throw, and He knelt down and prayed,
42 saying, "Father, if it is Your will, take this cup
away from Me; nevertheless [a]not My will, but
Yours, be done."
43 [1]Then [a]an angel appeared to Him from heaven,
strengthening Him.
44 [a]And being in agony, He prayed more earnestly. Then His sweat became like great drops of
blood falling down to the ground.
45 When He rose up from prayer, and had come
to His disciples, He found them sleeping from
sorrow.
46 Then He said to them, "Why [a]do you sleep?
Rise and [b]pray, lest you enter into temptation."
**47** And while He was still speaking, [a]behold, a
multitude; and he who was called [b]Judas, one of
the twelve, went before them and drew near to
Jesus to kiss Him.
48 But Jesus said to him, "Judas, are you betraying the Son of Man with a [a]kiss?"
49 When those around Him saw what was going
to happen, they said to Him, "Lord, shall we strike
with the sword?"
50 And [a]one of them struck the servant of the
high priest and cut off his right ear.
51 But Jesus answered and said, "Permit even
this." And He touched his ear and healed him.
52 [a]Then Jesus said to the chief priests, captains
of the temple, and the elders who had come to
Him, "Have you come out, as against a [b]robber,
with swords and clubs?
53 "When I was with you daily in the [a]temple,
you did not try to seize Me. But this is your [b]hour,
and the power of darkness."
**54** [a]Having arrested Him, they led *Him* and
brought Him into the high priest's house. [b]But
Peter followed at a distance.
55 [a]Now when they had kindled a fire in the
midst of the courtyard and sat down together,
Peter sat among them.
56 And a certain servant girl, seeing him as he sat
by the fire, looked intently at him and said, "This
man was also with Him."
57 But he denied [1]Him, saying, "Woman, I do not
know Him."
58 [a]And after a little while another saw him and
said, "You also are of them." But Peter said, "Man,
I am not!"
59 [a]Then after about an hour had passed, another
confidently affirmed, saying, "Surely this *fellow*
also was with Him, for he is a [b]Galilean."
60 But Peter said, "Man, I do not know what you
are saying!" Immediately, while he was still
speaking, [1]the rooster crowed.
61 And the Lord turned and looked at Peter.
Then [a]Peter remembered the word of the Lord,
how He had said to him, [b]"Before the rooster
[1]crows, you will deny Me three times."
62 So Peter went out and wept bitterly.
**63** [a]Now the men who held Jesus mocked Him
and [b]beat Him.
64 [1]And having blindfolded Him, they [a]struck
Him on the face and asked Him, saying, "Prophesy! Who is the one who struck You?"
65 And many other things they blasphemously
spoke against Him.
**66** [a]As soon as it was day, [b]the elders of the
people, both chief priests and scribes, came together and led Him into their council, saying,
67 [a]"If You are the Christ, tell us." But He said to
them, "If I tell you, you will [b]by no means believe.
68 "And if I [1]also ask *you,* you will by no means
answer [2]Me or let *Me* go.
69 [a]"Hereafter the Son of Man will sit on the
right hand of the power of God."
70 Then they all said, "Are You then the Son of
God?" So He said to them, [a]"You *rightly* say that I
am."
71 [a]And they said, "What further testimony do
we need? For we have heard it ourselves from His
own mouth."

### *Jesus Is Tried and Crucified*

**23** Then [a]the whole multitude of them arose
and led Him to [b]Pilate.
2 And they began to [a]accuse Him, saying, "We
found this *fellow* [b]perverting [1]the nation, and

**23** [a]John 13:22, 25
**24** [a]Mark 9:34
**25** [a]Mark 10:42–45
**26** [a][1 Pet. 5:3] [b]Luke 9:48
**27** [a][Luke 12:37] [b]Phil. 2:7
**28** [a][Heb. 2:18; 4:15]
**29** [a]Matt. 24:47
**30** [a][Matt. 8:11] [b][Rev. 3:21] [1]M mss. omit *in My kingdom*
**31** [a]1 Pet. 5:8 [b]Amos 9:9 [1]NU omits *And the Lord said*
**32** [a][John 17:9, 11, 15] [b]John 21:15–17
**34** [a]John 13:37, 38
**35** [a]Matt. 10:9
**37** [a]Is. 53:12 [1]*fulfilled*
**39** [a]John 18:1 [b]Luke 21:37
**40** [a]Mark 14:32–42
**41** [a]Matt. 26:39
**42** [a]John 4:34; 5:30; 6:38; 8:29
**43** [a]Matt. 4:11 [1]NU brackets vv. 43 and 44 as not in the original text.
**44** [a][Heb. 5:7]
**46** [a]Luke 9:32 [b]Luke 22:40
**47** [a]John 18:3–11 [b]Acts 1:16, 17
**48** [a][Prov. 27:6]
**50** [a]Matt. 26:51
**52** [a]Matt. 26:55 [b]Luke 23:32
**53** [a]Luke 19:47, 48 [b][John 12:27]
**54** [a]Matt. 26:57 [b]John 18:15
**55** [a]Mark 14:66–72
**57** [1]NU *it*
**58** [a]John 18:25
**59** [a]Mark 14:70 [b]Acts 1:11; 2:7
**60** [1]NU, M *a rooster*
**61** [a]Matt. 26:75 [b]John 13:38 [1]NU adds *today*
**63** [a]Ps. 69:1, 4, 7–9 [b]Is. 50:6
**64** [a]Zech. 13:7 [1]NU *And having blindfolded Him, they asked Him*
**66** [a]Matt. 27:1 [b]Acts 4:26
**67** [a]Matt. 26:63–66 [b]Luke 20:5–7
**68** [1]NU omits *also* [2]NU omits the rest of v. 68.
**69** [a]Heb. 1:3; 8:1
**70** [a]Matt. 26:64; 27:11
**71** [a]Mark 14:63

CHAPTER 23
**1** [a]John 18:28 [b]Luke 3:1; 13:1
**2** [a]Acts 24:2 [b]Acts 17:7 [1]NU *our*

[c]forbidding to pay taxes to Caesar, saying [d]that He Himself is Christ, a King."

**3** [a]Then Pilate asked Him, saying, "Are You the King of the Jews?" He answered him and said, "*It is as* you say."

4 So Pilate said to the chief priests and the crowd, [a]"I find no fault in this Man."

5 But they were the more fierce, saying, "He stirs up the people, teaching throughout all Judea, beginning from [a]Galilee to this place."

**6** When Pilate heard [1]of Galilee, he asked if the Man were a Galilean.

7 And as soon as he knew that He belonged to [a]Herod's jurisdiction, he sent Him to Herod, who was also in Jerusalem at that time.

8 Now when Herod saw Jesus, [a]he was exceedingly glad; for he had desired for a long *time* to see Him, because [b]he had heard many things about Him, and he hoped to see some miracle done by Him.

9 Then he questioned Him with many words, but He answered him [a]nothing.

10 And the chief priests and scribes stood and vehemently accused Him.

11 [a]Then Herod, with his [1]men of war, treated Him with contempt and mocked *Him,* arrayed Him in a gorgeous robe, and sent Him back to Pilate.

12 That very day [a]Pilate and Herod became friends with each other, for previously they had been at enmity with each other.

**13** [a]Then Pilate, when he had called together the chief priests, the rulers, and the people,

14 said to them, [a]"You have brought this Man to me, as one who misleads the people. And indeed, [b]having examined *Him* in your presence, I have found no fault in this Man concerning those things of which you accuse Him;

15 "no, neither did Herod, for [1]I sent you back to him; and indeed nothing deserving of death has been done by Him.

16 [a]"I will therefore chastise Him and release *Him*"

17 [a](for[1] it was necessary for him to release one to them at the feast).

18 And [a]they all cried out at once, saying, "Away with this *Man,* and release to us Barabbas"—

19 who had been thrown into prison for a certain rebellion made in the city, and for murder.

20 Pilate, therefore, wishing to release Jesus, again called out to them.

21 But they shouted, saying, "Crucify *Him,* crucify Him!"

22 Then he said to them the third time, "Why, what evil has He done? I have found no reason for death in Him. I will therefore chastise Him and let *Him* go."

23 But they were insistent, demanding with loud voices that He be crucified. And the voices of these men [1]and of the chief priests prevailed.

24 So [a]Pilate gave sentence that it should be as they requested.

25 [a]And he released [1]to them the one they requested, who for rebellion and murder had been thrown into prison; but he delivered Jesus to their will.

**26** [a]Now as they led Him away, they laid hold of a certain man, Simon a Cyrenian, who was coming from the country, and on him they laid the cross that he might bear *it* after Jesus.

27 And a great multitude of the people followed Him, and women who also mourned and lamented Him.

28 But Jesus, turning to them, said, "Daughters of Jerusalem, do not weep for Me, but weep for yourselves and for your children.

29 [a]"For indeed the days are coming in which they will say, 'Blessed *are* the barren, wombs that never bore, and breasts which never nursed!'

30 "Then they will begin [a]*'to say to the mountains, "Fall on us!" and to the hills, "Cover us!"'*

31 [a]"For if they do these things in the green wood, what will be done in the dry?"

32 [a]There were also two others, criminals, led with Him to be put to death.

33 And [a]when they had come to the place called Calvary, there they crucified Him, and the criminals, one on the right hand and the other on the left.

34 [1]Then Jesus said, "Father, [a]forgive them, for [b]they do not know what they do." And [c]they divided His garments and cast lots.

35 And [a]the people stood looking on. But even the [b]rulers with them sneered, saying, "He saved others; let Him save Himself if He is the Christ, the chosen of God."

36 The soldiers also mocked Him, coming and offering Him [a]sour wine,

37 and saying, "If You are the King of the Jews, save Yourself."

38 [a]And an inscription also was [1]written over Him in letters of Greek, Latin, and Hebrew:

THIS IS THE KING OF THE JEWS.

39 [a]Then one of the criminals who were hanged blasphemed Him, saying, [1]"If You are the Christ, save Yourself and us."

40 But the other, answering, rebuked him, saying, "Do you not even fear God, seeing you are under the same condemnation?

41 "And we indeed justly, for we receive the due reward of our deeds; but this Man has done [a]nothing wrong."

42 Then he said [1]to Jesus, "Lord, remember me when You come into Your kingdom."

43 And Jesus said to him, "Assuredly, I say to you, today you will be with Me in [a]Paradise."

**44** [a]Now it [1]was about the sixth hour, and there was darkness over all the earth until the ninth hour.

45 Then the sun was [1]darkened, and [a]the veil of the temple was torn in [2]two.

46 And when Jesus had cried out with a loud voice, He said, "Father, [a]*'into Your hands I commit My spirit.'*" [b]Having said this, He breathed His last.

47 [a]So when the centurion saw what had happened, he glorified God, saying, "Certainly this was a righteous Man!"

48 And the whole crowd who came together to that sight, seeing what had been done, beat their breasts and returned.

49 [a]But all His acquaintances, and the women who followed Him from Galilee, stood at a distance, watching these things.

**50** [a]Now behold, *there was* a man named Joseph, a council member, a good and just man.

51 He had not consented to their decision and deed. *He was* from Arimathea, a city of the Jews, [a]who[1] himself was also waiting for the kingdom of God.

2 [c]Matt. 17:27 [d]John 19:12
3 [a]1 Tim. 6:13
4 [a][1 Pet. 2:22]
5 [a]John 7:41
6 [1]NU omits *of Galilee*
7 [a]Luke 3:1; 9:7; 13:31
8 [a]Luke 9:9 [b]Matt. 14:1
9 [a]John 19:9
11 [a]Is. 53:3 [1]*troops*
12 [a]Acts 4:26, 27
13 [a]Mark 15:14
14 [a]Luke 23:1, 2 [b]Luke 23:4
15 [1]NU *he sent Him back to us*
16 [a]John 19:1
17 [a]John 18:39 [1]NU omits v. 17.
18 [a]Acts 3:13–15
23 [1]NU omits *and of the chief priests*
24 [a]Mark 15:15
25 [a]Is. 53:8 [1]NU, M omit *to them*
26 [a]Matt. 27:32
29 [a]Matt. 24:19
30 [a]Hos. 10:8; Rev. 6:16, 17; 9:6
31 [a][Jer. 25:29]
32 [a]Is. 53:9, 12
33 [a]John 19:17–24
34 [a]1 Cor. 4:12 [b]Acts 3:17 [c]Matt. 27:35 [1]NU brackets the first sentence as a later addition.
35 [a]Ps. 22:17 [b]Matt. 27:39
36 [a]Ps. 69:21
38 [a]John 19:19 [1]NU omits *written* and *in letters of Greek, Latin, and Hebrew*
39 [a]Mark 15:32 [1]NU *Are You not the Christ? Save*
41 [a][Heb. 7:26]
42 [1]NU *"Jesus, remember me*
43 [a][Rev. 2:7]
44 [a]Matt. 27:45–56 [1]NU adds *now*
45 [a]Matt. 27:51 [1]NU *obscured* [2]*the middle*
46 [a]Ps. 31:5 [b]John 19:30
47 [a]Mark 15:39
49 [a]Ps. 38:11
50 [a]Matt. 27:57–61
51 [a]Luke 2:25, 38 [1]NU *who was waiting*

52 This man went to Pilate and asked for the
body of Jesus.
53 [a]Then he took it down, wrapped it in linen,
and laid it in a tomb *that was* hewn out of the
rock, where no one had ever lain before.
54 That day was [a]the Preparation, and the Sabbath drew near.
55 And the women [a]who had come with Him
from Galilee followed after, and [b]they observed
the tomb and how His body was laid.
56 Then they returned and [a]prepared spices and
fragrant oils. And they rested on the Sabbath
[b]according to the commandment.

### *The Risen and Ascended Christ*

**24** Now [a]on the first *day* of the week, very
early in the morning, they, [1]and certain
*other women* with them, came to the tomb [b]bring-
ing the spices which they had prepared.
2 [a]But they found the stone rolled away from
the tomb.
3 [a]Then they went in and did not find the body
of the Lord Jesus.
4 And it happened, as they were [1]greatly perplexed about this, that [a]behold, two men stood by
them in shining garments.
5 Then, as they were afraid and bowed *their*
faces to the earth, they said to them, "Why do you
seek the living among the dead?
6 "He is not here, but is risen! [a]Remember how
He spoke to you when He was still in Galilee,
7 "saying, 'The Son of Man must be [a]delivered
into the hands of sinful men, and be crucified, and
the third day rise again.' "
8 And [a]they remembered His words.
9 [a]Then they returned from the tomb and told
all these things to the eleven and to all the rest.
10 It was Mary Magdalene, [a]Joanna, Mary *the
mother* of James, and the other *women* with them,
who told these things to the apostles.
11 [a]And their words seemed to them like [1]idle
tales, and they did not believe them.
12 [a]But Peter arose and ran to the tomb; and
stooping down, he saw the linen cloths [1]lying by
themselves; and he departed, marveling to himself
at what had happened.
**13** [a]Now behold, two of them were traveling that
same day to a village called Emmaus, which was
[1]seven miles from Jerusalem.
14 And they talked together of all these things
which had happened.
15 So it was, while they conversed and reasoned,
that [a]Jesus Himself drew near and went with
them.
16 But [a]their eyes were restrained, so that they
did not know Him.
17 And He said to them, "What kind of conversation *is* this that you have with one another as you
[1]walk and are sad?"
18 Then the one [a]whose name was Cleopas
answered and said to Him, "Are You the only
stranger in Jerusalem, and have You not known
the things which happened there in these days?"
19 And He said to them, "What things?" So they
said to Him, "The things concerning Jesus of
Nazareth, [a]who was a Prophet [b]mighty in deed
and word before God and all the people,
20 [a]"and how the chief priests and our rulers
delivered Him to be condemned to death, and
crucified Him.
21 "But we were hoping [a]that it was He who was
going to redeem Israel. Indeed, besides all this,
today is the third day since these things happened.
22 "Yes, and [a]certain women of our company,
who arrived at the tomb early, astonished us.
23 "When they did not find His body, they came
saying that they had also seen a vision of angels
who said He was alive.
24 "And [a]certain of those *who were* with us went
to the tomb and found *it* just as the women had
said; but Him they did not see."
25 Then He said to them, "O foolish ones, and
slow of heart to believe in all that the prophets
have spoken!
26 [a]"Ought not the Christ to have suffered these
things and to enter into His [b]glory?"
27 And beginning at [a]Moses and [b]all the Prophets, He [1]expounded to them in all the Scriptures
the things concerning Himself.
**28** Then they drew near to the village where they
were going, and [a]He [1]indicated that He would
have gone farther.
29 But [a]they constrained Him, saying, [b]"Abide
with us, for it is toward evening, and the day is far
spent." And He went in to stay with them.
30 Now it came to pass, as [a]He sat at the table
with them, that He took bread, blessed and broke
*it*, and gave it to them.
31 Then their eyes were opened and they knew
Him; and He vanished from their sight.
32 And they said to one another, "Did not our
heart burn within us while He talked with us on
the road, and while He opened the Scriptures to
us?"
33 So they rose up that very hour and returned to
Jerusalem, and found the eleven and those *who
were* with them gathered together,
34 saying, "The Lord is risen indeed, and [a]has
appeared to Simon!"
35 And they told about the things *that had happened* on the road, and how He was [1]known to
them in the breaking of bread.
**36** [a]Now as they said these things, Jesus Himself
stood in the midst of them, and said to them,
"Peace to you."
37 But they were terrified and frightened, and
supposed they had seen [a]a spirit.
38 And He said to them, "Why are you troubled?
And why do doubts arise in your hearts?
39 "Behold My hands and My feet, that it is I
Myself. [a]Handle Me and see, for a [b]spirit does not
have flesh and bones as you see I have."
40 [1]When He had said this, He showed them His
hands and His feet.
41 But while they still did not believe [a]for joy,
and marveled, He said to them, [b]"Have you any
food here?"
42 So they gave Him a piece of a broiled fish [1]and
some honeycomb.
43 [a]And He took *it* and ate in their presence.
**44** Then He said to them, [a]"These *are* the words
which I spoke to you while I was still with you,
that all things must be fulfilled which were written in the Law of Moses and *the* Prophets and *the*
Psalms concerning Me."
45 And [a]He opened their understanding, that
they might comprehend the Scriptures.
46 Then He said to them, [a]"Thus it is written,
[1]and thus it was necessary for the Christ to suffer
and to rise from the dead the third day,

53 [a]Mark 15:46
54 [a]Matt. 27:62
55 [a]Luke 8:2 [b]Mark 15:47
56 [a]Mark 16:1 [b]Ex. 20:10

CHAPTER 24
1 [a]John 20:1–8 [b]Luke 23:56 [1]NU omits *and certain other women with them*
2 [a]Mark 16:4
3 [a]Mark 16:5
4 [a]John 20:12 [1]NU omits *greatly*
6 [a]Luke 9:22
7 [a]Luke 9:44; 11:29, 30; 18:31–33
8 [a]John 2:19–22
9 [a]Mark 16:10
10 [a]Luke 8:3
11 [a]Luke 24:25 [1]*non-sense*
12 [a]John 20:3–6 [1]NU omits *lying*
13 [a]Mark 16:12 [1]Lit. *60 stadia*
15 [a][Matt. 18:20]
16 [a]John 20:14; 21:4
17 [1]NU *walk? And they stood still, looking sad.*
18 [a]John 19:25
19 [a]Matt. 21:11 [b]Acts 7:22
20 [a]Acts 13:27, 28
21 [a]Luke 1:68; 2:38
22 [a]Mark 16:10
24 [a]Luke 24:12
26 [a]Acts 17:2, 3 [b][1 Pet. 1:10–12]
27 [a][Deut. 18:15] [b][Is. 7:14; 9:6] [1]*ex-plained*
28 [a]Mark 6:48 [1]*acted as if*
29 [a]Gen. 19:2, 3 [b][John 14:23]
30 [a]Matt. 14:19
34 [a]1 Cor. 15:5
35 [1]*recognized*
36 [a]Mark 16:14
37 [a]Mark 6:49
39 [a]John 20:20, 27 [b][1 Cor. 15:50]
40 [1]Some printed New Testaments omit v. 40. It is found in nearly all Gr. mss.
41 [a]Gen. 45:26 [b]John 21:5
42 [1]NU omits *and some honeycomb*
43 [a]Acts 10:39–41
44 [a]Matt. 16:21; 17:22; 20:18
45 [a]Acts 16:14
46 [a]Acts 17:3 [1]NU *that the Christ should suffer and rise*

47 "and that repentance and [a]remission of sins should be preached in His name [b]to all nations, beginning at Jerusalem.
48 "And [a]you are witnesses of these things.
49 [a]"Behold, I send the Promise of My Father upon you; but tarry in the city [1]of Jerusalem until you are endued with power from on high."
**50** And He led them out [a]as far as Bethany, and He lifted up His hands and blessed them.
51 [a]Now it came to pass, while He blessed them, that He was parted from them and carried up into heaven.
52 [a]And they worshiped Him, and returned to Jerusalem with great joy,
53 and were continually [a]in the temple [1]praising and blessing God. [2]Amen.

**47** [a]Acts 5:31; 10:43; 13:38; 26:18 [b][Jer. 31:34]
**48** [a][Acts 1:8]
**49** [a]Joel 2:28 [1]NU omits *of Jerusalem*
**50** [a]Acts 1:12
**51** [a]Mark 16:19
**52** [a]Matt. 28:9
**53** [a]Acts 2:46 [1]NU omits *praising and* [2]NU omits *Amen*

*The Gospel According to*

# JOHN

### *Testimony of John the Baptist*

IN the beginning [a]was the Word, and the [b]Word was [c]with God, and the Word was [d]God.
2 [a]He was in the beginning with God.
3 [a]All things were made through Him, and without Him nothing was made that was made.
4 [a]In Him was life, and [b]the life was the light of men.
5 And [a]the light shines in the darkness, and the darkness did not [1]comprehend it.
**6** There was a [a]man sent from God, whose name *was* John.
7 This man came for a [a]witness, to bear witness of the Light, that all through him might [b]believe.
8 He was not that Light, but *was sent* to bear witness of that [a]Light.
9 [a]That was the true Light which gives light to every man coming into the world.
10 He was in the world, and the world was made through Him, and [a]the world did not know Him.
11 [a]He came to His [1]own, and His [2]own did not receive Him.
12 But [a]as many as received Him, to them He gave the [1]right to become children of God, to those who believe in His name:
13 [a]who were born, not of blood, nor of the will of the flesh, nor of the will of man, but of God.
**14** [a]And the Word [b]became [c]flesh and dwelt among us, and [d]we beheld His glory, the glory as of the only begotten of the Father, [e]full of grace and truth.
15 [a]John bore witness of Him and cried out, saying, "This was He of whom I said, [b]'He who comes after me [1]is preferred before me, [c]for He was before me.' "
16 [1]And of His [a]fullness we have all received, and grace for grace.
17 For [a]the law was given through Moses, *but* [b]grace and [c]truth came through Jesus Christ.
18 [a]No one has seen God at any time. [b]The only begotten [1]Son, who is in the bosom of the Father, He has declared *Him*.
**19** Now this is [a]the testimony of John, when the Jews sent priests and Levites from Jerusalem to ask him, "Who are you?"
20 [a]He confessed, and did not deny, but confessed, "I am not the Christ."
21 And they asked him, "What then? Are you Elijah?" He said, "I am not." "Are you [a]the Prophet?" And he answered, "No."
22 Then they said to him, "Who are you, that we may give an answer to those who sent us? What do you say about yourself?"
23 He said: [a]"I *am*

[b]*'The voice of one crying in the wilderness:*
*"Make straight the way of the* LORD,*" '*

as the prophet Isaiah said."
24 Now those who were sent were from the Pharisees.
25 And they asked him, saying, "Why then do you baptize if you are not the Christ, nor Elijah, nor the Prophet?"
26 John answered them, saying, [a]"I baptize with water, [b]but there stands One among you whom you do not know.
27 [a]"It is He who, coming after me, [1]is preferred before me, whose sandal strap I am not worthy to loose."
28 These things were done [a]in [1]Bethabara beyond the Jordan, where John was baptizing.
**29** The next day John saw Jesus coming toward him, and said, "Behold! [a]The Lamb of God [b]who takes away the sin of the world!
30 "This is He of whom I said, 'After me comes a Man who [1]is preferred before me, for He was before me.'
31 "I did not know Him; but that He should be revealed to Israel, [a]therefore I came baptizing with water."
32 [a]And John bore witness, saying, "I saw the Spirit descending from heaven like a dove, and He remained upon Him.
33 "I did not know Him, but He who sent me to baptize with water said to me, 'Upon whom you see the Spirit descending, and remaining on Him, [a]this is He who baptizes with the Holy Spirit.'
34 "And I have seen and testified that this is the [a]Son of God."
**35** Again, the next day, John stood with two of his disciples.
36 And looking at Jesus as He walked, he said, [a]"Behold the Lamb of God!"
37 The two disciples heard him speak, and they [a]followed Jesus.
38 Then Jesus turned, and seeing them following, said to them, "What do you seek?" They said to Him, "Rabbi" (which is to say, when translated, Teacher), "where are You staying?"
39 He said to them, "Come and see." They came and saw where He was staying, and remained

CHAPTER 1
**1** [a]1 John 1:1 [b]Rev. 19:13 [c][John 17:5] [d][1 John 5:20]
**2** [a]Gen. 1:1
**3** [a][Col. 1:16, 17]
**4** [a][1 John 5:11] [b]John 8:12; 9:5; 12:46
**5** [a][John 3:19] [1]Or *overcome*
**6** [a]Matt. 3:1–17
**7** [a]John 3:25–36; 5:33–35 [b][John 3:16]
**8** [a]Is. 9:2; 49:6
**9** [a]Is. 49:6
**10** [a]Heb. 1:2
**11** [a][Luke 19:14] [1]His own things or domain [2]His own people
**12** [a]Gal. 3:26 [1]*authority*
**13** [a][1 Pet. 1:23]
**14** [a]Rev. 19:13 [b]Gal. 4:4 [c]Heb. 2:11 [d]Is. 40:5 [e][John 8:32; 14:6; 18:37]
**15** [a]John 3:32 [b][Matt. 3:11] [c][Col. 1:17] [1]*ranks higher than I*
**16** [a][Col. 1:19; 2:9] [1]NU *For*
**17** [a][Ex. 20:1] [b][Rom. 5:21; 6:14] [c][John 8:32; 14:6; 18:37]
**18** [a]Ex. 33:20 [b]1 John 4:9 [1]NU *God*
**19** [a]John 5:33
**20** [a]Luke 3:15
**21** [a]Deut. 18:15, 18
**23** [a]Matt. 3:3 [b]Is. 40:3
**26** [a]Matt. 3:11 [b]Mal. 3:1
**27** [a]Acts 19:4 [1]*ranks higher than I*
**28** [a]Judg. 7:24 [1]NU, M *Bethany*
**29** [a]Rev. 5:6–14 [b][1 Pet. 2:24]
**30** [1]*ranks higher than I*
**31** [a]Matt. 3:6
**32** [a]Mark 1:10
**33** [a]Matt. 3:11
**34** [a]John 11:27
**36** [a]John 1:29
**37** [a]Matt. 4:20, 22

with Him that day (now it was about the tenth
hour).
40 One of the two who heard John *speak,* and
followed Him, was [a]Andrew, Simon Peter's
brother.
41 He first found his own brother Simon, and said
to him, "We have found the [1]Messiah" (which is
translated, the Christ).
42 And he brought him to Jesus. Now when Jesus
looked at him, He said, "You are Simon the son of
[1]Jonah. [a]You shall be called Cephas" (which is
translated, [2]A Stone).
**43** The following day Jesus wanted to go to
Galilee, and He found [a]Philip and said to him,
"Follow Me."
44 Now [a]Philip was from Bethsaida, the city of
Andrew and Peter.
45 Philip found [a]Nathanael and said to him, "We
have found Him of whom [b]Moses in the law, and
also the [c]prophets, wrote—Jesus [d]of Nazareth, the
[e]son of Joseph."
46 And Nathanael said to him, [a]"Can anything
good come out of Nazareth?" Philip said to him,
"Come and see."
47 Jesus saw Nathanael coming toward Him, and
said of him, "Behold, [a]an Israelite indeed, in whom
is no deceit!"
48 Nathanael said to Him, "How do You know
me?" Jesus answered and said to him, "Before
Philip called you, when you were under the fig
tree, I saw you."
49 Nathanael answered and said to Him, "Rabbi,
[a]You are the Son of God! You are [b]the King of
Israel!"
50 Jesus answered and said to him, "Because I
said to you, 'I saw you under the fig tree,' do you
believe? You will see greater things than these."
51 And He said to him, "Most assuredly, I say to
you, [a]hereafter[1] you shall see heaven open, and
the angels of God ascending and descending upon
the Son of Man."

### *Jesus' First Miracle at Cana*

**2** On the third day there was a [a]wedding in
[b]Cana of Galilee, and the [c]mother of Jesus was
there.
2 Now both Jesus and His disciples were invited
to the wedding.
3 And when they ran out of wine, the mother of
Jesus said to Him, "They have no wine."
4 Jesus said to her, [a]"Woman, [b]what does your
concern have to do with Me? [c]My hour has not yet
come."
5 His mother said to the servants, "Whatever He
says to you, do *it.*"
6 Now there were set there six waterpots of
stone, [a]according to the manner of purification of
the Jews, containing twenty or thirty gallons
apiece.
7 Jesus said to them, "Fill the waterpots with
water." And they filled them up to the brim.
8 And He said to them, "Draw *some* out now,
and take *it* to the master of the feast." And they
took *it.*
9 When the master of the feast had tasted [a]the
water that was made wine, and did not know
where it came from (but the servants who had
drawn the water knew), the master of the feast
called the bridegroom.
10 And he said to him, "Every man at the beginning sets out the good wine, and when the *guests*
have well drunk, then the inferior. You have kept
the good wine until now!"
11 This [a]beginning of signs Jesus did in Cana of
Galilee, [b]and [1]manifested His glory; and His disciples believed in Him.
12 After this He went down to [a]Capernaum, He,
His mother, [b]His brothers, and His disciples; and
they did not stay there many days.
**13** [a]Now the Passover of the Jews was at hand,
and Jesus went up to Jerusalem.
14 [a]And He found in the temple those who sold
oxen and sheep and doves, and the moneychangers [1]doing business.
15 When He had made a whip of cords, He drove
them all out of the temple, with the sheep and the
oxen, and poured out the changers' money and
overturned the tables.
16 And He said to those who sold doves, "Take
these things away! Do not make [a]My Father's
house a house of merchandise!"
17 Then His disciples remembered that it was
written, [a]*"Zeal for Your house [1]has eaten Me up."*
18 So the Jews answered and said to Him, [a]"What
sign do You show to us, since You do these
things?"
19 Jesus answered and said to them, [a]"Destroy
this temple, and in three days I will raise it up."
20 Then the Jews said, "It has taken forty-six
years to build this temple, and will You raise it up
in three days?"
21 But He was speaking [a]of the temple of His
body.
22 Therefore, when He had risen from the dead,
[a]His disciples remembered that He had said this
[1]to them; and they believed the Scripture and the
word which Jesus had said.
**23** Now when He was in Jerusalem at the [a]Pass-
over, during the feast, many believed in His name
when they saw the signs which He did.
24 But Jesus did not commit Himself to them,
because He [a]knew all *men,*
25 and had no need that anyone should testify of
man, for [a]He knew what was in man.

### *You Must Be Born Again*

**3** There was a man of the Pharisees named
Nicodemus, a ruler of the Jews.
2 [a]This man came to Jesus by night and said to
Him, "Rabbi, we know that You are a teacher
come from God; for [b]no one can do these signs
that You do unless [c]God is with him."
3 Jesus answered and said to him, "Most assuredly, I say to you, [a]unless one is born [1]again, he
cannot see the kingdom of God."
4 Nicodemus said to Him, "How can a man be
born when he is old? Can he enter a second time
into his mother's womb and be born?"
5 Jesus answered, "Most assuredly, I say to you,
[a]unless one is born of water and the Spirit, he
cannot enter the kingdom of God.
6 "That which is born of the flesh is [a]flesh, and
that which is born of the Spirit is spirit.
7 "Do not marvel that I said to you, 'You must
be born again.'
8 [a]"The wind blows where it wishes, and you
hear the sound of it, but cannot tell where it
comes from and where it goes. So is everyone who
is born of the Spirit."
9 Nicodemus answered and said to Him, [a]"How
can these things be?"

**40** [a]Matt. 4:18
**41** [1]Lit. *Anointed One*
**42** [a]Matt. 16:18 [1]NU *John* [2]Gk. *Petros,* usually translated *Peter*
**43** [a]John 6:5; 12:21, 22; 14:8, 9
**44** [a]John 12:21
**45** [a]John 21:2 [b]Luke 24:27 [c][Zech. 6:12] [d][Matt. 2:23] [e]Luke 3:23
**46** [a]John 7:41, 42, 52
**47** [a]Ps. 32:2; 73:1
**49** [a]Matt. 14:33 [b]Matt. 21:5
**51** [a]Gen. 28:12 [1]NU omits *hereafter*

CHAPTER 2
**1** [a][Heb. 13:4] [b]Josh. 19:28 [c]John 19:25
**4** [a]John 19:26 [b]2 Sam. 16:10 [c]John 7:6, 8, 30; 8:20
**6** [a][Mark 7:3]
**9** [a]John 4:46
**11** [a]John 4:54 [b][John 1:14] [1]*revealed*
**12** [a]Matt. 4:13 [b]Matt. 12:46; 13:55
**13** [a]Deut. 16:1–6
**14** [a]Mark 11:15, 17 [1]Lit. *sitting*
**16** [a]Luke 2:49
**17** [a]Ps. 69:9 [1]NU, M *will eat*
**18** [a]Matt. 12:38
**19** [a]Matt. 26:61; 27:40
**21** [a][1 Cor. 3:16; 6:19]
**22** [a]Luke 24:8 [1]NU, M omit *to them*
**23** [a][Acts 2:22]
**24** [a]Rev. 2:23
**25** [a]Matt. 9:4

CHAPTER 3
**2** [a]John 7:50; 19:39 [b]John 9:16, 33 [c][Acts 10:38]
**3** [a][1 Pet. 1:23] [1]Or *from above*
**5** [a][Acts 2:38]
**6** [a]1 Cor. 15:50
**8** [a]Eccl. 11:5
**9** [a]John 6:52, 60

10 Jesus answered and said to him, "Are you the
teacher of Israel, and do not know these things?
11 [a]"Most assuredly, I say to you, We speak what
We know and testify what We have seen, and
[b]you do not receive Our witness.
12 "If I have told you earthly things and you do
not believe, how will you believe if I tell you
heavenly things?
13 [a]"No one has ascended to heaven but He who
came down from heaven, *that is,* the Son of Man
[1]who is in heaven.
14 [a]"And as Moses lifted up the serpent in the
wilderness, even so [b]must the Son of Man be
lifted up,
15 "that whoever [a]believes in Him should [1]not
perish but [b]have eternal life.
16 [a]"For God so loved the world that He gave His
only begotten [b]Son, that whoever believes in Him
should not perish but have everlasting life.
17 [a]"For God did not send His Son into the world
to condemn the world, but that the world through
Him might be saved.
18 [a]"He who believes in Him is not condemned;
but he who does not believe is condemned already, because he has not believed in the name of
the only begotten Son of God.
19 "And this is the condemnation, [a]that the light
has come into the world, and men loved darkness
rather than light, because their deeds were evil.
20 "For [a]everyone practicing evil hates the light
and does not come to the light, lest his deeds
should be exposed.
21 "But he who does the truth comes to the light,
that his deeds may be clearly seen, that they have
been [a]done in God."
**22** After these things Jesus and His disciples
came into the land of Judea, and there He remained with them [a]and baptized.
23 Now John also was baptizing in Aenon near
[a]Salim, because there was much water there. [b]And
they came and were baptized.
24 For [a]John had not yet been thrown into
prison.
25 Then there arose a dispute between *some* of
John's disciples and the Jews about purification.
26 And they came to John and said to him,
"Rabbi, He who was with you beyond the Jordan,
[a]to whom you have testified—behold, He is baptizing, and all [b]are coming to Him!"
27 John answered and said, [a]"A man can receive
nothing unless it has been given to him from
heaven.
28 "You yourselves bear me witness, that I said,
[a]'I am not the Christ,' but, [b]'I have been sent
before Him.'
29 [a]"He who has the bride is the bridegroom; but
[b]the friend of the bridegroom, who stands and
hears him, rejoices greatly because of the bridegroom's voice. Therefore this joy of mine is fulfilled.
30 [a]"He must increase, but I *must* decrease.
31 [a]"He who comes from above [b]is above all; [c]he
who is of the earth is earthly and speaks of the
earth. [d]He who comes from heaven is above all.
32 "And [a]what He has seen and heard, that He
testifies; and no one receives His testimony.
33 "He who has received His testimony [a]has
certified that God is true.
34 [a]"For He whom God has sent speaks the
words of God, for God does not give the Spirit [b]by
measure.
35 [a]"The Father loves the Son, and has given all
things into His hand.
36 [a]"He who believes in the Son has everlasting
life; and he who does not believe the Son shall not
see life, but the [b]wrath of God abides on him."

### *Jesus in Samaria and Galilee*

4 Therefore, when the Lord knew that the
Pharisees had heard that Jesus made and
[a]baptized more disciples than John
2 (though Jesus Himself did not baptize, but His
disciples),
3 He left Judea and departed again to Galilee.
4 But He needed to go through Samaria.
5 So He came to a city of Samaria which is
called Sychar, near the plot of ground that [a]Jacob
[b]gave to his son Joseph.
6 Now Jacob's well was there. Jesus therefore,
being wearied from *His* journey, sat thus by the
well. It was about the sixth hour.
7 A woman of Samaria came to draw water.
Jesus said to her, "Give Me a drink."
8 For His disciples had gone away into the city
to buy food.
9 Then the woman of Samaria said to Him,
"How is it that You, being a Jew, ask a drink from
me, a Samaritan woman?" For [a]Jews have no
dealings with [b]Samaritans.
10 Jesus answered and said to her, "If you knew
the [a]gift of God, and who it is who says to you,
'Give Me a drink,' you would have asked Him, and
He would have given you [b]living water."
11 The woman said to Him, "Sir, You have nothing to draw with, and the well is deep. Where then
do You get that living water?
12 "Are You greater than our father Jacob, who
gave us the well, and drank from it himself, as
well as his sons and his livestock?"
13 Jesus answered and said to her, "Whoever
drinks of this water will thirst again,
14 "but [a]whoever drinks of the water that I shall
give him will never thirst. But the water that I
shall give him [b]will become in him a fountain of
water springing up into everlasting life."
15 [a]The woman said to Him, "Sir, give me this
water, that I may not thirst, nor come here to
draw."
16 Jesus said to her, "Go, call your husband, and
come here."
17 The woman answered and said, "I have no
husband." Jesus said to her, "You have well said,
'I have no husband,'
18 "for you have had five husbands, and the one
whom you now have is not your husband; in that
you spoke truly."
19 The woman said to Him, "Sir, [a]I perceive that
You are a prophet.
20 "Our fathers worshiped on [a]this mountain,
and you *Jews* say that in [b]Jerusalem is the place
where one ought to worship."
21 Jesus said to her, "Woman, believe Me, the
hour is coming [a]when you will neither on this
mountain, nor in Jerusalem, worship the Father.
22 "You worship [a]what you do not know; we
know what we worship, for [b]salvation is of the
Jews.
23 "But the hour is coming, and now is, when the
true worshipers will [a]worship the Father in [b]spirit
[c]and truth; for the Father is seeking such to
worship Him.
24 [a]"God *is* Spirit, and those who worship Him
must worship in spirit and truth."

11 [a][Matt. 11:27] [b]John 3:32; 8:14
13 [a]Eph. 4:9 [1]NU omits *who is in heaven*
14 [a]Num. 21:9 [b]John 8:28; 12:34; 19:18
15 [a]John 6:47 [b]John 3:36 [1]NU omits *not perish but*
16 [a]Rom. 5:8 [b][Is. 9:6]
17 [a]Luke 9:56
18 [a]John 5:24; 6:40, 47; 20:31
19 [a][John 1:4, 9–11]
20 [a]Eph. 5:11, 13
21 [a]1 Cor. 15:10
22 [a]John 4:1, 2
23 [a]1 Sam. 9:4 [b]Matt. 3:5, 6
24 [a]Matt. 4:12; 14:3
26 [a]John 1:7, 15, 27, 34 [b]Mark 2:2; 3:10; 5:24
27 [a]1 Cor. 3:5, 6; 4:7
28 [a]John 1:19–27 [b]Mal. 3:1
29 [a][2 Cor. 11:2] [b]Song 5:1
30 [a][Is. 9:7]
31 [a]John 3:13; 8:23 [b]Matt. 28:18 [c]1 Cor. 15:47 [d]John 6:33
32 [a]John 3:11; 15:15
33 [a]1 John 5:10
34 [a]John 7:16 [b]John 1:16
35 [a][Heb. 2:8]
36 [a]John 3:16, 17; 6:47 [b]Rom. 1:18

CHAPTER 4
1 [a]John 3:22, 26
5 [a]Gen. 33:19 [b]Gen. 48:22
9 [a]Acts 10:28 [b]2 Kin. 17:24
10 [a][Rom. 5:15] [b]Is. 12:3; 44:3
14 [a][John 6:35, 58] [b]John 7:37, 38
15 [a]John 6:34, 35; 17:2, 3
19 [a]Luke 7:16, 39; 24:19
20 [a]Judg. 9:7 [b]Deut. 12:5, 11
21 [a]1 Tim. 2:8
22 [a][2 Kin. 17:28–41] [b][Rom. 3:1; 9:4, 5]
23 [a][Heb. 13:10–14] [b]Phil. 3:3 [c][John 1:17]
24 [a]2 Cor. 3:17

25 The woman said to Him, "I know that Messiah
[a]is coming" (who is called Christ). "When He
comes, [b]He will tell us all things."
26 Jesus said to her, [a]"I who speak to you am
*He*."
**27** And at this *point* His disciples came, and they
marveled that He talked with a woman; yet no
one said, "What do You seek?" or, "Why are You
talking with her?"
28 The woman then left her waterpot, went her
way into the city, and said to the men,
29 "Come, see a Man [a]who told me all things that
I ever did. Could this be the Christ?"
30 Then they went out of the city and came to
Him.
31 In the meantime His disciples urged Him,
saying, "Rabbi, eat."
32 But He said to them, "I have food to eat of
which you do not know."
33 Therefore the disciples said to one another,
"Has anyone brought Him *anything* to eat?"
34 Jesus said to them, [a]"My food is to do the will
of Him who sent Me, and to [b]finish His work.
35 "Do you not say, 'There are still four months
and *then* comes [a]the harvest'? Behold, I say to
you, lift up your eyes and look at the fields, [b]for
they are already white for harvest!
36 [a]"And he who reaps receives wages, and gathers fruit for eternal life, that [b]both he who sows
and he who reaps may rejoice together.
37 "For in this the saying is true: [a]'One sows and
another reaps.'
38 "I sent you to reap that for which you have
not labored; [a]others have labored, and you have
entered into their labors."
**39** And many of the Samaritans of that city
believed in Him [a]because of the word of the
woman who testified, "He told me all that I *ever*
did."
40 So when the Samaritans had come to Him,
they urged Him to stay with them; and He stayed
there two days.
41 And many more believed because of His own
[a]word.
42 Then they said to the woman, "Now we believe, not because of what you said, for [a]we
ourselves have heard *Him* and we know that this
is indeed [1]the Christ, the Savior of the world."
**43** Now after the two days He departed from
there and went to Galilee.
44 For [a]Jesus Himself testified that a prophet has
no honor in his own country.
45 So when He came to Galilee, the Galileans
received Him, [a]having seen all the things He did in
Jerusalem at the feast; [b]for they also had gone to
the feast.
**46** So Jesus came again to Cana of Galilee [a]where
He had made the water wine. And there was a
certain [1]nobleman whose son was sick at Capernaum.
47 When he heard that Jesus had come out of
Judea into Galilee, he went to Him and implored
Him to come down and heal his son, for he was at
the point of death.
48 Then Jesus said to him, [a]"Unless you *people*
see signs and wonders, you will by no means
believe."
49 The nobleman said to Him, "Sir, come down
before my child dies!"
50 Jesus said to him, "Go your way; your son
lives." So the man believed the word that Jesus
spoke to him, and he went his way.
51 And as he was now going down, his servants
met him and told *him*, saying, "Your son lives!"
52 Then he inquired of them the hour when he
got better. And they said to him, "Yesterday at
the seventh hour the fever left him."
53 So the father knew that *it was* at the same
hour in which Jesus said to him, "Your son lives."
And he himself believed, and his whole household.
54 This again *is* the second sign Jesus did when
He had come out of Judea into Galilee.

### *Healing at the Bethesda Pool*

**5** After [a]this there was a feast of the Jews, and
Jesus [b]went up to Jerusalem.
2 Now there is in Jerusalem [a]by the Sheep *Gate*
a pool, which is called in Hebrew, [1]Bethesda,
having five porches.
3 In these lay a great multitude of sick people,
blind, lame, [1]paralyzed, [2]waiting for the moving of
the water.
4 For an angel went down at a certain time into
the pool and stirred up the water; then whoever
stepped in first, after the stirring of the water, was
made well of whatever disease he had.
5 Now a certain man was there who had an
infirmity thirty-eight years.
6 When Jesus saw him lying there, and knew
that he already had been *in that condition* a long
time, He said to him, "Do you want to be made
well?"
7 The sick man answered Him, "Sir, I have no
man to put me into the pool when the water is
stirred up; but while I am coming, another steps
down before me."
8 Jesus said to him, [a]"Rise, take up your bed and
walk."
9 And immediately the man was made well,
took up his bed, and walked. And [a]that day was
the Sabbath.
10 The Jews therefore said to him who was
cured, "It is the Sabbath; [a]it is not lawful for you
to carry your bed."
11 He answered them, "He who made me well
said to me, 'Take up your bed and walk.' "
12 Then they asked him, "Who is the Man who
said to you, 'Take up your bed and walk'?"
13 But the one who was [a]healed did not know
who it was, for Jesus had withdrawn, a multitude
being in *that* place.
14 Afterward Jesus found him in the temple, and
said to him, "See, you have been made well. [a]Sin
no more, lest a worse thing come upon you."
15 The man departed and told the Jews that it
was Jesus who had made him well.
**16** For this reason the Jews [a]persecuted Jesus,
[1]and sought to kill Him, because He had done
these things on the Sabbath.
17 But Jesus answered them, [a]"My Father has
been working until now, and I have been working."
18 Therefore the Jews [a]sought all the more to kill
Him, because He not only broke the Sabbath, but
also said that God was His Father, [b]making Himself equal with God.
19 Then Jesus answered and said to them, "Most
assuredly, I say to you, [a]the Son can do nothing of
Himself, but what He sees the Father do; for
whatever He does, the Son also does in like
manner.
20 "For [a]the Father loves the Son, and [b]shows
Him all things that He Himself does; and He will

**25** [a]Deut. 18:15 [b]John 4:29, 39
**26** [a]Dan. 9:25; Matt. 26:63, 64; Mark 14:61, 62
**29** [a]John 4:25
**34** [a]Ps. 40:7, 8; Heb. 10:9 [b]Job 23:12; [John 6:38; 17:4; 19:30]
**35** [a]Gen. 8:22 [b]Matt. 9:37; Luke 10:2
**36** [a]Dan. 12:3; Rom. 6:22 [b]1 Thess. 2:19
**37** [a]1 Cor. 3:5–9
**38** [a]Jer. 44:4; [1 Pet. 1:12]
**39** [a]John 4:29
**41** [a]Luke 4:32; [John 6:63]
**42** [a]John 17:8; 1 John 4:14 [1]NU omits *the Christ*
**44** [a]Matt. 13:57; Mark 6:4; Luke 4:24
**45** [a]John 2:13, 23; 3:2 [b]Deut. 16:16
**46** [a]John 2:1, 11 [1]*royal official*
**48** [a]John 6:30; Rom. 15:19; 1 Cor. 1:22; 2 Cor. 12:12; [2 Thess. 2:9]; Heb. 2:4

CHAPTER 5
**1** [a]Lev. 23:2; Deut. 16:16 [b]John 2:13
**2** [a]Neh. 3:1, 32; 12:39 [1]NU *Bethzatha*
**3** [1]*withered* [2]NU omits the rest of v. 3 and all of v. 4.
**8** [a]Matt. 9:6; Mark 2:11; Luke 5:24
**9** [a]John 9:14
**10** [a]Ex. 20:10; Neh. 13:19; Jer. 17:21, 22; Matt. 12:2; Mark 2:24; Luke 6:2
**13** [a]Luke 13:14; 22:51
**14** [a]Matt. 12:45; [Mark 2:5]; John 8:11
**16** [a]Luke 4:29; John 8:37; 10:39 [1]NU omits *and sought to kill Him*
**17** [a][John 9:4; 17:4]
**18** [a]John 7:1, 19 [b]John 10:30; Phil. 2:6
**19** [a]Matt. 26:39; John 5:30; 6:38; 8:28; 12:49; 14:10
**20** [a]Matt. 3:17; John 3:35; 2 Pet. 1:17 [b][Matt. 11:27]

show Him greater works than these, that you may
marvel.
21 "For as the Father raises the dead and gives
life to *them*, [a]even so the Son gives life to whom
He will.
22 "For the Father judges no one, but [a]has committed all judgment to the Son,
23 "that all should honor the Son just as they
honor the Father. [a]He who does not honor the Son
does not honor the Father who sent Him.
**24** "Most assuredly, I say to you, [a]he who hears
My word and believes in Him who sent Me has
everlasting life, and shall not come into judgment,
[b]but has passed from death into life.
25 "Most assuredly, I say to you, the hour is
coming, and now is, when [a]the dead will hear the
voice of the Son of God; and those who hear will
live.
26 "For [a]as the Father has life in Himself, so He
has granted the Son to have [b]life in Himself,
27 "and [a]has given Him authority to execute
judgment also, [b]because He is the Son of Man.
28 "Do not marvel at this; for the hour is coming
in which all who are in the graves will [a]hear His
voice
29 [a]"and come forth—[b]those who have done
good, to the resurrection of life, and those who
have done evil, to the resurrection of condemnation.
30 [a]"I can of Myself do nothing. As I hear, I
judge; and My judgment is righteous, because [b]I
do not seek My own will but the will of the Father
who sent Me.
**31** [a]"If I bear witness of Myself, My witness is not
[1]true.
32 [a]"There is another who bears witness of Me,
and I know that the witness which He witnesses
of Me is true.
33 "You have sent to John, [a]and he has borne
witness to the truth.
34 "Yet I do not receive testimony from man, but
I say these things that you may be saved.
35 "He was the burning and [a]shining lamp, and
[b]you were willing for a time to rejoice in his light.
36 "But [a]I have a greater witness than John's; for
[b]the works which the Father has given Me to
finish—the very [c]works that I do—bear witness of
Me, that the Father has sent Me.
37 "And the Father Himself, who sent Me, [a]has
testified of Me. You have neither heard His voice
at any time, [b]nor seen His form.
38 "But you do not have His word abiding in you,
because whom He sent, Him you do not believe.
39 [a]"You search the Scriptures, for in them you
think you have eternal life; and [b]these are they
which testify of Me.
40 [a]"But you are not willing to come to Me that
you may have life.
41 [a]"I do not receive honor from men.
42 "But I know you, that you do not have the
love of God in you.
43 "I have come in My Father's name, and you do
not receive Me; if another comes in his own name,
him you will receive.
44 [a]"How can you believe, who receive honor
from one another, and do not seek [b]the honor that
*comes* from the only God?
45 "Do not think that I shall accuse you to the
Father; [a]there is *one* who accuses you—Moses, in
whom you trust.
46 "For if you believed Moses, you would believe
Me; [a]for he wrote about Me.
47 "But if you [a]do not believe his writings, how
will you believe My words?"

## *Jesus Feeds Five Thousand*

**6** After [a]these things Jesus went over the Sea of
Galilee, which is *the Sea* of [b]Tiberias.
2 Then a great multitude followed Him, because
they saw His signs which He performed on those
who were [a]diseased.[1]
3 And Jesus went up on a mountain, and there
He sat with His disciples.
4 [a]Now the Passover, a feast of the Jews, was
near.
5 [a]Then Jesus lifted up *His* eyes, and seeing a
great multitude coming toward Him, He said to
[b]Philip, "Where shall we buy bread, that these
may eat?"
6 But this He said to test him, for He Himself
knew what He would do.
7 Philip answered Him, [a]"Two hundred denarii
worth of bread is not sufficient for them, that
every one of them may have a little."
8 One of His disciples, [a]Andrew, Simon Peter's
brother, said to Him,
9 "There is a lad here who has five barley loaves
and two small fish, [a]but what are they among so
many?"
10 Then Jesus said, "Make the people sit down."
Now there was much grass in the place. So the
men sat down, in number about five thousand.
11 And Jesus took the loaves, and when He had
given thanks He distributed *them* [1]to the disciples,
and the disciples to those sitting down; and likewise of the fish, as much as they wanted.
12 So when they were filled, He said to His
disciples, "Gather up the fragments that remain,
so that nothing is lost."
13 Therefore they gathered *them* up, and filled
twelve baskets with the fragments of the five
barley loaves which were left over by those who
had eaten.
14 Then those men, when they had seen the sign
that Jesus did, said, "This is truly [a]the Prophet
who is to come into the world."
**15** Therefore when Jesus perceived that they
were about to come and take Him by force to
make Him [a]king, He departed again to a mountain
by Himself alone.
16 [a]Now when evening came, His disciples went
down to the sea,
17 got into the boat, and went over the sea
toward Capernaum. And it was already dark, and
Jesus had not come to them.
18 Then the sea arose because a great wind was
blowing.
19 So when they had rowed about [1]three or four
miles, they saw Jesus walking on the sea and
drawing near the boat; and they were [a]afraid.
20 But He said to them, [a]"It is I; do not be afraid."
21 Then they willingly received Him into the
boat, and immediately the boat was at the land
where they were going.
**22** On the following day, when the people who
were standing on the other side of the sea saw
that there was no other boat there, except [1]that
one [2]which His disciples had entered, and that
Jesus had not entered the boat with His disciples,
but His disciples had gone away alone—
23 however, other boats came from Tiberias, near

21 [a][John 11:25]
22 [a][Acts 17:31]
23 [a]1 John 2:23
24 [a]John 3:16, 18; 6:47 [b][1 John 3:14]
25 [a][Col. 2:13]
26 [a]Ps. 36:9 [b]1 Cor. 15:45
27 [a][Acts 10:42; 17:31] [b]Dan. 7:13
28 [a][1 Thess. 4:15–17]
29 [a]Is. 26:19 [b]Dan. 12:2
30 [a]John 5:19 [b]Matt. 26:39
31 [a]John 8:14 [1]*valid* as testimony
32 [a][Matt. 3:17]
33 [a][John 1:15, 19, 27, 32]
35 [a]2 Pet. 1:19 [b]Mark 6:20
36 [a]1 John 5:9 [b]John 3:2; 10:25; 17:4 [c]John 9:16; 10:38
37 [a]Matt. 3:17 [b]1 John 4:12
39 [a]Is. 8:20; 34:16 [b]Luke 24:27
40 [a][John 1:11; 3:19]
41 [a]1 Thess. 2:6
44 [a]John 12:43 [b][Rom. 2:29]
45 [a]Rom. 2:12
46 [a]Deut. 18:15, 18
47 [a]Luke 16:29, 31

CHAPTER 6
1 [a]Mark 6:32 [b]John 6:23; 21:1
2 [a]Matt. 4:23; 8:16; 9:35; 14:36; 15:30; 19:2 [1]*sick*
4 [a]Deut. 16:1
5 [a]Matt. 14:14 [b]John 1:43
7 [a]Num. 11:21, 22
8 [a]John 1:40
9 [a]2 Kin. 4:43
11 [1]NU omits *to the disciples, and the disciples*
14 [a]Gen. 49:10
15 [a][John 18:36]
16 [a]Matt. 14:23
19 [a]Matt. 17:6 [1]Lit. *25 or 30 stadia*
20 [a]Is. 43:1, 2
22 [1]NU omits *that* [2]NU omits *which His disciples had entered*

the place where they ate bread after the Lord had
given thanks—
24 when the people therefore saw that Jesus was
not there, nor His disciples, they also got into
boats and came to Capernaum, [a]seeking Jesus.
25 And when they found Him on the other side of
the sea, they said to Him, "Rabbi, when did You
come here?"
26 Jesus answered them and said, "Most assuredly, I say to you, you seek Me, not because
you saw the signs, but because you ate of the
loaves and were filled.
27 [a]"Do not labor for the food which perishes, but
[b]for the food which endures to everlasting life,
which the Son of Man will give you, [c]because God
the Father has set His seal on Him."
28 Then they said to Him, "What shall we do,
that we may work the works of God?"
29 Jesus answered and said to them, [a]"This is the
work of God, that you believe in Him whom He
sent."
30 Therefore they said to Him, [a]"What sign will
You perform then, that we may see it and believe
You? What work will You do?
31 [a]"Our fathers ate the manna in the desert; as it
is written, [b]*'He gave them bread from heaven to
eat.'* "
32 Then Jesus said to them, "Most assuredly, I
say to you, Moses did not give you the bread from
heaven, but [a]My Father gives you the true bread
from heaven.
33 "For the bread of God is He who comes down
from heaven and gives life to the world."
34 [a]Then they said to Him, "Lord, give us this
bread always."
35 And Jesus said to them, [a]"I am the bread of
life. [b]He who comes to Me shall never hunger, and
he who believes in Me shall never [c]thirst.
36 [a]"But I said to you that you have seen Me and
yet [b]do not believe.
37 [a]"All that the Father gives Me will come to
Me, and [b]the one who comes to Me I will [1]by no
means cast out.
38 "For I have come down from heaven, [a]not to
do My own will, [b]but the will of Him who sent Me.
39 "This is the will of the Father who sent Me,
[a]that of all He has given Me I should lose nothing,
but should raise it up at the last day.
40 "And this is the will of Him who sent Me, [a]that
everyone who sees the Son and believes in Him
may have everlasting life; and I will raise him up
at the last day."
**41** The Jews then [1]complained against Him, because He said, "I am the bread which came down
from heaven."
42 And they said, [a]"Is not this Jesus, the son of
Joseph, whose father and mother we know? How
is it then that He says, 'I have come down from
heaven'?"
43 Jesus therefore answered and said to them,
[1]"Do not murmur among yourselves.
44 [a]"No one can come to Me unless the Father
who sent Me [b]draws him; and I will raise him up
at the last day.
45 "It is written in the prophets, [a]*'And they shall
all be taught by God.'* [b]Therefore everyone who
[1]has heard and learned from the Father comes
to Me.
46 [a]"Not that anyone has seen the Father, [b]ex-
cept He who is from God; He has seen the Father.
47 "Most assuredly, I say to you, [a]he who believes [1]in Me has everlasting life.
48 [a]"I am the bread of life.
49 [a]"Your fathers ate the manna in the wilderness, and are dead.
50 [a]"This is the bread which comes down from
heaven, that one may eat of it and not die.
51 "I am the living bread [a]which came down from
heaven. If anyone eats of this bread, he will live
forever; and [b]the bread that I shall give is My
flesh, which I shall give for the life of the world."
52 The Jews therefore [a]quarreled among themselves, saying, "How can this Man give us *His*
flesh to eat?"
53 Then Jesus said to them, "Most assuredly, I
say to you, unless [a]you eat the flesh of the Son of
Man and drink His blood, you have no life in you.
54 [a]"Whoever eats My flesh and drinks My blood
has eternal life, and I will raise him up at the last
day.
55 "For My flesh is [1]food indeed, and My blood is
[2]drink indeed.
56 "He who eats My flesh and drinks My blood
[a]abides in Me, and I in him.
57 "As the living Father sent Me, and I live
because of the Father, so he who feeds on Me will
live because of Me.
58 [a]"This is the bread which came down from
heaven—not [b]as your fathers ate the manna, and
are dead. He who eats this bread will live forever."
59 These things He said in the synagogue as He
taught in Capernaum.
**60** [a]Therefore many of His disciples, when they
heard *this,* said, "This is a [1]hard saying; who can
understand it?"
61 When Jesus knew in Himself that His disciples
complained about this, He said to them, "Does
this [1]offend you?
62 [a]"*What* then if you should see the Son of Man
ascend where He was before?
63 [a]"It is the Spirit who gives life; the [b]flesh
profits nothing. The [c]words that I speak to you are
spirit, and *they* are life.
64 "But [a]there are some of you who do not
believe." For [b]Jesus knew from the beginning who
they were who did not believe, and who would
betray Him.
65 And He said, "Therefore [a]I have said to you
that no one can come to Me unless it has been
granted to him by My Father."
66 [a]From that *time* many of His disciples went
[1]back and walked with Him no more.
67 Then Jesus said to the twelve, "Do you also
want to go away?"
68 But Simon Peter answered Him, "Lord, to
whom shall we go? You have [a]the words of eternal
life.
69 [a]"Also we have come to believe and know that
You are the [1]Christ, the Son of the living God."
70 Jesus answered them, [a]"Did I not choose you,
the twelve, [b]and one of you is a devil?"
71 He spoke of [a]Judas Iscariot, *the son* of Simon,
for it was he who would [b]betray Him, being one of
the twelve.

## *Jesus Teaches in the Temple*

**7** After these things Jesus walked in Galilee; for
He did not want to walk in Judea, [a]because the
[1]Jews sought to kill Him.
2 [a]Now the Jews' Feast of Tabernacles was at
hand.

**24** [a]Luke 4:42
**27** [a]Matt. 6:19 [b]John 4:14 [c]Acts 2:22
**29** [a][1 John 3:23]
**30** [a]Matt. 12:38; 16:1
**31** [a]Ex. 16:15 [b]Ex. 16:4, 15; Neh. 9:15; Ps. 78:24
**32** [a]John 3:13, 16
**34** [a]John 4:15
**35** [a]John 6:48, 58 [b]John 4:14; 7:37 [c]Is. 55:1, 2
**36** [a]John 6:26, 64; 15:24 [b]John 10:26
**37** [a]John 6:45 [b]2 Tim. 2:19 [1]*certainly not*
**38** [a]Matt. 26:39 [b]John 4:34
**39** [a]John 10:28; 17:12; 18:9
**40** [a]John 3:15, 16; 4:14; 6:27, 47, 54
**41** [1]*grumbled*
**42** [a]Matt. 13:55
**43** [1]*Stop grumbling*
**44** [a]Song 1:4 [b][Phil. 1:29; 2:12, 13]
**45** [a]Is. 54:13 [b]John 6:37 [1]M *hears and has learned*
**46** [a]John 1:18 [b]Matt. 11:27
**47** [a][John 3:16, 18] [1]NU omits *in Me*
**48** [a]John 6:33, 35
**49** [a]John 6:31, 58
**50** [a]John 6:51, 58
**51** [a]John 3:13 [b]Heb. 10:5
**52** [a]John 7:43; 9:16; 10:19
**53** [a]Matt. 26:26
**54** [a]John 4:14; 6:27, 40
**55** [1]NU *true food* [2]NU *true drink*
**56** [a][1 John 3:24; 4:15, 16]
**58** [a]John 6:49–51 [b]Ex. 16:14–35
**60** [a]John 6:66 [1]*difficult*
**61** [1]*make you stumble*
**62** [a]Acts 1:9; 2:32, 33
**63** [a]2 Cor. 3:6 [b]John 3:6 [c][John 6:68; 14:24]
**64** [a]John 6:36 [b]John 2:24, 25; 13:11
**65** [a]John 6:37, 44, 45
**66** [a]Luke 9:62 [1]Or *away;* lit. *to the back*
**68** [a]Acts 5:20
**69** [a]Luke 9:20 [1]NU *Holy One of God.*
**70** [a]Luke 6:13 [b][John 13:27]
**71** [a]John 12:4; 13:2, 26 [b]Matt. 26:14–16

CHAPTER 7
**1** [a]John 5:18; 7:19, 25; 8:37, 40 [1]The ruling authorities
**2** [a]Lev. 23:34

3 [a]His brothers therefore said to Him, "Depart
from here and go into Judea, that Your disciples
also may see the works that You are doing.
4 "For no one does anything in secret while he
himself seeks to be known openly. If You do these
things, show Yourself to the world."
5 For [a]even His [b]brothers did not believe in Him.
6 Then Jesus said to them, [a]"My time has not
yet come, but your time is always ready.
7 [a]"The world cannot hate you, but it hates Me
[b]because I testify of it that its works are evil.
8 "You go up to this feast. I am not [1]yet going
up to this feast, [a]for My time has not yet fully
come."
9 When He had said these things to them, He
remained in Galilee.
**10** But when His brothers had gone up, then He
also went up to the feast, not openly, but as it
were in secret.
11 Then [a]the Jews sought Him at the feast, and
said, "Where is He?"
12 And [a]there was much complaining among the
people concerning Him. [b]Some said, "He is good";
others said, "No, on the contrary, He deceives the
people."
13 However, no one spoke openly of Him [a]for fear
of the Jews.
14 Now about the middle of the feast Jesus went
up into the temple and [a]taught.
15 [a]And the Jews marveled, saying, "How does
this Man know letters, having never studied?"
16 [1]Jesus answered them and said, [a]"My doctrine
is not Mine, but His who sent Me.
17 [a]"If anyone wills to do His will, he shall know
concerning the doctrine, whether it is from God or
*whether* I speak on My own *authority*.
18 [a]"He who speaks from himself seeks his own
glory; but He who [b]seeks the glory of the One who
sent Him is true, and [c]no unrighteousness is in
Him.
19 [a]"Did not Moses give you the law, yet none of
you keeps the law? [b]Why do you seek to kill Me?"
20 The people answered and said, [a]"You have a
demon. Who is seeking to kill You?"
21 Jesus answered and said to them, "I did one
work, and you all marvel.
22 [a]"Moses therefore gave you circumcision (not
that it is from Moses, [b]but from the fathers), and
you circumcise a man on the Sabbath.
23 "If a man receives circumcision on the Sabbath, so that the law of Moses should not be
broken, are you angry with Me because [a]I made a
man completely well on the Sabbath?
24 [a]"Do not judge according to appearance, but
judge with righteous judgment."
**25** Now some of them from Jerusalem said, "Is
this not He whom they seek to [a]kill?
26 "But look! He speaks boldly, and they say
nothing to Him. [a]Do the rulers know indeed that
this is [1]truly the Christ?
27 [a]"However, we know where this Man is from;
but when the Christ comes, no one knows where
He is from."
28 Then Jesus cried out, as He taught in the
temple, saying, [a]"You both know Me, and you
know where I am from; and [b]I have not come of
Myself, but He who sent Me [c]is true, [d]whom you
do not know.
29 [1]"But [a]I know Him, for I am from Him, and He
sent Me."
30 Therefore [a]they sought to take Him; but [b]no
one laid a hand on Him, because His hour had not
yet come.
31 And [a]many of the people believed in Him, and
said, "When the Christ comes, will He do more
signs than these which this *Man* has done?"
**32** The Pharisees heard the crowd murmuring
these things concerning Him, and the Pharisees
and the chief priests sent officers to take Him.
33 Then Jesus said [1]to them, [a]"I shall be with you
a little while longer, and *then* I [b]go to Him who
sent Me.
34 "You [a]will seek Me and not find *Me*, and
where I am you [b]cannot come."
35 Then the Jews said among themselves,
"Where does He intend to go that we shall not
find Him? Does He intend to go to [a]the Dispersion
among the Greeks and teach the Greeks?
36 "What is this thing that He said, 'You will seek
Me and not find Me, and where I am you cannot
come'?"
**37** [a]On the last day, that great *day* of the feast,
Jesus stood and cried out, saying, [b]"If anyone
thirsts, let him come to Me and drink.
38 [a]"He who believes in Me, as the Scripture has
said, [b]out of his heart will flow rivers of living
water."
39 [a]But this He spoke concerning the Spirit,
whom those [1]believing in Him would receive; for
the [2]Holy Spirit was not yet *given*, because Jesus
was not yet [b]glorified.
**40** Therefore [1]many from the crowd, when they
heard this saying, said, "Truly this is [a]the
Prophet."
41 Others said, "This is [a]the Christ." But some
said, "Will the Christ come out of Galilee?
42 [a]"Has not the Scripture said that the Christ
comes from the seed of David and from the town
of Bethlehem, [b]where David was?"
43 So [a]there was a division among the people
because of Him.
44 Now [a]some of them wanted to take Him, but
no one laid hands on Him.
**45** Then the officers came to the chief priests and
Pharisees, who said to them, "Why have you not
brought Him?"
46 The officers answered, [a]"No man ever spoke
like this Man!"
47 Then the Pharisees answered them, "Are you
also deceived?
48 "Have any of the rulers or the Pharisees
believed in Him?
49 "But this crowd that does not know the law is
accursed."
50 Nicodemus [a](he who came to [1]Jesus [2]by night,
being one of them) said to them,
51 [a]"Does our law judge a man before it hears
him and knows what he is doing?"
52 They answered and said to him, "Are you also
from Galilee? Search and look, for [a]no prophet
[1]has arisen out of Galilee."
**53** [1]And everyone went to his *own* house.

### *Jesus the Light of the World*

**8** But Jesus went to the Mount of Olives.
2 Now [1]early in the morning He came again
into the temple, and all the people came to Him;
and He sat down and [a]taught them.
3 Then the scribes and Pharisees brought to
Him a woman caught in adultery. And when they
had set her in the midst,

**3** [a]Matt. 12:46
**5** [a]Ps. 69:8 [b]Mark 3:21
**6** [a]John 2:4; 8:20
**7** [a][John 15:19] [b]John 3:19
**8** [a]John 8:20 [1]NU omits *yet*
**11** [a]John 11:56
**12** [a]John 9:16; 10:19 [b]Luke 7:16
**13** [a][John 9:22; 12:42; 19:38]
**14** [a]Mark 6:34
**15** [a]Matt. 13:54
**16** [a]John 3:11 [1]NU, M *So Jesus*
**17** [a]John 3:21; 8:43
**18** [a]John 5:41 [b]John 8:50 [c][2 Cor. 5:21]
**19** [a]Deut. 33:4 [b]Matt. 12:14
**20** [a]John 8:48, 52
**22** [a]Lev. 12:3 [b]Gen. 17:9–14
**23** [a]John 5:8, 9, 16
**24** [a]Prov. 24:23
**25** [a]Matt. 21:38; 26:4
**26** [a]John 7:48 [1]NU omits *truly*
**27** [a]Luke 4:22
**28** [a]John 8:14 [b]John 5:43 [c]Rom. 3:4 [d]John 1:18; 8:55
**29** [a]Matt. 11:27 [1]NU, M omit *But*
**30** [a]Mark 11:18 [b]John 7:32, 44; 8:20; 10:39
**31** [a]Matt. 12:23
**33** [a]John 13:33 [b][1 Pet. 3:22] [1]NU, M omit *to them*
**34** [a]Hos. 5:6 [b][Matt. 5:20]
**35** [a]James 1:1
**37** [a]Lev. 23:36 [b][Is. 55:1]
**38** [a]Deut. 18:15 [b]Is. 12:3; 43:20; 44:3; 55:1
**39** [a]Is. 44:3 [b]John 12:16; 13:31; 17:5 [1]NU *who believed* [2]NU omits *Holy*
**40** [a]Deut. 18:15, 18 [1]NU *some*
**41** [a]John 4:42; 6:69
**42** [a]Mic. 5:2 [b]1 Sam. 16:1, 4
**43** [a]John 7:12
**44** [a]John 7:30
**46** [a]Luke 4:22
**50** [a]John 3:1, 2; 19:39 [1]Lit. *Him* [2]NU *before*
**51** [a]Deut. 1:16, 17; 19:15
**52** [a][Is. 9:1, 2] [1]NU *is to rise*
**53** [1]NU brackets 7:53 through 8:11 as not in the original text. They are present in over 900 mss. of John.

CHAPTER 8
**2** [a]John 8:20; 18:20 [1]M *very early*

4 they said to Him, "Teacher, [1]this woman was
caught in [a]adultery, in the very act.
5 [a]"Now [1]Moses, in the law, commanded us [2]that
such should be stoned. But what do You [3]say?"
6 This they said, testing Him, that they [a]might
have *something* of which to accuse Him. But
Jesus stooped down and wrote on the ground with
*His* finger, [1]as though He did not hear.
7 So when they continued asking Him, He
[1]raised Himself up and said to them, [a]"He who is
without sin among you, let him throw a stone at
her first."
8 And again He stooped down and wrote on the
ground.
9 Then those who heard *it*, [a]being[1] convicted by
*their* conscience, went out one by one, beginning
with the oldest *even* to the last. And Jesus was left
alone, and the woman standing in the midst.
10 When Jesus had raised Himself up [1]and saw no
one but the woman, He said to her, "Woman,
where are those accusers [2]of yours? Has no one
condemned you?"
11 She said, "No one, Lord." And Jesus said to
her, [a]"Neither do I condemn you; go [1]and [b]sin no
more."
12 Then Jesus spoke to them again, saying, [a]"I
am the light of the world. He who [b]follows Me
shall not walk in darkness, but have the light of
life."
**13** The Pharisees therefore said to Him, [a]"You
bear witness of Yourself; Your witness is not
[1]true."
14 Jesus answered and said to them, "Even if I
bear witness of Myself, My witness is true, for I
know where I came from and where I am going;
but [a]you do not know where I come from and
where I am going.
15 [a]"You judge according to the flesh; [b]I judge no
one.
16 "And yet if I do judge, My judgment is true;
for [a]I am not alone, but I *am* with the Father who
sent Me.
17 [a]"It is also written in your law that the testimony of two men is true.
18 "I am One who bears witness of Myself, and
[a]the Father who sent Me bears witness of Me."
19 Then they said to Him, "Where is Your Father?" Jesus answered, [a]"You know neither Me
nor My Father. [b]If you had known Me, you would
have known My Father also."
20 These words Jesus spoke in [a]the treasury, as
He taught in the temple; and [b]no one laid hands
on Him, for [c]His hour had not yet come.
**21** Then Jesus said to them again, "I am going
away, and [a]you will seek Me, and [b]will die in your
sin. Where I go you cannot come."
22 So the Jews said, "Will He kill Himself, because He says, 'Where I go you cannot come'?"
23 And He said to them, [a]"You are from beneath;
I am from above. [b]You are of this world; I am not
of this world.
24 [a]"Therefore I said to you that you will die in
your sins; [b]for if you do not believe that I am *He*,
you will die in your sins."
25 Then they said to Him, "Who are You?" And
Jesus said to them, "Just what I [a]have been saying
to you from the beginning.
26 "I have many things to say and to judge
concerning you, but [a]He who sent Me is true; and
[b]I speak to the world those things which I heard
from Him."
27 They did not understand that He spoke to
them of the Father.
28 Then Jesus said to them, "When you [a]lift[1] up
the Son of Man, [b]then you will know that I am *He*,
and [c]*that* I do nothing of Myself; but [d]as My
Father taught Me, I speak these things.
29 "And [a]He who sent Me is with Me. [b]The
Father has not left Me alone, [c]for I always do
those things that please Him."
30 As He spoke these words, [a]many believed in
Him.
**31** Then Jesus said to those Jews who believed
Him, "If you [a]abide in My word, you are My
disciples indeed.
32 "And you shall know the [a]truth, and [b]the truth
shall make you free."
33 They answered Him, [a]"We are Abraham's
descendants, and have never been in bondage to
anyone. How *can* you say, 'You will be made
free'?"
34 Jesus answered them, "Most assuredly, I say
to you, [a]whoever commits sin is a slave of sin.
35 "And [a]a slave does not abide in the house
forever, *but* a son abides forever.
36 [a]"Therefore if the Son makes you free, you
shall be free indeed.
**37** "I know that you are Abraham's descendants,
but [a]you seek to kill Me, because My word has no
place in you.
38 [a]"I speak what I have seen with My Father,
and you do what you have [1]seen with your father."
39 They answered and said to Him, [a]"Abraham is
our father." Jesus said to them, [b]"If you were
Abraham's children, you would do the works of
Abraham.
40 [a]"But now you seek to kill Me, a Man who has
told you the truth [b]which I heard from God.
Abraham did not do this.
41 "You do the deeds of your father." Then they
said to Him, "We were not born of fornication;
[a]we have one Father—God."
42 Jesus said to them, [a]"If God were your Father,
you would love Me, for [b]I proceeded forth and
came from God; [c]nor have I come of Myself, but
He sent Me.
43 [a]"Why do you not understand My speech?
Because you are not able to listen to My word.
44 [a]"You are of *your* father the devil, and the
[b]desires of your father you want to [c]do. He was a
murderer from the beginning, and [d]*does not* stand
in the truth, because there is no truth in him.
When he speaks a lie, he speaks from his own
*resources*, for he is a liar and the father of it.
45 "But because I tell the truth, you do not
believe Me.
46 "Which of you convicts Me of sin? And if I tell
the truth, why do you not believe Me?
47 [a]"He who is of God hears God's words; therefore you do not hear, because you are not of God."
**48** Then the Jews answered and said to Him, "Do
we not say rightly that You are a Samaritan and
[a]have a demon?"
49 Jesus answered, "I do not have a demon; but I
honor My Father, and [a]you dishonor Me.
50 "And [a]I do not seek My *own* glory; there is
One who seeks and judges.

**4** [a]Ex. 20:14 [1]M *we found this woman*
**5** [a]Lev. 20:10 [1]M *in our law Moses commanded* [2]NU, M *to stone such* [3]M adds *about her*
**6** [a]Matt. 22:15 [1]NU, M omit *as though He did not hear*
**7** [a]Deut. 17:7 [1]M *He looked up*
**9** [a]Rom. 2:22 [1]NU, M omit *being convicted by their conscience*
**10** [1]NU omits *and saw no one but the woman;* M *He saw her and said,* [2]NU, M omit *of yours*
**11** [a][John 3:17] [b][John 5:14] [1]NU, M add *from now on*
**12** [a]John 1:4; 9:5; 12:35 [b]1 Thess. 5:5
**13** [a]John 5:31 [1]*valid* as testimony
**14** [a]John 7:28; 9:29
**15** [a]John 7:24 [b][John 3:17; 12:47; 18:36]
**16** [a]John 16:32
**17** [a]Deut. 17:6; 19:15
**18** [a]John 5:37
**19** [a]John 16:3 [b]John 14:7
**20** [a]Mark 12:41, 43 [b]John 2:4; 7:30 [c]John 7:8
**21** [a]John 7:34; 13:33 [b]John 8:24
**23** [a]John 3:31 [b]1 John 4:5
**24** [a]John 8:21 [b][Mark 16:16]
**25** [a]John 4:26
**26** [a]John 7:28 [b]John 3:32; 15:15
**28** [a]John 3:14; 12:32; 19:18 [b][Rom. 1:4] [c]John 5:19, 30 [d]John 3:11 [1]Crucify
**29** [a]John 14:10 [b]John 8:16; 16:32 [c]John 4:34; 5:30; 6:38
**30** [a]John 7:31; 10:42; 11:45
**31** [a][John 14:15, 23]
**32** [a][John 1:14, 17; 14:6] [b][Rom. 6:14; 18, 22]
**33** [a][Matt. 3:9]
**34** [a]2 Pet. 2:19
**35** [a]Gal. 4:30
**36** [a]Gal. 5:1
**37** [a]John 7:19
**38** [a][John 3:32; 5:19, 30; 14:10, 24] [1]NU *heard from*
**39** [a]Matt. 3:9 [b][Rom. 2:28]
**40** [a]John 8:37 [b]John 8:26
**41** [a]Is. 63:16
**42** [a]1 John 5:1 [b]John 16:27; 17:8, 25 [c]Gal. 4:4
**43** [a][John 7:17]
**44** [a]Matt. 13:38 [b]1 John 2:16, 17 [c][1 John 3:8–10, 15] [d][Jude 6]
**47** [a]1 John 4:6
**48** [a]John 7:20; 10:20
**49** [a]John 5:41
**50** [a]John 5:41; 7:18

51 "Most assuredly, I say to you, [a]if anyone keeps
My word he shall never see death."
52 Then the Jews said to Him, "Now we know
that You [a]have a demon! [b]Abraham is dead, and
the prophets; and You say, 'If anyone keeps My
word he shall never taste death.'
53 "Are You greater than our father Abraham,
who is dead? And the prophets are dead. [a]Who do
You make Yourself out to be?"
54 Jesus answered, [a]"If I honor Myself, My honor
is nothing. [b]It is My Father who honors Me, of
whom you say that He is [1]your God.
55 "Yet [a]you have not known Him, but I know
Him. And if I say, 'I do not know Him,' I shall be a
liar like you; but I do know Him and [b]keep His
word.
56 "Your father Abraham [a]rejoiced to see My
day, [b]and he saw *it* and was glad."
57 Then the Jews said to Him, "You are not yet
fifty years old, and have You seen Abraham?"
58 Jesus said to them, "Most assuredly, I say to
you, [a]before Abraham was, [b]I AM."
59 Then [a]they took up stones to throw at Him;
but Jesus hid Himself and went out of the temple,
[b]going[1] through the midst of them, and so
passed by.

### *The Man Born Blind*

**9** Now as *Jesus* passed by, He saw a man who
was blind from birth.
2 And His disciples asked Him, saying, "Rabbi,
[a]who sinned, this man or his parents, that he was
born blind?"
3 Jesus answered, "Neither this man nor his
parents sinned, [a]but that the works of God should
be revealed in him.
4 [a]"I[1] must work the works of Him who sent Me
while it is [b]day; *the* night is coming when no one
can work.
5 "As long as I am in the world, [a]I am the light
of the world."
6 When He had said these things, [a]He spat on
the ground and made clay with the saliva; and He
anointed the eyes of the blind man with the clay.
7 And He said to him, "Go, wash [a]in the pool of
Siloam" (which is translated, Sent). So [b]he went
and washed, and came back seeing.
8 Therefore the neighbors and those who previously had seen that he was [1]blind said, "Is not this
he who sat and begged?"
9 Some said, "This is he." Others *said,* [1]"He is
like him." He said, "I am *he.*"
10 Therefore they said to him, "How were your
eyes opened?"
11 He answered and said, [a]"A Man called Jesus
made clay and anointed my eyes and said to me,
'Go to [1]the pool of Siloam and wash.' So I went
and washed, and I received sight."
12 Then they said to him, "Where is He?" He
said, "I do not know."
**13** They brought him who formerly was blind to
the Pharisees.
14 Now it was a Sabbath when Jesus made the
clay and opened his eyes.
15 Then the Pharisees also asked him again how
he had received his sight. He said to them, "He put
clay on my eyes, and I washed, and I see."
16 Therefore some of the Pharisees said, "This
Man is not from God, because He does not [1]keep
the Sabbath." Others said, [a]"How can a man who
is a sinner do such signs?" And [b]there was a
division among them.
17 They said to the blind man again, "What do
you say about Him because He opened your
eyes?" He said, [a]"He is a prophet."
18 But the Jews did not believe concerning him,
that he had been blind and received his sight, until
they called the parents of him who had received
his sight.
19 And they asked them, saying, "Is this your
son, who you say was born blind? How then does
he now see?"
20 His parents answered them and said, "We
know that this is our son, and that he was born
blind;
21 "but by what means he now sees we do not
know, or who opened his eyes we do not know.
He is of age; ask him. He will speak for himself."
22 His parents said these *things* because [a]they
feared the Jews, for the Jews had agreed already
that if anyone confessed *that* He *was* Christ, he
[b]would be put out of the synagogue.
23 Therefore his parents said, "He is of age; ask
him."
24 So they again called the man who was blind,
and said to him, [a]"Give God the glory! [b]We know
that this Man is a sinner."
25 He answered and said, "Whether He is a
sinner *or not* I do not know. One thing I know:
that though I was blind, now I see."
26 Then they said to him again, "What did He do
to you? How did He open your eyes?"
27 He answered them, "I told you already, and
you did not listen. Why do you want to hear *it*
again? Do you also want to become His disciples?"
28 Then they reviled him and said, "You are His
disciple, but we are Moses' disciples.
29 "We know that God [a]spoke to [b]Moses; *as for*
this *fellow,* [c]we do not know where He is from."
30 The man answered and said to them, [a]"Why,
this is a marvelous thing, that you do not know
where He is from; yet He has opened my eyes!
31 "Now we know that [a]God does not hear sinners; but if anyone is a worshiper of God and does
His will, He hears him.
32 "Since the world began it has been unheard of
that anyone opened the eyes of one who was born
blind.
33 [a]"If this Man were not from God, He could do
nothing."
34 They answered and said to him, [a]"You were
completely born in sins, and are you teaching us?"
And they [1]cast him out.
**35** Jesus heard that they had cast him out; and
when He had [a]found him, He said to him, "Do you
[b]believe in [c]the Son of [1]God?"
36 He answered and said, "Who is He, Lord, that
I may believe in Him?"
37 And Jesus said to him, "You have both seen
Him and [a]it is He who is talking with you."
38 Then he said, "Lord, I believe!" And he [a]wor-
shiped Him.
39 And Jesus said, [a]"For judgment I have come
into this world, [b]that those who do not see may
see, and that those who see may be made blind."
40 Then *some* of the Pharisees who were with
Him heard these words, [a]and said to Him, "Are we
blind also?"
41 Jesus said to them, [a]"If you were blind, you
would have no sin; but now you say, 'We see.'
Therefore your sin remains.

---

**51** [a]John 5:24; 11:26
**52** [a]John 7:20; 10:20 [b]Zech. 1:5
**53** [a]John 10:33; 19:7
**54** [a]John 5:31, 32 [b]Acts 3:13 [1]NU, M *our*
**55** [a]John 7:28, 29 [b][John 15:10]
**56** [a]Luke 10:24 [b]Heb. 11:13
**58** [a]Mic. 5:2 [b]Rev. 1:8
**59** [a]John 10:31; 11:8 [b]Luke 4:30 [1]NU omits the rest of v. 59.

CHAPTER 9
**2** [a]John 9:34
**3** [a]John 11:4
**4** [a][John 4:34; 5:19, 36; 17:4] [b]John 11:9, 10; 12:35 [1]NU *We*
**5** [a][John 1:5, 9; 3:19; 8:12; 12:35, 46]
**6** [a]Mark 7:33; 8:23
**7** [a]Neh. 3:15 [b]2 Kin. 5:14
**8** [1]NU *a beggar*
**9** [1]NU *No, but he is like him*
**11** [a]John 9:6, 7 [1]NU omits *the pool of*
**16** [a]John 3:2; 9:33 [b]John 7:12, 43; 10:19 [1]*observe*
**17** [a][John 4:19; 6:14]
**22** [a]Acts 5:13 [b]John 16:2
**24** [a]Josh. 7:19 [b]John 9:16
**29** [a]Num. 12:6–8 [b][John 5:45–47] [c]John 7:27, 28; 8:14
**30** [a]John 3:10
**31** [a]Zech. 7:13
**33** [a]John 3:2; 9:16
**34** [a]John 9:2 [1]Excommunicated him
**35** [a]John 5:14 [b]John 1:7; 16:31 [c]Matt. 14:33; 16:16 [1]NU *Man*
**37** [a]John 4:26
**38** [a]Matt. 8:2
**39** [a][John 3:17; 5:22, 27; 12:47] [b]Matt. 13:13; 15:14
**40** [a][Rom. 2:19]
**41** [a]John 15:22, 24

## *Jesus the Good Shepherd*

**10** "Most assuredly, I say to you, he who does
not enter the sheepfold by the door, but
climbs up some other way, the same is a thief and
a robber.
2 "But he who enters by the door is the shepherd of the sheep.
3 "To him the doorkeeper opens, and the sheep
hear his voice; and he calls his own sheep by
[a]name and leads them out.
4 "And when he brings out his own sheep, he
goes before them; and the sheep follow him, for
they know his voice.
5 "Yet they will by no means follow a [a]stranger,
but will flee from him, for they do not know the
voice of strangers."
6 Jesus used this illustration, but they did not
understand the things which He spoke to them.
**7** Then Jesus said to them again, "Most assuredly, I say to you, I am the door of the sheep.
8 "All who *ever* came [1]before Me are thieves and
robbers, but the sheep did not hear them.
9 [a]"I am the door. If anyone enters by Me, he
will be saved, and will go in and out and find
pasture.
10 "The thief does not come except to steal, and
to kill, and to destroy. I have come that they may
have life, and that they may have *it* more abundantly.
11 [a]"I am the good shepherd. The good shepherd
gives His life for the sheep.
12 "But a [1]hireling, *he who is* not the shepherd,
one who does not own the sheep, sees the wolf
coming and [a]leaves the sheep and flees; and the
wolf catches the sheep and scatters them.
13 "The hireling flees because he is a hireling and
does not care about the sheep.
14 "I am the good shepherd; and [a]I know My
*sheep,* and [b]am known by My own.
15 [a]"As the Father knows Me, even so I know the
Father; [b]and I lay down My life for the sheep.
16 "And [a]other sheep I have which are not of this
fold; them also I must bring, and they will hear
My voice; [b]and there will be one flock *and* one
shepherd.
17 "Therefore My Father [a]loves Me, [b]because I
lay down My life that I may take it again.
18 "No one takes it from Me, but I lay it down of
Myself. I [a]have power to lay it down, and I have
power to take it again. [b]This command I have
received from My Father."
19 Therefore [a]there was a division again among
the Jews because of these sayings.
20 And many of them said, [a]"He has a demon and
is [1]mad. Why do you listen to Him?"
21 Others said, "These are not the words of one
who has a demon. [a]Can a demon [b]open the eyes of
the blind?"
**22** Now it was the Feast of Dedication in Jerusalem, and it was winter.
23 And Jesus walked in the temple, [a]in Solomon's
porch.
24 Then the Jews surrounded Him and said to
Him, "How long do You keep us in [1]doubt? If You
are the Christ, tell us plainly."
25 Jesus answered them, "I told you, and you do
not believe. [a]The works that I do in My Father's
name, they [b]bear witness of Me.
26 "But [a]you do not believe, because you are not
of My sheep, [1]as I said to you.
27 [a]"My sheep hear My voice, and I know them,
and they follow Me.
28 "And I give them eternal life, and they shall
never perish; neither shall anyone snatch them
out of My hand.
29 [a]"My Father, [b]who has given *them* to Me, is
greater than all; and no one is able to snatch *them*
out of My Father's hand.
30 [a]"I and *My* Father are one."
**31** Then [a]the Jews took up stones again to stone
Him.
32 Jesus answered them, "Many good works I
have shown you from My Father. For which of
those works do you stone Me?"
33 The Jews answered Him, saying, "For a good
work we do not stone You, but for [a]blasphemy,
and because You, being a Man, [b]make Yourself
God."
34 Jesus answered them, "Is it not written in
your law, [a]*'I said, "You are gods"'*?
35 "If He called them gods, [a]to whom the word of
God came (and the Scripture [b]cannot be broken),
36 "do you say of Him [a]whom the Father sanctified and [b]sent into the world, 'You are blaspheming,' [c]because I said, 'I am [d]the Son of God'?
37 [a]"If I do not do the works of My Father, do not
believe Me;
38 "but if I do, though you do not believe Me,
[a]believe the works, that you may know and [1]be-
lieve [b]that the Father *is* in Me, and I in Him."
39 [a]Therefore they sought again to seize Him, but
He escaped out of their hand.
**40** And He went away again beyond the Jordan
to the place [a]where John was baptizing at first,
and there He stayed.
41 Then many came to Him and said, "John
performed no sign, [a]but all the things that John
spoke about this Man were true."
42 And many believed in Him there.

## *Jesus Raises Lazarus*

**11** Now a certain *man* was sick, Lazarus of
Bethany, the town of [a]Mary and her sister
Martha.
2 [a]It was *that* Mary who anointed the Lord with
fragrant oil and wiped His feet with her hair,
whose brother Lazarus was sick.
3 Therefore the sisters sent to Him, saying,
"Lord, behold, he whom You love is sick."
4 When Jesus heard *that,* He said, "This sickness is not unto death, but for the glory of God,
that the Son of God may be glorified through it."
5 Now Jesus loved Martha and her sister and
Lazarus.
6 So, when He heard that he was sick, [a]He
stayed two more days in the place where He was.
7 Then after this He said to *the* disciples, "Let us
go to Judea again."
8 *The* disciples said to Him, "Rabbi, lately the
Jews sought to [a]stone You, and are You going
there again?"
9 Jesus answered, "Are there not twelve hours
in the day? [a]If anyone walks in the day, he does
not stumble, because he sees the [b]light of this
world.
10 "But [a]if one walks in the night, he stumbles,
because the light is not in him."
11 These things He said, and after that He said to
them, "Our friend Lazarus [a]sleeps, but I go that I
may wake him up."
12 Then His disciples said, "Lord, if he sleeps he
will get well."
13 However, Jesus spoke of his death, but they

CHAPTER 10
3 [a]John 20:16
5 [a]2 Cor. 11:13–15
8 [1]M omits *before Me*
9 [a][Eph. 2:18]
11 [a]Is. 40:11
12 [a]Zech. 11:16, 17 [1]*hired man*
14 [a]2 Tim. 2:19 [b]2 Tim. 1:12
15 [a]Matt. 11:27 [b][John 15:13; 19:30]
16 [a]Is. 42:6; 56:8 [b]Eph. 2:13–18
17 [a]John 5:20 [b][Heb. 2:9]
18 [a][John 2:19; 5:26] [b][John 6:38; 14:31; 17:4; Acts 2:24, 32]
19 [a]John 7:43; 9:16
20 [a]John 7:20 [1]*insane*
21 [a][Ex. 4:11] [b]John 9:6, 7, 32, 33
23 [a]Acts 3:11; 5:12
24 [1]Suspense
25 [a]John 5:36; 10:38 [b]Matt. 11:4
26 [a][John 8:47] [1]NU omits *as I said to you*
27 [a]John 10:4, 14
29 [a]John 14:28 [b][John 17:2, 6, 12, 24]
30 [a]John 17:11, 21–24
31 [a]John 8:59
33 [a]John 5:18 [b]Matt. 9:3
34 [a]Ps. 82:6
35 [a]Matt. 5:17, 18 [b]1 Pet. 1:25
36 [a]John 6:27 [b]John 3:17 [c]John 5:17, 18 [d]Luke 1:35
37 [a]John 10:25; 15:24
38 [a]John 5:36 [b]John 14:10, 11 [1]NU *understand*
39 [a]John 7:30, 44
40 [a]John 1:28
41 [a][John 1:29, 36; 3:28–36; 5:33]

CHAPTER 11
1 [a]Luke 10:38, 39
2 [a]Matt. 26:7
6 [a]John 10:40
8 [a]John 8:59; 10:31
9 [a]John 9:4; 12:35 [b]Is. 9:2
10 [a]John 12:35
11 [a]Matt. 9:24

thought that He was speaking about taking rest in
sleep.
14 Then Jesus said to them plainly, "Lazarus is
dead.
15 "And I am glad for your sakes that I was not
there, that you may believe. Nevertheless let us go
to him."
16 Then [a]Thomas, who is called Didymus, said to
his fellow disciples, "Let us also go, that we may
die with Him."
**17** So when Jesus came, He found that he had
already been in the tomb four days.
18 Now Bethany was near Jerusalem, about [1]two
miles away.
19 And many of the Jews had joined the women
around Martha and Mary, to comfort them concerning their brother.
20 Then Martha, as soon as she heard that Jesus
was coming, went and met Him, but Mary was
sitting in the house.
21 Now Martha said to Jesus, "Lord, if You had
been here, my brother would not have died.
22 "But even now I know that [a]whatever You
ask of God, God will give You."
23 Jesus said to her, "Your brother will rise
again."
24 Martha said to Him, [a]"I know that he will rise
again in the resurrection at the last day."
25 Jesus said to her, "I am [a]the resurrection and
the life. [b]He who believes in Me, though he may
[c]die, he shall live.
26 "And whoever lives and believes in Me shall
never die. Do you believe this?"
27 She said to Him, "Yes, Lord, [a]I believe that
You are the Christ, the Son of God, who is to
come into the world."
**28** And when she had said these things, she went
her way and secretly called Mary her sister,
saying, "The Teacher has come and is calling for
you."
29 As soon as she heard *that,* she arose quickly
and came to Him.
30 Now Jesus had not yet come into the town,
but [1]was in the place where Martha met Him.
31 [a]Then the Jews who were with her in the
house, and comforting her, when they saw that
Mary rose up quickly and went out, followed her,
[1]saying, "She is going to the tomb to weep there."
32 Then, when Mary came where Jesus was, and
saw Him, she [a]fell down at His feet, saying to Him,
[b]"Lord, if You had been here, my brother would
not have died."
33 Therefore, when Jesus saw her weeping, and
the Jews who came with her weeping, He groaned
in the spirit and was troubled.
34 And He said, "Where have you laid him?"
They said to Him, "Lord, come and see."
35 [a]Jesus wept.
36 Then the Jews said, "See how He loved him!"
37 And some of them said, "Could not this Man,
[a]who opened the eyes of the blind, also have kept
this man from dying?"
**38** Then Jesus, again groaning in Himself, came
to the tomb. It was a cave, and a [a]stone lay
against it.
39 Jesus said, "Take away the stone." Martha,
the sister of him who was dead, said to Him,
"Lord, by this time there is a stench, for he has
been *dead* four days."
40 Jesus said to her, "Did I not say to you that if
you would believe you would [a]see the glory of
God?"
41 Then they took away the stone [1]*from the
place* where the dead man was lying. And Jesus
lifted up *His* eyes and said, "Father, I thank You
that You have heard Me.
42 "And I know that You always hear Me, but
[a]because of the people who are standing by I said
*this,* that they may believe that You sent Me."
43 Now when He had said these things, He cried
with a loud voice, "Lazarus, come forth!"
44 And he who had died came out bound hand
and foot with [a]graveclothes, and [b]his face was
wrapped with a cloth. Jesus said to them, "Loose
him, and let him go."
**45** Then many of the Jews who had come to
Mary, [a]and had seen the things Jesus did, believed
in Him.
46 But some of them went away to the Pharisees
and [a]told them the things Jesus did.
47 [a]Then the chief priests and the Pharisees
gathered a council and said, [b]"What shall we do?
For this Man works many signs.
48 "If we let Him alone like this, everyone will
believe in Him, and the Romans will come and
take away both our place and nation."
49 And one of them, [a]Caiaphas, being high priest
that year, said to them, "You know nothing at all,
50 [a]"nor do you consider that it is expedient for
[1]us that one man should die for the people, and
not that the whole nation should perish."
51 Now this he did not say on his own *authority;*
but being high priest that year he prophesied that
Jesus would die for the nation,
52 and [a]not for that nation only, but [b]also that He
would gather together in one the children of God
who were scattered abroad.
53 Then, from that day on, they plotted to [a]put
Him to death.
54 [a]Therefore Jesus no longer walked openly
among the Jews, but went from there into the
country near the wilderness, to a city called
[b]Ephraim, and there remained with His disciples.
55 [a]And the Passover of the Jews was near, and
many went from the country up to Jerusalem
before the Passover, to [b]purify themselves.
56 [a]Then they sought Jesus, and spoke among
themselves as they stood in the temple, "What do
you think—that He will not come to the feast?"
57 Now both the chief priests and the Pharisees
had given a command, that if anyone knew where
He was, he should report *it,* that they might [a]seize
Him.

### *Jesus Rides into Jerusalem*

**12** Then, six days before the Passover, Jesus
came to Bethany, [a]where Lazarus was [1]who
had been dead, whom He had raised from the
dead.
2 [a]There they made Him a supper; and Martha
served, but Lazarus was one of those who sat at
the table with Him.
3 Then [a]Mary took a pound of very costly oil of
[b]spikenard, anointed the feet of Jesus, and wiped
His feet with her hair. And the house was filled
with the fragrance of the oil.
4 But one of His disciples, [a]Judas Iscariot, Simon's *son,* who would betray Him, said,
5 "Why was this fragrant oil not sold for [1]three
hundred denarii and given to the poor?"
6 This he said, not that he cared for the poor,
but because he was a thief, and [a]had the money
box; and he used to take what was put in it.

**16** [a]John 14:5; 20:26–28
**18** [1]Lit. *15 stadia*
**22** [a][John 9:31; 11:41]
**24** [a][John 5:29]
**25** [a]John 5:21; 6:39, 40, 44 [b]1 John 5:10 [c]1 Cor. 15:22
**27** [a]Matt. 16:16
**30** [1]NU *was still*
**31** [a]John 11:19, 33 [1]NU *supposing that she was going*
**32** [a]Rev. 1:17 [b]John 11:21
**35** [a]Luke 19:41
**37** [a]John 9:6, 7
**38** [a]Matt. 27:60, 66
**40** [a][John 11:4, 23]
**41** [1]NU omits *from the place where the dead man was lying*
**42** [a]John 12:30; 17:21
**44** [a]John 19:40 [b]John 20:7
**45** [a]John 2:23; 10:42; 12:11, 18
**46** [a]John 5:15
**47** [a]Ps. 2:2 [b]Acts 4:16
**49** [a]Luke 3:2
**50** [a]John 18:14 [1]NU *you*
**52** [a]Is. 49:6 [b][Eph. 2:14–17]
**53** [a]Matt. 26:4
**54** [a]John 4:1, 3; 7:1 [b]2 Chr. 13:19
**55** [a]John 2:13; 5:1; 6:4 [b]Num. 9:10, 13; 31:19, 20
**56** [a]John 7:11
**57** [a]Matt. 26:14–16

CHAPTER 12
**1** [a]John 11:1, 43 [1]NU omits *who had been dead*
**2** [a]Mark 14:3; Luke 10:38–41
**3** [a]John 11:2 [b]Song 1:12
**4** [a]John 13:26
**5** [1]About one year's wages for a worker
**6** [a]John 13:29

7 But Jesus said, "Let her alone; [1]she has kept this for the day of My burial.
8 "For [a]the poor you have with you always, but Me you do not have always."
**9** Now a great many of the Jews knew that He was there; and they came, not for Jesus' sake only, but that they might also see Lazarus, [a]whom He had raised from the dead.
10 [a]But the chief priests plotted to put Lazarus to death also,
11 [a]because on account of him many of the Jews went away and believed in Jesus.
**12** [a]The next day a great multitude that had come to the feast, when they heard that Jesus was coming to Jerusalem,
13 took branches of palm trees and went out to meet Him, and cried out:

"Hosanna!
[a]'*Blessed is He who comes*
*in the name of the* LORD!'
The King of Israel!"

14 [a]Then Jesus, when He had found a young donkey, sat on it; as it is written:

15 *"Fear[a] not, daughter of Zion;*
*Behold, your King is coming,*
*Sitting on a donkey's colt."*

16 [a]His disciples did not understand these things at first; [b]but when Jesus was glorified, [c]then they remembered that these things were written about Him and *that* they had done these things to Him.
17 Therefore the people, who were with Him when He called Lazarus out of his tomb and raised him from the dead, bore witness.
18 [a]For this reason the people also met Him, because they heard that He had done this sign.
19 The Pharisees therefore said among themselves, [a]"You see that you are accomplishing nothing. Look, the world has gone after Him!"
**20** Now there [a]were certain Greeks among those [b]who came up to worship at the feast.
21 Then they came to Philip, [a]who was from Bethsaida of Galilee, and asked him, saying, "Sir, we wish to see Jesus."
22 Philip came and told Andrew, and in turn Andrew and Philip told Jesus.
23 But Jesus answered them, saying, [a]"The hour has come that the Son of Man should be glorified.
24 "Most assuredly, I say to you, [a]unless a grain of wheat falls into the ground and dies, it remains alone; but if it dies, it produces much [1]grain.
25 [a]"He who loves his life will lose it, and he who hates his life in this world will keep it for eternal life.
26 "If anyone serves Me, let him [a]follow Me; and [b]where I am, there My servant will be also. If anyone serves Me, him *My* Father will honor.
**27** [a]"Now My soul is troubled, and what shall I say? 'Father, save Me from this hour'? [b]But for this purpose I came to this hour.
28 "Father, glorify Your name." [a]Then a voice came from heaven, *saying,* "I have both glorified *it* and will glorify *it* again."
29 Therefore the people who stood by and heard *it* said that it had thundered. Others said, "An angel has spoken to Him."
30 Jesus answered and said, [a]"This voice did not come because of Me, but for your sake.
31 "Now is the judgment of this world; now [a]the ruler of this world will be cast out.
32 "And I, [a]if I am [1]lifted up from the earth, will draw [b]all *peoples* to Myself."
33 [a]This He said, signifying by what death He would die.
34 The people answered Him, [a]"We have heard from the law that the Christ remains forever; and how *can* You say, 'The Son of Man must be lifted up'? Who is this Son of Man?"
35 Then Jesus said to them, "A little while longer [a]the light is with you. [b]Walk while you have the light, lest darkness overtake you; [c]he who walks in darkness does not know where he is going.
36 "While you have the light, believe in the light, that you may become [a]sons of light." These things Jesus spoke, and departed, and [b]was hidden from them.
**37** But although He had done so many [a]signs before them, they did not believe in Him,
38 that the word of Isaiah the prophet might be fulfilled, which he spoke:

[a]*"Lord, who has believed our report?*
*And to whom has the arm*
*of the* LORD *been revealed?"*

39 Therefore they could not believe, because Isaiah said again:

40 *"He[a] has blinded their eyes and hardened*
*their hearts,*
[b]*Lest they should see with their eyes,*
*Lest they should understand with their*
*hearts and turn,*
*So that I should heal them."*

41 [a]These things Isaiah said [1]when he saw His glory and spoke of Him.
**42** Nevertheless even among the rulers many believed in Him, but [a]because of the Pharisees they did not confess *Him,* lest they should be put out of the synagogue;
43 [a]for they loved the praise of men more than the praise of God.
44 Then Jesus cried out and said, [a]"He who believes in Me, [b]believes not in Me [c]but in Him who sent Me.
45 "And [a]he who sees Me sees Him who sent Me.
46 [a]"I have come *as* a light into the world, that whoever believes in Me should not abide in darkness.
47 "And if anyone hears My words and does not [1]believe, [a]I do not judge him; for [b]I did not come to judge the world but to save the world.
48 [a]"He who rejects Me, and does not receive My words, has that which judges him—[b]the word that I have spoken will judge him in the last day.
49 "For [a]I have not spoken on My own *authority;* but the Father who sent Me gave Me a command, [b]what I should say and what I should speak.
50 "And I know that His command is everlasting life. Therefore, whatever I speak, just as the Father has told Me, so I [a]speak."

### *Disciples Must Be Servants*

**13** Now [a]before the feast of the Passover, when Jesus knew that [b]His hour had come that He should depart from this world to the Father, having loved His own who were in the world, He [c]loved them to the end.
2 And [1]supper being ended, [a]the devil having already put it into the heart of Judas Iscariot, Simon's *son,* to betray Him,

---

7 [1]NU *that she may keep*
8 [a]Mark 14:7
9 [a]John 11:43, 44
10 [a]Luke 16:31
11 [a]John 11:45; 12:18
12 [a]Matt. 21:4–9
13 [a]Ps. 118:25, 26
14 [a]Matt. 21:7
15 [a]Zech. 9:9
16 [a]Luke 18:34 [b]John 7:39; 12:23 [c][John 14:26]
18 [a]John 12:11
19 [a]John 11:47, 48
20 [a]Acts 17:4 [b]1 Kin. 8:41, 42
21 [a]John 1:43, 44; 14:8–11
23 [a]John 13:32
24 [a]1 Cor. 15:36 [1]Lit. *fruit*
25 [a]Mark 8:35
26 [a][Matt. 16:24] [b]John 14:3; 17:24
27 [a][Matt. 26:38, 39] [b]Luke 22:53
28 [a]Matt. 3:17; 17:5
30 [a]John 11:42
31 [a][2 Cor. 4:4]
32 [a]John 3:14; 8:28 [b][Rom. 5:18] [1]Crucified
33 [a]John 18:32; 21:19
34 [a]Mic. 4:7
35 [a][John 1:9; 7:33; 8:12] [b]Eph. 5:8 [c][1 John 2:9–11]
36 [a]Luke 16:8 [b]John 8:59
37 [a]John 11:47
38 [a]Is. 53:1
40 [a]Is. 6:9, 10 [b]Matt. 13:14
41 [a]Is. 6:1 [1]NU *because*
42 [a]John 7:13; 9:22
43 [a]John 5:41, 44
44 [a]Mark 9:37 [b][John 3:16, 18, 36; 11:25, 26] [c][John 5:24]
45 [a][John 14:9]
46 [a]John 1:4, 5; 8:12; 12:35, 36
47 [a]John 5:45 [b]John 3:17 [1]NU *keep them*
48 [a][Luke 10:16] [b]Deut. 18:18, 19
49 [a]John 8:38 [b]Deut. 18:18
50 [a]John 5:19; 8:28

CHAPTER 13
1 [a]Matt. 26:2 [b]John 12:23; 17:1 [c]John 15:9
2 [a]Luke 22:3 [1]NU *during supper*

3 Jesus, knowing [a]that the Father had given all
things into His hands, and that He [b]had come from
God and [c]was going to God,
4 [a]rose from supper and laid aside His garments,
took a towel and girded Himself.
5 After that, He poured water into a basin and
began to wash the disciples' feet, and to wipe
*them* with the towel with which He was girded.
6 Then He came to Simon Peter. And *Peter* said
to Him, [a]"Lord, are You washing my feet?"
7 Jesus answered and said to him, "What I am
doing you [a]do not understand now, [b]but you will
know after this."
8 Peter said to Him, "You shall never wash my
feet!" Jesus answered him, [a]"If I do not wash you,
you have no part with Me."
9 Simon Peter said to Him, "Lord, not my feet
only, but also *my* hands and *my* head!"
10 Jesus said to him, "He who is bathed needs
only to wash *his* feet, but is completely clean; and
[a]you are clean, but not all of you."
11 For [a]He knew who would betray Him; therefore He said, "You are not all clean."
**12** So when He had washed their feet, taken His
garments, and sat down again, He said to them,
"Do you [1]know what I have done to you?
13 [a]"You call Me Teacher and Lord, and you say
well, for *so* I am.
14 [a]"If I then, *your* Lord and Teacher, have
washed your feet, [b]you also ought to wash one
another's feet.
15 "For [a]I have given you an example, that you
should do as I have done to you.
16 [a]"Most assuredly, I say to you, a servant is not
greater than his master; nor is he who is sent
greater than he who sent him.
17 [a]"If you know these things, blessed are you if
you do them.
18 "I do not speak concerning all of you. I know
whom I have chosen; but that the [a]Scripture may
be fulfilled, [b]*'He who eats* [1]*bread with Me has
lifted up his heel against Me.'*
19 [a]"Now I tell you before it comes, that when it
does come to pass, you may believe that I am *He.*
20 [a]"Most assuredly, I say to you, he who receives whomever I send receives Me; and he who
receives Me receives Him who sent Me."
21 [a]When Jesus had said these things, [b]He was
troubled in spirit, and testified and said, "Most
assuredly, I say to you, [c]one of you will betray
Me."
22 Then the disciples looked at one another,
perplexed about whom He spoke.
23 Now [a]there was [1]leaning on Jesus' bosom one
of His disciples, whom Jesus loved.
24 Simon Peter therefore motioned to him to ask
who it was of whom He spoke.
25 Then, leaning [1]back on Jesus' breast, he said
to Him, "Lord, who is it?"
26 Jesus answered, "It is he to whom I shall give
a piece of bread when I have dipped *it.*" And
having dipped the bread, He gave *it* to [a]Judas
Iscariot, *the son* of Simon.
27 [a]Now after the piece of bread, Satan entered
him. Then Jesus said to him, "What you do, do
quickly."
28 But no one at the table knew for what reason
He said this to him.
29 For some thought, because [a]Judas had the
money box, that Jesus had said to him, "Buy *those
things* we need for the feast," or that he should
give something to the poor.
30 Having received the piece of bread, he then
went out immediately. And it was night.
**31** So, when he had gone out, Jesus said, [a]"Now
the Son of Man is glorified, and [b]God is glorified in
Him.
32 "If God is glorified in Him, God will also
glorify Him in Himself, and [a]glorify Him immediately.
33 "Little children, I shall be with you a [a]little
while longer. You will seek Me; [b]and as I said to
the Jews, 'Where I am going, you cannot come,'
so now I say to you.
34 [a]"A new commandment I give to you, that you
love one another; as I have loved you, that you
also love one another.
35 [a]"By this all will know that you are My disciples, if you have love for one another."
**36** Simon Peter said to Him, "Lord, where are
You going?" Jesus answered him, "Where I [a]am
going you cannot follow Me now, but [b]you shall
follow Me afterward."
37 Peter said to Him, "Lord, why can I not follow
You now? I will [a]lay down my life for Your sake."
38 Jesus answered him, "Will you lay down your
life for My sake? Most assuredly, I say to you, the
rooster shall not [a]crow till you have denied Me
three times.

### *Jesus Is the Way, the Truth, and the Life*

**14** "Let [a]not your heart be troubled; you believe in God, believe also in Me.
2 "In My Father's house are many [1]mansions; if
*it were* not *so,* [2]I would have told you. [a]I go to
prepare a place for you.
3 "And if I go and prepare a place for you, [a]I will
come again and receive you to Myself; that
[b]where I am, *there* you may be also.
4 "And where I go you know, and the way you
know."
5 [a]Thomas said to Him, "Lord, we do not know
where You are going, and how can we know the
way?"
6 Jesus said to him, "I am [a]the way, [b]the truth,
and [c]the life. [d]No one comes to the Father [e]except
through Me.
**7** [a]"If you had known Me, you would have
known My Father also; and from now on you
know Him and have seen Him."
8 Philip said to Him, "Lord, show us the Father,
and it is sufficient for us."
9 Jesus said to him, "Have I been with you so
long, and yet you have not known Me, Philip? [a]He
who has seen Me has seen the Father; so how can
you say, 'Show us the Father'?
10 "Do you not believe that [a]I am in the Father,
and the Father in Me? The words that I speak to
you [b]I do not speak on My own *authority;* but the
Father who dwells in Me does the works.
11 "Believe Me that I *am* in the Father and the
Father in Me, [a]or else believe Me for the sake of
the works themselves.
**12** [a]"Most assuredly, I say to you, he who believes in Me, the works that I do he will do also;
and greater *works* than these he will do, because I
go to My Father.
13 [a]"And whatever you ask in My name, that I
will do, that the Father may be [b]glorified in the
Son.
14 "If you [1]ask anything in My name, I will do *it.*
**15** [a]"If you love Me, [1]keep My commandments.

**3** [a]Acts 2:36 [b]John 8:42; 16:28 [c]John 17:11; 20:17
**4** [a][Luke 22:27]
**6** [a]Matt. 3:14
**7** [a]John 12:16; 16:12 [b]John 13:19
**8** [a][1 Cor. 6:11]
**10** [a][John 15:3]
**11** [a]John 6:64; 18:4
**12** [1]*understand*
**13** [a]Matt. 23:8, 10
**14** [a]Luke 22:27 [b][Rom. 12:10]
**15** [a][1 Pet. 2:21–24]
**16** [a]Matt. 10:24
**17** [a][James 1:25]
**18** [a]John 15:25; 17:12 [b]Ps. 41:9 [1]NU *My bread has*
**19** [a]John 14:29; 16:4
**20** [a]Matt. 10:40
**21** [a]Luke 22:21 [b]John 12:27 [c]1 John 2:19
**23** [a]John 19:26; 20:2; 21:7, 20 [1]*reclining*
**25** [1]NU, M add *thus*
**26** [a]John 6:70, 71; 12:4
**27** [a]Luke 22:3
**29** [a]John 12:6
**31** [a]John 12:23 [b][1 Pet. 4:11]
**32** [a]John 12:23
**33** [a]John 12:35; 14:19; 16:16–19 [b][John 7:34; 8:21]
**34** [a]1 Thess. 4:9
**35** [a]1 John 2:5
**36** [a]John 13:33; 14:2; 16:5 [b]2 Pet. 1:14
**37** [a]Mark 14:29–31
**38** [a]John 18:25–27

CHAPTER 14
**1** [a][John 14:27; 16:22, 24]
**2** [a]John 13:33, 36 [1]Lit. *dwellings* [2]NU *would I have told you that I go* or *I would have told you; for I go*
**3** [a][Acts 1:11] [b][John 12:26]
**5** [a]Matt. 10:3
**6** [a][Heb. 9:8; 10:19, 20] [b][John 1:14, 17; 8:32; 18:37] [c][John 11:25] [d]1 Tim. 2:5 [e][John 10:7–9]
**7** [a]John 8:19
**9** [a]Col. 1:15
**10** [a]John 10:38; 14:11, 20 [b]John 5:19; 14:24
**11** [a]John 5:36; 10:38
**12** [a]Luke 10:17
**13** [a]Matt. 7:7 [b]John 13:31

**14** [1]NU adds *Me*
**15** [a]1 John 5:3 [1]NU *you will keep*

16 "And I will pray the Father, and [a]He will give you another [1]Helper, that He may abide with you forever—

17 [a]"the Spirit of truth, [b]whom the world cannot receive, because it neither sees Him nor knows Him; but you know Him, for He dwells with you [c]and will be in you.

18 [a]"I will not leave you orphans; [b]I will come to you.

**19** "A little while longer and the world will see Me no more, but [a]you will see Me. [b]Because I live, you will live also.

20 "At that day you will know that [a]I *am* in My Father, and you in Me, and I in you.

21 [a]"He who has My commandments and keeps them, it is he who loves Me. And he who loves Me will be loved by My Father, and I will love him and [1]manifest Myself to him."

22 [a]Judas (not Iscariot) said to Him, "Lord, how is it that You will manifest Yourself to us, and not to the world?"

23 Jesus answered and said to him, "If anyone loves Me, he will keep My word; and My Father will love him, [a]and We will come to him and make Our home with him.

24 "He who does not love Me does not keep My words; and [a]the word which you hear is not Mine but the Father's who sent Me.

**25** "These things I have spoken to you while being present with you.

26 "But [a]the [1]Helper, the Holy Spirit, whom the Father will [b]send in My name, [c]He will teach you all things, and bring to your [d]remembrance all things that I said to you.

27 [a]"Peace I leave with you, My peace I give to you; not as the world gives do I give to you. Let not your heart be troubled, neither let it be afraid.

28 "You have heard Me [a]say to you, 'I am going away and coming *back* to you.' If you loved Me, you would rejoice because [1]I said, [b]'I am going to the Father,' for [c]My Father is greater than I.

29 "And [a]now I have told you before it comes, that when it does come to pass, you may believe.

30 "I will no longer talk much with you, [a]for the ruler of this world is coming, and he has [b]nothing in Me.

31 "But that the world may know that I love the Father, and [a]as the Father gave Me commandment, so I do. Arise, let us go from here.

### *Christ the True Vine*

**15** "I am the true vine, and My Father is the vinedresser.

2 [a]"Every branch in Me that does not bear fruit He [1]takes away; and every *branch* that bears fruit He prunes, that it may bear [b]more fruit.

3 [a]"You are already clean because of the word which I have spoken to you.

4 [a]"Abide in Me, and I in you. As the branch cannot bear fruit of itself, unless it abides in the vine, neither can you, unless you abide in Me.

5 "I am the vine, you *are* the branches. He who abides in Me, and I in him, bears much [a]fruit; for without Me you can do [b]nothing.

6 "If anyone does not abide in Me, [a]he is cast out as a branch and is withered; and they gather them and throw *them* into the fire, and they are burned.

7 "If you abide in Me, and My words [a]abide in you, [b]you[1] will ask what you desire, and it shall be done for you.

8 [a]"By this My Father is glorified, that you bear much fruit; [b]so you will be My disciples.

**9** "As the Father [a]loved Me, I also have loved you; abide in My love.

10 [a]"If you keep My commandments, you will abide in My love, just as I have kept My Father's commandments and abide in His love.

11 "These things I have spoken to you, that My joy may remain in you, and [a]*that* your joy may be full.

12 [a]"This is My [b]commandment, that you love one another as I have loved you.

13 [a]"Greater love has no one than this, than to lay down one's life for his friends.

14 [a]"You are My friends if you do whatever I command you.

15 "No longer do I call you servants, for a servant does not know what his master is doing; but I have called you friends, [a]for all things that I heard from My Father I have made known to you.

16 [a]"You did not choose Me, but I chose you and [b]appointed you that you should go and bear fruit, and *that* your fruit should remain, that whatever you ask the Father [c]in My name He may give you.

17 "These things I command you, that you love one another.

**18** [a]"If the world hates you, you know that it hated Me before *it hated* you.

19 [a]"If you were of the world, the world would love its own. Yet [b]because you are not of the world, but I chose you out of the world, therefore the world hates you.

20 "Remember the word that I said to you, [a]'A servant is not greater than his master.' If they persecuted Me, they will also persecute you. [b]If they kept My word, they will keep yours also.

21 "But [a]all these things they will do to you for My name's sake, because they do not know Him who sent Me.

22 [a]"If I had not come and spoken to them, they would have no sin, [b]but now they have no excuse for their sin.

23 [a]"He who hates Me hates My Father also.

24 "If I had not done among them [a]the works which no one else did, they would have no sin; but now they have [b]seen and also hated both Me and My Father.

25 "But *this happened* that the word might be fulfilled which is written in their law, [a]*'They hated Me without a cause.'*

**26** [a]"But when the [1]Helper comes, whom I shall send to you from the Father, the Spirit of truth who proceeds from the Father, [b]He will testify of Me.

27 "And [a]you also will bear witness, because [b]you have been with Me from the beginning.

### *Jesus Warns and Comforts His Disciples*

**16** "These things I have spoken to you, that you [a]should not be made to stumble.

2 [a]"They will put you out of the synagogues; yes, the time is coming [b]that whoever kills you will think that he offers God service.

3 "And [a]these things they will do [1]to you because they have not known the Father nor Me.

4 "But these things I have told you, that when [1]the time comes, you may remember that I told you of them. And these things I did not say to you at the beginning, because I was with you.

**16** [a]Rom. 8:15 [1]*Comforter,* Gr. *Parakletos*
**17** [a][1 John 4:6; 5:7] [b][1 Cor. 2:14] [c][1 John 2:27]
**18** [a][Matt. 28:20] [b][John 14:3, 28]
**19** [a]John 16:16, 22 [b][1 Cor. 15:20]
**20** [a]John 10:38; 14:11
**21** [a]1 John 2:5 [1]*reveal*
**22** [a]Luke 6:16
**23** [a]Rev. 3:20; 21:3
**24** [a]John 5:19
**26** [a]Luke 24:49 [b]John 15:26 [c]1 Cor. 2:13 [d]John 2:22; 12:16 [1]*Comforter,* Gr. *Parakletos*
**27** [a][Phil. 4:7]
**28** [a]John 14:3, 18 [b]John 16:16 [c][Phil. 2:6] [1]NU omits *I said*
**29** [a]John 13:19
**30** [a][John 12:31] [b][Heb. 4:15]
**31** [a]John 10:18

CHAPTER 15

**2** [a]Matt. 15:13 [b][Matt. 13:12] [1]Or *lifts up*
**3** [a][John 13:10; 17:17]
**4** [a][Col. 1:23]
**5** [a]Hos. 14:8 [b]2 Cor. 3:5
**6** [a]Matt. 3:10
**7** [a]1 John 2:14 [b]John 14:13; 16:23 [1]NU omits *you will*
**8** [a][Matt. 5:16] [b]John 8:31
**9** [a]John 5:20; 17:26
**10** [a]John 14:15
**11** [a]1 John 1:4
**12** [a]1 John 3:11 [b]Rom. 12:9
**13** [a]1 John 3:16
**14** [a][Matt. 12:50; 28:20]
**15** [a]Gen. 18:17
**16** [a]John 6:70; 13:18; 15:19 [b][Col. 1:6] [c]John 14:13; 16:23, 24
**18** [a]1 John 3:13
**19** [a]1 John 4:5 [b]John 17:14
**20** [a]John 13:16 [b]Ezek. 3:7
**21** [a]Matt. 10:22; 24:9
**22** [a]John 9:41; 15:24 [b][James 4:17]
**23** [a]1 John 2:23
**24** [a]John 3:2 [b]John 14:9
**25** [a]Ps. 35:19; 69:4; 109:3–5
**26** [a]Luke 24:49 [b]1 John 5:6 [1]*Comforter,* Gr. *Parakletos*
**27** [a]Luke 24:48 [b]Luke 1:2

CHAPTER 16

**1** [a]Matt. 11:6
**2** [a]John 9:22 [b]Acts 8:1

**3** [a]John 8:19; 15:21 [1]NU, M omit *to you*
**4** [1]NU *their*

5 "But now I [a]go away to Him who sent Me, and none of you asks Me, 'Where are You going?'

6 "But because I have said these things to you, [a]sorrow has filled your heart.

7 "Nevertheless I tell you the truth. It is to your advantage that I go away; for if I do not go away, the Helper will not come to you; but [a]if I depart, I will send Him to you.

8 "And when He has [a]come, He will convict the world of sin, and of righteousness, and of judgment:

9 [a]"of sin, because they do not believe in Me;

10 [a]"of righteousness, [b]because I go to My Father and you see Me no more;

11 [a]"of judgment, because [b]the ruler of this world is judged.

12 "I still have many things to say to you, [a]but you cannot bear *them* now.

13 "However, when He, [a]the Spirit of truth, has come, [b]He will guide you into all truth; for He will not speak on His own *authority*, but whatever He hears He will speak; and He will tell you things to come.

14 [a]"He will glorify Me, for He will take of what is Mine and declare *it* to you.

15 [a]"All things that the Father has are Mine. Therefore I said that He [1]will take of Mine and declare *it* to you.

16 "A [a]little while, and you will not see Me; and again a little while, and you will see Me, [b]because I go to the Father."

17 Then *some* of His disciples said among themselves, "What is this that He says to us, 'A little while, and you will not see Me; and again a little while, and you will see Me'; and, 'because I go to the Father'?"

18 They said therefore, "What is this that He says, 'A little while'? We do not [1]know what He is saying."

19 Now Jesus knew that they desired to ask Him, and He said to them, "Are you inquiring among yourselves about what I said, 'A little while, and you will not see Me; and again a little while, and you will see Me'?

20 "Most assuredly, I say to you that you will weep and [a]lament, but the world will rejoice; and you will be sorrowful, but your sorrow will be turned into [b]joy.

21 [a]"A woman, when she is in labor, has sorrow because her hour has come; but as soon as she has given birth to the child, she no longer remembers the anguish, for joy that a human being has been born into the world.

22 "Therefore you now have sorrow; but I will see you again and [a]your heart will rejoice, and your joy no one will take from you.

23 "And in that day you will ask Me nothing. [a]Most assuredly, I say to you, whatever you ask the Father in My name He will give you.

24 "Until now you have asked nothing in My name. Ask, and you will receive, [a]that your joy may be [b]full.

25 "These things I have spoken to you in figurative language; but the time is coming when I will no longer speak to you in figurative language, but I will tell you [a]plainly about the Father.

26 "In that day you will ask in My name, and I do not say to you that I shall pray the Father for you;

27 [a]"for the Father Himself loves you, because you have loved Me, and [b]have believed that I came forth from God.

28 [a]"I came forth from the Father and have come into the world. Again, I leave the world and go to the Father."

29 His disciples said to Him, "See, now You are speaking plainly, and using no figure of speech!

30 "Now we are sure that [a]You know all things, and have no need that anyone should question You. By this [b]we believe that You came forth from God."

31 Jesus answered them, "Do you now believe?

32 [a]"Indeed the hour is coming, yes, has now come, that you will be scattered, [b]each to his [1]own, and will leave Me alone. And [c]yet I am not alone, because the Father is with Me.

33 "These things I have spoken to you, that [a]in Me you may have peace. [b]In the world you [1]will have tribulation; but be of good cheer, [c]I have overcome the world."

### *Jesus Prays to God for His Disciples*

17 Jesus spoke these words, lifted up His eyes to heaven, and said: "Father, [a]the hour has come. Glorify Your Son, that Your Son also may glorify You,

2 [a]"as You have given Him authority over all flesh, that He [1]should give eternal life to as many [b]as You have given Him.

3 "And [a]this is eternal life, that they may know You, [b]the only true God, and Jesus Christ [c]whom You have sent.

4 [a]"I have glorified You on the earth. [b]I have finished the work [c]which You have given Me to do.

5 "And now, O Father, glorify Me together [1]with Yourself, with the glory [a]which I had with You before the world was.

6 [a]"I have [1]manifested Your name to the men [b]whom You have given Me out of the world. [c]They were Yours, You gave them to Me, and they have kept Your word.

7 "Now they have known that all things which You have given Me are from You.

8 "For I have given to them the words [a]which You have given Me; and they have received *them*, [b]and have known surely that I came forth from You; and they have believed that [c]You sent Me.

9 "I pray for them. [a]I do not pray for the world but for those whom You have given Me, for they are Yours.

10 "And all Mine are Yours, and [a]Yours are Mine, and I am glorified in them.

11 [a]"Now I am no longer in the world, but these are in the world, and I come to You. Holy Father, [b]keep[1] through Your name those whom You have given Me, that they may be one [c]as We *are*.

12 "While I was with them [1]in the world, [a]I kept them in [2]Your name. Those whom You gave Me I have kept; and [b]none of them is [3]lost [c]except the son of [4]perdition, [d]that the Scripture might be fulfilled.

13 "But now I come to You, and these things I speak in the world, that they may have My joy fulfilled in themselves.

14 "I have given them Your word; [a]and the world has hated them because they are not of the world, [b]just as I am not of the world.

15 "I do not pray that You should take them out

---

**16:5** [a]John 7:33; 13:33; 14:28; 17:11 **6** [a][John 16:20, 22] **7** [a]Acts 2:33 **8** [a]Acts 1:8; 2:1–4, 37 **9** [a]Acts 2:22 **10** [a]Acts 2:32 [b]John 5:32 **11** [a]Acts 26:18 [b][Luke 10:18] **12** [a]Mark 4:33 **13** [a][John 14:17] [b]John 14:26 **14** [a]John 15:26 **15** [a]Matt. 11:27 [1]NU, M *takes of Mine and will declare* **16** [a]John 7:33; 12:35; 13:33; 14:19; 19:40–42; 20:19 [b]John 13:3 **18** [1]*understand* **20** [a]Mark 16:10 [b]Luke 24:32, 41 **21** [a]Is. 13:8; 26:17; 42:14 **22** [a]1 Pet. 1:8 **23** [a]Matt. 7:7 **24** [a]John 17:13 [b]John 15:11 **25** [a]John 7:13 **27** [a][John 14:21, 23] [b]John 3:13 **28** [a]John 13:1, 3; 16:5, 10, 17 **30** [a]John 21:17 [b]John 17:8 **32** [a]Matt. 26:31, 56 [b]John 20:10 [c]John 8:29 [1]*own things* or *place* **33** [a][Eph. 2:14] [b]2 Tim. 3:12 [c]Rom. 8:37 [1]NU, M omit *will*

CHAPTER 17

**1** [a]John 12:23 **2** [a]John 3:35 [b]John 6:37, 39; 17:6, 9, 24 [1]M *shall* **3** [a]Jer. 9:23, 24 [b]1 Cor. 8:4 [c]John 3:34 **4** [a]John 13:31 [b]John 4:34; 19:30 [c]John 14:31 **5** [a]Phil. 2:6 [1]Lit. *alongside* **6** [a]Ps. 22:22 [b]John 6:37 [c]Ezek. 18:4 [1]*revealed* **8** [a]John 8:28 [b]John 8:42; 16:27, 30 [c]Deut. 18:15, 18 **9** [a][1 John 5:19] **10** [a]John 16:15 **11** [a]John 13:1 [b][1 Pet. 1:5] [c]John 10:30 [1]NU, M *keep them through Your name which You have given Me*

**12** [a]Heb. 2:13 [b]1 John 2:19 [c]John 6:70 [d]Ps. 41:9; 109:8 [1]NU omits *in the world* [2]NU *Your name which You gave Me. And I guarded them* (or *it*); [3]*destroyed* [4]*destruction*
**14** [a]John 15:19 [b]John 8:23

of the world, but [a]that You should keep them from
the evil *one.*
16 "They are not of the world, just as I am not of
the world.
17 [a]"Sanctify[1] them by Your truth. [b]Your word is
truth.
18 [a]"As You sent Me into the world, I also have
sent them into the world.
19 "And [a]for their sakes I sanctify Myself, that
they also may be sanctified by the truth.
**20** "I do not pray for these alone, but also for
those who [1]will believe in Me through their word;
21 [a]"that they all may be one, as [b]You, Father,
*are* in Me, and I in You; that they also may be one
in Us, that the world may believe that You
sent Me.
22 "And the [a]glory which You gave Me I have
given them, [b]that they may be one just as We are
one:
23 "I in them, and You in Me; [a]that they may be
made perfect in one, and that the world may
know that You have sent Me, and have loved
them as You have loved Me.
24 [a]"Father, I desire that they also whom You
gave Me may be with Me where I am, that they
may behold My glory which You have given Me;
[b]for You loved Me before the foundation of the
world.
25 "O righteous Father! [a]The world has not
known You, but [b]I have known You; and [c]these
have known that You sent Me.
26 [a]"And I have declared to them Your name,
and will declare *it,* that the love [b]with which You
loved Me may be in them, and I in them."

### *The Betrayal, Arrest, and Trial of Jesus*

**18** When Jesus had spoken these words, [a]He
went out with His disciples over [b]the Brook
Kidron, where there was a garden, which He and
His disciples entered.
2 And Judas, who betrayed Him, also knew the
place; [a]for Jesus often met there with His disciples.
3 [a]Then Judas, having received a detachment *of
troops,* and officers from the chief priests and
Pharisees, came there with lanterns, torches, and
weapons.
4 Jesus therefore, [a]knowing all things that
would come upon Him, went forward and said to
them, "Whom are you seeking?"
5 They answered Him, [a]"Jesus [1]of Nazareth."
Jesus said to them, "I am *He.*" And Judas, who
[b]betrayed Him, also stood with them.
6 Now when He said to them, "I am *He,*" they
drew back and fell to the ground.
7 Then He asked them again, "Whom are you
seeking?" And they said, "Jesus of Nazareth."
8 Jesus answered, "I have told you that I am *He.*
Therefore, if you seek Me, let these go their way,"
9 that the saying might be fulfilled which He
spoke, [a]"Of those whom You gave Me I have lost
none."
10 [a]Then Simon Peter, having a sword, drew it
and struck the high priest's servant, and cut off
his right ear. The servant's name was Malchus.
11 So Jesus said to Peter, "Put your sword into
the sheath. Shall I not drink [a]the cup which My
Father has given Me?"
**12** Then the detachment *of troops* and the captain and the officers of the Jews arrested Jesus
and bound Him.
13 And [a]they led Him away to [b]Annas first, for he
was the father-in-law of [c]Caiaphas who was high
priest that year.
14 [a]Now it was Caiaphas who advised the Jews
that it was [1]expedient that one man should die for
the people.
**15** [a]And Simon Peter followed Jesus, and so *did*
[b]another[1] disciple. Now that disciple was known
to the high priest, and went with Jesus into the
courtyard of the high priest.
16 [a]But Peter stood at the door outside. Then the
other disciple, who was known to the high priest,
went out and spoke to her who kept the door, and
brought Peter in.
17 Then the servant girl who kept the door said
to Peter, "You are not also *one* of this Man's
disciples, are you?" He said, "I am [a]not."
18 Now the servants and officers who had made a
fire of coals stood there, for it was cold, and they
warmed themselves. And Peter stood with them
and warmed himself.
**19** The high priest then asked Jesus about His
disciples and His doctrine.
20 Jesus answered him, [a]"I spoke openly to the
world. I always taught [b]in synagogues and [c]in the
temple, where [1]the Jews always meet, and in
secret I have said nothing.
21 "Why do you ask Me? Ask [a]those who have
heard Me what I said to them. Indeed they know
what I said."
22 And when He had said these things, one of the
officers who stood by [a]struck[1] Jesus with the palm
of his hand, saying, "Do You answer the high
priest like that?"
23 Jesus answered him, "If I have spoken evil,
bear witness of the evil; but if well, why do you
strike Me?"
24 [a]Then Annas sent Him bound to [b]Caiaphas the
high priest.
**25** Now Simon Peter stood and warmed himself.
[a]Therefore they said to him, "You are not also *one*
of His disciples, are you?" He denied *it* and said, "I
am not!"
26 One of the servants of the high priest, a
relative *of him* whose ear Peter cut off, said, "Did
I not see you in the garden with Him?"
27 Peter then denied again; and [a]immediately a
rooster crowed.
**28** [a]Then they led Jesus from Caiaphas to the
Praetorium, and it was early morning. [b]But they
themselves did not go into the [1]Praetorium, lest
they should be defiled, but that they might eat the
Passover.
29 [a]Pilate then went out to them and said, "What
accusation do you bring against this Man?"
30 They answered and said to him, "If He were
not [1]an evildoer, we would not have delivered Him
up to you."
31 Then Pilate said to them, "You take Him and
judge Him according to your law." Therefore the
Jews said to him, "It is not lawful for us to put
anyone to death,"
32 [a]that the saying of Jesus might be fulfilled
which He spoke, [b]signifying by what death He
would die.
33 [a]Then Pilate entered the [1]Praetorium again,
called Jesus, and said to Him, "Are You the King
of the Jews?"
34 Jesus answered him, "Are you speaking for
yourself about this, or did others tell you this
concerning Me?"
35 Pilate answered, "Am I a Jew? Your own

**15** [a]1 John 5:18
**17** [a][Eph. 5:26] [b]Ps. 119:9, 142, 151 [1]*Set them apart*
**18** [a]John 4:38; 20:21
**19** [a][Heb. 10:10]
**20** [1]NU, M omit *will*
**21** [a][Gal. 3:28] [b]John 10:38; 17:11, 23
**22** [a]1 John 1:3 [b][2 Cor. 3:18]
**23** [a][Col. 3:14]
**24** [a][1 Thess. 4:17] [b]John 17:5
**25** [a]John 15:21 [b]John 7:29; 8:55; 10:15 [c]John 3:17; 17:3, 8, 18, 21, 23
**26** [a]John 17:6 [b]John 15:9

CHAPTER 18
**1** [a]Mark 14:26, 32 [b]2 Sam. 15:23
**2** [a]Luke 21:37; 22:39
**3** [a]Luke 22:47–53
**4** [a]John 6:64; 13:1, 3; 19:28
**5** [a]Matt. 21:11 [b]Ps. 41:9 [1]Lit. *the Nazarene*
**9** [a][John 6:39; 17:12]
**10** [a]Matt. 26:51
**11** [a]Matt. 20:22; 26:39
**13** [a]Matt. 26:57 [b]Luke 3:2 [c]Matt. 26:3
**14** [a]John 11:50 [1]*advantageous*
**15** [a]Mark 14:54 [b]John 20:2–5 [1]M *the other*
**16** [a]Matt. 26:69
**17** [a]Matt. 26:34
**20** [a]Luke 4:15 [b]John 6:59 [c]Mark 14:49 [1]NU *all the Jews meet*
**21** [a]Mark 12:37
**22** [a]Jer. 20:2 [1]Lit. *gave Jesus a slap,*
**24** [a]Matt. 26:57 [b]John 11:49
**25** [a]Luke 22:58–62
**27** [a]John 13:38
**28** [a]Mark 15:1 [b]Acts 10:28; 11:3 [1]The governor's headquarters
**29** [a]Matt. 27:11–14
**30** [1]*a criminal*
**32** [a]Matt. 20:17–19; 26:2 [b]John 3:14; 8:28; 12:32, 33
**33** [a]Matt. 27:11 [1]The governor's headquarters

nation and the chief priests have delivered You to
me. What have You done?"
36 [a]Jesus answered, [b]"My kingdom is not of this
world. If My kingdom were of this world, My
servants would fight, so that I should not be
delivered to the Jews; but now My kingdom is not
from here."
37 Pilate therefore said to Him, "Are You a king
then?" Jesus answered, "You say *rightly* that I am
a king. For this cause I was born, and for this
cause I have come into the world, [a]that I should
bear [b]witness to the truth. Everyone who [c]is of the
truth [d]hears My voice."
38 Pilate said to Him, "What is truth?" And when
he had said this, he went out again to the Jews,
and said to them, [a]"I find no fault in Him at all."
**39** [a]"But you have a custom that I should release
someone to you at the Passover. Do you therefore
want me to release to you the King of the Jews?"
40 [a]Then they all cried again, saying, "Not this
Man, but Barabbas!" [b]Now Barabbas was a robber.

## *The Crucifixion and Burial of Jesus*

**19** So then [a]Pilate took Jesus and scourged
*Him.*
2 And the soldiers twisted a crown of thorns and
put *it* on His head, and they put on Him a purple
robe.
3 [1]Then they said, "Hail, King of the Jews!" And
they [a]struck Him with their hands.
4 Pilate then went out again, and said to them,
"Behold, I am bringing Him out to you, [a]that you
may know that I find no fault in Him."
**5** Then Jesus came out, wearing the crown of
thorns and the purple robe. And *Pilate* said to
them, "Behold the Man!"
6 [a]Therefore, when the chief priests and officers
saw Him, they cried out, saying, "Crucify *Him,*
crucify *Him!*" Pilate said to them, "You take Him
and crucify *Him,* for I find no fault in Him."
7 The Jews answered him, [a]"We have a law, and
according to [1]our law He ought to die, because
[b]He made Himself the Son of God."
8 Therefore, when Pilate heard that saying, he
was the more afraid,
9 and went again into the Praetorium, and said
to Jesus, "Where are You from?" [a]But Jesus gave
him no answer.
10 Then Pilate said to Him, "Are You not speaking to me? Do You not know that I have [1]power to
crucify You, and [1]power to release You?"
11 Jesus answered, [a]"You could have no power at
all against Me unless it had been given you from
above. Therefore [b]the one who delivered Me to
you has the greater sin."
12 From then on Pilate sought to release Him,
but the Jews cried out, saying, "If you let this Man
go, you are not Caesar's friend. [a]Whoever makes
himself a king speaks against Caesar."
13 [a]When Pilate therefore heard that saying, he
brought Jesus out and sat down in the judgment
seat in a place that is called *The* Pavement, but in
Hebrew, Gabbatha.
14 Now [a]it was the Preparation Day of the Passover, and about the sixth hour. And he said to the
Jews, "Behold your King!"
15 But they cried out, "Away with *Him,* away
with *Him!* Crucify Him!" Pilate said to them,
"Shall I crucify your King?" The chief priests
answered, [a]"We have no king but Caesar!"
16 [a]Then he delivered Him to them to be crucified. So they took Jesus [1]and led *Him* away.

**17** [a]And He, bearing His cross, [b]went out to a
place called *the Place* of a Skull, which is called in
Hebrew, Golgotha,
18 where they crucified Him, and [a]two others
with Him, one on either side, and Jesus in the
center.
19 [a]Now Pilate wrote a title and put *it* on the
cross. And the writing was:

JESUS OF NAZARETH,
THE KING OF THE JEWS.

20 Then many of the Jews read this title, for the
place where Jesus was crucified was near the city;
and it was written in Hebrew, Greek, *and* Latin.
21 Therefore the chief priests of the Jews said to
Pilate, "Do not write, 'The King of the Jews,' but,
'He said, "I am the King of the Jews." ' "
22 Pilate answered, "What I have written, I have
written."
23 [a]Then the soldiers, when they had crucified
Jesus, took His garments and made four parts, to
each soldier a part, and also the tunic. Now the
tunic was without seam, woven from the top in
one piece.
24 They said therefore among themselves, "Let
us not tear it, but cast lots for it, whose it shall
be," that the Scripture might be fulfilled which
says:

> [a]*"They divided My garments among them,*
> *And for My clothing they cast lots."*

Therefore the soldiers did these things.
**25** [a]Now there stood by the cross of Jesus His
mother, and His mother's sister, Mary the *wife* of
[b]Clopas, and Mary Magdalene.
26 When Jesus therefore saw His mother, and
[a]the disciple whom He loved standing by, He said
to His mother, [b]"Woman, behold your son!"
27 Then He said to the disciple, "Behold your
mother!" And from that hour that disciple took
her [a]to his own *home.*
**28** After this, Jesus, [1]knowing that all things were
now accomplished, [a]that the Scripture might be
fulfilled, said, "I thirst!"
29 Now a vessel full of sour wine was sitting
there; and [a]they filled a sponge with sour wine,
put *it* on hyssop, and put *it* to His mouth.
30 So when Jesus had received the sour wine, He
said, [a]"It is finished!" And bowing His head, He
gave up His spirit.
**31** [a]Therefore, because it was the Preparation
*Day,* [b]that the bodies should not remain on the
cross on the Sabbath (for that Sabbath was a
[c]high day), the Jews asked Pilate that their legs
might be broken, and *that* they might be taken
away.
32 Then the soldiers came and broke the legs of
the first and of the other who was crucified with
Him.
33 But when they came to Jesus and saw that He
was already dead, they did not break His legs.
34 But one of the soldiers pierced His side with a
spear, and immediately [a]blood and water came
out.
35 And he who has seen has testified, and his
testimony is [a]true; and he knows that he is telling
the truth, so that you may [b]believe.
36 For these things were done that the Scripture
should be fulfilled, [a]*"Not one of His bones shall be*
*broken."*
37 And again another Scripture says, [a]*"They shall*
*look on Him whom they pierced."*

**36** [a]1 Tim. 6:13 [b][Dan. 2:44; 7:14]
**37** [a][Matt. 5:17; 20:28] [b]Is. 55:4 [c][John 14:6] [d]John 8:47; 10:27
**38** [a]John 19:4, 6
**39** [a]Luke 23:17–25
**40** [a]Acts 3:14 [b]Luke 23:19

CHAPTER 19
**1** [a]Matt. 20:19; 27:26
**3** [a]Is. 50:6 [1]NU *And they came up to Him and said*
**4** [a]John 18:33, 38
**6** [a]Acts 3:13
**7** [a]Lev. 24:16 [b]Matt. 26:63–66 [1]NU *the law*
**9** [a]Is. 53:7
**10** [1]*authority*
**11** [a][Luke 22:53] [b]Rom. 13:1
**12** [a]Luke 23:2
**13** [a]1 Sam. 15:24
**14** [a]Matt. 27:62
**15** [a][Gen. 49:10]
**16** [a]Luke 23:24 [1]NU omits *and led Him away*
**17** [a]Mark 15:21, 22 [b]Num. 15:36
**18** [a]Is. 53:12
**19** [a]Matt. 27:37
**23** [a]Luke 23:34
**24** [a]Ps. 22:18
**25** [a]Mark 15:40 [b]Luke 24:18
**26** [a]John 13:23; 20:2; 21:7, 20, 24 [b]John 2:4
**27** [a]John 1:11; 16:32
**28** [a]Ps. 22:15 [1]M *seeing*
**29** [a]Matt. 27:48, 50
**30** [a]John 17:4
**31** [a]Mark 15:42 [b]Deut. 21:23 [c]Ex. 12:16
**34** [a][1 John 5:6, 8]
**35** [a]John 21:24 [b][John 20:31]
**36** [a][Ex. 12:46; Num. 9:12]; Ps. 34:20
**37** [a]Zech. 12:10; 13:6

38 [a]After this, Joseph of Arimathea, being a
disciple of Jesus, but secretly, [b]for fear of the Jews,
asked Pilate that he might take away the body of
Jesus; and Pilate gave *him* permission. So he came
and took the body of Jesus.
39 And [a]Nicodemus, who at first came to Jesus by
night, also came, bringing a mixture of [b]myrrh and
aloes, about a hundred pounds.
40 Then they took the body of Jesus, and [a]bound
it in strips of linen with the spices, as the custom
of the Jews is to bury.
41 Now in the place where He was crucified there
was a garden, and in the garden a new tomb in
which no one had yet been laid.
42 So [a]there they laid Jesus, [b]because of the Jews'
Preparation *Day*, for the tomb was nearby.

### *The Risen Christ*

**20** Now on the [a]first *day* of the week Mary
Magdalene went to the tomb early, while it
was still dark, and saw *that* the [b]stone had been
taken away from the tomb.
2 Then she ran and came to Simon Peter, and to
the [a]other disciple, [b]whom Jesus loved, and said to
them, "They have taken away the Lord out of the
tomb, and we do not know where they have laid
Him."
3 [a]Peter therefore went out, and the other disciple, and were going to the tomb.
4 So they both ran together, and the other
disciple outran Peter and came to the tomb first.
5 And he, stooping down and looking in, saw
[a]the linen cloths lying *there;* yet he did not go in.
6 Then Simon Peter came, following him, and
went into the tomb; and he saw the linen cloths
lying *there,*
7 and [a]the [1]handkerchief that had been around
His head, not lying with the linen cloths, but
folded together in a place by itself.
8 Then the [a]other disciple, who came to the
tomb first, went in also; and he saw and believed.
9 For as yet they did not [1]know the [a]Scripture,
that He must rise again from the dead.
10 Then the disciples went away again to their
own homes.
11 [a]But Mary stood outside by the tomb weeping,
and as she wept she stooped down *and looked* into
the tomb.
12 And she saw two angels in white sitting, one
at the head and the other at the feet, where the
body of Jesus had lain.
13 Then they said to her, "Woman, why are you
weeping?" She said to them, "Because they have
taken away my Lord, and I do not know where
they have laid Him."
14 [a]Now when she had said this, she turned
around and saw Jesus standing *there,* and [b]did not
know that it was Jesus.
15 Jesus said to her, "Woman, why are you
weeping? Whom are you seeking?" She, supposing Him to be the gardener, said to Him, "Sir, if
You have carried Him away, tell me where You
have laid Him, and I will take Him away."
16 Jesus said to her, [a]"Mary!" She turned and
said to [1]Him, "Rabboni!" (which is to say,
Teacher).
17 Jesus said to her, "Do not cling to Me, for I
have not yet [a]ascended to My Father; but go to
[b]My brethren and say to them, [c]'I am ascending to
My Father and your Father, and *to* [d]My God and
your God.'"

18 [a]Mary Magdalene came and told the [1]disciples
that she had seen the Lord, and *that* He had
spoken these things to her.
19 [a]Then, the same day at evening, being the first
*day* of the week, when the doors were shut where
the disciples were [1]assembled, for [b]fear of the
Jews, Jesus came and stood in the midst, and said
to them, [c]"Peace *be* with you."
20 When He had said this, He [a]showed them *His*
hands and His side. [b]Then the disciples were glad
when they saw the Lord.
21 So Jesus said to them again, "Peace to you!
[a]As the Father has sent Me, I also send you."
22 And when He had said this, He breathed on
*them,* and said to them, "Receive the Holy Spirit.
23 [a]"If you forgive the sins of any, they are
forgiven them; if you retain the *sins* of any, they
are retained."
24 Now Thomas, [a]called the Twin, one of the
twelve, was not with them when Jesus came.
25 The other disciples therefore said to him, "We
have seen the Lord." So he said to them, "Unless I
see in His hands the print of the nails, and put my
finger into the print of the nails, and put my hand
into His side, I will not believe."
26 And after eight days His disciples were again
inside, and Thomas with them. Jesus came, the
doors being shut, and stood in the midst, and said,
"Peace to you!"
27 Then He said to Thomas, "Reach your finger
here, and look at My hands; and [a]reach your hand
*here,* and put *it* into My side. Do not be [b]unbeliev-
ing, but believing."
28 And Thomas answered and said to Him, "My
Lord and my God!"
29 Jesus said to him, [1]"Thomas, because you have
seen Me, you have believed. [a]Blessed *are* those
who have not seen and *yet* have believed."
30 And [a]truly Jesus did many other signs in the
presence of His disciples, which are not written in
this book;
31 [a]but these are written that [b]you may believe
that Jesus [c]is the Christ, the Son of God, [d]and that
believing you may have life in His name.

### *A Breakfast by the Sea*

**21** After these things Jesus showed Himself
again to the disciples at the [a]Sea of Tiberias,
and in this way He showed *Himself:*
2 Simon Peter, [a]Thomas called Didymus, [b]Na-
thanael of [c]Cana in Galilee, [d]the *sons* of Zebedee,
and two others of His disciples were together.
3 Simon Peter said to them, "I am going fishing." They said to him, "We are going with you
also." They went out and [1]immediately got into
the boat, and that night they caught nothing.
4 But when the morning had now come, Jesus
stood on the shore; yet the disciples [a]did not know
that it was Jesus.
5 Then [a]Jesus said to them, "Children, have you
any food?" They answered Him, "No."
6 And He said to them, [a]"Cast the net on the
right side of the boat, and you will find *some.*" So
they cast, and now they were not able to draw it
in because of the multitude of fish.
7 Therefore [a]that disciple whom Jesus loved said
to Peter, "It is the Lord!" Now when Simon Peter
heard that it was the Lord, he put on *his* outer
garment (for he had removed it), and plunged into
the sea.
8 But the other disciples came in the little boat

**38** [a]Luke 23:50–56 [b][John 7:13; 9:22; 12:42]
**39** [a]John 3:1, 2; 7:50 [b]Matt. 2:11
**40** [a]John 20:5, 7
**42** [a]Is. 53:9 [b]John 19:14, 31

CHAPTER 20
**1** [a]Matt. 28:1–8 [b]Matt. 27:60, 66; 28:2
**2** [a]John 21:23, 24 [b]John 13:23; 19:26; 21:7, 20, 24
**3** [a]Luke 24:12
**5** [a]John 19:40
**7** [a]John 11:44 [1]*face cloth*
**8** [a]John 21:23, 24
**9** [a]Ps. 16:10 [1]*understand*
**11** [a]Mark 16:5
**14** [a]Matt. 28:9 [b]John 21:4
**16** [a]John 10:3 [1]NU adds *in Hebrew*
**17** [a]Heb. 4:14 [b]Heb. 2:11 [c]John 16:28; 17:11 [d]Eph. 1:17
**18** [a]Luke 24:10, 23 [1]NU *disciples, "I have seen the Lord,"*
**19** [a]Luke 24:36 [b]John 9:22; 19:38 [c]John 14:27; 16:16 [1]NU omits *assembled*
**20** [a]Acts 1:3 [b]John 16:20, 22
**21** [a]John 17:18, 19
**23** [a]Matt. 16:19; 18:18
**24** [a]John 11:16
**27** [a]1 John 1:1 [b]Mark 16:14
**29** [a]1 Pet. 1:8 [1]NU, M omit *Thomas*
**30** [a]John 21:25
**31** [a]Luke 1:4 [b]1 John 5:13 [c]Luke 2:11 [d]John 3:15, 16; 5:24

CHAPTER 21
**1** [a]John 6:1
**2** [a]John 20:24 [b]John 1:45–51 [c]John 2:1 [d]Matt. 4:21
**3** [1]NU omits *immediately*
**4** [a]John 20:14
**5** [a]Luke 24:41
**6** [a]Luke 5:4, 6, 7
**7** [a]John 13:23; 20:2

(for they were not far from land, but about two
hundred cubits), dragging the net with fish.
9 Then, as soon as they had come to land, they
saw a fire of coals there, and fish laid on it, and
bread.
10 Jesus said to them, "Bring some of the fish
which you have just caught."
11 Simon Peter went up and dragged the net to
land, full of large fish, one hundred and fifty-three;
and although there were so many, the net was not
broken.
12 Jesus said to them, [a]"Come *and* eat breakfast." Yet none of the disciples dared ask Him,
"Who are You?"—knowing that it was the Lord.
13 Jesus then came and took the bread and gave
it to them, and likewise the fish.
14 This *is* now [a]the third time Jesus showed
Himself to His disciples after He was raised from
the dead.
**15** So when they had eaten breakfast, Jesus said
to Simon Peter, "Simon, *son* of [1]Jonah, do you
love Me more than these?" He said to Him, "Yes,
Lord; You know that I [2]love You." He said to him,
[a]"Feed My lambs."
16 He said to him again a second time, "Simon,
*son* of [1]Jonah, do you love Me?" He said to Him,
"Yes, Lord; You know that I [2]love You." [a]He said
to him, "Tend My [b]sheep."
17 He said to him the third time, "Simon, *son* of
[1]Jonah, do you [2]love Me?" Peter was grieved
because He said to him the third time, "Do you
[2]love Me?" And he said to Him, "Lord, [a]You know
all things; You know that I [2]love You." Jesus said
to him, "Feed My sheep.
18 [a]"Most assuredly, I say to you, when you were
younger, you girded yourself and walked where
you wished; but when you are old, you will stretch
out your hands, and another will gird you and
carry *you* where you do not wish."
19 This He spoke, signifying [a]by what death he
would glorify God. And when He had spoken this,
He said to him, [b]"Follow Me."
**20** Then Peter, turning around, saw the disciple
[a]whom Jesus loved following, [b]who also had
leaned on His breast at the supper, and said,
"Lord, who is the one who betrays You?"
21 Peter, seeing him, said to Jesus, "But Lord,
what *about* this man?"
22 Jesus said to him, "If I [1]will that he remain [a]till
I come, what *is that* to you? You follow Me."
23 Then this saying went out among the brethren
that this disciple would not die. Yet Jesus did not
say to him that he would not die, but, "If I will
that he remain till I come, what *is that* to you?"
24 This is the disciple who [a]testifies of these
things, and wrote these things; and we know that
his testimony is true.
25 [a]And there are also many other things that
Jesus did, which if they were written one by one,
[b]I suppose that even the world itself could not
contain the books that would be written. Amen.

**12** [a]Acts 10:41
**14** [a]John 20:19, 26
**15** [a]Acts 20:28 [1]NU *John* [2]*have affection for*
**16** [a]Heb. 13:20 [b]Ps. 79:13 [1]NU *John* [2]*have affection for*
**17** [a]John 2:24, 25; 16:30 [1]NU *John* [2]*have affection for*
**18** [a]Acts 12:3, 4
**19** [a]2 Pet. 1:13, 14 [b][Matt. 4:19; 16:24]
**20** [a]John 13:23; 20:2 [b]John 13:25
**22** [a][Rev. 2:25; 3:11; 22:7, 20] [1]*desire*
**24** [a]John 19:35
**25** [a]John 20:30 [b]Amos 7:10

# THE ACTS

## *of the Apostles*

### *Jesus Ascends to Heaven*

THE former account I made, O [a]Theophilus, of
all that Jesus began both to do and teach,
2 [a]until the day in which [1]He was taken up,
after He through the Holy Spirit [b]had given commandments to the apostles whom He had chosen,
3 [a]to whom He also presented Himself alive
after His suffering by many [1]infallible proofs,
being seen by them during forty days and speaking of the things pertaining to the kingdom of
God.
**4** [a]And being assembled together with *them,* He
commanded them not to depart from Jerusalem,
but to wait for the Promise of the Father,
"which," *He said,* "you have [b]heard from Me;
5 [a]"for John truly baptized with water, [b]but you
shall be baptized with the Holy Spirit not many
days from now."
6 Therefore, when they had come together, they
asked Him, saying, "Lord, will You at this time
restore the kingdom to Israel?"
7 And He said to them, [a]"It is not for you to
[b]know times or seasons which the Father has put
in His own authority.
8 [a]"But you shall receive power [b]when the Holy
Spirit has come upon you; and [c]you shall be
[1]witnesses to Me in Jerusalem, and in all Judea
and [d]Samaria, and to the [e]end of the earth."
**9** [a]Now when He had spoken these things, while
they watched, [b]He was taken up, and a cloud
received Him out of their sight.
10 And while they looked steadfastly toward
heaven as He went up, behold, two men stood by
them [a]in white apparel,
11 who also said, "Men of Galilee, why do you
stand gazing up into heaven? This *same* Jesus,
who was taken up from you into heaven, [a]will so
come in like manner as you saw Him go into
heaven."
**12** [a]Then they returned to Jerusalem from the
mount called Olivet, which is near Jerusalem, a
Sabbath day's journey.
13 And when they had entered, they went up
[a]into the upper room where they were staying:
[b]Peter, James, John, and Andrew; Philip and
Thomas; Bartholomew and Matthew; James *the
son* of Alphaeus and [c]Simon the Zealot; and
[d]Judas *the son* of James.
14 [a]These all continued with one [1]accord in
prayer [2]and supplication, with [b]the women and
Mary the mother of Jesus, and with [c]His brothers.
**15** And in those days Peter stood up in the midst
of the [1]disciples (altogether the number [a]of names
was about a hundred and twenty), and said,
16 "Men *and* brethren, this Scripture had to be
fulfilled, [a]which the Holy Spirit spoke before by
the mouth of David concerning Judas, [b]who became a guide to those who arrested Jesus;

CHAPTER 1
**1** [a]Luke 1:3
**2** [a]Mark 16:19 [b]Matt. 28:19 [1]He ascended into heaven.
**3** [a]Mark 16:12, 14 [1]*unmistakable*
**4** [a]Luke 24:49 [b][John 14:16, 17, 26; 15:26]
**5** [a]Matt. 3:11 [b][Joel 2:28]
**7** [a]1 Thess. 5:1 [b]Matt. 24:36
**8** [a][Acts 2:1, 4] [b]Luke 24:49 [c]Luke 24:48 [d]Acts 8:1, 5, 14 [e]Col. 1:23 [1]NU *My witnesses*
**9** [a]Luke 24:50, 51 [b]Acts 1:2
**10** [a]John 20:12
**11** [a]Dan. 7:13
**12** [a]Luke 24:52
**13** [a]Acts 9:37, 39; 20:8 [b]Matt. 10:2–4 [c]Luke 6:15 [d]Jude 1
**14** [a]Acts 2:1, 46 [b]Luke 23:49, 55 [c]Matt. 13:55 [1]*purpose* or *mind* [2]NU omits *and supplication*
**15** [a]Rev. 3:4 [1]NU *brethren*
**16** [a]Ps. 41:9 [b]Luke 22:47

17 "for [a]he was numbered with us and obtained a
part in [b]this ministry."
18 [a](Now this man purchased a field with [b]the
[1]wages of iniquity; and falling headlong, he burst
open in the middle and all his [2]entrails gushed out.
19 And it became known to all those dwelling in
Jerusalem; so that field is called in their own
language, Akel Dama, that is, Field of Blood.)
20 "For it is written in the book of Psalms:

[a]*'Let his dwelling place be [1]desolate,*
*And let no one live in it';*

and,

[b]*'Let another take his [2]office.'*

21 "Therefore, of these men who have accompanied us all the time that the Lord Jesus went in
and out among us,
22 "beginning from the baptism of John to that
day when [a]He was taken up from us, one of these
must [b]become a witness with us of His resurrection."
23 And they proposed two: Joseph called [a]Barsa-
bas, who was surnamed Justus, and Matthias.
24 And they prayed and said, "You, O Lord, [a]who
know the hearts of all, show which of these two
You have chosen
25 [a]"to take part in this ministry and apostleship
from which Judas by transgression fell, that he
might go to his own place."
26 And they cast their lots, and the lot fell on
Matthias. And he was numbered with the eleven
apostles.

### *Peter's Sermon; the Coming of the Holy Spirit*

**2** When [a]the Day of Pentecost had fully come,
[b]they were all [1]with one accord in one place.
2 And suddenly there came a sound from
heaven, as of a rushing mighty wind, and [a]it filled
the whole house where they were sitting.
3 Then there appeared to them [1]divided tongues,
as of fire, and *one* sat upon each of them.
4 And [a]they were all filled with the Holy Spirit
and began [b]to speak with other tongues, as the
Spirit gave them utterance.
**5** And there were dwelling in Jerusalem Jews,
[a]devout men, from every nation under heaven.
6 And when this sound occurred, the [a]multitude
came together, and were confused, because everyone heard them speak in his own language.
7 Then they were all amazed and marveled,
saying to one another, "Look, are not all these
who speak [a]Galileans?
8 "And how *is it that* we hear, each in our own
[1]language in which we were born?
9 "Parthians and Medes and Elamites, those
dwelling in Mesopotamia, Judea and [a]Cappadocia,
Pontus and Asia,
10 "Phrygia and Pamphylia, Egypt and the parts
of Libya adjoining Cyrene, visitors from Rome,
both Jews and proselytes,
11 "Cretans and [1]Arabs—we hear them speaking
in our own tongues the wonderful works of God."
12 So they were all amazed and perplexed, saying
to one another, "Whatever could this mean?"
13 Others mocking said, "They are full of new
wine."
**14** But Peter, standing up with the eleven, raised
his voice and said to them, "Men of Judea and all
who dwell in Jerusalem, let this be known to you,
and heed my words.
15 "For these are not drunk, as you suppose,
[a]since it is *only* [1]the third hour of the day.
16 "But this is what was spoken by the prophet
Joel:

17 *'And[a] it shall come to pass in the last days, says God,*
[b]*That I will pour out of My Spirit on all flesh;*
*Your sons and [c]your daughters shall prophesy,*
*Your young men shall see visions,*
*Your old men shall dream dreams.*
18 *And on My menservants and on My maidservants*
*I will pour out My Spirit in those days;*
[a]*And they shall prophesy.*
19 [a]*I will show wonders in heaven above*
*And signs in the earth beneath:*
*Blood and fire and vapor of smoke.*
20 [a]*The sun shall be turned into darkness,*
*And the moon into blood,*
*Before the coming of the great and awesome day of the LORD.*
21 *And it shall come to pass*
*That [a]whoever calls on the name of the LORD*
*Shall be saved.'*

**22** "Men of Israel, hear these words: Jesus of
Nazareth, a Man attested by God to you [a]by
miracles, wonders, and signs which God did
through Him in your midst, as you yourselves also
know—
23 "Him, [a]being delivered by the determined
purpose and foreknowledge of God, [b]you [1]have
taken by lawless hands, have crucified, and put to
death;
24 [a]"whom God raised up, having [1]loosed the
[2]pains of death, because it was not possible that
He should be held by it.
25 "For David says concerning Him:

[a]*'I foresaw the LORD always before my face,*
*For He is at my right hand, that I may not be shaken.*
26 *Therefore my heart rejoiced, and my tongue was glad;*
*Moreover my flesh also will rest in hope.*
27 *For You will not leave my soul in Hades,*
*Nor will You allow Your Holy One to see [a]corruption.*
28 *You have made known to me the ways of life;*
*You will make me full of joy in Your presence.'*

29 "Men *and* brethren, let *me* speak freely to you
[a]of the patriarch David, that he is both dead and
buried, and his tomb is with us to this day.
30 "Therefore, being a prophet, [a]and knowing
that God had sworn with an oath to him that of
the fruit of his body, [1]according to the flesh, He
would raise up the Christ to sit on his throne,
31 "he, foreseeing this, spoke concerning the
resurrection of the Christ, [a]that His soul was not
left in Hades, nor did His flesh see corruption.
32 [a]"This Jesus God has raised up, [b]of which we
are all witnesses.
33 "Therefore [a]being exalted [1]to [b]the right hand
of God, and [c]having received from the Father the
promise of the Holy Spirit, He [d]poured out this
which you now see and hear.

---

**17** [a]Matt. 10:4 [b]Acts 1:25
**18** [a]Matt. 27:3–10 [b]Mark 14:21; 26:14, 15 [1]*reward of unrighteousness* [2]*intestines*
**20** [a]Ps. 69:25 [b]Ps. 109:8 [1]*deserted* [2]Gr. *episkopen, position of overseer*
**22** [a]Acts 1:9 [b]Acts 1:8; 2:32
**23** [a]Acts 15:22
**24** [a]1 Sam. 16:7
**25** [a]Acts 1:17

CHAPTER 2
**1** [a]Lev. 23:15 [b]Acts 1:14 [1]NU *together*
**2** [a]Acts 4:31
**3** [1]Or *tongues as of fire, distributed and resting on each*
**4** [a]Acts 1:5 [b]Mark 16:17
**5** [a]Acts 8:2
**6** [a]Acts 4:32
**7** [a]Acts 1:11
**8** [1]*dialect*
**9** [a]1 Pet. 1:1
**11** [1]*Arabians*
**15** [a]1 Thess. 5:7 [1]9 A.M.
**17** [a]Joel 2:28–32 [b]Acts 10:45 [c]Acts 21:9
**18** [a]1 Cor. 12:10
**19** [a]Joel 2:30
**20** [a]Matt. 24:29
**21** [a]Rom. 10:13
**22** [a]John 3:2; 5:6
**23** [a]Luke 22:22 [b]Acts 5:30 [1]NU omits *have taken*
**24** [a][Rom. 8:11] [1]*destroyed* or *abolished* [2]Lit. *birth pangs*
**25** [a]Ps. 16:8–11
**27** [a]Acts 13:30–37
**29** [a]Acts 13:36
**30** [a]Ps. 132:11 [1]NU *He would seat one on his throne,*
**31** [a]Ps. 16:10
**32** [a]Acts 2:24 [b]Acts 1:8; 3:15
**33** [a][Acts 5:31] [b][Heb. 10:12] [c][John 14:26] [d]Acts 2:1–11, 17; 10:45 [1]Possibly *by*

34 "For David did not ascend into the heavens,
but he says himself:

[a]*'The LORD said to my Lord,*
*"Sit at My right hand,*
35 *Till I make Your enemies Your footstool." '*

36 "Therefore let all the house of Israel know
assuredly that God has made this Jesus, whom
you crucified, both Lord and Christ."
37 Now when they heard *this,* [a]they were cut to
the heart, and said to Peter and the rest of the
apostles, "Men *and* brethren, what shall we do?"
38 Then Peter said to them, [a]"Repent, and let
every one of you be baptized in the name of Jesus
Christ for the [1]remission of sins; and you shall
receive the gift of the Holy Spirit.
39 "For the promise is to you and [a]to your children, and [b]to all who are afar off, as many as the
Lord our God will call."
**40** And with many other words he testified and
exhorted them, saying, "Be saved from this [1]per-
verse generation."
41 Then those who [1]gladly received his word
were baptized; and that day about three thousand
souls were added *to them.*
42 [a]And they continued steadfastly in the apostles' [1]doctrine and fellowship, in the breaking of
bread, and in prayers.
43 Then fear came upon every soul, and [a]many
wonders and signs were done through the apostles.
44 Now all who believed were together, and [a]had
all things in common,
45 and [1]sold their possessions and goods, and
[a]divided[2] them among all, as anyone had need.
46 [a]So continuing daily with one accord [b]in the
temple, and [c]breaking bread from house to house,
they ate their food with gladness and simplicity of
heart,
47 praising God and having favor with all the
people. And [a]the Lord added [1]to the church daily
those who were being saved.

### *A Lame Man Healed; Peter's Preaching*

**3** Now Peter and John went up together [a]to the
temple at the hour of prayer, [b]the ninth *hour.*
2 And [a]a certain man lame from his mother's
womb was carried, whom they laid daily at the
gate of the temple which is called Beautiful, [b]to
[1]ask alms from those who entered the temple;
3 who, seeing Peter and John about to go into
the temple, asked for alms.
4 And fixing his eyes on him, with John, Peter
said, "Look at us."
5 So he gave them his attention, expecting to
receive something from them.
6 Then Peter said, "Silver and gold I do not
have, but what I do have I give you: [a]In the name
of Jesus Christ of Nazareth, rise up and walk."
7 And he took him by the right hand and lifted
*him* up, and immediately his feet and ankle bones
received strength.
8 So he, [a]leaping up, stood and walked and
entered the temple with them—walking, leaping,
and praising God.
9 [a]And all the people saw him walking and
praising God.
10 Then they knew that it was he who [a]sat
begging alms at the Beautiful Gate of the temple;
and they were filled with wonder and amazement
at what had happened to him.

**34** [a]Ps. 68:18; 110:1
**37** [a]Luke 3:10, 12, 14
**38** [a]Luke 24:47 [1]*forgiveness*
**39** [a]Joel 2:28, 32 [b]Eph. 2:13
**40** [1]*crooked*
**41** [1]NU omits *gladly*
**42** [a]Acts 1:14 [1]*teaching*
**43** [a]Acts 2:22
**44** [a]Acts 4:32, 34, 37; 5:2
**45** [a]Is. 58:7 [1]*would sell* [2]*distributed*
**46** [a]Acts 1:14 [b]Luke 24:53 [c]Acts 2:42; 20:7
**47** [a]Acts 5:14 [1]NU omits *to the church*

CHAPTER 3
**1** [a]Acts 2:46 [b]Ps. 55:17
**2** [a]Acts 14:8 [b]John 9:8 [1]Beg
**6** [a]Acts 4:10
**8** [a]Is. 35:6
**9** [a]Acts 4:16, 21
**10** [a]John 9:8
**11** [a]John 10:23
**13** [a]John 5:30 [b]John 7:39; 12:23; 13:31 [c]Matt. 27:2 [d]Matt. 27:20
**14** [a]Mark 1:24 [b]Acts 7:52 [c]John 18:40
**15** [a]Acts 2:24 [b]Acts 2:32 [1]Or *Originator*
**16** [a]Matt. 9:22
**17** [a]Luke 23:34
**18** [a]Acts 26:22 [b]1 Pet. 1:10
**19** [a][Acts 2:38; 26:20]
**20** [1]NU, M *Christ Jesus* [2]NU, M *ordained for you before*
**21** [a]Acts 1:11 [b]Matt. 17:11 [c]Luke 1:70 [1]Or *time*
**22** [a]Deut. 18:15, 18, 19
**24** [a]Luke 24:25 [1]NU, M *proclaimed*
**25** [a][Rom. 9:4, 8] [b]Gen. 12:3; 18:18; 22:18; 26:4; 28:14
**26** [a][Rom. 1:16; 2:9] [b]Matt. 1:21

CHAPTER 4
**1** [a]Matt. 22:23

**11** Now as the lame man who was healed held on
to Peter and John, all the people ran together to
them in the porch [a]which is called Solomon's,
greatly amazed.
12 So when Peter saw *it,* he responded to the
people: "Men of Israel, why do you marvel at this?
Or why look so intently at us, as though by our
own power or godliness we had made this man
walk?
13 [a]"The God of Abraham, Isaac, and Jacob, the
God of our fathers, [b]glorified His Servant Jesus,
whom you [c]delivered up and [d]denied in the presence of Pilate, when he was determined to let
*Him* go.
14 "But you denied [a]the Holy One [b]and the Just,
and [c]asked for a murderer to be granted to you,
15 "and killed the [1]Prince of life, [a]whom God
raised from the dead, [b]of which we are witnesses.
16 [a]"And His name, through faith in His name,
has made this man strong, whom you see and
know. Yes, the faith which *comes* through Him
has given him this perfect soundness in the presence of you all.
17 "Yet now, brethren, I know that [a]you did *it* in
ignorance, as *did* also your rulers.
18 "But [a]those things which God foretold [b]by the
mouth of all His prophets, that the Christ would
suffer, He has thus fulfilled.
19 [a]"Repent therefore and be converted, that
your sins may be blotted out, so that times of
refreshing may come from the presence of the
Lord,
20 "and that He may send [1]Jesus Christ, who was
[2]preached to you before,
21 [a]"whom heaven must receive until the times
of [b]restoration of all things, [c]which God has
spoken by the mouth of all His holy prophets
since [1]the world began.
22 "For Moses truly said to the fathers, [a]*'The*
*LORD your God will raise up for you a Prophet like*
*me from your brethren. Him you shall hear in all*
*things, whatever He says to you.*
23 *'And it shall be that every soul who will not*
*hear that Prophet shall be utterly destroyed from*
*among the people.'*
24 "Yes, and [a]all the prophets, from Samuel and
those who follow, as many as have spoken, have
also [1]foretold these days.
25 [a]"You are sons of the prophets, and of the
covenant which God made with our fathers, saying to Abraham, [b]*'And in your seed all the families*
*of the earth shall be blessed.'*
26 "To you [a]first, God, having raised up His
Servant Jesus, sent Him to bless you, [b]in turning
away every one *of you* from your iniquities."

### *Peter and John Are Imprisoned*

**4** Now as they spoke to the people, the priests,
the captain of the temple, and the [a]Sadducees
came upon them,
2 being greatly disturbed that they taught the
people and preached in Jesus the resurrection
from the dead.
3 And they laid hands on them, and put *them* in
custody until the next day, for it was already
evening.
4 However, many of those who heard the word
believed; and the number of the men came to be
about five thousand.
**5** And it came to pass, on the next day, that
their rulers, elders, and scribes,

6 as well as [a]Annas the high priest, Caiaphas, John, and Alexander, and as many as were of the family of the high priest, were gathered together at Jerusalem.

7 And when they had set them in the midst, they asked, [a]"By what power or by what name have you done this?"

8 [a]Then Peter, filled with the Holy Spirit, said to them, "Rulers of the people and elders of Israel:

9 "If we this day are judged for a good deed *done* to *a* helpless man, by what means he has been made well,

10 "let it be known to you all, and to all the people of Israel, [a]that by the name of Jesus Christ of Nazareth, whom you crucified, [b]whom God raised from the dead, by Him this man stands here before you whole.

11 "This is the [a]*'stone which was rejected by you builders, which has become the chief cornerstone.'*

12 [a]"Nor is there salvation in any other, for there is no other name under heaven given among men by which we must be saved."

**13** Now when they saw the boldness of Peter and John, [a]and perceived that they were uneducated and untrained men, they marveled. And they realized that they had been with Jesus.

14 And seeing the man who had been healed [a]standing with them, they could say nothing against it.

15 But when they had commanded them to go aside out of the council, they conferred among themselves,

16 saying, [a]"What shall we do to these men? For, indeed, that a [1]notable miracle has been done through them *is* [b]evident[2] to all who dwell in Jerusalem, and we cannot deny *it.*

17 "But so that it spreads no further among the people, let us severely threaten them, that from now on they speak to no man in this name."

18 [a]So they called them and commanded them not to speak at all nor teach in the name of Jesus.

19 But Peter and John answered and said to them, [a]"Whether it is right in the sight of God to listen to you more than to God, you judge.

20 [a]"For we cannot but speak the things which [b]we have seen and heard."

21 So when they had further threatened them, they let them go, finding no way of punishing them, [a]because of the people, since they all [b]glorified God for [c]what had been done.

22 For the man was over forty years old on whom this miracle of healing had been performed.

**23** And being let go, [a]they went to their own *companions* and reported all that the chief priests and elders had said to them.

24 So when they heard that, they raised their voice to God with one accord and said: "Lord, [a]You *are* God, who made heaven and earth and the sea, and all that is in them,

25 "who [1]by the mouth of Your servant David have said:

[a]*'Why did the nations rage,*
*And the people plot vain things?*
26 *The kings of the earth took their stand,*
*And the rulers were gathered together*
*Against the* LORD *and against His Christ.'*

27 "For [a]truly against [b]Your holy Servant Jesus, [c]whom You anointed, both Herod and Pontius Pilate, with the Gentiles and the people of Israel, were gathered together

28 [a]"to do whatever Your hand and Your purpose determined before to be done.

29 "Now, Lord, look on their threats, and grant to Your servants [a]that with all boldness they may speak Your word,

30 "by stretching out Your hand to heal, [a]and that signs and wonders may be done [b]through the name of [c]Your holy Servant Jesus."

31 And when they had prayed, [a]the place where they were assembled together was shaken; and they were all filled with the Holy Spirit, [b]and they spoke the word of God with boldness.

**32** Now the multitude of those who believed [a]were of one heart and one soul; [b]neither did anyone say that any of the things he possessed was his own, but they had all things in common.

33 And with [a]great power the apostles gave [b]witness to the resurrection of the Lord Jesus. And [c]great grace was upon them all.

34 Nor was there anyone among them who lacked; [a]for all who were possessors of lands or houses sold them, and brought the proceeds of the things that were sold,

35 [a]and laid *them* at the apostles' feet; [b]and they distributed to each as anyone had need.

36 And [1]Joses, who was also named Barnabas by the apostles (which is translated Son of [2]Encouragement), a Levite of the country of Cyprus,

37 [a]having land, sold *it,* and brought the money and laid *it* at the apostles' feet.

### *Lying to the Holy Spirit*

**5** But a certain man named Ananias, with Sapphira his wife, sold a possession.

2 And he kept back *part* of the proceeds, his wife also being aware *of it,* and brought a certain part and laid *it* at the apostles' feet.

3 [a]But Peter said, "Ananias, why has [b]Satan filled your heart to lie to the Holy Spirit and keep back *part* of the price of the land for yourself?

4 "While it remained, was it not your own? And after it was sold, was it not in your own control? Why have you conceived this thing in your heart? You have not lied to men but to God."

5 Then Ananias, hearing these words, [a]fell down and breathed his last. So great fear came upon all those who heard these things.

6 And the young men arose and [a]wrapped him up, carried *him* out, and buried *him.*

7 Now it was about three hours later when his wife came in, not knowing what had happened.

8 And Peter answered her, "Tell me whether you sold the land for so much?" She said, "Yes, for so much."

9 Then Peter said to her, "How is it that you have agreed together [a]to test the Spirit of the Lord? Look, the feet of those who have buried your husband *are* at the door, and they will carry you out."

10 [a]Then immediately she fell down at his feet and breathed her last. And the young men came in and found her dead, and carrying *her* out, buried *her* by her husband.

11 [a]So great fear came upon all the church and upon all who heard these things.

**12** And [a]through the hands of the apostles many signs and wonders were done among the people. [b]And they were all with one accord in Solomon's Porch.

---

**6** [a]Luke 3:2
**7** [a]Matt. 21:23
**8** [a]Luke 12:11, 12
**10** [a]Acts 2:22; 3:6, 16 [b]Acts 2:24
**11** [a]Ps. 118:22
**12** [a][1 Tim. 2:5, 6]
**13** [a][1 Cor. 1:27]
**14** [a]Acts 3:11
**16** [a]John 11:47 [b]Acts 3:7–10 [1]*remarkable sign* [2]*well known*
**18** [a]Acts 5:28, 40
**19** [a]Acts 5:29
**20** [a]Acts 1:8; 2:32 [b][1 John 1:1, 3]
**21** [a]Acts 5:26 [b]Matt. 15:31 [c]Acts 3:7, 8
**23** [a]Acts 2:44–46; 12:12
**24** [a]Ex. 20:11
**25** [a]Ps. 2:1, 2 [1]NU *through the Holy Spirit, by the mouth of our father, Your servant David,*
**27** [a]Luke 22:2; 23:1, 8 [b][Luke 1:35] [c]John 10:36
**28** [a]Acts 2:23; 3:18
**29** [a]Acts 4:13, 31; 9:27; 13:46; 14:3; 19:8; 26:26
**30** [a]Acts 2:43; 5:12 [b]Acts 3:6, 16 [c]Acts 4:27
**31** [a]Acts 2:2, 4; 16:26 [b]Acts 4:29
**32** [a]Rom. 15:5, 6 [b]Acts 2:44
**33** [a][Acts 1:8] [b]Acts 1:22 [c]Rom. 6:15
**34** [a]Acts 2:45
**35** [a]Acts 4:37; 5:2 [b]Acts 2:45; 6:1
**36** [1]NU *Joseph* [2]Or *Consolation*
**37** [a]Acts 4:34, 35; 5:1, 2

CHAPTER 5
**3** [a]Deut. 23:21 [b]Luke 22:3
**5** [a]Acts 5:10, 11
**6** [a]John 19:40
**9** [a]Acts 5:3, 4
**10** [a]Acts 5:5
**11** [a]Acts 2:43; 5:5; 19:17
**12** [a]Acts 2:43; 4:30; 6:8; 14:3; 15:12 [b]Acts 3:11; 4:32

13 Yet [a]none of the rest dared join them, [b]but the
people esteemed them highly.
14 And believers were increasingly added to the
Lord, multitudes of both men and women,
15 so that they brought the sick out into the
streets and laid *them* on beds and couches, [a]that
at least the shadow of Peter passing by might fall
on some of them.
16 Also a multitude gathered from the surrounding cities to Jerusalem, bringing [a]sick people and
those who were tormented by unclean spirits, and
they were all healed.
**17** [a]Then the high priest rose up, and all those
who *were* with him (which is the sect of the
Sadducees), and they were filled with [1]indigna-
tion,
18 [a]and laid their hands on the apostles and put
them in the common prison.
19 But at night [a]an angel of the Lord opened the
prison doors and brought them out, and said,
20 "Go, stand in the temple and speak to the
people [a]all the words of this life."
21 And when they heard *that,* they entered the
temple early in the morning and taught. [a]But the
high priest and those with him came and called
the [1]council together, with all the [2]elders of the
children of Israel, and sent to the prison to have
them brought.
**22** But when the officers came and did not find
them in the prison, they returned and reported,
23 saying, "Indeed we found the prison shut
securely, and the guards standing [1]outside before
the doors; but when we opened them, we found
no one inside!"
24 Now when [1]the high priest, [a]the captain of the
temple, and the chief priests heard these things,
they wondered what the outcome would be.
25 So one came and told them, [1]saying, "Look,
the men whom you put in prison are standing in
the temple and teaching the people!"
26 Then the captain went with the officers and
brought them without violence, [a]for they feared
the people, lest they should be stoned.
27 And when they had brought them, they set
*them* before the council. And the high priest asked
them,
28 saying, [a]"Did we not strictly command you
not to teach in this name? And look, you have
filled Jerusalem with your doctrine, [b]and intend to
bring this Man's [c]blood on us!"
29 But Peter and the *other* apostles answered and
said: [a]"We ought to obey God rather than men.
30 [a]"The God of our fathers raised up Jesus
whom you murdered by [b]hanging on a tree.
31 [a]"Him God has exalted to His right hand *to be*
[b]Prince and [c]Savior, [d]to give repentance to Israel
and forgiveness of sins.
32 "And [a]we are His witnesses to these things,
and *so* also *is* the Holy Spirit [b]whom God has
given to those who obey Him."
**33** When they heard *this,* they were [a]furious[1] and
plotted to kill them.
34 Then one in the council stood up, a Pharisee
named [a]Gamaliel, a teacher of the law held in
respect by all the people, and commanded them to
put the apostles outside for a little while.
35 And he said to them: "Men of Israel, [1]take
heed to yourselves what you intend to do regarding these men.
36 "For some time ago Theudas rose up, claiming
to be somebody. A number of men, about four
hundred, [1]joined him. He was slain, and all who
obeyed him were scattered and came to nothing.
37 "After this man, Judas of Galilee rose up in the
days of the census, and drew away many people
after him. He also perished, and all who obeyed
him were dispersed.
38 "And now I say to you, keep away from these
men and let them alone; for if this plan or this
work is of men, it will come to nothing;
39 [a]"but if it is of God, you cannot overthrow it—
lest you even be found [b]to fight against God."
40 And they agreed with him, and when they had
[a]called for the apostles [b]and beaten *them,* they
commanded that they should not speak in the
name of Jesus, and let them go.
41 So they departed from the presence of the
council, [a]rejoicing that they were counted worthy
to suffer shame for [1]His name.
42 And daily [a]in the temple, and in every house,
[b]they did not cease teaching and preaching Jesus
*as* the Christ.

**13** [a]John 9:22 [b]Acts 2:47; 4:21
**15** [a]Acts 19:12
**16** [a]Mark 16:17, 18
**17** [a]Acts 4:1, 2, 6 [1]*jealousy*
**18** [a]Luke 21:12
**19** [a]Acts 12:7; 16:26
**20** [a][John 6:63, 68; 17:3]
**21** [a]Acts 4:5, 6 [1]Sanhedrin [2]*council of elders* or *senate*
**23** [1]NU, M omit *outside*
**24** [a]Acts 4:1; 5:26 [1]NU omits *the high priest*
**25** [1]NU, M omit *saying*
**26** [a]Matt. 21:26
**28** [a]Acts 4:17, 18 [b]Acts 2:23, 36 [c]Matt. 23:35
**29** [a]Acts 4:19
**30** [a]Acts 3:13, 15 [b][1 Pet. 2:24]
**31** [a][Acts 2:33, 36] [b]Acts 3:15 [c]Matt. 1:21 [d]Luke 24:47
**32** [a]John 15:26, 27 [b]Acts 2:4; 10:44
**33** [a]Acts 2:37; 7:54 [1]*cut to the quick*
**34** [a]Acts 22:3
**35** [1]*be careful*
**36** [1]*followed*
**39** [a]1 Cor. 1:25 [b]Acts 7:51; 9:5
**40** [a]Acts 4:18 [b]Matt. 10:17
**41** [a][1 Pet. 4:13–16] [1]NU *the name,* M *the name of Jesus*
**42** [a]Acts 2:46 [b]Acts 4:20, 29

CHAPTER 6
**1** [a]Acts 2:41; 4:4 [b]Acts 9:29; 11:20 [c]Acts 4:35; 11:29 [1]Jews who had adopted Greek culture
**2** [a]Ex. 18:17
**3** [a]1 Tim. 3:7 [b]1 Tim. 3:8–13
**4** [a]Acts 2:42
**5** [a]Acts 6:3; 11:24 [b]Acts 8:5, 26; 21:8 [c]Rev. 2:6, 15
**6** [a]Acts 1:24 [b][2 Tim. 1:6]
**7** [a]Acts 12:24 [b]John 12:42
**8** [a]Acts 2:43; 5:12; 8:15; 14:3 [1]NU *grace*
**10** [a]Luke 21:15
**11** [a]1 Kin. 21:10, 13
**13** [1]NU omits *blasphemous*
**14** [a]Acts 10:38; 25:8

### *Seven Chosen to Serve*

**6** Now in those days, [a]when *the number of* the
disciples was multiplying, there arose a complaint against the Hebrews by the [b]Hellenists,[1]
because their widows were neglected [c]in the daily
distribution.
2 Then the twelve summoned the multitude of
the disciples and said, [a]"It is not desirable that we
should leave the word of God and serve tables.
3 "Therefore, brethren, [a]seek out from among
you seven men of *good* reputation, full of the Holy
Spirit and wisdom, whom we may appoint over
this [b]business;
4 "but we [a]will give ourselves continually to
prayer and to the ministry of the word."
5 And the saying pleased the whole multitude.
And they chose Stephen, [a]a man full of faith and
the Holy Spirit, and [b]Philip, Prochorus, Nicanor,
Timon, Parmenas, and [c]Nicolas, a proselyte from
Antioch,
6 whom they set before the apostles; and [a]when
they had prayed, [b]they laid hands on them.
7 Then [a]the word of God spread, and the number of the disciples multiplied greatly in Jerusalem, and a great many [b]of the priests were obedient to the faith.
**8** And Stephen, full of [1]faith and power, did
great [a]wonders and signs among the people.
9 Then there arose some from what is called the
Synagogue of the Freedmen (Cyrenians, Alexan-
drians, and those from Cilicia and Asia), disputing
with Stephen.
10 And [a]they were not able to resist the wisdom
and the Spirit by which he spoke.
11 [a]Then they secretly induced men to say, "We
have heard him speak blasphemous words against
Moses and God."
12 And they stirred up the people, the elders, and
the scribes; and they came upon *him,* seized him,
and brought *him* to the council.
13 They also set up false witnesses who said,
"This man does not cease to speak [1]blasphemous
words against this holy place and the law;
14 [a]"for we have heard him say that this Jesus of
Nazareth will destroy this place and change the
customs which Moses delivered to us."
15 And all who sat in the council, looking steadfastly at him, saw his face as the face of an angel.

### *The Trial and Death of Stephen*

**7** Then the high priest said, "Are these things so?"

2 And he said, [a]"Brethren and fathers, listen: The [b]God of glory appeared to our father Abraham when he was in Mesopotamia, before he dwelt in [c]Haran,

3 "and said to him, [a]*'Get out of your country and from your relatives, and come to a land that I will show you.'*

4 "Then [a]he came out of the land of the Chaldeans and dwelt in Haran. And from there, when his father was [b]dead, He moved him to this land in which you now dwell.

5 "And *God* gave him no inheritance in it, not even *enough* to set his foot on. But even when *Abraham* had no child, [a]He promised to give it to him for a possession, and to his descendants after him.

6 "But God spoke in this way: [a]that his descendants would dwell in a foreign land, and that they would bring them into [b]bondage and oppress *them* four hundred years.

7 [a]*'And the nation to whom they will be in bondage I will* [b]*judge,'* said God, [c]*'and after that they shall come out and serve Me in this place.'*

8 [a]"Then He gave him the covenant of circumcision; [b]and so *Abraham* begot Isaac and circumcised him on the eighth day; [c]and Isaac *begot* Jacob, and [d]Jacob *begot* the twelve patriarchs.

**9** [a]"And the patriarchs, becoming envious, [b]sold Joseph into Egypt. [c]But God was with him

10 "and delivered him out of all his troubles, [a]and gave him favor and wisdom in the presence of Pharaoh, king of Egypt; and he made him governor over Egypt and all his house.

11 [a]"Now a famine and great [1]trouble came over all the land of Egypt and Canaan, and our fathers found no sustenance.

12 [a]"But when Jacob heard that there was grain in Egypt, he sent out our fathers first.

13 "And the [a]second *time* Joseph was made known to his brothers, and Joseph's family became known to the Pharaoh.

14 [a]"Then Joseph sent and called his father Jacob and [b]all his relatives to *him,* [1]seventy-five people.

15 [a]"So Jacob went down to Egypt; [b]and he died, he and our fathers.

16 "And [a]they were carried back to Shechem and laid in [b]the tomb that Abraham bought for a sum of money from the sons of Hamor, *the father* of Shechem.

**17** "But when [a]the time of the promise drew near which God had sworn to Abraham, [b]the people grew and multiplied in Egypt

18 "till another king [a]arose who did not know Joseph.

19 "This man dealt treacherously with our people, and oppressed our forefathers, [a]making them expose their babies, so that they might not live.

20 [a]"At this time Moses was born, and [b]was well pleasing to God; and he was brought up in his father's house for three months.

21 "But [a]when he was set out, [b]Pharaoh's daughter took him away and brought him up as her own son.

22 "And Moses was learned in all the wisdom of the Egyptians, and was [a]mighty in words and deeds.

23 [a]"Now when he was forty years old, it came into his heart to visit his brethren, the children of Israel.

24 "And seeing one of *them* suffer wrong, he defended and avenged him who was oppressed, and struck down the Egyptian.

25 "For he supposed that his brethren would have understood that God would deliver them by his hand, but they did not understand.

26 "And the next day he appeared to two of them as they were fighting, and *tried to* reconcile them, saying, 'Men, you are brethren; why do you wrong one another?'

27 "But he who did his neighbor wrong pushed him away, saying, [a]*'Who made you a ruler and a judge over us?*

28 *'Do you want to kill me as you did the Egyptian yesterday?'*

29 [a]"Then, at this saying, Moses fled and became a dweller in the land of Midian, where he [b]had two sons.

30 [a]"And when forty years had passed, an Angel [1]of the Lord appeared to him in a flame of fire in a bush, in the wilderness of Mount Sinai.

31 "When Moses saw *it,* he marveled at the sight; and as he drew near to observe, the voice of the Lord came to him,

32 "*saying,* [a]*'I am the God of your fathers—the God of Abraham, the God of Isaac, and the God of Jacob.'* And Moses trembled and dared not look.

33 [a]*'Then the* LORD *said to him, "Take your sandals off your feet, for the place where you stand is holy ground.*

34 *"I have surely* [a]*seen the oppression of My people who are in Egypt; I have heard their groaning and have come down to deliver them. And now come, I will* [b]*send you to Egypt."'*

35 "This Moses whom they rejected, saying, [a]*'Who made you a ruler and a judge?'* is the one God sent *to be* a ruler and a deliverer [b]by the hand of the Angel who appeared to him in the bush.

36 [a]"He brought them out, after he had [b]shown wonders and signs in the land of Egypt, [c]and in the Red Sea, [d]and in the wilderness forty years.

**37** "This is that Moses who said to the children of Israel, [a]*'The* LORD *your God will raise up for you a Prophet like me from your brethren.* [b]*Him*[1] *you shall hear.'*

38 [a]"This is he who was in the [1]congregation in the wilderness with [b]the Angel who spoke to him on Mount Sinai, and *with* our fathers, [c]the one who received the living [d]oracles[2] to give to us,

39 "whom our fathers [a]would not obey, but rejected. And in their hearts they turned back to Egypt,

40 "saying to Aaron, [a]*'Make us gods to go before us; as for this Moses who brought us out of the land of Egypt, we do not know what has become of him.'*

41 [a]"And they made a calf in those days, offered sacrifices to the idol, and [b]rejoiced in the works of their own hands.

42 "Then [a]God turned and gave them up to worship [b]the host of heaven, as it is written in the book of the Prophets:

[c]*'Did you offer Me slaughtered animals and*
*sacrifices during forty years in the*
*wilderness,*
*O house of Israel?*

43 *You also took up the tabernacle of Moloch,*
*And the star of your god Remphan,*
*Images which you made to worship;*

CHAPTER 7
2 [a]Acts 22:1 [b]Ps. 29:3 [c]Gen. 11:31, 32
3 [a]Gen. 12:1
4 [a]Gen. 11:31; 15:17 [b]Gen. 11:32
5 [a]Gen. 12:7; 13:15; 15:3, 18; 17:8; 26:3
6 [a]Gen. 15:13, 14, 16; 47:11, 12 [b]Ex. 1:8–14; 12:40, 41
7 [a]Gen. 15:14 [b]Ex. 14:13–31 [c]Ex. 3:12
8 [a]Gen. 17:9–14 [b]Gen. 21:1–5 [c]Gen. 25:21–26 [d]Gen. 29:31—30:24; 35:18, 22–26
9 [a]Gen. 37:4, 11, 28 [b]Gen. 37:28 [c]Gen. 39:2, 21, 23
10 [a]Gen. 41:38–44
11 [a]Gen. 41:54; 42:5 [1]*affliction*
12 [a]Gen. 42:1, 2
13 [a]Gen. 45:4, 16
14 [a]Gen. 45:9, 27 [b]Deut. 10:22 [1]Or *seventy,* Ex. 1:5
15 [a]Gen. 46:1–7 [b]Gen. 49:33
16 [a]Josh. 24:32 [b]Gen. 23:16
17 [a]Gen. 15:13 [b]Ex. 1:7–9
18 [a]Ex. 1:8
19 [a]Ex. 1:22
20 [a]Ex. 2:1, 2 [b]Heb. 11:23
21 [a]Ex. 2:3, 4 [b]Ex. 2:5–10
22 [a]Luke 24:19
23 [a]Ex. 2:11, 12
27 [a]Ex. 2:14
29 [a]Heb. 11:27 [b]Ex. 2:15, 21, 22; 4:20; 18:3
30 [a]Ex. 3:1–10 [1]NU omits *of the Lord*
32 [a]Ex. 3:6, 15
33 [a]Ex. 3:5, 7, 8, 10
34 [a]Ex. 2:24, 25 [b]Ps. 105:26
35 [a]Ex. 2:14 [b]Ex. 14:21
36 [a]Ex. 12:41; 33:1 [b]Ps. 105:27 [c]Ex. 14:21 [d]Ex. 16:1, 35
37 [a]Deut. 18:15, 18, 19 [b]Matt. 17:5 [1]NU, M omit *Him you shall hear*
38 [a]Ex. 19:3 [b]Gal. 3:19 [c]Deut. 5:27 [d]Heb. 5:12 [1]Gr. *ekklesia, assembly* or *church* [2]*sayings*
39 [a]Ps. 95:8–11
40 [a]Ex. 32:1, 23
41 [a]Deut. 9:16 [b]Ex. 32:6, 18, 19
42 [a][2 Thess. 2:11] [b]2 Kin. 21:3 [c]Amos 5:25–27

*And [a]I will carry you away beyond Babylon.'*

**44** "Our fathers had the tabernacle of witness in
the wilderness, as He appointed, instructing Moses [a]to make it according to the pattern that he
had seen,
45 [a]"which our fathers, having received it in turn,
also brought with Joshua into the land possessed
by the Gentiles, [b]whom God drove out before the
face of our fathers until the [c]days of David,
46 [a]"who found favor before God and [b]asked to
find a dwelling for the God of Jacob.
47 [a]"But Solomon built Him a house.
48 "However, [a]the Most High does not dwell in
temples made with hands, as the prophet says:

49 *'Heaven[a] is My throne,*
*And earth is My footstool.*
*What house will you build for Me? says the*
*LORD,*
*Or what is the place of My rest?*
50 *Has My hand not [a]made all these things?'*

**51** "*You* [a]stiff-necked[1] and [b]uncircumcised in
heart and ears! You always resist the Holy Spirit;
as your fathers *did*, so *do* you.
52 [a]"Which of the prophets did your fathers not
persecute? And they killed those who foretold
the coming of [b]the Just One, of whom you now
have become the betrayers and murderers,
53 [a]"who have received the law by the direction
of angels and have not kept *it*."
**54** [a]When they heard these things they were [1]cut
to the heart, and they gnashed at him with *their*
teeth.
55 But he, [a]being full of the Holy Spirit, gazed
into heaven and saw the [b]glory of God, and Jesus
standing at the right hand of God,
56 and said, "Look! [a]I see the heavens opened
and the [b]Son of Man standing at the right hand of
God!"
57 Then they cried out with a loud voice, stopped
their ears, and ran at him with one accord;
58 and they cast *him* out of the city and stoned
*him*. And [a]the witnesses laid down their clothes at
the feet of a young man named Saul.
59 And they stoned Stephen as he was calling on
*God* and saying, "Lord Jesus, [a]receive my spirit."
60 Then he knelt down and cried out with a loud
voice, [a]"Lord, do not charge them with this sin."
And when he had said this, he fell asleep.

## *Philip and the Ethiopian Eunuch*

**8** Now Saul was consenting to his death. At that
time a great persecution arose against the
church which was at Jerusalem; and [a]they were
all scattered throughout the regions of Judea and
Samaria, except the apostles.
2 And devout men carried Stephen *to his burial*,
and [a]made great lamentation over him.
3 As for Saul, [a]he made havoc of the church,
entering every house, and dragging off men and
women, committing *them* to prison.
**4** Therefore [a]those who were scattered went
everywhere preaching the word.
5 Then [a]Philip went down to [1]the city of Samaria and preached Christ to them.
6 And the multitudes with one accord heeded
the things spoken by Philip, hearing and seeing
the miracles which he did.
7 For [a]unclean spirits, crying with a loud voice,
came out of many who were possessed; and many
who were paralyzed and lame were healed.
8 And there was great joy in that city.
**9** But there was a certain man called Simon,
who previously [a]practiced [1]sorcery in the city and
[b]astonished the [2]people of Samaria, claiming that
he was someone great,
10 to whom they all gave heed, from the least to
the greatest, saying, "This man is the great power
of God."
11 And they heeded him because he had astonished them with his [1]sorceries for a long time.
12 But when they believed Philip as he preached
the things [a]concerning the kingdom of God and
the name of Jesus Christ, both men and women
were baptized.
13 Then Simon himself also believed; and when
he was baptized he continued with Philip, and was
amazed, seeing the miracles and signs which were
done.
**14** Now when the [a]apostles who were at Jerusalem heard that Samaria had received the word of
God, they sent Peter and John to them,
15 who, when they had come down, prayed for
them [a]that they might receive the Holy Spirit.
16 For [a]as yet He had fallen upon none of them.
[b]They had only been baptized in [c]the name of the
Lord Jesus.
17 Then [a]they laid hands on them, and they
received the Holy Spirit.
18 And when Simon saw that through the laying
on of the apostles' hands the Holy Spirit was
given, he offered them money,
19 saying, "Give me this power also, that anyone
on whom I lay hands may receive the Holy Spirit."
20 But Peter said to him, "Your money perish
with you, because [a]you thought that [b]the gift of
God could be purchased with money!
21 "You have neither part nor portion in this
matter, for your [a]heart is not right in the sight of
God.
22 "Repent therefore of this your wickedness,
and pray God [a]if perhaps the thought of your
heart may be forgiven you.
23 "For I see that you are [a]poisoned by bitterness
and bound by iniquity."
24 Then Simon answered and said, [a]"Pray to the
Lord for me, that none of the things which you
have spoken may come upon me."
25 So when they had testified and preached the
word of the Lord, they returned to Jerusalem,
preaching the gospel in many villages of the
Samaritans.
**26** Now an angel of the Lord spoke to [a]Philip,
saying, "Arise and go toward the south along the
road which goes down from Jerusalem to Gaza."
This is [1]desert.
27 So he arose and went. And behold, [a]a man of
Ethiopia, a eunuch of great authority under Can-
dace the queen of the Ethiopians, who had charge
of all her treasury, and [b]had come to Jerusalem to
worship,
28 was returning. And sitting in his chariot, he
was reading Isaiah the prophet.
29 Then the Spirit said to Philip, "Go near and
overtake this chariot."
30 So Philip ran to him, and heard him reading
the prophet Isaiah, and said, "Do you understand
what you are reading?"
31 And he said, "How can I, unless someone

43 [a]Jer. 25:9–12
44 [a][Heb. 8:5]
45 [a]Josh. 3:14; 18:1; 23:9 [b]Ps. 44:2 [c]2 Sam. 6:2–15
46 [a]2 Sam. 7:1–13 [b]1 Chr. 22:7
47 [a]1 Kin. 6:1–38; 8:20, 21
48 [a]1 Kin. 8:27
49 [a]Is. 66:1, 2
50 [a]Ps. 102:25
51 [a]Ex. 32:9 [b]Lev. 26:41 [1]*stubborn*
52 [a]2 Chr. 36:16 [b]Acts 3:14; 22:14
53 [a]Ex. 20:1
54 [a]Acts 5:33 [1]*furious*
55 [a]Acts 6:5 [b][Ex. 24:17]
56 [a]Matt. 3:16 [b]Dan. 7:13
58 [a]Acts 22:20
59 [a]Ps. 31:5
60 [a]Matt. 5:44

CHAPTER 8
1 [a]Acts 8:4; 11:19
2 [a]Gen. 23:2
3 [a]Phil. 3:6
4 [a]Matt. 10:23
5 [a]Acts 6:5; 8:26, 30 [1]Or *a*
7 [a]Mark 16:17
9 [a]Acts 8:11; 13:6 [b]Acts 5:36 [1]*magic* [2]Or *nation*
11 [1]*magic arts*
12 [a]Acts 1:3; 8:4
14 [a]Acts 5:12, 29, 40
15 [a]Acts 2:38; 19:2
16 [a]Acts 19:2 [b]Matt. 28:19 [c]Acts 10:48; 19:5
17 [a]Acts 6:6; 19:6
20 [a][Matt. 10:8] [b][Acts 2:38; 10:45; 11:17]
21 [a]Jer. 17:9
22 [a]2 Tim. 2:25
23 [a]Heb. 12:15
24 [a]James 5:16
26 [a]Acts 6:5 [1]Or *a deserted place*
27 [a]Ps. 68:31; 87:4 [b]John 12:20

guides me?" And he asked Philip to come up and
sit with him.
32 The place in the Scripture which he read was
this:

*[a]"He was led as a sheep to the slaughter;*
*And as a lamb is silent before its shearer,*
*[b]So He opened not His mouth.*
33 *In His humiliation His [a]justice was taken*
*away.*
*And who will declare His generation?*
*For His life is [b]taken from the earth."*

34 So the eunuch answered Philip and said, "I
ask you, of whom does the prophet say this, of
himself or of some other man?"
35 Then Philip opened his mouth, [a]and beginning
at this Scripture, preached Jesus to him.
36 Now as they went down the road, they came
to some water. And the eunuch said, "See, *here is*
water. [a]What hinders me from being baptized?"
37 [1]Then Philip said, [a]"If you believe with all your
heart, you may." And he answered and said, [b]"I
believe that Jesus Christ is the Son of God."
38 So he commanded the chariot to stand still.
And both Philip and the eunuch went down into
the water, and he baptized him.
39 Now when they came up out of the water, [a]the
Spirit of the Lord caught Philip away, so that the
eunuch saw him no more; and he went on his way
rejoicing.
40 But Philip was found at [1]Azotus. And passing
through, he preached in all the cities till he came
to [a]Caesarea.

## *Saul's Conversion and Preaching*

**9** Then [a]Saul, still breathing threats and murder
against the disciples of the Lord, went to the
high priest
2 and asked [a]letters from him to the synagogues
of Damascus, so that if he found any who were of
the Way, whether men or women, he might bring
them bound to Jerusalem.
3 [a]As he journeyed he came near Damascus, and
suddenly a light shone around him from heaven.
4 Then he fell to the ground, and heard a voice
saying to him, "Saul, Saul, [a]why are you persecuting Me?"
5 And he said, "Who are You, Lord?" Then the
Lord said, "I am Jesus, whom you are persecuting.
[1]*It is* hard for you to kick against the goads."
6 So he, trembling and astonished, said, "Lord,
what do You want me to do?" Then the Lord *said*
to him, "Arise and go into the city, and you will be
told what you must do."
7 And [a]the men who journeyed with him stood
speechless, hearing a voice but seeing no one.
8 Then Saul arose from the ground, and when
his eyes were opened he saw no one. But they led
him by the hand and brought *him* into Damascus.
9 And he was three days without sight, and
neither ate nor drank.
**10** Now there was a certain disciple at Damascus
[a]named Ananias; and to him the Lord said in a
vision, "Ananias." And he said, "Here I am, Lord."
11 So the Lord *said* to him, "Arise and go to the
street called Straight, and inquire at the house of
Judas for *one* called Saul [a]of Tarsus, for behold, he
is praying.
12 "And in a vision he has seen a man named
Ananias coming in and putting *his* hand on him,
so that he might receive his sight."
13 Then Ananias answered, "Lord, I have heard
from many about this man, [a]how much [1]harm he
has done to Your saints in Jerusalem.
14 "And here he has authority from the chief
priests to bind all [a]who call on Your name."
15 But the Lord said to him, "Go, for [a]he is a
chosen vessel of Mine to bear My name before
[b]Gentiles, [c]kings, and the [d]children[1] of Israel.
16 "For [a]I will show him how many things he
must suffer for My [b]name's sake."
17 [a]And Ananias went his way and entered the
house; and [b]laying his hands on him he said,
"Brother Saul, the Lord [1]Jesus, who appeared to
you on the road as you came, has sent me that
you may receive your sight and [c]be filled with the
Holy Spirit."
18 Immediately there fell from his eyes *something* like scales, and he received his sight at once;
and he arose and was baptized.
19 So when he had received food, he was
strengthened. [a]Then Saul spent some days with
the disciples at Damascus.
**20** Immediately he preached [1]the Christ in the
synagogues, that He is the Son of God.
21 Then all who heard were amazed, and said,
[a]"Is this not he who destroyed those who called
on this name in Jerusalem, and has come here for
that purpose, so that he might bring them bound
to the chief priests?"
22 But Saul increased all the more in strength,
[a]and confounded the Jews who dwelt in Damascus, proving that this *Jesus* is the Christ.
**23** Now after many days were past, [a]the Jews
plotted to kill him.
24 [a]But their plot became known to Saul. And
they watched the gates day and night, to kill him.
25 Then the disciples took him by night and [a]let
*him* down through the wall in a large basket.
**26** And [a]when Saul had come to Jerusalem, he
tried to join the disciples; but they were all afraid
of him, and did not believe that he was a disciple.
27 [a]But Barnabas took him and brought *him* to
the apostles. And he declared to them how he had
seen the Lord on the road, and that He had
spoken to him, [b]and how he had preached boldly
at Damascus in the name of Jesus.
28 So [a]he was with them at Jerusalem, coming in
and going out.
29 And he spoke boldly in the name of the Lord
Jesus and disputed against the [a]Hellenists,[1] [b]but
they attempted to kill him.
30 When the brethren found out, they brought
him down to Caesarea and sent him out to Tarsus.
**31** [a]Then the [1]churches throughout all Judea,
Galilee, and Samaria had peace and were [b]edified.[2]
And walking in the [c]fear of the Lord and in the
[d]comfort of the Holy Spirit, they were [e]multiplied.
**32** Now it came to pass, as Peter went [a]through
all *parts of the country,* that he also came down to
the saints who dwelt in Lydda.
33 There he found a certain man named Aeneas,
who had been bedridden eight years and was
paralyzed.
34 And Peter said to him, "Aeneas, [a]Jesus the
Christ heals you. Arise and make your bed." Then
he arose immediately.
35 So all who dwelt at Lydda and [a]Sharon saw
him and [b]turned to the Lord.
**36** At Joppa there was a certain disciple named

**32** [a]Is. 53:7, 8 [b]John 19:9
**33** [a]Luke 23:1–25 [b]Luke 23:33–46
**35** [a]Luke 24:27
**36** [a]Acts 10:47; 16:33
**37** [a][Mark 16:16] [b]Matt. 16:16 [1]NU, M omit v. 37. It is found in Western texts, including the Latin tradition.
**39** [a]Ezek. 3:12, 14
**40** [a]Acts 21:8 [1]Same as Heb. *Ashdod*

CHAPTER 9
**1** [a]Acts 7:57; 8:1, 3; 26:10, 11
**2** [a]Acts 22:5
**3** [a]1 Cor. 15:8
**4** [a][Matt. 25:40]
**5** [1]NU, M omit the rest of v. 5 and begin v. 6 with *But arise and go*
**7** [a][Acts 22:9; 26:13]
**10** [a]Acts 22:12
**11** [a]Acts 21:39; 22:3
**13** [a]Acts 9:1 [1]*bad things*
**14** [a]Acts 7:59; 9:2, 21
**15** [a]Eph. 3:7, 8 [b]Rom. 1:5; 11:13 [c]Acts 25:22, 23; 26:1 [d]Rom. 1:16; 9:1–5 [1]Lit. *sons*
**16** [a]Acts 20:23 [b]2 Cor. 4:11
**17** [a]Acts 22:12, 13 [b]Acts 8:17 [c]Acts 2:4; 4:31; 8:17; 13:52 [1]M omits *Jesus*
**19** [a]Acts 26:20
**20** [1]NU *Jesus*
**21** [a]Gal. 1:13, 23
**22** [a]Acts 18:28
**23** [a]2 Cor. 11:26
**24** [a]2 Cor. 11:32
**25** [a]Josh. 2:15
**26** [a]Acts 22:17–20; 26:20
**27** [a]Acts 4:36; 13:2 [b]Acts 9:20, 22
**28** [a]Gal. 1:18
**29** [a]Acts 6:1; 11:20 [b]2 Cor. 11:26 [1]Greek-speaking Jews
**31** [a]Acts 5:11; 8:1; 16:5 [b][Eph. 4:16, 29] [c]Ps. 34:9 [d]John 14:16 [e]Acts 16:5 [1]NU *church . . . was* [2]*built up*
**32** [a]Acts 8:14
**34** [a][Acts 3:6, 16; 4:10]
**35** [a]1 Chr. 5:16; 27:29 [b]Acts 11:21; 15:19

[1]Tabitha, which is translated [2]Dorcas. This woman
was full [a]of good works and charitable deeds
which she did.
37 But it happened in those days that she became
sick and died. When they had washed her, they
laid *her* in [a]an upper room.
38 And since Lydda was near Joppa, and the
disciples had heard that Peter was there, they sent
two men to him, imploring *him* not to delay in
coming to them.
39 Then Peter arose and went with them. When
he had come, they brought *him* to the upper room.
And all the widows stood by him weeping, showing the tunics and garments which Dorcas had
made while she was with them.
40 But Peter [a]put them all out, and [b]knelt down
and prayed. And turning to the body he [c]said,
"Tabitha, arise." And she opened her eyes, and
when she saw Peter she sat up.
41 Then he gave her *his* hand and lifted her up;
and when he had called the saints and widows, he
presented her alive.
42 And it became known throughout all Joppa,
[a]and many believed on the Lord.
43 So it was that he stayed many days in Joppa
with [a]Simon, a tanner.

### *No Distinction Between Jew and Greek*

**10** There was a certain man in [a]Caesarea called
Cornelius, a centurion of what was called
the Italian [1]Regiment,
2 [a]a devout *man* and one who [b]feared God with
all his household, who gave [1]alms generously to
the people, and prayed to God always.
3 About [1]the ninth hour of the day [a]he saw
clearly in a vision an angel of God coming in and
saying to him, "Cornelius!"
4 And when he observed him, he was afraid, and
said, "What is it, lord?" So he said to him, "Your
prayers and your alms have come up for a memorial before God.
5 "Now [a]send men to Joppa, and send for Simon
whose surname is Peter.
6 "He is lodging with [a]Simon, a tanner, whose
house is by the sea. [b]He[1] will tell you what you
must do."
7 And when the angel who spoke to him had
departed, Cornelius called two of his household
servants and a devout soldier from among those
who waited on him continually.
8 So when he had explained all *these* things to
them, he sent them to Joppa.
**9** The next day, as they went on their journey
and drew near the city, [a]Peter went up on the
housetop to pray, about [1]the sixth hour.
10 Then he became very hungry and wanted to
eat; but while they made ready, he fell into a
trance
11 and [a]saw heaven opened and an object like a
great sheet bound at the four corners, descending
to him and let down to the earth.
12 In it were all kinds of four-footed animals of
the earth, wild beasts, creeping things, and birds
of the air.
13 And a voice came to him, "Rise, Peter; kill and
eat."
14 But Peter said, "Not so, Lord! [a]For I have
never eaten anything common or unclean."
15 And a voice *spoke* to him again the second
time, [a]"What God has [1]cleansed you must not call
common."
16 This was done three times. And the object was
taken up into heaven again.
**17** Now while Peter [1]wondered within himself
what this vision which he had seen meant, behold,
the men who had been sent from Cornelius had
made inquiry for Simon's house, and stood before
the gate.
18 And they called and asked whether Simon,
whose surname was Peter, was lodging there.
19 While Peter thought about the vision, [a]the
Spirit said to him, "Behold, three men are seeking
you.
20 [a]"Arise therefore, go down and go with them,
doubting nothing; for I have sent them."
21 Then Peter went down to the men [1]who had
been sent to him from Cornelius, and said, "Yes, I
am he whom you seek. For what reason have you
come?"
22 And they said, "Cornelius *the* centurion, a just
man, one who fears God and [a]has a good reputation among all the nation of the Jews, was divinely instructed by a holy angel to summon you
to his house, and to hear words from you."
23 Then he invited them in and lodged *them.* On
the next day Peter went away with them, [a]and
some brethren from Joppa accompanied him.
**24** And the following day they entered Caesarea.
Now Cornelius was waiting for them, and had
called together his relatives and close friends.
25 As Peter was coming in, Cornelius met him
and fell down at his feet and worshiped *him.*
26 But Peter lifted him up, saying, [a]"Stand up; I
myself am also a man."
27 And as he talked with him, he went in and
found many who had come together.
28 Then he said to them, "You know how [a]un-
lawful it is for a Jewish man to keep company
with or go to one of another nation. But [b]God has
shown me that I should not call any man common
or unclean.
29 "Therefore I came without objection as soon
as I was sent for. I ask, then, for what reason have
you sent for me?"
30 So Cornelius said, [1]"Four days ago I was
fasting until this hour; and at the ninth hour I
prayed in my house, and behold, [a]a man stood
before me [b]in bright clothing,
31 "and said, 'Cornelius, [a]your prayer has been
heard, and [b]your [1]alms are remembered in the
sight of God.
32 'Send therefore to Joppa and call Simon here,
whose surname is Peter. He is lodging in the
house of Simon, a tanner, by the sea. [1]When he
comes, he will speak to you.'
33 "So I sent to you immediately, and you have
done well to come. Now therefore, we are all
present before God, to hear all the things commanded you by God."
**34** Then Peter opened *his* mouth and said: [a]"In
truth I perceive that God shows no partiality.
35 "But [a]in every nation whoever fears Him and
works righteousness is [b]accepted by Him.
36 "The word which *God* sent to the [1]children of
Israel, [a]preaching peace through Jesus Christ—
[b]He is Lord of all—
37 "that word you know, which was proclaimed
throughout all Judea, and [a]began from Galilee
after the baptism which John preached:
38 "how [a]God anointed Jesus of Nazareth with
the Holy Spirit and with power, who [b]went about

36 [a]1 Tim. 2:10 [1]Lit., in Aram., *Gazelle* [2]Lit., in Gr., *Gazelle*
37 [a]Acts 1:13; 9:39
40 [a]Matt. 9:25 [b]Acts 7:60 [c]Mark 5:41, 42
42 [a]John 11:45
43 [a]Acts 10:6

CHAPTER 10
1 [a]Acts 8:40; 23:23 [1]*Cohort*
2 [a]Acts 8:2; 9:22; 22:12 [b][Acts 10:22, 35; 13:16, 26] [1]*charitable gifts*
3 [a]Acts 10:30; 11:13 [1]3 P.M.
5 [a]Acts 11:13, 14
6 [a]Acts 9:43 [b]Acts 11:14 [1]NU, M omit the rest of v. 6.
9 [a]Acts 10:9–32; 11:5–14 [1]Noon
11 [a]Acts 7:56
14 [a]Deut. 14:3, 7
15 [a][Rom. 14:14] [1]Declared clean
17 [1]*was perplexed*
19 [a]Acts 11:12
20 [a]Acts 15:7–9
21 [1]NU, M omit *who had been sent to him from Cornelius*
22 [a]Acts 22:12
23 [a]Acts 10:45; 11:12
26 [a]Acts 14:14, 15
28 [a]John 4:9; 18:28 [b][Acts 10:14, 35; 15:8, 9]
30 [a]Acts 1:10 [b]Matt. 28:3 [1]NU *Four days ago to this hour, at the ninth hour*
31 [a]Dan. 10:12 [b]Heb. 6:10 [1]*charitable gifts*
32 [1]NU omits the rest of v. 32.
34 [a]Deut. 10:17
35 [a][Eph. 2:13] [b]Ps. 15:1, 2
36 [a]Is. 57:19 [b]Rom. 10:12 [1]Lit. *sons*
37 [a]Luke 4:14
38 [a]Luke 4:18 [b]Matt. 4:23

doing good and healing all who were oppressed by
the devil, [c]for God was with Him.
39 "And we are [a]witnesses of all things which He
did both in the land of the Jews and in Jerusalem,
whom [1]they [b]killed by hanging on a tree.
40 "Him [a]God raised up on the third day, and
showed Him openly,
41 [a]"not to all the people, but to witnesses chosen
before by God, *even* to us [b]who ate and drank
with Him after He arose from the dead.
42 "And [a]He commanded us to preach to the
people, and to testify [b]that it is He who was
ordained by God *to be* Judge [c]of the living and the
dead.
43 [a]"To Him all the prophets witness that,
through His name, [b]whoever believes in Him will
receive [c]remission[1] of sins."
**44** While Peter was still speaking these words,
[a]the Holy Spirit fell upon all those who heard the
word.
45 [a]And [1]those of the circumcision who believed
were astonished, as many as came with Peter,
[b]because the gift of the Holy Spirit had been
poured out on the Gentiles also.
46 For they heard them speak with tongues and
magnify God. Then Peter answered,
47 "Can anyone forbid water, that these should
not be baptized who have received the Holy Spirit
[a]just as we *have?*"
48 [a]And he commanded them to be baptized [b]in
the name of the Lord. Then they asked him to stay
a few days.

### *Peter Defends God's Grace*

**11** Now the apostles and brethren who were in
Judea heard that the Gentiles had also
received the word of God.
2 And when Peter came up to Jerusalem, [a]those
of the circumcision contended with him,
3 saying, [a]"You went in to uncircumcised men
[b]and ate with them!"
4 But Peter explained *it* to them [a]in order from
the beginning, saying:
5 [a]"I was in the city of Joppa praying; and in a
trance I saw a vision, an object descending like a
great sheet, let down from heaven by four corners; and it came to me.
6 "When I observed it intently and considered, I
saw four-footed animals of the earth, wild beasts,
creeping things, and birds of the air.
7 "And I heard a voice saying to me, 'Rise,
Peter; kill and eat.'
8 "But I said, 'Not so, Lord! For nothing common or unclean has at any time entered my
mouth.'
9 "But the voice answered me again from
heaven, 'What God has cleansed you must not call
common.'
10 "Now this was done three times, and all were
drawn up again into heaven.
11 "At that very moment, three men stood before
the house where I was, having been sent to me
from Caesarea.
12 "Then [a]the Spirit told me to go with them,
doubting nothing. Moreover [b]these six brethren
accompanied me, and we entered the man's
house.
13 [a]"And he told us how he had seen an angel
standing in his house, who said to him, 'Send men
to Joppa, and call for Simon whose surname is
Peter,
14 'who will tell you words by which you and all
your household will be saved.'
15 "And as I began to speak, the Holy Spirit fell
upon them, [a]as upon us at the beginning.
16 "Then I remembered the word of the Lord,
how He said, [a]'John indeed baptized with water,
but [b]you shall be baptized with the Holy Spirit.'
17 [a]"If therefore God gave them the same gift as
*He gave* us when we believed on the Lord Jesus
Christ, [b]who was I that I could withstand God?"
18 When they heard these things they became
silent; and they glorified God, saying, [a]"Then God
has also granted to the Gentiles repentance to
life."
**19** [a]Now those who were scattered after the
persecution that arose over Stephen traveled as
far as Phoenicia, Cyprus, and Antioch, preaching
the word to no one but the Jews only.
20 But some of them were men from Cyprus and
Cyrene, who, when they had come to Antioch,
spoke to [a]the Hellenists, preaching the Lord Jesus.
21 And [a]the hand of the Lord was with them, and
a great number believed and [b]turned to the Lord.
22 Then news of these things came to the ears of
the church in Jerusalem, and they sent out [a]Bar-
nabas to go as far as Antioch.
23 When he came and had seen the grace of God,
he was glad, and [a]encouraged them all that with
purpose of heart they should continue with the
Lord.
24 For he was a good man, [a]full of the Holy Spirit
and of faith. [b]And a great many people were added
to the Lord.
25 Then Barnabas departed for [a]Tarsus to seek
Saul.
26 And when he had found him, he brought him
to Antioch. So it was that for a whole year they
assembled with the church and taught a great
many people. And the disciples were first called
Christians in Antioch.
**27** And in these days [a]prophets came from Jerusalem to Antioch.
28 Then one of them, named [a]Agabus, stood up
and showed by the Spirit that there was going to
be a great famine throughout all the world, which
also happened in the days of [b]Claudius Caesar.
29 Then the disciples, each according to his
ability, determined to send [a]relief to the brethren
dwelling in Judea.
30 [a]This they also did, and sent it to the elders by
the hands of Barnabas and Saul.

### *Herod Kills James and Imprisons Peter*

**12** Now about that time Herod the king
stretched out *his* hand to harass some from
the church.
2 Then he killed James [a]the brother of John
with the sword.
3 And because he saw that it pleased the Jews,
he proceeded further to seize Peter also. Now it
was *during* [a]the Days of Unleavened Bread.
4 So [a]when he had arrested him, he put *him* in
prison, and delivered *him* to four [1]squads of soldiers to keep him, intending to bring him before
the people after Passover.
**5** Peter was therefore kept in prison, but [1]con-
stant prayer was offered to God for him by the
church.
6 And when Herod was about to bring him out,
that night Peter was sleeping, bound with two

**38** [c]John 3:2; 8:29
**39** [a]Acts 1:8 [b]Acts 2:23 [1]NU, M *they also*
**40** [a]Acts 2:24
**41** [a][John 14:17, 19, 22; 15:27] [b]Luke 24:30, 41–43
**42** [a]Matt. 28:19 [b]John 5:22, 27 [c]1 Pet. 4:5
**43** [a]Zech. 13:1 [b]Gal. 3:22 [c]Acts 13:38, 39 [1]*forgiveness*
**44** [a]Acts 4:31
**45** [a]Acts 10:23 [b]Acts 11:18 [1]The Jews
**47** [a]Acts 2:4; 10:44; 11:17; 15:8
**48** [a]1 Cor. 1:14–17 [b]Acts 2:38; 8:16; 19:5

CHAPTER 11
**2** [a]Acts 10:45
**3** [a]Acts 10:28 [b]Gal. 2:12
**4** [a]Luke 1:3
**5** [a]Acts 10:9
**12** [a][John 16:13] [b]Acts 10:23
**13** [a]Acts 10:30
**15** [a]Acts 2:1–4; 15:7–9
**16** [a]John 1:26, 33 [b]Is. 44:3
**17** [a][Acts 15:8, 9] [b]Acts 10:47
**18** [a]Rom. 10:12, 13; 15:9, 16
**19** [a]Acts 8:1, 4
**20** [a]Acts 6:1; 9:29
**21** [a]Luke 1:66 [b]Acts 9:35; 14:1
**22** [a]Acts 4:36; 9:27
**23** [a]Acts 13:43; 14:22
**24** [a]Acts 6:5 [b]Acts 5:14; 11:21
**25** [a]Acts 9:11, 30
**27** [a]1 Cor. 12:28
**28** [a]Acts 21:10 [b]Acts 18:2
**29** [a]1 Cor. 16:1
**30** [a]Acts 12:25

CHAPTER 12
**2** [a]Matt. 4:21; 20:23
**3** [a]Ex. 12:15; 23:15
**4** [a]John 21:18 [1]Gr. *tetrads, squads of four*
**5** [1]NU *constantly* or *earnestly*

chains between two soldiers; and the guards
before the door were [1]keeping the prison.
7 Now behold, [a]an angel of the Lord stood by
*him,* and a light shone in the prison; and he struck
Peter on the side and raised him up, saying, "Arise
quickly!" And his chains fell off *his* hands.
8 Then the angel said to him, "Gird yourself and
tie on your sandals"; and so he did. And he said to
him, "Put on your garment and follow me."
9 So he went out and followed him, and [a]did not
know that what was done by the angel was real,
but thought [b]he was seeing a vision.
10 When they were past the first and the second
guard posts, they came to the iron gate that leads
to the city, [a]which opened to them of its own
accord; and they went out and went down one
street, and immediately the angel departed from
him.
11 And when Peter had come to himself, he said,
"Now I know for certain that [a]the Lord has sent
His angel, and [b]has delivered me from the hand of
Herod and *from* all the expectation of the Jewish
people."
12 So, when he had considered *this,* [a]he came to
the house of Mary, the mother of [b]John whose
surname was Mark, where many were gathered
together [c]praying.
13 And as Peter knocked at the door of the gate,
a girl named Rhoda came to answer.
14 When she recognized Peter's voice, because of
*her* gladness she did not open the gate, but ran in
and announced that Peter stood before the gate.
15 But they said to her, "You are beside yourself!" Yet she kept insisting that it was so. So they
said, [a]"It is his angel."
16 Now Peter continued knocking; and when
they opened *the door* and saw him, they were
astonished.
17 But [a]motioning to them with his hand to keep
silent, he declared to them how the Lord had
brought him out of the prison. And he said, "Go,
tell these things to James and to the brethren."
And he departed and went to another place.
18 Then, as soon as it was day, there was no
small [1]stir among the soldiers about what had
become of Peter.
19 But when Herod had searched for him and not
found him, he examined the guards and commanded that *they* should be put to death. And he
went down from Judea to Caesarea, and stayed
*there.*
**20** Now Herod had been very angry with the
people of [a]Tyre and Sidon; but they came to him
with one accord, and having made Blastus [1]the
king's personal aide their friend, they asked for
peace, because [b]their country was [2]supplied with
food by the king's *country.*
21 So on a set day Herod, arrayed in royal apparel, sat on his throne and gave an oration to
them.
22 And the people kept shouting, "The voice of a
god and not of a man!"
23 Then immediately an angel of the Lord [a]struck
him, because [b]he did not give glory to God. And he
was eaten by worms and [1]died.
24 But [a]the word of God grew and multiplied.
**25** And [a]Barnabas and Saul returned [1]from Jerusalem when they had [b]fulfilled *their* ministry, and
they also [c]took with them [d]John whose surname
was Mark.

## *Paul and Barnabas Are Sent to the Gentiles*

**13** Now [a]in the church that was at Antioch
there were certain prophets and teachers:
[b]Barnabas, Simeon who was called Niger, [c]Lucius
of Cyrene, Manaen who had been brought up with
Herod the tetrarch, and Saul.
2 As they ministered to the Lord and fasted, the
Holy Spirit said, [a]"Now separate to Me Barnabas
and Saul for the work [b]to which I have called
them."
3 Then, [a]having fasted and prayed, and laid
hands on them, they sent *them* away.
**4** So, being sent out by the Holy Spirit, they
went down to Seleucia, and from there they sailed
to [a]Cyprus.
5 And when they arrived in Salamis, [a]they
preached the word of God in the synagogues of
the Jews. They also had [b]John as *their* assistant.
6 Now when they had gone through [1]the island
to Paphos, they found [a]a certain sorcerer, a false
prophet, a Jew whose name *was* Bar-Jesus,
7 who was with the proconsul, Sergius Paulus,
an intelligent man. This man called for Barnabas
and Saul and sought to hear the word of God.
8 But [a]Elymas the sorcerer (for so his name is
translated) [1]withstood them, seeking to turn the
proconsul away from the faith.
9 Then Saul, who also *is called* Paul, [a]filled with
the Holy Spirit, looked intently at him
10 and said, "O full of all deceit and all fraud,
[a]*you* son of the devil, *you* enemy of all righteousness, will you not cease perverting the straight
ways of the Lord?
11 "And now, indeed, [a]the hand of the Lord *is*
upon you, and you shall be blind, not seeing the
sun for a time." And immediately a dark mist fell
on him, and he went around seeking someone to
lead him by the hand.
12 Then the proconsul believed, when he saw
what had been done, being astonished at the
teaching of the Lord.
**13** Now when Paul and his party set sail from
Paphos, they came to Perga in Pamphylia; and
[a]John, departing from them, returned to Jerusalem.
14 But when they departed from Perga, they
came to Antioch in Pisidia, and [a]went into the
synagogue on the Sabbath day and sat down.
15 And [a]after the reading of the Law and the
Prophets, the rulers of the synagogue sent to
them, saying, "Men *and* brethren, if you have [b]any
word of [1]exhortation for the people, say on."
16 Then Paul stood up, and motioning with *his*
hand said, "Men of Israel, and [a]you who fear God,
listen:
17 "The God of this people [1]Israel [a]chose our
fathers, and exalted the people [b]when they dwelt
as strangers in the land of Egypt, and with [2]an
uplifted arm He [c]brought them out of it.
18 "Now [a]for a time of about forty years He put
up with their ways in the wilderness.
19 "And when He had destroyed [a]seven nations
in the land of Canaan, [b]He distributed their land to
them by allotment.
20 "After that [a]He gave *them* judges for about
four hundred and fifty years, [b]until Samuel the
prophet.
21 [a]"And afterward they asked for a king; so God
gave them [b]Saul the son of Kish, a man of the
tribe of Benjamin, for forty years.

**6** [1]*guarding*
**7** [a]Acts 5:19
**9** [a]Ps. 126:1 [b]Acts 10:3, 17; 11:5
**10** [a]Acts 5:19; 16:26
**11** [a][Ps. 34:7] [b]Job 5:19
**12** [a]Acts 4:23 [b]Acts 13:5, 13; 15:37 [c]Acts 12:5
**15** [a][Matt. 18:10]
**17** [a]Acts 13:16; 19:33; 21:40
**18** [1]*disturbance*
**20** [a]Matt. 11:21 [b]Ezek. 27:17 [1]*who was in charge of the king's bedchamber* [2]Lit. *nourished*
**23** [a]2 Sam. 24:16, 17 [b]Ps. 115:1 [1]*breathed his last*
**24** [a]Acts 6:7; 19:20
**25** [a]Acts 11:30 [b]Acts 11:30 [c]Acts 13:5, 13 [d]Acts 12:12; 15:37 [1]NU, M *to*

CHAPTER 13
**1** [a]Acts 14:26 [b]Acts 11:22 [c]Rom. 16:21
**2** [a]Gal. 1:15; 2:9 [b]Heb. 5:4
**3** [a]Acts 6:6
**4** [a]Acts 4:36
**5** [a][Acts 13:46] [b]Acts 12:25; 15:37
**6** [a]Acts 8:9 [1]NU *the whole island*
**8** [a]Ex. 7:11 [1]*opposed*
**9** [a]Acts 2:4; 4:8
**10** [a]Matt. 13:38
**11** [a]1 Sam. 5:6
**13** [a]Acts 15:38
**14** [a]Acts 16:13
**15** [a]Luke 4:16 [b]Heb. 13:22 [1]*encouragement*
**16** [a]Acts 10:35
**17** [a]Deut. 7:6–8 [b]Acts 7:17 [c]Ex. 14:8 [1]M omits *Israel* [2]Mighty power
**18** [a]Num. 14:34
**19** [a]Deut. 7:1 [b]Josh. 14:1, 2; 19:51
**20** [a]Judg. 2:16 [b]1 Sam. 3:20
**21** [a]1 Sam. 8:5 [b]1 Sam. 10:20–24

22 "And [a]when He had removed him, [b]He raised up for them David as king, to whom also He gave testimony and said, [c]'*I have found David* the *son* of Jesse, [d]*a man after My own heart,* who will do all My will.'

23 [a]"From this man's seed, according [b]to *the* promise, God raised up for Israel [c]a[1] Savior—Jesus—

24 [a]"after John had first preached, before His coming, the baptism of repentance to all the people of Israel.

25 "And as John was finishing his course, he said, [a]'Who do you think I am? I am not *He.* But behold, [b]there comes One after me, the sandals of whose feet I am not worthy to loose.'

26 "Men *and* brethren, sons of the [1]family of Abraham, and [a]those among you who fear God, [b]to you the [2]word of this salvation has been sent.

27 "For those who dwell in Jerusalem, and their rulers, [a]because they did not know Him, nor even the voices of the Prophets which are read every Sabbath, have fulfilled *them* in condemning *Him.*

28 [a]"And though they found no cause for death *in Him,* they asked Pilate that He should be put to death.

29 [a]"Now when they had fulfilled all that was written concerning Him, [b]they took *Him* down from the tree and laid *Him* in a tomb.

30 [a]"But God raised Him from the dead.

31 [a]"He was seen for many days by those who came up with Him from Galilee to Jerusalem, who are His witnesses to the people.

32 "And we declare to you glad tidings—[a]that promise which was made to the fathers.

33 "God has fulfilled this for us their children, in that He has raised up Jesus. As it is also written in the second Psalm:

> [a]*'You are My Son,*
> *Today I have begotten You.'*

34 "And that He raised Him from the dead, no more to return to [1]corruption, He has spoken thus:

> [a]*'I will give you the sure* [2]*mercies of David.'*

35 "Therefore He also says in another *Psalm:*

> [a]*'You will not allow Your Holy One to see*
> *corruption.'*

36 "For David, after he had served [1]his own generation by the will of God, [a]fell asleep, was buried with his fathers, and [2]saw corruption;

37 "but He whom God raised up [1]saw no corruption.

38 "Therefore let it be known to you, brethren, that [a]through this Man is preached to you the forgiveness of sins;

39 "and [a]by Him everyone who believes is justified from all things from which you could not be justified by the law of Moses.

40 "Beware therefore, lest what has been spoken in the prophets come upon you:

> 41 *'Behold,*[a] *you despisers,*
> *Marvel and perish!*
> *For I work a work in your days,*
> *A work which you will by no means believe,*
> *Though one were to declare it to you.'* "

**42** [1]So when the Jews went out of the synagogue, the Gentiles begged that these words might be preached to them the next Sabbath.

43 Now when the congregation had broken up, many of the Jews and devout proselytes followed Paul and Barnabas, who, speaking to them, [a]persuaded them to continue in [b]the grace of God.

44 On the next Sabbath almost the whole city came together to hear the word of God.

45 But when the Jews saw the multitudes, they were filled with envy; and contradicting and blaspheming, they [a]opposed the things spoken by Paul.

46 Then Paul and Barnabas grew bold and said, [a]"It was necessary that the word of God should be spoken to you first; but [b]since you reject it, and judge yourselves unworthy of everlasting life, behold, [c]we turn to the Gentiles.

47 "For so the Lord has commanded us:

> [a]*'I have set you as a light to the Gentiles,*
> *That you should be for salvation*
> *to the ends of the earth.'* "

48 Now when the Gentiles heard this, they were glad and glorified the word of the Lord. [a]And as many as had been appointed to eternal life believed.

49 And the word of the Lord was being spread throughout all the region.

50 But the Jews stirred up the devout and prominent women and the chief men of the city, [a]raised up persecution against Paul and Barnabas, and expelled them from their region.

51 [a]But they shook off the dust from their feet against them, and came to Iconium.

52 And the disciples [a]were filled with joy and [b]with the Holy Spirit.

### *Paul and Barnabas Are Persecuted*

**14** Now it happened in Iconium that they went together to the synagogue of the Jews, and so spoke that a great multitude both of the Jews and of the [a]Greeks believed.

2 But the unbelieving Jews stirred up the Gentiles and [1]poisoned their [2]minds against the brethren.

3 Therefore they stayed there a long time, speaking boldly in the Lord, [a]who was bearing witness to the word of His grace, granting signs and [b]wonders to be done by their hands.

4 But the multitude of the city was [a]divided: part sided with the Jews, and part with the [b]apostles.

5 And when a violent attempt was made by both the Gentiles and Jews, with their rulers, [a]to abuse and stone them,

6 they became aware of it and [a]fled to Lystra and Derbe, cities of Lycaonia, and to the surrounding region.

7 And they were preaching the gospel there.

**8** [a]And in Lystra a certain man without strength in his feet was sitting, a cripple from his mother's womb, who had never walked.

9 *This* man heard Paul speaking. [1]Paul, observing him intently and seeing that he had faith to be healed,

10 said with a loud voice, [a]"Stand up straight on your feet!" And he leaped and walked.

11 Now when the people saw what Paul had done, they raised their voices, saying in the Lycaonian *language,* [a]"The gods have come down to us in the likeness of men!"

12 And Barnabas they called [1]Zeus, and Paul, [2]Hermes, because he was the chief speaker.

13 Then the priest of Zeus, whose temple was in

---

**22** [a]1 Sam. 15:23, 26, 28 [b]1 Sam. 16:1, 12, 13 [c]Ps. 89:20 [d]1 Sam. 13:14
**23** [a]Is. 11:1 [b]Ps. 132:11 [c][Matt. 1:21] [1]M *salvation, after*
**24** [a][Luke 3:3]
**25** [a]Mark 1:7 [b]John 1:20, 27
**26** [a]Ps. 66:16 [b]Matt. 10:6 [1]*stock* [2]*message*
**27** [a]Luke 23:34
**28** [a]Matt. 27:22, 23
**29** [a]Luke 18:31 [b]Matt. 27:57–61
**30** [a]Matt. 12:39, 40; 28:6
**31** [a]Acts 1:3, 11
**32** [a][Gen. 3:15]
**33** [a]Ps. 2:7
**34** [a]Is. 55:3 [1]*the state of decay* [2]*blessings*
**35** [a]Ps. 16:10
**36** [a]Acts 2:29 [1]*in his* [2]*underwent decay*
**37** [1]*underwent no decay*
**38** [a]Jer. 31:34
**39** [a][Is. 53:11]
**41** [a]Hab. 1:5
**42** [1]Or *And when they went out of the synagogue of the Jews;* NU *And when they went out of the synagogue, they begged*
**43** [a]Acts 11:23 [b]Titus 2:11
**45** [a]1 Pet. 4:4
**46** [a]Rom. 1:16 [b]Ex. 32:10 [c]Acts 18:6
**47** [a]Is. 42:6; 49:6
**48** [a][Acts 2:47]
**50** [a]2 Tim. 3:11
**51** [a]Matt. 10:14
**52** [a]John 16:22 [b]Acts 2:4; 4:8, 31; 13:9

CHAPTER 14
**1** [a]Acts 18:4
**2** [1]*embittered* [2]Lit. *souls*
**3** [a]Heb. 2:4 [b]Acts 5:12
**4** [a]Luke 12:51 [b]Acts 13:2, 3
**5** [a]2 Tim. 3:11
**6** [a]Matt. 10:23
**8** [a]Acts 3:2
**9** [1]Lit. *Who*
**10** [a][Is. 35:6]
**11** [a]Acts 8:10; 28:6
**12** [1]*Jupiter* [2]*Mercury*

front of their city, brought oxen and garlands to
the gates, [a]intending to sacrifice with the multitudes.
14 But when the apostles Barnabas and Paul
heard this, [a]they tore their clothes and ran in
among the multitude, crying out
15 and saying, "Men, [a]why are you doing these
things? [b]We also are men with the same nature as
you, and preach to you that you should turn from
[c]these useless things [d]to the living God, [e]who
made the heaven, the earth, the sea, and all things
that are in them,
16 [a]"who in bygone generations allowed all nations to walk in their own ways.
17 [a]"Nevertheless He did not leave Himself without witness, in that He did good, [b]gave us rain
from heaven and fruitful seasons, filling our
hearts with [c]food and gladness."
18 And with these sayings they could scarcely
restrain the multitudes from sacrificing to them.
**19** [a]Then Jews from Antioch and Iconium came
there; and having persuaded the multitudes, [b]they
stoned Paul *and* dragged *him* out of the city,
supposing him to be [c]dead.
20 However, when the disciples gathered around
him, he rose up and went into the city. And the
next day he departed with Barnabas to Derbe.
**21** And when they had preached the gospel to
that city [a]and made many disciples, they returned
to Lystra, Iconium, and Antioch,
22 strengthening the souls of the disciples, [a]ex-
horting *them* to continue in the faith, and *saying,*
[b]"We must through many tribulations enter the
kingdom of God."
23 So when they had [a]appointed elders in every
church, and prayed with fasting, they commended
them to the Lord in whom they had believed.
24 And after they had passed through Pisidia,
they came to Pamphylia.
25 Now when they had preached the word in
Perga, they went down to Attalia.
26 From there they sailed to Antioch, where they
had been commended to the grace of God for the
work which they had completed.
27 Now when they had come and gathered the
church together, [a]they reported all that God had
done with them, and that He had [b]opened the door
of faith to the Gentiles.
28 So they stayed there a long time with the
disciples.

## *The Jerusalem Council*

**15** And [a]certain *men* came down from Judea
and taught the brethren, [b]"Unless you are
circumcised according to the custom of Moses,
you cannot be saved."
2 Therefore, when Paul and Barnabas had no
small dissension and dispute with them, they
determined that [a]Paul and Barnabas and certain
others of them should go up to Jerusalem, to the
apostles and elders, about this question.
3 So, [a]being sent on their way by the church,
they passed through Phoenicia and Samaria, [b]de-
scribing the conversion of the Gentiles; and they
caused great joy to all the brethren.
4 And when they had come to Jerusalem, they
were received by the church and the apostles and
the elders; and they reported all things that God
had done with them.
5 But some of the sect of the Pharisees who
believed rose up, saying, "It is necessary to circumcise them, and to command *them* to keep the
law of Moses."
**6** Now the apostles and elders came together to
consider this matter.
7 And when there had been much dispute, Peter
rose up and said to them: [a]"Men and brethren, you
know that a good while ago God chose among us,
that by my mouth the Gentiles should hear the
word of the gospel and believe.
8 "So God, [a]who knows the heart, [1]acknowl-
edged them by [b]giving them the Holy Spirit, just
as *He did* to us,
9 [a]"and made no distinction between us and
them, [b]purifying their hearts by faith.
10 "Now therefore, why do you test God [a]by
putting a yoke on the neck of the disciples which
neither our fathers nor we were able to bear?
11 "But [a]we believe that through the grace of the
Lord Jesus [1]Christ we shall be saved in the same
manner as they."
12 Then all the multitude kept silent and listened
to Barnabas and Paul declaring how many miracles and wonders God had [a]worked through
them among the Gentiles.
13 And after they had [1]become silent, [a]James
answered, saying, "Men *and* brethren, listen
to me:
14 [a]"Simon has declared how God at the first
visited the Gentiles to take out of them a people
for His name.
15 "And with this the words of the prophets
agree, just as it is written:

16 *'After[a] this I will return*
*And will rebuild the tabernacle of David,*
*which has fallen down;*
*I will rebuild its ruins,*
*And I will set it up;*
17 *So that the rest of mankind may seek the*
*LORD,*
*Even all the Gentiles who are called by My*
*name,*
*Says the [1]LORD who does all these things.'*

18 [1]"Known to God from eternity are all His
works.
19 "Therefore [a]I judge that we should not trouble
those from among the Gentiles who [b]are turning
to God,
20 "but that we [a]write to them to abstain [b]from
things polluted by idols, [c]*from* [1]sexual immorality,
[d]*from* things strangled, and *from* blood.
21 "For Moses has had throughout many generations those who preach him in every city, [a]being
read in the synagogues every Sabbath."
**22** Then it pleased the apostles and elders, with
the whole church, to send chosen men of their
own company to Antioch with Paul and Barnabas,
*namely,* Judas who was also named [a]Barsabas,[1]
and Silas, leading men among the brethren.
23 They wrote this *letter* by them:

The apostles, the elders, and the brethren,
To the brethren who are of the Gentiles in
Antioch, Syria, and Cilicia:
Greetings.

24 Since we have heard that [a]some who went
out from us have troubled you with words,
[b]unsettling your souls, [1]saying, "*You must* be
circumcised and keep the law"—to whom we
gave no *such* commandment—
25 it seemed good to us, being assembled with

13 [a]Dan. 2:46
14 [a]Matt. 26:65
15 [a]Acts 10:26 [b]James 5:17 [c]1 Cor. 8:4 [d]1 Thess. 1:9 [e]Rev. 14:7
16 [a]Ps. 81:12
17 [a]Rom. 1:19, 20 [b]Deut. 11:14 [c]Ps. 145:16
19 [a]Acts 13:45, 50; 14:2–5 [b]2 Cor. 11:25 [c][2 Cor. 12:1–4]
21 [a]Matt. 28:19
22 [a]Acts 11:23 [b][2 Tim. 2:12; 3:12]
23 [a]Titus 1:5
27 [a]Acts 15:4, 12 [b]2 Cor. 2:12

CHAPTER 15
1 [a]Gal. 2:12 [b]Phil. 3:2
2 [a]Gal. 2:1
3 [a]Rom. 15:24 [b]Acts 14:27; 15:4, 12
7 [a]Acts 10:20
8 [a]Acts 1:24 [b]Acts 2:4; 10:44, 47 [1]*bore witness to*
9 [a]Rom. 10:12 [b]Acts 10:15, 28
10 [a]Matt. 23:4
11 [a]Rom. 3:4; 5:15 [1]NU, M omit *Christ*
12 [a]Acts 14:27; 15:3, 4
13 [a]Acts 12:17 [1]*stopped speaking*
14 [a]Acts 15:7
16 [a]Amos 9:11, 12
17 [1]NU *Lord, who makes these things*
18 [1]NU (continuing v. 17) *known from eternity (of old).'*
19 [a]Acts 15:28; 21:25 [b]1 Thess. 1:9
20 [a]Acts 21:25 [b][1 Cor. 8:1; 10:20, 28] [c][1 Cor. 6:9] [d]Lev. 3:17 [1]Or *fornication*
21 [a]Acts 13:15, 27
22 [a]Acts 1:23 [1]NU, M *Barsabbas*
24 [a]Titus 1:10, 11 [b]Gal. 1:7; 5:10 [1]NU omits *saying, "You must be circumcised and keep the law"*

one [1]accord, to send chosen men to you with our beloved Barnabas and Paul,
26 [a]men who have risked their lives for the name of our Lord Jesus Christ.
27 We have therefore sent Judas and Silas, who will also report the same things by word of mouth.
28 For it seemed good to the Holy Spirit, and to us, to lay upon you no greater burden than these necessary things:
29 [a]that you abstain from things offered to idols, [b]from blood, from things strangled, and from [c]sexual[1] immorality. If you keep yourselves from these, you will do well.
Farewell.

**30** So when they were sent off, they came to Antioch; and when they had gathered the multitude together, they delivered the letter.
31 When they had read it, they rejoiced over its encouragement.
32 Now Judas and Silas, themselves being [a]prophets also, [b]exhorted and strengthened the brethren with many words.
33 And after they had stayed *there* for a time, they were [a]sent back with greetings from the brethren to [1]the apostles.
34 [1]However, it seemed good to Silas to remain there.
35 [a]Paul and Barnabas also remained in Antioch, teaching and preaching the word of the Lord, with many others also.
**36** Then after some days Paul said to Barnabas, "Let us now go back and visit our brethren in every city where we have preached the word of the Lord, *and see* how they are doing."
37 Now Barnabas [1]was determined to take with them [a]John called Mark.
38 But Paul insisted that they should not take with them [a]the one who had departed from them in Pamphylia, and had not gone with them to the work.
39 Then the contention became so sharp that they parted from one another. And so Barnabas took Mark and sailed to [a]Cyprus;
40 but Paul chose Silas and departed, [a]being [1]commended by the brethren to the grace of God.
41 And he went through Syria and Cilicia, [a]strengthening the churches.

### *The Mission to Macedonia*

**16** Then he came to [a]Derbe and Lystra. And behold, a certain disciple was there, [b]named Timothy, [c]*the* son of a certain Jewish woman who believed, but his father *was* Greek.
2 He was well spoken of by the brethren who were at Lystra and Iconium.
3 Paul wanted to have him go on with him. And he [a]took *him* and circumcised him because of the Jews who were in that region, for they all knew that his father was Greek.
4 And as they went through the cities, they delivered to them the [a]decrees to keep, [b]which were determined by the apostles and elders at Jerusalem.
5 [a]So the churches were strengthened in the faith, and increased in number daily.
**6** Now when they had gone through Phrygia and the region of [a]Galatia, they were forbidden by the Holy Spirit to preach the word in [1]Asia.
7 After they had come to Mysia, they tried to go into Bithynia, but the [1]Spirit did not permit them.
8 So passing by Mysia, they [a]came down to Troas.
9 And a vision appeared to Paul in the night. A [a]man of Macedonia stood and pleaded with him, saying, "Come over to Macedonia and help us."
10 Now after he had seen the vision, immediately we sought to go [a]to Macedonia, concluding that the Lord had called us to preach the gospel to them.
**11** Therefore, sailing from Troas, we ran a straight course to Samothrace, and the next *day* came to Neapolis,
12 and from there to [a]Philippi, which is the [1]foremost city of that part of Macedonia, a colony. And we were staying in that city for some days.
13 And on the Sabbath day we went out of the city to the riverside, where prayer was customarily made; and we sat down and spoke to the women who met *there.*
14 Now a certain woman named Lydia heard *us.* She was a seller of purple from the city of [a]Thyatira, who worshiped God. [b]The Lord opened her heart to heed the things spoken by Paul.
15 And when she and her household were baptized, she begged *us,* saying, "If you have judged me to be faithful to the Lord, come to my house and stay." So [a]she persuaded us.
**16** Now it happened, as we went to prayer, that a certain slave girl [a]possessed with a spirit of divination met us, who brought her masters [b]much profit by fortune-telling.
17 This girl followed Paul and us, and cried out, saying, "These men are the servants of the Most High God, who proclaim to us the way of salvation."
18 And this she did for many days. But Paul, [a]greatly [1]annoyed, turned and said to the spirit, "I command you in the name of Jesus Christ to come out of her." [b]And he came out that very hour.
19 But [a]when her masters saw that their hope of profit was gone, they seized Paul and Silas and [b]dragged *them* into the marketplace to the authorities.
20 And they brought them to the magistrates, and said, "These men, being Jews, [a]exceedingly trouble our city;
21 "and they teach customs which are not lawful for us, being Romans, to receive or observe."
22 Then the multitude rose up together against them; and the magistrates tore off their clothes [a]and commanded *them* to be beaten with rods.
23 And when they had laid many stripes on them, they threw *them* into prison, commanding the jailer to keep them securely.
24 Having received such a charge, he put them into the inner prison and fastened their feet in the stocks.
**25** But at midnight Paul and Silas were praying and singing hymns to God, and the prisoners were listening to them.
26 [a]Suddenly there was a great earthquake, so that the foundations of the prison were shaken; and immediately [b]all the doors were opened and everyone's chains were loosed.
27 And the keeper of the prison, awaking from sleep and seeing the prison doors open, supposing the prisoners had fled, drew his sword and was about to kill himself.

**25** [1]*purpose* or *mind*
**26** [a]Acts 13:50; 14:19
**29** [a]Acts 15:20; 21:25 [b]Lev. 17:14 [c]Col. 3:5 [1]Or *fornication*
**32** [a]Eph. 4:11 [b]Acts 14:22; 18:23
**33** [a]Heb. 11:31 [1]NU *those who had sent them*
**34** [1]NU, M omit v. 34.
**35** [a]Acts 13:1
**37** [a]Acts 12:12, 25 [1]*resolved*
**38** [a]Acts 13:13
**39** [a]Acts 4:36; 13:4
**40** [a]Acts 11:23; 14:26 [1]*committed*
**41** [a]Acts 16:5

CHAPTER 16
**1** [a]Acts 14:6 [b]Rom. 16:21 [c]2 Tim. 1:5; 3:15
**3** [a][Gal. 2:3; 5:2]
**4** [a]Acts 15:19–21 [b]Acts 15:28, 29
**5** [a]Acts 2:47; 15:41
**6** [a]Gal. 1:1, 2 [1]The Roman province of Asia
**7** [1]NU adds *of Jesus*
**8** [a]2 Cor. 2:12
**9** [a]Acts 10:30
**10** [a]2 Cor. 2:13
**12** [a]Phil. 1:1 [1]Lit. *first*
**14** [a]Rev. 1:11; 2:18, 24 [b]Luke 24:45
**15** [a]Judg. 19:21
**16** [a]1 Sam. 28:3, 7 [b]Acts 19:24
**18** [a]Mark 1:25, 34 [b]Mark 16:17 [1]*distressed*
**19** [a]Acts 16:16; 19:25, 26 [b]Matt. 10:18
**20** [a]Acts 17:8
**22** [a]1 Thess. 2:2
**26** [a]Acts 4:31 [b]Acts 5:19; 12:7, 10

28 But Paul called with a loud voice, saying, "Do
yourself no harm, for we are all here."
29 Then he called for a light, ran in, and fell down
trembling before Paul and Silas.
30 And he brought them out and said, [a]"Sirs,
what must I do to be saved?"
31 So they said, [a]"Believe on the Lord Jesus
Christ, and you will be saved, you and your
household."
32 Then they spoke the word of the Lord to him
and to all who were in his house.
33 And he took them the same hour of the night
and washed *their* stripes. And immediately he and
all his family were baptized.
34 Now when he had brought them into his
house, [a]he set food before them; and he rejoiced,
having believed in God with all his household.
**35** And when it was day, the magistrates sent the
[1]officers, saying, "Let those men go."
36 So the keeper of the prison reported these
words to Paul, saying, "The magistrates have sent
to let you go. Now therefore depart, and go in
peace."
37 But Paul said to them, "They have beaten us
openly, uncondemned [a]Romans, *and* have thrown
*us* into prison. And now do they put us out
secretly? No indeed! Let them come themselves
and get us out."
38 And the officers told these words to the magistrates, and they were afraid when they heard that
they were Romans.
39 Then they came and pleaded with them and
brought *them* out, and [a]asked *them* to depart from
the city.
40 So they went out of the prison [a]and entered
*the house of* Lydia; and when they had seen the
brethren, they encouraged them and departed.

## *Paul at Thessalonica, Berea, and Athens*

**17** Now when they had passed through Am-
phipolis and Apollonia, they came to [a]Thes-
salonica, where there was a synagogue of the
Jews.
2 Then Paul, as his custom was, [a]went in to
them, and for three Sabbaths [b]reasoned with them
from the Scriptures,
3 explaining and demonstrating [a]that the Christ
had to suffer and rise again from the dead, and
*saying,* "This Jesus whom I preach to you is the
Christ."
4 [a]And some of them were persuaded; and a
great multitude of the devout Greeks, and not a
few of the leading women, joined Paul and [b]Silas.
**5** But the Jews [1]who were not persuaded, [2]be-
coming [a]envious, took some of the evil men from
the marketplace, and gathering a mob, set all the
city in an uproar and attacked the house of
[b]Jason, and sought to bring them out to the
people.
6 But when they did not find them, they dragged
Jason and some brethren to the rulers of the city,
crying out, [a]"These who have turned the world
upside down have come here too.
7 "Jason has [1]harbored them, and these are all
acting contrary to the decrees of Caesar, [a]saying
there is another king—Jesus."
8 And they troubled the crowd and the rulers of
the city when they heard these things.
9 So when they had taken security from Jason
and the rest, they let them go.
**10** Then [a]the brethren immediately sent Paul and
Silas away by night to Berea. When they arrived,
they went into the synagogue of the Jews.
11 These were more [1]fair-minded than those in
Thessalonica, in that they received the word with
all readiness, and [a]searched the Scriptures daily *to
find out* whether these things were so.
12 Therefore many of them believed, and also not
a few of the Greeks, prominent women as well as
men.
13 But when the Jews from Thessalonica learned
that the word of God was preached by Paul at
Berea, they came there also and stirred up the
crowds.
14 [a]Then immediately the brethren sent Paul
away, to go to the sea; but both Silas and Timothy
remained there.
15 So those who conducted Paul brought him to
Athens; and [a]receiving a command for Silas and
Timothy to come to him with all speed, they
departed.
**16** Now while Paul waited for them at Athens,
[a]his spirit was provoked within him when he saw
that the city was [1]given over to idols.
17 Therefore he reasoned in the synagogue with
the Jews and with the *Gentile* worshipers, and in
the marketplace daily with those who happened
to be there.
18 [1]Then certain Epicurean and Stoic philosophers encountered him. And some said, "What
does this [2]babbler want to say?" Others said, "He
seems to be a proclaimer of foreign gods," because
he preached to them [a]Jesus and the resurrection.
19 And they took him and brought him to the
[1]Areopagus, saying, "May we know what this new
doctrine *is* of which you speak?
20 "For you are bringing some strange things to
our ears. Therefore we want to know what these
things mean."
21 For all the Athenians and the foreigners who
were there spent their time in nothing else but
either to tell or to hear some new thing.
**22** Then Paul stood in the midst of the [1]Areopa-
gus and said, "Men of Athens, I perceive that in all
things you are very religious;
23 "for as I was passing through and considering
the objects of your worship, I even found an altar
with this inscription:

TO THE UNKNOWN GOD.

Therefore, the One whom you worship without
knowing, Him I proclaim to you:
24 [a]"God, who made the world and everything in
it, since He is [b]Lord of heaven and earth, [c]does not
dwell in temples made with hands.
25 "Nor is He worshiped with men's hands, as
though He needed anything, since He [a]gives to all
life, breath, and all things.
26 "And He has made from one [1]blood every
nation of men to dwell on all the face of the earth,
and has determined their preappointed times and
[a]the boundaries of their dwellings,
27 [a]"so that they should seek the Lord, in the
hope that they might grope for Him and find Him,
[b]though He is not far from each one of us;
28 "for [a]in Him we live and move and have our
being, [b]as also some of your own poets have said,
'For we are also His offspring.'
29 "Therefore, since we are the offspring of God,
[a]we ought not to think that the Divine Nature is
like gold or silver or stone, something shaped by
art and man's devising.

**30** [a]Luke 3:10; Acts 2:37; 9:6; 22:10
**31** [a][John 3:16, 36; 6:47; Acts 13:38, 39; Rom. 10:9–11; 1 John 5:10]
**34** [a]Matt. 5:4; Luke 5:29; 19:6
**35** [1]*lictors,* lit. *rod bearers*
**37** [a]Acts 22:25–29
**39** [a]Matt. 8:34
**40** [a]Acts 16:14

CHAPTER 17
**1** [a]Acts 17:11, 13; 20:4; 27:2; Phil. 4:16; 1 Thess. 1:1; 2 Thess. 1:1; 2 Tim. 4:10
**2** [a]Luke 4:16; Acts 9:20; 13:5, 14; 14:1; 16:13; 19:8 [b]1 Thess. 2:1–16
**3** [a]Luke 24:26, 46; Acts 18:5, 28; Gal. 3:1
**4** [a]Acts 28:24 [b]Acts 15:22, 27, 32, 40
**5** [a]Acts 13:45 [b]Acts 17:6, 7, 9; Rom. 16:21 [1]NU omits *who were not persuaded* [2]M omits *becoming envious*
**6** [a][Acts 16:20]
**7** [a]Luke 23:2; John 19:12; 1 Pet. 2:13 [1]*welcomed*
**10** [a]Acts 9:25; 17:14
**11** [a]Is. 34:16; Luke 16:29; John 5:39 [1]Lit. *noble*
**14** [a]Matt. 10:23
**15** [a]Acts 18:5
**16** [a]2 Pet. 2:8 [1]*full of idols*
**18** [a]1 Cor. 15:12 [1]NU, M add *also* [2]Lit. *seed picker,* an idler who makes a living picking up scraps
**19** [1]Lit. *Hill of Ares,* or *Mars Hill*
**22** [1]Lit. *Hill of Ares,* or *Mars Hill*
**24** [a]Is. 42:5; Acts 14:15 [b]Deut. 10:14; Ps. 115:16; Matt. 11:25 [c]1 Kin. 8:27; Acts 7:48–50
**25** [a]Gen. 2:7; Is. 42:5; Dan. 5:23
**26** [a]Deut. 32:8; Job 12:23; Dan. 4:35 [1]NU omits *blood*
**27** [a][Rom. 1:20] [b]Deut. 4:7; Ps. 139:7, 10; Jer. 23:23, 24; [Acts 14:17]
**28** [a][Col. 1:17; Heb. 1:3] [b]Titus 1:12
**29** [a]Ps. 115:4–7; Is. 40:18, 19; Rom. 1:23

30 "Truly, [a]these times of ignorance God overlooked, but [b]now commands all men everywhere
to repent,
31 "because He has appointed a day on which
[a]He will judge the world in righteousness by the
Man whom He has ordained. He has given assurance of this to all by [b]raising Him from the dead."
32 And when they heard of the resurrection of
the dead, some mocked, while others said, "We
will hear you again on this *matter.*"
33 So Paul departed from among them.
34 However, some men joined him and believed,
among them Dionysius the Areopagite, a woman
named Damaris, and others with them.

### *Paul at Corinth and Ephesus*

**18** After these things Paul departed from Athens and went to Corinth.
2 And he found a certain Jew named [a]Aquila,
born in Pontus, who had recently come from Italy
with his wife Priscilla (because Claudius had
commanded all the Jews to depart from Rome);
and he came to them.
3 So, because he was of the same trade, he
stayed with them [a]and worked; for by occupation
they were tentmakers.
4 [a]And he reasoned in the synagogue every
Sabbath, and persuaded both Jews and Greeks.
5 [a]When Silas and Timothy had come from
Macedonia, Paul was [b]compelled [1]by the Spirit,
and testified to the Jews *that* Jesus *is* the Christ.
6 But [a]when they opposed him and blasphemed,
[b]he shook *his* garments and said to them, [c]"Your
blood *be* upon your *own* heads; [d]I *am* clean. [e]From
now on I will go to the Gentiles."
7 And he departed from there and entered the
house of a certain *man* named [1]Justus, *one* who
worshiped God, whose house was next door to the
synagogue.
8 [a]Then Crispus, the ruler of the synagogue,
believed on the Lord with all his household. And
many of the Corinthians, hearing, believed and
were baptized.
9 Now [a]the Lord spoke to Paul in the night by a
vision, "Do not be afraid, but speak, and do not
keep silent;
10 [a]"for I am with you, and no one will attack
you to hurt you; for I have many people in this
city."
11 And he continued *there* a year and six months,
teaching the word of God among them.
12 When Gallio was proconsul of Achaia, the
Jews with one accord rose up against Paul and
brought him to the [1]judgment seat,
13 saying, "This *fellow* persuades men to worship
God contrary to the law."
14 And when Paul was about to open *his* mouth,
Gallio said to the Jews, "If it were a matter of
wrongdoing or wicked crimes, O Jews, there
would be reason why I should bear with you.
15 "But if it is a [a]question of words and names
and your own law, look *to it* yourselves; for I do
not want to be a judge of such *matters.*"
16 And he drove them from the judgment seat.
17 Then [1]all the Greeks took [a]Sosthenes, the ruler
of the synagogue, and beat *him* before the judgment seat. But Gallio took no notice of these
things.
**18** So Paul still remained [1]a good while. Then he
took leave of the brethren and sailed for Syria,
and Priscilla and Aquila *were* with him. [a]He had
*his* hair cut off at [b]Cenchrea, for he had taken a
vow.
19 And he came to Ephesus, and left them there;
but he himself entered the synagogue and reasoned with the Jews.
20 When they asked *him* to stay a longer time
with them, he did not consent,
21 but took leave of them, saying, [a]"I[1] must by all
means keep this coming feast in Jerusalem; but I
will return again to you, [b]God willing." And he
sailed from Ephesus.
22 And when he had landed at [a]Caesarea, and
[1]gone up and greeted the church, he went down to
Antioch.
23 After he had spent some time *there,* he departed and went over the region of [a]Galatia and
Phrygia [1]in order, [b]strengthening all the disciples.
**24** [a]Now a certain Jew named Apollos, born at
Alexandria, an eloquent man *and* mighty in the
Scriptures, came to Ephesus.
25 This man had been instructed in the way of
the Lord; and being [a]fervent in spirit, he spoke and
taught accurately the things of the Lord, [b]though
he knew only the baptism of John.
26 So he began to speak boldly in the synagogue.
When Aquila and Priscilla heard him, they took
him aside and explained to him the way of God
more accurately.
27 And when he desired to cross to Achaia, the
brethren wrote, exhorting the disciples to receive
him; and when he arrived, [a]he greatly helped
those who had believed through grace;
28 for he vigorously refuted the Jews publicly,
[a]showing from the Scriptures that Jesus is the
Christ.

### *Paul's Preaching Causes a Riot at Ephesus*

**19** And it happened, while [a]Apollos was at
Corinth, that Paul, having passed through
[b]the upper regions, came to Ephesus. And finding
some disciples
2 he said to them, "Did you receive the Holy
Spirit when you believed?" So they said to him,
[a]"We have not so much as heard whether there is
a Holy Spirit."
3 And he said to them, "Into what then were
you baptized?" So they said, [a]"Into John's baptism."
4 Then Paul said, [a]"John indeed baptized with a
baptism of repentance, saying to the people that
they should believe on Him who would come after
him, that is, on Christ Jesus."
5 When they heard *this,* they were baptized [a]in
the name of the Lord Jesus.
6 And when Paul had [a]laid hands on them, the
Holy Spirit came upon them, and [b]they spoke with
tongues and prophesied.
7 Now the men were about twelve in all.
8 [a]And he went into the synagogue and spoke
boldly for three months, reasoning and persuading
[b]concerning the things of the kingdom of God.
9 But [a]when some were hardened and did not
believe, but spoke evil [b]of the Way before the
multitude, he departed from them and withdrew
the disciples, reasoning daily in the school of
Tyrannus.
10 And [a]this continued for two years, so that all
who dwelt in Asia heard the word of the Lord
Jesus, both Jews and Greeks.
**11** Now [a]God worked unusual miracles by the
hands of Paul,

---

**30** [a][Rom. 3:25] [b][Titus 2:11, 12]
**31** [a]Acts 10:42 [b]Acts 2:24

CHAPTER 18
**2** [a]1 Cor. 16:19
**3** [a]Acts 20:34
**4** [a]Acts 17:2
**5** [a]Acts 17:14, 15 [b]Acts 18:28 [1]Or *in his spirit* or *in the Spirit*
**6** [a]Acts 13:45 [b]Neh. 5:13 [c]2 Sam. 1:16 [d][Ezek. 3:18, 19] [e]Acts 13:46–48; 28:28
**7** [1]NU *Titius Justus*
**8** [a]1 Cor. 1:14
**9** [a]Acts 23:11
**10** [a]Jer. 1:18, 19
**12** [1]Gr. *bema*
**15** [a]Acts 23:29; 25:19
**17** [a]1 Cor. 1:1 [1]NU *they all*
**18** [a]Acts 21:24 [b]Rom. 16:1 [1]Lit. *many days*
**21** [a]Acts 19:21; 20:16 [b]1 Cor. 4:19 [1]NU omits *I must by all means keep this coming feast in Jerusalem*
**22** [a]Acts 8:40 [1]To Jerusalem
**23** [a]Gal. 1:2 [b]Acts 14:22; 15:32, 41 [1]*successively*
**24** [a]Titus 3:13
**25** [a]Rom. 12:11 [b]Acts 19:3
**27** [a]1 Cor. 3:6
**28** [a]Acts 9:22; 17:3; 18:5

CHAPTER 19
**1** [a]1 Cor. 1:12; 3:5, 6 [b]Acts 18:23
**2** [a]1 Sam. 3:7
**3** [a]Acts 18:25
**4** [a]Matt. 3:11
**5** [a]Acts 8:12, 16; 10:48
**6** [a]Acts 6:6; 8:17 [b]Acts 2:4; 10:46
**8** [a]Acts 17:2; 18:4 [b]Acts 1:3; 28:23
**9** [a]2 Tim. 1:15 [b]Acts 9:2; 19:23; 22:4; 24:14
**10** [a]Acts 19:8; 20:31
**11** [a]Mark 16:20

12 [a]so that even handkerchiefs or aprons were
brought from his body to the sick, and the diseases left them and the evil spirits went out of
them.
13 [a]Then some of the itinerant Jewish exorcists
[b]took it upon themselves to call the name of the
Lord Jesus over those who had evil spirits, saying,
[1]"We [2]exorcise you by the Jesus whom Paul
[c]preaches."
14 Also there were seven sons of Sceva, a Jewish
chief priest, who did so.
15 And the evil spirit answered and said, "Jesus I
know, and Paul I know; but who are you?"
16 Then the man in whom the evil spirit was
leaped on them, [1]overpowered them, and prevailed
against [2]them, so that they fled out of that house
naked and wounded.
17 This became known both to all Jews and
Greeks dwelling in Ephesus; and [a]fear fell on them
all, and the name of the Lord Jesus was magnified.
18 And many who had believed came [a]confessing
and telling their deeds.
19 Also, many of those who had practiced magic
brought their books together and burned *them* in
the sight of all. And they counted up the value of
them, and *it* totaled fifty thousand *pieces* of silver.
20 [a]So the word of the Lord grew mightily and
prevailed.
**21** [a]When these things were accomplished, Paul
[b]purposed in the Spirit, when he had passed
through [c]Macedonia and Achaia, to go to Jerusalem, saying, "After I have been there, [d]I must also
see Rome."
22 So he sent into Macedonia two of those who
ministered to him, [a]Timothy and [b]Erastus, but he
himself stayed in Asia for a time.
23 And [a]about that time there arose a great
commotion about [b]the Way.
24 For a certain man named Demetrius, a silversmith, who made silver shrines of [1]Diana, brought
[a]no small profit to the craftsmen.
25 He called them together with the workers of
similar occupation, and said: "Men, you know that
we have our prosperity by this trade.
26 "Moreover you see and hear that not only at
Ephesus, but throughout almost all Asia, this Paul
has persuaded and turned away many people,
saying that [a]they are not gods which are made
with hands.
27 "So not only is this trade of ours in danger of
falling into disrepute, but also the temple of the
great goddess Diana may be despised and [1]her
magnificence destroyed, whom all Asia and the
world worship."
28 Now when they heard *this,* they were full of
wrath and cried out, saying, "Great *is* Diana of the
Ephesians!"
29 So the whole city was filled with confusion,
and rushed into the theater with one accord,
having seized [a]Gaius and [b]Aristarchus, Macedonians, Paul's travel companions.
30 And when Paul wanted to go in to the people,
the disciples would not allow him.
31 Then some of the [1]officials of Asia, who were
his friends, sent to him pleading that he would not
venture into the theater.
32 Some therefore cried one thing and some
another, for the assembly was confused, and most
of them did not know why they had come together.
33 And they drew Alexander out of the multitude, the Jews putting him forward. And [a]Alex-
ander [b]motioned with his hand, and wanted to
make his defense to the people.
34 But when they found out that he was a Jew,
all with one voice cried out for about two hours,
"Great *is* Diana of the Ephesians!"
35 And when the city clerk had quieted the
crowd, he said: "Men of Ephesus, what man is
there who does not know that the city of the
Ephesians is temple guardian of the great goddess
[1]Diana, and of the *image* which fell down from
[2]Zeus?
36 "Therefore, since these things cannot be denied, you ought to be quiet and do nothing rashly.
37 "For you have brought these men here who
are neither robbers of temples nor blasphemers of
[1]your goddess.
38 "Therefore, if Demetrius and his fellow craftsmen have a [1]case against anyone, the courts are
open and there are proconsuls. Let them bring
charges against one another.
39 "But if you have any other inquiry to make, it
shall be determined in the lawful assembly.
40 "For we are in danger of being [1]called in
question for today's uproar, there being no reason
which we may give to account for this disorderly
gathering."
41 And when he had said these things, he dismissed the assembly.

### *Ministries in Greece; the Ephesian Elders*

**20** After the uproar had ceased, Paul called the
disciples to *himself,* embraced *them,* and
[a]departed to go to Macedonia.
2 Now when he had gone over that region and
encouraged them with many words, he came to
[a]Greece
3 and stayed three months. And [a]when the Jews
plotted against him as he was about to sail to
Syria, he decided to return through Macedonia.
4 And Sopater of Berea accompanied him to
Asia—also [a]Aristarchus and Secundus of the
Thessalonians, and [b]Gaius of Derbe, and [c]Timo-
thy, and [d]Tychicus and [e]Trophimus of Asia.
5 These men, going ahead, waited for us at
[a]Troas.
6 But we sailed away from Philippi after [a]the
Days of Unleavened Bread, and in five days joined
them [b]at Troas, where we stayed seven days.
**7** Now on [a]the first *day* of the week, when the
disciples came together [b]to break bread, Paul,
ready to depart the next day, spoke to them and
continued his message until midnight.
8 There were many lamps [a]in the upper room
where [1]they were gathered together.
9 And in a window sat a certain young man
named Eutychus, who was sinking into a deep
sleep. He was overcome by sleep; and as Paul
continued speaking, he fell down from the third
story and was taken up dead.
10 But Paul went down, [a]fell on him, and embracing *him* said, [b]"Do not trouble yourselves, for his
life is in him."
11 Now when he had come up, had broken bread
and eaten, and talked a long while, even till
daybreak, he departed.
12 And they brought the young man in alive, and
they were not a little comforted.
**13** Then we went ahead to the ship and sailed to
Assos, there intending to take Paul on board; for

12 [a]Acts 5:15
13 [a]Matt. 12:27 [b]Mark 9:38 [c]1 Cor. 1:23; 2:2 [1]NU *I* [2]*adjure,* solemnly command
16 [1]M *and they overpowered them* [2]NU *both of them*
17 [a]Luke 1:65; 7:16
18 [a]Matt. 3:6
20 [a]Acts 6:7; 12:24
21 [a]Rom. 15:25 [b]Acts 20:22 [c]Acts 20:1 [d]Rom. 1:13; 15:22–29
22 [a]1 Tim. 1:2 [b]Rom. 16:23
23 [a]2 Cor. 1:8 [b]Acts 9:2
24 [a]Acts 16:16, 19 [1]Gr. *Artemis*
26 [a]Is. 44:10–20
27 [1]NU *she be deposed from her magnificence*
29 [a]Rom. 16:23 [b]Col. 4:10
31 [1]*Asiarchs, rulers of Asia,* the province
33 [a]2 Tim. 4:14 [b]Acts 12:17
35 [1]Gr. *Artemis* [2]*heaven*
37 [1]NU *our*
38 [1]Lit. *matter*
40 [1]Or *charged with rebellion concerning today*

CHAPTER 20
1 [a]1 Tim. 1:3
2 [a]Acts 17:15; 18:1
3 [a]2 Cor. 11:26
4 [a]Col. 4:10 [b]Acts 19:29 [c]Acts 16:1 [d]Eph. 6:21 [e]2 Tim. 4:20
5 [a]2 Tim. 4:13
6 [a]Ex. 12:14, 15 [b]2 Tim. 4:13
7 [a]1 Cor. 16:2 [b]Acts 2:42, 46; 20:11
8 [a]Acts 1:13 [1]NU, M *we*
10 [a]1 Kin. 17:21 [b]Matt. 9:23, 24

so he had [1]given orders, intending himself to go on foot.
14 And when he met us at Assos, we took him on board and came to Mitylene.
15 We sailed from there, and the next *day* came opposite Chios. The following *day* we arrived at Samos and stayed at Trogyllium. The next *day* we came to Miletus.
16 For Paul had decided to sail past Ephesus, so that he would not have to spend time in Asia; for [a]he was hurrying [b]to be at Jerusalem, if possible, on [c]the Day of Pentecost.
**17** From Miletus he sent to Ephesus and called for the elders of the church.
18 And when they had come to him, he said to them: "You know, [a]from the first day that I came to Asia, in what manner I always lived among you,
19 "serving the Lord with all humility, with many tears and trials which happened to me [a]by the plotting of the Jews;
20 "how [a]I kept back nothing that was helpful, but proclaimed it to you, and taught you publicly and from house to house,
21 [a]"testifying to Jews, and also to Greeks, [b]repentance toward God and faith toward our Lord Jesus Christ.
22 "And see, now [a]I go bound in the spirit to Jerusalem, not knowing the things that will happen to me there,
23 "except that [a]the Holy Spirit testifies in every city, saying that chains and tribulations await me.
24 [1]"But [a]none of these things move me; nor do I count my life dear to myself, [b]so that I may finish my [2]race with joy, [c]and the ministry [d]which I received from the Lord Jesus, to testify to the gospel of the grace of God.
25 "And indeed, now I know that you all, among whom I have gone preaching the kingdom of God, will see my face no more.
26 "Therefore I testify to you this day that I *am* [a]innocent[1] of the blood of all *men*.
27 "For I have not [1]shunned to declare to you [a]the whole counsel of God.
28 [a]"Therefore take heed to yourselves and to all the flock, among which the Holy Spirit [b]has made you overseers, to shepherd the church [1]of God [c]which He purchased [d]with His own blood.
29 "For I know this, that after my departure [a]savage wolves will come in among you, not sparing the flock.
30 "Also [a]from among yourselves men will rise up, speaking [1]perverse things, to draw away the disciples after themselves.
31 "Therefore watch, and remember that [a]for three years I did not cease to warn everyone night and day with tears.
32 "So now, brethren, I commend you to God and [a]to the word of His grace, which is able [b]to build you up and give you [c]an inheritance among all those who are sanctified.
33 "I have coveted no one's silver or gold or apparel.
34 [1]"Yes, you yourselves know [a]that these hands have provided for my necessities, and for those who were with me.
35 "I have shown you in every way, [a]by laboring like this, that you must support the weak. And remember the words of the Lord Jesus, that He said, 'It is more blessed to give than to receive.' "
36 And when he had said these things, he knelt down and prayed with them all.
37 Then they all [a]wept [1]freely, and [b]fell on Paul's neck and kissed him,
38 sorrowing most of all for the words which he spoke, that they would see his face no more. And they accompanied him to the ship.

## *Paul Is Arrested at Jerusalem*

**21** Now it came to pass, that when we had departed from them and set sail, running a straight course we came to Cos, the following *day* to Rhodes, and from there to Patara.
2 And finding a ship sailing over to Phoenicia, we went aboard and set sail.
3 When we had sighted Cyprus, we passed it on the left, sailed to Syria, and landed at Tyre; for there the ship was to unload her cargo.
4 And finding [1]disciples, we stayed there seven days. [a]They told Paul through the Spirit not to go up to Jerusalem.
5 When we had come to the end of those days, we departed and went on our way; and they all accompanied us, with wives and children, till *we were* out of the city. And [a]we knelt down on the shore and prayed.
6 When we had taken our leave of one another, we boarded the ship, and they returned [a]home.
7 And when we had finished *our* voyage from Tyre, we came to Ptolemais, greeted the brethren, and stayed with them one day.
8 On the next *day* we [1]who were Paul's companions departed and came to [a]Caesarea, and entered the house of Philip [b]the evangelist, [c]who was *one* of the seven, and stayed with him.
9 Now this man had four virgin daughters [a]who prophesied.
10 And as we stayed many days, a certain prophet named [a]Agabus came down from Judea.
11 When he had come to us, he took Paul's belt, bound his *own* hands and feet, and said, "Thus says the Holy Spirit, [a]'So shall the Jews at Jerusalem bind the man who owns this belt, and deliver *him* into the hands of the Gentiles.' "
12 Now when we heard these things, both we and those from that place pleaded with him not to go up to Jerusalem.
13 Then Paul answered, [a]"What do you mean by weeping and breaking my heart? For I am ready not only to be bound, but also to die at Jerusalem for the name of the Lord Jesus."
14 So when he would not be persuaded, we ceased, saying, [a]"The will of the Lord be done."
**15** And after those days we [1]packed and went up to Jerusalem.
16 Also some of the disciples from Caesarea went with us and brought with them a certain Mnason of Cyprus, an early disciple, with whom we were to lodge.
17 [a]And when we had come to Jerusalem, the brethren received us gladly.
18 On the following *day* Paul went in with us to [a]James, and all the elders were present.
19 When he had greeted them, [a]he told in detail those things which God had done among the Gentiles [b]through his ministry.
20 And when they heard *it*, they glorified the Lord. And they said to him, "You see, brother, how many myriads of Jews there are who have believed, and they are all [a]zealous for the law;
21 "but they have been informed about you that

**13** [1]*arranged it*
**16** [a]Acts 18:21; 19:21; 21:4 [b]Acts 24:17 [c]Acts 2:1
**18** [a]Acts 18:19; 19:1, 10; 20:4, 16
**19** [a]Acts 20:3
**20** [a]Acts 20:27
**21** [a]Acts 18:5; 19:10 [b]Mark 1:15
**22** [a]Acts 19:21
**23** [a]Acts 21:4, 11
**24** [a]Acts 21:13 [b]2 Tim. 4:7 [c]Acts 1:17 [d]Gal. 1:1 [1]NU *But I do not count my life of any value or dear to myself* [2]*course*
**26** [a]Acts 18:6 [1]Lit. *clean*
**27** [a]Luke 7:30 [1]*avoided declaring*
**28** [a]1 Pet. 5:2 [b]1 Cor. 12:28 [c]Eph. 1:7, 14 [d]Heb. 9:14 [1]M *of the Lord and God*
**29** [a]Matt. 7:15
**30** [a]1 Tim. 1:20 [1]*misleading*
**31** [a]Acts 19:8, 10; 24:17
**32** [a]Heb. 13:9 [b]Acts 9:31 [c][Heb. 9:15]
**34** [a]Acts 18:3 [1]NU, M omit *Yes*
**35** [a]Rom. 15:1
**37** [a]Acts 21:13 [b]Gen. 45:14 [1]Lit. *much*

CHAPTER 21
**4** [a][Acts 20:23; 21:12] [1]NU *the disciples*
**5** [a]Acts 9:40; 20:36
**6** [a]John 1:11
**8** [a]Acts 8:40; 21:16 [b]Eph. 4:11 [c]Acts 6:5 [1]NU omits *who were Paul's companions*
**9** [a]Joel 2:28
**10** [a]Acts 11:28
**11** [a]Acts 20:23; 21:33; 22:25
**13** [a]Acts 20:24, 37
**14** [a]Luke 11:2; 22:42
**15** [1]*made preparations*
**17** [a]Acts 15:4
**18** [a]Gal. 1:19; 2:9
**19** [a]Rom. 15:18, 19 [b]Acts 1:17; 20:24
**20** [a]Acts 15:1; 22:3

you teach all the Jews who are among the Gentiles to forsake Moses, saying that they ought not to circumcise *their* children nor to walk according to the customs.
22 [1]"What then? The assembly must certainly meet, for they will hear that you have come.
23 "Therefore do what we tell you: We have four men who have taken a vow.
24 "Take them and be purified with them, and pay their expenses so that they may [a]shave *their* heads, and that all may know that those things of which they were informed concerning you are nothing, but *that* you yourself also walk orderly and keep the law.
25 "But concerning the Gentiles who believe, [a]we have written *and* decided [1]that they should observe no such thing, except that they should keep themselves from *things* offered to idols, from blood, from things strangled, and from [2]sexual immorality."
**26** Then Paul took the men, and the next day, having been purified with them, [a]entered the temple [b]to announce the [1]expiration of the days of purification, at which time an offering should be made for each one of them.
27 Now when the seven days were almost ended, [a]the Jews from Asia, seeing him in the temple, stirred up the whole crowd and [b]laid hands on him,
28 crying out, "Men of Israel, help! This is the man [a]who teaches all *men* everywhere against the people, the law, and this place; and furthermore he also brought Greeks into the temple and has defiled this holy place."
29 (For they had [1]previously seen [a]Trophimus the Ephesian with him in the city, whom they supposed that Paul had brought into the temple.)
30 And [a]all the city was disturbed; and the people ran together, seized Paul, and dragged him out of the temple; and immediately the doors were shut.
31 Now as they were [a]seeking to kill him, news came to the commander of the [1]garrison that all Jerusalem was in an uproar.
32 [a]He immediately took soldiers and centurions, and ran down to them. And when they saw the commander and the soldiers, they stopped beating Paul.
33 Then the [a]commander came near and took him, and [b]commanded *him* to be bound with two chains; and he asked who he was and what he had done.
34 And some among the multitude cried one thing and some another. So when he could not ascertain the truth because of the tumult, he commanded him to be taken into the barracks.
35 When he reached the stairs, he had to be carried by the soldiers because of the violence of the mob.
36 For the multitude of the people followed after, crying out, [a]"Away with him!"
**37** Then as Paul was about to be led into the barracks, he said to the commander, "May I speak to you?" He replied, "Can you speak Greek?
38 [a]"Are you not the Egyptian who some time ago stirred up a rebellion and led the four thousand assassins out into the wilderness?"
39 But Paul said, [a]"I am a Jew from Tarsus, in Cilicia, a citizen of no [1]mean city; and I implore you, permit me to speak to the people."
40 So when he had given him permission, Paul stood on the stairs and [a]motioned with his hand to the people. And when there was a great silence, he spoke to *them* in the [b]Hebrew language, saying,

22 [1]NU *What then is to be done? They will certainly hear*
24 [a]Acts 18:18
25 [a]Acts 15:19, 20, 29 [1]NU omits *that they should observe no such thing, except* [2]*fornication*
26 [a]Acts 21:24; 24:18 [b]Num. 6:13 [1]*completion*
27 [a]Acts 20:19; 24:18 [b]Acts 26:21
28 [a]Acts 6:13; 24:6
29 [a]Acts 20:4 [1]M omits *previously*
30 [a]Acts 16:19; 26:21
31 [a]2 Cor. 11:23 [1]*cohort*
32 [a]Acts 23:27; 24:7
33 [a]Acts 24:7 [b]Acts 20:23; 21:11
36 [a]John 19:15
38 [a]Acts 5:36
39 [a]Acts 9:11; 22:3 [1]*insignificant*
40 [a]Acts 12:17 [b]Acts 22:2

CHAPTER 22
1 [a]Acts 7:2
2 [a]Acts 21:40
3 [a]2 Cor. 11:22 [b]Deut. 33:3 [c]Acts 5:34 [d]Acts 23:6; 26:5 [e]Gal. 1:14 [f][Rom. 10:2]
4 [a]1 Tim. 1:13
5 [a]Acts 23:14; 24:1; 25:15 [b]Luke 22:66 [c]Acts 9:2
6 [a]Acts 9:3; 26:12, 13
9 [a]Acts 9:7 [1]NU omits *and were afraid*
12 [a]Acts 9:17 [b]Acts 10:22 [c]1 Tim. 3:7
14 [a]Acts 3:13; 5:30 [b]Acts 9:15; 26:16 [c]Acts 3:14; 7:52 [d]1 Cor. 9:1; 15:8 [e]Gal. 1:12
15 [a]Acts 23:11 [b]Acts 4:20; 26:16
16 [a]Heb. 10:22 [b]Rom. 10:13
17 [a]Acts 9:26; 26:20
18 [a]Acts 22:14 [b]Matt. 10:14
19 [a]Acts 8:3; 22:4 [b]Matt. 10:17
20 [a]Acts 7:54—8:1 [b]Luke 11:48 [1]NU omits *to his death*
21 [a]Acts 9:15

## *Paul's Defense at Jerusalem*

**22** Brethren[a] and fathers, hear my defense before you now."
2 And when they heard that he spoke to them in the [a]Hebrew language, they kept all the more silent. Then he said:
3 [a]"I am indeed a Jew, born in Tarsus of Cilicia, but brought up in this city [b]at the feet of [c]Gamaliel, taught [d]according to the strictness of our fathers' law, and [e]was zealous toward God [f]as you all are today.
4 [a]"I persecuted this Way to the death, binding and delivering into prisons both men and women,
5 "as also the high priest bears me witness, and [a]all the council of the elders, [b]from whom I also received letters to the brethren, and went to Damascus [c]to bring in chains even those who were there to Jerusalem to be punished.
6 "Now [a]it happened, as I journeyed and came near Damascus at about noon, suddenly a great light from heaven shone around me.
7 "And I fell to the ground and heard a voice saying to me, 'Saul, Saul, why are you persecuting Me?'
8 "So I answered, 'Who are You, Lord?' And He said to me, 'I am Jesus of Nazareth, whom you are persecuting.'
9 "And [a]those who were with me indeed saw the light [1]and were afraid, but they did not hear the voice of Him who spoke to me.
10 "So I said, 'What shall I do, Lord?' And the Lord said to me, 'Arise and go into Damascus, and there you will be told all things which are appointed for you to do.'
11 "And since I could not see for the glory of that light, being led by the hand of those who were with me, I came into Damascus.
12 "Then [a]a certain Ananias, a devout man according to the law, [b]having a good testimony with all the [c]Jews who dwelt *there*,
13 "came to me; and he stood and said to me, 'Brother Saul, receive your sight.' And at that same hour I looked up at him.
14 "Then he said, [a]'The God of our fathers [b]has chosen you that you should [c]know His will, and [d]see the Just One, [e]and hear the voice of His mouth.
15 [a]'For you will be His witness to all men of [b]what you have seen and heard.
16 'And now why are you waiting? Arise and be baptized, [a]and wash away your sins, [b]calling on the name of the Lord.'
17 "Now [a]it happened, when I returned to Jerusalem and was praying in the temple, that I was in a trance
18 "and [a]saw Him saying to me, [b]'Make haste and get out of Jerusalem quickly, for they will not receive your testimony concerning Me.'
19 "So I said, 'Lord, [a]they know that in every synagogue I imprisoned and [b]beat those who believe on You.
20 [a]'And when the blood of Your martyr Stephen was shed, I also was standing by [b]consenting [1]to his death, and guarding the clothes of those who were killing him.'
21 "Then He said to me, 'Depart, [a]for I will send you far from here to the Gentiles.'"
**22** And they listened to him until this word, and

*then* they raised their voices and said, [a]"Away
with such a *fellow* from the earth, for [b]he is not fit
to live!"
23 Then, as they cried out and [1]tore off *their*
clothes and threw dust into the air,
24 the commander ordered him to be brought
into the barracks, and said that he should be
examined under scourging, so that he might know
why they shouted so against him.
25 And as they bound him with thongs, Paul said
to the centurion who stood by, [a]"Is it lawful for
you to scourge a man who is a Roman, and
uncondemned?"
26 When the centurion heard *that,* he went and
told the commander, saying, "Take care what you
do, for this man is a Roman."
27 Then the commander came and said to him,
"Tell me, are you a Roman?" He said, "Yes."
28 The commander answered, "With a large sum
I obtained this citizenship." And Paul said, "But I
was born *a citizen.*"
29 Then immediately those who were about to
examine him withdrew from him; and the commander was also afraid after he found out that he
was a Roman, and because he had bound him.
**30** The next day, because he wanted to know for
certain why he was accused by the Jews, he
released him from *his* bonds, and commanded the
chief priests and all their council to appear, and
brought Paul down and set him before them.

### *The Jerusalem Jews Plot to Kill Paul*

**23** Then Paul, looking earnestly at the council,
said, "Men *and* brethren, [a]I have lived in all
good conscience before God until this day."
2 And the high priest Ananias commanded
those who stood by him [a]to strike him on the
mouth.
3 Then Paul said to him, "God will strike you,
*you* whitewashed wall! For you sit to judge me
according to the law, and [a]do you command me to
be struck contrary to the law?"
4 And those who stood by said, "Do you revile
God's high priest?"
5 Then Paul said, [a]"I did not know, brethren,
that he was the high priest; for it is written, [b]*'You*
*shall not speak evil of a ruler of your people.'* "
6 But when Paul perceived that one part were
Sadducees and the other Pharisees, he cried out in
the council, "Men *and* brethren, [a]I am a Pharisee,
the son of a Pharisee; [b]concerning the hope and
resurrection of the dead I am being judged!"
7 And when he had said this, a dissension arose
between the Pharisees and the Sadducees; and the
assembly was divided.
8 [a]For Sadducees say that there is no resurrection—and no angel or spirit; but the Pharisees
confess both.
9 Then there arose a loud outcry. And the
scribes of the Pharisees' party arose and protested,
saying, [a]"We find no evil in this man; [1]but [b]if a
spirit or an angel has spoken to him, [c]let us not
fight against God."
10 Now when there arose a great dissension, the
commander, fearing lest Paul might be pulled to
pieces by them, commanded the soldiers to go
down and take him by force from among them,
and bring *him* into the barracks.
**11** But [a]the following night the Lord stood by him
and said, [1]"Be of good cheer, Paul; for as you have
testified for Me in [b]Jerusalem, so you must also
bear witness at [c]Rome."
12 And when it was day, [a]some of the Jews
banded together and bound themselves under an
oath, saying that they would neither eat nor drink
till they had [b]killed Paul.
13 Now there were more than forty who had
formed this conspiracy.
14 They came to the chief priests and [a]elders, and
said, "We have bound ourselves under a great
oath that we will eat nothing until we have killed
Paul.
15 "Now you, therefore, together with the council, suggest to the commander that he be brought
down to you [1]tomorrow, as though you were
going to make further inquiries concerning him;
but we are ready to kill him before he comes
near."
16 So when Paul's sister's son heard of their
ambush, he went and entered the barracks and
told Paul.
17 Then Paul called one of the centurions to *him*
and said, "Take this young man to the commander, for he has something to tell him."
18 So he took him and brought *him* to the commander and said, "Paul the prisoner called me to
*him* and asked *me* to bring this young man to you.
He has something to say to you."
19 Then the commander took him by the hand,
went aside, and asked privately, "What is it that
you have to tell me?"
20 And he said, [a]"The Jews have agreed to ask
that you bring Paul down to the council tomorrow, as though they were going to inquire more
fully about him.
21 "But do not yield to them, for more than forty
of them lie in wait for him, men who have bound
themselves by an oath that they will neither eat
nor drink till they have killed him; and now they
are ready, waiting for the promise from you."
22 So the commander let the young man depart,
and commanded *him,* "Tell no one that you have
revealed these things to me."
**23** And he called for two centurions, saying,
"Prepare two hundred soldiers, seventy horsemen,
and two hundred spearmen to go to [a]Caesarea at
the third hour of the night;
24 "and provide mounts to set Paul on, and bring
*him* safely to Felix the governor."
25 He wrote a letter in the following manner:

**26** Claudius Lysias,
To the most excellent governor Felix:
Greetings.
27 [a]This man was seized by the Jews and was
about to be killed by them. Coming with the
troops I rescued him, having learned that he
was a Roman.
28 [a]And when I wanted to know the reason
they accused him, I brought him before their
council.
29 I found out that he was accused [a]concerning
questions of their law, [b]but had nothing
charged against him deserving of death or
chains.
30 And [a]when it was told me that [1]the Jews lay
in wait for the man, I sent him immediately
to you, and [b]also commanded his accusers to
state before you the charges against him.
Farewell.

**22** [a]Acts 21:36; 1 Thess. 2:16 [b]Acts 25:24
**23** [1]Lit. *threw*
**25** [a]Acts 16:37

CHAPTER 23
**1** [a]Acts 24:16; 1 Cor. 4:4; 2 Cor. 1:12; 4:2; 2 Tim. 1:3; Heb. 13:18
**2** [a]1 Kin. 22:24; Jer. 20:2; John 18:22
**3** [a]Lev. 19:35; Deut. 25:1, 2; John 7:51
**5** [a]Lev. 5:17, 18 [b]Ex. 22:28; Eccl. 10:20; 2 Pet. 2:10
**6** [a]Acts 26:5; Phil. 3:5 [b]Acts 24:15, 21; 26:6; 28:20
**8** [a]Matt. 22:23; Mark 12:18; Luke 20:27
**9** [a]Acts 25:25; 26:31 [b]John 12:29; Acts 22:6, 7, 17, 18 [c]Acts 5:39 [1]NU *what if a spirit or an angel has spoken to him?* omitting the last clause
**11** [a]Acts 18:9; 27:23, 24 [b]Acts 21:18, 19; 22:1–21 [c]Acts 28:16, 17, 23 [1]*Take courage*
**12** [a]Acts 23:21, 30; 25:3 [b]Acts 9:23, 24; 25:3; 26:21; 27:42; 1 Thess. 2:15
**14** [a]Acts 4:5, 23; 6:12; 22:5; 24:1; 25:15
**15** [1]NU omits *tomorrow*
**20** [a]Acts 23:12
**23** [a]Acts 8:40; 23:33
**27** [a]Acts 21:30, 33; 24:7
**28** [a]Acts 22:30
**29** [a]Acts 18:15; 25:19 [b]Acts 25:25; 26:31
**30** [a]Acts 23:20 [b]Acts 24:8; 25:6 [1]NU *there would be a plot against the man*

**31** Then the soldiers, as they were commanded, took Paul and brought *him* by night to Antipatris.
32 The next day they left the horsemen to go on with him, and returned to the barracks.
33 When they came to [a]Caesarea and had delivered the [b]letter to the governor, they also presented Paul to him.
34 And when the governor had read *it,* he asked what province he was from. And when he understood that *he was* from [a]Cilicia,
35 he said, [a]"I will hear you when your accusers also have come." And he commanded him to be kept in [b]Herod's [1]Praetorium.

### *Paul's Defense Before Felix*

**24** Now after [a]five days [b]Ananias the high priest came down with the elders and a certain orator *named* Tertullus. These gave evidence to the governor against Paul.
2 And when he was called upon, Tertullus began his accusation, saying: "Seeing that through you we enjoy great peace, and [1]prosperity is being brought to this nation by your foresight,
3 "we accept *it* always and in all places, most noble Felix, with all thankfulness.
4 "Nevertheless, not to be tedious to you any further, I beg you to hear, by your [1]courtesy, a few words from us.
5 [a]"For we have found this man *a* plague, a creator of dissension among all the Jews throughout the world, and a ringleader of the sect of the Nazarenes.
6 [a]"He even tried to profane the temple, and we seized him, [1]and wanted [b]to judge him according to our law.
7 [a]"But the commander Lysias came by and with great violence took *him* out of our hands,
8 [a]"commanding his accusers to come to you. By examining him yourself you may ascertain all these things of which we accuse him."
9 And the Jews also [1]assented, maintaining that these things were so.
**10** Then Paul, after the governor had nodded to him to speak, answered: "Inasmuch as I know that you have been for many years a judge of this nation, I do the more cheerfully answer for myself,
11 "because you may ascertain that it is no more than twelve days since I went up to Jerusalem [a]to worship.
12 [a]"And they neither found me in the temple disputing with anyone nor inciting the crowd, either in the synagogues or in the city.
13 "Nor can they prove the things of which they now accuse me.
14 "But this I confess to you, that according to [a]the Way which they call a sect, so I worship the [b]God of my fathers, believing all things which are written in [c]the Law and in the Prophets.
15 [a]"I have hope in God, which they themselves also accept, [b]that there will be a resurrection [1]of *the* dead, both of *the* just and *the* unjust.
16 [a]"This *being* so, I myself always strive to have a conscience without offense toward God and men.
17 "Now after many years [a]I came to bring alms and offerings to my nation,
18 [a]"in the midst of which some Jews from Asia found me [b]purified in the temple, neither with a mob nor with tumult.
19 [a]"They ought to have been here before you to object if they had anything against me.
20 "Or else let those who are *here* themselves say [1]if they found any wrongdoing in me while I stood before the council,
21 "unless *it is* for this one statement which I cried out, standing among them, [a]'Concerning the resurrection of the dead I am being judged by you this day.' "
**22** But when Felix heard these things, having more accurate knowledge of *the* [a]Way, he adjourned the proceedings and said, "When [b]Lysias the commander comes down, I will make a decision on your case."
23 So he commanded the centurion to keep Paul and to let *him* have liberty, and [a]told him not to forbid any of his friends to provide for or visit him.
24 And after some days, when Felix came with his wife Drusilla, who was Jewish, he sent for Paul and heard him concerning the [a]faith in Christ.
25 Now as he reasoned about righteousness, self-control, and the judgment to come, Felix was afraid and answered, "Go away for now; when I have a convenient time I will call for you."
26 Meanwhile he also hoped that [a]money would be given him by Paul, [1]that he might release him. Therefore he sent for him more often and conversed with him.
27 But after two years Porcius Festus succeeded Felix; and Felix, [a]wanting to do the Jews a favor, left Paul bound.

### *Paul Appeals to Caesar*

**25** Now when Festus had come to the province, after three days he went up from [a]Caesarea to Jerusalem.
2 [a]Then the [1]high priest and the chief men of the Jews informed him against Paul; and they petitioned him,
3 asking a favor against him, that he would summon him to Jerusalem—[a]while *they* lay in ambush along the road to kill him.
4 But Festus answered that Paul should be kept at Caesarea, and that he himself was going *there* shortly.
5 "Therefore," he said, "let those who have authority among you go down with *me* and accuse this man, to see [a]if there is any fault in him."
6 And when he had remained among them more than ten days, he went down to Caesarea. And the next day, sitting on the judgment seat, he commanded Paul to be brought.
7 When he had come, the Jews who had come down from Jerusalem stood about [a]and laid many serious complaints against Paul, which they could not prove,
8 while he answered for himself, [a]"Neither against the law of the Jews, nor against the temple, nor against Caesar have I offended in anything at all."
9 But Festus, [a]wanting to do the Jews a favor, answered Paul and said, [b]"Are you willing to go up to Jerusalem and there be judged before me concerning these things?"
10 So Paul said, "I stand at Caesar's judgment seat, where I ought to be judged. To the Jews I have done no wrong, as you very well know.
11 [a]"For if I am an offender, or have committed anything deserving of death, I do not object to dying; but if there is nothing in these things of

---

**33** [a]Acts 8:40 [b]Acts 23:26–30
**34** [a]Acts 6:9; 21:39
**35** [a]Acts 24:1, 10; 25:16 [b]Matt. 27:27 [1]Headquarters

CHAPTER 24
**1** [a]Acts 21:27 [b]Acts 23:2, 30, 35; 25:2
**2** [1]Or *reforms are*
**4** [1]*graciousness*
**5** [a]1 Pet. 2:12, 15
**6** [a]Acts 21:28 [b]John 18:31 [1]NU ends the sentence here and omits the rest of v. 6, all of v. 7, and the first clause of v. 8.
**7** [a]Acts 21:33; 23:10
**8** [a]Acts 23:30
**9** [1]NU, M *joined the attack*
**11** [a]Acts 21:15, 18, 26, 27; 24:17
**12** [a]Acts 25:8; 28:17
**14** [a]Acts 9:2; 24:22 [b]2 Tim. 1:3 [c]Acts 26:22; 28:23
**15** [a]Acts 23:6; 26:6, 7; 28:20 [b][Dan. 12:2] [1]NU omits *of the dead*
**16** [a]Acts 23:1
**17** [a]Rom. 15:25–28
**18** [a]Acts 21:27; 26:21 [b]Acts 21:26
**19** [a][Acts 23:30; 25:16]
**20** [1]NU, M *what wrongdoing they found*
**21** [a][Acts 23:6; 24:15; 28:20]
**22** [a]Acts 9:2; 18:26; 19:9, 23; 22:4 [b]Acts 23:26; 24:7
**23** [a]Acts 23:16; 27:3; 28:16
**24** [a][Rom. 10:9]
**26** [a]Ex. 23:8 [1]NU omits *that he might release him*
**27** [a]Acts 12:3; 23:35; 25:9, 14

CHAPTER 25
**1** [a]Acts 8:40; 25:4, 6, 13
**2** [a]Acts 24:1; 25:15 [1]NU *chief priests*
**3** [a]Acts 23:12, 15
**5** [a]Acts 18:14; 25:18
**7** [a]Acts 24:5, 13
**8** [a]Acts 6:13; 24:12; 28:17
**9** [a]Acts 12:2; 24:27 [b]Acts 25:20
**11** [a]Acts 18:14; 23:29; 25:25; 26:31

which these men accuse me, no one can deliver
me to them. [b]I appeal to Caesar."
12 Then Festus, when he had conferred with the
council, answered, "You have appealed to Caesar?
To Caesar you shall go!"
**13** And after some days King Agrippa and Bernice came to Caesarea to greet Festus.
14 When they had been there many days, Festus
laid Paul's case before the king, saying: [a]"There is
a certain man left a prisoner by Felix,
15 [a]"about whom the chief priests and the elders
of the Jews informed *me,* when I was in Jerusalem, asking for a judgment against him.
16 [a]"To them I answered, 'It is not the custom of
the Romans to deliver any man [1]to destruction
before the accused meets the accusers face to
face, and has opportunity to answer for himself
concerning the charge against him.'
17 "Therefore when they had come together,
[a]without any delay, the next day I sat on the
judgment seat and commanded the man to be
brought in.
18 "When the accusers stood up, they brought no
accusation against him of such things as I [1]sup-
posed,
19 [a]"but had some questions against him about
their own religion and about a certain Jesus, who
had died, whom Paul affirmed to be alive.
20 "And because I was uncertain of such questions, I asked whether he was willing to go to
Jerusalem and there be judged concerning these
matters.
21 "But when Paul [a]appealed to be reserved for
the decision of Augustus, I commanded him to be
kept till I could send him to Caesar."
22 Then [a]Agrippa said to Festus, "I also would
like to hear the man myself." "Tomorrow," he
said, "you shall hear him."
23 So the next day, when Agrippa and Bernice
had come with great [1]pomp, and had entered the
auditorium with the commanders and the prominent men of the city, at Festus' command [a]Paul
was brought in.
24 And Festus said: "King Agrippa and all the
men who are here present with us, you see this
man about whom [a]the whole assembly of the Jews
petitioned me, both at Jerusalem and here, crying
out that he was [b]not fit to live any longer.
25 "But when I found that [a]he had committed
nothing deserving of death, [b]and that he himself
had appealed to Augustus, I decided to send him.
26 "I have nothing certain to write to my lord
concerning him. Therefore I have brought him
out before you, and especially before you, King
Agrippa, so that after the examination has taken
place I may have something to write.
27 "For it seems to me unreasonable to send a
prisoner and not to specify the charges against
him."

### *Paul's Defense Before Agrippa*

**26** Then Agrippa said to Paul, "You are permitted to speak for yourself." So Paul stretched
out his hand and answered for himself:
2 "I think myself [a]happy, King Agrippa, because
today I shall answer [b]for myself before you concerning all the things of which I am [c]accused by
the Jews,
3 "especially because you are expert in all customs and questions which have to do with the
Jews. Therefore I beg you to hear me patiently.
4 "My manner of life from my youth, which was
spent from the beginning among my own nation
at Jerusalem, all the Jews know.
5 "They knew me from the first, if they were
willing to testify, that according to [a]the strictest
sect of our religion I lived a Pharisee.
6 [a]"And now I stand and am judged for the hope
of [b]the promise made by God to our fathers.
7 "To this *promise* [a]our twelve tribes, earnestly
serving *God* [b]night and day, [c]hope to attain. For
this hope's sake, King Agrippa, I am accused by
the Jews.
8 "Why should it be thought incredible by you
that God raises the dead?
9 [a]"Indeed, I myself thought I must do many
things [1]contrary to the name of [b]Jesus of Nazareth.
10 [a]"This I also did in Jerusalem, and many of the
saints I shut up in prison, having received authority [b]from the chief priests; and when they were
put to death, I cast my vote against *them.*
11 [a]"And I punished them often in every synagogue and compelled *them* to blaspheme; and
being exceedingly enraged against them, I persecuted *them* even to foreign cities.
**12** [a]"While thus occupied, as I journeyed to
Damascus with authority and commission from
the chief priests,
13 "at midday, O king, along the road I saw a
light from heaven, brighter than the sun, shining
around me and those who journeyed with me.
14 "And when we all had fallen to the ground, I
heard a voice speaking to me and saying in the
Hebrew language, 'Saul, Saul, why are you persecuting Me? *It is* hard for you to kick against the
goads.'
15 "So I said, 'Who are You, Lord?' And He said,
'I am Jesus, whom you are persecuting.
16 'But rise and stand on your feet; for I have
appeared to you for this purpose, [a]to make you a
minister and a witness both of the things which
you have seen and of the things which I will yet
reveal to you.
17 'I will [1]deliver you from the *Jewish* people, as
well as *from* the Gentiles, [a]to whom I [2]now send
you,
18 [a]'to open their eyes, *in order* [b]to turn *them*
from darkness to light, and *from* the power of
Satan to God, [c]that they may receive forgiveness
of sins and [d]an inheritance among those who are
[e]sanctified[1] by faith in Me.'
**19** "Therefore, King Agrippa, I was not disobedient to the heavenly vision,
20 "but [a]declared first to those in Damascus and
in Jerusalem, and throughout all the region of
Judea, and *then* to the Gentiles, that they should
repent, turn to God, and do [b]works befitting
repentance.
21 "For these reasons the Jews seized me in the
temple and tried to kill *me.*
22 "Therefore, having obtained help from God, to
this day I stand, witnessing both to small and
great, saying no other things than those [a]which
the prophets and [b]Moses said would come—
23 [a]"that the Christ would suffer, [b]that He would
be the first to rise from the dead, and [c]would
proclaim light to the *Jewish* people and to the
Gentiles."
**24** Now as he thus made his defense, Festus said
with a loud voice, "Paul, [a]you are beside yourself!
Much learning is driving you mad!"

---

**11** [b]Acts 26:32; 28:19
**14** [a]Acts 24:27
**15** [a]Acts 24:1; 25:2, 3
**16** [a]Acts 25:4, 5 [1]NU omits *to destruction,* although it is implied
**17** [a]Acts 25:6, 10
**18** [1]*suspected*
**19** [a]Acts 18:14, 15; 23:29
**21** [a]Acts 25:11, 12
**22** [a]Acts 9:15
**23** [a]Acts 9:15 [1]*pageantry*
**24** [a]Acts 25:2, 3, 7 [b]Acts 21:36; 22:22
**25** [a]Acts 23:9, 29; 26:31 [b]Acts 25:11, 12

CHAPTER 26
**2** [a][1 Pet. 3:14; 4:14] [b][1 Pet. 3:15, 16] [c]Acts 21:28; 24:5, 6
**5** [a]Phil. 3:5
**6** [a]Acts 23:6 [b]Acts 13:32
**7** [a]James 1:1 [b]1 Thess. 3:10 [c]Phil. 3:11
**9** [a]1 Tim. 1:12, 13 [b]Acts 2:22; 10:38 [1]*against*
**10** [a]Acts 8:1–3; 9:13 [b]Acts 9:14
**11** [a]Acts 22:19
**12** [a]Acts 9:3–8; 22:6–11; 26:12–18
**16** [a]Acts 22:15
**17** [a]Acts 22:21 [1]*rescue* [2]NU, M omit *now*
**18** [a]Is. 35:5; 42:7, 16 [b]1 Pet. 2:9 [c]Luke 1:77 [d]Col. 1:12 [e]Acts 20:32 [1]*set apart*
**20** [a]Acts 9:19, 20, 22; 11:26 [b]Matt. 3:8
**22** [a]Rom. 3:21 [b]John 5:46
**23** [a]Luke 24:26 [b]1 Cor. 15:20, 23 [c]Luke 2:32
**24** [a][1 Cor. 1:23; 2:13, 14; 4:10]

25 But he said, "I am not [1]mad, most noble Festus, but speak the words of truth and reason.

26 "For the king, before whom I also speak freely, [a]knows these things; for I am convinced that none of these things escapes his attention, since this thing was not done in a corner.

27 "King Agrippa, do you believe the prophets? I know that you do believe."

28 Then Agrippa said to Paul, "You almost persuade me to become a Christian."

29 And Paul said, [a]"I would to God that not only you, but also all who hear me today, might become both almost and altogether such as I am, except for these chains."

30 When he had said these things, the king stood up, as well as the governor and Bernice and those who sat with them;

31 and when they had gone aside, they talked among themselves, saying, [a]"This man is doing nothing deserving of death or chains."

32 Then Agrippa said to Festus, "This man might have been set [a]free [b]if he had not appealed to Caesar."

### *Paul's Voyage to Rome*

**27** And when [a]it was decided that we should sail to Italy, they delivered Paul and some other prisoners to *one* named Julius, a centurion of the Augustan Regiment.

2 So, entering a ship of Adramyttium, we put to sea, meaning to sail along the coasts of Asia. [a]Aristarchus, a Macedonian of Thessalonica, was with us.

3 And the next *day* we landed at Sidon. And Julius [a]treated Paul kindly and gave *him* liberty to go to his friends and receive care.

4 When we had put to sea from there, we sailed under *the shelter of* Cyprus, because the winds were contrary.

5 And when we had sailed over the sea which is off Cilicia and Pamphylia, we came to Myra, *a city* of Lycia.

6 There the centurion found [a]an Alexandrian ship sailing to Italy, and he put us on board.

7 When we had sailed slowly many days, and arrived with difficulty off Cnidus, the wind not permitting us to proceed, we sailed under *the shelter of* [a]Crete off Salmone.

8 Passing it with difficulty, we came to a place called Fair Havens, near the city *of* Lasea.

**9** Now when much time had been spent, and sailing was now dangerous [a]because [1]the Fast was already over, Paul advised them,

10 saying, "Men, I perceive that this voyage will end with disaster and much loss, not only of the cargo and ship, but also our lives."

11 Nevertheless the centurion was more persuaded by the helmsman and the owner of the ship than by the things spoken by Paul.

12 And because the harbor was not suitable to winter in, the majority advised to set sail from there also, if by any means they could reach Phoenix, a harbor of Crete opening toward the southwest and northwest, *and* winter *there.*

**13** When the south wind blew softly, supposing that they had obtained *their* desire, putting out to sea, they sailed close by Crete.

14 But not long after, a tempestuous head wind arose, called [1]Euroclydon.

15 So when the ship was caught, and could not head into the wind, we let *her* [1]drive.

16 And running under *the shelter of* an island called [1]Clauda, we secured the skiff with difficulty.

17 When they had taken it on board, they used cables to undergird the ship; and fearing lest they should run aground on the [1]Syrtis *Sands,* they struck sail and so were driven.

18 And because we were exceedingly tempest-tossed, the next *day* they lightened the ship.

19 On the third *day* [a]we threw the ship's tackle overboard with our own hands.

20 Now when neither sun nor stars appeared for many days, and no small tempest beat on *us,* all hope that we would be saved was finally given up.

21 But after long abstinence from food, then Paul stood in the midst of them and said, "Men, you should have listened to me, and not have sailed from Crete and incurred this disaster and loss.

22 "And now I urge you to take [1]heart, for there will be no loss of life among you, but only of the ship.

23 [a]"For there stood by me this night an angel of the God to whom I belong and [b]whom I serve,

24 "saying, 'Do not be afraid, Paul; you must be brought before Caesar; and indeed God has granted you all those who sail with you.'

25 "Therefore take heart, men, [a]for I believe God that it will be just as it was told me.

26 "However, [a]we must run aground on a certain island."

27 Now when the fourteenth night had come, as we were driven up and down in the Adriatic *Sea,* about midnight the sailors sensed that they were drawing near some land.

28 And they took soundings and found *it* to be twenty fathoms; and when they had gone a little farther, they took soundings again and found *it* to be fifteen fathoms.

29 Then, fearing lest we should run aground on the rocks, they dropped four anchors from the stern, and [1]prayed for day to come.

30 And as the sailors were seeking to escape from the ship, when they had let down the skiff into the sea, under pretense of putting out anchors from the prow,

31 Paul said to the centurion and the soldiers, "Unless these men stay in the ship, you cannot be saved."

32 Then the soldiers cut away the ropes of the skiff and let it fall off.

33 And as day was about to dawn, Paul implored *them* all to take food, saying, "Today is the fourteenth day you have waited and continued without food, and eaten nothing.

34 "Therefore I urge you to take nourishment, for this is for your survival, [a]since not a hair will fall from the head of any of you."

35 And when he had said these things, he took bread and [a]gave thanks to God in the presence of them all; and when he had broken *it* he began to eat.

36 Then they were all encouraged, and also took food themselves.

37 And in all we were two hundred and seventy-six [a]persons on the ship.

38 So when they had eaten enough, they lightened the ship and threw out the wheat into the sea.

**39** When it was day, they did not recognize the land; but they observed a bay with a beach, onto which they planned to run the ship if possible.

40 And they [1]let go the anchors and left *them* in

---

**25** [1]*out of my mind*
**26** [a]Acts 26:3
**29** [a]1 Cor. 7:7
**31** [a]Acts 23:9, 29; 25:25
**32** [a]Acts 28:18 [b]Acts 25:11

CHAPTER 27
**1** [a]Acts 25:12, 25
**2** [a]Acts 19:29
**3** [a]Acts 24:23; 28:16
**6** [a]Acts 28:11
**7** [a]Acts 2:11; 27:12, 21; Titus 1:5, 12
**9** [a]Lev. 16:29–31; 23:27–29; Num. 29:7 [1]The Day of Atonement, late September or early October
**14** [1]A southeast wind that stirs up broad waves; NU *Euraquilon,* a northeaster
**15** [1]*be driven*
**16** [1]NU *Cauda*
**17** [1]M *Syrtes*
**19** [a]Jon. 1:5
**22** [1]*courage*
**23** [a]Acts 18:9; 23:11; 2 Tim. 4:17 [b]Dan. 6:16; Rom. 1:9; 2 Tim. 1:3
**25** [a]Luke 1:45; Rom. 4:20, 21; 2 Tim. 1:12
**26** [a]Acts 28:1
**29** [1]Or *wished*
**34** [a]1 Kin. 1:52; [Matt. 10:30; Luke 12:7; 21:18]
**35** [a]1 Sam. 9:13; Matt. 15:36; Mark 8:6; John 6:11; [1 Tim. 4:3, 4]
**37** [a]Acts 2:41; 7:14; Rom. 13:1; 1 Pet. 3:20
**40** [1]*cast off*

the sea, meanwhile loosing the rudder ropes; and
they hoisted the mainsail to the wind and made
for shore.
41 But striking [1]a place where two seas met,
[a]they ran the ship aground; and the prow stuck
fast and remained immovable, but the stern was
being broken up by the violence of the waves.
42 And the soldiers' plan was to kill the prisoners,
lest any of them should swim away and escape.
43 But the centurion, wanting to save Paul, kept
them from *their* purpose, and commanded that
those who could swim should jump *overboard*
first and get to land,
44 and the rest, some on boards and some on
*parts* of the ship. And so it was [a]that they all
escaped safely to land.

### *Paul's Ministry on Malta and at Rome*

**28** Now when they had escaped, they then
found out that [a]the island was called Malta.
2 And the [a]natives[1] showed us unusual kindness; for they kindled a fire and made us all
welcome, because of the rain that was falling and
because of the cold.
3 But when Paul had gathered a bundle of sticks
and laid *them* on the fire, a viper came out because of the heat, and fastened on his hand.
4 So when the natives saw the creature hanging
from his hand, they said to one another, "No
doubt this man is a murderer, whom, though he
has escaped the sea, yet justice does not allow to
live."
5 But he shook off the creature into the fire and
[a]suffered no harm.
6 However, they were expecting that he would
swell up or suddenly fall down dead. But after
they had looked for a long time and saw no harm
come to him, they changed their minds and [a]said
that he was a god.
7 In that region there was an estate of the
[1]leading citizen of the island, whose name was
Publius, who received us and entertained us courteously for three days.
8 And it happened that the father of Publius lay
sick of a fever and dysentery. Paul went in to him
and [a]prayed, and [b]he laid his hands on him and
healed him.
9 So when this was done, the rest of those on
the island who had diseases also came and were
healed.
10 They also honored us in many [a]ways; and
when we departed, they provided such things as
were [b]necessary.
11 After three months we sailed in [a]an Alexandrian ship whose figurehead was the [1]Twin Brothers, which had wintered at the island.
12 And landing at Syracuse, we stayed three
days.
13 From there we circled round and reached
Rhegium. And after one day the south wind blew;
and the next day we came to Puteoli,
14 where we found [a]brethren, and were invited to
stay with them seven days. And so we went
toward Rome.
15 And from there, when the brethren heard
about us, they came to meet us as far as Appii
Forum and Three Inns. When Paul saw them, he
thanked God and took courage.
16 Now when we came to Rome, the centurion
delivered the prisoners to the captain of the
guard; but [a]Paul was permitted to dwell by himself
with the soldier who guarded him.
17 And it came to pass after three days that Paul
called the leaders of the Jews together. So when
they had come together, he said to them: "Men
*and* brethren, [a]though I have done nothing
against our people or the customs of our fathers,
yet [b]I was delivered as a prisoner from Jerusalem
into the hands of the Romans,
18 "who, [a]when they had examined me, wanted
to let *me* go, because there was no cause for
putting me to death.
19 "But when the [1]Jews spoke against *it*, [a]I was
compelled to appeal to Caesar, not that I had
anything of which to accuse my nation.
20 "For this reason therefore I have called for
you, to see *you* and speak with *you*, because [a]for
the hope of Israel I am bound with [b]this chain."
21 Then they said to him, "We neither received
letters from Judea concerning you, nor have any
of the brethren who came reported or spoken any
evil of you.
22 "But we desire to hear from you what you
think; for concerning this sect, we know that [a]it is
spoken against everywhere."
23 So when they had appointed him a day, many
came to him at *his* lodging, [a]to whom he explained
and solemnly testified of the kingdom of God,
persuading them concerning Jesus [b]from both the
Law of Moses and the Prophets, from morning till
evening.
24 And [a]some were persuaded by the things
which were spoken, and some disbelieved.
25 So when they did not agree among themselves, they departed after Paul had said one
word: "The Holy Spirit spoke rightly through
Isaiah the prophet to [1]our fathers,
26 "saying,

[a]*'Go to this people and say:*
*"Hearing you will hear,*
*and shall not understand;*
*And seeing you will see, and not perceive;*
27 *For the hearts of this people*
*have grown dull.*
*Their ears are hard of hearing,*
*And their eyes they have closed,*
*Lest they should see with their eyes and hear*
*with their ears,*
*Lest they should understand with their*
*hearts and turn,*
*So that I should heal them."'*

28 "Therefore let it be known to you that the
salvation of God has been sent [a]to the Gentiles,
and they will hear it!"
29 [1]And when he had said these words, the Jews
departed and had a great dispute among themselves.
30 Then Paul dwelt two whole years in his own
rented house, and received all who came to him,
31 [a]preaching the kingdom of God and teaching
the things which concern the Lord Jesus Christ
with all confidence, no one forbidding him.

---

**41** [a]2 Cor. 11:25 [1]A reef
**44** [a]Acts 27:22, 31

CHAPTER 28
**1** [a]Acts 27:26
**2** [a]Acts 28:4; Rom. 1:14; 1 Cor. 14:11; Col. 3:11 [1]Lit. *barbarians*
**5** [a]Mark 16:18; Luke 10:19
**6** [a]Acts 12:22; 14:11
**7** [1]Magistrate
**8** [a]Acts 9:40; [James 5:14, 15] [b]Matt. 9:18; Mark 5:23; 6:5; 7:32; 16:18; Luke 4:40; Acts 19:11, 12; [1 Cor. 12:9, 28]
**10** [a]Matt. 15:6; 1 Tim. 5:17 [b][Phil. 4:19]
**11** [a]Acts 27:6 [1]Gr. *Dioskouroi*, Zeus's sons Castor and Pollux
**14** [a]Rom. 1:8
**16** [a]Acts 23:11; 24:25; 27:3
**17** [a]Acts 23:29; 24:12, 13; 26:31 [b]Acts 21:33
**18** [a]Acts 22:24; 24:10; 25:8; 26:32
**19** [a]Acts 25:11, 21, 25 [1]The ruling authorities
**20** [a]Acts 26:6, 7 [b]Acts 26:29; Eph. 3:1; 4:1; 6:20; 2 Tim. 1:8, 16; Philem. 10, 13
**22** [a]Luke 2:34; Acts 24:5, 14; [1 Pet. 2:12; 3:16; 4:14, 16]
**23** [a]Luke 24:27; [Acts 17:3; 19:8] [b]Acts 26:6, 22
**24** [a]Acts 14:4; 19:9
**25** [1]NU *your*
**26** [a]Is. 6:9, 10; Jer. 5:21; Ezek. 12:2; Matt. 13:14, 15; Mark 4:12; Luke 8:10; John 12:40, 41; Rom. 11:8
**28** [a]Is. 42:1, 6; 49:6; Matt. 21:41; Luke 2:32; Rom. 11:11
**29** [1]NU omits v. 29.
**31** [a]Acts 4:31; Eph. 6:19

*The Epistle of Paul the Apostle to the*

# ROMANS

## *Paul's Ministry of the Gospel of Christ*

PAUL, a bondservant of Jesus Christ, [a]called
*to be* an apostle, [b]separated to the gospel of
God
2 [a]which He promised before [b]through His prophets in the Holy Scriptures,
3 concerning His Son Jesus Christ our Lord,
who [1]was [a]born of the seed of David according to
the flesh,
4 *and* [a]declared *to be* the Son of God with power
according [b]to the Spirit of holiness, by the resurrection from the dead.
5 Through Him [a]we have received grace and
apostleship for [b]obedience to the faith among all
nations [c]for His name,
6 among whom you also are the called of Jesus
Christ;

7 To all who are in Rome, beloved of God,
[a]called *to be* saints:

[b]Grace to you and peace from God our Father
and the Lord Jesus Christ.
**8** First, [a]I thank my God through Jesus Christ
for you all, that [b]your faith is spoken of throughout the whole world.
9 For [a]God is my witness, [b]whom I serve [1]with
my spirit in the gospel of His Son, that [c]without
ceasing I make mention of you always in my
prayers,
10 making request if, by some means, now at last
I may find a way in the will of God to come to
you.
11 For I long to see you, that [a]I may impart to
you some spiritual gift, so that you may be established—
12 that is, that I may be encouraged together
with you by [a]the mutual faith both of you and me.
13 Now I do not want you to be unaware, brethren, that I often planned to come to you (but [a]was
hindered until now), that I might have some [b]fruit
among you also, just as among the other Gentiles.
14 I am a debtor both to Greeks and to barbarians, both to wise and to unwise.
15 So, as much as is in me, *I am* ready to preach
the gospel to you who are in Rome also.
**16** For [a]I am not ashamed of the gospel [1]of Christ,
for [b]it is the power of God to salvation for everyone who believes, [c]for the Jew first and also for
the Greek.
17 For [a]in it the righteousness of God is revealed
from faith to faith; as it is written, [b]*"The just shall
live by faith."*
**18** [a]For the wrath of God is revealed from heaven
against all ungodliness and [b]unrighteousness of
men, who [1]suppress the truth in unrighteousness,
19 because [a]what may be known of God is [1]mani-
fest [2]in them, for [b]God has shown *it* to them.
20 For since the creation of the world [a]His invisible *attributes* are clearly seen, being understood
by the things that are made, *even* His eternal
power and [1]Godhead, so that they are without
excuse,
21 because, although they knew God, they did
not glorify *Him* as God, nor were thankful, but
[a]became futile in their thoughts, and their foolish
hearts were darkened.
22 [a]Professing to be wise, they became fools,
23 and changed the glory of the [a]incorruptible
[b]God into an image made like [1]corruptible man—
and birds and four-footed animals and creeping
things.
24 [a]Therefore God also gave them up to uncleanness, in the lusts of their hearts, [b]to dishonor their
bodies [c]among themselves,
25 who exchanged [a]the truth of God [b]for the lie,
and worshiped and served the creature rather
than the Creator, who is blessed forever. Amen.
26 For this reason God gave them up to [a]vile
passions. For even their [1]women exchanged the
natural use for what is against nature.
27 Likewise also the [1]men, leaving the natural
use of the [2]woman, burned in their lust for one
another, [1]men with [1]men committing what is
shameful, and receiving in themselves the penalty
of their error which was due.
28 And even as they did not like to retain God in
*their* knowledge, God gave them over to a de-
based mind, to do those things [a]which are not
fitting;
29 being filled with all unrighteousness, [1]sexual
immorality, wickedness, [2]covetousness, [3]mali-
ciousness; full of envy, murder, strife, deceit, evil-
mindedness; *they are* whisperers,
30 backbiters, haters of God, violent, proud,
boasters, inventors of evil things, disobedient to
parents,
31 [1]undiscerning, untrustworthy, unloving, [2]un-
forgiving, unmerciful;
32 who, [a]knowing the righteous judgment of
God, that those who practice such things [b]are
deserving of death, not only do the same but also
[c]approve of those who practice them.

## *The Fairness of God's Judgment*

**2** Therefore you are [a]inexcusable, O man, whoever you are who judge, [b]for in whatever you
judge another you condemn yourself; for you who
judge practice the same things.
2 But we know that the judgment of God is
according to truth against those who practice
such things.
3 And do you think this, O man, you who judge
those practicing such things, and doing the same,
that you will escape the judgment of God?
4 Or do you despise [a]the riches of His goodness,
[b]forbearance, and [c]longsuffering, [d]not knowing
that the goodness of God leads you to repentance?
5 But in accordance with your hardness and
your [1]impenitent heart [a]you are [2]treasuring up for
yourself wrath in the day of wrath and revelation
of the righteous judgment of God,
6 who [a]*"will render to each one according to his
deeds"*:
7 eternal life to those who by patient continu-
ance in doing good seek for glory, honor, and
immortality;
8 but to those who are self-seeking and [a]do not
obey the truth, but obey unrighteousness—indignation and wrath,
9 tribulation and anguish, on every soul of man
who does evil, of the Jew [a]first and also of the
[1]Greek;

CHAPTER 1
**1** [a]1 Tim. 1:11 [b]Acts 9:15; 13:2
**2** [a]Acts 26:6 [b]Gal. 3:8
**3** [a]Gal. 4:4 [1]*came*
**4** [a]Acts 9:20; 13:33 [b][Heb. 9:14]
**5** [a]Eph. 3:8 [b]Acts 6:7 [c]Acts 9:15
**7** [a]1 Cor. 1:2, 24 [b]1 Cor. 1:3
**8** [a]1 Cor. 1:4 [b]Rom. 16:19
**9** [a]Rom. 9:1 [b]Acts 27:23 [c]1 Thess. 3:10 [1]Or *in*
**11** [a]Rom. 15:29
**12** [a]Titus 1:4
**13** [a][1 Thess. 2:18] [b]Phil. 4:17
**16** [a]Ps. 40:9, 10 [b]1 Cor. 1:18, 24 [c]Acts 3:26 [1]NU omits *of Christ*
**17** [a]Rom. 3:21; 9:30 [b]Hab. 2:4
**18** [a][Acts 17:30] [b]2 Thess. 2:10 [1]*hold down*
**19** [a][Acts 14:17; 17:24] [b][John 1:9] [1]*evident* [2]*among*
**20** [a]Ps. 19:1–6 [1]*divine nature, deity*
**21** [a]Jer. 2:5
**22** [a]Jer. 10:14
**23** [a]1 Tim. 1:17; 6:15, 16 [b]Deut. 4:16–18 [1]*perishable*
**24** [a]Eph. 4:18, 19 [b]1 Cor. 6:18 [c]Lev. 18:22
**25** [a]1 Thess. 1:9 [b]Is. 44:20
**26** [a]Lev. 18:22 [1]Lit. *females*
**27** [1]Lit. *males* [2]Lit. *female*
**28** [a]Eph. 5:4
**29** [1]NU omits *sexual immorality* [2]*greed* [3]*malice*
**31** [1]*without understanding* [2]NU omits *unforgiving*
**32** [a][Rom. 2:2] [b][Rom. 6:21] [c]Hos. 7:3

CHAPTER 2
**1** [a][Rom. 1:20] [b][Matt. 7:1–5]
**4** [a][Eph. 1:7, 18; 2:7] [b][Rom. 3:25] [c]Ex. 34:6 [d]Is. 30:18
**5** [a][Deut. 32:34] [1]*unrepentant* [2]*storing*
**6** [a]Ps. 62:12; Prov. 24:12
**8** [a][2 Thess. 1:8]
**9** [a]1 Pet. 4:17 [1]*Gentile*

10 [a]but glory, honor, and peace to everyone who
works what is good, to the Jew first and also to
the Greek.
11 For [a]there is no partiality with God.
12 For as many as have sinned without law will
also perish without law, and as many as have
sinned in the law will be judged by the law
13 (for [a]not the hearers of the law *are* just in the
sight of God, but the doers of the law will be
justified;
14 for when Gentiles, who do not have the law,
by nature do the things in the law, these, although
not having the law, are a law to themselves,
15 who show the [a]work of the law written in
their hearts, their [b]conscience also bearing witness, and between themselves *their* thoughts
accusing or else excusing *them*)
16 [a]in the day when God will judge the secrets of
men [b]by Jesus Christ, [c]according to my gospel.
**17** [1]Indeed [a]you are called a Jew, and [b]rest[2] on the
law, [c]and make your boast in God,
18 and [a]know *His* will, and [b]approve the things
that are excellent, being instructed out of the law,
19 and [a]are confident that you yourself are a
guide to the blind, a light to those who are in
darkness,
20 an instructor of the foolish, a teacher of babes,
[a]having the form of knowledge and truth in the
law.
21 [a]You, therefore, who teach another, do you
not teach yourself? You who preach that a man
should not steal, do you steal?
22 You who say, "Do not commit adultery," do
you commit adultery? You who abhor idols, [a]do
you rob temples?
23 You who [a]make your boast in the law, do you
dishonor God through breaking the law?
24 For [a]*"the name of God is* [b]*blasphemed among
the Gentiles because of you,"* as it is written.
**25** [a]For circumcision is indeed profitable if you
keep the law; but if you are a breaker of the law,
your circumcision has become uncircumcision.
26 Therefore, [a]if an uncircumcised man keeps the
righteous requirements of the law, will not his
uncircumcision be counted as circumcision?
27 And will not the physically uncircumcised, if
he fulfills the law, [a]judge you who, *even* with *your*
[1]written *code* and circumcision, *are* a transgressor
of the law?
28 For [a]he is not a Jew who *is one* outwardly, nor
*is* circumcision that which *is* outward in the flesh;
29 but *he is* a Jew [a]who *is one* inwardly; and
[b]circumcision *is that* of the heart, [c]in the Spirit,
not in the letter; [d]whose [1]praise *is* not from men
but from God.

## *Justification by Faith, Not by the Law*

**3** What advantage then has the Jew, or what *is*
the profit of circumcision?
2 Much in every way! Chiefly because [a]to them
were committed the [1]oracles of God.
3 For what if [a]some did not believe? [b]Will their
unbelief make the faithfulness of God without
effect?
4 [a]Certainly not! Indeed, let [b]God be [1]true but
[c]every man a liar. As it is written:

[d]*"That You may be justified in Your words,*
*And may overcome when You are judged."*

5 But if our unrighteousness demonstrates the
righteousness of God, what shall we say? *Is* God
unjust who inflicts wrath? [a](I speak as a man.)
6 Certainly not! For then [a]how will God judge
the world?
7 For if the truth of God has increased through
my lie to His glory, why am I also still judged as a
sinner?
8 And *why* not *say,* [a]"Let us do evil that good
may come"?—as we are slanderously reported and
as some affirm that we say. Their [1]condemnation
is just.
**9** What then? Are we better *than they?* Not at
all. For we have previously charged both Jews and
Greeks that [a]they are all under sin.
10 As it is written:

[a]*"There is none righteous, no, not one;*
11 *There is none who understands;*
*There is none who seeks after God.*
12 *They have all turned aside;*
*They have together become unprofitable;*
*There is none who does good, no, not one."*
13 *"Their*[a] *throat is an open* [1]*tomb;*
*With their tongues they have practiced*
*deceit";*
[b]*"The poison of asps is under their lips";*
14 *"Whose*[a] mouth *is full of cursing and*
*bitterness."*
15 *"Their*[a] *feet are swift to shed blood;*
16 *Destruction and misery are in their ways;*
17 *And the way of peace they have not*
*known."*
18 *"There*[a] *is no fear of God before their eyes."*

19 Now we know that whatever [a]the law says, it
says to those who are under the law, that [b]every
mouth may be stopped, and all the world may
become [1]guilty before God.
20 Therefore [a]by the deeds of the law no flesh will
be justified in His sight, for by the law *is* the
knowledge of sin.
**21** But now [a]the righteousness of God apart from
the law is revealed, [b]being witnessed by the Law
[c]and the Prophets,
22 even the righteousness of God, through faith
in Jesus Christ, to all [1]and on all who believe. For
[a]there is no difference;
23 for [a]all have sinned and fall short of the glory
of God,
24 being justified [1]freely [a]by His grace [b]through
the redemption that is in Christ Jesus,
25 whom God set forth [a]*as* a [1]propitiation [b]by His
blood, through faith, to demonstrate His righteousness, because in His forbearance God had
passed over [c]the sins that were previously committed,
26 to demonstrate at the present time His righteousness, that He might be just and the justifier
of the one who has faith in Jesus.
**27** [a]Where *is* boasting then? It is excluded. By
what law? Of works? No, but by the law of faith.
28 Therefore we conclude [a]that a man is [1]justified
by faith apart from the deeds of the law.
29 Or *is He* the God of the Jews only? *Is He* not
also the God of the Gentiles? Yes, of the Gentiles
also,
30 since [a]*there is* one God who will justify the
circumcised by faith and the uncircumcised
through faith.
31 Do we then make void the law through faith?
Certainly not! On the contrary, we establish the
law.

**10** [a][1 Pet. 1:7] **11** [a]Deut. 10:17 **13** [a][James 1:22, 25] **15** [a]1 Cor. 5:1 [b]Acts 24:25 **16** [a][Matt. 25:31] [b]Acts 10:42; 17:31 [c]1 Tim. 1:11 **17** [a]John 8:33 [b]Mic. 3:11 [c]Is. 48:1, 2 [1]NU *But if* [2]*rely* **18** [a]Deut. 4:8 [b]Phil. 1:10 **19** [a]Matt. 15:14 **20** [a][2 Tim. 3:5] **21** [a]Matt. 23:3 **22** [a]Mal. 3:8 **23** [a]Rom. 2:17; 9:4 **24** [a]Ezek. 16:27 [b]Is. 52:5; Ezek. 36:22 **25** [a][Gal. 5:3] **26** [a][Acts 10:34] **27** [a]Matt. 12:41 [1]Lit. *letter* **28** [a][Gal. 6:15] **29** [a][1 Pet. 3:4] [b]Phil. 3:3 [c]Deut. 30:6 [d][1 Cor. 4:5] [1]A play on words—*Jew* is literally *praise.*

CHAPTER 3
**2** [a]Deut. 4:5–8 [1]*sayings,* Scriptures **3** [a]Heb. 4:2 [b][2 Tim. 2:13] **4** [a]Job 40:8 [b][John 3:33] [c]Ps. 62:9 [d]Ps. 51:4 [1]Found true **5** [a]Gal. 3:15 **6** [a][Gen. 18:25] **8** [a]Rom. 5:20 [1]Lit. *judgment* **9** [a]Gal. 3:22 **10** [a]Ps. 14:1–3; 53:1–3; Eccl. 7:20 **13** [a]Ps. 5:9 [b]Ps. 140:3 [1]*grave* **14** [a]Ps. 10:7 **15** [a]Prov. 1:16; Is. 59:7, 8 **18** [a]Ps. 36:1 **19** [a]John 10:34 [b]Job 5:16 [1]*accountable* **20** [a][Gal. 2:16] **21** [a]Acts 15:11 [b]John 5:46 [c]1 Pet. 1:10 **22** [a][Col. 3:11] [1]NU omits *and on all* **23** [a]Gal. 3:22 **24** [a][Eph. 2:8] [b][Heb. 9:12, 15] [1]*without any cost* **25** [a]Lev. 16:15 [b]Col. 1:20 [c]Acts 14:16; 17:30 [1]*mercy seat* **27** [a][1 Cor. 1:29] **28** [a]Gal. 2:16 [1]*declared righteous* **30** [a][Gal. 3:8, 20]

## Abraham Was Justified by Faith

4 What then shall we say that [a]Abraham our
[b]father[1] has found according to the flesh?
2 For if Abraham was [a]justified by works, he has
*something* to boast about, but not before God.
3 For what does the Scripture say? [a]"*Abraham*
*believed God, and it was* [1]*accounted to him for*
*righteousness.*"
4 Now [a]to him who works, the wages are not
counted [1]as grace but [1]as debt.
5 But to him who [a]does not work but believes on
Him who justifies [b]the ungodly, his faith is accounted for righteousness,
6 just as David also [a]describes the blessedness of
the man to whom God imputes righteousness
apart from works:

7 "*Blessed*[a] *are those whose lawless deeds are*
*forgiven,*
*And whose sins are covered;*
8 *Blessed is the man to whom the* LORD *shall*
*not impute sin.*"

9 *Does* this blessedness then *come* upon the
circumcised *only*, or upon the uncircumcised also?
For we say that faith was accounted to Abraham
for righteousness.
10 How then was it accounted? While he was
circumcised, or uncircumcised? Not while circumcised, but while uncircumcised.
11 And [a]he received the sign of circumcision, a
seal of the righteousness of the faith which *he had*
*while still* uncircumcised, that [b]he might be the
father of all those who believe, though they are
uncircumcised, that righteousness might be imputed to them also,
12 and the father of circumcision to those who
not only *are* of the circumcision, but who also
walk in the steps of the faith which our father
[a]Abraham *had while still* uncircumcised.
13 For the promise that he would be the [a]heir of
the world *was* not to Abraham or to his seed
through the law, but through the righteousness of
faith.
14 For [a]if those who are of the law *are* heirs, faith
is made void and the promise made of no effect,
15 because [a]the law brings about wrath; for
where there is no law *there is* no transgression.
16 Therefore *it is* of faith that *it might be* [a]accord-
ing to grace, [b]so that the promise might be [1]sure to
all the seed, not only to those who are of the law,
but also to those who are of the faith of Abraham,
[c]who is the father of us all
17 (as it is written, [a]"*I have made you a father of*
*many nations*") in the presence of Him whom he
believed—God, [b]who gives life to the dead and
calls those [c]things which do not exist as though
they did;
18 who, contrary to hope, in hope believed, so
that he became the father of many nations, according to what was spoken, [a]"*So shall your*
*descendants be.*"
19 And not being weak in faith, [a]he did not
consider his own body, already dead (since he was
about a hundred years old), [b]and the deadness of
Sarah's womb.
20 He did not waver at the promise of God
through unbelief, but was strengthened in faith,
giving glory to God,
21 and being fully convinced that what He had
promised [a]He was also able to perform.
22 And therefore [a]"*it was accounted to him for*
*righteousness.*"
23 Now [a]it was not written for his sake alone that
it was imputed to him,
24 but also for us. It shall be imputed to us who
believe [a]in Him who raised up Jesus our Lord from
the dead,
25 [a]who was delivered up because of our offenses,
and [b]was raised because of our justification.

## Death in Adam, Life in Christ

5 Therefore, [a]having been justified by faith, [1]we
have [b]peace with God through our Lord Jesus
Christ,
2 [a]through whom also we have access by faith
into this grace [b]in which we stand, and [c]rejoice in
hope of the glory of God.
3 And not only *that,* but [a]we also glory in
tribulations, [b]knowing that tribulation produces
[1]perseverance;
4 [a]and perseverance, [1]character; and character,
hope.
5 [a]Now hope does not disappoint, [b]because the
love of God has been poured out in our hearts by
the Holy Spirit who was given to us.
6 For when we were still without strength, [1]in
due time [a]Christ died for the ungodly.
7 For scarcely for a righteous man will one die;
yet perhaps for a good man someone would even
dare to die.
8 But [a]God demonstrates His own love toward
us, in that while we were still sinners, Christ died
for us.
9 Much more then, having now been justified
[a]by His blood, we shall be saved [b]from wrath
through Him.
10 For [a]if when we were enemies [b]we were reconciled to God through the death of His Son, much
more, having been reconciled, we shall be saved
[c]by His life.
11 And not only *that,* but we also [a]rejoice in God
through our Lord Jesus Christ, through whom we
have now received the reconciliation.
12 Therefore, just as [a]through one man sin entered the world, and [b]death through sin, and thus
death spread to all men, because all sinned—
13 (For until the law sin was in the world, but [a]sin
is not imputed when there is no law.
14 Nevertheless death reigned from Adam to
Moses, even over those who had not sinned according to the likeness of the transgression of
Adam, [a]who is a type of Him who was to come.
15 But the free gift *is* not like the [1]offense. For if
by the one man's offense many died, much more
the grace of God and the gift by the grace of the
one Man, Jesus Christ, abounded [a]to many.
16 And the gift *is* not like *that which came*
through the one who sinned. For the judgment
*which came* from one *offense resulted* in condemnation, but the free gift *which came* from many
[1]offenses *resulted* in justification.
17 For if by the one man's [1]offense death reigned
through the one, much more those who receive
abundance of grace and of the gift of righteousness will reign in life through the One, Jesus
Christ.)
18 Therefore, as through [1]one man's offense *judg-*
*ment* came to all men, resulting in condemnation,
even so through [a]one[2] Man's righteous act *the free*
*gift came* [b]to all men, resulting in justification of
life.

CHAPTER 4
1 [a]Is. 51:2 [b]James 2:21 [1]Or *(fore)father according to the flesh has found*
2 [a]Rom. 3:20, 27
3 [a]Gen. 15:6 [1]*imputed, credited, reckoned, counted*
4 [a]Rom. 11:6 [1]*according to*
5 [a][Eph. 2:8, 9] [b]Josh. 24:2
6 [a]Ps. 32:1, 2
7 [a]Ps. 32:1, 2
11 [a]Gen. 17:10 [b]Luke 19:9
12 [a]Rom. 4:18–22
13 [a]Gen. 17:4–6; 22:17
14 [a]Gal. 3:18
15 [a]Rom. 3:20
16 [a][Rom. 3:24] [b][Gal. 3:22] [c]Is. 51:2 [1]*certain*
17 [a]Gen. 17:5 [b][Rom. 8:11] [c]Rom. 9:26
18 [a]Gen. 15:5
19 [a]Gen. 17:17 [b]Heb. 11:11
21 [a][Heb. 11:19]
22 [a]Gen. 15:6
23 [a]Rom. 15:4
24 [a]Acts 2:24
25 [a]Is. 53:4, 5 [b][1 Cor. 15:17]

CHAPTER 5
1 [a]Is. 32:17 [b][Eph. 2:14] [1]Some ancient mss. *let us have*
2 [a][Eph. 2:18; 3:12] [b]1 Cor. 15:1 [c]Heb. 3:6
3 [a]Matt. 5:11, 12 [b]James 1:3 [1]*endurance*
4 [a][James 1:12] [1]*approved character*
5 [a]Phil. 1:20 [b]2 Cor. 1:22
6 [a][Rom. 4:25; 5:8; 8:32] [1]*at the right time*
8 [a][John 3:16; 15:13]
9 [a]Eph. 2:13 [b]1 Thess. 1:10
10 [a][Rom. 8:32] [b]2 Cor. 5:18 [c]John 14:19
11 [a][Gal. 4:9]
12 [a][1 Cor. 15:21] [b]Gen. 2:17
13 [a]1 John 3:4
14 [a][1 Cor. 15:21, 22]
15 [a][Is. 53:11] [1]*trespass* or *false step*
16 [1]*trespasses*
17 [1]*trespass*
18 [a][1 Cor. 15:21, 45] [b][John 12:32] [1]Or *one trespass* [2]Or *one righteous act*

19 For as by one man's disobedience many were
made sinners, so also by [a]one Man's obedience
many will be made righteous.
20 Moreover [a]the law entered that the offense
might abound. But where sin abounded, grace
[b]abounded much more,
21 so that as sin reigned in death, even so grace
might reign through righteousness to eternal life
through Jesus Christ our Lord.

### *Dead to Sin, Alive to God*

**6** What shall we say then? [a]Shall we continue in
sin that grace may abound?
2 Certainly not! How shall we who [a]died to sin
live any longer in it?
3 Or do you not know that [a]as many of us as
were baptized into Christ Jesus [b]were baptized
into His death?
4 Therefore we were [a]buried with Him through
baptism into death, that [b]just as Christ was raised
from the dead by [c]the glory of the Father, [d]even so
we also should walk in newness of life.
5 [a]For if we have been united together in the
likeness of His death, certainly we also shall be *in
the likeness* of *His* resurrection,
6 knowing this, that [a]our old man was crucified
with *Him,* that [b]the body of sin might be [1]done
away with, that we should no longer be slaves of
sin.
7 For [a]he who has died has been [1]freed from sin.
8 Now [a]if we died with Christ, we believe that
we shall also live with Him,
9 knowing that [a]Christ, having been raised from
the dead, dies no more. Death no longer has
dominion over Him.
10 For *the death* that He died, [a]He died to sin
once for all; but *the life* that He lives, [b]He lives to
God.
11 Likewise you also, [1]reckon yourselves to be
[a]dead indeed to sin, but [b]alive to God in Christ
Jesus our Lord.
12 [a]Therefore do not let sin reign in your mortal
body, that you should obey it in its lusts.
13 And do not present your [a]members *as* [1]instru-
ments of unrighteousness to sin, but [b]present
yourselves to God as being alive from the dead,
and your members *as* [1]instruments of righteousness to God.
14 For [a]sin shall not have dominion over you, for
you are not under law but under grace.
**15** What then? Shall we sin [a]because we are not
under law but under grace? Certainly not!
16 Do you not know that [a]to whom you present
yourselves slaves to obey, you are that one's
slaves whom you obey, whether of sin *leading* to
death, or of obedience *leading* to righteousness?
17 But God be thanked that *though* you were
slaves of sin, yet you obeyed from the heart [a]that
form of doctrine to which you were [1]delivered.
18 And [a]having been set free from sin, you became slaves of righteousness.
19 I speak in human *terms* because of the weakness of your flesh. For just as you presented your
members *as* slaves of uncleanness, and of lawlessness *leading* to *more* lawlessness, so now present
your members *as* slaves *of* righteousness [1]for
holiness.
20 For when you were [a]slaves of sin, you were
free in regard to righteousness.
21 [a]What fruit did you have then in the things of
which you are now ashamed? For [b]the end of
those things *is* death.
22 But now [a]having been set free from sin, and
having become slaves of God, you have your fruit
[1]to holiness, and the end, everlasting life.
23 For [a]the wages of sin *is* death, but [b]the [1]gift of
God *is* eternal life in Christ Jesus our Lord.

### *Law Cannot Save from Sin*

**7** Or do you not know, brethren (for I speak to
those who know the law), that the law [1]has
dominion over a man as long as he lives?
2 For [a]the woman who has a husband is bound
by the law to *her* husband as long as he lives. But
if the husband dies, she is released from the law of
*her* husband.
3 So then [a]if, while *her* husband lives, she marries another man, she will be called an adulteress;
but if her husband dies, she is free from that law,
so that she is no adulteress, though she has
married another man.
4 Therefore, my brethren, you also have become
[a]dead to the law through the body of Christ, that
you may be married to another—to Him who was
raised from the dead, that we should [b]bear fruit to
God.
5 For when we were in the flesh, the sinful
passions which were aroused by the law [a]were at
work in our members [b]to bear fruit to death.
6 But now we have been delivered from the law,
having died to what we were held by, so that we
should serve [a]in the newness of the Spirit and not
*in* the oldness of the letter.
**7** What shall we say then? *Is* the law sin? Certainly not! On the contrary, [a]I would not have
known sin except through the law. For I would
not have known covetousness unless the law had
said, [b]*"You shall not covet."*
8 But [a]sin, taking opportunity by the commandment, produced in me all *manner of evil* desire.
For [b]apart from the law sin *was* dead.
9 I was alive once without the law, but when
the commandment came, sin revived and I died.
10 And the commandment, [a]which *was* to *bring*
life, I found to *bring* death.
11 For sin, taking occasion by the commandment, deceived me, and by it killed *me.*
12 Therefore [a]the law *is* holy, and the commandment holy and just and good.
**13** Has then what is good become death to me?
Certainly not! But sin, that it might appear sin,
was producing death in me through what is good,
so that sin through the commandment might
become exceedingly sinful.
14 For we know that the law is spiritual, but I am
carnal, [a]sold under sin.
15 For what I am doing, I do not understand.
[a]For what I will to do, that I do not practice; but
what I hate, that I do.
16 If, then, I do what I will not to do, I agree with
the law that *it is* good.
17 But now, *it is* no longer I who do it, but sin
that dwells in me.
18 For I know that [a]in me (that is, in my flesh)
nothing good dwells; for to will is present with me,
but *how* to perform what is good I do not find.
19 For the good that I will *to do,* I do not do; but
the evil I will not *to do,* that I practice.
20 Now if I do what I will not *to do,* it is no longer
I who do it, but sin that dwells in me.

**19** [a][Phil. 2:8]
**20** [a]John 15:22 [b]1 Tim. 1:14

CHAPTER 6
**1** [a]Rom. 3:8; 6:15
**2** [a][Gal. 2:19]
**3** [a][Gal. 3:27] [b][1 Cor. 15:29]
**4** [a]Col. 2:12 [b]1 Cor. 6:14 [c]John 2:11 [d][Gal. 6:15]
**5** [a]Phil. 3:10
**6** [a]Gal. 2:20; 5:24; 6:14 [b]Col. 2:11 [1]*rendered inoperative*
**7** [a]1 Pet. 4:1 [1]*cleared*
**8** [a]2 Tim. 2:11
**9** [a]Rev. 1:18
**10** [a]Heb. 9:27 [b]Luke 20:38
**11** [a][Rom. 6:2; 7:4, 6] [b][Gal. 2:19] [1]*consider*
**12** [a]Ps. 19:13
**13** [a]Col. 3:5 [b]1 Pet. 2:24; 4:2 [1]Or *weapons*
**14** [a][Gal. 5:18]
**15** [a]1 Cor. 9:21
**16** [a]2 Pet. 2:19
**17** [a]2 Tim. 1:13 [1]*entrusted*
**18** [a]John 8:32
**19** [1]*unto sanctification*
**20** [a]John 8:34
**21** [a]Rom. 7:5 [b]Rom. 1:32
**22** [a]Rom. 6:18; 8:2 [1]*unto sanctification*
**23** [a]Gen. 2:17 [b]1 Pet. 1:4 [1]*free gift*

CHAPTER 7
**1** [1]*rules*
**2** [a]1 Cor. 7:39
**3** [a][Matt. 5:32]
**4** [a]Gal. 2:19; 5:18 [b]Gal. 5:22
**5** [a]Rom. 6:13 [b]James 1:15
**6** [a]Rom. 2:29
**7** [a]Rom. 3:20 [b]Ex. 20:17; Deut. 5:21
**8** [a]Rom. 4:15 [b]1 Cor. 15:56
**10** [a]Lev. 18:5
**12** [a]Ps. 19:8
**14** [a]2 Kin. 17:17
**15** [a][Gal. 5:17]
**18** [a][Gen. 6:5; 8:21]

21 I find then a law, that evil is present with me,
the one who wills to do good.
22 For I [a]delight in the law of God according to
[b]the inward man.
23 But [a]I see another law in [b]my members, warring against the law of my mind, and bringing me
into captivity to the law of sin which is in my
members.
24 O wretched man that I am! Who will deliver
me [a]from this body of death?
25 [a]I thank God—through Jesus Christ our Lord!
So then, with the mind I myself serve the law of
God, but with the flesh the law of sin.

### *Salvation from Sin, Death, and Suffering*

**8** *There is* therefore now no condemnation to
those who are in Christ Jesus, [a]who[1] do not
walk according to the flesh, but according to the
Spirit.
2 For [a]the law of [b]the Spirit of life in Christ
Jesus has made me free from [c]the law of sin and
death.
3 For [a]what the law could not do in that it was
weak through the flesh, [b]God *did* by sending His
own Son in the likeness of sinful flesh, on account
of sin: He condemned sin in the flesh,
4 that the righteous requirement of the law
might be fulfilled in us who [a]do not walk according to the flesh but according to the Spirit.
5 For [a]those who live according to the flesh set
their minds on the things of the flesh, but those
*who live* according to the Spirit, [b]the things of the
Spirit.
6 For [a]to be [1]carnally minded *is* death, but to be
spiritually minded *is* life and peace.
7 Because [a]the [1]carnal mind *is* enmity against
God; for it is not subject to the law of God, [b]nor
indeed can be.
8 So then, those who are in the flesh cannot
please God.
9 But you are not in the flesh but in the Spirit, if
indeed the Spirit of God dwells in you. Now if
anyone does not have the Spirit of Christ, he is
not His.
10 And if Christ *is* in you, the body *is* dead
because of sin, but the Spirit *is* life because of
righteousness.
11 But if the Spirit of [a]Him who raised Jesus from
the dead dwells in you, [b]He who raised Christ from
the dead will also give life to your mortal bodies
[1]through His Spirit who dwells in you.
**12** [a]Therefore, brethren, we are debtors—not to
the flesh, to live according to the flesh.
13 For [a]if you live according to the flesh you will
die; but if by the Spirit you [b]put to death the deeds
of the body, you will live.
14 For [a]as many as are led by the Spirit of God,
these are sons of God.
15 For [a]you did not receive the spirit of bondage
again [b]to fear, but you received the [c]Spirit of
adoption by whom we cry out, [d]"Abba,[1] Father."
16 [a]The Spirit Himself bears witness with our
spirit that we are children of God,
17 and if children, then [a]heirs—heirs of God and
joint heirs with Christ, [b]if indeed we suffer with
*Him,* that we may also be glorified together.
**18** For I consider that [a]the sufferings of this
present time are not worthy *to be compared* with
the glory which shall be revealed in us.
19 For [a]the earnest expectation of the creation
eagerly waits for the revealing of the sons of God.
20 For [a]the creation was subjected to futility, not
willingly, but because of Him who subjected *it* in
hope;
21 because the creation itself also will be delivered from the bondage of [1]corruption into the
glorious [a]liberty of the children of God.
22 For we know that the whole creation [a]groans
and labors with birth pangs together until now.
23 Not only that, but we also who have [a]the
firstfruits of the Spirit, [b]even we ourselves groan
[c]within ourselves, eagerly waiting for the adoption, the [d]redemption of our body.
24 For we were saved in this hope, but [a]hope that
is seen is not hope; for why does one still hope for
what he sees?
25 But if we hope for what we do not see, we
eagerly wait for *it* with perseverance.
26 Likewise the Spirit also helps in our weaknesses. For [a]we do not know what we should pray
for as we ought, but [b]the Spirit Himself makes
intercession [1]for us with groanings which cannot
be uttered.
27 Now [a]He who searches the hearts knows what
the mind of the Spirit *is,* because He makes
intercession for the saints [b]according to *the will of*
God.
28 And we know that all things work together for
good to those who love God, to those [a]who are the
called according to *His* purpose.
29 For whom [a]He foreknew, [b]He also predestined
[c]*to be* conformed to the image of His Son, [d]that
He might be the firstborn among many brethren.
30 Moreover whom He predestined, these He also
[a]called; whom He called, these He also [b]justified;
and whom He justified, these He also [c]glorified.
**31** What then shall we say to these things? [a]If
God *is* for us, who *can be* against us?
32 [a]He who did not spare His own Son, but
[b]delivered Him up for us all, how shall He not with
Him also freely give us all things?
33 Who shall bring a charge against God's elect?
[a]*It is* God who justifies.
34 [a]Who *is* he who condemns? *It is* Christ who
died, and furthermore is also risen, [b]who is even at
the right hand of God, [c]who also makes intercession for us.
35 Who shall separate us from the love of Christ?
*Shall* tribulation, or distress, or persecution, or
famine, or nakedness, or peril, or sword?
36 As it is written:

[a]*"For Your sake we are killed all day long;*
*We are accounted as sheep*
*for the slaughter."*

37 [a]Yet in all these things we are more than
conquerors through Him who loved us.
38 For I am persuaded that neither death nor life,
nor angels nor [a]principalities nor powers, nor
things present nor things to come,
39 nor height nor depth, nor any other created
thing, shall be able to separate us from the love of
God which is in Christ Jesus our Lord.

### *God's Mercy Is on Whom He Chooses*

**9** I [a]tell the truth in Christ, I am not lying, my
conscience also bearing me witness in the
Holy Spirit,
2 [a]that I have great sorrow and continual grief
in my heart.
3 For [a]I could wish that I myself were accursed

---

22 [a]Ps. 1:2 [b][2 Cor. 4:16]
23 [a][Gal. 5:17] [b]Rom. 6:13, 19
24 [a][1 Cor. 15:51, 52]
25 [a]1 Cor. 15:57

CHAPTER 8
1 [a]Gal. 5:16 [1]NU omits the rest of v. 1.
2 [a]Rom. 6:18, 22 [b][1 Cor. 15:45] [c]Rom. 7:24, 25
3 [a]Acts 13:39 [b][2 Cor. 5:21]
4 [a]Gal. 5:16, 25
5 [a]John 3:6 [b][Gal. 5:22–25]
6 [a]Gal. 6:8 [1]*fleshly*
7 [a]James 4:4 [b]1 Cor. 2:14 [1]*fleshly*
11 [a]Acts 2:24 [b]1 Cor. 6:14 [1]Or *because of*
12 [a][Rom. 6:7, 14]
13 [a]Gal. 6:8 [b]Eph. 4:22
14 [a][Gal. 5:18]
15 [a]Heb. 2:15 [b]2 Tim. 1:7 [c][Is. 56:5] [d]Mark 14:36 [1]Lit., in Aram., *Father*
16 [a]Eph. 1:13
17 [a]Acts 26:18 [b]Phil. 1:29
18 [a]2 Cor. 4:17
19 [a][2 Pet. 3:13]
20 [a]Gen. 3:17–19
21 [a][2 Cor. 3:17] [1]*decay*
22 [a]Jer. 12:4, 11
23 [a]2 Cor. 5:5 [b]2 Cor. 5:2, 4 [c][Luke 20:36] [d]Eph. 1:14; 4:30
24 [a]Heb. 11:1
26 [a]Matt. 20:22 [b]Eph. 6:18 [1]NU omits *for us*
27 [a]1 Chr. 28:9 [b]1 John 5:14
28 [a]2 Tim. 1:9
29 [a]2 Tim. 2:19 [b]Eph. 1:5, 11 [c][2 Cor. 3:18] [d]Heb. 1:6
30 [a][1 Pet. 2:9; 3:9] [b][Gal. 2:16] [c]John 17:22
31 [a]Num. 14:9
32 [a]Rom. 5:6, 10 [b][Rom. 4:25]
33 [a]Is. 50:8, 9
34 [a]John 3:18 [b]Mark 16:19 [c]Heb. 7:25; 9:24
36 [a]Ps. 44:22
37 [a]1 Cor. 15:57
38 [a][Eph. 1:21]

CHAPTER 9
1 [a]2 Cor. 1:23
2 [a]Rom. 10:1
3 [a]Ex. 32:32

from Christ for my brethren, my [1]countrymen
according to the flesh,
4 who are Israelites, [a]to whom *pertain* the adoption, [b]the glory, [c]the covenants, [d]the giving of the
law, [e]the service *of God,* and [f]the promises;
5 [a]of whom *are* the fathers and from [b]whom,
according to the flesh, Christ *came,* [c]who is over
all, *the* eternally blessed God. Amen.
**6** [a]But it is not that the word of God has taken
no effect. For [b]they *are* not all Israel who *are* of
Israel,
7 [a]nor *are they* all children because they are the
seed of Abraham; but, [b]*"In Isaac your seed shall*
*be called."*
8 That is, those who *are* the children of the
flesh, these *are* not the children of God; but [a]the
children of the promise are counted as the seed.
9 For this *is* the word of promise: [a]*"At this time*
*I will come and Sarah shall have a son."*
10 And not only *this,* but when [a]Rebecca also had
conceived by one man, *even* by our father Isaac
11 (for *the children* not yet being born, nor
having done any good or evil, that the purpose of
God according to election might stand, not of
works but of [a]Him who calls),
12 it was said to her, [a]*"The older shall serve the*
*younger."*
13 As it is written, [a]*"Jacob I have loved, but Esau*
*I have hated."*
**14** What shall we say then? [a]*Is there* unrighteousness with God? Certainly not!
15 For He says to Moses, [a]*"I will have mercy on*
*whomever I will have mercy, and I will have*
*compassion on whomever I will have compas-*
*sion."*
16 So then *it is* not of him who wills, nor of him
who runs, but of God who shows mercy.
17 For [a]the Scripture says to the Pharaoh, [b]*"For*
*this very purpose I have raised you up, that I may*
*show My power in you, and that My name may be*
*declared in all the earth."*
18 Therefore He has mercy on whom He wills,
and whom He wills He [a]hardens.
19 You will say to me then, "Why does He still
find fault? For [a]who has resisted His will?"
20 But indeed, O man, who are you to reply
against God? [a]Will the thing formed say to him
who formed *it,* "Why have you made me like
this?"
21 Does not the [a]potter have power over the clay,
from the same lump to make [b]one vessel for honor
and another for dishonor?
22 *What* if God, wanting to show *His* wrath and
to make His power known, endured with much
longsuffering [a]the vessels of wrath [b]prepared for
destruction,
23 and that He might make known [a]the riches of
His glory on the vessels of mercy, which He had
[b]prepared beforehand for glory,
24 *even* us whom He [a]called, [b]not of the Jews
only, but also of the Gentiles?
25 As He says also in Hosea:

[a]*"I will call them My people,*
*who were not My people,*
*And her beloved, who was not beloved."*
26 *"And[a] it shall come to pass in the place where*
*it was said to them,*
*'You are not My people,'*
*There they shall be called sons*
*of the living God."*

27 Isaiah also cries out concerning Israel:

[a]*"Though the number of the children of Israel*
*be as the sand of the sea,*
[b]*The remnant will be saved.*
28 *For He will finish the work*
*and cut it short in righteousness,*
[a]*Because the* LORD *will* [1]*make a short work*
*upon the earth."*

29 And as Isaiah said before:

[a]*"Unless the* LORD *of* [1]Sabaoth
*had left us a seed,*
[b]*We would have become like Sodom,*
*And we would have been made like*
*Gomorrah."*

**30** What shall we say then? [a]That Gentiles, who
did not pursue righteousness, have attained to
righteousness, [b]even the righteousness of faith;
31 but Israel, [a]pursuing the law of righteousness,
[b]has not attained to the law [1]of righteousness.
32 Why? Because *they did* not *seek it* by faith,
but as it were, [1]by the works of the law. For [a]they
stumbled at that stumbling stone.
33 As it is written:

[a]*"Behold, I lay in Zion a stumbling stone and*
*rock of offense,*
*And* [b]*whoever believes on Him will not be*
*put to shame."*

## *Salvation Is Open to All*

**10** Brethren, my heart's desire and prayer to
God for [1]Israel is that they may be saved.
2 For I bear them witness [a]that they have a zeal
for God, but not according to knowledge.
3 For they being ignorant of [a]God's righteousness, and seeking to establish their own [b]righ-
teousness, have not submitted to the righteousness of God.
4 For [a]Christ *is* the end of the law for righteousness to everyone who believes.
5 For Moses writes about the righteousness
which is of the law, [a]*"The man who does those*
*things shall live by them."*
6 But the righteousness of faith speaks in this
way, [a]*"Do not say in your heart, 'Who will ascend*
*into heaven?' "* (that is, to bring Christ down *from*
*above*)
7 or, [a]*" 'Who will descend into the abyss?' "*
(that is, to bring Christ up from the dead).
8 But what does it say? [a]*"The word is near you,*
*in your mouth and in your heart"* (that is, the
word of faith which we preach):
9 that [a]if you confess with your mouth the Lord
Jesus and believe in your heart that God has
raised Him from the dead, you will be saved.
10 For with the heart one believes unto righteousness, and with the mouth confession is made
unto salvation.
11 For the Scripture says, [a]*"Whoever believes on*
*Him will not be put to shame."*
12 For [a]there is no distinction between Jew and
Greek, for [b]the same Lord over all [c]is rich to all
who call upon Him.
13 For [a]*"whoever calls* [b]*on the name of the* LORD
*shall be saved."*
**14** How then shall they call on Him in whom they
have not believed? And how shall they believe in
Him of whom they have not heard? And how shall
they hear [a]without a preacher?

**3** [1]Or *relatives*
**4** [a]Ex. 4:22 [b]1 Sam. 4:21 [c]Acts 3:25 [d]Ps. 147:19 [e]Heb. 9:1, 6 [f][Acts 2:39; 13:32]
**5** [a]Deut. 10:15 [b][Luke 1:34, 35; 3:23] [c]Jer. 23:6
**6** [a]Num. 23:19 [b][Gal. 6:16]
**7** [a][Gal. 4:23] [b]Gen. 21:12
**8** [a]Gal. 4:28
**9** [a]Gen. 18:10, 14
**10** [a]Gen. 25:21
**11** [a][Rom. 4:17; 8:28]
**12** [a]Gen. 25:23
**13** [a]Mal. 1:2, 3
**14** [a]Deut. 32:4
**15** [a]Ex. 33:19
**17** [a]Gal. 3:8 [b]Ex. 9:16
**18** [a]Ex. 4:21
**19** [a]2 Chr. 20:6
**20** [a]Is. 29:16
**21** [a]Prov. 16:4 [b]2 Tim. 2:20
**22** [a][1 Thess. 5:9] [b][1 Pet. 2:8]
**23** [a][Col. 1:27] [b][Rom. 8:28–30]
**24** [a][Rom. 8:28] [b]Rom. 3:29
**25** [a]Hos. 2:23
**26** [a]Hos. 1:10
**27** [a]Is. 10:22, 23 [b]Rom. 11:5
**28** [a]Is. 10:23; 28:22 [1]NU *finish the work and cut it short*
**29** [a]Is. 1:9 [b]Is. 13:19 [1]Lit., in Heb., *Hosts*
**30** [a]Rom. 4:11 [b]Rom. 1:17; 3:21; 10:6
**31** [a][Rom. 10:2–4] [b][Gal. 5:4] [1]NU omits *of righteousness*
**32** [a][1 Cor. 1:23] [1]NU *by works,* omitting *of the law*
**33** [a]Is. 8:14; 28:16 [b]Rom. 5:5; 10:11

CHAPTER 10
**1** [1]NU *them*
**2** [a]Acts 21:20
**3** [a][Rom. 1:17] [b][Phil. 3:9]
**4** [a][Gal. 3:24; 4:5]
**5** [a]Lev. 18:5
**6** [a]Deut. 30:12–14
**7** [a]Deut. 30:13
**8** [a]Deut. 30:14
**9** [a]Luke 12:8
**11** [a]Is. 28:16
**12** [a]Rom. 3:22, 29 [b]Acts 10:36 [c]Eph. 1:7
**13** [a]Joel 2:32 [b]Acts 9:14
**14** [a]Titus 1:3

15 And how shall they preach unless they are
sent? As it is written:

[a]*"How beautiful are the feet of those who*
*[1]preach the gospel of peace,*
*Who bring glad tidings of good things!"*

16 But they have not all obeyed the gospel. For
Isaiah says, [a]*"Lord, who has believed our report?"*
17 So then faith *comes* by hearing, and hearing
by the word of God.
18 But I say, have they not heard? Yes indeed:

[a]*"Their sound has gone out to all the earth,*
*[b]And their words to the ends of the world."*

19 But I say, did Israel not know? First Moses
says:

[a]*"I will provoke you to jealousy*
*by those who are not a nation,*
*I will move you to anger by a [b]foolish*
*nation."*

20 But Isaiah is very bold and says:

[a]*"I was found by those who did not seek Me;*
*I was made manifest to those*
*who did not ask for Me."*

21 But to Israel he says:

[a]*"All day long I have stretched out My hands*
*To a disobedient and contrary people."*

### *Jews and Gentiles Grafted into One Tree*

11 I say then, [a]has God cast away His people?
[b]Certainly not! For [c]I also am an Israelite, of
the seed of Abraham, *of* the tribe of Benjamin.
2 God has not cast away His people whom [a]He
foreknew. Or do you not know what the Scripture
says of Elijah, how he pleads with God against
Israel, saying,
3 [a]*"LORD, they have killed Your prophets and*
*torn down Your altars, and I alone am left, and*
*they seek my life"*?
4 But what does the divine response say to him?
[a]*"I have reserved for Myself seven thousand men*
*who have not bowed the knee to Baal."*
5 [a]Even so then, at this present time there is a
remnant according to the election of grace.
6 And [a]if by grace, then *it is* no longer of works;
otherwise grace is no longer grace. [1]But if *it is* of
works, it is no longer grace; otherwise work is no
longer work.
7 What then? [a]Israel has not obtained what it
seeks; but the elect have obtained it, and the rest
were [b]blinded.
8 Just as it is written:

[a]*"God has given them a spirit of stupor,*
*[b]Eyes that they should not see*
*And ears that they should not hear,*
*To this very day."*

9 And David says:

[a]*"Let their table become a snare and a trap,*
*A stumbling block and*
*a recompense to them.*
10 *Let their eyes be darkened,*
*so that they do not see,*
*And bow down their back always."*

11 I say then, have they stumbled that they
should fall? Certainly not! But [a]through their [1]fall,
to provoke them to [b]jealousy, salvation *has come*
to the Gentiles.
12 Now if their [1]fall *is* riches for the world, and
their failure riches for the Gentiles, how much
more their fullness!
13 For I speak to you Gentiles; inasmuch as [a]I am
an apostle to the Gentiles, I magnify my ministry,
14 if by any means I may provoke to jealousy
*those who are* my flesh and [a]save some of them.
15 For if their being cast away *is* the reconciling
of the world, what *will* their acceptance *be* [a]but
life from the dead?
16 For if [a]the firstfruit *is* holy, the lump *is* also
*holy;* and if the root *is* holy, so *are* the branches.
17 And if [a]some of the branches were broken off,
[b]and you, being a wild olive tree, were grafted in
among them, and with them became a partaker of
the root and [1]fatness of the olive tree,
18 [a]do not boast against the branches. But if you
do boast, *remember that* you do not support the
root, but the root supports you.
19 You will say then, "Branches were broken off
that I might be grafted in."
20 Well *said.* Because of [a]unbelief they were
broken off, and you stand by faith. Do not be
haughty, but fear.
21 For if God did not spare the natural branches,
He may not spare you either.
22 Therefore consider the goodness and severity
of God: on those who fell, severity; but toward
you, [1]goodness, [a]if you continue in *His* goodness.
Otherwise [b]you also will be cut off.
23 And they also, [a]if they do not continue in
unbelief, will be grafted in, for God is able to graft
them in again.
24 For if you were cut out of the olive tree which
is wild by nature, and were grafted contrary to
nature into a cultivated olive tree, how much
more will these, who *are* natural *branches,* be
grafted into their own olive tree?
25 For I do not desire, brethren, that you should
be ignorant of this mystery, lest you should be
[a]wise in your own [1]opinion, that [b]blindness in part
has happened to Israel [c]until the fullness of the
Gentiles has come in.
26 And so all Israel will be [1]saved, as it is written:

[a]*"The Deliverer will come out of Zion,*
*And He will turn away ungodliness from*
*Jacob;*
27 *For [a]this is My covenant with them,*
*When I take away their sins."*

28 Concerning the gospel *they are* enemies for
your sake, but concerning the election *they are*
[a]beloved for the sake of the fathers.
29 For the gifts and the calling of God *are* [a]irrevo-
cable.
30 For as you [a]were once disobedient to God, yet
have now obtained mercy through their disobedience,
31 even so these also have now been disobedient,
that through the mercy shown you they also may
obtain mercy.
32 For God has [1]committed them [a]all to disobedience, that He might have mercy on all.
33 Oh, the depth of the riches both of the wisdom
and knowledge of God! How unsearchable *are* His
judgments and His ways past finding out!

34 *"For who has known the [a]mind of the LORD?*
*Or [b]who has become His counselor?"*

15 [a]Is. 52:7; Nah. 1:15 [1]NU omits *preach the gospel of peace, Who*
16 [a]Is. 53:1
18 [a]Ps. 19:4 [b]1 Kin. 18:10
19 [a]Deut. 32:21 [b]Titus 3:3
20 [a]Is. 65:1
21 [a]Is. 65:2

CHAPTER 11
1 [a]Jer. 46:28 [b]1 Sam. 12:22 [c]2 Cor. 11:22
2 [a][Rom. 8:29]
3 [a]1 Kin. 19:10, 14
4 [a]1 Kin. 19:18
5 [a]Rom. 9:27
6 [a]Rom. 4:4 [1]NU omits the rest of v. 6.
7 [a]Rom. 9:31 [b]2 Cor. 3:14
8 [a]Is. 29:10, 13 [b]Deut. 29:3, 4
9 [a]Ps. 69:22, 23
11 [a]Is. 42:6, 7 [b]Rom. 10:19 [1]*trespass*
12 [1]*trespass*
13 [a]Acts 9:15; 22:21
14 [a]1 Cor. 9:22
15 [a][Is. 26:16–19]
16 [a]Lev. 23:10
17 [a]Jer. 11:16 [b][Eph. 2:12] [1]*richness*
18 [a][1 Cor. 10:12]
20 [a]Heb. 3:19
22 [a]1 Cor. 15:2 [b][John 15:2] [1]NU adds *of God*
23 [a][2 Cor. 3:16]
25 [a]Rom. 12:16 [b]2 Cor. 3:14 [c]Luke 21:24 [1]*estimation*
26 [a]Is. 59:20, 21 [1]Or *delivered*
27 [a]Is. 27:9
28 [a]Deut. 7:8; 10:15
29 [a]Num. 23:19
30 [a][Eph. 2:2]
32 [a][Gal. 3:22] [1]*shut them all up in*
34 [a]Is. 40:13; Jer. 23:18 [b]Job 36:22

35 *"Or*[a] *who has first given to Him*
*And it shall be repaid to him?"*

36 For [a]of Him and through Him and to Him *are*
all things, [b]to whom *be* glory forever. Amen.

### *Christians Should Lead Transformed Lives*

**12** I [a]beseech[1] you therefore, brethren, by the
mercies of God, that you present your bodies [b]a living sacrifice, holy, acceptable to God,
*which is* your [2]reasonable service.
2 And [a]do not be conformed to this world, but
[b]be transformed by the renewing of your mind,
that you may [c]prove what *is* that good and acceptable and perfect will of God.
**3** For I say, [a]through the grace given to me, to
everyone who is among you, [b]not to think *of*
*himself* more highly than he ought to think, but to
think soberly, as God has dealt [c]to each one a
measure of faith.
4 For [a]as we have many members in one body,
but all the members do not have the same function,
5 so [a]we, *being* many, are one body in Christ,
and individually members of one another.
6 Having then gifts differing according to the
grace that is [a]given to us, *let us use them:* if
prophecy, *let us* [b]*prophesy* in proportion to our
faith;
7 or ministry, *let us use it* in *our* ministering; [a]he
who teaches, in teaching;
8 [a]he who exhorts, in exhortation; [b]he who
gives, with liberality; [c]he who leads, with diligence; he who shows mercy, [d]with cheerfulness.
**9** [a]*Let* love *be* without hypocrisy. [b]Abhor what is
evil. Cling to what is good.
10 [a]*Be* kindly affectionate to one another with
brotherly love, [b]in honor giving preference to one
another;
11 not lagging in diligence, fervent in spirit,
serving the Lord;
12 [a]rejoicing in hope, [b]patient[1] in tribulation,
[c]continuing steadfastly in prayer;
13 [a]distributing to the needs of the saints, [b]given[1]
to hospitality.
14 [a]Bless those who persecute you; bless and do
not curse.
15 [a]Rejoice with those who rejoice, and weep
with those who weep.
16 [a]Be of the same mind toward one another. [b]Do
not set your mind on high things, but associate
with the humble. Do not be wise in your own
opinion.
17 [a]Repay no one evil for evil. [b]Have[1] regard for
good things in the sight of all men.
18 If it is possible, as much as depends on you,
[a]live peaceably with all men.
19 Beloved, [a]do not avenge yourselves, but *rather*
give place to wrath; for it is written, [b]*"Vengeance*
*is Mine, I will repay,"* says the Lord.
20 Therefore[a]

*"If your enemy hungers, feed him;*
*If he thirsts, give him a drink;*
*For in so doing you will heap coals*
*of fire on his head."*

21 Do not be overcome by evil, but [a]overcome
evil with good.

### *Obey Authorities; Love Your Neighbor; Put on Christ*

**13** Let every soul be [a]subject to the governing
authorities. For there is no authority except
from God, and the authorities that exist are
appointed by God.
2 Therefore whoever resists [a]the authority resists the ordinance of God, and those who resist
will [1]bring judgment on themselves.
3 For rulers are not a terror to good works, but
to evil. Do you want to be unafraid of the authority? [a]Do what is good, and you will have praise
from the same.
4 For he is God's minister to you for good. But if
you do evil, be afraid; for he does not bear the
sword in vain; for he is God's minister, an avenger
to *execute* wrath on him who practices evil.
5 Therefore [a]*you* must be subject, not only
because of wrath [b]but also for conscience' sake.
6 For because of this you also pay taxes, for
they are God's ministers attending continually to
this very thing.
7 [a]Render therefore to all their due: taxes to
whom taxes *are due,* customs to whom customs,
fear to whom fear, honor to whom honor.
**8** Owe no one anything except to love one
another, for [a]he who loves another has fulfilled
the law.
9 For the commandments, [a]*"You shall not com-*
*mit adultery," "You shall not murder," "You shall*
*not steal,"* [1]*"You shall not bear false witness,"*
*"You shall not covet,"* and if *there is* any other
commandment, are *all* summed up in this saying,
namely, [b]*"You shall love your neighbor as your-*
*self."*
10 Love does no harm to a neighbor; therefore
[a]love *is* the fulfillment of the law.
**11** And *do* this, knowing the time, that now *it is*
high time [a]to awake out of sleep; for now our
salvation *is* nearer than when we *first* believed.
12 The night is far spent, the day is at hand.
[a]Therefore let us cast off the works of darkness,
and [b]let us put on the armor of light.
13 [a]Let us walk [1]properly, as in the day, [b]not in
revelry and drunkenness, [c]not in lewdness and
lust, [d]not in strife and envy.
14 But [a]put on the Lord Jesus Christ, and [b]make
no provision for the flesh, to *fulfill its* lusts.

### *The Law of Liberty and the Law of Love*

**14** Receive[a] one who is weak in the faith, *but*
not to disputes over doubtful things.
2 For one believes he [a]may eat all things, but he
who is weak eats *only* vegetables.
3 Let not him who eats despise him who does
not eat, and [a]let not him who does not eat judge
him who eats; for God has received him.
4 [a]Who are you to judge another's servant? To
his own master he stands or falls. Indeed, he will
be made to stand, for God is able to make him
stand.
5 [a]One person esteems *one* day above another;
another esteems every day *alike.* Let each be fully
convinced in his own mind.
6 He who [a]observes the day, observes *it* to the
Lord; [1]and he who does not observe the day, to the
Lord he does not observe *it.* He who eats, eats to
the Lord, for [b]he gives God thanks; and he who
does not eat, to the Lord he does not eat, and
gives God thanks.

---

35 [a]Job 41:11
36 [a]Heb. 2:10 [b]Heb. 13:21

CHAPTER 12
1 [a]2 Cor. 10:1–4 [b]Heb. 10:18, 20 [1]*urge* [2]*rational*
2 [a]1 John 2:15 [b]Eph. 4:23 [c][1 Thess. 4:3]
3 [a]Gal. 2:9 [b]Prov. 25:27 [c][Eph. 4:7]
4 [a]1 Cor. 12:12–14
5 [a][1 Cor. 10:17]
6 [a][John 3:27] [b]Acts 11:27
7 [a]Eph. 4:11
8 [a]Acts 15:32 [b][Matt. 6:1–3] [c][Acts 20:28] [d]2 Cor. 9:7
9 [a]1 Tim. 1:5 [b]Ps. 34:14
10 [a]Heb. 13:1 [b]Phil. 2:3
12 [a]Luke 10:20 [b]Luke 21:19 [c]Luke 18:1 [1]*persevering*
13 [a]1 Cor. 16:1 [b]1 Tim. 3:2 [1]Lit. *pursuing*
14 [a][Matt. 5:44]
15 [a][1 Cor. 12:26]
16 [a][Phil. 2:2; 4:2] [b]Jer. 45:5
17 [a][Matt. 5:39] [b]2 Cor. 8:21 [1]Or *Provide good*
18 [a]Heb. 12:14
19 [a]Lev. 19:18 [b]Deut. 32:35
20 [a]Prov. 25:21, 22
21 [a][Rom. 12:1, 2]

CHAPTER 13
1 [a]1 Pet. 2:13
2 [a][Titus 3:1] [1]Lit. *receive*
3 [a]1 Pet. 2:14
5 [a]Eccl. 8:2 [b][1 Pet. 2:13, 19]
7 [a]Matt. 22:21
8 [a][Gal. 5:13, 14]
9 [a]Ex. 20:13–17; Deut. 5:17–21 [b]Lev. 19:18 [1]NU omits *You shall not bear false witness*
10 [a][Matt. 7:12; 22:39, 40]
11 [a][1 Cor. 15:34]
12 [a]Eph. 5:11 [b][Eph. 6:11, 13]
13 [a]Phil. 4:8 [b]Prov. 23:20 [c][1 Cor. 6:9] [d]James 3:14 [1]*decently*
14 [a]Gal. 3:27 [b][Gal. 5:16]

CHAPTER 14
1 [a][1 Cor. 8:9; 9:22]
2 [a][Titus 1:15]
3 [a][Col. 2:16]
4 [a]James 4:11, 12
5 [a]Gal. 4:10
6 [a]Gal. 4:10 [b][1 Tim. 4:3] [1]NU omits the rest of this sentence.

7 For [a]none of us lives to himself, and no one dies to himself.
8 For if we [a]live, we live to the Lord; and if we die, we die to the Lord. Therefore, whether we live or die, we are the Lord's.
9 For [a]to this end Christ died [1]and rose and lived again, that He might be [b]Lord of both the dead and the living.
10 But why do you judge your brother? Or why do you show contempt for your brother? For [a]we shall all stand before the judgment seat of [1]Christ.
11 For it is written:

[a]*"As I live, says the* LORD,
*Every knee shall bow to Me,*
*And every tongue shall confess to God."*

12 So then [a]each of us shall give account of himself to God.
13 Therefore let us not judge one another [1]anymore, but rather resolve this, [a]not to put a stumbling block or a cause to fall in *our* brother's way.
**14** I know and am convinced by the Lord Jesus [a]that *there is* nothing unclean of itself; but to him who considers anything to be unclean, to him *it is* unclean.
15 Yet if your brother is grieved because of *your* food, you are no longer walking in love. [a]Do not destroy with your food the one for whom Christ died.
16 [a]Therefore do not let your good be spoken of as evil;
17 [a]for the kingdom of God is not eating and drinking, but righteousness and [b]peace and joy in the Holy Spirit.
18 For he who serves Christ in [1]these things [a]*is* acceptable to God and approved by men.
19 [a]Therefore let us pursue the things *which make* for peace and the things by which [b]one may [1]edify another.
20 [a]Do not destroy the work of God for the sake of food. [b]All things indeed *are* pure, [c]but *it is* evil for the man who eats with [1]offense.
21 *It is* good neither to eat [a]meat nor drink wine nor *do anything* by which your brother stumbles [1]or is offended or is made weak.
22 [1]Do you have faith? Have *it* to yourself before God. [a]Happy *is* he who does not condemn himself in what he approves.
23 But he who doubts is condemned if he eats, because *he does* not *eat* from faith; for [a]whatever *is* not from faith is [1]sin.

### *Paul's Ministry to the Gentiles*

**15** We [a]then who are strong ought to bear with the [1]scruples of the weak, and not to please ourselves.
2 [a]Let each of us please *his* neighbor for *his* good, leading to [1]edification.
3 [a]For even Christ did not please Himself; but as it is written, [b]*"The reproaches of those who reproached You fell on Me."*
4 For [a]whatever things were written before were written for our learning, that we through the [1]patience and comfort of the Scriptures might have hope.
5 [a]Now may the God of patience and comfort grant you to be like-minded toward one another, according to Christ Jesus,
6 that you may [a]with one mind *and* one mouth glorify the God and Father of our Lord Jesus Christ.
7 Therefore [a]receive one another, just [b]as Christ also received [1]us, to the glory of God.
8 Now I say that [a]Jesus Christ has become a [1]servant to the circumcision for the truth of God, [b]to confirm the promises *made* to the fathers,
9 and [a]that the Gentiles might glorify God for *His* mercy, as it is written:

[b]*"For this reason I will confess*
*to You among the Gentiles,*
*And sing to Your name."*

10 And again he says:

[a]*"Rejoice, O Gentiles, with His people!"*

11 And again:

[a]*"Praise the* LORD, *all you Gentiles!*
*Laud Him, all you peoples!"*

12 And again, Isaiah says:

[a]*"There shall be a root of Jesse;*
*And He who shall rise to reign*
*over the Gentiles,*
*In Him the Gentiles shall hope."*

13 Now may the God of hope fill you with all [a]joy and peace in believing, that you may abound in hope by the power of the Holy Spirit.
**14** Now [a]I myself am confident concerning you, my brethren, that you also are full of goodness, [b]filled with all knowledge, able also to admonish [1]one another.
15 Nevertheless, brethren, I have written more boldly to you on *some* points, as reminding you, [a]because of the grace given to me by God,
16 that [a]I might be a minister of Jesus Christ to the Gentiles, ministering the gospel of God, that the [b]offering [1]of the Gentiles might be acceptable, sanctified by the Holy Spirit.
17 Therefore I have reason to glory in Christ Jesus [a]in the things *which pertain* to God.
18 For I will not dare to speak of any of those things [a]which Christ has not accomplished through me, in word and deed, [b]to make the Gentiles obedient—
19 [a]in mighty signs and wonders, by the power of the Spirit of God, so that from Jerusalem and round about to Illyricum I have fully preached the gospel of Christ.
20 And so I have made it my aim to preach the gospel, not where Christ was named, [a]lest I should build on another man's foundation,
21 but as it is written:

[a]*"To whom He was not announced,*
*they shall see;*
*And those who have not heard*
*shall understand."*

**22** For this reason [a]I also have been much hindered from coming to you.
23 But now no longer having a place in these parts, and [a]having a great desire these many years to come to you,
24 whenever I journey to Spain, [1]I shall come to you. For I hope to see you on my journey, [a]and to be helped on my way there by you, if first I may [b]enjoy your *company* for a while.
25 But now [a]I am going to Jerusalem to [1]minister to the saints.

**7** [a][Gal. 2:20]
**8** [a]2 Cor. 5:14, 15
**9** [a]2 Cor. 5:15 [b]Acts 10:36 [1]NU omits *and rose*
**10** [a]2 Cor. 5:10 [1]NU *God*
**11** [a]Is. 45:23
**12** [a]1 Pet. 4:5
**13** [a]1 Cor. 8:9 [1]*any longer*
**14** [a]1 Cor. 10:25
**15** [a]1 Cor. 8:11
**16** [a][Rom. 12:17]
**17** [a]1 Cor. 8:8 [b][Rom. 8:6]
**18** [a]2 Cor. 8:21 [1]NU *this thing*
**19** [a]Rom. 12:18 [b]1 Cor. 14:12 [1]*build up*
**20** [a]Rom. 14:15 [b]Acts 10:15 [c]1 Cor. 8:9–12 [1]A feeling of giving offense
**21** [a]1 Cor. 8:13 [1]NU omits the rest of v. 21.
**22** [a][1 John 3:21] [1]NU *The faith which you have—have*
**23** [a]Titus 1:15 [1]M puts Rom. 16:25–27 here.

CHAPTER 15
**1** [a][Gal. 6:1, 2] [1]*weaknesses*
**2** [a]1 Cor. 9:22; 10:24, 33 [1]*building up*
**3** [a]Matt. 26:39 [b]Ps. 69:9
**4** [a]1 Cor. 10:11 [1]*perseverance*
**5** [a]1 Cor. 1:10
**6** [a]Acts 4:24
**7** [a]Rom. 14:1, 3 [b]Rom. 5:2 [1]NU, M *you*
**8** [a]Matt. 15:24 [b]2 Cor. 1:20 [1]*minister*
**9** [a]John 10:16 [b]2 Sam. 22:50; Ps. 18:49
**10** [a]Deut. 32:43
**11** [a]Ps. 117:1
**12** [a]Is. 11:1, 10
**13** [a]Rom. 12:12; 14:17
**14** [a]2 Pet. 1:12 [b]1 Cor. 1:5; 8:1, 7, 10 [1]M *others*
**15** [a]Rom. 1:5; 12:3
**16** [a]Rom. 11:13 [b][Is. 66:20] [1]Consisting of
**17** [a]Heb. 2:17; 5:1
**18** [a]Acts 15:12; 21:19 [b]Rom. 1:5
**19** [a]Acts 19:11
**20** [a][2 Cor. 10:13, 15, 16]
**21** [a]Is. 52:15
**22** [a]Rom. 1:13
**23** [a]Acts 19:21; 23:11
**24** [a]Acts 15:3 [b]Rom. 1:12 [1]NU omits *I shall come to you* and joins *Spain* with the next sentence.

**25** [a]Acts 19:21 [1]*serve*

26 For [a]it pleased those from Macedonia and
Achaia to make a certain contribution for the
poor among the saints who are in Jerusalem.
27 It pleased them indeed, and they are their
debtors. For [a]if the Gentiles have been partakers
of their spiritual things, [b]their duty is also to
minister to them in material things.
28 Therefore, when I have performed this and
have sealed to them [a]this fruit, I shall go by way of
you to Spain.
29 [a]But I know that when I come to you, I shall
come in the fullness of the blessing [1]of the gospel
of Christ.
30 Now I beg you, brethren, through the Lord
Jesus Christ, and [a]through the love of the Spirit,
[b]that you strive together with me in prayers to
God for me,
31 [a]that I may be delivered from those in Judea
who [1]do not believe, and that [b]my service for
Jerusalem may be acceptable to the saints,
32 [a]that I may come to you with joy [b]by the will
of God, and may [c]be refreshed together with you.
33 Now [a]the God of peace *be* with you all. Amen.

*Final Commendations and Greetings*

**16** I commend to you Phoebe our sister, who is
a servant of the church in [a]Cenchrea,
2 [a]that you may receive her in the Lord [b]in a
manner worthy of the saints, and assist her in
whatever business she has need of you; for indeed
she has been a helper of many and of myself also.
3 Greet [a]Priscilla and Aquila, my fellow workers
in Christ Jesus,
4 who risked their own necks for my life, to
whom not only I give thanks, but also all the
churches of the Gentiles.
5 Likewise *greet* [a]the church that is in their
house. Greet my beloved Epaenetus, who is [b]the
firstfruits of [1]Achaia to Christ.
6 Greet Mary, who labored much for us.
7 Greet Andronicus and Junia, my countrymen
and my fellow prisoners, who are of note among
the [a]apostles, who also [b]were in Christ before me.
8 Greet Amplias, my beloved in the Lord.
9 Greet Urbanus, our fellow worker in Christ,
and Stachys, my beloved.
10 Greet Apelles, approved in Christ. Greet those
who are of the *household* of Aristobulus.
11 Greet Herodion, my [1]countryman. Greet those
who are of the *household* of Narcissus who are in
the Lord.
12 Greet Tryphena and Tryphosa, who have labored in the Lord. Greet the beloved Persis, who
labored much in the Lord.
13 Greet Rufus, [a]chosen in the Lord, and his
mother and mine.
14 Greet Asyncritus, Phlegon, Hermas, Patrobas,
Hermes, and the brethren who are with them.
15 Greet Philologus and Julia, Nereus and his
sister, and Olympas, and all the saints who are
with them.
16 [a]Greet one another with a holy kiss. [1]The
churches of Christ greet you.
17 Now I urge you, brethren, note those [a]who
cause divisions and offenses, contrary to the
doctrine which you learned, and [b]avoid them.
18 For those who are such do not serve our Lord
[1]Jesus Christ, but [a]their own belly, and [b]by smooth
words and flattering speech deceive the hearts of
the simple.
19 For [a]your obedience has become known to all.
Therefore I am glad on your behalf; but I want
you to be [b]wise in what is good, and [1]simple
concerning evil.
20 And [a]the God of peace [b]will crush Satan under
your feet shortly. [c]The grace of our Lord Jesus
Christ *be* with you. Amen.
21 [a]Timothy, my fellow worker, and [b]Lucius,
[c]Jason, and [d]Sosipater, my countrymen, greet you.
22 I, Tertius, who wrote *this* epistle, greet you in
the Lord.
23 [a]Gaius, my host and *the host* of the whole
church, greets you. [b]Erastus, the treasurer of the
city, greets you, and Quartus, a brother.
24 [a]The[1] grace of our Lord Jesus Christ *be* with
you all. Amen.
25 [1]Now [a]to Him who is able to establish you
[b]according to my gospel and the preaching of
Jesus Christ, [c]according to the revelation of the
mystery [d]kept secret since the world began
26 but [a]now has been made manifest, and by the
prophetic Scriptures has been made known to all
nations, according to the commandment of the
everlasting God, for [b]obedience to the faith—
27 to [a]God, alone wise, *be* glory through Jesus
Christ forever. Amen.

26 [a]1 Cor. 16:1
27 [a]Rom. 11:17 [b]1 Cor. 9:11
28 [a]Phil. 4:17
29 [a][Rom. 1:11] [1]NU omits *of the gospel*
30 [a]Phil. 2:1 [b]2 Cor. 1:11
31 [a]2 Tim. 3:11; 4:17 [b]2 Cor. 8:4 [1]*are disobedient*
32 [a]Rom. 1:10 [b]Acts 18:21 [c]1 Cor. 16:18
33 [a]1 Cor. 14:33

CHAPTER 16
1 [a]Acts 18:18
2 [a]Phil. 2:29 [b]Phil. 1:27
3 [a]Acts 18:2, 18, 26
5 [a]1 Cor. 16:19 [b]1 Cor. 16:15 [1]NU *Asia*
7 [a]Acts 1:13, 26 [b]Gal. 1:22
11 [1]Or *relative*
13 [a]2 John 1
16 [a]1 Cor. 16:20 [1]NU *All the churches*
17 [a][Acts 15:1] [b][1 Cor. 5:9]
18 [a]Phil. 3:19 [b]Col. 2:4 [1]NU, M omit *Jesus*
19 [a]Rom. 1:8 [b]Matt. 10:16 [1]*innocent*
20 [a]Rom. 15:33 [b]Gen. 3:15 [c]1 Cor. 16:23
21 [a]Acts 16:1 [b]Acts 13:1 [c]Acts 17:5 [d]Acts 20:4
23 [a]1 Cor. 1:14 [b]Acts 19:22
24 [a]1 Thess. 5:28 [1]NU omits v. 24.
25 [a][Eph. 3:20] [b]Rom. 2:16 [c]Eph. 1:9 [d]Col. 1:26; 2:2; 4:3 [1]M puts Rom. 16:25–27 after Rom. 14:23.
26 [a]Eph. 1:9 [b]Rom. 1:5
27 [a]Jude 25

*The First Epistle of Paul the Apostle to the*

# CORINTHIANS

*Divisions in the Church Condemned*

PAUL, [a]called *to be* an apostle of Jesus Christ
[b]through the will of God, and [c]Sosthenes *our*
brother,

2 To the church of God which is at Corinth, to
those who [a]are [1]sanctified in Christ Jesus, [b]called
*to be* saints, with all who in every place call on the
name of Jesus Christ [c]our Lord, [d]both theirs and
ours:

3 [a]Grace to you and peace from God our Father
and the Lord Jesus Christ.

4 [a]I thank my God always concerning you for
the grace of God which was given to you by
Christ Jesus,
5 that you were enriched in everything by Him
[a]in all [1]utterance and all knowledge,
6 even as [a]the testimony of Christ was confirmed [1]in you,
7 so that you come short in no gift, eagerly
[a]waiting for the revelation of our Lord Jesus
Christ,
8 [a]who will also confirm you to the end, [b]*that
you may be* blameless in the day of our Lord Jesus
Christ.

CHAPTER 1
1 [a]Rom. 1:1 [b]2 Cor. 1:1 [c]Acts 18:17
2 [a][Acts 15:9] [b]Rom. 1:7 [c][1 Cor. 8:6] [d][Rom. 3:22] [1]*set apart*
3 [a]Rom. 1:7
4 [a]Rom. 1:8
5 [a][1 Cor. 12:8] [1]*speech*
6 [a]2 Tim. 1:8 [1]Or *among*
7 [a]Phil. 3:20
8 [a]1 Thess. 3:13; 5:23 [b]Col. 1:22; 2:7

9 [a]God *is* faithful, by whom you were called into [b]the fellowship of His Son, Jesus Christ our Lord.
**10** Now I plead with you, brethren, by the name of our Lord Jesus Christ, [a]that you all [1]speak the same thing, and *that* there be no [2]divisions among you, but *that* you be perfectly joined together in the same mind and in the same judgment.
11 For it has been declared to me concerning you, my brethren, by those of Chloe's *household,* that there are [1]contentions among you.
12 Now I say this, that [a]each of you says, "I am of Paul," or "I am of [b]Apollos," or "I am of [c]Cephas," or "I am of Christ."
13 [a]Is Christ divided? Was Paul crucified for you? Or were you baptized in the name of Paul?
14 I thank God that I baptized [a]none of you except [b]Crispus and [c]Gaius,
15 lest anyone should say that I had baptized in my own name.
16 Yes, I also baptized the household of [a]Stephanas. Besides, I do not know whether I baptized any other.
17 For Christ did not send me to baptize, but to preach the gospel, [a]not with wisdom of words, lest the cross of Christ should be made of no effect.
**18** For the [1]message of the cross is [a]foolishness to [b]those who are perishing, but to us [c]who are being saved it is the [d]power of God.
19 For it is written:

[a]*"I will destroy the wisdom of the wise,*
*And bring to nothing the understanding of*
*the prudent."*

20 [a]Where *is* the wise? Where *is* the scribe? Where *is* the [1]disputer of this age? [b]Has not God made foolish the wisdom of this world?
21 For since, in the [a]wisdom of God, the world through wisdom did not know God, it pleased God through the foolishness of the message preached to save those who believe.
22 For [a]Jews request a sign, and Greeks seek after wisdom;
23 but we preach Christ crucified, [a]to the Jews a [1]stumbling block and to the [2]Greeks [b]foolishness,
24 but to those who are called, both Jews and Greeks, Christ [a]the power of God and [b]the wisdom of God.
25 Because the foolishness of God is wiser than men, and the weakness of God is stronger than men.
**26** For [1]you see your calling, brethren, [a]that not many wise according to the flesh, not many mighty, not many [2]noble, *are called.*
27 But [a]God has chosen the foolish things of the world to put to shame the wise, and God has chosen the weak things of the world to put to shame the things which are mighty;
28 and the [1]base things of the world and the things which are despised God has chosen, and the things which are not, to bring to nothing the things that are,
29 that no flesh should glory in His presence.
30 But of Him you are in Christ Jesus, who became for us wisdom from God—and [a]righteousness and sanctification and redemption—
31 that, as it is written, [a]*"He who glories, let him glory in the* Lord."

## *Christ Crucified; Spiritual Wisdom*

**2** And I, brethren, when I came to you, did not come with excellence of speech or of wisdom declaring to you the [1]testimony of God.
2 For I determined not to know anything among you [a]except Jesus Christ and Him crucified.
3 [a]I was with you [b]in weakness, in fear, and in much trembling.
4 And my speech and my preaching [a]*were* not with persuasive words of [1]human wisdom, [b]but in demonstration of the Spirit and of power,
5 that your faith should not be in the wisdom of men but in the [a]power of God.
**6** However, we speak wisdom among those who are mature, yet not the wisdom of this age, nor of the rulers of this age, who are coming to nothing.
7 But we speak the wisdom of God in a mystery, the hidden *wisdom* which God [1]ordained before the ages for our glory,
8 which none of the rulers of this age knew; for [a]had they known, they would not have [b]crucified the Lord of glory.
9 But as it is written:

[a]*"Eye has not seen, nor ear heard,*
*Nor have entered into the heart of man*
*The things which God has prepared for those*
*who love Him."*

10 But [a]God has revealed *them* to us through His Spirit. For the Spirit searches all things, yes, the deep things of God.
11 For what man knows the things of a man except the [a]spirit of the man which is in him? [b]Even so no one knows the things of God except the Spirit of God.
12 Now we have received, not the spirit of the world, but [a]the Spirit who is from God, that we might know the things that have been freely given to us by God.
13 These things we also speak, not in words which man's wisdom teaches but which the [1]Holy Spirit teaches, comparing spiritual things with spiritual.
14 [a]But the natural man does not receive the things of the Spirit of God, for they are foolishness to him; nor can he know *them,* because they are spiritually discerned.
15 But he who is spiritual judges all things, yet he himself is *rightly* judged by no one.
16 For [a]*"who has known the mind of the* Lord *that he may instruct Him?"* [b]But we have the mind of Christ.

## *Jesus Christ Is the Only Foundation*

**3** And I, brethren, could not speak to you as to spiritual *people* but as to carnal, as to [a]babes in Christ.
2 I fed you with [a]milk and not with solid food; [b]for until now you were not able *to receive it,* and even now you are still not able;
3 for you are still carnal. For where *there are* envy, strife, and divisions among you, are you not carnal and [1]behaving like *mere* men?
4 For when one says, "I am of Paul," and another, "I *am* of Apollos," are you not carnal?
**5** Who then is Paul, and who *is* Apollos, but [a]ministers through whom you believed, as the Lord gave to each one?
6 [a]I planted, [b]Apollos watered, [c]but God gave the increase.
7 So then [a]neither he who plants is anything, nor he who waters, but God who gives the increase.
8 Now he who plants and he who waters are

**9** [a]Is. 49:7 [b][John 15:4] **10** [a]2 Cor. 13:11 [1]Have a uniform testimony [2]*schisms* or *dissensions* **11** [1]*quarrels* **12** [a]1 Cor. 3:4 [b]Acts 18:24 [c]John 1:42 **13** [a]2 Cor. 11:4 **14** [a]John 4:2 [b]Acts 18:8 [c]Rom. 16:23 **16** [a]1 Cor. 16:15, 17 **17** [a][1 Cor. 2:1, 4, 13] **18** [a]2 Cor. 2:15 [b]Acts 17:18 [c][1 Cor. 2:14; 15:2] [d]Rom. 1:16 [1]Lit. *word* **19** [a]Is. 29:14 **20** [a]Is. 19:12; 33:18 [b]Job 12:17 [1]*debater* **21** [a]Dan. 2:20 **22** [a]Matt. 12:38 **23** [a]Luke 2:34 [b][1 Cor. 2:14] [1]Gr. *skandalon, offense* [2]NU *Gentiles* **24** [a][Rom. 1:4] [b]Col. 2:3 **26** [a]John 7:48 [1]*consider* [2]*well-born* **27** [a]Matt. 11:25 **28** [1]*insignificant* or *lowly* **30** [a][2 Cor. 5:21] **31** [a]Jer. 9:23, 24

CHAPTER 2
**1** [1]NU *mystery* **2** [a]Gal. 6:14 **3** [a]Acts 18:1 [b][2 Cor. 4:7] **4** [a]2 Pet. 1:16 [b]Rom. 15:19 [1]NU omits *human* **5** [a]1 Thess. 1:5 **7** [1]*predetermined* **8** [a]Luke 23:34 [b]Matt. 27:33–50 **9** [a][Is. 64:4; 65:17] **10** [a]Matt. 11:25; 13:11; 16:17 **11** [a][James 2:26] [b]Rom. 11:33 **12** [a][Rom. 8:15] **13** [1]NU omits *Holy* **14** [a]Matt. 16:23 **16** [a]Is. 40:13 [b][John 15:15]

CHAPTER 3
**1** [a]Heb. 5:13 **2** [a]1 Pet. 2:2 [b]John 16:12 **3** [1]Lit. *walking according to man* **5** [a]2 Cor. 3:3, 6; 4:1; 5:18; 6:4 **6** [a]Acts 18:4 [b]Acts 18:24–27 [c][2 Cor. 3:5] **7** [a][Gal. 6:3]

one, [a]and each one will receive his own reward
according to his own labor.
9 For [a]we are God's fellow workers; you are
God's field, *you are* [b]God's building.
10 [a]According to the grace of God which was
given to me, as a wise master builder I have laid
[b]the foundation, and another builds on it. But let
each one take heed how he builds on it.
11 For no other foundation can anyone lay than
[a]that which is laid, [b]which is Jesus Christ.
12 Now if anyone builds on this foundation *with*
gold, silver, precious stones, wood, hay, straw,
13 each one's work will become clear; for the Day
[a]will declare it, because [b]it will be revealed by fire;
and the fire will test each one's work, of what sort
it is.
14 If anyone's work which he has built on *it*
endures, he will receive a reward.
15 If anyone's work is burned, he will suffer loss;
but he himself will be saved, yet so as through fire.
16 [a]Do you not know that you are the temple of
God and *that* the Spirit of God dwells in you?
17 If anyone [1]defiles the temple of God, God will
destroy him. For the temple of God is holy, which
*temple* you are.
**18** [a]Let no one deceive himself. If anyone among
you seems to be wise in this age, let him become a
fool that he may become wise.
19 For the wisdom of this world is foolishness
with God. For it is written, [a]*"He catches the wise
in their own craftiness"*;
20 and again, [a]*"The LORD knows the thoughts of
the wise, that they are futile."*
21 Therefore let no one boast in men. For [a]all
things are yours:
22 whether Paul or Apollos or Cephas, or the
world or life or death, or things present or things
to come—all are yours.
23 And [a]you *are* Christ's, and Christ *is* God's.

### *Caretakers of the Mysteries of God*

**4** Let a man so consider us, as [a]servants of
Christ [b]and stewards of the mysteries of God.
2 Moreover it is required in stewards that one be
found faithful.
3 But with me it is a very small thing that I
should be judged by you or by a human [1]court. In
fact, I do not even judge myself.
4 For I know of nothing against myself, yet I am
not justified by this; but He who judges me is the
Lord.
5 [a]Therefore judge nothing before the time,
until the Lord comes, who will both bring to [b]light
the hidden things of darkness and [c]reveal the
[1]counsels of the hearts. [d]Then each one's praise
will come from God.
**6** Now these things, brethren, I have figuratively transferred to myself and Apollos for your
sakes, that you may learn in us not to think
beyond what is written, that none of you may be
[1]puffed up on behalf of one against the other.
7 For who [1]makes you differ *from another?* And
[a]what do you have that you did not receive? Now
if you did indeed receive *it,* why do you boast as if
you had not received *it?*
8 You are already full! [a]You are already rich!
You have reigned as kings without us—and indeed I could wish you did reign, that we also
might reign with you!
9 For I think that God has displayed us, the
apostles, last, as men condemned to death; for we
have been made [1]a [a]spectacle to the world, both to
angels and to men.
10 We *are* [a]fools for Christ's sake, but you *are*
wise in Christ! [b]We *are* weak, but you *are* strong!
You *are* distinguished, but we *are* dishonored!
11 To the present hour we both hunger and
thirst, and we are poorly clothed, and beaten, and
homeless.
12 [a]And we labor, working with our own hands.
[b]Being reviled, we bless; being persecuted, we
endure;
13 being defamed, we [1]entreat. [a]We have been
made as the filth of the world, the offscouring of
all things until now.
**14** I do not write these things to shame you, but
[a]as my beloved children I warn *you.*
15 For though you might have ten thousand
instructors in Christ, yet *you do* not *have* many
fathers; for [a]in Christ Jesus I have begotten you
through the gospel.
16 Therefore I urge you, [a]imitate me.
17 For this reason I have sent [a]Timothy to you,
[b]who is my beloved and faithful son in the Lord,
who will [c]remind you of my ways in Christ, as I
[d]teach everywhere [e]in every church.
18 [a]Now some are [1]puffed up, as though I were
not coming to you.
19 [a]But I will come to you shortly, [b]if the Lord
wills, and I will know, not the word of those who
are puffed up, but the power.
20 For [a]the kingdom of God *is* not in word but in
[b]power.
21 What do you want? [a]Shall I come to you with
a rod, or in love and a spirit of gentleness?

### *Immorality in the Church Must Be Judged*

**5** It is actually reported *that there is* sexual
immorality among you, and such sexual immorality as is not even [1]named among the Gentiles—that a man has his father's [a]wife!
2 [a]And you are [1]puffed up, and have not rather
[b]mourned, that he who has done this deed might
be taken away from among you.
3 [a]For I indeed, as absent in body but present in
spirit, have already judged (as though I were
present) him who has so done this deed.
4 In the [a]name of our Lord Jesus Christ, when
you are gathered together, along with my spirit,
[b]with the power of our Lord Jesus Christ,
5 [a]deliver such a one to [b]Satan for the destruction of the flesh, that his spirit may be saved in the
day of the Lord [1]Jesus.
6 [a]Your glorying *is* not good. Do you not know
that [b]a little leaven leavens the whole lump?
7 Therefore [1]purge out the old leaven, that you
may be a new lump, since you truly are unleavened. For indeed [a]Christ, our [b]Passover, was sacrificed [2]for us.
8 Therefore [a]let us keep the feast, [b]not with old
leaven, nor [c]with the leaven of malice and wickedness, but with the unleavened *bread* of sincerity
and truth.
**9** I wrote to you in my epistle [a]not to [1]keep
company with sexually immoral people.
10 Yet *I* certainly *did* not *mean* with the sexually
immoral people of this world, or with the covetous, or extortioners, or idolaters, since then you
would need to go [a]out of the world.
11 But now I have written to you not to keep
company [a]with anyone named a brother, who is

8 [a]Ps. 62:12
9 [a]2 Cor. 6:1 [b][Eph. 2:20–22]
10 [a]Rom. 1:5 [b]1 Cor. 4:15
11 [a]Is. 28:16 [b]Eph. 2:20
13 [a]1 Pet. 1:7 [b]Luke 2:35
16 [a]2 Cor. 6:16
17 [1]*destroys*
18 [a]Prov. 3:7
19 [a]Job 5:13
20 [a]Ps. 94:11
21 [a][2 Cor. 4:5]
23 [a]2 Cor. 10:7

CHAPTER 4
1 [a]Col. 1:25 [b]Titus 1:7
3 [1]Lit. *day*
5 [a]Matt. 7:1 [b]Matt. 10:26 [c]1 Cor. 3:13 [d]Rom. 2:29 [1]*motives*
6 [1]*arrogant*
7 [a]John 3:27 [1]*distinguishes you*
8 [a]Rev. 3:17
9 [a]Heb. 10:33 [1]Lit. *theater*
10 [a]Acts 17:18; 26:24 [b]2 Cor. 13:9
12 [a]Acts 18:3; 20:34 [b]Matt. 5:44
13 [a]Lam. 3:45 [1]*exhort, encourage*
14 [a]1 Thess. 2:11
15 [a]Gal. 4:19
16 [a][1 Cor. 11:1]
17 [a]Acts 19:22 [b]1 Tim. 1:2, 18 [c]1 Cor. 11:2 [d]1 Cor. 7:17 [e]1 Cor. 14:33
18 [a]1 Cor. 5:2 [1]*arrogant*
19 [a]Acts 19:21; 20:2 [b]Acts 18:21
20 [a]1 Thess. 1:5 [b]1 Cor. 2:4
21 [a]2 Cor. 10:2

CHAPTER 5
1 [a]Lev. 18:6–8 [1]NU omits *named*
2 [a]1 Cor. 4:18 [b]2 Cor. 7:7–10 [1]*arrogant*
3 [a]Col. 2:5
4 [a][Matt. 18:20] [b][John 20:23]
5 [a]1 Tim. 1:20 [b][Acts 26:18] [1]NU omits *Jesus*
6 [a]1 Cor. 3:21 [b]Gal. 5:9
7 [a]Is. 53:7 [b]John 19:14 [1]*clean out* [2]NU omits *for us*
8 [a]Ex. 12:15 [b]Deut. 16:3 [c]Matt. 16:6
9 [a]2 Cor. 6:14 [1]*associate*
10 [a]John 17:15
11 [a]Matt. 18:17

sexually immoral, or covetous, or an idolater, or a
reviler, or a drunkard, or an extortioner—[b]not
even to eat with such a person.
12 For what *have* I *to do* with judging those also
who are outside? Do you not judge those who are
inside?
13 But those who are outside God judges. Therefore [a]*"put away from yourselves the evil person."*

### *Do Not Behave Like Worldly People*

**6** Dare any of you, having a matter against
another, go to law before the unrighteous, and
not before the [a]saints?
2 Do you not know that [a]the saints will judge
the world? And if the world will be judged by you,
are you unworthy to judge the smallest matters?
3 Do you not know that we shall [a]judge angels?
How much more, things that pertain to this life?
4 If then you have [1]judgments concerning
things pertaining to this life, do you appoint those
who are least esteemed by the church to judge?
5 I say this to your shame. Is it so, that there is
not a wise man among you, not even one, who
will be able to judge between his brethren?
6 But brother goes to law against brother, and
that before unbelievers!
7 Now therefore, it is already an utter failure for
you that you go to law against one another. [a]Why
do you not rather accept wrong? Why do you not
rather *let yourselves* be cheated?
8 No, you yourselves do wrong and cheat, and
*you do* these things *to your* brethren!
9 Do you not know that the unrighteous will
not inherit the kingdom of God? Do not be deceived. [a]Neither fornicators, nor idolaters, nor
adulterers, nor [1]homosexuals, nor [2]sodomites,
10 nor thieves, nor covetous, nor drunkards, nor
revilers, nor extortioners will inherit the kingdom
of God.
11 And such were [a]some of you. [b]But you were
washed, but you were [1]sanctified, but you were
justified in the name of the Lord Jesus and by the
Spirit of our God.
**12** [a]All things are lawful for me, but all things are
not [1]helpful. All things are lawful for me, but I will
not be brought under the power of [2]any.
13 [a]Foods for the stomach and the stomach for
foods, but God will destroy both it and them. Now
the body *is* not for [b]sexual immorality but [c]for the
Lord, [d]and the Lord for the body.
14 And [a]God both raised up the Lord and will also
raise us up [b]by His power.
15 Do you not know that [a]your bodies are members of Christ? Shall I then take the members of
Christ and make *them* members of a harlot?
Certainly not!
16 Or do you not know that he who is joined to a
harlot is one body *with her?* For [a]*"the two,"* He
says, *"shall become one flesh."*
17 [a]But he who is joined to the Lord is one spirit
*with Him.*
18 [a]Flee sexual immorality. Every sin that a man
does is outside the body, but he who commits
sexual immorality sins [b]against his own body.
19 Or [a]do you not know that your body is the
temple of the Holy Spirit *who is* in you, whom you
have from God, [b]and you are not your own?
20 For [a]you were bought at a price; therefore
glorify God in your body [1]and in your spirit, which
are God's.

11 [b]Gal. 2:12
13 [a]Deut. 13:5; 17:7, 12; 19:19; 21:21; 22:21, 24; 24:7

CHAPTER 6
1 [a]Dan. 7:22
2 [a]Ps. 49:14
3 [a]2 Pet. 2:4
4 [1]*courts*
7 [a][Prov. 20:22]
9 [a]Gal. 5:21 [1]*catamites,* those submitting to homosexuals [2]*male homosexuals*
11 [a][1 Cor. 12:2] [b]Heb. 10:22 [1]*set apart*
12 [a]1 Cor. 10:23 [1]*profitable* [2]Or *anything*
13 [a]Matt. 15:17 [b]Gal. 5:19 [c]1 Thess. 4:3 [d][Eph. 5:23]
14 [a]2 Cor. 4:14 [b]Eph. 1:19
15 [a]Rom. 12:5
16 [a]Gen. 2:24
17 [a][John 17:21–23]
18 [a]Heb. 13:4 [b]Rom. 1:24
19 [a]2 Cor. 6:16 [b]Rom. 14:7
20 [a]2 Pet. 2:1 [1]NU omits the rest of v. 20.

CHAPTER 7
1 [a]1 Cor. 7:8, 26
3 [a]Ex. 21:10
5 [a]Joel 2:16 [b]1 Thess. 3:5
6 [a]2 Cor. 8:8
7 [a]Acts 26:29
8 [a]1 Cor. 7:1, 26
9 [a]1 Tim. 5:14
10 [a]Mark 10:6–10 [b][Matt. 5:32]
14 [a]Mal. 2:15
15 [a]Rom. 12:18
16 [a]1 Pet. 3:1
17 [a]1 Cor. 4:17 [1]*direct*
18 [a]Acts 15:1
19 [a][Gal. 3:28; 5:6; 6:15] [b][John 15:14]
22 [a][John 8:36] [b]1 Pet. 2:16
23 [a]1 Pet. 1:18, 19

### *Principles of Marriage*

**7** Now concerning the things of which you
wrote to me: [a]*It is* good for a man not to touch
a woman.
2 Nevertheless, because of sexual immorality,
let each man have his own wife, and let each
woman have her own husband.
3 [a]Let the husband render to his wife the affection due her, and likewise also the wife to her
husband.
4 The wife does not have authority over her
own body, but the husband *does.* And likewise the
husband does not have authority over his own
body, but the wife *does.*
5 [a]Do not deprive one another except with
consent for a time, that you may give yourselves
to fasting and prayer; and come together again so
that [b]Satan does not tempt you because of your
lack of self-control.
6 But I say this as a concession, [a]not as a
commandment.
7 For [a]I wish that all men were even as I myself.
But each one has his own gift from God, one in
this manner and another in that.
8 But I say to the unmarried and to the widows:
[a]It is good for them if they remain even as I am;
9 but [a]if they cannot exercise self-control, let
them marry. For it is better to marry than to burn
*with passion.*
**10** Now to the married I command, *yet* not I but
the [a]Lord: [b]A wife is not to depart from *her*
husband.
11 But even if she does depart, let her remain
unmarried or be reconciled to *her* husband. And a
husband is not to divorce *his* wife.
12 But to the rest I, not the Lord, say: If any
brother has a wife who does not believe, and she is
willing to live with him, let him not divorce her.
13 And a woman who has a husband who does
not believe, if he is willing to live with her, let her
not divorce him.
14 For the unbelieving husband is sanctified by
the wife, and the unbelieving wife is sanctified by
the husband; otherwise [a]your children would be
unclean, but now they are holy.
15 But if the unbeliever departs, let him depart; a
brother or a sister is not under bondage in such
*cases.* But God has called us [a]to peace.
16 For how do you know, O wife, whether you
will [a]save *your* husband? Or how do you know, O
husband, whether you will save *your* wife?
**17** But as God has distributed to each one, as the
Lord has called each one, so let him walk. And [a]so
I [1]ordain in all the churches.
18 Was anyone called while circumcised? Let him
not become uncircumcised. Was anyone called
while uncircumcised? [a]Let him not be circumcised.
19 [a]Circumcision is nothing and uncircumcision
is nothing, but [b]keeping the commandments of
God *is what matters.*
20 Let each one remain in the same calling in
which he was called.
21 Were you called *while* a slave? Do not be
concerned about it; but if you can be made free,
rather use *it.*
22 For he who is called in the Lord *while* a slave
is [a]the Lord's freedman. Likewise he who is called
*while* free is [b]Christ's slave.
23 [a]You were bought at a price; do not become
slaves of men.

24 Brethren, let each one remain with [a]God in
that *state* in which he was called.
**25** Now concerning virgins: [a]I have no commandment from the Lord; yet I give judgment as one
[b]whom the Lord in His mercy *has made* [c]trustwor-
thy.
26 I suppose therefore that this is good because
of the present distress—[a]that *it is* good for a man
to remain as he is:
27 Are you bound to a wife? Do not seek to be
loosed. Are you loosed from a wife? Do not seek a
wife.
28 But even if you do marry, you have not
sinned; and if a virgin marries, she has not sinned.
Nevertheless such will have trouble in the flesh,
but I would spare you.
29 But [a]this I say, brethren, the time *is* short, so
that from now on even those who have wives
should be as though they had none,
30 those who weep as though they did not weep,
those who rejoice as though they did not rejoice,
those who buy as though they did not possess,
31 and those who use this world as not [a]misusing
*it.* For [b]the form of this world is passing away.
32 But I want you to be without [1]care. [a]He who is
unmarried [2]cares for the things of the Lord—how
he may please the Lord.
33 But he who is married cares about the things
of the world—how he may please *his* wife.
34 There [1]is a difference between a wife and a
virgin. The unmarried woman [a]cares about the
things of the Lord, that she may be holy both in
body and in spirit. But she who is married cares
about the things of the world—how she may
please *her* husband.
35 And this I say for your own profit, not that I
may put a leash on you, but for what is proper,
and that you may serve the Lord without distrac-
tion.
36 But if any man thinks he is behaving improp-
erly toward his [1]virgin, if she is past the flower of
youth, and thus it must be, let him do what he
wishes. He does not sin; let them marry.
37 Nevertheless he who stands steadfast in his
heart, having no necessity, but has power over his
own will, and has so determined in his heart that
he will keep his [1]virgin, does well.
38 [a]So then he who gives [1]*her* in marriage does
well, but he who does not give *her* in marriage
does better.
39 [a]A wife is bound by law as long as her husband
lives; but if her husband dies, she is at liberty to be
married to whom she wishes, [b]only in the Lord.
40 But she is happier if she remains as she is,
[a]according to my judgment—and [b]I think I also
have the Spirit of God.

### *Be Sensitive to Conscience*

**8** Now [a]concerning things offered to idols: We
know that we all have [b]knowledge. [c]Knowl-
edge [1]puffs up, but love [2]edifies.
2 And [a]if anyone thinks that he knows anything, he knows nothing yet as he ought to know.
3 But if anyone loves God, this one is known by
Him.
4 Therefore concerning the eating of things
offered to idols, we know that [a]an idol *is* nothing
in the world, [b]and that *there is* no other God but
one.
5 For even if there are [a]so-called gods, whether
in heaven or on earth (as there are many gods and
many lords),
6 yet [a]for us *there is* one God, the Father, [b]of
whom *are* all things, and we for Him; and [c]one
Lord Jesus Christ, [d]through whom *are* all things,
and [e]through whom we *live.*
7 However, *there is* not in everyone that knowledge; for some, [a]with consciousness of the idol,
until now eat *it* as a thing offered to an idol; and
their conscience, being weak, is [b]defiled.
8 But [a]food does not commend us to God; for
neither if we eat are we the better, nor if we do
not eat are we the worse.
9 But [a]beware lest somehow this liberty of yours
become [b]a [1]stumbling block to those who are
weak.
10 For if anyone sees you who have knowledge
eating in an idol's temple, will not [a]the conscience
of him who is weak be emboldened to eat those
things offered to idols?
11 And [a]because of your knowledge shall the
weak brother perish, for whom Christ died?
12 But [a]when you thus sin against the brethren,
and wound their weak conscience, you sin against
Christ.
13 Therefore, [a]if food makes my brother stumble,
I will never again eat meat, lest I make my
brother stumble.

### *Serving All Men*

**9** Am [a]I not an apostle? Am I not free? [b]Have I
not seen Jesus Christ our Lord? [c]Are you not
my work in the Lord?
2 If I am not an apostle to others, yet doubtless
I am to you. For you are [a]the [1]seal of my apostleship in the Lord.
3 My defense to those who examine me is this:
4 [a]Do we have no [1]right to eat and drink?
5 Do we have no right to take along [1]a believing
wife, as *do* also the other apostles, [a]the brothers of
the Lord, and [b]Cephas?
6 Or *is it* only Barnabas and I [a]*who* have no
right to refrain from working?
7 Who ever [a]goes to war at his own expense?
Who [b]plants a vineyard and does not eat of its
fruit? Or who [c]tends a flock and does not drink of
the milk of the flock?
8 Do I say these things as a *mere* man? Or does
not the law say the same also?
9 For it is written in the law of Moses, [a]*"You
shall not muzzle an ox while it treads out the
grain."* Is it oxen God is concerned about?
10 Or does He say *it* altogether for our sakes? For
our sakes, no doubt, *this* is written, that [a]he who
plows should plow in hope, and he who threshes
in hope should be partaker of his hope.
11 [a]If we have sown spiritual things for you, *is it*
a great thing if we reap your material things?
12 If others are partakers of *this* right over you,
*are* we not even more? [a]Nevertheless we have not
used this right, but endure all things [b]lest we
hinder the gospel of Christ.
13 [a]Do you not know that those who minister the
holy things eat *of the things* of the [b]temple, and
those who serve at the altar partake of *the offerings of* the altar?
14 Even so [a]the Lord has commanded [b]that those
who preach the gospel should live from the gospel.

**24** [a][Col. 3:22–24]
**25** [a]2 Cor. 8:8 [b]1 Tim. 1:13, 16 [c]1 Tim. 1:12
**26** [a]1 Cor. 7:1, 8
**29** [a]1 Pet. 4:7
**31** [a]1 Cor. 9:18 [b][1 John 2:17]
**32** [a]1 Tim. 5:5 [1]*concern* [2]*is concerned about*
**34** [a]Luke 10:40 [1]NU *is also*
**36** [1]Or *virgin daughter*
**37** [1]Or *virgin daughter*
**38** [a]Heb. 13:4 [1]NU *his own virgin*
**39** [a]Rom. 7:2 [b]2 Cor. 6:14
**40** [a]1 Cor. 7:6, 25 [b]1 Thess. 4:8

CHAPTER 8
**1** [a]Acts 15:20 [b]Rom. 14:14 [c]Rom. 14:3 [1]*makes arrogant* [2]*builds up*
**2** [a][1 Cor. 13:8–12]
**4** [a]Is. 41:24 [b]Deut. 4:35, 39; 6:4
**5** [a][John 10:34]
**6** [a]Mal. 2:10 [b]Acts 17:28 [c]John 13:13 [d]John 1:3 [e]Rom. 5:11
**7** [a][1 Cor. 10:28] [b]Rom. 14:14, 22
**8** [a][Rom. 14:17]
**9** [a]Gal. 5:13 [b]Rom. 12:13, 21 [1]*cause of offense*
**10** [a]1 Cor. 10:28
**11** [a]Rom. 14:15, 20
**12** [a]Matt. 25:40
**13** [a]Rom. 14:21

CHAPTER 9
**1** [a]Acts 9:15 [b]1 Cor. 15:8 [c]1 Cor. 3:6; 4:15
**2** [a]2 Cor. 12:12 [1]*certification*
**4** [a][1 Thess. 2:6, 9] [1]*authority*
**5** [a]Matt. 13:55 [b]Matt. 8:14 [1]Lit. *a sister, a wife*
**6** [a]Acts 4:36
**7** [a]2 Cor. 10:4 [b]Deut. 20:6 [c]John 21:15
**9** [a]Deut. 25:4
**10** [a]2 Tim. 2:6
**11** [a]Rom. 15:27
**12** [a][Acts 18:3; 20:33] [b]2 Cor. 11:12
**13** [a]Lev. 6:16, 26; 7:6, 31 [b]Num. 18:8–31
**14** [a]Matt. 10:10 [b]Rom. 10:15

15 But [a]I have used none of these things, nor
have I written these things that it should be done
so to me; for [b]it *would be* better for me to die than
that anyone should make my boasting void.
16 For if I preach the gospel, I have nothing to
boast of, for [a]necessity is laid upon me; yes, woe is
me if I do not preach the gospel!
17 For if I do this willingly, [a]I have a reward; but
if against my will, [b]I have been entrusted with a
stewardship.
18 What is my reward then? That [a]when I preach
the gospel, I may present the gospel [1]of Christ
without charge, that I [b]may not abuse my authority in the gospel.
**19** For though I am [a]free from all *men,* [b]I have
made myself a servant to all, [c]that I might win the
more;
20 and [a]to the Jews I became as a Jew, that I
might win Jews; to those *who are* under the law,
as under the [1]law, that I might win those *who are*
under the law;
21 [a]to [b]those *who are* without law, as without law
[c](not being without [1]law toward God, but under
[2]law toward Christ), that I might win those *who
are* without law;
22 [a]to the weak I became [1]as weak, that I might
win the weak. [b]I have become all things to all
*men,* [c]that I might by all means save some.
23 Now this I do for the gospel's sake, that I may
be partaker of it with *you.*
**24** Do you not know that those who run in a race
all run, but one receives the prize? [a]Run in such a
way that you may [1]obtain *it.*
25 And everyone who competes *for the prize* [1]is
temperate in all things. Now they *do it* to obtain a
perishable crown, but we *for* [a]an imperishable
*crown.*
26 Therefore I run thus: [a]not with uncertainty.
Thus I fight: not as *one who* beats the air.
27 [a]But I discipline my body and [b]bring *it* into
subjection, lest, when I have preached to others, I
myself should become [c]disqualified.

### *Do All to God's Glory*

**10** Moreover, brethren, I do not want you to be
unaware that all our fathers were under
[a]the cloud, all passed through [b]the sea,
2 all were baptized into Moses in the cloud and
in the sea,
3 all ate the same [a]spiritual food,
4 and all drank the same [a]spiritual drink. For
they drank of that spiritual Rock that followed
them, and that Rock was Christ.
5 But with most of them God was not well
pleased, for *their bodies* [a]were scattered in the
wilderness.
6 Now these things became our examples, to the
intent that we should not lust after evil things as
[a]they also lusted.
7 [a]And do not become idolaters as *were* some of
them. As it is written, [b]*"The people sat down to
eat and drink, and rose up to play."*
8 [a]Nor let us commit sexual immorality, as
[b]some of them did, and [c]in one day twenty-three
thousand fell;
9 nor let us [1]tempt Christ, as [a]some of them also
tempted, and [b]were destroyed by serpents;
10 nor complain, as [a]some of them also complained, and [b]were destroyed by [c]the destroyer.
11 Now [1]all these things happened to them as
examples, and [a]they were written for our [2]admonition, [b]upon whom the ends of the ages have come.
12 Therefore [a]let him who thinks he stands take
heed lest he fall.
13 No temptation has overtaken you except such
as is common to man; but [a]God *is* faithful, [b]who
will not allow you to be tempted beyond what you
are able, but with the temptation will also make
the way of escape, that you may be able to
[1]bear *it.*
**14** Therefore, my beloved, [a]flee from idolatry.
15 I speak as to [a]wise men; judge for yourselves
what I say.
16 [a]The cup of blessing which we bless, is it not
the [1]communion of the blood of Christ? [b]The
bread which we break, is it not the communion of
the body of Christ?
17 For [a]we, *though* many, are one bread *and* one
body; for we all partake of that one bread.
18 Observe [a]Israel [b]after the flesh: [c]Are not those
who eat of the sacrifices [1]partakers of the altar?
19 What am I saying then? [a]That an idol is anything, or what is offered to idols is anything?
20 Rather that the things which the Gentiles
[a]sacrifice [b]they sacrifice to demons and not to
God, and I do not want you to have fellowship
with demons.
21 [a]You cannot drink the cup of the Lord and
[b]the cup of demons; you cannot partake of the
[c]Lord's table and of the table of demons.
22 Or do we [a]provoke the Lord to jealousy? [b]Are
we stronger than He?
**23** All things are lawful [1]for me, but not all things
are [a]helpful; all things are lawful [1]for me, but not
all things [2]edify.
24 Let no one seek his own, but each one [a]the
other's *well-being.*
25 [a]Eat whatever is sold in the meat market,
asking no questions for conscience' sake;
26 for [a]*"the earth is the* LORD'*s, and all its fullness."*
27 If any of those who do not believe invites you
*to dinner,* and you desire to go, [a]eat whatever is
set before you, asking no question for conscience'
sake.
28 But if anyone says to you, "This was offered to
idols," do not eat it [a]for the sake of the one who
told you, and for conscience' sake; [1]for [b]*"the earth
is the* LORD'*s, and all its fullness."*
29 "Conscience," I say, not your own, but that of
the other. For [a]why is my liberty judged by another *man's* conscience?
30 But if I partake with thanks, why am I evil
spoken of for *the food* [a]over which I give thanks?
31 [a]Therefore, whether you eat or drink, or whatever you do, do all to the glory of God.
32 [a]Give no offense, either to the Jews or to the
Greeks or to the church of God,
33 just [a]as I also please all *men* in all *things,* not
seeking my own profit, but the *profit* of many,
that they may be saved.

**15** [a]Acts 18:3; 20:33 [b]2 Cor. 11:10
**16** [a][Rom. 1:14]
**17** [a]1 Cor. 3:8, 14; 9:18 [b]Gal. 2:7
**18** [a]1 Cor. 10:33 [b]1 Cor. 7:31; 9:12 [1]NU omits *of Christ*
**19** [a]1 Cor. 9:1 [b]Gal. 5:13 [c]Matt. 18:15
**20** [a]Acts 16:3; 21:23–26 [1]NU adds *though not being myself under the law*
**21** [a][Gal. 2:3; 3:2] [b][Rom. 2:12, 14] [c][1 Cor. 7:22] [1]NU *God's law* [2]NU *Christ's law*
**22** [a]Rom. 14:1; 15:1 [b]1 Cor. 10:33 [c]Rom. 11:14 [1]NU omits *as*
**24** [a]Gal. 2:2 [1]*win*
**25** [a]James 1:12 [1]*exercises self-control*
**26** [a]2 Tim. 2:5
**27** [a][Rom. 8:13] [b][Rom. 6:18] [c]Jer. 6:30

CHAPTER 10
**1** [a]Ex. 13:21, 22 [b]Ex. 14:21, 22, 29
**3** [a]Ex. 16:4, 15, 35
**4** [a]Ex. 17:5–7
**5** [a]Num. 14:29, 37; 26:65
**6** [a]Num. 11:4, 34
**7** [a]1 Cor. 5:11; 10:14 [b]Ex. 32:6
**8** [a]Rev. 2:14 [b]Num. 25:1–9 [c]Ps. 106:29
**9** [a]Ex. 17:2, 7 [b]Num. 21:6–9 [1]*test*
**10** [a]Ex. 16:2 [b]Num. 14:37 [c]Ex. 12:23
**11** [a]Rom. 15:4 [b]Phil. 4:5 [1]NU omits *all* [2]*instruction*
**12** [a]Rom. 11:20
**13** [a]1 Cor. 1:9 [b]Ps. 125:3 [1]*endure*
**14** [a]2 Cor. 6:17
**15** [a]1 Cor. 8:1
**16** [a]Matt. 26:26–28 [b]Acts 2:42 [1]*fellowship* or *sharing*
**17** [a]1 Cor. 12:12, 27
**18** [a]Rom. 4:12 [b]Rom. 4:1 [c]Lev. 3:3; 7:6, 14 [1]*fellowshippers* or *sharers*
**19** [a]1 Cor. 8:4
**20** [a]Lev. 17:7 [b]Deut. 32:17
**21** [a]2 Cor. 6:15, 16 [b]Deut. 32:38 [c][1 Cor. 11:23–29]
**22** [a]Deut. 32:21 [b]Ezek. 22:14
**23** [a]1 Cor. 6:12 [1]NU omits *for me* [2]*build up*

**24** [a]Phil. 2:4
**25** [a][1 Tim. 4:4]
**26** [a]Ps. 24:1
**27** [a]Luke 10:7, 8
**28** [a][1 Cor. 8:7, 10, 12] [b]Deut. 10:14 [1]NU omits the rest of v. 28.
**29** [a]Rom. 14:16
**30** [a]Rom. 14:6
**31** [a]Col. 3:17
**32** [a]Rom. 14:13
**33** [a]Rom. 15:2

### *Worship and the Lord's Supper*

**11** Imitate[a] me, just as I also *imitate* Christ.
2 Now I praise you, brethren, that you
remember me in all things and keep the traditions
just as I delivered *them* to you.
3 But I want you to know that [a]the head of
every man is Christ, [b]the head of woman *is* man,
and [c]the head of Christ *is* God.
4 Every man praying or [a]prophesying, having
*his* head covered, dishonors his head.
5 But every woman who prays or prophesies
with *her* head uncovered dishonors her head, for
that is one and the same as if her head were
[a]shaved.
6 For if a woman is not covered, let her also be
shorn. But if it is [a]shameful for a woman to be
shorn or shaved, let her be covered.
7 For a man indeed ought not to cover *his* head,
since [a]he is the image and glory of God; but
woman is the glory of man.
8 For man is not from woman, but woman [a]from
man.
9 Nor was man created for the woman, but
woman [a]for the man.
10 For this reason the woman ought to have *a*
*symbol of* authority on *her* head, because of the
angels.
11 Nevertheless, [a]neither *is* man independent of
woman, nor woman independent of man, in the
Lord.
12 For as woman *came* from man, even so man
also *comes* through woman; but all things are
from God.
13 Judge among yourselves. Is it proper for a
woman to pray to God with her head uncovered?
14 Does not even nature itself teach you that if a
man has long hair, it is a dishonor to him?
15 But if a woman has long hair, it is a glory to
her; for *her* hair is given [1]to her for a covering.
16 But [a]if anyone seems to be contentious, we
have no such custom, [b]nor *do* the churches of
God.
**17** Now in giving these instructions I do not
praise *you,* since you come together not for the
better but for the worse.
18 For first of all, when you come together as a
church, [a]I hear that there are divisions among
you, and in part I believe it.
19 For [a]there must also be factions among you,
[b]that those who are approved may be [1]recognized
among you.
20 Therefore when you come together in one
place, it is not to eat the Lord's Supper.
21 For in eating, each one takes his own supper
ahead of *others;* and one is hungry and [a]another is
drunk.
22 What! Do you not have houses to eat and
drink in? Or do you despise [a]the church of God
and [b]shame [1]those who have nothing? What shall
I say to you? Shall I praise you in this? I do not
praise *you.*
**23** For [a]I received from the Lord that which I also
delivered to you: [b]that the Lord Jesus on the *same*
night in which He was betrayed took bread;
24 and when He had given thanks, He broke *it*
and said, [1]"Take, eat; this is My body which is
[2]broken for you; do this in remembrance of Me."
25 In the same manner *He* also *took* the cup after
supper, saying, "This cup is the new covenant in
My blood. This do, as often as you drink *it,* in
remembrance of Me."
26 For as often as you eat this bread and drink
this cup, you proclaim the Lord's death [a]till He
comes.
**27** Therefore whoever eats [a]this bread or drinks
*this* cup of the Lord in an unworthy manner will
be guilty of the body and [1]blood of the Lord.
28 But [a]let a man examine himself, and so let him
eat of the bread and drink of the cup.
29 For he who eats and drinks [1]in an unworthy
manner eats and drinks judgment to himself, not
discerning the [2]Lord's body.
30 For this reason many *are* weak and sick
among you, and many [1]sleep.
31 For [a]if we would judge ourselves, we would
not be judged.
32 But when we are judged, [a]we are chastened by
the Lord, that we may not be condemned with the
world.
33 Therefore, my brethren, when you [a]come together to eat, wait for one another.
34 But if anyone is hungry, let him eat at home,
lest you come together for judgment. And the rest
I will set in order when I come.

### *Spiritual Unity of Believers*

**12** Now [a]concerning spiritual *gifts,* brethren, I
do not want you to be ignorant:
2 You know [a]that[1] you were Gentiles, carried
away to these [b]dumb[2] idols, however you were led.
3 Therefore I make known to you that no one
speaking by the Spirit of God calls Jesus [1]ac-
cursed, and [a]no one can say that Jesus is Lord
except by the Holy Spirit.
4 [a]There are [1]diversities of gifts, but [b]the same
Spirit.
5 [a]There are differences of ministries, but the
same Lord.
6 And there are diversities of activities, but it is
the same God [a]who works [1]all in all.
7 But the manifestation of the Spirit is given to
each one for the profit *of all:*
8 for to one is given [a]the word of wisdom
through the Spirit, to another [b]the word of knowledge through the same Spirit,
9 [a]to another faith by the same Spirit, to another
[b]gifts of healings by [1]the same Spirit,
10 [a]to another the working of miracles, to another [b]prophecy, to another [c]discerning of spirits,
to another [d]*different* kinds of tongues, to another
the interpretation of tongues.
11 But one and the same Spirit works all these
things, [a]distributing to each one individually [b]as
He wills.
**12** For [a]as the body is one and has many members, but all the members of that one body, being
many, are one body, [b]so also *is* Christ.
13 For [a]by one Spirit we were all baptized into
one body—[b]whether Jews or Greeks, whether
slaves or free—and [c]have all been made to drink
[1]into one Spirit.
14 For in fact the body is not one member but
many.
15 If the foot should say, "Because I am not a
hand, I am not of the body," is it therefore not of
the body?
16 And if the ear should say, "Because I am not
an eye, I am not of the body," is it therefore not of
the body?
17 If the whole body *were* an eye, where *would*
*be* the hearing? If the whole *were* hearing, where
*would be* the smelling?

CHAPTER 11
**1** [a]Eph. 5:1
**3** [a]Eph. 1:22; 4:15; 5:23 [b]Gen. 3:16 [c]John 14:28
**4** [a]1 Cor. 12:10
**5** [a]Deut. 21:12
**6** [a]Num. 5:18
**7** [a]Gen. 1:26, 27; 5:1; 9:6
**8** [a]Gen. 2:21–23
**9** [a]Gen. 2:18
**11** [a][Gal. 3:28]
**15** [1]M omits *to her*
**16** [a]1 Tim. 6:4 [b]1 Cor. 7:17
**18** [a]1 Cor. 1:10–12; 3:3
**19** [a]1 Tim. 4:1 [b][Deut. 13:3] [1]Lit. *manifest, evident*
**21** [a]Jude 12
**22** [a]1 Cor. 10:32 [b]James 2:6 [1]The poor
**23** [a]1 Cor. 15:3 [b]Matt. 26:26–28
**24** [1]NU omits *Take, eat* [2]NU omits *broken*
**26** [a]John 14:3
**27** [a][John 6:51] [1]NU, M *the blood*
**28** [a]2 Cor. 13:5
**29** [1]NU omits *in an unworthy manner* [2]NU omits *Lord's*
**30** [1]Are dead
**31** [a][1 John 1:9]
**32** [a]Ps. 94:12
**33** [a]1 Cor. 14:26

CHAPTER 12
**1** [a]1 Cor. 12:4; 14:1, 37
**2** [a]Eph. 2:11 [b]Ps. 115:5 [1]NU, M *that when* [2]*mute, silent*
**3** [a]Matt. 16:17 [1]Gr. *anathema*
**4** [a]Rom. 12:3–8 [b]Eph. 4:4 [1]*allotments* or *various kinds*
**5** [a]Rom. 12:6
**6** [a]1 Cor. 15:28 [1]*all things in*
**8** [a]1 Cor. 2:6, 7 [b]Rom. 15:14
**9** [a]2 Cor. 4:13 [b]Mark 3:15; 16:18 [1]NU *one*
**10** [a]Mark 16:17 [b]Rom. 12:6 [c]1 John 4:1 [d]Acts 2:4–11
**11** [a]Rom. 12:6 [b][John 3:8]
**12** [a]Rom. 12:4, 5 [b][Gal. 3:16]
**13** [a][Rom. 6:5] [b]Col. 3:11 [c][John 7:37–39] [1]NU omits *into*

18 But now [a]God has set the members, each one of them, in the body [b]just as He pleased.

19 And if they *were* all one member, where *would* the body *be?*

20 But now indeed *there are* many members, yet one body.

21 And the eye cannot say to the hand, "I have no need of you"; nor again the head to the feet, "I have no need of you."

22 No, much rather, those members of the body which seem to be weaker are necessary.

23 And those *members* of the body which we think to be less honorable, on these we bestow greater honor; and our unpresentable *parts* have greater modesty,

24 but our presentable *parts* have no need. But God composed the body, having given greater honor to that *part* which lacks it,

25 that there should be no [1]schism in the body, but *that* the members should have the same care for one another.

26 And if one member suffers, all the members suffer with *it;* or if one member is honored, all the members rejoice with *it.*

27 Now [a]you are the body of Christ, and [b]members individually.

28 And [a]God has appointed these in the church: first [b]apostles, second [c]prophets, third teachers, after that [d]miracles, then [e]gifts of healings, [f]helps, [g]administrations, varieties of tongues.

29 *Are* all apostles? *Are* all prophets? *Are* all teachers? *Are* all workers of miracles?

30 Do all have gifts of healings? Do all speak with tongues? Do all interpret?

31 But [a]earnestly desire the [1]best gifts. And yet I show you a more excellent way.

## *The Greatest Spiritual Gift*

**13** Though I speak with the tongues of men and of angels, but have not love, I have become sounding brass or a clanging cymbal.

2 And though I have *the gift of* [a]prophecy, and understand all mysteries and all knowledge, and though I have all faith, [b]so that I could remove mountains, but have not love, I am nothing.

3 And [a]though I bestow all my goods to feed *the poor,* and though I give my body [1]to be burned, but have not love, it profits me nothing.

4 [a]Love suffers long *and* is [b]kind; love [c]does not envy; love does not parade itself, is not [1]puffed up;

5 does not behave rudely, [a]does not seek its own, is not provoked, [1]thinks no evil;

6 [a]does not rejoice in iniquity, but [b]rejoices in the truth;

7 [a]bears all things, believes all things, hopes all things, endures all things.

8 Love never fails. But whether *there are* prophecies, they will fail; whether *there are* tongues, they will cease; whether *there is* knowledge, it will vanish away.

9 [a]For we know in part and we prophesy in part.

10 But when that which is [1]perfect has come, then that which is in part will be done away.

11 When I was a child, I spoke as a child, I understood as a child, I thought as a child; but when I became a man, I put away childish things.

12 For [a]now we see in a mirror, dimly, but then [b]face to face. Now I know in part, but then I shall know just as I also am known.

13 And now abide faith, hope, love, these three; but the greatest of these *is* love.

## *Principles Concerning Spiritual Gifts*

**14** Pursue love, and [a]desire spiritual *gifts,* [b]but especially that you may prophesy.

2 For he who [a]speaks in a tongue does not speak to men but to God, for no one understands *him;* however, in the spirit he speaks mysteries.

3 But he who prophesies speaks [a]edification and [b]exhortation and comfort to men.

4 He who speaks in a tongue edifies himself, but he who prophesies edifies the church.

5 I wish you all spoke with tongues, but even more that you prophesied; [1]for he who prophesies *is* greater than he who speaks with tongues, unless indeed he interprets, that the church may receive edification.

**6** But now, brethren, if I come to you speaking with tongues, what shall I profit you unless I speak to you either by [a]revelation, by knowledge, by prophesying, or by teaching?

7 Even things without life, whether flute or harp, when they make a sound, unless they make a distinction in the sounds, how will it be known what is piped or played?

8 For if the trumpet makes an uncertain sound, who will prepare for battle?

9 So likewise you, unless you utter by the tongue words easy to understand, how will it be known what is spoken? For you will be speaking into the air.

10 There are, it may be, so many kinds of languages in the world, and none of them *is* without [1]significance.

11 Therefore, if I do not know the meaning of the language, I shall be a [1]foreigner to him who speaks, and he who speaks *will be* a foreigner to me.

12 Even so you, since you are [1]zealous for spiritual *gifts, let it be* for the [2]edification of the church *that* you seek to excel.

13 Therefore let him who speaks in a tongue pray that he may [a]interpret.

14 For if I pray in a tongue, my spirit prays, but my understanding is unfruitful.

15 What is *the conclusion* then? I will pray with the spirit, and I will also pray with the understanding. [a]I will sing with the spirit, and I will also sing [b]with the understanding.

16 Otherwise, if you bless with the spirit, how will he who occupies the place of the uninformed say "Amen" [a]at your giving of thanks, since he does not understand what you say?

17 For you indeed give thanks well, but the other is not edified.

18 I thank my God I speak with tongues more than you all;

19 yet in the church I would rather speak five words with my understanding, that I may teach others also, than ten thousand words in a tongue.

**20** Brethren, [a]do not be children in understanding; however, in malice [b]be babes, but in understanding be mature.

21 [a]In the law it is written:

[b]*"With men of other tongues and other lips*
*I will speak to this people;*
*And yet, for all that, they will not hear Me,"*

says the Lord.

22 Therefore tongues are for a [a]sign, not to those who believe but to unbelievers; but prophesying is not for unbelievers but for those who believe.

---

**18** [a]1 Cor. 12:28 [b]Rom. 12:3
**25** [1]*division*
**27** [a]Rom. 12:5 [b]Eph. 5:30
**28** [a]Eph. 4:11 [b][Eph. 2:20; 3:5] [c]Acts 13:1 [d]1 Cor. 12:10, 29 [e]1 Cor. 12:9, 30 [f]Num. 11:17 [g]Rom. 12:8
**31** [a]1 Cor. 14:1, 39 [1]NU *greater*

CHAPTER 13
**2** [a]1 Cor. 12:8–10, 28; 14:1 [b]Matt. 17:20; 21:21
**3** [a]Matt. 6:1, 2 [1]NU *so I may boast*
**4** [a]Prov. 10:12; 17:9 [b]Eph. 4:32 [c]Gal. 5:26 [1]*arrogant*
**5** [a]1 Cor. 10:24 [1]*keeps no accounts of evil*
**6** [a]Rom. 1:32 [b]2 John 4
**7** [a]Gal. 6:2
**9** [a]1 Cor. 8:2; 13:12
**10** [1]*complete*
**12** [a]Phil. 3:12 [b][1 John 3:2]

CHAPTER 14
**1** [a]1 Cor. 12:31; 14:39 [b]Num. 11:25, 29
**2** [a]Acts 2:4; 10:46
**3** [a]Rom. 14:19; 15:2 [b]1 Tim. 4:13
**5** [1]NU *and*
**6** [a]1 Cor. 14:26
**10** [1]*meaning*
**11** [1]Lit. *barbarian*
**12** [1]*eager* [2]*building up*
**13** [a]1 Cor. 12:10
**15** [a]Col. 3:16 [b]Ps. 47:7
**16** [a]1 Cor. 11:24
**20** [a]Ps. 131:2 [b][1 Pet. 2:2]
**21** [a]John 10:34 [b]Is. 28:11, 12
**22** [a]Mark 16:17

23 Therefore if the whole church comes together
in one place, and all speak with tongues, and there
come in *those who are* uninformed or unbelievers,
[a]will they not say that you are [1]out of your mind?
24 But if all prophesy, and an unbeliever or an
uninformed person comes in, he is convinced by
all, he is convicted by all.
25 [1]And thus the secrets of his heart are revealed;
and so, falling down on *his* face, he will worship
God and report [a]that God is truly among you.
**26** How is it then, brethren? Whenever you come
together, each of you has a psalm, [a]has a teaching,
has a tongue, has a revelation, has an interpretation. [b]Let all things be done for [1]edification.
27 If anyone speaks in a tongue, *let there be* two
or at the most three, *each* in turn, and let one
interpret.
28 But if there is no interpreter, let him keep
silent in church, and let him speak to himself and
to God.
29 Let two or three prophets speak, and [a]let the
others judge.
30 But if *anything* is revealed to another who sits
by, [a]let the first keep silent.
31 For you can all prophesy one by one, that all
may learn and all may be encouraged.
32 And [a]the spirits of the prophets are subject to
the prophets.
33 For God is not *the author* of [1]confusion but of
peace, [a]as in all the churches of the saints.
34 [a]Let [1]your women keep silent in the churches,
for they are not permitted to speak; but *they are*
to be submissive, as the [b]law also says.
35 And if they want to learn something, let them
ask their own husbands at home; for it is shameful
for women to speak in church.
36 Or did the word of God come *originally* from
you? Or *was it* you only that it reached?
37 [a]If anyone thinks himself to be a prophet or
spiritual, let him acknowledge that the things
which I write to you are the commandments of
the Lord.
38 But [1]if anyone is ignorant, let him be ignorant.
39 Therefore, brethren, [a]desire earnestly to
prophesy, and do not forbid to speak with
tongues.
40 [a]Let all things be done decently and in order.

### *Christ's Resurrection and Our Resurrection*

**15** Moreover, brethren, I declare to you the
gospel [a]which I preached to you, which also
you received and [b]in which you stand,
2 [a]by which also you are saved, if you hold fast
that word which I preached to you—unless [b]you
believed in vain.
3 For [a]I delivered to you first of all that [b]which I
also received: that Christ died for our sins [c]accord-
ing to the Scriptures,
4 and that He was buried, and that He rose
again the third day [a]according to the Scriptures,
5 [a]and that He was seen by [1]Cephas, then [b]by
the twelve.
6 After that He was seen by over five hundred
brethren at once, of whom the greater part remain
to the present, but some have [1]fallen asleep.
7 After that He was seen by James, then [a]by all
the apostles.
8 [a]Then last of all He was seen by me also, as by
one born out of due time.
9 For I am [a]the least of the apostles, who am not
worthy to be called an apostle, because [b]I persecuted the church of God.
10 But [a]by the grace of God I am what I am, and
His grace toward me was not in vain; but I labored
more abundantly than they all, [b]yet not I, but the
grace of God *which was* with me.
11 Therefore, whether *it was* I or they, so we
preach and so you believed.
**12** Now if Christ is preached that He has been
raised from the dead, how do some among you say
that there is no resurrection of the dead?
13 But if there is no resurrection of the dead,
[a]then Christ is not risen.
14 And if Christ is not risen, then our preaching
*is* empty and your faith *is* also empty.
15 Yes, and we are found false witnesses of God,
because [a]we have testified of God that He raised
up Christ, whom He did not raise up—if in fact the
dead do not rise.
16 For if *the* dead do not rise, then Christ is not
risen.
17 And if Christ is not risen, your faith *is* futile;
[a]you are still in your sins!
18 Then also those who have [1]fallen [a]asleep in
Christ have perished.
19 [a]If in this life only we have hope in Christ, we
are of all men the most pitiable.
**20** But now [a]Christ is risen from the dead, *and*
has become [b]the firstfruits of those who have
[1]fallen asleep.
21 For [a]since by man *came* death, [b]by Man also
*came* the resurrection of the dead.
22 For as in Adam all die, even so in Christ all
shall [a]be made alive.
23 But [a]each one in his own order: Christ the
firstfruits, afterward those *who are* Christ's at His
coming.
24 Then *comes* the end, when He delivers [a]the
kingdom to God the Father, when He puts an end
to all rule and all authority and power.
25 For He must reign [a]till He has put all enemies
under His feet.
26 [a]The last enemy *that* will be destroyed *is*
death.
27 For [a]*"He has put all things under His feet."*
But when He says "all things are put under *Him*,"
*it is* evident that He who put all things under Him
is excepted.
28 [a]Now when all things are made subject to
Him, then [b]the Son Himself will also be subject to
Him who put all things under Him, that God may
be all in all.
**29** Otherwise, what will they do who are baptized
for the dead, if the dead do not rise at all? Why
then are they baptized for the dead?
30 And [a]why do we stand in [1]jeopardy every
hour?
31 I affirm, by [a]the boasting in you which I have
in Christ Jesus our Lord, [b]I die daily.
32 If, in the manner of men, [a]I have fought with
beasts at Ephesus, what advantage *is it* to me? If
*the* dead do not rise, [b]*"Let us eat and drink, for
tomorrow we die!"*
33 Do not be deceived: [a]"Evil company corrupts
good habits."
34 [a]Awake to righteousness, and do not sin; [b]for
some do not have the knowledge of God. [c]I speak
*this* to your shame.
**35** But someone will say, [a]"How are the dead
raised up? And with what body do they come?"

**23** [a]Acts 2:13 [1]*insane*
**25** [a]Is. 45:14 [1]NU omits *And thus*
**26** [a]1 Cor. 12:8–10; 14:6 [b][2 Cor. 12:19] [1]*build-ing up*
**29** [a]1 Cor. 12:10
**30** [a][1 Thess. 5:19, 20]
**32** [a]1 John 4:1
**33** [a]1 Cor. 11:16 [1]*disor-der*
**34** [a]1 Tim. 2:11 [b]Gen. 3:16 [1]NU omits *your*
**37** [a]2 Cor. 10:7
**38** [1]NU *if anyone does not recognize this, he is not recognized*
**39** [a]1 Cor. 12:31
**40** [a]1 Cor. 14:33

CHAPTER 15
**1** [a][Gal. 1:11] [b][Rom. 5:2; 11:20]
**2** [a]Rom. 1:16 [b]Gal. 3:4
**3** [a]1 Cor. 11:2, 23 [b][Gal. 1:12] [c]Ps. 22:15
**4** [a]Ps. 16:9–11; 68:18; 110:1
**5** [a]Luke 24:34 [b]Matt. 28:17 [1]Peter
**6** [1]Died
**7** [a]Acts 1:3, 4
**8** [a][Acts 9:3–8; 22:6–11; 26:12–18]
**9** [a]Eph. 3:8 [b]Acts 8:3
**10** [a]Eph. 3:7, 8 [b]Phil. 2:13
**13** [a][1 Thess. 4:14]
**15** [a]Acts 2:24
**17** [a][Rom. 4:25]
**18** [a]Job 14:12 [1]Died
**19** [a]2 Tim. 3:12
**20** [a]1 Pet. 1:3 [b]Acts 26:23 [1]Died
**21** [a]Rom. 5:12; 6:23 [b]John 11:25
**22** [a][John 5:28, 29]
**23** [a][1 Thess. 4:15–17]
**24** [a][Dan. 2:44; 7:14, 27]
**25** [a]Ps. 110:1
**26** [a][2 Tim. 1:10]
**27** [a]Ps. 8:6
**28** [a][Phil. 3:21] [b]1 Cor. 3:23; 11:3; 12:6
**30** [a]2 Cor. 11:26 [1]*danger*
**31** [a]1 Thess. 2:19 [b]Rom. 8:36
**32** [a]2 Cor. 1:8 [b]Is. 22:13; 56:12
**33** [a][1 Cor. 5:6]
**34** [a]Rom. 13:11 [b][1 Thess. 4:5] [c]1 Cor. 6:5
**35** [a]Ezek. 37:3

36 Foolish one, [a]what you sow is not made alive unless it dies.
37 And what you sow, you do not sow that body that shall be, but mere grain—perhaps wheat or some other *grain.*
38 But God gives it a body as He pleases, and to each seed its own body.
39 All flesh *is* not the same flesh, but *there is* one *kind* [1]of flesh of men, another flesh of animals, another of fish, *and* another of birds.
40 *There are* also [1]celestial bodies and [2]terrestrial bodies; but the glory of the celestial *is* one, and the *glory* of the terrestrial *is* another.
41 *There is* one glory of the sun, another glory of the moon, and another glory of the stars; for *one* star differs from *another* star in glory.
42 [a]So also *is* the resurrection of the dead. *The body* is sown in corruption, it is raised in incorruption.
43 [a]It is sown in dishonor, it is raised in glory. It is sown in weakness, it is raised in power.
44 It is sown a natural body, it is raised a spiritual body. There is a natural body, and there is a spiritual body.
45 And so it is written, [a]*"The first man Adam became a living being."* [b]The last Adam *became* [c]a life-giving spirit.
46 However, the spiritual is not first, but the natural, and afterward the spiritual.
47 [a]The first man *was* of the earth, [b]*made*[1] of dust; the second Man *is* [2]the Lord [c]from heaven.
48 As *was* the [1]*man* of dust, so also *are* those *who are* [1]*made* of dust; [a]and as *is* the heavenly *Man,* so also *are* those *who are* heavenly.
49 And [a]as we have borne the image of the *man* of dust, [b]we[1] shall also bear the image of the heavenly *Man.*
**50** Now this I say, brethren, that [a]flesh and blood cannot inherit the kingdom of God; nor does corruption inherit incorruption.
51 Behold, I tell you a [1]mystery: [a]We shall not all sleep, [b]but we shall all be changed—
52 in a moment, in the twinkling of an eye, at the last trumpet. [a]For the trumpet will sound, and the dead will be raised incorruptible, and we shall be changed.
53 For this corruptible must put on incorruption, and [a]this mortal *must* put on immortality.
54 So when this corruptible has put on incorruption, and this mortal has put on immortality, then shall be brought to pass the saying that is written: [a]*"Death is swallowed up in victory."*

55 *"O*[a1] *Death, where is your sting?*
*O Hades, where is your victory?"*

56 The sting of death *is* sin, and [a]the strength of sin *is* the law.
57 [a]But thanks *be* to God, who gives us [b]the victory through our Lord Jesus Christ.
58 [a]Therefore, my beloved brethren, be steadfast, immovable, always abounding in the work of the Lord, knowing [b]that your labor is not in vain in the Lord.

36 [a]John 12:24
39 [1]NU, M omit *of flesh*
40 [1]*heavenly* [2]*earthly*
42 [a][Dan. 12:3]
43 [a][Phil. 3:21]
45 [a]Gen. 2:7 [b][Rom. 5:14] [c]John 5:21; 6:57
47 [a]John 3:31 [b]Gen. 2:7; 3:19 [c]John 3:13 [1]*earthy* [2]NU omits *the Lord*
48 [a]Phil. 3:20 [1]*earthy*
49 [a]Gen. 5:3 [b]Rom. 8:29 [1]NU *let us also bear*
50 [a][John 3:3, 5]
51 [a][1 Thess. 4:15] [b][Phil. 3:21] [1]*hidden truth*
52 [a]Matt. 24:31
53 [a]2 Cor. 5:4
54 [a]Is. 25:8
55 [a]Hos. 13:14 [1]NU *O Death, where is your victory? O Death, where is your sting?*
56 [a][Rom. 3:20; 4:15; 7:8]
57 [a][Rom. 7:25] [b][1 John 5:4]
58 [a]2 Pet. 3:14 [b][1 Cor. 3:8]

CHAPTER 16
1 [a]Gal. 2:10
2 [a]Acts 20:7
3 [a]2 Cor. 3:1; 8:18
4 [a]2 Cor. 8:4, 19
5 [a]2 Cor. 1:15, 16
6 [a]Acts 15:3
7 [a]James 4:15
8 [a]Lev. 23:15–22
9 [a]Acts 14:27 [b]Acts 19:9
10 [a]Acts 19:22 [b]Phil. 2:20
11 [a]1 Tim. 4:12 [b]Acts 15:33
12 [a]1 Cor. 1:12; 3:5
13 [a]Matt. 24:42 [b]Phil. 1:27; 4:1 [c][Eph. 3:16; 6:10]
14 [a][1 Pet. 4:8]
15 [a]1 Cor. 1:16 [b]Rom. 16:5 [c]2 Cor. 8:4
16 [a]Heb. 13:17 [b][Heb. 6:10]
17 [a]2 Cor. 11:9
18 [a]Col. 4:8 [b]Phil. 2:29
19 [a]Rom. 16:5
20 [a]Rom. 16:16
21 [a]Col. 4:18

## *Final Instructions, Personal Plans, and Greetings*

**16** Now concerning [a]the collection for the saints, as I have given orders to the churches of Galatia, so you must do also:
2 [a]On the first *day* of the week let each one of you lay something aside, storing up as he may prosper, that there be no collections when I come.
3 And when I come, [a]whomever you approve by *your* letters I will send to bear your gift to Jerusalem.
4 [a]But if it is fitting that I go also, they will go with me.
**5** Now I will come to you [a]when I pass through Macedonia (for I am passing through Macedonia).
6 And it may be that I will remain, or even spend the winter with you, that you may [a]send me on my journey, wherever I go.
7 For I do not wish to see you now on the way; but I hope to stay a while with you, [a]if the Lord permits.
8 But I will tarry in Ephesus until [a]Pentecost.
9 For [a]a great and effective door has opened to me, and [b]*there are* many adversaries.
10 And [a]if Timothy comes, see that he may be with you without fear; for [b]he does the work of the Lord, as I also *do.*
11 [a]Therefore let no one despise him. But send him on his journey [b]in peace, that he may come to me; for I am waiting for him with the brethren.
12 Now concerning *our* brother [a]Apollos, I strongly urged him to come to you with the brethren, but he was quite unwilling to come at this time; however, he will come when he has a convenient time.
**13** [a]Watch, [b]stand fast in the faith, be brave, [c]be strong.
14 [a]Let all *that* you *do* be done with love.
15 I urge you, brethren—you know [a]the household of Stephanas, that it is [b]the firstfruits of Achaia, and *that* they have devoted themselves to [c]the ministry of the saints—
16 [a]that you also submit to such, and to everyone who works and [b]labors with *us.*
17 I am glad about the coming of Stephanas, Fortunatus, and Achaicus, [a]for what was lacking on your part they supplied.
18 [a]For they refreshed my spirit and yours. Therefore [b]acknowledge such men.
**19** The churches of Asia greet you. Aquila and Priscilla greet you heartily in the Lord, [a]with the church that is in their house.
20 All the brethren greet you. [a]Greet one another with a holy kiss.
21 [a]The salutation with my own hand—Paul's.
22 If anyone [a]does not love the Lord Jesus Christ, [b]let him be [1]accursed. [c]O[2] Lord, come!
23 [a]The grace of our Lord Jesus Christ *be* with you.
24 My love *be* with you all in Christ Jesus. Amen.

22 [a]Eph. 6:24 [b]Gal. 1:8, 9 [c]Jude 14, 15 [1]Gr. *anathema* [2]Aram. *Marana tha* or *Maranatha;* possibly *Maran atha, Our Lord has come*
23 [a]Rom. 16:20

*The Second Epistle of Paul the Apostle to the*

# CORINTHIANS

### *Paul Comforts the Believers*

PAUL, [a]an apostle of Jesus Christ by the will
of God, and [b]Timothy *our* brother,

To the church of God which is at Corinth,
[c]with all the saints who are in all Achaia:

2 [a]Grace to you and peace from God our Father
and the Lord Jesus Christ.
**3** [a]Blessed *be* the God and Father of our Lord
Jesus Christ, the Father of mercies and God of all
comfort,
4 who [a]comforts us in all our tribulation, that
we may be able to comfort those who are in any
[1]trouble, with the comfort with which we ourselves are comforted by God.
5 For as [a]the sufferings of Christ abound in us,
so our [1]consolation also abounds through Christ.
6 Now if we are afflicted, [a]*it is* for your consolation and salvation, which is effective for enduring
the same sufferings which we also suffer. Or if we
are comforted, *it is* for your consolation and
salvation.
7 And our hope for you *is* steadfast, because we
know that [a]as you are partakers of the sufferings,
so also *you will partake* of the consolation.
**8** For we do not want you to be ignorant, brethren, of [a]our [1]trouble which came to us in Asia: that
we were burdened beyond measure, above
strength, so that we despaired even of life.
9 Yes, we had the sentence of death in ourselves, that we should [a]not trust in ourselves but
in God who raises the dead,
10 [a]who delivered us from so great a death, and
[1]does deliver us; in whom we trust that He will
still deliver *us*,
11 you also [a]helping together in prayer for us,
that thanks may be given by many persons on
[1]our behalf [b]for the gift *granted* to us through
many.
**12** For our boasting is this: the testimony of our
conscience that we conducted ourselves in the
world in [1]simplicity and [a]godly sincerity, [b]not with
fleshly wisdom but by the grace of God, and more
abundantly toward you.
13 For we are not writing any other things to you
than what you read or understand. Now I trust
you will understand, even to the end
14 (as also you have understood us in part), [a]that
we are your boast as [b]you also *are* ours, in the day
of the Lord Jesus.
**15** And in this confidence [a]I intended to come to
you before, that you might have [b]a second benefit—
16 to pass by way of you to Macedonia, [a]to come
again from Macedonia to you, and be helped by
you on my way to Judea.
17 Therefore, when I was planning this, did I do
it lightly? Or the things I plan, do I plan [a]accord-
ing to the flesh, that with me there should be Yes,
Yes, and No, No?
18 But *as* God *is* [a]faithful, our [1]word to you was
not Yes and No.
19 For [a]the Son of God, Jesus Christ, who was
preached among you by us—by me, [b]Silvanus, and
[c]Timothy—was not Yes and No, [d]but in Him was
Yes.
20 [a]For all the promises of God in Him *are* Yes,
and in Him Amen, to the glory of God through us.
21 Now He who establishes us with you in Christ
and [a]has anointed us *is* God,
22 who [a]also has sealed us and [b]given us the
Spirit in our hearts as a guarantee.
23 Moreover [a]I call God as witness against my
soul, [b]that to spare you I came no more to Corinth.
24 Not [a]that we [1]have dominion over your faith,
but are fellow workers for your joy; for [b]by faith
you stand.

### *Paul Urges Forgiveness*

**2** But I determined this within myself, [a]that I
would not come again to you in sorrow.
2 For if I make you [a]sorrowful, then who is he
who makes me glad but the one who is made
sorrowful by me?
**3** And I wrote this very thing to you, lest, when
I came, [a]I should have sorrow over those from
whom I ought to have joy, [b]having confidence in
you all that my joy is *the joy* of you all.
4 For out of much [1]affliction and anguish of
heart I wrote to you, with many tears, [a]not that
you should be grieved, but that you might know
the love which I have so abundantly for you.
5 But [a]if anyone has caused grief, he has not
[b]grieved me, but all of you to some extent—not to
be too severe.
6 This punishment which *was inflicted* [a]by the
majority *is* sufficient for such a man,
7 [a]so that, on the contrary, you *ought* rather to
forgive and comfort *him*, lest perhaps such a one
be swallowed up with too much sorrow.
8 Therefore I urge you to reaffirm *your* love to
him.
9 For to this end I also wrote, that I might put
you to the test, whether you are [a]obedient in all
things.
10 Now whom you forgive anything, I also *forgive.* For [1]if indeed I have forgiven anything, I
have forgiven that one for your sakes in the
presence of Christ,
11 lest Satan should take advantage of us; for we
are not ignorant of his devices.
**12** Furthermore, [a]when I came to Troas to *preach*
Christ's gospel, and [b]a [1]door was opened to me by
the Lord,
13 [a]I had no rest in my spirit, because I did not
find Titus my brother; but taking my leave of
them, I departed for Macedonia.
14 Now thanks *be* to God who always leads us in
triumph in Christ, and through us [1]diffuses the
fragrance of His knowledge in every place.
15 For we are to God the fragrance of Christ
[a]among those who are being saved and [b]among
those who are perishing.
16 [a]To the one *we are* the aroma of death *leading*
to death, and to the other the aroma of life *leading*
to life. And [b]who *is* sufficient for these things?
17 For we are not, as [1]so many, [a]peddling[2] the
word of God; but as [b]of sincerity, but as from God,
we speak in the sight of God in Christ.

CHAPTER 1
**1** [a]2 Tim. 1:1 [b]1 Cor. 16:10 [c]Col. 1:2
**2** [a]Rom. 1:7
**3** [a]1 Pet. 1:3
**4** [a]Is. 51:12; 66:13 [1]*tribulation*
**5** [a]2 Cor. 4:10 [1]*comfort*
**6** [a]2 Cor. 4:15; 12:15
**7** [a][Rom. 8:17]
**8** [a]Acts 19:23 [1]*tribulation*
**9** [a]Jer. 17:5, 7
**10** [a][2 Pet. 2:9] [1]NU *shall*
**11** [a]Rom. 15:30 [b]2 Cor. 4:15; 9:11 [1]NU *your behalf*
**12** [a]2 Cor. 2:17 [b][1 Cor. 2:4] [1]The opposite of duplicity
**14** [a]2 Cor. 5:12 [b]Phil. 2:16
**15** [a]1 Cor. 4:19 [b]Rom. 1:11; 15:29
**16** [a]1 Cor. 16:3–6
**17** [a]2 Cor. 10:2; 11:18
**18** [a]1 John 5:20 [1]*message*
**19** [a]Mark 1:1 [b]1 Pet. 5:12 [c]2 Cor. 1:1 [d][Heb. 13:8]
**20** [a][Rom. 15:8, 9]
**21** [a][1 John 2:20, 27]
**22** [a][Eph. 4:30] [b][Eph. 1:14]
**23** [a]Gal. 1:20 [b]1 Cor. 4:21
**24** [a][1 Pet. 5:3] [b]Rom. 11:20 [1]*rule*

CHAPTER 2
**1** [a]2 Cor. 1:23
**2** [a]2 Cor. 7:8
**3** [a]2 Cor. 12:21 [b]Gal. 5:10
**4** [a][2 Cor. 2:9; 7:8, 12] [1]*tribulation*
**5** [a][1 Cor. 5:1] [b]Gal. 4:12
**6** [a]1 Cor. 5:4, 5
**7** [a]Gal. 6:1
**9** [a]2 Cor. 7:15; 10:6
**10** [1]NU *indeed, what I have forgiven, if I have forgiven anything, I did it for your sakes*
**12** [a]Acts 16:8 [b]1 Cor. 16:9 [1]Opportunity
**13** [a]2 Cor. 7:6, 13; 8:6
**14** [1]*manifests*
**15** [a][1 Cor. 1:18] [b][2 Cor. 4:3]
**16** [a]Luke 2:34 [b][1 Cor. 15:10]
**17** [a]2 Pet. 2:3 [b]2 Cor. 1:12 [1]M *the rest* [2]*adulterating for gain*

### *The New Covenant Written on Hearts*

3 Do [a]we begin again to commend ourselves? Or do we need, as some *others*, [b]epistles of commendation to you or *letters* of commendation from you?

2 [a]You are our epistle written in our hearts, known and read by all men;

3 clearly *you are* an epistle of Christ, [a]ministered by us, written not with ink but by the Spirit of the living God, not [b]on tablets of stone but [c]on tablets of flesh, *that is*, of the heart.

4 And we have such trust through Christ toward God.

5 [a]Not that we are sufficient of ourselves to think of anything as *being* from ourselves, but [b]our sufficiency *is* from God,

6 who also made us sufficient as [a]ministers of [b]the new covenant, not [c]of the letter but of the [1]Spirit; for [d]the letter kills, [e]but the Spirit gives life.

7 But if [a]the ministry of death, [b]written *and* engraved on stones, was glorious, [c]so that the children of Israel could not look steadily at the face of Moses because of the glory of his countenance, which *glory* was passing away,

8 how will [a]the ministry of the Spirit not be more glorious?

9 For if the ministry of condemnation *had* glory, the ministry [a]of righteousness exceeds much more in glory.

10 For even what was made glorious had no glory in this respect, because of the glory that excels.

11 For if what is passing away *was* glorious, what remains *is* much more glorious.

12 Therefore, since we have such hope, [a]we use great boldness of speech—

13 unlike Moses, [a]*who* put a veil over his face so that the children of Israel could not look steadily at [b]the end of what was passing away.

14 But [a]their minds were blinded. For until this day the same veil remains unlifted in the reading of the Old Testament, because the *veil* is taken away in Christ.

15 But even to this day, when Moses is read, a veil lies on their heart.

16 Nevertheless [a]when one turns to the Lord, [b]the veil is taken away.

17 Now [a]the Lord is the Spirit; and where the Spirit of the Lord *is*, there *is* [b]liberty.

18 But we all, with unveiled face, beholding [a]as in a mirror [b]the glory of the Lord, [c]are being transformed into the same image from glory to glory, just as [1]by the Spirit of the Lord.

### *Paul's Zeal in Preaching the Gospel*

4 Therefore, since we have this ministry, [a]as we have received mercy, we [b]do not lose heart.

2 But we have renounced the hidden things of shame, not walking in craftiness nor [1]handling the word of God deceitfully, but by manifestation of the truth [a]commending ourselves to every man's conscience in the sight of God.

3 But even if our gospel is veiled, [a]it is veiled to those who are perishing,

4 whose minds [a]the god of this age [b]has blinded, who do not believe, lest [c]the light of the gospel of the glory of Christ, [d]who is the image of God, should shine on them.

5 [a]For we do not preach ourselves, but Christ Jesus the Lord, and [b]ourselves your bondservants for Jesus' sake.

6 For it is the God [a]who commanded light to shine out of darkness, who has [b]shone in our hearts to *give* the light of the knowledge of the glory of God in the face of Jesus Christ.

7 But we have this treasure in earthen vessels, [a]that the excellence of the power may be of God and not of us.

8 *We are* [a]hard pressed on every side, yet not crushed; *we are* perplexed, but not in despair;

9 persecuted, but not [a]forsaken; [b]struck down, but not destroyed—

10 [a]always carrying about in the body the dying of the Lord Jesus, [b]that the life of Jesus also may be manifested in our body.

11 For we who live [a]are always delivered to death for Jesus' sake, that the life of Jesus also may be manifested in our mortal flesh.

12 So then death is working in us, but life in you.

13 And since we have [a]the same spirit of faith, according to what is written, [b]*"I believed and therefore I spoke,"* we also believe and therefore speak,

14 knowing that [a]He who raised up the Lord Jesus will also raise us up with Jesus, and will present *us* with you.

15 For [a]all things *are* for your sakes, that [b]grace, having spread through the many, may cause thanksgiving to abound to the glory of God.

16 Therefore we [a]do not lose heart. Even though our outward man is perishing, yet the inward *man* is [b]being renewed day by day.

17 For [a]our light affliction, which is but for a moment, is working for us a far more exceeding *and* eternal weight of glory,

18 [a]while we do not look at the things which are seen, but at the things which are not seen. For the things which are seen *are* temporary, but the things which are not seen *are* eternal.

### *Paul's Hope of Eternal Glory*

5 For we know that if [a]our earthly [1]house, *this* tent, is destroyed, we have a building from God, a house [b]not made with hands, eternal in the heavens.

2 For in this [a]we groan, earnestly desiring to be clothed with our [1]habitation which is from heaven,

3 if indeed, [a]having been clothed, we shall not be found naked.

4 For we who are in *this* tent groan, being burdened, not because we want to be unclothed, [a]but further clothed, that mortality may be swallowed up by life.

5 Now He who has prepared us for this very thing *is* God, who also [a]has given us the Spirit as [1]a guarantee.

6 So *we are* always confident, knowing that while we are at home in the body we are absent from the Lord.

7 For [a]we walk by faith, not by sight.

8 We are confident, yes, [a]well pleased rather to be absent from the body and to be present with the Lord.

9 Therefore we make it our aim, whether present or absent, to be well pleasing to Him.

10 [a]For we must all appear before the judgment seat of Christ, [b]that each one may receive the things *done* in the body, according to what he has done, whether good or bad.

11 Knowing, therefore, [a]the terror of the Lord, we persuade men; but we are well known to God,

CHAPTER 3
1 [a]2 Cor. 5:12; 10:12, 18; 12:11 [b]Acts 18:27
2 [a]1 Cor. 9:2
3 [a]1 Cor. 3:5 [b]Ex. 24:12; 31:18; 32:15 [c]Ps. 40:8
5 [a][John 15:5] [b]1 Cor. 15:10
6 [a]1 Cor. 3:5 [b]Jer. 31:31 [c]Rom. 2:27 [d]Gal. 3:10 [e]John 6:63 [1]Or *spirit*
7 [a]Rom. 7:10 [b]Ex. 34:1 [c]Ex. 34:29
8 [a][Gal. 3:5]
9 [a][Rom. 1:17; 3:21]
12 [a]Eph. 6:19
13 [a]Ex. 34:33–35 [b][Gal. 3:23]
14 [a]Acts 28:26
16 [a]Rom. 11:23 [b]Is. 25:7
17 [a][1 Cor. 15:45] [b]Gal. 5:1, 13
18 [a]1 Cor. 13:12 [b][2 Cor. 4:4, 6] [c][Rom. 8:29, 30] [1]Or *from the Lord, the Spirit*

CHAPTER 4
1 [a]1 Cor. 7:25 [b]2 Cor. 4:16
2 [a]2 Cor. 5:11 [1]*adulterating the word of God*
3 [a][1 Cor. 1:18]
4 [a]John 12:31 [b]John 12:40 [c][2 Cor. 3:8, 9] [d][John 1:18]
5 [a]1 Cor. 1:13 [b]1 Cor. 9:19
6 [a]Gen. 1:3 [b]2 Pet. 1:19
7 [a]1 Cor. 2:5
8 [a]2 Cor. 1:8; 7:5
9 [a]Ps. 37:24 [b][Heb. 13:5]
10 [a]Phil. 3:10 [b]Rom. 8:17
11 [a]Rom. 8:36
13 [a]2 Pet. 1:1 [b]Ps. 116:10
14 [a][Rom. 8:11]
15 [a]Col. 1:24 [b]2 Cor. 1:11
16 [a]2 Cor. 4:1 [b][Is. 40:29, 31]
17 [a]Rom. 8:18
18 [a][Heb. 11:1, 13]

CHAPTER 5
1 [a]Job 4:19 [b]Mark 14:58 [1]Physical body
2 [a]Rom. 8:23 [1]*dwelling*
3 [a]Rev. 3:18
4 [a]1 Cor. 15:53
5 [a]Rom. 8:23 [1]*down payment, earnest*
7 [a]Heb. 11:1
8 [a]Phil. 1:23
10 [a]Rom. 2:16; 14:10, 12 [b]Eph. 6:8
11 [a][Heb. 10:31; 12:29]

and I also trust are well known in your con-
sciences.
**12** For [a]we do not commend ourselves again to
you, but give you opportunity [b]to boast on our
behalf, that you may have *an answer* for those
who boast in appearance and not in heart.
13 For [a]if we are beside ourselves, *it is* for God; or
if we are of sound mind, *it is* for you.
14 For the love of Christ compels us, because we
judge thus: that [a]if One died for all, then all died;
15 and He died for all, [a]that those who live should
live no longer for themselves, but for Him who
died for them and rose again.
16 [a]Therefore, from now on, we regard no one
according to the flesh. Even though we have
known Christ according to the flesh, [b]yet now we
know *Him thus* no longer.
17 Therefore, if anyone [a]*is* in Christ, *he is* [b]a new
creation; [c]old things have passed away; behold, all
things have become [d]new.
18 Now all things *are* of God, [a]who has reconciled
us to Himself through Jesus Christ, and has given
us the ministry of reconciliation,
19 that is, that [a]God was in Christ reconciling the
world to Himself, not [1]imputing their trespasses to
them, and has committed to us the word of reconciliation.
20 Now then, we are [a]ambassadors for Christ, as
though God were pleading through us: we implore
*you* on Christ's behalf, be reconciled to God.
21 For [a]He made Him who knew no sin *to be* sin
for us, that we might become [b]the righteousness
of God in Him.

### *Paul's Sufferings in His Ministry*

**6** We then, *as* [a]workers together *with Him* also
[b]plead with *you* not to receive the grace of
God in vain.
2 For He says:

[a]*"In an acceptable time I have heard you,*
*And in the day of salvation I have helped*
*you."*

Behold, now *is* the accepted time; behold, now *is*
the day of salvation.
3 [a]We give no offense in anything, that our
ministry may not be blamed.
4 But in all *things* we commend ourselves [a]as
ministers of God: in much [1]patience, in tribulations, in needs, in distresses,
5 [a]in stripes, in imprisonments, in tumults, in
labors, in sleeplessness, in fastings;
6 by purity, by knowledge, by longsuffering, by
kindness, by the Holy Spirit, by [1]sincere love,
7 [a]by the word of truth, by [b]the power of God,
by [c]the armor of righteousness on the right hand
and on the left,
8 by honor and dishonor, by evil report and
good report; as deceivers, and *yet* true;
9 as unknown, and [a]*yet* well known; [b]as dying,
and behold we live; [c]as chastened, and *yet* not
killed;
10 as sorrowful, yet always rejoicing; as poor, yet
making many [a]rich; as having nothing, and *yet*
possessing all things.
**11** O Corinthians! [1]We have spoken openly to
you, [a]our heart is wide open.
12 You are not restricted by us, but [a]you are
restricted by your *own* affections.
13 Now in return for the same [a](I speak as to
children), you also be open.
14 [a]Do not be unequally yoked together with
unbelievers. For [b]what [1]fellowship has righteousness with lawlessness? And what [2]communion has
light with darkness?
15 And what accord has Christ with Belial? Or
what part has a believer with an unbeliever?
16 And what agreement has the temple of God
with idols? For [a]you[1] are the temple of the living
God. As God has said:

[b]*"I will dwell in them*
*And walk among them.*
*I will be their God,*
*And they shall be My people."*

17 Therefore

[a]*"Come out from among them*
*And be separate, says the Lord.*
*Do not touch what is unclean,*
*And I will receive you."*
18 *"I* [a]*will be a Father to you,*
*And you shall be My* [b]*sons and daughters,*
*Says the LORD Almighty."*

### *The Corinthians' Repentance*

**7** Therefore,[a] having these promises, beloved, let
us cleanse ourselves from all filthiness of the
flesh and spirit, perfecting holiness in the fear of
God.
2 Open *your hearts* to us. We have wronged no
one, we have corrupted no one, [a]we have cheated
no one.
3 I do not say *this* to condemn; for [a]I have said
before that you are in our hearts, to die together
and to live together.
4 [a]Great *is* my boldness of speech toward you,
[b]great *is* my boasting on your behalf. [c]I am filled
with comfort. I am exceedingly joyful in all our
tribulation.
5 For indeed, [a]when we came to Macedonia, our
bodies had no rest, but [b]we were troubled on every
side. [c]Outside *were* conflicts, inside *were* fears.
6 Nevertheless [a]God, who comforts the downcast, comforted us by [b]the coming of Titus,
7 and not only by his coming, but also by the
[1]consolation with which he was comforted in you,
when he told us of your earnest desire, your
mourning, your zeal for me, so that I rejoiced
even more.
8 For even if I made you [a]sorry with my letter, I
do not regret it; [b]though I did regret it. For I
perceive that the same epistle made you sorry,
though only for a while.
9 Now I rejoice, not that you were made sorry,
but that your sorrow led to repentance. For you
were made sorry in a godly manner, that you
might suffer loss from us in nothing.
10 For [a]godly sorrow produces repentance *lead-*
*ing* to salvation, not to be regretted; [b]but the
sorrow of the world produces death.
11 For observe this very thing, that you sorrowed
in a godly manner: What diligence it produced in
you, *what* [a]clearing *of yourselves, what* indignation, *what* fear, *what* vehement desire, *what* zeal,
*what* vindication! In all *things* you proved yourselves to be [b]clear in this matter.
12 Therefore, although I wrote to you, *I did* not
*do it* for the sake of him who had done the wrong,
nor for the sake of him who suffered wrong, [a]but
that our care for you in the sight of God might
appear to you.

**12** [a]2 Cor. 3:1 [b]2 Cor. 1:14
**13** [a]2 Cor. 11:1, 16; 12:11
**14** [a][Rom. 5:15; 6:6]
**15** [a][Rom. 6:11]
**16** [a]2 Cor. 10:3 [b][Matt. 12:50]
**17** [a][John 6:63] [b][Rom. 8:9] [c]Is. 43:18; 65:17 [d][Rom. 6:3–10]
**18** [a]Rom. 5:10
**19** [a][Rom. 3:24] [1]*reckoning*
**20** [a]Eph. 6:20
**21** [a]Is. 53:6, 9 [b][Rom. 1:17; 3:21]

CHAPTER 6
**1** [a]1 Cor. 3:9 [b]2 Cor. 5:20
**2** [a]Is. 49:8
**3** [a]Rom. 14:13
**4** [a]1 Cor. 4:1 [1]*endurance*
**5** [a]2 Cor. 11:23
**6** [1]Lit. *unhypocritical*
**7** [a]2 Cor. 7:14 [b]1 Cor. 2:4 [c]2 Cor. 10:4
**9** [a]2 Cor. 4:2; 5:11 [b]1 Cor. 4:9, 11 [c]Ps. 118:18
**10** [a][2 Cor. 8:9]
**11** [a]2 Cor. 7:3 [1]Lit. *Our mouth is open*
**12** [a]2 Cor. 12:15
**13** [a]1 Cor. 4:14
**14** [a]1 Cor. 5:9 [b]Eph. 5:6, 7, 11 [1]*in common* [2]*fellowship*
**16** [a][1 Cor. 3:16, 17; 6:19] [b]Lev. 26:12; Jer. 31:33; 32:38; Ezek. 37:26, 27 [1]NU *we*
**17** [a]Is. 52:11
**18** [a]2 Sam. 7:14 [b][Rom. 8:14]

CHAPTER 7
**1** [a][1 John 3:3]
**2** [a]Acts 20:33
**3** [a]2 Cor. 6:11, 12
**4** [a]2 Cor. 3:12 [b]1 Cor. 1:4 [c]Phil. 2:17
**5** [a]2 Cor. 2:13 [b]2 Cor. 4:8 [c]Deut. 32:25
**6** [a]2 Cor. 1:3, 4 [b]2 Cor. 2:13; 7:13
**7** [1]*comfort*
**8** [a]2 Cor. 2:2 [b]2 Cor. 2:4
**10** [a]Matt. 26:75 [b]Prov. 17:22
**11** [a]Eph. 5:11 [b]2 Cor. 2:5–11
**12** [a]2 Cor. 2:4

**13** Therefore we have been comforted in your
comfort. And we rejoiced exceedingly more for
the joy of Titus, because his spirit [a]has been
refreshed by you all.
14 For if in anything I have boasted to him about
you, I am not ashamed. But as we spoke all things
to you in truth, even so our boasting to Titus was
found true.
15 And his affections are greater for you as he
remembers [a]the obedience of you all, how with
fear and trembling you received him.
16 Therefore I rejoice that [a]I have confidence in
you in everything.

### *Excel in Giving*

**8** Moreover, brethren, we make known to you
the grace of God bestowed on the churches of
Macedonia:
2 that in a great trial of affliction the abundance
of their joy and [a]their deep poverty abounded in
the riches of their liberality.
3 For I bear witness that according to *their*
ability, yes, and beyond *their* ability, *they were*
freely willing,
4 imploring us with much urgency [1]that we
would receive the gift and [a]the fellowship of the
ministering to the saints.
5 And not *only* as we had hoped, but they first
[a]gave themselves to the Lord, and *then* to us by
the [b]will of God.
6 So [a]we urged Titus, that as he had begun, so
he would also complete this grace in you as well.
7 But as [a]you abound in everything—in faith, in
speech, in knowledge, in all diligence, and in your
love for us—*see* [b]that you abound in this grace
also.
**8** [a]I speak not by commandment, but I am
testing the sincerity of your love by the diligence
of others.
9 For you know the grace of our Lord Jesus
Christ, [a]that though He was rich, yet for your
sakes He became poor, that you through His
poverty might become [b]rich.
10 And in this [a]I give advice: [b]It is to your advantage not only to be doing what you began and
[c]were desiring to do a year ago;
11 but now you also must complete the doing *of*
*it;* that as *there was* a readiness to desire *it,* so
*there* also *may be* a completion out of what *you*
have.
12 For [a]if there is first a willing mind, *it is* accepted according to what one has, *and* not according to what he does not have.
13 For *I do* not *mean* that others should be eased
and you burdened;
14 but by an equality, *that* now at this time your
abundance *may supply* their lack, that their abundance also may supply your lack—that there may
be equality.
15 As it is written, [a]*"He who gathered much had
nothing left over, and he who gathered little had
no lack."*
**16** But thanks *be* to God who [1]puts the same
earnest care for you into the heart of Titus.
17 For he not only accepted the exhortation, but
being more diligent, he went to you of his own
accord.
18 And we have sent with him [a]the brother
whose praise *is* in the gospel throughout all the
churches,
19 and not only *that,* but who was also [a]chosen
by the churches to travel with us with this gift,
which is administered by us [b]to the glory of the
Lord Himself and *to show* your ready mind,
20 avoiding this: that anyone should blame us in
this lavish gift which is administered by us—
21 [a]providing honorable things, not only in the
sight of the Lord, but also in the sight of men.
22 And we have sent with them our brother
whom we have often proved diligent in many
things, but now much more diligent, because of
the great confidence which *we have* in you.
23 If *anyone inquires* about [a]Titus, *he is* my
partner and fellow worker concerning you. Or if
our brethren *are inquired about, they are* [b]mes-
sengers[1] of the churches, the glory of Christ.
24 Therefore show to them, [1]and before the
churches the proof of your love and of our [a]boast-
ing on your behalf.

### *The Importance of Giving Cheerfully*

**9** Now concerning [a]the ministering to the saints,
it is superfluous for me to write to you;
2 for I know your willingness, about which I
boast of you to the Macedonians, that Achaia was
ready a [a]year ago; and your zeal has stirred up the
majority.
3 [a]Yet I have sent the brethren, lest our boasting of you should be in vain in this respect, that,
as I said, you may be ready;
4 lest if *some* Macedonians come with me and
find you unprepared, we (not to mention you!)
should be ashamed of this [1]confident boasting.
5 Therefore I thought it necessary to [1]exhort the
brethren to go to you ahead of time, and prepare
your generous gift beforehand, which *you had*
previously promised, that it may be ready as *a
matter of* generosity and not as a [2]grudging
obligation.
**6** [a]But this *I say:* He who sows sparingly will
also reap sparingly, and he who sows [1]bountifully
will also reap [1]bountifully.
7 *So let* each one *give* as he purposes in his
heart, [a]not grudgingly or of [1]necessity; for [b]God
loves a cheerful giver.
8 [a]And God *is* able to make all grace abound
toward you, that you, always having all sufficiency in all *things,* may have an abundance for
every good work.
9 As it is written:

[a]*"He has dispersed abroad,*
*He has given to the poor;*
*His righteousness endures forever."*

10 Now [1]may He who [a]supplies seed to the sower,
and bread for food, [2]supply and multiply the seed
you have *sown* and increase the fruits of your
[b]righteousness,
11 while *you are* enriched in everything for all
liberality, [a]which causes thanksgiving through us
to God.
12 For the administration of this service not only
[a]supplies the needs of the saints, but also is
abounding through many thanksgivings to God,
13 while, through the proof of this ministry, they
[a]glorify God for the obedience of your confession
to the gospel of Christ, and for *your* liberal [b]shar-
ing with them and all *men,*
14 and by their prayer for you, who long for you
because of the exceeding [a]grace of God in you.
15 Thanks *be* to God [a]for His indescribable gift!

**13** [a]Rom. 15:32
**15** [a]2 Cor. 2:9
**16** [a]2 Thess. 3:4

CHAPTER 8
**2** [a]Mark 12:44
**4** [a]Rom. 15:25, 26 [1]NU, M omit *that we would receive,* thus changing text to *urgency for the favor and fellowship*
**5** [a][Rom. 12:1, 2] [b][Eph. 6:6]
**6** [a]2 Cor. 8:17; 12:18
**7** [a][1 Cor. 1:5; 12:13] [b]2 Cor. 9:8
**8** [a]1 Cor. 7:6
**9** [a]Phil. 2:6, 7 [b]Rom. 9:23
**10** [a]1 Cor. 7:25, 40 [b][Heb. 13:16] [c]2 Cor. 9:2
**12** [a]Mark 12:43, 44
**15** [a]Ex. 16:18
**16** [1]NU *has put*
**18** [a]2 Cor. 12:18
**19** [a]1 Cor. 16:3, 4 [b]2 Cor. 4:15
**21** [a]Rom. 12:17
**23** [a]2 Cor. 7:13, 14 [b]Phil. 2:25 [1]Lit. *apostles,* "sent ones"
**24** [a]2 Cor. 7:4, 14; 9:2 [1]NU, M omit *and*

CHAPTER 9
**1** [a]Gal. 2:10
**2** [a]2 Cor. 8:10
**3** [a]2 Cor. 8:6, 17
**4** [1]NU *confidence.*
**5** [1]*encourage* [2]Lit. *covetousness*
**6** [a]Prov. 11:24; 22:9 [1]*with blessings*
**7** [a]Deut. 15:7 [b]Rom. 12:8 [1]*compulsion*
**8** [a][Prov. 11:24]
**9** [a]Ps. 112:9
**10** [a]Is. 55:10 [b]Hos. 10:12 [1]NU omits *may* [2]NU *will supply*
**11** [a]2 Cor. 1:11
**12** [a]2 Cor. 8:14
**13** [a][Matt. 5:16] [b][Heb. 13:16]
**14** [a]2 Cor. 8:1
**15** [a][James 1:17]

### *Paul's Warfare and Authority*

**10** Now [a]I, Paul, myself am pleading with you
by the meekness and gentleness of Christ—
[b]who in presence *am* lowly among you, but being
absent am bold toward you.
2 But I beg *you* [a]that when I am present I may
not be bold with that confidence by which I
intend to be bold against some, who think of us as
if we walked according to the flesh.
3 For though we walk in the flesh, we do not
war according to the flesh.
4 [a]For the weapons [b]of our warfare *are* not
[1]carnal but [c]mighty in God [d]for pulling down
strongholds,
5 [a]casting down arguments and every high thing
that exalts itself against the knowledge of God,
bringing every thought into captivity to the obedience of Christ,
6 [a]and being ready to punish all disobedience
when [b]your obedience is fulfilled.
**7** [a]Do you look at things according to the outward appearance? [b]If anyone is convinced in
himself that he is Christ's, let him again consider
this in himself, that just as he *is* Christ's, even [1]so
[c]we *are* Christ's.
8 For even if I should boast somewhat more
[a]about our authority, which the Lord gave [1]us for
[2]edification and not for your destruction, [b]I shall
not be ashamed—
9 lest I seem to terrify you by letters.
10 "For *his* letters," they say, "*are* weighty and
powerful, but [a]*his* bodily presence *is* weak, and *his*
[b]speech contemptible."
11 Let such a person consider this, that what we
are in word by letters when we are absent, such
*we will* also *be* in deed when we are present.
**12** [a]For we dare not class ourselves or compare
ourselves with those who commend themselves.
But they, measuring themselves by themselves,
and comparing themselves among themselves, are
not wise.
13 [a]We, however, will not boast beyond measure,
but within the limits of the sphere which God
appointed us—a sphere which especially includes
you.
14 For we are not overextending ourselves (as
though *our authority* did not extend to you), [a]for
it was to you that we came with the gospel of
Christ;
15 not boasting of things beyond measure, *that
is*, [a]in other men's labors, but having hope, *that* as
your faith is increased, we shall be greatly enlarged by you in our sphere,
16 to preach the gospel in the *regions* beyond
you, *and* not to boast in another man's sphere of
accomplishment.
17 But [a]*"he who glories, let him glory in the
LORD."*
18 For [a]not he who commends himself is approved, but [b]whom the Lord commends.

### *The Danger of Being Deceived*

**11** Oh, that you would bear with me in a little
[a]folly—and indeed you do bear with me.
2 For I am [a]jealous for you with godly jealousy.
For [b]I have betrothed you to one husband, [c]that I
may present *you* [d]as a chaste virgin to Christ.
3 But I fear, lest somehow, as [a]the serpent
deceived Eve by his craftiness, so your minds
[b]may be corrupted from the [1]simplicity that is in
Christ.

CHAPTER 10
**1** [a]Rom. 12:1 [b]1 Thess. 2:7
**2** [a]1 Cor. 4:21
**4** [a]Eph. 6:13 [b]1 Tim. 1:18 [c]Acts 7:22 [d]Jer. 1:10 [1]*of the flesh*
**5** [a]1 Cor. 1:19
**6** [a]2 Cor. 13:2, 10 [b]2 Cor. 7:15
**7** [a][John 7:24] [b]1 Cor. 1:12; 14:37 [c]1 Cor. 3:23 [1]NU *as we are.*
**8** [a]2 Cor. 13:10 [b]2 Cor. 7:14 [1]NU omits *us* [2]*building up*
**10** [a]Gal. 4:13 [b]2 Cor. 11:6
**12** [a]2 Cor. 5:12
**13** [a]2 Cor. 10:15
**14** [a]1 Cor. 3:5, 6
**15** [a]Rom. 15:20
**17** [a]Jer. 9:24
**18** [a]Prov. 27:2 [b]Rom. 2:29

CHAPTER 11
**1** [a]2 Cor. 11:4, 16, 19
**2** [a]Gal. 4:17 [b]Hos. 2:19 [c]Col. 1:28 [d]Lev. 21:13
**3** [a]Gen. 3:4, 13 [b]Eph. 6:24 [1]NU adds *and purity*
**4** [a]Gal. 1:6–8
**5** [a]2 Cor. 12:11
**6** [a][1 Cor. 1:17] [b][Eph. 3:4] [c][2 Cor. 12:12] [1]NU omits *been*
**7** [a]1 Cor. 9:18 [1]*putting myself down*
**9** [a]Acts 20:33 [b]Phil. 4:10
**10** [a]Rom. 1:9; 9:1 [b]1 Cor. 9:15
**11** [a]2 Cor. 6:11; 12:15
**12** [a]1 Cor. 9:12
**13** [a]Phil. 1:15 [b]Phil. 3:2
**14** [a]Gal. 1:8
**15** [a][Phil. 3:19]
**17** [a]1 Cor. 7:6
**19** [a]1 Cor. 4:10
**20** [a][Gal. 2:4; 4:3, 9; 5:1]
**21** [a]2 Cor. 10:10 [b]Phil. 3:4
**22** [a]Phil. 3:4–6
**23** [a]1 Cor. 15:10 [b]Acts 9:16 [c]1 Cor. 15:30
**24** [a]Deut. 25:3 [b]2 Cor. 6:5
**25** [a]Acts 16:22, 23; 21:32 [b]Acts 14:5, 19 [c]Acts 27:1–44
**26** [a]Acts 9:23, 24; 13:45, 50; 17:5, 13 [b]Acts 14:5, 19; 19:23; 27:42

4 For if he who comes preaches another Jesus
whom we have not preached, or *if* you receive a
different spirit which you have not received, or a
[a]different gospel which you have not accepted—
you may well put up with it!
**5** For I consider that [a]I am not at all inferior to
the most eminent apostles.
6 Even though [a]*I am* untrained in speech, yet *I
am* not [b]in knowledge. But [c]we have [1]been thoroughly manifested among you in all things.
7 Did I commit sin in [1]humbling myself that you
might be exalted, because I preached the gospel of
God to you [a]free of charge?
8 I robbed other churches, taking wages *from
them* to minister to you.
9 And when I was present with you, and in
need, [a]I was a burden to no one, for what I lacked
[b]the brethren who came from Macedonia supplied.
And in everything I kept myself from being burdensome to you, and so I will keep *myself*.
10 [a]As the truth of Christ is in me, [b]no one shall
stop me from this boasting in the regions of
Achaia.
11 Why? [a]Because I do not love you? God knows!
12 But what I do, I will also continue to do, [a]that
I may cut off the opportunity from those who
desire an opportunity to be regarded just as we
are in the things of which they boast.
13 For such [a]*are* false apostles, [b]deceitful workers, transforming themselves into apostles of
Christ.
14 And no wonder! For Satan himself transforms
himself into [a]an angel of light.
15 Therefore *it is* no great thing if his ministers
also transform themselves into ministers of righteousness, [a]whose end will be according to their
works.
**16** I say again, let no one think me a fool. If
otherwise, at least receive me as a fool, that I also
may boast a little.
17 What I speak, [a]I speak not according to the
Lord, but as it were, foolishly, in this confidence of
boasting.
18 Seeing that many boast according to the flesh,
I also will boast.
19 For you put up with fools gladly, [a]since you
*yourselves* are wise!
20 For you put up with it [a]if one brings you into
bondage, if one devours *you*, if one takes *from
you*, if one exalts himself, if one strikes you on the
face.
21 To *our* shame [a]I say that we were too weak for
that! But [b]in whatever anyone is bold—I speak
foolishly—I am bold also.
**22** Are they [a]Hebrews? So *am* I. Are they Israelites? So *am* I. Are they the seed of Abraham? So
*am* I.
23 Are they ministers of Christ?—I speak as a
fool—I *am* more: [a]in labors more abundant, [b]in
stripes above measure, in prisons more frequently,
[c]in deaths often.
24 From the Jews five times I received [a]forty
[b]*stripes* minus one.
25 Three times I was [a]beaten with rods; [b]once I
was stoned; three times I [c]was shipwrecked; a
night and a day I have been in the deep;
26 *in* journeys often, *in* perils of waters, *in* perils
of robbers, [a]*in* perils of *my own* countrymen, [b]*in*
perils of the Gentiles, *in* perils in the city, *in* perils
in the wilderness, *in* perils in the sea, *in* perils
among false brethren;

27 in weariness and toil, [a]in sleeplessness often, [b]in hunger and thirst, in [c]fastings often, in cold and nakedness—
28 besides the other things, what comes upon me daily: [a]my deep concern for all the churches.
29 [a]Who is weak, and I am not weak? Who is made to stumble, and I do not burn with indignation?
30 If I must boast, [a]I will boast in the things which concern my [1]infirmity.
31 [a]The God and Father of our Lord Jesus Christ, [b]who is blessed forever, knows that I am not lying.
32 [a]In Damascus the governor, under Aretas the king, was guarding the city of the Damascenes with a garrison, desiring to arrest me;
33 but I was let down in a basket through a window in the wall, and escaped from his hands.

## *Paul's Love for the Church*

12 It is [1]doubtless not profitable for me to boast. I will come to [a]visions and [b]revelations of the Lord:
2 I know a man [a]in Christ who fourteen years ago—whether in the body I do not know, or whether out of the body I do not know, God knows—such a one [b]was caught up to the third heaven.
3 And I know such a man—whether in the body or out of the body I do not know, God knows—
4 how he was caught up into [a]Paradise and heard inexpressible words, which it is not lawful for a man to utter.
5 Of such a one I will boast; yet of myself I will not [a]boast, except in my infirmities.
6 For though I might desire to boast, I will not be a fool; for I will speak the truth. But I refrain, lest anyone should think of me above what he sees me *to be* or hears from me.
7 And lest I should be exalted above measure by the abundance of the revelations, a [a]thorn in the flesh was given to me, [b]a messenger of Satan to [1]buffet me, lest I be exalted above measure.
8 [a]Concerning this thing I pleaded with the Lord three times that it might depart from me.
9 And He said to me, "My grace is sufficient for you, for My strength is made perfect in weakness." Therefore most gladly [a]I will rather boast in my infirmities, [b]that the power of Christ may rest upon me.
10 Therefore [a]I take pleasure in infirmities, in reproaches, in needs, in persecutions, in distresses, for Christ's sake. [b]For when I am weak, then I am strong.
11 I have become [a]a fool [1]in boasting; you have compelled me. For I ought to have been commended by you; for [b]in nothing was I behind the most eminent apostles, though [c]I am nothing.
12 [a]Truly the signs of an apostle were accomplished among you with all perseverance, in signs and [b]wonders and mighty [c]deeds.
13 For what is it in which you were inferior to other churches, except that I myself was not burdensome to you? Forgive me this wrong!
14 [a]Now *for* the third time I am ready to come to you. And I will not be burdensome to you; for [b]I do not seek yours, but you. [c]For the children ought not to lay up for the parents, but the parents for the children.
15 And I will very gladly spend and be spent [a]for your souls; though [b]the more abundantly I love you, the less I am loved.
16 But be that *as it may,* [a]I did not burden you. Nevertheless, being crafty, I caught you by cunning!
17 Did I take advantage of you by any of those whom I sent to you?
18 I urged Titus, and sent our [a]brother with *him.* Did Titus take advantage of you? Did we not walk in the same spirit? Did *we* not *walk* in the same steps?
19 [a]Again,[1] do you think that we excuse ourselves to you? [b]We speak before God in Christ. [c]But *we do* all things, beloved, for your edification.
20 For I fear lest, when I come, I shall not find you such as I wish, and *that* [a]I shall be found by you such as you do not wish; lest *there be* contentions, jealousies, outbursts of wrath, selfish ambitions, backbitings, whisperings, conceits, tumults;
21 lest, when I come again, my God [a]will humble me among you, and I shall mourn for many [b]who have sinned before and have not repented of the uncleanness, [c]fornication, and lewdness which they have practiced.

## *Paul's Warning; Greetings and Benediction*

13 This *will be* [a]the third *time* I am coming to you. [b]*"By the mouth of two or three witnesses every word shall be established."*
2 [a]I have told you before, and foretell as if I were present the second time, and now being absent [1]I write to those [b]who have sinned before, and to all the rest, that if I come again [c]I will not spare—
3 since you seek a proof of Christ [a]speaking in me, who is not weak toward you, but mighty [b]in you.
4 [a]For though He was crucified in weakness, yet [b]He lives by the power of God. For [c]we also are weak in Him, but we shall live with Him by the power of God toward you.
5 Examine yourselves *as to* whether you are in the faith. Test yourselves. Do you not know yourselves, [a]that Jesus Christ is in you?—unless indeed you [1]are [b]disqualified.
6 But I trust that you will know that we are not disqualified.
7 Now [1]I pray to God that you do no evil, not that we should appear approved, but that you should do what is honorable, though [a]we may seem disqualified.
8 For we can do nothing against the truth, but for the truth.
9 For we are glad [a]when we are weak and you are strong. And this also we pray, [b]that you may be made complete.
10 [a]Therefore I write these things being absent, lest being present I should use sharpness, according to the [b]authority which the Lord has given me for edification and not for destruction.
11 Finally, brethren, farewell. Become complete. [a]Be of good comfort, be of one mind, live in peace; and the God of love [b]and peace will be with you.
12 [a]Greet one another with a holy kiss.
13 All the saints greet you.
14 [a]The grace of the Lord Jesus Christ, and the love of God, and [b]the [1]communion of the Holy Spirit *be* with you all. Amen.

**12** [a]Rom. 16:16
**14** [a]Rom. 16:24 [b]Phil. 2:1 [1]*fellowship*

**27** [a]Acts 20:31 [b]1 Cor. 4:11 [c]Acts 9:9; 13:2, 3; 14:23
**28** [a]Acts 20:18
**29** [a][1 Cor. 8:9, 13; 9:22]
**30** [a][2 Cor. 12:5, 9, 10] [1]*weakness*
**31** [a]1 Thess. 2:5 [b]Rom. 9:5
**32** [a]Acts 9:19–25

CHAPTER 12

**1** [a]Acts 16:9; 18:9; 22:17, 18; 23:11; 26:13–15; 27:23 [b][Gal. 1:12; 2:2] [1]NU *necessary, though not profitable, to boast*
**2** [a]Rom. 16:7 [b]Acts 22:17
**4** [a]Luke 23:43
**5** [a]2 Cor. 11:30
**7** [a]Ezek. 28:24 [b]Job 2:7 [1]*beat*
**8** [a]Matt. 26:44
**9** [a]2 Cor. 11:30 [b][1 Pet. 4:14]
**10** [a][Rom. 5:3; 8:35] [b]2 Cor. 13:4
**11** [a]2 Cor. 5:13; 11:1, 16; 12:6 [b]2 Cor. 11:5 [c]1 Cor. 3:7; 13:2; 15:9 [1]NU omits *in boasting*
**12** [a]Rom. 15:18 [b]Acts 15:12 [c]Acts 14:8–10; 16:16–18; 19:11, 12; 20:6–12; 28:1–10
**14** [a]2 Cor. 1:15; 13:1, 2 [b][1 Cor. 10:24–33] [c]1 Cor. 4:14
**15** [a][2 Tim. 2:10] [b]2 Cor. 6:12, 13
**16** [a]2 Cor. 11:9
**18** [a]2 Cor. 8:18
**19** [a]2 Cor. 5:12 [b][Rom. 9:1, 2] [c]1 Cor. 10:33 [1]NU *You have been thinking for a long time that we*
**20** [a]1 Cor. 4:21
**21** [a]2 Cor. 2:1, 4 [b]2 Cor. 13:2 [c]1 Cor. 5:1

CHAPTER 13

**1** [a]2 Cor. 12:14 [b]Deut. 17:6; 19:15
**2** [a]2 Cor. 10:2 [b]2 Cor. 12:21 [c]2 Cor. 1:23; 10:11 [1]NU omits *I write*
**3** [a]Matt. 10:20 [b][1 Cor. 9:2]
**4** [a][1 Pet. 3:18] [b][Rom. 1:4; 6:4] [c][2 Cor. 10:3, 4]
**5** [a][Gal. 4:19] [b]1 Cor. 9:27 [1]*do not stand the test*
**7** [a]2 Cor. 6:9 [1]NU *we*
**9** [a]1 Cor. 4:10 [b][1 Thess. 3:10]
**10** [a]1 Cor. 4:21 [b]2 Cor. 10:8
**11** [a]Rom. 12:16, 18 [b]Rom. 15:33

*The Epistle of Paul the Apostle to the*

# GALATIANS

### *Paul's Gospel Is from God*

PAUL, an apostle (not from men nor through
man, but [a]through Jesus Christ and God the
Father [b]who raised Him from the dead),
2 and all the brethren who are with me,

To the churches of Galatia:

3 Grace to you and peace from God the Father
and our Lord Jesus Christ,
4 [a]who gave Himself for our sins, that He might
deliver us [b]from this present evil age, according to
the will of our God and Father,
5 to whom *be* glory forever and ever. Amen.
**6** I marvel that you are turning away so soon
[a]from Him who called you in the grace of Christ,
to a different gospel,
7 [a]which is not another; but there are some
[b]who trouble you and want to [c]pervert[1] the gospel
of Christ.
8 But even if [a]we, or an angel from heaven,
preach any other gospel to you than what we
have preached to you, let him be [1]accursed.
9 As we have said before, so now I say again, if
anyone preaches any other gospel to you [a]than
what you have received, let him be accursed.
10 For [a]do I now [b]persuade men, or God? Or [c]do I
seek to please men? For if I still pleased men, I
would not be a bondservant of Christ.
**11** [a]But I make known to you, brethren, that the
gospel which was preached by me is not according
to man.
12 For [a]I neither received it from man, nor was I
taught *it,* but *it came* [b]through the revelation of
Jesus Christ.
13 For you have heard of my former conduct in
Judaism, how [a]I persecuted the church of God
beyond measure and [b]*tried to* destroy it.
14 And I advanced in Judaism beyond many of
my contemporaries in my own nation, [a]being
more exceedingly zealous [b]for the traditions of my
fathers.
15 But when it pleased God, [a]who separated me
from my mother's womb and called *me* through
His grace,
16 [a]to reveal His Son in me, that [b]I might preach
Him among the Gentiles, I did not immediately
confer with [c]flesh and blood,
17 nor did I go up to Jerusalem to those *who
were* apostles before me; but I went to Arabia, and
returned again to Damascus.
**18** Then after three years [a]I went up to Jerusalem
to see [1]Peter, and remained with him fifteen days.
19 But [a]I saw none of the other apostles except
[b]James, the Lord's brother.
20 (Now *concerning* the things which I write to
you, indeed, before God, I do not lie.)
21 [a]Afterward I went into the regions of Syria
and Cilicia.
22 And I was unknown by face to the churches of
Judea which [a]*were* in Christ.
23 But they were [a]hearing only, "He who formerly [b]persecuted us now preaches the faith
which he once *tried to* destroy."
24 And they [a]glorified God in me.

CHAPTER 1
1 [a]Acts 9:6 [b]Acts 2:24
4 [a][Matt. 20:28] [b]Heb. 2:5
6 [a]Gal. 1:15; 5:8
7 [a]2 Cor. 11:4 [b]Gal. 5:10, 12 [c]2 Cor. 2:17 [1]*distort*
8 [a]1 Cor. 16:22 [1]Gr. *anathema*
9 [a]Deut. 4:2
10 [a]1 Thess. 2:4 [b]1 Sam. 24:7 [c]1 Thess. 2:4
11 [a]1 Cor. 15:1
12 [a]1 Cor. 15:1 [b][Eph. 3:3–5]
13 [a]Acts 9:1 [b]Acts 8:3; 22:4, 5
14 [a]Acts 26:9 [b]Jer. 9:14
15 [a]Is. 49:1, 5
16 [a][2 Cor. 4:5–7] [b]Acts 9:15 [c]Matt. 16:17
18 [a]Acts 9:26 [1]NU *Cephas*
19 [a]1 Cor. 9:5 [b]Matt. 13:55
21 [a]Acts 9:30
22 [a]Rom. 16:7
23 [a]Acts 9:20, 21 [b]Acts 8:3
24 [a]Acts 11:18

CHAPTER 2
1 [a]Acts 15:2
2 [a]Acts 15:1–4 [b]Phil. 2:16 [1]*because of*
4 [a]Acts 15:1, 24 [b]Gal. 3:25; 5:1, 13 [c]Gal. 4:3, 9
5 [a][Gal. 1:6; 2:14; 3:1]
6 [a]Gal. 2:9; 6:3 [b]Acts 10:34 [c]2 Cor. 11:5; 12:11 [1]Lit. *does not receive the face of a man*
7 [a]Acts 9:15; 13:46; 22:21 [b]1 Thess. 2:4
8 [a]1 Pet. 1:1 [b]Acts 9:15 [c][Gal. 3:5]
9 [a]Matt. 16:18 [b]Rom. 1:5 [c]Acts 13:3 [1]Peter
10 [a]Acts 11:30
11 [a]Acts 15:35 [1]NU *Cephas* [2]*opposed*
12 [a][Acts 10:28; 11:2, 3] [1]Jewish Christians
14 [a]Gal. 1:6; 2:5 [b]1 Tim. 5:20 [c][Acts 10:28] [1]NU *how can you* [2]Some interpreters stop the quotation here.
15 [a][Acts 15:10] [b]Matt. 9:11
16 [a]Acts 13:38, 39 [b]Rom. 1:17 [c]Ps. 143:2 [1]*declared righteous*
17 [a][1 John 3:8]

### *No Return to the Law*

**2** Then after fourteen years [a]I went up again to
Jerusalem with Barnabas, and also took Titus
with *me.*
2 And I went up [1]by revelation, and communicated to them that gospel which I preach among
the Gentiles, but [a]privately to those who were of
reputation, lest by any means [b]I might run, or had
run, in vain.
3 Yet not even Titus who *was* with me, being a
Greek, was compelled to be circumcised.
4 And *this occurred* because of [a]false brethren
secretly brought in (who came in by stealth to spy
out our [b]liberty which we have in Christ Jesus,
[c]that they might bring us into bondage),
5 to whom we did not yield submission even for
an hour, that [a]the truth of the gospel might
continue with you.
6 But from those [a]who seemed to be something—whatever they were, it makes no difference to me; [b]God [1]shows personal favoritism to no
man—for those who seemed *to be something*
[c]added nothing to me.
7 But on the contrary, [a]when they saw that the
gospel for the uncircumcised [b]had been committed to me, as *the gospel* for the circumcised
*was* to Peter
8 (for He who worked effectively in Peter for the
apostleship to the [a]circumcised [b]also [c]worked
effectively in me toward the Gentiles),
9 and when James, [1]Cephas, and John, who
seemed to be [a]pillars, perceived [b]the grace that
had been given to me, they gave me and Barnabas
the right hand of fellowship, [c]that we *should go* to
the Gentiles and they to the circumcised.
10 *They desired* only that we should remember
the poor, [a]the very thing which I also was eager
to do.
**11** [a]Now when [1]Peter had come to Antioch, I
[2]withstood him to his face, because he was to be
blamed;
12 for before certain men came from James, [a]he
would eat with the Gentiles; but when they came,
he withdrew and separated himself, fearing [1]those
who were of the circumcision.
13 And the rest of the Jews also played the
hypocrite with him, so that even Barnabas was
carried away with their hypocrisy.
14 But when I saw that they were not straightforward about [a]the truth of the gospel, I said to
Peter [b]before *them* all, [c]"If you, being a Jew, live
in the manner of Gentiles and not as the Jews,
[1]why do you compel Gentiles to live as [2]Jews?
15 [a]"We *who are* Jews by nature, and not [b]sin-
ners of the Gentiles,
16 [a]"knowing that a man is not [1]justified by the
works of the law but [b]by faith in Jesus Christ,
even we have believed in Christ Jesus, that we
might be justified by faith in Christ and not [c]by
the works of the law; for by the works of the law
no flesh shall be justified.
17 "But if, while we seek to be justified by Christ,
we ourselves also are found [a]sinners, *is* Christ
therefore a minister of sin? Certainly not!
18 "For if I build again those things which I
destroyed, I make myself a transgressor.

19 "For I [a]through the law [b]died to the law that I might [c]live to God.

20 "I have been [a]crucified with Christ; it is no longer I who live, but Christ lives in me; and the *life* which I now live in the flesh [b]I live by faith in the Son of God, [c]who loved me and gave Himself for me.

21 "I do not set aside the grace of God; for [a]if righteousness *comes* through the law, then Christ died [1]in vain."

### *Justification by Faith*

3 O foolish Galatians! Who has bewitched you [1]that you should not obey the truth, before whose eyes Jesus Christ was clearly portrayed [2]among you as crucified?

2 This only I want to learn from you: Did you receive the Spirit by the works of the law, [a]or by the hearing of faith?

3 Are you so foolish? [a]Having begun in the Spirit, are you now being made perfect by [b]the flesh?

4 [a]Have you suffered so [1]many things in vain—if indeed *it was* in vain?

5 Therefore He who supplies the Spirit to you and works miracles among you, *does He do it* by the works of the law, or by the hearing of faith?—

6 just as Abraham [a]*"believed God, and it was accounted to him for righteousness."*

7 Therefore know that *only* [a]those who are of faith are sons of Abraham.

8 And [a]the Scripture, foreseeing that God would justify the Gentiles by faith, preached the gospel to Abraham beforehand, *saying,* [b]*"In you all the nations shall be blessed."*

9 So then those who *are* of faith are blessed with believing Abraham.

**10** For as many as are of the works of the law are under the curse; for it is written, [a]*"Cursed is everyone who does not continue in all things which are written in the book of the law, to do them."*

11 But that no one is [1]justified by the law in the sight of God *is* evident, for [a]*"the just shall live by faith."*

12 Yet [a]the law is not of faith, but [b]*"the man who does them shall live by them."*

13 [a]Christ has redeemed us from the curse of the law, having become a curse for us (for it is written, [b]*"Cursed is everyone who hangs on a tree"*),

14 [a]that the blessing of Abraham might come upon the [b]Gentiles in Christ Jesus, that we might receive [c]the promise of the Spirit through faith.

**15** Brethren, I speak in the manner of men: [a]Though *it is* only a man's covenant, yet *if it is* confirmed, no one annuls or adds to it.

16 Now to Abraham and his Seed were the promises made. He does not say, "And to seeds," as of many, but as of [a]one, [b]*"And to your Seed,"* who is [c]Christ.

17 And this I say, *that* the law, [a]which was four hundred and thirty years later, cannot annul the covenant that was confirmed before by God [1]in Christ, [b]that it should make the promise of no effect.

18 For if [a]the inheritance *is* of the law, [b]*it is* no longer of promise; but God gave *it* to Abraham by promise.

**19** What purpose then *does* the law *serve?* [a]It was added because of transgressions, till the [b]Seed should come to whom the promise was made; *and it was* [c]appointed through angels by the hand [d]of a mediator.

20 Now a mediator does not *mediate* for one *only,* [a]but God is one.

21 *Is* the law then against the promises of God? Certainly not! For if there had been a law given which could have given life, truly righteousness would have been by the law.

22 But the Scripture has confined [a]all under sin, [b]that the promise by faith in Jesus Christ might be given to those who believe.

23 But before faith came, we were kept under guard by the law, [1]kept for the faith which would afterward be revealed.

24 Therefore [a]the law was our [1]tutor *to bring us* to Christ, [b]that we might be justified by faith.

25 But after faith has come, we are no longer under a tutor.

**26** For you [a]are all sons of God through faith in Christ Jesus.

27 For [a]as many of you as were baptized into Christ [b]have put on Christ.

28 [a]There is neither Jew nor Greek, [b]there is neither slave nor free, there is neither male nor female; for you are all [c]one in Christ Jesus.

29 And [a]if you *are* Christ's, then you are Abraham's [b]seed, and [c]heirs according to the promise.

### *Sons and Heirs Through Christ*

4 Now I say *that* the heir, as long as he is a child, does not differ at all from a slave, though he is master of all,

2 but is under guardians and stewards until the time appointed by the father.

3 Even so we, when we were children, [a]were in bondage under the elements of the world.

4 But [a]when the fullness of the time had come, God sent forth His Son, [b]born[1] [c]of a woman, [d]born under the law,

5 [a]to redeem those who were under the law, [b]that we might receive the adoption as sons.

6 And because you are sons, God has sent forth [a]the Spirit of His Son into your hearts, crying out, [1]"Abba, Father!"

7 Therefore you are no longer a slave but a son, [a]and if a son, then an heir [1]of God [2]through Christ.

**8** But then, indeed, [a]when you did not know God, [b]you served those which by nature are not gods.

9 But now [a]after you have known God, or rather are known by God, [b]how *is it that* you turn again to [c]the weak and beggarly elements, to which you desire again to be in bondage?

10 [a]You observe days and months and seasons and years.

11 I am afraid for you, [a]lest I have labored for you in vain.

12 Brethren, I urge you to become like me, for I *became* like you. [a]You have not injured me at all.

13 You know that [a]because of physical infirmity I preached the gospel to you at the first.

14 And my trial which was in my flesh you did not despise or reject, but you received me [a]as an [1]angel of God, [b]*even* as Christ Jesus.

---

**19** [a]Rom. 8:2 [b][Rom. 6:2, 14; 7:4] [c][Rom. 6:11]
**20** [a][Rom. 6:6] [b]2 Cor. 5:15 [c]Eph. 5:2
**21** [a]Heb. 7:11 [1]*for nothing*

CHAPTER 3
**1** [1]NU omits *that you should not obey the truth* [2]NU omits *among you*
**2** [a]Rom. 10:16, 17
**3** [a][Gal. 4:9] [b]Heb. 7:16
**4** [a]Heb. 10:35 [1]Or *great*
**6** [a]Gen. 15:6
**7** [a]John 8:39
**8** [a]Rom. 9:17 [b]Gen. 12:3; 18:18; 22:18; 26:4; 28:14
**10** [a]Deut. 27:26
**11** [a]Hab. 2:4 [1]*declared righteous*
**12** [a]Rom. 4:4, 5 [b]Lev. 18:5
**13** [a][Rom. 8:3] [b]Deut. 21:23
**14** [a][Rom. 4:1–5, 9, 16] [b]Rom. 3:29, 30 [c]Is. 32:15
**15** [a]Heb. 9:17
**16** [a]Gen. 22:18 [b]Gen. 12:3, 7; 13:15; 24:7 [c][1 Cor. 12:12]
**17** [a]Ex. 12:40 [b][Rom. 4:13] [1]NU omits *in Christ*
**18** [a][Rom. 8:17] [b]Rom. 4:14
**19** [a]John 15:22 [b]Gal. 4:4 [c]Acts 7:53 [d]Ex. 20:19
**20** [a][Rom. 3:29]
**22** [a]Rom. 11:32 [b]Rom. 4:11
**23** [1]Lit. *confined*
**24** [a]Rom. 10:4 [b]Acts 13:39 [1]In a household, the guardian responsible for the care and discipline of the children
**26** [a]John 1:12
**27** [a][Rom. 6:3] [b]Rom. 10:12; 13:14
**28** [a]Col. 3:11 [b][1 Cor. 12:13] [c][Eph. 2:15, 16]
**29** [a]Gen. 21:10 [b]Rom. 4:11 [c]Rom. 8:17

CHAPTER 4
**3** [a]Col. 2:8, 20
**4** [a][Gen. 49:10] [b][John 1:14] [c]Gen. 3:15 [d]Luke 2:21, 27 [1]Or *made*
**5** [a][Matt. 20:28] [b][John 1:12]
**6** [a][Rom. 5:5; 8:9, 15, 16] [1]Lit., in Aram., *Father*
**7** [a][Rom. 8:16, 17] [1]NU *through God* [2]NU omits *through Christ*
**8** [a]Eph. 2:12 [b]Rom. 1:25
**9** [a][1 Cor. 8:3] [b]Col. 2:20 [c]Heb. 7:18
**10** [a]Rom. 14:5
**11** [a]1 Thess. 3:5
**12** [a]2 Cor. 2:5
**13** [a]1 Cor. 2:3
**14** [a]Mal. 2:7 [b][Luke 10:16] [1]Or *messenger*

15 [1]What then was the blessing you *enjoyed?* For
I bear you witness that, if possible, you would
have plucked out your own eyes and given them
to me.
16 Have I therefore become your enemy because
I tell you the truth?
17 They [a]zealously court you, *but* for no good;
yes, they want to exclude you, that you may be
zealous for them.
18 But it is good to be zealous in a good thing
always, and not only when I am present with you.
19 [a]My little children, for whom I labor in birth
again until Christ is formed in you,
20 I would like to be present with you now and to
change my tone; for I have doubts about you.
**21** Tell me, you who desire to be under the law,
do you not hear the law?
22 For it is written that Abraham had two sons:
[a]the one by a bondwoman, [b]the other by a freewoman.
23 But he *who was* of the bondwoman [a]was born
according to the flesh, [b]and he of the freewoman
through promise,
24 which things are symbolic. For these are [1]the
two covenants: the one from Mount [a]Sinai which
gives birth to bondage, which is Hagar—
25 for this Hagar is Mount Sinai in Arabia, and
corresponds to Jerusalem which now is, and is in
bondage with her children—
26 but the [a]Jerusalem above is free, which is the
mother of us all.
27 For it is written:

[a]*"Rejoice, O barren,*
*You who do not bear!*
*Break forth and shout,*
*You who are not in labor!*
*For the desolate has many more children*
*Than she who has a husband."*

28 Now [a]we, brethren, as Isaac *was,* are [b]children
of promise.
29 But, as [a]he who was born according to the
flesh then persecuted him *who was born* according to the Spirit, [b]even so *it is* now.
30 Nevertheless what does [a]the Scripture say?
[b]*"Cast out the bondwoman and her son, for* [c]*the*
*son of the bondwoman shall not be heir with the*
*son of the freewoman."*
31 So then, brethren, we are not children of the
bondwoman but of the free.

## *The Works of the Flesh and of the Spirit*

**5** Stand[a1] fast therefore in the liberty by which
Christ has made us free, and do not be entangled again with a [b]yoke of bondage.
2 Indeed I, Paul, say to you that [a]if you become
circumcised, Christ will profit you nothing.
3 And I testify again to every man who becomes
circumcised [a]that he is [1]a debtor to keep the whole
law.
4 [a]You have become estranged from Christ, you
who *attempt to* be justified by law; [b]you have
fallen from grace.
5 For we through the Spirit eagerly [a]wait for the
hope of righteousness by faith.
6 For [a]in Christ Jesus neither circumcision nor
uncircumcision avails anything, but [b]faith working through love.
**7** You [a]ran well. Who hindered you from obeying the truth?
8 This persuasion does not *come* from Him who
calls you.
9 [a]A little leaven leavens the whole lump.
10 I have confidence in you, in the Lord, that you
will have no other mind; but he who troubles you
shall bear his judgment, whoever he is.
11 And I, brethren, if I still preach circumcision,
[a]why do I still suffer persecution? Then [b]the
offense of the cross has ceased.
12 [a]I could wish that those [b]who trouble you
would even [1]cut themselves off!
13 For you, brethren, have been called to liberty;
only [a]do not *use* liberty as an [b]opportunity for the
flesh, but [c]through love serve one another.
14 For [a]all the law is fulfilled in one word, *even* in
this: [b]*"You shall love your neighbor as yourself."*
15 But if you bite and devour one another, beware lest you be consumed by one another!
**16** I say then: [a]Walk in the Spirit, and you shall
not fulfill the lust of the flesh.
17 For [a]the flesh lusts against the Spirit, and the
Spirit against the flesh; and these are contrary to
one another, [b]so that you do not do the things that
you wish.
18 But [a]if you are led by the Spirit, you are not
under the law.
19 Now [a]the works of the flesh are evident, which
are: [1]adultery, [2]fornication, uncleanness, lewdness,
20 idolatry, sorcery, hatred, contentions, jealousies, outbursts of wrath, selfish ambitions, dissensions, heresies,
21 envy, [1]murders, drunkenness, revelries, and
the like; of which I tell you beforehand, just as I
also told *you* in time past, that [a]those who practice
such things will not inherit the kingdom of God.
22 But [a]the fruit of the Spirit is [b]love, joy, peace,
longsuffering, kindness, [c]goodness, [d]faithfulness,
23 [1]gentleness, self-control. [a]Against such there is
no law.
24 And those *who are* Christ's [a]have crucified the
flesh with its passions and desires.
25 [a]If we live in the Spirit, let us also walk in the
Spirit.
26 [a]Let us not become conceited, provoking one
another, envying one another.

## *Bear and Share Burdens*

**6** Brethren, if a man is [1]overtaken in any trespass, you who *are* spiritual restore such a one
in a spirit of [a]gentleness, considering yourself lest
you also be tempted.
2 [a]Bear one another's burdens, and so fulfill [b]the
law of Christ.
3 For [a]if anyone thinks himself to be something,
when [b]he is nothing, he deceives himself.
4 But [a]let each one examine his own work, and
then he will have rejoicing in himself alone, and
[b]not in another.
5 For [a]each one shall bear his own load.
**6** [a]Let him who is taught the word share in all
good things with him who teaches.
7 Do not be deceived, God is not mocked; for
[a]whatever a man sows, that he will also reap.
8 For he who sows to his flesh will of the flesh
reap corruption, but he who sows to the Spirit will
of the Spirit reap [a]everlasting life.
9 And [a]let us not grow weary while doing good,
for in due season we shall reap [b]if we do not lose
heart.

**15** [1]NU *Where*
**17** [a]Rom. 10:2
**19** [a]1 Cor. 4:15
**22** [a]Gen. 16:15 [b]Gen. 21:2
**23** [a]Rom. 9:7, 8 [b]Heb. 11:11
**24** [a]Deut. 33:2 [1]NU, M omit *the*
**26** [a][Is. 2:2]
**27** [a]Is. 54:1
**28** [a]Gal. 3:29 [b]Acts 3:25
**29** [a]Gen. 21:9 [b]Gal. 5:11
**30** [a][Gal. 3:8, 22] [b]Gen. 21:10, 12 [c][John 8:35]

CHAPTER 5
**1** [a]Phil. 4:1 [b]Acts 15:10 [1]NU *For freedom Christ has made us free; stand fast therefore, and*
**2** [a]Acts 15:1
**3** [a][Rom. 2:25] [1]*obligated*
**4** [a][Rom. 9:31] [b]Heb. 12:15
**5** [a]Rom. 8:24
**6** [a][Gal. 6:15] [b]1 Thess. 1:3
**7** [a]1 Cor. 9:24
**9** [a]1 Cor. 5:6
**11** [a]1 Cor. 15:30 [b][1 Cor. 1:23]
**12** [a]Josh. 7:25 [b]Acts 15:1, 2 [1]*mutilate themselves*
**13** [a]1 Cor. 8:9 [b]1 Pet. 2:16 [c]1 Cor. 9:19
**14** [a]Matt. 7:12; 22:40 [b]Lev. 19:18
**16** [a]Rom. 6:12
**17** [a]Rom. 7:18, 22, 23; 8:5 [b]Rom. 7:15
**18** [a][Rom. 6:14; 7:4; 8:14]
**19** [a]Eph. 5:3, 11 [1]NU omits *adultery* [2]*sexual immorality*
**21** [a]1 Cor. 6:9, 10 [1]NU omits *murders*
**22** [a][John 15:2] [b][Col. 3:12–15] [c]Rom. 15:14 [d]1 Cor. 13:7
**23** [a]1 Tim. 1:9 [1]*meekness*
**24** [a]Rom. 6:6
**25** [a][Rom. 8:4, 5]
**26** [a]Phil. 2:3

CHAPTER 6
**1** [a]Eph. 4:2 [1]*caught*
**2** [a]Rom. 15:1 [b][James 2:8]
**3** [a]Rom. 12:3 [b][2 Cor. 3:5]
**4** [a]1 Cor. 11:28 [b]Luke 18:11
**5** [a][Rom. 2:6]
**6** [a]1 Cor. 9:11, 14
**7** [a][Rom. 2:6]
**8** [a][Rom. 6:8]
**9** [a]1 Cor. 15:58 [b][James 5:7, 8]

10 [a]Therefore, as we have opportunity, [b]let us do
good to all, [c]especially to those who are of the
household of faith.
11 See with what large letters I have written to
you with my own hand!
12 As many as desire to make a good showing in
the flesh, these *would* compel you to be circumcised, [a]only that they may not suffer persecution
for the cross of Christ.
13 For not even those who are circumcised keep
the law, but they desire to have you circumcised
that they may boast in your flesh.
14 But God forbid that I should boast except in
the [a]cross of our Lord Jesus Christ, by [1]whom the
world has been crucified to me, and [b]I to the
world.
15 For [a]in Christ Jesus neither circumcision nor
uncircumcision avails anything, but a new creation.
16 And as many as walk according to this rule,
peace and mercy *be* upon them, and upon the
Israel of God.
17 From now on let no one trouble me, for I bear
in my body the marks of the Lord Jesus.
18 Brethren, the grace of our Lord Jesus Christ
*be* with your spirit. Amen.

10 [a]Prov. 3:27 [b]Titus 3:8 [c]Rom. 12:13
12 [a]Gal. 5:11
14 [a][1 Cor. 1:18] [b]Col. 2:20 [1]Or *which,* the cross
15 [a]1 Cor. 7:19

*The Epistle of Paul the Apostle to the*

# EPHESIANS

## *Redemption in Christ*

PAUL, an apostle of Jesus Christ by the will of
God,
To the saints who are in Ephesus, and faithful
in Christ Jesus:
2 Grace to you and peace from God our Father
and the Lord Jesus Christ.
3 [a]Blessed *be* the God and Father of our Lord
Jesus Christ, who has blessed us with every
spiritual blessing in the heavenly *places* in Christ,
4 just as [a]He chose us in Him [b]before the foundation of the world, that we should [c]be holy and
without blame before Him in love,
5 [a]having predestined us to [b]adoption as sons by
Jesus Christ to Himself, [c]according to the good
pleasure of His will,
6 to the praise of the glory of His grace, [a]by
which He [1]made us accepted in [b]the Beloved.
7 [a]In Him we have redemption through His
blood, the forgiveness of sins, according to [b]the
riches of His grace
8 which He made to abound toward us in all
wisdom and [1]prudence,
9 [a]having made known to us the mystery of His
will, according to His good pleasure [b]which He
purposed in Himself,
10 that in the dispensation of [a]the fullness of the
times [b]He might gather together in one [c]all things
in Christ, [1]both which are in heaven and which
are on earth—in Him.
11 [a]In Him also we have obtained an inheritance,
being predestined according to [b]the purpose of
Him who works all things according to the counsel of His will,
12 [a]that we [b]who first trusted in Christ should be
to the praise of His glory.
13 In Him you also *trusted,* after you heard [a]the
word of truth, the gospel of your salvation; in
whom also, having believed, [b]you were sealed
with the Holy Spirit of promise,
14 [a]who[1] is the [2]guarantee of our inheritance
[b]until the redemption of [c]the purchased possession, [d]to the praise of His glory.
15 Therefore I also, [a]after I heard of your faith in
the Lord Jesus and your love for all the saints,
16 [a]do not cease to give thanks for you, making
mention of you in my prayers:
17 that [a]the God of our Lord Jesus Christ, the
Father of glory, [b]may give to you the spirit of
wisdom and revelation in the knowledge of Him,
18 [a]the eyes of your [1]understanding being enlightened; that you may know what is [b]the hope of
His calling, what are the riches of the glory of His
inheritance in the saints,
19 and what *is* the exceeding greatness of His
power toward us who believe, [a]according to the
working of His mighty power
20 which He worked in Christ when [a]He raised
Him from the dead and [b]seated *Him* at His right
hand in the heavenly *places,*
21 [a]far above all [b]principality[1] and [2]power and
[3]might and dominion, and every name that is
named, not only in this age but also in that which
is to come.
22 And [a]He put all *things* under His feet, and
gave Him [b]*to be* head over all *things* to the
church,
23 [a]which is His body, [b]the fullness of Him [c]who
fills all in all.

## *Salvation by Grace Through Faith in Christ*

2 And [a]you *He made alive,* [b]who were dead in
trespasses and sins,
2 [a]in which you once walked according to the
[1]course of this world, according to [b]the prince of
the power of the air, the spirit who now works in
[c]the sons of disobedience,
3 [a]among whom also we all once conducted
ourselves in [b]the lusts of our flesh, fulfilling the
desires of the flesh and of the mind, and [c]were by
nature children of wrath, just as the others.
4 But God, [a]who is rich in mercy, because of His
[b]great love with which He loved us,
5 [a]even when we were dead in trespasses, [b]made
us alive together with Christ (by grace you have
been saved),
6 and raised *us* up together, and made *us* sit
together [a]in the heavenly *places* in Christ Jesus,
7 that in the ages to come He might show the

CHAPTER 1
3 [a]2 Cor. 1:3
4 [a]Rom. 8:28 [b]1 Pet. 1:2 [c]Luke 1:75
5 [a][Rom. 8:29] [b]John 1:12 [c][1 Cor. 1:21]
6 [a][Rom. 3:24] [b]Matt. 3:17 [1]Lit. *bestowed grace (favor) upon us*
7 [a][Heb. 9:12] [b][Rom. 3:24, 25]
8 [1]*understanding*
9 [a][Rom. 16:25] [b][2 Tim. 1:9]
10 [a]Gal. 4:4 [b]1 Cor. 3:22 [c][Col. 1:16, 20] [1]NU, M omit *both*
11 [a]Rom. 8:17 [b]Is. 46:10
12 [a]2 Thess. 2:13 [b]James 1:18
13 [a]John 1:17 [b][2 Cor. 1:22]
14 [a]2 Cor. 5:5 [b]Rom. 8:23 [c][Acts 20:28] [d]1 Pet. 2:9 [1]NU *which* [2]*down payment, earnest*
15 [a]Col. 1:4
16 [a]Rom. 1:9
17 [a]John 20:17 [b]Col. 1:9
18 [a]Acts 26:18 [b]Eph. 2:12 [1]NU, M *hearts*
19 [a]Col. 2:12
20 [a]Acts 2:24 [b]Ps. 110:1
21 [a]Phil. 2:9, 10 [b][Rom. 8:38, 39] [1]*rule* [2]*authority* [3]*power*
22 [a]Ps. 8:6; 110:1 [b]Heb. 2:7
23 [a]Rom. 12:5 [b]Col. 2:9 [c][1 Cor. 12:6]

CHAPTER 2
1 [a]Col. 2:13 [b]Eph. 4:18
2 [a]Col. 1:21 [b]Eph. 6:12 [c]Col. 3:6 [1]Gr. *aion,* aeon
3 [a]1 Pet. 4:3 [b]Gal. 5:16 [c][Ps. 51:5]
4 [a]Rom. 10:12 [b]John 3:16
5 [a]Rom. 5:6, 8 [b][Rom. 6:4, 5]
6 [a]Eph. 1:20

exceeding riches of His grace in [a]His kindness
toward us in Christ Jesus.
8 [a]For by grace you have been saved [b]through
faith, and that not of yourselves; [c]*it is* the gift of
God,
9 not of [a]works, lest anyone should [b]boast.
10 For we are [a]His workmanship, created in
Christ Jesus for good works, which God prepared
beforehand that we should walk in them.
**11** Therefore remember that you, once Gentiles
in the flesh—who are called Uncircumcision by
what is called [a]the Circumcision made in the flesh
by hands—
12 that at that time you were without Christ,
being aliens from the commonwealth of Israel and
strangers from the covenants of promise, having
no hope and without God in the world.
13 But now in Christ Jesus you who once were
far off have been brought near by the blood of
Christ.
**14** For He Himself is our peace, who has made
both one, and has broken down the middle wall of
separation,
15 having abolished in His flesh the enmity, *that
is,* the law of commandments *contained* in ordinances, so as to create in Himself one [a]new man
*from* the two, *thus* making peace,
16 and that He might [a]reconcile them both to
God in one body through the cross, thereby [b]put-
ting to death the enmity.
17 And He came and preached peace to you who
were afar off and to those who were near.
18 For [a]through Him we both have access [b]by one
Spirit to the Father.
**19** Now, therefore, you are no longer strangers
and foreigners, but fellow citizens with the saints
and members of the household of God,
20 having been [a]built [b]on the foundation of the
[c]apostles and prophets, Jesus Christ Himself being
[d]the chief corner*stone,*
21 in whom the whole building, being fitted together, grows into [a]a holy temple in the Lord,
22 [a]in whom you also are being built together for
a [b]dwelling place of God in the Spirit.

### *The Gentiles Are Fellow Heirs*

**3** For this reason I, Paul, the prisoner of Christ
Jesus for you Gentiles—
2 if indeed you have heard of the [1]dispensation
of the grace of God [a]which was given to me for
you,
3 [a]how that by revelation [b]He made known to
me the mystery (as I have briefly written already,
4 by which, when you read, you may understand my knowledge in the mystery of Christ),
5 which in other ages was not made known to
the sons of men, as it has now been revealed by
the Spirit to His holy apostles and prophets:
6 that the Gentiles [a]should be fellow heirs, of the
same body, and partakers of His promise in Christ
through the gospel,
7 [a]of which I became a minister [b]according to
the gift of the grace of God given to me by [c]the
effective working of His power.
**8** To me, [a]who am less than the least of all the
saints, this grace was given, that I should preach
among the Gentiles [b]the unsearchable riches of
Christ,
9 and to make all see what *is* the [1]fellowship of
the mystery, which from the beginning of the ages
has been hidden in God who [a]created all things
[2]through Jesus Christ;
10 [a]to the intent that now [b]the [1]manifold wisdom
of God might be made known by the church [c]to
the [2]principalities and powers in the heavenly
*places,*
11 [a]according to the eternal purpose which He
accomplished in Christ Jesus our Lord,
12 in whom we have boldness and access [a]with
confidence through faith in Him.
13 [a]Therefore I ask that you do not lose heart at
my tribulations for you, [b]which is your glory.
**14** For this reason I bow my knees to the [a]Father
[1]of our Lord Jesus Christ,
15 from whom the whole family in heaven and
earth is named,
16 that He would grant you, [a]according to the
riches of His glory, [b]to be strengthened with might
through His Spirit in [c]the inner man,
17 [a]that Christ may dwell in your hearts through
faith; that you, [b]being rooted and grounded in
love,
18 [a]may be able to comprehend with all the saints
[b]what *is* the width and length and depth and
height—
19 to know the love of Christ which passes
knowledge; that you may be filled [a]with all the
fullness of God.
20 Now [a]to Him who is able to do exceedingly
abundantly [b]above all that we ask or think, [c]ac-
cording to the power that works in us,
21 [a]to Him *be* glory in the church by Christ Jesus
to all generations, forever and ever. Amen.

### *One Church, Many Parts*

**4** I, therefore, the prisoner [1]of the Lord, [2]beseech
you to [a]walk worthy of the calling with which
you were called,
2 with all lowliness and gentleness, with longsuffering, bearing with one another in love,
3 endeavoring to keep the unity of the Spirit [a]in
the bond of peace.
4 [a]*There is* one body and one Spirit, just as you
were called in one hope of your calling;
5 [a]one Lord, [b]one faith, [c]one baptism;
6 [a]one God and Father of all, who *is* above all,
and [b]through all, and in [1]you all.
**7** But [a]to each one of us grace was given according to the measure of Christ's gift.
8 Therefore He says:

[a]*"When He ascended on high,*
*He led captivity captive,*
*And gave gifts to men."*

9 [a](Now this, *"He ascended"*—what does it
mean but that He also [1]first descended into the
lower parts of the earth?
10 He who descended is also the One [a]who ascended far above all the heavens, [b]that He might
fill all things.)
11 And He Himself gave some *to be* apostles,
some prophets, some evangelists, and some pastors and teachers,
12 for the equipping of the saints for the work of
ministry, [a]for the [1]edifying of [b]the body of Christ,
13 till we all come to the unity of the faith [a]and of
the knowledge of the Son of God, to [b]a perfect
man, to the measure of the stature of the fullness
of Christ;
14 that we should no longer be [a]children, tossed
to and fro and carried about with every wind of

**7** [a]Titus 3:4
**8** [a][2 Tim. 1:9] [b]Rom. 4:16 [c][John 1:12, 13]
**9** [a]Rom. 4:4, 5; 11:6 [b]Rom. 3:27
**10** [a]Is. 19:25
**11** [a][Col. 2:11]
**15** [a]Gal. 6:15
**16** [a][Col. 1:20–22] [b][Rom. 6:6]
**18** [a]John 10:9 [b]1 Cor. 12:13
**20** [a]1 Pet. 2:4 [b]Matt. 16:18 [c]1 Cor. 12:28 [d]Ps. 118:22
**21** [a]1 Cor. 3:16, 17
**22** [a]1 Pet. 2:5 [b]John 17:23

CHAPTER 3
**2** [a]Acts 9:15 [1]*stewardship*
**3** [a]Acts 22:17, 21; 26:16 [b][Rom. 11:25; 16:25]
**6** [a]Gal. 3:28, 29
**7** [a]Rom. 15:16 [b]Rom. 1:5 [c]Rom. 15:18
**8** [a][1 Cor. 15:9] [b][Col. 1:27; 2:2, 3]
**9** [a]Heb. 1:2 [1]NU, M *stewardship (dispensation)* [2]NU omits *through Jesus Christ*
**10** [a]1 Pet. 1:12 [b][1 Tim. 3:16] [c]Col. 1:16; 2:10, 15 [1]*variegated* or *many-sided* [2]*rulers*
**11** [a][Eph. 1:4, 11]
**12** [a]Heb. 4:16; 10:19, 35
**13** [a]Phil. 1:14 [b]2 Cor. 1:6
**14** [a]Eph. 1:3 [1]NU omits *of our Lord Jesus Christ*
**16** [a][Phil. 4:19] [b]Col. 1:11 [c]Rom. 7:22
**17** [a]John 14:23 [b]Col. 1:23
**18** [a]Eph. 1:18 [b]Rom. 8:39
**19** [a]Eph. 1:23
**20** [a]Rom. 16:25 [b]1 Cor. 2:9 [c]Col. 1:29
**21** [a]Rom. 11:36

CHAPTER 4
**1** [a]1 Thess. 2:12 [1]Lit. *in* [2]*exhort, encourage*
**3** [a]Col. 3:14
**4** [a]Rom. 12:5
**5** [a]1 Cor. 1:13 [b]Jude 3 [c][Heb. 6:6]
**6** [a]Mal. 2:10 [b]Rom. 11:36 [1]NU omits *you;* M *us*
**7** [a][1 Cor. 12:7, 11]
**8** [a]Ps. 68:18
**9** [a]John 3:13; 20:17 [1]NU omits *first*
**10** [a]Acts 1:9 [b][Eph. 1:23]
**12** [a]1 Cor. 14:26 [b]Col. 1:24 [1]*building up*
**13** [a]Col. 2:2 [b]1 Cor. 14:20

**14** [a]1 Cor. 14:20

doctrine, by the trickery of men, in the cunning
craftiness of [b]deceitful plotting,
15 but, speaking the truth in love, may grow up
in all things into Him who is the [a]head—Christ—
16 [a]from whom the whole body, joined and knit
together by what every joint supplies, according
to the effective working by which every part does
its share, causes growth of the body for the
edifying of itself in love.
**17** This I say, therefore, and testify in the Lord,
that you should [a]no longer walk as [1]the rest of the
Gentiles walk, in the futility of their mind,
18 having their understanding darkened, being
alienated from the life of God, because of the
ignorance that is in them, because of the [a]blind-
ness of their heart;
19 [a]who, being past feeling, [b]have given themselves over to lewdness, to work all uncleanness
with greediness.
20 But you have not so learned Christ,
21 if indeed you have heard Him and have been
taught by Him, as the truth is in Jesus:
22 that you [a]put off, concerning your former
conduct, the old man which grows corrupt according to the deceitful lusts,
23 and [a]be renewed in the spirit of your mind,
24 and that you [a]put on the new man which was
created according to God, in true righteousness
and holiness.
**25** Therefore, putting away lying, [a]*"Let each one
of you speak truth with his neighbor,"* for [b]we are
members of one another.
26 [a]*"Be angry, and do not sin"*: do not let the sun
go down on your wrath,
27 [a]nor give [1]place to the devil.
28 Let him who stole steal no longer, but rather
[a]let him labor, working with *his* hands what is
good, that he may have something [b]to give him
who has need.
29 [a]Let no corrupt word proceed out of your
mouth, but [b]what is good for necessary [1]edifica-
tion, [c]that it may impart grace to the hearers.
30 And [a]do not grieve the Holy Spirit of God, by
whom you were sealed for the day of redemption.
31 [a]Let all bitterness, wrath, anger, [1]clamor, and
[b]evil speaking be put away from you, [c]with all
malice.
32 And [a]be kind to one another, tenderhearted,
[b]forgiving one another, even as God in Christ
forgave you.

### *Walk in Love, Light, and Wisdom*

**5** Therefore[a] be imitators of God as dear [b]chil-
dren.
2 And [a]walk in love, [b]as Christ also has loved us
and given Himself for us, an offering and a sacrifice to God [c]for a sweet-smelling aroma.
3 But fornication and all [a]uncleanness or [b]covet-
ousness, let it not even be named among you, as is
fitting for saints;
4 [a]neither filthiness, nor [b]foolish talking, nor
coarse jesting, [c]which are not fitting, but rather
[d]giving of thanks.
5 For [1]this you know, that no fornicator, unclean person, nor covetous man, who is an idolater, has any [a]inheritance in the kingdom of
Christ and God.
6 Let no one deceive you with empty words, for
because of these things the wrath of God comes
upon the sons of disobedience.
7 Therefore do not be [a]partakers with them.
8 For you were once darkness, but now *you are*
[a]light in the Lord. Walk as children of light
9 (for [a]the fruit of the [1]Spirit *is* in all goodness,
righteousness, and truth),
10 [a]finding out what is acceptable to the Lord.
11 And have [a]no fellowship with the unfruitful
works of darkness, but rather [1]expose *them.*
12 [a]For it is shameful even to speak of those
things which are done by them in secret.
13 But [a]all things that are [1]exposed are made
manifest by the light, for whatever makes manifest is light.
14 Therefore He says:

[a]"Awake, you who sleep,
Arise from the dead,
And Christ will give you light."

**15** [a]See then that you walk [1]circumspectly, not as
fools but as wise,
16 [a]redeeming the time, [b]because the days are
evil.
17 [a]Therefore do not be unwise, but [b]understand
[c]what the will of the Lord *is.*
18 And [a]do not be drunk with wine, in which is
dissipation; but be filled with the Spirit,
19 speaking to one another [a]in psalms and hymns
and spiritual songs, singing and making [b]melody
in your heart to the Lord,
20 [a]giving thanks always for all things to God the
Father [b]in the name of our Lord Jesus Christ,
21 [a]submitting to one another in the fear of [1]God.
**22** Wives, [a]submit to your own husbands, as to
the Lord.
23 For [a]the husband is head of the wife, as also
[b]Christ is head of the church; and He is the Savior
of the body.
24 Therefore, just as the church is subject to
Christ, so *let* the wives *be* to their own husbands
[a]in everything.
25 [a]Husbands, love your wives, just as Christ also
loved the church and [b]gave Himself for her,
26 that He might [1]sanctify and cleanse her [a]with
the washing of water [b]by the word,
27 [a]that He might present her to Himself a glorious church, [b]not having spot or wrinkle or any
such thing, but that she should be holy and
without blemish.
28 So husbands ought to love their own wives as
their own bodies; he who loves his wife loves
himself.
29 For no one ever hated his own flesh, but
nourishes and cherishes it, just as the Lord *does*
the church.
30 For [a]we are members of His body, [1]of His flesh
and of His bones.
31 [a]*"For this reason a man shall leave his father
and mother and be joined to his wife, and the* [b]*two
shall become one flesh."*
32 This is a great mystery, but I speak concerning Christ and the church.
33 Nevertheless [a]let each one of you in particular
so love his own wife as himself, and let the wife
*see* that she [b]respects *her* husband.

### *Family Responsibilities; the Christian's Armor*

**6** Children, [a]obey your parents in the Lord, for
this is right.
2 [a]*"Honor your father and mother,"* which is
the first commandment with promise:

**14** [b]Rom. 16:18 **15** [a]Eph. 1:22 **16** [a]Col. 2:19 **17** [a]Eph. 2:2; 4:22 [1]NU omits *the rest of* **18** [a]Rom. 1:21 **19** [a]1 Tim. 4:2 [b]1 Pet. 4:3 **22** [a]Col. 3:8 **23** [a][Rom. 12:2] **24** [a][Rom. 6:4; 7:6; 12:2] **25** [a]Zech. 8:16 [b]Rom. 12:5 **26** [a]Ps. 4:4; 37:8 **27** [a][Rom. 12:19] [1]*an opportunity* **28** [a]Acts 20:35 [b]Luke 3:11 **29** [a]Col. 3:8 [b]1 Thess. 5:11 [c]Col. 3:16 [1]*building up* **30** [a]Is. 7:13 **31** [a]Col. 3:8, 19 [b]James 4:11 [c]Titus 3:3 [1]*loud quarreling* **32** [a]2 Cor. 6:10 [b][Mark 11:25]

CHAPTER 5

**1** [a]Luke 6:36 [b]1 Pet. 1:14–16 **2** [a]1 Thess. 4:9 [b]Gal. 1:4 [c]2 Cor. 2:14, 15 **3** [a]Col. 3:5–7 [b][Luke 12:15] **4** [a]Matt. 12:34, 35 [b]Titus 3:9 [c]Rom. 1:28 [d]Phil. 4:6 **5** [a]1 Cor. 6:9, 10 [1]NU *know this* **7** [a]1 Tim. 5:22 **8** [a]1 Thess. 5:5 **9** [a]Gal. 5:22 [1]NU *light* **10** [a][Rom. 12:1, 2] **11** [a]2 Cor. 6:14 [1]*reprove* **12** [a]Rom. 1:24 **13** [a][John 3:20, 21] [1]*reproved* **14** [a][Is. 26:19; 60:1] **15** [a]Col. 4:5 [1]*carefully* **16** [a]Col. 4:5 [b]Eccl. 11:2 **17** [a]Col. 4:5 [b][Rom. 12:2] [c]1 Thess. 4:3 **18** [a]Prov. 20:1; 23:31 **19** [a]Acts 16:25 [b]James 5:13 **20** [a]Ps. 34:1 [b][1 Pet. 2:5] **21** [a][Phil. 2:3] [1]NU *Christ* **22** [a]Col. 3:18—4:1 **23** [a][1 Cor. 11:3] [b]Col. 1:18 **24** [a]Titus 2:4, 5 **25** [a]Col. 3:19 [b]Acts 20:28 **26** [a]John 3:5 [b][John 15:3; 17:17] [1]*set it apart* **27** [a]Col. 1:22 [b]Song 4:7 **30** [a]Gen. 2:23 [1]NU omits the rest of v. 30. **31** [a]Gen. 2:24 [b][1 Cor. 6:16] **33** [a]Col. 3:19 [b]1 Pet. 3:1, 6

CHAPTER 6

**1** [a]Col. 3:20 **2** [a]Deut. 5:16

3 *"that it may be well with you and you may live long on the earth."*
4 And [a]you, fathers, do not provoke your children to wrath, but [b]bring them up in the training and admonition of the Lord.
**5** [a]Bondservants, be obedient to those who are your masters according to the flesh, [b]with fear and trembling, [c]in sincerity of heart, as to Christ;
6 [a]not with eyeservice, as men-pleasers, but as bondservants of Christ, doing the will of God from the heart,
7 with good will doing service, as to the Lord, and not to men,
8 [a]knowing that whatever good anyone does, he will receive the same from the Lord, whether *he is* a slave or free.
9 And you, masters, do the same things to them, giving up threatening, knowing that [1]your own [a]Master also is in heaven, and [b]there is no partiality with Him.
**10** Finally, my brethren, be strong in the Lord and in the power of His might.
11 [a]Put on the whole armor of God, that you may be able to stand against the [1]wiles of the devil.
12 For we do not wrestle against flesh and blood, but against [a]principalities, against powers, against [b]the rulers of [1]the darkness of this age, against spiritual *hosts* of wickedness in the heavenly *places.*
13 [a]Therefore take up the whole armor of God, that you may be able to withstand [b]in the evil day, and having done all, to stand.
14 Stand therefore, [a]having girded your waist with truth, [b]having put on the breastplate of righteousness,
15 [a]and having shod your feet with the preparation of the gospel of peace;
16 above all, taking [a]the shield of faith with which you will be able to quench all the fiery darts of the wicked one.
17 And [a]take the helmet of salvation, and [b]the sword of the Spirit, which is the word of God;
18 [a]praying always with all prayer and supplication in the Spirit, [b]being watchful to this end with all perseverance and [c]supplication for all the saints—
19 and for me, that utterance may be given to me, [a]that I may open my mouth boldly to make known the mystery of the gospel,
20 for which [a]I am an ambassador in chains; that in it I may speak boldly, as I ought to speak.
**21** But that you also may know my affairs *and* how I am doing, [a]Tychicus, a beloved brother and [b]faithful minister in the Lord, will make all things known to you;
22 [a]whom I have sent to you for this very purpose, that you may know our affairs, and *that* he may [b]comfort your hearts.
23 Peace to the brethren, and love with faith, from God the Father and the Lord Jesus Christ.
24 Grace *be* with all those who love our Lord Jesus Christ in sincerity. Amen.

**4** [a]Col. 3:21 [b]Gen. 18:19
**5** [a][1 Tim. 6:1] [b]2 Cor. 7:15 [c]1 Chr. 29:17
**6** [a]Col. 3:22
**8** [a]Rom. 2:6
**9** [a]Col. 4:1 [b]Rom. 2:11 [1]NU *He who is both their Master and yours is*
**11** [a][2 Cor. 6:7] [1]*schemings*
**12** [a]Rom. 8:38 [b]Luke 22:53 [1]NU *this darkness,*
**13** [a][2 Cor. 10:4] [b]Eph. 5:16
**14** [a]Is. 11:5 [b]Is. 59:17
**15** [a]Is. 52:7
**16** [a]1 John 5:4
**17** [a]1 Thess. 5:8 [b][Heb. 4:12]
**18** [a]Luke 18:1 [b][Matt. 26:41] [c]Phil. 1:4
**19** [a]Col. 4:3
**20** [a]2 Cor. 5:20
**21** [a]Acts 20:4 [b]1 Cor. 4:1, 2
**22** [a]Col. 4:8 [b]2 Cor. 1:6

*The Epistle of Paul the Apostle to the*

# PHILIPPIANS

### *Paul's Thankfulness and Prayer to God*

PAUL and Timothy, bondservants of Jesus Christ,

To all the saints in Christ Jesus who are in Philippi, with the [1]bishops and [a]deacons:

2 Grace to you and peace from God our Father and the Lord Jesus Christ.
**3** [a]I thank my God upon every remembrance of you,
4 always in [a]every prayer of mine making request for you all with joy,
5 [a]for your fellowship in the gospel from the first day until now,
6 being confident of this very thing, that He who has begun [a]a good work in you will complete *it* until the day of Jesus Christ;
7 just as it is right for me to think this of you all, because I have you in my heart, inasmuch as both in my chains and in the defense and confirmation of the gospel, you all are partakers with me of grace.
8 For God is my witness, how greatly I long for you all with the affection of Jesus Christ.
9 And this I pray, that your love may abound still more and more in knowledge and all discernment,
10 that you may approve the things that are excellent, that you may be sincere and without offense till the day of Christ,
11 being filled with the fruits of righteousness [a]which *are* by Jesus Christ, [b]to the glory and praise of God.
**12** But I want you to know, brethren, that the things *which happened* to me have actually turned out for the furtherance of the gospel,
13 so that it has become evident [a]to the whole [1]palace guard, and to all the rest, that my chains are in Christ;
14 and most of the brethren in the Lord, having become confident by my chains, are much more bold to speak the word without fear.
15 Some indeed preach Christ even from envy and strife, and some also from goodwill:
16 [1]The former preach Christ from selfish ambition, not sincerely, supposing to add affliction to my chains;
17 but the latter out of love, knowing that I am appointed for the defense of the gospel.
18 What then? Only *that* in every way, whether in pretense or in truth, Christ is preached; and in this I rejoice, yes, and will rejoice.
**19** For I know that [a]this will turn out for my deliverance through your prayer and the supply of the Spirit of Jesus Christ,
20 according to my earnest expectation and hope that in nothing I shall be ashamed, but [a]with all

CHAPTER 1
**1** [a][1 Tim. 3:8–13] [1]Lit. *overseers*
**3** [a]1 Cor. 1:4
**4** [a]Eph. 1:16; 1 Thess. 1:2
**5** [a][Rom. 12:13]
**6** [a][John 6:29]
**11** [a][Eph. 2:10]; Col. 1:6 [b]John 15:8
**13** [a]Phil. 4:22 [1]Or *Praetorium*
**16** [1]NU reverses vv. 16 and 17.
**19** [a]Job 13:16, LXX
**20** [a]Eph. 6:19, 20

boldness, as always, so now also Christ will be
magnified in my body, whether by life [b]or by
death.
21 For to me, to live *is* Christ, and to die *is* gain.
22 But if *I* live on in the flesh, this *will mean* fruit
from *my* labor; yet what I shall choose I [1]cannot
tell.
23 [1]For I am hard pressed between the two,
having a [a]desire to depart and be with Christ,
*which is* [b]far better.
24 Nevertheless to remain in the flesh *is* more
needful for you.
25 And being confident of this, I know that I
shall remain and continue with you all for your
progress and joy of faith,
26 that [a]your rejoicing for me may be more
abundant in Jesus Christ by my coming to you
again.
**27** Only [a]let your conduct be worthy of the gospel
of Christ, so that whether I come and see you or
am absent, I may hear of your affairs, that you
stand fast in one spirit, [b]with one mind [c]striving
together for the faith of the gospel,
28 and not in any way terrified by your adversaries, which is to them a proof of perdition, but [1]to
you of salvation, and that from God.
29 For to you [a]it has been granted on behalf of
Christ, [b]not only to believe in Him, but also to
[c]suffer for His sake,
30 [a]having the same conflict [b]which you saw in
me and now hear *is* in me.

### *Love, Unity, and Humility Recommended*

**2** Therefore if *there is* any [1]consolation in Christ,
if any comfort of love, if any fellowship of the
Spirit, if any [a]affection and mercy,
2 [a]fulfill my joy [b]by being like-minded, having
the same love, *being* of [c]one accord, of one mind.
3 [a]*Let* nothing *be done* through selfish ambition
or conceit, but [b]in lowliness of mind let each
esteem others better than himself.
4 [a]Let each of you look out not only for his own
interests, but also for the interests of [b]others.
**5** [a]Let this mind be in you which was also in
Christ Jesus,
6 who, [a]being in the form of God, did not consider it [1]robbery to be equal with God,
7 [a]but [1]made Himself of no reputation, taking
the form [b]of a bondservant, *and* [c]coming in the
likeness of men.
8 And being found in appearance as a man, He
humbled Himself and [a]became [b]obedient to *the
point of* death, even the death of the cross.
9 [a]Therefore God also [b]has highly exalted Him
and [c]given Him the name which is above every
name,
10 [a]that at the name of Jesus every knee should
bow, of those in heaven, and of those on earth,
and of those under the earth,
11 and [a]*that* every tongue should confess that
Jesus Christ *is* Lord, to the glory of God the
Father.
**12** Therefore, my beloved, [a]as you have always
obeyed, not as in my presence only, but now much
more in my absence, [b]work out your own salvation with [c]fear and trembling;
13 for [a]it is God who works in you both to will
and to do [b]for *His* good pleasure.
14 Do all things [a]without [1]complaining and [b]dis-
puting,[2]
15 that you may become blameless and [1]harm-
less, children of God without fault in the midst of
a crooked and perverse generation, among whom
you shine as [a]lights in the world,
16 holding fast the word of life, so that [a]I may
rejoice in the day of Christ that [b]I have not run in
vain or labored in [c]vain.
17 Yes, and if [a]I am being poured out *as a drink
offering* on the sacrifice [b]and service of your faith,
[c]I am glad and rejoice with you all.
18 For the same reason you also be glad and
rejoice with me.
**19** But I trust in the Lord Jesus to send [a]Timothy
to you shortly, that I also may be encouraged
when I know your [1]state.
20 For I have no one [a]like-minded, who will
sincerely care for your state.
21 For all seek their own, not the things which
are of Christ Jesus.
22 But you know his proven character, [a]that as a
son with *his* father he served with me in the
gospel.
23 Therefore I hope to send him at once, as soon
as I see how it goes with me.
24 But I trust in the Lord that I myself shall also
come shortly.
**25** Yet I considered it necessary to send to you
[a]Epaphroditus, my brother, fellow worker, and
[b]fellow soldier, [c]but your messenger and [d]the one
who ministered to my need;
26 [a]since he was longing for you all, and was
distressed because you had heard that he was
sick.
27 For indeed he was sick almost unto death; but
God had mercy on him, and not only on him but
on me also, lest I should have sorrow upon sorrow.
28 Therefore I sent him the more eagerly, that
when you see him again you may rejoice, and I
may be less sorrowful.
29 Receive him therefore in the Lord with all
gladness, and hold such men in esteem;
30 because for the work of Christ he came close
to death, [1]not regarding his life, [a]to supply what
was lacking in your service toward me.

### *All for Christ*

**3** Finally, my brethren, [a]rejoice in the Lord. For
me to write the same things to you *is* not
tedious, but for you *it is* safe.
2 [a]Beware of dogs, beware of [b]evil workers,
[c]beware of the mutilation!
3 For we are [a]the circumcision, [b]who worship
[1]God in the Spirit, rejoice in Christ Jesus, and
have no confidence in the flesh,
4 though [a]I also might have confidence in the
flesh. If anyone else thinks he may have confidence in the flesh, I [b]more so:
5 circumcised the eighth day, of the stock of
Israel, [a]*of* the tribe of Benjamin, [b]a Hebrew of the
Hebrews; concerning the law, [c]a Pharisee;
6 concerning zeal, [a]persecuting the church; concerning the righteousness which is in the law,
blameless.
7 But [a]what things were gain to me, these I have
counted loss for Christ.
8 Yet indeed I also count all things loss [a]for the
excellence of the knowledge of Christ Jesus my
Lord, for whom I have suffered the loss of all

**20** [b][Rom. 14:8]
**22** [1]*do not know*
**23** [a][2 Cor. 5:2, 8] [b][Ps. 16:11] [1]NU, M *But*
**26** [a]2 Cor. 1:14
**27** [a]Eph. 4:1 [b]Eph. 4:3 [c]Jude 3
**28** [1]NU *of your salvation*
**29** [a][Matt. 5:11, 12] [b]Eph. 2:8 [c][2 Tim. 3:12]
**30** [a]Col. 1:29; 2:1 [b]Acts 16:19–40

CHAPTER 2
**1** [a]Col. 3:12 [1]Or *encouragement*
**2** [a]John 3:29 [b]Rom. 12:16 [c]Phil. 4:2
**3** [a]Gal. 5:26 [b]Rom. 12:10
**4** [a]1 Cor. 13:5 [b]Rom. 15:1, 2
**5** [a][Matt. 11:29]
**6** [a]2 Cor. 4:4 [1]Or *something to be held onto to be equal*
**7** [a]Ps. 22:6 [b]Is. 42:1 [c][John 1:14] [1]*emptied Himself* of His privileges
**8** [a]Matt. 26:39 [b]Heb. 5:8
**9** [a]Heb. 2:9 [b]Acts 2:33 [c]Eph. 1:21
**10** [a]Is. 45:23
**11** [a]John 13:13
**12** [a]Phil. 1:5, 6; 4:15 [b]John 6:27, 29 [c]Eph. 6:5
**13** [a]Heb. 13:20, 21 [b]Eph. 1:5
**14** [a]1 Pet. 4:9 [b]Rom. 14:1 [1]*grumbling* [2]*arguing*
**15** [a]Matt. 5:15, 16 [1]*innocent*
**16** [a]2 Cor. 1:14 [b]Gal. 2:2 [c]1 Thess. 3:5
**17** [a]2 Tim. 4:6 [b]Rom. 15:16 [c]2 Cor. 7:4
**19** [a]Rom. 16:21 [1]*condition*
**20** [a]2 Tim. 3:10
**22** [a]1 Cor. 4:17
**25** [a]Phil. 4:18 [b]Philem. 2 [c]2 Cor. 8:23 [d]2 Cor. 11:9
**26** [a]Phil. 1:8
**30** [a]1 Cor. 16:17 [1]*risking*

CHAPTER 3
**1** [a]1 Thess. 5:16
**2** [a]Gal. 5:15 [b]Ps. 119:115 [c]Rom. 2:28
**3** [a]Deut. 30:6 [b]Rom. 7:6 [1]NU, M *in the Spirit of God*
**4** [a]2 Cor. 5:16; 11:18 [b]2 Cor. 11:22, 23
**5** [a]Rom. 11:1 [b]2 Cor. 11:22 [c]Acts 23:6
**6** [a]Acts 8:3; 22:4, 5; 26:9–11
**7** [a]Matt. 13:44
**8** [a]Jer. 9:23

things, and count them as rubbish, that I may
gain Christ
9 and be found in Him, not having [a]my own
righteousness, which *is* from the law, but [b]that
which *is* through faith in Christ, the righteousness
which is from God by faith;
10 that I may know Him and the [a]power of His
resurrection, and [b]the fellowship of His sufferings,
being conformed to His death,
11 if, by any means, I may [a]attain[1] to the resurrection from the dead.
**12** Not that I have already [a]attained,[1] or am
already [b]perfected; but I press on, that I may lay
hold of that for which Christ Jesus has also laid
hold of me.
13 Brethren, I do not count myself to have [1]ap-
prehended; but one thing *I do,* [a]forgetting those
things which are behind and [b]reaching forward to
those things which are ahead,
14 [a]I press toward the goal for the prize of [b]the
upward call of God in Christ Jesus.
15 Therefore let us, as many as are [a]mature,
[b]have this mind; and if in anything you think
otherwise, [c]God will reveal even this to you.
16 Nevertheless, to *the degree* that we have
already [1]attained, [a]let us walk [b]by the same [2]rule,
let us be of the same mind.
**17** Brethren, [a]join in following my example, and
note those who so walk, as [b]you have us for a
pattern.
18 For many walk, of whom I have told you
often, and now tell you even weeping, *that they
are* [a]the enemies of the cross of Christ:
19 [a]whose end *is* destruction, [b]whose god *is their*
belly, and [c]*whose* glory *is* in their shame—[d]who
set their mind on earthly things.
20 For [a]our citizenship is in heaven, [b]from which
we also [c]eagerly wait for the Savior, the Lord
Jesus Christ,
21 [a]who will transform our lowly body that it
may be [b]conformed to His glorious body, [c]accord-
ing to the working by which He is able even to
[d]subdue all things to Himself.

## *Be Anxious for Nothing; Think These Thoughts*

**4** Therefore, my beloved and [a]longed-for brethren, [b]my joy and crown, so [c]stand fast in the
Lord, beloved.
**2** I implore Euodia and I implore Syntyche [a]to
be of the same mind in the Lord.
3 [1]And I urge you also, true companion, help
these women who [a]labored with me in the gospel,
with Clement also, and the rest of my fellow
workers, whose names *are* in [b]the Book of Life.
4 [a]Rejoice in the Lord always. Again I will say,
rejoice!

**9** [a]Rom. 10:3 [b]Rom. 1:17
**10** [a]Eph. 1:19, 20 [b][Rom. 6:3–5]
**11** [a]Acts 26:6–8 [1]Lit. *arrive at*
**12** [a][1 Tim. 6:12, 19] [b]Heb. 12:23 [1]*obtained it*
**13** [a]Luke 9:62 [b]Heb. 6:1 [1]*laid hold of it*
**14** [a]2 Tim. 4:7 [b]Heb. 3:1
**15** [a]1 Cor. 2:6 [b]Gal. 5:10 [c]Hos. 6:3
**16** [a]Gal. 6:16 [b]Rom. 12:16; 15:5 [1]*arrived* [2]NU omits *rule* and the rest of v. 16.
**17** [a][1 Cor. 4:16; 11:1] [b]Titus 2:7, 8
**18** [a]Gal. 1:7
**19** [a]2 Cor. 11:15 [b]1 Tim. 6:5 [c]Hos. 4:7 [d]Rom. 8:5
**20** [a]Eph. 2:6, 19 [b]Acts 1:11 [c]1 Cor. 1:7
**21** [a][1 Cor. 15:43–53] [b]1 John 3:2 [c]Eph. 1:19 [d][1 Cor. 15:28]

CHAPTER 4
**1** [a]Phil. 1:8 [b]2 Cor. 1:14 [c]Phil. 1:27
**2** [a]Phil. 2:2; 3:16
**3** [a]Rom. 16:3 [b]Luke 10:20 [1]NU, M *Yes*
**4** [a]Rom. 12:12
**5** [a][James 5:7–9] [1]*graciousness* or *forbearance*
**6** [a]Matt. 6:25 [b][1 Thess. 5:17, 18]
**7** [a][John 14:27]
**8** [a]Eph. 4:25 [b]2 Cor. 8:21 [c]Deut. 16:20 [d]1 Thess. 5:22 [e]1 Cor. 13:4–7
**9** [a]Rom. 15:33
**10** [a]2 Cor. 11:9 [1]*you have revived your care*
**11** [a]1 Tim. 6:6, 8
**12** [a]1 Cor. 4:11 [1]*live humbly* [2]*live in prosperity*
**13** [a]John 15:5 [1]NU *Him who*
**14** [a]Phil. 1:7
**15** [a]2 Cor. 11:8, 9

5 Let your [1]gentleness be known to all men.
[a]The Lord *is* at hand.
6 [a]Be anxious for nothing, but in everything by
prayer and supplication, with [b]thanksgiving, let
your requests be made known to God;
7 and [a]the peace of God, which surpasses all
understanding, will guard your hearts and minds
through Christ Jesus.
**8** Finally, brethren, whatever things are [a]true,
whatever things *are* [b]noble, whatever things *are*
[c]just, [d]whatever things *are* pure, whatever things
*are* [e]lovely, whatever things *are* of good report, if
*there is* any virtue and if *there is* anything praiseworthy—meditate on these things.
9 The things which you learned and received
and heard and saw in me, these do, and [a]the God
of peace will be with you.
**10** But I rejoiced in the Lord greatly that now at
last [a]your[1] care for me has flourished again;
though you surely did care, but you lacked opportunity.
11 Not that I speak in regard to need, for I have
learned in whatever state I am, [a]to be content:
12 [a]I know how to [1]be abased, and I know how to
[2]abound. Everywhere and in all things I have
learned both to be full and to be hungry, both to
abound and to suffer need.
13 I can do all things [a]through [1]Christ who
strengthens me.
14 Nevertheless you have done well that [a]you
shared in my distress.
15 Now you Philippians know also that in the
beginning of the gospel, when I departed from
Macedonia, [a]no church shared with me concerning giving and receiving but you only.
16 For even in Thessalonica you sent *aid* once
and again for my necessities.
17 Not that I seek the gift, but I seek [a]the fruit
that abounds to your account.
18 Indeed I [1]have all and abound. I am full,
having received from [a]Epaphroditus the things
*sent* from you, [b]a sweet-smelling aroma, [c]an acceptable sacrifice, well pleasing to God.
19 And my God [a]shall supply all your need according to His riches in glory by Christ Jesus.
20 [a]Now to our God and Father *be* glory forever
and ever. Amen.
**21** Greet every saint in Christ Jesus. The brethren
[a]who are with me greet you.
22 All the saints greet you, but especially those
who are of Caesar's household.
23 The grace of our Lord Jesus Christ be with
[1]you all. Amen.

**17** [a]Titus 3:14
**18** [a]Phil. 2:25 [b]Heb. 13:16 [c]2 Cor. 9:12 [1]Or *have received all*
**19** [a]Ps. 23:1
**20** [a]Rom. 16:27
**21** [a]Gal. 1:2
**23** [1]NU *your spirit*

*The Epistle of Paul the Apostle to the*

# COLOSSIANS

### *Devotion to Christ Above All*

PAUL, [a]an apostle of Jesus Christ by the will
of God, and Timothy our brother,
2 To the saints [a]and faithful brethren in Christ
*who are* in Colosse:

[b]Grace to you and peace from God our Father
[1]and the Lord Jesus Christ.
**3** [a]We give thanks to the God and Father of our
Lord Jesus Christ, praying always for you,
4 [a]since we heard of your faith in Christ Jesus
and of [b]your love for all the saints;
5 because of the hope [a]which is laid up for you
in heaven, of which you heard before in the word
of the truth of the gospel,
6 which has come to you, [a]as *it has* also in all
the world, and [b]is bringing forth [1]fruit, as *it is* also
among you since the day you heard and knew [c]the
grace of God in truth;
7 as you also learned from [a]Epaphras, our dear
fellow servant, who is [b]a faithful minister of Christ
on your behalf,
8 who also declared to us your [a]love in the
Spirit.
**9** [a]For this reason we also, since the day we
heard it, do not cease to pray for you, and to ask
[b]that you may be filled with [c]the knowledge of His
will [d]in all wisdom and spiritual understanding;
10 [a]that you may walk worthy of the Lord, [b]fully
pleasing *Him*, [c]being fruitful in every good work
and increasing in the [d]knowledge of God;
11 [a]strengthened with all might, according to His
glorious power, [b]for all patience and longsuffering
[c]with joy;
12 [a]giving thanks to the Father who has qualified
us to be partakers of [b]the inheritance of the saints
in the light.
13 He has delivered us from [a]the power of darkness [b]and [1]conveyed *us* into the kingdom of the
Son of His love,
14 [a]in whom we have redemption [1]through His
blood, the forgiveness of sins.
15 He is [a]the image of the invisible God, [b]the
firstborn over all creation.
16 For [a]by Him all things were created that are in
heaven and that are on earth, visible and invisible,
whether thrones or [b]dominions or [1]principalities
or [2]powers. All things were created [c]through Him
and for Him.
17 [a]And He is before all things, and in Him [b]all
things consist.
18 And [a]He is the head of the body, the church,
who is the beginning, [b]the firstborn from the dead,
that in all things He may have the preeminence.
**19** For it pleased *the Father that* [a]in Him all the
fullness should dwell,
20 and [a]by Him to reconcile [b]all things to Himself,
by Him, whether things on earth or things in
heaven, [c]having made peace through the blood of
His cross.
21 And you, [a]who once were alienated and enemies in your mind [b]by wicked works, yet now He
has [c]reconciled
22 [a]in the body of His flesh through death, [b]to
present you holy, and blameless, and above reproach in His sight—
23 if indeed you continue [a]in the faith, grounded
and steadfast, and are [b]not moved away from the
hope of the gospel which you heard, [c]which was
preached to every creature under heaven, [d]of
which I, Paul, became a minister.
**24** [a]I now rejoice in my sufferings [b]for you, and
fill up in my flesh [c]what is lacking in the afflictions
of Christ, for [d]the sake of His body, which is the
church,
25 of which I became a minister according to [a]the
[1]stewardship from God which was given to me for
you, to fulfill the word of God,
26 [a]the [1]mystery which has been hidden from
ages and from generations, [b]but now has been
revealed to His saints.
27 [a]To them God willed to make known what are
[b]the riches of the glory of this mystery among the
Gentiles: [1]which is [c]Christ in you, [d]the hope of
glory.
28 Him we preach, [a]warning every man and
teaching every man in all wisdom, [b]that we may
present every man perfect in Christ Jesus.
29 To this *end* I also labor, striving according to
His working which works in me [a]mightily.

### *Neither Philosophy nor Legalism, but Christ*

**2** For I want you to know what a great [a]conflict[1]
I have for you and those in Laodicea, and *for*
as many as have not seen my face in the flesh,
2 that their hearts may be encouraged, being
knit together in love, and *attaining* to all riches of
the full assurance of understanding, to the knowledge of the mystery of God, [1]both of the Father
and of Christ,
3 [a]in whom are hidden all the treasures of wisdom and knowledge.
4 Now this I say [a]lest anyone should deceive
you with persuasive words.
5 For [a]though I am absent in the flesh, yet I am
with you in spirit, rejoicing [1]to see [b]your *good*
order and the [c]steadfastness of your faith in
Christ.
6 [a]As you therefore have received Christ Jesus
the Lord, so walk in Him,
7 [a]rooted and built up in Him and established in
the faith, as you have been taught, abounding [1]in
it with thanksgiving.
8 Beware lest anyone [1]cheat you through philosophy and empty deceit, according to [a]the tradition of men, according to the [b]basic principles of
the world, and not according to Christ.
9 For [a]in Him dwells all the fullness of the
Godhead [1]bodily;
10 and you are complete in Him, who is the [a]head
of all [1]principality and power.
**11** In Him you were also [a]circumcised with the
circumcision made without hands, by [b]putting off
the body [1]of the sins of the flesh, by the circumcision of Christ,

CHAPTER 1
**1** [a]Eph. 1:1
**2** [a]1 Cor. 4:17 [b]Gal. 1:3 [1]NU omits *and the Lord Jesus Christ*
**3** [a]Phil. 1:3
**4** [a]Eph. 1:15 [b][Heb. 6:10]
**5** [a][1 Pet. 1:4]
**6** [a]Matt. 24:14 [b]John 15:16 [c]Eph. 3:2 [1]NU, M add *and growing*
**7** [a]Philem. 23 [b]2 Cor. 11:23
**8** [a]Rom. 15:30
**9** [a]Eph. 1:15–17 [b]1 Cor. 1:5 [c][Rom. 12:2] [d]Eph. 1:8
**10** [a]Eph. 4:1 [b]1 Thess. 4:1 [c]Heb. 13:21 [d]2 Pet. 3:18
**11** [a][Eph. 3:16; 6:10] [b]Eph. 4:2 [c][Acts 5:41]
**12** [a][Eph. 5:20] [b]Eph. 1:11
**13** [a]Eph. 6:12 [b]2 Pet. 1:11 [1]*transferred*
**14** [a]Eph. 1:7 [1]NU, M omit *through His blood*
**15** [a]2 Cor. 4:4 [b]Rev. 3:14
**16** [a]Heb. 1:2, 3 [b][Eph. 1:20, 21] [c]Heb. 2:10 [1]*rulers* [2]*authorities*
**17** [a][John 17:5] [b]Heb. 1:3
**18** [a]Eph. 1:22 [b]Rev. 1:5
**19** [a]John 1:16
**20** [a]Eph. 2:14 [b]2 Cor. 5:18 [c]Eph. 1:10
**21** [a][Eph. 2:1] [b]Titus 1:15 [c]2 Cor. 5:18, 19
**22** [a]2 Cor. 5:18 [b][Eph. 5:27]
**23** [a]Eph. 3:17 [b][John 15:6] [c]Col. 1:6 [d]Col. 1:25
**24** [a]2 Cor. 7:4 [b]Eph. 3:1, 13 [c][2 Cor. 1:5; 12:15] [d]Eph. 1:23
**25** [a]Gal. 2:7 [1]*dispensation* or *administration*
**26** [a][1 Cor. 2:7] [b][2 Tim. 1:10] [1]*secret* or *hidden truth*
**27** [a]2 Cor. 2:14 [b]Rom. 9:23 [c][Rom. 8:10, 11] [d]1 Tim. 1:1 [1]M *who*
**28** [a]Acts 20:20 [b]Eph. 5:27
**29** [a]Eph. 3:7

CHAPTER 2
**1** [a]Phil. 1:30 [1]*struggle*
**2** [1]NU omits *both of the Father and*
**3** [a]1 Cor. 1:24, 30
**4** [a]Rom. 16:18
**5** [a]1 Thess. 2:17 [b]1 Cor. 14:40 [c]1 Pet. 5:9 [1]Lit. *and seeing*
**6** [a]1 Thess. 4:1
**7** [a]Eph. 2:21 [1]NU omits *in it*
**8** [a]Gal. 1:14 [b]Gal. 4:3, 9, 10 [1]Lit. *plunder you* or *take you captive*
**9** [a][John 1:14] [1]*in bodily form*
**10** [a][Eph. 1:20, 21] [1]*rule and authority*
**11** [a]Deut. 10:16 [b]Rom. 6:6; 7:24 [1]NU omits *of the sins*

12 [a]buried with Him in baptism, in which you also
were raised with *Him* through [b]faith in the working of God, [c]who raised Him from the dead.
13 And you, being dead in your trespasses and
the uncircumcision of your flesh, He has made
alive together with Him, having forgiven you all
trespasses,
14 [a]having wiped out the [1]handwriting of requirements that was against us, which was contrary to
us. And He has taken it out of the way, having
nailed it to the cross.
15 [a]Having disarmed [b]principalities and powers,
He made a public spectacle of them, triumphing
over them in it.
16 So let no one [a]judge you in food or in drink, or
regarding a [1]festival or a new moon or sabbaths,
17 [a]which are a shadow of things to come, but
the [1]substance is of Christ.
18 Let no one cheat you of your reward, taking
delight in *false* humility and worship of angels,
intruding into those things which he has [1]not
seen, vainly puffed up by his fleshly mind,
19 and not holding fast to [a]the Head, from whom
all the body, nourished and knit together by joints
and ligaments, [b]grows with the increase *that is*
from God.
20 [1]Therefore, if you [a]died with Christ from the
basic principles of the world, [b]why, as *though*
living in the world, do you subject yourselves to
regulations—
21 [a]"Do not touch, do not taste, do not handle,"
22 which all concern things which perish with
the using—[a]according to the commandments and
doctrines of men?
23 [a]These things indeed have an appearance of
wisdom in self-imposed religion, *false* humility,
and [1]neglect of the body, *but are* of no value
against the indulgence of the flesh.

### *Character of the Christian Life and Home*

**3** If then you were [a]raised with Christ, seek
those things which are above, [b]where Christ is,
sitting at the right hand of God.
2 Set your mind on things above, not on things
on the [a]earth.
3 [a]For you died, [b]and your life is hidden with
Christ in God.
4 [a]When Christ *who is* [b]our life appears, then
you also will appear with Him in [c]glory.
5 [a]Therefore put to death [b]your members which
are on the earth: [c]fornication, uncleanness, passion, evil desire, and covetousness, [d]which is
idolatry.
6 [a]Because of these things the wrath of God is
coming upon [b]the sons of disobedience,
7 [a]in which you yourselves once walked when
you lived in them.
8 [a]But now you yourselves are to put off all
these: anger, wrath, malice, blasphemy, filthy
language out of your mouth.
9 Do not lie to one another, since you have put
off the old man with his deeds,
10 and have put on the new *man* who [a]is renewed
in knowledge [b]according to the image of Him who
[c]created him,
11 where there is neither [a]Greek nor Jew, circumcised nor uncircumcised, barbarian, Scythian,
slave *nor* free, [b]but Christ *is* all and in all.
**12** Therefore, [a]as *the* elect of God, holy and
beloved, [b]put on tender mercies, kindness, humility, meekness, longsuffering;
13 [a]bearing with one another, and forgiving one
another, if anyone has a complaint against another; even as Christ forgave you, so you also
*must do.*
14 [a]But above all these things [b]put on love, which
is the [c]bond of perfection.
15 And let [a]the peace of God rule in your hearts,
[b]to which also you were called [c]in one body; and
[d]be thankful.
16 Let the word of Christ dwell in you richly in all
wisdom, teaching and admonishing one another
[a]in psalms and hymns and spiritual songs, singing
with grace in your hearts to the Lord.
17 And [a]*whatever* you do in word or deed, *do* all
in the name of the Lord Jesus, giving thanks to
God the Father through Him.
**18** [a]Wives, submit to your own husbands, [b]as is
fitting in the Lord.
19 [a]Husbands, love your wives and do not be
[b]bitter toward them.
20 [a]Children, obey your parents [b]in all things, for
this is well pleasing to the Lord.
21 [a]Fathers, do not provoke your children, lest
they become discouraged.
22 [a]Bondservants, obey in all things your masters
according to the flesh, not with eyeservice, as
men-pleasers, but in sincerity of heart, fearing
God.
23 [a]And whatever you do, do it heartily, as to the
Lord and not to men,
24 [a]knowing that from the Lord you will receive
the reward of the inheritance; [b]for[1] you serve the
Lord Christ.
25 But he who does wrong will be repaid for what
he has done, and [a]there is no partiality.

### *Christian Graces; Final Greetings*

**4** Masters,[a] give your bondservants what is just
and fair, knowing that you also have a Master
in heaven.
2 [a]Continue earnestly in prayer, being vigilant in
it [b]with thanksgiving;
3 [a]meanwhile praying also for us, that God
would [b]open to us a door for the word, to speak
[c]the [1]mystery of Christ, [d]for which I am also in
chains,
4 that I may make it manifest, as I ought to
speak.
5 [a]Walk in [b]wisdom toward those *who are* outside, [c]redeeming the time.
6 *Let* your speech always *be* [a]with grace, [b]sea-
soned with salt, [c]that you may know how you
ought to answer each one.
**7** [a]Tychicus, a beloved brother, faithful minister,
and fellow servant in the Lord, will tell you all the
news about me.
8 [a]I am sending him to you for this very purpose, that [1]he may know your circumstances and
comfort your hearts,
9 with [a]Onesimus, a faithful and beloved
brother, who is *one* of you. They will make known
to you all things which *are happening* here.
10 [a]Aristarchus my fellow prisoner greets you,
with [b]Mark the cousin of Barnabas (about whom
you received instructions: if he comes to you,
welcome him),
11 and Jesus who is called Justus. These *are my*

**12** [a]Rom. 6:4 [b]Eph. 1:19, 20 [c]Acts 2:24
**14** [a][Eph. 2:15, 16] [1]*certificate of debt with its*
**15** [a][Is. 53:12] [b]Eph. 6:12
**16** [a]Rom. 14:3 [1]*feast day*
**17** [a]Heb. 8:5; 10:1 [1]Lit. *body*
**18** [1]NU omits *not*
**19** [a]Eph. 4:15 [b]Eph. 1:23; 4:16
**20** [a]Rom. 6:2–5 [b]Gal. 4:3, 9 [1]NU, M omit *Therefore*
**21** [a]1 Tim. 4:3
**22** [a]Titus 1:14
**23** [a]1 Tim. 4:8 [1]*severe treatment, asceticism*

CHAPTER 3
**1** [a]Col. 2:12 [b]Eph. 1:20
**2** [a][Matt. 6:19–21]
**3** [a][Rom. 6:2] [b][2 Cor. 5:7]
**4** [a][1 John 3:2] [b]John 14:6 [c]1 Cor. 15:43
**5** [a][Rom. 8:13] [b][Rom. 6:13] [c]Eph. 5:3 [d]Eph. 4:19; 5:3, 5
**6** [a]Rom. 1:18 [b][Eph. 2:2]
**7** [a]1 Cor. 6:11
**8** [a]Eph. 4:22
**10** [a]Rom. 12:2 [b][Rom. 8:9] [c][Eph. 2:10]
**11** [a]Gal. 3:27, 28 [b]Eph. 1:23
**12** [a][1 Pet. 1:2] [b]1 John 3:17
**13** [a][Mark 11:25]
**14** [a]1 Pet. 4:8 [b][1 Cor. 13] [c]Eph. 4:3
**15** [a][John 14:27] [b]1 Cor. 7:15 [c]Eph. 4:4 [d][1 Thess. 5:18]
**16** [a]Eph. 5:19
**17** [a]1 Cor. 10:31
**18** [a]1 Pet. 3:1 [b][Eph. 5:22—6:9]
**19** [a][Eph. 5:25] [b]Eph. 4:31
**20** [a]Eph. 6:1 [b]Eph. 5:24
**21** [a]Eph. 6:4
**22** [a]Eph. 6:5
**23** [a][Eccl. 9:10]
**24** [a]Eph. 6:8 [b]1 Cor. 7:22 [1]NU omits *for*
**25** [a]Rom. 2:11

CHAPTER 4
**1** [a]Eph. 6:9
**2** [a]Luke 18:1 [b]Col. 2:7
**3** [a]Eph. 6:19 [b]1 Cor. 16:9 [c]Eph. 3:3, 4; 6:19 [d]Eph. 6:20 [1]*hidden truth*
**5** [a]Eph. 5:15 [b][Matt. 10:16] [c]Eph. 5:16
**6** [a]Eccl. 10:12 [b]Mark 9:50 [c]1 Pet. 3:15
**7** [a]2 Tim. 4:12

**8** [a]Eph. 6:22 [1]NU *you may know our circumstances and he may comfort*
**9** [a]Philem. 10
**10** [a]Acts 19:29; 20:4; 27:2 [b]2 Tim. 4:11

only fellow workers for the kingdom of God who
are of the circumcision; they have proved to be a
comfort to me.
12 [a]Epaphras, who is *one* of you, a bondservant of
Christ, greets you, always [b]laboring fervently for
you in prayers, that you may stand [c]perfect and
[1]complete in all the will of God.
13 For I bear him witness that he has a great
[1]zeal for you, and those who are in Laodicea, and
those in Hierapolis.
14 [a]Luke the beloved physician and [b]Demas greet
you.
15 Greet the brethren who are in Laodicea, and
[1]Nymphas and [a]the church that *is* in [2]his house.
**16** Now when [a]this epistle is read among you, see
that it is read also in the church of the Laodiceans,
and that you likewise read the epistle from Laodicea.
17 And say to [a]Archippus, "Take heed to [b]the
ministry which you have received in the Lord,
that you may fulfill it."
18 [a]This salutation by my own hand—Paul. [b]Re-
member my chains. Grace *be* with you. Amen.

12 [a]Philem. 23 [b]Rom. 15:30 [c]Matt. 5:48 [1]NU *fully assured*
13 [1]NU *concern*
14 [a]2 Tim. 4:11 [b]2 Tim. 4:10
15 [a]Rom. 16:5 [1]NU *Nympha* [2]NU *her*
16 [a]1 Thess. 5:27
17 [a]Philem. 2 [b]2 Tim. 4:5
18 [a]1 Cor. 16:21 [b]Heb. 13:3

*The First Epistle of Paul the Apostle to the*

# THESSALONIANS

### *The Good Example of the Thessalonians*

**P**AUL, [a]Silvanus, and Timothy,

To the church of the [b]Thessalonians in God the
Father and the Lord Jesus Christ:

Grace to you and peace [1]from God our Father
and the Lord Jesus Christ.
**2** [a]We give thanks to God always for you all,
making mention of you in our prayers,
3 remembering without ceasing [a]your work of
faith, [b]labor of love, and patience of hope in our
Lord Jesus Christ in the sight of our God and
Father,
4 knowing, beloved brethren, [a]your election by
God.
5 For [a]our gospel did not come to you in word
only, but also in power, [b]and in the Holy Spirit
[c]and in much assurance, as you know what kind
of men we were among you for your sake.
6 And [a]you became followers of us and of the
Lord, having received the word in much affliction,
[b]with joy of the Holy Spirit,
7 so that you became examples to all in Macedonia and Achaia who believe.
8 For from you the word of the Lord [a]has
sounded forth, not only in Macedonia and Achaia,
but also [b]in every place. Your faith toward God
has gone out, so that we do not need to say
anything.
9 For they themselves declare concerning us
[a]what manner of entry we had to you, [b]and how
you turned to God from idols to serve the living
and true God,
10 and [a]to wait for His Son from heaven, whom
He raised from the dead, *even* Jesus who delivers
us [b]from the wrath to come.

### *The Thessalonians' Conversion*

**2** For you yourselves know, brethren, that our
coming to you was not in vain.
2 But [1]even after we had suffered before and
were spitefully treated at [a]Philippi, as you know,
we were [b]bold in our God to speak to you the
gospel of God in much conflict.
3 [a]For our exhortation *did* not *come* from error
or uncleanness, nor *was it* in deceit.
4 But as [a]we have been approved by God [b]to be
entrusted with the gospel, even so we speak, [c]not
as pleasing men, but God [d]who tests our hearts.
5 For [a]neither at any time did we use flattering
words, as you know, nor a [1]cloak for covetousness—[b]God *is* witness.
6 [a]Nor did we seek glory from men, either from
you or from others, when [b]we might have [c]made
demands [d]as apostles of Christ.
7 But [a]we were gentle among you, just as a
nursing *mother* cherishes her own children.
8 So, affectionately longing for you, we were
well pleased [a]to impart to you not only the gospel
of God, but also [b]our own lives, because you had
become dear to us.
9 For you remember, brethren, our [a]labor and
toil; for laboring night and day, [b]that we might not
be a burden to any of you, we preached to you the
gospel of God.
10 [a]You *are* witnesses, and God *also*, [b]how de-
voutly and justly and blamelessly we behaved
ourselves among you who believe;
11 as you know how we exhorted, and comforted, and [1]charged every one of you, as a father
*does* his own children,
12 [a]that you would walk worthy of God [b]who
calls you into His own kingdom and glory.
**13** For this reason we also thank God [a]without
ceasing, because when you [b]received the word of
God which you heard from us, you welcomed *it*
[c]not *as* the word of men, but as it is in truth, the
word of God, which also effectively [d]works in you
who believe.
14 For you, brethren, became imitators [a]of the
churches of God which are in Judea in Christ
Jesus. For [b]you also suffered the same things from
your own countrymen, just as they *did* from the
Judeans,
15 [a]who killed both the Lord Jesus and [b]their own
prophets, and have persecuted us; and they do not
please God [c]and are [1]contrary to all men,
16 [a]forbidding us to speak to the Gentiles that
they may be saved, so as always [b]to fill up *the
measure of* their sins; [c]but wrath has come upon
them to the uttermost.
**17** But we, brethren, having been taken away
from you for a short time [a]in presence, not in

CHAPTER 1
1 [a]1 Pet. 5:12 [b]Acts 17:1–9 [1]NU omits *from God our Father and the Lord Jesus Christ*
2 [a]Rom. 1:8
3 [a]John 6:29 [b]Rom. 16:6
4 [a]Col. 3:12
5 [a]Mark 16:20 [b]2 Cor. 6:6 [c]Heb. 2:3
6 [a]1 Cor. 4:16; 11:1 [b]Acts 5:41; 13:52
8 [a]Rom. 10:18 [b]Rom. 1:8; 16:19
9 [a]1 Thess. 2:1 [b]1 Cor. 12:2
10 [a][Rom. 2:7] [b]Rom. 5:9

CHAPTER 2
2 [a]Acts 14:5; 16:19–24 [b]Acts 17:1–9 [1]NU, M omit *even*
3 [a]2 Cor. 7:2
4 [a]1 Cor. 7:25 [b]Titus 1:3 [c]Gal. 1:10 [d]Prov. 17:3
5 [a]2 Cor. 2:17 [b]Rom. 1:9 [1]*pretext for greed*
6 [a]1 Tim. 5:17 [b]1 Cor. 9:4 [c]2 Cor. 11:9 [d]1 Cor. 9:1
7 [a]1 Cor. 2:3
8 [a]Rom. 1:11 [b]2 Cor. 12:15
9 [a]Acts 18:3; 20:34, 35 [b]2 Cor. 12:13
10 [a]1 Thess. 1:5 [b]2 Cor. 7:2
11 [1]NU, M *implored*
12 [a]Eph. 4:1 [b]1 Cor. 1:9
13 [a]1 Thess. 1:2, 3 [b]Mark 4:20 [c][Gal. 4:14] [d][1 Pet. 1:23]
14 [a]Gal. 1:22 [b]Acts 17:5
15 [a]Acts 2:23 [b]Matt. 5:12; 23:34, 35 [c]Esth. 3:8 [1]*hostile*
16 [a]Luke 11:52 [b]Gen. 15:16 [c]Matt. 24:6
17 [a]1 Cor. 5:3

heart, endeavored more eagerly to see your face
with great desire.
18 Therefore we wanted to come to you—even I,
Paul, time and again—but [a]Satan hindered us.
19 For [a]what *is* our hope, or joy, or [b]crown of
rejoicing? *Is it* not even you in the [c]presence of
our Lord Jesus Christ [d]at His coming?
20 For you are our glory and joy.

### *Paul's Concern and Prayer for the Church*

**3** Therefore, when we could no longer endure it,
we thought it good to be left in Athens alone,
2 and sent [a]Timothy, our brother and minister of
God, and our fellow laborer in the gospel of Christ,
to establish you and encourage you concerning
your faith,
3 [a]that no one should be shaken by these afflictions; for you yourselves know that [b]we are
appointed to this.
4 [a]For, in fact, we told you before when we were
with you that we would suffer tribulation, just as
it happened, and you know.
5 For this reason, when I could no longer endure it, I sent to know your faith, [a]lest by some
means the tempter had tempted you, and [b]our
labor might be in vain.
**6** [a]But now that Timothy has come to us from
you, and brought us good news of your faith and
love, and that you always have good remembrance of us, greatly desiring to see us, [b]as we also
*to see* you—
7 therefore, brethren, in all our affliction and
distress [a]we were comforted concerning you by
your faith.
8 For now we live, if you [a]stand fast in the Lord.
9 For what thanks can we render to God for
you, for all the joy with which we rejoice for your
sake before our God,
10 night and day praying exceedingly that we
may see your face [a]and perfect what is lacking in
your faith?
**11** Now may our God and Father Himself, and
our Lord Jesus Christ, [a]direct our way to you.
12 And may the Lord make you increase and
[a]abound in love to one another and to all, just as
we *do* to you,
13 so that He may establish [a]your hearts blameless in holiness before our God and Father at the
coming of our Lord Jesus Christ with all His
saints.

### *The Resurrection and Christ's Second Coming*

**4** Finally then, brethren, we urge and exhort in
the Lord Jesus [a]that you should abound more
and more, [b]just as you received from us how you
ought to walk and to please God;
2 for you know what commandments we gave
you through the Lord Jesus.
3 For this is [a]the will of God, [b]your sanctification: [c]that you should abstain from sexual immorality;
4 [a]that each of you should know how to possess
his own vessel in sanctification and honor,
5 [a]not in passion of lust, [b]like the Gentiles [c]who
do not know God;
6 that no one should take advantage of and
defraud his brother in this matter, because the
Lord [a]*is* the avenger of all such, as we also fore-
warned you and testified.
7 For God did not call us to uncleanness, [a]but in
holiness.
8 [a]Therefore he who rejects *this* does not reject
man, but God, [b]who[1] has also given us His Holy
Spirit.
**9** But concerning brotherly love you have no
need that I should write to you, for [a]you yourselves are taught by God [b]to love one another;
10 and indeed you do so toward all the brethren
who are in all Macedonia. But we urge you,
brethren, [a]that you increase more and more;
11 that you also aspire to lead a quiet life, [a]to
mind your own business, and [b]to work with your
own hands, as we commanded you,
12 [a]that you may walk properly toward those
who are outside, and *that* you may lack nothing.
**13** But I do not want you to be ignorant, brethren, concerning those who have fallen [1]asleep, lest
you sorrow [a]as others [b]who have no hope.
14 For [a]if we believe that Jesus died and rose
again, even so God will bring with Him [b]those who
[1]sleep in Jesus.
15 For this we say to you [a]by the word of the
Lord, that [b]we who are alive *and* remain until the
coming of the Lord will by no means precede
those who are [1]asleep.
16 For [a]the Lord Himself will descend from
heaven with a shout, with the voice of an archangel, and with [b]the trumpet of God. [c]And the dead
in Christ will rise first.
17 [a]Then we who are alive *and* remain shall be
caught up together with them [b]in the clouds to
meet the Lord in the air. And thus [c]we shall
always be with the Lord.
18 [a]Therefore comfort one another with these
words.

### *The Day of the Lord*

**5** But concerning [a]the times and the seasons,
brethren, you have no need that I should write
to you.
2 For you yourselves know perfectly that [a]the
day of the Lord so comes as a thief in the night.
3 For when they say, "Peace and safety!" then
[a]sudden destruction comes upon them, [b]as labor
pains upon a pregnant woman. And they shall not
escape.
4 [a]But you, brethren, are not in darkness, so that
this Day should overtake you as a thief.
5 You are all [a]sons of light and sons of the day.
We are not of the night nor of darkness.
6 [a]Therefore let us not sleep, as others *do,* but
[b]let us watch and be [1]sober.
7 For [a]those who sleep, sleep at night, and those
who get drunk [b]are drunk at night.
8 But let us who are of the day be sober, [a]put-
ting on the breastplate of faith and love, and *as* a
helmet the hope of salvation.
9 For [a]God did not appoint us to wrath, [b]but to
obtain salvation through our Lord Jesus Christ,
10 [a]who died for us, that whether we wake or
sleep, we should live together with Him.
11 Therefore [1]comfort each other and [2]edify one
another, just as you also are doing.
**12** And we urge you, brethren, [a]to recognize
those who labor among you, and are over you in
the Lord and [1]admonish you,

**18** [a]Rom. 1:13; 15:22
**19** [a]2 Cor. 1:14 [b]Prov. 16:31 [c]Jude 24 [d]1 Cor. 15:23

CHAPTER 3
**2** [a]Rom. 16:21
**3** [a]Eph. 3:13 [b]Acts 9:16; 14:22
**4** [a]Acts 20:24
**5** [a]1 Cor. 7:5 [b]Gal. 2:2
**6** [a]Acts 18:5 [b]Phil. 1:8
**7** [a]2 Cor. 1:4
**8** [a]Phil. 4:1
**10** [a]2 Cor. 13:9
**11** [a]Mark 1:3
**12** [a]Phil. 1:9
**13** [a]2 Thess. 2:17

CHAPTER 4
**1** [a]1 Cor. 15:58 [b]Phil. 1:27
**3** [a][Rom. 12:2] [b]Eph. 5:27 [c][1 Cor. 6:15–20]
**4** [a]Rom. 6:19
**5** [a]Col. 3:5 [b]Eph. 4:17, 18 [c]1 Cor. 15:34
**6** [a]2 Thess. 1:8
**7** [a]Lev. 11:44
**8** [a]Luke 10:16 [b]1 Cor. 2:10 [1]NU *who also gives*
**9** [a][Jer. 31:33, 34] [b]Matt. 22:39
**10** [a]1 Thess. 3:12
**11** [a]2 Thess. 3:11 [b]Acts 20:35
**12** [a]Rom. 13:13
**13** [a]Lev. 19:28 [b][Eph. 2:12] [1]Died
**14** [a]1 Cor. 15:13 [b]1 Cor. 15:20, 23 [1]Or *through Jesus sleep*
**15** [a]1 Kin. 13:17; 20:35 [b]1 Cor. 15:51, 52 [1]Dead
**16** [a][Matt. 24:30, 31] [b][1 Cor. 15:52] [c][1 Cor. 15:23]
**17** [a][1 Cor. 15:51–53] [b]Acts 1:9 [c]John 14:3; 17:24
**18** [a]1 Thess. 5:11

CHAPTER 5
**1** [a]Matt. 24:3
**2** [a][2 Pet. 3:10]
**3** [a]Is. 13:6–9 [b]Hos. 13:13
**4** [a]1 John 2:8
**5** [a]Eph. 5:8
**6** [a]Matt. 25:5 [b][1 Pet. 5:8] [1]*self-controlled*
**7** [a][Luke 21:34] [b]Acts 2:15
**8** [a]Eph. 6:14
**9** [a]Rom. 9:22 [b][2 Thess. 2:13]
**10** [a]2 Cor. 5:15
**11** [1]Or *encourage* [2]*build one another up*
**12** [a]1 Cor. 16:18 [1]*instruct* or *warn*

13 and to esteem them very highly in love for
their work's sake. [a]Be at peace among yourselves.
14 Now we [1]exhort you, brethren, [a]warn those
who are [2]unruly, [b]comfort the fainthearted, [c]uphold the weak, [d]be patient with all.
15 [a]See that no one renders evil for evil to anyone, but always [b]pursue what is good both for
yourselves and for all.
16 [a]Rejoice always,
17 [a]pray without ceasing,
18 in everything give thanks; for this is the will of
God in Christ Jesus for you.
19 [a]Do not quench the Spirit.
20 [a]Do not despise prophecies.
21 [a]Test all things; [b]hold fast what is good.
22 Abstain from every form of evil.

13 [a]Mark 9:50
14 [a]2 Thess. 3:6, 7, 11 [b]Heb. 12:12 [c]Rom. 14:1; 15:1 [d]Gal. 5:22 [1]*encourage* [2]*insubordinate* or *idle*
15 [a]Lev. 19:18 [b]Gal. 6:10
16 [a][2 Cor. 6:10]
17 [a]Eph. 6:18
19 [a]Eph. 4:30
20 [a]1 Cor. 14:1, 31
21 [a]1 John 4:1 [b]Phil. 4:8

23 Now may [a]the God of peace Himself [b]sanctify[1]
you completely; and may your whole spirit, soul,
and body [c]be preserved blameless at the coming of
our Lord Jesus Christ.
24 He who calls you *is* [a]faithful, who also will
[b]do *it.*
25 Brethren, pray for us.
26 Greet all the brethren with a holy kiss.
27 I charge you by the Lord that this [1]epistle be
read to all the [2]holy brethren.
28 The grace of our Lord Jesus Christ *be* with
you. Amen.

23 [a]Phil. 4:9 [b]1 Thess. 3:13 [c]1 Cor. 1:8, 9 [1]*set you apart*
24 [a][1 Cor. 10:13] [b]Phil. 1:6
27 [1]*letter* [2]NU omits *holy*

*The Second Epistle of Paul the Apostle to the*

# THESSALONIANS

### *God's Final Judgment and Glory*

PAUL, Silvanus, and Timothy,

To the church of the Thessalonians in God our
Father and the Lord Jesus Christ:

2 [a]Grace to you and peace from God our Father
and the Lord Jesus Christ.
3 We are bound to thank God always for you,
brethren, as it is fitting, because your faith grows
exceedingly, and the love of every one of you all
abounds toward each other,
4 so that [a]we ourselves boast of you among the
churches of God [b]for your patience and faith [c]in
all your persecutions and [1]tribulations that you
endure,
5 *which is* [a]manifest[1] evidence of the righteous
judgment of God, that you may be counted worthy of the kingdom of God, [b]for which you also
suffer;
6 [a]since *it is* a righteous thing with God to repay
with [1]tribulation those who trouble you,
7 and to *give* you who are troubled [a]rest with us
when [b]the Lord Jesus is revealed from heaven
with His mighty angels,
8 in flaming fire taking vengeance on those who
do not know God, and on those who do not obey
the gospel of our Lord Jesus Christ.
9 [a]These shall be punished with everlasting
destruction from the presence of the Lord and
[b]from the glory of His power,
10 when He comes, in that Day, [a]to be [b]glorified
in His saints and to be admired among all those
who [1]believe, because our testimony among you
was believed.
11 Therefore we also pray always for you that
our God would [a]count you worthy of *this* calling,
and fulfill all the good pleasure of *His* goodness
and [b]the work of faith with power,
12 [a]that the name of our Lord Jesus Christ may
be glorified in you, and you in Him, according to
the grace of our God and the Lord Jesus Christ.

CHAPTER 1
2 [a]1 Cor. 1:3
4 [a]2 Cor. 7:4 [b]1 Thess. 1:3 [c]1 Thess. 2:14 [1]*afflictions*
5 [a]Phil. 1:28 [b]1 Thess. 2:14 [1]*plain*
6 [a]Rev. 6:10 [1]*affliction*
7 [a]Rev. 14:13 [b]Jude 14
9 [a]Phil. 3:19 [b]Deut. 33:2
10 [a]Matt. 25:31 [b]John 17:10 [1]NU, M *have believed*
11 [a]Col. 1:12 [b]1 Thess. 1:3
12 [a][Col. 3:17]

CHAPTER 2
1 [a][1 Thess. 4:15–17] [b]Matt. 24:31
2 [a]Matt. 24:4 [1]NU *the Lord*
3 [a]1 Tim. 4:1 [b]Dan. 7:25; 8:25; 11:36 [c]John 17:12 [1]NU *lawlessness*
4 [a]Is. 14:13, 14 [b]1 Cor. 8:5 [1]NU omits *as God*
7 [a]1 John 2:18 [1]*hidden truth* [2]Or *he*
8 [a]Dan. 7:10 [b]Is. 11:4 [c]Heb. 10:27
9 [a]John 8:41 [b]Deut. 13:1
10 [a]2 Cor. 2:15 [b]1 Cor. 16:22
11 [a]Rom. 1:28 [b]1 Tim. 4:1
12 [a]Rom. 1:32
13 [a]Eph. 1:4 [b]1 Thess. 1:4 [c][1 Pet. 1:2] [1]*under obligation* [2]*being set apart by*
14 [a]1 Pet. 5:10

### *Falling Away from Christ*

2 Now, brethren, [a]concerning the coming of our
Lord Jesus Christ [b]and our gathering together
to Him, we ask you,
2 [a]not to be soon shaken in mind or troubled,
either by spirit or by word or by letter, as if from
us, as though the day of [1]Christ had come.
3 Let no one deceive you by any means; for *that
Day will not come* [a]unless the falling away comes
first, and [b]the man of [1]sin is revealed, [c]the son of
perdition,
4 who opposes and [a]exalts himself [b]above all
that is called God or that is worshiped, so that he
sits [1]as God in the temple of God, showing himself
that he is God.
5 Do you not remember that when I was still
with you I told you these things?
6 And now you know what is restraining, that
he may be revealed in his own time.
7 For [a]the [1]mystery of lawlessness is already at
work; only [2]He who now restrains *will do* so until
[2]He is taken out of the way.
8 And then the lawless one will be revealed,
[a]whom the Lord will consume [b]with the breath of
His mouth and destroy [c]with the brightness of His
coming.
9 The coming of the *lawless one* is [a]according to
the working of Satan, with all power, [b]signs, and
lying wonders,
10 and with all unrighteous deception among
[a]those who perish, because they did not receive
[b]the love of the truth, that they might be saved.
11 And [a]for this reason God will send them
strong delusion, [b]that they should believe the lie,
12 that they all may be condemned who did not
believe the truth but [a]had pleasure in unrighteousness.
13 But we are [1]bound to give thanks to God
always for you, brethren beloved by the Lord,
because God [a]from the beginning [b]chose you for
salvation [c]through [2]sanctification by the Spirit
and belief in the truth,
14 to which He called you by our gospel, for [a]the
obtaining of the glory of our Lord Jesus Christ.

15 Therefore, brethren, [a]stand fast and hold [b]the
traditions which you were taught, whether by
word or our [1]epistle.
16 Now may our Lord Jesus Christ Himself, and
our God and Father, [a]who has loved us and given
*us* everlasting consolation and [b]good hope by
grace,
17 comfort your hearts [a]and [1]establish you in
every good word and work.

### *Paul Asks Their Prayers, Warns Against Idleness*

**3** Finally, brethren, [a]pray for us, that the word of
the Lord may run *swiftly* and be glorified, just
as *it is* with you,
2 and [a]that we may be delivered from unreasonable and wicked men; [b]for not all have faith.
3 But [a]the Lord is faithful, who will establish
you and [b]guard *you* from the evil one.
4 And [a]we have confidence in the Lord concerning you, both that you do and will do the things
we command you.
5 Now may [a]the Lord direct your hearts into the
love of God and into the patience of Christ.
**6** But we command you, brethren, in the name
of our Lord Jesus Christ, [a]that you withdraw
[b]from every brother who walks [c]disorderly and
not according to the tradition which [1]he received
from us.
7 For you yourselves know how you ought to
follow us, for we were not disorderly among you;
8 nor did we eat anyone's bread [1]free of charge,
but worked with [a]labor and toil night and day,
that we might not be a burden to any of you,
9 not because we do not have [a]authority, but to
make ourselves an example of how you should
follow us.
10 For even when we were with you, we commanded you this: If anyone will not work, neither
shall he eat.
11 For we hear that there are some who walk
among you in a disorderly manner, not working at
all, but are [a]busybodies.
12 Now those who are such we command and
[1]exhort through our Lord Jesus Christ [a]that they
work in quietness and eat their own bread.
13 But *as for* you, brethren, [a]do not grow weary
*in* doing good.
14 And if anyone does not obey our word in this
[1]epistle, note that person and [a]do not keep company with him, that he may be ashamed.
15 [a]Yet do not count *him* as an enemy, [b]but
[1]admonish *him* as a brother.
**16** Now may [a]the Lord of peace Himself give you
peace always in every way. The Lord *be* with you
all.
17 [a]The salutation of Paul with my own hand,
which is a sign in every [1]epistle; so I write.
18 [a]The grace of our Lord Jesus Christ *be* with
you all. Amen.

15 [a]1 Cor. 16:13 [b]1 Cor. 11:2 [1]*letter*
16 [a][Rev. 1:5] [b]1 Pet. 1:3
17 [a]1 Cor. 1:8 [1]*strengthen*
CHAPTER 3
1 [a]Eph. 6:19
2 [a]Rom. 15:31 [b]Acts 28:24
3 [a]1 Cor. 1:9 [b]John 17:15
4 [a]2 Cor. 7:16
5 [a]1 Chr. 29:18
6 [a]Rom. 16:17 [b]1 Cor. 5:1 [c]1 Thess. 4:11 [1]NU, M *they*
8 [a]1 Thess. 2:9 [1]Lit. *for nothing*
9 [a]1 Cor. 9:4, 6–14
11 [a]1 Pet. 4:15
12 [a]Eph. 4:28 [1]*encourage*
13 [a]Gal. 6:9
14 [a]Matt. 18:17 [1]*letter*
15 [a]Lev. 19:17 [b]Titus 3:10 [1]*warn*
16 [a]Rom. 15:33
17 [a]1 Cor. 16:21 [1]*letter*
18 [a]Rom. 16:20, 24

## *The First Epistle of Paul the Apostle to*

# TIMOTHY

### *Keep the Faith of the Gospel*

PAUL, an apostle of Jesus Christ, by the
commandment of God our Savior and the
Lord Jesus Christ, our hope,

2 To Timothy, a [a]true son in the faith:

[b]Grace, mercy, *and* peace from God our Father
and Jesus Christ our Lord.
**3** As I urged you [a]when I went into Macedonia—remain in Ephesus that you may [1]charge
some [b]that they teach no other doctrine,
4 [a]nor give heed to fables and endless genealogies, which cause disputes rather than godly
edification which is in faith.
5 Now [a]the purpose of the commandment is love
[b]from a pure heart, *from* a good conscience, and
*from* [1]sincere faith,
6 from which some, having strayed, have turned
aside to [a]idle talk,
7 desiring to be teachers of the law, understanding neither what they say nor the things which
they affirm.
8 But we know that the law *is* [a]good if one uses
it lawfully,
9 knowing this: that the law is not made for a
righteous person, but for *the* lawless and insubordinate, for *the* ungodly and for sinners, for *the*
unholy and profane, for murderers of fathers and
murderers of mothers, for manslayers,
10 for fornicators, for sodomites, for kidnappers,
for liars, for perjurers, and if there is any other
thing that is [1]contrary to sound doctrine,
11 according to the glorious gospel of the
[a]blessed God which was [b]committed to my trust.
**12** And I thank Christ Jesus our Lord who has
[a]enabled me, [b]because He counted me faithful,
[c]putting *me* into the ministry,
13 although [a]I was formerly a blasphemer, a
persecutor, and an [1]insolent man; but I obtained
mercy because [b]I did *it* ignorantly in unbelief.
14 [a]And the grace of our Lord was exceedingly
abundant, [b]with faith and love which are in Christ
Jesus.
15 [a]This *is* a faithful saying and worthy of all
acceptance, that [b]Christ Jesus came into the
world to save sinners, of whom I am chief.
16 However, for this reason I obtained mercy,
that in me first Jesus Christ might show all longsuffering, as a pattern to those who are going to
believe on Him for everlasting life.
17 Now to [a]the King eternal, [b]immortal, [c]invisible,
to [1]God [d]who alone is wise, [e]*be* honor and glory
forever and ever. Amen.
**18** This [1]charge I commit to you, son Timothy,
according to the prophecies previously made
concerning you, that by them you may wage the
good warfare,
19 having faith and a good conscience, which
some having rejected, concerning the faith have
suffered shipwreck,

CHAPTER 1
2 [a]Titus 1:4 [b]Gal. 1:3
3 [a]Acts 20:1, 3 [b]Gal. 1:6, 7 [1]*command*
4 [a]Titus 1:14
5 [a]Rom. 13:8–10 [b]Eph. 6:24 [1]Lit. *unhypocritical*
6 [a]1 Tim. 6:4, 20
8 [a]Rom. 7:12, 16
10 [1]*opposed*
11 [a]1 Tim. 6:15 [b]1 Cor. 9:17
12 [a]1 Cor. 15:10 [b]1 Cor. 7:25 [c]Col. 1:25
13 [a]Acts 8:3 [b]John 4:21 [1]*violently arrogant*
14 [a]Rom. 5:20 [b]2 Tim. 1:13; 2:22
15 [a]2 Tim. 2:11 [b]Matt. 1:21; 9:13
17 [a]Ps. 10:16 [b]Rom. 1:23 [c]Heb. 11:27 [d]Rom. 16:27 [e]1 Chr. 29:11 [1]NU *the only God,*
18 [1]*command*

20 of whom are [a]Hymenaeus and [b]Alexander,
whom I delivered to Satan that they may learn
not to [c]blaspheme.

### *Pray for Everyone*

**2** Therefore I [1]exhort first of all that supplications, prayers, intercessions, *and* giving of
thanks be made for all men,
2 [a]for kings and [b]all who are in [1]authority, that
we may lead a quiet and peaceable life in all
godliness and [2]reverence.
3 For this *is* [a]good and acceptable in the sight
[b]of God our Savior,
4 [a]who desires all men to be saved [b]and to come
to the knowledge of the truth.
5 [a]For *there is* one God and [b]one Mediator
between God and men, *the* Man Christ Jesus,
6 [a]who gave Himself a ransom for all, to be
testified in due time,
7 [a]for which I was appointed a preacher and an
apostle—I am speaking the truth [1]in Christ *and*
not lying—[b]a teacher of the Gentiles in faith and
truth.
**8** I desire therefore that the men pray [a]every-
where, [b]lifting up holy hands, without wrath and
doubting;
9 in like manner also, that the [a]women adorn
themselves in modest apparel, with propriety and
[1]moderation, not with braided hair or gold or
pearls or costly clothing,
10 [a]but, which is proper for women professing
godliness, with good works.
11 Let a woman learn in silence with all submission.
12 And [a]I do not permit a woman to teach or to
have authority over a man, but to be in silence.
13 For Adam was formed first, then Eve.
14 And Adam was not deceived, but the woman
being deceived, fell into transgression.
15 Nevertheless she will be saved in childbearing
if they continue in faith, love, and holiness, with
self-control.

### *Qualifications of Church Officers*

**3** This *is* a faithful saying: If a man desires the
position of a [1]bishop, he desires a good work.
2 A bishop then must be blameless, the husband
of one wife, temperate, sober-minded, of good
behavior, hospitable, able to teach;
3 not [1]given to wine, not violent, [2]not greedy for
money, but gentle, not quarrelsome, not [3]covet-
ous;
4 one who rules his own house well, having *his*
children in submission with all reverence
5 (for if a man does not know how to rule his
own house, how will he take care of the church of
God?);
6 not a [1]novice, lest being puffed up with pride
he fall into the *same* condemnation as the devil.
7 Moreover he must have a good testimony
among those who are outside, lest he fall into
reproach and the [a]snare of the devil.
**8** Likewise deacons *must be* reverent, not
double-tongued, [a]not given to much wine, not
greedy for money,
9 holding the [1]mystery of the faith with a pure
conscience.
10 But let these also first be tested; then let them
serve as deacons, being *found* blameless.
11 Likewise, *their* wives *must be* reverent, not
[1]slanderers, temperate, faithful in all things.
12 Let deacons be the husbands of one wife,
ruling *their* children and their own houses well.
13 For those who have served well as deacons
[a]obtain for themselves a good standing and great
boldness in the faith which is in Christ Jesus.
**14** These things I write to you, though I hope to
come to you shortly;
15 but if I am delayed, *I write* so that you may
know how you ought to conduct yourself in the
house of God, which is the church of the living
God, the pillar and [1]ground of the truth.
16 And without controversy great is the [1]mystery
of godliness:

[a]God[2] was manifested in the flesh,
[b]Justified in the Spirit,
[c]Seen by angels,
[d]Preached among the Gentiles,
[e]Believed on in the world,
[f]Received up in glory.

### *Be Faithful to Your Spiritual Calling*

**4** Now the Spirit [1]expressly says that in latter
times some will depart from the faith, giving
heed [a]to deceiving spirits and doctrines of demons,
2 [a]speaking lies in hypocrisy, having their own
conscience [b]seared with a hot iron,
3 forbidding to marry, *and commanding* to abstain from foods which God created to be received
with thanksgiving by those who believe and know
the truth.
4 For every creature of God *is* good, and nothing is to be refused if it is received with thanksgiving;
5 for it is [1]sanctified by the word of God and
prayer.
**6** If you instruct the brethren in these things,
you will be a good minister of Jesus Christ, [a]nour-
ished in the words of faith and of the good doctrine which you have carefully followed.
7 But [a]reject profane and old wives' fables, and
[b]exercise yourself toward godliness.
8 For [a]bodily exercise profits a little, but godliness is profitable for all things, [b]having promise of
the life that now is and of that which is to come.
9 This *is* a faithful saying and worthy of all
acceptance.
10 For to this *end* [1]we both labor and suffer
reproach, because we trust in the living God, [a]who
is *the* Savior of all men, especially of those who
believe.
11 These things command and teach.
**12** Let no one [1]despise your youth, but be an
[a]example to the believers in word, in conduct, in
love, [2]in spirit, in faith, in purity.
13 Till I come, give attention to reading, to
exhortation, to [1]doctrine.
14 [a]Do not neglect the gift that is in you, which
was given to you by prophecy [b]with the laying on
of the hands of the eldership.
15 Meditate on these things; give yourself entirely to them, that your progress may be evident
to all.
16 Take heed to yourself and to the doctrine.
Continue in them, for in doing this you will save
both yourself and those who hear you.

### *Treatment of Church Members and Officers*

**5** Do not rebuke an older man, but exhort *him*
as a father, younger men as brothers,
2 older women as mothers, younger women as
sisters, with all purity.

---

**20** [a]2 Tim. 2:17, 18 [b]2 Tim. 4:14 [c]Acts 13:45

CHAPTER 2
**1** [1]*encourage*
**2** [a]Ezra 6:10 [b][Rom. 13:1] [1]*a prominent place* [2]*dignity*
**3** [a]Rom. 12:2 [b]2 Tim. 1:9
**4** [a]Ezek. 18:23, 32 [b][John 17:3]
**5** [a]Gal. 3:20 [b][Heb. 9:15]
**6** [a]Mark 10:45
**7** [a]Eph. 3:7, 8 [b][Gal. 1:15, 16] [1]NU omits *in Christ*
**8** [a]Luke 23:34 [b]Ps. 134:2
**9** [a]1 Pet. 3:3 [1]*discretion*
**10** [a]1 Pet. 3:4
**12** [a]1 Cor. 14:34

CHAPTER 3
**1** [1]Lit. *overseer*
**3** [1]*addicted* [2]NU omits *not greedy for money* [3]*loving money*
**6** [1]*new convert*
**7** [a]2 Tim. 2:26
**8** [a]Ezek. 44:21
**9** [1]*hidden truth*
**11** [1]*malicious gossips*
**13** [a]Matt. 25:21
**15** [1]*foundation, mainstay*
**16** [a][John 1:14] [b][Matt. 3:16] [c]Matt. 28:2 [d]Rom. 10:18 [e]Col. 1:6, 23 [f]Luke 24:51 [1]*hidden truth* [2]NU *Who*

CHAPTER 4
**1** [a]Rev. 16:14 [1]*explicitly*
**2** [a]Matt. 7:15 [b]Eph. 4:19
**5** [1]*set apart*
**6** [a]2 Tim. 3:14
**7** [a]2 Tim. 2:16 [b]Heb. 5:14
**8** [a]1 Cor. 8:8 [b]Ps. 37:9
**10** [a]Ps. 36:6 [1]NU *we labor and strive,*
**12** [a]1 Pet. 5:3 [1]*look down on your youthfulness* [2]NU omits *in spirit*
**13** [1]*teaching*
**14** [a]2 Tim. 1:6 [b]Acts 6:6

**3** Honor widows who are really widows.
4 But if any widow has children or grandchildren, let them first learn to show piety at home and [a]to repay their parents; for this is [1]good and acceptable before God.
5 Now she who is really a widow, and left alone, trusts in God and continues in supplications and prayers [a]night and day.
6 But she who lives in [1]pleasure is dead while she lives.
7 And these things command, that they may be blameless.
8 But if anyone does not provide for his own, [a]and especially for those of his household, [b]he has denied the faith [c]and is worse than an unbeliever.
9 Do not let a widow under sixty years old be taken into the number, *and not unless* she has been the wife of one man,
10 well reported for good works: if she has brought up children, if she has lodged strangers, if she has washed the saints' feet, if she has relieved the afflicted, if she has diligently followed every good work.
11 But [1]refuse *the* younger widows; for when they have begun to grow wanton against Christ, they desire to marry,
12 having condemnation because they have cast off their first [1]faith.
13 And besides they learn *to be* idle, wandering about from house to house, and not only idle but also gossips and busybodies, saying things which they ought not.
14 Therefore I desire that *the* younger *widows* marry, bear children, manage the house, give no opportunity to the adversary to speak reproachfully.
15 For some have already turned aside after Satan.
16 If any believing [1]man or woman has widows, let them [2]relieve them, and do not let the church be burdened, that it may relieve those who are really widows.
**17** Let the elders who rule well be counted worthy of double honor, especially those who labor in the word and doctrine.
18 For the Scripture says, [a]*"You shall not muzzle an ox while it treads out the grain,"* and, [b]"The laborer *is* worthy of his wages."
19 Do not receive an accusation against an elder except [a]from two or three witnesses.
20 Those who are sinning rebuke in the presence of all, that the rest also may fear.
21 I charge *you* before God and the Lord Jesus Christ and the [1]elect angels that you observe these things without [a]prejudice, doing nothing with partiality.
22 Do not lay hands on anyone hastily, nor [a]share in other people's sins; keep yourself pure.
23 No longer drink only water, but use a little wine for your stomach's sake and your frequent [1]infirmities.
24 Some men's sins are [a]clearly evident, preceding *them* to judgment, but those of some *men* follow later.
25 Likewise, the good works *of some* are clearly evident, and those that are otherwise cannot be hidden.

## *Christian Conduct in the World*

**6** Let as many [a]bondservants as are under the yoke count their own masters worthy of all honor, so that the name of God and *His* doctrine may not be blasphemed.
2 And those who have believing masters, let them not despise *them* because they are brethren, but rather serve *them* because those who are benefited are believers and beloved. Teach and exhort these things.
**3** If anyone teaches otherwise and does not consent to [a]wholesome words, *even* the words of our Lord Jesus Christ, [b]and to the [1]doctrine which accords with godliness,
4 he is proud, knowing nothing, but is obsessed with disputes and arguments over words, from which come envy, strife, reviling, evil suspicions,
5 [1]useless wranglings of men of corrupt minds and destitute of the truth, who suppose that godliness is a *means of* gain. [2]From [a]such withdraw yourself.
6 Now godliness with [a]contentment is great gain.
7 For we brought nothing into *this* world, [1]*and it is* [a]certain we can carry nothing out.
8 And having food and clothing, with these we shall be [a]content.
9 But those who desire to be rich fall into temptation and a snare, and *into* many foolish and harmful lusts which drown men in destruction and perdition.
10 For the love of money is a root of all *kinds of* evil, for which some have strayed from the faith in their greediness, and pierced themselves through with many sorrows.
**11** But you, O man of God, flee these things and pursue righteousness, godliness, faith, love, patience, gentleness.
12 Fight the good fight of faith, lay hold on eternal life, to which you were also called and have confessed the good confession in the presence of many witnesses.
13 I urge you in the sight of God who gives life to all things, and *before* Christ Jesus [a]who witnessed the good confession before Pontius Pilate,
14 that you keep *this* commandment without spot, blameless until our Lord Jesus Christ's appearing,
15 which He will manifest in His own time, *He who is* the blessed and only [1]Potentate, the King of kings and Lord of lords,
16 who alone has immortality, dwelling in [a]unapproachable light, [b]whom no man has seen or can see, to whom *be* honor and everlasting power. Amen.
**17** Command those who are rich in this present age not to be haughty, nor to trust in uncertain [a]riches but in the living God, who gives us richly all things [b]to enjoy.
18 *Let them* do good, that they be rich in good works, ready to give, willing to share,
19 [a]storing up for themselves a good foundation for the time to come, that they may lay hold on eternal life.
**20** O Timothy! [a]Guard what was committed to your trust, [b]avoiding the profane *and* [1]idle babble and contradictions of what is falsely called knowledge—
21 by professing it some have strayed concerning the faith. Grace *be* with you. Amen.

CHAPTER 5
**4** [a]Gen. 45:10 [1]NU, M omit *good and*
**5** [a]Acts 26:7
**6** [1]*indulgence*
**8** [a]Is. 58:7; 2 Cor. 12:14 [b]2 Tim. 3:5 [c]Matt. 18:17
**11** [1]Refuse to enroll
**12** [1]Or *solemn promise*
**16** [1]NU omits *man or* [2]*give aid to*
**18** [a]Deut. 25:4; 1 Cor. 9:7–9 [b]Lev. 19:13; Deut. 24:15; Matt. 10:10; Luke 10:7; 1 Cor. 9:14
**19** [a]Deut. 17:6; 19:15; Matt. 18:16
**21** [a]Deut. 1:17 [1]*chosen*
**22** [a]Eph. 5:6, 7; 2 John 11
**23** [1]*illnesses*
**24** [a]Gal. 5:19–21

CHAPTER 6
**1** [a]Eph. 6:5; Titus 2:9; 1 Pet. 2:18
**3** [a]2 Tim. 1:13 [b]Titus 1:1 [1]*teaching*
**5** [a]2 Tim. 3:5 [1]NU, M *constant friction* [2]NU omits the rest of v. 5.
**6** [a]Phil. 4:11; Heb. 13:5
**7** [a]Job 1:21; Ps. 49:17; Eccl. 5:15 [1]NU omits *and it is certain*
**8** [a]Prov. 30:8, 9
**13** [a]Matt. 27:2; John 18:36, 37
**15** [1]*Sovereign*
**16** [a]Dan. 2:22 [b]John 6:46
**17** [a]Jer. 9:23; 48:7 [b]Eccl. 5:18, 19
**19** [a][Matt. 6:20, 21; 19:21]
**20** [a][2 Tim. 1:12, 14] [b]Titus 1:14 [1]*empty chatter*

The Second Epistle of Paul the Apostle to

# TIMOTHY

### Be Loyal to the Faith

PAUL, an apostle of [1]Jesus Christ by the will
of God, according to the [a]promise of life
which is in Christ Jesus,

2 To Timothy, a [a]beloved son:

Grace, mercy, *and* peace from God the Father
and Christ Jesus our Lord.
**3** I thank God, whom I serve with a pure conscience, as *my* [a]forefathers *did,* as without ceasing
I remember you in my prayers night and day,
4 greatly desiring to see you, being mindful of
your tears, that I may be filled with joy,
5 when I call to remembrance [a]the [1]genuine
faith that is in you, which dwelt first in your
grandmother Lois and [b]your mother Eunice, and I
am persuaded is in you also.
6 Therefore I remind you [a]to stir up the gift of
God which is in you through the laying on of my
hands.
7 For [a]God has not given us a spirit of fear, [b]but
of power and of love and of a sound mind.
**8** [a]Therefore do not be ashamed of [b]the testimony of our Lord, nor of me [c]His prisoner, but
share with me in the sufferings for the gospel
according to the power of God,
9 who has saved us and called *us* with a holy
calling, [a]not according to our works, but [b]accord-
ing to His own purpose and grace which was
given to us in Christ Jesus [c]before time began,
10 but [a]has now been revealed by the appearing
of our Savior Jesus Christ, *who* has abolished
death and brought life and immortality to light
through the gospel,
11 [a]to which I was appointed a preacher, an
apostle, and a teacher [1]of the Gentiles.
12 For this reason I also suffer these things;
nevertheless I am not ashamed, [a]for I know whom
I have believed and am persuaded that He is able
to keep what I have committed to Him until that
Day.
**13** [a]Hold fast [b]the pattern of [c]sound words which
you have heard from me, in faith and love which
are in Christ Jesus.
14 That good thing which was committed to you,
keep by the Holy Spirit who dwells in us.
15 This you know, that all those in Asia have
turned away from me, among whom are Phygellus
and Hermogenes.
16 The Lord grant mercy to the [a]household of
Onesiphorus, for he often refreshed me, and was
not ashamed of my chain;
17 but when he arrived in Rome, he sought me
out very zealously and found *me.*
18 The Lord [a]grant to him that he may find
mercy from the Lord [b]in that Day—and you know
very well how many ways he [c]ministered to me at
Ephesus.

### Be Strong in Grace

**2** You therefore, [a]my son, [b]be strong in the grace
that is in Christ Jesus.
2 And the things that you have heard from me
among many witnesses, commit these to faithful
men who will be able to teach others also.

CHAPTER 1
**1** [a]Titus 1:2 [1]NU, M *Christ Jesus*
**2** [a]1 Tim. 1:2
**3** [a]Acts 24:14
**5** [a]1 Tim. 1:5; 4:6 [b]Acts 16:1 [1]Lit. *unhypocritical*
**6** [a]1 Tim. 4:14
**7** [a]Rom. 8:15 [b][Acts 1:8]
**8** [a][Rom. 1:16] [b]1 Tim. 2:6 [c]Eph. 3:1
**9** [a][Rom. 3:20] [b]Rom. 8:28 [c]Rom. 16:25
**10** [a]Eph. 1:9
**11** [a]Acts 9:15 [1]NU omits *of the Gentiles*
**12** [a]1 Pet. 4:19
**13** [a]Titus 1:9 [b]Rom. 2:20; 6:17 [c]1 Tim. 6:3
**16** [a]2 Tim. 4:19
**18** [a]Mark 9:41 [b]2 Thess. 1:10 [c]Heb. 6:10

CHAPTER 2
**1** [a]1 Tim. 1:2 [b]Eph. 6:10
**3** [a]2 Tim. 4:5 [b]1 Tim. 1:18 [1]NU *share*
**4** [a][2 Pet. 2:20]
**5** [a][1 Cor. 9:25]
**7** [a]Prov. 2:6 [1]NU *the Lord will give you*
**8** [a]Rom. 1:3, 4 [b]1 Cor. 15:4 [c]Rom. 2:16
**9** [a]Acts 9:16 [b]Eph. 3:1 [c]Acts 28:31
**10** [a]Eph. 3:13 [b]2 Cor. 1:6 [1]*chosen ones*
**11** [a]Rom. 6:5, 8
**12** [a][Rom. 5:17; 8:17] [b]Matt. 10:33
**13** [a]Num. 23:19
**14** [a]Titus 3:9 [1]*battle*
**15** [a]2 Pet. 1:10
**16** [1]*empty chatter* [2]*lead*
**17** [a]1 Tim. 1:20
**18** [a]1 Cor. 15:12
**19** [a][1 Cor. 3:11] [b][Nah. 1:7] [1]NU, M *the Lord*
**20** [a]Rom. 9:21
**21** [a]2 Tim. 3:17 [1]*set apart*
**22** [a]1 Tim. 6:11
**24** [a]Titus 3:2 [b]Titus 1:9 [c]1 Tim. 3:3
**25** [a]Gal. 6:1 [b]Acts 8:22 [c]1 Tim. 2:4

3 You therefore must [a]endure[1] hardship [b]as a
good soldier of Jesus Christ.
4 [a]No one engaged in warfare entangles himself
with the affairs of *this* life, that he may please him
who enlisted him as a soldier.
5 And also [a]if anyone competes in athletics, he is
not crowned unless he competes according to the
rules.
6 The hard-working farmer must be first to
partake of the crops.
7 Consider what I say, and [1]may the Lord [a]give
you understanding in all things.
8 Remember that Jesus Christ, [a]of the seed of
David, [b]was raised from the dead [c]according to my
gospel,
9 [a]for which I suffer trouble as an evildoer,
[b]*even* to the point of chains; [c]but the word of God
is not chained.
10 Therefore [a]I endure all things for the sake of
the [1]elect, [b]that they also may obtain the salvation
which is in Christ Jesus with eternal glory.
11 *This is* a faithful saying:

For [a]if we died with *Him,*
We shall also live with *Him.*
12 [a]If we endure,
We shall also reign with *Him.*
[b]If we deny *Him,*
He also will deny us.
13 If we are faithless,
He remains faithful;
He [a]cannot deny Himself.

**14** Remind *them* of these things, [a]charging *them*
before the Lord not to [1]strive about words to no
profit, to the ruin of the hearers.
15 [a]Be diligent to present yourself approved to
God, a worker who does not need to be ashamed,
rightly dividing the word of truth.
16 But shun profane *and* [1]idle babblings, for they
will [2]increase to more ungodliness.
17 And their message will spread like cancer.
[a]Hymenaeus and Philetus are of this sort,
18 who have strayed concerning the truth, [a]say-
ing that the resurrection is already past; and they
overthrow the faith of some.
19 Nevertheless [a]the solid foundation of God
stands, having this seal: "The Lord [b]knows those
who are His," and, "Let everyone who names the
name of [1]Christ depart from iniquity."
20 But in a great house there are not only [a]vessels
of gold and silver, but also of wood and clay, some
for honor and some for dishonor.
21 Therefore if anyone cleanses himself from the
latter, he will be a vessel for honor, [1]sanctified and
useful for the Master, [a]prepared for every good
work.
22 [a]Flee also youthful lusts; but pursue righteousness, faith, love, peace with those who call on the
Lord out of a pure heart.
23 But avoid foolish and ignorant disputes, knowing that they generate strife.
24 And [a]a servant of the Lord must not quarrel
but be gentle to all, [b]able to teach, [c]patient,
25 [a]in humility correcting those who are in opposition, [b]if God perhaps will grant them repentance,
[c]so that they may know the truth,

26 and *that* they may come to their senses *and*
[a]*escape* the snare of the devil, having been taken
captive by him to *do* his will.

### *Dangerous Times Are Coming*

**3** But know this, that [a]in the last days [1]perilous
times will come:
2 For men will be lovers of themselves, lovers of
money, boasters, proud, blasphemers, disobedient
to parents, unthankful, unholy,
3 unloving, [1]unforgiving, slanderers, without
self-control, brutal, despisers of good,
4 [a]traitors, headstrong, haughty, lovers of pleasure rather than lovers of God,
5 [a]having a form of godliness but [b]denying its
power. And [c]from such people turn away!
6 For [a]of this sort are those who creep into
households and make captives of gullible women
loaded down with sins, led away by various lusts,
7 always learning and never able [a]to come to the
knowledge of the truth.
8 [a]Now as Jannes and Jambres resisted Moses,
so do these also resist the truth: [b]men of corrupt
minds, [c]disapproved concerning the faith;
9 but they will progress no further, for their
folly will be manifest to all, [a]as theirs also was.
**10** [a]But you have carefully followed my doctrine,
manner of life, purpose, faith, longsuffering, love,
perseverance,
11 persecutions, afflictions, which happened to
me [a]at Antioch, [b]at Iconium, [c]at Lystra—what
persecutions I endured. And [d]out of *them* all the
Lord delivered me.
12 Yes, and [a]all who desire to live godly in Christ
Jesus will suffer persecution.
13 [a]But evil men and impostors will grow worse
and worse, deceiving and being deceived.
14 But you must [a]continue in the things which
you have learned and been assured of, knowing
from whom you have learned *them*,
15 and that from childhood you have known [a]the
Holy Scriptures, which are able to make you wise
for salvation through faith which is in Christ
Jesus.
16 [a]All Scripture *is* given by inspiration of God,
[b]and *is* profitable for doctrine, for reproof, for
correction, for [1]instruction in righteousness,
17 [a]that the man of God may be complete, [b]thor-
oughly equipped for every good work.

### *Preach the Word*

**4** I [a]charge *you* [1]therefore before God and the
Lord Jesus Christ, [b]who will judge the living
and the dead [2]at His appearing and His kingdom:
2 Preach the word! Be ready in season *and* out
of season. [a]Convince, [b]rebuke, [c]exhort, with all
longsuffering and teaching.
3 [a]For the time will come when they will not
endure [b]sound doctrine, [c]but according to their
own desires, *because* they have itching ears, they
will heap up for themselves teachers;
4 and they will turn *their* ears away from the
truth, and [a]be turned aside to fables.
5 But you be watchful in all things, [a]endure
afflictions, do the work of [b]an evangelist, fulfill
your ministry.
**6** For [a]I am already being poured out as a drink
offering, and the time of [b]my departure is at hand.
7 [a]I have fought the good fight, I have finished
the race, I have kept the faith.
8 Finally, there is laid up for me [a]the crown of
righteousness, which the Lord, the righteous
[b]Judge, will give to me [c]on that Day, and not to
me only but also to all who have loved His appearing.
**9** Be diligent to come to me quickly;
10 for [a]Demas has forsaken me, [b]having loved
this present world, and has departed for Thessalonica—Crescens for Galatia, Titus for Dalmatia.
11 Only Luke is with me. Get [a]Mark and bring
him with you, for he is useful to me for ministry.
12 And [a]Tychicus I have sent to Ephesus.
13 Bring the cloak that I left with Carpus at
Troas when you come—and the books, especially
the parchments.
14 [a]Alexander the coppersmith did me much
harm. May the Lord repay him according to his
works.
15 You also must beware of him, for he has
greatly resisted our words.
16 At my first defense no one stood with me, but
all forsook me. [a]May it not be charged against
them.
**17** [a]But the Lord stood with me and strengthened
me, [b]so that the message might be preached fully
through me, and *that* all the Gentiles might hear.
Also I was delivered [c]out of the mouth of the lion.
18 [a]And the Lord will deliver me from every evil
work and preserve *me* for His heavenly kingdom.
[b]To Him *be* glory forever and ever. Amen!
**19** Greet [a]Prisca and Aquila, and the household of
[b]Onesiphorus.
20 [a]Erastus stayed in Corinth, but [b]Trophimus I
have left in Miletus sick.
21 Do your utmost to come before winter. Eubulus greets you, as well as Pudens, Linus, Claudia,
and all the brethren.
**22** The Lord [1]Jesus Christ be with your spirit.
Grace be with you. Amen.

**26** [a]1 Tim. 3:7

CHAPTER 3
**1** [a]1 Tim. 4:1 [1]*times of stress*
**3** [1]*irreconcilable*
**4** [a]2 Pet. 2:10
**5** [a]Titus 1:16 [b]1 Tim. 5:8 [c]2 Thess. 3:6
**6** [a]Matt. 23:14
**7** [a]1 Tim. 2:4
**8** [a]Ex. 7:11, 12, 22; 8:7; 9:11 [b]1 Tim. 6:5 [c]Rom. 1:28
**9** [a]Ex. 7:11, 12; 8:18; 9:11
**10** [a]1 Tim. 4:6
**11** [a]Acts 13:44–52 [b]Acts 14:1–6, 19 [c]Acts 14:8–20 [d]Ps. 34:19
**12** [a][Ps. 34:19]
**13** [a]2 Thess. 2:11
**14** [a]2 Tim. 1:13
**15** [a]John 5:39
**16** [a][2 Pet. 1:20] [b]Rom. 4:23; 15:4 [1]*training, discipline*
**17** [a]1 Tim. 6:11 [b]2 Tim. 2:21

CHAPTER 4
**1** [a]1 Tim. 5:21 [b]Acts 10:42 [1]NU omits *therefore* [2]NU *and by*
**2** [a]Titus 2:15 [b]1 Tim. 5:20 [c]1 Tim. 4:13
**3** [a]2 Tim. 3:1 [b]1 Tim. 1:10 [c]2 Tim. 3:6
**4** [a]1 Tim. 1:4
**5** [a]2 Tim. 1:8 [b]Acts 21:8
**6** [a]Phil. 2:17 [b][Phil. 1:23]
**7** [a]1 Cor. 9:24–27
**8** [a]James 1:12 [b]John 5:22 [c]2 Tim. 1:12
**10** [a]Col. 4:14 [b]1 John 2:15
**11** [a]Acts 12:12, 25; 15:37–39
**12** [a]Acts 20:4
**14** [a]1 Tim. 1:20
**16** [a]Acts 7:60
**17** [a]Acts 23:11 [b]Acts 9:15 [c]1 Sam. 17:37
**18** [a]Ps. 121:7 [b]Rom. 11:36
**19** [a]Acts 18:2 [b]2 Tim. 1:16
**20** [a]Rom. 16:23 [b]Acts 20:4; 21:29
**22** [1]NU omits *Jesus Christ*

*The Epistle of Paul the Apostle to*

# TITUS

### *Qualifications and Duties of Elders*

**1** PAUL, a bondservant of God and an apostle of Jesus Christ, according to the faith of God's elect and [a]the acknowledgment of the truth [b]which accords with godliness,
2 in hope of eternal life which God, who [a]cannot lie, promised before time began,
3 but has in due time manifested His word through preaching, which was committed to me according to the commandment of God our Savior;

4 To [a]Titus, a true son in *our* common faith:

Grace, mercy, *and* peace from God the Father and [1]the Lord Jesus Christ our Savior.
**5** For this reason I left you in Crete, that you should [a]set in order the things that are lacking, and appoint elders in every city as I commanded you—
6 if a man is blameless, the husband of one wife, [a]having faithful children not accused of [1]dissipation or insubordination.
7 For a [1]bishop must be blameless, as a steward of God, not self-willed, not quick-tempered, [a]not given to wine, not violent, not greedy for money,
8 but hospitable, a lover of what is good, soberminded, just, holy, self-controlled,
9 holding fast the faithful word as he has been taught, that he may be able, by sound doctrine, both to exhort and convict those who contradict.
**10** For there are many insubordinate, both idle [a]talkers and deceivers, especially those of the circumcision,
11 whose mouths must be stopped, who subvert whole households, teaching things which they ought not, [a]for the sake of dishonest gain.
12 [a]One of them, a prophet of their own, said, "Cretans *are* always liars, evil beasts, lazy gluttons."
13 This testimony is true. [a]Therefore rebuke them sharply, that they may be sound in the faith,
14 not giving heed to Jewish fables and [a]commandments of men who turn from the truth.
15 [a]To the pure all things are pure, but to those who are defiled and unbelieving nothing is pure; but even their mind and conscience are defiled.
16 They profess to [a]know God, but [b]in works they deny Him, being [1]abominable, disobedient, [c]and disqualified for every good work.

### *Qualities of a Sound Church*

**2** But as for you, speak the things which are proper for sound doctrine:
2 that the older men be sober, reverent, temperate, sound in faith, in love, in patience;
3 the older women likewise, that they be reverent in behavior, not slanderers, not given to much wine, teachers of good things—
4 that they admonish the young women to love their husbands, to love their children,
5 to be discreet, chaste, [a]homemakers, good, [b]obedient to their own husbands, [c]that the word of God may not be blasphemed.
6 Likewise, exhort the young men to be soberminded,
7 in all things showing yourself *to be* [a]a pattern of good works; in doctrine *showing* integrity, reverence, [b]incorruptibility,[1]
8 sound speech that cannot be condemned, that one who is an opponent may be ashamed, having nothing evil to say of [1]you.
9 *Exhort* [a]bondservants to be obedient to their own masters, to be well pleasing in all *things,* not answering back,
10 not [1]pilfering, but showing all good [2]fidelity, that they may adorn the doctrine of God our Savior in all things.
**11** For [a]the grace of God that brings salvation has appeared to all men,
12 teaching us that, denying ungodliness and worldly lusts, we should live soberly, righteously, and godly in the present age,
13 [a]looking for the blessed [b]hope and glorious appearing of our great God and Savior Jesus Christ,
14 [a]who gave Himself for us, that He might redeem us from every lawless deed [b]and purify for Himself [c]*His* own special people, zealous for good works.
15 Speak these things, [a]exhort, and rebuke with all authority. Let no one despise you.

### *Graces of the Heirs of Grace*

**3** Remind them [a]to be subject to rulers and authorities, to obey, [b]to be ready for every good work,
2 to speak evil of no one, to be peaceable, gentle, showing all humility to all men.
3 For [a]we ourselves were also once foolish, disobedient, deceived, serving various lusts and pleasures, living in malice and envy, hateful and hating one another.
4 But when [a]the kindness and the love of [b]God our Savior toward man appeared,
5 [a]not by works of righteousness which we have done, but according to His mercy He saved us, through [b]the washing of regeneration and renewing of the Holy Spirit,
6 [a]whom He poured out on us abundantly through Jesus Christ our Savior,
7 that having been justified by His grace [a]we should become heirs according to the hope of eternal life.
8 [a]This is a faithful saying, and these things I want you to affirm constantly, that those who have believed in God should be careful to maintain good works. These things are good and profitable to men.
**9** But [a]avoid foolish disputes, genealogies, contentions, and strivings about the law; for they are unprofitable and useless.
10 [a]Reject a divisive man after the first and second [1]admonition,
11 knowing that such a person is warped and sinning, being self-condemned.
**12** When I send Artemas to you, or [a]Tychicus, be

CHAPTER 1
**1** [a]2 Tim. 2:25 [b][1 Tim. 3:16]
**2** [a]Num. 23:19
**4** [a]2 Cor. 2:13; 8:23; Gal. 2:3; 2 Tim. 4:10 [1]NU *Christ Jesus*
**5** [a]1 Cor. 11:34
**6** [a]1 Tim. 3:2–4; Titus 1:6–8 [1]*debauchery,* lit. *incorrigibility*
**7** [a]Lev. 10:9 [1]Lit. *overseer*
**10** [a]James 1:26
**11** [a]1 Tim. 6:5
**12** [a]Acts 17:28
**13** [a]2 Cor. 13:10; 2 Tim. 4:2
**14** [a]Is. 29:13
**15** [a]Luke 11:41; Rom. 14:14, 20; 1 Cor. 6:12
**16** [a]Matt. 7:20–23; 25:12; 1 John 2:4 [b][2 Tim. 3:5, 7] [c]Rom. 1:28 [1]*detestable*

CHAPTER 2
**5** [a]1 Tim. 5:14 [b]1 Cor. 14:34; 1 Tim. 2:11 [c]Rom. 2:24
**7** [a]Phil. 3:17; 1 Tim. 4:12 [b]Eph. 6:24 [1]NU omits *incorruptibility*
**8** [1]NU, M *us*
**9** [a]Eph. 6:5; 1 Tim. 6:1
**10** [1]*thieving* [2]*honesty*
**11** [a][Rom. 5:15]
**13** [a]1 Cor. 1:7 [b][Col. 3:4]
**14** [a]Is. 53:12; Gal. 1:4 [b]Ezek. 37:23; [Heb. 1:3; 9:14; 1 John 1:7] [c]Ex. 15:16
**15** [a]1 Tim. 4:13; 5:20; 2 Tim. 4:2

CHAPTER 3
**1** [a][Rom. 13:1]; 1 Pet. 2:13 [b]Col. 1:10
**3** [a]1 Cor. 6:11; 1 Pet. 4:3
**4** [a]Titus 2:11 [b]1 Tim. 2:3
**5** [a][Rom. 3:20]; Eph. 2:4–9 [b]John 3:3
**6** [a]Ezek. 36:25
**7** [a][Matt. 25:34]; Mark 10:17; [Rom. 8:17, 23, 24; Titus 1:2]
**8** [a]1 Tim. 1:15
**9** [a]1 Tim. 1:4; 2 Tim. 2:23
**10** [a]Matt. 18:17 [1]*warning*
**12** [a]Acts 20:4; Eph. 6:21; Col. 4:7; 2 Tim. 4:12

diligent to come to me at Nicopolis, for I have
decided to spend the winter there.
13 Send Zenas the lawyer and [a]Apollos on their
journey with haste, that they may lack nothing.
14 And let our *people* also learn to maintain good
works, to *meet* urgent needs, that they may not be
unfruitful.
15 All who *are* with me greet you. Greet those
who love us in the faith. Grace *be* with you all.
Amen.

13 [a]Acts 18:24; 1 Cor. 16:12

*The Epistle of Paul the Apostle to*

# PHILEMON

### *Paul's Concern for a Slave*

PAUL, a [a]prisoner of Christ Jesus, and Timothy *our* brother,

To Philemon our beloved *friend* and fellow
laborer,
2 to [1]the beloved Apphia, [a]Archippus our fellow
soldier, and to the church in your house:

3 Grace to you and peace from God our Father
and the Lord Jesus Christ.
4 [a]I thank my God, making mention of you
always in my prayers,
5 [a]hearing of your love and faith which you
have toward the Lord Jesus and toward all the
saints,
6 that the sharing of your faith may become
effective [a]by the acknowledgment of [b]every good
thing which is in [1]you in Christ Jesus.
7 For we [1]have great [2]joy and [3]consolation in
your love, because the [4]hearts of the saints have
been refreshed by you, brother.
8 Therefore, though I might be very bold in
Christ to command you what is fitting,
9 *yet* for love's sake I rather appeal *to you*—
being such a one as Paul, the aged, and now also a
prisoner of Jesus Christ—
10 I appeal to you for my son [a]Onesimus, whom I
have begotten *while* in my chains,
11 who once was unprofitable to you, but now is
profitable to you and to me.
12 I am sending him [1]back. You therefore receive
him, that is, my own [2]heart,
13 whom I wished to keep with me, that on your
behalf he might minister to me in my chains for
the gospel.
14 But without your consent I wanted to do
nothing, [a]that your good deed might not be by
compulsion, as it were, but voluntary.
15 For perhaps he departed for a while for this
*purpose*, that you might receive him forever,
16 no longer as a slave but more than a slave—a
beloved brother, especially to me but how much
more to you, both in the [a]flesh and in the Lord.
17 If then you count me as a partner, receive him
as *you would* me.
18 But if he has wronged you or owes anything,
put that on my account.
19 I, Paul, am writing with my own [a]hand. I will
repay—not to mention to you that you owe me
even your own self besides.
20 Yes, brother, let me have joy from you in the
Lord; refresh my heart in the Lord.
21 [a]Having confidence in your obedience, I write
to you, knowing that you will do even more than I
say.
22 But, meanwhile, also prepare a guest room for
me, for [a]I trust that [b]through your prayers I shall
be granted to you.
23 [a]Epaphras, my fellow prisoner in Christ Jesus,
greets you,
24 *as do* [a]Mark, [b]Aristarchus, [c]Demas, [d]Luke, my
fellow laborers.
25 [a]The grace of our Lord Jesus Christ *be* with
your spirit. Amen.

1 [a]Eph. 3:1
2 [a]Col. 4:17 [1]NU *our sister Apphia*
4 [a]2 Thess. 1:3
5 [a]Col. 1:4
6 [a]Phil. 1:9 [b][1 Thess. 5:18] [1]NU, M *us*
7 [1]NU *had* [2]M *thanksgiving* [3]*comfort* [4]Lit. *inward parts,* heart, liver, and lungs
10 [a]Col. 4:9
12 [1]NU *back to you in person, that is, my own heart,* [2]See v. 7.
14 [a]2 Cor. 9:7
16 [a]Col. 3:22
19 [a]1 Cor. 16:21
21 [a]2 Cor. 7:16
22 [a]Phil. 1:25; 2:24 [b]2 Cor. 1:11
23 [a]Col. 1:7; 4:12
24 [a]Acts 12:12, 25; 15:37–39 [b]Acts 19:29; 27:2 [c]Col. 4:14 [d]2 Tim. 4:11
25 [a]2 Tim. 4:22

*The Epistle to the*

# HEBREWS

### *Christ the Fullest Revelation of God*

GOD, who [1]at various times and [a]in various
ways spoke in time past to the fathers by
the prophets,
2 has in these last days spoken to us by *His* Son,
whom He has appointed heir of all things, through
whom also He made the [1]worlds;
3 [a]who being the brightness of *His* glory and the
express [b]image of His person, and [c]upholding all
things by the word of His power, [d]when He had
[1]by Himself [2]purged [3]our sins, [e]sat down at the
right hand of the Majesty on high,
4 having become so much better than the angels, as [a]He has by inheritance obtained a more
excellent name than they.
5 For to which of the angels did He ever say:

[a]*"You are My Son,*
*Today I have begotten You"*?

And again:

[b]*"I will be to Him a Father,*
*And He shall be to Me a Son"*?

CHAPTER 1
1 [a]Num. 12:6, 8 [1]Or *in many portions*
2 [1]Or *ages,* Gr. *aiones,* aeons
3 [a]John 1:14 [b]2 Cor. 4:4 [c]Col. 1:17 [d][Heb. 7:27] [e]Ps. 110:1 [1]NU omits *by Himself* [2]*cleansed* [3]NU omits *our*
4 [a][Phil. 2:9, 10]

5 [a]Ps. 2:7; Acts 13:33; Heb. 5:5 [b]2 Sam. 7:14

6 But when He again brings [a]the firstborn into
the world, He says:

[b]*"Let all the angels of God worship Him."*

7 And of the angels He says:

[a]*"Who makes His angels spirits*
*And His ministers a flame of fire."*

8 But to the Son *He says:*

[a]*"Your throne, O God, is forever and ever;*
*A* [1]*scepter of righteousness is the scepter of*
*Your kingdom.*
9 *You have loved righteousness and hated*
*lawlessness;*
*Therefore God, Your God,* [a]*has anointed You*
*With the oil of gladness more than Your*
*companions."*

10 And:

[a]*"You,* LORD*, in the beginning laid*
*the foundation of the earth,*
*And the heavens are the work*
*of Your hands.*
11 [a]*They will perish, but You remain;*
*And* [b]*they will all grow old like a garment;*
12 *Like a cloak You will fold them up,*
*And they will be changed.*
*But You are the* [a]*same,*
*And Your years will not fail."*

13 But to which of the angels has He ever said:

[a]*"Sit at My right hand,*
*Till I make Your enemies Your footstool"*?

14 [a]Are they not all ministering spirits sent forth
to minister for those who will [b]inherit salvation?

### *Christ Has Dominion over the World*

**2** Therefore we must give [1]the more earnest
heed to the things we have heard, lest we drift
away.
2 For if the word [a]spoken through angels proved
steadfast, and [b]every transgression and disobedience received a just [1]reward,
3 [a]how shall we escape if we neglect so great a
salvation, [b]which at the first began to be spoken
by the Lord, and was [c]confirmed to us by those
who heard *Him,*
4 [a]God also bearing witness [b]both with signs and
wonders, with various miracles, and [c]gifts[1] of the
Holy Spirit, [d]according to His own will?
5 For He has not put [a]the world to come, of
which we speak, in subjection to angels.
6 But one testified in a certain place, saying:

[a]*"What is man that You are mindful of him,*
*Or the son of man that You*
*take care of him?*
7 *You have made him* [1]*a little lower*
*than the angels;*
*You have crowned him with glory and*
*honor,*
[2]*And set him over the works of Your hands.*
8 [a]*You have put all things*
*in subjection under his feet."*

For in that He put all in subjection under him, He
left nothing *that is* not put under him. But now
[b]we do not yet see all things put under him.
9 But we see Jesus, [a]who was made [1]a little
lower than the angels, for the suffering of death
[b]crowned with glory and honor, that He, by the
grace of God, might taste death [c]for everyone.
10 For it was fitting for Him, [a]for whom *are* all
things and by whom *are* all things, in bringing
many sons to glory, to make the captain of their
salvation [b]perfect through sufferings.
11 For [a]both He who [1]sanctifies and those who
are being sanctified [b]*are* all of one, for which
reason [c]He is not ashamed to call them brethren,
12 saying:

[a]*"I will declare Your name to My brethren;*
*In the midst of the assembly*
*I will sing praise to You."*

13 And again:

[a]*"I will put My trust in Him."*

And again:

[b]*"Here am I and the children*
*whom God has given Me."*

14 Inasmuch then as the children have partaken
of flesh and blood, He [a]Himself likewise shared in
the same, [b]that through death He might destroy
him who had the power of [c]death, that is, the
devil,
15 and release those who [a]through fear of death
were all their lifetime subject to bondage.
16 For indeed He does not [1]give aid to angels, but
He does [2]give aid to the seed of Abraham.
17 Therefore, in all things He had [a]to be made
like *His* brethren, that He might be [b]a merciful and
faithful High Priest in things *pertaining* to God, to
make propitiation for the sins of the people.
18 [a]For in that He Himself has suffered, being
[1]tempted, He is able to aid those who are tempted.

### *Christ Our Model of Faithfulness*

**3** Therefore, holy brethren, partakers of the
heavenly calling, consider the Apostle and
High Priest of our confession, Christ Jesus,
2 who was faithful to Him who appointed Him,
as [a]Moses also *was faithful* in all His house.
3 For this One has been counted worthy of more
glory than Moses, inasmuch as [a]He who built the
house has more honor than the house.
4 For every house is built by someone, but [a]He
who built all things *is* God.
5 [a]And Moses indeed *was* faithful in all His
house as [b]a servant, [c]for a testimony of those
things which would be spoken *afterward,*
6 but Christ as [a]a Son over His own house,
[b]whose house we are [c]if we hold fast the confidence and the rejoicing of the hope [1]firm to the
end.
7 Therefore, as [a]the Holy Spirit says:

[b]*"Today, if you will hear His voice,*
8 *Do not harden your hearts*
*as in the rebellion,*
*In the day of trial in the wilderness,*
9 *Where your fathers tested Me, tried Me,*
*And saw My works forty years.*
10 *Therefore I was angry with that generation,*
*And said, 'They always go astray*
*in their heart,*
*And they have not known My ways.'*
11 *So I swore in My wrath,*
*'They shall not enter My rest.' "*

12 Beware, brethren, lest there be in any of you
an evil heart of unbelief in departing from the
living God;

**6** [a][Rom. 8:29] [b]Deut. 32:43, LXX, DSS; Ps. 97:7
**7** [a]Ps. 104:4
**8** [a]Ps. 45:6, 7 [1]A ruler's staff
**9** [a]Is. 61:1, 3
**10** [a]Ps. 102:25–27
**11** [a][Is. 34:4] [b]Is. 50:9; 51:6
**12** [a]Heb. 13:8
**13** [a]Ps. 110:1
**14** [a]Ps. 103:20 [b]Rom. 8:17

CHAPTER 2
**1** [1]*all the more careful attention*
**2** [a]Acts 7:53 [b]Num. 15:30 [1]*retribution* or *penalty*
**3** [a]Heb. 10:28 [b]Matt. 4:17 [c]Luke 1:2
**4** [a]Mark 16:20 [b]Acts 2:22, 43 [c]1 Cor. 12:4, 7, 11 [d]Eph. 1:5, 9 [1]*distributions*
**5** [a][2 Pet. 3:13]
**6** [a]Ps. 8:4–6
**7** [1]Or *for a little while* [2]NU, M omit the rest of v. 7.
**8** [a]Matt. 28:18 [b]1 Cor. 15:25, 27
**9** [a]Phil. 2:7–9 [b]Acts 2:33; 3:13 [c][John 3:16] [1]Or *for a little while*
**10** [a]Col. 1:16 [b]Heb. 5:8, 9; 7:28
**11** [a]Heb. 10:10 [b]Acts 17:26 [c]Matt. 28:10 [1]*sets apart*
**12** [a]Ps. 22:22
**13** [a]2 Sam. 22:3; Is. 8:17 [b]Is. 8:18
**14** [a]John 1:14 [b]Col. 2:15 [c]2 Tim. 1:10
**15** [a][Luke 1:74]
**16** [1]Or *take on* the nature of [2]Or *take on*
**17** [a]Phil. 2:7 [b][Heb. 4:15; 5:1–10]
**18** [a][Heb. 4:15, 16] [1]*tested*

CHAPTER 3
**2** [a]Num. 12:7
**3** [a]Zech. 6:12, 13
**4** [a][Eph. 2:10]
**5** [a]Heb. 3:2 [b]Ex. 14:31 [c]Deut. 18:15, 18, 19
**6** [a]Heb. 1:2 [b][1 Cor. 3:16] [c][Matt. 10:22] [1]NU omits *firm to the end*
**7** [a]Acts 1:16 [b]Ps. 95:7–11

13 but [1]exhort one another daily, while it is called
*"Today,"* lest any of you be hardened through the
deceitfulness of sin.
14 For we have become partakers of Christ if we
hold the beginning of our confidence steadfast to
the end,
15 while it is said:

[a]*"Today, if you will hear His voice,*
*Do not harden your hearts as in the*
*rebellion."*

16 [a]For who, having heard, rebelled? Indeed, *was*
*it* not all who came out of Egypt, *led* by Moses?
17 Now with whom was He angry forty years?
*Was it* not with those who sinned, [a]whose corpses
fell in the wilderness?
18 And [a]to whom did He swear that they would
not enter His rest, but to those who did not obey?
19 So we see that they could not enter in because
of [a]unbelief.

### *Be Sure to Enter the Promised Rest*

**4** Therefore, since a promise remains of entering
His rest, [a]let us fear lest any of you seem to
have come short of it.
2 For indeed the gospel was preached to us as
well as to them; but the word which they heard
did not profit them, [1]not being mixed with faith in
those who heard *it.*
3 For we who have believed do enter that rest,
as He has said:

[a]*"So I swore in My wrath,*
*'They shall not enter My rest,' "*

although the works were finished from the foundation of the world.
4 For He has spoken in a certain place of the
seventh *day* in this way: [a]*"And God rested on the*
*seventh day from all His works"*;
5 and again in this *place:* [a]*"They shall not enter*
*My rest."*
6 Since therefore it remains that some *must*
enter it, and those to whom it was first preached
did not enter because of disobedience,
7 again He designates a certain day, saying in
David, *"Today,"* after such a long time, as it has
been said:

[a]*"Today, if you will hear His voice,*
*Do not harden your hearts."*

8 For if [1]Joshua had [a]given them rest, then He
would not afterward have spoken of another day.
9 There remains therefore a rest for the people
of God.
10 For he who has entered His rest has himself
also ceased from his works as God *did* from His.
11 [a]Let us therefore be diligent to enter that rest,
lest anyone fall according to the same example of
disobedience.
12 For the word of God *is* [a]living and powerful,
and [b]sharper than any [c]two-edged sword, piercing
even to the division of soul and spirit, and of joints
and marrow, and is [d]a discerner of the thoughts
and intents of the heart.
13 [a]And there is no creature hidden from His
sight, but all things *are* [b]naked and open to the
eyes of Him to whom we *must give* account.
14 Seeing then that we have a great [a]High Priest
who has passed through the heavens, Jesus the
Son of God, [b]let us hold fast *our* confession.
15 For [a]we do not have a High Priest who cannot
sympathize with our weaknesses, but [b]was in all
*points* tempted as *we are,* [c]*yet* without sin.
16 [a]Let us therefore come boldly to the throne of
grace, that we may obtain mercy and find grace to
help in time of need.

### *Christ Our High Priest Forever*

**5** For every high priest taken from among men
[a]is appointed for men in things *pertaining* to
God, that he may offer both gifts and sacrifices for
sins.
2 He can [1]have compassion on those who are
ignorant and going astray, since he himself is also
subject to [a]weakness.
3 Because of this he is required as for the people,
so also for [a]himself, to offer *sacrifices* for sins.
4 And no man takes this honor to himself, but
he who is called by God, just as [a]Aaron *was.*
5 [a]So also Christ did not glorify Himself to
become High Priest, *but it* was He who said to
Him:

[b]*"You are My Son,*
*Today I have begotten You."*

6 As *He* also *says* in another *place:*

[a]*"You are a priest forever*
*According to the order of Melchizedek"*;

7 who, in the days of His flesh, when He had
[a]offered up prayers and supplications, [b]with vehement cries and tears to Him [c]who was able to save
Him from death, and was heard [d]because of His
godly fear,
8 though He was a Son, *yet* He learned [a]obedi-
ence by the things which He suffered.
9 And [a]having been perfected, He became the
author of eternal salvation to all who obey Him,
10 called by God as High Priest [a]*"according to*
*the order of Melchizedek,"*
11 of whom [a]we have much to say, and hard to
explain, since you have become [b]dull of hearing.
12 For though by this time you ought to be
teachers, you need *someone* to teach you again
the first principles of the [1]oracles of God; and you
have come to need [a]milk and not solid food.
13 For everyone who partakes *only* of milk *is*
unskilled in the word of righteousness, for he is [a]a
babe.
14 But solid food belongs to those who are [1]of full
age, *that is,* those who by reason of [2]use have
their senses exercised [a]to discern both good and
evil.

### *Be Faithful Because God Is Faithful*

**6** Therefore, [a]leaving the discussion of the ele-
mentary *principles* of Christ, let us go on to
[1]perfection, not laying again the foundation of
repentance from [b]dead works and of faith toward
God,
2 [a]of the doctrine of baptisms, [b]of laying on of
hands, [c]of resurrection of the dead, [d]and of eternal
judgment.
3 And this [1]we will do if God permits.
4 For *it is* impossible for those who were once
enlightened, and have tasted [a]the heavenly gift,
and [b]have become partakers of the Holy Spirit,
5 and have tasted the good word of God and the
powers of the age to come,
6 [1]if they fall away, to renew them again to
repentance, [a]since they crucify again for them-

13 [1]*encourage*
15 [a]Ps. 95:7, 8
16 [a]Num. 14:2, 11, 30
17 [a]Num. 14:22, 23
18 [a]Num. 14:30
19 [a]1 Cor. 10:11, 12

CHAPTER 4
1 [a]Heb. 12:15
2 [1]NU, M *since they were not united by faith with those who heeded it*
3 [a]Ps. 95:11
4 [a]Gen. 2:2
5 [a]Ps. 95:11
7 [a]Ps. 95:7, 8
8 [a]Josh. 22:4 [1]Gr. *Jesus,* same as Heb. *Joshua*
11 [a]2 Pet. 1:10
12 [a]Ps. 147:15 [b]Is. 49:2 [c]Eph. 6:17 [d]1 Cor. 14:24, 25
13 [a]Ps. 33:13–15; 90:8 [b]Job 26:6
14 [a]Heb. 2:17; 7:26 [b]Heb. 10:23
15 [a]Is. 53:3–5 [b]Luke 22:28 [c]2 Cor. 5:21
16 [a][Eph. 2:18]

CHAPTER 5
1 [a]Heb. 2:17; 8:3
2 [a]Heb. 7:28 [1]*deal gently with*
3 [a]Lev. 9:7; 16:6
4 [a]Ex. 28:1
5 [a]John 8:54 [b]Ps. 2:7
6 [a]Ps. 110:4
7 [a]Matt. 26:39, 42, 44 [b]Ps. 22:1 [c]Matt. 26:53 [d]Matt. 26:37
8 [a]Phil. 2:8
9 [a]Heb. 2:10
11 [a][John 16:12] [b][Matt. 13:15]
12 [a]1 Cor. 3:1–3 [1]*sayings,* Scriptures
13 [a]Eph. 4:14
14 [a]Is. 7:15 [1]*mature* [2]*practice*

CHAPTER 6
1 [a]Heb. 5:12 [b][Heb. 9:14] [1]*maturity*
2 [a]Acts 19:3–5 [b][Acts 8:17] [c]Acts 17:31 [d]Acts 24:25
3 [1]M *let us do*
4 [a][John 4:10] [b][Gal. 3:2, 5]
6 [a]Heb. 10:29 [1]Or *and have fallen away*

selves the Son of God, and put *Him* to an open
shame.
7 For the earth which drinks in the rain that
often comes upon it, and bears herbs useful for
those by whom it is cultivated, [a]receives blessing
from God;
8 [a]but if it bears thorns and briers, *it is* rejected
and near to being cursed, whose end *is* to be
burned.
**9** But, beloved, we are confident of better things
concerning you, yes, things that accompany salvation, though we speak in this manner.
10 For [a]God *is* not unjust to forget [b]your work
and [1]labor of love which you have shown toward
His name, *in that* you have [c]ministered to the
saints, and do minister.
11 And we desire that each one of you show the
same diligence [a]to the full assurance of hope until
the end,
12 that you do not become [1]sluggish, but imitate
those who through faith and patience [a]inherit the
promises.
**13** For when God made a promise to Abraham,
because He could swear by no one greater, [a]He
swore by Himself,
14 saying, [a]*"Surely blessing I will bless you, and*
*multiplying I will multiply you."*
15 And so, after he had patiently endured, he
obtained the [a]promise.
16 For men indeed swear by the greater, and [a]an
oath for confirmation *is* for them an end of all
dispute.
17 Thus God, determining to show more abundantly to [a]the heirs of promise [b]the [1]immutability
of His counsel, [2]confirmed *it* by an oath,
18 that by two [1]immutable things, in which it *is*
impossible for God to [a]lie, we [2]might have strong
consolation, who have fled for refuge to lay hold
of the hope [b]set before *us.*
19 This *hope* we have as an anchor of the soul,
both sure and steadfast, [a]and which enters the
Presence *behind* the veil,
20 [a]where the forerunner has entered for us, *even*
Jesus, [b]having become High Priest forever according to the order of Melchizedek.

### *Melchizedek a Picture of Christ*

**7** For this [a]Melchizedek, king of Salem, priest of
the Most High God, who met Abraham returning from the slaughter of the kings and blessed
him,
2 to whom also Abraham gave a tenth part of
all, first being translated "king of righteousness,"
and then also king of Salem, meaning "king of
peace,"
3 without father, without mother, without genealogy, having neither beginning of days nor end of
life, but made like the Son of God, remains a priest
continually.
4 Now consider how great this man *was,* to
whom even the patriarch Abraham gave a tenth
of the [1]spoils.
5 And indeed [a]those who are of the sons of Levi,
who receive the priesthood, have a commandment
to receive tithes from the people according to the
law, that is, from their brethren, though they have
come from the loins of Abraham;
6 but he whose genealogy is not derived from
them received tithes from Abraham [a]and blessed
[b]him who had the promises.
7 Now beyond all contradiction the lesser is
blessed by the better.
8 Here mortal men receive tithes, but there he
*receives them,* [a]of whom it is witnessed that he
lives.
9 Even Levi, who receives tithes, paid tithes
through Abraham, so to speak,
10 for he was still in the loins of his father when
Melchizedek met him.
**11** [a]Therefore, if perfection were through the
Levitical priesthood (for under it the people received the law), what further need *was there* that
another priest should rise according to the order
of Melchizedek, and not be called according to the
order of Aaron?
12 For the priesthood being changed, of necessity
there is also a change of the law.
13 For He of whom these things are spoken
belongs to another tribe, from which no man has
[1]officiated at the altar.
14 For *it is* evident that [a]our Lord arose from
[b]Judah, of which tribe Moses spoke nothing concerning [1]priesthood.
15 And it is yet far more evident if, in the likeness
of Melchizedek, there arises another priest
16 who has come, not according to the law of a
fleshly commandment, but according to the power
of an endless life.
17 For [1]He testifies:

[a]*"You are a priest forever*
*According to the order of Melchizedek."*

18 For on the one hand there is an annulling of
the former commandment because of [a]its weakness and unprofitableness,
19 for [a]the law made nothing [1]perfect; on the
other hand, *there is the* bringing in of [b]a better
hope, through which [c]we draw near to God.
**20** And inasmuch as *He was* not *made priest*
without an oath
21 (for they have become priests without an
oath, but He with an oath by Him who said to
Him:

[a]*"The LORD has sworn*
*And will not relent,*
*'You are a priest [1]forever*
*According to the order of Melchizedek'* "),

22 by so much more Jesus has become a [1]surety
of a [a]better covenant.
23 Also there were many priests, because they
were prevented by death from continuing.
24 But He, because He continues forever, has an
unchangeable priesthood.
25 Therefore He is also [a]able to save [1]to the
uttermost those who come to God through Him,
since He always lives [b]to make intercession for
them.
26 For such a High Priest was fitting for us, [a]*who*
*is* holy, [1]harmless, undefiled, separate from sinners, [b]and has become higher than the heavens;
27 who does not need daily, as those high priests,
to offer up sacrifices, first for His [a]own sins and
then for the people's, for this He did once for all
when He offered up Himself.
28 For the law appoints as high priests men who
have weakness, but the word of the oath, which
came after the law, *appoints* the Son who has
been perfected forever.

7 [a]Ps. 65:10
8 [a]Is. 5:6
10 [a]Rom. 3:4 [b]1 Thess. 1:3 [c]Rom. 15:25 [1]NU omits *labor of*
11 [a]Col. 2:2
12 [a]Heb. 10:36 [1]*lazy*
13 [a]Gen. 22:16, 17
14 [a]Gen. 22:16, 17
15 [a]Gen. 12:4; 21:5
16 [a]Ex. 22:11
17 [a]Heb. 11:9 [b]Rom. 11:29 [1]*unchangeableness of His purpose* [2]*guaranteed*
18 [a]Num. 23:19 [b][Col. 1:5] [1]*unchangeable* [2]M omits *might*
19 [a]Lev. 16:2, 15
20 [a][Heb. 4:14] [b]Heb. 3:1; 5:10, 11

CHAPTER 7
1 [a]Gen. 14:18–20
4 [1]*plunder*
5 [a]Num. 18:21–26
6 [a]Gen. 14:19, 20 [b][Rom. 4:13]
8 [a]Heb. 5:6; 6:20
11 [a]Heb. 7:18; 8:7
13 [1]*served*
14 [a]Is. 1:1 [b]Matt. 1:2 [1]NU *priests*
17 [a]Ps. 110:4 [1]NU *it is testified*
18 [a][Rom. 8:3]
19 [a][Acts 13:39] [b]Heb. 6:18, 19 [c]Rom. 5:2 [1]*complete*
21 [a]Ps. 110:4 [1]NU ends the quotation after *forever.*
22 [a]Heb. 8:6 [1]*guarantee*
25 [a]Jude 24 [b]Rom. 8:34 [1]*completely* or *forever*
26 [a]Heb. 4:15 [b]Eph. 1:20 [1]*innocent*
27 [a]Lev. 9:7; 16:6

## *The New Priest and the New Covenant*

**8** Now *this is* the main point of the things we are saying: We have such a High Priest, [a]who is seated at the right hand of the throne of the Majesty in the heavens,
2 a Minister of [a]the [1]sanctuary and of [b]the true tabernacle which the Lord erected, and not man.
3 For [a]every high priest is appointed to offer both gifts and sacrifices. Therefore [b]*it is* necessary that this One also have something to offer.
4 For if He were on earth, He would not be a priest, since there are priests who offer the gifts according to the law;
5 who serve [a]the copy and [b]shadow of the heavenly things, as Moses was divinely instructed when he was about to make the tabernacle. For He said, [c]*"See that you make all things according to the pattern shown you on the mountain."*
6 But now [a]He has obtained a more excellent ministry, inasmuch as He is also Mediator of a [b]better covenant, which was established on better promises.
7 For if that [a]first *covenant* had been faultless, then no place would have been sought for a second.
8 Because finding fault with them, He says: [a]*"Behold, the days are coming, says the* LORD, *when I will make a new covenant with the house of Israel and with the house of Judah—*
9 *"not according to the covenant that I made with their fathers in the day when I took them by the hand to lead them out of the land of Egypt; because they did not continue in My covenant, and I disregarded them, says the* LORD.
10 *"For this is the covenant that I will make with the house of Israel after those days, says the* [a]LORD: *I will put My laws in their mind and write them on their hearts; and* [b]*I will be their God, and they shall be My people.*
11 [a]*"None of them shall teach his neighbor, and none his brother, saying, 'Know the* [b]LORD,*' for all shall know Me, from the least of them to the greatest of them.*
12 *"For I will be merciful to their unrighteousness,* [a]*and their sins* [1]*and their lawless deeds I will remember no more."*
13 [a]In that He says, *"A new covenant,"* He has made the first obsolete. Now what is becoming obsolete and growing old is ready to vanish away.

## *The Greatness of Christ's Sacrifice*

**9** Then indeed, even the first *covenant* had ordinances of divine service and [a]the earthly sanctuary.
2 For a tabernacle was prepared: the first *part,* in which *was* the lampstand, the table, and the showbread, which is called the [1]sanctuary;
3 [a]and behind the second veil, the part of the tabernacle which is called the Holiest of All,
4 which had the [a]golden censer and [b]the ark of the covenant overlaid on all sides with gold, in which *were* [c]the golden pot that had the manna, [d]Aaron's rod that budded, and [e]the tablets of the covenant;
5 and [a]above it were the cherubim of glory overshadowing the mercy seat. Of these things we cannot now speak in detail.
6 Now when these things had been thus prepared, [a]the priests always went into the first part of the tabernacle, performing *the services.*
7 But into the second part the high priest *went* alone [a]once a year, not without blood, which he offered for [b]himself and *for* the people's sins *committed* in ignorance;
8 the Holy Spirit indicating this, that [a]the way into the Holiest of All was not yet made manifest while the first tabernacle was still standing.
9 It *was* symbolic for the present time in which both gifts and sacrifices are offered [a]which cannot make him who performed the service perfect in regard to the conscience—
10 *concerned* only with [a]foods and drinks, [b]various [1]washings, [c]and fleshly ordinances imposed until the time of reformation.
**11** But Christ came *as* High Priest of [a]the good things [1]to come, with the greater and more perfect tabernacle not made with hands, that is, not of this creation.
12 Not [a]with the blood of goats and calves, but [b]with His own blood He entered the Most Holy Place [c]once for all, [d]having obtained eternal redemption.
13 For if [a]the blood of bulls and goats and [b]the ashes of a heifer, sprinkling the unclean, [1]sanctifies for the [2]purifying of the flesh,
14 how much more shall the blood of Christ, who through the eternal Spirit offered Himself without [1]spot to God, [a]cleanse your conscience from [b]dead works [c]to serve the living God?
15 And for this reason [a]He is the Mediator of the new covenant, by means of death, for the redemption of the transgressions under the first covenant, that [b]those who are called may receive the promise of the eternal inheritance.
**16** For where there *is* a testament, there must also of necessity be the death of the testator.
17 For [a]a testament *is* in force after men are dead, since it has no power at all while the testator lives.
18 [a]Therefore not even the first *covenant* was dedicated without blood.
19 For when Moses had spoken every [1]precept to all the people according to the law, [a]he took the blood of calves and goats, [b]with water, scarlet wool, and hyssop, and sprinkled both the book itself and all the people,
20 saying, [a]*"This is the* [b]*blood of the covenant which God has commanded you."*
21 Then likewise [a]he sprinkled with blood both the tabernacle and all the vessels of the ministry.
22 And according to the law almost all things are [1]purified with blood, and [a]without shedding of blood there is no [2]remission.
**23** Therefore *it was* necessary that [a]the copies of the things in the heavens should be [1]purified with these, but the heavenly things themselves with better sacrifices than these.
24 For [a]Christ has not entered the holy places made with hands, *which are* [1]copies of [b]the true, but into heaven itself, now [c]to appear in the presence of God for us;
25 not that He should offer Himself often, as [a]the high priest enters the Most Holy Place every year with blood of another—
26 He then would have had to suffer often since the foundation of the world; but now, once at the end of the ages, He has appeared to put away sin by the sacrifice of Himself.
27 [a]And as it is appointed for men to die once, [b]but after this the judgment,
28 so [a]Christ was [b]offered once to bear the sins [c]of many. To those who [d]eagerly wait for Him He

CHAPTER 8
**1** [a]Col. 3:1
**2** [a]Heb. 9:8, 12 [b]Heb. 9:11, 24 [1]Lit. *holies*
**3** [a]Heb. 5:1; 8:4 [b][Eph. 5:2]
**5** [a]Heb. 9:23, 24 [b]Col. 2:17 [c]Ex. 25:40
**6** [a][2 Cor. 3:6–8] [b]Heb. 7:22
**7** [a]Ex. 3:8; 19:5
**8** [a]Jer. 31:31–34
**10** [a]Jer. 31:33 [b]Zech. 8:8
**11** [a]Is. 54:13 [b]Jer. 31:34
**12** [a]Rom. 11:27 [1]NU omits *and their lawless deeds*
**13** [a][2 Cor. 5:17]

CHAPTER 9
**1** [a]Ex. 25:8
**2** [1]*holy place,* lit. *holies*
**3** [a]Ex. 26:31–35; 40:3
**4** [a]Lev. 16:12 [b]Ex. 25:10 [c]Ex. 16:33 [d]Num. 17:1–10 [e]Ex. 25:16; 34:29
**5** [a]Lev. 16:2
**6** [a]Num. 18:2–6; 28:3
**7** [a]Ex. 30:10 [b]Heb. 5:3
**8** [a][John 14:6]
**9** [a]Heb. 7:19
**10** [a]Col. 2:16 [b]Num. 19:7 [c]Eph. 2:15 [1]Lit. *baptisms*
**11** [a]Heb. 10:1 [1]NU *that have come*
**12** [a]Heb. 10:4 [b]Eph. 1:7 [c]Zech. 3:9 [d][Dan. 9:24]
**13** [a]Lev. 16:14, 15 [b]Num. 19:2 [1]*sets apart* [2]*cleansing*
**14** [a]1 John 1:7 [b]Heb. 6:1 [c]Luke 1:74 [1]*blemish*
**15** [a]Rom. 3:25 [b]Heb. 3:1
**17** [a]Gal. 3:15
**18** [a]Ex. 24:6
**19** [a]Ex. 24:5, 6 [b]Lev. 14:4, 7 [1]*command*
**20** [a][Matt. 26:28] [b]Ex. 24:3–8
**21** [a]Ex. 29:12, 36
**22** [a]Lev. 17:11 [1]*cleansed* [2]*forgiveness*
**23** [a]Heb. 8:5 [1]*cleansed*
**24** [a]Heb. 6:20 [b]Heb. 8:2 [c]Rom. 8:34 [1]*representations*
**25** [a]Heb. 9:7
**27** [a]Gen. 3:19 [b][2 Cor. 5:10]
**28** [a]Rom. 6:10 [b]1 Pet. 2:24 [c]Matt. 26:28 [d]Titus 2:13

will appear a second time, apart from sin, for
salvation.

### *Justified by Faith in Christ's Sacrifice*

**10** For the law, having a [a]shadow of the good
things to come, *and* not the very image of
the things, [b]can never with these same sacrifices,
which they offer continually year by year, make
those who approach perfect.
2 For then would they not have ceased to be
offered? For the worshipers, once [1]purified, would
have had no more consciousness of sins.
3 But in those *sacrifices there is* a reminder of
sins every year.
4 For [a]*it is* not possible that the blood of bulls
and goats could take away sins.
**5** Therefore, when He came into the world, He
said:

[a]*"Sacrifice and offering You did not desire,*
*But a body You have prepared for Me.*
6 *In burnt offerings and sacrifices for sin*
*You had no pleasure.*
7 *Then I said, 'Behold, I have come—*
*In the volume of the book*
*it is written of Me—*
*To do Your will, O God.'"*

8 Previously saying, *"Sacrifice and offering,*
*burnt offerings, and offerings for sin You did not*
*desire, nor had pleasure in them"* (which are
offered according to the law),
9 then He said, *"Behold, I have come to do Your*
*will,* [1]*O God."* He takes away the first that He may
establish the second.
10 [a]By that will we have been [1]sanctified
[b]through the offering of the body of Jesus Christ
once *for all.*
**11** And every priest stands [a]ministering daily and
offering repeatedly the same sacrifices, which can
never take away sins.
12 [a]But this Man, after He had offered one sacrifice for sins forever, sat down [b]at the right hand of
God,
13 from that time waiting [a]till His enemies are
made His footstool.
14 For by one offering He has perfected forever
those who are being [1]sanctified.
15 But the Holy Spirit also witnesses to us; for
after He had said before,
16 [a]*"This is the covenant that I will make with*
*them after those days, says the* LORD: *I will put*
*My laws into their hearts, and in their minds I will*
*write them,"*
17 *then He adds,* [a]*"Their sins and their lawless*
*deeds I will remember no more."*
18 Now where there is [1]remission of these, *there*
*is* no longer an offering for sin.
**19** Therefore, brethren, having [a]boldness[1] to enter
[b]the Holiest by the blood of Jesus,
20 by a new and [a]living way which He consecrated for us, through the veil, that is, His flesh,
21 and *having* a High Priest over the house of
God,
22 let us [a]draw near with a true heart [b]in full
assurance of faith, having our hearts sprinkled
from an evil conscience and our bodies washed
with pure water.
23 Let us hold fast the confession of *our* hope
without wavering, for [a]He who promised *is* faithful.
24 And let us consider one another in order to stir
up love and good works,

CHAPTER 10
**1** [a]Heb. 8:5 [b]Heb. 7:19; 9:9
**2** [1]*cleansed*
**4** [a]Mic. 6:6, 7
**5** [a]Ps. 40:6–8
**9** [1]NU, M omit *O God*
**10** [a]John 17:19 [b][Heb. 9:12] [1]*set apart*
**11** [a]Num. 28:3
**12** [a]Col. 3:1 [b]Ps. 110:1
**13** [a]Ps. 110:1
**14** [1]*set apart*
**16** [a]Jer. 31:33, 34
**18** [1]*forgiveness*
**19** [a][Eph. 2:18] [b]Heb. 9:8, 12 [1]*confidence*
**20** [a]John 14:6
**22** [a]Heb. 7:19; 10:1 [b]Eph. 3:12
**23** [a]1 Cor. 1:9; 10:13
**25** [a]Acts 2:42 [b]Rom. 13:11 [c]Phil. 4:5
**26** [a]Num. 15:30 [b]2 Pet. 2:20 [c]Heb. 6:6
**27** [a]Zeph. 1:18
**28** [a]Deut. 17:2–6; 19:15
**29** [a][Heb. 2:3] [b]1 Cor. 11:29 [c][Matt. 12:31]
**30** [a]Deut. 32:35 [b]Deut. 32:36 [1]NU omits *says the Lord*
**31** [a][Luke 12:5]
**32** [a]Gal. 3:4 [1]*enlightened*
**33** [a]1 Cor. 4:9 [b]Phil. 1:7
**34** [a]2 Tim. 1:16 [b]Matt. 5:12 [c]Matt. 6:20 [1]NU *the prisoners* instead of *me in my chains* [2]*possessions* [3]NU omits *in heaven*
**35** [a]Matt. 5:12
**36** [a]Luke 21:19 [b][Col. 3:24]
**37** [a]Luke 18:8 [b]Hab. 2:3, 4 [1]*delay*
**38** [a]Rom. 1:17 [1]NU *my just one*
**39** [a]2 Pet. 2:20 [b]Acts 16:31 [1]*destruction*

CHAPTER 11
**1** [a]Rom. 8:24 [1]*realization* [2]Or *confidence*
**3** [a]Ps. 33:6 [1]Or *ages,* Gr. *aiones,* aeons
**4** [a]Gen. 4:3–5 [b]Heb. 12:24
**5** [a]Gen. 5:21–24

25 [a]not forsaking the assembling of ourselves
together, as *is* the manner of some, but exhorting
*one another,* and [b]so much the more as you see
[c]the Day approaching.
**26** For [a]if we sin willfully [b]after we have received
the knowledge of the truth, there [c]no longer
remains a sacrifice for sins,
27 but a certain fearful expectation of judgment,
and [a]fiery indignation which will devour the adversaries.
28 Anyone who has rejected Moses' law dies
without mercy on the testimony of two or three
[a]witnesses.
29 [a]Of how much worse punishment, do you
suppose, will he be thought worthy who has
trampled the Son of God underfoot, [b]counted the
blood of the covenant by which he was sanctified
a common thing, [c]and insulted the Spirit of grace?
30 For we know Him who said, [a]*"Vengeance is*
*Mine, I will repay,"* [1]says the Lord. And again,
[b]*"The* LORD *will judge His people."*
31 [a]It is a fearful thing to fall into the hands of
the living God.
32 But [a]recall the former days in which, after you
were [1]illuminated, you endured a great struggle
with sufferings:
33 partly while you were made [a]a spectacle both
by reproaches and tribulations, and partly while
[b]you became companions of those who were so
treated;
34 for you had compassion on [1]me [a]in my chains,
and [b]joyfully accepted the plundering of your
[2]goods, knowing that [c]you have a better and an
enduring possession for yourselves [3]in heaven.
35 Therefore do not cast away your confidence,
[a]which has great reward.
36 [a]For you have need of endurance, so that after
you have done the will of God, [b]you may receive
the promise:

37 *"For*[a] [b]*yet a little while,*
*And He who is coming will come*
*and will not* [1]*tarry.*
38 *Now* [a]*the*[1] *just shall live by faith;*
*But if anyone draws back,*
*My soul has no pleasure in him."*

39 But we are not of those [a]who draw back to
[1]perdition, but of those who [b]believe to the saving
of the soul.

### *The Honor Roll of the Faithful*

**11** Now faith is the [1]substance of things hoped
for, the [2]evidence [a]of things not seen.
2 For by it the elders obtained a *good* testimony.
3 By faith we understand that [a]the [1]worlds were
framed by the word of God, so that the things
which are seen were not made of things which are
visible.
**4** By faith [a]Abel offered to God a more excellent
sacrifice than Cain, through which he obtained
witness that he was righteous, God testifying of
his gifts; and through it he being dead still
[b]speaks.
5 By faith Enoch was taken away so that he did
not see death, [a]*"and was not found, because God*
*had taken him"*; for before he was taken he had
this testimony, that he pleased God.
6 But without faith *it is* impossible to please
*Him,* for he who comes to God must believe that
He is, and *that* He is a rewarder of those who
diligently seek Him.

7 By faith [a]Noah, being divinely warned of
things not yet seen, moved with godly fear, [b]pre-
pared an ark for the saving of his household, by
which he condemned the world and became heir
of [c]the righteousness which is according to faith.
**8** By faith [a]Abraham obeyed when he was called
to go out to the place which he would receive as
an inheritance. And he went out, not knowing
where he was going.
9 By faith he dwelt in the land of promise as *in* a
foreign country, [a]dwelling in tents with Isaac and
Jacob, [b]the heirs with him of the same promise;
10 for he waited for [a]the city which has foundations, [b]whose builder and maker *is* God.
11 By faith [a]Sarah herself also received strength
to conceive seed, and [b]she[1] bore a child when she
was past the age, because she judged Him [c]faithful
who had promised.
12 Therefore from one man, and him as good as
[a]dead, were born *as many* as the [b]stars of the sky
in multitude—innumerable as the sand which is
by the seashore.
**13** These all died in faith, [a]not having received
the [b]promises, but [c]having seen them afar off
[1]were assured of them, embraced *them* and [d]con-
fessed that they were strangers and pilgrims on
the earth.
14 For those who say such things [a]declare plainly
that they seek a homeland.
15 And truly if they had called to mind [a]that
*country* from which they had come out, they
would have had opportunity to return.
16 But now they desire a better, that is, a heavenly *country*. Therefore God is not ashamed [a]to be
called their God, for He has [b]prepared a city for
them.
**17** By faith Abraham, [a]when he was tested, offered up Isaac, and he who had received the
promises offered up his only begotten *son*,
18 [1]of whom it was said, [a]*"In Isaac your seed
shall be called,"*
19 concluding that God [a]*was* able to raise *him* up,
even from the dead, from which he also received
him in a figurative sense.
20 By faith [a]Isaac blessed Jacob and Esau concerning things to come.
21 By faith Jacob, when he was dying, [a]blessed
each of the sons of Joseph, and worshiped, *leaning*
on the top of his staff.
22 By faith [a]Joseph, when he was dying, made
mention of the departure of the children of Israel,
and gave instructions concerning his bones.
**23** By faith [a]Moses, when he was born, was hidden three months by his parents, because they
saw *he was* a beautiful child; and they were not
afraid of the king's [b]command.
24 By faith [a]Moses, when he became of age,
refused to be called the son of Pharaoh's daughter,
25 choosing rather to suffer affliction with the
people of God than to enjoy the [1]passing pleasures
of sin,
26 esteeming [a]the [1]reproach of Christ greater
riches than the treasures [2]in Egypt; for he looked
to the [b]reward.
27 By faith [a]he forsook Egypt, not fearing the
wrath of the king; for he endured as seeing Him
who is invisible.
28 By faith [a]he kept the Passover and the sprinkling of blood, lest he who destroyed the firstborn
should touch them.
29 By faith [a]they passed through the Red Sea as
by dry *land, whereas* the Egyptians, attempting *to
do* so, were drowned.
**30** By faith [a]the walls of Jericho fell down after
they were encircled for seven days.
31 By faith [a]the harlot Rahab did not perish with
those who [1]did not believe, when [b]she had received the spies with peace.
32 And what more shall I say? For the time
would fail me to tell of [a]Gideon and [b]Barak and
[c]Samson and [d]Jephthah, also *of* [e]David and [f]Sam-
uel and the prophets:
33 who through faith subdued kingdoms, worked
righteousness, obtained promises, [a]stopped the
mouths of lions,
34 [a]quenched the violence of fire, escaped the
edge of the sword, out of weakness were made
strong, became valiant in battle, turned to flight
the armies of the aliens.
35 [a]Women received their dead raised to life
again. Others were [b]tortured, not accepting deliverance, that they might obtain a better resurrection.
36 Still others had trial of mockings and scourg-
ings, yes, and [a]of chains and imprisonment.
37 [a]They were stoned, they were sawn in two,
[1]were tempted, were slain with the sword. [b]They
wandered about [c]in sheepskins and goatskins,
being destitute, afflicted, tormented—
38 of whom the world was not worthy. They
wandered in deserts and mountains, [a]*in* dens and
caves of the earth.
39 And all these, [a]having obtained a good testimony through faith, did not receive the promise,
40 God having provided something better for
us, that they should not be [a]made perfect apart
from us.

### *Renew Your Spiritual Life*

**12** Therefore we also, since we are surrounded
by so great a cloud of witnesses, [a]let us lay
aside every weight, and the sin which so easily
ensnares *us*, and [b]let us run [c]with endurance the
race that is set before us,
2 looking unto Jesus, the [1]author and [2]finisher
of *our* faith, [a]who for the joy that was set before
Him [b]endured the cross, despising the shame, and
[c]has sat down at the right hand of the throne of
God.
**3** [a]For consider Him who endured such hostility
from sinners against Himself, [b]lest you become
weary and discouraged in your souls.
4 [a]You have not yet resisted to bloodshed, striving against sin.
5 And you have forgotten the exhortation
which speaks to you as to sons:

[a]*"My son, do not despise the [1]chastening of the*
*LORD,*
*Nor be discouraged when you are rebuked by*
*Him;*
6 *For [a]whom the LORD loves He chastens,*
*And scourges every son whom He receives."*

7 [a]If[1] you endure chastening, God deals with
you as with sons; for what [b]son is there whom a
father does not chasten?
8 But if you are without chastening, [a]of which
all have become partakers, then you are illegitimate and not sons.
9 Furthermore, we have had human fathers who

**7** [a]Gen. 6:13–22 [b]1 Pet. 3:20 [c]Rom. 3:22
**8** [a]Gen. 12:1–4
**9** [a]Gen. 12:8; 13:3, 18; 18:1, 9 [b]Heb. 6:17
**10** [a][Heb. 12:22; 13:14] [b][Rev. 21:10]
**11** [a]Gen. 17:19; 18:11–14; 21:1, 2 [b]Luke 1:36 [c]Heb. 10:23 [1]NU omits *she bore a child*
**12** [a]Rom. 4:19 [b]Gen. 15:5; 22:17; 32:12
**13** [a]Heb. 11:39 [b]Gen. 12:7 [c]John 8:56 [d]Ps. 39:12 [1]NU, M omit *were assured of them*
**14** [a]Heb. 13:14
**15** [a]Gen. 11:31
**16** [a]Ex. 3:6, 15; 4:5 [b][Rev. 21:2]
**17** [a]James 2:21
**18** [a]Gen. 21:12 [1]*to*
**19** [a]Rom. 4:17
**20** [a]Gen. 27:26–40
**21** [a]Gen. 48:1, 5, 16, 20
**22** [a]Gen. 50:24, 25
**23** [a]Ex. 2:1–3 [b]Ex. 1:16, 22
**24** [a]Ex. 2:11–15
**25** [1]*temporary*
**26** [a]Heb. 13:13 [b]Rom. 8:18 [1]*reviling because of* [2]NU, M *of*
**27** [a]Ex. 10:28
**28** [a]Ex. 12:21
**29** [a]Ex. 14:22–29
**30** [a]Josh. 6:20
**31** [a]Josh. 2:9; 6:23 [b]Josh. 2:1 [1]*were disobedient*
**32** [a]Judg. 6:11; 7:1–25 [b]Judg. 4:6–24 [c]Judg. 13:24—16:31 [d]Judg. 11:1–29; 12:1–7 [e]1 Sam. 16; 17 [f]1 Sam. 7:9–14
**33** [a]Dan. 6:22
**34** [a]Dan. 3:23–28
**35** [a]1 Kin. 17:22 [b]Acts 22:25
**36** [a]Gen. 39:20
**37** [a]1 Kin. 21:13 [b]2 Kin. 1:8 [c]Zech. 13:4 [1]NU omits *were tempted*
**38** [a]1 Kin. 18:4, 13; 19:9
**39** [a]Heb. 11:2, 13
**40** [a]Heb. 5:9

CHAPTER 12
**1** [a]Col. 3:8 [b]1 Cor. 9:24 [c]Rom. 12:12
**2** [a]Luke 24:26 [b]Phil. 2:8 [c]Ps. 110:1 [1]*originator* [2]*perfecter*
**3** [a]Matt. 10:24 [b]Gal. 6:9
**4** [a][1 Cor. 10:13]
**5** [a]Prov. 3:11, 12 [1]*discipline*
**6** [a]Rev. 3:19
**7** [a]Deut. 8:5; 2 Sam. 7:14 [b]Prov. 13:24; 19:18; 23:13 [1]NU, M *It is for discipline that you endure; God*
**8** [a]1 Pet. 5:9

corrected *us*, and we paid *them* respect. Shall we not much more readily be in subjection to [a]the Father of spirits and live?
10 For they indeed for a few days chastened *us* as seemed *best* to them, but He for *our* profit, [a]that *we* may be partakers of His holiness.
11 Now no [1]chastening seems to be joyful for the present, but painful; nevertheless, afterward it yields [a]the peaceable fruit of righteousness to those who have been trained by it.
**12** Therefore [a]strengthen the hands which hang down, and the feeble knees,
13 and make straight paths for your feet, so that what is lame may not be *dislocated*, but rather be healed.
14 [a]Pursue peace with all *people*, and holiness, [b]without which no one will see the Lord:
15 looking carefully lest anyone [a]fall short of the grace of God; lest any [b]root of bitterness springing up cause trouble, and by this many become defiled;
16 lest there *be* any [a]fornicator or [1]profane person like Esau, [b]who for one morsel of food sold his birthright.
17 For you know that afterward, when he wanted to inherit the blessing, he was [a]rejected, for he found no place for repentance, though he sought it diligently with tears.
**18** For you have not come [1]to [a]the mountain that may be touched and that burned with fire, and to blackness and [2]darkness and tempest,
19 and the sound of a trumpet and the voice of words, so that those who heard *it* [a]begged that the word should not be spoken to them anymore.
20 (For they could not endure what was commanded: [a]*"And if so much as a beast touches the mountain, it shall be stoned* [1]*or shot with an arrow."*
21 And so terrifying was the sight *that* Moses said, [a]*"I am exceedingly afraid* and trembling.")
22 But you have come to Mount Zion and to the city of the living God, the heavenly Jerusalem, to an innumerable company of angels,
23 to the [1]general assembly and church of [a]the firstborn [b]*who are* registered in heaven, to God [c]the Judge of all, to the spirits of just men [d]made perfect,
24 to Jesus [a]the Mediator of the new covenant, and to [b]the blood of sprinkling that speaks better things [c]than *that of* Abel.
**25** See that you do not refuse Him who speaks. For [a]if they did not escape who refused Him who spoke on earth, much more *shall we not escape* if we turn away from Him who *speaks* from heaven,
26 whose voice then shook the earth; but now He has promised, saying, [a]*"Yet once more I* [1]*shake not only the earth, but also heaven."*
27 Now this, *"Yet once more,"* indicates the [a]removal of those things that are being shaken, as of things that are made, that the things which cannot be shaken may remain.
28 Therefore, since we are receiving a kingdom which cannot be shaken, let us have grace, by which we [1]may [a]serve God acceptably with reverence and godly fear.
29 For [a]our God *is* a consuming fire.

### *Final Moral and Spiritual Directions*

**13** Let [a]brotherly love continue.
2 [a]Do not forget to entertain strangers, for by so *doing* [b]some have unwittingly entertained angels.

9 [a][Job 12:10]
10 [a]Lev. 11:44
11 [a]James 3:17, 18 [1]*discipline*
12 [a]Is. 35:3
14 [a]Ps. 34:14 [b]Matt. 5:8
15 [a]Heb. 4:1 [b]Deut. 29:18
16 [a][1 Cor. 6:13–18] [b]Gen. 25:33 [1]*godless*
17 [a]Gen. 27:30–40
18 [a]Deut. 4:11; 5:22 [1]NU *to that which* [2]NU *gloom*
19 [a]Ex. 20:18–26
20 [a]Ex. 19:12, 13 [1]NU, M omit the rest of v. 20.
21 [a]Deut. 9:19
23 [a][James 1:18] [b]Luke 10:20 [c]Ps. 50:6; 94:2 [d][Phil. 3:12] [1]*festal gathering*
24 [a]Heb. 8:6; 9:15 [b]Ex. 24:8 [c]Gen. 4:10
25 [a]Heb. 2:2, 3
26 [a]Hag. 2:6 [1]NU *will shake*
27 [a][Is. 34:4; 54:10; 65:17]
28 [a]Heb. 13:15, 21 [1]M omits *may*
29 [a]Ex. 24:17

CHAPTER 13
1 [a]Rom. 12:10
2 [a]Matt. 25:35 [b]Gen. 18:1–22; 19:1
3 [a]Matt. 25:36
4 [a]Prov. 5:18, 19 [b]1 Cor. 6:9
5 [a]Deut. 31:6, 8; Josh. 1:5
6 [a]Ps. 27:1; 118:6
7 [1]*lead*
8 [a]Heb. 1:12
9 [1]NU, M *away*
12 [1]*set apart*
13 [a]1 Pet. 4:14
15 [a]Eph. 5:20 [b]Lev. 7:12 [c]Hos. 14:2 [1]Lit. *confessing*
16 [a]Rom. 12:13 [b]Phil. 4:18
17 [a]Phil. 2:29 [b]Ezek. 3:17 [1]*lead*
18 [a]Eph. 6:19 [b]Acts 23:1
20 [a]Rom. 5:1, 2, 10; 15:33 [b]Rom. 4:24 [c]1 Pet. 2:25; 5:4 [d]Zech. 9:11
21 [a]Phil. 2:13 [1]*perfect* [2]NU, M *us*
24 [1]*lead*

3 [a]Remember the prisoners as if chained with them—those who are mistreated—since you yourselves are in the body also.
4 [a]Marriage *is* honorable among all, and the bed undefiled; [b]but fornicators and adulterers God will judge.
5 *Let your* conduct *be* without covetousness; *be* content with such things as you have. For He Himself has said, [a]*"I will never leave you nor forsake you."*
6 So we may boldly say:

[a]*"The* LORD *is my helper;*
*I will not fear.*
*What can man do to me?"*

7 Remember those who [1]rule over you, who have spoken the word of God to you, whose faith follow, considering the outcome of *their* conduct.
8 Jesus Christ *is* [a]the same yesterday, today, and forever.
9 Do not be carried [1]about with various and strange doctrines. For *it is* good that the heart be established by grace, not with foods which have not profited those who have been occupied with them.
10 We have an altar from which those who serve the tabernacle have no right to eat.
11 For the bodies of those animals, whose blood is brought into the sanctuary by the high priest for sin, are burned outside the camp.
12 Therefore Jesus also, that He might [1]sanctify the people with His own blood, suffered outside the gate.
13 Therefore let us go forth to Him, outside the camp, bearing [a]His reproach.
14 For here we have no continuing city, but we seek the one to come.
15 [a]Therefore by Him let us continually offer [b]the sacrifice of praise to God, that is, [c]the fruit of *our* lips, [1]giving thanks to His name.
16 [a]But do not forget to do good and to share, for [b]with such sacrifices God is well pleased.
17 [a]Obey those who [1]rule over you, and be submissive, for [b]they watch out for your souls, as those who must give account. Let them do so with joy and not with grief, for that would be unprofitable for you.
**18** [a]Pray for us; for we are confident that we have [b]a good conscience, in all things desiring to live honorably.
19 But I especially urge *you* to do this, that I may be restored to you the sooner.
**20** Now may [a]the God of peace [b]who brought up our Lord Jesus from the dead, [c]that great Shepherd of the sheep, [d]through the blood of the everlasting covenant,
21 make you [1]complete in every good work to do His will, [a]working in [2]you what is well pleasing in His sight, through Jesus Christ, to whom *be* glory forever and ever. Amen.
22 And I appeal to you, brethren, bear with the word of exhortation, for I have written to you in few words.
23 Know that *our* brother Timothy has been set free, with whom I shall see you if he comes shortly.
24 Greet all those who [1]rule over you, and all the saints. Those from Italy greet you.
25 Grace *be* with you all. Amen.

# *The Epistle of*
# JAMES

## *Faith Works in Trial*

JAMES, [a]a bondservant of God and of the Lord
Jesus Christ,

To the twelve tribes which are scattered
abroad:

Greetings.
2 My brethren, [a]count it all joy [b]when you fall
into various trials,
3 [a]knowing that the testing of your faith produces [1]patience.
4 But let patience have *its* perfect work, that
you may be [1]perfect and complete, lacking nothing.
5 [a]If any of you lacks wisdom, [b]let him ask of
God, who gives to all liberally and without reproach, and [c]it will be given to him.
6 [a]But let him ask in faith, with no doubting, for
he who doubts is like a wave of the sea driven and
tossed by the wind.
7 For let not that man suppose that he will
receive anything from the Lord;
8 *he is* [a]a double-minded man, unstable in all his
ways.
**9** Let the lowly brother glory in his exaltation,
10 but the rich in his humiliation, because [a]as a
flower of the field he will pass away.
11 For no sooner has the sun risen with a burning
heat than it withers the grass; its flower falls, and
its beautiful appearance perishes. So the rich man
also will fade away in his pursuits.
**12** [a]Blessed *is* the man who endures temptation;
for when he has been approved, he will receive
[b]the crown of life [c]which the Lord has promised to
those who love Him.
13 Let no one say when he is tempted, "I am
tempted by God"; for God cannot be tempted by
evil, nor does He Himself tempt anyone.
14 But each one is tempted when he is drawn
away by his own desires and enticed.
15 Then, [a]when desire has conceived, it gives
birth to sin; and sin, when it is full-grown, [b]brings
forth death.
16 Do not be deceived, my beloved brethren.
17 [a]Every good gift and every perfect gift is from
above, and comes down from the Father of lights,
[b]with whom there is no variation or shadow of
turning.
18 [a]Of His own will He brought us forth by the
[b]word of truth, [c]that we might be a kind of
firstfruits of His creatures.
**19** [1]So then, my beloved brethren, let every man
be swift to hear, [a]slow to speak, [b]slow to wrath;
20 for the wrath of man does not produce the
righteousness of God.
**21** Therefore [a]lay aside all filthiness and [1]overflow
of wickedness, and receive with meekness the
implanted word, [b]which is able to save your souls.
22 But [a]be doers of the word, and not hearers
only, deceiving yourselves.
23 For [a]if anyone is a hearer of the word and not
a doer, he is like a man observing his natural face
in a mirror;
24 for he observes himself, goes away, and immediately forgets what kind of man he was.
25 But [a]he who looks into the perfect law of
liberty and continues *in it,* and is not a forgetful
hearer but a doer of the work, [b]this one will be
blessed in what he does.
26 If anyone [1]among you thinks he is religious,
and [a]does not bridle his tongue but deceives his
own heart, this one's religion *is* useless.
27 [a]Pure and undefiled religion before God and
the Father is this: [b]to visit orphans and widows in
their trouble, [c]*and* to keep oneself unspotted from
the world.

## *Faith Without Works Is Dead*

2 My brethren, do not hold the faith of our Lord
Jesus Christ, [a]*the Lord* of glory, with [b]partial-
ity.
2 For if there should come into your assembly a
man with gold rings, in [1]fine apparel, and there
should also come in a poor man in [2]filthy clothes,
3 and you [1]pay attention to the one wearing the
fine clothes and say to him, "You sit here in a
good place," and say to the poor man, "You stand
there," or, "Sit here at my footstool,"
4 have you not [1]shown partiality among yourselves, and become judges with evil thoughts?
5 Listen, my beloved brethren: [a]Has God not
chosen the poor of this world *to be* [b]rich in faith
and heirs of the kingdom [c]which He promised to
those who love Him?
6 But [a]you have dishonored the poor man. Do
not the rich oppress you [b]and drag you into the
courts?
7 Do they not blaspheme that noble name by
which you are [a]called?
8 If you really fulfill *the* royal law according to
the Scripture, [a]*"You shall love your neighbor as*
*yourself,"* you do well;
9 but if you [1]show partiality, you commit sin,
and are convicted by the law as [a]transgressors.
10 For whoever shall keep the whole law, and yet
[a]stumble in one *point,* [b]he is guilty of all.
11 For He who said, [a]*"Do not commit adultery,"*
also said, *"Do not murder."* Now if you do not
commit adultery, but you do murder, you have
become a transgressor of the law.
12 So speak and so do as those who will be
judged by [a]the law of liberty.
13 For [a]judgment is without mercy to the one
who has shown [b]no [c]mercy. [d]Mercy triumphs over
judgment.
**14** [a]What *does it* profit, my brethren, if someone
says he has faith but does not have works? Can
faith save him?
15 [a]If a brother or sister is naked and destitute of
daily food,
16 and [a]one of you says to them, "Depart in
peace, be warmed and filled," but you do not give
them the things which are needed for the body,
what *does it* profit?
17 Thus also faith by itself, if it does not have
works, is dead.
18 But someone will say, "You have faith, and I
have works." [a]Show me your faith without [1]your
works, [b]and I will show you my faith by [2]my
works.

CHAPTER 1
**1** [a]Acts 12:17
**2** [a]Acts 5:41 [b]2 Pet. 1:6
**3** [a]Rom. 5:3–5 [1]*endurance* or *perseverance*
**4** [1]*mature*
**5** [a]1 Kin. 3:9 [b]Matt. 7:7 [c]Jer. 29:12
**6** [a][Mark 11:23, 24]
**8** [a]James 4:8
**10** [a]Job 14:2
**12** [a]James 5:11 [b][1 Cor. 9:25] [c]Matt. 10:22
**15** [a]Job 15:35 [b][Rom. 5:12; 6:23]
**17** [a]John 3:27 [b]Num. 23:19
**18** [a]John 1:13 [b][1 Pet. 1:3, 23] [c][Eph. 1:12, 13]
**19** [a]Prov. 10:19; 17:27 [b]Prov. 14:17; 16:32 [1]NU *Know this* or *This you know*
**21** [a]Col. 3:8 [b]Acts 13:26 [1]*abundance*
**22** [a]Matt. 7:21–28
**23** [a]Luke 6:47
**25** [a]James 2:12 [b]John 13:17
**26** [a]Ps. 34:13 [1]NU omits *among you*
**27** [a]Matt. 25:34–36 [b]Is. 1:17 [c][Rom. 12:2]

CHAPTER 2
**1** [a]1 Cor. 2:8 [b]Lev. 19:15
**2** [1]*bright* [2]*vile*
**3** [1]Lit. *look upon*
**4** [1]*differentiated*
**5** [a]1 Cor. 1:27 [b]Luke 12:21 [c]Ex. 20:6
**6** [a]1 Cor. 11:22 [b]Acts 13:50
**7** [a]1 Pet. 4:16
**8** [a]Lev. 19:18
**9** [a]Deut. 1:17 [1]Lit. *receive the face*
**10** [a]Gal. 3:10 [b]Deut. 27:26
**11** [a]Ex. 20:13, 14; Deut. 5:17, 18
**12** [a]James 1:25
**13** [a]Job 22:6 [b]Prov. 21:13 [c]Mic. 7:18 [d]Rom. 12:8
**14** [a]Matt. 7:21–23, 26; 21:28–32
**15** [a]Luke 3:11
**16** [a][1 John 3:17, 18]
**18** [a]Heb. 6:10 [b]James 3:13 [1]NU omits *your* [2]NU omits *my*

19 You believe that there is one God. You do
well. Even the demons believe—and tremble!
20 But do you want to know, O foolish man, that
faith without works is [1]dead?
21 Was not Abraham our father justified by
works [a]when he offered Isaac his son on the altar?
22 Do you see [a]that faith was working together
with his works, and by [b]works faith was made
[1]perfect?
23 And the Scripture was fulfilled which says,
[a]*"Abraham believed God, and it was* [1]*accounted to*
*him for righteousness."* And he was called [b]the
friend of God.
24 You see then that a man is justified by works,
and not by faith only.
25 Likewise, [a]was not Rahab the harlot also
justified by works when she received the messengers and sent *them* out another way?
26 For as the body without the spirit is dead, so
faith without works is dead also.

## *The Tongue Cannot Be Tamed*

**3** My brethren, [a]let not many of you become
teachers, [b]knowing that we shall receive a
stricter judgment.
2 For [a]we all stumble in many things. [b]If anyone
does not stumble in word, [c]he *is* a [1]perfect man,
able also to bridle the whole body.
3 [1]Indeed, [a]we put bits in horses' mouths that
they may obey us, and we turn their whole body.
4 Look also at ships: although they are so large
and are driven by fierce winds, they are turned by
a very small rudder wherever the pilot desires.
5 Even so [a]the tongue is a little member and
[b]boasts great things. See how great a forest a little
fire kindles!
6 And [a]the tongue *is* a fire, a world of [1]iniquity.
The tongue is so set among our members that it
[b]defiles the whole body, and sets on fire the course
of [2]nature; and it is set on fire by [3]hell.
7 For every kind of beast and bird, of reptile and
creature of the sea, is tamed and has been tamed
by mankind.
8 But no man can tame the tongue. *It is* an
unruly evil, [a]full of deadly poison.
9 With it we bless our God and Father, and with
it we curse men, who have been made [a]in the
[1]similitude of God.
10 Out of the same mouth proceed blessing and
cursing. My brethren, these things ought not to
be so.
11 Does a spring send forth fresh *water* and bitter
from the same opening?
12 Can a [a]fig tree, my brethren, bear olives, or a
grapevine bear figs? [1]Thus no spring yields both
salt water and fresh.
**13** [a]Who *is* wise and understanding among you?
Let him show by good conduct *that* his works *are*
*done* in the meekness of wisdom.
14 But if you have [a]bitter envy and [1]self-seeking
in your hearts, [b]do not boast and lie against the
truth.
15 [a]This wisdom does not descend from above,
but *is* earthly, sensual, demonic.
16 For [a]where envy and self-seeking *exist,* confusion and every evil thing *are* there.
17 But [a]the wisdom that is from above is first
pure, then peaceable, gentle, willing to yield, full
of mercy and good fruits, [b]without partiality [c]and
without hypocrisy.
18 [a]Now the fruit of righteousness is sown in
peace by those who make peace.

## *Dangers of Pride, Judging, and Presumption*

**4** Where do [1]wars and fights *come* from among
you? Do *they* not *come* from your *desires for*
pleasure [a]that war in your members?
2 You lust and do not have. You murder and
covet and cannot obtain. You fight and [1]war. [2]Yet
you do not have because you do not ask.
3 [a]You ask and do not receive, [b]because you ask
amiss, that you may spend *it* on your pleasures.
4 [1]Adulterers and adulteresses! Do you not
know that [a]friendship with the world is enmity
with God? [b]Whoever therefore wants to be a
friend of the world makes himself an enemy of
God.
5 Or do you think that the Scripture says in
vain, [a]"The Spirit who dwells in us yearns jeal-
ously"?
6 But He gives more grace. Therefore He says:

[a]*"God resists the proud,*
*But gives grace to the humble."*

7 Therefore submit to God. [a]Resist the devil and
he will flee from you.
8 [a]Draw near to God and He will draw near to
you. [b]Cleanse *your* hands, *you* sinners; and [c]purify
*your* hearts, *you* double-minded.
9 [a]Lament and mourn and weep! Let your
laughter be turned to mourning and *your* joy to
gloom.
10 [a]Humble yourselves in the sight of the Lord,
and He will lift you up.
**11** [a]Do not speak evil of one another, brethren.
He who speaks evil of a brother [b]and judges his
brother, speaks evil of the law and judges the law.
But if you judge the law, you are not a doer of the
law but a judge.
12 There is one [1]Lawgiver, [a]who is able to save
and to destroy. [b]Who[2] are you to judge [3]another?
**13** Come now, you who say, "Today or tomorrow
[1]we will go to such and such a city, spend a year
there, buy and sell, and make a profit";
14 whereas you do not know what *will happen*
tomorrow. For what *is* your life? [a]It is even a
vapor that appears for a little time and then
vanishes away.
15 Instead you *ought* to say, [a]"If the Lord wills,
we shall live and do this or that."
16 But now you boast in your arrogance. [a]All
such boasting is evil.
17 Therefore, [a]to him who knows to do good and
does not do *it,* to him it is sin.

## *Danger of Riches; Patience and Prayer*

**5** Come now, *you* [a]rich, weep and howl for your
miseries that are coming upon *you!*
2 Your [a]riches [1]are corrupted, and [b]your garments are moth-eaten.
3 Your gold and silver are corroded, and their
corrosion will be a witness against you and will
eat your flesh like fire. [a]You have heaped up
treasure in the last days.
4 Indeed [a]the wages of the laborers who mowed
your fields, which you kept back by fraud, cry out;
and [b]the cries of the reapers have reached the ears
of the Lord of [1]Sabaoth.
5 You have lived on the earth in pleasure and
[1]luxury; you have [2]fattened your hearts [3]as in a
day of slaughter.

---

**20** [1]NU *useless*
**21** [a]Gen. 22:9, 10, 12, 16–18
**22** [a]Heb. 11:17 [b]John 8:39 [1]*complete*
**23** [a]Gen. 15:6 [b]2 Chr. 20:7 [1]*credited*
**25** [a]Heb. 11:31

CHAPTER 3
**1** [a][Matt. 23:8] [b]Luke 6:37
**2** [a]1 Kin. 8:46 [b]Ps. 34:13 [c][Matt. 12:34–37] [1]*mature*
**3** [a]Ps. 32:9 [1]NU *Now if*
**5** [a]Prov. 12:18; 15:2 [b]Ps. 12:3; 73:8
**6** [a]Prov. 16:27 [b][Matt. 12:36; 15:11, 18] [1]*unrighteousness* [2]*existence* [3]Gr. *Gehenna*
**8** [a]Ps. 140:3
**9** [a]Gen. 1:26; 5:1; 9:6 [1]*likeness*
**12** [a]Matt. 7:16–20 [1]NU *Neither can a salty spring produce fresh water.*
**13** [a]Gal. 6:4
**14** [a]Rom. 13:13 [b]Rom. 2:17 [1]*selfish ambition*
**15** [a]Phil. 3:19
**16** [a]1 Cor. 3:3
**17** [a]1 Cor. 2:6, 7 [b]James 2:1 [c]Rom. 12:9
**18** [a]Prov. 11:18

CHAPTER 4
**1** [a]Rom. 7:23 [1]*battles*
**2** [1]*battle* [2]NU, M omit *Yet*
**3** [a]Job 27:8, 9 [b][Ps. 66:18]
**4** [a]1 John 2:15 [b]Gal. 1:4 [1]NU omits *Adulterers and*
**5** [a]Gen. 6:5
**6** [a]Prov. 3:34
**7** [a][Eph. 4:27; 6:11]
**8** [a]2 Chr. 15:2 [b]Is. 1:16 [c]1 Pet. 1:22
**9** [a]Matt. 5:4
**10** [a]Job 22:29
**11** [a]1 Pet. 2:1–3 [b][Matt. 7:1–5]
**12** [a][Matt. 10:28] [b]Rom. 14:4 [1]NU adds *and Judge* [2]NU, M *But who* [3]NU *a neighbor*
**13** [1]M *let us*
**14** [a]Job 7:7
**15** [a]Acts 18:21
**16** [a]1 Cor. 5:6
**17** [a][Luke 12:47]

CHAPTER 5
**1** [a][Luke 6:24]
**2** [a]Matt. 6:19 [b]Job 13:28 [1]*have rotted*
**3** [a]Rom. 2:5
**4** [a]Lev. 19:13 [b]Deut. 24:15 [1]Lit., in Heb., *Hosts*
**5** [1]*indulgence* [2]Lit. *nourished* [3]NU omits *as*

6 You have condemned, you have murdered the
just; he does not resist you.
**7** Therefore be patient, brethren, until the coming of the Lord. See *how* the farmer waits for the
precious fruit of the earth, waiting patiently for it
until it receives the early and latter rain.
8 You also be patient. Establish your hearts, for
the coming of the Lord [1]is at hand.
9 Do not [1]grumble against one another, brethren, lest you be [2]condemned. Behold, the Judge is
standing at the door!
10 [a]My brethren, take the prophets, who spoke in
the name of the Lord, as an example of suffering
and [b]patience.
11 Indeed [a]we count them blessed who [b]endure.
You have heard of [c]the perseverance of Job and
seen [d]the end *intended by* the Lord—that [e]the
Lord is very compassionate and merciful.
12 But above all, my brethren, [a]do not swear,
either by heaven or by earth or with any other
oath. But let your "Yes" be "Yes," and *your* "No,"
"No," lest you fall into [1]judgment.
**13** Is anyone among you suffering? Let him [a]pray.
Is anyone cheerful? [b]Let him sing psalms.
14 Is anyone among you sick? Let him call for the
elders of the church, and let them pray over him,
[a]anointing him with oil in the name of the Lord.
15 And the prayer of faith will save the sick, and
the Lord will raise him up. [a]And if he has committed sins, he will be forgiven.
16 [1]Confess *your* trespasses to one another, and
pray for one another, that you may be healed.
[a]The effective, [2]fervent prayer of a righteous man
avails much.
17 Elijah was a man [a]with a nature like ours, and
[b]he prayed earnestly that it would not rain; and it
did not rain on the land for three years and six
months.
18 And he prayed [a]again, and the heaven gave
rain, and the earth produced its fruit.
**19** Brethren, if anyone among you wanders from
the truth, and someone [a]turns him back,
20 let him know that he who turns a sinner from
the error of his way [a]will save [1]a soul from death
and [b]cover a multitude of sins.

**8** [1]*has drawn near* **9** [1]Lit. *groan* [2]NU, M *judged* **10** [a]Matt. 5:12 [b]Heb. 10:36 **11** [a][Ps. 94:12] [b][James 1:12] [c]Job 1:21, 22; 2:10 [d]Job 42:10 [e]Num. 14:18 **12** [a]Matt. 5:34–37 [1]M *hypocrisy* **13** [a]Ps. 50:14, 15 [b]Eph. 5:19 **14** [a]Mark 6:13; 16:18 **15** [a]Is. 33:24 **16** [a]Num. 11:2 [1]NU *Therefore confess your sins* [2]*supplication* **17** [a]Acts 14:15 [b]1 Kin. 17:1; 18:1 **18** [a]1 Kin. 18:1, 42 **19** [a]Gal. 6:1 **20** [a]Rom. 11:14 [b][1 Pet. 4:8] [1]NU *his soul*

*The First Epistle of*

# PETER

### *Prophets Foretold Salvation in Christ*

PETER, an apostle of Jesus Christ,

To the [1]pilgrims [a]of the Dispersion in Pontus,
Galatia, Cappadocia, Asia, and Bithynia,
2 [a]elect [b]according to the foreknowledge of God
the Father, [c]in sanctification of the Spirit, for
[d]obedience and [e]sprinkling of the blood of Jesus
Christ:

[f]Grace to you and peace be multiplied.

**3** [a]Blessed *be* the God and Father of our Lord
Jesus Christ, who [b]according to His abundant
mercy [c]has begotten us again to a living hope
[d]through the resurrection of Jesus Christ from the
dead,
4 to an inheritance [1]incorruptible and undefiled
and that does not fade away, [a]reserved in heaven
for you,
5 [a]who are kept by the power of God through
faith for salvation ready to be revealed in the last
time.
6 [a]In this you greatly rejoice, though now [b]for a
little while, if need be, [c]you have been [1]grieved by
various trials,
7 that [a]the genuineness of your faith, *being*
much more precious than gold that perishes,
though [b]it is tested by fire, [c]may be found to
praise, honor, and glory at the revelation of Jesus
Christ,
8 [a]whom having not [1]seen you love. [b]Though
now you do not see *Him,* yet believing, you rejoice
with joy inexpressible and full of glory,
9 receiving the end of your faith—the salvation
of *your* souls.
10 Of this salvation the prophets have inquired
and searched carefully, who prophesied of the
grace *that would come* to you,
11 searching what, or what manner of time, [a]the
Spirit of Christ who was in them was indicating
when He testified beforehand the sufferings of
Christ and the glories that would follow.
12 To them it was revealed that, not to themselves, but to [1]us they were ministering the things
which now have been reported to you through
those who have preached the gospel to you by the
Holy Spirit sent from heaven—things which [a]an-
gels desire to look into.
**13** Therefore gird up the loins of your mind, be
sober, and rest *your* hope fully upon the grace
that is to be brought to you at the revelation of
Jesus Christ;
14 as obedient children, not [a]conforming yourselves to the former lusts, *as* in your ignorance;
15 [a]but as He who called you *is* holy, you also be
holy in all *your* conduct,
16 because it is written, [a]*"Be holy, for I am holy."*
17 And if you call on the Father, who [a]without
partiality judges according to each one's work,
conduct yourselves throughout the time of your
[1]stay *here* in fear;
18 knowing that you were not redeemed with
[1]corruptible things, *like* silver or gold, from your
aimless conduct *received* by tradition from your
fathers,
19 but [a]with the precious blood of Christ, [b]as of a
lamb without blemish and without spot.
20 [a]He indeed was foreordained before the foundation of the world, but was [1]manifest [b]in these
last times for you
21 who through Him believe in God, [a]who raised
Him from the dead and [b]gave Him glory, so that
your faith and hope are in God.

CHAPTER 1
**1** [a]James 1:1 [1]*sojourners,* temporary residents **2** [a]Eph. 1:4 [b][Rom. 8:29] [c]2 Thess. 2:13 [d]Rom. 1:5 [e]Heb. 10:22; 12:24 [f]Rom. 1:7 **3** [a]Eph. 1:3 [b]Gal. 6:16 [c][John 3:3, 5] [d]1 Cor. 15:20 **4** [a]Col. 1:5 [1]*imperishable* **5** [a]John 10:28 **6** [a]Matt. 5:12 [b]2 Cor. 4:17 [c]James 1:2 [1]*distressed* **7** [a]James 1:3 [b]Job 23:10 [c][Rom. 2:7] **8** [a]1 John 4:20 [b]John 20:29 [1]M *known* **11** [a]2 Pet. 1:21 **12** [a]Eph. 3:10 [1]NU, M *you* **14** [a][Rom. 12:2] **15** [a][2 Cor. 7:1] **16** [a]Lev. 11:44, 45; 19:2; 20:7 **17** [a]Acts 10:34 [1]*sojourning, dwelling* as resident aliens **18** [1]*perishable* **19** [a]Acts 20:28 [b]Ex. 12:5 **20** [a]Rom. 3:25 [b]Gal. 4:4 [1]*revealed* **21** [a]Acts 2:24 [b]Acts 2:33

**22** Since you [a]have purified your souls in obeying
the truth [1]through the Spirit in [2]sincere [b]love of
the brethren, love one another fervently with a
pure heart,
23 [a]having been born again, not of [1]corruptible
seed but [2]incorruptible, [b]through the word of God
which lives and abides [3]forever,
24 because

[a]*"All flesh is as grass,*
*And all [1]the glory of man*
*as the flower of the grass.*
*The grass withers,*
*And its flower falls away,*
25 [a]*But the [1]word of the LORD endures forever."*

[b]Now this is the word which by the gospel was
preached to you.

### *Our Inheritance Through Christ's Blood*

**2** Therefore, [a]laying aside all malice, all deceit,
hypocrisy, envy, and all evil speaking,
2 [a]as newborn babes, desire the pure [b]milk of the
word, that you may grow [1]thereby,
3 if indeed you have [a]tasted that the Lord *is*
gracious.
**4** Coming to Him *as to* a living stone, [a]rejected
indeed by men, but chosen by God *and* precious,
5 you also, as living stones, are being built up a
spiritual house, a holy priesthood, to offer up
spiritual sacrifices acceptable to God through
Jesus Christ.
6 Therefore it is also contained in the Scripture,

[a]*"Behold, I lay in Zion*
*A chief cornerstone, elect, precious,*
*And he who believes on Him will by no*
*means be put to shame."*

7 Therefore, to you who believe, *He is* precious;
but to those who [1]are disobedient,

[a]*"The stone which the builders rejected*
*Has become the chief cornerstone,"*

8 and

[a]*"A stone of stumbling*
*And a rock of offense."*

[b]They stumble, being disobedient to the word, [c]to
which they also were appointed.
9 But you *are* a chosen generation, a royal
priesthood, a holy nation, His own special people,
that you may proclaim the praises of Him who
called you out of [a]darkness into His marvelous
light;
10 [a]who once *were* not a people but *are* now the
people of God, who had not obtained mercy but
now have obtained mercy.
**11** Beloved, I beg *you* as sojourners and pilgrims,
abstain from fleshly lusts [a]which war against the
soul,
12 [a]having your conduct honorable among the
Gentiles, that when they speak against you as
evildoers, [b]they may, by *your* good works which
they observe, glorify God in the day of visitation.
**13** [a]Therefore submit yourselves to every [1]ordi-
nance of man for the Lord's sake, whether to the
king as supreme,
14 or to governors, as to those who are sent by
him for the punishment of evildoers and *for the*
praise of those who do good.
15 For this is the will of God, that by doing good
you may put to silence the ignorance of foolish
men—

**22** [a]Acts 15:9 [b]Heb. 13:1 [1]NU omits *through the Spirit* [2]Lit. *unhypocritical*
**23** [a]John 1:13 [b]James 1:18 [1]*perishable* [2]*imperishable* [3]NU omits *forever*
**24** [a]Is. 40:6–8 [1]NU *its glory as*
**25** [a]Is. 40:8 [b][John 1:1] [1]*spoken word*

CHAPTER 2
**1** [a]Heb. 12:1
**2** [a][Matt. 18:3; 19:14] [b]1 Cor. 3:2 [1]NU adds *up to salvation*
**3** [a]Heb. 6:5
**4** [a]Ps. 118:22
**6** [a]Is. 28:16
**7** [a]Ps. 118:22 [1]NU *disbelieve*
**8** [a]Is. 8:14 [b]1 Cor. 1:23 [c]Rom. 9:22
**9** [a][Acts 26:18]
**10** [a]Hos. 1:9, 10; 2:23
**11** [a]James 4:1
**12** [a]Phil. 2:15 [b]Matt. 5:16; 9:8
**13** [a]Matt. 22:21 [1]*institution*
**16** [a]Rom. 6:14, 20, 22 [b]Gal. 5:13 [1]*wickedness*
**17** [a]Prov. 24:21
**18** [a]Eph. 6:5–8
**19** [a]Matt. 5:10
**20** [a]Luke 6:32–34
**21** [a]Matt. 16:24 [b][1 John 2:6] [1]NU *you* [2]NU, M *you*
**22** [a]Is. 53:9
**23** [a]Is. 53:7 [b]Luke 23:46
**24** [a][Heb. 9:28] [b]Rom. 7:6 [c]Is. 53:5 [1]*wounds*
**25** [a]Is. 53:5, 6 [b][Ezek. 34:23] [1]Gr. *Episkopos*

CHAPTER 3
**1** [a]Eph. 5:22 [b]1 Cor. 7:16 [c]Matt. 18:15
**2** [a]1 Pet. 2:12; 3:6
**3** [a]1 Tim. 2:9
**4** [a]Rom. 2:29 [1]*imperishable*
**6** [a]Gen. 18:12
**7** [a][Eph. 5:25] [b]1 Cor. 12:23 [c]Job 42:8
**8** [1]NU *humble*
**9** [a][Prov. 17:13] [b]Matt. 5:44 [c]Matt. 25:34
**10** [a]Ps. 34:12–16 [b]James 1:26 [1]*restrain*
**11** [a]Ps. 37:27 [b]Rom. 12:18

16 [a]as free, yet not [b]using liberty as a cloak for
[1]vice, but as bondservants of God.
17 Honor all *people.* Love the brotherhood. Fear
[a]God. Honor the king.
**18** [a]Servants, *be* submissive to *your* masters with
all fear, not only to the good and gentle, but also
to the harsh.
19 For this *is* [a]commendable, if because of conscience toward God one endures grief, suffering
wrongfully.
20 For [a]what credit *is it* if, when you are beaten
for your faults, you take it patiently? But when
you do good and suffer, if you take it patiently,
this *is* commendable before God.
21 For [a]to this you were called, because Christ
also suffered for [1]us, [b]leaving [2]us an example, that
you should follow His steps:

22 *"Who[a] committed no sin,*
*Nor was deceit found in His mouth";*

23 [a]who, when He was reviled, did not revile in
return; when He suffered, He did not threaten, but
[b]committed *Himself* to Him who judges righteously;
24 [a]who Himself bore our sins in His own body on
the tree, [b]that we, having died to sins, might live
for righteousness—[c]by whose [1]stripes you were
healed.
25 For [a]you were like sheep going astray, but
have now returned [b]to the Shepherd and [1]Over-
seer of your souls.

### *Serving and Suffering for God's Glory*

**3** Wives, likewise, *be* [a]submissive to your own
husbands, that even if some do not obey the
word, [b]they, without a word, may [c]be won by the
conduct of their wives,
2 [a]when they observe your chaste conduct *accompanied* by fear.
3 [a]Do not let your adornment be *merely* outward—arranging the hair, wearing gold, or putting on *fine* apparel—
4 rather *let it be* [a]the hidden person of the heart,
with the [1]incorruptible *beauty* of a gentle and
quiet spirit, which is very precious in the sight of
God.
5 For in this manner, in former times, the holy
women who trusted in God also adorned themselves, being submissive to their own husbands,
6 as Sarah obeyed Abraham, [a]calling him lord,
whose daughters you are if you do good and are
not afraid with any terror.
**7** [a]Husbands, likewise, dwell with *them* with
understanding, giving honor to the wife, [b]as to the
weaker vessel, and as *being* heirs together of the
grace of life, [c]that your prayers may not be hindered.
**8** Finally, all *of you be* of one mind, having
compassion for one another; love as brothers, *be*
tenderhearted, *be* [1]courteous;
9 [a]not returning evil for evil or reviling for
reviling, but on the contrary [b]blessing, knowing
that you were called to this, [c]that you may inherit
a blessing.
10 For

[a]*"He who would love life*
*And see good days,*
[b]*Let him [1]refrain his tongue from evil,*
*And his lips from speaking deceit.*
11 *Let him [a]turn away from evil and do good;*
[b]*Let him seek peace and pursue it.*

12 *For the eyes of the* L*ORD*
*are on the righteous,*
[a]*And His ears are open to their prayers;*
*But the face of the* L*ORD is against those*
*who do evil."*

**13** [a]And who *is* he who will harm you if you
become followers of what is good?
14 [a]But even if you should suffer for righteousness' sake, *you are* blessed. [b]*"And do not be afraid*
*of their threats, nor be troubled."*
15 But [1]sanctify [2]the Lord God in your hearts,
and always [a]*be* ready to *give* a defense to everyone who asks you a reason for the [b]hope that is in
you, with meekness and fear;
16 [a]having a good conscience, that when they
defame you as evildoers, those who revile your
good conduct in Christ may be ashamed.
17 For *it is* better, if it is the will of God, to suffer
for doing good than for doing evil.
**18** For Christ also suffered once for sins, the just
for the unjust, that He might bring [1]us to God,
being put to death in the flesh but made alive by
the Spirit,
19 by whom also He went and preached to the
spirits in prison,
20 who formerly were disobedient, [1]when once
the Divine longsuffering waited in the days of
Noah, while *the* ark was being prepared, in which
a few, that is, eight souls, were saved through
water.
21 [a]There is also an antitype which now saves
us—baptism [b](not the removal of the filth of the
flesh, [c]but the answer of a good conscience toward
God), through the resurrection of Jesus Christ,
22 who has gone into heaven and [a]is at the right
hand of God, [b]angels and authorities and powers
having been made subject to Him.

## *Christ's Example to Be Followed*

**4** Therefore, since Christ suffered [1]for us in the
flesh, arm yourselves also with the same mind,
for he who has suffered in the flesh has ceased
from sin,
2 that he no longer should live the rest of *his*
time in the flesh for the lusts of men, [a]but for the
will of God.
3 For we *have spent* enough of our past [1]life-
time in doing the will of the Gentiles—when we
walked in lewdness, lusts, drunkenness, revelries,
drinking parties, and abominable idolatries.
4 In regard to these, they think it strange that
you do not run with *them* in the same flood of
dissipation, speaking evil of *you.*
5 They will give an account to Him who is ready
[a]to judge the living and the dead.
6 For this reason [a]the gospel was preached also
to those who are dead, that they might be judged
according to men in the flesh, but [b]live according
to God in the spirit.
**7** But [a]the end of all things is at hand; therefore
be serious and watchful in your prayers.
8 And above all things have fervent love for one
another, for [a]*"love will cover a multitude of sins."*
9 [a]*Be* hospitable to one another [b]without grumbling.
10 [a]As each one has received a gift, minister it to
one another, [b]as good stewards of [c]the manifold
grace of God.
11 [a]If anyone speaks, *let him speak* as the [1]ora-
cles of God. If anyone ministers, *let him do it* as
with the ability which God supplies, that [b]in all
things God may be glorified through Jesus Christ,
to whom belong the glory and the [2]dominion
forever and ever. Amen.
**12** Beloved, do not think it strange concerning
the fiery trial which is to try you, as though some
strange thing happened to you;
13 but rejoice [a]to the extent that you partake of
Christ's sufferings, that [b]when His glory is revealed, you may also be glad with exceeding joy.
14 If you are [1]reproached for the name of Christ,
[a]blessed *are you,* for the Spirit of glory and of God
rests upon you. [2]On their part He is blasphemed,
[b]but on your part He is glorified.
15 But let none of you suffer as a murderer, a
thief, an evildoer, or as a [1]busybody in other
people's matters.
16 Yet if *anyone suffers* as a Christian, let him
not be ashamed, but let him glorify God in this
[1]matter.
17 For the time *has come* [a]for judgment to begin
at the house of God; and if *it begins* with us first,
[b]what will *be* the end of those who do not obey
the gospel of God?
18 Now

[a]*"If the righteous one is scarcely saved,*
*Where will the ungodly and the sinner*
*appear?"*

19 Therefore let those who suffer according to
the will of God [a]commit their souls *to Him* in
doing good, as to a faithful Creator.

## *Instructions and Final Greeting*

**5** The elders who are among you I exhort, I who
am a fellow elder and a [a]witness of the sufferings of Christ, and also a partaker of the [b]glory
that will be revealed:
2 [a]Shepherd the flock of God which is among
you, serving as overseers, [b]not by compulsion but
[1]willingly, [c]not for dishonest gain but eagerly;
3 nor as [a]being [1]lords over [b]those entrusted to
you, but [c]being examples to the flock;
4 and when [a]the Chief Shepherd appears, you
will receive [b]the crown of glory that does not fade
away.
**5** Likewise you younger people, submit yourselves to *your* elders. Yes, [a]all of *you* be submissive to one another, and be clothed with humility,
for

[b]*"God resists the proud,*
*But* [c]*gives grace to the humble."*

6 Therefore humble yourselves under the
mighty hand of God, that He may exalt you in due
time,
7 casting all your care upon Him, for He cares
for you.
8 Be [1]sober, be [2]vigilant; [3]because your adversary the devil walks about like a roaring lion,
seeking whom he may devour.
9 Resist him, steadfast in the faith, knowing
that the same sufferings are experienced by your
brotherhood in the world.
10 But [1]may the God of all grace, [a]who called [2]us
to His eternal glory by Christ Jesus, after you
have suffered a while, [3]perfect, establish,
strengthen, and settle *you.*
11 [a]To Him *be* the glory and the dominion forever
and ever. Amen.

**12** [a]John 9:31
**13** [a]Prov. 16:7
**14** [a]James 1:12 [b]Is. 8:12
**15** [a]Ps. 119:46 [b][Titus 3:7] [1]*set apart* [2]NU *Christ as Lord*
**16** [a]Heb. 13:18
**18** [1]NU, M *you*
**20** [1]NU, M *when the longsuffering of God waited patiently*
**21** [a]Eph. 5:26 [b][Titus 3:5] [c][Rom. 10:10]
**22** [a]Ps. 110:1 [b]Rom. 8:38

CHAPTER 4
**1** [1]NU omits *for us*
**2** [a]John 1:13
**3** [1]NU *time*
**5** [a]Acts 10:42
**6** [a]1 Pet. 1:12; 3:19 [b][Rom. 8:9, 13]
**7** [a]Rom. 13:11
**8** [a][Prov. 10:12]
**9** [a]Heb. 13:2 [b]2 Cor. 9:7
**10** [a]Rom. 12:6–8 [b]1 Cor. 4:1, 2 [c][1 Cor. 12:4]
**11** [a]Eph. 4:29 [b][1 Cor. 10:31] [1]*utterances* [2]*sovereignty*
**13** [a]James 1:2 [b]2 Tim. 2:12
**14** [a]Matt. 5:11 [b]Matt. 5:16 [1]*insulted* or *reviled* [2]NU omits the rest of v. 14.
**15** [1]*meddler*
**16** [1]NU *name*
**17** [a]Is. 10:12 [b]Luke 10:12
**18** [a]Prov. 11:31
**19** [a]2 Tim. 1:12

CHAPTER 5
**1** [a]Matt. 26:37 [b]Rom. 8:17, 18
**2** [a]Acts 20:28 [b]1 Cor. 9:17 [c]1 Tim. 3:3 [1]NU adds *according to God*
**3** [a]Ezek. 34:4 [b]Ps. 33:12 [c]Phil. 3:17 [1]*masters*
**4** [a]Heb. 13:20 [b]2 Tim. 4:8
**5** [a]Eph. 5:21 [b]Prov. 3:34 [c]Is. 57:15
**8** [1]*self-controlled* [2]*watchful* [3]NU, M omit *because*
**10** [a]1 Cor. 1:9 [1]NU *the God of all grace,* [2]NU, M *you* [3]NU *will perfect*
**11** [a]Rev. 1:6

**12** By [a]Silvanus, our faithful brother as I consider
him, I have written to you briefly, exhorting and
testifying [b]that this is the true grace of God in
which you stand.

12 [a]2 Cor. 1:19 [b]Acts 20:24
13 [a]Acts 12:12, 25; 15:37, 39

13 She who is in Babylon, elect together with
*you,* greets you; and *so does* [a]Mark my son.
14 Greet one another with a kiss of love. Peace to
you all who are in Christ Jesus. Amen.

*The Second Epistle of*

# PETER

## *Grow in Christian Character*

SIMON PETER, a bondservant and [a]apostle of
Jesus Christ,

To those who have [1]obtained [b]like[2] precious
faith with us by the righteousness of our God and
Savior Jesus Christ:

2 [a]Grace and peace be multiplied to you in the
knowledge of God and of Jesus our Lord,
3 as His [a]divine power has given to us all things
that *pertain* to life and godliness, through the
knowledge of Him [b]who called us by glory and
virtue,
4 [a]by which have been given to us exceedingly
great and precious promises, that through these
you may be [b]partakers of the divine nature, having escaped the [1]corruption *that is* in the world
through lust.
**5** But also for this very reason, [a]giving all diligence, add to your faith virtue, to virtue [b]knowl-
edge,
6 to knowledge self-control, to self-control [1]per-
severance, to perseverance godliness,
7 to godliness brotherly kindness, and [a]to brotherly kindness love.
8 For if these things are yours and abound, *you
will be* neither [1]barren [a]nor unfruitful in the
knowledge of our Lord Jesus Christ.
9 For he who lacks these things is [a]shortsighted,
even to blindness, and has forgotten that he was
cleansed from his old sins.
10 Therefore, brethren, be even more diligent [a]to
make your call and election sure, for if you do
these things you will never stumble;
11 for so an entrance will be supplied to you
abundantly into the everlasting kingdom of our
Lord and Savior Jesus Christ.
**12** For this reason [a]I will not be negligent to
remind you always of these things, [b]though you
know and are established in the present truth.
13 Yes, I think it is right, [a]as long as I am in this
[1]tent, [b]to stir you up by reminding *you,*
14 [a]knowing that shortly I *must* [1]put off my tent,
just as [b]our Lord Jesus Christ showed me.
15 Moreover I will be careful to ensure that you
always have a reminder of these things after my
[1]decease.
**16** For we did not follow [a]cunningly devised
fables when we made known to you the [b]power
and [c]coming of our Lord Jesus Christ, but were
[d]eyewitnesses of His majesty.
17 For He received from God the Father honor
and glory when such a voice came to Him from
the Excellent Glory: [a]"This is My beloved Son, in
whom I am well pleased."
18 And we heard this voice which came from
heaven when we were with Him on [a]the holy
mountain.
19 [1]And so we have the prophetic word confirmed, which you do well to heed as a [a]light that
shines in a dark place, [b]until [c]the day dawns and
the morning star rises in your [d]hearts;
20 knowing this first, that [a]no prophecy of Scripture is of any private [1]interpretation,
21 for [a]prophecy never came by the will of man,
[b]but [1]holy men of God spoke *as they were* moved
by the Holy Spirit.

## *False Teaching and False Teachers*

**2** But there were also false prophets among the
people, even as there will be [a]false teachers
among you, who will secretly bring in destructive
heresies, even denying the Lord who bought
them, *and* bring on themselves swift destruction.
2 And many will follow their destructive ways,
because of whom the way of truth will be blasphemed.
3 By covetousness they will exploit you with
deceptive words; for a long time their judgment
has not been idle, and their destruction [1]does not
slumber.
**4** For if God did not spare the angels who
sinned, but cast *them* down to [1]hell and delivered
*them* into chains of darkness, to be reserved for
judgment;
5 and did not spare the ancient world, but saved
Noah, *one of* eight *people,* a preacher of righteousness, bringing in the flood on the world of the
ungodly;
6 and turning the cities of [a]Sodom and Gomorrah into ashes, condemned *them* to destruction,
making *them* an example to those who afterward
would live ungodly;
7 and [a]delivered righteous Lot, *who was* oppressed by the filthy conduct of the wicked
8 (for that righteous man, dwelling among
them, [a]tormented *his* righteous soul from day to
day by seeing and hearing *their* lawless deeds)—
9 *then* [a]the Lord knows how to deliver the godly
out of temptations and to reserve the unjust
under punishment for the day of judgment,
10 and especially [a]those who walk according to
the flesh in the lust of uncleanness and despise
authority. [b]*They are* presumptuous, self-willed.
They are not afraid to speak evil of [1]dignitaries,
11 whereas [a]angels, who are greater in power and
might, do not bring a reviling accusation against
them before the Lord.
**12** But these, [a]like natural brute beasts made to
be caught and destroyed, speak evil of the things

CHAPTER 1
1 [a]Gal. 2:8 [b]Eph. 4:5 [1]*received* [2]*faith of the same value*
2 [a]Dan. 4:1
3 [a]1 Pet. 1:5 [b]1 Thess. 2:12
4 [a]2 Cor. 1:20; 7:1 [b][2 Cor. 3:18] [1]*depravity*
5 [a]2 Pet. 3:18 [b]1 Pet. 3:7
6 [1]*patience*
7 [a]Gal. 6:10
8 [a][John 15:2] [1]*useless*
9 [a]1 John 2:9–11
10 [a]1 John 3:19
12 [a]Phil. 3:1 [b]1 Pet. 5:12
13 [a][2 Cor. 5:1, 4] [b]2 Pet. 3:1 [1]Body
14 [a][2 Tim. 4:6] [b]John 13:36; 21:18, 19 [1]Die and leave this body
15 [1]Lit. *exodus, departure*
16 [a]1 Cor. 1:17 [b][Eph. 1:19–22] [c][1 Pet. 5:4] [d]Matt. 17:1–5
17 [a]Matt. 17:5
18 [a]Matt. 17:1
19 [a][John 1:4, 5, 9] [b]Prov. 4:18 [c]Rev. 2:28; 22:16 [d][2 Cor. 4:5–7] [1]Or *We also have the more sure prophetic word*
20 [a][Rom. 12:6] [1]Or *origin*
21 [a][2 Tim. 3:16] [b]2 Sam. 23:2 [1]NU *men spoke from God*

CHAPTER 2
1 [a]1 Tim. 4:1, 2
3 [1]M *will not*
4 [1]Lit. *Tartarus*
6 [a]Gen. 19:1–26
7 [a]Gen. 19:16, 29
8 [a]Ps. 119:139
9 [a]Ps. 34:15–19
10 [a]Jude 4, 7, 8 [b]Jude 8 [1]*glorious ones,* lit. *glories*
11 [a]Jude 9
12 [a]Jude 10

they do not understand, and will utterly perish in
their own corruption,
13 [a]*and* will receive the wages of unrighteousness, *as* those who count it pleasure [b]to [1]carouse
in the daytime. [c]*They are* spots and blemishes,
[2]carousing in their own deceptions while [d]they
feast with you,
14 having eyes full of [1]adultery and that cannot
cease from sin, enticing unstable souls. [a]*They
have* a heart trained in covetous practices, *and are*
accursed children.
15 They have forsaken the right way and gone
astray, following the way of [a]Balaam the *son* of
Beor, who loved the wages of unrighteousness;
16 but he was rebuked for his iniquity: a dumb
donkey speaking with a man's voice restrained
the madness of the prophet.
17 [a]These are wells without water, [1]clouds carried
by a tempest, for whom is reserved the blackness
of darkness [2]forever.
**18** For when they speak great swelling *words* of
emptiness, they allure through the lusts of the
flesh, through lewdness, the ones who [1]have
actually escaped from those who live in error.
19 While they promise them liberty, they themselves are slaves of [1]corruption; [a]for by whom a
person is overcome, by him also he is brought into
[2]bondage.
20 For if, after they [a]have escaped the pollutions
of the world through the knowledge of the Lord
and Savior Jesus Christ, they are [b]again entangled
in them and overcome, the latter end is worse for
them than the beginning.
21 For [a]it would have been better for them not to
have known the way of righteousness, than having known *it,* to turn from the holy commandment delivered to them.
22 But it has happened to them according to the
true proverb: [a]*"A dog returns to his own vomit,"*
and, "a sow, having washed, to her wallowing in
the mire."

### *The Coming Day of the Lord*

**3** Beloved, I now write to you this second epistle
(in *both of* which [a]I stir up your pure minds by
way of reminder),
2 that you may be mindful of the words [a]which
were spoken before by the holy prophets, [b]and of
the commandment of [1]us, the apostles of the Lord
and Savior,
3 knowing this first: that scoffers will come in
the last days, [a]walking according to their own
lusts,
4 and saying, "Where is the promise of His
coming? For since the fathers fell asleep, all things
continue as *they were* from the beginning of
[a]creation."
5 For this they willfully forget: that [a]by the
word of God the heavens were of old, and the
earth [b]standing out of water and in the water,
6 [a]by which the world *that* then existed perished, being flooded with water.
7 But [a]the heavens and the earth *which* now
*exist* are kept in store by the same word, reserved
for [b]fire until the day of judgment and [1]perdition
of ungodly men.
8 But, beloved, do not forget this one thing, that
with the Lord one day *is* as a thousand years, and
[a]a thousand years as one day.
9 [a]The Lord is not slack concerning *His* promise,
as some count slackness, but [b]is longsuffering
toward [1]us, [c]not willing that any should perish but
[d]that all should come to repentance.
**10** But [a]the day of the Lord will come as a thief in
the night, in which [b]the heavens will pass away
with a great noise, and the elements will melt with
fervent heat; both the earth and the works that
are in it will be [1]burned up.
11 Therefore, since all these things will be dissolved, what manner *of persons* ought you to be
[a]in holy conduct and godliness,
12 [a]looking for and hastening the coming of the
day of God, because of which the heavens will [b]be
dissolved, being on fire, and the elements will
[c]melt with fervent heat?
13 Nevertheless we, according to His promise,
look for [a]new heavens and a [b]new earth in which
righteousness dwells.
**14** Therefore, beloved, looking forward to these
things, be diligent [a]to be found by Him in peace,
without spot and blameless;
15 and consider *that* [a]the longsuffering of our
Lord *is* salvation—as also our beloved brother
Paul, according to the wisdom given to him, has
written to you,
16 as also in all his [a]epistles, speaking in them of
these things, in which are some things hard to
understand, which untaught and unstable *people*
twist to their own destruction, as *they do* also the
[b]rest of the Scriptures.
17 You therefore, beloved, [a]since you know *this*
beforehand, [b]beware lest you also fall from your
own steadfastness, being led away with the error
of the wicked;
18 [a]but grow in the grace and knowledge of our
Lord and Savior Jesus Christ. [b]To Him *be* the
glory both now and forever. Amen.

**13** [a]Phil. 3:19 [b]Rom. 13:13 [c]Jude 12 [d]1 Cor. 11:20, 21 [1]*revel* [2]*reveling* **14** [a]Jude 11 [1]Lit. *an adulteress* **15** [a]Num. 22:5, 7 **17** [a]Jude 12, 13 [1]NU *and mists* [2]NU omits *forever* **18** [1]NU *are barely escaping* **19** [a]John 8:34 [1]*depravity* [2]*slavery* **20** [a]Matt. 12:45 [b][Heb. 6:4–6] **21** [a]Luke 12:47 **22** [a]Prov. 26:11

CHAPTER 3
**1** [a]2 Pet. 1:13 **2** [a]2 Pet. 1:21 [b]Jude 17 [1]NU, M *the apostles of your Lord and Savior* or *your apostles of the Lord and Savior* **3** [a]2 Pet. 2:10 **4** [a]Gen. 6:1–7 **5** [a]Gen. 1:6, 9 [b]Ps. 24:2; 136:6 **6** [a]Gen. 7:11, 12, 21–23 **7** [a]2 Pet. 3:10, 12 [b][2 Thess. 1:8] [1]*destruction* **8** [a]Ps. 90:4 **9** [a]Hab. 2:3 [b]Is. 30:18 [c]Ezek. 33:11 [d][Rom. 2:4] [1]NU *you* **10** [a]Rev. 3:3; 16:15 [b]Ps. 102:25, 26 [1]NU *laid bare,* lit. *found* **11** [a]1 Pet. 1:15 **12** [a]1 Cor. 1:7, 8 [b]Ps. 50:3 [c]Mic. 1:4 **13** [a]Is. 65:17; 66:22 [b]Rev. 21:1 **14** [a]1 Cor. 1:8; 15:58 **15** [a]Rom. 2:4 **16** [a]1 Cor. 15:24 [b]2 Tim. 3:16 **17** [a]Mark 13:23 [b]Eph. 4:14 **18** [a]Eph. 4:15 [b]2 Tim. 4:18

# *The First Epistle of* JOHN

### *Fellowship with the Father and the Son*

THAT [a]which was from the beginning, which
we have heard, which we have [b]seen with
our eyes, [c]which we have looked upon, and
[d]our hands have handled, concerning the [e]Word of
life—
2 [a]the life [b]was manifested, and we have seen,
[c]and bear witness, and declare to you that eternal
life which was [d]with the Father and was manifested to us—
3 that which we have seen and heard we declare
to you, that you also may have fellowship with us;

CHAPTER 1
**1** [a][John 1:1] [b]John 1:14 [c]2 Pet. 1:16 [d]Luke 24:39 [e][John 1:1, 4, 14]

**2** [a]John 1:4; [1 John 3:5, 8; 5:20] [b]Rom. 16:26; 1 Tim. 3:16 [c]John 21:24 [d][John 1:1, 18; 16:28]

and truly our fellowship *is* [a]with the Father and
with His Son Jesus Christ.
4 And these things we write to you [a]that [1]your
joy may be full.
**5** [a]This is the message which we have heard
from Him and declare to you, that [b]God is light
and in Him is no darkness at all.
6 [a]If we say that we have fellowship with Him,
and walk in darkness, we lie and do not practice
the truth.
7 But if we [a]walk in the light as He is in the
light, we have fellowship with one another, and
[b]the blood of Jesus Christ His Son cleanses us
from all sin.
8 If we say that we have no sin, we deceive
ourselves, and the truth is not in us.
9 If we [a]confess our sins, He is [b]faithful and just
to forgive us *our* sins and to [c]cleanse us from all
unrighteousness.
10 If we say that we have not sinned, we [a]make
Him a liar, and His word is not in us.

### *The Test of Knowing Christ*

**2** My little children, these things I write to you,
so that you may not sin. And if anyone sins,
[a]we have an Advocate with the Father, Jesus
Christ the righteous.
2 And [a]He Himself is the propitiation for our
sins, and not for ours only but [b]also for the whole
world.
**3** Now by this we know that we know Him, if
we keep His commandments.
4 He who says, "I know Him," and does not
keep His commandments, is a [a]liar, and the truth
is not in him.
5 But [a]whoever keeps His word, truly the love of
God [1]is perfected [b]in him. By this we know that we
are in Him.
6 [a]He who says he abides in Him [b]ought himself
also to walk just as He walked.
7 [1]Brethren, I write no new commandment to
you, but an old commandment which you have
had [a]from the beginning. The old commandment
is the word which you heard [2]from the beginning.
8 Again, [a]a new commandment I write to you,
which thing is true in Him and in you, [b]because
the darkness is passing away, and [c]the true light is
already shining.
9 [a]He who says he is in the light, and hates his
brother, is in darkness until now.
10 [a]He who loves his brother abides in the light,
and [b]there is no cause for stumbling in him.
11 But he who [a]hates his brother is in darkness
and [b]walks in darkness, and does not know where
he is going, because the darkness has blinded his
eyes.
**12** I write to you, little children,
Because [a]your sins are forgiven you for His
name's sake.
13 I write to you, fathers,
Because you have known Him
*who is* [a]from the beginning.
I write to you, young men,
Because you have overcome
the wicked one.
I write to you, little children,
Because you have [b]known the Father.
14 I have written to you, fathers,
Because you have known Him
*who is* from the beginning.
I have written to you, young men,
Because [a]you are strong, and the word
of God abides in you,
And you have overcome the wicked one.
**15** [a]Do not love the world or the things in the
world. [b]If anyone loves the world, the love of the
Father is not in him.
16 For all that *is* in the world—the lust of the
flesh, [a]the lust of the eyes, and the pride of life—is
not of the Father but is of the world.
17 And [a]the world is passing away, and the lust of
it; but he who does the will of God abides forever.
**18** [a]Little children, [b]it is the last hour; and as you
have heard that [c]the[1] Antichrist is coming, [d]even
now many antichrists have come, by which we
know [e]that it is the last hour.
19 [a]They went out from us, but they were not of
us; for [b]if they had been of us, they would have
continued with us; but *they went out* [c]that they
might be made manifest, that none of them were
of us.
20 But [a]you have an anointing [b]from the Holy
One, and [c]you[1] know all things.
21 I have not written to you because you do not
know the truth, but because you know it, and that
no lie is of the truth.
22 [a]Who is a liar but he who denies that [b]Jesus is
the Christ? He is antichrist who denies the Father
and the Son.
23 [a]Whoever denies the Son does not have the
[b]Father either; [c]he who acknowledges the Son has
the Father also.
**24** Therefore let that abide in you [a]which you
heard from the beginning. If what you heard from
the beginning abides in you, [b]you also will abide in
the Son and in the Father.
25 [a]And this is the promise that He has promised
us—eternal life.
26 These things I have written to you concerning
those who *try to* [1]deceive you.
27 But the [a]anointing which you have received
from Him abides in you, and [b]you do not need that
anyone teach you; but as the same anointing
[c]teaches you concerning all things, and is true,
and is not a lie, and just as it has taught you, you
[1]will abide in Him.
**28** And now, little children, abide in Him, that
[1]when He appears, we may have [a]confidence and
not be ashamed before Him at His coming.
29 [a]If you know that He is righteous, you know
that [b]everyone who practices righteousness is
born of Him.

### *The Command to Love*

**3** Behold [a]what manner of love the Father has
bestowed on us, that [b]we should be called
children of [1]God! Therefore the world does not
know [2]us, [c]because it did not know Him.
2 Beloved, [a]now we are children of God; and [b]it
has not yet been revealed what we shall be, but
we know that when He is revealed, [c]we shall be
like Him, for [d]we shall see Him as He is.
3 [a]And everyone who has this hope in Him
purifies himself, just as He is pure.

**3** [a]1 Cor. 1:9
**4** [a]John 15:11; 16:24 [1]NU, M *our*
**5** [a]1 John 3:11 [b][1 Tim. 6:16]
**6** [a][1 John 2:9–11]
**7** [a]Is. 2:5 [b][1 Cor. 6:11]
**9** [a]Prov. 28:13 [b][Rom. 3:24–26] [c]Ps. 51:2
**10** [a]1 John 5:10

CHAPTER 2
**1** [a]Heb. 7:25; 9:24
**2** [a][Rom. 3:25] [b]John 1:29
**4** [a]Rom. 3:4
**5** [a]John 14:21, 23 [b][1 John 4:12] [1]*has been completed*
**6** [a]John 15:4 [b]1 Pet. 2:21
**7** [a]1 John 3:11, 23; 4:21 [1]NU *Beloved* [2]NU omits *from the beginning*
**8** [a]John 13:34; 15:12 [b]Rom. 13:12 [c][John 1:9; 8:12; 12:35]
**9** [a][1 Cor. 13:2]
**10** [a][1 John 3:14] [b]2 Pet. 1:10
**11** [a][1 John 2:9; 3:15; 4:20] [b]John 12:35
**12** [a][1 Cor. 6:11]
**13** [a]John 1:1 [b][Rom. 8:15–17]
**14** [a]Eph. 6:10
**15** [a][Rom. 12:2] [b]James 4:4
**16** [a][Eccl. 5:10, 11
**17** [a]1 Cor. 7:31
**18** [a]John 21:5 [b]1 Pet. 4:7 [c]2 Thess. 2:3 [d]2 John 7 [e]1 Tim. 4:1 [1]NU omits *the*
**19** [a]Deut. 13:13 [b]Matt. 24:24 [c]1 Cor. 11:19
**20** [a]2 Cor. 1:21 [b]Acts 3:14 [c][John 16:13] [1]NU *you all know.*
**22** [a]2 John 7 [b]1 John 4:3
**23** [a]John 15:23 [b]John 5:23 [c]1 John 4:15; 5:1
**24** [a]2 John 6, 7 [b]John 14:23
**25** [a]John 3:14–16; 6:40; 17:2, 3
**26** [1]*lead you astray*
**27** [a][John 14:16; 16:13] [b][Jer. 31:33] [c][John 14:16] [1]NU omits *will*
**28** [a]1 John 3:21; 4:17; 5:14 [1]NU *if*
**29** [a]Acts 22:14 [b]1 John 3:7, 10

CHAPTER 3
**1** [a][John 3:16; Eph. 2:4–7; 1 John 4:10] [b][John 1:12] [c]John 15:18, 21; 16:3 [1]NU adds *And we are.* [2]M *you*
**2** [a][Is. 56:5; Rom. 8:15, 16] [b][Rom. 8:18, 19, 23] [c]Rom. 8:29; 2 Pet. 1:4 [d][Ps. 16:11]
**3** [a]1 John 4:17

4 Whoever commits sin also commits lawlessness, and [a]sin is lawlessness.
5 And you know [a]that He was manifested [b]to
take away our sins, and [c]in Him there is no sin.
6 Whoever abides in Him does not sin. Whoever
sins has neither seen Him nor known Him.
7 Little children, let no one deceive you. He who
practices righteousness is righteous, just as He is
righteous.
8 [a]He who sins is of the devil, for the devil has
sinned from the beginning. For this purpose the
Son of God was manifested, [b]that He might destroy the works of the devil.
9 Whoever has been [a]born of God does not sin,
for [b]His seed remains in him; and he cannot sin,
because he has been born of God.
**10** In this the children of God and the children of
the devil are manifest: Whoever does not practice
righteousness is not of God, nor *is* he who does
not love his brother.
11 For this is the message that you heard from
the beginning, [a]that we should love one another,
12 not as [a]Cain *who* was of the wicked one and
murdered his brother. And why did he murder
him? Because his works were evil and his brother's righteous.
13 Do not marvel, my brethren, if [a]the world
hates you.
14 We know that we have passed from death to
life, because we love the brethren. He who does
not love [1]*his* brother abides in death.
15 [a]Whoever hates his brother is a murderer, and
you know that [b]no murderer has eternal life
abiding in him.
**16** [a]By this we know love, [b]because He laid down
His life for us. And we also ought to lay down *our*
lives for the brethren.
17 But [a]whoever has this world's goods, and sees
his brother in need, and shuts up his heart from
him, how does the love of God abide in him?
18 My little children, [a]let us not love in word or in
tongue, but in deed and in truth.
19 And by this we [1]know [a]that we are of the
truth, and shall [2]assure our hearts before Him.
20 [a]For if our heart condemns us, God is greater
than our heart, and knows all things.
21 Beloved, if our heart does not condemn us, [a]we
have confidence toward God.
22 And [a]whatever we ask we receive from Him,
because we keep His commandments [b]and do
those things that are pleasing in His sight.
23 And this is His commandment: that we should
believe on the name of His Son Jesus Christ [a]and
love one another, as He gave [1]us commandment.
**24** Now [a]he who keeps His commandments
[b]abides in Him, and He in him. And [c]by this we
know that He abides in us, by the Spirit whom He
has given us.

### *Love for God and One Another*

**4** Beloved, do not believe every spirit, but [a]test
the spirits, whether they are of God; because
[b]many false prophets have gone out into the
world.
2 By this you know the Spirit of God: [a]Every
spirit that confesses that Jesus Christ has come in
the flesh is of God,
3 and every spirit that does not confess [1]that
Jesus [2]Christ has come in the flesh is not of God.
And this is the *spirit* of the Antichrist, which you
have heard was coming, and is now already in the
world.
4 You are of God, little children, and have
overcome them, because He who is in you is
greater than [a]he who is in the world.
5 [a]They are of the world. Therefore they speak
*as* of the world, and [b]the world hears them.
6 We are of God. He who knows God hears us;
he who is not of God does not hear us. [a]By this we
know the spirit of truth and the spirit of error.
**7** [a]Beloved, let us love one another, for love is of
God; and everyone who [b]loves is born of God and
knows God.
8 He who does not love does not know God, for
God is love.
9 [a]In this the love of God was manifested
toward us, that God has sent His only begotten
[b]Son into the world, that we might live through
Him.
10 In this is love, [a]not that we loved God, but that
He loved us and sent His Son [b]*to be* the propitiation for our sins.
11 Beloved, [a]if God so loved us, we also ought to
love one another.
**12** [a]No one has seen God at any time. If we love
one another, God abides in us, and His love has
been perfected in us.
13 [a]By this we know that we abide in Him, and
He in us, because He has given us of His Spirit.
14 And [a]we have seen and testify that [b]the Father
has sent the Son *as* Savior of the world.
15 [a]Whoever confesses that Jesus is the Son of
God, God abides in him, and he in God.
16 And we have known and believed the love
that God has for us. God is love, and [a]he who
abides in love abides in God, and God [b]in him.
**17** Love has been perfected among us in this: that
[a]we may have boldness in the day of judgment;
because as He is, so are we in this world.
18 There is no fear in love; but perfect love casts
out fear, because fear involves torment. But he
who fears has not been made perfect in love.
19 [a]We love [1]Him because He first loved us.
**20** [a]If someone says, "I love God," and hates his
brother, he is a liar; for he who does not love his
brother whom he has seen, [1]how can he love God
[b]whom he has not seen?
21 And [a]this commandment we have from Him:
that he who loves God *must* love his brother also.

### *Obedience by Faith*

**5** Whoever believes that [a]Jesus is the Christ is
[b]born of God, and everyone who loves Him
who begot also loves him who is begotten of Him.
2 By this we know that we love the children of
God, when we love God and [a]keep His commandments.
3 [a]For this is the love of God, that we keep His
commandments. And [b]His commandments are not
burdensome.
4 For [a]whatever is born of God overcomes the
world. And this is the victory that [b]has overcome
the world—[1]our faith.
5 Who is he who overcomes the world, but [a]he
who believes that Jesus is the Son of God?
**6** This is He who came [a]by water and blood—
Jesus Christ; not only by water, but by water and
blood. [b]And it is the Spirit who bears witness,
because the Spirit is truth.

**4** [a]Rom. 4:15
**5** [a]1 John 1:2; 3:8 [b]John 1:29 [c][2 Cor. 5:21]
**8** [a]Matt. 13:38 [b]Luke 10:18
**9** [a]John 1:3; 3:3 [b]1 Pet. 1:23
**11** [a][John 13:34; 15:12]
**12** [a]Gen. 4:4, 8
**13** [a][John 15:18; 17:14]
**14** [1]NU omits *his brother*
**15** [a]Matt. 5:21 [b][Gal. 5:20, 21]
**16** [a][John 3:16] [b]John 10:11; 15:13
**17** [a]Deut. 15:7
**18** [a]Ezek. 33:31
**19** [a]John 18:37 [1]NU *shall know* [2]*persuade, set at rest*
**20** [a][1 Cor. 4:4, 5]
**21** [a][1 John 2:28; 5:14]
**22** [a]Ps. 34:15 [b]John 8:29
**23** [a]Matt. 22:39 [1]M omits *us*
**24** [a]John 14:23 [b]John 14:21; 17:21 [c]Rom. 8:9, 14, 16

CHAPTER 4
**1** [a]1 Cor. 14:29 [b]Matt. 24:5
**2** [a]1 Cor. 12:3
**3** [1]NU omits *that* [2]NU omits *Christ has come in the flesh*
**4** [a]John 14:30; 16:11
**5** [a]John 3:31 [b]John 15:19; 17:14
**6** [a][1 Cor. 2:12–16]
**7** [a]1 John 3:10, 11, 23 [b]1 Thess. 4:9
**9** [a]Rom. 5:8 [b]John 3:16
**10** [a]Titus 3:5 [b]1 John 2:2
**11** [a]Matt. 18:33
**12** [a]John 1:18
**13** [a]John 14:20
**14** [a]John 1:14 [b]John 3:17; 4:42
**15** [a][Rom. 10:9]
**16** [a][1 John 3:24] [b][John 14:23]
**17** [a]1 John 2:28
**19** [a]1 John 4:10 [1]NU omits *Him*
**20** [a][1 John 2:4] [b]1 John 4:12 [1]NU *he cannot*
**21** [a][Matt. 5:43, 44; 22:37]

CHAPTER 5
**1** [a]1 John 2:22; 4:2, 15 [b]John 1:13
**2** [a]John 15:10
**3** [a]John 14:15 [b]Matt. 11:30; 23:4
**4** [a]John 16:33 [b]1 John 2:13; 4:4 [1]M *your*
**5** [a]1 Cor. 15:57
**6** [a]John 1:31–34 [b][John 14:17]

7 For there are three that bear witness [1]in
heaven: the Father, [a]the Word, and the Holy
Spirit; [b]and these three are one.
8 And there are three that bear witness on
earth: [a]the Spirit, the water, and the blood; and
these three agree as one.
9 If we receive [a]the witness of men, the witness
of God is greater; [b]for this is the witness of [1]God
which He has testified of His Son.
10 He who believes in the Son of God [a]has the
witness in himself; he who does not believe God
[b]has made Him a liar, because he has not believed
the testimony that God has given of His Son.
11 And this is the testimony: that God has given
us eternal life, and this life is in His Son.
12 [a]He who has the Son has [1]life; he who does not
have the Son of God does not have [1]life.
13 These things I have written to you who believe in the name of the Son of God, that you may
know that you have eternal life, [1]and that you
may *continue to* believe in the name of the Son of
God.
**14** Now this is the confidence that we have in
Him, that [a]if we ask anything according to His
will, He hears us.

**7** [a][John 1:1] [b]John 10:30 [1]NU, M omit the words from *in heaven* (v. 7) through *on earth* (v. 8). Only 4 or 5 very late mss. contain these words in Greek.
**8** [a]John 15:26
**9** [a]John 5:34, 37; 8:17, 18 [b][Matt. 3:16, 17] [1]NU, *God, that*
**10** [a][Rom. 8:16] [b]John 3:18, 33
**12** [a][John 3:15, 36; 6:47; 17:2, 3] [1]Or *the life*
**13** [1]NU omits the rest of v. 13.
**14** [a][1 John 2:28; 3:21, 22]
**16** [a]Job 42:8 [b][Matt. 12:31] [c]Jer. 7:16; 14:11
**17** [a]1 John 3:4

15 And if we know that He hears us, whatever we
ask, we know that we have the petitions that we
have asked of Him.
16 If anyone sees his brother sinning a sin *which*
*does* not *lead* to death, he will ask, and [a]He will
give him life for those who commit sin not *leading*
to death. [b]There is sin *leading* to death. [c]I do not
say that he should pray about that.
17 [a]All unrighteousness is sin, and there is sin not
*leading* to death.
**18** We know that [a]whoever is born of God does
not sin; but he who has been born of God [b]keeps[1]
[2]himself, and the wicked one does not touch him.
19 We know that we are of God, and [a]the whole
world lies *under the sway of* the wicked one.
20 And we know that the [a]Son of God has come
and [b]has given us an understanding, [c]that we may
know Him who is true; and we are in Him who is
true, in His Son Jesus Christ. [d]This is the true God
[e]and eternal life.
21 Little children, keep yourselves from idols.
Amen.

**18** [a][1 Pet. 1:23] [b]James 1:27 [1]*guards* [2]NU *him*
**19** [a]Gal. 1:4
**20** [a]1 John 4:2 [b]Luke 24:45 [c]John 17:3 [d]Is. 9:6 [e]1 John 5:11, 12

*The Second Epistle of*

# JOHN

### *Obey Christ's Commandments; Beware of Deceivers*

THE ELDER,

To the [1]elect lady and her children, whom I
love in truth, and not only I, but also all those who
have known [a]the truth,
2 because of the truth which abides in us and
will be with us forever:

3 [a]Grace, mercy, *and* peace will be with [1]you
from God the Father and from the Lord Jesus
Christ, the Son of the Father, in truth and love.
**4** I [a]rejoiced greatly that I have found *some* of
your children walking in truth, as we received
commandment from the Father.
5 And now I plead with you, lady, not as though
I wrote a new commandment to you, but that
which we have had from the beginning: [a]that we
love one another.
6 [a]This is love, that we walk according to His
commandments. This is the commandment, that
[b]as you have heard from the beginning, you
should walk in it.
7 For [a]many deceivers have gone out into the
world [b]who do not confess Jesus Christ *as* coming
in the flesh. [c]This is a deceiver and an antichrist.
8 [a]Look to yourselves, [b]that [1]we do not lose
those things we worked for, but *that* [1]we may
receive a full reward.
9 [a]Whoever [1]transgresses and does not abide in
the doctrine of Christ does not have God. He who
abides in the doctrine of Christ has both the
Father and the Son.
10 If anyone comes to you and [a]does not bring
this doctrine, do not receive him into your house
nor greet him;
11 for he who greets him shares in his evil deeds.
**12** [a]Having many things to write to you, I did not
wish *to do so* with paper and ink; but I hope to
come to you and speak face to face, [b]that our joy
may be full.
13 [a]The children of your elect sister greet you.
Amen.

**1** [a]Col. 1:5 [1]*chosen*
**3** [a]1 Tim. 1:2 [1]NU, M *us*
**4** [a]3 John 3, 4
**5** [a][John 13:34, 35; 15:12, 17]
**6** [a]1 John 2:5; 5:3 [b]1 John 2:24
**7** [a]1 John 2:19; 4:1 [b]1 John 4:2 [c]1 John 2:22
**8** [a]Mark 13:9 [b]Gal. 3:4 [1]NU *you*
**9** [a]John 7:16; 8:31 [1]NU *goes ahead*
**10** [a]Rom. 16:17
**12** [a]3 John 13, 14 [b]John 17:13
**13** [a]1 Pet. 5:13

*The Third Epistle of*

# JOHN

### *Gaius, Diotrephes, and Demetrius*

THE ELDER,

To the beloved Gaius, [a]whom I love in
truth:

2 Beloved, I pray that you may prosper in all
things and be in health, just as your soul prospers.
3 For I [a]rejoiced greatly when brethren came
and testified of the truth *that is* in you, just as you
walk in the truth.
4 I have no greater [a]joy than to hear that [b]my
children walk in [1]truth.
**5** Beloved, you do faithfully whatever you do for
the brethren [1]and for strangers,
6 who have borne witness of your love before
the church. *If* you send them forward on their
journey in a manner worthy of God, you will do
well,
7 because they went forth for His name's sake,
[a]taking nothing from the Gentiles.
8 We therefore ought to [a]receive[1] such, that we
may become fellow workers for the truth.
**9** I wrote to the church, but Diotrephes, who
loves to have the preeminence among them, does
not receive us.
10 Therefore, if I come, I will call to mind his
deeds which he does, [a]prating[1] against us with
malicious words. And not content with that, he
himself does not receive the brethren, and forbids
those who wish to, putting *them* out of the
church.
11 Beloved, [a]do not imitate what is evil, but what
is good. [b]He who does good is of God, [1]but he who
does evil has not seen [c]God.
12 Demetrius [a]has a *good* testimony from all, and
from the truth itself. And we also [1]bear witness,
[b]and you know that our testimony is true.
**13** [a]I had many things to write, but I do not wish
to write to you with pen and ink;
14 but I hope to see you shortly, and we shall
speak face to face. Peace to you. Our friends greet
you. Greet the friends by name.

**1** [a]2 John 1
**3** [a]2 John 4
**4** [a]1 Thess. 2:19, 20 [b][1 Cor. 4:15] [1]NU *the truth*
**5** [1]NU *and especially for*
**7** [a]1 Cor. 9:12, 15
**8** [a]Matt. 10:40 [1]NU *support*
**10** [a]Prov. 10:8, 10 [1]*talking nonsense*
**11** [a]Ps. 34:14; 37:27 [b][1 John 2:29; 3:10] [c][1 John 3:10] [1]NU, M omit *but*
**12** [a]1 Tim. 3:7 [b]John 19:35; 21:24 [1]*testify*
**13** [a]2 John 12

*The Epistle of*

# JUDE

### *Maintain Your Life with God*

JUDE, a bondservant of Jesus Christ, and
[a]brother of James,

To those who are [b]called, [1]sanctified by God
the Father, and [c]preserved in Jesus Christ:

2 Mercy, [a]peace, and love be multiplied to you.
**3** Beloved, while I was very diligent to write to
you [a]concerning our common salvation, I found it
necessary to write to you exhorting [b]you to contend earnestly for the faith which was once for all
delivered to the saints.
4 For certain men have crept in unnoticed, who
long ago were marked out for this condemnation,
ungodly men, who turn the grace of our God into
lewdness and deny the only Lord [1]God and our
Lord Jesus Christ.
**5** But I want to remind you, though you once
knew this, that [a]the Lord, having saved the people
out of the land of Egypt, afterward destroyed
those who did not believe.
6 And the angels who did not keep their [1]proper
domain, but left their own abode, He has reserved
in everlasting chains under darkness for the judgment of the great day;
7 as [a]Sodom and Gomorrah, and the cities
around them in a similar manner to these, having
given themselves over to sexual immorality and
gone after strange flesh, are set forth as an example, suffering the [1]vengeance of eternal fire.
8 [a]Likewise also these dreamers defile the flesh,
reject authority, and [b]speak evil of [1]dignitaries.
9 Yet Michael the archangel, in [1]contending
with the devil, when he disputed about the body
of Moses, dared not bring against him a reviling
accusation, but said, [a]"The Lord rebuke you!"
10 [a]But these speak evil of whatever they do not
know; and whatever they know naturally, like
brute beasts, in these things they corrupt themselves.
11 Woe to them! For they have gone in the way
[a]of Cain, [b]have run greedily in the error of Balaam
for profit, and perished [c]in the rebellion of Korah.
**12** These are [1]spots in your love feasts, while they
feast with you without fear, serving *only* themselves. *They are* clouds without water, carried
[2]about by the winds; late autumn trees without
fruit, twice dead, pulled up by the roots;
13 [a]raging waves of the sea, [b]foaming up their
own shame; wandering stars [c]for whom is reserved the blackness of darkness forever.
14 Now Enoch, the seventh from Adam, prophesied about these men also, saying, "Behold, the
Lord comes with ten thousands of His saints,
15 "to execute judgment on all, to convict all
who are ungodly among them of all their ungodly deeds which they have committed in an
ungodly way, and of all the [a]harsh things which
ungodly sinners have spoken against Him."
**16** These are grumblers, complainers, walking
according to their own lusts; and they [a]mouth
great swelling *words,* [b]flattering people to gain
advantage.
17 [a]But you, beloved, remember the words which
were spoken before by the apostles of our Lord
Jesus Christ:
18 how they told you that [a]there would be mock-

**1** [a]Acts 1:13 [b]Rom. 1:7 [c]John 17:1 [1]NU *beloved*
**2** [a]1 Pet. 1:2; 2 Pet. 1:2
**3** [a]Titus 1:4 [b]Phil. 1:27
**4** [1]NU omits *God*
**5** [a]Ex. 12:51; 1 Cor. 10:5–10; Heb. 3:16
**6** [1]*own*
**7** [a]Gen. 19:24; 2 Pet. 2:6 [1]*punishment*
**8** [a]2 Pet. 2:10 [b]Ex. 22:28 [1]*glorious ones,* lit. *glories*
**9** [a]Zech. 3:2 [1]*arguing*
**10** [a]2 Pet. 2:12
**11** [a]Gen. 4:3–8; Heb. 11:4; 1 John 3:12 [b]Num. 31:16; 2 Pet. 2:15; Rev. 2:14 [c]Num. 16:1–3, 31–35
**12** [1]*stains,* or *hidden reefs* [2]NU, M *along*
**13** [a]Is. 57:20 [b][Phil. 3:19] [c]2 Pet. 2:17; Jude 6
**15** [a]1 Sam. 2:3
**16** [a]2 Pet. 2:18 [b]Prov. 28:21
**17** [a]2 Pet. 3:2
**18** [a]Acts 20:29; [1 Tim. 4:1]; 2 Tim. 3:1; 4:3; 2 Pet. 3:3

ers in the last time who would walk according to
their own ungodly lusts.
19 These are [1]sensual persons, who cause divisions, not having the Spirit.
**20** But you, beloved, [a]building yourselves up on
your most holy faith, [b]praying in the Holy Spirit,
21 keep yourselves in the love of God, [a]looking
for the mercy of our Lord Jesus Christ unto
eternal life.
22 And on some have compassion, [1]making a
distinction;
23 but [a]others save [1]with fear, [b]pulling *them* out
of the [2]fire, hating even [c]the garment defiled by
the flesh.

**19** [1]*soulish* or *worldly*
**20** [a]Col. 2:7 [b][Rom. 8:26]
**21** [a]Titus 2:13
**22** [1]NU *who are doubting* (or *making distinctions*)
**23** [a]Rom. 11:14 [b]Amos 4:11 [c][Zech. 3:4, 5] [1]NU omits *with fear* [2]NU adds *and on some have mercy with fear*

**24** [a]Now to Him who is able
to keep [1]you from stumbling,
And [b]to present *you* faultless
Before the presence of His glory
with exceeding joy,
25 To [1]God our Savior,
[2]Who alone is wise,
*Be* glory and majesty,
Dominion and [3]power,
Both now and forever.
Amen.

**24** [a][Eph. 3:20] [b]Col. 1:22 [1]M *them*
**25** [1]NU *the only God our* [2]NU *Through Jesus Christ our Lord, Be glory* [3]NU adds *Before all time,*

# THE REVELATION

## *of Jesus Christ*

### *John's Vision of Christ*

THE Revelation of Jesus Christ, [a]which God
gave Him to show His servants—things
which must [1]shortly take place. And [b]He sent
and signified *it* by His angel to His servant John,
2 [a]who bore witness to the word of God, and to
the testimony of Jesus Christ, to all things [b]that
he saw.
3 [a]Blessed *is* he who reads and those who hear
the words of this prophecy, and keep those things
which are written in it; for [b]the time *is* near.
**4** John, to the seven churches which are in Asia:
Grace to you and peace from Him [a]who is and
[b]who was and who is to come, [c]and from the seven
Spirits who are before His throne,
5 and from Jesus Christ, [a]the faithful [b]witness,
the [c]firstborn from the dead, and [d]the ruler over
the kings of the earth. To Him [e]who [1]loved us [f]and
washed us from our sins in His own blood,
6 and has [a]made us [1]kings and priests to His God
and Father, [b]to Him *be* glory and dominion forever and ever. Amen.
7 Behold, He is coming with [a]clouds, and every
eye will see Him, even [b]they who pierced Him.
And all the tribes of the earth will mourn because
of Him. Even so, Amen.
8 [a]"I am the Alpha and the Omega, [1]*the* Beginning and *the* End," says the [2]Lord, [b]"who is and
who was and who is to come, the [c]Almighty."
**9** I, John, [1]both your brother and [a]companion in
the tribulation and [b]kingdom and patience of
Jesus Christ, was on the island that is called
Patmos for the word of God and for the testimony
of Jesus Christ.
10 [a]I was in the Spirit on [b]the Lord's Day, and I
heard behind me [c]a loud voice, as of a trumpet,
11 saying, [1]"I am the Alpha and the Omega, the
First and the Last," and, "What you see, write in a
book and send *it* to the seven churches [2]which are
in Asia: to Ephesus, to Smyrna, to Pergamos, to
Thyatira, to Sardis, to Philadelphia, and to Laodicea."
12 Then I turned to see the voice that spoke with
me. And having turned [a]I saw seven golden lampstands,

CHAPTER 1
**1** [a]John 3:32 [b]Rev. 22:6 [1]*quickly* or *swiftly*
**2** [a]1 Cor. 1:6 [b]1 John 1:1
**3** [a]Luke 11:28 [b]James 5:8
**4** [a]Ex. 3:14 [b]John 1:1 [c][Is. 11:2]
**5** [a]John 8:14 [b]Is. 55:4 [c][Col. 1:18] [d]Rev. 17:14 [e]John 13:34 [f]Heb. 9:14 [1]NU, M *loves us and freed*
**6** [a]1 Pet. 2:5, 9 [b]1 Tim. 6:16 [1]NU, M *a kingdom*
**7** [a]Matt. 24:30 [b]Zech. 12:10–14
**8** [a]Is. 41:4 [b]Rev. 4:8; 11:17 [c]Is. 9:6 [1]NU, M omit *the Beginning and the End* [2]NU, M *Lord God*
**9** [a]Phil. 1:7 [b][2 Tim. 2:12] [1]NU, M omit *both*
**10** [a]Acts 10:10 [b]Acts 20:7 [c]Rev. 4:1
**11** [1]NU, M omit *"I am the Alpha and Omega, the First and the Last," and* [2]NU, M omit *which are in Asia*
**12** [a]Ex. 25:37
**13** [a]Rev. 2:1 [b]Ezek. 1:26 [c]Dan. 10:5 [d]Rev. 15:6
**14** [a]Dan. 7:9 [b]Dan. 10:6
**15** [a]Ezek. 1:7 [b]Ezek. 1:24; 43:2
**16** [a]Rev. 1:20; 2:1; 3:1 [b]Is. 49:2 [c]Matt. 17:2
**17** [a]Ezek. 1:28 [b]Dan. 8:18; 10:10, 12 [c]Is. 41:4; 44:6; 48:12 [1]NU, M omit *to me*

13 [a]and in the midst of the seven lampstands
[b]*One* like the Son of Man, [c]clothed with a garment
down to the feet and [d]girded about the chest with
a golden band.
14 His head and [a]hair *were* white like wool, as
white as snow, and [b]His eyes like a flame of fire;
15 [a]His feet *were* like fine brass, as if refined in a
furnace, and [b]His voice as the sound of many
waters;
16 [a]He had in His right hand seven stars, [b]out of
His mouth went a sharp two-edged sword, [c]and
His countenance *was* like the sun shining in its
strength.
17 And [a]when I saw Him, I fell at His feet as
dead. But [b]He laid His right hand on me, saying [1]to
me, "Do not be afraid; [c]I am the First and the Last.
18 [a]"I *am* He who lives, and was dead, and behold, [b]I am alive forevermore. Amen. And [c]I have
the keys of [1]Hades and of Death.
19 [1]"Write the things which you have [a]seen, [b]and
the things which are, [c]and the things which will
take place after this.
20 "The [1]mystery of the seven stars which you
saw in My right hand, and the seven golden
lampstands: The seven stars are [a]the [2]angels of the
seven churches, and [b]the seven lampstands [3]which
you saw are the seven churches.

### *Christ's Letters to Four Churches*

**2** "To the [1]angel of the church of Ephesus write,
'These things says [a]He who holds the seven
stars in His right hand, [b]who walks in the midst of
the seven golden lampstands:
2 [a]"I know your works, your labor, your [1]pa-
tience, and that you cannot [2]bear those who are
evil. And [b]you have tested those [c]who say they are
apostles and are not, and have found them liars;
3 "and you have persevered and have patience,

**18** [a]Rom. 6:9 [b]Rev. 4:9 [c]Ps. 68:20 [1]Lit. *Unseen;* the unseen realm
**19** [a]Rev. 1:9–18 [b]Rev. 2:1 [c]Rev. 4:1 [1]NU, M *Therefore, write*
**20** [a]Rev. 2:1 [b]Zech. 4:2 [1]*hidden truth* [2]Or *messengers* [3]NU, M omit *which you saw*

CHAPTER 2
**1** [a]Rev. 1:16 [b]Rev. 1:13 [1]Or *messenger*
**2** [a]Ps. 1:6 [b]1 John 4:1 [c]2 Cor. 11:13 [1]*perseverance* [2]*endure*

and have labored for My name's sake and have [a]not become weary.

4 "Nevertheless I have *this* against you, that you have left your first love.

5 "Remember therefore from where you have fallen; repent and do the first works, [a]or else I will come to you quickly and remove your lampstand from its place—unless you repent.

6 "But this you have, that you hate the deeds of the Nicolaitans, which I also hate.

7 [a]"He who has an ear, let him hear what the Spirit says to the churches. To him who overcomes I will give [b]to eat from [c]the tree of life, which is in the midst of the Paradise of God." '

8 "And to the [1]angel of the church in Smyrna write,

'These things says [a]the First and the Last, who was dead, and came to life:

9 "I know your works, tribulation, and poverty (but you are [a]rich); and *I know* the blasphemy of [b]those who say they are Jews and are not, [c]but *are* a [1]synagogue of Satan.

10 [a]"Do not fear any of those things which you are about to suffer. Indeed, the devil is about to throw *some* of you into prison, that you may be tested, and you will have tribulation ten days. [b]Be faithful until death, and I will give you [c]the crown of life.

11 [a]"He who has an ear, let him hear what the Spirit says to the churches. He who overcomes shall not be hurt by [b]the second death." '

12 "And to the [1]angel of the church in Pergamos write,

'These things says [a]He who has the sharp two-edged sword:

13 "I know your works, and where you dwell, where Satan's throne *is.* And you hold fast to My name, and did not deny My faith even in the days in which Antipas *was* My faithful martyr, who was killed among you, where Satan dwells.

14 "But I have a few things against you, because you have there those who hold the doctrine of [a]Balaam, who taught Balak to put a stumbling block before the children of Israel, [b]to eat things sacrificed to idols, [c]and to commit sexual immorality.

15 "Thus you also have those who hold the doctrine of the Nicolaitans, [1]which thing I hate.

16 "Repent, or else I will come to you quickly and [a]will fight against them with the sword of My mouth.

17 "He who has an ear, let him hear what the Spirit says to the churches. To him who overcomes I will give some of the hidden [a]manna to eat. And I will give him a white stone, and on the stone [b]a new name written which no one knows except him who receives *it.*" '

18 "And to the [1]angel of the church in Thyatira write,

'These things says the Son of God, [a]who has eyes like a flame of fire, and His feet like fine brass:

19 [a]"I know your works, love, [1]service, faith, and your [2]patience; and *as* for your works, the last *are* more than the first.

20 "Nevertheless I have [1]a few things against you, because you allow [2]that woman [a]Jezebel, who calls herself a prophetess, [3]to teach and seduce My servants [b]to commit sexual immorality and eat things sacrificed to idols.

21 "And I gave her time [a]to [1]repent of her sexual immorality, and she did not repent.

22 "Indeed I will cast her into a sickbed, and those who commit adultery with her into great tribulation, unless they repent of [1]their deeds.

23 "I will kill her children with death, and all the churches shall know that I am He who [a]searches[1] the minds and hearts. And I will give to each one of you according to your works.

24 "Now to you I say, [1]and to the rest in Thyatira, as many as do not have this doctrine, who have not known the [a]depths of Satan, as they say, [b]I [2]will put on you no other burden.

25 "But hold fast [a]what you have till I come.

26 "And he who overcomes, and keeps [a]My works until the end, [b]to him I will give power over the nations—

27 *'He[a] shall rule them with a rod of iron;*
*They shall be dashed to pieces*
*like the potter's vessels'—*

as I also have received from My Father;

28 "and I will give him [a]the morning star.

29 "He who has an ear, let him hear what the Spirit says to the churches." '

## *Christ's Letters to Three Churches*

**3** "And to the [1]angel of the church in Sardis write,

'These things says He who [a]has the seven Spirits of God and the seven stars: "I know your works, that you have a name that you are alive, but you are dead.

2 "Be watchful, and strengthen the things which remain, that are ready to die, for I have not found your works perfect before [1]God.

3 [a]"Remember therefore how you have received and heard; hold fast and [b]repent. [c]Therefore if you will not watch, I will come upon you [d]as a thief, and you will not know what hour I will come upon you.

4 [1]"You have [a]a few names [2]even in Sardis who have not [b]defiled their garments; and they shall walk with Me [c]in white, for they are worthy.

5 "He who overcomes [a]shall be clothed in white garments, and I will not [b]blot out his name from the [c]Book of Life; but [d]I will confess his name before My Father and before His angels.

6 [a]"He who has an ear, let him hear what the Spirit says to the churches." '

7 "And to the [1]angel of the church in Philadelphia write,

'These things says [a]He who is holy, [b]He who is true, [c]*"He who has the key of David,* [d]*He who opens and no one shuts, and* [e]*shuts and no one opens"*:

8 [a]"I know your works. See, I have set before you [b]an open door, [1]and no one can shut it; for you have a little strength, have kept My word, and have not denied My name.

9 "Indeed I will make [a]*those* of the synagogue of Satan, who say they are Jews and are not, but lie—indeed [b]I will make them come and worship before your feet, and to know that I have loved you.

**2:3** [a]Gal. 6:9
**5** [a]Matt. 21:41
**7** [a]Matt. 11:15 [b][Rev. 22:2, 14] [c][Gen. 2:9; 3:22]
**8** [a]Rev. 1:8, 17, 18 [1]Or *messenger*
**9** [a]Luke 12:21 [b]Rom. 2:17 [c]Rev. 3:9 [1]*congregation*
**10** [a]Matt. 10:22 [b]Matt. 24:13 [c]James 1:12
**11** [a]Rev. 13:9 [b][Rev. 20:6, 14; 21:8]
**12** [a]Rev. 1:16; 2:16 [1]Or *messenger*
**14** [a]Num. 31:16 [b]Acts 15:29 [c]1 Cor. 6:13
**15** [1]NU, M *likewise.*
**16** [a]2 Thess. 2:8
**17** [a]Ex. 16:33, 34 [b]Rev. 3:12
**18** [a]Rev. 1:14, 15 [1]Or *messenger*
**19** [a]Rev. 2:2 [1]NU, M *faith, service* [2]*perseverance*
**20** [a]1 Kin. 16:31; 21:25 [b]Ex. 34:15 [1]NU, M *against you that you tolerate* [2]M *your wife Jezebel* [3]NU, M *and teaches and seduces*
**21** [a]Rev. 9:20; 16:9, 11 [1]NU, M *repent, and she does not want to repent of her sexual immorality.*
**22** [1]NU, M *her*
**23** [a]Jer. 11:20; 17:10 [1]*examines*
**24** [a]2 Tim. 3:1–9 [b]Acts 15:28 [1]NU, M omit *and* [2]NU, M omit *will*
**25** [a]Rev. 3:11
**26** [a][John 6:29] [b][Matt. 19:28]
**27** [a]Ps. 2:8, 9
**28** [a]2 Pet. 1:19

CHAPTER 3
**1** [a]Rev. 1:4, 16 [1]Or *messenger*
**2** [1]NU, M *My God*
**3** [a]1 Tim. 6:20 [b]Rev. 3:19 [c]Matt. 24:42, 43 [d][Rev. 16:15]
**4** [a]Acts 1:15 [b][Jude 23] [c]Rev. 4:4; 6:11 [1]NU, M *Nevertheless you* [3]NU, M omit *even*
**5** [a][Rev. 19:8] [b]Ex. 32:32 [c]Phil. 4:3 [d]Luke 12:8
**6** [a]Rev. 2:7
**7** [a]Acts 3:14 [b]1 John 5:20 [c]Is. 9:7; 22:22 [d][Matt. 16:19; Rev. 1:18] [e]Job 12:14 [1]Or *messenger*
**8** [a]Rev. 3:1 [b]1 Cor. 16:9 [1]NU, M *which no one can shut*
**9** [a]Rev. 2:9 [b]Is. 45:14; 49:23; 60:14

10 "Because you have kept [1]My command to persevere, [a]I also will keep you from the hour of trial which shall come upon [b]the whole world, to test those who dwell [c]on the earth.
11 [1]"Behold, [a]I am coming quickly! [b]Hold fast what you have, that no one may take [c]your crown.
12 "He who overcomes, I will make him [a]a pillar in the temple of My God, and he shall [b]go out no more. [c]I will write on him the name of My God and the name of the city of My God, the [d]New Jerusalem, which [e]comes down out of heaven from My God. [f]And *I will write on him* My new name.
13 [a]"He who has an ear, let him hear what the Spirit says to the churches." '
14 "And to the [1]angel of the church [2]of the Laodiceans write,

[a]'These things says the Amen, [b]the Faithful and True Witness, [c]the Beginning of the creation of God:
15 [a]"I know your works, that you are neither cold nor hot. I could wish you were cold or hot.
16 "So then, because you are lukewarm, and neither [1]cold nor hot, I will vomit you out of My mouth.
17 "Because you say, [a]'I am rich, have become wealthy, and have need of nothing'—and do not know that you are wretched, miserable, poor, blind, and naked—
18 "I counsel you [a]to buy from Me gold refined in the fire, that you may be rich; and [b]white garments, that you may be clothed, *that* the shame of your nakedness may not be revealed; and anoint your eyes with eye salve, that you may see.
19 [a]"As many as I love, I rebuke and [b]chasten.[1] Therefore be [2]zealous and repent.
20 "Behold, [a]I stand at the door and knock. [b]If anyone hears My voice and opens the door, [c]I will come in to him and dine with him, and he with Me.
21 "To him who overcomes [a]I will grant to sit with Me on My throne, as I also overcame and sat down with My Father on His throne.
22 [a]"He who has an ear, let him hear what the Spirit says to the churches." ' "

### *John's Vision of God's Throne*

4 After these things I looked, and behold, a door *standing* [a]open in heaven. And the first voice which I heard *was* like a [b]trumpet speaking with me, saying, "Come up here, and I will show you things which must take place after this."
2 Immediately [a]I was in the Spirit; and behold, [b]a throne set in heaven, and *One* sat on the throne.
3 [1]And He who sat there was [a]like a jasper and a sardius stone in appearance; [b]and *there was a* rainbow around the throne, in appearance like an emerald.
4 [a]Around the throne *were* twenty-four thrones, and on the thrones I saw twenty-four elders sitting, [b]clothed in white [1]robes; and they had crowns of gold on their heads.
5 And from the throne proceeded [a]lightnings, [1]thunderings, and voices. [b]Seven lamps of fire *were* burning before the throne, which are [c]the[2] seven Spirits of God.
6 Before the throne *there* [1]*was* [a]a sea of glass, like crystal. [b]And in the midst of the throne, and around the throne, *were* four living creatures full of eyes in front and in back.
7 [a]The first living creature *was* like a lion, the second living creature like a calf, the third living creature had a face like a man, and the fourth living creature *was* like a flying eagle.
8 *The* four living creatures, each having [a]six wings, were full of eyes around and within. And they do not rest day or night, saying:

[b]"Holy,[1] holy, holy,
[c]Lord God Almighty,
[d]Who was and is and is to come!"

9 Whenever the living creatures give glory and honor and thanks to Him who sits on the throne, [a]who lives forever and ever,
10 [a]the twenty-four elders fall down before Him who sits on the throne and worship Him who lives forever and ever, and cast their crowns before the throne, saying:

11 "You[a] are worthy, [1]O Lord,
To receive glory and honor and power;
[b]For You created all things,
And by [c]Your will they [2]exist
and were created."

### *Worthy Is the Lamb*

5 And I saw in the right *hand* of Him who sat on the throne [a]a scroll written inside and on the back, [b]sealed with seven seals.
2 Then I saw a strong angel proclaiming with a loud voice, [a]"Who is worthy to open the scroll and to loose its seals?"
3 And no one in heaven or on the earth or under the earth was able to open the scroll, or to look at it.
4 So I wept much, because no one was found worthy to open [1]and read the scroll, or to look at it.
5 But one of the elders said to me, "Do not weep. Behold, [a]the Lion of the tribe of [b]Judah, [c]the Root of David, has [d]prevailed to open the scroll [e]and [1]to loose its seven seals."
6 And I looked, [1]and behold, in the midst of the throne and of the four living creatures, and in the midst of the elders, stood [a]a Lamb as though it had been slain, having seven horns and [b]seven eyes, which are [c]the seven Spirits of God sent out into all the earth.
7 Then He came and took the scroll out of the right hand [a]of Him who sat on the throne.
8 Now when He had taken the scroll, [a]the four living creatures and the twenty-four elders fell down before the Lamb, each having a harp, and golden bowls full of incense, which are the [b]prayers of the saints.
9 And [a]they sang a new song, saying:

[b]"You are worthy to take the scroll,
And to open its seals;
For You were slain,
And [c]have redeemed us to God
[d]by Your blood
Out of every tribe and tongue
and people and nation,

**3:10** [a]2 Pet. 2:9 [b]Luke 2:1 [c]Is. 24:17 [1]Lit. *the word of My patience*
**11** [a]Phil. 4:5 [b]Rev. 2:25 [c][Rev. 2:10] [1]NU, M omit *Behold*
**12** [a]1 Kin. 7:21 [b]Ps. 23:6 [c][Rev. 14:1; 22:4] [d][Heb. 12:22] [e]Rev. 21:2 [f][Rev. 2:17; 22:4]
**13** [a]Rev. 2:7
**14** [a]2 Cor. 1:20 [b]Rev. 1:5; 3:7; 19:11 [c][Col. 1:15] [1]Or *messenger* [2]NU, M *in Laodicea*
**15** [a]Rev. 3:1
**16** [1]NU, M *hot nor cold*
**17** [a]Hos. 12:8
**18** [a]Is. 55:1 [b]2 Cor. 5:3
**19** [a]Job 5:17 [b]Heb. 12:6 [1]*discipline* [2]*eager*
**20** [a]Song 5:2 [b]Luke 12:36, 37 [c][John 14:23]
**21** [a]Matt. 19:28
**22** [a]Rev. 2:7

CHAPTER 4
**1** [a]Ezek. 1:1 [b]Rev. 1:10
**2** [a]Rev. 1:10 [b]Is. 6:1
**3** [a]Rev. 21:11 [b]Ezek. 1:28 [1]M omits *And He who sat there was,* making the following a description of the throne.
**4** [a]Rev. 11:16 [b]Rev. 3:4, 5 [1]NU, M *robes, with crowns*
**5** [a]Rev. 8:5; 11:19; 16:18 [b]Ex. 37:23 [c][Rev. 1:4] [1]NU, M *voices, and thunderings.* [2]M omits *the*
**6** [a]Rev. 15:2 [b]Ezek. 1:5 [1]NU, M add *something like*
**7** [a]Ezek. 1:10; 10:14
**8** [a]Is. 6:2 [b]Is. 6:3 [c]Rev. 1:8 [d]Rev. 1:4 [1]M has *holy* nine times.
**9** [a]Rev. 1:18
**10** [a]Rev. 5:8, 14; 7:11; 11:16; 19:4
**11** [a]Rev. 1:6; 5:12 [b]Gen. 1:1 [c]Col. 1:16 [1]NU, M *Our Lord and God* [2]NU, M *existed*

CHAPTER 5
**1** [a]Ezek. 2:9, 10 [b]Is. 29:11
**2** [a]Rev. 4:11; 5:9
**4** [1]NU, M omit *and read*
**5** [a]Gen. 49:9 [b]Heb. 7:14 [c]Is. 11:1, 10 [d]Rev. 3:21 [e]Rev. 6:1 [1]NU, M omit *to loose*
**6** [a][John 1:29] [b]Zech. 3:9; 4:10 [c]Rev. 1:4; 3:1; 4:5 [1]NU, M *saw,* omitting *and behold*
**7** [a]Rev. 4:2
**8** [a]Rev. 4:8–10; 19:4 [b]Rev. 8:3
**9** [a]Rev. 14:3 [b]Rev. 4:11 [c]John 1:29 [d][Heb. 9:12]

10 And have made [1]us [a]kings[2] and [b]priests to
our God;
And [3]we shall reign on the earth."

11 Then I looked, and I heard the voice of many
angels around the throne, the living creatures,
and the elders; and the number of them was ten
thousand times ten thousand, and thousands of
thousands,
12 saying with a loud voice:

"Worthy is the Lamb who was slain
To receive power and riches and wisdom,
And strength and honor and glory
and blessing!"

13 And [a]every creature which is in heaven and on
the earth and under the earth and such as are in
the sea, and all that are in them, I heard saying:

[b]"Blessing and honor and glory and power
*Be* to Him [c]who sits on the throne,
And to the Lamb, forever and [1]ever!"

14 Then the four living creatures said, "Amen!"
And the [1]twenty-four elders fell down and worshiped [2]Him who lives forever and ever.

## *The Six Seals*

6 Now [a]I saw when the Lamb opened one of the
[1]seals; and I heard [b]one of the four living
creatures saying with a voice like thunder, "Come
and see."
2 And I looked, and behold, [a]a white horse. [b]He
who sat on it had a bow; [c]and a crown was given
to him, and he went out [d]conquering and to
conquer.
3 When He opened the second seal, [a]I heard the
second living creature saying, "Come [1]and see."
4 [a]Another horse, fiery red, went out. And it was
granted to the one who sat on it to [b]take peace
from the earth, and that *people* should kill one
another; and there was given to him a great
sword.
5 When He opened the third seal, [a]I heard the
third living creature say, "Come and see." So I
looked, and behold, [b]a black horse, and he who sat
on it had a pair of [c]scales[1] in his hand.
6 And I heard a voice in the midst of the four
living creatures saying, "A [1]quart of wheat for a
[2]denarius, and three quarts of barley for a denarius; and [a]do not harm the oil and the wine."
7 When He opened the fourth seal, [a]I heard the
voice of the fourth living creature saying, "Come
and see."
8 [a]So I looked, and behold, a pale horse. And the
name of him who sat on it was Death, and Hades
followed with him. And [1]power was given to them
over a fourth of the earth, [b]to kill with sword, with
hunger, with death, [c]and by the beasts of the
earth.
9 When He opened the fifth seal, I saw under
[a]the altar [b]the souls of those who had been slain
[c]for the word of God and for [d]the testimony which
they held.
10 And they cried with a loud voice, saying,
[a]"How long, O Lord, [b]holy and true, [c]until You
judge and avenge our blood on those who dwell
on the earth?"
11 Then a [a]white robe was given to each of them;
and it was said to them [b]that they should rest a
little while longer, until both *the number of* their
fellow servants and their brethren, who would be
killed as they *were*, was completed.
12 I looked when He opened the sixth seal, [a]and
[1]behold, there was a great earthquake; and [b]the
sun became black as sackcloth of hair, and the
[2]moon became like blood.
13 [a]And the stars of heaven fell to the earth, as a
fig tree drops its late figs when it is shaken by a
mighty wind.
14 [a]Then the sky [1]receded as a scroll when it is
rolled up, and [b]every mountain and island was
moved out of its place.
15 And the [a]kings of the earth, the great men,
[1]the rich men, the commanders, the mighty men,
every slave and every free man, [b]hid themselves in
the caves and in the rocks of the mountains,
16 [a]and said to the mountains and rocks, "Fall on
us and hide us from the face of Him who [b]sits on
the throne and from the wrath of the Lamb!
17 "For the great day of His wrath has come,
[a]and who is able to stand?"

## *The Servants of God Sealed*

7 After these things I saw four angels standing
at the four corners of the earth, [a]holding the
four winds of the earth, [b]that the wind should not
blow on the earth, on the sea, or on any tree.
2 Then I saw another angel ascending from the
east, having the seal of the living God. And he
cried with a loud voice to the four angels to whom
it was granted to harm the earth and the sea,
3 saying, [a]"Do not harm the earth, the sea, or
the trees till we have sealed the servants of our
God [b]on their foreheads."
4 [a]And I heard the number of those who were
sealed. [b]One hundred *and* forty-four thousand [c]of
all the tribes of the children of Israel *were* sealed:

5 of the tribe of Judah
twelve thousand *were* sealed;
of the tribe of Reuben
twelve thousand *were* [1]sealed;
of the tribe of Gad
twelve thousand *were* sealed;
6 of the tribe of Asher
twelve thousand *were* sealed;
of the tribe of Naphtali
twelve thousand *were* sealed;
of the tribe of Manasseh
twelve thousand *were* sealed;
7 of the tribe of Simeon
twelve thousand *were* sealed;
of the tribe of Levi
twelve thousand *were* sealed;
of the tribe of Issachar
twelve thousand *were* sealed;
8 of the tribe of Zebulun
twelve thousand *were* sealed;
of the tribe of Joseph
twelve thousand *were* sealed;
of the tribe of Benjamin
twelve thousand *were* sealed.

9 After these things I looked, and behold, [a]a
great multitude which no one could number, [b]of
all nations, tribes, peoples, and tongues, standing
before the throne and before the Lamb, [c]clothed
with white robes, with palm branches in their
hands,
10 and crying out with a loud voice, saying,
[a]"Salvation *belongs* to our God [b]who sits on the
throne, and to the Lamb!"

**10** [a]Ex. 19:6 [b]Is. 61:6 [1]NU, M *them* [2]NU *a kingdom* [3]NU, M *they*
**13** [a]Phil. 2:10 [b]1 Chr. 29:11 [c]Rev. 4:2, 3; 6:16; 20:11 [1]M adds *Amen*
**14** [1]NU, M omit *twenty-four* [2]NU, M omit *Him who lives forever and ever*

CHAPTER 6
**1** [a][Rev. 5:5–7, 12; 13:8] [b]Rev. 4:7 [1]NU, M *seven seals*
**2** [a]Zech. 1:8; 6:3 [b]Ps. 45:4, 5, LXX [c]Zech. 6:11 [d]Matt. 24:5
**3** [a]Rev. 4:7 [1]NU, M omit *and see*
**4** [a]Zech. 1:8; 6:2 [b]Matt. 24:6, 7
**5** [a]Rev. 4:7 [b]Zech. 6:2, 6 [c]Matt. 24:7 [1]*balances*
**6** [a]Rev. 7:3; 9:4 [1]Gr. *choinix*, about 1 quart [2]About 1 day's wage for a worker
**7** [a]Rev. 4:7
**8** [a]Zech. 6:3 [b]Ezek. 5:12, 17; 14:21; 29:5 [c]Lev. 26:22 [1]*authority*
**9** [a]Rev. 8:3 [b][Rev. 20:4] [c]Rev. 1:2, 9 [d]2 Tim. 1:8
**10** [a]Zech. 1:12 [b]Rev. 3:7 [c]Rev. 11:18
**11** [a]Rev. 3:4, 5; 7:9 [b]Heb. 11:40
**12** [a]Matt. 24:7 [b]Joel 2:10, 31; 3:15 [1]NU, M omit *behold* [2]NU, M *whole moon*
**13** [a]Rev. 8:10; 9:1
**14** [a]Is. 34:4 [b]Rev. 16:20 [1]Or *split apart*
**15** [a]Ps. 2:2–4 [b]Is. 2:10, 19, 21; 24:21 [1]NU, M *the commanders, the rich men*
**16** [a]Luke 23:29, 30 [b]Rev. 20:11
**17** [a]Zeph. 1:14

CHAPTER 7
**1** [a]Dan. 7:2 [b]Rev. 7:3; 8:7; 9:4
**3** [a]Rev. 6:6 [b]Rev. 22:4
**4** [a]Rev. 9:16 [b]Rev. 14:1, 3 [c]Gen. 49:1–27
**5** [1]NU, M omit *sealed* in vv. 5b–8b.
**9** [a]Rom. 11:25 [b]Rev. 5:9 [c]Rev. 3:5, 18; 4:4; 6:11
**10** [a]Ps. 3:8 [b]Rev. 5:13

11 [a]All the angels stood around the throne and
the elders and the four living creatures, and fell on
their faces before the throne and [b]worshiped God,
12 [a]saying:

"Amen! Blessing and glory and wisdom,
Thanksgiving and honor and power and
might,
*Be* to our God forever and ever.
Amen."

13 Then one of the elders answered, saying to
me, "Who are these arrayed in [a]white robes, and
where did they come from?"
14 And I said to him, [1]"Sir, you know." So he said
to me, [a]"These are the ones who come out of the
great tribulation, and [b]washed their robes and
made them white in the blood of the Lamb.
15 "Therefore they are before the throne of God,
and serve Him day and night in His temple. And
He who sits on the throne will [a]dwell among them.
16 [a]"They shall neither hunger anymore nor
thirst anymore; [b]the sun shall not strike them, nor
any heat;
17 "for the Lamb who is in the midst of the
throne [a]will shepherd them and lead them to
[1]living fountains of waters. [b]And God will wipe
away every tear from their eyes."

### *The Seventh Seal and Four Trumpets*

8 When[a] He opened the seventh seal, there was
silence in heaven for about half an hour.
2 [a]And I saw the seven angels who stand before
God, [b]and to them were given seven trumpets.
3 Then another angel, having a golden censer,
came and stood at the altar. He was given much
incense, that he should offer *it* with [a]the prayers of
all the saints upon [b]the golden altar which was
before the throne.
4 And [a]the smoke of the incense, with the prayers of the saints, ascended before God from the
angel's hand.
5 Then the angel took the censer, filled it with
fire from the altar, and threw *it* to the earth. And
[a]there were noises, thunderings, [b]lightnings, [c]and
an earthquake.
6 So the seven angels who had the seven trumpets prepared themselves to sound.
7 The first angel sounded: [a]And hail and fire
followed, mingled with blood, and they were
thrown [b]to the [1]earth. And a third [c]of the trees
were burned up, and all green grass was burned
up.
8 Then the second angel sounded: [a]And *something* like a great mountain burning with fire was
thrown into the sea, [b]and a third of the sea
[c]became blood.
9 [a]And a third of the living creatures in the sea
died, and a third of the ships were destroyed.
10 Then the third angel sounded: [a]And a great
star fell from heaven, burning like a torch, [b]and it
fell on a third of the rivers and on the springs of
water.
11 [a]The name of the star is Wormwood. [b]A third
of the waters became wormwood, and many men
died from the water, because it was made bitter.
12 [a]Then the fourth angel sounded: And a third of
the sun was struck, a third of the moon, and a
third of the stars, so that a third of them were
darkened. A third of the day [1]did not shine, and
likewise the night.

11 [a]Rev. 4:6 [b]Rev. 4:11; 5:9, 12, 14; 11:16
12 [a]Rev. 5:13, 14
13 [a]Rev. 7:9
14 [a]Rev. 6:9 [b][Heb. 9:14] [1]NU, M *My lord*
15 [a]Is. 4:5, 6
16 [a]Is. 49:10 [b]Ps. 121:6
17 [a]Ps. 23:1 [b]Rev. 21:4 [1]NU, M *fountains of the waters of life*

CHAPTER 8
1 [a]Rev. 6:1
2 [a][Matt. 18:10] [b]2 Chr. 29:25–28
3 [a]Rev. 5:8 [b]Ex. 30:1
4 [a]Ps. 141:2
5 [a]Rev. 11:19; 16:18 [b]Rev. 4:5 [c]2 Sam. 22:8
7 [a]Ezek. 38:22 [b]Rev. 16:2 [c]Rev. 9:4, 15–18 [1]NU, M add *and a third of the earth was burned up*
8 [a]Jer. 51:25 [b]Ex. 7:17 [c]Ezek. 14:19
9 [a]Rev. 16:3
10 [a]Is. 14:12 [b]Rev. 14:7; 16:4
11 [a]Ruth 1:20 [b]Ex. 15:23
12 [a]Is. 13:10 [1]*had no light*
13 [a]Rev. 14:6; 19:17 [b]Rev. 9:12; 11:14; 12:12 [1]NU, M *eagle*

CHAPTER 9
1 [a]Rev. 8:10 [b]Luke 8:31 [1]Lit. *shaft of the abyss*
2 [a]Joel 2:2, 10
3 [a]Judg. 7:12
4 [a]Rev. 6:6 [b]Rev. 8:7 [c]Rev. 7:2, 3
5 [a][Rev. 9:10; 11:7] [1]The locusts
6 [a]Jer. 8:3
7 [a]Joel 2:4 [b]Nah. 3:17 [c]Dan. 7:8
8 [a]Joel 1:6
9 [a]Joel 2:5–7
11 [a]Eph. 2:2 [1]Lit. *Destruction* [2]Lit. *Destroyer*
12 [a]Rev. 8:13; 11:14
13 [a]Rev. 8:3
14 [a]Rev. 16:12
15 [a]Rev. 8:7–9; 9:18
16 [a]Dan. 7:10 [b]Ezek. 38:4 [c]Rev. 7:4
17 [a]Is. 5:28, 29
19 [a]Is. 9:15 [1]NU, M *the power of the horses*

13 And I looked, [a]and I heard an [1]angel flying
through the midst of heaven, saying with a loud
voice, [b]"Woe, woe, woe to the inhabitants of the
earth, because of the remaining blasts of the
trumpet of the three angels who are about to
sound!"

### *The Fifth and Sixth Trumpets*

9 Then the fifth angel sounded: [a]And I saw a
star fallen from heaven to the earth. To him
was given the key to [b]the [1]bottomless pit.
2 And he opened the bottomless pit, and smoke
arose out of the pit like the smoke of a great
furnace. So the [a]sun and the air were darkened
because of the smoke of the pit.
3 Then out of the smoke locusts came upon the
earth. And to them was given power, [a]as the
scorpions of the earth have power.
4 They were commanded [a]not to harm [b]the
grass of the earth, or any green thing, or any tree,
but only those men who do not have [c]the seal of
God on their foreheads.
5 And [1]they were not given *authority* to kill
them, [a]but to torment them *for* five months. Their
torment *was* like the torment of a scorpion when
it strikes a man.
6 In those days [a]men will seek death and will
not find it; they will desire to die, and death will
flee from them.
7 [a]The shape of the locusts was like horses
prepared for battle. [b]On their heads were crowns
of something like gold, [c]and their faces *were* like
the faces of men.
8 They had hair like women's hair, and [a]their
teeth were like lions' *teeth.*
9 And they had breastplates like breastplates of
iron, and the sound of their wings *was* [a]like the
sound of chariots with many horses running into
battle.
10 They had tails like scorpions, and there were
stings in their tails. Their power *was* to hurt men
five months.
11 And they had as king over them [a]the angel of
the bottomless pit, whose name in Hebrew *is*
[1]Abaddon, but in Greek he has the name [2]Apol-
lyon.
12 [a]One woe is past. Behold, still two more woes
are coming after these things.
13 Then the sixth angel sounded: And I heard a
voice from the four horns of the [a]golden altar
which is before God,
14 saying to the sixth angel who had the trumpet,
"Release the four angels who are bound [a]at the
great river Euphrates."
15 So the four angels, who had been prepared for
the hour and day and month and year, were
released to kill a [a]third of mankind.
16 Now [a]the number of the army [b]of the horsemen *was* two hundred million; [c]I heard the number of them.
17 And thus I saw the horses in the vision: those
who sat on them had breastplates of fiery red,
hyacinth blue, and sulfur yellow; [a]and the heads of
the horses *were* like the heads of lions; and out of
their mouths came fire, smoke, and brimstone.
18 By these three *plagues* a third of mankind was
killed—by the fire and the smoke and the brimstone which came out of their mouths.
19 For [1]their power is in their mouth and in their
tails; [a]for their tails *are* like serpents, having
heads; and with them they do harm.

20 But the rest of mankind, who were not killed
by these plagues, [a]did not repent of the works of
their hands, that they should not worship [b]de-
mons, [c]and idols of gold, silver, brass, stone, and
wood, which can neither see nor hear nor walk.
21 And they did not repent of their murders [a]or
their [1]sorceries or their sexual immorality or their
thefts.

## *The Little Book*

**10** I saw still another mighty angel coming
down from heaven, clothed with a cloud.
[a]And a rainbow *was* on [b]his head, his face *was* like
the sun, and [c]his feet like pillars of fire.
2 He had a little book open in his hand. [a]And he
set his right foot on the sea and *his* left *foot* on the
land,
3 and cried with a loud voice, as *when* a lion
roars. When he cried out, [a]seven thunders uttered
their voices.
4 Now when the seven thunders [1]uttered their
voices, I was about to write; but I heard a voice
from heaven saying [2]to me, [a]"Seal up the things
which the seven thunders uttered, and do not
write them."
5 The angel whom I saw standing on the sea
and on the land [a]raised up his [1]hand to heaven
6 and swore by Him who lives forever and ever,
[a]who created heaven and the things that are in it,
the earth and the things that are in it, and the sea
and the things that are in it, [b]that there should be
delay no longer,
7 but [a]in the days of the sounding of the seventh
angel, when he is about to sound, the mystery of
God would be finished, as He declared to His
servants the prophets.
**8** Then the voice which I heard from heaven
spoke to me again and said, "Go, take the little
book which is open in the hand of the angel who
stands on the sea and on the earth."
9 So I went to the angel and said to him, "Give
me the little book." And he said to me, [a]"Take and
eat it; and it will make your stomach bitter, but it
will be as sweet as honey in your mouth."
10 Then I took the little book out of the angel's
hand and ate it, [a]and it was as sweet as honey in
my mouth. But when I had eaten it, [b]my stomach
became bitter.
11 And [1]he said to me, "You must prophesy again
about many peoples, nations, tongues, and kings."

## *The Two Witnesses; the Seventh Trumpet*

**11** Then I was given [a]a reed like a measuring
rod. [1]And the angel stood, saying, [b]"Rise
and measure the temple of God, the altar, and
those who worship there.
2 "But leave out [a]the court which is outside the
temple, and do not measure it, [b]for it has been
given to the Gentiles. And they will [c]tread the
holy city underfoot *for* [d]forty-two months.
3 "And I will give *power* to my two [a]witnesses,
[b]and they will prophesy [c]one thousand two hundred and sixty days, clothed in sackcloth."
4 These are the [a]two olive trees and the two
lampstands standing before the [1]God of the earth.
5 And if anyone wants to harm them, [a]fire
proceeds from their mouth and devours their
enemies. [b]And if anyone wants to harm them, he
must be killed in this manner.
6 These [a]have power to shut heaven, so that no
rain falls in the days of their prophecy; and they
have power over waters to turn them to blood,
and to strike the earth with all plagues, as often as
they desire.
7 When they [a]finish their testimony, [b]the beast
that ascends [c]out of the bottomless pit [d]will make
war against them, overcome them, and kill them.
8 And their dead bodies *will lie* in the street of
[a]the great city which spiritually is called Sodom
and Egypt, [b]where also [1]our Lord was crucified.
9 [a]Then *those* from the peoples, tribes, tongues,
and nations [1]will see their dead bodies three-and-
a-half days, [b]and not allow their dead bodies to be
put into graves.
10 [a]And those who dwell on the earth will rejoice
over them, make merry, [b]and send gifts to one
another, [c]because these two prophets tormented
those who dwell on the earth.
**11** [a]Now after the three-and-a-half days [b]the
breath of life from God entered them, and they
stood on their feet, and great fear fell on those
who saw them.
12 And [1]they heard a loud voice from heaven
saying to them, "Come up here." [a]And they ascended to heaven [b]in a cloud, [c]and their enemies
saw them.
13 In the same hour [a]there was a great earthquake, [b]and a tenth of the city fell. In the earthquake seven thousand people were killed, and the
rest were afraid [c]and gave glory to the God of
heaven.
14 [a]The second woe is past. Behold, the third woe
is coming quickly.
**15** Then [a]the seventh angel sounded: [b]And there
were loud voices in heaven, saying, [c]"The [1]king-
doms of this world have become *the kingdoms* of
our Lord and of His Christ, [d]and He shall reign
forever and ever!"
16 And [a]the twenty-four elders who sat before
God on their thrones fell on their faces and
[b]worshiped God,
17 saying:

"We give You thanks, O Lord God Almighty,
The One [a]who is and who was
[1]and who is to come,
Because You have taken Your great power
[b]and reigned.
18 The nations were [a]angry,
And Your [1]wrath has come,
And the time of the [b]dead,
that they should be judged,
And that You should reward Your servants
the prophets and the saints,
And those who fear Your name,
small and great,
And should destroy those
who destroy the earth."

**19** Then [a]the temple of God was opened in
heaven, and the ark of [1]His covenant was seen in
His temple. And [b]there were lightnings, noises,
thunderings, an earthquake, [c]and great hail.

## *The Woman, the Child, and the Dragon*

**12** Now a great sign appeared in heaven: a
woman clothed with the sun, with the moon
under her feet, and on her head a garland of
twelve stars.

**20** [a]Deut. 31:29 [b]1 Cor. 10:20 [c]Dan. 5:23
**21** [a]Rev. 21:8; 22:15 [1]NU, M *drugs*

CHAPTER 10
**1** [a]Rev. 4:3 [b]Rev. 1:16 [c]Rev. 1:15
**2** [a]Matt. 28:18
**3** [a]Ps. 29:3–9
**4** [a]Dan. 8:26; 12:4, 9 [1]NU, M *sounded,* [2]NU, M omit *to me*
**5** [a]Dan. 12:7 [1]NU, M *right hand*
**6** [a]Rev. 4:11 [b]Rev. 16:17
**7** [a]Rev. 11:15
**9** [a]Jer. 15:16
**10** [a]Ezek. 3:3 [b]Ezek. 2:10
**11** [1]NU, M *they*

CHAPTER 11
**1** [a]Ezek. 40:3—42:20 [b]Num. 23:18 [1]NU, M omit *And the angel stood*
**2** [a]Ezek. 40:17, 20 [b]Ps. 79:1 [c]Dan. 8:10 [d]Rev. 12:6; 13:5
**3** [a]Rev. 20:4 [b]Rev. 19:10 [c]Rev. 12:6
**4** [a]Zech. 4:2, 3, 11, 14 [1]NU, M *Lord*
**5** [a]2 Kin. 1:10–12 [b]Num. 16:29
**6** [a]1 Kin. 17:1
**7** [a]Luke 13:32 [b]Rev. 13:1, 11; 17:8 [c]Rev. 9:1, 2 [d]Dan. 7:21
**8** [a]Rev. 14:8 [b]Heb. 13:12 [1]NU, M *their*
**9** [a]Rev. 17:15 [b]Ps. 79:2, 3 [1]NU, M *see . . . and will not allow*
**10** [a]Rev. 12:12 [b]Esth. 9:19, 22 [c]Rev. 16:10
**11** [a]Rev. 11:9 [b]Ezek. 37:5, 9, 10
**12** [a]Is. 14:13 [b]Acts 1:9 [c]2 Kin. 2:1 [1]M *I*
**13** [a]Rev. 6:12; 8:5; 11:19; 16:18 [b]Rev. 16:19 [c]Rev. 14:7; 16:9; 19:7
**14** [a]Rev. 8:13; 9:12
**15** [a]Rev. 8:2; 10:7 [b]Is. 27:13 [c]Rev. 12:10 [d]Ex. 15:18 [1]NU, M *kingdom . . . has become the kingdom*
**16** [a]Rev. 4:4 [b]Rev. 4:11; 5:9, 12, 14; 7:11
**17** [a]Rev. 16:5 [b]Rev. 19:6 [1]NU, M omit *and who is to come*
**18** [a]Ps. 2:1 [b]Dan. 7:10 [1]*anger*

**19** [a]Rev. 4:1; 15:5, 8 [b]Rev. 8:5 [c]Rev. 16:21 [1]M *the covenant of the Lord*

2 Then being with child, she cried out [a]in labor
and in pain to give birth.
3 And another sign appeared in heaven: behold,
[a]a great, fiery red dragon having seven heads and
ten horns, and seven diadems on his heads.
4 [a]His tail drew a third [b]of the stars of heaven
[c]and threw them to the earth. And the dragon
stood [d]before the woman who was ready to give
birth, [e]to devour her Child as soon as it was born.
5 She bore a male Child [a]who was to rule all
nations with a rod of iron. And her Child was
[b]caught up to God and His throne.
6 Then [a]the woman fled into the wilderness,
where she has a place prepared by God, that they
should feed her there [b]one thousand two hundred
and sixty days.
7 And war broke out in heaven: [a]Michael and
his angels fought [b]with the dragon; and the
dragon and his angels fought,
8 but they [1]did not prevail, nor was a place
found for [2]them in heaven any longer.
9 So [a]the great dragon was cast out, [b]that serpent of old, called the Devil and Satan, [c]who
deceives the whole world; [d]he was cast to the
earth, and his angels were cast out with him.
10 Then I heard a loud voice saying in heaven,
[a]"Now salvation, and strength, and the kingdom
of our God, and the power of His Christ have
come, for the accuser of our brethren, [b]who
accused them before our God day and night, has
been cast down.
11 "And [a]they overcame him by the blood of the
Lamb and by the word of their testimony, [b]and
they did not love their lives to the death.
12 "Therefore [a]rejoice, O heavens, and you who
dwell in them! [b]Woe to the inhabitants of the
earth and the sea! For the devil has come down to
you, having great wrath, [c]because he knows that
he has a short time."
13 Now when the dragon saw that he had been
cast to the earth, he persecuted [a]the woman who
gave birth to the male *Child.*
14 [a]But the woman was given two wings of a
great eagle, [b]that she might fly [c]into the wilderness to her place, where she is nourished [d]for a
time and times and half a time, from the presence
of the serpent.
15 So the serpent [a]spewed water out of his mouth
like a flood after the woman, that he might cause
her to be carried away by the flood.
16 But the earth helped the woman, and the
earth opened its mouth and swallowed up the
flood which the dragon had spewed out of his
mouth.
17 And the dragon was enraged with the woman,
and he went to make war with the rest of her
offspring, who keep the commandments of God
and have the testimony of Jesus [1]Christ.

### *The Beast from the Sea and the Beast from the Land*

**13** Then [1]I stood on the sand of the sea. And I
saw [a]a beast rising up out of the sea, [b]hav-
ing [2]seven heads and ten horns, and on his horns
ten crowns, and on his heads a [c]blasphemous
name.
2 Now the beast which I saw was like a leopard,
his feet were like *the feet of* a bear, and his mouth
like the mouth of a lion. The [a]dragon gave him his
power, his throne, and great authority.
3 And *I saw* one of his heads [a]as if it had been
mortally wounded, and his deadly wound was
healed. And [b]all the world marveled and followed
the beast.
4 So they worshiped the dragon who gave authority to the beast; and they worshiped the beast,
saying, [a]"Who *is* like the beast? Who is able to
make war with him?"
5 And he was given [a]a mouth speaking great
things and blasphemies, and he was given authority to [1]continue for [b]forty-two months.
6 Then he opened his mouth in blasphemy
against God, to blaspheme His name, [a]His tabernacle, and those who dwell in heaven.
7 It was granted to him [a]to make war with the
saints and to overcome them. And [b]authority was
given him over every [1]tribe, tongue, and nation.
8 All who dwell on the earth will worship him,
[a]whose names have not been written in the Book
of Life of the Lamb slain [b]from the foundation of
the world.
9 [a]If anyone has an ear, let him hear.
10 [a]He who leads into captivity shall go into
captivity; [b]he who kills with the sword must be
killed with the sword. [c]Here is the [1]patience and
the faith of the saints.
11 Then I saw another beast [a]coming up out of
the earth, and he had two horns like a lamb and
spoke like a dragon.
12 And he exercises all the authority of the first
beast in his presence, and causes the earth and
those who dwell in it to worship the first beast,
[a]whose deadly wound was healed.
13 [a]He performs great signs, [b]so that he even
makes fire come down from heaven on the earth
in the sight of men.
14 [a]And he deceives [1]those who dwell on the
earth [b]by those signs which he was granted to do
in the sight of the beast, telling those who dwell
on the earth to make an image to the beast who
was wounded by the sword [c]and lived.
15 He was granted *power* to give breath to the
image of the beast, that the image of the beast
should both speak [a]and cause as many as would
not worship the image of the beast to be killed.
16 He causes all, both small and great, rich and
poor, free and slave, [a]to receive a mark on their
right hand or on their foreheads,
17 and that no one may buy or sell except one
who has [1]the mark or [a]the name of the beast, [b]or
the number of his name.
18 [a]Here is wisdom. Let him who has [b]under-
standing calculate [c]the number of the beast, [d]for it
is the number of a man: His number *is* 666.

### *The 144,000; Two Harvests*

**14** Then I looked, and behold, [1]a [a]Lamb standing on Mount Zion, and with Him [b]one
hundred *and* forty-four thousand, [2]having His
Father's name [c]written on their foreheads.
2 And I heard a voice from heaven, [a]like the
voice of many waters, and like the voice of loud
thunder. And I heard the sound of [b]harpists playing their harps.
3 They sang as it were a new song before the
throne, before the four living creatures, and the
elders; and no one could learn that song [a]except
the hundred *and* forty-four thousand who were
redeemed from the earth.
4 These are the ones who were not defiled with

CHAPTER 12
**2** [a]Is. 26:17; 66:6–9
**3** [a]Rev. 13:1; 17:3, 7, 9
**4** [a]Rev. 9:10, 19 [b]Rev. 8:7, 12 [c]Dan. 8:10 [d]Rev. 12:2 [e]Matt. 2:16
**5** [a]Ps. 2:9 [b]Acts 1:9–11
**6** [a]Rev. 12:4, 14 [b]Rev. 11:3; 13:5
**7** [a]Dan. 10:13, 21; 12:1 [b]Rev. 20:2
**8** [1]*were not strong enough* [2]M *him*
**9** [a]John 12:31 [b]Gen. 3:1, 4 [c]Rev. 20:3 [d]Rev. 9:1
**10** [a]Rev. 11:15 [b]Zech. 3:1
**11** [a]Rom. 16:20 [b]Luke 14:26
**12** [a]Ps. 96:11 [b]Rev. 8:13 [c]Rev. 10:6
**13** [a]Rev. 12:5
**14** [a]Ex. 19:4 [b]Rev. 12:6 [c]Rev. 17:3 [d]Dan. 7:25; 12:7
**15** [a]Is. 59:19
**17** [1]NU, M omit *Christ*

CHAPTER 13
**1** [a]Dan. 7:2, 7 [b]Rev. 12:3 [c]Rev. 17:3 [1]NU *he* [2]NU, M *ten horns and seven heads*
**2** [a]Rev. 12:3, 9; 13:4, 12
**3** [a]Rev. 13:12, 14 [b]Rev. 17:8
**4** [a]Rev. 18:18
**5** [a]Dan. 7:8, 11, 20, 25; 11:36 [b]Rev. 11:2 [1]M *make war*
**6** [a][Col. 2:9]
**7** [a]Dan. 7:21 [b]Rev. 11:18 [1]NU, M add *and people*
**8** [a]Ex. 32:32 [b]Rev. 17:8
**9** [a]Rev. 2:7
**10** [a]Is. 33:1 [b]Gen. 9:6 [c]Rev. 14:12 [1]*perseverance*
**11** [a]Rev. 11:7
**12** [a]Rev. 13:3, 4
**13** [a]Matt. 24:24 [b]1 Kin. 18:38
**14** [a]Rev. 12:9 [b]2 Thess. 2:9 [c]2 Kin. 20:7 [1]M *my own people*
**15** [a]Rev. 16:2
**16** [a]Rev. 7:3; 14:9; 20:4
**17** [a]Rev. 14:9–11 [b]Rev. 15:2 [1]NU, M *the mark, the name*
**18** [a]Rev. 17:9 [b][1 Cor. 2:14] [c]Rev. 15:2 [d]Rev. 21:17

CHAPTER 14
**1** [a]Rev. 5:6 [b]Rev. 7:4; 14:3 [c]Rev. 7:3; 22:4 [1]NU, M *the* [2]NU, M add *His name and*
**2** [a]Rev. 1:15; 19:6 [b]Rev. 5:8
**3** [a]Rev. 5:9

women, [a]for they are virgins. These are the ones
[b]who follow the Lamb wherever He goes. These
[c]were [1]redeemed from *among* men, [d]*being* firstfruits to God and to the Lamb.
5 And [a]in their mouth was found no [1]deceit, for
[b]they are without fault [2]before the throne of God.
**6** Then I saw another angel [a]flying in the midst
of heaven, [b]having the everlasting gospel to
preach to those who dwell on the earth—[c]to every
nation, tribe, tongue, and people—
7 saying with a loud voice, [a]"Fear God and give
glory to Him, for the hour of His judgment has
come; [b]and worship Him who made heaven and
earth, the sea and springs of water."
8 And another angel followed, saying, [a]"Babylon[1] is fallen, is fallen, that great city, because [b]she
has made all nations drink of the wine of the
wrath of her fornication."
9 Then a third angel followed them, saying with
a loud voice, [a]"If anyone worships the beast and
his image, and receives *his* [b]mark on his forehead
or on his hand,
10 "he himself [a]shall also drink of the wine of the
wrath of God, which is [b]poured out full strength
into [c]the cup of His indignation. [d]He shall be
tormented with [e]fire and brimstone in the presence of the holy angels and in the presence of the
Lamb.
11 "And [a]the smoke of their torment ascends
forever and ever; and they have no rest day or
night, who worship the beast and his image, and
whoever receives the mark of his name."
12 [a]Here is the [1]patience of the saints; [b]here[2] *are*
those who keep the commandments of God and
the faith of Jesus.
13 Then I heard a voice from heaven saying [1]to
me, "Write: [a]'Blessed *are* the dead [b]who die in the
Lord from now on.' " "Yes," says the Spirit, [c]"that
they may rest from their labors, and their works
follow [d]them."
**14** Then I looked, and behold, a white cloud, and
on the cloud sat *One* like the Son of Man, having
on His head a golden crown, and in His hand a
sharp sickle.
15 And another angel [a]came out of the temple,
crying with a loud voice to Him who sat on the
cloud, [b]"Thrust in Your sickle and reap, for the
time has come [1]for You to reap, for the harvest [c]of
the earth is ripe."
16 So He who sat on the cloud thrust in His sickle
on the earth, and the earth was reaped.
**17** Then another angel came out of the temple
which is in heaven, he also having a sharp sickle.
18 And another angel came out from the altar,
[a]who had power over fire, and he cried with a loud
cry to him who had the sharp sickle, saying,
[b]"Thrust in your sharp sickle and gather the
clusters of the vine of the earth, for her grapes are
fully ripe."
19 So the angel thrust his sickle into the earth
and gathered the vine of the earth, and threw *it*
into [a]the great winepress of the wrath of God.
20 And [a]the winepress was trampled [b]outside the
city, and blood came out of the winepress, [c]up to
the horses' bridles, for one thousand six hundred
[1]furlongs.

### *Prelude to the Bowl Judgments*

**15** Then [a]I saw another sign in heaven, great
and marvelous: [b]seven angels having the
seven last plagues, [c]for in them the wrath of God
is complete.
2 And I saw *something* like [a]a sea of glass
[b]mingled with fire, and those who have the victory
over the beast, [c]over his image and [1]over his mark
*and* over the [d]number of his name, standing on
the sea of glass, [e]having harps of God.
3 They sing [a]the song of Moses, the servant of
God, and the song of the [b]Lamb, saying:

[c]"Great and marvelous *are* Your works,
Lord God Almighty!
[d]Just and true *are* Your ways,
O King of the [1]saints!
4 [a]Who shall not fear You, O Lord,
and glorify Your name?
For *You* alone *are* [b]holy.
For [c]all nations shall come and worship
before You,
For Your judgments have been manifested."

5 After these things I looked, and [1]behold, [a]the
[2]temple of the tabernacle of the testimony in
heaven was opened.
6 And out of the [1]temple came the seven angels
having the seven plagues, [a]clothed in pure bright
linen, and having their chests girded with golden
bands.
7 [a]Then one of the four living creatures gave to
the seven angels seven golden bowls full of the
wrath of God [b]who lives forever and ever.
8 [a]The temple was filled with smoke [b]from the
glory of God and from His power, and no one was
able to enter the temple till the seven plagues of
the seven angels were completed.

### *The Seven Bowls*

**16** Then I heard a loud voice from the temple
saying [a]to the seven angels, "Go and pour
out the [1]bowls [b]of the wrath of God on the earth."
**2** So the first went and poured out his bowl
[a]upon the earth, and a [1]foul and [b]loathsome sore
came upon the men [c]who had the mark of the
beast and those [d]who worshiped his image.
**3** Then the second angel poured out his bowl [a]on
the sea, and [b]it became blood as of a dead *man;*
[c]and every living creature in the sea died.
**4** Then the third angel poured out his bowl [a]on
the rivers and springs of water, [b]and they became
blood.
5 And I heard the angel of the waters saying:

[a]"You are righteous, [1]O Lord,
The One [b]who is and who [2]was
and who is to be,
Because You have judged these things.
6 For [a]they have shed the blood
[b]of saints and prophets,
[c]And You have given them blood to drink.
[1]For it is their just due."

7 And I heard [1]another from the altar saying,
"Even so, [a]Lord God Almighty, [b]true and righteous *are* Your judgments."
**8** Then the fourth angel poured out his bowl [a]on
the sun, [b]and power was given to him to scorch
men with fire.

**4** [a][2 Cor. 11:2] [b]Rev. 3:4; 7:17 [c]Rev. 5:9 [d]James 1:18 [1]M adds *by Jesus*
**5** [a]Ps. 32:2 [b]Eph. 5:27 [1]NU, M *falsehood* [2]NU, M omit the rest of v. 5.
**6** [a]Rev. 8:13 [b]Eph. 3:9 [c]Rev. 13:7
**7** [a]Rev. 11:18 [b]Neh. 9:6
**8** [a]Is. 21:9 [b]Jer. 51:7 [1]NU, M *Babylon the great is fallen, because*
**9** [a]Rev. 13:14, 15; 14:11 [b]Rev. 13:16
**10** [a]Ps. 75:8 [b]Rev. 18:6 [c]Rev. 16:19 [d]Rev. 20:10 [e]2 Thess. 1:7
**11** [a]Is. 34:8–10
**12** [a]Rev. 13:10 [b]Rev. 12:17 [1]*steadfastness, perseverance* [2]NU, M omit *here are those*
**13** [a]Eccl. 4:1, 2 [b]1 Cor. 15:18 [c]Heb. 4:9, 10 [d][1 Cor. 3:11–15; 15:58] [1]NU, M omit *to me*
**15** [a]Rev. 16:17 [b]Joel 3:13 [c]Jer. 51:33 [1]NU, M omit *for You*
**18** [a]Rev. 16:8 [b]Joel 3:13
**19** [a]Rev. 19:15
**20** [a]Is. 63:3 [b]Heb. 13:12 [c]Is. 34:3 [1]Lit. *stadia,* about 184 miles in all

CHAPTER 15
**1** [a]Rev. 12:1, 3 [b]Rev. 21:9 [c]Rev. 14:10
**2** [a]Rev. 4:6 [b][Matt. 3:11] [c]Rev. 13:14, 15 [d]Rev. 13:17 [e]Rev. 5:8 [1]NU, M omit *over his mark*
**3** [a]Ex. 15:1–21 [b]Rev. 15:3 [c]Deut. 32:3, 4 [d]Ps. 145:17 [1]NU, M *nations*
**4** [a]Ex. 15:14 [b]Lev. 11:44 [c]Is. 66:23
**5** [a]Num. 1:50 [1]NU, M omit *behold* [2]*sanctuary,* the inner shrine
**6** [a]Ex. 28:6 [1]*sanctuary,* the inner shrine
**7** [a]Rev. 4:6 [b]1 Thess. 1:9
**8** [a]Ex. 19:18; 40:34 [b]2 Thess. 1:9

CHAPTER 16
**1** [a]Rev. 15:1 [b]Rev. 14:10 [1]NU, M *seven bowls*

**2** [a]Rev. 8:7 [b]Ex. 9:9–11 [c]Rev. 13:15–17; 14:9 [d]Rev. 13:14 [1]*severe and malignant,* lit. *bad and evil*
**3** [a]Rev. 8:8; 11:6 [b]Ex. 7:17–21 [c]Rev. 8:9
**4** [a]Rev. 8:10 [b]Ex. 7:17–20
**5** [a]Rev. 15:3, 4 [b]Rev. 1:4, 8 [1]NU, M omit *O Lord* [2]NU, M *was, the Holy One*
**6** [a]Matt. 23:34 [b]Rev. 11:18 [c]Is. 49:26 [1]NU, M omit *For*
**7** [a]Rev. 15:3 [b]Rev. 13:10; 19:2 [1]NU, M omit *another from*
**8** [a]Rev. 8:12 [b]Rev. 9:17, 18

9 And men were scorched with great heat, and
they [a]blasphemed the name of God who has
power over these plagues; [b]and they did not
repent [c]and give Him glory.
**10** Then the fifth angel poured out his bowl [a]on
the throne of the beast, [b]and his kingdom became
full of darkness; [c]and they gnawed their tongues
because of the pain.
11 They blasphemed the God of heaven because
of their pains and their sores, and did not repent of
their deeds.
**12** Then the sixth angel poured out his bowl [a]on
the great river Euphrates, [b]and its water was dried
up, [c]so that the way of the kings from the east
might be prepared.
13 And I saw three unclean [a]spirits like frogs
*coming* out of the mouth of [b]the dragon, out of the
mouth of the beast, and out of the mouth of [c]the
false prophet.
14 For they are spirits of demons, [a]performing
signs, *which* go out to the kings [1]of the earth and
of [b]the whole world, to gather them to [c]the battle
of that great day of God Almighty.
15 [a]"Behold, I am coming as a thief. Blessed *is* he
who watches, and keeps his garments, [b]lest he
walk naked and they see his shame."
16 [a]And they gathered them together to the place
called in Hebrew, [1]Armageddon.
**17** Then the seventh angel poured out his bowl
into the air, and a loud voice came out of the
temple of heaven, from the throne, saying, [a]"It is
done!"
18 And [a]there were noises and thunderings and
lightnings; [b]and there was a great earthquake,
such a mighty and great earthquake [c]as had not
occurred since men were on the earth.
19 Now [a]the great city was divided into three
parts, and the cities of the nations fell. And [b]great
Babylon [c]was remembered before God, [d]to give
her the cup of the wine of the fierceness of His
wrath.
20 Then [a]every island fled away, and the mountains were not found.
21 And great hail from heaven fell upon men,
*each hailstone* about the weight of a talent. Men
blasphemed God because of the plague of the hail,
since that plague was exceedingly great.

### *The Scarlet Woman and the Scarlet Beast*

**17** Then [a]one of the seven angels who had the
seven bowls came and talked with me,
saying [1]to me, "Come, [b]I will show you the judgment of [c]the great harlot [d]who sits on many
waters,
2 [a]"with whom the kings of the earth committed
fornication, and [b]the inhabitants of the earth were
made drunk with the wine of her fornication."
3 So he carried me away in the Spirit [a]into the
wilderness. And I saw a woman sitting [b]on a
scarlet beast *which was* full of [c]names of blasphemy, having seven heads and ten horns.
4 The woman [a]was arrayed in purple and scarlet, [b]and adorned with gold and precious stones
and pearls, [c]having in her hand a golden cup [d]full
of abominations and the filthiness of [1]her fornication.
5 And on her forehead a name *was* written:

[a]MYSTERY,
BABYLON THE GREAT,
THE MOTHER OF HARLOTS
AND OF THE ABOMINATIONS
OF THE EARTH.

6 I saw [a]the woman, drunk [b]with the blood of
the saints and with the blood of [c]the martyrs of
Jesus. And when I saw her, I marveled with great
amazement.
**7** But the angel said to me, "Why did you marvel? I will tell you the [1]mystery of the woman and
of the beast that carries her, which has the seven
heads and the ten horns.
8 "The beast that you saw was, and is not, and
[a]will ascend out of the bottomless pit and [b]go to
[1]perdition. And those who [c]dwell on the earth [d]will
marvel, [e]whose names are not written in the Book
of Life from the foundation of the world, when
they see the beast that was, and is not, and [2]yet is.
9 [a]"Here *is* the mind which has wisdom: [b]The
seven heads are seven mountains on which the
woman sits.
10 There are also seven kings. Five have fallen,
one is, *and* the other has not yet come. And when
he comes, he must [a]continue a short time.
11 "The [a]beast that was, and is not, is himself also
the eighth, and is of the seven, and is going to
[1]perdition.
12 [a]"The ten horns which you saw are ten kings
who have received no kingdom as yet, but they
receive authority for one hour as kings with the
beast.
13 "These are of one mind, and they will give
their power and authority to the beast.
14 [a]"These will make war with the Lamb, and the
Lamb will [b]overcome them, [c]for He is Lord of lords
and King of kings; [d]and those *who are* with Him
*are* called, chosen, and faithful."
15 Then he said to me, [a]"The waters which you
saw, where the harlot sits, [b]are peoples, multitudes, nations, and tongues.
16 "And the ten horns which you [1]saw on the
beast, [a]these will hate the harlot, make her [b]deso-
late [c]and naked, eat her flesh and [d]burn her with
fire.
17 [a]"For God has put it into their hearts to fulfill
His purpose, to be of one mind, and to give their
kingdom to the beast, [b]until the words of God are
fulfilled.
18 "And the woman whom you saw [a]is that great
city [b]which reigns over the kings of the earth."

### *The Fall of Babylon the Great*

**18** After[a] these things I saw another angel
coming down from heaven, having great
authority, [b]and the earth was illuminated with his
glory.
2 And he cried [1]mightily with a loud voice,
saying, [a]"Babylon the great is fallen, is fallen, and
[b]has become a dwelling place of demons, a prison
for every foul spirit, and [c]a cage for every unclean
and hated bird!
3 "For all the nations [a]have drunk of the wine of
the wrath of her fornication, the kings of the
earth have committed fornication with her, [b]and
the merchants of the earth have become rich
through the [1]abundance of her luxury."

**9** [a]Rev. 16:11 [b]Dan. 5:22 [c]Rev. 11:13
**10** [a]Rev. 13:2 [b]Rev. 8:12; 9:2 [c]Rev. 11:10
**12** [a]Rev. 9:14 [b]Jer. 50:38 [c]Is. 41:2, 25; 46:11
**13** [a]1 John 4:1 [b]Rev. 12:3, 9 [c]Rev. 13:11, 14; 19:20; 20:10
**14** [a]2 Thess. 2:9 [b]Luke 2:1 [c]Rev. 17:14; 19:19; 20:8 [1]NU, M omit *of the earth and*
**15** [a]Matt. 24:43 [b]2 Cor. 5:3
**16** [a]Rev. 19:19 [1]Lit. *Mount Megiddo,* M *Megiddo*
**17** [a]Rev. 10:6; 21:6
**18** [a]Rev. 4:5 [b]Rev. 11:13 [c]Dan. 12:1
**19** [a]Rev. 14:8 [b]Rev. 17:5, 18 [c]Rev. 14:8; 18:5 [d]Is. 51:17
**20** [a]Rev. 6:14; 20:11

CHAPTER 17
**1** [a]Rev. 1:1; 21:9 [b]Rev. 16:19 [c]Nah. 3:4 [d]Jer. 51:13 [1]NU, M omit *to me*
**2** [a]Rev. 2:22; 18:3, 9 [b]Jer. 51:7
**3** [a]Rev. 12:6, 14; 21:10 [b]Rev. 12:3 [c]Rev. 13:1
**4** [a]Rev. 18:12, 16 [b]Dan. 11:38 [c]Jer. 51:7 [d]Rev. 14:8 [1]M *the fornication of the earth*
**5** [a]2 Thess. 2:7
**6** [a]Rev. 18:24 [b]Rev. 13:15 [c]Rev. 6:9, 10
**7** [1]*hidden truth*
**8** [a]Rev. 11:7 [b]Rev. 13:10; 17:11 [c]Rev. 3:10 [d]Rev. 13:3 [e]Rev. 13:8 [1]*destruction* [2]NU, M *shall be present*
**9** [a]Rev. 13:18 [b]Rev. 13:1
**10** [a]Rev. 13:5
**11** [a]Rev. 13:3, 12, 14; 17:8 [1]*destruction*
**12** [a]Dan. 7:20
**14** [a]Rev. 16:14; 19:19 [b]Rev. 19:20 [c]1 Tim. 6:15 [d]Jer. 50:44
**15** [a]Is. 8:7 [b]Rev. 13:7
**16** [a]Jer. 50:41 [b]Rev. 18:17, 19 [c]Ezek. 16:37, 39 [d]Rev. 18:8 [1]NU, M *saw, and the beast*
**17** [a]2 Thess. 2:11 [b]Rev. 10:7
**18** [a]Rev. 11:8; 16:19 [b]Rev. 12:4

CHAPTER 18
**1** [a]Rev. 17:1, 7 [b]Ezek. 43:2
**2** [a]Is. 13:19; 21:9 [b]Is. 13:21; 34:11, 13–15 [c]Is. 14:23 [1]NU, M omit *mightily*
**3** [a]Rev. 14:8 [b]Is. 47:15 [1]Lit. *strengths*

4 And I heard another voice from heaven saying, [a]"Come out of her, my people, lest you share
in her sins, and lest you receive of her plagues.
5 [a]"For her sins have reached to heaven, and
[b]God has remembered her iniquities.
6 [a]"Render to her just as she rendered [1]to you,
and repay her double according to her works; [b]in
the cup which she has mixed, [c]mix double for her.
7 [a]"In the measure that she glorified herself and
lived [1]luxuriously, in the same measure give her
torment and sorrow; for she says in her heart, 'I
sit *as* [b]queen, and am no widow, and will not see
sorrow.'
8 "Therefore her plagues will come [a]in one
day—death and mourning and famine. And [b]she
will be utterly burned with fire, [c]for strong *is* the
Lord God who [1]judges her.
**9** [a]"The kings of the earth who committed fornication and lived luxuriously with her [b]will weep
and lament for her, [c]when they see the smoke of
her burning,
10 "standing at a distance for fear of her torment,
saying, [a]'Alas, alas, that great city Babylon, that
mighty city! [b]For in one hour your judgment has
come.'
11 "And [a]the merchants of the earth will weep
and mourn over her, for no one buys their merchandise anymore:
12 [a]"merchandise of gold and silver, precious
stones and pearls, fine linen and purple, silk and
scarlet, every kind of citron wood, every kind of
object of ivory, every kind of object of most
precious wood, bronze, iron, and marble;
13 "and cinnamon and incense, fragrant oil and
frankincense, wine and oil, fine flour and wheat,
cattle and sheep, horses and chariots, and bodies
and [a]souls of men.
14 "The fruit that your soul longed for has gone
from you, and all the things which are rich and
splendid have [1]gone from you, and you shall find
them no more at all.
15 "The merchants of these things, who became
rich by her, will stand at a distance for fear of her
torment, weeping and wailing,
16 "and saying, 'Alas, alas, [a]that great city [b]that
was clothed in fine linen, purple, and scarlet, and
adorned with gold and precious stones and pearls!
17 [a]'For in one hour such great riches [1]came to
nothing.' [b]Every shipmaster, all who travel by
ship, sailors, and as many as trade on the sea,
stood at a distance
18 [a]"and cried out when they saw the smoke of
her burning, saying, [b]'What *is* like this great city?'
19 [a]"They threw dust on their heads and cried
out, weeping and wailing, and saying, 'Alas, alas,
that great city, in which all who had ships on the
sea became rich by her wealth! [b]For in one hour
she [1]is made desolate.'
20 [a]"Rejoice over her, O heaven, and *you* [1]holy
apostles and prophets, for [b]God has avenged you
on her!"
**21** Then a mighty angel took up a stone like a
great millstone and threw *it* into the sea, saying,
[a]"Thus with violence the great city Babylon shall
be thrown down, and [b]shall not be found anymore.
22 [a]"The sound of harpists, musicians, flutists,
and trumpeters shall not be heard in you anymore. No craftsman of any craft shall be found in
you anymore, and the sound of a millstone shall
not be heard in you anymore.
23 [a]"The light of a lamp shall not shine in you
anymore, [b]and the voice of bridegroom and bride
shall not be heard in you anymore. For [c]your
merchants were the great men of the earth, [d]for
by your sorcery all the nations were deceived.
24 "And [a]in her was found the blood of prophets
and saints, and of all who [b]were slain on the
earth."

### *The Marriage of the Lamb*

**19** After these things [a]I [1]heard a loud voice of a
great multitude in heaven, saying, "Alleluia!
[b]Salvation and glory and honor and power *belong*
to the Lord [2]our God!
2 "For [a]true and righteous *are* His judgments,
because He has judged the great harlot who
corrupted the earth with her fornication; and He
[b]has avenged on her the blood of His servants
*shed* by her."
3 Again they said, "Alleluia! [a]Her smoke rises up
forever and ever!"
4 And [a]the twenty-four elders and the four
living creatures fell down and worshiped God who
sat on the throne, saying, [b]"Amen! Alleluia!"
5 Then a voice came from the throne, saying,
[a]"Praise our God, all you His servants and those
who fear Him, [b]both[1] small and great!"
6 [a]And I heard, as it were, the voice of a great
multitude, as the sound of many waters and as the
sound of mighty thunderings, saying, "Alleluia!
For [b]the[1] Lord God Omnipotent reigns!
7 "Let us be glad and rejoice and give Him
glory, for [a]the marriage of the Lamb has come,
and His wife has made herself ready."
8 And [a]to her it was granted to be arrayed in
fine linen, clean and bright, [b]for the fine linen is
the righteous acts of the saints.
9 Then he said to me, "Write: [a]'Blessed *are* those
who are called to the marriage supper of the
Lamb!' " And he said to me, [b]"These are the true
sayings of God."
10 And [a]I fell at his feet to worship him. But he
said to me, [b]"See *that you do* not *do that!* I am
your [c]fellow servant, and of your brethren [d]who
have the testimony of Jesus. Worship God! For
the [e]testimony of Jesus is the spirit of prophecy."
**11** [a]Now I saw heaven opened, and behold, [b]a
white horse. And He who sat on him *was* called
[c]Faithful and True, and [d]in righteousness He
judges and makes war.
12 [a]His eyes *were* like a flame of fire, and on His
head *were* many crowns. [b]He [1]had a name written
that no one knew except Himself.
13 [a]He *was* clothed with a robe dipped in blood,
and His name is called [b]The Word of God.
14 [a]And the armies in heaven, [b]clothed in [1]fine
linen, white and clean, followed Him on white
horses.
15 Now [a]out of His mouth goes a [1]sharp sword,
that with it He should strike the nations. And [b]He
Himself will rule them with a rod of iron. [c]He
Himself treads the winepress of the fierceness and
wrath of Almighty God.
16 And [a]He has on *His* robe and on His thigh a
name written:

**4** [a]Is. 48:20
**5** [a]Gen. 18:20 [b]Rev. 16:19
**6** [a]Ps. 137:8 [b]Rev. 14:10 [c]Rev. 16:19 [1]NU, M omit *to you*
**7** [a]Ezek. 28:2–8 [b]Is. 47:7, 8 [1]*sensually*
**8** [a]Rev. 18:10 [b]Rev. 17:16 [c]Jer. 50:34 [1]NU, M *has judged*
**9** [a]Ezek. 26:16; 27:35 [b]Jer. 50:46 [c]Rev. 19:3
**10** [a]Is. 21:9 [b]Rev. 18:17, 19
**11** [a]Ezek. 27:27–34
**12** [a]Rev. 17:4
**13** [a]Ezek. 27:13
**14** [1]NU, M *been lost to you*
**16** [a]Rev. 17:18 [b]Rev. 17:4
**17** [a]Rev. 18:10 [b]Is. 23:14 [1]*have been laid waste*
**18** [a]Ezek. 27:30 [b]Rev. 13:4
**19** [a]Josh. 7:6 [b]Rev. 18:8 [1]*have been laid waste*
**20** [a]Jer. 51:48 [b]Luke 11:49 [1]NU, M *saints and apostles*
**21** [a]Jer. 51:63, 64 [b]Rev. 12:8; 16:20
**22** [a]Jer. 7:34; 16:9; 25:10
**23** [a]Jer. 25:10 [b]Jer. 7:34; 16:9 [c]Is. 23:8 [d]2 Kin. 9:22
**24** [a]Rev. 16:6; 17:6 [b]Jer. 51:49

CHAPTER 19
**1** [a]Rev. 11:15; 19:6 [b]Rev. 4:11 [1]NU, M add *something like* [2]NU, M omit *the Lord*
**2** [a]Rev. 15:3; 16:7 [b]Deut. 32:43
**3** [a]Is. 34:10
**4** [a]Rev. 4:4, 6, 10 [b]1 Chr. 16:36
**5** [a]Ps. 134:1 [b]Rev. 11:18 [1]NU, M omit *both*
**6** [a]Ezek. 1:24 [b]Rev. 11:15 [1]NU, M *our*
**7** [a][Matt. 22:2; 25:10]
**8** [a]Ezek. 16:10 [b]Ps. 132:9
**9** [a]Luke 14:15 [b]Rev. 22:6
**10** [a]Rev. 22:8 [b]Acts 10:26 [c][Heb. 1:14] [d]1 John 5:10 [e]Luke 24:27
**11** [a]Rev. 15:5 [b]Rev. 6:2; 19:19, 21 [c]Rev. 3:7, 14 [d]Is. 11:4
**12** [a]Rev. 1:14 [b]Rev. 2:17; 19:16 [1]M adds *names written, and*
**13** [a]Is. 63:2, 3 [b][John 1:1, 14]
**14** [a]Rev. 14:20 [b]Matt. 28:3 [1]NU, M *clean white linen*
**15** [a]Is. 11:4 [b]Ps. 2:8, 9 [c]Is. 63:3–6 [1]M *sharp two-edged*
**16** [a]Rev. 2:17; 19:12

[b]KING OF KINGS
AND LORD OF LORDS.

17 Then I saw an angel standing in the sun; and he cried with a loud voice, saying to all the birds that fly in the midst of heaven, [a]"Come and gather together for the [1]supper of the great God,
18 [a]"that you may eat the flesh of kings, the flesh of captains, the flesh of mighty men, the flesh of horses and of those who sit on them, and the flesh of all *people,* [1]free and slave, both small and great."
19 [a]And I saw the beast, the kings of the earth, and their armies, gathered together to make war against Him who sat on the horse and against His army.
20 [a]Then the beast was captured, and with him the false prophet who worked signs in his presence, by which he deceived those who received the mark of the beast and [b]those who worshiped his image. [c]These two were cast alive into the lake of fire [d]burning with brimstone.
21 And the rest [a]were killed with the sword which proceeded from the mouth of Him who sat on the horse. [b]And all the birds [c]were filled with their flesh.

## *Satan Bound; the Thousand-Year Reign; Final Judgment*

**20** Then I saw an angel coming down from heaven, [a]having the key to the bottomless pit and a great chain in his hand.
2 He laid hold of [a]the dragon, that serpent of old, who is *the* Devil and Satan, and bound him for a thousand years;
3 and he cast him into the bottomless pit, and shut him up, and [a]set a seal on him, [b]so that he should deceive the nations no more till the thousand years were finished. But after these things he must be released for a little while.
4 And I saw [a]thrones, and they sat on them, and [b]judgment was committed to them. Then *I saw* [c]the souls of those who had been beheaded for their witness to Jesus and for the word of God, [d]who had not worshiped the beast [e]or his image, and had not received *his* mark on their foreheads or on their hands. And they [f]lived and [g]reigned with Christ for [1]a thousand years.
5 But the rest of the dead did not live again until the thousand years were finished. This *is* the first resurrection.
6 Blessed and holy *is* he who has part in the first resurrection. Over such [a]the second death has no power, but they shall be [b]priests of God and of Christ, [c]and shall reign with Him a thousand years.
7 Now when the thousand years have expired, Satan will be released from his prison
8 and will go out [a]to deceive the nations which are in the four corners of the earth, [b]Gog and Magog, [c]to gather them together to battle, whose number *is* as the sand of the sea.
9 [a]They went up on the breadth of the earth and surrounded the camp of the saints and the beloved city. And fire came down from God out of heaven and devoured them.
10 The devil, who deceived them, was cast into the lake of fire and brimstone [a]where[1] the beast and the false prophet *are.* And they [b]will be tormented day and night forever and ever.
11 Then I saw a great white throne and Him who sat on it, from whose face [a]the earth and the heaven fled away. [b]And there was found no place for them.
12 And I saw the dead, [a]small and great, standing before [1]God, [b]and books were opened. And another [c]book was opened, which is *the Book* of Life. And the dead were judged [d]according to their works, by the things which were written in the books.
13 The sea gave up the dead who were in it, [a]and Death and Hades delivered up the dead who were in them. [b]And they were judged, each one according to his works.
14 Then [a]Death and Hades were cast into the lake of fire. [b]This is the second [1]death.
15 And anyone not found written in the Book of Life [a]was cast into the lake of fire.

## *The New Jerusalem*

**21** Now [a]I saw a new heaven and a new earth, [b]for the first heaven and the first earth had passed away. Also there was no more sea.
2 Then I, [1]John, saw [a]the holy city, New Jerusalem, coming down out of heaven from God, prepared [b]as a bride adorned for her husband.
3 And I heard a loud voice from heaven saying, "Behold, [a]the tabernacle of God *is* with men, and He will dwell with them, and they shall be His people. God Himself will be with them *and be* their God.
4 [a]"And God will wipe away every tear from their eyes; [b]there shall be no more death, [c]nor sorrow, nor crying. There shall be no more pain, for the former things have passed away."
5 Then [a]He who sat on the throne said, [b]"Behold, I make all things new." And He said [1]to me, "Write, for [c]these words are true and faithful."
6 And He said to me, [a]"It[1] is done! [b]I am the Alpha and the Omega, the Beginning and the End. [c]I will give of the fountain of the water of life freely to him who thirsts.
7 "He who overcomes [1]shall inherit all things, and [a]I will be his God and he shall be My son.
8 [a]"But the cowardly, [1]unbelieving, abominable, murderers, sexually immoral, sorcerers, idolaters, and all liars shall have their part in [b]the lake which burns with fire and brimstone, which is the second death."
9 Then one of [a]the seven angels who had the seven bowls filled with the seven last plagues came [1]to me and talked with me, saying, "Come, I will show you [b]the [2]bride, the Lamb's wife."
10 And he carried me away [a]in the Spirit to a great and high mountain, and showed me [b]the [1]great city, the [2]holy Jerusalem, descending out of heaven from God,
11 [a]having the glory of God. Her light *was* like a most precious stone, like a jasper stone, clear as crystal.
12 Also she had a great and high wall with [a]twelve gates, and twelve angels at the gates, and names written on them, which are *the names* of the twelve tribes of the children of Israel:
13 [a]three gates on the east, three gates on the north, three gates on the south, and three gates on the west.

16 [b]Dan. 2:47
17 [a]Ezek. 39:17 [1]NU, M *great supper of God*
18 [a]Ezek. 39:18–20 [1]NU, M *both free*
19 [a]Rev. 16:13–16
20 [a]Rev. 16:13 [b]Rev. 13:8, 12, 13 [c]Dan. 7:11 [d]Rev. 14:10
21 [a]Rev. 19:15 [b]Rev. 19:17, 18 [c]Rev. 17:16

CHAPTER 20
1 [a]Rev. 1:18; 9:1
2 [a]2 Pet. 2:4
3 [a]Dan. 6:17 [b]Rev. 12:9; 20:8, 10
4 [a]Dan. 7:9 [b][1 Cor. 6:2, 3] [c]Rev. 6:9 [d]Rev. 13:12 [e]Rev. 13:15 [f]John 14:19 [g]Rom. 8:17 [1]M *the*
6 [a][Rev. 2:11; 20:14] [b]Is. 61:6 [c]Rev. 20:4
8 [a]Rev. 12:9; 20:3, 10 [b]Ezek. 38:2; 39:1, 6 [c]Rev. 16:14
9 [a]Ezek. 38:9, 16
10 [a]Rev. 19:20; 20:14, 15 [b]Rev. 14:10 [1]NU, M *where also*
11 [a]2 Pet. 3:7 [b]Dan. 2:35
12 [a]Rev. 19:5 [b]Dan. 7:10 [c]Ps. 69:28 [d]Matt. 16:27 [1]NU, M *the throne*
13 [a]Rev. 1:18; 6:8; 21:4 [b]Rev. 2:23; 20:12
14 [a]1 Cor. 15:26 [b]Rev. 21:8 [1]NU, M *death, the lake of fire.*
15 [a]Rev. 19:20

CHAPTER 21
1 [a][2 Pet. 3:13] [b]Rev. 20:11
2 [a]Is. 52:1 [b]2 Cor. 11:2 [1]NU, M omit *John,*
3 [a]Lev. 26:11
4 [a]Is. 25:8 [b]1 Cor. 15:26 [c]Is. 35:10; 51:11; 65:19
5 [a]Rev. 4:2, 9; 20:11 [b]Is. 43:19 [c]Rev. 19:9; 22:6 [1]NU, M omit *to me*
6 [a]Rev. 10:6; 16:17 [b]Rev. 1:8; 22:13 [c]John 4:10 [1]M omits *It is done*
7 [a]Zech. 8:8 [1]M *I shall give him these things*
8 [a]1 Cor. 6:9 [b]Rev. 20:14 [1]M adds *and sinners,*

9 [a]Rev. 15:1 [b]Rev. 19:7; 21:2 [1]NU, M omit *to me* [2]NU, M *woman, the Lamb's bride*
10 [a]Rev. 1:10 [b]Ezek. 48 [1]NU, M omit *great* [2]NU, M *holy city, Jerusalem*
11 [a]Rev. 15:8; 21:23; 22:5
12 [a]Ezek. 48:31–34
13 [a]Ezek. 48:31–34

14 Now the wall of the city had twelve foundations, and [a]on them were the [1]names of the twelve
apostles of the Lamb.
15 And he who talked with me [a]had a gold reed to
measure the city, its gates, and its wall.
16 The city is laid out as a square; its length is as
great as its breadth. And he measured the city
with the reed: twelve thousand [1]furlongs. Its
length, breadth, and height are equal.
17 Then he measured its wall: one hundred *and*
forty-four cubits, *according* to the measure of a
man, that is, of an angel.
18 The construction of its wall was *of* jasper; and
the city *was* pure gold, like clear glass.
19 [a]The foundations of the wall of the city *were*
adorned with all kinds of precious stones: the first
foundation *was* jasper, the second sapphire, the
third chalcedony, the fourth emerald,
20 the fifth sardonyx, the sixth sardius, the seventh chrysolite, the eighth beryl, the ninth topaz,
the tenth chrysoprase, the eleventh jacinth, and
the twelfth amethyst.
21 The twelve gates *were* twelve [a]pearls: each
individual gate was of one pearl. [b]And the street of
the city *was* pure gold, like transparent glass.
**22** [a]But I saw no temple in it, for the Lord God
Almighty and the Lamb are its temple.
23 [a]The city had no need of the sun or of the
moon to shine [1]in it, for the [2]glory of God illuminated it. The Lamb *is* its light.
24 [a]And the nations [1]of those who are saved shall
walk in its light, and the kings of the earth bring
their glory and honor [2]into it.
25 [a]Its gates shall not be shut at all by day [b](there
shall be no night there).
26 [a]And they shall bring the glory and the honor
of the nations into [1]it.
27 But [a]there shall by no means enter it anything
[1]that defiles, or causes an abomination or a lie, but
only those who are written in the Lamb's [b]Book of
Life.

### *Jesus Is Coming Quickly*

**22** And he showed me [a]a [1]pure river of water of
life, clear as crystal, proceeding from the
throne of God and of the Lamb.
2 [a]In the middle of its street, and on either side
of the river, *was* [b]the tree of life, which bore
twelve fruits, each *tree* yielding its fruit every
month. The leaves of the tree *were* [c]for the healing of the nations.
3 And [a]there shall be no more curse, [b]but the
throne of God and of the Lamb shall be in it, and
His [c]servants shall serve Him.
4 [a]They shall see His face, and [b]His name *shall
be* on their foreheads.
5 [a]There shall be no night there: They need no
lamp nor [b]light of the sun, for [c]the Lord God gives
them light. [d]And they shall reign forever and ever.
**6** Then he said to me, [a]"These words *are* faithful
and true." And the Lord God of the [1]holy prophets
[b]sent His angel to show His servants the things
which must [c]shortly take place.
7 [a]"Behold, I am coming quickly! [b]Blessed *is* he
who keeps the words of the prophecy of this
book."
8 Now I, John, [1]saw and heard these things. And
when I heard and saw, [a]I fell down to worship
before the feet of the angel who showed me these
things.
9 Then he said to me, [a]"See *that you do* not *do
that.* [1]For I am your fellow servant, and of your
brethren the prophets, and of those who keep the
words of this book. Worship God."
10 [a]And he said to me, "Do not seal the words of
the prophecy of this book, [b]for the time is at hand.
11 "He who is unjust, let him be unjust still; he
who is filthy, let him be filthy still; he who is
righteous, let him [1]be righteous still; he who is
holy, let him be holy still."
**12** "And behold, I am coming quickly, and [a]My
reward *is* with Me, [b]to give to every one according
to his work.
13 [a]"I am the Alpha and the Omega, *the* [1]Begin-
ning and *the* End, the First and the Last."
14 [a]Blessed *are* those who [1]do His commandments, that they may have the right [b]to the tree of
life, [c]and may enter through the gates into the
city.
15 [1]But [a]outside *are* [b]dogs and sorcerers and
sexually immoral and murderers and idolaters,
and whoever loves and practices a lie.
16 [a]"I, Jesus, have sent My angel to testify to you
these things in the churches. [b]I am the Root and
the Offspring of David, [c]the Bright and Morning
Star."
17 And the Spirit and [a]the bride say, "Come!"
And let him who hears say, "Come!" [b]And let him
who thirsts come. Whoever desires, let him take
the water of life freely.
**18** [1]For I testify to everyone who hears the words
of the prophecy of this book: [a]If anyone adds to
these things, [2]God will add to him the plagues that
are written in this book;
19 and if anyone takes away from the words of
the book of this prophecy, [a]God[1] shall take away
his part from the [2]Book of Life, from the holy city,
and *from* the things which are written in this
book.
**20** He who testifies to these things says, "Surely I
am coming quickly." Amen. Even so, come, Lord
Jesus!
21 The grace of our Lord Jesus Christ *be* [1]with
you all. Amen.

**14** [a]Eph. 2:20 [1]NU, M *twelve names*
**15** [a]Ezek. 40:3
**16** [1]Lit. *stadia,* about 1,380 miles in all
**19** [a]Is. 54:11
**21** [a]Matt. 13:45, 46 [b]Rev. 22:2
**22** [a]John 4:21, 23
**23** [a]Is. 24:23; 60:19, 20 [1]NU, M omit *in it* [2]M *very glory*
**24** [a]Is. 60:3, 5; 66:12 [1]NU, M omit *of those who are saved* [2]M *of the nations to Him*
**25** [a]Is. 60:11 [b]Is. 60:20
**26** [a]Rev. 21:24 [1]M adds *that they may enter in.*
**27** [a]Joel 3:17 [b]Phil. 4:3 [1]NU, M *profane, nor one who causes*

CHAPTER 22
**1** [a]Ezek. 47:1 [1]NU, M omit *pure*
**2** [a]Ezek. 47:12 [b]Gen. 2:9 [c]Rev. 21:24
**3** [a]Zech. 14:11 [b]Ezek. 48:35 [c]Rev. 7:15
**4** [a][Matt. 5:8] [b]Rev. 14:1
**5** [a]Rev. 21:23 [b]Rev. 7:15 [c]Ps. 36:9 [d]Dan. 7:18, 27
**6** [a]Rev. 19:9 [b]Rev. 1:1 [c]Heb. 10:37 [1]NU, M *spirits of the prophets*
**7** [a][Rev. 3:11] [b]Rev. 1:3
**8** [a]Rev. 19:10 [1]NU, M *am the one who heard and saw*
**9** [a]Rev. 19:10 [1]NU, M omit *For*
**10** [a]Dan. 8:26 [b]Rev. 1:3
**11** [1]NU, M *do right*
**12** [a]Is. 40:10; 62:11 [b]Rev. 20:12
**13** [a]Is. 41:4 [1]NU, M *First and the Last, the Beginning and the End*
**14** [a]Dan. 12:12 [b][Prov. 11:30] [c]Rev. 21:27 [1]NU *wash their robes,*
**15** [a]1 Cor. 6:9 [b]Phil. 3:2 [1]NU, M omit *But*
**16** [a]Rev. 1:1 [b]Rev. 5:5 [c]Num. 24:17
**17** [a][Rev. 21:2, 9] [b]Is. 55:1
**18** [a]Deut. 4:2; 12:32 [1]NU, M omit *For* [2]M *may God add*
**19** [a]Ex. 32:33 [1]M *may God take away* [2]NU, M *tree of life*
**21** [1]NU *with all;* M *with all the saints*

# Harmony of the Gospels

| Date | Event | Location | Matthew | Mark | Luke | John | Related References |
|---|---|---|---|---|---|---|---|
| | Luke's Introduction | | | | 1:1–4 | | Acts 1:1 |
| | Pre-fleshly state of Christ | | | | | 1:1–18 | Heb. 1:1–14 |
| | Genealogy of Jesus Christ | | 1:1–17 | | 3:23–38 | | Ruth 4:18–22<br>1 Chr. 1:1–4 |
| **BIRTH, INFANCY, AND ADOLESCENCE OF JESUS AND JOHN THE BAPTIST IN 17 EVENTS** | | | | | | | |
| 7 B.C. | (1) Announcement of Birth of John | Jerusalem (Temple) | | | 1:5–25 | | Num. 6:3 |
| 7 or 6 B.C. | (2) Announcement of Birth of Jesus to the Virgin | Nazareth | | | 1:26–38 | | Is. 7:14 |
| c. 5 B.C. | (3) Song of Elizabeth to Mary | Hill Country of Judea | | | 1:39–45 | | |
| | (4) Mary's Song of Praise | | | | 1:46–56 | | Ps. 103:17 |
| 5 B.C. | (5) Birth, Infancy, and Purpose for Future of John the Baptist | Judea | | | 1:57–80 | | Mal. 3:1 |
| | (6) Announcement of Jesus' Birth to Joseph | Nazareth | 1:18–25 | | | | Is. 9:6, 7 |
| 5–4 B.C. | (7) Birth of Jesus Christ | Bethlehem | 1:24, 25 | | 2:1–7 | | Is. 7:14 |
| | (8) Proclamation by the Angels | Near Bethlehem | | | 2:8–14 | | 1 Tim. 3:16 |
| | (9) The Visit of Homage by Shepherds | Bethlehem | | | 2:15–20 | | |
| | (10) Jesus' Circumcision | Bethlehem | | | 2:21 | | Lev. 12:3 |
| 4 B.C. | (11) First Temple Visit with Acknowledgments by Simeon and Anna | Jerusalem | | | 2:22–38 | | Ex. 13:2<br>Lev. 12 |
| | (12) Visit of the Wise Men | Jerusalem & Bethlehem | 2:1–12 | | | | Num. 24:17 |
| | (13) Flight into Egypt and Massacre of Innocents | Bethlehem, Jerusalem & Egypt | 2:13–18 | | | | Jer. 31:15 |
| | (14) From Egypt to Nazareth with Jesus | | 2:19–23 | | 2:39 | | |
| Afterward | (15) Childhood of Jesus | Nazareth | | | 2:40, 51 | | |
| A.D. 7–8 | (16) Jesus, 12 Years Old, Visits the Temple | Jerusalem | | | 2:41–50 | | Deut. 16:1–8 |
| Afterward | (17) 18-Year Account of Jesus' Adolescence and Adulthood | Nazareth | | | 2:51, 52 | | 1 Sam. 2:26 |
| **TRUTHS ABOUT JOHN THE BAPTIST** | | | | | | | |
| c. A.D. 25–27 | John's Ministry Begins | Judean Wilderness | 3:1 | 1:1–4 | 3:1, 2 | 1:19–28 | Mal. 3:1 |
| | Man and Message | | 3:2–12 | 1:2–8 | 3:3–14 | | Is. 40:3 |
| | His Picture of Jesus | | 3:11, 12 | 1:7, 8 | 3:15–18 | 1:26, 27 | Acts 2:38 |
| | His Courage | | 14:4–12 | | 3:19, 20 | | |
| **BEGINNING OF JESUS' MINISTRY IN 12 EVENTS** | | | | | | | |
| c. A.D. 27 | (1) Jesus Baptized | Jordan River | 3:13–17 | 1:9–11 | 3:21–23 | 1:29–34 | Ps. 2:7 |
| | (2) Jesus Tempted | Wilderness | 4:1–11 | 1:12, 13 | 4:1–13 | | Ps. 91:11 |
| | (3) Calls First Disciples | Beyond Jordan | | | | 1:35–51 | |
| | (4) The First Miracle | Cana in Galilee | | | | 2:1–11 | |
| | (5) First Stay in Capernaum | (Capernaum is "His" city) | | | | 2:12 | |
| A.D. 27 | (6) First Cleansing of the Temple | Jerusalem | | | | 2:13–22 | Ps. 69:9 |
| | (7) Received at Jerusalem | Judea | | | | 2:23–25 | |
| | (8) Teaches Nicodemus about Second Birth | Judea | | | | 3:1–21 | Num. 21:8, 9 |
| | (9) Co-Ministry with John | Judea | | | | 3:22–30 | |

| Date | Event | Location | Matthew | Mark | Luke | John | Related References |
|---|---|---|---|---|---|---|---|
| A.D. 27 | (10) Leaves for Galilee | Judea | 4:12 | 1:14 | 4:14 | 4:1–4 | |
| | (11) Samaritan Woman at Jacob's Well | Samaria | | | | 4:5–42 | Josh. 24:32 |
| | (12) Returns to Galilee | | | 1:15 | 4:15 | 4:43–45 | |
| **A.D. 27–29** | **THE GALILEAN MINISTRY OF JESUS IN 55 EVENTS** | | | | | | |
| A.D. 27 | (1) Healing of the Nobleman's Son | Cana | | | | 4:46–54 | |
| | (2) Rejected at Nazareth | Nazareth | | | 4:16–30 | | Is. 61:1, 2 |
| | (3) Moved to Capernaum | Capernaum | 4:13–17 | | | | Is. 9:1, 2 |
| | (4) Four Become Fishers of Men | Sea of Galilee | 4:18–22 | 1:16–20 | 5:1–11 | | Ps. 33:9 |
| | (5) Demoniac Healed on the Sabbath Day | Capernaum | | 1:21–28 | 4:31–37 | | |
| | (6) Peter's Mother-in-Law Cured, Plus Others | Capernaum | 8:14–17 | 1:29–34 | 4:38–41 | | Is. 53:4 |
| c. A.D. 27 | (7) First Preaching Tour of Galilee | Galilee | 4:23–25 | 1:35–39 | 4:42–44 | | |
| | (8) Leper Healed and Response Recorded | Galilee | 8:1–4 | 1:40–45 | 5:12–16 | | Lev. 13:49 |
| | (9) Paralytic Healed | Capernaum | 9:1–8 | 2:1–12 | 5:17–26 | | Rom. 3:23 |
| | (10) Matthew's Call and Reception Held | Capernaum | 9:9–13 | 2:13–17 | 5:27–32 | | Hos. 6:6 |
| | (11) Disciples Defended via a Parable | Capernaum | 9:14–17 | 2:18–22 | 5:33–39 | | |
| A.D. 28 | (12) Goes to Jerusalem for Second Passover; Heals Lame Man | Jerusalem | | | | 5:1–47 | Ex. 20:10 |
| | (13) Plucked Grain Precipitates Sabbath Controversy | En Route to Galilee | 12:1–8 | 2:23–28 | 6:1–5 | | Deut. 5:14 |
| | (14) Withered Hand Healed Causes Another Sabbath Controversy | Galilee | 12:9–14 | 3:1–6 | 6:6–11 | | |
| | (15) Multitudes Healed | Sea of Galilee | 12:15–21 | 3:7–12 | 6:17–19 | | |
| | (16) Twelve Apostles Selected After a Night of Prayer | Near Capernaum | | 3:13–19 | 6:12–16 | | |
| | (17) Sermon on the Mt. | Near Capernaum | 5:1—7:29 | | 6:20–49 | | |
| | (18) Centurion's Servant Healed | Capernaum | 8:5–13 | | 7:1–10 | | Is. 49:12, 13 |
| | (19) Raises Widow's Son from Dead | Nain | | | 7:11–17 | | Job 19:25 |
| | (20) Jesus Allays John's Doubts | Galilee | 11:2–19 | | 7:18–35 | | Mal. 3:1 |
| | (21) Woes Upon the Privileged | | 11:20–30 | | | | Gen. 19:24 |
| | (22) A Sinful Woman Anoints Jesus | Simon's House, Capernaum | | | 7:36–50 | | |
| | (23) Another Tour of Galilee | Galilee | | | 8:1–3 | | |
| | (24) Jesus Accused of Blasphemy | Capernaum | 12:22–37 | 3:20–30 | 11:14–23 | | |
| | (25) Jesus' Answer to a Demand for a Sign | Capernaum | 12:38–45 | | 11:24–26, 29–36 | | |
| | (26) Mother, Brothers Seek Audience | Capernaum | 12:46–50 | 3:31–35 | 8:19–21 | | |
| | (27) Famous Parables of Sower, Seed, Tares, Mustard Seed, Leaven, Treasure, Pearl, Dragnet, Lamp Told | By Sea of Galilee | 13:1–52 | 4:1–34 | 8:4–18 | | Joel 3:13 |
| | (28) Sea Made Serene | Sea of Galilee | 8:23–27 | 4:35–41 | 8:22–25 | | |
| | (29) Gadarene Demoniac Healed | E. Shore of Galilee | 8:28–34 | 5:1–20 | 8:26–39 | | |
| | (30) Jairus' Daughter Raised and Woman with Hemorrhage Healed | | 9:18–26 | 5:21–43 | 8:40–56 | | |
| | (31) Two Blind Men's Sight Restored | | 9:27–31 | | | | |

| Date | Event | Location | Matthew | Mark | Luke | John | Related References |
|---|---|---|---|---|---|---|---|
| A.D. 28 | (32) Mute Demoniac Healed | | 9:32–34 | | | | |
| | (33) Nazareth's Second Rejection of Christ | Nazareth | 13:53–58 | 6:1–6 | | | |
| | (34) Twelve Sent Out | | 9:35—11:1 | 6:6–13 | 9:1–6 | | 1 Cor. 9:14 |
| | (35) Fearful Herod Beheads John | Galilee | 14:1–12 | 6:14–29 | 9:7–9 | | |
| Spring A.D. 29 | (36) Return of 12, Jesus Withdraws, 5000 Fed | Near Bethsaida | 14:13–21 | 6:30–44 | 9:10–17 | 6:1–14 | |
| | (37) Walks on the Water | Sea of Galilee | 14:22–33 | 6:45–52 | | 6:15–21 | |
| | (38) Sick of Gennesaret Healed | Gennesaret | 14:34–36 | 6:53–56 | | | |
| | (39) Peak of Popularity Passes in Galilee | Capernaum | | | | 6:22–71 7:1 | Is. 54:13 |
| A.D. 29 | (40) Traditions Attacked | | 15:1–20 | 7:1–23 | | | Ex. 21:17 |
| | (41) Aborted Retirement in Phoenicia: Syro-Phoenician Healed | Phoenicia | 15:21–28 | 7:24–30 | | | |
| | (42) Afflicted Healed | Decapolis | 15:29–31 | 7:31–37 | | | |
| | (43) 4000 Fed | Decapolis | 15:32–39 | 8:1–9 | | | |
| | (44) Pharisees Increase Attack | Magdala | 16:1–4 | 8:10–13 | | | |
| | (45) Disciples' Carelessness Condemned; Blind Man Healed | | 16:5–12 | 8:14–26 | | | Jer. 5:21 |
| | (46) Peter Confesses Jesus Is the Christ | Near Caesarea Philippi | 16:13–20 | 8:27–30 | 9:18–21 | | |
| | (47) Jesus Foretells His Death | Caesarea Philippi | 16:21–26 | 8:31–37 | 9:22–25 | | |
| | (48) Kingdom Promised | | 16:27, 28 | 9:1 | 9:26, 27 | | Prov. 24:12 |
| | (49) The Transfiguration | Mountain Unnamed | 17:1–13 | 9:2–13 | 9:28–36 | | Is. 42:1 |
| | (50) Epileptic Healed | Mt. of Transfiguration | 17:14–21 | 9:14–29 | 9:37–42 | | |
| | (51) Again Tells of Death, Resurrection | Galilee | 17:22, 23 | 9:30–32 | 9:43–45 | | |
| | (52) Taxes Paid | Capernaum | 17:24–27 | | | | Ex. 30:11–15 |
| | (53) Disciples Contend About Greatness; Jesus Defines; also Patience, Loyalty, Forgiveness | Capernaum | 18:1–35 | 9:33–50 | 9:46–62 | | |
| | (54) Jesus Rejects Brothers' Advice | Galilee | | | | 7:2–9 | |
| c. Sept. A.D. 29 | (55) Galilee Departure and Samaritan Rejection | | 19:1 | | 9:51–56 | 7:10 | |

## A.D. 29–30 LAST JUDEAN AND PEREAN MINISTRY OF JESUS IN 42 EVENTS

| Date | Event | Location | Matthew | Mark | Luke | John | Related References |
|---|---|---|---|---|---|---|---|
| Oct. A.D. 29 | (1) Feast of Tabernacles | Jerusalem | | | | 7:2, 11–52 | |
| | (2) Forgiveness of Adulteress | Jerusalem | | | | 7:53—8:11 | Lev. 20:10 |
| A.D. 29 | (3) Christ—the Light of the World | Jerusalem | | | | 8:12–20 | |
| | (4) Pharisees Can't Meet the Prophecy Thus Try to Destroy the Prophet | Jerusalem—Temple | | | | 8:12–59 | Is. 6:9 |
| | (5) Man Born Blind Healed; Following Consequences | Jerusalem | | | | 9:1–41 | |
| | (6) Parable of the Good Shepherd | Jerusalem | | | | 10:1–21 | |
| | (7) The Service of the Seventy | Probably Judea | | | 10:1–24 | | |
| | (8) Lawyer Hears the Story of the Good Samaritan | Judea (?) | | | 10:25–37 | | |
| | (9) The Hospitality of Martha and Mary | Bethany | | | 10:38–42 | | |
| | (10) Another Lesson on Prayer | Judea (?) | | | 11:1–13 | | |

| Date | Event | Location | Matthew | Mark | Luke | John | Related References |
|---|---|---|---|---|---|---|---|
| A.D. 29 | (11) Accused of Connection with Beelzebub | | | | 11:14–36 | | |
| | (12) Judgment Against Lawyers and Pharisees | | | | 11:37–54 | | Mic. 6:8 |
| | (13) Jesus Deals with Hypocrisy, Covetousness, Worry, and Alertness | | | | 12:1–59 | | Mic. 7:6 |
| | (14) Repent or Perish | | | | 13:1–5 | | |
| | (15) Barren Fig Tree | | | | 13:6–9 | | |
| | (16) Crippled Woman Healed on Sabbath | | | | 13:10–17 | | Deut. 5:12–15 |
| | (17) Parables of Mustard Seed and Leaven | Probably Perea | | | 13:18–21 | | |
| Winter A.D. 29 | (18) Feast of Dedication | Jerusalem | | | | 10:22–39 | Ps. 82:6 |
| | (19) Withdrawal Beyond Jordan | | | | | 10:40–42 | |
| | (20) Begins Teaching Return to Jerusalem with Special Words About Herod | Perea | | | 13:22–35 | | Ps. 6:8 |
| | (21) Meal with a Pharisee Ruler Occasions Healing Man with Dropsy; Parables of Ox, Best Places, and Great Supper | | | | 14:1–24 | | |
| | (22) Demands of Discipleship | Perea | | | 14:25–35 | | |
| | (23) Parables of Lost Sheep, Coin, Son | | | | 15:1–32 | | 1 Pet. 2:25 |
| | (24) Parables of Unjust Steward, Rich Man and Lazarus | | | | 16:1–31 | | |
| | (25) Lessons on Service, Faith, Influence | | | | 17:1–10 | | |
| | (26) Resurrection of Lazarus | Perea to Bethany | | | | 11:1–44 | |
| | (27) Reaction to It: Withdrawal of Jesus | | | | | 11:45–54 | |
| A.D. 30 | (28) Begins Last Journey to Jerusalem via Samaria & Galilee | Samaria, Galilee | | | 17:11 | | |
| | (29) Heals Ten Lepers | | | | 17:12–19 | | Lev. 13:45, 46 |
| | (30) Lessons on the Coming Kingdom | | | | 17:20–37 | | Gen. 6—7 |
| | (31) Parables: Persistent Widow, Pharisee and Tax Collector | | | | 18:1–14 | | |
| | (32) Doctrine on Divorce | | 19:1–12 | 10:1–12 | | | Deut. 24:1–4 Gen. 2:23–25 |
| | (33) Jesus Blesses Children: Objections | Perea | 19:13–15 | 10:13–16 | 18:15–17 | | Ps. 131:2 |
| | (34) Rich Young Ruler | Perea | 19:16–30 | 10:17–31 | 18:18–30 | | Ex. 20:1–17 |
| | (35) Laborers of the 11th Hour | | 20:1–16 | | | | |
| | (36) Foretells Death and Resurrection | Near Jordan | 20:17–19 | 10:32–34 | 18:31–34 | | Ps. 22 |
| | (37) Ambition of James and John | | 20:20–28 | 10:35–45 | | | |
| | (38) Blind Bartimaeus Healed | Jericho | | 10:46–52 | 18:35–43 | | |
| | (39) Interview with Zacchaeus | Jericho | | | 19:1–10 | | |
| | (40) Parable: the Minas | Jericho | | | 19:11–27 | | |
| | (41) Returns to Home of Mary and Martha | Bethany | | | | 11:55—12:1 | |
| | (42) Plot to Kill Lazarus | Bethany | | | | 12:9–11 | |
| Spring A.D. 30 | **JESUS' FINAL WEEK OF WORK AT JERUSALEM IN 41 EVENTS** | | | | | | |
| Sunday | (1) Triumphal Entry | Bethany, Jerusalem, Bethany | 21:1–9 | 11:1–11 | 19:28–44 | 12:12–19 | Zech. 9:9 |

| Date | Event | Location | Matthew | Mark | Luke | John | Related References |
|---|---|---|---|---|---|---|---|
| **Monday** | (2) Fig Tree Cursed and Temple Cleansed | Bethany to Jerusalem | 21:10–19 | 11:12–18 | 19:45–48 | | Jer. 7:11 |
| | (3) The Attraction of Sacrifice | Jerusalem | | | | 12:20–50 | Is. 6:10 |
| **Tuesday** | (4) Withered Fig Tree Testifies | Bethany to Jerusalem | 21:20–22 | 11:19–26 | | | |
| | (5) Sanhedrin Challenges Jesus. Answered by Parables: Two Sons, Wicked Vinedressers and Marriage Feast | Jerusalem | 21:23—22:14 | 11:27—12:12 | 20:1–19 | | Is. 5:1, 2 |
| | (6) Tribute to Caesar | Jerusalem | 22:15–22 | 12:13–17 | 20:20–26 | | |
| | (7) Sadducees Question the Resurrection | Jerusalem | 22:23–33 | 12:18–27 | 20:27–40 | | Ex. 3:6 |
| | (8) Pharisees Question Commandments | Jerusalem | 22:34–40 | 12:28–34 | | | |
| | (9) Jesus and David | Jerusalem | 22:41–46 | 12:35–37 | 20:41–44 | | Ps. 110:1 |
| | (10) Jesus' Last Sermon | Jerusalem | 23:1–39 | 12:38–40 | 20:45–47 | | |
| | (11) Widow's Mite | Jerusalem | | 12:41–44 | 21:1–4 | | Lev. 27:30 |
| | (12) Jesus Tells of the Future | Mt. Olives | 24:1–51 | 13:1–37 | 21:5–36 | | Dan. 12:1 |
| | (13) Parables: Ten Virgins, Talents. The Day of Judgment | Mt. Olives | 25:1–46 | | | | Zech. 14:5 |
| | (14) Jesus Tells Date of Crucifixion | | 26:1–5 | 14:1, 2 | 22:1, 2 | | |
| | (15) Anointing by Mary at Simon's Feast | Bethany | 26:6–13 | 14:3–9 | | 12:2–8 | |
| | (16) Judas Contracts the Betrayal | | 26:14–16 | 14:10, 11 | 22:3–6 | | Zech. 11:12 |
| **Thursday** | (17) Preparation for the Passover | Jerusalem | 26:17–19 | 14:12–16 | 22:7–13 | | Ex. 12:14–28 |
| **Thursday P.M.** | (18) Passover Eaten, Jealousy Rebuked | Jerusalem | 26:20 | 14:17 | 22:14–16, 24–30 | | |
| | (19) Feet Washed | Upper Room | | | | 13:1–20 | |
| | (20) Judas Revealed, Defects | Upper Room | 26:21–25 | 14:18–21 | 22:21–23 | 13:21–30 | Ps. 41:9 |
| | (21) Jesus Warns About Further Desertion; Cries of Loyalty | Upper Room | 26:31–35 | 14:27–31 | 22:31–38 | 13:31–38 | Zech. 13:7 |
| | (22) Institution of the Lord's Supper | Upper Room | 26:26–29 | 14:22–25 | 22:17–20 | | 1 Cor. 11:23–34 |
| | (23) Last Speech to the Apostles and Intercessory Prayer | Jerusalem | | | | 14:1—17:26 | Ps. 35:19 |
| **Thursday-Friday** | (24) The Grief of Gethsemane | Mt. Olives | 26:30, 36–46 | 14:26, 32–42 | 22:39–46 | 18:1 | Ps. 42:6 |
| **Friday** | (25) Betrayal, Arrest, Desertion | Gethsemane | 26:47–56 | 14:43–52 | 22:47–53 | 18:2–12 | |
| | (26) First Examined by Annas | Jerusalem | | | | 18:12–14, 19–23 | |
| | (27) Trial by Caiaphas and Council; Following Indignities | Jerusalem | 26:57, 59–68 | 14:53, 55–65 | 22:54, 63–65 | 18:24 | Lev. 24:16 |
| | (28) Peter's Triple Denial | Jerusalem | 26:58, 69–75 | 14:54, 66–72 | 22:54–62 | 18:15–18, 25–27 | |
| | (29) Condemnation by the Council | Jerusalem | 27:1 | 15:1 | 22:66–71 | | Ps. 110:1 |
| | (30) Suicide of Judas | Jerusalem | 27:3–10 | | | | Acts 1:18, 19 |
| | (31) First Appearance Before Pilate | Jerusalem | 27:2, 11–14 | 15:1–5 | 23:1–7 | 18:28–38 | |
| | (32) Jesus Before Herod | Jerusalem | | | 23:6–12 | | |
| | (33) Second Appearance Before Pilate | Jerusalem | 27:15–26 | 15:6–15 | 23:13–25 | 18:39—19:16 | Deut. 21:6–9 |
| | (34) Mockery by Roman Soldiers | Jerusalem | 27:27–30 | 15:16–19 | | | |
| | (35) Led to Golgotha | Jerusalem | 27:31–34 | 15:20–23 | 23:26–33 | 19:16, 17 | Ps. 69:21 |
| | (36) 6 Events of First 3 Hours on Cross | Calvary | 27:35–44 | 15:24–32 | 23:33–43 | 19:18–27 | Ps. 22:18 |
| | (37) Last 3 Hours on Cross | Calvary | 27:45–50 | 15:33–37 | 23:44–46 | 19:28–30 | Ps. 22:1 |
| | (38) Events Attending Jesus' Death | | 27:51–56 | 15:38–41 | 23:45, 47–49 | | |
| | (39) Burial of Jesus | Jerusalem | 27:57–60 | 15:42–46 | 23:50–54 | 19:31–37 | Ex. 12:46 |
| **Friday-Saturday** | (40) Tomb Sealed | Jerusalem | 27:61–66 | | 23:55, 56 | | Ex. 20:8–11 |
| | (41) Women Watch | Jerusalem | | 15:47 | | | |

| Date | Event | Location | Matthew | Mark | Luke | John | Related References |
|---|---|---|---|---|---|---|---|
| **A.D. 30** | **THE RESURRECTION THROUGH THE ASCENSION IN 12 EVENTS** | | | | | | |
| **Dawn of First Day (Sunday, "Lord's Day")** | (1) Women Visit the Tomb | Near Jerusalem | 28:1–10 | 16:1–8 | 24:1–11 | | |
| | (2) Peter and John See the Empty Tomb | | | | 24:12 | 20:1–10 | |
| | (3) Jesus' Appearance to Mary Magdalene | Jerusalem | | 16:9–11 | | 20:11–18 | |
| | (4) Jesus' Appearance to the Other Women | Jerusalem | 28:9, 10 | | | | |
| | (5) Guards' Report of the Resurrection | | 28:11–15 | | | | |
| **Sunday Afternoon** | (6) Jesus' Appearance to Two Disciples on Way to Emmaus | | | 16:12, 13 | 24:13–35 | | 1 Cor. 15:5 |
| **Late Sunday** | (7) Jesus' Appearance to Ten Disciples Without Thomas | Jerusalem | | 16:14 | 24:36–43 | 20:19–25 | |
| **One Week Later** | (8) Appearance to Disciples with Thomas | Jerusalem | | | | 20:26–31 | |
| **During 40 Days until Ascension** | (9) Jesus' Appearance to Seven Disciples by Sea of Galilee | Galilee | | | | 21:1–25 | |
| | (10) Appearance to 500 | Mt. in Galilee | | | | | 1 Cor. 15:6 |
| | (11) Great Commission | | 28:16–20 | 16:15–18 | 24:44–49 | | |
| | (12) The Ascension | Mt. Olivet | | 16:19, 20 | 24:50–53 | | Acts 1:4–11 |

# *The Jewish Calendar*

The Jews used two kinds of calendars:
*Civil Calendar*—official calendar of kings, childbirth, and contracts.
*Sacred Calendar*—from which festivals were computed.

| NAMES OF MONTHS | CORRESPONDS WITH | NO. OF DAYS | MONTH OF CIVIL YEAR | MONTH OF SACRED YEAR |
|---|---|---|---|---|
| **TISHRI** | Sept.–Oct. | 30 days | 1st | 7th |
| **HESHVAN** | Oct.–Nov. | 29 or 30 | 2nd | 8th |
| **CHISLEV** | Nov.–Dec. | 29 or 30 | 3rd | 9th |
| **TEBETH** | Dec.–Jan. | 29 | 4th | 10th |
| **SHEBAT** | Jan.–Feb. | 30 | 5th | 11th |
| **ADAR** | Feb.–Mar. | 29 or 30 | 6th | 12th |
| **NISAN** | Mar.–Apr. | 30 | 7th | 1st |
| **IYAR** | Apr.–May | 29 | 8th | 2nd |
| **SIVAN** | May–June | 30 | 9th | 3rd |
| **TAMMUZ** | June–July | 29 | 10th | 4th |
| **AB** | July–Aug. | 30 | 11th | 5th |
| ***ELUL** | Aug.–Sept. | 29 | 12th | 6th |

The Jewish day was from sunset to sunset, in 8 equal parts:

**FIRST WATCH** ..... SUNSET TO 9 P.M.
**SECOND WATCH** ... 9 P.M. TO MIDNIGHT
**THIRD WATCH** ..... MIDNIGHT TO 3 A.M.
**FOURTH WATCH** ... 3 A.M. TO SUNRISE

---

**FIRST WATCH** ..... SUNRISE TO 9 A.M.
**SECOND WATCH** ... 9 A.M. TO NOON
**THIRD WATCH** ..... NOON TO 3 P.M.
**FOURTH WATCH** ... 3 P.M. TO SUNSET

*Hebrew months were alternately 30 and 29 days long. Their year, shorter than ours, had 354 days. Therefore, about every 3 years (7 times in 19 years) an extra 29-day-month, VEADAR, was added between ADAR and NISAN.

# THE CHRISTIAN'S GUIDE TO THE NEW LIFE

*The Christian's Guide to the New Life* offers a complete doctrinal overview of the Bible to assist you in a practical, simplified way to study your Bible. The six main areas of study, described below, are further amplified; these systematically cover all the important areas of biblical theology. This unique study feature places before the Bible student an exegesis of Scripture with hundreds of scriptural references.

For the student just beginning Bible study, this guide covers in a fundamental way how to become a Christian, then steps the believer through the Christian life. The easy-to-use references and cross-references lead the reader toward a comprehensive, practical knowledge of God's Word.

The general organization of *The Christian's Guide to the New Life* includes six main areas of study:

Knowing God's Word
Understanding God's Being
Beginning the New Life
Growing in the New Life
Facing Problems in the New Life
Recognizing God's Institutions

These areas of study are subdivided into twenty-eight individual guides with appropriate Bible references. All the material is organized in a simple format to assist you in more easily understanding the Bible, the inspired Word of God. Each includes several discussions of Bible texts. For example, within the main area of study **Knowing God's Word** is Christian's Guide (1) **How God's Word Came to Us.** There are three discussions concerning how God's Word came to us: **Revelation of God's Word; Inspiration of God's Word;** and **Illumination of God's Word.**

*The Christian's Guide to the New Life* can be used in three easy ways:

- Monthly study—once a day for twenty-eight days study one of the Christian's Guides. Read each of the discussions and look up the listed references.
- Daily study—once a day for 105 days study a single discussion in the Bible text. Read the complete discussion and look up the listed references.
- Topical study—study individual Christian's Guides and discussions as the need arises.

You are now ready to begin using *The Christian's Guide to the New Life.* For each of the six main areas of study a synopsis is provided.

## Knowing God's Word

*Synopsis*

Christians should know the Bible for many reasons, but the primary one is because God is its author. All Bible students know that God is Creator (Gen. 1:1), Redeemer (Is. 60:16), and Judge (Gen. 18:25), but do we think of Him as the author of the Bible? Human writers feel it vital that we read their books; it is much more important that we read God's book, the Bible.

About fourteen centuries before Christ, our Bible had its beginnings in the Sinai desert. In this arid place God spoke to Moses, who had once been a prince in Egypt and was nearly 120 years old at the time. At the Lord's command, Moses began writing Scripture's first five books, Genesis through Deuteronomy. More than 1,500 years later, the divine manuscript was completed on a lonely, windswept island in the Mediterranean Sea by a former fisherman, John the apostle. From Genesis through Revelation, the final biblical book, there are sixty-six divinely inspired books. Over the centuries, approximately forty men and women—representing varied backgrounds and writing styles—served as channels for God's Word. Yet in spite of these variations in time and talent, the completed work displays a marvelous historical, theological, geographical, topical, and biographical unity.

The Bible's practical benefits for us may well be summarized under two headings: knowing and growing. The Bible proclaims the good news of the gospel that we might know God; it explains the will of God that all of us may grow spiritually before Him.

Scripture also reveals our place within God's program and answers crucial questions pertaining to our origin, purpose, and destiny. Because God has revealed His unchanging truths, the Christian faith provides real answers and guidance to every generation. Although we cannot grasp how individual events fit into God's program (Eccl. 11:5), we can understand God's basic plan in order to come to know and serve Him. Few joys can compare with realizing our places in God's program and working to fulfill our destinies.

### How God's Word Came to Us

**Deuteronomy 29:29. Revelation of God's Word—** Revelation may be defined as that process by which God imparted to man truths which he otherwise could not know. The details of creation in Genesis 1 and 2 are an example of revelation. As man was not created until the sixth day, we could not have possibly known the events occurring prior to this until God gave the facts to Moses.

We know God spoke to the human authors of our Bible; but just how did He speak? Was it in Hebrew? Greek? Angelic language? He spoke to them in their own language. God's call to young Samuel in the temple (1 Sam. 3:1–10) proves this, for the boy at first mistook God's voice for that of the aged priest Eli. Sometimes God spoke through angels: Gabriel was sent from heaven to tell Mary she would give birth to the Messiah

(Luke 1:26–37). On other occasions the Lord spoke directly to a man, as He did to Noah concerning the Great Flood (Gen. 6:13–21).

One of God's methods of communication in Scripture is to reveal His message through dreams and visions: The wise men (Matt. 2:12) were warned in a dream not to return to Herod, while Peter was later instructed in a vision to minister to Cornelius (Acts 10:10–16). God has communicated in many different ways. He revealed Himself to Moses from a burning bush (Ex. 3:4) and to Moses, Aaron, and Miriam out of a cloud (Num. 12:4, 5).

One of the most important ways that divine truths were given in the Old Testament was through the Angel of the Lord. Most Bible students perceive this heavenly messenger to be the preincarnate Christ Himself. For example, it is the Angel of the Lord who reassured Joshua on the eve of a battle (Josh. 5:13–15).

**Isaiah 59:21. Inspiration of God's Word**—The word *inspiration* is found but once in the New Testament. This occurs in 2 Timothy 3:16, where Paul says "All Scripture *is* given by inspiration of God," literally "God-breathed." Divine inspiration logically follows divine revelation. In revelation God speaks to man's ear while by inspiration He guides the pen to ensure that the imparted message is correctly written down.

There are several ideas about the process of inspiration. One is called the natural theory. This says that the Bible authors were inspired in the same sense that William Shakespeare was inspired. Another theory, called the content theory, suggests that God merely gave the writer the main content or idea, allowing him to choose his own words to express that concept. In contrast, Jesus Himself said that the very letters of the words were also chosen by God (Matt. 5:18). This position is referred to as the plenary-verbal view, which says that all (plenary) the very words (verbal) of the Bible are inspired by God. Jesus once told the devil that the Christian is to live by each of these inspired words (Matt. 4:4). The Bible authors understood that their writings were being guided by the Spirit of God, even as they wrote them. Peter said this was true of the Old Testament authors (2 Pet. 1:20, 21). He then stated that his own letters (1 and 2 Pet.) were inspired by God (2 Pet. 3:1, 2). Finally, he pointed out that this was also true concerning Paul's writings (2 Pet. 3:15, 16).

One final thing should be said about inspiration. Plenary-verbal inspiration does not guarantee the inspiration of any translation, but only of the original Hebrew and Greek manuscripts.

**Proverbs 6:23. Illumination of God's Word**—Illumination is the last of three important steps taken by God in communicating His Word to us. The first step was revelation which occurred when God spoke to the Bible authors. The second step was inspiration, that process whereby God guided them in correctly writing or uttering His message. But now a third step is needed to provide understanding for men and women as they hear God's revealed and inspired message. This vital step is illumination, that divine process whereby God causes the written revelation to be understood by the human heart.

This third step is needed because unsaved man is blinded both by his fallen, fleshly nature (1 Cor. 2:14) and by Satan himself (2 Cor. 4:3, 4).

The Person behind this illumination is the Holy Spirit. Just prior to His crucifixion, Christ promised to send the Holy Spirit, who would illuminate both unsaved people (John 16:8–11) and Christians (John 14:26; 16:13, 14).

An important example of the Holy Spirit's using God's Word to illuminate sinners is seen at Pentecost, where three thousand people are saved after hearing Simon Peter preach about Christ and the Cross (Acts 2:36–41).

But Christians also need this illumination to help them fully grasp the marvelous message in God's Word. Paul tells us that the Holy Spirit will show these tremendous truths to us as we read the Scriptures (1 Cor. 2:10; 2 Cor. 4:6).

## What God's Word Does

**Nehemiah 8:9. God's Word Convicts**—One of the great proofs that the Bible is really God's inspired Word is its unique ability to convict men and women of their sins. Let us consider but a few Old and New Testament examples which demonstrate the lifesaving power of the Scriptures.

*Old Testament examples:*

a. Josiah, a young and godly Judean king who ruled the Lord's people more than six centuries before Christ, succeeds a wicked ruler who hated righteousness. At the beginning of Josiah's rule a copy of God's Word is found in the temple. When it is read to the king, both he and his people are convicted of their sins in not keeping God's law. A great revival takes place (2 Chr. 34:18–21).
b. Nehemiah returns to help the returning Jews rebuild the gates in the Jerusalem wall. This great wall builder thinks the Word of God to be so important that he assembles the people and has the Scriptures read to them for three hours per day. This soon causes them to confess their sins (Neh. 9:3).

*New Testament examples:* Before Jesus left this earth He promised that the Holy Spirit would soon come upon the apostles. "And when He has come, He will convict the world of sin, and of righteousness, and of judgment" (John 16:8). There are many instances in the New Testament where we see the Holy Spirit using God's Word to convict people of their sin. At Pentecost Peter uses the Scriptures to rebuke Israel for crucifying its Messiah. This sermon results in three thousand souls being convicted and accepting Christ (Acts 2:37, 41).

**Psalm 17:4. God's Word Corrects**—Many symbols for God's Word can be found in the Bible itself. It can be thought of as a mirror (James 1:23–25), a seed (1 Pet. 1:23), a lamp (Ps. 119:105), a sword (Eph. 6:17), and even as food (Heb. 5:12–14). But the Bible also serves as a measuring rod or ruler. Many teachers have used wooden rulers in their classes not only to give the right measurement but, on occasion, to correct a misbehaving pupil. God's Word likewise can do both of these things. It should be used as a standard against which to measure our beliefs. What about certain religious groups that claim Christ was not God, or that the Bible is filled with silly tales? Immediately we can reject such claims by using our divine written ruler to discover that such arguments simply do not measure up.

Sometimes our heavenly teacher uses His written ruler to correct us when we are in the wrong. Israel's great king David once experienced this. "You have dealt well with Your servant, O LORD, according to Your word. . . . Before I was afflicted I went astray, but now I keep Your word" (Ps. 119:65, 67).

At times God's Word can correct believers when they are in honest and unintentional error. Aquila and Priscilla, a godly Christian couple, use the Scriptures to help a powerful young preacher named Apollos (Acts 18:24–26). Paul does the same thing for some former disciples of John the Baptist he meets in the city of Ephesus (Acts 19:1–7).

**Psalm 119:9. God's Word Cleanses**—One of the pieces of furniture in the Old Testament tabernacle was called the bronze laver (Ex. 38:8). It consisted of a huge upright bronze bowl filled with water, resting upon a pedestal. The priests would often stop at this laver and wash. The Word of God may be thought of in terms of that laver, for it too has the power to cleanse. The Old Testament laver could only remove the physical dirt from human hands, but the Scriptures can take away our moral filth (1 Pet. 1:22).

"If we confess our sins, He is faithful and just to forgive us *our* sins and to cleanse us from all unrighteousness" (1 John 1:9). What areas of my life can the Bible cleanse?

It can cleanse me from wrong thoughts. Sometimes we are tempted to think critically of others; God's Word can prevent this (Ps. 1:2). On other occasions fearful thoughts may race through our minds; the Scriptures will prevent this also (Josh. 1:8). In fact, the Bible will establish our total thought-life if we but allow it to do so (Phil. 4:8, 9; 2 Pet. 1:5–10).

It can cleanse me from wrong words. Of all the Bible authors, James seems to be God's expert on the sins of the human tongue. In the first chapter of his book, he deals with this very thing and shows the absolute necessity of dependence upon the Scriptures to keep our words true (James 1:22–26). See also Psalm 119:172.

It can cleanse me from wrong actions. Jesus promised us this would be the case: "You are already clean because of the word which I have spoken to you" (John 15:3).

Finally, God's Word will keep us from wrong thoughts, words, and actions; or else wrong thoughts, words, and actions will keep us from God's Word.

**John 8:31. God's Word Confirms**—To confirm means to fully establish a truth or fact. The Bible should be used to confirm the truth in our own hearts.

a. It confirms our salvation. Often Christians are troubled with doubts about their conversion experience. Did God really save them when they asked Him to do so? Are they still saved today? A number of verses may be used to confirm our salvation. One of the strongest is Jesus' own words in the gospel of John: "Most assuredly, I say to you, he who hears My word and believes in Him who sent Me has everlasting life, and shall not come into judgment, but has passed from death into life" (John 5:24). Compare John 3:16; 6:27, 35, 37, 40; 10:27–29; Romans 8:1.
b. It confirms the hand of God in all of life's bitter disappointments. Undoubtedly a most important verse of reassurance and comfort in the hour of great need is Romans 8:28: "And we know that all things work together for good to those who love God, to those who are the called according to *His* purpose."
c. It confirms our forgiveness when we sin. Sometimes believers carry with them an unnecessary burden of guilt over past sins and failures. Even though these have been confessed, they have difficulty believing God has truly forgiven and cleansed them. But time and again the Bible assures us that all confessed sin is instantly and eternally forgiven (Ps. 32:5, 103:12; Is. 38:17).

**Proverbs 22:21. God's Word Equips**—In a general sense it can be said that the Bible was written to convict sinners of sin and to equip believers for service.

a. It equips for evangelism. Philip the evangelist uses the fifty-third chapter of Isaiah to point the Ethiopian eunuch to Christ (Acts 8:26–35).
b. It equips for counseling others. In his two letters to Timothy, Paul constantly urges this young man to preach the Word of God (1 Tim. 1:3, 18; 4:13–15; 2 Tim. 2:1, 2, 15). "If you instruct the brethren in these things, you will be a good minister of Jesus Christ, nourished in the words of faith and of the good doctrine which you have carefully followed" (1 Tim. 4:6).
c. It equips one to use spiritual gifts that come from God. A spiritual gift is an ability given by the Holy Spirit to the believer for the purpose of edifying the church and glorifying God. In Ephesians 1:17–19 and 4:7, 11–14 Paul says a knowledge of God's Word will provide us with the maturity we need to use our gifts in the most effective way.
d. It equips us for doing battle with Satan. In Ephesians 6:10–17 Paul likens the believers' armor to that used by Roman foot soldiers. In this comparison the Word of God is likened to the soldier's sword (Eph. 6:17).

## How We Benefit from God's Word

**Daniel 11:32. We Know God Through His Word**—One of the most vital teachings of Scripture is that God can be known. The highest knowledge to which men and women can attain is a personal knowledge of God (Jer. 9:24). People do not naturally possess this knowledge (Rom. 3:10, 11), even though they know that He exists (Ps. 14:1; Rom. 1:19, 20). Knowing that God exists is not the same as knowing God personally, just as knowing about the president does not mean that you necessarily know him personally. This knowledge of God is crucial, however, since to know God personally is to be saved and have eternal life (John 17:3). People should rejoice in the fact that God earnestly wants them to attain this knowledge. That is why He has spoken to us in His Word, revealing Himself and disclosing the means by which we may know Him.

While God surely can be known, there is always more

to be learned about Him. There are many Scriptures which teach that our knowledge of God is partial. It is said to be "too wonderful" (Ps. 139:6), "unsearchable" (Ps. 145:3; Rom. 11:33), and "infinite" (Ps. 147:5). Since our knowledge of God is incomplete, we must increase it through spiritual growth. Paul, for example, prays to know God better (Phil. 3:10). We are even commanded to grow in the knowledge of Christ (2 Pet. 3:18). The development of one's intimate knowledge of God constitutes one of the greatest delights of the Christian life.

The Bible also reveals that God cannot be known personally apart from His Word. It contains the gospel which must be believed (Eph. 1:13), and the gospel brings forth saving faith in itself (Rom. 10:17). The gospel can therefore be called "the power of God to salvation" (Rom. 1:16). The part that the Scriptures and the gospel contained within them play in bringing men to know God is described in three important illustrations: the gospel is the agent of the new birth (James 1:18), that is, it is like the implanted seed without which the conception of new life cannot occur; it is also a cleansing agent through which God gives the believing sinner a spiritual bath that results in salvation (Eph. 5:26); the Scriptures are like an educator bringing the wisdom that leads to salvation (2 Tim. 3:15).

**Psalm 40:8. We Know God's Will Through His Word**—Knowing the will of God must not be thought of merely as finding a certain vocation in life. That aspect represents only a small part of God's will. Rather, the will of God is for everyone to live in conformity to His revealed will in His Word.

a. First of all, and most important, the will of God means believing Christ (John 6:40). If we do not take this first step in doing God's will, we will not be saved from judgment (Matt. 7:21; 12:50); if we do, we will live forever (1 John 2:17).
b. Second, clear statements of Scripture teach that God's will for every Christian includes sanctification (1 Thess. 4:13), giving thanks to God (1 Thess. 5:18), doing good (1 Pet. 2:15), and suffering for doing the right thing (1 Pet. 3:17).
c. Third, the Bible is God's will and must be applied to our lives (Deut. 29:29). This fact involves commands to be obeyed, principles to be followed, prohibitions of things to be avoided, and living examples to be imitated or shunned. An attitude of delightful desire should fill all attempts to do God's will (Ps. 40:8). God takes great joy in those who cheerfully do His will.

Although the Bible is a complete revelation of God's will, there are always decisions we must make that are not covered by specific statements of Scripture. In order to know God's will in such instances we must be in fellowship with the Lord (1 John 1:6, 7), seek principles from the Word (1 Cor. 10:6), obtain advice from godly counselors (Prov. 11:14; 15:22; 24:6), use common sense, and remember that God works through our own minds and desires to do His will (Phil. 2:13). When none of these principles seem to work, we must simply make the best possible decision, realizing that God will shut the door if it is not His will. Paul, for example, planned to go and see the Roman Christians, although not knowing if God would actually permit it in His will (Rom. 15:22–32). In most cases, however, the believer who thoroughly searches the Word will find the basis for an intelligent decision.

## What God's Word Tells Us About God's Program

**Deuteronomy 32:7. God's Work in the Past**—The Bible's revelation of God's work in the past provides an informative and exciting panorama of centuries of divine activity toward man.

First, it gives man an *education* in truths unknowable apart from divine revelation. For example, the creation of man described in Genesis 1 and 2 answers man's most basic questions: "Who am I?" and "Where did I come from?" Only, God Himself could disclose these facts.

Second, the Bible sets forth a mass of historical *evidence* for the truthfulness of the Christian faith. The most outstanding of these evidences are fulfilled prophecy, the miracles of Christ, and Christ's death and resurrection. The believer's faith is thus grounded in historical events and is far removed from what some have called "a leap into the dark."

Third, the Bible records *examples* to help present-day Christians. Various failures of Israel and the resulting judgments of God are often cited in the New Testament as things to avoid, for example, their idolatry and grumbling in the wilderness (1 Cor. 10:11), and their unbelief at Kadesh (Heb. 4:11). Paul is said to be a living example for believers to follow (1 Cor. 4:16; 11:1), as is Jesus' humility in the midst of suffering (1 Pet. 2:21).

Fourth, the Bible provides *encouragement* for Christians in their life and witness. If God could use an adulterer and murderer like David, then God can certainly use a struggling Christian today if he possesses David's devotion to the Lord. Likewise, if God saved Saul of Tarsus, the chief enemy of the early church (Acts 9:1–31), then surely He can save the people with whom Christians daily share their faith.

**Psalm 139:14. God's Work in Our Lives**—All people possess an inward desire that their work should have meaning and permanence (Ps. 90:16, 17). If man's work is not to be lost in the vastness of eternity, however, it must conform to the work God has designed for man. This work for the present day can be known only from God's Word.

According to the Word of God, the initial work of God is for us to believe in Jesus Christ (John 6:29; Rom. 6:17, 18). Apart from entering into this vital relationship with God, man cannot even begin to work for God. After coming to know Christ, the new Christian discovers God's program for the present from the Scriptures. It is, first of all, His work in the Christian himself. Regeneration is only the beginning of God's work in the believer. It actually introduces a process of becoming like Christ which God promises ultimately to bring to perfection (Phil. 1:6). The Christian's cheerful obedience to God's will as revealed in His Word helps speed this work along.

Second, no Christian can overlook God's work in the world. Jesus' command to spread the good news of the gospel to all men appears near the end of all four Gospels and at the beginning of the Book of Acts. God's method is that men proclaim the gospel and that the Holy Spirit convict (John 16:8–11).

Finally, God's work is in and through the church, the organism ordained by Christ for this age (Matt. 16:18). God works in the church through the Spirit and through spiritually gifted people to strengthen and bless it (Eph. 4:11–13).

## What God's Word Tells Us About God's Covenants

**Genesis 2:15–17. The Edenic Covenant**—The covenant in Eden is the first of the general or universal covenants. In it, Adam is charged to: (1) populate the earth (Gen. 1:28); (2) subdue the earth (Gen. 1:28); (3) exercise dominion over the animal creation (Gen. 1:28); (4) care for the Garden of Eden and enjoy its fruit (Gen 1:29; 2:15); and (5) refrain from eating the fruit of the tree of the knowledge of good and evil, under penalty of death (Gen. 2:16, 17). The Edenic Covenant was terminated by man's disobedience, when Adam and Eve ate of the fruit of the tree of the knowledge of good and evil, resulting in their spiritual and physical deaths. This failure necessitated the establishment of the covenant with Adam (Gen. 3:14–21).

**Genesis 3:14–21. The Adamic Covenant**—The covenant with Adam is the second general or universal covenant. It could be called the covenant with mankind, for it sets forth the conditions which will hold sway until the curse of sin is lifted (Is. 11:6–10; Rom. 8:18–23). According to the covenant, the conditions which will prevail are:

a. The serpent, the tool used by Satan to effect the fall of man, is cursed. The curse affects not only the instrument, the serpent, but also the indwelling energizer, Satan. Great physical changes took place in the serpent. Apparently it was upright; now it will go on its belly (v. 14). It was the most desirable animal of the animal creation; now it is the most loathsome. The sight or thought of a snake should be an effective reminder of the devastating effects of sin.
b. Satan is judged—he will enjoy limited success ("you shall bruise His heel," v. 15), but ultimately he will be judged ("He shall bruise your head," v. 15).
c. The first prophecy of the coming of the Messiah is given (v. 15).
d. There will be a multiplication of conception, necessitated by the introduction of death into the human race (v. 16).
e. There will be pain in childbirth (v. 16).
f. The woman is made subject to her husband (v. 16).
g. The ground is cursed and will bring forth weeds among the food which man must eat for his existence (vv. 17–19).
h. Physical change takes place in man; he will perspire when he works. He will have to work all his life long (v. 19).
i. In sinning, man dies spiritually, and ultimately will die physically. His flesh will decay until it returns to dust from which it was originally taken (v. 19).

**Genesis 9:1–19. The Noahic Covenant**—The covenant with Noah is the third general or universal covenant. Noah has just passed through the universal flood in which all the world's population had been wiped out. Only Noah, his wife, his three sons, and their wives—eight people—constitute the world's population. Noah might have thought that the things provided by the covenant with Adam had now been changed. However, God gives the Noahic Covenant so that Noah and all the human race to follow might know that the provisions made in the Adamic Covenant remain in effect with one notable addition: the principle of human government which includes the responsibility of suppressing the outbreak of sin and violence, so that it will not be necessary to destroy the earth again by a flood. The provisions of the covenant are:

a. The responsibility to populate the earth is reaffirmed (v. 1).
b. The subjection of the animal kingdom to man is reaffirmed (v. 2).
c. Man is permitted to eat the flesh of animals. However, he is to refrain from eating blood (vv. 3, 4).
d. The sacredness of human life is established. Whatever sheds man's blood, whether man or beast, must be put to death (vv. 5, 6).
e. This covenant is confirmed to Noah, all mankind, and every living creature on the face of the earth (vv. 9, 10).
f. The promise is given never to destroy the earth again by a universal flood (v. 11). The next time God destroys the earth, He will do so by fire (2 Pet. 3:10).
g. The rainbow is designated as a testimony of the existence of this covenant and the promise never to destroy the earth by flood. As long as we can see the rainbow we will know that the Noahic Covenant is in existence (vv. 12–17).

**Genesis 12:1–3. The Abrahamic Covenant**—The covenant with Abraham is the first of the theocratic covenants (pertaining to the rule of God). It is unconditional, depending solely upon God who obligates Himself in grace, indicated by the unconditional declaration, "I will," to bring to pass the promised blessings. The Abrahamic Covenant is the basis of all the other theocratic covenants and provides for blessings in three areas: (1) national—"I will make you a great nation," (2) personal—"I will bless you and make your name great; and you shall be a blessing," and (3) universal—"in you all families of the earth shall be blessed." This covenant was first given in broad outline and was later confirmed to Abraham in greater detail (cf. Gen. 13:14–17; 15:1–7, 18–21; 17:1–8). The Abrahamic Covenant constitutes an important link in all that God began to do, has done throughout history, and will continue to do until the consummation of history. It is the one purpose of God for humans into which all of God's programs and works fit. The personal aspects of the Abrahamic Covenant are fourfold: (1) to be the father of a great nation, (2) to receive personal blessing, (3) to receive personal honor and reputation, and (4) to be the source of blessing to others. The universal aspects of the covenant are threefold: (1) blessings for those people and nations which bless Abraham and the nation which comes from him; (2) cursings upon those people and nations which curse Abraham and Israel; and (3) blessings upon all the families of the earth through the Messiah, who, according to the flesh, is Abraham's son and provides salvation for the entire world.

**Exodus 19:5–8. The Mosaic Covenant**—The covenant with Moses is the second of the theocratic covenants (pertaining to the rule of God) and is conditional. It is introduced by the conditional formula, "if you will indeed obey My voice . . . then you shall be a special treasure." This covenant was given to the nation Israel so that those who believed God's promise given to Abraham in the Abrahamic Covenant (Gen. 12:1–3) would know how they should conduct themselves. The Mosaic Covenant in its entirety governs three areas of their lives: (1) the commandments governed their personal lives particularly as they related to God (Ex. 20:1–26); (2) the judgments governed their social lives particularly as they related to one another (Ex. 21:1—24:11); and (3) the ordinances governed their religious lives so that the people would know how to approach God on the terms that He dictates (Ex. 24:12—31:18). The Mosaic Covenant in no way replaced or set aside the Abrahamic Covenant. Its function is clearly set forth by Paul (Gal. 3:17–19), who points out that the law, the Mosaic Covenant, came 430 years after the Abrahamic Covenant. The Mosaic Covenant was added alongside the Abrahamic Covenant so that the people of Israel would know how to conduct their lives until "the seed," the Christ, comes and makes the complete and perfect sacrifice, toward which the sacrifices of the Mosaic Covenant only point. The Mosaic Covenant was never given so that by keeping it people could be saved, but so that they might realize that they cannot do what God wants them to do even when God writes it down on tablets of stone. The law was given that man might realize that he is helpless and hopeless when left to himself, and realize that his only hope is to receive the righteousness of God by faith in Jesus (Gal. 3:22–24).

**Deuteronomy 29:10–15; 30:11–20. The Palestinian Covenant**—The covenant concerning Palestine is the third of the theocratic covenants (pertaining to the rule of God). The Palestinian Covenant has two aspects: (1) the legal aspects which are immediate and conditional (Deut. 27—29); and (2) the grace aspects which are future and unconditional (Deut. 30:1–9). The enjoyment of the immediate blessings are introduced by the conditional formula: "if you diligently obey the voice of the LORD your God . . . the LORD your God will set you high above all nations of the earth" (Deut. 28:1). Sadly, Israel did not meet the condition of obedience, and is still experiencing God's curses and punishment for their disobedience (Deut. 28:15–68). The unconditional grace aspects of the Palestinian Covenant have yet to be realized. God will regather the scattered people of Israel and establish them in the land He has promised unconditionally to give them. Deuteronomy concludes the Palestinian Covenant with a final warning and challenge for obedience (Deut. 30:1–20).

**2 Samuel 7:4–17. The Davidic Covenant**—The covenant with David is the fourth of the theocratic covenants (pertaining to the rule of God). In this covenant David is promised three things: (1) a land forever (v. 10); (2) an unending dynasty (vv. 11, 16); and (3) an everlasting kingdom (vv. 13, 16). The birth of Solomon, David's son who is to succeed him, is predicted (v. 12). His particular role is to establish the throne of the Davidic Kingdom forever (v. 13). His throne continues, though his seed is cursed in the person of Jeconiah (Coniah), who was the king under whom the nation was carried captive to Babylon. Jeremiah prophesies that no one whose genealogical descent could be traced back to David through Jeconiah and Solomon would ever sit on David's throne (Jer. 22:24–30). Joseph, the legal, but not physical, father of Jesus traces his lineage to David through Jeconiah (Matt. 1:1–17). David, however, had another son, Nathan. His line was not cursed. Mary, the physical mother of Jesus, traces her lineage back to David through Nathan (Luke 3:23–38). Notice the care and the extent to which God goes to keep His word and to preserve its truthfulness. The virgin birth was absolutely essential not only to assure the sinless character of Jesus but also to fulfill the Davidic Covenant. Jesus receives His "blood right" to David's throne through His earthly mother, Mary, and His "legal right" to David's throne through His adoptive earthly father, Joseph. The virgin birth guarantees that one of David's line will sit on David's throne and rule forever, while at the same time preserving intact the curse and restriction on the line of descent through Jeconiah.

**Jeremiah 31:31–34. The New Covenant**—The New Covenant is the fifth and last of the theocratic covenants (pertaining to the rule of God). Four provisions are made in this covenant: (1) regeneration—God will put His law in their inward parts and write it in their hearts, 31:33; (2) a national restoration—Yahweh will be their God and the nation will be His people, 31:33; (3) personal ministry of the Holy Spirit—they will all be taught individually by God, 31:34; and (4) full justification—their sins will be forgiven and completely removed, 31:34. The New Covenant is made sure by the blood that Jesus shed on Calvary's cross. That blood which guarantees to Israel its New Covenant also provides for the forgiveness of sins for the believers who comprise the church. Jesus' payment for sins is more than adequate to pay for the sins of all who will believe in Him. The New Covenant is called "new" in contrast to the covenant with Moses which is called "old" (Jer. 31:32; Heb. 8:6–13) because it actually accomplishes what the Mosaic Covenant could only point to, that is, the child of God living in a manner that is consistent with the character of God.

## Understanding God's Being

*Synopsis*

The Bible reveals the nature of God as spirit, unity, and trinity. He is a spirit—a personal, infinite being (John 4:24); He is one—one in substance or nature and incapable of being divided into separate parts (Deut. 6:4); and He is three—eternally existing in three coequal persons (Matt. 28:19). While great mystery surrounds God's nature, it is reassuring to know that our God is above us.

God's attributes are merely words we use to describe how God is and how He acts toward us. Among these attributes are love, holiness, constancy, justice, truth, eternality, omniscience (all-knowing), omnipresence (all-present), and omnipotence (all-powerful). The fact that we can grasp and understand this much about God is evidence of God's desire that all peoples may know Him.

The word *Father* is variously applied in the Bible. When God is spoken of as the Father of all men, it is as Creator; as the Father of Christ, it expresses an eternal, unique relationship; as the Father of believers, it denotes a relationship established by grace; and as Father of Israel, it means a bond established by covenant. However Father is used, it is a deliberately chosen word to communicate to men one of the primary ways God wants us to conceive of Him.

The title *Son of God* is one which Jesus never directly applied to Himself, but when others applied it to Him Jesus willingly accepted it as a claim to His own deity (John 10:24–38). Jesus often referred to Himself as "the Son," which was certainly an abbreviation for the Son of God. How significant is this term to the Christian? It is very important, because it helps establish some major truths without which we would be left with little evidence that the words of Jesus Christ were actually true. It can be said that as our relationship with the Son of God determines whether we will become Christians, our relationship with the Spirit of God determines what kind of believers we will be.

## God the Father

**Malachi 2:10. God the Father of All**—The Fatherhood of God applies in a general sense to everyone since all men and women are created by God in His image. Thus their creaturehood is derived from His Fatherhood. This fact is demonstrated by Hebrews 12:9, which speaks of God as "the God of the spirits" (cf. Num. 16:22; Eccl. 12:7). Paul even agrees with a heathen poet that all men are God's offspring (Acts 17:28). He does not mean, of course, that everyone will have eternal life but that all men and women are the offspring of God in their created natures. James says that men still bear this image (James 3:9).

God is also the Father of all as sustainer of life. Every person is an object of His fatherly care (Matt. 18:10) and a candidate for His kingdom (Luke 18:16). Furthermore, God is not willing that any should perish (Matt. 18:14; 1 Tim. 2:4). Even when men and women reject God He still provides for them as He does believers with rain, fruitful seasons, food, and gladness (Matt. 5:45; Acts 14:17).

**Matthew 3:17. God the Father of Christ**—Every new Christian eventually wonders in what sense God may be called the Father of Christ and Christ the Son of God. The answer to this question is not a simple one.

First, one must recognize that the title Son of God does not speak of physical nature, for God is Spirit (John 4:24), and Christ was the Son of God before He assumed a human body in Bethlehem (John 3:16; Gal. 4:4). Passages which use terms implying physical origin must be taken in a figurative sense (Heb. 1:5).

Second, the title expresses a unique relationship. Christ distinguished His sonship from that of His disciples (John 20:17). He is begotten of God in a sense that no one else is (John 1:14; 3:16). Some call it "eternal generation," signifying the timelessness of this "God from God" relationship.

Third, the title describes a relationship of equality. The Son of God is no less than God. When Jesus claimed to be "one" with the Father, He was speaking of a unity of "substance" with the Father and thus equality in all the attributes of deity (John 10:30). The Jews certainly understood this claim, for they took up stones to stone Him, protesting that "You . . . make Yourself God" (John 10:33).

Fourth, the title especially emphasizes Christ's role as the revealer of God. He alone possesses the knowledge of the Father (John 14:6–9; 1 John 1:2) and He is the sole mediator of that knowledge (1 Tim. 2:5). Therefore no one can know the Father except through the Son (John 14:6). The narrowness of this way to God should be a sober incentive to take to all the world the message that the Son of God has come to impart to every person the life of the Father.

**Romans 8:15. God the Father of Believers**—God is the Father of all who believe in Christ in a special sense not shared by unbelievers. God is called their Father, first of all, because they have a new standing before Him. While unbelievers are the offspring of God because He created them (Acts 17:28, 29), they do not have the standing of sons. Their standing is rather as condemned sinners before God the Judge (John 3:18; Rev. 20:11). When a person believes in Christ as Savior, his estate is wonderfully changed from grim condemnation to privileged sonship. This new standing grants to all believers the legal right and spiritual privileges of divine sonship: "heirs of God and joint heirs with Christ" (Rom. 8:17).

God is the Father of believers also in the sense that He gives them new life (John 3:3). This relationship then is a family one involving many of the same realities that exist between an earthly father and child: birth of the child (John 3:3); partaking of the father's nature (2 Pet. 1:4); the father's care for the child (Matt. 6:32, 33; 7:9–11); and the father's discipline of the child (Heb. 12:6–8). Furthermore, this new Father-child relationship carries with it new brothers and sisters (Heb. 13:1).

To obtain God as Father is not a result of one's own merit but a result of Christ's. The one who believes in Christ as Savior enters into the blessed Father-child relationship with God solely on the grounds of Christ's sonship (Rom. 8:17; Heb. 2:17). It is the grand privilege and calling of those who know God as Father to graciously invite unbelievers to meet God as Father and not as Judge.

## The Son of God

**Isaiah 9:6. The Person of the Son of God**—It is crucial to remember that the existence of the Son of God did not commence with His birth in Bethlehem. He is spoken of as the Son before He became a man (Is. 9:6; Gal. 4:4). Micah prophesies of His birth, but yet states that

His "goings forth *have been* from of old, from everlasting" (Mic. 5:2). John says that He existed "in the beginning" before anything was created (John 1:1–3).

Even before He was born of Mary, He appeared to men in the Old Testament as the "Angel of the LORD." It is clear that this Angel is no ordinary angel because He is identified as God (Ex. 3:1, 4); He pardons sin (Ex. 23:20, 21); and He is worshiped (Josh. 5:13–15). While these passages do not say that this member of the Godhead was the preincarnate Christ, we may conclude that they are the same person since their work is the same.

While Christ was preexistent and appeared occasionally to men in the Old Testament, He took on a body permanently when He was conceived in Mary's womb. This incomparable event of God's becoming man in Jesus Christ is called the Incarnation. This miracle was prophesied hundreds of years previously (Is. 7:14) and was fulfilled historically in Mary in whose womb the Holy Spirit's power conceived a child (Matt. 1:23; Luke 1:35). Thus Christ, the sinless God-Man, was qualified to become our Redeemer (2 Cor. 5:21).

Having been born of a woman, Jesus Christ was fully man apart from sin (John 1:14). As a man He experienced the normal physical, mental, social, and spiritual growth as others did (Luke 2:52). He suffered pain, hunger, thirst, fatigue, temptation, pleasure, and rest. Because of His complete humanity He can be sympathetic and compassionate toward us (Heb. 4:15).

While Christ was fully man He was also fully God, as these facts indicate: He is called God (John 1:1; Heb. 1:8); He did works that only God could do, such as forgive sins (Mark 2:7) and create (Col. 1:16); He had attributes that only God could have, such as truth (John 14:6) and omniscience, all-knowing (John 2:24, 25); and He claimed equality with God (John 10:30).

The question may then be raised as to whether Christ lost anything of deity when He became a man (Phil. 2:6–8). While there is an inscrutable mystery involved in this unparalleled act of condescension, one can be certain that He lost none of God's attributes, because He was still God (John 20:28). He was fully God and fully man united in one person forever. Even now, at the right hand of God, He is the God-Man (1 Tim. 2:5). The great condescension of the Son of God's becoming a man serves eternally as a perfect model of humility and self-giving love (Phil. 2:5).

**John 10:10. The Earthly Life of the Son of God—** Since the gospel narratives are mainly concerned with Jesus' earthly ministry, it is important that the main aspects of His teaching be recognized. The most important of these are: the kingdom of God (Matt. 5—7; 24—25); His divine authority over men (Matt. 7:28, 29; Mark 2:10); His own role as God and Messiah demonstrated by miracles and signs (Matt. 16:15–20); the significance of His death and resurrection (Matt. 16:21; Luke 24:26); the relationship which His disciples and subsequent believers are to share with Him (John 13—16); and the urgency of His commission to believers to make disciples (Matt. 28:19, 20).

Of the many events of His earthly life the most significant, without a doubt, are His death and resurrection. On these two pivotal, historical incidents rests the validity of the entire Christian faith (1 Cor. 15:14). It is vital then to understand the nature of these two events. The death of Christ was first of all a humiliating physical death (John 19:18, 33). More than that, for a brief time it constituted a spiritual separation from God (Matt. 27:46). Within this moment there occurred the inexplicable mystery of the Father punishing the Son for the sins of the world (1 Pet. 3:18; 2 Cor. 5:21). This event, though it was the greatest crime of human history, was in the plan of God (Acts 2:23), and thus became the basis of salvation for sinners (Is. 53:5).

The power of the death of Christ would be nullified without His bodily resurrection. Though it does not justify us, the Resurrection demonstrated that His death, by which believing sinners are justified, was valid (1 Cor. 15:12–20). While skeptics have denied the bodily resurrection of Christ, the historical evidence for it is overwhelming: the many separate accounts of post-resurrection appearances, the empty tomb, and the transformed disciples. Every life that has been dramatically and wonderfully changed by believing in Christ since the first century is a testimony to its historical reality. Furthermore, it is the power of the Resurrection that marvelously empowers Christians today to live the Christian life (Eph. 1:19, 20; Phil. 3:10).

**Mark 10:45. The Ministry of the Son of God—**The ministry of Christ is threefold:

a. He is Savior. The title *Savior* implies many important and interrelated truths: the need of sinful men to be saved (1 Tim. 1:15); the qualifications of Christ as God-Man to be our Savior (John 10:18); the humiliating death He experienced to become our Savior (John 19:18); the victorious, bodily resurrection He experienced as a sure guarantee of our salvation (1 Cor. 15:13–22); and the glorious results of salvation (John 5:24). It is no wonder that in light of these precious realities Paul speaks of Christ as "our great God and Savior" (Titus 2:13).

b. He is High Priest. The high priest was of supreme importance in the Old Testament. It was on the basis of his mediation for the people before God on the Day of Atonement that they were brought near to God and protected from judgment (Lev. 16:16). Therefore his qualifications were exacting: appointed by God, physically perfect, ceremonially pure, and so on (Lev. 21). Jesus is eminently qualified to be our High Priest: He was appointed by God (Heb. 5:5); He is eternal (Heb. 7:24, 25); He is sinless (Heb. 7:26); His offering was final (Heb. 9:28); and His mediation is effective (Rom. 8:34; Heb. 7:25; 1 John 2:1). As the only qualified High Priest for men and women, Jesus Christ thus constitutes the only way to God (1 Tim. 2:5).

c. He is King. The position of king implies sovereign authority and rule over all. The Scriptures clearly teach that this right belongs only to Jesus Christ, who is called "the King of Kings and Lord of Lords" (Rev. 19:16). This title means that He is destined to rule as King and that every knee must ultimately bow and acknowledge His authority (Phil. 2:10). Those who acknowledge Christ as King and Lord in this life will reign with Him; those who do not will be judged by Him (Rev. 20:11–15). The weight of eternity hangs on this solemn decision.

## The Holy Spirit

**Ephesians 4:3. The Person of the Holy Spirit—** One of the most serious errors in the minds of many people concerning the Holy Spirit is that He is simply a principle or an influence. On the contrary, the Holy Spirit is as much a person (individual existence of a conscious being) as the Father and the Son.

a. The personality of the Holy Spirit. The Bible speaks of the mind (Rom. 8:27) and will (1 Cor. 12:11) of the Holy Spirit. He is often described as speaking directly to men in the Book of Acts. During Paul's second missionary journey the apostle was forbidden by the Spirit to visit a certain mission field (Acts 16:6, 7) and then was instructed to proceed toward another field of service (Acts 16:10). It was God's Spirit who spoke directly to Christian leaders in the Antioch church, commanding them to send Paul and Barnabas on their first missionary journey (Acts 13:2).

b. The deity of the Holy Spirit. He is not only a real person, but He is also God. As is God the Father, He too is everywhere at once (Ps. 139:7). As the Son is eternal, the Holy Spirit has also existed forever (Heb. 9:14). He is often referred to as God in the Bible. See Acts 5:3, 4. Finally, the Holy Spirit is equal with the Father and Son. This is seen during the baptism of Christ (Matt. 3:16, 17) and is mentioned by Jesus Himself just prior to His ascension from the Mount of Olives (Matt. 28:19, 20).

**Titus 3:5. The Work of the Holy Spirit in Salvation—**There are three wonderful works performed by the Holy Spirit in preparing unsaved people to become Christians.

a. The work of the Holy Spirit in restraining. Satan would enjoy nothing more than to destroy people before they make their decision to accept Christ as Savior. But the Holy Spirit prevents this from occurring (Is. 59:19).

b. The work of the Holy Spirit in convicting. Mankind's sin and righteousness are exposed by the Holy Spirit (John 16:8). There are two well-known examples of sinners being convicted by the Holy Spirit in the Book of Acts. Felix, a Roman governor, actually trembles under conviction as he hears Paul preach (Acts 24:25). The other case involves King Agrippa who responds to a gospel message by saying: "You almost persuade me to become a Christian" (Acts 26:28).

c. The work of the Holy Spirit in regenerating. When a repenting sinner accepts Christ as Savior he is given a new nature by the Holy Spirit. See 2 Corinthians 5:17. Jesus carefully explained this ministry of the Holy Spirit to Nicodemus (John 3:3–7).

**1 Corinthians 6:19. The Work of the Holy Spirit in Christian Living—**As a loving and wise mother tenderly watches over her child, so the Holy Spirit cares for the children of God.

a. The Holy Spirit indwells Christians. The Bible teaches that all believers are indwelt by the Holy Spirit (1 Cor. 6:19). The purpose of this indwelling ministry is to control the newly created nature given at conversion (2 Cor. 5:17; Eph. 3:16).

b. The Holy Spirit fills believers. We are admonished to "be filled with the Spirit" (Eph. 5:18). The word *fill* means "to be controlled." The filling does not mean that the Christian gets more of the Holy Spirit, but rather, He gets more of us!

c. The Holy Spirit sanctifies the believer (Rom. 15:16; 2 Thess. 2:13).

d. The Holy Spirit produces fruit in the life of the believer. This fruit is described by Paul: "But the fruit of the Spirit is love, joy, peace, longsuffering, kindness, goodness, faithfulness, gentleness, self-control" (Gal. 5:22, 23).

e. The Holy Spirit imparts gifts to Christians (Rom. 12:6–8; 1 Cor. 12:1–11; Eph. 4:7–12). A spiritual gift is an ability imparted to every Christian (1 Cor. 7:7; 1 Pet. 4:10). The purpose of these gifts is twofold, namely, to glorify God (Rev. 4:11) and to edify the body of Christ (Eph. 4:12, 13).

f. The Holy Spirit teaches believers. He will instruct us in all spiritual things as we read the Word of God (John 14:26) and abide in the Son of God (1 John 2:24–27).

# Beginning the New Life

*Synopsis*

Mankind is by nature sinful and needs the righteousness of God. We must be separated from sin and set apart to righteousness. If we are to approach God, we must do so on God's terms—we must have new lives in which our sins have been forgiven and obliterated.

It is one thing to be convinced of the need for the new life, but it is an entirely different thing to acquire the new life. When we are "saved" we are said to be new creatures (2 Cor. 5:17); to have passed from death to life (John 5:24); to have been transferred from the rule of darkness to the kingdom of God's Son (Col. 1:13); to have been born again (John 3:3); and to have been adopted by God (Gal. 4:4, 5). These wonderful results of having new life in Christ are offered freely to all who trust in Christ for salvation.

One of the most thrilling benefits of finding new life in Christ is "everlasting [eternal] life." We enter a new, personal relationship with God that gives us a fullness of spiritual vitality, and this new life is a gift which will never die. God can accomplish a life-changing transformation for all who truly believe in Christ.

## Need for the New Life

**Isaiah 6:3. Holiness of God—**Our greatest failing is in not realizing who God is and what His character is like. God is NOT human. He is God, and as such there is an infinite gap between the highest in us and the lowest in God. The gap between God and us is unbridgeable from our side. If the gap is to be bridged, it must be from God's side—for God is holy. To be holy means "to be set apart." God is set apart from the power, practice, and presence of sin, and is set apart to absolute righteousness and goodness. There is no sin in God and God can have nothing to do with sin. If we are to approach God, we must do so on God's terms. Somehow, we must be made holy—just as holy as God is. Any holiness which falls short of God's holiness will not be able to stand in the presence of God. Therefore, because of the holiness of God, we must have a new life in which our sins have been forgiven and done away with so that we actually can be as separated from sin as God is. This is the good news of the gospel—that Christ died for our sins, having taken them upon Himself, and has set us apart from them. This is our position before God which will never change. Because of what God has done, we can enter boldly into the presence of God.

**Genesis 3:6, 7. Adam's Sin**—Adam's sin does not seem to be a very great sin from man's perspective. All he did was take a bite of some fruit. Adam's sin is serious in that the fruit was of the tree of the knowledge of good and evil, of which God said that he was not to eat under penalty of death (Gen. 2:17). Up to this time Adam was morally innocent. When he sinned, he by nature became a sinner. As such he died. He died spiritually immediately and began to die physically. Adam was the first man ever to live upon the face of the earth. From Adam and Eve come every other human being who ever has lived upon the face of the earth. Thus Adam is the "federal head" from whom every other man came. Like begets like. Apples beget apples. Dogs beget dogs. Human beings beget human beings. Since Adam became a sinner before Eve conceived a child, every human being descended from him is a sinner just like him except Christ. Because of Adam's sin, death entered into the human race (Rom. 5:12–14); every human being needs to have the new life.

**Ecclesiastes 7:20. Individual Sin**—Each individual man, woman, and child who composes mankind is a sinner. Paul points out in Romans 3:13–16 that "their throat *is* an open tomb . . . the poison of asps [small, deadly poisonous snakes] *is* under their lips; whose mouth *is* full of cursing and bitterness. Their feet *are* swift to shed blood [consider the high incidence of violent crime, murder, and abortion that infects our society]; destruction and misery *are* in their ways [whatever man touches he corrupts]." All of this shows that there is no person who seeks after God and no person does what is right (Rom. 3:10, 11). Each individual man, woman, and child needs the righteousness of God. Without God's righteousness no one can ever enter or stand in God's presence. Plainly, every man, woman, and child needs to have a new life because each is a sinner.

## Way to the New Life

**Romans 6:23. New Life: A Free Gift**—You can work for sin but it is a cruel master. When it pays you off, its wage is death—separation from God forever. In stark contrast, God does not pay wages. He has a free gift to offer—eternal life. There is nothing that one can do to earn this gift. If one could earn it, it would not be a gift; it would be wages. Eternal life is just that—eternal—it never ceases. The basic concept underlying life is *union.* There are three kinds of life mentioned in the Bible: (1) physical life—union of the soul with the body; (2) spiritual life—union of the soul with God; and (3) eternal life—eternal union of the soul with God. Jesus said, "My sheep hear My voice . . . And I give them eternal life, and they shall never perish" (John 10:27, 28). The gift of God is eternal life. One receives this gift when he believes in Jesus as his own personal Savior. Having eternal life, he will never perish.

**Colossians 1:22. New Life: Based on Christ's Death**—Salvation is free, but it is not cheap. Salvation is a gift and costs me nothing, but it cost God everything—it cost Jesus His life. The wages of sin is death (separation from God). God's gift is eternal life (eternal union of the soul with God). This is possible because of the death of Jesus on Calvary's cross (Rom. 6:23). Jesus actually took sin's penalty for every man, woman, and child who ever has lived or ever will live. As He hung upon the cross He cried, "Eli, Eli, lama sabachthani?" Being interpreted, He cried, "My God, My God, why have You forsaken Me?" (Matt. 27:46). Jesus was separated from God the Father so that you and I do not have to be. This is the heart of the atonement. The marvel of it all is that He did this while we were His enemies: "But God demonstrates His own love toward us, in that while we were still sinners, Christ died for us" (Rom. 5:8).

**Acts 16:31. New Life: Received by Faith**—The words spoken to the Philippian jailer are the best news human ears have ever heard, for they clearly tell how we receive God's gift of eternal life. When we receive God's gift of eternal life we are said to be "saved." The basic concept underlying "salvation" or "being saved" is deliverance. We are delivered from the penalty of sin (death, separation from God) and from the power of sin. Ultimately we will be delivered from the very presence of sin and will be delivered into the very presence of God. We receive new life by faith—believing that Jesus died for our sins, that His death was in our place, and that His payment for sin is fully acceptable in God's sight. Faith can be summarized in the acrostic:

F orsaking
A ll
I
T ake
H im

According to Acts 20:21, we are to forsake all (repent of our sins) and to take Him (by faith turn to God for our salvation.

## Results of the New Life

**John 5:24. Everlasting Life**—One benefit of finding new life in Christ is called in the Bible "everlasting [eternal] life." The character of this great reality may be summarized by carefully looking at each word. The word *life* stresses the quality of this new relationship to God (John 10:10). It does not mean, of course, that we are not physically alive before salvation; it simply stresses the fact that we enter a new, personal relationship with God that gives us a fullness of spiritual vitality that we lacked before (John 17:3).

The word *everlasting* emphasizes life without end. Though it will not be completely fulfilled until our future bodily redemption (Rom. 8:23), it is still a present possession that can never perish (John 10:28).

Everlasting life must not be conceived of as an exclusively future possession. Rather, its possession is clearly seen in our actions. Thus, "no murderer has eternal life abiding in him" (1 John 3:15). Indeed, love is the confirming evidence that we do, in fact, have eternal life (1 John 3:14).

The greatness of this spiritual reality constitutes a wonderful incentive to vigorously proclaim the gospel to those who are still "dead in trespasses and sins" (Eph. 2:1).

**2 Corinthians 5:17. New Nature**—The term *new nature* refers to the spiritual transformation that occurs within the inner man when a person believes in Christ as Savior. The Christian is now a *new man* as opposed to the *old man* that he was before he became a Christian (Rom. 6:6; Eph 2:15; 4:22–24; Col. 3:9, 10). This concept of *newness* may be traced to an important choice between two Greek words, both meaning "new." One word means "new" in the sense of renovation (to repair), the other in the sense of fresh existence. It is the latter that is used to describe the Christian. He is not the old man renovated or refreshed; he is a brand-new man with a new family, a new set of values, new motivations, and new possessions.

The old man is still present in the new life and expresses himself in corrupting deeds such as lying (Eph. 4:22; Col. 3:9). The new man, to be visible, must be *put on* as one would put on a new suit of clothes (Col. 3:10). In other words, the new nature must be cultivated or nurtured by spiritual decisiveness to grow in Christ. We must not revert to putting on the *old suit* of the former life; rather, we must continue to grow in this new life (Eph. 5:8).

The message of the new nature is a message of supreme hope: the Spirit of God can accomplish a life-changing transformation for all who will only believe in Christ.

**Isaiah 61:10. Christ's Righteousness**—One of the most awesome requirements God made upon men and women is that they be righteous, that is, conform to His ethical and moral standards (Ps. 15:2; Mic. 6:8). Since God is holy, He cannot allow sinners into His presence (Is.6:3–5). Since all persons are sinners, they could not be saved apart from the supernatural intervention of God (Rom. 3:10, 23). The righteous demands of God coupled with the inability of man might present an insoluble dilemma. God Himself, however, has graciously solved the problem. He sent Christ, who never sinned, to die for our sins and thus satisfy His own wrath toward us. Simply put, it means that God, at the cross, treated Christ as though He had committed our sins even though He was righteous. On the other hand, when we believe in Christ, He treats us as though we were as righteous as Christ (2 Cor. 5:21). The Bible calls this type of righteousness "imputed righteousness" (Rom. 4:6). That simply means that God puts to our spiritual account the very worth of Christ, much as though He were a banker adding an inexhaustible deposit to our bank account. There are, sadly, many people who still refuse to believe that such an abundant blessing can be theirs as a free gift (Eph. 2:8, 9). Nevertheless, the Bible clearly urges all men to trust in Jesus Christ as Savior and thus be reckoned as righteous by God (Rom. 4:24).

**1 John 3:2. Placed into God's Family**—In a general sense all men and women are the offspring of God in that He is the Creator (Acts 17: 28, 29). This relationship, however, is not sufficient to offset the penalty of sin, because all persons are sinners separated from God (Rom 3:23). Therefore, for a sinful person to become a child of God, a miraculous transformation must take place. The Bible refers to this change as being "born again" (John 3:3). When an individual places his faith in Christ as Savior, he is born again into a new, spiritual, family relationship with God (Gal. 3:26). He gains God as Father (Eph. 4:6) and other Christians as brothers and sisters (Heb. 3:1). It is significant to note that the term "brotherly love," which Christians are commanded to have for each other (Heb. 13:1), is never used in the Greek language to refer to loving others as though they were your brothers. Rather, it is always used of loving those who actually are your brothers. So it is in the Christian faith: we actually are brothers and sisters with other Christians.

Not only are Christians the children of God by spiritual birth; they are adopted as well (Eph. 1:5). This figure implies a dramatic transformation of status from slave to son (Gal. 4:1–5). One is no longer in bondage to the master but becomes a free son possessing all the rights and privileges of sonship. One of these benefits is the right to call God *Abba*, an affectionate term meaning "Father" (Rom. 8:15). This marvelous relationship carries responsibilities with it, as well as privileges. Everyone who has the hope of having his sonship perfected someday is presently purifying his own life. Since he bears the family relationship to God, he must also exhibit the family character.

**Acts 1:8. Empowered by God**—One of the most common excuses for not becoming a Christian is the fear of failure to live the Christian life. Besides overlooking the fact that men cannot be saved on the basis of good works (Titus 3:5), this objection neglects the truth that God provides the power to live the Christian life. Before Christ was crucified He promised the coming of the Holy Spirit to help believers (John 16:13, 14). The subsequent events of the Book of Acts supply ample evidence of the fulfillment of this prophecy (Acts 4:7, 33; 6:8).

The power of the Holy Spirit was not designed solely for the first-century church. Rather, all Christians are indwelt by the Spirit and thus have His power available (1 Cor. 6:19). However, living the Christian life under the Spirit's power must not be thought of as simply allowing the Spirit to take control while the believer does nothing. The believer still must live the Christian life, though he does it through the Spirit's power. Romans 8:13 says, "if by the Spirit you put to death the deeds of the body, you will live." It is you who are to put to death the sinful deeds of the body, but you are to do it through the Spirit's power.

The Christian who struggles in his own strength to live the Christian life will fail. He must by faith appropriate daily the power of the Holy Spirit (Rom. 8:4, 5). Described practically, this means that the believer trusts the Spirit to empower him in specific instances such as sharing his faith with others, resisting temptation, being faithful, and so on. There is no *secret formula* that makes the Spirit's power available. It is simply a reliance on the Spirit to help.

## Assurance of the New Life

**Titus 1:2. Promise of God**—Often the Christian will doubt his salvation simply because he doesn't feel saved, not understanding that the basis for that salvation is the promise of God and not emotional feelings. In fact, the entire Trinity is involved in this.

a. The promise and work of the Father in our salvation. He has promised to graciously accept in Christ all repenting sinners (Eph. 1:6; Col. 3:3). This means a Christian has the right to be in heaven someday, for he is in Christ. God guarantees to us that He will work out all things for our good (Rom. 8:28).
b. The promise and work of the Son. He has promised us eternal life (John 5:24) and abundant life (John 10:10). This covers not only our final destiny in heaven, but also our present Christian service here on earth. He is, in fact, right now praying for us and ministering to us at His Father's right hand (Heb. 8:1; 9:24).
c. The promise and work of the Holy Spirit. The Holy Spirit is said to indwell the believer (John 14:16). In addition, He places all believing sinners into the body of Christ, thus assuring us of union with God Himself (1 Cor. 12:13).

**1 John 3:24. Witness of the Spirit**—While it is true that one need not always feel spiritual to have new life in Christ, nevertheless, feelings and emotions do play a vital role in our salvation. Both Paul (Rom. 8:16) and John (1 John 3:24) inform us we can experience that inner witness of the Holy Spirit to our spirit. What does this mean? It means we can enjoy the quiet confidence given by the Spirit that we have indeed passed from death unto life. It means we can now approach the mighty Creator of the vast universe and refer to Him as "Abba, Father" (Rom. 8:15). *Abba* is a very personal and intimate term for one's father. Prior to Pentecost only Christ had used the title for God (Mark 14:36). It is almost akin to our modern title *daddy*, or *papa*. It not only means we can approach the throne of grace with a holy boldness (Heb. 4:16), but we can also experience the blessing of knowing that the Father will hear and answer our prayers (1 John 3:22).

The apostle Paul experiences this witness during a crisis in his life while preaching in Corinth. See Acts 18:9, 10.

**1 Corinthians 6:11. Changed Life**—The first stanza of a famous Christian song begins: "What a wonderful change in my life has been wrought since Jesus came into my heart."

Without doubt the greatest proof of the new birth is a changed life. The child of God now suddenly loves the following:

a. He loves Jesus. Before conversion the sinner might hold Christ in high esteem, but after conversion he loves the Savior (1 John 5:1, 2).
b. He loves the Bible. We should love God's Word as the psalmist did in Psalm 119. He expresses his great love for God's Word no less than seventeen times! See verses 24, 40, 47, 48, 72, 97, 103, 111, 113, 127, 129, 140, 143, 159, 162, 165, 168.
c. He loves other Christians. "We know that we have passed from death to life, because we love the brethren" (1 John 3:14).
d. He loves his enemies. See Matthew 5:43–45.
e. He loves the souls of all people. Like Paul, he too can cry out for the conversion of loved ones. "Brethren, my heart's desire and prayer to God for Israel is that they may be saved" (Rom 10:1). See also 2 Corinthians 5:14.
f. He loves the pure life. John says if one loves the world, the love of the Father is not in him (1 John 2:15–17). See also 1 John 5:4.
g. He loves to talk to God. "Speaking to one another in psalms and hymns and spiritual songs, singing and making melody in your heart to the Lord" (Eph. 5:19).

## Growing in the New Life

*Synopsis*

Knowing how to grow in the new life is essential. The old adage is ever true: "Sin will keep you from God's Word, and God's Word will keep you from sin."

No factor in Christian growth is more important than prayer. Prayer may be defined as talking with and listening to God. We talk to Him with our lips and heart, and He talks to us through His will. It involves a two-way conversation. Spiritual maturity is impossible without systematic prayer.

Worship is essential also to spiritual growth. Worship involves honor and respect toward God, the ceremony of private and public worship, and the joyful service of Christians to their Lord. Christians who submit to the Lordship of Christ in reverence and service will grow in their spiritual lives.

The Bible describes Christian life as "[walking] in the Spirit" (Gal. 5:16). Walking best represents the step-by-step character of the spiritual life. Living by the Spirit's power is a moment-by-moment yielding to the Spirit's will and control. The evidence that we are walking in the Spirit is simply the display of the fruit of the Spirit (Gal. 5:22, 23). Walking in the Spirit involves confession of sin, yielding to God, and being filled with or controlled by the Spirit.

### Bible Study

**Nehemiah 8:3. Reading God's Word**—The person who can read well has a much better opportunity of knowing and understanding God's Word than the person who has to rely upon what others tell him about the Word of God. Reading the Word of God is a very important part of communicating God's Word to God's people. Public Scripture reading was a regular part of the worship services in Israel and in the early church. Today we are blessed above all people in history, for not only does nearly everyone know how to read, but there also are enough copies of the Bible available so that everyone may have a personal copy. Here are some suggestions to aid you in receiving the greatest benefit from reading the Bible:

a. Read the Bible prayerfully. Ask the Spirit of God to meet your heart's need as you read (Ps. 119:18).
b. Read the Bible thoughtfully. Think about the

meaning and implications of what you are reading.

c. Read the Bible carefully. Take note not only of the words that are used but also of how they relate to one another.
d. Read the Bible repeatedly. It may be of great help to read the same portion over daily for a month's time. This is a good way for its words to take root in your heart. If you are reading a short book, read it every day. Divide longer books into manageable portions of two or three chapters and read that portion through every day.
e. Read the Bible extensively. Sometimes it is of great help to read large portions of the Word of God through at one sitting. If you do this, do it at a time when you are alert and not likely to be disturbed during your reading.
f. Read the Bible regularly. It is good to have a particular time every day when you habitually give yourself to the reading of the Word of God.
g. Read the Bible faithfully. Inevitably there will be days when you will fail to read the Bible. Do not let your momentary lapse discourage you. Faithfully resume your practice of reading God's Word.
h. Read the Bible obediently. Because the Bible is God's Word written to you, it is essential to obey it (Ex. 24:3).

**Job 22:22. Memorizing God's Word**—You are not always able to study the Bible by reading it. If you have memorized a portion of the Word of God, you are able to gain insights into its meaning at times when a Bible is not readily available. The Bible recognizes the importance of Scripture memorization. The following benefits can be cited:

a. It keeps the child of God from sinning (Ps. 119:11).
b. It provides comfort in time of trouble (Ps. 119:52, 92).
c. It fixes your mind upon God (Ps. 43:3).
d. It provides daily sustenance for the spiritual life (Deut. 8:3).
e. It provides continual and ready guidance in all the situations of life (Prov. 6:20–23).
f. It provides the basis for formal and informal instruction of your children (Deut. 6:6, 7).

**Joshua 1:8. Meditating upon God's Word**—Joshua had just succeeded Moses in the leadership of the nation Israel. Moses had led the nation for forty years and had the benefit that all the wisdom and culture of Egypt and the king's household could provide. Moses was a seasoned, multi-talented man who had walked closely with God. Joshua, by contrast, was relatively untried. He was assuming an awesome responsibility in taking command of two-and-a-half million people. If anyone needed a formula for success, Joshua did. Likely there were many well-meaning people with all kinds of advice and formulas to help Joshua in the seemingly impossible task that lay ahead. What comfort and assurance it must have been as the Lord (Yahweh) spoke directly to Joshua, assuring him of His presence with him as He had been with Moses (Josh. 1:5), and giving him the key to success—meditating upon God's Word.

Joshua is to meditate upon the Word of God day and night (i.e., at all times), and is promised (1) prosperity and (2) good success in the God-given task that lies ahead. Reading and memorizing God's Word provide the basis for meditating upon God's Word. You meditate upon the Word of God by rehearsing its thoughts over and over in order to understand its implications for the situations of life. Meditating upon the Word of God will guarantee prosperity and success in the new life.

**Deuteronomy 31:12. Obedience to God's Word**—Reading, memorizing, and meditating upon the Word of God are of no value without obedience to the Word of God. To obey the Word of God, you do what the Word of God indicates should be done in any situation. Obedience to the Word of God is the only way that the child of God can be pleasing to God in the new life. Obedience to God's Word results in: being treasured by God (Ex. 19:5); blessedness (happiness) in life (Ps. 119:2); not being ashamed (Ps. 119:4–6); understanding (Ps. 119:100); avoidance of evil (Ps. 119:101); guidance for life (Ps. 119:105); safety and freedom from anxiety (Prov. 1:33); life (Prov. 19:16; Ezek. 18:19; John 8:51); God's blessing (Is. 1:19); greatness in the kingdom of heaven (Matt. 5:19); bearing fruit for God (Matt. 13:23); manifesting love for God (John 14:23; 1 John 2:5); promise of God's presence (John 14:23; 2 John 9); abiding in the love of God (John 15:10); evidence of the doctrine that has been taught (Rom. 6:17); assurance of salvation (1 John 2:3); eternal life (1 John 2:17); dwelling in God (1 John 3:24); love of God's children (1 John 5:2); and entrance into heaven (Rev. 22:7).

## Prayer

**Psalm 150:1. Praise**—To praise God is to acknowledge the glories of His excellent person. It differs somewhat from thanksgiving, which describes what God has done rather than what He is. Here are some facts about praise.

a. God alone is worthy of our praise (Ps. 18:3; 113:3).
b. It is His will for us that we praise Him (Ps. 50:23; Is. 43:21).
c. This praise should be continuous (Ps. 34:1; 71:6) and also public (Ps. 22:25).
d. We are to praise God for His holiness (2 Chr. 20:21), grace (Eph. 1:6), goodness (Ps. 135:3), and kindness (Ps. 138:2).
e. All nature praises God (Ps. 148:7–10).
f. The sun, moon, and stars praise Him (Ps. 19:1; 143:3).
g. The angels praise Him (Ps. 148:2).

In fact, we are told that on occasion God uses even the wrath of men to praise Him (Ps. 76:10). An example of this is seen in the selling of Joseph by his brothers into slavery (Gen. 37:28). God later uses this cruel act to promote Joseph as second ruler over all Egypt. As Joseph would remind his brothers: "But as for you, you meant evil against me; *but* God meant it for good, in order to bring it about as *it is* this day, to save many people alive" (Gen. 50:20).

**1 John 1:9. Confession**—One of the most remarkable chapters in the Old Testament is Psalm 51. This Psalm contains the actual words of confession uttered by King David after his great sins of adultery and murder (2 Sam. 11).

This prayer can serve as a pattern to the Christian when he is guilty of sin in his life today.

a. David begins his prayer by freely admitting his sin (Ps. 51:3, 4). This honesty is vital in our confession. God will graciously forgive all our sins, but not on account of our excuses.
b. He then displays real sorrow over his sin (Ps. 51:17). Paul writes (2 Cor. 7:10) that the main characteristic of true confession is godly sorrow.
c. He asks God's forgiveness (Ps. 51:1, 7–9).
d. He believes that God has heard him and will restore him (Ps. 51:12–15).

In the New Testament the most important single verse concerning confession is 1 John 1:9. In essence John tells us the means of forgiveness and cleansing is the blood of Christ, while the method of this forgiveness and cleansing is the confession of the Christian.

Like David, we must admit our sin, regret the actions of our sin, plead the blood of Christ, and believe that God has indeed done what He promised, namely, to cleanse us from sin and restore us to fellowship and service.

**1 Samuel 1:17. Petition—**One great difference between Christianity and all other religions is that the believer has a prayer-hearing and prayer-answering God. In the Old Testament during a contest with Elijah, the priests of Baal make desperate efforts to speak with their god by crying out and cutting themselves, but to no avail. "But *there was* no voice; no one answered" (1 Kin. 18:26). How different from these words are those of the Psalmist: "*But* certainly God has heard *me;* He has attended to the voice of my prayer" (Ps. 66:19).

a. The nature of our petitions. First of all, God has commanded us to pray (Matt. 7:7, 8; 1 Tim. 2:8). When we pray, our petitions should be made by faith (James 1:6) in the name of Jesus (John 14:13). If these simple rules are followed, we can rest assured our prayers are being heard (1 John 3:22; 5:14, 15).
b. The objects of our prayers. For whom or what should we pray? First of all, we need to pray for ourselves, because unless we are in God's will, He cannot hear our petitions about other things. Thus we should begin by asking for cleansing (1 John 1:9) and wisdom (James 1:5). Other areas of our petitions concern spiritual leaders (Col. 4:3), sick believers (James 5:14, 15), rulers (1 Tim. 2:1–3), and even for our enemies (Matt. 5:44).

**Philippians 4:6. Thanksgiving—**The importance and spiritual benefits of thanksgiving in our prayer life cannot be overemphasized. The Bible tells us God resists the proud, but gives grace to the humble (James 4:6). But the question is, How do you become humble? It is done by being thankful! A good rule is to "be anxious [worried] for nothing" (Phil. 4:6), be prayerful in all things (1 Thess. 5:18), and be thankful for anything. It was the sin of thanklessness that caused the ancient world to plunge into the terrible depths of sexual depravity (Rom. 1:21). In the Old Testament a special group of priests was appointed to do nothing else but praise and thank the Lord (2 Chr. 31:2).

There are two main things we are to thank God for:

a. We are to thank Him for His work in Creation. David reminds us concerning this area of thanksgiving in Psalm 100. Later, John the apostle tells us we will thank God for His work in Creation throughout all eternity. Note the words of this song of praise: "You are worthy, O Lord, to receive glory and honor and power; for You created all things, and by Your will they exist and were created" (Rev. 4:11).
b. We are to thank Him for His work in redemption. John also informs us that our second song in heaven will feature thanksgiving for God's work in redemption: "And they sang a new song, saying, 'You are worthy to take the scroll, and to open its seals; for You were slain, and have redeemed us to God by Your blood'" (Rev. 5:9).

**Proverbs 16:3. Commitment—**Dedication is the foundation of commitment. Without it the believer is unable to offer God anything else. Paul explains this dedication process in Romans 12:1 and 2. He emphasizes three things. First, it is our body which is to be dedicated as a living sacrifice to God. Second, we are to avoid being conformed to this world, but to strive to be transformed by the Word. Finally, by doing this we can discover God's perfect will for our lives.

After the dedication of our bodies, what are we to commit? We are to commit our salvation to God (2 Tim. 1:12). Second, we are to commit our works (Prov. 16:3). Then, our goals in life are to be given to Him (Job 5:8; Ps. 37:5). It is difficult but vital to commit our suffering experiences to God (1 Pet. 4:19). Our Lord Jesus did this very thing when He was on earth (1 Pet. 2:23). Finally, in the hour of death we can with confidence commit our very souls to God (Ps. 31:5). Paul the apostle assures us that any and all such commitments to the Lord will be accepted and honored. See 1 Corinthians 15:58.

## Stewardship

**1 Corinthians 12:1–10. Using Spiritual Gifts—**Spiritual gifts are discussed in detail in four passages of the New Testament: Romans 12:3–8; 1 Corinthians 12:1–10, 28–31; Ephesians 4:11, 12; and 1 Peter 4:10, 11. These lists are to be regarded as representative of spiritual gifts. Spiritual gifts are those gifts given by the Spirit of God for the accomplishment of God's purpose in the world and for the edification of the church, the body of Christ. Two things are important to remember concerning spiritual gifts: (1) every believer has been given spiritual gifts (Rom. 12:5, 6; 1 Cor. 12:7; 1 Pet. 4:10); and (2) the gifts belong to God and are given for the believer to use for the glory of God (1 Pet. 4:11).

**Galatians 5:13. Serving—**God intended that the Christian life should be dynamic, not static. We should sit under the teaching of the Word of God, understand and apply its meaning and implications, and serve God and our fellow believers. The Spirit of God has given us spiritual gifts, but those gifts are worthless unless they are put to use in the service of God and His church. Paul often uses the figure of the human body to show the dependence of the members of the body upon one another and the importance of each member serving the other (Rom. 12:4, 5; 1 Cor. 12:12–31). While some members of the body have more prominent places of service than others, all are equally important. The worst thing that can happen to the human body is for one of its members to become nonfunctioning. Paralysis, sickness, deterioration, and sometimes death occur when a body member ceases to serve the other members of the body in the particular way that God intended. To maintain strength, health, and vitality, every member of the body must function and serve all the other members of the body. This is also true of the spiritual or new life. We will grow in the new life, become strong, and maintain good spiritual health as we use the talents and abilities that God has given us to meet the needs of the other members of the body.

**2 Corinthians 9:6–8. Giving**—There is no better indicator of growth in the new life than in the area of giving. This passage deals with the attitude one should have in his giving—it should be cheerful. When giving is cheerful, it will also be generous. The important rule of thumb is not how much is given, but how much is left after the giving. God is not primarily occupied with the amount of the gift, but with the motive that lies behind it. All the money in the world belongs to God. My gift to Him does not make Him any richer; it makes me richer spiritually because of the realization that everything I have is His and that I am giving because I love Him and want to give.

The formula for giving is found in 1 Corinthians 16:2 where three principles can be seen: (1) my giving is to be regular, "on the first *day* of the week"; (2) my giving is to be systematic, "let each one of you lay something aside"; and (3) my giving is to be proportionate, "as he may prosper."

Failure to give of the money which God has given is a serious matter. The person who fails to honor God with his money actually robs God (Mal. 3:8), not because it impoverishes God but because it denies the God-ordained means for the support of His work and His ministers. For the child of God who honors God with his money God promises abundant blessing (Mal. 3:10; Luke 6:38) and the provision of his every need (Phil. 4:19). Giving, then, is a key to growth in the new life.

## Worship

**1 Chronicles 16:29. The Meaning of Worship**—Worship refers to the supreme honor or veneration given either in thought or deed to a person or thing. The Bible teaches that God alone is worthy of worship (Ps. 29:2), but it also sadly records accounts of those who worshiped other objects. Among those were people (Dan. 2:46), false gods (2 Kin. 10:19), images and idols (Is. 2:8; Dan. 3:5), heavenly bodies (2 Kin. 21:3), Satan (Rev. 13:4), and demons (Rev. 9:20). It is indeed tragic that many worshiped gods they could carry and not the God who could carry them. God Almighty alone is worthy of worship (Rev. 4:11).

True worship involves at least three important elements:

a. Worship requires reverence. This includes the honor and respect directed toward the Lord in thought and feeling. It is one thing to obey a superior unwillingly; it is quite another to commit one's thoughts and emotions in that obedience. Jesus said that those who worship God must do so "in spirit and truth" (John 4:24). The term *spirit* speaks of the personal nature of worship: It is from my person to God's person and involves the intellect, emotions, and will. The word *truth* speaks of the content of worship: God is pleased when we worship Him, understanding His true character.
b. Worship includes public expression. This was particularly prevalent in the Old Testament because of the sacrificial system. For example, when a believer received a particular blessing for which he wanted to thank God, it was not sufficient to say it privately; he expressed his thanks publicly with a thank-offering (Lev. 7:12).
c. Worship means service. These two concepts are often linked together in Scripture (Deut. 8:19). Furthermore, the words for worship in both Testaments originally referred to the labor of slaves for the master. Worship especially includes the joyful service which Christians render to Christ their Master. The concept of worship must not be restricted to church attendance, but should embrace an entire life of obedience to God.

**Hebrews 13:15. The Expressions of Worship**—Since worship encompasses thought, feeling, and deed, there are many expressions of it. Worship especially includes praise and thanksgiving which may be expressed privately or publicly, either by grateful declarations (Heb. 13:15) or by joyful singing (Ps. 100:2; Eph. 5:19; Col. 3:16). Portions of early Christian hymns of worship actually may be preserved in the New Testament (1 Tim. 3:16; 2 Tim. 2:11–13).

One very important expression of worship for the church is remembering the death of Christ through the Lord's Supper (1 Cor. 11:26). The Lord's Supper was instituted by Christ Himself (Matt. 26:26–28) and judged by Paul not to be taken lightly (1 Cor. 11:28–32).

Since worship means giving something to God, the cheerful giving of money to God's work is certainly an act of worship (2 Cor. 9:7). The giving of one's time to the Lord's work may be considered worship as well. The use of one's spiritual gifts in ministry to the body of Christ constitutes an example of worship as service (1 Cor. 12), as does faithfully occupying a church office (Eph. 4:11; 1 Tim. 3:1–13; Titus 1:5–9). Ministry in edifying saints and evangelizing sinners both likewise constitute services of worship.

The single most important act of worship for the Christian is the unqualified presentation of himself to God as an obedient servant. This dedication involves the body and the mind (Rom. 12:1, 2): the body because it contains the tools by which the will of God is carried out; the mind because it coordinates the actions to be executed by the body. When these are gladly devoted to God, they become instruments by which He effects His will on the earth. Such faithful and joyous service makes one's entire life a performance of worship.

**2 Chronicles 7:3. The Reasons for Worship**—The first reason for worship is simply that God commands it (1 Chr. 16:29; Matt. 4:10). The first four of the Ten Commandments, which are also the longest, clearly charge men to worship the one true God and Him alone (Ex. 20:3–10). To allow any person or thing to usurp the position of lordship over us constitutes gross disobedience to the will of God and incurs His terrible wrath (Ex. 20:5; Deut. 27:15). All people are destined to pay homage to God anyway, even if unwilling (Phil. 2:10).

An equally important reason for worship is that God deserves our worship. He alone possesses the attributes that merit our worship and service. Among these are goodness (Ps. 100:4, 5), mercy (Ex. 4:31), holiness (Ps. 99:5, 9), and creative power (Rev. 4:11). When men of biblical times clearly saw the unveiled glory of God, they could not help but fall prostrate in worship. Examples of this response can be seen in the actions of Moses (Ex. 34:5–8), Paul (Acts 9:3–6), and John (Rev. 1:9–17).

A final reason for worship is that men need to give it. People cannot find personal fulfillment apart from the glad submission of themselves in worshipful obedience to God. He is the Creator and they are the creatures (Rev. 4:11). People who adopt as their master anything less than God are building their lives on quicksand. They will be no stronger than the object they worship (Ps. 115:4–8). One who worships God, however, not only participates in the occupation of heaven (Rev. 7:9–12), but finds joyful satisfaction for the present (Rom. 12:2; Col. 3:24).

## Participation in the Local Church

**Romans 16:5. Definition of the Local Church—**The local church is a geographically located, temporally limited, and visibly evident manifestation of the universal church, the body of Christ. In the early New Testament days the local church met in the Jewish synagogue and had a very simple organization (James 2:2). A little later the church met in the homes of believers (Rom. 16:5), and it was not uncommon to have a number of churches in an area (Gal. 1:2). The idea of meeting in a building constructed for that exclusive purpose is a post-New Testament idea. (For a more complete discussion of the church read Acts 7:38 and the section The Meaning of the Church.)

**Hebrews 10:25. The Reason for Participation in the Local Church—**The ultimate reason that we should participate in a local church is because it is specifically commanded by God. Even in New Testament days there were those who yielded to the temptation of absenting themselves from the worship services of the local church. The writer of Hebrews points out that members of a local church have an obligation to one another. They are to provoke one another to good works and to exhort one another to live consistent lives worthy of God. This can best be done within the context of a local church: so believers are commanded not to forsake assembling together.

**Acts 2:42–47. Benefits of Participation in the Local Church—**The benefits of participation in a local church are immediately apparent. This passage records the first meeting of the first local church. From this passage seven benefits of participation in the local church are immediately apparent: instruction—"continued steadfastly in the apostles' doctrine"; fellowship—"and fellowship"; observance of the ordinances—"breaking of bread"; corporate prayer—"prayers"; effective outreach—"fear came upon every soul"; common cause—"had all things in common"; and mutual assistance—"divided them among all, as anyone had need." In addition to these, four other benefits of participation in the local church are clear: worship (Acts 20:7); discipline (Matt. 18:15–17; 2 Cor. 13:1–10); pastoral oversight (1 Pet. 5:1–3); and obedience to God's command (Heb. 10:25). Participation in the local church is not optional for the child of God. It is imperative and yields eternal benefits.

## Sharing Our Faith

**Matthew 28:19. Sharing Our Faith: Why?—**There are at least six compelling reasons for sharing our faith in Christ with those who have not experienced new life in Christ.

a. Because God has commanded us to do so. The final words of Jesus while on earth (Acts 1:8) and also the Bible (Rev. 22:17) speak concerning this.
b. Because it demonstrates our love for God. Christ said that if we truly loved Him we would keep His commandments (John 14:15).
c. Because all are lost (Rom. 3:10, 23).
d. Because our sharing is God's chosen method to tell all people. He could have used angels, but He didn't. Only redeemed sinners can tell lost sinners about Christ. See Romans 10:14–17; Acts 8:3.
e. Because God desires to save all people (Acts 4:12; 2 Pet. 3:9; 1 Tim. 2:4).
f. Because someone once shared his faith with us. It may have been a faithful Bible teacher, or a godly pastor, or a praying parent. In other words, they have the right to expect that we will do for others what they have done for us.

**1 Corinthians 15:3, 4. Sharing Our Faith: What?—**Before discussing just what is to be shared concerning our faith, let us mention a few things we are not to do. We are not commanded to force Christian standards upon the unbelieving world (1 Cor. 5:12). We are not to confuse people by allowing them to believe that church membership, tithing, or any good works are somehow connected with becoming a Christian (Eph. 2:8–10).

Actually, we have but one thing to share with the unsaved, and that is the gospel of Christ. According to Paul it involves the death and resurrection of Christ (1 Cor. 15:1–4). A plan for sharing your faith might be as follows:

a. God's Word says all are sinners, condemned to hell (Is. 53:6; Rom. 3:10, 11, 23; 5:8, 12; Rev. 20:15).
b. There is nothing a lost person can do on his own to save himself (Is. 64:6; Eph. 2:9).
c. Christ was born, crucified, and resurrected to save lost people from their sin (John 3:16; 1 Tim. 1:15).
d. To be saved a sinner must believe God's Word and invite Christ into his heart by faith (John 5:24; Acts 16:31).

**1 Thessalonians 1:5. Sharing Our Faith: How?—**In order to share our faith successfully, we must keep the following rules in mind.

a. First, we must be clean vessels. God reminds Isaiah the prophet of this, "Be clean, you who bear the vessels of the Lord" (Is. 52:11). David the sinner prays for forgiveness and cleansing. Upon receiving this he states, "*Then* I will teach transgressors Your ways, and sinners shall be converted to You" (Ps. 51:13). While God does not demand golden or silver vessels, He does require clean ones.

b. We must be able to clearly give out the simple facts of the gospel without getting bogged down with profound theological concepts. Philip the evangelist demonstrated how to do this when he dealt with a sinner in the desert. "Then Philip opened his mouth, and beginning at this Scripture, preached Jesus to him" (Acts 8:35).
c. We must avoid arguments and stick to the basic issues of man's sin and Christ's blood. Often unbelievers will attempt to sidestep the gospel by asking unrelated questions, such as "Where did Cain get his wife?"
d. We must use the Word of God. Paul's tremendous success as an evangelist can be linked directly to his constant use of God's Word. See Acts 17:2; 18:28; 2 Timothy 2:15; 3:14–17.
e. We must depend upon the Spirit of God. See John 3:15; Acts 6:10; 1 Corinthians 2:4.

**2 Timothy 4:2. Sharing Our Faith: When?**—A famous evangelist once ended a revival meeting in Chicago by advising the unbelievers who were present that night to go home and seriously consider the claims of the gospel, and then return on the following night prepared to make a decision for Christ. But on that same night, October 8, 1871, the tragic Chicago fire broke out. Before it was finally extinguished nearly four miles of buildings were consumed, along with 250 human fatalities. The evangelist then vowed never to end a service without giving an invitation to accept Christ immediately.

The question as to when we should share our faith is directly tied to when a sinner should accept Christ. The Bible is clear that God's accepted time is today. See Hebrews 3:15; 4:7; 2 Corinthians 6:2; Isaiah 55:6. The reason for this is very simple—a sinner has no assurance whatsoever that he will live to see tomorrow. See Proverbs 27:1; Luke 12:19; James 4:13–15.

Thus, we are to witness any time, all the time, in any place and in all places. The apostle Paul shows us how this should be done. He witnesses everywhere, in a prison at midnight (Acts 16:25–31), and even on a sinking ship during a dark and stormy day (Acts 27:20–25).

## Walking in the Spirit

**Psalm 73:1. Walking in the Spirit: Confession**—An important prerequisite to walking in the Spirit is the confession of sin. Sin must be confessed in order to restore fellowship and to continue receiving God's power (1 John 1:5–10). Confession means that we agree with God about our sin. This involves much more than simply acknowledging the sin. Confession requires an attitude of sorrow for the sin and a willingness to turn from it. It does not mean that we will never commit the same sin again, but it does mean that the attitude of repentance is present.

Confession should be made at the moment the Christian becomes aware of sin. Apart from this rule, moreover, the Scriptures mention two specific times for confession: before the close of the day (Eph. 4:26) and before the Lord's Supper is observed (1 Cor. 11:27–32). Failure to do the latter is a special cause for discipline from the Lord.

Confession of sin should normally involve only those who have knowledge of the sin. This means that private sins should be confessed privately (1 John 1:9); sins between individuals confessed between those involved (Matt. 5:23, 24); and public sins confessed publicly (Matt. 18:17). Public confession normally is made for the edification of the church (1 Cor. 14:26).

**Romans 12:1. Walking in the Spirit: Yielding**—Confession of sin in itself is not enough to enable the believer to automatically walk in the Spirit. He must then become a yielded instrument for God's service. What is to be yielded is simply himself (Rom. 6:13; James 4:7). This involves both the body (Rom. 12:1; 1 Cor. 6:20) and the mind (Rom. 12:2), since it is with the body that actions conceived in the mind are carried out and with the mind that they are formulated. Stated another way, that which is conceived in the mind is carried out in the body; thus, one's whole being must be presented by a decisive act of the will to God for His service. Yielding must not be thought of simply as a willingness to do some specific thing. Rather, it consists of dedication by a person to do whatever God commands.

Yielding leads not only to dedication but also can result in separation: "do not be conformed to this world" (Rom. 12:2). Since the world is resolutely opposed to God, one cannot revel in its lusts and at the same time do the will of God (1 John 2:15–17).

Finally, yielding includes transformation of the mind. This work is said to be accomplished through a lifetime of "renewing" the mind. Man's mind has been darkened by sin (Rom. 8:7; Col. 1:21) and must be brought to the place where it thinks as God thinks (Eph. 4:23). This renewing is said to come especially through prayer to God in everything (Phil. 4:6, 7) and through constant meditation on the Word of God (Ps. 119:1). This transformation is a lifelong process that will not be completed until we are with Christ (Phil. 1:6; 1 John 3:2). Along life's way, however, it brings a peace and delight that can only come from having embraced the mind of Christ.

**Ephesians 5:18. Walking in the Spirit: Filling**—To be filled with the Spirit is to be controlled by the Spirit and is therefore crucial to successfully living the Christian life. Unlike the indwelling of the Spirit, filling is a repeated experience. This is underscored by the use of the present tense ("be filled") as well as by biblical examples of Christians who were filled more than once (Acts 2:4; 4:31). Just as important, we must observe that filling is a command to be obeyed, not an option.

The next most important question is, How can someone be filled with the Spirit? The prerequisites are simply confession of sin and yielding to God. The former means to agree with God about the person's sin; the latter means primarily dedication of himself to God. As the believer chooses to obey in these areas, he is filled with the Spirit and enabled to manifest Christlike character. This obedience may be accompanied by prayer but is not necessarily so.

The certainty of being filled with the Spirit may be

confirmed by the believer's faith and life. The believer must, of course, believe God's Word that meeting the conditions will result in the filling. The Spirit-filled person will exhibit the Christlike character described in Galatians 5:22, 23 as the fruit of the Spirit. Included in that list are all the vibrant, attractive qualities desired by all Christians. How delightful it is that any Christian may possess them and be transformed by the filling of the Spirit.

## Facing Problems in the New Life

*Synopsis*

Just as we have problems in our physical lives, we also experience problems in our spiritual or new lives. We are strengthened and grow as we face and conquer difficulties, whether those problems are physical or spiritual. As we grow in our new strength, we bring glory to God as He demonstrates His faithfulness and that His grace is sufficient for every need (2 Cor. 12:9). Some of the problems that are common in the new life are sin, temptation, suffering, struggling to know the will of God, and doubt.

A believer must be especially wary of places, situations, and times in which he or she may be vulnerable to temptation. Certainly the best antidote to temptation is to be a growing Christian. The mind that is occupied with the things of the Lord cannot at the same time be susceptible to temptation.

Of all the possible sins against God, the most serious is that of self-will. This sin led to the fall of Satan (Is. 14:12–14), and it can be said to be the root of Adam's transgression (Gen. 3:1–7). It is, therefore, of utmost importance that the child of God find His will and perform it.

The dismissal of doubt and strengthening of faith are best accomplished by reading and understanding the Word of God (Rom. 10:17). The Holy Spirit will convict the willing heart of its power. Growing in the Word produces growth in faith; reading and understanding the Word are like planting seeds of faith in the heart. They will bear the mature fruit of faith.

### Sin

**Psalm 51:2. What Sin Is**—In dealing with sin it is important to know what sin is. If asked to define sin, people will come up with many different definitions as to what sin is—usually the things that the individual does not like. One of the most common definitions of sin is *missing the mark*—a failure to live up to an expected standard. The problem with this definition is that it fails to take into account that when the mark is missed, something is hit. Another definition of sin is found in 1 John 3:4, "sin is lawlessness." Put simply, according to this verse, sin is anything that is contrary to what the Word of God commands or forbids. This definition, however, does not take into account those things about which the Word of God is silent. The best definition for sin is found in 1 John 5:17, "All unrighteousness is sin."

**Isaiah 59:2. What Sin Does**—Sin, regardless of its degree, always has an effect—separation. Sin separates one from God. This separation from God is death. Adam was told that if he ate of the tree of the knowledge of good and evil that he would die (Gen. 3:3). Adam ate of the tree and immediately died spiritually—his soul was separated from God—and he began to die physically. The entrance of sin into the human race brought with it death (Rom. 5:12; 6:23). That man is a sinner is proven by the fact that he dies—where there is death, there is sin. Sin's penalty, death, can be remedied by life—union with God. This is achieved by belief in Jesus, who died to pay the penalty of man's sin (Rom. 5:21). For the one who believes in Jesus, the penalty of sin is broken. Yes, he will die physically (unless he is alive when Jesus returns to take all believers to heaven with Himself, (1 Thess. 5:14–18), but physical death for him is only the doorway into the presence of God. Sin, however, does have an effect upon the believer, for it mars his fellowship with God. Sin in the believer's life is a terrible thing and is not to be tolerated. While it is probable that the believer will sin, it is never necessary for him to do so (1 John 2:1).

**Psalm 32:5. What Should Be Done About Sin**—The believer should never condone or attempt to excuse his sin. There are only two things that should be done about sin: confess it and forsake it. The Old and New Testaments are agreed on this. David confessed his sin and experienced the Lord's forgiveness. John agrees as he points out: "If we confess our sins, He is faithful and just to forgive us *our* sins and to cleanse us from all unrighteousness" (1 John 1:9). To "confess" means *to acknowledge* or *to say the same thing as*. The believer is instructed that he is to say the same thing as God says about his sin, "It is sin." When the believer confesses his sin he has the assurance that God "is faithful" (He can be counted upon to keep His word) and "just" (He is just in dealing with our sins because He paid the price for them) "to forgive us *our* sins and to cleanse us from all unrighteousness." There is no sin too great and no sin too small—God is able to cleanse us completely from anything that is inconsistent with His own moral character. Having received forgiveness and cleansing, the believer is to forsake his sin and yield himself completely to God. In doing this the believer is restored to full fellowship with God.

### Temptation

**1 John 2:15. Temptation by the World**—The term *world* does not always refer to the universe as created by God. It often is used to describe the community of sinful humanity that possesses a spirit of rebellion against God (1 John 5:19). Because of its opposition to God, the world values those things which are contrary to God's will: "the lust of the flesh, the lust of the eyes, and the pride of life" (1 John 2:16). Its temptations to the believer are thus twofold: lust for the sensual and pride in mastery of his own life.

The attraction of the world is amplified by Satan who is head of its system. He is called the "ruler of this world" (John 12:31; 14:30; 16:11), and the whole world is said to be under his power (1 John 5:19).

Some of the tragic effects that love of the world will produce in the believer's life are:

a. A turning away from the Lord's work and other believers (2 Tim. 4:10);
b. Alienation from God (James 4:4);
c. Corrupting sins (2 Pet. 1:4; 1 John 2:15–17);
d. Deception by false teachers (1 John 4:1; 2 John 7).

The solution to the love of the world is to have a greater love for the Father (1 John 2:15). The Christian who seeks daily to please God in everything and who strives for spiritual growth through prayer, study of God's Word, and witnessing need not fall prey to the temptations of the world.

**Mark 14:38. Temptation by the Flesh**—*Flesh* in the Bible often means something other than the substance of the human body. It is used constantly to refer to the carnal, sinful principle within man that is opposed to God (Rom 8:7). The actions produced by the flesh are given in detail in Galatians 5:19–21. Among these are all types of sexual immorality, impurity, hatred, anger, false religions, envy, and drunkenness. A person whose life is characterized by these sins cannot be a true Christian and is under the wrath of God (Gal. 5:21; Eph. 2:3).

Though the flesh is not eradicated for the Christian, he does not have to obey it (Rom. 7:15–25). He possesses a new nature empowered by the Holy Spirit. Since the flesh and the Spirit are totally opposed to each other, the one whom the believer allows to dominate him will take charge in his life and produce its own fruit. The solution to the urges of the flesh lies in acknowledging that the power of sin was nullified by Jesus' death (Rom. 6:11) and in living under the control of the Spirit's power (Gal. 5:16). The latter is a moment-by-moment dependence in faith on the Spirit's power. The believer must choose by an act of his will to benefit from the Spirit's enablement.

**1 Chronicles 21:1. Temptation by Satan**—The role of Satan against the Christian is well summed up by the meaning of the name Satan—"adversary." He is also called "the devil," meaning "accuser." He can appear as a hideous dragon (Rev. 12:3, 4, 9) or as a beautifully deceptive "angel of light" (2 Cor. 11:14). He stands hatefully opposed to all the work of God and resourcefully promotes defiance among men (Mark 4:15; Job 2:4, 5).

When Satan sinned he was expelled from heaven (Luke 10:18), although apparently he still had some access to God (Job 1:6). A multitude of angels cast in their lot with him in his fall and subsequently became the demons mentioned often in the Bible (Matt. 12:24; Rev. 12:7). Although Satan's doom was secured by Jesus' death on the cross (John 16:11), he will continue to hinder God's program until he and his angels are cast into the lake of fire (Matt. 25:41; Rev. 20:10).

The terrifying work of Satan in the unbeliever is described in Scripture as follows: he blinds their minds (2 Cor. 4:4); he takes the Word of God from their hearts (Luke 8:12); and he controls them (Acts 13:8). In regard to Christians, Satan may accuse them (Rev. 12:10), devour their testimony for Christ (1 Pet. 5:8), deceive them (2 Cor. 11:14), hinder their work (1 Thess. 2:18), tempt them to immorality (1 Cor. 7:5), and even be used by God to discipline Christians (1 Cor. 5:5; 2 Cor. 12:7).

The Christian's response to Satan is to recognize his power and deception (2 Cor. 2:11; Eph. 6:11), to adhere steadfastly to the faith (1 Pet. 5:9), to resist him openly (James 4:7), and not to give him opportunities (Eph. 4:27). In practice, the best way to oppose him is to be a growing Christian. Also, in the light of his tremendous power to blind men to the gospel, Christians must always be aggressively and compassionately witnessing to the lost in order to snatch them from Satan's control (Acts 26:18). Believers can respond to temptation by Satan with confidence. We know that nothing can separate us from the love of God (Rom. 8:28–39).

## Suffering

**1 Peter 3:17. Kinds of Suffering**—There are three basic kinds of suffering, all of which can bring about much pain and discomfort to the believer.

a. Physical suffering. This, of course, occurs when a part of our body is injured or begins to malfunction, resulting in a disharmony between it and the rest of the body. Several factors can be involved in physical suffering. It can be caused by an accident or by carelessness (2 Sam. 4:4). It can be due to birth deformities (John 9:1). It can result from internal disorders (Luke 8:43). Finally, physical suffering may actually be caused by Satan (Job 2:7; Luke 13:16).
b. Mental suffering. In many ways this suffering is even more intense than physical suffering. Justified or unjustified concern over some matter can easily produce mental anguish. Paul himself experienced "fear and trembling" and "anguish of heart" (1 Cor. 2:3; 2 Cor. 1:8; 2:4, 13; 7:5).
c. Spiritual suffering. Spiritual suffering can come from the world (1 John 2:15–17), the flesh (Rom. 7:18–24), or the devil. Often it is the latter. See Acts 13:8–11; 16:16–18; 1 Thessalonians 2:18.

**Job 2:7. Purposes of Suffering**—Perhaps the most painful question confronting the believer is the problem of suffering. Why does a loving and wise God permit His children to suffer? The Scriptures offer a number of reasons for this:

a. To produce fruit. If we allow suffering to accomplish its purpose, it can bring forth patience (Heb. 10:36; James 1:3), joy (Ps. 30:5; 126:6), knowledge (Ps. 94:12), and maturity (1 Pet. 5:10).
b. To silence the devil. Satan once accused Job of merely serving God for the material blessings involved. But the Lord allowed the devil to torment Job to demonstrate that His servant loved God because of who He was, and not for what he could get from Him (Job 1:9–12; 2:3–7).
c. To glorify God (John 9:1–3; 11:1–4).
d. To make us like Jesus: "That I may know Him and the power of His resurrection, and the fellowship of His sufferings, being conformed to His death" (Phil. 3:10).
e. To teach us dependence. This is brought out by both Christ (John 15:1–5) and the apostle Paul (2 Cor. 12:1–10).
f. To refine our lives (Ps. 66:10–12; Prov. 17:3; 1 Pet. 1:6, 7).
g. To rebuke our sin (1 Pet. 2:20; 3:17; 4:15). As a faithful earthly father must in love punish his

erring child, so does our heavenly Father (Heb. 12:5–9).

h. To enlarge our ministry toward others (2 Cor. 1:3–7). It has been observed that he who has suffered much speaks many languages (understands others).

**Job 1:21. Response to Suffering**—In the hour of suffering the Christian should attempt to determine first of all just why he may be suffering. One can suffer because of his position or his disposition. Peter brings this truth out in his first epistle: "Servants, *be* submissive to *your* masters with all fear, not only to the good and gentle, but also to the harsh. For this *is* commendable, if because of conscience toward God one endures grief, suffering wrongfully" (1 Pet. 2:18, 19).

Suffering is often a two-sided coin. On the one side suffering may be viewed as coming from God to bring out the best in us. See Genesis 22:1, 2, 15–18; Hebrews 11:17. On the other side Satan attempts to use the same temptation and suffering to bring out the worst in us (James 1:13, 14). Finally, the believer can react to suffering in three different ways:

a. Despise it, that is, treat it too lightly, as did Esau his birthright (Heb. 12:5, 16).
b. Faint under it, that is, treat it too seriously (Heb. 12:5).
c. Be exercised by it, that is, receive instruction from it. This is the reaction desired by God (Heb. 12:11–13).

During this time both Peter and Paul advise us to commit our pain and suffering to God, realizing He is faithful to work out all things for our good and God's glory (Rom. 8:28; 1 Pet. 4:19). James tells us to "count it all joy" when we experience these dark hours (James 1:2).

**Jeremiah 37:15. Examples of Suffering**—In the Word of God there are four great examples of believers' suffering for the sake of righteousness. These are: Joseph, Job, Jeremiah, and Paul.

*The sufferings of Joseph:* he was hated by his brothers (Gen. 37:4, 5, 8); he was sold into slavery (Gen. 37:28); he was severely tempted (Gen. 39:7); and he was imprisoned (Gen. 39:20).

*The sufferings of Job:* his oxen and donkeys were stolen and his farmhands killed (Job 1:14, 15); his sheep and herdsmen were burned by a fire (Job 1:16); his camels were stolen and his servants killed (Job 1:17); his sons and daughters died in a windstorm (Job 1:18, 19); and he was struck with boils (Job 2:7).

*The sufferings of Jeremiah:* he was persecuted by his own family (Jer. 12:6); he was plotted against by his own hometown (Jer. 11:18–23); he was rejected and ridiculed by his religious peers (Jer. 20:1–3, 7–9); and he was arrested, beaten, and accused of treason (Jer. 37:11–16).

*The sufferings of Paul:* he was plotted against (Acts 9:23, 29; 20:3; 21:30; 23:10, 12; 25:3); he was stoned and left for dead (Acts 14:19); he was subjected to satanic pressure (1 Thess. 2:18); he was beaten and jailed at Philippi (Acts 16:19–24); he was ridiculed (Acts 17:16–18; 26:24); he was falsely accused (Acts 21:21, 28; 24:5–9); he endured a number of violent storms at sea (2 Cor. 11:25; Acts 27:14–20); he was bitten by a serpent (Acts 28:3, 4); and he was forsaken by all (2 Tim. 4:10, 16).

## Knowing the Will of God

**2 Kings 23:3. Knowing the Will of God Through the Scriptures**—The best way to study a subject often begins with a definition of that subject. What do we mean by the will of God? It is that holy and stated purpose of the Father to make His dear children as much like Christ as possible.

Without doubt the most important factor in finding God's will is the Bible itself. God speaks to us not in some loud voice, but through the Scriptures. *First,* the Scriptures declare He does have a definite will for my life. "The steps of a *good* man are ordered by the LORD" (Ps. 37:23). "I will instruct you and teach you in the way you should go" (Ps. 32:8). See also Ephesians 2:10; Hebrews 12:1. *Second,* God desires us to know this will for our lives. "Therefore do not be unwise, but understand what the will of the Lord *is*" (Eph. 5:17). *Third,* this will is continuous. It does not begin when I am thirty years of age. God has a will for children, young people, adults, and senior citizens. See Isaiah 58:11. *Fourth,* God's will is specific. "Your ears shall hear a word behind you, saying, 'This *is* the way, walk in it' " (Is. 30:21). "But the way of the upright *is* a highway" (Prov. 15:19). *Fifth,* God's will is profitable (Josh. 1:8; Ps. 1:1–3).

What is the will of God for us? As we have already noted, it differs from believer to believer. But here are four aspects in the will of God which apply to every Christian:

a. It is His will that we learn more about God (Col. 1:9).
b. It is His will that we grow in grace (1 Thess. 4:3).
c. It is His will that we study His Word (2 Tim. 3:14–17).
d. It is His will that we share our faith (Acts 1:8; 1 Tim. 2:4; 2 Pet. 3:9).

**Daniel 9:3, 4. Knowing the Will of God Through Prayer and Fasting**—Soon after Israel had invaded Palestine in the days of Joshua, the Israelites were tricked into signing an unscriptural peace treaty with a group of deceitful pagans. The cause for this tragic error is clearly stated in God's Word, "Then the men . . . did not ask counsel of the LORD" (Josh. 9:14). These pagans, the Gibeonites, brought only trouble to Israel. See Joshua 10:4–15; 2 Samuel 21:1–14.

It therefore becomes immediately obvious that one of the most important factors in knowing God's will for our lives is to pray. "If any of you lacks wisdom, let him ask of God, who gives to all liberally and without reproach, and it will be given to him" (James 1:5). See also Psalm 143:8, 10; James 4:2.

In the light of these passages it is evident a Christian must pray to know God's will. In other Bible verses fasting is linked with prayer.

a. Meaning of fasting: to fast is to abstain for a period of time from some important and necessary activity in our lives.
b. Purpose of fasting: this is done that we might spend that time in prayer before God.
c. Kinds of fasting: one may, for a time, refrain from sleep (2 Cor. 6:5; 11:27), marital sex (1 Cor. 7:1–5), or food (Matt. 4:1, 2).
d. Examples of biblical fasting: Moses (Deut. 9:9, 18,

25–29); Elijah (1 Kin. 19:8); Daniel (Dan. 9:3; 10:3); Ezra (Ezra 10:6); Nehemiah (Neh. 1:4); and Paul (2 Cor. 6:5; 11:27).

**Isaiah 6:8. Knowing the Will of God Through Submission to the Spirit**—The moment a repenting sinner receives Christ by faith into his heart the Holy Spirit immediately does five things for him:

a. He regenerates the believer, that is, He gives him a new nature (John 3:5, 6; Titus 3:5).
b. He baptizes the believer into the body of Christ (1 Cor. 12:13).
c. He indwells the believer (Rom. 8:9; 1 Cor. 6:19).
d. He seals the believer (Eph. 1:13; 4:30).
e. He fills the believer (Acts 2:4; 4:8; 7:55; 13:52).

All five of these ministries often occur at conversion. The fifth ministry, however, should be asked for as needed. See Ephesians 5:18; Galatians 5:16. Actually the word *control* is a better term than *fill* in describing this fifth ministry. It does not mean that we get more of the Spirit, but rather that He gets more of us. The fifth ministry is lost when the believer either quenches (1 Thess. 5:19) or grieves (Eph. 4:30) the Holy Spirit. The fifth ministry can be regained by following the command of 1 John 1:9, "If we confess our sins, He is faithful and just to forgive us *our* sins and to cleanse us from all unrighteousness."

How can a Christian be certain that he is indeed controlled by the Holy Spirit on a daily basis? First, he must consecrate his body as a living sacrifice to the Holy Spirit (Rom. 12:1, 2). Second, he must depend upon the Holy Spirit to convict him of sin (Ps. 139:23, 24; 19:12–14). Finally, he must look to the Holy Spirit for divine power in serving Christ (Acts 1:8; Gal. 5:16, 17; Eph. 3:16).

**Proverbs 24:6. Knowing the Will of God Through Circumstances and Counsel**—While the Christian is to live above his circumstances, he is not to be unaware of them. God often works through circumstances in revealing His perfect will for us. Certainly Paul's wonderful statement that "all things work together for good to those who love God" (Rom. 8:28) takes into account our circumstances. A number of biblical examples can be given to illustrate this.

a. God directed Abraham to substitute a ram, whose horns had somehow become entangled in a thicket, for the life of Isaac (Gen. 22:13).
b. God arranged for Pharaoh's daughter to be bathing in the river Nile at the exact time the baby Moses floated by in a little ark of bulrushes (Ex. 2:1–10).
c. Paul's young nephew happened to overhear a plot to kill his famous uncle. He then reported it to the authorities, thus saving the apostle's life (Acts 23:12–22).

Surely the above circumstances were providentially arranged. So the Christian should ask, when attempting to discover God's will, Is the Lord showing me something through my circumstances?

Counselors also play an important role in finding God's will. "In a multitude of counselors *there is* safety" (Prov. 24:6). However, three things must be kept in mind at this point:

a. Counsel must come from a godly source. "Confidence in an unfaithful *man* in time of trouble *is like* a bad tooth and a foot out of joint" (Prov. 25:19).
b. Sometimes even the godliest person can unknowingly give us wrong advice. Nathan the prophet did this when he encouraged David to build the temple (2 Sam. 7:1–13).
c. In the final analysis, each person is responsible for knowing God's revealed purpose for his own life.

## Doubt

**Lamentations 5:20. Occasions of Doubt**—Doubt may be defined as an uncertainty of belief or lack of confidence in something. Applied to the Christian life, doubt refers to the unbelief in God and His Word that Christians occasionally exhibit. It is possible that in a moment of infirmity a Christian may doubt the existence of God in spite of the fact that it is not reasonable for a person to disbelieve this obvious truth (Ps. 14:1). A Christian is more likely to doubt his salvation after sinning or after a spiritual defeat. A misunderstanding of such verses as 1 John 3:9 contributes to this doubt: "Whoever has been born of God does not sin." It is crucial to note that this verse speaks of a life-style of sin, not instances of sin.

A Christian may also doubt God's sovereignty or His goodness. In such circumstances as sickness, suffering, injustice, opposition, economic problems, family problems, national calamity, or apparently unanswered prayer, a Christian may be tempted to doubt the goodness of God. One must remember that it is not always possible to discern God's good hand in the affairs of life. The person of faith believes God even when circumstances appear to the contrary.

All doubt may be traced ultimately to unbelief in the Word of God, which affirms beyond question the existence and character of God. To regard doubt as the sin of unbelief and then confess it to God as sin is therefore the first step toward conquering it.

**Habakkuk 1:2. Sources of Doubt**—One of the most potent sources of doubt is introduced in the early chapters of Genesis. It is Satan himself who causes Eve to doubt God by questioning His Word: "Has God indeed said, 'You shall not eat of every tree of the garden'?" (Gen. 3:1). Satan even tries to get the long-suffering Job to curse God (Job 1:11). Satan is said to be seeking to devour Christians (1 Pet. 5:8). This statement must not be taken literally, but means that Satan wants to devour the Christian's commitment to God and testimony before others. One way he does this is by introducing doubt into the mind.

The world system is another source of doubt. Since it has its own set of values and objectives that are opposed to God, it also has its own worldly wisdom (1 Cor. 2:6). This wisdom stands in direct opposition to the wisdom of God taught by the Holy Spirit (1 Cor. 2:13). It is clearly revealed, for example, in the opposition of the evolutionary theory to the truth of the creation of man (1 Tim. 6:20).

Probably the greatest source of doubt Christians face is simply their own spiritual immaturity. James traces doubting in prayer to double-mindedness and instability (James 1:8). Paul explains that when Christians doubt sound doctrine, it is because they are children in the faith and thus are easily deceived (Eph. 4:14). Conquering this kind of doubt demands a growing, obedient relationship with God.

**1 Kings 18:21. Cure for Doubt**—The cure for doubt depends to some extent on the thing doubted. However, the real problem is not in the object doubted but in the subject who doubts. Therefore, the following steps should be taken by the doubting Christian:

a. Confess the doubt to God as sin. Doubt is basically unbelief in God and His Word and is therefore sin (Rom. 14:23; Heb. 11:6). God has promised to hear our confession of even the darkest unbelief.
b. Study the evidence for the Christian faith. Christians have nothing to fear by looking into the facts from any source of knowledge. The greatest evidence for the validity of Christianity, the resurrection of Christ, is attested by many proofs. Among these are the empty tomb, post-resurrection appearances, and transformed disciples. Since the Resurrection is true, it verifies everything the Bible says.
c. Make certain of your salvation. Paul exhorts Christians to examine themselves to make sure they are Christians (2 Cor. 13:5). So did the author of Hebrews (Heb. 6:1–9). Salvation from sin is by simple trust in Jesus Christ. Until you are assured of your salvation you will be troubled by enormous doubts.
d. Faithfully study the Word of God. "Faith *comes* by hearing, and hearing by the word of God" (Rom. 10:17). Through study and application of the Bible, our faith is strengthened and matured. Most especially, we must master the doctrines or basic teachings of the Bible if we are to be stable, mature Christians (1 Tim. 4:13, 16; 2 Tim. 3:16; Titus 2:1, 10).
e. Pray. The surest way to face doubts when they come is to have an extensive past history of answered prayer. The more a Christian prays with faith, the more that Christian sees God answer prayer; the more a person sees God answer prayer, the stronger that person's faith becomes while the doubt becomes less.

## Recognizing God's Institutions

*Synopsis*

God gave humanity four basic institutions: the family, human government, Israel, and the church. It may be observed that each of these institutions demonstrates a characteristic or attribute of God.

- The family illustrates the unity of God (Gen. 2:24; Deut. 6:4).
- Human government illustrates the judgment of God (Rom. 13:1, 2).
- Israel illustrates the election of God (Rom. 9:1–18; 11:1–5).
- The church illustrates the love of God (Eph. 5:22–27).

The family was the first human institution God created. Through the family God illustrates visibly the relationships which exist in the Godhead and the relationship which exists between Christ and His church. Through the family God sought to bring into proper relationship the world with Himself. He created all of the heavens and earth and the things in them that they might prepare the way for and sustain the crown of His creation—humanity.

God's purpose in human government is that it serve as both a custodian and an enforcer of His eternal law. It has been correctly noted that all the thousands of good and practical laws passed by hundreds of legislative bodies and rulers throughout history are in reality only amplifications of the Ten Commandments.

God's selection of Israel as a special nation may puzzle the Bible student, but His choice becomes obvious through study. When God promised Abraham that he would become the father of a great nation, He also promised that He would bless all peoples through that nation (Gen. 12:1–3). Israel was to be a channel of blessing as well as a recipient.

The church, illustrating God's love for us, is the fourth institution through which God works. The universal church—the body of Christ (Col. 1:18)—comprises all believers since the institution of the church.

### The Family

**Genesis 2:18–25. How the Family Began**—Genesis 2:18–25 fills in the details of the simple statement in Genesis 1:27: "Male and female He created them." This account particularly amplifies the "and female" part of the statement and shows how woman was created. Three observations can be made on the passage that will help us to understand how the family began:

a. The need for woman (vv. 18–20). Woman is absolutely essential in God's plan. It was God who observed, "*It is* not good that man should be alone" (v. 18), and determined to make a "helper" for Adam. Woman's role in the will of God was to be a "helper" who was suitable to man in every particular mental, spiritual, emotional, social, and physical need. God undertook an orientation program to show man the need that He alone had observed. He brought to man the birds and beasts He had created, so that man should exercise his dominion over them (v. 28) and name them (v. 19). However, in verse 20 it is noted that for Adam there was no "helper" similar to himself.
b. The provision of woman for man (vv. 21–24). God caused Adam to go to sleep, and God removed one of his "ribs." Exactly what God removed is not known, but it was adequate for His purpose. He "made" (lit., *built*) a woman (v. 22) whom Adam recognized as being his equal, "bone of my bones and flesh of my flesh." This resulted in what has become known as the universal law of marriage (v. 24), in which it can be seen that: (1) the responsibility for marriage is on the man's shoulders—he is to "leave his father and mother"; (2) the responsibility for keeping the union together is on the man's shoulders—he is to "be joined to" his wife;

and (3) the union is indissoluble—"they shall become one flesh."

c. The state of the first man and woman (v. 25). From the beginning the man and woman were "naked" in each other's presence and "were not ashamed." There is no shame in nudity when it occurs within the right context—the marital union. This passage clearly teaches that (1) sex was God's idea and is not sinful; (2) sex came before the Fall, and if the Fall had never taken place there still would be sexual relations between a man and his wife; and (3) propagation of the species is one, but not the exclusive, purpose for sex. The Bible gives two other reasons for sex: (1) to promote love between the husband and wife (Heb. 13:4), and (2) to prevent fornication—the unlawful satisfaction of the God-given sexual desire (1 Cor. 7:2).

**Deuteronomy 6:4–9. Three Essentials for a Christian Home**—A new generation of Israel is gathered on the plains of Moab to hear Moses review the law in preparation for their entrance to the Promised Land. The previous generation had died in unbelief in the wilderness. Moses begins his instruction by telling the people of Israel what a home is all about. He sets forth three components which must be true if the home is rightly related to God:

a. There must be a revelation of God (6:4). God revealed three things about Himself: (1) His eternality (Jehovah; Hebrew *YHWH,* The Eternal); (2) His plurality (*Elohim,* Hebrew plural of God, there are three Persons in the Godhead); and (3) His unity—"one LORD"—the three Persons of the Godhead constitute one God; each is essential.

b. There must be a response to God's revelation (6:5). The response is to be a total response of love with all one's being, heart, soul, and mind. This is the only fitting response to the eternal God who has revealed Himself.

c. There must be a threefold responsibility (6:6–9). This threefold responsibility acts as a check upon the proper response. If the earthly father responds to God with love he will be fulfilling his threefold responsibility. If he fails in any particular, confession of sin is necessary because he does not love God with all his heart, soul, and mind. The threefold responsibility is: (1) to have God's truth govern his heart (6:6)—there must be heart reality, not mere external conformity or ceremony; (2) to have God's truth govern his home—this is evidenced by the fact that the father teaches the truths of God's revelation to his children by both formal (teach diligently) and informal (talk of them) instruction; and (3) to have God's truth govern his habits and conduct personally, privately, and publicly. In short, the home is to be a divine school in which the father is to be the teacher, under Christ.

**1 Peter 3:1–6. The Role of the Wife**—In this passage the wife's only responsibility in the family is to "*be* submissive" to her husband. A woman is to submit to her husband, not to mankind in general. To be in subjection to her husband does not imply any kind of natural inferiority on the part of the wife to the husband. In marriage two people become one. Therefore there are two intellects, two sets of emotions, and two wills that have been joined to constitute one. To keep the union from fracturing and destroying itself, one of those persons is charged with leadership in the relationship, and one is charged with submission.

The wife's submission to her husband is her "adorning," which makes her truly beautiful (3:3). This inner beauty is of great value in God's sight (3:4). The believing women of the Old Testament who hoped to be the human channel for the Messiah to come into the world made themselves beautiful by being in subjection to their own husbands. This is supremely illustrated in the relationship between Sarah and Abraham. Wives are exhorted to do what Sarah did, to be in subjection to their husbands, letting the consequences rest with God, and thus become Sarah's daughters (3:6). For the wife who will do this God promises that, if her husband is either an unbeliever or out of fellowship with God, her subjection can be the very means God will use to bring her husband into a proper relationship with Him (3:1, 2). The wife's subjection may lead to the husband's salvation.

**Colossians 3:19. The Role of the Husband**—Paul tells the husband to love his wife (Eph. 5:25), while Peter tells the husband to dwell together with his wife (1 Pet. 3:7). The husband cannot live with his wife as Peter says unless he loves her in the way Paul means. The love that the husband is commanded to have for the wife is not primarily sexual or emotional (though both of those are involved). It is a love that loves in spite of the response (or lack of it) in the one loved. It is the kind of love that God has for the world (John 3:16) and is the fruit of the Spirit (Gal. 5:22). A husband can only love his wife properly if he is a Christian and under the control of the Holy Spirit.

The two responsibilities the husband has in the family are to dwell with his wife according to knowledge, and to render to his wife the honor which is due her because she is his wife. To "dwell together" with his wife means that the husband must take his wife into *every* aspect of his life. There are to be no areas of his life where there are signs that say, "Private, husband only—wife keep out."

The husband is to perform his two duties for a spiritual purpose: "that your prayers may not be hindered." The man who is not taking his wife into every aspect of his life and rendering to her the honor which is due her because she is his wife cannot communicate with her in the way that God intended; hence, he cannot communicate with God either. To make sure that the channel of communication with God is open, the husband must make sure that the channel of communication with his wife is open. Only in this way can he truly love his wife as God intended and manifest his headship properly.

**Proverbs 1:8. The Role of Children**—Both the Old and New Testaments agree that children have only one responsibility in the family—to obey their parents. The admonition of Solomon is more fully explained by Paul in Ephesians 6:1–3: "Children, obey your parents in the Lord, for this is right. 'Honor your father and mother,' which is the first commandment with promise: 'that it may be well with you and you may live long on the earth.' " "Children" is an inclusive term. It is not a matter of either sex or age that is involved.

Twice in Scripture God has intervened and directly stated what He would have children do. The last time was nearly two thousand years ago when He gave a revelation to Paul for the church. The first time was nearly thiry-four hundred years ago when He gave a revelation to Moses and Israel in which He commanded, "Honor your father and your mother." God's will for children is that they are to obey their parents. The expression "in the Lord" does not limit the responsibility only to the circumstances where the parents are believers. Colossians 3:20 clearly points out that children are to obey their parents "in all things," not just in those things pertaining to Christian living. "In the Lord" more properly is understood to mean by the Lord or because it is the Lord's directive (this is what God says children are to do). For children to obey their parents is righteous or Godlike. Such obedience is perfectly illustrated by God the Son who was completely obedient to God the Father, even though that obedience resulted in His death (Phil. 2:6–8).

Two things are promised to children who obey their parents: it will be well with them—they will have a happy life; and they will have a long life. These are the two things that children want most, and obedience to parents is the only way to assure them. That is why this is the first commandment with promise; from it springs all the other important issues of life. The child who has not learned to obey his parents, who are God's representatives in the family, will not learn to obey God.

**Ephesians 6:4. The Role of the Parents**—The father is the parent responsible for setting the pattern for the child's obedience in the family. Any disciplining the mother does is an extension of the father's authority in the home. The husband and the father must take leadership in this area of the family, and the wife and mother must be in submission. The father's responsibility is set forth in two ways: First, what the father is *not* to do—"do not provoke your children to wrath." He is not to over-discipline them or reign in terror, with the result that his children can only react in blind outbreaks of rage. Second, what the father *is* to do—"but bring them up in the training and admonition of the Lord." To "bring them up" involves three ideas:

a. It is a continuous job. As long as the child is a dependent, the father is to be responsible for providing for the child so that he becomes what God wants him to be.
b. It is a loving job. To "bring up" means literally *to nourish tenderly;* children should be objects of tender, loving care.
c. It is a twofold job involving nurture (lit., *child-training*)—all that a child needs for his development physically, mentally, and spiritually—and admonition (lit., *corrective* discipline) of the Lord.

The father is God's constituted home authority who is to discipline the child when he does not obey as God intends. The father who does not discipline his children is a father who is undisciplined himself and disobedient to God's will. A child's disobedience is not to be tolerated. See Exodus 21:15–17; Deuteronomy 21:18–21; Proverbs 13:24; 19:18; 22:15; 23:13, 14; 29:15–17.

**Proverbs 22:6. A Prescription for Rearing Children**—This verse reveals two ingredients in the prescription for rearing children: first, the command, "Train up a child in the way he should go"; and second, the promise, "when he is old he will not depart from it."

The command involves three parts:

a. The concept of training—"Train up." This does not denote corporal punishment but rather includes three ideas: *Dedication*—this is the consistent meaning of the word in its other Old Testament occurrences (Deut. 20:5; 1 Kin. 8:63; 2 Chr. 7:5). Child training must begin with dedication of the child to God; parents must realize that the child belongs exclusively to God and is given to them only as a stewardship. *Instruction*—this is the meaning of this word as it is used in the Jewish writings; the parents are to instruct or cause their children to learn everything essential in pleasing God. *Motivation*—this is the meaning of the word in Arabic, as it is used to describe the action of a midwife who stimulates the palate of the newborn babe so it will take nourishment. Parents are to create a taste or desire within the child so that he is internally motivated (rather than externally compelled) to do what God wants him to do.
b. The recipient of training—"a child." This is one of seven Hebrew words translated by the English word *child* and would better be translated by our word *dependent.* As long as the child is dependent on his parents he is to be the recipient of training, regardless of his age.
c. The content of the training—"in the way that he should go." The thought is that at each stage of his development the parents or guardians are to dedicate, instruct, and motivate the child to do what God evidently has best equipped the child to do for Him. This is graphically illustrated by Joshua when he said, "But as for me and my house, we will serve the LORD" (Josh. 24:15).

If the command has been kept, the promise can be claimed. The promise includes the time of realization—"when he is old"—this is best understood as being parallel with "a child," hence, "when he is independent," i.e., no longer economically dependent upon his parents, referring to the time when he leaves their home to establish his own. The promise includes the certainty of realization—"he will not depart from it." If the command has been kept, the promise will be realized. If the command has not been kept, the promise will not be realized. Rearing children is not an overnight occurrence; it takes careful forethought and conscious obedience on the part of the parents.

## Human Government

**Genesis 9:5. The Origin of Human Government**—It has been assumed that human government was officially instituted after the great Flood in Genesis 9. However, some form of law and order undoubtedly existed prior to this period. This is strongly suggested by both Jesus and Jude. Jesus in Luke 17:26, 27 says that prior to the Flood in Noah's day people conducted their affairs in much the same manner as we do today. Jude gives us the text of a message Enoch preached to sinners prior to the Flood (Jude 14, 15). We learn that one of the main factors which brought about the Flood was man's disobedience to the revealed law of God.

At any rate, there is certainly no doubt concerning the source of human government. God Himself is its divine author. Two individuals give testimony to this fact. Daniel reminds King Nebuchadnezzar that "the Most High rules in the kingdom of men, and gives it to whomever He chooses" (Dan. 4:25). The apostle Paul exhorts Christians to be subject to the laws of human government because all earthly powers exist through God's divine permission (Rom. 13).

If one rightly understands the origin of human government, then the conclusion is reached that lawless anarchy is not only rebellion against human authority, but actual blasphemy against the divine Creator Himself.

**Romans 13:1–4. The Function of Human Government**—The general function of human government, as instituted by God, may be said to be threefold: to protect, punish, and promote.

a. The Function of Protection: The moment Adam sinned it was obvious that civilizations would need some form of restraint and rule to protect citizens from themselves. An example of this function is seen in Acts 21:27–37 where Roman soldiers step in and save Paul from being murdered by his own enraged countrymen in Jerusalem.
b. The Function of Punishment: Both Paul and Peter bring this out. Paul writes that duly appointed human officials are to be regarded as God's servants to "bear the sword," that is, to impose punishment upon criminals (vv. 3, 4). Peter tells us that governors are "sent by him for the punishment of evildoers" (1 Pet. 2:13, 14).
c. The Function of Promotion: Human government is to promote the general welfare of the community where its laws are in effect. Paul commands us to pray for human leaders "that we may lead a quiet and peaceable life in all godliness and reverence" (1 Tim. 2:1, 2).

**1 Peter 2:13. Our Responsibility to Human Government**—It is impossible for a believer to be a good Christian and a bad citizen at the same time. As children of God our responsibility to human government is threefold.

a. We are to recognize and accept that the powers that be are ordained by God. "Let every soul be subject to the governing authorities. For there is no authority except from God, and the authorities that exist are appointed by God" (Rom. 13:1). This truth applies even to atheistic human governments unless, of course, the law is anti-scriptural. In that situation the believer must obey God rather than man (Acts 4:18–20). In fact, when Paul wrote those words in Romans 13:1, the evil emperor Nero was on the throne. See also Titus 3:1.
b. We are to pay our taxes to human government (Matt. 17:24–27; 22:21; Rom. 13:7).
c. We are to pray for the leaders in human government. "Therefore I exhort first of all that supplications, prayers, intercessions, *and* giving of thanks be made for all men, for kings and all who are in authority, that we may lead a quiet and peaceable life in all godliness and reverence. For this *is* good and acceptable in the sight of God our Savior" (1 Tim. 2:1–3).

Paul exhorts us to pray that those who are in authority may lead a quiet life. We are to pray that they hold their offices in godliness and honesty (1 Tim. 2:1–3).

## Israel

**Amos 3:2. Selection of Israel**—The selection of Israel as a special nation to God was part of God's plan (Rom. 11:2). Historically, the selection of Israel began with the Lord's promise to Abraham, "I will make you a great nation" (Gen. 12:2). The name *Israel* actually is from the new name which God gave to Abraham's grandson, Jacob. It was occasioned by Jacob's spiritual victory at the ford of Jabbok (Gen. 32:28). This fact explains why his descendants are often called the children of Israel.

The motivation for the Lord's choice of Israel as His select nation did not lie in any special attraction it possessed. Its people were, in fact, the least in number among all the nations (Deut. 7:6–8). Rather, the Lord chose them because of His love for them and because of His covenant with Abraham. This fact does not mean that God did not love other nations, because it was through Israel that He intended to bring forth the Savior and to bless the entire world (Gen. 12:3).

**Psalm 78:4. History of Israel**—The biblical history of Israel covers 1,800 years and represents a marvelous panorama of God's gracious working through promise, miracle, blessing, and judgment. Israel begins as only a promise to Abraham (Gen. 12:2). For over four hundred years the people of Israel rely on that promise, especially during the period of bondage to Egypt. Finally, in God's perfect timing, He brings the nation out of Egypt with the greatest series of miracles known in the entire Old Testament (Ex. 7—15). This event is called the Exodus, meaning *a going out.* Since it constitutes the miraculous birth of the nation, it is to this great act of redemption that the nation always looks back as the foremost example of God's care for His people (Ps. 77:14–20; 78:12–55; Hos. 11:1).

Once God has redeemed Israel He establishes His covenant with them at Mount Sinai (Ex. 19:5–8). From that point forward the nation is truly the Lord's possession, and He is their God. The covenant foretells gracious blessings for obedience and severe judgments for disobedience. The rest of Israel's history demonstrates the certainty of that prophecy. Through the periods of conquest, judges, monarchy, exile, restoration, and gentile domination, Israel is blessed when she obeys and judged when she disobeys. The nation is finally destroyed in A.D. 70, although this event is not described in the New Testament. Many prophecies, however, promise a future redemption for Israel (Rom. 11:26).

The practical value of studying Israel's history is threefold:

a. It sets forth examples to be followed or avoided (1 Cor. 10:6).
b. It shows God's control of all historical events, in

that He was able to deal with Israel as He chose (Ps. 78).

c. It serves as a model for all ages of God's kindness and mercy toward His people (Ps. 103:14).

**Deuteronomy 14:2. Purpose of Israel**—The modern-day student of the Bible may well ask why so much of Scripture is taken up with the history of a single nation. Certainly many Christians wonder why one nation should be called "God's chosen people." The answer to this question is bound up in God's purpose for Israel. When God promised Abraham that he would become the father of a great nation, He also promised that He would bless all peoples through that nation (Gen. 12:1–3). Therefore Israel was to be a channel of blessing as well as a recipient. Even their deliverance from Egypt was partially designed to show other nations that Israel's God was the only true God (Ex. 7:5; 14:18; Josh. 2:9–11). It was further prophesied by Isaiah that the Messiah would bring salvation to the Gentiles (Is. 49:6). Also in the Psalms there are many invitations to other nations to come and worship the Lord in Israel (Ps. 2:10–12; 117:1). Ruth the Moabitess is an example of a foreigner who believed in Israel's God.

It is clear that God's promise to Abraham to bless the whole world through him is still being fulfilled. The life, ministry, and death of Jesus Christ, and the existence and influence of the church today, all came about through God's choice of Israel. All whom the church wins to Christ, whether Jew or Gentile, enter into those great blessings channeled through Israel.

**1 Chronicles 28:4–6. Government of Israel**—The government of Israel may be considered under two important headings: the laws, and the leaders.

*The laws:*

a. The "commandments," especially the Ten Commandments, revealed God's holiness and set up a divine standard of righteousness for the people to follow (Ex. 20:1–17).
b. The judgments governed the social life of the people and concerned masters and servants (Ex. 21:1–11), physical injuries (Ex. 21:12–36), protection of property rights (Ex. 22:1–15), and so on.
c. The ordinances included the sacrifices that showed that blood must be shed for sinners to be forgiven (Lev. 1—17).

*The leaders:* At first Moses was the sole leader; then he was replaced by Joshua. After Joshua's death the nation was governed for many years by judges, who were usually raised up by God to oppose a specific enemy. Finally, at the people's request, God granted them a king, thus establishing the monarchy (1 Sam. 8:5, 22). Under the monarchy there were four key leaders:

a. The *king* was the Lord's representative who ruled the people, but only as the Lord's servant. He led in war (1 Sam. 8:20) and made judicial decisions (2 Sam. 15:2); but he could not make law, since he himself was under the law (Deut. 17:19). His relationship was so close to the Lord that he was adopted by the Lord (2 Sam. 7:14; Ps. 2:7).
b. The *priest* taught the Lord's law and officiated at the offering of the sacrifices (Lev. 1:5; Jer. 18:18).
c. The *prophet* was the man of God who spoke for God and gave divine pronouncements for the present (forthtelling) or for the future (foretelling).
d. The *wise man* produced literary works stressing practical wisdom (Prov. 1:1), taught discipline of character to the young (Prov. 22:17), and gave counsel to the king (2 Sam. 16:20). The choice of these men indicates an important biblical principle: God uses people to reach other people, a principle that is also evident in the Great Commission given to Christians (Matt. 28:19, 20).

**Psalm 29:2. Worship by Israel**—The central aspect of Israel's worship was the object of their worship, the Lord. While other nations paid homage to many gods (Deut. 29:18), only Israel worshiped the one true God (Ex. 20:3). This worship could be private (Ex. 34:8), as a family (Gen. 22:5), or corporate (1 Chr. 29:20), as a congregation.

Since so much of the Bible is devoted to Israel's public worship, it deserves special notice. It included offering sacrifices (1 Sam. 1:3), adopting a reverent posture (2 Chr. 7:6), verbal praise—either spoken (1 Chr. 16:36) or sung (Ps. 57:7), instrumental praise (Ps. 150:3–5), prayer (2 Chr. 6:14–42), and the great feasts (Lev. 23; 25). One need only read the Psalms to see the excellent form and spirit in which the godly of Israel worshiped.

The first place of worship for the people of Israel was the tabernacle constructed by Moses (Ex. 25—27; 30; 31; 35—40) and later the magnificent temple constructed by Solomon (1 Chr. 22:5). These structures served to localize the worship of the entire nation. This geographic limitation stands in bold contrast to the privilege of immediate and direct access to God now available to the New Testament believer who himself is the temple of God (Heb. 4:16; 1 Cor. 6:19).

## The Church

**Acts 7:38. The Meaning of the Church**—In modern English the word *church* is used in five ways: (1) a building designated as a place of worship, i.e., a church building; (2) all who profess faith in Christ regardless of particular theological beliefs; (3) a denomination; (4) a single organized Christian group, i.e., a local church; and (5) the body of Christ, i.e., the universal church. While all of these are legitimate uses for modern English, the word *church* is used in the New Testament in only the last two senses—a local church, or the body of Christ, the universal church. At its root, the word *church* means a "called-out group." It is used of the nation Israel (Acts 7:38), which was a group of people who were called out of the rest of the people of the world to have a special national relationship to God. It is used of a local church (1 Thess. 1:1, church of the Thessalonians; (Rev. 2:1, church of Ephesus, etc.), and of the universal church, the body of Christ (Col. 1:18). The universal church comprises all believers from the Day of Pentecost until the time God takes the church out of the world, and at which time His program for the church will be complete. The local church is a local, visible, temporal manifestation of the universal church. At one point in history the local and universal churches were identical (Acts 2:41). The universal church will not meet until "we all get to heaven" and once in session will never cease.

**Matthew 16:18. The Origin of the Church**—The church was a mystery (i.e., hidden, not revealed) in the Old Testament. It was first prophesied in these words spoken to Peter, "on this rock I will build My church." In this prophecy there is a play on the word *rock* which also happens to be Peter's name. Jesus said, "you are Peter [masculine, *petros*]" and "on this rock [feminine, *petra*] I will build My church." But when did the church actually begin? Again, many suggestions are offered for varying reasons. The simplest view is to understand the New Testament church as beginning on the Day of Pentecost in response to Peter's Pentecostal sermon when "about three thousand souls were added *to them* [i.e., the apostles]" (Acts 2:41). This group for the first time is called "the church" in Acts 2:47, and God added to their number daily those who were saved.

**Ephesians 3:21. The Purpose of the Church**—The ultimate purpose of the church is to bring honor and glory to its Head, Jesus Christ. It does this as it fulfills its two purposes related to God's program for the world.

The one purpose of the church, as it relates to the world, is evangelism. This program is spelled out in the Great Commission (Matt. 28:19, 20), which has never been rescinded. The program is to "make disciples of all the nations." The way this is to be done is twofold: by "baptizing them in the name of the Father and of the Son and of the Holy Spirit," and by "teaching them to observe all things that I have commanded you." Baptism is not an optional afterthought. It is a vital part of evangelism and making disciples. By baptism, one indicates that he has been identified with Christ in His death, burial, and resurrection (i.e., he is a member of the universal church, the body of Christ) and wishes to be identified with the local church. A responsible parent not only brings a child into the world, but also provides what is necessary for the child's growth. So in the church, teaching must accompany evangelism so that the child of God can learn all that God expects of him and has provided for him.

Another purpose of the church, as it relates to the world, is edification. According to Ephesians 4:12 the saints need to be edified (built up) for two goals: "for the equipping of the saints for the work of ministry." The believers who compose the church's membership need to be built up so that they may realize all that God has provided for Christian living and that they may come to spiritual maturity. They also need to be equipped to perform that work in the body of Christ that God wants them to perform. In a real sense each member of the church is to be a Christian worker so that the work that God wants to perform through the local church can be accomplished.

**1 Timothy 3:1–13. The Offices of the Church**—The New Testament uses four terms to describe the leadership of the church: (1) "elder" (Gr., *presbuteros*), which places emphasis upon the authority that the leadership has to teach or rule in the church; (2) "bishop" (Gr., *episkopos*—overseer), which emphasizes the fact that the leadership is charged with overseeing the local church and as such is responsible for the spiritual well-being of those in the church; (3) "pastor" (Gr., *poimen*—shepherd), which places emphasis upon the responsibility of the leadership of the church to shepherd the flock. No shepherd has ever given birth to his sheep. It is the responsibility of those in leadership to do for the sheep what they cannot do for themselves and to make sure that they are in good spiritual condition so that they can do what comes naturally, that is, beget other sheep; (4) "deacon" (Gr., *diakonos*—minister), which places emphasis upon the attitude that the leaders are to have in their leading. They are not to "lord it over" the flock, but are to realize that they are the ministers or servants of those whom the Lord has put under their care.

The function of the office of elder is twofold: (1) teaching and (2) ruling (1 Tim. 5:17). An elder is to be able to teach his people what the Word of God teaches and to give direction as to how that is to be accomplished in and through the local church.

The qualifications for the office of deacon are essentially the same as those for the elder except that the deacon need not be "able to teach." The deacons are to be spiritually in tune with the elders and are to seek to assist them in implementing the goals that the elders feel the Spirit of God is leading them to pursue through the local church.

**Ephesians 5:25–29. The Relationship of the Church to Christ**—The wonderful relationship that exists between Christ and the church was initiated by Christ who loved the church and gave Himself for it. The intimacies of that relationship are described with seven figures:

a. "The shepherd and the sheep" emphasizes both the warm leadership and protection of Christ and the helplessness and dependency of believers (John 10:1–18).
b. "The vine and the branches" points out the necessity for Christians to depend on Christ's sustaining strength for growth (John 15:1–8).
c. "Christ as High Priest" and "the church as a kingdom of priests" stresses the joyful worship, fellowship, and service which the church can render to God through Christ (Heb. 5:1–10; 7:1; 8:6; 1 Pet. 2:5–9; Rev. 1:6).
d. "The cornerstone and building stones" accents the foundational value of Christ to everything the church is and does, as well as Christ's value to the unity of believers. Love is to be the mortar which solidly holds the living stones together (1 Cor. 3:9; 13:1–13; Eph. 2:19–22; 1 Pet. 2:5).
e. "The head and many-membered body" is frequently used in Scripture to illustrate several tremendous truths: the church is a vibrant organism, not merely an organization; it draws its vitality and direction from Christ, the Head; and each believer has a unique and necessary place in its growth (1 Cor. 12:12, 13, 27; Eph. 4:4).
f. "The last Adam and new creation" presents Christ as the initiator of a new creation of believers as Adam was of the old creation (1 Cor. 15:22, 45; 2 Cor. 5:17).
g. "The bridegroom and bride" beautifully emphasizes the intimate fellowship and co-ownership existing between Christ and the church (Eph. 5:25–33; Rev. 19:7, 8; 21:9).

# PEOPLE AND PLACES OF THE BIBLE

This article identifies the most outstanding people and places whose proper names occur in the Bible, excluding the deuterocanonical books. The names are set out alphabetically as they are spelled in the New King James Version. People and places bearing the same name in Scripture are treated under separate entries with personal names listed first. Variant spellings are enclosed in brackets [ ], and the meaning of the name is then given in parentheses (). Under each entry, various individuals or places bearing this name are differentiated by boldface brackets, like this: **[1]; [2];** and so on. Then follows a description of the entry with several Bible verses listed where the name occurs. (Not all verses are given. If the reader is considering a passage that is not cited in the section, he must choose the name that would most likely be identical with the person or place in his passage.)

No attempt has been made to designate each person as a Palite, Harodite, Gileadite, and so on. Many of these designations refer to the ancestor of an individual. In other cases, they refer to the person's city, district, or distinctive clan. It is often a guess as to which meaning is intended.

The meanings of the names are not infallibly accurate. They are simply interesting possibilities.

Many people and places in Scripture bear the same name. In dozens of cases, it cannot be determined whether an individual or place in one book is identical with the same use of the name in another book. In the ancient world, a person was often called by more than one name. Many of the place names are pre-Israelite, and their history is obscure and uncertain. Different names were used to refer to certain sites in different periods of history (e.g., Acco and Ptolemais). These are grouped under the most familiar biblical name with the other names cross referenced to it. Modern place names are given under most of the biblical names.

In the transmission of Scripture, copyists occasionally made errors. Surely Reuel was not also called Deuel, nor Jemuel called Nemuel, and so on. Yet which is original? Only in a few cases do we have any clues.

We find variant forms and contractions of names throughout the Bible. They probably presented little difficulty to an ancient reader. But this further complicates the identification problem for us. Often a Hebrew name refers to both a person and a place.

The Hebrew genealogies are abbreviated at many points. At times it is difficult to distinguish a man from his ancestor. Consider also the problem of trying to match an abbreviated list with a fuller list. Either the names in the abbreviated list are independent of the longer list or they are already included in it. In other words, we may find the same person included in two lists or two different people in two lists.

In a few cases, our English versions use the same word to transliterate several similar Hebrew names. In these instances, we have recorded a separate entry for each Hebrew name (e.g., Iddo).

## A

**Aaron** ("enlightened, rich, mountaineer"), the brother of Moses. He became the first high priest of Israel (Ex. 4:14, 30; 7:2, 19; 17:9–12; 29; Num. 12; 17).

**Abdon** ("service, servile"). **[1]** A judge of Israel for eight years (Judg. 12:13, 15). *See* Bedan. **[2]** A descendant of Benjamin who dwelt in Jerusalem (1 Chr. 8:23). **[3]** Firstborn son of Jehiel, mentioned in Chronicles (1 Chr. 8:30; 9:36). **[4]** One sent to Huldah to inquire of the meaning of the Law (2 Chr. 34:20). He is called Achbor in Second Kings 22:12. Possibly he is identical with [2].

**Abdon** ("servile"), a city belonging to the tribe of Asher, located at the present site of Khirbet Abdeh (Josh. 21:30; 1 Chr. 6:74). It was once called Hebron; *see* Hebron [2].

**Abed-Nego** ("servant of Nebo; servant of Ishtar"), name given to Azariah, one of the three friends of Daniel who were carried captive to Babylon. He was thrown into a fiery furnace (Dan. 1:7; 2:49; 3:12–30).

**Abel** ("a breath, vapor; shepherd"), second son of Adam and Eve, slain by his brother Cain (Gen. 4:1–10; Heb. 11:4; 12:24).

**Abel Acacia Grove** ("meadow [brook] of Acacias"), largest campsite of the wandering Israelites, located on the plains of Moab (Num. 33:49).

**Abez** ("lofty"), a town in northern Palestine apportioned to the tribe of Issachar (Josh. 19:20).

**Abi-Albon** ("father of strength"), one of David's "valiant men" (2 Sam. 23:31). Also called Abiel (1 Chr. 11:32).

**Abiasaph [Ebiasaph]** ("my father has gathered"), a Levite whose descendants were gatekeepers of the tabernacle (Ex. 6:24; 1 Chr. 6:23; 9:19).

**Abiathar** ("father of super-excellence or preeminence"), the only priest to escape Saul's massacre at Nob; he was a high priest in David's time. He was deposed by Solomon (1 Sam. 22:20–23; 1 Kin. 2:27; 1 Chr. 15:11, 12). First Samuel 21 says that Ahimelech [1] was the high priest when David ate the showbread, yet Mark 2:26 states this occurred in the days of Abiathar the high priest. Abiathar may have been assisting his father as high priest and thus could be so designated. Or, since Abiathar was more prominent in history than was his father Ahimelech, he is so mentioned here instead of Ahimelech. If this is so (and it seems to be), then Abiathar is called the "high priest" before he actually assumed that office.

**Abigail** ("father [i.e., cause] of delight"). **[1]** A wife of Nabal and afterward of David (1 Sam. 25:3, 14–44). **[2]** Mother of Amasa, whom Absalom made captain (2 Sam. 17:25; 1 Chr. 2:16, 17).

**Abihu** ("he is my father"), a son of Aaron, destroyed with his brother for offering strange fire to God (Ex. 6:23; Lev. 10:1).

**Abijah [Abijam]** ("Jehovah is my father"). **[1]** A son of Samuel and wicked judge of Israel (1 Sam. 8:2; 1 Chr. 6:28). **[2]** The wife of Hezron (1 Chr. 2:24). **[3]** Son of Rehoboam and successor to the throne of Judah, an ancestor of Christ (1 Chr. 3:10; 2 Chr. 11:20—14:1; Matt. 1:7). He was also known as Abijam (1 Kin. 15:1). **[4]** The seventh son of Becher the son of Benjamin (1 Chr. 7:8). **[5]** A descendant of Aaron appointed by David in connection with the priestly courses (1 Chr. 24:10; cf. Luke 1:5). **[6]** A son of Jeroboam I of Israel (1 Kin. 14:1–8). **[7]** A priest of Nehemiah's time who sealed the covenant (Neh. 10:7). Possibly the same as the priest mentioned in Nehemiah 12:1, 4, 17.

**Abijam** ("father of the sea [or west]"). *See* Abijah [3].

**Abimelech** ("father of the king"). **[1]** Many scholars believe the King(s) Abimelech(s) of Gerar in Genesis 20, 21, and 26 are not proper names but a royal title borne by the Philistine kings. The Psalm 34 title mentions Abimelech where Achish should occur. Since the story of Achish was well known, it seems improbable to regard this as a mistake, but rather a royal title of Achish, king of Gath. **[2]** A son of Gideon who tried to become king of Israel, and did reign for three years (Judg. 8:30—10:1). **[3]** *See* Ahimelech [2].

**Abinadab** ("father or source of liberality or willingness"). **[1]** A man of Judah in whose house the ark was placed (1 Sam. 7:1; 2 Sam. 6:3, 4; 1 Chr. 13:7). **[2]** A brother of David (1 Sam. 16:8; 17:13; 1 Chr. 2:13). **[3]** Son of Saul slain by the Philistines (1 Sam. 31:2; 1 Chr. 8:33; 9:39; 10:2). **[4]** Father of one of Solomon's officers (1 Kin. 4:11).

**Abiram** ("father of elevation"). **[1]** One who conspired against Moses and was destroyed (Num. 16:27; Ps. 106:17). **[2]** Firstborn son of Hiel who died when his father began to rebuild Jericho (1 Kin. 16:34; cf. Josh. 6:26).

**Abishag** ("my father was a wanderer"), a beautiful woman chosen to nurse the aged David (1 Kin. 1:3, 15; 2:17, 21, 22). This woman may also be the heroine of the Song of Solomon, where she is simply called "the Shulamite."

**Abishai** ("my father is Jesse; source of wealth"), a son of David's sister, Zeruiah. He was one of David's mighty men (1 Sam. 26:6–9; 2 Sam. 2:18; 10:10; 23:18).

**Abner [Abiner]** ("my father of light"), a shortened form of *Abiner;* the captain of the host under Saul and Ishbosheth (1 Sam. 14:50, 51; 26:5, 7; 2 Sam. 2; 3).

**Abraham [Abram],** the founder of the Jewish nation and an ancestor of Christ. His name was changed from Abram ("the father is exalted") to Abraham ("father of multitudes") (Gen. 11—26; Matt. 1:1, 2).

**Absalom** ("father of peace"), a son of David who tried to usurp the throne from his father (2 Sam. 3:3; 13—19).

**Acco** ("compressed"), a town on the coast of Palestine about 40 km. (25 mi.) south of Tyre, apportioned to the tribe of Asher (Judg. 1:31); also called Ptolemais in Acts 21:7.

**Achan [Achar]** ("trouble"), one who stole part of the spoil of Jericho and brought "trouble" on his people. He was killed for this (Josh. 7:1–24). In First Chronicles 2:7, he is called *Achar*.

**Achim** ("woes"), ancestor of Christ (Matt. 1:14).

**Achish** ("serpent-charmer"). **[1]** A king of Gath to whom David fled for safety (1 Sam. 21; 27—29). **[2]** Another king of Gath who bore the same name but reigned during Solomon's time (1 Kin. 2:39, 40). However, many believe the kings to be identical.

**Achor** ("trouble"), a valley south of Jericho, in which Achan was stoned (Josh. 7:24); and which formed the northern boundary of Judah (Josh. 15:7).

**Achzib [Chezib]** ("false"). **[1]** A Canaanite city in the lowlands of Judah, captured by Joshua (Gen. 38:5; Josh. 15:44). **[2]** A seashore town on the northern side of Galilee near the Lebanon border (Josh. 19:29; Judg. 1:31).

**Adam** ("of the ground; firm"), the first man. His sin caused a curse to fall upon all the race (Gen. 2—3; 1 Cor. 15:22, 45). He is listed in the genealogy of Christ (Luke 3:38).

**Adam** ("red; of the earth"), a city on the east bank of the Jordan River that was given to the tribe of Reuben (Josh. 3:16).

**Adino** ("ornament"), a chief of David's mighty men (2 Sam. 23:8). Some identify him with Jashobeam [1]; others deny this.

**Admah** ("redness"), one of the Cities of the Plain that God destroyed with Sodom and Gomorrah (Gen. 19:25–29); its location may now be submerged by the southern end of the Dead Sea.

**Adnah** ("pleasure"). **[1]** A captain who joined David at Ziklag (1 Chr. 12:20). **[2]** A chief captain of Jehoshaphat (2 Chr. 17:14).

**Adonijah** ("Jehovah is my lord"). **[1]** A son of David, executed by Solomon for trying to usurp the throne (2 Sam. 3:4; 1 Kin. 1:2). **[2]** One sent by Jehoshaphat to teach the law (2 Chr. 17:8). **[3]** One who sealed the new covenant with God after the Exile (Neh. 10:14–16).

**Adoni-Zedek** ("lord of justice or righteousness"), a king of Jerusalem defeated by Joshua (Josh. 10:1–27).

**Adramyttium** ("from Adramys, brother of Craesus"), a port city of Mysia in the northwestern part of the Roman province of Asia (Acts 27:2; cf. 16:7).

**Adriatic** ("from [the city] Adria of Italy"), originally a name referring to the sea east of Italy. In later times, the term included the Mediterranean between Greece and Sicily (Acts 27:27).

**Adullam** ("refuge"), a town of Judah near Succoth. David made the headquarters of his rebellion against Saul in a cave near this town (Josh. 12:7–15; 1 Sam. 22; 2 Sam. 23:13).

**Aeneas** ("praise"), the paralytic of Lydda who was healed by Peter (Acts 9:33, 34).

**Aenon** ("fountains"), a place noted for its abundant supply of water, where John baptized his converts. Most likely this site was at the head of the Valley of Shechem (John 3:23).

**Agabus** ("locust"), a prophet of Jerusalem who foretold suffering for Paul if he went to Jerusalem (Acts 11:28; 21:10).

**Agag** ("high; warlike"), a name or title of the kings of Amalek; it is probably not a proper name. However, if it is a proper name, it is used to refer to two persons: **[1]** A king mentioned by Balaam (Num. 24:7). **[2]** A king that Saul spared, but who was later executed by Samuel (1 Sam. 15).

**Agrippa.** *See* Herod.

**Agur** ("gathered"), a sage who wrote Proverbs 30.

**Ahab** ("father's brother [uncle]"). **[1]** The seventh king of Israel. He was wicked and idolatrous and married a woman of the same character—Jezebel (1 Kin. 16:28—22:40). **[2]** A false prophet killed by Nebuchadnezzar (Jer. 29:21, 22).

**Ahasuerus.** **[1]** The king of Persia whom Esther married. He is known as Xerxes to historians (Esth. 1:1; 2:16; 10:3). **[2]** The father of Darius the Mede (Dan. 9:1). **[3]** Another name for Cambyses, king of Persia (Ezra 4:6).

**Ahaz** ("he holds"). **[1]** The eleventh king of Judah and an ancestor of Christ (2 Kin. 15:38—16:20; Matt. 1:9). **[2]** A descendant of Benjamin (1 Chr. 8:35, 36; 9:41, 42).

**Ahaziah [Azariah]** ("Jehovah holds or sustains"). **[1]** The eighth king of Israel. He was weak and idolatrous (1 Kin. 22:51—2 Kin. 1:18). **[2]** The sixth king of Judah; he reigned only one year (2 Kin. 8:24–29; 9:16f.). He was also known as Jehoahaz (2 Chr. 21:17; 25:23). His being called Azariah in Second Chronicles 22:6 is an error; over fifteen Hebrew manuscripts and all recent versions read Ahaziah. *See* Jehoahaz.

**Ahiezer** ("helping brother"). **[1]** A prince of Dan who helped Moses take a census (Num. 1:12; 2:25; 7:66). **[2]** One who joined David at Ziklag (1 Chr. 12:3).

**Ahihud** ("brother of honor"). **[1]** A prince of Asher (Num. 34:27). **[2]** A member of the family of Ehud, descended from Benjamin (1 Chr. 8:7).

**Ahijah** ("Jehovah is brother; my brother is Jehovah"). **[1]** A prophet who prophesied the splitting away of the ten tribes (1 Kin. 11:29, 30; 14:2, 4, 5). **[2]** Father of Baasha who conspired against Nadab (1 Kin. 15:27, 33; 21:22). **[3]** A son of Jerahmeel (1 Chr. 2:25). **[4]** One of David's mighty men (1 Chr. 11:36). **[5]** One who sealed the new covenant with God after the Exile (Neh. 10:26). **[6]** One set over the temple treasures (1 Chr. 26:20). *See also* Ahimelech.

**Ahimaaz** ("powerful brother"). **[1]** Father of Ahinoam, wife of Saul (1 Sam. 14:50). **[2]** One of Solomon's officers (1 Kin. 4:15). **[3]** Son of Zadok who remained loyal to David (2 Sam. 15:27, 36; 17:17, 20; 18:19–29).

**Ahimelech** ("brother of the king; my brother is king"). **[1]** A Hittite friend of David (1 Sam. 26:6). **[2]** A priest, son of Abiathar and grandson of [3] (2 Sam. 8:17; 1 Chr. 24:6). Some think the readings in these passages have been transposed (i.e., they speak of Ahimelech the son of Abiathar instead of Abiathar the son of Ahimelech). But this seems unlikely, especially in First Chronicles 24. He is called Abimelech in First Chronicles 18:16. The Septuagint has Ahimelech here also. **[3]** One of the priests of Nob slain for helping David (1 Sam. 21:1–8; 22:9–20). *See also* Abimelech; Ahijah.

**Ahinoam** ("pleasant brother"). **[1]** Wife of King Saul (1 Sam. 14:50). **[2]** A woman of Jezreel who married David (1 Sam. 25:43; 27:3; 1 Chr. 3:1).

**Ahithophel** ("brother of foolishness"), the real leader of Absalom's rebellion against David. When he saw that victory was impossible, he committed suicide (2 Sam. 15—17).

**Ahitub** ("a good brother; my brother is goodness"). **[1]** A son of Phinehas (1 Sam. 14:3; 22:9, 11, 12, 20). **[2]** Father of Zadok the high priest (2 Sam. 8:17; 15:27; 1 Chr. 6:7, 8). **[3]** A high priest of the same family who served during Nehemiah's time (1 Chr. 6:11; 9:11; Neh. 11:11).

**Aholibamah** ("tent of the high place"). **[1]** A wife of Esau (Gen. 36:2, 5, 14, 18). **[2]** A duke of Edom (Gen. 36:41). *See also* Esau's Wives.

**Ai [Aiath; Aija]** ("heap of ruins"). **[1]** One of the strongest Canaanite cities, located east of Bethel (Josh. 7:2; Neh. 11:31). In Isaiah 10:28 the Hebrew feminine form of the name (Aiath) occurs. **[2]** A city of the Ammonites, probably located near Heshbon (Jer. 49:3).

**Aijalon [Ajalon]** ("place of harts"). **[1]** A town located 22.5 km. (14 mi.) northwest of Jerusalem, designated as a Levitical city (Josh. 19:42; 21:24; 2 Chr. 28:18). **[2]** A site belonging to the tribe of Zebulun west of the Sea of Galilee, where the judge Elon was buried (Judg. 12:12). Its exact location is unknown.

**Ain** ("eye"). **[1]** A town of Judah near Rimmon, assigned to the Levites serving the tribe of Simeon (Josh. 15:32; 19:7; 21:16; 1 Chr. 4:32). **[2]** A site on the boundary line of the Promised Land, west of Riblah (Num. 34:11). Its exact location is unknown.

**Akel Dama [Potter's Field]** ("field of blood"), a field purchased by the priests of Jerusalem with the 30 pieces of silver that bought the betrayal of Jesus (Acts 1:19); also called Potter's Field (Matt. 27:7).

**Alexander** ("helper of man"). **[1]** A son of the Simon who bore Christ's cross (Mark 15:21). **[2]** A kinsman of Annas and a leading man in Jerusalem (Acts 4:6). **[3]** A Christian with Paul when the Ephesians had a riot (Acts 19:33). Perhaps the same as [1]. **[4]** A convert who apostatized (1 Tim. 1:20). **[5]** A person who did much harm to Paul (2 Tim. 4:14). Perhaps the same as [4].

**Alexandria** ("city of Alexander the Great"), a city on the Mediterranean coast of Egypt, which served as Egypt's capital city for many years (Acts 27:6; 28:11–13).

**Almon Diblathaim** ("hiding place of two fig sacks"), a site between the Arnon River and Shittim where the Israelites camped during their wandering in the wilderness (Num. 33:46).

**Alphaeus** ("leader; chief"). **[1]** The father of Levi (Matthew) (Mark 2:14). **[2]** The father of the apostle James (Matt. 10:3; Mark 3:18; Acts 1:13). Some identify him with Clopas. *See* Clopas.

**Alush** ("crowd"), a site where the Israelites camped on their journey from Egypt to Mount Sinai (Num. 33:14).

**Amalek** ("warlike; dweller in the vale"), a son of Eliphaz and progenitor of the Amalekites (Gen. 36:12, 16; 1 Chr. 1:36; cf. Ex. 17:8, 9).

**Amana** ("forth"), a range of mountains in Lebanon, probably south of the Amana [Abana] River (Song 4:8).

**Amasa** ("burden-bearer; people of Jesse"). **[1]** A nephew of David who became the commander of Absalom's army (2 Sam. 17:25; 19:13; 20:4–12). **[2]** One who opposed making slaves of captured Jews (2 Chr. 28:12).

**Amaziah** ("Jehovah has strength"). **[1]** Son and successor of Joash to the throne of Judah. He was murdered at

Lachish (2 Kin. 12:21—14:20). [2] A man of the tribe of Simeon (1 Chr. 4:34). [3] A Levite descendant from Merari (1 Chr. 6:45). [4] An idolatrous priest of Bethel (Amos 7:10, 12, 14).

**Amittai** ("truthful"), father of the prophet Jonah (2 Kin. 14:25; Jon. 1:1).

**Ammiel** ("my people are strong; my kinsman is God"). [1] One of those who spied out the Promised Land (Num. 13:12). [2] Father of Machir, David's friend (2 Sam. 9:4, 5; 17:27). [3] A porter of the tabernacle in the time of David (1 Chr. 26:5).

**Amminadab [Aminadab]** ("my people are willing or noble"). [1] Aaron's father-in-law (Ex. 6:23). [2] A prince of Judah and ancestor of Christ (Num. 1:7; 2:3; Ruth 4:19, 20; Matt. 1:4). [3] A son of Kohath (1 Chr. 6:22). [4] One who helped to bring the ark of the covenant from the house of Obed-Edom (1 Chr. 15:10, 11).

**Ammon.** *See* Ben-Ammi.

**Amnon** ("upbringing; faithful"). [1] Eldest son of David, by Ahinoam, slain by Absalom (2 Sam. 3:2; 13:1-39). [2] A son of Shimon of the family of Caleb (1 Chr. 4:20).

**Amon** ("workman" or "trustworthy"). [1] Governor of Samaria in Ahab's time (1 Kin. 22:26; 2 Chr. 18:25). [2] Son and successor of Manasseh to the throne of Judah; an ancestor of Christ (2 Kin. 21:19–25; Jer. 1:2; Zeph. 1:1; Matt. 1:10).

**Amos** ("burden-bearer; burdensome"). [1] A prophet during the reigns of Uzziah and Jeroboam (Amos 1:1; 7:10–12, 14). [2] An ancestor of Christ (Luke 3:25).

**Amoz** ("strong"), father of the prophet Isaiah (2 Kin. 19:2, 20; Is. 1:1; 2:1; 13:1).

**Amram** ("people exalted; red"). [1] A descendant of Levi and father or ancestor of Aaron, Moses, and Miriam (Ex. 6:18, 20; Num. 3:19; 26:58, 59). [2] One who had taken a foreign wife (Ezra 10:34).

**Ananiah** ("Jehovah has covered"), a town inhabited by the tribe of Benjamin after the Exile (Neh. 11:32).

**Ananias** ("Jehovah is gracious"). [1] A disciple struck dead for trying to deceive the apostles (Acts 5:1, 3, 5). [2] A disciple of Damascus who helped Paul after receiving a vision (Acts 9:10–17; 22:12). [3] A high priest in Jerusalem who opposed Paul (Acts 23:2; 24:1).

**Anathoth** ("answer"), a town of the tribe of Benjamin, located about 4 km. (2.5 mi.) northeast of Jerusalem (Josh. 21:18; Ezra 2:23); the birthplace of the prophet Jeremiah (Jer. 1:1; 11:21).

**Andrew** ("manly; conqueror"), the brother of Peter and one of the twelve apostles (Matt. 4:18; 10:2; John 1:40, 44; 6:8).

**Anna** ("grace"), a prophetess of the tribe of Asher in Christ's time (Luke 2:36).

**Annas** ("grace of Jehovah"), high priest of the Jews who first tried Christ (Luke 3:2; John 18:13, 24; Acts 4:6).

**Antioch** ("speedy as a chariot"). [1] A Syrian city on the south side of the Orontes River, where the followers of Jesus were first called Christians (Acts 11:19–26). [2] A city of Phrygia near the border of Pisidia, visited by Paul and Barnabas on their missionary journey (Acts 13:14).

**Antipas**, a Christian martyr of Pergamos (Rev. 2:13).

**Aphek [Aphik]** ("strength"). [1] A city north of Sidon (Josh. 13:4). [2] A town assigned to the tribe of Asher but never captured from the Canaanites; located just southeast of Acco (Josh. 19:30; Judg.1:31). [3] A town on the Plain of Sharon northeast of Joppa, whose king was killed by Joshua (Josh. 12:18). [4] A town between Shunem and Jezreel, whose soldiers fought in the war between Saul and the Philistines (1 Sam. 28:4; 29:1, 11; 31:1). This may have been the town where Ben-Hadad fought Ahab (1 Kin. 20:26–30), and where "Jehoash" of Israel would defeat the Syrians (2 Kin. 13:14–19). However, these two passages may refer to Aphek in Golan, about 5 km. (3 mi.) east of the Sea of Galilee.

**Apollonia** ("city of Apollo"), a Macedonian town visited by Paul on his way to Thessalonica (Acts 17:1).

**Apollos** ("a destroyer"), a Jewish Christian, mighty in the Scriptures, who came to Ephesus and was instructed by Aquila and Priscilla (Acts 18:24; 19:1; 1 Cor. 1:12; 3:4–6; Titus 3:13).

**Appii Forum** ("marketplace of Appius"), a town in Italy about 64 km. (40 mi.) from Rome. Roman Christians met Paul here when he was brought to plead his case before Caesar (Acts 28:15).

**Aquila** ("eagle"), a pious Jewish Christian, husband of Priscilla and friend of Paul (Acts 18:2, 18, 26; Rom. 16:3; 1 Cor. 16:19).

**Arab** ("ambush"), a town in the hills of Judah east of Dumah (Josh. 15:52).

**Arabah** ("steppe"), the depression of land holding the Sea of Galilee and the Dead Sea (Josh. 18:18). The "valley" of Joshua 11:2 probably refers to the Arabah.

**Arabia** ("desert"), a large peninsula bounded on the east by the Persian Gulf and the Gulf of Oman, on the west by the Red Sea, and on the south by the Indian Ocean. It was the home of many nomadic tribes, and was sometimes called the "East Country" (2 Chr. 21:16; Is. 13:20).

**Ararat** ("high land"), a mountainous, hilly land in western Asia (Jer. 51:27) later known as Armenia (Is. 37:38; 2 Kin. 19:37). Noah's ark rested on mountains in this area (Gen. 8:4).

**Araunah** ("Jehovah is firm"). *See also* Ornan.

**Archelaus** ("people's chief"), the son of Herod the Great who succeeded his father as the ruler of Idumea, Judea, and Samaria (Matt. 2:22).

**Archippus** ("chief groom"), a "fellow-soldier" whom Paul addresses (Col. 4:17; Philem. 2).

**Areopagus** ("hill of Ares [Mars]"), a hill west of the acropolis in Athens, where Paul addressed several Greek philosophers; also known as Mars's Hill (Acts 17:19–34).

**Aretas** ("pleasing; virtuous"), Aretas IV, Philopatris. King of the Nabataeans whose deputy tried to seize Paul (2 Cor. 11:32).

**Arimathea** ("heights"), the home of a businessman named Joseph, who gained permission to bury the body of Jesus (Matt. 27:57; Luke 23:51). Its exact location is not known, but is generally believed to have been about 16 km. (10 mi.) northeast of Lydda on the western edge of the hill country of Ephraim. *See also* Ramah.

**Aristarchus** ("the best ruler"), a faithful companion who accompanied Paul on his third missionary journey (Acts 19:29; 20:4; Col. 4:10).

**Aristobulus** ("best counselor"), a person in Rome whose household Paul saluted (Rom. 16:10).

**Armageddon** (Hebrew, *Har Megiddo*—"hill of Megiddo"), the site of the final battle between Christ and Satan (Rev. 16:16).

**Armenia.** *See* Ararat.

**Arnon** ("rushing water"), a river that pours into the Dead Sea (Num. 21:13; Josh. 13:16).

**Artaxerxes** ("fervent to spoil"). **[1]** A king of Persia, Artaxerxes I Longimanus, at whose court Ezra and Nehemiah were officials (Ezra 7:1, 7, 11, 12; Neh. 2:1; 5:14). **[2]** Some suppose that Ezra 4:7 uses "Artaxerxes" to refer to the pseudo-Smerdis king of Persia, but the reference is probably to [1].

**Asa** ("physician; healer"). **[1]** The third king of Judah and an ancestor of Christ (1 Kin. 15:8—16:29; Matt. 1:7, 8). **[2]** Head of a Levite family (1 Chr. 9:16).

**Asahel** ("God is doer; God has made"). **[1]** A son of David's sister, Zeruiah. He was slain by Abner (2 Sam. 2:18–32; 3:27, 30). **[2]** A Levite sent to teach the Law (2 Chr. 17:8). **[3]** A Levite employed as an officer of the offerings and tithes (2 Chr. 31:13). **[4]** Father of Jonathan, appointed to take a census of foreign wives (Ezra 10:15).

**Asaph** ("collector; gatherer"). **[1]** One of David's three chief musicians (1 Chr. 6:39; 15:17, 19). Author of Psalms 50, 73—83. **[2]** Father of Joah the recorder to Hezekiah (2 Kin. 18:18, 37; 2 Chr. 29:13). **[3]** A Levite whose descendants lived in Jerusalem (1 Chr. 9:15). **[4]** One whose descendants were porters in David's time (1 Chr. 26:1). The text should possibly read Abiasaph (q.v.). **[5]** A keeper of the royal forests in Judah (Neh. 2:8).

**Asenath** ("dedicated to [the deity] Neit"), the Egyptian wife of Joseph (Gen. 41:45, 50; 46:20).

**Ashdod** ("stronghold"), one of the five chief Canaanite cities; the seat of the worship of the fish god Dagon; located halfway between present-day Jaffa and Gaza (Josh. 11:22; 1 Sam. 5:1). In the N.T. the city is called Azotus (Acts 8:40).

**Asher [Aser]** ("happy"), the eighth son of Jacob and an ancestor of one of the twelve tribes of Israel (Gen. 30:13; 35:26; 46:17; 49:20; 1 Chr. 2:2).

**Ashkelon [Askelon]** ("wandering"), one of the five chief Canaanite cities, the seat of the worship of the goddess Derceto; located about 19 km. (12 mi.) north of the present-day city of Gaza (Josh. 13:3; Jer. 47:5).

**Ashkenaz** ("a fire that spreads"), a son of Gomer (Gen. 10:3; 1 Chr. 1:6). Possibly a race or tribe who dwelt near Ararat and Minni in eastern Armenia.

**Ashpenaz,** prince of Nebuchadnezzar's eunuchs who had charge of the captives from Judah (Dan. 1:3).

**Asia** ("eastern"), the term used by the Bible to refer to Asia Minor (1 Cor. 16:19; Acts 2:9). It is sometimes used to refer to a Roman province in Asia Minor (Acts 19:10; Rev. 1:4).

**Askelon.** *See* Ashkelon.

**Asshur [Assur]** ("level plain"). **[1]** A son of Shem (Gen. 10:22; 1 Chr. 1:17). Possibly the people of Assyria are intended. **[2]** Genesis 10:11, if denoting a person, refers to a son of Ham or to [1]. However, many scholars translate: "From that land he [Nimrod] went into Assyria [Asshur]."

**Asshur [Assur]** ("level plain"), a city in Assyria which was sometimes the capital, or the nation itself may be referred to (Num. 24:22, 24).

**Assur.** *See* Asshur.

**Assyria** ("country of Assur"), a Semitic nation on the Tigris River, whose capital was Nineveh (Gen. 2:14; 2 Kin. 15:10, 20).

**Atad** ("a thorn"), the campsite near Hebron used by Joseph and his brothers as they prepared to take Jacob's body back to Canaan (Gen. 50:11). The new name given the site was a pun: the Canaanites saw the mourning [Hebrew, *ēbhel*] of the Egyptians and called the place *Abel* [Hebrew, *ābhel*]—"meadow"; *Mizraim*—"of the Egyptians."

**Ataroth Addar [Ataroth Adar]** ("crown of Addar"), a village on the southern frontier of Ephraim (Josh. 16:5; 18:13). The town is probably to be identified with Ataroth (Josh. 16:2).

**Athaliah** ("whom Jehovah has afflicted; Jehovah is strong"). **[1]** The daughter of Jezebel, wife of King Jehoram, and afterwards ruler of Israel for six years (2 Kin. 8:26; 11:1–20; 2 Chr. 22:2—23:21). **[2]** A son of Jeroham (1 Chr. 8:26). **[3]** Father of a returned exile (Ezra 8:7).

**Athens** ("city of Athena"), the greatest city of classical Greece, capital of the Greek city-state of Attica, where Paul founded a Christian church (Acts 17:15–18).

**Attai** ("seasonable; timely"). **[1]** One who joined David at Ziklag (1 Chr. 12:11). **[2]** A son of King Rehoboam (2 Chr. 11:20). **[3]** Descendant of Pharez (1 Chr. 2:35, 36).

**Augustus** (i.e., "consecrated" or "holy"). Acts 25:21, 25; 27:1 use the Greek rendering of the title "reverend" in this fashion, since Augustus had been dead many years.

**Augustus Caesar,** the imperial name of Octavian, a nephew of Julius Caesar who became emperor of Rome. During his reign, Christ was born (Luke 2:1).

**Azarel [Azareel]** ("God is helper"). **[1]** One who joined David at Ziklag (1 Chr. 12:6). **[2]** One who ministered in the song service of the temple (1 Chr. 25:18). **[3]** A prince of Dan (1 Chr. 27:22). **[4]** One who took a foreign wife (Ezra 10:41). **[5]** A priest of the family of Immer (Neh. 11:13). **[6]** One who played the trumpet at the dedication of the new temple (Neh. 12:36).

**Azariah** ("Jehovah has helped"). **[1]** *See* Uzziah. **[2]** A ruler of Solomon's officers (1 Kin. 4:5). **[3]** A descendant of David's high priest (1 Kin. 4:2). **[4]** A descendant of Judah (1 Chr. 2:8). **[5]** A descendant of Jerahmeel (1 Chr. 2:38, 39). **[6]** A son of Ahimaaz (1 Chr. 6:9). **[7]** A high priest and grandson of [6] (1 Chr. 6:10, 11). **[8]** A son of Hilkiah the high priest under Josiah (1 Chr. 6:13, 14; 9:11; Ezra 7:1). **[9]** An ancestor of Samuel the prophet (1 Chr. 6:36). **[10]** A prophet who went to Asa (2 Chr. 15:1). **[11], [12]** Two sons of King Jehoshaphat (2 Chr. 21:2). **[13]** *See* Ahaziah [2]. **[14]** A captain who helped to place Joash on the throne (2 Chr. 23:1). **[15]** Another man who helped Joash (2 Chr. 23:1). **[16]** A high priest who opposed Uzziah (2 Chr. 26:17, 20). **[17]** A chief of Ephraim (2 Chr. 28:12). **[18]** A descendant of Kohath and father of Joel (2 Chr. 29:12). **[19]** One who helped cleanse the temple (2 Chr. 29:12). **[20]** A chief of the family of Zadok, priest in Hezekiah's time (2 Chr. 31:10, 13). **[21]** Ancestor of Zadok and Ezra (Ezra 7:3). **[22]** One who repaired the wall of Jerusalem (Neh. 3:23, 24). **[23]** One who came up to Jerusalem with Zerubbabel (Neh. 7:7). Perhaps this is another name of Seraiah (Ezra 2:2); if not, his name is omitted in this passage. **[24]** A priest who explained the Law (Neh. 8:7). **[25]** *See* Ezra [1]. **[26]** A prince of Judah (Neh. 12:33). **[27]** One who charged Jeremiah with false prophecy (Jer. 43:2). **[28]** A captive carried to Babylon with Daniel (Dan. 1:6, 7, 11, 19; 2:17). *See* Abed-Nego.

**Azubah** ("forsaken"). **[1]** The mother of King Jehoshaphat (1 Kin. 22:42; 2 Chr. 20:31). **[2]** Wife of Caleb, the son of Hezron (1 Chr. 2:18, 19)

## B

**Baal** ("master; lord"). **[1]** A descendant of Reuben (1 Chr. 5:5). **[2]** The fourth of ten sons of Jehiel (1 Chr. 8:29, 30; 9:36).

**Baal** ("master"), a city of Simeon, identical with Baalath Beer (1 Chr. 4:33).

**Baalath Beer** ("mistress of a well"), a border town of the tribe of Simeon, sometimes called "Ramah of the south" (Josh. 19:8). It is identical with Baal (q.v.).

**Baal Gad** ("the lord of fortune; Gad is lord"), a town at the foot of Mount Hermon that marked the northern limit of Joshua's conquest (Josh. 11:17; 12:7).

**Baal Hazor** ("lord of Hazor [enclosure]"), the place near Ephraim where Absalom had Amnon killed (2 Sam. 13:23); the probable site is about 7 km. (4.5 mi.) northeast of Bethel.

**Baal Hermon** ("lord of Hermon"), the site of Canaanite rituals on the eastern slope of Mount Hermon, which marked the northwest boundary of the half-tribe of Manasseh (Judg. 3:3; 1 Chr. 5:23).

**Baalis** ("lord of joy"), the king of the Ammonites after Jerusalem was taken (Jer. 40:14).

**Baal Tamar** ("lord of palms"), a place near Gibeah and Bethel in the territory of Benjamin, where the Israelites repelled the army of Gibeah (Judg. 20:33).

**Baana [Baanah]** ("son of grief; patient"). **[1]** One of Solomon's royal merchants (1 Kin. 4:12). **[2]** Another merchant of Solomon, responsible for Asher (1 Kin. 4:16). **[3]** Father of Zadok, the builder of the temple (Neh. 3:4). **[4]** Father of one of David's mighty men (2 Sam. 23:29; 1 Chr. 11:30). **[5]** A captain in Ishbosheth's army (2 Sam. 4:2, 5, 6, 9). **[6]** One who returned from the Exile with Zerubbabel (Ezra 2:2; Neh. 7:7; 10:27).

**Baasha** ("boldness"), the third king of Israel; war and wickedness characterized his reign (1 Kin. 15:16—16:13).

**Babylon** (meaning unknown). **[1]** The capital city of the Babylonian Empire, famous for its hanging gardens; a focal point of the Jewish captivity beginning in 586 B.C. (2 Kin. 17:24, 25; Is. 39:3, 6, 7). **[2]** Most scholars believe the references in First Peter 5:13 and Revelation 14:8; 18:2, 10–21 are to Rome. However, some believe Peter refers to [1].

**Balaam** ("a pilgrim; lord [Baal] of the people"), a prophet that the king of Moab induced to curse Israel. Instead, God put words of blessing in his mouth (Num. 22—24; 31:8).

**Balak** ("void; empty"), the king of Moab that hired Balaam to curse Israel (Num. 22—24; Josh. 24:9).

**Bani** ("posterity"). **[1]** One of David's mighty men (2 Sam. 23:36). **[2]** A descendant of Merari (1 Chr. 6:46). **[3]** A descendant of Pharez (1 Chr. 9:4). **[4]** Father of a family that returned from the Babylonian Captivity (Ezra 2:10; 10:29). In Nehemiah 7:15, he is called Binnui. **[5]** One whose descendants had taken foreign wives during the Exile (Ezra 10:34). **[6]** A descendant of [5] who took a foreign wife during the Exile (Ezra 10:38). **[7]** A Levite who helped to repair the wall of Jerusalem (Neh. 3:17; 8:7). **[8]** A Levite who assisted in the devotions of the people (Neh. 9:4; 10:13). **[9]** One who sealed the new covenant with God after the Exile (Neh. 10:14). **[10]** A Levite whose son was an overseer of the Levites after the Exile. Perhaps the same as [7] or [8] (Neh. 11:22). **[11], [12], [13]** Three Levites who participated in the temple worship (Neh. 9:4, 5).

**Bar,** Aramaic for the Hebrew "bēn," "son." "Bar" and "ben" are frequently prefixed to names to indicate direct relationship. Thus Peter is called Bar-Jonah (son of Jonah) because his father was named Jonah (Matt. 16:17) and perhaps Nathanael was called Bartholomew (son of Tolmai) because his father was named Tolmai.

**Barabbas** ("father's son"), a murderer whom the people demanded that Pontius Pilate should release instead of Christ (Matt. 27:17, 20, 21, 26; Mark 15:7). *See* Bar.

**Barak** ("lightning"), the general of the judge Deborah; he helped to defeat Sisera (Judg. 4:6—5:15).

**Barnabas** ("son of consolation"), a Jewish Christian who traveled widely with Paul (Acts 4:36; 9:27; 11:22–30; Gal. 2:1). His original name was Joses, but he was named Barnabas by the apostles (Acts 4:36); obviously they considered him to be *their* consoler. *See* Bar.

**Barsabas** ("son of Saba"). *See* Bar; Joseph [11]; Juda [12].

**Bartholomew** ("son of Tolmai"), one of Jesus' twelve apostles (Matt. 10:3; Mark 3:18; Acts 1:13). He is probably the same as Nathanael (q.v.). *See* Bar.

**Bartimaeus** (Aramaic *bar*, "son" and Greek *timaios*, "honorable"), a blind beggar healed by Christ (Mark 10:46–52). *See* Bar.

**Baruch** ("blessed"). **[1]** Jeremiah's friend and scribe (Jer. 32:12, 13, 16; 36). **[2]** One who helped to rebuild the wall of Jerusalem (Neh. 3:20; 10:6). **[3]** A descendant of Perez who returned from the Exile (Neh. 11:5).

**Barzillai** ("strong"). **[1]** One who befriended David when he fled from Absalom (2 Sam. 17:27; 19:31–39). **[2]** Husband of Merab, Saul's eldest daughter, and father of Adriel (2 Sam. 21:8). **[3]** A priest whose genealogy was lost during the Exile (Ezra 2:61; Neh. 7:63).

**Basemath** ("fragrant"). **[1]** A daughter of Solomon (1 Kin. 4:15). **[2]** A wife of Esau (Gen. 26:34). *See also* Esau. **[3]** Another wife of Esau, whom he married to appease his father (Gen. 36:3, 4, 10, 13). *See also* Esau's Wives.

**Bathsheba** ("the seventh daughter; daughter of the oath"), the beautiful wife of Uriah the Hittite, and afterward the wife of David (2 Sam. 11:3; 12:24; 1 Kin. 1:11—2:19). She was the mother of Solomon and an ancestor of Christ (Matt. 1:6). She is called Bathshua in First Chronicles 3:5.

**Bathshua** ("daughter of prosperity"). **[1]** Another name of Bathsheba (q.v.). **[2]** The wife of Judah. In Genesis 38:2 and First Chronicles 2:3, the KJV incorrectly renders her name as "daughter of Shua"; Bathshua is really a proper name.

**Beautiful Gate,** a portion of the east gate of Jerusalem where Peter and John healed a lame man (Acts 3:2).

**Bedan** ("son of judgment"). **[1]** A leader of Israel mentioned as a deliverer of the nation (1 Sam. 12:11). The Septuagint, Syriac, and Arabic read *Barak* instead; however, many think this is a reference to Abdon. **[2]** A descendant of Manasseh (1 Chr. 7:17).

**Beeliada** ("the lord knows"), a son of David (1 Chr. 14:7) also known as Eliada (2 Sam. 5:16; 1 Chr. 3:8).

**Beer** ("a well"). **[1]** A temporary encampment of the Israelites in the wilderness (Num. 21:16-18); possibly the same as Beer Elim (Is. 15:8). **[2]** A place where Jotham sought refuge from his brother Abimelech (Judg. 9:21); possibly the same as Beeroth.

**Beer Lahai Roi** ("well of the living one who sees me"), the well of Hagar, located between Kadesh and Bered on the road to Shur, about 80 km. (50 mi.) southwest of Beersheba (Gen. 16:14).

**Beersheba** ("well of oaths"), a city in southern Judah, site of Abraham's covenant with Abimelech; it is located about 45 km. (28 mi.) southwest of Hebron (Gen. 21:14, 22–31; Josh. 15:28).

**Belshazzar** (Hebrew form of the Babylonian name *Bel-shar-usur*—"[the god] Bel has protected the king [ship]"), the son of Nabonidus and co-regent in Babylon. He witnessed strange handwriting on the wall of his palace before his kingdom was overthrown by Persia (Dan. 5; 7:1; 8:1).

**Belteshazzar** (Hebrew form of the Babylonian name, Balat-usu-usur—"Protect his life!"), the name given to Daniel in Babylon (Dan. 1:7). *See* Daniel.

**Benaiah** ("Jehovah has built"). **[1]** The third leader of David's army, counselor to the kings, and loyal friend of both David and Solomon (2 Sam. 8:18; 20:23; 1 Kin. 1:8—2:46). **[2]** One of David's mighty men (2 Sam. 23:30; 1 Chr. 11:31). **[3]** Head of a family of the tribe of Simeon (1 Chr. 4:36). **[4]** One of David's priests (1 Chr. 15:18, 20, 24; 16:5, 6). **[5]** Father of one of David's counselors (1 Chr. 27:34). **[6]** The grandfather of Jahaziel (2 Chr. 20:14). **[7]** An overseer of the temple during Hezekiah's reign (2 Chr. 31:13). **[8], [9], [10], [11]** Four men who married foreign wives during the Exile (Ezra 10:25, 30, 35, 43). **[12]** Father of Pelatiah, a prince of Judah (Ezek. 11:1, 13).

**Ben-Ammi** ("son of my people"), the ancestor of the Ammonites (Gen. 19:38), born to Lot and his daughter.

**Ben-Hadad** ("son of [the god] Hadad"). **[1]** Ben-Hadad I, the king of Syria who made a league with Asa of Judah and invaded Israel (1 Kin. 15:18, 20; 2 Chr. 10:2, 4). **[2]** Ben-Hadad II, another king of Syria defeated by Ahab; he eventually laid siege to Samaria itself (1 Kin. 20; 2 Kin. 6:24; 8:7, 9). **[3]** The son of Hazael who reigned over Syria as the empire disintegrated (2 Kin. 13:3, 24, 25; Amos 1:4). **[4]** Possibly a general title of the Syrian kings (Jer. 49:27).

**Benjamin** ("son of the right hand"). **[1]** The youngest son of Jacob; his descendants became one of the twelve tribes of Israel (Gen. 35:18, 24; 42:4, 36; 43—45). **[2]** A descendant of Benjamin (1 Chr. 7:10). **[3]** A descendant of Harim (Ezra 10:32). **[4]** One who helped to repair the wall of Jerusalem (Neh. 3:23). **[5]** One who helped to dedicate the wall of Jerusalem (Neh. 12:34).

**Ben-Oni** ("son of my sorrow"), name given to Rachel's child as she died bearing him; Jacob changed his name to Benjamin (q.v.).

**Bernice** ("victorious"), the immoral daughter of Herod Agrippa I. She and her brother Agrippa (with whom she was living in incest) sat in judgment on Paul (Acts 25:13, 23; 26:30).

**Berothah [Berothai; Chun]** ("of a well"), a town in northern Palestine between Hamath and Damascus, captured by David; also called Chun (2 Sam. 8:8; 1 Chr. 18:8; Ezek. 47:16).

**Bethabara** ("house at the ford"), a place on the eastern side of the Jordan River where John the Baptist baptized his converts (John 1:28). The majority of Greek manuscripts read Bethany here instead; however, this city was not identical with Bethany proper.

**Bethany** ("house of affliction; place of unripe figs"), a settlement on the hill leading to the Mount of Olives, about 2.6 km. (1.6 mi.) from Jerusalem (Mark 11:1; Luke 19:29).

**Beth Aven** ("house of idols"), a town of the tribe of Benjamin, located in the wilderness near Ai (Josh. 7:2; 18:12; 1 Sam. 13:5).

**Bethel** ("house of God"). A town located about 18 km. (11 mi.) north of Jerusalem; an important site throughout the history of Israel (cf. Gen. 13:3; 28:18, 19; Josh. 16:2; Judg. 21:19). It was formerly called Luz. The modern town of Bertin is located near the ruins.

**Bethesda** ("house of outpouring or overflowing water"), a pool near the Sheep Gate of Jerusalem reputed to have healing qualities (John 5:2, 3).

**Beth Horon** ("cave house"), twin towns located on the boundary between the territories of Ephraim and Benjamin. Upper Beth Horon was situated on a mountain pass between Jerusalem and the plain to the west. Lower Beth Horon was about 2 km. (1.5 mi.) farther northwest (Josh. 16:3; 18:13; 2 Chr. 8:5; 1 Kin. 9:17). The modern names for these towns are Beit 'Ur et Tahta (Lower) and Beit 'Ur el Foka (Upper).

**Bethlehem** ("house of bread"). **[1]** A town about 10 km. (6 mi.) south of Jerusalem; birthplace of Jesus Christ (Matt. 2:5) and Ephrath (Gen. 35:16, 19; Ruth 4:11; cf. Mic. 5:2). Only in later times was it known as Bethlehem. It was originally called Ephrathah (Ephrath) (Ruth 4:11; Gen. 35:16). **[2]** A city of the tribe of Zebulun located about 11 km. (7 mi.) northwest of Nazareth (Josh. 19:15).

**Beth Nimrah** ("house of the leopardess"), a fortified city built by the tribe of Gad east of the Jordan River (Num. 32:36); also called Nimrah (Num. 32:3).

**Beth Peor** ("house of Peor"), a site near Pisgah where the Israelites placed their main camp while warring against Og (Deut. 3:29; 4:46).

**Bethphage** ("house of unripe figs"), a settlement near Bethany on the road from Jerusalem to Jericho, probably at the descent from the Mount of Olives (Matt. 21:1; Mark 11:1).

**Bethsaida** ("fish house"), a fishing town on the Sea of Galilee; birthplace of Philip, Andrew, and Simon (Matt. 11:21; Luke 9:10; Mark 6:45).

**Beth Shean [Beth Shan]** ("house of rest"), the southern border town of the region of Galilee; largest of the ten cities of the Decapolis (Josh. 17:11; 1 Chr. 7:29).

**Beth Shemesh** ("house of the sun"). **[1]** A town on the road from Ashkelon and Ashdod to Jerusalem; it is located about 38 km. (24 mi.) west of Jerusalem (Josh. 15:10). [2] A Canaanite city in the territory of Naphtali (Josh. 19:38; Judg. 1:33). [3] A city of the tribe of Issachar, probably on the Jordan River near the Sea of Galilee (Josh. 19:22). [4] Another name for the Egyptian city of Heliopolis (Jer. 43:13).

**Bethuel** ("dweller in God"), a son of Nahor, Abraham's brother (Gen. 22:22, 23; 28:5).

**Beulah** ("married"), Isaiah's name for the Promised Land after the Babylonian Captivity (Is. 62:4).

**Bezalel** ("God is protection"). [1] A chief worker and designer of the tabernacle (Ex. 31:2; 35:30; 36:1, 2). [2] One who had married a foreign wife (Ezra 10:30).

**Bigvai** ("happy; of the people"). [1] Head of one of the families who returned with Zerubbabel (Ezra 2:2, 14; 8:14; Neh. 7:7, 19). [2] One who sealed the covenant with Nehemiah (Neh. 10:16).

**Bildad** ("lord Adad; son of contention"), one of Job's three "friends" (Job 2:11; 8:1; 18:1; 25:1; 42:9).

**Bilhah** ("tender"), the handmaid of Rachel and mother of Dan and Naphtali (Gen. 29:29; 30:3–5, 7).

**Boanerges,** the surname bestowed upon James and John, the sons of Zebedee. It means "sons of thunder" (Mark 3:17).

**Boaz** ("fleetness; strength"), a Bethlehemite of Judah who became the husband of Ruth and an ancestor of Christ (Ruth 2—4; Matt. 1:5; Luke 3:32).

**Bochim** ("weepers"), a site near Gilgal where the Israelites repented of their sins (Judg. 2:1–5).

**Brook of the Willows.** *See* Willows, Brook of the.

**Buz** ("contempt"). [1] The second son of Nahor, the brother of Abraham (Gen. 22:21). [2] A descendant of Gad (1 Chr. 5:14).

**Buzi** ("despised by Jehovah"), a descendant of Aaron and father of Ezekiel (Ezek. 1:3).

## C

**Caesar,** the name of a branch of the aristocratic family of the Julii, which gained control of the Roman government; afterward it became a formal title of the Roman emperors. *See* Augustus Caesar; Tiberius Caesar; Claudius Caesar.

**Caesarea** ("city of Caesar"), a coastal city of Palestine that served as capital of the Roman province (Acts 8:40). Built by Herod the Great, it is located 37 km. (23 mi.) from the foot of Mount Carmel; also called Caesarea Maritima.

**Caesarea Philippi** ("Caesar's city of Philippi"), a town located at the foot of Mount Hermon; the northernmost extent of Jesus' ministry (Matt. 16:13–20).

**Caiaphas** ("depression"), the high priest who took a leading role in the trial of Jesus (Matt. 26:3, 57–68; John 11:49).

**Cain** ("acquired; spear"), the eldest son of Adam who killed his brother Abel (Gen. 4:1–25).

**Caleb [Chelubai]** ("impetuous; raging with madness"). [1] One of the spies sent out by Moses to see the Promised Land (Num. 13:6; Josh. 14—15). [2] A son of Hezron and grandfather of [1] (1 Chr. 2:18, 19, 42).

**Calvary.** *See* Golgotha.

**Cana** ("reeds"), a village of Galilee where Jesus performed the miracle of changing water into wine. It is located 16 km. (10 mi.) northeast of Nazareth (John 2:1, 11; 4:46).

**Canaan** ("low"), a son of Ham and grandson of Noah (Gen. 10:6–19; 1 Chr. 1:8, 13). Possibly a reference to the inhabitants of Canaan.

**Canaan** ("purple"), the native name of Palestine, the land given to Abraham and his descendants (Gen. 11:31; Ex. 6:4).

**Capernaum** ("village of Nahum"), a town on the northwest shore of the Sea of Galilee; an important center of Jesus' ministry (Matt. 4:13; Luke 4:31).

**Carchemish** ("city [fortress] of Chemosh"), a city west of the Euphrates River; the eastern capital of the Hittites (2 Chr. 35:20; Is. 10:9; Jer. 46:2).

**Carmel** ("orchard"). [1] A string of mountains that runs about 24 km. (15 mi.) through central Palestine and juts into the Mediterranean Sea (Jer. 46:18). [2] A town in the mountains of Judah about 14 km. (9 mi.) south-southeast of Hebron (Josh. 15:55; 1 Sam. 25:5); modern Kermel. [3] *See* Rachal.

**Cephas.** *See* Peter.

**Chaldea** ("demons"), the southern region of the Babylonian Empire (Jer. 50:10; Ezek. 11:24).

**Cherith** ("gorge"), a small stream east of the Jordan River, where birds fed the prophet Elijah (1 Kin. 17:3–5).

**Chidon [Nachon]** ("javelin"), the place where Uzzah was struck dead for touching the ark of the covenant (1 Chr. 13:9); in Second Samuel 6:6 the place is called Nachon. Its exact location is unknown.

**Chileab** ("restraint of father"), a son of David (2 Sam. 3:3); probably also called Daniel (1 Chr. 3:1).

**Chilion** ("pining"), son of Naomi and husband of Orpah (Ruth 1:2, 5).

**Chinnereth [Chinneroth]** ("harps"). [1] Another name for the Sea of Galilee (Num. 34:11; Josh. 12:3). [2] A city on the north shore of the Sea of Galilee (Deut. 3:17). [3] The region surrounding the city of Chinnereth (1 Kin. 15:20).

**Chloe** ("a tender sprout"), a Corinthian woman or an Ephesian woman who knew of the problems at Corinth (1 Cor. 1:11).

**Chorazin** ("secret"), a coastal city of the Sea of Galilee where Jesus Christ performed many miracles (Matt. 11:21; Luke 10:13).

**Christ.** *See* Jesus Christ.

**Chun** ("founding"). *See* Berothah.

**Cilicia** ("rolling"), a district of southeast Asia Minor. Paul was born in Tarsus, the principal city of this district (Acts 21:39).

**Cities of Refuge,** six Levitical cities set aside as sanctuaries for certain criminals: Bezer, Ramoth Gilead, Golan, Kedesh, Shechem, and Kirjath Arba (Deut. 4:41–43; Josh. 20:7–9).

**Cities of the Plain,** five cities located on the Plain of Jordan: Sodom, Gomorrah, Admah, Zeboim, and Zoar (Gen. 10:19; 13:10).

**City of David.** [1] Jebusite city of Zion captured by David's men. David made it his royal city and renamed it Jerusalem (2 Sam. 5:6–9; 1 Chr. 11:5, 7). [2] *See* Bethlehem.

**City of Salt,** a city in the wilderness of Judah near En Gedi (Josh. 15:62).

**Claudia** ("lame"), a Roman Christian who sent greetings to Timothy (2 Tim. 4:21).

**Claudius Caesar** ("lame ruler"), Roman emperor who banished the Jews from Rome (Acts 18:2).

**Claudius Lysias** ("lame dissolution"), a Roman officer, chief captain in Jerusalem (Acts 23:26).

**Clement** ("mild"), a co-worker with Paul at Philippi (Phil. 4:3).

**Cleopas** ("renowned father"), one of the disciples whom Jesus met on the way to Emmaus (Luke 24:18). *See also* Clopas.

**Clopas** ("renowned"), the husband of one of the Marys who followed Jesus (John 19:25); possibly the same as Alphaeus (q.v.). *See also* Alphaeus; Cleopas.

**Colosse** ("punishment"), a city in the district of Phrygia in Asia Minor (Col. 1:2).

**Corinth** ("ornament"), a Greek city located on the isthmus between the Peloponnesus and mainland Greece, about 64 km. (40 mi.) west of Athens (Acts 18:1; 1 Cor. 1:2).

**Cornelius** ("of a horn"), a Roman centurion who was converted to Christianity (Acts 10:1–31).

**Corner Gate,** a gate near the northwest corner of the wall of Jerusalem (2 Kin. 14:13).

**Crete** ("carnal"), a large island southeast of Greece (Titus 1:5).

**Crispus** ("curled"), a ruler of the Jewish synagogue at Corinth who was converted to Christ (Acts 18:7, 8; 1 Cor. 1:14).

**Cush** ("black"). [1] Eldest son of Ham (Gen. 10:6-8; 1 Chr. 1:8-10). [2] A descendant of Benjamin and enemy of David (Ps. 7, title).

**Cyprus** ("fairness"), an island in the northeastern Mediterranean Sea about 96 km. (60 mi.) east of Syria (Acts 13:4; 15:39).

**Cyrus,** founder of the Persian Empire; he returned the Jews to their land (Ezra 1:1–4, 7; 3:7; Is. 44:28; 45:1–4; Dan. 6:28).

## D

**Dalmanutha** ("bucket"), a fishing village on the western coast of the Sea of Galilee (Mark 8:10).

**Damascus** ("sackful of blood"), an important Syrian trade center; Paul was converted on the road from Jerusalem to this city (Gen. 14:15; Acts 9:2).

**Dan** ("judge"), the fifth son of Jacob and ancestor of one of the twelve tribes of Israel (Gen. 30:6; 49:16, 17).

**Dan** ("judge"), a town of the tribe of Dan in the northwest portion of Palestine (Josh. 19:47; Judg. 20:1).

**Daniel** ("God is my judge"). [1] A prophet at the time of Nebuchadnezzar and Cyrus. His wisdom and faith earned him a position of esteem under Nebuchadnezzar and Darius (Dan. 1:1–6; 2; 6:1, 2). [2] One of the sons of David (1 Chr. 3:1). *See* Chileab. [3] A Levite of the line of Ithamar (Ezra 8:2; Neh. 10:6).

**Darius** ("he that informs himself"). [1] The sub-king of Cyrus who received the kingdom of Belshazzar (Dan. 5:30—6:28); also known as Darius the Mede. [2] The fourth king of Persia (Ezra 4:5; Hag. 1:1; Zech. 1:1); also called Hystaspis. [3] Darius II (Nothus) who ruled Persia and Babylon (Neh. 12:22).

**Dathan** ("fount"), a chief of the tribe of Reuben who tried to overthrow Moses and Aaron (Num. 16; 26:9; Deut. 11:6).

**David** ("beloved"), the great statesman, general, and king of Israel. He united the divided tribes of Israel and made many preparations for the temple, which his son Solomon would complete (1 Sam. 16—1 Kin. 2:11). He was an ancestor of Christ (Matt. 1:6).

**Dead Sea.** *See* Salt Sea.

**Deborah** ("bee"). [1] The nurse of Rebekah (Gen. 24:59; 35:8). [2] Prophetess and judge of Israel who helped to deliver her people from Jabin and Sisera (Judg. 4:4–14; 5).

**Decapolis** ("ten cities"), a league of ten cities forming a Roman district on the Plain of Esdraelon and the Upper Jordan Valley (Matt. 4:25).

**Delaiah** ("Jehovah has raised; Jehovah is deliverer"). [1] One of David's priests (1 Chr. 24:18). [2] A prince who urged Jehoiakim not to destroy the roll containing Jeremiah's prophecies (Jer. 36:12, 25). [3] Ancestor of a post-exilic family that had lost its genealogy (Ezra 2:60; Neh. 7:62). [4] The father of Shemaiah (Neh. 6:10).

**Delilah** ("longing; dainty one"), a woman whom the Philistines paid to find Samson's source of strength (Judg. 16).

**Demetrius** ("belonging to Demeter"). [1] A Christian praised by John (3 John 12). [2] A silversmith who led the opposition against Paul at Ephesus (Acts 19:24–41).

**Derbe** ("sting"), a city of southeastern Asia Minor, where Paul sought refuge after being stoned at Lystra (Acts 14:6–20).

**Deuel** ("knowledge of God"), father of Eliasaph (Num. 1:14). He is called Reuel in Numbers 2:14; we do not know which name is original.

**Didymus.** *See* Thomas.

**Dinah** ("justice"), the daughter of Jacob and Leah who was violated by Shechem; this resulted in a tribal war (Gen. 34).

**Dionysius** ("Bacchus"), a member of the supreme court at Athens converted by Paul (Acts 17:34).

**Doeg** ("anxious; cared for"), a servant of King Saul who executed the priests of Nob on Saul's orders (1 Sam. 21:7; 22:9–19).

**Dorcas.** *See* Tabitha.

**Dothan** ("two wells"), a city of the tribe of Manasseh west of the Jordan River and northeast of Samaria, near Mount Gilboa; here Joseph was sold into slavery (Gen. 37:17; 2 Kin. 6:13).

**Drusilla** ("watered by dew"), a Jewess, the daughter of Herod Agrippa I and wife of Felix; she and Felix heard a powerful message of Paul's (Acts 24:24, 25).

**Dura** ("fortress"), the Babylonian plain where King Nebuchadnezzar set up a golden idol (Dan. 3:1).

## E

**Ebal** ("stone"), a mountain beside Mount Gerizim (Deut. 27:12, 13); modern Jebel Eslamiyeh.

**Ebed-Melech** ("the king's servant"), an Ethiopian eunuch who rescued Jeremiah (Jer. 38:7–12; 39:16).

**Ebenezer** ("stone of help"). [1] The site of the defeat of Israel by the Philistines (1 Sam. 4:1–22). It was in the north of Sharon near Aphek. [2] Name of a stone Samuel erected to commemorate his victory over the Philistines (1 Sam. 7:12). The stone was possibly named after [1] to give the idea that Israel's defeat there had been reversed.

**Eber** ("the other side; across"). **[1]** A descendant of Shem and an ancestor of Christ (Gen. 10:21, 24, 25; 11:14–17; Luke 3:35). Possibly the Hebrews and certain Aramean people are intended. **[2]** A descendant of Benjamin (1 Chr. 8:12). **[3]** Head of a priestly family (Neh. 12:20). *See* Heber.

**Eden** ("pleasure"). **[1]** The garden that God created as the first residence of man (Gen. 2:15); its exact location is unknown. It may have been between the Tigris and Euphrates Rivers near the head of the Persian Gulf. **[2]** A region in Mesopotamia (2 Kin. 19:12; Is. 37:12).

**Edom** ("red"), name given to Esau, the elder son of Isaac, because of the red stew for which he sold his birthright (Gen. 25:30). *See* Esau; Obed-Edom.

**Edom** ("red"), a mountainous region south of Moab, which stretches from the Dead Sea to the Gulf of Aqabah. It was settled by the descendants of Esau, the Edomites (Gen. 32:3; Ex. 15:15).

**Eglah** ("calf"), one of David's wives (2 Sam. 3:5; 1 Chr. 3:3).

**Eglon** ("circle"), a king of Moab who oppressed Israel in the days of the judges (Judg. 3:12–17).

**Egypt** ("land of the soul of Ptah"), northeast corner of Africa where the Israelites were held in bondage until Moses led them to the Promised Land (Gen. 45:9; 47:6).

**Ehud** ("strong"). **[1]** A judge who delivered Israel from the oppression of Eglon of Moab (Judg. 3:15–30). **[2]** Great-grandson of Benjamin (1 Chr. 7:10; 8:6); perhaps the same as [1].

**Elah** ("oak"). **[1]** A chieftain of Edom (Gen. 36:41; 1 Chr. 1:52). **[2]** Father of a commissary officer under Solomon (1 Kin. 4:18). **[3]** The son and successor of Baasha, king of Israel. He was murdered by Zimri (1 Kin. 16:6–14). **[4]** The father of Hoshea, last king of Israel (2 Kin. 15:30; 17:1). **[5]** A son of Caleb, son of Jephunneh (1 Chr. 4:15). **[6]** A descendant of Benjamin (1 Chr. 9:8).

**El Bethel** ("God of Bethel"), name Jacob gave the scene of his vision at Luz (Bethel) (Gen. 35:7).

**Eldad** ("God is a friend"), one of two elders who received the prophetic powers of Moses (Num. 11:26, 27).

**Eleazar** ("God is helper"). **[1]** Third son of Aaron and successor to the high priest's office (Ex. 6:23; Num. 3:32; 20:28). **[2]** One sanctified to keep the ark of the covenant (1 Sam. 7:1). **[3]** One of David's mighty men (2 Sam. 23:9; 1 Chr. 11:12). **[4]** A descendant of Merari who had no sons (1 Chr. 23:21, 22; 24:28). **[5]** A priest who accompanied Ezra when he returned to Jerusalem (Ezra 8:33). **[6]** A priest who assisted at the dedication of the walls of Jerusalem (Neh. 12:42); possibly the same as [5]. **[7]** An ancestor of Jesus (Matt. 1:15).

**Eli** ("Jehovah is high"), high priest at Shiloh and judge of Israel. He is remembered for his lack of firmness (1 Sam. 1—4).

**Eliakim** ("God is setting up"). **[1]** Successor of Shebna as master of Hezekiah's household (2 Kin. 18:18, 26; Is. 22:20). **[2]** Original name of King Jehoiakim (q.v.). **[3]** A priest in Nehemiah's time (Neh. 12:41). **[4]** An ancestor of Christ (Matt. 1:13).

**Eliezer** ("God is help"). **[1]** Abraham's chief servant (Gen. 15:2). **[2]** The second son of Moses and Zipporah (Ex. 18:4; 1 Chr. 23:15, 17). **[3]** A descendant of Benjamin (1 Chr. 7:8). **[4]** A priest who assisted with bringing the ark of the covenant to Jerusalem (1 Chr. 15:24). **[5]** A prince of Reuben in the time of David (1 Chr. 27:16). **[6]** A prophet who rebuked Jehoshaphat (2 Chr. 20:37). **[7]** A leader who induced others to return to Jerusalem (Ezra 8:16). **[8], [9], [10]** Three men who took foreign wives during the Exile (Ezra 10:18, 23, 31). **[11]** An ancestor of Christ (Luke 3:29).

**Elihu** ("God himself"). **[1]** One who joined David at Ziklag (1 Chr. 12:20). **[2]** A porter at the tabernacle at the time of David (1 Chr. 26:7). **[3]** The youngest "friend" of Job (Job 32:2, 4–6).

**Elijah** ("Jehovah is my God"). **[1]** A great prophet of God, he strenuously opposed idolatry. He was caught up in a chariot of fire to heaven (1 Kin. 17:1—2 Kin. 2:11; Matt. 17:3). **[2]** A chief of the tribe of Benjamin (1 Chr. 8:27). **[3]** One who married a foreign wife during the Exile (Ezra 10:26). **[4]** Another who took a foreign wife during the Exile (Ezra 10:21).

**Elimelech** ("my God is King"), the husband of Naomi and father-in-law of Ruth. He died in Moab (Ruth 1:2, 3; 2:1, 3; 4:3, 9).

**Eliphaz** ("God is dispenser"). **[1]** The leader of Job's three "friends" who confronted him (Job 2:11; 4:1; 15:1). **[2]** A son of Esau (Gen. 36:4, 10–12; 1 Chr. 1:35, 36).

**Eliphelet [Elpelet]** ("God is escape"). **[1]** The last of David's thirteen sons (2 Sam. 5:16; 1 Chr. 3:8; 14:7). **[2]** Another of David's sons (1 Chr. 3:6); called Elpelet in First Chronicles 14:5. **[3]** One of David's mighty men (2 Sam. 23:34).

**Elisha [Elishah]** ("God is Savior"). **[1]** The disciple and successor of Elijah; he held the prophetic office for 55 years (1 Kin. 19:16, 17, 19; 2 Kin. 2—6; Luke 4:27). **[2]** Eldest son of Javan and great-grandson of Noah (Gen. 10:4). Possibly the people of Cyprus or the inhabitants of Alasiya, a country near Cilicia. Others suggest it includes the Italians and Peloponnesians.

**Elishama** ("God is hearer"). **[1]** Grandfather of Joshua (Num. 1:10; 2:18; 1 Chr. 7:26). **[2]** A son of King David (2 Sam. 5:16; 1 Chr. 3:8). **[3]** Another son of David (1 Chr. 3:6); also called Elishua in Second Samuel 5:15 and First Chronicles 14:5. **[4]** A descendant of Judah (1 Chr. 2:41). **[5]** One of the "royal seed" and grandfather of Gedaliah (Jer. 41:1; 2 Kin. 25:25). **[6]** A scribe or secretary of Jehoiakim (Jer. 36:12, 20, 21). **[7]** A priest sent by Jehoshaphat to teach the Law (2 Chr. 17:8).

**Elizabeth** ("God is swearer; oath of God"), the wife of Zacharias and mother of John the Baptist (Luke 1:5–57).

**Elkanah [Elkonah]** ("God is possessing"). **[1]** Grandson of Korah (Ex. 6:24; 1 Chr. 6:23). **[2]** Father of the prophet Samuel and a descendant of [1] (1 Sam. 1:1–23; 2:11, 20). **[3]** A descendant of Levi (1 Chr. 6:25, 36). **[4]** A descendant of Levi (1 Chr. 6:26, 35); perhaps the same as [3]. **[5]** A Levite ancestor of Berechiah (1 Chr. 9:16). **[6]** One who joined David at Ziklag (1 Chr. 12:6). **[7]** A doorkeeper of the ark of the covenant (1 Chr. 15:23); perhaps the same as [6]. **[8]** An officer of King Ahaz (2 Chr. 28:7).

**Elymas** ("a sorcerer"), a false prophet who opposed Saul and Barnabas at Paphos (Acts 13:8); he was also called Bar-Jesus (v. 6).

**Emmaus** ("despised people"), a settlement about 16

km. (10 mi.) west of Jerusalem (Luke 24:13); its exact location is unknown.

**En Dor** ("fountain of habitation"), a town of the tribe of Manasseh where Saul consulted a witch about his future (Josh. 17:11); probably modern Indur on the northeastern shoulder of the Little Hermon Mountain, 10 km. (6 mi.) southeast of Nazareth.

**En Gedi** ("fountain of the goat"), a town on the western shore of the Dead Sea assigned to the tribe of Judah; originally called Hazazon Tamar (2 Chr. 20:2; Josh. 15:62).

**Enoch** ("teacher"). [1] The eldest son of Cain (Gen. 4:17, 18). [2] A son of Jared and an ancestor of Christ (Gen. 5:18, 19, 21; 1 Chr. 1:3; Luke 3:37; Heb. 11:5).

**Enoch** ("initiated"), a city built by Cain (Gen. 4:17).

**Enos [Enosh]** ("mortal"), son of Seth and ancestor of Christ (Gen. 4:26; 5:6–11; 1 Chr. 1:1; Luke 3:38).

**Enosh.** *See* Enos.

**Epaphras** (shortened form of *Epaphroditus*—"lovely"), a Christian worker with Paul who served as missionary to Colosse (Col. 1:7; 4:12; Philem. 23).

**Epaphroditus** ("lovely"), a Philippian Christian who worked so strenuously that he lost his health (Phil. 2:25; 4:18).

**Ephesus** ("desirable"), a town on the western coast of Asia Minor between Miletus and Smyrna; an important trading center (Acts 19:1).

**Ephod** ("oracular"), father of a prince of the tribe of Manasseh (Num. 34:23).

**Ephraim** ("doubly fruitful"), the second son of Joseph by Asenath. Although Ephraim was the younger of the two sons of Joseph, he received the firstborn's blessing. He was an ancestor of one of the twelve tribes of Israel (Gen. 41:52; 46:20; 48; 50:23).

**Ephraim** ("fruitful"). [1] The territory allotted to the tribe of Ephraim in the Promised Land (Num. 1:33). [2] A city near Baal Hazor, probably the same as "Ephraim near the wilderness" (2 Sam. 13:23; John 11:54). It is identified with modern et-Taiyibeh, about 6 km. (4 mi.) northeast of Bethel. [3] A gate on the north wall of old Jerusalem (2 Kin. 14:13; 2 Chr. 25:23). [4] A rough area (not forest) where Absalom was slain (2 Sam. 18:6). [5] A mountain allotted to the tribe of Ephraim (1 Sam. 1:1).

**Ephrathah [Ephrath]** ("fertility"), the second wife of Caleb (1 Chr. 2:19, 50; 4:4).

**Ephron** ("strong"), a Hittite from whom Abraham bought a field with a cave, which became Sarah's burial place (Gen. 23:8, 10, 13, 14; 49:30).

**Erastus** ("beloved"). [1] Christian sent with Timothy into Macedonia while Paul stayed in Asia (Acts 19:22). [2] An important person in Corinth sending greetings to Rome (Rom. 16:23). [3] One who remained at Corinth (2 Tim. 4:20). Perhaps some or all of the above are identical.

**Esarhaddon** ("Ashur has given a brother"), the son of Sennacherib and a powerful king of Assyria (2 Kin. 19:37; Ezra 4:2; Is. 37:38).

**Esau** ("hairy"), eldest son of Isaac and twin brother of Jacob. He is the progenitor of the tribe of Edom (Gen. 25:25). He sold his birthright to Jacob (Gen. 25:26–34; 27; 36).

**Esau's Wives.** There are two lists of Esau's wives—Genesis 26:34; 28:9 list them in this fashion: [1] Judith, the daughter of Beeri the Hittite, [2] Basemath, daughter of Elon the Hittite, and [3] Mahalath, the daughter of Ishmael, Abraham's son. The other list in Genesis 36:2, 3 runs thus: [1] Aholibamah, the daughter of Anah the daughter of Zibeon, [2] Adah, the daughter of Elon the Hittite, and [3] Basemath, the daughter of Ishmael. Some scholars suppose we are dealing with six women, but this seems unlikely. In the ancient world, many women received new names at marriage and this fact would account for the different names. Thus, [1] Judith is Aholibamah, [2] Basemath is Adah, and [3] Mahalath is Basemath. As far as Judith is concerned, Beeri might be her father and Anah her mother; or perhaps Anah is another name of Beeri. Some even think Beeri ("man of the springs") is a nickname rather than a proper name.

**Esther** ("star; [the goddess] Ishtar"), the Persian name of Hadassah, who was chosen by Ahasuerus to be his queen. The book of Esther tells her story.

**Ethan** ("ancient"). [1] A wise man in the days of Solomon (1 Kin. 4:31; Ps. 89, title). [2] A descendant of Judah (1 Chr. 2:6, 8). He is possibly identical with [1]. [3] *See* Jeduthun. [4] A descendant of Levi (1 Chr. 6:42).

**Ethbaal** ("Baal's man; with Baal"), king of Sidon and father of Ahab's wife Jezebel (1 Kin. 16:31).

**Ethiopia [Cush?]** ("burnt face"), a nation located in the upper region of the Nile River (Ps. 68:31; Is. 18:1). It is not the same as modern Ethiopia. *See also* Cush.

**Eubulus** ("of good counsel"), one of the Roman Christians that remained loyal to Paul (2 Tim. 4:21).

**Eunice** ("conquering well"), the pious mother of Timothy (2 Tim. 1:5; cf. Acts 16:1).

**Euphrates** (meaning unknown), a major river of western Asia, which begins in Armenia and joins the Tigris River before flowing into the Persian Gulf. It formed the western boundary of Mesopotamia (Gen. 2:14; 15:18).

**Eutychus** ("fortunate"), a young man at Troas whom Paul restored to life (Acts 20:6–12).

**Eve** ("life; life-giving"), the first woman, Adam's wife (Gen. 3:20; 4:1; 2 Chr. 11:3).

**Evil-Merodach** (Babylonian, Arvil-Marduk—"the man of [the god] Marduk"), the king of Babylon who released Jehoiachin from imprisonment. He succeeded his father, Nebuchadnezzar (2 Kin. 25:27–30; Jer. 52:31).

**Ezekiel** ("God strengthens"), a prophet of a priestly family carried captive to Babylon. He prophesied to the exiles in Mesopotamia by the river Chebar, and is the author of the book bearing his name (Ezek. 1:3; 24:24).

**Ezra** ("help"). [1] Head of one of the courses of priests that returned from the Exile (Neh. 12:1). The full form of his name, *Azariah*, occurs in Nehemiah 10:2. [2] A descendant of Judah through Caleb (1 Chr. 4:17). [3] A prominent scribe and priest descended from Hilkiah the high priest (Ezra 7:1–12; 10:1; Neh. 8:1–13). *See* Azariah.

## F

**Felix** ("happy"), Roman governor of Judea that presided over the trial of Paul at Caesarea (Acts 23:23–27; 24:22–27).

**Festus** ("swine-like"), successor of Felix to the governorship of Judea. He continued the trial of Paul begun under Felix (Acts 25; 26).

**Fortunatus** ("fortunate"), a Corinthian Christian

who cheered and comforted Paul at Ephesus (1 Cor. 16:17, 18).

## G

**Gad** ("fortune"). [1] The seventh son of Jacob and an ancestor of one of the twelve tribes (Gen. 30:11; 49:19). [2] David's seer who frequently advised him (1 Sam. 22:5; 1 Chr. 21:9–19).

**Gad** ("lot; fortune"), the territory settled by the tribe of Gad, east of the Jordan River (1 Sam. 13:7; Josh. 13:24).

**Gadara** ("walls"), a town located east of the Jordan River, 11 km. (7 mi.) south of the Sea of Galilee (Mark 5:1; Luke 8:26). It was one of the Decapolis cities (q.v.).

**Gaddiel** ("fortune of God"), one of the spies (Num. 13:10).

**Gaius** ("lord"). [1] One to whom John's third epistle is addressed (3 John 1). [2] A native of Macedonia and a companion of Paul (Acts 19:29). [3] A man of Derbe who accompanied Paul as far as Asia (Acts 20:4). [4] The host to Paul when he wrote to the Romans (Rom. 16:23). [5] A convert whom Paul baptized at Corinth (1 Cor. 1:14); some think he is identical with [4].

**Galatia** ("land of Galli"), a district of central Asia Minor (Acts 16:6).

**Galilee** ("circle"), one of the largest Roman districts of Palestine; the primary region of Jesus' ministry (Luke 3:1; 23:6).

**Galilee, Sea of,** a large lake in northern Palestine, fed by the Jordan River; several of Jesus' disciples worked as fishermen on this lake (John 6:1). The lake was also known as the Sea of Chinnereth (q.v.), the Sea of Tiberias, and the Sea of Gennesaret (q.v.). *See also* Chinnereth [1] and Gennesaret [2].

**Gallio** (meaning unknown), Roman proconsul of Achaia before whom Paul was tried in Corinth (Acts 18:12–17).

**Gamaliel** ("reward or recompense of God"). [1] A prince of the tribe of Manasseh (Num. 1:10; 2:20). [2] A great Jewish teacher of the Law. He persuaded his fellow Jews to let the apostles go free (Acts 5:33–40; 22:3).

**Gath** ("winepress"), one of the five chief Philistine cities; home of the giant Goliath (1 Sam. 17:4; 2 Kin. 12:17; 2 Chr. 26:6). Its exact location is not known.

**Gaza** ("strong"). [1] The southernmost of the five chief Philistine cities, located 72 km. (44.5 mi.) south of modern Jaffa and 4 km. (2.4 mi.) from the Mediterranean Sea. It was the scene of Samson's exploits (Josh. 11:22; Judg. 16:1–3; 2 Kin. 18:8; Jer. 25:20). [2] A town of the tribe of Ephraim located on a small plain near Shiloh (1 Chr. 7:28).

**Gehazi** ("valley of vision; diminisher"), the dishonest servant of Elisha (2 Kin. 4:12–37; 5:20–27; 8:4).

**Gennesaret** ("garden of the prince"). [1] The region on the northwest shore of the Sea of Galilee (Matt. 14:34). [2] Another name for the Sea of Galilee (Luke 5:1).

**Gergesa** ("pilgrims"), a town or district which would have been located on the eastern side of the Sea of Galilee. Its location is not certain, but some have suggested modern-day Kersa (Matt. 8:28).

**Gerizim** ("cutters; wasteland"), a steep mountain in central Palestine facing Mount Ebal (Deut. 11:29); its peak is 872 m. (2,840 ft.) above sea level.

**Gershom** ("exile"). [1] Firstborn son of Moses and Zipporah (Ex. 2:22; 18:3). [2] *See* Gershon. [3] A descendant of Phinehas (Ezra 8:2). [4] Father of Jonathan, a Levite during the time of the judges (Judg. 18:30).

**Gershon [Gershom]** ("exile"), the eldest son of Levi (Gen. 46:11; Ex. 6:16; 1 Chr. 6:1). He is also called Gershom (1 Chr. 6:16, 17, 20; 15:7).

**Gethsemane** ("oil press"), a garden east of Jerusalem, beyond the brook Kidron at the foot of Mount Olivet; the site of Christ's betrayal (Matt. 26:36–56).

**Geuel** ("salvation of God"), the spy sent out from Gad to bring back word about Canaan (Num. 13:15).

**Gibeah** ("hill"). [1] A Judean town about 16 km. (10 mi.) northwest of Hebron (Josh. 15:57). [2] A town midway between Jerusalem and Ramah; home and capital of King Saul (1 Sam. 10:26; 15:34). The town is called Gibeath in Joshua 18:28. [3] A town or hill in the territory of Ephraim (Josh. 24:33); probably near Timnah [1]. [4] A hill in Kirjath Jearim on which was located the house of Abinadad (2 Sam. 6:3, 4).

**Gibeon** ("hill height"), the chief city of the Hivites, assigned to the tribe of Benjamin; located 9 km. (5.5 mi.) north-northwest of Jerusalem (Josh. 11:19; 2 Sam. 20:1–9). Its modern name is El-Jib.

**Gideon** ("feller [i.e., great warrior]"), the great judge of Israel who delivered his people from Midian (Judg. 6—8); he was given the name Jerubbaal (q.v.).

**Gihon** ("stream; bursting forth"). [1] One of the four rivers of Eden [1] (Gen. 2:13). [2] An intermittent spring outside the walls of Jerusalem, south of the temple area (1 Kin. 1:38–45; 2 Chr. 32:30).

**Gilead** ("strong; rocky"). [1] A son of Machir (Num. 26:29, 30). [2] Father of Jephthah the judge (Judg. 11:1, 2). [3] A descendant of Gad (1 Chr. 5:14).

**Gilead** ("strong; rocky; rough"). [1] A region east of the Jordan River, stretching from Moab to the Yarmuk River (Deut. 3:16, 17). [2] A mountain jutting onto the Plain of Jezreel (Judg.7:3). [3] A city in the region of Gilead (Hos. 6:8).

**Gilgal** ("rolling"). [1] The first campsite of the Israelites after they crossed the Jordan River into Canaan, probably near Jericho (Josh. 4:19–24). [2] A village 11 km. (7 mi.) northeast of Bethel, from which Elijah and Elisha began their journey (2 Kin. 2:1–4; 4:38); present-day Jiljilia. [3] A town on the edge of the Plain of Sharon, about 8 km. (5 mi.) north-northeast of Antipatris (Josh. 10:6–9, 15). [4] A place on the northern boundary of Judah, near Debir (Josh. 15:7).

**Gog** ("high; mountain"). [1] A descendant of Reuben (1 Chr. 5:4). [2] A prince of Rosh, Meshech, and Tubal (Ezek. 38:2; 39:1, 11). In Revelation 20:8 Gog appears to have become a nation as is Magog, thus indicating the name is to be understood symbolically. *See also* Magog.

**Golan** ("passage"), a city of Bashan east of the Jordan River, assigned to the Levites as a city of refuge (Deut. 4:43; Josh. 21:27). It is probably the site of modern Sahem el-Jaulan, 27 km. (17 mi.) east of the Sea of Galilee.

**Golgotha [Calvary]** ("skull"), a hill just outside the walls of ancient Jerusalem; the site of Jesus' crucifixion (Matt. 27:33; John 19:17). Its exact location is unknown, but it was probably inside the walls of what is now called the "old city."

**Goliath** ("an exile or soothsayer"). [1] The Philistine

giant who was slain by David (1 Sam. 17:4–54). [2] Another giant, possibly the son of [1] (2 Sam. 21:19).

**Gomer.** [1] Eldest son of Japheth (Gen. 10:2, 3; 1 Chr. 1:5, 6). Possibly a people inhabiting the north, probably including or identical with the Cimmerians of classical history. [2] The immoral wife of Hosea (Hos. 1:3; 3:1–4).

**Gomorrah** ("submersion"), one of the five Cities of the Plain destroyed along with Sodom (Gen. 18:20; 19:24, 28). Many scholars believe it was submerged by the southeastern tip of the Dead Sea.

**Goshen** ("drawing near"). [1] A cattle-raising district of the Nile delta assigned to the Israelites before they were placed in bondage (Gen. 46:28). [2] A town in the hill country of Judah (Josh. 15:51); probably modern Dahariyeh, about 21 km. (13 mi.) southwest of Hebron. [3] A region of Judah that probably derived its name from the town of Goshen (Josh. 10:41; 11:16).

**Greece** (meaning uncertain), a country of Southern Europe between Italy and Asia Minor; one of the most powerful nations of the ancient world (Dan. 8:21; Zech. 9:13; Acts 20:2).

## H

**Habakkuk** ("love's embrace"), a prophet during the reigns of Jehoiakim and Josiah (Hab. 1:1; 3:1).

**Hadadezer [Hadarezer]** ("[the god] Hadad is my help"), the king of Zobah in Syria that warred against David and Joab (2 Sam. 8:3–12). His name is also written Hadarezer; perhaps this is a dialectal variant (2 Sam. 10:16; 1 Chr. 18:3–10).

**Hadarezer.** *See* Hadadezer.

**Hagar** ("wandering"), an Egyptian servant of Sarah; she became the mother of Ishmael by Abraham (Gen. 16:1–16; 21:14–17).

**Haggai** ("festive"), the first of the prophets who prophesied after the Babylonian Captivity (Ezra 5:1; Hag. 1:1, 3, 12).

**Haggith** ("festal"), the fifth wife of David and mother of Adonijah (2 Sam. 3:4; 1 Kin. 1:5, 11).

**Ham,** the youngest son of Noah. Because of his wickedness, his son Canaan was cursed (Gen. 5:32; 9:22–27).

**Ham.** [1] A name for Egypt used only in poetry (Ps. 78:51). [2] A place between Ashteroth Karnaim in Bashan and the Moabite country (Gen. 14:5). Possibly modern Ham about 5 mi. south of Irbid in the 'Ajlūn district.

**Haman** ("celebrated Human [Humban]"), the prime minister of Ahasuerus who plotted against the Jews (Esth. 3—9).

**Hamath** ("anger"). [1] A Hittite city on the Orontes River about 200 km. (125 mi.) north of Damascus; a supply base for Solomon's armies (2 Chr. 8:4). [2] The ideal northern boundary of Israel (Num. 13:21; 34:8).

**Hamon Gog** ("multitude of Gog"), the valley where Gog and his armies will be defeated in their final struggle against God's people (Ezek. 39:11–15).

**Hamor** ("ass"), the prince of Shechem whose son Shechem brought destruction on himself and his family (Gen. 33:19; 34:2–26).

**Hanani** ("gracious"). [1] A musician and head of one of the courses of the temple services (1 Chr. 25:4, 25). [2] The father of the prophet Jehu; cast into prison by Asa (1 Kin. 16:1, 7; 2 Chr. 16:7–10). [3] A priest who married a foreign wife (Ezra 10:20). [4] A brother of Nehemiah and a governor of Jerusalem under him (Neh. 1:2; 7:2). [5] A priest and musician who helped to purify the walls of Jerusalem (Neh. 12:36).

**Hananiah** ("Jehovah is gracious"). [1] A descendant of Benjamin (1 Chr. 8:24). [2] An officer of Uzziah (2 Chr. 26:11). [3] The father of a prince under Jehoiakim (Jer. 36:12). [4] The leader of the sixteenth division of David's musicians (1 Chr. 25:4, 23). [5] The grandfather of Irijah (Jer. 37:13). [6] A false prophet who opposed Jeremiah (Jer. 28). [7] One of Daniel's friends at Babylon (Dan. 1:7, 11, 19). *See also* Shadrach. [8] A son of Zerubbabel (1 Chr. 3:19, 21). [9] A Levite who married a foreign wife during the Exile (Ezra 10:28). [10] A druggist and priest who helped to rebuild the wall of Jerusalem (Neh. 3:8). [11] One who helped to rebuild the gate of Jerusalem (Neh. 3:30); perhaps the same as [10]. [12] A faithful Israelite placed in charge of Jerusalem (Neh. 7:2). [13] One who sealed the new covenant with God after the Exile (Neh. 10:23). [14] A priest present at the dedication of the walls of Jerusalem (Neh. 12:12, 41).

**Hannah** ("grace"), a prophetess, the mother of Samuel (1 Sam. 1).

**Hanòch [Enoch]** ("dedicated"). [1] A grandson of Abraham (Gen. 25:4). [2] The eldest son of Reuben, and founder of the Hanochite clan (Gen. 46:9; 1 Chr. 5:3). [3] Enoch, the son of Jared (1 Chr. 1:3).

**Haran** ("strong; enlightened"). [1] A brother of Abraham who died before his father (Gen. 11:26–31). [2] A descendant of Levi (1 Chr. 23:9). [3] A son of Caleb (1 Chr. 2:46).

**Haran** ("mountains"), a Mesopotamian city located 386 km. (240 mi.) northwest of Nineveh and 450 km. (280 mi.) north-northeast of Damascus (Gen. 11:31; 12:4, 5).

**Hashabiah** ("Jehovah is associated"). [1] A descendant of Levi (1 Chr. 6:45). [2] Another descendant of Levi (1 Chr. 9:14). [3] A son of Jeduthun (1 Chr. 25:3). [4] A descendant of Kohath (1 Chr. 26:30). [5] A son of Kemuel who was a prince of the Levites (1 Chr. 27:17). [6] A chief of a Levite clan (2 Chr. 35:9). [7] A Levite who returned with Ezra from Babylon (Ezra 8:19). [8] A chief of the family of Kohath (Ezra 8:24). [9] One who repaired the wall of Jerusalem (Neh. 3:17). [10] One who sealed the covenant with Nehemiah (Neh. 10:11). [11] A Levite in charge of certain temple functions (Neh. 11:15). [12] An attendant of the temple (Neh. 11:22). [13] A priest in the days of Jeshua (Neh. 12:21). [14] A chief Levite (Neh. 12:24). [Note: It is quite possible that [9], [12], and [14] refer to the same person.]

**Hattush** ("contender"). [1] Descendant of the kings of Judah, perhaps of Shechaniah (1 Chr. 3:22). [2] A descendant of David who returned from the Exile with Ezra (Ezra 8:2). [3] A priest who returned from the Exile with Zerubbabel (Neh. 12:2). [4] One who helped to rebuild the wall of Jerusalem (Neh. 3:10). [5] A priest who signed the covenant (Neh. 10:1, 4). [Note: Entries [1], [2], [3], and [5] may refer to the same person.]

**Hazael** ("God sees"), the murderer of Ben-Hadad II who usurped the throne of Syria (1 Kin. 19:15, 17; 2 Kin. 8:8–29).

**Hazor** ("enclosure"). [1] The capital of the Canaanite kingdom, later included in the territory of Naphtali in northern Palestine (Josh. 11:1, 10, 13); site of a major archaeological excavation. [2] A place in extreme southern Judah (Josh. 15:23); possibly modern el-Jebariyeh. [3] Another city in southern Judah (Josh. 15:25). Hezron was a district or region of the city or another name for the city itself (verse 25). [4] A village of the tribe of Benjamin, to which the Jewish exiles returned (Neh. 11:33); modern Khirbet Hazzur, 6 km. (4 mi.) north-northwest of Jerusalem. [5] A region of the Arabian Desert east of Palestine (Jer. 49:28, 30, 33).

**Heber** (properly Eber—"the other side; across"), head of a family of Gad (1 Chr. 5:13).

**Heber** ("companion"). [1] A descendant of Asher (Gen. 46:17; 1 Chr. 7:31, 32). [2] The husband of Jael, who killed Sisera (Judg. 4:11, 17, 21; 5:24). [3] Head of a clan of Judah (1 Chr. 4:18). [4] A descendant of Benjamin (1 Chr. 8:17). [5] Used in Luke 3:35 to refer to Eber [1].

**Hebron** ("ford; company"). [1] A son of Kohath (Ex. 6:18; Num. 3:19; 1 Chr. 6:2, 18). [2] A descendant of Caleb (1 Chr. 2:42, 43).

**Hebron** ("friendship"). [1] A city in the hills of Judah, 32 km. (20 mi.) south of Jerusalem (Gen. 13:18; Num. 13:22). [2] A town of the tribe of Asher, more frequently called Abdon (Josh. 21:30).

**Hell** ("conceal"), the place of woe for the departed. "Hades" is the New Testament name for "Sheol," which was conceived as a place where the souls of all dead resided (Ps. 16:10; Matt. 11:23; Acts 2:27). The KJV also has *hell* as its translation of *Gehenna*, a valley outside Jerusalem that Jesus used as a symbol of woe for lost souls.

**Heman** ("faithful"). [1] A musician and seer appointed by David as a leader in the temple's vocal and instrumental music (1 Chr. 6:33; 15:17; 2 Chr. 5:12; 35:15). [2] A wise man with whom Solomon was compared (1 Kin. 4:31; 1 Chr. 2:6). He composed a meditative Psalm (Ps. 88, title).

**Hermon** ("devoted to destruction"), the highest mountain of the Anti-Lebanon range, marking the northeast boundary of Palestine (Deut. 3:8; Josh. 11:17; 1 Chr. 5:23).

**Herod** ("heroic"). [1] Herod the Great, the sly king of Judea when Christ was born. In order to maintain power, he murdered the children of Bethlehem, thinking that he would be killing the Messiah (Matt. 2:1–22; Luke 1:5). [2] Herod Antipas, son of the former, was tetrarch of Galilee and Perea. He was the murderer of John the Baptist (Matt. 14:1–10; Luke 13:31, 32; 23:7–12). [3] Herod Philip, son of Herod the Great, was tetrarch of Iturea and Trachonitis (Luke 3:1). [4] Herod Philip, another son of Herod the Great, is the Philip whose wife Herod Antipas lured away (Matt. 14:3). [5] Herod Agrippa I, tetrarch of Galilee and eventual ruler of his grandfather's (i.e., Herod the Great's) old realm. He bitterly persecuted Christians (Acts 12:1–23). [6] Herod Agrippa II, son of Agrippa I and king of various domains, witnessed the preaching of Paul (Acts 25:13–26; 26:1–32). *See also* Archelaus; Bernice; Drusilla.

**Herodias** ("heroic"), granddaughter of Herod the Great, wife of Antipas, and ultimate cause of John the Baptist's death (Matt. 14:3–9; Luke 3:19).

**Hezekiah** ("Jehovah is strength"). [1] One who returned from Babylon (Ezra 2:16; Neh. 7:21). He, or his representative, is called Hizkijah (a form of Hezekiah) in Nehemiah 10:17. [2] The twelfth king of Judah; an ancestor of Christ. He instituted religious reform and improved the overall safety and prosperity of the nation (2 Kin. 18—20; 2 Chr. 29—32; Matt. 1:9, 10). [3] A son of Neariah, a descendant of the royal family of Judah (1 Chr. 3:23).

**Hiddekel** ("sound"), an archaic name for the Tigris River (Gen. 2:14; Dan. 10:4). It is narrower than the Euphrates, but carries more water. It joins the Euphrates 100 miles from the Persian Gulf at Al Qurna.

**Hiel** ("God is living"), a man who rebuilt Jericho (1 Kin. 16:34) and sacrificed his sons, in fulfillment of Joshua's curse (Josh. 6:26).

**Hilkiah** ("Jehovah is protection" or "my portion"). [1] One who stood with Ezra at the reading of the Law (Neh. 8:4). [2] A Levite who kept the children of the temple officials (1 Chr. 6:45). [3] A gatekeeper of the tabernacle (1 Chr. 26:11). [4] Master of the household of King Hezekiah (2 Kin. 18:18, 26; Is. 22:20; 36:3). [5] A priest of Anathoth and father of Jeremiah (Jer. 1:1). [6] High priest and the discoverer of the Book of the Law in the days of Josiah (2 Kin. 22:4, 8; 23:4). [7] The father of Gemariah (Jer. 29:3). [8] A chief of priests who returned from captivity (Neh. 12:7) and his later descendants (Neh. 12:12, 21).

**Hinnom**, an unknown person who had a son(s) after whom a valley near Jerusalem was named. Human sacrifices took place there in Jeremiah's day, and garbage was later incinerated in this defiled place (Josh. 15:8; 18:16; Neh. 11:30; Jer. 7:31, 32).

**Hinnom** ("their riches"), a narrow valley southwest of Jerusalem (Josh. 15:8; 18:16; 2 Chr. 28:3).

**Hiram [Huram]** (abbreviated form of Ahiram, "My brother is the exalted"). [1] A king of Tyre who befriended David and Solomon (2 Sam. 5:11; 1 Kin. 5; 9:11; 10:11). [2] The skillful worker in brass whom Solomon secured from King Hiram (1 Kin. 7:13, 40, 45; 2 Chr. 4:11, 16). [3] A descendant of Benjamin (1 Chr. 8:5).

**Hobab** ("beloved"), the father-in-law or brother-in-law of Moses (Num. 10:29; Judg. 4:11). The phrase "father-in-law" in Judges 4:11 may possibly mean nothing more than "in-law," or perhaps Jethro was also named Hobab; but the identity is uncertain. *See also* Jethro.

**Horeb** ("desert"), a range of mountains on the Sinai Peninsula, of which Mount Sinai is the highest (Ex. 17:6); now called the Serbal range.

**Hosea** ("help"; i.e., "Jehovah is help"), a prophet of Israel; he denounced the idolatries of Israel and Samaria (Hos. 1:1, 2).

**Hoshea [Hosea]** ("Jehovah is help or salvation"). [1] A chief of the tribe of Ephraim in the days of David (1 Chr. 27:20). [2] The last king of Israel; he was imprisoned by Sargon of Assyria (2 Kin. 15:30; 17:1, 4, 6; 18:1). [3] One who sealed the covenant with Nehemiah (Neh. 10:23). [3] The original name of Joshua (q.v.).

**Hur** ("free; noble"). [1] One of the men who held up Moses' arms during the battle with Amalek (Ex. 17:10, 12; 24:14). [2] A son of Caleb (Ex. 31:2; 35:30; 38:22; 1 Chr. 2:19, 50; 4:1, 4). [3] A Midianite king slain by Israel (Num. 31:8; Josh. 13:21). [4] An officer of Solomon on Mount Ephraim (1 Kin. 4:8). [5] The ruler of half of Jerusalem under Nehemiah (Neh. 3:9).

**Huram.** *See* Hiram.

**Hushai** ("quick"), a friend and counselor of David (2 Sam. 15:32, 37; 16:16–18; 17:5–15).

**Hymenaeus** ("nuptial"), an early Christian who fell into apostasy and error (1 Tim. 1:20; 2 Tim. 2:17).

## I

**Ibzan** ("famous; splendid"), a Bethlehemite who judged Israel for seven years (Judg. 12:8–10).

**Iconium** ("coming"), capital of the province of Lycaonia in Asia Minor (Acts 13:51; 14:1).

**Iddo** ("honorable; happy"), the official of Casiphia who provided Levites for Ezra (Ezra 8:17).

**Iddo** ("beloved"). [1] Captain of the tribe of Manasseh in Gilead (1 Chr. 27:21). [2] A descendant of Gershon (1 Chr. 6:21); called Adaiah in First Chronicles 6:41.

**Iddo** ("timely"). [1] Father of Abinadab (1 Kin. 4:14). [2] Grandfather of the prophet Zechariah (Zech. 1:7; Ezra 5:1).

**Iddo** ("adorned"). [1] A prophet who wrote about the kings of Israel (2 Chr. 9:29; 2 Chr. 12:15). [2] A priest who returned to Jerusalem with Zerubbabel (Neh. 12:4); perhaps the same as [1].

**Igal** ("Jehovah redeems"). [1] One of the twelve spies sent to search out Canaan (Num. 13:7). [2] One of David's heroes (2 Sam. 23:36). [3] A descendant of the royal house of Judah (1 Chr. 3:22).

**Illyricum** ("joy"), a Roman province on the east coast of the Adriatic Sea, stretching from Italy on the north to Macedonia on the south (Rom. 15:19). It was later renamed Dalmatia (q.v.).

**Immer** ("loquacious; prominent"). [1] A priest in the time of David (1 Chr. 24:14). [2] A priest of Jeremiah's time (Jer. 20:1). [3] The father of Zadok (Neh. 3:29). [4] A family of priests who gave their name to the sixteenth course of the temple service (1 Chr. 9:12; Ezra 2:37; Neh. 7:40).

**Imna [Jimna; Jimnah; Imnah]** ("lugging"). [1] A descendant of Asher (Gen. 46:17; 1 Chr. 7:35). [2] A son of Asher (Num. 26:44; 1 Chr. 7:30). [3] Father of Kore in Hezekiah's reign (2 Chr. 31:14).

**Imnah.** *See* Imna.

**India** (meaning unknown), a land on the eastern limit of the Persian Empire, surrounding the Indus River (Esth. 1:1; 8:9).

**Ira** ("watchful"). [1] A priest of David (2 Sam. 20:26). [2] One of David's thirty mighty men (1 Chr. 11:28; 2 Sam. 23:38) and a captain of the temple guard (1 Chr. 27:9). [3] Another of David's thirty (1 Chr. 11:40; 2 Sam. 23:26).

**Isaac** ("laughter"), the son of Abraham and Sarah, born to them in their old age. He was the father of Jacob and Esau and an ancestor of Christ (Gen. 21—25; Matt. 1:2).

**Isaiah** ("salvation of Jehovah"), called the "prince of prophets"; his career lasted over sixty years. He foretold the coming of Christ (Is. 1:1; 7:14; 9:6; 52:12–53).

**Iscariot.** *See* Judah [8].

**Ishbosheth** ("man of shame"), son and successor of King Saul. He reigned two years before being defeated by David (2 Sam. 2:8–15; 3:8, 14, 15; 4:5–12). He also was known as Esh-Baal (1 Chr. 8:33; 9:39).

**Ishmael** ("God hears"). [1] Son of Abraham and Hagar; his descendants are the Arabian nomads (Gen. 16:11–16; 17:18–26; 25:9–17; 28:9; 36:3). [2] The cunning son of Nethaniah and traitor of Israel (Jer. 40:8—41:18). [3] A descendant of Benjamin (1 Chr. 8:38). [4] Father of Zebadiah (2 Chr. 19:11). [5] A captain in the time of Jehoiada and Joash (2 Chr. 23:1). [6] A Levite who married a foreign wife during the Exile (Ezra 10:22).

**Israel.** *See* Jacob.

**Israel** ("who prevails with God"), the northern kingdom of the Hebrews in Palestine, inhabited by the ten tribes that followed Ishbosheth and Jeroboam. The cities of Jericho and Gezer marked its southern boundary (2 Chr. 35:18; cf. Gen. 32:32).

**Issachar** ("reward"). [1] Ninth son of Jacob and ancestor of one of the twelve tribes of Israel (Gen. 30:17, 18; 49:14, 15). [2] A tabernacle porter (1 Chr. 26:5).

**Italy** ("abounding with calves"), the peninsula jutting from the Alps into the Mediterranean Sea, bounded on the south by the straits of Messina (Acts 18:2; 27:1).

## J

**Jabesh** ("dry place"), father of Shallum, who killed Zechariah and reigned in his place (2 Kin. 15:10–14).

**Jabesh Gilead** ("dry"), a city of Gilead (Judg. 21:8; 1 Sam. 11:1). It may have been located at a site now called Wadi Yabis, about 32 km. (20 mi.) south of the Sea of Galilee.

**Jabin** ("intelligent; observed"). [1] A king of Hazor defeated by Joshua (Josh. 11:1). [2] Another king of Hazor who oppressed Israel and was defeated by Deborah (Judg. 4).

**Jachin** ("founding" or "he will establish"). [1] A son of Simeon (Gen. 46:10; Ex. 6:15; Num. 26:12). He is called Jarib in First Chronicles 4:24. [2] A priest in Jerusalem after the Babylonian Captivity (1 Chr. 9:10; Neh. 11:10). [3] Head of a family of Aaron (1 Chr. 24:17). *See* Jarib.

**Jachin** ("God establishes"), the right hand pillar of Solomon's porch on the temple of Jerusalem (1 Kin. 7:21).

**Jacob** ("supplanter; following after"). [1] Son of Isaac, twin of Esau, and an ancestor of Christ. He bought Esau's birthright and became the father of the Jewish nation (Gen. 25—50; Matt. 1:2). God changed his name from Jacob to Israel ("God strives"; Gen. 32:28; 35:10). [2] The father of Joseph, the husband of Mary (Matt. 1:15, 16).

**Jaddua** ("very knowing; known"). [1] One who sealed the covenant (Neh. 10:21). [2] The last high priest mentioned in the Old Testament (Neh. 12:11, 22).

**Jael** ("a wild goat"), wife of Heber who killed Sisera (Judg. 4:17–22; 5:6, 24).

**Jahaziel** ("God reveals"). [1] One who joined David at Ziklag (1 Chr. 12:4). [2] A priest who helped bring the ark of the covenant into Jerusalem (1 Chr. 16:6). [3] Son of Hebron (1 Chr. 23:19; 24:23). [4] A Levite who encouraged Jehoshaphat's army against the Moabites (2 Chr. 20:14). [5] A chief man whose son returned from Babylon (Ezra 8:5).

**Jair** ("Jehovah enlightens"). [1] A descendant of Judah through his father and of Manasseh through his mother (Num. 32:41; Deut. 3:14; 1 Kin. 4:13; 1 Chr. 2:22). [2] Judge of Israel for twenty-three years (Judg. 10:3–5). [3]

The father of Mordecai, Esther's cousin (Esth. 2:5). [4] *See* Jaare-Oregim.

**Jairus** ("enlightened"), a ruler of a synagogue near Capernaum whose daughter Jesus raised from the dead (Luke 8:41).

**Jambres,** one of the Egyptian magicians who opposed Moses (Ex. 7:9–13; 2 Tim. 3:8).

**James** (Greek form of Jacob). [1] The son of Zebedee and brother of John called to be one of the Twelve. He was slain by Herod Agrippa I (Matt. 4:21; Mark 5:37; Luke 9:54; Acts 12:2). [2] The son of Alphaeus, another of the twelve apostles. He is probably the same as James "the less," the son of Mary. By "the less" is meant his age or height in relation to James the son of Zebedee (Matt. 10:3; Mark 15:40; Acts 1:13). [3] The brother of Jesus (Matt. 13:55). After Christ's resurrection, he became a believer (1 Cor. 15:7) and a leader of the church at Jerusalem (Acts 12:17; Gal. 1:19; 2:9). He wrote the epistle of James (James 1:1). [4] Unknown person mentioned as "the brother of Judas." Most view this as an incorrect translation and would render "Judas, the son of James" (Luke 6:16; Acts 1:13).

**Jannes** ("he who seduces"), an Egyptian magician who opposed Moses (2 Tim. 3:8, 9; cf. Ex. 7:9–13).

**Japheth** ("the extender; fair; enlarged"), second son of Noah, considered the father of the Indo-European races (Gen. 5:32; 6:10; 7:13; 9:18, 23, 27; 1 Chr. 1:4, 5).

**Jarib** ("striving"). [1] A chief man under Ezra (Ezra 8:16). [2] A priest who took a foreign wife during the Exile (Ezra 10:18). [3] *See* Jachin [1].

**Jasher** ("upright"), one who wrote a now lost book (Josh. 10:13; 2 Sam. 1:18).

**Jason** ("healing"). [1] Paul's host during his stay at Thessalonica (Acts 17:5–9). [2] A Jewish Christian kinsman of Paul who sent salutations to Rome (Rom. 16:21). The men are possibly identical.

**Jebus** ("manager"), another name for Jerusalem (Judg. 19:10, 11).

**Jeconiah**. *See* Jehoiachin.

**Jedaiah** ("Jehovah is knowing"). [1] A priest of Jerusalem (1 Chr. 9:10; 24:7; Ezra 2:36; Neh. 7:39). [2] A priest who returned with Zerubbabel (Neh. 11:10; 12:6, 19). [3] Another priest who came up with Zerubbabel (Neh. 12:7, 21). [4] One who brought gifts to the temple (Zech. 6:10, 14).

**Jediael** ("God knows"). [1] A son of Benjamin (1 Chr. 7:6, 10, 11). Possibly the same as Ashbel (1 Chr. 8:1). [2] One of David's mighty men (1 Chr. 11:45). [3] One who joined David at Ziklag (1 Chr. 12:20). [4] A descendant of Korah, son of Meshelemiah (1 Chr. 26:2).

**Jedidiah** ("beloved of Jehovah"), the name God gave Solomon through Nathan (2 Sam. 12:25).

**Jeduthun** ("a choir of praise"). [1] One of the three chief musicians of the service of song (1 Chr. 9:16; 25:1–6; Neh. 11:17). He was also named Ethan (1 Chr. 6:44; 15:17, 19). [2] The father of Obed-Edom (1 Chr. 16:38). Some believe him identical with [1].

**Jehoahaz** ("Jehovah upholds"). [1] Son and successor of Jehu on the throne of Israel. His reign was one of disaster (2 Kin. 10:35; 13:2–25). [2] The son of Josiah and ruler of Judah for three months before he was deposed by Pharaoh Necho (2 Kin. 23:30–34; 2 Chr. 36:1–4). He was also called Shallum before becoming king (1 Chr. 3:15; Jer. 22:11). [3] *See* Ahaziah [2].

**Jehoash [Joash]** ("Jehovah has given; Jehovah supports"). [1] The ninth king of Judah. Until the time of Jehoiada the priest's death Jehoash followed God; afterward, he brought idolatry and disaster to his country (2 Kin. 11:21—12:21). He is more frequently called by the shortened form of his name, Joash. [2] The twelfth king of Israel; he was successful in many military campaigns (2 Kin. 13:9—14:16). He is most frequently called Joash, an abbreviated form of his name.

**Jehoiachin** ("Jehovah establishes"), ruler of Judah when it was captured by Nebuchadnezzar. He was an ancestor of Christ (2 Kin. 24:8–16; 2 Chr. 36:9, 10; Matt. 1:11, 12). Jeconiah ("Jehovah is able") is an altered form of his name (1 Chr. 3:16, 17; Jer. 24:1) as is Coniah ("Jehovah is creating"; Jer. 22:24, 28; 37:1).

**Jehoiada** ("Jehovah knows"). [1] The father of one of David's officers (2 Sam. 8:18; 1 Kin. 1:8, 26). [2] The chief priest of the temple for many years of the monarchy. He hid Joash from Athaliah for 6 years (2 Kin. 11—12:9). [3] One who joined David at Ziklag (1 Chr. 12:27). [4] A counselor of David (1 Chr. 27:34). [5] One who helped to repair a gate of Jerusalem (Neh. 3:6). [6] A priest replaced by Zephaniah (Jer. 29:26). *See* Joiada.

**Jehoiakim** ("Jehovah sets up" or "Jehovah has established"), the name given to Eliakim by Pharaoh Necho when he made him king of Judah. The name probably means that Necho claimed Jehovah had authorized him to put Eliakim on the throne (2 Kin. 23:34—24:6). Not to be confused with Joiakim.

**Jehonadab [Jonadab]** ("Jehovah is liberal"). [1] Descendant of Rechab, who forbade his followers and descendants to drink wine and live in houses (Jer. 35:6–19; 2 Kin. 10:15, 23). [2] The sly son of David's brother, Shimeah (2 Sam. 13:3, 5, 32, 35).

**Jehoram [Joram]** ("Jehovah is high"), Joram is a shortened form of the name. [1] Son and successor of Jehoshaphat to the throne of Judah and an ancestor of Christ (2 Kin. 8:16–24; Matt. 1:8). [2] The ninth king of Israel, slain by Jehu (2 Kin. 1:17; 3:1–6; 9:24). [3] A priest commissioned to teach the people (2 Chr. 17:8).

**Jehoshaphat [Joshaphat]** ("Jehovah is judge"). [1] The recorder of David (2 Sam. 8:16; 20:24; 1 Kin. 4:3). [2] An officer of Solomon (1 Kin. 4:17). [3] Father of Jehu, who conspired against Joram (2 Kin. 9:2, 14). [4] A priest who helped to bring the ark of the covenant from Obed-Edom (1 Chr. 15:24). [5] Faithful king of Judah and an ancestor of Christ (1 Kin. 22:41–50; Matt. 1:8).

**Jehoshaphat** ("judged of God"), the valley where the Last Judgment will take place (Joel 3:2); tradition identifies it as the Kidron Valley (q.v.).

**Jehu** ("Jehovah is he"). [1] The prophet who brought tidings of disaster to Baasha of Israel (1 Kin. 16:1–12; 2 Chr. 19:2). [2] The tenth king of Israel (1 Kin. 19:16, 17; 2 Kin. 9; 10). His corrupt leadership weakened the nation. [3] A descendant of Hezron (1 Chr. 2:38). [4] A descendant of Simeon (1 Chr. 4:35). [5] One who joined David at Ziklag (1 Chr. 12:3).

**Jeiel [Jehiel]** ("God snatches away"). [1] A chief of the tribe of Reuben (1 Chr. 5:7). [2] An ancestor of Saul (1 Chr. 9:35). [3] One of David's mighty men (1 Chr. 11:44). [4] A singer and gatekeeper of the tabernacle (1 Chr.

15:18, 21; 16:5). [5] A descendant of Asaph (2 Chr. 20:14). [6] A scribe or recorder of Uzziah (2 Chr. 26:11). [7] A Levite in Hezekiah's time (2 Chr. 29:13). [8] A chief Levite in the days of Josiah (2 Chr. 35:9). [9] One who returned to Jerusalem with Ezra (Ezra 8:13). [10] One who married a foreign wife during the Exile (Ezra 10:43).

**Jephthah** ("an opposer"), a judge of Israel who delivered his people from Ammon (Judg. 11—12:7).

**Jeremiah** ("Jehovah is high"). [1] A woman of Libnah whose daughter married King Josiah (2 Kin. 23:31; Jer. 52:1). [2] Head of a family of the tribe of Manasseh (1 Chr. 5:24). [3] One who joined David at Ziklag (1 Chr. 12:4). [4] A man of Gad who joined David at Ziklag (1 Chr. 12:10). 5] Another who joined David at Ziklag (1 Chr. 12:13). [6] A priest who sealed the new covenant with God after the Exile (Neh. 10:2; 12:1, 12). [7] A descendant of Jonadab (Jer. 35:3). [8] A prophet whose activity covered the reigns of the last five kings of Judah. He denounced the policies and idolatries of his nation (Jer. 1; 20; 26; 36).

**Jericho** ("his sweet smell"), a fortified city of Canaan located about 8 km. (5 mi.) from the north end of the Dead Sea and 27 km. (17 mi.) west of the Jordan River (Num. 22:1; Deut. 32:49). Today it is the oldest continually inhabited city in the world.

**Jeroboam** ("enlarger; he pleads the people's cause"). [1] The first king of Israel after the division of the kingdom. He reigned for 22 years (1 Kin. 11:26–40; 12:1—14:20). [2] The thirteenth king of Israel; his Israel was strong but overtly idolatrous (2 Kin. 14:23–29).

**Jeroham** ("loved"). [1] A Levite, the grandfather of Samuel (1 Sam. 1:1; 1 Chr. 6:27). [2] A descendant of Benjamin (1 Chr. 9:8). [3] Head of a family of Benjamin (1 Chr. 8:27). [4] A priest whose son lived in Jerusalem after the Exile (1 Chr. 9:12; Neh. 11:12). [5] Father of two who joined David at Ziklag (1 Chr. 12:7). [6] Father of Azareel, prince of Dan (1 Chr. 27:22). [7] Father of one who helped Jehoiada to set Joash on the throne of Judah (2 Chr. 23:1).

**Jerubbaal** ("let Baal contend" or possibly "let Baal show himself great"), the name given to Gideon by his father (Judg. 6:32; 7:1; 8:29).

**Jerubbesheth** ("contender with the idol"), name given to Jerubbaal (Gideon) by those who wanted to avoid pronouncing Baal (2 Sam. 11:21).

**Jerusalem** ("possession of peace"), capital of the southern kingdom of Judah, located 48 km. (30 mi.) from the Mediterranean Sea and 29 km. (18 mi.) west of the Jordan River (Josh. 10:1; 2 Sam. 5:5).

**Jeshurun** ("blessed"), a symbolic name for Israel (Deut. 32:15; Is. 44:2).

**Jesse** ("Jehovah exists; wealthy"), father of David and an ancestor of Christ (Ruth 4:17, 22; 1 Sam. 17:17; Matt. 1:5, 6).

**Jesus** (Greek form of Joshua). [1] A Christian who, with Paul, sent greetings to the Colossians (Col. 4:11); he was also called Justus. [2] *See* Joshua.

**Jesus Christ** (*Jesus*—"Jehovah is salvation," *Christ*—"the anointed one"), God's Son born of the Virgin Mary who came to earth to fulfill the prophecies of the King who would die for the sins of His people. The account of His ministry is found in the Gospels of Matthew, Mark, Luke, and John.

**Jethro** ("preeminence"), the father-in-law of Moses. He advised Moses to delegate the time-consuming administration of justice (Ex. 3:1; 4:18; 18:1–12). He is called Reuel in Exodus 2:18. In Numbers 10:29, the KJV calls him Raguel; but the Hebrew text reads Reuel.

**Jezebel** ("unexalted; unhusbanded"). [1] The wicked, idolatrous queen of Israel (1 Kin. 16:31; 18:4—21:25; 2 Kin. 9:7–37). [2] A false prophetess at Thyatira (Rev. 2:20). Possibly the name is symbolic and not the prophetess's real name.

**Jezreel** ("seed of God"). [1] A city on the Plain of Jezreel between Mount Gilboa and Mount Carmel (Josh. 19:18; 1 Kin. 21:1). [2] A town in Judah's hill country (Josh. 15:56); probably modern Khirbet Terrama on the Plain of Dibleh.

**Jimna.** *See* Imna.

**Joab** ("Jehovah is father"). [1] A son of Zeruiah, David's sister. He was captain of David's army (2 Sam. 2:13–32; 3:23–31; 18; 1 Kin. 2:22, 23). [2] A descendant of Judah (1 Chr. 2:54). Some scholars believe a city of Judah is referred to here. The name would include the four words that follow in the KJV and be written: Atroth Beth Joab. [3] One of the tribe of Judah (1 Chr. 4:14). [4] An ancestor of returned captives (Ezra 2:6; 8:9; Neh. 7:11).

**Joanna [Joannas]** ("God-given"). [1] An ancestor of Christ (Luke 3:27). [2] The wife of Chuza, Herod's steward, who ministered to Christ and the apostles (Luke 8:3; 24:10).

**Joash** (abbreviated form of Jehoash). [1] A man of Judah (1 Chr. 4:22). [2] Father of Gideon the judge (Judg. 6:11–32). [3] A son of Ahab (1 Kin. 22:26; 2 Chr. 18:25). [4] One who joined David at Ziklag (1 Chr. 12:3). [5] *See* Jehoash [1]. [6] *See* Jehoash [2].

**Joash** ("Jehovah has aided"). [1] A son of Becher, a descendant of Benjamin (1 Chr. 7:8). [2] The keeper of David's stores of oil (1 Chr. 27:28).

**Job** ("hated; persecuted"). [1] A pious man of Uz. His endurance in fierce trial resulted in marvelous blessing (Job 1—3; 42; Ezek. 14:14, 20). [2] The third son of Issachar (Gen. 46:13); he is also called Jashub (Num. 26:24; 1 Chr. 7:1).

**Jochebed** ("Jehovah is honor or glory"), a descendant of Levi and mother of Moses (Ex. 6:20; Num. 26:59).

**Joel** ("Jehovah is God"). [1] The firstborn son of Samuel the prophet (1 Sam. 8:2; 1 Chr. 6:33; 15:17). [2] A descendant of Simeon (1 Chr. 4:35). [3] The father of Shemaiah, a descendant of Reuben (1 Chr. 5:4, 8). [4] A chief of the tribe of Gad (1 Chr. 5:12). [5] An ancestor of the prophet Samuel (1 Chr. 6:36). [6] A descendant of Tola (1 Chr. 7:3). [7] One of David's mighty men (1 Chr. 11:38). [8] A Levite in David's time (1 Chr. 15:7, 11; 23:8). [9] A keeper of the treasures of the Lord's house (1 Chr. 6:22). [10] A prince of Manasseh west of the Jordan (1 Chr. 27:20). [11] A Levite who aided in cleansing the temple (2 Chr. 29:12). [12] One who married a foreign wife during the Exile (Ezra 10:43). [13] An overseer of the descendants of Benjamin in Jerusalem (Neh. 11:9). [14] A prophet in the days of Uzziah (Joel 1:1; Acts 2:16).

**Johanan** ("Jehovah is gracious"). [1] A captain who allied with Gedaliah after the fall of Jerusalem (2 Kin. 25:23; Jer. 40:8, 13). [2] Eldest son of Josiah, king of Judah (1 Chr. 3:15). [3] A son of Elioenai (1 Chr. 3:24). [4]

Father of a priest in Solomon's time (1 Chr. 6:9, 10). **[5], [6]** Two valiant men who joined David at Ziklag (1 Chr. 12:4, 12). **[7]** One who opposed making slaves of Judean captives in Ahaz's time (2 Chr. 28:12). **[8]** A returned exile (Ezra 8:12). **[9]** A priest who beckoned the exiles to Jerusalem (Ezra 10:6). **[10]** A son of Tobiah the Ammonite (Neh. 6:18). **[11]** A priest in the days of Joiakim (Neh. 12:22, 23).

**John** (a contraction of Jehohanan, "gift of God"). **[1]** The son of Zacharias and Elizabeth who came to prepare the way for the Messiah. He was called John the Baptist and was beheaded by Herod (Matt. 3; 11:7–18; 14:1–10; Luke 1:13–17). **[2]** A son of Zebedee and one of the twelve apostles. He is traditionally accorded the authorship of the Revelation, the Fourth Gospel, and the three epistles bearing his name (Matt. 4:21; 10:2; Acts 1:13; Gal. 2:9; Rev. 1:1). **[3]** A relative of the high priest Annas, who sat in judgment on Peter (Acts 4:6). **[4]** A missionary better known by his surname, Mark (q.v.). *See also* Johanan.

**Joiada** ("Jehovah knows"), a descendant of the priest Jeshua (Neh. 12:10, 11, 22; 13:28). *See* Jehoiada.

**Joiakim** ("Jehovah sets up"), the son of Jeshua who returned from the Babylonian Captivity (Neh. 12:10, 12, 26). Not to be confused with Jehoiakim.

**Joiarib** ("Jehovah knows"). **[1]** One whom Ezra sent to persuade ministers to return to the land of Israel (Ezra 8:16). **[2]** An ancestor of a family living in Jerusalem (Neh. 11:5). **[3]** A priest who returned from captivity (Neh. 11:10; 12:6, 19). He is called Jehoiarib in First Chronicles 9:10.

**Joktan,** a son of Eber of Shem's line (Gen. 10:25, 26; 1 Chr. 1:19, 20, 23). Perhaps the reference is to an Arabian tribe from which many other Arabian groups sprang.

**Jonadab.** *See* Jehonadab.

**Jonah [Jonas]** ("a dove"). **[1]** The father of Simon Peter (John 1:42; 21:15–17). **[2]** A Hebrew prophet sent to preach to Nineveh in the days of Jeroboam II. He was the first Hebrew prophet sent to a heathen nation (2 Kin. 14:25; Jon. 1:1, 3, 5, 17; 2:10; Matt. 12:39–41).

**Jonathan** ("Jehovah is given"). **[1]** A priest of an idol shrine in the territory of Ephraim (Judg. 18:30). **[2]** A son of Abiathar the high priest (2 Sam. 15:27, 36; 17:17; 1 Kin. 1:42). **[3]** A son of Shimea, David's brother (2 Sam. 21:21; 1 Chr. 20:7). **[4]** One of David's mighty men (2 Sam. 23:32; 1 Chr. 11:34). **[5]** A grandson of Onam (1 Chr. 2:32, 33). **[6]** An uncle of David (1 Chr. 27:32). **[7]** Father of one who returned with Ezra (Ezra 8:6). **[8]** One involved with the foreign wife controversy (Ezra 10:15). **[9]** A descendant of Jeshua the high priest (Neh. 12:11). **[10]** A priest (Neh. 12:14). **[11]** A scribe in whose house Jeremiah was kept prisoner (Jer. 37:15, 20; 38:26). **[12]** One who joined Gedaliah after the fall of Jerusalem (Jer. 40:8). **[13]** A son of Saul and close friend of David (1 Sam. 14; 18:1–4; 31:2).

**Joppa** ("beauty"), a town on the coast of Palestine (2 Chr. 2:16; Acts 9:36).

**Jordan** (meaning uncertain), the major river of Palestine. It rises in a valley between Mount Lebanon and Hermon. It follows a twisting route to enter the north end of the Dead Sea (Gen. 13:10; Josh. 2:7).

**Jose,** an ancestor of Christ (Luke 3:29). Not to be confused with Joses.

**Joseph** ("increaser"). **[1]** The son of Jacob and Rachel. He was sold into slavery but became the prime minister of Egypt (Gen. 37; 39—50). **[2]** Father of one of the spies sent into Canaan (Num. 13:7). **[3]** A son of Asaph (1 Chr. 25:2, 9). **[4]** One who married a foreign wife during the Exile (Ezra 10:42). **[5]** A priest of the family of Shebaniah (Neh. 12:14). **[6]** The husband of Mary, mother of Jesus (Matt. 1:16–24; 2:13; Luke 1:27; 2:4). **[7]** A converted Jew of Arimathea in whose tomb Jesus was laid (Matt. 27:57, 59; Luke 15:43). **[8]** An ancestor of Christ (Luke 3:24). **[9]** Another ancestor of Christ (Luke 3:26). **[10]** Yet another ancestor of Christ (Luke 3:30). **[11]** A disciple considered to take the place of Judas Iscariot (Acts 1:23). He was also known as Barsabas and Justus.

**Joses** ("helped"). **[1]** One of the brothers of Christ (Matt. 13:55; Mark 6:3). **[2]** The son of Mary, the wife of Clopas (Matt. 27:56; Mark 15:40, 47). Not to be confused with Jose.

**Joshaphat.** *See* Jehoshaphat.

**Joshua [Hoshea]** ("Jehovah is salvation"). **[1]** The successor of Moses; the general who led the conquest of the Promised Land (Ex. 17:9–14; 24:13; Deut. 31:1–23; 34:9). Moses changed his name from Hoshea ("Jehovah is help"), to Joshua. **[2]** A native of Beth Shemesh in the days of Eli (1 Sam. 6:14, 18). **[3]** The governor of Jerusalem under Josiah (2 Kin. 23:8). **[4]** High priest at the rebuilding of the temple (Hag. 1:1, 12, 14; 2:2, 4; Zech. 3:1, 3, 6).

**Josiah** ("Jehovah supports"). **[1]** Godly king of Judah during whose reign the Book of the Law was found (1 Kin. 13:2; 2 Kin. 22:1—23:30). He was an ancestor of Christ (Matt. 1:10, 11). **[2]** A son of Zephaniah living in Jerusalem (Zech. 6:10).

**Jotham** ("Jehovah is perfect"). **[1]** The son of Gideon who managed to escape from Abimelech (Judg. 9:5, 7, 21, 57). **[2]** A son of Jahdai (1 Chr. 2:47). **[3]** The twelfth king of Judah and an ancestor of Christ (2 Kin. 15:5–38; Is. 1:1; 7:1; Matt. 1:9).

**Judah [Judas; Jude]** ("praise"). **[1]** A son of Jacob by Leah and an ancestor of Christ. He acquired the birthright Reuben lost. His descendants became one of the twelve tribes of Israel (Gen. 29:35; 37:26–28; 43:3–10; Matt. 1:2, 3; Luke 3:33). **[2]** An ancestor of one who helped to rebuild the temple (Ezra 3:9). **[3]** One who married a foreign wife during the Exile (Ezra 10:23). **[4]** Second in authority over Jerusalem after the Exile (Neh. 11:9). **[5]** One who came up to Jerusalem with Zerubbabel (Neh. 12:8). **[6]** A prince of Judah (Neh. 12:34). **[7]** A priest and musician (Neh. 12:36). **[8]** One of the twelve apostles. He betrayed his Lord and hanged himself (Matt. 10:4; 26:14, 25, 47; 27:3; Luke 6:16; 22:3, 47, 48). He was called Iscariot, apparently meaning "a man of Kerioth," a town 19 km. (12 mi.) from Hebron. **[9]** One of the brothers of Jesus (Matt. 13:55; Mark 6:3). He wrote the epistle bearing his name (Jude 1). **[10]** A Galilean who caused a rebellion against Rome (Acts 5:37). **[11]** One with whom Paul stayed at Damascus (Acts 9:11). **[12]** A prophet sent to Antioch with Silas (Acts 15:22, 27); he was surnamed Barsabas. **[13]** *See* Thaddaeus. **[14], [15]** Two ancestors of Christ (Luke 3:26, 30).

**Judah** ("the praise of the Lord"), the territory of one of the original twelve tribes. Judah, along with Benjamin, formed the southern kingdom after Solomon's death.

The uncertain border between Israel and Judah ran between Bethel in Israel and Ramah in Judah. Jerusalem was its capital (2 Chr. 13:18; 15:8).

**Judea** ("the praise of the Lord"), first mentioned as a Persian province (Ezra 5:8). Later it became a Roman province (Matt. 2:1). Its northern boundary was Joppa on the west to a point 16.1 km. (10 mi.) north of the Dead Sea on the east. Its southern boundary was about 7 miles southwest of Gaza, through Beersheba, to the southern end of the Dead Sea.

**Justus** ("just"). **[1]** A believer in Corinth with whom Paul lodged (Acts 18:7). **[2]** *See* Jesus [2]. **[3]** *See* Joseph [11].

## K

**Kadesh.** *See* Kadesh Barnea; also Meribah [2].

**Kadesh Barnea** ("holy"), a wilderness on Palestine's southern frontier. It was on the border between the wilderness of Paran on the south and the wilderness of Zin on the north of the Sinai Peninsula (Num. 32:8; 34:4). It is also called simply Kadesh (Num. 13:26; 20:1). In Genesis 14:7 the region is called En Mishpat.

**Kedesh** ("holy"). **[1]** A city of the Canaanites near the northern border, defeated by Joshua (Josh. 12:22; 19:37). **[2]** Levitical city of refuge in Naphtali. It was sometimes called Kedesh Naphtali (Josh. 20:7; Judg. 4:6, 9). It is probably modern Kades, about 7.2 km. (4.5 mi.) northwest of Lake Huleh. **[3]** A Levitical city in Issachar (1 Chr. 6:72). **[4]** A city of Judah near Hazor and Ithan (Josh. 15:23).

**Keilah** ("fortress"), a town in the lowlands of Judah (1 Sam. 23:1, 13; Josh. 15:44). It is 8.5 mi. north of Hebron at Khirbet Kila.

**Kemuel** ("God stands" or "God's mound"). **[1]** A son of Nahor and a nephew of Abraham (Gen. 22:21). **[2]** A prince of Ephraim (Num. 34:24). **[3]** A Levite (1 Chr. 27:17).

**Kenaz [Kenez]** ("side" or "hunting"). **[1]** A duke of Edom (Gen. 36:42; 1 Chr. 1:53). **[2]** The fourth son of Eliphaz (Gen. 36:11, 15; 1 Chr. 1:36); perhaps the same as [1]. **[3]** Father of Othniel the judge (Josh. 15:17; Judg. 1:13). **[4]** A grandson of Caleb (1 Chr. 4:15).

**Kidron** ("obscure; making black or sad"), a valley in Jerusalem between the Mount of Ophel and the Mount of Olives (2 Sam. 15:23; John 18:1). Today it is called Wadi Sitti Maryan.

**Kirjath Arba** ("fourth city"), an early name for the city of Hebron (Gen. 23:2; Josh. 14:15). *See* Hebron.

**Kirjath Jearim** ("city of woods"), originally one of the cities of the Gibeonites located at the northwestern boundary of Judah (Josh. 9:17; Judg. 18:12). It is identical with Baalah (Josh. 15:9); Kirjath Arim (Ezra 2:25), Kirjath Baal (Josh. 18:14), and Baale Judah (2 Sam. 6:2). It is thought to be modern Deir el-Azhar, about 13.4 km. (8.3 mi.) northwest of Jerusalem.

**Kish [Cis]** ("bow; power"). **[1]** A son of Gibeon (1 Chr. 8:30; 9:36). **[2]** A Levite in David's time (1 Chr. 23:21; 24:29). **[3]** A descendant of Levi who assisted in the cleansing of the temple under Hezekiah (2 Chr. 29:12). **[4]** Great-grandfather of Mordecai (Esth. 2:5). **[5]** The father of King Saul (1 Sam. 9:1, 3; 14:51; Acts 13:21).

**Kishon [Kison]** ("bending; crooked"), a river in central Palestine which rises in Mount Tabor and, flowing westward, drains the valley of Esdraelon [Jezreel] (Judg. 4:7, 13; 1 Kin. 18:40; Ps. 83:9). Next to the Jordan, it is the most important river in Palestine.

**Korah** ("baldness"). **[1]** A son of Esau by Aholibamah (Gen. 36:5, 14, 18; 1 Chr. 1:35). **[2]** A son of Eliphaz (Gen. 36:16). **[3]** A son of Hebron (1 Chr. 2:43). **[4]** Grandson of Kohath and ancestor of some sacred musicians (1 Chr. 6:22; Ps. 42, 45, 46 titles). He was one of the leaders of the rebellion against Moses and Aaron; the earth swallowed them up (Num. 16:1–35).

**Kore** ("one who proclaims; quail"). **[1]** A Levite in charge of the freewill offerings in Hezekiah's time (2 Chr. 31:14). **[2]** A son of Asaph whose descendants were gatekeepers at the tabernacle (1 Chr. 9:19; 26:1, 19).

## L

**Laban** ("white; glorious"), the brother of Rebekah and father of Rachel and Leah. Jacob served him for seven years in order to marry Rachel, but Laban tricked him by substituting Leah at the wedding festivals (Gen. 24—31).

**Lamech** ("strong youth; overthrower"). **[1]** Father of Noah and ancestor of Christ (Gen. 5:25–31; Luke 3:36). **[2]** Father of Jabal and Jubal; he is the first recorded polygamist (Gen. 4:18–26).

**Laodicea** ("just people"), a chief city of Phrygia in Asia Minor (Col. 2:1; 4:15; Rev. 1:11). It is located on the Lycos River, a tributary of the Meander.

**Lazarus** (abridged form of Eleazar, "God has helped"). **[1]** The brother of Mary and Martha whom Jesus raised from the dead (John 11:1—12:17). **[2]** A believing beggar who was carried to Abraham's bosom (Luke 16:19–31).

**Leah** ("weary"), Jacob's wife through the deception of her father, Laban (Gen. 29—31).

**Lebbaeus.** *See* Thaddaeus.

**Lebanon** ("white"), one of two ranges of mountains in northern Palestine (Deut. 1:7; Josh. 1:4). The second is called the Anti-Lebanons; Mount Hermon is its highest peak. Running for about 161 km. (100 mi.), the chain begins about 24.1 km. (15 mi.) southeast of Sidon and runs north to about 19.3 km. (12 mi.) north-northeast of Tripolis in Syria.

**Lemuel** ("Godward; dedicated"), an unknown king often supposed to be Solomon or Hezekiah, whose words are recorded in Proverbs 31:1–9.

**Levi** ("joined"). **[1]** The third son of Jacob who avenged Dinah's wrong (Gen. 34:25–31), and went to Egypt with his father (Gen. 29:34; Ex. 6:16). His descendants became the priests of Israel. **[2]** An ancestor of Christ (Luke 3:24). **[3]** An ancestor of Christ (Luke 3:29). **[4]** Another name of Matthew (q.v.).

**Libya** ("heart of the sea"), the Greek name for the continent of Africa, west of Egypt (Acts 2:10). The Hebrews called this region Phut [Put]. Even though the Hebrew text of Ezekiel 30:5 and 38:5 read Phut, the KJV rendered the word *Libya. See also* Lubim.

**Lois** ("pleasing; better"), the pious grandmother of Timothy (2 Tim. 1:5).

**Lot** ("veiled"), Abraham's nephew who escaped from wicked Sodom (Gen. 13:1–14; Gen. 19).

**Lubim** ("dwellers in a thirsty land"), the North African continent west of Egypt (Nah. 3:9). *See also* Libya.

**Lucifer** (Latin, "light-bearer"), an epithet for the king of Babylon (Is. 14:12). Lucifer translates a Hebrew word meaning "light-bearer." The title came to be applied to Satan.

**Lucius** ("morning born; of light"). **[1]** A prophet or teacher from Cyrene ministering at Antioch (Acts 13:1). **[2]** A Jewish Christian who saluted the community at Rome (Rom. 16:21). Perhaps the same as [1].

**Luke** ("light-giving"), evangelist, physician, and author of the Third Gospel and Acts (Col. 4:14; 2 Tim. 4:11; Philem. 24).

**Lycaonia** ("she-wolf"), an inland district of Asia Minor. Paul twice visited in the cities of Derbe and Lystra here (Acts 14:6–11). It was bordered on the north by Galatia and on the south by Cilicia.

**Lydda** ("a standing pool"), a town located on the plains of Sharon (Acts 9:32). It is identical with Lod (q.v.).

**Lydia** ("native of Lydia"), a woman convert of Thyatira (Acts 16:14, 15).

**Lydia** ("Lydus land"), a country and people in Northern Africa, west of Egypt (Ezek. 30:5).

**Lysias.** *See* Claudius Lysias.

**Lystra** ("that dissolves"), a city of Lycaonia in central Asia Minor. Paul was stoned here (Acts 14:6–21).

## M

**Maachah [Maacah]** ("depression"). **[1]** The son of Nahor, Abraham's brother (Gen. 22:24). **[2]** One of David's wives and mother of Absalom (2 Sam. 3:3; 1 Chr. 3:2). **[3]** A king of Maachah (2 Sam. 10:6). Some translate "the king of Maachah." **[4]** Father of Achish, king of Gath (1 Kin. 2:39). He is called Maoch in First Samuel 27:2. **[5]** The mother of Asa, king of Judah (1 Kin. 15:10, 13; 2 Chr. 15:16). She is called Michaiah (2 Chr. 13:2). **[6]** Concubine of Caleb (1 Chr. 2:48). **[7]** Wife of Machir, son of Manasseh (1 Chr. 7:15, 16). **[8]** Wife of Jehiel (1 Chr. 8:29; 9:35). **[9]** Father of one of David's warriors (1 Chr. 11:43). **[10]** Father of Shephatiah, ruler of Simeon (1 Chr. 27:16).

**Macedonia** (meaning unknown), a nation lying to the north of Greece proper (Acts 16:9; 18:5).

**Magdala** ("tower"), a village located on the western edge of the Sea of Galilee (Matt. 15:39). It is present-day el-Mejdel, 4.8 km. (3 mi.) north-northwest of Tiberias.

**Magog** ("covering; roof"), the second son of Japheth (Gen. 10:2; 1 Chr. 1:5). Possibly a people inhabiting the north land. The name may denote the Scythians or be a comprehensive term for northern barbarians.

**Magog** ("region of Gog"), a country of undetermined location, generally described as being in a northerly direction from Palestine (Ezek. 38:2; 39:6). The first-century Jewish historian Josephus identified the land with the Scythians.

**Mahalaleel [Mahalalel]** ("God is splendor"). **[1]** Son of Cainan and an ancestor of Christ (Gen. 5:12, 13, 15; Luke 3:37). **[2]** One whose descendants lived at Jerusalem (Neh. 11:4).

**Maher-Shalal-Hash-Baz** ("the spoil hastens, the prey speeds"), symbolic name of Isaiah's son (Is. 8:1–4).

**Mahlon** ("mild; sickly"), the first husband of Ruth who died in Moab (Ruth 1:2–5).

**Malachi** ("messenger of Jehovah" or "my messenger"), the last of the prophets recorded in the Old Testament; he was contemporary with Nehemiah (Mal. 1:1).

**Malchiah [Malchijah; Melchiah]** ("Jehovah is king"). **[1]** A leader of singing under David's reign (1 Chr. 6:40). **[2]** An Aaronite whose descendants dwelt in Jerusalem after the Captivity (1 Chr. 9:12; Neh. 11:12). **[3]** Head of a priestly family (1 Chr. 24:9). **[4], [5], [6]** Three who married foreign wives during the Exile (Ezra 10:25, 31). **[7], [8], [9]** Three who helped to rebuild the wall of Jerusalem (Neh. 3:11, 14, 31). **[10]** A prince or Levite who stood beside Ezra as he read the Law (Neh. 8:4). **[11]** A priest who helped to purify the wall of Jerusalem (Neh. 10:3; 12:42). **[12]** Father of Pashhur (Jer. 21:1; 38:1).

**Malchijah.** *See* Malchiah.

**Malchishua.** *See* Melchishua.

**Malluch** ("counselor; ruling"). **[1]** A descendant of Levi (1 Chr. 6:44). **[2], [3]** Two who took foreign wives during the Exile (Ezra 10:29, 32). **[4]** A priest who sealed the covenant (Neh. 10:4). **[5]** A leader who sealed the new covenant with God after the Exile (Neh. 10:27). **[6]** One of the priests who returned with Zerubbabel (Neh. 12:2); he is called Melichu in verse 14.

**Malta** ("affording honey"), an island located in the Mediterranean Sea (Acts 28:1). It is 96.5 km. (60 mi.) south of Sicily.

**Mamre** ("firmness; vigor"), an Amorite chief who allied with Abram (Gen. 14:13, 24).

**Manasseh** ("causing forgetfulness"). **[1]** The first son of Joseph (Gen. 41:51). His descendants became one of the twelve tribes of Israel and occupied both sides of the Jordan (Josh. 16:4–9; 17). **[2]** The idolatrous successor of Hezekiah to the throne of Israel. He was an ancestor of Christ (2 Kin. 21:1–18; Matt. 1:10). **[3]** One whose descendants set up graven images at Laish (Judg. 18:30). Most scholars suggest that we should read Moses here instead. Perhaps a scribe felt an idolatrous descendant would cast reproach on the great lawgiver. A few manuscripts of the Septuagint, Old Latin, and the Vulgate read Moses here. **[4], [5]** Two who had taken foreign wives (Ezra 10:30, 33).

**Manoah** ("rest"), the father of Samson the judge (Judg. 13:1–23).

**Marah** ("bitter"), the fountain of bitter water in the wilderness of Shur where the Israelites first halted after crossing the Red Sea (Ex. 15:23; Num. 33:8). The traditional site is 'Ain Hawarah, about 75.6 km. (47 mi.) from Suez.

**Mark** ("polite; shining"), a Christian convert and missionary companion of Paul (Acts 12:12, 25; 15:37, 39; Col. 4:10). Mark is his Latin name, John his Hebrew name. He wrote the Gospel bearing his name.

**Martha** ("lady"), sister of Mary and Lazarus in Bethany (Luke 10:38, 40, 41; John 11:1–39).

**Mary** (Greek form of Miriam, "strong"). **[1]** The mother of Jesus Christ; her song of faith (Luke 1:46–55) reveals her deep faith (Matt. 1:16–20; cf. John 2:1–11). **[2]** Mary the sister of Martha. She anointed the Lord with ointment and received His approval (Luke 10:39, 42; John 11:1–45). **[3]** A woman of Magdala in Galilee. She had been converted after having "seven demons" cast out of her (Matt. 27:56, 61; 28:1; Luke 8:2; John 19:25). **[4]** The mother of John Mark (Acts 12:12). **[5]** A Roman Christian to whom Paul sent greetings (Rom. 16:6). **[6]** Mary, the mother of Joses (Mark 15:47) and

James (Luke 24:10), the "other Mary" (Matt. 28:1), and the Mary, wife of Clopas (John 19:25), are possibly to be identified as the same person (Mark 15:40).

**Massah** ("temptation"), the name of a spot in the vicinity of Horeb where the Israelites tempted God (Ex. 17:7; Deut. 6:16). *See also* Meribah [1].

**Mattaniah** ("gift of Jehovah"). **[1]** The original name of King Zedekiah (2 Kin. 24:17). **[2]** A descendant of Asaph whose family dwelt at Jerusalem (1 Chr. 9:15; 2 Chr. 20:14; Neh. 11:17, 22; 13:13). **[3]** A son of Heman the singer (1 Chr. 25:4, 16). **[4]** One who helped to cleanse the temple (2 Chr. 29:13). **[5], [6], [7], [8]** Four who married foreign wives during the Exile (Ezra 10:26, 27, 30, 37). **[9]** One of the gatekeepers (Neh. 12:25).

**Matthat** ("gift"). **[1]** Grandfather of Joseph and ancestor of Jesus (Luke 3:24). **[2]** Another ancestor of Jesus (Luke 3:29).

**Matthew** ("gift of God"), one of the twelve apostles; he was a tax collector before his call. He was also known as Levi (Matt. 9:9; 10:3; Mark 2:14). He wrote the Gospel bearing his name.

**Matthias** ("God's gift"), a Christian chosen to become an apostle to fill the place of Judas (Acts 1:23, 26).

**Mattithiah** ("gift of Jehovah"). **[1]** A Levite in charge of "things that were baked in the pans" (1 Chr. 9:31). **[2]** A Levite singer and gatekeeper (1 Chr. 15:18, 21; 16:5). **[3]** A son of Jeduthun (1 Chr. 25:3, 21). **[4]** One who took a foreign wife during the Exile (Ezra 10:43). **[5]** One who stood with Ezra when he read the Law (Neh. 8:4).

**Medad** ("love"), one of the elders of the Hebrews on whom the Spirit fell (Num. 11:26, 27).

**Media** ("middle land"), a country of Asia located south of the Caspian Sea, west of Parthia, north of Elam, and east of the Yagros Mountains. During the 400s B.C. the Persians and Medes had a powerful empire here (Esth. 1:3, 14, 18; Dan. 8:20).

**Melchishua [Malchishua]**, the third son of King Saul (1 Sam. 14:49; 31:2; 1 Chr. 8:33).

**Melchizedek [Melchisedec]** ("king of righteousness"), king and high priest of Salem. He was a prophetic symbol or "type" of Christ (Gen. 14:18–20; Ps. 110:4; Heb. 5—7).

**Memphis** ("abode of the good"), an ancient Egyptian city located on the western bank of the Nile in the central portion of the country (Hos. 9:6). It was also called Noph (Jer. 2:16).

**Menahem** ("comforter"), the idolatrous and cruel usurper of the throne of Israel who killed Shallum (2 Kin. 15:14–23).

**Mephibosheth** ("idol breaker"). **[1]** Son of Saul by his concubine Rizpah (2 Sam. 21:8). **[2]** A grandson of Saul. He was loyal to David, even though Ziba told David he was a traitor (2 Sam. 4:4; 9:6–13). He was also called Merib-Baal ("Baal contends") (1 Chr. 8:34; 9:40).

**Merab** ("increase"), daughter of Saul promised to David but given to Adriel (1 Sam. 14:49; 18:17, 19). Apparently she was a sister of Michal.

**Meremoth** ("strong; firm"). **[1]** A priest who weighed the gold and silver vessels of the temple (Ezra 8:33; Neh. 3:4, 21). **[2]** One who took a foreign wife during the Exile (Ezra 10:36). **[3]** One who sealed the new covenant with God after the Exile (Neh. 10:5; 12:3).

**Meribah** ("quarrel"). **[1]** The desert location where Moses struck the rock (Ex. 17:7). **[2]** Another name for Kadesh Barnea in the Wilderness of Zin, where the Hebrew people rebelled against Moses (Num. 20:13). In Deuteronomy 32:51 the place is called Meribah Kadesh.

**Meribah Kadesh.** *See* Meribah [2].

**Mesha** ("freedom"). **[1]** A king of Moab who rebelled against Ahaziah (2 Kin. 3:4). **[2]** Eldest son of Caleb (1 Chr. 2:42). **[3]** A descendant of Benjamin (1 Chr. 8:9).

**Meshach** ("the shadow of the prince; who is this?"), the name given to Mishael after he went into Babylonian captivity. He was delivered from the fiery furnace (Dan. 1:7; 3:12–30).

**Meshullam** ("associate; friend"). **[1]** Grandfather of Shaphan, a scribe (2 Kin. 22:3). **[2]** A descendant of King Jehoiakim (1 Chr. 3:19). **[3]** Head of a family of Gad (1 Chr. 5:13). **[4]** A descendant of Benjamin (1 Chr. 8:17). **[5]** One whose son lived in Jerusalem (1 Chr. 9:7). **[6]** One who lived in Jerusalem (1 Chr. 9:8). **[7]** A descendant of Aaron and an ancestor of Ezra (1 Chr. 9:11; Neh. 11:11). He is also called Shallum (Ezra 7:2; 1 Chr. 6:12, 13). **[8]** A priest (1 Chr. 9:12). **[9]** An overseer of the temple work (2 Chr. 34:12). **[10]** A chief man who returned with Ezra to Jerusalem (Ezra 8:16). **[11]** One who assisted in taking account of those who had foreign wives after the Exile (Ezra 10:15). **[12]** One who took a foreign wife during the Exile (Ezra 10:29). **[13], [14]** Two who rebuilt part of the wall of Jerusalem (Neh. 3:4, 6, 30; 6:18). **[15]** A prince or priest who stood with Ezra while he read the Law (Neh. 8:4). **[16]** A priest who sealed the new covenant with God after the Exile (Neh. 10:7). **[17]** One who sealed the new covenant with God after the Exile (Neh. 10:20). **[18]** One whose descendants lived in Jerusalem (Neh. 11:7). **[19]** A priest who assisted in the dedication of the wall of Jerusalem (Neh. 12:13, 33). **[20]** A descendant of Ginnethon (Neh. 12:16). **[21]** A Levite and gatekeeper after the Exile (Neh. 12:25).

**Mesopotamia** ("between two rivers"), a region located between the Tigris and Euphrates Rivers (Gen. 24:10; Deut. 23:4), excluding the mountain regions where the rivers take their rise and the low-lying plains of Babylon.

**Methuselah**, the longest living human recorded in the Bible, the grandfather of Noah and an ancestor of Christ (Gen. 5:21–27; Luke 3:37).

**Micah [Micha, Michah**—all probably contractions of Micaiah**]. [1]** Owner of a small private sanctuary (Judg. 17:1–5). **[2]** A descendant of Reuben (1 Chr. 5:5). **[3]** A son of Merib-Baal, Mephibosheth in Second Samuel 4:4 (1 Chr. 8:34). **[4]** A descendant of Kohath, son of Levi (1 Chr. 23:20; 24:24). **[5]** The father of Abdon (2 Chr. 34:20). He is called Michaiah in Second Kings 22:12. **[6]** A prophet (Jer. 26:18; Mic. 1:1). **[7]** The son of Zichri (1 Chr. 9:15; Neh. 11:17). **[8]** One who signed the covenant (Neh. 10:11).

**Michael** ("who is like God?"). **[1]** One sent to spy out the land of Canaan (Num. 13:13). **[2]** A descendant of Gad (1 Chr. 5:13). **[3]** Another descendant of Gad (1 Chr. 5:14). **[4]** An ancestor of Asaph (1 Chr. 6:40). **[5]** A chief of the tribe of Issachar (1 Chr. 7:3). **[6]** One residing in Jerusalem (1 Chr. 8:16). **[7]** A warrior who joined David at Ziklag (1 Chr. 12:20). **[8]** Father of Omri, a prince of Issachar (1 Chr. 27:18). **[9]** A son of Jehoshaphat (2 Chr.

21:2). [10] An ancestor of one who returned from the Exile (Ezra 8:8).

**Michaiah [Micaiah]** ("who is like Jehovah?"). [1] Wife of Rehoboam (2 Chr. 13:2). She is also called Maachah (1 Kin. 15:2; 2 Chr. 11:20). *See* Maachah [5]. [2] *See* Micah [5]. [3] A prince of Judah (2 Chr. 17:7). [4] The son of Zaccur (Neh. 12:35). [5] One present at the dedication of the wall (Neh. 12:41). [6] A prophet who predicted Ahab's downfall (1 Kin. 22:8–28; 2 Chr. 18:7–27).

**Michal** ("who is like God?"), a daughter of Saul whom David married (1 Sam. 14:49). Michal "had no children to the day of her death" (2 Sam. 6:23). Yet Second Samuel 21:8 states she had five sons. The KJV rendering, "whom she brought up for Adriel," is not a permissible translation—the Hebrew text states she bore them. A few Hebrew, Greek, and Syriac manuscripts read: "the five sons of Merab" instead of Michal, which seems a plausible solution to the problem. See First Samuel 18:19.

**Midian** ("contention"), a son of Abraham by Keturah and founder of the Midianites (Gen. 25:2, 4; 36:35; 1 Chr. 1:32).

**Midian** ("contention"), the land of the descendants of Midian beyond the Jordan. It included Edom, the Sinai Peninsula, and Arabian Petra (Ex. 2:15, 16; Judg. 6:1; Acts 7:29).

**Miletus** ("scarlet"), a coastal city of Ionia (Acts 20:15; 2 Tim. 4:20). It was 57.9 km. (36 mi.) south of Ephesus.

**Miphkad,** a gate in or near the northern end of the east wall of Jerusalem (Neh. 3:31).

**Miriam** ("fat; thick; strong"). [1] The sister of Moses and Aaron. She rebelled against Moses with Aaron at Hazeroth (Ex. 2:4–10; Num. 12:1–15; 20:1). [2] A woman descendant of Judah (1 Chr. 4:17).

**Mishael** ("who is what God is?"). [1] One who carried away the dead Nadab and Abihu (Ex. 6:22; Lev. 10:4). [2] One who stood with Ezra at the reading of the Law (Neh. 8:4). [3] One of the companions of Daniel in Babylon (Dan. 1:6, 7, 11, 19). *See* Meshach.

**Mithredath** ("given by [the god] Mithra"). [1] The treasurer of Cyrus through whom he restored the temple vessels (Ezra 1:8). [2] One who wrote to the king of Persia protesting the restoration of Jerusalem (Ezra 4:7).

**Mizpah** ("a watchtower"). [1] A mound of stones on Mount Gilead (Gen. 31:49). [2] A Hivite settlement in northern Palestine at the foot of Mount Hermon (Josh. 11:3). [3] A city in the lowlands of Judah (Josh. 15:38). It was just north of Eleutheropolis [Beit Jibrin]. [4] A town in Gilead east of the Jordan (Judg. 11:34). It is possibly identical with Ramath Mizpah. [5] A town of Benjamin just north of Jerusalem (Josh. 18:26; 1 Kin. 15:22). The exact site is uncertain. [6] A place in Moab (1 Sam. 22:3); perhaps modern Rujm el-Meshrefeh west-southwest of Madaba.

**Moab** ("from my father"), the son of Lot by his daughter and an ancestor of the Moabites (Gen. 19:34–37).

**Moab,** a land that consisted of the plateau east of the Dead Sea between the wadis Arnon and Zered, though at certain periods extending to the north of the Arnon (Deut. 1:5; Num. 22—25).

**Mordecai** ("dedicated to Mars"). [1] A Jewish exile who became a vizier of Persia. He helped save the Jews from destruction (Esth. 2—10). [2] A leader who returned from the Babylonian Captivity (Ezra 2:2; Neh. 7:7).

**Moreh** ("stretching"). [1] The first stopping place of Abram after he entered Canaan (Gen. 12:6). It was near Shechem. [2] A hill lying at the foot of the valley of Jezreel (Judg. 7:1). It is probably modern Jebel Dahy or Little Hermon about 12.9 km. (8 mi.) northwest of Mount Gilboa.

**Moriah** ("bitterness of the Lord"). [1] An elevation in Jerusalem on which Solomon built the temple (2 Chr. 3:1). Probably the same hilltop was used as the threshing floor of Araunah. The name Moriah was possibly ascribed by the Chronicler because of its traditional meaning (2 Sam. 24:18; 2 Chr. 3:1). [2] The hill on which Abraham was prepared to sacrifice Isaac (Gen. 22:2). The site is uncertain, but Samaritans identify Moriah with Moreh [1]. This seems unlikely.

**Moses** ("drawer-out; child; one-born"), the great prophet and lawgiver of Israel. He led his people from Egyptian bondage. The book of Exodus tells his story. He wrote the first five books of the Bible.

## N

**Naamah** ("pleasant"). [1] Daughter of Lamech and Zillah (Gen. 4:22). [2] A wife of Solomon and mother of Rehoboam (1 Kin. 14:21; 2 Chr. 12:13).

**Naamah** ("beautiful"), a town in the southwestern lowlands of Judah (Josh. 15:41). It is probably modern Khirbet Fered near Arak Ma'aman.

**Naaman** ("pleasantness"). [1] A Syrian general who was healed of leprosy by bathing in the Jordan (2 Kin. 5; Luke 4:27). [2] Grandson of Benjamin (Gen. 26:38, 40). [3] A son of Benjamin and founder of a tribal family (Gen. 46:21).

**Naarai** ("youthful"), one of David's valiant men (1 Chr. 11:37). Probably the same as Paarai (2 Sam. 23:35).

**Nabal** ("foolish; wicked"), a wealthy Carmelite who refused David and his men food (1 Sam. 25).

**Naboth** ("a sprout"), the owner whom Jezebel had killed in order to obtain his vineyard (1 Kin. 21:1–18).

**Nachon** ("stroke"). Scripture refers to the threshing floor of Nachon/Chidon (2 Sam. 6:6; 1 Chr. 13:9). This is either the combined name of two individuals, of two place names, or a combination of both. *Chidon* possibly means "destruction or a javelin."

**Nachon.** *See* Chidon.

**Nadab** ("liberal"). [1] Firstborn son of Aaron, struck dead for offering "profane fire" to God (Ex. 6:23; Lev. 10:1–3). [2] A descendant of Jerahmeel (1 Chr. 2:28, 30). [3] A brother of Gibeon (1 Chr. 8:30). [4] Son of Jeroboam I; he ruled Israel for two years (1 Kin. 15:25–31).

**Naggai** ("splendor"), ancestor of Jesus (Luke 3:25).

**Nahash** ("oracle" or "serpent"). [1] The father of Abigail and Zeruiah (2 Sam. 17:25). [2] An Ammonite king that was defeated by Saul (1 Sam. 11:1, 2; 12:12). [3] Another king of Ammon (2 Sam. 10:2; 17:27; 1 Chr. 19:1, 2). Not to be confused with Ir-Nahash.

**Nahbi** ("Jehovah is protection"), the spy of Naphtali whom Moses sent out to explore Canaan (Num. 13:14).

**Nahor** ("piercer"). [1] Grandfather of Abraham and ancestor of Christ (Gen. 11:22–25; Luke 3:34). [2] A brother of Abraham (Gen. 11:26, 27, 29; 22:20, 23; Josh. 24:2).

**Nahor,** a city mentioned in Genesis 24:10. This is possibly Haran, so-called after Abraham's brother, Nahor.

**Nahshon [Naashon; Naasson]** ("oracle"), a descendant of Judah and ancestor of Christ. Perhaps Aaron's brother-in-law (Ex. 6:23; Num. 1:7; Matt. 1:4).

**Nahum** ("comforter"). **[1]** One of the later prophets; he prophesied against Nineveh (Nah. 1:1). **[2]** An ancestor of Christ (Luke 3:25).

**Nain** ("beauty"), a village in Galilee where Christ resurrected a widow's son (Luke 7:11). It is located 3.2 km. (2 mi.) south of Mount Tabor and a little southwest of the Sea of Galilee.

**Naioth** ("habitation"), the place in Ramah where a community of prophets gathered around Samuel (1 Sam. 19:18–23; 20:1). Its location is not clearly identified. *See also* Ramah [2].

**Naomi** ("pleasantness; my joy"), mother-in-law to Ruth (Ruth 1:2—4:17).

**Naphtali** ("wrestling"), the sixth son of Jacob (Gen. 30:7, 8). His descendants became one of the twelve tribes.

**Naphtali [Nephthalim]** ("that struggles"), a territory assigned to the tribe of Naphtali, located in mountainous northern Palestine (Josh. 19:32–39; Matt. 4:13). It was bounded on the east by the Upper Jordan River and the Sea of Galilee and on the west by the territories of Zebulun and Asher.

**Nathan** ("gift"). **[1]** Prophet and royal advisor to David (2 Sam. 7:2–17; 12:1–25). **[2]** A son of King David and ancestor of Christ (2 Sam. 5:14; 1 Chr. 3:5; Luke 3:31). **[3]** Father of Igal (2 Sam. 23:36). **[4]** A descendant of Jerahmeel (1 Chr. 2:36). **[5]** A companion of Ezra (Ezra 8:16). **[6]** One of those who had married a foreign wife (Ezra 10:39). **[7]** Brother of Joel, one of David's valiant men (1 Chr. 11:38). **[8]** Father of Solomon's chief officer (1 Kin. 4:5). **[9]** A chief man of Israel (Zech. 12:12).

**Nathanael** ("God has given"), a Galilean called by Christ to be a disciple. He is probably to be identified with Bartholomew (John 1:45–49; 21:2; Acts 1:13). *See also* Bartholomew.

**Nazareth** ("sanctified"), the hometown of Jesus in lower Galilee, north of the Plain of Esdraelon [Jezreel] (Matt. 4:13; Mark 1:9). It is 8 km. (5 mi.) west-southwest of Tiberias, 32.2 km. (20 mi.) southwest of modern Tell Hum [Capernaum] and 141.6 km. (88 mi.) north of Jerusalem.

**Neapolis** ("the new city"), a seaport of Philippi in Macedonia (Acts 16:11; cf. 20:6). It is on the Strymonian Gulf 16.1 km. (10 mi.) east-southeast of Philippi.

**Nebat** ("cultivation"), father of Jeroboam I (1 Kin. 11:26).

**Nebo** ("that prophesies"). **[1]** The mountain from which Moses saw the Promised Land (Deut. 32:49; 34:1). It is a peak in the Abarim Mountains east of the Jordan, opposite Jericho; probably modern Jebel en Neba 12.9 km. (8 mi.) east of the mouth of the Jordan. On a clear day, all of Palestine can be seen from this peak. **[2]** A city of Reuben that fell again to the Moabites (Num. 32:3, 38; 33:47). It is probably modern Khirbet el-Mekhayyet, south of Mount Nebo. **[3]** A city in Judah (Ezra 2:29; Neh. 7:33), probably modern Beth-Nube, near Lydda.

**Nebuchadnezzar [Nebuchadrezzar]**(Babylonian, *Nabur-kudurri-utsur*—"may [the god] Nabu guard my boundary stones"), great king of the Babylonian Empire; he captured Jerusalem three times and carried Judah into captivity (2 Kin. 24:1, 10, 11; 25:1, 8, 22; Dan. 1—4).

**Nebushasban** ("Nabu delivers me"), a Babylonian prince (Jer. 39:13).

**Nebuzaradan** (Babylonian, "[the god] Nabu has given seed"), a Babylonian captain of the guard at the siege of Jerusalem (2 Kin. 25:8, 11, 20).

**Necho,** pharaoh of Egypt who fought Josiah at Megiddo (2 Chr. 35:20).

**Nehemiah** ("Jehovah is consolation"). **[1]** Governor of Jerusalem; he helped rebuild the fallen city (Neh. 1:1; 8:9; 12:47). **[2]** A chief man who returned from the Exile (Ezra 2:2; Neh. 7:7). **[3]** One who repaired the wall of Jerusalem (Neh. 3:16).

**Nehushta** ("basis; ground"), wife of Jehoiakim; mother of Jehoiachin (2 Kin. 24:8).

**Nekeb** ("cave"), a town on the boundary of the territory of Naphtali (Josh. 19:33); perhaps the same as Adami (q.v.).

**Nemuel** ("God is speaking"). **[1]** A descendant of Reuben (Num. 26:9). **[2]** A son of Simeon (Num. 26:12; 1 Chr. 4:24). In Genesis 46:10 and Exodus 6:15, he is called Jemuel.

**Nepheg** ("sprout; shoot"). **[1]** A brother of Korah (Ex. 6:21). **[2]** A son of David (2 Sam. 5:15; 1 Chr. 3:7; 14:6).

**Ner** ("light"). **[1]** An uncle (?) of Saul, father of Abner (1 Sam. 14:50). **[2]** Grandfather of Saul (1 Chr. 8:33; 9:39). These relationships are unclear. Abner may have been Saul's uncle. If so, Ner [1] and [2] are the same. He is also called Abiel (1 Sam. 9:1). It is also possible that Ner [2] (Abiel) had sons named Ner [1] and Kish, the father of Saul.

**Nergal-Sharezer** ("May the god Nergal defend the prince"), a Babylonian officer who released Jeremiah (Jer. 39:3, 13, 14).

**Neri** ("whose lamp is Jehovah"), ancestor of Christ (Luke 3:27).

**Nethanel** ("God gives"). **[1]** Chief of Issachar whom Moses sent to spy out the land of Canaan (Num. 1:8; 2:5; 7:18, 23; 10:15). **[2]** Fourth son of Jesse (1 Chr. 2:14). **[3]** One of the trumpet blowers when the ark of the covenant was brought up (1 Chr. 15:24). **[4]** A Levite (1 Chr. 24:6). **[5]** A son of Obed-Edom and gatekeeper of the tabernacle (1 Chr. 26:4). **[6]** A prince commissioned by Jehoshaphat to teach the people (2 Chr. 17:7). **[7]** A Levite in the days of Josiah (2 Chr. 35:9). **[8]** A priest who married a foreign wife (Ezra 10:22). **[9]** A priest in the days of Joiakim (Neh. 12:21). **[10]** Levite musician at the purification ceremony (Neh. 12:36).

**Nicanor** ("conqueror"), one of the seven chosen in the ministry to the poor (Acts 6:5).

**Nicodemus** ("innocent blood"), a Pharisee and ruler of the Jews who assisted in Christ's burial (John 3:1–15; 7:50–52; 19:39–42).

**Nicolas** ("conqueror of the people"), one of the seven chosen to aid in the ministration to the poor (Acts 6:5).

**Nicopolis** ("the city of victory"). **[1]** A town in Epirus in western Greece about 6.4 km. (4 mi.) north of Actium. **[2]** A city on both sides of the Nestus River, the boundary between Thrace and Macedonia. Paul referred to one of the above in Titus 3:12; the first is preferred.

**Nile** ("dark blue"), the greatest river of Egypt and the world's longest. It is simply referred to in Scripture as "the river" (Ex. 2:3; 7:21). The Nile is about 6,669.3 km. (4,145 mi.) long.

**Nimrah.** *See* Beth-Nimrah.

**Nimrim** ("bitterness"), a brook in Moab (Is. 15:6; Jer. 48:34). The name still exists in Wadi en-Nemeirah near the southeast end of the Dead Sea.

**Nimrod** ("valiant; strong"), a son of Cush (Gen. 10:8, 9; 1 Chr. 1:10). His kingdom included Babel, Erech, Accad, and Calneh, cities in Shinar, but also included Assyria.

**Nineveh [Nineve]** (meaning unknown), the capital of the Kingdom of Assyria (Nah. 1:1; cf. 3:1; Luke 11:32; Zeph. 2:13). It was located east of the Tigris River in the area north of the point the Tigris joins the Upper Zab. The ruins are now called Tell Kuyunjik and Tell Nebi Yunus.

**No** ("stirring up"), an Egyptian city better known as Thebes (Ezek. 30:14–16; Jer. 46:25). It was the capital of Upper Egypt.

**Noah** ("rest"), son of Lamech; the patriarch chosen to build the ark. Only his family survived the Flood (Gen. 5:28–32; 6:8–22; 7—10). He was an ancestor of Christ (Luke 3:36).

**Noah** ("flattery; movement"), a daughter of Zelophehad (Num. 26:33; Josh. 17:3).

**Nob** ("prophecy"), a city of the tribe of Benjamin located northeast of Jerusalem, within sight of the city (1 Sam. 21:1; 22:19).

**Nod** ("vagabond"), an unidentified land east of Eden to which Cain fled after the murder of Abel (Gen. 4:16). Some suppose it to be China, but this is speculation.

**Noph.** *See* Memphis.

**Nun [Non]** ("continuation; fish"). [1] A descendant of Ephraim (1 Chr. 7:27); possibly the same as [2]. [2] The father of Joshua (Ex. 33:11; 1 Kin. 16:34).

**Nymphas** ("bridegroom"), a Christian of Laodicea to whom Paul sends greetings (Col. 4:15). Some manuscripts read Nympha, which would make this individual a woman.

## O

**Obadiah** ("servant of Jehovah")[1] The governor or prime minister of Ahab who tried to protect the prophets against Jezebel (1 Kin. 18:3–16). [2] A descendant of David (1 Chr. 3:21). [3] A chief of the tribe of Issachar (1 Chr. 7:3). [4] A descendant of King Saul (1 Chr. 8:38; 9:44). [5] A man of the tribe of Zebulun (1 Chr. 27:19). [6] A chief of the Gadites who joined David at Ziklag (1 Chr. 12:9). [7] One of the princes whom Jehoshaphat commissioned to teach the Law (2 Chr. 17:7–9). [8] A Levite overseer in work done on the temple (2 Chr. 34:12). [9] The chief of a family that returned to Jerusalem (Ezra 8:9). [10] One who sealed the covenant with Nehemiah (Neh. 10:5). [11] A gatekeeper for the sanctuary of the temple (Neh. 12:25). [12] The fourth of the "minor prophets." His message was directed against Edom (Obad. 1).

**Obed** ("servant"). [1] A son of Boaz and Ruth, father of Jesse, and ancestor of Christ (Ruth 4:17; Matt. 1:5; Luke 3:32). [2] A descendant of Judah (1 Chr. 2:37, 38). [3] One of David's warriors (1 Chr. 11:47). [4] A Levite gatekeeper in David's time (1 Chr. 26:7). [5] Father of Azariah, who helped make Joash king of Judah (2 Chr. 23:1).

**Obed-Edom** ("servant of [the god] Edom"). [1] A man who housed the ark for three months (2 Sam. 6:10–12; 1 Chr. 13:13, 14). [2] One of the chief Levitical singers and doorkeepers (1 Chr. 15:18, 21, 24; 16:5, 38; 26:4, 8, 15). [3] A temple treasurer or official, or perhaps the tribe that sprang from [2] (2 Chr. 25:24).

**Oded** ("aiding" or "restorer"). [1] Father of Azariah the prophet (2 Chr. 15:1). [2] A prophet of Samaria who persuaded the northern army to free their Judean slaves (2 Chr. 28:9–15).

**Og** ("giant"), the giant king of Bashan, defeated at Edrei (Num. 21:33–35; Deut. 3:1–13).

**Olives, Mount of [Mount of Corruption; Olivet],** a ridge east of Jerusalem and separated from Jerusalem by the Kidron Valley (2 Sam. 15:30; Mark 11:1; Acts 1:12). It is called the Mount of Corruption in Second Kings 23:13.

**Omri** ("Jehovah apportions; pupil"). [1] The sixth king of Israel and founder of the third dynasty. He founded Samaria and made it Israel's capital (1 Kin. 16:15–28). [2] A descendant of Benjamin, the son of Becher (1 Chr. 7:8). [3] A descendant of Perez living at Jerusalem (1 Chr. 9:4). [4] A prince of Issachar in the days of David (1 Chr. 27:18).

**On** ("strength"), an ancient city of Lower Egypt situated on the Nile Delta (Gen. 41:45, 50). It is identical with Beth Shemesh [4], 30.6 km. (19 mi.) north of Memphis.

**Onan** ("vigorous"), the second son of Judah. He was slain by God for disobedience (Gen. 38:4–10; Num. 26:19).

**Onesimus** ("useful"), a slave on whose behalf Paul wrote an epistle to his master, Philemon (Col. 4:9; Philem. 10, 15).

**Onesiphorus** ("profit-bringer"), a loyal friend of Paul's who often refreshed him in prison (2 Tim. 1:16; 4:19).

**Ono** ("grief of him"), a city of Benjamin (1 Chr. 8:12; Ezra 2:33). It is probably modern Kafr 'Ana 11.3 km. (7 mi.) southeast of Joppa.

**Ophel** ("small white cloud"), a hill in southeastern Jerusalem (2 Chr. 27:3; Neh. 3:26; 11:21). It was near the Water Gate, Horse Gate, Pool of Siloam, the east court of the temple, and the Kidron Valley.

**Ophir** ("fruitful region"), a region where Solomon mined gold (1 Kin. 9:28; 1 Chr. 29:4). The location is highly uncertain. Josephus thought it was India, but the African coast in modern Somaliland is more probable.

**Ophrah** ("a fawn"). [1] A city of Benjamin (Josh. 18:23; 1 Sam. 13:17). It is probably modern eṭ-Ṭaiyibeh, about 6.4 km. (4 mi.) east-northeast of Bethel. [2] A city in Manasseh (Judg. 6:11, 24; 9:5). It is now called Arrabeh.

**Oreb** ("a raven"), the rock east of Jordan near Beth Barah where the Midianite chieftain Oreb died (Judg. 7:25; Is. 10:26). It is now called Ash-el-Ghorab.

**Ornan** ("active"), a Jebusite from whom David bought a piece of land, on which Solomon's temple was erected

(1 Chr. 21:15–25). He is called Araunah in Second Samuel 24:16.

**Orpah** ("fawn; youthful freshness"), daughter-in-law of Naomi (Ruth 1:4–14).

**Osnapper,** one who brought men from Susa and Elam to Samaria (Ezra 4:9). Formerly believed to be Esarhaddon, he is now believed to have been Ashurbanipal, king of Assyria, and Esarhaddon's son.

**Othniel** ("God is power"), Caleb's younger brother who liberated Israel from foreign rule (Judg. 1:13; 3:8–11; 1 Chr. 27:15).

**Ozem** ("strength"). **[1]** A brother of David (1 Chr. 2:15). **[2]** A son of Jerahmeel of Judah (1 Chr. 2:25).

## P

**Padan Aram [Padan]** ("plain [tableland] of Aram"), the plain region of Mesopotamia from the Lebanon Mountains to beyond the Euphrates, and from the Taurus Mountains on the north to beyond Damascus on the south (Gen. 25:20; 28:2; 31:18). It is called simply Padan in Genesis 48:7.

**Palestine [Palestina]** ("which is covered"), an ill-defined region between the Jordan River and the Dead Sea on the east and the Mediterranean on the west (Ex. 15:14; Joel 3:4; Gen. 15:18). Its northern border is roughly the Lebanon Mountain range. It stretches in a southwesterly triangle to the Gulf of Aqaba on the Red Sea.

**Palti** ("Jehovah delivers"). **[1]** The man selected from Benjamin to spy out the land (Num. 13:9). **[2]** *See* Paltiel [2].

**Paltiel** ("God delivers"). **[1]** A prince of the tribe of Issachar (Num. 34:26). **[2]** The man who married David's wife (2 Sam. 3:15). He is called Phalti in First Samuel 25:44.

**Pamphylia** ("a nation made up of every tribe"), a southern coastal area in Asia Minor; its main city is Perga (Acts 13:13; 14:24; 27:5).

**Paphos** ("that which boils"), a town on the southwest extremity of Cyprus; it was visited by Paul and Barnabas (Acts 13:6–13). It is modern Baffa.

**Paradise** ("pleasure ground; park"), figurative name for the place where God dwells (2 Cor. 12:4) and the abode of the righteous (Luke 23:43; Rev. 2:7).

**Paran** ("beauty"), a wilderness seven days' march from Mount Sinai (Gen. 21:21; Num. 10:12; 1 Sam. 25:1). It is located east of the wilderness of Beersheba and Shurj, and it merges with the Wilderness of Sin with no clearly marked boundary. The area borders on Edom and Midian; it is sometimes called Mount Paran (Hab. 3:3) and El Paran (Gen. 14:6).

**Parbar** ("a suburb"), an area on the west side of the temple containing officials' chambers and cattle stalls (1 Chr. 26:18).

**Parmenas** ("steadfast"), one of the seven deacons (Acts 6:5).

**Parvaim** ("eastern"), a place where gold was obtained for the decoration of Solomon's temple (2 Chr. 3:6). It may be modern Sak el-Farwain in southern Arabia.

**Pashhur** ("splitter; cleaver"). **[1]** Head of a priestly family (Ezra 2:38; 10:22; Neh. 7:41). **[2]** A priest who sealed the covenant with God after the Exile (Neh. 10:1, 3). Possibly identical with [1]. **[3]** A priest, the "chief governor in the house of the LORD," who persecuted Jeremiah (Jer. 20:1–6). **[4]** Son of Melchiah, whose family returned to Jerusalem (1 Chr. 9:12; Neh. 11:12; Jer. 21:1; 38:1).

**Patmos** ("mortal"), a barren island to which John was banished (Rev. 1:9). It is in the Greek archipelagos and is now called Patino.

**Patrobas** ("paternal"), a Roman Christian (Rom. 16:14).

**Paul** (Latin, *Paulus*—"little"), the Roman name of Saul of Tarsus, a Pharisee who studied Jewish law under Gamaliel (Acts 21:39). He was converted and made an apostle to the Gentiles (Acts 26:12–20). Perhaps he used his Roman name in humility. The Book of Acts tells of his missionary journeys.

**Pedaiah** ("Jehovah delivers"). **[1]** Father of Joel (1 Chr. 27:20). **[2]** Grandfather of King Josiah (2 Kin. 23:36). **[3]** Son or grandson of Jeconiah (1 Chr. 3:18, 19). **[4]** One who helped to rebuild the wall of Jerusalem (Neh. 3:25). **[5]** One who stood with Ezra when he read the Law (Neh. 8:4; 13:13). **[6]** A descendant of Benjamin (Neh. 11:7).

**Pekah** ("opening"), a usurper of the throne of Israel; he ruled for twenty years (2 Kin. 15:25–31).

**Pekahiah** ("Jehovah watches"), a son and successor of Menahem on the throne of Israel. He was murdered by Pekah (2 Kin. 15:22–26).

**Pelatiah** ("Jehovah delivers"). **[1]** One who sealed the new covenant with God after the Exile (Neh. 10:22). **[2]** A descendant of David (1 Chr. 3:21). **[3]** A captain of Simeon (1 Chr. 4:42, 43). **[4]** A wicked prince seen in Ezekiel's vision (Ezek. 11:1, 13).

**Peleg** ("division"), son of Eber and ancestor of Christ (Gen. 10:25; 11:16; Luke 3:35).

**Peniel.** *See* Penuel.

**Peninnah** ("coral; pearl"), second wife of Elkanah, father of Samuel (1 Sam. 1:2, 4).

**Penuel** ("face of God"). **[1]** A descendant of Benjamin (1 Chr. 8:25). **[2]** A chief or father of Gedar (1 Chr. 4:4).

**Penuel [Peniel]** ("face of God"), an encampment of the Hebrews east of Jordan (Gen. 32:30, 31; Judg. 8:8, 17). It derived its name from the fact that Jacob had seen God face-to-face there.

**Peor** ("opening"), a mountain peak near Pisgah in Moab (Num. 23:28). It stood across the Jordan River from Jericho.

**Perez** ("bursting through"), eldest son of Judah and an ancestor of Christ (1 Chr. 27:3; Neh. 11:4). He is also called Pharez (Gen. 38:29; 46:12; Luke 3:33).

**Perez Uzzah** ("breech of Uzzah"), the name David gave to the place Uzzah was struck by God (2 Sam. 6:8).

**Perga** ("very earthy"), the capital of Pamphylia in Asia Minor during the Roman period (Acts 13:13).

**Pergamos** ("elevation"), a city of Mysia in northwest Asia Minor and the site of one of the seven churches of Asia (Rev. 2:12–17).

**Persia** ("cuts or divides"), a great empire including all of western Asia and parts of Europe and Africa (Ezek. 38:5; Ezra 1:8). Persia proper corresponded to what is now the province of Fars in Iran.

**Persis** ("Persian"), a Christian woman at Rome (Rom. 16:12).

**Peter** ("stone; rock"), a fisherman called to be an apostle of Christ. He became one of the leaders of the early church (Matt. 4:18–20; 16:15–19; Acts 2). Christ changed this man's name from Simon to a name meaning "rock" (*Cephas* in Aramaic, *Peter* in Greek).

**Pethor** ("soothsayer"), the residence of Balaam (Num. 22:5; Deut. 23:4). The town was near the Euphrates River and the mountains of Aram. It was a few kilometers south of Carchemish.

**Pethuel** ("God's opening"), father of Joel the prophet (Joel 1:1).

**Pharaoh** ("inhabitant of the palace"), royal title of Egyptian kings, equivalent to our word *king* (Gen. 12:15; 37:36; Ex. 2:15; 1 Kin. 3:1; Is. 19:11).

**Pharpar** ("that produces fruit"), one of the two rivers of Damascus (2 Kin. 5:12). It is probably the modern Nahr el-'A'waj.

**Philadelphia** ("love of a brother"), a town of Lydia in Asia Minor. It was the site of one of the seven churches of Asia (Rev. 1:11; 3:7–13). It was 45.5 km. (28.3 mi.) southeast of Sardis.

**Philemon** ("friendship"), a convert at Colosse to whom Paul wrote an epistle on behalf of his runaway servant, Onesimus (Philem. 1, 5–7).

**Philetus** ("amiable"), a convert who was condemned by Paul because of his stand on the Resurrection (2 Tim. 2:17).

**Philip** ("lover of horses"). [1] One of the twelve apostles of Christ (Matt. 10:3; John 1:44–48; 6:5–9). [2] An evangelist mentioned several times in Acts (Acts 6:5; 8:5–13). [3] *See* Herod [3], [4].

**Philippi** ("the same"), a city of Macedonia founded by Philip the Great and named for him (Acts 16:12; 20:3–6). It lies inland about 16.1 km. (10 mi.) northwest of its seaport, Neapolis.

**Philistia** ("land of sojourners"), an area on the southwest coast of Palestine (Ps. 60:8; 87:4; 108:9). This land, which was the home of traditional enemies of Israel, was 80 km. (50 mi.) long and only 24 km. (15 mi.) wide.

**Philologus** ("a lover of learning"), a Roman Christian to whom Paul sent greetings (Rom. 16:15).

**Phinehas** ("mouth of brass"). [1] Grandson of Aaron and high priest (Ex. 6:25; Num. 25:6–18; 1 Chr. 6:4; 9:20). [2] Younger son of Eli; he was a priest who abused his office (1 Sam. 1:3; 2:22–24, 34). [3] Father of Eleazar (Ezra 8:33).

**Phlegon** ("burning"), a Roman Christian (Rom. 16:14).

**Phoebe** ("shining"), a servant of the church at Corinth or Cenchrea who helped Paul (Rom. 16:1).

**Phoenicia** ("land of palm trees"), a thin strip of territory between the Mediterranean Sea on the west and on the east the mountains of Lebanon (Acts 21:2; 11:19; 15:3). It included the hills running south from those mountains.

**Phoenix** ("land of palm trees"). [1] A harbor in southern Crete (Acts 27:12). [2] *See* Phoenicia.

**Phrygia** ("barren"), a large and important inland province of Asia Minor (Acts 2:10; 16:6).

**Phut [Put]** ("bow"), the third son of Ham (Gen. 10:6; 1 Chr. 1:8). Possibly a reference to a people related to the Egyptians. Many consider the reference to be to a people related to the Libyans.

**Phut.** *See* Libya.

**Phygellus** ("fugitive"), one who deserted Paul in Asia (2 Tim. 1:15).

**Pi Hahiroth** ("the mouth"), the location of the final Israelite encampment prior to crossing the Red Sea (Ex. 14:2, 9; Num. 33:7, 8). The site is uncertain, but it may be the swamps of Jeneffeh at the edge of the pass between Baal Zephon and the Great Bitter Lake.

**Pilate.** *See* Pontius Pilate.

**Pisgah** ("fortress"), the mountain ranges from which Moses viewed the Promised Land (Num. 21:20; Deut. 3:27). This part of the Abarim Range is near the northeast end of the Dead Sea.

**Pishon** ("changing"), a river of Eden (Gen. 2:11). It has traditionally been identified with the Phasis (modern Rion) or the Kur, a tributary of the Araxes. The Palla Copas canal has been suggested also.

**Pisidia** ("pitch"), an inland district of Asia Minor with Antioch as its capital (Acts 13:14).

**Pithom** ("their mouthful"), an Egyptian store-city built by the Israelites (Ex. 1:11). It was located in the valley connecting the Nile and Lake Timsah. The ruins are at Tell el-Maskhutah.

**Pontius Pilate** (Latin, *Pontius Pilatus*—"marine dart-carrier"), a Roman procurator of Judea. When Christ was brought before him for judgment, Pilate, fearing the Jews, turned Him over to the people even though he found Him not guilty (Matt. 27:2–24; John 18:28–40).

**Pontus** ("the sea"), a district in northeastern Asia Minor on the Pontus Euxinus (Acts 2:9; 1 Pet. 1:1).

**Porcius Festus.** *See* Festus.

**Potiphar** ("belonging to the sun-god"), Egyptian captain of the guard who became the master of Joseph (Gen. 37:36; 39:1).

**Poti-Pherah** ("given of the sun-god"), a priest of On; father-in-law of Joseph (Gen. 41:45, 50).

**Potter's Field.** *See* Akel Dama.

**Praetorium.** The Praetorium was originally the headquarters of a Roman camp, but in the provinces the name was used to designate the official residence. Jesus was brought to Pilate's Praetorium in Jerusalem (Mark 15:16).

**Prisca,** shortened form of Priscilla (q.v.).

**Priscilla [Prisca]** ("ancient one"), the wife of Aquila; a Jewish Christian deeply loyal to her faith (Acts 18:2, 18, 26; Rom. 16:3).

**Prochorus** ("choir leader"), one of the seven deacons (Acts 6:5).

**Ptolemais.** *See* Acco.

**Publius** ("common; first"), governor of Malta who courteously received Paul and his company when they were shipwrecked (Acts 28:1–10).

**Pudens** ("shame faced"), a Roman Christian (2 Tim. 4:21).

**Pul.** *See* Tiglath-Pileser.

**Pul** ("Lord"), a country of undetermined location (Is. 66:19), sometimes considered to be Libya.

**Put.** *See* Phut.

**Put.** *See* Libya.

## Q

**Quartus** ("fourth"), a Corinthian Christian who sent greetings to the church in Rome (Rom. 16:23).

**Quirinius** ("of Cyrene"), the governor of Syria (Luke 2:2).

## R

**Raamah** ("to constrain, humiliate"), a place near Ma'in in southwest Arabia (Ezek. 27:22). It is called Regma in inscriptions from that area.

**Raamses** ("child of the sun"), one of the cities the Israelites built for the Egyptians (Ex. 1:11). It is thought to be San el-Hazar or modern Kantir.

**Rabbah** ("great"). **[1]** The chief city of the Ammonites (Deut. 3:11; Josh. 13:25). It was located 37 km. (23 mi.) east of the Jordan River at the headwaters of the Jabbok. **[2]** A city in Judah near Kirjath Jearim (Josh. 15:60).

**Rabmag.** This is not a proper name, but an official position of some sort. It is unclear whether it is a high religious or governmental position (Jer. 39:3, 13). Nergal-Sharezer of Babylonia bore this title.

**Rabsaris,** not a proper name, but an official position in the Babylonian and Assyrian governments. Its precise nature is unknown (Jer. 39:3, 13; 1 Kin. 18:17).

**Rabshakeh,** the title of an office in the Assyrian government. Its precise function is unknown, but suggestions include that of a field marshal or governor of the Assyrian provinces east of Haran (2 Kin. 18:17–28; 19:4, 8).

**Rachal** ("to whisper"), a town in Judah (1 Sam. 30:29). Some believe the text should read Carmel and would be identical with Carmel [2].

**Rachel** ("ewe"), daughter of Laban, wife of Jacob, and mother of Joseph and Benjamin (Gen. 29—35).

**Raddai** ("Jehovah subdues" or "beating down"), brother of David (1 Chr. 2:14).

**Raguel.** *See* Jethro.

**Rahab** ("broad"), the harlot of Jericho who helped the Hebrew spies and who became an ancestor of Christ (Josh. 2:1–21; 6:17–25; Matt. 1:5).

**Raham** ("pity; love"), a descendant of Caleb (1 Chr. 2:44).

**Ram [Aram]** ("exalted"). **[1]** An ancestor of David and of Christ (Ruth 4:19; Matt. 1:3, 4; Luke 3:33). **[2]** Son of Jerahmeel of Judah (1 Chr. 2:27). **[3]** Head of the family of Elihu (Job 32:2).

**Ramah** ("elevated"). **[1]** A town in Benjamin near Gibeah, Geba, and Bethel (Josh. 18:25; Judg. 4:5; Is. 10:29; Matt. 2:18). It has been identified as modern Er-Ram 8 km. (5 mi.) north of Jerusalem. **[2]** The town where Samuel was born (1 Sam. 1:1). It is also called Ramathaim Zophim (1 Sam. 1:1). Its location is uncertain but has been identified with Ramah [1] and modern-day Rentis, about 14.5 km. (9 mi.) northeast of Lydda. It may be Arimathea. **[3]** A frontier town of Asher (Josh. 19:29). If not the same as Ramah [4] it may be Rameh, about 20.9 km. (13 mi.) south-southeast of Tyre. **[4]** A fortified city of Naphtali (Josh. 19:36). The site may be modern Rameh 27.4 km. (17 mi.) east-northeast of Acco. **[5]** *See* Ramoth Gilead. **[6]** *See* Ramath.

**Ramath [Ramoth]** ("height, elevation"), a city of Simeon called "Ramah of the South" (Josh. 19:8). It is now Kurnab. It is also called "Ramoth" in First Samuel 30:27.

**Ramathaim Zophim.** *See* Ramah [2].

**Ramath Mizpah** ("place of the watchtower"), a city of Gad in Gilead (Josh. 13:26). It was 24 km. (15 mi.) northwest of Rabbah of Ammon, at the Jabbok. It may be identical with Mizpah [4].

**Rameses** ("child of the sun"), a fertile district of Egypt where the Israelites settled (Gen. 47:11; Ex. 12:37). It was possibly the Land of Goshen.

**Ramoth** ("high places" or "heights"). **[1]** A Levitical city of Gilead in Gad (Deut. 4:43; Josh. 20:8). It is identical with Ramoth Gilead. **[2]** A city of Levi in Issachar (1 Chr. 6:37). It is identical with Jarmuth [2] and Remeth (q.v.). **[3]** *See* Ramath.

**Ramoth Gilead [Ramoth]** ("heights of Gilead"), the chief city of Gad. It was a city of refuge ascribed to the Levites (1 Kin. 4:13; 22:4). Sometimes it is called simply Ramoth (Deut. 4:43; Josh. 20:8). It has been identified with both Tell Ramith and Tell el-Hush.

**Rapha** ("fearful"). **[1]** The fifth son of Benjamin (1 Chr. 8:2). He is called Rephaiah in First Chronicles 9:43. **[2]** A descendant of King Saul (1 Chr. 8:37).

**Rebecca,** Greek form of Rebekah (q.v.).

**Rebekah [Rebecca]** ("flattering"), wife of Isaac and mother of Jacob and Esau (Gen. 22:23; 24—28).

**Rechab** ("companionship"). **[1]** A descendant of Benjamin who murdered Ishbosheth (2 Sam. 4:2, 5–9). **[2]** Founder of a tribe called Rechabites (2 Kin. 10:15; Jer. 35). **[3]** A descendant of Hemath (1 Chr. 2:55). **[4]** One who helped to build the wall of Jerusalem (Neh. 3:14).

**Red Sea,** a sea that divides Egypt and Arabia. It was across this body of water that the Israelites escaped from Egypt (Ex. 10:19). The Hebrews called it the Sea of Deliverance; others called it the Sea of Reeds.

**Refuge, Cities of.** *See* Cities of Refuge.

**Refuse Gate.** A gate in the southwest wall of Jerusalem (Neh. 2:13; 12:31).

**Rehoboam** ("freer of the people"), the son of Solomon; when he was king, ten tribes revolted from him and he set up the southern kingdom of Judah (1 Kin. 11:43; 12; 14). He was an ancestor of Christ (Matt. 1:7).

**Rehoboth** ("spaces"). **[1]** A well dug by Isaac in the Valley of Gerar (Gen. 26:22). It is probably modern Wadi Ruheibeh, 30.6 km. (19 mi.) southwest of Beersheba. **[2]** a suburb of Nineveh (Gen. 10:11). **[3]** A city somewhere in northern Edom (Gen. 36:37; 1 Chr. 1:48). Its location is unidentified.

**Remaliah** ("Jehovah increases" or "whom Jehovah has adorned"), father of Pekah (2 Kin. 15:25–37). This is perhaps not a proper name, but a slur on Pekah's impoverished background.

**Rephaim, Valley of** ("valley of the giants"), the site in Judah where David defeated the Philistines (Is. 17:5; 2 Sam. 5:18). It lies between Jerusalem and Bethlehem, southwest of Jerusalem and the Valley of Hinnom. It is probably the present-day Valley el-Bukaa.

**Rephidim** ("beds"), an Israelite encampment between the Wilderness of Sin and Mount Sinai (Ex. 17:1, 8). It may be the Wadi Refayid, northwest of Jebel Musa.

**Reu** ("friendship"), son of Peleg and ancestor of Christ (Gen. 11:18–21; Luke 3:35).

**Reuben** ("behold, a son"), eldest son of Jacob and Leah; he lost his birthright through sin against his father (Gen. 29:32; 35:22; 37:29). His descendants became one of the twelve tribes of Israel.

**Reuel** ("God is his friend"). [1] A son of Esau by Basemath (Gen. 36:4; 1 Chr. 1:35, 37). [2] Descendant of Benjamin (1 Chr. 9:8). [3] *See* Jethro. [4] *See* Deuel.

**Rezin** ("dominion"). [1] The last king of Syria who, along with Pekah, fought Judah (2 Kin. 15:37; 16:5–10). [2] One whose descendants returned from the Babylonian Captivity (Ezra 2:48; Neh. 7:50).

**Rezon** ("prince; noble"), a Syrian rebel who set up his own government in Damascus (1 Kin. 11:23). Many scholars think Rezon simply is a title denoting a prince and identify him with Hezion (q.v.).

**Rhegium** ("fracture"), a town located in southern Italy (Acts 28:13). It was opposite Messina in Sicily and is now called Reggio.

**Rhesa** ("head"), an ancestor of Christ (Luke 3:27).

**Rhoda** ("rose"), a maid in the house of Mary (Acts 12:12–15).

**Rhodes** ("rose"), an island located off the coast of Caria in southwest Asia Minor (Acts 21:1).

**Riblah** ("quarrel"). [1] A city on the Orontes where the sons of Zedekiah were slain (Jer. 39:5–7; 2 Kin. 23:33). It was 80 km. (50 mi.) south of Hamath. It may be modern Ribleh in the Plain of Coelesyria. [2] A border city of the Promised Land (Num. 34:11). It is perhaps modern Harmel northeast of the source of the Orontes.

**Rimmon** ("pomegranate"), a father of Ishbosheth's murderers (2 Sam. 4:2–9).

**Rimmon.** [1] A town in southern Judah (Josh. 15:32; 1 Chr. 4:32; Zech. 14:10). It is identified with Khirbet Umm er-Ramāmīn, about 9 mi. from Beersheba. [2] A rock near Gibeah (Judg. 20:45-47; 21:13). It is possibly a limestone projection 3 mi. east of Bethel. [3] A border town of Zebulun (1 Chr. 6:77). The town is called Dimnah in Joshua 21:35, a reading many scholars consider a corruption of Rimmon. The site is referred to in Joshua 19:13 as Rimmon. Many translate verse 13: " [the border] goes out to Ittah-Kazin and goes to Kemmon and bends [methoar] to Neah."

**Rome** ("city of Romulus"), the capital of the great Roman Empire (Acts 23:11). It is located in Italy on the Tiber River.

**Rufus** ("red"). [1] A son of Simon of Cyrene (Mark 15:21). He was probably well known to those to whom Mark wrote his Gospel. [2] A Roman Christian (Rom. 16:13); some identify him with [1].

**Ruth** ("friendship; companion"), Moabite wife of Mahlon and Boaz; she was the great-grandmother of David and an ancestor of Christ (Ruth 1:4, 5, 14–16; 4:10; Matt. 1:5).

## S

**Salah** ("petition; sprout"), a son of Arphaxad and ancestor of Christ (Gen. 10:24; 11:12). He is called Shelah in First Chronicles 1:18, 24 and Luke 3:35.

**Salamis** ("shaken"), a town located on the east end of Cyprus (Acts 13:5). It is 4.8 km. (3 mi.) northwest of modern Famagusta.

**Salem** ("perfect peace"), the city of Melchizedek (Gen. 14:18; Ps. 76:2). It is possibly modern Salim; however, many believe it to be Jerusalem.

**Salim** ("path"), the place where John baptized (John 3:23). It is near the waters of Aenon, which were probably north of Shechem, although the site is uncertain.

**Salma [Salmon]** ("strength; clothing"). [1] A son of Caleb, son of Hur (1 Chr. 2:51, 54). [2] Father of Boaz and ancestor of Christ (Ruth 4:20, 21; Matt. 1:4, 5; Luke 3:32). Not to be confused with Zalmon.

**Salmone** ("peace"), the easternmost point of the island of Crete (Acts 27:7). It is now known as Cape Sidero.

**Salome** ("clothing; strength"). [1] One of the women who saw the Crucifixion (Mark 15:40; 16:1). Matthew 27:56 mentions that the mother of the sons of Zebedee was present; she is probably to be identified with Salome. John 19:25 lists the sister of Jesus' mother among those near the cross; some scholars identify her with Salome, but others deny this. [2] The daughter of Herodias who danced before Herod (Matt. 14:6; Mark 6:22).

**Salt, City of.** *See* City of Salt.

**Salt Sea [Dead Sea; East Sea]**, the body of water at the southern end of the Jordan Valley, which contains no marine life because of its heavy mineral contents (Gen. 14:3; Num. 34:12). Its modern name is the Dead Sea.

**Salt, Valley of,** a plain traditionally located at the lower end of the Dead Sea (2 Sam. 8:13). Another such valley, the Wadi el-Milh (salt), is east of Beersheba, and may be the site of the defeat of the Edomites.

**Samaria** ("watch mountain"). [1] The capital of the northern kingdom of Israel (1 Kin. 20:1; 2 Chr. 18:2; Jer. 41:5). It was 67.6 km. (42 mi.) north of Jerusalem. [2] Another name for the kingdom of Israel (1 Kin. 13:32; 2 Kin. 17:24). [3] A district of Palestine in Christ's time (Luke 17:11–19). Galilee was on its north and Judea on the south.

**Samgar-Nebo**, a Babylonian officer who sat with other officials in the middle gate of Jerusalem (Jer. 39:3). Some take this as a proper name (perhaps meaning "be gracious, Nebo"). Others views it as a title of Nergal-Sharezer.

**Samos** ("full of gravel"), an island of Greece (Acts 20:15). It is off the western coast of Asia Minor southwest of Ephesus.

**Samothrace** ("of the Samians and Thracians"), a small island in the Aegean Sea off the southern coast of Thrace (Acts 16:11).

**Samson** ("distinguished; strong"), judge of Israel for 20 years. His great strength and moral weakness have made him famous (Judg. 13:24; 14—16).

**Samuel [Shemuel]** ("asked of God; heard of God"), prophet and last judge of Israel. He anointed Saul and later David as king (1 Sam. 1:20; 3—13; 15; 16; 19; 25:1; Heb. 11:32).

**Sanballat** ("strong"), a leading opponent of the Jews at the time they were rebuilding the walls of Jerusalem (Neh. 2:10; 4:1, 7; 6:1–14).

**Sapphira** ("beautiful; sapphire"), the dishonest wife of Ananias, who was struck dead by God (Acts 5:1–10).

**Sarah [Sarai]** ("princess"), the wife of Abraham and mother of Isaac (Gen. 17—18; 20—21; Heb. 11:11; 1 Pet. 3:6). Her name was changed from Sarai ("Jehovah is prince") to Sarah ("princess") because she would be the progenitor of a great nation (Gen. 17:15). *See* Serah.

**Sarai.** *See* Sarah.

**Sardis** ("prince of joy"), the capital city of Lydia where a church was located (Rev. 1:11; 3:1, 4). It was on the east bank of the Pactolus River about 80.5 km. (50 mi.) east of Smyrna.

**Sargon** ("[the god] has established the king [ship]"), an important king of Assyria who finished the siege of Samaria and carried away Israel. He is called by name only once in Scripture (Is. 20:1).

**Saul [Shaul]** ("asked"). **[1]** The first king of Israel; God eventually gave him up. He tried several times to slay David, but was killed himself at Gilboa (1 Sam. 9—31). **[2]** The original name of Paul (q.v.). **[3]** The sixth king of Edom (Gen. 36:37, 38; 1 Chr. 1:48, 49).

**Sceva** ("fitted"), a Jewish priest at Ephesus whose sons attempted to cast out a demon, but were wounded by it instead (Acts 19:14–16).

**Seba** (meaning unknown), an African nation bordering the land of Cush (Ps. 72:10; Is. 43:3). There is some confusion between Sheba and Seba, but they are probably two distinct locations.

**Secundus** ("second"), a Thessalonian Christian and friend of Paul (Acts 20:4).

**Seir** ("tempest"). **[1]** The valley and mountains of Aravah from the Dead Sea south to the Elanitic Gulf (Gen. 14:6; 32:3). Seir was the name of the mountain range in Edom and the name came to include the entire territory. **[2]** A ridge on Judah's border west of Kirjath Jearim (Josh. 15:10).

**Sela** ("a rock"). **[1]** The capital of Edom, located between the Dead Sea and the Gulf of Aqaba (2 Kin. 14:7; Is. 16:1). It is also called Petra. **[2]** A rock formation about 1,160 m. (3,800 ft.) above sea level, which dominates the city of Petra (cf. Judg. 1:36). It is now called Ummel-Bizarah.

**Seleucia** ("beaten by the waves"), a Syrian seaport from which Paul and Barnabas began their first missionary journey (Acts 13:4). It is located 8 km. (5 mi.) north of the mouth of the Orontes River.

**Sennacherib** (Babylonian, *Sin-ahi-eriba*—"[the god] Sin has substituted for my brother"), an Assyrian king who killed his brother to usurp the throne. He unsuccessfully invaded Judah. The amazing story of the destruction of his army is told in Second Kings 19 (2 Kin. 18:13; Is. 36:1; 37:17, 21, 37).

**Serah** ("extension"), a daughter of Asher (Gen. 46:17; 1 Chr. 7:30; Num. 26:46).

**Seraiah** ("Jehovah is prince; Jehovah has prevailed"). **[1]** A scribe of David (2 Sam. 8:17). In Second Samuel 20:25, he is called Sheva and Shavsha in First Chronicles 18:16. He is also called Shisha in First Kings 4:3. **[2]** Chief priest of Jerusalem (2 Kin. 25:18; 1 Chr. 6:14; Ezra 7:1). **[3]** One whom Gedaliah advised to submit to Chaldea (2 Kin. 25:23; Jer. 40:8). **[4]** The brother of Othniel (1 Chr. 4:13, 14). **[5]** A descendant of Simeon (1 Chr. 4:35). **[6]** A priest that returned to Jerusalem with Zerubbabel (Ezra 2:2). **[7]** A leader sent to capture Jeremiah (Jer. 36:26). **[8]** A prince of Judah who went to Babylon (Jer. 51:59, 61). **[9]** A son of Hilkiah dwelling in Jerusalem after the Exile (Neh. 11:11). **[10]** A chief of the priests who returned from Babylon (Neh. 12:1, 7).

**Sergius Paulus,** the Roman deputy of Cyprus who was converted because Elymas was struck blind (Acts 13:7).

**Serpent Well,** a well located between the Refuse Gate and the Valley Gate of Jerusalem (Neh. 2:13).

**Serug** ("strength; firmness"), father of Nahor and ancestor of Christ (Gen. 11:20, 21; Luke 3:35).

**Seth [Sheth]** ("compensation; sprout"), son of Adam and Eve, and an ancestor of Christ (Gen. 4:25, 26; 1 Chr. 1:1; Luke 3:38).

**Shabbethai** ("sabbath-born"). **[1]** An assistant to Ezra (Ezra 10:15). **[2]** One who explained the Law to the people (Neh. 8:7). **[3]** A chief Levite in Jerusalem (Neh. 11:16). All three may be identical.

**Shadrach** ("servant of [the god] Sin"), the name given to Hananiah at Babylon. He was cast into a fiery furnace and rescued (Dan. 1:7; 3).

**Shallum [Shallun]** ("recompenser"). **[1]** The youngest son of Naphtali (1 Chr. 7:13). He is also called Shillem (Gen. 46:24; Num. 26:49). **[2]** A descendant of Simeon (1 Chr. 4:25). **[3]** A descendant of Judah (1 Chr. 2:40, 41). **[4]** One who usurped the throne of Israel and reigned for one month (2 Kin. 15:10–15). **[5]** Husband of Huldah the prophetess (2 Kin. 22:14; 2 Chr. 34:22). **[6]** *See* Jehoahaz [2]. **[7]** *See* Meshullam [7]. **[8]** A gatekeeper of the tabernacle (1 Chr. 9:17–19, 31; Ezra 2:42; Neh. 7:45). **[9]** Father of Jehizkiah (2 Chr. 28:12). **[10], [11]** Two who married foreign wives during the Exile (Ezra 10:24, 42). **[12]** One who helped to repair the wall of Jerusalem (Neh. 3:12). **[13]** One who helped to repair the gate of Jerusalem (Neh. 3:15). **[14]** An uncle of Jeremiah (Jer. 32:7). **[15]** Father of one who was a temple officer in the days of Jehoiakim (Jer. 35:4).

**Shalman,** the king who sacked Beth Arbel (Hos. 10:14). Perhaps he was either Shalmaneser V of Assyria or Shalman king of Moab.

**Shalmaneser** (Babylonian, *Shulmaner-asharidu*—"[the god] Shulman is chief"). The King of Assyria to whom Hoshea became subject was Shalmaneser V (2 Kin. 17:3). Either Shalmaneser or Sargon, his successor, was the king to whom Samaria fell after a long siege (2 Kin. 17:6; 18:9).

**Shamgar** ("cupbearer; fleer"), judge of Israel who rescued his people from the Philistines (Judg. 3:31; 5:6).

**Shammah** ("fame; renown"). **[1]** A grandson of Esau (Gen. 36:13, 17; 1 Chr. 1:37). **[2]** A son of Jesse (1 Sam. 16:9; 17:13). He is also called Shimeah or Shimea (2 Sam. 13:3; 21:21; 1 Chr. 20:7; 2:13). **[3]** One of David's mighty men or the father of one of David's mighty men (2 Sam. 23:11). **[4]** Another of David's mighty men (2 Sam. 23:33), called Shammoth in First Chronicles 11:27. **[5]** Yet another of David's mighty men (2 Sam. 23:25).

**Shammua** ("famous"). **[1]** One sent to spy out the land of Canaan (Num. 13:4). **[2]** One of David's sons (2 Sam. 5:14; 1 Chr. 14:4). In First Chronicles 3:5, he is called Shimea. **[3]** A Levite who led the temple worship after the Exile (Neh. 11:17). He is also called Shemaiah (1 Chr. 9:16). **[4]** The head of a priestly family in Nehemiah's day (Neh. 12:18).

**Shaphan** ("prudent; sly"). **[1]** A scribe of Josiah who read him the Law (2 Kin. 22:3; 2 Chr. 34:8–21). **[2]** Father of a chief officer under Josiah (2 Kin. 22:12; 2 Chr. 34:20). **[3]** Father of Elasah (Jer. 29:3). **[4]** Father of Jaazaniah whom Ezekiel saw in a vision (Ezek. 8:11). Many scholars consider all of the above to be identical.

**Shaphat** ("judge"). **[1]** One sent to spy out the land of Canaan (Num. 13:5). **[2]** Father of Elisha the prophet (1 Kin. 19:16, 19; 2 Kin. 3:11; 6:31). **[3]** One of the family of David (1 Chr. 3:22). **[4]** A chief of Gad (1 Chr. 5:12). **[5]** One over David's herds in the valley (1 Chr. 27:29).

**Sharezer** (Babylonian, *Sharutsur*—"he has protected the king"). [1] A son of the Assyrian king Sennacherib who, with his brother, killed their father (2 Kin. 19:37; Is. 37:38). [2] One sent to consult the priests and prophets (Zech. 7:2).

**Sharon** ("his song"). [1] A region that lies between the Mediterranean Sea from Joppa to Carmel and the central portion of Palestine (1 Chr. 27:29; Acts 9:35). [2] A district east of the Jordan occupied by the tribe of Gad (1 Chr. 5:16).

**Shaul [Saul]** (variant form of Saul). [1] A descendant of Levi (1 Chr. 6:24). [2] A son of Simeon found in several lists (Gen. 46:10; Ex. 6:15; 1 Chr. 4:24).

**Shealtiel** ("lent by God"), father of Zerubbabel and an ancestor of Christ (Ezra 3:2, 8; 5:2; Hag. 1:1, 12; Matt. 1:12).

**Shear-Jashub** ("a remnant returns"), symbolic name given a son of Isaiah (Is. 7:3).

**Sheba** ("oath; covenant"). [1] A chief of Gad (1 Chr. 5:13). [2] One who rebelled against David and was beheaded for it (2 Sam. 20). [3] A grandson of Abraham (Gen. 25:3; 1 Chr. 1:32). [4] A descendant of Shem (Gen. 10:28; 1 Chr. 1:22). Some scholars identify [5] with [4]. They believe Sheba is a tribe or people and stress that close genealogical ties account for the occurrence of the name in both Ham's and Shem's genealogy. [5] A descendant of Ham (Gen. 10:7; 1 Chr. 1:9).

**Sheba** ("oath"). [1] A country in southwest Arabia (1 Kin. 10:1–13; 2 Chr. 9:1–12). Its capital was Ma'rib, which was about 60 miles east-northeast of San'a, the present capital of Yemen. [2] A town of Simeon mentioned after Beersheba (Josh. 19:2). Its location is uncertain.

**Shechaniah [Shecaniah]** ("Jehovah is a neighbor"). [1] Head of a family of the house of David (1 Chr. 3:21, 22). [2], [3] Two whose descendants returned from the Babylonian Captivity (Ezra 8:3, 5). [4] One who took a foreign wife during the Exile (Ezra 10:2). [5] Father of one who repaired the wall of Jerusalem (Neh. 3:29). [6] Father-in-law to one who opposed Nehemiah (Neh. 6:18). [7] A priest who returned from the Exile (Neh. 12:3). [8] A priest in the time of David (1 Chr. 24:11). [9] A priest in Hezekiah's day (2 Chr. 31:15).

**Shechem** ("shoulder"). [1] Son of Hamor who defiled Dinah; he and his family were soon destroyed for that act (Gen. 33:19; 34). [2] A descendant of Manasseh (Num. 26:31; Josh. 17:2). [3] Another descendant of Manasseh (1 Chr. 7:19).

**Shechem** ("portion"), an ancient city in central Palestine (Gen. 12:6; 33:18; Josh. 24:32; Acts 7:16), in the hill country of Ephraim. It is present-day Nablus, located about 66 km. (41 mi.) north of Jerusalem between Mount Ebal and Mount Gerizim.

**Shelah** ("peace"). [1] The youngest son of Judah (Gen. 38:5–26; 1 Chr. 2:3; 4:21). [2] *See* Salah.

**Shelomith** ("peacefulness"). [1] Mother of one stoned for blasphemy in the wilderness (Lev. 24:11). [2] Daughter of Zerubbabel (1 Chr. 3:19). [3] A descendant of Gershon (1 Chr. 23:9). [4] A descendant of Levi and Kohath (1 Chr. 23:18). [5] One over the treasures in the days of David (1 Chr. 26:25–28). [6] Child of Rehoboam (2 Chr. 11:20). [7] An ancestor of a family that returned from the Exile (Ezra 8:10). Not to be confused with Shelomoth.

**Shem** ("name; renown"), son of Noah and ancestor of Christ (Gen. 5:32; 6:10; 10:1; Luke 3:36).

**Shemaiah** ("Jehovah is fame" or "Jehovah hears"). [1] A prophet who warned Rehoboam against war (1 Kin. 12:22; 2 Chr. 11:2). [2] A descendant of David (1 Chr. 3:22). [3] Head of a family of Simeon (1 Chr. 4:37). [4] Son of Joel (1 Chr. 5:4). [5] A descendant of Merari (1 Chr. 9:14; Neh. 11:15). [6] One who helped to bring the ark of the covenant to the temple (1 Chr. 15:8, 11). [7] A Levite who recorded the allotment in David's day (1 Chr. 24:6). [8] A gatekeeper for the tabernacle (1 Chr. 26:4, 6, 7). [9] A Levite whom Jehoshaphat sent to teach the people (2 Chr. 17:8). [10] One who helped to cleanse the temple (2 Chr. 29:14). [11] A Levite in Hezekiah's day (2 Chr. 31:15). [12] A chief Levite in Josiah's day (2 Chr. 35:9). [13] One who returned with Ezra (Ezra 8:13). [14] A person sent to Iddo to enlist ministers (Ezra 8:16). [15], [16] Two who married foreign wives during the Exile (Ezra 10:21, 31). [17] One who helped to repair the wall of Jerusalem (Neh. 3:29). [18] One who tried to intimidate Nehemiah (Neh. 6:10). [19] One who sealed the new covenant with God after the Exile (Neh. 10:8). [20] One who helped to purify the wall of Jerusalem (Neh. 12:36). [21] One at the dedication of the wall of Jerusalem (Neh. 12:42). [22] Father of the prophet Urijah (Jer. 26:20). [23] One who wanted the priests to reprimand Jeremiah (Jer. 29:24, 31). [24] Father of a prince of the Jews (Jer. 36:12). [25] *See* Shammua [3]. [26] A prince of Judah who took part in the dedication of the wall (Neh. 12:34). [27] A Levite of the line of Asaph (Neh. 12:35). [28] A chief of the priests who returned with Zerubbabel (Neh. 12:6, 7).

**Shemariah [Shamariah]** ("whom Jehovah guards"). [1] One who joined David at Ziklag (1 Chr. 12:5). [2] A son of King Rehoboam (2 Chr. 11:19). [3], [4] Two who married foreign wives during the Exile (Ezra 10:32, 41).

**Shemer** ("watch"), owner of the hill which Omri bought and on which he built Samaria (1 Kin. 16:24).

**Shemuel** (variant form of Samuel—"asked of God"). [1] One appointed to divide the land of Canaan (Num. 34:20). [2] Head of a family of Issachar (1 Chr. 7:2). [3] *See* Samuel.

**Shen** ("tooth"), a place near which Samuel erected a stone memorial to the victory over the Philistines (1 Sam. 7:12).

**Shephatiah** ("Jehovah is judge"). [1] A son of David by Abital (2 Sam. 3:4; 1 Chr. 3:3). [2] Father of Meshullam who dwelt in Jerusalem (1 Chr. 9:8). [3] A valiant man who joined David at Ziklag (1 Chr. 12:5). [4] A prince of Simeon (1 Chr. 27:16). [5] A son of Jehoshaphat (2 Chr. 21:2). [6] An ancestor of returned captives (Ezra 2:4; Neh. 7:9). [7] One of Solomon's servants whose descendants returned from the Babylonian Captivity (Ezra 2:57; Neh. 7:59). [8] An ancestor of returned captives (Ezra 8:8). He is possibly identical with [6]. [9] A descendant of Perez whose descendants dwelt in Jerusalem (Neh. 11:4). [10] A prince of Judah in Zedekiah's time (Jer. 38:1).

**Shepherds, The,** the location where the royal family of King Ahaziah of Judah were slaughtered (2 Kin. 10:12–14). The Hebrew name is *Beth 'eked*; the site is probably

Beit Kad, about 25.7 km. (16 mi.) north-northeast of Samaria.

**Sheshbazzar** ("O Shamash [the god], protect the father"), the prince of Judah into whose hands Cyrus placed the temple vessels. Many believe he is the same as Zerubbabel, but others deny this. They claim Sheshbazzar was governor under Cyrus and Zerubbabel under Darius (Ezra 1:8, 11; 5:14–16).

**Shihor [Sihor]** ("blackness"), the east branch of the Nile River (1 Chr. 13:5; Jer. 2:18). Ideally, this was to be Israel's southern boundary.

**Shiloah [Shelah]** ("sent"), a waterway of Jerusalem (Is. 8:6; Neh. 3:15). It carried water from the spring of Gihon to the Pool of Shelah to irrigate the Kidron Valley outside the city. It is identical with Siloam [1].

**Shiloh** ("peace"), a town in Ephraim (Josh. 18:1–10; Judg. 21:19). It is halfway between Shechem and Bethel.

**Shimea [Shimeah]** ("[God] has heard [a prayer]"). **[1]** A descendant of Merari (1 Chr. 6:30). **[2]** Father of Berachiah (1 Chr. 6:39). **[3]** *See* Shammah [2]. **[4]** *See* Shammua [2]. **[5]** One of the family of King Saul whose descendants dwelt in Jerusalem (1 Chr. 8:32; 9:38). In the latter passage he is called Shimeam.

**Shimei [Shimi]** ("Jehovah is fame; Jehovah hear me"). **[1]** A son of Gershon and a grandson of Gershon (Ex. 6:17; Num. 3:18, 21; Zech. 12:13). **[2]** A descendant of Benjamin who cursed David when he was fleeing from Absalom (2 Sam. 16:5–13; 19:16–23). **[3]** A loyal officer of David (1 Kin. 1:8). **[4]** An officer of Solomon (1 Kin. 4:18). **[5]** Grandson of King Jeconiah (1 Chr. 3:19). **[6]** A man who had sixteen sons and six daughters (1 Chr. 4:26, 27). **[7]** A descendant of Reuben (1 Chr. 5:4). **[8]** A son of Libni (1 Chr. 6:29). **[9]** Father of a chief of Judah (1 Chr. 8:21). **[10]** A Levite (1 Chr. 23:9). **[11]** A Levite in the temple song service in the days of David (1 Chr. 25:17). **[12]** One in charge of many vineyards (1 Chr. 27:27). **[13]** One who helped to cleanse the temple (2 Chr. 29:14). **[14]** A Levite in charge of the temple offerings under Hezekiah (2 Chr. 31:12, 13). **[15], [16], [17]** Three men who took foreign wives during the Exile (Ezra 10:23, 33, 38). **[18]** Grandfather of Mordecai (Esth. 2:5).

**Shimri** ("Jehovah is watching"). **[1]** Head of a family of Simeon (1 Chr. 4:37). **[2]** Father of one of David's mighty men (1 Chr. 11:45). **[3]** Gatekeeper of the tabernacle in David's day (1 Chr. 26:10). **[4]** One who helped to cleanse the temple (2 Chr. 29:13).

**Shimrith** ("watch"), a woman of Moab,. mother of Jehozabad who killed Joash (2 Chr. 24:26). She is called Shomer in Second Kings 12:21.

**Shimshai** ("Jehovah is splendor"), a scribe who, with Rehum, wrote to the king of Persia opposing the rebuilding of the wall of Jerusalem (Ezra 4:8, 9, 17, 23).

**Shinar** ("watch of him that sleeps"), the plains later known as Babylonia or Chaldea, through which the Tigris and Euphrates Rivers flow (Gen. 10:10; Is. 11:11).

**Shiphrah** ("beauty"), one of the Hebrew midwives at the time of the birth of Moses (Ex. 1:15).

**Shishak,** another name for Shishak I, king of Egypt. He sheltered Jeroboam against Solomon and in later years invaded Judah (1 Kin. 11:40; 14:25; 2 Chr. 12).

**Shittim [Acacia Grove]** ("thorns"). **[1]** The final Israelite encampment before crossing the Jordan. Here Moses bade farewell and the Law was completed (Num. 25:1; Josh. 2:1). It was in Moab, east of Jordan, opposite Jericho. **[2]** A dry and unfruitful valley (Joel 3:18). The name may not denote any particular valley, but it may refer to the Kidron Wadi which starts northwest of Jerusalem, moves toward the east and runs toward the Dead Sea. It may also be a portion of the Arabah around the Dead Sea.

**Shobab** ("returning"). **[1]** A son of David (2 Sam. 5:14; 1 Chr. 3:5). **[2]** A son of Caleb (1 Chr. 2:18).

**Shua** ("prosperity"). **[1]** A daughter of Heber (1 Chr. 7:32). **[2]** A Canaanite whose daughter Judah married (Gen. 38:2, 12; 1 Chr. 2:3).

**Shuah [Shuhah]** ("depression"). **[1]** A son of Abraham by Keturah (Gen. 25:2; 1 Chr. 1:32). **[2]** A brother of Chelub; descendant of Caleb (1 Chr. 4:11).

**Shunem** ("their sleep"), a town near Jezreel that was allotted to the tribe of Issachar (Josh. 19:18; 1 Sam. 28:4). It was opposite Mount Gilboa. The site is present-day Solem or Sulam.

**Shur** ("wall"), a desert in the northwest part of the Sinai Peninsula (Gen. 16:7; 25:18). It was outside the eastern border of Egypt and was probably a caravan route between Egypt and Beersheba.

**Shushan [Susa]** ("a lily"), the capital of Elam inhabited by the Babylonians; later a royal residence and capital of the Persian Empire (Neh. 1:1; Dan. 8:2). The city was also known as Susa. The site is modern Shush on the Ulai River.

**Sibbechai** ("Jehovah is intervening"), a mighty man who killed a Philistine giant (2 Sam. 21:18; 1 Chr. 11:29; 20:4). He is called Mebunnai in Second Samuel 23:27.

**Siddim** ("the tilled field"), a valley near the Dead Sea (Gen. 14:3, 8, 10), full of bitumen pits.

**Sidon** ("fortress"), eldest son of Canaan, son of Ham (Gen. 10:15). He is called Zidon in First Chronicles 1:13. Possibly a reference to the ancestor of the inhabitants of the ancient city of Sidon.

**Sidon** ("hunting"), an ancient city of Canaan (Gen. 10:15, 19; Josh. 11:8; Luke 4:26).

**Sihon** ("great; bold"), an Amorite king that was defeated by Israel (Num. 21:21–31; Deut. 1:4; 2:24–32; Josh. 13:15–28).

**Sihor.** *See* Shihor.

**Silas [Silvanus]** ("forest; woody; third; asked"), an eminent member of the early church who traveled with Paul through Asia Minor and Greece and was imprisoned with him at Philippi (Acts 15:22, 32–34; 2 Cor. 1:19; 1 Thess. 1:1).

**Siloam** ("sent"). **[1]** A famous pool of Jerusalem at the south end of Hezekiah's tunnel (John 9:7). It is identical with Shiloah (q.v.). **[2]** A tower on the Ophel ridge near Siloam (Luke 13:4).

**Silvanus.** *See* Silas.

**Simeon [Simon]** ("hearing"). **[1]** The second son of Jacob by Leah (Gen. 29:33; 34:25; 48:5; 49:5). His descendants became one of the twelve tribes of Israel. **[2]** A devout Jew who blessed the Christ child in the temple (Luke 2:25–34). **[3]** An ancestor of Jesus (Luke 3:30). **[4]** A disciple and prophet at Antioch (Acts 13:1); he was surnamed Niger ("black"). **[5]** Original name of Peter (q.v.). Simon is but another form of Simeon. Not to be confused with Shimeon.

**Simon** ("hearing"). [1] Original name of the apostle Peter (Matt. 4:18; 16:16, 17; Luke 4:38; Acts 10:18). [2] Another of the twelve apostles, called Simon the Canaanite, indicating his fierce loyalty either to Israel or to his faith (Matt. 10:4; Mark 3:18; Luke 6:15; Acts 1:13). [3] One of Christ's brothers (Matt. 13:55; Mark 6:3). [4] A leper of Bethany in whose house Christ was anointed (Matt. 26:6; Mark 14:3). [5] A Cyrenian who was forced to bear the cross of Christ (Matt. 27:32; Mark 15:21). [6] A Pharisee in whose house the feet of Christ were anointed (Luke 7:40, 43, 44). [7] The father of Judas Iscariot (John 6:71; 12:4; 13:2). [8] A sorcerer who tried to buy the gifts of the Holy Spirit (Acts 8:9, 13, 18, 24). [9] A tanner of Joppa with whom Peter lodged (Acts 9:43; 10:6, 17, 32).

**Sin** ("bush"). [1] A city on the eastern side of the Nile (Ezek. 30:15, 16). It is possibly Pelusium; but is also identified with Syene, which is present-day Aswan at the first cataract of the Nile. [2] A wilderness area located between the Gulf of Suez and Sinai (Ex. 16:1; Num. 33:11, 12).

**Sinai** ("a bush"). [1] An area in the center of the peninsula that lies between the horns of the Red Sea, the Gulf of Suez, and the Gulf of Aqaba (Ex. 16:1; Acts 7:30–38). [2] A mountain, called also Horeb, where the Israelites received the Ten Commandments (Ex. 19:18). The location of the site is uncertain, although it is generally agreed to be in central Sinai. The traditional site is Jebel Musa, but other possibilities are Mount Serbal and Ras es-Safsafeh.

**Sinim** ("south country"), a land from which the scattered Israelites were again to be gathered (Is. 49:12). It probably refers to Syene on the southern Egyptian frontier where there was a Jewish garrison. Earlier scholars believed that China was indicated, but that view has been abandoned.

**Sion** ("breastplate"). [1] Another name for Mount Hermon (Deut. 4:48). [2] *See* Zion.

**Sirion** ("breastplate"), the name given to Mount Hermon by the Sidonians (Deut. 3:9; Ps. 29:6).

**Sisera** ("mediation; array"). [1] Captain of the army of Jabin who was murdered by Jael (Judg. 4:1–22; 5:26, 28). [2] One whose descendants returned (Ezra 2:53; Neh. 7:55).

**Smyrna** ("myrrh"), a city on the western coast of Asia Minor (Rev. 2:8–11). It is 64.4 km. (40 mi.) north of Ephesus.

**So** ("vizier"), a king of Egypt, either Osorkon IV or Tefnakht. Others believe this name is a reference to a city (2 Kin. 17:3–7).

**Sodom** ("their secret"), one of the five Cities of the Plain (Gen. 10:19; Rom. 9:29), destroyed because of its wickedness. The exact location of the site is unknown, but it is in the Dead Sea area.

**Solomon** ("peace"), son of David by Bathsheba and king of a united, strong Israel for forty years. His wisdom and carnal sin stand out in his multi-faceted character (1 Kin. 1:11; 2:11). He was an ancestor of Christ (Matt. 1:6, 7).

**Solomon's Pools,** a repository of water built by Solomon near Bethlehem (Eccl. 2:6).

**Solomon's Porch,** a colonnade built by Solomon on the east side of the temple (John 10:23; Acts 3:11).

**Sopater** ("one who defends the father"), a man of Berea who accompanied Paul to Asia (Acts 20:4). Perhaps the same as Sosipater (q.v.).

**Sorek** ("vine"), a valley in Gaza where Delilah lived (Judg. 16:4). It is modern Wadi es-Sarar, which begins 20.9 km. (13 mi.) southwest of Jerusalem and twists northwest toward the Mediterranean.

**Sosipater** ("one who defends the father"), one who sent greetings to the Roman Christians (Rom. 16:21). He was Jewish (a "kinsman" of Paul) and is possibly the same as Sopater (q.v.).

**Sosthenes** ("strong; powerful"). [1] Chief ruler of the synagogue at Corinth, beaten by the Greeks (Acts 18:17). [2] A believer who united with Paul in addressing the Corinthian church (1 Cor. 1:1). Some believe he was [1] after conversion.

**Spain** ("rain"), a peninsula in southwestern Europe (Rom. 15:24). The nation was known as Hispania to the Romans.

**Stachys** ("ear of corn"), a believer of Rome to whom Paul sent greetings (Rom. 16:9).

**Stephanas** ("crown"), one of the first believers of Achaia (1 Cor. 1:16; 16:15–17).

**Stephen** ("crown"), one of the seven deacons. He became the first martyr of the church after Christ (Acts 6:5–9; 7:59; 8:2).

**Succoth** ("tents"). [1] A town where Jacob built himself a house (Gen. 33:17; Josh. 13:27). It was east of the Jordan between Peniel and Shechem. Its probable location is Deir 'Alla, about 1.6 km. (1 mi.) west of where the Jabbok bulges and turns south. [2] The first camping ground of the Israelites after leaving Egypt (Ex. 12:37; 13:20).

**Supply Cities [Treasure House],** designated cities at which the kings of the ancient world kept their treasures and tithes (Ex. 1:11; Ezra 5:17).

**Sur** ("rebellion"), a gate in Jerusalem, possibly leading from the king's palace to the temple (2 Kin. 11:6). The parallel passage calls it the Gate of the Foundation (2 Chr. 23:5).

**Susa.** *See* Shushan.

**Susanna** ("lily"), one of the women who ministered to Christ and was His follower (Luke 8:3).

**Sychar** ("end"), a town of Samaria near Jacob's well (John 4:5).

**Syntyche** ("fortunate"), a woman of the church at Philippi (Phil. 4:2).

**Syracuse** ("that draws violently"), a city on the east coast of Sicily (Acts 28:12).

**Syria** (a form of the word *Assyria*), the country lying north and east of Palestine (Judg. 10:6; 1 Kin. 10:29; Acts 15:23). It stretched far inland from the Mediterranean and was bounded by the Taurus Mountains to the north.

**Syrtis Sands** ("shallows"), two shoals off the coast of Africa between Carthage and Cyrene (Acts 27:17). The greater Syrtis is now called the Gulf of Sidra, the lesser Syrtis the Gulf of Gabes.

## T

**Tabel** ("God is good"). [1] Father of a man the kings of Israel and Damascus planned to make king of Judah (Is.

7:6). [2] A Persian official who tried to hinder the rebuilding of the wall of Jerusalem (Ezra 4:7).

**Taberah** ("burning"), a place three days north of Mount Sinai where Israel was punished for murmuring against God (Num. 11:3; Deut. 9:22).

**Tabitha** ("gazelle"), the Christian woman of Joppa whom Peter raised from the dead (Acts 9:36–42). Dorcas is the Greek form of the name.

**Tabor** ("purity"). [1] A mountain located in the northern part of the Valley of Jezreel (Judg. 4:6, 12, 14; Ps. 89:12). It is now called Jebel el-Tur and is 8.8 km. (5.5 mi.) southeast of Nazareth. [2] A town of Zebulun given to the Levites (1 Chr. 6:77). Its location is uncertain. It may be the Chisloth Tabor of Joshua 19:12 or Khirbet Dabural, which is on a hill between Tabor and Nazareth. [3] A terebinth (not a plain as in KJV) in Benjamin (1 Sam. 10:3).

**Tadmor** ("bitterness"), a city known to the Greeks and Romans as Palmyra; it facilitated trade with the East (1 Kin. 9:18; 2 Chr. 8:4). Its ruin is Tadmar in an oasis east-northeast of Damascus about midway between the city and the Euphrates. Some believe the reading in First Kings should be *Tamar;* the Masoretic Hebrew scholars read *Tadmor* in the margin but *Tamar* in the text. If we read Tamar then the reference is to a city probably in southern Judah.

**Tahpanhes [Tehaphnehes]** ("secret temptation"), an Egyptian city on the Pelusiac channel of the Nile (Jer. 2:16; 43:7–9; 44:1; Ezek. 30:18). It is identified with modern Tell Defneh.

**Tahpenes,** an Egyptian queen, wife of the pharaoh, who received the fleeing Hadad, an enemy of Solomon (1 Kin. 11:18–20).

**Talmai** ("bold; spirited"). [1] A man or clan defeated by Caleb (Num. 13:22; Josh. 15:14; Judg. 1:10). [2] King of Geshur and father-in-law of David (2 Sam. 3:3; 13:27).

**Talmon** ("oppressor; violent"), a Levite in Ezra's day; a temple gatekeeper (1 Chr. 9:17; Ezra 2:42; Neh. 7:45).

**Tamar** ("palm"). [1] The wife of Er, mother of Perez, and an ancestor of Christ (Gen. 38:6, 11, 13; Ruth 4:12; Matt. 1:3). [2] The daughter of David violated by Amnon (2 Sam. 13:1–32). [3] A daughter of Absalom (2 Sam. 14:27).

**Tamar** ("palm tree"), a place somewhere to the southwest of the Dead Sea; some identify the site with the village of Thamara, near Kurnub and Ain el-Arūs. Others deny this (Ezek. 47:18, 19; 48:28).

**Tarshish [Tarshishah; Tharshish]** ("hard"). [1] A son of Javan and grandson of Noah (Gen. 10:4; 1 Chr. 1:7). Possibly a people who inhabited a region in Spain (Tartessus), near Gibraltar. [2] One of the seven princes of Persia (Esth. 1:14). [3] A descendant of Benjamin (1 Chr. 7:10).

**Tarshish** ("contemplation"), a city in southern Spain with which the Phoenicians traded (Jer. 10:9; Ezek. 27:12; 1 Kin. 10:22). It is believed to be modern Tartessus near Gibraltar.

**Tarsus** ("winged"), the most prominent city of Cilicia located on the river Cydnus in Asia Minor; it was the birthplace of Paul (Acts 9:11).

**Tartan** (meaning unknown), the title of a high Assyrian officer. There is evidence that the office was second only to the king. There are two Tartans mentioned in Scripture (2 Kin. 18:17; Is. 20:1).

**Tattenai** ("gift"), a Persian governor of Samaria in the days of Zerubbabel (Ezra 5:3; 6:6, 13).

**Tekoa** ("that is confirmed"), a town of Judah on the hills near Hebron (2 Sam. 14:2; Jer. 6:1). It is modern Taku 'ais, a ruined village 9.7 km. (6 mi.) south of Bethlehem.

**Tel Abib** ("heap of new grain"), a town of Babylonia near the river Chebar where Jewish exiles were placed (Ezek. 3:15).

**Telassar** ("taking away"), a city near Haran and Orfa in western Mesopotamia (2 Kin. 19:12; Is. 37:12).

**Tema** ("south; south country; sunburnt"), a son of Ishmael (Gen. 25:15). The place his descendants dwelt was also called Tema (Job 6:19). It was located in Arabia midway between Damascus and Mecca.

**Temple.** The structure in which the Israelites worshiped and offered sacrifices to God. There were three temples: Solomon's, Zerubbabel's, and Herod's.

**Terah** ("turning; duration"), the father of Abraham and ancestor of Christ (Gen. 11:27–32; Luke 3:34).

**Tertius** ("third"), the scribe to whom the epistle to the Romans was dictated (Rom. 16:22). Some conjecture that he is Silas (q.v.).

**Tertullus** ("third"), an orator hired by the Jews to state skillfully their case against Paul before Felix (Acts 24:1–8).

**Thaddaeus** (a name derived from an Aramaic word for the female breast), one of the twelve apostles (Matt. 10:3; Mark 3:18). He is the same as Judas, the brother of James (Luke 6:16; John 14:22; Acts 1:13). He was also named Lebbaeus ("heart").

**Thebez** ("muddy"), a place in the district of Neapolis (Judg. 9:50). It was 20.9 km. (13 mi.) southwest of Scythopolis [Beth Shean].

**Theophilus** ("loved by God"), an unknown person, possibly a Roman official, to whom Luke addressed his Gospel and Acts (Luke 1:3; Acts 1:1).

**Thessalonica** ("victory at sea"), a city situated on the Macedonian coast at the head of the Thermaic Gulf (Acts 17:1, 11, 13; 27:2). It is known as Salonika today.

**Theudas** ("the gift of God"), instigator of a rebellion against the Romans, which was crushed by them (Acts 5:36).

**Thomas** ("twin"), one of the twelve apostles of Jesus. When Christ rose from the dead, Thomas was most skeptical (Matt. 10:3; Mark 3:18; John 20:24–29). His Aramaic name is Didymus in Greek.

**Three Inns,** a station on the Appian Way near the modern city of Cisterna (Acts 28:15).

**Thyatira** ("sacrifice of labor"), a city between Pergamos and Sardis (Acts 16:14; Rev. 2:18–29). It was in Lydia in Asia Minor.

**Tiberias** ("good vision"), a city on the west coast of the Sea of Galilee (John 6:1; 21:1).

**Tiberius** ("son of [the river] Tiber"), third emperor of the Roman Empire (Luke 3:1).

**Tibni** ("intelligent"), one who rivaled Omri for the throne of Israel (1 Kin. 16:21, 22).

**Tidal** ("splendor; renown"), king of Goyim who, with his allies, invaded the cities of the plain (Gen. 14:1, 9).

**Tiglath-Pileser** (Babylonian, *Tukulti-apil-Esharra—*

"my trust is in the son of Asharra"), a king of Assyria who invaded Naphtali during the time of Pekah of Israel. He conquered northern Palestine and deported many from Naphtali (2 Kin. 15:29; 16:7, 10; 1 Chr. 5:6, 26). His native name was Pul (2 Kin. 15:19). Realizing he bore two names, we should translate First Chronicles 5:26, " God stirred Pul king of Assyria, that is, [not *and*] Tiglath-Pileser king of Assyria."

**Timaeus** ("honorable"), father of the blind Bartimaeus (Mark 10:46).

**Timon** ("honorable"), one of the seven deacons (Acts 6:1–6).

**Timothy** ("honored of God"), a young friend and convert of Paul; he traveled extensively with the apostle. He was from Lystra and was the son of Eunice, a Jewess, and a Greek father (Acts 16:1; 17:14, 15; 1 Tim. 1:2, 18; 6:20).

**Tirhakah,** a king of Ethiopia and Egypt who aided Hezekiah in his fight against Sennacherib (2 Kin. 19:9; Is. 37:9).

**Tirzah** ("delight"), youngest daughter of Zelophehad (Num. 26:33; 27:1; Josh. 17:3).

**Titus** ("pleasant"), a converted Grecian entrusted with a mission to Crete (2 Cor. 2:13; Gal. 2:1; Titus 1:4).

**Tob** ("good"), an area east of the Jordan between Gilead and the eastern deserts (Judg. 11:3, 5).

**Tobiah [Tobijah]** ("Jehovah is good"). **[1]** A Levite sent by Jehoshaphat to teach the Law (2 Chr. 17:8). **[2]** An ancestor of returning captives who had lost their genealogy (Ezra 2:60; Neh. 7:62). **[3]** An Ammonite servant of Sanballat who opposed Nehemiah (Neh. 2:10–20). **[4]** A leader who returned from the Babylonian Captivity (Zech. 6:10, 14).

**Tobijah.** *See* Tobiah.

**Togarmah** ("all bone"), a country that supplied horses and mules to the Tyrians and soldiers to the army of Gog (Ezek. 27:14; 38:6). Many identify this land with Armenia.

**Toi [Tou]** ("error; wandering"), a king of Hamath who sent his son to congratulate David on his victory over Hadadezer (2 Sam. 8:9, 10; 1 Chr. 18:9, 10).

**Tophel** ("ruin"), an area north of Bozra, toward the southeast corner of the Dead Sea (Deut. 1:1). It is perhaps Tafileh.

**Tophet [Topheth]** ("a drum"), once a part of a king's garden in Hinnom; it became a place where people in Jerusalem sacrificed their children (Is. 30:33; Jer. 19:6, 11–14; 2 Kin. 23:10).

**Trachonitis** ("strong"), a Roman province south of Damascus and north of Jordan (Luke 3:1). It is now called al-Seja.

**Troas** ("penetrated"), an important city on the coast of Mysia (Acts 16:8; 2 Tim. 4:13). It was in northern Asia Minor and is also called Alexandria.

**Trogyllium** ("fruit port"), a rocky projection of the ridge of Mycale and a town (Acts 20:15). They were both located on the western coast of Asia Minor opposite the island of Samos.

**Trophimus** ("a foster child"), a Christian convert and afterward a companion-in-travel with Paul (Acts 20:4; 21:29; 2 Tim. 4:20).

**Tryphena** ("dainty; shining"), a Christian woman of Rome to whom Paul sent greetings (Rom. 16:12).

**Tryphosa** ("disdain; shining"), a Christian woman at Rome sent greetings by Paul (Rom. 16:12).

**Tubal,** a son of Japheth (Gen. 10:2; 1 Chr. 1:5). Possibly a reference to a people in eastern Asia Minor; they are called Tabal in Assyrian inscriptions.

**Tubal-Cain,** one of the sons of Lamech and expert metalsmith (Gen. 4:22).

**Tychicus** ("fortunate"), a disciple and messenger of Paul (Acts 20:4; Eph. 6:21; 2 Tim. 4:12).

**Tyrannus** ("tyrant"), a Greek rhetorician or Jewish rabbi in whose school Paul taught at Ephesus (Acts 19:9).

**Tyre** ("rock"), a city on the central coast of Phoenicia noted for its commercial activity (Josh. 19:29; 2 Sam. 5:11; Jer. 25:22). It is located halfway between Acco and Sidon.

## U

**Ulai** ("pure water"), a river surrounding Shushan in Persia (Dan. 8:2, 16). It is now called Kerah or Kerkhah.

**Ur** ("flame; light"), father of one of David's mighty men (1 Chr. 11:35).

**Ur,** the city which Abram left to go to Haran (Gen. 11:28, 31). Ur is generally identified as ancient Ur (Uri), modern Tell el-Muqayyar located on the Euphrates in south Iraq.

**Urbanus** ("pleasant; witty"), a faithful Roman Christian whom Paul greeted (Rom. 16:9).

**Uriah [Urijah]** ("Jehovah is my light"). **[1]** A Hittite soldier in David's army. He was killed in a fierce battle, for David, desiring to marry his wife, Bathsheba, had placed him on the front battle line (2 Sam. 11). **[2]** A priest under Ahaz who built a pagan altar on the king's command; then placed it in the temple (2 Kin. 16:10–16). **[3]** A prophet whose message of judgment so offended Jehoiakim that he murdered him (Jer. 26:20–23). **[4]** A priest, the father of Meremoth (Ezra 8:33; Neh. 3:4, 21). **[5]** A man who stood by Ezra when he read the Law (Neh. 8:4). Possibly the same as [4]. **[6]** A priest whom Isaiah took as a witness (Is. 8:2).

**Urijah.** *See* Uriah.

**Uz [Huz]** ("counsel; firmness"). **[1]** Eldest son of Aram (Gen. 10:23). Possibly the name refers to an Aramean tribe or people. **[2]** A son of Shem (1 Chr. 1:17). The Septuagint makes this Uz identical with [1] naming Aram as his father. It is also possible the Hebrew text was abbreviated here. **[3]** A son of Dishan, son of Seir (Gen. 36:28). **[4]** The son of Nahor by Milcah (Gen. 22:21).

**Uz** ("counsel; firmness"). **[1]** The country where Job lived (Job 1:1). The two most likely locations are Hauran, south of Damascus, and the area between Edom and north Arabia. **[2]** A kingdom not far from Edom (Jer. 25:20; Lam. 4:21). Perhaps identical with [1].

**Uzza [Uzzah]** ("strength"). **[1]** A man who was struck dead by God when he touched the ark of the covenant (2 Sam. 6:2–7; 1 Chr. 13:6–10). **[2]** A descendant of Merari (1 Chr. 6:29). **[3]** A descendant of Ehud (1 Chr. 8:7). **[4]** An ancestor of a Nethinim family that returned from Babylon (Ezra 2:49; Neh. 7:51).

**Uzza, Garden of** ("strength"), the place where Manasseh, king of Judah, and Amon, his son, were buried (2 Kin. 21:18, 26).

**Uzzah.** *See* Uzza.

**Uzziah** ("Jehovah is strong" or "my strength is Jehovah"). **[1]** The eleventh king of Judah. When he attempted to offer incense unlawfully, God struck him with leprosy. He was also called Azariah (2 Kin. 15:1–8; 2 Chr. 26). He was an ancestor of Christ (Matt. 1:8, 9). **[2]** A Levite descended from Kohath and ancestor of Samuel (1 Chr. 6:24). **[3]** Father of Jehonathan (1 Chr. 27:25). **[4]** A priest who had married a foreign wife (Ezra 10:21). **[5]** A descendant of Judah (Neh. 11:4).

**Uzziel** ("God is my strength" or "God is strong"). **[1]** The ancestor of the Uzzielites; the son of Kohath (Ex. 6:18). **[2]** Captain of the sons of Simeon (1 Chr. 4:42). **[3]** A son of Bela and grandson to Benjamin (1 Chr. 7:7). **[4]** An assistant wall-builder (Neh. 3:8). **[5]** A Levite, son of Jeduthun, who helped to cleanse the temple (2 Chr. 29:14). **[6]** A musician set by David over the service of song in the temple (1 Chr. 25:4). Uzziel is the same as Azarel in verse 18.

## V

**Valley Gate,** a gate in the southwest wall of Jerusalem leading to the Hinnom Valley (Neh. 2:13).

**Vashti** ("beautiful woman; best"), the queen of Persia who was divorced by King Ahasuerus because she refused to come to his great feast (Esth. 1:10–22).

## W

**Water Gate,** a gate on the east side of Jerusalem, above the spring of Gihon (Neh. 8:1, 3).

**Wilderness,** the area in which the Israelites wandered for 40 years before entering Canaan (Deut. 1:1; Josh. 5:6). Several places are encompassed in the designation Wilderness; these are listed under their individual names (e.g., Paran, Zin, etc.).

**Willows, Brook of the,** a small stream that marks the boundary between Moab and Edom (Is. 15:7). It is possibly the lower course of Wadi el-Hesa where it meets the upper course of Seil el-Kerahi.

## Z

**Zacchaeus** ("pure"), a publican with whom Jesus lodged during His stay at Jericho (Luke 19:1–10).

**Zacharias** (Greek form of Zechariah—"memory of the Lord"). **[1]** The prophet whom the Jews stoned (Matt. 23:35; Luke 11:51). Some believe this prophet to be identical with Zechariah [11] or [16], though it is possible the reference is to an unknown prophet. **[2]** A priest, father of John the Baptist (Luke 1).

**Zadok** ("righteous"). **[1]** A high priest in the time of David (2 Sam. 8:17; 15:24–36; 1 Kin. 1:8–45). **[2]** Father of Jerusha, wife of Uzziah and mother of Jotham, both kings of Israel (2 Kin. 15:33; 2 Chr. 27:1). **[3]** Son of Ahitub and father of Shallum or Meshullam (1 Chr. 6:12, 13; Ezra 7:2). **[4]** A young man of valor (1 Chr. 12:28). **[5], [6]** Two who repaired the wall of Jerusalem (Neh. 3:4, 29). **[7]** One who sealed the covenant with Nehemiah (Neh. 10:21). **[8]** A scribe under Nehemiah (Neh. 13:13). **[9]** An ancestor of Christ (Matt. 1:14).

**Zalmon** ("terrace; accent"), the Ahohite who was one of David's guards (2 Sam. 23:28). He is called Ilai ("exalted") in First Chronicles 11:29. Not to be confused with Salmon.

**Zalmon** ("shady"), a wooded area in Shechem (Judg. 9:48, 49; Ps. 68:14).

**Zalmunna** ("withdrawn from protection"), a Midianite king slain by Gideon (Judg. 8:5–21).

**Zaphnath-Paaneah** ("savior of the world; revealer of secrets"), name given to Joseph by Pharaoh (Gen. 41:45).

**Zarephath** ("smelting place"), a town located near Zidon (Sidon) that was the residence of Elijah (1 Kin. 17:9).

**Zealot, The.** *See* Simon [2].

**Zebedee** ("the gift of Jehovah"), a fisherman of Galilee, husband of Salome, and father of the apostles James and John (Matt. 4:21; 27:56; Mark 1:19, 20).

**Zeboiium [Zeboim]** ("gazelles"). **[1]** One of the five Cities of the Plain (Gen. 10:19; 14:2, 9). **[2]** A valley between Michmash and the wilderness to the east (1 Sam. 13:16–18). **[3]** A Benjamite town (Neh. 11:34). It is probably north of Lydda, perhaps at Khirbet Sabeyah.

**Zebulun** ("dwelling"), tenth son of Jacob and ancestor of one of the twelve tribes (Gen. 30:20; 49:13; 1 Chr. 2:1).

**Zebulun** ("dwelling"), the territory given to the tribe of Zebulun (Josh. 19:27, 34). It was north of Issachar, east of Asher, and southwest of Naphtali.

**Zechariah** ("Jehovah my righteousness"). **[1]** A chief of the tribe of Reuben (1 Chr. 5:7). **[2]** A Levite gatekeeper in the days of David (1 Chr. 9:21; 26:2, 14). **[3]** A Levite set over the service of song in the days of David (1 Chr. 15:18, 20; 16:5). **[4]** A priest in the days of David (1 Chr. 15:24). **[5]** A descendant of Levi through Kohath (1 Chr. 24:25). **[6]** A descendant of Levi through Merari (1 Chr. 26:11). **[7]** Father of Iddo (1 Chr. 27:21). **[8]** A prince of Jehoshaphat sent to teach the people (2 Chr. 17:7). **[9]** A Levite who encouraged Jehoshaphat against Moab (2 Chr. 20:14). **[10]** A son of Jehoshaphat (2 Chr. 21:2). **[11]** A son of Jehoiada who was stoned (2 Chr. 24:20). Also mentioned in Matthew 23:35 and Luke 11:51. **[12]** Prophet in the days of Uzziah (2 Chr. 26:5). **[13]** A Levite who helped to cleanse the temple (2 Chr. 29:13). **[14]** A descendant of Levi (2 Chr. 34:12). **[15]** A prince of Judah in the days of Josiah (2 Chr. 35:8). **[16]** A prophet in the days of Ezra. His book still exists (Ezra 5:1; 6:14; Zech. 1:1, 7; 7:1, 8). **[17]** A chief man of Israel (Ezra 8:3). **[18]** One who returned from the Exile (Ezra 8:11). The chief man in Ezra 8:16 was probably [17] or [18]. **[19]** One who took a foreign wife during the Exile (Ezra 10:26). **[20]** A prince with Ezra (Neh. 8:4). **[21]** A descendant of Perez (Neh. 11:4). **[22]** One whose descendants dwelt in Jerusalem (Neh. 11:5). **[23]** A priest (Neh. 11:12). **[24]** A Levite trumpeter (Neh. 12:35, 36). **[25]** A priest who took part in the dedication ceremony (Neh. 12:41). **[26]** One whom Isaiah took as a witness (Is. 8:2). **[27]** Father of Abi or Abijah, mother of Hezekiah (2 Kin. 18:2). **[28]** Son and successor of Jeroboam II. He reigned only six months (2 Kin. 18:2).

**Zedekiah** ("Jehovah my righteousness; Jehovah is might"). **[1]** A false prophet who encouraged Ahab to attack the Syrians at Ramoth Gilead (1 Kin. 22:11, 24; 2 Chr. 18:10, 23). **[2]** A false prophet (Jer. 29:21–23). **[3]** A prince of Judah in the days of Jehoiakim (Jer. 36:12). **[4]** The last king of Judah; his rebellion spelled the doom of Judah (2 Kin. 24:18—25:7; 2 Chr. 36:11–21). He is probably referred to in First Chronicles 3:16 as a "son" or successor of Jeconiah. *See* Mattaniah [1].

**Zelophehad** ("firstborn"), grandson of Gilead (Num. 26:33; 27:1, 7; Josh. 17:3).

**Zenas** ("living"), a Christian who had been a teacher of the Law (Titus 3:13).

**Zephaniah** ("Jehovah is darkness; Jehovah has treasured"). **[1]** A prophet in the days of Josiah (Zeph. 1:1). **[2]** A Levite or priest, ancestor of Samuel (1 Chr. 6:36). Possibly the same as Uriel [1]. **[3]** Son of Josiah the priest (Zech. 6:10, 14). **[4]** A priest who opposed Babylonian rule (2 Kin. 25:18; Jer. 21:1; 37:3).

**Zered** ("brook"), a brook and valley that marks the greatest limit of the Hebrews' wandering in the wilderness (Num. 21:12; Deut. 2:13, 14). It was south of the Arnon, probably Wadi el-Hesa.

**Zerubbabel** ("seed of Babylon"). **[1]** The leader of a group who returned from exile; he began the rebuilding of the temple (Ezra 3—5; Neh. 7:7; 12:1, 47). He was an ancestor of Christ (Matt. 1:12, 13). **[2]** An ancestor of Christ (Luke 3:27); perhaps the same as [1].

**Zeruiah** ("balm"), a daughter of Jesse and David's sister (1 Sam. 26:6; 2 Sam. 2:13, 18).

**Ziklag** ("measure pressed down"), a city in the south of Judah (1 Sam. 30:1; 2 Sam. 1:1; 4:10). It is probably Tell el-Khutweilfel about 16.1 km. (10 mi.) north of Beersheba.

**Zillah** ("protection; screen"), one of the wives of Lamech (Gen. 4:19, 22, 23).

**Zilpah** ("myrrh dropping"), mother of Gad and Asher (Gen. 29:24; 30:9–13; 35:26).

**Zimran** ("celebrated"), a son of Abraham by Keturah (Gen. 25:2; 1 Chr. 1:32).

**Zimri** ("celebrated"). **[1]** A disobedient Israelite slain by Phinehas (Num. 25:14). **[2]** A captain who slew Elah (1 Kin. 16:9–20). **[3]** A son of Zerah of Judah (1 Chr. 2:6). **[4]** A descendant of Benjamin (1 Chr. 8:36; 9:42).

**Zin** ("swelling"), a wilderness on the southern border of Canaan, not to be confused with the Wilderness of Sin. It was either a part of the Wilderness of Paran or bordered on the wilderness which contained Kadesh Barnea (Num. 20:1; 27:14; Josh. 15:1–3).

**Zion [Sion]** ("monument; fortress; set up"), one of the hills on which Jerusalem stood. It came to be applied to the temple and the whole of Jerusalem and its people as a community whose destiny depends on God (2 Sam. 5:7; Is. 8:18; Ps. 48:11; Joel 2:23). Zion also is a symbol of heaven (Rev. 14:1).

**Ziphron** ("rejoicing"), a place specified by Moses as the northern boundary of the Promised Land (Num. 34:9). It is probably Za'feranh southeast of Restan.

**Zippor** ("bird"), father of Balak, king of Moab (Num. 22:2, 4, 10, 16).

**Zipporah** ("little bird"), the wife of Moses and daughter of Reuel (Ex. 2:21; 4:25; 18:2).

**Zoan** ("motion"), a city on the eastern bank of the Nile Delta on the Tanitic branch of the river (Ezek. 30:14). It was known to the Greeks as Tanis and is now San el-Hagar.

**Zoar** ("small"), one of the five Cities of the Plain of the Jordan (Gen. 14:2; 19:22). It probably was located at the southeast end of the Dead Sea near es-Safi. The original site is believed to be under the Dead Sea's waters.

**Zohar** ("nobility; distinction"). **[1]** Father of Ephron, from whom Abraham bought a field (Gen. 23:8; 25:9). **[2]** A son of Simeon of Judah (Gen. 46:10; Ex. 6:15). He is also called Zerah (1 Chr. 4:24).

**Zophim** ("place for a watchman"), a place on top of Pisgah where Balaam viewed the Israelite camp (Num. 23:14). It is possibly Tal'al es-Safa.

# CONCORDANCE

## A

**ABASED**
I know how to be *a* . . . . . . . . .Phil 4:12

**ABBA**
And He said, "*A* . . . . . . . . .Mark 14:36
whom we cry out, "*A* . . . . . . .Rom 8:15

**ABHOR**
Therefore I *a* myself . . . . . . . . .Job 42:6

**ABHORRED**
*a* His own inheritance . . . . . .Ps 106:40

**ABIDE**
the Most High shall *a* . . . . . . . .Ps 91:1
Him, "If you *a* . . . . . . . . . . . .John 8:31
"If you *a* in Me . . . . . . . . . . . .John 15:7
*a* in My love . . . . . . . . . . . . . .John 15:9

**ABIDES**
He who *a* in Me . . . . . . . . . . .John 15:5
will of God *a* forever . . . . . .1 John 2:17

**ABIDING**
do not have His word *a*. . . . . .John 5:38

**ABILITY**
according to his own *a*. . . . .Matt 25:15
*a* which God supplies. . . . . . .1 Pet 4:11

**ABLE**
shall give as he is *a* . . . . . . .Deut 16:17
God whom we serve is *a* . . . . .Dan 3:17
God is *a* to raise up . . . . . . . . .Matt 3:9
fear Him who is *a* . . . . . . . .Matt 10:28
Are you *a* to drink the . . . . .Matt 20:22
persuaded that He is *a* . . . . .2 Tim 1:12
learning and never *a* . . . . . . .2 Tim 3:7
that God was *a* to. . . . . . . . . .Heb 11:19

**ABOLISHED**
having *a* in His flesh. . . . . . . .Eph 2:15
Christ, who has *a* . . . . . . . . .2 Tim 1:10

**ABOMINABLE**
they deny Him, being *a*. . . . .Titus 1:16
unbelieving, *a* . . . . . . . . . . . . .Rev 21:8

**ABOMINATION**
yes, seven are an *a* . . . . . . . . .Prov 6:16
the scoffer is an *a* . . . . . . . . . .Prov 24:9
prayer shall be an *a* . . . . . . . .Prov 28:9
and place there the *a*. . . . . . .Dan 11:31
the *a* of desolation. . . . . . . . .Dan 12:11
the '*a of desolation*,' . . . . . . .Matt 24:15

**ABOMINATIONS**
delights in their *a*. . . . . . . . . . . .Is 66:3
a golden cup full of *a* . . . . . . . .Rev 17:4

**ABOUND**
the offense might *a*. . . . . . . . .Rom 5:20
sin that grace may *a*. . . . . . . . .Rom 6:1
to make all grace *a* . . . . . . . . .2 Cor 9:8
and I know how to *a* . . . . . . . .Phil 4:12

**ABOUNDED**
But where sin *a* . . . . . . . . . . .Rom 5:20

**ABOUNDING**
immovable, always *a* . . . . .1 Cor 15:58

**ABOVE**
that is in heaven *a*. . . . . . . . . . .Ex 20:4
*A* it stood seraphim. . . . . . . . . . . .Is 6:2
"He who comes from *a* . . . . . .John 3:31
I am from *a*. . . . . . . . . . . . . . . .John 8:23
been given you from *a* . . . . .John 19:11
things which are *a* . . . . . . . . . . .Col 3:1
perfect gift is from *a* . . . . . .James 1:17

**ABSENT**
in the body we are *a* . . . . . . . .2 Cor 5:6

**ABSTAIN**
we write to them to *a* . . . . . .Acts 15:20
*A* from every form . . . . . . .1 Thess 5:22

**ABUNDANCE**
put in out of their *a*. . . . . . .Mark 12:44
not consist in the *a* . . . . . . .Luke 12:15

**ABUNDANT**
in labors more *a* . . . . . . . . .2 Cor 11:23

**ABUNDANTLY**
*a* satisfied with the . . . . . . . . . .Ps 36:8
may have it more *a* . . . . . . .John 10:10
to do exceedingly *a* . . . . . . . . .Eph 3:20

**ACCEPT**
offering, I will not *a* . . . . . . . .Jer 14:12
Should I *a* this from . . . . . . . .Mal 1:13

**ACCEPTABLE**
*a* time I have heard. . . . . . . . . . .Is 49:8
proclaim the *a* year. . . . . . . . . . .Is 61:2
*proclaim the a year*. . . . . . . .Luke 4:19
is that good and *a*. . . . . . . . . .Rom 12:2

**ACCEPTABLY**
we may serve God *a*. . . . . . . .Heb 12:28

**ACCEPTED**
Behold, now is the *a* . . . . . . . .2 Cor 6:2
which He made us *a* . . . . . . . . .Eph 1:6

**ACCESS**
whom also we have *a* . . . . . . . .Rom 5:2

**ACCOMPLISHED**
all things were now *a*. . . . . .John 19:28

**ACCORD**
continued with one *a* . . . . . . .Acts 1:14

**ACCOUNT**
they will give *a* . . . . . . . . . .Matt 12:36
put that on my *a* . . . . . . . . . .Philem 18

**ACCOUNTED**
in the LORD, and He *a*. . . . . . .Gen 15:6
his faith is *a* . . . . . . . . . . . . . . .Rom 4:5
*God, and it was a* . . . . . . . . . . .Gal 3:6
*God, and it was a*. . . . . . . . .James 2:23

**ACCURSED**
not know the law is *a*. . . . . . .John 7:49
of God calls Jesus *a*. . . . . . . .1 Cor 12:3
to you, let him be *a*. . . . . . . . . . .Gal 1:8

**ACCUSATION**
over His head the *a* . . . . . . .Matt 27:37
they might find an *a* . . . . . . . .Luke 6:7

**ACCUSE**
they began to *a* Him . . . . . . .Luke 23:2

**ACCUSED**
while He was being *a*. . . . . .Matt 27:12

**ACCUSER**
*a* of our brethren . . . . . . . . . .Rev 12:10

**ACCUSING**
their thoughts *a* . . . . . . . . . . .Rom 2:15

**ACKNOWLEDGE**
*a* my transgressions . . . . . . . . .Ps 51:3
in all your ways *a*. . . . . . . . . . .Prov 3:6

**ACKNOWLEDGES**
*a* the Son has the. . . . . . . . .1 John 2:23

**ACQUAINT**
*a* yourself with Him. . . . . . . .Job 22:21

**ACQUAINTED**
a Man of sorrows and *a*. . . . . . . .Is 53:3

**ACQUIT**
at all *a* the wicked. . . . . . . . . . .Nah 1:3

**ACT**
in the very *a*. . . . . . . . . . . . . . .John 8:4

**ACTIONS**
by Him *a* are weighed . . . . . .1 Sam 2:3

**ACTS**
of Your awesome *a* . . . . . . . . . .Ps 145:6

**ADD**
Do not *a* to His words . . . . . . .Prov 30:6

**ADDED**
And the Lord *a* to the . . . . . .Acts 2:47
It was *a* because of. . . . . . . . . .Gal 3:19

**ADMONISH**
*a* him as a . . . . . . . . . . . . .2 Thess 3:15

**ADMONITION**
were written for our *a* . . . . .1 Cor 10:11
in the training and *a*. . . . . . . . .Eph 6:4

**ADOPTION**
the Spirit of *a* . . . . . . . . . . . . .Rom 8:15
waiting for the *a*. . . . . . . . . . .Rom 8:23
to whom pertain the *a* . . . . . . .Rom 9:4

**ADORN**
also, that the women *a* . . . . . .1 Tim 2:9

**ADORNED**
God also *a* themselves . . . . . . .1 Pet 3:5
prepared as a bride *a* . . . . . . . .Rev 21:2

**ADRIFT**
*a* among the dead. . . . . . . . . . . .Ps 88:5

**ADULTERER**
The eye of the *a*. . . . . . . . . . . .Job 24:15

**ADULTERERS**
nor idolaters, nor *a* . . . . . . . . .1 Cor 6:9
*a* God will judge . . . . . . . . . . .Heb 13:4

**ADULTEROUS**
*a* generation. . . . . . . . . . . . .Matt 12:39

**ADULTERY**
You shall not commit *a* . . . . . .Ex 20:14
already committed *a* . . . . . . .Matt 5:28
is divorced commits *a* . . . . . .Matt 5:32
another commits *a* . . . . . . .Mark 10:11
and those who commit *a* . . . . .Rev 2:22

**ADVANTAGE**
*a* that I go away . . . . . . . . . . .John 16:7
Satan should take *a* . . . . . . .2 Cor 2:11

**ADVERSARIES**
and there are many *a* . . . . . .1 Cor 16:9
terrified by your *a*. . . . . . . . . .Phil 1:28

**ADVERSARY**
"Agree with your *a* . . . . . . . .Matt 5:25
opportunity to the *a* . . . . . . .1 Tim 5:14
*a* the devil walks . . . . . . . . . . .1 Pet 5:8

**ADVERSITY**
I shall never be in *a* . . . . . . . . . .Ps 10:6
the day of *a* consider . . . . . . .Eccl 7:14

**ADVICE**
in this I give my *a* . . . . . . . . .2 Cor 8:10

**ADVOCATE**
sins, we have an *A* . . . . . . . .1 John 2:1

**AFAR**
and not a God *a*. . . . . . . . . . . . .Jer 23:23
to you who were *a* . . . . . . . . . .Eph 2:17
but having seen them *a*. . . . .Heb 11:13

**AFFAIRS**
himself with the *a* . . . . . . . . .2 Tim 2:4

**AFFECTION**
to his wife the *a* . . . 1 Cor 7:3

**AFFECTIONATE**
Be kindly *a* to one . . . Rom 12:10

**AFFIRM**
you to *a* constantly . . . Titus 3:8

**AFFLICT**
*a* Your heritage . . . Ps 94:5
For He does not *a* . . . Lam 3:33

**AFFLICTED**
To him who is *a* . . . Job 6:14
hears the cry of the *a* . . . Job 34:28
days of the *a* are evil . . . Prov 15:15
smitten by God, and *a* . . . Is 53:4
"O you *a* one . . . Is 54:11
being destitute, *a* . . . Heb 11:37

**AFFLICTING**
*a* the just and taking . . . Amos 5:12

**AFFLICTION**
is, the bread of *a* . . . Deut 16:3
*a* take hold of me . . . Job 30:16
and it is an evil *a* . . . Eccl 6:2
For our light *a* . . . 2 Cor 4:17
supposing to add *a* . . . Phil 1:16

**AFRAID**
garden, and I was *a* . . . Gen 3:10
saying, "Do not be *a* . . . Gen 15:1
none will make you *a* . . . Lev 26:6
ungodliness made me *a* . . . Ps 18:4
Whenever I am *a* . . . Ps 56:3
one will make them *a* . . . Is 17:2
do not be *a* . . . Matt 14:27
if you do evil, be *a* . . . Rom 13:4
do good and are not *a* . . . 1 Pet 3:6

**AFTERWARD**
*a* receive me to glory . . . Ps 73:24
you shall follow Me *a* . . . John 13:36

**AGAIN**
'You must be born *a* . . . John 3:7
having been born *a* . . . 1 Pet 1:23

**AGAINST**
come to '*set a man a* . . . Matt 10:35
or house divided *a* . . . Matt 12:25
Me is *a* Me . . . Matt 12:30
*a* the Spirit will not . . . Matt 12:31
*lifted up his heel a* . . . John 13:18
*LORD and a His Christ* . . . Acts 4:26
to kick *a* the goads . . . Acts 9:5
*a* the promises of God . . . Gal 3:21
we do not wrestle *a* . . . Eph 6:12
I have a few things *a* . . . Rev 2:20

**AGE**
the grave at a full *a* . . . Job 5:26
and in the *a* to come . . . Mark 10:30

**AGED**
a one as Paul, the *a* . . . Philem 9

**AGES**
ordained before the *a* . . . 1 Cor 2:7

**AGONY**
And being in *a* . . . Luke 22:44

**AGREE**
that if two of you *a* . . . Matt 18:19

**AGREED**
unless they are *a* . . . Amos 3:3

**AGREEMENT**
what *a* has the temple . . . 2 Cor 6:16

**AIR**
the birds of the *a* . . . Gen 1:26
of the *a* have nests . . . Luke 9:58
of the power of the *a* . . . Eph 2:2
meet the Lord in the *a* . . . 1 Thess 4:17

**ALIENATED**
darkened, being *a* . . . Eph 4:18
you, who once were *a* . . . Col 1:21

**ALIENS**
*A* have devoured his . . . Hos 7:9
Christ, being *a* . . . Eph 2:12

**ALIKE**
esteems every day *a* . . . Rom 14:5

**ALIVE**
I kill and I make *a* . . . Deut 32:39
son was dead and is *a* . . . Luke 15:24
presented Himself *a* . . . Acts 1:3
indeed to sin, but *a* . . . Rom 6:11
all shall be made *a* . . . 1 Cor 15:22
that we who are *a* . . . 1 Thess 4:15
and behold, I am *a* . . . Rev 1:18
These two were cast *a* . . . Rev 19:20

**ALLELUIA**
Again they said, "*A* . . . Rev 19:3

**ALLOW**
*a* Your Holy One . . . Ps 16:10
*a* My faithfulness . . . Ps 89:33
*a Your Holy One* . . . Acts 2:27

**ALLURE**
of emptiness, they *a* . . . 2 Pet 2:18

**ALMOND**
*a* tree blossoms . . . Eccl 12:5

**ALMOST**
*a* persuade me to . . . Acts 26:28

**ALOES**
mixture of myrrh and *a* . . . John 19:39

**ALPHA**
"I am the *A* and the . . . Rev 1:8
"I am the *A* and the . . . Rev 22:13

**ALTAR**
Then Noah built an *a* . . . Gen 8:20
'An *a* of earth you . . . Ex 20:24
it to you upon the *a* . . . Lev 17:11
your gift to the *a* . . . Matt 5:23
swears by the *a* . . . Matt 23:18
I even found an *a* . . . Acts 17:23
We have an *a* from . . . Heb 13:10

**ALTARS**
Even Your *a*, O LORD . . . Ps 84:3
*and torn down Your a* . . . Rom 11:3

**ALTERED**
of His face was *a* . . . Luke 9:29

**ALWAYS**
delight, rejoicing *a* . . . Prov 8:30
the poor with you *a* . . . Matt 26:11
lo, I am with you *a* . . . Matt 28:20
to them, that men *a* . . . Luke 18:1
immovable, *a* . . . 1 Cor 15:58
Rejoice in the Lord *a* . . . Phil 4:4
thus we shall *a* . . . 1 Thess 4:17
*a* be ready to give a . . . 1 Pet 3:15

**AM**
to Moses, "I *A* WHO I . . . Ex 3:14
First and I *a* the Last . . . Is 44:6
in My name, I *a* . . . Matt 18:20
*a* the bread of life . . . John 6:35
*a* the light of the . . . John 8:12
I *a* from above . . . John 8:23
Abraham was, I *A* . . . John 8:58
"I *a* the door . . . John 10:9
*a* the good shepherd . . . John 10:11
*a* the resurrection . . . John 11:25
to him, "I *a* the way . . . John 14:6
of God I *a* what I *a* . . . 1 Cor 15:10

**AMBASSADOR**
for which I am an *a* . . . Eph 6:20

**AMBASSADORS**
we are *a* for Christ . . . 2 Cor 5:20

**AMBITION**
Christ from selfish *a* . . . Phil 1:16

**AMEN**
are Yes, and in Him *A* . . . 2 Cor 1:20
creatures said, "*A* . . . Rev 5:14

**ANCHOR**
hope we have as an *a* . . . Heb 6:19

**ANCIENT**
Do not remove the *a* . . . Prov 23:10
"until the *A* of Days . . . Dan 7:22

**ANGEL**
"Behold, I send an *A* . . . Ex 23:20
Manoah said to the *A* . . . Judg 13:17
the *A* of His Presence . . . Is 63:9
things, behold, an *a* . . . Matt 1:20
for an *a* of the Lord . . . Matt 28:2
Then an *a* of the Lord . . . Luke 1:11
And behold, an *a* . . . Luke 2:9
*a* appeared to Him from . . . Luke 22:43
For an *a* went down at . . . John 5:4
*a* has spoken to Him . . . John 12:29
But at night an *a* . . . Acts 5:19
*A* who appeared to him . . . Acts 7:35
Then immediately an *a* . . . Acts 12:23
himself into an *a* . . . 2 Cor 11:14
even if we, or an *a* . . . Gal 1:8
Then I saw a strong *a* . . . Rev 5:2
Jesus, have sent My *a* . . . Rev 22:16

**ANGELS**
if He charges His *a* . . . Job 4:18
lower than the *a* . . . Ps 8:5
He shall give His *a* . . . Ps 91:11
*He shall give His a* . . . Matt 4:6
not even the *a* . . . Matt 24:36
and all the holy *a* . . . Matt 25:31
twelve legions of *a* . . . Matt 26:53
And she saw two *a* . . . John 20:12
and worship of *a* . . . Col 2:18
much better than the *a* . . . Heb 1:4
entertained *a* . . . Heb 13:2
things which *a* desire . . . 1 Pet 1:12
did not spare the *a* . . . 2 Pet 2:4
*a* who did not keep . . . Jude 6

**ANGER**
For His *a* is but for a . . . Ps 30:5
gracious, slow to *a* . . . Ps 103:8
Nor will He keep His *a* . . . Ps 103:9
around at them with *a* . . . Mark 3:5
bitterness, wrath, *a* . . . Eph 4:31

**ANGRY**
Cain, "Why are you *a* . . . Gen 4:6
"Let not the Lord be *a* . . . Gen 18:30
the Son, lest He be *a* . . . Ps 2:12
*a* man stirs up strife . . . Prov 29:22
right for you to be *a* . . . Jon 4:4
you that whoever is *a* . . . Matt 5:22
"*Be a, and do not* . . . Eph 4:26

**ANGUISH**
longer remembers the *a* . . . John 16:21
tribulation and *a* . . . Rom 2:9

**ANIMAL**
of every clean *a* . . . Gen 7:2
set him on his own *a* . . . Luke 10:34

**ANIMALS**
of *a* after their kind . . . . . . . . Gen 6:20
of four-footed *a* . . . . . . . . . . Acts 10:12

**ANNUL**
years later, cannot *a* . . . . . . . . Gal 3:17

**ANNULS**
is confirmed, no one *a* . . . . . . . Gal 3:15

**ANOINT**
*a* my head with oil . . . . . . . . . . . Ps 23:5
when you fast, *a* . . . . . . . . . . . Matt 6:17
*a* My body for burial . . . . . . . Mark 14:8
*a* your eyes with eye . . . . . . . . . Rev 3:18

**ANOINTED**
"Surely the LORD'S *a* . . . . . 1 Sam 16:6
destroy the LORD'S *a* . . . . . . 2 Sam 1:14
"Do not touch My *a* . . . . . . . 1 Chr 16:22
*because He has a* . . . . . . . . . . Luke 4:18
but this woman has *a* . . . . . . Luke 7:46
*a* the eyes of the . . . . . . . . . . . John 9:6
It was that Mary who *a* . . . . . John 11:2
Jesus, whom You *a* . . . . . . . . . Acts 4:27
and has *a* us is God . . . . . . . . 2 Cor 1:21

**ANOINTING**
But you have an *a* . . . . . . . . 1 John 2:20

**ANOTHER**
that you love one *a* . . . . . . . . John 13:34

**ANSWER**
call, and I will *a* . . . . . . . . . . . Job 13:22
how shall I *a* Him . . . . . . . . . . . Job 31:14
the day that I call, *a* . . . . . . . . . Ps 102:2
In Your faithfulness *a* . . . . . . . Ps 143:1
*a* turns away wrath . . . . . . . . Prov 15:1
*a* a fool according . . . . . . . . . Prov 26:4
or what you should *a* . . . . . . Luke 12:11
that you may have an *a* . . . . . 2 Cor 5:12

**ANT**
Go to the *a* . . . . . . . . . . . . . . . Prov 6:6

**ANTICHRIST**
have heard that the *A* . . . . . 1 John 2:18
*a* who denies the . . . . . . . . . 1 John 2:22
is a deceiver and an *a* . . . . . . . . 2 John 7

**ANTITYPE**
*a* which now saves us . . . . . . . 1 Pet 3:21

**ANXIETIES**
the multitude of my *a* . . . . . . . Ps 94:19

**ANXIETY**
*A* in the heart of man . . . . . Prov 12:25

**ANXIOUS**
Be *a* for nothing . . . . . . . . . . . . Phil 4:6

**APART**
justified by faith *a* . . . . . . . . . Rom 3:28

**APOSTLE**
called to be an *a* . . . . . . . . . . . . Rom 1:1
consider the *A* . . . . . . . . . . . . . . Heb 3:1

**APOSTLES**
of the twelve *a* . . . . . . . . . . . Matt 10:2
whom He also named *a* . . . . . Luke 6:13
am the least of the *a* . . . . . . . 1 Cor 15:9
none of the other *a* . . . . . . . . . . Gal 1:19
gave some to be *a* . . . . . . . . . . Eph 4:11

**APOSTLESHIP**
in this ministry and *a* . . . . . . Acts 1:25
are the seal of my *a* . . . . . . . . . 1 Cor 9:2

**APPAREL**
gold rings, in fine *a* . . . . . . . . James 2:2
or putting on fine *a* . . . . . . . . . 1 Pet 3:3

**APPEAL**
love's sake I rather *a* . . . . . . . . Philem 9

**APPEAR**
and let the dry land *a* . . . . . . . . Gen 1:9
also outwardly *a* . . . . . . . . . Matt 23:28
kingdom of God would *a* . . . Luke 19:11
For we must all *a* . . . . . . . . . . 2 Cor 5:10

**APPEARANCE**
Do not look at his *a* . . . . . . . 1 Sam 16:7
judge according to *a* . . . . . . . . John 7:24
those who boast in *a* . . . . . . . 2 Cor 5:12
found in *a* as a man . . . . . . . . . . Phil 2:8

**APPEARED**
an angel of the Lord *a* . . . . . Luke 1:11
who *a* in glory and . . . . . . . . . Luke 9:31
brings salvation has *a* . . . . . Titus 2:11
of the ages, He has *a* . . . . . . . . Heb 9:26

**APPEARING**
Lord Jesus Christ's *a* . . . . . . 1 Tim 6:14
and the dead at His *a* . . . . . . . 2 Tim 4:1
who have loved His *a* . . . . . . . 2 Tim 4:8

**APPEARS**
can stand when He *a* . . . . . . . . . Mal 3:2
who is our life *a* . . . . . . . . . . . . . Col 3:4
the Chief Shepherd *a* . . . . . . . . 1 Pet 5:4
in Him, that when He *a* . . . 1 John 2:28

**APPETITE**
are a man given to *a* . . . . . . . . Prov 23:2

**APPLE**
and my law as the *a* . . . . . . . . . Prov 7:2

**APPLES**
fitly spoken is like *a* . . . . . . . Prov 25:11

**APPLIED**
*a* my heart to know . . . . . . . . . Eccl 7:25

**APPOINT**
For God did not *a* . . . . . . . . . 1 Thess 5:9

**APPOINTED**
And as it is *a* for men . . . . . . . Heb 9:27

**APPROACH**
year, make those who *a* . . . . . Heb 10:1

**APPROACHING**
as you see the Day *a* . . . . . . Heb 10:25

**APPROVE**
do the same but also *a* . . . . . Rom 1:32

**APPROVED**
to God and *a* by men . . . . . . Rom 14:18
to present yourself *a* . . . . . . . 2 Tim 2:15

**ARBITRATOR**
Me a judge or an *a* . . . . . . . . Luke 12:14

**ARCHANGEL**
with the voice of an *a* . . . . 1 Thess 4:16

**ARGUMENTS**
casting down *a* and . . . . . . . . 2 Cor 10:5

**ARISE**
*A*, shine . . . . . . . . . . . . . . . . . . . . Is 60:1
but the LORD will *a* . . . . . . . . . . . Is 60:2
you who sleep, *a* . . . . . . . . . . . Eph 5:14

**ARK**
"Make yourself an *a* . . . . . . . . Gen 6:14
him, she took an *a* . . . . . . . . . . . . Ex 2:3
Bezalel made the *a* . . . . . . . . . . . Ex 37:1
in heaven, and the *a* . . . . . . . Rev 11:19

**ARM**
with an outstretched *a* . . . . . . . . Ex 6:6
Have you an *a* like God . . . . . Job 40:9
strength with His *a* . . . . . . . . . Luke 1:51
*a* yourselves also with . . . . . . . 1 Pet 4:1

**ARMED**
a strong man, fully *a* . . . . . Luke 11:21

**ARMIES**
And he sent out his *a* . . . . . . . Matt 22:7
surrounded by *a* . . . . . . . . . . Luke 21:20
And the *a* in heaven . . . . . . . . Rev 19:14
the earth, and their *a* . . . . . . Rev 19:19

**ARMOR**
Put on the whole *a* . . . . . . . . . . Eph 6:11

**ARMS**
are the everlasting *a* . . . . . . Deut 33:27
took Him up in his *a* . . . . . . . Luke 2:28

**AROMA**
the one we are the *a* . . . . . . . . 2 Cor 2:16
for a sweet-smelling *a* . . . . . . . . . Eph 5:2

**AROUSED**
the LORD was greatly *a* . . . . Num 11:10
Then Joseph, being *a* . . . . . . . Matt 1:24

**ARRAYED**
his glory was not *a* . . . . . . . . . Matt 6:29
"Who are these *a* . . . . . . . . . . . Rev 7:13

**ARROGANCE**
pride and *a* and the . . . . . . . . Prov 8:13

**ARROW**
*a* that flies by day . . . . . . . . . . . Ps 91:5

**ARROWS**
*a* pierce me deeply . . . . . . . . . . . Ps 38:2
Like *a* in the hand of . . . . . . . . Ps 127:4

**ASCEND**
Who may *a* into the . . . . . . . . . . . Ps 24:3
If I *a* into heaven . . . . . . . . . . . Ps 139:8
'I will *a* into heaven . . . . . . . . . Is 14:13
see the Son of Man *a* . . . . . . . John 6:62

**ASCENDED**
You have *a* on high . . . . . . . . . . Ps 68:18
"No one has *a* . . . . . . . . . . . . . John 3:13
*"When He a on high* . . . . . . . . . . Eph 4:8

**ASCENDING**
the angels of God *a* . . . . . . . . John 1:51

**ASCRIBE**
*A* strength to God . . . . . . . . . . Ps 68:34

**ASHAMED**
Let me not be *a* . . . . . . . . . . . . . . Ps 25:2
and Israel shall be *a* . . . . . . . . Hos 10:6
For whoever is *a* . . . . . . . . . . Mark 8:38
am not *a* of the gospel . . . . . . . Rom 1:16
Therefore God is not *a* . . . . . . Heb 11:16

**ASHES**
become like dust and *a* . . . . . . Job 30:19
in sackcloth and *a* . . . . . . . . Luke 10:13

**ASIDE**
of you lay something *a* . . . . . 1 Cor 16:2
lay *a* all filthiness . . . . . . . . James 1:21
Therefore, laying *a* . . . . . . . . . . 1 Pet 2:1

**ASK**
when your children *a* . . . . . . . . Josh 4:6
"*A* a sign for yourself . . . . . . . . . Is 7:11
whatever things you *a* . . . . . . Matt 21:22
*a*, and it will be . . . . . . . . . . . . Luke 11:9
that whatever You *a* . . . . . . . . John 11:22
*a* anything in My name . . . John 14:14
in that day you will *a* . . . . . . John 16:23
above all that we *a* . . . . . . . . . Eph 3:20
wisdom, let him *a* . . . . . . . . . James 1:5
But let him *a* in faith . . . . . . . James 1:6
because you do not *a* . . . . . . . James 4:2

**ASKS**
For everyone who *a* . . . . . . . . . Matt 7:8
you who, if his son *a* . . . . . . . . Matt 7:9
Or if he *a* for a fish . . . . . . . Luke 11:11

**ASLEEP**
But He was *a* . . . . . . . . . . . . . Matt 8:24
but some have fallen *a* . . . . . 1 Cor 15:6
those who are *a* . . . . . . . . . 1 Thess 4:15

**ASSEMBLING**
not forsaking the *a* ... Heb 10:25

**ASSEMBLY**
*a* I will praise You ... Ps 22:22
fast, call a sacred *a* ... Joel 1:14
*a I will sing praise* ... Heb 2:12
to the general *a* ... Heb 12:23

**ASSURANCE**
riches of the full *a* ... Col 2:2
Spirit and in much *a* ... 1 Thess 1:5
to the full *a* of hope ... Heb 6:11

**ASSURE**
*a* our hearts before ... 1 John 3:19

**ASSURED**
learned and been *a* ... 2 Tim 3:14

**ASTONISHED**
Just as many were *a* ... Is 52:14
who heard Him were *a* ... Luke 2:47

**ASTRAY**
and one of them goes *a* ... Matt 18:12
like sheep going *a* ... 1 Pet 2:25

**ATONEMENT**
the blood that makes *a* ... Lev 17:11
for it is the Day of *A* ... Lev 23:28
there will be no *a* ... Is 22:14

**ATTAIN**
It is high, I cannot *a* ... Ps 139:6
worthy to *a* that age ... Luke 20:35
by any means, I may *a* ... Phil 3:11

**ATTENTION**
My son, give *a* to my ... Prov 4:20

**ATTENTIVE**
Let Your ears be *a* ... Ps 130:2

**ATTESTED**
a Man *a* by God to you ... Acts 2:22

**AUSTERE**
because you are an *a* ... Luke 19:21

**AUTHOR**
For God is not the *a* ... 1 Cor 14:33
unto Jesus, the *a* ... Heb 12:2

**AUTHORITIES**
*a* that exist are ... Rom 13:1

**AUTHORITY**
them as one having *a* ... Matt 7:29
"All *a* has been given ... Matt 28:18
*a* I will give You ... Luke 4:6
and has given Him *a* ... John 5:27
You have given Him *a* ... John 17:2
the flesh, reject *a* ... Jude 8

**AUTUMN**
*a* trees without fruit ... Jude 12

**AVAILS**
of a righteous man *a* ... James 5:16

**AVENGE**
Beloved, do not *a* ... Rom 12:19
*a* our blood on those ... Rev 6:10

**AVENGER**
the Lord is the *a* ... 1 Thess 4:6

**AWAKE**
be satisfied when I *a* ... Ps 17:15
it is high time to *a* ... Rom 13:11
*A* to righteousness ... 1 Cor 15:34

**AWAY**
the wind drives *a* ... Ps 1:4
Do not cast me *a* ... Ps 51:11
a time to cast *a* ... Eccl 3:5
fair one, and come *a* ... Song 2:10
minded to put her *a* ... Matt 1:19
and earth will pass *a* ... Matt 24:35
"I am going *a* ... John 8:21
they cried out, "*A* ... John 19:15
unless the falling *a* ... 2 Thess 2:3
in Asia have turned *a* ... 2 Tim 1:15
heard, lest we drift *a* ... Heb 2:1
if they fall *a* ... Heb 6:6
which can never take *a* ... Heb 10:11
the world is passing *a* ... 1 John 2:17
if anyone takes *a* ... Rev 22:19

**AWESOME**
*a* is this place ... Gen 28:17
God, the great and *a* ... Deut 7:21
By *a* deeds in ... Ps 65:5
O God, You are more *a* ... Ps 68:35
Your great and *a* name ... Ps 99:3

**AWL**
his ear with an *a* ... Ex 21:6

**AX**
If the *a* is dull ... Eccl 10:10
And even now the *a* ... Matt 3:10

## B

**BABBLER**
"What does this *b* ... Acts 17:18

**BABBLINGS**
the profane and idle *b* ... 1 Tim 6:20

**BABE**
the *b* leaped in my ... Luke 1:44
You will find a *B* ... Luke 2:12
for he is a *b* ... Heb 5:13

**BABES**
Out of the mouth of *b* ... Ps 8:2
revealed them to *b* ... Matt 11:25
'*Out of the mouth of b* ... Matt 21:16
as to carnal, as to *b* ... 1 Cor 3:1
as newborn *b* ... 1 Pet 2:2

**BACK**
for the fool's *b* ... Prov 26:3
I gave My *b* to those ... Is 50:6
plow, and looking *b* ... Luke 9:62
of those who draw *b* ... Heb 10:39
someone turns him *b* ... James 5:19

**BACKBITERS**
*b*, haters of God ... Rom 1:30

**BACKBITING**
*b* tongue an angry ... Prov 25:23

**BACKSLIDER**
The *b* in heart will be ... Prov 14:14

**BACKSLIDINGS**
and I will heal your *b* ... Jer 3:22

**BACKWARD**
shadow ten degrees *b* ... 2 Kin 20:11

**BAD**
*b* tree bears *b* fruit ... Matt 7:17

**BAG**
"nor *b* for your ... Matt 10:10

**BAKED**
*b* unleavened cakes ... Ex 12:39

**BAKER**
the butler and the *b* ... Gen 40:1

**BALANCE**
small dust on the *b* ... Is 40:15

**BALANCES**
falsifying the *b* ... Amos 8:5

**BALD**
every head shall be *b* ... Jer 48:37

**BALDHEAD**
Go up, you *b* ... 2 Kin 2:23

**BALM**
no *b* in Gilead ... Jer 8:22

**BANDAGED**
him and *b* his wounds ... Luke 10:34

**BANKERS**
my money with the *b* ... Matt 25:27

**BANNERS**
we will set up our *b* ... Ps 20:5
as an army with *b* ... Song 6:4

**BANQUET**
*b* that I have prepared ... Esth 5:4

**BANQUETING**
He brought me to the *b* ... Song 2:4

**BAPTISM**
coming to his *b* ... Matt 3:7
*b* that I am baptized ... Matt 20:22
"But I have a *b* ... Luke 12:50
said, "Into John's *b* ... Acts 19:3
Lord, one faith, one *b* ... Eph 4:5
buried with Him in *b* ... Col 2:12

**BAPTISMS**
of the doctrine of *b* ... Heb 6:2

**BAPTIZE**
"I indeed *b* you with ... Matt 3:11
Himself did not *b* ... John 4:2

**BAPTIZED**
*b* will be saved ... Mark 16:16
every one of you be *b* ... Acts 2:38
all his family were *b* ... Acts 16:33
Arise and be *b* ... Acts 22:16
were *b* into Christ ... Rom 6:3
I thank God that I *b* ... 1 Cor 1:14
Spirit we were all *b* ... 1 Cor 12:13

**BAPTIZING**
*b* them in the name of ... Matt 28:19

**BARBARIAN**
nor uncircumcised, *b* ... Col 3:11

**BARLEY**
here who has five *b* ... John 6:9

**BARN**
the wheat into my *b* ... Matt 13:30

**BARNS**
reap nor gather into *b* ... Matt 6:26
I will pull down my *b* ... Luke 12:18

**BARREN**
But Sarai was *b* ... Gen 11:30
"Sing, O *b* ... Is 54:1

**BASE**
and the *b* things of ... 1 Cor 1:28

**BASIN**
poured water into a *b* ... John 13:5

**BASKET**
and put it under a *b* ... Matt 5:15
I was let down in a *b* ... 2 Cor 11:33

**BASKETS**
they took up twelve *b* ... Matt 14:20

**BATHED**
to him, "He who is *b* ... John 13:10

**BATS**
to the moles and *b* ... Is 2:20

**BATTLE**
*b* is the LORD'S ... 1 Sam 17:47
the *b* to the strong ... Eccl 9:11
became valiant in *b* ... Heb 11:34

**BEAR**
greater than I can *b* ... Gen 4:13
whom Sarah shall *b* ... Gen 17:21

not *b* false witness .......... Ex 20:16
*b* their iniquities .......... Is 53:11
*child, and b a Son* .......... Matt 1:23
A good tree cannot *b* .......... Matt 7:18
how long shall I *b* .......... Matt 17:17
by, to *b* His cross .......... Mark 15:21
And whoever does not *b* .......... Luke 14:27
are strong ought to *b* .......... Rom 15:1
*B* one another's .......... Gal 6:2
*b* the sins of many .......... Heb 9:28

**BEARD**
the edges of your *b* .......... Lev 19:27
running down on the *b* .......... Ps 133:2

**BEARING**
goes forth weeping, *b* .......... Ps 126:6
And He, *b* His cross .......... John 19:17
the camp, *b* His reproach .......... Heb 13:13

**BEARS**
Every branch that *b* .......... John 15:2

**BEAST**
You preserve man and *b* .......... Ps 36:6
And I saw a *b* rising .......... Rev 13:1
the mark of the *b* .......... Rev 19:20

**BEASTS**
like brute *b* .......... Jude 10

**BEAT**
*b* their swords into .......... Is 2:4
spat in His face and *b* .......... Matt 26:67

**BEATEN**
Three times I was *b* .......... 2 Cor 11:25

**BEAUTIFUL**
*B* in elevation .......... Ps 48:2
has made everything *b* .......... Eccl 3:11
my love, you are as *b* .......... Song 6:4
How *b* upon the .......... Is 52:7
indeed appear *b* .......... Matt 23:27

**BEAUTIFY**
*b* the place of My .......... Is 60:13

**BEAUTY**
"The *b* of Israel is .......... 2 Sam 1:19
to behold the *b* .......... Ps 27:4
see the King in His *b* .......... Is 33:17
no *b* that we should .......... Is 53:2

**BECAME**
*b* a living being .......... Gen 2:7
to the Jews I *b* .......... 1 Cor 9:20

**BED**
I remember You on my *b* .......... Ps 63:6
if I make my *b* in hell .......... Ps 139:8
"Arise, take up your *b* .......... Matt 9:6
be two men in one *b* .......... Luke 17:34
and the *b* undefiled .......... Heb 13:4

**BEDS**
sing aloud on their *b* .......... Ps 149:5

**BEFOREHAND**
up, do not worry *b* .......... Mark 13:11
told you all things *b* .......... Mark 13:23
when He testified *b* .......... 1 Pet 1:11

**BEG**
*b* you as sojourners .......... 1 Pet 2:11

**BEGAN**
since the world *b* .......... Luke 1:70

**BEGGAR**
there was a certain *b* .......... Luke 16:20

**BEGGARLY**
weak and *b* elements .......... Gal 4:9

**BEGINNING**
*b* God created the .......... Gen 1:1
In the *b* was the Word .......... John 1:1
a murderer from the *b* .......... John 8:44
True Witness, the *B* .......... Rev 3:14
and the Omega, the *B* .......... Rev 21:6

**BEGOTTEN**
I have *b* You .......... Ps 2:7
glory as of the only *b* .......... John 1:14
loves him who is *b* .......... 1 John 5:1

**BEGUILING**
*b* unstable souls .......... 2 Pet 2:14

**BEGUN**
Having *b* in the Spirit .......... Gal 3:3

**BEHALF**
you on Christ's *b* .......... 2 Cor 5:20

**BEHAVE**
does not *b* rudely .......... 1 Cor 13:5

**BEHAVED**
and blamelessly we *b* .......... 1 Thess 2:10

**BEHAVIOR**
of good *b*, hospitable .......... 1 Tim 3:2

**BEHEADED**
he sent and had John *b* .......... Matt 14:10

**BEHOLD**
*B*, the virgin shall .......... Is 7:14
Judah, "*B* your God .......... Is 40:9
*B* the Lamb of God .......... John 1:36
to them, "*B* the Man .......... John 19:5
*B* what manner of love .......... 1 John 3:1

**BEHOLDING**
with unveiled face, *b* .......... 2 Cor 3:18

**BEING**
move and have our *b* .......... Acts 17:28
who, *b* in the form of .......... Phil 2:6

**BELIEVE**
tears, "Lord, I *b* .......... Mark 9:24
have no root, who *b* .......... Luke 8:13
and slow of heart to *b* .......... Luke 24:25
to those who *b* .......... John 1:12
this, that they may *b* .......... John 11:42
written that you may *b* .......... John 20:31
the Lord Jesus and *b* .......... Rom 10:9
Christ, not only to *b* .......... Phil 1:29
comes to God must *b* .......... Heb 11:6
*b* that there is one .......... James 2:19
Even the demons *b* .......... James 2:19

**BELIEVED**
And he *b* in the LORD .......... Gen 15:6
Who has *b* our report .......... Is 53:1
seen Me, you have *b* .......... John 20:29
*"Abraham b God* .......... Rom 4:3
I know whom I have *b* .......... 2 Tim 1:12

**BELIEVERS**
be an example to the *b* .......... 1 Tim 4:12

**BELIEVES**
The simple *b* every .......... Prov 14:15
that whoever *b* in Him .......... John 3:16
"He who *b* in the Son .......... John 3:36
with the heart one *b* .......... Rom 10:10

**BELIEVING**
you ask in prayer, *b* .......... Matt 21:22

**BELLY**
on your *b* you shall go .......... Gen 3:14
And Jonah was in the *b* .......... Jon 1:17
whose god is their *b* .......... Phil 3:19

**BELOVED**
so He gives His *b* .......... Ps 127:2
My *b* is mine .......... Song 2:16
"This is My *b* .......... Matt 3:17
us accepted in the *B* .......... Eph 1:6
Luke the *b* physician .......... Col 4:14
"This is My *b* .......... 2 Pet 1:17

**BELT**
with a leather *b* .......... Matt 3:4

**BEND**
The wicked *b* their bow .......... Ps 11:2

**BENEATH**
"You are from *b* .......... John 8:23

**BENEFACTORS**
them are called '*b* .......... Luke 22:25

**BENEFIT**
might have a second *b* .......... 2 Cor 1:15

**BESEECH**
*b* you therefore .......... Rom 12:1

**BESIDE**
He leads me *b* the .......... Ps 23:2
"Paul, you are *b* .......... Acts 26:24

**BEST**
earnestly desire the *b* .......... 1 Cor 12:31

**BESTOWED**
love the Father has *b* .......... 1 John 3:1

**BETRAY**
you, one of you will *b* .......... Matt 26:21

**BETRAYED**
Man is about to be *b* .......... Matt 17:22

**BETRAYER**
See, My *b* is at .......... Matt 26:46

**BETRAYING**
"Judas, are you *b* .......... Luke 22:48

**BETRAYS**
who is the one who *b* .......... John 21:20

**BETROTH**
"I will *b* you to Me .......... Hos 2:19

**BETROTHED**
to a virgin *b* to a man .......... Luke 1:27

**BETTER**
*b* than sacrifice .......... 1 Sam 15:22
It is *b* to trust in .......... Ps 118:8
For it is *b* to marry .......... 1 Cor 7:9
Christ, which is far *b* .......... Phil 1:23
*b* than the angels .......... Heb 1:4
*b* things concerning .......... Heb 6:9

**BEWARE**
"*B* of false prophets .......... Matt 7:15

**BEWITCHED**
*b* you that you should .......... Gal 3:1

**BEYOND**
advanced in Judaism *b* .......... Gal 1:14

**BILLOWS**
*b* have gone over me .......... Ps 42:7

**BIND**
and whatever you *b* .......... Matt 16:19
*B* him hand and foot .......... Matt 22:13

**BIRD**
soul, "Flee as a *b* .......... Ps 11:1

**BIRDS**
*b* make their nests .......... Ps 104:17
"Look at the *b* .......... Matt 6:26
"Foxes have holes and *b* .......... Matt 8:20

**BIRTH**
the day of one's *b* .......... Eccl 7:1
Now the *b* of Jesus .......... Matt 1:18
will rejoice at his *b* .......... Luke 1:14
conceived, it gives *b* .......... James 1:15

**BIRTHDAY**
which was Pharaoh's *b* .......... Gen 40:20

**BIRTHRIGHT**
Esau despised his *b* .......... Gen 25:34

**BISHOP**
the position of a *b* .......... 1 Tim 3:1
*b* must be blameless ........ Titus 1:7

**BIT**
and they *b* the people ....... Num 21:6

**BITE**
A serpent may *b* .......... Eccl 10:11
But if you *b* and ............ Gal 5:15

**BITTER**
*b* herbs they ................ Ex 12:8
and do not be *b* ............. Col 3:19
But if you have *b* ......... James 3:14

**BITTERLY**
And Hezekiah wept *b* ...... 2 Kin 20:3
he went out and wept *b* .... Matt 26:75

**BITTERNESS**
you are poisoned by *b* ....... Acts 8:23
*b* springing up cause ....... Heb 12:15

**BLACK**
one hair white or *b* ......... Matt 5:36
a *b* horse .................. Rev 6:5
and the sun became *b* ....... Rev 6:12

**BLACKNESS**
whom is reserved the *b* ....... Jude 13

**BLACKSMITH**
I have created the *b* .......... Is 54:16

**BLADE**
first the *b* ............... Mark 4:28

**BLAME**
be holy and without *b* ........ Eph 1:4

**BLAMELESS**
and that man was *b* .......... Job 1:1
body be preserved *b* ...... 1 Thess 5:23

**BLAMELESSLY**
*b* we behaved ........... 1 Thess 2:10

**BLASPHEME**
*b* Your name forever ......... Ps 74:10
compelled them to *b* ....... Acts 26:11
*b* that noble name ......... James 2:7

**BLASPHEMED**
who passed by *b* Him ...... Matt 27:39
great heat, and they *b* ....... Rev 16:9

**BLASPHEMER**
I was formerly a *b* ......... 1 Tim 1:13

**BLASPHEMES**
*b* the name of the LORD .... Lev 24:16
"This Man *b* ............... Matt 9:3

**BLASPHEMIES**
is this who speaks *b* ....... Luke 5:21

**BLASPHEMY**
men, but the *b* against ..... Matt 12:31
was full of names of *b* ....... Rev 17:3

**BLEATING**
"What then is this *b* ..... 1 Sam 15:14

**BLEMISH**
be holy and without *b* ....... Eph 5:27
as of a lamb without *b* ...... 1 Pet 1:19

**BLEMISHED**
to the Lord what is *b* ........ Mal 1:14

**BLESS**
*b* those who *b* you .......... Gen 12:3
You go unless You *b* ........ Gen 32:26
"The LORD *b* you and ...... Num 6:24
*b* the LORD at all ............ Ps 34:1
*b* You while I live ............ Ps 63:4
*b* His holy name ............ Ps 103:1
*b* those who curse ......... Luke 6:28
*B* those who persecute ..... Rom 12:14
Being reviled, we *b* ........ 1 Cor 4:12

**BLESSED**
*B* is the man who walks ........ Ps 1:1
*B* is the man to whom ........ Ps 32:2
*B* is the nation whose ........ Ps 33:12
*B* is he who comes ......... Ps 118:26
rise up and call her *b* ...... Prov 31:28
*B* are the poor in ........... Matt 5:3
*B* are those who mourn ...... Matt 5:4
*B* are the meek ............ Matt 5:5
*B* are those who hunger ...... Matt 5:6
*B* are the merciful .......... Matt 5:7
*B* are the pure in ........... Matt 5:8
*B* are the peacemakers ...... Matt 5:9
*B* are those who are ........ Matt 5:10
*b is He who comes* ......... Matt 21:9
'It is more *b* to give ........ Acts 20:35
*B* be the God and ............ Eph 1:3
*B* are the dead who ........ Rev 14:13

**BLESSING**
and you shall be a *b* ......... Gen 12:2
before you today a *b* ....... Deut 11:26
shall be showers of *b* ...... Ezek 34:26
and you shall be a *b* ........ Zech 8:13
that the *b* of Abraham ....... Gal 3:14
with every spiritual *b* ........ Eph 1:3

**BLIND**
To open *b* eyes ............... Is 42:7
His watchmen are *b* ......... Is 56:10
*b* leads the *b* ............. Matt 15:14
to Him, "Are we *b* ......... John 9:40
miserable, poor, *b* ........... Rev 3:17

**BLINDED**
and the rest were *b* ......... Rom 11:7

**BLINDS**
a bribe, for a bribe *b* ....... Deut 16:19

**BLOOD**
of your brother's *b* .......... Gen 4:10
*b* shall be shed ............. Gen 9:6
*b* that makes atonement .... Lev 17:11
hands are full of *b* ............ Is 1:15
and the moon into *b* ......... Joel 2:31
For this is My *b* .......... Matt 26:28
His *b* be on us and ........ Matt 27:25
new covenant in My *b* .... Luke 22:20
were born, not of *b* ......... John 1:13
*b* has eternal life .......... John 6:54
with His own *b* ........... Acts 20:28
propitiation by His *b* ....... Rom 3:25
justified by His *b* ........... Rom 5:9
through His *b* ............. Eph 1:7
brought near by the *b* ....... Eph 2:13
against flesh and *b* ......... Eph 6:12
peace through the *b* ......... Col 1:20
with the precious *b* ........ 1 Pet 1:19
*b* of Jesus Christ His ....... 1 John 1:7
our sins in His own *b* ......... Rev 1:5
us to God by Your *b* .......... Rev 5:9
them white in the *b* ......... Rev 7:14
overcame him by the *b* ...... Rev 12:11
a robe dipped in *b* ......... Rev 19:13

**BLOODSHED**
Deliver me from the guilt of *b* . Ps 51:14

**BLOODTHIRSTY**
The LORD abhors the *b* ....... Ps 5:6

**BLOSSOM**
and *b* as the rose ............ Is 35:1

**BLOT**
from my sins, and *b* .......... Ps 51:9
and I will not *b* ............. Rev 3:5

**BLOTTED**
your sins may be *b* ......... Acts 3:19

**BLOW**
with a very severe *b* ........ Jer 14:17

**BLOWS**
"The wind *b* where it ........ John 3:8

**BOAST**
puts on his armor *b* ....... 1 Kin 20:11
and make your *b* ........... Rom 2:17
lest anyone should *b* ......... Eph 2:9

**BOASTERS**
God, violent, proud, *b* ....... Rom 1:30

**BOASTING**
Where is *b* then ........... Rom 3:27

**BODIES**
*b* a living sacrifice ......... Rom 12:1
not know that your *b* ....... 1 Cor 6:15
wives as their own *b* ........ Eph 5:28

**BODILY**
*b* form like a dove ......... Luke 3:22
of the Godhead *b* ............ Col 2:9

**BODY**
of the *b* is the eye .......... Matt 6:22
those who kill the *b* ....... Matt 10:28
this is My *b* ............. Matt 26:26
of the temple of His *b* ....... John 2:21
deliver me from this *b* ...... Rom 7:24
redemption of our *b* ........ Rom 8:23
many members in one *b* ..... Rom 12:4
But I discipline my *b* ....... 1 Cor 9:27
*b* which is broken ........ 1 Cor 11:24
baptized into one *b* ....... 1 Cor 12:13
are the *b* of Christ ........ 1 Cor 12:27
though I give my *b* ........ 1 Cor 13:3
It is sown a natural *b* ..... 1 Cor 15:44
in the *b* of His flesh ......... Col 1:22
our sins in His own *b* ...... 1 Pet 2:24

**BOILS**
Job with painful *b* ........... Job 2:7

**BOLDLY**
therefore come *b* ........... Heb 4:16

**BOLDNESS**
in whom we have *b* ......... Eph 3:12
that we may have *b* ...... 1 John 4:17

**BOND**
love, which is the *b* .......... Col 3:14

**BONDAGE**
out of the house of *b* ........ Ex 13:14
again with a yoke of *b* ........ Gal 5:1

**BONDS**
"Let us break Their *b* ......... Ps 2:3

**BONDSERVANTS**
*B*, be obedient to ............ Eph 6:5
Masters, give your *b* .......... Col 4:1

**BONDWOMAN**
the one by a *b* .............. Gal 4:22

**BONE**
*b* clings to my skin ......... Job 19:20

**BONES**
I can count all My *b* ......... Ps 22:17
and my *b* waste away ....... Ps 31:10
I kept silent, my *b* ........... Ps 32:3
the wind, or how the *b* ....... Eccl 11:5
say to them, 'O dry *b* ...... Ezek 37:4
of dead men's *b* ........... Matt 23:27
*b shall be broken* ......... John 19:36

**BOOK**
*are written in the b* ......... Gal 3:10
in the Lamb's *B* ........... Rev 21:27
the prophecy of this *b* ...... Rev 22:18

**BOOKS**
b there is no end .......... Eccl 12:12
not contain the b .......... John 21:25
God, and b were opened .......... Rev 20:12

**BOOTH**
of Zion is left as a b .......... Is 1:8

**BORDERS**
and enlarge the b .......... Matt 23:5

**BORE**
and to Sarah who b .......... Is 51:2
b the sin of many .......... Is 53:12
*b our sicknesses* .......... Matt 8:17
who Himself b our sins .......... 1 Pet 2:24
b a male Child who was .......... Rev 12:5

**BORN**
A time to be b .......... Eccl 3:2
unto us a Child is b .......... Is 9:6
b Jesus who is called .......... Matt 1:16
unless one is b again .......... John 3:3
"That which is b .......... John 3:6
having been b again .......... 1 Pet 1:23
who loves is b of God .......... 1 John 4:7

**BORROWER**
b is servant to the .......... Prov 22:7

**BORROWS**
The wicked b and does .......... Ps 37:21

**BOSOM**
angels to Abraham's b .......... Luke 16:22
Son, who is in the b .......... John 1:18

**BOTTOMLESS**
ascend out of the b .......... Rev 17:8
the key to the b .......... Rev 20:1

**BOUGHT**
b the threshing floor .......... 2 Sam 24:24
all that he had and b .......... Matt 13:46
For you were b at a .......... 1 Cor 6:20
denying the Lord who b .......... 2 Pet 2:1

**BOUND**
on earth will be b .......... Matt 16:19
And see, now I go b .......... Acts 20:22
who has a husband is b .......... Rom 7:2
Are you b to a wife .......... 1 Cor 7:27
Devil and Satan, and b .......... Rev 20:2

**BOUNTIFULLY**
and he who sows b .......... 2 Cor 9:6

**BOW**
"You shall not b .......... Ex 23:24
let us worship and b .......... Ps 95:6
who sat on it had a b .......... Rev 6:2

**BOWED**
stood all around and b .......... Gen 37:7
And they b the knee .......... Matt 27:29

**BOWL**
and poured out his b .......... Rev 16:2

**BOWLS**
Go and pour out the b .......... Rev 16:1

**BOX**
Judas had the money b .......... John 13:29

**BOYS**
shall be full of b .......... Zech 8:5

**BRAIDED**
not with b hair or .......... 1 Tim 2:9

**BRANCH**
raise to David a B .......... Jer 23:5
forth My Servant the B .......... Zech 3:8
b that bears fruit He .......... John 15:2

**BRANCHES**
vine, you are the b .......... John 15:5

**BRASS**
become sounding b .......... 1 Cor 13:1

**BRAVE**
in the faith, be b .......... 1 Cor 16:13

**BREAD**
of Salem brought out b .......... Gen 14:18
shall eat unleavened b .......... Ex 23:15
not live by b alone .......... Deut 8:3
b eaten in secret is .......... Prov 9:17
B gained by deceit is .......... Prov 20:17
Cast your b upon the .......... Eccl 11:1
for what is not b .......... Is 55:2
these stones become b .......... Matt 4:3
*not live by b alone* .......... Matt 4:4
this day our daily b .......... Matt 6:11
eating, Jesus took b .......... Matt 26:26
"I am the b of life .......... John 6:48
He was betrayed took b .......... 1 Cor 11:23

**BREADTH**
is as great as its b .......... Rev 21:16

**BREAK**
covenant I will not b .......... Ps 89:34
together to b bread .......... Acts 20:7

**BREAKING**
in the b of bread .......... Acts 2:42
b bread from house to .......... Acts 2:46

**BREAKS**
Until the day b .......... Song 2:17

**BREAST**
back on Jesus' b .......... John 13:25

**BREASTPLATE**
righteousness as a b .......... Is 59:17
having put on the b .......... Eph 6:14

**BREASTS**
Your two b are like .......... Song 4:5
b which nursed You .......... Luke 11:27

**BREATH**
nostrils the b of life .......... Gen 2:7
that there was no b .......... 1 Kin 17:17
Man is like a b .......... Ps 144:4
everything that has b .......... Ps 150:6
Surely I will cause b .......... Ezek 37:5
gives to all life, b .......... Acts 17:25
power to give b .......... Rev 13:15

**BREATHES**
indeed he b his last .......... Job 14:10

**BRETHREN**
and you are all b .......... Matt 23:8
least of these My b .......... Matt 25:40
firstborn among many b .......... Rom 8:29
thus sin against the b .......... 1 Cor 8:12
over five hundred b .......... 1 Cor 15:6
perils among false b .......... 2 Cor 11:26
sincere love of the b .......... 1 Pet 1:22
because we love the b .......... 1 John 3:14
our lives for the b .......... 1 John 3:16

**BRIBE**
you shall take no b .......... Ex 23:8
b blinds the eyes .......... Deut 16:19

**BRIBES**
hand is full of b .......... Ps 26:10

**BRICK**
people straw to make b .......... Ex 5:7

**BRICKS**
"Come, let us make b .......... Gen 11:3

**BRIDE**
I will show you the b .......... Rev 21:9
the Spirit and the b .......... Rev 22:17

**BRIDEGROOM**
and as the b rejoices .......... Is 62:5
mourn as long as the b .......... Matt 9:15
went out to meet the b .......... Matt 25:1
the friend of the b .......... John 3:29

**BRIDLE**
b the whole body .......... James 3:2

**BRIER**
b shall come up the .......... Is 55:13

**BRIERS**
there shall come up b .......... Is 5:6

**BRIGHTER**
a light from heaven, b .......... Acts 26:13

**BRIGHTNESS**
and kings to the b .......... Is 60:3
who being the b .......... Heb 1:3

**BRIMSTONE**
the lake of fire and b .......... Rev 20:10

**BRING**
b back his soul .......... Job 33:30
b My righteousness .......... Is 46:13
Who shall b a charge .......... Rom 8:33
b Christ down from .......... Rom 10:6
even so God will b .......... 1 Thess 4:14

**BROAD**
b is the way that .......... Matt 7:13

**BROKE**
b them at the foot of .......... Ex 32:19
He blessed and b .......... Matt 14:19
b the legs of the .......... John 19:32

**BROKEN**
this stone will be b .......... Matt 21:44
Scripture cannot be b .......... John 10:35
is My body which is b .......... 1 Cor 11:24

**BROKENHEARTED**
He heals the b and .......... Ps 147:3

**BRONZE**
So Moses made a b .......... Num 21:9
b walls against the .......... Jer 1:18
a third kingdom of b .......... Dan 2:39

**BROOD**
"B of vipers .......... Matt 12:34
as a hen gathers her b .......... Luke 13:34

**BROOK**
disciples over the B .......... John 18:1

**BROOKS**
for the water b .......... Ps 42:1

**BROTHER**
"Where is Abel your b .......... Gen 4:9
b offended is harder .......... Prov 18:19
b will deliver up .......... Matt 10:21
how often shall my b .......... Matt 18:21
b will rise again .......... John 11:23
b goes to law against .......... 1 Cor 6:6
Whoever hates his b .......... 1 John 3:15

**BROTHER'S**
Am I my b keeper .......... Gen 4:9
at the speck in your b .......... Matt 7:3

**BROTHERHOOD**
Love the b .......... 1 Pet 2:17

**BROTHERLY**
b love continue .......... Heb 13:1

**BROTHERS**
is My mother, or My b .......... Mark 3:33
b are these who hear .......... Luke 8:21

**BRUISE**
He shall b your head .......... Gen 3:15
the LORD to b Him .......... Is 53:10

**BRUISED**
He was b for our .......... Is 53:5
*b reed He will not* .......... Matt 12:20

**BUCKLER**
be your shield and b .......... Ps 91:4

**BUFFET**
of Satan to *b* me. . . . . . . . . . .2 Cor 12:7
**BUILD**
*b* ourselves a city . . . . . . . . . .Gen 11:4
"Would you *b* a house. . . . . . .2 Sam 7:5
labor in vain who *b* . . . . . . . . .Ps 127:1
down, and a time to *b* . . . . . . . .Eccl 3:3
'This man began to *b* . . . . .Luke 14:30
*What house will you b* . . . . . .Acts 7:49
"For if I *b* again . . . . . . . . . . .Gal 2:18
**BUILDER**
foundations, whose *b*. . . . . . .Heb 11:10
**BUILDING**
in whom the whole *b*. . . . . . . .Eph 2:21
**BUILDS**
one take heed how he *b* . . . . .1 Cor 3:10
**BUILT**
Wisdom has *b* her house . . . . .Prov 9:1
to a wise man who *b* . . . . . . .Matt 7:24
having been *b* on the. . . . . . . .Eph 2:20
**BULLS**
For if the blood of *b* . . . . . . . . .Heb 9:13
**BULWARKS**
Mark well her *b* . . . . . . . . . . . .Ps 48:13
**BUNDLE**
each man's *b* of money . . . . .Gen 42:35
**BURDEN**
Cast your *b* on the . . . . . . . . . .Ps 55:22
easy and My *b* is light . . . . .Matt 11:30
we might not be a *b* . . . . . . .1 Thess 2:9
on you no other *b* . . . . . . . . . . .Rev 2:24
**BURDENS**
For they bind heavy *b* . . . . . .Matt 23:4
Bear one another's *b* . . . . . . . . .Gal 6:2
**BURDENSOME**
I myself was not *b* . . . . . . . .2 Cor 12:13
commandments are not *b* . . .1 John 5:3
**BURIAL**
she did it for My *b* . . . . . . .Matt 26:12
for the day of My *b* . . . . . . . . .John 12:7
**BURIED**
Therefore we were *b* . . . . . . . . .Rom 6:4
and that He was *b* . . . . . . . . .1 Cor 15:4
*b* with Him in baptism. . . . . . .Col 2:12
**BURN**
the bush does not *b* . . . . . . . . . . .Ex 3:3
"Did not our heart *b* . . . . . .Luke 24:32
**BURNED**
If anyone's work is *b* . . . . . . .1 Cor 3:15
I give my body to be *b* . . . . . .1 Cor 13:3
**BURNING**
*b* torch that passed . . . . . . . .Gen 15:17
*b* fire shut up in my . . . . . . . . .Jer 20:9
plucked from the *b* . . . . . . . .Amos 4:11
**BURNT**
lamb for a *b* offering . . . . . . . .Gen 22:7
delight in *b* offering. . . . . . . . .Ps 51:16
**BURST**
the new wine will *b* . . . . . . . .Luke 5:37
**BURY**
and let the dead *b* . . . . . . . . .Matt 8:22
**BUSH**
from the midst of a *b* . . . . . . . . . .Ex 3:2
**BUSINESS**
about My Father's *b* . . . . . . .Luke 2:49
**BUSYBODIES**
at all, but are *b* . . . . . . . . .2 Thess 3:11
**BUTLER**
*b* did not remember. . . . . . . .Gen 40:23
**BUTTER**
were smoother than *b* . . . . . . .Ps 55:21
**BUY**
Yes, come, *b* wine and. . . . . . . . .Is 55:1
"I counsel you to *b* . . . . . . . . . .Rev 3:18
and that no one may *b* . . . . . .Rev 13:17
**BUYS**
has and *b* that field . . . . . . .Matt 13:44
**BYWORD**
But He has made me a *b* . . . . .Job 17:6

## C

**CAGE**
foul spirit, and a *c* . . . . . . . . . .Rev 18:2
**CAKE**
Ephraim is a *c* . . . . . . . . . . . . . .Hos 7:8
**CAKES**
and love the raisin *c*. . . . . . . . . .Hos 3:1
**CALAMITY**
will laugh at your *c* . . . . . . . .Prov 1:26
**CALCULATED**
*c* the dust of the. . . . . . . . . . . . .Is 40:12
**CALDRON**
this city is the *c* . . . . . . . . . . .Ezek 11:3
**CALF**
and made a molded *c*. . . . . . . . .Ex 32:4
And bring the fatted *c*. . . . .Luke 15:23
**CALL**
*c* upon Him while He . . . . . . . . .Is 55:6
*c* His name JESUS. . . . . . . . .Matt 1:21
*c* the righteous . . . . . . . . . . .Matt 9:13
Lord our God will *c* . . . . . . . .Acts 2:39
*c them My people*. . . . . . . . . .Rom 9:25
*c* and election sure . . . . . . . .2 Pet 1:10
**CALLED**
*c* the light Day. . . . . . . . . . . . . .Gen 1:5
*c* his wife's name Eve . . . . . . .Gen 3:20
I have *c* you by your . . . . . . . . . .Is 43:1
*"Out of Egypt I c* . . . . . . . . . .Matt 2:15
city *c* Nazareth . . . . . . . . . . .Matt 2:23
For many are *c*. . . . . . . . . . .Matt 20:16
to those who are the *c*. . . . . . .Rom 8:28
these He also *c* . . . . . . . . . . . .Rom 8:30
*c* children of God . . . . . . . . . .1 John 3:1
**CALLING**
the gifts and the *c*. . . . . . . . .Rom 11:29
For you see your *c* . . . . . . . . .1 Cor 1:26
remain in the same *c*. . . . . . .1 Cor 7:20
**CALLS**
*c* them all by name. . . . . . . . . .Ps 147:4
David himself *c*. . . . . . . . . .Mark 12:37
*c* his own sheep . . . . . . . . . . .John 10:3
**CALM**
there was a great *c*. . . . . . . . .Matt 8:26
**CAMEL**
it is easier for a *c* . . . . . . . . .Matt 19:24
**CAMP**
to Him, outside the *c*. . . . . . .Heb 13:13
**CAN**
I *c* do all things . . . . . . . . . . . .Phil 4:13
**CANCER**
will spread like *c* . . . . . . . . .2 Tim 2:17
**CANOPY**
His *c* around Him was . . . . . . .Ps 18:11
**CAPSTONE**
bring forth the *c*. . . . . . . . . . . .Zech 4:7
**CAPTAIN**
which, having no *c*. . . . . . . . . .Prov 6:7
**CAPTIVE**
and be led away *c*. . . . . . . . .Luke 21:24
*He led captivity c* . . . . . . . . . . .Eph 4:8
**CAPTIVES**
households and make *c* . . . . .2 Tim 3:6
**CAPTIVITY**
every thought into *c* . . . . . . .2 Cor 10:5
**CARCASS**
For wherever the *c* . . . . . . . .Matt 24:28
**CARE**
"Lord, do You not *c* . . . . . . .Luke 10:40
how will he take *c*. . . . . . . . . .1 Tim 3:5
**CARED**
he said, not that he *c* . . . . . . .John 12:6
**CAREFULLY**
I shall walk *c* all my . . . . . . . . .Is 38:15
**CARELESS**
but he who is *c* . . . . . . . . . . .Prov 19:16
**CARES**
no one *c* for my soul . . . . . . . . .Ps 142:4
for He *c* for you. . . . . . . . . . . . .1 Pet 5:7
**CARNAL**
*c* mind is enmity. . . . . . . . . . . .Rom 8:7
**CARNALLY**
*c* minded is death . . . . . . . . . . .Rom 8:6
**CAROUSE**
count it pleasure to *c* . . . . . . .2 Pet 2:13
**CARPENTER**
"Is this not the *c* . . . . . . . . . . .Mark 6:3
**CARRIED**
and *c* our sorrows . . . . . . . . . . . .Is 53:4
**CARRY**
for you to *c* your bed. . . . . . . .John 5:10
it is certain we can *c*. . . . . . . . .1 Tim 6:7
**CARRYING**
a man will meet you *c*. . . . .Mark 14:13
**CASE**
Festus laid Paul's *c*. . . . . . . .Acts 25:14
**CASSIA**
myrrh and aloes and *c*. . . . . . . .Ps 45:8
**CAST**
Why are you *c* down. . . . . . . . . .Ps 42:5
whole body to be *c* . . . . . . . . .Matt 5:29
In My name they will *c*. . . .Mark 16:17
by no means *c* out. . . . . . . . . .John 6:37
*c* their crowns before . . . . . . . .Rev 4:10
the great dragon was *c*. . . . . . .Rev 12:9
**CASTING**
*c* down arguments. . . . . . . . .2 Cor 10:5
*c* all your care . . . . . . . . . . . . .1 Pet 5:7
**CASTS**
perfect love *c* out . . . . . . . . .1 John 4:18
**CATCH**
*c* Him in His words. . . . . . .Mark 12:13
From now on you will *c* . . . . .Luke 5:10
**CATCHES**
and the wolf *c* the. . . . . . . . .John 10:12
*c the wise in their* . . . . . . . . .1 Cor 3:19
**CAUGHT**
behind him was a ram *c* . . . .Gen 22:13
her Child was *c* up . . . . . . . . . .Rev 12:5
**CAUSE**
*hated Me without a c* . . . . . .John 15:25
For this *c* I was born. . . . . . .John 18:37
**CAVES**
in dens and *c* of the . . . . . . . .Heb 11:38
**CEASE**
and night shall not *c*. . . . . . . .Gen 8:22

He makes wars *c* ... Ps 46:9
tongues, they will *c* ... 1 Cor 13:8

**CEASING**
pray without *c* ... 1 Thess 5:17

**CEDAR**
dwell in a house of *c* ... 2 Sam 7:2

**CEDARS**
the LORD breaks the *c* ... Ps 29:5

**CELESTIAL**
but the glory of the *c* ... 1 Cor 15:40

**CENSER**
Aaron, each took his *c* ... Lev 10:1

**CERTAINTY**
you may know the *c* ... Luke 1:4

**CERTIFICATE**
a man to write a *c* ... Mark 10:4

**CHAFF**
be chased like the *c* ... Is 17:13
He will burn up the *c* ... Matt 3:12

**CHAIN**
pit and a great *c* ... Rev 20:1

**CHAINED**
of God is not *c* ... 2 Tim 2:9

**CHAINS**
And his *c* fell off ... Acts 12:7
am, except for these *c* ... Acts 26:29

**CHAMBERS**
brought me into his *c* ... Song 1:4

**CHAMPION**
And a *c* went out from ... 1 Sam 17:4

**CHANGE**
now and to *c* my tone ... Gal 4:20
there is also a *c* ... Heb 7:12

**CHANGED**
*c* the glory of the ... Rom 1:23
but we shall all be *c* ... 1 Cor 15:51

**CHANGERS'**
and poured out the *c* ... John 2:15

**CHANGES**
*c* the times and the ... Dan 2:21

**CHANNELS**
*c* of the sea were seen ... Ps 18:15

**CHARIOT**
that suddenly a *c* ... 2 Kin 2:11

**CHARIOTS**
Some trust in *c* ... Ps 20:7

**CHARITABLE**
you do not do your *c* ... Matt 6:1
*c* deeds which she ... Acts 9:36

**CHARM**
*C* is deceitful and ... Prov 31:30

**CHARMS**
women who sew magic *c* ... Ezek 13:18

**CHASE**
Five of you shall *c* ... Lev 26:8

**CHASTE**
may present you as a *c* ... 2 Cor 11:2

**CHASTEN**
a father does not *c* ... Heb 12:7
I love, I rebuke and *c* ... Rev 3:19

**CHASTENED**
*c* us as seemed best ... Heb 12:10

**CHASTENING**
do not despise the *c* ... Job 5:17
Now no *c* seems to be ... Heb 12:11

**CHASTENS**
*the LORD loves He c* ... Heb 12:6

**CHASTISEMENT**
the *c* for our peace ... Is 53:5

**CHATTER**
*c* leads only to ... Prov 14:23

**CHEAT**
Beware lest anyone *c* ... Col 2:8

**CHEATED**
let yourselves be *c* ... 1 Cor 6:7

**CHEEK**
on your right *c* ... Matt 5:39

**CHEEKBONE**
my enemies on the *c* ... Ps 3:7

**CHEEKS**
His *c* are like a bed ... Song 5:13

**CHEER**
"Son, be of good *c* ... Matt 9:2

**CHEERFUL**
for God loves a *c* ... 2 Cor 9:7

**CHEERFULNESS**
shows mercy, with *c* ... Rom 12:8

**CHEESE**
and curdle me like *c* ... Job 10:10

**CHERISHES**
but nourishes and *c* ... Eph 5:29

**CHERUBIM**
above it were the *c* ... Heb 9:5

**CHIEF**
of whom I am *c* ... 1 Tim 1:15
*Zion a c cornerstone* ... 1 Pet 2:6

**CHILD**
Train up a *c* in the ... Prov 22:6
For unto us a *C* ... Is 9:6
*virgin shall be with c* ... Matt 1:23
of God as a little *c* ... Mark 10:15
So the *c* grew and ... Luke 1:80
When I was a *c* ... 1 Cor 13:11
She bore a male *C* ... Rev 12:5

**CHILDBEARING**
she will be saved in *c* ... 1 Tim 2:15

**CHILDBIRTH**
pain as a woman in *c* ... Is 13:8

**CHILDHOOD**
*c* you have known ... 2 Tim 3:15

**CHILDLESS**
give me, seeing I go *c* ... Gen 15:2
this man down as *c* ... Jer 22:30

**CHILDREN**
*c* are a heritage ... Ps 127:3
*c* rise up and call her ... Prov 31:28
and become as little *c* ... Matt 18:3
"Let the little *c* ... Matt 19:14
the right to become *c* ... John 1:12
now we are *c* of God ... 1 John 3:2

**CHOOSE**
therefore *c* life ... Deut 30:19
"You did not *c* ... John 15:16

**CHOSE**
just as He *c* us in Him ... Eph 1:4

**CHOSEN**
servant whom I have *c* ... Is 43:10
I know whom I have *c* ... John 13:18
*c* the foolish things ... 1 Cor 1:27
Has God not *c* the poor ... James 2:5

**CHRIST**
Jesus who is called *C* ... Matt 1:16
"You are the *C* ... Matt 16:16
a Savior, who is *C* ... Luke 2:11
It is *C* who died ... Rom 8:34
to be justified by *C* ... Gal 2:17
been crucified with *C* ... Gal 2:20
*C* is head of the ... Eph 5:23
to me, to live is *C* ... Phil 1:21
which is *C* in you ... Col 1:27
*C* who is our ... Col 3:4
Jesus *C* is the same ... Heb 13:8
*C* His Son cleanses us ... 1 John 1:7
that Jesus is the *C* ... 1 John 5:1

**CHRISTIAN**
anyone suffers as a *C* ... 1 Pet 4:16

**CHRISTIANS**
were first called *C* ... Acts 11:26

**CHRISTS**
"For false *c* and ... Matt 24:24

**CHURCH**
rock I will build My *c* ... Matt 16:18
*c* daily those who were ... Acts 2:47
Himself a glorious *c* ... Eph 5:27
as the Lord does the *c* ... Eph 5:29
body, which is the *c* ... Col 1:24
general assembly and *c* ... Heb 12:23

**CHURCHES**
these things in the *c* ... Rev 22:16

**CIRCLE**
who sits above the *c* ... Is 40:22

**CIRCUMCISE**
is necessary to *c* them ... Acts 15:5

**CIRCUMCISED**
among you shall be *c* ... Gen 17:10
who will justify the *c* ... Rom 3:30
if you become *c* ... Gal 5:2

**CIRCUMCISION**
*c* is that of the heart ... Rom 2:29
*C* is nothing and ... 1 Cor 7:19
Christ Jesus neither *c* ... Gal 5:6

**CIRCUMSPECTLY**
then that you walk *c* ... Eph 5:15

**CISTERN**
from your own *c* ... Prov 5:15

**CITIES**
He overthrew those *c* ... Gen 19:25
three parts, and the *c* ... Rev 16:19

**CITIZEN**
But I was born a *c* ... Acts 22:28

**CITIZENS**
but fellow *c* with the ... Eph 2:19

**CITIZENSHIP**
For our *c* is in heaven ... Phil 3:20

**CITY**
shall make glad the *c* ... Ps 46:4
*c* has become a harlot ... Is 1:21
How lonely sits the *c* ... Lam 1:1
*c* that is set on a ... Matt 5:14
He has prepared a *c* ... Heb 11:16
have no continuing *c* ... Heb 13:14
John, saw the holy *c* ... Rev 21:2

**CLAP**
of the field shall *c* ... Is 55:12

**CLAY**
pit, out of the miry *c* ... Ps 40:2
we are the *c* ... Is 64:8
blind man with the *c* ... John 9:6
have power over the *c* ... Rom 9:21

**CLEAN**
He who has *c* hands and ... Ps 24:4
make yourselves *c* ... Is 1:16
*c* out His threshing floor ... Matt 3:12
You can make me *c* ... Matt 8:2
"You are not all *c* ... John 13:11
"You are already *c* ... John 15:3

**CLEANSE**
*C* me from secret . . . Ps 19:12
and *c* me from my sin . . . Ps 51:2
How can a young man *c* . . . Ps 119:9
might sanctify and *c* . . . Eph 5:26
us our sins and to *c* . . . 1 John 1:9

**CLEANSED**
Were there not ten *c* . . . Luke 17:17

**CLEANSES**
Jesus Christ His Son *c* . . . 1 John 1:7

**CLEAR**
of life, *c* as crystal . . . Rev 22:1

**CLIFF**
secret places of the *c* . . . Song 2:14

**CLIMBS**
*c* up some other way . . . John 10:1

**CLING**
*C* to what is good . . . Rom 12:9

**CLINGS**
and My tongue *c* . . . Ps 22:15

**CLOAK**
let him have your *c* . . . Matt 5:40
using liberty as a *c* . . . 1 Pet 2:16

**CLODS**
The *c* of the valley . . . Job 21:33

**CLOSE**
*c* friends abhor me . . . Job 19:19

**CLOSED**
the deep *c* around me . . . Jon 2:5

**CLOTH**
a piece of unshrunk *c* . . . Matt 9:16

**CLOTHE**
He not much more *c* . . . Matt 6:30

**CLOTHED**
of skin, and *c* them . . . Gen 3:21
A man *c* in soft . . . Matt 11:8
I was naked and you *c* . . . Matt 25:36
legion, sitting and *c* . . . Mark 5:15
desiring to be *c* . . . 2 Cor 5:2
that you may be *c* . . . Rev 3:18

**CLOTHES**
*c* became shining . . . Mark 9:3
many spread their *c* . . . Luke 19:36
a poor man in filthy *c* . . . James 2:2

**CLOTHING**
*c* they cast lots . . . Ps 22:18
do you worry about *c* . . . Matt 6:28
to you in sheep's *c* . . . Matt 7:15
*c they cast lots* . . . John 19:24

**CLOTHS**
wrapped in swaddling *c* . . . Luke 2:12

**CLOUD**
My rainbow in the *c* . . . Gen 9:13
day in a pillar of *c* . . . Ex 13:21
He led them with the *c* . . . Ps 78:14
behold, a bright *c* . . . Matt 17:5
of Man coming in a *c* . . . Luke 21:27
*c* received Him out of . . . Acts 1:9
by so great a *c* . . . Heb 12:1

**CLOUDS**
of Man coming on the *c* . . . Matt 24:30
with them in the *c* . . . 1 Thess 4:17
are *c* without water . . . Jude 12
He is coming with *c* . . . Rev 1:7

**CLOUDY**
them by day with a *c* . . . Neh 9:12

**CLOVEN**
chew the cud or have *c* . . . Deut 14:7

**CLUSTER**
beloved is to me a *c* . . . Song 1:14

**COAL**
in his hand a live *c* . . . Is 6:6

**COALS**
*doing you will heap c* . . . Rom 12:20

**COBRA**
the lion and the *c* . . . Ps 91:13

**COBRA'S**
shall play by the *c* . . . Is 11:8

**COFFIN**
and he was put in a *c* . . . Gen 50:26
and touched the open *c* . . . Luke 7:14

**COIN**
if she loses one *c* . . . Luke 15:8

**COLD**
and harvest, *c* and . . . Gen 8:22
of many will grow *c* . . . Matt 24:12
that you are neither *c* . . . Rev 3:15

**COLLECTION**
concerning the *c* . . . 1 Cor 16:1

**COLT**
on a donkey, a *c* . . . Zech 9:9
*on a donkey, a c* . . . Matt 21:5

**COME**
He will *c* and save you . . . Is 35:4
who have no money, *c* . . . Is 55:1
Your kingdom *c* . . . Matt 6:10
"*C* to Me . . . Matt 11:28
"I have *c* in My . . . John 5:43
thirsts, let him *c* . . . John 7:37
*c* as a light into the . . . John 12:46
O Lord, *c* . . . 1 Cor 16:22
the door, I will *c* . . . Rev 3:20

**COMELINESS**
He has no form or *c* . . . Is 53:2

**COMES**
Lord's death till He *c* . . . 1 Cor 11:26

**COMFORT**
and Your staff, they *c* . . . Ps 23:4
yes, *c* My people . . . Is 40:1
*c* each other and edify . . . 1 Thess 5:11

**COMFORTED**
So Isaac was *c* after . . . Gen 24:67
refusing to be *c* . . . Jer 31:15

**COMFORTER**
she had no *c* . . . Lam 1:9

**COMFORTS**
I, even I, am He who *c* . . . Is 51:12

**COMING**
see the Son of Man *c* . . . Mark 13:26
mightier than I is *c* . . . Luke 3:16
are Christ's at His *c* . . . 1 Cor 15:23
Behold, I am *c* . . . Rev 3:11
"Surely I am *c* . . . Rev 22:20

**COMMAND**
*c* I have received . . . John 10:18
And I know that His *c* . . . John 12:50
if you do whatever I *c* . . . John 15:14

**COMMANDED**
not endure what was *c* . . . Heb 12:20

**COMMANDMENT**
*c* of the LORD is pure . . . Ps 19:8
which is the great *c* . . . Matt 22:36
"A new *c* I give to . . . John 13:34
which is the first *c* . . . Eph 6:2
And this is His *c* . . . 1 John 3:23

**COMMANDMENTS**
covenant, the Ten *C* . . . Ex 34:28
*as doctrines the c* . . . Matt 15:9
*c* hang all the Law . . . Matt 22:40
"He who has My *c* . . . John 14:21

**COMMANDS**
with authority He *c* . . . Mark 1:27

**COMMEND**
But food does not *c* . . . 1 Cor 8:8

**COMMENDABLE**
patiently, this is *c* . . . 1 Pet 2:20

**COMMENDED**
*c* the unjust steward . . . Luke 16:8

**COMMENDS**
but whom the Lord *c* . . . 2 Cor 10:18

**COMMIT**
"You shall not *c* . . . Ex 20:14
*into Your hands I c* . . . Luke 23:46

**COMMITS**
sin also *c* lawlessness . . . 1 John 3:4

**COMMITTED**
*c* Himself to Him who . . . 1 Pet 2:23

**COMMON**
*c* people heard Him . . . Mark 12:37
had all things in *c* . . . Acts 2:44
concerning our *c* . . . Jude 3

**COMMOTION**
there arose a great *c* . . . Acts 19:23

**COMMUNED**
I *c* with my heart . . . Eccl 1:16

**COMMUNION**
*c* of the Holy Spirit . . . 2 Cor 13:14

**COMPANION**
a man my equal, My *c* . . . Ps 55:13

**COMPANIONS**
while you became *c* . . . Heb 10:33

**COMPANY**
great was the *c* . . . Ps 68:11
to an innumerable *c* . . . Heb 12:22

**COMPARE**
*c* ourselves with those . . . 2 Cor 10:12

**COMPARED**
are not worthy to be *c* . . . Rom 8:18

**COMPASSION**
are a God full of *c* . . . Ps 86:15
He was moved with *c* . . . Matt 9:36
*whomever I will have c* . . . Rom 9:15
He can have *c* on those . . . Heb 5:2

**COMPASSIONATE**
the Lord is very *c* . . . James 5:11

**COMPASSIONS**
because His *c* fail not . . . Lam 3:22

**COMPEL**
*c* them to come in . . . Luke 14:23

**COMPELS**
the love of Christ *c* . . . 2 Cor 5:14

**COMPLAINED**
as some of them also *c* . . . 1 Cor 10:10

**COMPLAINERS**
These are grumblers, *c* . . . Jude 16

**COMPLAINING**
all things without *c* . . . Phil 2:14

**COMPLAINT**
for the LORD has a *c* . . . Mic 6:2

**COMPLETE**
work in you will *c* ........ Phil 1:6
and you are *c* in Him ........ Col 2:10
of God may be *c*. ........ 2 Tim 3:17

**COMPLETELY**
Himself sanctify you *c*. ... 1 Thess 5:23

**COMPOSED**
But God *c* the body ........ 1 Cor 12:24

**COMPREHEND**
which we cannot *c* ........ Job 37:5
the darkness did not *c* ........ John 1:5

**CONCEAL**
of God to *c* a matter ........ Prov 25:2

**CONCEALED**
than love carefully *c* ........ Prov 27:5

**CONCEIT**
selfish ambition or *c* ........ Phil 2:3

**CONCEITED**
Let us not become *c* ........ Gal 5:26

**CONCEIVE**
the virgin shall *c* ........ Is 7:14
And behold, you will *c* ..... Luke 1:31

**CONCEIVED**
in sin my mother *c* ........ Ps 51:5

**CONCERN**
Neither do I *c* myself ........ Ps 131:1

**CONCERNED**
Is it oxen God is *c*. ........ 1 Cor 9:9

**CONCESSION**
But I say this as a *c* ........ 1 Cor 7:6

**CONCLUSION**
Let us hear the *c* ........ Eccl 12:13

**CONDEMN**
world to *c* the world ........ John 3:17

**CONDEMNATION**
can you escape the *c*. ....... Matt 23:33
And this is the *c* ........ John 3:19
Their *c* is just ........ Rom 3:8
therefore now no *c*. ........ Rom 8:1

**CONDEMNED**
does not believe is *c* ........ John 3:18
*c* sin in the flesh ........ Rom 8:3

**CONDEMNS**
Who is he who *c* ........ Rom 8:34

**CONDUCT**
from your aimless *c* ........ 1 Pet 1:8
may be won by the *c*. ........ 1 Pet 3:1

**CONFESS**
*c* my transgressions. ........ Ps 32:5
that if you *c* with ........ Rom 10:9
*every tongue shall c* ........ Rom 14:11
If we *c* our sins. ........ 1 John 1:9

**CONFESSED**
*c* that He was Christ ........ John 9:22

**CONFESSES**
*c* that Jesus is the ........ 1 John 4:15

**CONFESSION**
with the mouth *c* ........ Rom 10:10
High Priest of our *c*. ........ Heb 3:1
let us hold fast our *c* ........ Heb 4:14

**CONFIDENCE**
*c* shall be your. ........ Is 30:15
Jesus, and have no *c* ........ Phil 3:3

**CONFINED**
the Scripture has *c*. ........ Gal 3:22

**CONFIRM**
who will also *c*. ........ 1 Cor 1:8

**CONFIRMED**
covenant that was *c* ........ Gal 3:17
*c* it by an oath ........ Heb 6:17

**CONFIRMING**
*c* the word through the .... Mark 16:20

**CONFLICT**
to know what a great *c* ........ Col 2:1

**CONFLICTS**
Outside were *c*. ........ 2 Cor 7:5

**CONFORMED**
predestined to be *c* ........ Rom 8:29
And do not be *c* ........ Rom 12:2

**CONFUSE**
*c* their language ........ Gen 11:7

**CONFUSED**
for the assembly was *c* ..... Acts 19:32

**CONGREGATION**
nor sinners in the *c* ........ Ps 1:5
God stands in the *c* ........ Ps 82:1

**CONQUER**
conquering and to *c* ........ Rev 6:2

**CONQUERORS**
we are more than *c* ........ Rom 8:37

**CONSCIENCE**
convicted by their *c* ........ John 8:9
strive to have a *c*. ........ Acts 24:16

**CONSECRATED**
*c* this house which you ...... 1 Kin 9:3

**CONSENT**
and does not *c* to ........ 1 Tim 6:3

**CONSENTED**
He had not *c* to their ..... Luke 23:51

**CONSENTING**
Now Saul was *c* to his ........ Acts 8:1

**CONSIDER**
When I *c* Your heavens ........ Ps 8:3
My people do not *c*. ........ Is 1:3
*C* the lilies of the ........ Matt 6:28
"*C* the ravens ........ Luke 12:24
*c* Him who endured ........ Heb 12:3

**CONSIST**
in Him all things *c*. ........ Col 1:17

**CONSOLATION**
if there is any *c* ........ Phil 2:1
given us everlasting *c* .... 2 Thess 2:16

**CONSOLE**
*c* those who mourn ........ Is 61:3

**CONSTANT**
*c* prayer was ........ Acts 12:5

**CONSUME**
whom the Lord will *c*. ..... 2 Thess 2:8

**CONSUMED**
but the bush was not *c*. ........ Ex 3:2
mercies we are not *c* ........ Lam 3:22
beware lest you be *c* ........ Gal 5:15

**CONSUMING**
our God is a *c* fire ........ Heb 12:29

**CONTAIN**
of heavens cannot *c*. ........ 2 Chr 2:6
*c* the books that would .... John 21:25

**CONTEMPT**
and be treated with *c* ...... Mark 9:12

**CONTEMPTIBLE**
and his speech *c* ........ 2 Cor 10:10

**CONTEND**
*c* earnestly for the ........ Jude 3

**CONTENT**
state I am, to be *c* ........ Phil 4:11
covetousness; be *c* ........ Heb 13:5

**CONTENTIONS**
sorcery, hatred, *c* ........ Gal 5:20

**CONTENTIOUS**
anyone seems to be *c*. ..... 1 Cor 11:16

**CONTENTMENT**
*c* is great gain. ........ 1 Tim 6:6

**CONTINUAL**
a merry heart has a *c*. ..... Prov 15:15
*c* coming she weary me ..... Luke 18:5

**CONTINUALLY**
heart was only evil *c* ........ Gen 6:5
will give ourselves *c* ........ Acts 6:4
remains a priest *c* ........ Heb 7:3

**CONTINUE**
Shall we *c* in sin that ........ Rom 6:1
*C* earnestly in prayer ........ Col 4:2
Let brotherly love *c* ........ Heb 13:1

**CONTINUED**
*c* steadfastly in the ........ Acts 2:42

**CONTRADICTIONS**
idle babble and *c*. ........ 1 Tim 6:20

**CONTRARY**
to worship God *c* ........ Acts 18:13

**CONTRIBUTION**
to make a certain *c*. ....... Rom 15:26

**CONTRITE**
a broken and a *c*. ........ Ps 51:17
poor and of a *c* spirit ........ Is 66:2

**CONTROVERSY**
for the LORD has a *c* ........ Jer 25:31

**CONVERSION**
describing the *c* ........ Acts 15:3

**CONVERTED**
unless you are *c* ........ Matt 18:3

**CONVICT**
He has come, He will *c*. ..... John 16:8

**CONVICTS**
"Which of you *c* ........ John 8:46

**CONVINCED**
Let each be fully *c* ........ Rom 14:5

**COOKED**
*c* their own children ........ Lam 4:10

**COOL**
water and *c* my tongue .... Luke 16:24

**COPIES**
necessary that the *c* ........ Heb 9:23

**COPPER**
sold for two *c* coins. ........ Luke 12:6

**COPPERSMITH**
*c* did me much harm. ....... 2 Tim 4:14

**COPY**
who serve the *c* ........ Heb 8:5

**CORD**
this line of scarlet *c* ........ Josh 2:18

**CORDS**
had made a whip of *c* ........ John 2:15

**CORNER**
was not done in a *c* ........ Acts 26:26

**CORNERSTONE**
*become the chief c* ........ Matt 21:42
*in Zion a chief c* ........ 1 Pet 2:6

**CORRECT**
*C* your son ........ Prov 29:17

**CORRECTED**
human fathers who *c* ... Heb 12:9

**CORRECTION**
Do not withhold *c* ... Prov 23:13
for reproof, for *c* ... 2 Tim 3:16

**CORRECTS**
the LORD loves He *c* ... Prov 3:12

**CORRODED**
and silver are *c* ... James 5:3

**CORRUPT**
in these things they *c* ... Jude 10

**CORRUPTED**
for all flesh had *c* ... Gen 6:12
Your riches are *c* ... James 5:2

**CORRUPTIBLE**
redeemed with *c* things ... 1 Pet 1:18

**CORRUPTION**
Your Holy One to see *c* ... Ps 16:10
*c* inherit incorruption ... 1 Cor 15:50
having escaped the *c* ... 2 Pet 1:4

**COST**
and count the *c* ... Luke 14:28

**COULD**
*c* remove mountains ... 1 Cor 13:2
which no one *c* number ... Rev 7:9

**COUNCILS**
deliver you up to *c* ... Mark 13:9

**COUNSEL**
who walks not in the *c* ... Ps 1:1
We took sweet *c* ... Ps 55:14
guide me with Your *c* ... Ps 73:24
according to the *c* ... Eph 1:11
immutability of His *c* ... Heb 6:17
"I *c* you to buy from ... Rev 3:18

**COUNSELOR**
be called Wonderful, *C* ... Is 9:6

**COUNSELORS**
*c* there is safety ... Prov 11:14

**COUNT**
*c* my life dear to ... Acts 20:24
His promise, as some *c* ... 2 Pet 3:9

**COUNTED**
Even a fool is *c* ... Prov 17:28
who rule well be *c* ... 1 Tim 5:17

**COUNTENANCE**
the LORD lift up His *c* ... Num 6:26
with a sad *c* ... Matt 6:16
His *c* was like ... Matt 28:3
of the glory of his *c* ... 2 Cor 3:7

**COUNTRY**
"Get out of your *c* ... Gen 12:1
that is, a heavenly *c* ... Heb 11:16

**COURAGE**
strong and of good *c* ... Deut 31:6

**COURT**
They zealously *c* ... Gal 4:17

**COURTEOUS**
be tenderhearted, be *c* ... 1 Pet 3:8

**COURTS**
and into His *c* ... Ps 100:4

**COVENANT**
I will establish My *c* ... Gen 6:18
day the LORD made a *c* ... Gen 15:18
will show them His *c* ... Ps 25:14
sons will keep My *c* ... Ps 132:12
I will make a new *c* ... Jer 31:31
the Messenger of the *c* ... Mal 3:1
This cup is the new *c* ... Luke 22:20
He says, *"A new c* ... Heb 8:13
Mediator of the new *c* ... Heb 12:24
of the everlasting *c* ... Heb 13:20

**COVENANTS**
the glory, the *c* ... Rom 9:4

**COVER**
He shall *c* you with ... Ps 91:4
*c* a multitude of sins ... James 5:20

**COVERED**
whose sin is *c* ... Ps 32:1
*c* all their sin ... Ps 85:2
For there is nothing *c* ... Matt 10:26

**COVERING**
spread a cloud for a *c* ... Ps 105:39

**COVERINGS**
and made themselves *c* ... Gen 3:7

**COVET**
"You shall not *c* ... Ex 20:17

**COVETED**
*c* no one's silver ... Acts 20:33

**COVETOUS**
nor thieves, nor *c* ... 1 Cor 6:10

**COVETOUSNESS**
heed and beware of *c* ... Luke 12:15

**COWARDLY**
the *c*, unbelieving ... Rev 21:8

**CRAFTILY**
His people, to deal *c* ... Ps 105:25

**CRAFTINESS**
deceived Eve by his *c* ... 2 Cor 11:3
in the cunning *c* ... Eph 4:14

**CRAFTSMAN**
instructor of every *c* ... Gen 4:22

**CRAFTY**
the devices of the *c* ... Job 5:12
Nevertheless, being *c* ... 2 Cor 12:16

**CREAM**
were bathed with *c* ... Job 29:6

**CREATE**
peace and *c* calamity ... Is 45:7

**CREATED**
So God *c* man in His ... Gen 1:27
Has not one God *c* ... Mal 2:10
*c* in Christ Jesus ... Eph 2:10
new man which was *c* ... Eph 4:24

**CREATION**
know that the whole *c* ... Rom 8:22
Christ, he is a new *c* ... 2 Cor 5:17
anything, but a new *c* ... Gal 6:15

**CREATOR**
Remember now your *C* ... Eccl 12:1
God, the LORD, the *C* ... Is 40:28
rather than the *C* ... Rom 1:25

**CREATURE**
the gospel to every *c* ... Mark 16:15

**CREATURES**
firstfruits of His *c* ... James 1:18

**CREDIT**
For what *c* is it if ... 1 Pet 2:20

**CREDITOR**
There was a certain *c* ... Luke 7:41

**CREEP**
sort are those who *c* ... 2 Tim 3:6

**CREEPING**
*c* thing and beast of ... Gen 1:24

**CREPT**
For certain men have *c* ... Jude 4

**CRIB**
donkey its master's *c* ... Is 1:3

**CRIED**
the poor who *c* out ... Job 29:12
of the depths I have *c* ... Ps 130:1

**CRIES**
your brother's blood *c* ... Gen 4:10

**CRIMES**
land is filled with *c* ... Ezek 7:23

**CRIMINALS**
also two others, *c* ... Luke 23:32

**CROOKED**
*c* places shall be made ... Is 40:4
in the midst of a *c* ... Phil 2:15

**CROSS**
does not take his *c* ... Matt 10:38
to bear His *c* ... Matt 27:32
come down from the *c* ... Matt 27:40
lest the *c* of Christ ... 1 Cor 1:17
boast except in the *c* ... Gal 6:14
the enemies of the *c* ... Phil 3:18
Him endured the *c* ... Heb 12:2
shall not follow a *c* ... Ex 23:2

**CROWN**
*c* the year with Your ... Ps 65:11
they had twisted a *c* ... Matt 27:29
obtain a perishable *c* ... 1 Cor 9:25
laid up for me the *c* ... 2 Tim 4:8
on His head a golden *c* ... Rev 14:14

**CROWNED**
angels, and You have *c* ... Ps 8:5
athletics, he is not *c* ... 2 Tim 2:5

**CROWNS**
His head were many *c* ... Rev 19:12

**CRUCIFIED**
"Let Him be *c* ... Matt 27:22
Calvary, there they *c* ... Luke 23:33
lawless hands, have *c* ... Acts 2:23
that our old man was *c* ... Rom 6:6
Jesus Christ and Him *c* ... 1 Cor 2:2
"I have been *c* ... Gal 2:20

**CRUCIFY**
out again, "*C* Him ... Mark 15:13

**CRUEL**
hate me with *c* hatred ... Ps 25:19

**CRUELTY**
the haunts of *c* ... Ps 74:20

**CRUSH**
of peace will *c* ... Rom 16:20

**CRUSHED**
every side, yet not *c* ... 2 Cor 4:8

**COUNTRYMEN**
for my brethren, my *c* ... Rom 9:3

**CRUST**
man is reduced to a *c* ... Prov 6:26

**CRY**
and their *c* came up to ... Ex 2:23
Does not wisdom *c* ... Prov 8:1
at midnight a *c* ... Matt 25:6
His own elect who *c* ... Luke 18:7

**CRYING**
nor sorrow, nor *c* ... Rev 21:4

**CRYSTAL**
a sea of glass, like *c* ... Rev 4:6

**CUBIT**
worrying can add one *c* . . . . .Matt 6:27

**CUNNING**
the serpent was more *c* . . . . . . .Gen 3:1
*c* craftiness of deceitful . . . . . .Eph 4:14

**CUP**
my *c* runs over . . . . . . . . . . . . . .Ps 23:5
Then He took the *c*. . . . . . . .Matt 26:27
possible, let this *c* . . . . . . . .Matt 26:39
*c* is the new covenant . . . . .Luke 22:20
You cannot drink the *c* . . . .1 Cor 10:21
*c* is the new covenant . . . . .1 Cor 11:25

**CURE**
and to *c* diseases . . . . . . . . . . .Luke 9:1

**CURES**
demons and perform *c*. . . . .Luke 13:32

**CURSE**
*c* the ground for man's. . . . . . .Gen 8:21
*C* God and die . . . . . . . . . . . . . . .Job 2:9
"I will send a *c*. . . . . . . . . . . . . .Mal 2:2
law are under the *c* . . . . . . . . .Gal 3:10

**CURSED**
*c* more than all cattle . . . . . . .Gen 3:14
'Depart from Me, you *c* . . . .Matt 25:41

**CURSES**
I will curse him who *c*. . . . . . .Gen 12:3

**CURTAIN**
the heavens like a *c* . . . . . . . . .Ps 104:2

**CUSTOM**
according to the *c* . . . . . . . . .Acts 15:1

**CUT**
evildoers shall be *c*. . . . . . . . . . .Ps 37:9
the wicked will be *c* . . . . . . . .Prov 2:22

**CYMBAL**
or a clanging *c*. . . . . . . . . . . .1 Cor 13:1

## D

**DAILY**
Give us this day our *d* . . . . . .Matt 6:11
take up his cross *d*. . . . . . . . .Luke 9:23
the Scriptures *d* . . . . . . . . . .Acts 17:11

**DANCE**
mourn, and a time to *d* . . . . . . .Eccl 3:4
and you did not *d* . . . . . . . . . .Matt 11:17

**DANCED**
Then David *d* before . . . . . .2 Sam 6:14

**DANCING**
saw the calf and the *d* . . . . . . .Ex 32:19
he heard music and *d* . . . . .Luke 15:25

**DARE**
someone would even *d* . . . . . . .Rom 5:7

**DARK**
I tell you in the *d* . . . . . . . . .Matt 10:27
shines in a *d* place . . . . . . . . .2 Pet 1:19

**DARKENED**
their understanding *d* . . . . . .Eph 4:18

**DARKNESS**
*d* He called Night . . . . . . . . . . .Gen 1:5
Those who sat in *d*. . . . . . . . . .Ps 107:10
*d* have seen a. . . . . . . . . . . . . . . . .Is 9:2
and deep *d* the people . . . . . . . . .Is 60:2
body will be full of *d* . . . . . . .Matt 6:23
cast out into outer *d*. . . . . . . .Matt 8:12
*d* rather than light. . . . . . . . .John 3:19
For you were once *d*. . . . . . . . . .Eph 5:8
called you out of *d* . . . . . . . . . .1 Pet 2:9
*d* is reserved. . . . . . . . . . . . . .2 Pet 2:17
and in Him is no *d*. . . . . . . . .1 John 1:5
*d* is passing away . . . . . . . . .1 John 2:8

**DARTS**
quench all the fiery *d* . . . . . . .Eph 6:16

**DASH**
You shall *d* them to . . . . . . . . . . .Ps 2:9
*lest you d your foot*. . . . . . . . . .Matt 4:6

**DASHED**
infants shall be *d*. . . . . . . . . .Hos 13:16

**DAUGHTER**
Rejoice greatly, O *d* . . . . . . . . .Zech 9:9
*"Fear not, d of Zion* . . . . . . .John 12:15
the son of Pharaoh's *d*. . . . . .Heb 11:24

**DAUGHTERS**
of God saw the *d* . . . . . . . . . . . .Gen 6:2
*d shall prophesy* . . . . . . . . . . .Acts 2:17

**DAY**
God called the light *D*. . . . . . . .Gen 1:5
and *d* and night. . . . . . . . . . . .Gen 8:22
"Remember the Sabbath *d* . . . .Ex 20:8
For a *d* in Your courts . . . . . . .Ps 84:10
*d* the LORD has . . . . . . . . . . .Ps 118:24
not strike you by *d*. . . . . . . . . .Ps 121:6
For the *d* of the LORD . . . . . . . .Joel 2:11
who can endure the *d* . . . . . . . .Mal 3:2
*d* our daily bread . . . . . . . . . .Matt 6:11
sent Me while it is *d*. . . . . . . . .John 9:4
person esteems one *d* . . . . . . .Rom 14:5
*D* will declare it. . . . . . . . . . .1 Cor 3:13
again the third *d*. . . . . . . . . .1 Cor 15:4
with the Lord one *d* . . . . . . . . .2 Pet 3:8

**DAYS**
*d* are swifter than a . . . . . . . . . .Job 7:6
of woman is of few *d* . . . . . . . . .Job 14:1
The *d* of our lives are . . . . . . . .Ps 90:10
before the difficult *d*. . . . . . . .Eccl 12:1
had shortened those *d* . . . .Mark 13:20
raise it up in three *d* . . . . . . .John 2:20

**DAYSPRING**
with which the *D*. . . . . . . . . .Luke 1:78

**DEACONS**
with the bishops and *d* . . . . . . .Phil 1:1
*d* must be reverent . . . . . . . . .1 Tim 3:8
*d* be the husbands . . . . . . . .1 Tim 3:12

**DEAD**
but the *d* know nothing . . . . . .Eccl 9:5
*d* bury their own *d*. . . . . . . . .Matt 8:22
not the God of the *d* . . . . . . .Matt 22:32
for this my son was *d*. . . . . .Luke 15:24
*d* will hear the voice . . . . . . .John 5:25
was raised from the *d*. . . . . . . .Rom 6:4
yourselves to be *d*. . . . . . . . . .Rom 6:11
be Lord of both the *d*. . . . . . . .Rom 14:9
resurrection of the *d* . . . . . .1 Cor 15:12
And the *d* in Christ . . . . . .1 Thess 4:16
without works is *d*. . . . . . . .James 2:26
And the *d* were judged. . . . . .Rev 20:12

**DEADLY**
they drink anything *d* . . . .Mark 16:18
evil, full of *d* poison . . . . . . . .James 3:8

**DEADNESS**
the *d* of Sarah's womb . . . . . .Rom 4:19

**DEAF**
*d* shall be unstopped. . . . . . . . . .Is 35:5
are cleansed and the *d*. . . . . .Matt 11:5

**DEAL**
My Servant shall *d*. . . . . . . . . .Is 52:13

**DEATH**
*d* parts you and me . . . . . . . .Ruth 1:17
and the shadow of *d* . . . . . . . . .Job 10:21
I sleep the sleep of *d*. . . . . . . . . .Ps 13:3
of the shadow of *d* . . . . . . . . . . .Ps 23:4
house leads down to *d* . . . . . .Prov 2:18
who hate me love *d* . . . . . . . .Prov 8:36
swallow up *d* forever. . . . . . . . . .Is 25:8
no pleasure in the *d*. . . . . . .Ezek 18:32
who shall not taste *d* . . . . . .Matt 16:28
but has passed from *d* . . . . . .John 5:24
Nevertheless *d* reigned . . . . .Rom 5:14
*D* no longer has. . . . . . . . . . . .Rom 6:9
the wages of sin is *d* . . . . . . . .Rom 6:23
proclaim the Lord's *d* . . . . .1 Cor 11:26
since by man came *d*. . . . . .1 Cor 15:21
*D is swallowed up in* . . . . . .1 Cor 15:54
The sting of *d* is sin. . . . . . .1 Cor 15:56
is sin leading to *d* . . . . . . . .1 John 5:16
Be faithful until *d* . . . . . . . . . .Rev 2:10
shall be no more *d* . . . . . . . . . .Rev 21:4
which is the second *d*. . . . . . . .Rev 21:8

**DEBTOR**
I am a *d* both to. . . . . . . . . . . .Rom 1:14
that he is a *d* to keep . . . . . . . . .Gal 5:3

**DEBTORS**
as we forgive our *d*. . . . . . . . .Matt 6:12
of his master's *d* . . . . . . . . . .Luke 16:5
brethren, we are *d* . . . . . . . . .Rom 8:12

**DECEIT**
nor was any *d* in His. . . . . . . . . .Is 53:9
philosophy and empty *d*. . . . . . .Col 2:8
*no sin, nor was d* . . . . . . . . . .1 Pet 2:22
mouth was found no *d* . . . . . . .Rev 14:5

**DECEITFUL**
deliver me from the *d*. . . . . . . . .Ps 43:1
"The heart is *d* . . . . . . . . . . . . .Jer 17:9
are false apostles, *d* . . . . . .2 Cor 11:13

**DECEITFULLY**
an idol, nor sworn *d* . . . . . . . . . .Ps 24:4
the word of God *d* . . . . . . . . . .2 Cor 4:2

**DECEITFULNESS**
this world and the *d*. . . . . . .Matt 13:22

**DECEIVE**
rise up and *d* many . . . . . . .Matt 24:11
Let no one *d* you with . . . . . . . .Eph 5:6
we have no sin, we *d* . . . . . . .1 John 1:8

**DECEIVED**
"The serpent *d* . . . . . . . . . . . .Gen 3:13
by the commandment, *d*. . . . .Rom 7:11
deceiving and being *d* . . . . .2 Tim 3:13

**DECEIVER**
how that *d* said . . . . . . . . . .Matt 27:63
This is a *d* and an. . . . . . . . . . . .2 John 7

**DECEIVES**
heed that no one *d* . . . . . . . . .Matt 24:4

**DECENTLY**
all things be done *d*. . . . . . .1 Cor 14:40

**DECEPTIVE**
you with *d* words . . . . . . . . . . .2 Pet 2:3

**DECISION**
in the valley of *d* . . . . . . . . . . .Joel 3:14

**DECLARE**
The heavens *d* the . . . . . . . . . . .Ps 19:1
*d* Your name to My . . . . . . . . .Ps 22:22
seen and heard we *d* . . . . . . .1 John 1:3

**DECLARED**
and *d* to be the Son of . . . . . . . .Rom 1:4

**DECREE**
"I will declare the *d*. . . . . . . . . . .Ps 2:7
in those days that a *d* . . . . . . .Luke 2:1

**DEDICATION**
it was the Feast of *D*. . . . . . .John 10:22

**DEED**
you do in word or *d* . . . . . . . . . .Col 3:17

**DEEDS**
because their *d* . . . John 3:19
"You do the *d* . . . John 8:41
*one according to his d*. . . Rom 2:6
you put to death the *d*. . . Rom 8:13

**DEEP**
LORD God caused a *d* . . . Gen 2:21
*d* uttered its voice . . . Hab 3:10
"Launch out into the *d* . . . Luke 5:4
I have been in the *d*. . . 2 Cor 11:25

**DEEPER**
*D* than Sheol . . . Job 11:8

**DEEPLY**
But He sighed *d* . . . Mark 8:12

**DEER**
As the *d* pants for the. . . Ps 42:1
shall leap like a *d* . . . Is 35:6

**DEFEATED**
and Israel was *d*. . . 1 Sam 4:10

**DEFEND**
*d* the fatherless . . . Is 1:17

**DEFENSE**
For wisdom is a *d* . . . Eccl 7:12
am appointed for the *d* . . . Phil 1:17
be ready to give a *d* . . . 1 Pet 3:15

**DEFILE**
also these dreamers *d*. . . Jude 8

**DEFILED**
lest they should be *d* . . . John 18:28
and conscience are *d*. . . Titus 1:15

**DEFILES**
mouth, this *d* a man . . . Matt 15:11
it anything that *d* . . . Rev 21:27

**DEFRAUD**
*d* his brother in this. . . 1 Thess 4:6

**DEGREES**
go forward ten *d* . . . 2 Kin 20:9

**DELICACIES**
of the king's *d* . . . Dan 1:5

**DELICATE**
a lovely and *d* woman. . . Jer 6:2

**DELIGHT**
But his *d* is in the. . . Ps 1:2
I *d* to do Your will. . . Ps 40:8
and I was daily His *d* . . . Prov 8:30
and let your soul *d* . . . Is 55:2
call the Sabbath a *d* . . . Is 58:13
For I *d* in the law of. . . Rom 7:22

**DELIGHTS**
for the LORD *d* in you . . . Is 62:4

**DELIVER**
Let Him *d* Him . . . Ps 22:8
I will *d* him and honor . . . Ps 91:15
into temptation, but *d*. . . Matt 6:13
let Him *d* Him now if. . . Matt 27:43
And the Lord will *d* . . . 2 Tim 4:18
*d* the godly out of . . . 2 Pet 2:9

**DELIVERANCE**
not accepting *d* . . . Heb 11:35

**DELIVERED**
who was *d* up because . . . Rom 4:25
was once for all *d*. . . Jude 3

**DELIVERER**
*D will come out of*. . . Rom 11:26

**DELIVERS**
dead, even Jesus who *d* . . . 1 Thess 1:10

**DELUSION**
send them strong *d* . . . 2 Thess 2:11

**DEMON**
Jesus rebuked the *d*. . . Matt 17:18
Samaritan and have a *d* . . . John 8:48

**DEMONIC**
is earthly, sensual, *d*. . . James 3:15

**DEMONS**
authority over all *d*. . . Luke 9:1
even the *d* are subject . . . Luke 10:17
Even the *d* believe. . . James 2:19

**DEMONSTRATE**
faith, to *d* His . . . Rom 3:25

**DEMONSTRATES**
*d* His own love toward . . . Rom 5:8

**DEN**
cast him into the *d* . . . Dan 6:16
it a '*d of thieves* . . . Matt 21:13

**DENARIUS**
the laborers for a *d*. . . Matt 20:2

**DENIED**
before men will be *d* . . . Luke 12:9
Peter then *d* again. . . John 18:27
*d* the Holy One and the. . . Acts 3:14
things cannot be *d* . . . Acts 19:36
household, he has *d* . . . 1 Tim 5:8

**DENIES**
But whoever *d*. . . Matt 10:33
*d* that Jesus is the. . . 1 John 2:22

**DENY**
let him *d* himself. . . Matt 16:24
He cannot *d* Himself . . . 2 Tim 2:13

**DENYING**
but *d* its power . . . 2 Tim 3:5
*d* the Lord who bought. . . 2 Pet 2:1

**DEPART**
scepter shall not *d*. . . Gen 49:10
on the left hand, '*D* . . . Matt 25:41
will *d* from the faith. . . 1 Tim 4:1

**DEPARTING**
heart of unbelief in *d* . . . Heb 3:12

**DEPARTURE**
*d* savage wolves will. . . Acts 20:29
and the time of my *d* . . . 2 Tim 4:6

**DEPRESSION**
of man causes *d* . . . Prov 12:25

**DEPTH**
nor height nor *d* . . . Rom 8:39
Oh, the *d* of the. . . Rom 11:33

**DEPTHS**
our sins into the *d* . . . Mic 7:19

**DERISION**
shall hold them in *d*. . . Ps 2:4

**DESCEND**
*d* now from the cross. . . Mark 15:32
Lord Himself will *d*. . . 1 Thess 4:16

**DESCENDANTS**
"We are Abraham's *d* . . . John 8:33

**DESCENDED**
He who *d* is also the . . . Eph 4:10

**DESCENDING**
of God ascending and *d* . . . John 1:51
the holy Jerusalem, *d* . . . Rev 21:10

**DESERT**
*d* shall rejoice . . . Is 35:1
'Look, He is in the *d*. . . Matt 24:26

**DESERTED**
*d* place by Himself. . . Matt 14:13

**DESERTS**
They wandered in *d*. . . Heb 11:38

**DESIGN**
with an artistic *d* . . . Ex 26:31

**DESIRABLE**
the eyes, and a tree *d* . . . Gen 3:6

**DESIRE**
*d* shall be for your . . . Gen 3:16
Behold, You *d* truth in. . . Ps 51:6
"Father, I *d* that. . . John 17:24
all manner of evil *d* . . . Rom 7:8
Brethren, my heart's *d*. . . Rom 10:1
*d* the best gifts . . . 1 Cor 12:31
the two, having a *d*. . . Phil 1:23

**DESIRED**
*d* are they than gold. . . Ps 19:10
One thing I have *d*. . . Ps 27:4

**DESIRES**
shall give you the *d* . . . Ps 37:4
the devil, and the *d* . . . John 8:44
not come from your *d*. . . James 4:1

**DESOLATE**
any more be termed *D* . . . Is 62:4
house is left to you *d* . . . Matt 23:38

**DESOLATION**
the '*abomination of d* . . . Matt 24:15

**DESPAIRED**
strength, so that we *d* . . . 2 Cor 1:8

**DESPISE**
one and *d* the other . . . Matt 6:24
*d* the riches of His. . . Rom 2:4

**DESPISED**
He is *d* and rejected . . . Is 53:3
the things which are *d* . . . 1 Cor 1:28

**DESPISES**
*d* his neighbor sins. . . Prov 14:21

**DESPISING**
the cross, *d* the shame. . . Heb 12:2

**DESTITUTE**
of corrupt minds and *d*. . . 1 Tim 6:5

**DESTROY**
why should you *d* . . . Eccl 7:16
shall not hurt nor *d*. . . Is 11:9
I did not come to *d* . . . Matt 5:17
Him who is able to *d* . . . Matt 10:28
Barabbas and *d* Jesus . . . Matt 27:20
to save life or to *d* . . . Luke 6:9
*d* men's lives but to . . . Luke 9:56
*d the wisdom of the* . . . 1 Cor 1:19
able to save and to *d* . . . James 4:12

**DESTROYED**
*d* all living things. . . Gen 7:23
house, this tent, is *d* . . . 2 Cor 5:1

**DESTRUCTION**
You turn man to *d* . . . Ps 90:3
*d* that lays waste . . . Ps 91:6
your life from *d* . . . Ps 103:4
Pride goes before *d*. . . Prov 16:18
whose end is *d*. . . Phil 3:19
with everlasting *d*. . . 2 Thess 1:9

**DESTRUCTIVE**
bring in *d* heresies. . . 2 Pet 2:1

**DETERMINED**
*d* their preappointed . . . Acts 17:26
For I *d* not to know . . . 1 Cor 2:2

**DEVICE**
there is no work or *d*. . . Eccl 9:10

**DEVICES**
not ignorant of his *d* . . . 2 Cor 2:11

**DEVIL**
to be tempted by the *d*. . . Matt 4:1
prepared for the *d* . . . Matt 25:41

of your father the *d* . . . . . . . .John 8:44
give place to the *d*. . . . . . . . . .Eph 4:27
the snare of the *d* . . . . . . . . .2 Tim 2:26
the works of the *d* . . . . . . . . .1 John 3:8

**DEVIOUS**
crooked, and who are *d* . . . . .Prov 2:15

**DEVISES**
*d* wickedness on his. . . . . . . . . .Ps 36:4
But a generous man *d*. . . . . . . . . .Is 32:8

**DEVOID**
He who is *d* of wisdom . . . . .Prov 11:12

**DEVOTED**
Your servant, who is *d*. . . . . .Ps 119:38

**DEVOUR**
For you *d* widows' . . . . . . . .Matt 23:14
bite and *d* one another. . . . . . .Gal 5:15
seeking whom he may *d* . . . . .1 Pet 5:8
*d* her Child as . . . . . . . . . . . .Rev 12:4

**DEVOURED**
Some wild beast has *d* . . . . .Gen 37:20
birds came and *d* them . . . . .Matt 13:4
of heaven and *d* them . . . . . . .Rev 20:9

**DEVOUT**
man was just and *d*. . . . . . . .Luke 2:25
*d* soldier from among . . . . . . .Acts 10:7

**DEW**
God give you of the *d*. . . . . . .Gen 27:28

**DIADEMS**
ten horns, and seven *d*. . . . . . .Rev 12:3

**DIAMOND**
*d* it is engraved. . . . . . . . . . . . .Jer 17:1

**DICTATES**
according to the *d*. . . . . . . . . .Jer 23:17

**DIE**
it you shall surely *d* . . . . . . . .Gen 2:17
but a person shall *d* . . . . . . .2 Chr 25:4
I shall not *d* . . . . . . . . . . . . .Ps 118:17
born, and a time to *d*. . . . . . . . . .Eccl 3:2
eat of it and not *d*. . . . . . . . . .John 6:50
to you that you will *d*. . . . . . .John 8:24
though he may *d* . . . . . . . . .John 11:25
that one man should *d*. . . . .John 11:50
the flesh you will *d*. . . . . . . . .Rom 8:13
For as in Adam all *d* . . . . . .1 Cor 15:22
and to *d* is gain . . . . . . . . . . . .Phil 1:21
for men to *d* once . . . . . . . . . .Heb 9:27
are the dead who *d*. . . . . . . . .Rev 14:13

**DIED**
And all flesh *d*. . . . . . . . . . . . .Gen 7:21
in due time Christ *d*. . . . . . . . . .Rom 5:6
Christ *d* for us . . . . . . . . . . . . .Rom 5:8
Now if we *d* with. . . . . . . . . . . .Rom 6:8
and He *d* for all . . . . . . . . . . .2 Cor 5:15
for if we *d* with Him . . . . . . .2 Tim 2:11

**DIES**
made alive unless it *d*. . . . .1 Cor 15:36

**DIFFERS**
for one star *d* from. . . . . . . .1 Cor 15:41

**DILIGENCE**
*d* it produced in you. . . . . . . .2 Cor 7:11

**DILIGENT**
*d* makes rich . . . . . . . . . . . . .Prov 10:4

**DILIGENTLY**
*d* lest anyone fall. . . . . . . . . .Heb 12:15

**DIM**
His eyes were not *d* . . . . . . . .Deut 34:7

**DIMLY**
we see in a mirror, *d* . . . . .1 Cor 13:12

**DINE**
come in to him and *d* . . . . . . . .Rev 3:20

**DINNER**
invites you to *d* . . . . . . . . . .1 Cor 10:27

**DIP**
*d* your piece of bread . . . . . . .Ruth 2:14

**DIPPED**
clothed with a robe *d* . . . . . . .Rev 19:13

**DIRECT**
Now may the Lord *d* . . . . . .2 Thess 3:5

**DIRT**
cast up mire and *d* . . . . . . . . . .Is 57:20

**DISARMED**
*d* principalities. . . . . . . . . . . . .Col 2:15

**DISASTER**
voyage will end with *d* . . . . .Acts 27:10

**DISCERN**
*d* the face of the sky . . . . . . .Matt 16:3
senses exercised to *d* . . . . . . . .Heb 5:14

**DISCERNED**
they are spiritually *d* . . . . . .1 Cor 2:14

**DISCERNER**
*d* of the thoughts . . . . . . . . . . .Heb 4:12

**DISCERNS**
a wise man's heart *d*. . . . . . . . .Eccl 8:5

**DISCIPLE**
he cannot be My *d*. . . . . . . .Luke 14:26
*d* whom Jesus loved . . . . . . . .John 21:7

**DISCIPLES**
My word, you are My *d* . . . . .John 8:31
but we are Moses' *d* . . . . . . . .John 9:28

**DISCIPLINES**
but he who loves him *d* . . . .Prov 13:24

**DISCORD**
and one who sows *d* . . . . . . . .Prov 6:19

**DISCOURAGED**
lest they become *d* . . . . . . . . . .Col 3:21
you become weary and *d*. . . . .Heb 12:3

**DISCRETION**
*d* will preserve you. . . . . . . . .Prov 2:11

**DISFIGURE**
*d* their faces that . . . . . . . . . .Matt 6:16

**DISGUISES**
and he *d* his face. . . . . . . . . . .Job 24:15

**DISHONOR**
My Father, and you *d* Me. . . .John 8:49
*d* their bodies among . . . . . . .Rom 1:24
It is sown in *d*. . . . . . . . . . .1 Cor 15:43

**DISHONORED**
But you have *d* the . . . . . . . .James 2:6

**DISHONORS**
For son *d* father . . . . . . . . . . . . .Mic 7:6

**DISOBEDIENT**
*out My hands to a d* . . . . . . . .Rom 10:21

**DISORDERLY**
for this *d* gathering . . . . . . .Acts 19:40

**DISPENSATION**
*d* of the fullness of. . . . . . . . . . .Eph 1:10

**DISPERSION**
the pilgrims of the *D* . . . . . . . .1 Pet 1:1

**DISPLEASE**
LORD see it, and it *d* . . . . . .Prov 24:18

**DISPLEASED**
they were greatly *d* . . . . . . .Matt 20:24
it, He was greatly *d* . . . . . . .Mark 10:14

**DISPUTE**
Now there was also a *d* . . . .Luke 22:24

**DISPUTER**
Where is the *d* of this . . . . . .1 Cor 1:20

**DISPUTES**
But avoid foolish *d* . . . . . . . . .Titus 3:9

**DISQUALIFIED**
myself should become *d* . . . .1 Cor 9:27

**DISQUIETED**
And why are you *d*. . . . . . . . . . .Ps 42:5

**DISSENSION**
had no small *d* and. . . . . . . . .Acts 15:2

**DISSIPATION**
not accused of *d*. . . . . . . . . . . .Titus 1:6

**DISSOLVED**
the heavens will be *d*. . . . . . .2 Pet 3:12

**DISTINCTION**
compassion, making a *d* . . . . . .Jude 22

**DISTRESS**
*d* them in His deep. . . . . . . . . . . .Ps 2:5
tribulation, or *d* . . . . . . . . . . .Rom 8:35

**DISTRESSED**
troubled and deeply *d*. . . . .Mark 14:33

**DISTRESSES**
bring me out of my *d* . . . . . . . .Ps 25:17

**DISTRIBUTED**
and they *d* to each as . . . . . . .Acts 4:35

**DISTRIBUTING**
*d* to the needs of the . . . . . . .Rom 12:13

**DITCH**
will fall into a *d*. . . . . . . . . .Matt 15:14

**DIVERSITIES**
There are *d* . . . . . . . . . . . . . .1 Cor 12:4

**DIVIDE**
*d* the spoil with the . . . . . . .Prov 16:19
"Take this and *d* . . . . . . . . .Luke 22:17

**DIVIDED**
and the waters were *d*. . . . . . .Ex 14:21
death they were not *d* . . . . .2 Sam 1:23
"Every kingdom *d*. . . . . . . .Matt 12:25
Is Christ *d*. . . . . . . . . . . . . . .1 Cor 1:13

**DIVIDES**
at home *d* the spoil. . . . . . . . . .Ps 68:12

**DIVIDING**
rightly *d* the word of. . . . . . .2 Tim 2:15

**DIVINATION**
shall you practice *d* . . . . . . . .Lev 19:26
a spirit of *d* met us . . . . . . . .Acts 16:16

**DIVINE**
*d* service and the . . . . . . . . . . . .Heb 9:1

**DIVISION**
So there was a *d*. . . . . . . . . . .John 7:43

**DIVISIONS**
note those who cause *d*. . . . .Rom 16:17
persons, who cause *d*. . . . . . . . .Jude 19

**DIVISIVE**
Reject a *d* man after . . . . . . .Titus 3:10

**DIVORCE**
her a certificate of *d*. . . . . . . .Deut 24:1
a certificate of *d* . . . . . . . . . .Mark 10:4

**DO**
men to *d* to you, *d*. . . . . . . . . .Matt 7:12
He sees the Father *d* . . . . . . .John 5:19
without Me you can *d* . . . . . .John 15:5
"Sirs, what must I *d*. . . . . . .Acts 16:30
*d* evil that good may. . . . . . . . .Rom 3:8
or whatever you *d*, *d* . . . . . .1 Cor 10:31

**DOCTRINE**
What new *d* is this . . . . . . . .Mark 1:27
"My *d* is not Mine . . . . . . . . .John 7:16
with every wind of *d* . . . . . . . .Eph 4:14
is contrary to sound *d*. . . . . .1 Tim 1:10

is profitable for *d* . . . . . . . . .2 Tim 3:16
not endure sound *d*. . . . . . . . .2 Tim 4:3

**DOCTRINES**
the commandments and *d* . . . .Col 2:22
various and strange *d*. . . . . . .Heb 13:9

**DOERS**
But be *d* of the word. . . . . . .James 1:22

**DOG**
*d* is better than a . . . . . . . . . . .Eccl 9:4
*d returns to his own* . . . . . . .2 Pet 2:22

**DOGS**
what is holy to the *d* . . . . . . . .Matt 7:6
*d* eat the crumbs which. . . .Matt 15:27
But outside are *d*. . . . . . . . . .Rev 22:15

**DOMINION**
let them have *d*. . . . . . . . . . . .Gen 1:26
*d* is an everlasting . . . . . . . . .Dan 4:34
sin shall not have *d* . . . . . . . .Rom 6:14
glory and majesty, *d* . . . . . . . . .Jude 25

**DONKEY**
*d* its master's crib . . . . . . . . . . . . .Is 1:3
and riding on a *d* . . . . . . . . . . .Zech 9:9
*colt, the foal of a d* . . . . . . . . .Matt 21:5
*d* speaking with a . . . . . . . . .2 Pet 2:16

**DOOM**
for the day of *d*. . . . . . . . . . . .Prov 16:4

**DOOR**
stone against the *d* . . . . . . .Matt 27:60
to you, I am the *d*. . . . . . . . . .John 10:7
before you an open *d* . . . . . . . . .Rev 3:8
I stand at the *d*. . . . . . . . . . . . .Rev 3:20

**DOORKEEPER**
I would rather be a *d* . . . . . . . .Ps 84:10

**DOORPOSTS**
write them on the *d*. . . . . . . . .Deut 6:9

**DOORS**
up, you everlasting *d*. . . . . . . . .Ps 24:7

**DOUBLE**
from the LORD'S hand *d*. . . . . . .Is 40:2
worthy of *d* honor . . . . . . . . .1 Tim 5:17

**DOUBLE-MINDED**
he is a *d* man . . . . . . . . . . . . .James 1:8

**DOUBT**
faith, why did you *d*. . . . . . .Matt 14:31

**DOUBTING**
in faith, with no *d* . . . . . . . . .James 1:6

**DOUBTS**
And why do *d* arise in . . . . .Luke 24:38
for I have *d* about you . . . . . . .Gal 4:20

**DOVE**
*d* found no resting. . . . . . . . . . .Gen 8:9
descending like a *d* . . . . . . . .Matt 3:16

**DOVES**
and harmless as *d* . . . . . . . .Matt 10:16

**DOWNCAST**
who comforts the *d* . . . . . . . . .2 Cor 7:6

**DRAGNET**
*d* that was cast. . . . . . . . . . .Matt 13:47

**DRAGON**
they worshiped the *d*. . . . . . . .Rev 13:4
He laid hold of the *d*. . . . . . . . .Rev 20:2

**DRAINED**
all faces are *d* . . . . . . . . . . . . . .Joel 2:6

**DRANK**
them, and they all *d* . . . . . .Mark 14:23

**DRAW**
*d* honey from the rock . . . . .Deut 32:13
me to *d* near to God . . . . . . . . .Ps 73:28
and the years *d*. . . . . . . . . . . .Eccl 12:1
will *d* all peoples . . . . . . . . .John 12:32
*D* near to God and He . . . . . .James 4:8

**DRAWS**
your redemption *d*. . . . . . . .Luke 21:28

**DREAM**
Now Joseph had a *d* . . . . . . . .Gen 37:5
your old men shall *d* . . . . . . . .Joel 2:28
to Joseph in a *d* . . . . . . . . . . .Matt 2:13
things today in a *d*. . . . . . . .Matt 27:19

**DREAMERS**
*d* defile the flesh . . . . . . . . . . . . .Jude 8

**DREAMS**
Nebuchadnezzar had *d*. . . . . . .Dan 2:1

**DRIED**
of her blood was *d*. . . . . . . . .Mark 5:29
saw the fig tree *d* . . . . . . . .Mark 11:20

**DRIFT**
have heard, lest we *d*. . . . . . . . .Heb 2:1

**DRINK**
gave me vinegar to *d*. . . . . . . .Ps 69:21
lest they *d* and forget . . . . . .Prov 31:5
follow intoxicating *d*. . . . . . . . . .Is 5:11
*d* the milk of the . . . . . . . . . . . .Is 60:16
bosom, that you may *d* . . . . . . .Is 66:11
"Bring wine, let us *d* . . . . . . .Amos 4:1
that day when I *d*. . . . . . . . .Matt 26:29
mingled with gall to *d*. . . . .Matt 27:34
with myrrh to *d* . . . . . . . . .Mark 15:23
to her, "Give Me a *d* . . . . . . . . .John 4:7
him come to Me and *d* . . . . . .John 7:37
do, as often as you *d* . . . . . .1 Cor 11:25
No longer *d* only water. . . . .1 Tim 5:23

**DRINKS**
to her, "Whoever *d*. . . . . . . . .John 4:13
*d* My blood has. . . . . . . . . . . .John 6:54
For he who eats and *d* . . . . .1 Cor 11:29

**DRIPPING**
His lips are lilies, *d*. . . . . . . .Song 5:13

**DROSS**
purge away your *d* . . . . . . . . . . .Is 1:25

**DROUGHT**
in the year of *d* . . . . . . . . . . . . .Jer 17:8
For I called for a *d*. . . . . . . . . .Hag 1:11

**DROVE**
So He *d* out the man . . . . . . . .Gen 3:24
temple of God and *d*. . . . . . .Matt 21:12

**DROWN**
nor can the floods *d* . . . . . . . . .Song 8:7
harmful lusts which *d* . . . . . .1 Tim 6:9

**DROWSINESS**
*d* will clothe a. . . . . . . . . . . .Prov 23:21

**DRUNK**
of the wine and was *d* . . . . . . .Gen 9:21
the guests have well *d*. . . . . .John 2:10
For these are not *d* . . . . . . . . .Acts 2:15
and another is *d* . . . . . . . . .1 Cor 11:21
I saw the woman, *d* . . . . . . . . .Rev 17:6

**DRUNKARD**
to and fro like a *d* . . . . . . . . . . .Is 24:20
or a reviler, or a *d* . . . . . . . . .1 Cor 5:11

**DRUNKEN**
I am like a *d* man . . . . . . . . . . .Jer 23:9

**DRUNKENNESS**
will be filled with *d*. . . . . . .Ezek 23:33
not in revelry and *d* . . . . . . .Rom 13:13
envy, murders, *d* . . . . . . . . . . .Gal 5:21

**DRY**
place, and let the *d* . . . . . . . . . .Gen 1:9
made the sea into *d*. . . . . . . . .Ex 14:21
It was *d* on the fleece . . . . . . .Judg 6:40
will be done in the *d* . . . . . .Luke 23:31

**DUE**
pay all that was *d* . . . . . . . .Matt 18:34
*d* time Christ died . . . . . . . . . .Rom 5:6
*d* season we shall. . . . . . . . . . . .Gal 6:9
exalt you in *d* time. . . . . . . . . .1 Pet 5:6

**DULL**
heart of this people *d* . . . . . . . . .Is 6:10
people have grown *d* . . . . . .Matt 13:15

**DUMB**
the tongue of the *d* . . . . . . . . . . .Is 35:6

**DUST**
formed man of the *d* . . . . . . . . .Gen 2:7
*d* you shall return . . . . . . . . . .Gen 3:19
and repent in *d*. . . . . . . . . . . . . .Job 42:6
that we are *d* . . . . . . . . . . . . .Ps 103:14
counted as the small *d* . . . . . . .Is 40:15
city, shake off the *d* . . . . . . .Matt 10:14
image of the man of *d* . . . . .1 Cor 15:49

**DUTY**
done what was our *d* . . . . . .Luke 17:10

**DWELL**
Who may *d* in Your holy . . . . . .Ps 15:1
"I *d* in the high and . . . . . . . . .Is 57:15
*"I will d in them* . . . . . . . . . .2 Cor 6:16
that Christ may *d*. . . . . . . . . . .Eph 3:17
men, and He will *d* . . . . . . . . .Rev 21:3

**DWELLING**
built together for a *d*. . . . . . . .Eph 2:22
a foreign country, *d*. . . . . . . . .Heb 11:9

**DWELLS**
He who *d* in the secret . . . . . . . .Ps 91:1
but the Father who *d* . . . . . .John 14:10
*d* all the fullness. . . . . . . . . . . . .Col 2:9
which righteousness *d* . . . . .2 Pet 3:13
you, where Satan *d* . . . . . . . . .Rev 2:13

**DWELT**
became flesh and *d* . . . . . . . .John 1:14
By faith he *d* in the . . . . . . . . .Heb 11:9

**DYING**
in the body the *d* . . . . . . . . . .2 Cor 4:10

## E

**EAGLE**
fly away like an *e* . . . . . . . . . .Prov 23:5
the way of an *e* . . . . . . . . . . .Prov 30:19
like a flying *e*. . . . . . . . . . . . . . . .Rev 4:7

**EAGLES**
up with wings like *e* . . . . . . . . .Is 40:31
*e* will be gathered . . . . . . . .Matt 24:28

**EAGLES'**
how I bore you on *e* . . . . . . . . . .Ex 19:4

**EAR**
shall pierce his *e* . . . . . . . . . . . .Ex 21:6
and the *e* of the wise. . . . . . .Prov 18:15
*e* is uncircumcised . . . . . . . . . .Jer 6:10
what you hear in the *e*. . . . .Matt 10:27
cut off his right *e* . . . . . . . . .John 18:10
*not seen, nor e heard* . . . . . . . .1 Cor 2:9
"He who has an *e*. . . . . . . . . . . .Rev 2:7

**EARLY**
Very *e* in the morning. . . . . .Mark 16:2
arrived at the tomb *e*. . . . . .Luke 24:22

**EARNESTLY**
He prayed more *e*. . . . . . . . .Luke 22:44
*e* that it would not . . . . . . . .James 5:17
you to contend *e*. . . . . . . . . . . . . .Jude 3

**EARS**
and hear with their *e* . . . . . . . . .Is 6:10
"He who has *e* . . . . . . . . . . .Matt 11:15
they have itching *e*. . . . . . . . .2 Tim 4:3

**EARTH**
coming to judge the *e* . . . . .1 Chr 16:33
foundations of the *e* . . . . . . . . .Job 38:4
*e* is the LORD'S. . . . . . . . . . . . . .Ps 24:1
You had formed the *e* . . . . . . . . .Ps 90:2
there was ever an *e*. . . . . . . . .Prov 8:23
*e* abides forever . . . . . . . . . . . . .Eccl 1:4
for the meek of the *e* . . . . . . . . . .Is 11:4
*e* is My footstool . . . . . . . . . . . . .Is 66:1
I will darken the *e* . . . . . . . . .Amos 8:9
shall inherit the *e* . . . . . . . . . .Matt 5:5
heaven and *e* pass away . . . . .Matt 5:18
*e* as it is in heaven . . . . . . . . .Matt 6:10
treasures on *e* . . . . . . . . . . . .Matt 6:19
then shook the *e*. . . . . . . . . . .Heb 12:26
new heaven and a new *e*. . . . . .Rev 21:1

**EARTHLY**
If I have told you *e* . . . . . . . . .John 3:12
we know that if our *e* house . .2 Cor 5:1
their mind on *e* things . . . . . .Phil 3:19
from above, but is *e* . . . . . . .James 3:15

**EARTHQUAKE**
after the wind an *e* . . . . . . .1 Kin 19:11
there was a great *e*. . . . . . . . .Matt 28:2

**EARTHQUAKES**
And there will be *e* . . . . . . . .Mark 13:8

**EASIER**
"Which is *e*, to say . . . . . . . . .Mark 2:9
"It is *e* for a camel. . . . . . . .Mark 10:25

**EAST**
goes toward the *e*. . . . . . . . . . .Gen 2:14
wise men from the *E* . . . . . . . .Matt 2:1
many will come from *e* . . . . .Matt 8:11
will come from the *e* . . . . . .Luke 13:29

**EAT**
you may freely *e* . . . . . . . . . . .Gen 2:16
'You shall not *e* . . . . . . . . . . . .Gen 3:17
*e* this scroll. . . . . . . . . . . . . . .Ezek 3:1
life, what you will *e* . . . . . . . .Matt 6:25
give us His flesh to *e* . . . . . . .John 6:52
one believes he may *e* . . . . . . .Rom 14:2
*e* meat nor drink wine . . . . .Rom 14:21
I will never again *e* . . . . . . . .1 Cor 8:13
neither shall he *e*. . . . . . . .2 Thess 3:10

**EATEN**
Have you *e* from the . . . . . . . .Gen 3:11
And he was *e* by worms. . . . .Acts 12:23

**EATS**
receives sinners and *e* . . . . . .Luke 15:2
"Whoever *e* My flesh . . . . . . .John 6:54
*e* this bread will live . . . . . . .John 6:58
He who *e*, *e* to the . . . . . . . . . .Rom 14:6
an unworthy manner *e* . . . .1 Cor 11:29

**EDIFICATION**
has given me for *e* . . . . . . . .2 Cor 13:10
rather than godly *e*. . . . . . . . .1 Tim 1:4

**EDIFIES**
puffs up, but love *e* . . . . . . . . .1 Cor 8:1

**EDIFY**
but not all things *e* . . . . . . .1 Cor 10:23

**EDIFYING**
of the body for the *e*. . . . . . . . .Eph 4:16

**ELDER**
against an *e* except. . . . . . . .1 Tim 5:19

**ELDERS**
the tradition of the *e* . . . . . . .Matt 15:2
be rejected by the *e* . . . . . . . .Luke 9:22
they had appointed *e* . . . . . .Acts 14:23
*e* who rule well be. . . . . . . . .1 Tim 5:17
lacking, and appoint *e*. . . . . . .Titus 1:5
*e* obtained a good. . . . . . . . . . .Heb 11:2
*e* who are among you I . . . . . . .1 Pet 5:1
I saw twenty-four *e* . . . . . . . . . .Rev 4:4

**ELDERSHIP**
of the hands of the *e* . . . . . . .1 Tim 4:14

**ELECT**
gather together His *e*. . . . . .Matt 24:31
*e* have obtained it . . . . . . . . . .Rom 11:7
*e* according to the. . . . . . . . . . .1 Pet 1:2
*a chief cornerstone, e*. . . . . . . .1 Pet 2:6

**ELECTION**
call and *e* sure . . . . . . . . . . . .2 Pet 1:10

**ELEMENTS**
weak and beggarly *e* . . . . . . . . .Gal 4:9
*e* will melt with . . . . . . . . . . .2 Pet 3:10

**ELEVEN**
numbered with the *e*. . . . . . . .Acts 1:26

**ELOQUENT**
an *e* man and mighty in . . . .Acts 18:24

**EMBALM**
to *e* his father. . . . . . . . . . . . . .Gen 50:2

**ENCOURAGED**
is, that I may be *e* . . . . . . . . . .Rom 1:12
and all may be *e* . . . . . . . . .1 Cor 14:31

**END**
make me to know my *e* . . . . . . .Ps 39:4
shall keep it to the *e*. . . . . . . .Ps 119:33
*e* is the way of death . . . . . .Prov 14:12
Declaring the *e* . . . . . . . . . . . . .Is 46:10
what shall be the *e* . . . . . . . . .Dan 12:8
the harvest is the *e* . . . . . . .Matt 13:39
always, even to the *e* . . . . . .Matt 28:20
He loved them to the *e* . . . . . .John 13:1
For Christ is the *e*. . . . . . . . . .Rom 10:4
But the *e* of all . . . . . . . . . . . . .1 Pet 4:7
the latter *e* is worse . . . . . . . .2 Pet 2:20
My works until the *e* . . . . . . . .Rev 2:26
Beginning and the *E* . . . . . . .Rev 22:13

**ENDLESS**
and *e* genealogies . . . . . . . . . .1 Tim 1:4
to the power of an *e* . . . . . . . . .Heb 7:16

**ENDURANCE**
*e* the race that . . . . . . . . . . . .Heb 12:1

**ENDURE**
as the sun and moon *e* . . . . . . . .Ps 72:5
His name shall *e* . . . . . . . . . . .Ps 72:17
being persecuted, we *e* . . . . .1 Cor 4:12

**ENDURED**
he had patiently *e* . . . . . . . . . .Heb 6:15
*e* as seeing Him who is . . . . .Heb 11:27
For consider Him who *e*. . . . . .Heb 12:3

**ENDURES**
And His truth *e* . . . . . . . . . . . .Ps 100:5
For His mercy *e* . . . . . . . . . . . .Ps 136:1
But he who *e* to the . . . . . . .Matt 10:22
*e* only for a while . . . . . . . . .Matt 13:21
for the food which *e* . . . . . . . .John 6:27
he has built on it *e*. . . . . . . . .1 Cor 3:14
hopes all things, *e*. . . . . . . . .1 Cor 13:7
*the word of the LORD e*. . . . . .1 Pet 1:25

**ENDURING**
the LORD is clean, *e*. . . . . . . . . .Ps 19:9

**ENEMIES**
the presence of my *e*. . . . . . . . . .Ps 23:5
*e* will lick the dust . . . . . . . . . . .Ps 72:9
to you, love your *e* . . . . . . . . .Matt 5:44
*e will be those* . . . . . . . . . . .Matt 10:36
*e* we were reconciled . . . . . . . .Rom 5:10
till He has put all *e* . . . . . . .1 Cor 15:25
were alienated and *e* . . . . . . . . .Col 1:21
His *e* are made His . . . . . . . .Heb 10:13

**ENEMY**
If your *e* is hungry . . . . . . . .Prov 25:21
rejoice over me, my *e* . . . . . . . . .Mic 7:8
and hate your *e* . . . . . . . . . . .Matt 5:43
last *e* that will be . . . . . . . .1 Cor 15:26
become your *e* because. . . . . . .Gal 4:16
not count him as an *e*. . . . .2 Thess 3:15
makes himself an *e* . . . . . . . .James 4:4

**ENJOY**
richly all things to *e*. . . . . . .1 Tim 6:17
than to *e* the passing . . . . . . .Heb 11:25

**ENJOYMENT**
So I commended *e* . . . . . . . . . .Eccl 8:15

**ENLIGHTEN**
*E* my eyes. . . . . . . . . . . . . . . . . .Ps 13:3

**ENLIGHTENED**
those who were once *e* . . . . . . . .Heb 6:4

**ENMITY**
And I will put *e* . . . . . . . . . . . .Gen 3:15
the carnal mind is *e* . . . . . . . . .Rom 8:7
in His flesh the *e* . . . . . . . . . . .Eph 2:15

**ENRAPTURED**
and always be *e* . . . . . . . . . . .Prov 5:19

**ENRICHED**
while you are *e* . . . . . . . . . . .2 Cor 9:11

**ENSNARED**
The wicked is *e*. . . . . . . . . . .Prov 12:13

**ENSNARES**
sin which so easily *e* . . . . . . . .Heb 12:1

**ENTER**
*E* into His gates. . . . . . . . . . . .Ps 100:4
you will by no means *e*. . . . . .Matt 5:20
"*E* by the narrow . . . . . . . . . .Matt 7:13
*e* the kingdom of God. . . . . .Matt 19:24
*E* into the joy of your . . . . . .Matt 25:21
and pray, lest you *e* . . . . . . .Matt 26:41
"Strive to *e* through . . . . . .Luke 13:24
who have believed do *e* . . . . . . .Heb 4:3
*e* the temple till the . . . . . . . . .Rev 15:8

**ENTERED**
Then Satan *e* Judas. . . . . . . .Luke 22:3
through one man sin *e* . . . . . .Rom 5:12
*ear heard, nor have e*. . . . . . . .1 Cor 2:9
the forerunner has *e* . . . . . . . .Heb 6:20
*e* the Most Holy Place . . . . . . .Heb 9:12

**ENTERS**
If anyone *e* by Me . . . . . . . . . .John 10:9

**ENTHRONED**
You are holy, *e* in . . . . . . . . . . . .Ps 22:3

**ENTIRELY**
give yourself *e* . . . . . . . . . . .1 Tim 4:15

**ENTREAT**
being defamed, we *e* . . . . . . .1 Cor 4:13

**ENTREATED**
*e* our God for this . . . . . . . . . .Ezra 8:23

**ENVIOUS**
patriarchs, becoming *e*. . . . . . .Acts 7:9

**ENVY**
*e* slays a simple. . . . . . . . . . . . . .Job 5:2
*e* is rottenness . . . . . . . . . . .Prov 14:30
not let your heart *e*. . . . . . . .Prov 23:17
full of *e* . . . . . . . . . . . . . . . . . .Rom 1:29
not in strife and *e* . . . . . . . . .Rom 13:13
love does not *e* . . . . . . . . . . . .1 Cor 13:4
*e*, murders . . . . . . . . . . . . . . . . .Gal 5:21
living in malice and *e* . . . . . . .Titus 3:3

**EPISTLE**
You are our *e* written .......2 Cor 3:2

**EPISTLES**
as also in all his *e*..........2 Pet 3:16

**ERR**
My people Israel to *e*........Jer 23:13

**ERROR**
a sinner from the *e*........James 5:20
led away with the *e* ........2 Pet 3:17
run greedily in the *e* .........Jude 11

**ERRORS**
can understand his *e* ........Ps 19:12

**ESCAPE**
*e* all these things.........Luke 21:36
same, that you will *e* ........Rom 2:3
also make the way of *e* ....1 Cor 10:13
how shall we *e* if we..........Heb 2:3

**ESCAPED**
after they have *e* ..........2 Pet 2:20

**ESTABLISH**
seeking to *e* their own ......Rom 10:3
faithful, who will *e* .......2 Thess 3:3
*E* your hearts.............James 5:8
a while, perfect, *e*..........1 Pet 5:10

**ESTABLISHED**
Your throne is *e* .............Ps 93:2
built up in Him and *e*.........Col 2:7
covenant, which was *e*........Heb 8:6

**ESTEEM**
and we did not *e*..............Is 53:3
*e* others better than .........Phil 2:3

**ESTEEMED**
For what is highly *e*.......Luke 16:15

**ESTEEMS**
One person *e* one day .......Rom 14:5

**ETERNAL**
*e* God is your refuge.......Deut 33:27
For man goes to his *e* .......Eccl 12:5
and inherit *e* life .........Matt 19:29
in the age to come, *e* ......Mark 10:30
not perish but have *e* .......John 3:15
you think you have *e* .......John 5:39
And I give them *e* life......John 10:28
"And this is *e* life..........John 17:3
the gift of God is *e*..........Rom 6:23
are not seen are *e*..........2 Cor 4:18
lay hold on *e* life ..........1 Tim 6:12
*e* life which was...........1 John 1:2

**ETERNITY**
Also He has put *e* ..........Eccl 3:11
One who inhabits *e*...........Is 57:15

**EUNUCH**
of Ethiopia, a *e* ............Acts 8:27

**EUNUCHS**
have made themselves *e* . . .Matt 19:12

**EVANGELIST**
of Philip the *e* .............Acts 21:8
do the work of an *e* .........2 Tim 4:5

**EVANGELISTS**
some prophets, some *e*.......Eph 4:11

**EVERLASTING**
from *E* is Your name.........Is 63:16
awake, some to *e* life........Dan 12:2
not perish but have *e* .......John 3:16
Him who sent Me has *e* .....John 5:24
endures to *e* life ...........John 6:27
in Him may have *e*.........John 6:40
believes in Me has *e*........John 6:47
*e* destruction from the .....2 Thess 1:9

**EVIDENCE**
*e* of things not seen .........Heb 11:1

**EVIDENT**
*e* that our Lord arose........Heb 7:14

**EVIL**
of good and *e* ...............Gen 2:9
knowing good and *e* .........Gen 3:5
his heart was only *e* .........Gen 6:5
I will fear no *e* ..............Ps 23:4
*e* more than good ............Ps 52:3
To do *e* is like sport........Prov 10:23
*e* will bow before the.......Prov 14:19
keeping watch on the *e*......Prov 15:3
*e* all the days of her .......Prov 31:12
to those who call *e*............Is 5:20
of peace and not of *e* ........Jer 29:11
Seek good and not *e* .......Amos 5:14
deliver us from the *e* .......Matt 6:13
If you then, being *e* ........Matt 7:11
*e* treasure brings .........Matt 12:35
everyone practicing *e*.......John 3:20
done any good or *e* .........Rom 9:11
Repay no one *e* for.........Rom 12:17
provoked, thinks no *e* ......1 Cor 13:5

**EVILDOER**
"If He were not an *e*.......John 18:30
suffer trouble as an *e* .......2 Tim 2:9

**EVILDOERS**
*e* shall be cut off.............Ps 37:9
Depart from me, you *e*.....Ps 119:115
iniquity, a brood of *e* ..........Is 1:4
against you as *e* ...........1 Pet 2:12

**EXALT**
*e* His name together...........Ps 34:3
*E* the humble............Ezek 21:26
and he shall *e* himself.......Dan 8:25

**EXALTATION**
who rejoice in My *e* ...........Is 13:3
brother glory in his *e*.......James 1:9

**EXALTED**
Let God be *e*............2 Sam 22:47
I will be *e* among the ........Ps 46:10
You are *e* far above...........Ps 97:9
His name alone is *e* ........Ps 148:13
valley shall be *e* .............Is 40:4
"Him God has *e* ...........Acts 5:31
And lest I should be *e* ......2 Cor 12:7
also has highly *e*............Phil 2:9

**EXALTS**
Righteousness *e*..........Prov 14:34
high thing that *e*..........2 Cor 10:5
*e* himself above all........2 Thess 2:4

**EXAMINE**
But let a man *e* ..........1 Cor 11:28
But let each one *e*............Gal 6:4

**EXAMPLE**
to make her a public *e* ......Matt 1:19
I have given you an *e* ......John 13:15
youth, but be an *e*.........1 Tim 4:12
us, leaving us an *e* .........1 Pet 2:21
are set forth as an *e*...........Jude 7

**EXAMPLES**
happened to them as *e*.....1 Cor 10:11
to you, but being *e* ..........1 Pet 5:3

**EXCHANGE**
give in *e* for his soul......Matt 16:26

**EXCHANGED**
nor can it be *e*.............Job 28:17
*e* the truth of God for .......Rom 1:25

**EXCUSE**
but now they have no *e*.....John 15:22
they are without *e*..........Rom 1:20

**EXCUSES**
accord began to make *e*....Luke 14:18

**EXECUTE**
*e* judgment also ...........John 5:27
*e* wrath on him who ........Rom 13:4

**EXECUTES**
*e* justice for me..............Mic 7:9

**EXERCISE**
*e* yourself toward ..........1 Tim 4:7

**EXHORT**
*e* him as a father...........1 Tim 5:1
Speak these things, *e* ......Titus 2:15
*e* one another..............Heb 3:13

**EXHORTATION**
he who exhorts, in *e* ........Rom 12:8
to reading, to *e* ...........1 Tim 4:13

**EXHORTED**
as you know how we *e* ....1 Thess 2:11

**EXIST**
by Your will they *e*..........Rev 4:11

**EXPECT**
an hour you do not *e* ......Luke 12:40

**EXPECTATION**
the people were in *e*........Luke 3:15
a certain fearful *e* .........Heb 10:27

**EXPLAIN**
was no one who could *e* .....Gen 41:24
"*E* this parable to us ......Matt 15:15
to say, and hard to *e*.........Heb 5:11

**EXPLAINED**
He *e* all things to His ......Mark 4:34

**EXPOSED**
his deeds should be *e* .......John 3:20

**EXPOUNDED**
He *e* to them in all........Luke 24:27

**EXPRESS**
of His glory and the *e* ........Heb 1:3

**EXTORTION**
they are full of *e*..........Matt 23:25

**EXTORTIONERS**
*e* will inherit .............1 Cor 6:10

**EYE**
the ear, but now my *e*........Job 42:5
guide you with My *e*..........Ps 32:8
*e* is not satisfied ............Eccl 1:8
the apple of His *e* ...........Zech 2:8
if your right *e*.............Matt 5:29
*it was said, 'An e* ...........Matt 5:38
plank in your own *e*.........Matt 7:3
*e* causes you to sin .........Matt 18:9
Or is your *e* evil ..........Matt 20:15
through the *e* of a needle. . .Luke 18:25
the twinkling of an *e*......1 Cor 15:52
every *e* will see Him .........Rev 1:7
your eyes with *e* salve .......Rev 3:18

**EYES**
*e* will be opened.............Gen 3:5
and my *e* shall behold.......Job 19:27
*e* are ever toward the ........Ps 25:15
The *e* of the LORD are .......Ps 34:15
I will lift up my *e* ...........Ps 121:1
but the *e* of a fool .........Prov 17:24
be wise in his own *e* ........Prov 26:5
You have dove's *e* ..........Song 1:15
*e* have seen the King...........Is 6:5
who have *e* and see ..........Jer 5:21
rims were full of *e* .........Ezek 1:18
You are of purer *e* ..........Hab 1:13

But blessed are your e . . . . .Matt 13:16
"He put clay on my e . . . . . . .John 9:15
*e they have closed* . . . . . . . . .Acts 28:27
*e that they should not* . . . . . . .Rom 11:8
have seen with our e . . . . . . .1 John 1:1
the lust of the e . . . . . . . . . .1 John 2:16
as snow, and His e . . . . . . . . . .Rev 1:14
creatures full of e. . . . . . . . . . . .Rev 4:6
horns and seven e. . . . . . . . . . . .Rev 5:6

**EYESERVICE**
not with e. . . . . . . . . . . . . . . . . . .Eph 6:6

**EYEWITNESSES**
the beginning were e. . . . . . . .Luke 1:2
e of His majesty . . . . . . . . . . .2 Pet 1:16

# F

**FABLES**
nor give heed to f . . . . . . . . . .1 Tim 1:4
cunningly devised f. . . . . . . .2 Pet 1:16

**FACE**
"For I have seen God f. . . . . .Gen 32:30
f shone while he. . . . . . . . . . . . .Ex 34:29
sins have hidden His f . . . . . . . .Is 59:2
f shone like the sun . . . . . . .Matt 17:2
dimly, but then f . . . . . . . . .1 Cor 13:12
with unveiled f . . . . . . . . . .2 Cor 3:18
withstood him to his f . . . . . . .Gal 2:11
They shall see His f. . . . . . . . .Rev 22:4

**FADE**
we all f as a leaf. . . . . . . . . . . . . .Is 64:6
rich man also will f. . . . . . .James 1:11
and that does not f. . . . . . . . . .1 Pet 1:4

**FADES**
withers, the flower f . . . . . . . . . .Is 40:7

**FAIL**
tittle of the law to f . . . . . . .Luke 16:17
faith should not f. . . . . . . . .Luke 22:32
they will f . . . . . . . . . . . . . . .1 Cor 13:8
*Your years will not f* . . . . . . . .Heb 1:12

**FAILING**
"men's hearts f . . . . . . . . . .Luke 21:26

**FAILS**
Love never f. . . . . . . . . . . . . .1 Cor 13:8

**FAINT**
shall walk and not f . . . . . . . . .Is 40:31

**FAINTS**
My soul f for Your. . . . . . . . . .Ps 119:81
and the whole heart f . . . . . . . . . .Is 1:5
the earth, neither f. . . . . . . . . .Is 40:28

**FAITH**
shall live by his f. . . . . . . . . . . .Hab 2:4
you, O you of little f. . . . . . . . .Matt 6:30
not found such great f . . . . . .Matt 8:10
that you have no f. . . . . . . . .Mark 4:40
"Increase our f. . . . . . . . . . . .Luke 17:5
will He really find f. . . . . . .Luke 18:8
are sanctified by f. . . . . . . . .Acts 26:18
God is revealed from f . . . . . .Rom 1:17
f apart from the deeds . . . . . .Rom 3:28
his f is accounted for. . . . . . . . .Rom 4:5
those who are of the f. . . . . . .Rom 4:16
f which we preach. . . . . . . . . .Rom 10:8
f comes by hearing . . . . . . . .Rom 10:17
and you stand by f . . . . . . . .Rom 11:20
in proportion to our f . . . . . . .Rom 12:6
Do you have f . . . . . . . . . . . .Rom 14:22
though I have all f. . . . . . . . .1 Cor 13:2
And now abide f. . . . . . . . . .1 Cor 13:13
For we walk by f . . . . . . . . . . .2 Cor 5:7
the flesh I live by f. . . . . . . . . .Gal 2:20
f are sons of Abraham . . . . . . . .Gal 3:7
But after f has come. . . . . . . . .Gal 3:25
of the household of f. . . . . . . . .Gal 6:10
been saved through f. . . . . . . . .Eph 2:8
one Lord, one f. . . . . . . . . . . . . .Eph 4:5
taking the shield of f. . . . . . . .Eph 6:16
ceasing your work of f . . . . .1 Thess 1:3
for not all have f. . . . . . . . . .2 Thess 3:2
the mystery of the f . . . . . . . .1 Tim 3:9
I have kept the f . . . . . . . . . . .2 Tim 4:7
in our common f . . . . . . . . . . .Titus 1:4
not being mixed with f . . . . . . .Heb 4:2
f is the substance. . . . . . . . . . .Heb 11:1
without f it is. . . . . . . . . . . . . .Heb 11:6
someone says he has f . . . . .James 2:14
Show me your f . . . . . . . . . .James 2:18
and not by f only . . . . . . . . .James 2:24
f will save the sick . . . . . . . .James 5:15
add to your f virtue . . . . . . . . .2 Pet 1:5
the patience and the f . . . . . .Rev 13:10

**FAITHFUL**
God, He is God, the f . . . . . . . .Deut 7:9
LORD preserves the f. . . . . . . .Ps 31:23
eyes shall be on the f . . . . . . . .Ps 101:6
but who can find a f. . . . . . . .Prov 20:6
the Holy One who is f. . . . . . .Hos 11:12
"Who then is a f. . . . . . . . . .Matt 24:45
good and f servant . . . . . . . .Matt 25:23
"He who is f in what . . . . . .Luke 16:10
have judged me to be f . . . . .Acts 16:15
God is f . . . . . . . . . . . . . . . . . . .1 Cor 1:9
is my beloved and f. . . . . . . .1 Cor 4:17
But as God is f. . . . . . . . . . . .2 Cor 1:18
f brethren in Christ . . . . . . . . . .Col 1:2
He who calls you is f . . . . .1 Thess 5:24
This is a f saying and . . . . . .1 Tim 1:15
f High Priest in . . . . . . . . . . . . .Heb 2:17
He who promised is f. . . . . . .Heb 10:23
He is f and just to . . . . . . . . .1 John 1:9
Be f until death . . . . . . . . . . . .Rev 2:10
words are true and f. . . . . . . . .Rev 21:5

**FAITHFULNESS**
I have declared Your f . . . . . . .Ps 40:10
Your f also surrounds. . . . . . . . .Ps 89:8
f endures to all. . . . . . . . . . . .Ps 119:90
great is Your f. . . . . . . . . . . . .Lam 3:23
unbelief make the f . . . . . . . . .Rom 3:3

**FAITHLESS**
"O f generation . . . . . . . . . . .Mark 9:19
If we are f . . . . . . . . . . . . . . .2 Tim 2:13

**FALL**
a deep sleep to f. . . . . . . . . . . .Gen 2:21
Let them f by their. . . . . . . . . . . .Ps 5:10
a righteous man may f. . . . .Prov 24:16
but the wicked shall f. . . . . .Prov 24:16
the blind, both will f . . . . . .Matt 15:14
the stars will f . . . . . . . . . . .Matt 24:29
"I saw Satan f . . . . . . . . . . .Luke 10:18
take heed lest he f. . . . . . . .1 Cor 10:12
if they f away . . . . . . . . . . . . . .Heb 6:6
lest anyone f short of. . . . . . .Heb 12:15
and rocks, "F on us . . . . . . . . .Rev 6:16

**FALLEN**
"Babylon is f. . . . . . . . . . . . . . . .Is 21:9
you have f from grace. . . . . . . . .Gal 5:4
"Babylon is f . . . . . . . . . . . . . .Rev 14:8

**FALLING**
great drops of blood f. . . . . .Luke 22:44
f away comes first . . . . . . . .2 Thess 2:3

**FALSE**
"You shall not bear f. . . . . . . .Ex 20:16
I hate every f way. . . . . . . . .Ps 119:104
f witness shall perish. . . . . .Prov 21:28
"Beware of f prophets . . . . . .Matt 7:15
f christs and f. . . . . . . . . . . .Matt 24:24
and we are found f. . . . . . . .1 Cor 15:15
of f brethren . . . . . . . . . . . . . . . .Gal 2:4
f prophets have gone . . . . . . .1 John 4:1
mouth of the f prophet . . . . . .Rev 16:13

**FALSEHOOD**
for their deceit is f . . . . . . . .Ps 119:118
offspring of f . . . . . . . . . . . . . . . .Is 57:4

**FALSELY**
of evil against you f. . . . . . . .Matt 5:11
f called knowledge . . . . . . . .1 Tim 6:20

**FAMILIES**
in you all the f. . . . . . . . . . . . .Gen 12:3
the God of all the f. . . . . . . . . . .Jer 31:1
*in your seed all the f*. . . . . . . .Acts 3:25

**FAMILY**
shall mourn, every f. . . . . . .Zech 12:12
f were baptized . . . . . . . . . . .Acts 16:33

**FAMINES**
And there will be f. . . . . . . . .Matt 24:7

**FAMISH**
righteous soul to f . . . . . . . . .Prov 10:3

**FAMISHED**
honorable men are f . . . . . . . . . .Is 5:13

**FAR**
Your judgments are f. . . . . . . . .Ps 10:5
Be not f from Me . . . . . . . . . . .Ps 22:11
The LORD is f from the . . . .Prov 15:29
*their heart is f from* . . . . . . .Matt 15:8
going to a f country . . . . . .Mark 13:34
though He is not f. . . . . . . . .Acts 17:27
you who once were f . . . . . . . .Eph 2:13

**FARMER**
The hard-working f . . . . . . . .2 Tim 2:6
See how the f waits . . . . . . . .James 5:7

**FASHIONED**
have made me and f. . . . . . . . . .Job 10:8

**FASHIONS**
He f their hearts . . . . . . . . . . .Ps 33:15

**FAST**
f as you do this day . . . . . . . . . .Is 58:4
f that I have chosen. . . . . . . . . .Is 58:5
"Moreover, when you f. . . . . . .Matt 6:16
disciples do not f . . . . . . . . . .Matt 9:14
'I f twice a week. . . . . . . . . .Luke 18:12

**FASTED**
'When you f and . . . . . . . . . . . .Zech 7:5
And when He had f . . . . . . . . .Matt 4:2

**FASTING**
except by prayer and f . . . . .Matt 17:21
give yourselves to f. . . . . . . . .1 Cor 7:5

**FASTINGS**
in sleeplessness, in f. . . . . . . .2 Cor 6:5

**FAT**
and you will eat the f. . . . . . .Gen 45:18
f is the LORD'S. . . . . . . . . . . . . .Lev 3:16

**FATHER**
man shall leave his f. . . . . . . . .Gen 2:24
and you shall be a f. . . . . . . . . .Gen 17:4
I was a f to the poor. . . . . . . . .Job 29:16
A f of the fatherless . . . . . . . . . .Ps 68:5
f pities his children . . . . . . . .Ps 103:13
God, everlasting F . . . . . . . . . . .Is 9:6
You, O LORD, are our F. . . . . . .Is 63:16
time cry to Me, 'My F . . . . . . . . .Jer 3:4
for I am a F to Israel . . . . . . . .Jer 31:9
"A son honors his f . . . . . . . . . .Mal 1:6
Have we not all one F . . . . . . .Mal 2:10
Our F in heaven. . . . . . . . . . . . .Matt 6:9
"He who loves f . . . . . . . . . . .Matt 10:37

does anyone know the F . . . Matt 11:27
*'He who curses f.* . . . Matt 15:4
for One is your F . . . Matt 23:9
F will be divided . . . Luke 12:53
F loves the Son . . . John 3:35
F raises the dead . . . John 5:21
F judges no one . . . John 5:22
He has seen the F . . . John 6:46
F who sent Me bears . . . John 8:18
we have one F . . . John 8:41
of your f the devil . . . John 8:44
"I and My F are one . . . John 10:30
'I am going to the F . . . John 14:28
came forth from the F . . . John 16:28
that he might be the f . . . Rom 4:11
one God and F of all . . . Eph 4:6
*"I will be to Him a F* . . . Heb 1:5
comes down from the F . . . James 1:17
if you call on the F . . . 1 Pet 1:17
and testify that the F . . . 1 John 4:14

**FATHER'S**
you in My F kingdom . . . Matt 26:29
I must be about My F . . . Luke 2:49
F house are many . . . John 14:2
that a man has his f . . . 1 Cor 5:1

**FATHERLESS**
the helper of the f . . . Ps 10:14
He relieves the f . . . Ps 146:9
do not defend the f . . . Is 1:23
they may rob the f . . . Is 10:2
You the f finds mercy . . . Hos 14:3

**FATHERS**
the LORD God of our f . . . Ezra 7:27
f trusted in You . . . Ps 22:4
our ears, O God, our f . . . Ps 44:1
f ate the manna . . . John 6:31
of whom are the f . . . Rom 9:5
unaware that all our f . . . 1 Cor 10:1

**FATNESS**
of the root and f . . . Rom 11:17

**FAULT**
I have found no f . . . Luke 23:14
does He still find f . . . Rom 9:19
of God without f . . . Phil 2:15

**FAULTLESS**
covenant had been f . . . Heb 8:7
to present you f . . . Jude 24

**FAULTS**
"I remember my f . . . Gen 41:9
me from secret f . . . Ps 19:12

**FAVOR**
granted me life and f . . . Job 10:12
His f is for life . . . Ps 30:5
A good man obtains f . . . Prov 12:2
and stature, and in f . . . Luke 2:52
God and having f . . . Acts 2:47

**FAVORED**
"Rejoice, highly f . . . Luke 1:28

**FAVORITISM**
do not show personal f . . . Luke 20:21
God shows personal f . . . Gal 2:6

**FEAR**
live, for I f God . . . Gen 42:18
to put the dread and f . . . Deut 2:25
said, "Does Job f . . . Job 1:9
Yes, you cast off f . . . Job 15:4
The f of the LORD is . . . Ps 19:9
of death, I will f . . . Ps 23:4
whom shall I f . . . Ps 27:1
Oh, f the LORD . . . Ps 34:9
there is no f of God . . . Ps 36:1
The f of the LORD is . . . Ps 111:10
The f of man brings a . . . Prov 29:25
F God and keep His . . . Eccl 12:13
let Him be your f . . . Is 8:13
"Be strong, do not f . . . Is 35:4
who would not f . . . Jer 10:7
f Him who is able . . . Matt 10:28
"Do not f . . . Luke 12:32
"Do you not even f . . . Luke 23:40
And walking in the f . . . Acts 9:31
given us a spirit of f . . . 2 Tim 1:7
those who through f . . . Heb 2:15
because of His godly f . . . Heb 5:7
F God . . . 1 Pet 2:17
love casts out f . . . 1 John 4:18

**FEARED**
He is also to be f . . . 1 Chr 16:25
f God more than . . . Neh 7:2
Yourself, are to be f . . . Ps 76:7
Then those who f . . . Mal 3:16

**FEARFUL**
It is a f thing to . . . Heb 10:31

**FEARFULLY**
f and wonderfully made . . . Ps 139:14

**FEARING**
sincerity of heart, f . . . Col 3:22
forsook Egypt, not f . . . Heb 11:27

**FEARS**
upright man, one who f . . . Job 1:8
me from all my f . . . Ps 34:4
every nation whoever f . . . Acts 10:35
f has not been made . . . 1 John 4:18

**FEAST**
and you shall keep a f . . . Num 29:12
hate, I despise your f . . . Amos 5:21
every year at the F . . . Luke 2:41
when you give a f . . . Luke 14:13
Now the Passover, a f . . . John 6:4
great day of the f . . . John 7:37

**FEASTING**
go to the house of f . . . Eccl 7:2

**FEASTS**
the best places at f . . . Luke 20:46
spots in your love f . . . Jude 12

**FED**
and f you with manna . . . Deut 8:3
f you with milk and . . . 1 Cor 3:2

**FEEBLE**
strengthened the f . . . Job 4:4
and there was none f . . . Ps 105:37
and my flesh is f . . . Ps 109:24
hang down, and the f . . . Heb 12:12

**FEED**
ravens to f you there . . . 1 Kin 17:4
and f your flocks . . . Is 61:5
to him, "F My lambs . . . John 21:15
*your enemy hungers, f* . . . Rom 12:20
my goods to f the poor . . . 1 Cor 13:3

**FEEDS**
your heavenly Father f . . . Matt 6:26

**FEET**
all things under his f . . . Ps 8:6
He makes my f like the . . . Ps 18:33
You have set my f . . . Ps 31:8
for their f run to . . . Prov 1:16
Her f go down to death . . . Prov 5:5
mountains are the f . . . Is 52:7
place of My f glorious . . . Is 60:13
in that day His f . . . Zech 14:4
two hands or two f . . . Matt 18:8
began to wash His f . . . Luke 7:38
wash the disciples' f . . . John 13:5
*f are swift to shed* . . . Rom 3:15
*beautiful are the f* . . . Rom 10:15
*all things under His f* . . . 1 Cor 15:27
and having shod your f . . . Eph 6:15
fell at His f as dead . . . Rev 1:17

**FELLOW**
begins to beat his f . . . Matt 24:49
f citizens with the . . . Eph 2:19
Gentiles should be f . . . Eph 3:6
I am your f servant . . . Rev 19:10

**FELLOWSHIP**
doctrine and f . . . Acts 2:42
were called into the f . . . 1 Cor 1:9
f has righteousness . . . 2 Cor 6:14
the right hand of f . . . Gal 2:9
And have no f with the . . . Eph 5:11
of love, if any f . . . Phil 2:1
and the f of His . . . Phil 3:10
we say that we have f . . . 1 John 1:6
the light, we have f . . . 1 John 1:7

**FERVENT**
f prayer of a . . . James 5:16
will melt with f . . . 2 Pet 3:10

**FERVENTLY**
love one another f . . . 1 Pet 1:22

**FEW**
let your words be f . . . Eccl 5:2
and there are f . . . Matt 7:14
but the laborers are f . . . Matt 9:37
called, but f chosen . . . Matt 20:16
"Lord, are there f . . . Luke 13:23

**FIDELITY**
but showing all good f . . . Titus 2:10

**FIELD**
let the f be joyful . . . Ps 96:12
"The f is the world . . . Matt 13:38
and buys that f . . . Matt 13:44
you are God's f . . . 1 Cor 3:9

**FIERY**
LORD sent f serpents . . . Num 21:6
shall make them as a f . . . Ps 21:9
burning f furnace . . . Dan 3:6
concerning the f . . . 1 Pet 4:12

**FIG**
f leaves together . . . Gen 3:7
"Look at the f . . . Luke 21:29
'I saw you under the f . . . John 1:50

**FIGHT**
"The LORD will f . . . Ex 14:14
Our God will f for us . . . Neh 4:20
My servants would f . . . John 18:36
to him, let us not f . . . Acts 23:9
F the good f . . . 1 Tim 6:12
have fought the good f . . . 2 Tim 4:7

**FIGHTS**
your God is He who f . . . Josh 23:10
because my lord f . . . 1 Sam 25:28
f come from among you . . . James 4:1

**FIGS**
from thornbushes or f . . . Matt 7:16
or a grapevine bear f . . . James 3:12

**FILL**
f the earth and subdue . . . Gen 1:28
"do I not f heaven . . . Jer 23:24
f this temple with . . . Hag 2:7
"F the waterpots . . . John 2:7
that He might f . . . Eph 4:10

**FILLED**
the whole earth be f . . . Ps 72:19
for they shall be f . . . Matt 5:6
let the children be f . . . Mark 7:27
he would gladly have f . . . Luke 15:16

being *f* with all............Rom 1:29
but be *f* with the ...........Eph 5:18
peace, be warmed and *f*....James 2:16

**FILTHY**
with *f* garments............Zech 3:3
poor man in *f* clothes.......James 2:2
oppressed by the *f* ..........2 Pet 2:7
let him be *f*...............Rev 22:11

**FIND**
sure your sin will *f* .......Num 32:23
waters, for you will *f*........Eccl 11:1
seek, and you will *f* .........Matt 7:7
*f* a Babe wrapped...........Luke 2:12
*f* no fault in this Man ......Luke 23:4
*f* grace to help in ...........Heb 4:16

**FINDS**
*f* me *f* life.................Prov 8:35
*f* a wife *f* a good...........Prov 18:22
and he who seeks *f*..........Matt 7:8
*f* his life will lose .........Matt 10:39
and he who seeks *f*.......Luke 11:10

**FINGER**
written with the *f* ..........Ex 31:18
dip the tip of his *f* ........Luke 16:24
"Reach your *f*............John 20:27

**FINISH**
he has enough to *f*........Luke 14:28
has given Me to *f*..........John 5:36

**FINISHED**
*f* the work which You.......John 17:4
He said, "It is *f*...........John 19:30
I have *f* the race ...........2 Tim 4:7

**FIRE**
rained brimstone and *f*.....Gen 19:24
to him in a flame of *f* .........Ex 3:2
God who answers by *f* ....1 Kin 18:24
LORD was not in the *f* ....1 Kin 19:12
we went through *f*..........Ps 66:12
*f* goes before Him............Ps 97:3
burns as the *f*...............Is 9:18
you walk through the *f*.......Is 43:2
*f* that burns all the...........Is 65:5
He break out like *f*.........Amos 5:6
for conflict by *f*............Amos 7:4
like a refiner's *f*............Mal 3:2
the Holy Spirit and *f*.......Matt 3:11
*f is not quenched* ........Mark 9:44
"I came to send *f*.........Luke 12:49
tongues, as of *f*..............Acts 2:3
*f* taking vengeance .......2 Thess 1:8
and that burned with *f*.....Heb 12:18
And the tongue is a *f*.......James 3:6
vengeance of eternal *f* ........Jude 7
into the lake of *f* ..........Rev 20:14

**FIRM**
of the hope *f* to the ...........Heb 3:6

**FIRMAMENT**
Thus God made the *f*.........Gen 1:7
*f* shows His handiwork .......Ps 19:1

**FIRST**
*f* father sinned..............Is 43:27
desires to be *f*............Matt 20:27
*f* shall be slave ..........Mark 10:44
And the gospel must *f*.....Mark 13:10
evil, of the Jew *f* ............Rom 2:9
*f man Adam became a*.....1 Cor 15:45
that we who *f* trusted .......Eph 1:12
love Him because He *f* ....1 John 4:19
I am the *F* and the ..........Rev 1:17
you have left your *f* ..........Rev 2:4
is the *f* resurrection.........Rev 20:5

**FIRSTBORN**
LORD struck all the *f* .......Ex 12:29
brought forth her *f*.........Matt 1:25
that He might be the *f* ......Rom 8:29
invisible God, the *f*..........Col 1:15
the beginning, the *f* .........Col 1:18
witness, the *f* from...........Rev 1:5

**FIRSTFRUITS**
also who have the *f*.........Rom 8:23
and has become the *f*......1 Cor 15:20
Christ the *f* .............1 Cor 15:23

**FISH**
had prepared a great *f*.......Jon 1:17
belly of the great *f*........Matt 12:40
five loaves and two *f* ......Matt 14:17
and likewise the *f*.........John 21:13

**FISHERS**
and I will make you *f*.......Matt 4:19

**FIVE**
*f* smooth stones .........1 Sam 17:40
about *f* thousand men .....Matt 14:21
and *f* were foolish..........Matt 25:2

**FIXED**
is a great gulf *f* ..........Luke 16:26

**FLAME**
appeared to him in a *f*.........Ex 3:2
am tormented in this *f* ....Luke 16:24
*and His ministers a f*.........Heb 1:7
and His eyes like a *f*.........Rev 1:14

**FLAMES**
the LORD divides the *f*........Ps 29:7

**FLAMING**
*f* sword which turned .......Gen 3:24
in *f* fire taking...........2 Thess 1:8

**FLATTER**
They *f* with their .............Ps 5:9

**FLATTERED**
Nevertheless they *f* .........Ps 78:36

**FLATTERING**
*f* speech deceive ..........Rom 16:18
swelling words, *f*............Jude 16

**FLATTERS**
*f* his neighbor spreads ......Prov 29:5

**FLATTERY**
shall corrupt with *f*........Dan 11:32

**FLAVOR**
the salt loses its *f*..........Matt 5:13

**FLAX**
*f He will not quench* ......Matt 12:20

**FLEE**
Or where can I *f*............Ps 139:7
and the shadows *f* .........Song 2:17
who are in Judea *f*........Matt 24:16
*F* sexual immorality .......1 Cor 6:18
*f* these things and.........1 Tim 6:11
devil and he will *f* .........James 4:7

**FLESH**
bone of my bones and *f* ......Gen 2:23
shall become one *f*..........Gen 2:24
*f* had corrupted their........Gen 6:12
*f* I shall see God ..........Job 19:26
my *f* also will rest in .........Ps 16:9
is wearisome to the *f*......Eccl 12:12
and all *f* shall see it...........Is 40:5
"All *f* is grass ................Is 40:6
out My Spirit on all *f*........Joel 2:28
Simon Bar-Jonah, for *f* ....Matt 16:17
*two shall become one f*......Matt 19:5
were shortened, no *f*.......Matt 24:22
*two shall become one f* .....Mark 10:8
And the Word became *f* .....John 1:14
I shall give is My *f*.........John 6:51
*f* profits nothing............John 6:63
of God, but with the *f* .......Rom 7:25
on the things of the *f*.........Rom 8:5
to the *f* you will die.........Rom 8:13
*f* should glory in His .......1 Cor 1:29
*"shall become one f*.........1 Cor 6:16
For the *f* lusts..............Gal 5:17
have crucified the *f* .........Gal 5:24
may boast in your *f* .........Gal 6:13
the lust of the *f* ..........1 John 2:16
has come in the *f*..........1 John 4:2

**FLESHLY**
*f* wisdom but by the........2 Cor 1:12
*f* lusts which .............1 Pet 2:11

**FLIES**
Dead *f* putrefy the..........Eccl 10:1

**FLOAT**
and he made the iron *f* ......2 Kin 6:6

**FLOCK**
lead Joseph like a *f*...........Ps 80:1
He will feed His *f* ...........Is 40:11
you do not feed the *f*........Ezek 34:3
my God, "Feed the *f*........Zech 11:4
*sheep of the f* ............Matt 26:31
"Do not fear, little *f*.......Luke 12:32
there will be one *f*.........John 10:16
Shepherd the *f* of God........1 Pet 5:2
examples to the *f* ............1 Pet 5:3

**FLOOD**
the waters of the *f* ..........Gen 7:10
them away like a *f* ...........Ps 90:5
the days before the *f*......Matt 24:38
bringing in the *f* ...........2 Pet 2:5
of his mouth like a *f*.......Rev 12:15

**FLOODS**
me, and the *f* of..............Ps 18:4
*f* on the dry ground............Is 44:3
rain descended, the *f* ......Matt 7:25

**FLOURISH**
the righteous shall *f* .........Ps 72:7

**FLOW**
of his heart will *f*..........John 7:38

**FLOWER**
as a *f* of the field...........Ps 103:15
beauty is a fading *f*...........Is 28:4
grass withers, the *f*...........Is 40:7
*of man as the f*............1 Pet 1:24

**FLOWERS**
*f* appear on the earth.......Song 2:12

**FLOWING**
'a land *f* with milk..........Deut 6:3
the Gentiles like a *f* .........Is 66:12

**FLUTE**
play the harp and *f*.........Gen 4:21

**FLUTES**
instruments and *f* ..........Ps 150:4

**FLUTISTS**
harpists, musicians, *f*......Rev 18:22

**FLY**
soon cut off, and we *f*........Ps 90:10

**FOLLOW**
*f* You wherever You go ......Matt 8:19
He said to him, "*F* ..........Matt 9:9
up his cross, and *f*..........Mark 8:34
will by no means *f* ..........John 10:5
serves Me, let him *f*.......John 12:26
that you should *f* ..........1 Pet 2:21
*f* the Lamb wherever He .....Rev 14:4
and their works *f*..........Rev 14:13

**FOLLOWED**
*f* the LORD my God..........Josh 14:8
we have left all and *f* .....Mark 10:28

**FOLLOWS**
*f* Me shall not walk . . . . . . . . John 8:12

**FOLLY**
taken much notice of *f* . . . . . . Job 35:15
not turn back to *f* . . . . . . . . . . . . Ps 85:8
*F* is joy to him who is . . . . . . Prov 15:21
*f* is set in great . . . . . . . . . . . . Eccl 10:6

**FOOD**
you it shall be for *f*. . . . . . . . . . Gen 1:29
that lives shall be *f*. . . . . . . . . . Gen 9:3
*f* which you eat shall . . . . . . . Ezek 4:10
the fields yield no *f* . . . . . . . . . Hab 3:17
that there may be *f* . . . . . . . . . Mal 3:10
to give them *f*. . . . . . . . . . . . Matt 24:45
and you gave Me *f* . . . . . . . . Matt 25:35
and he who has *f* . . . . . . . . . . Luke 3:11
have you any *f* . . . . . . . . . . . . John 21:5
they ate their *f* . . . . . . . . . . . . Acts 2:46
our hearts with *f*. . . . . . . . . . Acts 14:17
destroy with your *f*. . . . . . . . Rom 14:15
*f* makes my brother. . . . . . . . 1 Cor 8:13
the same spiritual *f*. . . . . . . . 1 Cor 10:3
sower, and bread for *f* . . . . . . 2 Cor 9:10
And having *f* and . . . . . . . . . . 1 Tim 6:8
and not solid *f* . . . . . . . . . . . . . Heb 5:12
But solid *f* belongs to. . . . . . . . Heb 5:14
of *f* sold his. . . . . . . . . . . . . . . Heb 12:16
destitute of daily *f*. . . . . . . . James 2:15

**FOODS**
*f* which God . . . . . . . . . . . . . . 1 Tim 4:3

**FOOL**
*f* has said in his . . . . . . . . . . . . . Ps 14:1
is like sport to a *f*. . . . . . . . . Prov 10:23
*f* is right in his own . . . . . . . Prov 12:15
is too lofty for a *f*. . . . . . . . . . . Prov 24:7
whoever says, 'You *f*. . . . . . . . Matt 5:22
I have become a *f*. . . . . . . . . 2 Cor 12:11

**FOOLISH**
I was so *f* and . . . . . . . . . . . . . . Ps 73:22
*f* pulls it down with . . . . . . . . Prov 14:1
*f* man squanders it . . . . . . . . Prov 21:20
Has not God made *f*. . . . . . . . 1 Cor 1:20
O *f* Galatians . . . . . . . . . . . . . . . Gal 3:1
were also once *f*. . . . . . . . . . . . Titus 3:3
But avoid *f* disputes . . . . . . . . Titus 3:9

**FOOLISHLY**
I speak *f*. . . . . . . . . . . . . . . . 2 Cor 11:21

**FOOLISHNESS**
*F* is bound up in the . . . . . . . Prov 22:15
devising of *f* is sin. . . . . . . . . . Prov 24:9
of the cross is *f*. . . . . . . . . . . . 1 Cor 1:18
Because the *f* of God . . . . . . . 1 Cor 1:25

**FOOLS**
*f* despise wisdom . . . . . . . . . . . Prov 1:7
folly of *f* is deceit . . . . . . . . . . Prov 14:8
*F* mock at sin . . . . . . . . . . . . . Prov 14:9
We are *f* for Christ's . . . . . . . 1 Cor 4:10

**FOOT**
will not allow your *f*. . . . . . . . . Ps 121:3
*f* will not stumble. . . . . . . . . . Prov 3:23
From the sole of the *f*. . . . . . . . . . . Is 1:6
*f* causes you to sin . . . . . . . . . Matt 18:8
*you dash your f* . . . . . . . . . . . Luke 4:11
If the *f* should say . . . . . . . . 1 Cor 12:15

**FOOTSTOOL**
Your enemies Your *f*. . . . . . . . . Ps 110:1
*Your enemies Your f*. . . . . . . Matt 22:44

**FORBID**
said, "Do not *f*. . . . . . . . . . . . Mark 9:39
"Can anyone *f*. . . . . . . . . . . . Acts 10:47
prophesy, and do not *f*. . . . . 1 Cor 14:39
*f* that I should boast. . . . . . . . . Gal 6:14

**FORBIDDING**
*f* to marry . . . . . . . . . . . . . . . . 1 Tim 4:3

**FOREFATHERS**
conscience, as my *f*. . . . . . . . . 2 Tim 1:3

**FOREHEADS**
put a mark on the *f* . . . . . . . . . Ezek 9:4
seal of God on their *f* . . . . . . . . . Rev 9:4
his mark on their *f*. . . . . . . . . . Rev 20:4

**FOREIGNER**
"I am a *f* and a. . . . . . . . . . . . . Gen 23:4
of me, since I am a *f*. . . . . . . . Ruth 2:10
to God except this *f* . . . . . . . Luke 17:18

**FOREIGNERS**
*f* who were there spent . . . . . Acts 17:21
longer strangers and *f*. . . . . . . Eph 2:19

**FOREKNEW**
For whom He *f* . . . . . . . . . . . . Rom 8:29
His people whom He *f*. . . . . . . Rom 11:2

**FOREKNOWLEDGE**
purpose and *f* of God. . . . . . . . Acts 2:23

**FOREORDAINED**
He indeed was *f* . . . . . . . . . . . 1 Pet 1:20

**FORESAW**
*'I f the LORD* . . . . . . . . . . . . . . Acts 2:25

**FORESEEING**
*f* that God would . . . . . . . . . . . . Gal 3:8

**FORESEES**
A prudent man *f*. . . . . . . . . . . Prov 22:3

**FORETOLD**
have also *f* these days. . . . . . . Acts 3:24
killed those who *f*. . . . . . . . . . Acts 7:52

**FOREVER**
and eat, and live *f*. . . . . . . . . . Gen 3:22
to our children *f*. . . . . . . . . . Deut 29:29
LORD sits as King *f*. . . . . . . . . Ps 29:10
Do not cast us off *f*. . . . . . . . . . Ps 44:23
throne, O God, is *f*. . . . . . . . . . . Ps 45:6
"You are a priest *f*. . . . . . . . . . Ps 110:4
His mercy endures *f* . . . . . . . . Ps 136:1
of our God stands *f*. . . . . . . . . . . Is 40:8
My salvation will be *f* . . . . . . . . Is 51:6
will not cast off *f* . . . . . . . . . . Lam 3:31
like the stars *f* . . . . . . . . . . . . Dan 12:3
and the glory *f*. . . . . . . . . . . . Matt 6:13
the Christ remains *f* . . . . . . John 12:34
who is blessed *f*. . . . . . . . . . 2 Cor 11:31
to whom be glory *f*. . . . . . . . . . . Gal 1:5
generation, *f* and ever. . . . . . . Eph 3:21
and Father be glory *f* . . . . . . . Phil 4:20
*throne, O God, is f*. . . . . . . . . . Heb 1:8
lives and abides *f*. . . . . . . . . . 1 Pet 1:23
of darkness *f*. . . . . . . . . . . . . . . Jude 13
power, both now and *f*. . . . . . . . Jude 25
And they shall reign *f*. . . . . . . Rev 22:5

**FOREVERMORE**
Blessed be the LORD *f* . . . . . . . Ps 89:52
this time forth and *f*. . . . . . . . . Ps 113:2
behold, I am alive *f* . . . . . . . . . Rev 1:18

**FORGAVE**
to repay, he freely *f* . . . . . . . Luke 7:42
God in Christ *f* . . . . . . . . . . . . Eph 4:32
even as Christ *f* . . . . . . . . . . . . Col 3:13

**FORGET**
*f* the LORD who brought . . . . Deut 6:12
I will not *f* Your word . . . . . . Ps 119:16
If I *f* you . . . . . . . . . . . . . . . . . . Ps 137:5
My son, do not *f* . . . . . . . . . . . Prov 3:1
*f* the LORD your Maker. . . . . . . Is 51:13
*f* your work and labor . . . . . . Heb 6:10

**FORGETFULNESS**
in the land of *f* . . . . . . . . . . . . Ps 88:12

**FORGETS**
and immediately *f*. . . . . . . . James 1:24

**FORGETTING**
*f* those things which . . . . . . . . Phil 3:13

**FORGIVE**
*f* their sin and heal . . . . . . . . 2 Chr 7:14
good, and ready to *f* . . . . . . . . . . Ps 86:5
And *f* us our debts . . . . . . . . . Matt 6:12
Father will also *f* . . . . . . . . . . Matt 6:14
his heart, does not *f*. . . . . . . Matt 18:35
Who can *f* sins but God. . . . . . Mark 2:7
*f* the sins of any . . . . . . . . . . John 20:23
you ought rather to *f*. . . . . . . . 2 Cor 2:7
*F* me this wrong . . . . . . . . . 2 Cor 12:13
*f* us our sins and to . . . . . . . . 1 John 1:9

**FORGIVEN**
*sins be f them* . . . . . . . . . . . . Mark 4:12
to whom little is *f* . . . . . . . . . Luke 7:47
*f* you all trespasses. . . . . . . . . . Col 2:13
your sins are *f* . . . . . . . . . . . 1 John 2:12

**FORGIVENESS**
But there is *f* with . . . . . . . . . . Ps 130:4
preached to you the *f*. . . . . . . Acts 13:38
they may receive *f* . . . . . . . . Acts 26:18
His blood, the *f* . . . . . . . . . . . . . Eph 1:7

**FORGIVES**
*f* all your iniquities . . . . . . . . . Ps 103:3
"Who is this who even *f*. . . . Luke 7:49

**FORGIVING**
tenderhearted, *f* . . . . . . . . . . . Eph 4:32
and *f* one another . . . . . . . . . . . Col 3:13

**FORGOT**
remember Joseph, but *f* . . . . Gen 40:23
They soon *f* His works . . . . . . Ps 106:13

**FORGOTTEN**
*f* the God who fathered. . . . . Deut 32:18
not one of them is *f* . . . . . . . Luke 12:6
*f* the exhortation . . . . . . . . . . . Heb 12:5
*f* that he was cleansed . . . . . . . 2 Pet 1:9

**FORM**
earth was without *f*. . . . . . . . . . Gen 1:2
Who would *f* a god or. . . . . . . . . Is 44:10
*f* the light and create . . . . . . . . . Is 45:7
descended in bodily *f*. . . . . . . Luke 3:22
time, nor seen His *f* . . . . . . . . John 5:37
For the *f* of this . . . . . . . . . . . 1 Cor 7:31
who, being in the *f* . . . . . . . . . . Phil 2:6
Abstain from every *f*. . . . . 1 Thess 5:22
having a *f* of . . . . . . . . . . . . . . 2 Tim 3:5

**FORMED**
And the LORD God *f* . . . . . . . . . Gen 2:7
*f* my inward parts . . . . . . . . . Ps 139:13
say of him who *f* . . . . . . . . . . . . Is 29:16
"Before I *f* you in. . . . . . . . . . . . . Jer 1:5
Will the thing *f*. . . . . . . . . . . . Rom 9:20
until Christ is *f* . . . . . . . . . . . . Gal 4:19

**FORMER**
*f* days better than . . . . . . . . . . Eccl 7:10
*f* rain to the earth . . . . . . . . . . . Hos 6:3
*f* prophets preached . . . . . . . . . Zech 1:4
your *f* conduct . . . . . . . . . . . . . Eph 4:22
*f* things have passed . . . . . . . . Rev 21:4

**FORMS**
clay say to him who *f* . . . . . . . . . Is 45:9
*f* the spirit of man . . . . . . . . . Zech 12:1

**FORNICATION**
We were not born of *f* . . . . . . . John 8:41
of the wrath of her *f*. . . . . . . . . Rev 14:8

**FORNICATOR**
you know, that no *f* . . . . . . . . . . Eph 5:5
lest there be any *f* . . . . . . . . . Heb 12:16

**FORNICATORS**
but *f* and adulterers ... Heb 13:4

**FORSAKE**
But I did not *f* ... Ps 119:87
father, and do not *f* ... Prov 1:8
of you does not *f* ... Luke 14:33
*never leave you nor f* ... Heb 13:5

**FORSAKEN**
My God, why have You *f* ... Ps 22:1
seen the righteous *f* ... Ps 37:25
a mere moment I have *f* ... Is 54:7
*My God, why have You f* ... Matt 27:46
persecuted, but not *f* ... 2 Cor 4:9
for Demas has *f* ... 2 Tim 4:10

**FORSAKING**
*f* the assembling ... Heb 10:25

**FORSOOK**
*f* God who made him ... Deut 32:15
all the disciples *f* ... Matt 26:56
with me, but all *f* ... 2 Tim 4:16

**FORTRESS**
LORD is my rock, my *f* ... 2 Sam 22:2
my rock of refuge, a *f* ... Ps 31:2

**FOUND**
*f* a helper comparable ... Gen 2:20
a thousand I have *f* ... Eccl 7:28
LORD while He may be *f* ... Is 55:6
fruit on it and *f* none ... Luke 13:6
he was lost and is *f* ... Luke 15:24
*f* the Messiah" (which ... John 1:41
and be *f* in Him ... Phil 3:9

**FOUNDATION**
Of old You laid the *f* ... Ps 102:25
the earth without a *f* ... Luke 6:49
loved Me before the *f* ... John 17:24
I have laid the *f* ... 1 Cor 3:10
*f* can anyone lay than ... 1 Cor 3:11
us in Him before the *f* ... Eph 1:4
not laying again the *f* ... Heb 6:1
Lamb slain from the *f* ... Rev 13:8

**FOUNDATIONS**
when I laid the *f* ... Job 38:4
And the *f* of the wall ... Rev 21:19

**FOUNTAIN**
will become in him a *f* ... John 4:14

**FOUNTAINS**
on that day all the *f* ... Gen 7:11
lead them to living *f* ... Rev 7:17

**FRAGRANCE**
was filled with the *f* ... John 12:3
we are to God the *f* ... 2 Cor 2:15

**FREE**
'You will be made *f* ... John 8:33
And having been set *f* ... Rom 6:18
Jesus has made me *f* ... Rom 8:2
is neither slave nor *f* ... Gal 3:28
Christ has made us *f* ... Gal 5:1
he is a slave or *f* ... Eph 6:8

**FREED**
has died has been *f* ... Rom 6:7

**FREEDMAN**
slave is the Lord's *f* ... 1 Cor 7:22

**FREELY**
the garden you may *f* ... Gen 2:16
*F* you have received ... Matt 10:8
*f* give us all ... Rom 8:32
the water of life *f* ... Rev 22:17

**FRIEND**
of Abraham Your *f* ... 2 Chr 20:7
*f* who sticks closer ... Prov 18:24
a *f* of tax collectors ... Matt 11:19
of you shall have a *f* ... Luke 11:5
*f* Lazarus sleeps ... John 11:11
he was called the *f* ... James 2:23
wants to be a *f* ... James 4:4

**FRIENDS**
My *f* scorn me ... Job 16:20
the rich has many *f* ... Prov 14:20
one's life for his *f* ... John 15:13
I have called you *f* ... John 15:15
to forbid any of his *f* ... Acts 24:23

**FROGS**
your territory with *f* ... Ex 8:2
*f* coming out of the ... Rev 16:13

**FRUIT**
and showed them the *f* ... Num 13:26
brings forth its *f* ... Ps 1:3
*f* is better than gold ... Prov 8:19
with good by the *f* ... Prov 12:14
like the first *f* ... Is 28:4
does not bear good *f* ... Matt 3:10
good tree bears good *f* ... Matt 7:17
not drink of this *f* ... Matt 26:29
and blessed is the *f* ... Luke 1:42
life, and bring no *f* ... Luke 8:14
and he came seeking *f* ... Luke 13:6
'And if it bears *f* ... Luke 13:9
branch that bears *f* ... John 15:2
that you bear much *f* ... John 15:8
should go and bear *f* ... John 15:16
God, you have your *f* ... Rom 6:22
that we should bear *f* ... Rom 7:4
But the *f* of the ... Gal 5:22
yields the peaceable *f* ... Heb 12:11
Now the *f* of ... James 3:18
autumn trees without *f* ... Jude 12
tree yielding its *f* ... Rev 22:2

**FRUITFUL**
them, saying, "Be *f* ... Gen 1:22
wife shall be like a *f* ... Ps 128:3
pleasing Him, being *f* ... Col 1:10

**FRUITS**
Therefore bear *f* ... Matt 3:8
know them by their *f* ... Matt 7:16
of mercy and good *f* ... James 3:17
which bore twelve *f* ... Rev 22:2

**FULFILL**
for us to *f* all ... Matt 3:15
*f* the law of Christ ... Gal 6:2
*f* my joy by being ... Phil 2:2
and *f* all the good ... 2 Thess 1:11
If you really *f* ... James 2:8

**FULFILLED**
the law till all is *f* ... Matt 5:18
of the Gentiles are *f* ... Luke 21:24
all things must be *f* ... Luke 24:44
of the law might be *f* ... Rom 8:4
loves another has *f* ... Rom 13:8
For all the law is *f* ... Gal 5:14

**FULFILLMENT**
love is the *f* of the ... Rom 13:10

**FULL**
and it was *f* of bones ... Ezek 37:1
whole body will be *f* ... Matt 6:22
that your joy may be *f* ... John 15:11
You are already *f* ... 1 Cor 4:8
learned both to be *f* ... Phil 4:12

**FULLNESS**
*f* we have all received ... John 1:16
But when the *f* of the ... Gal 4:4
filled with all the *f* ... Eph 3:19
Him dwells all the *f* ... Col 2:9

**FURNACE**
you out of the iron *f* ... Deut 4:20
of a burning fiery *f* ... Dan 3:6
cast them into the *f* ... Matt 13:42
the smoke of a great *f* ... Rev 9:2

**FURY**
Thus will I spend My *f* ... Ezek 6:12
in anger and *f* on the ... Mic 5:15

## G

**GAIN**
and to die is *g* ... Phil 1:21
rubbish, that I may *g* ... Phil 3:8
is a means of *g* ... 1 Tim 6:5
contentment is great *g* ... 1 Tim 6:6
for dishonest *g* ... 1 Pet 5:2

**GAINED**
*g* five more talents ... Matt 25:20

**GAINS**
*g* the whole world ... Matt 16:26

**GALL**
They also gave me *g* ... Ps 69:21
wine mingled with *g* ... Matt 27:34

**GAP**
and stand in the *g* ... Ezek 22:30

**GARDEN**
LORD God planted a *g* ... Gen 2:8
*g* enclosed is my ... Song 4:12
Eden, the *g* of God ... Ezek 28:13
where there was a *g* ... John 18:1
*g* a new tomb in which ... John 19:41

**GARMENT**
the hem of His *g* ... Matt 9:20
have on a wedding *g* ... Matt 22:11
cloth on an old *g* ... Mark 2:21
*all grow old like a g* ... Heb 1:11
hating even the *g* ... Jude 23

**GARMENTS**
*g* did not wear out on ... Deut 8:4
They divide My *g* ... Ps 22:18
from Edom, with dyed *g* ... Is 63:1
Take away the filthy *g* ... Zech 3:4
man clothed in soft *g* ... Matt 11:8
spread their *g* on the ... Matt 21:8
and divided His *g* ... Matt 27:35
by them in shining *g* ... Luke 24:4
*g* are moth-eaten ... James 5:2
be clothed in white *g* ... Rev 3:5

**GATE**
by the narrow *g* ... Matt 7:13
by the Sheep *G* a pool ... John 5:2
laid daily at the *g* ... Acts 3:2
suffered outside the *g* ... Heb 13:12

**GATES**
up your heads, O you *g* ... Ps 24:7
The LORD loves the *g* ... Ps 87:2
is known in the *g* ... Prov 31:23
go through the *g* ... Is 62:10
and the *g* of Hades ... Matt 16:18
wall with twelve *g* ... Rev 21:12
*g* were twelve pearls ... Rev 21:21
*g* shall not be shut ... Rev 21:25

**GATHER**
and a time to *g* stones ... Eccl 3:5
*g* the lambs with His ... Is 40:11
*g* His wheat into the ... Matt 3:12
sow nor reap nor *g* ... Matt 6:26
Do men *g* grapes from ... Matt 7:16
*g* where I have not ... Matt 25:26
*g* together His ... Mark 13:27

**GATHERED**
g some of every kind ...... Matt 13:47
the nations will be g ...... Matt 25:32

**GATHERING**
g together of the ........... Gen 1:10
g together to Him ........ 2 Thess 2:1

**GATHERS**
The Lord GOD, who g ......... Is 56:8
together, as a hen g ....... Matt 23:37

**GAVE**
to be with me, she g ......... Gen 3:12
g You this authority ....... Matt 21:23
that He g His only ......... John 3:16
Those whom You g ........ John 17:12
but God g the increase ...... 1 Cor 3:6
g Himself for our sins ........ Gal 1:4
g Himself for me ........... Gal 2:20
g Himself for it ............ Eph 5:25

**GENERATION**
One g passes away .......... Eccl 1:4
who will declare His g ........ Is 53:8
and adulterous g ......... Matt 12:39
this g will by no .......... Matt 24:34
from this perverse g ........ Acts 2:40
But you are a chosen g ....... 1 Pet 2:9

**GENERATIONS**
be remembered in all g ...... Ps 45:17
g will call me blessed ...... Luke 1:48

**GENEROUS**
no longer be called g .......... Is 32:5

**GENTILES**
G were separated .......... Gen 10:5
as a light to the G ............ Is 42:6
G shall come to your .......... Is 60:3
all these things the G ...... Matt 6:32
into the way of the G ....... Matt 10:5
revelation to the G ........ Luke 2:32
G are fulfilled ........... Luke 21:24
bear My name before G ..... Acts 9:15
poured out on the G ....... Acts 10:45
*a light to the G* ........... Acts 13:47
also the God of the G ....... Rom 3:29
mystery among the G ........ Col 1:27
a teacher of the G .......... 1 Tim 2:7

**GENTLE**
from Me, for I am g ....... Matt 11:29
But we were g among ..... 1 Thess 2:7
to be peaceable, g .......... Titus 3:2
only to the good and g ...... 1 Pet 2:18
ornament of a g ............ 1 Pet 3:4

**GENTLENESS**
love and a spirit of g ....... 1 Cor 4:21
g, self-control .............. Gal 5:23
all lowliness and g .......... Eph 4:2
Let your g be known to ....... Phil 4:5
love, patience, g .......... 1 Tim 6:11

**GHOST**
supposed it was a g ........ Mark 6:49

**GIFT**
it is the g of God ........... Eccl 3:13
is Corban"—'(that is, a g ... Mark 7:11
If you knew the g .......... John 4:10
but the g of God is ......... Rom 6:23
each one has his own g ...... 1 Cor 7:7
though I have the g ....... 1 Cor 13:2
it is the g of God ............ Eph 2:8
Do not neglect the g ....... 1 Tim 4:14
you to stir up the g ......... 2 Tim 1:6
tasted the heavenly g ........ Heb 6:4
Every good g and every ... James 1:17

**GIFTS**
You have received g ......... Ps 68:18
and Seba will offer g ........ Ps 72:10
how to give good g ......... Matt 7:11
rich putting their g ........ Luke 21:1
g differing ................ Rom 12:6
are diversities of g ......... 1 Cor 12:4
and desire spiritual g ...... 1 Cor 14:1
*captive, and gave g* .......... Eph 4:8

**GIRD**
G Your sword upon Your ...... Ps 45:3
and another will g ........ John 21:18
Therefore g up the ......... 1 Pet 1:13

**GIRDED**
a towel and g Himself ...... John 13:4

**GIVE**
g you the desires ............ Ps 37:4
Yes, the LORD will g ........ Ps 85:12
G me understanding ....... Ps 119:34
"G to him who asks ........ Matt 5:42
G us this day our .......... Matt 6:11
what you have and g ...... Matt 19:21
authority I will g ........... Luke 4:6
g them eternal life ........ John 10:28
A new commandment I g ... John 13:34
but what I do have I g ........ Acts 3:6
g us all things ............. Rom 8:32
G no offense ............. 1 Cor 10:32
g him who has need ........ Eph 4:28
g thanks to God always ... 2 Thess 2:13
g yourself entirely ........ 1 Tim 4:15

**GIVEN**
to him more will be g ...... Matt 13:12
has, more will be g ........ Matt 25:29
to whom much is g ........ Luke 12:48
g Me I should lose .......... John 6:39
Spirit was not yet g ........ John 7:39

**GIVES**
g life to the world .......... John 6:33
All that the Father g ....... John 6:37
The good shepherd g ...... John 10:11
not as the world g ......... John 14:27
g us richly all things ...... 1 Tim 6:17
who g to all liberally ....... James 1:5
*g grace to the humble* ...... James 4:6

**GLAD**
streams shall make g ........ Ps 46:4
I was g when they said ....... Ps 122:1
make merry and be g ..... Luke 15:32
he saw it and was g ........ John 8:56

**GLADNESS**
me hear joy and g ............ Ps 51:8
Serve the LORD with g ...... Ps 100:2

**GLORIFIED**
and they g the God of ...... Matt 15:31
Jesus was not yet g ........ John 7:39
when Jesus was g ......... John 12:16
By this My Father is g ...... John 15:8
"I have g You on the ....... John 17:4
g His Servant Jesus ........ Acts 3:13
these He also g ............ Rom 8:30
things God may be g ....... 1 Pet 4:11

**GLORIFY**
g your Father in .......... Matt 5:16
"Father, g Your name ...... John 12:28
"He will g Me ........... John 16:14
And now, O Father, g ....... John 17:5
what death he would g ..... John 21:19
therefore g God in ......... 1 Cor 6:20
also Christ did not g ......... Heb 5:5
ashamed, but let him g ..... 1 Pet 4:16

**GLORIOUS**
G things are spoken .......... Ps 87:3
g splendor of Your .......... Ps 145:5
habitation, holy and g ........ Is 63:15
it to Himself a g ........... Eph 5:27
be conformed to His g ....... Phil 3:21
g appearing of our ........ Titus 2:13

**GLORY**
Please, show me Your g ..... Ex 33:18
g has departed from ...... 1 Sam 4:21
Who is this King of g ........ Ps 24:8
Your power and Your g ....... Ps 63:2
wise shall inherit g ........ Prov 3:35
It is the g of God to ........ Prov 25:2
g I will not give ............ Is 42:8
that they may have g ....... Matt 6:2
the power and the g ........ Matt 6:13
g was not arrayed ......... Matt 6:29
Man will come in the g .... Matt 16:27
with power and great g .... Matt 24:30
"G to God in the .......... Luke 2:14
and we beheld His g ....... John 1:14
and manifested His g ...... John 2:11
I do not seek My own g ..... John 8:50
"Give God the g ........... John 9:24
g which I had with You ..... John 17:5
g which You gave Me I .... John 17:22
he did not give g .......... Acts 12:23
doing good seek for g ........ Rom 2:7
fall short of the g .......... Rom 3:23
in faith, giving g .......... Rom 4:20
the adoption, the g .......... Rom 9:4
the riches of His g ......... Rom 9:23
God, alone wise, be g ...... Rom 16:27
*who glories, let him g* ...... 1 Cor 1:31
*who glories, let him g* .... 2 Cor 10:17
to His riches in g .......... Phil 4:19
appear with Him in g ........ Col 3:4
For you are our g ........ 1 Thess 2:20
many sons to g ............ Heb 2:10
*grass, and all the g* ........ 1 Pet 1:24
to whom belong the g ...... 1 Pet 4:11
for the Spirit of g ......... 1 Pet 4:14
the presence of His g ........ Jude 24
O Lord, to receive g ......... Rev 4:11
g of God illuminated ....... Rev 21:23

**GLORYING**
Your g is not good .......... 1 Cor 5:6

**GLUTTON**
you say, 'Look, a g ......... Luke 7:34

**GLUTTONS**
g shames his .............. Prov 28:7
evil beasts, lazy g ......... Titus 1:12

**GNASHING**
will be weeping and g ...... Matt 8:12

**GO**
'Let My people g ............. Ex 5:1
for wherever you g ......... Ruth 1:16
Those who g down to ....... Ps 107:23
Where can I g from ......... Ps 139:7
to whom shall we g ........ John 6:68
g you cannot come ......... John 8:21
I g to prepare a place ....... John 14:2
and he shall g out no more ... Rev 3:12

**GOADS**
to kick against the g ......... Acts 9:5

**GOAL**
I press toward the g ........ Phil 3:14

**GOATS**
his sheep from the g ....... Matt 25:32
with the blood of g .......... Heb 9:12
g could take away .......... Heb 10:4

**GOD**
G created the heavens ........ Gen 1:1
Abram of G Most High ..... Gen 14:19
and I will be their G ........ Gen 17:8

I am the LORD your *G* . . . . . . . .Ex 20:2
*G* is a consuming fire. . . . . . .Deut 4:24
If the LORD is *G* . . . . . . . . .1 Kin 18:21
*G* is greater than all . . . . . . . .2 Chr 2:5
You have been My *G* . . . . . . . .Ps 22:10
*G* is our refuge . . . . . . . . . . . . . .Ps 46:1
*G* is in the midst of. . . . . . . . . . .Ps 46:5
me a clean heart, O *G* . . . . . . .Ps 51:10
Our *G* is the *G* . . . . . . . . . . . . .Ps 68:20
Who is so great a *G* . . . . . . . . .Ps 77:13
Restore us, O *G* . . . . . . . . . . . . .Ps 80:7
You alone are *G* . . . . . . . . . . . .Ps 86:10
Exalt the LORD our *G* . . . . . . . .Ps 99:9
Yes, our *G* is merciful . . . . . . .Ps 116:5
For *G* is in heaven . . . . . . . . . . .Eccl 5:2
Counselor, Mighty *G* . . . . . . . . . .Is 9:6
*G* is my salvation . . . . . . . . . . . .Is 12:2
stricken, smitten by *G* . . . . . . . .Is 53:4
"*G* with us . . . . . . . . . . . . . . .Matt 1:23
in *G* my Savior . . . . . . . . . . .Luke 1:47
the Word was with *G* . . . . . . . .John 1:1
"For *G* so loved the. . . . . . . . .John 3:16
"*G* is Spirit. . . . . . . . . . . . . . .John 4:24
"My Lord and my *G*. . . . . . .John 20:28
Christ is the Son of *G* . . . . . . .Acts 8:37
Indeed, let *G* be true. . . . . . . . .Rom 3:4
If *G* is for us . . . . . . . . . . . . . .Rom 8:31
*G* is faithful. . . . . . . . . . . . . . .1 Cor 1:9
*G* shall supply all . . . . . . . . . .Phil 4:19
*and I will be their G* . . . . . . . .Heb 8:10
*G* is a consuming fire . . . . . .Heb 12:29
for *G* is love . . . . . . . . . . . . . .1 John 4:8
No one has seen *G*. . . . . . . .1 John 4:12
*G* Himself will be . . . . . . . . . .Rev 21:3
and I will be his *G* . . . . . . . . . .Rev 21:7

**GODDESS**
after Ashtoreth the *g* . . . . . .1 Kin 11:5
of the great *g* Diana . . . . . . .Acts 19:35

**GODHEAD**
eternal power and *G*. . . . . . . .Rom 1:20
the fullness of the *G*. . . . . . . . . .Col 2:9

**GODLINESS**
is the mystery of *g* . . . . . . . .1 Tim 3:16
Now *g* with contentment . . . .1 Tim 6:6
having a form of *g* . . . . . . . . .2 Tim 3:5
to perseverance *g*. . . . . . . . . . .2 Pet 1:6

**GODLY**
who desire to live *g*. . . . . . . .2 Tim 3:12
reverence and *g* fear . . . . . . .Heb 12:28
to deliver the *g*. . . . . . . . . . . . .2 Pet 2:9

**GODS**
your God is God of *g*. . . . . . .Deut 10:17
I said, "You are *g* . . . . . . . . . . . .Ps 82:6
yourselves with *g* . . . . . . . . . . . .Is 57:5
If He called them *g*. . . . . . . .John 10:35
*g* have come down to us . . . .Acts 14:11

**GOLD**
*g* I do not have. . . . . . . . . . . . . .Acts 3:6
with braided hair or *g* . . . . . .1 Tim 2:9
a man with *g* rings . . . . . . . .James 2:2
Your *g* and silver are . . . . . . .James 5:3
more precious than *g*. . . . . . . .1 Pet 1:7
like silver or *g* . . . . . . . . . . . .1 Pet 1:18
of the city was pure *g*. . . . . . .Rev 21:21

**GONE**
like sheep have *g*. . . . . . . . . . . . .Is 53:6

**GOOD**
God saw that it was *g* . . . . . . .Gen 1:10
but God meant it for *g*. . . . . .Gen 50:20
indeed accept *g*. . . . . . . . . . . . .Job 2:10
is none who does *g* . . . . . . . . . . .Ps 14:1
Truly God is *g* to . . . . . . . . . . . .Ps 73:1
*g* word makes it glad . . . . . .Prov 12:25
on the evil and the *g*. . . . . . . . .Prov 15:3
A merry heart does *g* . . . . . .Prov 17:22
learn to do *g* . . . . . . . . . . . . . . . .Is 1:17
talked to me, with *g*. . . . . . . .Zech 1:13
they may see your *g*. . . . . . . . .Matt 5:16
"A *g* man out of the . . . . . . .Matt 12:35
No one is *g* but One . . . . . . .Matt 19:17
For she has done a *g*. . . . . . .Matt 26:10
on earth peace, *g*. . . . . . . . . .Luke 2:14
*g* works I have shown. . . . . .John 10:32
who went about doing *g* . . . .Acts 10:38
*g* man someone would . . . . . . .Rom 5:7
in my flesh) nothing *g* . . . . . .Rom 7:18
overcome evil with *g*. . . . . . .Rom 12:21
Jesus for *g* works. . . . . . . . . . .Eph 2:10
fruitful in every *g*. . . . . . . . . . .Col 1:10
know that the law is *g* . . . . . .1 Tim 1:8
For this is *g* and . . . . . . . . . . .1 Tim 2:3
bishop, he desires a *g* . . . . . . .1 Tim 3:1
for this is *g* and. . . . . . . . . . . .1 Tim 5:4
prepared for every *g*. . . . . . .2 Tim 2:21
Every *g* gift and every. . . . .James 1:17

**GOODNESS**
"I will make all My *g* . . . . . . .Ex 33:19
and abounding in *g*. . . . . . . . . .Ex 34:6
"You are my Lord, my *g*. . . . . . .Ps 16:2
Surely *g* and mercy . . . . . . . . . .Ps 23:6
that I would see the *g*. . . . . . . .Ps 27:13
the riches of His *g*. . . . . . . . . . .Rom 2:4
consider the *g* and . . . . . . . .Rom 11:22
kindness, *g*. . . . . . . . . . . . . . . .Gal 5:22

**GOSPEL**
The beginning of the *g* . . . . . .Mark 1:1
and believe in the *g* . . . . . . .Mark 1:15
*g* must first be . . . . . . . . . .Mark 13:10
separated to the *g*. . . . . . . . . . .Rom 1:1
not ashamed of the *g* . . . . . . .Rom 1:16
to a different *g* . . . . . . . . . . . . .Gal 1:6
the everlasting *g* . . . . . . . . . . .Rev 14:6

**GOVERNMENT**
and the *g* will be upon. . . . . . . . . .Is 9:6

**GRACE**
But Noah found *g* . . . . . . . . . . .Gen 6:8
*g* is poured upon Your . . . . . . . .Ps 45:2
The LORD will give *g*. . . . . . . .Ps 84:11
the Spirit of *g*. . . . . . . . . . . .Zech 12:10
and the *g* of God was . . . . . . .Luke 2:40
*g* and truth came . . . . . . . . . .John 1:17
And great *g* was upon. . . . . . .Acts 4:33
receive abundance of *g*. . . . . .Rom 5:17
*g* is no longer *g* . . . . . . . . . . .Rom 11:6
For you know the *g* . . . . . . . . .2 Cor 8:9
*g* is sufficient. . . . . . . . . . . . .2 Cor 12:9
The *g* of the Lord . . . . . . . . .2 Cor 13:14
you have fallen from *g* . . . . . . . .Gal 5:4
to the riches of His *g* . . . . . . . . .Eph 1:7
*g* you have been. . . . . . . . . . . . .Eph 2:8
*g* was given according. . . . . . . .Eph 4:7
*G* be with all those . . . . . . . . .Eph 6:24
shaken, let us have *g*. . . . . . . .Heb 12:28
But He gives more *g* . . . . . . .James 4:6
but grow in the *g* . . . . . . . . . .2 Pet 3:18

**GRACIOUS**
he said, "God be *g* . . . . . . . . .Gen 43:29
I will be *g* to whom I . . . . . . . .Ex 33:19
at the *g* words which . . . . . . .Luke 4:22
that the Lord is *g* . . . . . . . . . . .1 Pet 2:3

**GRAFTED**
in unbelief, will be *g*. . . . . . .Rom 11:23

**GRAIN**
it treads out the *g*. . . . . . . . . .Deut 25:4
be revived like *g* . . . . . . . . . . .Hos 14:7
to pluck heads of *g* . . . . . . . . .Matt 12:1
unless a *g* of wheat. . . . . . . .John 12:24

**GRAPES**
brought forth wild *g* . . . . . . . . . . .Is 5:2
have eaten sour *g*. . . . . . . . . . .Ezek 18:2
Do men gather *g* . . . . . . . . . .Matt 7:16
*g* are fully ripe . . . . . . . . . . . .Rev 14:18

**GRASS**
The *g* withers . . . . . . . . . . . . . . .Is 40:7
so clothes the *g*. . . . . . . . . . . .Matt 6:30
*"All flesh is as g*. . . . . . . . . . . .1 Pet 1:24

**GRAVE**
my soul up from the *g* . . . . . . . .Ps 30:3
And they made His *g* . . . . . . . . .Is 53:9
the power of the *g*. . . . . . . . . .Hos 13:14

**GRAVES**
and the *g* were opened . . . . .Matt 27:52
*g* which are not . . . . . . . . . .Luke 11:44
*g* will hear His voice . . . . . . .John 5:28

**GRAY**
the man of *g* hairs . . . . . . . .Deut 32:25

**GREAT**
and make your name *g* . . . . . .Gen 12:2
For the LORD is *g* . . . . . . . .1 Chr 16:25
Who does *g* things . . . . . . . . . . .Job 5:9
*g* is the Holy One. . . . . . . . . . . . .Is 12:6
*g* is Your faithfulness. . . . . . .Lam 3:23
he shall be called *g* . . . . . . . .Matt 5:19
one pearl of *g* price . . . . . . .Matt 13:46
desires to become *g* . . . . . . .Matt 20:26
*g* drops of blood . . . . . . . . . .Luke 22:44
appearing of our *g*. . . . . . . . . .Titus 2:13
*g* men, the rich men. . . . . . . . .Rev 6:15
Mystery, Babylon the *G*. . . . . .Rev 17:5
the dead, small and *g*. . . . . . .Rev 20:12

**GREATER**
kingdom of heaven is *g* . . . .Matt 11:11
place there is One *g* . . . . . . . .Matt 12:6
*g* than Jonah is here . . . . . .Matt 12:41
*g* than Solomon is here . . . .Matt 12:42
a servant is not *g* . . . . . . . . .John 13:16
*G* love has no one . . . . . . . . .John 15:13
'A servant is not *g* . . . . . . . .John 15:20
he who prophesies is *g*. . . . . .1 Cor 14:5
condemns us, God is *g*. . . . .1 John 3:20
witness of God is *g* . . . . . . . .1 John 5:9

**GREATEST**
little child is the *g* . . . . . . . . .Matt 18:4
but the *g* of these is . . . . . . .1 Cor 13:13

**GREATNESS**
is the exceeding *g* . . . . . . . . . .Eph 1:19

**GREED**
part is full of *g*. . . . . . . . . . .Luke 11:39

**GREEDINESS**
all uncleanness with *g* . . . . . .Eph 4:19

**GREEDY**
of everyone who is *g* . . . . . . . .Prov 1:19
not violent, not *g*. . . . . . . . . . .1 Tim 3:3

**GREEK**
written in Hebrew, *G*. . . . . .John 19:20
and also for the *G* . . . . . . . . . .Rom 1:16
is neither Jew nor *G*. . . . . . . . .Gal 3:28

**GREEN**
lie down in *g* pastures . . . . . . . .Ps 23:2

**GRIEF**
and acquainted with *g* . . . . . . . .Is 53:3
joy and not with *g* . . . . . . . . .Heb 13:17

**GRIEVE**
*g* the Holy Spirit . . . . . . . . . . .Eph 4:30

**GRIEVED**
earth, and He was *g* . . . . . . . . .Gen 6:6

*g* His Holy Spirit ... Is 63:10
with anger, being *g* ... Mark 3:5

**GROAN**
even we ourselves *g* ... Rom 8:23
who are in this tent *g* ... 2 Cor 5:4

**GROANING**
I am weary with my *g* ... Ps 6:6
Then Jesus, again *g* ... John 11:38

**GROANINGS**
*g* which cannot ... Rom 8:26

**GROUND**
"Cursed is the *g* ... Gen 3:17
you stand is holy *g* ... Ex 3:5
up your fallow *g* ... Jer 4:3
others fell on good *g* ... Matt 13:8
bought a piece of *g* ... Luke 14:18
God, the pillar and *g* ... 1 Tim 3:15

**GROUNDED**
being rooted and *g* ... Eph 3:17

**GROW**
truth in love, may *g* ... Eph 4:15
but *g* in the grace and ... 2 Pet 3:18

**GRUDGINGLY**
in his heart, not *g* ... 2 Cor 9:7

**GUARANTEE**
in our hearts as a *g* ... 2 Cor 1:22
us the Spirit as a *g* ... 2 Cor 5:5
who is the *g* of our ... Eph 1:14

**GUIDE**
He will be our *g* ... Ps 48:14
*g* our feet into the ... Luke 1:79
has come, He will *g* ... John 16:13

**GUIDES**
to you, blind *g* ... Matt 23:16

**GUILT**
of your fathers' *g* ... Matt 23:32

**GUILTLESS**
*g* who takes His name ... Ex 20:7
have condemned the *g* ... Matt 12:7

**GUILTY**
"We are truly *g* ... Gen 42:21
the world may become *g* ... Rom 3:19
in one point, he is *g* ... James 2:10

**GULF**
you there is a great *g* ... Luke 16:26

## H

**HABITATION**
Is God in His holy *h* ... Ps 68:5
but He blesses the *h* ... Prov 3:33
Jerusalem, a quiet *h* ... Is 33:20
from His holy *h* ... Zech 2:13
be clothed with our *h* ... 2 Cor 5:2

**HADES**
be brought down to *H* ... Matt 11:23
*H* shall not ... Matt 16:18
being in torments in *H* ... Luke 16:23
*not leave my soul in H* ... Acts 2:27
I have the keys of *H* ... Rev 1:18
*H* were cast into the ... Rev 20:14

**HAIL**
of the plague of the *h* ... Rev 16:21

**HAIR**
you cannot make one *h* ... Matt 5:36
"But not a *h* of your ... Luke 21:18
not with braided *h* ... 1 Tim 2:9
*h* like women's *h* ... Rev 9:8

**HAIRS**
"But the very *h* ... Matt 10:30

**HALLOWED**
the Sabbath day and *h* ... Ex 20:11
who is holy shall be *h* ... Is 5:16
heaven, *h* be Your name ... Matt 6:9

**HAND**
the *h* of God was very ... 1 Sam 5:11
My times are in Your *h* ... Ps 31:15
"Sit at My right *h* ... Ps 110:1
heart is in the *h* ... Prov 21:1
Whatever your *h* ... Eccl 9:10
is at his right *h* ... Eccl 10:2
do not withhold your *h* ... Eccl 11:6
My *h* has laid the ... Is 48:13
Behold, the LORD's *h* ... Is 59:1
are the work of Your *h* ... Is 64:8
Am I a God near at *h* ... Jer 23:23
of heaven is at *h* ... Matt 3:2
if your right *h* ... Matt 5:30
do not let your left *h* ... Matt 6:3
*h* causes you to sin ... Mark 9:43
sitting at the right *h* ... Mark 14:62
at the right *h* of God ... Acts 7:55
The Lord is at *h* ... Phil 4:5
*"Sit at My right h* ... Heb 1:13
down at the right *h* ... Heb 10:12

**HANDIWORK**
firmament shows His *h* ... Ps 19:1

**HANDLE**
*H* Me and see ... Luke 24:39
do not taste, do not *h* ... Col 2:21

**HANDLED**
and our hands have *h* ... 1 John 1:1

**HANDS**
took his life in his *h* ... 1 Sam 19:5
but His *h* make whole ... Job 5:18
They pierced My *h* ... Ps 22:16
*h* formed the dry land ... Ps 95:5
than having two *h* ... Matt 18:8
"Behold My *h* and My ... Luke 24:39
*h* the print of the ... John 20:25
his *h* what is good ... Eph 4:28
the laying on of the *h* ... 1 Tim 4:14
to fall into the *h* ... Heb 10:31

**HANDWRITING**
having wiped out the *h* ... Col 2:14

**HANGED**
and went and *h* himself ... Matt 27:5

**HANGS**
*h* the earth on nothing ... Job 26:7
*is everyone who h* ... Gal 3:13

**HAPPY**
*H* is the man who has ... Ps 127:5

**HARD**
I knew you to be a *h* ... Matt 25:24
This is a *h* saying ... John 6:60
are some things *h* ... 2 Pet 3:16

**HARDEN**
But I will *h* his heart ... Ex 4:21
*h your hearts as* ... Heb 3:8

**HARDENED**
But Pharaoh *h* his ... Ex 8:32
their heart was *h* ... Mark 6:52
*eyes and h their hearts* ... John 12:40
lest any of you be *h* ... Heb 3:13

**HARDENS**
and whom He wills He *h* ... Rom 9:18

**HARDSHIP**
*h* as a good soldier ... 2 Tim 2:3

**HARLOT**
of a *h* named Rahab ... Josh 2:1
*h* is one body with her ... 1 Cor 6:16
*h* Rahab did not perish ... Heb 11:31
of the great *h* who ... Rev 17:1

**HARLOTRIES**
Let her put away her *h* ... Hos 2:2

**HARLOTRY**
are the children of *h* ... Hos 2:4
for the spirit of *h* ... Hos 5:4

**HARLOTS**
*h* enter the ... Matt 21:31
Great, The Mother of *H* ... Rev 17:5

**HARP**
Lamb, each having a *h* ... Rev 5:8

**HARPS**
We hung our *h* upon the ... Ps 137:2

**HARVEST**
seedtime and *h* ... Gen 8:22
"The *h* is past ... Jer 8:20
*h* truly is plentiful ... Matt 9:37
sickle, because the *h* ... Mark 4:29
already white for *h* ... John 4:35

**HASTENS**
and he sins who *h* ... Prov 19:2

**HASTILY**
lay hands on anyone *h* ... 1 Tim 5:22

**HASTY**
Do you see a man *h* ... Prov 29:20

**HATE**
love the LORD, *h* evil ... Ps 97:10
*h* every false way ... Ps 119:104
*h* the double-minded ... Ps 119:113
I *h* and abhor lying ... Ps 119:163
love, and a time to *h* ... Eccl 3:8
You who *h* good and ... Mic 3:2
either he will *h* ... Matt 6:24

**HATED**
but Esau I have *h* ... Mal 1:3
And you will be *h* ... Matt 10:22
have seen and also *h* ... John 15:24
*but Esau I have h* ... Rom 9:13
For no one ever *h* ... Eph 5:29

**HATEFUL**
*h* woman when she is ... Prov 30:23
in malice and envy, *h* ... Titus 3:3

**HATERS**
backbiters, *h* of God ... Rom 1:30

**HATES**
six things the LORD *h* ... Prov 6:16
lose it, and he who *h* ... John 12:25
"If the world *h* ... John 15:18
*h* his brother is ... 1 John 2:11

**HAUGHTY**
bring down *h* looks ... Ps 18:27
my heart is not *h* ... Ps 131:1
*h* spirit before a fall ... Prov 16:18

**HEAD**
He shall bruise your *h* ... Gen 3:15
and gave Him to be *h* ... Eph 1:22
For the husband is *h* ... Eph 5:23

**HEAL**
O LORD, *h* me ... Ps 6:2
*h* your backslidings ... Jer 3:22
torn, but He will *h* ... Hos 6:1
"*H* the sick ... Matt 10:8
*so that I should h* ... Matt 13:15
*sent Me to h the* ... Luke 4:18
Physician, *h* yourself ... Luke 4:23

**HEALED**
and return and be *h* ... Is 6:10

- His stripes we are *h* ... Is 53:5
- When I would have *h* ... Hos 7:1
- and He *h* them ... Matt 4:24
- that you may be *h* ... James 5:16
- his deadly wound was *h* ... Rev 13:3

**HEALING**
- shall arise with *h* ... Mal 4:2
- and *h* all kinds of ... Matt 4:23
- tree were for the *h* ... Rev 22:2

**HEALINGS**
- to another gifts of *h* ... 1 Cor 12:9

**HEALS**
- *h* all your diseases ... Ps 103:3
- Jesus the Christ *h* ... Acts 9:34

**HEALTH**
- all things and be in *h* ... 3 John 2

**HEAR**
- "*H*, O Israel ... Deut 6:4
- Him you shall *h* ... Deut 18:15
- *H* me when I call ... Ps 4:1
- O You who *h* prayer ... Ps 65:2
- ear, shall He not *h* ... Ps 94:9
- *h* rather than to give ... Eccl 5:1
- *'Hearing you will h* ... Matt 13:14
- "Take heed what you *h* ... Mark 4:24
- that God does not *h* ... John 9:31
- And how shall they *h* ... Rom 10:14
- man be swift to *h* ... James 1:19
- *h* what the Spirit says ... Rev 2:7

**HEARD**
- *h* their cry because of ... Ex 3:7
- that they will be *h* ... Matt 6:7
- *h* the word believed ... Acts 4:4
- *not seen, nor ear h* ... 1 Cor 2:9
- things that you have *h* ... 2 Tim 2:2
- the word which they *h* ... Heb 4:2
- which we have *h* ... 1 John 1:1
- Lord's Day, and I *h* ... Rev 1:10

**HEARER**
- if anyone is a *h* ... James 1:23

**HEARERS**
- for not the *h* of the ... Rom 2:13
- of the word, and not *h* ... James 1:22

**HEARING**
- 'Keep on *h* ... Is 6:9
- *h* they do not ... Matt 13:13
- *h they may hear* ... Mark 4:12
- or by the *h* of faith ... Gal 3:2

**HEARS**
- out, and the LORD *h* ... Ps 34:17
- of God *h* God's words ... John 8:47
- "And if anyone *h* ... John 12:47
- who is of the truth *h* ... John 18:37
- He who knows God *h* ... 1 John 4:6
- And let him who *h* ... Rev 22:17

**HEART**
- *h* was only evil ... Gen 6:5
- *h* rejoices in the LORD ... 1 Sam 2:1
- God gave him another *h* ... 1 Sam 10:9
- LORD looks at the *h* ... 1 Sam 16:7
- his wives turned his *h* ... 1 Kin 11:4
- He pierces my *h* ... Job 16:13
- My *h* also instructs me ... Ps 16:7
- *h* is overflowing ... Ps 45:1
- *h* shall depart from me ... Ps 101:4
- look and a proud *h* ... Ps 101:5
- with my whole *h* ... Ps 111:1
- as he thinks in his *h* ... Prov 23:7
- *h* reveals the man ... Prov 27:19
- trusts in his own *h* ... Prov 28:26
- The *h* of the wise is ... Eccl 7:4
- and a wise man's *h* ... Eccl 8:5
- *h* yearned for him ... Song 5:4
- and the whole *h* ... Is 1:5
- the yearning of Your *h* ... Is 63:15
- *h* is deceitful above ... Jer 17:9
- I will give them a *h* ... Jer 24:7
- and take the stony *h* ... Ezek 11:19
- get yourselves a new *h* ... Ezek 18:31
- are the pure in *h* ... Matt 5:8
- is, there your *h* ... Matt 6:21
- of the *h* proceed evil ... Matt 15:19
- *h* will flow rivers ... John 7:38
- "Let not your *h* ... John 14:1
- Satan filled your *h* ... Acts 5:3
- *h* that God has raised ... Rom 10:9
- refresh my *h* in the ... Philem 20
- and shuts up his *h* ... 1 John 3:17

**HEARTILY**
- you do, do it *h* ... Col 3:23

**HEARTS**
- God tests the *h* ... Ps 7:9
- And he will turn the *h* ... Mal 4:6
- *h* failing them from ... Luke 21:26
- will guard your *h* ... Phil 4:7
- of God rule in your *h* ... Col 3:15

**HEATHEN**
- repetitions as the *h* ... Matt 6:7

**HEAVEN**
- called the firmament *H* ... Gen 1:8
- LORD looks down from *h* ... Ps 14:2
- word is settled in *h* ... Ps 119:89
- For God is in *h* ... Eccl 5:2
- "*H* is My throne ... Is 66:1
- for the kingdom of *h* ... Matt 3:2
- your Father in *h* ... Matt 5:16
- on earth as it is in *h* ... Matt 6:10
- "*H* and earth will ... Matt 24:35
- from Him a sign from *h* ... Mark 8:11
- have sinned against *h* ... Luke 15:18
- you shall see *h* ... John 1:51
- one has ascended to *h* ... John 3:13
- the true bread from *h* ... John 6:32
- a voice came from *h* ... John 12:28
- sheet, let down from *h* ... Acts 11:5
- laid up for you in *h* ... Col 1:5
- there was silence in *h* ... Rev 8:1
- Now I saw a new *h* ... Rev 21:1

**HEAVENLY**
- your *h* Father will ... Matt 6:14
- *h* host praising God ... Luke 2:13
- if I tell you *h* things ... John 3:12
- blessing in the *h* ... Eph 1:3
- a better, that is, a *h* ... Heb 11:16
- the living God, the *h* ... Heb 12:22

**HEAVENS**
- and the highest *h* ... Deut 10:14
- *h* cannot contain ... 1 Kin 8:27
- *h* declare the glory ... Ps 19:1
- For as the *h* are high ... Ps 103:11
- behold, I create new *h* ... Is 65:17
- and behold, the *h* ... Matt 3:16
- *h* will be shaken ... Matt 24:29
- *h are the work of Your* ... Heb 1:10
- *h* will pass away ... 2 Pet 3:10

**HEEDS**
- *h* counsel is wise ... Prov 12:15

**HEEL**
- you shall bruise His *h* ... Gen 3:15
- has lifted up his *h* ... Ps 41:9
- *Me has lifted up his h* ... John 13:18

**HEIGHT**
- nor *h* nor depth ... Rom 8:39
- length and depth and *h* ... Eph 3:18

**HEIR**
- He has appointed *h* ... Heb 1:2
- the world and became *h* ... Heb 11:7

**HEIRS**
- if children, then *h* ... Rom 8:17
- should be fellow *h* ... Eph 3:6

**HELL**
- shall be turned into *h* ... Ps 9:17
- go down alive into *h* ... Ps 55:15
- *H* and Destruction are ... Prov 27:20
- be in danger of *h* fire ... Matt 5:22
- to be cast into *h* ... Matt 18:9
- the condemnation of *h* ... Matt 23:33
- power to cast into *h* ... Luke 12:5

**HELMET**
- And take the *h* of ... Eph 6:17
- and love, and as a *h* ... 1 Thess 5:8

**HELP**
- May He send you *h* ... Ps 20:2
- A very present *h* ... Ps 46:1
- He is their *h* and ... Ps 115:9
- Our *h* is in the name ... Ps 124:8
- *h* my unbelief ... Mark 9:24
- and find grace to *h* ... Heb 4:16

**HELPED**
- fall, but the LORD *h* ... Ps 118:13
- of salvation I have *h* ... Is 49:8
- *h* His servant Israel ... Luke 1:54

**HELPER**
- I will make him a *h* ... Gen 2:18
- Behold, God is my *h* ... Ps 54:4
- give you another *H* ... John 14:16
- "But when the *H* ... John 15:26
- *"The LORD is my h* ... Heb 13:6

**HELPFUL**
- all things are not *h* ... 1 Cor 6:12

**HELPS**
- the Spirit also *h* ... Rom 8:26

**HEM**
- and touched the *h* ... Matt 9:20

**HERE**
- Then I said, "*H* am I ... Is 6:8

**HERESIES**
- dissensions, *h* ... Gal 5:20

**HERITAGE**
- for that is his *h* ... Eccl 3:22
- This is the *h* of the ... Is 54:17
- of My people, My *h* ... Joel 3:2
- the flock of Your *h* ... Mic 7:14

**HIDDEN**
- and my sins are not *h* ... Ps 69:5
- Your word I have *h* ... Ps 119:11
- *h* that will not ... Matt 10:26
- the *h* wisdom which God ... 1 Cor 2:7
- bring to light the *h* ... 1 Cor 4:5
- have renounced the *h* ... 2 Cor 4:2
- rather let it be the *h* ... 1 Pet 3:4
- give some of the *h* ... Rev 2:17

**HIDE**
- *H* me under the shadow ... Ps 17:8
- You shall *h* them in ... Ps 31:20
- You *h* Your face ... Ps 104:29
- darkness shall not *h* ... Ps 139:12
- You are God, who *h* ... Is 45:15
- "Fall on us and *h* ... Rev 6:16

**HIDES**
- He *h* His face ... Ps 10:11

**HIDING**
- You are my *h* place ... Ps 32:7

**HIGH**
priest of God Most *H* . . . . . . . Gen 14:18
For the LORD Most *H* . . . . . . . . Ps 47:2
"I dwell in the *h* . . . . . . . . . . . . Is 57:15
know that the Most *H* . . . . . . . Dan 4:17
up on a *h* mountain by . . . . . . Matt 17:1
your mind on *h* things . . . . . Rom 12:16
*h* thing that exalts . . . . . . . . 2 Cor 10:5
and faithful *H* Priest . . . . . . . . Heb 2:17

**HIGHER**
you, 'Friend, go up *h* . . . . . . Luke 14:10

**HIGHWAY**
in the desert a *h* . . . . . . . . . . . . . Is 40:3

**HIGHWAYS**
*h* shall be elevated . . . . . . . . . . Is 49:11
go into the *h* . . . . . . . . . . . . . . Matt 22:9

**HILL**
My King on My holy *h* . . . . . . . . . Ps 2:6
*h* cannot be hidden . . . . . . . . Matt 5:14
*and h brought low* . . . . . . . . . . Luke 3:5

**HILLS**
of the everlasting *h* . . . . . . . . Gen 49:26
of the *h* are His also . . . . . . . . . . Ps 95:4
up my eyes to the *h* . . . . . . . . . Ps 121:1

**HINDER**
all things lest we *h* . . . . . . . . 1 Cor 9:12

**HINDERED**
Who *h* you from obeying . . . . . . Gal 5:7
prayers may not be *h* . . . . . . . . 1 Pet 3:7

**HOLD**
right hand shall *h* . . . . . . . . . Ps 139:10
*h* fast that word which . . . . . 1 Cor 15:2
*h* fast and repent . . . . . . . . . . . . Rev 3:3

**HOLIER**
near me, for I am *h* . . . . . . . . . . . Is 65:5

**HOLIEST**
the way into the *H* . . . . . . . . . . . Heb 9:8

**HOLINESS**
You, glorious in *h* . . . . . . . . . . Ex 15:11
I have sworn by My *h* . . . . . . . . Ps 89:35
the Highway of *H* . . . . . . . . . . . . Is 35:8
to the Spirit of *h* . . . . . . . . . . . Rom 1:4
spirit, perfecting *h* . . . . . . . . . 2 Cor 7:1
uncleanness, but in *h* . . . . . 1 Thess 4:7
be partakers of His *h* . . . . . . . Heb 12:10

**HOLY**
where you stand is *h* . . . . . . . . . . Ex 3:5
day, to keep it *h* . . . . . . . . . . . . . Ex 20:8
the LORD your God am *h* . . . . . Lev 19:2
*h* seed is mixed . . . . . . . . . . . . . Ezra 9:2
God sits on His *h* . . . . . . . . . . . . Ps 47:8
God, in His *h* mountain . . . . . . . Ps 48:1
"*H*, *h*, *h* . . . . . . . . . . . . . . . . . . . . . Is 6:3
child of the *H* Spirit . . . . . . . . Matt 1:18
baptize you with the *H* . . . . . . Mark 1:8
who speak, but the *H* . . . . . Mark 13:11
*H* Spirit will come . . . . . . . . . Luke 1:35
*H* Spirit descended . . . . . . . . Luke 3:22
Father give the *H* . . . . . . . . Luke 11:13
*H* Spirit will teach . . . . . . . Luke 12:12
*H* Spirit was not . . . . . . . . . . . John 7:39
*H* Spirit has come . . . . . . . . . . . Acts 1:8
all filled with the *H* . . . . . . . . . Acts 2:4
receive the *H* Spirit . . . . . . . . Acts 19:2
peace and joy in the *H* . . . . . Rom 14:17
*H* Spirit teaches . . . . . . . . . . 1 Cor 2:13
that we should be *h* . . . . . . . . . . Eph 1:4
were sealed with the *H* . . . . . . Eph 1:13
partakers of the *H* . . . . . . . . . . . Heb 6:4
*H* Spirit sent from . . . . . . . . . 1 Pet 1:12
it is written, "*Be h* . . . . . . . . . 1 Pet 1:16
moved by the *H* Spirit . . . . . . 2 Pet 1:21
anointing from the *H* . . . . . 1 John 2:20
says He who is *h* . . . . . . . . . . . . . Rev 3:7
For You alone are *h* . . . . . . . . . Rev 15:4
is *h*, let him be *h* . . . . . . . . . . Rev 22:11

**HOME**
sparrow has found a *h* . . . . . . . . Ps 84:3
to his eternal *h* . . . . . . . . . . . . Eccl 12:5
that while we are at *h* . . . . . . . 2 Cor 5:6
to show piety at *h* . . . . . . . . . . 1 Tim 5:4

**HOMEMAKERS**
be discreet, chaste, *h* . . . . . . . . Titus 2:5

**HONEY**
and with *h* from the . . . . . . . . . Ps 81:16
was locusts and wild *h* . . . . . . . Matt 3:4

**HONEYCOMB**
than honey and the *h* . . . . . . . . Ps 19:10
fish and some *h* . . . . . . . . . . Luke 24:42

**HONOR**
*H* your father and your . . . . . . Ex 20:12
will deliver him and *h* . . . . . . . Ps 91:15
*H* and majesty are . . . . . . . . . . . Ps 96:6
*H* the LORD with your . . . . . . . Prov 3:9
before *h* is humility . . . . . . . Prov 15:33
spirit will retain *h* . . . . . . . . . Prov 29:23
Father, where is My *h* . . . . . . . . Mal 1:6
is not without *h* . . . . . . . . . . Matt 13:57
*H your father and your* . . . . . Matt 15:4
*h* the Son just as they . . . . . . . John 5:23
"I do not receive *h* . . . . . . . . . John 5:41
but I *h* My Father . . . . . . . . . . John 8:49
"If I *h* Myself . . . . . . . . . . . . . John 8:54
him My Father will *h* . . . . . . John 12:26
to whom fear, *h* . . . . . . . . . . . . Rom 13:7
sanctification and *h* . . . . . . . 1 Thess 4:4
alone is wise, be *h* . . . . . . . . . 1 Tim 1:17
and clay, some for *h* . . . . . . . 2 Tim 2:20
no man takes this *h* . . . . . . . . . . Heb 5:4
from God the Father *h* . . . . . . 2 Pet 1:17
give glory and *h* . . . . . . . . . . . . . Rev 4:9

**HONORABLE**
His work is *h* and . . . . . . . . . . . Ps 111:3
holy day of the LORD *h* . . . . . . . Is 58:13
providing *h* things . . . . . . . . 2 Cor 8:21
Marriage is *h* among . . . . . . . . Heb 13:4
having your conduct *h* . . . . . . 1 Pet 2:12

**HONORS**
*'This people h Me* . . . . . . . . . . Mark 7:6
It is My Father who *h* . . . . . . . John 8:54

**HOPE**
*h* He has uprooted . . . . . . . . . Job 19:10
also will rest in *h* . . . . . . . . . . . . Ps 16:9
My *h* is in You . . . . . . . . . . . . . . Ps 39:7
For You are my *h* . . . . . . . . . . . . Ps 71:5
I *h* in Your word . . . . . . . . . . Ps 119:147
good that one should *h* . . . . . . Lam 3:26
to *h*, in *h* believed . . . . . . . . . . Rom 4:18
*h* does not disappoint . . . . . . . . Rom 5:5
were saved in this *h* . . . . . . . . Rom 8:24
And now abide faith, *h* . . . . 1 Cor 13:13
life only we have *h* . . . . . . . . 1 Cor 15:19
may know what is the *h* . . . . . Eph 1:18
were called in one *h* . . . . . . . . . . Eph 4:4
Christ in you, the *h* . . . . . . . . . Col 1:27
Jesus Christ, our *h* . . . . . . . . . 1 Tim 1:1
for the blessed *h* . . . . . . . . . . Titus 2:13
to lay hold of the *h* . . . . . . . . . . Heb 6:18
in of a better *h* . . . . . . . . . . . . . Heb 7:19
who has this *h* in Him . . . . . . 1 John 3:3

**HOPED**
substance of things *h* . . . . . . . Heb 11:1

**HORSE**
and behold, a white *h* . . . . . . . . Rev 6:2
and behold, a white *h* . . . . . . Rev 19:11

**HOSANNA**
*H* in the highest . . . . . . . . . . . Matt 21:9

**HOSPITABLE**
Be *h* to one another . . . . . . . . . 1 Pet 4:9

**HOSTS**
The LORD of *h* is with . . . . . . . . Ps 46:7
praise Him, all His *h* . . . . . . . . Ps 148:2
against spiritual *h* . . . . . . . . . Eph 6:12

**HOUR**
Man is coming at an *h* . . . . . Matt 24:44
"But the *h* is coming . . . . . . . John 4:23
save Me from this *h* . . . . . . . John 12:27
keep you from the *h* . . . . . . . . . Rev 3:10

**HOUSE**
But as for me and my *h* . . . . Josh 24:15
Through wisdom a *h* . . . . . . . Prov 24:3
better to go to the *h* . . . . . . . . . . Eccl 7:2
*h* was filled with . . . . . . . . . . . . . Is 6:4
*h* divided against . . . . . . . . . Matt 12:25
*h shall be called a* . . . . . . . . Matt 21:13
not make My Father's *h* . . . . . John 2:16
*h* are many mansions . . . . . . John 14:2
publicly and from *h* . . . . . . . Acts 20:20
who rules his own *h* . . . . . . . . 1 Tim 3:4
the church in your *h* . . . . . . . . Philem 2
For every *h* is built . . . . . . . . . . Heb 3:4
His own *h*, whose *h* . . . . . . . . . . Heb 3:6

**HOUSEHOLD**
over the ways of her *h* . . . . . . Prov 31:27
*be those of his own h* . . . . . . Matt 10:36
*h* were baptized . . . . . . . . . . Acts 16:15
saved, you and your *h* . . . . . . Acts 16:31
who are of Caesar's *h* . . . . . . . Phil 4:22

**HOUSEHOLDER**
*h* who brings out of . . . . . . . Matt 13:52

**HOUSES**
*H* and riches are an . . . . . . . Prov 19:14
who has left *h* or . . . . . . . . . Matt 19:29
you devour widows' *h* . . . . . . Matt 23:14

**HOVERING**
Spirit of God was *h* . . . . . . . . . . Gen 1:2

**HUMBLE**
man Moses was very *h* . . . . . Num 12:3
the cry of the *h* . . . . . . . . . . . . . . Ps 9:12
*h* shall hear of it and . . . . . . . . . Ps 34:2
contrite and *h* spirit . . . . . . . . . Is 57:15
a meek and *h* people . . . . . . . Zeph 3:12
associate with the *h* . . . . . . . Rom 12:16
*gives grace to the h* . . . . . . . . James 4:6
*H* yourselves in the . . . . . . . James 4:10
*gives grace to the h* . . . . . . . . . 1 Pet 5:5
*h* yourselves under the . . . . . . 1 Pet 5:6

**HUMBLED**
as a man, He *h* Himself . . . . . . Phil 2:8

**HUMBLES**
*h* Himself to behold . . . . . . . . . Ps 113:6

**HUMILITY**
the Lord with all *h* . . . . . . . . Acts 20:19
delight in false *h* . . . . . . . . . . . Col 2:18
mercies, kindness, *h* . . . . . . . . . Col 3:12
*h* correcting those . . . . . . . . 2 Tim 2:25
gentle, showing all *h* . . . . . . . . Titus 3:2
and be clothed with *h* . . . . . . . . 1 Pet 5:5

**HUNGER**
They shall neither *h* . . . . . . . . . Is 49:10
are those who *h* . . . . . . . . . . . . Matt 5:6
for you shall *h* . . . . . . . . . . . . Luke 6:25

to Me shall never *h* . . . . . . . .John 6:35
present hour we both *h* . . . . .1 Cor 4:11
They shall neither *h* . . . . . . . .Rev 7:16

**HUNGRY**
and fills the *h*. . . . . . . . . . . . . .Ps 107:9
gives food to the *h* . . . . . . . . . .Ps 146:7
'for I was *h* and you . . . . . . .Matt 25:35
when did we see You *h*. . . . .Matt 25:37
to be full and to be *h* . . . . . . . . .Phil 4:12

**HUNTER**
Nimrod the mighty *h* . . . . . . .Gen 10:9
Esau was a skillful *h* . . . . . .Gen 25:27

**HURT**
*h* a woman with child . . . . . . .Ex 21:22
but I was not *h* . . . . . . . . . . .Prov 23:35
another to his own *h* . . . . . . . . .Eccl 8:9
They shall not *h* . . . . . . . . . . . . .Is 11:9
it will by no means *h* . . . . .Mark 16:18
shall not be *h* by the. . . . . . . . .Rev 2:11

**HUSBAND**
She also gave to her *h* . . . . . . . .Gen 3:6
*h* safely trusts her . . . . . . . .Prov 31:11
your Maker is your *h* . . . . . . . . .Is 54:5
now have is not your *h*. . . . . .John 4:18
you will save your *h* . . . . . . .1 Cor 7:16
the *h* of one wife . . . . . . . . . . .1 Tim 3:2

**HUSBANDS**
*H*, love your wives. . . . . . . . . .Eph 5:25
Let deacons be the *h*. . . . . . .1 Tim 3:12

**HYMN**
when they had sung a *h*. . . .Matt 26:30

**HYMNS**
praying and singing *h* . . . . .Acts 16:25
in psalms and *h*. . . . . . . . . . . .Eph 5:19

**HYPOCRISY**
you are full of *h* . . . . . . . . . .Matt 23:28
Pharisees, which is *h* . . . . . .Luke 12:1
Let love be without *h* . . . . . . .Rom 12:9
away with their *h*. . . . . . . . . . .Gal 2:13
and without *h* . . . . . . . . . . .James 3:17
malice, all deceit, *h* . . . . . . . . .1 Pet 2:1

**HYPOCRITE**
and the joy of the *h* . . . . . . . . . .Job 20:5
for everyone is a *h* . . . . . . . . . . . .Is 9:17
also played the *h* . . . . . . . . . . .Gal 2:13

**HYPOCRITES**
not be like the *h*. . . . . . . . . . . .Matt 6:5
do you test Me, you *h* . . . . . .Matt 22:18
and Pharisees, *h* . . . . . . . . .Matt 23:13


## I


**IDLE**
*i* person will suffer . . . . . . . .Prov 19:15
*i* word men may speak. . . . .Matt 12:36
saw others standing *i*. . . . . . .Matt 20:3
they learn to be *i*. . . . . . . . . .1 Tim 5:13

**IDOL**
thing offered to an *i*. . . . . . . . .1 Cor 8:7
That an *i* is anything . . . . .1 Cor 10:19

**IDOLATER**
or covetous, or an *i* . . . . . . . .1 Cor 5:11

**IDOLATERS**
fornicators, nor *i* . . . . . . . . . . .1 Cor 6:9
and murderers and *i* . . . . . . .Rev 22:15

**IDOLATRIES**
and abominable *i*. . . . . . . . . . .1 Pet 4:3

**IDOLATRY**
beloved, flee from *i* . . . . . . .1 Cor 10:14
*i*, sorcery . . . . . . . . . . . . . . . . .Gal 5:20

**IDOLS**
land is also full of *i* . . . . . . . . . . . .Is 2:8
in the room of his *i*. . . . . . . . .Ezek 8:12
who regard worthless *i* . . . . . . .Jon 2:8
You who abhor *i* . . . . . . . . . . .Rom 2:22
keep yourselves from *i* . . . .1 John 5:21
worship demons, and *i*. . . . . . .Rev 9:20

**IGNORANCE**
that you did it in *i*. . . . . . . . . .Acts 3:17
*i* God overlooked. . . . . . . . . .Acts 17:30
sins committed in *i* . . . . . . . . . .Heb 9:7

**IGNORANTLY**
because I did it *i* . . . . . . . . . .1 Tim 1:13

**ILLUMINATED**
after you were *i* . . . . . . . . . .Heb 10:32
and the earth was *i* . . . . . . . . .Rev 18:1
for the glory of God *i* . . . . . . .Rev 21:23

**IMAGE**
Us make man in Our *i* . . . . . .Gen 1:26
since he is the *i* . . . . . . . . . .1 Cor 11:7
He is the *i* of the . . . . . . . . . . . .Col 1:15
and not the very *i* . . . . . . . . . .Heb 10:1
the beast and his *i* . . . . . . . . . .Rev 14:9

**IMAGINATION**
the proud in the *i*. . . . . . . . . .Luke 1:51

**IMITATE**
as I also *i* Christ . . . . . . . . . .1 Cor 11:1

**IMMANUEL**
shall call His name *I*. . . . . . . . . .Is 7:14
*shall call His name I* . . . . . . .Matt 1:23

**IMMORAL**
murderers, sexually *i* . . . . . . .Rev 21:8

**IMMORALITY**
except sexual *i*. . . . . . . . . . . .Matt 5:32
abstain from sexual *i* . . . . .1 Thess 4:3

**IMMORTAL**
to the King eternal, *i* . . . . . .1 Tim 1:17

**IMMORTALITY**
mortal must put on *i* . . . . . .1 Cor 15:53
who alone has *i*. . . . . . . . . . .1 Tim 6:16

**IMMOVABLE**
be steadfast, *i* . . . . . . . . . . .1 Cor 15:58

**IMMUTABLE**
that by two *i* things. . . . . . . . .Heb 6:18

**IMPART**
that it may *i* grace. . . . . . . . . .Eph 4:29

**IMPENITENT**
*i* heart you are . . . . . . . . . . . . .Rom 2:5

**IMPOSSIBLE**
God nothing will be *i*. . . . . . .Luke 1:37
without faith it is *i* . . . . . . . . .Heb 11:6

**IMPUTE**
the LORD does not *i* . . . . . . . . . .Ps 32:2

**IMPUTED**
might be *i* to them . . . . . . . . .Rom 4:11
but sin is not *i*. . . . . . . . . . . . .Rom 5:13

**IMPUTES**
*i* righteousness apart . . . . . . . .Rom 4:6

**INCORRUPTIBLE**
the glory of the *i*. . . . . . . . . . .Rom 1:23
dead will be raised *i* . . . . . .1 Cor 15:52
to an inheritance *i* . . . . . . . . . .1 Pet 1:4

**INCORRUPTION**
corruption inherit *i*. . . . . . .1 Cor 15:50

**INCREASE**
Of the *i* of His . . . . . . . . . . . . . . .Is 9:7
Lord, "*I* our faith. . . . . . . . . .Luke 17:5
"He must *i* . . . . . . . . . . . . . . .John 3:30
but God gave the *i*. . . . . . . . . .1 Cor 3:6

**INCREASES**
who have no might He *i* . . . . . .Is 40:29

**INCURABLE**
Your sorrow is *i*. . . . . . . . . . . .Jer 30:15

**INDIGNATION**
*i* which will devour . . . . . . . .Heb 10:27
into the cup of His *i* . . . . . . . .Rev 14:10

**INEXCUSABLE**
Therefore you are *i* . . . . . . . . . .Rom 2:1

**INEXPRESSIBLE**
Paradise and heard *i*. . . . . . .2 Cor 12:4
you rejoice with joy *i* . . . . . . . .1 Pet 1:8

**INFALLIBLE**
suffering by many *i* . . . . . . . . .Acts 1:3

**INFIRMITIES**
*"He Himself took our i* . . . . .Matt 8:17

**INHERIT**
love me to *i* wealth . . . . . . . . .Prov 8:21
*i* the kingdom prepared. . . .Matt 25:34
unrighteous will not *i*. . . . . . .1 Cor 6:9
who overcomes shall *i* . . . . . . .Rev 21:7

**INHERITANCE**
"You shall have no *i*. . . . . . .Num 18:20
is the place of His *i*. . . . . . . . .Deut 32:9
the portion of my *i* . . . . . . . . . . .Ps 16:5
*i* shall be forever . . . . . . . . . . .Ps 37:18
He will choose our *i* . . . . . . . . . .Ps 47:4
will arise to your *i*. . . . . . . . .Dan 12:13
And God gave him no *i*. . . . . . .Acts 7:5
and give you an *i*. . . . . . . . . .Acts 20:32
For if the *i* is of the . . . . . . . . . .Gal 3:18
we have obtained an *i*. . . . . . .Eph 1:11
be partakers of the *i*. . . . . . . . .Col 1:12
receive as an *i* . . . . . . . . . . . .Heb 11:8
*i* incorruptible . . . . . . . . . . . . .1 Pet 1:4

**INIQUITIES**
*i* have overtaken me . . . . . . . .Ps 40:12
forgives all your *i*. . . . . . . . . . .Ps 103:3
LORD, should mark *i*. . . . . . . .Ps 130:3
was bruised for our *i*. . . . . . . . . .Is 53:5
He shall bear their *i* . . . . . . . . .Is 53:11
*i* have separated you. . . . . . . . . .Is 59:2

**INIQUITY**
God, visiting the *i* of the . . . . . .Ex 20:5
was brought forth in *i* . . . . . . . .Ps 51:5
If I regard *i* in my. . . . . . . . . . .Ps 66:18
*i* have dominion. . . . . . . . . .Ps 119:133
*i* will reap sorrow. . . . . . . . . .Prov 22:8
a people laden with *i*. . . . . . . . . . .Is 1:4
*i* is taken away . . . . . . . . . . . . . . .Is 6:7
has laid on Him the *i* . . . . . . . . .Is 53:6
will remember their *i* . . . . . . . .Hos 9:9
to those who devise *i* . . . . . . . . .Mic 2:1
like You, pardoning *i*. . . . . . . .Mic 7:18
all you workers of *i* . . . . . . .Luke 13:27
a fire, a world of *i*. . . . . . . . . .James 3:6

**INJUSTICE**
*i* have your fathers . . . . . . . . . . .Jer 2:5

**INN**
room for them in the *i* . . . . . . .Luke 2:7
brought him to an *i*. . . . . . . .Luke 10:34

**INNOCENCE**
washed my hands in *i* . . . . . . .Ps 73:13

**INNOCENT**
because I was found *i* . . . . . . .Dan 6:22
saying, "I am *i*. . . . . . . . . . .Matt 27:24
this day that I am *i*. . . . . . . .Acts 20:26

**INQUIRED**
Therefore David *i* ... 1 Sam 23:2
the prophets have *i* ... 1 Pet 1:10

**INQUIRY**
shall make careful *i* ... Deut 19:18

**INSANE**
images, and they are *i* ... Jer 50:38

**INSPIRATION**
is given by *i* of God ... 2 Tim 3:16

**INSTRUCT**
I will *i* you and teach ... Ps 32:8
*the LORD that he may i* ... 1 Cor 2:16

**INSTRUCTED**
This man had been *i* ... Acts 18:25
are excellent, being *i* ... Rom 2:18
Moses was divinely *i* ... Heb 8:5

**INSTRUCTION**
seeing you hate *i* ... Ps 50:17
Hear *i* and be wise ... Prov 8:33
Give *i* to a wise man ... Prov 9:9
for correction, for *i* ... 2 Tim 3:16

**INSTRUCTS**
My heart also *i* ... Ps 16:7

**INSTRUMENTS**
your members as *i* ... Rom 6:13

**INSUBORDINATE**
for the lawless and *i* ... 1 Tim 1:9

**INSUBORDINATION**
of dissipation or *i* ... Titus 1:6

**INSULTED**
will be mocked and *i* ... Luke 18:32
*i* the Spirit of grace ... Heb 10:29

**INSULTS**
nor be afraid of their *i* ... Is 51:7

**INTEGRITY**
In the *i* of my heart ... Gen 20:5
in doctrine showing *i* ... Titus 2:7

**INTERCEDE**
the LORD, who will *i* ... 1 Sam 2:25

**INTERCESSION**
of many, and made *i* ... Is 53:12
Spirit Himself makes *i* ... Rom 8:26
always lives to make *i* ... Heb 7:25

**INTERCESSOR**
that there was no *i* ... Is 59:16

**INTEREST**
collected it with *i* ... Luke 19:23

**INTERPRET**
Do all *i*? ... 1 Cor 12:30
pray that he may *i* ... 1 Cor 14:13

**INTERPRETATION**
to another the *i* ... 1 Cor 12:10
of any private *i* ... 2 Pet 1:20

**INTERPRETATIONS**
Do not *i* belong to God ... Gen 40:8

**INVISIBLE**
of the world His *i* ... Rom 1:20
is the image of the *i* ... Col 1:15
eternal, immortal, *i* ... 1 Tim 1:17
as seeing Him who is *i* ... Heb 11:27

**INWARD**
You have formed my *i* ... Ps 139:13
God according to the *i* ... Rom 7:22
*i* man is being renewed ... 2 Cor 4:16

**INWARDLY**
*i* they are ... Matt 7:15
is a Jew who is one *i* ... Rom 2:29

**IRON**
*i* sharpens *i* ... Prov 27:17
its feet partly of *i* ... Dan 2:33

**ISRAEL**
"Hear, O *I* ... Deut 6:4
For they are not all *I* ... Rom 9:6
and upon the *I* of God ... Gal 6:16

**ITCHING**
they have *i* ears ... 2 Tim 4:3

## J

**JEALOUS**
God, am a *j* God ... Ex 20:5
a consuming fire, a *j* ... Deut 4:24
For I am *j* for you ... 2 Cor 11:2

**JEALOUSY**
They provoked Him to *j* ... Deut 32:16
as strong as death, *j* ... Song 8:6
for you with godly *j* ... 2 Cor 11:2

**JEOPARDY**
stand in *j* every hour ... 1 Cor 15:30

**JESTING**
talking, nor coarse *j* ... Eph 5:4

**JESUS**
*J* Christ was as ... Matt 1:18
shall call His name *J* ... Matt 1:21
*J* was led up by the ... Matt 4:1
and laid hands on *J* ... Matt 26:50
Barabbas and destroy *J* ... Matt 27:20
*J* withdrew with His ... Mark 3:7
*J* went into Jerusalem ... Mark 11:11
as they were eating, *J* ... Mark 14:22
and he delivered *J* ... Mark 15:15
truth came through *J* ... John 1:17
*J* lifted up His eyes ... John 6:5
*J* wept ... John 11:35
*J* was crucified ... John 19:20
This *J* God has raised ... Acts 2:32
of Your holy Servant *J* ... Acts 4:30
believed on the Lord *J* ... Acts 11:17
your mouth the Lord *J* ... Rom 10:9
among you except *J* ... 1 Cor 2:2
perfect in Christ *J* ... Col 1:28
But we see *J* ... Heb 2:9
looking unto *J* ... Heb 12:2
Revelation of *J* Christ ... Rev 1:1
so, come, Lord *J* ... Rev 22:20

**JOIN**
of the rest dared *j* ... Acts 5:13

**JOINED**
and mother and be *j* ... Gen 2:24
what God has *j* ... Matt 19:6
whom the whole body, *j* ... Eph 4:16

**JOINT**
*j* as He wrestled ... Gen 32:25
My bones are out of *j* ... Ps 22:14
*j* heirs with Christ ... Rom 8:17

**JOINTS**
and knit together by *j* ... Col 2:19
and spirit, and of *j* ... Heb 4:12

**JOT**
one *j* or one tittle ... Matt 5:18

**JOY**
is fullness of *j* ... Ps 16:11
*j* comes in the morning ... Ps 30:5
*j* you will draw ... Is 12:3
ashes, the oil of *j* ... Is 61:3
shall sing for *j* ... Is 65:14
receives it with *j* ... Matt 13:20
Enter into the *j* ... Matt 25:21
in my womb for *j* ... Luke 1:44
there will be more *j* ... Luke 15:7
did not believe for *j* ... Luke 24:41
My *j* may remain in you ... John 15:11
they may have My *j* ... John 17:13
the Spirit is love, *j* ... Gal 5:22
are our glory and *j* ... 1 Thess 2:20
*j* that was set before ... Heb 12:2
count it all *j* ... James 1:2
with exceeding *j* ... 1 Pet 4:13

**JOYFUL**
Make a *j* shout to the ... Ps 100:1
and make them *j* ... Is 56:7

**JUDGE**
The LORD *j* between you ... Gen 16:5
coming to *j* the earth ... 1 Chr 16:33
sword the LORD will *j* ... Is 66:16
deliver you to the *j* ... Matt 5:25
"*J* not ... Matt 7:1
"Man, who made Me a *j* ... Luke 12:14
*j* who did not fear God ... Luke 18:2
As I hear, I *j* ... John 5:30
"Do not *j* according ... John 7:24
I *j* no one ... John 8:15
*j* the world but to ... John 12:47
this, O man, you who *j* ... Rom 2:3
Therefore let us not *j* ... Rom 14:13
Christ, who will *j* ... 2 Tim 4:1
But if you *j* the law ... James 4:11

**JUDGES**
He makes the *j* of the ... Is 40:23
For the Father *j* ... John 5:22
he who is spiritual *j* ... 1 Cor 2:15
*j* me is the Lord ... 1 Cor 4:4
Him who *j* righteously ... 1 Pet 2:23

**JUDGMENT**
Teach me good *j* ... Ps 119:66
from prison and from *j* ... Is 53:8
be in danger of the *j* ... Matt 5:21
shall not come into *j* ... John 5:24
and My *j* is righteous ... John 5:30
if I do judge, My *j* ... John 8:16
"Now is the *j* ... John 12:31
the righteous *j* ... Rom 1:32
*j* which came from one ... Rom 5:16
appear before the *j* ... 2 Cor 5:10
after this the *j* ... Heb 9:27
time has come for *j* ... 1 Pet 4:17
a long time their *j* ... 2 Pet 2:3
darkness for the *j* ... Jude 6

**JUDGMENTS**
The *j* of the LORD are ... Ps 19:9
unsearchable are His *j* ... Rom 11:33

**JUST**
Noah was a *j* man ... Gen 6:9
*j* man who perishes ... Eccl 7:15
*j* shall live by his ... Hab 2:4
her husband, being a *j* ... Matt 1:19
resurrection of the *j* ... Luke 14:14
*j* persons who need no ... Luke 15:7
the Holy One and the *J* ... Acts 3:14
dead, both of the *j* ... Acts 24:15
*j shall live by faith* ... Rom 1:17
that He might be *j* ... Rom 3:26
*j* men made perfect ... Heb 12:23
have murdered the *j* ... James 5:6
He is faithful and *j* ... 1 John 1:9

**JUSTICE**
*j* as the noonday ... Ps 37:6
and Your poor with *j* ... Ps 72:2
*j* the measuring line ... Is 28:17
the LORD is a God of *j* ... Is 30:18
He will bring forth *j* ... Is 42:1

*J* is turned back ... Is 59:14
I, the LORD, love *j* ... Is 61:8
truth, and His ways *j* ... Dan 4:37
'Execute true *j* ... Zech 7:9
"Where is the God of *j* ... Mal 2:17
*and He will declare j* ... Matt 12:18
*His humiliation His j* ... Acts 8:33

**JUSTIFICATION**
because of our *j* ... Rom 4:25
offenses resulted in *j* ... Rom 5:16

**JUSTIFIED**
Me that you may be *j* ... Job 40:8
words you will be *j* ... Matt 12:37
But wisdom is *j* ... Luke 7:35
*j* rather than the ... Luke 18:14
who believes is *j* ... Acts 13:39
*"That You may be j* ... Rom 3:4
law no flesh will be *j* ... Rom 3:20
*j* freely by His grace ... Rom 3:24
having been *j* by ... Rom 5:1
these He also *j* ... Rom 8:30
that we might be *j* ... Gal 2:16
no flesh shall be *j* ... Gal 2:16
the harlot also *j* ... James 2:25

**JUSTIFIES**
He who *j* the wicked ... Prov 17:15
It is God who *j* ... Rom 8:33

**JUSTIFY**
wanting to *j* himself ... Luke 10:29
"You are those who *j* ... Luke 16:15
is one God who will *j* ... Rom 3:30

## K

**KEEP**
*k* you wherever you go ... Gen 28:15
day, to *k* it holy ... Ex 20:8
Let all the earth *k* ... Hab 2:20
*k* the commandments ... Matt 19:17
If you love Me, *k* ... John 14:15
*k* through Your name ... John 17:11
orderly and *k* the law ... Acts 21:24
*k* the unity of the ... Eph 4:3
*k* His commandments ... 1 John 2:3

**KEEPER**
Am I my brother's *k* ... Gen 4:9
The LORD is your *k* ... Ps 121:5

**KEEPS**
*k* truth forever ... Ps 146:6
*k* the commandment ... Prov 19:16
none of you *k* the law ... John 7:19
born of God *k* himself ... 1 John 5:18
and *k* his garments ... Rev 16:15

**KEPT**
For I have *k* the ways ... 2 Sam 22:22
these things I have *k* ... Matt 19:20
love, just as I have *k* ... John 15:10
*k* back part of the ... Acts 5:2
I have *k* the faith ... 2 Tim 4:7
who are *k* by the power ... 1 Pet 1:5

**KEY**
have taken away the *k* ... Luke 11:52
*"He who has the k* ... Rev 3:7

**KEYS**
I will give you the *k* ... Matt 16:19
And I have the *k* ... Rev 1:18

**KILL**
*k* the Passover ... Ex 12:21
I *k* and I make alive ... Deut 32:39
"Am I God, to *k* ... 2 Kin 5:7
a time to *k* ... Eccl 3:3
of them they will *k* ... Luke 11:49
afraid of those who *k* ... Luke 12:4
Why do you seek to *k* ... John 7:19
*k* and eat ... Acts 10:13

**KILLED**
Abel his brother and *k* ... Gen 4:8
for Your sake we are *k* ... Ps 44:22
and scribes, and be *k* ... Matt 16:21
Siloam fell and *k* them ... Luke 13:4
*k* the Prince of life ... Acts 3:15
*"For Your sake we are k* ... Rom 8:36
who *k* both the Lord ... 1 Thess 2:15

**KILLS**
the one who *k* the ... Matt 23:37
for the letter *k* ... 2 Cor 3:6

**KIND**
animals after their *k* ... Gen 6:20
*k* can come out by ... Mark 9:29
suffers long and is *k* ... 1 Cor 13:4
And be *k* to one ... Eph 4:32

**KINDLY**
Julius treated Paul *k* ... Acts 27:3
*k* affectionate to one ... Rom 12:10

**KINDNESS**
For His merciful *k* ... Ps 117:2
*k* shall not depart ... Is 54:10
I remember you, the *k* ... Jer 2:2
by longsuffering, by *k* ... 2 Cor 6:6
longsuffering, *k* ... Gal 5:22
and to brotherly *k* ... 2 Pet 1:7

**KING**
Yet I have set My *K* ... Ps 2:6
The LORD is *K* forever ... Ps 10:16
And the *K* of glory ... Ps 24:7
For God is my *K* ... Ps 74:12
when your *k* is a child ... Eccl 10:16
and the everlasting *K* ... Jer 10:10
the LORD shall be *K* ... Zech 14:9
He who has been born *K* ... Matt 2:2
This Is Jesus the *K* ... Matt 27:37
"Behold your *K* ... John 19:14
Now to the *K* eternal ... 1 Tim 1:17
only Potentate, the *K* ... 1 Tim 6:15
this Melchizedek, *k* ... Heb 7:1
*K* of Kings and Lord of ... Rev 19:16

**KINGDOM**
Yours is the *k* ... 1 Chr 29:11
*k* is the LORD's ... Ps 22:28
the scepter of Your *k* ... Ps 45:6
is an everlasting *k* ... Ps 145:13
*k* which shall never be ... Dan 2:44
High rules in the *k* ... Dan 4:17
"Repent, for the *k* ... Matt 3:2
for Yours is the *k* ... Matt 6:13
But seek first the *k* ... Matt 6:33
the mysteries of the *k* ... Matt 13:11
are the sons of the *k* ... Matt 13:38
of such is the *k* ... Matt 19:14
back, is fit for the *k* ... Luke 9:62
against nation, and *k* ... Luke 21:10
he cannot see the *k* ... John 3:3
he cannot enter the *k* ... John 3:5
If My *k* were of this ... John 18:36
for the *k* of God is ... Rom 14:17
will not inherit the *k* ... Gal 5:21
*the scepter of Your k* ... Heb 1:8
we are receiving a *k* ... Heb 12:28

**KINGDOMS**
the *k* were moved ... Ps 46:6
showed Him all the *k* ... Matt 4:8
have become the *k* ... Rev 11:15

**KINGS**
The *k* of the earth set ... Ps 2:2
By me *k* reign ... Prov 8:15
before governors and *k* ... Matt 10:18
*k* have desired to see ... Luke 10:24
You have reigned as *k* ... 1 Cor 4:8
and has made us *k* ... Rev 1:6
that the way of the *k* ... Rev 16:12

**KISS**
*K* the Son ... Ps 2:12
"You gave Me no *k* ... Luke 7:45
one another with a *k* ... 1 Pet 5:14

**KISSED**
And they *k* one another ... 1 Sam 20:41
and *k* Him ... Matt 26:49
and she *k* His feet and ... Luke 7:38

**KNEE**
that to Me every *k* ... Is 45:23
*have not bowed the k* ... Rom 11:4
of Jesus every *k* ... Phil 2:10

**KNEES**
make firm the feeble *k* ... Is 35:3
this reason I bow my *k* ... Eph 3:14
and the feeble *k* ... Heb 12:12

**KNEW**
in the womb I *k* ... Jer 1:5
to them, 'I never *k* ... Matt 7:23
*k* what was in man ... John 2:25
For He made Him who *k* ... 2 Cor 5:21

**KNIT**
be encouraged, being *k* ... Col 2:2

**KNOCK**
*k*, and it will be ... Matt 7:7
at the door and *k* ... Rev 3:20

**KNOW**
*k* good and evil ... Gen 3:22
*k* that I am the LORD ... Ex 6:7
*k* that my Redeemer ... Job 19:25
make me to *k* wisdom ... Ps 51:6
Who can *k* it ... Jer 17:9
saying, '*K* the LORD ... Jer 31:34
*k* what hour your Lord ... Matt 24:42
an oath, "I do not *k* ... Matt 26:72
the world did not *k* ... John 1:10
We speak what We *k* ... John 3:11
*k* that You are ... John 6:69
hear My voice, and I *k* ... John 10:27
If you *k* these things ... John 13:17
*k* whom I have chosen ... John 13:18
we are sure that You *k* ... John 16:30
*k* that I love You ... John 21:15
*k* times or seasons ... Acts 1:7
and said, "Jesus I *k* ... Acts 19:15
wisdom did not *k* ... 1 Cor 1:21
nor can he *k* them ... 1 Cor 2:14
For we *k* in part and ... 1 Cor 13:9
*k* the love of Christ ... Eph 3:19
*k* whom I have believed ... 2 Tim 1:12
we *k* that we *k* Him ... 1 John 2:3
and you *k* all things ... 1 John 2:20
By this we *k* love ... 1 John 3:16
*k* that He abides ... 1 John 3:24
*k* that we are of God ... 1 John 5:19
"I *k* your works ... Rev 2:2

**KNOWLEDGE**
and the tree of the *k* ... Gen 2:9
unto night reveals *k* ... Ps 19:2
*k* is too wonderful ... Ps 139:6
Wise people store up *k* ... Prov 10:14
*k* spares his words ... Prov 17:27
and he who increases *k* ... Eccl 1:18
*k* is that wisdom ... Eccl 7:12
*k* shall increase ... Dan 12:4
having more accurate *k* ... Acts 24:22
having the form of *k* ... Rom 2:20
law is the *k* of sin ... Rom 3:20
whether there is *k* ... 1 Cor 13:8

Christ which passes *k* . . . . . . .Eph 3:19
is falsely called *k* . . . . . . . . .1 Tim 6:20
in the grace and *k* . . . . . . . . .2 Pet 3:18

**KNOWN**
If you had *k* Me. . . . . . . . . . . .John 8:19
My sheep, and am *k* . . . . . . .John 10:14
The world has not *k* . . . . . . .John 17:25
*peace they have not k* . . . . . . .Rom 3:17
*"For who has k* . . . . . . . . . . .Rom 11:34
after you have *k* . . . . . . . . . . . .Gal 4:9
requests be made *k* . . . . . . . . . .Phil 4:6
*k* the Holy Scriptures . . . . . .2 Tim 3:15

**KNOWS**
"For God *k* that in . . . . . . . . . . .Gen 3:5
*k* what is in the . . . . . . . . . . . .Dan 2:22
*k* the things you have . . . . . . .Matt 6:8
and hour no one *k* . . . . . . . .Matt 24:36
but God *k* your hearts . . . . .Luke 16:15
searches the hearts *k* . . . . . . .Rom 8:27
*k* the things of God . . . . . . . .1 Cor 2:11
*k* those who are His . . . . . . .2 Tim 2:19
to him who *k* to do . . . . . . . .James 4:17
and *k* all things. . . . . . . . . .1 John 3:20

## L

**LABOR**
Six days you shall *l* . . . . . . . . . .Ex 20:9
things are full of *l* . . . . . . . . . . .Eccl 1:8
has man for all his *l* . . . . . . . .Eccl 2:22
He shall see the *l*. . . . . . . . . . . .Is 53:11
to Me, all you who *l* . . . . . . .Matt 11:28
"Do not *l* for the . . . . . . . . . . .John 6:27
knowing that your *l* . . . . . .1 Cor 15:58
but rather let him *l* . . . . . . . . .Eph 4:28
mean fruit from my *l* . . . . . . .Phil 1:22
your work of faith, *l*. . . . . . .1 Thess 1:3
forget your work and *l*. . . . . . .Heb 6:10
your works, your *l* . . . . . . . . . . .Rev 2:2

**LABORED**
*l* more abundantly than . . .1 Cor 15:10
for you, lest I have *l* . . . . . . . . .Gal 4:11

**LABORERS**
but the *l* are few . . . . . . . . . . .Matt 9:37

**LABORING**
*l* night and day . . . . . . . . . .1 Thess 2:9

**LABORS**
entered into their *l*. . . . . . . . .John 4:38
creation groans and *l* . . . . . . .Rom 8:22
*l* more abundant . . . . . . . . .2 Cor 11:23
may rest from their *l* . . . . . . .Rev 14:13

**LACK**
What do I still *l* . . . . . . . . . .Matt 19:20
"One thing you *l*. . . . . . . . .Mark 10:21

**LADDER**
and behold, a *l*. . . . . . . . . . . .Gen 28:12

**LAID**
the place where they *l*. . . . . .Mark 16:6
Where have you *l*. . . . . . . . .John 11:34

**LAKE**
cast alive into the *l* . . . . . . . .Rev 19:20

**LAMB**
but where is the *l*. . . . . . . . . . .Gen 22:7
He was led as a *l* . . . . . . . . . . . . .Is 53:7
The *L* of God who takes . . . . .John 1:29
the elders, stood a *L*. . . . . . . . . .Rev 5:6
"Worthy is the *L* . . . . . . . . . . .Rev 5:12
by the blood of the *L*. . . . . . . .Rev 12:11

**LAME**
*l* shall leap like a . . . . . . . . . . . .Is 35:6
blind see and the *l* . . . . . . . . .Matt 11:5
And a certain man *l* . . . . . . . . .Acts 3:2

**LAMENTATION**
*was heard in Ramah, l*. . . . . .Matt 2:18
and made great *l*. . . . . . . . . . . .Acts 8:2

**LAMP**
Your word is a *l* . . . . . . . . . .Ps 119:105
the *l* of the wicked . . . . . . . . .Prov 13:9
his *l* will be put out . . . . . . .Prov 20:20
Nor do they light a *l*. . . . . . . .Matt 5:15
"The *l* of the body. . . . . . . . . .Matt 6:22
when he has lit a *l* . . . . . . . . .Luke 8:16
*l* gives you light. . . . . . . . . .Luke 11:36
does not light a *l* . . . . . . . . . .Luke 15:8
burning and shining *l* . . . . . .John 5:35

**LAMPS**
he made its seven *l* . . . . . . . . .Ex 37:23
and trimmed their *l*. . . . . . . .Matt 25:7

**LAMPSTAND**
branches of the *l* . . . . . . . . . . .Ex 25:32
a basket, but on a *l*. . . . . . . . .Matt 5:15
and remove your *l* . . . . . . . . . . .Rev 2:5

**LAND**
*l* that I will show you. . . . . . . .Gen 12:1
*l* flowing with milk . . . . . . . . . . .Ex 3:8
they will see the *l* . . . . . . . . . . .Is 33:17
*Bethlehem, in the l* . . . . . . . . .Matt 2:6

**LANGUAGE**
whole earth had one *l* . . . . . . .Gen 11:1
speak in his own *l*. . . . . . . . . . .Acts 2:6
blasphemy, filthy *l* . . . . . . . . . . .Col 3:8

**LANGUAGES**
according to their *l* . . . . . . . .Gen 10:20

**LAST**
He shall stand at *l* . . . . . . . . .Job 19:25
First and I am the *L* . . . . . . . . . .Is 44:6
*l* will be first . . . . . . . . . . . .Matt 20:16
the First and the *L*. . . . . . . . . .Rev 1:11

**LATTER**
*l* times some will . . . . . . . . . .1 Tim 4:1

**LAUGH**
Why did Sarah *l* . . . . . . . . . .Gen 18:13
Woe to you who *l* . . . . . . . . . .Luke 6:25

**LAUGHS**
The Lord *l* at him. . . . . . . . . . .Ps 37:13

**LAUGHTER**
your *l* be turned to. . . . . . . . .James 4:9

**LAW**
stones a copy of the *l*. . . . . . . .Josh 8:32
The *l* of the LORD is . . . . . . . . . .Ps 19:7
I delight in Your *l*. . . . . . . . . .Ps 119:70
Oh, how I love Your *l* . . . . . . .Ps 119:97
And Your *l* is truth. . . . . . . .Ps 119:142
*l* will proceed from Me . . . . . . . .Is 51:4
in whose heart is My *l* . . . . . . . .Is 51:7
the *L* is no more . . . . . . . . . . . .Lam 2:9
The *l* of truth was in . . . . . . . . .Mal 2:6
to destroy the *L* . . . . . . . . . . .Matt 5:17
for this is the *L*. . . . . . . . . . . .Matt 7:12
hang all the *L* and the . . . . .Matt 22:40
"The *l* and the . . . . . . . . . . .Luke 16:16
*l* was given through. . . . . . . .John 1:17
"Does our *l* judge a. . . . . . . . .John 7:51
*l* is the knowledge. . . . . . . . . .Rom 3:20
because the *l* brings . . . . . . . .Rom 4:15
when there is no *l* . . . . . . . . . .Rom 5:13
you are not under *l* . . . . . . . . .Rom 6:14
For what the *l* could . . . . . . . . .Rom 8:3
*l* that I might live . . . . . . . . . .Gal 2:19
under guard by the *l* . . . . . . . .Gal 3:23
born under the *l*. . . . . . . . . . . . .Gal 4:4
*l* is fulfilled in one . . . . . . . . . .Gal 5:14
into the perfect *l* . . . . . . . . . .James 1:25
fulfill the royal *l* . . . . . . . . . . .James 2:8

**LAWFUL**
Is it *l* to pay taxes. . . . . . . . .Matt 22:17
All things are *l* . . . . . . . . . . .1 Cor 6:12

**LAWGIVER**
There is one *L* . . . . . . . . . . .James 4:12

**LAWLESS**
*l* one will be revealed. . . . . .2 Thess 2:8

**LAWLESSNESS**
Me, you who practice *l*. . . . . .Matt 7:23
*l* is already at work . . . . . . .2 Thess 2:7

**LAWYERS**
Woe to you also, *l*. . . . . . . . .Luke 11:46

**LAY**
nowhere to *l* His head . . . . . .Matt 8:20
*l* hands may receive . . . . . . . .Acts 8:19

**LAZINESS**
*l* the building decays. . . . . . .Eccl 10:18

**LAZY**
*l* man will be put to . . . . . . .Prov 12:24
wicked and *l* servant . . . . . .Matt 25:26
liars, evil beasts, *l*. . . . . . . . .Titus 1:12

**LEAD**
*L* me in Your truth and . . . . . . .Ps 25:5
And do not *l* us into . . . . . . . .Matt 6:13
"Can the blind *l*. . . . . . . . . . .Luke 6:39

**LEADS**
He *l* me in the paths. . . . . . . . . .Ps 23:3
And if the blind *l* . . . . . . . . .Matt 15:14

**LEAF**
plucked olive *l*. . . . . . . . . . . . .Gen 8:11

**LEAN**
all your heart, and *l*. . . . . . . . .Prov 3:5

**LEAP**
Then the lame shall *l* . . . . . . . . .Is 35:6

**LEARN**
*l* to do good . . . . . . . . . . . . . . . .Is 1:17
My yoke upon you and *l*. . . .Matt 11:29

**LEARNED**
Me the tongue of the *l*. . . . . . . . .Is 50:4
have not so *l* Christ. . . . . . . . .Eph 4:20
in all things I have *l* . . . . . . . .Phil 4:12

**LEARNING**
*l* is driving you mad . . . . . . .Acts 26:24

**LEAST**
so, shall be called *l*. . . . . . . . .Matt 5:19

**LEAVE**
a man shall *l* his . . . . . . . . . . .Gen 2:24
For You will not *l* . . . . . . . . . . .Ps 16:10
*"I will never l* . . . . . . . . . . . . .Heb 13:5

**LEAVEN**
of heaven is like *l*. . . . . . . . .Matt 13:33
*l* leavens the whole . . . . . . . . . .Gal 5:9

**LEAVES**
and they sewed fig *l*. . . . . . . . . .Gen 3:7
The *l* of the tree . . . . . . . . . . . .Rev 22:2

**LED**
*l* them forth by the. . . . . . . . . .Ps 107:7
For as many as are *l* . . . . . . . .Rom 8:14

**LEFT**
*l* hand know what your . . . . . .Matt 6:3

**LEND**
"And if you *l* . . . . . . . . . . . .Luke 6:34

**LENDER**
is servant to the *l* . . . . . . . . . .Prov 22:7

**LENDS**
ever merciful, and *l* . . . . . . . . .Ps 37:26

**LENGTH**
is your life and the *l* . . . . . . . Deut 30:20

**LEOPARD**
or the *l* its spots . . . . . . . . . . . . Jer 13:23

**LEPERS**
"And many *l* were in . . . . . . . Luke 4:27

**LET**
"*L* there be light" . . . . . . . . . . . Gen 1:3

**LETTER**
for the *l* kills . . . . . . . . . . . . . . 2 Cor 3:6
or by word or by *l* . . . . . . . . . 2 Thess 2:2

**LETTERS**
does this Man know *l* . . . . . . . John 7:15

**LEVIATHAN**
"Can you draw out *L* . . . . . . . . Job 41:1

**LEVITE**
"Likewise a *L* . . . . . . . . . . . Luke 10:32

**LEWDNESS**
wickedness, deceit, *l* . . . . . . . Mark 7:22

**LIAR**
for he is a *l* and the . . . . . . . . . John 8:44
but every man a *l* . . . . . . . . . . . Rom 3:4
we make Him a *l* . . . . . . . . . 1 John 1:10
his brother, he is a *l* . . . . . . . 1 John 4:20

**LIARS**
"All men are *l* . . . . . . . . . . . . Ps 116:11
*l* shall have their . . . . . . . . . . . Rev 21:8

**LIBERALITY**
he who gives, with *l* . . . . . . . . Rom 12:8

**LIBERALLY**
who gives to all *l* . . . . . . . . . . James 1:5

**LIBERTY**
year, and proclaim *l* . . . . . . . . Lev 25:10
*'to proclaim l to the* . . . . . . . Luke 4:18
into the glorious *l* . . . . . . . . . . Rom 8:21
Lord is, there is *l* . . . . . . . . . . 2 Cor 3:17
therefore in the *l* . . . . . . . . . . . Gal 5:1

**LIE**
Do not *l* to one . . . . . . . . . . . . . . Col 3:9
God, who cannot *l* . . . . . . . . . . Titus 1:2
an abomination or a *l* . . . . . . Rev 21:27

**LIED**
You have not *l* to men . . . . . . . . Acts 5:4

**LIES**
sin *l* at the door . . . . . . . . . . . . . Gen 4:7
speaking *l* in . . . . . . . . . . . . . . 1 Tim 4:2

**LIFE**
the breath of *l* . . . . . . . . . . . . . . Gen 2:7
'For the *l* of the . . . . . . . . . . . . Lev 17:11
before you today *l* . . . . . . . . . Deut 30:15
He will redeem their *l* . . . . . . . Ps 72:14
word has given me *l* . . . . . . . . Ps 119:50
She is a tree of *l* . . . . . . . . . . . Prov 3:18
finds me finds *l* . . . . . . . . . . . . Prov 8:35
*L* is more than . . . . . . . . . . . Luke 12:23
*l* was the light . . . . . . . . . . . . . John 1:4
so the Son gives *l* . . . . . . . . . . John 5:21
spirit, and they are *l* . . . . . . . John 6:63
have the light of *l* . . . . . . . . . . John 8:12
and I lay down My *l* . . . . . . . John 10:15
resurrection and the *l* . . . . . John 11:25
you lay down your *l* . . . . . . . John 13:38
*l* which I now live . . . . . . . . . . . Gal 2:20
*l* is hidden with . . . . . . . . . . . . . . Col 3:3
For what is your *l* . . . . . . . . James 4:14
*l* was manifested . . . . . . . . . . 1 John 1:2
and the pride of *l* . . . . . . . . . 1 John 2:16
has given us eternal *l* . . . . . 1 John 5:11
the Lamb's Book of *L* . . . . . . Rev 21:27
right to the tree of *l* . . . . . . . . Rev 22:14
the water of *l* freely . . . . . . . . Rev 22:17
from the Book of *L* . . . . . . . . . Rev 22:19

**LIFT**
I will *l* up my eyes to . . . . . . . . Ps 121:1
Lord, and He will *l* . . . . . . . . James 4:10

**LIFTED**
your heart is *l* . . . . . . . . . . . . Ezek 28:2
in Hades, he *l* up his . . . . . . Luke 16:23
the Son of Man be *l* . . . . . . . . John 3:14
"And I, if I am *l* . . . . . . . . . . John 12:32

**LIGHT**
"Let there be *l* . . . . . . . . . . . . . . Gen 1:3
The LORD is my *l* . . . . . . . . . . . . Ps 27:1
and a *l* to my path . . . . . . . . Ps 119:105
The *l* of the righteous . . . . . . . Prov 13:9
The LORD gives *l* . . . . . . . . . Prov 29:13
Truly the *l* is sweet . . . . . . . . . Eccl 11:7
let us walk in the *l* . . . . . . . . . . . . Is 2:5
*l* shall break forth . . . . . . . . . . . . Is 58:8
"You are the *l* . . . . . . . . . . . . Matt 5:14
"Let your *l* so shine . . . . . . . . Matt 5:16
than the sons of *l* . . . . . . . . . . Luke 16:8
and the life was the *l* . . . . . . . . John 1:4
darkness rather than *l* . . . . . . John 3:19
saying, "I am the *l* . . . . . . . . . John 8:12
God who commanded *l* . . . . . . 2 Cor 4:6
Walk as children of *l* . . . . . . . . . Eph 5:8
You are all sons of *l* . . . . . . . 1 Thess 5:5
into His marvelous *l* . . . . . . . . 1 Pet 2:9
to you, that God is *l* . . . . . . . . 1 John 1:5
*l* as He is in the . . . . . . . . . . . 1 John 1:7
says he is in the *l* . . . . . . . . . . 1 John 2:9
The Lamb is its *l* . . . . . . . . . . Rev 21:23

**LIGHTNING**
"For as the *l* . . . . . . . . . . . . . Matt 24:27
countenance was like *l* . . . . . Matt 28:3

**LIGHTNINGS**
the throne proceeded *l* . . . . . . . . Rev 4:5

**LIGHTS**
"Let there be *l* . . . . . . . . . . . . . Gen 1:14
whom you shine as *l* . . . . . . . . Phil 2:15

**LIKENESS**
according to Our *l* . . . . . . . . . . Gen 1:26
carved image—or any *l* . . . . . . . Ex 20:4
when I awake in Your *l* . . . . . . Ps 17:15
and coming in the *l* . . . . . . . . . . Phil 2:7

**LILY**
the *l* of the valleys . . . . . . . . . . Song 2:1

**LIMIT**
to the sea its *l* . . . . . . . . . . . . Prov 8:29

**LINE**
upon precept, *l* upon . . . . . . . . . Is 28:10
I am setting a plumb *l* . . . . . . Amos 7:8

**LINEN**
wrapped Him in the *l* . . . . . Mark 15:46

**LINGER**
salvation shall not *l* . . . . . . . . . Is 46:13

**LION**
*l* shall eat straw . . . . . . . . . . . . . Is 11:7

**LIONS**
the mouths of *l* . . . . . . . . . . . . Heb 11:33

**LIPS**
off all flattering *l* . . . . . . . . . . . Ps 12:3
The *l* of the righteous . . . . . Prov 10:21
but the *l* of knowledge . . . . . Prov 20:15
am a man of unclean *l* . . . . . . . . . Is 6:5
*other l I will speak* . . . . . . . 1 Cor 14:21
*from evil, and his l* . . . . . . . . . 1 Pet 3:10

**LISTEN**
you are not able to *l* . . . . . . . . John 8:43
you who fear God, *l* . . . . . . . . Acts 13:16

**LISTENS**
but whoever *l* to me . . . . . . . . Prov 1:33

**LITTLE**
though you are *l* . . . . . . . . . . . . . Mic 5:2
*l* ones only a cup . . . . . . . . . . Matt 10:42
"O you of *l* faith . . . . . . . . . . . Matt 14:31
to whom *l* is forgiven . . . . . . . Luke 7:47
faithful in a very *l* . . . . . . . . Luke 19:17

**LIVE**
eat, and *l* forever . . . . . . . . . . . Gen 3:22
a man does, he shall *l* . . . . . . . Lev 18:5
"Seek Me and *l* . . . . . . . . . . . . Amos 5:4
but the just shall *l* . . . . . . . . . . . Hab 2:4
*l by bread alone* . . . . . . . . . . . . Matt 4:4
"for in Him we *l* . . . . . . . . . . Acts 17:28
*l* peaceably with all . . . . . . . Rom 12:18
the life which I now *l* . . . . . . . . Gal 2:20
If we *l* in the Spirit . . . . . . . . . . Gal 5:25
to me, to *l* is Christ . . . . . . . . . Phil 1:21

**LIVED**
died and rose and *l* . . . . . . . . . Rom 14:9
And they *l* and reigned . . . . . . Rev 20:4

**LIVES**
but man *l* by every . . . . . . . . . . Deut 8:3
but Christ *l* in me . . . . . . . . . . . Gal 2:20
to lay down our *l* . . . . . . . . . 1 John 3:16
"I am He who *l* . . . . . . . . . . . . . Rev 1:18

**LIVING**
and man became a *l* . . . . . . . . . Gen 2:7
in the light of the *l* . . . . . . . . . . Ps 56:13
the dead, but of the *l* . . . . . . Matt 22:32
Why do you seek the *l* . . . . . . Luke 24:5
the word of God is *l* . . . . . . . . . Heb 4:12
*l* creature was like a . . . . . . . . . Rev 4:7

**LOATHSOME**
but a wicked man is *l* . . . . . . . Prov 13:5

**LOAVES**
have here only five *l* . . . . . . . Matt 14:17
you ate of the *l* . . . . . . . . . . . . John 6:26

**LOCUST**
What the chewing *l* . . . . . . . . . . . Joel 1:4

**LOCUSTS**
and his food was *l* . . . . . . . . . . . Matt 3:4

**LOFTY**
Wisdom is too *l* . . . . . . . . . . . . Prov 24:7

**LONG**
your days may be *l* . . . . . . . . . Deut 5:16
who *l* for death . . . . . . . . . . . . . . Job 3:21
I *l* for Your salvation . . . . . . Ps 119:174
go around in *l* robes . . . . . . Mark 12:38

**LONGSUFFERING**
is love, joy, peace, *l* . . . . . . . . . . Gal 5:22
and gentleness, with *l* . . . . . . . . Eph 4:2
for all patience and *l* . . . . . . . . . Col 1:11
might show all *l* . . . . . . . . . . 1 Tim 1:16
when once the Divine *l* . . . . . 1 Pet 3:20
and consider that the *l* . . . . . . 2 Pet 3:15

**LOOK**
A proud *l* . . . . . . . . . . . . . . . . Prov 6:17
"*L* to Me . . . . . . . . . . . . . . . . . . Is 45:22
*l* on Me whom they . . . . . . . . Zech 12:10
say to you, '*L* here . . . . . . . . Luke 17:23
while we do not *l* . . . . . . . . . . 2 Cor 4:18

**LOOKED**
For He *l* down from the . . . . . Ps 102:19
He *l* for justice . . . . . . . . . . . . . . . . Is 5:7
the Lord turned and *l* . . . . . Luke 22:61
for he *l* to the reward . . . . . . . Heb 11:26

**LOOKING**
the plow, and *l* back . . . . . . . . Luke 9:62
*l* for the blessed hope . . . . . . . Titus 2:13
*l* unto Jesus . . . . . . . . . . . . . . . Heb 12:2

*l* carefully lest . . . . . . . . . . . .Heb 12:15
*l* for the mercy of . . . . . . . . . . Jude 21

**LOOKS**
The lofty *l* of man . . . . . . . . . . . .Is 2:11
to you that whoever *l*. . . . . . .Matt 5:28

**LOOSE**
and whatever you *l* . . . . . . .Matt 16:19
said to them, "*L* him . . . . . .John 11:44

**LOOSED**
the silver cord is *l* . . . . . . . . . .Eccl 12:6

**LORD**
*L* is my strength . . . . . . . . . . . .Ex 15:2
*L* our God, the *L*. . . . . . . . . . . .Deut 6:4
You alone are the *L* . . . . . . . . . .Neh 9:6
The *L* of hosts. . . . . . . . . . . . . .Ps 24:10
Gracious is the *L* . . . . . . . . . . .Ps 116:5
*L* surrounds His people . . . . . .Ps 125:2
The *L* is righteous . . . . . . . . . .Ps 129:4
*L* is near to all who . . . . . . . .Ps 145:18
*L* is a God of justice. . . . . . . . . .Is 30:18
*L* Our Righteousness . . . . . . . .Jer 23:6
"the *L* is one. . . . . . . . . . . . . .Zech 14:9
*shall not tempt the L*. . . . . . . .Matt 4:7
*shall worship the L* . . . . . . . .Matt 4:10
Son of Man is also *L* . . . . . . .Mark 2:28
who is Christ the *L* . . . . . . . .Luke 2:11
*L* is risen indeed . . . . . . . . .Luke 24:34
call me Teacher and *L* . . . . .John 13:13
He is *L* of all . . . . . . . . . . . . .Acts 10:36
with your mouth the *L* . . . . . .Rom 10:9
say that Jesus is *L*. . . . . . . . .1 Cor 12:3
second Man is the *L* . . . . . .1 Cor 15:47
the Spirit of the *L* . . . . . . . . .2 Cor 3:17
that Jesus Christ is *L* . . . . . . .Phil 2:11
and deny the only *L* . . . . . . . . . .Jude 4
*L* God Omnipotent . . . . . . . . .Rev 19:6

**LORDS**
for He is Lord of *l* . . . . . . . . . .Rev 17:14

**LOSE**
save his life will *l*. . . . . . . . .Matt 16:25

**LOSES**
but if the salt *l* . . . . . . . . . . .Matt 5:13
and *l* his own soul . . . . . . . .Matt 16:26

**LOSS**
count all things *l*. . . . . . . . . . . .Phil 3:8

**LOST**
save that which was *l* . . . . .Matt 18:11
and none of them is *l* . . . . . .John 17:12
You gave Me I have *l* . . . . . . .John 18:9

**LOTS**
garments, casting *l* . . . . . .Mark 15:24
And they cast their *l*. . . . . . . .Acts 1:26

**LOUD**
cried out with a *l* . . . . . . . . .Matt 27:46
I heard behind me a *l*. . . . . . . .Rev 1:10

**LOVE**
*l* your neighbor as . . . . . . . . .Lev 19:18
*l* the LORD your God . . . . . . . .Deut 6:5
Oh, *l* the LORD. . . . . . . . . . . . .Ps 31:23
he has set his *l* . . . . . . . . . . . . .Ps 91:14
Oh, how I *l* Your law . . . . . . .Ps 119:97
*l* covers all sins. . . . . . . . . . .Prov 10:12
a time to *l* . . . . . . . . . . . . . . . . .Eccl 3:8
banner over me was *l*. . . . . . . .Song 2:4
*l* is as strong as . . . . . . . . . . .Song 8:6
do justly, to *l* mercy . . . . . . . . .Mic 6:8
to you, *l* your enemies . . . . . .Matt 5:44
which of them will *l* . . . . . . .Luke 7:42
you do not have the *l* . . . . . . .John 5:42
if you have *l* for one . . . . . . .John 13:35
"If you *l* Me . . . . . . . . . . . . .John 14:15
and My Father will *l* . . . . . .John 14:23
*l* one another as I . . . . . . . . . .John 15:12
*l* has no one than this . . . . .John 15:13
because the *l* of God . . . . . . . . .Rom 5:5
to *l* one another. . . . . . . . . . . .Rom 13:8
*L* suffers long and is . . . . . . .1 Cor 13:4
*L* never fails . . . . . . . . . . . . .1 Cor 13:8
greatest of these is *l* . . . . . .1 Cor 13:13
For the *l* of Christ . . . . . . . . .2 Cor 5:14
of the Spirit is *l* . . . . . . . . . . . .Gal 5:22
Husbands, *l* your wives . . . . .Eph 5:25
the commandment is *l* . . . . . .1 Tim 1:5
For the *l* of money is . . . . . . .1 Tim 6:10
Let brotherly *l*. . . . . . . . . . . . .Heb 13:1
having not seen you *l*. . . . . . . .1 Pet 1:8
for "*l will cover a* . . . . . . . . . .1 Pet 4:8
brotherly kindness *l* . . . . . . . .2 Pet 1:7
By this we know *l* . . . . . . . .1 John 3:16
Beloved, let us *l*. . . . . . . . . . .1 John 4:7
know God, for God is *l*. . . . . .1 John 4:8
There is no fear in *l*. . . . . . .1 John 4:18
*l* Him because He first . . . .1 John 4:19
who loves God must *l* . . . . .1 John 4:21
For this is the *l* . . . . . . . . . . .1 John 5:3
have left your first *l*. . . . . . . . . .Rev 2:4

**LOVED**
*L* one and friend You . . . . . . . .Ps 88:18
Yet Jacob I have *l*. . . . . . . . . . . .Mal 1:2
forgiven, for she *l*. . . . . . . . . .Luke 7:47
so *l* the world that . . . . . . . . .John 3:16
whom Jesus *l* . . . . . . . . . . . .John 13:23
"As the Father *l* . . . . . . . . . . .John 15:9
*l* them as You have. . . . . . . .John 17:23
the Son of God, who *l* . . . . . . . .Gal 2:20
*l* the church and gave . . . . . . .Eph 5:25
Beloved, if God so *l* . . . . . . .1 John 4:11
To Him who *l* us and . . . . . . . . .Rev 1:5

**LOVELY**
he is altogether *l* . . . . . . . . . .Song 5:16
whatever things are *l* . . . . . . . .Phil 4:8

**LOVES**
"He who *l* father or . . . . . . .Matt 10:37
*l* his life will lose . . . . . . . . .John 12:25
*l* Me will be loved. . . . . . . . .John 14:21
*l* a cheerful giver. . . . . . . . . . .2 Cor 9:7
If anyone *l* the world . . . . . .1 John 2:15
*l* God must love his . . . . . . .1 John 4:21

**LOVINGKINDNESS**
to declare Your *l*. . . . . . . . . . . . .Ps 92:2

**LOWER**
*made him a little l*. . . . . . . . . . .Heb 2:7

**LOWLINESS**
with all *l* and. . . . . . . . . . . . . . .Eph 4:2

**LOWLY**
for I am gentle and *l*. . . . . . .Matt 11:29
in presence am *l* . . . . . . . . . .2 Cor 10:1
*l* brother glory . . . . . . . . . . . .James 1:9

**LUKEWARM**
because you are *l* . . . . . . . . . . .Rev 3:16

**LUST**
looks at a woman to *l*. . . . . . .Matt 5:28
not fulfill the *l* . . . . . . . . . . . . .Gal 5:16
You *l* and do not have. . . . . . .James 4:2
the *l* of the flesh. . . . . . . . . .1 John 2:16

**LUSTS**
to fulfill its *l* . . . . . . . . . . . . .Rom 13:14
also youthful *l* . . . . . . . . . . .2 Tim 2:22
and worldly *l* . . . . . . . . . . . . .Titus 2:12
to the former *l* . . . . . . . . . . . .1 Pet 1:14
abstain from fleshly *l* . . . . . .1 Pet 2:11
to their own ungodly *l*. . . . . . . . .Jude 18

**LUTE**
Praise Him with the *l* . . . . . . .Ps 150:3

**LUXURY**
in pleasure and *l* . . . . . . . . . .James 5:5
the abundance of her *l*. . . . . . .Rev 18:3

**LYING**
I hate and abhor *l* . . . . . . . .Ps 119:163
righteous man hates *l* . . . . . .Prov 13:5
not trust in these *l* . . . . . . . . . . . .Jer 7:4
signs, and *l* wonders . . . . . .2 Thess 2:9

## M

**MADE**
*m* the stars also. . . . . . . . . . . .Gen 1:16
things My hand has *m* . . . . . . . .Is 66:2
All things were *m* . . . . . . . . . .John 1:3

**MADNESS**
*m* is in their hearts. . . . . . . . . .Eccl 9:3

**MAGIC**
*m* brought their books . . . . .Acts 19:19

**MAGNIFIED**
So let Your name be *m*. . . . .2 Sam 7:26
the Lord Jesus was *m* . . . . . .Acts 19:17
also Christ will be *m* . . . . . . .Phil 1:20

**MAGNIFIES**
"My soul *m* the Lord . . . . . . .Luke 1:46

**MAGNIFY**
*m* the LORD with me . . . . . . . . .Ps 34:3

**MAIDSERVANT**
"Behold the *m* . . . . . . . . . . . .Luke 1:38

**MAIDSERVANTS**
*m I will pour out My*. . . . . . . .Acts 2:18

**MAJESTY**
right hand of the *M*. . . . . . . . . .Heb 1:3
eyewitnesses of His *m* . . . . . .2 Pet 1:16
wise, be glory and *m* . . . . . . . . .Jude 25

**MAKE**
Let Us *m* man in Our . . . . . . .Gen 1:26
*m* you a great nation. . . . . . . .Gen 12:2
"You shall not *m* . . . . . . . . . . . .Ex 20:4
*m* Our home with him . . . . .John 14:23

**MAKER**
*M* is your husband . . . . . . . . . . .Is 54:5
has forgotten his *M* . . . . . . . . .Hos 8:14
builder and *m* is God . . . . . . .Heb 11:10

**MALICE**
however, in *m* be babes . . . .1 Cor 14:20
laying aside all *m* . . . . . . . . . .1 Pet 2:1

**MAN**
"Let Us make *m* . . . . . . . . . . .Gen 1:26
*m* that You are mindful . . . . . . . .Ps 8:4
coming of the Son of *M* . . . .Matt 24:27
"Behold the *M* . . . . . . . . . . . .John 19:5
since by *m* came death . . . .1 Cor 15:21
though our outward *m* . . . . .2 Cor 4:16
that the *m* of God may . . . . .2 Tim 3:17
is the number of a *m* . . . . . .Rev 13:18

**MANGER**
and laid Him in a *m* . . . . . . . .Luke 2:7

**MANIFEST**
*m* Myself to him. . . . . . . . . .John 14:21

**MANIFESTATION**
But the *m* of the . . . . . . . . . .1 Cor 12:7

**MANIFESTED**
"I have *m* Your name. . . . . . .John 17:6
God was *m* in the flesh. . . . .1 Tim 3:16
the life was *m* . . . . . . . . . . . .1 John 1:2

**MANIFOLD**
the *m* wisdom of God. . . . . . . .Eph 3:10

**MANNA**
of Israel ate *m* . . . . . . . . . . . . Ex 16:35
Our fathers ate the *m* . . . . . . John 6:31

**MANNER**
Is this the *m* of man . . . . . . . 2 Sam 7:19
in an unworthy *m* . . . . . . . . 1 Cor 11:27
Behold what *m* of love . . . . . 1 John 3:1

**MANSIONS**
house are many *m* . . . . . . . . John 14:2

**MANTLE**
Then he took the *m* . . . . . . . . 2 Kin 2:14

**MARK**
And the LORD set a *m* . . . . . . . Gen 4:15
whoever receives the *m* . . . . . Rev 14:11

**MARRED**
so His visage was *m* . . . . . . . . . Is 52:14

**MARRIAGE**
*M* is honorable among . . . . . . . Heb 13:4

**MARRIED**
But he who is *m* . . . . . . . . . . . 1 Cor 7:33

**MARRY**
they neither *m* nor are . . . . . Matt 22:30
forbidding to *m* . . . . . . . . . . . 1 Tim 4:3

**MARRYING**
and drinking, *m* . . . . . . . . . . Matt 24:38

**MARTYRS**
the blood of the *m* . . . . . . . . . . Rev 17:6

**MARVELED**
Jesus heard it, He *m* . . . . . . . Matt 8:10
so that Pilate *m* . . . . . . . . . . Mark 15:5

**MARVELOUS**
It is *m* in our eyes . . . . . . . . . . Ps 118:23
of darkness into His *m* . . . . . . 1 Pet 2:9

**MASTER**
a servant like his *m* . . . . . . . Matt 10:25
not greater than his *m* . . . . . John 15:20
and useful for the *M* . . . . . . . 2 Tim 2:21

**MASTERS**
can serve two *m* . . . . . . . . . . Luke 16:13
who have believing *m* . . . . . . 1 Tim 6:2

**MATTERS**
the weightier *m* . . . . . . . . . . Matt 23:23

**MATURE**
in understanding be *m* . . . . 1 Cor 14:20
us, as many as are *m* . . . . . . . Phil 3:15

**MEANT**
but God *m* it for good . . . . . . . Gen 50:20

**MEASURE**
a perfect and just *m* . . . . . . . Deut 25:15
give the Spirit by *m* . . . . . . . . John 3:34
to each one a *m* . . . . . . . . . . . Rom 12:3

**MEASURED**
*m* the waters in the . . . . . . . . . . Is 40:12
you use, it will be *m* . . . . . . . . . Matt 7:2

**MEASURES**
your house differing *m* . . . . Deut 25:14

**MEASURING**
behold, a man with a *m* . . . . . . Zech 2:1
*m* themselves by . . . . . . . . . 2 Cor 10:12

**MEAT**
will never again eat *m* . . . . . 1 Cor 8:13

**MEDIATOR**
by the hand of a *m* . . . . . . . . . . . Gal 3:19
is one God and one *M* . . . . . . . 1 Tim 2:5
to Jesus the *M* of the . . . . . . . Heb 12:24

**MEDICINE**
does good, like *m* . . . . . . . . . Prov 17:22

**MEDICINES**
you will use many *m* . . . . . . . . Jer 46:11

**MEDITATE**
but you shall *m* . . . . . . . . . . . . . Josh 1:8
*M* within your heart on . . . . . . . . Ps 4:4
I will *m* on Your . . . . . . . . . . . Ps 119:15
*m* beforehand on what . . . . Luke 21:14
*m* on these things . . . . . . . . . . . Phil 4:8

**MEDITATES**
in His law he *m* . . . . . . . . . . . . . . . Ps 1:2

**MEDITATION**
of my mouth and the *m* . . . . . . Ps 19:14
It is my *m* all the day . . . . . . . Ps 119:97

**MEDIUM**
or a woman who is a *m* . . . . . Lev 20:27

**MEDIUM'S**
shall be like a *m* . . . . . . . . . . . . Is 29:4

**MEDIUMS**
Seek those who are *m* . . . . . . . . . Is 8:19

**MEEK**
with equity for the *m* . . . . . . . . . Is 11:4
Blessed are the *m* . . . . . . . . . . Matt 5:5

**MEEKNESS**
are done in the *m* . . . . . . . . . James 3:13

**MEET**
prepare to *m* your God . . . . . Amos 4:12
*m* the Lord in the air . . . . . 1 Thess 4:17

**MELODY**
singing and making *m* . . . . . . Eph 5:19

**MELT**
the elements will *m* . . . . . . . . 2 Pet 3:10

**MEMBER**
the body is not one *m* . . . . . . 1 Cor 12:14

**MEMBERS**
you that one of your *m* . . . . . Matt 5:29
do not present your *m* . . . . . . . Rom 6:13
neighbor, for we are *m* . . . . . . . Eph 4:25

**MEMORIAL**
and this is My *m* . . . . . . . . . . . . Ex 3:15
also be told as a *m* . . . . . . . . Matt 26:13

**MEMORY**
The *m* of the righteous . . . . . Prov 10:7

**MEN**
*m* began to call on the . . . . . . . Gen 4:26
make you fishers of *m* . . . . . . Matt 4:19
goodwill toward *m* . . . . . . . . Luke 2:14
from heaven or from *m* . . . . . Luke 20:4
Likewise also the *m* . . . . . . . . Rom 1:27
the Lord, and not to *m* . . . . . . . . Eph 6:7
between God and *m* . . . . . . . . 1 Tim 2:5

**MENSERVANTS**
And also on My *m* . . . . . . . . . . . Joel 2:29
*And on My m and on My* . . . . Acts 2:18

**MERCHANDISE**
house a house of *m* . . . . . . . . . John 2:16

**MERCIES**
*give you the sure m* . . . . . . . Acts 13:34

**MERCIFUL**
LORD, the LORD God, *m* . . . . . . Ex 34:6
He is ever *m* . . . . . . . . . . . . . . . Ps 37:26
Blessed are the *m* . . . . . . . . . . Matt 5:7
saying, 'God be *m* . . . . . . . . Luke 18:13
*For I will be m* . . . . . . . . . . . . . Heb 8:12

**MERCY**
but showing *m* to . . . . . . . . . . . . Ex 20:6
and abundant in *m* . . . . . . . Num 14:18
*m* endures forever . . . . . . . . 1 Chr 16:34
*M* and truth have met . . . . . . Ps 85:10
*m* is everlasting . . . . . . . . . . . . Ps 100:5
Let not *m* and truth . . . . . . . . . Prov 3:3
For I desire *m* and not . . . . . . . . Hos 6:6
do justly, to love *m* . . . . . . . . . . . Mic 6:8
*'I desire m and not* . . . . . . . . . Matt 9:13
And His *m* is on those . . . . . . Luke 1:50
*"I will have m* . . . . . . . . . . . . . Rom 9:15
that He might have *m* . . . . . Rom 11:32
*m* has made trustworthy . . . 1 Cor 7:25
as we have received *m* . . . . . . . 2 Cor 4:1
God, who is rich in *m* . . . . . . . . Eph 2:4
but I obtained *m* . . . . . . . . . . . 1 Tim 1:13
him that he may find *m* . . . . 2 Tim 1:18
to His *m* He saved us . . . . . . . Titus 3:5
that we may obtain *m* . . . . . . . Heb 4:16

**MERRY**
*m* heart makes a . . . . . . . . . . Prov 15:13
that we should make *m* . . . . Luke 15:32

**MESSENGER**
"Behold, I send My *m* . . . . . . . . Mal 3:1
*'Behold, I send My m* . . . . . . Matt 11:10

**MESSIAH**
until *M* the Prince . . . . . . . . . Dan 9:25
"We have found the *M* . . . . . . John 1:41

**MIDST**
God is in the *m* . . . . . . . . . . . . . . Ps 46:5
I am there in the *m* . . . . . . . Matt 18:20

**MIGHT**
'My power and the *m* . . . . . . . Deut 8:17
'Not by *m* nor by . . . . . . . . . . . . Zech 4:6
in the power of His *m* . . . . . . . Eph 6:10
honor and power and *m* . . . . . . Rev 7:12

**MIGHTIER**
coming after me is *m* . . . . . . . Matt 3:11

**MIGHTY**
He was a *m* hunter . . . . . . . . . Gen 10:9
How the *m* have fallen . . . . . 2 Sam 1:19
the LORD *m* in battle . . . . . . . . . . Ps 24:8
their Redeemer is *m* . . . . . . . Prov 23:11
*m* has done great . . . . . . . . . . Luke 1:49
the flesh, not many *m* . . . . . . 1 Cor 1:26
the working of His *m* . . . . . . . Eph 1:19

**MILK**
come, buy wine and *m* . . . . . . . . Is 55:1
shall flow with *m* . . . . . . . . . . . Joel 3:18
have come to need *m* . . . . . . . . Heb 5:12
desire the pure *m* . . . . . . . . . . . 1 Pet 2:2

**MILLSTONE**
*m* were hung around his . . . . Matt 18:6
a stone like a great *m* . . . . . . Rev 18:21

**MIND**
put wisdom in the *m* . . . . . . . . Job 38:36
perfect peace, whose *m* . . . . . . . . Is 26:3
nor have an anxious *m* . . . . Luke 12:29
*m* I myself serve the . . . . . . . . Rom 7:25
*who has known the m* . . . . . Rom 11:34
Be of the same *m* . . . . . . . . . . Rom 12:16
convinced in his own *m* . . . . . Rom 14:5
*"Who has known the m* . . . . . 1 Cor 2:16
you are out of your *m* . . . . . 1 Cor 14:23
Let this *m* be in you . . . . . . . . . Phil 2:5
love and of a sound *m* . . . . . . . 2 Tim 1:7

**MINDFUL**
is man that You are *m* . . . . . . . . . Ps 8:4
for you are not *m* . . . . . . . . . Matt 16:23
*is man that You are m* . . . . . . . . . Heb 2:6

**MINDS**
put My law in their *m* . . . . . . . Jer 31:33
I stir up your pure *m* . . . . . . . . 2 Pet 3:1

**MINISTER**
for he is God's *m* . . . . . . . . . . . Rom 13:4
you will be a good *m* . . . . . . . . 1 Tim 4:6

**MINISTERS**
for they are God's *m* ........Rom 13:6
If anyone *m* ..............1 Pet 4:11

**MINISTRIES**
are differences of *m*........1 Cor 12:5

**MINISTRY**
But if the *m* of death........2 Cor 3:7
since we have this *m*........2 Cor 4:1
and has given us the *m*.....2 Cor 5:18
for the work of *m*...........Eph 4:12
fulfill your *m* .............2 Tim 4:5
a more excellent *m* ..........Heb 8:6

**MIRACLE**
no one who works a *m*......Mark 9:39

**MIRACLES**
God worked unusual *m* ....Acts 19:11
the working of *m*.........1 Cor 12:10

**MISERY**
and remember his *m* .......Prov 31:7

**MITES**
widow putting in two *m* ....Luke 21:2

**MOCK**
Fools *m* at sin..............Prov 14:9
to the Gentiles to *m*.......Matt 20:19

**MOCKED**
at noon, that Elijah *m* ....1 Kin 18:27
deceived, God is not *m*........Gal 6:7

**MOCKER**
Wine is a *m*...............Prov 20:1

**MOCKS**
He who *m* the poor .........Prov 17:5

**MODERATION**
with propriety and *m*.......1 Tim 2:9

**MOMENT**
In a *m* they die ............Job 34:20
in a *m*, in the............1 Cor 15:52

**MONEY**
be redeemed without *m* .......Is 52:3
and you who have no *m*........Is 55:1
and hid his lord's *m* ......Matt 25:18
promised to give him *m* ...Mark 14:11
"Carry neither *m* .........Luke 10:4
I sent you without *m* ......Luke 22:35
be purchased with *m* .......Acts 8:20
not greedy for *m* ...........1 Tim 3:3
*m* is a root of all ..........1 Tim 6:10

**MONEYCHANGERS**
the tables of the *m*........Matt 21:12

**MOON**
until the *m* is no more .......Ps 72:7
*m* will not give its........Mark 13:24

**MORNING**
Evening and *m* and at .......Ps 55:17
Lucifer, son of the *m* .........Is 14:12
very early in the *m* ........Luke 24:1
the Bright and *M* Star......Rev 22:16

**MORTAL**
sin reign in your *m*.........Rom 6:12
and this *m* must put ......1 Cor 15:53

**MORTALITY**
*m* may be swallowed........2 Cor 5:4

**MOTH**
where *m* and rust..........Matt 6:19

**MOTHER**
because she was the *m* ......Gen 3:20
*leave his father and m*......Matt 19:5
"Behold your *m* ..........John 19:27
The *M* of Harlots ...........Rev 17:5

**MOUNT**
come up to *M* Sinai .........Ex 19:23
they shall *m* up with.........Is 40:31

**MOUNTAIN**
to Horeb, the *m* ..............Ex 3:1
let us go up to the *m* ...........Is 2:3
image became a great *m*.....Dan 2:35
Who are you, O great *m*......Zech 4:7
you will say to this *m*......Matt 17:20
with Him on the holy *m*.....2 Pet 1:18

**MOUNTAINS**
*m* were brought forth.........Ps 90:2
*m* shall depart and the .......Is 54:10
in Judea flee to the *m* .....Matt 24:16
that I could remove *m*......1 Cor 13:2

**MOURN**
a time to *m* ................Eccl 3:4
are those who *m*............Matt 5:4
of the earth will *m*...........Rev 1:7

**MOURNED**
and have not rather *m*.......1 Cor 5:2

**MOURNING**
shall be a great *m* ........Zech 12:11
be turned to *m* and ........James 4:9

**MOUTH**
"Who has made man's *m* .....Ex 4:11
Out of the *m* of babes..........Ps 8:2
knowledge, but the *m* .....Prov 10:14
The *m* of an immoral ......Prov 22:14
and a flattering *m* ........Prov 26:28
*m* speaking pompous ........Dan 7:8
*m* defiles a man ..........Matt 15:11
*m* I will judge you ........Luke 19:22
I will give you a *m*........Luke 21:15
*m* confession is made ......Rom 10:10
*m* great swelling words.......Jude 16
vomit you out of My *m*.......Rev 3:16

**MOVED**
she shall not be *m* ...........Ps 46:5
spoke as they were *m*.......2 Pet 1:21

**MUCH**
*m* study is ...............Eccl 12:12
to whom *m* is given .......Luke 12:48

**MULTIPLIED**
of the disciples *m* ...........Acts 6:7
word of God grew and *m*....Acts 12:24

**MULTIPLY**
"Be fruitful and *m* .........Gen 1:22
*m* the descendants .........Jer 33:22

**MULTITUDE**
stars of heaven in *m*........Deut 1:10
In the *m* of words sin ......Prov 10:19
compassion on the *m* ......Matt 15:32
with the angel a *m* ........Luke 2:13
*"love will cover a m* .........1 Pet 4:8
and behold, a great *m* .........Rev 7:9

**MURDER**
"You shall not *m* ...........Ex 20:13
*'You shall not m*...........Matt 5:21
You *m* and covet and .......James 4:2

**MURDERED**
up Jesus whom you *m*.......Acts 5:30

**MURDERER**
He was a *m* from the .......John 8:44
his brother is a *m* ........1 John 3:15

**MURDERERS**
and profane, for *m* .........1 Tim 1:9
abominable, *m*.............Rev 21:8

**MURDERS**
evil thoughts, *m*..........Matt 15:19

**MUSING**
while I was *m*...............Ps 39:3

**MUTILATION**
beware of the *m*.............Phil 3:2

**MUZZLE**
*"You shall not m*..........1 Tim 5:18

**MYSTERIES**
to you to know the *m* ......Matt 13:11
and understand all *m* ......1 Cor 13:2

**MYSTERY**
given to know the *m*.......Mark 4:11
wisdom of God in a *m* .......1 Cor 2:7
Behold, I tell you a *m* .....1 Cor 15:51
made known to us the *m*......Eph 1:9
the *m* of godliness ........1 Tim 3:16

## N

**NAILED**
*n* it to the cross.............Col 2:14

**NAKED**
And they were both *n* .......Gen 2:25
knew that they were *n*........Gen 3:7
*N* I came from my...........Job 1:21
'I was *n* and you..........Matt 25:36
but all things are *n* .........Heb 4:13
brother or sister is *n* ......James 2:15
poor, blind, and *n*...........Rev 3:17

**NAKEDNESS**
or famine, or *n* ............Rom 8:35
*n* may not be revealed .......Rev 3:18

**NAME**
Abram called on the *n*.......Gen 13:4
Israel shall be your *n* ......Gen 35:10
This is My *n* forever .........Ex 3:15
shall not take the *n*..........Ex 20:7
glorious and awesome *n*....Deut 28:58
excellent is Your *n* ............Ps 8:1
*n* will put their trust .........Ps 9:10
be His glorious *n* ...........Ps 72:19
do not call on Your *n* .........Ps 79:6
to Your *n* give glory .........Ps 115:1
above all Your *n*............Ps 138:2
A good *n* is to be...........Prov 22:1
what is His Son's *n*.........Prov 30:4
be called by a new *n* ..........Is 62:2
Everlasting is Your *n* ........Is 63:16
They will call on My *n* ......Zech 13:9
to you who fear My *n*.........Mal 4:2
hallowed be Your *n* .........Matt 6:9
prophesied in Your *n* .......Matt 7:22
*n Gentiles will trust* ......Matt 12:21
together in My *n* .........Matt 18:20
many will come in My *n* ....Matt 24:5
who believe in His *n* .......John 1:12
comes in his own *n*.........John 5:43
his own sheep by *n*.........John 10:3
through faith in His *n* ......Acts 3:16
there is no other *n*..........Acts 4:12
which is above every *n* .......Phil 2:9
deed, do all in the *n* .........Col 3:17
a more excellent *n*...........Heb 1:4
you hold fast to My *n* ........Rev 2:13
*n* that you are alive ..........Rev 3:1
having His Father's *n* .......Rev 14:1
and glorify Your *n* ..........Rev 15:4
*n* written that no one.......Rev 19:12

**NAME'S**
saved them for His *n* ........Ps 106:8

**NAMED**
I have *n* you................Is 45:4

**NARROW**
"Enter by the *n* gate ....... Matt 7:13

**NATION**
make you a great *n* ......... Gen 12:2
exalts a *n* ............... Prov 14:34
*n* that was not called.......... Is 65:1
I will make them one *n* .... Ezek 37:22
since there was a *n* ......... Dan 12:1
*n* will rise against ......... Matt 24:7
for he loves our *n* ........... Luke 7:5
*those who are not a n* ...... Rom 10:19
tribe, tongue, and *n*......... Rev 13:7

**NATIONS**
Why do the *n* rage ............ Ps 2:1
I will give You the *n*........... Ps 2:8
*n* shall serve Him .......... Ps 72:11
disciples of all the *n*....... Matt 28:19
who was to rule all *n* ........ Rev 12:5
the healing of the *n* ......... Rev 22:2

**NATURAL**
women exchanged the *n*..... Rom 1:26
the men, leaving the *n* ...... Rom 1:27
did not spare the *n* ........ Rom 11:21
*n* man does not receive ..... 1 Cor 2:14
It is sown a *n* body........ 1 Cor 15:44

**NATURE**
We who are Jews by *n* ....... Gal 2:15
by *n* children of wrath........ Eph 2:3
of the divine *n* ............. 2 Pet 1:4

**NEAR**
But the word is very *n* ..... Deut 30:14
upon Him while He is *n* ....... Is 55:6
know that it is *n*.......... Matt 24:33
kingdom of God is *n* ...... Luke 21:31
*"The word is n* ............ Rom 10:8
to those who were *n*......... Eph 2:17
for the time is *n* ............. Rev 1:3

**NEARER**
now our salvation is *n* ..... Rom 13:11

**NEED**
the things you have *n* ....... Matt 6:8
supply all your *n*.......... Phil 4:19
to help in time of *n* ........ Heb 4:16

**NEGLECT**
if we *n* so great a ............ Heb 2:3

**NEGLECTED**
*n* the weightier .......... Matt 23:23

**NEIGHBOR**
you shall love your *n* ....... Lev 19:18
*You shall love your n* ....... Matt 5:43
"And who is my *n* ........ Luke 10:29
*You shall love your n* ....... Rom 13:9

**NEVER**
in Me shall *n* thirst ........ John 6:35
in Me shall *n* die ......... John 11:26
Love *n* fails .............. 1 Cor 13:8
*n* take away sins .......... Heb 10:11
*"I will n leave you* .......... Heb 13:5
for prophecy *n* came by ..... 2 Pet 1:21

**NEW**
and there is nothing *n*........ Eccl 1:9
For behold, I create *n* ........ Is 65:17
*n* every morning........... Lam 3:23
wine into *n* wineskins ...... Matt 9:17
of the *n* covenant ......... Matt 26:28
*n* commandment I give .... John 13:34
he is a *n* creation .......... 2 Cor 5:17
*when I will make a n*......... Heb 8:8
*n* heavens and a *n* ......... 2 Pet 3:13
*n* name written which....... Rev 2:17
And they sang a *n* ........... Rev 5:9
And I saw a *n* heaven........ Rev 21:1
I make all things *n* ......... Rev 21:5

**NEWNESS**
also should walk in *n* ........ Rom 6:4

**NIGHT**
darkness He called *N* ........ Gen 1:5
It is a *n* of solemn .......... Ex 12:42
pillar of fire by *n* ........... Ex 13:22
gives songs in the *n* ........ Job 35:10
and continued all *n* ........ Luke 6:12
man came to Jesus by *n*...... John 3:2
*n* is coming when no ........ John 9:4
came to Jesus by *n* ........ John 19:39
as a thief in the *n*......... 1 Thess 5:2
there shall be no *n* ......... Rev 21:25

**NINETY-NINE**
he not leave the *n*......... Matt 18:12

**NOTHING**
I can of Myself do *n* ........ John 5:30
Me you can do *n* ........... John 15:5
men, it will come to *n* ....... Acts 5:38
have not love, I am *n*....... 1 Cor 13:2
Be anxious for *n* ............ Phil 4:6
For we brought *n* .......... 1 Tim 6:7

**NOURISHED**
"I have *n* and................. Is 1:2

**NOURISHES**
*n* and cherishes it .......... Eph 5:29

**NUMBER**
if a man could *n*........... Gen 13:16
teach us to *n* our days ....... Ps 90:12
which no one could *n* ......... Rev 7:9
His *n* is 666 .............. Rev 13:18


## O


**OATH**
for the sake of your *o*......... Eccl 8:2
he denied with an *o* ....... Matt 26:72
*o* which He swore.......... Luke 1:73

**OATHS**
shall perform your *o* ....... Matt 5:33

**OBEDIENCE**
*o* many will be made ....... Rom 5:19
captivity to the *o*.......... 2 Cor 10:5
yet He learned *o* ........... Heb 5:8

**OBEDIENT**
you are willing and *o* ......... Is 1:19
of the priests were *o* ......... Acts 6:7
to make the Gentiles *o* ..... Rom 15:18
Himself and became *o* ....... Phil 2:8
as *o* children ............. 1 Pet 1:14

**OBEY**
God and *o* His voice ........ Deut 4:30
His voice we will *o* ........ Josh 24:24
*o* is better than ......... 1 Sam 15:22
*o* God rather than men ..... Acts 5:29
and do not *o* the truth........ Rom 2:8
yourselves slaves to *o*....... Rom 6:16
*o* your parents in all......... Col 3:20
Bondservants, *o* in all ....... Col 3:22
on those who do not *o*...... 2 Thess 1:8
*O* those who rule .......... Heb 13:17

**OBEYED**
of sin, yet you *o*............ Rom 6:17
they have not all *o* ........ Rom 10:16
By faith Abraham *o* ......... Heb 11:8

**OBSERVATION**
does not come with *o* ...... Luke 17:20

**OBSERVE**
teaching them to *o* all ..... Matt 28:20

**OBTAIN**
they also may *o* mercy ..... Rom 11:31
*o* salvation through....... 1 Thess 5:9

**OBTAINED**
*o* a part in this ............ Acts 1:17
yet have now *o* mercy ...... Rom 11:30
endured, he *o* the........... Heb 6:15

**OBTAINS**
*o* favor from the LORD ...... Prov 8:35

**OFFEND**
lest we *o* them ........... Matt 17:27
than that he should *o* ...... Luke 17:2
them, "Does this *o*......... John 6:61

**OFFENDED**
So they were *o* at Him ..... Matt 13:57

**OFFENSE**
and a rock of *o*.............. Is 8:14
You are an *o* to Me ........ Matt 16:23
by the one man's *o* ......... Rom 5:17
the *o* of the cross............ Gal 5:11
sincere and without *o* ....... Phil 1:10
*and a rock of o* ............ 1 Pet 2:8

**OFFENSES**
For *o* must come........... Matt 18:7
impossible that no *o* ....... Luke 17:1

**OFFER**
come and *o* your gift ....... Matt 5:24
let us continually *o* ........ Heb 13:15

**OFFERED**
to eat those things *o* ....... 1 Cor 8:10
so Christ was *o* ............ Heb 9:28
*o* one sacrifice ............ Heb 10:12

**OFFERING**
*o* You did not require ......... Ps 40:6
You make His soul an *o* ...... Is 53:10
Himself for us, an *o*.......... Eph 5:2
*o You did not* .............. Heb 10:5
*o* He has perfected......... Heb 10:14

**OFFERINGS**
and offered burnt *o* ......... Gen 8:20
*In burnt o and* ............. Heb 10:6

**OFFICE**
sitting at the tax *o* .......... Matt 9:9

**OFFSPRING**
wife and raise up *o*........ Matt 22:24
For we are also His *o*....... Acts 17:28
am the Root and the *O*...... Rev 22:16

**OFTEN**
*o* I wanted to gather ...... Luke 13:34
as *o* as you eat this ....... 1 Cor 11:26

**OIL**
a bin, and a little *o* ....... 1 Kin 17:12
very costly fragrant *o* ...... Matt 26:7
anointing him with *o* ..... James 5:14
and do not harm the *o* ........ Rev 6:6

**OLD**
young, and now am *o* ........ Ps 37:25
was said to those of *o* ...... Matt 5:21
but when you are *o*........ John 21:18
*your o men shall dream* ..... Acts 2:17
*o* man was crucified ......... Rom 6:6
*o* things have passed....... 2 Cor 5:17
have put off the *o* man ........ Col 3:9
that serpent of *o*............ Rev 20:2

**OLDER**
*o* shall serve the .......... Gen 25:23
not rebuke an *o* man........ 1 Tim 5:1

**OLDEST**
beginning with the *o* ........ John 8:9

**OLIVE**
a freshly plucked *o* ... Gen 8:11
*o* tree which is wild ... Rom 11:24

**OMNIPOTENT**
For the Lord God *O* ... Rev 19:6

**ONCE**
died, He died to sin *o* ... Rom 6:10
for men to die *o* ... Heb 9:27
also suffered *o* ... 1 Pet 3:18

**ONE**
*O* thing you lack ... Mark 10:21
*o* thing is needed ... Luke 10:42
I and My Father are *o* ... John 10:30
Me, that they may be *o* ... John 17:11
*o* accord in the temple ... Acts 2:46
for you are all *o* ... Gal 3:28
to create in Himself *o* ... Eph 2:15
*o* Lord ... Eph 4:5
*o* faith ... Eph 4:5
*o* baptism ... Eph 4:5
*o* God and Father of ... Eph 4:6
For there is *o* God and ... 1 Tim 2:5
*o* Mediator between God ... 1 Tim 2:5
a thousand years as *o* ... 2 Pet 3:8

**OPENED**
*o* not His mouth ... Is 53:7
*o* the Scriptures ... Luke 24:32
*o* their understanding ... Luke 24:45
Now I saw heaven *o* ... Rev 19:11

**OPENS**
him the doorkeeper *o* ... John 10:3
*and shuts and no one o* ... Rev 3:7

**OPINION**
be wise in your own *o* ... Rom 11:25

**OPINIONS**
falter between two *o* ... 1 Kin 18:21

**OPPORTUNITY**
But sin, taking *o* ... Rom 7:8
as we have *o* ... Gal 6:10
but you lacked *o* ... Phil 4:10

**OPPRESS**
he loves to *o* ... Hos 12:7
*o* the widow or the ... Zech 7:10
Do not the rich *o* ... James 2:6

**OPPRESSED**
for all who are *o* ... Ps 103:6
The tears of the *o* ... Eccl 4:1
He was *o* and He was ... Is 53:7
healing all who were *o* ... Acts 10:38

**OPPRESSES**
*o* the poor reproaches ... Prov 14:31

**OPPRESSION**
have surely seen the *o* ... Ex 3:7
their life from *o* ... Ps 72:14
brought low through *o* ... Ps 107:39
Redeem me from the *o* ... Ps 119:134
considered all the *o* ... Eccl 4:1
*o* destroys a wise ... Eccl 7:7
justice, but behold, *o* ... Is 5:7
*surely seen the o* ... Acts 7:34

**ORACLES**
received the living *o* ... Acts 7:38
were committed the *o* ... Rom 3:2
principles of the *o* ... Heb 5:12

**ORDAINED**
*o* you a prophet ... Jer 1:5
the Man whom He has *o* ... Acts 17:31

**ORDER**
done decently and in *o* ... 1 Cor 14:40

**ORDERS**
*o* his conduct aright I ... Ps 50:23

**ORDINANCE**
resists the *o* of God ... Rom 13:2

**ORDINANCES**
and fleshly *o* imposed ... Heb 9:10

**ORPHANS**
I will not leave you *o* ... John 14:18
to visit *o* and widows ... James 1:27

**OUGHT**
These you *o* to have ... Matt 23:23
pray for as we *o* ... Rom 8:26
persons *o* you to be ... 2 Pet 3:11

**OUTCAST**
they called you an *o* ... Jer 30:17

**OUTCASTS**
will assemble the *o* ... Is 11:12

**OUTRAN**
the other disciple *o* ... John 20:4

**OUTSIDE**
and dish, that the *o* ... Matt 23:26
Pharisees make the *o* ... Luke 11:39
toward those who are *o* ... Col 4:5
to Him, *o* the camp ... Heb 13:13
But *o* are dogs and ... Rev 22:15

**OUTSTRETCHED**
and with an *o* arm ... Deut 26:8

**OUTWARD**
at the *o* appearance ... 1 Sam 16:7
your adornment be merely *o* ... 1 Pet 3:3

**OUTWARDLY**
not a Jew who is one *o* ... Rom 2:28

**OVERCAME**
My throne, as I also *o* ... Rev 3:21
"And they *o* him by ... Rev 12:11

**OVERCOME**
good cheer, I have *o* ... John 16:33
and the Lamb will *o* ... Rev 17:14

**OVERCOMES**
of God *o* the world ... 1 John 5:4
*o* I will give to eat ... Rev 2:7
*o* shall not be hurt ... Rev 2:11
*o* shall inherit all ... Rev 21:7

**OVERSEER**
to the Shepherd and *O* ... 1 Pet 2:25

**OVERSEERS**
you, serving as *o* ... 1 Pet 5:2

**OVERSHADOW**
of the Highest will *o* ... Luke 1:35

**OVERTHREW**
As God *o* Sodom and ... Jer 50:40

**OVERTHROW**
*o* the faith of some ... 2 Tim 2:18

**OVERTHROWN**
and Nineveh shall be *o* ... Jon 3:4

**OVERTHROWS**
and *o* the mighty ... Job 12:19
*o* them in the night ... Job 34:25
*o* the words of the ... Prov 22:12

**OVERWHELM**
*o* the fatherless ... Job 6:27

**OVERWHELMED**
and my spirit was *o* ... Ps 77:3
my spirit is *o* within ... Ps 143:4

**OVERWORK**
Do not *o* to be rich ... Prov 23:4

**OWE**
*O* no one anything ... Rom 13:8

**OWED**
*o* him ten thousand ... Matt 18:24

**OWN**
He came to His *o* ... John 1:11
having loved His *o* ... John 13:1
world would love its *o* ... John 15:19
and you are not your *o* ... 1 Cor 6:19
But each one has his *o* ... 1 Cor 7:7
For all seek their *o* ... Phil 2:21
from our sins in His *o* ... Rev 1:5

**OX**
shall not muzzle an *o* ... Deut 25:4
*o* knows its owner ... Is 1:3
Sabbath loose his *o* ... Luke 13:15
*shall not muzzle an o* ... 1 Cor 9:9

## P

**PACIFIES**
A gift in secret *p* ... Prov 21:14

**PAIN**
*p* you shall bring ... Gen 3:16
*p* as a woman in ... Is 13:8
Why is my *p* perpetual ... Jer 15:18
shall be no more *p* ... Rev 21:4

**PAINED**
My heart is severely *p* ... Ps 55:4
I am *p* in my very ... Jer 4:19

**PAINFUL**
for the present, but *p* ... Heb 12:11

**PAINS**
The *p* of death ... Ps 116:3
having loosed the *p* ... Acts 2:24

**PAINT**
your eyes with *p* ... Jer 4:30

**PALACE**
enter the King's *p* ... Ps 45:15
guards his own *p* ... Luke 11:21
evident to the whole *p* ... Phil 1:13

**PALACES**
out of the ivory *p* ... Ps 45:8

**PALE**
behold, a *p* horse ... Rev 6:8

**PALM**
*p* branches in their ... Rev 7:9

**PALMS**
struck Him with the *p* ... Matt 26:67

**PAMPERS**
*p* his servant from ... Prov 29:21

**PANGS**
The *p* of death ... Ps 18:4
labors with birth *p* ... Rom 8:22

**PARABLE**
do You speak this *p* ... Luke 12:41

**PARABLES**
rest it is given in *p* ... Luke 8:10

**PARADISE**
will be with Me in *P* ... Luke 23:43
in the midst of the *P* ... Rev 2:7

**PARDON**
He will abundantly *p* ... Is 55:7
*p* all their iniquities ... Jer 33:8

**PARDONING**
is a God like You, *p* ... Mic 7:18

**PARENTS**
will rise up against *p* ... Matt 10:21
has left house or *p* ... Luke 18:29
disobedient to *p* ... Rom 1:30

**PART**
has chosen that good p . . . .Luke 10:42
you, you have no p . . . . . . . . . .John 13:8
For we know in p . . . . . . . . . .1 Cor 13:9
shall take away his p. . . . . . .Rev 22:19

**PARTAKE**
for we all p of that . . . . . . . .1 Cor 10:17

**PARTAKER**
in hope should be p . . . . . . . .1 Cor 9:10
Christ, and also a p . . . . . . . . .1 Pet 5:1

**PARTAKERS**
Gentiles have been p . . . . . .Rom 15:27
know that as you are p . . . . . .2 Cor 1:7
qualified us to be p. . . . . . . . . .Col 1:12

**PARTIAL**
You shall not be p. . . . . . . . . .Lev 19:15

**PARTIALITY**
that God shows no p . . . . . . .Acts 10:34
doing nothing with p . . . . . .1 Tim 5:21
good fruits, without p . . . . .James 3:17

**PASS**
I will p over you. . . . . . . . . . .Ex 12:13
When you p through the. . . . . . .Is 43:2
and earth will p. . . . . . . . . .Matt 24:35

**PASSED**
forbearance God had p . . . . . .Rom 3:25
High Priest who has p. . . . . . .Heb 4:14
We know that we have p . . .1 John 3:14

**PASSES**
of Christ which p. . . . . . . . . . .Eph 3:19

**PASSION**
uncleanness, p . . . . . . . . . . . . . .Col 3:5

**PASSIONS**
gave them up to vile p . . . . . .Rom 1:26

**PASSOVER**
It is the LORD'S P . . . . . . . . . .Ex 12:11
I will keep the P. . . . . . . . . .Matt 26:18
indeed Christ, our P . . . . . . . .1 Cor 5:7
By faith he kept the P . . . . .Heb 11:28

**PASTORS**
and some p and . . . . . . . . . . . .Eph 4:11

**PASTURE**
the sheep of Your p. . . . . . . . . . .Ps 74:1
in and out and find p . . . . . . .John 10:9

**PASTURES**
to lie down in green p. . . . . . . . .Ps 23:2

**PATH**
You will show me the p . . . . . .Ps 16:11

**PATHS**
He leads me in the p. . . . . . . . . .Ps 23:3
*make His p straight* . . . . . . . .Matt 3:3
and make straight p . . . . . . .Heb 12:13

**PATIENCE**
'Master, have p . . . . . . . . . .Matt 18:26
and bear fruit with p. . . . . . .Luke 8:15
labor of love, and p. . . . . . . .1 Thess 1:3
faith, love, p . . . . . . . . . . . . .1 Tim 6:11
your faith produces p. . . . . . .James 1:3
p have its perfect . . . . . . . . . .James 1:4
in the kingdom and p. . . . . . . . . .Rev 1:9

**PATIENT**
rejoicing in hope, p. . . . . . . .Rom 12:12
uphold the weak, be p . . . .1 Thess 5:14

**PATIENTLY**
if you take it p . . . . . . . . . . . .1 Pet 2:20

**PATRIARCHS**
begot the twelve p. . . . . . . . . . .Acts 7:8

**PATTERN**
p which you were shown . . . . .Ex 26:30
as you have us for a p . . . . . . .Phil 3:17
*p shown you on the* . . . . . . . . . .Heb 8:5

**PEACE**
you, and give you p . . . . . . . .Num 6:26
both lie down in p. . . . . . . . . . . . . .Ps 4:8
p have those who love . . . . .Ps 119:165
I am for p . . . . . . . . . . . . . . . . .Ps 120:7
war, and a time of p. . . . . . . . . .Eccl 3:8
Father, Prince of P . . . . . . . . . . . .Is 9:6
keep him in perfect p . . . . . . . . .Is 26:3
p they have not . . . . . . . . . . . . . .Is 59:8
slightly, saying, 'P . . . . . . . . . .Jer 6:14
place I will give p . . . . . . . . . . .Hag 2:9
is worthy, let your p . . . . . . .Matt 10:13
that I came to bring p . . . . .Matt 10:34
and on earth p . . . . . . . . . . . . .Luke 2:14
if a son of p is there . . . . . . . .Luke 10:6
that make for your p . . . . . .Luke 19:42
I leave with you, My p . . . . .John 14:27
in Me you may have p . . . . .John 16:33
Grace to you and p . . . . . . . . . .Rom 1:7
by faith, we have p . . . . . . . . . .Rom 5:1
God has called us to p . . . . . .1 Cor 7:15
p will be with you . . . . . . . . .2 Cor 13:11
Spirit is love, joy, p. . . . . . . . . .Gal 5:22
He Himself is our p. . . . . . . . . .Eph 2:14
and the p of God . . . . . . . . . . . .Phil 4:7
And let the p of God . . . . . . . . .Col 3:15
faith, love, p . . . . . . . . . . . . .2 Tim 2:22
meaning "king of p," . . . . . . . . .Heb 7:2

**PEACEABLE**
is first pure, then p . . . . . . .James 3:17

**PEACEABLY**
depends on you, live p. . . . . .Rom 12:18

**PEACEFUL**
in a p habitation . . . . . . . . . . . .Is 32:18

**PEACEMAKERS**
Blessed are the p . . . . . . . . . . .Matt 5:9

**PEARL**
he had found one p. . . . . . . .Matt 13:46

**PEARLS**
nor cast your p. . . . . . . . . . . . .Matt 7:6
gates were twelve p . . . . . . . .Rev 21:21

**PENTECOST**
P had fully come. . . . . . . . . . . .Acts 2:1

**PEOPLE**
will take you as My p . . . . . . . . .Ex 6:7
p shall be my p . . . . . . . . . . .Ruth 1:16
p who know the joyful . . . . . . .Ps 89:15
We are His p and the . . . . . . . .Ps 100:3
Blessed is Egypt My p . . . . . . .Is 19:25
to make ready a p . . . . . . . . .Luke 1:17
take out of them a p . . . . . . .Acts 15:14
*who were not My p* . . . . . . . . .Rom 9:25
*and they shall be My p* . . . . .2 Cor 6:16
*LORD will judge His p*. . . . . .Heb 10:30
but are now the p . . . . . . . . . .1 Pet 2:10
tribe and tongue and p . . . . . . .Rev 5:9
they shall be His p. . . . . . . . . .Rev 21:3

**PERCEIVE**
seeing, but do not p. . . . . . . . . . . .Is 6:9
*they may see and not p* . . . . .Mark 4:12

**PERDITION**
except the son of p . . . . . . . .John 17:12
revealed, the son of p. . . . . .2 Thess 2:3
who draw back to p . . . . . . . .Heb 10:39

**PERFECT**
Noah was a just man, p. . . . . . .Gen 6:9
Father in heaven is p . . . . . . .Matt 5:48
they may be made p . . . . . . .John 17:23
and p will of God. . . . . . . . . . . .Rom 12:2
when that which is p. . . . . .1 Cor 13:10
present every man p. . . . . . . . . .Col 1:28
good gift and every p . . . . . .James 1:17
in word, he is a p . . . . . . . . . .James 3:2
p love casts out fear. . . . . . .1 John 4:18

**PERFECTED**
third day I shall be p . . . . . .Luke 13:32
or am already p. . . . . . . . . . . .Phil 3:12
the Son who has been p . . . . . .Heb 7:28

**PERFECTION**
let us go on to p . . . . . . . . . . . . .Heb 6:1

**PERISH**
so that we may not p . . . . . . . . . .Jon 1:6
little ones should p . . . . . . .Matt 18:14
in Him should not p . . . . . . . .John 3:16
and they shall never p . . . . .John 10:28
among those who p . . . . . .2 Thess 2:10
that any should p. . . . . . . . . . . .2 Pet 3:9

**PERISHABLE**
do it to obtain a p. . . . . . . . . .1 Cor 9:25

**PERISHED**
Truth has p and has . . . . . . . . .Jer 7:28

**PERISHING**
We are p . . . . . . . . . . . . . . . . .Matt 8:25

**PERMIT**
And I do not p a woman . . . .1 Tim 2:12

**PERMITS**
we will do if God p. . . . . . . . . . .Heb 6:3

**PERMITTED**
p no one to do them . . . . . . . .Ps 105:14
we are p . . . . . . . . . . . . . . . . . .2 Cor 4:8

**PERSECUTE**
when they revile and p . . . . .Matt 5:11

**PERSECUTED**
If they p Me . . . . . . . . . . . . .John 15:20
p, but not forsaken . . . . . . . . .2 Cor 4:9

**PERSECUTES**
wicked in his pride p . . . . . . . . .Ps 10:2

**PERSECUTION**
p arises because of. . . . . . . .Matt 13:21
At that time a great p. . . . . . . .Acts 8:1
do I still suffer p. . . . . . . . . . . .Gal 5:11

**PERSECUTOR**
a blasphemer, a p . . . . . . . . .1 Tim 1:13

**PERSEVERANCE**
tribulation produces p . . . . . . .Rom 5:3

**PERSEVERE**
kept My command to p . . . . . .Rev 3:10

**PERSISTENCE**
p he will rise and. . . . . . . . . .Luke 11:8

**PERSON**
do not regard the p. . . . . . . .Matt 22:16
express image of His p . . . . . . .Heb 1:3

**PERSUADE**
"You almost p me . . . . . . . . .Acts 26:28

**PERSUADED**
neither will they be p . . . . .Luke 16:31
p that He is able . . . . . . . . . .2 Tim 1:12

**PERSUASIVE**
p words of human . . . . . . . . . .1 Cor 2:4

**PERVERSE**
because your way is p . . . . .Num 22:32
p man sows strife . . . . . . . . .Prov 16:28
from this p generation . . . . . .Acts 2:40

**PERVERT**
"You shall not *p* justice . . . .Deut 16:19
*p* the gospel of Christ. . . . . . . . .Gal 1:7

**PERVERTING**
will you not cease *p*. . . . . . . .Acts 13:10

**PERVERTS**
*p* his ways will become. . . . . .Prov 10:9

**PESTILENCE**
from the perilous *p*. . . . . . . . . . .Ps 91:3
Before Him went *p* . . . . . . . . . .Hab 3:5

**PESTILENCES**
will be famines, *p* . . . . . . . . .Matt 24:7

**PETITIONS**
*p* that we have asked. . . . . .1 John 5:15

**PHARISEE**
to pray, one a *P* . . . . . . . . . .Luke 18:10

**PHILOSOPHERS**
*p* encountered him . . . . . . . .Acts 17:18

**PHILOSOPHY**
cheat you through *p* . . . . . . . . . .Col 2:8

**PHYSICIAN**
have no need of a *p*. . . . . . . . .Matt 9:12

**PHYSICIANS**
her livelihood on *p*. . . . . . . . .Luke 8:43

**PIECES**
*they took the thirty p* . . . . . .Matt 27:9

**PIERCE**
a sword will *p* . . . . . . . . . . . .Luke 2:35

**PIERCED**
*p* My hands and My feet . . . . .Ps 22:16
on Me whom they have *p* . . .Zech 12:10
of the soldiers *p* . . . . . . . . . .John 19:34
*p* themselves through . . . . .1 Tim 6:10
and they also who *p* . . . . . . . . . .Rev 1:7

**PIERCING**
*p* even to the division . . . . . . .Heb 4:12

**PILGRIMAGE**
heart is set on *p* . . . . . . . . . . . . .Ps 84:5
In the house of my *p*. . . . . . . .Ps 119:54

**PILGRIMS**
we are aliens and *p*. . . . . . .1 Chr 29:15
were strangers and *p*. . . . . . .Heb 11:13

**PILLAR**
and she became a *p* . . . . . . . .Gen 19:26
and by night in a *p* . . . . . . . . .Ex 13:21
the living God, the *p*. . . . . . .1 Tim 3:15

**PILLARS**
break their sacred *p* . . . . . . . .Ex 34:13
blood and fire and *p*. . . . . . . . .Joel 2:30
and his feet like *p* . . . . . . . . . .Rev 10:1

**PIT**
who go down to the *p* . . . . . . . . .Ps 28:1
a harlot is a deep *p* . . . . . . . .Prov 23:27
my life in the *p* . . . . . . . . . . . .Lam 3:53
up my life from the *p* . . . . . . . . .Jon 2:6
into the bottomless *p* . . . . . . . .Rev 20:3

**PITIABLE**
of all men the most *p*. . . . . .1 Cor 15:19

**PITS**
The proud have dug *p* . . . . . .Ps 119:85

**PITY**
for someone to take *p*. . . . . . . .Ps 69:20
*p* He redeemed them. . . . . . . . . .Is 63:9
just as I had *p*. . . . . . . . . . .Matt 18:33

**PLACE**
Come, see the *p* . . . . . . . . . .Matt 28:6
My word has no *p*. . . . . . . . . .John 8:37
I go to prepare a *p* . . . . . . . . .John 14:2
might go to his own *p* . . . . . . .Acts 1:25

**PLACES**
and the rough *p*. . . . . . . . . . . . . .Is 40:4
They love the best *p*. . . . . . . .Matt 23:6
in the heavenly *p*. . . . . . . . . . . .Eph 1:3

**PLAGUE**
bring yet one more *p* . . . . . . . . .Ex 11:1

**PLAGUES**
*p* that are written . . . . . . . . .Rev 22:18

**PLANK**
First remove the *p*. . . . . . . . . .Matt 7:5

**PLANS**
He makes the *p* of the . . . . . . .Ps 33:10
that devises wicked *p*. . . . . . .Prov 6:18

**PLANT**
a time to *p*. . . . . . . . . . . . . . . .Eccl 3:2
Him as a tender *p* . . . . . . . . . . . .Is 53:2
*p* of an alien vine . . . . . . . . . . .Jer 2:21
*p* which My heavenly . . . . .Matt 15:13

**PLANTED**
shall be like a tree *p* . . . . . . . . . .Ps 1:3
by the roots and be *p* . . . . . . .Luke 17:6
I *p*, Apollos watered . . . . . . . .1 Cor 3:6

**PLANTS**
neither he who *p* . . . . . . . . . . .1 Cor 3:7

**PLATTER**
head here on a *p*. . . . . . . . . . .Matt 14:8

**PLEASANT**
food, that it was *p* . . . . . . . . . . .Gen 3:6
how good and how *p*. . . . . . . . .Ps 133:1

**PLEASANTNESS**
Her ways are ways of *p*. . . . . .Prov 3:17

**PLEASE**
in the flesh cannot *p*. . . . . . . . .Rom 8:8
*p* his neighbor for his . . . . . . .Rom 15:2
how he may *p* the Lord . . . . .1 Cor 7:32
is impossible to *p* Him. . . . . . .Heb 11:6

**PLEASED**
Then You shall be *p* . . . . . . . . .Ps 51:19
in whom I am well *p* . . . . . . .Matt 3:17
God was not well *p* . . . . . . . .1 Cor 10:5
testimony, that he *p* . . . . . . . .Heb 11:5

**PLEASES**
Whatever the LORD *p* . . . . . . .Ps 135:6

**PLEASING**
sacrifice, well *p*. . . . . . . . . . . .Phil 4:18
for this is well *p* . . . . . . . . . . . .Col 3:20
in you what is well *p* . . . . . . .Heb 13:21

**PLEASURE**
Do good in Your good *p* . . . . . .Ps 51:18
*p* will be a poor man. . . . . . .Prov 21:17
shall perform all My *p* . . . . . . .Is 44:28
your Father's good *p* . . . . . .Luke 12:32
to the good *p* of His . . . . . . . . . .Eph 1:5
*for sin You had no p*. . . . . . . . .Heb 10:6
*back, My soul has no p* . . . . .Heb 10:38
*p* that war in your . . . . . . . . .James 4:1

**PLEASURES**
Your right hand are *p* . . . . . . .Ps 16:11
cares, riches, and *p* . . . . . . . .Luke 8:14
to enjoy the passing *p* . . . . . .Heb 11:25

**PLOW**
put his hand to the *p* . . . . . . .Luke 9:62

**PLOWED**
You have *p* wickedness . . . . .Hos 10:13

**PLOWMAN**
*p* shall overtake the . . . . . . .Amos 9:13

**PLUCK**
*p* the heads of grain . . . . . . .Mark 2:23

**PLUCKED**
cheeks to those who *p* . . . . . . . . .Is 50:6
And His disciples *p* . . . . . . . . .Luke 6:1
you would have *p* . . . . . . . . . . .Gal 4:15

**PLUNDER**
*p* the Egyptians. . . . . . . . . . . . .Ex 3:22
the *p* of the poor is. . . . . . . . . . . .Is 3:14
house and *p* his goods . . . . .Matt 12:29

**PLUNDERED**
a people robbed and *p* . . . . . . . .Is 42:22
"And when you are *p* . . . . . . . .Jer 4:30

**PLUNDERING**
me because of the *p*. . . . . . . . . . .Is 22:4
accepted the *p* of your . . . . . .Heb 10:34

**POETS**
some of your own *p* . . . . . . . .Acts 17:28

**POISON**
*"The p of asps is* . . . . . . . . . . .Rom 3:13

**POISONED**
*p* by bitterness . . . . . . . . . . . .Acts 8:23

**POLLUTIONS**
have escaped the *p*. . . . . . . . .2 Pet 2:20

**POMP**
had come with great *p* . . . . .Acts 25:23

**POMPOUS**
and a mouth speaking *p* . . . . . .Dan 7:8

**PONDER**
*P* the path of your. . . . . . . . . .Prov 4:26

**PONDERED**
*p* them in her heart . . . . . . . .Luke 2:19

**PONDERS**
*p* all his paths. . . . . . . . . . . . .Prov 5:21

**POOR**
*p* will never cease . . . . . . . .Deut 15:11
So the *p* have hope . . . . . . . . . .Job 5:16
I delivered the *p* . . . . . . . . . . .Job 29:12
*p* shall eat and be. . . . . . . . . . .Ps 22:26
But I am *p* and needy. . . . . . . .Ps 40:17
Let the *p* and needy . . . . . . . . .Ps 74:21
He raises the *p*. . . . . . . . . . . . .Ps 113:7
a slack hand becomes *p* . . . . .Prov 10:4
*p* man is hated even . . . . . . .Prov 14:20
who has mercy on the *p* . . . .Prov 14:21
He who oppresses the *p* . . . .Prov 14:31
*p* reproaches his Maker . . . . .Prov 17:5
Do not rob the *p* . . . . . . . . . .Prov 22:22
remembered that same *p* . . . .Eccl 9:15
the alien or the *p* . . . . . . . . . .Zech 7:10
"Blessed are the *p* . . . . . . . . . .Matt 5:3
*p* have the gospel . . . . . . . . . .Matt 11:5
For you have the *p* . . . . . . . .Matt 26:11
your sakes He became *p* . . . . .2 Cor 8:9
should remember the *p* . . . . . .Gal 2:10
God not chosen the *p* . . . . . . .James 2:5
wretched, miserable, *p* . . . . . .Rev 3:17

**PORTION**
O LORD, You, are the *p* . . . . . . .Ps 16:5
heart and my *p* forever . . . . . .Ps 73:26
You are my *p* . . . . . . . . . . . . .Ps 119:57
I will divide Him a *p*. . . . . . . . .Is 53:12
rejoice in their *p* . . . . . . . . . . . . .Is 61:7
The *P* of Jacob is not . . . . . . . .Jer 10:16
"The LORD is my *p*. . . . . . . . .Lam 3:24
and appoint him his *p* . . . . .Matt 24:51
to give them their *p*. . . . . . .Luke 12:42
Father, give me the *p*. . . . . .Luke 15:12

**POSSESS**
descendants shall *p*. . . . . . . .Gen 22:17
*p* the land which. . . . . . . . . . .Josh 1:11
By your patience *p* . . . . . . .Luke 21:19
*p* his own vessel. . . . . . . . . .1 Thess 4:4

**POSSESSED**
"The LORD *p* me at . . . . . . . .Prov 8:22

**POSSESSING**
and yet p all things ... 2 Cor 6:10

**POSSESSION**
as an everlasting p ... Gen 17:8
and an enduring p ... Heb 10:34

**POSSESSIONS**
and sold their p ... Acts 2:45

**POSSIBLE**
God all things are p ... Matt 19:26
p that the blood ... Heb 10:4

**POUR**
p My Spirit on your ... Is 44:3
P out Your fury ... Jer 10:25
that I will p out My ... Joel 2:28
"And I will p ... Zech 12:10
angels, "Go and p ... Rev 16:1

**POURED**
I am p out like water ... Ps 22:14
grace is p upon Your ... Ps 45:2
strong, because He p ... Is 53:12
and My fury will be p ... Jer 7:20
broke the flask and p ... Mark 14:3
I am already being p ... 2 Tim 4:6
whom He p out on us ... Titus 3:6

**POVERTY**
leads only to p ... Prov 14:23
p put in all the ... Luke 21:4
and their deep p ... 2 Cor 8:2
p might become rich ... 2 Cor 8:9
tribulation, and p ... Rev 2:9

**POWER**
that I may show My p ... Ex 9:16
him who is without p ... Job 26:2
p who can understand ... Job 26:14
p belongs to God ... Ps 62:11
p Your enemies shall ... Ps 66:3
gives strength and p ... Ps 68:35
a king is, there is p ... Eccl 8:4
No one has p over the ... Eccl 8:8
Not by might nor by p ... Zech 4:6
the kingdom and the p ... Matt 6:13
the Son of Man has p ... Matt 9:6
Scriptures nor the p ... Matt 22:29
p went out from Him ... Luke 6:19
you are endued with p ... Luke 24:49
I have p to lay it ... John 10:18
"You could have no p ... John 19:11
you shall receive p ... Acts 1:8
as though by our own p ... Acts 3:12
man is the great p ... Acts 8:10
"Give me this p ... Acts 8:19
for it is the p ... Rom 1:16
saved it is the p ... 1 Cor 1:18
Greeks, Christ the p ... 1 Cor 1:24
that the p of Christ ... 2 Cor 12:9
greatness of His p ... Eph 1:19
the Lord and in the p ... Eph 6:10
to His glorious p ... Col 1:11
the glory of His p ... 2 Thess 1:9
of fear, but of p ... 2 Tim 1:7
by the word of His p ... Heb 1:3
p of death, that ... Heb 2:14
as His divine p ... 2 Pet 1:3
dominion and p ... Jude 25
to him I will give p ... Rev 2:26
honor and glory and p ... Rev 5:13

**POWERFUL**
of the LORD is p ... Ps 29:4
of God is living and p ... Heb 4:12

**POWERS**
principalities and p ... Col 2:15
word of God and the p ... Heb 6:5

**PRAISE**
p shall be of You in ... Ps 22:25
the people shall p ... Ps 45:17
P is awaiting You ... Ps 65:1
let all the peoples p ... Ps 67:3
p shall be continually ... Ps 71:6
And the heavens will p ... Ps 89:5
Seven times a day I p ... Ps 119:164
that has breath p ... Ps 150:6
Let another man p ... Prov 27:2
let her own works p ... Prov 31:31
and your gates P ... Is 60:18
He makes Jerusalem a p ... Is 62:7
for You are my p ... Jer 17:14
Me a name of joy, a p ... Jer 33:9
give you fame and p ... Zeph 3:20
*You have perfected p* ... Matt 21:16
of men more than the p ... John 12:43
p is not from men but ... Rom 2:29
Then each one's p ... 1 Cor 4:5
should be to the p ... Eph 1:12
to the glory and p ... Phil 1:11
*I will sing p to You* ... Heb 2:12
the sacrifice of p ... Heb 13:15
and for the p of those ... 1 Pet 2:14
saying, "P our God ... Rev 19:5

**PRAISED**
daily He shall be p ... Ps 72:15
LORD'S name is to be p ... Ps 113:3
and greatly to be p ... Ps 145:3
the Most High and p ... Dan 4:34

**PRAISES**
it is good to sing p ... Ps 147:1
husband also, and he p ... Prov 31:28

**PRAISEWORTHY**
if there is anything p ... Phil 4:8

**PRAISING**
they will still be p ... Ps 84:4
of the heavenly host p ... Luke 2:13
in the temple p ... Luke 24:53

**PRAY**
at noon I will p ... Ps 55:17
who hate you, and p ... Matt 5:44
"And when you p ... Matt 6:5
manner, therefore, p ... Matt 6:9
"Watch and p ... Matt 26:41
"Lord, teach us to p ... Luke 11:1
"And I will p ... John 14:16
I do not p for the ... John 17:9
"I do not p for ... John 17:20
p without ceasing ... 1 Thess 5:17
Brethren, p for us ... 1 Thess 5:25
Let him p ... James 5:13
to one another, and p ... James 5:16
say that he should p ... 1 John 5:16

**PRAYED**
p more earnestly ... Luke 22:44
p earnestly that it ... James 5:17

**PRAYER**
p made in this place ... 2 Chr 7:15
and my p is pure ... Job 16:17
a p to the God of my ... Ps 42:8
p also will be made ... Ps 72:15
He shall regard the p ... Ps 102:17
to the LORD, but the p ... Prov 15:8
not go out except by p ... Matt 17:21
all night in p to God ... Luke 6:12
continually to p ... Acts 6:4
where p was ... Acts 16:13
steadfastly in p ... Rom 12:12
to fasting and p ... 1 Cor 7:5
always with all p ... Eph 6:18
but in everything by p ... Phil 4:6
the word of God and p ... 1 Tim 4:5
And the p of faith ... James 5:15

**PRAYERS**
though you make many p ... Is 1:15
a pretense make long p ... Matt 23:14
fervently for you in p ... Col 4:12
p may not be hindered ... 1 Pet 3:7
which are the p ... Rev 5:8

**PREACH**
time Jesus began to p ... Matt 4:17
you hear in the ear, p ... Matt 10:27
*p the gospel to the* ... Luke 4:18
And how shall they p ... Rom 10:15
p Christ crucified ... 1 Cor 1:23
was I or they, so we p ... 1 Cor 15:11
P the word ... 2 Tim 4:2

**PREACHED**
p that people ... Mark 6:12
out and p everywhere ... Mark 16:20
of sins should be p ... Luke 24:47
p Christ to them ... Acts 8:5
lest, when I have p ... 1 Cor 9:27
than what we have p ... Gal 1:8
the gospel was p ... Heb 4:2
also He went and p ... 1 Pet 3:19

**PREACHER**
they hear without a p ... Rom 10:14
I was appointed a p ... 1 Tim 2:7

**PREACHES**
the Jesus whom Paul p ... Acts 19:13
p another Jesus whom ... 2 Cor 11:4
p any other gospel ... Gal 1:9
p the faith which he ... Gal 1:23

**PREACHING**
p Jesus as the ... Acts 5:42
not risen, then our p ... 1 Cor 15:14

**PRECEPTS**
all His p are sure ... Ps 111:7
how I love Your p ... Ps 119:159

**PRECIOUS**
P in the sight of the ... Ps 116:15
She is more p than ... Prov 3:15
p things shall not ... Is 44:9
if you take out the p ... Jer 15:19
farmer waits for the p ... James 5:7
more p than gold ... 1 Pet 1:7
who believe, He is p ... 1 Pet 2:7
p in the sight of ... 1 Pet 3:4

**PREDESTINED**
He foreknew, He also p ... Rom 8:29
having p us to ... Eph 1:5
inheritance, being p ... Eph 1:11

**PREEMINENCE**
He may have the p ... Col 1:18
loves to have the p ... 3 John 9

**PREFERENCE**
in honor giving p ... Rom 12:10

**PREJUDICE**
these things without p ... 1 Tim 5:21

**PREMEDITATE**
p what you will ... Mark 13:11

**PREPARATION**
Now it was the P ... John 19:14
your feet with the p ... Eph 6:15

**PREPARE**
p a table before me in ... Ps 23:5
*P the way of the LORD* ... Mark 1:3
p a place for you ... John 14:2

**PREPARED**
for whom it is p ... Matt 20:23
which You have p ... Luke 2:31

mercy, which He had *p* ...... Rom 9:23
*things which God has p* ..... 1 Cor 2:9
Now He who has *p* .......... 2 Cor 5:5
*p* beforehand that we ....... Eph 2:10
God, for He has *p* .......... Heb 11:16

**PRESENCE**
themselves from the *p* ........ Gen 3:8
went out from the *p* ......... Gen 4:16
*P* will go with you .......... Ex 33:14
afraid in any man's *p* ....... Deut 1:17
*p* is fullness of joy ........... Ps 16:11
shall dwell in Your *p* ....... Ps 140:13
not tremble at My *p* ......... Jer 5:22
shall shake at My *p* ....... Ezek 38:20
and drank in Your *p* ...... Luke 13:26
*full of joy in Your p* ......... Acts 2:28
but his bodily *p* .......... 2 Cor 10:10
obeyed, not as in my *p* ...... Phil 2:12

**PRESENT**
we are all *p* before ......... Acts 10:33
evil is *p* with me ........... Rom 7:21
*p* your bodies a living ....... Rom 12:1
or death, or things *p* ....... 1 Cor 3:22
absent in body but *p* ........ 1 Cor 5:3
that He might *p* ............ Eph 5:27
*p* you faultless ............... Jude 24

**PRESERVE**
He shall *p* your soul ......... Ps 121:7
The LORD shall *p* ........... Ps 121:8
loses his life will *p* ........ Luke 17:33
every evil work and *p* ...... 2 Tim 4:18

**PRESERVED**
soul, and body be *p* ...... 1 Thess 5:23

**PRESERVES**
For the LORD *p* the .......... Ps 31:23
*p* the souls of His ........... Ps 97:10
he who keeps his way *p* .... Prov 16:17

**PRETENSE**
*p* make long prayers ...... Matt 23:14

**PRICE**
one pearl of great *p* ....... Matt 13:46
you were bought at a *p* ..... 1 Cor 6:20

**PRIDE**
*p* serves as ................. Ps 73:6
By *p* comes nothing ....... Prov 13:10
*P* goes before ............ Prov 16:18
and her daughter had *p* .... Ezek 16:49
was hardened in *p* .......... Dan 5:20
For the *p* of the ............ Zech 11:3
evil eye, blasphemy, *p* ...... Mark 7:22
*p* he fall into the ........... 1 Tim 3:6
of the eyes, and the *p* ...... 1 John 2:16

**PRIEST**
he was the *p* of God ........ Gen 14:18
*p* forever according ......... Ps 110:4
so He shall be a *p* .......... Zech 6:13
and faithful High *P* ......... Heb 2:17
we have a great High *P* ...... Heb 4:14
*p forever according* .......... Heb 5:6
Christ came as High *P* ...... Heb 9:11

**PRIESTHOOD**
*p* being changed ........... Heb 7:12
has an unchangeable *p* ...... Heb 7:24
generation, a royal *p* ........ 1 Pet 2:9

**PRIESTS**
to Me a kingdom of *p* ......... Ex 19:6
her *p* teach for pay .......... Mic 3:11
made us kings and *p* ......... Rev 1:6

**PRINCE**
is the house of the *p* ........ Job 21:28
everlasting Father, *P* .......... Is 9:6

until Messiah the *P* ........ Dan 9:25
days without king or *p* ........ Hos 3:4
*p* asks for gifts .............. Mic 7:3
and killed the *P* ........... Acts 3:15
His right hand to be *P* ...... Acts 5:31
the *p* of the power ........... Eph 2:2

**PRINCES**
to put confidence in *p* ........ Ps 118:9
He brings the *p* ............. Is 40:23

**PRISON**
and put him into the *p* ..... Gen 39:20
Bring my soul out of *p* ....... Ps 142:7
in darkness from the *p* ........ Is 42:7
the opening of the *p* .......... Is 61:1
John had heard in *p* ........ Matt 11:2
I was in *p* and you ........ Matt 25:36

**PRIZE**
the goal for the *p* ........... Phil 3:14

**PROCEED**
of the same mouth *p* ...... James 3:10

**PROCEEDED**
for I *p* forth ............... John 8:42

**PROCEEDS**
by every word that *p* ........ Deut 8:3
*by every word that p* ........ Matt 4:4
Spirit of truth who *p* ...... John 15:26

**PROCLAIM**
began to *p* it freely ........ Mark 1:45
knowing, Him I *p* ......... Acts 17:23
drink this cup, you *p* ...... 1 Cor 11:26

**PROCLAIMED**
*p* the good news ............. Ps 40:9
he went his way and *p* ...... Luke 8:39

**PROCLAIMER**
"He seems to be a *p* ........ Acts 17:18

**PROCLAIMS**
good news, who *p* ............ Is 52:7

**PRODIGAL**
with *p* living ............ Luke 15:13

**PROFANE**
and priest are *p* ............ Jer 23:11
tried to *p* the temple ........ Acts 24:6
But reject *p* and old ........ 1 Tim 4:7

**PROFANED**
and *p* My Sabbaths ........ Ezek 22:8

**PROFANENESS**
of Jerusalem *p* has ......... Jer 23:15

**PROFANING**
*p* the covenant of the ........ Mal 2:10

**PROFESS**
They *p* to know God ........ Titus 1:16

**PROFIT**
For what *p* is it to ......... Matt 16:26
For what will it *p* ......... Mark 8:36
"For what *p* is it to ........ Luke 9:25
her masters much *p* ....... Acts 16:16
brought no small *p* ........ Acts 19:24
what is the *p* of circumcision? . Rom 3:1
not seeking my own *p* ..... 1 Cor 10:33
Christ will *p* you ............ Gal 5:2
about words to no *p* ........ 2 Tim 2:14
them, but He for our *p* ..... Heb 12:10
What does it *p* ........... James 2:14
and sell, and make a *p* ..... James 4:13

**PROFITABLE**
It is doubtless not *p* ........ 2 Cor 12:1
of God, and is *p* ........... 2 Tim 3:16

**PROFITS**
have not love, it *p* ......... 1 Cor 13:3

**PROMISE**
Behold, I send the *P* ...... Luke 24:49
but to wait for the *P* ......... Acts 1:4
"For the *p* is to you ......... Acts 2:39
for the hope of the *p* ........ Acts 26:6
*p* might be sure ............ Rom 4:16
Therefore, since a *p* .......... Heb 4:1
to the heirs of *p* ............ Heb 6:17
did not receive the *p* ....... Heb 11:39

**PROMISED**
Him faithful who had *p* .... Heb 11:11

**PROMISES**
For all the *p* of God ........ 2 Cor 1:20
his Seed were the *p* ......... Gal 3:16
having received the *p* ...... Heb 11:13
great and precious *p* ........ 2 Pet 1:4

**PROPER**
you, but for what is *p* ....... 1 Cor 7:35
but, which is *p* ........... 1 Tim 2:10

**PROPERLY**
Let us walk *p* ............ Rom 13:13

**PROPHECY**
miracles, to another *p* ..... 1 Cor 12:10
for *p* never came by the ..... 2 Pet 1:21
is the spirit of *p* ........... Rev 19:10
of the book of this *p* ........ Rev 22:19

**PROPHESIED**
Lord, have we not *p* ........ Matt 7:22
prophets and the law *p* .... Matt 11:13

**PROPHESIES**
*p* edifies the church ........ 1 Cor 14:4

**PROPHESY**
prophets, "Do not *p* .......... Is 30:10
the prophets *p* falsely ........ Jer 5:31
your daughters shall *p* ...... Joel 2:28
Who can but *p* ............. Amos 3:8
saying, "*P* to us .......... Matt 26:68
*your daughters shall p* ...... Acts 2:17
know in part and we *p* ...... 1 Cor 13:9

**PROPHET**
raise up for you a *P* ....... Deut 18:15
"I alone am left a *p* ...... 1 Kin 18:22
I ordained you a *p* ............. Jer 1:5
The *p* is a fool .............. Hos 9:7
nor was I a son of a *p* ...... Amos 7:14
send you Elijah the *p* ......... Mal 4:5
*p* shall receive a .......... Matt 10:41
*p* is not without honor ..... Matt 13:57
by Daniel the *p* .......... Mark 13:14
is not a greater *p* .......... Luke 7:28
it cannot be that a *p* ..... Luke 13:33
Nazareth, who was a *P* ... Luke 24:19
"Are you the *P* ............ John 1:21
"This is truly the *P* ........ John 6:14
with him the false *p* ........ Rev 19:20

**PROPHETIC**
*p* word confirmed .......... 2 Pet 1:19

**PROPHETS**
the Law or the *P* .......... Matt 5:17
is the Law and the *P* ...... Matt 7:12
or one of the *p* ........... Matt 16:14
the tombs of the *p* ....... Matt 23:29
indeed, I send you *p* ...... Matt 23:34
one who kills the *p* ....... Matt 23:37
Then many false *p* ....... Matt 24:11
have Moses and the *p* ..... Luke 16:29
You are sons of the *p* ........ Acts 3:25
*p* did your fathers not ....... Acts 7:52
To Him all the *p* ......... Acts 10:43
do you believe the *p* ...... Acts 26:27
by the Law and the *P* ....... Rom 3:21
*have killed Your p* ......... Rom 11:3
to be apostles, some *p* ....... Eph 4:11

this salvation the *p* ........1 Pet 1:10
because many false *p* ......1 John 4:1
found the blood of *p* ........Rev 18:24

**PROPITIATION**
set forth as a *p* ............Rom 3:25
to God, to make *p* ..........Heb 2:17
He Himself is the *p* ........1 John 2:2
His Son to be the *p* .......1 John 4:10

**PROPRIETY**
modest apparel, with *p* .....1 Tim 2:9

**PROSPER**
they *p* who love you .........Ps 122:6
of the LORD shall *p*..........Is 53:10
against you shall *p*..........Is 54:17
storing up as he may *p* .....1 Cor 16:2
I pray that you may *p*........3 John 2

**PROSPERED**
since the LORD has *p* ......Gen 24:56

**PROSPERING**
His ways are always *p* ........Ps 10:5

**PROSPERITY**
*p* all your days ............Deut 23:6
*p* the destroyer ............Job 15:21
Now in my *p* I said...........Ps 30:6
has pleasure in the *p*........Ps 35:27
when I saw the *p* ............Ps 73:3
I pray, send now *p*..........Ps 118:25
that we have our *p* ........Acts 19:25

**PROSPEROUS**
will make your way *p*........Josh 1:8

**PROSPERS**
just as your soul *p* ..........3 John 2

**PROUD**
tongue that speaks *p*.........Ps 12:3
and fully repays the *p* .......Ps 31:23
does not respect the *p*.........Ps 40:4
a haughty look and a *p* ......Ps 101:5
*p* He knows from afar .......Ps 138:6
Everyone *p*................Prov 16:5
by wine, he is a *p*...........Hab 2:5
He has scattered the *p*.....Luke 1:51
*"God resists the p* ..........1 Pet 5:5

**PROVERB**
of a drunkard is a *p* ........Prov 26:9
one shall take up a *p* .........Mic 2:4
to the true *p*..............2 Pet 2:22

**PROVERBS**
spoke three thousand *p* ....1 Kin 4:32
in order many *p*............Eccl 12:9

**PROVIDE**
"My son, God will *p* ........Gen 22:8
"*P* neither gold nor ........Matt 10:9
if anyone does not *p* ........1 Tim 5:8

**PROVIDED**
these hands have *p*........Acts 20:34
*p* something better ........Heb 11:40

**PROVISION**
no *p* for the flesh..........Rom 13:14

**PROVOKE**
"Do they *p* Me to............Jer 7:19
you, fathers, do not *p*.........Eph 6:4

**PROVOKED**
*p* the Most High............Ps 78:56
his spirit was *p*...........Acts 17:16
seek its own, is not *p*.......1 Cor 13:5

**PRUDENCE**
to give *p* to the .............Prov 1:4
wisdom, dwell with *p*......Prov 8:12
us in all wisdom and *p* .......Eph 1:8

**PRUDENT**
*p* man covers shame.......Prov 12:16
A *p* man conceals.........Prov 12:23
The wisdom of the *p*........Prov 14:8
*p* considers well ..........Prov 14:15
heart will be called *p*......Prov 16:21
*p* man foresees evil.........Prov 22:3
Therefore the *p*...........Amos 5:13
from the wise and *p*.......Matt 11:25

**PRUDENTLY**
Servant shall deal *p* .........Is 52:13

**PRUNES**
that bears fruit He *p* .......John 15:2

**PSALM**
each of you has a *p* .......1 Cor 14:26

**PSALMIST**
and the sweet *p* ..........2 Sam 23:1

**PSALMS**
to one another in *p* .........Eph 5:19
Let him sing *p*............James 5:13

**PUNISH**
*p* the righteous is.........Prov 17:26
Shall I not *p* them for .........Jer 5:9

**PUNISHED**
*p* them often in every ......Acts 26:11
These shall be *p*..........2 Thess 1:9

**PUNISHES**
will you say when He *p*......Jer 13:21

**PUNISHMENT**
*p* is greater than I..........Gen 4:13
you do in the day of *p*.........Is 10:3
*p* they shall perish .........Jer 10:15
not turn away its *p* .........Amos 1:3
into everlasting *p* ........Matt 25:46
*p* which was inflicted .......2 Cor 2:6
Of how much worse *p* ......Heb 10:29
sent by him for the *p* .......1 Pet 2:14
the unjust under *p*..........2 Pet 2:9

**PURE**
a mercy seat of *p* gold .......Ex 25:17
'My doctrine is *p*............Job 11:4
that he could be *p*..........Job 15:14
of the LORD are *p*.............Ps 12:6
ways of a man are *p* ........Prov 16:2
a generation that is *p*......Prov 30:12
things indeed are *p*........Rom 14:20
whatever things are *p*........Phil 4:8
keep yourself *p*...........1 Tim 5:22
*p* all things are *p*..........Titus 1:15
above is first *p*...........James 3:17
babes, desire the *p*..........1 Pet 2:2
just as He is *p* ............1 John 3:3

**PURER**
*p* eyes than to behold .......Hab 1:13

**PURGE**
*P* me with hyssop............Ps 51:7

**PURGED**
away, and your sin *p* ...........Is 6:7

**PURIFICATION**
with the water of *p*........Num 31:23

**PURIFIED**
all things are *p* ............Heb 9:22
Since you have *p* ..........1 Pet 1:22

**PURIFIES**
hope in Him *p* himself .....1 John 3:3

**PURIFY**
and *p* your hearts .........James 4:8

**PURIFYING**
*p* their hearts by ..........Acts 15:9
sanctifies for the *p*..........Heb 9:13

**PURIM**
called these days *P*.........Esth 9:26

**PURITY**
spirit, in faith, in *p*........1 Tim 4:12

**PURPOSE**
a time for every *p* ...........Eccl 3:1
But for this *p* I came ......John 12:27
by the determined *p* ........Acts 2:23
to fulfill His *p* ............Rev 17:17

**PURSUE**
*p* righteousness ............Rom 9:30
*P* love..................1 Cor 14:1

**PURSUES**
flee when no one *p* .........Prov 28:1

## Q

**QUAIL**
and it brought *q*..........Num 11:31

**QUARREL**
*He will not q nor cry* .......Matt 12:19
of the Lord must not *q* .....2 Tim 2:24

**QUARRELSOME**
but gentle, not *q* ...........1 Tim 3:3

**QUEEN**
heart, 'I sit as *q* ............Rev 18:7

**QUENCH**
Many waters cannot *q*.......Song 8:7
*flax He will not q*..........Matt 12:20
*q* all the fiery...............Eph 6:16
Do not *q* the Spirit.......1 Thess 5:19

**QUENCHED**
that shall never be *q*.......Mark 9:43

**QUESTIONS**
and asking them *q* ........Luke 2:46

**QUICKLY**
with your adversary *q*......Matt 5:25
Surely I am coming *q* ......Rev 22:20

**QUIET**
aspire to lead a *q*........1 Thess 4:11
a gentle and *q* spirit.........1 Pet 3:4

**QUIETNESS**
a handful with *q*............Eccl 4:6
in *q* and confidence.........Is 30:15
of righteousness, *q* ..........Is 32:17
that they work in *q* ......2 Thess 3:12

## R

**RABBI**
be called by men, '*R*........Matt 23:7

**RACA**
to his brother, '*R* ..........Matt 5:22

**RACE**
man to run its *r* .............Ps 19:5
*r* is not to the swift .........Eccl 9:11
I have finished the *r*........2 Tim 4:7
with endurance the *r*........Heb 12:1

**RAGE**
Why do the nations *r* ..........Ps 2:1
*'Why did the nations r* ......Acts 4:25

**RAIN**
had not caused it to *r*.........Gen 2:5
And the *r* was on the ........Gen 7:12
I will *r* down on him .....Ezek 38:22
given you the former *r*.......Joel 2:23

the good, and sends *r* . . . . . . . Matt 5:45
"and the *r* descended . . . . . . . Matt 7:25
*r* that often comes . . . . . . . . . . Heb 6:7
that it would not *r* . . . . . . . . James 5:17

**RAINBOW**
"I set My *r* in the . . . . . . . . . . Gen 9:13
and there was a *r* . . . . . . . . . . . Rev 4:3

**RAINED**
*r* fire and brimstone . . . . . . Luke 17:29

**RAINS**
*r* righteousness . . . . . . . . . . . Hos 10:12

**RAISE**
third day He will *r* . . . . . . . . . . . Hos 6:2
in three days I will *r* . . . . . . . John 2:19
and I will *r* him up at . . . . . . . John 6:40
and the Lord will *r* . . . . . . . . James 5:15

**RAISED**
be killed, and be *r* . . . . . . . . Matt 16:21
just as Christ was *r* . . . . . . . . . Rom 6:4
Spirit of Him who *r* . . . . . . . . Rom 8:11
"How are the dead *r* . . . . . . 1 Cor 15:35
and the dead will be *r* . . . . . 1 Cor 15:52
and *r* us up together . . . . . . . . . Eph 2:6

**RAISES**
For as the Father *r* . . . . . . . . . John 5:21
but in God who *r* . . . . . . . . . . . 2 Cor 1:9

**RAN**
You *r* well . . . . . . . . . . . . . . . . . . Gal 5:7

**RANSOM**
to give His life a *r* . . . . . . . . Mark 10:45
who gave Himself a *r* . . . . . . . 1 Tim 2:6

**RANSOMED**
and the *r* of the LORD . . . . . . . . Is 35:10
redeemed Jacob, and *r* . . . . . . Jer 31:11

**RASH**
Do not be *r* with your . . . . . . . . Eccl 5:2

**RASHLY**
and do nothing *r* . . . . . . . . . . Acts 19:36

**RAVENOUS**
inwardly they are *r* . . . . . . . . Matt 7:15

**RAVENS**
"Consider the *r* . . . . . . . . . . Luke 12:24

**REACHING**
*r* forward to those . . . . . . . . . . Phil 3:13

**READ**
day, and stood up to *r* . . . . . . . Luke 4:16
hearts, known and *r* . . . . . . . . 2 Cor 3:2

**READER**
let the *r* understand . . . . . . Mark 13:14

**READINESS**
the word with all *r* . . . . . . . . Acts 17:11

**READING**
*r* the prophet Isaiah . . . . . . . . Acts 8:30

**READS**
Blessed is he who *r* . . . . . . . . . . Rev 1:3

**READY**
and those who were *r* . . . . . . Matt 25:10
"Lord, I am *r* . . . . . . . . . . . Luke 22:33
Be *r* in season and out . . . . . . 2 Tim 4:2
and always be *r* . . . . . . . . . . . 1 Pet 3:15

**REAP**
they neither sow nor *r* . . . . . . Matt 6:26
you knew that I *r* . . . . . . . . . Matt 25:26

**REAPED**
you have *r* iniquity . . . . . . . . Hos 10:13

**REAPERS**
*r* are the angels . . . . . . . . . . Matt 13:39

**REAPING**
*r* what I did not . . . . . . . . . . Luke 19:22

**REAPS**
One sows and another *r* . . . . . John 4:37

**REASON**
Come now, and let us *r* . . . . . . . . Is 1:18
who asks you a *r* . . . . . . . . . . 1 Pet 3:15

**REASONED**
for three Sabbaths *r* . . . . . . . . Acts 17:2

**REBEL**
if you refuse and *r* . . . . . . . . . . . . Is 1:20

**REBELLING**
more against Him by *r* . . . . . . . Ps 78:17

**REBELLION**
*hearts as in the r* . . . . . . . . . . . . Heb 3:8

**REBELLIOUS**
day long to a *r* people . . . . . . . . . Is 65:2

**REBUILD**
God, to *r* its ruins . . . . . . . . . . . Ezra 9:9
*r* it as in the days of . . . . . . . Amos 9:11

**REBUKE**
Turn at my *r* . . . . . . . . . . . . . . Prov 1:23
*r* a wise man . . . . . . . . . . . . . . . Prov 9:8
*r* is better than love . . . . . . . . Prov 27:5
*r* the oppressor . . . . . . . . . . . . . . Is 1:17
sins against you, *r* . . . . . . . . . Luke 17:3
Do not *r* an older man . . . . . . . 1 Tim 5:1
who are sinning *r* . . . . . . . . . 1 Tim 5:20
The Lord *r* you . . . . . . . . . . . . . . . Jude 9
As many as I love, I *r* . . . . . . . . Rev 3:19

**REBUKED**
*r* the winds and the . . . . . . . . Matt 8:26
*r* their unbelief . . . . . . . . . . Mark 16:14
but he was *r* for his . . . . . . . . 2 Pet 2:16

**REBUKES**
ear that hears the *r* . . . . . . . Prov 15:31

**RECEIVE**
believing, you will *r* . . . . . . . Matt 21:22
and His own did not *r* . . . . . . . John 1:11
will come again and *r* . . . . . . John 14:3
the world cannot *r* . . . . . . . . John 14:17
Ask, and you will *r* . . . . . . . . John 16:24
*R* the Holy Spirit . . . . . . . . . John 20:22
"Lord Jesus, *r* . . . . . . . . . . . . . Acts 7:59
*r* the Holy Spirit . . . . . . . . . . . Acts 19:2
*R* one who is weak . . . . . . . . . Rom 14:1
*r* the Spirit by the . . . . . . . . . . . . Gal 3:2
suppose that he will *r* . . . . . . James 1:7

**RECEIVED**
But as many as *r* . . . . . . . . . . John 1:12
for God has *r* him . . . . . . . . . . Rom 14:3
For I *r* from the Lord . . . . . . 1 Cor 11:23
*r* Christ . . . . . . . . . . . . . . . . . . . Col 2:6
*r* up in glory . . . . . . . . . . . . . 1 Tim 3:16

**RECEIVES**
*r* you *r* Me . . . . . . . . . . . . . . Matt 10:40
and whoever *r* Me . . . . . . . . . Mark 9:37

**RECONCILE**
and that He might *r* . . . . . . . . Eph 2:16

**RECONCILED**
First be *r* to your . . . . . . . . . . Matt 5:24
were enemies we were *r* . . . . . Rom 5:10
Christ's behalf, be *r* . . . . . . . 2 Cor 5:20

**RECONCILIATION**
now received the *r* . . . . . . . . . Rom 5:11
to us the word of *r* . . . . . . . . . 2 Cor 5:19

**RECONCILING**
cast away is the *r* . . . . . . . . . Rom 11:15
God was in Christ *r* . . . . . . . . 2 Cor 5:19

**REDEEM**
But God will *r* my soul . . . . . . Ps 49:15
*r* their life from . . . . . . . . . . . . Ps 72:14
was going to *r* Israel . . . . . . Luke 24:21
*r* those who were . . . . . . . . . . . . Gal 4:5
us, that He might *r* . . . . . . . . . Titus 2:14

**REDEEMED**
Let the *r* of the LORD . . . . . . . . Ps 107:2
*r* shall walk there . . . . . . . . . . . . Is 35:9
sea a road for the *r* . . . . . . . . . . Is 51:10
and you shall be *r* . . . . . . . . . . . . Is 52:3
and *r* His people . . . . . . . . . . Luke 1:68
Christ has *r* us from . . . . . . . . Gal 3:13
that you were not *r* . . . . . . . . . 1 Pet 1:18
were slain, and have *r* . . . . . . . . Rev 5:9

**REDEEMER**
For I know that my *R* . . . . . . . Job 19:25
our *R* from Everlasting . . . . . . Is 63:16

**REDEEMING**
*r* the time . . . . . . . . . . . . . . . . . Eph 5:16

**REDEMPTION**
those who looked for *r* . . . . . . Luke 2:38
your *r* draws near . . . . . . . . Luke 21:28
grace through the *r* . . . . . . . . Rom 3:24
the adoption, the *r* . . . . . . . . . Rom 8:23
sanctification and *r* . . . . . . . . 1 Cor 1:30
In Him we have *r* . . . . . . . . . . . Eph 1:7
for the day of *r* . . . . . . . . . . . . . Eph 4:30
obtained eternal *r* . . . . . . . . . . Heb 9:12

**REED**
*r* He will not break . . . . . . . . . . . Is 42:3
*r* shaken by the wind . . . . . . . Matt 11:7

**REFINED**
us as silver is *r* . . . . . . . . . . . . . Ps 66:10

**REFINER**
He will sit as a *r* . . . . . . . . . . . . Mal 3:3

**REFORMATION**
until the time of *r* . . . . . . . . . . Heb 9:10

**REFRESH**
*r* my heart in the Lord . . . . . Philem 20

**REFRESHED**
his spirit has been *r* . . . . . . . 2 Cor 7:13
for he often *r* . . . . . . . . . . . . . 2 Tim 1:16

**REFRESHES**
*r* the soul of his . . . . . . . . . . . Prov 25:13

**REFRESHING**
*r* may come from the . . . . . . . . Acts 3:19

**REFUGE**
eternal God is your *r* . . . . . . Deut 33:27
God is our *r* and . . . . . . . . . . . . . Ps 46:1
who have fled for *r* . . . . . . . . . . Heb 6:18

**REGARD**
*r* iniquity in my heart . . . . . . . Ps 66:18
did not fear God nor *r* . . . . . . Luke 18:2

**REGARDED**
my hand and no one *r* . . . . . . . Prov 1:24
*r* the lowly state . . . . . . . . . . Luke 1:48

**REGARDS**
*r* a rebuke will be . . . . . . . . . Prov 13:18

**REGENERATION**
to you, that in the *r* . . . . . . . Matt 19:28
the washing of *r* . . . . . . . . . . . Titus 3:5

**REGISTERED**
So all went to be *r* . . . . . . . . . . Luke 2:3

**REGRETTED**
but afterward he *r* . . . . . . . . Matt 21:29

**REGULATIONS**
yourselves to *r* . . . . . . . . . . . . . Col 2:20

**REIGN**
"And He will *r* . . . . . . . . . . . . Luke 1:33
righteousness will *r* . . . . . . . . Rom 5:17
so grace might *r* . . . . . . . . . . . Rom 5:21
do not let sin *r* . . . . . . . . . . . . Rom 6:12

For He must *r* till He ..... 1 Cor 15:25
of Christ, and shall *r* ..... Rev 20:6

**REIGNED**
so that as sin *r* ..... Rom 5:21
You have *r* as kings ..... 1 Cor 4:8
And they lived and *r* ..... Rev 20:4

**REIGNS**
to Zion, "Your God *r* ..... Is 52:7
Lord God Omnipotent *r* ..... Rev 19:6

**REJECT**
"All too well you *r* ..... Mark 7:9
*R* a divisive man ..... Titus 3:10

**REJECTED**
He is despised and *r* ..... Is 53:3
*r has become the chief* ..... Matt 21:42
many things and be *r* ..... Luke 17:25
This Moses whom they *r* ..... Acts 7:35
to a living stone, *r* ..... 1 Pet 2:4

**REJECTION**
you shall know My *r* ..... Num 14:34

**REJECTS**
he who *r* Me *r* ..... Luke 10:16

**REJOICE**
*R* in the LORD ..... Ps 33:1
of Your wings I will *r* ..... Ps 63:7
Let them *r* before God ..... Ps 68:3
Let the heavens *r* ..... Ps 96:11
Let the earth *r* ..... Ps 97:1
we will *r* and be glad ..... Ps 118:24
she shall *r* in time to ..... Prov 31:25
*R*, O young man ..... Eccl 11:9
your heart shall *r* ..... Is 66:14
Do not *r* over me ..... Mic 7:8
Nevertheless do not *r* ..... Luke 10:20
loved Me, you would *r* ..... John 14:28
but the world will *r* ..... John 16:20
and your heart will *r* ..... John 16:22
*R* with those who ..... Rom 12:15
and in this I *r* ..... Phil 1:18
faith, I am glad and *r* ..... Phil 2:17
*R* in the Lord always ..... Phil 4:4
*R* always ..... 1 Thess 5:16
yet believing, you *r* ..... 1 Pet 1:8

**REJOICED**
and my spirit has *r* ..... Luke 1:47
In that hour Jesus *r* ..... Luke 10:21
Your father Abraham *r* ..... John 8:56

**REJOICES**
glad, and my glory *r* ..... Ps 16:9
but *r* in the truth ..... 1 Cor 13:6

**REJOICING**
come again with *r* ..... Ps 126:6
he went on his way *r* ..... Acts 8:39
confidence and the *r* ..... Heb 3:6

**RELENT**
sworn and will not *r* ..... Ps 110:4
*sworn and will not r* ..... Heb 7:21

**RELENTED**
and God *r* from the ..... Jon 3:10

**RELENTING**
I am weary of *r* ..... Jer 15:6

**RELIGION**
in self-imposed *r* ..... Col 2:23
and undefiled *r* ..... James 1:27

**RELIGIOUS**
things you are very *r* ..... Acts 17:22

**REMAIN**
you, that My joy may *r* ..... John 15:11
your fruit should *r* ..... John 15:16
If I will that he *r* ..... John 21:22
the greater part *r* ..... 1 Cor 15:6
we who are alive and *r* ..... 1 Thess 4:15
the things which *r* ..... Rev 3:2

**REMAINS**
"While the earth *r* ..... Gen 8:22
Therefore your sin *r* ..... John 9:41
There *r* therefore a ..... Heb 4:9

**REMEMBER**
*R* the Sabbath day ..... Ex 20:8
but we will *r* the name ..... Ps 20:7
*r* Your name in the ..... Ps 119:55
*R* now your Creator ..... Eccl 12:1
*r* the former things ..... Is 43:18
and their sin I will *r* ..... Jer 31:34
in wrath *r* mercy ..... Hab 3:2
and to *r* His holy ..... Luke 1:72
"*R* Lot's wife ..... Luke 17:32
*r* the words of the ..... Acts 20:35
*R* that Jesus Christ ..... 2 Tim 2:8
*R* those who rule ..... Heb 13:7

**REMEMBERED**
Then God *r* Noah ..... Gen 8:1
*r* His covenant with ..... Ex 2:24
*r* His covenant forever ..... Ps 105:8
yea, we wept when we *r* ..... Ps 137:1
And Peter *r* the word ..... Matt 26:75
*r* the word of the Lord ..... Acts 11:16

**REMEMBRANCE**
*r* my song in the night ..... Ps 77:6
Put Me in *r* ..... Is 43:26
do this in *r* of Me ..... Luke 22:19
do this in *r* of Me ..... 1 Cor 11:24

**REMISSION**
repentance for the *r* ..... Mark 1:4
Jesus Christ for the *r* ..... Acts 2:38
where there is *r* ..... Heb 10:18

**REMNANT**
The *r* will return ..... Is 10:21
time there is a *r* ..... Rom 11:5

**REMORSEFUL**
been condemned, was *r* ..... Matt 27:3

**REMOVE**
*r* this cup from Me ..... Luke 22:42
*r* your lampstand ..... Rev 2:5

**REMOVED**
Though the earth be *r* ..... Ps 46:2
and the hills be *r* ..... Is 54:10
this mountain, 'Be *r* ..... Matt 21:21

**REND**
So *r* your heart ..... Joel 2:13

**RENDER**
What shall I *r* to the ..... Ps 116:12
*R* therefore to Caesar ..... Matt 22:21

**RENEW**
*r* a steadfast ..... Ps 51:10
on the LORD shall *r* ..... Is 40:31

**RENEWED**
that your youth is *r* ..... Ps 103:5
inward man is being *r* ..... 2 Cor 4:16
and be *r* in the spirit ..... Eph 4:23

**RENEWING**
transformed by the *r* ..... Rom 12:2

**RENOWN**
were of old, men of *r* ..... Gen 6:4

**REPAID**
Shall evil be *r* ..... Jer 18:20

**REPAY**
again, I will *r* ..... Luke 10:35
because they cannot *r* ..... Luke 14:14
*R* no one evil for evil ..... Rom 12:17
*is Mine, I will r* ..... Rom 12:19
*r* their parents ..... 1 Tim 5:4

**REPAYS**
the LORD, who fully *r* ..... Is 66:6

**REPENT**
I abhor myself, and *r* ..... Job 42:6
"*R*, for the kingdom ..... Matt 3:2
you *r* you will all ..... Luke 13:3
said to them, "*R* ..... Acts 2:38
men everywhere to *r* ..... Acts 17:30
be zealous and *r* ..... Rev 3:19

**REPENTANCE**
you with water unto *r* ..... Matt 3:11
a baptism of *r* for the ..... Mark 1:4
persons who need no *r* ..... Luke 15:7
renew them again to *r* ..... Heb 6:6
found no place for *r* ..... Heb 12:17
all should come to *r* ..... 2 Pet 3:9

**REPENTED**
it, because they *r* ..... Matt 12:41

**REPETITIONS**
*r* as the heathen do ..... Matt 6:7

**REPORT**
Who has believed our *r* ..... Is 53:1
things are of good *r* ..... Phil 4:8

**REPROACH**
*R* has broken my heart ..... Ps 69:20
with dishonor comes *r* ..... Prov 18:3
not remember the *r* ..... Is 54:4
because I bore the *r* ..... Jer 31:19
these things You *r* ..... Luke 11:45
lest he fall into *r* ..... 1 Tim 3:7
esteeming the *r* ..... Heb 11:26
and without *r* ..... James 1:5

**REPROACHED**
If you are *r* for the ..... 1 Pet 4:14

**REPROACHES**
is not an enemy who *r* ..... Ps 55:12
in infirmities, in *r* ..... 2 Cor 12:10

**REPROOF**
for doctrine, for *r* ..... 2 Tim 3:16

**REPROOFS**
*r* of instruction are ..... Prov 6:23

**REPUTATION**
seven men of good *r* ..... Acts 6:3
made Himself of no *r* ..... Phil 2:7

**REQUEST**
He gave them their *r* ..... Ps 106:15
For Jews *r* a sign ..... 1 Cor 1:22

**REQUESTS**
*r* be made known ..... Phil 4:6

**REQUIRE**
offering You did not *r* ..... Ps 40:6
what does the LORD *r* ..... Mic 6:8

**REQUIRED**
your soul will be *r* ..... Luke 12:20
him much will be *r* ..... Luke 12:48

**REQUIREMENTS**
keeps the righteous *r* ..... Rom 2:26
*r* that was against us ..... Col 2:14

**RESERVED**
*"I have r for Myself* ..... Rom 11:4
*r* in heaven for you ..... 1 Pet 1:4
habitation, He has *r* ..... Jude 6

**RESIST**
*r* an evil person ..... Matt 5:39
*r* the Holy Spirit ..... Acts 7:51
*R* the devil and he ..... James 4:7

**RESISTED**
For who has *r* His will ..... Rom 9:19

for he has greatly *r* . . . . . . . .2 Tim 4:15
You have not yet *r* . . . . . . . . . .Heb 12:4

**RESISTS**
*"God r the proud* . . . . . . . . . .James 4:6
for *"God r the proud*. . . . . . . . .1 Pet 5:5

**RESPECT**
of the law held in *r* . . . . . . . . .Acts 5:34
and we paid them *r* . . . . . . . . .Heb 12:9

**RESPECTED**
And the LORD *r* Abel . . . . . . . .Gen 4:4

**REST**
is the Sabbath of *r*. . . . . . . . . .Ex 31:15
to build a house of *r* . . . . . . .1 Chr 28:2
*R* in the LORD . . . . . . . . . . . . . .Ps 37:7
fly away and be at *r* . . . . . . . . . .Ps 55:6
"This is the *r*. . . . . . . . . . . . . . .Is 28:12
is the place of My *r* . . . . . . . . . . .Is 66:1
and I will give you *r*. . . . . . .Matt 11:28
*shall not enter My r* . . . . . . . .Heb 3:11
remains therefore a *r* . . . . . . . .Heb 4:9
that they should *r* . . . . . . . . . .Rev 6:11
"that they may *r* . . . . . . . . . .Rev 14:13
But the *r* of the dead . . . . . . . .Rev 20:5

**RESTED**
He had done, and He *r*. . . . . . . .Gen 2:2
*"And God r on the* . . . . . . . . . . .Heb 4:4

**RESTORATION**
until the times of *r* . . . . . . . . .Acts 3:21

**RESTORE**
*R* to me the joy . . . . . . . . . . . . .Ps 51:12
"So I will *r* to you . . . . . . . . . .Joel 2:25
and will *r* all things. . . . . . .Matt 17:11
You at this time *r* . . . . . . . . . . .Acts 1:6
who are spiritual *r*. . . . . . . . . . .Gal 6:1

**RESTORES**
He *r* my soul. . . . . . . . . . . . . . . .Ps 23:3

**RESTRAINS**
only He who now *r*. . . . . . . .2 Thess 2:7

**RESTRAINT**
they break all *r* . . . . . . . . . . . . .Hos 4:2

**RESTS**
*r* quietly in the heart . . . . . .Prov 14:33

**RESURRECTION**
to her, "I am the *r*. . . . . . . . .John 11:25
them Jesus and the *r* . . . . . .Acts 17:18
the likeness of His *r* . . . . . . . . .Rom 6:5
say that there is no *r* . . . . . .1 Cor 15:12
and the power of His *r*. . . . . . .Phil 3:10
obtain a better *r* . . . . . . . . . .Heb 11:35
This is the first *r* . . . . . . . . . . .Rev 20:5

**RETAIN**
*r* the sins of any . . . . . . . . . .John 20:23

**RETURN**
womb, naked shall he *r*. . . . . .Eccl 5:15
let him *r* to the LORD . . . . . . . . .Is 55:7
me, and I will *r* . . . . . . . . . . . .Jer 31:18
"*R* to Me. . . . . . . . . . . . . . . . . .Zech 1:3
he says, 'I will *r* . . . . . . . . .Matt 12:44

**RETURNED**
astray, but have now *r* . . . . . .1 Pet 2:25

**RETURNING**
*r* evil for evil or. . . . . . . . . . . . .1 Pet 3:9

**RETURNS**
As a dog *r* to his own . . . . . .Prov 26:11
*"A dog r to his own* . . . . . . . .2 Pet 2:22

**REVEAL**
the Son wills to *r* Him . . . . .Matt 11:27
*r* His Son in me . . . . . . . . . . . .Gal 1:16

**REVEALED**
things which are *r* . . . . . . . .Deut 29:29
righteousness to be *r* . . . . . . . . .Is 56:1
the Son of Man is *r* . . . . . . .Luke 17:30
the wrath of God is *r*. . . . . . . .Rom 1:18
glory which shall be *r*. . . . . . .Rom 8:18
the Lord Jesus is *r* . . . . . . . .2 Thess 1:7
lawless one will be *r* . . . . . .2 Thess 2:8
ready to be *r* in the. . . . . . . . . .1 Pet 1:5
when His glory is *r* . . . . . . . .1 Pet 4:13
*r* what we shall be. . . . . . . . .1 John 3:2

**REVEALER**
Lord of kings, and a *r* . . . . . . .Dan 2:47

**REVEALING**
waits for the *r* . . . . . . . . . . . . .Rom 8:19

**REVEALS**
as a talebearer *r*. . . . . . . . . .Prov 20:19
*r* His secret to His. . . . . . . . . .Amos 3:7

**REVELATION**
Where there is no *r*. . . . . . . .Prov 29:18
it came through the *r*. . . . . . . .Gal 1:12
spirit of wisdom and *r*. . . . . . .Eph 1:17
*r* He made known to . . . . . . . . .Eph 3:3
and glory at the *r*. . . . . . . . . . .1 Pet 1:7

**REVERENCE**
and *r* My sanctuary. . . . . . . .Lev 19:30
God acceptably with *r*. . . . . .Heb 12:28

**REVERENT**
man who is always *r* . . . . . .Prov 28:14
their wives must be *r*. . . . . . .1 Tim 3:11

**REVILE**
are you when they *r*. . . . . . . .Matt 5:11
*r* God's high priest . . . . . . . . .Acts 23:4

**REVILED**
crucified with Him *r*. . . . . .Mark 15:32
who, when He was *r*. . . . . . . .1 Pet 2:23

**REVIVAL**
give us a measure of *r* . . . . . . .Ezra 9:8

**REVIVE**
Will You not *r* us . . . . . . . . . . . .Ps 85:6
two days He will *r* . . . . . . . . . . .Hos 6:2

**REVIVED**
came, sin *r* and I died . . . . . . . .Rom 7:9

**REWARD**
exceedingly great *r* . . . . . . . . .Gen 15:1
look, and see the *r* . . . . . . . . . . .Ps 91:8
behold, His *r* is with . . . . . . . . .Is 40:10
for great is your *r*. . . . . . . . . .Matt 5:12
you, they have their *r* . . . . . . .Matt 6:2
by no means lose his *r* . . . . .Matt 10:42
we receive the due *r*. . . . . . .Luke 23:41
will receive his own *r* . . . . . . .1 Cor 3:8
cheat you of your *r* . . . . . . . . . .Col 2:18
for he looked to the *r* . . . . . . .Heb 11:26
quickly, and My *r*. . . . . . . . . .Rev 22:12

**REWARDS**
Whoever *r* evil for . . . . . . . .Prov 17:13
and follows after *r*. . . . . . . . . . . .Is 1:23

**RICH**
Abram was very *r* . . . . . . . . . .Gen 13:2
The *r* and the poor . . . . . . . . .Prov 22:2
*r* rules over the poor. . . . . . . .Prov 22:7
*r* man is wise in his . . . . . . .Prov 28:11
do not curse the *r* . . . . . . . . .Eccl 10:20
it is hard for a *r* . . . . . . . . . .Matt 19:23
to you who are *r*. . . . . . . . . . .Luke 6:24
from the *r* man's table. . . . .Luke 16:21
for he was very *r* . . . . . . . . .Luke 18:23
You are already *r*. . . . . . . . . . .1 Cor 4:8
though He was *r* . . . . . . . . . . .2 Cor 8:9

who desire to be *r* . . . . . . . . . . .1 Tim 6:9
of this world to be *r* . . . . . . . .James 2:5
you say, 'I am *r*. . . . . . . . . . . . .Rev 3:17

**RICHES**
*R* and honor are . . . . . . . . . . .Prov 8:18
*R* do not profit . . . . . . . . . . . .Prov 11:4
in his *r* will fall . . . . . . . . . .Prov 11:28
of the wise is their *r* . . . . . . .Prov 14:24
and *r* are an . . . . . . . . . . . . .Prov 19:14
of the LORD are *r* . . . . . . . . . .Prov 22:4
*r* are not forever . . . . . . . . . .Prov 27:24
do you despise the *r* . . . . . . . . .Rom 2:4
might make known the *r* . . . .Rom 9:23
what are the *r* . . . . . . . . . . . . .Eph 1:18
show the exceeding *r*. . . . . . . . .Eph 2:7
the unsearchable *r* . . . . . . . . . .Eph 3:8
*r* than the treasures . . . . . . .Heb 11:26
to receive power and *r* . . . . . . .Rev 5:12

**RICHLY**
Christ dwell in you *r* . . . . . . . .Col 3:16
God, who gives us *r* . . . . . . .1 Tim 6:17

**RIGHT**
the *r* of the firstborn . . . . . .Deut 21:17
"Is your heart *r*. . . . . . . . . .2 Kin 10:15
Lord, "Sit at My *r* . . . . . . . . . .Ps 110:1
is a way which seems *r*. . . . .Prov 14:12
clothed and in his *r*. . . . . . . . .Mark 5:15
to them He gave the *r*. . . . . . .John 1:12
your heart is not *r*. . . . . . . . . .Acts 8:21
seven stars in His *r* . . . . . . . . . .Rev 2:1

**RIGHTEOUS**
also destroy the *r*. . . . . . . . . .Gen 18:23
and they justify the *r*. . . . . . .Deut 25:1
that he could be *r* . . . . . . . . . .Job 15:14
"The *r* see it and. . . . . . . . . . .Job 22:19
*r* shows mercy and . . . . . . . . . .Ps 37:21
I have not seen the *r*. . . . . . . . .Ps 37:25
the LORD loves the *r* . . . . . . . .Ps 146:8
*r* is a well of life . . . . . . . . . .Prov 10:11
*r* will be gladness. . . . . . . . .Prov 10:28
*r* will be delivered . . . . . . . .Prov 11:21
*r* will be recompensed . . . . .Prov 11:31
the prayer of the *r*. . . . . . . . .Prov 15:29
*r* are bold as a lion . . . . . . . . .Prov 28:1
*r* considers the cause . . . . . . .Prov 29:7
Do not be overly *r* . . . . . . . . . .Eccl 7:16
event happens to the *r* . . . . . . .Eccl 9:2
with My *r* right hand . . . . . . . .Is 41:10
By His knowledge My *r* . . . . . .Is 53:11
The *r* perishes. . . . . . . . . . . . . . .Is 57:1
they sell the *r* . . . . . . . . . . . . .Amos 2:6
not come to call the *r* . . . . . . .Matt 9:13
*r* men desired to see. . . . . . .Matt 13:17
*r* will shine forth as . . . . . . .Matt 13:43
that they were *r*. . . . . . . . . . . .Luke 18:9
"Certainly this was a *r* . . . .Luke 23:47
*"There is none r* . . . . . . . . . . .Rom 3:10
*r* man will one die. . . . . . . . . . .Rom 5:7
Jesus Christ the *r* . . . . . . . . .1 John 2:1

**RIGHTEOUSLY**
should live soberly, *r*. . . . . . .Titus 2:12
to Him who judges *r* . . . . . . .1 Pet 2:23

**RIGHTEOUSNESS**
it to him for *r*. . . . . . . . . . . . . .Gen 15:6
I put on *r*. . . . . . . . . . . . . . . . .Job 29:14
I call, O God of my *r*. . . . . . . . . . .Ps 4:1
from the LORD, and *r*. . . . . . . . . .Ps 24:5
shall speak of Your *r* . . . . . . . .Ps 35:28
the good news of *r* . . . . . . . . . . .Ps 40:9
heavens declare His *r* . . . . . . . . .Ps 50:6
*r* and peace have . . . . . . . . . . .Ps 85:10
*R* will go before Him . . . . . . . .Ps 85:13
*r* endures forever . . . . . . . . . . .Ps 111:3
*r* delivers from death . . . . . . .Prov 10:2

The *r* of the blameless ...... Prov 11:5
the way of *r* is life ......... Prov 12:28
*R* exalts a nation ......... Prov 14:34
He who follows *r* .......... Prov 21:21
*r* lodged in it ............... Is 1:21
in the LORD I have *r* ........ Is 45:24
*r* will be forever ............. Is 51:8
I will declare your *r* ......... Is 57:12
*r* as a breastplate ........... Is 59:17
*r* goes forth as .............. Is 62:1
The Lord Our *R* ............ Jer 23:6
to David a Branch of *r* ...... Jer 33:15
The *r* of the righteous ..... Ezek 18:20
who turn many to *r* ......... Dan 12:3
to fulfill all *r* ............. Matt 3:15
exceeds the *r* of the ........ Matt 5:20
to you in the way of *r* ...... Matt 21:32
For in it the *r* .............. Rom 1:17
even the *r* of God .......... Rom 3:22
*accounted to him for r* ..... Rom 4:22
*r* will reign in life ......... Rom 5:17
might reign through *r* ...... Rom 5:21
ignorant of God's *r* ......... Rom 10:3
we might become the *r* ..... 2 Cor 5:21
the breastplate of *r* ......... Eph 6:14
not having my own *r* ......... Phil 3:9
*r* which we have ........... Titus 3:5
does not produce the *r* ..... James 1:20
a preacher of *r* ............. 2 Pet 2:5
a new earth in which *r* ...... 2 Pet 3:13
who practices *r* .......... 1 John 2:29
He who practices *r* ........ 1 John 3:7

**RIGHTLY**
wise uses knowledge *r* ...... Prov 15:2
*r* dividing the word ........ 2 Tim 2:15

**RISE**
for He makes His sun *r* ..... Matt 5:45
third day He will *r* ........ Matt 20:19
third day He will *r* ........ Luke 18:33
be the first to *r* ........... Acts 26:23
in Christ will *r* .......... 1 Thess 4:16

**RISEN**
women there has not *r* ..... Matt 11:11
disciples that He is *r* ....... Matt 28:7
"The Lord is *r* ........... Luke 24:34
then Christ is not *r* ....... 1 Cor 15:13
if Christ is not *r* .......... 1 Cor 15:17
But now Christ is *r* ....... 1 Cor 15:20

**RIVER**
peace to her like a *r* .......... Is 66:12
he showed me a pure *r* ....... Rev 22:1

**RIVERS**
By the *r* of Babylon ......... Ps 137:1
All the *r* run into the ........ Eccl 1:7
his heart will flow *r* ........ John 7:38

**ROAR**
The LORD also will *r* ........ Joel 3:16

**ROARING**
and the waves *r* .......... Luke 21:25
walks about like a *r* ......... 1 Pet 5:8

**ROARS**
"The LORD *r* from .......... Amos 1:2
as when a lion *r* ............ Rev 10:3

**ROB**
"Will a man *r* God ........... Mal 3:8

**ROBBED**
*r* other churches .......... 2 Cor 11:8

**ROBBER**
is a thief and a *r* ........... John 10:1
Now Barabbas was a *r* ..... John 18:40

**ROBBERS**
also crucified two *r* ....... Mark 15:27
Me are thieves and *r* ....... John 10:8

**ROBBERY**
did not consider it *r* .......... Phil 2:6

**ROBE**
'Bring out the best *r* ...... Luke 15:22
on Him a purple *r* .......... John 19:2
Then a white *r* was ......... Rev 6:11

**ROBES**
have stained all My *r* ......... Is 63:3
to go around in long *r* ..... Luke 20:46
clothed with white *r* ......... Rev 7:9

**ROCK**
you shall strike the *r* ......... Ex 17:6
and struck the *r* .......... Num 20:11
For their *r* is not .......... Deut 32:31
"The LORD is my *r* ....... 2 Sam 22:2
And who is a *r* .......... 2 Sam 22:32
Blessed be my *R* ........ 2 Sam 22:47
For You are my *r* ........... Ps 31:3
*r* that is higher than ......... Ps 61:2
been mindful of the *R* ........ Is 17:10
shadow of a great *r* ........... Is 32:2
his house on the *r* .......... Matt 7:24
*r* I will build My ......... Matt 16:18
*stumbling stone and r* ...... Rom 9:33
*R* that followed them ...... 1 Cor 10:4

**ROD**
Your *r* and Your staff ......... Ps 23:4
shall come forth a *R* .......... Is 11:1
*rule them with a r* .......... Rev 2:27

**ROOM**
you a large upper *r* ....... Mark 14:15
no *r* for them in the ........ Luke 2:7
into the upper *r* ............ Acts 1:13

**ROOT**
day there shall be a *R* ........ Is 11:10
because they had no *r* ...... Matt 13:6
of money is a *r* ............ 1 Tim 6:10
lest any *r* of ............. Heb 12:15
I am the *R* and the ......... Rev 22:16

**ROOTED**
*r* and built up in Him ......... Col 2:7

**ROSE**
end Christ died and *r* ....... Rom 14:9
buried, and that He *r* ...... 1 Cor 15:4
that Jesus died and *r* ..... 1 Thess 4:14

**RULE**
and he shall *r* ............. Gen 3:16
puts an end to all *r* ....... 1 Cor 15:24
let the peace of God *r* ........ Col 3:15
Let the elders who *r* ....... 1 Tim 5:17
Remember those who *r* ...... Heb 13:7

**RULER**
to Me the One to be *r* ......... Mic 5:2
by Beelzebub, the *r* ....... Matt 12:24
the *r* of this world .......... John 12:31
*'Who made you a r* ......... Acts 7:27

**RULERS**
and the *r* take counsel ......... Ps 2:2
"You know that the *r* ...... Matt 20:25
which none of the *r* .......... 1 Cor 2:8
powers, against the *r* ....... Eph 6:12

**RULES**
that the Most High *r* ........ Dan 4:17
that the Most High *r* ........ Dan 4:32
*r* his own house well ........ 1 Tim 3:4

**RULING**
*r* their children ........... 1 Tim 3:12

**RUMORS**
hear of wars and *r* ......... Matt 24:6

**RUN**
*r* and not be weary .......... Is 40:31
us, and let us *r* ............ Heb 12:1

# S

**SABAOTH**
*S had left us a* ............. Rom 9:29
ears of the Lord of *S* ....... James 5:4

**SABBATH**
"Remember the *S* ........... Ex 20:8
*S* was made for man ....... Mark 2:27

**SABBATHS**
*S* you shall keep ........... Ex 31:13

**SACRIFICE**
to the LORD than *s* ......... Prov 21:3
For the LORD has a *s* .......... Is 34:6
of My offerings they *s* ....... Hos 8:13
LORD has prepared a *s* ...... Zeph 1:7
*desire mercy and not s* ..... Matt 9:13
an offering and a *s* ........... Eph 5:2
put away sin by the *s* ........ Heb 9:26
no longer remains a *s* ...... Heb 10:26
offer the *s* of praise ........ Heb 13:15

**SACRIFICED**
*s* their sons and their ....... Ps 106:37

**SACRIFICES**
The *s* of God are a ........... Ps 51:17
multitude of your *s* ........... Is 1:11
priests, to offer up *s* ......... Heb 7:27
*s* God is well pleased ...... Heb 13:16

**SAFE**
he has received him *s* ..... Luke 15:27

**SAFELY**
make them lie down *s* ....... Hos 2:18

**SAFETY**
say, "Peace and *s* ......... 1 Thess 5:3

**SAINTS**
*s* who are on the earth ....... Ps 16:3
does not forsake His *s* ....... Ps 37:28
is the death of His *s* ........ Ps 116:15
war against the *s* .......... Dan 7:21
Jesus, called to be *s* ......... 1 Cor 1:2
the least of all the *s* .......... Eph 3:8
be glorified in His *s* ..... 2 Thess 1:10
all delivered to the *s* .......... Jude 3
shed the blood of *s* ......... Rev 16:6

**SALT**
shall season with *s* ......... Lev 2:13
"You are the *s* ............ Matt 5:13
*s* loses its flavor .......... Mark 9:50

**SALVATION**
still, and see the *s* .......... Ex 14:13
*S* belongs to the LORD ......... Ps 3:8
is my light and my *s* ......... Ps 27:1
God is the God of *s* .......... Ps 68:20
joy in the God of my *s* ....... Hab 3:18
raised up a horn of *s* ....... Luke 1:69
"Nor is there *s* ............ Acts 4:12
the power of God to *s* ........ Rom 1:16
and is the day of *s* .......... 2 Cor 6:2
work out your own *s* ........ Phil 2:12
chose you for *s* .......... 2 Thess 2:13
neglect so great a *s* .......... Heb 2:3

**SAMARITAN**
a drink from me, a *S* ........ John 4:9

**SANCTIFICATION**
will of God, your *s* ........ 1 Thess 4:3

**SANCTIFIED**
they also may be *s* ........ John 17:19
washed, but you were *s* ..... 1 Cor 6:11
for it is *s* by the ............ 1 Tim 4:5

**SANCTIFIES**
For both He who *s* .......... Heb 2:11

**SANCTIFY**
*s* My great name . . . . . . . . . Ezek 36:23
*S* them by Your truth . . . . . . John 17:17
that He might *s* . . . . . . . . . . . . Eph 5:26

**SANCTUARY**
let them make Me a *s* . . . . . . . . Ex 25:8
and the earthly *s* . . . . . . . . . . . . Heb 9:1

**SAND**
descendants as the *s* . . . . . . . Gen 32:12
innumerable as the *s* . . . . . . . Heb 11:12

**SAT**
up into heaven, and *s* . . . . . Mark 16:19
And He who *s* there was . . . . . . Rev 4:3

**SATAN**
before the LORD, and *S* . . . . . . . Job 1:6
"Away with you, *S* . . . . . . . . . Matt 4:10
"Get behind Me, *S* . . . . . . . . Matt 16:23
"How can *S* cast out . . . . . . . Mark 3:23
*S* has asked for you . . . . . . . Luke 22:31
to the working of *S* . . . . . . . 2 Thess 2:9
known the depths of *S* . . . . . . . Rev 2:24
years have expired, *S* . . . . . . . Rev 20:7

**SATIATED**
*s* the weary soul . . . . . . . . . . . Jer 31:25

**SATISFIED**
I shall be *s* when I . . . . . . . . . . Ps 17:15
that are never *s* . . . . . . . . . . Prov 30:15
of His soul, and be *s* . . . . . . . . . Is 53:11

**SATISFIES**
*s* the longing soul . . . . . . . . . . . Ps 107:9

**SATISFY**
*s* us early with Your . . . . . . . . . Ps 90:14
long life I will *s* . . . . . . . . . . . . Ps 91:16
for what does not *s* . . . . . . . . . . . Is 55:2

**SAVE**
Oh, *s* me for Your . . . . . . . . . . . . . Ps 6:4
*s* the children of the . . . . . . . . . . Ps 72:4
*s* the souls of the . . . . . . . . . . . . Ps 72:13
that I cannot *s* . . . . . . . . . . . . . . . Is 59:1
*s* you and deliver you . . . . . . . Jer 15:20
other, that he may *s* . . . . . . . . Hos 13:10
JESUS, for He will *s* . . . . . . . . Matt 1:21
*s* his life will . . . . . . . . . . . . Matt 16:25
*s* that which was . . . . . . . . . Matt 18:11
let Him *s* Himself if . . . . . . . Luke 23:35
but to *s* the world . . . . . . . . . John 12:47
the world to *s* sinners . . . . . . 1 Tim 1:15

**SAVED**
"He *s* others . . . . . . . . . . . . . Matt 27:42
that we should be *s* . . . . . . . . Luke 1:71
"Your faith has *s* . . . . . . . . . . Luke 7:50
through Him might be *s* . . . . John 3:17
them, saying, "Be *s* . . . . . . . . . Acts 2:40
what must I do to be *s* . . . . . . Acts 16:30
which also you are *s* . . . . . . . 1 Cor 15:2
grace you have been *s* . . . . . . . . Eph 2:8
to His mercy He *s* . . . . . . . . . . Titus 3:5
of those who are *s* . . . . . . . . . . Rev 21:24

**SAVES**
antitype which now *s* . . . . . . . 1 Pet 3:21

**SAVIOR**
I, the LORD, am your *S* . . . . . . . Is 60:16
rejoiced in God my *S* . . . . . . . Luke 1:47
the city of David a *S* . . . . . . . Luke 2:11
up for Israel a *S* . . . . . . . . . . Acts 13:23
God, who is the *S* . . . . . . . . . 1 Tim 4:10
God and *S* Jesus Christ . . . . Titus 2:13

**SAWN**
stoned, they were *s* . . . . . . . . Heb 11:37

**SAY**
"But I *s* to you that . . . . . . . . Matt 5:22
"But who do you *s* . . . . . . . . Matt 16:15

**SAYING**
This is a faithful *s* . . . . . . . . 1 Tim 1:15

**SAYINGS**
whoever hears these *s* . . . . . . Matt 7:24

**SCALES**
on it had a pair of *s* . . . . . . . . . . Rev 6:5

**SCARLET**
your sins are like *s* . . . . . . . . . . . Is 1:18

**SCATTER**
I will *s* you among the . . . . . . Lev 26:33

**SCATTERED**
Israel is like *s* sheep . . . . . . . . Jer 50:17
*the sheep will be s* . . . . . . . . Mark 14:27

**SCATTERS**
not gather with Me *s* . . . . . . Matt 12:30

**SCEPTER**
*s* shall not depart . . . . . . . . . Gen 49:10

**SCHEMER**
will be called a *s* . . . . . . . . . . . Prov 24:8

**SCHEMES**
have sought out many *s* . . . . . Eccl 7:29

**SCHISM**
there should be no *s* . . . . . . . 1 Cor 12:25

**SCHOOL**
daily in the *s* of . . . . . . . . . . . . Acts 19:9

**SCOFF**
They *s* at kings . . . . . . . . . . . . Hab 1:10

**SCOFFER**
"He who corrects a *s* . . . . . . . . . Prov 9:7
*s* is an abomination . . . . . . . . Prov 24:9

**SCOFFERS**
*s* will come in the . . . . . . . . . . . 2 Pet 3:3

**SCORCHED**
And men were *s* with . . . . . . . . Rev 16:9

**SCORN**
My friends *s* me . . . . . . . . . . . Job 16:20

**SCORNS**
He *s* the scornful . . . . . . . . . . Prov 3:34

**SCORPIONS**
on serpents and *s* . . . . . . . . . Luke 10:19
They had tails like *s* . . . . . . . . . Rev 9:10

**SCOURGE**
will mock Him, and *s* . . . . . Mark 10:34

**SCOURGES**
*s every son whom* . . . . . . . . . . Heb 12:6

**SCRIBES**
"Beware of the *s* . . . . . . . . . Mark 12:38

**SCRIPTURE**
*S* cannot be broken . . . . . . . John 10:35
All *S* is given by . . . . . . . . . . 2 Tim 3:16

**SCRIPTURES**
*S* must be fulfilled . . . . . . . Mark 14:49

**SCROLL**
eat this *s* . . . . . . . . . . . . . . . . . Ezek 3:1
the sky receded as a *s* . . . . . . . Rev 6:14

**SEA**
drowned in the Red *S* . . . . . . . . Ex 15:4
who go down to the *s* . . . . . . Ps 107:23
and the *s* obey Him . . . . . . . . Matt 8:27
throne there was a *s* . . . . . . . . . . Rev 4:6
there was no more *s* . . . . . . . . . Rev 21:1

**SEAL**
stands, having this *s* . . . . . . 2 Tim 2:19

**SEALED**
by whom you were *s* . . . . . . . . Eph 4:30

**SEAM**
tunic was without *s* . . . . . . . John 19:23

**SEANCE**
"Please conduct a *s* . . . . . . . 1 Sam 28:8

**SEARCH**
glory of kings is to *s* . . . . . . . . Prov 25:2
*s* the Scriptures . . . . . . . . . . . John 5:39

**SEARCHED**
*s* the Scriptures . . . . . . . . . . Acts 17:11

**SEARCHES**
For the Spirit *s* . . . . . . . . . . . 1 Cor 2:10

**SEASON**
Be ready in *s* and out . . . . . . . 2 Tim 4:2

**SEASONED**
how shall it be *s* . . . . . . . . . . . Matt 5:13

**SEASONS**
the times and the *s* . . . . . . . 1 Thess 5:1

**SEAT**
shall make a mercy *s* . . . . . . . Ex 25:17
before the judgment *s* . . . . . 2 Cor 5:10

**SEATS**
at feasts, the best *s* . . . . . . . . Matt 23:6

**SECRET**
*s* things belong . . . . . . . . . . Deut 29:29
in the *s* place of His . . . . . . . . . . Ps 27:5
Father who is in the *s* . . . . . . . . Matt 6:6

**SECRETLY**
He lies in wait *s* . . . . . . . . . . . . . Ps 10:9

**SECRETS**
For He knows the *s* . . . . . . . . . . Ps 44:21
God will judge the *s* . . . . . . . . Rom 2:16

**SECT**
to the strictest *s* . . . . . . . . . . Acts 26:5

**SECURELY**
nation that dwells *s* . . . . . . . . Jer 49:31

**SEDUCED**
flattering lips she *s* . . . . . . . . Prov 7:21

**SEE**
in my flesh I shall *s* . . . . . . . . Job 19:26
for they shall *s* God . . . . . . . . . Matt 5:8
seeing they do not *s* . . . . . . . Matt 13:13
rejoiced to *s* My day . . . . . . . . John 8:56
They shall *s* His face . . . . . . . . Rev 22:4

**SEED**
He shall see His *s* . . . . . . . . . . . Is 53:10
*S* were the promises . . . . . . . . . Gal 3:16
you are Abraham's *s* . . . . . . . . Gal 3:29

**SEEDS**
the good *s* are the . . . . . . . . . Matt 13:38

**SEEK**
and pray and *s* My face . . . . . 2 Chr 7:14
*S* the LORD while He . . . . . . . . . Is 55:6
*s*, and you will find . . . . . . . . . Matt 7:7
of Man has come to *s* . . . . . . Luke 19:10
"You will *s* Me and . . . . . . . . . John 7:34
For all *s* their own . . . . . . . . . . Phil 2:21
*s* those things that . . . . . . . . . . . Col 3:1

**SEEKING**
like a roaring lion, *s* . . . . . . . . 1 Pet 5:8

**SEEKS**
*there is none who s* . . . . . . . . . Rom 3:11

**SEEMS**
There is a way which *s* . . . . . Prov 14:12

**SEEN**
*s* God face to face . . . . . . . . . . Gen 32:30
No one has *s* God at . . . . . . . . John 1:18
*s* Me has *s* the . . . . . . . . . . . . . John 14:9
things which are not *s* . . . . . . 2 Cor 4:18

**SEES**
*s* his brother in need ...... 1 John 3:17

**SELF-CONFIDENT**
a fool rages and is *s* ...... Prov 14:16

**SELF-CONTROL**
gentleness, *s* ...... Gal 5:23
to knowledge *s* ...... 2 Pet 1:6

**SELF-CONTROLLED**
just, holy, *s* ...... Titus 1:8

**SELF-SEEKING**
where envy and *s* exist ...... James 3:16

**SELL**
*s* whatever you have ...... Mark 10:21

**SEND**
"Behold, I *s* you out ...... Matt 10:16
has sent Me, I also *s* ...... John 20:21

**SENSES**
of use have their *s* ...... Heb 5:14

**SENSIBLY**
men who can answer *s* ...... Prov 26:16

**SENSUAL**
but is earthly, *s* ...... James 3:15

**SENT**
unless they are *s* ...... Rom 10:15

**SEPARATED**
it pleased God, who *s* ...... Gal 1:15

**SEPARATES**
who repeats a matter *s* ...... Prov 17:9

**SEPARATION**
the middle wall of *s* ...... Eph 2:14

**SERAPHIM**
Above it stood *s* ...... Is 6:2

**SERIOUS**
therefore be *s* and ...... 1 Pet 4:7

**SERPENT**
*s* was more cunning ...... Gen 3:1
"Make a fiery *s* ...... Num 21:8
Moses lifted up the *s* ...... John 3:14

**SERPENTS**
Therefore be wise as *s* ...... Matt 10:16

**SERVANT**
*s* will rule over a son ...... Prov 17:2
good and faithful *s* ...... Matt 25:21

**SERVANTS**
"We are unprofitable *s* ...... Luke 17:10

**SERVE**
to be served, but to *s* ...... Matt 20:28
but through love *s* ...... Gal 5:13

**SERVES**
"If anyone *s* Me ...... John 12:26

**SERVICE**
is your reasonable *s* ...... Rom 12:1
with good will doing *s* ...... Eph 6:7

**SERVING**
fervent in spirit, *s* ...... Rom 12:11

**SET**
"See, I have *s* ...... Deut 30:15
*s* aside the grace ...... Gal 2:21

**SETTLE**
"Therefore *s* it in ...... Luke 21:14

**SETTLED**
O LORD, Your word is *s* ...... Ps 119:89

**SEVEN**
*s* churches which are ...... Rev 1:4

**SEVENTY**
*S* weeks are ...... Dan 9:24

**SEVERE**
not to be too *s* ...... 2 Cor 2:5

**SEVERITY**
the goodness and *s* ...... Rom 11:22

**SHADE**
may nest under its *s* ...... Mark 4:32

**SHADOW**
in the *s* of His hand ...... Is 49:2
the law, having a *s* ...... Heb 10:1

**SHAKE**
*s* the earth ...... Is 2:19
I will *s* all nations ...... Hag 2:7

**SHAKEN**
not to be soon *s* ...... 2 Thess 2:2

**SHAKES**
*s* the Wilderness ...... Ps 29:8

**SHAME**
never be put to *s* ...... Joel 2:26
to put to *s* the wise ...... 1 Cor 1:27
glory is in their *s* ...... Phil 3:19

**SHAMEFUL**
For it is *s* even to ...... Eph 5:12

**SHARE**
to do good and to *s* ...... Heb 13:16

**SHARING**
for your liberal *s* ...... 2 Cor 9:13

**SHARP**
*s* as a two-edged sword ...... Prov 5:4

**SHARPEN**
*s* their tongue like a ...... Ps 64:3

**SHARPENS**
my adversary *s* His ...... Job 16:9

**SHARPNESS**
present I should use *s* ...... 2 Cor 13:10

**SHEATH**
your sword into the *s* ...... John 18:11

**SHEAVES**
bringing his *s* ...... Ps 126:6
gather them like *s* ...... Mic 4:12

**SHED**
which is *s* for many ...... Matt 26:28

**SHEDDING**
blood, and without *s* ...... Heb 9:22

**SHEEP**
*s* will be scattered ...... Zech 13:7
having a hundred *s* ...... Luke 15:4
and I know My *s* ...... John 10:14
*"He was led as a s* ...... Acts 8:32

**SHEEPFOLDS**
lie down among the *s* ...... Ps 68:13

**SHEET**
object like a great *s* ...... Acts 10:11

**SHELTER**
the LORD will be a *s* ...... Joel 3:16

**SHELTERS**
*s* him all the day long ...... Deut 33:12

**SHEOL**
not leave my soul in *S* ...... Ps 16:10
the belly of *S* I cried ...... Jon 2:2

**SHEPHERD**
The LORD is my *s* ...... Ps 23:1
His flock like a *s* ...... Is 40:11
*'I will strike the S* ...... Matt 26:31
"I am the good *s* ...... John 10:11
the dead, that great *S* ...... Heb 13:20
*S* the flock of God ...... 1 Pet 5:2
when the Chief *S* ...... 1 Pet 5:4

**SHEPHERDS**
And I will give you *s* ...... Jer 3:15
*s* have led them astray ...... Jer 50:6

**SHIELD**
I am your *s* ...... Gen 15:1
truth shall be your *s* ...... Ps 91:4
all, taking the *s* ...... Eph 6:16

**SHINE**
LORD make His face *s* ...... Num 6:25
among whom you *s* ...... Phil 2:15

**SHINED**
them a light has *s* ...... Is 9:2

**SHINES**
heed as a light that *s* ...... 2 Pet 1:19

**SHINING**
light is already *s* ...... 1 John 2:8

**SHIPS**
down to the sea in *s* ...... Ps 107:23

**SHIPWRECK**
faith have suffered *s* ...... 1 Tim 1:19

**SHOOT**
they *s* out the lip ...... Ps 22:7

**SHORT**
have sinned and fall *s* ...... Rom 3:23

**SHORTENED**
those days were *s* ...... Matt 24:22

**SHOUT**
from heaven with a *s* ...... 1 Thess 4:16

**SHOW**
a land that I will *s* ...... Gen 12:1
*s* Him greater works ...... John 5:20

**SHOWBREAD**
*s* which was not lawful ...... Matt 12:4

**SHOWERS**
make it soft with *s* ...... Ps 65:10

**SHREWDLY**
because he had dealt *s* ...... Luke 16:8

**SHRINES**
who made silver *s* ...... Acts 19:24

**SHRIVELED**
You have *s* me up ...... Job 16:8

**SHUFFLES**
with his eyes, he *s* ...... Prov 6:13

**SHUNNED**
feared God and *s* evil ...... Job 1:1

**SHUT**
For you *s* up the ...... Matt 23:13

**SHUTS**
*s* his eyes from seeing ...... Is 33:15
*who opens and no one s* ...... Rev 3:7

**SICK**
I was *s* and you ...... Matt 25:36
faith will save the *s* ...... James 5:15

**SICKLE**
"Thrust in Your *s* ...... Rev 14:15

**SICKNESS**
will sustain him in *s* ...... Prov 18:14
"This *s* is not unto ...... John 11:4

**SICKNESSES**
*and bore our s* ...... Matt 8:17

**SIDE**
The LORD is on my *s* ...... Ps 118:6

**SIFT**
*s* the nations with the ...... Is 30:28

**SIGH**
our years like a *s* ...... Ps 90:9

**SIGHING**
For my *s* comes before . . . . . . . Job 3:24

**SIGHT**
and see this great *s* . . . . . . . . . . . Ex 3:3
by faith, not by *s* . . . . . . . . . . . 2 Cor 5:7

**SIGN**
will give you a *s* . . . . . . . . . . . . . Is 7:14
seeks after a *s* . . . . . . . . . . . Matt 12:39
For Jews request a *s* . . . . . . . 1 Cor 1:22

**SIGNS**
and let them be for *s* . . . . . . . . Gen 1:14
cannot discern the *s* . . . . . . . . Matt 16:3
Jesus did many other *s* . . . . John 20:30

**SILENCE**
that You may *s* . . . . . . . . . . . . . . . Ps 8:2
seal, there was *s* . . . . . . . . . . . . . Rev 8:1

**SILENT**
season, and am not *s* . . . . . . . . . Ps 22:2

**SILK**
and covered you with *s* . . . . Ezek 16:10

**SILLY**
They are *s* children . . . . . . . . . . Jer 4:22

**SILVER**
may buy the poor for *s* . . . . . . Amos 8:6
him thirty pieces of *s* . . . . . . Matt 26:15

**SIMILITUDE**
been made in the *s* . . . . . . . . . James 3:9

**SIMPLE**
making wise the *s* . . . . . . . . . . . Ps 19:7

**SIMPLICITY**
corrupted from the *s* . . . . . . . 2 Cor 11:3

**SIN**
and be sure your *s* . . . . . . . . Num 32:23
Be angry, and do not *s* . . . . . . . . . Ps 4:4
*s* is always before me . . . . . . . . . Ps 51:3
soul an offering for *s* . . . . . . . . . Is 53:10
and He bore the *s* . . . . . . . . . . . Is 53:12
who takes away the *s* . . . . . . . John 1:29
"He who is without *s* . . . . . . . . John 8:7
convict the world of *s* . . . . . . . John 16:8
*s* entered the world . . . . . . . . . Rom 5:12
*s* is not imputed . . . . . . . . . . . Rom 5:13
*s* shall not have . . . . . . . . . . . . Rom 6:14
Shall we *s* because we . . . . . . Rom 6:15
made Him who knew no *s* . . . 2 Cor 5:21
man of *s* is revealed . . . . . . . 2 Thess 2:3
we are, yet without *s* . . . . . . . . Heb 4:15
do it, to him it is *s* . . . . . . . . James 4:17
say that we have no *s* . . . . . . 1 John 1:8
and he cannot *s* . . . . . . . . . . . 1 John 3:9

**SINCERE**
and from *s* faith . . . . . . . . . . . 1 Tim 1:5

**SINCERITY**
simplicity and godly *s* . . . . . . 2 Cor 1:12

**SINFUL**
from me, for I am a *s* . . . . . . . . Luke 5:8
become exceedingly *s* . . . . . . . Rom 7:13

**SING**
Let him *s* psalms . . . . . . . . . James 5:13

**SINGERS**
The *s* went before . . . . . . . . . . . Ps 68:25

**SINGING**
His presence with *s* . . . . . . . . . Ps 100:2
and spiritual songs, *s* . . . . . . . Eph 5:19

**SINISTER**
who understands *s* . . . . . . . . . Dan 8:23

**SINK**
I *s* in deep mire . . . . . . . . . . . . . . Ps 69:2
to *s* he cried out . . . . . . . . . . Matt 14:30

**SINNED**
You only, have I *s* . . . . . . . . . . . . Ps 51:4
"Father, I have *s* . . . . . . . . . Luke 15:18
for all have *s* and . . . . . . . . . . Rom 3:23
say that we have not *s* . . . . . 1 John 1:10

**SINNER**
*s* who repents than . . . . . . . . Luke 15:7
*the ungodly and the s* . . . . . . 1 Pet 4:18

**SINNERS**
in the path of *s* . . . . . . . . . . . . . . . Ps 1:1
the righteous, but *s* . . . . . . . . Matt 9:13
while we were still *s* . . . . . . . . . Rom 5:8
many were made *s* . . . . . . . . . . Rom 5:19
the world to save *s* . . . . . . . . 1 Tim 1:15
such hostility from *s* . . . . . . . . Heb 12:3

**SINS**
from presumptuous *s* . . . . . . . . Ps 19:13
You, our secret *s* . . . . . . . . . . . . . Ps 90:8
the soul who *s* shall . . . . . . . . Ezek 18:4
if your brother *s* . . . . . . . . . . Matt 18:15
*s* according to the . . . . . . . . . 1 Cor 15:3
the forgiveness of *s* . . . . . . . . . . Eph 1:7
If we confess our *s* . . . . . . . . . 1 John 1:9
propitiation for our *s* . . . . . . . 1 John 2:2

**SISTER**
is My brother and *s* . . . . . . . Matt 12:50

**SIT**
but to *s* on My right . . . . . . . Matt 20:23
*"S at My right hand* . . . . . . . . Heb 1:13
I will grant to *s* . . . . . . . . . . . . Rev 3:21

**SITS**
It is He who *s* above . . . . . . . . . Is 40:22
so that he *s* as God . . . . . . . . 2 Thess 2:4

**SITTING**
where Christ is, *s* . . . . . . . . . . . . Col 3:1

**SKILL**
hand forget its *s* . . . . . . . . . . . . Ps 137:5

**SKILLFULNESS**
guided them by the *s* . . . . . . . . Ps 78:72

**SKIN**
God made tunics of *s* . . . . . . . . Gen 3:21
LORD and said, "*S* . . . . . . . . . . . Job 2:4
Ethiopian change his *s* . . . . . . Jer 13:23

**SKIP**
He makes them also *s* . . . . . . . . Ps 29:6

**SKIPPING**
upon the mountains, *s* . . . . . . . Song 2:8

**SKULL**
to say, Place of a *S* . . . . . . . Matt 27:33

**SKY**
*s* receded as a scroll . . . . . . . . . Rev 6:14

**SLACK**
The Lord is not *s* . . . . . . . . . . . 2 Pet 3:9

**SLAIN**
is the Lamb who was *s* . . . . . . . Rev 5:12

**SLANDER**
and whoever spreads *s* . . . . . Prov 10:18

**SLANDERERS**
be reverent, not *s* . . . . . . . . . 1 Tim 3:11

**SLANDEROUSLY**
as we are *s* reported . . . . . . . . . Rom 3:8

**SLAUGHTER**
led as a lamb to the *s* . . . . . . . . . . Is 53:7
*as sheep for the s* . . . . . . . . . . . Rom 8:36

**SLAVE**
commits sin is a *s* . . . . . . . . . . John 8:34

**SLAVES**
should no longer be *s* . . . . . . . . Rom 6:6

**SLAY**
*s* the righteous . . . . . . . . . . . Gen 18:25

**SLEEP**
God caused a deep *s* . . . . . . . . Gen 2:21
neither slumber nor *s* . . . . . . . Ps 121:4
He gives His beloved *s* . . . . . . . Ps 127:2
among you, and many *s* . . . 1 Cor 11:30
We shall not all *s* . . . . . . . . . 1 Cor 15:51

**SLEEPERS**
gently the lips of *s* . . . . . . . . . . Song 7:9

**SLEEPING**
"Are you still *s* . . . . . . . . . . . Matt 26:45

**SLEEPLESSNESS**
in labors, in *s* . . . . . . . . . . . . . . 2 Cor 6:5

**SLEEPS**
"Our friend Lazarus *s* . . . . . John 11:11

**SLEPT**
I lay down and *s* . . . . . . . . . . . . . . Ps 3:5

**SLIGHTED**
is the one who is *s* . . . . . . . . . . Prov 12:9

**SLING**
he had, and his *s* . . . . . . . . 1 Sam 17:40

**SLIP**
their foot shall *s* . . . . . . . . . . Deut 32:35

**SLIPPERY**
set them in *s* places . . . . . . . . . Ps 73:18

**SLOOPS**
all the beautiful *s* . . . . . . . . . . . . Is 2:16

**SLOW**
hear, *s* to speak, *s* . . . . . . . . . James 1:19

**SLUGGARD**
will you slumber, O *s* . . . . . . . . Prov 6:9

**SLUMBERING**
upon men, while *s* . . . . . . . . . Job 33:15

**SMALL**
And I saw the dead, *s* . . . . . . . Rev 20:12

**SMELL**
and he smelled the *s* . . . . . . . Gen 27:27

**SMELLS**
*s* the battle from afar . . . . . . . Job 39:25

**SMITTEN**
Him stricken, *s* . . . . . . . . . . . . . . Is 53:4

**SMOKE**
was filled with *s* . . . . . . . . . . . . Rev 15:8

**SMOOTH**
and the rough places *s* . . . . . . . . Is 40:4

**SMOOTH-SKINNED**
man, and I am a *s* . . . . . . . . . Gen 27:11

**SNAIL**
*s* which melts away as . . . . . . . . Ps 58:8

**SNARE**
is a fowler's *s* . . . . . . . . . . . . . . . Hos 9:8
it will come as a *s* . . . . . . . . Luke 21:35
and escape the *s* . . . . . . . . . . 2 Tim 2:26

**SNARED**
all of them are *s* . . . . . . . . . . . . Is 42:22

**SNARES**
who seek my life lay *s* . . . . . . . Ps 38:12

**SNATCH**
neither shall anyone *s* . . . . . John 10:28

**SNATCHES**
*s* away what was . . . . . . . . . Matt 13:19

**SNEER**
and you *s* at it . . . . . . . . . . . . . Mal 1:13

**SNIFFED**
they *s* at the wind . . . . . . . . . . . Jer 14:6

**SNORTING**
*s* strikes terror . . . . . . . . . . . .Job 39:20

**SNOW**
shall be whiter than *s* . . . . . . . .Ps 51:7
shall be as white as *s* . . . . . . . . .Is 1:18

**SOAKED**
their land shall be *s* . . . . . . . . . .Is 34:7

**SOAP**
lye, and use much *s*. . . . . . . . . .Jer 2:22

**SOBER**
the older men be *s* . . . . . . . . . .Titus 2:2

**SOBERLY**
think, but to think *s*. . . . . . . .Rom 12:3

**SODA**
and like vinegar on *s* . . . . . .Prov 25:20

**SODOMITES**
nor homosexuals, nor *s* . . . . . .1 Cor 6:9

**SOJOURNER**
But no *s* had to lodge . . . . . . .Job 31:32

**SOJOURNERS**
are strangers and *s* . . . . . . . .Lev 25:23

**SOLD**
*s* his birthright . . . . . . . . . . .Gen 25:33
*s* all that he had. . . . . . . . . .Matt 13:46
but I am carnal, *s*. . . . . . . . . .Rom 7:14

**SOLDIER**
hardship as a good *s*. . . . . . . .2 Tim 2:3

**SOLDIERS**
*s* twisted a crown. . . . . . . . .John 19:2

**SOLITARILY**
heritage, who dwell *s*. . . . . . . .Mic 7:14

**SOLITARY**
God sets the *s* in. . . . . . . . . . . .Ps 68:6

**SOMEBODY**
up, claiming to be *s* . . . . . . . .Acts 5:36

**SOMETHING**
thinks himself to be *s* . . . . . . . .Gal 6:3

**SON**
Me, 'You are My *S* . . . . . . . . . . . .Ps 2:7
is born, unto us a *S*. . . . . . . . . . . .Is 9:6
fourth is like the *S* . . . . . . . . .Dan 3:25
will bring forth a *S* . . . . . . . .Matt 1:21
"This is My beloved *S* . . . . . .Matt 3:17
Jesus, You *S* of God . . . . . . . .Matt 8:29
are the Christ, the *S* . . . . . .Matt 16:16
Whose *S* is He . . . . . . . . . . .Matt 22:42
coming of the *S* of Man . . . .Matt 24:37
'I am the *S* of God . . . . . . . .Matt 27:43
of Jesus Christ, the *S* . . . . . . .Mark 1:1
out, the only *s* . . . . . . . . . . . .Luke 7:12
The only begotten *S*. . . . . . . . .John 1:18
that this is the *S* . . . . . . . . . .John 1:34
of the only begotten *S* . . . . . .John 3:18
*S* can do nothing . . . . . . . . . .John 5:19
*s* abides forever . . . . . . . . . .John 8:35
you believe in the *S* . . . . . . . .John 9:35
I said, 'I am the *S*. . . . . . . . .John 10:36
"Woman, behold your *s* . . . .John 19:26
Jesus Christ is the *S*. . . . . . . .Acts 8:37
by sending His own *S*. . . . . . . .Rom 8:3
not spare His own *S* . . . . . . . .Rom 8:32
live by faith in the *S* . . . . . . . .Gal 2:20
God sent forth His *S* . . . . . . . . .Gal 4:4
the knowledge of the *S* . . . . . .Eph 4:13
*"You are My S* . . . . . . . . . . . . . .Heb 1:5
though He was a *S*. . . . . . . . . . .Heb 5:8
but made like the *S*. . . . . . . . . .Heb 7:3
"This is My beloved *S* . . . . . .2 Pet 1:17
Whoever denies the *S* . . . . .1 John 2:23
One like the *S* of Man . . . . . . .Rev 1:13

**SONG**
Sing to Him a new *s*. . . . . . . . . .Ps 33:3
He has put a new *s*. . . . . . . . . . .Ps 40:3
I will sing a new *s* . . . . . . . . . .Ps 144:9
They sang a new *s* . . . . . . . . . . .Rev 5:9

**SONGS**
my Maker, who gives *s*. . . . . .Job 35:10
and spiritual *s*. . . . . . . . . . . . .Eph 5:19

**SONS**
*s* shall come from afar . . . . . . . .Is 60:4
He will purify the *s* . . . . . . . . . .Mal 3:3
that you may become *s*. . . . .John 12:36
who are of faith are *s* . . . . . . . . .Gal 3:7
the adoption as *s* . . . . . . . . . . . .Gal 4:5
in bringing many *s* . . . . . . . . .Heb 2:10
speaks to you as to *s* . . . . . . . .Heb 12:5

**SOON**
for it is *s* cut off. . . . . . . . . . . .Ps 90:10

**SOOTHED**
or bound up, or *s* . . . . . . . . . . . . .Is 1:6

**SORCERER**
But Elymas the *s* . . . . . . . . . .Acts 13:8

**SORCERERS**
outside are dogs and *s* . . . . . .Rev 22:15

**SORCERESS**
shall not permit a *s*. . . . . . . . . .Ex 22:18

**SORCERY**
idolatry, *s*. . . . . . . . . . . . . . . . . .Gal 5:20

**SORES**
and putrefying *s* . . . . . . . . . . . . . .Is 1:6

**SORROW**
multiply your *s* . . . . . . . . . . . .Gen 3:16
*s* is continually . . . . . . . . . . . .Ps 38:17
and He adds no *s* . . . . . . . . .Prov 10:22
Your *s* is incurable . . . . . . . . .Jer 30:15
them sleeping from *s*. . . . . .Luke 22:45
*s* will be turned . . . . . . . . . . .John 16:20
*s* produces repentance. . . . . .2 Cor 7:10
*s* as others who have . . . . .1 Thess 4:13
no more death, nor *s* . . . . . . . .Rev 21:4

**SORROWFUL**
But I am poor and *s* . . . . . . . . .Ps 69:29
saying, he went away *s* . . . .Matt 19:22
soul is exceedingly *s* . . . . . .Matt 26:38
and I may be less *s* . . . . . . . . .Phil 2:28

**SORROWS**
*s* shall be multiplied . . . . . . . . .Ps 16:4
by men, a Man of *s* . . . . . . . . . . .Is 53:3
are the beginning of *s* . . . . . .Matt 24:8

**SORRY**
*s* that He had made man. . . . . .Gen 6:6
For you were made *s* . . . . . . . .2 Cor 7:9

**SOUGHT**
I *s* the LORD. . . . . . . . . . . . . . . . .Ps 34:4
*s* what was lost . . . . . . . . . . .Ezek 34:4

**SOUL**
with all your *s* . . . . . . . . . . . . .Deut 6:5
"My *s* loathes life . . . . . . . . . . .Job 10:1
*s* draws near the Pit . . . . . . . .Job 33:22
will not leave my *s*. . . . . . . . . . .Ps 16:10
converting the *s*. . . . . . . . . . . . . .Ps 19:7
He restores my *s* . . . . . . . . . . . .Ps 23:3
you cast down, O my *s* . . . . . . . .Ps 42:5
Let my *s* live . . . . . . . . . . . . .Ps 119:175
no one cares for my *s* . . . . . . . .Ps 142:4
me wrongs his own *s* . . . . . . . .Prov 8:36
When You make His *s*. . . . . . . . .Is 53:10
*s* delight itself. . . . . . . . . . . . . . .Is 55:2
the *s* of the father as. . . . . . . .Ezek 18:4
able to destroy both *s*. . . . . .Matt 10:28
and loses his own *s* . . . . . . . .Matt 16:26
*with all your s* . . . . . . . . . . .Matt 22:37
your whole spirit, *s* . . . . . . .1 Thess 5:23
to the saving of the *s* . . . . . . .Heb 10:39
his way will save a *s* . . . . . .James 5:20
health, just as your *s* . . . . . . . .3 John 2

**SOULS**
and will save the *s* . . . . . . . . . .Ps 72:13
and he who wins *s* . . . . . . . .Prov 11:30
unsettling your *s* . . . . . . . . .Acts 15:24
is able to save your *s* . . . . . .James 1:21

**SOUND**
voice was like the *s* . . . . . . . .Ezek 43:2
do not *s* a trumpet . . . . . . . . . .Matt 6:2
*s* words which you . . . . . . . .2 Tim 1:13

**SOUNDNESS**
him this perfect *s* . . . . . . . . . .Acts 3:16

**SOUNDS**
a distinction in the *s* . . . . . . .1 Cor 14:7

**SOW**
*s* trouble reap . . . . . . . . . . . . . . .Job 4:8
Those who *s* in tears . . . . . . . .Ps 126:5
Blessed are you who *s*. . . . . . . .Is 32:20
"They *s* the wind . . . . . . . . . . . .Hos 8:7
*s* is not made alive. . . . . . . .1 Cor 15:36

**SOWER**
"Behold, a *s* went. . . . . . . . . .Matt 13:3

**SOWN**
*s* spiritual things . . . . . . . . .1 Cor 9:11
of righteousness is *s* . . . . . .James 3:18

**SOWS**
*s* the good seed is the . . . . .Matt 13:37
'One *s* and another. . . . . . . . .John 4:37
for whatever a man *s* . . . . . . . . .Gal 6:7

**SPARE**
He who did not *s* . . . . . . . . . . .Rom 8:32
if God did not *s*. . . . . . . . . . . . .2 Pet 2:4

**SPARES**
*s* his rod hates his . . . . . . . .Prov 13:24

**SPARK**
the work of it as a *s* . . . . . . . . . . .Is 1:31

**SPARKLES**
it is red, when it *s*. . . . . . . . .Prov 23:31

**SPARKS**
to trouble, as the *s* . . . . . . . . . . .Job 5:7

**SPARROW**
*s* has found a home. . . . . . . . . . .Ps 84:3

**SPARROWS**
more value than many *s* . . .Matt 10:31

**SPAT**
Then they *s* on Him . . . . . . .Matt 27:30

**SPEAK**
only the word that I *s*. . . . . .Num 22:35
oh, that God would *s*. . . . . . . . .Job 11:5
and a time to *s*. . . . . . . . . . . . . .Eccl 3:7
*s* anymore in His name. . . . . . .Jer 20:9
or what you should *s* . . . . . .Matt 10:19
to you when all men *s* . . . . . .Luke 6:26
*s* what I have seen . . . . . . . . .John 8:38
He hears He will *s* . . . . . . . .John 16:13
Spirit and began to *s* . . . . . . . .Acts 2:4
So *s* and so do as. . . . . . . . . .James 2:12

**SPEAKING**
envy, and all evil *s* . . . . . . . . . .1 Pet 2:1

**SPEAKS**
to face, as a man *s* . . . . . . . . . .Ex 33:11
He whom God has sent *s* . . . .John 3:34
When he *s* a lie. . . . . . . . . . . .John 8:44
he being dead still *s* . . . . . . . .Heb 11:4
of sprinkling that *s* . . . . . . . .Heb 12:24

**SPEAR**
His side with a *s*. . . . . . . . . . .John 19:34

**SPEARS**
and their *s* into ... Is 2:4

**SPECK**
do you look at the *s* ... Matt 7:3

**SPECTACLE**
you were made a *s* ... Heb 10:33

**SPEECH**
one language and one *s* ... Gen 11:1
and his *s* contemptible ... 2 Cor 10:10
*s* always be with grace ... Col 4:6

**SPEECHLESS**
your mouth for the *s* ... Prov 31:8

**SPEED**
they shall come with *s* ... Is 5:26

**SPEEDILY**
I call, answer me *s* ... Ps 102:2

**SPEND**
Why do you *s* money for ... Is 55:2
amiss, that you may *s* ... James 4:3

**SPENT**
"But when he had *s* ... Luke 15:14

**SPEW**
nor hot, I will *s* ... Rev 3:16

**SPIDER**
*s* skillfully grasps ... Prov 30:28

**SPIES**
men who had been *s* ... Josh 6:23

**SPIN**
neither toil nor *s* ... Matt 6:28

**SPINDLE**
her hand holds the *s* ... Prov 31:19

**SPIRIT**
And the *S* of God was ... Gen 1:2
*S* shall not strive ... Gen 6:3
*S* that is upon you and ... Num 11:17
portion of your *s* ... 2 Kin 2:9
Then a *s* passed before ... Job 4:15
hand I commit my *s* ... Ps 31:5
The *s* of a man is the ... Prov 20:27
*s* will return to God ... Eccl 12:7
*S* has gathered them ... Is 34:16
I have put My *S* ... Is 42:1
"The *S* of the Lord ... Is 61:1
*S* entered me when He ... Ezek 2:2
new heart and a new *s* ... Ezek 18:31
"I will put My *S* ... Ezek 36:27
walk in a false *s* ... Mic 2:11
and He saw the *S* ... Matt 3:16
*I will put My S* ... Matt 12:18
*S* descending upon Him ... Mark 1:10
*s* indeed is willing ... Mark 14:38
go before Him in the *s* ... Luke 1:17
manner of *s* you are of ... Luke 9:55
*hands I commit My s* ... Luke 23:46
they had seen a *s* ... Luke 24:37
"God is *S* ... John 4:24
I speak to you are *s* ... John 6:63
"the *S* of truth ... John 14:17
but if a *s* or an angel ... Acts 23:9
the flesh but in the *S* ... Rom 8:9
does not have the *S* ... Rom 8:9
*s* that we are children ... Rom 8:16
what the mind of the *S* ... Rom 8:27
to us through His *S* ... 1 Cor 2:10
gifts, but the same *S* ... 1 Cor 12:4
but the *S* gives life ... 2 Cor 3:6
Now the Lord is the *S* ... 2 Cor 3:17
Having begun in the *S* ... Gal 3:3
has sent forth the *S* ... Gal 4:6
with the Holy *S* ... Eph 1:13
the unity of the *S* ... Eph 4:3
stand fast in one *s* ... Phil 1:27
*S* expressly says that ... 1 Tim 4:1
*S* who dwells in us ... James 4:5
made alive by the *S* ... 1 Pet 3:18
do not believe every *s* ... 1 John 4:1
By this you know the *S* ... 1 John 4:2
has given us of His *S* ... 1 John 4:13
*S* who bears witness ... 1 John 5:6
not having the *S* ... Jude 19
I was in the *S* on the ... Rev 1:10
him hear what the *S* ... Rev 2:7
And the *S* and the ... Rev 22:17

**SPIRITS**
who makes His angels *s* ... Ps 104:4
heed to deceiving *s* ... 1 Tim 4:1

**SPIRITUAL**
*s* judges all things ... 1 Cor 2:15
However, the *s* is not ... 1 Cor 15:46
*s* restore such a one ... Gal 6:1

**SPIRITUALLY**
*s* minded is life ... Rom 8:6

**SPITEFULLY**
for those who *s* ... Matt 5:44

**SPITTING**
face from shame and *s* ... Is 50:6

**SPLENDOR**
on the glorious *s* ... Ps 145:5

**SPOIL**
He shall divide the *s* ... Is 53:12

**SPOILER**
I have created the *s* ... Is 54:16

**SPOKE**
"No man ever *s* ... John 7:46
I was a child, I *s* ... 1 Cor 13:11
in various ways *s* ... Heb 1:1
*s* as they were moved ... 2 Pet 1:21

**SPOKEN**
I have not *s* in secret ... Is 45:19
why am I evil *s* ... 1 Cor 10:30

**SPOKESMAN**
So he shall be your *s* ... Ex 4:16

**SPONGE**
them ran and took a *s* ... Matt 27:48

**SPOT**
church, not having *s* ... Eph 5:27
Himself without *s* ... Heb 9:14

**SPOTS**
These are *s* in your ... Jude 12

**SPREAD**
Then the word of God *s* ... Acts 6:7

**SPREADS**
*s* them out like a tent ... Is 40:22

**SPRING**
Truth shall *s* out of ... Ps 85:11
*s* send forth fresh ... James 3:11

**SPRINGING**
a fountain of water *s* ... John 4:14

**SPRINGS**
and the thirsty land *s* ... Is 35:7

**SPRINKLE**
"Then I will *s* ... Ezek 36:25

**SPRINKLED**
having our hearts *s* ... Heb 10:22

**SPRINKLING**
*s* that speaks ... Heb 12:24

**SPROUT**
and the seed should *s* ... Mark 4:27

**SQUARES**
voice in the open *s* ... Prov 1:20

**STAFF**
this Jordan with my *s* ... Gen 32:10
Your rod and Your *s* ... Ps 23:4
on the top of his *s* ... Heb 11:21

**STAGGER**
they will drink and *s* ... Jer 25:16

**STAGGERS**
as a drunken man *s* ... Is 19:14

**STAKES**
*s* will ever be removed ... Is 33:20

**STALLS**
be no herd in the *s* ... Hab 3:17

**STAMMERERS**
*s* will be ready ... Is 32:4

**STAMMERING**
*s* tongue that you ... Is 33:19

**STAMPING**
At the noise of the *s* ... Jer 47:3

**STAND**
one shall be able to *s* ... Deut 7:24
lives, and He shall *s* ... Job 19:25
ungodly shall not *s* ... Ps 1:5
not lack a man to *s* ... Jer 35:19
And who can *s* when He ... Mal 3:2
that kingdom cannot *s* ... Mark 3:24
he will be made to *s* ... Rom 14:4
Watch, *s* fast in the ... 1 Cor 16:13
for by faith you *s* ... 2 Cor 1:24
having done all, to *s* ... Eph 6:13
*S* therefore ... Eph 6:14
of God in which you *s* ... 1 Pet 5:12
"Behold, I *s* at the ... Rev 3:20

**STANDARD**
LORD will lift up a *s* ... Is 59:19

**STANDING**
they love to pray *s* ... Matt 6:5
and the Son of Man *s* ... Acts 7:56

**STANDS**
him who thinks he *s* ... 1 Cor 10:12

**STAR**
For we have seen His *s* ... Matt 2:2
Bright and Morning *S* ... Rev 22:16

**STARS**
He made the *s* also ... Gen 1:16
born as many as the *s* ... Heb 11:12

**STATE**
learned in whatever *s* ... Phil 4:11

**STATURE**
in wisdom and *s* ... Luke 2:52

**STATUTE**
shall be a perpetual *s* ... Lev 3:17

**STATUTES**
the *s* of the LORD are ... Ps 19:8
Teach me Your *s* ... Ps 119:12

**STAY**
*S* here and watch with ... Matt 26:38

**STEADFAST**
beloved brethren, be *s* ... 1 Cor 15:58
soul, both sure and *s* ... Heb 6:19
Resist him, *s* in the ... 1 Pet 5:9

**STEADFASTLY**
*s* set His face to go ... Luke 9:51
And they continued *s* ... Acts 2:42

**STEADFASTNESS**
good order and the *s* ... Col 2:5

**STEADILY**
could not look *s* . . . . . 2 Cor 3:13

**STEADY**
and his hands were *s* . . . . . Ex 17:12

**STEAL**
"You shall not *s* . . . . . Ex 20:15
thieves break in and *s* . . . . . Matt 6:19
night and *s* Him away . . . . . Matt 27:64

**STEM**
forth a Rod from the *s* . . . . . Is 11:1

**STENCH**
there will be a *s* . . . . . Is 3:24
this time there is a *s* . . . . . John 11:39

**STEP**
*s* has turned from the . . . . . Job 31:7

**STEPS**
The *s* of a good man . . . . . Ps 37:23
and established my *s* . . . . . Ps 40:2
the LORD directs his *s* . . . . . Prov 16:9
should follow His *s* . . . . . 1 Pet 2:21

**STEWARD**
be blameless, as a *s* . . . . . Titus 1:7

**STEWARDS**
of Christ and *s* . . . . . 1 Cor 4:1

**STEWARDSHIP**
entrusted with a *s* . . . . . 1 Cor 9:17

**STICK**
'For Joseph, the *s* . . . . . Ezek 37:16

**STICKS**
a man gathering *s* . . . . . Num 15:32

**STIFF**
rebellion and your *s* . . . . . Deut 31:27

**STIFF-NECKED**
"You *s* and . . . . . Acts 7:51

**STILL**
When I awake, I am *s* . . . . . Ps 139:18
sea, "Peace, be *s* . . . . . Mark 4:39

**STILLBORN**
burial, I say that a *s* . . . . . Eccl 6:3

**STINGS**
like a serpent, and *s* . . . . . Prov 23:32

**STIR**
I remind you to *s* . . . . . 2 Tim 1:6

**STIRRED**
So the LORD *s* up the . . . . . Hag 1:14

**STIRS**
it *s* up the dead for . . . . . Is 14:9

**STOCKS**
*s* that were in the . . . . . Jer 20:2

**STOIC**
and *S* philosophers . . . . . Acts 17:18

**STOMACH**
Foods for the *s* . . . . . 1 Cor 6:13

**STOMACH'S**
little wine for your *s* . . . . . 1 Tim 5:23

**STONE**
him, a pillar of *s* . . . . . Gen 35:14
*s* shall be a witness . . . . . Josh 24:27
*s* which the builders . . . . . Ps 118:22
I lay in Zion a *s* . . . . . Is 28:16
take the heart of *s* . . . . . Ezek 36:26
will give him a *s* . . . . . Matt 7:9
*s* will be broken . . . . . Matt 21:44
*s which the builders* . . . . . Luke 20:17
those works do you *s* . . . . . John 10:32
Him as to a living *s* . . . . . 1 Pet 2:4

**STONED**
*s* Stephen as he was . . . . . Acts 7:59
They were *s* . . . . . Heb 11:37

**STONES**
Abraham from these *s* . . . . . Matt 3:9
command that these *s* . . . . . Matt 4:3

**STONY**
Some fell on *s* ground . . . . . Mark 4:5

**STOOPED**
And again He *s* down . . . . . John 8:8

**STOPPED**
her flow of blood *s* . . . . . Luke 8:44

**STORE**
exist are kept in *s* . . . . . 2 Pet 3:7

**STORK**
*s* has her home in the . . . . . Ps 104:17

**STORM**
He calms the *s* . . . . . Ps 107:29
for a shelter from *s* . . . . . Is 4:6

**STRAIGHT**
make *s* in the desert a . . . . . Is 40:3
and make *s* paths for . . . . . Heb 12:13

**STRAIGHTFORWARD**
that they were not *s* . . . . . Gal 2:14

**STRAIN**
"Blind guides, who *s* . . . . . Matt 23:24

**STRAITS**
and desperate *s* . . . . . Deut 28:53

**STRANGE**
*s* thing happened . . . . . 1 Pet 4:12

**STRANGER**
and loves the *s* . . . . . Deut 10:18
I was a *s* and you took . . . . . Matt 25:35

**STRANGERS**
know the voice of *s* . . . . . John 10:5
you are no longer *s* . . . . . Eph 2:19

**STRANGLING**
that my soul chooses *s* . . . . . Job 7:15

**STRAP**
than I, whose sandal *s* . . . . . Mark 1:7

**STRAW**
stones, wood, hay, *s* . . . . . 1 Cor 3:12

**STRAY**
who make my people *s* . . . . . Mic 3:5

**STRAYED**
yet I have not *s* . . . . . Ps 119:110
for which some have *s* . . . . . 1 Tim 6:10

**STREAM**
like a flowing *s* . . . . . Is 66:12

**STREAMS**
He also brought *s* . . . . . Ps 78:16

**STREET**
In the middle of its *s* . . . . . Rev 22:2

**STREETS**
You taught in our *s* . . . . . Luke 13:26

**STRENGTH**
*s* no man shall . . . . . 1 Sam 2:9
The LORD is the *s* . . . . . Ps 27:1
is our refuge and *s* . . . . . Ps 46:1
They go from *s* to . . . . . Ps 84:7
*S* and honor are her . . . . . Prov 31:25
might He increases *s* . . . . . Is 40:29
O LORD, my *s* and my . . . . . Jer 16:19
were still without *s* . . . . . Rom 5:6
*s* is made perfect . . . . . 2 Cor 12:9

**STRENGTHEN**
and He shall *s* . . . . . Ps 27:14
*S* the weak hands . . . . . Is 35:3
*s* your brethren . . . . . Luke 22:32
*s* the things . . . . . Rev 3:2

**STRENGTHENED**
unbelief, but was *s* . . . . . Rom 4:20
stood with me and *s* . . . . . 2 Tim 4:17

**STRENGTHENING**
*s* the souls of the . . . . . Acts 14:22

**STRENGTHENS**
through Christ who *s* . . . . . Phil 4:13

**STRETCH**
are old, you will *s* . . . . . John 21:18

**STRETCHED**
I have *s* out my hands . . . . . Ps 88:9
*"All day long I have s* . . . . . Rom 10:21

**STRETCHES**
For he *s* out his hand . . . . . Job 15:25

**STRICKEN**
of My people He was *s* . . . . . Is 53:8

**STRIFE**
man stirs up *s* . . . . . Prov 15:18
even from envy and *s* . . . . . Phil 1:15
which come envy, *s* . . . . . 1 Tim 6:4

**STRIKE**
The sun shall not *s* . . . . . Ps 121:6
"*S* the Shepherd . . . . . Zech 13:7
*'I will s the Shepherd* . . . . . Matt 26:31

**STRINGED**
of your *s* instruments . . . . . Amos 5:23

**STRIP**
*s* yourselves . . . . . Is 32:11

**STRIPES**
*s* we are healed . . . . . Is 53:5
*s* you were healed . . . . . 1 Pet 2:24

**STRIVE**
My Spirit shall not *s* . . . . . Gen 6:3
"*S* to enter through . . . . . Luke 13:24
the Lord not to *s* . . . . . 2 Tim 2:14

**STRIVING**
for a man to stop *s* . . . . . Prov 20:3

**STROKE**
with a mighty *s* . . . . . Jer 14:17

**STRONG**
The LORD *s* and mighty . . . . . Ps 24:8
*s* is Your hand . . . . . Ps 89:13
"When a *s* man . . . . . Luke 11:21
We then who are *s* . . . . . Rom 15:1
I am weak, then I am *s* . . . . . 2 Cor 12:10
my brethren, be *s* . . . . . Eph 6:10
weakness were made *s* . . . . . Heb 11:34

**STRONGHOLD**
of my salvation, my *s* . . . . . Ps 18:2

**STRUCK**
*s* the rock twice . . . . . Num 20:11
the hand of God has *s* . . . . . Job 19:21
Behold, He *s* the rock . . . . . Ps 78:20
in My wrath I *s* . . . . . Is 60:10
*s* the head from the . . . . . Hab 3:13
took the reed and *s* . . . . . Matt 27:30

**STUBBLE**
do wickedly will be *s* . . . . . Mal 4:1

**STUBBORN**
If a man has a *s* . . . . . Deut 21:18

**STUBBORN-HEARTED**
"Listen to Me, you *s* . . . . . Is 46:12

**STUBBORNNESS**
do not look on the *s* . . . . . Deut 9:27

**STUDIED**
having never *s* . . . . . . . . . . . .John 7:15

**STUMBLE**
have caused many to *s* . . . . . . .Mal 2:8
you will be made to *s* . . . . . .Matt 26:31
immediately they *s*. . . . . . . . .Mark 4:17
who believe in Me to *s*. . . . . .Mark 9:42
For we all *s* in many . . . . . . .James 3:2

**STUMBLED**
*s* that they should. . . . . . . . .Rom 11:11

**STUMBLES**
word, immediately he *s* . . . .Matt 13:21

**STUMBLING**
but a stone of *s* . . . . . . . . . . . . . .Is 8:14
Behold, I will lay *s* . . . . . . . . . .Jer 6:21
*I lay in Zion a s*. . . . . . . . . . . .Rom 9:33
this, not to put a *s*. . . . . . . . . .Rom 14:13
of yours become a *s* . . . . . . . . .1 Cor 8:9
and *"A stone of s* . . . . . . . . . . .1 Pet 2:8
to keep you from *s* . . . . . . . . . . .Jude 24

**STUMBLINGBLOCK**
the deaf, nor put a *s* . . . . . . . .Lev 19:14

**STUPID**
who hates correction is *s* . . . .Prov 12:1

**SUBDUE**
*s* all things to . . . . . . . . . . . . .Phil 3:21

**SUBJECT**
for it is not *s* . . . . . . . . . . . . . . .Rom 8:7
Let every soul be *s* . . . . . . . . .Rom 13:1
all their lifetime *s* . . . . . . . . . .Heb 2:15

**SUBJECTED**
because of Him who *s*. . . . . . .Rom 8:20

**SUBJECTION**
*put all things in s* . . . . . . . . . . .Heb 2:8

**SUBMISSION**
his children in *s* . . . . . . . . . . .1 Tim 3:4

**SUBMISSIVE**
Yes, all of you be *s* . . . . . . . . . .1 Pet 5:5

**SUBMIT**
Therefore *s* to God . . . . . . . . .James 4:7
*s* yourselves to every . . . . . . .1 Pet 2:13

**SUBSIDED**
and the waters *s* . . . . . . . . . . . .Gen 8:1

**SUBSTANCE**
Bless his *s* . . . . . . . . . . . . . .Deut 33:11

**SUCCESS**
please give me *s* . . . . . . . . . .Gen 24:12
but wisdom brings *s* . . . . . . .Eccl 10:10

**SUCCESSFUL**
Joseph, and he was a *s*. . . . . . .Gen 39:2

**SUDDENLY**
*s* there was with the . . . . . . .Luke 2:13

**SUE**
*s* you and take away. . . . . . . .Matt 5:40

**SUFFER**
for the Christ to *s* . . . . . . . .Luke 24:46
Christ, if indeed we *s* . . . . . . .Rom 8:17
in Him, but also to *s* . . . . . . . .Phil 1:29

**SUFFERED**
*s* these things and to . . . . . .Luke 24:26
for whom I have *s* . . . . . . . . . . .Phil 3:8
after you have *s* . . . . . . . . . . .1 Pet 5:10

**SUFFERING**
Is anyone among you *s* . . . .James 5:13

**SUFFERINGS**
I consider that the *s* . . . . . . . .Rom 8:18
perfect through *s*. . . . . . . . . . .Heb 2:10

**SUFFERS**
Love *s* long and is . . . . . . . . .1 Cor 13:4

**SUFFICIENCY**
but our *s* is from God. . . . . . . .2 Cor 3:5

**SUFFICIENT**
*S* for the day is its . . . . . . . . .Matt 6:34

**SUM**
How great is the *s* . . . . . . . . .Ps 139:17

**SUMMED**
commandment, are all *s*. . . . .Rom 13:9

**SUMMER**
and heat, winter and *s* . . . . . .Gen 8:22

**SUMPTUOUSLY**
fine linen and fared *s* . . . . .Luke 16:19

**SUN**
So the *s* stood still. . . . . . . . .Josh 10:13
*s* shall not strike you . . . . . . . .Ps 121:6
*s* returned ten degrees . . . . . . . .Is 38:8
the *s* and moon grow . . . . . . . .Joel 2:10
*s* shall go down on the . . . . . . . .Mic 3:6
for He makes His *s*. . . . . . . . .Matt 5:45
the *s* was darkened . . . . . . .Luke 23:45
do not let the *s* . . . . . . . . . . . . .Eph 4:26
*s* became black as . . . . . . . . . .Rev 6:12
had no need of the *s* . . . . . . . .Rev 21:23

**SUPPER**
to eat the Lord's *S* . . . . . . . .1 Cor 11:20
took the cup after *s* . . . . . . .1 Cor 11:25
together for the *s* . . . . . . . . . .Rev 19:17

**SUPPLICATION**
by prayer and *s* . . . . . . . . . . . . .Phil 4:6

**SUPPLIES**
by what every joint *s*. . . . . . . .Eph 4:16

**SUPPLY**
And my God shall *s* . . . . . . . .Phil 4:19

**SUPPORT**
this, that you must *s*. . . . . . .Acts 20:35

**SUPREME**
to the king as *s*. . . . . . . . . . . .1 Pet 2:13

**SURE**
*s* your sin will find. . . . . . . .Num 32:23
call and election *s* . . . . . . . . .2 Pet 1:10

**SURETY**
Be *s* for Your servant . . . . . .Ps 119:122
Jesus has become a *s*. . . . . . . .Heb 7:22

**SURROUND**
LORD, mercy shall *s* . . . . . . . .Ps 32:10

**SURROUNDED**
also, since we are *s* . . . . . . . . .Heb 12:1

**SURVIVOR**
was no refugee or *s*. . . . . . . . .Lam 2:22

**SUSPICIONS**
reviling, evil *s*. . . . . . . . . . . . .1 Tim 6:4

**SUSTAIN**
*S* me with cakes of. . . . . . . . . .Song 2:5

**SWADDLING**
Him in *s* cloths . . . . . . . . . . . .Luke 2:7

**SWALLOW**
a gnat and *s* a camel . . . . . .Matt 23:24

**SWEAR**
'You shall not *s*. . . . . . . . . . . .Matt 5:33
began to curse and *s* . . . . . .Matt 26:74

**SWEARING**
By *s* and lying . . . . . . . . . . . . . .Hos 4:2

**SWEARS**
but whoever *s* by the . . . . . .Matt 23:18

**SWEAT**
Then His *s* became like. . . .Luke 22:44

**SWEET**
*s* are Your words. . . . . . . . . .Ps 119:103
but it will be as *s* . . . . . . . . . . .Rev 10:9

**SWEETNESS**
mouth like honey in *s* . . . . . . .Ezek 3:3

**SWELLING**
they speak great *s* . . . . . . . . .2 Pet 2:18

**SWIFT**
let every man be *s* . . . . . . . .James 1:19

**SWIM**
night I make my bed *s*. . . . . . . . .Ps 6:6

**SWOON**
as they *s* like the. . . . . . . . . . .Lam 2:12

**SWORD**
*s* which turned every . . . . . . .Gen 3:24
The *s* of the LORD is . . . . . . . . . .Is 34:6
'A *s* is sharpened . . . . . . . . . .Ezek 21:9
Bow and *s* of battle I . . . . . . . . .Hos 2:18
to bring peace but a *s*. . . . . .Matt 10:34
for all who take the *s* . . . . . .Matt 26:52
the *s* of the Spirit. . . . . . . . . . .Eph 6:17
than any two-edged *s* . . . . . . .Heb 4:12
mouth goes a sharp *s*. . . . . . .Rev 19:15

**SWORDS**
shall beat their *s*. . . . . . . . . . . . . .Is 2:4

**SWORE**
*So I s in My wrath* . . . . . . . . . .Heb 3:11

**SWORN**
By Myself I have *s*. . . . . . . . .Gen 22:16
*"The LORD has s* . . . . . . . . . . .Heb 7:21

**SYMBOLIC**
which things are *s* . . . . . . . . . .Gal 4:24

**SYMPATHIZE**
Priest who cannot *s*. . . . . . . . .Heb 4:15

**SYMPATHY**
My *s* is stirred . . . . . . . . . . . . .Hos 11:8

**SYNAGOGUE**
but are a *s* of Satan . . . . . . . . . .Rev 2:9

## T

**TABERNACLE**
*t* He shall hide me . . . . . . . . . . .Ps 27:5
I will abide in Your *t* . . . . . . . . .Ps 61:4
*and will rebuild the t* . . . . . .Acts 15:16
and more perfect *t* . . . . . . . . . .Heb 9:11

**TABERNACLES**
Feast of *T* was at hand. . . . . . .John 7:2

**TABLE**
prepare a *t* before me . . . . . . . . .Ps 23:5
dogs under the *t* . . . . . . . . . .Mark 7:28
of the Lord's *t*. . . . . . . . . . . .1 Cor 10:21

**TABLES**
and overturned the *t* . . . . . .Matt 21:12

**TABLET**
is engraved on the *t*. . . . . . . . . .Jer 17:1

**TAIL**
*t* drew a third of the . . . . . . . . .Rev 12:4

**TAKE**
*t* Your Holy Spirit. . . . . . . . . . .Ps 51:11
*T* My yoke upon you and . . .Matt 11:29
and *t* up his cross . . . . . . . . .Mark 8:34
My life that I may *t* . . . . . . . .John 10:17

**TAKEN**
He was *t* from prison. . . . . . . . . .Is 53:8

one will be *t* and the ... Matt 24:40
until He is *t* out of ... 2 Thess 2:7

**TALEBEARER**
*t* reveals secrets ... Prov 11:13

**TALENT**
went and hid your *t* ... Matt 25:25

**TALK**
shall *t* of them when ... Deut 6:7

**TALKED**
within us while He *t* ... Luke 24:32

**TALKERS**
both idle *t* and ... Titus 1:10

**TAMBOURINE**
The mirth of the *t* ... Is 24:8

**TARES**
the *t* also appeared ... Matt 13:26

**TARGET**
You set me as Your *t* ... Job 7:20

**TARRY**
*come and will not t* ... Heb 10:37

**TASK**
this burdensome *t* ... Eccl 1:13

**TASTE**
Oh, *t* and see that the ... Ps 34:8
might *t* death for ... Heb 2:9

**TASTED**
*t* the heavenly gift ... Heb 6:4

**TAUGHT**
as His counselor has *t* ... Is 40:13
from man, nor was I *t* ... Gal 1:12

**TAUNT**
and a byword, a *t* ... Jer 24:9

**TAX**
*t* collectors do the ... Matt 5:46

**TAXES**
*t* to whom *t* ... Rom 13:7

**TEACH**
"Can anyone *t* ... Job 21:22
*t* me Your paths ... Ps 25:4
*t* you the fear of the ... Ps 34:11
*t* transgressors Your ... Ps 51:13
So *t* us to number our ... Ps 90:12
*t* you again the first ... Heb 5:12

**TEACHER**
for One is your *T* ... Matt 23:8
know that You are a *t* ... John 3:2
named Gamaliel, a *t* ... Acts 5:34
a *t* of the Gentiles in ... 1 Tim 2:7

**TEACHERS**
understanding than all my *t* . Ps 119:99
prophets, third *t* ... 1 Cor 12:28
and some pastors and *t* ... Eph 4:11
desiring to be *t* ... 1 Tim 1:7
there will be false *t* ... 2 Pet 2:1

**TEACHES**
the Holy Spirit *t* ... 1 Cor 2:13
the same anointing *t* ... 1 John 2:27

**TEACHING**
*t* them to observe all ... Matt 28:20
*t* every man in all ... Col 1:28

**TEAR**
I, even I, will *t* ... Hos 5:14
will wipe away every *t* ... Rev 21:4

**TEARS**
my couch with my *t* ... Ps 6:6
mindful of your *t* ... 2 Tim 1:4
it diligently with *t* ... Heb 12:17

**TEETH**
You have broken the *t* ... Ps 3:7

**TELL**
"Who can *t* if God ... Jon 3:9
*t* him his fault ... Matt 18:15
whatever they *t* ... Matt 23:3
He comes, He will *t* ... John 4:25

**TEMPERATE**
prize is *t* in all ... 1 Cor 9:25
husband of one wife, *t* ... 1 Tim 3:2

**TEMPEST**
And suddenly a great *t* ... Matt 8:24

**TEMPLE**
So Solomon built the *t* ... 1 Kin 6:14
LORD is in His holy *t* ... Ps 11:4
One greater than the *t* ... Matt 12:6
"Destroy this *t* ... John 2:19
your body is the *t* ... 1 Cor 6:19
grows into a holy *t* ... Eph 2:21
sits as God in the *t* ... 2 Thess 2:4
and the Lamb are its *t* ... Rev 21:22

**TEMPLES**
*t* made with hands ... Acts 7:48

**TEMPORARY**
which are seen are *t* ... 2 Cor 4:18

**TEMPT**
*t the LORD your God* ... Matt 4:7
nor does He Himself *t* ... James 1:13

**TEMPTATION**
do not lead us into *t* ... Matt 6:13
the man who endures *t* ... James 1:12

**TEMPTED**
forty days, *t* by Satan ... Mark 1:13
lest you also be *t* ... Gal 6:1
in all points *t* ... Heb 4:15

**TEMPTER**
Now when the *t* came to ... Matt 4:3

**TENDER**
your heart was *t* ... 2 Kin 22:19

**TENDERHEARTED**
to one another, *t* ... Eph 4:32

**TENDS**
*t* a flock and does not ... 1 Cor 9:7

**TENT**
earthly house, this *t* ... 2 Cor 5:1

**TENTMAKERS**
occupation they were *t* ... Acts 18:3

**TENTS**
than dwell in the *t* ... Ps 84:10

**TERRESTRIAL**
bodies and *t* bodies ... 1 Cor 15:40

**TERRIBLE**
is great and very *t* ... Joel 2:11

**TERRIFIED**
and not in any way *t* ... Phil 1:28

**TERRIFY**
me with dreams and *t* ... Job 7:14

**TERRIFYING**
*t* was the sight ... Heb 12:21

**TERROR**
are nothing, you see *t* ... Job 6:21
not be afraid of the *t* ... Ps 91:5

**TERRORS**
consumed with *t* ... Ps 73:19

**TEST**
said, "Why do you *t* ... Matt 22:18
*T* all things ... 1 Thess 5:21
but *t* the spirits ... 1 John 4:1

**TESTAMENT**
where there is a *t* ... Heb 9:16

**TESTED**
God *t* Abraham ... Gen 22:1
*where your fathers t* ... Heb 3:9
though it is *t* by fire ... 1 Pet 1:7

**TESTIFIED**
he who has seen has *t* ... John 19:35
of God which He has *t* ... 1 John 5:9

**TESTIFIES**
that the Holy Spirit *t* ... Acts 20:23

**TESTIFY**
*t* what We have ... John 3:11
*t* that the Father ... 1 John 4:14

**TESTIFYING**
was righteous, God *t* ... Heb 11:4

**TESTIMONIES**
those who keep His *t* ... Ps 119:2
*t* are my meditation ... Ps 119:99

**TESTIMONY**
two tablets of the *T* ... Ex 31:18
under your feet as a *t* ... Mark 6:11
no one receives His *t* ... John 3:32
has not believed the *t* ... 1 John 5:10
For the *t* of Jesus is ... Rev 19:10

**TESTING**
came to Him, *t* Him ... Matt 19:3

**TESTS**
men, but God who *t* ... 1 Thess 2:4

**THANK**
"I *t* You, Father ... Matt 11:25
*t* You that I am not ... Luke 18:11

**THANKFUL**
Him as God, nor were *t* ... Rom 1:21

**THANKFULNESS**
Felix, with all *t* ... Acts 24:3

**THANKS**
the cup, and gave *t* ... Matt 26:27
*T* be to God for His ... 2 Cor 9:15

**THANKSGIVING**
His presence with *t* ... Ps 95:2
into His gates with *t* ... Ps 100:4
supplication, with *t* ... Phil 4:6

**THEATER**
and rushed into the *t* ... Acts 19:29

**THIEF**
do not despise a *t* ... Prov 6:30
because he was a *t* ... John 12:6
Lord will come as a *t* ... 2 Pet 3:10

**THIEVES**
and companions of *t* ... Is 1:23

**THINGS**
in heaven give good *t* ... Matt 7:11
kept all these *t* ... Luke 2:51
share in all good *t* ... Gal 6:6

**THINK**
*t* you have eternal ... John 5:39
not to *t* of himself ... Rom 12:3

**THINKS**
yet the LORD *t* upon me ... Ps 40:17
for as he *t* in his ... Prov 23:7
*t* he stands take heed ... 1 Cor 10:12

**THIRST**
those who hunger and *t* ... Matt 5:6
in Me shall never *t* ... John 6:35
anymore nor *t* anymore ... Rev 7:16

**THIRSTS**
My soul *t* for God ... Ps 42:2
saying, "If anyone *t* ... John 7:37
freely to him who *t* ... Rev 21:6

**THIRSTY**
I was *t* and you gave. . . . . . .Matt 25:35

**THISTLES**
or figs from *t* . . . . . . . . . . . . .Matt 7:16

**THORN**
a *t* in the flesh was . . . . . . . .2 Cor 12:7

**THORNBUSHES**
gather grapes from *t* . . . . . . .Matt 7:16

**THORNS**
Both *t* and thistles it . . . . . . . .Gen 3:18
And some fell among *t*. . . . . .Matt 13:7
wearing the crown of *t*. . . . . .John 19:5

**THOUGHT**
You understand my *t* . . . . . . . .Ps 139:2
I *t* as a child . . . . . . . . . . . . .1 Cor 13:11

**THOUGHTS**
The LORD knows the *t* . . . . . . .Ps 94:11
unrighteous man his *t* . . . . . . . .Is 55:7
"For My *t* are not your . . . . . . . .Is 55:8
Jesus, knowing their *t*. . . . . . .Matt 9:4
heart proceed evil *t* . . . . . . .Matt 15:19
*"The LORD knows the t*. . . . .1 Cor 3:20

**THREAT**
shall flee at the *t*. . . . . . . . . . . .Is 30:17

**THREATEN**
suffered, He did not *t* . . . . . . .1 Pet 2:23

**THREATENING**
to them, giving up *t*. . . . . . . . . .Eph 6:9

**THREATS**
still breathing *t* . . . . . . . . . . . .Acts 9:1

**THREE**
hope, love, these *t* . . . . . . . .1 Cor 13:13

**THRESH**
it is time to *t* her . . . . . . . . . . .Jer 51:33

**THRESHING**
*t* shall last till the . . . . . . . . . .Lev 26:5

**THROAT**
*t is an open tomb* . . . . . . . . . .Rom 3:13

**THRONE**
Your *t*, O God, is. . . . . . . . . . . . .Ps 45:6
Lord sitting on a *t* . . . . . . . . . . . . .Is 6:1
"Heaven is My *t* . . . . . . . . . . . . .Is 66:1
for it is God's *t* . . . . . . . . . . . .Matt 5:34
will give Him the *t* . . . . . . . .Luke 1:32
*"Your t, O God, is*. . . . . . . . . . . .Heb 1:8
come boldly to the *t* . . . . . . . . .Heb 4:16
My Father on His *t*. . . . . . . . . .Rev 3:21
I saw a great white *t* . . . . . . .Rev 20:11

**THRONES**
invisible, whether *t* . . . . . . . . .Col 1:16

**THRONG**
house of God in the *t* . . . . . . . .Ps 55:14

**THROW**
*t* Yourself down . . . . . . . . . . . .Matt 4:6

**THROWN**
neck, and he were *t*. . . . . . . .Mark 9:42

**THRUST**
and rose up and *t*. . . . . . . . . .Luke 4:29

**THUNDER**
The voice of Your *t* . . . . . . . . . .Ps 77:18
the voice of loud *t*. . . . . . . . . . .Rev 14:2

**THUNDERED**
"The LORD *t* from . . . . . . .2 Sam 22:14

**THUNDERINGS**
the sound of mighty *t*. . . . . . . .Rev 19:6

**THUNDERS**
the God of glory *t* . . . . . . . . . . .Ps 29:3

**TIDINGS**
I bring you good *t*. . . . . . . . . .Luke 2:10

**TILL**
no man to *t* the ground . . . . . . .Gen 2:5

**TILLER**
but Cain was a *t* . . . . . . . . . . . .Gen 4:2

**TILLS**
*t* his land will have. . . . . . . .Prov 28:19

**TIME**
pray to You in a *t* . . . . . . . . . . . .Ps 32:6
for the *t* is near. . . . . . . . . . . . . .Rev 1:3

**TIMES**
the signs of the *t*. . . . . . . . . . .Matt 16:3
not for you to know *t*. . . . . . . . .Acts 1:7
last days perilous *t*. . . . . . . . .2 Tim 3:1

**TITHE**
And he gave him a *t* . . . . . . .Gen 14:20
For you pay *t* of mint . . . . . .Matt 23:23

**TITHES**
and to bring the *t* . . . . . . . . .Neh 10:37
Bring all the *t* . . . . . . . . . . . . .Mal 3:10

**TITHING**
the year of *t* . . . . . . . . . . . .Deut 26:12

**TITLE**
Now Pilate wrote a *t* . . . . . .John 19:19

**TITTLE**
away, one jot or one *t* . . . . . .Matt 5:18

**TODAY**
*t* I have begotten You . . . . . . . . . .Ps 2:7
*t* you will be with Me. . . . . .Luke 23:43
*"T, if you will hear* . . . . . . . . . .Heb 3:7
the same yesterday, *t*. . . . . . . .Heb 13:8

**TOIL**
*t* you shall eat of . . . . . . . . . . .Gen 3:17

**TOILED**
"Master, we have *t*. . . . . . . . . .Luke 5:5

**TOLD**
Behold, I have *t* . . . . . . . . . . .Matt 28:7
so, I would have *t* . . . . . . . . . .John 14:2

**TOLERABLE**
you, it will be more *t* . . . . . .Matt 10:15

**TOMB**
in the garden a new *t* . . . . . .John 19:41

**TOMBS**
like whitewashed *t* . . . . . . .Matt 23:27

**TOMORROW**
drink, for *t* we die . . . . . . . . . . .Is 22:13
do not worry about *t*. . . . . . . .Matt 6:34
what will happen *t* . . . . . . .James 4:14

**TONGUE**
remember you, let my *t* . . . . . .Ps 137:6
forever, but a lying *t*. . . . . . .Prov 12:19
*t* breaks a bone . . . . . . . . . . .Prov 25:15
*t* should confess that . . . . . . . .Phil 2:11
does not bridle his *t* . . . . . . .James 1:26
no man can tame the *t*. . . . . .James 3:8
every nation, tribe, *t* . . . . . . . .Rev 14:6

**TONGUES**
from the strife of *t* . . . . . . . . . .Ps 31:20
will speak with new *t* . . . . .Mark 16:17
divided *t*, as of fire . . . . . . . . . .Acts 2:3
I speak with the *t* . . . . . . . . .1 Cor 13:1

**TOOTH**
*eye for an eye and a t* . . . . . . .Matt 5:38

**TOPHET**
the high places of *T* . . . . . . . . .Jer 7:31

**TORCH**
and like a fiery *t*. . . . . . . . . . .Zech 12:6

**TORCHES**
When he had set the *t* . . . . . .Judg 15:5
come with flaming *t* . . . . . . . . .Nah 2:3

**TORMENT**
You come here to *t* . . . . . . . . .Matt 8:29
*t* ascends forever . . . . . . . . . .Rev 14:11

**TORMENTED**
And they will be *t* . . . . . . . . .Rev 20:10

**TORMENTS**
"And being in *t* . . . . . . . . . .Luke 16:23

**TORN**
of the temple was *t*. . . . . . . .Matt 27:51

**TORTURED**
Others were *t*. . . . . . . . . . . . .Heb 11:35

**TOSSED**
*t* to and fro and . . . . . . . . . . . .Eph 4:14

**TOTTER**
drunkard, and shall *t* . . . . . . . .Is 24:20

**TOUCH**
If only I may *t*. . . . . . . . . . . . .Matt 9:21

**TOUCHED**
*t* my mouth with it . . . . . . . . . . . .Is 6:7

**TOUCHES**
He *t* the hills . . . . . . . . . . . . .Ps 104:32

**TOWER**
*t* whose top is in the. . . . . . . . .Gen 11:4
a watchman in the *t* . . . . . . . . . .Is 21:5

**TRACKED**
*t* our steps so that we . . . . . . .Lam 4:18

**TRADERS**
are princes, whose *t* . . . . . . . . . .Is 23:8

**TRADITION**
transgress the *t* . . . . . . . . . . .Matt 15:2
according to the *t* . . . . . . . . . . . .Col 2:8

**TRAIN**
*T* up a child in the . . . . . . . . .Prov 22:6

**TRAINED**
those who have been *t*. . . . . .Heb 12:11

**TRAINING**
bring them up in the *t*. . . . . . . .Eph 6:4

**TRAITOR**
also became a *t* . . . . . . . . . . .Luke 6:16

**TRAITORS**
*t*, headstrong . . . . . . . . . . . . .2 Tim 3:4

**TRAMPLE**
serpent you shall *t* . . . . . . . . . .Ps 91:13
swine, lest they *t* . . . . . . . . . . .Matt 7:6

**TRAMPLED**
*t* the Son of God . . . . . . . . . . .Heb 10:29
the winepress was *t* . . . . . . . .Rev 14:20

**TRANCE**
*t* I saw a vision . . . . . . . . . . . .Acts 11:5

**TRANSFIGURED**
and was *t* before them . . . . . .Matt 17:2

**TRANSFORMED**
this world, but be *t* . . . . . . . . .Rom 12:2

**TRANSGRESS**
do Your disciples *t* . . . . . . . . .Matt 15:2

**TRANSGRESSED**
Yes, all Israel has *t* . . . . . . . . .Dan 9:11
*t* your commandment . . . . .Luke 15:29

**TRANSGRESSES**
Whoever *t* and does not . . . . . .2 John 9

**TRANSGRESSION**
no law there is no *t* . . . Rom 4:15
deceived, fell into *t* . . . 1 Tim 2:14

**TRANSGRESSIONS**
mercies, blot out my *t* . . . Ps 51:1
For I acknowledge my *t* . . . Ps 51:3
was wounded for our *t* . . . Is 53:5
for the *t* of My people . . . Is 53:8

**TRANSGRESSOR**
I make myself a *t* . . . Gal 2:18

**TRANSGRESSORS**
Then I will teach *t* . . . Ps 51:13
numbered with the *t* . . . Is 53:12

**TRAP**
of Israel, as a *t* . . . Is 8:14

**TRAPS**
for me, and from the *t* . . . Ps 141:9

**TRAVEL**
For you *t* land and sea . . . Matt 23:15

**TRAVELER**
*t* who turns aside . . . Jer 14:8

**TRAVELING**
lie waste, the *t* . . . Is 33:8

**TREACHEROUS**
are insolent, *t* . . . Zeph 3:4

**TREACHEROUSLY**
"This man dealt *t* . . . Acts 7:19

**TREAD**
You shall *t* upon the . . . Ps 91:13

**TREADS**
*an ox while it t* . . . 1 Tim 5:18
*t* the winepress . . . Rev 19:15

**TREASURE**
and you will have *t* . . . Matt 19:21
"So is he who lays up *t* . . . Luke 12:21
But we have this *t* . . . 2 Cor 4:7

**TREASURED**
*t* the words of His . . . Job 23:12

**TREASURER**
Erastus, the *t* of the . . . Rom 16:23

**TREASURES**
it more than hidden *t* . . . Job 3:21
I will give you the *t* . . . Is 45:3
for yourselves *t* . . . Matt 6:19
are hidden all the *t* . . . Col 2:3
riches than the *t* . . . Heb 11:26

**TREATY**
Now Solomon made a *t* . . . 1 Kin 3:1

**TREE**
you eaten from the *t* . . . Gen 3:11
*t* planted by the . . . Ps 1:3
like a native green *t* . . . Ps 37:35
*t* bears good fruit . . . Matt 7:17
His own body on the *t* . . . 1 Pet 2:24
the river, was the *t* . . . Rev 22:2

**TREES**
late autumn *t* without . . . Jude 12
the sea, or the *t* . . . Rev 7:3

**TREMBLE**
that the nations may *t* . . . Is 64:2
they shall fear and *t* . . . Jer 33:9

**TREMBLED**
Then everyone who *t* . . . Ezra 9:4
the earth shook and *t* . . . Ps 18:7
and indeed they *t* . . . Jer 4:24

**TREMBLING**
in fear, and in much *t* . . . 1 Cor 2:3
*t* you received . . . 2 Cor 7:15
flesh, with fear and *t* . . . Eph 6:5

**TRENCH**
and he made a *t* . . . 1 Kin 18:32

**TRESPASSES**
forgive men their *t* . . . Matt 6:14
not imputing their *t* . . . 2 Cor 5:19
who were dead in *t* . . . Eph 2:1

**TRIAL**
concerning the fiery *t* . . . 1 Pet 4:12

**TRIBE**
the Lion of the *t* . . . Rev 5:5
blood out of every *t* . . . Rev 5:9

**TRIBES**
*t* which are scattered . . . James 1:1

**TRIBULATION**
there will be great *t* . . . Matt 24:21
world you will have *t* . . . John 16:33
with her into great *t* . . . Rev 2:22
out of the great *t* . . . Rev 7:14

**TRIBULATIONS**
*t* enter the kingdom . . . Acts 14:22
but we also glory in *t* . . . Rom 5:3
*t* that you endure . . . 2 Thess 1:4

**TRIED**
a *t* stone, a precious . . . Is 28:16

**TRIMMED**
and *t* their lamps . . . Matt 25:7

**TRIUMPH**
always leads us in *t* . . . 2 Cor 2:14

**TRIUMPHED**
the LORD, for He has *t* . . . Ex 15:1

**TRODDEN**
*t* the winepress alone . . . Is 63:3

**TROUBLE**
few days and full of *t* . . . Job 14:1
*t* He shall hide me . . . Ps 27:5
not in *t* as other men . . . Ps 73:5
will be with him in *t* . . . Ps 91:15
Savior in time of *t* . . . Jer 14:8
there are some who *t* . . . Gal 1:7

**TROUBLED**
you are worried and *t* . . . Luke 10:41
shaken in mind or *t* . . . 2 Thess 2:2

**TROUBLES**
out of all their *t* . . . Ps 25:22
will be famines and *t* . . . Mark 13:8
him out of all his *t* . . . Acts 7:10

**TROUBLING**
wicked cease from *t* . . . Job 3:17

**TRUE**
He who sent Me is *t* . . . John 7:28
Indeed, let God be *t* . . . Rom 3:4
whatever things are *t* . . . Phil 4:8
may know Him who is *t* . . . 1 John 5:20
for these words are *t* . . . Rev 21:5

**TRUMPET**
deed, do not sound a *t* . . . Matt 6:2
*t* makes an uncertain . . . 1 Cor 14:8
For the *t* will sound . . . 1 Cor 15:52

**TRUST**
*T* in the LORD . . . Ps 37:3
*T* in the LORD with all . . . Prov 3:5
Do not *t* in a friend . . . Mic 7:5
who *t* in riches . . . Mark 10:24

**TRUSTED**
"He *t* in the LORD . . . Ps 22:8
"He *t* in God . . . Matt 27:43

**TRUSTS**
but he who *t* in the . . . Ps 32:10

**TRUTH**
led me in the way of *t* . . . Gen 24:48
Behold, You desire *t* . . . Ps 51:6
*t* shall be your shield . . . Ps 91:4
and Your law is *t* . . . Ps 119:142
*t* is fallen in the . . . Is 59:14
called the City of *T* . . . Zech 8:3
you shall know the *t* . . . John 8:32
"I am the way, the *t* . . . John 14:6
He, the Spirit of *t* . . . John 16:13
to Him, "What is *t* . . . John 18:38
who suppress the *t* . . . Rom 1:18
but, speaking the *t* . . . Eph 4:15
your waist with *t* . . . Eph 6:14
I am speaking the *t* . . . 1 Tim 2:7
they may know the *t* . . . 2 Tim 2:25
the knowledge of the *t* . . . 2 Tim 3:7
that we are of the *t* . . . 1 John 3:19
the Spirit is *t* . . . 1 John 5:6

**TRY**
which is to *t* you . . . 1 Pet 4:12

**TUMULT**
Your enemies make a *t* . . . Ps 83:2

**TUNIC**
Also he made him a *t* . . . Gen 37:3

**TUNICS**
the LORD God made *t* . . . Gen 3:21

**TURBAN**
"Remove the *t* . . . Ezek 21:26

**TURN**
you shall not *t* . . . Deut 17:11
"Repent, *t* away from . . . Ezek 14:6
on your right cheek, *t* . . . Matt 5:39
*t* them from darkness . . . Acts 26:18

**TURNED**
The wicked shall be *t* . . . Ps 9:17
of Israel, they have *t* . . . Is 1:4
to you, and how you *t* . . . 1 Thess 1:9

**TURNING**
marvel that you are *t* . . . Gal 1:6
or shadow of *t* . . . James 1:17

**TURNS**
A soft answer *t* . . . Prov 15:1
him know that he who *t* . . . James 5:20

**TURTLEDOVE**
*t* is heard in our land . . . Song 2:12

**TUTOR**
the law was our *t* . . . Gal 3:24

**TWIST**
and unstable people *t* to . . . 2 Pet 3:16

**TWO**
*T* are better than one . . . Eccl 4:9
*t shall become one* . . . Matt 19:5
one new man from the *t* . . . Eph 2:15

**TYPE**
of Adam, who is a *t* . . . Rom 5:14

## U

**UNAFRAID**
Do you want to be *u* . . . Rom 13:3

**UNBELIEF**
because of their *u* . . . Matt 13:58
help my *u* . . . Mark 9:24
did it ignorantly in *u* . . . 1 Tim 1:13
enter in because of *u* . . . Heb 3:19

**UNBELIEVERS**
yoked together with *u* . . . 2 Cor 6:14

**UNBELIEVING**
Do not be *u* . . . . . . . . . . . . . .John 20:27
*u* nothing is pure. . . . . . . . . . .Titus 1:15
But the cowardly, *u* . . . . . . . . .Rev 21:8

**UNCIRCUMCISED**
not the physically *u* . . . . . . . .Rom 2:27

**UNCLEAN**
I am a man of *u* lips . . . . . . . . . . .Is 6:5
any man common or *u* . . . . .Acts 10:28
there is nothing *u*. . . . . . . . .Rom 14:14
that no fornicator, *u* . . . . . . . . .Eph 5:5

**UNCLEANNESS**
men's bones and all *u* . . . . .Matt 23:27
flesh in the lust of *u*. . . . . . . .2 Pet 2:10

**UNCLOTHED**
we want to be *u* . . . . . . . . . . . .2 Cor 5:4

**UNCOVERS**
*u* deep things out of . . . . . . . .Job 12:22

**UNDEFILED**
incorruptible and *u* . . . . . . . . .1 Pet 1:4

**UNDERMINE**
and you *u* your friend. . . . . . . .Job 6:27

**UNDERSTAND**
if there are any who *u* . . . . . . . .Ps 14:2
hearing, but do not *u*. . . . . . . . . . .Is 6:9
Why do you not *u* . . . . . . . . . .John 8:43
*lest they should u* . . . . . . . . .Acts 28:27
some things hard to *u* . . . . . .2 Pet 3:16

**UNDERSTANDING**
His *u* is infinite . . . . . . . . . . . .Ps 147:5
lean not on your own *u*. . . . . . .Prov 3:5
*u* will find good . . . . . . . . . . .Prov 19:8
His *u* is unsearchable. . . . . . . .Is 40:28
also still without *u* . . . . . . .Matt 15:16
also pray with the *u* . . . . . .1 Cor 14:15
the Lord give you *u*. . . . . . . . .2 Tim 2:7
Who is wise and *u* . . . . . . . .James 3:13

**UNDERSTANDS**
*there is none who u*. . . . . . . . .Rom 3:11

**UNDERSTOOD**
Then I *u* their end . . . . . . . . . .Ps 73:17
clearly seen, being *u* . . . . . . .Rom 1:20

**UNDESIRABLE**
gather together, O *u*. . . . . . . . .Zeph 2:1

**UNDIGNIFIED**
I will be even more *u* . . . . . .2 Sam 6:22

**UNDISCERNING**
*u*, untrustworthy . . . . . . . . . .Rom 1:31

**UNDONE**
"Woe is me, for I am *u*. . . . . . . . . .Is 6:5

**UNEDUCATED**
that they were *u* . . . . . . . . . . .Acts 4:13

**UNFAITHFUL**
way of the *u* is hard . . . . . . .Prov 13:15

**UNFAITHFULLY**
back and acted *u* . . . . . . . . . . .Ps 78:57

**UNFORGIVING**
unloving, *u*. . . . . . . . . . . . . . .Rom 1:31

**UNFORMED**
substance, being yet *u*. . . . . .Ps 139:16

**UNFRUITFUL**
and it becomes *u*. . . . . . . . . .Mark 4:19

**UNGODLINESS**
heaven against all *u*. . . . . . . .Rom 1:18

**UNGODLY**
*u* shall not stand . . . . . . . . . . . . .Ps 1:5
Christ died for the *u* . . . . . . . . .Rom 5:6

**UNHOLY**
between the holy and *u* . . . .Ezek 22:26

**UNINFORMED**
the place of the *u*. . . . . . . . .1 Cor 14:16

**UNINTENTIONALLY**
kills his neighbor *u* . . . . . . . .Deut 4:42

**UNITE**
*u* my heart to fear . . . . . . . . . .Ps 86:11

**UNITY**
to dwell together in *u*. . . . . . . .Ps 133:1
to keep the *u* of the . . . . . . . . . .Eph 4:3

**UNJUST**
master commended the *u* . . .Luke 16:8
of the just and the *u* . . . . . . .Acts 24:15
For God is not *u* . . . . . . . . . . . .Heb 6:10

**UNJUSTLY**
long will you judge *u* . . . . . . . . .Ps 82:2

**UNKNOWN**
To The *U* God . . . . . . . . . . . .Acts 17:23

**UNLEAVENED**
the Feast of *U* Bread . . . . . . . .Ex 12:17

**UNLOVING**
untrustworthy, *u* . . . . . . . . . .Rom 1:31

**UNMERCIFUL**
unforgiving, *u* . . . . . . . . . . . .Rom 1:31

**UNPREPARED**
with me and find you *u* . . . . . .2 Cor 9:4

**UNPRESENTABLE**
*u* parts have greater . . . . . .1 Cor 12:23

**UNPROFITABLE**
'We are *u* servants. . . . . . . .Luke 17:10
for that would be *u* . . . . . . . .Heb 13:17

**UNPUNISHED**
wicked will not go *u* . . . . . . .Prov 11:21

**UNQUENCHABLE**
up the chaff with *u* . . . . . . . .Matt 3:12

**UNRESTRAINED**
that the people were *u*. . . . . . .Ex 32:25

**UNRIGHTEOUS**
*u* man his thoughts. . . . . . . . . . .Is 55:7
*u* will not inherit the. . . . . . . .1 Cor 6:9

**UNRIGHTEOUSNESS**
all ungodliness and *u*. . . . . . .Rom 1:18
cleanse us from all *u* . . . . . . .1 John 1:9
All *u* is sin. . . . . . . . . . . . . .1 John 5:17

**UNRULY**
warn those who are *u* . . . .1 Thess 5:14

**UNSEARCHABLE**
*u* are His judgments. . . . . . .Rom 11:33

**UNSKILLED**
only of milk is *u*. . . . . . . . . . .Heb 5:13

**UNSPOTTED**
to keep oneself *u* . . . . . . . . .James 1:27

**UNSTABLE**
*U* as water. . . . . . . . . . . . . . . .Gen 49:4

**UNSTOPPED**
of the deaf shall be *u*. . . . . . . . . .Is 35:5

**UNTAUGHT**
which *u* and unstable . . . . . .2 Pet 3:16

**UNTRUSTWORTHY**
undiscerning, *u* . . . . . . . . . . .Rom 1:31

**UNWASHED**
eat bread with *u* hands. . . . . .Mark 7:5

**UNWISE**
Therefore do not be *u*. . . . . . . .Eph 5:17

**UNWORTHY**
*u* manner will be. . . . . . . . .1 Cor 11:27

**UPHOLD**
*U* me according to Your . . .Ps 119:116

**UPHOLDING**
*u* all things by the . . . . . . . . . . .Heb 1:3

**UPHOLDS**
LORD *u* all who fall . . . . . . . .Ps 145:14

**UPPER**
show you a large *u* . . . . . . .Mark 14:15

**UPRIGHT**
*u* is His delight. . . . . . . . . . . .Prov 15:8

**UPRIGHTNESS**
princes for their *u* . . . . . . . .Prov 17:26

**UPROOT**
*u* the wheat with them . . . .Matt 13:29

**URIM**
Thummim and Your *U* . . . . .Deut 33:8

**US**
"God with *u*, . . . . . . . . . . . . .Matt 1:23
If God is for *u* . . . . . . . . . . . . .Rom 8:31
none of them were of *u* . . . .1 John 2:19

**USE**
who spitefully *u* you . . . . . . .Matt 5:44
*u* liberty as an . . . . . . . . . . . . .Gal 5:13

**USELESS**
one's religion is *u*. . . . . . . . .James 1:26

**USES**
if one *u* it lawfully . . . . . . . . .1 Tim 1:8

**USING**
*u* liberty as a . . . . . . . . . . . . .1 Pet 2:16

**USURY**
'Take no *u* or . . . . . . . . . . . . .Lev 25:36

**UTTER**
*u* dark sayings of old . . . . . . . . .Ps 78:2

**UTTERANCE**
the Spirit gave them *u* . . . . . . .Acts 2:4

**UTTERED**
which cannot be *u* . . . . . . . .Rom 8:26

**UTTERMOST**
*u* those who come . . . . . . . . . .Heb 7:25

**UTTERS**
Day unto day *u* speech. . . . . . . .Ps 19:2

## V

**VAGABOND**
*v* you shall be on the . . . . . . . .Gen 4:12

**VAIN**
the people plot a *v* . . . . . . . . . . . .Ps 2:1
you believed in *v* . . . . . . . . . .1 Cor 15:2

**VALIANT**
They are not *v* for the . . . . . . . . .Jer 9:3

**VALIANTLY**
God we will do *v*. . . . . . . . . . . .Ps 60:12

**VALLEY**
*v* shall be exalted . . . . . . . . . . . .Is 40:4

**VALOR**
a mighty man of *v* . . . . . . .1 Sam 16:18

**VALUE**
of more *v* than they . . . . . . . .Matt 6:26

**VALUED**
It cannot be *v* in the . . . . . . . .Job 28:16

**VANISH**
knowledge, it will *v*. . . . . . . .1 Cor 13:8

**VANISHED**
and He *v* from their. . . . . . .Luke 24:31

**VANITY**
of vanities, all is *v* ... Eccl 1:2

**VAPOR**
best state is but *v* ... Ps 39:5
It is even a *v* that ... James 4:14

**VARIATION**
whom there is no *v* ... James 1:17

**VEGETABLES**
and let them give us *v* ... Dan 1:12
is weak eats only *v* ... Rom 14:2

**VEHEMENT**
of fire, a most *v* ... Song 8:6

**VEIL**
*v* of the temple was ... Matt 27:51
Presence behind the *v* ... Heb 6:19

**VENGEANCE**
*V* is Mine ... Deut 32:35

**VENOM**
it becomes cobra *v* ... Job 20:14

**VESSEL**
like a potter's *v* ... Ps 2:9
for he is a chosen *v* ... Acts 9:15

**VESSELS**
treasure in earthen *v* ... 2 Cor 4:7

**VEXED**
grieved, and I was *v* ... Ps 73:21

**VICE**
as a cloak for *v* ... 1 Pet 2:16

**VICTIM**
and plucked the *v* ... Job 29:17

**VICTORY**
*v* that has overcome ... 1 John 5:4

**VIEW**
"Go, *v* the land ... Josh 2:1

**VIGILANT**
Be sober, be *v* ... 1 Pet 5:8

**VIGOR**
nor his natural *v* ... Deut 34:7

**VILE**
them up to *v* passions ... Rom 1:26

**VINDICATED**
know that I shall be *v* ... Job 13:18

**VINDICATION**
Let my *v* come from ... Ps 17:2

**VINE**
"I am the true *v* ... John 15:1

**VINEDRESSER**
and My Father is the *v* ... John 15:1

**VINEGAR**
As *v* to the teeth and ... Prov 10:26

**VINES**
foxes that spoil the *v* ... Song 2:15

**VINEYARD**
Who plants a *v* and ... 1 Cor 9:7

**VIOLENCE**
was filled with *v* ... Gen 6:11
of heaven suffers *v* ... Matt 11:12

**VIOLENT**
haters of God, *v* ... Rom 1:30

**VIPER**
and stings like a *v* ... Prov 23:32

**VIPERS**
to them, "Brood of *v* ... Matt 3:7

**VIRGIN**
*v* shall conceive ... Is 7:14
*"Behold, the v shall* ... Matt 1:23

**VIRGINS**
*v* who took their lamps ... Matt 25:1

**VIRTUE**
to your faith *v* ... 2 Pet 1:5

**VISAGE**
*v* was marred more than ... Is 52:14

**VISIBLE**
that are on earth, *v* ... Col 1:16

**VISION**
in a trance I saw a *v* ... Acts 11:5
to the heavenly *v* ... Acts 26:19

**VISIONS**
young men shall see *v* ... Joel 2:28

**VISIT**
*v* orphans and widows ... James 1:27

**VISITATION**
God in the day of *v* ... 1 Pet 2:12

**VISITED**
Israel, for He has *v* ... Luke 1:68

**VISITING**
*v* the iniquity of the fathers ... Ex 20:5

**VISITOR**
am a foreigner and a *v* ... Gen 23:4

**VITALITY**
*v* was turned into the ... Ps 32:4

**VOICE**
fire a still small *v* ... 1 Kin 19:12
if you will hear His *v* ... Ps 95:7
*"The v of one crying* ... Matt 3:3
And suddenly a *v* ... Matt 3:17
for they know his *v* ... John 10:4
the truth hears My *v* ... John 18:37
If anyone hears My *v* ... Rev 3:20

**VOICES**
and there were loud *v* ... Rev 11:15

**VOID**
they are a nation *v* ... Deut 32:28
heirs, faith is made *v* ... Rom 4:14

**VOLUME**
*in the v of the book* ... Heb 10:7

**VOLUNTEERS**
Your people shall be *v* ... Ps 110:3

**VOMIT**
*returns to his own v* ... 2 Pet 2:22

**VOW**
for he had taken a *v* ... Acts 18:18

**VOWS**
to reconsider his *v* ... Prov 20:25

## W

**WAGE**
*w* the good warfare ... 1 Tim 1:18

**WAGES**
For the *w* of sin is ... Rom 6:23
Indeed the *w* of the ... James 5:4

**WAIL**
"Son of man, *w* ... Ezek 32:18

**WAILING**
There will be *w* ... Matt 13:42

**WAIT**
*w* patiently for Him ... Ps 37:7
those who *w* on the ... Is 40:31
To those who eagerly *w* ... Heb 9:28

**WAITED**
*w* patiently for the ... Ps 40:1
Divine longsuffering *w* ... 1 Pet 3:20

**WAITING**
ourselves, eagerly *w* ... Rom 8:23
from that time *w* ... Heb 10:13

**WAITS**
the creation eagerly *w* ... Rom 8:19

**WAKE**
us, that whether we *w* ... 1 Thess 5:10

**WALK**
*w* before Me and be ... Gen 17:1
Yea, though I *w* ... Ps 23:4
*W* prudently when you ... Eccl 5:1
"This is the way, *w* ... Is 30:21
be weary, they shall *w* ... Is 40:31
*w* humbly with your God ... Mic 6:8
*W* while you have the ... John 12:35
so we also should *w* ... Rom 6:4
For we *w* by faith ... 2 Cor 5:7
*W* in the Spirit ... Gal 5:16
And *w* in love ... Eph 5:2
that you may *w* worthy ... Col 1:10
and they shall *w* ... Rev 3:4

**WALKED**
Methuselah, Enoch *w* ... Gen 5:22
The people who *w* ... Is 9:2
in which you once *w* ... Eph 2:2

**WALKING**
not *w* in craftiness ... 2 Cor 4:2

**WALKS**
the LORD your God *w* ... Deut 23:14
is the man who *w* ... Ps 1:1
he who *w* in darkness ... John 12:35
adversary the devil *w* ... 1 Pet 5:8

**WALL**
then the *w* of the city ... Josh 6:5
you, you whitewashed *w* ... Acts 23:3
a window in the *w* ... 2 Cor 11:33
Now the *w* of the city ... Rev 21:14

**WALLS**
By faith the *w* of ... Heb 11:30

**WANDER**
they have loved to *w* ... Jer 14:10

**WANDERED**
They *w* in deserts and ... Heb 11:38

**WANDERERS**
and they shall be *w* ... Hos 9:17

**WANDERING**
*w* stars for whom is ... Jude 13

**WANDERS**
if anyone among you *w* ... James 5:19

**WANT**
I shall not *w* ... Ps 23:1

**WANTING**
balances, and found *w* ... Dan 5:27

**WANTON**
have begun to grow *w* ... 1 Tim 5:11

**WAR**
There is a noise of *w* ... Ex 32:17
*w* may rise against ... Ps 27:3
shall they learn *w* ... Is 2:4
king, going to make *w* ... Luke 14:31
You fight and *w* ... James 4:2
fleshly lusts which *w* ... 1 Pet 2:11
He judges and makes *w* ... Rev 19:11

**WARFARE**
to her, that her *w* ... Is 40:2
*w* entangles ... 2 Tim 2:4

**WARMED**
Depart in peace, be *w* . . . . .James 2:16

**WARMING**
when she saw Peter *w*. . . . .Mark 14:67

**WARMS**
*w* them in the dust . . . . . . . . .Job 39:14

**WARN**
*w* those who are unruly. . .1 Thess 5:14

**WARNED**
Then, being divinely *w* . . . . .Matt 2:12
Who *w* you to flee. . . . . . . . . . .Matt 3:7

**WARNING**
*w* every man and . . . . . . . . . . .Col 1:28

**WARPED**
such a person is *w* . . . . . . . . .Titus 3:11

**WARRING**
*w* against the law of . . . . . . . .Rom 7:23

**WARRIOR**
He runs at me like a *w* . . . . . .Job 16:14

**WARS**
And you will hear of *w*. . . . . .Matt 24:6
Where do *w* and fights. . . . . .James 4:1

**WASH**
*w* myself with snow . . . . . . . . .Job 9:30
*W* me thoroughly . . . . . . . . . . . .Ps 51:2
*w* His feet with her . . . . . . . .Luke 7:38
said to him, "Go, *w* . . . . . . . . .John 9:7
*w* the disciples' . . . . . . . . . . .John 13:5
*w* away your sins . . . . . . . . .Acts 22:16

**WASHED**
*w* his hands before the. . . . .Matt 27:24
But you were *w* . . . . . . . . . . .1 Cor 6:11
Him who loved us and *w* . . . . . .Rev 1:5

**WASHING**
us, through the *w* . . . . . . . . . .Titus 3:5

**WASHINGS**
and drinks, various *w* . . . . . . .Heb 9:10

**WASTE**
the cities are laid *w*. . . . . . . . . .Is 6:11
"Why this *w*. . . . . . . . . . . . . .Matt 26:8

**WASTED**
this fragrant oil *w* . . . . . . . .Mark 14:4

**WASTELAND**
*w* shall be glad . . . . . . . . . . . . .Is 35:1

**WASTING**
that this man was *w* . . . . . . .Luke 16:1

**WATCH**
is past, and like a *w* . . . . . . . . . .Ps 90:4
"*W* therefore . . . . . . . . . . . .Matt 24:42

**WATCHED**
come, he would have *w* . . . .Matt 24:43

**WATCHES**
Blessed is he who *w* . . . . . . . .Rev 16:15

**WATCHFUL**
But you be *w* in all . . . . . . . . .2 Tim 4:5

**WATCHING**
he comes, will find *w*. . . . . .Luke 12:37

**WATCHMAN**
I have made you a *w* . . . . . . .Ezek 3:17

**WATCHMEN**
I have set *w* on your . . . . . . . . . .Is 62:6

**WATER**
Eden to *w* the garden . . . . . . .Gen 2:10
I am poured out like *w*. . . . . . .Ps 22:14
For I will pour *w* . . . . . . . . . . . . .Is 44:3
given you living *w* . . . . . . . . .John 4:10
rivers of living *w* . . . . . . . . . .John 7:38
can yield both salt *w* . . . . . .James 3:12
the Spirit, the *w* . . . . . . . . . .1 John 5:8
are clouds without *w*. . . . . . . . .Jude 12
let him take the *w* . . . . . . . . .Rev 22:17

**WATERED**
I planted, Apollos *w* . . . . . . . .1 Cor 3:6

**WATERS**
me beside the still *w* . . . . . . . . .Ps 23:2
though its *w* roar and . . . . . . . .Ps 46:3
your bread upon the *w* . . . . . .Eccl 11:1
thirsts, come to the *w* . . . . . . . . .Is 55:1
fountain of living *w* . . . . . . . . .Jer 2:13
living fountains of *w* . . . . . . . .Rev 7:17

**WAVE**
its fruit shall *w* . . . . . . . . . . . .Ps 72:16

**WAVER**
He did not *w* at the . . . . . . . . .Rom 4:20

**WAVERING**
of our hope without *w* . . . . . .Heb 10:23

**WAVES**
sea, tossed by the *w* . . . . . . .Matt 14:24

**WAX**
My heart is like *w* . . . . . . . . . .Ps 22:14

**WAY**
As for God, His *w*. . . . . . . .2 Sam 22:31
the LORD knows the *w*. . . . . . . . .Ps 1:6
Teach me Your *w* . . . . . . . . . . .Ps 27:11
in the *w* everlasting. . . . . . . .Ps 139:24
*w* that seems right. . . . . . . .Prov 14:12
The *w* of the just is . . . . . . . . . . .Is 26:7
wicked forsake his *w*. . . . . . . . . .Is 55:7
and pervert the *w* . . . . . . . . . .Amos 2:7
he will prepare the *w* . . . . . . . .Mal 3:1
and broad is the *w* . . . . . . . . .Matt 7:13
*will prepare Your w* . . . . . . .Matt 11:10
to him, "I am the *w* . . . . . . . .John 14:6
explained to him the *w*. . . . .Acts 18:26
*w* which He consecrated . . . .Heb 10:20
to have known the *w* . . . . . . .2 Pet 2:21

**WAYS**
for all His *w* are . . . . . . . . . . .Deut 32:4
transgressors Your *w*. . . . . . . .Ps 51:13
*w* please the LORD . . . . . . . . .Prov 16:7
"Stand in the *w*. . . . . . . . . . . . .Jer 6:16
and owns all your *w* . . . . . . . .Dan 5:23
*w* are everlasting . . . . . . . . . . .Hab 3:6
unstable in all his *w* . . . . . . .James 1:8
and true are Your *w*. . . . . . . . .Rev 15:3

**WEAK**
gives power to the *w* . . . . . . . . .Is 40:29
knee will be as *w* . . . . . . . . . .Ezek 7:17
but the flesh is *w* . . . . . . . . .Matt 26:41
Receive one who is *w* . . . . . . .Rom 14:1
God has chosen the *w* . . . . . .1 Cor 1:27
We are *w* . . . . . . . . . . . . . . . .1 Cor 4:10
*w* I became as *w* . . . . . . . . . .1 Cor 9:22
For when I am *w* . . . . . . . . .2 Cor 12:10

**WEAKENED**
*w* my strength in the . . . . . . .Ps 102:23

**WEAKENS**
*w* the hands of the men. . . . . . .Jer 38:4

**WEAKER**
the wife, as to the *w* . . . . . . . . .1 Pet 3:7

**WEAKNESS**
*w* were made strong . . . . . .Heb 11:34

**WEAKNESSES**
also helps in our *w* . . . . . . . . .Rom 8:26

**WEALTH**
*W* gained by dishonesty. . . .Prov 13:11

**WEALTHY**
am rich, have become *w* . . . . .Rev 3:17

**WEANED**
*w* child shall put his . . . . . . . . . .Is 11:8

**WEAPON**
*w* formed against you . . . . . . . .Is 54:17

**WEAPONS**
For the *w* of our . . . . . . . . . . .2 Cor 10:4

**WEAR**
'What shall we *w* . . . . . . . . . .Matt 6:31

**WEARIED**
you have *w* Me with . . . . . . . . .Is 43:24
therefore, being *w* . . . . . . . . . .John 4:6

**WEARINESS**
say, 'Oh, what a *w* . . . . . . . . . .Mal 1:13

**WEARISOME**
and much study is *w* . . . . . . .Eccl 12:12

**WEARY**
shall run and not be *w* . . . . . . .Is 40:31
continual coming she *w* . . . .Luke 18:5
And let us not grow *w* . . . . . . . .Gal 6:9
do not grow *w* in . . . . . . . .2 Thess 3:13

**WEATHER**
'It will be fair *w* . . . . . . . . . . .Matt 16:2

**WEDDING**
day there was a *w*. . . . . . . . . . .John 2:1

**WEEK**
the first day of the *w* . . . . . . .Matt 28:1

**WEEKS**
*w* are determined . . . . . . . . . .Dan 9:24

**WEEP**
a time to *w* . . . . . . . . . . . . . . . .Eccl 3:4
you shall *w* no more . . . . . . . . .Is 30:19
Blessed are you who *w* . . . . .Luke 6:21
of Jerusalem, do not *w*. . . . .Luke 23:28
*w* with those who *w* . . . . . . .Rom 12:15

**WEEPING**
the noise of the *w* . . . . . . . . . .Ezra 3:13
They shall come with *w* . . . . . .Jer 31:9
There will be *w* . . . . . . . . . . .Matt 8:12
outside by the tomb *w* . . . . .John 20:11

**WEIGH**
O Most Upright, You *w* . . . . . . . .Is 26:7

**WEIGHED**
You have been *w* . . . . . . . . . . .Dan 5:27

**WEIGHS**
eyes, but the LORD *w* . . . . . . .Prov 16:2

**WEIGHT**
us lay aside every *w* . . . . . . . .Heb 12:1

**WEIGHTIER**
have neglected the *w*. . . . . .Matt 23:23

**WELFARE**
does not seek the *w* . . . . . . . . . .Jer 38:4

**WELL**
daughters have done *w* . . . .Prov 31:29
wheel broken at the *w*. . . . . . .Eccl 12:6
"Those who are *w* . . . . . . . . .Matt 9:12
said to him, '*W* done . . . . .Matt 25:21

**WELL-BEING**
each one the other's *w* . . . . .1 Cor 10:24

**WELLS**
These are *w* without . . . . . . .2 Pet 2:17

**WENT**
They *w* out from us . . . . . . .1 John 2:19

**WEPT**
out and *w* bitterly . . . . . . . .Matt 26:75
He saw the city and *w* . . . . .Luke 19:41
Jesus *w*. . . . . . . . . . . . . . . . .John 11:35

**WET**
his body was *w* with . . . . . . . .Dan 4:33

**WHEAT**
*w* falls into the . . . . . . . . . . . John 12:24

**WHEEL**
in the middle of a *w* . . . . . . . . Ezek 1:16

**WHEELS**
noise of rattling *w*. . . . . . . . . . . Nah 3:2

**WHERE**
not knowing *w* he was. . . . . . . Heb 11:8

**WHIP**
A *w* for the horse . . . . . . . . . . Prov 26:3

**WHIRLWIND**
Job out of the *w*. . . . . . . . . . . . . Job 38:1
has His way in the *w*. . . . . . . . . Nah 1:3

**WHISPER**
my ear received a *w* . . . . . . . . . Job 4:12

**WHISPERER**
*w* separates the best. . . . . . . Prov 16:28

**WHISPERERS**
they are *w*. . . . . . . . . . . . . . . . Rom 1:29

**WHISPERINGS**
backbitings, *w*. . . . . . . . . . . 2 Cor 12:20

**WHITE**
clothed in *w* garments . . . . . . . . Rev 3:5
behold, a *w* horse . . . . . . . . . . . . Rev 6:2
and made them *w* . . . . . . . . . . Rev 7:14

**WHOLE**
*w* body were an eye . . . . . . 1 Cor 12:17

**WHOLESOME**
not consent to *w* words . . . . . . 1 Tim 6:3

**WHOLLY**
*w* followed the LORD . . . . . . . Deut 1:36

**WICKED**
*w* shall be silent. . . . . . . . . . . 1 Sam 2:9
*w* shall be no more . . . . . . . . . . Ps 37:10
if there is any *w* . . . . . . . . . . . Ps 139:24
*w* forsake his way . . . . . . . . . . . . Is 55:7
and desperately *w*. . . . . . . . . . . Jer 17:9
the sway of the *w*. . . . . . . . . 1 John 5:19

**WICKEDLY**
God will never do *w* . . . . . . . . Job 34:12

**WICKEDNESS**
LORD saw that the *w*. . . . . . . . . Gen 6:5
in the tents of *w* . . . . . . . . . . . . Ps 84:10
man repented of his *w* . . . . . . . . Jer 8:6
is full of greed and *w*. . . . . Luke 11:39
sexual immorality, *w* . . . . . . . Rom 1:29
and overflow of *w*. . . . . . . . . James 1:21

**WIDE**
shall open your hand *w* . . . . . Deut 15:8
*w* is the gate and . . . . . . . . . . Matt 7:13
to you, our heart is *w*. . . . . . . 2 Cor 6:11

**WIDOW**
the fatherless and *w*. . . . . . . . . Ps 146:9
How like a *w* is she. . . . . . . . . . Lam 1:1
Then one poor *w* . . . . . . . . . Mark 12:42
*w* has children or . . . . . . . . . . 1 Tim 5:4

**WIDOW'S**
and I caused the *w* . . . . . . . . . Job 29:13

**WIDOWS**
*w* were neglected . . . . . . . . . . . Acts 6:1
to visit orphans and *w*. . . . . James 1:27

**WIFE**
and be joined to his *w* . . . . . . . Gen 2:24
*w* finds a good thing. . . . . . . Prov 18:22
but a prudent *w* . . . . . . . . . . Prov 19:14
"Go, take yourself a *w*. . . . . . . . Hos 1:2
"Whoever divorces his *w* . . Mark 10:11
'I have married a *w*. . . . . . Luke 14:20
"Remember Lot's *w*. . . . . . Luke 17:32
so love his own *w*. . . . . . . . . . . Eph 5:33
the husband of one *w*. . . . . . . . Titus 1:6
bride, the Lamb's *w* . . . . . . . . . Rev 21:9

**WILD**
olive tree which is *w*. . . . . . . Rom 11:24

**WILDERNESS**
I will make the *w* . . . . . . . . . . . Is 41:18
*of one crying in the w* . . . . . . . Matt 3:3
the serpent in the *w* . . . . . . . . John 3:14

**WILES**
to stand against the *w* . . . . . . Eph 6:11

**WILL**
*w* be done on earth as . . . . . . Matt 6:10
but he who does the *w* . . . . . . Matt 7:21
on earth peace, good *w* . . . . . Luke 2:14
nevertheless not My *w* . . . . Luke 22:42
flesh, nor of the *w*. . . . . . . . . . John 1:13
not to do My own *w* . . . . . . . . John 6:38
*w* is present with me . . . . . . . Rom 7:18
and perfect *w* of God. . . . . . . . Rom 12:2
works in you both to *w* . . . . . . Phil 2:13
according to His own *w*. . . . . . . Heb 2:4
good work to do His *w* . . . . . . Heb 13:21

**WILLFULLY**
For if we sin *w* . . . . . . . . . . . Heb 10:26
For this they *w*. . . . . . . . . . . . . 2 Pet 3:5

**WILLING**
If you are *w* and . . . . . . . . . . . . . Is 1:19
The spirit indeed is *w* . . . . . Matt 26:41
*w* that any should . . . . . . . . . . 2 Pet 3:9

**WILLINGLY**
by compulsion but *w* . . . . . . . . 1 Pet 5:2

**WILLOWS**
our harps upon the *w*. . . . . . . . Ps 137:2

**WILLS**
to whom the Son *w*. . . . . . . . Matt 11:27
it is not of him who *w* . . . . . . . Rom 9:16
say, "If the Lord *w* . . . . . . . . James 4:15

**WIN**
to all, that I might *w*. . . . . . . 1 Cor 9:19

**WIND**
the chaff which the *w*. . . . . . . . . . Ps 1:4
A reed shaken by the *w* . . . . . Matt 11:7
"The *w* blows where. . . . . . . . . John 3:8
of a rushing mighty *w* . . . . . . . Acts 2:2

**WINDOWS**
not open for you the *w* . . . . . . . Mal 3:10

**WINDS**
be, that even the *w*. . . . . . . . . Matt 8:27

**WINDSTORM**
And a great *w* arose . . . . . . . Mark 4:37

**WINE**
*W* is a mocker. . . . . . . . . . . . . Prov 20:1
love is better than *w* . . . . . . . . Song 1:2
Yes, come, buy *w*. . . . . . . . . . . . . Is 55:1
they gave Him sour *w* . . . . . Matt 27:34
do not be drunk with *w*. . . . . . Eph 5:18
not given to much *w* . . . . . . . . Titus 2:3

**WINEBIBBERS**
Do not mix with *w* . . . . . . . . Prov 23:20

**WINEPRESS**
"I have trodden the *w*. . . . . . . . . Is 63:3
into the great *w* . . . . . . . . . . Rev 14:19
Himself treads the *w*. . . . . . . Rev 19:15

**WINESKINS**
new wine into old *w*. . . . . . . . Matt 9:17

**WING**
One *w* of the cherub . . . . . . . 1 Kin 6:24

**WINGS**
the shadow of Your *w*. . . . . . . . . Ps 36:7
with healing in His *w* . . . . . . . . Mal 4:2

**WINNOW**
You shall *w* them . . . . . . . . . . . Is 41:16

**WINS**
*w* souls is wise . . . . . . . . . . . Prov 11:30

**WINTER**
For lo, the *w* is past . . . . . . . Song 2:11
flight may not be in *w* . . . . . Matt 24:20

**WIPE**
*w* away every tear . . . . . . . . . . Rev 21:4

**WISDOM**
for this is your *w* . . . . . . . . . . . Deut 4:6
is the man who finds *w* . . . . . Prov 3:13
Get *w* . . . . . . . . . . . . . . . . . . . . . Prov 4:5
is the beginning of *w* . . . . . . . Prov 9:10
*w* is justified by her . . . . . . . Matt 11:19
Jesus increased in *w* . . . . . . . Luke 2:52
riches both of the *w* . . . . . . . Rom 11:33
the gospel, not with *w*. . . . . . . 1 Cor 1:17
For the *w* of this world. . . . . . 1 Cor 3:19
not with fleshly *w* . . . . . . . . . 2 Cor 1:12
all the treasures of *w* . . . . . . . . . Col 2:3
If any of you lacks *w* . . . . . . . James 1:5
power and riches and *w* . . . . . . Rev 5:12

**WISE**
Do not be *w* in your . . . . . . . . . Prov 3:7
he who wins souls is *w*. . . . . Prov 11:30
Therefore be *w* as. . . . . . . . . Matt 10:16
five of them were *w* . . . . . . . . Matt 25:2
to God, alone *w*. . . . . . . . . . . Rom 16:27
Where is the *w*. . . . . . . . . . . . 1 Cor 1:20
not as fools but as *w* . . . . . . . . Eph 5:15
are able to make you *w*. . . . . 2 Tim 3:15

**WISELY**
you do not inquire *w* . . . . . . . . Eccl 7:10

**WISER**
he was *w* than all men . . . . . 1 Kin 4:31
of God is *w* than men. . . . . . . 1 Cor 1:25

**WISH**
*w* it were already. . . . . . . . . Luke 12:49

**WISHED**
Then he *w* death for . . . . . . . . . . Jon 4:8

**WITCHCRAFT**
is as the sin of *w*. . . . . . . . . 1 Sam 15:23

**WITHDRAW**
From such *w* yourself. . . . . . . 1 Tim 6:5

**WITHER**
also shall not *w* . . . . . . . . . . . . . . Ps 1:3

**WITHERS**
The grass *w*. . . . . . . . . . . . . . . . . Is 40:7
*The grass w* . . . . . . . . . . . . . . 1 Pet 1:24

**WITHHELD**
and your sins have *w* . . . . . . . . Jer 5:25

**WITHHOLD**
good thing will He *w* . . . . . . . . Ps 84:11

**WITHOUT**
pray *w* ceasing. . . . . . . . . . 1 Thess 5:17
*w* works is dead . . . . . . . . . . James 2:26

**WITHSTAND**
you may be able to *w*. . . . . . . . Eph 6:13

**WITHSTOOD**
I *w* him to his face . . . . . . . . . . Gal 2:11

**WITNESS**
all the world as a *w* . . . . . . Matt 24:14
This man came for a *w*. . . . . . . John 1:7
do not receive Our *w* . . . . . . . John 3:11
Christ, the faithful *w* . . . . . . . . Rev 1:5
beheaded for their *w* . . . . . . . . Rev 20:4

**WITNESSED**
is revealed, being *w* . . . . . . . . Rom 3:21

**WITNESSES**
"You are My *w* ... Is 43:10
the presence of many *w* ... 1 Tim 6:12
so great a cloud of *w* ... Heb 12:1

**WIVES**
Husbands, love your *w* ... Eph 5:25
*w* must be reverent ... 1 Tim 3:11

**WOLF**
The *w* and the lamb ... Is 65:25

**WOLVES**
out as lambs among *w* ... Luke 10:3
my departure savage *w* ... Acts 20:29

**WOMAN**
she shall be called *W* ... Gen 2:23
whoever looks at a *w* ... Matt 5:28
Then the *w* of Samaria ... John 4:9
"*W*, behold your ... John 19:26
natural use of the *w* ... Rom 1:27
His Son, born of a *w* ... Gal 4:4
*w* being deceived ... 1 Tim 2:14
*w* clothed with the sun ... Rev 12:1

**WOMB**
nations are in your *w* ... Gen 25:23
in the *w* I knew you ... Jer 1:5
is the fruit of your *w* ... Luke 1:42

**WOMEN**
O fairest among *w* ... Song 1:8
*w* will be grinding ... Matt 24:41
are you among *w* ... Luke 1:28
admonish the young *w* ... Titus 2:4
times, the holy *w* ... 1 Pet 3:5

**WONDER**
marvelous work and a *w* ... Is 29:14

**WONDERFUL**
things too *w* for me ... Job 42:3
name will be called *W* ... Is 9:6

**WONDERFULLY**
fearfully and *w* made ... Ps 139:14

**WONDERS**
"And I will show *w* ... Joel 2:30
signs, and lying *w* ... 2 Thess 2:9

**WONDROUS**
*w* works declare that ... Ps 75:1

**WONDROUSLY**
God, who has dealt *w* ... Joel 2:26

**WOOD**
precious stones, *w* ... 1 Cor 3:12

**WOODCUTTERS**
but let them be *w* ... Josh 9:21

**WOOL**
they shall be as *w* ... Is 1:18
hair were white like *w* ... Rev 1:14

**WORD**
*w* is very near you ... Deut 30:14
*w* I have hidden ... Ps 119:11
*w* is a lamp to my feet ... Ps 119:105
Every *w* of God is pure ... Prov 30:5
the *w* of our God ... Is 40:8
for every idle *w* ... Matt 12:36
The seed is the *w* ... Luke 8:11
beginning was the *W* ... John 1:1
*W* became flesh and ... John 1:14
Your *w* is truth ... John 17:17
Let the *w* of Christ ... Col 3:16
come to you in *w* only ... 1 Thess 1:5
by the *w* of His power ... Heb 1:3
For the *w* of God is ... Heb 4:12
does not stumble in *w* ... James 3:2
through the *w* of God ... 1 Pet 1:23
let us not love in *w* ... 1 John 3:18
name is called The *W* ... Rev 19:13

**WORDS**
Let the *w* of my mouth ... Ps 19:14
The *w* of the wise are ... Eccl 12:11
pass away, but My *w* ... Matt 24:35
You have the *w* of ... John 6:68
not with wisdom of *w* ... 1 Cor 1:17
those who hear the *w* ... Rev 1:3

**WORK**
day God ended His *w* ... Gen 2:2
people had a mind to *w* ... Neh 4:6
the *w* of Your fingers ... Ps 8:3
Man goes out to his *w* ... Ps 104:23
*w* is honorable and ... Ps 111:3
God will bring every *w* ... Eccl 12:14
For I will *w* a *w* ... Hab 1:5
could do no mighty *w* ... Mark 6:5
This is the *w* of God ... John 6:29
"I must *w* the works ... John 9:4
*w* which You have given ... John 17:4
know that all things *w* ... Rom 8:28
*w* is no longer *w* ... Rom 11:6
Do not destroy the *w* ... Rom 14:20
abounding in the *w* ... 1 Cor 15:58
If anyone will not *w* ... 2 Thess 3:10
but a doer of the *w* ... James 1:25

**WORKED**
which He *w* in Christ ... Eph 1:20

**WORKER**
*w* is worthy of his ... Matt 10:10
*w* who does not need ... 2 Tim 2:15

**WORKERS**
we are God's fellow *w* ... 1 Cor 3:9

**WORKING**
My Father has been *w* ... John 5:17
through faith in the *w* ... Col 2:12

**WORKMANSHIP**
For we are His *w* ... Eph 2:10

**WORKS**
are Your wonderful *w* ... Ps 40:5
and let her own *w* ... Prov 31:31
For I know their *w* ... Is 66:18
show Him greater *w* ... John 5:20
*w* that I do he will do ... John 14:12
might stand, not of *w* ... Rom 9:11
is the same God who *w* ... 1 Cor 12:6
not justified by the *w* ... Gal 2:16
Now the *w* of the flesh ... Gal 5:19
not of *w*, lest anyone ... Eph 2:9
for it is God who *w* ... Phil 2:13
but does not have *w* ... James 2:14
also justified by *w* ... James 2:25
"I know your *w* ... Rev 2:2
their *w* follow them ... Rev 14:13
according to their *w* ... Rev 20:12

**WORLD**
"The field is the *w* ... Matt 13:38
He was in the *w* ... John 1:10
For God so loved the *w* ... John 3:16
His Son into the *w* ... John 3:17
*w* cannot hate you ... John 7:7
You are of this *w* ... John 8:23
I have overcome the *w* ... John 16:33
*w* may become guilty ... Rom 3:19
be conformed to this *w* ... Rom 12:2
loved this present *w* ... 2 Tim 4:10
Do not love the *w* ... 1 John 2:15
*w* is passing away ... 1 John 2:17

**WORLDS**
also He made the *w* ... Heb 1:2

**WORM**
But I am a *w* ... Ps 22:6
*w does not die and the* ... Mark 9:44

**WORMS**
And he was eaten by *w* ... Acts 12:23

**WORMWOOD**
of the star is *W* ... Rev 8:11

**WORRY**
to you, do not *w* ... Matt 6:25

**WORRYING**
*w* can add one ... Matt 6:27

**WORSE**
*w* than their fathers ... Jer 7:26

**WORSHIP**
and have come to *w* Him ... Matt 2:2
*w* what you do not know ... John 4:22
*the angels of God w* ... Heb 1:6

**WORSHIPED**
on their faces and *w* ... Rev 11:16

**WORSHIPER**
if anyone is a *w* ... John 9:31

**WORTH**
and make my speech *w* ... Job 24:25

**WORTHLESS**
Indeed they are all *w* ... Is 41:29

**WORTHLESSNESS**
long will you love *w* ... Ps 4:2

**WORTHY**
present time are not *w* ... Rom 8:18
to walk *w* ... Eph 4:1
the world was not *w* ... Heb 11:38
*W* is the Lamb who ... Rev 5:12

**WOUND**
and my *w* incurable ... Jer 15:18
and his deadly *w* ... Rev 13:3

**WOUNDED**
But He was *w* for our ... Is 53:5

**WOUNDING**
killed a man for *w* ... Gen 4:23

**WOUNDS**
Faithful are the *w* ... Prov 27:6

**WRANGLINGS**
useless *w* of men of ... 1 Tim 6:5

**WRATH**
speak to them in His *w* ... Ps 2:5
Surely the *w* of man ... Ps 76:10
So I swore in My *w* ... Ps 95:11
*W* is cruel and anger a ... Prov 27:4
in My *w* I struck you ... Is 60:10
*w* remember mercy ... Hab 3:2
For the *w* of God is ... Rom 1:18
up for yourself *w* ... Rom 2:5
nature children of *w* ... Eph 2:3
sun go down on your *w* ... Eph 4:26
Let all bitterness, *w* ... Eph 4:31
holy hands, without *w* ... 1 Tim 2:8
*So I swore in My w* ... Heb 3:11
not fearing the *w* ... Heb 11:27
for the *w* of man does ... James 1:20
of the wine of the *w* ... Rev 14:8
for in them the *w* ... Rev 15:1
fierceness of His *w* ... Rev 16:19

**WRATHFUL**
*w* man stirs up strife ... Prov 15:18

**WRESTLE**
For we do not *w* ... Eph 6:12

**WRETCHED**
*w* man that I am ... Rom 7:24
know that you are *w* ... Rev 3:17

**WRETCHEDNESS**
do not let me see my *w*. . . . .Num 11:15

**WRINGING**
*w* the nose produces . . . . . . .Prov 30:33

**WRINKLE**
not having spot or *w* . . . . . . . .Eph 5:27

**WRITE**
*w them on their hearts* . . . . . .Heb 8:10

**WRITING**
the *w* was the *w*. . . . . . . . . . . .Ex 32:16

**WRITINGS**
do not believe his *w* . . . . . . . .John 5:47

**WRITTEN**
tablets of stone, *w* . . . . . . . . . .Ex 31:18
your names are *w* . . . . . . . .Luke 10:20
"What I have *w* . . . . . . . . . .John 19:22

**WRONG**
Man has done nothing *w*. . .Luke 23:41
But he who does *w* . . . . . . . . . .Col 3:25

**WRONGED**
We have *w* no one . . . . . . . . . .2 Cor 7:2

**WRONGS**
me *w* his own soul . . . . . . . . .Prov 8:36

**WROTE**
stooped down and *w*. . . . . . . . .John 8:6

**WROUGHT**
And skillfully *w*. . . . . . . . . . .Ps 139:15

## Y

**YEAR**
the acceptable *y* . . . . . . . . . . . . .Is 61:2
of sins every *y* . . . . . . . . . . . . .Heb 10:3

**YEARS**
and for days and *y*. . . . . . . . . .Gen 1:14
lives are seventy *y*. . . . . . . . . .Ps 90:10
when He was twelve *y*. . . . . .Luke 2:42
with Him a thousand *y* . . . . . .Rev 20:6

**YES**
let your '*Y*' be '*Y*,' . . . . . . . . .Matt 5:37

**YESTERDAY**
for we are but of *y*. . . . . . . . . . . .Job 8:9

**YOKE**
"Take My *y* upon you. . . . . .Matt 11:29

**YOKED**
Do not be unequally *y*. . . . . .2 Cor 6:14

**YOUNG**
I have been *y* . . . . . . . . . . . . . .Ps 37:25
she may lay her *y*. . . . . . . . . . . .Ps 84:3
I write to you, *y*. . . . . . . . . .1 John 2:13

**YOUNGER**
Likewise you *y* people . . . . . . .1 Pet 5:5

**YOURS**
the battle is not *y* . . . . . . . .2 Chr 20:15
*Y* is the kingdom . . . . . . . . . .Matt 6:13
And all Mine are *Y* . . . . . . .John 17:10
for I do not seek *y*. . . . . . . . .2 Cor 12:14

**YOUTH**
the sins of my *y* . . . . . . . . . . . . .Ps 25:7
and *y* are vanity . . . . . . . . . .Eccl 11:10
I have kept from my *y* . . . . .Matt 19:20

**YOUTHFUL**
Flee also *y* lusts . . . . . . . . . .2 Tim 2:22

**YOUTHS**
*y* shall faint and be . . . . . . . . . .Is 40:30

## Z

**ZEAL**
The *z* of the LORD of . . . . . .2 Kin 19:31
"*Z for Your house has* . . . . . .John 2:17
that they have a *z*. . . . . . . . . .Rom 10:2

**ZEALOUS**
*z* for good works. . . . . . . . . . .Titus 2:14